牛津高階
英漢雙解詞典
Oxford Advanced Learner's English-Chinese Dictionary

Eighth edition
第八版

英語原文版

原著：**A S Hornby**（霍恩比）

策劃編輯：**Joanna Turnbull**

總編輯：Diana Lea

編輯主任：Dilys Parkinson

編輯：Patrick Phillips
Ben Francis
Suzanne Webb
Victoria Bull

語音編輯：Michael Ashby

英漢雙解版

總顧問：陸谷孫

審訂：石孝殊

翻譯：趙翠蓮　鄒曉玲等

OXFORD
UNIVERSITY PRESS
牛津大學出版社

OXFORD
UNIVERSITY PRESS

Oxford University Press is a department of the University of Oxford. It furthers the University's objective of excellence in research, scholarship, and education by publishing worldwide. Oxford is a registered trade mark of Oxford University Press in the UK and in certain other countries

Published in Hong Kong by
Oxford University Press (China) Limited
18th Floor, Warwick House East, Taikoo Place, 979 King's Road, Quarry Bay, Hong Kong

Oxford Advanced Learner's English-Chinese Dictionary (Eighth edition)
English-Chinese edition (Orthodox characters)

English text originally published as Oxford Advanced Learner's Dictionary (Eighth edition)

ISBN: 978-0-19-396634-5 (paperback)
ISBN: 978-0-19-398612-1 (paperback/CD pack)
ISBN: 978-0-19-396635-2 (pocket flexicover)
ISBN: 978-0-19-398613-8 (CD-ROM)

This impression (lowest digit)
10 9 8 7 6 5 4 3 2 1

Contents 目錄

Advisers of the English Edition
英文版顧問名單

Advisory Board 顧問小組

Dr Keith Brown
Prof Guy Cook
Dr Alan Cruse
Ruth Gairns
Moira Runcie
Prof Gabriele Stein
Dr Norman Whitney
Prof Henry Widdowson

Consultants 特約顧問

Dr Maggie Charles
(Writing Tutor Consultant)
Prof Choong Bae Kim
Prof Paul Gunashekar
Prof Hirosada Iwasaki
Prof Masanori Toyota
Sally Wehmeier
(Chief Editor, 6th and 7th editions)

American English 美式英語顧問

Jamie Greene
Stephanie Hirschman
Karen Stern

Advisers on World English 世界各地英語顧問

Dr Modupe M Alimi (*West African*)
Tony Deverson (*New Zealand*)
Heather Fitzgerald (*Canadian*)
Prof Paul Gunashekar (*Indian*)
Megan Hall (*South African*)
Leah Kariuki (*East African*)
Dr Bruce Moore (*Australian*)
John Muitung'u (*East African*)
Joseph Noble (*South African*)

Advisers on scientific words 科技詞彙顧問

Dr James Mendelssohn
Dr Geoffrey Neuss

出版説明

2013 年，《牛津高階英語詞典》(Oxford Advanced Learner's Dictionary) 出版 65 週年，英語版銷量至今已經超過 3 500 萬冊，其最新第八版的英漢雙解版也在這個時候出版了。

曾編寫包括著名的《英語用法指南》(Practical English Usage) 等多本英語語法書籍的 Michael Swan 替本書的英語原文版撰寫序言。他説，大力促成《牛津高階英語詞典》出版的霍恩比 (A S Hornby) 不僅編纂詞典，還編寫了英語教學用書，説明詞類所屬的結構，並探討了詞彙和語法之間的銜接。霍恩比的思想和工作孕育出今天的學習型詞典——提供讀音、主要詞義、語法標識、搭配、動詞和句法模式、同義詞辨析、用法規則、基礎文化知識等等。

經過近七十年的演化和修訂，《牛津高階》第八版的釋義更準確簡潔，並從語料庫選錄真實的例證。新版全書內容較上一版增加 20%。正文修訂超過 5 000 項，增收新詞 1 000 條，包括 cloud computing、microblogging、passive-aggressive 等等，並廣泛收錄美國英語單詞和外來語（從別的語言吸收來的英語詞語）。

牛津詞典增收的新詞必須得到廣泛應用，詞條釋義則力求全面，例如第八版增修尤其在北美地區常用的 kick-ass，其他一些英語詞典只收錄 powerful and aggressive 義，本詞典還收錄 extremely good and successful 一義，並附例證，幫助讀者更好地掌握新詞新義。

詞典編輯在修纂第八版之前，針對教師和學生作了廣泛的調研。很多受訪者表示，最希望詞典能幫助他們學習英語寫作，以及增加詞彙量。《牛津高階》第八版新收錄的寫作指南 (Writing Tutor) 講解多種常用文體的寫作技巧，並設置範文，提供各種文體常用的詞彙和表達方式。此外，「寫作指南」也收錄了幫助學生準備口頭報告的單元，解説製作和準備演講材料的步驟和訣竅。

本書另備光碟版，可與 Microsoft Word、Outlook、Internet Explorer 等應用軟件配合使用。除附詞典正文全文檢索的功能外，光碟還收錄涵蓋十多種文體的英語寫作互動學習軟件 iWriter：從構思、起草、寫作到檢查，每個步驟都附詳細説明，協助學生逐步實踐各種文體的寫作。iWriter 跟詞典中的「寫作指南」互相配合使用，效果更佳。

《牛津高階》第八版其他主要的增修內容還包括圖解詞彙擴充 (Visual Vocabulary Builder)、詞語搭配 (Collocations) 和學術詞彙表 (Academic Word List)。配合牛津 3000 詞彙 (Oxford 3000™) 一起學習，可以把詞彙量提升至超過 7 500 個。

坊間其他針對非英語為母語讀者的學習型詞典 (learner's dictionary) 編纂的理念皆源自於《牛津高階英語詞典》。較諸其他同類型英漢詞典，《牛津高階英漢雙解詞典》第八版對學生提供更多的學習支援，是一本提升英語運用水平重要的工具書。

詞典編輯工作繁複瑣碎，疏漏之處在所難免，尚祈廣大讀者不吝指正為感。

牛津大學出版社（中國）有限公司
二〇一三年二月

Advisory Board and Editorial Team of the English-Chinese Edition
英漢雙解版顧問及編輯人員名單

Publisher 出版人	Ben Mak 麥嘉隆	
General Adviser 總顧問	Lu Gusun 陸谷孫	
Reviewers 審訂	Shi Xiaoshu 石孝殊	Harry Yu 于海江
Translators 翻譯	Zou Xiaoling 鄒曉玲	Zhao Cuilian 趙翠蓮
	Wang Yuzhang 王玉章	Shi Xiaoshu 石孝殊
	Xiang Xiaolin 向小林	Zhang Yaoping 張耀平
	Wang Shengyin 王升印	Ma Hongqi 馬紅旗
Consultant Editor 特約編輯	Hugo Tseng 曾泰元	
	Oxford University Press (China) 牛津大學出版社（中國）	**The Commercial Press (Beijing)** 商務印書館（北京）
Managing Editors 策劃編輯	Franky Lau 劉浩賢	Luan Qi 欒奇
Executive Editors 責任編輯	Kelly Li 李潔萍	Liu Tong 劉彤
Editors 編輯	Benny Chan 陳文浩	
	Clement Chak 翟善銘	
	Sophia Loh 羅兆欣	
	Billy Wan 温沛恒	
	Natalie Lui 呂昇人	
	Windy Wong 黃雪孟	
Proofreaders 校對	Wong Hou-tin 黃浩天	The Commercial Press (Beijing) Proofreading Team 商務印書館（北京）校對科
	Lee Mung-yim 李夢艷	
	Andrew Lam 林耀輝	
	Dawn Chow 周曉彤	

陸谷孫序

填過一首詞，最後兩句："哪堪地裂天崩，還有詞人吐鳳"，自表不甘應和而退出公共文字領域的意思。兼之替牛津系的學習型詞典多次作序，說來說去，無非就是這麼幾句話，產生了文字疲勞和序言恐懼症，這篇八版的序言是推了又推的，並早早求他們另請高明，別到時誤了事。誰知截稿期限逼近，他們透過不同途徑，傳過話來，依然瞄準了我。我怕誤了人家的生意，雖無搏虎之力，也只好再做一回馮婦了。

出於各種各樣不同的目的，管它有沒有"英語帝國主義"，學英文的人只增不減，恐怕是個不爭的事實；學習過程中使用何種詞典為好，也是被問到最多的問題之一。在我本人學英語的時代（上世紀 50 年代），《牛津高階》還是罕有的佳品，偶見少數幾位僑生使用。當時坊間還鮮有牛津的重量級競爭對手，缺厄敧危之時，尤以物稀為貴，個人發現這部詞典針對非母語學生的"動詞模式"特別富創意且有用，雖說查了正文還要到書前去細看動詞的實際用法，二次查閱，不甚方便。後來，盜版上市，購來手擁一冊，更成為用英語造句作文不可或缺的良師益友。只是"狎生蔑"(familiarity breeds contempt)，用得多了，漸漸發現編者 A.S. Hornby 的模式涵蓋不足——恐怕所有模式化的條條框框都無法把活生生的客觀事物一網打盡。好在牛津的詞典人也有與時俱進的起碼常識，一版一版修訂，動詞類別的劃分所本，從早年語法學家 Harold E. Palmer 和 Otto Jespersen 等演進到 Randolph Quirk 這樣的交際派，《高階》教學 + 描記 + 實用的編纂初衷，得到更好的貫徹並發展，以至於《牛津高階》的影響基本上仍是常年不衰。如果說，當年中國學英語的學生非寫不可的英文句子，如"某某某領導我們從勝利走向勝利"(XXX leads us to march from victory to victory)，其用法是否地道，第一版還不置一詞的話，到了第八版，就早已解決了。一百十幾歲的 Hornby 先生地下有知，不必在墳墓裏輾轉翻側了。而當年以 [VN-ADJ] 和 [VN-N] 之類的二次查閱指示標記，為以 ~ sb/sth + adj.，sb/sth + noun，sb/sth + adj./noun 這樣一目瞭然的模式所替代，不能不說更有利於學生直觀對號運用。看來，編雙語詞典，這個 sb/sth 是個誰也不能棄置不用的縮略代用語。英語教師怕就怕，時至今日，學生用得順手了，在不該出現縮略語的自己產出的文本上，一樣任 sb/sth 滿天飛——還有 esp(ecially).、usu(ally) 等等——我把這稱之為詞典文體的侵害。關於這一點，讀者諸君可以翻翻八版另備的 iWriter，看看簡縮式和縮略詞如何使用才算得體。

iWriter 再往後，我欣賞八版編者把具象和抽象詞彙分開處理的用心，因為具象有一目瞭然之效，而抽象則非花費（有時是大量的）筆墨無可窮盡其義。具象詞彙包含在一個小杜登式分門別類的 78 頁圖解內（正文插圖因此得以大減），而以抽象為主的學科專業詞彙則以陰文 AW (academic word) 遍佈詞典正文各處。所謂的文學評論專業用詞，撮其要者，撐滿 4 頁，似乎是作為一個抽象詞彙的非窮盡性範本而陳列於附錄。如此分佈，有助於凸顯詞彙教學中，同樣是實詞，抽象遠遠難於具象。譬如電腦的"鼠"啊"貓"啊的，都有可視特質，但有誰能把 catharsis（疏泄、宣洩之類意思）畫得出來？

儘管我們在課堂裏教的是書寫語——即便是對話也形諸文字——可語言學家有個共識，那就是所有的人類語言首先就是口口相傳的有聲交際方式。以前的詞典"啞"的居多（包括鄙人敗絮自擁的上海譯文版《英漢大詞典》）。《牛津高階》以及競爭對手各家早配備了有聲光碟，有的連數以萬計的例證也容於其中。下載之後，聽着模仿，目接加上耳聞，多感官地接受信息，若能持之以恆，詞彙、語用和句法知識長進的同時，讀音也會朝着"母語化"接近。有些北方同學說到"dead"、"get"等詞時，起首的輔音往往來個衝擊式的"硬爆破"，而 /ai/ 這樣的雙母音又總是讀不到位，y 變成了類乎中文"喂"的聲音；來自南方的同學則不習慣於"dead"、"get"等結尾輔音的"隱爆破"，習慣性地把最後單個輔音拖長，讀出音節，聽着像是"dead(er)"、"get(ter)"等。至於音調可能問題更多。根據本人經驗，改進語音，靠別人正音固然不是完全無用，但主要的還是靠自己聽着樣本複讀模仿。記得我們那時學英語，只有一架破舊的鋼絲答錄機放出"靈格風"The record is on the gramophone; The gramophone is on the table 和 The table is on the floor 等單調內容，或許正是因為內容沒有什麼“含金量”，千百次地跟着張口出聲而不過心，日長月久，那腔調便成了外語語感的一部份。學語音，確實需要一點“小和尚念經，有口無心”那種“一根筋”似的傻勁兒。詞典過去被稱作“無聲的教師”，現在有聲了，理應受到“小和尚”們歡迎。

歐美有一部份語言學家繼承 1980 年代開始“政治正確”的文化多元論，也有提出語言多元論的。因而才有書名從 The Story of English 到 The Stories of English 以及提法從 World English 到 World Englishes，從不同“品類”(varieties) 到所謂“三個同心圓”(詳見印籍語言學家 Braj Kachru 著作) 的漸變。在這些語言學家們看來，如中國式 (包括香港) 的典型英語表達錯誤，如 to emphasise/stress on the importance (受 emphasis/stress 作名詞用的“傳染”)、to be lack of (受 for lack of 的“傳染”?)，於交際目的無損，可算是 one of Englishes。這種“寬容”態度對於我們這樣對英語而論的“他者”來說，可能值得歡迎。只是不復拘檢，不再苛求，也得有個度。在一味強調流利達意的課堂裏，待到學生不分 interesting 和 interested，一抬手大剌剌寫出“I'm interesting in physics”之類句子，那可真是交際悲劇，在“同心圓”的最外層是否還能穩佔一席之地，也成問題。為了保證最低限度的準確性和語用不出逆反效果，《牛津高階》八版的“Which Word?”、“Vocabulary Building”、“Language Bank”、“Collocations”、“More About”等欄目，因為預設的針對性較強，我認為還是相當有用的，沒有偏離《高階》教學 + 描記 + 實用的編纂初衷。

我先前常說，編詞典要“給讀者正確的信息，而不是試圖把所有正確的信息都給讀者”(譬如 AAA 必須註明是 American Automobile Association 的縮寫，至於在美國一般都讀作 triple A 則屬可有可無的或然信息)。現在看來這話說得不完整，應補充成為“給讀者預設中他們所需要的正確信息”。高階讀者既非 fools 又非 saints，預設他們之所需當然不能像入海計沙，成功無期。但取法乎上，僅得其中，可能是個不壞的設計思路。

陸谷孫 1940 年生，浙江余姚人。1965 年復旦大學外文系研究生畢業。曾任復旦大學外國語言文學學院院長，現為復旦大學傑出教授。1970 年參加《新英漢詞典》的編寫，是主要設計者和定稿人之一；1976 年起，主編《英漢大詞典》及其《補編》和第二版；發表關於莎士比亞、雙語詞典編纂、英語教學、翻譯等中英文論文 90 餘篇，出版《莎士比亞專輯》、《莎士比亞十講》、《雙語詞典編纂特性之研究》等學術專著；英譯漢《幼獅》(上下卷)、《錢商》(合譯)、《二號街的囚徒》、《鯊腭》、《星期一的故事》(合譯)、《一江流過水悠悠》、《生活曾經這樣》、《胡謅詩集》、《毛姆短篇小說》(合譯) 等；漢譯英《明式傢具》、《清玉》等。著有《餘墨集》等；發表書評、雜文不計，部份收入《餘墨集》和《餘墨二集》。

劉紹銘序

上世紀五十年代中我在台灣唸大學，常找藉口到夏濟安 (1916–1965) 老師住的温州街教職員單身宿舍聊天。話題總離不開文學作品的欣賞和英文寫作的甘苦。言談間他一再重複老話：學英文不能指望什麼「名師」指引，一切只能靠自己。老師在上海唸大學時曾患過肺病，迫得呆在家中休養了一段時間。我問他病中怎樣打發日子。他説躺在牀上抱着韋氏詞典背生字。

夏老師寫得一手漂亮的英文，全靠自修磨練得來。已故 *Oxford Advanced Learner's Dictionary*（《牛津高階英語詞典》）主編 A.S. Hornby 明確的認識到學生要學好一種語文，首先要建立一個足夠日常使用的詞彙。濟安先生在牀上背字典，雖然是環境使然，但實際上對他掌握 a working vocabulary 大有幫助。Vocabulary 是由一堆各不相關的單字湊成。一個單字的意義要看放在什麼 context 中才能決定。"Go down, Moses, let my people go" 在這句中的 "down" 是「副詞」(adverb)。但在 "The duck was plucking at the down under her wings" 這句中，鴨子翅膀下的 down 是「絨毛」。

一般詞典的功能是釋義。修讀英語的人如立志寫作，光靠背誦生字不能成事。夏濟安經過了「捧詞典背生字」階段後的另一個自修途徑是一本接一本的追讀十九世紀英國名家小説，特別是狄更斯的作品。狄更斯的故事讓他讀得如醉如痴，但因為他有志寫作，他讀得更為用心的是狄更斯多樣化的敍事文體 (variety of expressions)。

第八版《牛津高階》新增了不少有關寫作的專頁。在 Vocabulary Building 欄目下出現的例句可讓我們看到刻板的表述怎樣轉變為生動語言的過程。文章忌見同一詞語在同一的敍事空間中反複出現。且看出現在下面六個句子的單字 approximately 怎樣演變：

(1) The tickets cost *approximately* £20 each.（票每張約 20 英鎊。）

(2) How much will it cost, *approximately*?（這個大概多少錢？）

(3) We are expecting *approximately* thirty people to come.（我們預計會來三十人左右。）

(4) Profits have fallen by *approximately* 15%.（利潤下降了大約 15%。）

(5) You can expect to earn *approximately* £40,000 a year.（你可望每年賺 4 萬英鎊左右。）

(6) She earns *approximately* £25,000.（她大約賺 25,000 英鎊。）

Approximately 是「大約」、「接近」、「差不多」。以上六個例句，從內容看，全可用上 approximately 作為「大約」的正式譯文。但如每個句子中的「大約」全由 approximately 來負擔，達意雖然沒有問題，文字未免太呆板了。因此在 Vocabulary Building 這一欄內，我們看到了與 approximately 同義的多種不同説法。

(1) The tickets cost *about* £20 each.

(2) How much will it cost, *more or less*?

(3) We are expecting thirty *or so* people to come.

(4) Profits have fallen by *roughly* 15%

(5) You can expect to earn *round about* £40,000 a year.

(6) She earns *somewhere in the region of* £25,000.

新版《牛津高階》有別於同類詞典的最大特色是於正文 (The Dictionary) 外增設的參考資料。Oxford Writing Tutor（牛津寫作指南）這個附件包含了十四個有關寫作的項目。在 What makes writing formal?（撰寫正式文章的要素）這一輯內，有這麼一個提示：Use suitable synonyms for common words such as do, put, get, make。為什麼不用 do, put, get, make 這些顯淺的字眼？因為這都是口語。在 formal writing 中，“Several operations were done” 不合規矩，應説 “Several operations were carried out” 或 “Several operations were performed”。

新版詞典所列的參考資料，互相發明。不想一再使用 interesting 形容這個故事多「有趣」，有多個同義詞給你選擇，如 fascinating, compelling, stimulating, gripping, absorbing 等。要注意的是，有些字在解釋上雖然同義，但用法卻有不同。answer 和 reply 究竟有什麼分別？新版詞典在 Which Word（詞語辨析）這個欄目下提供了答案。Answer 回覆的對象，可以是人、問題、或信件，後面不用 to。Reply 後面則要用 to。試看下面例句：I'm writing to answer your questions（特此函覆貴方提問）。如要改用 reply，就應這麼説：I am writing to reply to your questions。

新版《牛津高階》除了做足釋義的基本要求外，同時也兼顧英文書寫的各種規矩。「牛津寫作指南」教我們怎樣寫議論文、長篇論文、學位論文、書評和文評等。每一類文體略加討論後就列舉一個示範樣本。這本新詞典在內容取材上確做到了巨細無遺、取捨有道。什麼是 dangling participle？一般詞典不會收入這一條，因為這是一個語言學的問題，只合留在文法專書討論。此説雖然言之成理，但事實上這種「半吊子分詞」經常出現，連英語是母語的人也一樣犯錯。喜見新版《牛津高階》收了這一條：

> 'Dangling participles' are not considered correct. In the sentence 'While walking home, my phone rang', 'walking' is a dangling participle. A correct form of the sentence would be 'while I was walking home, my phone rang'.

“While walking home” 為什麼是「半吊子分詞」？因為分詞「六神無主」，我們不知道誰在走路回家。修讀英文，如果能得「名師」指點，當然再好不過，但如迫於環境，一切都得靠自己時，憑着苦心與毅力，一樣可以修成「正果」。濟安先生在這方面的成就，給我們豎立了一個「有志事竟成」的好榜樣。而靠自己自學英文，一本好的詞典是一大助力。喜見如今的英語學習型詞典為學英語的人設想越來越周到，此新版《牛津高階》就是其中的佼佼者。

劉紹銘　1934 年生，廣東惠陽人，生於香港。1960 年畢業於台灣大學外文系。1966 年得美國印第安那大學比較文學博士學位。曾先後任教香港中文大學、新加坡國立大學、夏威夷大學和美國威斯康辛大學。現為香港嶺南大學榮休教授。

蘇正隆序

1940 年代之前英美出版的英語詞典都只是為本國人編纂的，很少考慮到非母語學習者的需求。譬如，名詞可數不可數的問題，動詞類型和句構的關係，形容詞作為修飾語和作為補語的不同，都是非母語學習者難以掌握的。因此，牛津大學出版社 1948 年推出 *A Learner's Dictionary of Current English* 後，立即大受歡迎，成為全世界最暢銷的英語學習詞典。

我自己中學時曾經在台北牯嶺街舊書鋪裏買了由 A.S. Hornby, Gatenby 和 Wakefield 合編，1942 年出版的 *Idiomatic and Syntactic Dictionary of English*，就是它的前身。高中畢業那年，台灣東華書局出版了根據 1963 年牛津 ALDCE 第二版翻譯的雙解版。我英文老師胡治國教授參與編輯工作，所以書一問世，馬上買了一本。OALDCE 雙解版第三版出版前，負責校訂的張先信教授邀我參觀，我大膽提出幾個以往詞典中常見的誤譯，如把 eat one's word 誤為「食言、背信」，把 a miss is as good as a mile 誤為「失之毫釐，謬以千里」的例子，張教授馬上據以改正，因此《牛津高階英漢雙解詞典》第三版算是海峽兩岸第一本把這類民初以來誤譯的成語給予正確中譯的英漢詞典。因為和《牛津高階英漢雙解詞典》有這麼一點淵源，因此牛津詞典編輯部邀我為第八版寫一段話，我覺得與有榮焉。

《牛津高階英漢雙解詞典》第八版有不少特色：我自己頗喜歡的是 Visual Vocabulary Builder（圖解詞彙擴充），共有 42 個主題，從「城市和鄉村」、「樹、植物和花」、「動物界」到「服裝」、「地球和太陽系」等。每個領域除了透過精美的彩圖介紹 50 到 80 個中英對應詞彙，還有言簡意賅的背景知識及近似詞彙辨析，對學英文、從事翻譯工作很有幫助。以往編詞典的人不知道 living room 是「客廳」，所以把它直譯為「起居室」；不知道 vise/vice 就是放在工作桌上方便夾住加工物的工具「台鉗」(又稱「虎鉗」或「萬力」)，把它誤譯為夾斷鐵絲、拔釘子「老虎鉗」，諸如此類，不勝枚舉。現在透過情境圖解，讀者一目瞭然，不會再混淆不清了。

除了這些主題式的圖解詞彙之外，詞典正文中也穿插許多為英文學習者貼心設計的插圖，譬如，在 bar 詞條下，從「吧枱」(bar)、「一塊肥皂」(bar of soap)、「條碼」(bar code)、「橫梁」(crossbar) 到「樂譜的小節」(bar of music)，就有 10 個小圖片圖解。此外，新增「牛津寫作指南」(Oxford Writing Tutor)，從寫作過程、撰寫摘要、應用信函、學術論文、電子郵件，到簡歷的寫作，都有簡明扼要的介紹，可有效提升英文寫作能力。

近廿年來語料庫及搜尋工具的發達，讓我們方便大量搜集語料，因此對語言的使用就有了更客觀的描述和分析。這些成果都反映在《牛津高階英漢雙解詞典》編輯上。譬如穿插在詞典正文裏有不少用法說明：according to 項下的 Language Bank（用語庫），就說明它和 For X, X's view is that, X takes the view that, in X's view, X is of the opinion that, X believed that 都是「陳述某人的觀點」，但所介紹的其他英文表達方式會讓我們的寫作、翻譯更多采多姿、更有變化。

這部詞典對翻譯也相當有幫助，具體表現在搭配 (Collocations)、詞語辨析 (Which Words?)、同義詞辨析 (Synonyms) 及中英雙語釋義上。我在《用 Google 統計檢驗英文用法》一文提到：國人很喜歡把「我們創造了經濟奇蹟」譯成 "We have created economic miracles." 但英文的習慣 miracle 不與 create 搭配，而是與 perform 或 work 搭配。這在《牛津高階英漢雙解詞典》第八版的例子裏剛好都有體現。

早期的英漢詞典大多只着重在幫助讀者理解的層次，對於如何增強表達方面——説、寫、譯的能力，往往用處有限。《牛津高階英漢雙解詞典》在提升學習者表達能力的功能，本來就相當不錯，第八版在這方面更加用心。除前面提到的 Language Bank（用語庫）外，Collocations（詞語搭配）的例子也比前一版更豐富，編排也更有系統。同一主題常用詞語的搭配全都匯聚在一起，再按依其子題排列。譬如，International relations（國際關係）主題下，分為 Trade（貿易），Conflict（衝突），Aid（援助）等。與「貿易」有關的詞語搭配有 impose/life/raise/remove import tariffs **徵收／取消／提高／廢除**進口關税等 9 個句式，24 種搭配；與「衝突」有關的詞語搭配有 compromise/endanger/protect national security **損害／危及／保護**國家安全等 7 個句式，26 種搭配；與「援助」有關的則有 deliver/distribute medical supplies **運送／分發**醫療用品等 6 個句式，14 種搭配。學習者若能把這本詞典裏所有的「詞語搭配」欄仔細研讀一遍，英文寫作及中翻英的功力當可立即提升一甲子，光這一點就值回買這部詞典的票價了！

蘇正隆　1975 年台灣大學外文系畢業。1977 年創立書林出版公司，並擔任總編輯。長期致力於翻譯教學與研究工作，主要研究領域在英漢與漢英翻譯、詞典學、英語常見錯誤分析、動植物名詞。2006–2009 年擔任台灣翻譯學學會理事長，2010 年起擔任執行長。曾參與多本英文及英漢詞典編輯、校訂，如《麥克米倫高階英漢雙解詞典》、《柯林斯英語圖畫字典》、《書林易解英語詞典》等；曾擔任英國普茲茅斯大學、廈門理工學院、香港城市大學等院校的訪問學人或客座教授，並擔任台灣多個官方機構的學術評鑑委員。

編譯者序

舉世公認的權威英語學習工具書 *Oxford Advanced Learner's Dictionary (8th Edition)* 於二〇一〇年春以嶄新的面目展現於世。

正如策劃編輯喬安娜 • 特恩布爾 (Joanna Turnbull) 所説，編者們首先在全球範圍進行了調研，邀請世界各地師生反饋英語教學中的具體艱巨任務、重點和難點，以及他們最需要的幫助。針對反映的情況，編者們目的明確，編寫出內容貼切、重點突出、充分滿足廣大師生最迫切需要的這版詞典。

牛津大學出版社 (中國) 隨即着手準備製作英漢雙解版。牛津詞典編輯部仔細對比了八版和七版的區別，發現八版的主要特色如下：

新增新詞約 1 000 條；非正文部份大幅修訂，新增 Oxford Writing Tutor (牛津寫作指南) 和 Visual Vocabulary Builder (圖解詞彙擴充)；另備的光盤裏有 iWriter 互動學習軟件，協助學生互動寫作；強化 Oxford 3000™ (牛津 3000 核心詞)，核心詞詞條後用 0┳ 標示，常用義項的序號後用小 0┳ 標示；新增 **AW** 標識，表示屬於 Academic Word List (學術詞彙)，以方便各不同學科學生學習；在 Notes on usage (用法説明框) 中新增兩類：Language Bank (用語庫) 和 Collocations (詞語搭配)，進一步提高助學功能。

第八版以上諸多特色使學習者倍感親切，愛不釋手。以新增的 Oxford Writing Tutor 為例，頁數廖廖，豐富全面，精簡扼要，畫龍點睛，舉一反三，字字珠璣；再加上光盤中的 iWriter，如虎添翼。

牛津編輯部根據八版具體內容，邀請了以下譯者。

趙翠蓮教授負責翻譯正文新增詞條、非正文部份和 iWriter 部份；鄒曉玲教授負責翻譯正文修訂內容、用法説明和正文插圖。兩位譯者都經歷了六、七兩版的磨煉，看似駕輕就熟，實則新的挑戰：所譯部份多為新增材料。所以他們仍然謙虛謹慎，兢兢業業，如期保質完成。

陸谷孫教授負責審訂新增詞條的翻譯，石孝殊教授負責審訂所有非正文部份的翻譯。審稿者認真負責，一絲不苟，反複查證，亦如期保質完成。

台灣的曾泰元教授煞費苦心為新增詞條提供了台灣用語的譯法。

詞典翻譯實屬不易，一詞之譯，輒旬月躊躇。以 tagine 一詞為例，趙翠蓮教授費盡心思，多方檢索；接着在譯審過程中又數次修改，始譯為：1. 塔吉鍋炖菜 (燜炖加調料的肉菜)；2. 塔吉鍋 (陶製、尖蓋、用於烹飪和上菜，源於北非)。又如，Lough Foyle 是"湖"還是"灣"? 現有的英漢詞典各説不一。最後，根據事實確定為"福伊爾潟湖"。再如，potty-mouthed 譯為"爆粗口的"，slugger 譯為"拚命三郎"等等都經過或啟發或長久思索查閱的歷程。

鄒曉玲教授的肺腑之言，道出了譯者的心聲："在翻譯過程中，必然會接觸到各個領域的詞彙。為了準確地理解原文，並把英語表示的意義準確地用漢語表達出來，常常要查閱許多書籍，不斷學習新的知識。有時候一個詞語或句子英語很容易理解，但由於文化差異，很難用漢語表達出來，或者絞盡腦汁也只能譯出其表面意思，難以將其中真正的內涵傳達給讀者。遇到這種情況，必須反複思考，仔細斟酌，找到兩種語言和文化的差異點，甚至是經過無數個日日夜夜和一次又一次的打磨才將其譯成讀者能接受的東西。這個過程可以説是身心疲憊。只有經歷過這個過程的譯者才深深體會到詞典翻譯的辛苦。"

整個編輯出版工作由牛津大學出版社 (中國) 編輯部和北京商務印書館英語編輯室精心規劃，詳細安排，具體部署。

全書的編輯加工和校對、發排、出版分以下幾個階段：

第一階段（二〇一〇年四月至八月）：項目籌組

1. 牛津編輯部比較第八版與第七版的內容，為翻譯工作定調，把新增內容分成幾個類別：新增詞條、作了修訂的內容、幾乎全新編寫的非正文部份及新增的用法説明。
2. 甄選譯者、約稿、試稿。
3. 制訂翻譯體例、各式編輯加工文件，包括字表、統一譯文等。
4. 發稿。

第二階段（二〇一〇年九月至二〇一一年十二月）：翻譯、建立項目的數據庫

1. 兩位譯者分批交稿，牛津編輯部抽查譯文質量。
2. 審訂人審訂譯稿。
3. 詞典內容編訂與排版全採用數據庫處理。在這段期間，編輯與數據工程人員緊密合作，做數據轉換和版面設計。

第三階段（二〇一一年十一月至二〇一二年三月）：編輯加工

1. 牛津編輯部收到審訂人校正的稿件後，與北京商務印書館英語編輯室合作進行編輯加工。
2. 牛津編輯部負責將各審訂人、商務印書館編輯及牛津編輯部提出的修訂作最後核對、整合、修改，然後進行校對。
3. 對於專科詞彙，尤其細心考證，翻閱百科全書，中國全國科學技術名詞審訂委員會公佈的譯名，參閱網絡上不同界別的官方或權威網站的信息。

第四階段（二〇一一年八月至二〇一三年三月）校對、出版

1. 校對詞典內容：牛津編輯部和北京商務印書館校對科分別對全書進行嚴格仔細的校對；校對工作分四輪，每一輪各有側重，按既定工序嚴格進行。
2. 除第八版全新翻譯的內容外，編輯同時仔細校閱第七版保留的內容，對原文已顯過時或譯文錯誤或不盡完善之處重新修訂、補遺。與英語版編輯保持聯繫，確保英文行文、注音等正確。

幾十位編譯校等人員從仔細項目籌組，認真翻譯審訂，精心建立項目數據庫，全方位編輯加工，輪番校對到發排出版，又是一個緊張有序，辛勤勞動的三年。

《牛津高階英漢雙解詞典》第八版即將出版問世了。我們深信，這部詞典將是群星燦爛中明亮耀眼的那一顆。

我們綆短汲深，錯誤不足之處希望廣大讀者不吝賜教指正。

石孝殊
重慶大學
二〇一二年十二月

石孝殊 1928 年生，重慶大學英語教授。早年畢業於中央大學（現南京大學）、四川外國語學院研究生班。曾任教於四川外國語學院、重慶第四十三中學、南岸區教師進修學校、重慶建築大學、重慶大學。從事外語教學凡四十多年，兼通英語、俄語。英語教學曾執教於非英語專業初中、高中、大學專科、本科、研究生、大學教師進修班、出國留學培訓班等，英語專業大學專科、本科、中學英語教師等。曾參與多部教材和詞典的編譯工作，包括主編《（許國璋主編）英語自學手冊》第一、二、三、四冊，北京商務印書館，1983 至 1987 年。

Foreword

Michael Swan

When A S Hornby began the work that was ultimately to lead to this 8th edition of the *Oxford Advanced Learner's Dictionary*, language teaching was in a transitional phase. The old bias towards teaching the written language, with heavy use of translation, was being replaced in many quarters by a focus on teaching speech without recourse to the mother tongue – a movement in which Hornby was heavily involved. However, the emphasis was still largely on presenting and practising forms rather than on training learners to deploy them in natural communication. Our profession was, at that time, decidedly better at teaching languages than at teaching people to use them.

In the intervening seventy years there have been profound changes, whose nature and scale Hornby could hardly have foreseen. The communicative language teaching movement and its offshoots have encouraged us to analyse and teach 'language in use'. We have become skilled at bridging the gap between the classroom and the world outside, and at producing learners who are able to use the languages they have studied for 'real life' purposes. The danger is that, as we concentrate on teaching learners to do things with language, we may lose our focus on the actual language that is needed to do these things. Discourse skills, negotiation for meaning, communication strategies, task performance, pragmatic competence and our various other current concerns may well be important, but the fundamental priorities have not changed. Language teaching is, ultimately, teaching language. Grammar, lexis and phonology remain central, and an adequate command of these is as necessary as it has ever been for efficient and effective communication. Today's learners of English, just like Hornby's students, need well-planned teaching and reference material to underpin their study.

Hornby's mission was to provide such material. He was by no means only a lexicographer. He wrote a widely-used three-level course, the *Oxford Progressive English Course*. His *Guide to Patterns and Usage in English*, which provided information about the structures into which individual nouns, verbs and adjectives enter, explored the interface between lexis and grammar long before electronic corpora made this an easy task. But Hornby was well aware that, of all the knowledge and skills which a language learner must master, the most important element, and the one involving the heaviest learning load, is an adequate working vocabulary. In this connection he saw clearly that, along with a good learner's grammar, a student of English can benefit enormously from a well-produced, pedagogically-oriented monolingual dictionary. Such a work has the space to provide detailed practical information about the most important words of the language: pronunciations, key meanings, collocations, grammatical patterning, synonym comparisons, constraints on usage and so on. Hornby was that rare combination, a scholar-pedagogue who was equally at home analysing language and teaching a class, and he was the ideal person to produce a dictionary of this very special kind. It was perhaps inevitable that this gifted lexicographer should ultimately find himself in partnership with the world's most experienced dictionary publisher. The rest is history.

Hornby would have had no difficulty in recognizing this 8th edition as a continuation of his work. It has all the features that he regarded as essential: accurate simple definitions, realistic examples, information on pronunciation, guidance on the grammatical and collocational patterns that words enter into, and notes on synonym distinctions and other aspects of usage. At the same time, it contains a wealth of additional features that Hornby might not have foreseen, but would certainly have welcomed. The clarity of definitions is rigorously controlled with the help of a list of 3000 keyword families. There are various useful appendices, including pictorial vocabulary-building materials. There is even a 49-page 'Writing Tutor', with language banks for different genres and further interactive guidance on the CD-ROM. The electronic version of the dictionary also provides additional examples, etymologies, and thesaurus-type information. Hornby would, I believe, have been surprised and delighted at the character of his braingrandchild (if I may be allowed to infiltrate a new word into this lexicographical heartland).

This new edition of a classic dictionary brings together, once again, the work of a distinguished pedagogic lexicographer and an outstanding reference publisher, and in doing so makes an invaluable contribution to the central business of language teaching – teaching the language.

英文版序言（譯文）

霍恩比着手編寫《牛津高階英語詞典》(Oxford Advanced Learner's Dictionary) 時，語言教學正處於過渡階段。霍恩比的工作最終讓這部第八版得以面世。舊時偏好大量借助翻譯來教授書面語，在很多地方這做法正逐漸被取代，教學的重點轉向不依賴母語去教授口語——霍恩比深入參與了這一運動。然而，語言教學所強調的大致依然是描述和操練，而不是訓練學習者如何在自然交際中運用語言。那時候，教師顯然善於教人語言多於教人怎麼使用語言。

七十年來發生的巨大變化，性質和規模乃霍恩比所難預見的。交際法語言教學運動及其分支學説倡導分析和教授「活的語言」。我們已經掌握技巧，填補課堂和外面世界之間的隔閡，培養學生將所學的語言知識運用於「現實生活」之中。然而，這也有其危險之處：我們專注於教導學生運用語言作什麼用途，卻忽略在這些用途所需要的真實語言。話語技巧、意義協商、交際策略、任務表現、語用能力，以及我們目前所關注的各種其他問題可能都很重要，但是根本的重點沒有改變，語言教學歸根到底是教授語言。語法、詞彙和語音依然是核心。一如既往，充分掌握這些技能才能達成有效且成功的交際。如今學習英語的人就如霍恩比的學生，需要精心設計的教學和參考資料作為學習的基礎。

霍恩比的使命就是要提供這樣的材料，他絕不只是詞典編纂人，他撰寫了廣為使用的三階教程——《牛津進階英語教程》(Oxford Progressive English Course)。他的《英語句型與用法指南》(Guide to Patterns and Usage in English) 除説明各個名詞、動詞和形容詞所屬的結構之外，還探討了詞彙與語法之間的銜接。這類工作採用電子語料庫做容易很多，但霍恩比在很早以前已經在做。不過，霍恩比很清楚，環顧學習語言的人必須掌握的所有知識和技能，足夠的應用詞彙是最重要且學習負擔最重的。他由此清楚地認識到一本精心編纂、以教學為本的英語單語詞典，同好的學生語法書一樣，能讓學英語的人獲益良多。這樣的詞典闢出空間為英語中最重要的詞語提供詳細的實用信息：讀音、主要詞義、搭配、語法模式、同義詞辨析、用法規則等等。霍恩比正是那種少有的兼才，是既精於分析語言又熟悉課堂教學的學者型教師，由他編寫這種別具一格的詞典合適不過。這位才華橫溢的詞典編纂者最終能夠與世界上最資深的詞典出版社合作或許是必然的事。後事發展便眾所周知了。

霍恩比應該不難看出，這《牛津高階英語詞典》第八版是他作品的延續。本詞典擁有他認為所有不可或缺的特點：準確簡潔的釋義、真實的例證、讀音信息、單詞的語法與搭配模式，以及同義詞辨析等用法説明。同時，它包含了大量其他的特點，這些特點霍恩比或許預見不到，但一定會贊成。詞條的釋義清晰，有嚴格的把控，主要借助 3 000 關鍵詞彙表寫成。本詞典收錄多種實用附錄，包括圖解詞彙擴充資料，甚至還有 32 頁的「寫作指南」。配套的光盤中有針對不同寫作體裁的用語庫和更全面的交互式指導材料。電子版詞典提供更多的例證、詞源和同義詞方面的信息 *。我相信，霍恩比對於他的「智生孫」(braingrandchild，請允許我將一個新詞混入這一詞典編纂腹地) 的特色會感到驚喜。

這部經典詞典的新版本再一次將一位著名教學詞典學家的作品和一家傑出的工具書出版社結合在一起。與此同時，它對於語言教學的核心任務——教授語言——作出了重大的貢獻。

Michael Swan

* 只限於英語版的配套光盤

The Hornby Trust

The A S Hornby Educational Trust was set up by A S Hornby in 1961 and he generously gave a large part of his income to it. Today, a royalty from every copy of the *OALD* sold still goes to the Trust. Thanks to the Trust, in conjunction with the British Council, hundreds of teachers have had the opportunity to take part in regional ELT workshops around the world. Each year a number of Hornby scholarships are offered by the British Council, allowing teachers and teacher trainers from countries around the world to spend a year studying linguistics and ELT at British universities. Dr Amol Padwad was a Hornby scholar from 1999 to 2000.

Being a Hornby Scholar

The Hornby scholarship and the year of study at the University of Leeds are perhaps the most significant turning points in my personal and professional life. Personally, living in a different country and culture enriched my understanding and broadened my perspectives. Professionally, I gained a deeper understanding of my profession, saw my own context in a different light, and developed a greater sense of purpose and commitment. It was amazing and extremely helpful to join the global ELT community, and the fabulous Hornby Alumni family, with networking and contacts all over the world. I am still reaping the rich benefits of this membership.

Upon returning home to India, the contribution I could make to the ELT community in my area was more satisfying than the personal gains of prestige, recognition and career advancement. If asked for specific instances, I would like to list three: raising the awareness of the teachers of English in my area about ELT; promoting networking opportunities and the professional association for teachers; and launching some innovative initiatives in teacher development.

While trying to organize the first-ever ELT conference in 2003 in my district, I had to first explain what ELT meant, as it was an unknown term in that area a few years ago. The subsequent annual ELT conferences and other events over the years have changed the situation remarkably. Most teachers are now aware of ELT – our annual conferences attract a wide range of teachers and a variety of presentations related to ELT.

The national association ELTAI (English Language Teachers' Association of India) too was unheard of in my region, nor was there any awareness about joining professional associations for one's development. I was able to set up an ELTAI chapter in the region, now one of the most vibrant ones in India, which organizes ELT conferences and other events and promotes research in ELT.

Perhaps the most direct relation between my being a Hornby scholar and my contributions to the local ELT community is the ongoing 'English Teachers' Clubs (ETCs)' experiment. Taking my cue from a small voluntary group of young teachers from my town, who frequently met to tackle some of their urgent crises, I encouraged them to form an ETC as a long-term and sustainable professional development enterprise. It was the Hornby Trust which supported the ETC idea at the pilot stage and later as a larger project. Thanks to this project several ETCs in different parts of India are promoting the professional development of the member teachers, as well as strengthening ELT activities in the region. An informal online group of teachers from over 25 countries is at present trying out the experiment in their own contexts. Two masters-level studies (at the University of Exeter and the Institute of Education, London) have studied this experiment.

Six former Hornby Scholars from India, including me, were supported by the Hornby Trust in a unique nationwide project on the adaptation of prescribed course material for effective teaching, with Prof. N S Prabhu as the consultant. This project trained over 400 teachers in adapting prescribed materials to their diverse contexts, and also involved compiling a handbook for teachers based on the insights from the project.

It is difficult to fully convey the tremendous value a Hornby scholarship adds to a person and a community. I salute the great A S Hornby for his vision and his endowment. One way of repaying the great debt we owe to him is to continue working for the empowerment of teachers of English and to take the Hornby legacy further.

Dr. Amol Padwad
Head, Department of English, J M Patel College, Bhandara, India.
Hornby Scholar 1999-2000

霍恩比信託基金

霍恩比於 1961 年設立了霍恩比教育信託基金，並慷慨捐獻了其收入的一大部份。今天，每售出一冊《牛津高階英語詞典》(OALD) 所得的一部份版稅仍然捐給該信託基金。該信託基金聯同英國文化協會讓數百名教師有機會參加世界各地的地區性英語教學研習會。英國文化協會每年都提供一批霍恩比獎學金，讓來自世界各國的教師和教師培訓者在英國的大學學習語言學和英語教學，為期一年。阿莫爾 • 帕德沃德博士 (Dr Amol Padwad) 是 1999 至 2000 年霍恩比獎學金學人。

霍恩比獎學金學人的話

霍恩比獎學金和在利茲大學 (University of Leeds) 學習的一年，也許是我個人生活和專業領域中最重要的轉折點。對於個人而言，在異國文化中生活使我增長了見識，擴闊了視野。在專業方面，我更加瞭解自己的專業，從不同的角度看待自己所處的環境，並增強了目標感和使命感。加入全球英語教學界並成為絕妙的霍恩比獎學金學人的一分子，因而與世界各地建立信息交流，這令人驚喜，對我也大有助益。我目前仍然因為曾是霍恩比獎學金學人而受益甚豐。

回到印度之後，與聲望、讚譽和職業晉升等個人所得比較，我對我的地區英語教學界付出所得的成績給予我的滿足感更大。如果需要具體舉例說明，我會列舉三條：提高我所在地區的英語教師對英語教學的認識，促進教師交流信息的機會和推動教師專業協會，並提出一些有創意的師資培訓方案。

2003 年，我試圖在我所在地區組織有史以來第一次英語教學研討會時，我得首先解釋「英語教學」(ELT) 的意思，因為幾年前英語教學在那裏還鮮為人知。隨後舉辦年度英語教學研討會等活動，大大改變了這種狀況。如今大多數教師知道英語教學是什麼——我們的年度研討會吸引了許多英語教師和各類與英語教學相關的人士發言。

我所在地區過去對印度英語教師協會 (ELTAI – English Language Teacher's Association of India) 這一全國性協會也聞所未聞，也不曉得加入專業協會可以提高自身的水平。我在區內組建了該教師協會的分會，如今是印度最活躍的分會之一，負責舉辦英語教學研討會等活動，並促進英語教學研究。

作為霍恩比獎學金學人，還有我對本地英語教學界的貢獻，這兩者之間最直接的關係或許是正在進行的「英語教師會」(ETCs – English Teacher's Clubs) 實驗計劃。我所在的城鎮有一個青年教師自發組織的小組，他們經常碰頭處理一些亟待解決的難題。我從中得到啟發，鼓勵他們組建英語教師會，作為一項長期而可持續的職業發展規劃。在試驗階段以至後來英語教師會這一想法得以擴展，都有賴霍恩比信託基金的支持。由於這一項目，印度各地的幾個英語教師會正在推進其成員教師的專業發展，並加強區內的英語教學活動。超過 25 個國家的教師組成非正式在線小組，目前正在所屬地區進行這一實驗計劃。有兩項碩士學位研究（在埃克塞特大學 (University of Exeter) 和倫敦教育學院 (Institute of Education, London)）分別對本實驗計劃進行調研。

包括我在內的六名印度前霍恩比獎學金學人由霍恩比信託基金資助，參與了一個特別的全國性項目，對指定教材進行改編以達到理想的教學成果。這個項目由 N S 普拉布教授 (Prof. N S Prabhu) 擔任顧問，培訓了 400 多名教師，根據各自不同的環境，改編指定的教材，並根據該項目的研究結果編寫教師手冊。

霍恩比獎學金給個人和社區帶來的巨大價值難以言表。我向偉大的霍恩比的遠見卓識和無私捐贈致敬。報答霍氏偉大恩惠的一種方式，就是繼續為加強英語師資力量而努力，把霍恩比的遺產發揚光大。

Dr. Amol Padwad
印度　彭達拉
J M 帕特爾學院 (J M Patel College) 英語系主任
1999–2000 霍恩比獎學金學人

Abbreviations used in the dictionary
本詞典使用的縮寫

abbr.	abbreviation 縮寫
adj.	adjective 形容詞
adv.	adverb 副詞
C	countable noun 可數名詞
conj.	conjunction 連詞
det.	determiner 限定詞
I	intransitive verb 不及物動詞
n.	noun 名詞
pl.	plural 複數
pp	past participle 過去分詞
prep.	preposition 介詞
pron.	pronoun 代詞
pt	past tense 過去時
sb	somebody 某人
sing.	singular 單數
sth	something 某事物
symb.	symbol 符號
T	transitive verb 及物動詞
U	uncountable noun 不可數名詞
v.	verb 動詞
AustralE	Australian English 澳大利亞英語
BrE	British English 英式英語
CanE	Canadian English 加拿大英語
EAfrE	East African English 東非英語
IndE	Indian English 印度英語
IrishE	Irish English 愛爾蘭英語
NAmE	North American English 美式英語
NEngE	English from Northern England 英格蘭北部英語
NZE	New Zealand English 新西蘭英語
SAfrE	South African English 南非英語
ScotE	Scottish English 蘇格蘭英語
SEAsianE	South-East Asian English 東南亞英語
US	English from the United States 美國英語
WAfrE	West African English 西非英語
WelshE	Welsh English 威爾士英語

→ To see how the abbreviations are used to show how different types of verbs and nouns are used, look at pages **R6–12** and **R16–19**. 關於縮寫表示不同動詞和名詞的用法，見 **R6–12** 和 **R16–19** 頁。

Symbols used in the dictionary
本詞典使用的符號

~	replaces the headword of an entry 代替詞目
■	shows new part of speech in an entry 表示詞條中不同的詞類
▸	derivative(s) section of an entry 詞條中的派生詞部份
·	in headword (**af·fect**), shows where a word can be broken 指詞目中的分隔點（如 **af·fect**），表示單詞可斷開處
↔	in phrasal verbs, shows that the object may come either before or after the particle 用於短語動詞，表示賓語放在小品詞前後均可
OPP	shows an opposite 表示反義詞
SYN	shows a synonym 表示同義詞
IDM	idiom(s) section of an entry 詞條中的習語部份
PHR V	phrasal verb(s) section of an entry 詞條中的短語動詞部份
🔑	shows a word from the *Oxford 3000* (see page R60) 表示牛津 3000 詞彙表中的詞彙（見 R60 頁）
AW	shows word is from the Academic Word List (see page R62) 表示學術詞彙表中的詞彙（見 R62 頁）
*	separator of English text and translation 詞典原文與漢譯分隔符

Labels used in the dictionary 本詞典使用的標識

The following labels are used with words that express a particular attitude or are appropriate in a particular situation. 下列標識表示有關用語反映特定態度或適用於特定場合。

approving expressions show that you feel approval or admiration, for example *feisty*, *petite*. 褒義詞表示贊同或讚賞，如 feisty（堅決而據理力爭的）、petite（嬌小的）。

disapproving expressions show that you feel disapproval or contempt, for example *blinkered*, *newfangled*. 貶義詞表示反對或藐視，如 blinkered（目光狹窄的；心胸隘窄的）、newfangled（新奇怪異的；時髦複雜的）。

figurative language is used in a non-literal or metaphorical way, as in 比喻指用比擬或隱喻方式表達，如：*He didn't want to cast a shadow on* (= spoil) *their happiness*. 他不想給他們的幸福蒙上陰影。

formal expressions are usually only used in serious or official language and would not be appropriate in normal everyday conversation. Examples are *admonish*, *besmirch*. 正式用語通常只用於莊重或正式場合，不宜用於日常會話中，如 admonish（告誡；警告）、besmirch（詆譭；敗壞…的名聲）。

humorous expressions are intended to be funny, for example *ignoramus*, *lurgy*. 幽默語目的是為了增加趣味，如 ignoramus（無知識的人）、lurgy（小恙；小病）。

informal expressions are used between friends or in a relaxed or unofficial situation. They are not appropriate for formal situations. Examples are *bonkers*, *dodgy*. 非正式用語用於朋友之間以及輕鬆或非正式場合，不宜用於正式場合，如 bonkers（瘋狂；愚蠢透頂）、dodgy（狡詐的）。

ironic language uses words to mean the opposite of the meaning that they seem to have, as in *You're a great help, I must say!* (= no help at all). 反語指說與表面意義相反的話，如：*You're a great help, I must say!* (= no help at all). 我得說，你可沒少幫忙！（= 根本沒幫忙）

literary language is used mainly in literature and imaginative writing, for example *aflame*, *halcyon*. 文學用語主要用於文學和創造性的寫作中，如 aflame（在燃燒）、halcyon（平安幸福的）。

offensive expressions are used by some people to address or refer to people in a way that is very insulting, especially in connection with their race, religion, sex or disabilities, for example *half-caste*, *slut*. You should not use these words. 冒犯語指以侮辱的方式對人說話或提及某人，尤指與種族、宗教、性或殘疾等有關的問題，如 half-caste（混血兒）、slut（蕩婦；邋遢女人）。這些詞不應使用。

slang is very informal language, sometimes restricted to a particular group of people, for example people of the same age or those who have the same interests or do the same job. Examples are *dingbat*, *dosh*. 俚語指很不正式的用語，有時只限於某一特定群體，如同齡人、興趣相同的人或同行，如 dingbat（笨蛋；蠢貨；傻瓜）、dosh（錢）。

taboo expressions are likely to be thought by many people to be obscene or shocking. You should not use them. Examples are *bloody*, *shit*. 禁忌語指許多人認為猥褻或惡毒的用語，應該避免使用，如 bloody（該死）、shit（他媽的）。

technical language is used by people who specialize in particular subject areas, for example *accretion*, *adipose*. 術語指某特定學科領域的人使用的專門詞語，如 accretion（積聚層；堆積層；堆積、積聚過程）、adipose（身體組織用於貯存脂肪的）。

The following labels show other restrictions on the use of words. 下列標識表明詞彙使用的其他限制。

dialect describes expressions that are mainly used in particular regions of the British Isles, not including Ireland, Scotland or Wales, for example *beck*, *nowt*. 方言（dialect）指主要用於不包括愛爾蘭、蘇格蘭或威爾士在內的不列顛群島某些特定地區的詞語，如 beck（小溪）、nowt（無；沒有什麼）。

old-fashioned expressions are passing out of current use, for example *balderdash*, *beanfeast*. 老式用法（old-fashioned）指逐漸過時的用語，如 balderdash（胡說）、beanfeast（聚會；喜慶）。

old use describes expressions that are no longer in current use, for example *ere*, *perchance*. 舊用法（old use）指現已不再使用的詞語，如 ere（在…之前）、perchance（也許；可能）。

saying describes a well-known fixed or traditional phrase, such as a proverb, that is used to make a comment, give advice, etc, for example *actions speak louder than words*. 諺語、格言或警句（saying）指眾所周知的固定說法或傳統說法，用作評論、建議等，如 actions speak louder than words（行動比言語更為響亮）。

TM shows a trademark of a manufacturing company, for example *Band-Aid*, *Frisbee*. 表示生產廠家的商標，如 Band-Aid（邦迪牌創可貼）、Frisbee（弗里斯比飛盤）。

Key to dictionary entries
本詞典詞條用法

Finding the word 查找單詞

Information in the dictionary is given in entries, arranged in alphabetical order of **headwords. Compound words** are in separate entries, also arranged alphabetically.
本詞典的詞條按詞目的字母順序排列。複合詞作獨立詞條列出，仍按字母順序排列。

headwords 詞目

entry 詞條

book·bind·er /ˈbʊkbaɪndə(r)/ *noun* a person whose job is fastening the pages of books together and putting covers on them 裝訂工人 ▸ **book·bind·ing** *noun* [U]

book·case /ˈbʊkkeɪs/ *noun* a piece of furniture with shelves for keeping books on 書架；書櫃 ➲ VISUAL VOCAB page V21

ˈbook club *noun* **1** an organization that sells books cheaply to its members 讀書俱樂部（會員購書享受打折優惠） **2** = BOOK GROUP

Some headwords can have more than one part of speech.
有些詞目可能有兩個或以上的詞類。

Squares show where the information on each part of speech begins.
方塊標示每種詞類信息的起始。

headword and all possible parts of speech
詞目和各種可能的詞類

blind·fold /ˈblaɪndfəʊld; *NAmE* -foʊld/ *noun, verb, adj., adv.*
▪ *noun* something that is put over sb's eyes so they cannot see 障眼物；眼罩
▪ *verb* **~ sb** to cover sb's eyes with a piece of cloth or other covering so that they cannot see （用布等）蒙住眼睛：*The hostages were tied up and blindfolded.* 人質被捆綁起來並蒙上了眼睛。
▪ *adj., adv.* (*BrE*) (also **blind·fold·ed** *BrE, NAmE*) with the eyes covered 被蒙住眼睛：*The reporter was taken blindfold to a secret location.* 那位記者被蒙着眼睛帶到了一處

There are some words in English that have the same spelling as each other but different pronunciations.
英語中有些詞拼法相同，但讀音不同。

The small **homonym number** shows that this is the first of two headwords spelled *gill*.
同形異義詞旁的小號碼表示兩個拼法相同的詞目 gill 中的第一個。

Different pronunciation is given at each headword. 每個詞目後給出不同的讀音。

gill[1] /ɡɪl/ *noun* [usually pl.] one of the openings on the side of a fish's head that it breathes through 鰓 ➲ VISUAL VOCAB page V12
IDM **to the ˈgills** (*informal*) completely full （完全）滿了，飽了；滿滿當當：*I was stuffed to the gills with chocolate cake.* 我吃巧克力蛋糕都撐到嗓子眼兒了。

gill[2] /dʒɪl/ *noun* a unit for measuring liquids. There are four gills in a pint. 及耳（液量單位，一品脱為四及耳）

There are also some words in English that have more than one possible spelling, and both spellings are acceptable. Information about these words is given at the most frequent spelling.
英語中還有些詞可能有兩種或以上的拼法，而這些拼法都可接受。這類詞的相關信息在使用頻率最高的拼法下給出。

The variant spelling is given in brackets.
不同拼法在括號中給出。

ban·is·ter (also **ban·nis·ter**) /ˈbænɪstə(r)/ *noun* (*BrE* also **ban·is·ters** [pl.]) the posts and rail which you can hold for support when going up or down stairs （樓梯的）欄杆，扶手：*to hold on to the banister/banisters* 緊抓住

At the entry for the less frequent spelling a cross-reference directs you to the main entry.
在使用頻率較低的拼法詞條下，以相互參照的詮釋引向主詞條。

ban·nis·ter = BANISTER

Irregular forms of verbs are treated in the same way.
不規則動詞的各種形式以相同方式處理。

Some words that are **derivatives** of other words do not have their own entry in the dictionary because they can be easily understood from the meaning of the word from which they are derived (the root word). They are given in the same entry as the root word, in a specially marked section.
有些詞是其他詞的派生詞，在本詞典中沒有單獨的條目，因為從派生它們的源詞（根詞）很容易便可理解其含義。這些詞置於根詞詞條內，以特定符號標示。

be·lated /bɪˈleɪtɪd/ *adj.* coming or happening late 遲來的；晚出現的： *a belated birthday present* 遲來的生日禮物 ▸ **be·lated·ly** *adv.*

The blue triangle shows where the derivative section starts.
藍色三角形標示派生詞部份的起始。

You can find **idioms** and **phrasal verbs** in separate sections, marked with special symbols.
習語和短語動詞部份分別列出，以特定符號標示。

fetch 0━ /fetʃ/ *verb*
1 0━ (*especially BrE*) to go to where sb/sth is and bring them/it back （去）拿來；（去）請來： **~ sb/sth** *to fetch help / a doctor* 去請人幫助；去請醫生 ◊ *The inhabitants have to walk a mile to fetch water.* 居民得走一英里路去取水。◊ *She's gone to fetch the kids from school.* 她去學校接孩子了。◊ **~ sb sth** *Could you fetch me my bag?* 你能幫我去取我的包嗎？ **2 ~ sth** to be sold for a particular price 售得，賣得（某價） SYN **sell for**： *The painting is expected to fetch $10 000 at auction.* 這幅畫預計拍賣可得 10 000 元。
IDM **fetch and ˈcarry (for sb)** to do a lot of little jobs for sb as if you were their servant （為某人）打雜，當聽差，跑腿
PHR V **ˌfetch ˈup** (*informal, especially BrE*) to arrive somewhere without planning to 偶然來到；意外到達： *And then, a few years later, he somehow fetched up in Rome.* 後來，過了幾年，他不知怎麼到了羅馬。

phrasal verbs section with symbol PHR V (see pages R13–15)
以符號 PHR V 提示的短語動詞部份（見 R13–15 頁）

idioms section with symbol IDM (see pages R22–23)
以符號 IDM 提示的習語部份（見 R22–23 頁）

Finding the meaning 查找詞義

Some words have very long entries. It is not usually necessary to read the whole entry from the beginning, if you already know something about the general meaning that you are looking for.
有些詞條目很長，如果你對所查詞語的大意有所瞭解，通常不必從頭開始將整個詞條都看一遍。

spin 🔑 /spɪn/ *verb, noun*
■ *verb* (**spin·ning, spun, spun** /spʌn/)
▸ TURN ROUND QUICKLY 快速旋轉 **1** 🔑 [I, T] to turn round and round quickly; to make sth do this（使）快速旋轉：(**+ adv./prep.**) *The plane was spinning out of control.* 飛機失去控制，不停地旋轉。◇ *a spinning ice skater* 做旋轉動作的溜冰者 ◇ *My head is spinning* (= I feel as if my head is going around and I can't balance). 我覺得天旋地轉。◇ **~ (round/around)** *The dancers spun round and round.* 舞者不停地旋轉。◇ **~ sth (round/around)** *to spin a ball/coin/wheel* 轉動球／硬幣／輪子 **2** 🔑 [I, T] **~ (sb) round/around | + adv./prep.** to turn round quickly once; to make sb do this（使）急轉身，猛轉回頭，急轉彎：*He spun around to face her.* 他猛地回過身來，面對着她。
▸ MAKE THREAD 紡線 **3** [I, T] to make thread from wool, cotton, silk, etc. by twisting it 紡（線）；紡（紗）：

Short cuts show the context or general meaning.
義項提示表示語境或大意。

Meanings that are closely related share the same short cut.
含義相近的詞義在同一義項提示內。

Understanding and using the word 詞彙理解和使用

aban·doned 🔑 AW /əˈbændənd/ *adj.*
1 🔑 left and no longer wanted, used or needed 被離棄的；被遺棄的；被拋棄的：*an abandoned car/house* 被拋棄的轎車；棄置的房子 ◇ *The child was found abandoned but unharmed.* 該棄兒被人們發現時安然無恙。 **2** (of people or their behaviour 人或行為) wild; not following accepted standards 放縱的；墮落的

Words printed in larger type and with a 🔑 symbol are part of the **Oxford 3000** list of important words (see pages **R60–61**). Small keys indicate which parts of the entry are most important.
字體較大、標有符號 🔑 的單詞是牛津 3000 重要詞表中的單詞（見 **R60–61** 頁）。小鑰匙符號標示詞條中最重要的義項。

Words from the Academic Word List are marked with **AW** (see pages **R62–63**).
學術詞彙表中的單詞以符號 **AW** 標示（見 **R62–63** 頁）。

aard·vark /ˈɑːdvɑːk; *NAmE* ˈɑːrdvɑːrk/ *noun* an animal from southern Africa that has a long nose and tongue and that eats insects 土豚（非洲食蟻獸）

pronunciation, with American pronunciation where it is different (see pages **R64–68**)
讀音：與英式讀音不同的美式讀音會標註出來（見 **R64–68** 頁）

ˌ**baby** ˈ**grand** *noun* a small GRAND PIANO 小型平台鋼

Stress marks show stress on compounds.
重音符號表示複合詞的重讀。

Irregular forms of verbs, with their pronunciations. Irregular plurals of nouns are also shown.
不規則動詞的形式及讀音。亦給出不規則名詞的複數形式。

examples of use in *italic type*
斜體字為用法例證

cling /klɪŋ/ *verb* (**clung**, **clung** /klʌŋ/) **1** [I] to hold on tightly to sb/sth 抓緊；緊握；緊抱：**~ to sb/sth** *survivors clinging to a raft* 緊緊抓住救生筏的幸存者 ◇ **~ on to sb/sth** *She clung on to her baby.* 她緊緊抱住她的嬰兒。◇ **~ on** *Cling on tight!* 緊緊抓住！◇ **~ together** *They clung together, shivering with cold.* 他們緊緊地抱在一起，冷得直發抖。➲ SYNONYMS at HOLD **2** [I] to stick to sth 粘住；附着：*a dress that clings* (= fits closely and shows the shape of your body) 緊身連衣裙 ◇ **~ to sth** *The wet shirt clung to his chest.* 濕襯衫緊貼在他的胸部。◇ *The smell of smoke still clung to her clothes.* 煙味仍附着在她的衣服上不散。**3** [I] **~ (to sb)** (usually *disapproving*) to stay close to sb, especially because you need them emotionally（尤指因感情需要而）依戀，依附：*After her*

prepositions, adverbs and structures that can be used with this word
可與詞目搭配的介詞、副詞和結構

label giving information about usage (see page XX)
用法說明標識（見 xx 頁）

comparatives and superlatives of adjectives
形容詞的比較級和最高級

hearty /ˈhɑːti; *NAmE* ˈhɑːrti/ *adj., noun*

■ ***adj.*** (**heart·ier**, **hearti·est**) **1** [usually before noun] showing friendly feelings for sb 親切的；友好的：*a hearty welcome* 熱情的歡迎 **2** (sometimes *disapproving*) loud, cheerful and full of energy 喧鬧而活潑的；吵鬧快活且精力充沛的：*a hearty and boisterous fellow* 活潑愛吵鬧的傢伙 ◇ *a hearty voice* 響亮的嗓子 **3** [only before noun] (of

information on use of adjectives (see pages **R18–19**)
形容詞用法說明（見 **R18–19** 頁）

dock /dɒk; *NAmE* dɑːk/ *noun, verb*

■ ***noun*** **1** [C] a part of a port where ships are repaired, or where goods are put onto or taken off them 船塢；船埠；碼頭：*dock workers* 碼頭工人 ◇ *The ship was* ***in dock.*** 船泊在船塢。➲ see also DRY DOCK **2 docks** [pl.] a group of docks in a port and the buildings around them that are used for repairing ships, storing goods, etc. 港區 **3** [C] (*NAmE*) = JETTY **4** [C] (*NAmE*) a raised platform for loading vehicles or trains（供運貨汽車或鐵路貨車裝卸貨物的）月台 **5** [C] the part of a court where the person who has been accused of a crime stands or sits during a trial（法庭的）被告席：*He's been* ***in the dock*** (= on trial for a crime) *several times already.* 他已受審多次。➲ COLLOCATIONS at JUSTICE **6** [U] a wild plant of northern Europe with large thick leaves that can be rubbed on skin that has been stung by NETTLES to make it less painful 酸模（北歐闊葉野草，可用來揉擦被蕁麻刺傷的皮膚以止痛）：*dock leaves* 酸模葉

■ ***verb*** **1** [I, T] **~ (sth)** if a ship **docks** or you **dock** a ship, it sails into a HARBOUR and stays there（使船）進港，停靠碼頭，進入船塢：*The ferry is expected to dock at 6.* 渡船預計在 6 點停靠碼頭。**2** [I, T] **~ (sth)** if two SPACECRAFT **dock**, or **are docked**, they are joined together in space（使太空船在外層空間）對接：*Next year, a*

fixed form of noun
名詞的固定形式

information on different types of noun (see pages **R16–18**)
各類名詞的說明（見 **R16–18** 頁）

common phrase in **bold type** in example (see pages **R20–21**)
例證中用黑體表示通用短語（見 **R20–21** 頁）

verb codes and frames (see pages **R6–12**)
動詞代碼和框架（見 **R6–12** 頁）

word used in definition that is not in the **Oxford 3000**
釋義中牛津 3000 詞彙表以外的詞

Build your vocabulary 擴充詞彙

The dictionary also contains a lot of information that will help you increase your vocabulary and use the language productively.
本詞典亦包括許多有助於擴充詞彙和加強英語運用能力的信息。

stable 0‑ᴗ AW /ˈsteɪbl/ *adj., noun, verb*
■ *adj.* **1** 0‑ᴗ firmly fixed; not likely to move, change or fail 穩定的；穩固的；牢固的 SYN **steady**：*stable prices* 穩定的價格 ◊ *a stable relationship* 穩定的關係 ◊ *This ladder doesn't seem very stable.* 這架梯子好像不太穩。◊ *The patient's condition is stable* (= it is not getting worse). 患者病情穩定。 **2** 0‑ᴗ (of a person 人) calm and reasonable; not easily upset 穩重的；沉穩的；持重的 SYN **balanced**：*Mentally, she is not very stable.* 她的心理狀態不十分穩定。 **3** (*technical* 術語) (of a substance 物質) staying in the same chemical or ATOMIC state （化學狀態或原子狀態）穩定的：*chemically stable* 化學狀態穩定的 OPP **unstable** ▸ **sta·bly** /ˈsteɪbli/ *adv.*

WORD FAMILY
stable *adj.* (≠ unstable)
stability *noun* (≠ instability)
stabilize *verb*

Special symbols show synonyms and opposites.
特定符號表示同義詞和反義詞。

Word families show words related to the headword.
詞族顯示與詞目相關的詞。

Notes help you choose the right word, and also help with difficult grammar points. They are all listed on pages **R24–28**.
用法説明幫助讀者正確選擇詞彙和理解語法難點，該部份列表見 **R24–28** 頁。

Synonyms 同義詞辨析

valuable

precious • priceless • irreplaceable

These words all describe sth that is worth a lot of money or very important to sb. 以上各詞均用以形容物品值錢、寶貴。

valuable worth a lot of money 指值錢的、貴重的：*The thieves took three pieces of valuable jewellery.* 竊賊盜走了三件貴重的首飾。

precious rare and worth a lot of money; loved or valued very much 指珍稀的、珍貴的、寶貴的：*a precious Chinese vase, valued at half a million pounds* 價值 50 萬英鎊的稀世中國花瓶 ◊ *precious memories of our time together* 我們共度時光的珍貴回憶

priceless extremely valuable; loved or valued very much 指無價的、極珍貴的、極寶貴的：*a priceless collection of antiques* 價值連城的古文物收藏

irreplaceable too valuable or special to be replaced 指因貴重或獨特而不能替代的

PATTERNS
- valuable/precious/priceless/irreplaceable **possessions**
- valuable/precious/priceless **antiques/jewels/jewellery**

words listed in order of how frequent they are
詞彙按使用頻率順序列出

Cross-references refer you to information in other parts of the dictionary.
相互參照的詮釋引導讀者去查閱本詞典中其他部份的信息。

bear 0‑ᴗ /beə(r); *NAmE* ber/ *verb, noun*
■ *noun* **1** a heavy wild animal with thick fur and sharp CLAWS (= pointed parts on the ends of its feet). There are many types of bear. 熊：*a black bear* 黑熊 ➲ see also GRIZZLY BEAR, POLAR BEAR, TEDDY BEAR **2** (*finance* 財) a person who sells shares in a company, etc., hoping to buy them back later at a lower price （在證券市場等）賣空的人 ➲ compare BULL (3) ➲ see also BEARISH
IDM **like a bear with a sore 'head** (*informal*) bad-tempered or in a bad-tempered way 急性子；脾氣暴躁

Compare refers you to a word with a contrasting meaning.
比照 (compare) 引導讀者去查閱詞義形成對照的詞。

See also refers you to a word with a similar or related meaning.
另見 (see also) 引導讀者去查閱具有相似或相關意義的詞。

Numbers 數字

10000-foot view /ˌten ˈθaʊznd ˈfʊt ˈvjuː/ *noun*（*business* 商）a broad general view or description of a problem 概況；概述 **SYN** HELICOPTER VIEW, OVERVIEW: *Let me give you the 10000-foot view.* 我來介紹一下大致情況。

1040 form /ˌten ˈfɔːti fɔːm; *NAmE* ˈfɔːrti fɔːrm/ *noun* (in the US) an official document in which you give details of the amount of money that you have earned so that the government can calculate how much tax you have to pay （美國）個人收入申報表

12 /twelv/ *noun* (in Britain) a label that is given to a film/movie to show that it can be watched legally only by people who are at least twelve years old; a film/movie that has this label （英國）12 歲可看影片（標籤）: *I can take the kids too—it's a 12.* 我可以把孩子們也帶去——這是供 12 歲以上的人觀看的影片。

1471 /ˈwʌn fɔː sevn wʌn; *NAmE* fɔːr/ (in Britain) the telephone number you can use to find out the telephone number of the person who called you most recently, and the time the call was made（英國）用以查詢最近一個來電號碼和時間的電話號碼

15 /ˌfɪfˈtiːn/ *noun* (in Britain) a label that is given to a film/movie to show that it can be watched legally only by people who are at least fifteen years old; a film/movie that has this label （英國）15 歲可看影片（標籤）

18 /ˌeɪˈtiːn/ *noun* (in Britain) a label that is given to a film/movie to show that it can be watched legally only by people who are at least eighteen years old; a film/movie that has this label （英國）18 歲可看影片（標籤）

18-wheeler /ˌeɪtiːn ˈwiːlə(r)/ *noun* (*NAmE*) a very large truck with nine wheels on each side * 18 輪大卡車

20/20 vision /ˌtwenti twenti ˈvɪʒn/ *noun* the ability to see perfectly without using glasses or CONTACT LENSES 標準視力；正常視力

2.1 /ˌtuː ˈwʌn/ *noun* the upper level of the second highest standard of degree given by a British or an Australian university（英國或澳大利亞大學的學位成績）B 等 A 級：*I got a 2.1.* 我獲得 B 等 A 級。

2.2 /ˌtuː ˈtuː/ *noun* the lower level of the second highest standard of degree given by a British or an Australian university（英國或澳大利亞大學的學位成績）B 等 B 級

24-hour clock /ˌtwenti fɔːr aʊə ˈklɒk; *NAmE* aʊər ˈklɑːk/ *noun* the system of using twenty four numbers to talk about the hours of the day, instead of dividing it into two units of twelve hours * 24 小時制

24/7 /ˌtwenti fɔː ˈsevən; *NAmE* fɔːr/ *adv.* (*informal*) twenty-four hours a day, seven days a week (used to mean 'all the time') 一週 7 天一天 24 小時；全時間：*She's with me all the time—24/7.* 她白天黑夜都和我在一起。

3-D (also **three-D**) /ˌθriː ˈdiː/ *noun* [U] the quality of having, or appearing to have, length, width and depth 三維；立體：*These glasses allow you to see the film in 3-D.* 這種眼鏡可看立體影片。

3G /ˌθriː ˈdʒiː/ *abbr.* third generation (used to describe a level of performance for MOBILE/CELL PHONES that makes it possible to move data to and from the Internet) * 3G，第三代移動通信：*3G technology* * 3G 技術

35mm /ˌθɜːtifaɪv ˈmɪlimiːtə(r); *NAmE* ˌθɜːrti-/ *noun* the size of film that is usually used in cameras for taking photographs and making films/movies * 35 毫米膠片

360-degree feedback /ˈθriː hʌndrəd ən sɪksti dɪˈgriː ˈfiːdbæk/ (also **360-degree appraisal**) *noun* [U]（*business* 商）information provided by all the people that an employee deals with, used as a way of deciding how well the employee does their job（用於評估雇員績效的）360 度反饋；360 度績效考核：*360-degree feedback assessments* * 360 度績效評估

4 × 4 /ˌfɔː baɪ ˈfɔː; *NAmE* ˌfɔːr baɪ ˈfɔːr/ *noun* a vehicle with a system in which power is applied to all four wheels, making it easier to control 四輪驅動汽車

411 /ˌfɔː wʌn ˈwʌn; *NAmE* ˌfɔːr/ *noun* **1** [U] the telephone number of the service that you use in the US to find out a person's telephone number（美國）查號電話號碼：*Call 411.* 撥 411 查號。 **2 the 411** [sing.] (*NAmE, informal*) the true facts about a situation or the information you need 實情；需要瞭解的情況：*He'll give us the 411 on what to expect.* 他會就可能發生的情況向我們介紹的。

7/7 /ˌsevn ˈsevn/ *noun* (*BrE*) the abbreviation for the date 7 July, 2005, when several bomb attacks took place in London 七月七日（即 2005 年 7 月 7 日，那天倫敦遭到幾次炸彈襲擊）

the $64,000 question /ˌsɪksti fɔː ˌθaʊznd ˌdɒlə ˈkwestʃən; *NAmE* fɔːr, ˌdɑːlər/ *noun* (*informal*) the thing that people most want to know, or that is most important 人們最想知道的事；最重要的事：*It's a clever plan, but the sixty-four thousand dollar question is: will it work?* 這是個絕妙的計劃，但最重要的是，行得通嗎？

9/11 /ˌnaɪn ɪˈlevn/ *noun* the abbreviation for the date September 11, 2001, when terrorists flew planes into the World Trade Center in New York, the Pentagon in Washington, D.C., and a field in Pennsylvania, killing thousands of people 九一一（即 2001 年 9 月 11 日，那天恐怖分子駕駛飛機撞向紐約世貿大廈、華盛頓特區的五角大樓和賓夕法尼亞州野外，導致幾千人死亡）

911 /ˌnaɪn wʌn ˈwʌn/ the telephone number used in the US to call the police, fire or ambulance services in an emergency 美國緊急求救電話號碼：(*NAmE*) *Call 911.* 撥 911 報警。

99 /ˌnaɪntiˈnaɪn/ *noun* (*BrE*) an ice cream in a cone with a stick of chocolate in the top 巧克力棒蛋捲冰淇淋

999 /ˌnaɪn naɪn ˈnaɪn/ the telephone number used in Britain to call the police, fire or ambulance services in an emergency 英國緊急求救電話號碼：(*BrE*) *Dial 999.* 撥 999 報警。

Aa

A /eɪ/ *noun, symbol, abbr.*

■ ***noun*** (also **a**) (*pl.* **As**, **A's**, **a's** /eɪz/) **1** [C, U] the first letter of the English alphabet 英語字母表的第 1 個字母：*'Apple' begins with (an) A/'A'.* * apple 一詞以字母 a 開頭。 **2 A** [C, U] (*music* 音) the 6th note in the SCALE of C MAJOR * A 音（C 大調的第 6 音或音符） **3** [C, U] the highest mark/grade that a student can get for a piece of work or course of study（學業成績）第一等，優，甲：*She got (an)* ***A in/for*** *Biology.* 她生物科成績得 A。◇ *He had* ***straight A's*** (= nothing but A's) *all through high school.* 他讀中學時成績全部是 A。 **4 A** [U] used to represent the first of two or more possibilities（表示兩個或更多可能性中的）第一個：*Shall we go for plan A or plan B?* 我們採用第一方案還是第二方案？ **5 A** [U] used to represent a person, for example in an imagined situation or to hide their identity（代表一個假設的或不指名的人）甲：*Assume A knows B is guilty.* 假定甲知道乙應負罪責。 ➲ see also A-FRAME, A LEVEL, A-ROAD

IDM **from A to B** from one place to another 從一地到另一地：*For me a car is just a means of getting from A to B.* 在我看來，汽車只不過是從一地到另一地的代步工具。 **from A to Z** including everything there is to know about sth 從頭到尾；徹底地；完全：*He knew his subject from A to Z.* 他通曉自己的學科。

■ ***symbol*** **1** used in Britain before a number to refer to a particular important road * A 級公路，幹線公路（英國公路代號，後接數字）：*the A34 to Newbury* 通往紐伯里的 A34 號（幹線）公路 **2** used (but not in the US) before numbers which show standard METRIC sizes of paper（除美國外，用於數字前表示標準紙張尺寸）A …號紙（尺寸）：*a sheet of* ***A4*** *paper* (= 297×210mm) 一張 A4 號紙（= 297 × 210 毫米）◇ ***A3*** (= 420×297mm) * A3 號紙（= 420 × 297 毫米）◇ ***A5*** (= 210×148mm) * A5 號紙（= 210 × 148 毫米）

■ ***abbr.*** (in writing) AMP(S)（書寫形式）安，安培（電流單位）

a 🔑 /ə; *strong form* eɪ/ (also **an** /ən; *strong form* æn/) *indefinite article*

HELP The form **a** is used before consonant sounds and the form **an** before vowel sounds. When saying abbreviations like 'FM' or 'UN', use **a** or **an** according to how the first letter is said. For example, **F** is a consonant, but begins with the sound /e/ and so you say: *an FM radio.* **U** is a vowel but begins with /j/ and so you say: *a UN declaration.* * a 用於輔音前，an 用於元音前。在 FM、UN 等縮略語前，用 a 還是用 an，需視首字母如何發音而定。如 F 是輔音字母，但其發音以 /e/ 開頭，故應說：an FM radio。U 是元音字母，但其發音以 /j/ 開頭，故應說：a UN declaration。 **1** 🔑 used before countable or singular nouns referring to people or things that have not already been mentioned（用於可數名詞或單數名詞前，表示未曾提到的）一（人、事、物）：*a man/horse/unit* 一個人；一匹馬；一個單位◇ *an aunt/egg/hour/x-ray* 一位姑母；一顆雞蛋；一小時；一張 X 光片◇ *I can only carry two at a time.* 我一次只能帶兩個。◇ *There's a visitor for you.* 有位客人找你。◇ *She's a friend of my father's* (= one of my father's friends). 她是我父親的朋友。 **2** 🔑 used before uncountable nouns when these have an adjective in front of them, or phrase following them（用於前有形容詞或後有短語的不可數名詞前）：*a good knowledge of French* 精通法語◇ *a sadness that won't go away* 揮之不去的悲愁 **3** 🔑 any; every 任何一；每一：*A lion is a dangerous animal.* 獅子是猛獸。 **4** 🔑 used to show that sb/sth is a member of a group or profession（表示為某一群體或職業中的一員）：*Their new car's a BMW.* 他們的新轎車是輛寶馬。◇ *She's a Buddhist.* 她是佛教徒。◇ *He's a teacher.* 他是教師。◇ *Is that a Monet* (= a painting by Monet)? 那是莫奈的畫嗎？ **5** used in front of two nouns that are seen as a single unit（用於視為一體的兩個名詞之前）：*a knife and fork* 一副刀叉 **6** used instead of *one* before some numbers（用於某些數字前，代替 one）：*A thousand people were there.* 那裏有一千人。 **7** used when talking about prices, quantities and rates（用於價格、數量、比率等）一，每一 **SYN** **per**：*They cost 50p a kilo.* 其價錢是一公斤 50 便士。◇ *I can type 50 words a minute.* 我每分鐘能打 50 個單詞。◇ *He was driving at 50 miles an hour.* 當時他正以每小時 50 英里的速度駕車。 **8** a person like sb 像（某人）的人；…式的人物：*She's a little Hitler.* 她是個小希特勒。 **9** used before sb's name to show that the speaker does not know the person（用於某人姓名前，表示說話者不認識此人）有個：*There's a Mrs Green to see you.* 有位格林太太要見你。 **10** used before the names of days of the week to talk about one particular day（用於一星期中某天的名稱前，表示具體某一天）：*She died on a Tuesday.* 她是在某個星期二去世的。

a- /eɪ/ *prefix* (in nouns, adjectives and adverbs 構成名詞、形容詞和副詞) not; without 非；不；無；沒有：*atheist* 無神論者◇ *atypical* 非典型的◇ *asexually* 無性地

A1 /ˌeɪ ˈwʌn/ *adj.* (*informal*) very good 很棒的；極好的：*The car was in A1 condition.* 汽車狀況好極了。

A2 (level) /ˌeɪ ˈtuː levl/ *noun* [C, U] a British exam usually taken in Year 13 of school or college (= the final year) when students are aged 18. Students must first have studied a subject at AS level before they can take an A2 exam. Together AS and A2 level exams form the A-level qualification, which is needed for entrance to universities. * A2 證書考試（英國中學生在 18 歲時參加，之前必須修完高級補充程度考試的同一門課，通過這兩種考試才有資格入讀大學）：*A2 exams* * A2 證書考試 ◇ *Students will normally take three A2 subjects.* 學生通常要選三門 A2 證書考試科目。◇ *He's* ***doing an A2 (level)*** *in History.* 他正為參加 A2 證書考試修讀歷史。◇ *More than 20 subjects are on offer* ***at A2 level*** *at our college.* 本校提供 20 多門 A2 證書考試課程。

AA /ˌeɪ ˈeɪ/ *abbr.* **1** (usually **the AA**) Automobile Association (a British organization which provides services for car owners) 汽車協會（英國一個為車主提供服務的組織） **2** ALCOHOLICS ANONYMOUS

AAA /ˌeɪ eɪ ˈeɪ/ *abbr.* **1** American Automobile Association (an American organization which provides services for car owners) 美國汽車協會（美國一個為車主提供服務的組織） **2** (in the UK) Amateur Athletic Association（英國）業餘體育協會

A & E /ˌeɪ ənd ˈiː/ *abbr.* ACCIDENT AND EMERGENCY（醫院）急診室

A & R /ˌeɪ ənd ˈɑː(r)/ *abbr.* artists and repertoire (the department in a record company that is responsible for finding new singers and bands and getting them to sign a contract with the company)（唱片公司的）藝人及音樂產品部

aard·vark /ˈɑːdvɑːk; *NAmE* ˈɑːrdvɑːrk/ *noun* an animal from southern Africa that has a long nose and tongue and that eats insects 土豚（非洲食蟻獸）

aargh /ɑː; *NAmE* ɑːr/ *exclamation* used to express fear, anger, or some other strong emotion（表示恐懼、憤怒等強烈情感）啊：*Aargh—get that cat off the table!* 啊，把那貓從桌上趕走！

aback /əˈbæk/ *adv.*

IDM **be taken aˈback (by sb/sth)** to be shocked or surprised by sb/sth（被…）嚇了一跳；大吃一驚；震驚：*She was completely taken aback by his anger.* 他的憤怒把她嚇了一大跳。 ➲ see also TAKE SB ABACK at TAKE ➲ **SYNONYMS** at SURPRISE

aba·cus /ˈæbəkəs/ *noun* (*pl.* **aba·cuses** /-kəsɪz/) a frame with small balls which slide along wires. It is used as a tool or toy for counting. 算盤

aba·lone /ˌæbəˈləʊni; *NAmE* -ˈloʊ-/ *noun* [C, U] a SHELLFISH that can be eaten and whose shell contains MOTHER-OF-PEARL 鮑魚

aban·don 🔑 **AW** /əˈbændən/ *verb, noun*

■ ***verb*** **1** 🔑 to leave sb, especially sb you are responsible for, with no intention of returning（不顧責任、義務等）離棄，遺棄，拋棄：**~ sb** *The baby had been abandoned by its mother.* 這個嬰兒被母親遺棄了。◇ **~ sb to sth** *The study showed a deep fear among the elderly of being abandoned to the care of strangers.* 研究表明，

老人十分害怕被丟給陌生人照管。**2** to leave a thing or place, especially because it is impossible or dangerous to stay （不得已而）捨棄，丟棄，離開 **SYN** **leave**：**~ sth** *Snow forced many drivers to abandon their vehicles.* 大雪迫使許多駕駛者棄車步行。◇ *He gave the order to* ***abandon ship*** (= to leave the ship because it was sinking). 他下令棄船（因船快要沉沒）。◇ **~ sth to sb/sth** *They had to abandon their lands to the invading forces.* 他們不得不捨棄土地，讓侵略軍佔領。**3** **~ sth** to stop doing sth, especially before it is finished; to stop having sth 中止；放棄；不再有：*They abandoned the match because of rain.* 因為下雨，他們中止了比賽。◇ *She abandoned hope of any reconciliation.* 她對和解已不再抱有希望。**4** to stop supporting or helping sb; to stop believing in sth 停止（支持或幫助）；放棄（信念）：**~ sb** *The country abandoned its political leaders after the war.* 戰後該國人民不再擁護他們的政治領袖。◇ **~ sth** *By 1930 he had abandoned his Marxist principles.* * 1930 年時他已放棄了馬克思主義信念。**5** **~ yourself to sth** (*literary*) to feel an emotion so strongly that you can feel nothing else 陷入，沉湎於（某種情感）：*He abandoned himself to despair.* 他陷入絕望。

■ ***noun*** [U] (*formal*) an uncontrolled way of behaving that shows that sb does not care what other people think 放任；放縱：*He signed cheques with careless abandon.* 他無所顧忌地亂開支票。**IDM** see GAY *adj.*

aban·doned **AW** /əˈbændənd/ *adj.* **1** left and no longer wanted, used or needed 被離棄的；被遺棄的；被拋棄的：*an abandoned car/house* 被拋棄的轎車；棄置的房子 ◇ *The child was found abandoned but unharmed.* 該棄兒被人們發現時安然無恙。**2** (of people or their behaviour 人或行為) wild; not following accepted standards 放縱的；墮落的

aban·don·ment **AW** /əˈbændənmənt/ *noun* [U] (*formal*) **1** the act of leaving a person, thing or place with no intention of returning 離棄；遺棄；拋棄 **2** the act of giving up an idea or stopping an activity with no intention of returning to it 放棄；中止：*the government's abandonment of its new economic policy* 政府對新經濟政策的放棄

abase /əˈbeɪs/ *verb* **~ yourself** (*formal*) to act in a way that shows that you accept sb's power over you 表現卑微；卑躬屈節；屈從 ▸ **abase·ment** *noun* [U]

abashed /əˈbæʃt/ *adj.* [not before noun] embarrassed and ashamed because of sth that you have done 羞愧；窘迫；尷尬 **OPP** **unabashed**

abate /əˈbeɪt/ *verb* [I, T] (*formal*) to become less strong; to make sth less strong （使）減弱，減退，減輕，減少：*The storm showed no signs of abating.* 暴風雨沒有減弱的跡象。◇ **~ sth** *Steps are to be taken to abate pollution.* 將會採取措施減少污染。▸ **abate·ment** *noun* [U]

ab·at·toir /ˈæbətwɑː(r)/ *noun* (*BrE*) = SLAUGHTERHOUSE

abaya /əˈbeɪjə; *NAmE* əˈbaɪjə/ *noun* a full-length piece of clothing worn over other clothes by Arab men or women 阿拉伯罩袍

abba /ˈʌbə/ (also **appa**) *noun* (*IndE*) (especially as a form of address 尤用於稱呼) a father 阿爸；爸爸

ab·bess /ˈæbes/ *noun* a woman who is the head of a CONVENT 女修院院長

abbey /ˈæbi/ *noun* a large church together with a group of buildings in which MONKS or NUNS live or lived in the past （大）隱修院；（曾為大隱修院的）大教堂：*Westminster Abbey* 威斯敏斯特教堂 ◇ *a ruined abbey* 破敗不堪的教堂

abbot /ˈæbət/ *noun* a man who is the head of a MONASTERY or an ABBEY 男修院院長

ab·bre·vi·ate /əˈbriːvieɪt/ *verb* [usually passive] **~ sth (to sth)** to make a word, phrase or name shorter by leaving out letters or using only the first letter of each word 縮略；把詞語、名稱縮寫（成…）**SYN** **shorten**：*the Jet Propulsion Laboratory* (*usually abbreviated to JPL*) 噴氣推進實驗室（通常縮寫成 JPL）▸ **ab·bre·vi·ated** *adj.*：*Where appropriate, abbreviated forms are used.* 適當的地方用縮寫形式。

ab·bre·vi·ation /əˌbriːviˈeɪʃn/ *noun* **1** [C] **~ (of/for sth)** a short form of a word, etc. 略語；縮寫詞；縮寫形式：*What's the abbreviation for 'Saint'?* * Saint 的縮寫形式是什麼？**2** [U] the process of abbreviating sth 縮略；縮寫

ABC /ˌeɪ biː ˈsiː/ *noun, abbr.*

■ ***noun*** [sing.] (*BrE*) (*NAmE* **ABCs** [pl.]) **1** all the letters of the alphabet, especially as they are learnt by children 字母表（尤指兒童學習的全部字母）：*Do you know your ABC?* 你認識所有的字母嗎？**2** the basic facts about a subject （某學科的）基礎知識，入門：*the ABC of gardening* 園藝入門 **IDM** see EASY *adj.*

■ ***abbr.*** **1** American Broadcasting Company (a large national American television company) 美國廣播公司（美國一家全國性的大型電視廣播公司）**2** Australian Broadcasting Corporation (the Australian national public broadcasting company) 澳大利亞廣播公司

ABD /ˌeɪ biː ˈdiː/ *abbr.* (*NAmE*) all but dissertation (having completed all the work for a higher degree except the DISSERTATION)（課業修畢）僅差學位論文即可畢業；僅欠畢業論文：*ABD students may apply.* 僅欠畢業論文的學生可以申請。

ab·di·cate /ˈæbdɪkeɪt/ *verb* **1** [I, T] to give up the position of being king or queen 退位；遜位：*He abdicated in favour of his son.* 他把王位讓給了兒子。◇ **~ sth** *She was forced to abdicate the throne of Spain.* 她被迫讓出西班牙的王位。**2** [T] **~ responsibility/your responsibilities** to fail or refuse to perform a duty 失職；放棄職責 ▸ **ab·di·ca·tion** /ˌæbdɪˈkeɪʃn/ *noun* [U, C]

ab·do·men /ˈæbdəmən/ *noun* **1** the part of the body below the chest that contains the stomach, BOWELS, etc. 腹（部）**2** the end part of an insect's body that is attached to its THORAX （昆蟲的）腹部 ➲ **VISUAL VOCAB** page V13

ab·dom·inal /æbˈdɒmɪnl; *NAmE* -ˈdɑːm-/ *adj., noun*

■ ***adj.*** [only before noun] (*anatomy* 解) relating to or connected with the abdomen 腹部的；肚子的：*abdominal pains* 腹痛

■ ***noun*** **abdominals** (also *informal* **abs**) [pl.] the muscles of the abdomen 腹肌

ab·duct /æbˈdʌkt/ *verb* **~ sb** to take sb away illegally, especially using force 誘拐；劫持；綁架 **SYN** **kidnap** ▸ **ab·duc·tion** /æbˈdʌkʃn/ *noun* [U, C]

ab·duct·ee /ˌæbdʌkˈtiː/ *noun* a person who has been abducted 被劫持者；被綁架者；肉票

ab·duct·or /æbˈdʌktə(r)/ *noun* **1** a person who abducts sb 劫持者；綁架者；綁匪 **2** (also **abˈductor muscle**) (*anatomy* 解) a muscle that moves a body part away from the middle of the body or from another part 展肌 ➲ compare ADDUCTOR

abed /əˈbed/ *adv.* (*old use*) in bed 在牀上

Aber·do·nian /ˌæbəˈdəʊniən; *NAmE* ˌæbərˈdoʊ-/ *noun* a person from Aberdeen in Scotland （蘇格蘭）阿伯丁人，阿伯丁居民 ▸ **Aber·do·nian** *adj.*

ab·er·rant /æˈberənt/ *adj.* (*formal*) not usual or not socially acceptable 違反常規的；反常的；異常的：*aberrant behaviour* 反常行為

ab·er·ra·tion /ˌæbəˈreɪʃn/ *noun* [C, U] (*formal*) a fact, an action or a way of behaving that is not usual, and that may be unacceptable 脫離常規；反常現象；異常行為

abet /əˈbet/ *verb* (**-tt-**) **~ sb** to help or encourage sb to do sth wrong 教唆；唆使；煽動；慫恿：*He was abetted in the deception by his wife.* 他行騙是受了妻子的慫恿。**IDM** see AID *v.*

abey·ance /əˈbeɪəns/ *noun* [U] **IDM** **in abeyance** (*formal*) not being used, or being stopped for a period of time 擱置；暫停使用；暫時中止

ABH /ˌeɪ biː ˈeɪtʃ/ *abbr.* (*BrE, law* 律) ACTUAL BODILY HARM 實際身體傷害（罪）

abhor /əbˈhɔː(r)/ *verb* (**-rr-**) (not used in the progressive tenses 不用於進行時) **~ sth** (*formal*) to hate sth, for example a way of behaving or thinking, especially for moral reasons （尤指因道德原因而）憎恨，厭惡，憎惡 **SYN** **detest, loathe**

A

ab·hor·rence /əbˈhɒrəns; NAmE -ˈhɔːr-; -ˈhɑːr-/ *noun* [U, sing.] (*formal*) a feeling of strong hatred, especially for moral reasons（尤指因道德原因的）憎恨，厭惡，憎惡

ab·hor·rent /əbˈhɒrənt; NAmE -ˈhɔːr-; -ˈhɑːr-/ *adj.* **~ (to sb)** (*formal*) causing hatred, especially for moral reasons（尤指因道德原因）令人憎恨的，令人厭惡的，令人憎惡的 SYN **repugnant**： *Racism is abhorrent to a civilized society.* 文明社會憎惡種族主義。

abide /əˈbaɪd/ *verb* (**abided**, **abided**) HELP In sense 2 **abode** is also used for the past tense and past participle. 作第 2 義時過去時和過去分詞也用 abode。 **1** [T] **can't/couldn't abide sb/sth** to dislike sb/sth so much that you hate having to be with or deal with them（十分厭惡而）不能容忍，無法容忍 SYN **bear, stand**： *I can't abide people with no sense of humour.* 我討厭和沒有幽默感的人打交道。◇ *He couldn't abide the thought of being cooped up in an office.* 一想到關在辦公室裏工作，他就覺得受不了。 **2** [I] **+ adv./prep.** (*old use* or *formal*) to stay or live in a place 逗留；停留；居留；居住： *May joy and peace abide in us all.* 願我們大家都歡樂平安。

PHR V **aˈbide by sth** (*formal*) to accept and act according to a law, an agreement, etc. 遵守，遵循（法律、協議、協定等）： *You'll have to abide by the rules of the club.* 你必須遵守俱樂部的規定。◇ *We will abide by their decision.* 我們願意遵從他們的決定。

abid·ing /əˈbaɪdɪŋ/ *adj.* (*formal*) (of a feeling or belief 感情或信念) lasting for a long time and not changing 持久的；長久的；始終不渝的

abil·ity 🔑 /əˈbɪləti/ *noun* (*pl.* **-ies**)
1 🔑 [sing.] **~ to do sth** the fact that sb/sth is able to do sth 能力： *The system has the ability to run more than one program at the same time.* 該系統能夠同時運行一個以上的程序。◇ *Everyone has the right to good medical care regardless of their ability to pay.* 無論支付能力如何，每個人都有權得到良好的醫療照顧。◇ *A gentle form of exercise will increase your ability to relax.* 和緩的運動鍛煉會提高自我放鬆的能力。 OPP **inability** **2** 🔑 [C, U] a level of skill or intelligence 才能；本領；才智： *Almost everyone has some musical ability.* 幾乎人人都有一些音樂才能。◇ *He was a man of extraordinary abilities.* 他才幹卓著。◇ *students of mixed abilities* 能力各不相同的學生 ◇ *A woman of her ability will easily find a job.* 有她那樣才能的婦女找工作不難。◇ *I try to do my job* ***to the best of my ability*** (= as well as I can). 我盡全力做好我的工作。

-ability, -ibility ➲ -ABLE

abi·ot·ic /ˌeɪbaɪˈɒtɪk; NAmE -ˈɑːtɪk/ *adj.* (*technical* 術語) not involving biology or living things 與生物無關的；非生物的： *abiotic processes* 非生物過程

ab·ject /ˈæbdʒekt/ *adj.* [usually before noun] (*formal*) **1** terrible and without hope 悲慘絕望的；淒慘的： ***abject poverty/misery/failure*** 赤貧；淒慘；慘敗 **2** without any pride or respect for yourself 下賤的；卑躬屈節的；自卑的： *an abject apology* 低聲下氣的道歉 ▸ **ab·ject·ly** *adv.*

ab·jure /əbˈdʒʊə(r); NAmE əbˈdʒʊr/ *verb* **~ sth** (*formal*) to promise publicly that you will give up or reject a belief or a way of behaving 公開保證放棄，聲明放棄（信念、行為、活動） SYN **renounce**

ab·la·tion /əˈbleɪʃn/ *noun* [U] (*geology* 地) the loss of material from a large mass of ice, snow or rock as a result of the action of the sun, wind or rain（冰、雪的）消融；（岩石的）磨蝕

ab·la·tive /ˈæblətɪv/ *noun* (*grammar* 語法) (in some languages 用於某些語言) the form that a noun, a pronoun or an adjective can take to show, for example, who or what sth is done by or where sth comes from（詞的）奪格，離格 ➲ compare ACCUSATIVE, DATIVE, GENITIVE, NOMINATIVE, VOCATIVE ▸ **ab·la·tive** *adj.*

ablaze /əˈbleɪz/ *adj.* [not before noun] **1** burning quickly and strongly 猛烈燃燒： *The whole building was soon ablaze.* 整棟大樓很快就熊熊燃燒起來。◇ *Cars and buses were* ***set ablaze*** *during the riot.* 暴亂中許多輛車和公共汽車被縱火焚燒。 **2** full of bright light or colours 閃耀；發光；明亮；色彩鮮豔： *There were lights still ablaze as they drove up to the house.* 他們駕車到了屋前時，（屋內）燈火仍然通明。◇ **~ with sth** *The trees were ablaze with the colours of autumn.* 樹木披上了絢麗的秋裝。 **3 ~ (with sth)** full of strong emotion or excitement 充滿激情的；情緒激動的： *He turned to her, his eyes ablaze with anger.* 他轉過身來，怒目圓睜瞪着她。

able 🔑 /ˈeɪbl/ *adj.*

> **WORD FAMILY**
> **able** *adj.* (≠ unable)
> **ably** *adv.*
> **ability** *noun* (≠ inability)
> **disabled** *adj.*
> **disability** *noun*

1 🔑 **~ to do sth** (used as a modal verb 用作情態動詞) to have the skill, intelligence, opportunity, etc. needed to do sth 能；能夠： *You must be able to speak French for this job.* 幹這項工作你得會說法語。◇ *A viral illness left her barely able to walk.* 一場病毒引起的疾病使她走路都十分困難。◇ *I didn't feel able to disagree with him.* 我覺得無法不同意他的意見。◇ *Will you be able to come?* 你能來嗎？ OPP **unable** ➲ note at CAN[1] **2** (**abler** /ˈeɪblə(r)/, **ablest** /ˈeɪblɪst/) intelligent; good at sth 有才智的；有才能的；（某方面）擅長的： *the ablest student in the class* 班上最有才華的學生 ◇ *We aim to help the less able in society to lead an independent life.* 我們的宗旨是幫助社會上能力較弱的人獨立生活。 ➲ see also ABLY

-able, -ible *suffix* (in adjectives 構成形容詞) **1** that can or must be 可…的；能…的；應…的： *calculable* 能計算的 ◇ *taxable* 應納稅的 **2** having the quality of 具有…性質的： *fashionable* 時髦的 ◇ *comfortable* 舒適的 ◇ *changeable* 易變的 ▸ **-ability, -ibility** (in nouns 構成名詞)： *capability* 能力 ◇ *responsibility* 責任 **-ably, -ibly** (in adverbs 構成副詞)： *noticeably* 顯著地 ◇ *incredibly* 令人難以置信地

ˌable-ˈbodied *adj.* physically healthy, fit and strong in contrast to sb who is weak or disabled 健康的；健壯的；體格健全的

ˌable ˈseaman *noun* a sailor of lower rank in the British navy（英國海軍）一等水兵

ab·lu·tions /əˈbluːʃnz/ *noun* [pl.] (*formal* or *humorous*) the act of washing yourself 沐浴；淨體（禮）；淨手（禮）

ably /ˈeɪbli/ *adv.* skilfully and well 能幹地： *We were ably assisted by a team of volunteers.* 我們得到一批志願者的大力協助。 ➲ see also ABLE (2)

ABM /ˌeɪ biː ˈem/ *noun* (*CanE*) the abbreviation for 'automated banking machine' 自動櫃員機（全寫為 automated banking machine） ➲ CASH MACHINE

ab·neg·ation /ˌæbnɪˈɡeɪʃn/ *noun* [U] (*formal*) the act of not allowing yourself to have sth that you want; the act of rejecting sth 克制；自制；拒絕；放棄 ▸ **ab·neg·ate** /ˈæbnɪɡeɪt/ *verb* **~ sth**

ab·nor·mal AW /æbˈnɔːml; NAmE -ˈnɔːrml/ *adj.* different from what is usual or expected, especially in a way that is worrying, harmful or not wanted 不正常的；反常的；變態的；畸形的： *abnormal levels of sugar in the blood* 血糖值不正常 ◇ *They thought his behaviour was abnormal.* 他們認為他行為反常。 OPP **normal** ▸ **ab·nor·mal·ly** AW /æbˈnɔːməli; NAmE -ˈnɔːrm-/ *adv.*： *abnormally high blood pressure* 異常高的血壓

ab·nor·mal·ity /ˌæbnɔːˈmæləti; NAmE -nɔːrˈm-/ *noun* (*pl.* **-ies**) [C, U] a feature or characteristic in a person's body or behaviour that is not usual and may be harmful, worrying or cause illness（身體、行為等）不正常，反常，變態，畸形： *abnormalities of the heart* 心臟異常 ◇ ***congenital/foetal abnormality*** 先天性 / 胎兒畸形

Abo /ˈæbəʊ; NAmE ˈæboʊ/ *noun* (*pl.* **-os**) (*AustralE, taboo, informal*) an extremely offensive word for an Aborigine（對澳大利亞土著的蔑稱）土鬼，土包子

aboard /əˈbɔːd; NAmE əˈbɔːrd/ *adv., prep.* on or onto a ship, plane, bus or train 在（船、飛機、公共汽車、火車等）上；上（船、飛機、公共汽車、火車等） SYN **on board**： *We went aboard.* 我們上了船。◇ *He was already aboard the plane.* 他已經登機了。◇ *The plane crashed, killing all 157 passengers aboard.* 飛機墜毀，機上 157 名乘客全部遇難。◇ ***All aboard!*** (= the bus, boat, etc. is leaving soon) 請大家上車（或船等）！（表示馬上就要開了）◇ ***Welcome aboard!*** (= used to welcome passengers or a person joining a new organization, etc.) 歡迎各位乘客！；歡迎加盟（新組織等）！

abode /əˈbəʊd; *NAmE* əˈboʊd/ *noun* [usually sing.] (*formal* or *humorous*) the place where sb lives 住所；家：*homeless people* ***of no fixed abode*** (= with no permanent home) 無家可歸的人（沒有固定居所）◇ *You are most welcome to my humble abode.* 竭誠歡迎光臨寒舍。➲ see also ABIDE (2), RIGHT OF ABODE

abol·ish /əˈbɒlɪʃ; *NAmE* əˈbɑːl-/ *verb* **~ sth** to officially end a law, a system or an institution 廢除，廢止（法律、制度、習俗等）：*This tax should be abolished.* 這種稅應該取消。

abo·li·tion /ˌæbəˈlɪʃn/ *noun* [U] the ending of a law, a system or an institution （法律、制度、習俗等的）廢除，廢止：*the abolition of slavery* 奴隸制的廢除

abo·li·tion·ist /ˌæbəˈlɪʃənɪst/ *noun* a person who is in favour of the abolition of sth 主張廢除…的人

ˈA-bomb *noun* = ATOM BOMB

abom·in·able /əˈbɒmɪnəbl; *NAmE* əˈbɑːm-/ *adj.* extremely unpleasant and causing disgust 令人憎惡的；令人厭惡的；極其討厭的 **SYN** **appalling, disgusting**：*The judge described the attack as an abominable crime.* 法官稱那次襲擊為令人髮指的罪行。◇ *We were served the most abominable coffee.* 給我們喝的是最劣質的咖啡。 ▸ **abom·in·ably** /əˈbɒmɪnəbli; *NAmE* əˈbɑːm-/ *adv.*：*She treated him abominably.* 她待他極其惡劣。

A͵bominable ˈSnowman *noun* = YETI

abom·in·ate /əˈbɒmɪneɪt; *NAmE* əˈbɑːm-/ *verb* (not used in the progressive tenses 不用於進行時) **~ sth/sb** (*formal*) to feel hatred or disgust for sth/sb 憎恨；憎惡；厭惡；極其討厭

abom·in·ation /əˌbɒmɪˈneɪʃn; *NAmE* əˌbɑːm-/ *noun* (*formal*) a thing that causes disgust and hatred, or is considered extremely offensive 令人憎恨的事物；可惡的東西

abo·ri·ginal /ˌæbəˈrɪdʒənl/ *adj., noun*

■ ***adj.*** **1** (usually **Aboriginal**) relating to the original people living in Australia 澳大利亞土著的：*the issue of Aboriginal land rights* 澳大利亞土著土地權問題 **2** relating to the original people, animals, etc. of a place and to a period of time before Europeans arrived （歐洲人到來之前某地區的人、動物等）土著的，土生土長的：*the aboriginal peoples of Canada* 加拿大土著◇ *aboriginal art/culture* 土著藝術／文化

■ ***noun*** (usually **Aboriginal**) a member of a race of people who were the original people living in a country, especially Australia （尤指澳大利亞的）土著，土人 ➲ see also KOORI

abo·ri·gine /ˌæbəˈrɪdʒəni/ *noun* **1** a member of a race of people who were the original people living in a country 原住居民；土著；土人 **2** **Aborigine** a member of the race of people who were the original people of Australia 澳大利亞土著 ➲ see also KOORI

abort /əˈbɔːt; *NAmE* əˈbɔːrt/ *verb* **1** [T] **~ sth** to end a PREGNANCY early in order to prevent a baby from developing and being born alive 使流產：*to* ***abort a child/pregnancy/foetus*** 使嬰兒流產；終止妊娠；墮胎 **2** [I] (*technical* 術語) to give birth to a child or young animal too early for it to survive 流產；小產：*The virus can cause pregnant animals to abort.* 這種病毒可能導致懷孕動物流產。➲ see also MISCARRY (1) **3** [I, T, often passive] to end or cause sth to end before it has been completed, especially because it is likely to fail （使）夭折，中止（尤指很可能失敗的事情）：(*computing* 計) *If the wrong password is given the program aborts.* 如果鍵入錯誤的密碼，程序即會中止。◇ **~ sth** *We had no option but to abort the mission.* 我們毫無選擇，只有取消這項任務。◇ *The plan was aborted at the last minute.* 計劃在最後一刻取消了。

abor·tion /əˈbɔːʃn; *NAmE* əˈbɔːrʃn/ *noun* **1** [U] the deliberate ending of a PREGNANCY at an early stage 人工流產；墮胎；打胎：*to* ***support/oppose abortion*** 支持／反對墮胎◇ *a woman's right to abortion* 婦女做人工流產的權利◇ *abortion laws* 墮胎法◇ *I've always been anti-abortion.* 我一直反對墮胎。**2** [C] a medical operation to end a PREGNANCY at an early stage 人工流產手術；墮胎手術：*She decided to* ***have an abortion.*** 她決定做人工流產。**SYN** **termination** ➲ compare MISCARRIAGE

abor·tion·ist /əˈbɔːʃənɪst; *NAmE* əˈbɔːrʃ-/ *noun* a person who performs abortions, especially illegally （尤指非法）為人墮胎者

abort·ive /əˈbɔːtɪv; *NAmE* əˈbɔːrtɪv/ *adj.* (*formal*) (of an action 行動) not successful; failed 不成功的；失敗的 **SYN** **unsuccessful**：*an abortive military coup* 一次流產的軍事政變◇ *abortive attempts to divert the course of the river* 河流改道不遂的嘗試

abound /əˈbaʊnd/ *verb* [I] to exist in great numbers or quantities 大量存在；有許多：*Stories about his travels abound.* 有關他遊歷的故事多得很。

PHR V **aˈbound with/in sth** to have sth in great numbers or quantities 有大量；富於：*The lakes abound with fish.* 這些湖泊盛產魚。➲ see also ABUNDANCE, ABUNDANT

about 🔑 /əˈbaʊt/ *adv., prep., adj.*

■ ***adv.*** **1** 🔑 a little more or less than; a little before or after 大約；左右 **SYN** **approximately**：*It costs about $10.* 這大約要花 10 元錢。◇ *They waited (for) about an hour.* 他們等了一小時左右。◇ *He arrived (at) about ten.* 他是十點鐘左右到的。**2** 🔑 nearly; very close to 將近；幾乎：*I'm just about ready.* 我就要準備好了。◇ *This is about the best we can hope for.* 這差不多是我們所能希望的最好結果。**3** 🔑 (*especially BrE*) in many directions; here and there 到處；處處；各處：*The children were rushing about in the garden.* 孩子們在花園裏跑來跑去。**4** 🔑 (*especially BrE*) in no particular order; in various places 凌亂地；四處；到處：*Her books were lying about on the floor.* 她的書在地板上東一本西一本地放着。**5** (*especially BrE*) doing nothing in particular 閒着；無所事事：*People were standing about in the road.* 人們在路上閒站着。**6** (*especially BrE*) able to be found in a place 在某地；附近；周圍：*There was nobody about.* 附近沒有人。◇ *There's a lot of flu about.* 這一帶流感肆虐。**7** (*technical* 術語 or *formal*) facing the opposite direction 向後轉；掉轉方向；掉頭：*He brought the ship about.* 他掉轉船頭。➲ note at AROUND

IDM **that's about ˈall | that's about ˈit** used to say that you have finished telling sb about sth and there is nothing to add 我要說的就是這些；我的話完了：*'Anything else?' 'No, that's about it for now.'* "還有什麼要說的嗎？" "沒有了，現在我要說的就是這些。" ➲ more at JUST *adv.*, OUT *adv.*

■ ***prep.*** **1** 🔑 on the subject of sb/sth; in connection with sb/sth 關於；對於：*a book about flowers* 一本關於花卉的書◇ *Tell me* ***all about*** *it.* 把這件事全部告訴我。◇ *What's she so angry about?* 她為什麼生這麼大的氣？◇ *There's something strange about him.* 他有點怪。◇ *I don't know what you're* ***on about*** (= talking about). 我不懂你在談什麼。◇ *There's nothing you can do about it now.* 現在你對此毫無辦法。**2** 🔑 used to describe the purpose or an aspect of sth 目的是；為了；涉及…方面：*Movies are* ***all about*** *making money these days.* 當今電影就是只顧賺錢。◇ ***What was all that about?*** (= what was the reason for what has just happened?) 這到底是怎麼回事？**3** 🔑 busy with sth; doing sth 忙於；從事於：*Everywhere people were going about their daily business.* 無論哪裏，人們都在忙着幹日常工作。◇ *And* ***while you're about it*** … (= while you're doing that) 在你幹這件事的同時，順便… **4** (*especially BrE*) in many directions in a place; here and there 在…到處；在…各處：*We wandered about the town for an hour or so.* 我們在城裏到處遊逛了一個小時左右。◇ *He looked about the room.* 他在房間裏四下看了看。**5** (*especially BrE*) in various parts of a place; here and there 在…四處：*The papers were strewn about the room.* 房間裏四處亂扔着文件。**6** (*especially BrE*) next to a place or person; in the area mentioned 在…附近；在…地方：*She's somewhere about the office.* 她在辦公室裏某處。**7** (*literary*) surrounding sb/sth 圍繞：*She wore a shawl about her shoulders.* 她披了一件披肩。

IDM **how/what about …?** **1** 🔑 used when asking for information about sb/sth （詢問消息）怎麼樣，如何：

How about Ruth? Have you heard from her? 露絲怎麼樣了？你有她的消息嗎？◇ *I'm having fish. What about you?* 我吃魚，你呢？ **2** used to make a suggestion（建議時説）怎麼樣，好嗎：*How about going for a walk?* 去散散步怎麼樣？◇ (*especially NAmE*) *How about we go for a walk?* 我們去散散步怎麼樣？◇ *What about a break?* 休息一下如何？

■ ***adj.***

IDM **be about to do sth** to be close to doing sth; to be going to do sth very soon 即將，行將，正要（做某事）：*I was just about to ask you the same thing.* 我剛才正要問你同一件事情。 **not be about to do sth** to not be willing to do sth; to not intend to do sth 不願，無意（做某事）：*I've never done any cooking and I'm not about to start now.* 我從來沒有做過飯，也不想從現在開始做起來。

Language Bank 用語庫

about

Saying what a text is about 描述文章的內容

- The book **is about** homeless people in the cities. 這本書寫的是城市中無家可歸的人們。
- The report **deals with** the issue of homelessness in London. 這篇報道是關於倫敦的無家可歸問題。
- The writer **discusses** the problems faced by homeless people. 作者討論了無家可歸者面臨的種種問題。
- The article **presents an overview of** the issues surrounding homelessness. 這篇文章概述了有關無家可歸的種種問題。
- The novel **explores** the theme of friendship among homeless people. 這部小説探究了無家可歸的人之間的友誼這個主題。
- The first chapter **examines** the relationship between homelessness and drug addiction. 第一章考察了無家可歸與吸毒成癮之間的關係。
- The paper **considers** the question of why so many young people become homeless. 這篇論文論述了為何如此多的年輕人變得無家可歸的問題。

a,bout-'turn (*BrE*) (also **a,bout-'face** *NAmE, BrE*) *noun* [sing.] a complete change of opinion, plan or behaviour（意見、計劃、行為的）徹底改變：*The government did an about-turn over nuclear energy.* 政府對核能的態度來了個 180 度的大轉變。

above /ə'bʌv/ *prep., adv., adj.*

■ ***prep.*** **1** at or to a higher place or position than sth/sb 在（或向）…上面：*The water came above our knees.* 水淹過了我們的膝蓋。◇ *We were flying above the clouds.* 我們在雲層上面飛行。◇ *the people in the apartment above mine* 我樓上那套公寓裏的人們◇ *A captain in the navy ranks above a captain in the army.* 海軍的 captain（上校）軍銜比陸軍的 captain（上尉）高。◇ *They finished the year six places above their local rivals.* 這一年結束，他們的排名比當地競爭對手超前六個名次。 **2** more than sth; greater in number, level or age than sb/sth（數目、數量、水平、年齡）超過，多於，大於：*Inflation is above 6%.* 通貨膨脹超過 6%。◇ *Temperatures have been above average.* 氣溫一直比平均溫度高。◇ *We cannot accept children above the age of 10.* 我們不能接受 10 歲以上的兒童。 **3** of greater importance or of higher quality than sb/sth（重要性、質量）超過，勝過：*I rate her above most other players of her age.* 我認為她優於大多數同齡參賽者。 **4** too good or too honest to do sth（因善良或誠實正直而）不至於，不屑於（做某事）：*She's not above lying when it suits her.* 她在適當時機還是會説謊的。◇ *He's above suspicion* (= he is completely trusted). 他無可置疑。 **5** (of a sound 聲音) louder or clearer than another sound（音量或清晰度）超過（另一種聲音）：*I couldn't hear her above the noise of the traffic.* 交通嘈雜，我聽不見她的聲音。

IDM **above 'all** most important of all; especially 最重要的是；尤其是：*Above all, keep in touch.* 最要緊的是保持聯繫。 ➲ LANGUAGE BANK at EMPHASIS **a'bove yourself** (*disapproving*) having too high an opinion of yourself 自高自大；妄自尊大 ➲ more at OVER *prep.*

■ ***adv.*** **1** at or to a higher place 在（或向）上面；在（或向）較高處：*Put it on the shelf above.* 把它放到上面的擱板上。◇ *Seen from above the cars looked tiny.* 從高處往下看，車輛顯得很小。◇ *They were acting on instructions from above* (= from sb in a higher position of authority). 他們是在按照上級的指示辦事。 **2** greater in number, level or age（數目、數量、水平、年齡）超過，更多，更大：*increases of 5% and above* 增加 5% 或以上◇ *A score of 70 or above will get you an 'A'.* * 70 分或以上就可以得"優"。◇ *children aged 12 and above* * 12 歲或以上的孩子 **3** earlier in sth written or printed 上文；前文：*As was stated above …* 如上所述…◇ *See above, page 97.* 見前文，第 97 頁。

■ ***adj.*** [only before noun] mentioned or printed previously in a letter, book, etc. 前文述及的；上述的：*Please write to us at the above address.* 請按上述地址來函。 ▸ **the above** *noun* [sing.+sing./pl. v.] : *Please notify us if the above is not correct.* 如果上面所説的不正確，請通知我們。◇ *All the above* (= people mentioned above) *have passed the exam.* 以上各人都通過了考試。

Which Word? 詞語辨析

above / over

- **Above** and **over** can both be used to describe a position higher than something. * above 和 over 均可表示位置高於…或在…上：*They built a new room above/over the garage.* 他們在汽車房上面加建了一個房間。 When you are talking about movement from one side of something to the other, you can only use **over**. 表示從某物的一邊移至另一邊只能用 over：*They jumped over the stream.* 他們跳過了小溪。 **Over** can also mean 'covering'. * over 亦可表示覆蓋着：*He put a blanket over the sleeping child.* 他把毯子蓋在睡着了的孩子身上。
- **Above** and **over** can also mean 'more than'. **Above** is used in relation to a minimum level or a fixed point. * above 和 over 亦可表示多於。above 與最低限度或某固定點關聯：*2 000 feet above sea level* 海拔 2 000 英尺◇ *Temperatures will not rise above zero tonight.* 今天夜間的溫度不會高於零度。 **Over** is used with numbers, ages, money and time. * over 與數目、年齡、金錢和時間連用：*He's over 50.* 他已年過半百。◇ *It costs over £100.* 這個值 100 英鎊以上。◇ *We waited over 2 hours.* 我們等了兩個多小時。

a,bove 'board *adj., adv.* legal and honest; in a legal and honest way 合法而坦誠（的）；開誠佈公（的）：*Don't worry; the deal was completely above board.* 別擔心，交易是完全合法的。 **ORIGIN** If card players keep their hands above the table (the board), other players can see what they are doing. 源於紙牌遊戲。如果玩牌者將手放在桌上，其動作就會被其他玩牌者看得一清二楚。

a,bove-'mentioned *adj.* [only before noun] mentioned or named earlier in the same letter, book, etc. 前文述及的；上述的

a,bove-the-'fold *adj.* in a position where it is seen first, for example on the top half of the front page of a newspaper or in the part of a web page that you see first when you open it（報紙頭版、網頁等）居於上端的，位置明顯的，第一眼看到的：*above-the-fold images* 位置醒目的圖像◇ *The company logo must be placed in an above-the-fold position.* 公司標誌必須放在顯眼的位置。 ➲ compare BELOW-THE-FOLD **IDM** see FOLD *n.*

abra·ca·dabra /,æbrəkə'dæbrə/ *exclamation* a word that people say when they do a magic trick, in order to make it successful（表演魔術、施魔法時所唸的咒語）阿布拉卡達布拉

ab·rade /ə'breɪd/ *verb* **~ sth** (*technical* 術語) to rub the surface of sth, such as rock or skin, and damage it or make it rough 磨損（岩石等）；擦傷（皮膚等）

A

ab·ra·sion /ə'breɪʒn/ *noun* (*technical* 術語) **1** [C] a damaged area of the skin where it has been rubbed against sth hard and rough （皮膚、表皮）擦傷處；（表層）磨損處：*He suffered cuts and abrasions to the face.* 他的臉上有許多傷口和擦傷。 **2** [U] damage to a surface caused by rubbing sth very hard against it 磨損：*Diamonds have extreme resistance to abrasion.* 鑽石極抗磨損。

abra·sive /ə'breɪsɪv/ *adj., noun*
■ ***adj.*** **1** an **abrasive** substance is rough and can be used to clean a surface or to make it smooth 有研磨作用的；研磨的：*abrasive kitchen cleaners* 廚房擦洗去污劑 **2** (of a person or their manner 人或行為方式、態度) rude and unkind; acting in a way that may hurt other people's feelings 生硬粗暴的；粗魯的；傷人感情的 ▸ **abra·sive·ly** *adv.* **abra·sive·ness** *noun* [U]
■ ***noun*** a substance used for cleaning surfaces or for making them smooth （用來擦洗表面或使表面光滑的）磨料

abreast /ə'brest/ *adv.* next to sb/sth and facing the same way 並列；並排；並肩：*cycling two abreast* 兩輛自行車並排而行 ◇ **~ of sb/sth** *A police car **drew abreast** of us and signalled us to stop.* 一輛警車開過來與我們並列，示意我們停下來。
IDM **keep abreast of sth** to make sure that you know all the most recent facts about a subject 瞭解最新情況；跟上（某事物的發展）：*It is almost impossible to keep abreast of all the latest developments in computing.* 要跟上計算機領域所有最新的發展幾乎不可能。

abridge /ə'brɪdʒ/ *verb* **~ sth** to make a book, play, etc. shorter by leaving parts out 刪節，節略（書籍、劇本等） ▸ **abridged** *adj.*: *an **abridged edition/version*** 節版；節本 **OPP** **unabridged** **abridge·ment** (also **abridg·ment**) *noun* [U, C]

abroad 0‑ᵂ /ə'brɔːd/ *adv.* (*especially BrE*)
1 0‑ᵂ in or to a foreign country 在國外；到國外：*to **be/go/travel/live abroad*** 在外國；出國；到國外旅行；在外國居住 ◇ *She worked abroad for a year.* 她在國外工作了一年。◇ *imports of cheap food from abroad* 國外廉價食物的進口 ◇ *He was famous, both **at home and abroad*** (= in his own country and in other countries). 他享譽國內外。 **2** (*formal*) being talked about or felt by many people 廣為流傳：*There was news abroad that a change was coming.* 盛傳即將有一個變動。 **3** (*old use*) outside; outdoors 在室外；到室外；戶外

ab·ro·gate /'æbrəgeɪt/ *verb* **~ sth** (*technical* 術語) to officially end a law, an agreement, etc. 廢除，廢止，撤銷（法律、協議等） **SYN** **repeal** ▸ **ab·ro·ga·tion** /ˌæbrə'geɪʃn/ *noun* [U]

ab·rupt /ə'brʌpt/ *adj.* **1** sudden and unexpected, often in an unpleasant way 突然的；意外的：*an **abrupt change/halt/departure*** 突然改變；驟然停頓；拂袖而去 **2** speaking or acting in a way that seems unfriendly and rude; not taking time to say more than is necessary （言語、行為）粗魯的，莽撞的，唐突的；生硬的 **SYN** **brusque**, **curt**：*an abrupt manner* 唐突的舉止 ◇ *She was very abrupt with me in our meeting.* 我們會面時，她跟我說話非常生硬。 ▸ **ab·rupt·ly** *adv.* **ab·rupt·ness** *noun* [U]

ABS /ˌeɪ biː 'es/ *abbr.* anti-lock braking system 防抱死裝置 ➲ see also ANTI-LOCK

abs /æbz/ *noun* [pl.] (*informal*) = ABDOMINALS *n.*

ab·scess /'æbses/ *noun* a swollen and infected area on your skin or in your body, full of a thick yellowish liquid (called PUS) 膿腫

ab·scissa /æb'sɪsə/ (*pl.* **ab·scissae** /-siː/ or **ab·scissas**) *noun* (*mathematics* 數) the COORDINATE that gives the distance along the horizontal AXIS 橫坐標 ➲ compare ORDINATE

ab·scond /əb'skɒnd; *NAmE* əb'skɑːnd/ *verb* [I] **1 ~ (from sth)** to escape from a place that you are not allowed to leave without permission 逃走；逃遁 **2 ~ (with sth)** to leave secretly and take with you sth, especially money, that does not belong to you （攜款）潛逃：*He absconded with the company funds.* 他捲走公司的資金潛逃了。

ab·seil /'æbseɪl/ (*BrE*) (*NAmE* **rap·pel**) *verb* [I] **~ (down, off, etc. sth)** to go down a steep CLIFF or rock while attached to a rope, pushing against the slope or rock with your feet 繞繩下降（用繩纏繞着身體，雙腳蹬陡坡或峭壁自己放繩下滑） ➲ VISUAL VOCAB page V49 ▸ **ab·seil** (*BrE*) (*NAmE* **rap·pel**) *noun*

ab·sence 0‑ᵂ /'æbsəns/ *noun*
1 0‑ᵂ [U, C] the fact of sb being away from a place where they are usually expected to be; the occasion or period of time when sb is away 缺席；不在：*The decision was made **in my absence*** (= while I was not there). 這個決定是我不在的時候作出的。◇ *We did not receive any news during his long absence.* 我們在他長期離開的時候沒有得到一點消息。◇ **~ from** … *absence from work* 缺勤 ◇ *repeated absences from school* 一再缺課 ➲ see also LEAVE **2** 0‑ᵂ [U] the fact of sb/sth not existing or not being available; a lack of sth 不存在；缺乏：*The case was dismissed **in the absence of** any definite proof.* 此案因缺乏確鑿證據而不予受理。◇ *the absence of any women on the board of directors* 董事會成員中沒有婦女的現象 **OPP** **presence**
IDM ˌ**absence makes the heart grow** ˈ**fonder** (*saying*) used to say that when you are away from sb that you love, you love them even more 不相見，倍思念 ➲ more at CONSPICUOUS

ab·sent 0‑ᵂ *adj., verb*
■ ***adj.*** /'æbsənt/ **1** 0‑ᵂ **~ (from …)** not in a place because of illness, etc. 缺席；不在：*to be absent from work* 缺勤 **OPP** **present** **2** 0‑ᵂ **~ (from sth)** not present in sth 不存在；缺少：*Love was totally absent from his childhood.* 他童年時根本沒有受到疼愛。 **OPP** **present** **3** showing that you are not really looking at or thinking about what is happening around you 心不在焉的；出神的：*an absent expression* 心不在焉的神情 ➲ see also ABSENTLY
■ ***verb*** /æb'sent/ **~ yourself (from sth)** (*formal*) to not go to or be in a place where you are expected to be 缺席；不參加；不在：*He had absented himself from the office for the day.* 這一天他沒有去辦公室上班。

ab·sen·tee /ˌæbsən'tiː/ *noun* a person who is not at a place where they were expected to be 缺席者；缺勤者；缺課者

ˌ**absentee** ˈ**ballot** (*NAmE*) (*BrE* ˈ**postal vote**) *noun* a vote in an election that you can send when you cannot be present 郵寄的選票；郵寄投票

ab·sen·tee·ism /ˌæbsən'tiːɪzəm/ *noun* [U] the fact of being frequently away from work or school, especially without good reasons （經常性無故的）曠工，曠課

ˌ**absentee** ˈ**landlord** *noun* a person who rents their property to sb, but does not live in it and rarely visits it 在外業主，在外地主（不在產業內居住也很少來看管）

ab·sen·tia ➲ IN ABSENTIA

ab·sent·ly /'æbsəntli/ *adv.* in a way that shows you are not looking at or thinking about what is happening around you 心不在焉地；出神地：*He nodded absently, his attention absorbed by the screen.* 他全神注視着屏幕，只是心不在焉地點了點頭。

ˌ**absent-**ˈ**minded** *adj.* tending to forget things, perhaps because you are not thinking about what is around you, but about sth else 健忘的；心不在焉的 **SYN** **forgetful** ▸ ˌ**absent-**ˈ**minded·ly** *adv.* ˌ**absent-**ˈ**minded·ness** *noun* [U]

ab·sinthe /'æbsɪnθ/ *noun* [U] a very strong green alcoholic drink that tastes of ANISEED 苦艾酒（帶茴香味的綠色烈性酒）

ab·so·lute 0‑ᵂ /'æbsəluːt/ *adj., noun*
■ ***adj.*** **1** 0‑ᵂ total and complete 完全的；全部的；絕對的：*a class for absolute beginners* 零起點班 ◇ *absolute confidence/trust/silence/truth* 充滿信心；絕對信任；萬籟俱寂；絕對真實 ◇ *'You're wrong,' she said with absolute certainty.* "你錯了。"她斬釘截鐵地說。 **2** 0‑ᵂ [only before noun] used, especially in spoken English, to give emphasis to what you are saying （英語口語中尤用以強調）道地的，確實的，十足的：*There's absolute rubbish*

on television tonight. 今晚的電視節目簡直糟糕透頂。◇ *He must earn an absolute fortune.* 他準是賺了一大筆錢。**3** definite and without any doubt or confusion 肯定的；無疑的；明確的：*There was no absolute proof.* 沒有確鑿的證據。◇ *He taught us that the laws of physics were absolute.* 他教導我們說，物理定律是確實存在的。◇ *The divorce became absolute last week.* 離婚在上週已成定局。➲ see also DECREE ABSOLUTE **4** not limited or restricted 不受限制的；不受約束的：***absolute power/authority*** 無上權力；絕對權威 ◇ *an* ***absolute ruler/monarchy*** (= one with no limit to their power) 獨裁統治者；專制君主 **5** existing or measured independently and not in relation to sth else 獨立的；絕對的：*Although prices are falling* ***in absolute terms****, energy is still expensive.* 儘管能源的絕對售價在下降，但仍然昂貴。◇ *Beauty cannot be measured by any absolute standard.* 美是不可能用任何絕對標準來衡量的。➲ compare RELATIVE *adj.*

■ ***noun*** an idea or a principle that is believed to be true or valid in any circumstances 絕對真理（指思想或原理）：*Right and wrong are, for her, moral absolutes.* 她認為，是與非是道德上的絕對準則。

ab·so·lute·ly 🗝 /ˈæbsəluːtli/ *adv.*
1 🗝 used to emphasize that sth is completely true（強調真實無誤）絕對地，完全地：*You're absolutely right.* 你完全正確。◇ *He made it absolutely clear.* 他把此事講得一清二楚。**2** 🗝 **absolutely no ..., absolutely nothing** used to emphasize sth negative 絕對不；完全沒有：*She did absolutely no work.* 她一點活兒也沒有幹。◇ *There's absolutely nothing more the doctors can do.* 醫生的確再也無計可施了。**3** 🗝 used with adjectives or verbs that express strong feelings or extreme qualities to mean 'extremely' 極其：*I was absolutely furious with him.* 我被他氣死了。◇ *She absolutely adores you.* 她極為崇拜你。◇ *He's an absolutely brilliant cook.* 他的廚藝精湛至極。**4** 🗝 /ˌæbsəˈluːtli/ used to emphasize that you agree with sb, or to give sb permission to do sth（強調同意或允許）當然，對極了：*'They could have told us, couldn't they?' 'Absolutely!'* "他們本來可以告訴我們的，不是嗎？" "當然！" ◇ *'Can we leave a little early?' 'Absolutely!'* "我們可以早一點離開嗎？" "完全可以！" **5** 🗝 **absolutely not** used to emphasize that you strongly disagree with sb, or to refuse permission（強調很不同意或不允許）當然不，絕對不行：*'Was it any good?' 'No, absolutely not.'* "那有什麼好處嗎？" "絕對沒有。"

ˌabsolute maˈjority *noun* more than half of the total number of votes or winning candidates 絕對多數（指超過半數的選票或競選席位）

ˌabsolute ˈtemperature *noun* [U, C] temperature measured from absolute zero in degrees KELVIN 絕對溫度

ˌabsolute ˈzero *noun* [U] the lowest temperature that is thought to be possible 絕對零度

ab·so·lu·tion /ˌæbsəˈluːʃn/ *noun* [U] (especially in the Christian Church 尤指基督教中的) a formal statement that a person is forgiven for what he or she has done wrong 赦罪；赦免；解罪

ab·so·lut·ism /ˈæbsəluːtɪzəm/ *noun* [U] **1** a political system in which a ruler or government has total power at all times 專制制度；專制政體 **2** belief in a political, religious or moral principle which is thought to be true in all circumstances（政治、宗教、道德上的）絕對主義，絕對論，絕對原則 ▸ **ab·so·lut·ist** *noun, adj.*

ab·solve /əbˈzɒlv; *NAmE* əbˈzɑːlv/ *verb (formal)* **1 ~ sb (of/from sth)** to state formally that sb is not guilty or responsible for sth 宣告…無罪；免除…的責任：*The court absolved him of all responsibility for the accident.* 法院宣告他對該事故不負任何責任。**2 ~ sb (from/of sth)** to give ABSOLUTION to sb 赦免…的罪：*I absolve you from all your sins.* 我赦免你所有的罪過。

ab·sorb 🗝 /əbˈsɔːb; -ˈzɔːb; *NAmE* -ˈsɔːrb; -ˈzɔːrb/ *verb*
▸ **LIQUID/GAS** 液體；氣體 **1** 🗝 to take in a liquid, gas or other substance from the surface or space around 吸收（液體、氣體等）：**~ sth** *Plants absorb carbon dioxide from the air.* 植物吸收空氣中的二氧化碳。◇ **~ sth into sth** *The cream is easily absorbed into the skin.* 這種乳霜皮膚易吸收。
▸ **MAKE PART OF STH LARGER** 使併入 **2** [often passive] to make sth smaller become part of sth larger 使併入；吞併；同化：**~ sth** *The country simply cannot absorb this influx of refugees.* 這個國家實在沒有能力接納這麼多湧入的難民。◇ **~ sth into sth** *The surrounding small towns have been absorbed into the city.* 四周的小城鎮已併入這座城市。
▸ **INFORMATION** 信息 **3** 🗝 **~ sth** to take sth into the mind and learn or understand it 理解；掌握 **SYN take in**：*It's a lot of information to absorb all at once.* 要一下子消化這些資料，真是很多。
▸ **INTEREST SB** 引起興趣 **4 ~ sb** to interest sb very much so that they pay no attention to anything else 吸引全部注意力；使全神貫注 **SYN engross**：*This work had absorbed him for several years.* 這項工作曾使他沉迷了好幾年。
▸ **HEAT/LIGHT/ENERGY** 熱；光；能 **5 ~ sth** to take in and keep heat, light, energy, etc. instead of reflecting it 吸收（熱、光、能等）：*Black walls absorb a lot of heat during the day.* 黑色牆壁在白天吸收大量的熱。
▸ **SHOCK/IMPACT** 震動；撞擊 **6 ~ sth** to reduce the effect of a blow, hit, etc. 減輕（打擊、碰擊等的）作用：*This tennis racket absorbs shock on impact.* 這款網球拍能減輕撞擊所產生的劇烈震動。➲ see also SHOCK ABSORBER
▸ **MONEY/TIME/CHANGES** 金錢；時間；變化 **7 ~ sth** to use up a large supply of sth, especially money or time 耗費，耗去（大量金錢、時間等）：*The new proposals would absorb $80 billion of the federal budget.* 這些新提案將耗費 800 億元聯邦政府預算。**8 ~ sth** to deal with changes, effects, costs, etc. 承受，承擔，對付（變化、結果、費用等）：*The company is unable to absorb such huge losses.* 公司無法承受如此巨大的損失。

ab·sorb·able /əbˈsɔːbəbl; -ˈzɔːb-; *NAmE* -ˈsɔːrb-; -ˈzɔːrb-/ *adj.* able to be absorbed, especially into the body 可吸收的；能被身體吸收的：*absorbable gases* 可吸收的氣體

ab·sor·bance /əbˈsɔːbəns; -ˈzɔːb-; *NAmE* -ˈsɔːrb-; -ˈzɔːrb-/ *noun* (*physics* 物) the ability of a substance to absorb light（光）吸收度；吸光度

ab·sorbed /əbˈsɔːbd; -ˈzɔːbd; *NAmE* -ˈsɔːrbd; -ˈzɔːrbd/ *adj.* [not usually before noun] **~ in sth/sb** very interested in sth/sb so that you are not paying attention to anything else 被…吸引住；專心致志；全神貫注：*She seemed totally absorbed in her book.* 她好像完全被這本書迷住了。

ab·sorb·ent /əbˈsɔːbənt; -ˈzɔːb-; *NAmE* -ˈsɔːrb-; -ˈzɔːrb-/ *adj.* able to take in sth easily, especially liquid 易吸收（液體等）的：***absorbent paper/materials*** 吸水紙；吸收性材料 ▸ **ab·sorb·ency** /-ənsi/ *noun* [U]

ab·sorb·ing /əbˈsɔːbɪŋ; -ˈzɔːb-; *NAmE* -ˈsɔːrb-; -ˈzɔːrb-/ *adj.* interesting and enjoyable and holding your attention completely 十分吸引人的；引人入勝的；精彩的：*an absorbing book/game* 一本引人入勝的書；一場極有趣的遊戲 ➲ **SYNONYMS** at INTERESTING

ab·sorp·tion /əbˈsɔːpʃn; -ˈzɔːp-; *NAmE* -ˈsɔːrp-; -ˈzɔːrp-/ *noun* [U] **1** the process of a liquid, gas or other substance being taken in（液體、氣體等的）吸收：*Vitamin D is necessary to aid the absorption of calcium from food.* 從食物中吸取鈣需靠維生素 D 的幫助。**2** the process of a smaller group, country, etc. becoming part of a larger group or country 併入；同化：*the absorption of immigrants into the host country* 移民融入移居國 **3 ~ (in sth)** the fact of sb being very interested in sth so that it takes all their attention 專心致志；全神貫注；着迷：*His work suffered because of his total absorption in sport.* 他痴迷於體育運動而影響了工作。

ab·stain /əbˈsteɪn/ *verb* [I] **1 ~ (from sth)** to choose not to use a vote, either in favour of or against sth（投票時）棄權：*Ten people voted in favour, five against and two abstained.* 十人投票贊成，五人反對，兩人棄權。**2 ~ (from sth)** to decide not to do or have sth, especially sth you like or enjoy, because it is bad for your health or considered morally wrong 戒；戒除：*to abstain from alcohol/sex/drugs* 戒酒；禁慾；戒毒 **3 ~ (from sth)** (*IndE*) to stay away from sth 離開；迴避：*The workers who abstained from work yesterday have been suspended.*

昨天曠工的工人被暫時停職。➲ see also ABSTENTION, ABSTINENCE

ab·stain·er /əbˈsteɪnə(r)/ *noun* **1** a person who chooses not to vote either in favour of or against sth（投票）棄權者 **2** a person who never drinks alcohol 滴酒不沾的人

ab·ste·mi·ous /əbˈstiːmiəs/ *adj.* (*formal*) not allowing yourself to have much food or alcohol, or to do things that are enjoyable 飲食有度的；有節制的

ab·sten·tion /əbˈstenʃn/ *noun* **1** [C, U] **~ (from sth)** an act of choosing not to use a vote either in favour of or against sth 棄權（不投票）：*The voting was 15 in favour, 3 against and 2 abstentions.* 表決結果是 15 人贊成，3 人反對，2 人棄權。 **2** [U] (*formal*) the act of not allowing yourself to have or do sth enjoyable or sth that is considered bad 戒；戒除 ➲ see also ABSTAIN

ab·stin·ence /ˈæbstɪnəns/ *noun* [U] **~ (from sth)** (*formal*) the practice of not allowing yourself sth, especially food, alcoholic drinks or sex, for moral, religious or health reasons（因道德、宗教或健康原因對飲食、酒、色等的）節制；禁慾：*total abstinence from strong drink* 戒絕烈性酒 ➲ see also ABSTAIN

ab·stin·ent /ˈæbstɪnənt/ *adj.* not allowing yourself sth, especially alcoholic drinks, for moral, religious or health reasons（因道德、宗教或健康原因對酒等）節制的；禁慾的

ab·stract **AW** *adj., noun, verb*

■ ***adj.*** /ˈæbstrækt/ **1** based on general ideas and not on any particular real person, thing or situation 抽象的（與個別情況相對）；純理論的：***abstract knowledge/principles*** 理論知識；抽象原理 ◇ *The research shows that pre-school children are capable of thinking in abstract terms.* 研究顯示，學前兒童具有抽象思維的能力。➲ compare CONCRETE *adj.* (2) **2** existing in thought or as an idea but not having a physical reality 抽象的（與具體經驗相對）：*We may talk of beautiful things but beauty itself is abstract.* 我們儘可談論美的事物，但美本身卻是抽象的。 **3** (of art 藝術) not representing people or things in a realistic way, but expressing the artist's ideas about them 抽象（派）的 ➲ compare FIGURATIVE (2), REPRESENTATIONAL (1) ▸ **ab·stract·ly** **AW** *adv.*

■ ***noun*** /ˈæbstrækt/ **1** an abstract work of art 抽象派藝術作品 **2** a short piece of writing containing the main ideas in a document（文獻等的）摘要，概要 **SYN** **summary**

IDM **in the ˈabstract** in a general way, without referring to a particular real person, thing or situation 抽象地；理論上

■ ***verb*** /æbˈstrækt/ **1 ~ sth (from sth)** to remove sth from somewhere 把…抽象出；提取；抽取；分離：*She abstracted the main points from the argument.* 她把論據概括成要點。◇ *a plan to abstract 8 million gallons of water from the river* 從這條河中抽取 800 萬加侖水的計劃 **2 ~ sth** (*technical* 術語) to make a written summary of a book, etc. 寫出（書等的）摘要

ab·stract·ed /æbˈstræktɪd/ *adj.* (*formal*) thinking deeply about sth and not paying attention to what is around you 出神的；心神專注的 ▸ **ab·stract·ed·ly** *adv.*

ˌabstract exˈpressionism *noun* [U] a style and movement in abstract art that developed in New York in the middle of the 20th century and tries to express the feelings of the artist rather than showing a physical object 抽象表現主義（20 世紀中期源於紐約，旨在表現藝術家之情感而非現實形體）▸ **ˌabstract exˈpressionist** *noun*：*abstract expressionists like Jackson Pollock* 抽象表現派畫家如傑克遜•波洛克 **ˌabstract exˈpressionist** *adj.* [usually before noun]：*abstract expressionist art* 抽象表現主義藝術

ab·strac·tion **AW** /æbˈstrækʃn/ *noun* **1** [C, U] (*formal*) a general idea not based on any particular real person, thing or situation; the quality of being abstract 抽象概念；抽象 **2** [U] (*formal*) the state of thinking deeply about sth and not paying attention to what is around you 出神；心神專注 **3** [U, C] (*technical* 術語) the action of removing sth from sth else; the process of being removed from sth else 提取；抽取；分離：*water abstraction from rivers* 從河流中抽取水

ab·strac·tion·ism /æbˈstrækʃnɪzəm/ *noun* [U] **1** (*technical* 術語) the principles and practices of ABSTRACT art 抽象（藝術）主義 **2** the expression of ideas in an abstract way（思想的）抽象表達；抽象主義創作 ▸ **ab·strac·tion·ist** *noun, adj.* [usually before noun]

ˌabstract ˈnoun *noun* (*grammar* 語法) a noun, for example *goodness* or *freedom*, that refers to an idea or a general quality, not to a physical object 抽象名詞 ➲ compare COMMON NOUN, PROPER NOUN

ab·struse /əbˈstruːs; æb-/ *adj.* (*formal*, often *disapproving*) difficult to understand 難解的；深奧的：*an abstruse argument* 玄奧的論點

ab·surd /əbˈsɜːd; *NAmE* əbˈsɜːrd/ *adj.* **1** completely ridiculous; not logical and sensible 荒謬的；荒唐的；怪誕不經的 **SYN** **ridiculous**：*That uniform makes the guards look absurd.* 警衛們穿着那種制服看起來怪模怪樣的。◇ *Of course it's not true, what an absurd idea.* 那當然不合乎事實，這個想法太荒唐了！ **2 the absurd** *noun* [sing.] things that are or that seem to be absurd 荒誕的事物；悖理的東西：*He has a good sense of the absurd.* 他對荒誕事物有較強的識別能力。▸ **ab·surd·ity** *noun* [U, C] (*pl.* **-ies**)：*It was only later that she could see the absurdity of the situation.* 要到後來她才看出了那種局面的荒唐。 **ab·surd·ly** *adv.* **SYN** **ridiculously**：*The paintings were sold for absurdly high prices.* 那些畫以高得出奇的價格售出。

ab·surd·ism /əbˈsɜːdɪzəm; *NAmE* -ˈsɜːrd-/ *noun* [U] the belief that humans exist in a world with no purpose or order 荒誕主義（認為人存在於無序宇宙之中）▸ **ab·surd·ist** *noun* **ab·surd·ist** *adj.* [usually before noun]：*absurdist literature* 荒誕派文學

ABTA /ˈæbtə/ *abbr.* Association of British Travel Agents (an organization in Britain that protects customers, for example by giving them back the money for their tickets if a travel agent goes BANKRUPT) 英國旅行社協會（保障旅行社客戶權益的機構）

abun·dance /əˈbʌndəns/ *noun* [sing., U] **~ (of sth)** (*formal*) a large quantity that is more than enough 大量；豐盛；充裕

IDM **in abundance** in large quantities 大量；豐盛；充裕：*Fruit and vegetables grew in abundance on the island.* 該島盛產水果和蔬菜。

abun·dant /əˈbʌndənt/ *adj.* (*formal*) existing in large quantities; more than enough 大量的；豐盛的；充裕的 **SYN** **plentiful**：*Fish are abundant in the lake.* 湖裏魚很多。◇ *We have abundant evidence to prove his guilt.* 我們有充分的證據證明他有罪。

abun·dant·ly /əˈbʌndəntli/ *adv.* **1 ~ clear** very clear 十分清楚；非常明白：*She made her wishes abundantly clear.* 她充分表明了她的意願。 **2** in large quantities 大量地；豐盛地；充裕地：*Calcium is found most abundantly in milk.* 奶含鈣最豐富。

abuse 🔑 *noun, verb*

■ ***noun*** /əˈbjuːs/ **1** 🔑 [U, sing.] the use of sth in a way that is wrong or harmful 濫用；妄用 **SYN** **misuse**：***alcohol/drug/solvent abuse*** 酗酒；嗜毒；嗜吸膠毒 ◇ *The system of paying cash bonuses is* ***open to abuse*** (= might be used in the wrong way). 支付現金紅利制度可能被人鑽空子。◇ **~ of sth** *He was arrested on charges of corruption and* ***abuse of power***. 他因被控貪污腐化和濫用職權而遭逮捕。◇ *What she did was an abuse of her position as manager.* 她的所作所為是濫用經理職權。 **2** 🔑 [U, pl.] unfair, cruel or violent treatment of sb 虐待：*child abuse* 虐待兒童 ◇ *sexual abuse* 性虐待 ◇ *reported abuses by the secret police* 已舉報的秘密警察虐待行為 ◇ *She suffered years of physical abuse.* 她遭受了多年的肉體摧殘。 **3** 🔑 [U] rude and offensive remarks, usually made when sb is very angry 辱罵；惡語 **SYN** **insults**：*to* ***scream/hurl/shout abuse*** 高聲謾罵；破口大罵；大聲辱罵 ◇ *a* ***stream/torrent of abuse*** 不斷辱罵；劈頭蓋臉一通臭罵

■ ***verb*** /əˈbjuːz/ **1** 🔑 **~ sth** to make bad use of sth, or to use so much of sth that it harms your health 濫用：*to* ***abuse alcohol/drugs*** 酗酒；嗜毒 ◇ *He systematically abused his body with heroin and cocaine.* 他因吸服海洛

因和可卡因一步一步地把身體搞垮了。 **2** ⊶ **~ sth** to use power or knowledge unfairly or wrongly 濫用，妄用（權力、所知所聞）：*She abused her position as principal by giving jobs to her friends.* 她濫用自己作為校長的職權，把工作安排給朋友們。◇ *He felt they had abused his trust by talking about him to the press* (= tricked him, although he had trusted them). 他覺得他們向報界透露有關他的情況是辜負了他的信任。 **3** ⊶ **~ sb/sth** to treat a person or an animal in a cruel or violent way, especially sexually 虐待；性虐待；傷害：*All the children had been physically and emotionally abused.* 所有這些兒童的身心都受到了摧殘。◇ *He had abused his own daughter* (= had sex with her). 他曾姦污了自己的親生女兒。◇ *The boy had been sexually abused.* 這個男孩曾遭受過性虐待。 **4 ~ sb** to make rude or offensive remarks to or about sb 辱罵；惡語傷人；詆譭 **SYN insult**：*The referee had been threatened and abused.* 裁判遭到了恐嚇和謾罵。▸ **ab·user** *noun*：*a drug abuser* 嗜毒者 ◇ *a child abuser* 虐待兒童者

abu·sive /əˈbjuːsɪv/ *adj.* **1** (of speech or of a person 言語或人) rude and offensive; criticizing rudely and unfairly 辱罵的；惡語的；譭謗的：***abusive language/remarks*** 穢言惡語；惡言謾罵 ◇ *He became abusive when he was drunk.* 他喝醉時就滿口髒話罵人了。 **2** (of behaviour 行為) involving violence 虐待的：*an abusive relationship* 虐待關係 ▸ **abu·sive·ly** *adv.*

abut /əˈbʌt/ *verb* (**-tt-**) [I, T] **~ (on/onto) sth** (*formal*) (of land or a building 土地或建築物) to be next to sth or to have one side touching the side of sth 鄰接；毗連；緊靠：*His land abuts onto a road.* 他的土地緊靠公路。

abys·mal /əˈbɪzməl/ *adj.* extremely bad or of a very low standard 極壞的；糟透的 **SYN terrible** ▸ **abys·mal·ly** *adv.*

abyss /əˈbɪs/ *noun* [usually sing.] (*formal* or *literary*) a very deep wide space or hole that seems to have no bottom 深淵：*Ahead of them was a gaping abyss.* 他們前面是一個巨大的深淵。◇ (*figurative*) *an* ***abyss of ignorance/despair/loneliness*** 無知到極點；徹底絕望；無盡的孤寂 ◇ (*figurative*) *The country is stepping back from the edge of an abyss.* 該國臨淵而退。

AC /ˌeɪ ˈsiː/ *abbr.* **1** (also **ac**, **a/c**) (*especially NAmE*) AIR CONDITIONING **2** ALTERNATING CURRENT ➲ compare DIRECT CURRENT

a/c (in writing 書寫形式) *abbr.* **1** ACCOUNT 賬戶 **2** AIR CONDITIONING 空氣調節系統

aca·cia /əˈkeɪʃə/ (also **aˈcacia tree**) *noun* a tree with yellow or white flowers. There are several types of acacia tree, some of which produce a sticky liquid used in making glue. 金合歡樹（有些樹的樹汁用於製作黏膠）

aca·demia **AW** /ˌækəˈdiːmiə/ (also *formal* or *humorous* **aca·deme** /ˈækədiːm/) *noun* [U] the world of learning, teaching, research, etc. at universities, and the people involved in it 學術界

aca·dem·ic ⊶ **AW** /ˌækəˈdemɪk/ *adj.*, *noun*

■ ***adj.*** **1** ⊶ [usually before noun] connected with education, especially studying in schools and universities 學業的，教學的，學術的（尤指與學校教育有關）：*The students return in October for the start of the new academic year.* 學生於十月返校，開始新學年的學習。◇ *high/low academic standards* 高 / 低學術水平 ◇ *an academic career* 學術生涯 **2** ⊶ [usually before noun] involving a lot of reading and studying rather than practical or technical skills 學術的（與實踐性、技術性相對）：***academic subjects/qualifications*** 學科；學歷 **3** ⊶ good at subjects involving a lot of reading and studying 學習良好的：*She wasn't very academic and hated school.* 她學習不怎麼樣，而且討厭上學。 **4** not connected to a real or practical situation and therefore not important 純理論的；空談的；學究式的：*It is a purely academic question.* 這是一個純理論問題。◇ *The whole thing's academic now—we can't win anyway.* 現在這一切都是紙上談兵，反正我們贏不了。 ▸ **aca·dem·ic·al·ly** **AW** /-kli/ *adv.*：*You have to do well academically to get into medical school.* 你得學習成績優良才能入讀醫學院。

■ ***noun*** a person who teaches and/or does research at a university or college 高等院校教師；高校科研人員

acad·em·ician /əˌkædəˈmɪʃn; *NAmE* ˌækədəˈmɪʃn/ *noun* a member of an academy (2) 院士；學會會員

ˌacademic ˈyear *noun* the period of the year during which students go to school or university 學年

acad·emy **AW** /əˈkædəmi/ *noun* (*pl.* **-ies**) **1** a school or college for special training 專科院校：*the Royal Academy of Music* 皇家音樂學院 ◇ *a* ***police/military academy*** 警官 / 軍官學校 **2** (usually **Academy**) a type of official organization which aims to encourage and develop art, literature, science, etc. (藝術、文學、科學等的) 研究院，學會：*the Royal Academy of Arts* 皇家藝術學會 **3** a SECONDARY SCHOOL in Scotland (蘇格蘭) 中等學校，中學 **4** a private school in the US (美國) 私立學校 **5** a SECONDARY SCHOOL in England which has some independence from local authority control (英格蘭) 私立中等學校，私立中學

Aˌcademy Aˈward™ (also **Oscar™**) *noun* one of the awards given every year by the US Academy of Motion Picture Arts and Sciences for achievement in the making of films/movies 奧斯卡金像獎（美國電影藝術科學院頒發的年度電影成就獎）

Aca·dian /əˈkeɪdiən/ *noun* **1** a French-speaking Canadian from New Brunswick, and parts of Quebec near it, Nova Scotia or Prince Edward Island 阿卡迪亞人（操法語，居於加拿大新不倫瑞克省、鄰近的魁北克省部份地區、新斯科舍或愛德華島省） **2** (in the US) a person from Louisiana whose family originally came from the French COLONY of Acadia in what is now Nova Scotia（美國路易斯安那州的）阿卡迪亞法國殖民地移民後裔

a cap·pella /ˌæ kəˈpelə; ˌɑː/ *adj.* (of music 音樂) for singing voices alone, without musical instruments（合唱）無樂器伴奏的 ▸ **a cap·pella** *adv.*

ACAS /ˈeɪkæs/ *abbr.* (in Britain) Advisory, Conciliation and Arbitration Service (the organization that helps employers and employees settle disagreements) (英國) 咨詢調解與仲裁局（幫助雇主與雇員解決爭議的機構）

ac·cede /əkˈsiːd/ *verb* [I] (*formal*) **1 ~ (to sth)** to agree to a request, proposal, etc. 同意（請求、建議等）：*He acceded to demands for his resignation.* 他同意要他辭職的要求。 **2 ~ (to sth)** to achieve a high position, especially to become king or queen 就任；就職；（尤指君主）即位：*Queen Victoria acceded to the throne in 1837.* 維多利亞女王於 1837 年即位。➲ see also ACCESSION (1)

ac·cel·er·ate /əkˈseləreɪt/ *verb* **1** [I, T] to happen or to make sth happen faster or earlier than expected (使) 加速，加快：*Inflation continues to accelerate.* 通貨膨脹不斷加速。◇ **~ sth** *Exposure to the sun can accelerate the ageing process.* 暴露在日光下會加快老化過程。 **2** [I] (of a vehicle or person 車輛或人) to start to go faster 加速；加快：*The runners accelerated smoothly around the bend.* 賽跑運動員在轉彎處順勢加速。◇ *The car accelerated to overtake me.* 那輛汽車加速超過了我。 **OPP decelerate**

ac·cel·er·ation /əkˌseləˈreɪʃn/ *noun* **1** [U, sing.] **~ (in sth)** an increase in how fast sth happens 加速；加快：*an acceleration in the rate of economic growth* 經濟增長加速 **2** [U] the rate at which a vehicle increases speed (車輛) 加速能力，加速的幅度：*a car with good acceleration* 加速性能良好的汽車 **3** [U] (*physics* 物) the rate at which the VELOCITY (= speed in a particular direction) of an object changes 加速度

ac·cel·er·ator /əkˈseləreɪtə(r)/ *noun* **1** (*BrE*) (also **ˈgas pedal** *NAmE*, *BrE*) the PEDAL in a car or other vehicle that you press with your foot to control the speed of the engine（汽車等的）加速裝置，油門 ➲ COLLOCATIONS at DRIVING ➲ VISUAL VOCAB page V52 **2** (*physics* 物) a machine for making ELEMENTARY PARTICLES move at high speeds（基本粒子）加速器

acˈcelerator board (also **acˈcelerator card**) *noun* (*computing* 計) a CIRCUIT BOARD that can be put into a small computer to increase the speed at which it processes information（計算機）加速板，加速卡

A

ac·cel·er·om·eter /əkˌseləˈrɒmɪtə(r); *NAmE* -ˈrɑːm-/ *noun* (*physics* 物) an instrument for measuring ACCELERATION 加速度計

ac·cent *noun, verb*

■ ***noun*** /ˈæksent; -sənt/ **1** a way of pronouncing the words of a language that shows which country, area or social class a person comes from 口音；腔調；土音：*a northern/Dublin/Indian/Scottish accent* 北方 / 都柏林 / 印度 / 蘇格蘭口音 ◇ *a **strong/broad accent*** (= one that is very noticeable) 濃重的口音 ◇ *She spoke English **with an accent**.* 她說英語帶有口音。 ➲ compare DIALECT **2** the emphasis that you should give to part of a word when saying it 重音 SYN **stress**：*In 'today' the accent is on the second syllable.* * today 一詞的重音在第二音節。 **3** a mark on a letter to show that it should be pronounced in a particular way 讀音符號（標在字母上）：*Canapé has an accent on the 'e'.* * canapé 在 e 上面有尖音符號。 **4** [sing.] a special importance that is given to sth 着重點；強調 SYN **emphasis**：*In all our products **the accent is on** quality.* 我們的全部產品都是強調質量。

■ ***verb*** /ækˈsent/ **~ sth** to emphasize a part of sth 着重；強調；突出

ac·cent·ed /ˈæksentɪd/ *adj.* **1** spoken with a foreign accent 帶有異國口音的；帶有他鄉腔調的：*He spoke heavily accented English.* 他說英語帶有濃重的異國口音。 **2** (*technical* 術語) spoken with particular emphasis 重讀的：***accented vowels/syllables*** 重讀元音 / 音節 **3** (*technical* 術語) (of a letter of the alphabet 字母) written or printed with a special mark on it to show it should be pronounced in a particular way 帶有特定讀音符號的：***accented characters*** 標有特定讀音符號的字符

ac·cen·tu·ate /əkˈsentʃueɪt/ *verb* **~ sth** to emphasize sth or make it more noticeable 着重；強調；使突出 ▸ **ac·cen·tu·ation** /əkˌsentʃuˈeɪʃn/ *noun* [U]

ac·cept /əkˈsept/ *verb*

▸ **OFFER/INVITATION** 建議；邀請 **1** [I, T] to take willingly sth that is offered; to say 'yes' to an offer, invitation, etc. 收受；接受（建議、邀請等）：*He asked me to marry him and I accepted.* 他向我求婚，我答應了。◇ **~ sth** *Please accept our sincere apologies.* 請接受我們真誠的歉意。◇ *It was pouring with rain so I accepted his offer of a lift.* 天正下着瓢潑大雨，所以我領了他的情，搭了他的便車。◇ *She's decided not to accept the job.* 她決定不接受這項工作。◇ **~ sth from sb** *He is charged with accepting bribes from a firm of suppliers.* 他被控收受了一家供應商的賄賂。◇ **~ sth for sth** *She said she'd accept $15 for it.* 她說她要 15 元才賣。 OPP **refuse**

▸ **RECEIVE AS SUITABLE** 認為合適而接受 **2** [T] to receive sth as suitable or good enough（認為合適或足夠好而）接受：**~ sth** *This machine only accepts coins.* 這台機器只接受硬幣。◇ *Will you accept a cheque?* 你收支票嗎？◇ **~ sth for sth** *My article has been accepted for publication.* 我的文章已被採用準備發表。

▸ **AGREE** 同意 **3** [T] to agree to or approve of sth 同意；認可：**~ sth** *They accepted the court's decision.* 他們接受法院的判決。◇ *He accepted all the changes we proposed.* 他同意我們提出的全部修改方案。◇ **~ sth from sb** *She won't accept advice from anyone.* 她不會接受任何人的忠告。 OPP **reject** ➲ SYNONYMS at AGREE

▸ **RESPONSIBILITY** 責任 **4** [T] **~ sth** to admit that you are responsible or to blame for sth 承認，承擔（責任等）：*He accepts full responsibility for what happened.* 他承認對所發生的事負全部責任。◇ *You have to accept the consequences of your actions.* 你得對你的行為後果負責。

▸ **BELIEVE** 相信 **5** [T] to believe that sth is true 相信（某事屬實）：**~ sth** *I don't accept his version of events.* 我不相信他對事件的說法。◇ **~ sth as sth** *Can we accept his account as the true version?* 我們能相信他說的是事實嗎？◇ **~ that …** *I accept that this will not be popular.* 我認為這是不會受歡迎的。◇ **it is accepted that …** *It is generally accepted that people are motivated by success.* 普遍認為，成功催人奮進。◇ **it is accepted to be, have, etc. sth** *The workforce is generally accepted to have the best conditions in Europe.* 歐洲工人的勞動環境公認是最好的。

▸ **DIFFICULT SITUATION** 困境 **6** [T] to continue in a difficult situation without complaining, because you realize that you cannot change it 容忍，忍受（困境等）：**~ sth** *You just have to **accept the fact that** we're never going to be rich.* 你只得接受我們永遠也富不起來這個事實。◇ *Nothing will change as long as the workers continue to accept these appalling conditions.* 只要工人繼續容忍這種惡劣的勞動條件，情況就不會有任何改變。◇ **~ sth as sth** *They accept the risks as part of the job.* 他們甘冒風險，把這當成工作的一部份。◇ **~ that …** *He just refused to accept that his father was no longer there.* 他就是不肯接受他父親已不在的現實。

▸ **WELCOME** 歡迎 **7** [T] to make sb feel welcome and part of a group 歡迎；接納：**~ sb** *It may take years to be completely accepted by the local community.* 也許需要多年方能被當地居民完全接納。◇ **~ sb into sth** *She had never been accepted into what was essentially a man's world.* 她從未被這個基本上屬於男人的世界所接受。◇ **~ sb as sth** *He never really accepted her as his own child.* 他一直沒有真正接納她為自己的女兒。 OPP **reject**

▸ **ALLOW SB TO JOIN** 准許加入 **8** [T] to allow sb to join an organization, attend an institution, use a service, etc. 接納，接受（為成員、會員等）：**~ sb** *The college he applied to has accepted him.* 他申請的那所學院錄取了他。◇ **~ sb into sth** *She was disappointed not to be accepted into the club.* 她沒有獲准加入俱樂部，感到失望。◇ **~ sb as sth** *The landlord was willing to accept us as tenants.* 房東願意把房子租給我們住。◇ **~ sb to do sth** *She was accepted to study music.* 她獲准學習音樂。 OPP **reject**

ac·cept·able /əkˈseptəbl/ *adj.*

1 agreed or approved of by most people in a society（社會上）認同的，認可的：*Children must learn socially acceptable behaviour.* 兒童必須學會社會上認可的行為舉止。 **2** that sb agrees is of a good enough standard or allowed 可接受的；令人滿意的；可容許的：*For this course a pass in English at grade B is acceptable.* 英語成績達到 B 級就可以學習這門課程。◇ *Air pollution in the city had reached four times the acceptable levels.* 這座城市的空氣污染程度曾高達可接受標準的四倍。◇ **~ to sb** *We want a political solution that is acceptable to all parties.* 我們需要一個各方都可接受的政治解決方案。 **3** not very good but good enough 還可以的；尚可的；差強人意的：*The food was acceptable, but no more.* 食物還可以，但說不上很好。 OPP **unacceptable** ▸ **ac·cept·abil·ity** /əkˌseptəˈbɪləti/ *noun* [U] **ac·cept·ably** /-bli/ *adv.*

ac·cept·ance /əkˈseptəns/ *noun* **1** [U, C] the act of accepting a gift, an invitation, an offer, etc. 接受（禮物、邀請、建議等）：*Please confirm your acceptance of this offer in writing.* 請書面確認你接受這項建議。◇ *He made a short **acceptance speech/speech of acceptance**.* 他作了簡短演說，表示感謝。 **2** [U] the act of agreeing with sth and approving of it 同意；認可：*The new laws have **gained widespread acceptance**.* 新法律獲得廣泛贊同。 **3** [U] the process of allowing sb to join sth or be a member of a group 接納，接受（為成員、會員等）：*Your acceptance into the insurance plan is guaranteed.* 你參加保險計劃一事已有保證。◇ *Social acceptance is important for most young people.* 對大多數青年來說，重要的是要為社會所接納。 **4** [U] willingness to accept an unpleasant or difficult situation 無怨接受（逆境、困境等）；逆來順受：*acceptance of death/suffering* 接受死亡 / 苦難

ac·cess AW /ˈækses/ *noun, verb*

■ ***noun*** [U] **1** a way of entering or reaching a place 通道；通路；入徑：*The police **gained access** through a broken window.* 警察從一扇破窗戶鑽了進去。◇ **~ to sth** *The only access to the farmhouse is across the fields.* 去那農舍的唯一通路是穿過田野。◇ *Disabled visitors are welcome; there is good wheelchair access to most facilities.* 歡迎殘疾人士參觀，坐輪椅可以方便地到達多數設施。 ➲ compare EGRESS **2 ~ (to sth)** the opportunity or right to use sth or to see sb/sth（使用或見到的）機會，權利：*Students must **have access** to good resources.* 學生必須有機會使用好的資源。◇ *You need a password to **get access** to the computer system.* 使用這個計算機系統需要密碼。◇ *access to confidential information* 接觸機密情報的機會 ◇ *Journalists were **denied access*** *to the President.* 記者被擋住，無法見到總統。◇ *Many divorced fathers only have access to their children at weekends* (= they are allowed by law to see them only at weekends). 很多離婚父親只有在週末才有權見到自己的孩子。 ➲ compare VISITATION (1)

■ ***verb* 1 ~ sth** (*computing* 計) to open a computer file in order to get or add information 存取（計算機文件） **2 ~ sth** (*formal*) to reach, enter or use sth 到達；進入；使用：*The loft can be accessed by a ladder.* 搭梯子可以上閣樓。

ˈaccess course *noun* (*BrE*) a course of education that prepares students without the usual qualifications, in order that they can study at university or college 高考資格補習班（為沒有所需學歷者而設）

ac·cess·ible AW /əkˈsesəbl/ *adj.* **1** that can be reached, entered, used, seen, etc. 可到達的；可接近的；可進入的；可使用的；可見到的：*The remote desert area is accessible only by helicopter.* 只有乘直升機才能進入那遙遠的荒漠地區。◇ **~ to sb** *These documents are not accessible to the public.* 公眾無法看到這些文件。 **2** easy to understand 容易理解的；易懂的：*Her poetry is always very accessible.* 她的詩作總是非常通俗易懂。◇ **~ to sb** *a programme making science more accessible to young people* 一項使科學更容易為年輕人所瞭解的計劃 **3** (of a person 人) easy to talk to and to get to know 易接近的；易相處的；易打交道的 OPP **inaccessible** ▸ **ac·ces·si·bil·ity** AW /əkˌsesəˈbɪləti/ *noun* [U]

ac·ces·sion /ækˈseʃn/ *noun* **1** [U] **~ (to sth)** the act of becoming a ruler of a country（國家統治者的）就職，就任；（君主、帝王等的）登基，即位：*the accession of Queen Victoria to the throne* 維多利亞女王即位 ➲ see also ACCEDE (2) **2** [U] **~ (to sth)** the act of becoming part of an international organization 正式加入（國際組織）：*the accession of new member states to the EU in 2004* 新成員國在 2004 年正式加入歐盟 ◇ *the new* ***accession states*** *of the EU* 正式加入歐盟的新成員國 **3** [C] (*technical* 術語) a thing that is added to a collection of objects, paintings, etc. in a library or museum（圖書館、博物館的）新增項目，新增藏品，新增藏書

ac·ces·sor·ize (*BrE* also **-ise**) /əkˈsesəraɪz/ *verb* **~ sth** to add fashionable items or extra decorations to sth, especially to your clothes 加時髦配件；加裝飾物；加搭配服飾品

ac·ces·sory /əkˈsesəri/ *noun, adj.*

■ ***noun*** (*pl.* **-ies**) **1** [usually pl.] an extra piece of equipment that is useful but not essential or that can be added to sth else as a decoration 附件；配件；附屬物：*bicycle accessories* 自行車附件 ◇ *a range of furnishings and accessories for the home* 各種各樣的家居裝飾物及配件 **2** [usually pl.] a thing that you can wear or carry that matches your clothes, for example a belt or a bag（衣服的）配飾 ➲ VISUAL VOCAB pages V64, V65 **3** (*law* 律) a person who helps sb to commit a crime or who knows about it and protects the person from the police 同謀；從犯；幫兇：*an* ***accessory before/after the fact*** (= before/after the crime was committed) 事前／事後從犯◇ **~ to sth** *He was charged with being an accessory to murder.* 他被控為謀殺罪的從犯。

■ ***adj.*** (*technical* 術語) not the most important when compared to others 輔助的；副的：*the accessory muscles of respiration* 副呼吸肌

ˈaccess road *noun* a road used for driving into or out of a particular place（進出某處的）行車通道 ➲ compare SLIP ROAD

ˈaccess time *noun* [U, C] (*computing* 計) the time taken to obtain data stored on a computer 存取時間（取出計算機中貯存的數據所用的時間）

ac·ci·dent 🔑 /ˈæksɪdənt/ *noun*

1 🔑 [C] an unpleasant event, especially in a vehicle, that happens unexpectedly and causes injury or damage（交通）事故；意外遭遇；不測事件：*a* ***car/road/traffic accident*** 車禍；公路事故；交通事故 ◇ *He was killed* ***in an accident.*** 他死於車禍。◇ *One in seven accidents is caused by sleepy drivers.* 每七次交通事故就有一次是駕車者睏倦造成的。◇ *The accident happened at 3 p.m.* 事故發生於下午 3 點鐘。◇ *to* ***have an accident*** 出事故 ◇ *a* ***serious/minor accident*** 嚴重／輕微事故 ◇ *a* ***fatal accident*** (= in which sb is killed) 死亡事故 ◇ *accidents in the home* 家中發生的意外事件 ◇ *a* ***climbing/riding accident*** 登山／騎馬意外 ◇ *Take out* ***accident insurance*** *before you go on your trip.* 你去旅行前要辦理好意外保險。◇ *I didn't mean to break it—* ***it was an accident.*** 我不是故意打碎它的 —— 這是個意外。 **2** [C, U] something that happens unexpectedly and is not planned in advance 意外；偶然的事：*Their early arrival was just an accident.* 他們早到僅僅是偶然而已。◇ *It is* ***no accident*** *that men fill most of the top jobs in nursing.* 男人擔任護理中大多數最重要的工作絕非偶然。◇ *an* ***accident of birth/fate/history*** (= describing facts and events that are due to chance or circumstances) 出生／命運／歷史的偶然性 ➲ SYNONYMS at LUCK

IDM **ˌaccidents will ˈhappen** people say **accidents will happen** to tell sb who has had an accident, for example breaking sth, that it does not matter and they should not worry 出事是難免的 **by accident** 🔑 in a way that is not planned or organized 偶然；意外地：*We met by accident at the airport.* 我們在機場不期而遇。◇ *Helen got into acting purely by accident.* 海倫當演員完全出於偶然。 OPP **deliberately**, **on purpose** ➲ more at CHAPTER, WAIT *v.*

ac·ci·den·tal 🔑 /ˌæksɪˈdentl/ *adj.* happening by chance; not planned 意外的；偶然的：*a verdict of accidental death* 意外死亡的裁決 ◇ *I didn't think our meeting was accidental—he must have known I would be there.* 我認為我們相遇不是偶然的 —— 他肯定知道我要去那裏。 ▸ **ac·ci·den·tal·ly** 🔑 /-təli/ *adv.*：*As I turned around, I accidentally hit him in the face.* 我轉身時不經意撞了他的臉。◇ *The damage couldn't have been caused accidentally.* 這次損毀不可能是偶然因素造成的。

ˌaccident and eˈmergency (*abbr.* **A & E**) (*BrE*) *noun* [U] (*NAmE* **eˈmergency room**) the part of a hospital where people who need urgent treatment are taken（醫院）急診室：*the hospital accident and emergency department* 醫院的急診部 ➲ see also CASUALTY (3)

ˈaccident-prone *adj.* more likely to have accidents than other people（人）易出事故的

ac·claim /əˈkleɪm/ *verb, noun*

■ ***verb*** [usually passive] to praise or welcome sb/sth publicly 公開稱譽某人／某事物（為…）；給予高度評價：**~ sb/sth** *a* ***highly/widely acclaimed*** *performance* 受到高度／廣泛讚揚的演出 ◇ **~ sb/sth as sth** *The work was acclaimed as a masterpiece.* 該作品被譽為傑作。

■ ***noun*** [U] praise and approval for sb/sth, especially an artistic achievement（尤指對藝術成就的）稱譽，高度評價：***international/popular/critical acclaim*** 國際上的／公眾的／評論家的讚揚

ac·clam·ation /ˌækləˈmeɪʃn/ *noun* [U] **1** (*formal*) loud and enthusiastic approval or welcome 喝彩；歡呼；歡迎 **2** (*technical* 術語) the act of electing sb using a spoken not written vote（口頭表決）擁護，贊成：*The decision was taken* ***by acclamation.*** 該決議是經口頭表決而作出的。

ac·cli·mate /ˈækləmeɪt/ *verb* (*NAmE*) = ACCLIMATIZE ▸ **ac·cli·ma·tion** /ˌækləˈmeɪʃn/ *noun* [U]

ac·cli·ma·tize (*BrE* also **-ise**) /əˈklaɪmətaɪz/ (*NAmE* also **ac·cli·mate**) *verb* [I, T] to get used to a new place, situation or climate（使）習慣（新地方、新情況、新氣候）；（使）服水土：**~ (to sth)** *Arrive two days early in order to acclimatize.* 提前兩天到達以便適應新環境。◇ **~ yourself (to sth)** *She was fine once she had acclimatized herself to the cold.* 她習慣了寒冷以後身體立即就好了。 ▸ **ac·cli·ma·tiza·tion**, **-isa·tion** /əˌklaɪmətaɪˈzeɪʃn; *NAmE* -təˈz-/ *noun* [U]

ac·col·ade /ˈækəleɪd; ˌækəˈleɪd/ *noun* (*formal*) praise or an award for an achievement that people admire 讚揚；表揚；獎勵；獎賞；榮譽

ac·com·mo·date AW /əˈkɒmədeɪt; *NAmE* əˈkɑːm-/ *verb* **1** [T] **~ sb** to provide sb with a room or place to sleep, live or sit 提供住宿（或膳宿、座位等）：*The hotel can accommodate up to 500 guests.* 這家旅館可供 500 位旅客住宿。 **2** [T] **~ sb/sth** to provide enough space for sb/sth

A

容納；提供空間：*Over 70 minutes of music can be accommodated on one CD.* 一張激光唱片可以容納 70 多分鐘的音樂。 **3** [T] **~ sth** (*formal*) to consider sth, such as sb's opinion or a fact, and be influenced by it when you are deciding what to do or explaining sth 考慮到；顧及：*Our proposal tries to accommodate the special needs of minority groups.* 我們的提案盡量照顧到少數群體的特殊需要。 **4** [T] **~ sb (with sth)** (*formal*) to help sb by doing what they want 幫忙；給…提供方便 SYN **oblige**：*I have accommodated the press a great deal, giving numerous interviews.* 我多次接受採訪，已給了報界許多方便。 **5** [I, T] **~ (sth/yourself) to sth** (*formal*) to change your behaviour so that you can deal with a new situation better 順應，適應（新情況）：*I needed to accommodate to the new schedule.* 我需要適應新的時間表。

ac·com·mo·dat·ing /əˈkɒmədeɪtɪŋ; *NAmE* əˈkɑːm-/ *adj.* (*formal*) willing to help and do things for other people 樂於助人的；與人方便的 SYN **obliging**

ac·com·mo·da·tion 🔑 AW /əˌkɒməˈdeɪʃn; *NAmE* əˌkɑːm-/ *noun*
1 🔑 [U] (*BrE*) a place to live, work or stay in 住處；辦公處；停留處：***rented/temporary/furnished accommodation*** 租的 / 臨時的 / 有傢具的住處 ◇ *Hotel accommodation is included in the price of your holiday.* 你度假的價錢包括旅館住宿。◇ *The building plans include much needed new office accommodation.* 建築規劃包括緊缺的新辦公用房在內。◇ *First-class accommodation is available on all flights.* 所有班機都備有一等艙位。 **2 accommodations** [pl.] (*NAmE*) somewhere to live or stay, often also providing food or other services 住宿；膳宿：*More and more travelers are looking for bed and breakfast accommodations in private homes.* 愈來愈多的旅行者在尋找由私人住戶提供住宿加早餐的服務。 **3** [C, U] (*formal*) an agreement or arrangement between people or groups with different opinions which is acceptable to everyone; the process of reaching this agreement 和解；調解；調和：*They were forced to reach an accommodation with the rebels.* 他們被迫與叛亂分子達成調解協議。

ac·com·pani·ment AW /əˈkʌmpənimənt/ *noun* **1** [C, U] **~ (to sth)** music that is played to support singing or another instrument（音樂）伴奏：*traditional songs with piano accompaniment* 用鋼琴伴奏的傳統歌曲 **2** [C] **~ (to sth)** something that you eat, drink or use together with sth else 佐餐物；伴隨物：*The wine makes a good accompaniment to fish dishes.* 這種葡萄酒很適合作魚菜的佐餐酒。 **3** [C] **~ (to sth)** (*formal*) something that happens at the same time as another thing 伴隨發生的事情：*High blood pressure is a common accompaniment to this disease.* 這種病通常伴隨有高血壓。
IDM **to the accompaniment of sth 1** while a musical instrument is being played 在…的伴奏下：*They performed to the accompaniment of guitars.* 他們在吉他的伴奏下表演。 **2** while sth else is happening 在…發生時；伴隨有；同時有：*She made her speech to the accompaniment of loud laughter.* 她的演講不斷引起哄堂大笑。

ac·com·pan·ist /əˈkʌmpənɪst/ *noun* a person who plays a musical instrument, especially a piano, while sb else plays or sings the main part of the music 伴奏者；（尤指）鋼琴伴奏者

ac·com·pany 🔑 AW /əˈkʌmpəni/ *verb* (**ac·com·pan·ies, ac·com·pany·ing, ac·com·pan·ied, ac·com·pan·ied**)
1 🔑 **~ sb** (*formal*) to travel or go somewhere with sb 陪同；陪伴：*His wife accompanied him on the trip.* 那次旅行他由妻子陪同。 **2** 🔑 **~ sth** to happen or appear with sth else 伴隨；與…同時發生：*strong winds accompanied by heavy rain* 狂風夾着暴雨 ◇ *Each pack contains a book and accompanying CD.* 每包內裝書一本，並附光盤一張。 **3 ~ sb (at/on sth)** to play a musical instrument, especially a piano, while sb else sings or plays the main tune（尤指用鋼琴）為…伴奏：*The singer was accompanied on the piano by her sister.* 女歌手由她姐姐鋼琴伴奏。

ac·com·plice /əˈkʌmplɪs; *NAmE* əˈkɑːm-/ *noun* a person who helps another to commit a crime or to do sth wrong 幫兇；共犯；同謀

ac·com·plish /əˈkʌmplɪʃ; *NAmE* əˈkɑːm-/ *verb* **~ sth** to succeed in doing or completing sth 完成 SYN **achieve**：*The first part of the plan has been safely accomplished.* 計劃的第一部份已順利完成。◇ *I don't feel I've accomplished very much today.* 我覺得我今天沒幹成多少事。◇ *That's it. **Mission accomplished*** (= we have done what we aimed to do). 就這樣。大功告成。

ac·com·plished /əˈkʌmplɪʃt; *NAmE* əˈkɑːm-/ *adj.* very good at a particular thing; having a lot of skills 才華高的；技藝高超的；熟練的：*an accomplished artist/actor/chef* 技藝高超的藝術家 / 演員 / 廚師 ◇ *She was an elegant and accomplished woman.* 她是位優雅的才女。

ac·com·plish·ment /əˈkʌmplɪʃmənt; *NAmE* əˈkɑːm-/ *noun* **1** [C] an impressive thing that is done or achieved after a lot of work 成就；成績 SYN **achievement**：*It was one of the President's greatest accomplishments.* 那是總統最偉大的成就之一。 **2** [C, U] a skill or special ability 才藝；技藝；專長：*Drawing and singing were among her many accomplishments.* 她多才多藝，能歌善畫。◇ *a poet of rare accomplishment* 出類拔萃的詩人 **3** [U] (*formal*) the successful completing of sth 完成；成就：*Money will be crucial to the accomplishment of our objectives.* 要實現我們的目標，錢是至關重要的。

ac·cord /əˈkɔːd; *NAmE* əˈkɔːrd/ *noun, verb*
■ ***noun*** a formal agreement between two organizations, countries, etc. 協議；條約：*The two sides signed a **peace accord** last July.* 在剛過去的七月，雙方簽訂了和平條約。
IDM **in accord (with sth/sb)** (*formal*) in agreement with 與…一致（或相符合）：*This action would not be in accord with our policy.* 這一行動不會符合我們的方針。 **of your own acˈcord** without being asked, forced or helped 自願地；主動地：*He came back of his own accord.* 他主動回來了。◇ *The symptoms will clear up of their own accord.* 症狀將會自行消失。 **with ˌone acˈcord** (*BrE, formal*) if people do sth **with one accord**, they do it at the same time, because they agree with each other 全體一致；一致地
■ ***verb*** (*formal*) **1** [T] to give sb/sth authority, status or a particular type of treatment 給予，贈予，授予（權力、地位、某種待遇）：**~ sth to sb/sth** *Our society accords great importance to the family.* 我們的社會賦予家庭十分重要的地位。◇ **~ sb/sth sth** *Our society accords the family great importance.* 我們的社會賦予家庭十分重要的地位。 **2** [I] **~ (with sth)** to agree with or match sth（與…）一致，符合，配合：*These results accord closely with our predictions.* 這些結果和我們的預測相當一致。

ac·cord·ance /əˈkɔːdns; *NAmE* əˈkɔːrdns/ *noun*
IDM **in accordance with sth** (*formal*) according to a rule or the way that sb says that sth should be done 依照；依據：*in accordance with legal requirements* 根據法律要求

ac·cord·ing·ly /əˈkɔːdɪŋli; *NAmE* əˈkɔːrd-/ *adv.* **1** in a way that is appropriate to what has been done or said in a particular situation 照着；相應地：*We have to discover his plans and act accordingly.* 我們得找出他的計劃，照着辦。 **2** (used especially at the beginning of a sentence 尤用於句首) for that reason 因此；所以 SYN **therefore**：*The cost of materials rose sharply last year. Accordingly, we were forced to increase our prices.* 去年材料成本大幅度提高，因此我們被迫加價。

ac·cord·ing to 🔑 /əˈkɔːdɪŋ tə; *NAmE* əˈkɔːrdɪŋ/ *prep.*
1 🔑 as stated or reported by sb/sth 據（…所說）；按（…所報道）：*According to Mick, it's a great movie.* 據米克說，這是一部了不起的電影。◇ *You've been absent six times according to our records.* 根據我們的記錄，你已經缺席六次了。 ➲ LANGUAGE BANK at ILLUSTRATE **2** 🔑 following, agreeing with or depending on sth 依照；按照；根據：*The work was done according to her instructions.* 這項工作是依照她的指示辦的。◇ *Everything **went according to plan**.* 一切均按照計劃進行。◇ *The salary will be fixed according to qualifications and experience.* 薪金將依資歷和經驗而定。 IDM see COAT *n.*

Language Bank 用語庫

according to

Reporting someone's opinion 陳述某人的觀點

- Photography is, **according to** Vidal, the art form of untalented people. 據維達爾所言，攝影是沒有天賦的人的藝術形式。
- **For** Vidal, photography is the art form of untalented people. 對維達爾來說，攝影是沒有天賦的人的藝術形式。
- His **view is that** photography is not art but merely the mechanical reproduction of images. 他的觀點是攝影不是藝術，而只是機械地複製圖像。
- Smith **takes the view that** photography is both an art and a science. 史密斯所持的觀點是：攝影既是一門藝術也是一門科學。
- **In** Brown's **view**, photography should be treated as a legitimate art in its own right. 在布朗看來，攝影本身就應該被視為一種正當的藝術。
- James **is of the opinion that** a good painter can always be a good photographer if he or she so decides. 詹姆斯認為一個好的畫家定能成為一個好的攝影師，只要他／她一心這樣做。
- Emerson **believed that** a photograph should only reflect what the human eye can see. 埃默森認為照片應該只是反映人們肉眼所能見到的東西。

➲ Language Banks at ARGUE, OPINION

ac·cor·dion /ə'kɔːdiən; *NAmE* ə'kɔːrd-/ *noun* a musical instrument that you hold in both hands to produce sounds. You press the two ends together and pull them apart and press buttons and/or keys to produce the different notes. 手風琴 ➲ see also PIANO ACCORDION

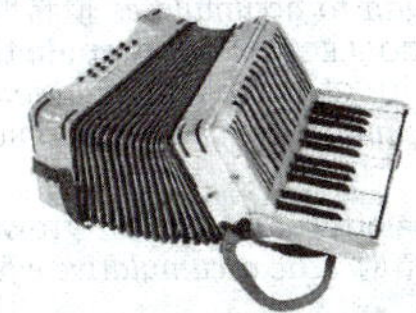

accordion 手風琴

concertina 六角形手風琴

ac·cost /ə'kɒst; *NAmE* ə'kɔːst; ə'kɑːst/ *verb* **~ sb** (*formal*) to go up to sb and speak to them, especially in a way that is rude or threatening （貿然）上前搭訕；（唐突地）走近談話： *She was accosted in the street by a complete stranger.* 在街上，一個完全陌生的人貿然走到她跟前搭訕。

ac·count 🔑 /ə'kaʊnt/ *noun, verb*

■ *noun*

▸ AT BANK 銀行 **1** 🔑 (*abbr.* **a/c**) an arrangement that sb has with a bank, etc. to keep money there, take some out, etc. 賬戶： *I don't have a bank account.* 我沒有銀行賬戶。◇ *to have an **account at/with** a bank* 在銀行有賬戶 ◇ *to **open/close an account*** 開立／結清賬戶 ◇ *What's your account number please?* 請問您的賬戶號碼？◇ *I paid the cheque into my savings account.* 我把支票存入我的儲蓄賬戶。◇ *a joint account* (= one in the name of more than one person) 聯合賬戶 ➲ COLLOCATIONS at FINANCE ➲ see also BUDGET ACCOUNT, CHECKING ACCOUNT, CURRENT ACCOUNT, DEPOSIT ACCOUNT

▸ BUSINESS RECORDS 商業記錄 **2** 🔑 [usually pl.] a written record of money that is owed to a business and of money that has been paid by it 賬目： *to do the accounts* 記賬 ◇ *the accounts department* 會計部門 ➲ see also EXPENSE ACCOUNT, PROFIT AND LOSS ACCOUNT

▸ WITH SHOP/STORE 商店 **3** (*BrE* also **'credit account**) (*NAmE* also **'charge account**) an arrangement with a shop/store or business to pay bills for goods or services at a later time, for example in regular amounts every month 賒銷賬；賒欠賬；賒購： *Put it on my account please.* 請記在我的賒購賬上。◇ *We have accounts with most of our suppliers.* 我們與大多數供應商都是實行賒購制。➲ SYNONYMS at BILL

▸ REGULAR CUSTOMER 老主顧 **4** (*business* 商) a regular customer 老主顧： *The agency has lost several of its most important accounts.* 這家代理機構失去了幾家最重要的老客戶。

▸ COMPUTING 計算機技術 **5** an arrangement that sb has with a company that allows them to use the Internet, send and receive messages by email, etc. （互聯網、電子郵件等的）賬戶，賬號： *an **Internet/email account*** 互聯網／電子郵件賬戶

▸ DESCRIPTION 描述 **6** a written or spoken description of sth that has happened 描述；敘述；報告： *She gave the police a full account of the incident.* 她向警方詳盡地敘述了所發生的事情。➲ SYNONYMS at REPORT **7** an explanation or a description of an idea, a theory or a process （思想、理論、過程的）解釋，說明，敘述： *the Biblical account of the creation of the world* 《聖經》對創世的解釋

IDM **by/from all accounts** according to what other people say 據說；根據報道： *I've never been there, but it's a lovely place, by all accounts.* 我從未去過那裏，但據說是個美麗的地方。 **by your own account** according to what you say yourself 根據某人自己所說： *By his own account he had an unhappy childhood.* 據他自己說，他童年不愉快。 **give a good/poor ac'count of yourself** (*BrE*) to do sth or perform well or badly, especially in a contest （尤指比賽中）表現好／不好，幹得出色／差勁： *The team gave a good account of themselves in the match.* 這個隊在比賽中表現出色。 **of no/little ac'count** (*formal*) not important 不重要；無足輕重 **on account** if you buy sth or pay **on account**, you pay nothing or only a small amount immediately and the rest later 掛賬；（先付小部份款額的）賒賬 **on sb's account** because of what you think sb wants 為了某人的緣故： *Please don't change your plans on my account.* 請別因為我而改變你的計劃。 **on account of sb/sth** 🔑 because of sb/sth 由於；因為： *She retired early on account of ill health.* 她體弱多病，所以提前退休。➲ LANGUAGE BANK at BECAUSE **on no account** | **not on any account** (used to emphasize sth 用於強調) not for any reason 決不；絕對不： *On no account should the house be left unlocked.* 離開住宅時千萬要鎖門。 **on your own ac'count** **1** for yourself 為自己： *In 2006 Smith set up in business on his own account.* * 2006 年史密斯開展自己的業務。 **2** because you want to and you have decided, not sb else 自願地： *No one sent me, I am here on my own account.* 沒有人派我，我自己來的。 **on this/that account** (*formal*) because of the particular thing that has been mentioned 由於這個／那個緣故： *Weather conditions were poor, but he did not delay his departure on that account.* 天氣不好，但他並沒有因此延期啟程。 **put/turn sth to good ac'count** (*formal*) to use sth in a good or helpful way 善用；利用 **take account of sth** | **take sth into account** to consider particular facts, circumstances, etc. when making a decision about sth 考慮到；顧及： *The company takes account of environmental issues wherever possible.* 這家公司總是盡量考慮到各方面的環境問題。◇ *Coursework is taken into account as well as exam results.* 除考試結果外，課程作業也要計入成績。◇ *The defendant asked for a number of other offences to be taken into account.* 被告要求考慮一些其他罪行。➲ more at BLOW *n.*, CALL *v.*, SETTLE *v.*

■ *verb* [usually passive] (*formal*) to have the opinion that sb/sth is a particular thing 認為是；視為： **~ sb/sth + adj.** *In English law a person is accounted innocent until they are proved guilty.* 按英格蘭法律，一個人未經證實有罪之前被視為無罪。◇ **~ sb/sth + noun** *The event was accounted a success.* 人們認為這次活動是成功的。

IDM **there's no accounting for 'taste** (*saying*) used to say how difficult it is to understand why sb likes sb/sth that you do not like at all 人的愛憎好惡是無法解釋的；人各有所好： *She thinks he's wonderful—oh well, there's* *no accounting for taste.* 她認為他了不起。嗯，算了，人各有所好嘛。

PHR V **ac'count for sth** **1** to be the explanation or cause of sth 是…的說明（或原因）**SYN** **explain**：*The poor weather may have accounted for the small crowd.* 天氣不好可能是人來得少的原因。◇ *Oh well, that accounts for it* (= I understand now why it happened). 哎呀，原來是這麼一回事。**2** to give an explanation of sth 解釋；說明 **SYN** **explain**：*How do you account for the show's success?* 你認為這次演出為何成功？**3** to be a particular amount or part of sth （數量上、比例上）佔：*The Japanese market accounts for 35% of the company's revenue.* 日本市場佔該公司收入的 35%。➲ LANGUAGE BANK at PROPORTION **ac'count for sb/sth** **1** to know where sb/sth is or what has happened to them, especially after an accident（尤指在事故之後）瞭解，查明：*All passengers have now been accounted for.* 現在所有乘客的情況均已查明。**2** (*informal*) to defeat or destroy sb/sth 打敗；破壞；摧毀；消滅：*Our anti-aircraft guns accounted for five enemy bombers.* 我們的高射炮擊落了五架敵人的轟炸機。**ac'count for sth (to sb)** to give a record of how the money in your care has been spent 報賬；出示經手款項的單據：*We have to account for every penny we spend on business trips.* 我們出公差所用的每一分錢都得報清楚。

ac·count·able /ə'kaʊntəbl/ *adj.* [not usually before noun] responsible for your decisions or actions and expected to explain them when you are asked（對自己的決定、行為）負有責任，有說明義務：**~ to sb** *Politicians are ultimately accountable to the voters.* 從政者最終是向選民負責。◇ **~ for sth** *Someone must be **held accountable** for the killings.* 必須有人要對這些兇殺事件負責。▸ **ac·count·abil·ity** /əˌkaʊntə'bɪləti/ *noun* [U]：(*formal*) *the accountability of a company's directors to the shareholders* 公司董事向股東所負之責

ac·count·ancy /ə'kaʊntənsi/ *noun* [U] the work or profession of an accountant 會計工作；會計職業

ac·count·ant /ə'kaʊntənt/ *noun* a person whose job is to keep or check financial accounts 會計；會計師

ac'count executive *noun* a business person, especially one working in advertising, who is responsible for dealing with one of the company's regular customers 客戶主任（在廣告公司等中負責為指定長期客戶提供服務）

ac·count·ing /ə'kaʊntɪŋ/ *noun* [U] the process or work of keeping financial accounts 會計：*a career in accounting* 會計職業 ◇ *accounting methods* 會計方法

acˌcounts 'payable *noun* [pl.] (*business* 商) money that is owed by a company（會計項目）應付款項，應付賬款

acˌcounts re'ceivable *noun* [pl.] (*business* 商) money that is owed to a company（會計項目）應收款項，應收賬款

ac·coutre·ments /ə'kuːtrəmənts/ (*US* also **ac·cou·ter·ments** /ə'kuːtərmənts/) *noun* [pl.] (*formal* or *humorous*) pieces of equipment that you need for a particular activity（某項活動所需的）裝備，配備

ac·credit /ə'kredɪt/ *verb* **1** [usually passive] (*formal*) to believe that sb is responsible for doing or saying sth 把…歸於；認為（某事為某人所說、所做）：**~ sth to sb** *The discovery of distillation is usually accredited to the Arabs of the 11th century.* 通常認為，蒸餾法是阿拉伯人在 11 世紀發明的。◇ **~ sb with sth** *The Arabs are usually accredited with the discovery of distillation.* 通常認為，阿拉伯人發明了蒸餾法。**2** [usually passive] **~ sb to …** (*technical* 術語) to choose sb for an official position, especially as an AMBASSADOR 委任，委派（某人為大使等）：*He was accredited to Madrid.* 他被委任為駐馬德里的大使。**3 ~ sth/sb** to officially approve sth/sb as being of an accepted quality or standard 正式認可：*Institutions that do not meet the standards will not be accredited for teacher training.* 沒有達標的大專院校不會獲得教師培訓的資格。

ac·credit·ation /əˌkredɪ'teɪʃn/ *noun* [U] official approval given by an organization stating that sb/sth has achieved a required standard 達到標準；證明合格：*a letter of accreditation* 一份合格證明書

ac·credit·ed /ə'kredɪtɪd/ *adj.* [usually before noun] **1** (of a person 人) officially recognized as sth; with official permission to be sth 官方認可的；獲正式承認的：*our accredited representative* 我們官方委任的代表 ◇ *Only accredited journalists were allowed entry.* 只有正式認可的記者才獲准入內。**2** officially approved as being of an accepted quality or standard 鑒定合格的；達到標準的：*a fully **accredited school/university/course*** 充分鑒定合格的學校／大學／課程

ac·cre·tion /ə'kriːʃn/ *noun* (*technical* 術語 or *formal*) **1** [C] a layer of a substance that is slowly added to sth 積聚層；堆積層 **2** [U] the process of new layers being slowly added to sth 堆積，積聚（過程）

ac·crue /ə'kruː/ *verb* (*formal*) **1** [I] to increase over a period of time（逐漸）增長，增加：*Interest will accrue if you keep your money in a savings account.* 如果把錢存入儲蓄賬戶，就會自然生息。◇ **~ (to sb) (from sth)** *economic benefits accruing to the country from tourism* 旅遊業為該國帶來的經濟效益 **2** [T] **~ sth** to allow a sum of money or debts to grow over a period of time 積累（錢款或債務）**SYN** **accumulate**：*The firm had accrued debts of over $6m.* 該公司已積欠了 600 多萬元的債務。▸ **ac·crual** /ə'kruːəl/ *noun* [U, C]：*the accrual of interest* 利息積累

ac·cul·tur·ate /ə'kʌltʃəreɪt/ *verb* [I, T] **~ (sb) (to sth)** (*formal*) to learn to live successfully in a different culture; to help sb to do this（使）適應新的文化習俗，融入…文化 ▸ **ac·cul·tur·ation** /əˌkʌltʃə'reɪʃn/ *noun* [U]

ac·cu·mu·late **AW** /ə'kjuːmjəleɪt/ *verb* **1** [T] **~ sth** to gradually get more and more of sth over a period of time 積累；積聚 **SYN** **amass**：*I seem to have accumulated a lot of books.* 我好像已經收集了很多書。◇ *By investing wisely she accumulated a fortune.* 她投資精明，積累了一筆財富。➲ SYNONYMS at COLLECT **2** [I] to gradually increase in number or quantity over a period of time（數量）逐漸增加；（數額）逐漸增長 **SYN** **build up**：*Debts began to accumulate.* 債務開始增加。➲ SYNONYMS at COLLECT ▸ **ac·cu·mu·la·tion** **AW** /əˌkjuːmjə'leɪʃn/ *noun* [U, C]：*the accumulation of wealth* 財富的積累 ◇ *an accumulation of toxic chemicals* 有毒化學物質的積聚

ac·cu·mu·la·tive /ə'kjuːmjələtɪv/ *adj.* (*formal*) growing by increasing gradually 累積的：*the accumulative effects of pollution* 污染的累積效應

ac·cu·mu·la·tor /ə'kjuːmjəleɪtə(r)/ *noun* **1** (*computing* 計) a section of a computer that is used for storing the results of what has been calculated 累加器 **2** (*BrE*) (*NAmE* **'storage battery**) a large battery that you can fill with electrical power (= that you can RECHARGE) 蓄電池 **3** (*BrE*) a bet on a series of races or other events, where the money won or originally bet is placed on the next race, etc. 累計下注（每贏一次即押於下一輪賭博）

ac·cur·acy **AW** /'ækjərəsi/ *noun* [U] the state of being exact or correct; the ability to do sth skilfully without making mistakes 準確（性）；精確（程度）：*They questioned the accuracy of the information in the file.* 他們懷疑檔案中信息的正確性。◇ *She hits the ball with great accuracy.* 她擊球十分準確。**OPP** **inaccuracy**

ac·cur·ate **AW** /'ækjərət/ *adj.*
1 correct and true in every detail 正確無誤的：*an accurate description/account/calculation* 準確的描述／敘述／計算 ◇ *accurate information/data* 正確無誤的情報／資料 ◇ *Accurate records must be kept.* 必須保存準確的記錄。**2** able to give completely correct information or to do sth in an exact way 精確的；準確的：*a highly accurate electronic compass* 高度精確的電子羅盤儀 ◇ *accurate to within 3 mm* 精確得誤差不超過 3 毫米 ◇ *My watch is not very accurate.* 我的錶走得不很準。**3** an **accurate** throw, shot, weapon, etc. hits or reaches the thing that it was aimed at 準確的（擲、射、擊等）**OPP** **inaccurate** ▸ **ac·cur·ate·ly** **AW** *adv.*：*The article accurately reflects public opinion.* 文章如實反映了公眾的意見。◇ *You need to hit the ball accurately.* 你必須準確擊球。

ac·cur·sed /ə'kɜːsɪd; *NAmE* -'kɜːrs-/ *adj.* (*old-fashioned*) having a CURSE (= a bad magic SPELL) on it 受詛咒的

ac·cus·ation /ˌækju'zeɪʃn/ *noun* [C, U] a statement saying that you think a person is guilty of doing sth wrong, especially of committing a crime; the fact of accusing sb 控告；起訴；告發；譴責：*I don't want to **make an accusation** until I have some proof.* 我要有一些證據以後才提出控告。◇ *There was a hint of accusation in her voice.* 她的語氣暗含譴責。◇ **~ of sth** *accusations of corruption/cruelty/racism* 對貪污腐化 / 殘暴行為 / 種族主義的控告 ◇ **~ against sb** *No one believed her wild accusations against her husband.* 無人相信她對丈夫的無端指責。◇ **~ that …** *He denied the accusation that he had ignored the problems.* 他否認別人說他忽視這些問題的指控。

ac·cusa·tive /ə'kjuːzətɪv/ *noun* (*grammar* 語法) (in some languages 用於某些語言) the form of a noun, a pronoun or an adjective when it is the DIRECT OBJECT of a verb, or connected with the DIRECT OBJECT 賓格；受格：*In the sentence, 'I saw him today', the word 'him' is **in the accusative**.* 在 I saw him today 一句中，him 一詞為賓格。➲ compare ABLATIVE, DATIVE, GENITIVE, NOMINATIVE, VOCATIVE ▸ **ac·cusa·tive** *adj.*

ac·cusa·tory /ə'kjuːzətəri; ˌækju'zeɪtəri; *NAmE* -tɔːri/ *adj.* (*formal*) suggesting that you think sb has done sth wrong 譴責的；指責的；控告的

ac·cuse 🔑 /ə'kjuːz/ *verb* **~ sb (of sth)** to say that sb has done sth wrong or is guilty of sth 控告；控訴；譴責：*to accuse sb of murder/theft* 控告某人謀殺 / 盜竊 ◇ *She accused him of lying.* 她指責他說謊。◇ *The government was accused of incompetence.* 政府被指責無能。◇ (*formal*) *They **stand accused** of crimes against humanity.* 他們被控違反人道罪。▸ **ac·cuser** *noun*

WORD FAMILY
accuse *verb*
accusation *noun*
accusing *adj.*
accusatory *adj.*
accused *noun*

the ac·cused /ə'kjuːzd/ *noun* (*pl.* **the ac·cused**) a person who is on trial for committing a crime （刑事）被告：*The accused was found innocent.* 被告被判定無罪。◇ *All the accused have pleaded guilty.* 所有被告都表示服罪。➲ compare DEFENDANT

ac·cus·ing /ə'kjuːzɪŋ/ *adj.* showing that you think sb has done sth wrong 譴責的；指責的：*an **accusing look/finger/tone*** 譴責的目光；指責的手指；責備的語調 ◇ *Her accusing eyes were fixed on him.* 她用責備的眼光盯着他。▸ **ac·cus·ing·ly** *adv.*

ac·cus·tom /ə'kʌstəm/ *verb*
PHR V **ac'custom yourself/sb to sth** to make yourself/sb familiar with sth or become used to it 使習慣於：*It took him a while to accustom himself to the idea.* 他過了一段時間才習慣這個想法。

ac·cus·tomed /ə'kʌstəmd/ *adj.* **1** (rather *formal*) familiar with sth and accepting it as normal or usual 習慣於 **SYN** **used to**：**~ to sth** *to **become/get accustomed** to sth* 習慣於某事物 ◇ *My eyes slowly **grew accustomed** to the dark.* 我的眼睛慢慢適應了黑暗。◇ **~ to doing sth** *She was a person accustomed to having eight hours' sleep a night.* 她是那種習慣每晚睡八個小時的人。**2** [usually before noun] (*formal*) usual 通常的；慣常的 **SYN** **habitual**：*He took his accustomed seat by the fire.* 他坐在爐火邊慣常坐的座位。**OPP** **unaccustomed**

AC/DC /eɪ siː 'diː siː/ *adj.* (*slang*) = BISEXUAL

ace /eɪs/ *noun, adj., verb*
■ **noun** **1** a PLAYING CARD with a large single symbol on it, which has either the highest or the lowest value in a particular card game * A 紙牌（亦稱"愛司"）：*the **ace of spades/hearts/diamonds/clubs*** 黑桃 / 紅心 / 方塊 / 梅花 A ➲ **VISUAL VOCAB** page V37 **2** (*informal*) a person who is very good at doing sth 擅長…的人；精於…的人：*a soccer/flying ace* 足球 / 飛行頂尖高手 ◇ *an ace marksman* 神槍手 **3** (in TENNIS 網球) a SERVE (= the first hit) that is so good that your opponent cannot reach the ball 發球得分；愛司球：*He served 20 aces in the match.* 他在這場比賽中發了 20 個愛司球。
IDM **an ace up your 'sleeve** (*BrE*) (*NAmE* **an ace in the 'hole**) (*informal*) a secret advantage, for example a piece of information or a skill, that you are ready to use if you need to 秘藏的王牌；應急的妙計；錦囊妙計 **hold all the aces** to have all the advantages in a situation 佔盡天時地利人和 **play your 'ace** to use your best argument, etc. in order to get an advantage in a situation 打出王牌；使出絕招 **within an ace of sth/of doing sth** (*BrE*) very close to sth 差一點兒；幾乎：*We came within an ace of victory.* 我們差一點兒就要勝利了。
■ **adj.** (*informal*) very good 第一流的；極好的：*We had an ace time.* 我們過得真痛快。
■ **verb** **~ sth** (*informal, especially NAmE*) to be successful in sth 在…中獲得成功：*He aced all his tests.* 他通過了對他的所有測試。

acel·lu·lar /ˌeɪ'seljələ(r)/ *adj.* (*biology* 生) not consisting of or divided into cells 無細胞的；非細胞（組成）的

acer /'eɪsə(r)/ *noun* [C, U] a tree or plant that is often grown for its attractive leaves and bright autumn/fall colours 槭屬植物，秋槭（常栽作風景樹）

acerb·ic /ə'sɜːbɪk; *NAmE* ə'sɜːrb-/ *adj.* (*formal*) (of a person or what they say 人或言語) critical in a direct and rather cruel way 尖刻的；嚴厲的：*The letter was written in her usual acerbic style.* 這封信是用她慣常的尖刻語調寫的。▸ **acerb·ity** /ə'sɜːbəti; *NAmE* ə'sɜːrb-/ *noun* [U]

acet·amino·phen /əˌsiːtə'mɪnəfen/ (*NAmE*) (*BrE* **para·ceta·mol**) *noun* [U, C] a drug used to reduce pain and fever 醋氨酚；撲熱息痛

acet·ate /'æsɪteɪt/ *noun* **1** [U] a chemical made from acetic acid, used in making plastics, etc. 醋酸鹽；醋酸酯 **2** [U] a chemical used to make FIBRES which are used to make clothes, etc. 醋酸纖維素 **3** [C] a transparent plastic sheet that you can write or print sth on and show on a screen using an OVERHEAD PROJECTOR 醋酸透明塑膠片；投影膠片

acet·ic acid /əˌsiːtɪk 'æsɪd/ *noun* [U] the acid in VINEGAR that gives it its taste and smell 乙酸；醋酸

acet·one /'æsɪtəʊn; *NAmE* -toʊn/ *noun* [U] a clear liquid with a strong smell used for cleaning things, making paint thinner and producing various chemicals 丙酮

acetyl·ene /ə'setəliːn/ (also **eth·yne**) *noun* [U] (*symb.* C_2H_2) a gas that burns with a very hot bright flame, used for cutting or joining metal 乙炔；電石氣

ach /ɑːx/ *exclamation* (*ScotE*) used to express the fact that you are surprised, sorry, etc.（表示驚奇、遺憾等）啊

ach·cha /ʌ'tʃɑː/ *exclamation* (*IndE, informal*) **1** used to show that the speaker agrees with, accepts, understands, etc. sth（表示同意、接受、明白等）嗯，唔，噢：*Achcha! We'll meet at eight.* 好吧！我們八點鐘見。**2** used to express surprise, happiness, etc.（表示驚奇、高興等）啊，哇，呵哈

ache /eɪk/ *verb, noun*
■ **verb** **1** [I] to feel a continuous dull pain 疼痛；隱痛 **SYN** **hurt**：*I'm aching all over.* 我周身疼痛。◇ **~ from sth** *Her eyes ached from lack of sleep.* 她的眼睛因睡眠不足而隱隱作痛。◇ (*figurative*) *It makes my heart ache* (= it makes me sad) *to see her suffer.* 看到她在受苦，我心裏真難過。➲ **SYNONYMS** at HURT **2** [I, T] (*formal*) to have a strong desire for sb/sth or to do sth 渴望 **SYN** **long**：**~ for sb/sth** *I was aching for home.* 我很想回家。◇ **~ to do sth** *He ached to see her.* 他渴望見到她。
■ **noun** (often in compounds 常構成複合詞) a continuous feeling of pain in a part of the body（身體某部位的）疼痛：*Mummy, I've got a tummy ache.* 媽媽，我肚子疼。◇ *Muscular **aches and pains** can be soothed by a relaxing massage.* 做放鬆按摩可以減輕肌肉疼痛。◇ (*figurative*) *an ache in my heart* (= a continuous sad feeling) 我心中的隱痛 ➲ see also ACHY, BELLYACHE, HEARTACHE

achieve 🔑 **AW** /ə'tʃiːv/ *verb*
1 🔑 [T] **~ sth** to succeed in reaching a particular goal, status or standard, especially by making an effort for a long time（憑長期努力）達到（某目標、地位、標準）**SYN** **attain**：*He had finally achieved success.* 他終於獲得了成功。◇ *They could not achieve their target of less than 3% inflation.* 他們未能達到通貨膨脹低於 3% 的目標。**2** [T] **~ sth** to succeed in doing sth or causing sth

A

to happen 完成 SYN **accomplish**：*I haven't achieved very much today.* 我今天沒做成多少事。◇ *All you've achieved is to upset my parents.* 你唯一做到的就是使我的父母難過。 **3** [I] to be successful 成功：*Their background gives them little chance of achieving at school.* 他們的家庭背景使他們很難有機會在學校學有所成。
▸ **achiev·able** AW *adj.*：*Profits of $20m look achievable.* *2 000 萬元的利潤看來是可以完成的。◇ *achievable goals* 可以達到的目標 OPP **unachievable**

achieve·ment 🔑 AW /əˈtʃiːvmənt/ *noun*
1 🔑 [C] a thing that sb has done successfully, especially using their own effort and skill 成就；成績；功績：*the greatest scientific achievement of the decade* 這十年最偉大的科學成就 ◇ *It was a remarkable achievement for such a young player.* 如此年輕的選手有這樣的成績真是了不起。◇ *They were proud of their children's achievements.* 他們對孩子們的成績感到自豪。 **2** 🔑 [U] the act or process of achieving sth 達到；完成：*the need to raise standards of achievement in education* 在教育中提高成績標準的必要性 ◇ *Even a small success gives you **a sense of achievement*** (= a feeling of pride). 即便是小小的成功也給人一種成就感。

achiever /əˈtʃiːvə(r)/ *noun* **1** a person who achieves a high level of success, especially in their career（尤指事業）成功者 **2** (after an adjective 用於形容詞之後) a person who achieves the particular level of success that is stated 取得…成績的人：*a low achiever* 成績平庸的人

Achil·les heel /əˌkɪliːz ˈhiːl/ *noun* [sing.] a weak point or fault in sb's character, which can be attacked by other people 致命弱點；致命的缺陷 ORIGIN Named after the Greek hero **Achilles**. When he was a small child, his mother held him below the surface of the river Styx to protect him against any injury. She held him by his heel, which therefore was not touched by the water. Achilles died after being wounded by an arrow in the heel. 源自希臘英雄阿喀琉斯（Achilles）的故事。傳說他年幼時，母親把他浸在斯提克斯冥河中，使他刀槍不入。由於母親提着他的腳踵，因此他的腳踵沒有沾上河水。後來他因腳踵中箭身亡。

Aˌchil·les ˈten·don (also **Achil·les**) *noun* the TENDON that connects the muscles at the back of the lower part of the leg to the heel 跟腱

ach·ing·ly /ˈeɪkɪŋli/ *adv.* (of qualities or feelings 品質或情感) very great and affecting you deeply 非常；極其；感人至深地：*an achingly beautiful song* 觸人靈魂的妙曲

ach·kan /ˈʌʃkən/ *noun* a piece of men's clothing that reaches to the knees, with buttons down the front, worn in S Asia 愛客坎（南亞男子的開衫長款上衣）

achy /ˈeɪki/ *adj.* (*informal*) suffering from a continuous slight pain 隱痛不止的：*I feel all achy.* 我感到渾身痠痛。◇ *an achy back* 背痛

acid 🔑 /ˈæsɪd/ *noun, adj.*
■ ***noun*** **1** 🔑 [U, C] (*chemistry* 化) a chemical, usually a liquid, that contains HYDROGEN and has a pH of less than seven. The HYDROGEN can be replaced by a metal to form a salt. Acids are usually sour and can often burn holes in or damage things they touch. 酸 ➲ compare ALKALI ➲ see also ACETIC ACID, AMINO ACID, ASCORBIC ACID, CITRIC ACID, HYDROCHLORIC ACID, LACTIC ACID, NITRIC ACID, NUCLEIC ACID, SULPHURIC ACID **2** [U] (*slang*) = LSD
■ ***adj.*** **1** (*technical* 術語) that contains acid or has the essential characteristics of an acid; that has a pH of less than seven 酸的；酸性的：*Rye is tolerant of poor, acid soils.* 黑麥耐貧瘠的酸性土壤。➲ compare ALKALINE **2** that has a bitter sharp taste 酸的；酸味的 SYN **sour**：*acid fruit* 酸水果 ➲ SYNONYMS at BITTER **3** (of a person's remarks 言辭) critical and unkind 尖刻的；尖酸的 SYN **sarcastic, cutting**：*an acid wit* 尖刻的俏皮話

ˈacid house *noun* [U] a type of electronic music with a strong steady beat, often played at parties where some people take harmful drugs 迷幻豪斯音樂（節奏強烈、平穩的電子音樂，常在有人服用迷幻藥的聚會上演奏）

acid·ic /əˈsɪdɪk/ *adj.* **1** very sour 很酸的：*Some fruit juices are very acidic.* 有些果汁酸得很。 **2** containing acid 酸性的：*acidic soil* 酸性土壤

acid·ify /əˈsɪdɪfaɪ/ *verb* (**acid·ifies, acid·ify·ing, acid·ified, acid·ified**) [I, T] **~ (sth)** (*technical* 術語) to become or make sth become an acid（使）變成酸，酸化

acid·ity /əˈsɪdəti/ *noun* [U] the state of having a sour taste or of containing acid 酸味；酸性

ˌacid ˈjazz *noun* [U] a type of dance music that combines JAZZ, FUNK, SOUL, and HIP HOP 迷幻爵士（結合爵士樂、放克樂、靈樂和嘻哈音樂成分的舞曲）

acid·ly /ˈæsɪdli/ *adv.* in an unpleasant or critical way 尖酸地；尖刻地：*'Thanks for nothing,' she said acidly.* "不用你費心。" 她挖苦地說。

ˌacid ˈrain *noun* [U] rain that contains harmful chemicals from factory gases and that damages trees, crops and buildings 酸雨 ➲ VISUAL VOCAB page V7

ˌacid ˈtest (also **ˈlitmus test** especially in *NAmE*) *noun* [sing.] a way of deciding whether sth is successful or true 決定性考驗；嚴峻的考驗：*The acid test of a good driver is whether he or she remains calm in an emergency.* 在緊急情況下能否保持冷靜是對好司機的嚴峻考驗。

ackee (also **akee**) /ˈæki/ *noun* **1** [C] a type of tree that produces bright red fruit, originally from W Africa 阿開基木（原產於西非，結鮮紅色果實） **2** [U] the fruit from this tree, which is poisonous to eat unless it is completely RIPE 阿開基木果實（未完全成熟時有毒）

ac·know·ledge 🔑 AW /əkˈnɒlɪdʒ; *NAmE* əkˈnɑːl-/ *verb*
▸ ADMIT 承認 **1** 🔑 to accept that sth is true 承認（屬實）：**~ sth** *She refuses to acknowledge the need for reform.* 她拒不承認改革的必要性。◇ *a generally acknowledged fact* 公認的事實 ◇ **~ that …** *I did not acknowledge that he had done anything wrong.* 我沒有承認他犯了什麼錯。◇ **~ sth to be, have, etc. sth** *It is generally acknowledged to be true.* 普遍認為那是真的。➲ SYNONYMS at ADMIT
▸ ACCEPT STATUS 承認地位 **2** 🔑 to accept that sb/sth has a particular authority or status 承認（權威、地位） SYN **recognize**：**~ sb/sth** *The country acknowledged his claim to the throne.* 這個國家承認了他繼承王位的權利。◇ **~ sb/sth as sth** *He is widely acknowledged as the best player in the world.* 普遍認為他是世界最佳球員。◇ **~ sb/sth to be, have, etc. sth** *He is widely acknowledged to be the best player in the world.* 普遍認為他是世界最佳球員。
▸ REPLY TO LETTER 覆信 **3 ~ sth** to tell sb that you have received sth that they sent to you 告知收悉：*All applications will be acknowledged.* 所有的申請都將得到覆函告知收悉。◇ *Please acknowledge receipt of this letter.* 信收到後請覆函告知。
▸ SMILE/WAVE 微笑；揮手 **4 ~ sb/sth** to show that you have noticed sb/sth by smiling, waving, etc.（微笑、揮手等）致意：*I was standing right next to her, but she didn't even acknowledge me.* 我就站在她身邊，可是她理都不理我。
▸ EXPRESS THANKS 表示感謝 **5 ~ sth** to publicly express thanks for help you have been given（公開）感謝：*I gratefully acknowledge financial support from several local businesses.* 我對幾家本地企業的資助表示感謝。

ac·know·ledge·ment AW (also **ac·know·ledg·ment**) /əkˈnɒlɪdʒmənt; *NAmE* əkˈnɑːl-/ *noun* **1** [sing., U] an act of accepting that sth exists or is true, or that sth is there（對事實、現實、存在的）承認：*This report is an acknowledgement of the size of the problem.* 這個報告承認了問題的嚴重性。◇ *She gave me a smile of acknowledgement* (= showed that she had seen and recognized me). 她向我微笑打招呼。 **2** [C, U] an act or a statement expressing thanks to sb; something that is given to sb as thanks 感謝；謝禮：*The flowers were a small acknowledgement of your kindness.* 這些花聊表謝意，感謝你的好心幫助。◇ *I was sent a free copy **in acknowledgement of** my contribution.* 我收到一本贈刊，表示對我投稿的謝意。 **3** [C] a letter saying that sth has been received 收件覆函：*I didn't receive an acknowledgement of my application.* 我的申請沒有得到覆信告知收悉。 **4** [C, usually pl.] a statement, especially at the beginning of a book, in which the writer expresses thanks to the people who have helped（尤指作者在卷首的）致謝，鳴謝

acme /ˈækmi/ *noun* [usually sing.] (*formal*) the highest stage of development or the most excellent example of sth 頂峰；頂點；典範 **SYN** **height**

acne /ˈækni/ *noun* [U] a skin condition, common among young people, that produces many PIMPLES (= spots), especially on the face and neck 痤瘡；粉刺：*to suffer from/have acne* 患痤瘡；長粉刺

aco·lyte /ˈækəlaɪt/ *noun* **1** (*formal*) a person who follows and helps a leader 侍從；隨員；助手 **2** (*technical* 術語) a person who helps a priest in some church ceremonies 輔祭；贊禮

acorn /ˈeɪkɔːn; *NAmE* -kɔːrn/ *noun* the small brown nut of the OAK tree, that grows in a base shaped like a cup 橡子；橡實 **IDM** see OAK ➲ VISUAL VOCAB page V10

acous·tic /əˈkuːstɪk/ *adj.* (*NAmE* also **acous·tic·al** /əˈkuːstɪkl/) **1** related to sound or to the sense of hearing 聲音的；音響的；聽覺的 **2** [usually before noun] (of a musical instrument or performance 樂器或演奏) designed to make natural sound, not sound produced by electrical equipment 原聲的；自然聲的 ➲ VISUAL VOCAB page V36 ▸ **acous·tic·al·ly** /-kli/ *adv.*

acous·tics /əˈkuːstɪks/ *noun* **1** [pl.] (also **acoustic** [sing.]) the shape, design, etc. of a room or theatre that make it good or bad for carrying sound（房間、戲院的）傳聲效果，音響效果：*The acoustics of the new concert hall are excellent.* 新音樂廳的傳聲效果極佳。 **2** [U] the scientific study of sound 聲學

ac·quaint /əˈkweɪnt/ *verb* **~ sb/yourself with sth** (*formal*) to make sb/yourself familiar with or aware of sth 使熟悉；使瞭解：*Please acquaint me with the facts of the case.* 請把這事的實情告訴我。◇ *You will first need to acquaint yourself with the filing system.* 你首先需要熟悉文件歸檔方法。

ac·quaint·ance /əˈkweɪntəns/ *noun* **1** [C] a person that you know but who is not a close friend 認識的人；泛泛之交；熟人：*Claire has a wide circle of* ***friends and acquaintances***. 克萊爾交遊很廣。◇ *He's just a business acquaintance.* 他只是業務上認識的人。 **2** [U, C] **~ (with sb)** (*formal*) slight friendship（與某人）認識，略有交情：*He hoped their acquaintance would develop further.* 他希望他們的交情會進一步發展。 **3** [U, C] **~ with sth** (*formal*) knowledge of sth（對某事物的）瞭解：*I had little acquaintance with modern poetry.* 我對現代詩所知甚少。

IDM **make sb's acquaintance | make the acquaintance of sb** (*formal*) to meet sb for the first time 與某人初次相見；結識某人：*I am delighted to make your acquaintance, Mrs Baker.* 貝克太太，我很高興與您相識。◇ *I made the acquaintance of several musicians around that time.* 大約在那段時間，我結識了幾位音樂家。 **of your acˈquaintance** (*formal*) that you know 所認識的；所瞭解的：*No one else of my acquaintance was as rich or successful.* 我所認識的人當中，沒有其他人如此富有或者成功。 **on first acˈquaintance** (*formal*) when you first meet sb 初次相見時：*Even on first acquaintance it was clear that he was not 'the right type'.* 初次見面就看出他顯然不是“對路子的人”。 ➲ more at NOD *v.*

acˈquaintance rape *noun* [U, C] (*especially NAmE*) the crime of RAPING sb, committed by a person he or she knows 熟人強姦（罪）；約會強暴

ac·quaint·ance·ship /əˈkweɪntənsʃɪp/ *noun* [U, C, usually sing.] (*formal*) a slight friendship with sb or knowledge of sth 泛泛之交；認識；瞭解：*It was unfair to judge her on such a brief acquaintanceship.* 你剛認識她就對她作出評價，這是不公平的。

ac·quaint·ed /əˈkweɪntɪd/ *adj.* [not before noun] **1 ~ with sth** (*formal*) familiar with sth, having read, seen or experienced it 熟悉；瞭解：*The students are already acquainted with the work of Shakespeare.* 這些學生已讀過莎士比亞的著作。◇ *Employees should be fully acquainted with emergency procedures.* 雇員應當十分熟悉應急措施。 **2** not close friends with sb, but having met a few times before（與某人）相識，熟悉：*We got acquainted at the conference* (= met and started to get to know each other). 我們在那次會議上相識了。◇ **~ with sb** *I am well acquainted with her family.* 我和她家裏的人很熟。

ac·qui·esce /ˌækwiˈes/ *verb* [I] **~ (in/to sth)** (*formal*) to accept sth without arguing, even if you do not really agree with it 默然接受；默認；默許；順從：*Senior government figures must have acquiesced in the cover-up.* 政府高級官員必然已經默許掩蓋真相。

ac·qui·es·cence /ˌækwiˈesns/ *noun* [U] (*formal*) the fact of being willing to do what sb wants and to accept their opinions, even if you are not sure that they are right 默然接受；默認；默許；順從：*There was general acquiescence in the UN sanctions.* 普遍默認了聯合國的制裁。 ▸ **ac·qui·es·cent** /-ˈesnt/ *adj.*

ac·quire **AW** /əˈkwaɪə(r)/ *verb* (*formal*) **1** **~ sth** to gain sth by your own efforts, ability or behaviour（通過努力、能力、行為表現）獲得，得到：*She has acquired a good knowledge of English.* 她英語已經學得很好。◇ *He has acquired a reputation for dishonesty.* 他得到了奸詐的名聲。◇ *I have recently* ***acquired a taste*** *for olives.* 我最近開始喜歡吃橄欖了。 **2** **~ sth** to obtain sth by buying or being given it 購得；獲得；得到：*The company has just acquired new premises.* 公司剛購得新辦公樓。◇ *I've suddenly acquired a stepbrother.* 我突然有了一個繼兄。

IDM **an acquired ˈtaste** a thing that you do not like much at first but gradually learn to like 養成的愛好：*Abstract art is an acquired taste.* 要慢慢培養才會欣賞抽象藝術。

ac·qui·si·tion **AW** /ˌækwɪˈzɪʃn/ *noun* **1** [U] the act of getting sth, especially knowledge, a skill, etc.（知識、技能等的）獲得，得到：*theories of child language acquisition* 幼兒語言習得的理論 **2** [C] something that sb buys to add to what they already own, usually sth valuable（多指貴重的）購得物：*His latest acquisition is a racehorse.* 他最近購得一匹賽馬。 **3** [C, U] (*business* 商) a company, piece of land, etc. bought by sb, especially another company; the act of buying it 購置物；收購的公司；購置的產業；購置；收購：*They have made acquisitions in several EU countries.* 他們在幾個歐盟國家購買了一些產業。◇ *the acquisition of shares by employees* 雇員購股

ac·quisi·tive /əˈkwɪzətɪv/ *adj.* (*formal, disapproving*) wanting very much to buy or get new possessions 渴求獲取財物的；貪婪的 ▸ **ac·quisi·tive·ness** *noun* [U]

ac·quit /əˈkwɪt/ *verb* (-tt-) **1 ~ sb (of sth)** to decide and state officially in court that sb is not guilty of a crime 宣判無罪：*The jury acquitted him of murder.* 陪審團裁決他謀殺罪不成立。 **OPP** **convict** **2 ~ yourself well, badly, etc.** (*formal*) to perform or behave well, badly, etc. 表現好（或壞等）：*He acquitted himself brilliantly in the exams.* 他在考試中表現出色。

ac·quit·tal /əˈkwɪtl/ *noun* [C, U] an official decision in court that a person is not guilty of a crime 宣告無罪；無罪的判決：*The case resulted in an acquittal.* 此案件最終作出無罪判決。◇ *The jury voted for acquittal.* 陪審團表決贊成判定無罪。 **OPP** **conviction** ➲ COLLOCATIONS at JUSTICE

acre /ˈeɪkə(r)/ *noun* a unit for measuring an area of land; 4 840 square yards or about 4 050 square metres 英畝（4 840 平方碼，約為 4 050 平方米）：*3 000 acres of parkland* * 3 000 英畝開闊綠地 ◇ *a three-acre wood* 一片三英畝的林地 ◇ (*informal*) *Each house has acres of space around it* (= a lot of space). 每座房屋四周都有大量空地。

acre·age /ˈeɪkərɪdʒ/ *noun* [U, C] an area of land measured in acres 英畝數

acrid /ˈækrɪd/ *adj.* having a strong, bitter smell or taste that is unpleasant（氣、味）辛辣的，難聞的，刺激的 **SYN** **pungent**：*acrid smoke from burning tyres* 燃燒輪胎產生的刺鼻氣味 ➲ SYNONYMS at BITTER

acri·mo·ni·ous /ˌækrɪˈməʊniəs; *NAmE* -ˈmoʊ-/ *adj.* (*formal*) (of an argument, etc. 爭論等) angry and full of strong bitter feelings and words 尖刻的；譏諷的；激烈的 **SYN** **bitter**：*His parents went through an*

A

acrimonious divorce. 他的父母在激烈爭吵中離了婚。
▸ **acri·mo·ni·ous·ly** *adv.*

acri·mony /ˈækrɪməni; *NAmE* -moʊni/ *noun* [U] (*formal*) angry bitter feelings or words （態度、言辭）尖刻，譏諷：*The dispute was settled without acrimony.* 沒有唇槍舌劍，這場糾紛就解決了。

acro·bat /ˈækrəbæt/ *noun* an entertainer who performs difficult acts such as balancing on high ropes, especially at a CIRCUS 雜技演員

acro·bat·ic /ˌækrəˈbætɪk/ *adj.* involving or performing difficult acts or movements with the body 雜技的；雜技般的；雜技演員的：*acrobatic feats* 雜技表演 ◇ *an acrobatic dancer* 特技舞蹈演員 ▸ **acro·bat·ic·al·ly** /-kli/ *adv.*

acro·bat·ics /ˌækrəˈbætɪks/ *noun* [pl.] acrobatic acts and movements 雜技：*acrobatics on the high wire* 走鋼絲雜技 ◇ (*figurative*) *vocal acrobatics* (= performing skilfully with the voice when singing) 高超的歌唱技巧

acro·nym /ˈækrənɪm/ *noun* a word formed from the first letters of the words that make up the name of sth, for example 'AIDS' is an acronym for 'acquired immune deficiency syndrome' 首字母縮略詞（如 AIDS 是由 acquired immune deficiency syndrome 的首字母組成）

acrop·olis /əˈkrɒpəlɪs; *NAmE* əˈkrɑːp-/ *noun* (in an ancient Greek city) a castle, or an area that is designed to resist attack, especially one on top of a hill 衞城（古希臘城邦中的城堡或具有防衞性質的地區，多建於山頂）

across 0⊶ /əˈkrɒs; *NAmE* əˈkrɔːs; əˈkrɑːs/ *adv., prep.*

■ ***adv.*** **HELP** For the special uses of **across** in phrasal verbs, look at the entries for the verbs. For example **come across** is in the phrasal verb section at **come**. * across 在短語動詞中的特殊用法見有關動詞詞條。如 come across 在詞條 come 的短語動詞部份。 **1** 0⊶ from one side to the other side 從一邊到另一邊；橫過；寬：*It's too wide. We can't swim across.* 這太寬了，我們游不過去。◇ *The yard measures about 50 feet across.* 庭院寬約 50 英尺。 **2** 0⊶ in a particular direction towards or at sb/sth 從…的一邊向…：*When my name was called, he looked across at me.* 當叫到我名字的時候，他從那邊朝我看過來。 **3** 0⊶ **across from** opposite 在對面；在對過：*There's a school just across from our house.* 有一所學校就在我們房子對面。 **4** (of an answer in a CROSSWORD 縱橫字謎謎底) written from side to side 橫寫的：*I can't do 3 across.* 我猜不出第 3 格橫寫的謎底。

■ ***prep.*** **1** 0⊶ from one side to the other side of sth 從…一邊到另一邊；橫過：*He walked across the field.* 他走過田地。◇ *I drew a line across the page.* 我在這一頁上畫了一條橫線。◇ *A grin spread across her face.* 她粲然一笑。◇ *Where's the nearest bridge across the river?* 過河最近的橋在哪兒？ **2** 0⊶ on the other side of sth 在…對面；在…對過：*There's a bank right across the street.* 街對面就有一家銀行。 **3** on or over a part of the body 在（身體某部位）上：*He hit him across the face.* 他打了他的臉。◇ *It's too tight across the back.* 背部太緊。 **4** in every part of a place, group of people, etc. 在…各處；遍及 **SYN** **throughout**：*Her family is scattered across the country.* 她家中的人散居全國各地。◇ *This view is common across all sections of the community.* 該社區所有階層的人普遍持有這種看法。

ac·ros·tic /əˈkrɒstɪk; *NAmE* -ˈkrɔːs-; -ˈkrɑːs-/ *noun* a poem or other piece of writing in which particular letters in each line, usually the first letters, can be read downwards to form a word or words 離合詩，離合詩體（各行的某些字，通常是開頭字母可組合成詞）

acryla·mide /əˈkrɪləmaɪd/ *noun* [U, C] a substance used in various industrial processes. Acrylamide is also found in food that has been cooked at high temperatures, and may be a cause of cancer. 丙烯酰胺（工業用物質，也見於高溫烹調的食物，可致癌）

acryl·ic /əˈkrɪlɪk/ *adj., noun*

■ ***adj.*** made of a substance produced by chemical processes from a type of acid 丙烯酸的：***acrylic paints/fibres*** 丙烯酸塗料／纖維 ◇ *an acrylic sweater* 一件丙烯酸運動衫

■ ***noun*** **1** [U] a type of FIBRE produced by chemical processes, used to make clothes, etc. 丙烯酸纖維 **2** [C, usually pl.] a type of paint used by artists（畫家用的）丙烯酸顏料

ACT /ˌeɪ siː ˈtiː/ *abbr.* American College Test (an exam that some HIGH SCHOOL students take before they go to college) 美國高等院校考試（一些高中生入高等院校前參加的考試）

act 0⊶ /ækt/ *noun, verb*

■ ***noun***

▸ **STH THAT SB DOES** 作為 **1** 0⊶ [C] a particular thing that sb does 行為；行動；所為：*a criminal act* 犯罪行為 ◇ **~ of sth** *an act of kindness* 善行 ◇ *acts of terrorism* 恐怖行動 ◇ **~ of sb** *The murder was the act of a psychopath.* 這次謀殺是精神變態者所為。 ➲ SYNONYMS at ACTION

▸ **LAW** 法律 **2** 0⊶ [C] a law that has been passed by a parliament（議會通過的）法案，法令：*an Act of Congress* 國會法案 ◇ *the Banking Act 2009* * 2009 年頒佈的銀行法

▸ **PRETENDING** 假裝 **3** 0⊶ [sing.] a way of behaving that is not sincere but is intended to have a particular effect on others 假裝：*Don't take her seriously—it's all an act.* 別跟她認真，這全是假戲一場。◇ *You could tell she was just **putting on an act**.* 你可以看出，她是在裝模作樣。

▸ **IN PLAY/ENTERTAINMENT** 戲劇；娛樂 **4** [C] one of the main divisions of a play, an OPERA, etc.（戲劇、歌劇等的）一幕：*a play in five acts* 一齣五幕劇 ◇ *The hero dies in Act 5, Scene 3.* 男主角在第 5 幕第 3 場死去。 **5** [C] one of several short pieces of entertainment in a show 一項表演：*a **circus/comedy/magic act*** 馬戲／喜劇／魔術表演 **6** [C] a performer or group of musicians 表演者；音樂人組合：*They were one of rock's most impressive live acts.* 他們是最富感染力的現場表演搖滾樂組合之一。

IDM **ˌact of ˈGod** (*law* 律) an event caused by natural forces beyond human control, such as a storm, a flood or an EARTHQUAKE 天災；不可抗力（如風暴、洪水、地震） **be/get in on the act** (*informal*) to be/become involved in an activity that sb else has started, especially to get sth for yourself 參與；插一手 **do, perform, stage a disapˈpearing/ˈvanishing act** (*informal*) to go away or be impossible to find when people need or want you 隱藏踪跡；潛踪隱跡 **get your ˈact together** (*informal*) to organize yourself and your activities in a more effective way in order to achieve sth 集中精力：*He needs to get his act together if he's going to pass.* 要是他想合格，就必須集中精力。 **a ˌhard/ˌtough act to ˈfollow** a person who is so good or successful at sth that it will be difficult for anyone else coming after them to be as good or successful 令人望塵莫及的人 **in the act (of doing sth)** while you are doing sth 正在（做某事）；當場：*He was **caught in the act** of stealing a car.* 他偷汽車時被當場逮個正着。 ➲ more at CLEAN *v.*, READ *v.*

■ ***verb***

▸ **DO STH** 做某事 **1** 0⊶ [I] to do sth for a particular purpose or in order to deal with a situation 做事；行動：*It is vital that we act to stop the destruction of the rainforests.* 至關緊要的是，我們應當採取行動制止破壞雨林。◇ *The girl's life was saved because the doctors acted so promptly.* 多虧醫生行動迅速，女孩的生命得救了。◇ *He claims he acted in self-defence.* 他聲稱他是出於自衞。

▸ **BEHAVE** 行為 **2** 0⊶ [I] to behave in a particular way 表現得：**+ adv.** *John's been acting very strangely lately.* 近來約翰的行為怪得很。◇ **~ like sb/sth** *Stop acting like spoilt children!* 別再像慣壞的孩子那樣胡鬧了！◇ **~ as if/though ...** *She was acting as if she'd seen a ghost.* 她的行為舉止像是見到幽靈一般。 **HELP** In spoken English people often use **like** instead of **as if** or **as though** in this meaning, especially in *NAmE*. 英語口語中，尤其是美式英語，常用 like 代替 as if 或 as though 表示此義：*She was acting like she'd seen a ghost.* This is not considered correct in written *BrE*. 英式英語的書面語中，此用法被視為不正確。

▸ **PRETEND** 假裝 **3** 0⊶ [I] to pretend by your behaviour to be a particular type of person 假裝：**+ noun** *He's been acting the devoted husband all day.* 他整天裝作模範丈夫的樣子。◇ **+ adj.** *I decided to act dumb.* 我決定裝啞。

▸ **PERFORM IN PLAY/MOVIE** 戲劇／電影表演 **4** 0⊶ [I, T] to perform a part in a play or film/movie 扮演（戲劇、電影中的角色）：*Have you ever acted?* 你演過戲嗎？◇ *Most of the cast act well.* 這齣戲大多數演員演得不錯。◇ **~ sth** *Who's acting (the part of) Hamlet?* 誰演哈姆雷特（這個角色）？◇ *The play was well acted.* 這齣戲演得不錯。

A

▸ **PERFORM FUNCTION** 起作用 **5** [I] to perform a particular role or function 充當；起作用：**~ as sth** *Can you act as interpreter?* 你能擔任口譯嗎？◇ **~ like sth** *hormones in the brain that act like natural painkillers* 大腦中起着天然止痛藥作用的荷爾蒙

▸ **HAVE EFFECT** 有作用 **6** [I] **~ (on sth)** to have an effect on sth（對…）有作用，有影響：*Alcohol acts quickly on the brain.* 酒精對大腦迅速產生影響。**IDM** see AGE *n.*, FOOL *n.*, OWN *v.*

PHR V **'act for/on behalf of sb** to be employed to deal with sb's affairs for them, for example by representing them in court（受雇）代表某人行事 **'act on/upon sth** to take action as a result of advice, information, etc. 根據（建議、信息等）行事：*Acting on information from a member of the public, the police raided the club.* 警察根據一個老百姓的報告，突然搜查了這家俱樂部。◇ *Why didn't you act on her suggestion?* 你為什麼沒有按照她的建議去做呢？ **ˌact sth↔'out 1** to perform a ceremony or show how sth happened, as if performing a play 履行（儀式）；將…表演出來：*The ritual of the party conference is acted out in the same way every year.* 該黨的大會程序年年照行如儀。◇ *The children started to act out the whole incident.* 孩子們開始表演整個事件。**2** to act a part in a real situation 充當（真實情況中的角色）：*She acted out the role of the wronged lover.* 她扮作一個受冤枉的情人。 **ˌact 'up** (*informal*) **1** to behave badly 表現不好；搗亂：*The kids started acting up.* 孩子們開始調皮搗蛋起來。**2** to not work as it should 出毛病：*How long has your ankle been acting up?* 你的腳踝受傷多久了？

Synonyms 同義詞辨析

action

measure • step • act • move

These are all words for a thing that sb does. 以上各詞均指行為、行動。

action a thing that sb does 指行動、動作：*Her quick action saved the child's life.* 她行動迅速，救了小孩的命。

measure an official action that is done in order to achieve a particular aim 指措施、方法：*Tougher measures against racism are needed.* 需要更強硬的反種族主義措施。

step one of a series of things that you do in order to achieve sth 指步驟、措施：*This was a first step towards a united Europe.* 這是向建立統一歐洲的目標邁出的最重要的一步。

act a thing that sb does 指行為、行動、所為：*an act of kindness* 善行

ACTION OR ACT? 用 action 還是 act？

These two words have the same meaning but are used in different patterns. An **act** is usually followed by *of* and/or used with an adjective. **Action** is not usually used with *of* but is often used with *his, her, etc.* 這兩個詞意義相同，但用於不同的句型。act 後常跟 of，而且和／或常與形容詞連用。action 通常不與 of 連用，但常與 his、her 等詞連用：*a heroic act of bravery* 英勇壯舉 ◇ ~~*a heroic action of bravery*~~ ◇ *his heroic actions/acts during the war* 他在戰爭中的英雄壯舉 **Action** often combines with *take* but **act** does not. * action 常與 take 搭配，act 則不能：~~*We shall take whatever acts are necessary.*~~

move (used especially in journalism) an action that you do or need to do to achieve sth（尤用於新聞）指為達到某目標而採取或需要採取的行動：*They are waiting for the results of the opinion polls before deciding their next move.* 他們在等待民意測驗的結果，然後再決定下一步行動。

PATTERNS

- to **take** action/measures/steps
- to **make** a step/move
- a **heroic/brave/daring** action/step/act/move

act·ing /'æktɪŋ/ *noun, adj.*

■ ***noun*** [U] the activity or profession of performing in plays, films/movies, etc.（戲劇、電影等中的）表演；演藝業

■ ***adj.*** [only before noun] doing the work of another person for a short time 臨時代理的 **SYN** **temporary**：*the acting manager* 代理經理

ac·tin·ium /æk'tɪniəm/ *noun* [U] (*symb.* **Ac**) a chemical element. Actinium is a RADIOACTIVE metal. 錒（放射性化學元素）

ac·tion 🔑 /'ækʃn/ *noun, verb*

■ ***noun***

▸ **WHAT SB DOES** 作為 **1** 🔑 [U] the process of doing sth in order to make sth happen or to deal with a situation 行動；行為過程：*The time has come for action if these beautiful animals are to survive.* 若要使這些美麗的動物能生存下去，現在就要行動起來。◇ *Firefighters* **took action** *immediately to stop the blaze spreading.* 消防隊員立即採取了行動制止大火蔓延。◇ *What is the best* **course of action** *in the circumstances?* 在這種情況下最佳行動方針是什麼？◇ *She began to explain her* **plan of action** *to the group.* 她開始向小組講解她的行動計劃。➲ see also DIRECT ACTION, INDUSTRIAL ACTION **2** 🔑 [C] a thing that sb does 所做之事；行為：*Her quick action saved the child's life.* 她行動迅速，救了小孩的命。◇ *Each of us must take responsibility for our own actions.* 我們每個人都必須對自己的行為負責。

▸ **LEGAL PROCESS** 訴訟程序 **3** 🔑 [C, U] a legal process to stop a person or company from doing sth, or to make them pay for a mistake, etc. 訴訟；起訴：*A libel action is being brought against the magazine that published the article.* 刊登該文章的雜誌將受到誹謗訴訟。◇ *He is considering taking legal action against the hospital.* 他正考慮起訴這家醫院。

▸ **IN WAR** 戰爭 **4** 🔑 [U] fighting in a battle or war 戰鬥；作戰：*military action* 軍事行動 ◇ *soldiers killed* **in action** 陣亡戰士

▸ **IN STORY/PLAY** 故事；戲劇 **5** [U] the events in a story, play, etc.（故事、戲劇等中的）情節：*The action takes place in France.* 這個故事發生在法國。

▸ **EXCITING EVENTS** 激動人心的事 **6** 🔑 [U] exciting events 激動人心的事：*I like films with plenty of action.* 我喜歡情節曲折離奇的動作片。◇ *New York is* **where the action is.** 紐約是個熱鬧活躍的地方。

▸ **EFFECT** 作用 **7** [U] **~ of sth (on sth)** the effect that one substance or chemical has on another（一種物質或化學品對另一種所起的）作用：*the action of sunlight on the skin* 陽光對皮膚的作用

▸ **OF PART OF THE BODY** 身體部位 **8** [U, C] (*technical* 術語) the way a part of the body moves or functions（身體部位的）動作，功能：*a study of the action of the liver* 對肝功能的研究

▸ **OF MACHINE** 機器 **9** [sing.] the MECHANICAL parts of a piano, gun, clock, etc. or the way the parts move（鋼琴、槍炮、鐘錶等的）機械裝置，活動部件；（機械部件的）活動方式 ➲ see also PUMP-ACTION

IDM **actions speak louder than 'words** (*saying*) what a person actually does means more than what they say they will do 行動勝於語言 **in 'action** 🔑 if sb/sth is **in action**, they are doing the activity or work that is typical for them 在活動中；在運轉：*Just press the button to see your favourite character in action.* 只要按一下按鍵就可以看到你喜歡的角色表演。◇ *I've yet to see all the players in action.* 我還得看所有參賽者的實地比賽。 **into 'action** 🔑 if you put an idea or a plan **into action**, you start making it happen or work 實行；實施：*The new plan for traffic control is being put into action on an experimental basis.* 新的交通管理方案正在試驗實施。 **out of 'action** not able to work or be used because of injury or damage 不能工作；失去作用；停止運轉：*Jon will be out of action for weeks with a broken leg.* 喬恩斷了一條腿，將有幾個星期不能走動。◇ *The photocopier is out of action today.* 複印機今天故障了。 **a piece/slice of the 'action** (*informal*) a share or role in an interesting or exciting activity, especially in order to make money 插手，參與（尤指為了賺錢）：*Foreign* *firms will all want a piece of the action if the new airport goes ahead.* 要是新機場開始修建，外國公司都會來插一手撈好處。➲ more at EVASIVE, SPRING *v.*, SWING *v.*

■ ***verb*** **~ sth** to make sure that sth is done or dealt with 務必做，確保處理（某事）：*Your request will be actioned.* 你的要求會處理的。

ac·tion·able /ˈækʃənəbl/ *adj.* giving sb a valid reason to bring a case to court 可予起訴的；可提起訴訟的

ac·tion·er /ˈækʃənə(r)/ *noun* (*NAmE, informal*) = ACTION MOVIE

ˈaction figure *noun* a DOLL representing a soldier or a character from a film/movie, TV show, etc.（仿影視等角色的）戰士玩偶，人偶

ˈaction film *noun* (*BrE*) = ACTION MOVIE

ˈaction group *noun* (often as part of a name 常作名稱的一部份) a group that is formed to work for social or political change（社會或政治改革的）行動小組：*the Child Poverty Action Group* 解除兒童貧困行動小組

ˈAction Man™ *noun* **1** a toy in the form of a soldier 機動人（一種玩具兵）**2** an active and aggressive man 進取型的男子：*The illness damaged his Action Man image.* 這場病損害了他那愛打拚的形象。

ˈaction movie (*BrE* also **ˈaction film**) (also *NAmE, informal* **ac·tion·er**) *noun* a film/movie that has a lot of exciting action and adventure 動作影片

ˈaction-packed *adj.* full of exciting events and activity 充滿令人興奮的活動的：*an action-packed weekend* 活動安排得滿滿的週末

ˈaction point *noun* a suggestion for action that must be taken, especially one that is made in a meeting（尤指在會議上達成的）行動方案

ˌaction ˈreplay *noun* (*BrE*) **1** (*NAmE* **ˌinstant ˈreplay**) part of sth, for example a sports game on television, that is immediately repeated, often more slowly, so that you can see a goal or another exciting or important moment again（體育比賽等電視畫面的）即時重放，慢鏡頭重放 **2** an event or a situation that repeats sth that has happened before（往事的）重演：*It was an action replay of the problems of his first marriage.* 這是他第一次婚姻問題的重演。

ˈaction research *noun* [U] studies done to improve the working methods of people who do a particular job or activity, especially in education（尤指教育界為改進工作方法等而開展的）行動研究

ˈaction stations *noun* [pl.] the positions to which soldiers go to be ready for fighting 戰鬥崗位

ac·ti·vate /ˈæktɪveɪt/ *verb* **~ sth** to make sth such as a device or chemical process start working 使活動；激活；使活化：*The burglar alarm is activated by movement.* 這防盜警報器一動就會響。◇ *The gene is activated by a specific protein.* 這種基因由一種特異性蛋白激活。▸ **ac·ti·vation** /ˌæktɪˈveɪʃn/ *noun* [U]

ac·tive 0‑ /ˈæktɪv/ *adj., noun*

■ ***adj.***

▸ BUSY 忙碌 **1** 0‑ always busy doing things, especially physical activities（尤指體力上）忙碌的，活躍的：*Although he's nearly 80, he is still very active.* 儘管快80歲了，他還是十分活躍。OPP **inactive**

▸ TAKING PART 參加 **2** 0‑ involved in sth; making a determined effort and not leaving sth to happen by itself 積極的：*They were both politically active.* 他們兩人在政治上都很積極。◇ ***active involvement/participation/support/resistance*** 積極參與／參加／支持／抵抗 ◇ *She takes an **active part** in school life.* 她積極參加學校活動。◇ *The parents were active in campaigning against cuts to the education budget.* 學生家長積極參加反對削減教育預算的活動。◇ *They took active steps to prevent the spread of the disease.* 他們採取積極措施，防止疾病蔓延。

▸ DOING AN ACTIVITY 活動 **3** 0‑ doing sth regularly; functioning 定期進行的；起作用的：*sexually active teenagers* 性慾旺盛的青少年 ◇ *animals that are active only at night* 僅在夜間活動的動物 ◇ *The virus is still active in the blood.* 這種病毒仍然在血液中起作用。◇ *an active volcano* (= likely to ERUPT) 活火山 OPP **inactive** ➲ compare DORMANT

▸ LIVELY 充滿活力 **4** lively and full of ideas 活躍的；（思想上）充滿活力的：*That child has a very active imagination.* 那個小孩想像力十分豐富。

▸ CHEMICAL 化學 **5** having or causing a chemical effect 起化學作用的；有效的：*What is the active ingredient in aspirin?* 什麼是阿司匹林中的有效成分？OPP **inactive**

▸ GRAMMAR 語法 **6** connected with a verb whose subject is the person or thing that performs the action 主動語態的：*In 'He was driving the car', the verb is active.* 在 He was driving the car 一句中，動詞是主動語態。➲ compare PASSIVE *adj.* (2)

▸ **ac·tive·ly** 0‑ *adv.*：*Your proposal is being actively considered.* 你的提議正得到認真考慮。◇ *She was actively looking for a job.* 她在積極找工作。

■ ***noun*** (also **ˌactive ˈvoice**) [sing.] the form of a verb in which the subject is the person or thing that performs the action 主動語態 ➲ compare PASSIVE *n.*

ˈactive list *noun* **1** a list of people that an organization may contact at any time, offering a service, providing information, or asking them to do sth 積極分子名單（可用於隨時聯繫以便提供服務、信息或尋求幫助等）：*Please email us to be removed from our active list of blood donors.* 假如你想把自己的名字從獻血聯繫人名單中刪去，請給我們發電子郵件。**2** a list of officers or former officers connected to one of the armed forces who can be called for duty 服役名冊（記錄現役或退役軍官）

ˌactive ˈservice (*NAmE* also **ˌactive ˈduty**) *noun* [U] the work of a member of the armed forces, especially during a war 現役；（尤指）戰時服役：*troops on active service* 現役部隊

ac·tiv·ist /ˈæktɪvɪst/ *noun* a person who works to achieve political or social change, especially as a member of an organization with particular aims 積極分子；活躍分子：*gay activists* 爭取男同性戀者權益的活動人士 ▸ **ac·tiv·ism** /ˈæktɪvɪzəm/ *noun* [U]

ac·tiv·ity 0‑ /ækˈtɪvəti/ *noun* (*pl.* **-ies**)

1 0‑ [U] a situation in which sth is happening or a lot of things are being done 活動；熱鬧狀況；活躍：*economic activity* 經濟活動 ◇ *The streets were noisy and full of activity.* 街上熙熙攘攘，車水馬龍。◇ *Muscles contract and relax during physical activity.* 身體活動時肌肉收縮放鬆。➲ compare INACTIVITY at INACTIVE **2** 0‑ [C, usually pl.] a thing that you do for interest or pleasure, or in order to achieve a particular aim（為興趣、娛樂或達到一定目的而進行的）活動：***leisure/outdoor/classroom activities*** 休閒／戶外／課堂活動 ◇ *The club provides a wide variety of activities including tennis, swimming and squash.* 這家俱樂部的活動豐富多彩，諸如網球、游泳、壁球等。◇ ***illegal/criminal activities*** 不法／犯罪活動

actor 0‑ /ˈæktə(r)/ *noun* a person who performs on the stage, on television or in films/movies, especially as a profession 演員

ˌactor-ˈmanager *noun* an actor who is in charge of a theatre company and acts in the plays that they perform 演員兼劇團總監

ac·tress 0‑ /ˈæktrəs/ *noun* a woman who performs on the stage, on television or in films/movies, especially as a profession 女演員 HELP Many women now prefer to be called **actors**, although when the context is not clear, **an actor** is usually understood to refer to a man. 雖然在上下文不明確時 actor 通常指男演員，但是現在很多女演員都喜歡被稱為 actor。➲ note at GENDER

ac·tual 0‑ /ˈæktʃuəl/ *adj.* [only before noun]

1 0‑ used to emphasize sth that is real or exists in fact 真實的；實際的：*What were his actual words?* 他的原話是什麼？◇ *The actual cost was higher than we expected.* 實際成本比我們預計的要高。◇ *James looks younger than his wife but **in actual fact** (= really) he is five years older.* 詹姆斯看起來比他妻子年輕，但實際上他還大了五歲。**2** 0‑ used to emphasize the most important part of sth（強調事情最重要的部份）真正的，…本身：*The wedding preparations take weeks but the actual ceremony* *takes less than an hour.* 準備婚禮要幾週，而婚禮儀式本身還不到一小時。

Which Word? 詞語辨析

actual / current / present

- **Actual** does not mean **current** or **present**. It means 'real' or 'exact', and is often used in contrast with something that is not seen as real or exact. * actual 與 current 或 present 意義不同，其含義為真實的或確實的，常與不真實或不確實的事物形成對比：*I need the actual figures, not an estimate.* 我需要確切的數字，而不是估計。
- **Present** means 'existing or happening now'. * present 意為現存、現行：*How long have you been in your present job?* 你幹現在這工作多長時間了？
- **Current** also means 'existing or happening now', but can suggest that the situation is temporary. * current 也指現存、現行，但含暫時之意：*The factory cannot continue its current level of production.* 這家工廠不能維持目前的生產水平。
- **Actually** does not mean 'at the present time'. Use **currently**, **at present** or **at the moment** instead. * actually 無現在、目前之意，表示此義用 currently、at present 或 at the moment。

➲ note at PRESENTLY

ˌactual ˌbodily ˈharm *noun* [U] (*abbr.* **ABH**) (*BrE*, *law* 律) the crime of causing sb physical injury 實際身體傷害（罪）➲ compare GRIEVOUS BODILY HARM

ac·tu·al·ity /ˌæktʃuˈæləti/ *noun* (*pl.* **-ies**) (*formal*) **1** [U] the state of sth existing in reality 真實；實際：*The building looked as impressive **in actuality** as it did in photographs.* 這棟大樓外觀雄偉，與照片中所見一模一樣。**2** [C, usually pl.] things that exist 真實情況；現實情況；事實 SYN **facts, realities**：*the grim actualities of prison life* 嚴酷的監獄生活現實

ac·tu·al·ize (*BrE* also **-ise**) /ˈæktʃuəlaɪz/ *verb* **~ sth** to make sth real; to make sth happen 實現；使發生：*He finally actualized his dream.* 他最終實現了自己的夢想。

ac·tu·al·ly 🔑 /ˈæktʃuəli/ *adv.* **1** 🔑 used in speaking to emphasize a fact or a comment, or that sth is really true（在口語中用於強調事實）的確，真實地，事實上：*What did she actually say?* 她到底是怎麼說的？◇ *It's not actually raining now.* 其實現在並沒有下雨。◇ *That's the only reason I'm actually going.* 這是我確實要走的唯一理由。◇ *There are lots of people there who can actually help you.* 那裏有很多人可以真正幫上你的忙。◇ *I didn't want to say anything without actually reading the letter first.* 在未確實讀信之前我什麼也不想說。**2** 🔑 used to show a contrast between what is true and what sb believes, and to show surprise about this contrast（表示想法與事實不一致因而驚奇）居然，竟然：*It was actually quite fun after all.* 這居然還很有趣。◇ *The food was not actually all that expensive.* 食品居然並不那麼昂貴。◇ *Our turnover actually increased last year.* 去年我們的營業額竟然增加了。**3** 🔑 used to correct sb in a polite way（禮貌地糾正他人）實際上，事實上：*We're not American, actually. We're Canadian.* 實際上我們不是美國人。我們是加拿大人。◇ *Actually, it would be much more sensible to do it later.* 事實上，以後再辦這件事可能要明智得多。◇ *They're not married, actually.* 他們實際上沒有結婚。**4** 🔑 used to get sb's attention, to introduce a new topic or to say sth that sb may not like, in a polite way（禮貌地引起注意、轉換話題、直言）確實，說實在的：*Actually, I'll be a bit late home.* 說真的，我回家會晚一點。◇ *Actually, I'm busy at the moment—can I call you back?* 說實在的，我這會兒正忙。我可以給你回電話嗎？➲ note at ACTUAL

ac·tu·ary /ˈæktʃuəri; *NAmE* -eri/ *noun* (*pl.* **-ies**) a person whose job involves calculating insurance risks and payments for insurance companies by studying how frequently accidents, fires, deaths, etc. happen 精算師（以研究事故、火災、死亡等發生的頻率為依據，為保險公司計算保險風險和保險費）▶ **ac·tu·ar·ial** /ˌæktʃuˈeəriəl; *NAmE* -ˈeriəl/ *adj.*

ac·tu·ate /ˈæktʃueɪt/ *verb* (*formal*) **1 ~ sth** to make a machine or device start to work 開動（機器、裝置等）SYN **activate** **2** [usually passive] **~ sb** to make sb behave in a particular way 激勵；驅使 SYN **motivate**：*He was actuated entirely by malice.* 他完全是出於惡意。

acu·ity /əˈkjuːəti/ *noun* [U] (*formal*) the ability to think, see or hear clearly（思維、視力、聽力的）敏度，敏銳

acu·men /ˈækjəmən; əˈkjuːmən/ *noun* [U] the ability to understand and decide things quickly and well 精明；敏銳：***business/commercial/financial acumen*** 生意上／商業上／理財精明強幹

acu·pres·sure /ˈækjupreʃə(r)/ (also **shi·atsu**) *noun* [U] a form of medical treatment, originally from Japan, in which pressure is applied to particular parts of the body using the fingers 指壓（源於日本的一種治療方式，以手指按壓身體特定部位）

acu·punc·ture /ˈækjupʌŋktʃə(r)/ *noun* [U] a Chinese method of treating pain and illness using special thin needles which are pushed into the skin in particular parts of the body 針刺療法

acu·punc·tur·ist /ˈækjupʌŋktʃərɪst/ *noun* a person who is trained to perform acupuncture 針療醫師

acute /əˈkjuːt/ *adj.* **1** very serious or severe 十分嚴重的：*There is an acute shortage of water.* 水嚴重短缺。◇ *acute pain* 劇痛 ◇ *the world's acute environmental problems* 全球十分嚴重的環境問題 ◇ *Competition for jobs is acute.* 求職競爭非常激烈。**2** an **acute** illness is one that has quickly become severe and dangerous（疾病）急性的：*acute appendicitis* 急性闌尾炎 OPP **chronic** **3** (of the senses 感官) very sensitive and well developed 靈敏的 SYN **keen**：*Dogs have an acute sense of smell.* 狗的嗅覺靈敏。**4** intelligent and quick to notice and understand things 敏銳的；有洞察力的：*He is an acute observer of the social scene.* 他是個敏銳的社會現狀觀察者。◇ *Her judgement is acute.* 她的判斷敏銳。**5** (*geometry* 幾何) (of an angle 角) less than 90° 銳角的 ▶ **acute·ness** *noun* [U]

aˌcute ˈaccent *noun* the mark placed over a vowel to show how it should be pronounced, as over the *e* in *fiancé* 尖音符號（標在元音上面）➲ compare CIRCUMFLEX, GRAVE², TILDE, UMLAUT

aˌcute ˈangle *noun* an angle of less than 90° 銳角 ➲ VISUAL VOCAB page V71 ➲ compare OBTUSE ANGLE, REFLEX ANGLE, RIGHT ANGLE

acute·ly /əˈkjuːtli/ *adv.* **1 ~ aware/conscious** noticing or feeling sth very strongly 深深感覺到；強烈意識到：*I am acutely aware of the difficulties we face.* 我十分清楚我們面臨的困難。**2** (describing unpleasant feelings) very; very strongly（描述不快的感覺）極其，強烈地：*acutely embarrassed* 極其尷尬

-acy ➲ -CY, -ACY

acyc·lic /ˌeɪˈsaɪklɪk/ *adj.* **1** (*technical* 術語) not occurring in cycles 非週期的；非循環的 **2** (*chemistry* 化) (of a COMPOUND or MOLECULE 化合物或分子) containing no rings of atoms 無環的；非環狀的

AD (*BrE*) (*NAmE* **A.D.**) /ˌeɪ ˈdiː/ *abbr.* used in the Christian CALENDAR to show a particular number of years since the year when Christ was believed to have been born (from Latin 'Anno Domini') 公元（源自拉丁語 Anno Domini）：*in (the year) AD 55* 公元 55 年 ◇ *in 55 AD* 公元 55 年 ◇ *in the fifth century AD* 公元 5 世紀 ➲ compare AH, BC, BCE, CE

ad 🔑 /æd/ *noun* (*informal*) = ADVERTISEMENT：*We put an ad in the local paper.* 我們在當地報紙上登了一則廣告。◇ *an ad for a new chocolate bar* 新品種巧克力棒的廣告 ➲ **SYNONYMS** at ADVERTISEMENT ➲ see also BANNER AD

adage /ˈædɪdʒ/ *noun* a well-known phrase expressing a general truth about people or the world 諺語；格言 SYN **saying**

A

A

ada·gio /ə'dɑːdʒiəʊ; *NAmE* -dʒioʊ/ *noun* (*pl.* **-os**) (*music* 音) a piece of music to be played slowly 柔板樂章；柔板 ▸ **ada·gio** *adj., adv.*

Adam /'ædəm/ *noun* IDM see KNOW *v.*

ad·am·ant /'ædəmənt/ *adj.* determined not to change your mind or to be persuaded about sth 堅決的；堅定不移的：*Eva was adamant that she would not come.* 伊娃堅決不來。▸ **ad·am·ant·ly** *adv.*：*His family were adamantly opposed to the marriage.* 他的家人堅決反對這門親事。

ad·am·ant·ine /ˌædə'mæntaɪn/ *adj.* (*literary*) very strong and impossible to break 堅韌的；剛勁的

ˌAdam's 'apple *noun* the lump at the front of the throat that sticks out, particularly in men, and moves up and down when you swallow 喉結

adapt 🔑 AW /ə'dæpt/ *verb*
1 🔑 [T] to change sth in order to make it suitable for a new use or situation 使適應，使適合（新用途、新情況）SYN **modify**：**~ sth** *These styles can be adapted to suit individual tastes.* 這些式樣可以修改，以適應個人不同愛好。◇ **~ sth for sth** *Most of these tools have been specially adapted for use by disabled people.* 這些工具多數已經過特別改裝，供殘疾人士使用。 **2** 🔑 [I, T] to change your behaviour in order to deal more successfully with a new situation 適應（新情況）SYN **adjust**：*It's amazing how soon you adapt.* 你這麼快就適應了，真是令人驚奇。◇ *The organisms were forced to adapt in order to survive.* 生物被迫適應，以求生存。◇ **~ to sth** *We have had to adapt quickly to the new system.* 我們不得不迅速適應了新制度。◇ *A large organization can be slow to adapt to change.* 大機構可能應變遲緩。◇ **~ yourself to sth** *It took him a while to adapt himself to his new surroundings.* 他過了好一陣子才適應了新環境。 **3** 🔑 [T] **~ sth (for sth) (from sth)** to change a book or play so that it can be made into a play, film/movie, television programme, etc. 改編；改寫：*Three of her novels have been adapted for television.* 她的長篇小說中有三部已改編成電視節目。

adapt·able AW /ə'dæptəbl/ *adj.* (*approving*) able to change or be changed in order to deal successfully with new situations 有適應能力的；能適應的：*Older workers can be as adaptable and quick to learn as anyone else.* 較年長的工人的適應能力和學習速度有時並不亞於其他任何人。◇ *Successful businesses are highly adaptable to economic change.* 成功的企業對於經濟轉變的適應能力很強。▸ **adapt·abil·ity** AW /əˌdæptə'bɪləti/ *noun* [U]

adap·ta·tion AW /ˌædæp'teɪʃn/ (also *less frequent* **adap·tion** /ə'dæpʃn/) *noun* **1** [C] a film/movie, book or play that is based on a particular piece of work but that has been changed for a new situation 改編本；改寫本：*a screen adaptation of Shakespeare's 'Macbeth'* 莎士比亞悲劇《麥克佩斯》的電影改寫本 **2** [U] the process of changing sth, for example your behaviour, to suit a new situation 適應：*the adaptation of desert species to the hot conditions* 沙漠物種對炎熱環境的適應

adap·tive AW /ə'dæptɪv/ *adj.* (*technical* 術語) concerned with changing; able to change when necessary in order to deal with different situations 適應的；有適應能力的

adap·tor (also **adap·ter**) /ə'dæptə(r)/ *noun* **1** a device for connecting pieces of electrical equipment that were not designed to fit together （電器設備的）轉接器，適配器 **2** (*BrE*) a device for connecting more than one piece of equipment to the same SOCKET (= a place in the wall where equipment is connected to the electricity supply) （供多個設備連接電源的）多頭插頭，多功能插頭

ADC /ˌeɪ diː 'siː/ *abbr.* AIDE-DE-CAMP

add 🔑 /æd/ *verb*
1 🔑 [T] to put sth together with sth else so as to increase the size, number, amount, etc. 增加；加添：**~ sth** *Next add the flour.* 接着加麪粉。◇ *The juice contains no added sugar.* 這種果汁沒有加糖。◇ *The plan has the added (= extra) advantage of bringing employment to rural areas.* 該計劃還有一個優點，就是給農村地區帶來了就業機會。◇ **~ sth to sth** *A new wing was added to the building.* 這棟大樓新添了一座配樓。◇ *Shall I add your name to the list?* 我可以把你的名字寫進名單嗎？ **2** 🔑 [I, T] to put numbers or amounts together to get a total 加：**~ A to B** *Add 9 to the total.* 總數再加上 9。◇ **~ A and B together** *If you add all these amounts together you get a huge figure.* 你把這些數量加在一起就會得到一個巨額數字。OPP **subtract** **3** 🔑 [T] to say sth more; to make a further remark 補充說；繼續說：**+ speech** *'And don't be late,' she added.* "還有別遲到。" 她補充說道。◇ **~ sth (to sth)** *I have nothing to add to my earlier statement.* 我對我早先說的話沒有什麼補充的。◇ **~ that …** *He added that they would return a week later.* 他接着說，他們一週以後會回來。 **4** [T] **~ sth (to sth)** to give a particular quality to an event, a situation, etc. 添加（特色）：*The suite will add a touch of class to your bedroom.* 這套傢具會給你的臥室增添一些典雅氣質。

IDM **add ˌinsult to 'injury** to make a bad relationship with sb worse by offending them even more 傷害之餘又侮辱；（冒犯別人）令關係惡化 **'added to this …** | **'add to this …** used to introduce another fact that helps to emphasize a point you have already made 此外（還…）：*Add to this the excellent service and you can see why it's the most popular hotel on the island.* 這再加上優質服務，你就能明白為何這家旅館在島上最受歡迎。

PHR V **ˌadd sth↔'in** to include sth with sth else 把…加進去；包括：*Remember to add in the cost of drinks.* 記住把飲料費加進去。 **ˌadd sth↔'on (to sth)** 🔑 to include or attach sth extra 附加；加上：*A service charge of 15% was added on to the bill.* 賬單上附加了 15% 的服務費。➲ related noun ADD-ON **'add to sth** to increase sth in size, number, amount, etc. 使（數量）增加；使（規模）擴大：*The bad weather only added to our difficulties.* 惡劣的天氣只是再增加了我們的困難。◇ *The house has been added to (= new rooms, etc. have been built on to it) from time to time.* 這座房子一次又一次地在擴建。 **ˌadd 'up** (*informal*) **1** (especially in negative sentences 尤用於否定句) to seem reasonable; to make sense 合乎情理；有道理：*His story just doesn't add up.* 他說的情況根本不合情理。 **2** (not used in the progressive tenses 不用於進行時) to increase by small amounts until there is a large total 積少成多：*When you're feeding a family of six the bills soon add up.* 你要養活一家六口，開支很快就大起來了。 **ˌadd 'up** | **ˌadd sth↔'up** 🔑 to calculate the total of two or more numbers or amounts 把…加起來：*The waiter can't add up.* 這個服務員不會算賬。◇ *Add up all the money I owe you.* 把我欠你的錢全部加起來。 **ˌadd 'up to sth** **1** 🔑 to make a total amount of sth 總共是；總計為：*The numbers add up to exactly 100.* 這些數字的總數恰好是 100。 **2** to lead to a particular result; to show sth 結果是；表示 SYN **amount to sth**：*These clues don't really add up to very much (= give us very little information).* 這些線索實際上說明不了什麼問題。

ADD /ˌeɪ diː 'diː/ *abbr.* ATTENTION DEFICIT DISORDER 注意缺陷障礙；多動症

ad·den·dum /ə'dendəm/ *noun* (*pl.* **ad·denda** /-də/) (*formal*) a section of extra information that is added to sth, especially to a book （尤指書籍的）補遺，補篇

adder /'ædə(r)/ *noun* a small poisonous snake, often with diamond-shaped marks on its back. Adders are the only poisonous snakes in Britain. 蝰蛇，寬蛇（英國僅有的一種毒蛇，背部有菱形斑）

ad·dict /'ædɪkt/ *noun* **1** a person who is unable to stop taking harmful drugs 吸毒成癮的人；癮君子：***a heroin/drug/nicotine addict*** 吸食海洛因／毒品／尼古丁成癮的人 **2** a person who is very interested in sth and spends a lot of their free time on it 對…入迷的人：*a video game addict* 遊戲機迷

ad·dict·ed /ə'dɪktɪd/ *adj.* [not before noun] **1 ~ (to sth)** unable to stop taking harmful drugs, or using or doing sth as a habit 上癮；成癮；有癮：*to become addicted to drugs/gambling* 吸毒成癮；嗜賭 **2 ~ (to sth)** spending all your free time doing sth because you are so interested in it 入迷：*He's addicted to computer games.* 他迷上了電腦遊戲。

ad·dic·tion /ə'dɪkʃn/ *noun* [U, C] the condition of being addicted to sth 癮；入迷；嗜好：*cocaine addiction* 可卡

因癮 ◇ **~ to sth** *He is now fighting his addiction to alcohol.* 他現在正努力戒酒。➲ COLLOCATIONS at ILL

ad·dict·ive /əˈdɪktɪv/ *adj.* **1** if a drug is **addictive**, it makes people unable to stop taking it 使人上癮的：*Heroin is highly addictive.* 海洛因很容易使人上癮。**2** if an activity or type of behaviour is **addictive**, people need to do it as often as possible because they enjoy it 使人入迷的：*I find jogging very addictive.* 我覺得慢跑鍛煉很使人着迷。

ˈadd-in *noun* (*computing* 計) **1** a computer program that can be added to a larger program to allow it do more things 附加程序；外加程序；附加程式 **2** = EXPANSION CARD ▸ **ˈadd-in** *adj.* [only before noun]：*add-in software* 附加軟件

Language Bank 用語庫

addition

Adding another item 補充說明

- Bilingual children do better in IQ tests than children who speak only one language. **In addition / What is more**, they seem to find it easier to learn third or even fourth languages. 講兩種語言的兒童比只講一種語言的兒童智商測試得分更高。此外／而且，講兩種語言的兒童似乎在學習第三甚至第四種語言時覺得更容易。
- Learning another language **not only** improves children's job prospects in later life, **but also** boosts their self-esteem. 學習另一種語言不僅可以提升兒童未來的職業前景，而且可以增強他們的自尊心。
- Teaching children a second language improves their job prospects in later life. **Other** benefits **include** increased self-esteem and greater tolerance of other cultures. 教兒童第二語言可以提升他們未來的職業前景。此外，還可以使他們獲得更強的自信心，對其他文化更包容。
- **Another / One further / One additional** reason for encouraging bilingual education is that it boosts children's self-esteem. 另一個鼓勵雙語教育的原因是它能增強兒童的自尊心。
- Studies suggest that bilingual children find it easier to learn additional languages. There is, **moreover**, increasing evidence that bilingual children perform better across a range of school subjects, not just foreign languages. 研究表明，講兩種語言的兒童學習其他語言覺得更容易。此外，越來越多的證據表明，講兩種語言的兒童不僅在外語學習上，同時在其他各門學科的學習上都表現得更好。
- His claim that children find bilingual education confusing is based on very little evidence. **Moreover**, the evidence he does provide is seriously flawed. 他認為雙語教育會使兒童感到迷惑的說法幾乎是沒有依據的。況且，他僅有的證據也是有嚴重缺陷的。
- Research has shown that first-language development is not impeded by exposure to a second language. **Furthermore**, there is no evidence to support the claim that children find bilingual education confusing. 研究已經表明，接觸第二語言不會妨礙第一語言的發展。而且，沒有證據支持雙語教育使兒童感到迷惑這種說法。

add·ition 🔑 /əˈdɪʃn/ *noun* **1** 🔑 [U] the process of adding two or more numbers together to find their total 加；加法：*children learning addition and subtraction* 學習加減的兒童 OPP **subtraction** **2** 🔑 [C] **~ (to sth)** a thing that is added to sth else 增加物；添加物：*the latest addition to our range of cars* 我們汽車系列新增加的款式 ◇ *an addition to the family* (= another child) 這家新添的一口人（又生了一個孩子） **3** 🔑 [U] **~ (of sth)** the act of adding sth to sth else 增加；添加：*Pasta's basic ingredients are flour and water, sometimes **with the addition of** eggs or oil.* 意大利麵製品的主要成分是麪粉和水，有時加雞蛋和食用油。**4** (*NAmE*) (*BrE* **extension**) [C] **~ (to sth)** a new part that is added to a building （建築物的）擴建部份，增建部份：*architects who specialize in home additions* 專門從事住宅擴建的建築師

IDM **in addition (to sb/sth)** 🔑 used when you want to mention another person or thing after sth else 除…以外（還）：*In addition to these arrangements, extra ambulances will be on duty until midnight.* 除了這些安排以外，另增救護車值班至午夜。◇ *There is, in addition, one further point to make.* 此外，還有一點要說。

add·ition·al 🔑 /əˈdɪʃənl/ *adj.* more than was first mentioned or is usual 附加的；額外的；外加的 SYN **extra**：*additional resources/funds/security* 額外資源；附加基金；外加保安措施 ◇ *The government provided an additional £25 million to expand the service.* 政府另撥了 2 500 萬英鎊用於擴展該服務。▸ **add·ition·al·ly** /-ʃənəli/ *adv.* SYN **in addition**：*Additionally, the bus service will run on Sundays, every two hours.* 此外，公共汽車將於星期天運行，每兩小時一班。

addi·tive /ˈædətɪv/ *noun* a substance that is added in small amounts to sth, especially food, in order to improve it, give it colour, make it last longer, etc. （尤指食品的）添加劑，添加物：*food additives* 食品添加劑 ◇ *additive-free orange juice* 不含添加劑的橙汁 ◇ *chemical additives in petrol* 汽油中的化學添加劑 ➲ COLLOCATIONS at DIET

addle /ˈædl/ *verb* **~ sth** to make sb unable to think clearly; to confuse sb 使不能清晰地思考；使糊塗：*Being in love must have addled your brain.* 墮入愛河必已使你神魂顛倒。

ad·dled /ˈædld/ *adj.* **1** (*old-fashioned*) confused; unable to think clearly 頭腦糊塗的；昏庸的：*his addled brain* 他糊塗的頭腦 **2** (*BrE*) (of an egg 蛋) not fresh; bad to eat 腐壞的；變質的

ˈadd-on *noun* a thing that is added to sth else 附加物；附加裝置：*The company offers scuba-diving as an add-on to the basic holiday price.* 這家公司提供戴水肺潛水活動，費用不含在基本度假費用內。◇ *add-on software* (= added to a computer) 計算機附加軟件

ad·dress 🔑 *noun, verb*

■ *noun* /əˈdres; *NAmE* əˈdres; ˈædres/ **1** 🔑 [C] details of where sb lives or works and where letters, etc. can be sent 住址；地址；通信處：*What's your **name and address**?* 你的姓名、住址？◇ *I'll give you my address and phone number.* 我會告訴你我的地址和電話號碼。◇ *Is that your **home address**?* 這是你的住址嗎？◇ *Please note my **change of address**.* 請注意我的地址變了。◇ *Police found him at an address* (= a house or flat/apartment) *in West London.* 警方在倫敦西區一處住所裏找到了他。◇ *people **of no fixed address*** (= with no permanent home) 沒有固定居所的人 ➲ see also FORWARDING ADDRESS **2** 🔑 [C] (*computing* 計) a series of words and symbols that tells you where you can find sth using a computer, for example on the Internet （互聯網等的）地址：*What's your **email address**?* 你的電郵地址是什麼？◇ *The project has a new **website address**.* 這個項目有個新的網址。**3** [C] a formal speech that is made in front of an audience 演說；演講：*tonight's televised presidential address* 今晚總統的電視演講 ➲ SYNONYMS at SPEECH ➲ COLLOCATIONS at VOTE **4** [U] **form/mode of ~** the correct title, etc. to use when you talk to sb 稱呼

■ *verb* /əˈdres/ **1** 🔑 [usually passive] to write on an envelope, etc. the name and address of the person, company, etc. that you are sending it to by mail 寫（收信人）姓名地址；致函：**~ sth** *The letter was correctly addressed, but delivered to the wrong house.* 信上的姓名地址寫得都對，但被錯投到另一家去了。◇ **~ sth to sb/sth** *Address your application to the Personnel Manager.* 把你的申請信寄給人事經理。➲ compare READDRESS ➲ see also SAE, SASE **2** to make a formal speech to a group of people 演說；演講：*to address a meeting* 在會議上發表演講 **3** (*formal*) to say sth directly to sb 向…說話：**~ sb** *I was surprised when he addressed me in English.* 他用英語跟我說話，我很詫異。◇ **~ sth to sb** *Any questions should be addressed to your teacher.* 任何問題都應該向你的老師求教。**4 ~ sb (as sth)** to use a particular name

A

or title for sb when you speak or write to them 稱呼（某人）；冠以（某種稱呼）：*The judge should be addressed as 'Your Honour'.* 對法官應該稱"法官大人"。**5** (*formal*) to think about a problem or a situation and decide how you are going to deal with it 設法解決；處理；對付：**~ sth** *Your essay does not address the real issues.* 你的論文沒有論證實質問題。◇ **~ yourself to sth** *We must address ourselves to the problem of traffic pollution.* 我們必須設法解決交通污染問題。

ad·dress·able /ə'dresəbl/ *adj.* **1** (of a problem or situation 問題或情況) that can be addressed 可處理的；可解決的；可對付的：*Let's start with the more easily addressable issues.* 我們先從較容易處理的問題着手。**2** (*computing* 計) (of a part of a computer system 計算機系統部件) that is identified using its own address 可尋址的；可定址的

ad'dress bar *noun* a line near the top of a page on an Internet BROWSER where you can type in the address of a website or where the website address is displayed（互聯網瀏覽器頂部的）地址欄，網址欄

ad'dress book *noun* **1** a book in which you keep addresses, phone numbers, etc. 通訊錄；通訊簿 **2** a computer file where you store email and Internet addresses（計算機）通訊錄

ad·dress·ee /ˌædre'siː/ *noun* a person that a letter, etc. is addressed to 收信人；收件人

ad·duce /ə'djuːs; *NAmE* ə'duːs/ *verb* [often passive] **~ sth** (*formal*) to provide evidence, reasons, facts, etc. in order to explain sth or to show that sth is true 引證，舉出（證據、理由、事實等）**SYN** **cite**：*Several factors have been adduced to explain the fall in the birth rate.* 有幾個因素已被援引來說明出生率降低的原因。

ad·duct·or /ə'dʌktə(r)/ (also **ad'ductor muscle**) *noun* (*anatomy* 解) a muscle that moves a body part towards the middle of the body or towards another part 內收肌 ➲ compare ABDUCTOR (2)

ad·en·oids /'ædənɔɪdz/ *noun* [pl.] pieces of soft TISSUE at the back of the nose and throat, that are part of the body's IMMUNE SYSTEM and that can swell up and cause breathing difficulties, especially in children 腺樣體，增殖體（尤指小兒的咽扁桃體）▶ **ad·en·oid·al** /ˌædə'nɔɪdl/ *adj.*

adept /ə'dept/ *adj.* **~ (at/in sth) | ~ (at/in doing sth)** good at doing sth that is quite difficult 內行的；熟練的；擅長的 **SYN** **skilful** ▶ **adept** /'ædept/ *noun* **adept·ly** *adv.*

ad·equate 🔑 **AW** /'ædɪkwət/ *adj.* enough in quantity, or good enough in quality, for a particular purpose or need 足夠的；合格的；合乎需要的：*an adequate supply of hot water* 熱水供應充足 ◇ *The room was small but adequate.* 房間雖小但夠用。◇ *There is a lack of adequate provision for disabled students.* 為殘疾學生提供的服務不夠。◇ *He didn't give an adequate answer to the question.* 他沒有對這個問題作出滿意的答覆。◇ **~ for sth** *The space available is not adequate for our needs.* 現有的空間不能滿足我們的需要。◇ **~ to do sth** *training that is adequate to meet the future needs of industry* 足以滿足未來工業需要的培訓 **OPP** **inadequate** ▶ **ad·equacy** **AW** /'ædɪkwəsi/ *noun* [U]：*The adequacy of the security arrangements has been questioned.* 有人質疑安全措施是否足夠。**OPP** **inadequacy** **ad·equate·ly** 🔑 **AW** *adv.*：*Are you adequately insured?* 你買夠保險了嗎？**OPP** **inadequately**

ADHD /ˌeɪ diː eɪtʃ 'diː/ *abbr.* ATTENTION DEFICIT HYPERACTIVITY DISORDER 注意缺陷障礙；多動症；過動症

ad·here /əd'hɪə(r); *NAmE* əd'hɪr/ *verb* [I] **~ (to sth)** (*formal*) to stick firmly to sth 粘附；附着：*Once in the bloodstream, the bacteria adhere to the surface of the red cells.* 細菌一進入血液裏，就附着在紅細胞表面上。

PHR V **ad'here to sth** (*formal*) to behave according to a particular law, rule, set of instructions, etc.; to follow a particular set of beliefs or a fixed way of doing sth 堅持，遵守，遵循（法律、規章、指示、信念等）：*For ten months he adhered to a strict no-fat low-salt diet.* 十個月來他嚴格堅持無脂肪少鹽飲食。◇ *She adheres to teaching methods she learned over 30 years ago.* 她依循她 30 多年前所學的教學法教學。

ad·her·ence /əd'hɪərəns; *NAmE* əd'hɪr-/ *noun* [U] the fact of behaving according to a particular rule, etc., or of following a particular set of beliefs, or a fixed way of doing sth 堅持；遵守；遵循：*strict adherence to the rules* 嚴格遵守規章制度

ad·her·ent /əd'hɪərənt; *NAmE* əd'hɪr-/ *noun* (*formal*) a person who supports a political party or set of ideas（政黨、思想的）擁護者，追隨者，信徒 **SYN** **supporter**

ad·he·sion /əd'hiːʒn/ *noun* [U] (*technical* 術語) the ability to stick or become attached to sth 粘附（力）；粘着（力）

ad·he·sive /əd'hiːsɪv; -'hiːz-/ *noun, adj.*

■ ***noun*** [C, U] a substance that you use to make things stick together 黏合劑；黏着劑

■ ***adj.*** that can stick to sth 粘合的；粘附的；有附着力的 **SYN** **sticky**：*adhesive tape* 黏膠帶 ➲ see also SELF-ADHESIVE

ad hoc /ˌæd 'hɒk; *NAmE* 'hɑːk/ *adj.* (from *Latin*) arranged or happening when necessary and not planned in advance 臨時安排的；特別的；專門的：*an ad hoc meeting to deal with the problem* 處理此問題的特別會議 ◇ *The meetings will be held* **on an ad hoc basis.** 會議將根據需要隨時舉行。▶ **ad hoc** *adv.*

ad hom·in·em /ˌæd 'hɒmɪnem; *NAmE* 'hɑːm-/ *adj., adv.* (*formal*) directed against a person's character rather than their argument 針對個人（而非理據）的：*an ad hominem attack* 人身攻擊

adieu /ə'djuː; *NAmE* ə'duː/ *exclamation* (*old use* or *literary*) goodbye 再見：*I bid you adieu.* 跟你說再見。

ad in·fin·itum /ˌæd ˌɪnfɪ'naɪtəm/ *adv.* (from *Latin*) without ever coming to an end; again and again 無止境地；無休止地：*You cannot stay here ad infinitum without paying rent.* 你不付房租就不能永遠住在這裏。◇ *The problem would be repeated ad infinitum.* 這個問題會一再出現。

adi·pose /'ædɪpəʊs; -z; *NAmE* -poʊ-/ *adj.* (*technical* 術語) (of body TISSUE 身體組織) used for storing fat 用於貯存脂肪的

ad·ja·cent **AW** /ə'dʒeɪsnt/ *adj.* (of an area, a building, a room, etc. 地區、建築、房間等) next to or near sth 與…毗連的；鄰近的：*The planes landed on adjacent runways.* 這些飛機在毗連的跑道上降落。◇ **~ to sth** *Our farm land was adjacent to the river.* 我們的農田在河邊。

aˌdjacent 'angle *noun* (*geometry* 幾何) one of the two angles formed on the same side of a straight line when another line meets it 鄰角

ad·jec·tive /'ædʒɪktɪv/ *noun* (*grammar* 語法) a word that describes a person or thing, for example *big*, *red* and *clever* in *a big house*, *red wine* and *a clever idea* 形容詞 ▶ **ad·jec·tival** /ˌædʒek'taɪvl/ *adj.*：*an adjectival phrase* 形容詞短語 **ad·jec·tival·ly** /-'taɪvəli/ *adv.*：*In 'bread knife', the word 'bread' is used adjectivally.* 在詞組 bread knife 中，bread 用作形容詞。

ad·join /ə'dʒɔɪn/ *verb* [T, I] **~ (sth)** (*formal*) to be next to or joined to sth 緊挨；鄰接；毗連：*A barn adjoins the farmhouse.* 一座穀倉緊靠着農舍。▶ **ad·join·ing** *adj.* [usually before noun]：*They stayed in adjoining rooms.* 他們住的房間緊挨着。◇ *We'll have more space if we knock down the adjoining wall* (= the wall between two rooms). 要是我們把這堵隔牆推倒，就會有更大的空間。

ad·journ /ə'dʒɜːn; *NAmE* ə'dʒɜːrn/ *verb* [I, T, often passive] (*formal*) to stop a meeting or an official process, especially a trial, for a period of time 休庭；休會；延期：*The court adjourned for lunch.* 午餐時間法庭休庭。◇ **~ sth** *The trial has been adjourned until next week.* 審判延期至下週。▶ **ad·journ·ment** *noun* [C, U]：*The judge granted us a short adjournment.* 法官允許我們暫時休庭。

PHR V **ad'journ to ...** (*formal* or *humorous*) to go to another place, especially in order to relax（尤指為了休息放鬆）到別處，換地方

ad·judge /ə'dʒʌdʒ/ *verb* [usually passive] (*formal*) to make a decision about sb/sth based on the facts that are available 宣判；裁決；判定：**~ sth + adj.** *The company was adjudged bankrupt.* 該公司被宣判破產。◇ **~ sth + noun** *The tour was adjudged a success.* 這次出行被認為是成功的。◇ **sth is adjudged to be, have, etc. sth** *The reforms were generally adjudged to have failed.* 人們普遍認為，改革已經失敗。

ad·ju·di·cate /ə'dʒu:dɪkeɪt/ *verb* **1** [I, T] to make an official decision about who is right in a disagreement between two groups or organizations 判決，裁決（爭執等）：**~ (on/upon/in sth)** *A special subcommittee adjudicates on planning applications.* 有一個特別小組委員會裁決規劃申請項目。◇ **~ (sth) (between A and B)** *Their purpose is to adjudicate disputes between employers and employees.* 他們的目的是裁決雇主與雇員之間的糾紛。 **2** [I] to be a judge in a competition（比賽中）裁判，評判：*Who is adjudicating at this year's contest?* 今年比賽誰當裁判？ ▶ **ad·ju·di·ca·tion** /ə,dʒu:dɪ'keɪʃn/ *noun* [U, C]：*The case was referred to a higher court for adjudication.* 該案件已提交上級法院裁決。 **ad·ju·di·ca·tor** *noun*：*You may refer your complaint to an independent adjudicator.* 你可以向獨立裁判投訴。

ad·junct /'ædʒʌŋkt/ *noun* **1** (*grammar* 語法) an adverb or a phrase that adds meaning to the verb in a sentence or part of a sentence 附加語；修飾成分：*In 'She went home yesterday' and 'He ran away in a panic', 'yesterday' and 'in a panic' are adjuncts.* 在 She went home yesterday 和 He ran away in a panic 兩句中，yesterday 和 in a panic 是修飾成分。 **2** (*formal*) a thing that is added or attached to sth larger or more important 附屬物；附件：*The memory expansion cards are useful adjuncts to the computer.* 內存擴充卡是計算機很有用的附件。

ad·jure /ə'dʒʊə(r); *NAmE* ə'dʒʊr/ *verb* **~ sb to do sth** (*formal*) to ask or to order sb to do sth 要求；命令：*He adjured them to tell the truth.* 他要求他們講真話。

ad·just 🔑 **AW** /ə'dʒʌst/ *verb*
1 🔑 [T] to change sth slightly to make it more suitable for a new set of conditions or to make it work better 調整；調節：**~ sth** *Watch out for sharp bends and adjust your speed accordingly.* 當心急轉彎並相應調整車速。◇ *This button is for adjusting the volume.* 這個按鈕是調節音量的。◇ **~ sth to sth** *Adjust your language to the age of your audience.* 要根據聽眾的年齡使用相應的語言。 **2** 🔑 [I, T] to get used to a new situation by changing the way you behave and/or think 適應；習慣 **SYN** **adapt**：*They'll be fine—they just need time to adjust.* 他們會好起來的，只是需要時間來適應。◇ **~ to sth** *After a while his eyes adjusted to the dark.* 過了一會兒他的眼睛習慣了黑暗。◇ **~ to doing sth** *It took her a while to adjust to living alone.* 她過了一段時間才適應獨自生活。◇ **~ yourself to sth** *You'll quickly adjust yourself to student life.* 你將很快適應學生生活。 **3** [T] **~ sth** to move sth slightly so that it looks neater or feels more comfortable 整理：*He smoothed his hair and adjusted his tie.* 他捋平頭髮，整了整領帶。 ➲ see also WELL ADJUSTED

ad·just·able /ə'dʒʌstəbl/ *adj.* that can be moved to different positions or changed in shape or size 可調整的；可調節的：*adjustable seat belts* 可調節的安全帶 ◇ *The height of the bicycle seat is adjustable.* 這輛自行車鞍座的高度可以調整。

,adjustable 'spanner (*BrE*) (also **'monkey wrench** *NAmE, BrE*) *noun* a tool that can be adjusted to hold and turn things of different widths 活動扳手 ➲ **VISUAL VOCAB** page V20 ➲ compare SPANNER, WRENCH *n.* (1)

ad·just·ment **AW** /ə'dʒʌstmənt/ *noun* [C, U] **1** a small change made to sth in order to correct or improve it 調整；調節：*I've made a few adjustments to the design.* 我已對設計作了幾處調整。◇ *Some adjustment of the lens may be necessary.* 可能需要調整一下鏡頭。 **2** a change in the way a person behaves or thinks（行為、思想的）調整，適應：*She went through a period of emotional adjustment after her marriage broke up.* 婚姻破裂後，她熬過了一段感情調整期。

ad·ju·tant /'ædʒʊtənt/ *noun* an army officer who does office work and helps other officers 副官

,Adjutant 'General *noun* (*pl.* **,Adjutants 'General**) **1** an officer of very high rank in the British army who is responsible for organization（英國陸軍）副官長 **2** the officer of very high rank in the US army who is in charge of organization（美國陸軍）官長，署長

ad-lib /,æd 'lɪb/ *verb* (**-bb-**) [I, T] to say sth in a speech or a performance that you have not prepared or practised 即席講話；即興表演 **SYN** **improvise**：*She abandoned her script and began ad-libbing.* 她拋開腳本即興表演起來。◇ **~ sth** *I lost my notes and had to ad-lib the whole speech.* 我把講稿弄丟了，只好臨時說了一通。 ▶ **ad lib** *noun*：*The speech was full of ad libs.* 講話中滿是即興之詞。 **ad lib** *adj.*：*an ad lib speech* 即興演講 **ad lib** *adv.*：*She delivered her lines ad lib.* 她的台詞是即興說出的。

adman /'ædmæn/ *noun* (*pl.* **-men** /-men/) (*informal*) a person who works in advertising 廣告商；廣告從業人員

admin /'ædmɪn/ *noun* [U] (*BrE, informal*) = ADMINISTRATION (1)：*a few admin problems* 一些行政問題 ◇ *She works in admin.* 她在行政部門工作。

ad·min·is·ter /əd'mɪnɪstə(r)/ *verb* **1** [often passive] **~ sth** to manage and organize the affairs of a company, an organization, a country, etc. 管理（公司、組織、機構）；治理（國家） **SYN** **manage**：*to administer a charity/fund/school* 管理一家慈善機構 / 一項基金 / 一所學校 ◇ *The pension funds are administered by commercial banks.* 養老基金由商業銀行經管。 **2 ~ sth** to make sure that sth is done fairly and in the correct way 施行；執行：*to* ***administer justice/the law*** 司法；執法 ◇ *The questionnaire was administered by trained interviewers.* 問卷調查是由經過訓練的採訪人員負責執行的。 **3 ~ sth (to sb)** (*formal*) to give or to provide sth, especially in a formal way 給予；提供：*The teacher has the authority to administer punishment.* 老師有權處罰。 **4** [often passive] (*formal*) to give drugs, medicine, etc. to sb 給予，施用（藥物等）：**~ sth** *Police believe his wife could not have administered the poison.* 警方認為他的妻子是不可能下毒的。◇ **~ sth to sb** *The dose was administered to the child intravenously.* 已給那孩子靜脈注射了一劑藥物。 **5 ~ a kick, a punch, etc. (to sb/sth)** (*formal*) to kick or to hit sb/sth 踢；打：*He administered a severe blow to his opponent's head.* 他朝着對手的頭部狠狠打了一拳。

ad·min·is·tra·tion **AW** /əd,mɪnɪ'streɪʃn/ *noun* **1** (also *BrE, informal* **admin**) [U] the activities that are done in order to plan, organize and run a business, school or other institution（企業、學校等的）管理，行政：*Administration costs are passed on to the customer.* 行政費用轉嫁給了消費者。◇ *the day-to-day administration of a company* 公司的日常管理工作 ◇ *I work in the Sales Administration department.* 我在銷售管理部門工作。 **2** [U] the process or act of organizing the way that sth is done 施行；執行：*the administration of justice* 司法 **3** [C] the people who plan, organize and run a business, an institution, etc.（企業、學校等的）管理部門，行政部門：*university administrations* 大學行政部門 **4** (often **Administration**) [C] the government of a country, especially the US（尤指美國）政府：*the Obama administration* 奧巴馬政府 ◇ *Successive administrations have failed to solve the country's economic problems.* 一屆又一屆政府均未能解決這個國家的經濟問題。 **5** [U] (*formal*) the act of giving a drug to sb（藥物的）施用：*the administration of antibiotics* 施用抗生素 **6** [U] (*BrE, AustralE, law* 律) a situation in which the financial affairs of a business that cannot pay its debts are managed by an independent administrator 行政接管（公司破產時由獨立管理人員負責其運營）：*If it cannot find extra funds, the company will* ***go into administration***. 如果公司籌不到額外資金就將進入行政接管程序。 ➲ compare CHAPTER 11

ad·min·is·tra·tive **AW** /əd'mɪnɪstrətɪv; *NAmE* -streɪtɪv/ *adj.* connected with organizing the work of a business or an institution 管理的；行政的：*an* ***administrative job/assistant/error*** 管理工作；行政助理；管理上的錯誤 ▶ **ad·min·is·tra·tive·ly** **AW** *adv.*

ad·min·is·tra·tor **AW** /əd'mɪnɪstreɪtə(r)/ *noun* a person whose job is to manage and organize the public or

A

business affairs of a company or an institution（公司、機構的）管理人員，行政人員：*a hospital administrator* 醫院管理人員

ad·mir·able /ˈædmərəbl/ *adj.* (*formal*) having qualities that you admire and respect 可欽佩的；值得讚賞的；令人羨慕的 SYN **commendable**：*Her dedication to her work was admirable.* 她對工作的奉獻精神可欽可佩。◇ *He made his points with admirable clarity.* 他闡述觀點明確，值得讚賞。▸ **ad·mir·ably** /-əbli/ *adv.*：*Joe coped admirably with a difficult situation.* 喬面對困境應付裕如。

ad·miral /ˈædmərəl/ *noun* an officer of very high rank in the navy 海軍將官；海軍上將；艦隊司令：*The admiral visited the ships under his command.* 艦隊司令視察了他所統率的軍艦。◇ *Admiral Lord Nelson* 海軍上將納爾遜勳爵 ➲ see also REAR ADMIRAL, RED ADMIRAL

ˌAdmiral of the ˈFleet (*BrE*) (*US* **ˈFleet Admiral**) *noun* an admiral of the highest rank in the navy（英國）海軍元帥；（美國）海軍五星上將

the Ad·mir·alty /ˈædmərəlti/ *noun* [sing.+sing./pl. v.] (in Britain in the past) the government department controlling the navy（英國舊時）海軍部

ad·mir·ation 0‑ /ˌædməˈreɪʃn/ *noun* [U] a feeling of respect and liking for sb/sth 欽佩；讚賞；羨慕：*to* ***watch/gaze in admiration*** 讚賞地觀看 / 凝視着 ◇ **~ for sb/sth** *I have great admiration for her as a writer.* 我十分欽佩她這個作家。

ad·mire 0‑ /ədˈmaɪə(r)/ *verb*
1 0‑ to respect sb for what they are or for what they have done 欽佩；讚賞；仰慕：**~ sb/sth** *I really admire your enthusiasm.* 我確實欽佩你的熱情。◇ *You have to* ***admire the way*** *he handled the situation.* 你不得不佩服他處理這個局面的手段。◇ **~ sb/sth for sth** *The school is widely admired for its excellent teaching.* 這所學校教學優秀，遠近稱譽。◇ **~ sb for doing sth** *I don't agree with her, but I admire her for sticking to her principles.* 我不同意她的意見，但是我讚賞她恪守原則。**2** 0‑ **~ sth** to look at sth and think that it is attractive and/or impressive 欣賞：*He stood back to admire his handiwork.* 他退後幾步欣賞他的手工製品。▸ **ad·mir·ing** *adj.*：*She was used to receiving admiring glances from men.* 她習慣了男人投來的讚賞目光。**ad·mir·ing·ly** *adv.*

ad·mirer /ədˈmaɪərə(r)/ *noun* **1 ~ of sb/sth** a person who admires sb/sth, especially a well-known person or thing 欽佩者；讚賞者：*He is a great admirer of Picasso's early paintings.* 他十分讚賞畢加索的早期畫作。**2** a man who is attracted to a woman and admires her 追求者，愛慕者（指愛慕女人的男人）：*She never married but had many admirers.* 她從未結婚，不過追求者不少。

ad·mis·sible /ədˈmɪsəbl/ *adj.* that can be allowed or accepted, especially in court（尤指法庭）可接受的，受理的 OPP **inadmissible** ▸ **ad·mis·si·bil·ity** /ədˌmɪsəˈbɪləti/ *noun* [U]

ad·mis·sion /ədˈmɪʃn/ *noun* **1** [U, C] the act of accepting sb into an institution, organization, etc.; the right to enter a place or to join an institution or organization（機構、組織等的）准許加入，加入權，進入權：*Hospital admission is not necessary in most cases.* 大多數情況下，病人無須住院。◇ *Hospital admissions for asthma attacks have doubled.* 哮喘發作入院人次已成倍增加。◇ *the university* ***admissions policy/office*** 大學招生政策 / 招生辦公室 ◇ *They tried to get into the club but were refused admission.* 他們試圖進入俱樂部，但遭到了拒絕。◇ *She failed to* ***gain admission*** *to the university of her choice.* 她未獲自己選擇的大學錄取。◇ **~ to sth** *countries applying for admission to the European Union* 申請加入歐洲聯盟的國家 ◇ *Last admissions to the park are at 4 p.m.* 公園最後的入園時間是下午 4 點。**2** [C] a statement in which sb admits that sth is true, especially sth wrong or bad that they have done（尤指對過錯、罪行的）承認，招認，招供：*He is a thief* ***by his own admission*** (= he has admitted it). 他自己供認是小偷。◇ **~ of sth** *an* ***admission of guilt/failure/defeat*** 承認有罪 / 失敗 / 被擊敗 ◇ **~ that ...** *The minister's resignation was an admission that she had lied.* 這位部長辭職等於承認她自己撒過謊。**3** [U] the amount of money that you pay to go into a building or to an event 入場費；門票費：***admission charges/prices*** 入場費 / 票價 ◇ *£5 admission* 入場費 5 英鎊 ◇ *What's the admission?* 門票多少錢？

Synonyms 同義詞辨析

admit

acknowledge • recognize • concede • confess

These words all mean to agree, often unwillingly, that sth is true. 以上各詞均含承認之意，常指不情願地承認某事屬實。

admit to agree, often unwillingly, that sth is true 指承認（常指不情願地承認某事屬實）：*It was a stupid thing to do, I admit.* 我承認，那次幹的是件蠢事。

acknowledge (*rather formal*) to accept that sth exists, is true or has happened 指承認某事物存在或屬實：*She refuses to acknowledge the need for reform.* 她拒不承認改革的必要性。

recognize to admit or be aware that sth exists or is true 指承認、意識到：*They recognized the need to take the problem seriously.* 他們承認這個問題需要嚴肅對待。

concede (*rather formal*) to admit, often unwillingly, that sth is true or logical 指承認（常指不情願地承認某事屬實或合乎邏輯）：*He was forced to concede (that) there might be difficulties.* 他被迫承認可能有困難。

ADMIT OR CONCEDE? 用 admit 還是 concede？

When sb **admits** sth, they are usually agreeing that sth which is generally considered bad or wrong is true or has happened, especially when it relates to their own actions. When sb **concedes** sth, they are usually accepting, unwillingly, that a particular fact or statement is true or logical. * admit 通常指承認普遍認為不好或錯誤的事情屬實或確實發生過，尤指與自己行為有關。concede 通常指勉強承認某事屬實或某種說法合乎邏輯。

confess (*rather formal*) to admit sth that you feel ashamed or embarrassed about 指承認自己感到羞愧或尷尬的事：*She was reluctant to confess her ignorance.* 她不願意承認自己無知。

PATTERNS

- to admit/acknowledge/recognize/concede/confess **that ...**
- to admit/confess **to sth**
- to admit/concede/confess sth **to sb**
- to admit/acknowledge/recognize **the truth**
- to admit/confess your **mistakes/ignorance**

admit 0‑ /ədˈmɪt/ *verb* (-tt-)
▸ **ACCEPT TRUTH** 承認事實 **1** 0‑ [I, T] **~ (to sb) (that ...)** to agree, often unwillingly, that sth is true（常指勉強）承認 SYN **confess**：*It was a stupid thing to do, I admit.* 我承認，那次幹的是件蠢事。◇ **+ speech** *'I'm very nervous,' she admitted reluctantly.* "我很緊張。" 她不願意地承認說。◇ **~ to sth** *Don't be afraid to admit to your mistakes.* 不要怕認錯。◇ **~ to doing sth** *She admits to being strict with her children.* 她承認對自己的孩子很嚴厲。◇ **~ sth** *He admitted all his mistakes.* 他承認了全部錯誤。◇ *She stubbornly refuses to admit the truth.* 她頑固地拒不承認事實。◇ *Why don't you just* ***admit defeat*** (= recognize that you cannot do sth) *and let someone else try?* 你幹嗎不乾脆承認自己不行，讓別人來試試？◇ *Admit it! You were terrified!* 承認了吧！你嚇壞了！◇ **~ (that) ...** *They freely admit (that) they still have a lot to learn.* 他們坦率承認，他們要學的東西還很多。◇ ***You must admit that*** *it all sounds very strange.* 你必須承認這一切聽起來很古怪。◇ **~ to sb that ...** *I couldn't admit to my parents that I was finding the course difficult.* 我無法向父母實話實說，我覺得這門課程很難。◇ **be admitted that ...** *It was generally admitted that the*

government had acted too quickly. 普遍認為，政府行動過急。◇ **be admitted to be, have, etc. sth** *The appointment is now generally admitted to have been a mistake.* 現在公認那次任命是一個錯誤。

▸ ACCEPT BLAME 承認責任 **2** [I, T] to say that you have done sth wrong or illegal 承認（過錯、罪行）；招認；招供 SYN **confess to**：**~ to sth** *He refused to admit to the other charges.* 他拒不承認其他指控。◇ **~ to doing sth** *She admitted to having stolen the car.* 她供認偷了那輛轎車。◇ **~ sth** *She admitted theft.* 她招認了偷竊行為。◇ *He refused to admit his guilt.* 他拒不認罪。◇ **~ doing sth** *She admitted having driven the car without insurance.* 她供認駕駛了這輛沒有保險的轎車。

▸ ALLOW TO ENTER/JOIN 准許進入／加入 **3** [T] (*formal*) to allow sb/sth to enter a place 准許進入（某處）：**~ sb/sth** *Each ticket admits one adult.* 每張票只准許一位成人入場。◇ **~ sb/sth to/into sth** *You will not be admitted to the theatre after the performance has started.* 演出開始後不許進入劇場。◇ *The narrow windows admit little light into the room.* 窗戶狹窄，只有少量光線可以照進房間。 **4** [T] (*formal*) to allow sb to become a member of a club, a school or an organization 准許…加入（俱樂部、組織）；接收（入學）：**~ sb** *The society admits all US citizens over 21.* 凡 21 歲以上的美國公民均可加入該社團。◇ **~ sb to/into sth** *Women were only admitted into the club last year.* 這家俱樂部去年才接納女會員。

▸ TO HOSPITAL 醫院 **5** [T, often passive] **~ sb to/into a hospital, an institution, etc.** (*formal*) to take sb to a hospital, or other institution where they can receive special care 接收入院；收治：*Two crash victims were admitted to the local hospital.* 兩位車禍受害者已送進當地醫院。

PHR V **ad'mit of sth** (*formal*) to show that sth is possible or probable as a solution, an explanation, etc. 容許，有…可能（指解決辦法、解釋等）

ad·mit·tance /əd'mɪtns/ *noun* [U] (*formal*) the right to enter or the act of entering a building, an institution, etc.（建築物、機構等的）進入權，進入：*Hundreds of people were unable to* ***gain admittance*** *to the hall.* 數以百計的人未能獲准進入大廳。

ad·mit·ted·ly /əd'mɪtɪdli/ *adv.* used, especially at the beginning of a sentence, when you are accepting that sth is true（尤用於句首）誠然，無可否認：*Admittedly, it is rather expensive but you don't need to use much.* 它的確很貴，但不需要用得很多。

ad·mix·ture /əd'mɪkstʃə(r)/ *noun* (*formal*) **1** a mixture 混合；摻和：*an admixture of aggression and creativity* 進取精神和創意的結合 **2** something, especially a small amount of sth, that is mixed with sth else 摻入物：*a French-speaking region with an admixture of German speakers* 摻雜說德語的人的法語地區

ad·mon·ish /əd'mɒnɪʃ; *NAmE* -'mɑːn-/ *verb* (*formal*) **1 ~ sb (for sth/for doing sth)** | **+ speech** to tell sb firmly that you do not approve of sth that they have done 責備；告誡；警告 SYN **reprove**：*She was admonished for chewing gum in class.* 她在課堂上嚼口香糖，受到了告誡。 **2 ~ sb (to do sth)** to strongly advise sb to do sth 力勸；忠告：*A warning voice admonished him not to let this happen.* 他耳邊響起警鐘，警告他別讓這種事情發生。

ad·mon·ition /ˌædmə'nɪʃn/ (also *less frequent* **ad·mon·ish·ment** /əd'mɒnɪʃmənt; *NAmE* -'mɑːn-/) *noun* [C, U] (*formal*) a warning to sb about their behaviour 警告；告誡 ▸ **ad·moni·tory** /əd'mɒnɪtri; *NAmE* -'mɑːn-/ *adj.*

ad nau·seam /ˌæd 'nɔːziæm/ *adv.* (from *Latin*) if a person says or does sth **ad nauseam**, they say or do it again and again so that it becomes boring or annoying 令人厭煩地：*Sports commentators repeat the same phrases ad nauseam.* 體育解說員翻來覆去說着同樣的詞語，真叫人膩煩。

ado /ə'duː/ *noun*

IDM **without further/more ado** (*old-fashioned*) without delaying; immediately 毫不遲延；乾脆；立即

adobe /ə'dəʊbi; *NAmE* ə'doʊbi/ *noun* [U] mud that is dried in the sun, mixed with STRAW and used as a building material（建築用）黏土；黏土坯

ado·les·cence /ˌædə'lesns/ *noun* [U] the time in a person's life when he or she develops from a child into an adult 青春期；青春 SYN **puberty** ➲ COLLOCATIONS at AGE

ado·les·cent /ˌædə'lesnt/ *noun* a young person who is developing from a child into an adult 青少年：*adolescents between the ages of 13 and 18 and the problems they face* * 13 至 18 歲的青少年以及他們面臨的問題 ▸ **ado·les·cent** *adj.*：***adolescent boys/girls/experiences*** 青春期的男孩／女孩／經歷

Ado·nis /ə'dəʊnɪs; *NAmE* ə'doʊ-/ *noun* an extremely attractive young man 英俊青年 ORIGIN From the name of the beautiful young man in ancient Greek myths, who was loved by both Aphrodite and Persephone. He was killed by a wild boar but Zeus ordered that he should spend the winter months in the underworld with Persephone and the summer months with Aphrodite. 源自希臘神話中的美少年阿多尼斯之名，他同時為阿佛洛狄忒和珀耳塞福涅所愛。被野豬咬死後，宙斯命其在陰間和珀耳塞福涅一起度過冬季，和阿佛洛狄忒一起度過夏季。

adopt /ə'dɒpt; *NAmE* ə'dɑːpt/ *verb*

▸ CHILD 小孩 **1** [I, T] to take sb else's child into your family and become its legal parent(s) 收養；領養：*a campaign to encourage childless couples to adopt* 鼓勵無子女夫婦領養孩子的運動 ◇ **~ sb** *to adopt a child* 領養孩子 ◇ *She was forced to have her baby adopted.* 她被迫把嬰兒給人收養。➲ COLLOCATIONS at CHILD ➲ compare FOSTER *v.* (2)

▸ METHOD 方法 **2** [T] **~ sth** to start to use a particular method or to show a particular attitude towards sb/sth 採用（某方法）；採取（某態度）：*All three teams adopted different approaches to the problem.* 三個隊處理這個問題的方法各不相同。

▸ SUGGESTION 建議 **3** [T] **~ sth** to formally accept a suggestion or policy by voting 正式通過，表決採納（建議、政策等）：*to adopt a resolution* 通過一項決議 ◇ *The council is expected to adopt the new policy at its next meeting.* 委員會有望在下次會議上正式通過這項新政策。

▸ NEW NAME/COUNTRY 新名字／國家 **4** [T] **~ sth** to choose a new name, a country, a custom, etc. and begin to use it as your own 選用（名字等）；移居（某國）；承襲（風俗）：*to* ***adopt a name/title/language*** 取名；襲用頭銜；採用某語言 ◇ *Early Christians in Europe adopted many of the practices of the older, pagan religions.* 歐洲早期的基督教徒承襲了更古老的一些異教的許多習俗。

▸ WAY OF BEHAVING 行為方式 **5** [T] **~ sth** (*formal*) to use a particular manner, way of speaking, expression, etc. 採用（某種舉止、說話方式等）：*He adopted an air of indifference.* 他擺出一副滿不在乎的樣子。

▸ CANDIDATE 候選人 **6** [T] **~ sb (as sth)** (*BrE, politics* 政) to choose sb as a candidate in an election or as a representative 選定，選舉（某人為候選人或代表）：*She was adopted as parliamentary candidate for Wood Green.* 她被推舉為伍德格林選區的議員候選人。

adopt·ed /ə'dɒptɪd; *NAmE* ə'dɑːp-/ *adj.* **1** an **adopted** child has legally become part of a family which is not the one in which he or she was born 收養的；領養的：*Danny is their adopted son.* 丹尼是他們的養子。 **2** an **adopted** country is one in which sb chooses to live although it is not the one they were born in 所選擇居住的；移居的

adop·ter /ə'dɒptə(r); *NAmE* ə'dɑːp-/ *noun* **1** a person who adopts a child 收養者 **2** a person who starts using a new technology（新技術）採用者：***early/late adopters*** *of DVD players* 早期／後來用 DVD 機的人

adop·tion /ə'dɒpʃn; *NAmE* ə'dɑːpʃn/ *noun* **1** [U, C] the act of adopting a child 收養；領養：*She put the baby up for adoption.* 她提出要讓人收養那個嬰兒。➲ COLLOCATIONS at CHILD **2** [U] the decision to start using sth such as an idea, a plan or a name 採用（想法、計劃、名字等）：*the adoption of new technology* 新技術的採用 **3** [U, C] (*BrE, politics* 政) the act of choosing sb as a candidate for an election 選定，推選，推舉（候選人）：

his adoption as the Labour candidate 他被選定為工黨候選人

adop·tive /əˈdɒptɪv; *NAmE* əˈdɑːp-/ *adj.* [usually before noun] an **adoptive** parent or family is one that has legally adopted a child 收養的；有收養關係的

ador·able /əˈdɔːrəbl/ *adj.* very attractive and easy to feel love for 可愛的；討人喜愛的：*What an adorable child!* 多可愛的小孩呀！▸ **ador·ably** /-əbli/ *adv.*

ad·or·ation /ˌædəˈreɪʃn/ *noun* [U] a feeling of great love or worship 熱愛；愛慕；敬慕；崇拜：*He gazed at her with pure adoration.* 他一往情深地注視着她。◇ *The painting is called 'Adoration of the Infant Christ'.* 這幅畫叫做"朝拜耶穌聖嬰"。

adore /əˈdɔː(r)/ *verb* (not used in the progressive tenses 不用於進行時) **1 ~ sb** to love sb very much 熱愛，愛慕（某人）：*It's obvious that she adores him.* 她顯然深深地愛着他。➲ SYNONYMS at LOVE **2** (*informal*) to like sth very much 喜愛，熱愛（某事物）：**~ sth** *I simply adore his music!* 我簡直太喜愛他的音樂了！◇ **~ doing sth** *She adores working with children.* 她熱愛參與兒童工作。➲ SYNONYMS at LIKE

ador·ing /əˈdɔːrɪŋ/ *adj.* [usually before noun] showing much love and admiration 熱愛的；愛慕的；敬慕的；崇拜的 ▸ **ador·ing·ly** *adv.*

adorn /əˈdɔːn; *NAmE* əˈdɔːrn/ *verb* [often passive] (*formal*) to make sth/sb look more attractive by decorating it or them with sth 裝飾；裝扮：**~ sth/sb** *Gold rings adorned his fingers.* 他的手指戴着幾枚金戒指。◇ (*ironic*) *Graffiti adorned the walls.* 這些牆遭到亂畫亂塗。◇ **~ sth/sb/yourself with sth** *The walls were adorned with paintings.* 牆上裝飾了繪畫。◇ *The children adorned themselves with flowers.* 孩子們佩戴着鮮花。▸ **adorn·ment** *noun* [U, C]：*A plain necklace was her only adornment.* 她身上的飾物就只有一串簡單的項鏈。

ad·renal gland /əˈdriːnl glænd/ *noun* either of the two small organs above the KIDNEYS that produce adrenaline and other HORMONES 腎上腺

adrena·line /əˈdrenəlɪn/ (also **adrena·lin**) *noun* [U] a substance produced in the body when you are excited, afraid or angry. It makes the heart beat faster and increases your energy and ability to move quickly. 腎上腺素（激動、害怕或憤怒時產生的體內分泌，使心跳加快，提升活動能力）：*The excitement at the start of a race can really **get the adrenaline flowing**.* 比賽起點的興奮確實能使人熱血沸騰。

adrift /əˈdrɪft/ *adj.* [not before noun] **1** if a boat or a person in a boat is **adrift**, the boat is not tied to anything or is floating without being controlled by anyone 漂浮；漂流：*The survivors were adrift in a lifeboat for six days.* 幸存者在救生艇上漂流了六天。**2** (*BrE*) (of a person 人) feeling alone and without a direction or an aim in life 漫無目的；隨波逐流；漂泊無依：*young people adrift in the big city* 在大城市四處漂泊的年輕人 **3** no longer attached or fixed in the right position 脫開；鬆開：*I nearly suffocated when the pipe on my breathing apparatus **came adrift**.* 我的呼吸器上的管子脫落時，我差一點窒息。◇ (*figurative*) *She had been **cut adrift** from everything she had known.* 她曾被迫與她熟悉的一切切斷關係。◇ (*figurative*) *Our plans had gone badly adrift.* 我們的計劃已嚴重受挫。**4 ~ (of sb/sth)** (*BrE*) (in sport 體育運動) behind the score or position of your opponents 分數落後；排名在後：*The team are now just six points adrift of the leaders.* 現在該隊得分比領先的隊只落後六分。

IDM **cast/set sb adrift** [usually passive] to leave sb to be carried away on a boat that is not being controlled by anyone 使漂流：(*figurative*) *Without language human beings are cast adrift.* 人無語言則茫然無依。

adroit /əˈdrɔɪt/ *adj.* (*formal*) skilful and clever, especially in dealing with people（尤指待人接物）精明的，幹練的，機敏的 SYN **skilful**：*an adroit negotiator* 談判老手 ▸ **adroit·ly** *adv.* **adroit·ness** *noun* [U]

ADSL /ˌeɪ diː es ˈel/ *abbr.* asymmetric digital subscriber line (a system for connecting a computer to the Internet using a telephone line) 非對稱數字用戶線路，非對稱數位式用戶線路（利用電話線上網）

ad·sorb /ədˈsɔːb; -ˈzɔːb; *NAmE* -ˈzɔːrb; -ˈsɔːrb/ *verb* **~ sth** (*technical* 術語) if sth **adsorbs** a liquid, gas or other substance, it holds it on its surface 吸附（液體、氣體等）：*The dye is adsorbed onto the fibre.* 染料已吸附在纖維上。

ADT /ˌeɪ diː ˈtiː/ *abbr.* ATLANTIC DAYLIGHT TIME

aduki /əˈduːki/ *noun* = ADZUKI

adu·la·tion /ˌædjuˈleɪʃn; *NAmE* ˌædʒəˈl-/ *noun* [U] (*formal*) admiration and praise, especially when this is greater than is necessary 稱讚；吹捧；奉承 ▸ **adu·la·tory** /ˌædjuˈleɪtəri; *NAmE* ˈædʒələtɔːri/ *adj.*

adult 0-w AW /ˈædʌlt; əˈdʌlt/ *noun, adj.*

■ *noun* **1** 0-w a fully grown person who is legally responsible for their actions（法律上指能為自己的行為負責的）成年人 SYN **grown-up**：*Children must be accompanied by an adult.* 兒童必須要有大人陪同。◇ *Why can't you two act like civilized adults?* 你們倆為什麼就不能像有教養的成年人那樣行事呢？**2** 0-w a fully grown animal 成年動物：*The fish return to the river as adults in order to breed.* 這種魚長成以後回到河中產卵。

■ *adj.* **1** 0-w fully grown or developed 成年的；發育成熟的：*preparing young people for adult life* 指導年輕人準備過成人生活 ◇ *the adult population* 成年人口 ◇ *adult monkeys* 長成的猴子 **2** behaving in an intelligent and responsible way; typical of what is expected of an adult（智力、思想、行為）成熟的，成人的 SYN **grown-up**：*When my parents split up, it was all very adult and open.* 我父母離異時，事情處理得很成熟、很開放。**3** [only before noun] intended for adults only, because it is about sex or contains violence 僅限成人的（因有色情或暴力內容）：*an adult movie* 僅供成人觀看的電影 ➲ see also ADULTHOOD

ˌadult eduˈcation (also **conˌtinuing eduˈcation**) *noun* [U] education for adults that is available outside the formal education system, for example at evening classes 成人教育

adul·ter·ate /əˈdʌltəreɪt/ *verb* [often passive] **~ sth (with sth)** to make food or drink less pure by adding another substance to it（在飲食中）摻雜，摻假 SYN **contaminate** ➲ see also UNADULTERATED (2) ▸ **adul·ter·ation** /əˌdʌltəˈreɪʃn/ *noun* [U]

adul·ter·er /əˈdʌltərə(r)/ *noun* (*formal*) a person who commits adultery 通姦者；姦夫

adul·ter·ess /əˈdʌltərəs/ *noun* (*formal*) a woman who commits adultery 姦婦

adul·tery /əˈdʌltəri/ *noun* [U] sex between a married person and sb who is not their husband or wife 通姦：*He was accused of **committing adultery**.* 他被控通姦。▸ **adul·ter·ous** /əˈdʌltərəs/ *adj.*：*an adulterous relationship* 通姦關係

adult·hood AW /ˈædʌlthʊd; əˈdʌlt-/ *noun* [U] the state of being an adult 成年：*a child reaching adulthood* 已成年的孩子

ad·um·brate /ˈædəmbreɪt; *NAmE* also əˈdem-/ *verb* **~ sth** (*formal*) to give a general idea or description of sth without details 概述；概括說明；勾畫輪廓 SYN **outline**

ad·vance 0-w /ədˈvɑːns; *NAmE* -ˈvæns/ *noun, verb, adj.*

■ *noun*

▸ FORWARD MOVEMENT 向前移動 **1** 0-w [C] the forward movement of a group of people, especially armed forces（尤指武裝部隊的）前進，行進：*We feared that an advance on the capital would soon follow.* 我們擔心接下來會馬上向首都推進。➲ COLLOCATIONS at WAR

▸ DEVELOPMENT 發展 **2** 0-w [C, U] **~ (in sth)** progress or a development in a particular activity or area of understanding 進步；進展：*recent advances in medical science* 醫學的最新進展 ◇ *We live in an age of rapid technological advance.* 我們生活在技術迅猛發展的時代。

▸ MONEY 金錢 **3** [C, usually sing.] money paid for work before it has been done or money paid earlier than expected 預付款：*They offered an advance of £5 000 after the signing of the contract.* 他們在合同簽訂後預付了 5 000 英鎊。◇ *She asked for an advance on her salary.* 她要求預支薪金。

▸ SEXUAL 兩性 **4 advances** [pl.] attempts to start a sexual relationship with sb 勾引；求愛；追求： *He had* ***made advances*** *to one of his students.* 他曾追求過他的一個學生。

▸ PRICE INCREASE 漲價 **5** [C] **~ (on sth)** (*business* 商) an increase in the price or value of sth （價格、價值的）上漲，提高： *Share prices showed significant advances.* 股票價格大幅上漲。

IDM **in advance (of sth)** **1** before the time that is expected; before sth happens （時間上）在…前；預先；事先： *a week/month/year in advance* 提前一星期／一個月／一年 ◇ *It's cheaper if you book the tickets in advance.* 預訂票要便宜一些。◇ *People were evacuated from the coastal regions in advance of the hurricane.* 颶風襲來之前，沿海地帶的人已經撤離。 **2** more developed than sb/sth else （發展上）超前： *Galileo's ideas were well in advance of the age in which he lived.* 伽利略的思想遠遠超越了他所處的時代。

■ *verb*

▸ MOVE FORWARD 向前移動 **1** [I] to move forward towards sb/sth, often in order to attack or threaten them or it（為了進攻、威脅等）前進，行進： *The troops were finally given the order to advance.* 部隊終於收到前進的命令。◇ *They had advanced 20 miles by nightfall.* 夜幕降臨時，他們已推進了 20 英里。◇ *the advancing Allied troops* 節節挺進的盟軍部隊 ◇ **~ on/towards sb/sth** *The mob advanced on us, shouting angrily.* 暴民憤怒地喊叫着向我們逼近。 ➲ compare RETREAT *v.* (1)

▸ DEVELOP 發展 **2** [I, T] if knowledge, technology, etc. **advances**, it develops and improves （知識、技術等）發展，進步： *Our knowledge of the disease has advanced considerably over recent years.* 近年來我們對這種疾病的瞭解深入多了。◇ **~ sth** *This research has done much to advance our understanding of language learning.* 這項研究大大提高了我們對語言學習的認識。

▸ HELP TO SUCCEED 促進 **3** [T] to help sth to succeed 促進；推動 SYN **further**： *Studying for new qualifications is one way of advancing your career.* 為提高學歷而進修是促進事業發展的一個辦法。◇ *They worked together to advance the cause of democracy.* 他們合力推動民主事業。

▸ MONEY 金錢 **4** [T] to give sb money before the time it would usually be paid 預付： **~ sth to sb** *We are willing to advance the money to you.* 我們願意預付款給你。◇ **~ sb sth** *We will advance you the money.* 我們將把款項預付給你。

▸ SUGGEST 建議 **5** [T] **~ sth** (*formal*) to suggest an idea, a theory, or a plan for other people to discuss 提出（想法、理論、計劃） SYN **put forward**： *The article advances a new theory to explain changes in the climate.* 這篇文章提出了一個解釋氣候變化的新理論。

▸ MAKE EARLIER 提前 **6** [T] **~ sth** (*formal*) to change the time or date of an event so that it takes place earlier 提前；提早 SYN **bring forward**： *The date of the trial has been advanced by one week.* 審判日期提前了一星期。 OPP **postpone**

▸ MOVE FORWARD 向前移動 **7** [I, T] (*formal*) to move forward to a later part of sth; to move sth forward to a later part 向前推（至下一步）；（使）向前移動： *Users advance through the program by answering a series of questions.* 用戶通過回答一系列問題，逐步完成整個程序。◇ **~ sth** *This button advances the tape to the beginning of the next track.* 這個按鈕可使錄音帶轉到下一首歌曲的開始。

▸ INCREASE 增加 **8** [I] (*business* 商) (of prices, costs, etc. 價格、成本等) to increase in price or amount 上漲；增加： *Oil shares advanced amid economic recovery hopes.* 在一片經濟復蘇的希望中石油股票價格上漲。

■ *adj.* [only before noun] **1** done or given before sth is going to happen 預先的；事先的： *Please give us* ***advance warning*** *of any changes.* 如有變動，請事先通知我們。◇ *We need* ***advance notice*** *of the numbers involved.* 我們需要事先得知涉及的數量。◇ *No* ***advance booking*** *is necessary on most departures.* 大多數起程票無須預訂。 **2 ~ party/team** a group of people who go somewhere first, before the main group 先遣隊；先頭部隊

ad·vanced /ədˈvɑːnst; *NAmE* -ˈvænst/ *adj.*
1 having the most modern and recently developed ideas, methods, etc. 先進的： *advanced technology* 先進技術 ◇ *advanced industrial societies* 先進的工業社會 **2** (of a course of study 課程) at a high or difficult level 高級的；高等的： *There were only three of us on the advanced course.* 只有我們三人學高級課程。◇ *an advanced student of English* 高階英語學生 **3** at a late stage of development （發展）晚期的，後期的： *the advanced stages of the disease* 疾病晚期

IDM **of advanced ˈyears | sb's advanced ˈage** used in polite expressions to describe sb as 'very old' 高齡；年事已高： *He was a man of advanced years.* 他年事已高。◇ (*humorous*) *Even at my advanced age I still know how to enjoy myself!* 我雖說是黃昏暮年，也還懂得如何找樂！

Adˌvanced ˈHigher *noun* (in Scotland) an exam in a particular subject at a higher level than HIGHER, taken by some school students at the age of around 18（蘇格蘭）學生高級進階證書考試（應試年齡在 18 歲左右）

adˈvanced level *noun* = A LEVEL： *For this course, you need two GCE Advanced Level passes.* 要學這門課程，就須要通過普通教育證書兩門學科的高級證書考試。

adˌvanced ˈplacement *noun* [U] (*abbr.* **AP**) an advanced course for high school students in the US by which students can gain college CREDITS before they actually go to college 先修課程，進階課程（美國中學生在上大學前所修習以獲得大學學分的課程）

adˈvance guard (also **adˈvanced guard**) *noun* [C+sing./pl. v.] a group of soldiers who go somewhere to make preparations before other soldiers arrive 先遣部隊

ad·vance·ment /ədˈvɑːnsmənt; *NAmE* -ˈvæns-/ *noun* (*formal*) **1** [U, C] the process of helping sth to make progress or succeed; the progress that is made 促進；推動；發展；前進： *the* ***advancement of knowledge/education/science*** 知識／教育／科學的發展 **2** [U] progress in a job, social class, etc. （工作、社會階級等的）提升，晉升： *There are good opportunities for advancement if you have the right skills.* 如果有合適的技能，就有很好的晉升機會。

ad·van·cing /ədˈvɑːnsɪŋ; *NAmE* -ˈvæns-/ *adj.* **~ years/age** used as a polite way of referring to the fact of time passing and of sb growing older 年事漸高： *She is still very active, in spite of her advancing years.* 她儘管年事漸高，仍然十分活躍。

ad·van·tage /ədˈvɑːntɪdʒ; *NAmE* -ˈvæn-/ *noun, verb*

■ *noun* [C, U] **1** a thing that helps you to be better or more successful than other people 有利條件；有利因素；優勢： *a* ***big/great/definite advantage*** 大的／很大的／確定的優勢 ◇ *an unfair advantage* (= sth that benefits you, but not your opponents) 不公平的有利因素（指有利於自己、但並不有利於對手）◇ *She* ***had the advantage of*** *a good education.* 她具有受過良好教育的有利條件。◇ *You will* ***be at an advantage*** (= have an advantage) *in the interview if you have thought about the questions in advance.* 如果你預先考慮過這些問題，面試就會處於優勢。◇ **~ over sb** *Being tall gave him an advantage over the other players.* 他個子高，比其他運動員有利。 OPP **disadvantage** **2** a quality of sth that makes it better or more useful 優點： *A small car* ***has the added advantage of*** *being cheaper to run.* 小型轎車還有一個優點是養護成本比較便宜。◇ *One advantage of/One of the advantages of living in the country is the fresh air.* 在鄉下居住的一個好處就是空氣清新。◇ *Each of these systems has its advantages and disadvantages.* 這些系統各有其優缺點。 OPP **disadvantage** **3** (in TENNIS 網球) the first point scored after a score of 40–40（局末平分後）佔先；優勢分： *Advantage Federer* 費德勒佔先

IDM **be/work to your adˈvantage** to give you an advantage; to change a situation in a way that gives you an advantage 對…有利： *It would be to your advantage to attend this meeting.* 參加這次會議會對你有利。◇ *Eventually, the new regulations will work to our advantage.* 新規章制度最終將對我們有利。 **take adˈvantage of sth/sb** **1** to make use of sth well; to make use of an opportunity 利用；利用（機會）： *She took advantage of the children's absence to tidy their rooms.* 她趁孩子們不在時收拾了他們的房間。◇ *We* ***took full advantage*** *of the hotel facilities.* 我們充分享用了旅館設施。 **2** to make use of sb/sth in a way that is unfair or dishonest 欺騙；佔…的便宜 **SYN** **exploit**： *He took advantage of my generosity* (= for example, by taking more than I had intended to give). 他利用我的慷慨佔了便宜。 **to (good/best) ad'vantage** in a way that shows the best of sth（十分 / 最）有效地，出色地；使優點突出： *The photograph showed him to advantage.* 他在這張照片中照得挺不錯的。 **turn sth to your ad'vantage** to use or change a bad situation so that it helps you 使轉為有利；變（不利）為有利；利用

■ *verb* **~ sb** (*formal*) to put sb in a better position than other people or than they were in before 使處於有利地位；有利於；有助於

ad·van·taged /əd'vɑːntɪdʒd; *NAmE* -'væn-/ *adj.* being in a good social or financial situation （在社會上或經濟上）處於優越地位的： *We aim to improve opportunities for the less advantaged in society.* 我們的宗旨是為社會地位比較低下的人增加機會。 **OPP** **disadvantaged**

ad·van·ta·geous /ˌædvən'teɪdʒəs/ *adj.* **~ (to sb)** good or useful in a particular situation 有利的；有好處的 **SYN** **beneficial**： *A free trade agreement would be advantageous to both countries.* 自由貿易協定對兩國都會有利。 **OPP** **disadvantageous** ▸ **ad·van·ta·geous·ly** *adv.*

ad·vent /'ædvent/ *noun* **1** [sing.] **the ~ of sth/sb** the coming of an important event, person, invention, etc. （重要事件、人物、發明等的）出現，到來： *the advent of new technology* 新技術的出現 **2 Advent** [U] (in the Christian religion) the period of approximately four weeks before Christmas （基督教）將臨節，降臨節（聖誕節前的四個星期左右）

'Advent calendar *noun* a piece of stiff paper with a picture and 24 small doors with numbers on. Children open a door each day during Advent and find a picture or a piece of chocolate behind each one. 基督降臨曆（兒童每天打開一扇編了號的小門，裏面有圖片或巧克力）

ad·ven·ti·tious /ˌædven'tɪʃəs/ *adj.* (*formal*) happening by accident; not planned 偶然發生的；非計劃中的

ad·ven·ture /əd'ventʃə(r)/ *noun*
1 [C] an unusual, exciting or dangerous experience, journey or series of events 冒險；冒險經歷；奇遇： *her adventures travelling in Africa* 她在非洲旅行時的冒險經歷 ◇ *When you're a child, life is one big adventure.* 在孩提時代，生活是一大不尋常的經歷。 ◇ *adventure stories* 歷險故事 **2** [U] excitement and the willingness to take risks, try new ideas, etc. 冒險的刺激；大膽開拓： *a **sense/spirit of adventure*** 冒險意識 / 精神

ad'venture game *noun* a type of computer game in which you play a part in an adventure （電腦）涉險遊戲，冒險遊戲

adˌventure 'playground *noun* (*BrE*) an area where children can play, with large structures, ropes, etc. for climbing on 奇遇遊樂場，冒險樂園（有大型結構、繩子等，供兒童玩耍攀登）

ad·ven·turer /əd'ventʃərə(r)/ *noun* **1** (*old-fashioned*) a person who enjoys exciting new experiences, especially going to unusual places 冒險者；冒險家 **2** (often *disapproving*) a person who is willing to take risks or act in a dishonest way in order to gain money or power 投機分子

ad·ven·ture·some /əd'ventʃəsəm; *NAmE* -tʃərs-/ *adj.* (*NAmE*) = ADVENTUROUS (1)

ad·ven·tur·ess /əd'ventʃəres/ *noun* **1** (*old-fashioned*) a woman who enjoys exciting new experiences, especially going to unusual places 女冒險家 **2** (often *disapproving*) a woman who is willing to take risks or act in a dishonest way in order to gain money or power 不擇手段的女人

ad·ven·tur·ism /əd'ventʃərɪzəm/ *noun* [U] (*disapproving*) a willingness to take risks in business or politics in order to gain sth for yourself（企業、政治等方面）冒險主義

ad·ven·tur·ous /əd'ventʃərəs/ *adj.* **1** (*NAmE* also **ad·ven·ture·some**) (of a person 人) willing to take risks and try new ideas; enjoying being in new, exciting situations 有冒險精神的；大膽開拓的： *For the more adventurous tourists, there are trips into the mountains with a local guide.* 對更願獵奇探險的旅遊者，有本地嚮導帶領進山遊覽。◇ *Many teachers would like to be more adventurous and creative.* 許多教師願意更加進取，更富創造性。 **2** including new and interesting things, methods and ideas（指事物、方法、思想）新奇的： *The menu contained traditional favourites as well as more adventurous dishes.* 這份菜單有受歡迎的傳統菜，也有較為新奇的菜肴。 **3** full of new, exciting or dangerous experiences 充滿新鮮事物的；刺激不斷的；驚險的： *an **adventurous trip/lifestyle*** 驚險的旅行；充滿刺激的生活方式 **OPP** **unadventurous** ▸ **ad·ven·tur·ous·ly** *adv.*

ad·verb /'ædvɜːb; *NAmE* -vɜːrb/ *noun* (*grammar* 語法) a word that adds more information about place, time, manner, cause or degree to a verb, an adjective, a phrase or another adverb 副詞： *In 'speak kindly', 'incredibly deep', 'just in time' and 'too quickly', 'kindly', 'incredibly', 'just' and 'too' are all adverbs.* 在 speak kindly、incredibly deep、just in time 和 too quickly 四個短語中，kindly、incredibly、just 和 too 都是副詞。 ➲ see also SENTENCE ADVERB ▸ **ad·ver·bial** /æd'vɜːbiəl; *NAmE* -'vɜːrb-/ *adj.*： *'Very quickly indeed' is an adverbial phrase.* * very quickly indeed 是副詞短語。

adˌverbial 'particle *noun* (*grammar* 語法) an adverb used especially after a verb to show position, direction of movement, etc. 副詞小詞，副詞小品詞（尤用於動詞後，表示位置、運動方向等）： *In 'come back', 'break down' and 'fall off', 'back', 'down' and 'off' are all adverbial particles.* 在 come back、break down 和 fall off 中，back、down 和 off 都是副詞小詞。

ad·ver·sar·ial /ˌædvə'seəriəl; *NAmE* -vər'seriəl/ *adj.* (*formal* or *technical* 術語) (especially of political or legal systems 尤指政治或法律制度) involving people who are in opposition and who make attacks on each other 對立的；敵對的： *the adversarial nature of the two-party system* 兩黨制的對抗性 ◇ *an adversarial system of justice* 審判對抗制

ad·ver·sary /'ædvəsəri; *NAmE* -vərseri/ *noun* (*pl.* **-ies**) (*formal*) a person that sb is opposed to and competing with in an argument or a battle （辯論、戰鬥中的）敵手，對手 **SYN** **opponent**

ad·verse /'ædvɜːs; əd'vɜːs; *NAmE* -vɜːrs/ *adj.* [usually before noun] negative and unpleasant; not likely to produce a good result 不利的；有害的；反面的： ***adverse change/circumstances/weather conditions*** 不利的變動；逆境；惡劣天氣 ◇ *Lack of money will have an **adverse effect** on our research programme.* 缺少資金將對我們的研究方案有不利影響。 ◇ *They have attracted strong adverse criticism.* 他們已招致強烈非難。 ◇ *This drug is known to have adverse side effects.* 眾所周知，這種藥具有不良副作用。 ▸ **ad·verse·ly** *adv.*： *Her health was **adversely affected** by the climate.* 那種氣候損害了她的健康。

ad·ver·sity /əd'vɜːsəti; *NAmE* -'vɜːrs-/ *noun* [U, C] (*pl.* **-ies**) (*formal*) a difficult or unpleasant situation 困境；逆境： *courage **in the face of adversity*** 面對逆境的勇氣 ◇ *He overcame many personal adversities.* 他克服了多次個人不幸。

ad·vert /'ædvɜːt; *NAmE* -vɜːrt/ *noun* (*BrE*) (*informal*) = ADVERTISEMENT (1), (3)： *the adverts on television* 電視廣告 ◇ *When the adverts came on I got up to put the kettle on.* 電視播放廣告時，我起身去燒了壺水。
➲ **SYNONYMS** at ADVERTISEMENT

ad·ver·tise /'ædvətaɪz; *NAmE* -vərt-/ *verb*
1 [I, T] to tell the public about a product or a service in order to encourage people to buy or to use it 做廣告；登廣告： *If you want to attract more customers, try advertising in the local paper.* 如果你要吸引更多顧客，就試試在當地報紙登廣告。 ◇ **~ sth (as sth)** *The cruise was advertised as the 'journey of a lifetime'.* 這次航行被宣傳為"終生難得的旅行"。 **2** [I, T] to let people know that sth is going to happen, or that a job is available by giving details about it in a newspaper, on a notice in a

public place, on the Internet, etc. （在報紙、公共場所公告牌、互聯網等上）公佈，徵聘：**~ (for sb/sth)** *We are currently advertising for a new sales manager.* 目前我們公開徵聘一位新的銷售經理。◇ **~ sth** *We advertised the concert quite widely.* 我們為這次音樂會作了相當廣泛的宣傳。 **3** [T] **~ sth** to show or tell sth about yourself to other people 展現，宣傳（自己的事） **SYN publicize**：*I wouldn't advertise the fact that you don't have a work permit.* 我不會向外聲張你沒有工作許可證這件事。

ad·ver·tise·ment 🔑 /əd'vɜːtɪsmənt; *NAmE* ˌædvər'taɪz-/ *noun*
1 🔑 [C] (also *informal* **ad**) (*BrE* also, *informal* **ad·vert**) **~ (for sth)** a notice, picture or film telling people about a product, job or service 廣告；啟事：*Put an advertisement in the local paper to sell your car.* 在當地報紙登一則廣告來出售你的汽車。➲ see also CLASSIFIED ADVERTISEMENTS **2** [C] (*BrE* also **ad·vert**) **~ for sth** an example of sth that shows its good qualities 廣告（樣）品：*Dirty streets and homelessness are no advertisement for a prosperous society.* 骯髒的街道和無家可歸現象絕不是繁榮社會的景象。 **3** [U] the act of advertising sth and making it public 廣告活動；廣告宣傳

Synonyms 同義詞辨析

advertisement

publicity • ad • commercial • promotion • trailer

These are all words for a notice, picture or film/movie telling people about a product, job or service. 以上各詞均指廣告、啟事。

advertisement a notice, picture or film/movie telling people about a product, job or service; an example of sth that shows its good qualities; the act of advertising sth and making it public 指廣告、宣傳的實例、廣告活動或廣告宣傳：*Put an advertisement in the local paper to sell your car.* 在當地報紙登一則廣告來出售你的汽車。◇ *Dirty streets are no advertisement for a prosperous society.* 骯髒的街道決不是繁榮社會的景象。

publicity [U] the business of attracting the attention of the public to sb/sth such as a company, book, film/movie, film/movie star or product; the things that are done to attract attention 指宣傳業、廣告宣傳工作或傳播工作：*She works in publicity.* 她從事宣傳工作。◇ *There has been a lot of advance publicity for her new film.* 她的新電影尚未上映即大加宣傳。

ad (*informal*) a notice, picture or film/movie telling people about a product, job or service 指廣告、啟事：*We put an ad in the local paper.* 我們在當地報紙上刊登了一則廣告。◇ *an ad for a new chocolate bar* 新品種巧克力棒的廣告

commercial an advertisement on television or on the radio 指電視或電台播放的廣告

promotion a set of advertisements for a particular product or service; activities done in order to increase the sales of a product or service 指廣告宣傳、促銷活動：*a special promotion of local products* 當地產品的特別促銷活動 ◇ *She works in sales and promotion.* 她從事銷售和推廣工作。

trailer (*especially BrE*) a series of short scenes from a film/movie or television programme, shown in advance to advertise it 指電影或電視節目的預告片。

PATTERNS

- (a/an) advertisement/publicity/ad/commercial/promotion/trailer **for** sth
- a **TV/television/radio/cinema** advertisement/ad/commercial/promotion
- to **run/show** a(n) advertisement/ad/commercial/trailer

ad·ver·tiser /'ædvətaɪzə(r); *NAmE* -vərt-/ *noun* a person or company that advertises 廣告商；廣告人員；廣告公司；登廣告者

ad·ver·tis·ing 🔑 /'ædvətaɪzɪŋ; *NAmE* -vərt-/ *noun* [U] the activity and industry of advertising things to people on television, in newspapers, on the Internet, etc. 廣告活動；廣告業；做廣告：*A good **advertising campaign** will increase our sales.* 良好的廣告宣傳活動會增加我們的銷售量。◇ *Cigarette advertising has been banned.* 香煙廣告已遭禁止。◇ ***radio/TV advertising*** 廣播／電視廣告 ◇ *Val works for an **advertising agency*** (= a company that designs advertisements). 瓦爾為一家廣告公司工作。◇ *a career in advertising* 廣告職業

ad·ver·tor·ial /ˌædvə'tɔːriəl; *NAmE* -vər't-/ *noun* an advertisement that is designed to look like an article in the newspaper or magazine in which it appears 社論式廣告

ad·vice 🔑 /əd'vaɪs/ *noun* [U] **~ (on sth)** an opinion or a suggestion about what sb should do in a particular situation 勸告；忠告；建議；意見：*advice on road safety* 有關道路安全的建議 ◇ *They **give advice** to people with HIV and AIDS.* 他們向艾滋病病毒攜帶者和艾滋病患者提供咨詢。◇ ***Ask** your teacher's **advice/Ask** your teacher **for advice** on how to prepare for the exam.* 向你的老師咨詢一下如何準備考試。◇ *We were advised to **seek legal advice**.* 有人勸我們找律師咨詢。◇ *Let me give you **a piece of advice**.* 讓我給你一個忠告。◇ ***A word of advice**. Don't wear that dress.* 一句忠告：別穿那件連衣裙。◇ ***Take my advice**. Don't do it.* 聽我的勸告，別幹這件事。◇ *I chose it **on his advice**.* 我這是照他的建議選擇的。

ad'vice column (*NAmE*) (*BrE* **'agony column**) *noun* part of a newspaper or magazine in which sb gives advice to readers who have sent letters about their personal problems （報紙或雜誌的）答問專欄

ad'vice columnist (*NAmE*) (*BrE* **'agony aunt/uncle**) *noun* a person who writes in a newspaper or magazine giving advice in reply to people's letters about their personal problems （報紙或雜誌的）答問專欄作者

ad·vis·able /əd'vaɪzəbl/ *adj.* [not usually before noun] sensible and a good idea in order to achieve sth 明智；可取：*Early booking is advisable.* 預訂宜早。◇ **~ to do sth** *It is advisable to book early.* 預訂宜早。 **OPP inadvisable** ▸ **ad·vis·abil·ity** /ədˌvaɪzə'bɪləti/ *noun* [U]

ad·vise 🔑 /əd'vaɪz/ *verb*
1 🔑 [I, T] to tell sb what you think they should do in a particular situation 勸告；忠告；建議：**~ (sb) against sth/against doing sth** *I would **strongly advise** against going out on your own.* 我要極力奉勸你別單獨外出。◇ **~ sb** *Her mother was away and couldn't advise her.* 她的母親不在身邊，無法向她提出勸告。◇ **~ sth** *I'd advise extreme caution.* 我建議要慎之又慎。◇ **+ speech** *'Get there early,' she advised (them).* "早點兒到那裏。" 她囑咐（他們）說。◇ **~ sb to do sth** *Police are advising people to stay at home.* 警方告誡民眾要留在家裏。◇ *I'd advise you not to tell him.* 我勸你別告訴他。◇ **~ that …** *They advise that a passport be carried with you at all times.* 他們建議護照要隨時帶在身邊。◇ (*BrE* also) *They advise that a passport should be carried with you at all times.* 他們建議護照要隨時帶在身邊。◇ **it is advised that …** *It is strongly advised that you take out insurance.* 奉勸你務必辦理保險。◇ **~ doing sth** *I'd advise buying your tickets well in advance if you want to travel in August.* 要是想在八月份去旅行，我建議及早購票。➲ see also ILL-ADVISED, WELL ADVISED ➲ SYNONYMS at RECOMMEND **2** 🔑 [I, T] to give sb help and information on a subject that you know a lot about 出主意；提出建議；提供咨詢：**~ (sb) on/about sth/about doing sth** *We employ an expert to advise on new technology.* 我們聘用了一位專家作新技術顧問。◇ *She advises the government on environmental issues.* 她是政府的環境問題顧問。◇ **~ (sb) what, which, whether, etc. …** *The pharmacist will advise which medicines are safe to take.* 藥劑師會建議服用哪些藥才安全。◇ *Your lawyer can advise you whether to take any action.* 你的律師可以告訴你是否起訴。
3 [T] (*formal*) to officially tell sb sth 通知；正式告知 **SYN inform**：**~ sb of sth** *Please advise us of any change of address.* 如地址有變，敬請告知。◇ **~ sb when, where, how, etc. …** *I will contact you later to advise you*

when to come. 稍後我會與你聯繫，通知你何時前來。◇ **~ sb that ...** *I regret to advise you that the course is now full.* 本課程已滿額，特此通知。

ad·vised·ly /əd'vaɪzədli/ *adv.* (*formal*) if you say that you are using a word **advisedly**, you mean that you have thought carefully before choosing it 經過認真思考；經過深思熟慮

ad·vise·ment /əd'vaɪzmənt/ *noun* [U] (*NAmE, formal*) advice 勸告；忠告；建議；意見：*the University Advisement Center* 大學咨詢中心

IDM **take sth under ad'visement** to think carefully about sth before making a decision about it 對某事作周密考慮；深思熟慮：*The judge has taken the matter under advisement.* 法官已經周密考慮這一事情。

ad·viser (also **ad·visor**) /əd'vaɪzə(r)/ *noun* a person who gives advice, especially sb who knows a lot about a particular subject 顧問；忠告者；提供意見者：*a financial adviser* 財務顧問◇ **~ (to sb) (on sth)** *a special adviser to the President on education* 總統的教育特別顧問

ad·vis·ory /əd'vaɪzəri/ *adj., noun*

■ ***adj.*** having the role of giving professional advice 顧問的；咨詢的：*an **advisory committee/body/service*** 顧問委員會／咨詢機構／服務◇ *He acted in an advisory capacity only.* 他僅以顧問身分工作。

■ ***noun*** (*pl.* **-ies**) (*NAmE*) an official warning that sth bad is going to happen 警報：*a tornado advisory* 龍捲風警報

ad·vo·cacy **AW** /'ædvəkəsi/ *noun* [U] **1 ~ (of sth)** (*formal*) the giving of public support to an idea, a course of action or a belief（對某思想、行動方針、信念的）擁護，支持，提倡 **2** (*technical* 術語) the work of lawyers who speak about cases in court（律師）出庭辯護；律師的工作

'advocacy group *noun* (*NAmE*) a group of people who work together to achieve sth, especially by putting pressure on the government, etc., usually on behalf of people who are unable to speak for themselves 倡議團體；翻請團；請願團體：*an advocacy group for the rights of the mentally ill* 代表精神病患者的維權團體 ➲ compare INTEREST GROUP, PRESSURE GROUP

ad·vo·cate **AW** *verb, noun*

■ ***verb*** /'ædvəkeɪt/ (*formal*) to support sth publicly 擁護；支持；提倡：**~ sth** *The group does not advocate the use of violence.* 該團體不支持使用暴力。◇ **~ (sb) doing sth** *Many experts advocate rewarding your child for good behaviour.* 很多專家主張對小孩的良好表現加以獎勵。◇ **~ that ...** *The report advocated that all buildings be fitted with smoke detectors.* 報告主張所有的建築物都應安裝煙火探測器。◇ (*BrE* also) *The report advocated that all buildings should be fitted with smoke detectors.* 報告主張所有的建築物都應安裝煙火探測器。➲ SYNONYMS at RECOMMEND

■ ***noun*** /'ædvəkət/ **1** a person who supports or speaks in favour of sb or of a public plan or action 擁護者；支持者；提倡者：**~ (for sth/sb)** *an advocate for hospital workers* 醫院工作人員的支持者◇ **~ (of sth/sb)** *a staunch advocate of free speech* 言論自由的堅定擁護者 ➲ see also DEVIL'S ADVOCATE **2** a person who defends sb in court 辯護律師；出庭辯護人 **3** (in Scotland) a lawyer who has the right to argue cases in higher courts（蘇格蘭）出庭律師，辯護律師，大律師 ➲ note at LAWYER

adze (*NAmE* also **adz**) /ædz/ *noun* a heavy tool with a curved blade at RIGHT ANGLES to the handle, used for cutting or shaping large pieces of wood 錛子（削平木料用的平頭斧）

ad·zuki /əd'zuːki/ (also **ad'zuki bean**, **aduki**) *noun* a type of small round dark red BEAN that you can eat 赤豆；紅豆

aegis /'iːdʒɪs/ *noun*

IDM **under the aegis of sb/sth** (*formal*) with the protection or support of a particular organization or person 在…保護（或支持）下

ae·olian (*especially US* **eo·lian**) /iː'əʊliən; *NAmE* iː'oʊ-/ *adj.* (*technical* 術語) connected with or caused by the action of the wind 風的；風成的

aeon (*BrE*) (also **eon** *NAmE, BrE*) /'iːən/ *noun* **1** (*formal*) an extremely long period of time; thousands of years 極漫長的時期；千萬年 **2** (*geology* 地) a major division of time, divided into ERAS 宙（地質學上的年代分期，下分代）：*aeons of geological history* 數以億萬年計的地質史

aer·ate /'eəreɪt; *NAmE* 'er-/ *verb* **1 ~ sth** to make it possible for air to become mixed with soil, water, etc. 使（土壤、水等）透氣：*Earthworms do the important job of aerating the soil.* 蚯蚓幹着使土壤透氣的重要工作。**2 ~ sth** to add a gas, especially CARBON DIOXIDE, to a liquid under pressure 充二氧化碳於，充氣於（液體）：*aerated water* 汽水 ▸ **aer·ation** /eə'reɪʃn; *NAmE* e'reɪ-/ *noun* [U]

aer·ial /'eəriəl; *NAmE* 'er-/ *noun, adj.*

■ ***noun*** (*BrE*) (also **an·tenna** *NAmE, BrE*) a piece of equipment made of wire or long straight pieces of metal for receiving or sending radio and television signals 天線 ➲ VISUAL VOCAB pages V17, V52

■ ***adj.*** **1** from a plane 從飛機上的：***aerial attacks/bombardment/photography*** 空中攻擊／轟炸／攝影◇ *an aerial view of Palm Island* 棕櫚島鳥瞰圖 **2** in the air; existing above the ground 空中的；空氣中的；地表以上的：*The banyan tree has aerial roots.* 榕樹有氣根。

aerie (*NAmE*) = EYRIE

aero- /'eərəʊ; *NAmE* 'eroʊ/ *combining form* (in nouns, adjectives and adverbs 構成名詞、形容詞和副詞) connected with air or aircraft 空氣的；空中的；飛行器的：*aerodynamic* 空氣動力的◇ *aerospace* 航空航天工業

aero·bat·ics /ˌeərə'bætɪks; *NAmE* ˌerə-/ *noun* [U+sing./pl. v.] exciting and skilful movements performed in an aircraft, such as flying upside down, especially in front of an audience 特技飛行 ▸ **aero·batic** *adj.*：*an aerobatic display* 特技飛行表演 ➲ VISUAL VOCAB page V53

aer·obic /eə'rəʊbɪk; *NAmE* e'roʊ-/ *adj.* **1** (*biology* 生) needing OXYGEN 需氧的；好氧的：*aerobic bacteria* 需氧細菌 **2** (of physical exercise 健身活動) especially designed to improve the function of the heart and lungs 有氧的；增強心肺功能的 **OPP** **anaerobic**

aer·obics /eə'rəʊbɪks; *NAmE* e'roʊ-/ *noun* [U] physical exercises intended to make the heart and lungs stronger, often done in classes, with music 有氧運動（通常在課堂上伴隨音樂進行的增強心肺功能的健身活動）：*to do aerobics* 做有氧運動

aero·drome /'eərədrəʊm; *NAmE* 'erədroʊm/ (*BrE*) (*US* **air·drome**) *noun* (*old-fashioned*) a small airport 小型飛機場

aero·dy·nam·ics /ˌeərəʊdaɪ'næmɪks; *NAmE* ˌeroʊ-/ *noun* **1** [pl.] the qualities of an object that affect the way it moves through the air 空氣動力（特性）：*Research has focused on improving the car's aerodynamics.* 研究的重點是改善轎車的流線型。**2** [U] the science that deals with how objects move through air 空氣動力學 ▸ **aero·dy·nam·ic** /-mɪk/ *adj.*：*the car's aerodynamic shape* (= making it able to move faster) 汽車的流線型 **aero·dy·nam·ic·al·ly** /-kli/ *adv.*

aero·foil /'eərəfɔɪl; *NAmE* 'er-/ (*BrE*) (*NAmE* **air·foil**) *noun* the basic curved structure of an aircraft's wing that helps to lift it into the air 翼型（指機翼在空氣中運動時能產生升力的型面）

aero·gramme (*BrE*) (*NAmE* **aero·gram**) /'eərəgræm; *NAmE* 'erə-/ (also **'air letter** *NAmE, BrE*) *noun* a sheet of light paper that can be folded and sent by air as a letter 航空郵簡（一張薄紙摺成，作航空信寄出）

aero·naut /'eərənɔːt; *NAmE* 'erə-/ *noun* a traveller in a HOT-AIR BALLOON or AIRSHIP 熱氣球（或飛艇）乘客

aero·naut·ics /ˌeərə'nɔːtɪks; *NAmE* ˌerə-/ *noun* [U] the science or practice of building and flying aircraft 航空學；飛行學；飛行術 ▸ **aero·naut·ic·al** /-'nɔːtɪkl/ *adj.*：*an aeronautical engineer* 航空工程師

aero·plane /'eərəpleɪn; *NAmE* 'erə-/ (*BrE*) (also **air·plane** especially in *NAmE*) (also **plane** *BrE, NAmE*) *noun* a flying vehicle with wings and one or more engines 飛機 ➲ VISUAL VOCAB page V53

aero·sol /'eərəsɒl; *NAmE* 'erəsɔːl; 'erəsɑːl/ *noun* a metal container in which a liquid such as paint or HAIRSPRAY is kept under pressure and released as a spray（噴油

漆、頭髮定型劑等的）噴霧器，霧化器；氣霧劑；氣溶膠：*ozone-friendly aerosols* 不損害臭氧層的氣霧劑 ◇ *an **aerosol can/spray*** 噴霧罐；氣霧噴霧器 ➲ VISUAL VOCAB page V33

aero·space /'eərəʊspeɪs; *NAmE* 'eroʊ-/ *noun* [U] the industry of building aircraft, vehicles and equipment to be sent into space 航空航天工業：*jobs in aerospace and defence* 航天與國防工作 ◇ *the aerospace industry* 航空航天工業

aero·stat /'eərəstæt; *NAmE* 'erə-/ *noun* (*technical* 術語) an aircraft filled with hot air, such as an AIRSHIP or HOT-AIR BALLOON （充注熱空氣的）浮空器，飛行器（如飛艇、熱氣球）

aes·thete (*NAmE* also **es·thete**) /'iːsθiːt; 'es-; *NAmE* 'es-/ *noun* (*formal*, sometimes *disapproving*) a person who has a love and understanding of art and beautiful things 審美家

aes·thet·ic (*NAmE* also **es·thet·ic**) /iːs'θetɪk; es-; *NAmE* es-/ *adj.*, *noun*

■ ***adj.*** **1** concerned with beauty and art and the understanding of beautiful things 審美的；有審美觀點的；美學的：*an aesthetic appreciation of the landscape* 用審美的眼光欣賞風景 ◇ *The benefits of conservation are both financial and aesthetic.* 保護自然環境在經濟上和美化環境上都有好處。 **2** made in an artistic way and beautiful to look at 美的；藝術的：*Their furniture was more aesthetic than functional.* 他們的傢具美觀多於實用。 ▸ **aes·thet·ic·al·ly** (*NAmE* also **es-**) /-kli/ *adv.*：*aesthetically pleasing colour combinations* 賞心悅目的色彩搭配

■ ***noun*** **1** [C] the aesthetic qualities and ideas of sth 美感；審美觀：*The students debated the aesthetic of the poems.* 學生就這些詩的美展開了辯論。 **2 aesthetics** [U] the branch of philosophy that studies the principles of beauty, especially in art 美學 ▸ **aes·theti·cism** (*NAmE* also **es-**) /iːs'θetɪsɪzəm; es-; *NAmE* es-/ *noun* [U]

aeti·ology (*BrE*) (*NAmE* **eti·ology**) /ˌiːti'ɒlədʒi; *NAmE* -'ɑːl-/ *noun* [U] (*medical* 醫) the scientific study of the causes of disease 病原學；病因學

afar /ə'fɑː(r)/ *adv.*

IDM **from a'far** (*literary*) from a long distance away 從遠處：*He loved her from afar* (= did not tell her he loved her). 他暗戀着她。

afara /ə'fɑːrə/ (also **limba**) *noun* **1** [C] a tall tree that grows in W Africa （西非）阿法拉樹，欖仁樹 **2** [U] the wood from this tree, often used for making furniture 阿法拉木，欖仁木（常用於製作傢具） **3** [C] (*WAfrE*) a bridge, usually made of wood 橋；（通常指）木橋

AFC /ˌeɪ ef 'siː/ *abbr.* **1** (*BrE*) Association Football Club 足球俱樂部；足球聯合會：*Leeds United AFC* 利茲聯隊足球俱樂部 **2** (*NAmE*) American Football Conference (one of the two groups of teams in the NFL) 美式足球聯盟（美國全國足球聯盟下兩大聯盟之一） **3** (*BrE*) Air Force Cross (an award given to members of the AIR FORCE, for being brave when flying rather than when fighting the enemy) 空軍十字勳章（獎勵飛行而非作戰的英勇表現） **4** automatic frequency control (a system which allows radios and televisions to continue to receive the same signal) 自動頻率控制

af·fable /'æfəbl/ *adj.* pleasant, friendly and easy to talk to 和藹可親的；易於交談的 SYN **genial** ▸ **af·fa·bil·ity** /ˌæfə'bɪləti/ *noun* [U] **af·fably** *adv.*

af·fair 🔑 /ə'feə(r); *NAmE* ə'fer/ *noun*

▸ PUBLIC/POLITICAL ACTIVITIES 公共 / 政治活動 **1** 🔑 **affairs** [pl.] events that are of public interest or political importance 公共事務；政治事務：***world/international/business affairs*** 世界 / 國際 / 商業事務 ◇ *an expert on foreign affairs* (= political events in other countries) 外事專家 ◇ *affairs of state* 國務 ➲ see also CURRENT AFFAIRS

▸ EVENT 事件 **2** 🔑 [C, usually sing.] an event that people are talking about or describing in a particular way 事件；事情：*The newspapers exaggerated the whole affair wildly.* 報章毫無根據地誇大了整個事件。◇ *The debate was a pretty disappointing affair.* 那次辯論使人頗感失望。◇ *She wanted the celebration to be a simple **family affair**.* 她希望慶祝活動簡簡單單的，僅限於家人參加。

▸ RELATIONSHIP 關係 **3** 🔑 [C] a sexual relationship between two people, usually when one or both of them are married to sb else（尤指已婚男女的）私通，風流韻事：*She **is having an affair** with her boss.* 她跟老闆有曖昧關係。➲ see also LOVE AFFAIR (1)

▸ PRIVATE BUSINESS 私人業務 **4** 🔑 **affairs** [pl.] matters connected with a person's private business and financial situation 私人業務：*I looked after my father's financial affairs.* 我照管父親的財務。◇ *She wanted to **put her affairs in order** before she died.* 她想在去世前把自己的事務安排妥當。 **5** [sing.] a thing that sb is responsible for (and that other people should not be concerned with) 個人的事 SYN **business**：*How I spend my money is my affair.* 我如何用錢是我自己的事。

▸ OBJECT 物品 **6** [C] (*old-fashioned*) (with an adjective 與形容詞連用) an object that is unusual or difficult to describe 不尋常之物；難描述的東西：*Her hat was an amazing affair with feathers and a huge brim.* 她的帽子嵌着羽毛，帽簷很寬，真是件奇物。 IDM see STATE *n.*

af·faire /ə'feə(r); *NAmE* ə'fer/ *noun* (from *French*, *literary*) a love affair 熱戀關係；風流韻事

af·fect 🔑 AW /ə'fekt/ *verb*

1 🔑 [often passive] **~ sb/sth** to produce a change in sb/sth 影響：*How will these changes affect us?* 這些變化對我們會有什麼影響？◇ *Your opinion will not affect my decision.* 你的意見不會影響我的決定。◇ *The south of the country was worst affected by the drought.* 該國南方旱情最嚴重。 **2** 🔑 [often passive] **~ sb/sth** (of a disease 疾病) to attack sb or a part of the body; to make sb become ill/sick 侵襲；感染：*The condition affects one in five women.* 每五個婦女就有一個人患有這種病。◇ *Rub the cream into the affected areas.* 把乳膏揉進患處。 **3 ~ sb** [often passive] to make sb have strong feelings of sadness, pity, etc.（感情上）深深打動；使悲傷（或憐憫等）：*They were deeply affected by the news of her death.* 她死亡的消息使他們唏噓不已。 **4 ~ (to do) sth** (*formal*) to pretend to be feeling or thinking sth 假裝：*She affected a calmness she did not feel.* 她強裝鎮靜。 **5 ~ sth** (*formal*, *disapproving*) to use or wear sth that is intended to impress other people 炫耀；做作 SYN **put on**：*I wish he wouldn't affect that ridiculous accent.* 但願他別故意裝出那種可笑的腔調。

> **Which Word? 詞語辨析**
>
> **affect / effect**
>
> - **affect** *verb* = 'to have an influence on sb/sth' * affect 動詞 = 影響某人 / 某事：*Does television affect children's behaviour?* 電視對孩子的行為有影響嗎？ It is not a noun. 該詞不作名詞。
> - **effect** *noun* = 'result, influence' * effect 名詞 = 作用；影響：*Does television have an effect on children's behaviour?* 電視對孩子的行為有影響嗎？
> - **effect** *verb* is quite rare and formal and means 'to achieve or produce'. * effect 作動詞罕見且正式，意為實現、產生：*They hope to effect a reconciliation.* 他們希望實現和解。

af·fect·ation /ˌæfek'teɪʃn/ *noun* [C, U] behaviour or an action that is not natural or sincere and that is often intended to impress other people 假裝；做作；裝模作樣：*His little affectations irritated her.* 他的裝腔作勢令她不快。◇ *Kay has no affectation at all.* 凱一點也不做作。◇ *He raised his eyebrows with an affectation of surprise* (= pretending to be surprised). 他揚起雙眉裝出一副驚奇的樣子。

af·fect·ed /ə'fektɪd/ *adj.* (of a person or their behaviour 人或行為) not natural or sincere 假裝的；做作的：*an **affected laugh/smile*** 假笑；不自然的微笑 OPP **unaffected** ▸ **af·fect·ed·ly** *adv.*

af·fect·ing /ə'fektɪŋ/ *adj.* (*formal*) producing strong feelings of sadness and sympathy 深深打動人的；感動人的；激起憐憫的

af·fec·tion 0-m /ə'fekʃn/ *noun*
1 0-m [U, sing.] the feeling of liking or loving sb/sth very much and caring about them 喜愛；鍾愛：*Children need lots of love and affection.* 孩子需要多多疼愛和關懷。◇ *He didn't* ***show*** *his wife any* ***affection****.* 他沒有向妻子表示一點愛。◇ *She was held in deep affection by all her students.* 她的學生都十分愛戴她。◇ **~ for sb/sth** *Mr Darcy's affection for his sister* 達西先生對他妹妹的關愛之情 ◇ *I have a great affection for New York.* 我很喜歡紐約。➲ COLLOCATIONS at MARRIAGE **2 affections** [pl.] (*formal* or *literary*) a person's feelings of love 愛情：*Anne had two men trying to win her affections.* 安妮有兩個男人追求。

af·fec·tion·ate /ə'fekʃənət/ *adj.* showing caring feelings and love for sb 表示關愛的 **SYN loving**：*He is very affectionate towards his children.* 他非常關愛他的孩子。◇ *an affectionate kiss* 親昵的一吻 ▸ **af·fec·tion·ate·ly** *adv.*：*William was affectionately known as Billy.* 人們親昵地稱威廉為比利。

af·fect·ive **AW** /ə'fektɪv/ *adj.* (*technical* 術語) connected with emotions and attitudes 感情的；情感的：*affective disorders* 情感障礙 ▸ **af·fect·ive·ly** **AW** *adv.*

af·fi·da·vit /ˌæfə'deɪvɪt/ *noun* (*law* 律) a written statement that you swear is true, and that can be used as evidence in court 附誓書面證詞；宣誓作證書

af·fili·ate *verb, noun*
■ **verb** /ə'fɪlieɪt/ **1** [T, usually passive] **~ sb/sth (with/to sb/sth)** to link a group, a company or an organization very closely with another, larger one 使隸屬，使併入（較大的團體、公司、組織）：*The hospital is affiliated with the local university.* 這家醫院附屬於當地大學。◇ *The group is not affiliated to any political party.* 該團體不隸屬任何政黨。**2** [T, I] **~ (yourself) (with sb/sth)** to join, to be connected with, or to work for an organization 加入；與…有關；為…工作：*The majority of people questioned affiliated themselves with a religious group.* 接受詢問的人大多數都加入了宗教團體。
■ **noun** /ə'fɪliət/ a company, an organization, etc. that is connected with or controlled by another, larger one 附屬機構；分支機構；分公司；分會

af·fili·ated /ə'fɪlieɪtɪd/ *adj.* [only before noun] closely connected to or controlled by a group or an organization 隸屬的：*All affiliated members can vote.* 所有隸屬成員都有投票權。◇ *a government-affiliated institute* 一家隸屬於政府的研究所 **OPP unaffiliated**

af·fili·ation /əˌfɪli'eɪʃn/ *noun* [U, C] (*formal*) **1** a person's connection with a political party, religion, etc.（與政黨、宗教等的）隸屬關係：*He was arrested because of his political affiliation.* 他因所屬政黨的關係而被捕。**2** one group or organization's official connection with another 隸屬；從屬

af·fin·ity /ə'fɪnəti/ *noun* (*pl.* **-ies**) (*formal*) **1** [sing.] **~ (for/with sb/sth)** | **~ (between A and B)** a strong feeling that you understand sb/sth and like them or it 喜好；喜愛 **SYN rapport**：*Sam was born in the country and had a deep affinity with nature.* 薩姆在鄉下出生，特別喜愛大自然。**2** [U, C] **~ (with sb/sth)** | **~ (between A and B)** a close relationship between two people or things that have similar qualities, structures or features 密切的關係；類同：*There is a close affinity between Italian and Spanish.* 意大利語和西班牙語關係密切。

af'finity card *noun* a CREDIT CARD printed with the name of an organization, for example a charity, which receives a small amount of money each time the card is used 認同卡（印有某機構名稱的信用卡，持卡人每次使用此卡，該機構均可獲得回饋金）

af'finity group *noun* (*especially NAmE*) a group of people who share the same interest or purpose（有共同利益或目的的）親和團體

af·firm /ə'fɜːm; *NAmE* ə'fɜːrm/ *verb* (*formal*) to state firmly or publicly that sth is true or that you support sth strongly 申明；斷言；公開支持 **SYN confirm**：**~ sth** *Both sides affirmed their commitment to the cease-fire.* 雙方均申明答應停火。◇ **~ that …** *I can affirm that no one will lose their job.* 我可以肯定，誰都不會丟掉工作。▸ **af·firm·ation** /ˌæfə'meɪʃn; *NAmE* ˌæfər'm-/ *noun* [U, C]：*She nodded in affirmation.* 她肯定地點了點頭。

af·firma·tive /ə'fɜːmətɪv; *NAmE* ə'fɜːrm-/ *adj., noun*
■ **adj.** (*formal*) an **affirmative** word or reply means 'yes' or expresses agreement 肯定的；同意的 **OPP negative** ▸ **af·firma·tive·ly** *adv.*：*90% voted affirmatively.* * 90% 投票贊成。
■ **noun** (*formal*) a word or statement that means 'yes'; an agreement or a CONFIRMATION 肯定；同意：*She answered* ***in the affirmative*** (= said 'yes'). 她作出了肯定的答覆。**OPP negative**

afˌfirmative 'action (*especially NAmE*) (*BrE* usually **ˌpositive disˌcrimin'ation**) *noun* [U] the practice or policy of making sure that a particular number of jobs, etc. are given to people from groups that are often treated unfairly because of their race, sex, etc. 積極區別對待政策（對因種族、性別等原因遭歧視的群體在就業等方面給予特別照顧）➲ compare REVERSE DISCRIMINATION

affix *verb, noun*
■ **verb** /ə'fɪks/ [often passive] **~ sth (to sth)** (*formal*) to stick or attach sth to sth else 粘上；貼上；附上：*The label should be firmly affixed to the package.* 這張標籤應該牢牢地貼在包裹上。
■ **noun** /'æfɪks/ (*grammar* 語法) a letter or group of letters added to the beginning or end of a word to change its meaning. The PREFIX *un-* in *unhappy* and the SUFFIX *-less* in *careless* are both affixes. 詞綴（unhappy 中的 un- 和 careless 中的 -less 都是詞綴）

af·flict /ə'flɪkt/ *verb* [often passive] (*formal*) to affect sb/sth in an unpleasant or harmful way 折磨；使痛苦：**~ sb/sth** *Aid will be sent to the afflicted areas.* 將向受災地區提供援助。◇ **be afflicted with sth** *About 40% of the country's population is afflicted with the disease.* 全國 40% 左右的人口患有這種疾病。

af·flic·tion /ə'flɪkʃn/ *noun* [U, C] (*formal*) pain and suffering or sth that causes it 折磨；痛苦

af·flu·ent /'æfluənt/ *adj.* (*formal*) having a lot of money and a good standard of living 富裕的 **SYN prosperous, wealthy**：*affluent Western countries* 富裕的西方國家 ◇ *a very affluent neighbourhood* 富人區 ➲ SYNONYMS at RICH ▸ **af·flu·ence** /'æfluəns/ *noun* [U] **SYN prosperity**

af·ford 0-m /ə'fɔːd; *NAmE* ə'fɔːrd/ *verb*
1 0-m [no passive] (usually used with *can*, *could* or *be able to*, especially in negative sentences or questions 通常與 can、could 或 be able to 連用，尤用於否定句或疑問句) to have enough money or time to be able to buy or to do sth 買得起；（有時間）做，能做：**~ sth** *Can we afford a new car?* 我們買得起一輛新車嗎？◇ *None of them could afford £50 for a ticket.* 他們中沒有哪個拿得出 50 英鎊買一張票。◇ *She felt she couldn't afford any more time off work.* 她覺得再也抽不出時間歇班了。◇ **~ to do sth** *We can't afford to go abroad this summer.* 今年夏天我們沒有足夠的錢去國外。◇ *She never took a taxi, even though she could afford to.* 儘管她坐得起出租汽車，但她從未坐過。◇ **~ sth to do sth** *He couldn't afford the money to go on the trip.* 他不夠錢去這次旅行。**2** 0-m [no passive] (usually used with *can* or *could*, especially in negative sentences and questions 通常與 can 或 could 連用，尤用於否定句或疑問句) if you say that you **can't afford** to do sth, you mean that you should not do it because it will cause problems for you if you do 承擔得起（後果）：**~ to do sth** *We cannot afford to ignore this warning.* 我們對這個警告絕不能等閒視之。◇ (*formal*) *They could* ***ill afford*** *to lose any more staff.* 他們再也不能損失員工了。◇ **~ sth** *We cannot afford any more delays.* 我們不能再有任何耽擱了。**3** (*formal*) to provide sb with sth 提供；給予：**~ sth** *The tree affords some shelter from the sun.* 這棵樹可以擋一擋太陽。◇ **~ sb sth** *The programme affords young people the chance to gain work experience.* 這項計劃給年輕人提供了獲得工作經驗的機會。▸ **af·ford·abil·ity** /əˌfɔːdə'bɪləti; *NAmE* əˌfɔːrd-/ *noun* [U] **af·ford·able** /ə'fɔːdəbl; *NAmE* ə'fɔːrd-/ *adj.*：*affordable prices/housing* 付得起的價格；買得起的住宅 **OPP unaffordable** ➲ SYNONYMS at CHEAP **af·ford·ably** *adv.*：*affordably priced apartments* 經濟型公寓住宅

Synonyms 同義詞辨析

afraid

frightened • scared • terrified • alarmed • paranoid

These words all describe feeling or showing fear. 以上各詞均形容害怕。

afraid [not before noun] feeling fear; worried that sth bad might happen 指害怕、擔心不幸的事可能發生： *There's nothing to be afraid of.* 沒有什麼要害怕的。◇ *Aren't you afraid (that) you'll fall?* 你不怕會跌倒嗎？

frightened feeling fear; worried that sth bad might happen 指害怕、擔心不幸的事可能發生： *a frightened child* 受驚的孩子 ◇ *She was frightened that the glass would break.* 她擔心玻璃會破碎。

scared (*rather informal*) feeling fear; worried that sth bad might happen 指害怕、擔心不幸的事可能發生： *The thieves got scared and ran away.* 小偷慌張起來，都跑掉了。

AFRAID, FRIGHTENED OR SCARED? 用 afraid、frightened 還是 scared？

Scared is more informal, more common in speech, and often describes small fears. **Afraid** cannot come before a noun. It can only take the preposition *of*, not *about*. If you are **afraid/frightened/scared of** sb/sth/doing sth or **afraid/frightened/scared to** do sth, you think you are in danger of being hurt or suffering in some way. If you are **frightened/scared about** sth/doing sth, it is less a fear for your personal safety and more a worry that sth unpleasant might happen.
* scared 較非正式，較常用於日常談話中，常指稍微害怕。afraid 不用於名詞前，只能與介詞 of 而非 about 連用。afraid/frightened/scared of sb/sth/doing sth 或 afraid/frightened/scared to do sth 均指擔心受到傷害或遭受痛苦。frightened/scared about sth/doing sth 較少指擔心個人安全，更多的是指害怕不快的事情發生。

terrified very frightened 指恐懼、很害怕： *I was terrified (that) she wouldn't come.* 我很害怕她不來。◇ *She looked at him with wide, terrified eyes.* 她看着他，雙目圓睜，充滿恐懼。

alarmed afraid that sth dangerous or unpleasant might happen 指擔心危險或不快的事情發生： *She was alarmed at the prospect of travelling alone.* 她一想到獨自旅行的情景就害怕。

paranoid (*rather informal*) afraid or suspicious of other people and believing that they are trying to harm you, in a way that is not reasonable 指多疑、不合情理的恐懼： *You're just being paranoid.* 你只是在疑神疑鬼。

PATTERNS

- afraid/frightened/scared **of** spiders, etc.
- frightened/scared/paranoid **about** ...
- afraid/frightened/scared/terrified **that** ...
- afraid/frightened/scared **to** open the door, etc.
- **Don't be** afraid/frightened/scared/alarmed.

af·for·est·ation /əˌfɒrɪˈsteɪʃn; *NAmE* əˌfɔːr-; əˌfɑːr-/ *noun* [U] (*technical* 術語) the process of planting areas of land with trees in order to form a forest 植樹造林 ➲ compare DEFORESTATION ▸ **af·for·est** /əˈfɒrɪst; *NAmE* əˈfɔːr-; əˈfɑːr-/ *verb* [usually passive] **~ sth**

af·fray /əˈfreɪ/ *noun* [C, usually sing., U] (*law* 律) a fight or violent behaviour in a public place （在公共場所）鬥毆，鬧事

af·fri·cate /ˈæfrɪkət/ *noun* (*phonetics* 語音) a speech sound that is made up of a PLOSIVE followed immediately by a FRICATIVE, for example /tʃ/ and /dʒ/ in *chair* and *jar* 塞擦音

af·front /əˈfrʌnt/ *noun, verb*

■ *noun* [usually sing.] **~ (to sb/sth)** a remark or an action that insults or offends sb/sth 侮辱；冒犯

■ *verb* [usually passive] **~ sb/sth** (*formal*) to insult or offend sb 侮辱；冒犯： *He hoped they would not feel affronted if they were not invited.* 他希望如果他們沒有獲得邀請也不要感到受辱。◇ *an affronted expression* 受到冒犯的表情

Afghan hound /ˌæfgæn ˈhaʊnd/ *noun* a tall dog with long soft hair and a pointed nose 阿富汗獵狗

afi·cion·ado /əˌfɪʃəˈnɑːdəʊ; *NAmE* -doʊ/ *noun* (*pl.* **-os**) a person who likes a particular sport, activity or subject very much and knows a lot about it 酷愛…者；迷

afield /əˈfiːld/ *adv.*

IDM **far/farther/further aˈfield** far away from home; to or in places that are not near 遠離家鄉；去遠處；在遠方： *You can hire a car if you want to explore further afield.* 假如你想逛更遠的地方，可以租輛汽車。◇ *Journalists came* ***from as far afield as*** *China.* 新聞記者來自遙遠的中國。

aflame /əˈfleɪm/ *adj.* [not before noun] (*literary*) **1** burning; on fire 在燃燒 SYN **ablaze**： *The whole building was soon aflame.* 整棟大樓很快就燃燒起來。 **2** full of bright colours and lights 五彩繽紛 SYN **ablaze**： *The woods were aflame with autumn colours.* 秋林斑斕絢麗。 **3** showing excitement or embarrassment 激動；窘迫： ***eyes/cheeks aflame*** 兩眼閃光；兩頰緋紅

AFL-CIO /ˌeɪ ef el siː aɪ ˈəʊ; *NAmE* ˈoʊ/ *abbr.* American Federation of Labor and Congress of Industrial Organizations (an organization of TRADE/LABOR UNIONS) 勞聯－產聯，美國勞工聯合會－產業工會聯合會（美國工會的一個聯合組織）

afloat /əˈfləʊt; *NAmE* əˈfloʊt/ *adj.* [not before noun] **1** floating on water （在水上）漂浮： *Somehow we kept the boat afloat.* 我們想辦法使船沒有下沉。 **2** (of a business, etc. 企業等) having enough money to pay debts; able to survive 有償債能力；能維持下去： *They will have to borrow £10 million next year, just to* ***stay afloat.*** 明年他們得舉債 1 000 萬英鎊才能維持下去。

afoot /əˈfʊt/ *adj.* [not before noun] being planned; happening 計劃中；進行中： *There are plans afoot to increase taxation.* 正在擬訂增稅方案。◇ *Changes were afoot.* 各種變革正在進行之中。

afore·men·tioned /əˌfɔːˈmenʃənd; *NAmE* əˌfɔːrˈm-/ (also **afore·said** /əˈfɔːsed; *NAmE* əˈfɔːrsed/) (also **said**) *adj.* [only before noun] (*formal* or *law* 律) mentioned before, in an earlier sentence 前面提到的；上述的： *The aforementioned person was seen acting suspiciously.* 有人看見前面提到的那個人行動可疑。

afore·thought /əˈfɔːθɔːt; *NAmE* əˈfɔːrθ-/ *adj.* IDM see MALICE

a for·ti·ori /ˌeɪ ˌfɔːtiˈɔːraɪ; *NAmE* ˌfɔːrt-/ *adv.* (*formal* or *law* 律) (from *Latin*) for or with an even stronger reason 更有理由；理由更充分

afoul /əˈfaʊl/ *adv.* (*NAmE*)

IDM **run aˈfoul of sth** to do sth that is not allowed by a law or rule, or to do sth that people in authority disapprove of （與法律、規章、當權者等）相抵觸，有衝突： *to run afoul of the law* 違犯法律

afraid 🔑 /əˈfreɪd/ *adj.* [not before noun]

1 🔑 feeling fear; frightened because you think that you might be hurt or suffer 害怕，畏懼（可能受傷害、受苦）： *Don't be afraid.* 別怕。◇ **~ of sb/sth** *It's all over. There's nothing to be afraid of now.* 一切都結束了。現在沒有什麼可怕的了。◇ *Are you afraid of spiders?* 你怕蜘蛛嗎？◇ **~ of doing sth** *I started to feel afraid of going out alone at night.* 我開始害怕夜間單獨外出了。◇ **~ to do sth** *She was afraid to open the door.* 她不敢開門。 **2** 🔑 worried about what might happen 擔心（會發生某事）： **~ of doing sth** *She was afraid of upsetting her parents.* 她擔心會使她父母不安。◇ **~ to do sth** *Don't be afraid to ask if you don't understand.* 你要是不懂，儘管問好了。◇ **~ (that ...)** *We were afraid (that) we were going to capsize the boat.* 我們擔心會把船弄翻。 **3 ~ for sb/sth** worried or frightened that sth unpleasant, dangerous, etc. will happen to a particular person or thing 擔心，生怕（將發生不快、不幸或危險的事）： *I'm not afraid for me, but for the baby.* 我擔心的不是自己，而是

嬰兒。◇ *They had already fired three people and he was afraid for his job.* 他們已經解雇了三人，所以他為他的工作擔憂。

IDM **I'm afraid** used as a polite way of telling sb sth that is unpleasant or disappointing, or that you are sorry about（禮貌地說出令人不快、失望或感到遺憾的事）我怕，恐怕，很遺憾，對不起：*I can't help you, I'm afraid.* 對不起，我幫不了你的忙。◇ *I'm afraid we can't come.* 很遺憾，我們來不了。◇ *I'm afraid that it's not finished yet.* 此事恐怕還沒有完。◇ *He's no better, **I'm afraid to say**.* 我很抱歉地說，他一點也不見好轉。◇ *'Is there any left?' '**I'm afraid not**.'* "還有剩的沒有？" "恐怕沒有。" ◇ *'Will it hurt?' '**I'm afraid so**.'* "那痛不痛？" "恐怕會痛。"

'A-frame (also **ˌA-frame 'house**) *noun* (*especially NAmE*) a house with very steep sides that meet at the top in the shape of the letter A * A 形房屋

'A-frame tent *noun* = RIDGE TENT

afresh /əˈfreʃ/ *adv.* (*formal*) again, especially from the beginning or with new ideas 從頭；重新；另行：*It was a chance to **start afresh**.* 這是個重新開始的機會。

Af·ri·can /ˈæfrɪkən/ *adj.*, *noun*
■ ***adj.*** of or connected with Africa 非洲的
■ ***noun*** a person from Africa, especially a black person 非洲人（尤指黑人）

ˌAfrican A'merican *noun* a person from America who is a member of a race of people who have dark skin, originally from Africa（非洲裔）美國黑人 ▶ **ˌAfrican A'merican** *adj.*

ˌAfrican Ca'nadian *noun* a Canadian citizen whose family was originally from Africa 非裔加拿大人 ▶ **ˌAfrican Ca'nadian** *adj.*

ˌAfrican re'naissance *noun* [sing.] a period of time when Africa will experience great development in its economy and culture. Some people believe that this started at the end of the 20th century. 非洲復興（非洲在經濟和文化方面將出現巨大發展的時期，有人認為這一趨勢始於 20 世紀末）

Af·ri·kaans /ˌæfrɪˈkɑːns/ *noun* [U] a language that has developed from Dutch, spoken in South Africa 阿非利堪斯語；南非荷蘭語

Af·ri·kaner /ˌæfrɪˈkɑːnə(r)/ *noun* a person from South Africa, usually of Dutch origin, whose first language is Afrikaans 阿非利卡人（以南非荷蘭語為第一語言的南非人，常為荷蘭裔）

Afro /ˈæfrəʊ; *NAmE* ˈæfroʊ/ *noun* (*pl.* **-os**) a HAIRSTYLE sometimes worn by black people and popular in the 1970s, in which the hair forms a round mass of tight curls 非洲式髮型（20 世紀 70 年代流行的某些黑人的圓形緊密鬈髮）

Afro- /ˈæfrəʊ; *NAmE* ˈæfroʊ/ *combining form* (in nouns and adjectives 構成名詞和形容詞) African 非洲人；非洲（人）的：*Afro-Asian* 亞非的

Afro·beat /ˈæfrəʊbiːt; *NAmE* ˈæfroʊ-/ *noun* [U] a type of music that combines traditional Nigerian rhythms and singing styles with JAZZ and FUNK 非洲節拍樂（將傳統尼日利亞節奏及歌唱風格與爵士樂、放克樂相融合）

ˌAfro-Carib'bean *noun* a person who comes, or whose family comes, from the Caribbean and who is a member of a group of people with dark skin who originally came from Africa 加勒比海黑人 ▶ **ˌAfro-Carib'bean** *adj.*

aft /ɑːft; *NAmE* æft/ *adv.* (*technical* 術語) in, near or towards the back of a ship or an aircraft 在（或向）船尾；在（或向）機尾 ▶ **aft** *adj.* ➲ compare FORE *adv.* (1)

after /ˈɑːftə(r); *NAmE* ˈæf-/ *prep.*, *conj.*, *adv.*, *adj.*
■ ***prep.*** **1** later than sth; following sth in time（時間）在…後：*We'll leave after lunch.* 我們將在午飯後動身。◇ *They arrived **shortly after** 5.* 他們是在 5 點鐘剛過到達的。◇ ***Not long after that** he resigned.* 那以後不久他就辭職了。◇ *Let's meet **the day after tomorrow/the week after next**.* 咱們後天／下下週再見。◇ *After winning the prize she became famous overnight.* 她獲獎後一夜之間成名了。◇ *After an hour I went home* (= when an hour had passed). 一小時之後我回家了。◇ (*NAmE*) *It's ten after seven in the morning* (= 7.10 a.m.) 現在是早上七點十分。 **2** **... after ...** used to show that sth happens many times or continuously（表示反複不斷或一個接着一個）：*day after day of hot weather* 日復一日的炎熱天氣 ◇ *I've told you time after time not to do that.* 我一再告訴過你不要幹那件事。➲ see also ONE AFTER ANOTHER at ONE **3** behind sb when they have left; following sb 跟隨；追趕；在…後面：*Shut the door after you.* 隨手關門。◇ *I'm always having to clean up after the children* (= clean the place after they have left it dirty and untidy). 孩子們離開以後，我總得打掃一番。◇ *He ran after her with the book.* 他拿着那本書在後面追趕她。◇ *She was left staring after him.* 她目不轉睛地望着他離去的背影。 **4** next to and following sb/sth in order or importance（按順序、重要性）在…後面，僅次於：*Your name comes after mine in the list.* 在名單上你的名字在我的後面。◇ *He's the tallest, after Richard.* 除了理查德，他的個子最高。◇ ***After you*** (= Please go first). 請先走。◇ ***After you with** the paper* (= Can I have it next?). 報紙你看完了給我看。 **5** in contrast to sth 與…對照；與…對比：*It was pleasantly cool in the house after the sticky heat outside.* 與戶外的濕熱相比，屋裏真是涼爽愜意。 **6** as a result of or because of sth that has happened 鑒於；由於：*I'll never forgive him after what he said.* 由於他說了那些話，我永遠也不會原諒他。 **7** despite sth; although sth has happened 儘管；即使某事之後：*I can't believe she'd do that, not after all I've done for her.* 在我為她做了這一切之後，我無法相信她會那樣做。 **8** trying to find or catch sb/sth 尋找；追捕：*The police are after him.* 警方正在追捕他。◇ *He's after a job at our place.* 他到我們這兒找工作。 **9** about sb/sth 關於：*She asked after you* (= how you were). 她問候你。 **10** in the style of sb/sth; following the example of sb/sth 模仿；依照：*a painting after Goya* 一幅仿戈雅的畫 ◇ *We named the baby 'Ena' after her grandmother.* 我們以嬰兒祖母的名字給嬰兒取名"埃娜"。 **11 after-** (in adjectives 構成形容詞) happening or done later than the time or event mentioned …後的：*after-hours drinking* (= after closing time) 打烊時間以後飲酒 ◇ *an after-school club* 課外活動俱樂部 ◇ *after-dinner mints* 餐後薄荷糖

IDM **ˌafter 'all** **1** despite what has been said or expected 畢竟；終歸：*So you made it after all!* 你畢竟成功了！ **2** used when you are explaining sth, or giving a reason（解釋或說明理由）別忘了，到底：*He should have paid. He suggested it, after all.* 他本來就應該付款，反正他自己也這麼提出。 **be after doing sth** (*IrishE*) **1** to be going to do sth soon; to be intending to do sth soon 正要做某事；打算就要做某事 **2** to have just done sth 剛做了某事
■ ***conj.*** at a time later than sth; when sth has finished 在…以後：*I'll call you after I've spoken to them.* 我和他們談了以後就給你打電話。◇ *Several years after they'd split up they met again by chance in Paris.* 他們離異幾年以後在巴黎又偶然相遇。
■ ***adv.*** later in time; afterwards 後來；以後：*That was in 1996. **Soon after**, I heard that he'd died.* 那是在 1996 年。不久以後我聽說他死了。◇ *I could come next week, or the week after.* 我可能下週來，或者再下一週。◇ *And they all **lived happily ever after**.* 從此以後他們都過着幸福的生活。
■ ***adj.*** [only before noun] (*old use*) following; later 後來的；以後的：*in after years* 在以後的歲月中

after·birth /ˈɑːftəbɜːθ; *NAmE* ˈæftərbɜːrθ/ *noun* (usually **the afterbirth**) [sing.] the material that comes out of a woman or female animal's body after a baby has been born, and which was necessary to feed and protect the baby 胞衣；胎盤及羊膜 SYN **placenta**

after·burn·er /ˈɑːftəbɜːnə(r); *NAmE* ˈæftərbɜːrnər/ *noun* (*technical* 術語) a device for increasing the power of a JET ENGINE（噴氣發動機的）加力燃燒裝置，後燃室，後燃器

after·care /ˈɑːftəkeə(r); *NAmE* ˈæftərker/ *noun* [U] **1** care or treatment given to a person who has just left hospital, prison, etc.（病人出院後的）護理，治療；（犯人出獄後的）安置，事後處理：*aftercare services* 出院後護理服務 **2** (*BrE*) service and advice that is offered by some companies to customers who have bought a car, WASHING MACHINE, etc. 售後服務

ˈafter-effect *noun* [usually pl.] the **after-effects** of a drug, an illness or an unpleasant event are the feelings that you experience later as a result of it （藥物的）後效，後作用；（疾病、不快事情的）後遺症，後果，事後

after·glow /ˈɑːftəɡləʊ; *NAmE* ˈæftərɡloʊ/ *noun* [usually sing.] (*literary*) **1** the light that is left in the sky after the sun has set （日落後的）餘暉，落照，晚霞 **2** a pleasant feeling after a good experience 美好的回憶

after·life /ˈɑːftəlaɪf; *NAmE* ˈæftərl-/ *noun* [sing.] a life that some people believe exists after death 陰世；死後（靈魂的）生活

after·math /ˈɑːftəmæθ; -mɑːθ; *NAmE* ˈæftərmæθ/ *noun* [usually sing.] the situation that exists as a result of an important (and usually unpleasant) event, especially a war, an accident, etc. （戰爭、事故、不快事情的）後果，創傷：*A lot of rebuilding took place **in the aftermath of** the war.* 戰後進行了大量的重建工作。◇ *the assassination of the Prime Minister and its immediate aftermath* 暗殺首相及其直接後果

after·noon 🔑 /ˌɑːftəˈnuːn; *NAmE* ˌæftərˈn-/ *noun* [U, C] the part of the day from 12 midday until about 6 o'clock 下午（中午 12 點至 6 點左右）：***this/ yesterday/tomorrow afternoon*** 今天 / 昨天 / 明天下午 ◇ ***In the afternoon** they went shopping.* 他們下午去購物了。◇ *She studies art two afternoons a week.* 她每週兩個下午學習藝術。◇ *Are you ready for this afternoon's meeting?* 今天下午的會議你準備好了沒有？◇ *The baby always has an afternoon nap.* 嬰兒午後總要睡一會兒。◇ *Come over on Sunday afternoon.* 星期天下午過來。◇ *Where were you **on the afternoon of** May 21?* * 5 月 21 日下午你在哪裏？ ➲ see also GOOD AFTERNOON

after·noons /ˌɑːftəˈnuːnz; *NAmE* ˌæftərˈn-/ *adv.* during the afternoon every day 每天下午：*Afternoons he works at home.* 每天下午他在家裏工作。

af·ters /ˈɑːftəz; *NAmE* ˈæftərz/ *noun* [U] (*BrE, informal*) a sweet dish that you eat at the end of a meal （正餐最後一道菜）甜食，後盤：*fruit salad for afters* 作為正餐後盤的水果色拉 ➲ see also DESSERT, PUDDING, SWEET *n.*

ˌafter-ˌsales ˈservice *noun* [U] the fact of providing help to customers after they have bought a product, usually involving doing repairs that are needed or giving advice on how to use the product 售後服務

after·shave /ˈɑːftəʃeɪv; *NAmE* ˈæftərʃ-/ *noun* [U, C] a liquid with a pleasant smell that men sometimes put on their faces after they shave （男人剃鬚後抹的）潤膚液；鬚後水；鬍後水

after·shock /ˈɑːftəʃɒk; *NAmE* ˈæftərʃɑːk/ *noun* a small EARTHQUAKE that happens after a bigger one （地震後的）餘震

after·taste /ˈɑːftəteɪst; *NAmE* ˈæftərt-/ *noun* [sing.] a taste (usually an unpleasant one) that stays in your mouth after you have eaten or drunk sth （飲食後留在口中且常難聞的）回味，餘味，苦味

after·thought /ˈɑːftəθɔːt; *NAmE* ˈæftərθ-/ *noun* [usually sing.] a thing that is thought of, said or added later, and is often not carefully planned 事後想法，事後添加的事物（常指未經周密考慮）：*They only invited Jack and Sarah **as an afterthought**.* 他們邀請傑克和薩拉不過是事後想起的補救辦法。

after·wards 🔑 /ˈɑːftəwədz; *NAmE* ˈæftərwərdz/ (*especially BrE*) (*NAmE* usually **after·ward**) *adv.* at a later time; after an event that has already been mentioned 以後；後來：*Afterwards she was sorry for what she'd said.* 後來她後悔說了那些話。◇ *Let's go out now and eat afterwards.* 咱們現在出去，然後再吃飯。◇ *Shortly afterwards he met her again.* 不久之後，他又遇到了她。

after·word /ˈɑːftəwɜːd; *NAmE* ˈæftərwɜːrd/ *noun* a section at the end of a book that says sth about the main text, and may be written by a different author 後記；跋 ➲ compare FOREWORD

ag /æx; ʌx/ *exclamation* (*SAfrE*) used when you are reacting to sth that has been said, or when you are angry or irritated by sth （對他人的話作出反應或表示生氣、惱怒）唔，啊，哎呀：*Ag, don't worry about it.* 哦，別擔心。◇ *Ag, no man!* 嘿，不行！

Aga™ /ˈɑːɡə/ *noun* (*BrE*) a type of British cooker/stove made of solid iron that is also used for heating. 'Aga saga' is a humorous name for a novel about the lives of British middle-class women, because Agas are very popular with this group. 雅家爐（實心鐵製，用於烹飪和取暖。"雅家爐小說"趣指描寫英國中產階級婦女生活的小說，因她們喜用此爐而得名）

again 🔑 /əˈɡen; əˈɡeɪn/ *adv.*

1 🔑 one more time; on another occasion 再一次；又一次：*Could you say it again, please?* 請再說一遍好嗎？◇ *When will I see you again?* 我何時能再見到你？◇ *This must never happen again.* 這種事再也不能發生了。◇ ***Once again** (= as had happened several times before), the train was late.* 火車又晚點了。◇ *I've told you **again and again** (= many times) not to do that.* 我一再告訴過你別幹那種事。◇ *I'll have to write it **all over again** (= again from the beginning).* 我得從頭再寫一遍。 **2** 🔑 showing that sb/sth is in the same place or state that they were in originally 返回原處；復原：*He was glad to be home again.* 他很高興又回到家了。◇ *She spends two hours a day getting to work and **back again**.* 她每天上班來回要花兩小時。◇ *You'll soon feel well again.* 你很快就會康復的。 **3** added to an amount that is already there 增加；多：*The cost is about **half as much again** as it was two years ago.* 現在的價格比兩年前提高約一半。◇ *I'd like **the same again** (= the same amount or the same thing).* 我想再來一份同樣的。 **4** used to show that a comment or fact is connected with what you have just said 再說；其次：*And again, we must think of the cost.* 再說，我們必須考慮成本。 **5 then/there ~** used to introduce a fact or an opinion that contrasts with what you have just said （引出相對照的事實或看法）再說，另一方面：*We might buy it but then again we might not.* 我們可能買，不過也可能不買。 **6** used when you ask sb to tell you sth or repeat sth that you think they have told you already 請再說一遍：*What was the name again?* 叫什麼名字，再說一遍好不好？ **IDM** see NOW *adv.*, SAME *pron.*, TIME *n.*

against 🔑 /əˈɡenst; əˈɡeɪnst/ *prep.*

HELP For the special uses of **against** in phrasal verbs, look at the entries for the verbs. For example **count against sb** is in the phrasal verb section at **count**. * against 在短語動詞中的特殊用法見有關動詞詞條。如 count against sb 在詞條 count 的短語動詞部份。

1 🔑 opposing or disagreeing with sb/sth 反對；與…相反；逆；違反：*the fight against terrorism* 反對恐怖主義的鬥爭 ◇ *We're playing against the league champions next week.* 下週我們要和聯賽冠軍隊比賽。◇ *We were rowing against the current.* 我們划船逆流而上。◇ *That's against the law.* 那是違法的。◇ *She was forced to marry against her will.* 她被迫違背自己的心願嫁了人。◇ *Are you for or against the death penalty?* 你贊成還是反對死刑？◇ *She is against seeing (= does not want to see) him.* 她不想見他。◇ *I'd advise you against doing that.* 我勸你別做那事。 **2** 🔑 not to the advantage or favour of sb/sth 對…不利：*The evidence is against him.* 證據對他不利。◇ *Her age is against her.* 她的年齡對她不利。 ➲ compare FOR *prep.* (7) **3** close to, touching or hitting sb/sth 緊靠；倚；碰；撞：*Put the piano there, against the wall.* 把鋼琴放在那兒，緊靠着牆。◇ *The rain beat against the windows.* 雨點擊打着窗戶。 **4** in order to prevent sth from happening or to reduce the damage caused by sth 以防：*an injection against rabies* 狂犬病預防注射 ◇ *They took precautions against fire.* 他們採取了防火措施。◇ *Are we insured against theft?* 我們保了盜竊險沒有？ **5** with sth in the background, as a contrast 以…為背景；襯托：*His red clothes stood out clearly against the snow.* 他的紅衣服在白雪中格外顯眼。◇ (*figurative*) *The love story unfolds against a background of civil war.* 這愛情故事以內戰為背景展開。 **6** used when you are comparing two things 和…相比：*You must weigh the benefits against the cost.* 你一定要權衡利益與成本二者的得失。◇ *Check your receipts against the statement.* 核對你的收據與結算單是否相符。◇ *What's the rate of exchange against*

A

Collocations 詞語搭配

The ages of life 年齡段

Childhood/youth 童年／青年時期

- **be born and raised/bred** in Oxford; into a wealthy/middle-class family 在牛津出生並長大；在一個富裕／中產階級家庭出生並長大
- **have** a happy/an unhappy/a tough childhood 有一個幸福／不幸／艱苦的童年
- **grow up** in a musical family/an orphanage; on a farm 成長於音樂之家／孤兒院／農場
- **be/grow up** an only child (= with no brothers or sisters) 是獨生子
- **reach/hit/enter/go through** adolescence/puberty 進入／經歷青春期
- **be in** your teens/early twenties/mid-twenties/late twenties 十幾歲；二十出頭；二十五歲左右；將近三十歲
- **undergo/experience** physical/psychological changes 經歷生理／心理變化
- **give in to/succumb to/resist** peer pressure 屈服於／頂住同輩的壓力
- **assert** your independence/individuality 維護獨立／個性

Adulthood 成年

- **leave** school/university/home 離開學校／大學／家
- **go out to** work (at sixteen) （16 歲）投身工作
- **get/find** a job/partner 找到工作／伴侶
- **be/get** engaged/married 訂婚；結婚
- **have/get** a wife/husband/mortgage/steady job 有妻子／丈夫／按揭貸款／穩定的工作
- **settle down and have** kids/children/a family 安定下來並生兒育女
- **begin/start/launch/build** a career (in politics/science/the music industry) 開始（政治／科學／音樂）職業生涯
- **prove** (**to be**)/**represent/mark/reach** a (major) turning point for sb/in your life/career 最終成為／代表／標誌／達到某人／某人人生／某人職業生涯的（重要）轉折點
- **reach/be well into/settle into** middle age 進入／安度中年
- **have/suffer/go through** a midlife crisis 經歷中年危機
- **take/consider** early retirement 提前退休；考慮提前退休
- **approach/announce/enjoy** your retirement 臨近／宣佈／享受退休

Old age 老年

- **have/see/spend time with** your grandchildren 有孫輩；與孫輩共度時光
- **take up/pursue/develop** a hobby 開始／追求／培養一種愛好
- **get/receive/draw/collect/live on** a pension 得到／提取／領取退休金；靠退休金生活
- **approach/save for/die from** old age 臨近晚年；存錢養老；老死
- **live to** a ripe old age 高壽
- **reach** the grand old age of 102/23 (*often ironic*) 活到 102／23 歲高齡（常作反語）
- **be/become/be getting/be going** senile (*often ironic*) 變得衰老（常作反語）
- **die** (**peacefully**)/**pass away** in your sleep/after a brief illness 睡夢中／患病不久（平靜地）離開人世

the dollar? 美元的兌換率是多少？ **IDM** see AS *conj.*, STACKED

agape /əˈɡeɪp/ *adj.* [not before noun] (*formal*) if a person's mouth is **agape**, it is wide open, especially because they are surprised or shocked（嘴巴因吃驚等）大張着

agar /ˈeɪɡɑː(r)/ (also **ˌagar-ˈagar**) *noun* [U] a substance like jelly, used by scientists for growing CULTURES 瓊脂；洋菜

agate /ˈæɡət/ *noun* [U, C] a hard stone with bands or areas of colour, used in jewellery 瑪瑙

agave /əˈɡeɪvi; -ˈɡɑːv-; *NAmE* əˈɡɑːvi/ *noun* a plant that grows in hot dry areas of N and S America, with sharp points on the leaves and tall groups of flowers 龍舌蘭（生長在南北美洲熱帶乾旱地區）

ag·bada /æɡˈbɑːdə/ *noun* a long ROBE (= long piece of clothing) worn by men in some parts of W Africa（西非）男式長袍

age 0‒ /eɪdʒ/ *noun, verb*

■ ***noun*** **1** 0‒ [C, U] the number of years that a person has lived or a thing has existed 年齡：*He left school **at the age of** 18.* 他 18 歲讀完中學。◇ *She needs more friends of her own age.* 她需要更多的同齡朋友。◇ *children from 5–10 **years of age*** * 5 至 10 歲的兒童 ◇ *Young people of all ages go there to meet.* 不同年齡的年輕人都去那裏聚會。◇ *When I was your age I was already married.* 我在你這個年紀時已經結婚了。◇ *He started playing the piano **at an early age**.* 他幼年開始彈鋼琴。◇ *All ages admitted.* 老幼均可入內。◇ *Children **over the age of** 12 must pay full fare.* * 12 歲以上兒童須購全票。◇ *She was beginning to **feel her age*** (= feel that she was getting old). 她開始感到自己上年紀了。◇ *He was tall **for his age*** (= taller than you would expect, considering his age). 以他的年齡，他算高個子。◇ *There's a big **age gap** between them* (= a big difference in their ages). 他們的年齡相差很大。◇ *ways of calculating the age of the earth* 計算地球年齡的方法 **2** 0‒ [U, C] a particular period of a person's life 年齡段：*middle age* 中年 ◇ *15 is an awkward age.* * 15 歲是個尷尬的年紀。◇ *He died of old age.* 他終其天年。➲ see also THE THIRD AGE **3** 0‒ [C] a particular period of history（歷史上的）時代，時期：*the nuclear age* 核時代 ◇ *the age of the computer* 計算機時代 ➲ see also BRONZE AGE, IRON AGE, NEW AGE, STONE AGE **4** 0‒ [U] the state of being old 老年；陳年；破舊；老化：*Wine improves **with age**.* 陳酒味濃。◇ *The jacket was showing signs of age.* 這件夾克已露出破舊的痕跡。◇ *the wisdom that comes with age* 隨着年齡而增加的智慧 **5** 0‒ **ages** [pl.] (also **an age** [sing.]) (*informal, especially BrE*) a very long time 很長時間：*I waited **for ages**.* 我等了好長時間。◇ *It'll probably **take ages** to find a parking space.* 大概得老半天才能找到停車位。◇ *Carlos left **ages ago**.* 卡洛斯老早就離開了。◇ *It's been an age since we've seen them.* 我們有很長一段時間沒有見到他們了。 **6** [C] (*geology* 地) a length of time which is a division of an EPOCH 期

IDM **ˌbe/ˌact your ˈage** to behave in a way that is suitable for sb of your age and not as though you were much younger 行為和年齡相稱；舉止不再有孩子氣 **ˌcome of ˈage 1** when a person **comes of age**, they reach the age when they have an adult's legal rights and responsibilities 成年；達到法定年齡 ➲ see also COMING OF AGE **2** if sth **comes of age**, it reaches the stage of development at which people accept and value it 成熟；發達 **ˌlook your ˈage** to seem as old as you really are and not younger or older 容貌與年齡相當 **ˌunder ˈage** not legally old enough to do a particular thing 未到法定年齡：*It is illegal to sell cigarettes to children who are under age.* 售香煙給未到法定年齡的兒童是非法的。 ➲ see also UNDERAGE ➲ more at ADVANCED, CERTAIN *adj.*, DAY, FEEL *v.*, GRAND *adj.*, RIPE

■ ***verb*** (**ag·ing**, **aged**, **aged**) **HELP** In *BrE* the present participle can also be spelled **age·ing**. 英式英語中，現在分詞也可拼作 ageing。 **1** [I] to become older 變老：*As he aged, his memory got worse.* 他隨着年事增高，記憶力就變差了。◇ *The population is aging* (= more people are living longer). 人口正在老齡化。 **2** [T] to make sb/sth look, feel or seem older 使顯老；使變老；使蒼老：**~ sb** *The shock has aged her.* 這次打擊讓她顯得蒼老了。◇

~ sth *Exposure to the sun ages the skin.* 太陽曝曬會使皮膚粗老。 **3** [I, T] to develop in flavour over a period of time; to allow sth to do this （使）成熟，變陳 **SYN** **mature**：*The cheese is left to age for at least a year.* 這種奶酪至少要擱一年才成熟。◇ **~ sth** *The wine is aged in oak casks.* 這種酒是用櫟木酒桶放陳的。

-age *suffix* (in nouns 構成名詞) **1** the action or result of（表示動作或結果）：*breakage* 破損 **2** a state or condition of（表示狀態或狀況）：*bondage* 奴役 **3** a set or group of（表示一套或一組）：*baggage* 行李 **4** an amount of（表示數量）：*mileage* 英里數 **5** the cost of（表示費用）：*postage* 郵費 **6** a place where（表示地方）：*anchorage* 泊地

aged 0-m *adj.*
1 0-m /eɪdʒd/ [not before noun] of the age of …歲：*They have two children aged six and nine.* 他們有兩個小孩，一個六歲，一個九歲。◇ *volunteers aged between 25 and 40* * 25 至 40 歲的志願者 **2** /ˈeɪdʒɪd/ (*formal*) very old 年邁的：*my aged aunt* 我年邁的嬸嬸 ➲ SYNONYMS at OLD **3 the aged** /ˈeɪdʒɪd/ *noun* [pl.] very old people（統稱）老人：*services for the sick and the aged* 為病人和老人提供的服務

ˈage group (also *less frequent* **ˈage bracket**) *noun* people of a similar age or within a particular range of ages 年齡組；年齡段：*men in the older age group* 較年長組別的男子 ◇ *education for the 16–18 age group* * 16 至 18 歲年齡段的教育 ◇ *Which age bracket are you? (Please tick the box.)* 你在哪個年齡段？（請在方格中打鈎。）

age·ing (*BrE*) (also **aging** *NAmE, BrE*) /ˈeɪdʒɪŋ/ *noun, adj.*
■ ***noun*** [U] the process of growing old 變老；蒼老；變舊；老化：*signs of ageing* 變老的跡象
■ ***adj.*** [usually before noun] becoming older and usually less useful, safe, healthy, etc. 變老的；老朽的；變舊的；老化的：*ageing equipment* 老化的設備 ◇ *an ageing rock star* 日益年邁的搖滾樂歌星

age·ism (*NAmE* also **agism**) /ˈeɪdʒɪzəm/ *noun* [U] unfair treatment of people because they are considered too old 對老年人的歧視；年齡歧視 ▶ **age·ist** *adj.* **age·ist** *noun*

age·less /ˈeɪdʒləs/ *adj.* (*literary*) **1** never looking old or never seeming to grow old 青春永駐的；永不顯老的 **SYN** **timeless**：*Her beauty appeared ageless.* 她的美顯得經久不衰。 **2** existing for ever; impossible to give an age to 永恆的 **SYN** **timeless**：*the ageless mystery of the universe* 宇宙永恆之謎

ˈage limit *noun* the oldest or youngest age at which you are allowed to do sth 年齡限制：*the **upper/lower age limit*** 年齡上限／下限

agency 0-m /ˈeɪdʒənsi/ *noun* (*pl.* **-ies**)
1 0-m a business or an organization that provides a particular service especially on behalf of other businesses or organizations 服務機構；（尤指）代理機構，經銷機構：*an **advertising/employment agency*** 廣告社；職業介紹所 ◇ *You can book at your local **travel agency**.* 你可以在當地的旅行社預訂。◇ ***international aid agencies** caring for refugees* 國際援助難民事務所 ➲ see also DATING AGENCY, NEWS AGENCY, PRESS AGENCY **2** 0-m (*especially NAmE*) a government department that provides a particular service（政府的）專門機構：*the Central Intelligence Agency (CIA)*（美國）中央情報局
IDM **through the agency of** (*formal*) as a result of the action of sb/sth 由於…的作用

agenda /əˈdʒendə/ *noun* a list of items to be discussed at a meeting（會議的）議程表，議事日程：*The next item **on the agenda** is the publicity budget.* 議程表上的下一項是宣傳預算。◇ *For the government, education is now **at the top of the agenda*** (= most important). 對政府來說，教育是當務之急。◇ *In our company, quality is **high on the agenda**.* 我們公司高度重視質量。◇ *Newspapers have been accused of trying to **set the agenda** for the government* (= decide what is important). 人們指責報章企圖替政府決定政務的輕重緩急。➲ see also HIDDEN AGENDA

Which Word? 詞語辨析

agenda / diary / schedule / timetable

■ A book with a space for each day where you write down things that you have to do in the future is called a **diary** or a **datebook** (*NAmE*) (not an *agenda*). You may also have a **calendar** on your desk or hanging up in your room, where you write down your appointments. A **diary** or a **journal** is also the record that some people keep of what has happened during the day. 記事簿用 diary 或 datebook（美式英語），不用 agenda。記錄約會等事宜也可用枱曆或掛曆（calendar）。diary 或 journal 亦指日記、日誌：*The Diary of Anne Frank*《安妮 • 弗蘭克的日記》

■ In *BrE* your **schedule** is a plan that lists all the work that you have to do and when you must do each thing and a **timetable** is a list showing the fixed times at which events will happen. 在英式英語中，schedule 指工作計劃、日程安排，timetable 指時間表、時刻表：*a bus/train timetable* 公共汽車／火車時刻表 In *NAmE* these are both called a **schedule**. 在美式英語中，上述兩種含義均用 schedule。

agent 0-m /ˈeɪdʒənt/ *noun*
1 0-m a person whose job is to act for, or manage the affairs of, other people in business, politics, etc.（企業、政治等的）代理人，經紀人：*an insurance agent* 保險經紀人 ◇ *Our agent in New York deals with all US sales.* 我們在紐約的代理商經辦在整個美國的銷售。➲ see also ESTATE AGENT, LAND AGENT, TRAVEL AGENT **2** 0-m a person whose job is to arrange work for an actor, musician, sports player, etc. or to find sb who will publish a writer's work（演員、音樂家、運動員、作家等的）代理人，經紀人：*a **theatrical/literary agent*** 劇院經紀人；文稿（出版）代理人 ➲ see also PRESS AGENT **3** = SECRET AGENT：*an enemy agent* 敵方特務 ➲ see also DOUBLE AGENT, SPECIAL AGENT **4** (*formal*) a person or thing that has an important effect on a situation 原動力，動因（指對事態起重要作用的人、事物）：*The charity has been an agent for social change.* 這個慈善機構一直推動社會變革。 **5** (*technical* 術語) a chemical or a substance that produces an effect or a change or is used for a particular purpose（化學）劑：***cleaning/oxidizing agents*** 去污劑；氧化劑 **6** (*grammar* 語法) the person or thing that does an action (expressed as the subject of an active verb, or in a 'by' phrase with a passive verb) 施事者；施動者；行為主體 ➲ compare PATIENT ➲ see also FREE AGENT

ˌAgent ˈGeneral *noun* (*pl.* **ˌAgents ˈGeneral**) the representative of an Australian state or Canadian PROVINCE in a foreign country（澳大利亞州或加拿大省的）駐外代表

agent pro·voca·teur /ˌæʒɒ̃ prəˌvɒkəˈtɜː(r); *NAmE* ˌɑːʒɑ̃ː proʊˌvɑːkəˈtɜːr/ (also **pro·voca·teur**) *noun* (*pl.* **agents pro·voca·teurs** /ˌæʒɒ̃ prəˌvɒkəˈtɜː(r); *NAmE* ˌɑːʒɑ̃ː proʊˌvɑːkəˈtɜːr/) (from *French*) a person who is employed by a government to encourage people in political groups to do sth illegal so that they can be arrested（受雇於政府，慫恿政治團體人士犯法以便將之逮捕的）密探，坐探

ˌage of conˈsent *noun* [sing.] the age at which sb is legally old enough to agree to have a sexual relationship 同意年齡，承諾年齡（可發生性關係的法定年齡）

ˌage-ˈold *adj.* [usually before noun] having existed for a very long time 古老的；已存在很久的：*an **age-old custom/problem*** 古老的風俗；由來已久的問題

ˈage-set *noun* (*EAfrE*) a group of boys or men of a similar age（男孩或男子的）同齡組

ag·glom·er·ate *verb, noun, adj.* (*formal*)
■ ***verb*** /əˈɡlɒməreɪt; *NAmE* əˈɡlɑːm-/ [I, T] to form into a mass or group; to collect things and form them into a mass or group（使）成團，聚結：*These small particles agglomerate together to form larger clusters.* 這些顆粒聚

A

結形成較大的團。◇ **~ sth** *They agglomerated many small pieces of research into a single large study.* 他們把許多小的研究課題彙集成一個大項目。

■ ***noun*** /ə'glɒmərət; *NAmE* ə'glɑːm-/ a mass or collection of things 大團；聚結物：*a multimedia agglomerate* (= group of companies) 一個多媒體集團

■ ***adj.*** /ə'glɒmərət; *NAmE* ə'glɑːm-/ formed into a mass or group 成團的；聚結的

ag·glom·er·ation /əˌglɒmə'reɪʃn; *NAmE* əˌglɑːm-/ *noun* [C, U] (*formal*) a group of things put together in no particular order or arrangement（雜亂聚集的）團，塊，堆；聚集

ag·glu·tin·ative /ə'gluːtɪnətɪv/ *adj.* (*linguistics* 語言) = SYNTHETIC (2)

ag·grand·ize·ment (*BrE* also **-ise·ment**) /ə'grændɪzmənt/ *noun* [U] (*formal, disapproving*) an increase in the power or importance of a person or country（個人或國家權力或重要性的）擴大，增加，提高：*Her sole aim is personal aggrandizement.* 她唯一的目的就是擴大個人權勢。

ag·gra·vate /'ægrəveɪt/ *verb* **1 ~ sth** to make an illness or a bad or unpleasant situation worse 使嚴重；使惡化 SYN **worsen**：*Pollution can aggravate asthma.* 污染會使哮喘加重。◇ *Military intervention will only aggravate the conflict even further.* 軍事介入只會使衝突加劇。**2 ~ sb** (*informal*) to annoy sb, especially deliberately（尤指故意地）激怒，惹惱 SYN **irritate** ▸ **ag·gra·vat·ing** *adj.* **ag·gra·va·tion** /ˌægrə'veɪʃn/ *noun* [U, C]：*I don't need all this aggravation at work.* 我工作時不需要這一切惱人的事。◇ *The drug may cause an aggravation of the condition.* 這種藥可能導致病情惡化。

ag·gra·vat·ed /'ægrəveɪtɪd/ *adj.* [only before noun] (*law* 律) an **aggravated** crime involves further unnecessary violence or unpleasant behaviour（罪行）嚴重的，加重的

ag·gre·gate AW *noun, adj., verb*

■ ***noun*** /'ægrɪgət/ **1** [C] a total number or amount made up of smaller amounts that are collected together 總數；合計 **2** [U, C] (*technical* 術語) sand or broken stone that is used to make concrete or for building roads, etc.（可成混凝土或修路等用的）骨料，集料

IDM **in (the) 'aggregate** (*formal*) added together as a total or single amount 總共；作為總體 **on 'aggregate** (*BrE, sport* 體) when the scores of a number of games are added together（各次比賽相加的）總分：*They won 4–2 on aggregate.* 他們以總分 4:2 獲勝。

■ ***adj.*** /'ægrɪgət/ [only before noun] (*economics* 經 or *sport* 體) made up of several amounts that are added together to form a total number 總數的；總計的：***aggregate demand/investment/turnover*** 總需求／投資／成交量 ◇ (*BrE*) *an aggregate win over their rivals* 以總分戰勝他們的對手

■ ***verb*** /'ægrɪgeɪt/ [usually passive] **~ sth (with sth)** (*formal* or *technical* 術語) to put together different items, amounts, etc. into a single group or total 總計；合計：*The scores were aggregated with the first round totals to decide the winner.* 此次得分與第一輪所得總分合計決出優勝者。▸ **ag·gre·ga·tion** AW /ˌægrɪ'geɪʃn/ *noun* [U, C]：*the aggregation of data* 資料彙集

ag·gre·ga·tor /'ægrɪgeɪtə(r)/ *noun* (*computing* 計) an Internet company that collects information about other companies' products and services and puts it on a single website 信息彙集公司（彙集互聯網其他公司的產品和服務信息並在單獨的網站上發佈）：*a news aggregator* 新聞彙總機構

ag·gres·sion /ə'greʃn/ *noun* [U] **1** feelings of anger and hatred that may result in threatening or violent behaviour 好鬥情緒；攻擊性：*The research shows that computer games may cause aggression.* 研究顯示，電腦遊戲可能引起好鬥情緒。**2** a violent attack or threats by one person against another person or by one country against another country 侵犯；挑釁；侵略：*unprovoked military aggression* 無端軍事侵犯

ag·gres·sive 0→ /ə'gresɪv/ *adj.* **1** 0→ angry, and behaving in a threatening way; ready to attack 好鬥的；挑釁的；侵略的；富於攻擊性的：*He gets aggressive when he's drunk.* 他喝醉了就喜歡尋釁滋事。◇ *a dangerous aggressive dog* 一條危險的惡犬 **2** 0→ acting with force and determination in order to succeed 氣勢洶洶的；聲勢浩大的；志在必得的：*an aggressive advertising campaign* 一場聲勢浩大的廣告宣傳活動 ◇ *A good salesperson has to be aggressive in today's competitive market.* 在當今競爭激烈的市場上，好的銷售員應該有進取精神。▸ **ag·gres·sive·ly** *adv.*：*'What do you want?' he demanded aggressively.* "你想怎麼樣？"他挑釁地問道。◇ *aggressively marketed products* 極力推銷的產品 **ag·gres·sive·ness** *noun* [U]

ag·gres·sor /ə'gresə(r)/ *noun* a person, country, etc. that attacks first 侵略者；挑釁者

ag·grieved /ə'griːvd/ *adj.* **1 ~ (at/by sth)** feeling that you have been treated unfairly 憤憤不平的；感到受委屈的 **2** (*law* 律) suffering unfair or illegal treatment and making a complaint 受害的；受委屈的：*the aggrieved party* (= person) in the case 案件中的受害方

aggro /'ægrəʊ; *NAmE* 'ægroʊ/ *noun* [U] (*BrE, informal*) **1** violent aggressive behaviour 暴力侵犯行為；鬧事；尋釁：*Don't give me any aggro or I'll call the police.* 不要對我使用暴力，不然我就叫警察。**2** problems and difficulties that are annoying 煩惱；麻煩：*I had a lot of aggro at the bank.* 我在銀行遇到了一大堆煩心的事。

aghast /ə'gɑːst; *NAmE* ə'gæst/ *adj.* [not before noun] filled with horror and surprise when you see or hear sth 驚恐；驚駭 SYN **horrified**：*Erica looked at him aghast.* 埃里卡驚恐地望着他。◇ **~ at sth** *He stood aghast at the sight of so much blood.* 他看見這麼多血，嚇得目瞪口呆。

agile /'ædʒaɪl; *NAmE* 'ædʒl/ *adj.* **1** able to move quickly and easily（動作）敏捷的，靈活的 SYN **nimble** **2** able to think quickly and in an intelligent way（思維）機敏的，機靈的：*an* ***agile mind/brain*** 敏捷的思維；靈活的頭腦 ▸ **agil·ity** /ə'dʒɪləti/ *noun* [U]：*He had the agility of a man half his age.* 他的敏捷趕得上歲數比他小一半的人。

aging, agism = AGEING, AGEISM

agi·tate /'ædʒɪteɪt/ *verb* **1** [I, T] to argue strongly for sth you want, especially for changes in a law, in social conditions, etc.（尤指為法律、社會狀況的改變而）激烈爭論，鼓動，煽動 SYN **campaign**：**~ (for/against sth)** *political groups agitating for social change* 鼓吹社會變革的政治團體 ◇ **~ to do sth** *Her family are agitating to have her transferred to a prison in the UK.* 她的家人正多方游說把她轉到英國監獄。**2** [T] **~ sb** to make sb feel angry, anxious or nervous 激怒；使不安；使激動 **3** [T] **~ sth** (*technical* 術語) to make sth, especially a liquid, move around by stirring or shaking it 攪動，搖動（液體等）

agi·tated /'ædʒɪteɪtɪd/ *adj.* showing in your behaviour that you are anxious and nervous 焦慮不安的；激動的：*Calm down! Don't get so agitated.* 冷靜下來！別那麼激動。

agi·ta·tion /ˌædʒɪ'teɪʃn/ *noun* **1** [U] worry and anxiety that you show by behaving in a nervous way 焦慮不安；憂慮；煩亂：*Dot arrived in a state of great agitation.* 多特到達時十分焦慮不安。**2** [U, C] **~ (for/against sth)** public protest in order to achieve political change 騷動；煽動；鼓動：*widespread agitation for social reform* 要求社會改革的大騷動 **3** [U] (*technical* 術語) the act of stirring or shaking a liquid（液體的）攪動，搖動

agi·ta·tor /'ædʒɪteɪtə(r)/ *noun* (*disapproving*) a person who tries to persuade people to take part in political protest（政治上的）煽動者，鼓動者

agit·prop /'ædʒɪtprɒp; *NAmE* -prɑːp/ *noun* [U] the use of art, films/movies, music, etc. to spread LEFT-WING political ideas（利用影視等藝術形式對左翼政見的）宣傳鼓動

aglow /ə'gləʊ; *NAmE* ə'gloʊ/ *adj.* [not before noun] (*literary*) shining with warmth and colour or happiness 光照融融；發紅光

AGM /ˌeɪ dʒiː 'em/ *abbr.* (*BrE*) annual general meeting (an important meeting which the members of an organization hold once a year in order to elect officers, discuss past and future activities and examine the accounts) 年會；年度大會

ag·nos·ia /æɡˈnəʊsiə; -ziə; *NAmE* æɡˈnoʊʒə/ *noun* [U] (*medical* 醫) the lack of the ability to recognize things and people 失認症；辨識不能

ag·nos·tic /æɡˈnɒstɪk; *NAmE* -ˈnɑːs-/ *noun* a person who believes that it is not possible to know whether God exists or not 不可知論者（認為上帝存在與否是不可知的）➲ compare ATHEIST ▸ **ag·nos·tic** *adj.* **ag·nos·ti·cism** /æɡˈnɒstɪsɪzəm; *NAmE* -ˈnɑːs-/ *noun* [U]

ago 0⊶ /əˈɡəʊ; *NAmE* əˈɡoʊ/ *adv.* used in expressions of time with the simple past tense to show how far in the past sth happened（與動詞簡單過去時連用）以前：*two weeks/months/years ago* 兩週／兩月／兩年以前 ◇ *The letter came a few days ago.* 這封信是幾天前寄來的。◇ *She was here just a minute ago.* 剛才她還在這兒。◇ *a short/long time ago* 不久／很久以前 ◇ *How long ago did you buy it?* 這東西你是多久以前買的？◇ *It was on TV not (so) long ago.* 電視不（很）久以前播出了這個節目。◇ *He stopped working some time ago* (= quite a long time ago). 好久以前他就停止工作了。◇ *They're getting married? It's not that long ago* (= it's only a short time ago) *that they met!* 他們要結婚啦？他們剛認識不久嘛！

agog /əˈɡɒɡ; *NAmE* əˈɡɑːɡ/ *adj.* [not before noun] excited and very interested to find out sth 興奮期待；急切瞭解

ag·on·ize (*BrE* also **-ise**) /ˈæɡənaɪz/ *verb* [I] ~ **(over/about sth)** to spend a long time thinking and worrying about a difficult situation or problem 苦苦思索；焦慮不已：*I spent days agonizing over whether to take the job or not.* 我用了好些天苦苦思考是否接受這個工作。

ag·on·ized (*BrE* also **-ised**) /ˈæɡənaɪzd/ *adj.* suffering or expressing severe pain or anxiety 十分痛苦的；很焦慮的：*agonized cries* 痛苦不堪的叫聲

ag·on·iz·ing (*BrE* also **-is·ing**) /ˈæɡənaɪzɪŋ/ *adj.* causing great pain, anxiety or difficulty 使人十分痛苦的；令人焦慮不安的；帶來巨大困難的：*his father's agonizing death* 他父親極度痛苦的死 ◇ *It was the most agonizing decision of her life.* 這是她一生中最難作的決定。

ag·on·iz·ing·ly (*BrE* also **-is·ing·ly**) /ˈæɡənaɪzɪŋli/ *adv.* used meaning 'extremely' to emphasize sth negative（強調反面事物）極其：*an agonizingly slow process* 極其緩慢的過程

agony /ˈæɡəni/ *noun* (*pl.* **-ies**) [U, C] extreme physical or mental pain（精神或肉體的）極度痛苦：*Jack collapsed* ***in agony*** *on the floor.* 傑克十分痛苦地癱倒在地板上。◇ *It was agony not knowing where the children were.* 孩子們下落不明真讓人揪心。◇ *She waited in an agony of suspense.* 她在懸念的煎熬中等待着。◇ *The worst agonies of the war were now beginning.* 戰爭最深重的苦難現在開始了。◇ *Tell me now! Don't* ***prolong the agony*** (= make it last longer). 現在就告訴我吧！別再要我心急如焚。 **IDM** see PILE *v.*

ˈagony aunt (*BrE*) (*NAmE* **adˈvice columnist**) *noun* a person who writes in a newspaper or magazine giving advice in reply to people's letters about their personal problems（報紙或雜誌的）答讀者問專欄作者；讀者來信專欄主筆 ➲ compare AGONY UNCLE

ˈagony column (*BrE*) (*NAmE* **adˈvice column**) *noun* part of a newspaper or magazine in which sb gives advice to readers who have sent letters about their personal problems（報紙或雜誌中為讀者個人疑難問題提供咨詢的）答讀者問專欄；讀者來信專欄

ˈagony uncle (*BrE*) (*NAmE* **adˈvice columnist**) *noun* a man who writes in a newspaper or magazine giving advice in reply to people's letters about their personal problems（報紙或雜誌的）答讀者問專欄男作者；讀者來信專欄男主筆 ➲ compare AGONY AUNT

agora /ˈæɡɒrə; *NAmE* ˈæɡərə/ *noun* (*pl.* **agorae** /-riː/ or **agoras**) in ancient Greece, an open space used for markets and public meetings（古希臘的）廣場；露天集市；露天聚會場所

agora·pho·bia /ˌæɡərəˈfəʊbiə; *NAmE* -ˈfoʊ-/ *noun* [U] (*technical* 術語) a fear of being in public places where there are many other people 廣場恐怖；曠野恐怖；恐曠症；公共場所恐懼（症）➲ compare CLAUSTROPHOBIA

agora·pho·bic /ˌæɡərəˈfəʊbɪk; *NAmE* -ˈfoʊ-/ *noun* a person who suffers from agoraphobia 廣場恐怖症患者；公共場所恐懼症患者 ▸ **agora·pho·bic** *adj.*

agrar·ian /əˈɡreəriən; *NAmE* əˈɡrer-/ *adj.* [usually before noun] (*technical* 術語) connected with farming and the use of land for farming 農業的；土地的；耕地的

aˌgrarian revoˈlution *noun* [sing.] (often **the Agrarian Revolution**) a period when farming in a country changes completely as a result of new methods or a change in who owns the land 農業革命；土地革命

Synonyms 同義詞辨析

agree

accept • approve • go along with sb/sth • consent

These words all mean to say that you will do what sb wants or that you will allow sth to happen. 以上各詞均含答應、同意之意。

agree to say that you will do what sb wants or that you will allow sth to happen 指答應、容許：*He agreed to let me go early.* 他同意讓我早走。

accept to be satisfied with sth that has been done, decided or suggested 指同意、接受、認可：*They accepted the court's decision.* 他們接受法院的判決。

approve to officially agree to a plan, suggestion or request 指批准、正式通過（計劃、建議或要求）：*The committee unanimously approved the plan.* 委員會一致通過了計劃。

go along with sb/sth (*rather informal*) to agree to sth that sb else has decided; to agree with sb else's ideas 指贊同某事，同意某人的觀點：*She just goes along with everything he suggests.* 他的一切建議她都贊同。

consent (*rather formal*) to agree to sth or give your permission for sth 指同意、准許、允許：*She finally consented to answer our questions.* 她最終同意回答我們的問題。

PATTERNS

- to agree/consent **to** sth
- to agree/consent **to do sth**
- to agree to/accept/approve/go along with/consent to a **plan/proposal**
- to agree to/accept/approve a **request**

agree 0⊶ /əˈɡriː/ *verb*

▸ SHARE OPINION 同意 **1** 0⊶ [I, T] to have the same opinion as sb; to say that you have the same opinion 同意；贊成：*When he said that, I had to agree.* 他說了那話，我只好同意。◇ **+ speech** *'That's true', she agreed.* "是這樣的。"她同意說。◇ **~ (with sb) (about/on sth)** *He agreed with them about the need for change.* 他同意他們需要變革的意見。◇ **~ with sth** *I agree with her analysis of the situation.* 我贊成她對形勢的分析。◇ **~ (that) …** *We agreed (that) the proposal was a good one.* 我們一致認為這個建議不錯。◇ *'It's terrible.'* ***'I couldn't agree more!'*** (= I completely agree) "太糟糕了。" "可不是嘛！" **OPP** **disagree** **2** 0⊶ [T] if people **are agreed** or sth **is agreed**, everyone has the same opinion about sth（對…）取得一致意見，一致同意：**be agreed (on/about sth)** *Are we all agreed on this?* 我們在這個問題上是不是全體意見一致？◇ **be agreed (that …)** *It was agreed (that) we should hold another meeting.* 大家一致同意我們應該再開一次會。

▸ SAY YES 應允 **3** 0⊶ [I, T] to say 'yes'; to say that you will do what sb wants or that you will allow sth to happen 應允；答應；同意：*I asked for a pay rise and she agreed.* 我要求提高工資，她答應了。◇ **~ to sth** *Do you think he'll agree to their proposal?* 你認為他會同意他們的建議嗎？◇ **~ (that) …** *She agreed (that) I could go early.* 她允許我早走。◇ **~ to do sth** *She agreed to let me go early.* 她同意讓我早走。

A

▸ DECIDE 決定 **4** [I, T] to decide with sb else to do sth or to have sth 商定；約定： **~ on sth** *Can we agree on a date?* 我們能否約定一個日期？◇ **~ sth** *They met at the agreed time.* 他們在約定的時間見面了。◇ *Can we agree a price?* 我們可不可以商定一個價格？◇ *They left at ten, as* **agreed**. 他們按照約好的時間在十點鐘離去。◇ **~ to do sth** *We agreed to meet on Thursday.* 我們約定在星期四見面。◇ **~ what, where, etc. …** *We couldn't agree what to do.* 關於應該怎麼辦我們各執己見。

▸ ACCEPT 認可 **5** [T] **~ sth** to officially accept a plan, request, etc. 批准，認可（計劃、要求等）SYN **approve**： *Next year's budget has been agreed.* 明年的預算已獲批准。

▸ BE THE SAME 相符 **6** [I] to be the same as sth（與…）相符，一致 SYN **tally**： *The figures do not agree.* 這些數字不相符。◇ **~ with sth** *Your account of the accident does not agree with hers.* 你對事故的敍述與她的敍述不一致。OPP **disagree**

▸ GRAMMAR 語法 **7** [I] **~ (with sth)** to match a word or phrase in NUMBER, GENDER or PERSON（在數、性或人稱上與…）一致： *In 'Tom likes jazz', the singular verb 'likes' agrees with the subject 'Tom'.* 在 Tom likes jazz 一句中，動詞單數形式 likes 與主語 Tom 一致。

IDM **a,gree to 'differ** if two people **agree to differ**, they accept that they have different opinions about sth, but they decide not to discuss it any longer 同意各自保留不同意見

PHR V **not a'gree with sb** (of food 食物) to make you feel ill/sick 使難受；不適合；不相宜： *I love strawberries, but they don't agree with me.* 我喜歡草莓，但吃了以後不舒服。

agree·able /ə'griːəbl/ *adj.* (*formal*) **1** pleasant and easy to like 愉悅的；討人喜歡的；宜人的： *We spent a most agreeable day together.* 我們在一起度過了非常愉快的一天。◇ *He seemed extremely agreeable.* 他似乎特別招人喜歡。OPP **disagreeable 2** [not before noun] **~ (to sth)** willing to do sth or allow sth 欣然同意： *Do you think they will be agreeable to our proposal?* 你認為他們會爽快同意我們的提議嗎？ **3 ~ (to sb)** able to be accepted by sb 可以接受的；適合的： *The deal must be agreeable to both sides.* 處理方法必須是雙方都可以接受的。

agree·ably /ə'griːəbli/ *adv.* (*formal*) in a pleasant, nice way 愉悅地；令人愉快地；愜意地： *an agreeably warm day* 暖洋洋的一天◇ *They were agreeably surprised by the quality of the food.* 他們對食物的質量感到又驚又喜。

agree·ment 0-w /ə'griːmənt/ *noun*
1 0-w [C] an arrangement, a promise or a contract made with sb 協定；協議；契約： *an international peace agreement* 國際和平協定◇ *The agreement* (= the document recording the agreement) *was signed during a meeting at the UN.* 這個協定是在聯合國的一次會議上簽訂的。◇ **~ with sb** *They have a free trade agreement with Australia.* 他們與澳大利亞簽有自由貿易協定。◇ **~ between A and B** *An agreement* **was finally reached** *between management and employees.* 勞資雙方終於達成了協議。◇ **~ to do sth** *They had made a verbal agreement to sell.* 他們達成了口頭售貨協定。◇ *They had an agreement never to talk about work at home.* 他們約定在家中絕不談工作。➲ see also GENTLEMAN'S AGREEMENT, PRENUPTIAL AGREEMENT **2** 0-w [U] the state of sharing the same opinion or feeling（意見或看法）一致： *The two sides failed to* **reach agreement**. 雙方未能取得一致意見。◇ **in ~** *Are we in agreement about the price?* 對這個價格我們是否意見一致？OPP **disagreement 3** 0-w [U] the fact of sb approving of sth and allowing it to happen 應允；同意： *You'll have to get your parents' agreement if you want to go on the trip.* 你要想去旅行就必須徵得你父母的同意。 **4** [U] **~ (with sth)** (*grammar* 語法) (of words in a phrase 短語中的單詞) the state of having the same NUMBER, GENDER or PERSON（在數、性或人稱方面的）一致 SYN **concord**： *In the sentence 'They live in the country', the plural form of the verb 'live' is in agreement with the plural subject 'they'.* 在 They live in the country 一句中，動詞複數形式 live 與複數主語 they 一致。

agri- ➲ AGRO-

agri·busi·ness /'ægrɪbɪznəs/ *noun* [U, C] (*technical* 術語) an industry concerned with the production and sale of farm products, especially involving large companies 農工聯合企業；農業綜合企業

agri·cul·tur·al·ist /ˌægrɪ'kʌltʃərəlɪst/ *noun* an expert in agriculture who gives advice to farmers 農學家；農業技術員；農藝師

agri·cul·ture /'ægrɪkʌltʃə(r)/ *noun* [U] the science or practice of farming 農業；農學；農藝： *The number of people employed in agriculture has fallen in the last decade.* 過去十年，農業從業人數已經下降。➲ COLLOCATIONS at TOWN ▸ **agri·cul·tural** /ˌægrɪ'kʌltʃərəl/ *adj.*： *agricultural policy/land/production/development* 農業政策/土地/生產/發展

agri·tour·ism /'ægrɪtʊərɪzəm; -tɔːr-; NAmE -tʊr-/ *noun* [U] holidays/vacations in which tourists visiting a country stay with local people who live in the countryside 農業旅遊；農家樂旅遊

agro- /'ægrəʊ; NAmE 'ægroʊ/ (also **agri-**) *combining form* (in nouns, adjectives and adverbs 構成名詞、形容詞和副詞) connected with farming 農業；農業的…： *agro-industry* 農用工業◇ *agriculture* 農業

agro·chem·ical /ˌægrəʊ'kemɪkl; NAmE ˌægroʊ-/ *noun* any chemical used in farming, especially for killing insects or for making plants grow better 農藥

ˌagro-'industry *noun* [U] industry connected with farming 農用工業 ▸ **ˌagro-in'dustrial** *adj.*

agrono·mist /ə'grɒnəmɪst; NAmE ə'grɑːn-/ *noun* a scientist who studies the relationship between crops and the environment 農學家 ▸ **agron·omy** *noun* [U]

aground /ə'graʊnd/ *adv.* if a ship **runs/goes aground**, it touches the ground in shallow water and cannot move（指船）擱淺 ▸ **aground** *adj.* [not before noun]

ague /'eɪgjuː/ *noun* [U] (*old-fashioned*) a disease such as MALARIA that causes fever and SHIVERING (= shaking of the body) 瘧疾

AH (*BrE*) (*US* **A.H.**) /ˌeɪ 'eɪtʃ/ *abbr.* used in the Muslim CALENDAR to show a particular number of years since the year when Muhammad left Mecca in AD 622 (from Latin 'Anno Hegirae') 伊斯蘭教紀元，回曆（從公元 622 年起算）： *a Koran dated 556 AH* 回曆 556 年的一部《古蘭經》➲ compare AD, BC, BCE, CE (2)

ah /ɑː/ *exclamation* used to express surprise, pleasure, admiration or sympathy, or when you disagree with sb（表示驚奇、高興、讚賞、同情或不同意）啊： *Ah, there you are!* 啊，你原來在這兒！◇ *Ah, this coffee is good.* 啊，這咖啡真好。◇ *Ah well, better luck next time.* 好啦好啦，祝你下次運氣好一些。◇ *Ah, but that may not be true.* 不過嘛，那可能不是真的。

aha /ɑː'hɑː/ *exclamation* used when you are expressing pleasure that you have understood sth or found sth out（表示瞭解或發現某事物的喜悅）啊哈： *Aha! So that's where I left it!* 啊哈！原來我把它丟在這兒了！

achoo /ɑː'tʃuː; ə'tʃuː/ *exclamation* = ATISHOO

ahead 0-w /ə'hed/ *adv.*

HELP For the special uses of **ahead** in phrasal verbs, look at the entries for the verbs. For example **press ahead (with sth)** is in the phrasal verb section at **press**.
* ahead 在短語動詞中的特殊用法見有關動詞詞條。如 press ahead (with sth) 在詞條 press 的短語動詞部份。

1 0-w further forward in space or time; in front（時間、空間）向前面，在前面： *I'll run ahead and warn them.* 我要跑在前頭，警告他們。◇ *The road ahead was blocked.* 前面的路被封了。◇ *We've got a lot of hard work ahead.* 我們往後還有很多艱苦工作要做。◇ *This will create problems in the months ahead.* 在以後的幾個月中這個就要出問題。◇ *He was looking straight ahead* (= straight forward, in front of him). 他逕直往前看去。 **2** 0-w earlier 提前；預先；提早 SYN **in advance**： *The party was planned weeks ahead.* 聚會提前幾個星期就已籌劃好了。 **3** 0-w winning; further advanced 佔優勢；領先： *Our team was ahead by six points.* 我們隊領先六分。◇ *You need to work hard to keep ahead.* 你要努力才能保持領先優勢。

a'head of *prep.* **1** further forward in space or time than sb/sth; in front of sb/sth（時間、空間）在…前面：*Two boys were ahead of us.* 有兩個男孩在我們前面。◇ *Ahead of us lay ten days of intensive training.* 我們還要進行十天的強化訓練。**2** earlier than sb/sth 早於：*I finished several days ahead of the deadline.* 我是在最後期限的前幾天完成的。**3** further advanced than sb/sth; in front of sb, for example in a race or competition 領先：*She was always* ***well ahead*** *of the rest of the class.* 她總是遙遙領先班上的同學。◇ *His ideas were way* ***ahead of their time*** (= very new and so not widely understood or accepted). 他的思想遠遠超越了他們那個時代。

ahem /ə'hem; ə'həm/ *exclamation* used in writing to show the sound of a short cough made by sb who is trying to get attention or to say sth that is difficult or embarrassing（書寫用語，表示引起注意或難以啟齒時發出的短促咳嗽聲）呃哼：*Ahem, can I make a suggestion?* 呃哼，我可以提個建議嗎？

ahis·tor·ic·al /ˌeɪhɪ'stɒrɪkl; *NAmE* -'stɔːr-; -'stɑːr-/ *adj.* (*formal*) not showing any knowledge of history or of what has happened before 非歷史的；沒有歷史背景的；不顧史實的

-aholic /ə'hɒlɪk; *NAmE* ə'hɔːl-; ə'hɑːl-/ *suffix* (in nouns 構成名詞) liking sth very much and unable to stop doing or using it 嗜好…的；對…成癮的：*a shopaholic* 購物成癖的人 ◇ *a chocaholic* 嗜食巧克力的人

ahoy /ə'hɔɪ/ *exclamation* used by people in boats to attract attention（船上的人用以引起注意）啊呵：*Ahoy there!* 啊呵！◇ *Ship ahoy!* (= there is a ship in sight) 啊，一條船！

AI /ˌeɪ 'aɪ/ *abbr.* **1** ARTIFICIAL INSEMINATION：*AID or artificial insemination by a donor* 供者人工授精 **2** ARTIFICIAL INTELLIGENCE

aid 0-w AW /eɪd/ *noun, verb*

■ ***noun*** **1** 0-w [U] money, food, etc. that is sent to help countries in difficult situations 援助；救援物資；援助款項：***economic/humanitarian/emergency aid*** 經濟／人道主義／緊急援助 ◇ *An extra £10 million in* ***foreign aid*** *has been promised.* 額外的 1 000 萬英鎊外國援助款項已得到保證。◇ ***aid agencies*** (= organizations that provide help) 救援機構 ◇ *medical aid programmes* 醫療援助計劃 ➲ COLLOCATIONS at INTERNATIONAL ➲ see also FINANCIAL AID, LEGAL AID **2** 0-w [U] help that you need to perform a particular task（完成某工作所需的）幫助，助手，輔助物：*He was breathing only* ***with the aid of*** *a ventilator.* 他只能靠呼吸器呼吸。◇ *This job would be impossible* ***without the aid of*** *a computer.* 這項工作不用計算機是不行的。**3** [U] (*formal*) help that is given to a person 幫助；援助：*One of the staff saw he was in difficulty and* ***came to his aid*** (= helped him). 一名工作人員見他有困難，便過來幫忙。➲ see also FIRST AID **4** [C] an object, a machine, etc. that you use to help you do sth 輔助設備：*a hearing aid* 助聽器 ◇ *Photos make useful teaching aids.* 照片可以成為有用的教具。

IDM **in aid of sth/sb** 0-w (*BrE*) in order to help sb/sth 為了幫助某人／某事物：*collecting money in aid of charity* 為資助慈善事業的募捐 **what's … in aid of?** (*BrE*) used to ask why sth is happening …究竟是為啥（發生）；…是做什麼用的：*What's all this crying in aid of?* 這哭叫聲究竟是為啥？

■ ***verb*** 0-w [I, T] (*formal*) to help sb/sth to do sth, especially by making it easier 幫助；援助 SYN **assist**：**~ (sb/sth) in sth/in doing sth** *The new test should aid in the early detection of the disease.* 新的化驗應該有助於早早檢查出這種疾病。◇ **~ sb (to do sth)** *This feature is designed to aid inexperienced users.* 這個特色裝置是為幫助沒有經驗的用戶而設計的。◇ **~ sth** *Aided by heat and strong winds, the fire quickly spread.* 乘着高溫和大風，火勢迅速蔓延。◇ *They were accused of aiding his escape.* 他們被控幫助他逃跑。◇ **~ sb/sth in sth/in doing sth** *They were accused of aiding him in his escape.* 他們被控幫助他逃跑。◇ **~ sb (with sth)** *Words will be displayed around the room to aid students with spelling.* 單詞會張貼在室內各處以幫助學生學習拼寫。

IDM **ˌaid and a'bet** (*law* 律) to help sb to do sth illegal or wrong 夥同作案；同謀：*She stands accused of aiding and abetting the crime.* 她被控協同犯罪。

aide /eɪd/ *noun* a person who helps another person, especially a politician, in their job（尤指從政者的）助手：*White House aides* 白宮助理

aide-de-camp /ˌeɪd də 'kɒ̃; *NAmE* 'kæmp/ *noun* (*pl.* **aides-de-camp** /ˌeɪd də 'kɒ̃; *NAmE* 'kæmp/) (*abbr.* **ADC**) an officer in the army or navy who helps a more senior officer（陸軍或海軍）副官，隨從參謀

aide-memoire /ˌeɪd mem'wɑː(r)/ *noun* (from *French*) (*pl.* **aides-memoire**, **aides-memoires** /ˌeɪd mem'wɑː(r)/) a thing, especially a book or document, that helps you to remember sth 幫助記憶的東西（尤指書、文檔）

AIDS (*BrE* usually **Aids**) /eɪdz/ *noun* [U] the abbreviation for 'Acquired Immune Deficiency Syndrome' (an illness which attacks the body's ability to resist infection and which usually causes death) 艾滋病，愛滋病（全寫為 Acquired Immune Deficiency Syndrome，獲得性免疫缺損綜合症）：***AIDS research/education/victims*** 艾滋病研究／教育／患者 ◇ *He developed* ***full-blown AIDS*** *five years after contracting HIV.* 他感染艾滋病病毒五年以後，患上了完全型艾滋病。

ai·kido /aɪ'kiːdəʊ; *NAmE* -doʊ/ *noun* [U] (from *Japanese*) a Japanese system of fighting in which you hold and throw your opponent 合氣道（以擒、摔為主的一種日本武術）

ail /eɪl/ *verb* **1 ~ sth** (*formal*) to cause problems for sb/sth 困擾；干擾；使麻煩：*They discussed the problems ailing the steel industry.* 他們討論了困擾鋼鐵工業的問題。**2 ~ sb** (*old use*) to make sb ill/sick 使患病；使不適：*What is ailing you?* 你哪裏不舒服？

ail·eron /'eɪlərɒn; *NAmE* -rɑːn/ *noun* (*technical* 術語) a part of the wing of a plane that moves up and down to control the plane's balance（飛機的）副翼 ➲ VISUAL VOCAB page V53

ail·ing /'eɪlɪŋ/ *adj.* (*formal*) **1** ill/sick and not improving 有病的；體弱的：*She looked after her ailing father.* 她照顧她有病的父親。**2** (of a business, government, etc. 企業、政府等) having problems and getting weaker 處境困難的；每況愈下的：*measures to help the ailing economy* 改善經濟不景氣的措施

ail·ment /'eɪlmənt/ *noun* an illness that is not very serious 輕病；小恙：***childhood/common/minor ailments*** 兒童期／常見／輕微小病 ➲ SYNONYMS at DISEASE

aim 0-w /eɪm/ *noun, verb*

■ ***noun*** **1** 0-w [C] the purpose of doing sth; what sb is trying to achieve 目的；目標：*the aims of the lesson* 本課教學目標 ◇ *She went to London* ***with the aim of*** *finding a job.* 她去倫敦是為了找工作。◇ *Our main aim is to increase sales in Europe.* 我們的主要目標是增加在歐洲的銷售量。◇ *Bob's one aim in life is to earn a lot of money.* 鮑勃唯一的人生目標就是掙很多的錢。◇ *Teamwork is required in order to* ***achieve these aims.*** 要達到這些目標需要齊心協力。◇ *She set out the company's* ***aims and objectives*** *in her speech.* 她在講話中提出了公司的各項目標。➲ SYNONYMS at PURPOSE **2** [U] the action or skill of pointing a weapon at sb/sth 瞄準：*Her aim was good and she hit the lion with her first shot.* 她瞄得準，第一槍就打中了獅子。◇ *The gunman* ***took aim*** (= pointed his weapon) *and fired.* 持槍歹徒瞄準後就射擊了。

IDM **take 'aim at sb/sth** (*NAmE*) to direct your criticism at sb/sth 把目標對準某人（或某事物）；把批評的矛頭指向某人（或某事物）

■ ***verb*** **1** 0-w [I, T] to try or plan to achieve sth 力求達到；力爭做到：*He has always* ***aimed high*** (= tried to achieve a lot). 他總是心氣很高。◇ **~ for sth** *We should aim for a bigger share of the market.* 我們應該以更大的市場份額為目標。◇ **~ at sth** *The government is aiming at a 50% reduction in unemployment.* 政府正着力減少 50% 的失業人數。◇ **~ to do sth** *They are aiming to reduce unemployment by 50%.* 他們正力求使失業人數下降 50%。◇ *We aim to be there around six.* 我們設法六點鐘左右到那裏。◇ **~ at doing sth** *They're aiming at training everybody by the end of the year.* 他們力求在年底前讓人人得到培訓。**2** 0-w [T] **be aimed at sth/at doing sth** to

A

have sth as an aim 目的是；旨在： *These measures are aimed at preventing violent crime.* 這些措施旨在防止暴力犯罪。 **3** [I, T] to point or direct a weapon, a shot, a kick, etc. at sb/sth 瞄準；對準： **~ at sb/sth** *I was aiming at the tree but hit the car by mistake.* 我對準樹射擊，不料誤中了汽車。◇ **~ for sb/sth** *Aim for the middle of the target.* 瞄準靶心。◇ **~ sth (at sb/sth)** *The gun was aimed at her head.* 槍瞄準了她的頭。 **4** [T, usually passive] **~ sth at sb** to say or do sth that is intended to influence or affect a particular person or group 針對；對象是： *The book is aimed at very young children.* 這本書的對象是幼童。◇ *My criticism wasn't aimed at you.* 我的批評不是針對你的。

aim·less /ˈemləs/ *adj.* having no direction or plan 沒有方向的；無目標的；無計劃的： *My life seemed aimless.* 我的生活似乎沒有目標。 ▸ **aim·less·ly** *adv.*： *He drifted aimlessly from one job to another.* 他漫無目的地換了一份又一份工作。 **aim·less·ness** *noun* [U]

ain't /emt/ *short form* (*non-standard* or *humorous*) **1** am not/is not/are not 不是： *Things ain't what they used to be.* 現在情況不比從前了。 **2** has not/have not 沒有： *I ain't got no money.* 我沒有錢。◇ *You ain't seen nothing yet.* 你什麼都沒有看到。

IDM **if it ain't ˌbroke, don't ˈfix it** (*informal*) used to say that if sth works well enough, it should not be changed 未損勿修；能用莫換

aioli /aɪˈəʊli; *NAmE* aɪˈoʊli/ *noun* [U] (from *French*) a thick cold sauce made of MAYONNAISE and GARLIC 蒜泥蛋黃醬

air /eə(r); *NAmE* er/ *noun, verb*

■ ***noun***

▸ **GAS** 氣體 **1** [U] the mixture of gases that surrounds the earth and that we breathe 空氣： *air pollution* 空氣污染 ◇ *Let's go out for some **fresh air**.* 咱們出去呼吸點新鮮空氣。◇ *I need to put some air in my tyres.* 我需要給我的輪胎打些氣。◇ *currents of warm air* 暖氣流

▸ **SPACE** 空間 **2** [U] (usually **the air**) the space above the ground or that is around things 空中；天空： *I kicked the ball high **in/into the air**.* 我把球高高地踢到空中。◇ *Spicy smells wafted **through the air**.* 空中飄來一陣陣辛辣的氣味。◇ *Music filled the night air.* 樂聲邊漾在夜空中。 ⇒ see also OPEN AIR

▸ **FOR PLANES** 飛機 **3** [U] the space above the earth where planes fly （飛行的）空中，天空： *It only takes three hours **by air*** (= in a plane). 乘飛機只要三個小時。◇ ***air travel/traffic*** 航空旅行；空中交通 ◇ *The temple was clearly visible from the air.* 從空中看去，那座廟宇清晰可辨。◇ *A surprise air attack* (= from aircraft) *was launched at night.* 夜間突然發起了空襲。

▸ **IMPRESSION** 印象 **4** [sing.] the particular feeling or impression that is given by sb/sth; the way sb does sth 感覺；印象；神態： *The room had an air of luxury.* 房間具有豪華的氣派。◇ *She looked at him with a defiant air.* 她用蔑視的神情望着他。

▸ **TUNE** 曲調 **5** [C] (*old-fashioned*) (often used in the title of a piece of music 常用於樂曲名) a tune 曲調： *Bach's Air on a G string* 巴赫的 G 弦上的曲調

▸ **BEHAVIOUR** 行為 **6 airs** [pl.] (*disapproving*) a way of behaving that shows that sb thinks that they are more important, etc. than they really are 擺架子；裝腔作勢： *I hate the way she **puts on airs**.* 我不喜歡她那裝腔作勢的樣子。

IDM **ˌairs and ˈgraces** (*BrE, disapproving*) a way of behaving that shows that sb thinks that they are more important, etc. than they really are 擺架子；裝腔作勢 SYN **airs float/walk on ˈair** to feel very happy 歡天喜地；得意揚揚 **in the ˈair** felt by a number of people to exist or to be happening 在傳播中；流行；可感覺到： *There's romance in the air.* 有種浪漫的氣氛。 **ˌon/ˌoff (the) ˈair** broadcasting or not broadcasting on television or radio （電視、廣播）正在／停止播送： *We will be back on air tomorrow morning at 7.* 明天早上 7 點本節目重新開播。◇ *The programme was taken off the air over the summer.* 這個節目在夏季停播。 **up in the ˈair** not yet decided 懸而未決： *Our travel plans are still up in the air.* 我們的旅行計劃尚未落實。 ⇒ more at BREATH, CASTLE, CLEAR *v.*, NOSE *n.*, PLUCK *v.*, THIN *adj.*

■ ***verb***

▸ **CLOTHES** 衣服 **1** [T, I] **~ (sth)** (*especially BrE*) to put clothing, etc. in a place that is warm or has plenty of air so that it dries completely and smells fresh; to be left to dry somewhere 晾；晾乾： *Air the sheets well.* 把這些牀單好好晾曬一下。◇ *Leave the towels out to air.* 把毛巾拿出去晾乾。

▸ **A ROOM** 房間 **2** [T, I] **~ (sth)** (*BrE*) (*NAmE* **ˌair (sth) ˈout**) to allow fresh air into a room or a building; to be filled with fresh air （使）通風，透風： *The rooms had all been cleaned and aired.* 所有的房間都已打掃乾淨並且通了風。

▸ **OPINIONS** 意見 **3** [T] **~ sth** to express your opinions publicly 公開發表 SYN **voice**： *The weekly meeting enables employees to **air their grievances**.* 週會可以讓雇員訴說他們的委屈。

▸ **RADIO/TV PROGRAMME** 廣播／電視節目 **4** [T, I] **~ (sth)** (*especially NAmE*) to broadcast a programme on the radio or on television; to be broadcast 播出；播送： *The show will be aired next Tuesday night.* 這個節目將在下週二夜間播出。◇ *The program aired last week.* 該節目已於上週播出。

PHR V **ˌair ˈout | ˌair sth↔ˈout** (*NAmE*) = AIR (2)

ˌair ˈambulance *noun* (*especially BrE*) an aircraft, especially a HELICOPTER, with special equipment, used for taking sick or injured people to a hospital, especially in cases where a road vehicle cannot get through or cannot make the journey quickly enough 救護機；（尤指）救護直升機 ⇒ compare MEDEVAC

air·bag /ˈeəbæg; *NAmE* ˈer-/ *noun* a safety device in a car that fills with air if there is an accident, to protect the people in the car 安全氣囊，安全氣袋（遇車禍時充氣保護車內的人）

air·base /ˈeəbeɪs; *NAmE* ˈerb-/ *noun* a place where military aircraft fly from and are kept, and where some staff live 空軍基地；航空基地

ˈair bed (*BrE*) (also **ˈair mattress** *NAmE, BrE*) *noun* a large plastic or rubber bag that can be filled with air and used as a bed 充氣牀墊 ⇒ VISUAL VOCAB page V23

air·borne /ˈeəbɔːn; *NAmE* ˈerbɔːrn/ *adj.* **1** [not before noun] (of a plane or passengers 飛機或乘客) in the air 升空： *Do not leave your seat until the plane is airborne.* 飛機升空時不要離開座位。 **2** [only before noun] carried through the air 空氣傳播的： ***airborne seeds/viruses*** 空氣傳播的種子／病毒 ⇒ compare WATERBORNE **3** [only before noun] (of soldiers 士兵) trained to jump out of aircraft onto enemy land in order to fight 空降的： *an airborne division* 空降師

ˈair brake *noun* a BRAKE in a vehicle that is worked by air pressure （車輛的）氣動剎車，氣閘，空氣制動器

ˈair bridge (*BrE*) (*NAmE* **Jet·way™**) *noun* a bridge that can be moved and put against the door of an aircraft, so people can get on and off 旅客登機（活動）橋

air·brush /ˈeəbrʌʃ; *NAmE* ˈerb-/ *noun, verb*

■ ***noun*** an artist's tool for spraying paint onto a surface, that works by air pressure （繪畫等用的）氣筆，噴槍

■ ***verb*** to paint sth with an airbrush; to change a detail in a photograph with an airbrush 用噴槍噴繪；用氣筆修改（照片）： **~ sth** *an airbrushed photograph of a model* 用氣筆修改過的模特兒照片 ◇ **~ sth out** *Somebody had been airbrushed out of the picture.* 畫面上有個人用氣筆給抹掉了。

Air·bus™ /ˈeəbʌs; *NAmE* ˈerbʌs/ *noun* a large plane that carries passengers over short and medium distances 空中客車，空中巴士（運送中、短途乘客的大型飛機）

ˌair chief ˈmarshal *noun* an officer of very high rank in the British AIR FORCE （英國）空軍上將： *Air Chief Marshal Sir Robin Hall* 空軍上將羅賓•霍爾爵士

ˌair ˈcommodore *noun* an officer of high rank in the British AIR FORCE （英國）空軍准將： *Air Commodore Peter Shaw* 空軍准將彼得•肖

ˈair conditioner *noun* a machine that cools and dries air 空調機；空調設備

ˈair conditioning (also **ˈair con**) *noun* [U] (*abbr.* **AC**, **a/c**) a system that cools and dries the air in a building or car 空氣調節系統 ▸ **ˈair-conditioned** *adj.*: *air-conditioned offices* 裝有空調的辦公室

ˈair-cooled *adj.* made cool by a current of air 風冷的；氣冷的

ˈair corridor *noun* an area in the sky that aircraft must stay inside when they fly over a country（飛機飛越外國領空時獲准使用的）空中走廊

ˈair cover *noun* [U] protection which aircraft give to soldiers and military vehicles on the land or sea 空中掩護

air·craft 🔑 /ˈeəkrɑːft; *NAmE* ˈerkræft/ *noun* (*pl.* **air·craft**) any vehicle that can fly and carry goods or passengers 飛機；航空器：***fighter/transport/military aircraft*** 戰鬥機；運輸機；軍用飛機 ➲ VISUAL VOCAB page V53 ➲ see also LIGHT AIRCRAFT

ˈaircraft carrier *noun* a large ship that carries aircraft which use it as a base to land on and take off from 航空母艦

air·craft·man /ˈeəkrɑːftmən; *NAmE* ˈerkræft-/, **air·craft·woman** /ˈeəkrɑːftwʊmən; *NAmE* ˈerkræft-/ *noun* (*pl.* **-men** /-mən/, **-women** /-wɪmɪn/) the lowest rank in the British AIR FORCE 空軍士兵（英國空軍最低軍階）：*Aircraftman John Green* 空軍士兵約翰•格林

air·crew /ˈeəkruː; *NAmE* ˈerk-/ *noun* [C+sing./pl. v.] the pilot and other people who fly a plane, especially in the air force（尤指空軍的）機組人員，空勤人員，空勤組

ˈair-dash *verb* [I] **+ adv./prep.** (*IndE, informal*) (especially of officials 尤指官員) to go somewhere by plane suddenly and/or quickly 空中急趕（突然或匆匆乘機前往）：*The minister air-dashed to Delhi because of the parliamentary crisis.* 部長因議會的危機立刻起程飛往德里。

air·drome /ˈeədrəʊm; *NAmE* ˈerdroʊm/ (*US*) (*BrE* **aero·drome**) *noun* (*old-fashioned*) a small airport 小型飛機場

air·drop /ˈeədrɒp; *NAmE* ˈerdrɑːp/ *noun* the act of dropping supplies, soldiers, etc. from an aircraft by PARACHUTE 空投；空降：*The UN has begun making airdrops of food to refugees.* 聯合國已開始向難民空投食物。 ▸ **air·drop** *verb* (**-pp-**) **~ sth**

air·fare /ˈeəfeə(r); *NAmE* ˈerfer/ *noun* the money that you pay to travel by plane 機票費用；飛機票價：*Take advantage of low-season airfares.* 利用淡季飛機票價。

air·field /ˈeəfiːld; *NAmE* ˈerf-/ *noun* an area of flat ground where military or private planes can take off and land 飛機場

air·flow /ˈeəfləʊ; *NAmE* ˈerfloʊ/ *noun* [U] the flow of air around a moving aircraft or vehicle（運行中的飛機或汽車周圍的）氣流

air·foil /ˈeəfɔɪl; *NAmE* ˈerf-/ (*NAmE*) (*BrE* **aero·foil**) *noun* the basic curved structure of an aircraft's wing that helps to lift it into the air 翼型（指機翼在空氣中運動時能產生升力的曲線型面）

ˈair force *noun* [C+sing./pl. v.] the part of a country's armed forces that fights using aircraft 空軍：*the US Air Force* 美國空軍 ◇ *air-force officers* 空軍軍官 ➲ COLLOCATIONS at WAR

ˌAir Force ˈOne *noun* the name given to a special aircraft in the US AIR FORCE when the US President is using it 空軍一號（美國總統的專用座機）

air·freight /ˈeəfreɪt; *NAmE* ˈerf-/ *noun* [U] goods that are transported by aircraft; the system of transporting goods by aircraft 空運的貨物；空中貨運 ▸ **air·freight** *verb* **~ sth**

ˈair freshener *noun* [C, U] a substance or device for making a place smell more pleasant 空氣清新劑；空氣清新機；空氣淨化器

ˈair guitar *noun* [C, U] used to describe the actions of a person playing an imaginary electric GUITAR, especially while listening to rock music 空氣吉他（尤指聽搖滾樂時佯裝彈吉他的動作）

ˈair·gun /ˈeəgʌn; *NAmE* ˈer-/ (also **ˈair rifle**) *noun* a gun that uses air pressure to fire small metal balls (called PELLETS) 氣槍；BB 槍

air·head /ˈeəhed; *NAmE* ˈerh-/ *noun* (*informal, disapproving*) a stupid person 笨蛋；傻瓜：*She's a total airhead!* 她完全是個大傻瓜！

ˈair hostess *noun* (*BrE, old-fashioned*) a female FLIGHT ATTENDANT（客機上的）女乘務員；空中小姐

air·ily /ˈeərəli; *NAmE* ˈer-/ *adv.* (*formal*) in a way that shows that you are not worried or that you are not treating sth as serious 無憂無慮地；無所謂地

air·ing /ˈeərɪŋ; *NAmE* ˈerɪŋ/ *noun* [sing.] **1** the expression or discussion of opinions in front of a group of people（意見等的）公開發表，公開討論：*an opportunity to give your views an airing* 公開發表你觀點的一次機會 ◇ *The subject got a thorough airing in the British press.* 這個問題在英國新聞界得到了充分討論。 **2** the act of allowing warm air to make clothes, beds, etc. fresh and dry 晾；晾曬；透風

ˈairing cupboard *noun* (*BrE*) a warm cupboard in which clean sheets, clothes, etc. are put to make sure they are completely dry（烘乾衣物的）烘櫃

ˈair kiss *noun* a way of saying hello or goodbye to sb by kissing them near the side of their face but not actually touching them（見面或道別時的）撮唇示吻 ▸ **ˈair-kiss** *verb* [T, I] **~ (sb/sth)**

air·less /ˈeələs; *NAmE* ˈerl-/ *adj.* not having any fresh or moving air or wind, and therefore unpleasant 沒有新鮮空氣的；沒有一絲風的；空氣沉悶的：*a stuffy, airless room* 空氣沉悶不通風的房間 ◇ *The night was hot and airless.* 夜晚很熱，沒有一絲風。

ˈair letter *noun* = AEROGRAMME

air·lift /ˈeəlɪft; *NAmE* ˈerl-/ *noun, verb*

▪ ***noun*** an operation to take people, soldiers, food, etc. to or from an area by aircraft, especially in an emergency or when roads are closed or dangerous 空運；空投

▪ ***verb* ~ sb/sth** to take sb/sth to or from an area by aircraft, especially in an emergency or when roads are closed or dangerous 空運，空投（人員或物資）：*Two casualties* ***were airlifted to safety.*** 兩名傷亡人員已空運到安全地區。 ➲ compare SEALIFT

air·line /ˈeəlaɪn; *NAmE* ˈerl-/ *noun* [C+sing./pl. v.] a company that provides regular flights to take passengers and goods to different places 航空公司：*international airlines* 國際航空公司 ◇ *an airline pilot* 航空公司飛機駕駛員 ➲ COLLOCATIONS at TRAVEL

air·liner /ˈeəlaɪnə(r); *NAmE* ˈerl-/ *noun* a large plane that carries passengers 大型客機；班機

air·lock /ˈeəlɒk; *NAmE* ˈerlɑːk/ *noun* **1** a small room with a tightly closed door at each end, which you go through to reach another area at a different air pressure, for example on a SPACECRAFT or SUBMARINE（航天器的）壓差隔離室；（潛艇的）氣閘 **2** a bubble of air that blocks the flow of liquid in a PUMP or pipe 氣塞

air·mail /ˈeəmeɪl; *NAmE* ˈerm-/ *noun* [U] the system of sending letters, etc. by air 航空郵遞：*Send it airmail/by airmail.* 將它空郵寄出。

air·man /ˈeəmən; *NAmE* ˈerm-/, **air·woman** /ˈeəwʊmən; *NAmE* ˈerw-/ *noun* (*pl.* **-men** /-mən/, **-women** /-wɪmɪn/) **1** a member of the British AIR FORCE, especially one below the rank of an officer（英國尤指軍階比軍官低的）空軍人員 **2** a member of one of the lowest ranks in the US AIR FORCE（美國空軍軍階最低的）空軍士兵：*Airman Brines* 空軍士兵布賴恩斯

ˈair marshal *noun* **1** an officer of very high rank in the British AIR FORCE（英國）空軍中將：*Air Marshal Gordon Black* 空軍中將戈登•布萊克 **2** (also **ˈsky marshal**) an armed guard, especially a government official, who travels on a plane with the passengers in order to protect the plane from TERRORISTS 空中反恐武裝警衛

ˈair mattress (*especially NAmE*) (*BrE* also **air·bed**) *noun* a large plastic or rubber bag that can be filled with air and used as a bed 充氣牀墊 ➲ VISUAL VOCAB page V23

ˈAir Miles™ *noun* [pl.] points that you collect by buying plane tickets and other products, which you can then use to pay for air travel 航空里程積分（可用來充抵機票費用）

air·miss /ˈeəmɪs; *NAmE* ˈerm-/ *noun* (*BrE*) an occasion when two or more aircraft fly too close to one another and a crash nearly happens 空中險情；飛機險撞

ˈair pistol *noun* a small gun that uses air pressure to fire small metal balls (called PELLETS) 氣手槍

air·plane /ˈeəpleɪn; *NAmE* ˈerp-/ *noun* (*especially NAmE*) = PLANE (1)：*They arrived in Belgium* ***by airplane***. 他們乘飛機到達比利時。◇ *an* ***airplane crash/flight*** 飛機墜毀／飛行 ◇ *a* ***commercial/jet/military airplane*** 商用／噴氣／軍用飛機

air·play /ˈeəpleɪ; *NAmE* ˈerp-/ *noun* [U] time that is spent broadcasting a particular record, performer, or type of music on the radio（唱片、歌手或某種音樂等的）電台播送時間：*The band is starting to get a lot of airplay.* 這支樂隊的歌曲已開始在電台熱播。

ˈair pocket *noun* **1** a closed area that becomes filled with air 氣窩 **2** an area of low air pressure that makes a plane suddenly drop while flying 氣阱，氣穴（使飛機突然下降的低氣壓區）

air·port 🔑 /ˈeəpɔːt; *NAmE* ˈerpɔːrt/ *noun* a place where planes land and take off and that has buildings for passengers to wait in 航空站；航空港；機場：*Gatwick Airport* 蓋特威克機場 ◇ *waiting in the airport lounge* 在機場候機廳等候

ˌairport ˈfiction *noun* [U] novels that are popular and easy to read, often bought by people at airports 機場小說（常指在機場購買的通俗消遣讀物）

ˈair power *noun* [U] military forces involving aircraft 空軍戰力

ˈair pump *noun* a piece of equipment for sending air into or out of sth 氣泵；抽氣機

ˈair quality *noun* [U] the degree to which the air is clean and free from pollution 空氣質量；空氣品質

ˈair quotes *noun* [pl.] imaginary quotation marks made in the air with your fingers when you are speaking, to show that you are using a word or phrase in an unusual way 手勢引號（用雙手手指比畫的引號，用以表示所用詞語非常規意義）

ˈair raid *noun* an attack by a number of aircraft dropping many bombs on a place 空襲：*The family was killed in an air raid.* 這家人在一次空襲中遇難。◇ *an* ***air-raid shelter/warning*** 防空洞；空襲警報

ˈair rifle *noun* = AIR GUN

ˌair-sea ˈrescue *noun* [C, U] (*especially BrE*) the process of rescuing people from the sea using aircraft（使用飛機的）海空救援

air·ship /ˈeəʃɪp; *NAmE* ˈerʃɪp/ *noun* a large aircraft without wings, filled with a gas which is lighter than air, and driven by engines 飛艇；飛船 ➲ VISUAL VOCAB page V53

ˈair show *noun* a show at which people can watch aircraft flying 航空表演；飛行表演

air·sick /ˈeəsɪk; *NAmE* ˈersɪk/ *adj.* [not usually before noun] feeling ill/sick when you are travelling on an aircraft 暈機 ▸ **air·sick·ness** *noun* [U]

air·space /ˈeəspeɪs; *NAmE* ˈers-/ *noun* [U] the part of the sky where planes fly, usually the part above a particular country that is legally controlled by that country 領空；（某國的）空域：*The jet entered Chinese airspace without permission.* 那架噴氣式飛機未經許可闖入中國領空。

air·speed /ˈeəspiːd; *NAmE* ˈer-/ *noun* the speed of an aircraft relative to the air through which it is moving（飛機的）空速 ➲ compare GROUND SPEED

air·stream /ˈeəstriːm; *NAmE* ˈerstriːm/ *noun* a movement of air, especially a strong one（尤指強烈的）氣流

ˈair strike *noun* an attack made by aircraft 空中打擊；空襲

air·strip /ˈeəstrɪp; *NAmE* ˈers-/ (also **ˈlanding strip**) *noun* a narrow piece of cleared land that an aircraft can land on 簡易機場；簡易跑道

ˈair support *noun* [U] help which aircraft give to soldiers and military vehicles on the land or sea 空中支援

ˈair terminal *noun* **1** a building at an airport that provides services for passengers travelling by plane（機場）候機大樓；機場大樓 **2** (*BrE*) an office in a city from which passengers can catch buses to the airport 城市中心民航班車站（設在市區，向乘客提供民航班車去機場）

air·tight /ˈeətaɪt; *NAmE* ˈert-/ *adj.* not allowing air to get in or out 密封的；不透氣的：*Store the cake in an airtight container.* 把蛋糕存放在密封容器裏。◇ (*figurative*) *an airtight alibi* (= one that cannot be proved to be false) 無懈可擊的不在犯罪現場的證據

air·time /ˈeətaɪm; *NAmE* ˈert-/ *noun* [U] **1** the amount of time that is given to a particular subject on radio or television（廣播或電視節目的）播放時間 **2** the amount of time that is paid for when you are using a mobile/cell phone（移動電話計費的）通話時間

ˌair-to-ˈair *adj.* [usually before noun] from one aircraft to another while they are both flying 空對空的：*an air-to-air missile* 空對空導彈

ˌair-to-ˈground *adj.* [usually before noun] directed or operating from an aircraft to the surface of the land 空對地的；從飛機對地面的：*air-to-ground weapons* 空對地武器

ˌair-to-ˈsurface *adj.* [usually before noun] moving or passing from a flying aircraft to the surface of the sea or land 空對面的；從飛機對海面（或地面）的：*air-to-surface missiles* 空對面導彈

ˌair traffic conˈtrol *noun* [U] **1** the activity of giving instructions by radio to pilots of aircraft so that they know when and where to take off or land 空中交通管制 **2** the group of people or the organization that provides an air traffic control service 空中交通管制人員（或管制站）：*The pilot was given clearance to land by air traffic control.* 飛行員得到空中交通管制站發出的着陸許可。

ˌair traffic conˈtroller *noun* a person whose job is to give instructions by radio to pilots of aircraft so that they know when and where to take off or land 空中交通管制員；航空調度員

ˌair vice-ˈmarshal *noun* an officer of very high rank in the British AIR FORCE（英國）空軍少將：*Air Vice-Marshal Andrew Burns* 空軍少將安德魯 • 伯恩斯

air·waves /ˈeəweɪvz; *NAmE* ˈerw-/ *noun* [pl.] radio waves that are used in broadcasting radio and television（廣播、電視使用的）無線電波；波段：*More and more TV and radio stations are crowding the airwaves.* 愈來愈多的電視台和廣播電台使無線電波段愈來愈擁擠。◇ *A well-known voice came* ***over the airwaves***. 電波傳來了一個大家熟悉的聲音。

air·way /ˈeəweɪ; *NAmE* ˈerweɪ/ *noun* **1** (*medical* 醫) the passage from the nose and throat to the lungs, through which you breathe 氣道 **2** (often used in names of AIRLINES 常用於航空公司名稱) a route regularly used by planes（飛機的）固定航線：*British Airways* 英國航空公司

air·worthy /ˈeəwɜːði; *NAmE* ˈerwɜːrði/ *adj.* (of aircraft 飛行器) safe to fly 適航的 ▸ **air·worthi·ness** *noun* [U]

airy /ˈeəri; *NAmE* ˈeri/ *adj.* (**air·ier**, **airi·est**) **1** with plenty of fresh air because there is a lot of space 通風的；空氣流通的：*The office was light and airy.* 辦公室又明亮又通風。**2** (*formal*) acting or done in a way that shows that you are not worried or that you are not treating sth as serious 無憂無慮的；無所謂的；漫不經心的：*He dismissed her with an airy wave.* 他隨意一揮手就把她打發走了。➲ see also AIRILY **3** (*formal, disapproving*) not serious or practical 不嚴肅的；不切實際的：***airy promises/speculation*** 輕率的諾言；無端猜測

ˌairy-ˈfairy *adj.* (*BrE, informal, disapproving*) not clear or practical 模糊的；不現實的；不切實際的

aisle /aɪl/ *noun* a passage between rows of seats in a church, theatre, train, etc., or between rows of shelves in a supermarket（教堂、戲院、火車等座位間或超級市場貨架間的）走道，過道：*an aisle seat* (= in a plane)（飛機上）緊靠過道的座位 ◇ *Coffee and tea are in the next aisle.* 下一個走道處有咖啡和茶。➲ compare GANGWAY (1)

IDM **go/walk down the 'aisle** (*informal*) to get married 結婚 ➲ more at ROLL *v.*

aitch /eɪtʃ/ *noun* the letter H written as a word 字母 H：*He spoke with a cockney accent and* ***dropped his aitches*** (= did not pronounce the letter H at the start of words). 他帶倫敦東區的口音，總是漏發詞首的 h 音。

ajar /əˈdʒɑː(r)/ *adj.* [not before noun] (of a door 門) slightly open 半開；微啟：*I'll leave the door ajar.* 我讓門半開着。

aka /ˌeɪ keɪ ˈeɪ/ *abbr.* also known as 又名；亦稱：*Antonio Fratelli, aka 'Big Tony'* 安東尼奧 • 弗拉泰利，又名"大托尼"

akimbo /əˈkɪmbəʊ; *NAmE* -boʊ/ *adv.*

IDM **(with) arms a'kimbo** with your hands on your hips and your elbows pointing away from your body 雙手叉腰

akin /əˈkɪn/ *adj.* **~ to sth** (*formal*) similar to 相似的；類似的：*What he felt was more akin to pity than love.* 他感受到的更像憐憫，而不是愛。

-al *suffix* **1** (in adjectives 構成形容詞) connected with 與…有關的：*magical* 魔術的 ◇ *verbal* 言語的 ➲ see also -ALLY **2** (in nouns 構成名詞) a process or state of（表示過程或狀態）：*survival* 幸存

à la /ˈɑː lɑː/ *prep.* (from *French*) in the same style as sb/sth else 按照…方式；仿照：*a new band that sings à la Beatles* 模仿披頭士樂隊唱歌的一支新樂隊

ala·bas·ter /ˈæləbɑːstə(r); *NAmE* -bæs-/ *noun* [U] a type of white stone that is often used to make statues and decorative objects 雪花石膏（常用於雕塑和裝飾品）：*an alabaster tomb* 雪花石膏墓 ◇ (*literary*) *her pale, alabaster* (= white and smooth) *skin* 她白淨光滑的皮膚

à la carte /ˌɑː lɑː ˈkɑːt; *NAmE* ˈkɑːrt/ *adj.*, *adv.* (from *French*) if food in a restaurant is **à la carte**, or if you eat **à la carte**, you choose from a list of dishes that have separate prices, rather than having a complete meal at a fixed price 按菜單點菜（與套餐相對）

alack /əˈlæk/ *exclamation* (*old use* or *humorous*) used to show you are sad or sorry（表示悲傷或遺憾）哎呀，唉：***Alas and alack****, we had missed our bus.* 唉，完了，我們沒趕上公共汽車。

alac·rity /əˈlækrəti/ *noun* [U] (*formal*) great willingness or enthusiasm 欣然同意；十分樂意：*They accepted the offer with alacrity.* 他們欣然接受了建議。

A,laddin's 'cave *noun* a place where there are many wonderful objects 阿拉丁的藏寶洞；寶庫

à la mode /ˌɑː lɑː ˈməʊd; *NAmE* ˈmoʊd/ *adj.*, *adv.* (from *French*) **1** [not before noun] (*old-fashioned*) fashionable; in the latest fashion 流行；時髦 **2** [after noun] (*NAmE*) served with ice cream 加有冰淇淋的：*apple pie à la mode* 蘋果餡餅加冰淇淋

alarm 🗝 /əˈlɑːm; *NAmE* əˈlɑːrm/ *noun*, *verb*

■ ***noun*** **1** 🗝 [U] fear and anxiety that sb feels when sth dangerous or unpleasant might happen 驚恐；驚慌；恐慌：*'What have you done?' Ellie cried* ***in alarm.*** "你幹了些什麼？"埃利驚恐地喊道。◇ *I felt a growing sense of alarm when he did not return that night.* 那天夜裏他沒有回家，我的恐慌感油然而生。◇ *The doctor said there was no* ***cause for alarm.*** 醫生說不必驚慌。➲ SYNONYMS at FEAR **2** 🗝 [C, usually sing.] a loud noise or a signal that warns people of danger or of a problem 警報：*She decided to* ***sound the alarm*** (= warn people that the situation was dangerous). 她決定發出警報。◇ *I hammered on all the doors to* ***raise the alarm.*** 我敲打所有的門讓大家警覺。➲ see also FALSE ALARM **3** 🗝 [C] a device that warns people of a particular danger 警報器：*a* ***burglar/fire/smoke alarm*** 防盜／防火／煙火警報器 ◇ *The cat* ***set off the alarm*** (= made it start ringing). 貓碰響了警鈴。◇ *A car* ***alarm went off*** *in the middle of the night* (= started ringing). 半夜裏一輛汽車的警報器突然響了起來。**4** = ALARM CLOCK：*The* ***alarm went off*** *at 7 o'clock.* 鬧鐘在 7 點鐘鬧鈴響了。

IDM **a'larm bells ring/start ringing** if you say that **alarm bells are ringing**, you mean that people are starting to feel worried and suspicious 警鐘敲響；發出危險信號

■ ***verb*** **1** 🗝 **~ sb** to make sb anxious or afraid 使驚恐；使害怕；使擔心 **SYN** **worry**：*The captain knew there was an engine fault but didn't want to alarm the passengers.* 船長知道一台發動機出了故障，不過他不想驚動乘客。➲ SYNONYMS at FRIGHTEN **2 ~ sth** to fit sth such as a door with a device that warns people when sb is trying to enter illegally 給（門等）安裝警報器

a'larm call *noun* **1** a telephone call which is intended to wake you up 催醒電話；叫醒電話：*Could I have an alarm call at 5.30 tomorrow, please?* 請在明天早晨 5:30 打電話叫醒我好嗎？ **2** a cry of warning made by a bird or animal（鳥獸遇險時發出的）告警聲

a'larm clock (also **alarm**) *noun* a clock that you can set to ring a bell, etc. at a particular time and wake you up 鬧鐘：*I set the alarm clock for 7 o'clock.* 我把鬧鐘定在 7 點鐘鬧響。➲ picture at CLOCK

alarmed 🗝 /əˈlɑːmd; *NAmE* əˈlɑːrmd/ *adj.*

1 🗝 **~ (at/by sth)** anxious or afraid that sth dangerous or unpleasant might happen 擔心；害怕：*She was alarmed at the prospect of travelling alone.* 她一想到獨自旅行的情景就害怕。➲ SYNONYMS at AFRAID **2** [not before noun] protected by an alarm 有警報裝置：*This door is alarmed.* 這扇門安裝了警報器。

alarm·ing 🗝 /əˈlɑːmɪŋ; *NAmE* əˈlɑːrm-/ *adj.* causing worry and fear 使人驚恐的；令人驚慌的；引起恐慌的：*an alarming increase in crime* 犯罪活動駭人的增加 ◇ *The rainforests are disappearing* ***at an alarming rate.*** 雨林正以驚人的速度消失。▸ **alarm·ing·ly** *adv.*：*Prices have risen alarmingly.* 價格漲得嚇人。

alarm·ist /əˈlɑːmɪst; *NAmE* əˈlɑːrm-/ *adj.* (*disapproving*) causing unnecessary fear and anxiety 危言聳聽的；駭人的：*A spokesperson for the food industry said the TV programme was alarmist.* 食品工業的一位發言人說這個電視節目危言聳聽。▸ **alarm·ist** *noun*

alas /əˈlæs/ *exclamation* (*old use* or *literary*) used to show you are sad or sorry（表示悲傷或遺憾）哎呀，唉：*For many people, alas, hunger is part of everyday life.* 唉，對很多人來說，挨餓是家常便飯。

al·ba·tross /ˈælbətrɒs; *NAmE* -trɔːs; -trɑːs/ *noun* **1** a very large white bird with long wings that lives in the Pacific and Southern Oceans 信天翁（白色長翼大海鳥，生活於太平洋和南半球海洋）➲ VISUAL VOCAB page V12 **2** [usually sing.] (*formal*) a thing that causes problems or prevents you from doing sth 惹麻煩的事；苦惱；障礙

al·beit **AW** /ˌɔːlˈbiːɪt/ *conj.* (*formal*) although 儘管；雖然：*He finally agreed, albeit reluctantly, to help us.* 儘管勉強，他最後還是同意幫助我們。

al·bin·ism /ˈælbɪnɪzəm/ *noun* [U] (*technical* 術語) the condition of being an albino 白化病

al·bino /ælˈbiːnəʊ; *NAmE* -ˈbaɪnoʊ/ *noun* (*pl.* **-os**) a person or an animal that is born with no colour (= PIGMENT) in the hair or skin, which are white, or in the eyes, which are pink 患白化病的人（或動物）▸ **al·bino** *adj.* [only before noun]

Al·bion /ˈælbiən/ *noun* [U] (*literary*) an ancient name for Britain or England 阿爾比恩（古時用以指不列顛或英格蘭）

album /ˈælbəm/ *noun* **1** a book in which you keep photographs, stamps, etc. 相冊；影集；集郵簿；集物簿冊：*a photo album* 相冊 ◇ *an online album* (= a website where you can store and view photographs) 網上相冊（可貯存和觀看照片的網站）➲ VISUAL VOCAB page V41 **2** a collection of pieces of music released as a single item, usually on a CD, CASSETTE, or on the Internet（唱片、盒式磁帶或網上的）音樂專輯，歌曲專輯：*the band's latest album* 這個樂隊的最新專輯 ◇ *an online album* (= an album that you can listen to on the

A

Internet) 網上專輯 ➲ COLLOCATIONS at MUSIC ➲ compare SINGLE *n.* (2)

al·bu·men /ˈælbjumɪn; *NAmE* ælˈbju:mən/ *noun* [U] (*technical* 術語) the clear inside part of an egg that is white when cooked 蛋白；蛋清 SYN **white** ➲ compare YOLK

Al·ca·traz /ˈælkətræz/ *noun* a small US island near San Francisco where there is a former prison 阿爾卡特拉斯島（三藩市附近的美屬小島，有一舊時的監獄）: *The clinic felt like Alcatraz. There was no escape.* 那家診所令人感覺像四面環水的監牢，無路可逃。

al·chem·ist /ˈælkəmɪst/ *noun* a person who studied alchemy 煉金術士

al·chemy /ˈælkəmi/ *noun* [U] **1** a form of chemistry studied in the Middle Ages which involved trying to discover how to change ordinary metals into gold 煉金術（見於中世紀，企圖把普通金屬煉成黃金） **2** (*literary*) a mysterious power or magic that can change things（改變事物的）神秘力量，魔力

al·cher·inga /ˌæltʃəˈrɪŋɡə/ (also **Dream·time**) *noun* [U] according to some Australian Aboriginals, the time when the first people were created（澳大利亞土著神話中的）世界發端，夢想期，夢幻時代

al·co·hol 0‑w /ˈælkəhɒl; *NAmE* -hɔ:l; -hɑ:l/ *noun* [U] **1** 0‑w drinks such as beer, wine, etc. that can make people drunk 含酒精飲料；酒: *He never drinks alcohol.* 他從來不喝酒。◇ *alcohol abuse* 酗酒 ➲ COLLOCATIONS at DIET **2** 0‑w the clear liquid that is found in drinks such as beer, wine, etc. and is used in medicines, cleaning products, etc. 酒精；乙醇: *Wine contains about 10% alcohol.* 葡萄酒含有約 10% 的酒精。◇ *levels of alcohol in the blood* 血液中酒精含量 ◇ *He pleaded guilty to driving with excess alcohol.* 他對過量飲酒後駕車一事表示服罪。◇ ***low-alcohol** beer* 酒精度低的啤酒 ◇ ***alcohol-free** beer* 不含酒精的啤酒

al·co·hol·ic 0‑w /ˌælkəˈhɒlɪk; *NAmE* -ˈhɔ:l-; -ˈhɑ:l-/ *adj., noun*

■ ***adj.*** **1** 0‑w connected with or containing alcohol 酒精的；含酒精的: *alcoholic drinks* 含酒精的飲料 OPP **non-alcoholic** ➲ see also SOFT DRINK **2** caused by drinking alcohol 飲酒引起的: *The guests left in an alcoholic haze.* 客人們醉醺醺地離去了。

■ ***noun*** 0‑w a person who regularly drinks too much alcohol and cannot easily stop drinking, so that it has become an illness 酒精中毒者；嗜酒如命者；酒鬼 ➲ see also LUSH *n.*

Alco,holics A'nonymous *noun* [U] (*abbr.* **AA**) an international organization, begun in Chicago in 1935, for people who are trying to stop drinking alcohol. They have meetings to help each other. 匿名戒酒會（1935 年成立於芝加哥的國際組織，成員不用全名）

al·co·hol·ism /ˈælkəhɒlɪzəm; *NAmE* -hɔ:l-; -hɑ:l-/ *noun* [U] the medical condition caused by drinking too much alcohol regularly 酒精中毒

al·co·pop /ˈælkəʊpɒp; *NAmE* -koʊpɑ:p/ *noun* (*BrE*) a sweet FIZZY (= with bubbles) drink that contains alcohol 泡泡甜酒

al·cove /ˈælkəʊv; *NAmE* -koʊv/ *noun* an area in a room that is formed by part of a wall being built farther back than the rest of the wall 壁凹，凹室，壁龕（房內牆壁凹進空間）: *The bookcase fits neatly into the alcove.* 書架正好放得進壁凹。

al dente /ˌæl ˈdenteɪ; -ti/ *adj.* (from *Italian*) (of cooked food, especially PASTA 尤指如意大利麪等煮過的食物) firm, but not hard, when bitten 筋道的；有韌性耐咀嚼的；有嚼勁的 ▸ **al dente** *adv.*

alder /ˈɔ:ldə(r)/ *noun* a tree like a BIRCH that grows in northern countries, usually in wet ground 榿木（多見於北方國家潮濕地區）

al·der·man /ˈɔ:ldəmən; *NAmE* -dərm-/ *noun* (*pl.* **-men** /-mən/) **1** (in England and Wales in the past) a senior member of a town, BOROUGH or county council, below the rank of a MAYOR, chosen by other members of the council（舊時英格蘭和威爾士的）高級市政官（職位低於市長） **2** (*feminine* **al·der·woman**, *pl.* **-women** /-wɪmɪn/) (in the US, Canada and Australia) an elected member of a town or city council（美國、加拿大、澳大利亞的）市政委員會委員: *Alderman Tim Evans* 市政委員會委員蒂姆•埃文斯

ale /eɪl/ *noun* **1** [U, C] a type of beer, usually sold in bottles or cans. There are several kinds of ale. 麥芽啤酒: ***brown/pale ale*** 深色 / 淺色麥芽啤酒 **2** [C] a glass, bottle or can of ale 一杯（或一瓶、一罐）麥芽啤酒: *Two light ales please.* 請來兩杯淡麥芽啤酒。 **3** [U] (*old-fashioned*) beer generally（泛指）啤酒 ➲ see also BROWN ALE, GINGER ALE, REAL ALE

alec, aleck ➲ SMART ALEC

ale·house /ˈeɪlhaʊs/ *noun* (*old-fashioned, BrE*) a place where people used to drink beer 啤酒店；酒館

alert /əˈlɜ:t; *NAmE* əˈlɜ:rt/ *adj., verb, noun*

■ ***adj.*** **1** able to think quickly; quick to notice things 警覺的；警惕的；戒備的: *Suddenly he found himself awake and fully alert.* 突然他發覺自己醒了過來，而且高度警覺。◇ *Two alert scientists spotted the mistake.* 兩個警覺的科學家發現了這個錯誤。 **2 ~ to sth** aware of sth, especially a problem or danger 意識到；注意到: *We must be alert to the possibility of danger.* 我們必須認識到危險的可能性。 ▸ **alert·ly** *adj.* **alert·ness** *noun* [U]

■ ***verb*** [often passive] **1 ~ sb (to do sth)** | **~ sb (that) …** to warn sb about a dangerous or urgent situation 向…報警；使警覺；使警惕；使戒備: *Neighbours quickly alerted the emergency services.* 鄰居很快向緊急情況中心報了警。◇ *Alerted by a noise downstairs, he sat up and turned on the light.* 樓下的響聲使他警覺，他坐起來打開燈。 **2 ~ sb to sth** to make sb aware of sth 使意識到；使認識到: *They had been alerted to the possibility of further price rises.* 他們已意識到價格可能繼續上漲。

■ ***noun*** **1** [sing., U] a situation in which people are watching for danger and ready to deal with it 警戒；戒備；警惕: *Police are warning the public to **be on the alert** for suspicious packages.* 警方警告公眾要警惕可疑包裹。◇ *More than 5 000 troops have been placed **on (full) alert**.* * 5 000 多名士兵已處於（全面）戒備狀態。 **2** [C] a warning of danger or of a problem 警報: ***a bomb/fire alert*** 炸彈 / 火警警報 ➲ see also RED ALERT

A level /ˈeɪ levl/ (also **ad'vanced level**) *noun* [C, U] a British exam taken in a particular subject, usually in the final year of school at the age of 18 高級證書考試（英國中學單科考試，通常在畢業年級進行）: *You need three A levels to get onto this university course.* 你要選修這門大學課程，就需要通過三科高級證書考試。◇ *What A levels are you doing?* 你在準備哪些科目的高級證書考試？◇ *I'm doing maths A level.* 我在準備數學高級證書考試。◇ *two A level passes/two passes at A level* 兩門高級證書考試及格 ➲ compare A2, AS, GCE, GCSE, GNVQ, NVQ

Alexander technique /ˌælɪɡˈzɑ:ndə tekni:k; *NAmE* -ˈzændər/ *noun* [sing., U] a method of improving sb's health by teaching them how to stand, sit and move correctly 亞歷山大技巧，亞歷山大健身技術（通過糾正不良的坐立姿勢、保持身體各部位的平衡以增進健康）

alex·an·drine /ˌælɪɡˈzɑ:ndrɪn; -aɪn; *NAmE* -ˈzæn-/ *adj.* (*technical* 術語) (of lines of poetry 詩行) containing six IAMBIC, FEET 亞歷山大詩體的；含六音步抑揚格的 ▸ **alex·an·drine** *noun*

al·fal·fa /ælˈfælfə/ *noun* [U] a plant with small divided leaves and purple flowers, grown as food for farm animals and as a salad vegetable 苜蓿

al fresco /æl ˈfreskəʊ; *NAmE* -koʊ/ *adj.* outdoors 在戶外的: *an al fresco lunch party* 戶外午餐會 ▸ **al·fresco** *adv.*: *eating al fresco* 在戶外用餐

algae /ˈældʒi:; ˈælɡi:/ *noun* [U, pl.] (*sing.* **alga** /ˈælɡə/) (*technical* 術語) very simple plants, such as SEAWEED, that have no real leaves, STEMS or roots, and that grow in or near water 藻；海藻 ▸ **algal** /ˈælɡəl/ *adj.* [only before noun]: ***algal blooms/growth*** 藻花；藻類生長

al·ge·bra /ˈældʒɪbrə/ *noun* [U] a type of mathematics in which letters and symbols are used to represent quantities 代數 ▸ **al·ge·bra·ic** /ˌældʒɪˈbreɪɪk/ *adj.*

al·go·rithm /ˈælɡərɪðəm/ *noun* (*computing* 計) a set of rules that must be followed when solving a particular problem 算法；計算程序

al·haja /æl'hædʒə/ *noun* (*WAfrE*) a woman who is a Muslim and has completed a religious journey to Mecca (often used as a title) 阿哈婭（朝覲過麥加的穆斯林女子，常用作稱謂）➲ compare ALHAJI

al·haji /æl'hædʒi/ *noun* (*WAfrE*) a man who is a Muslim and has completed a religious journey to Mecca (often used as a title) 阿哈吉（朝覲過麥加的穆斯林男子，常用作稱謂）➲ compare ALHAJA

-alia /-eɪliə/ *suffix* (in plural nouns 構成複數名詞) items connected with the particular area of activity or interest mentioned（與某活動或興趣範圍）有關的物品： *kitchenalia* 廚房用品

alias /'eɪliəs/ *adv., noun*

■ ***adv.*** used when a person, especially a criminal or an actor, is known by two names（罪犯、演員等）又名，亦名，別名，化名： *Mick Clark, alias Sid Brown* 米克•克拉克，又名錫德•布朗 ◇ *Hercule Poirot, alias David Suchet* (= David Suchet plays the part of Hercule Poirot) 赫爾克里•波洛，由大衞•蘇切特扮演 ◇ *David Suchet, alias Hercule Poirot of the famous TV series* 大衞•蘇切特，即著名電視連續劇中的赫爾克里•波洛

■ ***noun*** **1** a false or different name, especially one that is used by a criminal（尤指罪犯所用的）化名，別名： *He checked into the hotel under an alias.* 他用化名登記住進旅館。**2** (*computing* 計) a name that can be used instead of the actual name for a file, Internet address, etc.（檔案、互聯網地址等用的）別名，假名

alibi /'æləbaɪ/ *noun* **1** evidence that proves that a person was in another place at the time of a crime and so could not have committed it 不在犯罪現場證明： *The suspects all had alibis for the day of the robbery.* 嫌疑人均有證據證明搶劫當天不在犯罪現場。 **2** an excuse for sth that you have done wrong 藉口；託辭

Alice band /'ælɪs bænd/ *noun* (*BrE*) a band which holds your hair back away from your face, but lets it hang freely at the back 髮箍

ˌAlice in 'Wonder·land *noun* [U] used to describe a situation that is very strange, in which things happen that do not make any sense and are the opposite of what you would expect（事情悖理且與想像的截然相反的）怪異局面： *The country's economic system is pure Alice in Wonderland.* 這個國家的經濟制度實屬匪夷所思。 ▶ **Alice-in-Wonderland** *adj.* [only before noun]： *I felt I was in an Alice-in-Wonderland world.* 我感覺就像置身於奇幻世界之中。 **ORIGIN** From the title of a children's story by Lewis Carroll. 源自劉易思•卡羅爾所著的兒童小說《艾麗絲漫遊奇境記》。

alien /'eɪliən/ *adj., noun*

■ ***adj.*** **1 ~ (to sb/sth)** strange and frightening; different from what you are used to 陌生的；不熟悉 **SYN** **hostile**： *an alien environment* 陌生的環境 ◇ *In a world that had suddenly become alien and dangerous, he was her only security.* 在一個突然變得陌生而危險的世界裏，他是她唯一的守護神。 **2** (often *disapproving*) from another country or society; foreign 外國的；異域的： *an alien culture* 異族文化 **3** (*disapproving*) not usual or acceptable 不相容；相抵觸；格格不入： **~ to sb/sth** *The idea is alien to our religion.* 這種思想與我們的宗教不相容。◇ *Cruelty was quite alien to him.* 他絕無殘忍之心。 **4** connected with creatures from another world 外星的： *alien beings from outer space* 外星人

■ ***noun*** **1** (*NAmE* also **ˌnon-'citizen**) (*law* 律 or *technical* 術語) a person who is not a citizen of the country in which they live or work 外國人；外僑： *an illegal alien* 非法外僑 ➲ compare RESIDENT ALIEN **2** a creature from another world 外星生物： *aliens from outer space* 外星人

alien·ate /'eɪliəneɪt/ *verb* **1 ~ sb** to make sb less friendly or sympathetic towards you 使疏遠；使不友好；離間： *His comments have alienated a lot of young voters.* 他的評論使許多年輕選民離他而去。 **2 ~ sb (from sth/sb)** to make sb feel that they do not belong in a particular group 使（與某群體）格格不入；使疏遠： *Very talented children may feel alienated from the others in their class.* 天才出眾的孩子可能覺得與班上的同學格格不入。 ▶ **alien·ation** /ˌeɪliə'neɪʃn/ *noun* [U]： *The new policy resulted in the alienation of many voters.* 新政策導致許多選民疏遠了。◇ *Many immigrants suffer from a sense of alienation.* 許多移民因感到不容於社會而苦惱。

alight /ə'laɪt/ *adj., verb*

■ ***adj.*** [not before noun] **1** on fire 燃燒；着火： *A cigarette* ***set*** *the dry grass* ***alight****.* 一支香煙把乾草點燃了。◇ *Her dress* ***caught alight*** *in the fire.* 她的衣服讓火燒着了。 **2** (*formal*) (of faces or eyes 臉或眼) showing a feeling of happiness or excitement 容光煥發；興奮 **IDM** see WORLD

■ ***verb*** (*formal* or *literary*) **1** [I] **~ (in/on/upon sth)** (of a bird or an insect 鳥或昆蟲) to land in or on sth after flying to it 降落；飛落 **SYN** **land** **2** [I] **~ (from sth)** to get out of a bus, a train or other vehicle 從（公共汽車、火車等）下來 **SYN** **get off**： *Do not alight from a moving bus.* 公共汽車行駛時不要下車。

PHR V **a'light on/upon sth** to think of, find or notice sth, especially by chance（尤指偶然地）想到，發現，注意到： *Eventually, we alighted on the idea of seeking sponsorship.* 最後我們偶然想到了尋求贊助。◇ *Her eyes suddenly alighted on the bundle of documents.* 她的目光突然落到了這捆文件上。

align /ə'laɪn/ *verb* **1** [I, T] **~ (sth) (with sth)** to arrange sth in the correct position, or to be in the correct position, in relation to sth else, especially in a straight line 排列整齊；使對齊；（尤指）成一直線： *Make sure the shelf is aligned with the top of the cupboard.* 務必使擱架與櫥櫃頂端靠齊。◇ *The top and bottom line of each column on the page should align.* 版面每欄的頭一行和末一行要對齊。 **2** [T] **~ sth (with/to sth)** to change sth slightly so that it is in the correct relationship to sth else 使一致： *Domestic prices have been aligned with those in world markets.* 國內價格已調整到與世界市場一致。

PHR V **a'lign yourself with sb/sth** to publicly support an organization, a set of opinions or a person that you agree with 公開支持（某組織、意見、人）

align·ment /ə'laɪnmənt/ *noun* [U, C] **1** arrangement in a straight line 排成直線： *A bone in my spine was* ***out of alignment****.* 我的脊椎骨有一節脫位。 **2** political support given to one country or group by another（國家、團體間的）結盟： *Japan's alignment with the West* 日本與西方國家的結盟

alike /ə'laɪk/ *adj., adv.*

■ ***adj.*** [not before noun] very similar 相像；十分相似： *My sister and I do not look alike.* 我和妹妹外貌不相像。 ➲ compare UNLIKE

■ ***adv.*** **1** in a very similar way 十分相像地；很相似地： *They tried to treat all their children alike.* 他們盡量對自己的孩子一視同仁。 **2** used after you have referred to two people or groups, to mean 'both' or 'equally' 兩者都；同樣地： *Good management benefits employers and employees alike.* 良好的管理對雇主和雇員同樣有利。 **IDM** see GREAT *adj.*, SHARE *v.*

ali·men·tary canal /ˌælɪmentəri kə'næl/ *noun* the passage in the body that carries food from the mouth to the ANUS 消化道

ali·mony /'ælɪməni; *NAmE* -moʊni/ *noun* [U] (*especially NAmE*) the money that a court orders sb to pay regularly to their former wife or husband when the marriage is ended（離婚後一方給另一方的）生活費，撫養費 ➲ compare MAINTENANCE (3), PALIMONY

'A-line *adj.* (of a skirt or dress 裙子或連衣裙) wider at the bottom than at the top 呈 A 字型的；寬下襬的

ali·quot /'ælɪkwɒt; *NAmE* -kwɑːt/ *noun* **1** (*technical* 術語) a small amount of sth that is taken from a larger amount, especially when it is taken in order to do chemical tests on it（尤指化學實驗的）試樣 **2** (*mathematics* 數) a quantity which can be exactly divided into another 整除數

'A-list *adj.* [usually before noun] used to describe the group of people who are considered to be the most famous, successful or important 第一等的；最出名（或成功、重要）的： *He only invited* ***A-list celebrities*** *to his parties.* 他只邀請頭等名流參加他的聚會。 ➲ compare B-LIST

A

alive /ə'laɪv/ *adj.* [not before noun]
1 living; not dead 活着；在世：*We don't know whether he's alive or dead.* 我們不知道他是死是活。◇ *Is your mother **still alive**?* 你的母親還健在嗎？◇ *Doctors **kept** the baby **alive** for six weeks.* 醫生使嬰兒活了六週。◇ *I was glad to hear you're **alive and well**.* 聽說你健在我很高興。◇ *She had to steal food just to **stay alive**.* 她得偷食物才不至於餓死。◇ *He was **buried alive** in the earthquake.* 地震把他活埋了。 **2 ~ (with sth)** full of emotion, excitement, activity, etc. 情緒飽滿；激動興奮；有生氣；有活力：*Ed was alive with happiness.* 埃德高興得眉飛色舞。 **3** continuing to exist 繼續存在：*to **keep** a tradition **alive*** 繼承傳統 **4 ~ with sth** full of living or moving things 充滿（活的或動的東西）：*The pool was alive with goldfish.* 池塘裏滿是游來游去的金魚。 **5 ~ to sth** aware of sth; knowing sth exists and is important 意識到；認識到；注意到：*to be alive to the dangers/facts/possibilities* 意識到危險；認識到事實；注意到可能

IDM **a,live and 'kicking** very active, healthy or popular 充滿活力；活蹦亂跳；生氣勃勃；流行 **bring sth a'live** to make sth interesting 使有趣：*The pictures bring the book alive.* 圖片使得這本書生動有趣。 **come a'live 1** (of a subject or an event 主題或活動) to become interesting and exciting 引起興趣；生動起來 SYN **come to life**：*The game came alive in the second half.* 比賽在下半場變得有看頭了。 **2** (of a place 地方) to become busy and full of activity 熱鬧起來；活躍起來 SYN **come to life**：*The city starts to come alive after dark.* 這座城市天黑以後便熱鬧起來。 **3** (of a person 人) to show interest in sth and become excited about it 興致勃勃；有精神起來：*She came alive as she talked about her job.* 她一談到她的工作精神就來了。 ➲ more at EAT

al·kali /'ælkəlaɪ/ *noun* [C, U] (*chemistry* 化) a chemical substance that reacts with acids to form a salt and gives a SOLUTION with a pH of more than seven when it is dissolved in water 鹼 ➲ compare ACID *n.* (1)

al·ka·line /'ælkəlaɪn/ *adj.* **1** (*chemistry* 化) having the nature of an alkali 鹼性的 **2** (*technical* 術語) containing alkali 含鹼的：*alkaline soil* 鹼性土壤 ➲ compare ACID *adj.* (1)

al·ka·lin·ity /,ælkə'lɪnəti/ *noun* [U] the state of being or containing an ALKALI 鹼度；鹼性

al·kal·oid /'ælkəlɔɪd/ *noun* (*biology* 生 or *medical* 醫) a poisonous substance found in some plants. There are many different alkaloids and some are used as the basis for drugs. 生物鹼

al·kane /'ælkeɪn/ *noun* (*chemistry* 化) any of a series of COMPOUNDS that contain CARBON and HYDROGEN 鏈烷；烷烴：*Methane and propane are alkanes.* 甲烷和丙烷是鏈烷。

Alka-Seltzer™ /,ælkə 'seltsə(r)/ *noun* [C, U] a medicine that you mix with water to make a drink that helps with INDIGESTION 我可舒適發泡錠（一種水溶性胃藥片）

al·kene /'ælkiːn/ *noun* (*chemistry* 化) any of a series of gases that contain HYDROGEN and CARBON and that have a double BOND (= force of attraction) between two of the CARBON atoms 烯；鏈烯烴

all /ɔːl/ *det., pron., adv.*

■ ***det.* 1** (used with plural nouns. The noun may have *the, this, that, my, her, his,* etc. in front of it, or a number. 與複數名詞連用。名詞前可用 the、this、that、my、her、his 等，也可用數詞。) the whole number of 所有；全部；全體；一切：*All horses are animals, but not all animals are horses.* 所有的馬都是動物，但並不是所有的動物都是馬。◇ *Cars were coming from all directions* (= every direction). 汽車從四面八方駛來。◇ *All the people you invited are coming.* 你邀請的人都會來。◇ *All my plants have died.* 我的花草全死光了。◇ *All five men are hard workers.* 五個人全都工作努力。 **2** (used with uncountable nouns. The noun may have *the, this, that, my, her, his,* etc. in front of it. 與不可數名詞連用。名詞前可用 the、this、that、my、her、his 等。) the whole amount of 所有；全部；一切：*All wood tends to shrink.* 所有的木頭都會收縮。◇ *You've had all the fun and I've had all the hard work.* 你所有的快樂都享受了，我所有的辛苦都嚐盡了。◇ *All this mail must be answered.* 所有這些信件都必須回覆。◇ *He has lost all his money.* 他失去了所有的錢。 **3** used with singular nouns showing sth has been happening for a whole period of time（與單數名詞連用，表示某事在某段時間內持續發生）全部的，整個的：*He's worked hard all year.* 他一年到頭都在辛勤勞動。◇ *She was unemployed for all that time.* 那段時間她一直失業。 **4** the greatest possible 極度；盡量：*In all honesty* (= being as honest as I can), *I can't agree.* 說實在的，我不能同意。 **5** consisting or appearing to consist of one thing only 唯一；全是；僅僅：*The magazine was all advertisements.* 這份雜誌全是廣告。◇ *She was **all smiles*** (= smiling a lot). 她笑容滿面。 **6** any whatever 無論什麼；任何：*He denied all knowledge of the crime.* 他矢口否認對這樁罪案知情。

IDM **and all 'that (jazz, rubbish, etc.)** (*informal*) and other similar things 以及諸如此類的：*I'm bored by history—dates and battles and all that stuff.* 我厭煩歷史，盡是些年代啦戰爭啦什麼的。 **not all that good, well, etc.** not particularly good, well, etc. 不那麼好；不很好：*He doesn't sing all that well.* 他唱得並不特別好。 **not as bad(ly), etc. as all 'that** not as much as has been suggested 並非那麼壞（等）：*They're not as rich as all that.* 他們並不是那麼富有。 **of 'all people, things, etc.** (*informal*) used to express surprise because sb/sth seems the least likely person, example, etc. 在所有的…當中偏偏：*I didn't think you, of all people, would become a vegetarian.* 我真沒有想到，在所有的人當中偏偏你會成為素食者。 **of 'all the ...** (*informal*) used to express anger（表示生氣）真是，真氣人：*I've locked myself out. Of all the stupid things to do!* 我把自己鎖在門外了，真是蠢得很！ ➲ more at FOR *prep.*

■ ***pron.* 1** the whole number or amount 所有；全部；全體；一切：*All of the food has gone.* 食物全光了。◇ *They've eaten all of it.* 他們全吃光了。◇ *They've eaten it all.* 他們吃得一點也沒剩。◇ *I invited some of my colleagues but not all.* 我邀請了一些同事，並不是所有的。◇ *Not all of them were invited.* 他們當中並不是人人都受到邀請。◇ *All of them enjoyed the party.* 他們都喜歡那次聚會。◇ *They all enjoyed it.* 他們都喜歡。◇ *His last movie was best of all.* 他最近的那部電影是他所有電影中最好的一部。 **2** (followed by a relative clause, often without *that* 後接常不帶 that 的關係從句) the only thing; everything 唯一的事物；所有的事物；一切：*All I want is peace and quiet.* 我只要和平安寧。◇ *It was all that I had.* 那就是我擁有的一切。 ➲ note at ALTOGETHER

IDM **all in 'all** when everything is considered 從各方面考慮；總的說來：*All in all it had been a great success.* 總的說來，那是個巨大的成功。 **all in 'one** having two or more uses, functions, etc. 多功能；多用途：*It's a corkscrew and bottle-opener all in one.* 這是一物多用，既是瓶塞鑽，又是開瓶器。 **and 'all 1** also; included; in addition 而且；還；包括：*She jumped into the river, clothes and all* (= with her clothes on). 她連衣服也沒脫就跳進河中。 **2** (*informal*) as well; too 也：*'I'm freezing.' 'Yeah, me and all.'* "我都快凍僵了。" "對，我也是。" **(not) at all** in any way; to any degree 一點也（不）；完全（不）：*I didn't enjoy it at all.* 我一點也不喜歡。 **in all** as a total 總共；共計 SYN **altogether**：*There were twelve of us in all for dinner.* 我們一共十二人吃飯。◇ *That's £25.40 in all.* 總計 25.40 英鎊。 **,not at 'all** used as a polite reply to an expression of thanks（回答道謝的客套語）不用謝，哪兒的話：*'Thanks very much for your help.' 'Not at all, it was a pleasure.'* "多謝你幫了忙。" "別客氣，不用謝。" **your 'all** everything you have 所有的一切：*They gave their all* (= fought and died) *in the war.* 他們在戰爭中英勇犧牲，獻出了一切。 ➲ more at ABOVE *prep.*, AFTER *prep.*, END *v.*, END *n.*, FOR *prep.*, SIDE *n.*

■ ***adv.* 1** completely 完全：*She was dressed all in white.* 她穿得一身白。◇ *He lives all alone.* 他索居獨處。◇ *The coffee went all over my skirt.* 咖啡濺了我一裙子。 **2** (*informal*) very 很；十分；非常：*She was all excited.* 她非常激動。◇ *Now don't get all upset about it.* 別再為那件事那麼難過了。 **3 ~ too ...** used to show that sth is more than you would like 太；過分：*I'm all too aware of the problems.* 我實在太明白這些問題了。◇ *The end of* the trip came all too soon. 這次旅行結束得未免太快了。**4** (in sports and games 體育運動、比賽、遊戲) to each side 每方；各：*The score was four all.* 比分是四平。

IDM **all a'long** all the time; from the beginning 一直；始終：*I realized it was in my pocket all along.* 我發覺它一直就在我口袋裏。**all a'round** ➲ ALL ROUND **all the better, harder, etc.** so much better, harder, etc. 更好（或努力等）：*We'll have to work all the harder with two people off sick.* 有兩個人病了沒上班，所以我們得加把勁幹。**all but** **1** almost 幾乎；差不多：*The party was all but over when we arrived.* 我們到的時候，聚會都快要結束了。◇ *It was all but impossible to read his writing.* 他的筆跡幾乎沒法辨認。**2** everything or everyone except sth/sb 除…外全部：*All but one of the plates were damaged.* 除去一隻，盤子全打碎了。**all 'in** **1** physically tired 疲勞；疲憊 SYN **exhausted**：*At the end of the race he felt all in.* 他在賽跑結束時感到筋疲力盡。**2** (*BrE*) including everything 全部包括在內；總共：*The holiday cost £250 all in.* 假期總共花了 250 英鎊。➲ see also ALL-IN **all of sth** (often *ironic*) used to emphasize an amount, a size, etc. usually when it is very small（強調數量、體積等，而實際上通常很小）足足：*It must be all of 100 metres to the car!* 走到車那裏一定足足有 100 米呀！**all 'over** **1** everywhere 到處；處處：*We looked all over for the ring.* 我們到處找那枚戒指。**2** (*informal*) what you would expect of the person mentioned 正如所提到的人那樣；十分像；十足：*That sounds like my sister all over.* 這聽起來很像我的妹妹。**all 'round** (*BrE*) (*NAmE* **all a'round**) **1** in every way; in all respects 在各方面；全面：*a good performance all round* 從各方面看來都精彩的演出 **2** for each person 給每個人：*She bought drinks all round.* 她給每個人都買了飲料。**,all 'there** (*informal*) having a healthy mind; thinking clearly 心理健全；頭腦清醒：*He behaves very oddly at times—I don't think he's quite all there.* 他有時候怪裏怪氣的，我覺得他腦筋不大正常。**be all about sb/sth** used to say what the most important aspect of sth is 最重要的是；主要的是：*It's all about money these days.* 如今談的就是錢。**be all for sth/for doing sth** (*informal*) to believe strongly that sth should be done 堅信某事應完成；完全贊成：*They're all for saving money where they can.* 他們想盡一切辦法存錢。**be all 'over sb** (*informal*) to show a lot of affection for or enthusiasm about sb 向某人獻殷勤；討好某人；諂媚：*He was all over her at the party.* 他在聚會上向她大獻殷勤。**be all 'that** (*US, informal*) to be very attractive or impressive 魅力十足；美麗動人；十分出色：*He thinks he's all that.* 他覺得自己頗有魅力。**be all up (with sb)** (*old-fashioned, informal*) to be the end for sb（某人）完蛋了：*It looks as though it's all up with us now* (= we are ruined, have no further chances, etc.). 看來我們現在全完蛋了。

all- /ɔːl/ *combining form* (in adjectives and adverbs 構成形容詞和副詞) **1** completely 全部；完全；十足：*an all-British cast* 清一色的英國演員陣容 ◇ *an all-inclusive price* 全部包括在內的價格 **2** in the highest degree 最高程度；最：*all-important* 首要 ◇ *all-powerful* 最強大

,all-'action *adj.* [only before noun] having a lot of exciting events 充滿打鬥動作的；全動感的：*an all-action movie* 動作影片

Allah /'ælə/ *noun* the name of God among Muslims 安拉，真主（穆斯林信奉的神）

,all-A'merican *adj.* **1** having good qualities that people think are typically American 具有典型美國人優良素質的；典型美國人的：*a clean-cut all-American boy* 典型十足的美國男孩 **2** (of a sports player 運動員) chosen as one of the best players in the US（被譽為）全美最佳的

,all-a'round (*NAmE*) (*BrE* **,all-'round**) *adj.* [only before noun] **1** including many different subjects, skills, etc. 全面的；多方面的 **2** (of a person 人) with a wide range of skills or abilities 全能的；多才多藝的

allay /ə'leɪ/ *verb* **~ sth** (*formal*) to make sth, especially a feeling, less strong 減輕（尤指情緒）：*to **allay fears/concern/suspicion*** 減輕恐懼；減輕憂慮；減少懷疑

the 'All Blacks *noun* [pl.] the RUGBY team of New Zealand 全黑隊（指新西蘭國家橄欖球隊）

,all-Ca'nadian *adj.* **1** chosen as one of the best in, or representing the whole of, Canada, for example in sports（被選為）全加拿大最佳的；代表加拿大的 **2** having qualities that people think are typically Canadian 具有典型加拿大人素質的；典型加拿大人的

the ,all-'clear *noun* [sing.] **1** a signal (often a sound) which shows that a place or situation is no longer dangerous 解除警報；警報解除信號 **2** if a doctor gives sb **the all-clear**, they tell the person that he/she does not have any health problems 沒有疾病；完全健康 **3** permission to do sth 准許；許可：*The ship was given the all-clear to sail.* 這艘船獲得了航行許可。

,all-'comers *noun* [pl.] anyone who wants to take part in an activity or a competition 所有申請者；所有想參加者

,all-con'sum·ing *adj.* (of an interest 興趣) taking up all of your time or energy 耗盡時間（或精力）的；全身心投入的；令人着迷的：*an all-consuming love of jazz* 對爵士樂的迷戀

'all-day *adj.* [only before noun] continuing for the whole day 整整一天的；全天的：*an all-day meeting* 持續一天的會議

al·le·ga·tion /,ælə'geɪʃn/ *noun* a public statement that is made without giving proof, accusing sb of doing sth that is wrong or illegal（無證據的）說法，指控 SYN **accusation**：*to **investigate/deny/withdraw an allegation*** 調查／否認／撤回指控 ◇ **~ of sth** *Several newspapers **made allegations** of corruption in the city's police department.* 有幾家報紙聲稱該市警察部門腐敗。◇ **~ (of sth) against sb** *allegations of dishonesty against him* 關於他不誠實的多種說法 ◇ **~ about sb/sth** *The committee has made serious allegations about interference in its work.* 委員會嚴正指控其工作受到了干涉。◇ **~ that …** *an allegation that he had been dishonest* 一種關於他不誠實的說法 ➲ SYNONYMS at CLAIM

al·lege /ə'ledʒ/ *verb* [often passive] (*formal*) to state sth as a fact but without giving proof（未提出證據）斷言，指稱，聲稱：**~ (that)** … *The prosecution alleges (that) she was driving carelessly.* 控方指控她不小心駕駛。◇ **it is alleged (that)** … *It is alleged that he mistreated the prisoners.* 據稱他虐待犯人。◇ **be alleged to be, have, etc. sth** *He is alleged to have mistreated the prisoners.* 他被指控虐待犯人。◇ **~ sth** *This procedure should be followed in cases where dishonesty has been alleged.* 指控欺詐的案件應遵循本訴訟程序。▸ **al·leged** *adj.* [only before noun]：(*formal*) *the **alleged attacker/victim/killer*** (= that sb says is one) 涉嫌的襲擊者／受害者／殺人兇手 ◇ *the **alleged attack/offence/incident*** (= that sb says has happened) 聲稱的襲擊／罪行／事件 **al·leged·ly** /ə'ledʒɪdli/ *adv.*：*crimes allegedly committed during the war* 據說是戰爭期間所犯的罪行

al·le·giance /ə'liːdʒəns/ *noun* [U, C] a person's continued support for a political party, religion, ruler, etc.（對政黨、宗教、統治者的）忠誠，效忠，擁戴：*to **switch/transfer/change allegiance*** 轉變／轉移／改變擁戴對象 ◇ ***an oath/a vow/a statement of allegiance*** 效忠宣誓／誓約／聲明 ◇ *People of various party allegiances joined the campaign.* 各個不同政黨的擁護者都參加了這次活動。◇ **~ (to sb/sth)** *to **pledge/swear allegiance*** 宣誓；發誓 ◇ *He affirmed his allegiance to the president.* 他堅稱自己擁戴總統。

al·le·gory /'æləgəri; *NAmE* -gɔːri/ *noun* [C, U] (*pl.* **-ies**) a story, play, picture, etc. in which each character or event is a symbol representing an idea or a quality, such as truth, evil, death, etc.; the use of such symbols 寓言；諷喻；寓言體；諷喻法：*a political allegory* 政治諷喻 ◇ *the poet's use of allegory* 詩人的諷喻手法 ➲ see also FABLE (1) ▸ **al·le·gor·ic·al** /,ælə'gɒrɪkl; *NAmE* -'gɔːr-/ *adj.*：*an **allegorical figure/novel*** 寓言人物；諷喻小說 **al·le·gor·ic·al·ly** *adv.*

al·legro /ə'legrəʊ; *NAmE* -groʊ/ *noun* (*pl.* **-os**) (*music* 音) a piece of music to be played in a fast and lively manner 快板樂曲 ▸ **al·legro** *adj.*, *adv.*

al·lele /ə'liːl/ *noun* (*biology* 生) one of two or more possible forms of a GENE that are found at the same place on a CHROMOSOME 等位基因

al·le·luia /,ælɪ'luːjə/ *noun, exclamation* = HALLELUJAH

A

ˌall-emˈbracing *adj.* (*formal*) including everything 無所不包的；概括一切的

ˌall-enˈcompass·ing *adj.* (*formal*) including everything 包羅萬象的；總括的

Allen key™ /ˈælən kiː/ (*BrE*) (*NAmE* **ˈAllen wrench™**) *noun* a small tool used for turning an Allen screw 艾倫螺釘扳手；六角螺絲小扳手 ➲ picture at KEY

ˈAllen screw™ *noun* a screw with a hole that has six sides 艾倫螺釘，六角螺絲（頂端有六角形孔）

al·ler·gen /ˈælədʒən; *NAmE* ˈælərdʒən/ *noun* a substance that causes an allergy 過敏原，變應原（能引起變態反應或過敏的物質）

al·ler·gic /əˈlɜːdʒɪk; *NAmE* əˈlɜːrdʒɪk/ *adj.* **1** ~ (to sth) having an allergy to sth （對…）變態反應的，變應的，過敏的：*I like cats but unfortunately I'm allergic to them.* 我喜歡貓，但遺憾的是我對貓過敏。**2** caused by an allergy 變態反應性的；變應性的；過敏性的：*an* ***allergic reaction/rash*** 過敏性反應／皮疹 **3** [not before noun] ~ **to sth** (*informal, humorous*) having a strong dislike of sth/sb 對…十分反感；厭惡：*You could see he was allergic to housework.* 你可以看出他很討厭做家務。

al·lergy /ˈælədʒi; *NAmE* ˈælərdʒi/ *noun* (*pl.* **-ies**) ~ (**to sth**) a medical condition that causes you to react badly or feel ill/sick when you eat or touch a particular substance 變態反應；過敏反應：*I have an allergy to animal hair.* 我對動物毛過敏。

al·le·vi·ate /əˈliːvieɪt/ *verb* ~ **sth** to make sth less severe 減輕；緩和；緩解 SYN **ease**：*to alleviate suffering* 減輕苦難 ◇ *A number of measures were taken to alleviate the problem.* 採取了一系列措施緩解這個問題。▸ **al·le·vi·ation** /əˌliːviˈeɪʃn/ *noun* [U]

alley /ˈæli/ *noun* **1** (also **al·ley·way** /ˈæliweɪ/) a narrow passage behind or between buildings （建築群中間或後面的）小街，小巷，胡同：*a* ***narrow/dark alley*** 狹窄的／黑暗的小巷 ➲ VISUAL VOCAB page V3 ➲ see also BLIND ALLEY, BOWLING ALLEY **2** (*NAmE*) (*BrE* **tram·lines**) (*informal*) the pair of parallel lines on a TENNIS or BADMINTON COURT that mark the extra area that is used when four people are playing （網球或羽毛球球場兩側的）雙打線
IDM **(right) up your ˈalley** (*NAmE*) = (RIGHT) UP YOUR STREET at STREET

ˈalley cat *noun* a cat that lives on the streets 流浪貓；（街上的）野貓

al·li·ance /əˈlaɪəns/ *noun* **1** an agreement between countries, political parties, etc. to work together in order to achieve sth that they all want （國家、政黨等的）結盟，聯盟，同盟：*to* ***form/make an alliance*** 結成／締結同盟 ◇ ~ **with sb/sth** *The Social Democrats are now* ***in alliance with*** *the Greens.* 社會民主黨現在與綠黨結成聯盟。◇ ~ **between A and B** *an alliance between education and business to develop the use of technology in schools* 為在學校中發展技術應用而結成的校企聯盟 **2** a group of people, political parties, etc. who work together in order to achieve sth that they all want 結盟團體；聯盟

al·lied 🔑 *adj.*
1 🔑 /ˈælaɪd/ (often **Allied**) [only before noun] connected with countries that unite to fight a war together, especially the countries that fought together against Germany in the First and Second World Wars （國與國協同作戰）結盟的，聯盟的；（第一次世界大戰期間）協約國的；（第二次世界大戰期間）同盟國的：*Italy joined the war on the Allied side in 1915.* * 1915 年，意大利加入協約國參戰。◇ ***allied forces/troops*** 盟軍；盟軍部隊 **2** /ˈælaɪd; əˈlaɪd/ (*formal*) (of two or more things 兩個或以上事物) similar or existing together; connected with sth 類似的；共存的；有關聯的：*medicine, nursing, physiotherapy and other allied professions* 醫藥、護理、理療以及其他相關專業 ◇ ~ **to/with sth** *In this job you will need social skills allied with technical knowledge.* 這項工作需要社交能力和專業知識。➲ see also ALLY

al·li·ga·tor /ˈælɪɡeɪtə(r)/ *noun* a large REPTILE similar to a CROCODILE, with a long tail, hard skin and very big JAWS, that lives in rivers and lakes in N and S America and China 鈍吻鱷

ˈalligator clip *noun* (*especially NAmE*) = CROCODILE CLIP

ˌall-imˈport·ant *adj.* extremely important 極重要的

ˌall-ˈin *adj.* [only before noun] (*BrE*) including the cost of all parts of sth 包括所有費用的 SYN **inclusive**：*an all-in price of £500 with no extras to pay* 共 500 英鎊，無需支付額外費用的全包價格

ˌall-inˈclusive *adj.* including everything or everyone 包括一切的；無所不包的：*Our trips are all-inclusive—there are no hidden costs.* 我們的旅行費用全包，沒有任何隱含性費用。

ˌall-in-ˈone *adj.* [only before noun] (*BrE*) able to do the work of two or more things that are usually separate 多用途的；多功能的；幾合一的：*an all-in-one shampoo and conditioner* 二合一洗髮護髮劑 ▸ **ˌall-in-ˈone** *noun*：*We sell printers and scanners, and all-in-ones that combine the two.* 我們出售打印機、掃描儀，以及打印掃描二合一設備。

al·lit·er·ation /əˌlɪtəˈreɪʃn/ *noun* [U] (*technical* 術語) the use of the same letter or sound at the beginning of words that are close together, as in *sing a song of sixpence* 頭韻，頭韻法（相連單詞的開頭使用同樣的字母或語音）▸ **al·lit·era·tive** /əˈlɪtrətɪv; *NAmE* əˈlɪtəreɪtɪv/ *adj.*

al·lium /ˈæliəm/ *noun* (*technical* 術語) any plant that belongs to the same group as onions and GARLIC 蔥屬植物

ˌall-ˈnight *adj.* [only before noun] **1** (of a place 地方) open through the night 通宵開放的；通宵服務的：*an all-night cafe* 通宵營業的咖啡館 **2** (of an activity 活動) continuing through the night 通宵的：*an all-night party* 通宵聚會

ˌall-ˈnighter *noun* (*NAmE, informal*) a time when you stay awake all night studying 通宵學習；開通宵夜車

al·lo·cate AW /ˈæləkeɪt/ *verb* to give sth officially to sb/sth for a particular purpose 撥…（給）；劃…（歸）；分配…（給）：~ **sth (for sth)** *A large sum has been allocated for buying new books for the library.* 已劃撥了一大筆款子給圖書館購買新書。◇ ~ **sth (to sb/sth)** *They intend to allocate more places to mature students this year.* 今年他們打算給成人學生提供更多的學額。◇ *More resources are being allocated to the project.* 正在調撥更多的資源給這個項目。◇ ~ **sb/sth sth** *The project is being allocated more resources.* 這個項目正獲得更多的資源。

al·lo·ca·tion AW /ˌæləˈkeɪʃn/ *noun* **1** [C] an amount of money, space, etc. that is given to sb for a particular purpose 劃撥的款項；撥給的場地；分配的東西 **2** [U] the act of giving sth to sb for a particular purpose 劃；撥；分配：*the allocation of food to those who need it most* 分配糧食給最需要的人

allo·morph /ˈæləmɔːf; *NAmE* -mɔːrf/ *noun* (*linguistics* 語言) one possible form of a particular MORPHEME. The forms /s/, /z/ and /ɪz/ in *cats, dogs* and *horses* are allomorphs of the plural ending *s*. 語素變體（如 cats、dogs、horses 中的 /s/、/z/ 和 /ɪz/ 是複數詞尾 s 的變體）

allo·phone /ˈæləfəʊn; *NAmE* -foʊn/ *noun* **1** (*phonetics* 語音) a sound that is slightly different from another sound, although both sounds belong to the same PHONEME and the difference does not affect meaning. For example, the /l/ at the beginning of *little* is different from the /l/ at the end. 音位變體，同位音（同一音位有不同發音，如 little 中的第一個 /l/ 與結尾的 /l/ 發音不同）**2** (*CanE*) a person who comes to live in Canada, especially Quebec, from another country, whose first language is neither French nor English （尤指魁北克省）母語非法語（或英語）的加拿大人 ▸ **allo·phone** *adj.*：*Within French-speaking Quebec, anglophone, allophone and Aboriginal minorities also exist.* 在講法語的魁北克省境內也有少數說英語、母語非法語或英語的加拿大人以及土著。

ˌall-or-ˈnothing *adj.* used to describe two extreme situations which are the only possible ones （只可能出現兩

A

種極端局面）全贏或全輸的：*an all-or-nothing decision* (= one which could either be very good or very bad) 孤注一擲的決定

allo·saurus /ˌæləˈsɔːrəs/ *noun* a type of large DINOSAUR 異特龍（大型恐龍）

allot /əˈlɒt; *NAmE* əˈlɑːt/ *verb* (-tt-) to give time, money, tasks, etc. to sb/sth as a share of what is available 分配，配給（時間、錢財等）；分派（任務等）：**~ sth** *I completed the test within the* ***time allotted***. 我在限定的時間內完成了測試。◇ **~ sth to sb/sth** *How much money has been allotted to us?* 我們分到了多少撥款？◇ **~ sb/sth sth** *How much money have we been allotted?* 我們分到了多少撥款？

al·lot·ment /əˈlɒtmənt; *NAmE* əˈlɑːt-/ *noun* **1** [C] (*BrE*) a small area of land in a town which a person can rent in order to grow vegetables on it（城鎮居民可以租來種菜的）小塊土地 **2** [C, U] (*formal*) an amount of sth that sb is given or allowed to have; the process of giving sth to sb 分配物；分配量；份額；分配：*Water allotments to farmers were cut back in the drought.* 在乾旱時期配給農民的水量減少。◇ *the allotment of shares to company employees* 公司雇員股票分配

allo·trope /ˈælətrəʊp; *NAmE* -troʊp/ *noun* (*chemistry* 化) one of the different forms in which a chemical element exists. For example, diamond and GRAPHITE are allotropes of CARBON. 同素異形體

ˌall-ˈout *adj.* [only before noun] using or involving every possible effort and done in a very determined way 全力以赴的：*all-out war* 全面戰爭 ◇ *an all-out attack on the opposition* 向對方的全面進攻 ▸ **ˌall ˈout** *adv.*：*We're going all out to win.* 我們竭盡全力爭取勝利。

ˈall-over *adj.* [only before noun] covering the whole of sth 遍佈表面的：*an all-over tan* 全身曬黑的皮膚

allow 🔑 /əˈlaʊ/ *verb*

▸ **LET SB/STH DO STH 允許 1** 🔑 to let sb/sth do sth; to let sth happen or be done 允許；准許：**~ sb to do sth** *His parents won't allow him to stay out late.* 他的父母不會允許他在外待到很晚。◇ *He* ***is not allowed to*** *stay out late.* 他不可以在外待到很晚。◇ *They shouldn't be allowed to get away with it.* 不應就此放過他們。◇ **~ sth to do sth** *He allowed his mind to wander.* 他聽任自己的思緒信馬由韁。◇ **~ yourself to do sth** *She won't allow herself to be dictated to.* 她不會聽人擺佈的。◇ **~ sth** *Smoking is not allowed in the hall.* 大廳內不准吸煙。 **2** 🔑 **~ sb/yourself sth** to let sb have sth 給予：*You're allowed an hour to complete the test.* 你們有一個小時的時間來完成這次測驗。◇ *I'm not allowed visitors.* 我不可以接見來訪者。 **3** 🔑 [usually passive] to let sb/sth go into, through, out of, etc. a place 允許進入（或出去、通過）：**~ sth** *No dogs allowed* (= you cannot bring them in). 不准攜狗入內。◇ **~ sb/sth + adv./prep.** *The prisoners are* ***allowed out*** *of their cells for two hours a day.* 囚犯每天可以放風兩小時。◇ *The crowd parted to* ***allow her through***. 人群向兩旁閃開讓她通過。◇ *You won't be* ***allowed up*** (= out of bed) *for several days.* 你將有幾天不能下牀。

▸ **MAKE POSSIBLE 使可能 4** 🔑 **~ sth** to make sth possible 使可能：*A ramp allows easy access for wheelchairs.* 坡道便於輪椅進出。➲ LANGUAGE BANK at PROCESS

▸ **TIME/MONEY/FOOD, ETC. 時間；金錢；食物 5** 🔑 **~ sth (for sb/sth)** to make sure that you have enough of sth for a particular purpose（為某目的）留出，給出：*You need to allow three metres of fabric for the dress.* 這身衣服你需要用三米布料。

▸ **ACCEPT/ADMIT 接受；承認 6** (*formal*) to accept or admit sth; to agree that sth is true or correct 接受；承認；同意（某事屬實或正確）：**~ sth** *The judge allowed my claim.* 法官同意我的要求。◇ (in a court of law) *'Objection!' 'I'll allow it.'* "反對！" "反對有效。" ◇ **~ that ...** *He refuses to allow that such a situation could arise.* 他拒不承認這種情況可能發生。◇ **~ sb sth** *She was very helpful when my mother was ill—I'll allow you that.* 我母親生病時她幫了很大的忙，我同意你說的這一點。

➲ compare DISALLOW

IDM **alˌlow ˈme** used to offer help politely（禮貌地表示主動幫忙）讓我來 ➲ more at REIN *n.*

PHR V **alˈlow for sb/sth** 🔑 to consider or include sb/sth when calculating sth 考慮到；把…計算在內：*It will take about an hour to get there, allowing for traffic delays.* 考慮到交通阻塞，到那裏大約需要一小時。◇ *All these factors must be allowed for.* 所有這些因素都必須估計進去。 **alˈlow of sth** (*formal*) to make sth possible 容許；使有可能：*The facts allow of only one explanation.* 這些事實只可能有一種解釋。

al·low·able /əˈlaʊəbl/ *adj.* **1** that is allowed, especially by law or by a set of rules（法律、規章等）允許的，承認的，容許的 **2** (*BrE*) **allowable** amounts of money are amounts that you do not have to pay tax on 可減免的（稅收部份）

al·low·ance /əˈlaʊəns/ *noun* **1** an amount of money that is given to sb regularly or for a particular purpose 津貼；補貼；補助：*an allowance of $20 a day* 每天 20 元補貼 ◇ *a* ***clothing/living/travel allowance*** 服裝 / 生活 / 交通補貼 ◇ *Do you get an allowance for clothing?* 你有服裝補貼嗎？➲ see also ATTENDANCE ALLOWANCE **2** the amount of sth that is allowed in a particular situation 限額；定量：*a baggage allowance of 20 kilos* 行李限重 20 公斤 **3** (*BrE*) an amount of money that can be earned or received before you start paying tax 免稅額：*personal tax allowances* 個人所得免稅額 **4** (*especially NAmE*) = POCKET MONEY (1)

IDM **make allowance(s) for sth** to consider sth, for example when you are making a decision or planning sth 考慮到，估計到（如在制訂決策或計劃時）：*The budget made allowance for inflation.* 預算考慮到了通貨膨脹。◇ *The plan makes no allowance for people working at different rates.* 這個計劃沒有把人們工作速度不同考慮在內。 **make allowances (for sb)** to allow sb to behave in a way that you would not usually accept, because of a problem or because there is a special reason 體諒；諒解

alloy *noun, verb*

■ ***noun*** /ˈælɔɪ/ [C, U] a metal that is formed by mixing two types of metal together, or by mixing metal with another substance 合金：*Brass is an alloy of copper and zinc.* 黃銅是銅鋅合金。

■ ***verb*** /əˈlɔɪ/ **~ sth (with sth)** (*technical* 術語) to mix one metal with another, especially one of lower value 把…鑄成合金（尤指摻入一種價值低的金屬）

ˌall-ˈparty *adj.* [usually before noun] involving all political parties 所有政黨的；各黨派的；跨黨派的：*all-party support* 各黨派的支持

ˌall-points ˈbulletin *noun* (*abbr.* **APB**) (*US*) a radio message sent to every officer of a police force, giving details of people who are suspected of a crime, of stolen vehicles, etc. 全面通緝通告（警方無線電聯絡信息，通告嫌犯特徵、失竊詳情等）

ˌall-ˈpowerful *adj.* having complete power 有無上權力的；擁有全權的：*the all-powerful secret police* 權力無限的秘密警察

ˌall-ˈpurpose *adj.* [only before noun] having many different uses; able to be used in many situations 多用途的；通用的

ˌall-purpose ˈflour (*NAmE*) (*BrE* **ˌplain ˈflour**) *noun* [U] flour that does not contain BAKING POWDER（不含發酵粉的）普通麪粉 ➲ compare SELF-RISING FLOUR

all ˈright 🔑 (also *non-standard* or *informal* **al·right**) *adj., adv., exclamation*

■ ***adj., adv.* 1** 🔑 acceptable; in an acceptable manner 可接受（的）；滿意（的）**SYN** OK：*Is the coffee all right?* 這咖啡還滿意嗎？◇ *Are you getting along all right in your new job?* 你的新工作順利嗎？◇ *'They're off to Spain next week.' 'It's* ***all right for some****, isn't it?'* (= some people are lucky) "他們下週去西班牙。" "有些人就是幸運，是不是？" **2** 🔑 safe and well 安全健康（的）；平安無恙（的）**SYN** OK：*I hope the children are all right.* 我希望孩子們平安無事。◇ *Do you feel all right?* 你感覺還好嗎？➲ SYNONYMS at WELL **3** 🔑 only just good enough 尚可；還算可以 **SYN** OK：*Your work is all right but I'm sure you could do better.* 你的工作還算可以，但我相信你可以幹得更好。 **4** 🔑 that can be allowed 可允許（的）；可以（的）**SYN** OK：*Are you sure it's all right for me to leave early?* 你確定我早離開

A

沒問題嗎？ **5** (*informal*) used to emphasize that there is no doubt about sth（加強語氣）無疑，確實：*'Are you sure it's her?' 'Oh, it's her all right.'* "你肯定是她嗎？" "哦，確實是她。"

IDM **I'm all ˈright, Jack** (*BrE, informal*) used by or about sb who is happy with their own life and does not care about other people's problems 我過得很好（或愜意）（別人的事我是不管的） **it'll be all ˌright on the ˈnight** (*saying*) used to say that a performance, an event, etc. will be successful even if the preparations for it have not gone well（演出、活動等）到時候自會成功的；車到山前必有路 ➲ more at BIT

■ *exclamation* **1** 🔑 used to check that sb agrees or understands（確保對方同意或理解）如何，是不是 SYN **OK**：*We've got to get up early, all right?* 我們得早起牀，可以吧？ **2** 🔑 used to say that you agree（表示同意）好，行，可以 SYN **OK**：*'Can you do it?' 'Oh, all right.'* "你能幹好這件事嗎？" "噢，能。" **3** 🔑 used when accepting thanks for help or a favour, or when sb says they are sorry（回答對方的感謝或道歉）不要緊，沒什麼 SYN **OK**：*'I'm really sorry.' 'That's all right, don't worry.'* "實在對不起。" "沒啥，別操心。" **4** 🔑 used to get sb's attention（引起注意）哎 SYN **OK**：*All right class, turn to page 20.* 好啦，同學們，翻到第 20 頁。 **5** (*BrE, informal*) used to say hello（打招呼）你好：*'All right, Bill.' 'All right.'* "你好，比爾。" "你好。" **6 you're all right** (*BrE, slang*) used to refuse an offer or invitation, especially one that you think is unreasonable or not very good 不用啦（表示拒絕，尤其認為不合理或不太好的提議或邀請）：*'Could I interest you in our special offer?' 'No, you're all right, mate.'* "您要不要考慮一下我們的特價商品呢？" "不用啦，夥計。"

ˌall-ˈround (*BrE*) (*NAmE* **ˌall-aˈround**) *adj.* [only before noun] **1** including many different subjects, skills, etc. 全面的；多方面的：*an all-round education* 培養全面發展的教育 **2** (of a person 人) with a wide range of skills or abilities 全能的；多才多藝的：*She's a good all-round player.* 她是個優秀的全能選手。

all-ˈrounder *noun* (*BrE*) a person who has many different skills and abilities 多才多藝者；全才；通才

ˌAll ˈSaints' Day *noun* a Christian festival in honour of the SAINTS, held on 1 November 諸聖節，眾聖日（基督教節日，11 月 1 日）

ˌall-ˈsinging, ˌall-ˈdancing *adj.* [only before noun] (*BrE, informal*) (of a machine or system 機器或系統) having a lot of advanced technical features and therefore able to perform many different functions 先進的；多功能的

ˌAll ˈSouls' Day *noun* a Christian festival in honour of the dead, held on 2 November 萬靈節，追思節（基督教節日，11 月 2 日）

all·spice /ˈɔːlspaɪs/ *noun* [U] the dried BERRIES of a tree from the West Indies, used in cooking as a spice 多香果（西印度群島多香果的果乾，用作調味香料）

ˈall-star *adj.* [only before noun] including many famous actors, players, etc. 全明星（或演員、運動員等）組成的：*an all-star cast* 全明星陣容

ˌall-terrain ˈboard *noun* = MOUNTAINBOARD

ˌall-terrain ˈvehicle *noun* = ATV

ˌall-ˈticket *adj.* [usually before noun] for which tickets need to be obtained in advance 需預先購票的：*an all-ticket match* 全部憑票入場的比賽

ˈall-time *adj.* [only before noun] (used when you are comparing things or saying how good or bad sth is) of any time（用於比較或表示好壞程度）空前的，創紀錄的，一向的：*one of the all-time great players* 歷來最傑出的選手之一 ◊ *my all-time favourite song* 我一直喜愛的歌曲 ◊ *Unemployment reached an all-time record of 3 million.* 失業人數高達 300 萬的創紀錄數字。◊ *Profits are at an* ***all-time high/low***. 利潤空前地高／低。

al·lude /əˈluːd/ *verb*

PHR V **alˈlude to sb/sth** (*formal*) to mention sth in an indirect way 間接提到；暗指；影射 ➲ see also ALLUSION

al·lure /əˈlʊə(r); *NAmE* əˈlʊr/ *noun* [U] (*formal*) the quality of being attractive and exciting 誘惑力；引誘力；吸引力：*sexual allure* 性誘惑 ◊ *the allure of the big city* 大城市的吸引力

al·lur·ing /əˈlʊərɪŋ; *NAmE* əˈlʊrɪŋ/ *adj.* attractive and exciting in a mysterious way 誘人的；迷人的；有吸引力的：*an alluring smile* 迷人的微笑 ▸ **al·lur·ing·ly** *adv.*

al·lu·sion /əˈluːʒn/ *noun* [C, U] ~ (**to sb/sth**) (*formal*) something that is said or written that refers to or mentions another person or subject in an indirect way (= ALLUDES to it) 暗指；引喻；典故：*His statement was seen as an allusion to the recent drug-related killings.* 他的聲明被視為暗指最近與毒品有關的多起兇殺案。◊ *Her poetry is full of obscure literary allusion.* 她的詩隨處可見晦澀的文學典故。

al·lu·sive /əˈluːsɪv/ *adj.* (*formal*) containing allusions 間接提到的；暗指的；影射的；含典故的：*an allusive style of writing* 引經據典的寫作風格

al·lu·vial /əˈluːviəl/ *adj.* [usually before noun] (*geology* 地) made of sand and earth that is left by rivers or floods（河流、洪水）沖積的，淤積的

al·lu·vium /əˈluːviəm/ *noun* [U] (*geology* 地) sand and earth that is left by rivers or floods 沖積物；沖積層

ˌall-ˈweather *adj.* [usually before noun] suitable for all types of weather 適合各種氣候的；全天候的：*an all-weather football pitch* 全天候足球場

ˌall-wheel ˈdrive *noun* (*especially NAmE*) = FOUR-WHEEL DRIVE

ally 🔑 *noun, verb*

> **WORD FAMILY**
> **ally** *verb, noun*
> **allied** *adj.*
> **alliance** *noun*

■ *noun* /ˈælaɪ/ (*pl.* **-ies**) **1** 🔑 [C] a country that has agreed to help and support another country, especially in case of a war（尤指戰時的）同盟國 **2** 🔑 [C] a person who helps and supports sb who is in a difficult situation, especially a politician（尤指從政者的）盟友，支持者：*a close ally and friend of the prime minister* 首相的一個親密盟友和夥伴 **3 the Allies** [pl.] the group of countries including Britain and the US that fought together in the First and Second World Wars（第一次世界大戰中的）協約國；（第二次世界大戰中的）同盟國

■ *verb* 🔑 /əˈlaɪ/ (**al·lies**, **ally·ing**, **al·lied**, **al·lied**) [T, I] ~ (**yourself**) **with sb/sth** to give your support to another group or country 與…結盟：*The prince allied himself with the Scots.* 王子與蘇格蘭人結盟。

-ally *suffix* (makes adverbs from adjectives that end in *-al* 以 -al 結尾的形容詞加 ly 構成副詞)：*magically* 有魔力地 ◊ *sensationally* 轟動地

Alma Mater /ˌælmə ˈmɑːtə(r); ˈmeɪtə(r)/ (also **alma mater**) *noun* [sing.] (*especially NAmE*) the school, college or university that sb went to 母校

al·manac (also *less frequent* **al·man·ack**) /ˈɔːlmənæk; ˈæl-/ *noun* **1** a book that is published every year giving information for that year about a particular subject or activity 年鑒 **2** a book that gives information about the sun, moon, times of the TIDES (= the rise and fall of the sea level), etc. for each day of the year 曆書；年曆

al·mighty /ɔːlˈmaɪti/ *adj.* **1** (in prayers 祈禱時說) having complete power 全能的：*Almighty God, have mercy on us.* 全能的上主，請垂憐我們。 **2** [only before noun] (*informal*) very great or severe 極大的；十分嚴重的：*an* ***almighty bang/crash/roar*** 砰的／嘩啦／轟的一聲巨響 **3** (*taboo, offensive*) used in the expressions shown in the example, to express surprise or anger（表示驚奇或憤怒）全能的，有無限權力的：*Christ/God Almighty! What the hell do you think you are doing?* 全能的基督／上帝！你認為你究竟在幹什麼？ **4 the Almighty** *noun* [sing.] God 全能者（指上主）

al·mond /ˈɑːmənd/ *noun* the flat pale sweet nut of the **almond tree** used in cooking and to make almond oil 扁桃仁；杏仁（扁桃樹的果仁）：*ground almonds* 杏仁粉 ◊ ***blanched almonds*** (= with their skins removed) 去皮杏仁 ◊ *almond paste* 杏仁醬 ◊ *almond eyes* (= eyes shaped like almonds) 杏眼（形似杏仁的眼睛） ➲ VISUAL VOCAB page V32

al·most 🔑 /ˈɔːlməʊst; *NAmE* -moʊst/ *adv.* not quite 幾乎；差不多 SYN **nearly**：*I like almost all of them.* 我差不多所有的都喜歡。◊ *It's a mistake they* *almost always make.* 這是他們幾乎總要犯的錯誤。◇ *The story is almost certainly false.* 這個故事幾乎肯定是虛構的。◇ *It's almost time to go.* 是差不多該走的時候了。◇ *Dinner's almost ready.* 飯就要做好了。◇ *He slipped and almost fell.* 他滑了一下，險些跌倒。◇ *Their house is almost opposite ours.* 他們的房子幾乎正對着我們的房子。◇ *They'll eat almost anything.* 他們幾乎什麼都吃。◇ *Almost no one* (= hardly anyone) *believed him.* 幾乎沒人相信他的話。

Synonyms 同義詞辨析

almost / nearly / practically

These three words have similar meanings and are used frequently with the following words. 上述三個近義詞常與下列詞語連用：

almost ~	nearly ~	practically ~
certainly	(numbers)	all
all	all	every
every	always	no
entirely	every	nothing
impossible	finished	impossible
empty	died	anything

- They are used in positive sentences. 三詞均用於肯定句：*She almost/nearly/practically missed her train.* 她差點兒誤了火車。They can be used before words like *all, every* and *everybody.* 三詞均可用於 all、every、everybody 等詞前：*Nearly all the students have bikes.* 幾乎所有學生都有自行車。◇ *I've got practically every CD they've made.* 他們灌製的每張激光唱片我幾乎都有。**Practically** is used more in spoken than in written English. **Nearly** is the most common with numbers. * practically 多用於口語，少用於書面語。nearly 最常與數字連用：*There were nearly 200 people at the meeting.* 與會者有近 200 人。They can also be used in negative sentences but it is more common to make a positive sentence with **only just**. 三詞亦可用於否定句，但是用 only just 構成肯定句更常見：*We only just got there in time.* (or 或：*We almost/nearly didn't get there in time.*) 我們險些未能及時趕到那兒。
- **Almost** and **practically** can be used before words like *any, anybody, anything,* etc. * almost 和 practically 均可用於 any、anybody、anything 等詞前：*I'll eat almost anything.* 我幾乎吃什麼都行。You can also use them before *no, nobody, never,* etc. but it is much more common to use **hardly** or **scarcely** with *any, anybody, ever,* etc. 這兩個詞亦可用於 no、nobody、never 等詞前，但是這類情況更常用 hardly 或 scarcely 與 any、anybody、ever 等詞搭配：*She's hardly ever in.* (or 或：*She's almost never in.*) 她幾乎從來不在家。
- **Almost** can be used when you are saying that one thing is similar to another. 表示某物與另一物相似可用 almost：*The boat looked almost like a toy.* 這船看上去簡直像個玩具。
- In *BrE* you can use *very* and *so* before **nearly**. 在英式英語中，nearly 前可用 very 和 so：*He was very nearly caught.* 他差點兒被抓住。

➲ note at HARDLY

alms /ɑːmz/ *noun* [pl.] (*old-fashioned*) money, clothes and food that are given to poor people 施捨物（或金）；救濟金（或物）

alms·house /ˈɑːmzhaʊs/ *noun* (in the past in Britain) a house owned by a charity where poor people (usually the old) lived without paying rent （英國舊時的）救濟院，貧民所

aloe /ˈæləʊ; *NAmE* ˈæloʊ/ *noun* a tropical plant with thick leaves with sharp points that contain a lot of water. The juice of some types of aloe is used in medicine and COSMETICS. 蘆薈（有些品種的汁液可用於製藥和化妝品）

aloe vera /ˌæləʊ ˈvɪərə; *NAmE* ˌæloʊ ˈvɪrə/ *noun* **1** [U] a substance that comes from a type of aloe, used in products such as skin creams 蘆薈汁（用於生產護膚霜等） **2** [C] the aloe that this substance comes from 真蘆薈

aloft /əˈlɒft; *NAmE* əˈlɔːft/ *adv.* (*formal*) high in the air 在空中高處

aloha /əˈləʊhə; *NAmE* əˈloʊhə/ *exclamation* a Hawaiian word meaning 'love', used to say hello or gooodbye 你好，再見（夏威夷語意為"愛"）

a'loha shirt *noun* = HAWAIIAN SHIRT

Which Word? 詞語辨析

alone / lonely / lone

- **Alone**, and **on your own** / **by yourself** (which are less formal and are the normal phrases used in spoken English), describe a person or thing that is separate from others. They do not mean that the person is unhappy. * alone 和不太正式、常用於英語口語的 on your own、by yourself 均指獨自，但無孤獨之意：*I like being alone in the house.* 我喜歡獨自一人待在家裏。◇ *I'm going to London by myself next week.* 我準備下星期一個人去倫敦。◇ *I want to finish this on my own* (= without anyone's help). 我想獨自完成這項工作。
- **Lone/solitary/single** mean that there is only one person or thing there; **lone** and **solitary** may sometimes suggest that the speaker thinks the person involved is lonely. * lone、solitary、single 意為單獨；lone 和 solitary 有時可能暗示說話者認為談及的人孤單：*a lone jogger in the park* 在公園裏獨自慢跑的一個人◇ *long, solitary walks* 獨自一人長途行走
- **Lonely** (*NAmE* also **lonesome**) means that you are alone and sad. * lonely（美式英語亦作 lonesome）意為孤寂：*a lonely child* 孤寂的孩子◇ *Sam was very lonely when he first moved to New York.* 薩姆剛搬到紐約時非常寂寞。It can also describe places or activities that make you feel lonely. * lonely 還可描述使人感到孤寂的地方或活動：*a lonely house* 一座冷清的房子

alone 🔑 /əˈləʊn; *NAmE* əˈloʊn/ *adj.* [not before noun], *adv.*
1 🔑 without any other people 獨自：*I don't like going out alone at night.* 我不喜歡夜晚單獨外出。◇ *He lives alone.* 他獨居獨處。◇ *Finally the two of us were* ***alone together***. 最後只有我們兩人在一起。◇ *She was sitting* ***all alone*** *in the hall.* 她一個人坐在大廳裏。◇ *Tom is* ***not alone in*** *finding Rick hard to work with.* 並不只是湯姆一人認為里克難以共事。 **2** 🔑 without the help of other people or things 獨力；單獨：*It's hard bringing up children alone.* 一個人獨力撫養孩子是艱難的。◇ *The assassin said he had acted alone.* 暗殺者聲稱他當時單獨行動。 **3** 🔑 lonely and unhappy or without any friends 孤苦伶仃；無依無靠；孤獨；寂寞：*Carol felt all alone in the world.* 卡羅爾感到自己在世界上無依無靠。◇ *I've been so alone since you went away.* 你走了以後我一直很寂寞。 **4** used after a noun or pronoun to show that the person or thing mentioned is the only one （用於名詞或代詞後）唯一，只有：*You can't blame anyone else; you alone made the decision.* 你不能責怪任何人，是你一人做的決定。 **5** used after a noun or pronoun to emphasize one particular thing （用於名詞或代詞後以加強語氣）僅僅，單，只：*The shoes alone cost £200.* 僅鞋子一項就花了 200 英鎊。

IDM **go it a'lone** to do sth without help from anyone 獨力；獨自幹；單幹：*Andrew decided to go it alone and start his own business.* 安德魯決定獨力開辦自己的企業。 **leave/let sb alone** 🔑 to stop annoying sb or trying to

A

get their attention 不打擾；不驚動：*She's asked to be left alone but the press photographers follow her everywhere.* 她要求別打擾她，但是攝影記者到處都跟着她。**leave/let sth alone** to stop touching, changing, or moving sth 不碰；不變動；不移動：*I've told you before—leave my things alone!* 我告訴過你，別碰我的東西！**let alone** used after a statement to emphasize that because the first thing is not true or possible, the next thing cannot be true or possible either 更不用說：*There isn't enough room for us, let alone any guests.* 連我們都沒有足夠的空間，更不用說客人了。**stand a'lone** **1** to be independent or not connected with other people, organizations or ideas 單獨；獨立：*These islands are too small to stand alone as independent states.* 這些島嶼太小，不能算是獨立的國家。**2** to be not near other objects or buildings 孤零零地矗立：*The arch once stood alone at the entrance to the castle.* 拱門曾經孤零零地矗立在城堡的入口處。➲ more at TIME *n.*

along /ə'lɒŋ; *NAmE* ə'lɔːŋ; ə'lɑːŋ/ *prep., adv.*
■ ***prep.*** **1** from one end to or towards the other end of sth 沿着；順着：*They walked slowly along the road.* 他們沿公路慢慢走。◇ *I looked along the shelves for the book I needed.* 我在書架上一格一格地找我需要的那本書。**2** in a line that follows the side of sth long 靠着…邊：*Houses had been built along both sides of the river.* 沿河兩岸已蓋起了房屋。**3** at a particular point on or beside sth long 沿着…的某處（或旁邊）：*You'll find his office just along the corridor.* 沿着走廊你就可以找到他的辦公室。
■ ***adv.*** HELP For the special uses of **along** in phrasal verbs, look at the entries for the verbs. For example **get along with sb** is in the phrasal verb section at **get**. * along 在短語動詞中的特殊用法見有關動詞詞條。如 get along with sb 在詞條 get 的短語動詞部份。**1** forward 向前：*I was just walking along singing to myself.* 我獨自唱着歌向前走去。◇ *He pointed out various landmarks as we drove along.* 我們驅車前行時，他指出各種各樣的地標。**2** with sb（與某人）一道，一起：*We're going for a swim. Why don't you come along?* 我們要去游泳。你幹嗎不一起去？◇ *I'll be along* (= I'll join you) *in a few minutes.* 過一會兒我就來。**3** towards a better state or position 越來越（好）：*The book's coming along nicely.* 這本書愈來愈好看了。
IDM **along with sb/sth** in addition to sb/sth; in the same way as sb/sth 除…以外（還）；與…同樣地：*She lost her job when the factory closed, along with hundreds of others.* 工廠倒閉時，她和成百上千的其他人一樣失去了工作。

along·side /əˌlɒŋ'saɪd; *NAmE* əˌlɔːŋ-; əˌlɑːŋ-/ *prep.*
1 next to or at the side of sth 在…旁邊；沿着…的邊：*A police car pulled up alongside us.* 一輛警車在我們旁邊停了下來。**2** together with or at the same time as sth/sb 與…一起；與…同時：*Traditional beliefs still flourish alongside a modern urban lifestyle.* 現代城市生活方式盛行的同時，傳統信念仍然大行其道。▸ **along·side** *adv.*：*Nick caught up with me and rode alongside.* 尼克趕上了我，跟我並騎前進。

aloo (also **alu**) /'æluː/ *noun* [U] (*IndE*) potatoes 土豆

aloof /ə'luːf/ *adj.* [not usually before noun] not friendly or interested in other people 冷漠；冷淡 SYN **distant, remote** ▸ **aloof·ness** *noun* [U]
IDM **keep/hold (yourself) aloof | remain/stand aloof** to not become involved in sth; to show no interest in people 不參與；遠離；無動於衷；漠不關心：*The Emperor kept himself aloof from the people.* 這個皇帝對人民漠不關心。

alo·pe·cia /ˌæləˈpiːʃə/ *noun* [U] (*medical* 醫) loss of hair from the head and body, often caused by illness 脫髮，禿頭（常因疾病而起）

aloud /ə'laʊd/ *adv.*
1 in a voice that other people can hear 出聲地：*The teacher listened to the children **reading aloud**.* 老師聽着孩子們朗讀。◇ *He read the letter aloud to us.* 他把信大聲唸給我們聽。◇ *'What am I going to do?' she wondered aloud.* "我怎麼辦呢？" 她疑惑地說。➲ note at LOUD **2** in a loud voice 大聲地：*She cried aloud in protest.* 她大聲抗議。IDM see THINK *v.*

al·paca /æl'pækə/ *noun* **1** [C] a S American animal that is related to the LLAMA and has long hair 羊駝（南美長毛動物）**2** [U] a type of soft wool or cloth made from the hair of the alpaca, used especially for making expensive clothes 羊駝毛；羊駝呢：*an alpaca coat* 羊駝毛外衣

alpha /'ælfə/ *noun* the first letter of the Greek alphabet (Α, α) 希臘字母表的第 1 個字母

al·pha·bet /'ælfəbet/ *noun*
a set of letters or symbols in a fixed order used for writing a language（一種語言的）字母表，全部字母 ORIGIN From *alpha* and *beta*, the first two letters of the Greek alphabet. 源自希臘字母表的頭兩個字母 alpha 和 beta。

al·pha·bet·ic /ˌælfəˈbetɪk/ (also **al·pha·bet·ic·al**) *adj.* (of a written or printed character 手寫或印刷字符) being one of the letters of the alphabet, rather than a number or other symbol （屬於）字母的 ➲ compare NON-ALPHABETIC

al·pha·bet·ic·al /ˌælfəˈbetɪkl/ *adj.*
1 according to the correct order of the letters of the alphabet 按字母（表）順序的：*The names on the list are **in alphabetical order**.* 名單上的名字是按字母順序排列的。**2** = ALPHABETIC ▸ **al·pha·bet·ic·al·ly** /-kli/ *adv.*：***arranged/listed/stored alphabetically*** 按字母順序安排／列表／存貯

al·pha·bet·ize (*BrE* also **-ise**) /'ælfəbətaɪz/ *verb* **~ sth** to arrange a list of words in alphabetical order 按字母順序排列

ˌalphabet 'soup *noun* [U] **1** (*informal*) language that is extremely difficult to understand, especially because it contains many symbols or abbreviations（因含有許多符號或縮略語等而極難懂的）代號語言 **2** soup that contains PASTA in the shape of letters 字母湯（湯裏含有字母形麪食）

ˌalpha 'male *noun* [usually sing.] the man or male animal in a particular group who has the most power 老大（某一群體中最有權力的男子或雄性動物）

alpha·numer·ic /ˌælfənjuːˈmerɪk; *NAmE* -nuːˈm-/ (also **alpha·numer·ic·al** /-ɪkl/) *adj.* containing both letters and numbers 含有字母和數字的；字母與數字並用的：*an alphanumeric code* 含字母和數字的代碼

'alpha particle *noun* (*technical* 術語) the NUCLEUS of a HELIUM atom; a PARTICLE with a positive electrical charge passing through it, that is produced in a nuclear reaction * α 粒子

'alpha test *noun* (*technical* 術語) a test done by a company on a new product that they are developing * α 測試（公司試驗本身正在開發的新產品）➲ compare BETA TEST ▸ **'alpha-test** *verb* **~ sth**

al·pine /'ælpaɪn/ *adj., noun*
■ ***adj.*** existing in or connected with high mountains, especially the Alps in Central Europe 高山的；（尤指中歐）阿爾卑斯山的
■ ***noun*** any plant that grows best on mountains 高山植物

al·pi·nist /'ælpɪnɪst/ *noun* a person who climbs high mountains as a sport, especially in the Alps 登高山者（尤指阿爾卑斯山）▸ **al·pi·nism** /'ælpɪnɪzəm/ *noun* [U]

al·ready /ɔːl'redi/ *adv.*
1 before now or before a particular time in the past 已經；早已：*'Lunch?' 'No thanks, I've already eaten.'* "午餐？" "不，謝謝，我已吃過了。" ◇ *We got there early but Mike had already left.* 我們及早到了那裏，但是邁克已經離開了。**2** used to express surprise that sth has happened so soon or so early（表示驚奇）已經，都：*Is it 10 o'clock already?* 都 10 點鐘了？◇ *You're not leaving already, are you?* 你已經不打算走了，是不是？**3** used to emphasize that a situation or problem exists（強調情況或問題存在）已經：*I'm already late.* 我已經遲到了。◇ *There are far too many people already. We can't take any more.* 已經有太多的人了。我們再也接待不了啦。IDM see ENOUGH *pron.*

A

British/American 英式/美式英語

already / just / yet

- **Already** and **yet** are usually used with the present perfect tense, but in *NAmE* they can also be used with the simple past tense. * already 和 yet 通常與現在完成時連用，但在美式英語中還可與簡單過去時連用： *I already did it.* 我已經完成了。◇ *Did you eat yet?* 你吃飯了嗎？
- However, this is much more common in spoken than in written English and some Americans do not consider it acceptable, even in speech. The present perfect is more common in *NAmE* and almost always used in *BrE*. 不過，此用法多見於口語，而且有些美國人認為，即使在口語中此用法也不可取。在美式英語中較常用現在完成時，在英式英語中則幾乎總是用現在完成時表示： *I've already done it.* 我已經完成了。◇ *Have you eaten yet?* 你吃飯了嗎？
- **Just** is mostly used with the perfect tenses in *BrE* and with the simple past in *NAmE*. * just 在英式英語中多與完成時連用，在美式英語中則多與簡單過去時連用： *(BrE) I've just had some bad news.* ◇ *(NAmE) I just got some bad news.* 我剛得到一些壞消息。

al·right /ɔːlˈraɪt/ *adv.* *(informal)* = ALL RIGHT **HELP** Some people consider that this form should not be used in formal writing. 有人認為正式書面語中不應該用此形式。

Al·sa·tian /ælˈseɪʃn/ *(BrE)* (also ˌ**German** ˈ**shepherd** *NAmE, BrE*) *noun* a large dog, often trained to help the police, to guard buildings or (especially in the US) to help blind people find their way 德國牧羊犬（常訓練成警犬，看家護院，尤其在美國還給盲人帶路）

also 🔑 /ˈɔːlsəʊ; *NAmE* ˈɔːlsoʊ/ *adv.* (not used with negative verbs 不與否定動詞連用) in addition; too 而且；此外；也；同樣： *She's fluent in French and German. She also speaks a little Italian.* 她的法語和德語講得流利，也會説一點意大利語。◇ *rubella, **also known as** German measles* * rubella （風疹），亦稱 German measles（德國麻疹）◇ *I didn't like it that much. Also, it was much too expensive.* 我並不怎麼喜歡它，再説它太貴了。◇ *Jake's father had also been a doctor* (= both Jake and his father were doctors). 傑克和他的父親都是醫生。◇ *She was **not only** intelligent **but also** very musical.* 她不僅聰明，而且極具音樂天分。⊃ LANGUAGE BANK at ADDITION

Which Word? 詞語辨析

also / as well / too

- **Also** is more formal than **as well** and **too**, and it usually comes before the main verb or after *be*. * also 比 as well 和 too 正式，通常置於主要動詞之前或 be 之後： *I went to New York last year, and I also spent some time in Washington.* 我去年去了紐約，還在華盛頓待了些時間。 In *BrE* it is not usually used at the end of a sentence. **Too** is much more common in spoken and informal English. It is usually used at the end of a sentence. 在英式英語中，also 通常不置於句末。too 則多用於非正式的口語，且通常置於句末： *'I'm going home now.' 'I'll come too.'* "現在我要回家了。" "我也一塊兒去。" In *BrE* **as well** is used like **too**, but in *NAmE* it sounds formal or old-fashioned. 在英式英語中，as well 的用法同 too，但在美式英語中，as well 顯得正式或過時。
- When you want to add a second negative point in a negative sentence, use **not ... either**. 在否定句中要增加一個否定成分可用 not ... either： *She hasn't phoned and she hasn't written either.* 她沒來過電話，也沒有寫信。 If you are adding a negative point to a positive one, you can use **not ... as well/too**. 在肯定句中要增加一個否定成分可用 not ... as well/too： *You can have a burger, but you can't have fries as well.* 你可以吃漢堡包，但不可以同時又吃炸薯條。

ˈ**also-ran** *noun* a person who is not successful, especially in a competition or an election 失敗者；（尤指競賽或競選的）失利者

altar /ˈɔːltə(r)/ *noun* a holy table in a church or TEMPLE（教堂、廟宇的）聖壇，祭壇，祭台： *the high altar* (= the most important one in a particular church) 教堂正祭台

IDM **at/on the altar of sth** *(formal)* because of sth that you think is worth suffering for 因為，為了（值得為之受苦的事物）： *He was willing to sacrifice his happiness on the altar of fame.* 為了名聲，他心甘情願犧牲幸福。

ˈ**altar boy** *noun* a boy who helps the priest in church services, especially in the Roman Catholic church 輔祭（宗教禮儀中的輔助男童，尤見於羅馬天主教）

al·tar·piece /ˈɔːltəpiːs; *NAmE* -tərp-/ *noun* a painting or other piece of art, located near the ALTAR in a church 祭壇畫（教堂祭壇附近的裝飾結構）

alter 🔑 **AW** /ˈɔːltə(r)/ *verb*
1 🔑 [I, T] to become different; to make sb/sth different （使）改變，更改，改動： *Prices did not alter significantly during 2007.* * 2007 年間，價格沒有大的變化。◇ *He had altered so much I scarcely recognized him.* 他變得我幾乎認不出來了。◇ **~ sb/sth** *It doesn't alter the way I feel.* 這並沒有改變我的感受。◇ *Nothing can **alter the fact that** we are to blame.* 什麼也改變不了我們要受指責這個事實。◇ *The landscape has been radically altered, severely damaging wildlife.* 地貌徹底改變，嚴重損害了野生生物。 **2** 🔑 [T] **~ sth** to make changes to a piece of clothing so that it will fit you better 修改（衣服使更合身） ▸ **al·ter·able** **AW** *adj.* *(formal)* **OPP** **unalterable**

al·ter·ation **AW** /ˌɔːltəˈreɪʃn/ *noun* **1** [C] a change to sth that makes it different 改變；變化： ***major/minor alterations*** 大 / 小改變 ◇ *They are **making** some **alterations to** the house.* 他們正在對這棟房子做一些改動。◇ *an **alteration in** the baby's heartbeat* 這嬰兒心搏的變化 **2** [U] the act of making a change to sth 改變；更改；改動： *The dress will not need much alteration.* 這件衣服不需大改。

al·ter·ca·tion /ˌɔːltəˈkeɪʃn; *NAmE* -tərˈk-/ *noun* [C, U] *(formal)* a noisy argument or disagreement 爭論；爭辯；爭吵

alter ego /ˌæltər ˈiːɡəʊ; ˌɔːl-; *NAmE* ˈiːɡoʊ/ *noun* *(pl.* **alter egos**) (from *Latin*) **1** a person whose personality is different from your own but who shows or acts as another side of your personality 第二自我： *Superman's alter ego was Clark Kent.* 超人的第二自我是克拉克 • 肯特。 **2** a close friend who is very like yourself 至交；知己；摯友

al·ter·nate **AW** *adj., verb, noun*
■ *adj.* /ɔːlˈtɜːnət; *NAmE* ˈɔːltərnət/ [usually before noun] **1** (of two things 兩事物) happening or following one after the other regularly 交替的；輪流的： *alternate layers of fruit and cream* 水果層和奶油層相間 **2** if sth happens on **alternate** days, nights, etc. it happens on one day, etc. but not on the next 間隔的；每隔（…天等）的： *John has to work on alternate Sundays.* 約翰每隔一週就有一個星期日得上班。 **3** *(especially NAmE)* = ALTERNATIVE (1) ▸ **al·ter·nate·ly** *adv.*： *He felt alternately hot and cold.* 他感到忽冷忽熱。
■ *verb* /ˈɔːltəneɪt; *NAmE* -tərn-/ **1** [T] to make things or people follow one after the other in a repeated pattern 使交替；使輪流： **~ A and B** *Alternate cubes of meat and slices of red pepper.* 交替放置肉丁和紅辣椒片。◇ **~ A with B** *Alternate cubes of meat with slices of red pepper.* 交替放置肉丁和紅辣椒片。 **2** [I] (of things or people 事物或人) to follow one after the other in a repeated pattern 交替；輪流： *alternating dark and pale stripes* 深淺條紋相間 ◇ **~ with sth** *Dark stripes alternate with pale ones.* 深淺條紋相間。 **3** [I] **~ between A and B** to keep changing from one thing to another and back again 交替： *Her mood alternated between happiness and despair.* 她的心情一會兒高興一會兒絕望。 ▸ **al·ter·na·tion** /ˌɔːltəˈneɪʃn; *NAmE* -tərˈn-/ *noun* [U, C]： *the alternation of day and night* 日夜交替

A

■ **noun** /ˈɔːltɜːnət; NAmE -tərn-/ (NAmE) a person who does a job for sb who is away 代替者；代理人；候補者

al,ternate 'angles (also **'Z angles**) noun [pl.] (geometry 幾何) equal angles formed on opposite sides of a line that crosses two parallel lines, in the position of the inner angles of a Z（內）錯角 ➲ VISUAL VOCAB page V71 ➲ compare CORRESPONDING ANGLES

,alternating 'current noun [U, C] (abbr. **AC**) an electric current that changes its direction at regular intervals many times a second 交流電 ➲ compare DIRECT CURRENT

al·ter·na·tive 0-π AW /ɔːlˈtɜːnətɪv; NAmE -ˈtɜːrn-/ noun, adj.

■ **noun** 0-π a thing that you can choose to do or have out of two or more possibilities 可供選擇的事物：*You can be paid in cash weekly or by cheque monthly; those are the two alternatives.* 你的工資可以按週以現金支取，或按月以支票支取，二者可選其一。◇ *We had **no alternative but to** fire Gibson.* 我們別無他法，只有辭退吉布森。◇ *There is a vegetarian alternative on the menu every day.* 每天的菜單上另有素食餐點。➲ SYNONYMS at OPTION

■ **adj.** [only before noun] **1** 0-π (also **al·ter·nate** especially in NAmE) that can be used instead of sth else 可供替代的：*an alternative method of doing sth* 做某事的其他方法 ◇ *Do you have an alternative solution?* 你有沒有別的解決辦法？ **2** 0-π different from the usual or traditional way in which sth is done 非傳統的；另擇性的：***alternative comedy/lifestyles/values*** 非傳統喜劇／生活方式／價值 ◇ ***alternative energy*** (= electricity or power that is produced using the energy from the sun, wind, water, etc.) 替代能源（指太陽能、風能、水能等）

al,ternative 'fuel noun [C, U] fuel that can be used instead of FOSSIL FUELS such as coal and oil, and instead of nuclear fuel 代用燃料，替代燃料（可代替礦物燃料或核燃料）

al·ter·na·tive·ly 0-π AW /ɔːlˈtɜːnətɪvli; NAmE -ˈtɜːrn-/ adv. used to introduce a suggestion that is a second choice or possibility（引出第二種選擇或可能的建議）要不，或者：*The agency will make travel arrangements for you. Alternatively, you can organize your own transport.* 旅行社將為你安排旅行，或者你也可以自行安排交通工具。

al,ternative 'medicine noun [C, U] any type of treatment that does not use the usual scientific methods of Western medicine, for example one using plants instead of artificial drugs 另類醫療，替代醫學，另類療法（不用西醫通常使用的科學方法，而使用其他方法，如用草藥代替人造藥物）

al·ter·na·tor /ˈɔːltəneɪtə(r); NAmE -tərn-/ noun a device, used especially in a car, that produces an ALTERNATING CURRENT（尤指汽車上的）交流發電機

Which Word? 詞語辨析

although / even though / though

■ You can use these words to show contrast between two clauses or two sentences. **Though** is used more in spoken than in written English. You can use **although**, **even though** and **though** at the beginning of a sentence or clause that has a verb. Notice where the commas go. 在兩個從句或句子之間可用上述詞表示對比。though 多用於口語，although、even though 和 though 可用於句首或帶有動詞的從句開頭。注意逗號的位置：*Although/Even though/Though everyone played well, we lost the game.* 儘管每個人都打得不錯，我們還是輸了。◇ *We lost the game, although/even though/though everyone played well.* 我們輸了，儘管每個人都打得不錯。

■ You cannot use **even** on its own at the beginning of a sentence or clause instead of **although**, **even though** or **though**. * even 不能單獨置於句首或從句開頭以代替 although、even though 或 though：~~*Even everyone played well, we lost the game.*~~

al·though 0-π (also US informal **altho**) /ɔːlˈðəʊ; NAmE ɔːlˈðoʊ/ conj.

1 0-π used for introducing a statement that makes the main statement in a sentence seem surprising 雖然；儘管；即使 SYN **though**：*Although the sun was shining, it wasn't very warm.* 儘管太陽高照，卻不很暖和。◇ *Although small, the kitchen is well designed.* 廚房雖小，但設計巧妙。➲ LANGUAGE BANK at HOWEVER **2** 0-π used to mean 'but' or 'however' when you are commenting on a statement 不過；然而：*I felt he was wrong, although I didn't say so at the time.* 我覺得他錯了，不過我當時沒有說出來。

al·tim·eter /ˈæltɪmiːtə(r); NAmE ælˈtɪmətər/ noun an instrument for showing height above sea level, used especially in an aircraft（尤指用於飛行器中的）測高計，高度表

al·ti·tude /ˈæltɪtjuːd; NAmE -tuːd/ noun **1** [C, usually sing.] the height above sea level 海拔；海拔高度：*We are flying **at an altitude of** 6 000 metres.* 我們的飛行高度是 6 000 米。◇ *The plane made a dive to a lower altitude.* 飛機俯衝到較低高度。 **2** [C, usually pl., U] a place that is high above sea level（海拔高的）高處，高地：*Snow leopards live **at high altitudes**.* 雪豹生活在海拔高的地區。◇ *The athletes trained **at altitude** in Mexico City.* 田徑運動員在海拔高的墨西哥城受訓。

'altitude sickness noun [U] illness caused by a lack of OXYGEN, because of being very high above sea level, for example on a mountain 高原病，高山病（由缺氧引起）

Alt key /ˈɔːlt kiː/ (also **ALT key**) noun a key on a computer keyboard which you press while pressing other keys, in order to change their function（計算機鍵盤上的）替換鍵，功能擴展鍵

alto /ˈæltəʊ; NAmE ˈæltoʊ/ noun, adj.

■ **noun** (pl. **-os**) **1** (also **con·tralto**) [C] a singing voice with a lower range than that of a SOPRANO; a person with an alto voice 中音；中音歌手 **2** [sing.] a musical part that is written for an alto voice 中音聲部 ➲ compare BARITONE, BASS[1], COUNTERTENOR, TENOR

■ **adj.** [only before noun] (of a musical instrument 樂器) with the second highest range of notes in its group 中音的：*an alto saxophone* 中音薩克斯管 ➲ compare SOPRANO, TENOR

Which Word? 詞語辨析

altogether / all together

■ **Altogether** and **all together** do not mean the same thing. **Altogether** means 'in total' or (in BrE) 'completely'. * altogether 和 all together 含義不同。altogether 意為總共或完全地（英式英語）：*We have invited fifty people altogether.* 我們共邀請了五十人。◇ *I am not altogether convinced by this argument.* 我不完全信服這一論據。

■ **All together** means 'all in one place' or 'all at once'. * all together 意為全部在同一地方或同一時間：*Can you put your books all together in this box?* 你能把你的書都放進這個箱子裏嗎？◇ *Let's sing 'Happy Birthday'. All together now!* 咱們來唱"生日快樂"。現在一起唱！

al·together 0-π /,ɔːltəˈgeðə(r)/ adv., noun

■ **adv.** **1** 0-π (used to emphasize sth) completely; in every way（用以強調）完全，全部：*The train went slower and slower until it stopped altogether.* 火車愈來愈慢，最後完全停了。◇ *I don't altogether agree with you.* 我不完全同意你的意見。◇ *I am **not altogether** happy (= I am very unhappy) about the decision.* 我對這個決定很不滿意。◇ *It was an altogether different situation.* 這完全是另外一種情況。 **2** 0-π used to give a total number or amount（表示總數或總額）總共，一共：*You owe me £68 altogether.* 你一共欠我 68 英鎊。 **3** 0-π used to introduce a summary when you have mentioned a number of different things 總之；總而言之：*The food was good and we loved the music. Altogether it was a great evening.* 吃的不錯，音樂我們也喜歡。總之，那天晚上過得非常愉快。

■ ***noun***
IDM **in the alto'gether** (*old-fashioned, informal*) without any clothes on 一絲不掛；赤身裸體

al·tru·ism /ˈæltruɪzəm/ *noun* [U] (*formal*) the fact of caring about the needs and happiness of other people more than your own 利他主義；利他；無私 ▸ **al·tru·is·tic** /ˌæltruˈɪstɪk/ *adj.*：*altruistic behaviour* 利他行為

alu = ALOO

alum /ˈæləm/ *noun* [U] a substance formed from ALUMINIUM/ALUMINUM and another metal, used, for example, to prepare leather and to change the colour of things 明礬，白礬（用於製革、印染等）

alu·mina /əˈluːmɪnə/ *noun* [U] (*technical* 術語) a white substance found in many types of rock, especially CLAY 礬土

alu·min·ium /ˌæljəˈmɪniəm; ˌælə-/ (*BrE*) (*NAmE* **alu·mi·num** /əˈluːmɪnəm/) *noun* [U] (*symb.* **Al**) a chemical element. Aluminium is a light, silver-grey metal used for making pans, etc. 鋁：*aluminium saucepans/window frames* 鋁鍋 / 窗框 ◇ ***aluminium foil*** (= for example, for wrapping food in) 鋁箔（如用於包裹食物）

alumna /əˈlʌmnə/ *noun* (*pl.* **alum·nae** /-niː/) (*formal, especially NAmE*) a former woman student of a school, college or university 女校友；女畢業生

alumni /əˈlʌmnaɪ/ *noun* [pl.] (*especially NAmE*) the former male and female students of a school, college or university（統稱）校友，畢業生：*Harvard Alumni Association* 哈佛大學校友會

alum·nus /əˈlʌmnəs/ *noun* (*pl.* **alumni** /-naɪ/) (*formal, especially NAmE*) a former male student of a school, college or university 男校友；男畢業生

al·veo·lar /ælˈviːələ(r); *BrE* also ˌælviˈəʊlə(r)/ *noun* (*phonetics* 語音) a speech sound made with the tongue touching the part of the mouth behind the upper front teeth, for example /t/ and /d/ in *tie* and *die* 齒齦音 ▸ **al·veo·lar** *adj.*

al·veo·lus /ælˈviːələs; *BrE* also ˌælviˈəʊləs/ *noun* (*pl.* **al·veoli** /ælˈviːəlaɪ; -liː; *BrE* also ˌælviˈəʊlaɪ; -liː/) (*anatomy* 解) one of the many small spaces in each lung where gases can pass into or out of the blood 肺泡

al·ways 0‑ᵚ /ˈɔːlweɪz/ *adv.*
1 0‑ᵚ at all times; on every occasion 總是；每次都是：*There's always somebody at home in the evenings.* 晚上總有人在家。◇ *Always lock your car.* 每次都要把汽車鎖上。◇ *She always arrives at 7.30.* 她每次都是 7:30 到。◇ *The children always seem to be hungry.* 孩子們永遠都好像肚子餓。◇ *We're not always this busy!* 我們並不總是這麼忙！ **2** 0‑ᵚ for a long time; since you can remember 一直；一貫：*Pat has always loved gardening.* 帕特一直喜愛園藝。◇ *This is the way we've always done it.* 我們一直是這樣幹的。◇ *This painting is very good—Ellie always was very good at art* (= so it is not very surprising). 這幅畫很好 —— 埃利一直擅長繪畫。◇ *Did you always want to be an actor?* 你以前一直想當演員嗎？ **3** 0‑ᵚ for all future time（將）永遠：*I'll always love you.* 我將永遠愛你。 **4** 0‑ᵚ if you say a person is **always doing** sth, or sth is **always happening**, you mean that they do it, or it happens, very often, and that this is annoying（討厭地）老是，一再：*She's always criticizing me.* 她老是批評我。◇ *That phone's always ringing.* 那個電話總是響個不停。 **5 can/could always …, there's always …** used to suggest a possible course of action（建議可能的行動）總還，總還有：*If it doesn't fit, you can always take it back.* 要是它不合適，你總還可以把它退回去嘛。◇ *If he can't help, there's always John.* 如果他幫不上忙，總還有約翰呢。

IDM **as 'always** 0‑ᵚ as usually happens or is expected 和往常一樣；和料想的一樣 **SYN** **as usual**：*As always, Polly was late for school.* 波利和往常一樣，上學又遲到了。➲ more at ONCE *adv.*

Alz·heim·er's dis·ease /ˈæltshaməz dɪziːz; *NAmE* -ərz/ (also **Alz·heim·er's**) *noun* [U] a serious disease, especially affecting older people, that prevents the brain from functioning normally and causes loss of memory, loss of ability to speak clearly, etc. 阿爾茨海默氏病；早老性痴呆病 **SYN** **senile dementia**

AM /ˌeɪ ˈem/ *abbr.* **1** amplitude modulation (one of the main methods of broadcasting sound by radio) 調幅；振幅調制 **2** Assembly Member (a person who has been elected to represent an area of Wales in the Welsh Assembly, the parliament for Wales) 議員（威爾士議會成員）：*Peter Black AM* 彼得 • 布萊克議員 ◇ *Labour AMs* 工黨議員

am /əm; *strong form* æm/ ➲ BE

a.m. 0‑ᵚ (*NAmE* also **A.M.**) /ˌeɪ ˈem/ *abbr.* between midnight and midday (from Latin 'ante meridiem') 午夜至正午，上午，午前（源自拉丁語 ante meridiem）：*It starts at 10 a.m.* 上午 10 點開始。➲ compare P.M.

amah /ˈɑːmə/ *noun* (in S or E Asia) a woman employed by a family to clean, care for children, etc. 阿嬤（東亞或南亞國家的女傭、保母或奶媽）

amal·gam /əˈmælgəm/ *noun* **1** [C, usually sing.] **~ (of sth)** (*formal*) a mixture or combination of things 混合物；綜合體：*The film script is an amalgam of all three books.* 這個電影腳本由三本書合成的。 **2** [U] (*technical* 術語) a mixture of MERCURY and another metal, used especially to fill holes in teeth 汞合金，汞齊（尤用於補牙）

amal·gam·ate /əˈmælgəmeɪt/ *verb* **~ (sth) (with/into sth)**
1 [I, T] if two organizations **amalgamate** or **are amalgamated**, they join together to form one large organization（使）合併，聯合 **SYN** **merge**：*A number of colleges have amalgamated to form the new university.* 一些學院聯合組成了這所新大學。◇ **~ with/into sth** *The company has now amalgamated with another local firm.* 這家公司現在已與當地另一家公司合併了。◇ **~ sth** *They decided to amalgamate the two schools.* 他們決定將兩所學校合併。◇ **~ sth with/into sth** *The two companies were amalgamated into one.* 這兩家公司合併成一家公司。 **2** [T] **~ sth (into/with sth)** to put two or more things together so that they form one 使混合；使合併 **SYN** **merge**：*This information will be amalgamated with information obtained earlier.* 這個信息要與早先得到的信息綜合在一起。 ▸ **amal·gam·ation** /əˌmælgəˈmeɪʃn/ *noun* [U, C]：*the amalgamation of small farms into larger units* 小農場合併成大農場

amanu·en·sis /əˌmænjuˈensɪs/ *noun* (*pl.* **amanu·en·ses** /-siːz/) (*formal*) **1** a person who writes down your words when you cannot write, for example if you are injured and have an exam 代筆人；抄寫員 **2** an assistant, especially one who writes or types for sb 助手；（尤指）秘書

amar·yl·lis /ˌæməˈrɪlɪs/ *noun* [C, U] a tall white, pink or red flower shaped like a TRUMPET 孤挺花（喇叭狀白色、粉紅色或紅色高莖花）

amasi /əˈmɑːsi/ (also **maas**) *noun* [U] (*SAfrE*) sour milk 酸牛奶

amass /əˈmæs/ *verb* **~ sth** to collect sth, especially in large quantities（尤指大量）積累，積聚 **SYN** **accumulate**：*He amassed a fortune from silver mining.* 他靠開採銀礦積累了一筆財富。➲ SYNONYMS at COLLECT

ama·teur /ˈæmətə(r); -tʃə(r)/ *noun, adj.*
■ ***noun*** **1** a person who takes part in a sport or other activity for enjoyment, not as a job 業餘愛好者；業餘運動員：*The tournament is open to both amateurs and professionals.* 這次錦標賽業餘選手和職業選手均可參加。 **2** (usually *disapproving*) a person who is not skilled 生手；外行：*This work was done by a bunch of amateurs!* 這項工作是一夥外行幹的！ **OPP** **professional** ▸ **ama·teur·ism** /ˈæmətərɪzəm; -tʃə-/ *noun* [U]：*New rules on amateurism allow payment for promotional work.* 新的業餘條例規定，做促銷工作可獲得報酬。
■ ***adj.*** **1** [usually before noun] doing sth for enjoyment or interest, not as a job 業餘愛好的：*an amateur photographer* 業餘攝影愛好者 **2** [usually before noun] done for enjoyment, not as a job 業餘的：*amateur athletics* 業餘田徑運動 **3** (usually *disapproving*) = AMATEURISH **OPP** **professional**

ˌamateur draˈmatics *noun* [U] (*BrE*) the activity of producing and acting in plays for the theatre, by people who do it for enjoyment, not as a job 業餘戲劇愛好活動

A

ama·teur·ish /ˈæmətərɪʃ; -tʃə-/ (also **ama·teur**) *adj.* (usually *disapproving*) not done or made well or with skill 外行的；生手的；業餘的：*Detectives described the burglary as 'crude and amateurish'.* 偵探稱這次夜盜是拙劣的生手幹的。**OPP professional**

ama·tory /ˈæmətəri; *NAmE* -tɔːri/ *adj.* [only before noun] (*formal* or *humorous*) relating to or connected with sexual desire or activity 性慾的；性愛的：*his amatory exploits* 他傲人的風流韻事

amaze /əˈmeɪz/ *verb* to surprise sb very much 使驚奇；使驚愕；使驚詫：**~ sb** *Just the size of the place amazed her.* 僅僅地方之大就使她十分驚奇。◇ **~ sb what, how, etc. …** *It never ceases to amaze me what some people will do for money.* 有些人為了錢什麼都會幹得出來，這一直使我驚愕不已。◇ ***What amazes me is*** *how long she managed to hide it from us.* 使我驚詫的是，她竟然能把這件事瞞了我們這麼久。◇ **it amazes sb that …/to see, find, learn, etc.** *It amazed her that they could be so calm at such a time.* 在這個時候他們還能如此冷靜，真讓她感到驚訝。➲ SYNONYMS at SURPRISE

amazed /əˈmeɪzd/ *adj.* very surprised 大為驚奇：*an amazed silence* 驚愕得一片默然 ◇ **~ at sb/sth** *I was amazed at her knowledge of French literature.* 她的法國文學知識之豐富使我大為驚奇。◇ **~ by sb/sth** *We were amazed by his generosity.* 他的慷慨令我們喜出望外。◇ **~ (that) …** *I was banging so loudly I'm amazed (that) they didn't hear me.* 我把門敲得砰砰響。真奇怪，他們居然沒有聽見。◇ **~ how …** *She was amazed how little he had changed.* 她驚詫的是他竟然沒怎麼改變。◇ **~ to see, find, learn, etc.** *We were amazed to find that no one was hurt.* 我們很驚異地發現竟沒有人受傷。

amaze·ment /əˈmeɪzmənt/ *noun* [U] a feeling of great surprise 驚奇；驚愕；驚詫：***To my amazement,*** *he remembered me.* 使我大為驚奇的是他還記得我。◇ *She looked at him* ***in amazement.*** 她驚愕地望着他。

amaz·ing /əˈmeɪzɪŋ/ *adj.* very surprising, especially in a way that makes you feel pleasure or admiration 令人大為驚奇的；（尤指）令人驚喜（或驚羨、驚歎）的 **SYN astounding, incredible**：*an amazing achievement/discovery/success/performance* 驚人的成就／發現／成功／表演 ◇ *That's amazing, isn't it?* 真是令人驚歎，是不是？◇ ***It's amazing how*** *quickly people adapt.* 人適應環境的速度之快真是驚人。▶ **amaz·ing·ly** *adv.*：*Amazingly, no one noticed.* 令人驚奇的是，竟沒有人注意到。◇ *The meal was amazingly cheap.* 這餐飯便宜得出奇。

Amazon /ˈæməzən; *NAmE* also -zɑːn/ *noun* **1** (in ancient Greek stories) a woman from a group of female WARRIORS (= soldiers)（古希臘神話中的）亞馬孫族女戰士 **2 amazon** (*literary*) a tall strong woman 高大強悍的女人

am·bas·sador /æmˈbæsədə(r)/ *noun* an official who lives in a foreign country as the senior representative there of his or her own country 大使；使節：*the British Ambassador to Italy/in Rome* 英國駐意大利／羅馬大使 ◇ *a former ambassador to the UN* 前任駐聯合國大使 ◇ (*figurative*) *The best ambassadors for the sport are the players.* 這種運動最好的大使就是運動員。▶ **am·bas·sador·ial** /æmˌbæsəˈdɔːriəl/ *adj.*

amber /ˈæmbə(r)/ *noun* [U] **1** a hard clear yellowish-brown substance, used in making decorative objects or jewellery 琥珀：*amber beads* 琥珀珠子 **2** a yellowish-brown colour 琥珀色；黃褐色：*The traffic lights were on amber.* 交通信號黃燈亮了。▶ **amber** *adj.*

ˌamber ˈfluid (also **ˌamber ˈliquid**) *noun* [U] (*AustralE, informal*) beer 啤酒

am·ber·gris /ˈæmbəɡriːs; -ɡrɪs; *NAmE* ˈæmbər-/ *noun* [U] a substance that is used in making some PERFUMES. It is produced naturally by a type of WHALE. 龍涎香（抹香鯨分泌物，用以製香水）

ambi- /ˈæmbi/ *prefix* (in nouns, adjectives and adverbs 構成名詞、形容詞和副詞) referring to both of two 二者（都）：*ambidextrous* 左右手都靈巧的 ◇ *ambivalent* 矛盾情緒的

ambi·dex·trous /ˌæmbiˈdekstrəs/ *adj.* able to use the left hand or the right hand equally well 左右手都靈巧的；左右開弓的

am·bi·ence (also **am·bi·ance**) /ˈæmbiəns/ *noun* [sing.] the character and atmosphere of a place 環境；氣氛；格調：*the relaxed ambience of the city* 這座城市輕鬆的氛圍

am·bi·ent /ˈæmbiənt/ *adj.* **1** [only before noun] (*technical* 術語) relating to the surrounding area; on all sides 周圍環境的；周圍的：***ambient temperature/light/conditions*** 周圍的溫度／光線／環境 **2** (especially of music 尤指音樂) creating a relaxed atmosphere 產生輕鬆氛圍的：*a compilation of ambient electronic music* 氛圍電子音樂彙編 ◇ *soft, ambient lighting* 輕鬆柔和的照明

am·bi·gu·ity AW /ˌæmbɪˈɡjuːəti/ *noun* (*pl.* **-ies**) **1** [U] the state of having more than one possible meaning 歧義；一語多義：*Write clear definitions in order to avoid ambiguity.* 釋義要寫清楚以免產生歧義。**2** [C] a word or statement that can be understood in more than one way 模稜兩可的詞；含混不清的語句：*There were several inconsistencies and ambiguities in her speech.* 她的發言有幾處前後不一致和含混不清。**3** [U, C] the state of being difficult to understand or explain because of involving many different aspects 模稜兩可；不明確：*You must understand the ambiguity of my position.* 你必須理解我處的位置不明確。

am·bigu·ous AW /æmˈbɪɡjuəs/ *adj.* **1** that can be understood in more than one way; having different meanings 模稜兩可的；含混不清的：***an ambiguous word/term/statement*** 模稜兩可的詞／用語／說法 ◇ *Her account was deliberately ambiguous.* 她的陳述故意含混不清。**2** not clearly stated or defined 不明確的：*His role has always been ambiguous.* 他的角色一直不明確。**OPP unambiguous** ▶ **am·bigu·ous·ly** *adv.*：*an ambiguously worded agreement* 措辭含混的協議

ambit /ˈæmbɪt/ *noun* [sing.] (*formal*) the range of the authority or influence of sth（權力、影響的）範圍，界限：*This case falls clearly* ***within the ambit of*** *the 2001 act.* 這件案子顯然屬於 2001 年法案的範圍。

am·bi·tion /æmˈbɪʃn/ *noun*
1 [C] something that you want to do or achieve very much 追求的目標；夙願：*It had been her* ***lifelong ambition.*** 這是她終身追求的目標。◇ ***political/literary/sporting ambitions*** 政治抱負；文學夙願；運動目標 ◇ **~ of being/doing sth** *She never* ***achieved her ambition*** *of becoming a famous writer.* 她一直未能實現當名作家的夙願。◇ **~ to be/do sth** *His burning ambition was to study medicine.* 他夢寐以求的是學醫。**2** [U] the desire or determination to be successful, rich, powerful, etc. 野心；雄心；志向；抱負：*motivated by personal ambition* 為個人野心所驅使 ◇ *She was intelligent but suffered from a lack of ambition.* 她很聰明，但卻缺乏遠大志向。

am·bi·tious /æmˈbɪʃəs/ *adj.* **1** determined to be successful, rich, powerful, etc. 有野心的；有雄心的：*a fiercely ambitious young manager* 雄心勃勃的年輕經理 ◇ *They were very ambitious for their children* (= they wanted them to be successful). 他們望子成龍心切。**2** needing a lot of effort, money or time to succeed 費力的；耗資的；耗時的：*the government's ambitious plans for social reform* 政府耗資巨大的社會改革計劃 **OPP unambitious** ▶ **am·bi·tious·ly** *adv.*

am·biva·lent /æmˈbɪvələnt/ *adj.* **~ (about/towards sb/sth)** having or showing both good and bad feelings about sb/sth（憂喜參半、好壞參半等）矛盾情緒的：*She seems to feel ambivalent about her new job.* 她似乎對她的新工作憂喜參半。◇ *He has an ambivalent attitude towards her.* 他對她懷着矛盾的心情。▶ **am·biva·lence** *noun* [U, sing.]：**~ (about/towards sb/sth)** *Many people feel some ambivalence towards television and its effect on our lives.* 很多人以矛盾的態度對待電視及其對生活的影響。**am·biva·lent·ly** *adv.*

amble /ˈæmbl/ *verb* [I] **+ adv./prep.** to walk at a slow relaxed speed 緩行；漫步 **SYN stroll**：*We ambled down to the beach.* 我們漫步向海灘走去。

am·bro·sia /æm'brəʊziə; *NAmE* -'broʊ-/ *noun* [U] **1** (in ancient Greek and Roman stories 古希臘和羅馬神話) the food of the gods 神的食物；神肴；仙饈 **2** (*literary*) something that is very pleasant to eat 美味佳肴；珍饈

am·bu·lance 0-w /'æmbjələns/ *noun* a vehicle with special equipment, used for taking sick or injured people to a hospital 救護車：*the ambulance service* 救護車服務 ◇ *ambulance staff* 救護車全體人員 ◇ *Call an ambulance!* 叫一輛救護車！

'ambulance chaser *noun* (*informal, disapproving, especially NAmE*) a lawyer who earns money by encouraging people who have been in an accident to make claims in court 慫恿事故受害者提出訴訟的律師

am·bu·la·tory /'æmbjələtəri; *NAmE* -tɔːri/ *adj.* **1** (*formal*) related to or adapted for walking （適用於）步行的：*an ambulatory corridor* 迴廊 **2** (*formal*) that is not fixed in one place and can move around easily 非固定的；可移動的；流動的 **SYN** **mobile**：*an ambulatory care service* 流動護理服務

am·bush /'æmbʊʃ/ *noun, verb*

■ ***noun*** [C, U] the act of hiding and waiting for sb and then making a surprise attack on them 伏擊；埋伏：*Two soldiers were killed in a terrorist ambush.* 兩名士兵遭到恐怖分子伏擊而死亡。◇ *They were **lying in ambush**, waiting for the aid convoy.* 他們埋伏起來，等着襲擊援助車隊。

■ ***verb*** **~ sb/sth** to make a surprise attack on sb/sth from a hidden position 伏擊：*The guerrillas ambushed them near the bridge.* 游擊隊員在大橋附近伏擊了他們。◇ (*figurative*) *She was ambushed by reporters.* 記者突然一擁而上採訪她。

ameba, **ameb·ic** (*US*) = AMOEBA, AMOEBIC

ameli·or·ate /ə'miːliəreɪt/ *verb* **~ sth** (*formal*) to make sth better 改善；改進；改良：*Steps have been taken to ameliorate the situation.* 已經採取措施以改善局面。
▸ **ameli·or·ation** /əˌmiːliə'reɪʃn/ *noun* [U]

amen /ɑː'men; eɪ'men/ (also **Amen**) *exclamation, noun* a word used at the end of prayers and HYMNS, meaning 'may it be so' 阿門（用於祈禱或聖歌結束時，表示誠心所願）：*We ask this through our Lord, Amen.* 奉主之名而求，阿門。◇ *Amen to that* (= I certainly agree with that). 我當然同意那個意見。

amen·able /ə'miːnəbl/ *adj.* **1** (of people 人) easy to control; willing to be influenced by sb/sth 順從的；順服的：*They had three very amenable children.* 他們有三個很聽話的孩子。◇ **~ to sth** *He seemed most amenable to my idea.* 他似乎對我的想法十分佩服。 **2 ~ to sth** (*formal*) that you can treat in a particular way 可用某種方式處理的：*'Hamlet' is the least amenable of all Shakespeare's plays to being summarized.* 在莎士比亞所有的戲劇中，《哈姆雷特》最難概括。

amend **AW** /ə'mend/ *verb* **~ sth** to change a law, document, statement, etc. slightly in order to correct a mistake or to improve it 修正，修訂（法律、文件、聲明等）：*He asked to see the amended version.* 他要求看修訂本。

amend·ment **AW** /ə'mendmənt/ *noun* **1** [C, U] a small change or improvement that is made to a law or a document; the process of changing a law or a document（法律、文件的）改動，修正案，修改，修訂：*to **introduce/propose/table an amendment*** (= to suggest it) 提出一項修正案 ◇ *Parliament passed the bill without further amendment.* 議會未作進一步修改便通過了法案。◇ **~ to sth** *She made several minor amendments to her essay.* 她對自己的論文作了幾處小的修改。 **2 Amendment** [C] a statement of a change to the CONSTITUTION of the US（美國憲法的）修正案：*The 19th Amendment gave women the right to vote.* 第 19 次修正案賦予婦女選舉權。

amends /ə'mendz/ *noun* [pl.]
IDM **make amends (to sb) (for sth/for doing sth)** to do sth for sb in order to show that you are sorry for sth wrong or unfair that you have done（因某事向某人）賠償，補償，賠不是；將功補（過） **SYN** **make up for sth**

amen·ity /ə'miːnəti; *NAmE* ə'menəti/ *noun* [usually pl.] (*pl.* **-ies**) a feature that makes a place pleasant, comfortable or easy to live in 生活福利設施；便利設施：*The campsite is close to all **local amenities**.* 營地緊靠當地所有的便利設施。◇ *Many of the houses lacked even **basic amenities*** (= baths, showers, hot water, etc.). 很多房屋甚至缺乏基本的生活設施。

amen·or·rhoea (*BrE*) (*NAmE* **amen·or·rhea**) /əˌmenə'riːə; *NAmE* eɪˌmen-/ *noun* [U] (*medical* 醫) a condition in which an adult woman does not MENSTRUATE (= there is no flow of blood from her WOMB every month) 閉經；無月經；停經

Amer·asian /ˌæmə'reɪʃn; -'reɪʒn/ *noun* a person with one Asian parent and one parent from the US 美亞混血兒（父母一方為亞洲人，一方為美國人） ▸ **Amer·asian** *adj.*

Ameri·can /ə'merɪkən/ *noun, adj.*

■ ***noun*** **1** a person from America, especially the US 美洲人；（尤指）美國人 ➲ see also AFRICAN AMERICAN, NATIVE AMERICAN **2** (also **A'merican English**) the English language as spoken in the US 美國英語

■ ***adj.*** of or connected with N or S America, especially the US 美洲的；（尤指）美國的：*I'm American.* 我是美國人。◇ *American culture/tourists* 美國文化／遊客

IDM **as Aˌmerican as apple 'pie** used to say that sth is typical of America 典型美國式的；地道美國式的

More About 補充説明

America

- The continent of **America** is divided into **North America** and **South America**. The narrow region joining North and South America is **Central America**. 美洲（America）大陸劃分為北美洲（North America）和南美洲（South America），連接兩地的地峽為中美洲（Central America）。
- **North America**, which is a geographical term, consists of the **United States of America**, **Canada** and **Mexico**. **Latin America**, a cultural term, refers to the non-English speaking countries of Central and South America, where mainly Portuguese and Spanish are spoken. Mexico is part of Latin America. 北美洲（North America）是地理術語，由美國（United States of America）、加拿大（Canada）和墨西哥（Mexico）組成。拉丁美洲（Latin America）是文化術語，指中美洲和南美洲的非英語國家，那裏主要說葡萄牙語和西班牙語。墨西哥是拉丁美洲的一部份。
- The **United States of America** is usually shortened to the **USA**, the **US**, the **States** or simply **America**. * the United States of America（美國）通常簡稱為 the USA、the US、the States 或乾脆叫 America：*the US President* 美國總統 ◇ *Have you ever been to the States?* 你去過美國嗎？◇ *She emigrated to America in 1995.* 她 1995 年移民美國。Many people from other parts of the continent dislike this use of **America** to mean just the US, but it is very common. 雖然美洲大陸其他地方許多人不喜歡用 America 指美國，但此用法非常普遍。
- **American** is usually used to talk about somebody or something from the United States of America. * American 通常指美國的人或事物：*Do you have an American passport?* 你有美國護照嗎？◇ *American football* 美式足球 ◇ *I'm not American, I'm Canadian.* 我不是美國人，我是加拿大人。 **Latin American** and **South American** are used to refer to other parts of the continent. * Latin American（拉丁美洲的；拉丁美洲人）和 South American（南美洲的；南美洲人）指美洲大陸的其他部份：*Latin American dance music* 拉丁美洲舞曲 ◇ *Quite a lot of South Americans study here.* 相當多的南美洲人在這裏學習。

A

Ameri·cana /əˌmerɪˈkɑːnə/ *noun* [pl.] things connected with the US that are thought to be typical of it 典型美國事物

Aˌmerican ˈbreakfast *noun* a large breakfast which can include CEREAL and cooked food, such as eggs with HAM 美式早餐（量大，包括麥片粥、蛋、火腿等）➲ see also ENGLISH BREAKFAST, CONTINENTAL BREAKFAST

Aˌmerican ˈcheese *noun* [U] (*US*) a kind of orange cheese that is usually sold in thin slices wrapped in plastic 美式奶酪（橙色，通常切片用塑料包裝出售）

the Aˌmerican ˈdream *noun* [sing.] the values and social standards that people traditionally try to achieve in the US, such as DEMOCRACY, equal rights and wealth 美國夢（美國人傳統的價值觀和社會標準，如民主、權利平等和財富）

the Aˌmerican ˈeagle *noun* a bird with a white head and white tail feathers that is the national symbol of the US 白頭雕，白頭鷲，白頭鷹（美國的象徵）

Aˌmerican ˈfootball (*BrE*) (*NAmE* **foot·ball**) *noun* [U] a game played by two teams of 11 players, using an OVAL ball which players kick, throw, or carry. Teams try to put the ball over the other team's line. 美式足球，美式橄欖球（雙方隊員各 11 人，球呈橢圓形，球員可足踢、手傳或抱球奔跑，球越過對方端線得分）➲ VISUAL VOCAB page V44

Aˌmerican ˈIndian *noun* = NATIVE AMERICAN

Ameri·can·ism /əˈmerɪkənɪzəm/ *noun* **1** [C] a word, phrase or spelling that is typical of American English, used in another variety of English 美式英語單詞（或短語、拼法）**2** [U] the essential quality of being American 美國特色；美洲特色

Ameri·can·ize (*BrE* also **-ise**) /əˈmerɪkənaɪz/ *verb* **~ sb/sth** to make sb/sth American in character 使美國化 ▸ **Ameri·can·iza·tion**, **-isa·tion** /əˌmerəkənaɪˈzeɪʃn; *NAmE* -nəˈz-/ *noun* [U]

the Aˈmerican League *noun* (in the US) one of the two organizations for professional BASEBALL 美國職業棒球聯盟 ➲ see also NATIONAL LEAGUE

Aˌmerican ˈplan *noun* [U] = FULL BOARD

ameri·cium /ˌæməˈrɪsiəm; -ˈrɪʃi-/ *noun* [U] (*symb.* **Am**) a chemical element. Americium is a RADIOACTIVE metal. 鎇（放射性化學元素）

Amer·in·dian /ˌæməˈrɪndiən/ *noun* (*old-fashioned*) = NATIVE AMERICAN

ameth·yst /ˈæməθɪst/ *noun* [C, U] a purple SEMI-PRECIOUS stone, used in making jewellery 紫水晶；紫晶：*an amethyst ring* 紫水晶戒指

ami·able /ˈeɪmiəbl/ *adj.* pleasant; friendly and easy to like 和藹可親的；親切友好的 **SYN** **agreeable**：*an amiable tone of voice* 親切的聲調 ◇ *Her parents seemed very amiable.* 她的父母好像很和藹可親。▸ **ami·abil·ity** /ˌeɪmiəˈbɪləti/ *noun* [U] **ami·ably** *adv.*：*'That's fine,' he replied amiably.* "那很好。"他親切友好地回答道。

am·ic·able /ˈæmɪkəbl/ *adj.* done or achieved in a polite or friendly way and without arguing 心平氣和的；友善的：*an amicable relationship* 和睦的關係 ◇ *An amicable settlement was reached.* 已達成和解。▸ **am·ic·ably** *adv.*

amid /əˈmɪd/ (also **mid**, **amidst** /əˈmɪdst/) *prep.* (*formal*) **1** in the middle of or during sth, especially sth that causes excitement or fear 在…過程中；在…中：*He finished his speech amid tremendous applause.* 他在雷鳴般的掌聲中結束了演講。◇ *The firm collapsed amid allegations of fraud.* 該公司在一片指控其詐騙的聲音下倒閉了。**2** surrounded by sth 在…中；四周是：*The hotel was in a beautiful position amid lemon groves.* 旅館位於檸檬樹叢之中，優美宜人。

amid·ships /əˈmɪdʃɪps/ *adv.* (*technical* 術語) in or near the middle part of a ship 在（或靠近）船體中部

amino acid /əˌmiːnəʊ ˈæsɪd; *NAmE* -noʊ/ *noun* (*chemistry* 化) any of the substances that combine to form the basic structure of PROTEINS 氨基酸

amir = EMIR

the Amish /ˈɑːmɪʃ; *BrE* also ˈæmɪʃ/ *noun* [pl.] the members of a strict religious group in N America. The Amish live a simple farming life and reject some forms of modern technology. 阿曼門諾派（北美洲戒律嚴謹的宗教團體，過簡樸的農耕生活，拒絕使用某些現代技術）▸ **Amish** *adj.*

amiss /əˈmɪs/ *adj.*, *adv.*

■ ***adj.*** [not before noun] wrong; not as it should be 不對；不正常：*She sensed something was amiss and called the police.* 她覺得有點不對頭，就叫了警察。

■ ***adv.***

IDM **not come/go aˈmiss** (*BrE*) to be useful or pleasant in a particular situation 並非不稱心；並非不順當：*A little luck wouldn't go amiss right now!* 此刻若交點好運還是相當稱心的。**take sth aˈmiss** (*BrE*) to feel offended by sth, perhaps because you have understood it in the wrong way 見怪：*Would she take it amiss if I offered to help?* 我要是提出幫助，她會不會見怪？

amity /ˈæməti/ *noun* [U] (*formal*) a friendly relationship between people or countries 和睦；友好

amma /ˈʌmɑː/ *noun* (*IndE*) (especially as a form of address 尤用作稱謂) a mother 阿媽；媽媽

am·meter /ˈæmiːtə(r)/ *noun* an instrument for measuring the strength of an electric current 安培計；電流表

ammo /ˈæməʊ; *NAmE* ˈæmoʊ/ *noun* [U] (*old-fashioned, informal*) = AMMUNITION

am·mo·nia /əˈməʊniə; *NAmE* əˈmoʊ-/ *noun* [U] (*symb.* **NH_3**) a gas with a strong smell; a clear liquid containing ammonia, used as a cleaning substance 氨；氨水

ammonite 菊石

am·mon·ite /ˈæmənaɪt/ *noun* a FOSSIL of a simple sea creature which no longer exists, and which was related to SNAILS 菊石（已滅絕的頭足動物，與螺近緣）

am·mo·nium /əˈməʊniəm; *NAmE* əˈmoʊ-/ *noun* [U] (*chemistry* 化) a salt made from AMMONIA containing NITROGEN and HYDROGEN together with another element 銨

am·mu·ni·tion /ˌæmjuˈnɪʃn/ *noun* [U] **1** a supply of bullets, etc. to be fired from guns 彈藥 **2** information that can be used against another person in an argument（辯論中可攻擊對方的）信息，事實：*The letter gave her all the ammunition she needed.* 這封信給了她所需的一切有力證據。

am·nesia /æmˈniːziə; *NAmE* -ˈniːʒə/ *noun* [U] a medical condition in which sb partly or completely loses their memory 記憶缺失；遺忘（症）▸ **am·nesiac** /æmˈniːziæk; *NAmE* -ˈniːʒ-/ *noun*：*This new discovery helps amnesiacs keep their memory.* 這一新的發現有助於遺忘症患者保持記憶。

am·nesty /ˈæmnəsti/ *noun* (*pl.* **-ies**) **1** [C, usually sing., U] an official statement that allows people who have been put in prison for crimes against the state to go free（對政治犯的）赦免，大赦：*The president granted a general amnesty for all political prisoners.* 總統大赦了所有的政治犯。**2** [C, usually sing.] a period of time during which people can admit to a crime or give up weapons without being punished 赦免期（此期間交代罪行或交出武器可獲赦免）：*2 000 knives have been handed in during the month-long amnesty.* 在為期一個月的赦免期中交出的刀有 2 000 把。

ˌAmnesty Interˈnational *noun* an international human rights organization that works to help people who have been put in prison for their beliefs or race and not because they have committed a crime. It also works to prevent TORTURE and punishment by death. 大赦國際，國際特赦組織（國際人權組織，旨在幫助因信仰或種族而被關押者，並爭取制止酷刑和死刑）

am·nio·cen·tesis /ˌæmniəʊsenˈtiːsɪs; *NAmE* -nioʊ-/ *noun* [U, sing.] a medical test that involves taking some liquid from a pregnant woman's WOMB in order to find out if the baby has particular illnesses or health problems 羊膜穿刺術（經孕婦腹壁吸出液體檢查胎兒健康狀況）

am·ni·ot·ic fluid /ˌæmniɒtɪk ˈfluːɪd; *NAmE* -ɑːtɪk/ *noun* [U] the liquid that surrounds a baby inside the mother's WOMB 羊水

amn't /ˈæmənt/ *short form* (*ScotE, IrishE, non-standard*) am not 不是

amoeba (*US* also **ameba**) /əˈmiːbə/ *noun* (*pl.* **amoe·bas** or **amoe·bae** /-biː/) a very small living creature that consists of only one cell 阿米巴，變形蟲（單細胞生物）

amoeb·ic (*US* also **ameb·ic**) /əˈmiːbɪk/ *adj.* related to or similar to an amoeba 變形蟲的；變形蟲狀的

aˌmoebic ˈdysentery (*US* also **aˌmebic ˈdysentery**) *noun* [U] an infection of the INTESTINE caused by an amoeba 阿米巴痢疾

amok /əˈmɒk; *NAmE* əˈmɑːk/ *adv.*
IDM **run amok** to suddenly become very angry or excited and start behaving violently, especially in a public place（尤指在公共場所）發狂，狂暴，瘋狂

among 🔑 /əˈmʌŋ/ (also **amongst** /əˈmʌŋst/) *prep.* **1** 🔑 surrounded by sb/sth; in the middle of sb/sth 在…中；周圍是：*a house among the trees* 樹林中的一座房子 ◇ *They strolled among the crowds.* 他們在人群中信步而行。◇ *I found the letter amongst his papers.* 我在他的文件中找到這封信。◇ *It's OK, you're among friends now.* 好了，現在你的周圍都是朋友了。 **2** 🔑 being included or happening in groups of things or people 在（其）中；…之一：*A British woman was among the survivors.* 幸存者中有一位英國婦女。◇ *He was among the last to leave.* 他是最後離開者之一。◇ *This attitude is common among the under-25s.* 這種態度在 25 歲以下的青年中很普遍。◇ *'What was wrong with the job?' 'Well, the pay wasn't good,* ***among other things****.'* "這份工作有什麼不好嗎？" "嗯，別的不説，工資就不怎麼樣。" ◇ *Discuss it* ***among yourselves*** (= with each other) *first.* 你們自己先討論一下。 **3** 🔑 used when you are dividing or choosing sth, and three or more people or things are involved 在三者或以上中（分配或選擇）：*They divided the money up among their three children.* 他們把錢分給了他們的三個孩子。

amoral /ˌeɪˈmɒrəl; *NAmE* -ˈmɔːr-/ *adj.* not following any moral rules and not caring about right and wrong 不關道德的；不遵守道德準則的 ➲ compare IMMORAL, MORAL ▸ **amor·al·ity** /ˌeɪməˈræləti/ *noun* [U]

am·or·ous /ˈæmərəs/ *adj.* showing sexual desire and love towards sb 表示性愛的；含情脈脈的：*Mary rejected Tony's amorous advances.* 瑪麗拒絕了托尼的挑逗。 ▸ **am·or·ous·ly** *adv.*

amorph·ous /əˈmɔːfəs; *NAmE* -ˈmɔːrf-/ *adj.* [usually before noun] (*formal*) having no definite shape, form or structure 無固定形狀的；不規則的；無組織的 SYN **shapeless**：*an amorphous mass of cells with no identity at all* 不知何物的雜亂一團的細胞

amort·ize (*BrE* also **-ise**) /əˈmɔːtaɪz; *NAmE* ˈæmərtaɪz/ *verb* **~ sth** (*business* 商) to pay back a debt by making small regular payments over a period of time 分期償還，攤還（債款） ▸ **amort·iza·tion, -isa·tion** /əˌmɔːtaɪˈzeɪʃn; *NAmE* ˌæmərtəˈz-/ *noun* [U, C]

amount 🔑 /əˈmaʊnt/ *noun, verb*
■ **noun** [C, U] **1** 🔑 a sum of money 金額：*The insurance company will refund any amount due to you.* 保險公司將賠償你應得的所有款項。◇ *You will receive a bill for the full amount.* 你將收到一張全部金額的賬單。 **2** 🔑 **~ (of sth)** (used especially with uncountable nouns 尤與不可數名詞連用) a quantity of sth 數量；數額：*an amount of time/money/information* 一段時間；一筆錢；一些信息 ◇ *We've had an enormous amount of help from people.* 我們得到了人們大力幫助。◇ *The server is designed to store huge amounts of data.* 該服務器是為存貯大量數據設計的。
IDM **any amount of sth** a large quantity of sth 大量：*There's been any amount of research into the subject.* 對這個課題已進行了大量研究。 **no amount of sth** used for saying that sth will have no effect 即使再多（或再大）（也不）：*No amount of encouragement would make him jump into the pool.* 再怎樣鼓勵，他也不肯往游泳池裏跳。
■ ***verb***
PHR V **aˈmount to sth** **1** 🔑 to add up to sth; to make sth as a total 總計；共計：*His earnings are said to amount to £300 000 per annum.* 據説他每年的酬金高達 30 萬英鎊。◇ *They gave me some help in the beginning but it* ***did not amount to much*** (= they did not give me much help). 起初他們給了我一些幫助，但幫助不大。 **2** to be equal to or the same as sth 等於；相當於：*Her answer amounted to a complete refusal.* 她的答覆等於完全拒絕。◇ *Their actions amount to a breach of contract.* 他們的行為已屬違反合同。◇ *It'll cost a lot—well, take a lot of time, but it* ***amounts to the same thing****.* 付出會很多——哦，得花大量時間，不過反正都是一回事。

amour /əˈmʊə(r); *NAmE* əˈmʊr/ *noun* (*old-fashioned*, from *French*) a love affair, especially a secret one（尤指秘密的）戀愛；風流韻事

amour propre /ˌæmʊə ˈprɒprə; *NAmE* ˌɑːmʊr ˈproːprə/ *noun* [U] (*formal*, from *French*) a feeling of pride in your own character and abilities 自尊心

amp /æmp/ *noun* **1** (also **am·pere** /ˈæmpeə(r); *NAmE* ˈæmpɪr; -per/) (*abbr.* **A**) the unit for measuring electric current 安，安培（電流單位）：*a 13 amp fuse/plug* * 13 安保險絲 / 插頭 **2** (*informal*) = AMPLIFIER

amped /æmpt/ (also **ˌamped ˈup**) *adj.* (*NAmE, informal*) excited, especially because of an event 興奮的；激動的：*an amped audience of hardcore fans* 狂熱的鐵杆支持者觀眾 ◇ *I get pretty amped up before I compete.* 在比賽之前我激動得熱血沸騰。

am·per·age /ˈæmpərɪdʒ/ *noun* [U] the strength of an electric current, measured in AMPS（電流強度）安培數

am·per·sand /ˈæmpəsænd; *NAmE* -pərs-/ *noun* the symbol &, used to mean 'and'（表示 and 的符號）：*She works for Bond & Green.* 她在邦德—格林公司工作。

am·phet·amine /æmˈfetəmiːn/ *noun* [C, U] a drug that makes you feel excited and full of energy. Amphetamines are sometimes taken illegally. 苯丙胺（中樞興奮藥）；安非他明

am·phib·ian /æmˈfɪbiən/ *noun* any animal that can live both on land and in water. Amphibians have cold blood and skin without SCALES. FROGS, TOADS and NEWTS are all amphibians. 兩棲動物 ➲ COLLOCATIONS at LIFE ➲ VISUAL VOCAB page V13 ➲ compare REPTILE

am·phibi·ous /æmˈfɪbiəs/ *adj.* **1** able to live both on land and in water（生物）水陸兩棲的 **2** (of military operations 軍事行動) involving soldiers landing at a place from the sea 兩棲作戰的；登陸的 **3** suitable for use on land or water 水陸兩用的：*amphibious vehicles* 水陸兩用車輛

amphi·theatre (*especially US* **-ter**) /ˈæmfɪθɪətə(r); *NAmE* -θiːətər/ *noun* **1** a round building without a roof and with rows of seats that rise in steps around an open space. Amphitheatres were used especially in ancient Greece and Rome for public entertainments.（尤指古希臘和古羅馬的）圓形露天劇場，圓形露天競技場 ➲ VISUAL VOCAB page V15 **2** a room, hall or theatre with rows of seats that rise in steps 階梯式座位大廳（或劇場、室） **3** (*technical* 術語) an open space that is surrounded by high sloping land 圓形凹地

am·phora /ˈæmfərə; *NAmE* also æmˈfɔːrə/ *noun* (*pl.* **am·phorae** /ˈæmfəriː; *NAmE* also æmˈfɔːriː/ or **am·phoras**) a tall ancient Greek or Roman container with two handles and a narrow neck（古希臘或羅馬的）雙耳細頸瓶

ampi·cil·lin /ˌæmpɪˈsɪlɪn/ *noun* [U] a form of PENICILLIN that is used to treat certain infections 氨苄青黴素；氨必西林

ample /ˈæmpl/ *adj.* **1** enough or more than enough 足夠的；豐裕的 **SYN** **plenty of**：*ample opportunity/evidence/space/proof* 充分的機會；足夠的證據；寬敞的空間；充足的證明 ◊ *There was ample time to get to the airport.* 有足夠的時間到達機場。◊ *Ample free parking is available.* 有寬敞的免費停車場。 **2** (of a person's figure 人的體形) large, often in an attractive way 豐滿的；碩大的：*an ample bosom* 豐滿的胸脯 ▸ **amply** /ˈæmpli/ *adv.*：*His efforts were amply rewarded.* 他的努力得到了豐厚的回報。

am·pli·fier /ˈæmplɪfaɪə(r)/ (also *informal* **amp**) *noun* an electrical device or piece of equipment that makes sounds or radio signals louder 放大器；擴音器；揚聲器：*a 25 watt amplifier* 一台 25 瓦擴音器 ➲ VISUAL VOCAB page V36

amp·lify /ˈæmplɪfaɪ/ *verb* (**amp·li·fies**, **amp·li·fy·ing**, **amp·li·fied**, **amp·li·fied**) **1** [T] **~ sth** to increase sth in strength, especially sound 放大，增強（聲音等）：*to **amplify** a guitar/an electric current/a signal* 放大吉他聲音／電流／信號 **2** [I, T] (*formal*) to add details to a story, statement, etc. 進一步敘述，闡發（故事、事情、陳述等）：*She refused to amplify further.* 她拒絕提供詳情。◊ **~ sth** *You may need to amplify this point.* 你可能需要對這一點進一步予以說明。 ▸ **amp·li·fi·ca·tion** /ˌæmplɪfɪˈkeɪʃn/ *noun* [U]：*electronic amplification* 電子放大 ◊ *That comment needs some amplification.* 這個評論需要一些闡明。

amp·li·tude /ˈæmplɪtjuːd; *NAmE* -tuːd/ *noun* [U, C] (*physics* 物) the greatest distance that a wave, especially a sound or radio wave, VIBRATES (= moves up and down)（聲音、無線電波等的）振幅 ➲ picture at WAVELENGTH

amply *adv.* ➲ AMPLE

am·poule (*US* also **am·pule**) /ˈæmpuːl; *NAmE* also -pjuːl/ *noun* a small container, usually made of glass, containing a drug that will be used for an INJECTION 安瓿（裝針劑的小玻璃瓶）

am·pu·tate /ˈæmpjuteɪt/ *verb* [T, I] **~ (sth)** to cut off sb's arm, leg, finger or toe in a medical operation（用外科手術）切斷；截（肢）：*He had to have both legs amputated.* 他不得不鋸掉雙腿。◊ *They may have to amputate.* 他們可能不得不施行截肢手術。 ➲ COLLOCATIONS at INJURY ▸ **am·pu·ta·tion** /ˌæmpjuˈteɪʃn/ *noun* [U, C]

am·pu·tee /ˌæmpjuˈtiː/ *noun* a person who has had an arm or a leg amputated 被截肢者

amu·let /ˈæmjʊlət/ *noun* a piece of jewellery that some people wear because they think it protects them from bad luck, illness, etc. 護身符，驅邪物（為祛邪防病等佩戴的珠寶）

amuse 🔑 /əˈmjuːz/ *verb*
1 🔑 to make sb laugh or smile 逗笑；逗樂：**~ sb** *My funny drawings amused the kids.* 我的滑稽圖畫把孩子們逗樂了。◊ *This will amuse you.* 這個會逗你笑的。◊ **it amuses sb to do sth** *It amused him to think that they were probably talking about him at that very moment.* 想到就在這會兒他們大概正在談論他，他不禁笑了起來。 **2** 🔑 to make time pass pleasantly for sb/yourself（提供）消遣；（使）娛樂 **SYN** **entertain**：**~ sb** *She suggested several ideas to help Laura amuse the twins.* 她給勞拉出了一些主意，好逗這對雙胞胎開心。◊ **~ yourself** *I'm sure I'll be able to amuse myself for a few hours.* 我相信我能自娛自樂幾個小時。

amused 🔑 /əˈmjuːzd/ *adj.* thinking that sb/sth is funny, so that you smile or laugh 逗樂的；覺得好笑的：*There was an amused look on the President's face.* 總統面帶愉悅的神情。◊ *Janet was **not amused*** (= she was annoyed or angry). 珍妮特感到惱怒。◊ **~ at/by sth** *We were all amused at his stories.* 我們都被他的故事逗笑了。◊ **~ to see, find, learn, etc.** *He was amused to see how seriously she took the game.* 他看見她玩這個遊戲十分認真的樣子，覺得好笑。

IDM **keep sb aˈmused** to give sb interesting things to do, or to entertain them so that they do not become bored 使某人快樂；使某人消遣：*Playing with water can keep children amused for hours.* 嬉水可以使孩子們玩樂好幾個小時。

amuse·ment /əˈmjuːzmənt/ *noun* **1** [U] the feeling that you have when sth is funny or amusing, or it entertains you 可笑；愉悅；娛樂：*She could not hide her amusement at the way he was dancing.* 她見他跳舞的姿勢，不禁笑出聲來。◊ ***To my amusement** he couldn't get the door open.* 使我感到好笑的是，他竟然打不開門。◊ *Her eyes twinkled **with amusement**.* 她的眼睛閃耀着愉悅的光芒。 **2** [C, usually pl.] a game, an activity, etc. that provides entertainment and pleasure 娛樂活動；遊戲；消遣活動：*traditional seaside amusements including boats, go-karts and a funfair* 包括乘船、微型單座賽車和露天遊樂場的傳統海濱娛樂活動

aˈmusement arcade (*BrE*) (also **ar·cade** *NAmE, BrE*) *noun* a place where you can play games on machines which you use coins to operate 遊戲機廳；電動遊樂場

aˈmusement park *noun* a large park which has a lot of things that you can ride and play on and many different activities to enjoy 遊樂場；娛樂園

amus·ing 🔑 /əˈmjuːzɪŋ/ *adj.* funny and enjoyable 逗人笑的；有樂趣的；好笑的：*an amusing story/game/incident* 逗人笑的故事／遊戲／事件 ◊ *I didn't find the joke at all amusing.* 我認為這笑話一點也不可笑。 ➲ SYNONYMS at FUNNY ▸ **amus·ing·ly** *adv.*

amyg·dala /əˈmɪɡdələ/ *noun* (*pl.* **amyg·da·lae** /əˈmɪɡdəliː/) (*anatomy* 解) either of two areas in the brain that are linked to memory, the emotions and the sense of smell 杏仁核，杏仁體（大腦的兩個區域之一，與記憶、情緒及味覺有關）

amy·lase /ˈæmɪleɪz; *NAmE* ˈæməleɪs/ *noun* [U] (*chemistry* 化) an ENZYME (= a substance that helps a chemical change to take place) that allows the body to change some substances into simple sugars 澱粉酶

an *indefinite article* ➲ A

-an, -ana ➲ -IAN, -IANA

ana·bol·ic ster·oid /ˌænəbɒlɪk ˈsterɔɪd; ˈstɪə-; *NAmE* ˌænəbɑːlɪk ˈster-; ˈstɪr-/ *noun* an artificial HORMONE (= a chemical substance) that increases the size of the muscles. It is sometimes taken illegally by people who play sports. 合成代謝類固醇（人工合成激素，能增大肌肉，有時被運動員違禁使用） ➲ see also STEROID

an·achron·ism /əˈnækrənɪzəm/ *noun* **1** a person, a custom or an idea that seems old-fashioned and does not belong to the present 過時的人（或風俗、思想）：*The monarchy is seen by many people as an anachronism in the modern world.* 很多人認為君主制在現代世界不合時宜。 **2** something that is placed, for example in a book or play, in the wrong period of history 弄錯年代；時代錯誤 ▸ **ana·chron·is·tic** /əˌnækrəˈnɪstɪk/ *adj.*

ana·conda /ˌænəˈkɒndə; *NAmE* -ˈkɑːn-/ *noun* a large S American snake of the BOA family, that crushes other animals to death before eating them 水蚺（南美洲蟒蛇）

an·aemia (*BrE*) (*NAmE* **an·e·mia**) /əˈniːmiə/ *noun* [U] a medical condition in which sb has too few red cells in their blood, making them look pale and feel weak 貧血（症）

an·aemic (*BrE*) (*NAmE* **an·emic**) /əˈniːmɪk/ *adj.* **1** suffering from anaemia 貧血的；患貧血症的：*She looks anaemic.* 她看來像是有貧血症。 **2** weak and not having much effect 衰弱無力的；無生氣的 **SYN** **feeble**：*an anaemic performance* 一場有氣無力的表演

an·aer·obic /ˌæneəˈrəʊbɪk; *NAmE* ˌæneˈroʊ-/ *adj.* **1** (*biology* 生) not needing OXYGEN 厭氧的：*anaerobic bacteria* 厭氧菌 **2** (of physical exercise 身體鍛煉) not especially designed to improve the function of the heart and lungs 無氧的（不專為改善心肺功能） **OPP** **aerobic**

an·aes·the·sia /ˌænəsˈθiːziə/ (*especially US* **an·es·the·sia** /-ˈθiːʒə/) *noun* [U] **1** the use of anaesthetic during medical operations 麻醉 **2** (*technical* 術語) the state of being unable to feel anything, especially pain 感覺缺失；麻木

an·aes·thet·ic (*especially US* **an·es·thet·ic**) /ˌænəsˈθetɪk/ *noun, adj.*

■ ***noun*** [U, C] a drug that makes a person or an animal unable to feel anything, especially pain, either in the whole body or in a part of the body 麻醉藥；麻醉劑：*How long will I **be under anaesthetic**?* 我會給麻醉多長時間？◇ *They gave him a **general anaesthetic*** (= one that makes you become unconscious). 他們對他施行了全身麻醉。◇ *(a) **local anaesthetic*** (= one that affects only a part of the body) 局部麻醉

■ ***adj.*** [only before noun] containing a substance that makes a person or an animal unable to feel pain in all or part of the body 麻醉的：*an **anaesthetic drug/spray*** 麻醉藥／噴劑

an·aes·the·tist (*especially US* **an·es·the·tist**) /əˈniːsθətɪst/ *noun* a person who is trained to give anaesthetics to patients 麻醉師

an·aes·the·tize (*BrE* also **-ise**) (*especially US* **an·es·the·tize**) /əˈniːsθətaɪz/ *verb* **~ sb** to make a person unable to feel pain, etc., especially by giving them an anaesthetic before a medical operation 使麻醉；使麻木

ana·gram /ˈænəɡræm/ *noun* a word or phrase that is made by arranging the letters of another word or phrase in a different order 相同字母異序詞：*An anagram of 'Elvis' is 'lives'.* * lives 是 Elvis 的一個異序詞。

anal /ˈeɪnl/ *adj.* **1** connected with the ANUS 肛門的：*the anal region* 肛門區 **2** (also **ˌanal-reˈtentive**) (*disapproving*) caring too much about small details and about how things are organized 挑剔枝節的；專注小事的 ▸ **anal·ly** /-nəli/ *adv.*

an·al·gesia /ˌænəlˈdʒiːziə; *NAmE* -ʒə/ *noun* [U] (*medical* 醫) the loss of the ability to feel pain while still conscious 痛覺缺失

an·al·gesic /ˌænəlˈdʒiːzɪk/ *noun* (*medical* 醫) a substance that reduces pain 止痛藥；鎮痛劑 SYN **painkiller**：*Aspirin is a mild analgesic.* 阿司匹林是藥性平和的止痛藥。▸ **an·al·gesic** *adj.*：***analgesic drugs/effects*** 止痛藥／藥效

analo·gous AW /əˈnæləɡəs/ *adj.* (*formal*) **~ (to/with sth)** similar in some way to another thing or situation and therefore able to be compared with it 相似的；類似的：*Sleep has often been thought of as being in some way analogous to death.* 人們常常認為睡眠在某種意義上來說類似死亡。

ana·logue (*BrE*) (*NAmE* **ana·log**) /ˈænəlɒɡ; *NAmE* -lɔːɡ; -lɑːɡ/ *adj., noun*

■ ***adj.*** (*technical* 術語) **1** (of an electronic process 電子處理方法) using a continuously changing range of physical quantities to measure or store data 模擬的：*an **analogue circuit/computer/signal*** 模擬線路／計算機／信號 **2** (*BrE* also **ana·log**) (of a clock or watch 鐘錶) showing the time using hands on a DIAL and not with a display of numbers 指針式的 ➲ compare DIGITAL

■ ***noun*** (*formal* or *technical* 術語) a thing that is similar to another thing 相似物；類似事情：*Scientists are attempting to compare features of extinct animals with living analogues.* 科學家正試圖把已滅絕動物的特徵與現存類似動物的相比較。

ana·logy AW /əˈnælədʒi/ *noun* (*pl.* **-ies**) **1** [C] a comparison of one thing with another thing that has similar features; a feature that is similar 類比；比擬；相似之處：**~ (between A and B)** *The teacher **drew an analogy** between the human heart and a pump.* 老師打了個比喻，把人的心臟比作水泵。◇ **~ (with sth)** *There are no analogies with any previous legal cases.* 以往的法律案件沒有哪一宗可與此案類比。 **2** [U] the process of comparing one thing with another thing that has similar features in order to explain it 類推；比擬：*learning **by analogy*** 用類推法學習

an·al·pha·bet·ic /ˌænælfəˈbetɪk/ *adj.* **1** (*technical* 術語) completely unable to read or write 全文盲的；完全不懂讀寫的 **2** = NON-ALPHABETIC **3** (*linguistics* 語言) representing sounds with signs made of several parts rather than by single letters or symbols 非拼音的；非字母的

ˌanal-reˈtentive *adj.* (*disapproving*) = ANAL (2)

ana·lyse 🔑 AW (*BrE*) (*NAmE* **ana·lyze**) /ˈænəlaɪz/ *verb*

1 🔑 to examine the nature or structure of sth, especially by separating it into its parts, in order to understand or explain it 分析：**~ sth** *The job involves gathering and analysing data.* 這項工作包括搜集和分析資料。◇ *He tried to analyse his feelings.* 他試圖分析自己的感情。◇ **~ what, how, etc. …** *We need to analyse what went wrong.* 我們需要分析是什麼出了差錯。➲ SYNONYMS at EXAMINE **2 ~ sb** = PSYCHOANALYSE

an·aly·sis 🔑 AW /əˈnæləsɪs/ *noun* (*pl.* **an·aly·ses** /-siːz/)

1 🔑 [U, C] the detailed study or examination of sth in order to understand more about it; the result of the study（對事物的）分析，分析結果：*statistical analysis* 統計分析 ◇ *The book is an analysis of poverty and its causes.* 這本書分析了貧困及其原因。 **2** 🔑 [U, C] a careful examination of a substance in order to find out what it consists of（對物質的）分析：*The blood samples are sent to the laboratory **for analysis**.* 血樣要送往實驗室進行分析。◇ *You can ask for a chemical analysis of your tap water.* 你可以要求給你的自來水做化學分析。 **3** [U] = PSYCHOANALYSIS：*In analysis the individual resolves difficult emotional conflicts.* 在心理分析治療法中，個人可以化解嚴重的情感衝突。

IDM **in the ˌfinal/ˌlast aˈnalysis** used to say what is most important after everything has been discussed, or considered 歸根結底；總之：*In the final analysis, it's a matter of personal choice.* 歸根結底，這是個人的選擇。

ana·lyst AW /ˈænəlɪst/ *noun* **1** a person whose job involves examining facts or materials in order to give an opinion on them 分析者；化驗員：*a political/food analyst* 政治分析家；食物化驗員 ◇ *City analysts forecast huge profits this year.* 倫敦金融分析家預測今年的利潤非常豐厚。➲ see also SYSTEMS ANALYST **2** = PSYCHOANALYST

ana·lyt·ic AW /ˌænəˈlɪtɪk/ *adj.* **1** (also **isol·at·ing**) (*linguistics* 語言) (of languages 語言) using word order rather than word endings to show the functions of words in a sentence 分析的，分析型的（用詞序而非詞尾顯示詞在句中的功能）➲ compare SYNTHETIC *adj.* (2) **2** = ANALYTICAL

ana·lyt·ic·al AW /ˌænəˈlɪtɪkl/ (also **ana·lyt·ic**) *adj.* **1** using a logical method of thinking about sth in order to understand it, especially by looking at all the parts separately 分析的；解析的；分析性的：*She has a clear analytical mind.* 她頭腦清醒，善於分析。◇ *an analytic approach to the problem* 用分析方法處理這個問題 **2** using scientific analysis in order to find out about sth（科學）分析的：*analytical methods of research* 分析研究法 ▸ **ana·lyt·ic·al·ly** AW /-kli/ *adv.*

ana·lyze AW (*NAmE*) = ANALYSE

ana·paest /ˈænəpiːst; -pest/ (*BrE*) (*NAmE* **ana·pest** /ˈænəpest/) *noun* (*technical* 術語) a unit of sound in poetry consisting of two weak or short syllables followed by one strong or long syllable 抑抑揚格（詩歌中由兩輕一重或兩短一長音節組成的音步）▸ **ana·paes·tic, ana·pes·tic** /ˌænəˈpiːstɪk; -ˈpestɪk; *NAmE* ˌænəˈpestɪk/ *adj.*

anaphor /ˈænəfə(r); -fɔː(r)/ *noun* (*grammar* 語法) a word or phrase that refers back to an earlier word or phrase. For example, in the phrase 'My mother said she was leaving', 'she' is used as an anaphor for 'my mother' 照應語，回指語（返指上文中的詞或詞組）

anaph·ora /əˈnæfərə/ *noun* [U] the use of a word that refers to or replaces another word used earlier in a sentence, for example the use of 'does' in the sentence 'I disagree and so does John' 逆向照應（下文的詞返指或代替上文的詞）▸ **ana·phor·ic** /ˌænəˈfɒrɪk; *NAmE* -ˈfɔːr-; -ˈfɑːr-/ *adj.*

ana·phyl·axis /ˌænəfɪˈlæksɪs/ *noun* [U, C] (*pl.* **ana·phyl·axes** /ˌænəfɪˈlæksiːz/) (*medical* 醫) an extreme ALLERGIC reaction to sth that you eat or touch 過敏反應 ▸ **ana·phyl·ac·tic** /ˌænəfɪˈlæktɪk/ *adj.*：*anaphylactic shock* 過敏性休克

A

an·arch·ism /ˈænəkɪzəm; *NAmE* ˈænərk-/ *noun* [U] the political belief that laws and governments are not necessary 無政府主義

an·arch·ist /ˈænəkɪst; *NAmE* ˈænərk-/ *noun* a person who believes that laws and governments are not necessary 無政府主義者 ▶ **an·arch·is·tic** /ˌænəˈkɪstɪk; *NAmE* ˌænərˈk-/ *adj.*

an·archy /ˈænəki; *NAmE* ˈænərki/ *noun* [U] a situation in a country, an organization, etc. in which there is no government, order or control 無政府狀態；混亂；無法無天：*The overthrow of the military regime was followed by a period of anarchy.* 軍事統治政權被推翻以後，接着是一段時期的無政府狀態。◇ *There was complete anarchy in the classroom when their usual teacher was away.* 級任老師不在時，班上一片混亂。▶ **an·arch·ic** /əˈnɑːkɪk; *NAmE* əˈnɑːrkɪk/ (also *less frequent* **an·arch·ic·al** /-kl/) *adj.*

anath·ema /əˈnæθəmə/ *noun* [U, C, usually sing.] (*formal*) a thing or an idea which you hate because it is the opposite of what you believe 可憎的事物；可惡的想法：*Racial prejudice is (an) anathema to me.* 對我來說，種族歧視非常可惡。

anato·mist /əˈnætəmɪst/ *noun* a scientist who studies anatomy 解剖學家

anat·omy /əˈnætəmi/ *noun* (*pl.* **-ies**) **1** [U] the scientific study of the structure of human or animal bodies 解剖學 **2** [C, U] the structure of an animal or a plant （動植物的）結構，解剖：*the anatomy of the horse* 馬的身體構造 ◇ *human anatomy* 人體解剖 **3** [C] (*humorous*) a person's body 人體：*Various parts of his anatomy were clearly visible.* 他身體的各個部位都清晰可見。**4** [C] (*formal*) an examination of what sth is like or why it happens 剖析；解析：*an anatomy of the current recession* 對當前衰退的剖析 ▶ **ana·tom·ical** /ˌænəˈtɒmɪkl; *NAmE* -ˈtɑːm-/ *adj.*：*anatomical diagrams* 解剖示意圖 **ana·tom·ic·al·ly** /-kli/ *adv.*

ANC /ˌeɪ en ˈsiː/ *abbr.* African National Congress (= a political party in South Africa) 非洲人國民大會，非洲民族議會（南非政黨）

-ance, **-ence** *suffix* (in nouns 構成名詞) the action or state of （表示行動或狀況）：*assistance* 幫助 ◇ *confidence* 信心

an·ces·tor /ˈænsestə(r)/ *noun* **1** a person in your family who lived a long time ago 祖宗；祖先 SYN **forebear**：*His ancestors had come to America from Ireland.* 他的祖先從愛爾蘭來到美國。**2** an animal that lived in the past which a modern animal has developed from（動物的）原種：*a reptile that was the common ancestor of lizards and turtles* 作為蜥蜴和龜的共同原種的一種爬行動物 **3** an early form of a machine which later became more developed （機器的）原型 SYN **forerunner**：*The ancestor of the modern bicycle was called a penny-farthing.* 現代自行車的原型稱作 penny-farthing（一種前輪大後輪小的自行車）。➲ compare DESCENDANT ▶ **an·ces·tral** /ænˈsestrəl/ *adj.*：*her ancestral home* (= that had belonged to her ANCESTORS) 她的祖居

an·ces·try /ˈænsestri/ *noun* [C, usually sing., U] (*pl.* **-ies**) the family or the race of people that you come from （統稱）祖宗，祖先；列祖列宗：*to have Scottish ancestry* 祖籍蘇格蘭 ◇ *He was able to trace his ancestry back over 1 000 years.* 他可追祖溯宗至 1 000 年以前。

an·chor /ˈæŋkə(r)/ *noun, verb*

■ *noun* **1** [C, U] a heavy metal object that is attached to a rope or chain and dropped over the side of a ship or boat to keep it in one place 錨：*to* **drop anchor** 拋錨 ◇ *The ship lay* **at anchor** *two miles off the rocky coast.* 船在離岩岸兩英里處拋錨停泊。◇ *We* **weighed anchor** (= pulled it out of the water). 我們起錨。**2** [C] a person or thing that gives sb a feeling of safety 給以安全感的人（或物）；精神支柱；頂梁柱：*the anchor of the family* 全家的頂梁柱 **3** [C] (*especially NAmE*) = ANCHORMAN, ANCHORWOMAN

■ *verb* **1** [I, T] ~ (**sth**) to let an anchor down from a boat or ship in order to prevent it from moving away 拋錨；下錨：*We anchored off the coast of Spain.* 我們在西班牙沿海拋錨停泊。**2** [T] ~ **sth** to fix sth firmly in position so that it cannot move 使固定；扣牢；繫牢：*Make sure the table is securely anchored.* 務必要把桌子固定好。**3** [T, usually passive] ~ **sb/sth** (**in/to sth**) to firmly base sth on sth else 使扎根；使基於：*Her novels are anchored in everyday experience.* 她的小說取材自日常生活經驗。**4** [I, T] ~ (**sth**) (*NAmE*) to be the person who introduces reports or reads the news on television or radio 主持（電視、廣播節目）：*She anchored the evening news for seven years.* 她主持了七年晚間新聞報道。

anchor 錨

an·chor·age /ˈæŋkərɪdʒ/ *noun* [C, U] **1** a place where ships or boats can anchor （船的）錨地，停泊處 **2** a place where sth can be fastened to sth else 固定處；扣牢處；繫牢點：*anchorage points for a baby's car seat* 汽車上嬰兒座位的扣牢點

an·chor·man /ˈæŋkəmæn; *NAmE* -kərm-/, **an·chor·woman** /ˈæŋkəwʊmən; *NAmE* -kərw-/ *noun* (*pl.* **-men** /-men/, **-women** /-wɪmɪn/) (also **an·chor** especially in *NAmE*) a man or woman who presents a live radio or television programme and introduces reports by other people（電台、電視現場直播的）節目主持人

an·chovy /ˈæntʃəvi; *NAmE* -tʃoʊvi/ *noun* [C, U] (*pl.* **-ies**) a small fish with a strong salty flavour 鯷（鹹水小魚）：*a pizza topped with cheese and anchovies* 奶酪和鯷魚比薩餅

an·cient 🔑 /ˈeɪnʃənt/ *adj.*

1 🔑 belonging to a period of history that is thousands of years in the past 古代的 OPP **modern**：***ancient history/civilization*** 古代史／文明 ◇ *ancient Greece* 古希臘 **2** 🔑 very old; having existed for a very long time 古老的；很老的：*an ancient oak tree* 古橡樹 ◇ *ancient monuments* 古跡 ◇ (*humorous*) *He's ancient—he must be at least fifty!* 他老得很了 —— 肯定至少有五十歲！**3 the ancients** *noun* [pl.] the people who lived in ancient times, especially the Egyptians, Greeks and Romans （尤指埃及、希臘和羅馬的）古代人 ▶ **an·cient·ly** *adv.*：*the area where the market was anciently held* (= in ancient times) 古代集市所在地

an·cil·lary /ænˈsɪləri; *NAmE* ˈænsəleri/ *adj.* ~ (**to sth**) **1** providing necessary support to the main work or activities of an organization 輔助的；補充的 SYN **auxiliary**：***ancillary staff/services/equipment*** 輔助人員／服務設施／設備 ◇ ***ancillary workers*** *in the health service such as cooks and cleaners* 公共醫療部門中諸如廚師和清潔工之類的輔助人員 **2** in addition to sth else but not as important 附屬的；附加的：*ancillary rights* 附屬權益

-ancy, **-ency** *suffix* (in nouns 構成名詞) the state or quality of （表示狀況或性質）：*expectancy* 期待 ◇ *complacency* 自滿

and 🔑 /ənd; ən; *also* n; *especially after* /t/; /d/; *strong form* ænd/ *conj.* (used to connect words or parts of sentences 用於連接單詞或句中並列部份) **1** 🔑 also; in addition to 和；與；同；又；而：*bread and butter* 塗黃油的麵包 ◇ *a table, two chairs and a desk* 一張桌子、兩把椅子和一張辦公桌 ◇ *Sue and I left early.* 我和蘇早離開了。◇ *Do it slowly and carefully.* 要慢慢仔細地做。◇ *Can he read and write?* 他能讀會寫嗎？◇ *I cooked lunch. And I made a cake.* (= you are emphasizing how much you have done) 我做了午飯，還做了一個蛋糕。HELP When **and** is used in common phrases connecting two things or people that are closely linked, the determiner is not usually repeated before the second: *a knife and fork* ◇ *my father and mother*, but: *a knife and a spoon* ◇ *my* *father and my uncle.* 如果 and 在一般短語中連接兩個聯繫密切的人或事物，第二個單詞前的限定詞通常省略：a knife and fork、my father and mother，而 a knife and a spoon、my father and my uncle 則不省略。 **2** added to 加；加上 SYN **plus**：*5 and 5 makes 10.* * 5 加 5 等於 10。◇ *What's 47 and 16?* * 47 加 16 得多少？ HELP When numbers (but not dates) are spoken, **and** is used between the hundreds and the figures that follow: *2 264—two thousand, two hundred* **and** *sixty-four*, but: *1964—nineteen sixty-four*. 口語中說數字時（日期除外），and 用於百位數與緊跟的數之間：2 264 說 two thousand, two hundred and sixty-four，但 1964 年只說 nineteen sixty-four。 **3** then; following this 然後；接着：*She came in and took her coat off.* 她進來後脫了外衣。 **4** **go, come, try, stay, etc. ~** used before a verb instead of *to*, to show purpose（用於動詞前代替 to，表示目的）…為了：*Go and get me a pen please.* 請你去給我拿支鋼筆來。◇ *I'll come and see you soon.* 我很快就會來看你。◇ *We stopped and bought some bread.* 我們停下來買了一些麪包。 HELP In this structure **try** can only be used in the infinitive or to tell somebody what to do. 在此結構中，try 只能用於不定式或祈使句。 **5** used to introduce a comment or a question（引出說話或提問）那麼，於是：*'We talked for hours.' 'And what did you decide?'* "我們談了好幾小時。" "那麼你們作出了什麼決定？" **6** as a result（表示結果）結果是；那麼；就：*Miss another class and you'll fail.* 你再缺一次課就會不及格。 **7** used between repeated words to show that sth is repeated or continuing（連接相同的詞，表示反複或連續）接連，又，愈來愈：*He tried and tried but without success.* 他反複嘗試，但沒有成功。◇ *The pain got worse and worse.* 疼痛越來越厲害了。 **8** used between repeated words to show that there are important differences between things or people of the same kind.（連接相同的詞，強調差別）與…不同，各有不同：*I like city life but there are cities and cities.* 我喜歡城市生活，但城市之間也有差異。 ➲ see also AND/OR

an·dante /æn'dænteɪ/ *noun* (*music* 音) a piece of music to be played fairly slowly 行板樂曲（速度稍緩） ▸ **an·dante** *adv., adj.*

and/or *conj.* (*informal*) used when you say that two situations exist together, or as an alternative to each other 和（或）；以及（或者）；和 / 或：*There is no help for those with lots of luggage and/or small children.* 對於行李多而且（或者）有小孩的人一點幫助都沒有。

an·dro·gen /'ændrədʒən/ *noun* (*biology* 生) a male sex HORMONE, for example TESTOSTERONE 雄激素

an·drogy·nous /æn'drɒdʒənəs; *NAmE* -'drɑːdʒ-/ *adj.* having both male and female characteristics; looking neither strongly male nor strongly female 雌雄同體的；兼具兩性的

an·droid /'ændrɔɪd/ (also **droid**) *noun* a ROBOT that looks like a real person 人形機器人

an·ec·dotal /ˌænɪk'dəʊtl; *NAmE* -'doʊtl/ *adj.* based on anecdotes and possibly not true or accurate 佚事的；趣聞的；傳聞的：*anecdotal evidence* 傳聞的證據 ▸ **an·ec·dot·al·ly** /-təli/ *adv.*：*This reaction has been reported anecdotally by a number of patients.* 一些患者據稱有這種反應。

an·ec·dote /'ænɪkdəʊt; *NAmE* -doʊt/ *noun* [C, U] **1** a short, interesting or amusing story about a real person or event 佚事；趣聞：*amusing anecdotes about his brief career as an actor* 關於他短暫演員生涯的趣聞佚事 **2** a personal account of an event 傳聞：*This research is based on anecdote, not fact.* 這項研究是根據傳聞，而非事實。

an·emia, an·emic (*NAmE*) = ANAEMIA, ANAEMIC

an·emom·eter /ˌænɪ'mɒmɪtə(r); *NAmE* -'mɑːm-/ (also **'wind gauge**) *noun* an instrument for measuring the speed of the wind or of a current of gas 風速計；風速儀

anem·one /ə'neməni/ *noun* a small plant with white, red, blue or purple flowers that are shaped like cups and have dark centres 銀蓮花，風花（開杯形有黑心的白、紅、藍、紫花） ➲ see also SEA ANEMONE

an·es·the·sia, an·es·thet·ic, an·es·the·tist, an·es·the·tize (*NAmE*) = ANAESTHESIA, ANAESTHETIC, ANAESTHETIST, ANAESTHETIZE

an·es·the·sio·logist /ˌænəsˌθiːzi'ɒlədʒɪst; *NAmE* -'ɑːlə-/ *noun* (*NAmE*) a doctor who studies the use of anaesthetics 麻醉師

an·eur·ysm /'ænjərɪzəm/ *noun* (*medical* 醫) an area of extreme swelling on the wall of an ARTERY 動脈瘤

anew /ə'njuː; *NAmE* ə'nuː/ *adv.* (*formal*) if sb does sth **anew**, they do it again from the beginning or do it in a different way 重新；再：*They started life anew in Canada.* 他們在加拿大開始新生。

angel /'eɪndʒl/ *noun* **1** a spirit who is believed to be a servant of God, and is sent by God to deliver a message or perform a task. Angels are often shown dressed in white, with wings. 天使 ➲ see also GUARDIAN ANGEL **2** a person who is very good and kind; a child who behaves well 安琪兒（指善良的人或可愛的小孩）；善人：*John* **is no angel**, *believe me* (= he does not behave well). 相信我，約翰絕非善良之輩。 **3** (*informal*) used when you are talking to sb and you are grateful to them 大好人（感激某人時所說）：*Thanks Dad,* **you're an angel**. 謝謝爸爸，你是個大好人。◇ **Be an angel** *and make me a cup of coffee.* 行行好，給我泡杯咖啡。 IDM see FOOL *n.*

Angel·eno (also **Angel·ino**) /ˌændʒə'liːnəʊ; *NAmE* -'liːnoʊ/ *noun* (*pl.* **-os**) (*informal*) a person who lives in Los Angeles 洛杉磯人

angel·fish /'eɪndʒlfɪʃ/ *noun* (*pl.* **angel·fish** or **angel·fishes**) a type of brightly coloured FRESHWATER or SALTWATER fish with a thin deep body and long FINS 神仙魚

'angel food cake *noun* [U, C] (*NAmE*) a light cake made with the white part of eggs and without fat, often baked in a ring shape 天使蛋糕，安琪兒蛋糕（用蛋白做成的脫脂鬆軟蛋糕，常為環狀）

an·gel·ic /æn'dʒelɪk/ *adj.* good, kind or beautiful; like an angel 善良的；美麗的；天使般的：*an angelic smile* 天使般的微笑 ▸ **an·gel·ic·al·ly** *adv.* /-kli/

an·gel·ica /æn'dʒelɪkə/ *noun* [U] pieces of a plant with a sweet smell, that have been boiled in sugar and are used to decorate cakes 白芷（糖漬可作甜點配飾）

an·gelus /'ændʒələs/ (also **the Angelus**) *noun* [sing.] (in the Roman Catholic Church 羅馬天主教) prayers said in the morning, at midday and in the evening; a bell rung when it is time for these prayers 三鐘經（於晨、午、晚頌唸）；三鐘經的鳴鐘

anger /'æŋgə(r)/ *noun, verb*

▪ *noun* [U] the strong feeling that you have when sth has happened that you think is bad and unfair 怒；怒火；怒氣：*Jan slammed her fist on the desk* **in anger**. 簡氣憤地捶打桌子。◇ *the growing anger and frustration of young unemployed people* 年輕失業者日益增長的憤怒和沮喪 ◇ **~ at sb/sth** *He was filled with anger at the way he had been treated.* 他因遭受如此待遇而怒火滿腔。

▪ *verb* [often passive] **~ sb** to make sb angry 使發怒；激怒：*The question clearly angered him.* 這個問題顯然激怒了他。

an·gina /æn'dʒaɪnə/ (also *technical* 術語 **an·gina pec·toris** /ænˌdʒaɪnə 'pektərɪs/) *noun* [U] (*medical* 醫) severe pain in the chest caused by a low supply of blood to the heart during exercise because the ARTERIES are partly blocked 心絞痛

angio·plasty /'ændʒiəʊplæsti; *NAmE* 'ændʒioʊ-/ *noun* [C, U] (*pl.* **-ies**) (*medical* 醫) a medical operation to repair or open a blocked BLOOD VESSEL, especially either of the two ARTERIES that supply blood to the heart 血管成形術（修復或打開栓塞的冠狀動脈血管等）

angle /'æŋgl/ *noun, verb*

▪ *noun* **1** the space between two lines or surfaces that join, measured in degrees 角：*a 45° angle* * 45° 角 ➲ VISUAL VOCAB page V71 ➲ see also ACUTE ANGLE, ADJACENT ANGLE, CORRESPONDING ANGLES, OBTUSE ANGLE, RIGHT ANGLE, WIDE-ANGLE LENS **2** the direction that sth is leaning or pointing in when it is not in a vertical or horizontal line 斜角；角度：*The tower of Pisa leans **at an angle**.* 比薩斜塔塔身傾斜。◇ *The plane was coming in at a steep angle.* 飛機當時正俯衝降落。◇ *His hair was sticking up at all angles.* 他的頭髮都豎了起來，亂蓬蓬的。 **3** 0┳ a position from which you look at sth 角度：*The photo was taken from an unusual angle.* 這張照片是從不尋常角度拍攝的。 **4** 0┳ a particular way of presenting or thinking about a situation, problem, etc. 觀點；立場；角度：*We need a new angle for our next advertising campaign.* 我們需要從一個新的角度去展開下一次廣告活動。◇ *You can look at the issue from many different angles.* 你可以從很多不同的角度看這個問題。◇ *The article concentrates on the human angle* (= the part that concerns people's emotions) *of the story.* 這篇文章集中討論了故事中人的情感問題。

■ *verb* **1** [T] **~ sth** to move or place sth so that it is not straight or not directly facing sb/sth 斜移；斜置：*He angled his chair so that he could sit and watch her.* 他斜移了椅子，以便坐着觀察她。 **2** [T] **~ sth** to present information, a report, etc. based on a particular way of thinking or for a particular audience 以（某角度）報道；以（某觀點）提供信息：*The programme is angled towards younger viewers.* 這個節目的對象是較年輕的觀眾。 **3** (usually **go angling**) [I] to catch fish with a line and a hook 垂釣；釣魚

PHR V **'angle for sth** to try to get a particular reaction or response from sb, without directly asking for what you want 轉彎抹角地打聽；博取：*She was angling for sympathy.* 她有意博取同情。

'angle bracket *noun* [usually pl.] one of a pair of marks, < >, used around words or figures to separate them from the surrounding text 尖角括號

ang·ler /ˈæŋɡlə(r)/ *noun* a person who catches fish (= goes angling) as a hobby 垂釣者 ➲ compare FISHERMAN

An·gli·can /ˈæŋɡlɪkən/ *noun* a member of the Church of England or of a Church connected with it in another country 聖公會教徒 ▸ **An·gli·can** *adj.*：*the Anglican Church* 聖公會

An·gli·cism /ˈæŋɡlɪsɪzəm/ *noun* a word or phrase from the English language that is used in another language 英式用語，英式說法（指從英語中借用的詞語）：*Many French people try to avoid Anglicisms such as 'weekend' and 'shopping'.* 很多法國人盡量避免使用 weekend 和 shopping 之類的英式用語。

an·gli·cize (*BrE* also **-ise**) /ˈæŋɡlɪsaɪz/ *verb* **~ sb/sth** to make sb/sth English in character 使英語化；使英國化：*Gutmann anglicized his name to Goodman.* * Gutmann 把他的名字改為英語化的 Goodman。

an·gling /ˈæŋɡlɪŋ/ *noun* [U] (*BrE*) the art or sport of catching fish with a FISHING ROD, usually in rivers and lakes rather than in the sea 垂釣

Anglo /ˈæŋɡləʊ; *NAmE* ˈæŋɡloʊ/ *noun* (*pl.* **-os**) **1** (*especially US*) a white person of European origin 歐裔白人 **2** (*CanE, informal*) = ANGLOPHONE

Anglo- /ˈæŋɡləʊ; *NAmE* ˈæŋɡloʊ/ *combining form* (in nouns and adjectives 構成名詞和形容詞) English or British 英格蘭的；英國的：*Anglo-American* 英美的 ◇ *Anglophile* 親英者 ◇ *Anglo-Indian* 英印的

ˌAnglo-ˈCatholic *noun* a member of the part of the Church of England that is most similar to the Roman Catholic Church in its beliefs and practices 英國國教高派教會教徒（英國聖公會內一派的教徒，信仰與禮儀與羅馬天主教最相似）

anglo·mania /ˌæŋɡləʊˈmeɪniə; *NAmE* ˌæŋɡloʊ-/ *noun* [U] an extremely strong admiration for England or English customs 英國狂（對英國或英國習俗的迷戀）

ˌAnglo-ˈNorman *noun* [U] a form of Norman French spoken in England in the MIDDLE AGES 盎格魯－諾曼語，英國法語（指中世紀英格蘭人講的諾曼法語）

Anglo·phile /ˈæŋɡləʊfaɪl; *NAmE* ˈæŋɡloʊ-/ *noun* a person who is not British but who likes Britain or British things very much 親英者；崇英者

Anglo·pho·bia /ˌæŋɡləʊˈfəʊbiə; *NAmE* ˌæŋɡloʊˈfoʊbiə/ *noun* [U] hatred or fear of England or Britain 仇英；恐英 ▸ **Anglo·phobe** /ˈæŋɡləʊfəʊb; *NAmE* ˈæŋɡloʊfoʊb/ *noun*：*Her father was an Anglophobe.* 她父親是個仇英分子。 **Anglo·phobic** /ˌæŋɡləʊˈfəʊbɪk; *NAmE* ˌæŋɡloʊˈfoʊbɪk/ *adj.*

anglo·phone /ˈæŋɡləʊfəʊn; *NAmE* -oʊfoʊn/ *noun* a person who speaks English, especially in countries where English is not the only language that is spoken 講英語的人（尤指在英語非唯一語言的國家） ▸ **anglo·phone** *adj.*：*anglophone communities* 英語社區

ˌAnglo-ˈSaxon *noun* **1** [C] a person whose ANCESTORS were English 盎格魯－撒克遜人（英國血統的人） **2** [C] an English person of the period before the Norman Conquest（諾曼人征服以前的）英國人 **3** [U] the Old English language 盎格魯－撒克遜語；古英語 ▸ **ˌAnglo-ˈSaxon** *adj.*：*Anglo-Saxon kings* 盎格魯－撒克遜國王

the Anglo·sphere /ˈæŋɡləʊsfɪə(r); *NAmE* ˈæŋɡloʊsfɪr/ *noun* [sing.] the group of countries where English is the main language 英語文化圈

an·gora /æŋˈɡɔːrə/ *noun* **1** [C] a breed of cat, GOAT or RABBIT that has long smooth hair 安哥拉貓（或山羊、兔） **2** [U] a type of soft wool or cloth made from the hair of the angora GOAT or RABBIT 安哥拉山羊毛（織物）；安哥拉兔毛（織物）：*an angora sweater* 安哥拉羊毛套衫

An·gos·tura™ /ˌæŋɡəˈstjʊərə; *NAmE* -ˈstʊrə/ (also **ˌAngostura ˈbitters**) *noun* [U] a bitter liquid, flavoured with the BARK of a tropical tree, that is used to give flavour to alcoholic drinks 安戈斯圖拉液，芸香精油（一種熱帶樹皮調製的苦味液，用於酒精飲料調味）

angrez /ʌŋˈreɪz/ *noun* (*pl.* **angrez**) (*IndE, informal*) an English person 英國人；英國佬

angry 0┳ /ˈæŋɡri/ *adj.* (**an·grier**, **an·gri·est**) **HELP** You can also use **more angry** and **most angry**. 亦可用 more angry 和 most angry。

1 0┳ having strong feelings about sth that you dislike very much or about an unfair situation 發怒的；憤怒的；生氣的：*Her behaviour really **made me angry**.* 她的行為確實令我惱火。◇ *Thousands of angry demonstrators filled the square.* 廣場上聚滿了成千上萬的憤怒示威者。◇ *The comments provoked an angry response from union leaders.* 這些評論激起了工會領導人的憤怒。◇ **~ with/at sb** *Please don't **be angry** with me. It wasn't my fault.* 請別衝着我發脾氣，不是我的錯。◇ **~ with/at sb about/for sth** *I was very angry with myself for making such a stupid mistake.* 我很生自己的氣，竟犯了這樣愚蠢的錯誤。◇ **~ at/about/over sth** *He felt angry at the injustice of the situation.* 他對這種不公的現象感到憤憤不平。◇ *The passengers grew angry about the delay.* 延誤使乘客氣憤起來。 **2** (of a wound 傷口) red and infected 紅腫的；感染的；發炎的 **3** (*literary*) (of the sea or the sky 海或天空) dark and STORMY 狂風暴雨的；波濤洶湧的；天昏地暗的 ▸ **an·grily** 0┳ /-əli/ *adv.*：*Some senators reacted angrily to the President's remarks.* 一些參議員對總統的言辭感到憤怒，反應強烈。◇ *He swore angrily.* 他憤然咒罵。

angst /æŋst/ *noun* [U] (from *German*) a feeling of anxiety and worry about a situation, or about your life（對形勢、事態、生活的）憂慮，焦慮：*songs full of teenage angst* 充滿青少年焦慮的歌曲

ˈangst-ridden *adj.* having feelings of angst 憂慮的；焦慮的：*a generation of angst-ridden adolescents* 焦慮躁動的青少年一代

ang·strom /ˈæŋstrəm/ *noun* (*chemistry* 化, *physics* 物) a very small unit of length, equal to 1×10^{-10} metre, used for measuring WAVELENGTHS and the distance between atoms 埃（長度的單位，等於 10^{-10} 米，用於量度波長和原子間的距離）

angsty /ˈæŋsti/ *adj.* having or showing feelings of angst 憂慮的；焦慮的：*Stefan plays the role of a rebellious, angsty outsider who joins a terrorist cell.* 斯蒂芬扮演叛逆、焦躁的角色，不見容於社會，並加入了恐怖組織。◇ *angsty poetry/drama/lyrics* 格調憂鬱的詩歌／戲劇／歌詞

Synonyms 同義詞辨析

angry

mad • indignant • cross • irate

These words all describe people feeling and/or showing anger. 以上各詞均形容人憤怒和／或發怒。

angry feeling or showing anger 指憤怒、發怒：*Please don't be angry with me.* 請別生我的氣。◇ *Thousands of angry demonstrators filled the square.* 廣場上聚滿了成千上萬的憤怒示威者。

mad [not before noun] (*informal, especially NAmE*) angry 指憤怒或發怒：*He got **mad** and walked out.* 他大動肝火，憤然離去。◇ *She's **mad at me** for being late.* 我遲到了，她非常生氣。NOTE **Mad** is the usual word for 'angry' in informal American English. In British English, the phrase 'go mad' means 'very angry'. 在非正式的美式英語中，mad 為表示憤怒或發怒（angry）的常用詞。在英式英語中，短語 go mad 表示非常氣憤：*Dad'll go mad when he sees what you've done.* 父親看到你的所作所為會非常氣憤。'Go mad' can also mean 'go crazy' or 'get very excited'. * go mad 也可指發瘋、發狂或激動起來。

indignant feeling or showing anger and surprise because you think that you or sb else has been treated unfairly 指因遭遇或見到不公平的事而憤慨、憤怒：*She was very indignant at the way she had been treated.* 她對自己受到的待遇大為光火。

cross (*especially BrE, rather informal*) rather angry or annoyed 指十分憤怒、惱怒：*I was quite cross with him for being late.* 我因他遲到而十分生氣。NOTE This word is often used by or to children. 該詞常為兒童用語或對兒童的用語。

irate very angry 指極其憤怒的、暴怒的：*irate customers* 憤怒的顧客 ◇ *an irate letter* 言辭激憤的信 NOTE **Irate** is not usually followed by a preposition. * irate 後通常不跟介詞：~~*She was irate with me/about it.*~~

PATTERNS

- angry/mad/indignant/cross **about/at** sth
- angry/cross **with** sb (for doing sth)
- angry/mad/indignant/cross **that** ...
- to **get** angry/mad/cross
- to **make sb** angry/mad/cross

an·guish /'æŋɡwɪʃ/ *noun* [U] (*formal*) severe pain, mental suffering or unhappiness 劇痛；極度痛苦；苦惱：*He groaned in anguish.* 他痛苦地呻吟。◇ *Tears of anguish filled her eyes.* 她雙眸噙滿了傷心的淚水。▶ **an·guished** *adj.*：*anguished cries* 痛苦不堪的喊聲 ◇ *an anguished letter from her prison cell* 她從獄中寄來的一封悲痛欲絕的信

an·gu·lar /'æŋɡjələ(r)/ *adj.* **1** (of a person 人) thin and without much flesh so that the bones are noticeable 瘦骨嶙峋的；骨瘦如柴的：*an angular face* 瘦削的臉 ◇ *a tall angular woman* 又高又瘦的女人 **2** having angles or sharp corners 有稜角的；有尖角的：*a design of large angular shapes* 大稜角形的圖案

ani·mal 🔑 /'ænɪml/ *noun, adj.*

■ **noun 1** 🔑 a creature that is not a bird, a fish, a REPTILE, an insect or a human 獸；牲畜；動物（不包括鳥、魚、爬行動物、昆蟲和人）：*the animals and birds of South America* 南美的鳥獸 ◇ *a small furry animal* 毛茸茸的小動物 ◇ *Fish oils are less saturated than animal fats.* 魚油不如動物脂肪飽和。◇ *domestic animals such as dogs and cats* 狗貓之類的家畜 **2** 🔑 any living thing that is not a plant or a human 動物（不包括植物或人的生物）：*the animal kingdom* 動物界 ◇ *This product has not been tested on animals.* 這種產品尚未在動物身上試驗。➲ VISUAL VOCAB pages V12, V13 **3** 🔑 any living creature, including humans 動物（包括人）：*Humans are the only animals to have developed speech.* 人是唯一發展出語言的動物。➲ COLLOCATIONS at LIFE ➲ compare VEGETABLE (1) **4** a person who behaves in a cruel or unpleasant way, or who is very dirty 衣冠禽獸；殘暴的人；卑鄙下流的人：*The person who did this is an animal, a brute.* 幹這種事的人是畜生，是野獸。**5** a particular type of person, thing, organization, etc. 某類型的人（或事物、機構等）：*She's not a political animal.* 她不是搞政治的那種人。◇ *The government that followed the election was a very different animal.* 選舉後的政府與前一屆截然不同。➲ see also DUMB ANIMAL, HIGHER ANIMALS

■ **adj.** [only before noun] relating to the physical needs and basic feelings of people 肉體的；肉慾的；情慾的：***animal desires/passion/instincts*** 獸慾；肉慾激情；情慾本能 ◇ ***animal magnetism*** (= a quality in sb that other people find attractive, usually in a sexual way) 對異性的吸引力

ˌanimal conˈtrol officer *noun* (*NAmE, formal*) a person whose job is to catch animals that are walking freely in the streets and do not seem to have a home 流浪動物管理員 ➲ compare DOGCATCHER

ˌanimal ˈhusbandry *noun* [U] (*technical* 術語) farming that involves keeping animals to produce food 畜牧業

ˌanimal ˈrights *noun* [pl.] the rights of animals to be treated well, for example by not being hunted or used for medical research 動物權益（指獲得善待，如不能獵殺或用於醫學研究）：*His research work was attacked by **animal rights activists**.* 他的研究受到了動物權益維護者的抨擊。

an·im·ate *verb, adj.*

■ **verb** /'ænɪmeɪt/ **1 ~ sth** to make sth more lively or full of energy 使具活力；使生氣勃勃：*A smile suddenly animated her face.* 她嫣然一笑，立顯容光煥發。**2** [usually passive] **~ sth** to make models, toys, etc. seem to move in a film/movie by rapidly showing slightly different pictures of them in a series, one after another 把…製作成動畫片

■ **adj.** /'ænɪmət/ (*formal*) living; having life 有生命的；有活力的；有生氣的：*animate beings* 生物 OPP **inanimate**

ani·mated /'ænɪmeɪtɪd/ *adj.* **1** full of interest and energy 興致勃勃的；活躍的；生氣勃勃的 SYN **lively**：***an animated discussion/conversation*** 熱烈的討論；興致勃勃的交談 ◇ *Her face suddenly became animated.* 她的面孔突然變得生氣盎然。**2** (of pictures, drawings, etc. in a film/movie 電影的畫面、圖畫等) made to look as if they are moving 栩栩如生的；（似）能活動的：***animated cartoons/graphics/models*** 動畫片；活動圖形／模型 ▶ **ani·mated·ly** *adv.*：*People were talking animatedly.* 人們熱烈地交談著。

an·ima·teur /ˌænɪmə'tɜː(r)/ *noun* (from French) a person whose job is to organize or encourage artistic or social projects and activities（藝術或社會活動的）發起人，倡導者

ani·ma·tion /ˌænɪ'meɪʃn/ *noun* **1** [U] energy and enthusiasm in the way you look, behave or speak 生氣；活力；富有生命力：*His face was drained of all colour and animation.* 他面如死灰。➲ see also SUSPENDED ANIMATION **2** [U] the process of making films/movies, videos and computer games in which drawings or models of people and animals seem to move（電影、錄像、電腦遊戲的）動畫製作：***computer/cartoon animation*** 電腦動畫／動畫片製作 **3** [C] a film/movie in which drawings of people and animals seem to move 動畫片：*The electronic dictionary included some animations.* 電子詞典中有一些動畫片。

ani·ma·tor /'ænɪmeɪtə(r)/ *noun* a person who makes animated films 動畫片製作者；動畫片繪製者

anima·tron·ics /ˌænɪmə'trɒnɪks; *NAmE* -'trɑːn-/ *noun* [U] the process of making and operating ROBOTS that look like real people or animals, used in films/movies and other types of entertainment 電子動畫製作技術（電影等製作中機器人或動物的製造和操作）▶ **anima·tron·ic** *adj.*

anime /'ænɪmeɪ; 'ænɪmə/ *noun* [U] Japanese film/movie and television ANIMATION, often with a SCIENCE FICTION subject 日本動畫片（常以科幻為主題）

ani·mism /'ænɪmɪzəm/ *noun* [U] **1** the belief that plants, objects and natural things such as the weather have a living soul 泛靈論；萬物有靈論 **2** belief in a power that organizes and controls the universe 神力主宰論（認為有某種力量掌管宇宙）▸ **ani·mist** /'ænɪmɪst/ *noun* **ani·mis·tic** /ˌænɪ'mɪstɪk/ *adj.*

ani·mos·ity /ˌænɪ'mɒsəti; *NAmE* -'mɑːs-/ *noun* [U, C] (*pl.* **-ies**) a strong feeling of opposition, anger or hatred 仇恨；憤怒；敵意；憎惡 SYN **hostility**：**~ (toward(s) sb/sth)** *He felt no animosity towards his critics.* 他對批評他的人並不心懷怨恨。◇ **~ (between A and B)** *personal animosities between members of the two groups* 兩個集團成員之間的私仇

ani·mus /'ænɪməs/ *noun* [U, sing.] **~ (against sb/sth)** (*formal*) a strong feeling of opposition, anger or hatred 仇恨；憤怒；敵意

anion /'ænaɪən/ *noun* (*chemistry* 化, *physics* 物) an ION with a negative electrical CHARGE 負離子；陰離子 ➲ compare CATION

anise /'ænɪs/ *noun* [U] a plant with seeds that smell sweet 茴芹

ani·seed /'ænəsiːd/ *noun* [U] the dried seeds of the anise plant, used to give flavour to alcoholic drinks and sweets/candy 茴芹籽（用於酒精飲料及糖果）

ankh 安可

ankh /æŋk/ *noun* an object or design like a cross but with a LOOP instead of the top arm, sometimes worn as jewellery. The ankh was used in ancient Egypt as the symbol of life. 安可（頂部為環狀結構的"十"字，古埃及用以象徵生命）

ankle 🔑 /'æŋkl/ *noun* the joint connecting the foot to the leg 踝；踝關節：*to **sprain/break your ankle*** 扭傷 / 折斷你的踝關節 ◇ *My ankles have swollen.* 我的兩個腳腕子都腫了。◇ *We found ourselves **ankle-deep** in water* (= the water came up to our ankles). 水淹到了我們的腳踝。◇ ***ankle boots*** (= that cover the ankle) 及踝短筒靴 ➲ VISUAL VOCAB page V59

'ankle sock (*BrE*) (*US* **ank·let**) *noun* a type of very short sock 套襪，船襪（只及踝關節處）：*a girl in a blue dress and ankle socks* 身穿藍色連衣裙和套襪的女孩

ank·let /'æŋklət/ *noun* **1** a piece of jewellery worn around the ankle 腳鐲；踝環 **2** (*US*) (*BrE* **'ankle sock**) a type of very short sock 套襪，船襪（只及踝關節處）

an·ky·lo·saur /'æŋkɪləsɔː(r)/ *noun* a type of plant-eating DINOSAUR covered with hard plates made of bone for protection 甲龍（食草恐龍，全身披甲）

anna /'ʌnə/ *noun* (*IndE*) **1** an older brother 哥哥；兄長 **2** the leader of a group of young people who go around together and sometimes cause trouble 小混混頭兒；（青少年幫派的）老大

annals /'ænlz/ *noun* [pl.] **1** an official record of events or activities year by year; historical records 編年史；歷史記載：*His deeds went down **in the annals of** British history.* 他的事跡已載入英國編年史。 **2** used in the title of academic JOURNALS（用於學術雜誌的名稱）年報，年鑒：*Annals of Science, vol. viii*《科學年報》卷八

an·neal /ə'niːl/ *verb* **~ sth** (*technical* 術語) to heat metal or glass and allow it to cool slowly, in order to make it stronger or softer 給（金屬或玻璃）退火

annex /ə'neks/ *verb* **~ sth** (*formal*) to take control of a country, region, etc., especially by force 強佔，併吞（國家、地區等）SYN **occupy**：*Germany annexed Austria in 1938.* * 1938 年德國吞併了奧地利。▸ **an·nex·ation** /ˌænek'seɪʃn/ *noun* [U, C]

an·nexe (*BrE*) (also **annex** *NAmE, BrE*) /'æneks/ *noun* **1** a building that is added to, or is near, a larger one and that provides extra living or work space 附屬建築物；附加建築物：*Our rooms were in the annexe.* 我們的房間在附屬建築物裏。 **2** (*formal*) an extra section of a document（文件的）附件，附錄 SYN **appendix**

an·ni·hi·late /ə'naɪəleɪt/ *verb* **1 ~ sb/sth/yourself** to destroy sb/sth completely 消滅；殲滅；毀滅：*The human race has enough weapons to annihilate itself.* 人類有足夠的武器滅絕自己。 **2 ~ sb/sth** to defeat sb/sth completely 徹底擊敗：*She annihilated her opponent, who failed to win a single game.* 她大獲全勝，對方連一局也沒有贏。▸ **an·ni·hi·la·tion** /əˌnaɪə'leɪʃn/ *noun* [U]：*the annihilation of the whole human race* 全人類的毀滅

an·ni·ver·sary 🔑 /ˌænɪ'vɜːsəri; *NAmE* -'vɜːrs-/ *noun* (*pl.* **-ies**) a date that is an exact number of years after the date of an important or special event 週年紀念日：*on the anniversary of his wife's death* 在他妻子去世的週年忌日 ◇ *to celebrate your **wedding anniversary*** 慶祝結婚紀念日 ◇ *the theatre's 25th anniversary celebrations* 劇院 25 週年慶祝活動 ➲ COLLOCATIONS at MARRIAGE

an·no·tate /'ænəteɪt/ *verb* **~ sth** to add notes to a book or text, giving explanations or comments 給…作註解（或評註）▸ **an·no·ta·tion** /ˌænə'teɪʃn/ *noun* [C, U]：*It will be published with annotations and an index.* 這本書出版時將附有註釋和索引。 **an·no·tated** *adj.*：*an annotated edition* 附有註解的版本

an·nounce 🔑 /ə'naʊns/ *verb*

1 🔑 to tell people sth officially, especially about a decision, plans, etc. 宣佈，宣告（決定、計劃等）：**~ sth** *They haven't formally announced their engagement yet.* 他們還沒有正式宣佈訂婚。◇ (*figurative*) *A ring at the doorbell announced Jack's arrival.* 門鈴一響就知道傑克駕到。◇ **~ sth to sb** *The government yesterday announced to the media plans to create a million new jobs.* 政府在昨天向媒體宣佈了創造一百萬個新工作的計劃。 HELP You cannot 'announce somebody something'. 不能說 announce somebody something：~~*They announced us their decision.*~~ ◇ **~ that …** *We are pleased to announce that all five candidates were successful.* 我們高興地宣佈，五位候選人全都當選了。◇ **it is announced that …** *It was announced that new speed restrictions would be introduced.* 據宣佈，將推行新的速度限制。➲ SYNONYMS at DECLARE **2** 🔑 to give information about sth in a public place, especially through a LOUDSPEAKER（尤指通過廣播）通知：**~ sth** *Has our flight been announced yet?* 廣播宣佈了我們的航班沒有？◇ **+ speech** *'Now boarding flight 897, destination Seattle,' the loudspeaker announced.* "飛往西雅圖的 897 次航班現在開始登機。"廣播通知說。◇ **~ that …** *They announced that the flight would be delayed.* 廣播通知，該航班將誤點。 **3** 🔑 to say sth in a loud and/or serious way 聲稱；宣稱：**+ speech** *'I've given up smoking,' she announced.* "我戒煙了。"她鄭重其事地說。◇ **~ that …** *She announced that she'd given up smoking.* 她宣稱已戒煙。➲ SYNONYMS at DECLARE **4 ~ yourself/sb** to tell sb your name or sb else's name when you or they arrive at a place 宣佈（某人）到達；通報…的到來：*Would you announce the guests as they arrive?* (= call out their names, for example at a formal party) 客人到達時請你通報他們的姓名好嗎？ **5 ~ sth** to introduce, or to give information about, a programme on the radio or television（在廣播或電視中）播音，廣播

an·nounce·ment /ə'naʊnsmənt/ *noun* **1** [C] a spoken or written statement that informs people about sth（一項）公告，佈告，通告：*to **make an announcement*** 發表公告 ◇ *Today's announcement of a peace agreement came after weeks of discussion.* 經過幾週的討論之後，今天公佈了和平協議。◇ *Announcements of births, marriages and deaths appear in some newspapers.* 有些報紙刊登出生、結婚、死亡通告。➲ SYNONYMS at STATEMENT **2** [U] the act of publicly informing people about sth（指行動）宣佈，宣告：*Announcement of the verdict was accompanied by shouts and cheers.* 在一片喊叫和歡呼聲中宣佈了正式判決。

an·noun·cer /ə'naʊnsə(r)/ *noun* **1** a person who introduces, or gives information about, programmes on the radio or television（廣播、電視的）廣播員，播音員，節目主持人 ➲ see also HOST *n.* (3), PRESENTER (1) **2** a person who gives information about sth in a station, an airport, etc., especially through a LOUDSPEAKER（車站、機場等的）廣播員，播音員

annoy 🔑 /ə'nɔɪ/ *verb*
1 🔑 to make sb slightly angry 使惱怒；使生氣 SYN **irritate**：**~ sb** *His constant joking was beginning to annoy her.* 他不停地開玩笑，已開始惹她生氣。◇ **it annoys sb when …** *It really annoys me when people forget to say thank you.* 有人連謝謝都忘記說時我確實感到不愉快。◇ **~ sb to do sth** *It annoys me to see him getting ahead of me.* 我看見他領先於我就心裏不痛快。 **2** 🔑 **~ sb** to make sb uncomfortable or unable to relax 打擾；騷擾 SYN **bother**：*He swatted a fly that was annoying him.* 他猛力拍打一隻攪得他心煩的蒼蠅。

an·noy·ance /ə'nɔɪəns/ *noun* **1** [U] the feeling of being slightly angry 惱怒；生氣；煩惱 SYN **irritation**：*He could not conceal his annoyance at being interrupted.* 他因受攪而難掩怒色。◇ *Much* **to our annoyance**, *they decided not to come after all.* 他們終於決定不來，使我們很生氣。◇ *She stamped her foot* **in annoyance**. 她氣得直跺腳。 **2** [C] something that makes you slightly angry 使人煩惱的事；令人生氣的事物

annoy·ed 🔑 /ə'nɔɪd/ *adj.* [not usually before noun] slightly angry 惱怒；生氣；煩惱 SYN **irritated**：**~ (with sb) (at/about sth)** *He was beginning to get very annoyed with me about my carelessness.* 因為我粗心大意，他已開始惱火了。◇ *I was* **annoyed with myself** *for giving in so easily.* 我氣自己那麼輕易就讓步了。◇ *I bet she was annoyed at having to write it out again.* 我敢說她對不得不重寫一遍感到惱火。◇ **~ that …** *I was annoyed that they hadn't turned up.* 我惱怒的是他們沒有如期露面。◇ **~ to find, see, etc.** *He was annoyed to find himself going red.* 他因為發覺自己臉紅而懊惱。

annoy·ing 🔑 /ə'nɔɪɪŋ/ *adj.* making sb feel slightly angry 使惱怒的；使生氣的；使煩惱的 SYN **irritating**：*This interruption is very annoying.* 這樣打岔令人討厭。◇ *Her most annoying habit was eating with her mouth open.* 她最讓人討厭的習慣就是張着嘴吃東西。▸ **an·noy·ing·ly** *adv.*

an·nual 🔑 AW /'ænjuəl/ *adj., noun*
■ *adj.* [usually before noun] **1** 🔑 happening or done once every year 每年的；一年一次的；年度的：*an* ***annual meeting/event/report*** 年會；一年一度的大事；年度報告 **2** 🔑 relating to a period of one year 一年的：*an* ***annual income/subscription/budget*** 年收入；年度訂閱費；年度預算 ◇ *an average annual growth rate of 8%* 平均 8% 的年增長率 ◇ *annual rainfall* 年降雨量 ➲ compare BIANNUAL
■ *noun* **1** a book, especially one for children, that is published once a year, with the same title each time, but different contents 年刊；年報；年鑒 **2** any plant that grows and dies within one year or season 一年生植物；一季生植物 ➲ compare BIENNIAL *n.*, PERENNIAL *n.*

an·nu·al·ized (*BrE* also **-ised**) /'ænjuəlaɪzd/ *adj.* (*technical* 術語) calculated for a period of a year but based on the amounts for a shorter period 按年度計算的；折算成為年度總額的

an·nu·al·ly 🔑 AW /'ænjuəli/ *adv.* once a year 一年一次地：*The exhibition is held annually.* 這個展覽每年舉行一次。

an·nu·ity /ə'njuːəti; *NAmE* -'nuː-/ *noun* (*pl.* **-ies**) **1** a fixed amount of money paid to sb each year, usually for the rest of their life 年金（常為養老金） **2** a type of insurance that pays a fixed amount of money to sb each year 年金保險

annul /ə'nʌl/ *verb* (**-ll-**) **~ sth** to state officially that sth is no longer legally valid 廢除；取消；宣告無效：*Their marriage was annulled after just six months.* 他們的婚姻僅過半年就宣告取消。▸ **an·nul·ment** *noun* [C, U]

an·nu·lar /'ænjələ(r)/ *adj.* (*technical* 術語) shaped like a ring 環狀的；輪狀的

an·nun·ci·ation /əˌnʌnsi'eɪʃn/ *noun* [sing.] **the Annunciation** (in the Christian religion) the occasion when Mary was told that she was to be the mother of Christ, celebrated on 25 March（基督教）聖母領報，天使報喜（瑪利亞被告知將做基督的母親）；聖母領報節，天使報喜節（3 月 25 日）

anode /'ænəʊd; *NAmE* 'ænoʊd/ *noun* (*technical* 術語) the ELECTRODE in an electrical device where OXIDATION occurs; the positive electrode in an ELECTROLYTIC cell and the negative electrode in a battery 陽極；正極 ➲ compare CATHODE

ano·dize (*BrE* also **-ise**) /'ænədaɪz/ *verb* **~ sth** to cover a metal, especially ALUMINIUM/ALUMINUM, with a layer of OXIDE in order to protect it 對（鋁等金屬）作陽極氧化；陽極處理

ano·dyne /'ænədaɪn/ *adj.* (*formal*) unlikely to cause disagreement or offend anyone; not expressing strong opinions 不得罪人的；溫和的 SYN **bland**

anoint /ə'nɔɪnt/ *verb* **~ sb/sth (with sth)** to put oil or water on sb's head as part of a religious ceremony 傅（聖油、聖水）：*The priest anointed her with oil.* 神父為她傅油。

anom·al·ous /ə'nɒmələs; *NAmE* -'nɑːm-/ *adj.* (*formal*) different from what is normal or expected 異常的；反常的 ▸ **anom·al·ous·ly** *adv.*

anom·aly /ə'nɒməli; *NAmE* ə'nɑːm-/ *noun* (*pl.* **-ies**) **~ (in sth)** a thing, situation, etc. that is different from what is normal or expected 異常事物；反常現象：*the many anomalies in the tax system* 稅制中的許多破格現象 ◇ *the apparent anomaly that those who produced the wealth, the workers, were the poorest* 創造財富的工人最貧窮這一明顯不正常現象

an·omie (also **anomy**) /'ænəmi/ *noun* [U] (*formal*) a lack of social or moral standards 失範，無規範狀態（社會準則或價值觀的崩潰）

anon /ə'nɒn; *NAmE* ə'nɑːn/ *adv.* (*old-fashioned* or *literary*) soon 不久；很快：*See you anon.* 再見。

anon. /ə'nɒn; *NAmE* ə'nɑːn/ *abbr.* ANONYMOUS

ano·nym·ity /ˌænə'nɪməti/ *noun* [U] **1** the state of remaining unknown to most other people 匿名；不知姓名；名字不公開：*Names of people in the book were changed to preserve anonymity.* 為了姓名保密，書中的人用的都是化名。◇ *the anonymity of the city* (= where people do not know each other) 城市中的人互不相識的現象 ◇ (*especially NAmE*) *He agreed to give an interview* ***on condition of anonymity*** (= if his name was not mentioned). 他同意在不披露姓名的條件下接受採訪。 **2** the state of not having any unusual or interesting features 無特色；無個性特徵：*the anonymity of the hotel decor* 這家旅館毫無特色的裝飾風格

ano·nym·ize (*BrE* also **-ise**) /ə'nɒnɪmaɪz; *NAmE* ə'nɑːn-/ *verb* **1 ~ sth** (*technical* 術語) if you **anonymize** a test result, especially a medical test result, you remove any information that shows who it belongs to 隱匿（實驗結果的）對象信息；使匿名化 **2 ~ sth** (*computing* 計) if you **anonymize** data that is sent or received over the Internet, you remove any information that identifies which particular computer that data originally came from 匿名化處理（通過網絡發送或接收的數據信息）

an·onym·ous /ə'nɒnɪməs; *NAmE* ə'nɑːn-/ *adj.* **1** (of a person 人) with a name that is not known or that is not made public 不知姓名的；名字不公開的：*an anonymous donor* 不知姓名的捐贈者 ◇ *The money was donated by a local businessman who wishes to* ***remain anonymous***. 這筆款子是當地一位不願透露姓名的企業家捐贈的。 **2** (*abbr.* **anon.**) written, given, made, etc. by sb who does not want their name to be known or made public 匿名的；不具名的：*an anonymous letter* 匿名信 **3** without any unusual or interesting features 沒有特色的：*long stretches of dull and anonymous countryside* 大片大片千篇一律、枯燥平淡的鄉村 ▸ **an·onym·ous·ly** *adv.*

A

Which Word? 詞語辨析

answer / reply

Verbs 動詞

- **Answer** and **reply** are the most common verbs used for speaking or writing as a reaction to a question, letter, etc. * answer 和 reply 為口語或書面語中表示回答問題、覆信等最通用的動詞。
- Note that you **answer** a person, question or letter, not *answer to* them, but you **reply to** somebody or something. 表示回答或回覆時，answer 後不用 to，賓語可以是人，也可以是問題或信，而 reply 後要用 to：*I'm writing to answer your questions.* 特此函覆貴方提問。◇ *I'm writing to reply to your questions.* 特此函覆貴方提問。◇ ~~*I'm writing to answer to your questions.*~~
- **Answer** can be used with or without an object. * answer 既可帶賓語，也可不帶賓語：*I haven't answered her email yet.* 我還沒有回覆她的電郵。◇ *I knocked on the door but nobody answered.* 我敲了門，但無人應答。 **Reply** is often used with the actual words spoken. * reply 常帶直接引語：*'I won't let you down,' he replied.* "我不會讓你失望的。"他回答說。
- **Respond** is less common and more formal. * respond 較少用，且較正式：*The directors were unwilling to **respond to** questions.* 董事們不願意回答問題。
- You can only **answer** a door or a phone. 應門或接電話只能用 answer。

➲ see also REJOIN[2], RETORT, GET BACK TO SB at GET

Nouns 名詞

- Note the phrases **in answer to** and **in reply to**. 注意 in answer to 和 in reply to 的用法：*I'm writing in answer to your letter.* 特此函覆。

➲ see also RESPONSE (1), (2), REJOINDER, RETORT

a͵nonymous FT'P *noun* [U] (*computing* 計) a system that allows anybody to DOWNLOAD files from the Internet without having to give their name 匿名下載文件系統；不記名下載系統

ano·rak /ˈænəræk/ *noun* **1** (*especially BrE*) a short coat with a HOOD that is worn as protection against rain, wind and cold 帶帽防寒短上衣 ➲ VISUAL VOCAB page V61 **2** (*BrE, informal*) a person who spends a lot of time learning facts or collecting things that most other people think are boring 怪僻的搜集者（花大量時間瞭解或收集別人大多認為無聊的東西）

an·or·exia /ˌænəˈreksiə/ (also **an·or·exia ner·vosa** /ˌænəˌreksiə nɜːˈvəʊsə; *NAmE* nɜːrˈvoʊsə/) *noun* [U] an emotional DISORDER, especially affecting young women, in which there is an ABNORMAL fear of being fat, causing the person to stop eating, leading to dangerous weight loss（尤指年輕女子害怕肥胖而引起的）厭食，食慾缺乏，神經性厭食 ➲ COLLOCATIONS at DIET ➲ compare BULIMIA

an·or·exic /ˌænəˈreksɪk/ *noun* a person who is suffering from anorexia 厭食者；食慾缺乏者 ▸ **an·or·exic** *adj.*：*She's anorexic.* 她是厭食症患者。

an·other 0-ᵂ /əˈnʌðə(r)/ *det., pron.*
1 0-ᵂ one more; an extra thing or person 又一；再一；另一（事物或人）：*Would you like another drink?* 還想喝一杯嗎？◇ *'Finished?' 'No, I've got another three questions to do.'* "做完了？" "沒有，我還有三個問題要解答。" ◇ *We've still got another* (= a further) *forty miles to go.* 我們還要走四十英里。◇ *'It's a bill.' 'Oh no, not another!'* "這是帳單。" "哦，別又來一張！" ◇ *I got another of those calls yesterday.* 昨天我又接了一個那樣的電話。 HELP **Another** can be followed by a singular noun, by **of** and a plural noun, or by a number and a plural noun. * another 後可接單數名詞、of 加複數名詞或數字加複數名詞。 ➲ compare OTHER (1) ➲ LANGUAGE BANK at ADDITION **2** 0-ᵂ different; a different person or thing 另一；不同的（人或事物）：*Let's do it another time.* 咱們下次再辦這件事吧。◇ *We need another computer* (= a new one). 我們還需要一台電腦。◇ *We can try that—but whether it'll work is **another matter**.* 我們可以試試看，但行不行則是另一回事。◇ *The room's too small. Let's see if they've got **another one**.* 這房間太小。咱們看看他們有沒有另一間。◇ *I don't like this room. I'm going to ask for another.* 我不喜歡這個房間。我打算另要一間。 **3** a person or thing of a very similar type 類似的（人或事物）：*She's going to be another Madonna* (= as famous as her). 她就要變得跟麥當娜一般出名了。◇ *There'll never be another like him.* 不會再有像他那樣的人物了。 ➲ see also ONE ANOTHER
IDM **of one kind, sort, etc. or aˈnother** used when you are referring to various types of a thing, without saying exactly what you mean 各種不同的：*We've all got problems of one kind or another.* 我們都有這樣那樣的問題。 ➲ more at ONE *number, det.*

A. N. Other /ˌeɪ en ˈʌðə(r)/ *noun* [sing.] a person whose name is not known or not yet decided, for example in a list of players in a team（名單中）未指名者，某人，待定人選

an·swer 0-ᵂ /ˈɑːnsə(r); *NAmE* ˈæn-/ *noun, verb*
■ *noun* **1** 0-ᵂ something that you say, write or do to react to a question or situation 答覆；回答：*I rang the bell, but there was no answer.* 我按了門鈴，但沒有人應門。◇ **~ to sth** *I can't easily **give an answer** to your question.* 你的問題我難以回答。◇ *Have you had an answer to your letter?* 你那封信有回音沒有？◇ *As if **in answer to** our prayers, she offered to lend us £10 000.* 好像祈禱很靈驗似的，她提出借給我們 1 萬英鎊。◇ *She had no answer to the accusations.* 她對控告無以為答。 **2** 0-ᵂ something that you write or say in reply to a question in a test, an exam, an exercise, etc.; the correct reply to a question in a test, etc.（試題、練習等的）答案，正確答案：*Write your answers on the sheet provided.* 在所發的答題紙上寫下答案。◇ *Do you know the answer* (= the right one) *to question 12?* 你知道第 12 題的正確答案嗎？ **3** 0-ᵂ a solution to a problem （問題的）解決辦法，答案：*There is no easy answer.* 沒有容易的解決辦法。◇ *This could be the answer to all our problems.* 這可能就是我們全部問題的解決辦法。◇ *The obvious answer would be to cancel the party.* 明擺着的解決方法是取消聚會。 **4** a person or thing from one place that may be thought to be as good as a famous person or thing from another place 足以媲美的人；堪稱相當的事物：*The new theme park will be Britain's answer to Disneyland.* 英國新的主題樂園可與迪斯尼樂園媲美。
IDM **have/know all the ˈanswers** (*informal*, often *disapproving*) to be confident that you know sth, especially when you actually do not（自以為）全懂，什麼都精通：*He thinks he knows all the answers.* 他自以為什麼都知道。 ➲ more at NO *exclam.*
■ *verb* **1** 0-ᵂ [I, T] to say, write or do sth as a reaction to a question or situation 答覆；回答 SYN **reply**：*I repeated the question, but she didn't answer.* 我把問題重複了一遍，但是她仍沒有回答。◇ **~ sth** *You haven't **answered my question**.* 你沒有回答我的問題。◇ *to **answer a letter/an advertisement*** 覆信；對廣告作出反應 ◇ *to **answer the phone*** (= to pick up the phone when it rings) 接電話 ◇ *to **answer the door*** (= to open the door when sb knocks/rings) 應門（鈴）聲開門 ◇ *My **prayers have been answered*** (= I have got what I wanted). 我的祈禱應驗了。◇ *He refused to answer the charges against him.* 他拒絕對他的指控進行答辯。◇ **~ (sb)** *Come on, answer me! Where were you?* 快點，回答我！你到哪兒去了？◇ *He answered me with a smile.* 他對我報以微笑。◇ **+ speech** *'I'd prefer to walk,' she answered.* "我寧願步行。" 她答道。◇ **~ sb + speech** *'I'd prefer to walk,' she answered him.* "我寧願步行。" 她回答他道。◇ **~ (sb) that ...** *She answered that she would prefer to walk.* 她回答說她寧願步行。◇ **~ sb sth** *Answer me this: how did they know we were here?* 回答我這個問題：他們怎麼知道我們在這兒？ **2** [T] **~ sth** (*formal*) to be suitable for sth; to match sth 適合；符合；比得上；相配：*Does this answer your requirements?* 這個符合你的要求嗎？

IDM **answer to the name of sth** (especially of a pet animal 尤指寵物) to be called sth 名叫；叫做 ➲ more at DESCRIPTION

PHR V **,answer 'back** to defend yourself against criticism 為自己辯護；答辯： *He was given the chance to answer back in a radio interview.* 在一次廣播訪談中他得到了辯白的機會。 **,answer 'back | ,answer sb 'back** to speak rudely to sb in authority, especially when they are criticizing you or telling you to do sth 頂嘴；回嘴；還嘴： *Don't answer back!* 別回嘴！◇ *Stop answering your mother back!* 不准和母親頂嘴！ **'answer for sth** **1** to accept responsibility or blame for sth 對…負責；因…受到譴責： *You will have to answer for your behaviour one day.* 總有一天你要因你的行為承擔責任。◇ *This government* ***has a lot to answer for*** (= is responsible for a lot of bad things). 這屆政府對很多壞事都有責任。 **2** to promise that sb has a particular quality or can be relied on to do sth 擔保，保證（某人的品質等）： *I can answer for her honesty.* 我可以擔保她為人誠實。 **'answer for sb** (usually in negative sentences 通常用於否定句) to say that sb else will do sth or have a particular opinion 代表…講話；代表…的意見： *I agree, but I can't answer for my colleagues.* 我同意，但是我不能代表我同事們的意見。 **'answer to sb (for sth)** to have to explain your actions or decisions to sb 向某人（為某事）負責： *All sales clerks answer to the store manager.* 所有售貨員都向商店經理負責。

an·swer·able /'ɑːnsərəbl; *NAmE* 'æn-/ *adj.* **1** [not before noun] **~ to sb (for sth)** having to explain your actions to sb in authority over you 向某人（對某事）負責： *She was a free agent, answerable to no one for her behaviour.* 她是個自由分子，言行不受任何人約束。 **2** [not before noun] **~ (for sth)** responsible for sth and ready to accept punishment or criticism for it （為某事）承擔責任，承擔後果： *Ministers must be made answerable for their decisions.* 各部長必須對所做的決定承擔責任。 **3** (of a question 問題) that can be answered 可答覆的

'answering machine (*BrE* also **an·swer·phone**) *noun* a machine that you connect to your telephone to answer your calls and record any message left by the person calling 電話答錄機： *I called several times, but only got the answering machine.* 我打了幾次電話，但只有電話答錄機答話。

an·swer·phone /'ɑːnsəfəʊn; *NAmE* 'ænsərfoʊn/ *noun* (*BrE*) = ANSWERING MACHINE： *She left her name and number on his answerphone.* 她把自己的姓名和電話號碼留在他的電話答錄機上。

ant /ænt/ *noun* a small insect that lives in highly organized groups. There are many types of ant. 螞蟻： *an ants' nest* 蟻窩 ◇ *an ant colony* 蟻群 ➲ **VISUAL VOCAB** page V13 ➲ see also ANTHILL

IDM **have 'ants in your pants** (*informal*) to be very excited or impatient about sth and unable to stay still 焦躁不安；坐立不安

-ant, -ent *suffix* **1** (in adjectives 構成形容詞) that is or does sth 是…的；做…的： *significant* 有意義的 ◇ *different* 不同 **2** (in nouns 構成名詞) a person or thing that …人；…事物： *inhabitant* 居民 ◇ *deterrent* 具威懾性的事物

ant·acid /ænt'æsɪd/ *noun* a medicine that prevents or corrects ACIDITY, especially in the stomach 解酸藥；抗酸藥

an·tag·on·ism /æn'tægənɪzəm/ *noun* [U, pl.] **~ (to/toward(s) sb/sth) | ~ (between A and B)** feelings of hatred and opposition 對立情緒；對抗情緒；敵對；敵意 **SYN** **hostility**： *The antagonism he felt towards his old enemy was still very strong.* 他對宿敵的仇恨仍然十分強烈。◇ *the racial antagonisms in society* 社會上的種族對立情緒

an·tag·on·ist /æn'tægənɪst/ *noun* (*formal*) a person who strongly opposes sb/sth 對立者；對抗者；對手；敵人 **SYN** **opponent**

an·tag·on·is·tic /æn,tægə'nɪstɪk/ *adj.* **~ (to/toward(s) sb/sth)** (*formal*) showing or feeling opposition 對立情緒的；對抗的；敵對的；敵意的 **SYN** **hostile** ▸ **an·tag·on·is·tic·al·ly** /-kli/ *adv.*

an·tag·on·ize (*BrE* also **-ise**) /æn'tægənaɪz/ *verb* **~ sb** to do sth to make sb angry with you 使對立；使生氣： *Not wishing to antagonize her further, he said no more.* 他不願惹她更生氣，便不再說話。

the Ant·arc·tic /æn'tɑːktɪk; *NAmE* -'tɑːrk-/ *noun* [sing.] the regions of the world around the South Pole 南極地區 ▸ **Ant·arc·tic** *adj.* [only before noun]： *Antarctic explorers* 南極探險家 ➲ compare ARCTIC

the An,tarctic 'Circle *noun* [sing.] the line of LATITUDE 66° 33' South 南極圈 ➲ compare ARCTIC CIRCLE

ante /'ænti/ *noun* [sing.]

IDM **raise/up the 'ante** to increase the level of sth, especially demands or sums of money 提高要求；增加金額

ante- /'ænti/ *prefix* (in nouns, adjectives and verbs 構成名詞、形容詞和動詞) before; in front of 在…前；在…前面： *ante-room* 前廳 ◇ *antenatal* 產前 ◇ *antedate* 早於 ➲ compare POST-, PRE-

ant·eat·er /'æntiːtə(r)/ *noun* an animal with a long nose and tongue that eats ANTS 食蟻獸

ante·bellum /,ænti'beləm/ *adj.* [only before noun] (*formal*) connected with the years before a war, especially the American Civil War 戰前歲月的；（尤指）美國內戰前的： *the laws of the antebellum American South* 內戰前美國南方的法律

ante·ce·dent /,æntɪ'siːdnt/ *noun, adj.*

■ ***noun*** **1** [C] (*formal*) a thing or an event that exists or comes before another, and may have influenced it 前事；前情 **2** **antecedents** [pl.] (*formal*) the people in sb's family who lived a long time ago 祖先；先人 **SYN** **ancestors, forebears** **3** [C] (*grammar* 語法) a word or phrase to which the following word, especially a pronoun, refers 先行詞；先行語： *In 'He grabbed the ball and threw it in the air', 'ball' is the antecedent of 'it'.* 在 He grabbed the ball and threw it in the air 一句中，ball 是 it 的先行詞。

■ ***adj.*** (*formal*) previous 先前的： *antecedent events* 先前的事件

ante·cham·ber /'æntitʃeɪmbə(r)/ *noun* (*formal*) = ANTEROOM

ante·date /,ænti'deɪt/ *verb* **~ sth** = PREDATE

ante·di·lu·vian /,æntidɪ'luːviən/ *adj.* (*formal* or *humorous*) very old-fashioned 早已過時的；十分老式的

ante·lope /'æntɪləʊp; *NAmE* -loʊp/ *noun* (*pl.* **ante·lope** or **ante·lopes**) an African or Asian animal like a DEER, that runs very fast. There are many types of antelope. 羚；羚類動物

ante·natal /,ænti'neɪtl/ (*BrE*) (also **pre·natal** *NAmE, BrE*) *adj.* [only before noun] relating to the medical care given to pregnant women 產前的： ***antenatal care/classes/screening*** 產前保健／學習班／檢查 ◇ *an* ***antenatal clinic*** 產前檢查診所 ➲ compare POST-NATAL

an·tenna /æn'tenə/ *noun* **1** (*pl.* **an·ten·nae** /-niː/) either of the two long thin parts on the heads of some insects and some animals that live in shells, used to feel and touch things with 觸角；觸鬚 **SYN** **feeler**： (*figurative*) *The minister was praised for his acute political antennae* (= ability to understand complicated political situations). 這位部長以政治觸覺敏銳而為人稱道。 ➲ **VISUAL VOCAB** page V13 **2** (*pl.* **an·ten·nas** or **an·ten·nae**) (*especially NAmE*) (*BrE* also **aer·ial**) a piece of equipment made of wire or long straight pieces of metal for receiving or sending radio and television signals 天線： *radio antennas* 收音機天線 ➲ **VISUAL VOCAB** pages V17, V52

an·ter·ior /æn'tɪəriə(r); *NAmE* -'tɪr-/ *adj.* [only before noun] (*technical* 術語) (of a part of the body 身體部位) at or near the front 前部的；前面的 **OPP** **posterior**

ante·room /'æntiruːm; -rʊm/ (also *formal* **ante·cham·ber**) *noun* a room where people can wait before entering a larger room, especially in an important public building （尤指重要公共建築的）前廳，接待室

an·them /'ænθəm/ *noun* **1** a song that has a special importance for a country, an organization or a particular group of people, and is sung on special occasions 國歌；（組織或群體的）社歌，團歌：*The European anthem was played at the opening and closing ceremonies.* 歐洲頌歌在開幕禮和閉幕禮上演奏。➲ see also NATIONAL ANTHEM **2** a short religious song for a CHOIR (= a group of singers), often with an organ（宗教）頌歌（常由管風琴伴奏）

an·them·ic /æn'θiːmɪk/ *adj.* (*formal*) (of a piece of music 樂曲) that makes you feel happy and enthusiastic 歡樂的；激發熱情的

an·ther /'ænθə(r)/ *noun* (*biology* 生) the part of a flower at the top of a STAMEN that produces POLLEN 花藥（花的雄蕊頂端產生花粉的部份）➲ **VISUAL VOCAB** page V11

ant·hill /'ænthɪl/ *noun* a pile of earth formed by ANTS over their nests 蟻塚；蟻垤

an·tholo·gize (*BrE* also **-ise**) /æn'θɒlədʒaɪz; *NAmE* -'θɑːl-/ *verb* **~ sb/sth** to include a writer or piece of writing in an anthology 把（作者或作品）收入選集

an·thol·ogy /æn'θɒlədʒi; *NAmE* -'θɑːl-/ *noun* (*pl.* **-ies**) a collection of poems, stories, etc. that have been written by different people and published together in a book（不同作家作品的）選集

an·thra·cite /'ænθrəsaɪt/ *noun* [U] a very hard type of coal that burns slowly without producing a lot of smoke or flames 無煙煤

an·thrax /'ænθræks/ *noun* [U] a serious disease that affects sheep and cows and sometimes people, and can cause death 炭疽（牛羊疾病，人偶得，可致命）

an·thro·po- /'ænθrəpəʊ; *NAmE* -poʊ/ *combining form* (in nouns, adjectives and adverbs 構成名詞、形容詞和副詞) connected with humans 人的；人類的：*anthropology* 人類學

an·thro·po·cen·tric /ˌænθrəpə'sentrɪk/ *adj.* believing that humans are more important than anything else 人類中心論的；人本位的 ▸ **an·thro·po·cen·trism** /ˌænθrəpə'sentrɪzəm/ *noun* [U]

an·thro·poid /'ænθrəpɔɪd/ *adj.*, *noun* (*technical* 術語)
■ ***adj.*** (of an APE 猿) looking like a human 類人的；似人的
■ ***noun*** any type of APE that is similar to a human 類人猿

an·thro·polo·gist /ˌænθrə'pɒlədʒɪst; *NAmE* -'pɑːl-/ *noun* a person who studies anthropology 人類學家

an·thro·pol·ogy /ˌænθrə'pɒlədʒi; *NAmE* -'pɑːl-/ *noun* [U] the study of the human race, especially of its origins, development, customs and beliefs 人類學 ▸ **an·thro·po·logic·al** /ˌænθrəpə'lɒdʒɪkl; *NAmE* -'lɑːdʒ-/ *adj.*

an·thro·po·morph·ic /ˌænθrəpə'mɔːfɪk; *NAmE* -'mɔːrf-/ *adj.* (of beliefs or ideas 信念或思想) treating gods, animals or objects as if they had human qualities 人格化的；擬人化的 ▸ **an·thro·po·morph·ism** /ˌænθrəpə'mɔːfɪzəm; *NAmE* -'mɔːrf-/ *noun* [U]

anti /'ænti/ *prep.* (*informal*) if sb is **anti** sb/sth, they do not like or agree with that person or thing 反對 ➲ compare PRO *prep.*

anti- 🗝 /'ænti/ *prefix* (in nouns and adjectives 構成名詞和形容詞) **1** 🗝 opposed to; against 反；反對：*anti-tank weapons* 反坦克武器 ◇ *antisocial* 反社會 ➲ compare PRO- **2** 🗝 the opposite of 對立；對立面：*anti-hero* 反英雄 ◇ *anticlimax* 掃興的結局 **3** 🗝 preventing 防；防止：*antifreeze* 防凍劑

ˌanti-'aircraft *adj.* [only before noun] designed to destroy enemy aircraft 防空的：***anti-aircraft fire/guns/missiles*** 防空火力；高射炮；防空導彈

anti·bac·ter·ial /ˌæntibæk'tɪəriəl; *NAmE* -'tɪriəl/ *adj.* that kills bacteria 滅菌的；抗菌的：*antibacterial treatments* 抗菌處理

anti·bi·ot·ic /ˌæntibaɪ'ɒtɪk; *NAmE* -'ɑːtɪk/ *noun* [usually pl.] a substance, for example PENICILLIN, that can destroy or prevent the growth of bacteria and cure infections 抗菌素，抗生素（如青黴素）：*The doctor put her on antibiotics* (= told her to take them). 醫生要她服用抗生素。▸ **anti·bi·ot·ic** *adj.*：*an antibiotic drug* 抗菌素藥 ◇ *effective antibiotic treatment* 有效的抗生素治療

anti·body /'æntibɒdi; *NAmE* -bɑːdi/ *noun* (*pl.* **-ies**) a substance that the body produces in the blood to fight disease, or as a reaction when certain substances are put into the body 抗體（血液中抵抗疾病或當某些物質進入身體時產生反應的物質）

ˌanti-'choice *adj.* (*NAmE*, *disapproving*) against giving women the right to have an ABORTION 反對自由墮胎的 ➲ compare PRO-CHOICE

Anti·christ /'æntikraɪst/ (usually **the Antichrist**) *noun* [sing.] (in Christianity 基督教) the DEVIL; Christ's greatest enemy 假基督（指基督的大敵魔鬼）

an·tici·pate 🗝 **AW** /æn'tɪsɪpeɪt/ *verb*
1 🗝 to expect sth 預料；預期：**~ sth** *We don't anticipate any major problems.* 我們預料不會發生什麼大問題。◇ *Our anticipated arrival time is 8.30.* 我們預計抵達的時間是 8:30。◇ *The eagerly anticipated movie will be released next month.* 那齣觀眾翹首企盼的電影將於下月上映。◇ **~ doing sth** *They anticipate moving to bigger premises by the end of the year.* 他們預期年底前遷入較大的經營場址。◇ **~ sth doing sth** *I don't anticipate it being a problem.* 我不認為它會成為一個問題。◇ **~ that ...** *We anticipate that sales will rise next year.* 我們預料明年銷售量將會增加。◇ **it is anticipated that ...** *It is anticipated that inflation will stabilize at 3%.* 據預測，通貨膨脹將穩定在 3%。➲ compare UNANTICIPATED **2** 🗝 to see what might happen in the future and take action to prepare for it 預見，預計（並做準備）：**~ sth** *We need someone who can anticipate and respond to changes in the fashion industry.* 我們需要一個能預見時裝業變化並做相應安排的人。◇ **~ what, how, that, etc. ...** *Try and anticipate what the interviewers will ask.* 盡量設想面試主持者會提出什麼問題。**3 ~ (doing) sth | ~ (sth doing) sth** to think with pleasure and excitement about sth that is going to happen 期盼；期望：*We eagerly anticipated the day we would leave school.* 我們迫切地期盼着畢業離校的那一天。◇ *The more I anticipated arriving somewhere, the more disappointed I was.* 我越期盼在某方面有所成就，就越失望。**4 ~ sb (doing sth)** (*formal*) to do sth before it can be done by sb else 先於…做；早於…行動 **SYN** **forestall**：*When Scott reached the South Pole he found that Amundsen had anticipated him.* 斯科特到達南極時發現阿蒙森已先到過那裏。▸ **an·tici·pa·tory** /ænˌtɪsɪ'peɪtəri; *NAmE* æn'tɪsəpətɔːri/ *adj.*：(*formal*) *a fast anticipatory movement by the goalkeeper* 守門員的快速預期動作

an·tici·pa·tion **AW** /ænˌtɪsɪ'peɪʃn/ *noun* [U] **1** the fact of seeing that sth might happen in the future and perhaps doing sth about it now 預料；預期；預見；預計：*He bought extra food **in anticipation of** more people coming than he'd invited.* 他預料來的客人會比邀請的多，就多買了食物。**2** a feeling of excitement about sth (usually sth good) that is going to happen 期盼；期望：***happy/eager/excited anticipation*** 愉快的／殷切的／激動的期盼 ◇ *The courtroom was filled with anticipation.* 法庭上人們滿懷期望的心情。

anti·cler·ic·al /ˌænti'klerɪkl/ *adj.* opposed to priests and their influence in political life 反教權主義的：*anticlerical movements in the seventeenth century* 十七世紀的反教權主義運動 ▸ **anti·cler·ic·al·ism** /-ɪzəm/ *noun* [U]

anti·cli·max /ˌænti'klaɪmæks/ *noun* [C, U] a situation that is disappointing because it happens at the end of sth that was much more exciting, or because it is not as exciting as you expected 掃興的結局；掃興：*Travelling in Europe was something of an anticlimax after the years he'd spent in Africa.* 他在非洲生活了多年，到歐洲旅行真是有點太平淡了。◇ *a **sense/feeling of anticlimax*** 掃興感 ➲ compare CLIMAX *n.* ▸ **anti·cli·mac·tic** /ˌæntiklaɪ'mæktɪk/ *adj.*

anti·cline /'æntiklaɪn/ *noun* (*geology* 地) an area of ground where layers of rock in the earth's surface have been folded into a curve that is higher in the middle than at the ends 背斜（層）（指地球表面岩層疊起成弧狀、中間高於邊緣的區域）➲ compare SYNCLINE

anti·clock·wise /ˌænti'klɒkwaɪz; *NAmE* -'klɑːk-/ (*BrE*) (*NAmE* **coun·ter·clock·wise**) *adv.*, *adj.* in the opposite direction to the movement of the hands of a clock 逆時針方向（的）：*Turn the key anticlockwise/in* *an anticlockwise direction.* 朝逆時針方向轉動鑰匙。 **OPP clockwise**

anti·coagu·lant /ˌæntikəʊˈæɡjələnt; *NAmE* -koʊ-/ *noun* (*medical* 醫) a substance that stops the blood from becoming thick and forming CLOTS 抗凝（血）劑

anti·con·vul·sant /ˌæntikənˈvʌlsənt/ *noun* a drug used to prevent EPILEPTIC, FITS or similar illnesses 抗驚厥藥；抗癲癇藥；抗痙攣藥 ▸ **anti·con·vul·sant** *adj.*

antics /ˈæntɪks/ *noun* [pl.] **1** behaviour which is silly and funny in a way that people usually like 滑稽可笑的舉止： *The bank staff got up to all sorts of antics to raise money for charity.* 銀行職員使出各種可笑的花招為慈善事業籌款。 **2** behaviour which is ridiculous or dangerous 荒唐行為；危險舉動

anti·cyc·lone /ˌæntiˈsaɪkləʊn; *NAmE* -ˈkloʊn/ *noun* an area of high air pressure that produces calm weather conditions with clear skies 反氣旋，高氣壓（天氣晴朗平靜） ➲ compare DEPRESSION (5)

anti·depres·sant /ˌæntidɪˈpresnt/ *noun* a drug used to treat DEPRESSION 抗抑鬱藥；抗抑鬱劑 ▸ **anti·depres·sant** *adj.* [only before noun]：*antidepressant drugs* 抗抑鬱

anti·dote /ˈæntidəʊt; *NAmE* -doʊt/ *noun* **1 ~ (to sth)** a substance that controls the effects of a poison or disease 解毒藥；解毒劑： *There is no known antidote to the poison.* 這種毒的解藥尚未發現。 **2 ~ (to sth)** anything that takes away the effects of sth unpleasant 消除令人不快的事物；矯正方法： *A Mediterranean cruise was the perfect antidote to a long cold winter.* 到地中海航遊是度過漫長寒冬的絕妙辦法。

anti·freeze /ˈæntifriːz/ *noun* [U] a chemical that is added to the water in the RADIATOR of cars and other vehicles to stop it from freezing 防凍劑，抗凝劑（加入車輛散熱器的水中以防凍結）

anti·gen /ˈæntɪdʒən/ *noun* (*medical* 醫) a substance that enters the body and starts a process that can cause disease. The body then usually produces ANTIBODIES to fight the antigens. 抗原（能激發人體產生抗體）

anti·glob·al·iza·tion (*BrE* also **-isa·tion**) /ˌæntiˌɡləʊbəlaɪˈzeɪʃn; *NAmE* -ˌɡloʊbələˈz-/ *noun* [U] opposition to the increase in the power of large international companies and institutions because of the bad effects on the economies of individual countries, especially poorer ones 反全球化： *antiglobalization protests at the G8 summit* 八國峰會時的反全球化抗議 ◇ *the antiglobalization movement* 反全球化運動

anti·grav·ity /ˌæntiˈɡrævəti/ *noun* [U] (*physics* 物) an imaginary force that works against GRAVITY 反重力；反引力

ˈanti-hero *noun* the main character in a story, but one who does not have the qualities of a typical hero, and is either more like an ordinary person or is morally bad 反英雄（故事中不按傳統主角品格塑造的主人公）

anti·his·ta·mine /ˌæntiˈhɪstəmiːn/ *noun* [C, U] a drug used to treat ALLERGIES, especially HAY FEVER 抗組胺藥（抗枯草熱等過敏反應）： ***antihistamine cream/injections/shots*** 抗組胺乳膏／注射

ˌanti-inˈflam·ma·tory *adj.* (of a drug 藥) used to reduce INFLAMMATION 消炎的；抗炎的 ▸ **anti-inflam·ma·tory** *noun* (*pl.* **-ies**)

ˈanti-lock *adj.* [only before noun] **anti-lock** BRAKES stop the wheels of a vehicle locking if you have to stop suddenly, and so make the vehicle easier to control 防抱死的： *an anti-lock braking system or ABS* 防抱死裝置

anti·mat·ter /ˈæntimætə(r)/ *noun* [U] (*physics* 物) matter that is made up of antiparticles 反物質（由反粒子組成）

an·tim·ony /ˈæntɪməni; *NAmE* -moʊni/ *noun* [U] (*symb.* **Sb**) a chemical element. Antimony is a silver-white metal that breaks easily, used especially in making ALLOYS. 銻

anti·oxi·dant /ˌæntiˈɒksɪdənt; *NAmE* -ˈɑːks-/ *noun* **1** (*biology* 生) a substance such as VITAMIN C or E that removes dangerous MOLECULES, etc., such as FREE RADICALS from the body 抗氧化物質（如維生素 C 或 E，可消除體內自由基等有害分子） **2** (*chemistry* 化) a substance that helps prevent OXIDATION, especially one used to help prevent stored food products from going bad（尤用於食物保鮮的）抗氧化劑

anti·par·ticle /ˈæntipɑːtɪkl; *NAmE* -pɑːrt-/ *noun* (*physics* 物) a very small part of an atom that has the same mass as a normal PARTICLE but the opposite electrical CHARGE 反粒子（與基本粒子質量相同，但電荷相反）

anti·pasto /ˌæntiˈpæstəʊ; *NAmE* -oʊ/ *noun* (*pl.* **anti·pasti** /-ti/) (in Italian cooking 意大利烹飪) a small amount of food that you eat before the main part of a meal 開胃菜；開胃食物 **SYN appetizer, starter**

an·tip·athy /ænˈtɪpəθi/ *noun* [U, C, usually sing.] (*pl.* **-ies**) **~ (between A and B)** | **~ (to/toward(s) sb/sth)** (*formal*) a strong feeling of dislike 厭惡；反感 **SYN hostility**： ***personal/mutual antipathy*** 個人／相互反感 ◇ *a **growing antipathy** towards the idea* 對這個想法越來越多的反感 ▸ **anti·path·et·ic** /ˌæntɪpəˈθetɪk/ *adj.* ： **~ (to sb/sth)** *antipathetic to change* 厭惡變革

ˌanti-personˈnel *adj.* [only before noun] (of weapons 武器) designed to kill or injure people, not to destroy buildings or vehicles, etc. 專門用於殺傷人的；殺傷性的

anti·per·spir·ant /ˌæntiˈpɜːspərənt; *NAmE* -ˈpɜːrs-/ *noun* [U, C] a substance that people use, especially under their arms, to prevent or reduce sweat 止汗劑 ➲ see also DEODORANT

the An·tipo·des /ænˈtɪpədiːz/ *noun* [pl.] (*BrE*) a way of referring to Australia and New Zealand, often used in a humorous way（常作幽默）澳大利亞和新西蘭，澳新 ▸ **An·tipo·dean** /ˌæntɪpəˈdiːən/ *adj.*

anti·pro·ton /ˈæntiprəʊtɒn; *NAmE* -proʊtɑːn/ *noun* (*physics* 物) a PARTICLE that has the same mass as a PROTON, but a negative electrical CHARGE 反質子（與質子質量相同，但電荷相反）

anti·quar·ian /ˌæntɪˈkweəriən; *NAmE* -ˈkwer-/ *adj.*, *noun*

■ ***adj.*** [usually before noun] connected with the study, collection or sale of valuable old objects, especially books（尤指書籍）古文物的，古文物研究（或收藏、經營）的

■ ***noun*** (also *less frequent* **anti·quary** /ˈæntɪkwəri; *NAmE* -kweri/) a person who studies, collects or sells old and valuable objects 古文物研究者（或收藏家、經營者）

anti·quark /ˈæntikwɑːk; *NAmE* -kwɑːrk/ *noun* (*physics* 物) the ANTIPARTICLE of a QUARK 反夸克

anti·quated /ˈæntɪkweɪtɪd/ *adj.* (usually *disapproving*) (of things or ideas 事物或思想) old-fashioned and no longer suitable for modern conditions 過時的；陳舊的 **SYN outdated**

an·tique /ænˈtiːk/ *adj.*, *noun*

■ ***adj.*** [usually before noun] (of furniture, jewellery, etc. 傢具、珠寶等) old and often valuable 古老的；古董的： *an antique mahogany desk* 古紅木辦公桌

■ ***noun*** an object such as a piece of furniture that is old and often valuable 文物；古物；古董；古玩： *Priceless antiques were destroyed in the fire.* 無價之寶的古董在大火中焚燬。◇ *an antique shop* (= one that sells antiques) 古玩店 ◇ *an antique dealer/antiques dealer* (= a person who sells antiques) 古董商

an·tiquity /ænˈtɪkwəti/ *noun* (*pl.* **-ies**) **1** [U] the ancient past, especially the times of the Greeks and Romans 古代（尤指古希臘和古羅馬時期）： *The statue was brought to Rome **in antiquity**.* 這座雕像是古時運到羅馬的。 **2** [U] the state of being very old or ancient 古老；古： *A number of the monuments are of considerable antiquity.* 有些歷史遺跡相當古老。 **3** [C, usually pl.] an object from ancient times 文物；古物；古董；古跡： *Egyptian/Roman antiquities* 埃及／羅馬古物

anti·retro·viral /ˌæntiˌretrəʊˈvaɪrəl; *NAmE* -troʊ-/ *adj.* designed to stop viruses such as HIV damaging the body 抗逆轉錄病毒的；抗反轉錄病毒的： *antiretroviral drugs* 抗逆轉錄病毒藥物

ˌanti-ˈroll bar *noun* a metal bar that is part of a car's SUSPENSION, which stops the car from leaning too much when it goes around corners（汽車懸架的）橫向平衡桿，防傾斜桿

A

anti-Semitism /ˌænti ˈsemətɪzəm/ *noun* [U] hatred of Jews; unfair treatment of Jews 反猶太（主義）；排猶（主義）➲ COLLOCATIONS at RACE ▸ **anti-Semitic** /ˌænti səˈmɪtɪk/ *adj.*：*anti-Semitic propaganda* 反猶宣傳 **anti-Semite** /ˌænti ˈsiːmaɪt/ *noun*：*He was a notorious anti-Semite.* 他是臭名昭著的反猶主義者。

anti·sep·tic /ˌæntiˈseptɪk/ *noun, adj.*
■ **noun** [C, U] a substance that helps to prevent infection in wounds by killing bacteria 防腐劑；抗菌劑 SYN **disinfectant**
■ **adj.** **1** able to prevent infection 防腐的；抗菌的：***antiseptic cream/lotion/wipes*** 防腐乳膏／洗液／擦劑 **2** very clean and free from bacteria 無菌的；消過毒的 SYN **sterile**：*Cover the burn with an antiseptic dressing.* 在燒傷處包上無菌敷料。

anti·social /ˌæntiˈsəʊʃl; NAmE -ˈsoʊʃl/ *adj.* **1** harmful or annoying to other people, or to society in general 反社會的；危害社會的；令人討厭的：*antisocial behaviour* 反社會行為 **2** not wanting to spend time with other people 不合群的；孤僻的：*They'll think you're being antisocial if you don't go.* 要是你不去，他們就會認為你不合群。➲ compare SOCIABLE

anti-ˈtank *adj.* [only before noun] (of weapons 武器) for use against enemy tanks 反坦克的：*anti-tank missiles/mines* 反坦克導彈／地雷

an·tith·esis /ænˈtɪθəsɪs/ *noun* [usually sing.] (*pl.* **an·tith·eses** /ænˈtɪθəsiːz/) (*formal*) **1** the opposite of sth 對立（面）；對照：*Love is the antithesis of selfishness.* 愛是自私的對立面。◇ *Students finishing their education at 16 is the **very antithesis** of what society needs.* * 16 歲停止學業的學生並非社會所需要的。**2** a contrast between two things（二者間的）對比，對照：*There is an antithesis between the needs of the state and the needs of the people.* 政府的需要和人民的需要這二者出現了對立。
▸ **an·ti·thet·ic·al** /ˌæntɪˈθetɪkl/ *adj.* ~ **(to sth)**

anti·trust /ˌæntiˈtrʌst/ *adj.* [only before noun] (of laws 法律) preventing companies or groups of companies from controlling prices unfairly 反托拉斯的；反壟斷的

anti·viral /ˌæntiˈvaɪrəl/ *adj.* (of a drug 藥) used to treat infectious diseases caused by a virus 抗病毒的

anti·virus /ˈæntivaɪrəs/ *adj.* (*computing* 計) designed to find and destroy computer viruses 查殺病毒的；殺毒的：*antivirus software* 殺毒軟件

ant·ler /ˈæntlə(r)/ *noun* [usually pl.] one of the two horns that grow on the head of male DEER 鹿角 ➲ VISUAL VOCAB page V12

ant·onym /ˈæntənɪm/ *noun* (*technical* 術語) a word that means the opposite of another word 反義詞 SYN **opposite**：*'Old' has two possible antonyms: 'young' and 'new'.* * old 的反義詞可能有兩個：young 和 new。➲ compare SYNONYM

antsy /ˈæntsi/ *adj.* (*NAmE, informal*) impatient; not able to keep still 煩躁的；坐立不安的

anus /ˈeɪnəs/ *noun* (*anatomy* 解) the opening in a person's bottom through which solid waste leaves the body 肛門 ➲ VISUAL VOCAB page V59 ➲ see also ANAL (1)

anvil /ˈænvɪl/ *noun* an iron block on which a BLACKSMITH puts hot pieces of metal before shaping them with a HAMMER 鐵砧

anx·iety 🔑 /æŋˈzaɪəti/ *noun* (*pl.* **-ies**)
1 🔑 [U] ~ **(about/over sth)** the state of feeling nervous or worried that sth bad is going to happen 焦慮；憂慮：***acute/intense/deep anxiety*** 非常／極度／深深的憂慮 ◇ *Some hospital patients experience high levels of anxiety.* 有些住院病人十分焦慮不安。**2** 🔑 [C] a worry or fear about sth 擔心；憂慮；害怕：*If you're worried about your health, share your anxieties with your doctor.* 你要是擔心自己的健康，就把憂慮告訴醫生吧。**3** [U] a strong feeling of wanting to do sth or of wanting sth to happen 渴望：~ **to do sth** *the candidate's anxiety to win the vote* 候選人對選舉勝利的渴望 ◇ ~ **for sth** *the people's anxiety for the war to end* 人民對結束戰爭的渴望

anx·ious 🔑 /ˈæŋkʃəs/ *adj.*
1 🔑 feeling worried or nervous 焦慮；憂慮；擔心：~ **(about sth)** *He seemed anxious about the meeting.* 他似乎對這次會議憂心忡忡。◇ ~ **(for sb)** *Parents are naturally anxious for their children.* 父母自然為兒女擔心。➲ SYNONYMS at WORRIED **2** 🔑 causing anxiety; showing anxiety 令人焦慮的；流露出憂慮的：*There were a few anxious moments in the baseball game.* 那場棒球賽中有些時刻令人焦慮不安。◇ *an **anxious look/face/expression*** 憂慮的目光／面容／表情 **3** 🔑 wanting sth very much 渴望；非常希望：~ **to do sth** *She was anxious to finish school and get a job.* 她渴望畢業，然後找工作。◇ *He was **anxious not to** be misunderstood.* 他希望不被人誤解。◇ ~ **for sth** *There are plenty of graduates anxious for work.* 有大量畢業生渴求工作。◇ ~ **for sb to do sth** *I'm anxious for her to do as little as possible.* 我盼她盡量少幹。◇ ~ **that ...** *She was anxious that he should meet her father.* 她盼望他見她父親。▸ **anx·ious·ly** 🔑 *adv.*：*to **ask/look/wait anxiously*** 憂慮地問／瞧／等待 ◇ *Residents are anxiously awaiting a decision.* 居民焦慮地期待決定。

any 🔑 /ˈeni/ *det., pron., adv.*
■ **det.** **1** 🔑 used with uncountable or plural nouns in negative sentences and questions, after *if* or *whether*, and after some verbs such as *prevent, ban, forbid*, etc. to refer to an amount or a number of sth, however large or small（與不可數或複數名詞連用，用於否定句和疑問句，也用於 if 或 whether 之後，或緊接某些動詞如 prevent、ban、forbid 等）任何的，任一的：*I didn't eat any meat.* 我一點兒肉也沒吃。◇ *Are there any stamps?* 有郵票嗎？◇ *I've got hardly any money.* 我幾乎不名一文。◇ *You can't go out without any shoes.* 你不穿鞋不能出門。◇ *He forbids any talking in class.* 他嚴禁課堂上講話。◇ *She asked if we had any questions.* 她問我們有沒有問題。HELP In positive sentences **some** is usually used instead of **any**. 在肯定句中通常用 some 不用 any：*I've got some paper if you want it.* It is also used in questions that expect a positive answer. * some 還用於預期得到肯定回答的問句中：*Would you like some milk in your tea?* **2** 🔑 used with singular countable nouns to refer to one of a number of things or people, when it does not matter which one（與單數可數名詞連用）任一：*Take any book you like.* 你喜歡哪本書就拿哪本。◇ *Any colour will do.* 什麼顏色都行。◇ *Any teacher will tell you that students learn at different rates.* 任何老師都知道學生學習有快有慢。➲ see also IN ANY CASE at CASE *n.*, IN ANY EVENT at EVENT, AT ANY RATE at RATE *n.* **3 not just ~ sb/sth** used to show that sb/sth is special 非一般的；不尋常的：*It isn't just any day—it's my birthday!* 今天不是一般的日子，是我的生日！
■ **pron.** **1** 🔑 used in negative sentences and in questions and after *if* or *whether* to refer to an amount or a number, however large or small（用於否定句和疑問句中或 if、whether 後）任何數量，任一數額：*We need some more paint; there isn't any left.* 我們還需要一些油漆，已經用光了。◇ *I need some stamps. Are there any in your bag?* 我需要一些郵票。你包裏有嗎？◇ *Please let me know how many people are coming, if any.* 如果有人要來的話，請告訴我有多少。◇ *She spent hardly any of the money.* 這錢她幾乎一點兒都沒花。◇ *He returned home without any of the others.* 僅他一人回到了家。HELP In positive sentences **some** is usually used instead of **any**. It is also used in questions that expect a positive reply. 在肯定句中通常用 some 而非 any。some 還用於預期得到肯定回答的問句中：*I've got plenty of paper—would you like some?* **2** 🔑 one or more of a number of people or things, especially when it does not matter which 任一；任何一些：*I'll take any you don't want.* 你不要的我隨便拿一個。◇ *'Which colour do you want?' 'Any of them will do.'* "你要哪種顏色？" "隨便哪種都行。"
IDM **sb isn't having any (of it)** (*informal*) somebody is not interested or does not agree 某人不感興趣；某人不同意：*I suggested sharing the cost, but he wasn't having any of it.* 我提議分擔費用，可是他不同意。
■ **adv.** **1** 🔑 used to emphasize an adjective or adverb in negative sentences or questions, meaning 'at all'（用於否定句或疑問句中，加強形容詞或副詞的語氣）一點兒也（不），完全（不），絲毫：*He wasn't any good at French.* 他的法語糟透了。◇ *I can't run any faster.* 我不能

跑得更快了。◇ *Is your father feeling any better?* 你的父親身體好些了嗎？◇ *I don't want any more.* 我不再要了。◇ *If you don't tell them, nobody will be* **any the wiser** (= they will not find out about it). 如果你不告訴他們，誰也不會察覺。 **2** (*NAmE, informal*) used at the end of a negative sentence to mean 'at all' （用於否定句末）根本（不）： *That won't hurt you any.* 那根本不會傷害你。

any·body 🔑 /ˈenibɒdi; *NAmE* -bɑːdi; -bʌdi/ *pron.* = ANYONE： *Is there anybody who can help me?* 有人能幫我嗎？◇ *Anybody can use the pool—you don't need to be a member.* 任何人都可使用這個游泳池，不必是會員。◇ *She wasn't anybody before she got that job.* 她在獲得那個職位之前不過是個無名之輩。

any·how /ˈenihaʊ/ *adv.* **1** = ANYWAY **2** in a careless way; not arranged in an order 隨便地；雜亂無章地： *She piled the papers in a heap on her desk, just anyhow.* 她把文件在桌上隨便擱成一堆。

any ˈmore (*BrE*) (also **any·more** *NAmE, BrE*) *adv.* often used at the end of negative sentences and at the end of questions, to mean 'any longer' （常用於否定句和疑問句末）再也（不），（不）再： *She doesn't live here any more.* 她已經不在這裏住了。◇ *Why doesn't he speak to me any more?* 他為啥不再理我了？◇ *Now she won't have to go out to work any more.* 現在她不必再出去工作了。 **HELP** Do not use 'no more' with this meaning. 不能用 no more 表示此義： ~~*She doesn't live here no more.*~~

any·one 🔑 /ˈeniwʌn/ (also **any·body**) *pron.*
1 🔑 used instead of *someone* in negative sentences and in questions after *if / whether*; and after verbs such as *prevent, forbid, avoid*, etc. （用於否定句、疑問句，也用於 if 或 whether 之後，或緊接 prevent、forbid、avoid 等動詞，代替 someone）任何人： *Is anyone there?* 有人嗎？◇ *Does anyone else want to come?* 還有人想來嗎？◇ *Did anyone see you?* 有沒有人見到了你？◇ *Hardly anyone came.* 幾乎沒有人來。◇ *I forbid anyone to touch that clock.* 我不准任何人碰那台鐘。 **HELP** The difference between **anyone** and **someone** is the same as the difference between **any** and **some**. Look at the notes there. * anyone 和 someone 的區別與 any 和 some 的區別相同。參看該兩詞條下的註解。 **2** 🔑 any person at all; it does not matter who 隨便哪個人： *Anybody can see that it's wrong.* 隨便哪個人都可以看出這是錯的。◇ *The exercises are so simple that almost anyone can do them.* 練習十分簡單，幾乎誰都會做。 **3** (in negative sentences 用於否定句) an important person 重要人物： *She wasn't anyone before she got that job.* 她在獲得那個職位之前不過是個無名之輩。

any·place /ˈenipleɪs/ *adv.* (*NAmE*) = ANYWHERE

any·thing 🔑 /ˈeniθɪŋ/ *pron.*
1 🔑 used instead of *something* in negative sentences and in questions; after *if / whether*; and after verbs such as *prevent, ban, avoid*, etc. （用於否定句、疑問句，也用於 if 或 whether 之後，或緊接 prevent、ban、avoid 等動詞，代替 something）任何東西，任何事物： *Would you like anything else?* 你要點別的什麼嗎？◇ *There's never anything worth watching on TV.* 電視上根本沒有什麼值得看的節目。◇ *If you remember anything at all, please let us know.* 如果你還記得點兒什麼請告訴我們。◇ *We hope to prevent anything unpleasant from happening.* 我們希望防止任何不愉快的事發生。 **HELP** The difference between **anything** and **something** is the same as the difference between **any** and **some**. Look at the notes there. * anything 和 something 的區別與 any 和 some 的區別相同。參看該兩詞條下的註解。 **2** 🔑 any thing at all, when it does not matter which 隨便哪個東西；隨便什麼事物： *I'm so hungry, I'll eat anything.* 我餓慌了，隨便吃什麼都行。 **3** any thing of importance 重要東西；重要事物： *Is there anything* (= any truth) *in these rumours?* 這些傳聞中有沒有真實的東西？

IDM **anything but** definitely not 決不；根本不： *The hotel was anything but cheap.* 這家旅館根本不便宜。◇ *It wasn't cheap. Anything but.* 它不便宜。絕對不。 **anything like sb/sth** 🔑 (*informal*) (used in questions and negative statements 用於疑問句和否定陳述) similar to sb/sth 和…相像；與…相似： *He isn't anything like my first boss.* 他完全不像我的第一個老闆。 **as happy, quick, etc. as anything** (*informal*) very happy, quick, etc. 非常幸福（或迅速等）： *I felt as pleased as anything.* 我感到無比高興。 **like ˈanything** (*BrE, informal*) very much 非常；像什麼似的： *They're always slagging me off like anything.* 他們經常把我罵得狗血淋頭。 **not anything like as good, much, etc.** used to emphasize that sth is not as good, not enough, etc. 根本不，無論如何都不（好、夠等）： *The book wasn't anything like as good as her first one.* 這本書遠遠不如她的處女作。 **not for ˈanything** (*informal*) definitely not 決不；根本不： *I wouldn't give it up for anything.* 我決不放棄。 **or anything** (*informal*) or another thing of a similar type 或其他什麼類似的： *If you want to call a meeting or anything, just let me know.* 要是你想召集個會議什麼的，就請告訴我。

ˈany time (*BrE*) (also **any·time** *NAmE, BrE*) *adv.* at a time that is not fixed 在任何時候；隨便什麼時候： *Call me any time.* 隨時給我打電話。

IDM **ˌanytime ˈsoon** (*NAmE*) used in negative sentences and questions to refer to the near future （用於否定句和疑問句）即將，馬上： *Will she be back anytime soon?* 她會馬上回來嗎？

any·way 🔑 /ˈeniweɪ/ (also **any·how**) (also *NAmE, informal* **any·ways**) *adv.*
1 🔑 used when adding sth to support an idea or argument 而且；加之；反正 **SYN** **besides**： *It's too expensive and anyway the colour doesn't suit you.* 這個太貴，而且顏色也不適合你。◇ *It's too late now, anyway.* 反正現在已經太遲了。 **2** 🔑 despite sth; even so 儘管；即使這樣： *The water was cold but I took a shower anyway.* 水很冷，不過我還是沖了個淋浴。◇ *I'm afraid we can't come, but thanks for the invitation anyway.* 恐怕我們來不了，不過還是感謝邀請。 **3** 🔑 used when changing the subject of a conversation, ending the conversation or returning to a subject （轉換話題、結束談話或回到原話題時說）無論如何，反正： *Anyway, let's forget about that for the moment.* 咱們無論如何暫時不要再提這件事。◇ *Anyway, I'd better go now—I'll see you tomorrow.* 反正我現在還是走的好，明天見。 **4** 🔑 used to correct or slightly change what you have said （糾正或略微改變說過的話）至少： *She works in a bank. She did when I last saw her, anyway.* 她在銀行工作。至少我上次見到她時是這樣。

any·where 🔑 /ˈeniweə(r); *NAmE* -wer/ (*NAmE* also **any·place**) *adv.*
1 🔑 used in negative sentences and in questions instead of *somewhere* （用於否定句和疑問句，代替 somewhere）在任何地方： *I can't see it anywhere.* 我哪兒也見不到它。◇ *Did you go anywhere interesting?* 你去過任何有趣的地方嗎？◇ *Many of these animals are not found anywhere else.* 這些動物中有很多是其他地方沒有的。◇ *He's never been anywhere outside Britain.* 他從來沒有去過英國以外的任何地方。 **HELP** The difference between **anywhere** and **somewhere** is the same as the difference between **any** and **some**. Look at the notes there. * anywhere 和 somewhere 的區別與 any 和 some 的區別相同。參看該兩詞條下的註解。 **2** 🔑 in, at or to any place, when it does not matter where 在（或去）任何地方；隨便哪個地方： *Put the box down anywhere.* 把箱子隨便放在哪兒都可以。◇ *An accident can happen anywhere.* 任何地方都可能發生事故。 ▸ **any·where** 🔑 *pron.*： *I don't have anywhere to stay.* 我沒有可以待的地方。◇ *Do you know anywhere I can buy a second-hand computer?* 你知道我在哪兒可以買到二手計算機嗎？

AOB /ˌeɪ əʊ ˈbiː; *NAmE* oʊ/ *abbr.* any other business (the things that are discussed at the end of an official meeting that are not on the AGENDA) 其他事項（正式會議末尾所討論的未列入議程的事項）

A-OK /ˌeɪ əʊ ˈkeɪ; *NAmE* ˌeɪ oʊ ˈkeɪ/ *adj.* [not before noun] (*NAmE, informal*) in good condition; in an acceptable manner 狀況良好；過得去；還好： *Everything's A-OK now.* 現在一切都妥帖了。 ▸ **A-OK** *adv.*： *The party went off A-OK.* 聚會進行得還順利。

A

aorta /eɪ'ɔːtə; NAmE eɪ'ɔːrtə/ *noun* (*anatomy* 解) the main ARTERY that carries blood from the heart to the rest of the body once it has passed through the LUNGS 主動脈

Ao·tea·roa /aʊˌteɪə'rəʊə; NAmE -'roʊə/ *noun* (*NZE*) the Maori name for New Zealand, usually translated as 'the land of the long white cloud' 新西蘭（毛利語，意為"白雲綿綿之地"）

AP /ˌeɪ 'piː/ *abbr.* ASSOCIATED PRESS 美聯社

apace /ə'peɪs/ *adv.* (*formal*) at a fast speed; quickly 高速地；迅速地：*to* ***continue/grow/proceed/develop apace*** 繼續保持高速；迅速生長；進展迅速；高速發展

Apa·che /ə'pætʃi/ *noun* (*pl.* **Apa·che** or **Apa·ches**) a member of a Native American people, many of whom live in the south-western US 阿帕切人（美洲土著，多居於美國西南部）

apart 0‑ /ə'pɑːt; NAmE ə'pɑːrt/ *adv.*
1 0‑ separated by a distance, of space or time（指空間或時間）相隔，相距：*The two houses stood 500 metres apart.* 兩座房子相距 500 米。◇ *Their birthdays are only three days apart.* 他們的生日僅隔三日。◇ (*figurative*) *The two sides in the talks are still a long way apart* (= are far from reaching an agreement). 談判雙方的意見仍相去甚遠。**2** 0‑ not together; separate or separately 不在一起；分離；分開：*We're living apart now.* 我們現在不住在一起。◇ *Over the years, Rosie and I had* ***drifted apart***. 多年以來，我和羅西早已疏遠。◇ *She keeps herself apart from other people.* 她與其他人保持距離。◇ *I can't* ***tell*** *the twins* ***apart*** (= see the difference between them). 我分不出這一對雙胞胎中誰是誰。**3** 0‑ into pieces 成碎片：*The whole thing just* ***came apart*** *in my hands.* 這整件東西偏偏在我手裏破裂了。◇ *We had to* ***take*** *the engine* ***apart***. 我們不得不拆卸了引擎。◇ *When his wife died, his world* ***fell apart***. 他在妻子去世後萬念俱灰。**4** used to say that sb/sth is not included in what you are talking about（指所說的不包括在內）除外：*Victoria apart, not one of them seems suitable for the job.* 除了維多利亞，看來他們誰也不適合這個工作。IDM see JOKE *v.*, POLE *n.*, RIP *v.*, WORLD

a'part from 0‑ (also **a'side from** especially in *NAmE*) *prep.*
1 0‑ except for 除了…外（都）；要不是：*I've finished apart from the last question.* 除了最後一道題，我全做完了。➲ LANGUAGE BANK at EXCEPT **2** 0‑ in addition to; as well as 除了…外（還）；此外；加之：*Apart from their house in London, they also have a villa in Spain.* 他們在倫敦有一座房子，此外在西班牙還有一座別墅。◇ *It was a difficult time. Apart from everything else, we had financial problems.* 當時是困難時期。別的一切都不說，我們財政上也有問題。◇ *You've got to help. Apart from anything else you're my brother.* 你得幫忙。別的不說，你總歸是我兄弟。➲ note at BESIDES

apart·heid /ə'pɑːtaɪt; -eɪt; NAmE ə'pɑːrtaɪt; -eɪt/ *noun* [U] the former political system in South Africa in which only white people had full political rights and other people, especially black people, were forced to live away from white people, go to separate schools, etc. 種族隔離（前南非政府推行的政策）

apart·ment 0‑ /ə'pɑːtmənt; NAmE ə'pɑːrt-/ *noun*
1 0‑ (*especially NAmE*) a set of rooms for living in, usually on one floor of a building（通常指在同一樓層的）公寓套房 ➲ COLLOCATIONS at HOUSE ➲ compare CONDOMINIUM, FLAT (1) **2** 0‑ a set of rooms used for a holiday/vacation（度假用的）公寓套房：*self-catering holiday apartments* 自己開伙的度假租房 **3** [usually pl.] (*BrE*) a room in a house, especially a large or famous house（尤指巨屋、名宅的）房間：*You can visit the whole palace except for the private apartments.* 整座宮殿除內殿外均可參觀。

a'partment block (*BrE*) (*NAmE* **a'partment building**) *noun* a large building with flats/apartments on each floor 公寓大樓 ➲ VISUAL VOCAB page V16

a'partment house *noun* (*US*) a small apartment block（小的）公寓樓

apa·thet·ic /ˌæpə'θetɪk/ *adj.* showing no interest or enthusiasm 冷漠；淡漠；無動於衷：*The illness made her apathetic and unwilling to meet people.* 疾病使她冷漠，不願見人。▸ **apa·thet·ic·al·ly** /ˌæpə'θetɪkli/ *adv.*

ap·athy /'æpəθi/ *noun* [U] the feeling of not being interested in or enthusiastic about something, or things in general 冷漠；淡漠：*There is* ***widespread apathy*** *among the electorate.* 選民普遍態度冷淡。

apato·saurus /əˌpætə'sɔːrəs/ (also **bron·to·saurus**) *noun* a very large DINOSAUR with a long neck and tail 謬龍（長頸長尾的巨型恐龍）

APB /ˌeɪ piː 'biː/ *abbr.* (*NAmE*) ALL-POINTS BULLETIN 全面通緝通告

ape /eɪp/ *noun, verb*
■ ***noun*** a large animal like a MONKEY, with no tail. There are different types of ape. 類人猿；無尾猿：*the great apes* (= for example, ORANG-UTANS or CHIMPANZEES) 類人猿（如猩猩、黑猩猩）
IDM **go 'ape/'apeshit** (*slang, especially NAmE*) to become extremely angry or excited 暴跳如雷；激動異常
■ ***verb*** **1 ~ sb/sth** (*BrE, disapproving*) to do sth in the same way as sb else, especially when it is not done very well（尤指笨拙地）模仿，學…的樣子 SYN **imitate**：*For years the British film industry merely aped Hollywood.* 多年來，英國電影業一味模仿好萊塢。**2 ~ sb/sth** (*especially NAmE*) to copy the way sb else behaves or talks, in order to make fun of them（為了取笑）學…的樣，模仿 SYN **mimic**：*We used to ape the teacher's southern accent.* 我們過去常模仿老師的南方口音。

ape·man /'eɪpmæn/ *noun* (*pl.* **-men** /-men/) a large animal, half way between an APE and a human 猿人

aperi·tif /əˌperə'tiːf/ *noun* (*especially BrE*) a drink, usually one containing alcohol, that people sometimes have just before a meal（餐前）開胃酒

aper·ture /'æpətʃə(r); NAmE also -tʃʊr/ *noun* **1** (*formal*) a small opening in sth 小孔；縫隙 **2** (*technical* 術語) an opening that allows light to reach a LENS, especially in cameras（尤指攝影機等的光圈）孔徑：*For flash photography, set the aperture at f.5.6.* 用閃光照相，要把光圈孔徑定為 5.6。

ape·shit /'eɪpʃɪt/ *noun*
IDM **go 'apeshit** ➲ APE

Apex /'eɪpeks/ (also **APEX**) *abbr.* Advanced Purchase Excursion (a system that offers cheaper travel tickets when they are bought in advance) 預付款旅遊票優惠

apex /'eɪpeks/ *noun* [usually sing.] (*pl.* **apexes**) the top or highest part of sth 頂點；最高點：*the apex of the roof/triangle* 房頂；三角形的頂點 ◇ (*figurative*) *At 37, she'd reached the apex of her career.* 她在 37 歲時達到了事業的巔峰。

apha·sia /ə'feɪziə/ *noun* [U] (*medical* 醫) the loss of the ability to understand or produce speech, because of brain damage 失語症

aphid /'eɪfɪd/ *noun* a very small insect that is harmful to plants. There are several types of aphid, including, for example, GREENFLY. 蚜蟲（體小，植物害蟲）

aph·or·ism /'æfərɪzəm/ *noun* (*formal*) a short phrase that says sth true or wise 格言；警句 ▸ **aph·or·is·tic** /ˌæfə'rɪstɪk/ *adj.*

aph·ro·dis·iac /ˌæfrə'dɪziæk/ *noun* a food or drug that is said to give people a strong desire to have sex 春藥；激發性慾的食物 ▸ **aph·ro·dis·iac** *adj.*：*the aphrodisiac qualities of ginseng* 人參的催慾功效

api·ary /'eɪpiəri; NAmE -ieri/ *noun* (*pl.* **-ies**) a place where BEES are kept 養蜂場

apiece /ə'piːs/ *adv.* (used after a noun or number 用於名詞或數字後) having, costing or measuring a particular amount each 每人；每個；各：*Rooney and Walcott scored a goal apiece.* 魯尼和沃爾科特各進一球。◇ *The largest stones weigh over five tonnes apiece.* 最大的石頭每塊重五噸以上。

aplenty /ə'plenti/ *adv., adj.* [after noun] (*formal*) in large amounts, especially more than is needed 大量；充裕；綽綽有餘

aplomb /ə'plɒm; *NAmE* ə'plɑːm/ *noun* [U] (*formal*) if sb does sth **with aplomb**, they do it in a confident and successful way, often in a difficult situation 鎮定；沉着；泰然自若：*with* ***considerable/great/remarkable aplomb*** 相當的／十分的／非凡的鎮定 ◇ *He delivered the speech with his* ***usual aplomb***. 他以慣常的沉着語氣作了演講。

ap·noea (*BrE*) (*NAmE* **ap·nea**) /æp'niːə/ *noun* [U] (*medical* 醫) a condition in which sb stops breathing temporarily while they are sleeping 睡眠呼吸暫停

apoca·lypse /ə'pɒkəlɪps; *NAmE* ə'pɑːk-/ *noun* **1** [sing., U] the destruction of the world 世界毀滅：*Civilization is on the brink of apocalypse.* 文明已瀕臨毀滅的邊緣。**2 the Apocalypse** [sing.] the end of the world, as described in the Bible（《聖經》所述的）末世 **3** [sing.] a situation causing very serious damage and destruction 大動亂；大災變：*an environmental apocalypse* 環境大災變

apoca·lyp·tic /əˌpɒkə'lɪptɪk; *NAmE* əˌpɑːk-/ *adj.* **1** describing very serious damage and destruction in past or future events 描述（歷史）大動亂的；預示（未來）大災變的：*an apocalyptic view of history* 對歷史抱極其悲觀的觀點 ◇ *apocalyptic warnings of the end of society* 對社會末日駭人聽聞的預警 **2** like the end of the world 似末世的；像世界末日的：*an apocalyptic scene* 末世景象

apoc·rypha /ə'pɒkrɪfə; *NAmE* ə'pɑːk-/ *noun* [pl.] **1 Apocrypha** Christian religious texts that are related to the Bible but not officially considered to be part of it 外經，旁經（沒有列入正典《聖經》的經籍）**2** writings which are not considered to be genuine 贋文；偽書

apoc·ryph·al /ə'pɒkrɪfl; *NAmE* ə'pɑːk-/ *adj.* (of a story 傳說) well known, but probably not true 傳聞但不足為憑的；虛構的：*Most of the stories about him are apocryphal.* 關於他的傳聞多屬虛構。

apo·gee /'æpədʒiː/ *noun* [sing.] **1** (*formal*) the highest point of sth, where it is greatest or most successful 頂峰；頂點；最高點 **2** (*astronomy* 天) the point in the ORBIT of the moon, a planet or other object in space when it is furthest from the planet, for example the earth, around which it turns 遠地點（繞地運動的天體在軌道上離地球或其他行星的最遠點）➲ compare PERIGEE

apol·it·ical /ˌeɪpə'lɪtɪkl/ *adj.* **1** (of a person 人) not interested in politics; not thinking politics are important 不關心政治的；不重視政治的 **2** not connected with a political party 與政黨無關的

Apol·lo·nian /ˌæpə'ləʊniən; *NAmE* -'loʊ-/ *adj.* **1** connected with the ancient Greek god Apollo 阿波羅神的；日神的 **2** (*formal*) connected with the controlled and reasonable aspects of human nature 自制的；理性的 ➲ compare DIONYSIAC

apolo·get·ic /əˌpɒlə'dʒetɪk; *NAmE* əˌpɑːl-/ *adj.* feeling or showing that you are sorry for doing sth wrong or for causing a problem 道歉的；謝罪的；愧疚的：*'Sorry,' she said, with an apologetic smile.* "對不起。" 她說，歉然一笑。◇ **~ about/for sth** *They were very apologetic about the trouble they'd caused.* 他們對所惹的麻煩深感愧疚。▸ **apolo·get·ic·al·ly** /əˌpɒlə'dʒetɪkli; *NAmE* əˌpɑːl-/ *adv.*：*'I'm sorry I'm late,' he murmured apologetically.* "對不起，我遲到了。" 他小聲道歉說。

apo·lo·gia /ˌæpə'ləʊdʒiə; *NAmE* -'loʊ-/ *noun* (*formal*) a formal written defence of your own or sb else's actions or opinions 書面辯解；辯解書；辯解文：*His book was seen as an apologia for the war.* 他的著作被視為是對這場戰爭的辯護。

apolo·gist /ə'pɒlədʒɪst; *NAmE* ə'pɑːl-/ *noun* **~ (for sb/sth)** a person who tries to explain and defend sth, especially a political system or religious ideas（尤指政治或宗教方面的）辯護者，辯解者

apolo·gize (*BrE* also **-ise**) 🔑 /ə'pɒlədʒaɪz; *NAmE* ə'pɑːl-/ *verb* [I] **~ (to sb) (for sth)** to say that you are sorry for doing sth wrong or causing a problem 道歉；謝罪：*Why should I apologize?* 我為什麼要道歉？◇ *Go and apologize to her.* 去給她賠不是。◇ *We apologize for the late departure of this flight.* 本航班延誤離境，謹致歉意。

apol·ogy /ə'pɒlədʒi; *NAmE* ə'pɑːl-/ *noun* (*pl.* **-ies**) **1** [C, U] **~ (to sb) (for sth)** a word or statement saying sorry for sth that has been done wrong or that causes a problem 道歉；謝罪：*to* ***offer/make/demand/accept an apology*** 主動道歉；致歉；要求／接受道歉 ◇ *You* ***owe him an apology*** *for what you said.* 你要為你所說的話向他道歉。◇ *We should like to offer our apologies for the delay to your flight today.* 今天航班誤點，敬請原諒。◇ *We received a letter of apology.* 我們收到了一封道歉信。**2** [C, usually pl.] information that you cannot go to a meeting or must leave early（因不能赴會或提前離會的）致歉：*The meeting started with apologies* (= the names of people who said they could not go to the meeting). 會議一開始就宣佈了請假缺席者的名單。◇ (*formal*) *She* ***made her apologies*** *and left early.* 她致歉後就提前離開了。

IDM **make no a'pology/a'pologies for sth** if you say that you **make no apology/apologies for** sth, you mean that you do not feel that you have said or done anything wrong（對某事）無可道歉，無錯可認

apo·plec·tic /ˌæpə'plektɪk/ *adj.* **1** very angry 大怒的；十分生氣的：*He was apoplectic with rage at the decision.* 他對這個決定異常憤怒。**2** (*old-fashioned*) connected with apoplexy 中風的；卒中的：*an* ***apoplectic attack/fit*** 中風的發作

apo·plexy /'æpəpleksi/ *noun* [U] (*old-fashioned*) the sudden loss of the ability to feel or move caused by an injury in the brain 中風；卒中 SYN **a stroke**

aporia /ə'pɔːriə/ *noun* (*technical* 術語) a situation in which two or more parts of a theory or argument do not agree, meaning that the theory or argument cannot be true（理論或論據的）自相矛盾，不成立

apos·tate /ə'pɒsteɪt; *NAmE* ə'pɑːs-/ *noun* (*formal*) a person who has rejected their religious or political beliefs 叛教者；脫黨者；變節者 ▸ **apos·tasy** /ə'pɒstəsi; *NAmE* ə'pɑːs-/ *noun* [U]

a pos·teri·ori /ˌeɪ ˌpɒsteri'ɔːraɪ; *NAmE* ˌpɑːs-/ *adj.*, *adv.* (from *Latin*, *formal*) analysing sth by starting from known facts and then thinking about the possible causes of the facts, for example saying 'Look, the streets are wet so it must have been raining.' 從事實推斷原因；由果及因 ➲ compare A PRIORI

apos·tle /ə'pɒsl; *NAmE* ə'pɑːsl/ *noun* **1 Apostle** any one of the twelve men that Christ chose to tell people about him and his teachings 宗徒，使徒（耶穌十二門徒之一）**2 ~ (of sth)** (*formal*) a person who strongly believes in a policy or an idea and tries to make other people believe in it（政策或思想的）倡導者，鼓吹者：*an apostle of free enterprise* 自由企業的鼓吹者

apos·tolic /ˌæpə'stɒlɪk; *NAmE* -'stɑːlɪk/ *adj.* (*technical* 術語) **1** connected with the Apostles or their teaching 宗徒的；使徒的；傳自宗徒的 **2** connected with the Pope or Popes, who are considered to have had authority passed down to them from Christ's Apostles 羅馬教宗的；宗座的

apos·tro·phe /ə'pɒstrəfi; *NAmE* ə'pɑːs-/ *noun* **1** the mark (') used to show that one or more letters or numbers have been left out, as in *she's* for *she is* and *'63* for *1963* 撇號；省字符；省略符號 **2** the mark (') used before or after the letter 's' to show that sth belongs to sb, as in *Sam's watch* and *the horses' tails* 撇號；所有格符號 **3** the mark (') used before the letter 's' to show the plural of a letter or number, as in *How many 3's are there in 9?* and *There are two m's in 'comma'.* 撇號；複數符號

apos·tro·phize (*BrE* also **-ise**) /ə'pɒstrəfaɪz; *NAmE* ə'pɑːs-/ *verb* **1 ~ sb** to address what you are saying, or a poem, a speech in a play, etc. to a particular person 對…述說；向…誦詩（或台詞等）**2 ~ sth** to add apostrophes to a piece of writing 給…加撇號

apoth·ecary /ə'pɒθəkəri; *NAmE* ə'pɑːθəkeri/ *noun* (*pl.* **-ies**) a person who made and sold medicines in the past（舊時製藥兼售藥的）藥劑師，藥商

apothe·osis /əˌpɒθi'əʊsɪs; *NAmE* əˌpɑːθi'oʊ-/ *noun* [usually sing.] (*pl.* **apothe·oses** /-siːz/) (*formal*) **1** the highest or most perfect development of sth 鼎盛時期；發展頂峰；

A

完美階段 **2** the best time in sb's life or career（人生或事業的）巔峰 **3** a formal statement that a person has become a god（指人）冊封為神，尊奉為神，神化：*the apotheosis of a Roman emperor* 冊封羅馬皇帝為神

app /æp/ *abbr.* APPLICATION

appa /'ʌpə/ *noun* (*IndE*) = ABBA

appal (*BrE*) (*NAmE* **ap·pall**) /ə'pɔːl/ *verb* (**-ll-**) to shock sb very much 使大為震驚；使驚駭 SYN **horrify**：**~ sb** *The brutality of the crime has appalled the public.* 罪行之殘暴使公眾大為震驚。◇ *The idea of sharing a room appalled her.* 合住一個房間的想法使她驚駭。◇ **it appals sb that ... /to do sth** *It appalled me that they could simply ignore the problem.* 他們竟然把問題置之不理，令我非常詫異。

ap·palled /ə'pɔːld/ *adj.* feeling or showing horror or disgust at sth unpleasant or wrong 感到驚駭的；表示憎惡的 SYN **horrified**：*an* ***appalled expression/silence*** 驚恐的表情；嚇得說不出話 ◇ *We watched appalled as the child ran in front of the car.* 小孩在汽車前面跑過，我們看得心驚膽戰。◇ **~ at sth** *They were appalled at the waste of recyclable material.* 他們憎惡有人浪費可回收材料。

ap·pal·ling /ə'pɔːlɪŋ/ *adj.* **1** (*NAmE, formal* or *BrE*) shocking; extremely bad 令人震驚的；使人驚駭的；極為惡劣的：*The prisoners were living in appalling conditions.* 囚犯的居住條件極為惡劣。 **2** (*informal*) very bad 糟糕的；很不像話的：*The bus service is appalling now.* 現在公共汽車服務很差。▸ **ap·pal·ling·ly** *adv.*：***appallingly bad/difficult*** 極差；極為困難 ◇ *The essay was appallingly written.* 這文章寫得一塌糊塗。

ap·par·at /ˌæpə'rɑːt/ *noun* [usually sing.] the system of officials, offices, etc. that a government, especially a Communist government, uses to run a country（尤指共產黨的）政府體制，國家機器

ap·par·at·chik /ˌæpə'rɑːtʃɪk/ *noun* (from *Russian, disapproving* or *humorous*) an official in a large political organization（大政治機構的）官員：*party apparatchiks* 黨的官員

ap·par·atus /ˌæpə'reɪtəs; *NAmE* -'rætəs/ *noun* (*pl.* **ap·par·atuses**) **1** [U] the tools or other pieces of equipment that are needed for a particular activity or task 儀器；器械；裝置：*a piece of laboratory apparatus* 一件實驗室儀器 ◇ *Firefighters needed breathing apparatus to enter the burning house.* 消防隊員需要呼吸器以便進入燃燒中的大樓。➲ SYNONYMS at EQUIPMENT **2** [C, usually sing.] the structure of a system or an organization, particularly that of a political party or a government（尤指政黨或政府的）機構，組織，機關：*the power of the state apparatus* 國家機關的權力 **3** [C, usually sing.] (*technical* 術語) a system of organs in the body 器官：*the sensory apparatus* 感覺器官

ap·parel /ə'pærəl/ *noun* [U] **1** (*especially NAmE*) clothing, when it is being sold in shops/stores（商店出售的）衣服，服裝：*The store sells women's and children's apparel.* 這家商店出售女裝和童裝。 **2** (*old-fashioned* or *formal*) clothes, particularly those worn on a formal occasion（尤指正式場合穿的）衣服，服裝：*lords and ladies in fine apparel* 衣着漂亮的貴族和貴婦

ap·par·ent 🗝 AW /ə'pærənt/ *adj.*
1 🗝 [not usually before noun] easy to see or understand 顯而易見；明白易懂；顯然 SYN **obvious**：*Their devotion was apparent.* 他們的忠誠顯而易見。◇ *Then,* ***for no apparent reason****, the train suddenly stopped.* 接着，不知什麼原因，火車突然停了下來。◇ **~ (from sth) (that ...)** *It was apparent from her face that she was really upset.* 從面容上一眼就可以看出她確實心緒煩亂。◇ **~ (to sb) (that ...)** *It soon* ***became apparent*** *to everyone that he couldn't sing.* 很快大家就看出來他不會唱歌。➲ SYNONYMS at CLEAR ➲ LANGUAGE BANK at ILLUSTRATE **2** 🗝 [usually before noun] that seems to be real or true but may not be 貌似的；表面上的；未必真實的 SYN **seeming**：*My parents were concerned at my apparent lack of enthusiasm for school.* 我看來對上學不感興趣，使父母擔心。➲ see also APPEAR

ap·par·ent·ly 🗝 AW /ə'pærəntli/ *adv.* according to what you have heard or read; according to the way sth appears 據…所知；看來；顯然：*Apparently they are getting divorced soon.* 看樣子，他們很快就要離婚。◇ *I thought she had retired, but apparently she hasn't.* 我原以為她退休了，但顯然她還沒有退。◇ *He paused, apparently lost in thought.* 他停頓下來，顯然陷入了沉思。

ap·par·ition /ˌæpə'rɪʃn/ *noun* a GHOST or an image of a person who is dead（人死後的）鬼，鬼魂，幽靈

ap·peal 🗝 /ə'piːl/ *noun, verb*
■ ***noun*** **1** 🗝 [C, U] a formal request to a court or to sb in authority for a judgement or a decision to be changed 上訴；申訴：(*BrE*) *to lodge an appeal* 提出上訴 ◇ (*NAmE*) *to file an appeal* 提出上訴 ◇ (*BrE*) *an appeal court/judge* 上訴法庭／法官 ◇ (*NAmE*) *an appeals court/judge* 上訴法庭／法官 ◇ **~ against sth** *an appeal against the 3-match ban* 不服禁賽 3 場令的申訴 ➲ COLLOCATIONS at JUSTICE ➲ see also COURT OF APPEAL **2** 🗝 [U] a quality that makes sb/sth attractive or interesting 吸引力；感染力；魅力：***mass/wide/popular appeal*** 對大眾的／廣泛的／普遍的吸引力 ◇ *The Beatles have never really* ***lost their appeal.*** 披頭士樂隊的感染力經久不衰。◇ *The prospect of living in a city* ***holds little appeal*** *for me.* 住在城市裏的機會對我沒有什麼吸引力。➲ see also SEX APPEAL **3** 🗝 [C, U] an urgent and deeply felt request for money, help or information, especially one made by a charity or by the police（尤指慈善機構或警方的）呼籲，籲請，懇求：*a look of silent appeal* 默默懇求的目光 ◇ **~ (to sb) (for sth)** *to launch a TV appeal for donations to the charity* 通過電視呼籲為該慈善事業捐贈 ◇ *The child's mother made an emotional appeal on TV for his return.* 孩子的母親在電視上懇切地要求兒子回家。◇ **~ to sb to do sth** *The police made an appeal to the public to remain calm.* 警方籲請公眾保持鎮靜。 **4** [C] **~ to sth** an indirect suggestion that any good, fair or reasonable person would act in a particular way 啟發；打動：*I relied on an appeal to his finer feelings.* 我寄望能打動他的愛心。
■ ***verb*** **1** 🗝 [I] **~ (to sb/sth) (against sth)** to make a formal request to a court or to sb in authority for a judgement or a decision to be changed 上訴；申訴：*He said he would appeal after being found guilty on four counts of murder.* 法庭判決他犯有四項謀殺罪，他表示要上訴。◇ *The company is appealing against the ruling.* 公司正對判決提出申訴。HELP In North American English, the form **appeal (sth) (to sb/sth)** is usually used, without a preposition. 美式英語通常用 appeal (sth) (to sb/sth)，不加介詞：*The company has ten days to appeal the decision to the tribunal.* **2** 🗝 [I] to attract or interest sb 有吸引力；有感染力；引起興趣：*The prospect of a long wait in the rain did not appeal.* 想到要在雨中久等使人掃興。◇ **~ to sb** *The design has to appeal to all ages and social groups.* 設計得要雅俗共賞，老幼皆宜。 **3** 🗝 [I] to make a serious and urgent request 呼籲；籲請；懇求：*I am appealing* (= asking for money) *on behalf of the famine victims.* 我代表饑民籲請捐款。◇ **~ (to sb) (for sth)** *Community leaders appealed for calm* (= urged people to remain calm). 社區領導們呼籲保持冷靜。◇ *Police have appealed for witnesses to come forward.* 警方呼籲證人挺身而出。◇ **~ to sb to do sth** *Organizers appealed to the crowd not to panic.* 組織者呼籲人群不要驚慌。 **4** [I] **~ (to sth)** to try to persuade sb to do sth by suggesting that it is a fair, reasonable or honest thing to do 啟發；勸說；打動：*They needed to appeal to his sense of justice.* 他們需要激發他的正義感。

ap'peal court *noun* **1** = COURT OF APPEAL **2 Ap'peals Court** [C] (*US*) = COURT OF APPEALS

ap·peal·ing /ə'piːlɪŋ/ *adj.* **1** attractive or interesting 有吸引力的；有感染力的；令人感興趣的：*Spending the holidays in Britain wasn't a prospect that I found particularly appealing.* 在英國度假對我並不特別有吸引力。OPP **unappealing** **2** showing that you want people to help you or to show you pity or sympathy 懇求的；可憐的；希望同情的：*'Would you really help?' he said with an appealing look.* "你真的願意幫忙嗎？" 他滿臉懇求地說。▸ **ap·peal·ing·ly** *adv.*：*The dog looked up at her appealingly.* 狗可憐巴巴地望着她。

ap·pear 🔑 /ə'pɪə(r); *NAmE* ə'pɪr/ *verb*
▸ LOOK/SEEM 看來；好像 **1** 🔑 *linking verb* (not used in the progressive tenses 不用於進行時) to give the impression of being or doing sth 顯得；看來；似乎 SYN **seem**：+ **adj.** *She didn't appear at all surprised at the news.* 她聽到這消息時一點也沒有顯得吃驚。◇ *It appears unlikely that interest rates will fall further.* 看來利率不大會再降低。◇ + **noun** *He appears a perfectly normal person.* 他看上去完全是個正常的人。◇ **~ to do sth** *She appeared to be in her late thirties.* 看樣子她快四十歲了。◇ *They appeared not to know what was happening.* 他們似乎不知道正在發生的事。◇ *There appears to have been a mistake.* 看來一直有一個差錯。◇ **it appears (that)** ... *It appears that there has been a mistake.* 看來一直有一個差錯。◇ ***It would appear that*** *this was a major problem.* 看來這是個主要問題。➲ LANGUAGE BANK at PERHAPS ▸ BE SEEN 出現 **2** 🔑 [I] to start to be seen 出現；呈現；顯現：*Three days later a rash appeared.* 三天後出現了皮疹。◇ + **adv./prep.** *A bus appeared around the corner.* 一輛公共汽車出現在拐角處。◇ *Smoke appeared on the horizon.* 地平線上升起了煙霧。▸ BEGIN TO EXIST 起源；出現 **3** 🔑 [I] (+ **adv./prep.**) to begin to exist or be known or used for the first time 起源；出現；首次使用：*When did mammals appear on the earth?* 地球上的哺乳動物起源於何時？◇ *This problem first appeared in the inner cities.* 這個問題最初在市中心出現。▸ OF BOOK/PROGRAMME 書；節目 **4** [I] (+ **adv./prep.**) to be published or broadcast 出版；廣播：*His new book will be appearing in the spring.* 他的新書將於春季出版。◇ *It was too late to prevent the story from appearing in the national newspapers.* 要阻止全國性報紙刊登這件事情已為時太晚。▸ IN MOVIE/PLAY 電影；戲劇 **5** [I] (+ **adv./prep.**) to take part in a film/movie, play, television programme, etc. 演出：*He has appeared in over 60 movies.* 他在 60 多部電影中演出過。◇ *She regularly appears on TV.* 她經常在電視上露面。◇ *Next month he will be appearing as Obama in a new play on Broadway.* 下月他將在百老匯上演的一齣新戲中扮演奧巴馬。▸ ARRIVE 到達 **6** [I] (+ **adv./prep.**) to arrive at a place 抵達；來到：*By ten o'clock Lee still hadn't appeared.* 到十點鐘李仍然沒有露面。▸ BE WRITTEN/MENTIONED 記載；提及 **7** [I] (+ **adv./prep.**) to be written or mentioned somewhere 記載；提及：*Your name will appear at the front of the book.* 你的名字將出現在書的前頁。▸ IN COURT 法庭 **8** [I] (+ **adv./prep.**) to be present in court in order to give evidence or answer a charge 出庭（作證或答辯）：*A man will appear in court today charged with the murder.* 一個被控犯謀殺罪的男人今天將出庭受審。◇ *She appeared on six charges of theft.* 她因被控犯有六項盜竊罪而出庭受審。◇ *He has been asked to appear as a witness for the defence.* 他已被傳喚出庭為被告作證。**9** [I] **~ for/on behalf of sb** to act as sb's lawyer in court（作為律師）出庭；出庭當…的律師：*Cherie Booth is the lawyer appearing for the defendant.* 徹里 • 布思作為被告的辯護律師出庭。➲ compare DISAPPEAR ➲ see also APPARENT

ap·pear·ance 🔑 /ə'pɪərəns; *NAmE* ə'pɪr-/ *noun*
▸ WAY STH LOOKS/SEEMS 外觀 **1** 🔑 [C, U] the way that sb/sth looks on the outside; what sb/sth seems to be 外貌；外觀；外表：*the* ***physical/outward/external appearance*** *of sth* 某物的外觀 ◇ *She had never been greatly concerned about her appearance.* 她從來不怎麼注重外貌。◇ *The dog was similar in general appearance to a spaniel.* 這條狗總的來看像西班牙獵狗。◇ *He gave* ***every appearance of*** (= seemed very much to be) *enjoying himself.* 他處處表現得很快活。◇ *Judging by appearances can be misleading.* 單憑外表判斷可能出錯。◇ ***To all appearances*** (= as far as people could tell) *he was dead.* 從一切跡象來看，他已經死了。◇ *When she lost all her money, she was determined to* ***keep up appearances*** (= hide the true situation and pretend that everything was going well). 她把錢全虧光時，決意佯裝若無其事。▸ SB/STH ARRIVING 到達 **2** 🔑 [C, usually sing.] the fact of sb/sth arriving, especially when it is not expected（尤指突然的）抵達，到來：*The sudden appearance of a security guard caused them to drop the money and run.* 保安人員突然出現，他們丟下錢就跑了。◇ *I don't want to go to the party, but I suppose I'd better* ***put in an appearance*** (= go there for a short time). 我不想去參加這個聚會，不過我認為最好還是去露個面。**3** 🔑 [C, usually sing.] the moment at which sth begins to exist or starts to be seen or used 起源；出現；首次使用：*the early appearance of daffodils in spring* 春來早開的水仙 ◇ *the appearance of organic vegetables in the supermarkets* 有機蔬菜在超級市場上市 ▸ IN PUBLIC 公開 **4** [C] an act of appearing in public, especially as a performer, politician, etc., or in court 公開露面；演出；出庭：*The Dutch player will make his first appearance for Liverpool this Saturday.* 這名荷蘭球員將於本星期六在利物浦隊中首次亮相。◇ *The singer's first public appearance was at the age of eight.* 這位歌手八歲時初次登台演出。◇ *the defendant's appearance in court* 被告出庭 ▸ BEING PUBLISHED/BROADCAST 出版；廣播 **5** [C, usually sing.] an act of being published or broadcast 出版；廣播：*the appearance of claims about the minister's private life in the press* 關於這位大臣私生活的說法見諸報端

ap·pease /ə'pi:z/ *verb* (*formal*, usually *disapproving*) **1 ~ sb** to make sb calmer or less angry by giving them what they want 安撫；撫慰：*The move was widely seen as an attempt to appease critics of the regime.* 普遍認為，這一舉措是試圖安撫批評政權的人。**2 ~ sb/sth** to give a country what it wants in order to avoid war 綏靖（滿足另一國的要求以避免戰爭）▸ **ap·pease·ment** *noun* [U]：*a policy of appeasement* 綏靖政策

ap·pel·lant /ə'pelənt/ *noun* (*law* 律) a person who appeals against a decision made in court 上訴人

ap·pel·late court /ə'pelət kɔ:t; *NAmE* kɔ:rt/ *noun* (*technical* 術語) a court in which people can appeal against decisions made in other courts of law 上訴法庭

ap·pel·la·tion /ˌæpə'leɪʃn/ *noun* (*formal*) a name or title 名稱；稱呼；稱號

ap·pel·la·tive /ə'pelətɪv/ *adj., noun*
■ ***adj.*** (*formal*) relating to the giving of a name 命名的；稱謂的；名稱的
■ ***noun*** (*technical* 術語) a common noun that is used to address a person or thing, for example 'mother' or 'doctor' 稱呼詞（可作呼語的名詞）

ap·pend AW /ə'pend/ *verb* **~ sth (to sth)** (*formal*) to add sth to the end of a piece of writing（在文章後面）附加，增補：*Footnotes have been appended to the document.* 該文件附加了腳註。

ap·pend·age /ə'pendɪdʒ/ *noun* (*formal*) a smaller or less important part of sth larger 附加物；附屬物

ap·pend·ec·tomy /ˌæpen'dektəmi/ *noun* [C, U] (*pl.* **-ies**) (*medical* 醫) the removal of the APPENDIX by SURGERY 闌尾切除術

ap·pen·di·citis /əˌpendə'saɪtɪs/ *noun* [U] a painful swelling of the appendix that can be very serious 闌尾炎

ap·pen·dix AW /ə'pendɪks/ *noun* (*pl.* **ap·pen·di·ces** /-dɪsi:z/ or **ap·pen·dixes**) **1** a small bag of TISSUE that is attached to the large INTESTINE. In humans, the appendix has no clear function. 闌尾：*He had to have his appendix out* (= removed). 他不得不切除了闌尾。➲ VISUAL VOCAB page V59 **2** a section giving extra information at the end of a book or document（書、文件的）附錄：*Full details are given in Appendix 3.* 詳情見附錄 3。

ap·per·tain /ˌæpə'teɪn; *NAmE* -pər't-/ *verb*
PHR V **apper'tain to sb/sth** (*formal*) to belong or refer to sb/sth 屬於；涉及；關係到：*rights appertaining to the property* 產權 ◇ *These figures appertain to last year's sales.* 這些數字指的是去年的銷售額。

ap·pe·tite /'æpɪtaɪt/ *noun* **1** [U, C, usually sing.] physical desire for food 食慾；胃口：*He suffered from headaches and* ***loss of appetite****.* 他患有頭痛和食慾不振。◇ *The walk gave me a good appetite.* 散步使我胃口大開。◇ *Don't*

A

spoil your appetite by eating between meals. 不要在兩餐之間吃東西，以免影響胃口。 **2** [C] a strong desire for sth 強烈慾望： *sexual appetites* 性慾 ◇ *The preview was intended to **whet your appetite*** (= make you want more). 預告是為了吊胃口。◇ **~ for sth** *The public have an insatiable appetite for scandal.* 公眾對醜事總是喜聞樂道。

ap·pet·izer (*BrE* also **-iser**) /ˈæpɪtaɪzə(r)/ *noun* a small amount of food or a drink that you have before a meal（餐前的）開胃品，開胃飲料

ap·pe·tiz·ing (*BrE* also **-is·ing**) /ˈæpɪtaɪzɪŋ/ *adj.* (of food, etc. 食物等) that smells or looks attractive; making you feel hungry or thirsty 開胃的；引起食慾的；使渴的 OPP **unappetizing**

ap·plaud /əˈplɔːd/ *verb* **1** [I, T] to show your approval of sb/sth by clapping your hands 鼓掌： *He started to applaud and the others joined in.* 他開始鼓掌，其他人也跟着鼓起掌來。◇ **~ sb** *They rose to applaud the speaker.* 他們起立向演講者鼓掌。◇ *She was applauded as she came on stage.* 她出台時人們向她鼓掌。 **2** [T] (*formal*) to express praise for sb/sth because you approve of them or it 稱讚；讚許；讚賞： **~ sth** *We applaud her decision.* 我們稱讚她的決定。◇ *His efforts to improve the situation are to be applauded.* 他為改善狀況所作的努力應該受到讚許。◇ **~ sb (for sth)** *I applaud her for having the courage to refuse.* 我讚賞她敢於拒絕。

ap·plause /əˈplɔːz/ *noun* [U] the noise made by a group of people clapping their hands and sometimes shouting to show their approval or enjoyment 鼓掌；喝彩： *Give her a big **round of applause**!* 為她熱烈鼓掌！◇ *The audience broke into rapturous applause.* 聽眾中爆發出一片歡呼喝彩聲。

apple 🔑 /ˈæpl/ *noun* a round fruit with shiny red or green skin and firm white flesh 蘋果： *an apple pie* 蘋果餡餅 ◇ *apple sauce* 蘋果沙司 ◇ *a garden with three apple trees* 有三棵蘋果樹的花園 ➲ VISUAL VOCAB page V30 ➲ see also ADAM'S APPLE, BIG APPLE, COOKING APPLE, CRAB APPLE, EATING APPLE, TOFFEE APPLE
IDM **the apple doesn't fall/never falls far from the ˈtree** (*saying, especially NAmE*) a child usually behaves in a similar way to his or her parent(s) 有什麼樣的父母就有什麼樣的兒女；上行下效 **the ˌapple of sb's ˈeye** a person or thing that is loved more than any other 心肝寶貝；掌上明珠 **ˌapples and ˈoranges** (*NAmE*) used to describe a situation in which two people or things are completely different from each other 蘋果橘子兩碼事；截然不同： *They really are apples and oranges.* 他們確實是迥然不同。◇ *They are both great but **you can't compare apples and oranges**.* 他們倆都很棒，但是截然不同，無法比較。➲ more at AMERICAN *adj.*, ROTTEN *adj.*

ˈapple cart *noun* IDM see UPSET *v.*

ˌapple ˈpie *noun* **1** [C, U] apples baked in a dish with PASTRY on the bottom, sides and top 蘋果派；蘋果餡餅： *a slice of apple pie* 一片蘋果餡餅 **2** [U] (*NAmE*) used to represent an idea of perfect home life and comfort 完美的家庭生活；溫馨舒適： *Who could argue against **motherhood and apple pie**?* 誰會反對母性與家庭的溫馨呢？ IDM see AMERICAN *adj.*

ap·plet /ˈæplət/ *noun* (*computing* 計) a program that is run from within another program, for example from within an Internet BROWSER 小應用程序；小程序

ap·pli·ance /əˈplaɪəns/ *noun* a machine that is designed to do a particular thing in the home, such as preparing food, heating or cleaning （家用）電器，器具： ***electrical/household appliances*** 電器；家用器具 ◇ *They sell a wide range of **domestic appliances**—washing machines, dishwashers and so on.* 他們出售各種家用電器，如洗衣機、洗碗機等等。➲ VISUAL VOCAB page V25

ap·plic·able /əˈplɪkəbl; ˈæplɪkəbl/ *adj.* [not usually before noun] that can be said to be true in the case of sb/sth 適用；合適 SYN **relevant**： *Give details of children where applicable* (= if you have any). 如有子女請提供詳情。◇ **~ to sb/sth** *Much of the form was not applicable* (= did not apply) *to me.* 表格中很多部份不適用於我。
▸ **ap·plic·abil·ity** /əˌplɪkəˈbɪləti; ˌæplɪk-/ *noun* [U]： *The new approach had wide applicability to all sorts of different problems.* 新方法廣泛適用於解決各種各樣的問題。

ap·pli·cant /ˈæplɪkənt/ *noun* **~ (for sth)** a person who makes a formal request for sth (= applies for it), especially for a job, a place at a college or university, etc. 申請人（尤指求職、進高等學校等）： *There were over 500 applicants for the job.* 有 500 多人申請這份工作。

ap·pli·ca·tion 🔑 /ˌæplɪˈkeɪʃn/ *noun*
▸ **FOR JOB/COURSE** 求職；辦手續 **1** 🔑 [C, U] a formal (often written) request for sth, such as a job, permission to do sth or a place at a college or university 申請；請求；申請書；申請表： *a planning/passport application* 規劃 / 護照申請 ◇ *an **application form*** (= a piece of paper on which to apply for sth) 申請表 ◇ **~ for sth/to do sth** *an application for membership/a loan/a licence* 會籍 / 貸款 / 執照申請 ◇ **~ to sb (for sth/to do sth)** *His application to the court for bail has been refused.* 他向法庭申請保釋遭到拒絕。◇ *Further information is available **on application** to the principal.* 可向校長提交申請書索取更多信息。➲ COLLOCATIONS at JOB
▸ **PRACTICAL USE** 實用 **2** 🔑 [U, C] **~ (of sth) (to sth)** the practical use of sth, especially a theory, discovery, etc.（尤指理論、發現等的）應用，運用： *the application of new technology to teaching* 新技術在教學上的應用 ◇ *The invention would have a wide range of applications in industry.* 這項發明在工業中會有廣泛用途。
▸ **OF PAINT/CREAM** 油漆；乳劑 **3** [C, U] an act of putting or spreading sth, such as paint or medical creams, onto sth else 塗抹；敷用；施用： *lotion for external application only* (= to be put on the skin, not swallowed) 僅限外部敷用的乳液 ◇ *It took three applications of paint to cover the graffiti.* 刷了三道油漆才蓋住了塗鴉。
▸ **OF RULE/LAW** 規章；法律 **4** [U] the act of making a rule, etc. operate or become effective 運用；生效： *strict application of the law* 法律的嚴格執行
▸ **COMPUTING** 計算機技術 **5** [C] (*abbr.* **app**) a program designed to do a particular job; a piece of software 應用程序；應用軟件；應用程式；應用軟體： *a database application* 數據庫應用軟件 ◇ *to download an app* 下載一個應用軟件 ➲ VISUAL VOCAB page V67 ➲ see also KILLER APPLICATION
▸ **HARD WORK** 勤奮 **6** [U] (*formal*) determination to work hard at sth; great effort 勤奮；努力： *Success as a writer demands great application.* 作家要成功就得悉力以赴。

ap·pli·ca·tor /ˈæplɪkeɪtə(r)/ *noun* a small tool that is used to put a substance onto a surface, or to put sth into an object 敷抹器；充填器： *Use the applicator to apply cream to the affected area.* 用塗藥器把藥膏抹在患處。➲ VISUAL VOCAB page V60

ap·plied /əˈplaɪd/ *adj.* [usually before noun] (especially of a subject of study 尤指學科) used in a practical way; not THEORETICAL 應用的；實用的： *applied mathematics* (= as used by engineers, etc.) 應用數學 ➲ compare PURE (7)

apˌplied linˈguistics *noun* [U] the scientific study of language as it relates to practical problems, in areas such as teaching and dealing with speech problems 應用語言學

ap·pli·qué /əˈpliːkeɪ; *NAmE* ˌæpləˈkeɪ/ *noun* [U] a type of NEEDLEWORK in which small pieces of cloth are sewn or stuck in a pattern onto a larger piece（織物的）縫飾，嵌花，貼花 ▸ **ap·pli·quéd** *adj.*

apply 🔑 /əˈplaɪ/ *verb* (**ap·plies**, **ap·ply·ing**, **ap·plied**, **ap·plied**)
▸ **FOR JOB/COURSE** 求職；辦手續 **1** 🔑 [I, T] to make a formal request, usually in writing, for sth such as a job, a place at college, university, etc.（通常以書面形式）申請，請求： *You should **apply in person/by letter**.* 你應該當面 / 寫信申請。◇ **~ for sth** *to apply for a job/passport/grant* 申請工作 / 護照 / 撥款 ◇ **~ to sb/sth (for sth)** *to apply to a company/university* 向公司 / 大學申請 ◇ **~ to do sth** *He has applied to join the army.* 他已報名參軍。
▸ **USE** 用 **2** 🔑 [T] to use sth or make sth work in a particular situation 使用；應用： **~ sth** *to apply economic sanctions/political pressure* 採用經濟制裁；施加政治壓力 ◇ **~ sth to sth** *The new technology was applied to farming.* 這項新技術已應用於農業。

▸ **PAINT/CREAM** 油漆；乳劑 **3** 🔑 [T] **~ sth (to sth)** to put or spread sth such as paint, cream, etc. onto a surface 塗；敷；施：*Apply the cream sparingly to your face and neck.* 把乳霜薄薄地抹在臉和脖子上。

▸ **BE RELEVANT** 有關 **4** 🔑 [I, T] (not used in the progressive tenses 不用於進行時) to concern or relate to sb/sth 有關；涉及：*Special conditions apply if you are under 18.* * 18 歲以下者按特殊情況處理。◇ **~ to sb/sth** *What I am saying applies only to some of you.* 我所說的只涉及你們中的一些人。◇ **~ sth to sb/sth** *The word 'unexciting' could never be applied to her novels.* "乏味"這個詞絕對和她的小說沾不上邊兒。

▸ **WORK HARD** 勤奮 **5** [T] to work at sth or study sth very hard 勤奮工作；努力學習：**~ yourself** *You would pass your exams if you applied yourself.* 努力學習就會通過考試。◇ **~ yourself/sth to sth/to doing sth** *We applied our minds to finding a solution to our problem.* 我們絞盡腦汁尋求解決問題的辦法。

▸ **PRESS HARD** 用力壓 **6** [T] to press on sth hard with your hand, foot, etc. to make sth work or have an effect on sth 手壓；腳踩：**~ sth** *to apply the brakes (of a vehicle)* 踩剎車 ◇ **~ sth to sth** *Pressure applied to the wound will stop the bleeding.* 壓住傷口可以止血。

ap·point 🔑 /əˈpɔɪnt/ *verb*
1 🔑 to choose sb for a job or position of responsibility 任命；委任：**~ sb** *They have appointed a new head teacher at my son's school.* 我兒子讀書的學校任命了一位新校長。◇ **~ sb to sth** *She has recently been appointed to the committee.* 她最近獲委任為委員會成員。◇ **~ sb + noun** | **~ sb as sth** *They appointed him (as) captain of the English team.* 他們任命他為英格蘭隊隊長。◇ **~ sb to do sth** *A lawyer was appointed to represent the child.* 一名律師被指定為這個孩子的代理人。 **2** [usually passive] **~ sth** (*formal*) to arrange or decide on a time or place for doing sth 安排，確定（時間、地點）：*A date for the meeting is still to be appointed.* 會議日期尚待確定。◇ *Everyone was assembled at the* ***appointed time.*** 全體人員均按規定時間召集到場。

ap·point·ee /əˌpɔɪnˈtiː/ *noun* a person who has been chosen for a job or position of responsibility 被任命者；被委任者：*the new appointee to the post* 新委任此職務者

ap·point·ment 🔑 /əˈpɔɪntmənt/ *noun*
1 🔑 [C] a formal arrangement to meet or visit sb at a particular time, especially for a reason connected with their work 約會；預約；約定：*I've got a* ***dental appointment*** *at 3 o'clock.* 我約了下午 3 點看牙醫。◇ *to make/keep an appointment* 預約；守約 ◇ *Viewing is* ***by appointment only*** (= only at a time that has been arranged in advance). 參觀必須預約。◇ **~ with sb** *an appointment with my lawyer* 與我的律師的約定 ◇ **~ for sth** *an appointment for a blood test* 驗血預約 ◇ **~ for sb to do sth** *She* ***made an appointment*** *for her son to see the doctor.* 她為兒子約定了看醫生的時間。 **2** 🔑 [C, U] **~ (as/to sth)** the act of choosing a person for a job or position of responsibility; the fact of being chosen for a job, etc. 任命；委任：*her recent appointment to the post* 她新近獲此職位的任命 ◇ *his appointment as principal* 他擔任校長的任命 **3** [C] (*especially BrE*) a job or position of responsibility 職務；職位：*a permanent/first appointment* 固定職位；第一次任職 ➲ SYNONYMS at JOB

ap·por·tion /əˈpɔːʃn; *NAmE* əˈpɔːrʃn/ *verb* (*formal*) to divide sth among people; to give a share of sth to sb 分配；分攤；分派：**~ sth** *The programme gives the facts but does not* ***apportion blame.*** 這個節目只擺出事實，並不評論誰是誰非。◇ **~ sth among/between/to sb** *They apportioned the land among members of the family.* 他們把土地分給了家中各人。 ▸ **ap·por·tion·ment** *noun* [U, sing.] (*formal*)：*The apportionment of seats in the House of Representatives is based on the population of each state.* 眾議院的席位是根據各州的人口分配的。

ap·po·site /ˈæpəzɪt/ *adj.* **~ (to sth)** (*formal*) very appropriate for a particular situation or in relation to sth 很合適；很恰當

ap·pos·ition /ˌæpəˈzɪʃn/ *noun* [U] (*grammar* 語法) the use of a noun phrase immediately after another noun phrase that refers to the same person or thing 同位：*In the phrase 'Paris, the capital of France', 'the capital of France' is in apposition to 'Paris'.* 在短語 Paris, the capital of France 中，the capital of France 是 Paris 的同位語。

ap·prais·al /əˈpreɪzl/ *noun* [C, U] **1** a judgement of the value, performance or nature of sb/sth 評價；估價；估計；鑒定：*He had read many detailed critical appraisals of her work.* 他讀了許多詳細評論她的作品的文章。◇ *She was honest in her appraisal of her team's chances.* 她對自己隊獲勝機會的估計是中肯的。 **2** (*business* 商) (*BrE*) a meeting in which an employee discusses with their manager how well they have been doing their job; the system of holding such meetings（上司對雇員的）工作鑒定會；工作表現評估：***staff/performance appraisal*** 員工 / 工作表現評估 ◇ *I have my appraisal today.* 我今天與上司見面討論我的工作表現。

ap·praise /əˈpreɪz/ *verb* **1** **~ sb/sth** (*formal*) to consider or examine sb/sth and form an opinion about them or it 估量；估價：*an* ***appraising glance/look*** 打量的一瞥 / 目光 ◇ *His eyes coolly appraised the young woman before him.* 他雙眼冷靜地打量着面前的年輕女子。◇ *She stepped back to appraise her workmanship.* 她退後一步，看看她的作品是否完美。 **2** **~ sb** to make a formal judgement about the value of a person's work, usually after a discussion with them about it（對某人的工作）作出評價：*Managers must appraise all staff.* 經理必須對全體員工作出評價。

ap·prais·er /əˈpreɪzə(r)/ *noun* (*NAmE*) a person whose job is to examine a building and say how much it is worth（房地產）估價師

ap·pre·ciable AW /əˈpriːʃəbl/ *adj.* large enough to be noticed or thought important（大得）可以覺察到的，足以認為重要的；可觀的 SYN **considerable**：*The new regulations will not make an appreciable difference to most people.* 新的規定對大多數人將無大影響。◇ *an* ***appreciable effect/increase/amount*** 可觀的效果 / 增長 / 數量 ▸ **ap·pre·ciably** AW /-əbli/ *adv.*：*The risk of infection is appreciably higher among children.* 受到感染的危險在兒童中要高得多。

ap·preci·ate 🔑 AW /əˈpriːʃieɪt/ *verb*
1 🔑 [T] (not used in the progressive tenses 不用於進行時) **~ sb/sth** to recognize the good qualities of sb/sth 欣賞；賞識；重視：*You can't really appreciate foreign literature in translation.* 看翻譯作品不能真正欣賞到外國文學原著的美妙之處。◇ *His talents are not* ***fully appreciated*** *in that company.* 他的才幹在那家公司未受到充分賞識。◇ *Her family doesn't appreciate her.* 她的家人不重視她。 **2** 🔑 [T] (not usually used in the progressive tenses 通常不用於進行時) to be grateful for sth that sb has done; to welcome sth 感激；感謝；歡迎：**~ sth** *I'd appreciate some help.* 如果有人幫忙我將非常感激。◇ *Your support is greatly appreciated.* 十分感謝你的支持。◇ *Thanks for coming. I* ***appreciate it.*** 謝謝光臨。無任歡迎。◇ ***I would appreciate it if*** *you paid in cash.* 假如你支付現金的話，我會不勝感激。◇ **~ doing sth** *I don't appreciate being treated like a second-class citizen.* 我不願被人當作二等公民。◇ **~ sb doing sth** *We would appreciate you letting us know of any problems.* 如有任何問題，請告訴我們。 **3** [T] (not used in the progressive tenses 不用於進行時) to understand that sth is true 理解；意識到；領會 SYN **realize**：**~ sth** *What I failed to appreciate was the distance between the two cities.* 我沒有意識到這兩座城市間的距離。◇ **~ how, what, etc. …** *I don't think you appreciate how expensive it will be.* 我想你不瞭解它會有多昂貴。◇ **~ that …** *We didn't* ***fully appreciate*** *that he was seriously ill.* 我們沒有充分認識到他的病情很嚴重。 **4** [I] to increase in value over a period of time 增值；升值：*Their investments have appreciated over the years.* 他們的投資這些年來已經增值。 OPP **depreciate**

ap·pre·ci·ation AW /əˌpriːʃiˈeɪʃn/ *noun* **1** [U] pleasure that you have when you recognize and enjoy the good qualities of sb/sth 欣賞：*She shows little appreciation of good music.* 她感受不到美好音樂的妙處。◇ *The crowd murmured* ***in appreciation.*** 人群低聲讚歎着。 **2** [U, sing.] **~ of sth** a full or sympathetic understanding of sth, such as a situation or a problem, and of what it

A

involves 理解；體諒；同情：*I had no appreciation of the problems they faced.* 我沒有體諒到他們所面臨的困難。**3** [U] **~ (of/for sth)** the feeling of being grateful for sth 感激；感謝：*Please accept this gift **in appreciation of** all you've done for us.* 承蒙鼎力相助，不勝感激，謹備薄禮，敬請笑納。**4** [U, sing.] **~ (in sth)** increase in value over a period of time 增值；升值 OPP **depreciation** **5** [C] **~ (of sth)** (*formal*) a piece of writing or a speech in which the strengths and weaknesses of sb/sth, especially an artist or a work of art, are discussed and judged（尤指藝術方面的）鑒定，評價，評估

ap·pre·cia·tive /əˈpriːʃətɪv/ *adj.* **1 ~ (of sth)** feeling or showing that you are grateful for sth 感激的；感謝的：*The company was very appreciative of my efforts.* 公司對我的努力十分讚賞。**2** showing pleasure or enjoyment 欣賞的；賞識的：*an **appreciative audience/smile*** 有欣賞力的觀眾；會意的微笑 ◇ ***appreciative laughter/comments*** 讚賞的笑聲／議論 ▸ **ap·pre·cia·tive·ly** *adv.*

ap·pre·hend /ˌæprɪˈhend/ *verb* (*formal*) **1 ~ sb** (of the police 警方) to catch sb and arrest them 逮捕；拘押 **2 ~ sth** (*old-fashioned*) to understand or recognize sth 理解；認識到；領會

ap·pre·hen·sion /ˌæprɪˈhenʃn/ *noun* **1** [U, C] worry or fear that sth unpleasant may happen 憂慮；擔心；疑懼；恐懼 SYN **anxiety**：*There is growing apprehension that fighting will begin again.* 人們愈來愈擔心會重開戰火。◇ *He watched the election results **with some apprehension**.* 他不無憂慮地觀察選舉結果。**2** [U] (*formal*) the act of capturing or arresting sb, usually by the police 逮捕；拘押

ap·pre·hen·sive /ˌæprɪˈhensɪv/ *adj.* worried or frightened that sth unpleasant may happen 憂慮的；擔心的；疑懼的；恐懼的：*an **apprehensive face/glance/look*** 憂慮的面容／一瞥／目光 ◇ **~ about/of sth** *I was a little apprehensive about the effects of what I had said.* 我有點擔憂我說的話所帶來的影響。◇ *You have no reason to be apprehensive of the future.* 你不必憂慮未來。◇ **~ that ...** *She was deeply apprehensive that something might go wrong.* 她很擔心可能要出什麼差錯。▸ **ap·pre·hen·sive·ly** *adv.*

ap·pren·tice /əˈprentɪs/ *noun, verb*

■ ***noun*** a young person who works for an employer for a fixed period of time in order to learn the particular skills needed in their job 學徒；徒弟：*an apprentice electrician/chef* 電工／廚師學徒

■ ***verb*** [usually passive] **~ sb (to sb) (as sth)** (*old-fashioned*) to make sb an apprentice 使某人當（某人的）學徒

ap·pren·tice·ship /əˈprentɪʃɪp/ *noun* [C, U] a period of time working as an apprentice; a job as an apprentice 學徒期；學徒工作：*She was in the second year of her apprenticeship as a carpenter.* 她當木工學徒已是第二年了。◇ *He had **served his apprenticeship** as a plumber.* 他當過管子工學徒。

ap·prise /əˈpraɪz/ *verb* **~ sb of sth** (*formal*) to tell or inform sb of sth 通知；告知

ap·proach 🔑 AW /əˈprəʊtʃ; *NAmE* əˈproʊtʃ/ *verb, noun*

■ ***verb***

▸ MOVE NEAR 接近 **1** 🔑 [I, T] to come near to sb/sth in distance or time（在距離或時間上）靠近，接近：*We heard the sound of an approaching car/a car approaching.* 我們聽見一輛汽車駛近的聲音。◇ *Winter is approaching.* 冬天就要來臨。◇ **~ sb/sth** *As you approach the town, you'll see the college on the left.* 快到市鎮時就可以看見左邊的學院。

▸ OFFER/ASK 建議；要求 **2** 🔑 [T] to speak to sb about sth, especially to ask them for sth or to offer to do sth 接洽；建議；要求：**~ sb** *We have been approached by a number of companies that are interested in our product.* 一些對我們的產品感興趣的公司已和我們接洽。◇ *I'd like to ask his opinion but I find him difficult to approach* (= not easy to talk to in a friendly way). 我想徵求他的意見，但發現很難和他談得攏。◇ **~ sb for sth/about (doing) sth** *She approached the bank for a loan.* 她向銀行要求貸款。

▸ AMOUNT/QUALITY 數量；質量 **3** 🔑 [T] **~ sth** to come close to sth in amount, level or quality（在數額、水平或質量上）接近：*profits approaching 30 million dollars* 接近 3 000 萬元的利潤 ◇ *Few writers approach his richness of language.* 他語言之豐富很少有作家能望其項背。

▸ PROBLEM/TASK 問題；任務 **4** 🔑 [T] **~ sth** to start dealing with a problem, task, etc. in a particular way 着手處理；對付：*What's the best way of approaching this problem?* 什麼是處理這個問題的最佳方式？

■ ***noun***

▸ TO PROBLEM/TASK 問題；任務 **1** 🔑 [C] a way of dealing with sb/sth; a way of doing or thinking about sth such as a problem or a task（待人接物或思考問題的）方式，方法，態度：*She took the wrong approach in her dealings with them.* 她用錯誤的手段和他們打交道。◇ **~ to sth** *The school has decided to adopt a different approach to discipline.* 學校決定採取另外一種方式解決紀律問題。

▸ MOVEMENT NEARER 接近 **2** 🔑 [sing.] movement nearer to sb/sth in distance or time（在距離或時間上的）靠近，接近：*She hadn't heard his approach and jumped as the door opened.* 她沒有聽見他走近的聲音，所以門開時嚇了一跳。◇ *the approach of spring* 春天的來臨

▸ OFFER/REQUEST 建議；要求 **3** [C] the act of speaking to sb about sth, especially when making an offer or a request 接洽；建議；要求：*The club has **made an approach** to a local company for sponsorship.* 俱樂部已向當地一家公司尋求贊助。◇ *She resented his persistent approaches.* 她對他沒完沒了的糾纏極為反感。

▸ PATH/ROAD 小徑；道路 **4** [C] a path, road, etc. that leads to a place 通路；路徑；道路：*All the approaches to the palace were guarded by troops.* 通往宮殿的所有道路都有軍隊守衛。◇ *a new approach road to the port* 去港口的一條新通路

▸ OF AIRCRAFT 飛機 **5** [C] the part of an aircraft's flight immediately before landing 進場；進場着陸：*to begin the final approach to the runway* 開始進入跑道着陸

▸ STH SIMILAR 相似事物 **6** [sing.] a thing that is like sth else that is mentioned 相似（或近似）的事物：*That's the **nearest approach** to an apology you'll get from him.* 那是他所能作出的最似歉意的表示。IDM see CARROT

ap·proach·able AW /əˈprəʊtʃəbl; *NAmE* əˈproʊtʃ-/ *adj.* **1** friendly and easy to talk to; easy to understand 和藹可親的；易理解的：*Despite being a big star, she's very approachable.* 她雖然是個大明星，卻非常平易近人。◇ *an approachable piece of music* 淺顯易懂的樂曲 OPP **unapproachable** **2** [not before noun] that can be reached by a particular route or from a particular direction 可接近的；能達到的：*The summit was approachable only from the south.* 只有從南面才能到達山頂。

ap·pro·ba·tion /ˌæprəˈbeɪʃn/ *noun* [U] (*formal*) approval or agreement 認可；批准

ap·pro·pri·acy AW /əˈprəʊpriəsi; *NAmE* əˈproʊ-/ *noun* [U] **1** the extent to which sth is suitable or acceptable 適合性；恰當性 **2** (*linguistics* 語言) the extent to which a word or phrase sounds correct and natural in relation to the situation it is used in（詞語等的）得體；恰當用詞

ap·pro·pri·ate 🔑 AW *adj., verb*

■ ***adj.*** 🔑 /əˈprəʊpriət; *NAmE* əˈproʊ-/ suitable, acceptable or correct for the particular circumstances 合適的；恰當的：*an appropriate response/measure/method* 恰如其分的反應；恰當的措施／方法 ◇ *Now that the problem has been identified, appropriate action can be taken.* 現在既已找出問題的癥結，即可採取適當行動。◇ *Is now an appropriate time to make a speech?* 現在發表演講是不是時候？◇ *Please debit my Mastercard/Visa/American Express card* (***delete as appropriate***) (= cross out the options that do not apply). 請在我的萬事達／維薩／美國運通信用卡（刪除不適用者）賬戶中扣除。◇ **~ for sth** *Jeans are not appropriate for a formal party.* 正式聚會上穿牛仔褲不合適。◇ **~ to sth** *The book was written in a style appropriate to the age of the children.* 這本書的文體適合兒童閱讀。OPP **inappropriate** ▸ **ap·pro·pri·ate·ly** AW *adv.*：*The government has been accused of not responding appropriately to the needs of the homeless.* 政府未採取恰當的措施以應無家可歸者的需要，為此已受到譴責。◇ *The chain of volcanoes is known, **appropriately enough**, as the 'Ring of Fire'.* 人們把這鏈狀火山群很恰當地稱作"火環"。**ap·pro·pri·ate·ness** AW *noun* [U]

■ *verb* /ə'prəʊprieɪt; *NAmE* ə'proʊ-/ (*formal*) **1 ~ sth** to take sth, sb's ideas, etc. for your own use, especially illegally or without permission 盜用；挪用；佔用；侵吞：*He was accused of appropriating club funds.* 他被控盜用俱樂部資金。◇ *Some of the opposition party's policies have been appropriated by the government.* 反對黨的一些政策已被政府照搬照用。**2 ~ sth (for sth)** to take or give sth, especially money for a particular purpose 撥（專款等）：*Five million dollars have been appropriated for research into the disease.* 已撥款五百萬元用於這種疾病的研究。➲ compare MISAPPROPRIATE

ap·pro·pri·ation /əˌprəʊpri'eɪʃn; *NAmE* əˌproʊ-/ *noun* **1** [U, sing.] (*formal* or *law* 律) the act of taking sth that belongs to sb else, especially without permission 擅自調用；盜用；挪用；佔用；侵吞：*dishonest appropriation of property* 以欺騙的手法侵吞財產 ➲ compare MISAPPROPRIATION **2** [U, sing.] (*formal*) the act of keeping or saving money for a particular purpose 撥（專）款：*a meeting to discuss the appropriation of funds* 討論撥款的會議 **3** [C] (*formal*) a sum of money to be used for a particular purpose, especially by a government or company（尤指政府、公司的）所撥款項，專款：*an appropriation of £20 000 for payment of debts* 用於還債的 2 萬英鎊撥款

ap·prov·al 🔑 /ə'pruːvl/ *noun* **1** 🔑 [U] the feeling that sb/sth is good or acceptable; a positive opinion of sb/sth 贊成；同意：*She desperately wanted to win her father's approval.* 她急不可待地想贏得她父親的贊同。◇ *Do the plans* ***meet with your approval?*** 這些計劃你贊成嗎？◇ *Several people nodded* ***in approval.*** 好幾個人點頭表示同意。OPP **disapproval 2** 🔑 [U, C] agreement to, or permission for sth, especially a plan or request 批准，通過，認可（計劃、要求等）：*The plan will be submitted to the committee for official approval.* 該計劃將送交委員會正式批准。◇ ***parliamentary/congressional/government approval*** 議會的／國會的／政府的批准 ◇ *Senior management have given their* ***seal of approval*** (= formal approval) *to the plans.* 高層管理部門已經正式批准這些計劃。◇ *I can't agree to anything without my partner's approval.* 沒有合夥人的認可我什麼也不能答應。◇ *planning approvals*（建築）規劃的批准 ◇ *The proposal is* ***subject to approval*** *by the shareholders* (= they need to agree to it). 這項建議須得到股東的批准。◇ **~ (for sth) (from sb)** *They* ***required/received approval*** *for the proposal from the shareholders.* 他們要求／獲得股東對這項提議的批准。**3** [U] if you buy goods or if goods are sold **on approval**, you can use them for a time without paying, until you decide if you want to buy them or not（商品）試用，包退包換

ap·prove 🔑 /ə'pruːv/ *verb* **1** 🔑 [I] to think that sb/sth is good, acceptable or suitable 贊成；同意：*I told my mother I wanted to leave school but she didn't approve.* 我告訴母親我不想繼續上學，但是母親不同意。◇ **~ of sb/sth** *Do you approve of my idea?* 你同意我的想法嗎？◇ **~ of sb doing sth** *She doesn't approve of me leaving school this year.* 她不贊成我今年離校。◇ (*formal*) **~ of sb's doing sth** *She doesn't approve of my leaving school this year.* 她不贊成我今年離校。OPP **disapprove 2** 🔑 [T] **~ sth** to officially agree to a plan, request, etc. 批准，通過（計劃、要求等）：*The committee unanimously approved the plan.* 委員會一致通過了計劃。➲ SYNONYMS at AGREE **3** 🔑 [T, often passive] **~ sth** to say that sth is good enough to be used or is correct 認可；核准：*The course is approved by the Department for Education.* 課程已獲教育部核准。

ap'proved school *noun* (*BrE*) a school where young people who had committed crimes were sent in the past（舊時的）少年犯教養院，少年感化院

ap·prov·ing 🔑 /ə'pruːvɪŋ/ *adj.* showing that you believe that sb/sth is good or acceptable 贊成的；同意的：*He gave me an approving nod.* 他向我點頭表示同意。OPP **disapproving** ▸ **ap·prov·ing·ly** *adv.*: *She looked at him approvingly and smiled.* 她面帶微笑讚許地望着他。

approx *abbr.* APPROXIMATE, APPROXIMATELY

ap·proxi·mant /ə'prɒksɪmənt; *NAmE* ə'prɑːks-/ *noun* **1** (*phonetics* 語音) a speech sound made by bringing the parts of the mouth that produce speech close together but not actually touching, for example /r/ and /w/ in *right* and *wet* in many accents of English 近似音；無擦通音；無摩擦延續音 **2** (*mathematics* 數) a solution that is close to, but not exactly, the solution of a problem 逼近式

ap·proxi·mate 🔑 AW *adj.*, *verb*

■ *adj.* 🔑 /ə'prɒksɪmət; *NAmE* ə'prɑːk-/ (*abbr.* **approx**) almost correct or accurate, but not completely so 大約的；近似的；接近的：*an* ***approximate number/total/cost*** 約數；概算總額；約計成本 ◇ *The cost given is only approximate.* 所列成本僅係約計。◇ *Use these figures as an approximate guide in your calculations.* 在你的計算中把這些數字作為近似參考數值。OPP **exact**

Vocabulary Building 詞彙擴充

Ways of saying approximately 表示"大約"的方式

- The flight takes **approximately** three hours. 飛行大約需要三小時。
- The tickets cost **about** £20 each. 票每張約 20 英鎊。
- The repairs will cost $200, **give or take** a few dollars. 修理費要花 200 元，出入不過幾元。
- How much will it cost, **more or less**? 這個大概多少錢？
- We are expecting thirty **or so** people to come. 我們預計會來三十人左右。
- She must be 25 **or thereabouts**. 她肯定在 25 歲上下。
- Profits have fallen by **roughly** 15%. 利潤下降了大約 15%。
- You can expect to earn **round about** £40,000 a year. 你可望每年賺 4 萬英鎊左右。
- The price is **somewhere around** $800. 價格在 800 元上下。
- She earns **somewhere in the region of** £25,000. 她大約掙 25 000 英鎊。

All these words and phrases are used in both speaking and writing; **about** is the most common and **approximately** the most formal. 上述各詞和短語在口語和書面語中均可使用，about 最常用，approximately 最正式。

■ *verb* /ə'prɒksɪmeɪt; *NAmE* ə'prɑːk-/ (*formal*) **1** [T, I] to be similar or close to sth in nature, quality, amount, etc., but not exactly the same 近似；接近：**~ sth** *The animals were reared in conditions which approximated the wild as closely as possible.* 這些動物是在盡量近似自然的環境下飼養的。◇ *The total cost will approximate £15 billion.* 總費用將近 150 億英鎊。◇ **~ to sth** *His story approximates to the facts that we already know.* 他的陳述和我們已掌握的事實接近。**2** [T] **~ sth** to calculate or estimate sth fairly accurately 近似計算；概略估算：*a formula for approximating the weight of a horse* 估算一匹馬重量的公式

ap·proxi·mate·ly 🔑 AW /ə'prɒksɪmətli; *NAmE* ə'prɑːk-/ *adv.* used to show that sth is almost, but not completely, accurate or correct 大概；大約；約莫：*The journey took approximately seven hours.* 旅程大約花了七個小時。

ap·proxi·ma·tion AW /əˌprɒksɪ'meɪʃn; *NAmE* əˌprɑːk-/ *noun* **1** an estimate of a number or an amount that is almost correct, but not exact 近似值；粗略估算：*That's just an approximation, you understand.* 你知道那僅僅是近似值。**2 ~ (of/to sth)** a thing that is similar to sth else, but is not exactly the same 類似事物：*Our results should be a good approximation of the true state of affairs.* 我們的結果應該和實際情況相當接近。

A

ap·pur·ten·ance /əˈpɜːtɪnəns; *NAmE* əˈpɜːrt-/ *noun* [usually pl.] (*formal* or *humorous*) a thing that forms a part of sth larger or more important 附屬物；附加物

APR /ˌeɪ piː ˈɑː(r)/ *noun* [sing.] the abbreviation for 'annual percentage rate' (the amount of interest a bank charges on money that it lends, calculated for a period of a year) 年百分率（全寫為 annual percentage rate，指銀行貸款年百分率）：*a rate of 26.4% APR* 貸款年利率 26.4%

après-ski /ˌæpreɪ ˈskiː/ *noun* [U] (from *French*) social activities and entertainments that take place in hotels and restaurants after a day's SKIING（一整天）滑雪後的社交娛樂（在旅館、餐廳舉行）

apri·cot /ˈeɪprɪkɒt; *NAmE* ˈæprɪkɑːt/ *noun* **1** [C] a round fruit with yellow or orange skin and a large seed inside 杏子；杏：*dried apricots* 杏乾 **2** [U] a yellowish-orange colour 杏黃色 ▸ **apri·cot** *adj.*：*The room was painted apricot and white.* 房間漆成了杏黃色和白色。

April 0━ /ˈeɪprəl/ *noun* [U, C] (*abbr.* **Apr.**) the fourth month of the year, between March and May 四月：*She was born in April.* 她是四月出生的。◇ (*BrE*) *The meeting is on the fifth of April/April the fifth.* 會議日期是四月五日。◇ (*NAmE*) *The meeting is on April fifth.* 會議日期是四月五日。◇ *We went to Japan last April.* 四月我們去了日本。◇ *I arrived at the end of April.* 我是四月底到達的。◇ *last April's election* 上一個四月的選舉 ◇ *April showers* (= light rain that falls in the spring) 四月的陣雨 ◇ *an April wedding* 四月的婚禮

ˌApril ˈFool *noun* **1** a trick that is traditionally played on sb on 1 April (called **April Fool's Day** or **All Fools' Day**) 在愚人節開的玩笑 **2** a person who has a trick played on them on April Fool's Day 愚人節被愚弄的人

a pri·ori /ˌeɪ praɪˈɔːraɪ/ *adj., adv.* (from *Latin*, *formal*) using facts or principles that are known to be true in order to decide what the probable effects or results of sth will be, for example saying 'They haven't eaten anything all day so they must be hungry.' 從事實推斷結果；由因及果 ➲ compare A POSTERIORI

ap·ron /ˈeɪprən/ *noun* **1** a piece of clothing worn over the front of the body, from the chest or the waist down, and tied around the waist. Aprons are worn over other clothes to keep them clean, for example when cooking. 圍裙 ➲ compare PINAFORE (2) **2** (*technical* 術語) an area with a hard surface at an airport, where aircraft are turned around, loaded, etc.（機場的）停機坪 **3** (also **ˈapron stage**) (*technical* 術語) (in a theatre 劇院) the part of the stage that is in front of the curtain 台口（舞台幕前的部份）

IDM (**tied to**) **sb's apron strings** (too much under) the influence and control of sb（過分受）某人的影響（或控制）：*The British prime minister is too apt to cling to Washington's apron strings.* 英國首相對華府過於唯命是從。

apro·pos /ˌæprəˈpəʊ; *NAmE* -ˈpoʊ/ (also **apro·pos of**) *prep.* concerning or related to sb/sth 關於；至於：*Apropos (of) what you were just saying …* 至於你剛才所說的…

apse /æps/ *noun* a small area, often in the shape of a SEMICIRCLE, usually at the east end of a church（教堂東端的）半圓形小室

apt /æpt/ *adj.* **1** suitable or appropriate in the circumstances 恰當的；適當的：*a particularly* ***apt description/name/comment*** 特別恰當的描述／名字／評論 **2** likely or having a natural tendency to do sth 易於…；有…傾向：**~ to be …** *apt to be forgetful/careless* 健忘；常常粗心大意 ◇ **~ to do sth** *Babies are apt to put objects into their mouths.* 嬰兒愛把東西往嘴裏塞。 **3 ~ pupil** a person who has a natural ability to learn and understand 天資聰穎的人 ▸ **aptly** *adv.*：*the aptly named Grand Hotel* 名副其實的大飯店 **apt·ness** *noun* [U]

ap·ti·tude /ˈæptɪtjuːd; *NAmE* -tuːd/ *noun* [U, C] natural ability or skill at doing sth 天資；天生的才能；天賦 **SYN** **talent**：*an aptitude test* (= one designed to show whether sb has the natural ability for a particular job or course of education) 能力傾向測驗 ◇ **~ for sth** *She showed a natural aptitude for the work.* 她表現出了做這工作的天賦。◇ **~ for doing sth** *His aptitude for dealing with children got him the job.* 他善於和兒童打交道的本事使他得到了這份工作。

aqua /ˈækwə/ *noun* [U] **1** water (used especially on the labels on packages of food, drinks, medicines, etc. in order to show how much water they contain) 水（尤用於表示食物、飲料、藥物等的水含量）**2** a bluish-green colour 湖綠色

aqua·culture /ˈækwəkʌltʃə(r)/ *noun* [U] the growing of plants in water for food 水產養殖（業）

aqua·lung /ˈækwəlʌŋ/ *noun* a piece of breathing equipment that a DIVER wears on his/her back when swimming underwater 水肺；水下呼吸器

aqua·mar·ine /ˌækwəməˈriːn/ *noun* **1** [C, U] a pale greenish-blue SEMI-PRECIOUS stone 海藍寶石 **2** [U] a pale greenish-blue colour 海藍色；淺藍色 ▸ **aqua·mar·ine** *adj.*：*an aquamarine sea* 藍色的大海

aqua·plane /ˈækwəpleɪn/ *verb, noun*

■ *verb* **1** (*BrE*) (*NAmE* **hydro·plane**) [I] (of a motor vehicle 機動車輛) to slide out of control on a wet road 在潮濕路面上打滑失控 **2** [I] to stand on a board that is pulled along on water behind a SPEEDBOAT in the sport of aquaplaning 滑水

■ *noun* a board that sb stands on in the sport of aquaplaning 滑水板

aqua·plan·ing /ˈækwəpleɪnɪŋ/ *noun* [U] **1** the sport of being pulled along on a board behind a SPEEDBOAT on water（快艇牽引）滑水板運動 **2** (*BrE*) (*NAmE* **hydro·plan·ing**) the fact of a motor vehicle sliding on a wet surface, so that it is out of control（機動車輛在潮濕路面上的）打滑

aquar·ium /əˈkweəriəm; *NAmE* əˈkwer-/ *noun* (*pl.* **aquar·iums** or **aqua·ria** /-riə/) **1** a large glass container in which fish and other water creatures and plants are kept 養魚缸；水族玻璃槽 **2** a building where people can go to see fish and other water creatures 水族館

Aquar·ius /əˈkweəriəs; *NAmE* əˈkwer-/ (also **the ˈWater Bearer**, **the ˈWater Carrier**) *noun* **1** [U] the 11th sign of the ZODIAC 黃道第十一宮；寶瓶宮；寶瓶（星）座 **2** [sing.] a person born when the sun is in this sign, that is between 21 January and 19 February 屬寶瓶座的人（約出生於 1 月 21 日至 2 月 19 日）▸ **Aquar·ian** /əˈkweəriən; *NAmE* əˈkwer-/ *noun, adj.*

aqua·robics /ˌækwəˈrəʊbɪks; *NAmE* -ˈroʊ-/ *noun* [U] physical exercises that you do in water, often done in classes 水中有氧操（常為上課形式）➲ compare AEROBICS

aqua·tic /əˈkwætɪk/ *adj.* [usually before noun] **1** growing or living in, on or near water 水生的；水棲的：***aquatic plants/life/ecosystems*** 水生植物／動植物／生態系統 **2** connected with water 水的；水中的；水上的：*aquatic sports* 水上運動

aqua·tint /ˈækwətɪnt/ *noun* [U, C] (*technical* 術語) a method of producing a picture using acid on a metal plate; a picture produced using this method 凹版腐蝕法；凹版腐蝕畫；飛塵腐蝕法；飛塵腐蝕畫

aque·duct /ˈækwɪdʌkt/ *noun* a structure for carrying water, usually one built like a bridge across a valley or low ground 渡槽；高架渠 ➲ VISUAL VOCAB page V14

aque·ous /ˈeɪkwiəs/ *adj.* (*technical* 術語) containing water; like water 水的；含水的；水狀的

ˌaqueous ˈhumour (*especially US* **ˌaqueous ˈhumor**) *noun* [U] (*anatomy* 解) the clear liquid inside the front part of the eye 房水，眼房水（眼球的水狀液）➲ compare VITREOUS HUMOUR

aqui·fer /ˈækwɪfə(r)/ *noun* (*geology* 地) a layer of rock or soil that can absorb and hold water（岩石或土壤的）含水層，蓄水層

aquil·ine /ˈækwɪlaɪn/ *adj.* (*formal*) a person with an **aquiline nose** or **aquiline features** has a nose that is thin and curved, similar to the BEAK of an EAGLE 鉤狀的；鷹喙狀的

Arab /ˈærəb/ *noun, adj.*

■ *noun* **1** a person from the Middle East or N Africa, whose ANCESTORS lived in the Arabian Peninsula 阿拉

伯人 **2** a type of horse originally from Arabia 阿拉伯馬
■ ***adj.*** of or connected with Arabia or Arabs 阿拉伯的；阿拉伯人的：*Arab countries* 阿拉伯諸國

ar·ab·esque /ˌærəˈbesk/ *noun* **1** [C] (in BALLET 芭蕾舞) a position in which the dancer balances on one leg with the other leg lifted and stretched out behind parallel to the ground 阿拉貝斯克舞姿，迎風展翅（一腳着地，一條腿向後平伸）**2** [C, U] (in art 藝術) a type of design where lines wind around each other 阿拉伯花飾（互相交織的曲線圖案）

Ara·bian /əˈreɪbiən/ *adj.* of or connected with Arabia 阿拉伯的 **HELP** **Arabian** is used to describe places. * Arabian 用以描述地方：*the Arabian peninsula* 阿拉伯半島 The people are **Arabs** and the adjective to describe them is **Arab**. * Arabs 表示人，其形容詞為 Arab：*Arab children* 阿拉伯兒童 The language is **Arabic**. * Arabic 指語言：*Arabic script* 阿拉伯文字

Arab·ic /ˈærəbɪk/ *noun, adj.*
■ ***noun*** [U] the language of the Arabs 阿拉伯語
■ ***adj.*** of or connected with the literature and language of Arab people 阿拉伯文學的；阿拉伯語的：*Arabic poetry* 阿拉伯詩歌

ˌArabic ˈnumeral *noun* any of the symbols 0, 1, 2, 3, 4, etc. used for writing numbers in many countries 阿拉伯數字 ➲ compare ROMAN NUMERAL

ar·able /ˈærəbl/ *adj.* connected with growing crops such as WHEAT 耕作的；可耕的：***arable farming/farms/crops*** 耕作農業／農場／莊稼 ◇ ***arable land/fields*** (= used or suitable for growing crops) 可耕地／田

arach·nid /əˈræknɪd/ *noun* (*technical* 術語) any small creature of the class that includes spiders, SCORPIONS, MITES and TICKS 蛛形綱動物（包括蜘蛛、蠍子、蟎和蜱）➲ **VISUAL VOCAB** page V13 ➲ compare INSECT

arach·no·pho·bia /əˌræknəˈfəʊbiə; *NAmE* -ˈfoʊ-/ *noun* [U] an extreme fear of spiders 蜘蛛恐懼症

Aran /ˈærən/ *adj.* [only before noun] (*BrE*) (of knitted clothing 針織服飾) with a traditional pattern of lines and diamond shapes made by raised STITCHES 阿倫式的（有凸線和菱形圖案）：*an Aran sweater* 阿倫式針織套衫

ar·bi·ter /ˈɑːbɪtə(r); *NAmE* ˈɑːrb-/ *noun* **~ (of sth)** (*formal*) a person with the power or influence to make judgements and decide what will be done or accepted 仲裁人；公斷人；裁決人；決定者；權威人士：*The law is the final arbiter of what is considered obscene.* 何謂猥褻最終由法律裁決。◇ *an **arbiter of taste/style/fashion*** 鑒賞／款式／時裝權威

ar·bi·trage /ˈɑːbɪtrɑːʒ; -trɪdʒ; *NAmE* ˈɑːrbətrɑːʒ/ *noun* [U] (*business* 商) the practice of buying sth (for example, shares or foreign money) in one place and selling it in another place where the price is higher 套匯；套購；套利 ▸ **ar·bi·tra·geur** /ˌɑːbɪtrɑːˈʒɜː(r); *NAmE* ˌɑːrbətrɑːˈʒɜːr/ (also **ar·bi·trager** /ˈɑːbɪtrɪdʒə(r); *NAmE* ˈɑːrbətrɑːʒər/) *noun*

ar·bi·trary **AW** /ˈɑːbɪtrəri; ˈɑːbɪtri; *NAmE* ˈɑːrbətreri/ *adj.* **1** (of an action, a decision, a rule, etc. 行動、決定、規章等) not seeming to be based on a reason, system or plan and sometimes seeming unfair 任意的；武斷的；隨心所欲的：*The choice of players for the team seemed completely arbitrary.* 看來這個隊的隊員完全是隨意選定的。◇ *He makes unpredictable, arbitrary decisions.* 他做的決定難以預料，主觀武斷。**2** (*formal*) using power without restriction and without considering other people 專橫的；專制的：*the arbitrary powers of officials* 官員的專制權力 ▸ **ar·bi·trar·ily** **AW** /ˌɑːbɪˈtrerəli; ˈɑːbɪtrəli; *NAmE* ˌɑːrbəˈt-/ *adv.*：*The leaders of the groups were chosen arbitrarily.* 這些團體的領導人是任意挑選的。**ar·bi·trari·ness** **AW** *noun* [U]

ar·bi·trate /ˈɑːbɪtreɪt; *NAmE* ˈɑːrb-/ *verb* [I, T] to officially settle an argument or a disagreement between two people or groups 仲裁；公斷：**~ (in/on) (sth)** *to arbitrate in a dispute* 對一場糾紛進行仲裁 ◇ **~ between A and B** *A committee was created to arbitrate between management and the unions.* 已成立一個委員會在資方與工會之間進行仲裁。

ar·bi·tra·tion /ˌɑːbɪˈtreɪʃn; *NAmE* ˌɑːrb-/ *noun* [U] the official process of settling an argument or a disagreement by sb who is not involved 仲裁；公斷：*Both sides in the dispute have agreed to **go to arbitration**.* 爭執雙方已同意提請仲裁。

ar·bi·tra·tor /ˈɑːbɪtreɪtə(r); *NAmE* ˈɑːrb-/ *noun* a person who is chosen to settle a disagreement 仲裁人；公斷人

ar·bor·eal /ɑːˈbɔːriəl; *NAmE* ɑːrˈb-/ *adj.* (*technical* 術語) relating to trees; living in trees 樹木的；樹棲的

ar·bor·etum /ˌɑːbəˈriːtəm; *NAmE* ˌɑːrb-/ *noun* (*pl.* **ar·bor·etums** or **ar·bor·eta** /-tə/) a garden where many different types of tree are grown, for people to look at or for scientific study（供觀賞、科研的）樹木園，植物園

ar·bori·cul·ture /ˈɑːbərɪkʌltʃə(r); *NAmE* ˈɑːrb-/ *noun* [U] the study or practice of growing trees and SHRUBS 樹木栽培研究；樹木栽培 ▸ **ar·bori·cul·tural** /ˌɑːbərɪˈkʌltʃərəl; *NAmE* ˌɑːrb-/ *adj.*：*an arboricultural specialist* 樹木栽培專家 **ar·bori·cul·tur·ist** *noun*

ar·bor·ist /ˈɑːbərɪst; *NAmE* ˈɑːrb-/ *noun* (*formal*) = TREE SURGEON

ar·bour (*especially US* **arbor**) /ˈɑːbə(r); *NAmE* ˈɑːrb-/ *noun* a shelter in a garden/yard for people to sit under, made by growing climbing plants over a frame（花園、院子中由藤蔓在架子上攀緣而成的）棚架，涼棚

arc /ɑːk; *NAmE* ɑːrk/ *noun, verb*
■ ***noun*** **1** (*geometry* 幾何) part of a circle or a curved line 弧 ➲ **VISUAL VOCAB** page V71 **2** a curved shape 弧形：*the arc of a rainbow* 彩虹的弧形 ◇ *The beach swept around in an arc.* 海灘呈弧形伸展開來。**3** (*technical* 術語) an electric current passing across a space between two TERMINALS 電弧 ➲ see also ARC LAMP
■ ***verb*** (**arc·ing** /ˈɑːkɪŋ; *NAmE* ˈɑːrk-/, **arced**, **arced** /ɑːkt; *NAmE* ɑːrkt/) (*technical* 術語) **1** [I] to move in the shape of an arc 作弧形運動 **2** [I] to form an electric arc 形成電弧

ar·cade /ɑːˈkeɪd; *NAmE* ɑːrˈk-/ *noun* **1** a covered passage with ARCHES along the side of a row of buildings (usually a row of shops/stores) 拱廊，拱廊通道（常指一排商店門前的帶頂走道）**2** a covered passage between streets, with shops/stores on either side 拱廊商店街（設於兩街之間，兩側均有商店）➲ **VISUAL VOCAB** page V2, V3 **3** (also **ˈshopping arcade**) (both *BrE*) a large building with a number of shops/stores in it 商場；購物中心；商業中心 ➲ compare SHOPPING MALL **4** (*BrE* also **aˈmusement arcade**) a place where you can play games on machines which you use coins to operate 遊戲機廳；電動遊樂場：*arcade games* 遊戲機室遊戲

Ar·ca·dia /ɑːˈkeɪdiə; *NAmE* ɑːrˈk-/ *noun* [sing.] a part of southern Greece used in poetry and stories to represent an idea of perfect country life 阿卡迪亞（希臘南部地區，在詩歌和小說中常用來指代世外桃源）

Ar·ca·dian /ɑːˈkeɪdiən; *NAmE* ɑːrˈk-/ *adj.* of or connected with Arcadia or an idea of perfect country life 阿卡迪亞的；世外桃源式的

ar·ca·na /ɑːˈkeɪnə; *NAmE* ɑːrˈk-/ *noun* **1** [pl.] things that are secret or mysterious 秘密事件；神秘事物 **2** [sing.] either of the two groups of cards in a TAROT, PACK/DECK, the **major arcana** and the **minor arcana** 阿卡納牌（塔羅牌中的兩組牌之一，分大阿卡納和小阿卡納）

ar·cane /ɑːˈkeɪn; *NAmE* ɑːrˈk-/ *adj.* (*formal*) secret and mysterious and therefore difficult to understand 神秘的；晦澀難懂的

arch /ɑːtʃ; *NAmE* ɑːrtʃ/ *noun, verb, adj.*
■ ***noun*** **1** a curved structure that supports the weight of sth above it, such as a bridge or the upper part of a building 拱（支撐如橋梁或房屋上部的弧形結構）**2** a structure with a curved top that is supported by straight sides, sometimes forming an entrance or built as a MONUMENT 拱門：*Go through the arch and follow the path.* 穿過拱門沿小徑往前走。◇ *Marble Arch is a famous London landmark.* 大理石拱門是倫敦著名的地標。➲ **VISUAL VOCAB** page V14 **3** the raised part of the foot formed by a curved section of bones 足背；足弓

➲ VISUAL VOCAB page V59 **4** anything that forms a curved shape at the top 拱形；拱形物：*the delicate arch of her eyebrows* 她那彎彎的柳眉

■ ***verb*** **1** [T, I] **~ (sth)** if you **arch** part of your body, or if it **arches**, it moves and forms a curved shape（使）成弓形：*The cat arched its back and hissed.* 貓弓起背發出嘶嘶聲。**2** [I] to be in a curved line or shape across or over sth 呈拱形覆蓋；呈弧形橫跨：*Tall trees arched over the path.* 大樹呈拱形遮蔭了小道。

■ ***adj.*** [usually before noun] (often *disapproving*) seeming amused because you know more about a situation than other people 調皮的；淘氣的：*an arch tone of voice* 調皮的語氣 ▸ **arch·ly** *adv.*：*'Guess what?' she said archly.* "猜猜看？"她調皮地說道。

arch- /ɑːtʃ; *NAmE* ɑːrtʃ/ *combining form* (in nouns 構成名詞) main; most important or most extreme 主要的；最重要的；極端的：*archbishop* 大主教 ◇ *arch-enemy* 主要敵人

archae·olo·gist (*NAmE* also **arche·olo·gist**) /ˌɑːkiˈɒlədʒɪst; *NAmE* ˌɑːrkiˈɑːl-/ *noun* a person who studies archaeology 考古學家

archae·ology (*NAmE* also **arche·ology**) /ˌɑːkiˈɒlədʒi; *NAmE* ˌɑːrkiˈɑːl-/ *noun* [U] the study of cultures of the past, and of periods of history by examining the remains of buildings and objects found in the ground 考古學 ➲ see also INDUSTRIAL ARCHAEOLOGY ▸ **arch·aeo·logic·al** (*NAmE* also **arch·eo·logic·al**) /ˌɑːkiəˈlɒdʒɪkl; *NAmE* ˌɑːrkiəˈlɑːdʒ-/ *adj.*：***archaeological excavations/evidence*** 考古發掘/實證

archae·op·teryx /ˌɑːkiˈɒptərɪks; *NAmE* ˌɑːrkiˈɑːptərɪks/ *noun* the oldest known bird, which existed about 150 million years ago 始祖鳥（1.5 億年前存在）

ar·chaic /ɑːˈkeɪɪk; *NAmE* ɑːrˈk-/ *adj.* **1** old and no longer used 古體的；已不通用的：*'Thou art' is an archaic form of 'you are'.* * thou art 是 you are 的古體。**2** very old-fashioned 早已過時的；陳舊的 **SYN** **outdated**：*The system is archaic and unfair and needs changing.* 這個制度早已過時而且不公平，需要改變。**3** from a much earlier or ancient period of history 古代的；早期的：*archaic art* 古代藝術

archa·ism /ˈɑːkeɪɪzəm; *NAmE* ˈɑːrk-/ *noun* (*technical* 術語) a very old word or phrase that is no longer used 古詞；古語

arch·an·gel /ˈɑːkeɪndʒl; *NAmE* ˈɑːrk-/ *noun* an ANGEL of the highest rank 總領天使；天使長：*the Archangel Gabriel* 總領天使加俾額爾

arch·bishop /ˌɑːtʃˈbɪʃəp; *NAmE* ˌɑːrtʃ-/ *noun* a BISHOP of the highest rank, responsible for all the churches in a large area 大主教；總主教：*the Archbishop of Canterbury* (= the head of the Church of England) 坎特伯雷大主教（即英國國教會領袖）

arch·bish·op·ric /ˌɑːtʃˈbɪʃəprɪk; *NAmE* ˌɑːrtʃ-/ *noun* **1** the position of an archbishop 大主教職位 **2** the district for which an archbishop is responsible 大主教區

arch·deacon /ˌɑːtʃˈdiːkən; *NAmE* ˌɑːrtʃ-/ *noun* a priest just below the rank of BISHOP, especially in the Anglican Church（尤指聖公會的）會吏長

arch·dio·cese /ˌɑːtʃˈdaɪəsɪs; *NAmE* ˌɑːrtʃ-/ *noun* a district under the care of an ARCHBISHOP 大主教區

arch·duch·ess /ˌɑːtʃˈdʌtʃəs; *NAmE* ˌɑːrtʃ-/ *noun* (in the past) the wife of an archduke or a daughter of the EMPEROR of Austria 大公夫人；女大公（舊時奧地利公主）

arch·duke /ˌɑːtʃˈdjuːk; *NAmE* ˌɑːrtʃˈduːk/ *noun* (in the past) a son of the EMPEROR of Austria 大公（舊時奧地利皇太子）：*Archduke Franz Ferdinand* 弗蘭茨•斐迪南大公 ➲ compare GRAND DUKE

arched /ɑːtʃt; *NAmE* ɑːrtʃt/ *adj.* in the shape of an ARCH 拱形的；弧形的：*a chair with an arched back* 有拱形靠背的椅子

ˌarch-ˈenemy *noun* a person's main enemy 主要敵人；大敵；死敵

arche·olo·gist, **arche·ology** (*NAmE*) = ARCHAEOLOGIST, ARCHAEOLOGY

arch·er /ˈɑːtʃə(r); *NAmE* ˈɑːrtʃ-/ *noun* a person who shoots with a BOW and arrows 弓箭手；射箭運動員 ➲ VISUAL VOCAB page V40

arch·ery /ˈɑːtʃəri; *NAmE* ˈɑːrtʃ-/ *noun* [U] the art or sport of shooting arrows with a BOW 射箭術；射箭運動 ➲ VISUAL VOCAB page V40

arche·typal /ˌɑːkiˈtaɪpl; *NAmE* ˌɑːrki-/ *adj.* having all the important qualities that make sb/sth a typical example of a particular kind of person or thing 典型的：*The Beatles were the archetypal pop group.* 披頭士樂隊是典型的流行音樂樂隊。

arche·type /ˈɑːkitaɪp/ *noun* (*formal*) the most typical or perfect example of a particular kind of person or thing 典型：*She is the archetype of an American movie star.* 她是典型的美國影星。

archi·pel·ago /ˌɑːkɪˈpeləɡəʊ; *NAmE* ˌɑːrkɪˈpeləɡoʊ/ *noun* (*pl.* **-os** or **-oes**) a group of islands and the sea surrounding them 群島；列島；群島和周圍的海

archi·tect /ˈɑːkɪtekt; *NAmE* ˈɑːrk-/ *noun* **1** a person whose job is designing buildings, etc. 建築師 **2** a person who is responsible for planning or creating an idea, an event or a situation 設計師；締造者；創造者：*He was one of the principal architects of the revolution.* 他是那次革命的主要發動者之一。◇ *Jones was the architect of the team's first goal.* 瓊斯是球隊入第一球的發動者。

archi·tec·ton·ic /ˌɑːkɪtekˈtɒnɪk; *NAmE* ˌɑːrkɪtekˈtɑːnɪk/ *adj.* (*technical* 術語) of or connected with architecture or architects 建築（學）上的；建築師的

archi·tec·tural /ˌɑːkɪˈtektʃərəl; *NAmE* ˌɑːrk-/ *adj.* connected with architecture 建築學的；建築方面的：*architectural features* 建築特色 ▸ **archi·tec·tur·al·ly** *adv.*：*The house is of little interest architecturally.* 這座房子建築方面平淡無奇。

archi·tec·ture /ˈɑːkɪtektʃə(r); *NAmE* ˈɑːrk-/ *noun* **1** [U] the art and study of designing buildings 建築學：*to study architecture* 學習建築學 **2** [U] the design or style of a building or buildings 建築設計；建築風格：*the architecture of the eighteenth century* 十八世紀的建築風格 ◇ *modern architecture* 現代建築設計 ➲ VISUAL VOCAB page V14 **3** [C, U] (*computing* 計) the design and structure of a computer system 體系結構；(總體、層次) 結構

archi·trave /ˈɑːkɪtreɪv; *NAmE* ˈɑːrk-/ *noun* (*technical* 術語) the frame around a door or window（門、窗的）框緣

arch·ive /ˈɑːkaɪv; *NAmE* ˈɑːrk-/ *noun, verb*

■ ***noun*** (also **archives** [pl.]) a collection of historical documents or records of a government, a family, a place or an organization; the place where these records are stored 檔案；檔案館；檔案室：*the National Sound Archive* 國家音響檔案館 ◇ *archive film* 檔案膠片 ◇ *The BBC's archives are bulging with material.* 英國廣播公司的檔案庫材料極其豐富。

■ ***verb*** **1 ~ sth** to put or store a document or other material in an archive 把…存檔；把…歸檔 **2 ~ sth** (*computing* 計) to move information that is not often needed to a tape or disk to store it 存檔

arch·iv·ist /ˈɑːkɪvɪst; *NAmE* ˈɑːrk-/ *noun* a person whose job is to develop and manage an archive 檔案保管員

ˌarch-ˈrival *noun* a person's main opponent 主要競爭對手；主要敵手

arch·way /ˈɑːtʃweɪ; *NAmE* ˈɑːrtʃ-/ *noun* a passage or an entrance with an ARCH over it 拱道；拱門：*We went through a stone archway into the courtyard.* 我們穿過石拱門進入院子。

ˈarc lamp (also **ˈarc light**) *noun* a lamp that gives very bright light that is produced by an electric ARC 弧光燈

Arc·tic /ˈɑːktɪk; *NAmE* ˈɑːrk-/ *adj., noun*

■ ***adj.*** **1** [only before noun] related to or happening in the regions around the North Pole 北極的；北極地區的：*Arctic explorers* 北極探險者 ➲ compare ANTARCTIC **2 arctic** extremely cold 極冷的；嚴寒的：*TV pictures showed the arctic conditions.* 電視畫面顯示了嚴寒的環境。

■ ***noun*** [sing.] **the Arctic** the regions of the world around the North Pole 北極；北極地區

the ˌArctic ˈCircle *noun* [sing.] the line of LATITUDE 66° 33′ North 北極圈 ➲ compare ANTARCTIC CIRCLE

A

ar·dent /ˈɑːdnt; *NAmE* ˈɑːrdnt/ *adj.* [usually before noun] very enthusiastic and showing strong feelings about sth/sb 熱烈的；激情的 SYN **passionate** : *an ardent supporter of European unity* 歐洲統一的熱烈支持者 ▸ **ar·dent·ly** *adv.*

ar·dour (*especially US* **ardor**) /ˈɑːdə(r); *NAmE* ˈɑːrdər/ *noun* [U] (*formal*) very strong feelings of enthusiasm or love 激情；熱情 SYN **passion**

ar·du·ous /ˈɑːdjuəs; -dʒu-; *NAmE* ˈɑːrdʒuəs/ *adj.* involving a lot of effort and energy, especially over a period of time 艱苦的；艱難的： *an arduous journey across the Andes* 翻越安第斯山脈的艱苦之行 ◇ *The work was arduous.* 這項工作很艱巨。 ▸ **ar·du·ous·ly** *adv.*

are[1] /ə(r); *strong form* ɑː(r)/ ➲ BE

are[2] /eə(r); ɑː(r); *NAmE* er; ɑːr/ *noun* a unit for measuring an area of land; 100 square metres 公畝（等於 100 平方米）

area 🔑 AW /ˈeəriə; *NAmE* ˈeriə/ *noun*

▸ PART OF PLACE 地區 **1** 🔑 [C] part of a place, town, etc., or a region of a country or the world（地方、城市、國家、世界的）地區，地域： *mountainous/desert areas* 山區；荒漠地域 ◇ *rural/urban/inner-city areas* 農村／城市地區；內城區 ◇ *There is heavy traffic in the downtown area tonight.* 今夜商業鬧市區交通繁忙。 ◇ *She knows the **local area** very well.* 她非常瞭解這地區的情況。 ◇ *John is the London area manager.* 約翰是倫敦地區經理。 ◇ *Wreckage from the plane was scattered over a **wide area**.* 飛機失事殘骸散落在一個廣闊地域。 ◇ *The farm and **surrounding area** were flooded.* 農場和周圍地區遭洪水淹沒了。 ➲ see also CATCHMENT AREA, CONSERVATION AREA, DEVELOPMENT AREA, NO-GO AREA **2** 🔑 [C] a part of a room, building or particular space that is used for a special purpose（房間、建築物、處所劃為某用途的）地方，場地，區： *the hotel reception area* 旅館接待處 ◇ *a play/parking/dining area* 遊戲場地；停車場；用餐處 ➲ SYNONYMS at PLACE ➲ see also REST AREA, SERVICE AREA

▸ PARTICULAR PLACE 部位 **3** 🔑 [C] a particular place on an object（物體上的）區，部位： *Move the cursor to a blank area of the computer screen.* 把光標移至電腦屏幕的空區。 ◇ *The tumour had not spread to other areas of the body.* 腫瘤尚未擴散到身體其他部位。

▸ SUBJECT/ACTIVITY 學科；活動 **4** 🔑 [C] **~ (of sth)** a particular subject or activity, or an aspect of it 領域；方面： *the areas of training and development* 訓練和發展方面 ◇ *Finance is Mark's area.* 財務是馬克負責的範圍。 ◇ *The big **growth area** of recent years has been in health clubs.* 健身俱樂部是近年來發展迅速的領域。 ➲ see also GREY AREA

▸ MEASUREMENT 量度 **5** 🔑 [C, U] the amount of space covered by a flat surface or piece of land, described as a measurement 面積： *the area of a triangle* 三角形的面積 ◇ *The room is 12 square metres in area.* 這個房間面積是 12 平方米。

▸ FOOTBALL 足球 **6 the area** (*BrE*) (in football (SOCCER) 足球) = PENALTY AREA : *He shot from just outside the area.* 他就在禁區外邊拔腳射門。

ˈ**area code** *noun* the numbers for a particular area or city, which you use when you are making a telephone call from outside the local area（電話的）地區代碼，區號 ➲ compare DIALLING CODE

arena /əˈriːnə/ *noun* **1** a place with a flat open area in the middle and seats around it where people can watch sports and entertainment 圓形運動場；圓形劇場： *a concert at Wembley Arena* 在文布利運動場舉行的音樂會 **2** (*formal*) an area of activity that concerns the public, especially one where there is a lot of opposition between different groups or countries 鬥爭場所；競爭舞台；活動場所： *the **political/international arena*** 政治／國際舞台

aren't /ɑːnt; *NAmE* ɑːrnt/ *short form* **1** are not **2** (in questions 用於疑問句) am not : *Aren't I clever?* 難道我不聰明嗎？

areola /əˈriːələ/ *noun* (*pl.* **areo·lae** /-liː/) the round area of skin around the NIPPLE 乳暈

argon /ˈɑːɡɒn; *NAmE* ˈɑːrɡɑːn/ *noun* [U] (*symb.* **Ar**) a chemical element. Argon is a gas that does not react with anything and is used in electric lights. 氬；氬氣

argot /ˈɑːɡəʊ; *NAmE* ˈɑːrɡət; -ɡoʊ/ *noun* [sing., U] (from *French*) words and phrases that are used by a particular group of people and not easily understood by others 行話；暗語；黑話；切口 SYN **jargon**

ar·gu·able /ˈɑːɡjuəbl; *NAmE* ˈɑːrɡ-/ *adj.* (*formal*) **1** that you can give good reasons for 可論證的；有論據的： ***It is arguable that** giving too much detail may actually be confusing.* 過分詳細反而使人糊塗的說法是有道理的。 **2** not certain; that you do not accept without question 無把握的；可疑的 SYN **debatable** : *It is arguable whether the case should have ever gone to trial* (= perhaps it should not have). 這個案件原本是否應該審判還是個問題。

ar·gu·ably /ˈɑːɡjuəbli; *NAmE* ˈɑːrɡ-/ *adv.* used (often before a comparative or superlative adjective) when you are stating an opinion that you believe you could give reasons to support（常用於形容詞比較級或最高級前）可論證地，按理： *He is arguably the best actor of his generation.* 按理他是他那一代中最優秀的演員。

Language Bank 用語庫

argue

Verbs for reporting an opinion 陳述觀點的動詞

- Some critics **argue** that Picasso remained a great master all his life. 一些評論家認為畢加索畢生都是一位大師。
- Others **maintain** that there is a significant deterioration in quality in his post-war work. 其他人堅稱他戰後的作品質量明顯下降。
- Picasso himself **claimed** that good art is created, but great art is stolen. 畢加索自己聲稱，好的藝術是創造出來的，偉大的藝術卻是偷來的。
- As Smith **has noted**, Picasso borrowed imagery from African art. 正如史密斯所述，畢加索借用了非洲藝術的意象。
- As the author **points out**, Picasso borrowed imagery from African art. 正如作者指出的那樣，畢加索借用了非洲藝術的意象。
- The writer **challenges the notion that** Picasso's sculpture was secondary to his painting. 作者對這種觀點表示質疑，即畢加索的雕塑不及他的繪畫。
- **It has been suggested that** Picasso's painting was influenced by jazz music. 據說畢加索的繪畫受到爵士樂的影響。

➲ Language Banks at ABOUT, ACCORDING TO

argue 🔑 /ˈɑːɡjuː; *NAmE* ˈɑːrɡ-/ *verb* **1** 🔑 [I] to speak angrily to sb because you disagree with them 爭論；爭吵；爭辯： *My brothers are always arguing.* 我的兄弟們總是爭論不休。 ◇ **~ (with sb) (about/over sth)** *We're always arguing with each other about money.* 我們總是為錢吵嘴。 ◇ **~ with sb** *I don't want to argue with you—just do it!* 我不想和你爭辯，幹吧！ **2** 🔑 [I, T] to give reasons why you think that sth is right/wrong, true/not true, etc., especially to persuade people that you are right 論證；說理；爭辯： **~ for/against sth/doing sth** *They argued for the right to strike.* 他們據理力爭罷工權利。 ◇ **~ sth** *She argued the case for bringing back the death penalty.* 她為恢復死刑的主張提供論據。 ◇ *He was too tired to **argue the point*** (= discuss the matter). 他太倦了，不想討論這個問題。 ◇ *a well-argued article* 鑿鑿有據的文章 ◇ **~ that …** *He argued that they needed more time to finish the project.* 他提出理由說明他們需要更多的時間來完成該項目。 ◇ ***It could be argued that** laws are made by and for men.* 法律由人制訂，也是為人制訂的這一點頗有道理。 ➲ LANGUAGE BANK at NEVERTHELESS, PERHAPS **3** [T] **~ sth** (*formal*) to show clearly that sth exists or is true 證明；表明：*These latest developments argue a change in government policy.* 最近的事態發展表明政府改變了政策。

IDM **ˌargue the ˈtoss** (*BrE, informal*) to continue to disagree about a decision, especially when it is too late to change it or it is not very important （對決定）徒然反對，作無謂的爭執

PHR V **ˌargue sb ˈinto/ˈout of doing sth** to persuade sb to do/not do sth by giving them reasons 說服（某人）做 / 不做（某事）：*They argued him into withdrawing his complaint.* 他們說服他撤回了投訴。 **ˈargue with sth** (usually used in negative sentences 通常用於否定句) (*informal*) to disagree with a statement 不同意（說法）；不承認（表述）：*He's a really successful man—you can't argue with that.* 他是一個真正成功的人，你不得不承認這個事實。

ar·gu·ment 0‑w /ˈɑːɡjumənt; *NAmE* ˈɑːrɡ-/ *noun* **1** 0‑w [C, U] a conversation or discussion in which two or more people disagree, often angrily 爭論；爭吵；爭辯；辯論：*to* ***win/lose an argument*** 辯論贏了 / 輸了◇ *After some heated argument a decision was finally taken.* 激烈辯論以後終於作出了決定。◇ **~ (with sb) (about/over sth)** *We* ***had an argument*** *with the waiter about the bill.* 我們和服務員就賬單發生了爭吵。◇ **~ with sb** *She* ***got into an argument with*** *the teacher.* 她和老師爭論了起來。 **2** 0‑w [C] a reason or set of reasons that sb uses to show that sth is true or correct 論據；理由；論點：*Her main argument was a moral one.* 她的主要論據是道德上的。◇ **~ for/against sth** *There are strong* ***arguments for and against*** *euthanasia.* 對安樂死支持和反對的人都有強而有力的論據。◇ **~ that …** *His argument was that public spending must be reduced.* 他的論點是公共開支必須縮減。 ➲ WRITING TUTOR page WT13 **3** [U] **~ (about sth)** the act of disagreeing in a conversation or discussion using a reason or set of reasons 辯論：*Let's assume* ***for the sake of argument*** (= in order to discuss the problem) *that we can't start till March.* 為方便討論起見，先假定我們要到三月份才能開始。

ar·gu·men·ta·tion /ˌɑːɡjumənˈteɪʃn; *NAmE* ˌɑːrɡ-/ *noun* [U] logical arguments used to support a theory, an action or an idea 推論；論證；論據

ar·gu·men·ta·tive /ˌɑːɡjuˈmentətɪv; *NAmE* ˌɑːrɡ-/ *adj.* a person who is **argumentative** likes arguing or often starts arguing 好爭論的；愛辯論的

argy-bargy /ˌɑːdʒi ˈbɑːdʒi; *NAmE* ˌɑːrdʒi ˈbɑːrdʒi/ *noun* [U, C] (*pl.* **ˌargy-ˈbargies**) (*BrE, informal*) noisy disagreement 爭吵；吵嘴；拌嘴；吵鬧；抬槓

ar·gyle /ɑːˈɡaɪl; *NAmE* ˈɑːrɡaɪl/ *noun* [U] a knitted pattern of diamond shapes on a plain background, especially on a sweater or on socks （套衫、襪子等上的）菱形花紋，菱形圖案

aria /ˈɑːriə/ *noun* a song for one voice, especially in an OPERA or ORATORIO （尤指歌劇或清唱劇中的）詠歎調

-arian *suffix* (in nouns and adjectives 構成名詞和形容詞) believing in; practising 相信…的；實行…的：*humanitarian* 人道主義的◇ *disciplinarian* 嚴格執行紀律者

arid /ˈærɪd/ *adj.* **1** (of land or a climate 土地或氣候) having little or no rain; very dry 乾旱的；乾燥的：*arid and semi-arid deserts* 乾旱和半乾旱的沙漠 **2** (*formal*) with nothing new or interesting in it 枯燥的；乏味的；毫無新意的：*an arid discussion* 枯燥的討論 ▸ **arid·ity** /əˈrɪdəti/ *noun* [U]

Aries /ˈeəriːz; *NAmE* ˈeriːz/ *noun* **1** [U] the first sign of the ZODIAC, the RAM 黃道第一宮；白羊宮；白羊（星）座 **2** [sing.] a person born when the sun is in this sign, that is between 21 March and 20 April 屬白羊座的人（約出生於 3 月 21 日至 4 月 20 日）

aright /əˈraɪt/ *adv.* (*old-fashioned*) correctly 正確地；對

arise 0‑w /əˈraɪz/ *verb* (**arose** /əˈrəʊz; *NAmE* əˈroʊz/, **arisen** /əˈrɪzn/)
1 0‑w [I] (rather *formal*) (especially of a problem or a difficult situation 尤指問題或困境) to happen; to start to exist 發生；產生；出現 **SYN** **occur**：*A new crisis has arisen.* 新危機已經出現。◇ *We keep them informed of any changes as they arise.* 如有任何變化，我們隨時通知他們。◇ *Children should be disciplined* ***when the need arises*** (= when it is necessary). 必要時孩子應該受到管教。◇ *A storm arose during the night.* 夜間暴風雨大作。 **2** [I] **~ (out of/from sth)** (rather *formal*) to happen as a result of a particular situation （由…）引起；（因…）產生：*injuries arising out of a road accident* 道路交通事故造成的傷害◇ *Emotional or mental problems can arise from a physical cause.* 身體上的原因可以引起情緒或精神上的問題。◇ *Are there any* ***matters arising*** *from the minutes of the last meeting?* 根據上次會議記錄，有沒有什麼新情況出現？ **3** [I] (*formal*) to begin to exist or develop 出現；產生；發展：*Several new industries arose in the town.* 城裏出現了好幾種新行業。 **4** [I] (*old use* or *literary*) to get out of bed; to stand up 起牀；起立；起身：*He arose at dawn.* 他黎明即起。 **5** [I] **~ (against sb/sth)** (*old use*) to come together to protest about sth or to fight for sth 群起反對；奮起鬥爭：*The peasants arose against their masters.* 農民奮起反對奴役他們的人。 **6** [I] (*literary*) (of a mountain, a tall building, etc. 山、高大建築物等) to become visible gradually as you move towards it （隨着人走近而）逐漸顯現

ar·is·toc·racy /ˌærɪˈstɒkrəsi; *NAmE* -ˈstɑːk-/ *noun* [C+sing./pl. v.] (*pl.* **-ies**) (in some countries) people born in the highest social class, who have special titles （某些國家的）貴族 **SYN** **nobility**：*members of the aristocracy* 貴族成員

ar·is·to·crat /ˈærɪstəkræt; *NAmE* əˈrɪst-/ *noun* a member of the aristocracy （一個）貴族 ➲ compare COMMONER

ar·is·to·crat·ic /ˌærɪstəˈkrætɪk; *NAmE* əˌrɪstə-/ *adj.* belonging to or typical of the ARISTOCRACY 貴族的 **SYN** **noble**：*an* ***aristocratic name/family/lifestyle*** 貴族姓氏 / 家庭 / 生活方式

Ar·is·to·tel·ian /ˌærɪstəˈtiːliən/ *adj.* connected with Aristotle or his philosophy 亞里士多德（哲學）的

arith·met·ic /əˈrɪθmətɪk/ *noun* [U] **1** the type of mathematics that deals with the adding, multiplying, etc. of numbers 算術：*He's not very good at arithmetic.* 他不太擅長算術。 **2** sums involving the adding, multiplying, etc. of numbers 算術運算；四則運算：*a quick bit of* ***mental arithmetic*** (= sums you do in your head, without writing anything down) 心算◇ *I think there's something wrong with your arithmetic.* 我認為你的計算有錯。

arith·met·ic·al /ˌærɪθˈmetɪkl/ (also **arith·met·ic**) *adj.* relating to arithmetic 算術的：*an arithmetical calculation* 算術運算 ▸ **arith·met·ic·al·ly** /-kli/ *adv.*

arithˌmetic ˈmean *noun* (*mathematics* 數) = MEAN *n.* (2)

arithˌmetic proˈgression (also **arithˌmetic ˈseries**) *noun* a series of numbers that decrease or increase by the same amount each time, for example 2, 4, 6, 8 算術級數，等差級數（如 2、4、6、8） ➲ compare GEOMETRIC PROGRESSION

the ark /ɑːk; *NAmE* ɑːrk/ (also **ˌNoah's ˈark**) *noun* [sing.] (in the Bible《聖經》) a large boat which Noah built to save his family and two of every type of animal from the flood 方舟，諾亞方舟（諾亞為家人及一對對各種動物避洪水所造的大船）

IDM **out of the ˈark | sth went out with the ˈark** (*BrE, informal*) if sb says that an object or a custom is **out of the ark** or **went out with the ark**, they think that it is very old-fashioned 極古老；十分陳舊；過時

arm 0‑w /ɑːm; *NAmE* ɑːrm/ *noun, verb*

■ *noun* ➲ see also ARMS

▸ **PART OF BODY** 身體部位 **1** 0‑w either of the two long parts that stick out from the top of the body and connect the shoulders to the hands 臂；手臂；上肢：*He escaped with only a broken arm.* 他得以逃生，只是斷了一隻胳膊。◇ *She threw her arms around his neck.* 她張開雙臂摟住他的脖子。◇ *The officer grabbed him* ***by the arm*** (= grabbed his arm). 警察抓住了他的手臂。◇ *She touched him gently on the arm.* 她輕輕地碰了碰他的胳膊。◇ *He held the dirty rag* ***at arm's length*** (= as far away from his body as possible). 他拎着髒抹布，身子離得遠遠的。◇ *They walked along* ***arm in arm*** (= with the arm of one person linked with the arm of the other).

他們臂挽着臂一路走着。◇ *She cradled the child* ***in her arms***. 她懷抱着小孩。◇ *They fell asleep* ***in each other's arms*** (= holding each other). 他們互相摟抱着睡着了。◇ *He was carrying a number of files* ***under his arm*** (= between his arm and his body). 他腋下挾着一些卷宗。◇ *He walked in with a tall blonde* ***on his arm*** (= next to him and holding his arm). 他手挽着一個高個子金髮女郎走了進來。➲ **COLLOCATIONS** at PHYSICAL ➲ **VISUAL VOCAB** page V59

‣ **OF CLOTHING** 衣服 **2** ⊶ the part of a piece of clothing that covers the arm 袖子 **SYN** **sleeve**

‣ **OF CHAIR** 椅子 **3** the part of a chair, etc. on which you rest your arms 扶手 ➲ **VISUAL VOCAB** pages V21, V69

‣ **OF MACHINERY** 機器 **4** a long narrow part of an object or a piece of machinery, especially one that moves 臂狀物（尤指可移動的物體部份或機器部件）：*a robotic arm* 機械臂

‣ **OF WATER/LAND** 水；陸地 **5** a long narrow piece of water or land that is joined to a larger area 狹長港灣；（連接較大地區的）狹長地帶：*A small bridge spans the arm of the river.* 一座小橋橫跨河灣。

‣ **OF ORGANIZATION** 組織機構 **6** [usually sing.] **~ (of sth)** a section of a large organization that deals with one particular activity 分部；職能部門 **SYN** **wing**：*the research arm of the company* 公司的科研部門

IDM **cost/pay an ˌarm and a ˈleg** (*informal*) to cost/pay a lot of money（使）花一大筆錢 **keep sb at arm's length** to avoid having a close relationship with sb 與某人保持距離；不親近某人：*He keeps all his clients at arm's length.* 他不與任何委託人過分親密。➲ more at AKIMBO, BABE, BEAR *v.*, CHANCE *v.*, FOLD *v.*, LONG *adj.*, OPEN *adj.*, RIGHT *adj.*, SHOT *n.*, TWIST *v.*

■ ***verb*** **1** ⊶ [I, T] to provide weapons for yourself/sb in order to fight a battle or a war 武裝；裝備；備戰：*The country was arming against the enemy.* 這個國家正在備戰迎擊敵人。◇ **~ yourself/sb (with sth)** *The men armed themselves with sticks and stones.* 這些人以棍棒和石塊作為武器。◇ (*figurative*) *She had armed herself for the meeting with all the latest statistics.* 為了這次會議，她準備了所有最新統計資料。➲ see also ARMED **2** [T] **~ sth** to make a bomb, etc. ready to explode 使（炸彈等）隨時爆炸 ➲ compare DISARM

ar·mada /ɑːˈmɑːdə; *NAmE* ɑːrˈm-/ *noun* a large group of armed ships sailing together（大型）艦隊：*The Spanish Armada was sent to attack England in 1588.* * 1588 年西班牙無敵艦隊被派遣進攻英國。◇ (*figurative*) *a vast armada of football fans* 一大群足球迷

ar·ma·dillo /ˌɑːməˈdɪləʊ; *NAmE* ˌɑːrməˈdɪloʊ/ *noun* (*pl.* **-os**) an American animal with a hard shell made of pieces of bone 犰狳（美洲動物，體表覆蓋角質鱗片的護甲）

Ar·ma·ged·don /ˌɑːməˈgedn; *NAmE* ˌɑːrm-/ *noun* [sing., U] **1** (in the Bible《聖經》) a battle between good and evil at the end of the world 世界末日的善惡大決戰 **2** a terrible war that could destroy the world（足以毀滅世界的）大決戰

Ar·mag·nac /ˈɑːmənjæk; *NAmE* ˈɑːr-/ *noun* [U] a type of French BRANDY 阿馬涅克酒（法國白蘭地酒）

Ar·ma·lite™ /ˈɑːməlaɪt; *NAmE* ˈɑːrm-/ *noun* a type of light automatic RIFLE 阿瑪萊特自動步槍

ar·ma·ment /ˈɑːməmənt; *NAmE* ˈɑːrm-/ *noun* **1** [C, usually pl.] weapons, especially large guns, bombs, tanks, etc. 軍備；武器：*the armaments industry* 軍火工業 **2** [U] the process of increasing the amount of weapons an army or a country has, especially to prepare for war 武裝；戰備 ➲ compare DISARMAMENT

arma·ture /ˈɑːmətʃə(r); *NAmE* ˈɑːrm-/ *noun* (*technical* 術語) a frame that is covered to make a figure（塑像的）骨架，模架：*The figures are made from clay over a wire armature.* 這些塑像是將黏土貼在金屬絲骨架上製成的。

arm·band /ˈɑːmbænd; *NAmE* ˈɑːrm-/ *noun* **1** a cloth band worn around the arm as a sign of sth, for example that sb has an official position 臂章；袖章：*The stewards all wore armbands.* 乘務員都戴了臂章。◇ *Many people at the funeral service were wearing black armbands.* 葬禮上許多人戴着黑紗。 **2** either of two plastic rings that can be filled with air and worn around the arms by sb who is learning to swim（學游泳時用的可充氣）臂圈

ˈarm candy *noun* [U] (*informal*) a beautiful woman that a man takes with him when he goes to a public event in order to impress other people（男子參加社交活動時所帶的）掛臂美女

arm·chair *noun, adj.*

■ ***noun*** /ˈɑːmtʃeə(r); ɑːmˈtʃeə(r); *NAmE* ˈɑːrmtʃer; ɑːrmˈtʃer/ a comfortable chair with sides on which you can rest your arms 扶手椅：*to sit in an armchair* 坐在扶手椅上 ➲ **VISUAL VOCAB** page V21

■ ***adj.*** /ˈɑːmtʃeə(r); *NAmE* ˈɑːrmtʃer/ [only before noun] knowing about a subject through books and television, rather than by doing it for yourself 書本知識的；只說而沒有行動的：*an* ***armchair*** *critic/traveller* 不切實際的批評家；端坐家中的神遊旅行者

armed ⊶ /ɑːmd; *NAmE* ɑːrmd/ *adj.*

1 ⊶ involving the use of weapons 使用武器的；用武力的：*an armed robbery* 持械搶劫 ◇ *an international armed conflict* (= a war) 國際武裝衝突 **OPP** **unarmed** **2** ⊶ carrying a weapon, especially a gun 攜帶武器的；持槍的；荷槍實彈的：*The man is armed and dangerous.* 這個男子有槍，是個危險分子。◇ *armed guards* 武裝警衛 ◇ *Police were* ***heavily armed***. 警察全副武裝。◇ **~ with a gun, etc.** *He was armed with a rifle.* 他配有一支步槍。**OPP** **unarmed** **3 ~ (with sth)** knowing sth or carrying sth that you need in order to help you to perform a task 備有所需的：*He was armed with all the facts.* 他備有所需的全部事實材料。

IDM **ˌarmed to the ˈteeth** having many weapons 武裝到牙齒；全副武裝

the ˌarmed ˈforces (*BrE* also **the ˌarmed ˈservices**) *noun* [pl.] a country's army, navy and AIR FORCE（一國的）武裝部隊，武裝力量

arm·ful /ˈɑːmfʊl; *NAmE* ˈɑːrm-/ *noun* a quantity that you can carry in one or both arms 單臂（或雙臂）一抱的量；一抱

arm·hole /ˈɑːmhəʊl; *NAmE* ˈɑːrmhoʊl/ *noun* the place in a coat, shirt, dress, etc. that your arm goes through 袖孔

ar·mis·tice /ˈɑːmɪstɪs; *NAmE* ˈɑːrm-/ *noun* [sing.] a formal agreement during a war to stop fighting and discuss making peace 休戰；停戰；休戰條約；停戰協定 **SYN** **ceasefire**

arm·lock /ˈɑːmlɒk; *NAmE* ˈɑːrmlɑːk/ *noun* (in WRESTLING 摔跤運動) a way of holding an opponent's arm so that they cannot move 夾臂：*He had him in an armlock.* 他夾住了對手的手臂。

ar·moire /ɑːmˈwɑː(r); *NAmE* ɑːrmˈwɑːr/ *noun* (from *French*) a cupboard with drawers or shelves underneath, especially one that has a lot of decoration（常指華麗或精緻的）大衣櫥，大櫥櫃

ar·mor·ial /ɑːˈmɔːriəl; *NAmE* ɑːrˈm-/ *adj.* connected with HERALDRY 紋章的

ar·mour (*especially US* **armor**) /ˈɑːmə(r); *NAmE* ˈɑːrm-/ *noun* [U] **1** special metal clothing that soldiers wore in the past to protect their bodies while fighting 盔甲；甲冑：*a suit of armour* 一副盔甲 ◇ (*figurative*) *Monkeys do not have any kind of protective armour and use their brains to solve problems.* 猴子沒有任何防身的盔甲，就動腦筋解決問題。 **2** metal covers that protect ships and military vehicles such as tanks（軍艦、坦克等的）裝甲，防彈鋼板 **3** (*technical* 術語) military vehicles used in war 裝甲部隊；裝甲車輛：*an attack by infantry and armour* 步兵和裝甲兵的進攻 **IDM** see CHINK *n.*, KNIGHT *n.*

ar·moured (*especially US* **ar·mored**) /ˈɑːməd; *NAmE* ˈɑːrmərd/ *adj.* **1** (especially of a military vehicle 尤指軍用交通工具) protected by metal covers 有裝甲的：*The cruiser was heavily armoured.* 這艘巡洋艦有堅固的裝甲。◇ *an armoured car* 裝甲車 **2** using armoured vehicles 使用裝甲交通工具的：*an armoured division* 裝甲師

A

ˌarmoured ˈpersonnel ˈcarrier (*especially US* **ˌarmored ˈpersonnel ˈcarrier**) *noun* a military vehicle used to transport soldiers 裝甲運兵車

ar·mour·er (*especially US* **ar·mor·er**) /ˈɑːmərə(r); *NAmE* ˈɑːrm-/ *noun* a person who makes or repairs weapons and armour 軍械製造師；軍械維修工；軍械工

ˌarmour-ˈplated (*especially US* **armor-**) *adj.* (of vehicles 交通工具) covered with sheets of metal to provide protection against bullets, etc. 有裝甲的；由裝甲鋼板覆蓋的

ar·moury (*especially US* **ar·mory**) /ˈɑːməri; *NAmE* ˈɑːrm-/ *noun* (*pl.* **-ies**) **1** a place where weapons and armour are kept 軍械庫 SYN **arsenal** **2** (in the US or Canada) a building which is the HEADQUARTERS for training people who are not professional soldiers, for example the National Guard（美國或加拿大國民衛隊等的）總部大樓 **3** (*formal*) the things that sb has available to help them achieve sth 錦囊；寶庫：*Doctors have an armoury of drugs available.* 醫生都備有各種各樣的藥物。 **4** all the weapons and military equipment that a country has（一國的）軍事裝備：*Britain's nuclear armoury* 英國的核武器裝備

arm·pit /ˈɑːmpɪt; *NAmE* ˈɑːrm-/ (also *NAmE, informal* **pit**) *noun* the part of the body under the arm where it joins the shoulder 腋；腋窩 ➲ VISUAL VOCAB page V59 ➲ see also UNDERARM

IDM **the ˈarmpit of sth** (*informal, especially NAmE*) the most unpleasant or ugly place in a country or region 骯髒的角落；齷齪的地方：*The city has been called the armpit of America.* 這座城市被稱為美國最令人厭惡的地方。

arm·rest /ˈɑːmrest; *NAmE* ˈɑːrm-/ *noun* the part of some types of seat, especially in planes or cars, which supports your arm（飛機、汽車等座位的）靠手，扶手

arms 🔑 /ɑːmz; *NAmE* ɑːrmz/ *noun* [pl.]
1 🔑 (*formal*) weapons, especially as used by the army, navy, etc. 兵器；武器：*arms and ammunition* 兵器和彈藥 ◇ *Police officers in the UK do not usually* ***carry arms.*** 英國警察通常不攜帶武器。 ➲ see also FIREARM, SMALL ARMS **2** = COAT OF ARMS：*the King's Arms* (= used as the name of a pub) 國王盾形徽章（酒吧名）

IDM **be under ˈarms** (*formal*) to have weapons and be ready to fight in a war 處於備戰狀態；嚴陣以待；枕戈待旦 **lay down your ˈarms** (*formal*) to stop fighting 放下武器；停止作戰 **take up arms (against sb)** (*formal*) to prepare to fight 拿起武器；準備戰鬥 **(be) up in ˈarms (about/over sth)** (*informal*) (of a group of people 一群人) to be very angry about sth and ready to protest strongly about it 極力反對；強烈抗議 ➲ more at BEAR *v.*, PRESENT *v.*

ˈarms control *noun* [U] international agreements to destroy weapons or limit the number of weapons that countries have 軍備控制

ˈarms race *noun* [sing.] a situation in which countries compete to get the most and best weapons 軍備競賽

ˈarm-twisting *noun* [U] (*informal*) the use of a lot of pressure or even physical force to persuade sb to do sth 強迫；施加壓力

ˈarm-wrestling *noun* [U] a competition to find out which of two people is the strongest, in which they try to force each other's arm down onto a table 扳手腕；比腕力

army 🔑 /ˈɑːmi; *NAmE* ˈɑːrmi/ *noun* (*pl.* **-ies**)
1 🔑 [C+sing./pl. v.] a large organized group of soldiers who are trained to fight on land 陸上作戰軍隊；陸軍部隊：*The two opposing armies faced each other across the battlefield.* 敵對兩軍在戰場上嚴陣對峙。 **2** 🔑 **the army** [sing.+sing./pl. v.] the part of a country's armed forces that fights on land（一國的）陸軍：*Her husband is in* ***the army.*** 她的丈夫在陸軍服役。 ◇ *After leaving school, Mike* ***went into the army.*** 邁克在學校畢業後參加了陸軍。 ◇ *an army officer* 陸軍軍官 ➲ COLLOCATIONS at WAR **3** [C+sing./pl. v.] a large number of people or things, especially when they are organized in some way or involved in a particular activity 大批；大群：*an army of advisers/volunteers* 一大批顧問；志願者大軍 ◇ *An army of ants marched across the path.* 一大群螞蟻浩浩蕩蕩地穿過小徑。

ˌarmy ˈsurplus *noun* [U] clothing and equipment that the army no longer needs and is sold to the public（可公開出售的）剩餘軍用物資

ar·nica /ˈɑːnɪkə; *NAmE* ˈɑːrn-/ *noun* [U] a natural medicine made from a plant, used to treat BRUISES (= marks that appear on the skin after sb has fallen, been hit, etc.) 山金車酊（用於治療挫傷等的天然藥物）

ˈA-road *noun* (in Britain) a road that is less important than a MOTORWAY, but wider and straighter than a B-ROAD（英國）幹線公路，A 級公路（略次於高速公路，但較 B 級公路寬直）

aroma /əˈrəʊmə; *NAmE* əˈroʊmə/ *noun* a pleasant, noticeable smell 芳香；香味：*the aroma of fresh coffee* 新鮮咖啡的香味

aroma·ther·apy /əˌrəʊməˈθerəpi; *NAmE* əˌroʊmə-/ *noun* [U] the use of natural oils that smell sweet for controlling pain or for rubbing into the body during MASSAGE 芳香療法（用天然芳香油鎮痛或按摩時揉入體內）
▸ **aroma·ther·ap·ist** *noun*

aro·mat·ic /ˌærəˈmætɪk/ *adj.* having a pleasant noticeable smell 芳香的；有香味的 SYN **fragrant**：***aromatic oils/herbs*** 芳香油／草

arose *past tense of* ARISE

around 🔑 /əˈraʊnd/ *adv., prep.*
■ ***adv.*** HELP For the special uses of **around** in phrasal verbs, look at the entries for the verbs. For example **come around to sth** is in the phrasal verb section at **come.** * around 在短語動詞中的特殊用法見有關動詞詞條。如 come around to sth 在詞條 come 的短語動詞部份。 **1** 🔑 approximately 大約：*He arrived around five o'clock.* 他大約是五點鐘到的。 ◇ *The cost would be somewhere around £1 500.* 費用要在 1 500 英鎊上下。 **2** 🔑 on every side; surrounding sb/sth 周圍；四周：*I could hear laughter all around.* 我可以聽見周圍的笑聲。 ◇ *a yard with a fence* ***all around*** 四周圍着柵欄的院子 **3** 🔑 (*especially NAmE*) (*BrE* usually **round**) moving in a circle 圍繞；環繞：*How do you make the wheels go around?* 你怎樣使這些輪子轉動起來？ **4** 🔑 (*especially NAmE*) (*BrE* usually **round**) measured in a circle 以圓周計算：*an old tree that was at least ten feet around* 合抱至少十英尺的古樹 **5** 🔑 in or to many places 到處；向各處：*We were all running around trying to get ready in time.* 我們東奔西跑，望能按時準備就緒。 ◇ *This is our new office—Kay will show you around.* 這是我們的新辦公室，凱會帶你參觀一下。 ◇ *There were papers lying around all over the floor.* 地板上四處散亂着文件。 **6** 🔑 used to describe activities that have no real purpose 閒散地；無目的地：*There were several young people sitting around looking bored.* 有幾個年青人閒坐着，一副無聊的樣子。 **7** 🔑 present in a place; available 出現；現有；可用：*There was more money around in those days.* 那年頭比現在富裕。 ◇ *I knocked but there was no one around.* 我敲了門，但是沒有人應門。 ◇ *Digital television has been around for some time now.* 數字電視已經面市一段時間了。 **8** active and well known in a sport, profession, etc.（體育運動、專業等中）走紅的，活躍的：*a new tennis champion who could be around for a long time* 可能會走紅很長時期的新網球冠軍 ◇ *She's been around as a film director since the 1980s.* 自 20 世紀 80 年代以來她一直是活躍在影壇的著名導演。 **9** (*especially NAmE*) (*BrE* usually **round**) in a circle or curve to face another way or the opposite way 轉彎；掉轉；掉頭：*She turned the car around and drove off.* 她把轎車掉頭開走了。 ◇ *They looked around when he called.* 他呼喊時他們回頭張望。 ➲ see also ABOUT, ROUND

IDM **have been around** to have gained knowledge and experience of the world 閱歷世事；飽經世故

■ ***prep.*** (*especially NAmE*) (*BrE* usually **round**) **1** 🔑 surrounding sb/sth; on each side of sth 圍繞；環繞：*The house is built around a central courtyard.* 這房子是圍繞着中央的庭院而建的。 ◇ *He put his arms around her.* 他摟着她。 **2** 🔑 on, to or from the other side of sb/sth 在那邊；到那邊；從那邊：*Our house is just around the*

A

corner. 過了拐角就是我們的房子。◇ *The bus came around the bend.* 公共汽車從拐彎處駛來。◇ *There must be a way around the problem.* 肯定有解決這個問題的辦法。 **3** in a circle 繞着：*They walked around the lake.* 他們繞着湖邊行走。 **4** in or to many places in an area 到處；向各處：*They walked around the town looking for a place to eat.* 他們在城裏到處尋找吃飯的地方。 **5** to fit in with particular people, ideas, etc. 同…一致；適合；符合：*I can't arrange everything around your timetable!* 我不可能事事都按着你的時刻表安排！

Which Word? 詞語辨析

around / round / about

- **Around** and **round** can often be used with the same meaning in *BrE*, though **around** is more formal. 在英式英語中，around 和 round 近義，不過 around 較正式：*The earth goes round/around the sun.* 地球繞着太陽轉。◇ *They live round/around the corner.* 他們住在拐角附近。◇ *We travelled round/around India.* 我們在印度各地旅行。◇ *She turned round/around when I came in.* 我進來時她轉過身來。 In *NAmE* only **around** can be used in these meanings. 在美式英語中，表示上述意思只能用 around。
- **Around, round** and **about** can also sometimes be used with the same meaning in *BrE*. 在英式英語中，有時 around、round 和 about 的含義相同：*The kids were running around/round/about outside.* 孩子們在外面跑來跑去。◇ *I've been waiting around/round/about to see her all day.* 為了要見到她，我等了一整天。 In *NAmE* only **around** can be used in these meanings. 在美式英語中，表示上述意思只能用 around。 **About** or **around** can be used in both *BrE* and *NAmE* to mean 'approximately'. 在英式英語和美式英語中，about 或 around 均可表示大約：*We left around/about 8 o'clock.* 我們在 8 點鐘左右離開了。

a,round-the-'clock *adj.* = ROUND-THE-CLOCK

arouse /ə'raʊz/ *verb* **1 ~ sth** to make sb have a particular feeling or attitude 激起，引起（感情、態度）：*to **arouse sb's interest/curiosity/anger*** 引起某人的興趣／好奇心／怒氣 ◇ *Her strange behaviour aroused our suspicions.* 她的占怪行為引起了我們的懷疑。 **2 ~ sb** to make sb feel sexually excited 激起性慾 **SYN** **excite** **3 ~ sb** to make you feel more active and want to start doing sth 使行動起來；激發：*The whole community was aroused by the crime.* 這個罪行使整個社會行動起來。 **4 ~ sb (from sth)** (*formal*) to wake sb from sleep 喚醒 ⊃ see also ROUSE ▸ **arousal** /ə'raʊzl/ *noun* [U]：***emotional/sexual arousal*** 情緒激動；性衝動

ar·peg·gio /ɑː'pedʒiəʊ; *NAmE* ɑːr'pedʒioʊ/ *noun* (*pl.* **-os**) (*music* 音) the notes of a CHORD played quickly one after the other 琶音，琶音和弦（快速連續彈出和弦的音符）

arr. *abbr.* **1** (in writing) arrives; arrival （書寫形式）抵達，到達：*arr. London 06.00* 早晨 6 點抵達倫敦 ⊃ compare DEP. **2** (*music* 音) (in writing) arranged by （書寫形式）由…改編：*Handel, arr. Mozart* 莫扎特改編的亨德爾的樂曲

ar·raign /ə'reɪn/ *verb* [usually passive] **~ sb (for sth)** (*law* 律) to bring sb to court in order to formally accuse them of a crime 提訊；提審；控告：*He was arraigned for murder.* 他因謀殺罪而被提訊。◇ *He was arraigned on a charge of murder.* 他以謀殺罪名而受到提審。 ▸ **ar·raign·ment** *noun* [C, U]

ar·range /ə'reɪndʒ/ *verb*
1 [T, I] to plan or organize sth in advance 安排；籌備：**~ sth** *The party was arranged quickly.* 聚會很快就安排好了。◇ *She arranged a loan with the bank.* 她和銀行商定了一項貸款。◇ *Can I arrange an appointment for Monday?* 我可以安排星期一約見嗎？◇ *We met at six, **as arranged**.* 我們按時在六點鐘碰面。◇ **~ how, where, etc. …** *We've still got to arrange how to get to the airport.* 我們還得安排如何到達機場。◇ **~ to do sth** *Have you arranged to meet him?* 你安排好去見他了嗎？◇ **~ that …** *I've arranged that we can borrow their car.* 我已經說好了，我們可以借用他們的車。◇ **~ for sth (to do sth)** *We arranged for a car to collect us from the airport.* 我們安排了一輛轎車到機場接我們。◇ **~ with sb (about sth)** *I've arranged with the neighbours about feeding the cat while we are away.* 我們外出期間給貓餵食的事，我已和鄰居安排妥了。 **2** [T] **~ sth** to put sth in a particular order; to make sth neat or attractive 整理；排列；佈置：*The books are arranged alphabetically by author.* 這些書是按作者姓名字母順序排列的。◇ *I must arrange my financial affairs and make a will.* 我必須把我的財務安排好，並立下遺囑。◇ *She arranged the flowers in a vase.* 她用花瓶把花插好。 **3** [T] **~ sth (for sth)** to write or change a piece of music so that it is suitable for a particular instrument or voice 譜寫，改編（樂曲）：*He arranged traditional folk songs for the piano.* 他把傳統民歌改編成鋼琴曲。

ar,ranged 'marriage *noun* a marriage in which the parents choose the husband or wife for their child 包辦婚姻

ar·range·ment /ə'reɪndʒmənt/ *noun*
1 [C, usually pl.] a plan or preparation that you make so that sth can happen 安排；籌備：*travel arrangements* 旅行安排 ◇ **~ for sth** *I'll **make arrangements** for you to be met at the airport.* 我會安排人到機場接你。 **2** [C, usually pl.] the way things are done or organized 安排方式；佈置：*She's happy with her unusual living arrangements.* 她對自己不同尋常的生活安排方式感到很得意。◇ *new security arrangements* 新保安措施 ◇ *There are special arrangements for people working overseas.* 對赴海外工作的人員有特別安排。 **3** [C, U] an agreement that you make with sb that you can both accept 商定；約定：*We can **come to an arrangement** over the price.* 我們可以就價格問題達成一項協議。◇ **~ between A and B** *an arrangement between the school and the parents* 學校和家長的一項約定 ◇ **~ with sb (to do sth)** *You can cash cheques here **by prior arrangement** with the bank.* 你事先和銀行商妥，就可以在這裏兌現支票。◇ **~ that …** *They had an arrangement that the children would spend two weeks with each parent.* 他們商定，孩子們與父方母方各住兩個星期。 **4** [C, U] a group of things that are organized or placed in a particular order or position; the act of placing things in a particular order 整理好的東西；整理；排列；佈置：*plans of the possible seating arrangements* 幾種可行的座次安排方案 ◇ *the art of flower arrangement* 插花藝術 **5** [C, U] a piece of music that has been changed, for example for another instrument to play 改編樂曲

ar·ran·ger /ə'reɪndʒə/ *noun* **1** a person who arranges music that has been written by sb different 樂曲改編者 **2** a person who arranges things 籌備者；安排者：*arrangers of care services for the elderly* 安排照料老人的籌劃者

ar·rant /'ærənt/ *adj.* [only before noun] (*old-fashioned*) used to emphasize how bad sth/sb is （強調有多壞）十足的，壞透的：*arrant nonsense* 一派胡言

array /ə'reɪ/ *noun, verb*
■ ***noun*** **1** [usually sing.] a group or collection of things or people, often one that is large or impressive 大堆；大群；大量：*a vast array of bottles of different shapes and sizes* 一大批形狀大小不一的瓶子 ◇ *a dazzling array of talent* 耀眼的大批天才 **2** (*computing* 計) a way of organizing and storing related data in a computer memory 數組；陣列 **3** (*technical* 術語) a set of numbers, signs or values arranged in rows and columns 數組；陣列
■ ***verb*** [usually passive] (*formal*) **1 ~ sth** to arrange a group of things in a pleasing way or so that they are in order 佈置；排列：*Jars of all shapes and sizes were arrayed on the shelves.* 在擱架上整齊地排列着大大小小各式各樣的罐子。 **2 ~ sb** to arrange soldiers in a position from which they are ready to attack 配置（兵力）

array·ed /ə'reɪd/ *adj.* [not before noun] **~ (in sth)** (*literary*) dressed in a particular way, especially in beautiful clothes 穿戴（尤指漂亮衣服）：*She was arrayed in a black velvet gown.* 她穿着一件黑色天鵝絨長禮服。

A

ar·rears /əˈrɪəz; *NAmE* əˈrɪrz/ *noun* [pl.] money that sb owes that they have not paid at the right time 逾期欠款：*rent/mortgage/tax arrears* 拖欠租金／按揭貸款／稅款

IDM **be in arrears | get/fall into arrears** to be late in paying money that you owe 到期未付；拖欠：*We're two months in arrears with the rent.* 我們拖欠了兩個月的租金。 **in arrears** if money or a person is paid **in arrears** for work, the money is paid after the work has been done 後付；拖欠；拖延

ar·rest /əˈrest/ *verb, noun*

■ *verb* **1** [T, often passive] if the police **arrest** sb, the person is taken to a POLICE STATION and kept there because the police believe they may be guilty of a crime 逮捕；拘留：**~ sb** *A man has been arrested in connection with the robbery.* 一名男子因與這樁搶劫案有關已被逮捕。◇ **~ sb for sth** *She was arrested for drug-related offences.* 她因涉嫌毒品犯罪而被捕。◇ **~ sb for doing sth** *You could get arrested for doing that.* 你幹那種事可能要遭逮捕。➲ COLLOCATIONS at JUSTICE **2** [T] **~ sth** (*formal*) to stop a process or a development 阻止；中止：*They failed to arrest the company's decline.* 他們未能阻止公司的衰落。 **3** [T] **~ sth** (*formal*) to make sb notice sth and pay attention to it 吸引（注意）：*An unusual noise* ***arrested his attention.*** 一陣不尋常的嘈雜聲引起了他的注意。 **4** [I] (*medical* 醫) if sb **arrests**, their heart stops beating 心跳停止：*He arrested on the way to the hospital.* 他在送院途中停止了心跳。

■ *noun* [C, U] **1** the act of arresting sb 逮捕；拘捕：*The police made several arrests.* 警方逮捕了好幾人。◇ *She was* ***under arrest*** *on suspicion of murder.* 她因涉嫌謀殺而被逮捕。◇ *Opposition leaders were put under* ***house arrest*** (= not allowed to leave their houses). 反對黨領袖遭軟禁。➲ see also CITIZEN'S ARREST **2** an act of sth stopping or being interrupted 停止；中止：*He died after suffering a* ***cardiac arrest*** (= when his heart suddenly stopped). 他死於心搏停止。

arˌrestable ofˈfence *noun* (*law* 律) an offence for which sb can be arrested without a WARRANT from a judge 構成逮捕的罪行；應予逮捕的罪行

ar·rest·ing /əˈrestɪŋ/ *adj.* (*formal*) attracting a lot of attention; very attractive 引人注意的；很有吸引力的

ar·rival /əˈraɪvl/ *noun*

1 [U, C] an act of coming or being brought to a place 到達；抵達：*Guests receive dinner* ***on/upon arrival*** *at the hotel.* 旅客一到旅館即可就餐。◇ *We apologize for the late arrival of the train.* 我們為火車誤點表示歉意。◇ *the arrival of the mail in the morning* 上午送達的郵件◇ *daily arrivals of refugees* 每天到來的難民◇ *There are 120* ***arrivals and departures*** *every day.* 每天有 120 次航班離港和抵港。OPP **departure** **2** [C] a person or thing that comes to a place 到達者；抵達物：*The first arrivals at the concert got the best seats.* 最早來到音樂會的人坐上了最好的座位。◇ ***early/late/new arrivals*** 早到／晚到／新到者◇ *We're expecting* ***a new arrival*** (= a baby) *in the family soon.* 我們家很快就會添一個新生嬰兒。 **3** [U] the time when a new technology or idea is introduced（新技術、新思想的）引進，採用，推行：*the arrival of pay TV* 收費電視的引進 IDM see DEAD *adj.*

ar·rive /əˈraɪv/ *verb*

1 [I] (*abbr.* **arr.**) to get to a place, especially at the end of a journey 到達；抵達：*I'll wait until they arrive.* 我會一直等到他們來。◇ *I was pleased to hear you arrived home safely.* 聽說你平安到家我很高興。◇ *to* ***arrive early/late*** *for a meeting* 開會早到／遲到◇ *The police arrived to arrest him.* 警察趕來逮捕了他。◇ **~ at/in/on …** *She'll arrive in New York at noon.* 她將在正午抵達紐約。◇ *The train arrived at the station 20 minutes late.* 火車遲了 20 分鐘到站。◇ *By the time I* ***arrived on the scene****, it was all over.* 我來到現場時，一切都已結束。◇ *We didn't arrive back at the hotel until very late.* 我們很晚才回到了旅館。 **2** [I] (of things 東西) to be brought to sb 送達；寄到：*A letter arrived for you this morning.* 今天上午來了一封給你的信。◇ *Send your application to arrive by 31 October.* 申請信要在 10 月 31 日前寄到。◇ *We waited an hour for our lunch to arrive.* 我們等午飯等了一小時。◇ *The new product will arrive on supermarket shelves* (= be available) *early next year.* 明年初該新產品就會在超級市場上架。 **3** [I] (of an event or a moment 事件或時刻) to happen or to come, especially when you have been waiting for it 發生；到來：*The wedding day finally arrived.* 婚禮這一天終於到來。◇ *The baby arrived* (= was born) *early.* 嬰兒早早地出生了。

IDM **sb has arˈrived** (*informal*) somebody has become successful 某人成功了：*He knew he had arrived when he was shortlisted for the Booker prize.* 被列入布克小說作品獎決選名單後，他知道自己成功了。

PHR V **arˈrive at sth** to decide on or find sth, especially after discussion and thought 達成（協議）；作出（決議等）；得出（結論等） SYN **reach**：*to* ***arrive at an agreement/a decision/a conclusion*** 達成協議；作出決定；得出結論◇ *to arrive at the truth* 找到真理

ar·riv·iste /ˌæriːˈviːst/ *noun* (from *French, disapproving*) a person who is determined to be accepted as a member of a social group, etc. to which they do not really belong 攀龍附鳳的人

ar·ro·gance /ˈærəgəns/ *noun* [U] the behaviour of a person when they feel that they are more important than other people, so that they are rude to them or do not consider them 傲慢；自大

ar·ro·gant /ˈærəgənt/ *adj.* behaving in a proud, unpleasant way, showing little thought for other people 傲慢的；自大的 ▸ **ar·ro·gant·ly** *adv.*

ar·ro·gate /ˈærəgeɪt/ *verb*

PHR V **arrogate to yourself sth** (*formal*) to claim or take sth that you have no right to 妄稱；擅取：*I do not arrogate to myself the right to decide.* 我不擅自決定。

arrow /ˈærəʊ; *NAmE* ˈæroʊ/ *noun*

1 a thin stick with a sharp point at one end, which is shot from a BOW 箭：*a* ***bow and arrow*** 弓箭◇ ***to fire/shoot an arrow*** 射箭◇ *The road continues as straight as an arrow.* 公路筆直延伸。➲ VISUAL VOCAB page V40 **2** a mark or sign like an arrow (→), used to show direction or position 箭號；箭頭：*Follow the arrows.* 順着箭頭指示方向走。◇ *Use the arrow keys to move the cursor.* 用鍵盤上的箭頭鍵移動光標。

ar·row·head /ˈærəʊhed; *NAmE* ˈæroʊ-/ *noun* the sharp pointed end of an arrow 箭頭；箭鏃

ar·row·root /ˈærəʊruːt; *NAmE* ˈæroʊ-/ *noun* [U] a plant whose roots can be cooked and eaten or made into a type of flour, used especially to make sauces thick; the flour itself 竹芋（根狀莖可食用或用於烹飪，使調味汁變稠）；竹芋粉

ar·royo /əˈrɔɪəʊ; *NAmE* -oʊ/ *noun* (*pl.* **-os**) (from *Spanish*) a narrow channel with steep sides cut by a river in a desert region（沙漠地區的）旱谷，乾谷

arse /ɑːs; *NAmE* ɑːrs/ *noun, verb*

■ *noun* (*BrE, taboo, slang*) **1** (*NAmE* **ass**) the part of the body that you sit on; your bottom 屁股；腚：*Get off your arse!* (= stop sitting around doing nothing) 別閒坐着！ **2** (usually following an adjective 通常置於形容詞後) a stupid person 笨蛋；傻瓜 ➲ see also SMART-ARSE

IDM **My arse!** (*taboo, slang*) used by some people to show they do not believe what sb has said 我才不信這屁話 **work your ˈarse off** (*taboo, slang*) to work very hard 拚命幹 ➲ more at KISS *v.*, KNOW *v.*, LICK *v.*, PAIN *n.*

■ *verb*

IDM **can't be ˈarsed (to do sth)** (*BrE, taboo, slang*) to not want to do sth because it is too much trouble 不願（做麻煩事）：*I was supposed to do some work this weekend but I couldn't be arsed.* 這個週末我本應該幹點事，不過我不願去找那個麻煩。

PHR V **ˌarse aˈbout/aˈround** (*BrE, taboo, slang*) to waste time by behaving in a silly way 鬼混；閒混

arse·hole /ˈɑːshəʊl; *NAmE* ˈɑːrshoʊl/ (*BrE*) (*NAmE* **ass·hole**) *noun* (*taboo, slang*) **1** the ANUS 屁眼；肛門 **2** a stupid or unpleasant person 笨蛋；討厭鬼：*What an arsehole!* 真蠢得出奇！

ˈarse-licker (*BrE*) (*NAmE* **ˈass-licker**) *noun* (*taboo, slang*) a person who is too friendly to sb in authority and is always ready to do what they want 馬屁精 ▸ **ˈarse-licking** (*BrE*) (*NAmE* **ˈass-licking**) *noun* [U]

ar·senal /ˈɑːsənl; *NAmE* ˈɑːrs-/ *noun* **1** a collection of weapons such as guns and EXPLOSIVES（統稱）武器：*Britain's nuclear arsenal* 英國的核武器 **2** a building where military weapons and EXPLOSIVES are made or stored 兵工廠；武器庫；軍火庫

ar·senic /ˈɑːsnɪk; *NAmE* ˈɑːrs-/ *noun* [U] (*symb.* As) a chemical element. Arsenic is an extremely poisonous white powder. 砷

arsey /ˈɑːsi; *NAmE* ˈɑːrsi/ *noun* (*AustralE, informal*) very lucky 交鴻運的；運氣十足的

arson /ˈɑːsn; *NAmE* ˈɑːrsn/ *noun* [U] the crime of deliberately setting fire to sth, especially a building 縱火（罪）；放火（罪）：*to carry out an* ***arson attack*** 進行縱火襲擊 ➲ COLLOCATIONS at CRIME

ar·son·ist /ˈɑːsənɪst; *NAmE* ˈɑːrs-/ *noun* a person who commits the crime of arson 縱火犯；放火犯

art 🔑 /ɑːt; *NAmE* ɑːrt/ *noun, verb*

■ ***noun*** **1** 🔑 [U] the use of the imagination to express ideas or feelings, particularly in painting, drawing or SCULPTURE 藝術，美術（尤指繪畫、雕刻、雕塑）：*modern/contemporary/American art* 現代／當代／美國藝術 ◇ *an* ***art critic/historian/lover*** 藝術批評家／史家／愛好者 ◇ *Can we call television art?* 我們能把電視稱作藝術嗎？◇ *stolen* ***works of art*** 被盜藝術品 ◇ *Her performance displayed great art.* 她的表演展現了精湛的技藝。➲ see also CLIP ART, FINE ART **2** 🔑 [U] examples of objects such as paintings, drawings or SCULPTURES 藝術作品；美術作品：*an* ***art gallery/exhibition*** 美術館／展覽 ◇ *a collection of art and antiques* 一批收藏的藝術品和古董 **3** 🔑 [U] the skill of creating objects such as paintings and drawings, especially when you study it 藝術技巧：*She's good at art and design.* 她擅長美術和設計。◇ *an* ***art teacher/student/college/class*** 美術教師／學生／學院／班 **4** 🔑 **the arts** [pl.] art, music, theatre, literature, etc. when you think of them as a group（統稱）藝術：*lottery funding for the arts* 為藝術籌集資金的彩票 ➲ see also PERFORMING ARTS **5** [C] a type of VISUAL or performing art 表演藝術：*Dance is a very theatrical art.* 舞蹈是非常講究舞台感的一種藝術。 **6** 🔑 [C, usually pl.] the subjects you can study at school or university that are not scientific, such as languages, history or literature 人文科學，文科（如語言、歷史、文學）：*an arts degree* 文科學位 ➲ compare SCIENCE (3) **7** [C, U] an ability or a skill that you can develop with training and practice 技能；技術；技巧：*a therapist trained in the art of healing* 接受過治療技術訓練的治療員 ◇ *Letter-writing is a lost art nowadays.* 當今尺牘是一種已消失的技巧。◇ *Appearing confident at interviews is* ***quite an art***

Collocations 詞語搭配

Fine arts 藝術

Creating art 藝術創作

- **make** a work of art/a drawing/a sketch/a sculpture/a statue/engravings/etchings/prints 創作藝術品；繪畫；畫素描；創作雕塑／雕像／雕版印刷品／蝕刻畫／版畫
- **do** an oil painting/a self-portrait/a line drawing/a rough sketch 畫油畫／自畫像／線條畫／草圖
- **create** a work of art/an artwork/paintings and sculptures 創作一件藝術品／繪畫和雕塑
- **produce** paintings/portraits/oil sketches/his most celebrated work/a series of prints 創作繪畫／肖像畫／油畫速寫／他最知名的作品／一組版畫
- **paint** a picture/landscape/portrait/mural/in oils/in watercolours/(*especially US*) in watercolors/on canvas 畫畫／風景畫／肖像／壁畫／油畫／水彩畫／帆布畫
- **draw** a picture/a portrait/a cartoon/a sketch/a line/a figure/the human form/in charcoal/in ink 畫畫／肖像／漫畫／素描／線條／形體／人形／木炭畫／墨水畫
- **sketch** a preliminary drawing/a figure/a shape 勾勒草圖／形體／圖形
- **carve** a figure/an image/a sculpture/an altarpiece/reliefs/a block of wood 雕刻形體／形象／雕塑／祭壇畫／浮雕／一塊木頭
- **sculpt** a portrait bust/a statue/an abstract figure 雕刻半身像／塑像／抽象形體
- **etch** a line/a pattern/a design/a name into the glass 蝕刻線條／圖案／圖樣／名字在玻璃杯上
- **mix** colours/(*especially US*) colors/pigments/paints 調色；調顏料
- **add/apply** thin/thick layers of paint/colour/(*especially US*) color/pigment 加上薄薄／厚厚幾層顏料
- **use** oil pastels/charcoal/acrylic paint/a can of spray paint 使用彩筆／木炭筆／丙烯酸顏料／一罐噴霧顏料
- **work in** bronze/ceramics/stone/oils/pastels/watercolour/a wide variety of media 用青銅／陶瓷／石頭／油彩／蠟筆／水彩／各種各樣的材料製作藝術品

Describing art 描述藝術

- **paint/depict** a female figure/a biblical scene/a pastoral landscape/a domestic interior 描繪女性形體／與《聖經》有關的場景／田園風光／室內裝飾
- **depict/illustrate** a traditional/mythological/historical/religious theme 描述／闡釋傳統的／神話的／歷史的／宗教的主題
- **create** an abstract composition/a richly textured surface/a distorted perspective 設計抽象的藝術構圖／豐富的層次／視覺扭曲效果
- **paint** dark/rich/skin/flesh tones 漆成深色／濃重的顏色／膚色／肉色
- **use** broad brush strokes/loose brushwork/vibrant colours/a limited palette/simple geometric forms 用粗筆線條／散漫的筆法／鮮豔的顏色／有限的色調／簡單的幾何圖形
- **develop/adopt/paint in** a stylized manner/an abstract style 用非寫實手法／抽象方式闡明／採用／描繪

Showing and selling art 藝術品展示及銷售

- **commission** an altarpiece/a bronze bust of sb/a portrait/a religious work/an artist to paint sth 委託創作一幅祭壇畫／一座某人的半身銅像／一幅肖像畫／一件宗教藝術品；委託藝術家為某物作畫
- **frame** a painting/portrait 給一幅畫／肖像畫鑲框
- **hang** art/a picture/a painting 懸掛藝術品／圖畫／畫作
- **display/exhibit** modern art/sb's work/a collection/original artwork/drawings/sculptures/a piece 陳列／展出現代藝術品／某人的作品／收藏品／藝術真品／圖畫／雕塑／一件藝術品
- **be displayed/hung** in a gallery/museum 在美術館／博物館展出
- **install/place** a sculpture in/at/on sth 在某處安放一座雕塑
- **erect/unveil** a bronze/marble/life-size statue 豎立／揭幕一座銅像／大理石像／與真人一樣大的雕像
- **hold/host/mount/open/curate/see** (*especially BrE*) an exhibition/(*NAmE usually*) exhibit 舉辦／主持／籌辦／舉行／組織／觀看展覽
- **be/go on** (*BrE*) exhibition/(*NAmE*) exhibit 參展
- **feature/promote/showcase** a conceptual artist/contemporary works 重點介紹／宣傳／展示一位概念派藝術家／當代作品
- **collect** African art/modern British paintings/Japanese prints 收藏非洲藝術品／現代英國繪畫／日本版畫
- **restore/preserve** a fresco/great works of art 修復／保護濕壁畫／偉大的藝術品

A

(= rather difficult). 面試時表現出充滿信心是一門很高的藝術。IDM see FINE *adj.*

■ ***verb thou art*** (*old use*) used to mean 'you are', when talking to one person（即 you are，對一人講話時用）

art deco /ˌɑːt ˈdekəʊ; *NAmE* ˌɑːrt ˈdekoʊ/ (also **Art Deco**) *noun* [U] a popular style of decorative art in the 1920s and 1930s that has GEOMETRIC shapes with clear outlines and bright strong colours 裝飾派藝術（流行於 20 世紀 20 至 30 年代，呈幾何圖形，線條清晰，色彩鮮明）

ˈart director *noun* **1** the person who is responsible for the pictures, photos, etc. in a magazine（雜誌的）美術編輯 **2** the person who is responsible for the SETS and PROPS when a film/movie is being made（電影的）佈景師，美術指導

arte·fact (also **ar·ti·fact** especially in *NAmE*) /ˈɑːtɪfækt; *NAmE* ˈɑːrt-/ *noun* (*technical* 術語) an object that is made by a person, especially sth of historical or cultural interest 人工製品，手工藝品（尤指有歷史或文化價值的）

ar·teri·ole /ɑːˈtɪəriəʊl; *NAmE* ɑːrˈtɪrioʊl/ *noun* (*anatomy* 解) a thin branch of an ARTERY that leads off into CAPILLARIES 小動脈

ar·terio·scler·osis /ɑːˌtɪəriəʊskləˈrəʊsɪs; *NAmE* ɑːrˌtɪrioʊskləˈroʊsɪs/ *noun* [U] (*medical* 醫) a condition in which the walls of the arteries become thick and hard, making it difficult for blood to flow 動脈硬化

ar·tery /ˈɑːtəri; *NAmE* ˈɑːrt-/ *noun* (*pl.* **-ies**) **1** any of the tubes that carry blood from the heart to other parts of the body 動脈：*blocked arteries* 堵塞的動脈 ➲ COLLOCATIONS at ILL ➲ compare VEIN ➲ see also CORONARY ARTERY **2** a large and important road, river, railway/railroad line, etc. 幹線（指主要公路、河流、鐵路線等）▸ **ar·ter·ial** /ɑːˈtɪəriəl; *NAmE* ɑːrˈtɪr-/ *adj.* [only before noun]：***arterial blood/disease*** 動脈血／病 ◇ *an* ***arterial road*** 幹線公路

ar·te·sian well /ɑːˌtiːziən ˈwel; *NAmE* ɑːrˈtiːʒn/ *noun* a hole made in the ground through which water rises to the surface by natural pressure 自流井

ˈart form *noun* **1** [C] a particular type of artistic activity 藝術形式：*The short story is a difficult art form to master.* 短篇小說是一種很難掌握的藝術形式。**2** [sing.] an activity that sb does very well and gives them the opportunity to show imagination 擅長且可發揮想像力的活動：*She has elevated the dinner party into an art form.* 她把宴會辦得猶如一種藝術。

art·ful /ˈɑːtfl; *NAmE* ˈɑːrtfl/ *adj.* [usually before noun] **1** (*disapproving*) clever at getting what you want, sometimes by not telling the truth 施展巧計的；取巧的 SYN **crafty** **2** (of things or actions 事物或行動) designed or done in a clever way 精巧的；巧妙的 ▸ **art·ful·ly** /-fəli/ *adv.*

ˈart gallery (also **gal·lery**) *noun* a building where paintings and other works of art are shown to the public 美術館；藝術展覽館

ˌart ˈhistory *noun* [U] the study of the history of painting, SCULPTURE, etc. 藝術史

ˈart-house *adj.* [only before noun] **art-house** films/movies are usually made by small companies and are not usually seen by a wide audience（電影）實驗性的，不公開放映的

arth·ri·tic /ɑːˈθrɪtɪk; *NAmE* ɑːrˈθ-/ *adj.* suffering from or caused by arthritis 患關節炎的；關節炎引起的：***arthritic hands/pain*** 患關節炎的手；關節炎引起的疼痛

arth·ritis /ɑːˈθraɪtɪs; *NAmE* ɑːrˈθ-/ *noun* [U] a disease that causes pain and swelling in one or more joints of the body 關節炎 ➲ see also OSTEOARTHRITIS, RHEUMATOID ARTHRITIS

arthro·pod /ˈɑːθrəpɒd; *NAmE* ˈɑːrθrəpɑːd/ *noun* (*biology* 生) an INVERTEBRATE animal such as an insect, spider, or CRAB, that has its SKELETON on the outside of its body and has joints on its legs 節肢動物

Ar·thur·ian /ɑːˈθjʊəriən; *NAmE* ɑːrˈθʊr-/ *adj.* connected with the stories about Arthur, a king of ancient Britain, his Knights of the Round Table and COURT at Camelot 亞瑟王（及騎士和朝臣）故事的：*Arthurian legends* 亞瑟王傳奇故事

ar·ti·choke /ˈɑːtɪtʃəʊk; *NAmE* ˈɑːrtətʃoʊk/ *noun* [C, U] **1** (also ˌ**globe ˈarti·choke**) a round vegetable with a lot of thick green leaves. The bottom part of the leaves and the inside of the artichoke can be eaten when cooked. 洋薊，球薊（圓形蔬菜，綠色厚葉基部及莖內部均可食用）➲ VISUAL VOCAB page V31 **2** (*BrE*) = JERUSALEM ARTICHOKE

art·icle 🔑 /ˈɑːtɪkl; *NAmE* ˈɑːrt-/ *noun*
1 🔑 ~ (**on/about sth**) a piece of writing about a particular subject in a newspaper or magazine（報刊上的）文章，論文，報道：*Have you seen that article about young fashion designers?* 你見到了關於年輕時裝設計師的那篇文章沒有？➲ see also LEADING ARTICLE **2** 🔑 (*law* 律) a separate item in an agreement or a contract（協議、契約的）條款，項：*Article 10 of the European Convention guarantees free speech.*《歐洲公約》第 10 條保障言論自由。**3** 🔑 (*formal*) a particular item or separate thing, especially one of a set 物件，物品（尤指整套中的一件）SYN **item**：*articles of clothing* 衣物 ◇ *toilet articles such as soap and shampoo* 諸如肥皂和洗髮劑之類的梳妝用品 ◇ *The articles found in the car helped the police to identify the body.* 在汽車上發現的物品有助於警方辨認死者身分。**4** (*grammar* 語法) the words *a* and *an* (**the indefinite article**) or *the* (**the definite article**) 冠詞（a 和 an 為不定冠詞，the 為定冠詞）

art·icled /ˈɑːtɪkld; *NAmE* ˈɑːrt-/ *adj.* (*BrE*) employed by a group of lawyers, ARCHITECTS or ACCOUNTANTS while training to become qualified 簽約給（律師、建築師、會計師）當實習生的：*an articled clerk* (= sb who is training to be a SOLICITOR) 見習律師 ◇ *She* ***was articled to*** *a firm of solicitors.* 她與律師事務所簽了約當見習律師。

ˌarticle of ˈfaith *noun* (*pl.* **articles of faith**) something you believe very strongly, as if it were a religious belief 信條；信念

ar·ticu·late *verb*, *adj.*
■ ***verb*** /ɑːˈtɪkjuleɪt; *NAmE* ɑːrˈt-/ **1** [T] ~ **sth** (**to sb**) (*formal*) to express or explain your thoughts or feelings clearly in words 明確表達；清楚說明：*She struggled to articulate her thoughts.* 她竭力表明她的想法。**2** [I, T] to speak, pronounce or play sth in a clear way 口齒清楚；清晰吐（詞）；清晰發（音）：*He was too drunk to articulate properly.* 他醉得連話都說不清楚。◇ ~ **sth** *Every note was carefully articulated.* 每個音都唱得很認真，很清楚。**3** [I] ~ (**with sth**) (*formal*) to be related to sth so that together the two parts form a whole 與…合成整體：*These courses are designed to articulate with university degrees.* 這些課程旨在與大學學位接軌。**4** [I, T] (*technical* 術語) to be joined to sth else by a joint, so that movement is possible; to join sth in this way 用關節連接；鏈合；鉸接：~ (**with sth**) *bones that articulate with others* 與其他骨骼以關節相連的骨骼 ◇ ~ **sth** *a robot with articulated limbs* 關節型四肢機器人
■ ***adj.*** /ɑːˈtɪkjələt; *NAmE* ɑːrˈt-/ **1** (of a person 人) good at expressing ideas or feelings clearly in words 善於表達的 **2** (of speech 說話) clearly expressed or pronounced 口齒清楚的；發音清晰的：*All we could hear were loud sobs, but no articulate words.* 我們聽到的只是大聲啜泣，沒有清楚的話語。OPP **inarticulate** ▸ **ar·ticu·late·ly** *adv.*

ar·ticu·lated /ɑːˈtɪkjuleɪtɪd; *NAmE* ɑːrˈt-/ *adj.* (*BrE*) (of a vehicle 車輛) with two or more sections joined together in a way that makes it easier to turn corners 鉸接的：*an* ***articulated lorry/truck*** 鉸接式卡車 ➲ VISUAL VOCAB page V57 ➲ see also TRACTOR-TRAILER

ar·ticu·la·tion /ɑːˌtɪkjuˈleɪʃn; *NAmE* ɑːrˌt-/ *noun* **1** [U] (*formal*) the expression of an idea or a feeling in words（思想感情的）表達：*the articulation of his theory* 他的理論的表述 **2** [U] (*formal*) the act of making sounds in speech or music 說話；吐詞；發音：*The singer worked hard on the clear articulation of every note.* 歌手苦練每一個音都唱得清晰。**3** [U, C, usually sing.] (*technical* 術語) a joint or connection that allows movement 關節；關節連接；鉸接式接頭

A

ar·ti·fact (*especially NAmE*) = ARTEFACT

ar·ti·fice /ˈɑːtɪfɪs; *NAmE* ˈɑːrt-/ *noun* [U, C] (*formal*) the clever use of tricks to cheat sb 詭計；奸計 **SYN** **cunning**

ar·ti·fi·cial /ˌɑːtɪˈfɪʃl; *NAmE* ˌɑːrt-/ *adj.* **1** made or produced to copy sth natural; not real 人工的；人造的；假的：*an **artificial limb/flower/sweetener/fertilizer*** 假肢；假花；人造甜味劑；化肥 ◇ ***artificial lighting/light*** 人工照明；人造光 **2** created by people; not happening naturally 人為的；非自然的：*A job interview is a very artificial situation.* 求職面試是一個相當不自然的場面。◇ *the artificial barriers of race, class and gender* 種族、階級、性別的人為障礙 **3** not what it appears to be 虛假的；假裝的 **SYN** **fake**：*artificial emotion* 假裝的情感 ▸ **ar·ti·fi·ci·al·ity** /ˌɑːtɪˌfɪʃiˈæləti; *NAmE* ˌɑːrt-/ *noun* [U] **ar·ti·fi·cial·ly** /ˌɑːtɪˈfɪʃəli; *NAmE* ˌɑːrt-/ *adv.*：*artificially created lakes* 人工湖泊 ◇ *artificially low prices* 人為壓低的價格

Synonyms 同義詞辨析

artificial

synthetic • false • man-made • fake • imitation

These words all describe things that are not real, or not naturally produced or grown. 以上各詞均指假的、非天然的、人造的。

artificial made or produced to copy sth natural; not real 指人工的、人造的、假的：*artificial flowers* 假花 ◇ *artificial light* 人造光

synthetic made by combining chemical substances rather than being produced naturally by plants or animals 指人工合成的：*synthetic drugs* 合成藥物 ◇ *shoes with synthetic soles* 合成鞋底的鞋

false not natural 指非天然的、非天生的、假的：*false teeth* 假牙 ◇ *a false beard* 假鬍子

man-made made by people; not natural 指人造的、非天然的：*man-made fibres such as nylon* 尼龍之類的人造纖維

fake made to look like sth else; not real 指偽造的、冒充的、假的：*a fake-fur jacket* 一件人造毛皮的短上衣

imitation [only before noun] made to look like sth else; not real 指仿製的、人造的、假的：*She would never wear imitation pearls.* 她絕不會戴假珍珠。

PATTERNS

- artificial/synthetic/man-made **fabrics/fibres/materials/products**
- artificial/synthetic/fake/imitation **fur/leather**
- artificial/synthetic/false/fake/imitation **diamonds/pearls**

ˌartificial inseminˈation *noun* [U] (*abbr.* **AI**) the process of making a woman or female animal pregnant by an artificial method of putting male SPERM inside her, and not by sexual activity 人工授精：*artificial insemination by a donor, abbreviated to 'AID'* 非配偶人工授精（縮寫為 AID）

ˌartificial inˈtelligence *noun* [U] (*abbr.* **AI**) (*computing* 計) an area of study concerned with making computers copy intelligent human behaviour 人工智能；人工智慧

ˌartificial ˈlanguage *noun* a language invented for international communication or for use with computers（為國際交流目的的）人造語言；（用於計算機的）人工語言

ˌartificial respiˈration (*BrE* also **ˌartificial ventiˈlation**) *noun* [U] the process of helping a person who has stopped breathing begin to breathe again, usually by blowing into their mouth or nose 人工呼吸 ➲ compare MOUTH-TO-MOUTH RESUSCITATION

ar·til·lery /ɑːˈtɪləri; *NAmE* ɑːrˈt-/ *noun* **1** [U] large, heavy guns which are often moved on wheels（統稱）火炮：*The town is under heavy artillery fire.* 該市鎮處於密集的炮火之下。**2 the artillery** [sing.] the section of an army trained to use these guns 炮兵部隊

ar·ti·san /ˌɑːtɪˈzæn; *NAmE* ˈɑːrtəzn/ *noun* (*formal*) a person who does skilled work, making things with their hands 工匠；手藝人 **SYN** **craftsman**

art·ist /ˈɑːtɪst; *NAmE* ˈɑːrt-/ *noun* **1** a person who creates works of art, especially paintings or drawings 藝術家；（尤指）畫家：*an exhibition of work by contemporary British artists* 當代英國畫家作品展 ◇ *a graphic artist* 平面造型藝術家 ◇ *a make-up artist* 化妝師 ◇ *Police have issued an artist's impression of her attacker.* 警方公佈了襲擊她的人的模擬像。◇ (*figurative*) *Whoever made this cake is a real artist.* 製作這個蛋糕的人真是個藝術大師。➲ COLLOCATIONS at ART **2** (*especially BrE* **ar·tiste** /ɑːˈtiːst; *NAmE* ɑːrˈt-/) a professional entertainer such as a singer, a dancer or an actor 專業演員；藝人：*a **recording/solo artist*** 音像錄製藝術師；單人表演演員

ar·tis·tic /ɑːˈtɪstɪk; *NAmE* ɑːrˈt-/ *adj.* **1** connected with art or artists 藝術的；藝術家的：*the artistic works of the period* 該時期的藝術品 ◇ *a work of great artistic merit* 藝術價值很高的作品 ◇ *the artistic director of the theatre* 劇院藝術總監 **2** showing a natural skill in or enjoyment of art, especially being able to paint or draw well 有藝術天賦的；（尤指）有美術才能的：***artistic abilities/achievements/skills/talent*** 藝術才能／成就／技巧／天才 ◇ *She comes from a very artistic family.* 她出身於藝術世家。**3** done with skill and imagination; attractive or beautiful 有藝術性的；精美的：*an artistic arrangement of dried flowers* 富有藝術性的乾花插花 **IDM** see LICENCE ▸ **ar·tis·tic·al·ly** /ɑːˈtɪstɪkli; *NAmE* ɑːrˈt-/ *adv.*

arˌtistic diˈrector *noun* the person in charge of deciding which plays, OPERAS, etc. a theatre company will perform, and the general artistic policy of the company（劇團）藝術總監

art·is·try /ˈɑːtɪstri; *NAmE* ˈɑːrt-/ *noun* [U] the skill of an artist 藝術技巧：*He played the piece with effortless artistry.* 他遊刃有餘地演奏了這首樂曲。

art·less /ˈɑːtləs; *NAmE* ˈɑːrt-/ *adj.* (*formal*) **1** simple, natural and honest 天真的；直率的：*the artless sincerity of a young child* 幼童的天真爛漫 **2** made without skill or art 缺乏藝術性的；拙劣的

art nou·veau /ˌɑː(t) nuːˈvəʊ; *NAmE* ˌɑːr(t) nuːˈvoʊ/ (also **Art Nouveau**) *noun* [U] a style of decorative art and ARCHITECTURE popular in Europe and the US at the end of the 19th century and beginning of the 20th century that uses complicated designs and curved patterns based on natural shapes like leaves and flowers 新藝術（19 世紀末 20 世紀初流行於歐洲和美國的裝飾藝術和建築風格，採用基於花、葉等自然形狀的複雜設計和曲線圖案）

ˌarts and ˈcrafts *noun* [pl.] activities that need both artistic and practical skills, such as making cloth, jewellery and POTTERY 手工藝

artsy /ˈɑːtsi; *NAmE* ˈɑːrtsi/ (*NAmE*) (*BrE* **arty**) *adj.* (*informal*, usually *disapproving*) seeming or wanting to be very artistic or interested in the arts 附庸風雅的；似乎愛好藝術的

artsy-fartsy /ˌɑːtsi ˈfɑːtsi; *NAmE* ˌɑːrtsi ˈfɑːrtsi/ (*especially NAmE*) (*BrE* **arty-farty**) *adj.* (*informal, disapproving*) connected with, or having an interest in, the arts 附庸風雅的

ˌart ˈtherapy *noun* [U] a type of PSYCHOTHERAPY in which you are encouraged to express yourself using art materials 藝術治療（通過藝術形式表達自我以達到治療效果的心理療法）

art·work /ˈɑːtwɜːk; *NAmE* ˈɑːrtwɜːrk/ *noun* **1** [U] photographs and pictures prepared for books, magazines, etc.（書刊等上的）插圖，圖片 **2** [C] a work of art, especially one in a museum（尤指博物館裏的）藝術作品

arty /ˈɑːti; *NAmE* ˈɑːrti/ (*BrE*) (*NAmE* **artsy**) *adj.* (*informal*, usually *disapproving*) seeming or wanting to be very

A

artistic or interested in the arts 附庸風雅的；似乎愛好藝術的： *She hangs out with the arty types she met at drama school.* 她和一些在戲劇學校認識的附庸風雅的朋友常混在一起。

arty-farty /ˌɑːti ˈfɑːti; *NAmE* ˌɑːrti ˈfɑːrti/ (*BrE*) (*especially NAmE* **ˌartsy-ˈfartsy**) *adj.* (*informal, disapproving*) connected with, or having an interest in, the arts 附庸風雅的：*I expect he's out with his arty-farty friends.* 我想他去會他那幫玩藝術的朋友了。

aru·gula /æˈruːɡjʊlə/ (*NAmE*) (*BrE* **rocket**) *noun* [U] a plant with long green leaves that have a strong flavour and are eaten raw in salads 芝麻菜；火箭生菜

arum lily /ˈeərəm lɪli; *NAmE* ˈerəm/ *noun* (*especially BrE*) an African plant with large white PETALS 馬蹄蓮；水芋；海芋

arvo /ˈɑːvəʊ; *NAmE* ˈɑːrvoʊ/ *noun* (*pl.* **-os**) (*AustralE, NZE, informal*) afternoon 下午；午後： *See you this arvo!* 下午見！

-ary *suffix* (in adjectives and nouns 構成形容詞和名詞) connected with 與…有關（的）： *planetary* 行星的 ◇ *budgetary* 預算的

Aryan /ˈeəriən; *NAmE* ˈer-/ *noun* **1** a member of the group of people that went to S Asia in around 1500 BC 雅利安人（公元前 1 500 年前後到南亞） **2** a person who spoke any of the languages of the Indo-European group 講印歐系語言的人 **3** (especially according to the ideas of the German Nazi party) a member of a Caucasian, not Jewish, race of people, especially one with fair hair and blue eyes 屬於雅利安人種的人（尤指德國納粹黨認為的非猶太民族白種人） ▸ **Aryan** *adj.*

AS ➲ AS (LEVEL)

Which Word? 詞語辨析

as / like

You can use both **as** and **like** to say that things are similar. * as 和 like 均可表示相似。

- **Like** is a preposition and is used before nouns and pronouns. * like 為介詞，置於名詞和代詞前： *He has blue eyes like me.* 他和我一樣有雙藍眼睛。
- **As** is a conjunction and an adverb and is used before a clause, another adverb or a clause beginning with a preposition. * as 為連詞和副詞，置於從句、另一副詞或以介詞引導的從句前： *She enjoys all kinds of music, as I do.* 她和我一樣什麼音樂都喜歡。◇ *Repeat these five steps, as in the last exercise.* 照前面的練習一樣，重複這五個步驟。
- In informal English **like** is frequently used as a conjunction or an adverb instead of **as**. 在非正式英語中，like 常常代替 as，用作連詞或副詞： *Nobody understands him like I do.* 誰都不像我那麼瞭解他。◇ *I don't want to upset him again like before.* 我不願意再像過去那樣使他掃興。 It is also used instead of **as if**. * like 亦可用以代替 as if： *It looks like we're going to be late.* 看來我們要遲到了。 These uses of **like** are common but are not considered correct in formal written English. * like 的這類用法很常見，但在規範的書面英語中並不認為正確。

You will find more help on the use of **as** and **like** in the entries for particular verbs, such as *act, behave*, etc. 關於 as 和 like 的其他用法，參見 act、behave 等動詞詞條。

as 🗝 /əz; *strong form* æz/ *prep., adv., conj.*

■ ***prep.*** **1** 🗝 used to describe sb/sth appearing to be sb/sth else 像；如同： *They were all dressed as clowns.* 他們都打扮成小丑。◇ *The bomb was disguised as a package.* 炸彈偽裝成一個包裹。 **2** 🗝 used to describe the fact that sb/sth has a particular job or function 作為；當作： *She works as a courier.* 她的職業是導遊。◇ *Treat me as a friend.* 要把我當作朋友。◇ *I respect him as a doctor.* 我尊敬他這個醫生。◇ *You can use that glass as a vase.* 你可以把那個玻璃杯當作花瓶用。◇ *The news came as a shock.* 消息傳來，令人震驚。◇ *She had been there often as a child* (= when she was a child). 她小時候常去那裏。

■ ***adv.*** **1** 🗝 **as … as …** used when you are comparing two people or things, or two situations（比較時用）像…一樣，如同： *You're as tall as your father.* 你和你父親一樣高。◇ *He was as white as a sheet.* 他面無血色。◇ *She doesn't play as well as her sister.* 她演奏得不如她姐姐。◇ *I haven't known him as long as you* (= as you have known him). 我認識他的時間沒有你長。◇ *He doesn't earn as much as me.* 他掙的錢比我少。◇ *He doesn't earn as much as I do.* 他掙的錢不如我多。◇ *It's not as hard as I thought.* 這沒有我想像的那麼困難。◇ *Run as fast as you can.* 你盡量快跑。◇ *We'd like it as soon as possible.* 我們希望越快越好。 **2** 🗝 used to say that sth happens in the same way（指事情以同樣的方式發生）和…一樣： *As always, he said little.* 他和平時一樣，少言寡語。◇ *The 'h' in honest is silent, as in 'hour'.* * honest 中的 h 與 hour 中的 h 一樣都不發音。

■ ***conj.*** **1** 🗝 while sth else is happening 當…時；隨着： *He sat watching her as she got ready.* 他一直坐着看她準備停當。◇ *As she grew older she gained in confidence.* 隨着年齡的增長她的信心增強了。 ➲ LANGUAGE BANK at PROCESS **2** 🗝 in the way in which 照…方式： *They did as I had asked.* 他們是按照我的要求做的。◇ *Leave the papers as they are.* 別去動那些文件。◇ *She lost it, just as I said she would.* 我就說了吧，她把它丟失了。 **3** 🗝 used to state the reason for sth 因為；由於： *As you were out, I left a message.* 你不在，所以我留了一張字條兒。◇ *She may need some help as she's new.* 她是新來的，可能需要一些幫助。 **4** used to make a comment or to add information about what you have just said 正如；如同： *As you know, Julia is leaving soon.* 你是知道的，朱莉婭馬上要離開了。◇ *She's very tall, as is her mother.* 她個子很高，和她母親一樣。 **5** used to say that in spite of sth being true, what follows is also true 儘管；雖然；即使 **SYN** **though** ： *Happy as they were, there was something missing.* 儘管他們很快樂，但總缺少點什麼。◇ *Try as he might* (= however hard he tried), *he couldn't open the door.* 他想盡了辦法也沒能打開門。

IDM **as against sth** in contrast with sth 與…相對照；和…相比較： *They got 27% of the vote as against 32% at the last election.* 這次選舉他們得了 27% 的票，而上次他們得了 32%。 **ˌas and ˈwhen** used to say that sth may happen at some time in the future, but only when sth else has happened（用於在特定條件下才會發生的事情）將來…時，到時候： *We'll decide on the team as and when we qualify.* 將來我們具備了條件時就會決定成立這個隊。◇ *I'll tell you more as and when* (= as soon as I can). 我一有可能就會告訴你更多情況。 **as for sb/sth** 🗝 used to start talking about sb/sth 至於；關於 **SYN** **regarding** ： *As for Jo, she's doing fine.* 至於喬，她現在日子過得不錯。◇ *As for food for the party, that's all being taken care of.* 關於聚會要用的食物，都在置辦當中。 **as from …/as of …** used to show the time or date from which sth starts（指起始時間或日期）自…起： *Our fax number is changing as from May 12.* 我們的傳真號碼自 5 月 12 日起更改。 **as if/as though** 🗝 in a way that suggests sth 似乎；好像；彷彿： *He behaved as if nothing had happened.* 他表現得若無其事。◇ *It sounds as though you had a good time.* 聽起來你好像過得挺愉快。◇ *It's my birthday. As if you didn't know!* 今天是我的生日。你好像不知道似的！◇ *'Don't say anything.' '*As if I would!*'* (= surely you do not expect me to) "什麼也別說。" "我才不會說呢！" **ˌas it ˈis** considering the present situation; as things are 照現狀： *We were hoping to finish it by next week—as it is, it may be the week after.* 我們本希望在下週完成，看樣子可能要下下週才行。◇ *I can't help—I've got too much to do as it is* (= already). 我幫不了忙，我已經有太多的工作了。 **as it ˈwere** used when a speaker is giving his or her own impression of a situation or expressing sth in a particular way 可以說；在一定程度上： *Teachers must put the brakes on, as it were, when they notice students looking puzzled.* 當老師發現學生神色茫然時，就應該在一定程度上放慢速度。 **as to sth | as regards sth** used when you are referring to sth 關於；至於： *As to tax, that will be deducted from your salary.* 至於稅款，將從

你薪水中扣除。**as you 'do** used as a comment on sth that you have just said（對剛說過的話的評論）：*He smiled and I smiled back. As you do.* 他微笑，我也報以微笑。真所謂禮尚往來。➲ more at WELL *adv.*, YET *adv.*

ASA /ˌeɪ es ˈeɪ/ *abbr.* **1** Advertising Standards Authority (an organization in Britain that controls the standard of advertising)（英國）廣告標準局 **2** American Standards Association (used especially to show the speed of film) 美國標準協會（尤用於額定膠片感光度）：*a 400 ASA film* 美國標準 400 度膠片

asap /ˌeɪ es eɪ ˈpiː/ *abbr.* as soon as possible 儘快

as·bes·tos /æsˈbestəs/ *noun* [U] a soft grey mineral that does not burn, used especially in the past in building as a protection against fire or to prevent heat loss 石棉

as·bes·tosis /ˌæsbesˈtəʊsɪs; *NAmE* -ˈtoʊ-/ *noun* [U] a disease of the lungs caused by breathing in asbestos dust 石棉沉着病，石棉肺（因吸入石棉粉塵引起的肺病）

ASBO /ˈæzbəʊ; *NAmE* -boʊ/ *noun* the abbreviation for 'antisocial behaviour order' (in the UK, an order made by a court which says that sb must stop behaving in a harmful or annoying way to other people) 反社會行為令（全寫為 antisocial behaviour order，由英國法院發出的對傷害或騷擾他人行為的禁令）

as·cend /əˈsend/ *verb* [I, T] (*formal*) to rise; to go up; to climb up 上升；升高；登高：*The path started to ascend more steeply.* 小徑開始陡峭而上。◇ *The air became colder as we ascended.* 隨着我們往上攀登，空氣就寒冷起來。◇ *The results, ranked* ***in ascending order*** (= from the lowest to the highest) *are as follows:* 結果按由低到高的順序排列如下：◇ **~ from sth** *Mist ascended from the valley.* 薄霧從山谷升起。◇ **~ to sth** (*figurative*) *He ascended to the peak of sporting achievement.* 他達到了運動成就的頂峰。◇ **~ sth** *Her heart was thumping as she ascended the stairs.* 她上樓梯時，心怦怦跳個不停。◇ (*figurative*) *to ascend the throne* (= become king or queen) 登基 **OPP descend**

as·cend·ancy (also **as·cend·ency**) /əˈsendənsi/ *noun* [U] **~ (over sb/sth)** (*formal*) the position of having power or influence over sb/sth 支配地位；優勢；影響：***moral/political/intellectual ascendancy*** 道德影響；政治支配地位；智力優勢 ◇ *The opposition party was* ***in the ascendancy*** (= gaining control). 反對黨已漸佔優勢。

as·cend·ant (also **as·cend·ent**) /əˈsendənt/ *noun*
IDM **in the ascendant** (*formal*) being or becoming more powerful or popular（權力、影響等）越來越大；日益受歡迎

as·cen·sion /əˈsenʃn/ *noun* [sing.] **1 the Ascension** (in the Christian religion 基督教) the journey of Jesus from the earth into heaven 耶穌升天 **2** (*formal*) the act of moving up or of reaching a high position 上升；升高；登上：*her ascension to the throne* 她的登基

Asˈcension Day *noun* (in the Christian religion 基督教) the 40th day after Easter when Christians remember when Jesus left the earth and went into heaven 耶穌升天節（復活節後的第 40 天）

as·cent /əˈsent/ *noun* **1** [C, usually sing.] the act of climbing or moving up; an upward journey 上升；升高；登高：*the first ascent of Mount Everest* 首次攀登珠穆朗瑪峰 ◇ *The cart began its gradual ascent up the hill.* 運貨馬車開始緩緩上山。◇ *The rocket steepened its ascent.* 火箭飛速升空。**OPP descent** **2** [C, usually sing.] an upward path or slope 上坡；上坡路：*At the other side of the valley was a steep ascent to the top of the hill.* 山谷的那邊是直達山頂的陡坡。**OPP descent** **3** [U] (*formal*) the process of moving forward to a better position or of making progress 前進；提高；進步：*man's ascent to civilization* 人類向文明的進化

as·cer·tain /ˌæsəˈteɪn; *NAmE* ˌæsərˈt-/ *verb* (*formal*) to find out the true or correct information about sth 查明；弄清：**~ sth** *It can be difficult to ascertain the facts.* 可能難以查明事實真相。◇ **~ that …** *I ascertained that the driver was not badly hurt.* 我已查清，駕駛員傷勢不重。◇ **it is ascertained that …** ***It should be ascertained that*** *the plans comply with the law.* 須要弄清楚，這些計劃要合法。◇ **~ what, whether, etc. …** *The police are trying to ascertain what really happened.* 警方正設法查清到底發生了什麼事。◇ *Could you ascertain whether she will be coming to the meeting?* 請你弄清楚她來不來開會好嗎？◇ **it is ascertained what, whether, etc. …** ***It must be ascertained*** *if the land is still owned by the government.* 必須確定這塊土地是否仍屬於政府所有。▸ **as·cer·tain·able** /ˌæsəˈteɪnəbl; *NAmE* ˌæsərˈt-/ *adj.* **as·cer·tain·ment** /ˌæsəˈteɪnmənt; *NAmE* ˌæsərˈt-/ *noun* [U]

as·cet·ic /əˈsetɪk/ *adj.* [usually before noun] not allowing yourself physical pleasures, especially for religious reasons; related to a simple and strict way of living 過清苦生活的；（尤指）苦行的；禁慾的：*The monks lived a very ascetic life.* 僧侶過着很清苦的生活。▸ **as·cet·ic** *noun*：*monks, hermits and ascetics* 僧侶、隱士和苦行者 **as·ceti·cism** /əˈsetɪsɪzəm/ *noun* [U]

ASCII /ˈæski/ *noun* [U] (*computing* 計) the abbreviation for 'American Standard Code for Information Interchange' (a standard code used so that data can be moved between computers that use different programs) 美國信息交換用標準代碼（全寫為 American Standard Code for Information Interchange，使用不同程序的計算機可互相傳送數據的一種標準碼）

as·cor·bic acid /əsˌkɔːbɪk ˈæsɪd; *NAmE* -ˌkɔːrb-/ *noun* [U] = VITAMIN C

ascot /ˈæskɒt; *NAmE* ˈæskɑːt/ *noun* (*NAmE*) = CRAVAT

ascribe /əˈskraɪb/ *verb*
PHR V **aˈscribe sth to sb** to consider or state that a book, etc. was written by a particular person 認為…是（某人）所寫 **SYN attribute**：*This play is usually ascribed to Shakespeare.* 通常認為這部劇是莎士比亞所寫。**aˈscribe sth to sb/sth** (*formal*) **1** to consider that sth is caused by a particular thing or person 把…歸因於；認為…是由於：*He ascribed his failure to bad luck.* 他認為自己的失敗是運氣不好。**2** to consider that sb/sth has or should have a particular quality 認為…具有 **SYN attribute**：*We ascribe great importance to these policies.* 我們認為這些政策十分重要。▸ **ascrib·able** *adj.*：**~ to sb/sth** *Their success is ascribable to the quality of their goods.* 他們的成功在於商品的質量。**ascrip·tion** /əˈskrɪpʃn/ *noun* [U, C]：**~ (to sb/sth)** *the ascription of meaning to objects and events* 事物所賦有的內涵

ASEAN /ˈæsiæn/ *abbr.* Association of South East Asian Nations 東盟；東南亞國家聯盟

asep·tic /ˌeɪˈseptɪk/ *adj.* (*medical* 醫) free from harmful bacteria 無（病）菌的 **OPP septic**

asex·ual /ˌeɪˈsekʃuəl/ *adj.* **1** (*technical* 術語) not involving sex; not having sexual organs 無性的；無性器官的：*asexual reproduction* 無性生殖 **2** not having sexual qualities; not interested in sex 性缺乏的；性冷淡的：*the tendency to see old people as asexual* 認為老年人性缺乏的傾向 ▸ **asex·ual·ly** *adv.*：*to reproduce asexually* 無性生殖

ASH /æʃ/ *abbr.* Action on Smoking and Health (an organization in the UK that tries to make people stop smoking by showing how dangerous it is) 吸煙與健康行動組織，英國控煙組織（通過說明吸煙的危害性倡導戒煙）

ash /æʃ/ *noun* **1** [U] the grey or black powder that is left after sth, especially TOBACCO, wood or coal, has burnt 灰；灰燼：*cigarette ash* 香煙灰 ◇ *black volcanic ash* 黑色火山灰 **2 ashes** [pl.] what is left after sth has been destroyed by burning 灰燼；廢墟：*The town was reduced to ashes in the fighting.* 在戰鬥中這座城鎮已化為灰燼。◇ *the glowing ashes of the campfire* 營火剩下的灼熱餘燼 ◇ (*figurative*) *The party had risen, like a phoenix, from the ashes of electoral disaster.* 該黨像長生鳥一樣，從選舉慘敗的灰燼中重新崛起。**3 ashes** [pl.] the powder that is left after a dead person's body has been CREMATED (= burned) 骨灰：*She wanted her ashes to be scattered at sea.* 她希望自己的骨灰撒向大海。**4** [C, U] (also **ˈash tree**) a forest tree with grey BARK 梣；白蠟樹 ➲ VISUAL VOCAB page V10 ➲ see also MOUNTAIN ASH **5** [U] the hard pale wood of the ash tree 梣木 **6** (*technical* 術語) the letter æ, used in Old English, and

A

as a PHONETIC symbol to represent the vowel sound in *cat* * æ（古英語的一個字母，也為音標，表示如 cat 一詞中的元音）IDM see SACKCLOTH

ashamed /əˈʃeɪmd/ *adj.* [not before noun]
1 feeling shame or embarrassment about sb/sth or because of sth you have done 慚愧；羞愧；尷尬： **~ of sth** *She was deeply ashamed of her behaviour at the party.* 她對自己在聚會上的行為深感羞愧。◇ *Mental illness is **nothing to be ashamed of**.* 精神病並不羞愧。◇ **~ of sb** *His daughter looked such a mess that he was ashamed of her.* 他為女兒一副邋遢的樣子感到羞慚。◇ **~ of yourself** *You should be ashamed of yourself for telling such lies.* 你扯這種謊應該感到羞恥。◇ **~ that …** *I feel almost ashamed that I've been so lucky.* 真有點不好意思，我太幸運了。◇ **~ to be sth** *The football riots made me ashamed to be English.* 足球騷亂事件使我身為英國人汗顏得無地自容。 **2** **~ to do sth** unwilling to do sth because of shame or embarrassment 因慚愧而不情願；因尷尬而勉強： *I'm **ashamed to say** that I lied to her.* 我真不好意思說我向她撒了謊。◇ *I cried at the end and I'm not ashamed to admit it.* 最後我哭了，我並不恥於承認哭過。

Which Word? 詞語辨析

ashamed / embarrassed

- You feel **ashamed** when you feel guilty because of something wrong that you have deliberately done. 因明知故犯而感到羞愧用 ashamed： *You should be ashamed of treating your daughter like that.* 你這樣對待自己的女兒應該感到羞愧。Do not use **ashamed** when you are talking about something that is not very serious or important. 不很嚴重或不很重要的事情不要用 ashamed： *I am sorry that I forgot to buy the milk.* 對不起，我忘了買牛奶。◇ ~~*I am ashamed that I forgot to buy the milk.*~~
- You feel **embarrassed** when you have made a mistake or done something stupid or feel awkward in front of other people. 犯了錯誤、幹了傻事或在他人面前感到難為情用 embarrassed： *I was embarrassed about forgetting his name.* 我把他的名字忘了，感到尷尬。

ˌash ˈblonde *adj., noun*
■ *adj.* (also **ˌash ˈblond**) **1** (of hair 頭髮) very pale blonde in colour 淡褐色的 **2** (of a person 人) having ash blonde hair 頭髮淡褐色的
■ *noun* a woman with hair that is ash blonde in colour 頭髮淡褐色的女子 ➲ see also BLONDE

ashen /ˈæʃn/ *adj.* (usually of sb's face 通常指臉) very pale; without colour because of illness or fear 面色蒼白的；沒有血色的： *They listened ashen-faced to the news.* 他們聽着消息時面如死灰。◇ *His face was ashen and wet with sweat.* 他面如土色，汗如雨下。

Ash·ken·azi /ˌæʃkəˈnɑːzi/ *noun* (*pl.* **Ash·ken·azim** /-ɪm/) a Jew whose ANCESTORS came from central or eastern Europe（德系）猶太人（祖先居住在歐洲中部或東部）➲ compare SEPHARDI

ashore /əˈʃɔː(r)/ *adv.* towards, onto or on land, having come from an area of water such as the sea or a river 向（或在）岸上；向（或在）陸地： *to **come/go ashore*** ◇ *a drowned body found washed ashore on the beach* 沖到海灘上被人發現的一具溺水者屍體 ◇ *The cruise included several days ashore.* 這次航行包括幾天陸上行程。

ash·ram /ˈæʃrəm/ *noun* a place where Hindus who wish to live away from society live together as a group; a place where other Hindus go for a short time to say prayers before returning to society（印度教徒的）靜修處，隱修處

ash·tray /ˈæʃtreɪ/ *noun* a container into which people who smoke put ASH, cigarette ends, etc. 煙灰缸

ˌAsh ˈWednesday *noun* [U, C] the first day of Lent 聖灰星期三（基督教四旬期首日）➲ see also SHROVE TUESDAY

Asia Minor /ˌeɪʃə ˈmaɪnə(r)/ *noun* [sing.] the western PENINSULA of Asia, which now forms most of Turkey 小亞細亞（亞洲西部半島，現構成土耳其大部份國土）

Asian /ˈeɪʃn; ˈeɪʒn/ *noun, adj.*
■ *noun* a person from Asia, or whose family originally came from Asia 亞洲人： *British Asians* 英裔亞洲人 HELP In *BrE* **Asian** is used especially to refer to people from India, Pakistan and Bangladesh. In *NAmE* it is used especially to refer to people from the Far East. 英式英語中，Asian 尤指印度人、巴基斯坦人和孟加拉人。美式英語中，Asian 尤指遠東人。
■ *adj.* of or connected with Asia 亞洲的： *Asian music* 亞洲音樂

ˌAsian Aˈmerican *noun* a person from America whose family come from Asia, especially E Asia 亞裔美國人；（尤指）東亞裔美國人 ▶ **ˌAsian-Aˈmerican** *adj.*

Asi·at·ic /ˌeɪʃiˈætɪk; ˌeɪzi-/ *adj.* (*technical* 術語) of or connected with Asia 亞洲的： *the Asiatic tropics* 亞洲熱帶

ˈA-side *noun* the side of a pop record that was considered more likely to be successful（唱片的）A 面（錄有比 B 面可能更受歡迎的歌曲）➲ compare B-SIDE

aside /əˈsaɪd/ *adv., noun*
■ *adv.* **1** to one side; out of the way 到旁邊；在旁邊： *She pulled the curtain aside.* 她把窗簾拉向一邊。◇ ***Stand aside** and let these people pass.* 閃開，讓這些人過去。◇ *He **took me aside*** (= away from a group of people) *to give me some advice.* 他把我拉到一旁，給我出主意。◇ *(figurative)* ***Leaving aside*** (= not considering at this stage) *the cost of the scheme, let us examine its benefits.* 方案的費用暫且不理，咱們來審查方案的好處。◇ *All our protests were **brushed aside*** (= ignored). 我們的一切抗議均被置之不理。 **2** to be used later 留；存： *We **set aside** some money for repairs.* 我們存了一些錢作為修理費用。 **3** used after nouns to say that except for one thing, sth is true（用於名詞後）除…以外： *Money worries aside, things are going well.* 除了錢令人發愁外，事情進展順利。
■ *noun* **1** (in the theatre 戲劇) something that a character in a play says to the audience, but which the other characters on stage are not intended to hear 旁白 **2** a remark, often made in a low voice, which is not intended to be heard by everyone present 低聲說的話 **3** a remark that is not directly connected with the main subject that is being discussed 離題話： *I mention it only as an aside.* 我只是順便提及。

aˈside from *prep.* (*especially NAmE*) = APART FROM： *Aside from a few scratches, I'm OK.* 除了幾處擦傷外，我安然無恙。➲ LANGUAGE BANK at EXCEPT

as·in·ine /ˈæsɪnaɪn/ *adj.* (*formal*) stupid or silly 愚蠢的；笨的 SYN **ridiculous**

ask /ɑːsk; *NAmE* æsk/ *verb, noun*
■ *verb*
▸ **QUESTION** 問題 **1** [I, T] to say or write sth in the form of a question, in order to get information 問；詢問： *How old are you—if you don't **mind me/my asking**?* 要是你不介意我提問，你多大年紀了？◇ **~ about sb/sth** *He asked about her family.* 他詢問了她的家庭情況。◇ **~ sth** *Can I **ask a question**?* 我能提個問題嗎？◇ *Did you ask the price?* 你問了價錢沒有？◇ **+ speech** *'Where are you going?' she asked.* "你去哪裏？"她問道。◇ **~ sb + speech** *'Are you sure?' he asked her.* "你有把握嗎？"他問她。◇ **~ sb sth** *She asked the students their names.* 她問了學生們的姓名。◇ *I often **get asked** that!* 我常常被問到那件事！◇ **~ sb (about sth)** *The interviewer asked me about my future plans.* 採訪者問了我的未來計劃。◇ **~ where, what, etc. …** *He asked where I lived.* 他問我住在哪裏。◇ **~ sb where, what, etc. …** *I had to ask the teacher what to do next.* 我不得不問老師下一步做什麼。◇ *I was asked if/whether I could drive.* 有人問我會不會開車。HELP You cannot say 'ask to sb'. 不能說 ask to sb： ~~*I asked to my friend what had happened.*~~
▸ **REQUEST** 請求 **2** [T] to tell sb that you would like them to do sth or that you would like sth to happen 要求；請求： **~ sb to do sth** *All the students were asked*

to complete a questionnaire. 全體學生都被要求填一份調查表。◊ *Eric asked me to marry him.* 埃里克求我嫁給他。◊ **~ whether, what, etc. …** *I asked whether they could change my ticket.* 我問他們是否可以給我換票。◊ **~ sb whether, what, etc. …** *She asked me if I would give her English lessons.* 她問我願不願意給她上英語課。**~ that …** (*formal*) *She asked that she be kept informed of developments.* 她要求繼續向她報告事態發展情況。◊ (*BrE* also) *She asked that she should be kept informed.* 她要求繼續向她報告有關情況。**3** [I, T] to say that you would like sb to give you sth 請求，懇求（給予）；徵求：**~ for sth** *to ask for a job/a drink/an explanation* 求職；要一杯飲料；要求解釋 ◊ *I am writing to ask for some information about courses.* 我寫信是想瞭解關於課程的情況。◊ **~ sth** *Why don't you ask his advice?* 你為什麼不徵詢他的意見？◊ **~ sb for sth** *Why don't you ask him for his advice?* 你為什麼不徵求他的意見？◊ **~ sth of sb** *Can I ask a favour of you?* 能請你幫個忙嗎？◊ **~ sb sth** *Can I ask you a favour?* 我能請你幫個忙嗎？

▸ **PERMISSION** 准許 **4** [T] to request permission to do sth 請求允許；要求准許：**~ to do sth** *Did you ask to use the car?* 你是提出想用這輛車嗎？◊ *I asked to see the manager.* 我要求見經理。◊ **~ if, whether, etc. …** *I'll ask if it's all right to park here.* 我會問是否可以在這裏停車。◊ **~ sb if, whether, etc. …** *She asked her boss whether she could have the day off.* 她問老闆可不可以讓她請一天假。

▸ **INVITE** 邀請 **5** [T] to invite sb 請；邀請：**~ sb (+ adv./prep.)** *They've asked me to dinner.* 他們已邀請我吃飯。◊ *I didn't ask them in* (= to come into the house). 我沒有請他們進屋。◊ *We must ask the neighbours round* (= to our house). 我們得請鄰居到家裏來。◊ **~ sb to do sth** *She's asked him to come to the party.* 她已邀請他來參加聚會。

▸ **MONEY** 錢 **6** [T] **~ sth (for sth)** to request a particular amount of money for sth that you are selling 要價；索價：***He's asking £2 000 for the car.*** 這輛轎車他要價 2 000 英鎊。

▸ **EXPECT/DEMAND** 期望；要求 **7** [T] to expect or demand sth 期望；要求：**~ sth** *I know I'm asking a great deal.* 我知道我的要求很高。◊ **~ sth of sb** *You're asking too much of him.* 你對他要求過分了。◊ **~ sth to do sth** *I know it's asking a lot to expect them to win again.* 我知道期望他們再次獲勝未免要求太高了。➲ SYNONYMS at DEMAND

IDM **'ask for it** (*informal*) to deserve sth bad that happens to you or that sb does to you 罪有應得；自討苦吃；自找麻煩 **be 'asking for trouble | be 'asking for it** (*informal*) to behave in a way that is very likely to result in trouble 要自找麻煩；要自討苦吃 **,don't 'ask** (*informal*) if you say **don't ask** to sb, you mean that you do not want to reply to their question, because it would be awkward, embarrassing, etc. 不問為好；還是別問的好 **,don't ask 'me** (*informal*) if you say **don't ask me**, you mean that you do not know the answer to a question and are annoyed you have been asked（不知答案或拂意作答時說）別問我 **for the 'asking** if you can have sth **for the asking**, it is very easy for you to get it if you ask for it 只需要求，一經索取（便可獲得）：*The job is yours for the asking.* 只要開口，這份工作就是你的了。**I 'ask you** (*informal*) if you say **I ask you**, you are expressing disapproval, shock or anger about sth/sb（表示不贊成、震驚或氣憤）請問，真是，這還了得 **if you ask 'me** (*informal*) in my personal opinion 我認為；依我說：*Their marriage was a mistake, if you ask me.* 依我看，他們的婚姻是個錯誤。

PHR V **'ask after sb** (*BrE*) to say that you would like to know how sb is, what they are doing, etc. 問候；問好：*He always asks after you in his letters.* 他在信中常問你好。**,ask a'round** to speak to a number of different people in order to try and get some information 四處打聽；多方詢問：*I don't know of any vacancies in the company but I'll ask around.* 我不知道公司有沒有空缺，不過我會打聽打聽。**,ask sb 'back** (*especially BrE*) to invite sb to come back to your house when you are both out together 邀請（一起外出的人）回到家裏來：*I hoped he wouldn't ask me back.* 我本不希望他會邀請我回到他家去。**'ask for sb/sth** to say that you want to speak to sb or be directed to a place 說要找（某人）；問到（某處）的路：*When you arrive, ask for Jane.* 你到達後找簡。**,ask sb 'out** to invite sb to go out with you, especially as a way of starting a romantic relationship. 邀請外出（尤指男女交往約會之始）：*He's too shy to ask her out.* 他太靦腆，不好意思約她外出。

■ ***noun***

IDM **a big 'ask** (*informal*) a difficult thing to achieve or deal with 難以做到的事情；棘手的事：*Beating the world champions is certainly a big ask for the team.* 這個隊要打敗世界冠軍當然難度很大。

Synonyms 同義詞辨析

ask

enquire • demand

These words all mean to say or write sth in the form of a question, in order to get information. 以上各詞均含口頭或書面詢問之義。

ask to say or write sth in the form of a question, in order to get information 指口頭或書面提問、詢問：*'Where are you going?' she asked.* "你去哪？"她問道。◊ *She asked the students their names.* 她問了學生的姓名。◊ *Can I **ask a question**?* 我能提個問題嗎？

enquire/inquire (*rather formal*) to ask sb for information 指詢問、查詢：*I called the station to enquire about train times.* 我打電話到車站詢問了火車時刻。

demand to ask a question very firmly 指嚴正地問、質問：*'And where have you been?' he demanded angrily.* "那你去了哪裏？"他怒氣沖沖地質問道。

PATTERNS

- to ask/enquire **about/after** sb/sth
- to ask/enquire/demand sth **of** sb
- to ask/enquire/demand **what/who/how**, etc.
- to ask/enquire **politely**
- to ask/enquire/demand **angrily**

askance /əˈskæns/ *adv.*

IDM **look askance (at sb/sth) | look (at sb/sth) askance** to look at or react to sb/sth with suspicion or doubt, or in a critical way（懷疑或不滿地）斜眼看，瞟

ask·ari /əˈskɑːri/ *noun* (*EAfrE*) a person who is employed to guard a building, valuable things, etc.; a SECURITY GUARD 保安；警衛

askew /əˈskjuː/ *adv.*, *adj.* [not before noun] not in a straight or level position 歪；斜 **SYN** **crooked**：*His glasses had been knocked askew by the blow.* 他的眼鏡一下子被打歪了。◊ *Her hat was slightly askew.* 她的帽子戴得有點斜。

'asking price *noun* the price that sb wants to sell sth for 要價；索價 ➲ compare SELLING PRICE

aslant /əˈslɑːnt; *NAmE* əˈslænt/ *adv.* not exactly vertical or horizontal; at an angle 傾斜地；歪斜地：*The picture hung aslant.* 照片掛歪了。

asleep /əˈsliːp/ *adj.* [not before noun] sleeping 睡着：*The baby was **sound asleep** (= sleeping deeply) upstairs.* 嬰兒在樓上睡得很香。◊ *I waited until they were all **fast asleep** (= sleeping deeply).* 我一直等到他們都進入了夢鄉。◊ *He was so exhausted that he **fell asleep** at his desk.* 他太累了，竟伏在書桌上睡着了。◊ *She was still **half asleep** (= not fully awake) when she arrived at work.* 她到了上班地點時仍然睡眼惺忪。◊ *The police found him asleep in a garage.* 警察發現他在車庫裏睡着了。**OPP** **awake**

AS (level) /eɪ ˈes levl/ *noun* [C, U] Advanced Subsidiary (level); a British exam usually taken in Year 12 of school or college (= the year before the final year) when students are aged 17. Together with A2 exams, AS levels form the A-level qualification, which is

A

needed for entrance to universities. 高級補充程度考試（英國學生在 17 歲時參加，通過此考試及 A2 考試的學生才有資格入讀大學）：*AS exams* 高級補充程度考試 ◇ *Students will normally take four or five AS subjects.* 學生通常要選四門或五門高級補充程度考試學科。◇ *She's* ***doing an AS*** *(****level****) in French.* 她正為參加高級補充程度考試學習法語。◇ *More than 20 subjects are on offer* ***at AS level*** *at our college.* 本校提供 20 多門高級補充程度考試學科。

asp /æsp/ *noun* **1** a small poisonous snake found in SW Europe 小毒蛇（見於歐洲西南部）**2** a general name for various types of small poisonous snake found in N Africa 阿斯普蛇（見於北非的小毒蛇）

as·para·gus /əˈspærəɡəs/ *noun* [U] a plant whose young green or white STEMS are cooked and eaten as a vegetable 蘆筍；龍鬚菜 ➲ VISUAL VOCAB page V31

as·par·tame /əˈspɑːteɪm; *NAmE* ˈæspɑːrteɪm/ *noun* [U] a sweet substance used instead of sugar in drinks and food products, especially ones for people who are trying to lose weight 阿斯巴甜代糖（常用作減肥食品、飲料的人造甜味添加劑）

as·pect 🔑 **AW** /ˈæspekt/ *noun*
1 🔑 [C] a particular part or feature of a situation, an idea, a problem, etc.; a way in which it may be considered 方面；層面：*The book aims to cover all aspects of city life.* 這本書旨在涵蓋城市生活的各個方面。◇ *the most important aspect of the debate* 這場辯論最重要的方面 ◇ *She felt she had looked at the problem from every aspect.* 她覺得她已從各個角度去考慮了這個問題。◇ *This was one aspect of her character he hadn't seen before.* 這是他過去沒有瞭解到的她的性格的一個方面。
2 [sing., U] (*formal*) the appearance of a place, a situation or a person 樣子；外觀；外表：*Events began to take on a more sinister aspect.* 事情開始呈現較為不祥的徵兆。
3 [C, usually sing.] (*formal*) the direction in which a building, window, piece of land, etc. faces; the side of a building that faces a particular direction 朝向；方位 **SYN orientation** **4** [U, C] (*grammar* 語法) the form of a verb that shows, for example, whether the action happens once or repeatedly, is completed or still continuing（動詞的）體（如表示動作等發生一次或多次、已完成或正在進行）➲ see also PERFECT *adj.* (7), PROGRESSIVE *adj.* (3)

aspen /ˈæspən/ *noun* a type of POPLAR tree, with leaves that move even when there is very little wind （美洲）顫楊，大齒楊；（歐洲）山楊

Asperger's syndrome /ˈæspɜːɡəz sɪndrəʊm; *NAmE* ˈæspɜːrɡərz sɪndroʊm/ *noun* [U] a mild type of AUTISM (= a mental condition in which a person finds it very difficult to communicate or form relationships with others) 阿斯佩格綜合症，亞斯伯格症候群（一種輕度自閉症）

as·per·gill·osis /ˌæspədʒɪˈləʊsɪs; *NAmE* ˌæspərdʒɪˈloʊsɪs/ *noun* [U] a serious condition in which parts of the body, usually the lungs, become infected by FUNGI 曲黴病，麴菌病（由真菌引起的肺部感染）

as·per·ity /æˈsperəti/ *noun* [U] (*formal*) the fact of being rough or severe, especially in the way you speak to or treat sb（尤指語言、態度）粗暴，嚴厲 **SYN harshness**

as·per·sions /əˈspɜːʃnz; *NAmE* əˈspɜːrʒnz/ *noun* [pl.] (*formal*) critical or unpleasant remarks or judgements 批評意見；非難；中傷：*I wouldn't want to* ***cast aspersions on*** *your honesty.* 我可不想批評你的誠信。

as·phalt /ˈæsfælt; *NAmE* -fɔːlt/ *noun* [U] a thick black sticky substance used especially for making the surface of roads 瀝青；柏油

as·phyxia /æsˈfɪksiə; əsˈf-/ *noun* [U] the state of being unable to breathe, causing death or loss of CONSCIOUSNESS 窒息

as·phyxi·ate /əsˈfɪksieɪt/ *verb* **~ sb** to make sb become unconscious or die by preventing them from breathing 使窒息；悶死 **SYN suffocate** ▸ **as·phyxi·ation** /əsˌfɪksiˈeɪʃn/ *noun* [U]

aspic /ˈæspɪk/ *noun* [U] clear jelly which food can be put into when it is being served cold 肉凍：*chicken breast* ***in aspic*** 雞脯凍

as·pi·dis·tra /ˌæspɪˈdɪstrə/ *noun* a plant with broad green pointed leaves, often grown indoors 蜘蛛抱蛋（常為室內盆栽植物，綠葉寬而尖）

as·pir·ant /əˈspaɪərənt; ˈæspərənt/ *noun* **~ (to/for sth)** (*formal*) a person with a strong desire to achieve a position of importance or to win a competition 有抱負的人；有雄心壯志的人：*aspirants to the title of world champion* 有志奪取世界冠軍的人 ▸ **as·pir·ant** *adj.* [only before noun] = ASPIRING

as·pir·ate *noun, verb*
■ ***noun*** /ˈæspərət/ (*phonetics* 語音) the sound /h/, as in *house* * h 音；送氣音：*The word 'hour' is pronounced without an initial aspirate.* * hour 的首字母 h 不發送氣音。
■ ***verb*** /ˈæspəreɪt/ **1 ~ sth** (*medical* 醫) to remove liquid from a person's body with a machine（用吸引機）抽吸（體腔中的液體）**2 ~ sth** (*phonetics* 語音) to pronounce sth with an 'h' sound or with a breath 發 h 音；發送氣音

as·pir·ation /ˌæspəˈreɪʃn/ *noun* **1** [C, usually pl., U] a strong desire to have or do sth 渴望；抱負；志向：*I didn't realize you had political aspirations.* 我沒有意識到你有政治上的抱負。◇ **~ to do sth** *He has never had any aspiration to earn a lot of money.* 他從未企求賺很多錢。◇ **~ for sth** *What changes are needed to meet women's aspirations for employment?* 需要什麼樣的改革才能滿足女性對就業的渴望呢？**2** [U] (*phonetics* 語音) the action of pronouncing a word with a /h/ sound, as in *house* 發送氣音；送氣

as·pir·ation·al /ˌæspəˈreɪʃənl/ *adj.* wanting very much to achieve success in your career or to improve your social status and standard of living 渴望成功的；一心想提高社會地位和生活水平的

as·pire /əˈspaɪə(r)/ *verb* [I, T] to have a strong desire to achieve or to become sth 渴望（成就）；有志（成為）：**~ (to sth)** *She aspired to a scientific career.* 她有志於科學事業。◇ **~ to be/do sth** *He aspired to be their next leader.* 他渴望成為他們的下一屆領導人。

as·pirin /ˈæsprɪn; ˈæspərɪn/ *noun* [U, C] (*pl.* **as·pirin** or **as·pir·ins**) a drug used to reduce pain, fever and INFLAMMATION 阿司匹林（鎮痛解熱消炎藥）：*Do you have any aspirin?* 你有阿司匹林嗎？◇ *Take two aspirin(s) for a headache.* 頭痛服兩片阿司匹林。

as·pir·ing /əˈspaɪərɪŋ/ (also *less frequent* **as·pir·ant**) *adj.* [only before noun] **1** wanting to start the career or activity that is mentioned 渴望從事…的；有志成為…的：*Aspiring musicians need hours of practice every day.* 想當音樂家就要每天練許多小時。**2** wanting to be successful in life 有抱負的；有志向的：*He came from an aspiring working-class background.* 他出身於有抱負的工人階級家庭。

ass /æs/ *noun* **1** (*NAmE*) (*BrE* **arse**) (*taboo, slang*) the part of the body that you sit on; your bottom 屁股；腚 **2** (*BrE, informal*) a stupid person 蠢人；笨蛋 **SYN fool**：*Don't be such an ass!* 別那麼傻頭傻腦的！◇ ***I made an ass of myself*** *at the meeting—standing up and then forgetting the question.* 我在會議上出了個大洋相，站起來卻忘了要問的問題。**3** (*BrE, old use*) a DONKEY 驢
IDM **get your ˈass in gear | move your ˈass** (*slang, especially NAmE*) a rude way of telling sb to hurry 別磨磨蹭蹭的；趕快 **get your ˌass over/in ˈhere, etc.** (*slang, especially NAmE*) a rude way of telling sb to come here, etc. 滾過來（或進來等）➲ more at BLOW *v.*, COVER *v.*, KICK *v.*, KISS *v.*, PAIN *n.*

as·sa·gai = ASSEGAI

as·sail /əˈseɪl/ *verb* (*formal*) **1 ~ sb/sth** to attack sb/sth violently, either physically or with words 攻擊；襲擊；抨擊：*He was assailed with fierce blows to the head.* 他的頭遭到猛烈毆打。◇ *The proposal was assailed by the opposition party.* 提案遭到反對黨的抨擊。◇ (*figurative*) *A vile smell assailed my nostrils.* 一股惡臭十分刺鼻。**2** [usually passive] **~ sb** to disturb or upset sb severely 困擾；使苦惱：*to* ***be assailed by worries/doubts/fears*** 為焦慮／疑慮／擔心所困擾

as·sail·ant /ə'seɪlənt/ *noun* (*formal*) a person who attacks sb, especially physically 攻擊者；行兇者 SYN **attacker**

as·sas·sin /ə'sæsɪn; *NAmE* -sn/ *noun* a person who murders sb important or famous, for money or for political reasons（為金錢或政治目的的）暗殺者，行刺者

as·sas·sin·ate /ə'sæsɪneɪt; *NAmE* -sən-/ *verb* [often passive] **~ sb** to murder an important or famous person, especially for political reasons（尤為政治目的的）暗殺；行刺：*The prime minister was assassinated by extremists.* 首相遭極端分子暗殺。◇ *a plot to assassinate the president* 刺殺總統的陰謀 ▸ **as·sas·sin·ation** /əˌsæsɪ'neɪʃn; *NAmE* -sə'n-/ *noun* [U, C]：*The president survived a number of assassination attempts.* 總統在數次暗殺企圖中幸免於難。◇ *the assassination of John F. Kennedy* 暗殺約翰 • F • 肯尼迪

as·sault /ə'sɔːlt/ *noun, verb*

■ ***noun*** **1** [U, C] the crime of attacking sb physically 侵犯他人身體（罪）；侵犯人身罪：*Both men were charged with assault.* 兩人均被控侵犯他人身體罪。◇ *sexual assaults* 性攻擊（指強姦、猥褻）◇ **~ on/upon sb** *A significant number of* ***indecent assaults*** *on women go unreported.* 很大數量的猥褻婦女罪沒有舉報。➲ COLLOCATIONS at CRIME **2** [C] **~ (on/upon/against sb/sth)** (by an army, etc. 軍隊等) the act of attacking a building, an area, etc. in order to take control of it 攻擊；突擊；襲擊 SYN **attack**：*An assault on the capital was launched in the early hours of the morning.* 凌晨時分向首都發起了攻擊。 **3** [C] **~ (on/upon sth)** the act of trying to achieve sth that is difficult or dangerous（向困難或危險事物發起的）衝擊：*The government has mounted a new assault on unemployment.* 政府向失業發起新的攻勢。◇ *Three people died during an assault on the mountain* (= while trying to climb it). 登山過程中有三人死亡。**4** [C] an act of criticizing sb/sth severely 抨擊 SYN **attack**：*The suggested closures* ***came under assault*** *from all parties.* 關閉機構的建議受到各方嚴厲批評。◇ **~ on/upon/against sb/sth** *The paper's assault on the president was totally unjustified.* 這份報紙對總統的攻擊純屬無稽之談。

■ ***verb*** **1 ~ sb** to attack sb violently, especially when this is a crime 猛烈攻擊，襲擊，侵犯（尤指構成罪）：*He has been charged with assaulting a police officer.* 他被控襲擊警察。◇ *Four women have been* ***sexually assaulted*** *in the area recently.* 近來這個地區有四名婦女遭到強姦猥褻。 **2 ~ sth** (*formal*) to affect your senses in a way that is very unpleasant or uncomfortable 使（感官）難受：*Loud rock music assaulted our ears.* 喧鬧的搖滾樂直往我們耳朵裏鑽。

asˌsault and 'battery *noun* [U] (*law* 律) the crime of threatening to harm sb and then attacking them physically 毆打和侵犯人身（罪）；襲擊和暴力傷害（罪）

as'sault course (*BrE*) (*NAmE* **'obstacle course**) *noun* an area of land with many objects that are difficult to climb, jump over or go through, which is used, especially by soldiers, for improving physical skills and strength 近戰訓練場；障礙場

assay /ə'seɪ/ *noun* [C, U] (*technical* 術語) the testing of metals and chemicals for quality, often to see how pure they are（金屬、化學物質量的）鑒定，試驗，測定 ▸ **assay** *verb* **~ sth**

as·se·gai (also **as·sa·gai**) /'æsəgaɪ/ *noun* **1** a weapon consisting of a long stick with a sharp metal point on the end, used mainly in southern Africa（多為南非部落所用的）長矛，標槍 **2** a South African tree which produces hard wood（南非的）山茱萸樹

as·sem·blage /ə'semblɪdʒ/ *noun* (*formal, technical* 術語) a collection of things; a group of people（人、物的）聚集，集聚：*Tropical rainforests have the most varied assemblage of plants in the world.* 熱帶雨林聚集了世界上種類最繁多的植物。

as·sem·ble AW /ə'sembl/ *verb* **1** [I, T] to come together as a group; to bring people or things together as a group 聚集；集合；收集：*All the students were asked to assemble in the main hall.* 全體學生獲通知到大禮堂集合。◇ *She then addressed the* ***assembled company*** (= all the people there). 接着她向全體集合者講話。◇ **~ sth** *to assemble evidence/data* 收集證據 / 數據◇ *The manager has assembled a world-class team.* 經理已聚集了一個世界一流的團隊。 **2** [T] **~ sth** to fit together all the separate parts of sth, for example a piece of furniture 裝配；組裝：*The shelves are easy to assemble.* 擱架容易裝配。OPP **disassemble** ➲ SYNONYMS at BUILD

as·sem·bler /ə'semblə(r)/ *noun* **1** a person who assembles a machine or its parts 裝配工 **2** (*computing* 計) a program for changing instructions into MACHINE CODE 彙編程序，彙編器，組譯器（將指令轉變為機器碼）**3** (*computing* 計) = ASSEMBLY LANGUAGE

Asˌsemblies of 'God *noun* [pl.] the largest Pentecostal Church in the US (= one that emphasizes the gifts of the Holy Spirit, such as the power to heal people who are ill/sick) 神召會（美國規模最大的五旬節教派，強調醫治等神恩）

as·sem·bly AW /ə'sembli/ *noun* (*pl.* **-ies**) **1** (also **Assembly**) [C] a group of people who have been elected to meet together regularly and make decisions or laws for a particular region or country 立法機構；會議；議會：***state/legislative/federal/local assemblies*** 州眾議院；立法會議；聯邦 / 地方議會◇ *Power has been handed over to provincial and regional assemblies.* 權力已移交給省和地區議會。◇ *The national assembly has voted to adopt the budget.* 國民議會已表決通過預算。◇ *the California Assembly* 美國加利福尼亞州眾議院◇ *the UN General Assembly* 聯合國大會 **2** [U, C] the meeting together of a group of people for a particular purpose; a group of people who meet together for a particular purpose 集會；（統稱）集會者：*They were fighting for freedom of speech and freedom of assembly.* 他們為言論自由和集會自由而鬥爭。◇ *He was to address a public assembly on the issue.* 他要對公眾集會發表演說談論這個問題。◇ *an* ***assembly point*** (= a place where people have been asked to meet) 集會地點 **3** [C, U] a meeting of the teachers and students in a school, usually at the start of the day, to give information, discuss school events or say prayers together（全校師生的）晨會，朝會 **4** [U] the process of putting together the parts of sth such as a vehicle or piece of furniture 裝配；組裝；總成：*Putting the bookcase together should be a simple assembly job.* 組裝書櫥應該是個簡單的裝配活。◇ *a car assembly plant* 汽車裝配廠

as'sembly language *noun* [C, U] (also **as·sem·bler**) (*computing* 計) the language in which a program is written before it is changed into MACHINE CODE 彙編語言；組合語言

as'sembly line *noun* = PRODUCTION LINE：*workers on the assembly line* 裝配線上的工人

as·sem·bly·man /ə'sembliːmən/, **as·sem·bly·wo·man** /ə'sembliwʊmən/ *noun* (*pl.* **-men** /-mən/, **-wo·men** /-wɪmɪn/) a person who is an elected representative in a state assembly in the US（美國）州眾議院議員

as'sembly room *noun* [usually pl.] (*especially BrE*) a public room or building in which meetings and social events are held（供會議、社交活動等用的）禮堂

as·sent /ə'sent/ *noun, verb*

■ ***noun*** [U] **~ (to sth)** (*formal*) official agreement to or approval of sth 同意；贊成：*The director has* ***given her assent to*** *the proposals.* 負責人已表示同意提案。◇ *He nodded (his) assent.* 他點頭同意了。◇ *There were murmurs of both assent and dissent from the crowd.* 人群議論紛紛，贊成和反對的都有。◇ *The bill passed in Parliament has now* ***received*** *(****the****)* ***Royal Assent*** (= been approved by the king/queen). 議會通過的法案已獲御准。

■ ***verb*** [I] **~ (to sth)** | **(+ speech)** (*formal*) to agree to a request, an idea or a suggestion 同意，贊成（要求、想法或建議）：*Nobody would assent to the terms they proposed.* 誰也不會同意他們提出的條件。

as·sert /ə'sɜːt; *NAmE* ə'sɜːrt/ *verb* **1** to state clearly and firmly that sth is true 明確肯定；斷言：**~ that …** *She continued to assert that she was innocent.* 她仍然堅稱自己無辜。◇ **~ sth** *She continued to assert her innocence.* 她仍然堅稱自己無辜。◇ **+ speech** *'That is wrong,' he*

A

asserted. “那是錯的。”他斷言道。◇ **it is asserted that …** *It is commonly asserted that older people prefer to receive care from family members.* 人們普遍確認，老年人更願意由家人照顧。 **2 ~ yourself** to behave in a confident and determined way so that other people pay attention to your opinions 堅持自己的主張；表現堅定 **3 ~ sth** to make other people recognize your right or authority to do sth, by behaving firmly and confidently 維護自己的權利（或權威）：*to **assert** your **independence/rights*** 維護你的獨立／權利 ◇ *I was determined to **assert** my **authority** from the beginning.* 我決心一開始就維護我的權威。 **4 ~ itself** to start to have an effect 生效；起作用：*Good sense asserted itself.* 明智服人。

as·ser·tion /əˈsɜːʃn; *NAmE* əˈsɜːrʃn/ *noun* **1** [C] a statement saying that you strongly believe sth to be true 認定；斷言 SYN **claim**：*He was correct in his assertion that the minister had been lying.* 他認定部長說謊，事實果然如此。◇ *Do you have any evidence to support your assertions?* 你的斷言是否有真憑實據？ ➲ SYNONYMS at CLAIM **2** [U, C] the act of stating, using or claiming sth strongly 聲稱；使用；主張：*the assertion of his authority* 對他權威的維護 ◇ *The demonstration was an assertion of the right to peaceful protest.* 這次示威遊行行使了和平抗議權。

as·sert·ive /əˈsɜːtɪv; *NAmE* əˈsɜːrtɪv/ *adj.* expressing opinions or desires strongly and with confidence, so that people take notice 堅定自信的；堅決主張的：*You should try and be more assertive.* 你應該努力堅定信心。◇ *assertive behaviour* 堅定自信的行為 OPP **submissive** ▸ **as·sert·ive·ly** *adv.* **as·sert·ive·ness** *noun* [U]：*an assertiveness training course* 建立自信心訓練班

as·sess AW /əˈses/ *verb* **1** to make a judgement about the nature or quality of sb/sth 評估，評定（性質、質量）：**~ sb/sth** *It's difficult to assess the effects of these changes.* 這些變化帶來的效果難以評估。◇ *to assess a patient's needs* 判定病人的需要 ◇ **~ sb/sth as sth** *The young men were assessed as either safe or unsafe drivers.* 這些年輕人被評定為謹慎駕駛員和不謹慎駕駛員兩類。◇ *I'd assess your chances as low.* 我估計你的機會不大。◇ **~ whether, how, etc. …** *The committee assesses whether a building is worth preserving.* 該委員會評定一棟建築物是否值得保存。◇ *We are trying to assess how well the system works.* 我們正設法評估這個系統運行得是否順暢。 **2** to calculate the amount or value of sth 估算，估定，核定（數量、價值）SYN **estimate**：**~ sth** *They have assessed the amount of compensation to be paid.* 他們已經核定賠償額。◇ **~ sth at sth** *Damage to the building was assessed at £40 000.* 該建築物的損失估定為 4 萬英鎊。 ▸ **as·sess·able** AW *adj.*

as·sess·ment AW /əˈsesmənt/ *noun* **1** [C] an opinion or a judgement about sb/sth that has been thought about very carefully 看法；評價 SYN **evaluation**：*a detailed assessment of the risks involved* 對涉及的風險所作的詳細判斷 ◇ *his assessment of the situation* 他對形勢的看法 **2** [U] the act of judging or forming an opinion about sb/sth 評定；核定；判定：*written exams and other forms of assessment* 筆試及其他形式的考核 ◇ *Objective assessment of the severity of the problem was difficult.* 難以客觀判定該問題的嚴重性。 ➲ see also CONTINUOUS ASSESSMENT **3** [C] an amount that has been calculated and that must be paid 核定的付款額：*a tax assessment* 稅款核定額

aˈssessment centre (*BrE*) (*NAmE* **aˈssessment center**) *noun* (*business* 商) (*especially BrE*) an event where people applying for a job are given a number of tests and interviews to find out what their strengths and weaknesses are; the place where this happens 求職評估；求職評估中心；求職評量；求職評量中心：*After the first interview you may be asked back for an assessment centre.* 第一次面試之後可能要求你回來接受求職評估。

as·ses·sor /əˈsesə(r)/ *noun* **1** an expert in a particular subject who is asked by a court or other official group to give advice （法庭或官方團體的）顧問，襄審員 **2** a person who calculates the value or cost of sth or the amount of money to be paid（財產、費用等的）估價員：*an **insurance/tax assessor*** 保險估價員；估稅員 **3** a person who judges how well sb has done in an exam, a competition, etc.（考試、比賽等的）考核人，評判員：*College lecturers acted as external assessors of the exam results.* 學院講師是考試成績的校外考核人。

asset /ˈæset/ *noun* **1** a person or thing that is valuable or useful to sb/sth 有價值的人（或事物）；有用的人（或事物）：*In his job, patience is an invaluable asset.* 他幹的這份工作，耐心是無價之寶。◇ **~ to sb/sth** *She'll be an asset to the team.* 她將是這個隊的骨幹。 **2** [usually pl.] a thing of value, especially property, that a person or company owns, which can be used or sold to pay debts 資產；財產：*the net **asset value** of the company* 公司的資產淨值 ◇ *Her assets include shares in the company and a house in France.* 她的財產包括公司的股份和在法國的一座房子。◇ ***asset sales/management*** 資產銷售／管理 ◇ ***financial/capital assets*** 金融／資本資產 ➲ compare LIABILITY

ˈasset-stripping *noun* [U] (*business* 商) (usually *disapproving*) the practice of buying a company which is in financial difficulties at a low price and then selling everything that it owns in order to make a profit 資產倒賣，資產拆賣（以低價購進公司，再將其資產出售，以獲取利潤）

ass·hole /ˈæshəʊl; *NAmE* -hoʊl/ (*NAmE*) (*BrE* **arse·hole**) *noun* (*taboo, slang*) **1** the ANUS 屁眼；肛門 **2** a stupid or unpleasant person 笨蛋；討厭鬼

as·sidu·ous /əˈsɪdjuəs; *NAmE* -dʒuəs/ *adj.* (*formal*) working very hard and taking great care that everything is done as well as it can be 兢兢業業的；勤勤懇懇的 SYN **diligent** ▸ **as·si·du·ity** /ˌæsɪˈdjuːəti/ *noun* [U] **as·sidu·ous·ly** *adv.*

as·sign AW /əˈsaɪn/ *verb* **1** to give sb sth that they can use, or some work or responsibility 分配（某物）；分派，佈置（工作、任務等）：**~ sth (to sb)** *The two large classrooms have been assigned to us.* 這兩間大教室分配給了我們。◇ *The teacher assigned a different task to each of the children.* 老師給每個孩子都佈置了不同的作業。◇ **~ sb sth** *We have been assigned the two large classrooms.* 我們分得了這兩間大教室。◇ *The teacher assigned each of the children a different task.* 老師給每個孩子都佈置了不同的作業。 **2** to provide a person for a particular task or position 指定；指派：**~ sb (to sth/as sth)** *They've assigned their best man to the job.* 他們指派了最優秀的人擔任這項工作。◇ **~ sb to do sth** *British forces have been assigned to help with peacekeeping.* 英國軍隊被派遣協助維持和平。 **3** [usually passive] **~ sb to sb/sth** to send a person to work under the authority of sb or in a particular group 委派；派遣：*I was assigned to B platoon.* 我被派到 B 排工作。 **4** to say that sth has a particular value or function, or happens at a particular time or place 確定（價值、功能、時間、地點）：**~ sth to sth** *Assign a different colour to each different type of information.* 給每類信息分別確定一種顏色。◇ **~ sth sth** *The painting cannot be assigned an exact date.* 這幅畫的年代確定不了。 **5 ~ sth to sb** (*law* 律) to say that your property or rights now belong to sb else 轉讓，讓與（財產、權利）：*The agreement assigns copyright to the publisher.* 協議規定將版權轉讓給出版商。

as·sig·na·tion /ˌæsɪɡˈneɪʃn/ *noun* (*formal* or *humorous*) a meeting, especially a secret one, often with a lover 幽會；約會

as·sign·ment AW /əˈsaɪnmənt/ *noun* **1** [C, U] a task or piece of work that sb is given to do, usually as part of their job or studies （分派的）工作，任務：*You will need to complete three written assignments per semester.* 你每學期要完成三個書面作業。◇ *She is in Greece on an assignment for one of the Sunday newspapers.* 她在希臘為一家星期日報執行一項任務。◇ *one of our reporters **on assignment** in China* 我們派駐中國的一名記者 ◇ *I had set myself a tough assignment.* 我給自己定了一項艱巨任務。 **2** [U] the act of giving sth to sb; the act of giving sb a particular task （工作等的）分派，佈置：*his assignment to other duties in the same company* 他在同一公司內擔任的其他職務

A

as·simi·late /əˈsɪməleɪt/ *verb* **1** [T] **~ sth** to fully understand an idea or some information so that you are able to use it yourself 透徹理解；消化；吸收：*The committee will need time to assimilate this report.* 委員會需要時間來吃透這個報告。 **2** [I, T] to become, or allow sb to become, a part of a country or community rather than remaining in a separate group （使）同化：**~ (into/to sth)** *New arrivals find it hard to assimilate.* 新來者感到難以融入當地社會。◇ **~ sb (into/to sth)** *Immigrants have been successfully assimilated into the community.* 外來移民順利地融入當地社會。 **3** [T, often passive] **~ sth into/to sth** to make an idea, a person's attitude, etc. fit into sth or be acceptable 使吸收，使接受（想法、態度等）：*These changes were gradually assimilated into everyday life.* 這些改變逐漸滲進了日常生活。

as·simi·la·tion /əˌsɪməˈleɪʃn/ *noun* **1** [U] the act of assimilating sb or sth, or being assimilated 吸收；接受：*the rapid assimilation of new ideas* 對新思想的迅速吸收 ◇ *his assimilation into the community* 他融入社區 **2** [U, C] (*phonetics* 語音) the act of making two sounds in speech that are next to each other more similar to each other in certain ways, for example the pronunciation of the /t/ in *football* as a /p/; an example of this 同化（使相鄰的兩個音發音接近，如 football 中 t 的發音為 p）；同化現象

as·sist 🔑 AW /əˈsɪst/ *verb, noun*

■ *verb* (*formal*) **1** 🔑 [I, T] to help sb to do sth 幫助；協助；援助：*Anyone willing to assist can contact this number.* 凡願協助者可撥此號碼聯繫。◇ **~ in/with sth** *We are looking for people who would be willing to assist in the group's work.* 我們正尋找願意協助該團體工作的人。◇ **~ sb** *We'll do all we can to assist you.* 我們會盡量幫你。◇ *The play was directed by Mike Johnson, assisted by Sharon Gale.* 該劇由邁克•約翰遜導演，沙倫•蓋爾為助理導演。◇ **~ sb in doing sth** *We will assist you in finding somewhere to live.* 我們將幫你找個住的地方。◇ **~ sb in/with sth** *Two men* ***are assisting the police with their enquiries*** (= are being questioned by the police). 有兩個人正配合警方的詢問。◇ **~ sb to do sth** *a course to assist adults to return to the labour market* 成人重返勞工市場的輔導班 **2** 🔑 [T] **~ sth** to help sth to happen more easily 促進：*activities that will assist the decision-making process* 促進決策進程的活動

■ *noun* an action in HOCKEY, BASEBALL, etc. in which a player helps another player on the same team to score a goal or point（曲棍球等）助攻；（棒球等）助殺

as·sist·ance 🔑 AW /əˈsɪstəns/ *noun* [U] (*formal*) help or support 幫助；援助；支持：***technical/economic/military assistance*** 技術／經濟／軍事援助 ◇ ***financial assistance*** *for people on low incomes* 給低收入者的經濟援助 ◇ *Can I* ***be of any assistance?*** 我能幫上忙嗎？◇ *Despite his cries, no one* ***came to his assistance.*** 儘管他喊叫，卻沒有人來幫助他。◇ *He can walk only* ***with the assistance of*** *crutches.* 他只能靠一副拐杖走路。◇ **~ with sth** *She offered me practical assistance with my research.* 她給我的研究提供了實實在在的援助。◇ **~ in doing sth/to do sth** *The company provides advice and assistance in finding work.* 公司提供咨詢並幫助找工作。

as·sist·ant 🔑 AW /əˈsɪstənt/ *noun, adj.*

■ *noun* **1** 🔑 a person who helps or supports sb, usually in their job 助理；助手：*My assistant will now demonstrate the machine in action.* 現在我的助手將演示機器運轉情況。◇ *a senior research assistant* 高級研究助理 ➲ see also PDA, PERSONAL ASSISTANT, TEACHING ASSISTANT **2** 🔑 (*BrE*) = SALES CLERK, SHOP ASSISTANT：*a sales assistant in a department store* 一名百貨公司售貨員 **3** (*BrE*) a student at university or college who spends time in a foreign country teaching his or her own language in a school 助教（在國外留學的大學生，教授本國語）

■ *adj.* 🔑 [only before noun] (*abbr.* **Asst**) (often in titles 常用於頭銜) having a rank below a senior person and helping them in their work 助理的；副的：*the assistant manager* 協理 ◇ *Assistant Chief Constable Owen* 助理警察局長歐文 ◇ *Assistant Attorney General William Weld* 助理檢察總長威廉•韋爾德

asˌsistant proˈfessor *noun* (in the US and Canada) a teacher at a college or university who has a rank just below the rank of an ASSOCIATE PROFESSOR（美國和加拿大的）助理教授（職位比副教授低一級）

asˌsistant refeˈree (also **referee's assistant**) *noun* (in football (SOCCER) 足球) the official name for a LINESMAN (= an official who helps the REFEREE, for example in deciding whether or where a ball has passed outside the field of play) 助理裁判（邊線裁判員的正式名稱）

as·sis·tant·ship /əˈsɪstəntʃɪp/ *noun* **1** (*BrE*) the position of being an ASSISTANT (3) 助手職位；助理職位 **2** (*NAmE*) a paid position for a GRADUATE student that involves some teaching or research（研究生的）助教金職位，助研金職位

asˌsisted ˈliving *noun* [U] accommodation for people who need help, for example with tasks like washing and dressing themselves 贍養院；安養照護：*assisted living apartments* 贍養公寓

asˌsisted ˈsuicide *noun* [U] the act of a person killing himself/herself with the help of sb such as a doctor, especially because he/she is suffering from a disease that has no cure（假醫生等他人之手的）輔助自殺，協助自殺

as·sizes /əˈsaɪzɪz/ *noun* a court in the past which travelled to each county of England and Wales（英格蘭和威爾士舊時的）巡迴法庭 ▸ **as·size** *adj.* [only before noun]：*the assize court* 巡迴審判法庭

ˈass-kicking *adj.* = KICK-ASS

ˈass-licker (*NAmE*) (*BrE* **ˈarse-licker**) *noun* (*taboo, slang*) a person who is too friendly to sb in authority and is always ready to do what they want 馬屁精 ▸ **ˈass-licking** (*NAmE*) (*BrE* **ˈarse-licking**) *noun* [U]

Assoc. *abbr.* (in writing) ASSOCIATION（書寫形式）協會，社團，聯盟

as·so·ci·ate 🔑 *verb, adj., noun*

■ *verb* /əˈsəʊʃieɪt; -sieɪt; *NAmE* əˈsoʊ-/ **1** 🔑 [T] **~ sb/sth (with sb/sth)** to make a connection between people or things in your mind 聯想；聯繫：*I always associate the smell of baking with my childhood.* 一聞到烘烤食物的味道，我就想起了童年。◇ *He is closely associated in the public mind with horror movies.* 在公眾的心目中，他總是和恐怖電影緊密聯繫在一起。 **2** [I] **~ with sb** to spend time with sb, especially a person or people that sb else does not approve of 交往；（尤指）混在一起 SYN **mix**：*I don't like you associating with those people.* 我不喜歡你和那些人混在一起。 **3** [T] **~ yourself with sth** (*formal*) to show that you support or agree with sth 表明支持；表示同意：*I associate myself with the Prime Minister's remarks* (= I agree with them). 我贊同首相所言。 OPP **dissociate**

■ *adj.* /əˈsəʊʃiət; -siət; *NAmE* əˈsoʊ-/ [only before noun] **1** (often in titles 常用於頭銜) of a lower rank; having fewer rights in a particular profession or organization 非正式的；準的；副的：*associate membership of the European Union* 歐洲聯盟的非正式會員身分 ◇ *an associate member/director/editor* 準會員；副導演／主編 **2** joined to or connected with a profession or an organization 聯合的；有關聯的：*an associate company in Japan* 在日本的一家聯營公司

■ *noun* /əˈsəʊʃiət; *NAmE* əˈsoʊ-/ **1** a person that you work with, do business with or spend a lot of time with 同事；夥伴：*business associates* 業務夥伴 **2** (also **Associate**) an ASSOCIATE 合夥人 **3 Associate** (*US*) a person who has an Associate's degree (= one that is given after completing two years of study at a junior college) 準學士（獲得兩年制高校學位）

as·so·ci·ated 🔑 /əˈsəʊʃieɪtɪd; -sieɪt-; *NAmE* əˈsoʊ-/ *adj.*

1 🔑 if one thing is **associated with** another, the two things are connected because they happen together or one thing causes the other 有關聯的；相關的 SYN **connected**：*the risks associated with taking drugs* 與吸毒有關的危險 ◇ *Salaries and associated costs have risen substantially.* 薪金與相關費用大大增加。 **2** 🔑 if a person is **associated with** an organization, etc. they support it 有聯繫的：*He no longer wished to be associated with the party's policy on education.* 他不再願意與該黨的教育方針認同。 **3 Associated** used in the name of a business company that is made up of a number of smaller companies （用於聯合企業的名稱）聯合的：*Associated Newspapers* 聯合報業

As,sociated 'Press *noun* (*abbr.* **AP**) a US news service. Its offices throughout the world send news to its members which include newspapers and television and radio stations. （美國）聯合通訊社；美聯社

as,sociate pro'fessor *noun* (in the US and Canada) a teacher at a college or university who has a rank just below the rank of a professor （美國和加拿大的）副教授（職位比教授低一級）

as·so·ci·ation 🗝 /ə,səʊʃi'eɪʃn; -si'eɪ-; *NAmE* ə,soʊ-/ *noun*
1 🗝 [C+sing./pl. v.] (*abbr.* **Assoc.**) an official group of people who have joined together for a particular purpose 協會；社團；聯盟 SYN **organization**：*Do you belong to any professional or trade associations?* 你參加了專業學會或行業協會沒有？◇ *the Football Association* 足球協會 ◇ *a residents' association* 居民聯合會 ➲ see also HOUSING ASSOCIATION **2** 🗝 [C, U] **~ (with sb/sth)** a connection or relationship between people or organizations 聯合；合夥；關聯；交往：*his alleged association with terrorist groups* 他被指稱的與恐怖組織的關聯 ◇ *They have maintained a close association with a college in the US.* 他們和美國一所學院保持了密切聯繫。◇ *The book was published* ***in association with*** (= together with) *English Heritage.* 這本書是與英國文化遺產保護協會聯合出版的。◇ *She became famous through her association with the group of poets.* 她通過與這些詩人交往而成名。 **3** 🗝 [C, usually pl.] an idea or a memory that is suggested by sb/sth; a mental connection between ideas 聯想；聯繫：*The seaside had all sorts of pleasant associations with childhood holidays for me.* 海濱使我聯想起童年假期的各種愉快情景。◇ *The cat soon made the association between human beings and food.* 這隻貓很快就把人類與食物聯繫起來。 **4** 🗝 [C] a connection between things where one is caused by the other 因果關係：*a proven association between passive smoking and cancer* 已被證實的被動吸煙與癌症之間的因果關係

As,sociation 'football *noun* [U] (*BrE, formal*) = FOOTBALL (1)

as·so·cia·tive /ə'səʊʃiətɪv; *NAmE* ə'soʊ-/ *adj.* **1** relating to the association of ideas or things 聯想的 **2** (*mathematics* 數) giving the same result no matter what order the parts of a calculation are done, for example (a × b) × c = a × (b × c) 結合的

as·son·ance /'æsənəns/ *noun* [U] (*technical* 術語) the effect created when two syllables in words that are close together have the same vowel sound, but different consonants, or the same consonants but different vowels, for example, *sonnet* and *porridge* or *cold* and *killed* 準押韻，半諧韻，半諧音（靠得很近的單詞中有兩個音節元音相同而輔音不同，或輔音相同而元音不同）

as·sort·ed /ə'sɔːtɪd; *NAmE* ə'sɔːrtəd/ *adj.* of various different sorts 各種各樣的；混雜的；什錦的：*The meat is served with salad or assorted vegetables.* 端上的肉配有色拉或什錦蔬菜。◇ *The jumper comes in assorted colours.* 各種顏色的針織套衫一應俱全。

as·sort·ment /ə'sɔːtmənt; *NAmE* ə'sɔːrt-/ *noun* [usually sing.] a collection of different things or of different types of the same thing 各種各樣 SYN **mixture**：*a wide assortment of gifts to choose from* 各式各樣可供挑選的禮品 ◇ *He was dressed in an odd assortment of clothes.* 他穿着奇裝異服。

Asst (also **Asst.** especially in *NAmE*) *abbr.* (in writing) ASSISTANT （書寫形式）助理的，副的：*Asst Manager* 協理

as·suage /ə'sweɪdʒ/ *verb* **~ sth** (*formal*) to make an unpleasant feeling less severe 緩和，減輕（不快）

as·sume 🗝 AW /ə'sjuːm; *NAmE* ə'suːm/ *verb*
1 🗝 to think or accept that sth is true but without having proof of it 假定；假設；認為：**~ (that)** … *It is* ***reasonable to assume*** *(****that****) the economy will continue to improve.* 認為經濟將繼續好轉是有道理的。◇ ***Let us assume*** *for a moment that the plan succeeds.* 咱們暫時假設計劃成功。◇ *She would, he assumed, be home at the usual time.* 他認為，她會在通常時間回到家的。◇ **it is assumed (that)** … *It is generally assumed that stress is caused by too much work.* 普遍認為，緊張是工作過重所致。◇ **~ sth** *Don't always* ***assume the worst*** (= that sth bad has happened). 別總往最壞處想。◇ *In this example we have assumed a unit price of $10.* 在這個例子中，我們已假定單價為 10 元。◇ **~ sb/sth to be/have sth** *I had assumed him to be a Belgian.* 我本以為他是比利時人。 **2 ~ sth** (*formal*) to take or begin to have power or responsibility 承擔（責任）；就（職）；取得（權力） SYN **take**：*The court assumed responsibility for the girl's welfare.* 法庭承擔了保障這個女孩福利的責任。◇ *Rebel forces have assumed control of the capital.* 反叛武裝力量已控制了首都。 **3 ~ sth** (*formal*) to begin to have a particular quality or appearance 呈現（外觀、樣子）；顯露（特徵） SYN **take on**：*This matter has assumed considerable importance.* 這件事看來相當重要。◇ *In the story the god assumes the form of an eagle.* 在這個故事中神以鷹的形象出現。 **4 ~ sth** (*formal*) to pretend to have a particular feeling or quality 裝出；假裝 SYN **put on**：*He assumed an air of concern.* 他裝出關心的樣子。

as·sumed AW /ə'sjuːmd; *NAmE* ə'suːmd/ *adj.* [only before noun] that you suppose to be true or to exist 假定的；假設的：*the assumed differences between the two states* 兩種狀況的假定區別

as,sumed 'name *noun* a name that sb uses that is not their real name 化名 SYN **pseudonym**：*He was living* ***under an assumed name.*** 他過着隱姓埋名的生活。

as·sum·ing AW /ə'sjuːmɪŋ; *NAmE* ə'suːmɪŋ/ *conj.* **~ (that)** used to suppose that sth is true so that you can talk about what the results might be 假設…為真；假如：*Assuming (that) he's still alive, how old would he be now?* 假定他還活着，現在有多大年紀了？◇ *I hope to go to college next year,* ***always assuming*** *I pass my exams.* 我希望明年上大學，當然是在我通過考試的前提下。

as·sump·tion AW /ə'sʌmpʃn/ *noun* **1** [C] a belief or feeling that sth is true or that sth will happen, although there is no proof 假定；假設：*an* ***underlying/implicit assumption*** 設想；暗含的假定 ◇ *We need to challenge some of the basic assumptions of Western philosophy.* 我們有必要向西方哲學的某些基本假設提出質疑。◇ *We are working* ***on the assumption that*** *everyone invited will turn up.* 我們假定了每一個人都會應邀出席並正就此作出安排。◇ *It was impossible to* ***make assumptions about*** *people's reactions.* 臆斷人們的反應是不可能的。◇ *His actions were based on a false assumption.* 他的行為基於錯誤的設想。 **2** [C, U] **~ of sth** (*formal*) the act of taking or beginning to have power or responsibility （責任的）承擔；擔任；（權力的）獲得：*their* ***assumption of power/control*** 他們權力/控制的取得

as·sur·ance AW /ə'ʃʊərəns; -ʃɔːr-; *NAmE* ə'ʃʊr-/ *noun*
1 [C] a statement that sth will certainly be true or will certainly happen, particularly when there has been doubt about it 保證；擔保 SYN **guarantee, promise**：*They called for assurances that the government is committed to its education policy.* 他們要求政府保證切實執行其教育方針。◇ *Unemployment seems to be rising, despite repeated* ***assurances to the contrary.*** 儘管反複擔保減少失業，失業率看來卻在上升。 **2** (also **,self-as'surance**) [U] belief in your own abilities or strengths 自信 SYN **confidence**：*There was an air of easy assurance and calm about him.* 他表現出從容自信和冷靜。 **3** [U] (*BrE*) a type of insurance in which money is paid out when sb dies or after an agreed period of time 人壽保險：*a life assurance company* 人壽保險公司 ➲ see also QUALITY ASSURANCE

as·sure 🗝 AW /ə'ʃʊə(r); -ʃɔː(r); *NAmE* ə'ʃʊr/ *verb*
1 🗝 to tell sb that sth is definitely true or is definitely going to happen, especially when they have doubts about it 使確信；向…保證：**~ sb (that)** … *You think I did it deliberately, but I assure you (that) I did not.* 你認

為這是我故意幹的，不過我向你保證不是的。◇ *We were assured that everything possible was being done.* 我們確信是在盡一切努力。◇ *She's perfectly safe, **I can assure you**.* 我可以向你保證，她絕對安全。◇ **~ sb (of sth)** *We assured him of our support.* 我們向他保證給予支持。◇ **~ sb + speech** *'He'll come back,' Susan assured her.* "他會回來的。" 蘇珊安慰她道。 **2** (*formal*) to make yourself certain about sth 弄清；查明：**~ yourself of sth** *He assured himself of her safety.* 他確定她是安全的。◇ **~ yourself that …** *She assured herself that the letter was still in the drawer.* 她查清楚信仍然在抽屜裏。 **3** to make sth certain to happen 確保；使確定 **SYN** **guarantee**：**~ sth** *Victory would assure a place in the finals.* 勝利將確保能參加決賽。◇ **~ sb sth** *Victory would assure them a place in the finals.* 勝利將確保他們能參加決賽。 **4 ~ sth** (*BrE*) to INSURE sth, especially against sb's death 保險（尤指人壽險）：*What is the sum assured?* 人壽保險額是多少？ **IDM** see REST *v.*

as·sured **AW** /əˈʃʊəd; əˈʃɔːd; *NAmE* əˈʃʊrd/ *adj.* **1** (also **ˌself-asˈsured**) confident in yourself and your abilities 自信的；有把握的：*He spoke in a calm, assured voice.* 他冷靜自信地說。 **2** certain to happen 必將發生的；確定的 **SYN** **guaranteed**：*Success seemed assured.* 看來已必勝無疑。 **3 ~ of sth** (of a person 人) certain to get sth 肯定得到：*You are assured of a warm welcome at this hotel.* 你在這家旅館肯定會受到熱情歡迎。

as·sured·ly **AW** /əˈʃʊərədli; əˈʃɔːr-; *NAmE* əˈʃʊr-/ *adv.* (*formal*) certainly; definitely 肯定地；一定地

AST /ˌeɪ es ˈtiː/ *abbr.* ATLANTIC STANDARD TIME

as·ta·tine /ˈæstətiːn/ *noun* [U] (*symb.* **At**) a chemical element. Astatine is a RADIOACTIVE element which is found in small amounts in nature, and is produced artificially for use in medicine. 砹（放射性化學元素）

aster /ˈæstə(r)/ *noun* a garden plant that has pink, purple, blue or white flowers with many long narrow PETALS 紫菀（園藝植物）

as·ter·isk /ˈæstərɪsk/ *noun* the symbol (*) placed next to a particular word or phrase to make people notice it or to show that more information is given in another place 星號（置於詞語旁以引起注意或另有註釋）：*I've placed an asterisk next to the tasks I want you to do first.* 我在要你首先完成的任務旁邊標上了星號。 ▸ **as·ter·isk** *verb*：**~ sth** *I've asterisked the tasks I want you to do first.* 我在要你首先完成的任務旁邊標上了星號。

astern /əˈstɜːn; *NAmE* əˈstɜːrn/ *adv.* (*technical* 術語) **1** in, at or towards the back part of a ship or boat 在船尾；向船尾 **2** if a ship or boat is moving **astern**, it is moving backwards（指船）向後

as·ter·oid /ˈæstərɔɪd/ *noun* any one of the many small planets that go around the sun 小行星

asthma /ˈæsmə; *NAmE* ˈæzmə/ *noun* [U] a medical condition of the chest that makes breathing difficult 氣喘；哮喘：*a severe asthma attack* 哮喘嚴重發作

asth·mat·ic /æsˈmætɪk; *NAmE* æzˈmætɪk/ *noun* a person who suffers from asthma 氣喘患者；哮喘患者 ▸ **asth·mat·ic** *adj.*：*asthmatic patients* 哮喘患者 ◇ *an asthmatic attack* 哮喘發作

astig·ma·tism /əˈstɪɡmətɪzəm/ *noun* [U] (*medical* 醫) a fault in the shape of a person's eye that prevents them from seeing clearly 散光

as·ton·ish /əˈstɒnɪʃ; *NAmE* əˈstɑːn-/ *verb* to surprise sb very much 使十分驚訝；使大為驚奇；使吃驚 **SYN** **amaze** ➲ SYNONYMS at SURPRISE：**~ sb** *The news astonished everyone.* 這消息使大家十分驚訝。◇ *She astonished us by saying she was leaving.* 她說她要離開，令我們大為驚訝。◇ **it astonishes sb (that) …** *It astonishes me (that) he could be so thoughtless.* 我真沒有料到他會如此輕率。

as·ton·ished /əˈstɒnɪʃt; *NAmE* əˈstɑːn-/ *adj.* very surprised 感到十分驚訝；吃驚 **SYN** **amazed**：*The helicopter landed before our astonished eyes.* 直升機就降落在我們眼前，令人十分驚訝。◇ **~ at/by sth/sb** *My parents looked astonished at my news.* 我的父母聽到我的消息後顯得十分驚訝。◇ **~ (that) …** *She seemed astonished (that) I had never been to Paris.* 我從未去過巴黎，這似乎使她大為驚奇。◇ **~ to find/hear/learn/see …** *He was astonished to learn he'd won the competition.* 他聽說他比賽贏了，感到很驚訝。

as·ton·ish·ing /əˈstɒnɪʃɪŋ; *NAmE* əˈstɑːn-/ *adj.* very surprising; difficult to believe 令人十分驚訝的；使人大為驚奇的；難以置信的 **SYN** **amazing**：*She ran 100m in an astonishing 10.6 seconds.* 她以 10.6 秒的驚人速度跑完了 100 米。◇ *I find it absolutely astonishing that you didn't like it.* 你不喜歡它，我感到難以置信。 ▸ **as·ton·ish·ing·ly** *adv.*：*Jack took the news astonishingly well.* 傑克對這個消息表現得出奇地冷靜。◇ *Astonishingly, a crowd of several thousands turned out to hear him.* 令人十分驚異的是有幾千人來聽他講話。

as·ton·ish·ment /əˈstɒnɪʃmənt; *NAmE* əˈstɑːn-/ *noun* [U] a feeling of very great surprise 驚訝；驚異 **SYN** **amazement**：***To my utter astonishment**, she remembered my name.* 她竟記得我的名字，使我萬分驚訝。◇ *He stared **in astonishment** at the stranger.* 他驚愕地盯着那陌生人。

as·tound /əˈstaʊnd/ *verb* **~ sb** to surprise or shock sb very much 使震驚；使大驚 **SYN** **astonish**：*His arrogance astounded her.* 他的傲慢使她震驚。◇ *She was astounded by his arrogance.* 他的傲慢使她震驚。 ➲ note at SURPRISE

as·tound·ed /əˈstaʊndɪd/ *adj.* very surprised or shocked by sth, because it seems very unlikely 感到震驚的；大吃一驚的 **SYN** **astonished**：*an astounded expression* 大吃一驚的表情 ◇ *How can you say that? I'm absolutely astounded.* 你怎麼能說出那種話？我感到大為震驚。◇ **~ at/by sth** *She looked astounded at the news.* 她聽到那消息時顯得震驚。◇ **~ (that) …** *The doctors were astounded (that) he survived.* 醫生們十分驚愕的是他竟活過來了。◇ **~ to find/hear/learn/see …** *I was astounded to see her appear from the house.* 我看見她從房子裏出來，大吃一驚。

as·tound·ing /əˈstaʊndɪŋ/ *adj.* so surprising that it is difficult to believe 令人震驚的；使大吃一驚的 **SYN** **astonishing**：*There was an astounding 20% increase in sales.* 銷售量驚人地增加了 20%。 ▸ **as·tound·ing·ly** *adv.*

as·tra·khan /ˌæstrəˈkæn; *NAmE* ˈæstrəkən/ *noun* [U] a type of black tightly-curled cloth made from the wool of a particular type of young sheep, used especially for making coats and hats; a type of cloth that is made to look like this 阿斯特拉罕羔羊毛織物；仿阿斯特拉罕羔羊毛織物

as·tral /ˈæstrəl/ *adj.* [only before noun] **1** (*technical* 術語) connected with the stars 星的：*astral navigation* 星際航行 **2** connected with the spiritual rather than the physical world of existence 精神世界的：*the astral plane* 精神世界層面

astray /əˈstreɪ/ *adv.*

IDM **go aˈstray** **1** to become lost; to be stolen 丟失；被盜：*Several letters went astray or were not delivered.* 有幾封信丟失或未投遞。◇ *We locked up our valuables so they would not go astray.* 我們把貴重物品鎖了起來以免被盜。 **2** to go in the wrong direction or to have the wrong result 走錯方向；誤入歧途：*Fortunately the gunman's shots went astray.* 幸好持槍歹徒把子彈打偏了。◇ *Jack's parents thought the other boys might **lead him astray*** (= make him do things that are wrong). 傑克的父母認為，其他的男孩可能會把他引入歧途。

astride /əˈstraɪd/ *prep., adv.*

■ ***prep.*** with one leg on each side of sth 跨（或騎）在…上：*to sit **astride a horse/bike/chair*** 騎馬 / 自行車；跨坐在椅子上 ◇ (*figurative*) *a town astride the river* 跨河的城鎮

■ ***adv.*** **1** with legs or feet wide apart 叉開兩腿 **2** with one leg on each side 跨着；騎着

as·trin·gent /əˈstrɪndʒənt/ *adj., noun*

■ ***adj.*** **1** (*technical* 術語) (of a liquid or cream 液體或乳劑) able to make the skin feel less OILY or to stop the loss of blood from a cut（能使皮膚或傷口）收斂的，止血的 **2** (*formal*) critical in a severe or clever way 尖刻的；辛辣的：***astringent writers/comments*** 尖刻的作家 / 話 **3** (*formal*) (of a taste or smell 味道或氣味) slightly bitter

A

but fresh 微苦而清新的：*the astringent taste of lemon juice* 檸檬汁微苦卻清新的味道 ▸ **astrin·gency** /-ənsi/ *noun* [U]

■ **noun** a liquid or cream used in COSMETICS or medicine to make the skin less OILY or to stop the loss of blood from a cut（用於化妝品或藥物中的）收斂劑，止血劑

astro- /ˈæstrəʊ; *NAmE* ˈæstroʊ/ *combining form* (in nouns, adjectives and adverbs 構成名詞、形容詞和副詞) connected with the stars or outer space 星（的）；天體（的）；外層空間（的）；宇宙空間（的）：*astronaut* 宇航員 ◇ *astrophysics* 天體物理學

astro·labe /ˈæstrəleɪb/ *noun* (*astronomy* 天) a device used in the past for measuring the distances of stars, planets etc. and for calculating the position of a ship 星盤（舊時用於測量天體高度等）

as·trol·oger /əˈstrɒlədʒə(r); *NAmE* əˈstrɑːl-/ *noun* a person who uses astrology to tell people about their character, about what might happen to them in the future, etc. 占星家

as·trol·ogy /əˈstrɒlədʒi; *NAmE* əˈstrɑːl-/ *noun* [U] the study of the positions of the stars and the movements of the planets in the belief that they influence human affairs 占星術；占星學 ▸ **astro·logic·al** /ˌæstrəˈlɒdʒɪkl; *NAmE* -ˈlɑːdʒ-/ *adj.*：*astrological influences* 占星術的影響

astro·naut /ˈæstrənɔːt/ *noun* a person whose job involves travelling and working in a SPACECRAFT 宇航員；航天員；太空人

as·tron·omer /əˈstrɒnəmə(r); *NAmE* əˈstrɑːn-/ *noun* a scientist who studies astronomy 天文學家

astro·nom·ic·al /ˌæstrəˈnɒmɪkl; *NAmE* -ˈnɑːm-/ *adj.* **1** connected with ASTRONOMY 天文學的；天文的：*astronomical observations* 天文觀測 **2** (also **astro·nom·ic**) (*informal*) (of an amount, a price, etc. 數量、價格等) very large 極其巨大的：*the astronomical costs of land for building* 建築用地極其巨大的成本 ◇ *The figures are astronomical.* 這些都是天文數字。 ▸ **astro·nom·ic·al·ly** /-kli/ *adv.*：*Interest rates are astronomically high.* 利率極高。

astroˌnomical ˈunit *noun* (*abbr.* **AU**) (*astronomy* 天) a unit of measurement equal to 149.6 million kilometres, which is the distance from the centre of the earth to the sun 天文單位（即地球中心與太陽的距離，約合 1.496 億公里）

as·tron·omy /əˈstrɒnəmi; *NAmE* əˈstrɑːn-/ *noun* [U] the scientific study of the sun, moon, stars, planets, etc. 天文學

astro·phys·ics /ˌæstrəʊˈfɪzɪks; *NAmE* ˌæstroʊ-/ *noun* [U] the scientific study of the physical and chemical structure of the stars, planets, etc. 天體物理學 ▸ **astro·physi·cist** /-ˈfɪzɪsɪst/ *noun*

Astro·Turf™ /ˈæstrəʊtɜːf; *NAmE* ˈæstroʊtɜːrf/ *noun* [U] an artificial surface that looks like grass, for playing sports on 阿斯特羅人造草皮

ˈA student *noun* (*especially NAmE*) a student who gets or is likely to get the highest marks/grades in his/her work or exams 學業成績得 A 者；優等生

as·tute /əˈstjuːt; *NAmE* əˈstuːt/ *adj.* very clever and quick at seeing what to do in a particular situation, especially how to get an advantage 精明的；狡猾的 **SYN** **shrewd**：*an* ***astute businessman/politician/observer*** 精明的商人；狡猾的政客；敏鋭的觀察家 ◇ *It was an astute move to sell the shares then.* 那時出售股份是精明之舉。 ▸ **as·tute·ly** *adv.* **as·tute·ness** *noun* [U]

asun·der /əˈsʌndə(r)/ *adv.* (*old-fashioned* or *literary*) into pieces; apart 碎；散：*families* ***rent/torn asunder*** *by the revolution* 這場革命所拆散的家庭

asy·lum /əˈsaɪləm/ *noun* **1** (also *formal* **poˌlitical aˈsylum**) [U] protection that a government gives to people who have left their own country, usually because they were in danger for political reasons（政治）庇護，避難：***to seek/apply for/be granted asylum*** 尋求／申請／獲准政治避難 ◇ *There was a nationwide debate on whether the asylum laws should be changed.* 對是否應該修改政治避難法展開了一場全國性的大辯論。 **2** [C] (*old use*) a hospital where people who were mentally ill could be cared for, often for a long time 精神病院

aˈsylum seeker *noun* a person who has been forced to leave their own country because they are in danger and who arrives in another country asking to be allowed to stay there 尋求避難者；尋求庇護的移民 ➲ COLLOCATIONS at RACE

asym·met·ric /ˌeɪsɪˈmetrɪk/ (also **asym·met·ric·al** /ˌeɪsɪˈmetrɪkl/) *adj.* **1** having two sides or parts that are not the same in size or shape 不對稱的：*Most people's faces are asymmetric.* 大多數人的臉不對稱。 **OPP** **sym·metrical** **2** (*technical* 術語) not equal, for example in the way each side or part behaves 不對等的：*Linguists are studying the asymmetric use of Creole by parents and children* (= parents use one language and children reply in another). 語言學家正在研究父母和孩子使用克里奧爾混合語時的不對等現象（即父母使用一種語言而孩子用另一種語言回答）。 ▸ **asym·met·ric·al·ly** /-ɪkli/ *adv.* **asym·met·ry** /ˌeɪˈsɪmətri/ *noun* [C, U]

asymˌmetric ˈbars (*BrE*) (*NAmE* **unˌeven ˈbars**) *noun* [pl.] two bars on posts of different heights that are used by women for doing GYMNASTIC exercises on 高低槓（女子體操器械）

asymp·tom·at·ic /ˌeɪsɪmptəˈmætɪk/ *adj.* (*medical* 醫) (of a person or illness 人或疾病) having no SYMPTOMS 無症狀的

asyn·chron·ous /eɪˈsɪŋkrənəs/ *adj.* (*formal*) (of two or more objects or events 兩個或多個物體或事情) not existing or happening at the same time 不同時存在（或發生）的；非共時的 ▸ **asyn·chron·ous·ly** *adv.*

at 🔑 /ət; *strong form* æt/ *prep.*

1 🔑 used to say where sth/sb is or where sth happens 在（某處）：*at the corner of the street* 在街角 ◇ *We changed at Crewe.* 我們在克魯換的車。 ◇ *They arrived late at the airport.* 他們晚到了機場。 ◇ *At the roundabout take the third exit.* 在環島處走第三個出口。 ◇ *I'll be at home all morning.* 我一上午都在家。 ◇ *She's at Tom's* (= at Tom's house). 她在湯姆家中。 ◇ *I met her at the hospital.* 我在醫院遇見了她。 ◇ *How many people were there at the concert?* 音樂會上有多少人？ **2** 🔑 used to say where sb works or studies 在（表示學習或工作地點）：*He's been at the bank longer than anyone else.* 他在銀行工作的時間比任何人都長。 ◇ *She's at Yale* (= Yale University). 她上耶魯大學。 **3** 🔑 used to say when sth happens 在（某時間或時刻）：*We left at 2 o'clock.* 我們在兩點鐘離開的。 ◇ *at the end of the week* 在週末 ◇ *We woke at dawn.* 我們在黎明醒來。 ◇ *I didn't know at the time of writing* (= when I wrote). 我寫的時候並不知道。 ◇ *At night you can see the stars.* 夜晚可以看見星星。 ◇ (*BrE*) *What are you doing at the weekend?* 你打算週末幹什麼？ **4** 🔑 used to state the age at which sb does sth 在…歲時：*She got married at 25.* 她 25 歲結婚。 ◇ *He left school at the age of 16.* 他 16 歲便離開學校。 **5** 🔑 in the direction of or towards sb/sth 向；朝：*What are you looking at?* 你在看什麼？ ◇ *He pointed a gun at her.* 他把槍口對着她。 ◇ *Somebody threw paint at the prime minister.* 有人朝首相扔油漆。 **6** used after a verb to show that sb tries to do sth, or partly does sth, but does not succeed or complete it （用於動詞後，涉及未做成或未做完的事）：*He clutched wildly at the rope as he fell.* 他墜落時拚命想抓住繩子。 ◇ *She nibbled at a sandwich* (= ate only small bits of it). 她一小口一小口地吃三明治。 **7** 🔑 used to state the distance away from sth 在…遠；從相隔…遠的地方：*I held it at arm's length.* 我伸直胳膊提着它。 ◇ *Can you read a car number plate at fifty metres?* 在五十米遠處你能看清汽車牌嗎？ **8** 🔑 used to show the situation sb/sth is in, what sb is doing or what is happening 處於…狀態：*The country is now at war.* 這個國家正在打仗。 ◇ *I felt at a disadvantage.* 我覺得處於不利地位。 ◇ *I think Mr Harris is at lunch.* 我想哈里斯先生正在吃午飯。 **9** 🔑 used to show a rate, speed, etc. （用於速度、比率等）以，達：*He was driving at 70 mph.* 他以每小時 70 英里的速度駕車行駛。 ◇ *The noise came at two-minute intervals* (= once every two minutes). 每兩分鐘傳來一次響聲。 ◇ *Prices start at $1 000.* 起價 1 000 元 **10** 🔑 **~ sb's/sth's best/worst, etc.** used to say that sb/sth is as good, bad, etc. as they can be 處於最佳（或最差等）狀態；在全盛（或谷底等）時期：*This was Murray at his best.* 這是默里的最佳表現。◇ *The garden's at its most beautiful in June.* 六月的花園最美麗。 **11** used with adjectives to show how well sb does sth（與形容詞連用，表示狀況）在…方面：*I'm **good at** French.* 我的法語很好。◇ *She's hopeless at managing people.* 她對人事管理一竅不通。 **12** used with adjectives to show the cause of sth（與形容詞連用）因為，由於，對…：*They were impatient at the delay.* 他們對拖延不耐煩了。◇ *She was delighted at the result.* 對這個結果她感到高興。 **13** (*formal*) in response to sth 應…（而）；響應；回答：*They attended the dinner at the chairman's invitation.* 他們應董事長之邀出席了宴會。 **14** (*NAmE*) used when giving a telephone number（提供電話號碼時用）：*You can reach me at 637-2335, extension 354.* 你可以打 637-2335 這個電話號碼，轉分機 354 與我聯繫。 **15** (*computing* 計) the symbol (@) used in email addresses（用於電子郵箱地址中的符號 @）

IDM **at that** used when you are giving an extra piece of information（提供額外信息時）而且還：*He managed to buy a car after all—and a nice one at that.* 他終於設法買了一輛小轎車，而且還挺不錯的。 **be 'at it again** to be doing sth, especially sth bad 正在做某事（尤指壞事）：*Look at all that graffiti—those kids have been at it again.* 瞧瞧所有的那些塗鴉，又是那些孩子幹的好事。 **ˌwhere it's 'at** (*informal*) a place or an activity that is very popular or fashionable 盛大活動（場合）；流行活動（地方）：*Judging by the crowds waiting to get in, this seems to be where it's at.* 從等待入場的人群來看，這好像是個盛大活動。

at·av·is·tic /ˌætəˈvɪstɪk/ *adj.* (*formal*) related to the attitudes and behaviour of the first humans 返祖性的：*an **atavistic urge/instinct/fear*** 返祖傾向／本能；返祖性畏懼

ataxia /əˈtæksiə/ (also **ataxy** /əˈtæksi/) *noun* [U] (*medical* 醫) the loss of full control of the body's movements 共濟失調，協調不能，運動失調（表現為動作不穩、不協調）▸ **ataxic** *adj.*

ate *past tense* of EAT

-ate *suffix* **1** (in adjectives 構成形容詞) full of or having the quality of 充滿…的；有…性質的：*passionate* 充滿熱情的 ◇ *Italianate* 意大利風格的 **2** (in verbs 構成動詞) to give the thing or quality mentioned to 賦予某物；給予…性質：*hyphenate* 用連字符連接 ◇ *activate* 使活動 **3** (in nouns 構成名詞) the status or function of（表示地位或職能）：*a doctorate* 博士學位 **4** (in nouns 構成名詞) a group with the status or function of（表示有地位或職能的群體）：*the electorate* 全體選民 **5** (*chemistry* 化) (in nouns 構成名詞) a salt formed by the action of a particular acid（酸作用形成的）鹽：*sulphate* 硫酸鹽

'A-team *noun* [usually sing.] **1** the best sports team in a school, club, etc.（學校等的）最佳運動隊，甲隊 **2** a group of the best workers, soldiers, etc.（工人、士兵等的）精英小組

atel·ier /əˈteliei; *NAmE* ˌætlˈjeɪ/ *noun* a room or building in which an artist works（藝術家的）工作室，製作室 **SYN** studio

atem·poral /ˌeɪˈtempərəl/ *adj.* (*formal*) existing or considered without relation to time 非時間的；不受時間影響的

athe·ism /ˈeɪθiɪzəm/ *noun* [U] the belief that God does not exist 無神論 **OPP** theism ▸ **athe·is·tic** /ˌeɪθiˈɪstɪk/ *adj.*

athe·ist /ˈeɪθiɪst/ *noun* a person who believes that God does not exist 無神論者 ➲ compare AGNOSTIC

ath·lete /ˈæθliːt/ *noun* **1** a person who competes in sports 運動員：*Olympic athletes* 奧運會運動員 **2** (*BrE*) a person who competes in sports such as running and jumping 田徑運動員 **3** a person who is good at sports and physical exercise 擅長運動的人；健兒：*She is a natural athlete.* 她是個天生的運動健將。

ˌathlete's 'foot *noun* [U] an infectious skin disease that affects the feet, especially between the toes 腳癬

ath·let·ic /æθˈletɪk/ *adj.* **1** physically strong, fit and active 健壯的：*an **athletic figure/build*** 健壯的體形／體格 ◇ *a tall, slim athletic girl* 修長健美的姑娘 **2** [only before noun] (*BrE*) connected with sports such as running, jumping and throwing (= athletics) 體育運動的；田徑運動的：*an **athletic club/coach*** 運動員俱樂部／教練 ▸ **ath·let·ical·ly** /-ɪkli/ *adv.* **ath·leti·cism** /æθˈletɪsɪzəm/ *noun* [U]：*She moved with great athleticism about the court.* 她在球場上矯健地奔跑活動。

ath·let·ics /æθˈletɪks/ *noun* [U] **1** (*BrE*) (*NAmE* **ˌtrack and 'field**) sports that people compete in, such as running and jumping 田徑運動 ➲ VISUAL VOCAB page V46 **2** (*NAmE*) any sports that people compete in 體育運動：*students involved in all forms of college athletics* 參加各種大學體育運動的學生

ath'letic shoe *noun* (*NAmE*) = TENNIS SHOE

athˌletic sup'porter *noun* (*especially NAmE*) = JOCK-STRAP

at-'home *noun, adj.*

■ ***noun*** (*old-fashioned*) a party in sb's home 家中聚會：*We're having an at-home—can you come?* 我們要在家中聚會——你能來嗎？

■ ***adj.*** **ˌat-'home** [only before noun] **1** done or taking place at home 在家裏進行（或發生）的：*an at-home job* 一份在家裏做的工作 **2** (of a parent 父親或母親) staying at home rather than going out to work 在家的；不外出工作的：*at-home dads* 家庭全職爸爸

-athon /əθən; *NAmE* əθɑːn/ *suffix* (in nouns 構成名詞) an event in which a particular activity is done for a very long time, especially one organized to raise money for charity 持續時間很長的活動（尤指為慈善事業募集基金）：*a swimathon* 馬拉松式游泳

athwart /əˈθwɔːt; *NAmE* əˈθwɔːrt/ *prep.* (*literary* or *formal*) **1** across; from one side to the other 橫跨於：*They put a table athwart the doorway.* 他們把桌子橫放在門口。 **2** not agreeing with; opposite to 與…不一致；與…相反：*His statement ran athwart what was previously said.* 他講的話與先前所說的相抵觸。

-ation ➲ -ION

atish·oo /əˈtɪʃuː/ (*BrE*) (also **ah·choo** *NAmE, BrE*) *exclamation* the word for the sound people make when they SNEEZE 阿嚏（指噴嚏聲）

-ative *suffix* (in adjectives 構成形容詞) doing or tending to do sth 做…的；有…傾向的：*illustrative* 解說性的 ◇ *talkative* 愛說話的 ▸ **-atively** *suffix* (in adverbs 構成副詞)：*creatively* 有創造性

Atkins Diet™ /ˈætkɪnz daɪət/ *noun* a diet in which you eat foods that contain a high level of PROTEIN (meat, eggs, cheese, etc.) and avoid foods that contain a high level of CARBOHYDRATES (bread, rice, fruit, etc.) 阿特金斯規定飲食（高蛋白質、低碳水化合物）

Atˌlantic 'Daylight Time *noun* [U] (*abbr.* **ADT**) the time used in summer in an area that includes the east of Canada, Puerto Rico and the Virgin Islands, that is three hours earlier than GMT 大西洋日光節約時間，大西洋夏令時間（加拿大東部、波多黎各、美屬維爾京群島的夏季時間，比格林尼治平時早三個小時）

Atˌlantic 'Standard Time *noun* [U] (*abbr.* **AST**) (also **At'lantic time**) the time used in winter in an area that includes the east of Canada, Puerto Rico and the Virgin Islands, that is four hours earlier than GMT 大西洋標準時間（加拿大東部、波多黎各、美屬維爾京群島的冬季時間，比格林尼治平時早四個小時）

At·lan·tis /ætˈlæntɪs/ *noun* [U] (in stories 傳説) an island full of beauty and wealth, that was said to have been covered by the sea and lost. There are many stories about people's attempts to find it. 亞特蘭蒂斯，大西島（一座美麗富饒的海島，據説已沉入海底消失）

atlas /ˈætləs/ *noun* a book of maps 地圖冊；地圖集：*a world atlas* 世界地圖冊 ◇ *a road atlas of Europe* 歐洲道路地圖冊

ATM /ˌeɪ tiː ˈem/ *noun* the abbreviation for 'automated teller machine' 自動櫃員機，自動提款機（全寫為 automated teller machine）➲ CASH MACHINE

ˌAT'M card (*US*) (*BrE* **'cash card**) *noun* a plastic card used to get money from a CASH MACHINE (= a machine in or outside a bank) 現金卡；自動取款卡 ➲ compare CHEQUE CARD, CREDIT CARD, DEBIT CARD

at·mos·phere 0┳ /ˈætməsfɪə(r); NAmE -fɪr/ *noun* **1** 0┳ **the atmosphere** [sing.] the mixture of gases that surrounds the earth（圍繞地球的）大氣，大氣層，大氣圈：*the upper atmosphere* 高層大氣 ◇ *pollution of the atmosphere* 大氣污染 **2** 0┳ [C] a mixture of gases that surrounds another planet or a star（圍繞其他天體的）氣體：*Saturn's atmosphere* 土星的大氣 **3** 0┳ [C] the air in a room or in a confined space; the air around a place（房間、封閉空間或某處的）空氣：*a **smoky/stuffy atmosphere*** 煙霧瀰漫的／悶熱的空氣 ◇ *These plants love warm, humid atmospheres.* 這些植物喜歡溫暖潮濕的空氣。 **4** 0┳ [C, sing., U] the feeling or mood that you have in a particular place or situation; a feeling between two people or in a group of people 氣氛；氛圍：*a party atmosphere* 聚會的氣氛 ◇ *The hotel offers a friendly atmosphere and personal service.* 這家旅館服務周到，使客人感到賓至如歸。◇ *Use music and lighting to create a romantic atmosphere.* 用音樂和照明創造一種浪漫的氣氛。◇ *There was an atmosphere of mutual trust between them.* 他們之間以前有一種相互信任的氣氛。◇ *The children grew up in an atmosphere of violence and insecurity.* 這些孩子在暴力和無安全感的環境中長大。◇ *The old house is full of atmosphere* (= it's very interesting). 這座老房子情趣盎然。 **IDM** see HEAVY *adj.*

at·mos·pher·ic /ˌætməsˈferɪk/ *adj.* **1** [only before noun] related to the earth's atmosphere 大氣的；大氣層的：***atmospheric pollution/conditions/pressure*** 大氣污染／狀況／壓力 **2** creating an exciting or emotional mood 令人激動的；使人動感情的：*atmospheric music* 有感染力的音樂

at·mos·pher·ics /ˌætməsˈferɪks; NAmE also -ˈfɪr-/ *noun* [pl.] **1** qualities in sth that create a particular atmosphere 氣氛特徵 **2** noises that sometimes interrupt a radio broadcast 大氣干擾；天電

atoll /ˈætɒl; NAmE ˈætɔːl; -tɑːl/ *noun* an island made of CORAL and shaped like a ring with a lake of sea water (called a LAGOON) in the middle 環狀珊瑚島；環礁

atom 0┳ /ˈætəm/ *noun* the smallest part of a chemical element that can take part in a chemical reaction 原子：*the splitting of the atom* 原子的分裂 ◇ *Two atoms of hydrogen combine with one atom of oxygen to form a molecule of water.* 兩個氫原子和一個氧原子結合組成一個水分子。

ˈatom bomb (also **ˈA-bomb**) *noun* a bomb that explodes using the energy that is produced when an atom or atoms are split 原子彈

atom·ic /əˈtɒmɪk; NAmE əˈtɑːmɪk/ *adj.* [usually before noun] **1** connected with atoms or an atom 原子的；與原子有關的：*atomic structure* 原子結構 **2** related to the energy that is produced when atoms are split; related to weapons that use this energy 原子能的；原子武器的：***atomic energy/power*** 原子能／動力 ◇ *the atomic bomb* 原子彈

aˌtomic ˈclock *noun* an extremely accurate clock that uses the movement of atoms or MOLECULES to measure time 原子鐘（利用原子或分子運動計時，精確度極高）

atom·ic·ity /ˌætəmˈɪsɪti/ *noun* (*chemistry* 化) the number of atoms in one MOLECULE of a substance 原子價

aˌtomic ˈmass *noun* (*chemistry* 化) = RELATIVE ATOMIC MASS

aˌtomic ˈnumber *noun* (*chemistry* 化) the number of PROTONS in the NUCLEUS (= centre) of an atom, which is characteristic of a chemical element. Elements are placed in the PERIODIC TABLE according to their atomic numbers. 原子序數（指原子在元素週期表中的序號）

aˌtomic ˈtheory *noun* (*chemistry* 化, *physics* 物) the theory that all elements are made up of small PARTICLES called atoms which are made up of a central NUCLEUS surrounded by moving ELECTRONS 原子論

aˌtomic ˈweight *noun* (*chemistry* 化) = RELATIVE ATOMIC MASS

atom·ism /ˈætəmɪzəm/ *noun* [U] (*technical* 術語) the idea of analysing sth by separating it into its different parts 原子論（借助各個組成部份之間的差異等來分析整體）➲ compare HOLISM (1) ▸ **atom·is·tic** /ˌætəˈmɪstɪk/ *adj.*

atom·ize (*BrE* also **-ise**) /ˈætəmaɪz/ *verb* **~ sth** to reduce sth to atoms or very small pieces 使分裂成原子；使粉碎；使成微粒；使霧化

atom·izer (*BrE* also **-iser**) /ˈætəmaɪzə(r)/ *noun* a container that forces a liquid such as water or paint out as a very fine spray 霧化器；噴霧器

atonal /eɪˈtəʊnl; NAmE eɪˈtoʊnl/ *adj.* (of a piece of music 樂曲) not written in any particular KEY 無調的 **OPP** **tonal** ▸ **aton·al·ity** /ˌeɪtəʊˈnæləti; NAmE ˌeɪtoʊˈn-/ *noun* [U]

atone /əˈtəʊn; NAmE əˈtoʊn/ *verb* [I] **~ (for sth)** (*formal*) to act in a way that shows you are sorry for doing sth wrong in the past 贖（罪）；彌補（過錯）**SYN** **make amends**：*to atone for a crime* 贖罪 ▸ **atone·ment** *noun* [U]：*to make atonement for his sins* 贖他的罪過 ◇ *Yom Kippur, the Jewish day of atonement* 猶太教的贖罪日 Yom Kippur

atop /əˈtɒp; NAmE əˈtɑːp/ *prep.* (*especially NAmE*) (*BrE, old-fashioned* or *literary*) on top of; at the top of 在…頂上：*a flag high atop a pole* 高掛在旗杆頂端的旗子 ◇ *a scoop of ice cream atop a slice of apple pie* 一片蘋果餡餅上面的一勺冰淇淋

atopic /eɪˈtɒpɪk; NAmE -ˈtɑːp-/ *adj.* (*medical* 醫) relating to a form of ALLERGY where there is a reaction in a part of the body that does not have direct contact with the thing causing the ALLERGY 特應性的，異位的（指過敏部位並非直接接觸過敏原）

-ator *suffix* (in nouns 構成名詞) a person or thing that does sth 做…的人（或事物）：*creator* 創造者 ◇ *percolator* 咖啡滲濾器

A to Z /ˌeɪ tə ˈzed; NAmE ˌeɪ tə ˈziː/ *noun* [sing.] **1** (*BrE*) a book containing street maps of all the areas of a large city（標明各街道位置的）城市地圖冊 **2** a book containing all the information you need about a subject or place 指南大全：*an A to Z of needlework* 刺繡指南大全

ATP /ˌeɪ tiː ˈpiː/ *abbr.* (*BrE*) the abbreviation for 'automatic train protection' (a system for automatically stopping a train if the driver does not stop or go slower when a signal tells him/her to) 列車自動保護系統（全寫為 automatic train protection）

ˌat-ˈrisk *adj.* [only before noun] (of a person or group 人或群體) in danger of being attacked or hurt, especially in their own home（尤指居家時）處於危險中的，可能遭受傷害的：*Social services keep lists of **at-risk children**.* 社工組織保留有在家裏可能遭受傷害的孩子名單。

at·rium /ˈeɪtriəm/ *noun* **1** a large high space, usually with a glass roof, in the centre of a modern building（現代建築物中央通常帶有玻璃屋頂的）中庭，中廳 **2** an open space in the centre of an ancient Roman VILLA (= a large house)（古羅馬大宅的）天井 **3** (*anatomy* 解) either of the two upper spaces in the heart that are used in the first stage of sending the blood around the body 心房 **SYN** **auricle**

atro·cious /əˈtrəʊʃəs; NAmE əˈtroʊ-/ *adj.* **1** very bad or unpleasant 糟透的；十分討厭的 **SYN** **terrible**：*She speaks French with an atrocious accent.* 她講的法語帶有很難聽的口音。◇ *Isn't the weather atrocious?* 天氣不是糟透了嗎？ **2** very cruel and shocking 殘暴的；殘忍的；兇惡的：*atrocious acts of brutality* 殘暴的獸行 ▸ **atro·cious·ly** *adv.*

atro·city /əˈtrɒsəti; NAmE əˈtrɑːs-/ *noun* [C, usually pl., U] (*pl.* **-ies**) a cruel and violent act, especially in a war（尤指戰爭中的）殘暴行為

at·ro·phy /ˈætrəfi/ *noun, verb*

■ ***noun*** [U] (*medical* 醫) the condition of losing flesh, muscle, strength, etc. in a part of the body because it does not have enough blood 萎縮；衰退：(*figurative, formal*) *The cultural life of the country will sink into atrophy unless more writers and artists emerge.* 如果沒有更多的作家和藝術家出現，這個國家的文化生活將衰退。

■ ***verb*** (**at·ro·phies**, **at·ro·phy·ing**, **at·ro·phied**, **at·ro·phied**) [I] if a part of the body **atrophies**, it becomes weak

because it is not used or because it does not have enough blood 萎縮；衰退：(*figurative*) *Memory can atrophy through lack of use.* 記憶力不常使用就會衰退。
▸ **at·ro·phied** *adj.*：*atrophied muscles* 萎縮的肌肉 ◇ *atrophied religious values* 淡化的宗教價值觀念

at·ta·boy /ˈætəbɔɪ/ *exclamation* (*informal, especially NAmE*) used when you want to encourage sb or show your admiration of them, especially a boy or man（對男性表示鼓勵或欽佩）好樣的 ➲ see also ATTAGIRL

at·tach 🔑 **AW** /əˈtætʃ/ *verb*
1 🔑 [T] to fasten or join one thing to another 把…固定，把…附（在…上）：**~ sth** *I attach a copy of my notes for your information.* 我附上筆記一份供你參考。◇ *I attach a copy of the spreadsheet* (= send it with an email). 我隨電子郵件附上電子表格一份。◇ **~ sth to sth** *Attach the coupon to the front of your letter.* 把優惠券附在信的正面。◇ (*figurative*) *They have attached a number of conditions to the agreement* (= said that the conditions must be part of the agreement). 他們在協議上附加了一些條件。➲ compare DETACH **2** 🔑 [T] **~ importance, significance, value, weight, etc. (to sth)** to believe that sth is important or worth thinking about 認為有重要性（或意義、價值、分量等）；重視：*I attach great importance to this research.* 我認為這項研究十分重要。**3** [T] **~ yourself to sb** to join sb for a time, sometimes when you are not welcome or have not been invited（有時不受歡迎或未受邀請而）參加，和…在一起，纏着：*He attached himself to me at the party and I couldn't get rid of him.* 在聚會上他老是纏着我，我簡直無法擺脱他。**4** [I, T] (*formal*) to be connected with sb/sth; to connect sth to sth（使）與…有聯繫；與…有關連：**~ to sb/sth** *No one is suggesting that any health risks attach to this product.* 沒有人指出這個產品可能會危害健康。◇ *No blame attaches to you.* 你一點責任也沒有。◇ **~ sth to sb/sth** *This does not attach any blame to you.* 這事你一點責任也沒有。

at·taché /əˈtæʃeɪ; *NAmE* ˌætəˈʃeɪ/ *noun* a person who works at an EMBASSY, usually with a special responsibility for a particular area of activity（使館的）專員，隨員：*a cultural attaché* 文化專員

at'taché case *noun* a small hard flat case used for carrying business documents 公文包 ➲ VISUAL VOCAB page V64 ➲ compare BRIEFCASE

at·tached 🔑 **AW** /əˈtætʃt/ *adj.*
1 🔑 **~ (to sb/sth)** full of affection for sb/sth 依戀；愛慕：*I've never seen two people so attached to each other.* 我從未見過兩個人如此形影不離。◇ *We've grown very attached to this house.* 我們變得非常喜歡這座房子。➲ compare UNATTACHED **2** 🔑 [not before noun] **~ to sth** working for or forming part of an organization 附屬於；為…工作：*The research unit is attached to the university.* 這個研究單位附屬於大學。**3** 🔑 **~ (to sth)** joined to sth 所附的：*Please complete the attached application form.* 請填寫所附申請表。

at·tach·ment **AW** /əˈtætʃmənt/ *noun* **1** [C, U] a strong feeling of affection for sb/sth 依戀；愛慕：*a child's strong attachment to its parents* 孩子對父母的強烈依戀 **2** [C, U] belief in and support for an idea or a set of values 信念；信仰；忠誠；擁護：*the popular attachment to democratic government* 對民主政府的普遍擁護 **3** [C] a tool that you can fix onto a machine, to make it do another job（機器的）附件，附加裝置，附屬物：*an electric drill with a range of different attachments* 配有各種附件的電鑽 **4** [U, C] the act of joining one thing to another; a thing that joins two things together 連接；連接物：*All cars built since 1981 have points for the attachment of safety restraints.* 自 1981 年起生產的轎車都有安全保護裝置的連接點。◇ *They discussed the attachment of new conditions to the peace plans.* 他們討論把新條件加入到和平計劃中去。◇ *They had to check the strength of the seat attachments to the floor of the plane.* 他們需要檢查座椅與飛機艙面固定接頭的強度。**5** [U, C] (*BrE*) a short time spent working with an organization such as a hospital, school or part of the armed forces 暫時隸屬於（某醫院、學校、部隊等）；短期在…工作：*She's **on attachment** to the local hospital.* 她暫時在當地醫院工作。◇ *a 4-month training attachment* 為期 4 個月的培訓 **6** [C] (*computing* 計) a document that you send to sb using email（用電子郵件發送的）附件 ➲ COLLOCATIONS at EMAIL

at·tack 🔑 /əˈtæk/ *noun, verb*
■ *noun*
▸ **VIOLENCE** 暴力 **1** 🔑 [C, U] **~ (on sb)** an act of using violence to try to hurt or kill sb 襲擊；攻擊：*a series of racist attacks* 一連串的種族襲擊行為
▸ **IN WAR** 戰爭 **2** 🔑 [C, U] **~ (on sb/sth)** an act of trying to kill or injure the enemy in war, using weapons such as guns and bombs（在戰爭中使用武器的）進攻，攻擊：*to **launch/make/mount an attack*** 發起 / 進行攻擊；發動進攻 ◇ *The patrol came **under attack** from all sides.* 巡邏隊受到四面八方的攻擊。➲ COLLOCATIONS at WAR ➲ see also COUNTER-ATTACK
▸ **CRITICISM** 批評 **3** 🔑 [C, U] **~ (on sb/sth)** strong criticism of sb/sth in speech or in writing（口頭或書面的）抨擊，非難：*a scathing attack on the government's policies* 對政府政策的猛烈抨擊 ◇ *The school has come **under attack** for failing to encourage bright pupils.* 這所學校因未能鼓勵聰明學生而受到非難。
▸ **ACTION TO STOP STH** 制止 **4** 🔑 [C] **~ (on sth)** an action that you take to try to stop or change sth that you feel is bad 抑制；打擊；處理：*to launch **an all-out attack on** poverty/unemployment* 全力打擊貧窮 / 失業
▸ **OF ILLNESS** 疾病 **5** 🔑 [C] a sudden, short period of illness, usually severe, especially an illness that you have often（尤指常發疾病的）發作，侵襲：*to suffer an asthma attack* 哮喘發作 ◇ *an acute attack of food poisoning* 急性食物中毒 ◇ *a panic attack* 一陣恐慌 ◇ (*figurative*) *an attack of the giggles* 一陣咯咯傻笑 ➲ see also HEART ATTACK
▸ **OF EMOTION** 情感 **6** 🔑 [C] a sudden period of feeling an emotion such as fear（情感的）一陣突發：*an attack of nerves* 突然緊張不安
▸ **DAMAGE** 損害 **7** [U, C] the action of sth such as an insect, or a disease, that causes damage to sth/sb（病蟲等的）損害，傷害：*The roof timbers were affected by rot and insect attack.* 屋頂的木料已經腐朽並遭蟲害。
▸ **IN SPORT** 體育運動 **8** 🔑 [sing.] (*BrE*) (*NAmE* **of·fense**) the players in a team whose job is to try to score goals or points 進攻隊員：*Germany's attack has been weakened by the loss of some key players through injury.* 德國隊幾名主力隊員因傷不能上場，削弱了進攻力量。➲ compare DEFENCE (7) **9** 🔑 [C, U] the actions that players take to try to score a goal or win the game（隊員等的）進攻：*a sustained attack on the Arsenal goal* 向阿森納隊球門的持續進攻
■ *verb*
▸ **USE VIOLENCE** 使用暴力 **1** 🔑 [I, T, often passive] to use violence to try to hurt or kill sb 襲擊；攻擊：*Most dogs will not attack unless provoked.* 大多數的狗受到挑釁才會攻擊。◇ **~ sb** *A woman was attacked and robbed by a gang of youths.* 一名婦女遭到一夥年輕人襲擊和搶劫。◇ **~ sb with sth** *The man attacked him with a knife.* 那個男人持刀向他行兇。
▸ **IN WAR** 戰爭 **2** 🔑 [I, T] to use weapons, such as guns and bombs against an enemy in a war, etc.（在戰爭等中使用武器）進攻，攻擊：*The guerrillas attack at night.* 游擊隊在夜間發動襲擊。◇ **~ sb/sth** *At dawn the army attacked the town.* 軍隊在拂曉時向這座城鎮發動攻擊。
▸ **CRITICIZE** 批評 **3** 🔑 [T] to criticize sb/sth severely 抨擊；非難：**~ sb/sth** *a newspaper article attacking the England football manager* 報紙上的一篇抨擊英格蘭足球隊經理的文章 ◇ **~ sb/sth for sth/for doing sth** *She has been attacked for ignoring her own party members.* 她因漠視本黨黨員而受到非難。
▸ **DAMAGE** 損害 **4** 🔑 [T] **~ sth** to have a harmful effect on sth 侵襲；損害：*a disease that attacks the brain* 侵襲大腦的疾病 ◇ *The vines were attacked by mildew.* 葡萄藤受到了黴菌的侵害。
▸ **DO STH WITH ENERGY** 奮力做 **5** [T] **~ sth** to deal with sth with a lot of energy and determination 奮力處理；全力對付：*Let's attack one problem at a time.* 咱們每次全力處理一個問題。
▸ **IN SPORT** 體育運動 **6** [I] to go forward in a game in order to try to score goals or points 進攻 ➲ compare

A

DEFEND (3)： *Spain attacked more in the second half and deserved a goal.* 西班牙隊在下半場加強攻勢，攻進了一球。

at'tack dog *noun* **1** a dog that has been trained to attack people or other animals（經過訓練的）攻擊犬 **2** (*disapproving*) a person who often makes strong personal attacks on other people in public 言辭激烈的人身攻擊者；瘋狗： *His image has changed from statesman to attack dog.* 他的形象從政治家變成了見人就咬的惡狗。

at·tack·er /ə'tækə(r)/ *noun* a person who attacks sb 攻擊者；襲擊者；進攻者： *She didn't really see her attacker.* 她沒有看清楚襲擊她的人。

at·ta·girl /'ætəgɜːl; *NAmE* -gɜːrl/ *exclamation* (*informal, especially NAmE*) used when you want to encourage a girl or woman, or show your admiration of them（對女性表示鼓勵或欽佩）好樣的 ➲ see also ATTABOY

at·tain AW /ə'teɪn/ *verb* (*formal*) **1 ~ sth** to succeed in getting sth, usually after a lot of effort（通常經過努力）獲得，得到： *Most of our students attained five 'A' grades in their exams.* 我們多數學生的考試成績是五個優。 **2 ~ sth** to reach a particular age, level or condition 達到（某年齡、水平、狀況）： *The cheetah can attain speeds of up to 97 kph.* 獵豹的奔跑速度每小時可達 97 公里。

at·tain·able AW /ə'teɪnəbl/ *adj.* that you can achieve 可達到的；可獲得的： ***attainable goals/objectives/targets*** 可達到的目標 ◇ *This standard is easily attainable by most students.* 這個標準大多數學生都容易達到。 OPP **unattainable**

at·tain·ment AW /ə'teɪnmənt/ *noun* (*formal*) **1** [C, usually pl.] (*BrE*) something that you achieved 成就；造詣： *a young woman of impressive educational attainments* 一位學業成就斐然的年輕女子 **2** [U] success in achieving sth 達到；獲得： *The attainment of his ambitions was still a dream.* 他要實現的抱負仍然是一個夢想。◇ *attainment targets* (= for example in education) 學業成績目標

attar /'ætə(r)/ (also **otto**) *noun* an ESSENTIAL OIL usually made from ROSE PETALS（從玫瑰花瓣等中提取的）精油；玫瑰油

at·tempt 🔑 /ə'tempt/ *noun, verb*

■ ***noun*** **1** 🔑 [C, U] an act of trying to do sth, especially sth difficult, often with no success 企圖；試圖；嘗試： *I passed my driving test* ***at the first attempt.*** 我考汽車駕駛執照時一次就通過了。◇ **~ to do sth** *Two factories were closed* ***in an attempt*** *to cut costs.* 為削減費用，關閉了兩家工廠。◇ *They* ***made no attempt*** *to escape.* 他們沒有企圖逃跑。◇ **~ at sth/at doing sth** *The couple made an unsuccessful attempt at a compromise.* 這對夫婦試圖和解但未成功。 **2** 🔑 [C] **~ (on sb/sb's life)** an act of trying to kill sb 殺人企圖： *Someone has* ***made an attempt on*** *the President's* ***life.*** 有人企圖刺殺總統。 **3** 🔑 [C] **~ (on sth)** an effort to do better than sth, such as a very good performance in sport（為超越某事物的）嘗試，努力： *his attempt on the world land speed record* 他為創造陸上速度世界紀錄所作的嘗試

■ ***verb*** 🔑 to make an effort or try to do sth, especially sth difficult 努力；嘗試；試圖： **~ to do sth** *I will attempt to answer all your questions.* 我將努力回答你的全部問題。◇ *Do not attempt to repair this yourself.* 不要試圖自己修理這個東西。◇ **~ sth** *The prisoners attempted an escape, but failed.* 囚犯企圖逃跑，但失敗了。

at·tempted 🔑 /ə'temptɪd/ *adj.* [only before noun] (of a crime, etc. 犯罪等) that sb has tried to do but without success 未遂的： ***attempted rape/murder/robbery*** 企圖強姦／謀殺／搶劫

at·tend 🔑 /ə'tend/ *verb*

1 🔑 [I, T] (rather *formal*) to be present at an event 出席；參加： *We'd like as many people as possible to attend.* 我們希望出席的人越多越好。◇ **~ sth** *The meeting was attended by 90% of shareholders.* * 90% 的股東出席了會議。◇ *to attend a wedding/funeral* 參加婚禮／葬禮 **2** 🔑 [T] **~ sth** (*formal*) to go regularly to a place 經常去，定期去（某處）： *Our children attend the same school.* 我們的孩子上同一所學校。◇ *How many people attend church every Sunday?* 每個星期天有多少人去教堂？ **3** [I] **~ (to sb/sth)** (*formal*) to pay attention to what sb is saying or to what you are doing 注意；專心： *She hadn't been attending during the lesson.* 上課時她一直不專心。 **4** [T] **~ sth** (*formal*) to happen at the same time as sth 伴隨發生： *She dislikes the loss of privacy that attends TV celebrity.* 她不喜歡成為電視名人後隨之失去個人隱私。 **5** [T] **~ sb** (*formal*) to be with sb and help them 隨同；陪同： *The President was attended by several members of his staff.* 總統有幾名幕僚隨從。

PHR V **at'tend to sb/sth** 🔑 to deal with sb/sth; to take care of sb/sth 處理；對付；照料；關懷： *I have some urgent business to attend to.* 我有一些急事要處理。◇ *A nurse attended to his needs constantly.* 有一位護士經常照料他的需要。◇ (*BrE, formal*) *Are you being attended to, Sir?* (= for example, in a shop) 先生，有人接待你嗎？

at·tend·ance /ə'tendəns/ *noun* **1** [U, C] the act of being present at a place, for example at school 出席；參加；上學；到場： *Attendance at these lectures is not compulsory.* 這些課不是硬性規定要聽的。◇ *Teachers must keep a record of students' attendances.* 老師必須記錄學生的出席情況。 **2** [C, U] the number of people present at an organized event 出席人數： ***high/low/falling/poor attendances*** 出席的人數多／少／下降／很少◇ *There was an attendance of 42 at the meeting.* 有 42 人參加了會議。

IDM **be in at'tendance** (*formal*) to be present at a special event 出席（特別活動）： *Several heads of state were in attendance at the funeral.* 有幾位國家元首出席了葬禮。 **be in at'tendance (on sb)** (*formal*) to be with or near sb in order to help them if necessary 陪侍；隨侍（某人）左右；服侍： *He always has at least two bodyguards in attendance.* 他總有至少兩名保鏢護衛。 **take at'tendance** (*NAmE*) to check who is present and who is not present at a place and to mark this information on a list of names 點名 ➲ more at DANCE *v.*

at'tendance allowance *noun* [U] the money that a very sick or disabled older person receives from the government in Britain if they need sb to care for them at home nearly all the time 護理津貼（英國政府發給全日需要照料的病殘老年人）

at·tend·ant /ə'tendənt/ *noun, adj.*

■ ***noun*** **1** a person whose job is to serve or help people in a public place 服務員；侍者： *a* ***cloakroom/parking/museum attendant*** 衣帽間／停車服務員；博物館接待員 ➲ see also FLIGHT ATTENDANT **2** a person who takes care of and lives or travels with an important person or a sick or disabled person（要人的）侍從，隨從；（病人的）護理者

■ ***adj.*** [usually before noun] (*formal*) closely connected with sth that has just been mentioned 伴隨的；隨之而來的： ***attendant problems/risks/circumstances*** 隨之而來的問題／風險／情況◇ **~ upon sth** *We had all the usual problems attendant upon starting a new business.* 我們遇到了創業時通常會出現的所有問題。

at·tend·ee /ˌæten'diː/ *noun* a person who attends a meeting, etc. 出席者；在場者

at·tend·er /ə'tendə(r)/ (*especially BrE*) (*NAmE* usually **at·tend·ee**) *noun* a person who goes to a place or an event, often on a regular basis（常指經常的）出席者： *She's a regular attender at evening classes.* 她按時上夜校學習。

at·ten·tion 🔑 /ə'tenʃn/ *noun, exclamation*

■ ***noun***

▸ **LISTENING/LOOKING CAREFULLY** 注意聽／看 **1** 🔑 [U] the act of listening to, looking at or thinking about sth/sb carefully 注意；專心；留心；注意力： *the report's attention to detail* 報告對細節的注意◇ *He turned his attention back to the road again.* 他把注意力轉回到道路上。◇ *Small children have a very short* ***attention span.*** 幼兒的注意力持續時間很短。◇ *Please* ***pay attention*** (= listen carefully) *to what I am saying.* 請注意聽我講的話。◇ *Don't* ***pay any attention*** *to what they say* (= don't think that it is important). 別在意他們所說的話。◇ *She tried to* ***attract*** *the waiter's* ***attention.*** 她試圖引起服務員的注意。◇ *I tried not to* ***draw attention to*** (= make people notice) *the weak points in my argument.* 我盡量使人不察覺到我論證中的弱點。◇ *An article in the newspaper* *caught my attention.* 報上一篇文章引起了我的注意。◇ *I couldn't give the programme my* ***undivided attention.*** 我不能專心一意地關注這個方案。◇ (*formal*) *It* ***has come to my attention*** (= I have been informed) *that …* 我已獲悉… ◇ (*formal*) *He* ***called*** (***their***) ***attention*** *to the fact that many files were missing.* 他提請他們注意許多檔案已經遺失這一事實。◇ (*formal*) *Can I have your attention please?* 請注意聽我講話好嗎？ ➲ LANGUAGE BANK at EMPHASIS

▸ INTEREST 興趣 **2** [U] interest that people show in sb/sth 興趣；關注：*Films with big stars always* ***attract*** *great* ***attention.*** 有大明星演出的電影總是引起很大的興趣。◇ *As the youngest child, she was always* ***the centre of attention.*** 身為幼女，她一直是大家關注的中心。**3** [C, usually pl.] things that sb does to try to please you or to show their interest in you 殷勤；關心：*She tried to escape the unwanted attentions of her former boyfriend.* 她盡量避開她前男友多餘的殷勤。

▸ TREATMENT 處理 **4** [U] special care, action or treatment 特別照料（或行動、處理）：*She was in need of medical attention.* 她需要治療。◇ *The roof needs attention* (= needs to be repaired). 房頂需要修理了。◇ ***for the attention of …*** (= written on the envelope of an official letter to say who should deal with it) 由…辦理（正式信件信封上的用語）

▸ SOLDIERS 士兵 **5** [U] the position soldiers take when they stand very straight with their feet together and their arms at their sides 立正姿勢：*to* ***stand at/to attention*** 立正站着；立正 ➲ compare (STAND) AT EASE at EASE *n.*

■ *exclamation* **1** used for asking people to listen to sth that is being announced 注意：*Attention, please! Passengers for flight KL412 are requested to go to gate 21 immediately.* 請注意！請 KL412 航班的乘客立即到 21 號門登機。**2** used for ordering soldiers to stand to attention 立正

at'tention deficit disorder (also **at,tention ,deficit hyperac'tivity disorder**) *noun* [U] (*abbr.* **ADD, ADHD**) a medical condition, especially in children, that makes it difficult for them to pay attention to what they are doing, to stay still for long and to learn things 注意缺陷障礙，多動症，過動症（尤指兒童）

at·ten·tive /ə'tentɪv/ *adj.* **1** listening or watching carefully and with interest 注意的；專心的；留心的：*an attentive audience* 聚精會神的聽眾 **2** helpful; making sure that people have what they need 關心的；肯幫忙的：*The hotel staff are friendly and attentive.* 旅館人員友好而且照顧周到。◇ **~ to sb/sth** *Ministers should be more attentive to the needs of families.* 部長們應該更關懷家庭的需要。▸ **at·ten·tive·ly** *adv.* **at·ten·tive·ness** *noun* [U] OPP **inattentive**

at·tenu·ate /ə'tenjueɪt/ *verb* **~ sth** (*formal*) to make sth weaker or less effective 使減弱；使降低效力：*The drug attenuates the effects of the virus.* 這藥能減輕病毒的作用。▸ **at·tenu·ation** /ə,tenju'eɪʃn/ *noun* [U]

at·tenu·ated /ə'tenjueɪtɪd/ *adj.* (*formal*) **1** made weaker or less effective 減弱的：*an attenuated form of the virus* 毒性已衰減的病毒 **2** (of a person 人) very thin 消瘦的

at·tenu·ator /ə'tenjueɪtə(r)/ *noun* (*technical* 術語) a device consisting of a number of RESISTORS which reduce the strength of a radio sound or signal（信號）衰減器

at·test /ə'test/ *verb* (*formal*) **1** [I, T] **~ (to sth)** | **~ (that …)** | **~ (sth)** to show or prove that sth is true 證實；是…的證據 SYN **bear witness to**：*Contemporary accounts attest to his courage and determination.* 當時的報道證實了他的勇氣和決心。**2** [T] **~ (sth)** | **~ (that …)** to state that you believe that sth is true or genuine, for example in court 作證，證明（如在法庭上）：*to attest a will* 就遺囑作見證 ◇ *The signature was attested by two witnesses.* 這個簽名有兩名見證人。

attic /'ætɪk/ *noun* a room or space just below the roof of a house, often used for storing things（緊靠屋頂的）閣樓，頂樓：*furniture stored in the attic* 存放在閣樓的傢具 ◇ *an attic bedroom* 頂樓臥室 ➲ compare GARRET, LOFT (1)

at·tire /ə'taɪə(r)/ *noun* [U] (*formal*) clothes 服裝；衣服：*dressed in formal evening attire* 穿着晚禮服

at·tired /ə'taɪəd; *NAmE* ə'taɪərd/ *adj.* [not before noun] (*formal* or *literary*) dressed in a particular way 穿着…衣服

at·ti·tude 0-w AW /'ætɪtjuːd; *NAmE* 'ætɪtuːd/ *noun*
1 0-w [C] **~ (to/towards sb/sth)** the way that you think and feel about sb/sth; the way that you behave towards sb/sth that shows how you think and feel 態度；看法：*changes in public attitudes to marriage* 公眾對婚姻的看法的轉變 ◇ *the government's attitude towards single parents* 政府對單親的看法 ◇ *to* ***have a good/bad/positive/negative attitude towards sb/sth*** 對某人（或事物）持好的／壞的／肯定的／否定的態度 ◇ *Youth is simply an* ***attitude of mind.*** 青春僅僅是心態問題。◇ *If you want to pass your exams you'd better change your attitude!* 你若想通過考試就最好改變你的態度！◇ *You're taking a pretty selfish attitude over this, aren't you?* 你對這個問題的看法相當自私，對不對？◇ *A lot of drivers have a serious* ***attitude problem*** (= they do not behave in a way that is acceptable to other people). 許多駕車者有一種嚴重的動輒發火傾向。**2** [U] confident, sometimes aggressive behaviour that shows you do not care about other people's opinions and that you want to do things in an individual way 我行我素的做派：*a band* ***with attitude*** 一味只顧自我陶醉的樂隊 ◇ *You'd better get rid of that attitude and shape up, young man.* 年輕人，你最好改掉那種態度，學學好。**3** [C] (*formal*) a position of the body 姿勢：*Her hands were folded in an attitude of prayer.* 她雙手合攏成祈禱姿勢。IDM see STRIKE *v.*

at·ti·tu·din·al /,ætɪ'tjuːdɪnl; *NAmE* -'tuː-/ *adj.* (*formal*) related to the attitudes that people have 態度上的

attn (also **attn.** especially in *NAmE*) *abbr.* (*business* 商) (in writing) for the attention of（書寫形式）由…辦理：*Sales Dept, attn C Biggs* 銷售部，由 C•比格斯辦理 ➲ see also FAO

at·tor·ney 0-w /ə'tɜːni; *NAmE* ə'tɜːrni/ *noun*
1 0-w (*especially US*) a lawyer, especially one who can act for sb in court 律師（尤指代表當事人出庭者）➲ note at LAWYER ➲ see also DISTRICT ATTORNEY **2** a person who is given the power to act on behalf of another in business or legal matters（業務或法律事務上的）代理人：*She was made her father's attorney when he became ill.* 她在父親生病時代理父親的事務。➲ see also POWER OF ATTORNEY

At,torney 'General *noun* (*pl.* **Attorneys General** or **Attorney Generals**) **1** the most senior legal officer in some countries or states, for example the UK or Canada, who advises the government or head of state on legal matters（英國、加拿大等地的）總檢察長，首席檢察官 **2 the At,torney 'General** the head of the US Department of Justice and a member of the President's cabinet (= a group of senior politicians who advise the President)（美國的）司法部長

at·tract 0-w /ə'trækt/ *verb*
1 0-w [usually passive] if you are **attracted** by sth, it interests you and makes you want it; if you are **attracted** by sb, you like or admire them 吸引；使喜愛；引起…的好感（或愛慕）：**~ sb** *I had always been attracted by the idea of working abroad.* 我總是嚮往去國外工作。◇ **~ sb to sb/sth** *What first attracted me to her was her sense of humour.* 她首先吸引我的是她的幽默感。**2** 0-w **~ sb/sth (to sth)** to make sb/sth come somewhere or take part in sth 招引：*The warm damp air attracts a lot of mosquitoes.* 溫暖潮濕的空氣招來了大量蚊子。◇ *The exhibition has attracted thousands of visitors.* 展覽吸引了成千上萬的參觀者。**3** 0-w **~ sth** to make people have a particular reaction 引起（反應）：*This proposal has* ***attracted a lot of interest.*** 這個提案引起了很大的興趣。◇ *His comments were bound to* ***attract criticism.*** 他的說話必然會招致批評。◇ *She tried to* ***attract the attention*** *of the waiter.* 她試圖引起服務員的注意。**4** (*physics* 物) if a MAGNET or GRAVITY **attracts** sth, it makes it move towards it 吸引 OPP **repel** IDM see OPPOSITE *n.*

at·tract·ant /ə'træktənt/ *noun* (*technical* 術語) a substance that attracts sth, especially an animal（對動物

等的）引誘物，引誘劑：*This type of trap uses no bait or other attractant.* 這種陷阱不用誘餌或其他引誘物。

at·trac·tion /əˈtrækʃn/ *noun*
1 [sing., U] a feeling of liking sb, especially sexually（尤指兩性間的）愛慕，吸引：*She felt an immediate attraction for him.* 她立即對他產生了愛慕之情。◇ *Sexual attraction is a large part of falling in love.* 墮入愛河很大部份是由於性吸引。**2** [C] an interesting or enjoyable place to go or thing to do 嚮往的地方；有吸引力的事：*Buckingham Palace is a major **tourist attraction**.* 白金漢宮是重要的旅遊勝地。◇ *The **main attraction** at Giverny is Monet's garden.* 吉維尼主要的景點是莫奈花園。**3** [C, U] a feature, quality or person that makes sth seem interesting and enjoyable, and worth having or doing 有吸引力的特徵（或品質、人）：*I can't see the attraction of sitting on a beach all day.* 我看不出整天坐在海灘上有什麼樂趣。◇ *City life holds little attraction for me.* 我對城市生活不感興趣。◇ *She is the star attraction of the show.* 她是這個節目中耀眼的明星。**4** [U] (*physics* 物) a force that pulls things towards each other 吸引力：***gravitational/magnetic attraction*** 地心引力；磁力 ➲ compare REPULSION

at·tract·ive /əˈtræktɪv/ *adj.*
1 (of a person 人) pleasant to look at, especially in a sexual way 性感的；嫵媚的；英俊的；誘人的：*an attractive woman* 嫵媚的女人◇ *I like John but I don't **find him attractive** physically.* 我喜歡約翰，不過我認為他長得並不英俊。➲ SYNONYMS at BEAUTIFUL **2** (of a thing or a place 物或地方) pleasant 吸引人的；令人愉快的：*a big house with an attractive garden* 帶有美麗花園的一所巨宅◇ *That's one of the less attractive aspects of her personality.* 那是她個性中不太討人喜歡的一面。**3** having features or qualities that make sth seem interesting and worth having（事物）有吸引力的；誘人的 SYN **appealing**：*an attractive offer/proposition* 誘人的提議 OPP **unattractive** ▸ **at·tract·ive·ly** *adv.*：*The room is arranged very attractively.* 這個房間佈置得十分宜人。◇ *attractively priced hotel rooms* 價格誘人的旅館房間 **at·tract·ive·ness** *noun* [U]：*the attractiveness of travelling abroad* 國外旅遊的吸引力

at·trib·ut·able AW /əˈtrɪbjətəbl/ *adj.* [not before noun] **~ to sb/sth** probably caused by the thing mentioned 可歸因於；可能由於：*Their illnesses are attributable to a poor diet.* 他們的病可能是不良飲食所致。

at·tri·bute AW *verb, noun*
■ ***verb*** /əˈtrɪbjuːt/ **1 ~ sth to sth** to say or believe that sth is the result of a particular thing 把…歸因於；認為…是由於：*She attributes her success to hard work and a little luck.* 她認為她的成功來自勤勞和一點運氣。**2** to say or believe that sb is responsible for doing sth, especially for saying, writing or painting sth 認為是…所為（或說、寫、作）：**~ sth** *The committee refused to **attribute blame** without further information.* 如果沒有進一步的情況，委員會拒絕歸罪於任何人。◇ **~ sth to sb** *This play is usually attributed to Shakespeare.* 人們通常認為這齣戲劇是莎士比亞所寫。▸ **at·tri·bu·tion** AW /ˌætrɪˈbjuːʃn/ *noun* [U]：*The attribution of this painting to Rembrandt has never been questioned.* 從未有人懷疑這幅畫是倫勃朗所作。
■ ***noun*** /ˈætrɪbjuːt/ a quality or feature of sb/sth 屬性；性質；特徵：*Patience is one of the most important attributes in a teacher.* 耐心是教師最重要的品質之一。

at·tribu·tive /əˈtrɪbjətɪv/ *adj.* (*grammar* 語法) (of adjectives or nouns 形容詞或名詞) used before a noun to describe it（用於所修飾的名詞前）定語的：*In 'the blue sky' and 'a family business', 'blue' and 'family' are attributive.* 在 the blue sky 和 a family business 中，blue 和 family 是定語。➲ compare PREDICATIVE ▸ **at·tribu·tive·ly** *adv.*：*Some adjectives can only be used attributively.* 有些形容詞只能用作定語。

at·tri·tion /əˈtrɪʃn/ *noun* [U] (*formal*) **1** a process of making sb/sth, especially your enemy, weaker by repeatedly attacking them or creating problems for them（尤指給敵人造成的）削弱，消耗：*It was a **war of attrition**.* 這是一場消耗戰。**2** (*especially NAmE*) (*BrE* also **ˌnatural ˈwastage**) the process of reducing the number of people who are employed by an organization by, for example, not replacing people who leave their jobs 自然減員

at·tuned /əˈtjuːnd; *NAmE* əˈtuːnd/ *adj.* [not before noun] **~ (to sb/sth)** familiar with sb/sth so that you can understand or recognize them or it and act in an appropriate way 熟悉；適應；習慣：*She wasn't yet attuned to her baby's needs.* 她還沒有熟悉她寶寶的需要。

ATV /ˌeɪ tiː ˈviː/ *noun* (*especially NAmE*) the abbreviation for 'all-terrain vehicle' (a small open vehicle with one seat and four wheels with very thick tyres, designed especially for use on rough ground without roads) 全地形車（全寫為 all-terrain vehicle）➲ see also QUAD BIKE

atyp·ical /ˌeɪˈtɪpɪkl/ *adj.* not typical or usual 非典型的；反常的：*atypical behaviour* 反常行為 OPP **typical**

AU /ˌeɪ ˈjuː/ *abbr.* ASTRONOMICAL UNIT

au·ber·gine /ˈəʊbəʒiːn; *NAmE* ˈoʊbərʒiːn/ (*BrE*) (*NAmE* **egg·plant**) *noun* [C, U] a vegetable with shiny dark purple skin and soft white flesh 茄子 ➲ VISUAL VOCAB page V31

au·burn /ˈɔːbən; *NAmE* ˈɔːbərn/ *adj.* (of hair 毛髮) reddish-brown in colour 紅褐色的 ▸ **au·burn** *noun* [U]：*the rich auburn of her hair* 她頭髮的深紅褐色

auc·tion /ˈɔːkʃn; ˈɒk-; *NAmE* ˈɔːk-/ *noun, verb*
■ ***noun*** [C, U] a public event at which things are sold to the person who offers the most money for them 拍賣：*an auction of paintings* 繪畫拍賣會◇ *The house is **up for auction*** (= will be sold at an auction). 這所房子將被拍賣。◇ *A classic Rolls-Royce fetched* (= was sold for) ***£25 000 at auction**.* 一輛古典式勞斯萊斯轎車拍得 25 000 英鎊。◇ *an Internet auction site* 互聯網拍賣網站
■ ***verb*** [usually passive] **~ sth** to sell sth at an auction 拍賣：*The costumes from the movie are to be auctioned for charity.* 這部電影用過的服裝將用於慈善拍賣。
PHR V **ˌauction sth↔ˈoff** to sell sth at an auction, especially sth that is no longer needed or wanted 拍賣掉（尤指不再需要的物品）：*The Army is auctioning off a lot of surplus equipment.* 陸軍正在把大量剩餘設備拍賣掉。

auc·tion·eer /ˌɔːkʃəˈnɪə(r); ˌɒk-; *NAmE* ˌɔːkʃəˈnɪr/ *noun* a person whose job is to direct an auction and sell the goods 拍賣人；拍賣商

ˈauction house *noun* a company that sells things in auctions 拍賣行

ˈauction room *noun* a building in which AUCTIONS are held 拍賣廳

au·da·cious /ɔːˈdeɪʃəs/ *adj.* (*formal*) willing to take risks or to do sth shocking 敢於冒險的；大膽的 SYN **daring**：*an audacious decision* 大膽的決定 ▸ **au·da·cious·ly** *adv.*

au·da·city /ɔːˈdæsəti/ *noun* [U] brave but rude or shocking behaviour 魯莽；大膽無禮 SYN **nerve**：*He **had the audacity** to say I was too fat.* 他竟敢說我太肥胖。

aud·ible /ˈɔːdəbl/ *adj.* that can be heard clearly 聽得見的：*Her voice was **barely audible** above the noise.* 一片嘈雜，她的聲音只能勉強聽得見。OPP **inaudible** ▸ **audi·bil·ity** /ˌɔːdəˈbɪləti/ *noun* [U] **aud·ibly** /-əbli/ *adv.*

audi·ence /ˈɔːdiəns/ *noun*
1 [C+sing./pl. v.] the group of people who have gathered to watch or listen to sth (a play, concert, sb speaking, etc.)（戲劇、音樂會或演講等的）觀眾，聽眾：*The audience was/were clapping for 10 minutes.* 觀眾鼓掌 10 分鐘。◇ *an audience of 10 000* * 1 萬名觀眾◇ *The debate was televised in front of a **live audience**.* 這場辯論當着現場觀眾的面進行電視直播。**2** [C] a number of people or a particular group of people who watch, read or listen to the same thing（同一事物的）觀眾，讀者，聽眾：*An audience of millions watched the wedding on TV.* 幾百萬觀眾在電視上觀看了婚禮。◇ ***TV/cinema/movie audiences*** 電視／電影院／電影觀眾◇ *His book reached an even wider audience when it was made into a movie.* 他的書被搬上銀幕後贏得了更廣大的觀眾。◇ *The **target audience** for this advertisement was mainly teenagers.* 這個廣告的對象主要是十幾歲的青少年觀眾。

3 [C] a formal meeting with an important person（與要人的）會見；覲見；進見：*an audience with the Pope* 覲見教宗 ➲ SYNONYMS at INTERVIEW

audio /ˈɔːdiəʊ; *NAmE* ˈɔːdioʊ/ *adj.* [only before noun] connected with sound that is recorded 聲音的；錄音的：*audio and video cassettes* 盒式錄音帶和錄像帶 ▸ **audio** *noun* [U]

audio- /ˈɔːdiəʊ; *NAmE* ˈɔːdioʊ/ *combining form* (in nouns, adjectives and adverbs 構成名詞、形容詞和副詞) connected with hearing or sound 音的；聲的；聽的：*an audiobook* (= a reading of a book on CASSETTE, CD, etc.) 有聲讀物 ◇ *audio-visual* 視聽的

audi·ology /ˌɔːdiˈɒlədʒi; *NAmE* -ˈɑːl-/ *noun* [U] the science and medicine that deals with the sense of hearing 聽力（醫）學 ▸ **audi·ologist** *noun*

audi·om·etry /ˌɔːdiˈɒmətri; *NAmE* -ˈɑːm-/ *noun* [U] (*technical* 術語) the measurement of how good a person's sense of hearing is 測聽法；聽力測量

ˈaudio tape *noun* [U] MAGNETIC tape on which sound can be recorded 錄音帶

ˈaudio typist *noun* a person who types letters or other documents from recordings（根據錄音打字的）文字記錄員

ˌaudio-ˈvisual *adj.* (*abbr.* **AV**) using both sound and pictures 視聽的：*audio-visual aids for the classroom* 課堂視聽教具

audit /ˈɔːdɪt/ *noun, verb*

▪ *noun* [C, U] **1** an official examination of business and financial records to see that they are true and correct 審計；稽核：*an annual audit* 年度審計 ◇ *a tax audit* 稅項審計 **2** an official examination of the quality or standard of sth（質量或標準的）審查，檢查 ➲ see also GREEN AUDIT

▪ *verb* **1 ~ sth** to officially examine the financial accounts of a company 審計；稽核 **2 ~ sth** (*NAmE*) to attend a course at college or university but without taking any exams or receiving credit 旁聽（大學課程）

the ˈAudit Commission *noun* [sing.] (in Britain) an organization that checks that public money is being spent in the best way by local governments（英國的）審計署

au·di·tion /ɔːˈdɪʃn/ *noun, verb*

▪ *noun* a short performance given by an actor, a singer, etc., so that sb can decide whether they are suitable to act in a play, sing in a concert, etc.（擬進行表演者的）試演，試唱，試音

▪ *verb* **1** [I] **~ (for sth)** to take part in an audition 試演；試唱；試音：*She was auditioning for the role of Lady Macbeth.* 她試演了麥克佩斯夫人的角色。 **2** [T] **~ sb (for sth)** to watch, listen to and judge sb at an audition 對（某人）面試；讓（某人）試演（或試唱、試音）：*We auditioned over 200 children for the part.* 我們為這個角色面試了 200 多名兒童。

au·dit·or /ˈɔːdɪtə(r)/ *noun* **1** a person who officially examines the business and financial records of a company 審計員；稽核員 **2** (*NAmE*) a person who attends a college course, but without having to take exams and without receiving credit（大學課程的）旁聽生

audi·tor·ium /ˌɔːdɪˈtɔːriəm/ *noun* (*pl.* **audi·tor·iums** or **audi·toria** /-riə/) **1** the part of a theatre, concert hall, etc. in which the audience sits（劇院、音樂廳等的）聽眾席，觀眾席 **2** (*especially NAmE*) a large building or room in which public meetings, concerts, etc. are held 禮堂；會堂

audi·tory /ˈɔːdətri; *NAmE* -tɔːri/ *adj.* (*technical* 術語) connected with hearing 聽的；聽覺的：*auditory stimuli* 聽覺刺激

ˈaudit trail *noun* the detailed record of information on paper or on a computer that can be examined to prove what happened, for example what pieces of business were done and what decisions were made 審計軌跡（指用來進行審查的詳細記錄）

au fait /ˌəʊ ˈfeɪ; *NAmE* ˌoʊ/ *adj.* [not before noun] **~ (with sth)** (from *French*) completely familiar with sth 完全熟悉：*I'm new here so I'm not completely au fait with the system.* 我初來乍到，所以對這個系統還不完全熟悉。

Augean stables /ɔːˌdʒiːən ˈsteɪblz/ *noun* [pl.] (in ancient Greek stories 古希臘故事) the very large stables which Hercules cleaned in a day by making a river flow through them 奧吉亞斯的廐房（面積很大，赫拉克勒斯引河水一日沖洗乾淨）

auger /ˈɔːɡə(r)/ *noun* a tool for making holes in wood, that looks like a large CORKSCREW 木螺鑽，螺旋鑽（用於木材鑽孔）

aught /ɔːt/ *pron.* (*old use*) anything 任何事物

aug·ment /ɔːɡˈment/ *verb* **~ sth** (*formal*) to increase the amount, value, size, etc. of sth 增加；提高；擴大 ▸ **aug·men·ta·tion** /ˌɔːɡmenˈteɪʃn/ *noun* [U, C]

aug·men·ta·tive /ˌɔːɡˈmentətɪv/ *adj.* (*linguistics* 語言) (of an AFFIX or a word using an affix 詞綴或含詞綴詞) increasing a quality expressed in the original word, especially by meaning 'a large one of its kind' 增義的，增強詞義的（尤指表示巨大）

augur /ˈɔːɡə(r)/ *verb* [I] **~ well/badly** (*formal*) to be a sign that sth will be successful or not successful in the future 主（吉或凶）；是…的預兆 **SYN** **bode**：*Conflicts among the various groups do not augur well for the future of the peace talks.* 各派之間的衝突對和平談判不是一個好兆頭。

au·gury /ˈɔːɡjʊri/ *noun* (*pl.* **-ies**) (*literary*) a sign of what will happen in the future 預兆；徵兆 **SYN** **omen**

Au·gust 0➡ /ˈɔːɡəst/ *noun* [U, C] (*abbr.* **Aug.**) the 8th month of the year, between July and September 八月：(*BrE*) *August Bank Holiday* (= a public holiday on the last Monday in August in Britain) 八月銀行假日（英國公共假日，八月最後一個星期一） **HELP** To see how **August** is used, look at the examples at **April**. * August 的用法見詞條 April 下的示例。

au·gust /ɔːˈɡʌst/ *adj.* [usually before noun] (*formal*) impressive, making you feel respect 威嚴的；莊嚴的

Au·gust·an /ɔːˈɡʌstən/ *adj.* **1** connected with or happening during the time of the Roman EMPEROR Augustus（古羅馬帝國皇帝）奧古斯都的；奧古斯都時代的 **2** connected with English literature of the 17th and 18th centuries that was written in a style that was considered CLASSICAL 奧古斯都時代文學的（指 17、18 世紀的英國文學）；英國古典文學的

auk /ɔːk/ *noun* a northern bird with short narrow wings that lives near the sea 海雀（北方海鳥，翅短窄）

auld lang syne /ˌɔːld læŋ ˈsaɪn/ *noun* an old Scottish song expressing feelings of friendship, traditionally sung at midnight on New Year's Eve 美好往昔，友誼地久天長（古蘇格蘭民歌，按傳統在除夕午夜唱起）

au nat·urel /ˌəʊ ˌnætjuˈrel; *NAmE* ˌoʊ/ *adj., adv.* [not before noun] (from *French*) in a natural way 自然：*The fish is served au naturel, uncooked and with nothing added.* 這條魚是生吃的，未經蒸煮，也沒加任何調味品。

aunt 0➡ /ɑːnt; *NAmE* ænt/ *noun*

1 0➡ the sister of your father or mother; the wife of your uncle 姑母；姨母；伯母；嬸母；舅母：*Aunt Alice* 艾麗斯姨母 ◇ *My aunt lives in Canada.* 我的姑母住在加拿大。 **2** (*informal*) used by children, with a first name, to address a woman who is a friend of their parents（兒語）阿姨 ➲ see also AGONY AUNT

aun·tie (also **aunty**) /ˈɑːnti; *NAmE* ˈænti/ *noun* (*informal*) aunt 姑母；姨母；伯母；舅母；阿姨；嬸嬸：*Auntie Mary* 瑪麗嬸嬸

Aunt Sally /ˌɑːnt ˈsæli; *NAmE* ˌænt/ *noun* **1** (*BrE*) a game in which people throw balls at a model of a person's head to win prizes 薩利大嬸投擲遊戲，莎莉姑媽遊戲（用球投擲一人頭模型贏獎） **2** a person or thing that a lot of people criticize 遭眾人批評的人（或事物）：*The foreign minister has become everybody's favourite Aunt Sally.* 外交部長已成為眾矢之的。

au pair /ˌəʊ ˈpeə(r); *NAmE* ˌoʊ ˈper/ *noun* (*BrE*) a young person, usually a woman, who lives with a family in a foreign country in order to learn the language. An au pair helps in the house and takes care of children and

A

receives a small wage. 換工，“互裨”（女）生（住國外家庭，以勞動換取食宿並學習語言）

aura /ˈɔːrə/ *noun* ~ **(of sth)** a feeling or particular quality that is very noticeable and seems to surround a person or place 氣氛；氛圍；氣質：*She always has an aura of confidence.* 她總是滿有信心的樣子。

aural /ˈɔːrəl/ *adj.* (*technical* 術語) connected with hearing and listening 聽覺的；聽的：*aural and visual images* 視聽圖像 ◇ *aural comprehension tests* 聽力理解測驗 ▸ **aur·al·ly** /-əli/ *adv.*

aure·ate /ˈɔːriət/ *adj.* (*formal*) **1** decorated in a complicated way 華麗的：*an aureate style of writing* 華麗的文風 **2** made of gold or of the colour of gold 金的；金（黃）色的 SYN **golden**

aure·ole /ˈɔːriəʊl; *NAmE* -oʊl/ *noun* (*literary*) a circle of light 光環；光輪

au re·voir /ˌəʊ rəˈvwɑː(r); *NAmE* ˌoʊ/ *exclamation* (from *French*) goodbye (until we meet again) 再見

aur·icle /ˈɔːrɪkl/ *noun* (*anatomy* 解) **1** either of the two upper spaces in the heart used to send blood around the body 心耳 SYN **atrium** ➲ compare VENTRICLE (1) **2** the outer part of the ear 耳廓

aur·ora aus·tra·lis /ɔːˌrɔːrə ɒsˈtrɑːlɪs; ɔːsˈt-; *NAmE* ɔːsˈt-/ *noun* [sing.] = THE SOUTHERN LIGHTS

aur·ora bor·ealis /ɔːˌrɔːrə ˌbɔːriˈeɪlɪs/ *noun* [sing.] = THE NORTHERN LIGHTS

aus·pices /ˈɔːspɪsɪz/ *noun* [pl.]
IDM **under the auspices of sb/sth** with the help, support or protection of sb/sth 在…幫助（或支持、保護）下：*The community centre was set up under the auspices of a government initiative.* 在政府的大力支持下，社區中心建成了。

aus·pi·cious /ɔːˈspɪʃəs/ *adj.* (*formal*) showing signs that sth is likely to be successful in the future 吉利的；吉祥的 SYN **promising**：*an auspicious start to the new school year* 新學年的開門紅 OPP **inauspicious**

Aus·sie (also **Oz·zie**) /ˈɒzi; *NAmE* ˈɔːzi/ *noun* (*informal*) a person from Australia 澳大利亞人 ▸ **Aus·sie** *adj.*

aus·tere /ɒˈstɪə(r); ɔːˈst-; *NAmE* ɔːˈstɪr/ *adj.* **1** simple and plain; without any decorations 樸素的；簡陋的；無華飾的：*her austere bedroom with its simple narrow bed* 她那僅有一張窄牀的簡陋卧室 **2** (of a person 人) strict and serious in appearance and behaviour 嚴肅的；嚴厲的：*My father was a distant, austere man.* 我父親是個難以接近的嚴肅的人。 **3** allowing nothing that gives pleasure; not comfortable 苦行的；禁慾的：*the monks' austere way of life* 僧侶的苦行生活方式 ▸ **aus·tere·ly** *adv.*

aus·ter·ity /ɒˈsterəti; ɔːˈster-/ *noun* (*pl.* **-ies**) **1** [U] a situation when people do not have much money to spend because there are bad economic conditions（經濟的）緊縮；嚴格節制消費：*War was followed by many years of austerity.* 緊隨戰爭的是多年的經濟緊縮。 **2** [U] the quality of being austere 苦行；禁慾：*the austerity of the monks' life* 僧侶的禁慾生活 **3** [C, usually pl.] something that is part of an austere way of life 艱苦；樸素：*the austerities of wartime Europe* 戰時歐洲的艱苦生活

aus·tral /ˈɒstrəl; ˈɔːs-; *NAmE* ˈɔːs-/ *adj.* (*formal*) relating to the south 南的；南方的；南部的

Austra·la·sia /ˌɒstrəˈleɪʃə; -ˈleɪʒə; ˌɔːstrə-; *NAmE* ˌɔːstrə-/ *noun* the region including Australia, New Zealand and the islands of the SW Pacific 澳大拉西亞（包括澳大利亞、新西蘭及太平洋西南島嶼）▸ **Austra·la·sian** *adj.*, *noun*

Australia Day /ɒˈstreɪliə deɪ; *NAmE* ɔːˈstreɪljə; ɑːˈs-/ *noun* a national public holiday in Australia on 26 January, when people remember the founding of New South Wales on that date in 1788 澳大利亞日（1 月 26 日，澳大利亞國慶日，紀念 1788 年新南威爾士州成立）

Aus·tra·lian /ɒˈstreɪliən; ɔːˈstreɪ-/ *adj.*, *noun*
■ *adj.* of or connected with Australia 澳大利亞的
■ *noun* a person from Australia 澳大利亞人

Auˌstralian ˈRules (also **Australian ˌRules ˈfootball**) *noun* [U] an Australian game, played by two teams of 18 players, using an OVAL ball, which may be kicked, carried or hit with the hand 澳大利亞式橄欖球（兩隊各 18 人參賽，球呈橢圓形，可以足踢、抱傳或以手擊球）

Aus·tralo·pith·ecus /ˌɒstrələʊˈpɪθɪkəs; *NAmE* ˌɔːstrəloʊ-/ *noun* [U, C] a creature similar to humans and APES that existed over one million years ago in Africa 南方古猿（一百萬年前生活在非洲，與人類和類人猿相似）

Austro- /ˈɒstrəʊ-; *NAmE* ˈɔːstroʊ-/ *combining form* (in nouns and adjectives 構成名詞和形容詞) Austrian 奧地利（的）；奧地利人（的）：*the Austro-Hungarian border* 奧匈邊境

aut·archy (also **aut·arky**) /ˈɔːtɑːki; *NAmE* ˈɔːtɑːrki/ *noun* (*pl.* **-ies**) **1** [U, C] = AUTOCRACY **2** [U] (*economics* 經) economic independence 經濟獨立；自給自足 ▸ **aut·arch·ic** (also **aut·ark·ic**) /ɔːˈtɑːkɪk; *NAmE* -ˈtɑːrk-/ *adj.*

au·teur /əʊˈtɜː(r); ɔːˈt-; *NAmE* oʊˈt-/ *noun* a film/movie director who plays such an important part in making their films/movies that they are considered to be the author 主創導演；導演作者 ORIGIN From the French word *auteur*, meaning author. 源自法語 auteur，意為“作者”。

au·then·tic /ɔːˈθentɪk/ *adj.* **1** known to be real and genuine and not a copy 真正的；真品的；真跡的：*I don't know if the painting is authentic.* 我不知道這幅畫是不是真跡。 OPP **inauthentic** **2** true and accurate 真實的；真正的：*an authentic account of life in the desert* 對沙漠生活的真實描述 ◇ *the authentic voice of young black Americans* 年輕美國黑人的真實呼聲 OPP **inauthentic** **3** made to be exactly the same as the original 逼真的：*an authentic model of the ancient town* 古城的仿真模型 ▸ **au·then·tic·al·ly** /-kli/ *adv.*：*authentically flavoured Mexican dishes* 地道的墨西哥風味菜肴

au·then·ti·cate /ɔːˈθentɪkeɪt/ *verb* to prove that sth is genuine, real or true 證明…是真實的；證實：**~ sth** *The letter has been authenticated by handwriting experts.* 這封信已由筆跡專家證明是真的。◇ **~ sth as sth** *Experts have authenticated the writing as that of Byron himself.* 專家鑒定這字跡是拜倫的親筆。 ▸ **au·then·ti·ca·tion** /ɔːˌθentɪˈkeɪʃn/ *noun* [U]

au·then·ti·city /ˌɔːθenˈtɪsəti/ *noun* [U] the quality of being genuine or true 真實性；確實性

author 🔑 AW /ˈɔːθə(r)/ *noun*, *verb*
■ *noun* **1** 🔑 a person who writes books or the person who wrote a particular book 著者；作者；作家：*Who is your favourite author?* 你最喜歡哪位作家？◇ *He is the author of three books on art.* 他寫了三本藝術專著。◇ *best-selling author Paul Theroux* 暢銷書作家保羅•泰魯 ◇ *Who's the author?* 作者是誰？ ➲ COLLOCATIONS at LITERATURE **2** the person who creates or starts sth, especially a plan or an idea（尤指計劃或思想的）創造者，發起人：*As the author of the proposal I cannot agree with you.* 我作為提案的發起人，不能同意你的意見。
■ *verb* **~ sth** (*formal*) to be the author of a book, report, etc. 著作；寫作；編寫

author·ess /ˈɔːθəres/ *noun* (*old-fashioned*) a woman author 女著者；女作者；女作家

au·thor·ial /ɔːˈθɔːriəl/ *adj.* [usually before noun] (*technical* 術語) coming from or connected with the author of sth 著者的；作者的；作家的

author·ing /ˈɔːθərɪŋ/ *noun* [U] (*computing* 計) creating computer programs without using programming language, for use in MULTIMEDIA products 創作

au·thori·tar·ian /ɔːˌθɒrɪˈteəriən; *NAmE* əˌθɔːrəˈter-; əˌθɑːr-/ *adj.* believing that people should obey authority and rules, even when these are unfair, and even if it means that they lose their personal freedom 威權主義的；專制的：*an **authoritarian regime/government/state*** 威權主義的政體／政府／國家 ▸ **au·thori·tar·ian** *noun*：*Father was a strict authoritarian.* 父親是個嚴厲的專制主義者。 **au·thori·tar·ian·ism** *noun* [U]

au·thori·ta·tive AW /ɔːˈθɒrətətɪv; *NAmE* əˈθɔːrəteɪtɪv; əˈθɑːr-/ *adj.* **1** showing that you expect people to obey and respect you 命令式的；專斷的；權威式的：*an authoritative tone of voice* 命令式的口氣 **2** that you can trust and respect as true and correct 權威性的：*the most authoritative book on the subject* 這個學科最具權威的著作 ▸ **au·thori·ta·tive·ly** *adv.*

au·thor·ity AW /ɔːˈθɒrəti; *NAmE* əˈθɔːr-; əˈθɑːr-/ *noun* (*pl.* **-ies**)

▸ **POWER** 權力 **1** [U] the power to give orders to people 權力；威權；當權（地位）：*in a position of authority* 當權 ◇ *She now* **has authority over** *the people who used to be her bosses.* 她現在管轄着過去是她上司的那些人。◇ *Nothing will be done because no one* **in authority** (= who has a position of power) *takes the matter seriously.* 什麼也辦不了，因為掌權的誰也不認真對待這個問題。**2** [U] **~ (to do sth)** the power or right to do sth 權；職權：*Only the manager has the authority to sign cheques.* 只有經理才有權簽支票。

▸ **PERMISSION** 准許 **3** [U] official permission to do sth 批准；授權：*It was done without the principal's authority.* 做這件事未經校長批准。◇ *We acted* **under the authority of** *the UN.* 我們是經聯合國授權行動的。

▸ **ORGANIZATION** 組織機構 **4** [C, usually pl.] the people or an organization who have the power to make decisions or who have a particular area of responsibility in a country or region 當局；官方；當權者：*The health authorities are investigating the problem.* 衛生當局正在調查這個問題。◇ *I have to report this to the authorities.* 我得向官方報告此事。⊃ see also LOCAL AUTHORITY

▸ **KNOWLEDGE** 知識 **5** [U] the power to influence people because they respect your knowledge or official position 權威；威信；影響力：*He spoke* **with authority** *on the topic.* 他就這個課題發表權威意見。

▸ **EXPERT** 專家 **6** [C] **~ (on sth)** a person with special knowledge 專家；學術權威；泰斗 SYN **specialist**：*She's an authority on criminal law.* 她是刑法專家。

IDM **have sth on good au'thority** to be able to believe sth because you trust the person who gave you the information 有可靠的根據

au·thor·iza·tion (*BrE* also **-isa·tion**) /ˌɔːθəraɪˈzeɪʃn; *NAmE* ˌɔːθərəˈzeɪʃn/ *noun* **1** [U, C] official permission or power to do sth; the act of giving permission 批准；授權：*You may not enter the security area without authorization.* 未經批准不得進入警戒地區。◇ *Who gave the authorization to release the data?* 誰授權發表這些資料的？ **2** [C] a document that gives sb official permission to do sth 批准書；授權書：*Can I see your authorization?* 我能看你的授權書嗎？

au·thor·ize (*BrE* also **-ise**) /ˈɔːθəraɪz/ *verb* [often passive] to give official permission for sth, or for sb to do sth 批准；授權：**~ sth** *I can authorize payments up to £5 000.* 我有權批准的付款限額為 5 000 英鎊。◇ *an authorized biography* 經認可的傳記 ◇ **~ sb to do sth** *I have authorized him to act for me while I am away.* 我已授權他在我外出時代理我的職務。◇ *The soldiers were authorized to shoot at will.* 士兵得到允許可以隨意開槍。⊃ see also UNAUTHORIZED

ˌAuthorized 'Version *noun* [sing.] an English version of the Bible that was translated in 1611 on the instructions of King James I of England 《聖經》欽定英譯本（英王詹姆斯一世於 1611 年頒行）

author·ship AW /ˈɔːθəʃɪp; *NAmE* ˈɔːθərʃɪp/ *noun* [U] **1** the identity of the person who wrote sth, especially a book（尤指書的）作者，作者身分：*The authorship of the poem is unknown.* 這首詩的作者不詳。**2** the activity or fact of writing a book 寫作；著述

aut·ism /ˈɔːtɪzəm/ *noun* [U] a mental condition in which a person finds it very difficult to communicate or form relationships with others 自閉症；孤獨症 ▸ **aut·is·tic** /ɔːˈtɪstɪk/ *adj.*：***autistic behaviour/children*** 自閉症行為 / 兒童

auto /ˈɔːtəʊ; *NAmE* ˈɔːtoʊ/ *noun* (*pl.* **-os**) (*NAmE*) a car 汽車：*the auto industry* 汽車工業

auto- /ˈɔːtəʊ; *NAmE* ˈɔːtoʊ/ (also **aut-**) *combining form* (in nouns, adjectives and adverbs 構成名詞、形容詞和副詞) **1** of or by yourself 自己（的）；本身（的）：*autobiography* 自傳 **2** by itself without a person to operate it 由本身（的）；無人操作（的）：*automatic* 自動

auto·biog·raphy /ˌɔːtəbaɪˈɒɡrəfi; *NAmE* -ˈɑːɡ-/ *noun* [C, U] (*pl.* **-ies**) the story of a person's life, written by that person; this type of writing 自傳；自傳體寫作 ⊃ compare BIOGRAPHY ▸ **auto·bio·graph·ic·al** /ˌɔːtəˌbaɪəˈɡræfɪkl/ *adj.*：*an autobiographical novel* (= one that contains many of the writer's own experiences) 自傳體小説

'auto bra *noun* (*NAmE*) = BRA (2)

auto·clave /ˈɔːtəʊkleɪv; ˈɔːtə-; *NAmE* ˈɔːtoʊ-/ *noun* a strong closed container, used for processes that involve high temperatures or pressure 高壓釜，壓熱器（用於強熱高壓工序的密封堅固容器）

au·toc·racy /ɔːˈtɒkrəsi; *NAmE* ɔːˈtɑːk-/ *noun* (*pl.* **-ies**) (also **aut·archy**) **1** [U] a system of government of a country in which one person has complete power 獨裁政體；專制制度 **2** [C] a country that is ruled by one person who has complete power 獨裁國家；專制國家

auto·crat /ˈɔːtəkræt/ *noun* **1** a ruler who has complete power 獨裁者；專制統治者；專制君主 SYN **despot** **2** a person who expects to be obeyed by other people and does not care about their opinions or feelings 專橫的人；獨斷專行的人 ▸ **auto·crat·ic** /ˌɔːtəˈkrætɪk/ *adj.*：*an autocratic manager* 獨斷專行的經理 **auto·crat·ic·al·ly** /-kli/ *adv.*

auto·cross /ˈɔːtəʊkrɒs; *NAmE* ˈɔːtoʊkrɔːs; ˈɔːtoʊkrɑːs/ *noun* [U] a form of motor racing in which cars are driven over rough ground 汽車越野賽 ⊃ compare RALLYCROSS

Auto·cue™ /ˈɔːtəʊkjuː; *NAmE* ˈɔːtoʊ-/ (*BrE*) (also **tele·prompt·er** *NAmE, BrE*) *noun* a device used by people who are speaking in public, especially on television, which displays the words that they have to say 電子提詞器，自動提示器（尤用於電視廣播時向說話人提示講詞）

auto·didact /ˈɔːtəʊdɪdækt; *NAmE* ˈɔːtoʊ-/ *noun* (*formal*) a person who has taught himself or herself sth rather than having lessons 自學者；自修者 ▸ **auto·didac·tic** /ˌɔːtəʊdɪˈdæktɪk; *NAmE* ˌɔːtoʊ-/ *adj.*

ˌauto-e'rotic *adj.* relating to the practice of sb getting sexual excitement from their own body 自慰性行為的

ˌauto-ex'posure *noun* **1** [C] part of a camera that automatically adjusts the amount of light that reaches the film（照相機的）自動曝光裝置 **2** [U] the ability of a camera to do this（照相機的）自動曝光

auto·focus /ˌɔːtəʊˈfəʊkəs; *NAmE* ˌɔːtoʊˈfoʊkəs/ *noun* **1** [C] part of a camera that automatically adjusts itself, so that the picture will be clear（照相機的）自動聚焦裝置 **2** [U] the ability of a camera to do this（照相機的）自動聚焦

auto·genic /ˌɔːtəʊˈdʒenɪk; ˌɔːtə-; *NAmE* ˌɔːtoʊ-/ *adj.* (*formal*) created by or from the thing itself 自生的；自體的

ˌautogenic 'training *noun* [U] a way of relaxing and dealing with stress using positive thoughts and mental exercises 自生訓練（利用積極思維和心理訓練緩解壓力）

auto·graph /ˈɔːtəɡrɑːf; *NAmE* -ɡræf/ *noun, verb*

■ ***noun*** a famous person's signature, especially when sb asks them to write it（名人的）親筆簽名：*Could I have your autograph?* 我能請你簽個名嗎？

■ ***verb*** **~ sth** (of a famous person 名人) to sign your name on sth for sb to keep（在…上）簽名：*The whole team has autographed a football, which will be used as a prize.* 全體隊員在一個足球上簽了名，用作獎品。

auto·immune /ˌɔːtəʊɪˈmjuːn; *NAmE* ˌɔːtoʊ-/ *adj.* [only before noun] (*medical* 醫) an **autoimmune** disease or medical condition is one that is caused by substances that usually prevent illness 自體免疫的；自身免疫的

auto·maker /ˈɔːtəʊmeɪkə(r); *NAmE* ˈɔːtoʊ-/ *noun* (*NAmE*) a company that makes cars 汽車製造商

auto·mat /ˈɔːtəmæt/ *noun* (*US*) in the past, a restaurant in which food and drink were bought from machines 自動餐館（舊時用自動售賣機供應食物的餐館）

auto·mate AW /ˈɔːtəmeɪt/ *verb* [usually passive] **~ sth** to use machines and computers instead of people to do a job or task 使自動化：*The entire manufacturing process*

A

has been automated. 整個生產過程已自動化。◇ *The factory is now **fully automated**.* 這家工廠現在是全自動化。

ˌautomated ˈteller machine *noun* (*abbr.* ATM) = CASH MACHINE

auto·mat·ic AW /ˌɔːtəˈmætɪk/ *adj., noun*

■ ***adj.*** **1** (of a machine, device, etc. 機器、裝置等) having controls that work without needing a person to operate them 自動的：*automatic doors* 自動門 ◇ *a **fully automatic** driverless train* 全自動無人駕駛列車 ◇ *automatic transmission* (= in a car, etc.)（汽車等內的）自動變速器 ◇ *an automatic rifle* (= one that continues to fire as long as the TRIGGER is pressed) 自動步槍 **2** done or happening without thinking 無意識的；不假思索的 SYN **instinctive**：*Breathing is an automatic function of the body.* 呼吸是一種無意識的功能。◇ *My reaction was automatic.* 我的反應是不由自主的。**3** always happening as a result of a particular action or situation 必然的；當然的：*A fine for this offence is automatic.* 這種違法行為當然要罰款。▸ **auto·mat·ic·al·ly** AW /-kli/ *adv.* *The heating switches off automatically.* 該供暖系統可自動關閉。◇ *I turned left automatically without thinking.* 我不假思索地向左轉彎。◇ *You will automatically get free dental treatment if you are under 18.* * 18 歲以下的人一律免費得到牙科治療。

■ ***noun*** **1** a gun that can fire bullets continuously as long as the TRIGGER is pressed 自動手槍（或步槍）**2** (*BrE*) a car with a system of gears that operates without direct action from the driver 自動變速汽車；自動換擋汽車 ➲ compare STICK SHIFT

ˌautomatic ˈpilot (also **auto·pilot**) *noun* a device in an aircraft or a ship that keeps it on a fixed course without the need for a person to control it（飛機的）自動駕駛儀；（船的）自動操舵裝置

IDM **be on ˌautomatic ˈpilot** to do sth without thinking because you have done the same thing many times before 習慣性地做；機械性地做：*I got up and dressed on automatic pilot.* 我習慣性地起牀穿衣。

ˌautomatic transˈmission *noun* [U, C] a system in a vehicle that changes the gears for the driver automatically（機動車的）自動變速器

ˌautomatic ˈwriting *noun* [U] writing which is believed to have been done in an unconscious state or under a SUPERNATURAL influence（無意識狀態或在超自然力影響下的）自書動作

auto·ma·tion AW /ˌɔːtəˈmeɪʃn/ *noun* [U] the use of machines to do work that was previously done by people 自動化：*Automation meant the loss of many factory jobs.* 自動化意味着許多工廠工人失業。

au·toma·tism /ɔːˈtɒmətɪzəm; *NAmE* ɔːˈtɑːm-/ *noun* [U] (*art* 美術) a method of painting that avoids conscious thought and allows a free flow of ideas 自動主義，自縱畫法（避免意識思維、任憑想像力自由發揮的繪畫方法）

au·toma·ton /ɔːˈtɒmətən; *NAmE* ɔːˈtɑːm-/ *noun* (*pl.* **au·toma·tons** or **au·tom·ata** /-tə/) **1** a person who behaves like a machine, without thinking or feeling anything 不動腦筋機械行事的人 SYN **robot** **2** a machine that moves without human control; a small ROBOT 自動操作裝置；小機器人

auto·mo·bile /ˈɔːtəməbiːl/ *noun* (*NAmE*) a car 汽車：*the automobile industry* 汽車工業 ◇ *an automobile accident* 車禍

auto·mo·tive /ˌɔːtəˈməʊtɪv; *NAmE* -ˈmoʊ-/ *adj.* (*formal*) connected with vehicles that are driven by engines 汽車的；機動車的：*the automotive industry* 汽車工業

auto·nom·ic ner·vous sys·tem /ˌɔːtənɒmɪk ˈnɜːvəs sɪstəm; *NAmE* ˌɔːtənɑːmɪk ˈnɜːrvəs/ *noun* the part of your NERVOUS SYSTEM that controls processes which are unconscious, for example the process of your heart beating 自主神經系統，植物神經系統（控制心跳等無意識運動）

au·tono·mous /ɔːˈtɒnəməs; *NAmE* ɔːˈtɑːn-/ *adj.* **1** (of a country, a region or an organization 國家、地區、組織) able to govern itself or control its own affairs 自治的；有自治權的 SYN **independent**：*an autonomous republic/state/province* 自治共和國／州／省 **2** (of a person 人) able to do things and make decisions without help from anyone else 自主的；有自主權的 ▸ **au·tono·mous·ly** *adv.*

au·ton·omy /ɔːˈtɒnəmi; *NAmE* ɔːˈtɑːn-/ *noun* [U] (*formal*) **1** the freedom for a country, a region or an organization to govern itself independently 自治；自治權 SYN **independence**：*a campaign in Wales for greater autonomy* 威爾士爭取更大自治權的運動 **2** the ability to act and make decisions without being controlled by anyone else 自主；自主權：*giving individuals greater autonomy in their own lives* 給個人在生活中更大的自主權

auto·pilot /ˈɔːtəʊpaɪlət; *NAmE* ˈɔːtoʊ-/ *noun* = AUTOMATIC PILOT

aut·opsy /ˈɔːtɒpsi; *NAmE* ˈɔːtɑːpsi/ *noun* (*pl.* **-ies**) an official examination of a dead body by a doctor in order to discover the cause of death 驗屍；屍體解剖 SYN **post-mortem**：*an autopsy report* 驗屍報告 ◇ *to perform an autopsy* 進行屍體剖驗

ˈauto racing *noun* [U] (*NAmE*) = MOTOR RACING

ˈauto-rickshaw *noun* a covered motor vehicle with three wheels, a driver's seat in front and a seat for passengers at the back, used especially in some Asian countries 機動三輪拉客車，機動黃包車，摩的（主要在亞洲國家）

auto·save /ˈɔːtəʊseɪv; *NAmE* ˈɔːtoʊ-/ *noun* [sing.] (*computing* 計) the fact that changes to a document are saved automatically as you work 自動保存；自動貯存；自動存檔 ▸ **auto·save** *verb* **~ sth**

ˌauto-sugˈgestion *noun* [U] (*psychology* 心) a process that makes you believe sth or act in a particular way according to ideas that come from within yourself without you realizing it 自我暗示

auto·wind /ˈɔːtəʊwaɪnd; *NAmE* ˈɔːtoʊ-/ (also **auto·wind·er** /ˈɔːtəʊwaɪndə(r); *NAmE* ˈɔːtoʊ-/) *noun* **1** [sing.] part of a camera which automatically winds the film forwards so that you can take the next picture（照相機的）自動捲片裝置 **2** [U] the ability of a camera to do this（照相機的）自動捲片功能 ▸ **auto·wind** *verb* [I]

au·tumn /ˈɔːtəm/ (*especially BrE*) (*NAmE* usually **fall**) *noun* [U, C] the season of the year between summer and winter, when leaves change colour and the weather becomes colder 秋天；秋季：*in the autumn of 2010* 在 2010 年秋季 ◇ *in **early/late autumn*** 初／晚秋 ◇ *the autumn term* (= for example at a school or college in Britain) 秋季學期 ◇ ***autumn colours/leaves*** 秋色／葉 ◇ *It's been a very mild autumn this year.* 今年秋天一直很暖和。

au·tum·nal /ɔːˈtʌmnəl/ *adj.* [usually before noun] like or connected with autumn 秋天的；秋季的：*autumnal colours* 秋天的色彩

aux·il·iary /ɔːɡˈzɪliəri/ *adj., noun*

■ ***adj.*** **1** (of workers 工人) giving help or support to the main group of workers 輔助的 SYN **ancillary**：*auxiliary nurses/workers/services* 助理護士；輔助工／服務 **2** (*technical* 術語) (of a piece of equipment 設備) used if there is a problem with the main piece of equipment 備用的

■ ***noun*** (*pl.* **-ies**) **1** (also **auˌxiliary ˈverb**) (*grammar* 語法) a verb such as *be*, *do* and *have* used with main verbs to show tense, etc. and to form questions and negatives 助動詞 **2** a worker who gives help or support to the main group of workers 輔助工；輔助人員：*nursing auxiliaries* 護理輔助人員

auxin /ˈɔːksɪn/ *noun* [U] a HORMONE found in plants（植物）生長素

AV /ˌeɪ ˈviː/ *abbr.* AUDIO-VISUAL

avail /əˈveɪl/ *noun, verb*

■ ***noun***

IDM **to little/no aˈvail** (*formal*) with little or no success 沒有什麼效果；不成功：*The doctors tried everything to keep him alive but to no avail.* 醫生千方百計想使他活下來，但無濟於事。**of little/no aˈvail** (*formal*) of little or no use 沒有什麼用處；沒有用：*Your ability to argue* *is of little avail if the facts are wrong.* 如果論據是錯的，你的辯才也就沒有什麼用了。

■ **verb 1** [T] **~ sb (sth)** | **~ sth** (*formal* or *old-fashioned*) to be helpful or useful to sb 有幫助；有益；有用 **2** [T, I] (*IndE, non-standard*) to make use of sth, especially an opportunity or offer 利用（尤指機會、提議等）：**~ sth** *To avail all these benefits, just register online.* 要想得到所有這些好處，就在線註冊吧。◇ **~ of sth** *Why not avail of our special offers?* 為什麼不利用我們的特別優惠呢？

PHR V **a'vail yourself of sth** (*formal*) to make use of sth, especially an opportunity or offer 利用（尤指機會、提議等）：*Guests are encouraged to avail themselves of the full range of hotel facilities.* 旅館鼓勵旅客充分利用各種設施。

avail·able 🔑 **AW** /əˈveɪləbl/ *adj.* **1** 🔑 (of things 東西) that you can get, buy or find 可獲得的；可購得的；可找到的：*available resources/facilities* 可利用的資源／設備 ◇ ***readily/freely/publicly/generally available*** 可以容易／免費／讓公眾／普遍得到的 ◇ *Tickets are available free of charge from the school.* 學校有免費票。◇ *When will the information be **made available**?* 何時才可以瞭解到情況？◇ *Further information is available on request.* 詳情備索。◇ *This was the only room available.* 這是唯一可用的房間。◇ *We'll send you a copy as soon as it **becomes available**.* 一有貨我們就會給你寄一本去。◇ *Every available doctor was called to the scene.* 所有能找到的醫生都被召集到了現場。**2** 🔑 (of a person 人) free to see or talk to people 有空的：*Will she be available this afternoon?* 今天下午她有空嗎？◇ *The director was not available for comment.* 主管沒有時間發表意見。▶ **avail·abil·ity** **AW** /əˌveɪləˈbɪləti/ *noun* [U]：*the availability of cheap flights* 有廉價機票出售 ◇ (*BrE*)：*This offer is **subject to availability**.* 優惠至此產品售完為止。

ava·lanche /ˈævəlɑːnʃ; *NAmE* ˈævəlæntʃ/ (*NAmE* also **snow·slide**) *noun* a mass of snow, ice and rock that falls down the side of a mountain 雪崩；山崩：*alpine villages destroyed in an avalanche* 在一場雪崩中被摧毀的高山村莊 ◇ (*figurative*) *We received an avalanche of letters in reply to our advertisement.* 我們在登出廣告後收到了雪片般飛來的大批答覆信件。

avant- /ˈævɒ̃; *NAmE* ˈævɑ̃/ *combining form* (used especially with types of popular music 尤用於各類流行音樂) in a style that is modern and very different from what has been done before 前衛的：*experimental music like avant-rock* 前衛搖滾樂之類的實驗音樂 ◇ *avant-jazz* 前衛爵士樂 ◇ *avant-pop* 前衛流行樂

the avant-garde /ˌævɒ̃ ˈɡɑːd; *NAmE* ˌævɑ̃ː ˈɡɑːrd/ *noun* (from *French*) **1** [sing.] new and very modern ideas in art, music or literature that are sometimes surprising or shocking（藝術、音樂或文學方面的）前衛派思想 **2** [sing.+sing./pl. v.] a group of artists, etc. who introduce new and very modern ideas 前衛派（藝術家等）▶ **avant-garde** *adj.*

Grammar Point 語法說明

avenge / revenge

Avenge is a verb; **revenge** is (usually) a noun. * avenge 為動詞，revenge 通常作名詞。

- People **avenge** something or **avenge** themselves **on** somebody. 報某事之仇用 avenge something，向某人報仇用 avenge oneself on somebody：*She vowed to avenge her brother's death.* 她發誓要為哥哥之死報仇。◇ *He later avenged himself on his wife's killers.* 他後來向殺害他妻子的人報了仇。You **take revenge on** a person. 報復某人用 take revenge on。
- In more formal or literary English, **revenge** can also be a verb. People **revenge** themselves **on** somebody or **are revenged on** them (with the same meaning). 在較正式或文學用語中，revenge 亦可作動詞。revenge oneself on somebody 或 be revenged on somebody 意思相同，均表示向某人報仇：*He was later revenged on his wife's killers.* 他後來向殺害他妻子的人報了仇。You cannot **revenge** something. 不能說 revenge something：~~*She vowed to revenge her brother's death.*~~

avar·ice /ˈævərɪs/ *noun* [U] (*formal*) extreme desire for wealth（對錢財的）貪婪，貪心，貪得無厭 **SYN** **greed** ▶ **avar·icious** /ˌævəˈrɪʃəs/ *adj.*

ava·tar /ˈævətɑː(r)/ *noun* **1** (in Hinduism and Buddhism) a god appearing in a physical form 化身（印度教和佛教中化作人形或獸形的神）**2** a picture of a person or an animal that represents a particular computer user, on a computer screen, especially in a computer game or CHAT ROOM（尤指電腦遊戲或聊天室中代表使用者的）用戶頭像

Ave. (*NAmE* also **Av.**) *abbr.* (used in written addresses) AVENUE（用於書面地址）大街：*Fifth Ave.* 第五大街

avenge /əˈvendʒ/ *verb* (*formal*) to punish or hurt sb in return for sth bad or wrong that they have done to you, your family or friends 報（某事）之仇；向（某人）報仇：**~ sth** *He promised to avenge his father's murder.* 他發誓要報殺父之仇。◇ **~ yourself on sb** *She was determined to avenge herself on the man who had betrayed her.* 她決心向那個負心男人報仇。▶ **aven·ger** *noun*

av·enue /ˈævənjuː; *NAmE* -nuː/ *noun* **1** (*abbr.* **Ave.**, **Av.**) a street in a town or city（城鎮的）大街：*a hotel on Fifth Avenue* 第五大街上的一家旅館 **2** (*BrE*) a wide straight road with trees on both sides, especially one leading to a big house 林蔭道（尤指通往大住宅者）**3** a choice or way of making progress towards sth 選擇；途徑；手段：*Several avenues are open to us.* 有幾個辦法可以供我們選擇。◇ *We will explore every avenue until we find an answer.* 我們會探索一切途徑，直到找到答案為止。

aver /əˈvɜː(r)/ *verb* (**-rr-**) **~ that …** | **~ sth** | **+ speech** (*formal*) to state firmly and strongly that sth is true 斷言；確認 **SYN** **assert**, **declare**：*She averred that she had never seen the man before.* 她斬釘截鐵地說以前從未見過這個男人。

aver·age 🔑 /ˈævərɪdʒ/ *adj., noun, verb*

■ **adj. 1** 🔑 [only before noun] calculated by adding several amounts together, finding a total, and dividing the total by the number of amounts 平均的：*an **average rate/cost/price*** 平均費率／成本／價格 ◇ *Average earnings are around £20 000 per annum.* 年平均收入約為 2 萬英鎊。◇ *at an average speed of 100 miles per hour* 以平均每小時 100 英里的速度 **2** 🔑 typical or normal 典型的；正常的：*40 hours is a fairly average working week for most people.* 對大多數人來說，一週工作 40 小時是相當正常的。◇ *children of **above/below average** intelligence* 高於／低於一般智力的兒童 ◇ *£20 for dinner is about average.* 花 20 英鎊吃正餐算是價格一般。**3** 🔑 ordinary; not special 普通的；平常的；一般的：*I was just an average sort of student.* 我只是一個普通的學生。▶ **aver·age·ly** *adv.*：*He was attractive and averagely intelligent.* 他討人喜歡，智力一般。

■ **noun** [C, U] **1** 🔑 the result of adding several amounts together, finding a total, and dividing the total by the number of amounts 平均數：*The average of 4, 5 and 9 is 6.* * 4、5、9 三個數的平均數是 6。◇ *Parents spend **an average of** $220 a year on toys.* 父母為孩子買玩具的花費每年平均為 220 元。◇ *If I get an A on this essay, that will bring my average* (= average mark/grade) *up to a B+.* 如果我的這篇論文得 A，我的平均成績就會提高到 B+。⊃ see also GRADE POINT AVERAGE **2** 🔑 a level which is usual 平均水平；一般水準：*Temperatures are **above/below average** for the time of year.* 溫度高於／低於此時的年平均溫度。◇ *400 people a year die of this disease **on average**.* 平均每年有 400 人死於這種疾病。◇ *Class sizes in the school are below **the national average**.* 這所學校班上的人數少於全國平均數。**IDM** see LAW

■ **verb 1** [T] **~ sth** [no passive] to be equal to a particular amount as an average 平均為：*Economic growth is expected to average 2% next year.* 明年經濟增長預計平均可達 2%。◇ *Drivers in London can expect to average about 12 miles per hour* (= to have that as their average speed). 估計倫敦的駕車者平均時速為 12 英里。**2** [T, I] **~ (sth)** to calculate the average of sth 計算出…的平均數：*Earnings are averaged over the whole period.* 所計算的是整個時期的平均收入。

A

PHR V **,average 'out (at sth)** to result in an average amount over a period of time or when several things are considered 平均數為： *The cost should average out at about £6 per person.* 費用應該是平均每人約 6 英鎊。◇ *Sometimes I pay, sometimes he pays—it seems to average out* (= result in us paying the same amount). 有時我付錢，有時他付錢，看來兩相持平。 **,average sth↔'out (at sth)** to calculate the average of sth 計算出…的平均數

averse /ə'vɜːs; *NAmE* ə'vɜːrs/ *adj.* [not before noun] **1 not ~ to sth / to doing sth** liking sth or wanting to do sth; not opposed to doing sth 喜歡；想做；不反對做： *I mentioned it to Kate and she wasn't averse to the idea.* 我向凱特提起這個想法，她不反對。 **2 ~ to sth / to doing sth** (*formal*) not liking sth or wanting to do sth; opposed to doing sth 不喜歡；不想做；反對做： *He was averse to any change.* 他反對任何改變。

aver·sion /ə'vɜːʃn; *NAmE* ə'vɜːrʒn/ *noun* [C, U] a strong feeling of not liking sb/sth 厭惡；憎惡： *a strong aversion* 深深厭惡 ◇ **~ to sb/sth** *He had an aversion to getting up early.* 他十分討厭早起。

a'version therapy *noun* [U] a way of helping sb to lose a bad habit, by making the habit seem to be associated with an effect that is not pleasant 厭惡療法（通過令人不愉快的刺激，使接受治療者避免不良行為）

avert /ə'vɜːt; *NAmE* ə'vɜːrt/ *verb* **1 ~ sth** to prevent sth bad or dangerous from happening 防止，避免（危險、壞事）: *A disaster was narrowly averted.* 及時防止了一場災難。◇ *He did his best to avert suspicion.* 他盡量避嫌。 **2 ~ your eyes/gaze/face (from sth)** to turn your eyes, etc. away from sth that you do not want to see 轉移目光；背過臉： *She averted her eyes from the terrible scene in front of her.* 她背過臉，不去看面前可怕的場面。

avian /'eɪviən/ *adj.* [usually before noun] (*technical* 術語) of or connected with birds 鳥（類）的；關於鳥（類）的

'avian flu *noun* [U] (*formal*) = BIRD FLU

avi·ary /'eɪviəri; *NAmE* 'eɪvieri/ *noun* (*pl.* **-ies**) a large CAGE or building for keeping birds in, for example in a ZOO 大鳥籠，鳥舍（如動物園內的）

avi·ation /ˌeɪvi'eɪʃn/ *noun* [U] the designing, building and flying of aircraft 航空製造業；航空；飛行： ***civil/military aviation*** 民用／軍用航空 ◇ *the* ***aviation business/industry*** 航空業／工業

avi·ator /'eɪvieɪtə(r)/ *noun* (*old-fashioned*) a person who flies an aircraft 飛行員；飛機駕駛員

avid /'ævɪd/ *adj.* **1** [usually before noun] very enthusiastic about sth (often a hobby) 熱衷的；酷愛的 **SYN** **keen**： *an* ***avid reader/collector*** 酷愛閱讀／收藏的人 ◇ *She has* ***taken an avid interest in*** *the project* (= she is extremely interested in it). 她對這個項目入了迷。 **2 ~ for sth** wanting to get sth very much 渴望的；渴求的： *He was avid for more information.* 他渴望知道更多信息。 ▸ **avid·ity** /ə'vɪdəti/ *noun* [U] **avid·ly** *adv.* : *She reads avidly.* 她如飢如渴地閱讀。

avi·on·ics /ˌeɪvi'ɒnɪks; *NAmE* -'ɑːn-/ *noun* **1** [U] the science of ELECTRONICS when used in designing and making aircraft 航空電子學 **2** [pl.] the electronic devices in an aircraft or a SPACECRAFT 航空（或航天）電子設備 ▸ **avi·on·ic** *adj.*

avo·cado /ˌævə'kɑːdəʊ; *NAmE* -'kɑːdoʊ/ *noun* (*pl.* **-os**) (*BrE* also **,avocado 'pear**) a tropical fruit with hard, dark green skin, soft, light green flesh and a large seed inside. Avocados are not sweet and are sometimes eaten at the beginning of a meal. 油梨，鱷梨（熱帶水果，皮硬呈深綠色，肉軟呈淺綠色，核大） ➲ VISUAL VOCAB page V30

avo·ca·tion /ˌævəʊ'keɪʃn; *NAmE* ˌævoʊ-/ *noun* (*formal*) a hobby or other activity that you do for interest and enjoyment 業餘愛好

avo·cet /'ævəset/ *noun* a bird that lives on or near water, with long legs and black and white feathers 反嘴鷸（腿長、羽毛黑白相間的涉禽）

avoid 🔑 /ə'vɔɪd/ *verb* **1** 🔑 to prevent sth bad from happening 避免；防止： **~ sth** *The accident could have been avoided.* 這個事故本來是可以避免的。◇ *They* ***narrowly avoided*** *defeat.* 他們險些遭擊敗了。◇ *The name was changed to avoid confusion with another firm.* 改名是為了避免和另一家公司混淆。◇ **~ doing sth** *They built a wall to avoid soil being washed away.* 他們建了一堵牆防止土壤流失。 **2** 🔑 to keep away from sb/sth; to try not to do sth 迴避；避開；躲避： **~ sb/sth** *He's been avoiding me all week.* 整整一個星期他一直在迴避我。◇ *She kept avoiding my eyes* (= avoided looking at me). 她總是躲避我的目光。◇ *I left early to avoid the rush hour.* 我早早動身以避開交通高峰時刻。◇ **~ doing sth** *I've been avoiding getting down to work all day.* 我一整天都刻意不投入工作。◇ *You should avoid mentioning his divorce.* 你應該避免提及他離婚的事。 **3** 🔑 **~ sth** to prevent yourself from hitting sth 避免撞到（某物）： *The car swerved to avoid a cat.* 那輛車突然一個急轉彎以避免軋到一隻貓。

IDM **avoid sb/sth like the 'plague** (*informal*) to try very hard not to meet sb, do sth, etc. 像避瘟疫似地躲着某人（或某事物）；盡量避開某人（或某事物） ➲ more at TRAP *n.*

avoid·able /ə'vɔɪdəbl/ *adj.* that can be prevented 可以避免的： *Many deaths from heart disease are actually avoidable.* 許多因心臟病造成的死亡實際上是可以避免的。 **OPP** **unavoidable**

avoid·ance /ə'vɔɪdəns/ *noun* [U] **~ (of sth)** not doing sth; preventing sth from existing or happening 避免；防止；迴避；避開： *A person's health improves with the avoidance of stress.* 一個人只要避免緊張，健康狀況就會改善。 ➲ see also TAX AVOIDANCE

avoir·du·pois /ˌævədə'pɔɪz; ˌævwɑːdjuː'pwɑː; *NAmE* ˌævərdə'pɔɪz/ *noun* [U] the system of weights based on the pound 常衡（以磅為單位的衡制）

avow /ə'vaʊ/ *verb* **~ that ...** | **~ sth** | **+ speech** (*formal*) to say firmly and often publicly what your opinion is, what you think is true, etc. 聲明；公開宣稱： *An aide avowed that the President had known nothing of the deals.* 一位助理聲明，總統對那些交易毫不知情。 ▸ **avow·al** /ə'vaʊəl/ *noun* : (*formal*) *an avowal of love* 公開表示愛情

avowed /ə'vaʊd/ *adj.* [only before noun] (*formal*) that has been admitted or stated in public 公開承認的；公開宣稱的： *an avowed atheist* 公開宣稱的無神論者 ◇ *an* ***avowed aim/intention/objective/purpose*** 公開宣稱的宗旨／意圖／目標／目的 ▸ **avow·ed·ly** /ə'vaʊɪdli/ *adv.*

avun·cu·lar /ə'vʌŋkjələ(r)/ *adj.* (*formal*) behaving in a kind and friendly way towards young people, similar to the way an uncle treats his nieces or nephews 像伯伯（或叔叔）似的；諄諄長輩風範的；慈愛的

aw /ɔː/ *exclamation* (*especially NAmE*) used to express disapproval, protest or sympathy （表示不滿、抗議或同情等）呀： *Aw, come on, Andy!* 呀，行啦，安迪！

await /ə'weɪt/ *verb* (*formal*) **1 ~ sb/sth** to wait for sb/sth 等候；等待；期待： *He is in custody* ***awaiting trial.*** 他正被拘留候審。◇ *Her latest novel is eagerly awaited.* 人們正急切地期待着她的最新小說。 **2 ~ sb** to be going to happen to sb 將發生在，將降臨到（某人頭上）： *A warm welcome awaits all our guests.* 我們的客人都將受到熱烈歡迎。

awake 🔑 /ə'weɪk/ *adj.*, *verb*

■ ***adj.*** 🔑 [not before noun] not asleep (especially immediately before or after sleeping) 醒着（尤指入睡前或剛醒時）： *to be* ***half/fully awake*** 半睡半醒；睡意全無 ◇ *to be* ***wide awake*** (= fully awake) 毫無睡意 ◇ *I was still awake when he came to bed.* 他就寢時我還沒有入睡。◇ *The noise was* ***keeping*** *everyone* ***awake.*** 喧鬧聲吵得大家都睡不着。◇ *I was finding it hard to* ***stay awake.*** 我已睏得難熬。◇ *He* ***lies awake*** *at night worrying about his job.* 他擔心他的工作，夜晚躺在牀上睡不着。◇ *She was awake* (= not unconscious) *during the operation on her leg.* 給她的腿動手術時她一直醒着。

■ ***verb*** (**awoke** /ə'wəʊk; *NAmE* ə'woʊk/, **awoken** /ə'wəʊkən; *NAmE* ə'woʊkən/) (*formal*) **1** [I, T] to wake up; to make sb wake up（使）醒來： **~ (sb) (from/to sth)** *I awoke from a deep sleep.* 我從沉睡中醒來。◇ **~ to do sth** *He awoke to*

A

find her gone. 他醒來發現她已經走了。◇ **~ sb** *Her voice awoke the sleeping child.* 她的聲音驚醒了睡着的小孩。**2** [I, T] **~ (sth)** if an emotion **awakes** or sth **awakes** an emotion, you start to feel that emotion 喚起；被喚起：*His speech is bound to awake old fears and hostilities.* 他的發言必然要激起昔日的恐懼和敵對情緒。

PHR V **a'wake to sth** to become aware of sth and its possible effects or results 察覺到；意識到；醒悟到：*It took her some time to awake to the dangers of her situation.* 過了一些時間她才意識到她處境的危險。➲ compare WAKE

Which Word? 詞語辨析

awake / awaken / wake up / waken

- **Wake (up)** is the most common of these verbs. It can mean somebody has finished sleeping 上述動詞中 wake (up) 最通用，可表示睡醒：*What time do you usually wake up?* 你通常什麼時候醒來？ or that somebody or something has disturbed your sleep. 亦指弄醒、喚醒：*The children woke me up.* 孩子們把我吵醒了。◇ *I was woken (up) by the telephone.* 電話鈴聲把我吵醒了。
- The verb **awake** is usually only used in writing and in the past tense **awoke**. 動詞 awake 通常只用於書面語的過去時 awoke：*She awoke to a day of brilliant sunshine.* 她醒來時是陽光燦爛的一天。**Waken** and **awaken** are much more formal. **Awaken** is used especially in literature. * waken 和 awaken 要正式得多。awaken 尤用於文學作品：*The Prince awakened Sleeping Beauty with a kiss.* 王子的吻喚醒了睡美人。
- **Awake** is also an adjective. * awake 亦作形容詞：*I was awake half the night worrying.* 我憂心忡忡，半宿不能成眠。◇ *Is the baby awake yet?* 寶寶醒來了嗎？ **Waking** is not used in this way. * waking 不能這樣用。
- Look also at ASLEEP and the verb SLEEP

awaken /ə'weɪkən/ *verb* (*formal*) **1** [I, T, often passive] to wake up; to make sb wake up （使）醒來：**~ (sb) (from/to sth)** *She awakened to the sound of birds singing.* 她醒來聽到鳥的叫聲。◇ **~ to do sth** *We awakened to find the others gone.* 我們醒來發現其他人已經走了。◇ **~ sb** *He was awakened at dawn by the sound of crying.* 黎明時他被哭喊聲吵醒。➲ note at AWAKE **2** [I, T] **~ (sth)** if an emotion **awakens** or sth **awakens** an emotion, you start to feel that emotion 喚起；被喚起：*The dream awakened terrible memories.* 這個夢喚起了可怕的往事。

PHR V **a'waken (sb) to sth** to become aware or to make sb aware of sth and its possible effects or results （使）察覺到，意識到，醒悟到：*I gradually awakened to the realization that our marriage was over.* 我逐漸意識到我們的婚姻結束了。➲ compare WAKEN (2)

awak·en·ing /ə'weɪkənɪŋ/ *noun* **1** [C, usually sing.] an occasion when you realize sth or become aware of sth 醒悟；覺醒：*If they had expected a warm welcome, they were in for a* ***rude awakening*** (= they would soon realize that it would not be warm). 要是他們以為會受到熱烈歡迎，他們很快就會醒悟並非如此。**2** [C, U] the act of beginning to understand or feel sth; the act of sth starting or waking 認識；感到；被激起；被喚起：*sexual awakening* 性慾的萌動 ◇ *the awakening of interest in the environment* 對環境產生的興趣

award 🔑 /ə'wɔːd; *NAmE* ə'wɔːrd/ *noun, verb*

■ *noun* **1** 🔑 [C] (often in names of particular awards 常用於獎項名稱) a prize such as money, etc. for sth that sb has done 獎；獎品；獎金；獎狀：*He was nominated for the best actor award.* 他獲得最佳演員獎提名。◇ *an* ***award presentation/ceremony*** 頒獎；頒獎儀式 ◇ *the Housing Design Award* 住宅設計獎 ◇ **~ for sth** *to* ***win/receive/get an award*** *for sth* 因某事贏得／得到／獲得獎項 ➲ see also ACADEMY AWARD **2** [C] an increase in the amount of money sb earns （收入的）增加：*an annual pay award* 年工資增加 **3** [C, U] the amount of money that a court decides should be given to sb who has won a case; the decision to give this money （賠償）裁定額；（賠償）裁決：*an award of £600 000 in libel damages* * 60 萬英鎊的誹謗損害賠償 **4** [U] the official decision to give sth (such as a DIPLOMA) to sb （畢業證書等的）授予：*Satisfactory completion of the course will lead to the award of the Diploma of Social Work.* 合格完成此課程者將獲得社會福利工作文憑。**5** [C] (*BrE*) money that students get to help pay for living costs while they study or do research 獎學金；助學金

■ *verb* 🔑 [T] to make an official decision to give sth to sb as a payment, prize, etc. 授予；獎勵；判給：**~ sth (to sb)** *The judges awarded equal points to both finalists.* 裁判判定決賽雙方得分相等。◇ **~ (sb) sth** *The judges awarded both finalists equal points.* 裁判判定決賽雙方得分相等。◇ *He was awarded damages of £50 000.* 他判得損害賠償金 5 萬英鎊。

award·ee /əˌwɔːˈdiː; *NAmE* əˌwɔːrˈdiː/ *noun* a person who is awarded sth, such as a prize 受獎者；獲獎者

a'ward-winning *adj.* [only before noun] having won a prize 獲獎的：*the award-winning TV drama* 獲獎電視劇

aware 🔑 **AW** /ə'weə(r); *NAmE* ə'wer/ *adj.*

1 🔑 [not before noun] knowing or realizing sth 知道；意識到；明白：*As you're aware, this is not a new problem.* 正如你所瞭解的，這不是一個新問題。◇ ***As far as I'm aware****, nobody has done anything about it.* 據我所知，尚無人對此採取任何措施。◇ ***acutely/painfully*** (= very) ***aware*** 深切地／痛苦地認識到 ◇ **~ of sth** *I don't think people are really aware of just how much it costs.* 我認為人們並不真正明白這要花多少錢。◇ *He was* ***well aware*** *of the problem.* 他很清楚這個問題。◇ *Everybody should* ***be made aware of*** *the risks involved.* 應該讓人人都知道所涉及的風險。◇ **~ that …** *Were you aware that something was wrong?* 你有沒有意識到已經出了問題？ **2** 🔑 [not before noun] noticing that sth is present, or that sth is happening 察覺到；發覺；發現：**~ of sb/sth** *She slipped away without him being aware of it.* 她悄悄離開，沒有讓他發覺。◇ *They suddenly became aware of people looking at them.* 他們突然意識到有些人在瞧着他們。◇ **~ that …** *I was aware that she was trembling.* 我察覺到她在發抖。**3** (used with an adverb 與副詞連用) interested in and knowing about sth, and thinking it is important 對…有興趣的；有…意識的：*Young people are very environmentally aware.* 年輕人的環保意識很強。**OPP** **unaware**

aware·ness **AW** /ə'weənəs; *NAmE* ə'wer-/ *noun* [U, sing.] **~ (of sth)** | **~ (that …)** knowing sth; knowing that sth exists and is important; being interested in sth 知道；認識；意識；興趣：*an awareness of the importance of eating a healthy diet* 認識到健康飲食的重要性 ◇ *There was an almost complete* ***lack of awareness*** *of the issues involved.* 對有關問題幾乎是一無所知。◇ *It is important that students* ***develop an awareness of*** *how the Internet can be used.* 重要的是學生逐漸懂得如何使用互聯網。◇ *to* ***raise/heighten/increase*** *public* ***awareness*** *of sth* 加強／提高／增強公眾對某事物的意識 ◇ ***a greater/a growing/an increasing awareness*** *of sth* 對某事物更大的／日益增長的／愈來愈大的興趣 ◇ *environmental awareness* (= knowing that looking after the environment is important) 環境意識 ◇ *Energy Awareness Week* （節約）能源意識週 ◇ *There seems to be a general awareness that this is not the solution.* 似乎人們已普遍認識到這不是解決問題的辦法。

awash /ə'wɒʃ; *NAmE* ə'wɔːʃ; ə'wɑːʃ/ *adj.* [not before noun] **1 ~ (with water)** covered with water 被淹沒；被漫過；被水覆蓋 **2 ~ with sth** having sth in large quantities 充滿：*The city is awash with drugs.* 這座城市毒品泛濫。

away 🔑 /ə'weɪ/ *adv.*

HELP For the special uses of **away** in phrasal verbs, look at the entries for the verbs. For example **get away with sth** is in the phrasal verb section at **get**. * away 在短語動詞中的特殊用法見有關動詞詞條。如 get away with sth 在詞條 get 的短語動詞部份。**1** 🔑 to or at a distance from sb/sth in space or time （時間或空間上）離開（某距離），在（某距離）處：*The beach is a mile away.* 海灘在一英里外。◇ *Christmas is still months away.*

離聖誕節還有幾個月。◇ **~ from sb/sth** *The station is a few minutes' walk away from here.* 車站離這裏有步行幾分鐘的路程。 **2** to a different place or in a different direction 去別處；朝另一個方向： *Go away!* 走開！◇ *Put your toys away.* 把你的玩具收拾起來。◇ *The bright light made her look away.* 強光使她把視線轉向別處。 **3** not present 不在；離開 **SYN** **absent** ： *There were ten children away yesterday.* 昨天有十個孩子缺席。◇ *Sorry, he's away.* 對不起，他不在。◇ **~ from sb/sth** *She was away from work for a week.* 她有一個星期沒來上班。 **4** used after verbs to say that sth is done continuously or with a lot of energy（用於動詞後）持續地，勁頭十足地： *She was still writing away furiously when the bell went.* 鈴聲響時她還在不停地寫着。◇ *They were soon chatting away like old friends.* 他們很快就像老朋友一樣聊起天來。 **5** until disappearing completely 直到完全消失： *The water boiled away.* 水燒乾了。◇ *The music faded away.* 樂聲逐漸消失。◇ *They danced the night away* (= all night). 他們跳舞跳了一個通宵。 **6** (*sport* 體) at the opponent's ground or STADIUM 在客場： *Chelsea are playing away this Saturday.* 本星期六切爾西隊要在客場比賽。◇ *an* **away match/game** 客場比賽 ➲ compare HOME *adj.* (4)

IDM **away with …** (*literary*) used to say that you would like to be rid of sb/sth 讓（某人或事物）消失吧： *Away with all these rules and regulations!* 讓所有這些規章制度見鬼去吧！ ➲ more at COBWEBS, DANCE *v.*, FAR *adv.*, RIGHT *adv.*, STRAIGHT *adv.*

away·day /ˈəweɪdeɪ/ *noun* (*BrE, business* 商) a day that a group of workers spend together away from their usual place of work in order to discuss ideas or plans（不在工作場所的）外出研討日： *The management are having an awayday to discuss strategy.* 管理層今天外出商議策略。◇ *We talked about it at the awayday.* 我們外出開會那天說起過這事。

awe /ɔː/ *noun, verb*

■ ***noun*** [U] feelings of respect and slight fear; feelings of being very impressed by sth/sb 敬畏；驚歎： *awe and respect* 敬畏和尊敬 ◇ *awe and wonder* 敬畏和驚奇 ◇ *He speaks of her* **with awe**. 他談到她時肅然起敬。◇ *'It's magnificent,' she whispered* **in awe**. "真是壯麗。" 她小聲地驚歎道。

IDM **be/stand in ˈawe of sb/sth** to admire sb/sth and be slightly frightened of them/it 對…敬畏；對…望而生畏： *While Diana was in awe of her grandfather, she adored her grandmother.* 黛安娜敬畏她的祖父，但敬佩她的祖母。

■ ***verb*** **~ sb** [usually passive] (*formal*) to fill sb with awe 使敬畏；使驚歎： *She seemed awed by the presence of so many famous people.* 見到這麼多名人出席，似乎令她驚歎不已。 ▸ **awed** *adj.* : *We watched in awed silence.* 我們敬畏地默然觀看着。

ˈawe-inspir·ing *adj.* impressive; making you feel respect and admiration 令人驚歎的；使人敬佩的；令人敬慕的： *The building was awe-inspiring in size and design.* 這座建築的規模和設計氣勢宏偉。

awe·some /ˈɔːsəm/ *adj.* **1** very impressive or very difficult and perhaps rather frightening 令人驚歎的；使人驚懼的；很困難的；難得嚇人的： *an awesome sight* 驚人的奇觀 ◇ *awesome beauty/power* 天仙之美；大得嚇人的權力 ◇ *They had an awesome task ahead.* 他們就要有十分艱巨的任務。 **2** (*especially NAmE, informal*) very good, enjoyable, etc. 很好的（或極好玩的等）： *I just bought this awesome new CD!* 我剛買了這張特棒的新CD！◇ *Wow! That's totally awesome!* 哇！真是棒極了！ ➲ SYNONYMS at GREAT ▸ **awe·some·ly** *adv.* : *awesomely beautiful* 極其美麗

awe·struck /ˈɔːstrʌk/ *adj.* (*literary*) feeling very impressed by sth 驚歎的： *People were awestruck by the pictures the satellite sent back to Earth.* 人們對人造衞星送回地球的圖片歎為觀止。

awful /ˈɔːfl/ *adj., adv.*

■ ***adj.*** **1** (*informal*) very bad or unpleasant 很壞的；極討厭的： *That's an awful colour.* 那顏色難看得很。◇ *'They didn't even offer to pay.' 'Oh that's awful.'* "他們甚至不主動付錢。" "哦，那真不像話。" ◇ *It's awful, isn't it?* 糟糕透了，不是嗎？◇ *The weather last summer was awful.* 剛過去的夏季天氣真壞。◇ *I feel awful about forgetting her birthday.* 我忘了她的生日，感到很過意不去。◇ ***to look/feel awful*** (= to look/feel ill) 面帶病容；感到很不舒服 ◇ *There's an awful smell in here.* 這裏有股很難聞的味道。◇ *The awful thing is, it was my fault.* 糟糕的是，這是我的過失。 ➲ note at TERRIBLE **2** (*informal*) used to emphasize sth, especially that there is a large amount or too much of sth 非常的；很多的；過多的： *It's going to cost* ***an awful lot of*** *money.* 這要花非常多的錢。◇ *There's not an awful lot of room.* 沒有很多的空間。◇ *I feel an awful lot better than I did yesterday.* 我覺得身體比昨天好得多了。◇ (*BrE*) *I had an awful job persuading him to come* (= it was very difficult). 說服他來真是費勁死了。 **3** very shocking 駭人聽聞的；可怕的 **SYN** **terrible** ： *the awful horrors of war* 駭人聽聞的戰爭恐怖情形 ▸ **aw·ful·ness** *noun* [U] ： *the sheer awfulness of the situation* 糟透了的情況

■ ***adv.*** (*informal, especially NAmE*) very; extremely 非常；極其： *Clint is awful smart.* 克林特機靈極了。

aw·ful·ly /ˈɔːfli/ *adv.*
very; extremely 非常；極其 **SYN** **terribly** ： *I'm awfully sorry about that problem the other day.* 我對前幾天的那個問題感到非常遺憾。

awhile /əˈwaɪl/ *adv.* (*formal* or *literary*) for a short time 片刻；一會兒

awk·ward /ˈɔːkwəd; *NAmE* -wərd/ *adj.*
1 making you feel embarrassed 令人尷尬的；使人難堪的： *There was an awkward silence.* 一陣令人尷尬的沉默。 **2** difficult to deal with 難對付的；難處理的 **SYN** **difficult** ： *Don't ask awkward questions.* 不要問棘手的問題。◇ *You've put me in an awkward position.* 你使得我狼狽不堪。◇ *an awkward customer* (= a person who is difficult to deal with) 難對付的傢伙 ◇ *Please don't be awkward about letting him come.* 關於讓他來這事請你不要作梗。 **3** not convenient 不方便的 **SYN** **inconvenient** ： *Have I come at an awkward time?* 我來得不是時候吧？ **4** difficult or dangerous because of its shape or design（因形狀、設計而）產生困難的，危險的： *This box is very awkward for one person to carry.* 這隻箱子一個人很不好搬。 **5** not moving in an easy way; not comfortable（動作）笨拙的；不舒適的： *He tried to dance, but he was too clumsy and awkward.* 他試着跳舞，但是太笨拙，太彆扭。◇ *I must have slept in an awkward position—I'm aching all over.* 我肯定是睡的姿勢不當，我全身疼痛。 ▸ **awk·ward·ly** *adv.* : *'I'm sorry,' he said awkwardly.* "對不起。" 他局促不安地說。◇ *She fell awkwardly and broke her ankle.* 她重重地摔了一跤，摔斷了踝關節。◇ *an awkwardly shaped room* 形狀彆扭的房間 **awk·ward·ness** *noun* [U] ： *She laughed to cover up her feeling of awkwardness.* 她用笑聲掩飾她的難堪。

awl /ɔːl/ *noun* a small pointed tool used for making holes, especially in leather（尤指鑽皮革的）鑽子，錐子

awn·ing /ˈɔːnɪŋ/ *noun* a sheet of strong cloth that stretches out from above a door or window to keep off the sun or rain（門窗上面的）遮陽篷，雨篷 ➲ VISUAL VOCAB page V2, V3

awoke *past tense* of AWAKE

awoken *past part.* of AWAKE

AWOL /ˈeɪwɒl; *NAmE* ˈeɪwɔːl/ *abbr.* absent without leave (used especially in the armed forces when sb has left their group without permission) 擅離職守，無故離隊，開小差（尤用於軍隊）： *He's* ***gone AWOL*** *from his base.* 他從基地開了小差。◇ (*humorous*) *The guitarist went AWOL in the middle of the recording.* 在錄音過程當中吉他手溜走了。

awry /əˈraɪ/ *adv., adj.* **1** if sth **goes awry**, it does not happen in the way that was planned. 出錯；出岔子： *All my plans for the party had gone awry.* 我的聚會計劃全亂了套。 **2** not in the right position 歪；斜 **SYN** **untidy** ： *She rushed out, her hair awry.* 她披頭散髮衝了出來。

axe /æks/ *noun, verb*

■ ***noun*** (*especially BrE*) (*US* usually **ax**) **1** a tool with a wooden handle and a heavy metal blade, used for

A

chopping wood, cutting down trees, etc. 斧 ➲ see also BATTLEAXE, ICE AXE, PICKAXE **2 the axe** [sing.] (*informal*) (often used in newspapers 常用於報刊中) if sb gets **the axe**, they lose their job; if an institution or a project gets **the axe**, it is closed or stopped, usually because of a lack of money（遭）解雇；倒閉；被停業：*Up to 300 workers are* ***facing the axe*** *at a struggling Merseyside firm.* 默西賽德的一家艱苦掙扎的公司有多達 300 名工人面臨被解雇。◇ *Patients are delighted their local hospital has been saved from the axe.* 病人高興的是當地醫院得以免遭關閉。

IDM **ˌhave an ˈaxe to grind** to have private reasons for being involved in sth or for arguing for a particular cause 有私心；有個人打算：*She had no axe to grind and was only acting out of concern for their safety.* 她毫無私心，這樣做只是出於對他們安全的關懷。

■ *verb* (*BrE*) (*US* **ax**) [often passive] **1 ~ sth** (*informal*) (often used in newspapers 常用於報刊中) to get rid of a service, system, etc. or to reduce the money spent on it by a large amount 精簡（機構等）；大量削減（經費等）：*Other less profitable services are to be axed later this year.* 其他盈利較少的服務預計今年稍晚將大量削減。**2 ~ sb** (*informal*) (often used in newspapers 常用於報刊中) to remove sb from their job 解雇；開除：*Jones has been axed from the team.* 瓊斯已被開除出隊。**3 ~ sb** to kill sb with an axe 用斧把…砍死

axe 斧

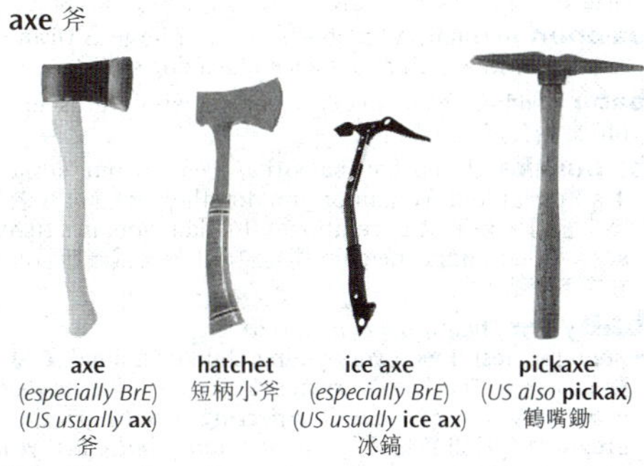

axe (*especially BrE*) (*US usually* **ax**) 斧 | **hatchet** 短柄小斧 | **ice axe** (*especially BrE*) (*US usually* **ice ax**) 冰鎬 | **pickaxe** (*US also* **pickax**) 鶴嘴鋤

axel /ˈæksl/ *noun* a jump in SKATING in which you jump from the front outside edge of one foot, turn in the air, and land on the outside edge of your other foot 阿克謝爾跳，前外一週半跳（溜冰時以一腳前外刃起跳旋轉後以另一腳外刃着地）

axe·man /ˈæksmən/ (*especially BrE*) (*NAmE* usually **axman**) (*pl.* **-men** /-mən/) *noun* (*informal*) a man who attacks other people with an axe 用斧砍人的人

axial /ˈæksiəl/ *adj.* of or related to an AXIS 軸的；軸線的：*an axial road* 軸路

axiom /ˈæksiəm/ *noun* (*formal*) a rule or principle that most people believe to be true 公理

axio·mat·ic /ˌæksiəˈmætɪk/ *adj.* [not usually before noun] (*formal*) true in such an obvious way that you do not need to prove it 公理；不證自明 SYN **self-evident**：*It is axiomatic that life is not always easy.* 生活並不總是一帆風順是明擺着的事實。▸ **axio·mat·ic·al·ly** *adv.*

axis /ˈæksɪs/ *noun* (*pl.* **axes** /ˈæksiːz/) **1** an imaginary line through the centre of an object, around which the object turns 軸（旋轉物體假想的中心線）：*Mars takes longer to revolve on its axis than the Earth.* 火星自轉一週的時間比地球長。**2** (*technical* 術語) a fixed line against which the positions of points are measured, especially points on a GRAPH（尤指圖表中的）固定參考軸線，坐標軸：*the* ***vertical/horizontal axis*** 縱／橫坐標軸 **3** (*geometry* 幾何) a line that divides a shape into two equal parts 對稱中心線（將物體平分為二）：*an axis of symmetry* 對稱軸 ◇ *The axis of a circle is its diameter.* 圓的對稱中心線就是直徑。**4** [usually sing.] (*formal*) an agreement or ALLIANCE between two or more countries 軸心（國與國之間的協議或聯盟）：*the Franco-German axis* 法德軸心

axis 對稱中心線

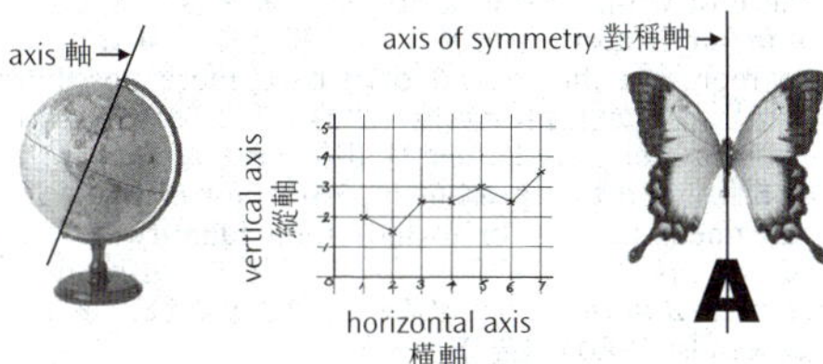

axle /ˈæksl/ *noun* a long straight piece of metal that connects a pair of wheels on a vehicle 車軸；輪軸：*the* ***front/rear axle*** 前／後車軸

axman (*US*) = AXEMAN

axon /ˈæksɒn; *NAmE* ˈæksɑːn/ *noun* (*biology* 生) the long thin part of a nerve cell along which signals are sent to other cells 軸突（神經細胞的突起，將信號發送到其他細胞）➲ compare DENDRITE

ayah /ˈaɪə/ *noun* (*IndE*) **1** a woman whose job is caring for children, doing domestic work, etc.（照看孩子、做家務等的）女傭，阿嬤 **2** a person whose job is caring for sb who is ill/sick（照料病人的）護理員，看護人員

aya·tol·lah /ˌaɪəˈtɒlə; *NAmE* -ˈtoʊlə/ *noun* a religious leader of Shiite Muslims in Iran 阿亞圖拉（伊朗伊斯蘭教什葉派宗教領袖）

aye /aɪ/ *exclamation* (*old use* or *dialect*) **1** yes 是；對：*'Did you see what happened?' 'Oh aye, I was there.'* "你看見了發生的事嗎？" "啊，是的，我在場。" **2** always; still 總是；仍然

ayes /aɪz/ *noun* [pl.] the total number of people voting 'yes' in a formal debate, for example in a parliament（議會等辯論中的）贊成票總數：*The ayes have it* (= more people have voted for sth than against it). 投票贊成的人佔多數。OPP **noes**

Ayur·vedic medicine /ˌaɪəveɪdɪk ˈmedsn; *NAmE* ˌɑːjʊr-/ *noun* [U] a type of traditional Hindu medicine that treats illnesses using a combination of foods, HERBS and breathing exercises 阿育吠陀醫學（結合食物、草藥和呼吸運動治療疾病的印度教傳統醫學）

aza·lea /əˈzeɪliə/ *noun* a plant or bush with large flowers that may be pink, purple, white or yellow, grown in a pot or in a garden 映山紅

azi·muth /ˈæzɪməθ/ *noun* (*astronomy* 天) an angle related to a distance around the earth's HORIZON, used to find out the position of a star, planet, etc. 地平經度，方位角（用以找出恒星、行星等的方位）

AZT™ /ˌeɪ zed ˈtiː; *NAmE* ziː/ *noun* [U] a drug that is used to treat AIDS 齊多夫定（用於治療艾滋病的藥）

azure /ˈæʒə(r); *BrE* also ˈæzjʊə(r)/ *adj.* bright blue in colour like the sky 天藍色的；蔚藍色的 ▸ **azure** *noun* [U]

Bb

B

B /biː/ *noun, symbol*

■ ***noun*** (also **b**) (*pl.* **Bs**, **B's**, **b's** /biːz/) **1** [C, U] the second letter of the English alphabet 英語字母表的第 2 個字母：*'Butter' begins with (a) B/'B'.* * butter 一詞以字母 b 開頭。**2 B** [C, U] (*music* 音) the 7th note in the SCALE of C MAJOR * B 音（C 大調的第 7 音或音符）**3 B** [C, U] the second highest mark/grade that a student can get for a piece of work（學業成績）第二等，良：*She got (a) B* ***in/for*** *History.* 她的歷史科成績是良。**4 B** [U] used to represent the second of two or more possibilities（表示兩個或兩個以上可能性中的）第二個：*Shall we go for plan A or plan B?* 我們選用第一方案還是第二方案？**5 B** [U] used to represent a person, for example in an imagined situation or to hide their identity（假設的或不指出姓名身分的第二人）乙，乙某：*Let's pretend A meets B in the park.* 假設甲某和乙某在公園裏相遇。➲ see also B-ROAD **IDM** see A

■ ***symbol*** used in Britain before a number to refer to a particular secondary road * B 級公路（英國公路代號，後接數字）：*the B1224 to York* 通往約克的 B1224 號公路

b. *abbr.* (in writing 書寫形式) born 出生：*Emily Clifton, b. 1800* 埃米莉・克利夫頓，1800 年生

B2B /ˌbiː tə ˈbiː/ *abbr.* BUSINESS-TO-BUSINESS 企業對企業

BA (*BrE*) (*NAmE* **B.A.**) /ˌbiː ˈeɪ/ *noun* the abbreviation for 'Bachelor of Arts' (a first university degree in an ARTS subject) 文學士（全寫為 Bachelor of Arts，大學文科的初級學位）：*to* ***be/have/do a BA*** 是文學士；有文學士學位；攻讀文學士 ◇ (*BrE*) *Darren Green BA* 文學士達倫・格林

baa /bɑː/ *noun* the sound made by sheep or LAMBS（羊叫聲）咩 ▸ **baa** *verb* [I] (**baa·ing**, **baaed** or **baa'd**)

baba /ˈbɑːbɑː/ *noun* **1** a small cake, often with RUM poured over it（常倒上朗姆酒的）鬆軟小蛋糕；婆婆蛋糕 **2** (*IndE, EAfrE*) a father (often also used as a title or form of address for any older man, showing respect) 阿爸，前輩（常用作對年長男子的敬稱）**3** (*IndE*) a holy man 聖潔的人；聖人 **4** (*IndE*) (used especially as a form of address 尤用作稱呼) a small child 寶寶；小孩子

Bab·bitt /ˈbæbɪt/ *noun* (*NAmE*) a person who is satisfied with a narrow set of values and thinks mainly about possessions and making money 巴比特式人物（滿足於一套狹隘的價值觀、只關心財富和賺錢）**ORIGIN** From the name of the main character in the novel *Babbitt* by Sinclair Lewis. 源自辛克萊・劉易斯的小說《巴比特》中主人公的名字。

bab·ble /ˈbæbl/ *noun, verb*

■ ***noun*** [sing.] **1** the sound of many people speaking at the same time 嘈雜的人聲：*a babble of voices* 人聲嘈雜 **2** talking that is confused or silly and is difficult to understand 含混不清的話；胡言亂語：*I can't listen to his constant babble.* 我聽不得他那沒完沒了的瞎扯。**3** the sounds a baby makes before beginning to say actual words（幼兒）咿呀學語聲 ➲ see also PSYCHOBABBLE

■ ***verb*** **1** [I, T] **~ (away/on) (sth)** to talk quickly in a way that is difficult to understand 含混不清地說；嘀里嘟嚕地說：*They were all babbling away in a foreign language.* 他們都嘰里咕嚕地說着外語。◇ *I realized I was babbling like an idiot.* 我意識到我像個傻瓜一樣在胡言亂語。**2** [I] to make the sound of water flowing over rocks, like a stream（水流過石塊）潺潺作響：*a babbling brook* 潺潺的小溪

babby /ˈbæbi/ *noun* (*pl.* **-ies**) (*BrE, dialect*) a baby 嬰兒

babe /beɪb/ *noun* **1** (*old use*) a baby 嬰兒 **2** (*slang*) a word used to address a young woman, or your wife, husband or lover, usually expressing affection but sometimes considered offensive if used by a man to a woman he does not know 寶貝兒，心肝兒（對年輕女子或愛人的昵稱。男子用以稱呼不相識的女子則有冒犯之嫌）：*What're you doing tonight, babe?* 你今晚做什麼，寶貝兒？**3** (*informal*) an attractive young woman 有魅力的年輕女子

IDM **a ˌbabe in ˈarms** (*old-fashioned*) a very small baby that cannot yet walk 襁褓中的嬰兒 ➲ more at MOUTH *n.*

babel /ˈbeɪbl/ *noun* [sing.] (*formal*) the sound of many voices talking at one time, especially when more than one language is being spoken 嘈雜聲（尤指講多種語言）**ORIGIN** From the Bible story in which God punished the people who were trying to build a tower to reach heaven (the **tower of Babel**) by making them unable to understand each others' languages. 源自《聖經》故事。世人擬建造通天的巴別塔（the tower of Babel），上帝為懲罰他們而使他們無法理解彼此的語言。

ˈbabe magnet *noun* (*slang, especially NAmE*) a man or a man's possession that is considered to be attractive to women 寶貝磁鐵（指吸引女性的男子或男性物品）：*Bob's such a babe magnet.* 鮑勃真是個吸引異性的萬人迷。◇ *A sports car like that is a complete babe magnet.* 那樣的跑車絕對吸引女性。

ˌbabes in the ˈwood *noun* [pl.] innocent people who are easily tricked or harmed 幼稚易受騙的人；易受傷害的人 **ORIGIN** From a children's story about a boy and a girl who are left alone in a wood where they die and a bird covers them with leaves. 源自童話，一雙男女孩童被棄於森林中。孩子死後，一隻鳥銜來樹葉將其掩埋。

ba·boon /bəˈbuːn; *NAmE* bæˈb-/ *noun* a large African or Asian MONKEY with a long face like a dog's 狒狒

babu /ˈbɑːbuː/ *noun* (*IndE*) a person who works in an office 辦公室職員；白領

ba·bushka /bəˈbʊʃkə; ˈbæbʊʃkə/ *noun* (from *Russian*) **1** a Russian old woman or grandmother（俄羅斯）老太婆，祖母，外婆 **2** a traditional Russian woman's HEADSCARF, tied under the chin 婆婆頭巾（傳統俄羅斯頭巾，在頦下打結）

baby 🔑 /ˈbeɪbi/ *noun, adj., verb*

■ ***noun*** (*pl.* **-ies**) **1** 🔑 a very young child or animal 嬰兒；動物幼崽：*The baby's crying!* 嬰兒在哭！◇ *a newborn baby* 新生兒 ◇ *My sister's* ***expecting a baby*** (= she is pregnant). 我姐姐懷孕了。◇ *She* ***had a baby*** *last year.* 她去年生了個孩子。◇ *a* ***baby boy/girl*** 男嬰；女嬰 ◇ ***baby food/clothes*** 嬰兒食品 / 服裝 ◇ *a baby monkey/blackbird* 幼猴；黑鸝雛 ➲ COLLOCATIONS at CHILD **2** (*informal*) the youngest member of a family or group（家庭或團體中）最年幼的成員：*He's the baby of the team.* 他在隊裏年紀最小。**3** (*disapproving*) a person who behaves like a young child and is easily upset 幼稚的人；孩子氣的人：*Stop crying and don't be such a baby.* 別哭了，別這麼孩子氣。**4** (*slang, especially NAmE*) a word used to address sb, especially your wife, husband or lover, in a way that expresses affection but that can be offensive if used by a man to a woman he does not know 寶貝兒，心肝兒（對愛人的昵稱。男子用以稱呼不相識的女子則有冒犯之嫌）

IDM **be your/sb's baby** (*informal*) to be a plan or project that sb is responsible for and cares about because they have created it（計劃或項目）就像某人的孩子一樣（因親自制訂而盡心負責）**leave sb holding the ˈbaby** (*informal*) to suddenly make sb responsible for sth important that is really your responsibility（突然）把重大責任推給某人：*He changed to another job and we were left holding the baby.* 他換了工作，把活兒甩給我們。**throw the baby out with the ˈbathwater** (*informal*) to lose sth that you want at the same time as you are trying to get rid of sth that you do not want 把嬰兒和洗澡水一起倒掉（丟棄不想要的東西的同時失去寶貴的東西）➲ more at CANDY, SLEEP *v.*

■ ***adj.*** [only before noun] **baby** vegetables are a very small version of particular vegetables, or are picked when they are very small（蔬菜）小型的，幼嫩的：*baby carrots* 小胡蘿蔔

■ ***verb*** (**ba·bies**, **baby·ing**, **ba·bied**, **ba·bied**) **~ sb** to treat sb with too much care, as if they were a baby 嬰兒般對待；百般呵護

ˌbaby ˈblue *adj.* very pale blue in colour 嬰兒藍的；淡藍色的 ▸ **ˌbaby ˈblue** *noun* [U]

ˈ**baby blues** *noun* [pl.] (*informal*) a depressed feeling that some women get after the birth of a baby 產後抑鬱 **SYN** **post-natal depression**

ˈ**baby boom** *noun* a period when many more babies are born than usual 生育高峰（期）

ˈ**baby boomer** (*NAmE* also **boom·er**) *noun* a person born during a baby boom, especially after the Second World War （尤指第二次世界大戰後）生育高峰期出生的人

ˈ**baby bouncer** *noun* (*BrE*) a type of seat that hangs from pieces of ELASTIC, in which a baby can sit and BOUNCE up and down 嬰兒搖椅

ˈ**baby buggy** *noun* **1** ˈ**Baby Buggy™** (*BrE*) = BUGGY (2) **2** (*old-fashioned*, *NAmE*) = BABY CARRIAGE

ˈ**baby carriage** (*NAmE*) (*BrE* **pram**) *noun* a small vehicle on four wheels for a baby to go out in, pushed by a person on foot 嬰兒車 ➲ picture at PUSHCHAIR

ˌ**baby-ˈdoll** *adj.* used to describe a style of women's dress or NIGHTDRESS that is short with a high waist and is similar to the type of dress traditionally worn by DOLLS（連衣裙或女睡袍）娃娃裝式的

ˈ**baby-faced** *adj.* with a face that looks young and innocent 長着稚氣的臉的；長着娃娃臉的

ˈ**baby fat** (*NAmE*) (*BrE* ˈ**puppy fat**) *noun* [U] fat on a child's body that disappears as the child grows older 嬰兒肥（長大後消失）

ˌ**baby ˈgrand** *noun* a small GRAND PIANO 小型平台鋼琴；小型三角鋼琴

Baby·gro™ /ˈbeɪbiɡrəʊ; *NAmE* -ɡroʊ/ *noun* (*pl.* **-os**) (*BrE*) a piece of clothing for babies, usually covering the whole body except the head and hands, made of a type of cloth that stretches easily（彈性）嬰兒連身服 ➲ compare ONESIES

ba·by·hood /ˈbeɪbihʊd/ *noun* [U] the period of your life when you are a baby 嬰兒期

baby·ish /ˈbeɪbiɪʃ/ *adj.* (usually *disapproving*) typical of or suitable for a baby 嬰兒的；嬰兒般的；稚氣的

ˈ**baby shower** *noun* (*especially NAmE*) a party given for a woman who is going to have a baby, at which her friends give her presents for the baby（為即將分娩的女子舉辦的）新生兒送禮會，產前派對

baby·sit /ˈbeɪbisɪt/ *verb* (**baby·sit·ting**, **baby·sat**, **baby·sat**) (also **sit**) [I, T] to take care of babies or children for a short time while their parents are out 代人臨時照看小孩；當臨時保母：**~ (for sb)** *She regularly babysits for us.* 她定期來為我們照看小孩。◇ **~ sb** *He's babysitting the neighbour's children.* 他在幫鄰居臨時照看小孩。▸ **baby·sit·ting** *noun* [U]

baby·sit·ter /ˈbeɪbisɪtə(r)/ (also **sit·ter** especially in *NAmE*) *noun* a person who takes care of babies or children while their parents are away from home and is usually paid to do this 臨時保母；代人臨時照看小孩的人：*I can't find a babysitter for tonight.* 我找不到人今天晚上幫我看小孩。➲ see also CHILDMINDER

ˈ**baby talk** *noun* [U] the words or sounds a baby says when it is learning to talk; the special language adults sometimes use when talking to babies 牙牙學語（聲）；（成人對嬰兒所用的）模仿兒語

ˈ**baby tooth** (*BrE* also ˈ**milk tooth**) *noun* any of the first set of teeth in young children that drop out and are replaced by others 乳牙；乳齒

ˈ**baby walker** (*BrE*) (*NAmE* **walk·er**) *noun* a frame with wheels and a HARNESS for a baby who can walk around a room, supported by the frame（幼兒）學步車

bac·ca·laur·eate /ˌbækəˈlɔːriət/ *noun* **1** the last SECONDARY SCHOOL exam in France and other countries, and in some international schools（法國等國家以及一些國際學校的）中學畢業會考：*to sit/take/pass/fail your baccalaureate* 參加／通過／未通過中學畢業會考 ➲ see also INTERNATIONAL BACCALAUREATE **2** (in the US) a religious service or talk for students who have completed HIGH SCHOOL or college（美國為中學或大學畢業生舉行的）宗教禮儀，佈道

bac·carat /ˈbækərɑː/ *noun* [U] a card game in which players hold two or three cards each and bet on whose cards will have the highest number left over when their value is divided by ten 巴卡拉紙牌遊戲，百家樂（玩牌者手持兩張或三張紙牌，賭誰的點數被十除後餘數最大）

bac·chan·al·ian /ˌbækəˈneɪliən/ *adj.* (*formal*) (of a party, etc. 聚會等) wild and involving large amounts of alcohol 縱酒狂歡的；歡鬧的 **ORIGIN** From the name of the Greek god **Bacchus** (also called Dionysus), the god of wine and wild enjoyment. 源自希臘酒神與狂歡之神巴克斯（Bacchus）的名字。

baccy /ˈbæki/ *noun* [U] (*BrE*, *informal*) TOBACCO 煙草

bach /bætʃ/ *noun* (*NZE*) a small holiday house 度假小別墅

bach·elor /ˈbætʃələ(r)/ *noun* **1** a man who has never been married 未婚男子；單身漢：*an eligible bachelor* (= one that many people want to marry, especially because he is rich) 合意單身男子（常因富有而為理想對象）◇ *a* ***confirmed bachelor*** (= a person who does not intend to marry; often used in newspapers to refer to a HOMOSEXUAL man) 信守獨身主義的單身漢（報章上常用來指同性戀男子）➲ compare SPINSTER **2** (usually **Bachelor**) a person who has a Bachelor's degree (= a first university degree) 學士：*a* ***Bachelor of Arts/Engineering/Science*** 文學士；工程學士；理學士 ➲ see also BA, BEd, BSc **3** (*CanE*) = BACHELOR APARTMENT

ˈ**bachelor apartment** *noun* a small flat/apartment suitable for a person living alone 單身套房；單身公寓房

ba·chelor·ette /ˌbætʃələˈret/ *noun* (*NAmE*) a young woman who is not married 單身女子；單身女郎

ˈ**bachelor girl** *noun* an independent young woman who is not married 獨立生活的年輕女子；單身女子

bach·elor·hood /ˈbætʃələhʊd; *NAmE* -lərh-/ *noun* [U] the time in a man's life before he is married 男子的未婚時期

ˈ**bachelor pad** *noun* a house or flat/apartment in which a man who is not married enjoys a lifestyle without family responsibilities 單身男子的窩；單身男子公寓；單身漢公寓

ˈ**bachelor party** (*NAmE*) (*BrE* ˈ**stag night**, ˈ**stag party**) *noun* a party that a man has with his male friends just before he gets married, often the night before 男子婚前聚會（常在結婚前一夜舉行，招待男性朋友）

ba·cil·lus /bəˈsɪləs/ *noun* (*pl.* **ba·cilli** /bəˈsɪlaɪ/) a type of bacteria. There are several types of bacillus, some of which cause disease. 桿菌（有些可致病）

back 🔑 /bæk/ *noun*, *adj.*, *adv.*, *verb*

■ ***noun***

▸ **PART OF BODY 身體部位** **1** 🔑 the part of the human body that is on the opposite side to the chest, between the neck and the tops of the legs; the part of an animal's body that CORRESPONDS to this（人體或動物的）背部，背；腰背：*Do you sleep on your back or your front?* 你睡覺是仰着還是趴着？◇ *He stood with his back to the door.* 他背對着門站着。◇ *They had their hands tied behind their backs.* 他們雙手被反剪起來。◇ *back pain* 背痛 ◇ *a back massage* 背部按摩 ◇ *A small boy rode on the elephant's back.* 一個小男孩騎在大象背上。➲ **COLLOCATIONS** at PHYSICAL ➲ **VISUAL VOCAB** page V59 ➲ see also BAREBACK, HORSEBACK **2** 🔑 the row of bones in the middle of the back 脊柱；脊梁骨 **SYN** **backbone**, **spine**：*She broke her back in a riding accident.* 她在一次騎馬事故中摔斷了脊梁骨。◇ *He* ***put his back out*** (= DISLOCATED sth in his back) *lifting the crates.* 他搬大木箱時脊椎脫了臼。

▸ **PART FURTHEST FROM FRONT 後部** **3** 🔑 [usually sing.] **~ (of sth)** the part or area of sth that is furthest from the front 後部；後面；末尾：*We could only get seats* ***at the back*** (= of the room). 我們只能找到後排的座位。◇ *I found some old photos at the back of the drawer.* 我從抽屜儘裏頭找到一些舊照片。◇ *He was shot in the back of the knee.* 他被子彈擊中了膕窩。◇ *The house has three bedrooms at the front and two* ***at the back***. 房屋正面有三間臥室，後面兩間。◇ (*BrE*) *There's room for three people* ***in the back***. 後排的空間可容三人。◇ (*NAmE*) *There's room for three people* ***in back*** (= of a car, etc.). 後排的

B

B

空間可容三人。◇ (*BrE*) *If you'd like to come* **round the back** (= to the area behind the house), *I'll show you the garden.* 請到屋子後面看看花園。➲ see also HARDBACK, PAPERBACK, SHORT BACK AND SIDES

▸ **OF PIECE OF PAPER** 紙張 **4** 🗝 [usually sing.] **~ (of sth)** the part of a piece of paper, etc. that is on the opposite side to the one that has information or the most important information on it （文件等的）背面：*Write your name on the back of the cheque.* 把你的名字寫在支票背面。

▸ **OF BOOK** 書刊 **5** 🗝 [usually sing.] **~ (of sth)** the last few pages of a book, etc. （書等的）最後幾頁，末尾：*The television guide is at the back of the paper.* 電視節目指南在報紙的末尾。

▸ **OF CHAIR** 椅子 **6** the part of a chair, etc. against which you lean your back （椅子等的）靠背 ➲ **VISUAL VOCAB** page V21

▸ **-BACKED** 靠背… **7** (in adjectives 構成形容詞) used to describe furniture that has the type of back mentioned （傢具）…靠背的：*a high-backed sofa* 高靠背沙發

▸ **IN SPORT** 體育運動 **8** (in sports 體育運動) a player whose main role is to defend their team's goal 後衛 ➲ compare FORWARD *n.* ➲ see also FULLBACK, HALFBACK

IDM **at/in the back of your mind** if a thought, etc. is **at the back of your mind**, you are aware of it but it is not what you are mainly thinking about 在潛意識裏；依稀記得 **the ˌback of beˈyond** (*informal*) a place that is a long way from other houses, towns, etc. 偏僻地方；邊遠地區 **ˌback to ˈback 1** if two people stand **back to back**, they stand with their backs facing or touching each other 背靠背；背對背 ➲ see also BACK-TO-BACK **2** if two or more things happen **back to back**, they happen one after the other 接連地；接二連三 **ˌback to ˈfront** 🗝 (*BrE*) (*NAmE* **back·wards**) if you put on a piece of clothing **back to front**, you make a mistake and put the back where the front should be （衣服）前後顛倒（或穿反）：*I think you've got that sweater on back to front.* 我覺得你把毛衣前後穿反了。➲ compare INSIDE OUT at INSIDE *n.* **be glad, etc. to see the back of sb/sth** (*informal, especially BrE*) to be happy that you will not have to deal with or see sb/sth again because you do not like them or it 慶幸終於擺脱（不喜歡的人或事物）：*Was I pleased to see the back of her!* 真高興不會再見到她了！ **behind sb's ˈback** 🗝 without sb's knowledge or permission 背着某人；背地裏；私下：*Have you been talking about me behind my back?* 你們是不是在背後說我的閒話？◇ *They went ahead and sold it behind my back.* 他們逕自背着我把它賣了。➲ compare TO SB'S FACE at FACE *n.* **be on sb's ˈback** (*informal*) to keep asking or telling sb to do sth that they do not want to do, in a way that they find annoying 纏磨；煩擾 **break the ˈback of sth** to finish the largest or most important part of a task 完成（任務等的）主要部份 **get/put sb's ˈback up** (*informal*) to annoy sb 惹惱：*That sort of attitude really gets my back up!* 那種態度實在叫我惱火！ **get off sb's ˈback** (*informal*) to stop annoying sb, for example by criticizing them, or asking them to do sth 不再煩擾某人（如停止批評或纏磨等）：*Just get off my back, will you!* 請別煩我了好嗎！ **have (got) sb's ˈback** (*NAmE, informal*) to protect and support sb 保護，支持（某人）：*Don't worry, I've got your back.* 別擔心，我支持你。 **have your ˌback to the ˈwall** (*informal*) to be in a difficult situation in which you are forced to do sth but are unable to make the choices that you would like 處於背水一戰的境地；沒有退路 **off the ˌback of a ˈlorry** (*BrE, informal, humorous*) goods that **fell off the back of a lorry** were probably stolen. People say or accept that they came 'off the back of a lorry' to avoid saying or asking where they really came from. （指貨物等）來路不明 **on the back of sth** as a result of an achievement or a success 由於（某項成就）：*The profits growth came on the back of a 26 per cent rise in sales.* 利潤增長來自 26% 的銷售額增長。 **(flat) on your back** (*informal*) in bed because you are ill/sick 因病臥牀；臥病：*She's been flat on her back for over a week now.* 她臥病有一個多星期了。◇ (*figurative*) *The UK market was flat on its back* (= business was very bad). （當時）英國的市場十分不景氣。 **put your ˈback into sth** to use a lot of effort and energy on a particular task 全力以赴 **turn your back** 🗝 to turn so that you are facing in the opposite direction 扭頭；轉身 **turn your back on sb/sth 1** 🗝 to move so that you are standing or sitting with your back facing sb/sth 轉身背對某人（或某物）：*When on stage, try not to turn your back on the audience.* 在舞台上盡量不要背對觀眾。 **2** 🗝 to reject sb/sth that you have previously been connected with 背棄；拋棄：*She turned her back on them when they needed her.* 他們需要她的時候，她卻背棄了他們。➲ more at COVER *v.*, EYE *n.*, KNOW *v.*, PAT *n.*, PAT *v.*, PUSH *v.*, ROD, SCRATCH *v.*, SHIRT, STAB *n.*, STAB *v.*, STRAW, WATER *n.*

■ ***adj.*** [only before noun]

▸ **AWAY FROM FRONT** 在後 **1** 🗝 located behind or at the back of sth 背後的；後面的；後部的：*We were sitting in the back row.* 我們坐在後排。◇ *back teeth* 臼齒 ◇ *a back room* (= one at the back of a building) 後室（位於建築物後部）◇ *the back page of a newspaper* 報紙最末一頁 ➲ compare FRONT *adj.* (1)

▸ **FROM PAST** 過去 **2** of or from a past time 過去的；舊時的：*a back number of the magazine* 一份過期雜誌

▸ **OWED** 拖欠 **3** owed for a time in the past 到期未付的；拖欠的：***back pay/taxes/rent*** 欠薪 / 稅 / 租金

▸ **PHONETICS** 語音 **4** (*phonetics* 語音) (of a vowel 元音) produced with the back of the tongue in a higher position than the front, for example /ɑː/ in English 舌後的，後位性的（舌高點位於口腔後部發音）➲ compare CENTRAL (5), FRONT *adj.* (2)

IDM **on the back ˈburner** (*informal*) (of an idea, a plan, etc. 主意、計劃等) left for the present time, to be done or considered later 暫時擱置 ➲ compare ON THE FRONT BURNER at FRONT *adj.* ➲ see also BACK-BURNER

■ ***adv.*** **HELP** For the special uses of **back** in phrasal verbs, look at the entries for the verbs. For example **pay sb back** is in the phrasal verb section at **pay**. * back 在短語動詞中的特殊用法見有關動詞詞條。如 pay sb back 在詞條 pay 的短語動詞部份。

▸ **AWAY FROM FRONT** 後面 **1** 🗝 away from the front or centre; behind you 向後；在後；在背面：*I stepped back to let them pass.* 我退後一步給他們讓路。◇ *Sit back and relax.* 靠椅背坐好，放鬆放鬆。◇ *You've combed your hair back.* 你把頭髮往後梳了。◇ *He turned and looked back.* 他轉身向後望。◇ *She fell back towards the end of the race.* 賽跑快結束時她落後了。**OPP** **forward**

▸ **AT A DISTANCE** 距離 **2** 🗝 at a distance away from sth 與（某物）有距離：*The barriers kept the crowd back.* 障礙物攔住了人群。◇ *Stand back and give me some room.* 站遠點兒，給我騰出些地方。

▸ **UNDER CONTROL** 受控制 **3** 🗝 under control; prevented from being expressed or coming out 控制住；忍住：*He could no longer hold back his tears.* 他再也無法控制住眼淚。

▸ **AS BEFORE** 像先前 **4** 🗝 to or into the place, condition, situation or activity where sb/sth was before 回原處；恢復原狀：*Put the book back on the shelf.* 把書放回書架上。◇ *Please give me my ball back.* 請把我的球還給我。◇ *He'll be back on Monday.* 他星期一會回來。◇ *It takes me an hour to walk* ***there and back***. 我步行往返要花一個小時。◇ *Could you go back to the beginning of the story?* 你能不能回到故事的開頭？◇ *She woke up briefly and then went back to sleep.* 她醒了片刻又睡了。◇ *We were right* ***back where we started***, *only this time without any money.* 我們回到了起點，只是這次一點錢也沒有。

▸ **IN PAST** 過去 **5** 🗝 in or into the past; ago 以前：*The village has a history going back to the Middle Ages.* 這個村子的歷史可追溯至中世紀。◇ *She left* ***back in*** *November.* 她十一月已經離開了。◇ *That was a few years back.* 那是幾年以前的事。

▸ **AT A PREVIOUS PLACE** 在原處 **6** 🗝 at a place previously left or mentioned 在曾去過（或提到過）的地方；在前面：*We should have turned left five kilometres back.* 我們在五公里之前就該左拐的。◇ *Back at home, her parents were worried.* 在家中，她的父母很擔心。◇ *I can't wait to get back home.* 我急不可待想趕回家。

▸ **IN RETURN** 回應 **7** 🗝 in return or reply 回報；回答：*If he kicks me, I'll kick him back.* 他要是踢我，我就踢他。◇ *Could you call back later, please?* 請稍後再打電話來好嗎？

IDM **ˌback and ˈforth** from one place to another and back again repeatedly 反複來回：*ferries sailing back and forth between the islands* 往返於島與島之間的渡船 **ˌback in the ˈday** in the past 過去；從前；舊時：*My dad's always talking about how great everything was back in the day.* 我爸爸總是講過去的一切如何如何的好。 **back of sth** (*NAmE, informal*) behind sth 在某物的背後（或背面）：*the houses back of the church* 位於教堂後面的房屋 ➲ more at EARTH *n.*, SQUARE *n.*

■ *verb*

▸ **MOVE BACKWARDS** 後退 **1** [I, T] to move or make sth move backwards（使）後退，倒退：**+ adv./prep.** *He backed against the wall, terrified.* 他退到牆邊，驚恐萬分。◇ **~ sth + adv./prep.** *If you can't drive in forwards, try backing it in.* 若不能開車正面駛入，不妨倒車進去。➲ compare REVERSE *v.* (6)

▸ **SUPPORT** 支持 **2** [T] **~ sb/sth** to give help or support to sb/sth 幫助；支持：*Her parents backed her in her choice of career.* 她父母支持她的職業選擇。◇ *Doctors have backed plans to raise the tax on cigarettes.* 醫生們對提高煙草稅計劃給予了支持。◇ *The programme of economic reform is backed* (= given financial support) *by foreign aid.* 經濟改革計劃得到外資援助。◇ *a United Nations-backed peace plan* 得到聯合國支持的和平計劃

▸ **BET MONEY** 下賭注 **3** [T] **~ sth** to bet money on a horse in a race, a team in a competition, etc. 下賭注於（賽馬、參賽隊伍等）：*I backed the winner and won fifty pounds.* 我押對了賭注，贏了五十英鎊。

▸ **MUSIC** 音樂 **4** [T] **~ sth** to play or sing music that supports the main singer or instrument 伴奏；伴唱 ➲ see also BACKING (3)

▸ **COVER BACK** 覆蓋背面 **5** [T] **~ sth (with sth)** [usually passive] to cover the back of sth in order to support or protect it（用某物）在…背後加固，給…加背襯

▸ **BE BEHIND** 在後面 **6** [T, usually passive] **~ sth** (*BrE*) to be located behind sth 位於（某物）的後面；在…後面：*The house is backed by fields.* 房子的後面是田野。

IDM **ˌback the wrong ˈhorse** (*BrE*) to support sb/sth that is not successful 下錯賭注（支持了失敗的一方或事情）

PHR V **ˌback aˈway (from sb/sth)** to move away backwards from sb/sth that is frightening or unpleasant; to avoid doing sth that is unpleasant 躲避（可怕或討厭的人或事物）；避免（做討厭的事）；退避 **ˌback ˈdown (on/from sth)** (*NAmE* also **ˌback ˈoff**) to take back a demand, an opinion, etc. that other people are strongly opposed to; to admit defeat 放棄（別人強烈反對的要求、主張等）；認輸：*She refused to back down on a point of principle.* 她在一個原則問題上拒絕讓步。 **ˌback ˈoff 1** to move backwards in order to get away from sb/sth frightening or unpleasant 退縮，退卻（以躲避可怕或討厭的人或事物）：*As the riot police approached, the crowd backed off.* 隨着防暴警察逼近，人群往後退卻了。 **2** to stop threatening, criticizing or annoying sb 停止威脅（或批評、騷擾）：*Back off! There's no need to yell at me.* 走開點！沒必要對我大喊大叫。◇ *The press have agreed to back off and leave the couple alone.* 新聞界同意退讓，不再攪擾這對夫婦。 **ˌback ˈoff (from sth)** to choose not to take action, in order to avoid a difficult situation 放棄（採取行動）；退讓：*The government backed off from a confrontation.* 政府放棄對抗。 **ˌback ˈonto sth** (*BrE*) (of a building 建築物) to have sth directly behind it 背向；背靠：*Our house backs onto the river.* 我們的房子背向河流。 **ˌback ˈout (of sth)** to decide that you are no longer going to take part in sth that has been agreed 退出；撤手：*He lost confidence and backed out of the deal at the last minute.* 他失去了信心，在最後一刻退出了協議。 **ˌback ˈup** | **ˌback sth↔ˈup** to move backwards, especially in a vehicle 後退；倒（車）：*You can back up another two feet or so.* 你可以再退兩英尺左右。◇ *I backed the car up to the door.* 我把車倒到門前。 **ˌback sb/sth↔ˈup 1** to support sb/sth; to say that what sb says, etc. is true 支持；證實（某人所言）：*I'll back you up if they don't believe you.* 如果他們不相信你，我會為你作證。◇ *The writer doesn't back up his opinions with examples.* 作者不用實例印證他的看法。 **2** to provide support for sb/sth 支持；支援：*two doctors backed up by a team of nurses* 由一組護士輔助的兩名醫生 ◇ *The rebels backed up their demands with threats.* 反叛者以恐嚇手段要挾。➲ related noun BACKUP (1) **ˌback sth↔ˈup** (*computing* 計) to prepare a second copy of a file, program, etc. that can be used if the main one fails or needs extra support 給（文件、程序等）做備份；備份 ➲ related noun BACKUP (2)

Which Word? 詞語辨析

at the back / at the rear / behind

- **At the back** and **at the rear** have a similar meaning, but **at the rear** is used more in formal or official language. * at the back 和 at the rear 意義相近，但 at the rear 多用於正式或官方語言：*What's that at the back of the fridge?* 冰箱儘裏頭那東西是什麼？◇ *Smoking is only allowed at the rear of the aircraft.* 只有飛機後艙允許抽煙。 It is more usual to talk about the **back door** of a house but the **rear exit** of an aircraft or public building. If something is **behind** something else it is near to the back of it but not part of it. 指房子的後門較常用 back door，但飛機或公共建築的後門較常用 rear exit。behind 指在後面，但不是其中的部份。Compare 比較：*Our room was at the back of the hotel.* 我們的房間在旅館靠後面的地方。 and 和 *There's a lovely wood just behind our hotel.* 在我們旅館的後面就有一片美麗的樹林。

back·ache /ˈbækeɪk/ *noun* [U, C] a continuous pain in the back 背痛；腰痛：(*BrE*) *to have backache/a backache* 背痛 ◇ (*NAmE*) *to have a backache* 背痛

ˌback ˈalley *noun* a narrow passage behind or between buildings 後巷；夾道

ˌback-ˈalley *adj.* [only before noun] happening or done secretly, often illegally （非法）秘密發生的，秘密進行的；偷偷摸摸的：*a back-alley abortion* 非法秘密墮胎

back·beat /ˈbækbiːt/ *noun* (*music* 音) a strong emphasis on one or two of the beats that are not normally emphasized, used especially in JAZZ and rock music 基調強節奏（尤見於爵士樂和搖滾樂）

ˌback ˈbench *noun* [usually pl.] (in the House of Commons in Britain, and in certain other parliaments) any of the seats for Members of Parliament who do not have senior positions in the government or the other parties（英國下院及其他某些國家議會的）後座議員席，普通議員席：*He resigned as Home Secretary and returned to the back benches.* 他辭去了內政大臣的職務，回到後座議員席。◇ *back-bench MPs* 下院普通議員 ➲ compare THE FRONT BENCH

back·bench·er /ˌbækˈbentʃə(r)/ *noun* (in the British and certain other parliaments) a member who sits in the rows of seats at the back, and who does not have an important position in the government or the opposition（英國和其他某些國家議會的）後座議員，普通議員，後排議員 ➲ compare FRONTBENCHER

back·bit·ing /ˈbækbaɪtɪŋ/ *noun* [U] unpleasant and unkind talk about sb who is not present 背後中傷；背後誹謗

back·board /ˈbækbɔːd; *NAmE* -bɔːrd/ *noun* the board behind the BASKET in the game of BASKETBALL（籃球）籃板

back·bone /ˈbækbəʊn; *NAmE* -boʊn/ *noun* **1** [C] the row of small bones that are connected together down the middle of the back 脊梁骨；脊柱 **SYN** **spine** ➲ **VISUAL VOCAB** page V59 **2** [sing.] the most important part of a system, an organization, etc. that gives it support and strength 支柱；骨幹；基礎：*Agriculture forms the backbone of the rural economy.* 農業是農村經濟的基礎。 **3** [U] the strength of character that you need to do sth difficult 毅力；骨氣：*He doesn't have the backbone to face the truth.* 他沒有面對現實的勇氣。

ˈback-breaking *adj.* (of physical work 體力勞動) very hard and tiring 艱苦繁重的；累死人的

B

ˌback-ˈburn·er *verb* **~ sth** (*informal, especially NAmE*) to leave an idea or a plan for a time, to be done or considered later 把…擱置一時 ➲ compare ON THE BACK BURNER at BACK *adj.*

ˈback catalogue (*NAmE* also **ˈback catalog**) *noun* all the recorded music previously produced by a musician（音樂家的）已發行全輯：*The entire Beatles' back catalogue has been put online.* 披頭士的全套作品都已經放到網上。

back·channel /ˈbæktʃænl/ *noun* **1** a secret or unusual way of passing information to other people（傳遞消息的）秘密渠道，特殊途徑 **2** (*linguistics* 語言) a sound or sign that sb makes to show that they are listening to the person who is talking to them 言語反饋示意，反輸，附應（以聲音或示意作為對說話人的反饋）

back·chat /ˈbæktʃæt/ (*BrE*) (*NAmE* **ˈback talk**) *noun* [U] (*informal*) a way of answering that shows no respect for sb in authority 頂嘴

back·cloth /ˈbækklɒθ; *NAmE* -klɔːθ; -klɑːθ/ *noun* (*BrE*) = BACKDROP

back·comb /ˈbækkəʊm; *NAmE* -koʊm/ (*BrE*) (*NAmE* **tease**) *verb* **~ sth** to COMB your hair in the opposite direction to the way it grows so that it looks thicker 反梳（頭髮）使之蓬起

ˌback ˈcopy *noun* (*BrE*) = BACK ISSUE

back·coun·try /ˈbækkʌntri/ *noun* [U] (*NAmE*) an area away from roads and towns, especially in the mountains（山中等）偏僻地區，偏遠地區

back·court /ˈbækkɔːt; *NAmE* -kɔːrt/ *noun* **1** (in TENNIS, BASKETBALL, etc. 網球、籃球等) the area at either end of the COURT 後場 **2** (in BASKETBALL 籃球) the players who form the defence 防守隊員 **3** (*ScotE*) an area surrounded by walls but with no roof at the back of a building 後院

back·crawl /ˈbækkrɔːl/ *noun* [U, sing.] (*BrE*) = BACKSTROKE

back·date /ˌbækˈdeɪt/ *verb* **1 ~ sth** to write a date on a cheque or other document that is earlier than the actual date 倒填日期（在支票等上簽寫比實際較早的日期）➲ compare POST-DATE (1) **2 ~ sth** (*BrE*) to make sth, especially a payment, take effect from an earlier date 使（付款等）在較早的日期開始生效：*Postal workers are getting a 5.2% pay rise, backdated to February.* 郵政員工的工資將提高 5.2%，追溯至二月份起算。

ˌback ˈdoor *noun* the door at the back or side of a building 後門；邊門

IDM **by/through the back door** in an unfair or indirect way 走後門：*He used his friends to help him get into the civil service by the back door.* 他利用朋友幫他開後門當上了公務員。

ˌback-ˈdoor *adj.* [only before noun] using indirect or secret means in order to achieve sth 後門的；不正當的

back·draught (also **back·draft**) /ˈbækdrɑːft; *NAmE* -dræft/ *noun* **1** a current of air that flows backwards down a CHIMNEY, pipe, etc.（煙囪、管道等的）倒煙，倒灌風，逆通風 **2** an explosion caused by more OXYGEN being supplied to a fire, for example by a door being opened（給火焰供氧過多引起的）回火，逆火

back·drop /ˈbækdrɒp; *NAmE* -drɑːp/ (*BrE* also **back·cloth**) *noun* **1** a painted piece of cloth that is hung behind the stage in a theatre as part of the SCENERY（舞台的）背景幕布 **2** everything that can be seen around an event that is taking place, but which is not part of that event（事件發生時）周圍陪襯景物：*The mountains provided a dramatic backdrop for our picnic.* 群山如畫，給我們的野餐平添景色。 **3** the general conditions in which an event takes place, which sometimes help to explain that event（事態或活動的）背景：*It was **against this backdrop** of racial tension that the civil war began.* 這場內戰肇端於種族之間的緊張狀態。

ˌback ˈend *noun* (*especially BrE*) **1** the end of a period or process（時段或過程的）結束，結尾：*the back end of last year* 去年年終 **2** the part of sth which is behind the part that you can see（物體的）後端，背面 **3** (*informal*) a person's bottom (= the part they sit on) 屁股

ˈback-end *adj.* [only before noun] **1** relating to the end of a period or process 結束的；結尾的 **2** (*computing* 計) (of a device or program 裝置或程序) not used directly by a user, but used by a program or computer 後端的，後台的（指不歸用戶直接使用，而由程序或電腦使用）➲ compare FRONT-END

back·er /ˈbækə(r)/ *noun* a person or company that gives support to sb/sth, especially financial support 支持者；資助者；贊助人

back·field /ˈbækfiːld/ *noun* [sing., U] **1** (in AMERICAN FOOTBALL 美式足球) the area of play behind the line of SCRIMMAGE 後場（爭球線後面的區域） **2** the players who play in or around this area 守衛隊員

back·fill /ˈbækfɪl/ *verb* **~ sth** to fill a hole with the material that has been dug out of it 回填（用挖出的材料重新填回洞穴）

back·fire /ˌbækˈfaɪə(r)/ *verb* **1** [I] **~ (on sb)** to have the opposite effect to the one intended, with bad or dangerous results 產生事與願違的不良（或危險）後果：*Unfortunately the plan backfired.* 不幸的是，計劃產生了適得其反的結果。 **2** [I] (of an engine or a vehicle 發動機或車輛) to make a sudden noise like an explosion 逆火；回火 ➲ compare MISFIRE

back·flip /ˈbækflɪp/ *noun* if sb does a **backflip**, they turn their body over backwards in the air and land on their feet again 後空翻

ˈback-formation *noun* [U, C] (*linguistics* 語言) a word formed by removing or changing the end of a word that already exists. For example, *commentate* is a back-formation from *commentator*. 逆構詞法（將已存在的詞通過去除或改變其後綴構成新詞。如 commentate 由 commentator 一詞逆構而成）

back·gam·mon /ˈbækgæmən; ˌbækˈgæmən/ *noun* [U] a game for two people played on a board marked with long thin triangles. Players throw DICE and move pieces around the board. 十五子棋戲（棋盤上有楔形小區，兩人玩，擲骰子決定走棋步數）➲ VISUAL VOCAB page V38

back·ground 🔑 /ˈbækgraʊnd/ *noun*

▸ **FAMILY/EDUCATION, ETC.** 家庭、教育等 **1** 🔑 [C] the details of a person's family, education, experience, etc. 出身背景；學歷；經歷：*a person's **family/social/cultural/educational/class background*** 一個人的出身／社會／文化／教育／階級背景 ◇ *The job would suit someone with a business background.* 這項工作適合有商務經驗的人。

▸ **PAST** 過去 **2** 🔑 [C, usually sing., U] the circumstances or past events that help explain why sth is how it is; information about these（事態發展等的）背景：*the historical background to the war* 這場戰爭的歷史背景 ◇ ***background information/knowledge*** 背景資料／知識 ◇ *The elections are taking place **against a background** of violence.* 選舉正在暴亂的情況下進行。◇ *Can you give me more background on the company?* 你能多提供一些這家公司的背景資料嗎？

▸ **OF PICTURE/PHOTO** 圖畫；照片 **3** 🔑 [C, usually sing.] the part of a picture, photograph or view behind the main objects, people, etc. 後景；背景：*a photograph with trees **in the background*** 以樹木為遠景的照片 ➲ SYNONYMS at ENVIRONMENT ➲ compare FOREGROUND *n.* (1)

▸ **LESS IMPORTANT POSITION** 次要位置 **4** 🔑 [sing.] a position in which people are not paying attention to sb/sth or not as much attention as they are paying to sb/sth else 不顯眼的位置；幕後：*He prefers to remain **in the background** and let his assistant talk to the press.* 他喜歡待在幕後，讓他的助理向新聞界發佈消息。◇ *A piano tinkled gently **in the background**.* 背景是悠揚的鋼琴聲。◇ ***background music*** 背景音樂 ◇ *There was a lot of **background noise*** (= that you could hear, but were not listening to). 背景噪音很多。➲ compare FOREGROUND *n.* (2)

▸ **COLOUR UNDER STH** 底色 **5** [C, usually sing.] a colour or design on which sth is painted, drawn, etc. 底色；底花；底子：*The name of the company is written in red on a white background.* 公司的名稱是用白底紅字寫的。

IDM **in the ˈbackground** (*computing* 計) (of a computer program 計算機程序) not being used at the present time and appearing on the screen behind programs that are being used 在後台；背景的 ➲ compare IN THE FOREGROUND at FOREGROUND *n.* ➲ more at MERGE

back·hand /ˈbækhænd/ *noun* [usually sing.] (in TENNIS, etc. 網球等) a stroke played with the back of the hand turned in the direction towards which the ball is hit 反手；反手擊球：*He has a good backhand* (= he can make good backhand strokes). 他的反手擊球很棒。◇ *a backhand volley/drive* 反手截擊／抽球 ➲ compare FOREHAND

back·han·ded /ˌbækˈhændɪd/ *adj.* having a meaning that is not directly or clearly expressed, or that is not intended 間接的；拐彎抹角的；有言外之意的

IDM **a ˌbackhanded ˈcompliment** (*NAmE* also **ˌleft-handed ˈcompliment**) a remark that seems to express admiration but could also be understood as an insult 隱含譏諷的恭維

back·hand·er /ˈbækhændə(r)/ *noun* (*BrE, informal*) a secret and illegal payment made to sb in exchange for a favour 賄賂 SYN **bribe**

ˌback-ˈheel *verb* **~ sth** to kick a ball using the heel 用腳跟踢（球）：*He back-heeled the ball towards goal.* 他用腳跟將球踢向球門。▸ **ˌback-ˈheel** *noun*

back·hoe /ˈbækhəʊ; *NAmE* -hoʊ/ *noun* a large vehicle with machinery for digging, used in building roads, etc. 反鏟挖土機

back·ing /ˈbækɪŋ/ *noun* **1** [U] help 幫助；協助 SYN **support**：*financial backing* 資助 ◇ *The police gave the proposals their full backing.* 警方對這些提案給予全力支持。 **2** [U, C] material attached to the back of sth in order to protect it or make it stronger 背襯 **3** [U, C, usually sing.] (especially in pop music) music that accompanies the main singer or tune（尤指流行音樂的）伴唱，伴奏：*a* ***backing group/singer/track*** 伴奏樂團；伴唱歌手；伴奏歌曲

ˌback ˈissue (*BrE* also **ˌback ˈcopy**, **ˌback ˈnumber**) *noun* a copy of a newspaper or magazine from a date in the past 過期的報紙（或雜誌）

back·lash /ˈbæklæʃ/ *noun* [sing.] **~ (against sth)** | **~ (from sb)** a strong negative reaction by a large number of people, for example to sth that has recently changed in society（對社會變動等的）強烈抵制，集體反對：*The government is facing an angry backlash from voters over the new tax.* 政府正面臨選民對新稅項的強烈反對。

back·less /ˈbækləs/ *adj.* (of a dress 連衣裙) not covering most of the back 露背的

back·light /ˈbæklaɪt/ *noun, verb*

▪ ***noun*** [U] light from behind sth in a photograph or painting（照片或繪畫的）背景光

▪ ***verb*** (*pt, pp* **-lit** or **-lighted**) **~ sth** to shine light on sth from behind 從背後照亮；背景照明；給…打背景燈 ▸ **back·lit** *adj.*：*a backlit photograph* 有背景光的照片

back·list /ˈbæklɪst/ *noun* the list of books that have been published by a company in the past and are still available（出版商的）存書目錄

back·log /ˈbæklɒg; *NAmE* -lɔːg; -lɑːg/ *noun* a quantity of work that should have been done already, but has not yet been done 積壓的工作

back·lot /ˈbæklɒt; *NAmE* -lɑːt/ *noun* an outdoor area in a film/movie studio, where pieces of SCENERY are made and some scenes are filmed（電影製片廠的）外景場地

back·mark·er /ˈbækmɑːkə(r); *NAmE* -mɑːrk-/ *noun* (*BrE*) the person, horse, etc. who is in last position in a race（賽跑、賽馬等）最後一名，末位

back·most /ˈbækməʊst; *NAmE* -moʊst/ *adj.* [usually before noun] furthest back 最後面的：*the backmost teeth* 最裏面的牙齒

ˌback ˈnumber *noun* (*BrE*) = BACK ISSUE

ˌback ˈoffice *noun* (*business* 商) the part of a business company which does not deal directly with the public 後勤部門

back·pack /ˈbækpæk/ *noun, verb*

▪ ***noun*** (*especially NAmE*) (*BrE* also **ruck·sack**) a large bag, often supported on a light metal frame, carried on the back and used especially by people who go climbing or walking（尤指登山者或遠足者使用的）背包，旅行包 ➲ VISUAL VOCAB pages V64, V70

▪ ***verb*** [I] (usually **go backpacking**) to travel on holiday/vacation carrying your equipment and clothes in a backpack 背包旅行：*They went backpacking in Spain last year.* 他們去年背着背包在西班牙旅行。▸ **back·pack·er** *noun*

ˌback ˈpassage *noun* (*BrE*) a polite way of referring to sb's RECTUM (= the part of the body where solid waste leaves the body)（委婉語）直腸

ˌback-ˈpedal *verb* (**-ll-**, *NAmE* **-l-**) **1** [I] **~ (on sth)** to change an earlier statement or opinion; to not do sth that you promised to do 收回（意見等）；（立場）軟化；出爾反爾：*The protests have forced the government to back-pedal on the new tax.* 抗議活動已迫使政府撤銷新的稅目。 **2** [I] to PEDAL backwards on a bicycle; to walk or run backwards 倒踩自行車的腳蹬；倒走；倒跑

back·plane /ˈbækpleɪn/ *noun* (*computing* 計) a CIRCUIT BOARD that other devices can be connected to 底板（可接其他裝置的電路板）

ˈback-projec·tion *noun* **1** [U] the process of shining an image onto the back of a screen 背面投影 **2** [C] an image that has been shone onto the back of a screen 背投影像

back·rest /ˈbækrest/ *noun* part of a seat that supports sb's back 靠背

ˌback ˈroom *noun* a room at the back of a building, away from the entrance, often where secret activities take place 後室；密室

ˈback-room boys *noun* [pl.] (*BrE*) people who do important work for a person or an organization but who are not well known themselves 默默無聞地從事重要工作的人；無名功臣

back·scratch·ing /ˈbækskrætʃɪŋ/ *noun* [U] (*informal, often disapproving*) the fact of giving sb help in return for help that they have given you, often in connection with sth that might be illegal 互開方便之門，互相利用（常指從事非法活動）

ˌback ˈseat *noun* a seat at the back of a vehicle（車輛的）後座

IDM **take a back seat** to allow sb else to play a more active and important role in a particular situation than you do 允許他人領先；甘願居於人下；退居幕後

ˌback-seat ˈdriver *noun* (*disapproving*) **1** a passenger in a vehicle who keeps giving advice to the driver about how he or she should drive 對駕駛者指手畫腳的乘客 **2** a person who wants to be in control of sth that is not really their responsibility 企圖越權者

back·sheesh = BAKSHEESH

back·shift /ˈbækʃɪft/ *noun* [U] (*linguistics* 語言) the changing of a tense when reporting what sb said, for example when reporting the words 'What *are* you doing?' as 'He asked me what I *was* doing'（轉成間接引語時的）時態後移

back·side /ˈbæksaɪd/ *noun* (*informal*) the part of the body that you sit on 屁股 SYN **behind**, **bottom**：*Get up off your backside and do some work!* 起來幹點活兒吧！ IDM see PAIN *n.*

back·slap·ping /ˈbækslæpɪŋ/ *noun* [U] loud and enthusiastic behaviour when people are praising each other for sth good they have done（熱情的）互相祝賀，互相打氣 ▸ **back·slap·ping** *adj.* [only before noun]：*backslapping tributes* 互勉的話

back·slash /ˈbækslæʃ/ *noun* a mark (\), used in computer commands 反斜槓（計算機符號）➲ compare FORWARD SLASH

back·slid·ing /ˈbækslaɪdɪŋ/ *noun* [U] the situation when sb fails to do sth that they agreed to do and returns to their former bad behaviour 倒退；故態復萌

back·space /ˈbækspeɪs/ *noun, verb*

▪ ***noun*** the key on the keyboard of a computer or TYPEWRITER which allows you to move backwards. On a computer keyboard this key also removes the last letter that you typed.（計算機或打字機的）回格鍵，回退鍵；（計算機的）回刪鍵

B

■ **verb** [I] to use the backspace key on a computer keyboard or on a TYPEWRITER 回格；回退；回刪

back·spin /ˈbækspɪn/ *noun* [U] a backward spinning movement of a ball that has been hit, which makes it go less far than it normally would（球的）迴旋，下旋

ˈback-stabbing *noun* [U] the action of criticizing sb when they are not there, while pretending to be their friend at other times 背後中傷；暗箭傷人

back·stage /ˌbækˈsteɪdʒ/ *adv.* **1** in the part of a theatre where the actors and artists get ready and wait to perform 在後台：*After the show, we were allowed to go backstage to meet the cast.* 表演結束之後，我們獲准到後台和演員們見面。 **2** away from the attention of the public; in secret 私下；秘密地：*I'd like to know what really goes on backstage in government.* 我想知道政府在幕後究竟幹些什麼。▶ **back·stage** *adj.*

back·stairs /ˈbæksteəz; *NAmE* -sterz/ *noun, adj.*

■ **noun** [pl.] stairs at the back or side of a building, sometimes used by servants 後樓梯，側樓梯（有時供僕人用）

■ **adj.** secret or dishonest 背地裏的；暗中的：*backstairs deals between politicians* 政客之間的幕後交易

back·stitch /ˈbækstɪtʃ/ *noun* [U, C] a method of sewing in which each STITCH begins at the middle of the previous one 回式針腳縫法；倒縫

back·story /ˈbækstɔːri/ *noun* (*pl.* **-ies**) [C, U] **1** the things that are supposed to have happened to the characters in a film/movie, novel, etc., before the film/movie, etc. starts（電影、小說等的）幕後故事，故事背景：*The film spends too long establishing the characters' backstories.* 這部電影對人物的背景故事着墨太多。 **2** (especially in journalism 尤用於新聞業) the background to a news story 新聞報道的背景：*First, some backstory: …* 首先講一些背景資料：…

back·street /ˈbækstriːt/ *noun, adj.*

■ **noun** a small quiet street, usually in a poor part of a town or city, away from main roads 偏僻街道，小巷（常位於貧民區）

■ **adj.** [only before noun] acting or happening secretly, often dishonestly or illegally 秘密的；偷偷摸摸的；暗地裏的：*backstreet dealers* 非法交易者 ◇ *backstreet abortions* 非法墮胎

back·stroke /ˈbækstrəʊk; *NAmE* -stroʊk/ (*BrE* also **back·crawl**) *noun* [U, sing.] a style of swimming in which you lie on your back 仰泳：*Can you do (the) backstroke?* 你會仰泳嗎？◇ *He won the 100 metres backstroke* (= the race). 他獲得 100 米仰泳比賽冠軍。➲ VISUAL VOCAB page V45

back·swing /ˈbækswɪŋ/ *noun* (*sport* 體) the backwards movement of your arm or arms before you hit the ball（擊球前）向後擺臂動作

ˈback talk (*NAmE*) (*BrE* **back·chat**) *noun* [U] (*informal*) a way of answering that shows no respect for sb in authority 頂嘴

ˌback-to-ˈback *noun* (*BrE*) a house in a row of houses that share walls with the houses on each side and behind 連排式房屋（側面和背面與其他房屋相連接）：*back-to-backs built for the poor in the 19th century* * 19 世紀為貧民建造的連排式房屋

back·track /ˈbæktræk/ *verb* **1** [I] to go back along the same route that you have just come along 原路返回；折回；折返 **2** [I] to change an earlier statement, opinion or promise because of pressure from sb/sth（屈於壓力而）改變聲明（或主張），出爾反爾；退縮

back·up /ˈbækʌp/ *noun* [U, C] **1** extra help or support that you can get if necessary 增援；後援：*The police had backup from the army.* 警方得到了軍方的增援。◇ *We can use him as a backup if one of the other players drops out.* 如果有參賽者退出，我們可以用他作為替補。◇ *a backup power supply* 備用電源 **2** (*computing* 計) a copy of a file, etc. that can be used if the original is lost or damaged（文件等的）備份：*Always make a backup of your work.* 所有文件都須要備份。◇ *a backup copy* 備份文件 ➲ see also BACK UP at BACK *v.*

ˈbackup light (*NAmE*) (*BrE* **reˈversing light**) *noun* a white light at the back of a vehicle that comes on when the vehicle moves backwards 倒車燈

back·ward 🔑 /ˈbækwəd; *NAmE* -wərd/ *adj.*

1 🔑 [only before noun] directed or moving towards the back 向後的；朝後的：*She strode past him **without a backward glance**.* 她大步從他身邊走過，都沒有回頭瞧他一眼。 **2** 🔑 moving in a direction that means that no progress is being made 倒退的；反向的 SYN **retrograde**：*She felt that going back to live in her home town would be a backward step.* 她覺得回到家鄉生活就是沒出息。 **3** having made less progress than normal; developing slowly 落後的；進步緩慢的：*a backward part of the country, with no paved roads and no electricity* 該國的一個落後地區，沒有鋪設馬路也沒有電力 ◇ *a backward child* 遲鈍兒童 ◇ (*BrE, informal*) *She's not **backward in coming forward*** (= she's not shy). 她勇敢地站出來。➲ compare FORWARD *adj.*

ˌbackward ˈclasses *noun* [pl.] (in India) the people in a CASTE (= division of society) or community who are recommended by each state authority for special help in education and employment 落後階級，落後種姓（印度各省當局建議在教育和就業方面給予優惠）

ˈbackward-looking *adj.* (*disapproving*) opposed to progress or change 反進步（或變革）的；滯後的；落後的

back·ward·ness /ˈbækwədnəs; *NAmE* -wərd-/ *noun* [U] the state of having made less progress than normal 落後狀況

back·wards 🔑 /ˈbækwədz; *NAmE* -wərdz/ (also **back·ward** especially in *NAmE*) *adv.*

1 🔑 towards a place or position that is behind 向後：*I lost my balance and fell backwards.* 我沒有站穩，仰面摔倒。◇ *He took a step backwards.* 他退後一步。 OPP **forward** **2** 🔑 in the opposite direction to the usual one 朝反方向；倒着：*'Ambulance' is written backwards so you can read it in the mirror.* * ambulance 是倒着寫的，以便在鏡中認讀。◇ *In the movie they take a journey backwards through time.* 影片中的人作逆時光旅行。 **3** 🔑 towards a worse state 每況愈下地：*I felt that going to live with my parents would be a step backwards.* 我覺得回去和我父母一同生活會更糟。 OPP **forward** **4** 🔑 (*NAmE*) (*BrE* **ˌback to ˈfront**) if you put on a piece of clothing **backwards**, you make a mistake and put the back where the front should be（衣服）前後顛倒（或穿反）

IDM **ˌbackward(s) and ˈforward(s)** 🔑 from one place or position to another and back again many times 來來回回：*She rocked backwards and forwards on her chair.* 她坐在搖椅上前後搖晃着。 **bend/lean over ˈbackwards (to do sth)** to make a great effort, especially in order to be helpful or fair 盡力；竭力：*I've bent over backwards to help him.* 我已盡最大努力幫助他。➲ more at KNOW *v.*

ˌbackwards comˈpatible (also **ˌbackward comˈpatible**) *adj.* (*computing* 計) able to be used with systems, machines or programs which are older 向後兼容的；兼容舊系統（或機器、程序）的

back·wash /ˈbækwɒʃ; *NAmE* -wɔːʃ; -wɑːʃ/ *noun* [sing.] **1** the unpleasant result of an event 惡果；餘波；不良後果 **2** waves caused by a boat moving through water; the movement of water back into the sea after a wave has hit the beach（行船激起的）反流，尾流；（波浪拍擊岸邊後的）退浪

back·water /ˈbækwɔːtə(r)/ *noun* **1** a part of a river away from the main part, where the water only moves slowly（河流的）滯水，壅水，回水 **2** (often *disapproving*) a place that is away from the places where most things happen, and is therefore not affected by events, progress, new ideas, etc. 與世隔絕的地區；落後地區：***a sleepy/quiet/rural backwater*** 沉寂的／寧靜的／鄉下的落後地區

back·woods /ˈbækwʊdz/ *noun* [pl.] a place that is away from any big towns and from the influence of modern life 邊遠落後地區

back·woods·man /ˈbækwʊdzmən/ *noun* (*pl.* **-men** /-mən/) (*NAmE*) a person who lives in a region far from towns where not many people live, especially one who does not have much education or good manners（尤指沒有文化或粗野的）邊遠地區的鄉下人

back·yard /ˌbækˈjɑːd; *NAmE* -ˈjɑːrd/ *noun* **1** (*BrE*) an area with a hard surface behind a house, often surrounded by a wall（屋後常有圍牆的）後院 **2** (*NAmE*) the whole area behind and belonging to a house, including an area of grass and the garden（包括草坪和花園的）屋後附屬地帶：*a backyard barbecue* 後院烤肉野宴 ➲ see also YARD (1), (2)

IDM **in your (own) backyard** in or near the place where you live or work 在自己生活（或工作）的地方附近；在自己的後院：*The residents didn't want a new factory in their backyard.* 居民不希望在他們附近建新工廠。◇ *The party leader is facing opposition in his own backyard* (= from his own members). 該黨領導面臨着黨內人士的反對。➲ see also NIMBY

bac·lava = BAKLAVA

bacon /ˈbeɪkən/ *noun* [U] meat from the back or sides of a pig that has been CURED (= preserved using salt or smoke), usually served in thin slices 鹹豬肉；熏豬肉：*a rasher of bacon* 一片鹹豬肉 ◇ *bacon and eggs* 鹹肉和雞蛋 ◇ ***smoked/unsmoked bacon*** 熏製／未熏製的豬肉 ➲ compare GAMMON, HAM *n.* (1), PORK **IDM** see HOME *adv.*, SAVE *v.*

bac·teria 0→ /bækˈtɪəriə; *NAmE* -ˈtɪr-/ *noun* [pl.] (*sing.* **bac·ter·ium** /-iəm/) the simplest and smallest forms of life. Bacteria exist in large numbers in air, water and soil, and also in living and dead creatures and plants, and are often a cause of disease. 細菌 ➲ COLLOCATIONS at LIFE ▸ **bac·ter·ial** /-riəl/ *adj.*：***bacterial infections/growth*** 細菌傳染／生長

bac·teri·ology /bækˌtɪəriˈɒlədʒi; *NAmE* -ˌtɪriˈɑːl-/ *noun* [U] the scientific study of bacteria 細菌學 ▸ **bac·terio·logic·al** /bækˌtɪəriəˈlɒdʒɪkl; *NAmE* -ˌtɪriəˈlɑːdʒ-/ *adj.* **bac·teri·olo·gist** *noun*

Vocabulary Building 詞彙擴充

Bad and very bad

Instead of saying that something is **bad** or **very bad**, try to use more precise and interesting adjectives to describe things. 表示不好或糟糕，除了用 bad 或 very bad 外，儘量用更貼切、更有意思的形容詞來描述：

- an **unpleasant**/a **foul**/a **disgusting** smell 令人不快的／難聞的／惡心的氣味
- **appalling/dreadful/severe** weather 糟透的／十分惡劣的／非常惡劣的天氣
- an **unpleasant**/a **frightening**/a **traumatic** experience 不愉快的／可怕的／痛苦難忘的經歷
- **poor/weak** eyesight 視力差
- a **terrible/serious/horrific** accident 重大的／嚴重的／可怕的事故
- a **wicked**/an **evil**/an **immoral** person 惡毒的／邪惡的／道德敗壞的人
- an **awkward**/an **embarrassing**/a **difficult** situation 令人尷尬的／使人難堪的／艱難的處境
- We were working in **difficult/appalling** conditions. 我們在艱苦的／惡劣的條件下工作。

To refer to your health, you can say 談及身體狀況可說：*I feel unwell/sick/terrible.* 我感到不舒服／惡心／難受極了。◇ *I don't feel* (*very*) *well.* 我感到不（太）舒服。

In conversation, words like **terrible**, **horrible**, **awful** and **dreadful** can be used in most situations to mean 'very bad'. 在口語中，terrible、horrible、awful、dreadful 等詞在多數情況下均可表示糟糕。

bad 0→ /bæd/ *adj.*, *noun*, *adv.*

■ **adj.** (**worse** /wɜːs; *NAmE* wɜːrs/, **worst** /wɜːst; *NAmE* wɜːrst/)

▸ UNPLEASANT 令人不快 **1** 0→ unpleasant; full of problems 令人不快的；問題成堆的；壞的：*bad news/weather/dreams/habits* 壞消息；壞天氣；噩夢；惡習 ◇ *I'm having a really bad day.* 我今天倒霉透了。◇ *It was the worst experience of her life.* 那是她一生中最糟糕的經歷。◇ *Smoking gives you bad breath.* 吸煙會引致口氣。◇ *Things are **bad enough** without our own guns shelling us.* 本來情況就夠糟的了，偏偏我們自己的大炮又向我們開起火來。

▸ POOR QUALITY 劣質 **2** 0→ of poor quality; below an acceptable standard 質量差的；不合格的：*bad conditions/driving* 惡劣的情況；拙劣的駕駛技術 ◇ *a bad copy/diet* 不清晰的複印本；劣質飲食 ◇ *I thought it was a very bad article.* 我以為那是一篇很低劣的文章。◇ *This isn't as bad as I thought.* 這沒我原來所想的那麼差。◇ *That's not a bad idea.* 那個主意不錯。

▸ NOT GOOD AT STH 不擅長 **3** 0→ **~ at sth/at doing sth** (of a person 人) not able to do sth well or in an acceptable way 拙於；不擅；不善於 **SYN** **poor**：*a bad teacher* 不稱職的教師 ◇ *You're a bad liar!* 你連說謊都不會！◇ *He's a bad loser* (= he complains when he loses a game). 他是個輸不起的人。◇ *She is so bad at keeping secrets.* 她一點都不會保守秘密。

▸ SERIOUS 嚴重 **4** 0→ serious; severe 嚴重的；劇烈的：*You're heading for a bad attack of sunburn.* 你會被嚴重曬傷的。◇ *The engagement was a bad mistake.* 這婚約是個大錯。◇ *My headache is getting worse.* 我頭痛越來越厲害了。

▸ NOT APPROPRIATE 不合適 **5** 0→ [only before noun] not appropriate in a particular situation 不適合的；不適當的：*I know that this is a bad time to ask for help.* 我知道在這時候要求幫助不合適。◇ *He now realized that it had been a bad decision on his part.* 他現在意識到是他作了一個不恰當的決定。

▸ WICKED 邪惡 **6** 0→ morally unacceptable 不道德的；邪惡的：*The hero gets to shoot all the bad guys.* 主人公結果射殺了所有的壞蛋。◇ *He said I must have done something bad to deserve it.* 他說我肯定是罪有應得。

▸ CHILDREN 兒童 **7** 0→ [usually before noun] (especially of children 尤指兒童) not behaving well 頑皮的；不乖的 **SYN** **naughty**：*Have you been a bad boy?* 你調皮了嗎？

▸ HARMFUL 有害 **8** 0→ [not before noun] **~ for sb/sth** harmful; causing or likely to cause damage 有害；招致損害：*Those shoes are bad for her feet.* 那雙鞋會傷她的腳。◇ *Weather like this is bad for business.* 這種天氣不利於做買賣。

▸ PAINFUL 疼痛 **9** [usually before noun] (of parts of the body 身體部位) not healthy; painful 有病的；疼痛的：*I've got a bad back.* 我背部疼痛。

▸ FOOD 食物 **10** not safe to eat because it has decayed 變質的；腐爛的：*Put the meat in the fridge so it doesn't **go bad**.* 把肉放進冰箱裏，免得壞了。

▸ TEMPER/MOOD 脾氣；情緒 **11** **~ temper/mood** the state of feeling annoyed or angry 發脾氣；壞情緒；惱怒：*It put me in a bad mood for the rest of the day.* 那事讓我餘下整天再也沒了好心情。

▸ GUILTY/SORRY 愧疚；遺憾 **12** **feel ~** to feel guilty or sorry about sth 感到愧疚（或遺憾）：*She felt bad about leaving him.* 她因離開他而感到歉疚。◇ *Why should I want to make you feel bad?* 我幹嗎要讓你難過呢？

▸ ILL/SICK 有病；不舒服 **13** **feel/look ~** to feel or look ill/sick 覺得不舒服；感到有病；面有病容；氣色不好：*I'm afraid I'm feeling pretty bad.* 很抱歉，我覺得很不舒服。

▸ EXCELLENT 極好 **14** (**bad·der**, **bad·dest**) (*slang, especially NAmE*) good; excellent 頂呱呱的；沒治

IDM Most idioms containing **bad** are at the entries for the nouns and verbs in the idioms, for example **be bad news** (**for sb/sth**) is at **news**. 大多數含 bad 的習語，都可在該等習語中的名詞及動詞相關詞條找到，如 be bad news (for sb/sth) 在詞條 news 下。**can't be bad** (*informal*) used to try to persuade sb to agree that sth is good（勸導時說）沒有什麼不好：*You'll save fifty dollars,*

B

B

which can't be bad, can it? 你會省下五十元錢，這就夠好了，對吧？ **have got it 'bad** (*informal, humorous*) to be very much in love 熱戀着；在熱戀中： *You're not seeing him again tonight, are you? That's five times this week—you've got it bad!* 你今天晚上不再和他見面了，是吧？這個星期都約會了五次，你們熱戀了！ **not 'bad** (*informal*) quite good; better than you expected 不錯；比預料的好：*'How are you?' 'Not too bad.'* "你怎麼樣？" "還不錯。" ◇ *That wasn't bad for a first attempt.* 第一次嘗試，還算不錯。 **too bad** (*informal*) **1** (*ironic*) used to say 'bad luck' or 'it's a shame' when you do not really mean it （等於說 "倒霉" 或 "可惜"，實際上並無同情之意）： *If sometimes they're the wrong decisions, too bad.* 如果有時這些決定是錯誤的，那可是太不幸了。 **2** a shame; a pity 遺憾；可惜： *Too bad every day can't be as good as this.* 可惜並不是每一天都像今天這麼好。 **3** (*old-fashioned*) annoying 令人生氣的；惱人的：*Really, it was too bad of you to be so late.* 你來得這麼晚實在不像話。

■ ***noun* the bad** [U] bad people, things, or events 壞人；壞事： *You will always have the bad as well as the good in the world.* 人生在世總是有苦有甜。

IDM **,go to the 'bad** (*old-fashioned*) to begin behaving in an immoral way 墮落： *I hate to see you going to the bad.* 我不願看到你墮落。 **'my bad** (*NAmE, informal*) used when you are admitting that sth is your fault or that you have made a mistake 是我的錯；我錯了： *I'm sorry—my bad.* 對不起，我錯了。 **take the ,bad with the 'good** to accept the bad aspects of sth as well as the good ones 接受人生的甘苦（或事物的好與壞） **to the 'bad** (*BrE*) used to say that sb now has a particular amount less money than they did before 虧損： *After the sale they were £300 to the bad.* 這筆買賣使他們虧損了 300 英鎊。

■ ***adv.*** (*NAmE, informal*) badly 很；非常：*She wanted it real bad.* 她確實很想得到它。◇ *Are you hurt bad?* 你傷得重嗎？

bad·ass /'bædæs/ *adj.* (*NAmE, informal*) (of a person 人) tough and aggressive 粗野蠻橫的 ▸ **bad·ass** *noun*

,bad 'breath *noun* [U] breath that smells unpleasant 難聞的呼氣；口臭 **SYN** **halitosis**：*Have I got bad breath?* 我有口臭嗎？

,bad 'debt *noun* [C, U] a debt that is unlikely to be paid 壞賬；呆賬；倒賬

baddy /'bædi/ *noun* (*pl.* **-ies**) (*BrE, informal*) a bad or evil character in a film/movie, book, play, etc. （電影、書、戲劇等中的）壞人，惡棍： *As usual, the cops get the baddies in the end.* 跟平常一樣，警察最後把壞人都抓起來了。 **OPP** **goody**

bade *past tense of* BID[2]

badge /bædʒ/ *noun* **1** a small piece of metal or plastic, with a design or words on it, that a person wears to show that they belong to an organization, support sth, have achieved sth, have a particular rank, etc. 徽章；獎章： *She wore a badge saying 'Vote for Coates'.* 她戴着一枚徽章，上面寫着 "投科茨一票"。◇ *All employees have to wear name badges.* 所有員工均須佩戴名牌。 ➲ VISUAL VOCAB page V65 ➲ compare BUTTON *n.* (4) **2** (*BrE*) (*NAmE* **patch**) a piece of material that you sew onto clothes as part of a uniform （制服上的）標記，標識： *the school badge* 校徽 **3** a small piece of metal that you carry or wear to prove who you are, used, for example, by police officers 證章；警徽： *He pulled out a badge and said he was a cop.* 他拿出工作證，說他是警察。 **4** (*formal*) something that shows that a particular quality is present 標記；象徵： *His gun was a badge of power for him.* 他的槍對他而言是權力的標誌。

badger /'bædʒə(r)/ *noun, verb*

■ ***noun*** an animal with grey fur and wide black and white lines on its head. Badgers are NOCTURNAL (= active mostly at night) and live in holes in the ground. 獾（挖洞居住，夜間活動）

■ ***verb*** to put pressure on sb by repeatedly asking them questions or asking them to do sth 糾纏，煩擾（反複提出問題或要求） **SYN** **pester**： **~ sb (into doing sth)** *I finally badgered him into coming with us.* 我終於磨着他和我們一起來了。◇ **~ sb about sth** *Reporters constantly badger her about her private life.* 記者經常糾纏着打聽她的私生活。◇ **~ sb to do sth** *His daughter was always badgering him to let her join the club.* 他女兒老纏着他讓她加入俱樂部。

,bad 'hair day *noun* (*informal*) a day on which everything seems to go wrong 很不順利的一天；倒霉的一天

bad·in·age /'bædɪnɑːʒ; *NAmE* ,bædən'ɑːʒ/ *noun* [U] (from *French, literary*) friendly joking between people 開玩笑；打趣 **SYN** **banter**

bad·lands /'bædlændz/ *noun* [pl.] **1** large areas of land that have been farmed too much with the result that plants will not grow there （耕作過度）劣地，惡地 **2 the Badlands** a large area of land in the western US where plants will not grow 巴德蘭茲地區（美國西部一處貧瘠地帶）

,bad 'language *noun* [U] words that many people find offensive 髒話；冒犯人（或咒罵人）的話 **SYN** **swear words**

badly /'bædli/ *adv.* (**worse, worst**)
1 not skilfully or not carefully 拙劣地；差；不認真仔細： *to play/sing badly* 表演 / 唱得不好◇ *badly designed/organized* 設計 / 組織得很差 **OPP** **well** **2** not successfully 不成功地；受挫： *Things have been going badly.* 事情進展得不順利。◇ *I did badly* (= was not successful) *in my exams.* 我考得不好。 **OPP** **well** **3** not in an acceptable way 未能令人滿意： *to behave/sleep badly* 表現差；睡得不好◇ *badly paid/treated* 報酬低微；受虐待 ◇ *The kids took the dog's death very badly* (= they were very unhappy). 孩子們對狗的死感到很難過。 **OPP** **well** **4** in a way that makes people get a bad opinion about sth 給人壞的印象；負面地： *The economic crisis reflects badly on the government's policies.* 經濟危機反映出政府政策不如人意的一面。◇ *She's only trying to help, so don't **think badly of** her.* 她只是想幫忙，所以別把她想得太壞。 **OPP** **well** **5** used to emphasize how much you want, need, etc. sb/sth 很；非常： *The building is **badly in need of** repair.* 這棟樓急需維修。◇ *They wanted to win so badly.* 他們求勝心切。◇ *I miss her badly.* 我十分想念她。 **6** used to emphasize how serious a situation or an event is 嚴重地；厲害地： ***badly damaged/injured/hurt*** 損壞 / 傷勢 / 傷害嚴重 ◇ *The country has been badly affected by recession.* 該國受到經濟衰退的嚴重影響。◇ *Everything's **gone badly wrong**!* 一切都糟透了！

badly 'off *adj.* (**worse 'off, worst 'off**) **1** not having much money 窮困的；拮据的 **SYN** **poor**： *We aren't too badly off but we can't afford a house like that.* 我們並不是一文不名，但我們負擔不起那樣的房子。 **OPP** **well off** **2** not in a good situation 境況不佳的： *I've got quite a big room so I'm not too badly off.* 我有一間蠻大的屋子，所以住得還不壞。 **OPP** **well off**

IDM **be badly 'off for sth** (*BrE*) to not have enough of sth 某物短少；缺乏某物

bad·mash /bʌd'mɑːʃ/ *noun* (*IndE*) a dishonest man 不誠實的男子；惡漢；流氓

bad·min·ton /'bædmɪntən/ *noun* [U] a game like TENNIS played by two or four people, usually indoors. Players hit a small light kind of ball, originally with feathers around it (= a SHUTTLECOCK) across a high net using a RACKET. 羽毛球運動 ➲ VISUAL VOCAB page V45

'bad-mouth *verb* **~ sb** (*informal*) to say unpleasant things about sb 說人壞話： *No one wants to employ somebody who bad-mouths their former employer.* 沒有人願意雇用說前雇主壞話的人。

bad·ness /'bædnəs/ *noun* [U] the fact of being morally bad 道德敗壞： *There was not a hint of badness in him.* 他道德十分高尚。

,bad-'tempered *adj.*
often angry; in an angry mood 易怒的；發脾氣的： *She gets very bad-tempered when she's tired.* 她累的時候就愛發脾氣。

Ba·fana Ba·fana /bə,fɑːnə bə'fɑːnə/ *noun* (*SAfrE*) a popular name for the South African national men's football (SOCCER) team 南非小子（南非國家男子足球隊的俗稱）

baf·fle /ˈbæfl/ *verb, noun*

■ ***verb*** to confuse sb completely; to be too difficult or strange for sb to understand or explain 使困惑；難住：**~ sb** *His behaviour baffles me.* 他的行為使我難以琢磨。◇ **be baffled (as to) why, how, where, etc.** ... *I'm baffled as to why she hasn't called.* 我不明白她為什麼沒打電話。◇ *I'm baffled why she hasn't called.* 我不明白她為什麼沒打電話。▸ **baffle·ment** *noun* [U]: *His reaction was one of bafflement.* 他的反應是迷惑不解。**baf·fling** *adj.*

■ ***noun*** (*technical* 術語) a screen used to control or prevent the flow of sound, light or liquid（控制聲、光、液體等流動的）隔板，擋板，反射板

BAFTA /ˈbæftə/ *abbr., noun*

■ ***abbr.*** British Academy of Film and Television Arts 英國電影電視藝術學院

■ ***noun*** an award presented by the British Academy of Film and Television Arts 英國電影電視藝術學院獎：*He won a BAFTA for the role.* 他演出這個角色獲得英國電影電視藝術學院獎。

bag 🔑 /bæg/ *noun, verb*

■ ***noun***

▸ **CONTAINER 容器 1** 🔑 [C] (often in compounds 常構成複合詞) a container made of paper or plastic, that opens at the top, used especially in shops/stores（尤指商店用的）紙袋，塑料袋：*a **plastic/polythene/paper bag*** 塑料／聚乙烯／紙袋 ◇ *a **laundry/mail bag*** 洗衣袋；郵袋 ◇ *a black plastic **rubbish/garbage bag*** 一個黑色塑料垃圾袋 **2** 🔑 [C] a strong container made from cloth, plastic, leather, etc., usually with one or two handles, used to carry things in when shopping or travelling 手提包；旅行袋：*a shopping bag* 購物袋 ◇ *a make-up bag* 化妝品提包 ◇ *He's upstairs unpacking his bags.* 他在樓上打開他的旅行袋取出東西。◇ *She opened her bag* (= her HANDBAG) *and took out her comb.* 她打開手提包，取出梳子。➲ **VISUAL VOCAB** pages V64, V70 ➲ see also AIRBAG, BEANBAG, BUMBAG, GOODY BAG, PUNCHBAG, SANDBAG *n.*, TEA BAG

▸ **AMOUNT 數量 3** [C] **~ (of sth)** the amount contained in a bag 一袋（的量）：*She ate a bag of chips.* 她吃了一袋炸土豆條。➲ **VISUAL VOCAB** page V33 ➲ see also MIXED BAG, RAGBAG **4 bags** [U, pl.] **~ (of sth)** (*BrE, informal*) a large amount or a large number of sth 大量；很多：*Get in! There's bags of room.* 進來吧！地方很空。

▸ **UNDER EYES 眼下方 5 bags** [pl.] dark circles or loose folds of skin under the eyes, as a result of getting old or lack of sleep 黑眼圈；眼袋

▸ **UNPLEASANT WOMAN 討厭的女人 6** [C] (*informal, especially BrE*) an insulting word for an unpleasant or bad-tempered older woman 醜婦，潑婦（指討厭或壞脾氣的年長女人）➲ see also RATBAG, SCUMBAG, WINDBAG

▸ **BIRDS/ANIMALS 鳥；動物 7** [C, usually sing.] all the birds, animals, etc. shot or caught on one occasion（一次）獵獲物 **HELP** There are many other compounds ending in **bag**. You will find them at their place in the alphabet. 以 bag 結尾的複合詞還有很多，可在各字母中的適當位置查到。

IDM ▸ **ˌbag and ˈbaggage** with all your possessions, especially secretly or suddenly（尤指秘密地或突然地）攜帶全部財產：*He threw her out onto the street, bag and baggage.* 他突然把她連人帶東西一股腦兒扔到大街上。**a ˌbag of ˈbones** (*informal*) a very thin person or animal 瘦骨嶙峋的人（或動物）；皮包骨 **be in the ˈbag** (*informal*) if sth is **in the bag**, it is almost certain to be won or achieved 十拿九穩；穩操勝券 **leave sb holding the ˈbag** (*NAmE, informal*) to suddenly make sb responsible for sth important, such as finishing a difficult job, that is really your responsibility 突然把重擔推給某人 **(not) sb's ˈbag** (*informal*) (not) sth that you are interested in or good at（非）愛好，特長：*Poetry isn't really my bag.* 我其實並不擅長詩歌。➲ more at CAT, NERVE *n.*, PACK *v.*, TRICK *n.*

■ ***verb*** (**-gg-**)

▸ **PUT INTO BAGS 裝進袋子 1 ~ sth (up)** to put sth into bags 把…裝進袋子：*The fruit is washed, sorted and bagged at the farm.* 水果在農場洗淨、分揀並裝袋。

▸ **CATCH ANIMAL 捕獵動物 2 ~ sth** (*informal*) to catch or kill an animal 捕獲，獵殺（動物）

▸ **IN SPORT 體育運動 3 ~ sth** (*informal*) to score a goal, point, etc. 得分：*Dublin bagged two goals in last night's win.* 在昨晚獲勝的那場比賽中都柏林隊射進了兩球。

▸ **CLAIM STH 聲稱擁有 4 ~ sth** (*BrE, informal*) to claim sth as yours before sb else claims it; to take sth before sb else can get it 搶佔；佔有：*Sally had managed to bag the two best seats.* 薩莉搶到了那兩個最好的位子。◇ *Quick, bag that table over there!* 快點佔住那邊的桌子！

▸ **CRITICIZE SB/STH 批評 5 ~ sb/sth** (*AustralE, NZE, informal*) to criticize sb/sth 批評；挑剔；指責

▸ **DECIDE NOT TO DO STH 決定不做 6 ~ sth** (*NAmE, informal*) to decide not to do sth because you think it will not be successful or because you think it will be better to do it later（認為不會成功或以後做會更好而）放棄，取消：*They decided to bag the trip because they were short of cash.* 因為缺錢，他們決定取消這次旅行。

IDM ▸ **bags (I)** ... (*BrE*) (*NAmE* **ˈdibs on** ...) (*informal*) used to claim sth as yours before sb else can claim it …是我的；我要求…：*Bags I sit in the front seat!* 我一定要坐前面的位子！

baga·telle /ˌbægəˈtel/ *noun* **1** [U] a game played on a board with small balls that you try to hit into holes 小型枱球 **2** [C, usually sing.] (*literary*) a small and unimportant thing or amount 瑣事；無足輕重的事；微量：*It cost a mere bagatelle.* 這個只花了一點錢。

bagel /ˈbeɪgl/ *noun* a hard bread roll shaped like a ring 百吉圈（硬麪包）

bag·gage 🔑 /ˈbægɪdʒ/ *noun* [U]

1 🔑 (*especially NAmE*) = LUGGAGE：*excess baggage* (= weighing more than the limit allowed on a plane) 超重行李（超出乘飛機所允許的重量）◇ *baggage handlers* (= people employed to load and unload baggage at airports)（機場）行李員 ◇ (*NAmE*) *We loaded our baggage into the car.* 我們把行李裝上了汽車。➲ **COLLOCATIONS** at TRAVEL **2** the beliefs and attitudes that sb has as a result of their past experiences（因閱歷而形成的）信仰，看法：*She was carrying a lot of **emotional baggage**.* 她背負着很多感情債。**IDM** ▸ see BAG *n.*

Which Word? 詞語辨析

baggage / luggage

- **Luggage** is the usual word in *BrE*, but **baggage** is also used, especially in the context of the bags and cases that passengers take on a flight. In *NAmE* **baggage** is usually used. 英式英語常用 luggage，但也用 baggage，尤指旅客乘飛機時所帶的行李。美式英語通常用 baggage。
- Both these words are uncountable nouns. 兩者均為不可數名詞：*Do you have a lot of luggage?* 你的行李多嗎？◇ *Two pieces of luggage have gone missing.* 有兩件行李丟失了。◇ *Never leave baggage unattended.* 別丟下行李不管。

ˈbaggage car (*NAmE*) (*BrE* **ˈluggage van**) *noun* a coach/car on a train for carrying passengers' luggage（火車的）行李車廂

ˈbaggage reclaim (*BrE*) (*NAmE* **ˈbaggage claim**) *noun* [U] the place at an airport where you get your suitcases, etc. again after you have flown（機場）行李提取處

Bag·gie™ /ˈbægi/ *noun* (*NAmE*) a small bag made of clear plastic that is used for storing SANDWICHES, etc. 巴吉袋（用於包三明治等的透明小塑料袋）

baggy /ˈbægi/ *adj.* (**bag·gier**, **bag·gi·est**) (of clothes 衣服) fitting loosely 寬鬆的；鬆垮的：*a baggy T-shirt* 寬鬆的 T 恤衫 **OPP** **tight**

ˈbag lady *noun* a woman who has no home and who walks around carrying her possessions with her（攜帶行囊露宿街頭的）流浪女人

ˈbag lunch *noun* (*NAmE*) a meal of SANDWICHES, fruit, etc. that you take to school, work, etc. in a bag 自備袋裝午餐 ➲ compare BOX LUNCH, PACKED LUNCH

B

bag·pipes /ˈbæɡpaɪps/ (also **pipes**) noun [pl.] (NAmE also **bag·pipe** [sing.]) a musical instrument played especially in Scotland. The player blows air into a bag held under the arm and then slowly forces the air out through pipes to produce a noise. 風笛 ➲ picture at PIPE ▸ **bag·pipe** adj.：*bagpipe music* 風笛樂

ba·guette /bæˈɡet/ noun **1** (also ˌ**French** ˈ**loaf**, ˌ**French** ˈ**stick**) a LOAF of white bread in the shape of a long thick stick that is crisp on the outside and soft inside（法國）脆皮白麪包棒 **2** a small baguette or part of one that is filled with food and eaten as a SANDWICH 脆皮夾餡麪包棒；三明治小麪包棒：*a cheese baguette* 奶酪夾心小麪包棒

bah /bɑː/ *exclamation* used to show a sound that people make to express disapproval（表示不贊成的聲音）

Baha'i (also **Bahai**) /bɑːˈhɑːi; bəˈhaɪ/ noun [U] a religion that teaches that people and religions are the same, and that there should be peace 巴哈教（其教義為人即宗教，並且應該建立和平）

Ba·hasa In·do·nesia /bəˌhɑːsə ɪndəˈniːʒə/ noun [U] the official language of Indonesia 印度尼西亞語（指該國官方語言）

Ba·hasa Ma·lay·sia /bəˌhɑːsə məˈleɪʒə/ noun [U] the official language of Malaysia 馬來西亞語（指該國官方語言）

bail /beɪl/ noun, verb

■ **noun 1** [U] money that sb agrees to pay if a person accused of a crime does not appear at their trial. When bail has been arranged, the accused person is allowed to go free until the trial. 保釋金；保釋：*Can anyone **put up bail** for you?* 有人保釋你嗎？◇ *She was released **on £2 000 bail**.* 她以 2 000 英鎊獲得保釋。◇ *Bail was set at $1 million.* 保釋金定為 100 萬元。◇ *He committed another offence while he was out **on bail*** (= after bail had been agreed). 他在具保候審期間又犯罪了。◇ *The judge **granted/refused bail**.* 法官准予／不准保釋。◇ *She **jumped/skipped bail*** (= did not appear at her trial). 她棄保潛逃（未如期到庭受審）。➲ COLLOCATIONS at JUSTICE **2** [C, usually pl.] (in CRICKET 板球) either of the two small pieces of wood on top of each set of three wooden posts (called STUMPS) 三柱門上的橫木

■ **verb** (BrE also **bale**) **1** [T] **~ sb (to do sth)** to release sb on bail 允許保釋（某人）：*He was **bailed to appear** in court on 15 March.* 他獲得保釋，定於 3 月 15 日到庭候審。 **2** [I] (NAmE, informal) to leave a place, especially quickly（尤指迅速地）離開：*Sorry, I really have to bail.* 對不起，我真得趕緊走了。 **3** [T] **~ sb (up)** (AustralE, NZE, informal) to approach sb and talk to them, often when they do not want this 接近某人並與之攀談（尤指對方不願意）

PHR V ˌ**bail** ˈ**out (of sth)** **1** to jump out of a plane that is going to crash（從即將墜毀的飛機中）跳傘 **2** to escape from a situation that you no longer want to be involved in 逃避，擺脫（不想再牽連其中的情況）：*I'd understand if you wanted to bail out of this relationship.* 如果你想從這種關係中擺脫出來，我可以理解。ˌ**bail** ˈ**out** | ˌ**bail (sth)**↔ˈ**out** to empty water from sth by lifting it out with your hand or a container（從…中）往外舀水：*He had to stop rowing to bail water out of the boat.* 他不得不停止划船，把船裏的水舀出去。◇ *The boat will sink unless we bail out.* 我們若不排水，船就要沉。ˌ**bail sb**↔ˈ**out** to pay sb's bail for them 保釋（某人）ˌ**bail sb**↔ˈ**out (of sth)** to rescue sb from a difficult situation 幫助（某人）脫離困境：*The government had to bail the company out of financial difficulty.* 政府只得幫助該公司渡過財政難關。◇ *Ryan's late goal bailed out his team.* 瑞安在比賽後階段得的一分拯救了他的球隊。➲ SYNONYMS at SAVE

bai·ley /ˈbeɪli/ noun the open area of a castle, inside the outer wall（城堡外廓內的）堡場

bail·iff /ˈbeɪlɪf/ noun **1** (BrE) a law officer whose job is to take the possessions and property of people who cannot pay their debts 執達員；執達官 **2** (BrE) a person employed to manage land or a large farm for sb else 莊園主管家 **3** (NAmE) an official who keeps order in court, takes people to their seats, watches prisoners, etc. 法警

bail·out /ˈbeɪlaʊt/ noun an act of giving money to a company, a foreign country, etc. that has very serious financial problems 緊急財政援助；金援

bain-marie /ˌbæn məˈriː/ noun (from French) a pan of hot water in which a bowl of food is cooked or warmed slowly 熱水燉鍋；熱水蒸鍋；雙層保溫鍋

bairn /beən; NAmE bern/ noun (ScotE, NEngE) a child 小孩

bait /beɪt/ noun, verb

■ **noun** [U, C] **1** food put on a hook to catch fish or in nets, traps, etc. to catch animals or birds 魚餌；誘餌：*The fish took the bait.* 魚咬了釣餌。 **2** a person or thing that is used to catch sb or to attract them, for example to make them do what you want 用作誘餌的人（或物）

■ **verb 1 ~ sth (with sth)** to place food on a hook, in a trap, etc. in order to attract or catch an animal 下誘餌；在（魚鈎上、陷阱中等）放誘餌：*He baited the trap with a piece of meat.* 他在陷阱中放了一片肉做誘餌。 **2 ~ sb** to deliberately try to make sb angry by making cruel or insulting remarks（故意以侮辱性言語）激怒 **3 -baiting** (in compound nouns 構成複合名詞) the activity of attacking a wild animal with dogs 縱犬襲擊（野獸）：*bear-baiting* 縱犬鬥熊

ˌ**bait-and-ˈswitch** noun [C, usually sing.] a selling method where advertisements for low-priced products are used to attract customers, who are then persuaded to buy sth more expensive 誘售法（以廉價商品招徠，再兜售較高價商品）

baize /beɪz/ noun [U] a type of thick cloth made of wool that is usually green, used especially for covering card tables and BILLIARD, SNOOKER or POOL tables 枱面呢，厚羊毛氈（通常綠色，尤用作牌桌、枱球枱面的襯墊）

bake 🔑 /beɪk/ verb

1 🔑 [T, I] to cook food in an oven without extra fat or liquid; to be cooked in this way（在烤爐裏）烘烤；焙：**~ (sth)** *baked apples* 烤蘋果 ◇ *the delicious smell of baking bread* 烤製麪包的香味 ◇ **~ sth for sb** *I'm baking a birthday cake for Alex.* 我在給亞歷克斯烤生日蛋糕。◇ **~ sb sth** *I'm baking Alex a cake.* 我在給亞歷克斯烤蛋糕。➲ COLLOCATIONS at COOKING ➲ VISUAL VOCAB page V27 **2** [I, T] to become or to make sth become hard by heating（將某物）烤硬：*The bricks are left in the kiln to bake.* 磚坯放在窯裏燒。◇ **~ sth (+ adj.)** *The sun had baked the ground hard.* 太陽把地面曬硬了。 **3** [I] (informal) to be or become very hot（變得）灼熱，炎熱：*We sat baking in the sun.* 我們坐在太陽底下曬得熱死了。➲ see also HALF-BAKED

baked Al·aska /ˌbeɪkt əˈlæskə/ noun [C, U] a DESSERT made of cake and ice cream covered in MERINGUE and cooked quickly in a very hot oven 烤脆皮冰淇淋蛋糕，火焰冰淇淋（將蛋糕冰淇淋裹上蛋糖，放入高温烤箱烤製）

baked ˈbeans noun [pl.] **1** (especially BrE) small white BEANS cooked in a tomato sauce and usually sold in cans 番茄醬烘豆（常製成罐頭） **2** (NAmE) = BOSTON BAKED BEANS

ˌ**baked poˈtato** (also ˌ**jacket poˈtato**) noun a potato cooked in its skin in an oven（帶皮）烤土豆：*a baked potato and beans* 一份烤土豆加烘豆

bake·house /ˈbeɪkhaʊs/ noun (old-fashioned) a building or an area where bread is made 麪包作坊；麪包房

Bake·lite™ /ˈbeɪkəlaɪt; NAmE also ˈbeɪkl-/ noun [U] a type of hard plastic used in the past for electrical equipment, etc. 貝克萊特酚醛樹脂；（酚醛）電木，膠木

baker /ˈbeɪkə(r)/ noun **1** a person whose job is baking and selling bread and cakes 麪包（糕餅）師傅；麪包店老闆 **2 baker's** (pl. **bakers**) (BrE) a shop that sells bread and cakes 麪包店：*I'm just going to the baker's.* 我正要去麪包店。

ˌ**baker's ˈdozen** noun [sing.] (old-fashioned) a group of thirteen (= one more than a dozen, which is twelve) 十三 ORIGIN This phrase comes from bakers' old custom of adding one extra loaf to an order of a dozen. 源自舊時麪包店老闆的習慣，即給所訂購的一打麪包搭送一條麪包。

bakery /ˈbeɪkəri/ *noun* (*pl.* **-ies**) (*NAmE* also **bake·shop**) a place where bread and cakes are made and/or sold 麵包（糕餅）店；麵包（糕餅）烘房；麵包廠

ˈ**bake sale** *noun* (*NAmE*) an event at which cakes, etc. are baked and sold to make money, usually for a school or charity 烤餅義賣（為學校或慈善事業等募集基金）

bake·shop /ˈbeɪkʃɒp; *NAmE* -ʃɑːp/ *noun* (*NAmE*) = BAKERY

bake·ware /ˈbeɪkweə(r); *NAmE* -wer/ *noun* [U] tins and other containers used for baking 烘焙用具

bak·ing /ˈbeɪkɪŋ/ *noun, adj.*

■ ***noun*** [U] the process of cooking using dry heat in an oven 烤製；烘焙：*a **baking dish/tin*** 烤盤；烤模

■ ***adj.*** (also ˌ**baking** ˈ**hot**) extremely hot 灼熱的；熾熱的

ˈ**baking flour** *noun* [U] (*US*) = SELF-RISING FLOUR

ˈ**baking powder** *noun* [U] a mixture of powders that are used to make cakes rise and become light as they are baked 發酵粉

ˈ**baking sheet** (also ˈ**baking tray**) (both *BrE*) (*NAmE* ˈ**cookie sheet**) *noun* a small sheet of metal used for baking food on （小片）烘烤板

ˈ**baking soda** *noun* [U] = SODIUM BICARBONATE

bak·kie /ˈbʌki/ *noun* (*SAfrE*) a motor vehicle with low sides and no roof at the back, used for transporting goods or people, or as a car（無後蓋的）小型輕便客貨車 ➲ compare PICKUP *n.* (1)

bak·lava (also **bac·lava**) /ˈbɑːkləvə; *NAmE* ˌbɑːkləˈvɑː/ *noun* [C, U] a sweet dish from the Middle East, made from very thin PASTRY, nuts, and HONEY 蜜糖果仁千層酥（中東薄脆甜點）

bak·sheesh (also **back·sheesh**) /ˌbækˈʃiːʃ/ *noun* [U] (*informal*) (in some Asian countries) a small amount of money that is given as a gift to poor people, or given to sb to thank them or to persuade them to help you（一些亞洲國家中的）施捨，小費

bala·clava /ˌbæləˈklɑːvə/ (also ˌ**balaclava** ˈ**helmet**) *noun* (*especially BrE*) a type of hat made of wool that covers most of the head, neck and face 巴拉克拉瓦盔式帽，巴拉克拉瓦羊毛頭罩（裹住頭、頸和臉的大部份）

bala·fon /ˈbæləfɒn; *NAmE* -fɑːn/ *noun* a large type of XYLOPHONE (= a musical instrument with rows of wooden bars that you hit) that is used in W African music 巴拉風；西非大木琴

bala·laika /ˌbæləˈlaɪkə/ *noun* a musical instrument like a GUITAR with a body shaped like a triangle and two, three, or four strings, popular especially in Russia 巴拉萊卡琴，三角琴（俄羅斯撥弦樂器，腹呈三角形，可有二弦、三弦或四弦）➲ VISUAL VOCAB page V36

bal·ance 🔑 /ˈbæləns/ *noun, verb*

■ ***noun***

▸ **EQUAL AMOUNTS** 等量 **1** 🔑 [U, sing.] a situation in which different things exist in equal, correct or good amounts 均衡；平衡；均勢：*This newspaper maintains a good balance in its presentation of different opinions.* 這份報紙不偏不倚地報道不同的意見。◇ *Tourists often disturb the delicate balance of nature on the island.* 觀光客常常干擾島上脆弱的自然生態平衡。◇ *His wife's death disturbed the **balance of his mind**.* 妻子的離世使他心神不寧。◇ **~ between A and B** *Try to keep a balance between work and relaxation.* 盡量保持工作與休閒均衡。➲ see also IMBALANCE

▸ **OF BODY** 身體 **2** 🔑 [U] the ability to keep steady with an equal amount of weight on each side of the body 平衡能力：*Athletes need a good sense of balance.* 運動員要有良好的平衡感。◇ *I struggled to **keep my balance** on my new skates.* 我穿着新溜冰鞋，努力保持平衡。◇ *She cycled round the corner, **lost her balance** and fell off.* 她騎車拐彎時失去平衡，摔了下來。

▸ **MONEY** 錢 **3** 🔑 [C, usually sing.] the amount that is left after taking numbers or money away from a total 餘額：*to check your **bank balance*** (= to find out how much money there is in your account) 核對銀行結存 **4** 🔑 [C, usually sing.] an amount of money still owed after some payment has been made 結欠：*The balance of $500 must be paid within 90 days.* * 500 元結欠款必須於 90 天之內付清。

▸ **INSTRUMENT FOR WEIGHING** 秤 **5** [C] an instrument for weighing things, with a bar that is supported in the middle and has dishes hanging from each end 天平；秤

IDM (**on**) **the balance of** ˈ**evidence/probaˈbility** (*formal*) (considering) the evidence on both sides of an argument, to find the most likely reason for or result of sth（從）總的來說；（考慮）正反兩方面；權衡雙方證據 (**be/hang**) **in the** ˈ**balance** if the future of sth/sb, or the result of sth is/hangs **in the balance**, it is uncertain（前途）不明朗；（結果）未定，懸而未決：*The long-term future of the space programme hangs in the balance.* 航天計劃的長遠前景尚未明朗。(**catch/throw sb**) **off** ˈ**balance** **1** to make sb/sth unsteady and in danger of falling 使失去平衡（而有跌落危險）：*I was thrown off balance by the sudden gust of wind.* 突如其來的一陣風差點兒把我吹倒。**2** to make sb surprised and no longer calm 使（毫無準備而）不知所措：*The senator was clearly caught off balance by the unexpected question.* 參議員顯然因這意想不到的問題而不知所措。**on** ˈ**balance** after considering all the information 總的來說：*On balance, the company has had a successful year.* 總的來說，公司這一年業績很好。➲ more at REDRESS *v.*, STRIKE *v.*, SWING *v.*, TIP *v.*

■ ***verb***

▸ **KEEP STEADY** 保持平衡 **1** 🔑 [I, T] to put your body or sth else into a position where it is steady and does not fall 使（在某物上）保持平衡；立穩：**~ (on sth)** *How long can you balance on one leg?* 你單腿能站多久？◇ **~ sth (on sth)** *The television was precariously balanced on top of a pile of books.* 電視機不穩地擺在一堆書上面。◇ *She balanced the cup on her knee.* 她把杯子在膝蓋上放穩。

▸ **BE/KEEP EQUAL** （使）相等 **2** 🔑 [I, T] to be equal in value, amount, etc. to sth else that has the opposite effect 相抵；抵消 **SYN** **offset**：**~ out** *The good and bad effects of any decision will usually balance out.* 任何決策的效果往往利弊互見。◇ **~ sth (out)** *This year's profits will balance our previous losses.* 本年度的贏利將可彌補我們之前的虧損。◇ *His lack of experience was balanced by a willingness to learn.* 他的好學彌補了他經驗的不足。**3** 🔑 [T] **~ A with/and B** to give equal importance to two contrasting things or parts of sth 同等重視（相對的兩個事物或方面）：*She tries to balance home life and career.* 她力圖兼顧家庭生活和事業。

▸ **COMPARE** 比較 **4** [T] **~ A against B** to compare the relative importance of two contrasting things 比較（兩個相對的事物）；權衡重要性：*The cost of obtaining legal advice needs to be balanced against its benefits.* 法律咨詢的費用與其效益需通盤考慮。

▸ **MONEY** 錢 **5** [T] **~ sth** (*finance* 財) to show that in an account the total money spent is equal to the total money received; to calculate the difference between the two totals 結平（賬目）

ˈ**balance beam** *noun* (*NAmE*) = BEAM *n.* (3)

bal·anced /ˈbælənst/ *adj.* [usually before noun] (*approving*) keeping or showing a balance so that different things or different parts of sth exist in equal or correct amounts 保持（或顯示）平衡的：*The programme presented a balanced view of the two sides of the conflict.* 節目公平地反映了衝突雙方的情況。◇ *a balanced diet* (= one with the quantity and variety of food needed for good health) 均衡飲食

ˌ**balance of** ˈ**payments** *noun* [sing.] the difference between the amount a country pays for imports and the amount it receives for exports in a particular period of time 國際收支差額（一國在某時期的進出口差額）

ˌ**balance of** ˈ**power** *noun* [sing.] **1** a situation in which political or military strength is divided between two countries or groups of countries（國際政治或軍事的）均勢 ➲ COLLOCATIONS at INTERNATIONAL **2** the power held by a small group which can give its support to either of two larger and equally strong groups 舉足輕重的力量（兩個較大團體勢力均衡時，小團體所具有的可改變均勢的力量）

ˌ**balance of** ˈ**trade** (also ˈ**trade balance**) *noun* [sing.] the difference in value between imports and exports

國際貿易差額：*a balance-of-trade deficit* (= when a country spends more on imports than it earns from exports) 國際貿易逆差

B

'balance sheet *noun (finance* 財) a written statement showing the amount of money and property that a company has and listing what has been received and paid out 資產負債表；決算表；資金平衡表

'bal·an·cing act *noun* a process in which sb tries to please two or more people or groups who want different things 平衡各方權益的行動：*The UN must perform a delicate balancing act between the different sides in the conflict.* 聯合國必須在各方衝突之間擔任公正的協調工作。

bal·cony /ˈbælkəni/ *noun (pl. -ies)* **1** a platform that is built on the upstairs outside wall of a building, with a wall or rail around it. You can get out onto a balcony from an upstairs room. 陽台 ➲ VISUAL VOCAB page V17 **2** an area of seats upstairs in a theatre （劇院的）樓廳，樓座 ➲ see also CIRCLE *n.* (4), FIRST BALCONY

bald /bɔːld/ *adj.* **1** having little or no hair on the head 禿頂的；禿頭的：*He started* ***going bald*** *in his twenties.* 他二十幾歲便開始謝頂。➲ VISUAL VOCAB page V60 **2** without any of the usual hair, marks, etc. covering the skin or surface of sth 無毛的；無茸毛的；光禿的：*Our dog has a bald patch on its leg.* 我們的狗腿上脫了一片毛。◇ *a bald tyre* (= a tyre whose surface has become smooth) 磨平了的輪胎 **3** without any extra explanation or detail to help you understand or accept what is being said 不加贅述的；簡單的；赤裸裸的：*The bald fact is that we don't need you any longer.* 事實很簡單，我們不再需要你了。◇ *The letter was a bald statement of our legal position.* 那封信直截了當地說出我們的法律立場。➲ see also BALDLY ▸ **bald·ness** *noun* [U]

IDM **(as) bald as a coot** *(BrE, informal)* completely bald 光禿禿

,bald 'eagle *noun* a N American BIRD OF PREY (= a bird that kills other creatures for food) with a white head and white tail feathers. It is used as a symbol of the US. 白頭雕，白頭鷲（北美食肉猛禽，頭尾羽毛呈白色，是美國的象徵）

bal·der·dash /ˈbɔːldədæʃ; *NAmE* -dərd-/ *noun* [U] *(old-fashioned)* nonsense 胡說；廢話

,bald-'faced *adj. (disapproving, especially NAmE)* making no attempt to hide your dishonest behaviour 赤裸裸的；公然的；厚顏無恥的 SYN **barefaced, blatant**：*bald-faced lies* 赤裸裸的謊話

bald·ing /ˈbɔːldɪŋ/ *adj.* starting to lose the hair on your head 開始脫髮的；變禿的：*a short balding man with glasses* 一個戴眼鏡的有些禿頂的小個子男人

bald·ly /ˈbɔːldli/ *adv.* in a few words with nothing extra or unnecessary 直截了當地；不加贅述地：*'You're lying,' he said baldly.* "你撒謊。"他直截了當地說。

baldy (also **baldie**) /ˈbɔːldi/ *noun (pl. -ies) (informal, offensive)* a person who has no hair or almost no hair on their head 禿頭；禿子

bale /beɪl/ *noun, verb*

■ ***noun*** a large amount of a light material pressed tightly together and tied up 大包，大捆（輕物品）：***bales of hay/straw/cotton/wool*** 大捆大捆的乾草／稻草／棉花／羊毛

■ ***verb*** **1 ~ sth** to make sth into bales 將…打成大包（或大捆）：*The waste paper is baled, then sent for recycling.* 廢紙被打成大包，然後送去回收再利用。 **2 ~ sb (to do sth)** *(BrE)* = BAIL *v.*

PHR V **,bale 'out | ,bale sth↔'out | ,bale sb↔'out** *(BrE)* = BAIL OUT, BAIL STH OUT, BAIL SB OUT

bale·ful /ˈbeɪlfl/ *adj. (literary)* threatening to do sth evil or to hurt sb 威嚇的；嚇唬的：*a* ***baleful look/influence*** 兇惡的外表／勢力 ▸ **bale·ful·ly** /ˈbeɪlfəli/ *adv.*

baler /ˈbeɪlə(r)/ *noun* a machine for making paper, cotton, HAY, etc. into BALES 打包機；壓捆機

balk *(especially NAmE)* = BAULK

Bal·kan·ize /ˈbɔːlkənaɪz; *BrE* also ˈbɒl-/ *verb* **~ sth** to divide a region into smaller regions which are unfriendly or aggressive towards each other 巴爾幹化（將某地區分裂成敵對區域）▸ **Bal·kan·iza·tion** /ˌbɔːlkənaɪˈzeɪʃn; *BrE* also ˌbɒl-/ *noun* [U]

the Bal·kans /ˈbɔːlkənz; *BrE* also ˈbɒl-/ *noun* [pl.] a region of SE Europe, including the countries to the south of the rivers Sava and Danube 巴爾幹（位於歐洲東南部，包括薩瓦河和多瑙河以南諸國）▸ **Bal·kan** *adj.*：*the Balkan Peninsula* 巴爾幹半島

balky /ˈbɔːlki; ˈbɔːki/ *adj. (NAmE)* (of a person or machine 人或機器) refusing or failing to do what you want them to do 倔強的；不聽使喚的

ball 🔑 /bɔːl/ *noun, verb*

■ ***noun*** **1** 🔑 a round object used for throwing, hitting or kicking in games and sports 球：*a* ***golf/tennis/cricket ball*** 高爾夫球；網球；板球 ◇ *Bounce the ball and try and hit it over the net.* 讓球反彈起來，然後試把它打過網。➲ VISUAL VOCAB page V44 **2** 🔑 a round object or a thing that has been formed into a round shape 球狀物：*The sun was a huge ball of fire low on the horizon.* 落在地平線上的太陽像個大火球。◇ *a ball of string* 一團線 ◇ *Some animals roll themselves into a ball for protection.* 有些動物會蜷縮成一團來保護自己。 **3** a kick, hit or throw of the ball in some sports 踢出（或擊出、投出）的一球：*He sent over a high ball.* 他投了一個高球。 **4** (in BASEBALL 棒球) a throw by the PITCHER that is outside the STRIKE ZONE (= the area between the BATTER's upper arms and knees)（投手投出的）壞球 **5 ~ of the foot/hand** the part underneath the big toe or the thumb 大腳趾球；拇指球；魚際；跖球 ➲ VISUAL VOCAB page V59 **6** [usually pl.] *(taboo, informal)* a TESTICLE 睾丸 ➲ see also BALLS *n.* (4) **7** a large formal party with dancing （大型正式的）舞會

IDM **a ,ball and 'chain** *(BrE)* a problem that prevents you from doing what you would like to do 羈絆；障礙 **the ball is in your/sb's 'court** it is your/sb's responsibility to take action next （球已經丟給你了）下一步就看你的了：*They've offered me the job, so the ball's in my court now.* 他們已答應把那份工作給我，下一步就看我怎麼辦了。 **a ,ball of 'fire** *(informal)* a person who is full of energy and enthusiasm 充滿活力和熱情的人；生龍活虎的人；朝氣蓬勃的人 **get/set/start/keep the ball 'rolling** to make sth start happening; to make sure that sth continues to happen 開始某事；繼續某事 **have a 'ball** *(informal)* to enjoy yourself a lot 狂歡；玩得痛快 **have something/a lot on the 'ball** *(US, informal)* to be capable of doing a job very well; to be intelligent 有能耐；有才智 **(be) on the 'ball** to be aware of and understand what is happening and able to react quickly 敏銳；機警：*The new publicity manager is really on the ball.* 新任宣傳部經理的確精明幹練。 **pick up/take the ,ball and 'run with it** *(especially NAmE)* to develop an idea or plan that already exists 採納（想法）並發揚光大；接手並發展（計劃）：*It's up to the private sector to take the ball and run with it.* 該輪到私營部門接手並發展它了。 **play 'ball (with sb)** **1** *(NAmE)* to play with a ball 玩球；耍球：*Chris was in the park playing ball with the kids.* 克里斯在公園裏和孩子們一起玩球。 **2** *(informal)* to be willing to work with other people in a helpful way, especially so that sb can get what they want （和某人）合作 **the whole ball of 'wax** *(NAmE, informal)* the whole thing; everything 整個；全部；一切：*I panicked, I cried—the whole ball of wax.* 我驚慌失措，我大喊大叫，所有的反應都做齊了。➲ more at CARRY, DROP *v.*, EYE *n.*

■ ***verb*** **1** [I, T] to form sth or be formed into the shape of a ball 做成球狀；使成團塊：**~ (into sth)** *Her hands balled into fists.* 她雙手攥拳。◇ **~ sth (into sth)** *My hands were balled into fists.* 我雙手攥成拳頭。 **2** [T] **~ sb** *(NAmE, taboo, slang)* (of a man 男性) to have sex with a woman 和（女性）交媾

bal·lad /ˈbæləd/ *noun* **1** a song or poem that tells a story 敘事詩；民歌；民謠：*a medieval ballad about a knight and a lady* 一首關於騎士和貴族小姐的中世紀謠曲 **2** a slow song about love （節奏緩慢的）情歌：*Her latest single is a ballad.* 她的最新單曲唱片是一首情歌。➲ COLLOCATIONS at MUSIC

bal·lad·eer /ˌbæləˈdɪə(r); *NAmE* -ˈdɪr/ *noun* a person who sings or writes ballads 敍事曲演唱者（或編寫者）；敍事詩作者

ball-and-socket joint 球窩關節

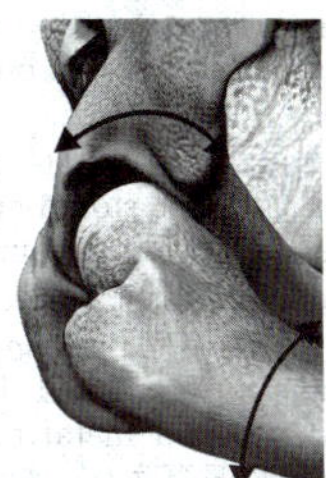

ˌball-and-ˈsocket joint *noun* (*anatomy* 解) a joint such as the hip joint, in which a ball-shaped part moves inside a curved hollow part 球窩關節；杵臼關節

bal·last /ˈbæləst/ *noun* [U] **1** heavy material placed in a ship or HOT-AIR BALLOON to make it heavier and keep it steady（船中保持平衡的）壓艙物；（熱氣球的）鎮重物 **2** a layer of stones that makes a strong base on which a road, railway/railroad, etc. can be built（用作公路或鐵路路基的）道砟

ball bearing 滾珠軸承

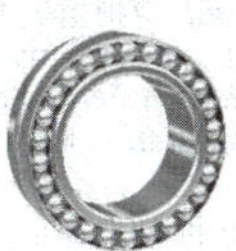

ˌball ˈbearing *noun* a ring of small metal balls used in a machine to enable the parts to turn smoothly; one of these small metal balls 滾珠軸承；滾珠

ball·boy /ˈbɔːlbɔɪ/ *noun* a boy who picks up the balls for the players in a TENNIS match（網球賽中替球手撿球的）球童 ➲ see also BALLGIRL

ˈball-breaker *noun* (*informal*) a sexually aggressive woman who destroys men's confidence（性慾旺盛，使男子甘拜下風的）女魔 ▸ **ˈball-breaking** *adj.*

ball·cock /ˈbɔːlkɒk; *NAmE* -kɑːk/ *noun* a device with a floating ball that controls the amount of water going into a container, for example the water tank of a toilet 浮球旋塞；浮球閥

bal·ler·ina /ˌbæləˈriːnə/ *noun* a female dancer in BALLET 芭蕾舞女演員 ➲ see also PRIMA BALLERINA

bal·let /ˈbæleɪ/ *noun* **1** [U] a style of dancing that tells a dramatic story with music but no talking or singing 芭蕾舞：*She wants to be a* ***ballet dancer****.* 她想當芭蕾舞演員。◇ *ballet shoes* 芭蕾舞鞋 **2** [C] a story or work of art performed by a group of ballet dancers 芭蕾舞劇：*'Swan Lake' is one of the great classical ballets.*《天鵝湖》是一部偉大的古典芭蕾舞劇。**3** [C+sing./pl. v.] a group of dancers who work and perform ballet together 芭蕾舞團：*members of the Royal Ballet* 皇家芭蕾舞團成員

bal·let·ic /bæˈletɪk/ *adj.* (*formal, approving*) smooth and elegant, like a movement or a dancer in ballet（動作）舒展優雅的，芭蕾舞風格的

ˈball game *noun* **1** any game played with a ball 球類運動 **2** (*NAmE*) a game of BASEBALL 棒球比賽：*Are you going to the ball game?* 你去看棒球賽嗎？

IDM **a (whole) different/new ˈball game** (*informal*) a completely different kind of situation 截然不同的新局面

ball·girl /ˈbɔːlɡɜːl; *NAmE* -ɡɜːrl/ *noun* a girl who picks up the balls for the players in a TENNIS match（網球賽中替球手撿球的）女球童 ➲ see also BALLBOY

ball·hawk /ˈbɔːlhɔːk/ *noun* (*US, informal*) a player who is good at getting or catching balls, especially in AMERICAN FOOTBALL, BASEBALL or BASKETBALL（尤指美式足球、棒球或籃球中的）爭球能手

ˈball hockey *noun* [U] (*CanE*) a version of ICE HOCKEY played on a hard surface without ice, and with a ball instead of a PUCK 旱地曲棍球；旱地冰球

bal·listic /bəˈlɪstɪk/ *adj.* connected with ballistics 彈道（學）的；發射的

IDM **go balˈlistic** (*informal*) to become very angry 大怒；暴怒：*He went ballistic when I told him.* 我告訴他時他勃然大怒。

balˌlistic ˈmissile *noun* a MISSILE that is fired into the air at a particular speed and angle in order to fall in the right place 彈道導彈

bal·lis·tics /bəˈlɪstɪks/ *noun* [U] the scientific study of things that are shot or fired through the air, such as bullets and MISSILES 彈道學；發射學

bal·loon /bəˈluːn/ *noun, verb*

■ ***noun*** **1** a small bag made of very thin rubber that becomes larger and rounder when you fill it with air or gas. Balloons are brightly coloured and used as decorations or toys. 氣球：***to blow up/burst/pop a balloon*** 吹起氣球；使氣球爆裂 ➲ compare TRIAL BALLOON **2** (also **hot-ˈair balloon**) a large balloon made of strong material that is filled with hot air or gas to make it rise in the air, usually carrying a BASKET for passengers 熱氣球 ➲ VISUAL VOCAB page V53

IDM **when the balˈloon goes up** (*BrE, informal*) when the trouble that you are expecting begins 意料中的麻煩出現時；（不出所料）出亂子時 ➲ more at LEAD[2]

■ ***verb*** **1** [I] **~ (out/up)** to suddenly swell out or get bigger（突然）膨脹，漲大：*Her skirt ballooned out in the wind.* 她的裙子讓風吹得鼓起來了。**2** [I] (usually **go ballooning**) to travel in a HOT-AIR BALLOON as a sport 乘熱氣球飛行

bal·loon·ist /bəˈluːnɪst/ *noun* a person who travels in a balloon as a sport 乘氣球飛行者

balˈloon whisk *noun* a WHISK that you hold in your hand, made of thin pieces of curved wire 氣球形手動攪拌器，打蛋器（用弧狀細金屬絲製成）

bal·lot /ˈbælət/ *noun, verb*

■ ***noun*** **1** [U, C] the system of voting in writing and usually in secret; an occasion on which a vote is held（無記名）投票選舉；投票表決：*The chairperson is chosen by* ***secret ballot****.* 主席是通過無記名投票選舉產生的。◇ *The union cannot call a strike unless it* ***holds a ballot*** *of members.* 工會未經會員投票表決不得發動罷工。➲ SYNONYMS at ELECTION ➲ COLLOCATIONS at VOTE **2** (*BrE* also **ˈballot paper**) [C] the piece of paper on which sb marks who they are voting for 選票：*What percentage of eligible voters* ***cast their ballots****?* 合資格選民的投票率是多少？**3 the ballot** [sing.] the total number of votes in an election（選舉中的）投票總數：*She won 58.8% of the ballot.* 她贏得了投票總數的 58.8%。➲ see also POLL *n.* (2), (3)

■ ***verb*** **1** [T] **~ sb (on sth)** to ask sb to vote in writing and secretly about sth 要求某人（對某事）無記名投票 SYN **poll**：*The union balloted its members on the proposed changes.* 工會要求會員對所提議的變革進行無記名投票。**2** [I] to vote secretly about sth 進行無記名投票：*The workers balloted for a strike.* 工人對是否罷工進行無記名投票表決。

ˈballot box *noun* **1** [C] a box in which people put their ballots after voting 投票箱 **2 the ballot box** [sing.] the system of voting in an election 投票選舉制：*The people make their wishes known through the ballot box.* 人們以投票方式表達他們的願望。

ˈballot paper *noun* (*BrE*) = BALLOT *n.* (2)

ball·park /ˈbɔːlpɑːk; *NAmE* -pɑːrk/ *noun* **1** [C] (*especially NAmE*) a place where BASEBALL is played 棒球場 **2** [sing.]

B

an area or a range within which an amount is likely to be correct or within which sth can be measured（數額的）變動範圍；可量範圍：*The offers for the contract were all **in the same ballpark**.* 就此合同的開價均在同一範圍內。◇ *If you said five million you'd be **in the ballpark**.* 如果你說的是五百萬，那就差不多了。◇ *Give me a **ballpark figure*** (= a number that is approximately right). 給我個大致恰當的數字。

ball·point /ˈbɔːlpɔɪnt/ (also **ˌballpoint ˈpen**) *noun* a pen with a very small metal ball at its point, that rolls ink onto the paper 圓珠筆；原子筆 ➲ VISUAL VOCAB page V69 ➲ compare BIRO

ball·room /ˈbɔːlruːm; -rʊm/ *noun* a very large room used for dancing on formal occasions 舞廳 ➲ compare DANCE HALL

ˌballroom ˈdancing *noun* [U] a type of dancing done with a partner and using particular fixed steps and movements to particular types of music such as the WALTZ 交際舞；交誼舞

balls /bɔːlz/ *noun*, *verb*

■ ***noun*** (*taboo, slang*) **1** [U] (*BrE*) nonsense 胡說；廢話：*That's a load of balls!* 那是一派胡言！ **2** [pl.] courage 勇氣：*She's got balls, I'll say that for her.* 我敢說她有膽量。◇ *It took a lot of balls to do that.* 那麼做需要很大的勇氣。 **3 Balls!** (*BrE*) *exclamation* used as a swear word when you are disagreeing with sth, or when you are angry about sth（粗俗話，表示不同意或惱怒） HELP Less offensive ways to express this are 'Nonsense!', or 'Come off it!' 較溫和的用語是 Nonsense! 或 Come off it! **4** [pl.] TESTICLES 睾丸

IDM **go ˈballs out** to do sth in a very determined or extreme way, especially when it means taking risks 豁出去；拚命幹：*The team went balls out in the final.* 決賽時這個隊拚得很兇。

■ ***verb***

PHR V **ˌballs sth↔ˈup** (*BrE, taboo, slang*) to spoil sth; to do sth very badly 把…搞糟；弄得一塌糊塗 ➲ related noun BALLS-UP HELP A more polite way of saying this is **foul sth up**, **mess sth up**, or **bungle sth**. 較禮貌的說法是 foul sth up、mess sth up 或 bungle sth。➲ see also BALL *n.* (6)

ˈballs-out *adj.* (*taboo, slang*) very determined or extreme 很堅決的；十分極端的：*a balls-out attack* 猛烈攻擊 ◇ *It's a balls-out shoot-'em-up action movie.* 那是一部火爆槍戰動作片。

ˈballs-up *noun* (*taboo, slang, especially BrE*) something that has been done very badly 混亂；一團糟：*I made a real balls-up of my exams.* 我考試考得一塌糊塗。

ballsy /ˈbɔːlzi/ *adj.* (*informal, especially NAmE*) showing a lot of courage and determination 有膽量的；有決心的；有種的：*She is one ballsy lady!* 她是個敢作敢為的女子！

bally·hoo /ˌbæliˈhuː; *NAmE* ˈbælihuː/ *noun* [U] (*informal, disapproving*) unnecessary noise and excitement 大吹大擂；喧囂

balm /bɑːm/ *noun* [U, C, usually sing.] **1** (also **bal·sam**) oil with a pleasant smell that is obtained from some types of trees and plants, used in the past to help heal wounds, for example 香脂油（昔日用於療傷等） **2** a liquid, cream, etc. that has a pleasant smell and is used to make wounds less painful or skin softer 鎮痛軟膏；護膚膏；香液：*lip balm* 護唇膏 **3** (*literary*) something that makes you feel calm or relaxed 令人感到安慰（或鎮定）的事物

bal·moral /bælˈmɒrəl; *NAmE* -ˈmɔːr-/ *noun* **1** a type of round hat without a BRIM, often with RIBBONS attached, worn by some Scottish soldiers as part of their uniform 巴爾莫勒爾帽（某些蘇格蘭士兵所戴、常綴絲帶的無邊圓帽） **2** a strong heavy walking boot 巴爾莫勒爾遠足靴

balmy /ˈbɑːmi/ *adj.* (*approving*) (of the air, weather, etc. 空氣、天氣等) warm and pleasant 溫暖愜意的 SYN **mild**：*a balmy summer evening* 清爽宜人的夏夜

ba·lo·ney /bəˈləʊni; *NAmE* -ˈloʊ-/ *noun* [U] **1** (*informal, especially NAmE*) nonsense; lies 胡說；謊話：*Don't give me that baloney!* 別對我講那些鬼話！ **2** (*NAmE*) = BOLOGNA

balsa /ˈbɔːlsə/ (also **ˈbalsa wood**) *noun* [U] the light wood of the tropical American **balsa tree**, used especially for making models 熱帶美洲輕木（尤用於製作模型）

bal·sam /ˈbɔːlsəm/ *noun* **1** [U, C] = BALM (1) **2** [C] any plant or tree from which BALM is obtained 產香脂的花草（或樹）

bal·sam·ic vin·egar /bɔːlˌsæmɪk ˈvɪnɪɡə(r)/ *noun* [U] a dark sweet Italian VINEGAR, stored in BARRELS (= round wooden containers) to give it flavour 香脂醋，意大利黑醋（黑色，味甜，貯存於木桶中以釀製出香味）

balti /ˈbɔːlti; ˈbɒlti; *NAmE* ˈbɑːlti/ *noun* [C, U] a type of meat or vegetable dish cooked in Pakistani style, usually served in a round metal pan which gives its name to the dish 巴爾蒂鍋菜（一種巴基斯坦式菜肴，通常用圓形平底鍋盛載）

Bal·tic /ˈbɔːltɪk/ *adj.* relating to the Baltic Sea in northern Europe and the countries surrounding it 波羅的海的；波羅的海各國的：*the Baltic republics of Estonia, Latvia and Lithuania* 愛沙尼亞、拉脫維亞和立陶宛等波羅的海共和國

bal·us·ter /ˈbæləstə(r)/ *noun* any of the short posts that form a balustrade 欄杆柱

bal·us·trade /ˌbæləˈstreɪd/ *noun* a row of posts, joined together at the top, built along the edge of a BALCONY, bridge, etc. to prevent people from falling off, or as a decoration（陽台、橋等的）欄杆

bam /bæm/ *exclamation* (*informal*) **1** used to represent the sound of a sudden loud hit or a gun being fired（表示突然的重擊聲或槍聲）嘭，砰：*She pointed the gun at him and—bam!* 她把槍對着他，然後——砰！ **2** used to show that sth happens very suddenly（表示突然）驀地：*I saw him yesterday and—bam!—I realized I was still in love with him.* 我昨天見到他，突然間，我意識到我還愛着他。

bam·boo /ˌbæmˈbuː/ *noun* [C, U] (*pl.* **-oos**) a tall tropical plant that is a member of the grass family and has hard hollow STEMS that are used for making furniture, poles, etc. 竹；竹子：*a bamboo grove* 竹林 ◇ *a bamboo chair* 竹椅 ◇ *bamboo shoots* (= young bamboo plants that can be eaten) 竹筍 ➲ VISUAL VOCAB page V11

bam·boo·zle /bæmˈbuːzl/ *verb* **~ sb** (*informal*) to confuse sb, especially by tricking them 迷惑；（尤指）哄騙，欺騙

ban 0→ /bæn/ *verb*, *noun*

■ ***verb*** (**-nn-**) **1** 0→ **~ sth** to decide or say officially that sth is not allowed 明令禁止；取締 SYN **prohibit**：*Chemical weapons are banned internationally.* 國際上禁止使用化學武器。 **2** 0→ [usually passive] to order sb not to do sth, go somewhere, etc., especially officially 禁止（某人）做某事（或去某處等）：**~ sb from sth** *He was banned from the meeting.* 他被取消了出席會議的資格。◇ **~ sb from doing sth** *She's been banned from leaving Greece while the allegations are investigated.* 當局對指控進行調查期間，禁止她離開希臘。◇ (*BrE*) *He was banned from driving for six months.* 他被禁止駕駛六個月。

■ ***noun*** 0→ **~ (on sth)** an official rule that says that sth is not allowed 禁令：*There is to be a total ban on smoking in the office.* 辦公室將徹底禁止吸煙。◇ *to **impose/lift a ban*** 頒佈／解除禁令

banal /bəˈnɑːl; *NAmE* also ˈbeɪnl/ *adj.* (*disapproving*) very ordinary and containing nothing that is interesting or important 平庸的；平淡乏味的；無關緊要的；陳腐的

ban·al·ity /bəˈnæləti/ *noun* (*pl.* **-ies**) [U, C] (*disapproving*) the quality of being banal; things, remarks, etc. that are banal 平庸；平淡乏味；陳腐的事物；陳詞濫調：*the banality of modern city life* 現代城市生活的單調乏味 ◇ *They exchanged banalities for a couple of minutes.* 他們彼此客套了幾分鐘。

ba·nana /bəˈnɑːnə; *NAmE* bəˈnænə/ *noun* a long curved fruit with a thick yellow skin and soft flesh, that grows on trees in hot countries 香蕉：*a bunch of bananas* 一串香蕉 ➲ VISUAL VOCAB page V30

IDM **go ba'nanas** (*slang*) to become angry, crazy or silly 發怒；發瘋；犯傻

ba'nana belt *noun* (*NAmE, informal*) a region where the weather is warm 香蕉帶（指氣候溫暖地帶）

ba,nana re'public *noun* (*disapproving, offensive*) a poor country with a weak government, that depends on foreign money 香蕉共和國（政府無能、依賴外援的貧窮國家）

ba'nana skin *noun* (*BrE, informal*) something that could cause difficulty or embarrassment, especially to sb in a public position 造成麻煩（或使人當眾出醜）的事物

ba,nana 'split *noun* a cold DESSERT (= a sweet dish) made from a BANANA that is cut in half along its length and filled with ice cream, nuts, etc. 香蕉聖代，香蕉船（將香蕉縱向剖開，加進冰淇淋、果仁等做成的甜食冷盤）

band 🔑 /bænd/ *noun, verb*

■ ***noun***

▸ GROUP OF MUSICIANS 樂隊 **1** 🔑 [C+sing./pl. v.] a small group of musicians who play popular music together, often with a singer or singers 流行音樂樂隊：*a **rock/jazz band*** 搖滾樂／爵士樂隊 ◇ *She's a singer with a band.* 她是一個樂隊的歌手。➲ see also BOY BAND, GIRL BAND **2** 🔑 [C+sing./pl. v.] a group of musicians who play BRASS and PERCUSSION instruments 管樂隊；鼓號樂隊：*a military band* 軍樂隊 ➲ see also BRASS BAND, MARCHING BAND, ONE-MAN BAND

▸ GROUP OF PEOPLE 人群；團夥 **3** 🔑 [C+sing./pl. v.] a group of people who do sth together or who have the same ideas 一夥人；一幫人：*a band of outlaws* 一幫歹徒 ◇ *He persuaded a small band of volunteers to help.* 他勸服了一小批志願者來幫忙。

▸ STRIP OF MATERIAL/COLOUR 帶子；顏色帶 **4** 🔑 [C] a thin flat strip or circle of any material that is put around things, for example to hold them together or to make them stronger 帶；箍：*She always ties her hair back in a band.* 她總是用一條帶子把頭髮紮在後面。◇ *All babies in the hospital have name bands on their wrists.* 醫院裏所有新生兒手腕上都套着寫有名字的手箍。◇ *She wore a simple band of gold (= a ring) on her finger.* 她戴着一枚淨面的金戒指。➲ VISUAL VOCAB page V65 ➲ see also ARMBAND, HAIRBAND, HATBAND, RUBBER BAND, SWEATBAND, WAISTBAND **5** 🔑 [C] a strip of colour or material on sth that is different from what is around it 條紋；條飾：*a white plate with a blue band around the edge* 帶藍邊的白盤子

▸ OF RADIO WAVES 無線電波 **6** (also **wave·band**) [C] a range of radio waves 頻帶；波段：*Short-wave radio uses the 20-50 metre band.* 短波收音機用的波段是 20–50 米。

▸ RANGE 範圍 **7** [C] a range of numbers, ages, prices, etc. within which people or things are counted or measured （數目、年齡、價格等的）範圍，段：*the 25-35 age band* * 25–35 歲的年齡段 ◇ *tax bands* 稅收等級

■ ***verb***

▸ WITH COLOUR/MATERIAL 色彩；材料 **1** [usually passive] **be banded** (+ **adj.**) to put a band of a different colour or material around sth 加彩條（或嵌條等）：*Many insects are banded black and yellow.* 很多昆蟲有黑色和黃色的條紋。

▸ PUT INTO RANGE 劃分範圍 **2** [usually passive] **~ sth** (*BrE*) to be organized into bands of price, income, etc. （將價格、收入等）劃分檔次，分等級：*Tax is banded according to income.* 賦稅是按收入劃分等級的。

PHR V **,band to'gether** to form a group in order to achieve sth 聯合；攜手：*Local people banded together to fight the drug dealers.* 當地人齊心協力打擊毒品販子。

ban·dage 🔑 /'bændɪdʒ/ *noun, verb*

■ ***noun*** 🔑 a strip of cloth used for tying around a part of the body that has been hurt in order to protect or support it 繃帶

■ ***verb*** 🔑 **~ sth** (**up**) to wrap a bandage around a part of the body in order to protect it because it is injured 用繃帶包紮 ➲ COLLOCATIONS at INJURY

'Band-Aid™ *noun* (*especially NAmE*) **1** (*BrE* also **plas·ter**, **'sticking plaster**) [C, U] material that can be stuck to the skin to protect a small wound or cut; a piece of this 膏藥；創可貼；護創膠布 **2** (*disapproving*) a temporary solution to a problem that does not really solve it at all 權宜之計

ban·dana (also **ban·danna**) /bæn'dænə/ *noun* a piece of brightly coloured cloth worn around the neck or head 色彩鮮豔的圍巾（或頭巾）

B and B (also **B & B**, **b and b**, **b & b**) /ˌbiː ən 'biː/ *abbr.* (*informal, especially BrE*) BED AND BREAKFAST

'band council *noun* (*CanE*) a local form of Aboriginal government in Canada, consisting of an elected chief and COUNCILLORS 社議會（加拿大土著的地方政府，由一名酋長和數名社議員組成）

ban·deau /'bændəʊ; *NAmE* -doʊ/ *noun* **1** a narrow band worn around the head to hold the hair in place 束髮帶 **2** a piece of women's clothing that is tied around the body to cover the breasts 管狀胸罩；狹帶式胸罩：*a bandeau bikini top* 管狀比基尼上裝

bandh /bʌnd/ *noun* (*IndE*) a general strike 總罷工

bandi·coot /'bændɪkuːt/ *noun* **1** a small Australasian animal with a long nose and long tail, which eats mainly insects 袋狸（澳大拉西亞長鼻長尾小動物，主食昆蟲） **2** (also **,bandicoot 'rat**) an Asian RAT 袋狸鼠

band·ing /'bændɪŋ/ (also **stream·ing** especially in *BrE*) *noun* [U] the policy of dividing school students into groups of the same level of ability （把學生按能力）分班（或分組）

ban·dit /'bændɪt/ *noun* a member of an armed group of thieves who attack travellers 土匪

ban·dito /bæn'diːtəʊ; *NAmE* -toʊ/ (also **ban·dido**) /-dəʊ; *NAmE* -doʊ/ *noun* (*NAmE*, from *Spanish*) (*pl.* **-os**) a Mexican BANDIT 墨西哥土匪

ban·dit·ry /'bændɪtri/ *noun* [U] (*formal*) acts of stealing and violence by bandits 土匪行為（或活動）

band·leader /'bændliːdə(r)/ *noun* a player who is in charge of a band, especially a JAZZ band （尤指爵士樂的）樂隊領隊

band·mas·ter /'bændmɑːstə(r); *NAmE* -mæs-/ *noun* a person who CONDUCTS a military or BRASS band 軍樂隊（或管樂隊）指揮

bando·bast /'bʌndəbʌst/ *noun* [U, C, usually sing.] (*IndE*) preparation or an arrangement for dealing with sth 準備；安排：*The **police bandobast** was very effective.* 警方的安排十分奏效。

ban·do·lier (also **ban·do·leer**) /ˌbændə'lɪə(r); *NAmE* -'lɪr/ *noun* a belt made for carrying bullets and worn over the shoulder （斜挎肩上的）子彈帶

bands·man /'bændzmən/ *noun* (*pl.* **-men** /-mən/) a musician who plays in a military or BRASS band 軍樂隊（或銅管樂隊）隊員

band·stand /'bændstænd/ *noun* a covered platform outdoors, where musicians, especially a BRASS or military band, can stand and play （室外有蓋的）樂隊演奏台

band·wagon /'bændwægən/ *noun* [usually sing.] an activity that more and more people are becoming involved in 風靡的活動；時尚：*The World Cup bandwagon is starting to roll.* 世界杯足球賽熱潮即將湧起。

IDM **climb/jump on the 'bandwagon** (*informal, disapproving*) to join others in doing sth that is becoming fashionable because you hope to become popular or successful yourself 趕時髦；追隨潮流：*politicians eager to jump on the environmental bandwagon* 急於隨大溜加入環保行列的政客們 **ORIGIN** In the US, political PARADES often included a band on a wagon. Political leaders would join them in the hope of winning popular support. 源自美國的政治宣傳遊行，常有樂隊彩車隨行。政治領袖參與遊行希望贏得民眾的廣泛支持。

band·width /'bændwɪdθ/ *noun* [C, U] (*computing* 計) **1** a band of FREQUENCIES used for sending electronic signals 帶寬；頻寬 **2** a measurement of the amount of information that a particular computer network or Internet connection can send in a particular time. It is often measured in BITS per second. 帶寬值，頻寬值

B

B

（計算機網絡或互聯網接口一定時間內傳送信息量的量度，按每秒傳送的字節數計）

bandy /ˈbændi/ *adj.*, *verb*

■ ***adj.*** (of the legs 雙腿) curving, with the knees wide apart 向外彎曲的；羅圈的： *to be bandy-legged* 有羅圈腿

■ ***verb*** (**ban·dies**, **bandy·ing**, **ban·died**, **ban·died**)

IDM **bandy ˈwords (with sb)** (*old-fashioned*) to argue with sb or speak rudely to them（與…）爭吵，發生口角

PHR V **ˌbandy sth↔aˈbout/aˈround** [usually passive] if a name, a word, a story, etc., is **bandied about/around**, it is mentioned frequently by many people 傳播；散佈： *His name was being bandied about as a future prime minister.* 人們紛紛傳說他是未來的首相。

bane /beɪn/ *noun* [sing.] **the ~ of sb/sth** something that causes trouble and makes people unhappy 造成困擾（或不快）的事物： *The neighbours' kids are the* ***bane of my life.*** 街坊鄰居的孩子們讓我生活得很不安寧。

bane·ful /ˈbeɪnfl/ *adj.* (*literary*) evil or causing evil 邪惡的；引起災禍的

bang /bæŋ/ *verb*, *noun*, *adv.*, *exclamation*

■ ***verb*** **1** [I, T] to hit sth in a way that makes a loud noise 猛敲；砸： **~ on sth** *She banged on the door angrily.* 她憤怒地砰砰打門。◇ **~ sth (with sth)** *The baby was banging the table with his spoon.* 嬰孩用調羹敲打着桌子。➲ **SYNONYMS** at HIT **2** [I, T] to close sth or to be closed with a loud noise（把…）砰地關上 **SYN** **slam**： *A window was banging somewhere* (= opening and closing noisily). 什麼地方有扇窗戶在砰砰地開開關關。◇ **+ adj.** *The door banged shut behind her.* 她出去時把門砰地一聲關上了。◇ **~ sth** *Don't bang the door when you go out!* 出去時別那麼砰一聲地關門！ **3** [T] **~ sth + adv./prep.** to put sth somewhere suddenly and violently 猛摔；砰地一扔 **SYN** **slam**： *He banged the money down on the counter.* 他把錢往櫃枱上砰地一擲。◇ *She banged saucepans around irritably.* 她暴躁地把鍋摔來摔去。 **4** [T] **~ sth (+ adv./prep.)** to hit sth, especially a part of the body, against sth by accident 碰撞；磕 **SYN** **bump**： *She tripped and banged her knee on the desk.* 她絆了一跤，膝蓋磕在桌子上。 **5** [T] **~ sb** (*taboo*, *slang*) (of a man 男性) to have sex with a woman 和（女性）性交

IDM see DRUM *n.*, HEAD *n.*

PHR V **ˌbang aˈbout/aˈround** to move around noisily 乒乓作響地來來去去： *We could hear the kids banging around upstairs.* 我們能聽到孩子們在樓上咚咚地跑來跑去。 **ˌbang ˈinto sth** to crash into or hit sth by mistake（不小心）撞着某物： *I banged into a chair and hurt my leg.* 我撞到椅子上，碰傷了腿。 **ˌbang ˈon about sth** (*BrE*, *informal*) to talk a lot about sth in a boring way 嘮叨；絮叨 **SYN** **go on**： *He keeps banging on about his new job.* 他沒完沒了地嘮叨他那份新工作。 **ˌbang sb↔ˈup** (*BrE*, *informal*) to put sb in prison 使某人鋃鐺入獄；把某人收監 **ˌbang sth↔ˈup** (*NAmE*, *informal*) to damage or injure sth 毀壞；損害

■ ***noun*** **1** a sudden loud noise 突然的巨響： *The door swung shut with a bang.* 門砰地一聲關上了。◇ *Suddenly there was a loud bang and a puff of smoke.* 突然一聲巨響，噴出了一股黑煙。 ➲ see also BIG BANG **2** a sudden painful blow on a part of the body（對身體部位的）猛撞，猛敲，猛擊： *a bang on the head* 頭被撞擊 **3** **bangs** [pl.] (*NAmE*) (*BrE* **fringe**) the front part of sb's hair that is cut so that it hangs over their FOREHEAD 額前短髮；劉海兒 ➲ **VISUAL VOCAB** page V60 **4** = BHANG **5** (*informal*, *computing* 計) the symbol (!) 歎號

IDM **ˌbang for your ˈbuck** (*especially NAmE*, *informal*) if you get more, better, etc. **bang for your buck**, you get better value for the money you spend or the effort you put in to sth 錢花得合算；所作的努力值得 **with a ˈbang** (*informal*) **1** very successfully 很成功： *The party went* ***with a bang.*** 聚會十分圓滿。 **2** in a way that everyone notices; with a powerful effect 引人注目；有強烈影響： *The team won their last four games, ending the season with a bang.* 該隊贏了最後四場比賽，給本賽季畫了一個亮麗的句號。➲ more at EARTH *n.*, SLAP *adv.*

■ ***adv.*** (*informal*, *especially BrE*) exactly; completely 正好；完全地： *Our computers are* ***bang up to date.*** 我們的電腦是最先進的。◇ *My estimate was bang on target.* 我的估計完全準確。◇ *You're bang on time, as usual.* 你像往常一樣，非常準時。➲ see also SLAP BANG at SLAP *adv.*

IDM **bang goes sth** (*BrE*, *informal*) used when you say that sth you hoped to have or achieve is no longer possible（希望等）破滅： *Bang went my hopes of promotion.* 我晉升的希望破滅了。 **go ˈbang** (*informal*) to burst or explode with a loud noise; to make a sudden loud noise 爆；爆炸；發出巨響： *A balloon suddenly went bang.* 一隻氣球突然砰地一聲爆了。 **IDM** see RIGHT *n.*

■ ***exclamation*** used to show the sound of sth loud, like a gun（表示槍聲等巨響）砰： *'Bang, bang, you're dead!' shouted the little boy.* "砰！砰！你死了！" 小男孩喊道。

ˌbanged ˈup *adj.* (*NAmE*, *informal*) injured or damaged 受傷的；損壞的： *Two days after the accident she still looked pretty banged up.* 事故過去兩天後她看上去傷勢仍然很重。

bang·er /ˈbæŋə(r)/ *noun* (*BrE*, *informal*) **1** a SAUSAGE 香腸： *bangers and mash* 香腸和土豆泥 **2** (*NAmE* **beat·er**) an old car that is in bad condition 破舊的汽車 **3** a FIREWORK that makes a loud noise when it explodes 爆竹；鞭炮

Bangla /ˈbʌŋlɑː/ *noun* [U] **1** the Bengali language 孟加拉語 **2** Bangladesh 孟加拉國

ban·gle /ˈbæŋɡl/ *noun* a piece of jewellery in the form of a large ring of gold, silver, etc. worn loosely around the wrist 手鐲 ➲ **VISUAL VOCAB** page V65

ˈbang-up *adj.* (*NAmE*, *informal*) very good 挺好的；很棒的

bania /ˈbʌnjə/ *noun* (*IndE*) **1** a person who sells things 商人 **2** (*disapproving*) a person who is interested in making money 財迷；貪財的人

ban·ish /ˈbænɪʃ/ *verb* **1** [usually passive] **~ sb (from …) (to …)** to order sb to leave a place, especially a country, as a punishment 放逐；流放；把（某人）驅逐出境 **SYN** **exile**： *He was banished to Australia, where he died five years later.* 他被流放到澳大利亞，五年後在那裏去世。◇ *The children were banished from the dining room.* 孩子們被趕出餐室。 **2** **~ sb/sth (from sth)** to make sb/sth go away; to get rid of sb/sth 趕走；驅除： *The sight of food banished all other thoughts from my mind.* 看到吃的，我別的什麼都忘記了。

ban·ish·ment /ˈbænɪʃmənt/ *noun* [U] the punishment of being sent away from a place, especially from a country 放逐；流放；驅逐出境

ban·is·ter (also **ban·nis·ter**) /ˈbænɪstə(r)/ *noun* (*BrE* also **ban·is·ters** [pl.]) the posts and rail which you can hold for support when going up or down stairs（樓梯的）欄杆，扶手： *to hold on to the banister/banisters* 緊抓住扶手 ➲ picture at STAIRCASE

banjo /ˈbændʒəʊ; *NAmE* ˈbændʒoʊ/ *noun* (*pl.* **-os**) a musical instrument like a GUITAR, with a long neck, a round body and four or more strings 班卓，班卓琴（撥弦樂器，長頸、圓身）➲ **VISUAL VOCAB** page V36

bank 0→ /bæŋk/ *noun*, *verb*

■ ***noun***

▸ **FOR MONEY** 金錢 **1** 0→ an organization that provides various financial services, for example keeping or lending money 銀行： *My salary is paid directly into my bank.* 我的工資直接撥到我的銀行。◇ *I need to go to the bank* (= the local office of a bank). 我得去趟銀行。◇ *a bank loan* 銀行貸款 ◇ *a bank manager* 銀行經理 ➲ **COLLOCATIONS** at FINANCE ➲ see also INVESTMENT BANK, MERCHANT BANK

▸ **IN GAMBLING** 賭博 **2** a supply of money or things that are used as money in some games, especially those in which gambling is involved（尤指賭博中的）籌碼；賭本

▸ **STH COLLECTED/STORED** 收集／貯存物 **3** an amount of sth that is collected; a place where sth is stored ready for use 庫存；庫： *a bank of knowledge* 知識寶庫 ◇ ***a blood/sperm bank*** 血庫；精子庫 ➲ see also DATABANK

▸ **OF RIVER/CANAL** 河；水道 **4** 0→ the side of a river, CANAL, etc. and the land near it 岸；河畔： *He jumped in and swam to the opposite bank.* 他跳下水，游到對岸。◇ *It's on the north bank of the Thames.* 它位於泰晤士河北岸。◇ *a house on the banks of the River Severn* (= on land near the river) 塞文河畔的一所房子

▸ **SLOPE** 斜坡 **5** a raised area of ground that slopes at the sides, often at the edge of sth or dividing sth 斜坡；

壟；埂：*There were low banks of earth between the rice fields.* 稻田之間有低矮的田埂。◇ *The girls ran down the steep grassy bank.* 女孩子們沿長滿青草的陡坡跑下去。**6** an artificial slope built at the side of a road, so that cars can drive fast around bends（路面拐彎處為方便車輛快速行駛而築起的）邊坡

▸ **OF CLOUD/SNOW, ETC.** 雲、雪等 **7** a mass of cloud, snow, etc., especially one formed by the wind（尤指風吹到一起的）積雲，積雪：*The sun disappeared behind a bank of clouds.* 太陽消失在一大片雲後面。

▸ **OF MACHINES, ETC.** 機器等 **8** a row or series of similar objects, especially machines 一排（同類物品）；一系列（機器等）：*a **bank of lights/switches/computers*** 一排燈／開關／計算機

IDM **not ˌbreak the ˈbank** (*informal, humorous*) if you say sth **won't break the bank**, you mean that it won't cost a lot of money, or more than you can afford 花費不太大；支付得起 ➲ more at LAUGH *v.*

■ ***verb***

▸ **MONEY** 錢 **1** [T] **~ sth** to put money into a bank account 把（錢）存入銀行：*She is believed to have banked* (= been paid) *£10 million in two years.* 據信她兩年內在銀行存了 1 000 萬英鎊。**2** [I] **~ (with/at ...)** to have an account with a particular bank（在某銀行）開賬戶，存款：*The family had banked with Coutts for generations.* 那家幾代人都在庫茨銀行存錢。

▸ **OF PLANE** 飛機 **3** [I] to travel with one side higher than the other when turning（轉彎時）傾斜飛行：*The plane banked steeply to the left.* 飛機向左作高度傾斜飛行。

▸ **FORM PILES** 堆積 **4** [T] **~ sth (up)** to form sth into piles 堆積（某物）：*They banked the earth (up) into a mound.* 他們把土堆成了一個土丘。

▸ **A FIRE** 爐火 **5** [T] **~ sth (up)** to pile coal, etc. on a fire so that the fire burns slowly for a long time（用煤等）封爐火：*The fire was banked up as high as if it were midwinter.* 爐火被封得很厚實，好像就是隆冬。

PHR V **ˈbank on sb/sth** to rely on sb/sth 依靠；指望：*I'm banking on your help.* 我還得靠你幫助呢。◇ *'I'm sure he'll help.' '**Don't bank on it** (= it is not likely to happen).'* "我相信他會幫忙的。" "那可不見得。" ◇ **~ to do sth** *I'm banking on you to help me.* 我還得靠你幫忙呢。◇ **~ doing sth** *I was banking on getting something to eat on the train.* 我指望在火車上能找到吃的。**ˌbank ˈup** to form into piles, especially because of the wind 堆積（尤指由於風吹）：*The snow had banked up against the wall.* 雪靠牆堆積起來了。

bank·able /ˈbæŋkəbl/ *adj.* (*informal*) likely to make money for sb 可賺錢的；可贏利的：*The movie's success has made her one of the world's most bankable stars.* 這部影片的成功使她成了世界上最有身價的明星之一。

ˈbank account *noun* an arrangement that you have with a bank that allows you to keep your money there, to pay in or take out money, etc. 銀行賬戶：*to **open/close a bank account*** 開立／結清銀行賬戶

ˈbank balance *noun* the amount of money that sb has in their bank account at a particular time 銀行存款餘額；銀行結存

ˈbank card *noun* **1** (also **ˈbanker's card**) (both *BrE*) a plastic card provided by your bank that may be used as a CHEQUE CARD or DEBIT CARD or to get money from your account out of a machine 支票保付卡；取款機提款卡 **2** (*NAmE*) a credit card provided by your bank, that can also be used as a DEBIT CARD and to get money from your account out of a machine 銀行信用卡；取款機提款卡

ˈbank draft (also **ˈbanker's draft**) *noun* a cheque paid by a bank to another bank or to a particular person or organization 銀行匯票

bank·er /ˈbæŋkə(r)/ *noun* **1** a person who owns a bank or has an important job at a bank 銀行老闆（或要員）；銀行家：*a merchant banker* 投資銀行家 **2** a person who is in charge of the money in particular games（某些賭博遊戲中的）莊家

ˌbanker's ˈorder *noun* (*BrE*) an instruction to your bank to pay money to sb directly from your bank account 付款委託，自動轉賬委託（讓銀行直接從賬戶付款）➲ compare STANDING ORDER

ˌbank ˈholiday (*BrE*) *noun* a public holiday, for example Christmas Day, New Year's Day, etc. 銀行假日（公共假日，如聖誕節、元旦等）：*Bank Holiday Monday* 銀行假日星期一 ◇ *a bank holiday weekend* (= a weekend followed by a Monday which is a holiday) 銀行假日週末（之後的星期一為假日的大週末）➲ compare LEGAL HOLIDAY, PUBLIC HOLIDAY ➲ see also HOLIDAY

bank·ing /ˈbæŋkɪŋ/ *noun* [U] the business activity of banks 銀行業：*She's thinking about a career in banking.* 她正在考慮從事銀行業。

bank·note /ˈbæŋknəʊt; *NAmE* -noʊt/ *noun* (*especially BrE*) = NOTE *n.* (6)：*forged* (= illegally copied) *banknotes* 偽鈔

ˈbank rate *noun* the rate of interest charged by a bank for lending money, which is fixed by a central bank in a country 銀行利率；銀行貼現率

bank·roll /ˈbæŋkrəʊl; *NAmE* -roʊl/ *verb, noun*

■ ***verb*** **~ sb/sth** (*informal, especially NAmE*) to support sb/sth by giving money 資助；提供資金 **SYN** **finance**：*They claimed his campaign had been bankrolled with drug money.* 他們聲稱他的競選活動是由販毒資金支持的。

■ ***noun*** (*especially NAmE*) a supply of money 資金：*He is the candidate with the biggest campaign bankroll.* 他是競選資金最雄厚的候選人。

bank·rupt /ˈbæŋkrʌpt/ *adj., noun, verb*

■ ***adj.*** **1** without enough money to pay what you owe 破產；倒閉 **SYN** **insolvent**：*They **went bankrupt** in 2009.* 他們於 2009 年破產。◇ *The company was **declared bankrupt** in the High Court.* 那家公司經高等法院宣告破產了。**2 ~ (of sth)** (*formal, disapproving*) completely lacking in anything that has value 完全缺乏（有價值的東西）：*a government bankrupt of new ideas* 完全缺乏新觀念的政府 ◇ *a society that is morally bankrupt* 道德淪喪的社會

■ ***noun*** (*law* 律) a person who has been judged by a court to be unable to pay his or her debts（經法院判決的）破產者

■ ***verb*** **~ sb** to make sb bankrupt 使破產：*The company was almost bankrupted by legal costs.* 這家公司為律師費用所累幾乎破產。

bank·rupt·cy /ˈbæŋkrʌptsi/ *noun* [U, C] (*pl.* **-ies**) the state of being bankrupt 破產 **SYN** **insolvency**：*The company **filed for bankruptcy*** (= asked to be officially bankrupt) *in 2009.* 這家公司於 2009 年提交了破產申請。◇ ***moral/political bankruptcy*** 道德的淪喪；政治的破產 ◇ *There could be further bankruptcies among small farmers.* 小農場主中可能還會有人破產。➲ COLLOCATIONS at BUSINESS

ˈbank statement (also **state·ment**) *noun* a printed record of all the money paid into and out of a customer's bank account within a particular period 銀行結單（某時期內存戶存取款項的清單）

ban·ner /ˈbænə(r)/ *noun* a long piece of cloth with a message on it that is carried between two poles or hung in a public place to show support for sth 橫幅；旗幡：*Protesters carried a banner reading 'Save our Wildlife'.* 抗議者打着"救救我們的野生生物"字樣的橫幅。➲ VISUAL VOCAB pages V2, V3

ˈbanner ad *noun* an advertisement across the top or bottom or down the side of a page on the Internet（互聯網上的）通欄廣告，橫幅廣告；網幅廣告

ˌbanner ˈheadline *noun* a line of words printed in large letters across the front page of a newspaper（報紙頭版的）通欄大標題

ˌbanner ˈyear *noun* (*NAmE*) a year in which sth is especially successful 輝煌的一年

ban·nis·ter = BANISTER

banns /bænz/ *noun* [pl.] a public statement in church that two people intend to marry each other（教堂裏的）結婚預告

B

ban·offi pie (also **ba,n·offee 'pie**) /bəˌnɒfi ˈpaɪ; *NAmE* bəˌnɔːfi; -ˌnɑːf-/ *noun* a sweet food made with TOFFEE, BANANAS and cream 香蕉太妃派（用乳脂糖、香蕉和奶油製成）

ban·quet /ˈbæŋkwɪt/ *noun* **1** a formal meal for a large number of people, usually for a special occasion, at which speeches are often made 宴會；盛宴： *a state banquet in honour of the visiting President* 為來訪總統舉辦的國宴 **2** a large impressive meal 筵席

ban·quet·ing /ˈbæŋkwɪtɪŋ/ *adj.* connected with banquets 宴會的： *a banqueting hall* 宴會廳

ban·quette /bæŋˈket/ *noun* a long soft seat along a wall in a restaurant, etc.（飯店等沿牆的）長軟座，長沙發

ban·shee /bænˈʃiː; ˈbænʃiː/ *noun* (in Irish stories) a female spirit who gives a long sad cry as a warning to people that sb in their family is going to die soon 猜女（愛爾蘭傳說中預報死訊的女妖）

ban·tam /ˈbæntəm/ *noun* a type of small chicken 矮腳雞

ban·tam·weight /ˈbæntəmweɪt/ *noun* a BOXER weighing between 51 and 53.5 kilograms, or a WRESTLER who weighs between 52 and 57 kilograms, heavier than a FLYWEIGHT 最輕量級拳擊運動員（體重為 51 到 53.5 公斤）；次輕量級摔跤運動員（體重為 52 到 57 公斤）： *a bantamweight champion* 最輕量級拳擊冠軍

ban·ter /ˈbæntə(r)/ *noun, verb*

■ ***noun*** [U] friendly remarks and jokes（善意的）玩笑，打趣： *He enjoyed exchanging banter with the customers.* 他喜歡和顧客開玩笑。

■ ***verb*** [I] **~ (with sb)** to joke with sb（和某人）開玩笑；逗樂： *He bantered with reporters and posed for photographers.* 他和記者們打趣，並擺姿勢讓他們拍照。

ban·ter·ing /ˈbæntərɪŋ/ *adj.* (of a way of talking 講話方式) amusing and friendly 風趣的；詼諧的： *There was a friendly, bantering tone in his voice.* 他的聲音裏流露着友好詼諧的語調。

ban·yan /ˈbænjən/ (also **ˈbanyan tree**) *noun* a S Asian tree with structures that grow down from the branches to the ground and then grow into new roots and TRUNKS 榕樹（見於南亞，樹枝上有氣根伸入土壤，變成新的樹幹）

bao·bab /ˈbeɪəʊbæb; *NAmE* ˈbeɪoʊ-/ *noun* a short thick tree, found especially in Africa and Australia, that lives for many years 猴麪包，瓶樹（尤見於非洲和澳大利亞，生命力強）

bap /bæp/ *noun* (*BrE*) a round flat bread roll 圓麪包 ➲ see also BUN (2)

bap·tism /ˈbæptɪzəm/ *noun* a Christian ceremony in which a few drops of water are poured on sb or they are covered with water, to welcome them into the Christian Church and often to name them（基督教的）洗禮，浸禮 ➲ compare CHRISTENING

IDM **a ˌbaptism of ˈfire** a difficult introduction to a new job or activity 重大的考驗；戰火的洗禮

bap·tis·mal /bæpˈtɪzməl/ *adj.* [only before noun] connected with baptism 洗禮的；浸禮的： ***a baptismal service/ceremony*** 洗禮儀式

Bap·tist /ˈbæptɪst/ *noun* a member of a Christian Protestant Church that believes that baptism should take place when a person is old enough to understand what it means, and not as a baby 浸禮會教徒 ▸ **Bap·tist** *adj.* [usually before noun]： *a Baptist church* 浸禮會教派

bap·tize (*BrE* also **-ise**) /bæpˈtaɪz/ *verb* [usually passive] **~ sb (+ noun)** to give sb BAPTISM 授洗；付洗；施洗： *She was baptized Mary.* 她受洗時取名為瑪麗。◇ *I was baptized a Catholic.* 我領洗成為天主教徒。➲ see also CHRISTEN (1)

Bapu /ˈbɑːpuː/ *noun* (*IndE*) **1** (used especially as a form of address 尤用作稱呼) a father 父親；爸爸 **2** a name by which Mahatma Gandhi is referred to, showing affection 巴普（對聖雄甘地的愛稱）

bars 吧枱；條；棒

bar 吧枱

sandwich bar 三明治櫃枱

five-bar gate 五根木的柵門

bars on a window 窗條

bar of chocolate 巧克力塊

bar of soap 肥皂塊

barcode 條碼

bars on an electric fire 電取暖器的電熱棒

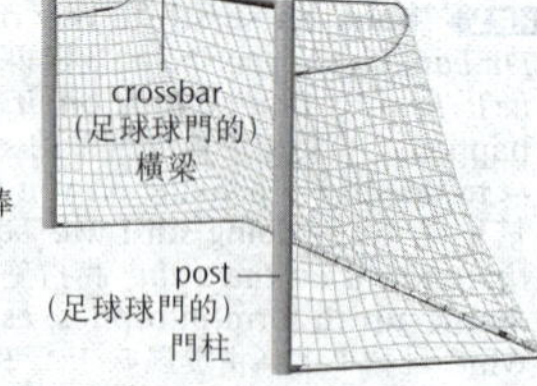

crossbar 橫梁

bar of music 樂譜的小節

bar 🔑 /bɑː(r)/ *noun, verb, prep.*

■ ***noun***

▸ **FOR DRINKS/FOOD** 飲食 **1** 🔑 [C] a place where you can buy and drink alcoholic and other drinks 酒吧： *We met at a bar called the Flamingo.* 我們在一家名為弗拉明戈的酒吧相遇。◇ *the island's only **licensed bar*** (= one that is allowed to sell alcoholic drinks) 島上唯一有酒類銷售許可證的酒吧 ◇ *a cocktail bar* 雞尾酒酒吧 ◇ (*BrE*) *I found David in the bar of the Red Lion* (= a room in a pub where drinks are served). 我在紅獅酒吧找到了戴維。➲ see also BARROOM, LOUNGE BAR, MINIBAR, PUBLIC BAR, SALOON BAR at SALOON (2) **2** 🔑 [C] a long wide wooden surface where drinks, etc. are served（出售飲料等的）櫃枱；吧枱： *She was sitting at the bar.* 她坐在吧枱那裏。◇ *It was so crowded I couldn't get to the bar.* 人太多了，我無法擠到吧枱那兒。 **3** 🔑 [C] (especially in compounds 尤用於構成複合詞) a place in which a particular kind of food or drink is the main thing that is served（專售某類飲食的）小吃店，館，處所： *a sandwich bar* 三明治店 ◇ *a coffee bar* 咖啡館 ➲ see also OXYGEN BAR, SNACK BAR, WINE BAR

▸ **OF CHOCOLATE/SOAP** 巧克力；肥皂 **4** 🔑 [C] a piece of sth with straight sides（長方形）條，塊： *a **bar of*** *chocolate/soap* 一條巧克力／肥皂◇*candy bars* 糖棒

▸ **OF METAL/WOOD 金屬；木材** **5** [C] a long straight piece of metal or wood. Bars are often used to stop sb from getting through a space. 長條，棒，欄杆（常用作護欄）：*He smashed the window with an iron bar.* 他用鐵棒敲碎了窗戶。◇*All the ground floor windows were fitted with bars.* 底層所有的窗戶都裝了鐵柵。◇*a five-bar gate* (= one made with five horizontal bars of wood) 用五根橫木條釘成的柵門 ➲ VISUAL VOCAB page V46 ➲ see also BULL BARS, ROLL BAR, SPACE BAR, TOW BAR

▸ **IN ELECTRIC FIRE 電熱爐** **6** [C] a piece of metal with wire wrapped around it that becomes red and hot when electricity is passed through it 電熱棒

▸ **IN SPORTS 體育運動** **7 the bar** [sing.] the CROSSBAR of a goal（球門的）橫梁：*His shot hit the bar.* 他射門擊中球門的橫梁。

▸ **OF COLOUR/LIGHT 顏色；光** **8** [C] a band of colour or light 條；帶：*Bars of sunlight slanted down from the tall narrow windows.* 一道道陽光從高高的狹窄窗口斜射下來。

▸ **THAT PREVENTS STH 障礙** **9** [C, usually sing.] ~ **(to sth)** a thing that stops sb from doing sth 障礙；羈絆：*At that time being a woman was a bar to promotion in most professions.* 那時在大多數職業中，身為女性就是晉升的障礙。➲ see also COLOUR BAR

▸ **IN MUSIC 音樂** **10** (*BrE*) (*NAmE* **meas·ure**) [C] one of the short sections of equal length that a piece of music is divided into, and the notes that are in it（樂譜的）小節：*four beats to the bar* 每小節四拍◇*the opening bars of a piece of music* 樂曲開頭的幾個小節 ➲ picture at MUSIC

▸ **LAW 法律** **11 the Bar** [sing.] (*BrE*) the profession of BARRISTER (= a lawyer in a higher court) 大律師專業（可出席高等法庭）：*to* ***be called to the Bar*** (= allowed to work as a qualified BARRISTER) 獲得大律師資格 **12 the Bar** [sing.] (*NAmE*) the profession of any kind of lawyer 律師專業

▸ **MEASUREMENT 度量** **13** a unit for measuring the pressure of the atmosphere, equal to a hundred thousand NEWTONS per square metre 巴（氣壓單位，等於 100 000 牛頓／平方米）➲ see also MILLIBAR

IDM **not have a 'bar of sth** (*AustralE, NZE*) to have nothing to do with sth 與（某事）無關；與（某事）毫不相干；不沾手：*If he tries to sell you his car, don't have a bar of it.* 他若是想要把車賣給你，你可別去理他。**be,hind 'bars** (*informal*) in prison 蹲班房；被監禁；坐牢：*The murderer is now safely behind bars.* 殺人犯現在被關在監獄裏，不會再造成危險了。**set the 'bar** to set a standard of quality or performance 設定標準：*The show really sets the bar for artistic invention.* 這場演出真正為藝術創新設立了標杆。➲ more at LOWER[1] *v.*, RAISE *v.*

■ ***verb*** **(-rr-)**

▸ **CLOSE WITH BARS 用鐵條等封住** **1** [usually passive] ~ **sth** to close sth with a bar or bars（用鐵條或木條）封，堵：*All the doors and windows were barred.* 所有的門、窗都加上了鐵條。

▸ **BLOCK 阻擋** **2** ~ **sth** to block a road, path, etc. so that nobody can pass 阻擋；攔住：*Two police officers were barring her exit.* 兩名警察擋着她的出路。◇*We found our way barred by rocks.* 我們發現大石塊擋住了我們的路。

▸ **PREVENT 阻止** **3** ~ **sb (from sth/from doing sth)** to ban or prevent sb from doing sth 禁止，阻止（某人做某事）：*The players are barred from drinking alcohol the night before a match.* 運動員在參賽前夜不得喝酒。**IDM** see HOLD *n.*

■ ***prep.*** (*especially BrE*) except for sb/sth 除…外：*The students all attended, bar two who were ill.* 除了兩人生病，所有的學生都到了。◇*It's the best result we've ever had,* ***bar none*** (= none was better). 這是我們所取得的前所未有的最好成績。**IDM** see SHOUTING

bar·aza /bəˈrɑːzə/ *noun* (*EAfrE*) a public meeting that is held in order to discuss important matters affecting the community 社區集會；社區大會

barb /bɑːb; *NAmE* bɑːrb/ *noun* **1** the point of an arrow or a hook that is curved backwards to make it difficult to pull out（箭、鉤的）倒鉤，倒刺 **2** a remark that is meant to hurt sb's feelings 挖苦（或傷人、帶刺）的話 ➲ see also BARBED

Vocabulary Building 詞彙擴充

A bar of chocolate

If you want to describe a whole unit of a particular substance, or a group of things that are normally together, for example when you buy them, you need to use the correct word. 指一件或一組東西（如購物時）須用恰當的量詞。

- a **bar** of soap/chocolate; a candy **bar** 一條肥皂／巧克力；糖果棒
- a **block** of ice/stone/wood 一大塊冰／石頭／木頭
- a **bolt/roll/length** of fabric 一匹／一捲／一段織物
- a **cube** of ice/sugar; an ice/sugar **cube** 一塊冰塊／方糖
- a **loaf** of bread 一條麪包
- a **roll** of film/carpet 一捲膠片／地毯
- a **slab** of marble/concrete 大理石板；混泥土板
- a **stick** of gum 一條口香糖
- a **bunch** of bananas/grapes 一串香蕉／葡萄
- a **bunch/bouquet** of flowers 一束花
- a **bundle** of sticks 一捆枝條
- a **set/bunch** of keys 一套／一串鑰匙
- a **set** of chairs/glasses/clothes/guitar strings 一套椅子／玻璃杯／衣服；一副吉他弦

bar·bar·ian /bɑːˈbeəriən; *NAmE* bɑːrˈber-/ *noun* **1** a person long ago in the past who belonged to a European people which was considered wild and UNCIVILIZED（古代歐洲原始部落的）野蠻人：*barbarian invasions of the fifth century* * 5 世紀時野蠻人的入侵 **2** a person who behaves very badly and has no respect for art, education, etc. 沒有文化的人；粗野的人

bar·bar·ic /bɑːˈbærɪk; *NAmE* bɑːrˈb-/ *adj.* **1** cruel and violent and not as expected from people who are educated and respect each other 殘暴的；野蠻的；沒有文化的：*a* ***barbaric act/custom/ritual*** 野蠻的行為／習俗／儀式◇*The way these animals are killed is barbaric.* 宰殺這些動物的手段很殘忍。**2** connected with BARBARIANS (1) 野蠻人的；原始部落人的 ▸ **bar·bar·ic·al·ly** /-kli/ *adv.*

bar·bar·ism /ˈbɑːbərɪzəm; *NAmE* ˈbɑːrb-/ *noun* [U] **1** a state of not having any education, respect for art, etc. 野蠻；未開化；不文明 **2** cruel or violent behaviour 殘暴的行為；殘酷：*the barbarism of war* 戰爭的殘酷

bar·bar·ity /bɑːˈbærəti; *NAmE* bɑːrˈb-/ *noun* (*pl.* **-ies**) [U, C] behaviour that deliberately causes extreme pain or suffering to others 暴行；殘忍

bar·bar·ous /ˈbɑːbərəs; *NAmE* ˈbɑːrb-/ *adj.* (*formal*) **1** extremely cruel and shocking 殘酷的；駭人聽聞的：*the barbarous treatment of these prisoners of war* 對這些戰犯的殘酷待遇 **2** showing a lack of education and good manners 缺乏教養的；粗野的 ▸ **bar·bar·ous·ly** *adv.*

bar·be·cue /ˈbɑːbɪkjuː; *NAmE* ˈbɑːrb-/ *noun, verb*

■ ***noun*** (*abbr.* **BBQ**) (also *informal* **bar·bie** *BrE, AustralE*) **1** a metal frame for cooking food on over an open fire outdoors（燒烤野餐用的）烤架：*I put another steak on the barbecue.* 我在烤架上又放了一塊肉排。◇*a barbecue sausage* (= cooked in this way) 烤香腸 ➲ VISUAL VOCAB pages V19, V27 **2** an outdoor meal or party when food is cooked in this way 燒烤野餐：*Let's have a barbecue!* 我們來一次戶外燒烤吧！➲ compare COOKOUT

■ ***verb*** [T, I] ~ **(sth)** to cook food on a barbecue 燒烤野餐 ➲ compare BROIL (1)

,barbecue 'sauce *noun* [C, U] a spicy sauce served with food that has been cooked on a barbecue 烤肉醬

barbed /bɑːbd; *NAmE* bɑːrbd/ *adj.* **1** (of an ARROW or a hook 箭或鉤) having a point that is curved backwards (called a BARB) 有倒鉤的 **2** (of a remark or comment

說話或評論) meant to hurt sb's feelings 挖苦的；傷人的；帶刺的

B

barbed wire 帶刺鐵絲網

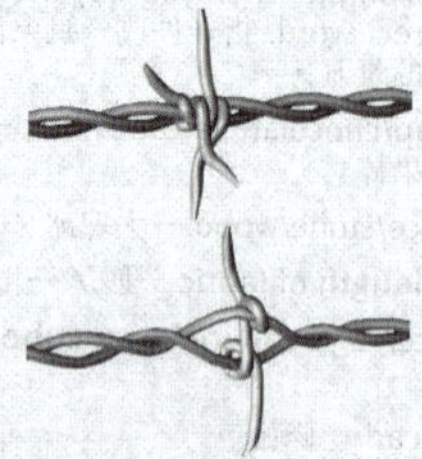

ˌ**barbed 'wire** *noun* [U] strong wire with short sharp points on it, used especially for fences 帶刺鐵絲網（尤用作圍欄）：*a barbed wire fence* 帶刺鐵絲網圍欄

bar·bell /'bɑːbel; *NAmE* 'bɑːrbel/ *noun* a long metal bar with weights at each end, used in the sport of WEIGHT-LIFTING and for exercise 槓鈴（舉重器械）➲ VISUAL VOCAB page V42

bar·ber /'bɑːbə(r); *NAmE* 'bɑːrb-/ *noun* **1** a person whose job is to cut men's hair and sometimes to shave them（兼刮鬍子的）理髮師 **2** (also **barber's**) (both *BrE*) (*pl.* **bar·bers**) a shop where men can have their hair cut（男子）理髮店 ➲ compare HAIRDRESSER

bar·ber·shop /'bɑːbəʃɒp; *NAmE* 'bɑːrbərʃɑːp/ *noun* **1** (*especially NAmE*) (*BrE* usually **barber's**) [C] a place where a barber works 理髮店 **2** [U] a type of light music for four parts sung by men, without instruments 理髮店四重唱（一種無樂器伴奏的男聲四重唱）：*a barbershop quartet* 男聲四重唱

ˌ**barber's 'pole** *noun* a pole painted with a SPIRAL of red and white that is traditionally hung outside a barber's shop 轉花筒（掛在理髮店外的紅白兩色旋轉彩柱，為理髮店傳統標誌）

bar·bie /'bɑːbi; *NAmE* 'bɑːrbi/ *noun* (*BrE, AustralE, informal*) = BARBECUE

'**Barbie doll™** (also **Barbie**) *noun* **1** a DOLL that looks like an attractive young woman 芭比娃娃 **2** (*informal*) a woman who is sexually attractive, especially one who is thought to be stupid or boring 芭比女郎（尤指愚蠢或俗氣的性感女子）

ˌ**bar 'billiards** *noun* [U] (*BrE*) a game played on a small table, in which you try to hit balls into holes without knocking down the small wooden objects that stand in front of the holes 酒吧枱球，酒吧撞球（小型枱球遊戲，須擊球入洞，不得撞倒洞口障礙木塊）

bar·bit·ur·ate /bɑː'bɪtʃʊrət; *NAmE* bɑːr'b-/ *noun* a powerful drug that makes you feel calm and relaxed or puts you to sleep. There are several types of barbiturate. 巴比土酸鹽，巴比妥酸鹽（用於鎮靜、催眠等）

Bar·bour™ /'bɑːbə(r); *NAmE* 'bɑːrbər/ *noun* a type of coat, usually dark green, made of special cotton with WAX on it that protects against rain and wind 巴伯風雨衣（通常為深綠色，用蠟棉布製成）

'**bar chart** (also '**bar graph**) *noun* a diagram that uses lines or narrow RECTANGLES (= bars) of different heights (but equal widths) to show different amounts, so that they can be compared 柱形圖（以不同長度的條形表示不同數量以作比較）➲ WRITING TUTOR page WT25 ➲ compare HISTOGRAM

bar·code /'bɑːkəʊd; *NAmE* 'bɑːrkoʊd/ *noun* a pattern of thick and thin lines that is printed on things you buy. It contains information that a computer can read. 條碼 ➲ picture at BAR

bard /bɑːd; *NAmE* bɑːrd/ *noun* (*literary*) a person who writes poems 詩人

bare /beə(r); *NAmE* ber/ *adj., verb*

■ ***adj.*** (**barer, bar·est**) **1** not covered by any clothes 裸體的；裸露的：*She likes to walk around in **bare feet**.* 她喜歡光着腳走來走去。➲ see also BAREFOOT **2** (of trees or countryside 樹木或村野) not covered with leaves; without plants or trees（樹木）光禿禿的；（土地）荒蕪的：*the bare branches of winter trees* 冬天樹木光禿禿的枝椏 ◇ *a bare mountainside* 光禿禿的山坡 **3** (of surfaces 表面) not covered with or protected by anything 無遮蓋的；沒有保護的：*bare wooden floorboards* 未鋪地毯的木地板 ◇ *Bare wires were sticking out of the cable.* 電纜露出了裸線。◇ *The walls were bare except for a clock.* 牆上除了一隻掛鐘什麼也沒有。**4** (of a room, cupboard, etc. 房間、櫃子等) empty 空的：*The fridge was completely bare.* 電冰箱裏什麼也沒有。◇ *bare shelves* 空蕩蕩的架子 **5** [only before noun] just enough; the most basic or simple 僅夠的；最基本的；最簡單的：*The family was short of even the **bare necessities** of life.* 那家人甚至沒有最起碼的生活所需。◇ *We only had the **bare essentials** in the way of equipment.* 我們只有最基本的設備。◇ *He did the **bare minimum** of work but still passed the exam.* 他只花了最少的工夫，卻仍然通過了考試。◇ *She gave me only the bare facts of the case.* 她只給我介紹了這個案件的一些基本資料。◇ *It was the barest hint of a smile.* 那是一個幾乎不露一絲痕跡的笑。➲ SYNONYMS at NAKED, PLAIN ▸ **bare·ness** *noun* [U]

IDM **the bare 'bones (of sth)** the basic facts 梗概；概要：*the bare bones of the story* 故事梗概 **with your bare 'hands** without weapons or tools 赤手空拳；徒手：*He was capable of killing a man with his bare hands.* 他赤手空拳就能取人性命。**lay sth 'bare** (*formal*) to show sth that was covered or to make sth known that was secret 暴露；揭露：*Every aspect of their private lives has been laid bare.* 他們的私生活全面曝光了。➲ more at CUPBOARD

■ ***verb* ~ sth** to remove the covering from sth, especially from part of the body 揭開；脫（衣服）：*She was paid several thousand dollars to **bare all** (= take all her clothes off) for the magazine.* 她獲得數千元報酬為那本雜誌作全裸畫頁。

IDM **bare your 'soul (to sb)** to tell sb your deepest and most private feelings （向某人）打開心扉，傾訴衷腸 **bare your 'teeth** to show your teeth in an aggressive and threatening way （兇狠地）齜牙咧嘴：*The dog bared its teeth and growled.* 那條狗齜牙咧嘴地低吼。

bare·back /'beəbæk; *NAmE* 'berb-/ *adj., adv.* on a horse without a SADDLE（騎馬）不用馬鞍（的）：*a bareback rider* 不用馬鞍的騎手 ◇ *riding bareback* 不用馬鞍騎馬

bare·faced /'beəfeɪst; *NAmE* 'berf-/ *adj.* [only before noun] (*disapproving*) showing that you do not care about offending sb or about behaving badly 厚顏無恥的；公然的；露骨的 **SYN** **bald-faced, blatant**：*a barefaced lie* 無恥的謊言 ◇ *barefaced cheek* 厚顏無恥

bare·foot /'beəfʊt; *NAmE* 'berf-/ (also *less frequent* **bare·foot·ed**) *adj., adv.* not wearing anything on your feet 赤腳（的）：*poor children going barefoot in the street* 光着腳流落街頭的窮孩子

bare·head·ed /ˌbeə'hedɪd; *NAmE* ˌber'h-/ *adj., adv.* not wearing anything to cover your head 頭上不戴東西（的）；光着頭（的）

ˌ**bare-'knuckle** (also ˌ**bare-'knuckled**) *adj.* [only before noun] (of a BOXER or BOXING match 拳擊手或拳擊比賽) without gloves 不戴拳擊手套的

bare·ly /'beəli; *NAmE* 'berli/ *adv.* **1** in a way that is just possible but only with difficulty 僅僅；剛剛；勉強可能：*The music was barely audible.* 音樂聲勉強能聽見。◇ *She was barely able to stand.* 她勉強能站立。◇ *We barely had time to catch the train.* 我們差點沒趕上火車。**2** in a way that almost does not happen or exist 幾乎不；幾乎沒有：*She barely acknowledged his presence.* 她只略微向他打了個招呼。◇ *There was barely any smell.* 幾乎沒有什麼氣味。**3** just; certainly not more than (a particular amount, age, time, etc.) 剛好；不超過（某個數量、年齡、時間等）：*Barely 50% of the population voted.* 僅有50%的人口投票。◇ *He was barely 20 years old and already running his own company.* 他只有20歲，卻已經

B

營起自己的公司了。◇ *They arrived barely a minute later.* 過了不到一分鐘他們就到了。 **4** only a very short time before 剛才；剛剛： *I had barely started speaking when he interrupted me.* 我剛剛開始講話，他便打斷了我。 ➲ note at HARDLY

barf /bɑːf; *NAmE* bɑːrf/ *verb* [I] (*NAmE, informal*) to VOMIT 嘔吐 ▸ **barf** *noun* [U]

bar·fly /ˈbɑːflaɪ; *NAmE* ˈbɑːr-/ *noun* (*pl.* **-ies**) (*informal*) a person who spends a lot of time drinking in bars 酒吧常客

bar·gain 0━ /ˈbɑːɡən; *NAmE* ˈbɑːrɡən/ *noun, verb*

■ ***noun*** **1** 0━ a thing bought for less than the usual price 減價品；便宜貨： *I picked up a few good bargains in the sale.* 我在減價期間買了幾樣挺不錯的便宜貨。◇ *The car was a bargain at that price.* 那輛車的價格真便宜。◇ *bargain prices* 廉價 ➲ COLLOCATIONS at SHOPPING **2** ~ (**with sb**) an agreement between two or more people or groups, to do sth for each other 協議；交易： *He and his partner had* ***made a bargain*** *to tell each other everything.* 他和他的合夥人約定，要互通信息，毫無保留。◇ *I've done what I promised and I expect you to* ***keep your side of the bargain*** (= do what you agreed in return). 我已經履約，希望你也能遵守協議。◇ *Finally the two sides* ***struck a bargain*** (= reached an agreement). 雙方最終達成了協議。

IDM **into the ˈbargain** (*BrE*) (*NAmE* **in the ˈbargain**) (used to emphasize an extra piece of information 強調額外的信息) also; as well 另外；而且；也： *Volunteers learn a lot and enjoy themselves into the bargain.* 志願者在學到很多東西的同時還能得到樂趣。 ➲ more at HARD *adj.*, STRIKE *v.*

■ ***verb*** [I] to discuss prices, conditions, etc. with sb in order to reach an agreement that is acceptable（與某人就某事）討價還價，商討條件 SYN **negotiate**： ~ (**with sb**) (**about/over/for sth**) *In the market dealers were bargaining with growers over the price of coffee.* 在市場上商人正和種植者就咖啡的價格進行商談。◇ *He said he wasn't prepared to bargain.* 他說他不願討價還價。

PHR V ˌ**bargain sth↔aˈway** to give sth away and not get sth of equal value in return 做虧本交易；賤賣： *They felt that their leaders had bargained away their freedom.* 他們認為他們的領導人以犧牲他們的自由做了交易。 ˈ**bargain for/on sth** (usually in negative sentences 通常用於否定句) to expect sth to happen and be prepared for it 預料到；料想到： *We hadn't bargained for this sudden change in the weather.* 我們沒有預料到這樣的天氣突變。◇ *When he agreed to answer a few questions,* ***he got more than he bargained for*** (= he got more questions, or more difficult ones, than he had expected). 他同意回答幾個問題，不料卻招來了一堆難以回答的問題。◇ ~ **doing sth** *I didn't bargain on finding them here as well.* 我沒想到還會在這裏遇到他們。◇ ~ **sb doing sth** *I hadn't bargained on them being here.* 我沒想到他們會在這裏。

ˌ**bargain ˈbasement** *noun* a part of a large shop/store, usually in the floor below street level, where goods are sold at reduced prices（商場的）地下減價商品部： *bargain-basement prices* 減價部的價格

ˈ**bargain hunter** *noun* a person who is looking for goods that are good value for money, usually because they are being sold at prices that are lower than usual 減價品搜尋者；專買便宜貨者 ▸ ˈ**bargain hunting** *noun* [U]

bar·gain·ing /ˈbɑːɡənɪŋ; *NAmE* ˈbɑːrɡ-/ *noun* [U] discussion of prices, conditions, etc. with the aim of reaching an agreement that is acceptable 討價還價；商談；商討 SYN **negotiation**： *After much* ***hard bargaining*** *we reached an agreement.* 經過一番艱難的討價還價，我們達成了協議。◇ *wage bargaining* 有關工資的談判 ◇ *Exporters are in a strong* ***bargaining position*** *at the moment.* 目前出口商在洽談中處於有利地位。 ➲ see also COLLECTIVE BARGAINING, PLEA-BARGAINING

ˈ**bargaining chip** (*BrE* also ˈ**bargaining counter**) *noun* a fact or a thing that a person or a group of people can use to get an advantage for themselves when they are trying to reach an agreement with another group 籌碼；談判中的有利條件

ˈ**bargaining power** *noun* [U] the amount of control a person or group has when trying to reach an agreement with another group in a business or political situation（談判中一方的）討價還價的能力

barge /bɑːdʒ; *NAmE* bɑːrdʒ/ *noun, verb*

■ ***noun*** a large boat with a flat bottom, used for carrying goods and people on CANALS and rivers 駁船（運河、河流上運載客貨的大型平底船）

■ ***verb*** [I, T] + **adv./prep.** to move in an awkward way, pushing people out of the way or crashing into them 衝撞；亂闖 SYN **push**： *He barged past me to get to the bar.* 他經過我的身邊向賣酒的櫃枱硬擠過去。◇ *They* ***barged their way*** *through the crowds.* 他們橫衝直撞地擠過人群。

PHR V ˌ**barge ˈin** (**on sb/sth**) to enter a place or join a group of people, rudely interrupting what sb else is doing or saying 闖入；插嘴；打岔： *I hope you don't mind me barging in like this.* 希望你不介意我如此冒昧打岔。◇ *He barged in on us while we were having a meeting.* 我們正在開會，他闖了進來。

barge·board /ˈbɑːdʒbɔːd; *NAmE* ˈbɑːrdʒbɔːrd/ *noun* a board that is fixed to the end of a roof to hide the ends of the wooden roof BEAMS 山牆封簷板

bar·gee /bɑːˈdʒiː; *NAmE* bɑːrˈdʒiː/ *noun* a person who controls or works on a BARGE 駁船船長；駁船船員

barge·pole /ˈbɑːdʒpəʊl; *NAmE* ˈbɑːrdʒpoʊl/ *noun* IDM see TOUCH *v.*

ˈ**bar graph** *noun* = BAR CHART

ˈ**bar-hop** *verb* [I] (**-pp-**) (*NAmE, informal*) to drink in a series of bars in a single day or evening 逐吧買醉（一天或一夜之中從一家酒吧喝到另一家）

bar·is·ta (also **Bar·is·ta**™) /bəˈriːstə; -ˈrɪs-/ *noun* a person who works in a COFFEE BAR 小咖啡廳服務生

bari·tone /ˈbærɪtəʊn; *NAmE* -toʊn/ *noun* **1** a man's singing voice with a range between TENOR and BASS; a man with a baritone voice 男中音；男中音歌手 **2** a musical instrument that is second lowest in PITCH in its family 上低音號 ▸ **bari·tone** *adj.* ➲ compare ALTO *n.* (1), BASS[1] *n.* (2), TENOR *n.* (1)

bar·ium /ˈbeəriəm; *NAmE* ˈber-/ *noun* [U] (*symb.* **Ba**) a chemical element that is a soft silver-white metal 鋇

ˌ**barium ˈmeal** *noun* a substance containing barium that a doctor gives sb to swallow before an X-RAY because it makes organs in the body easier to see 鋇液（X 光造影劑）

bark /bɑːk; *NAmE* bɑːrk/ *noun, verb*

■ ***noun*** [U, C] **1** the outer covering of a tree 樹皮 ➲ VISUAL VOCAB page V10 **2** the short loud sound made by dogs and some other animals（狗等的）吠聲，嗥叫聲 **3** a short loud sound made by a gun or a voice 槍聲；短促響亮的人聲： *a bark of laughter* 一聲大笑

IDM **sb's bark is worse than their bite** (*informal*) used to say that sb is not really as angry or as aggressive as they sound 嘴硬心軟；說話強硬，其實並不傷人；貌似兇狠

■ ***verb*** **1** [I] ~ (**at sb/sth**) when a dog **barks**, it makes a short loud sound（狗）吠叫： *The dog suddenly started barking at us.* 那條狗突然開始對我們汪汪叫。 **2** [T] to give orders, ask questions, etc. in a loud, unfriendly way 厲聲發令；厲聲質問： ~ **out sth** *She barked out an order.* 她厲聲下命令。◇ ~ **sth** (**at sb**) *He barked questions at her.* 他厲聲質問她。◇ + **speech** *'Who are you?' he barked.* "你是誰？" 他厲聲質問道。 **3** [T] ~ **sth** (*especially BrE*) to rub the skin off your knee, etc. by falling or by knocking against sth 擦破（或蹭掉）…的皮 SYN **graze**

IDM **be barking up the wrong ˈtree** (*informal*) to have the wrong idea about how to get or achieve sth 把方法搞錯（或想偏）；走錯路線： *You're barking up the wrong tree if you're expecting us to lend you any money.* 你要是指望我們借錢給你，你是走錯廟門了。 IDM see DOG *n.*

bark·er /ˈbɑːkə(r); *NAmE* ˈbɑːrk-/ *noun* a person who stands outside a place where there is entertainment and shouts to people to go in（在娛樂場所門外）大聲招徠顧客者，拉客者

B

ˌbark·ing ˈmad (also **bark·ing**) *adj.* (*BrE, informal*) completely crazy 瘋狂透頂的；完全發瘋的

bar·ley /ˈbɑːli; *NAmE* ˈbɑːrli/ *noun* [U] a plant grown for its grain that is used for making food, beer and WHISKY; the grains of this plant 大麥；大麥粒 ➲ VISUAL VOCAB page V32

ˈbarley sugar *noun* [U] a hard clear sweet/candy made from boiled sugar 大麥糖；麥芽糖

ˈbarley water *noun* [U] (*BrE*) a drink made by boiling BARLEY in water. It is usually flavoured with orange or lemon. 大麥茶（常以柑橘或檸檬調味）：*lemon barley water* 檸檬大麥茶

ˌbarley ˈwine *noun* [U] a strong English beer 大麥啤酒（英格蘭啤酒，酒精度高）

ˈbar line *noun* (*music* 音) a vertical line used in written music to mark a division between BARS/MEASURES 小節線

bar·maid /ˈbɑːmeɪd; *NAmE* ˈbɑːrm-/ (*BrE*) (*NAmE* **bar·tend·er**) *noun* a woman who works in a bar, serving drinks 酒吧女招待

bar·man /ˈbɑːmən; *NAmE* ˈbɑːrmən/ *noun* (*pl.* **-men** /-mən/) (*especially BrE*) (*NAmE* usually **bar·tend·er**) a man who works in a bar, serving drinks 酒吧男招待；酒吧男侍

bar mitz·vah /ˌbɑː ˈmɪtsvə; *NAmE* ˌbɑːr/ *noun* **1** a ceremony and celebration for a Jewish boy who has reached the age of 13, at which he accepts the religious responsibilities of an adult 受誡禮（為年滿 13 歲的猶太男孩舉行的成人儀式）**2** the boy who is celebrating this occasion 行受誡禮的猶太男孩 ➲ compare BAT MITZVAH

barmy /ˈbɑːmi; *NAmE* ˈbɑːrmi/ *adj.* (*BrE, informal*) slightly crazy 傻乎乎的；瘋瘋癲癲的

barn /bɑːn; *NAmE* bɑːrn/ *noun* **1** a large farm building for storing grain or keeping animals in 穀倉；畜棚；倉房：*a hay barn* 乾草棚 ◇ *They live in a converted barn* (= a barn that has been turned into a house). 他們住在由穀倉改成的房子裏。➲ VISUAL VOCAB pages V2, V3, V15 ➲ see also DUTCH BARN **2** a large plain ugly building 簡陋的大建築物：*They live in a great barn of a house.* 他們住在一所簡陋的大房子裏。**3** (*NAmE*) a building in which buses, trucks, etc. are kept when not being used（公共汽車、卡車等的）車庫

IDM **close, etc. the barn door after the horse has eˈscaped** (*NAmE*) ➲ STABLE DOOR

bar·nacle /ˈbɑːnəkl; *NAmE* ˈbɑːrn-/ *noun* a small SHELLFISH that attaches itself to objects underwater, for example to rocks and the bottoms of ships 藤壺（小甲殼動物，附着於水下岩石或船底等）

Bar·nardo's /bəˈnɑːdəʊz; *NAmE* bərˈnɑːrdoʊz/ *noun* a British charity that helps children with social, physical and mental problems 巴納多基金會（英國慈善機構，向有社交、身體和智力問題的兒童提供幫助）ORIGIN From Dr Thomas Barnardo, who opened a home for poor children without parents in London in 1870. 源自托馬斯・巴納多博士（Dr Thomas Barnardo），他於 1870 年在倫敦設立了一所孤兒院。

ˈbarn dance *noun* an informal social event at which people dance traditional COUNTRY DANCES 穀倉舞會（跳鄉村舞的非正式社交聚會）

bar·net /ˈbɑːnɪt; *NAmE* ˈbɑːrn-/ *noun* (*BrE, informal*) a person's hair 頭髮

bar·ney /ˈbɑːni; *NAmE* ˈbɑːrni/ *noun* (*BrE, informal*) an argument 鬥嘴

ˈbarn owl *noun* a BIRD OF PREY (= a bird that kills other creatures for food) of the OWL family, that often makes its nest in BARNS and other buildings 倉鴞（常築巢於穀倉等的貓頭鷹）➲ VISUAL VOCAB page V12

barn·storm /ˈbɑːnstɔːm; *NAmE* ˈbɑːrnstɔːrm/ *verb* [I, T] **~ (sth)** (*especially NAmE*) to travel quickly through an area making political speeches, or getting a lot of attention for your organization, ideas, etc. 作巡迴政治演說（或宣傳、游說等）：*He barnstormed across the southern states in an attempt to woo the voters.* 他在南方各州作巡迴演說，企圖拉選票。

barn·storm·ing /ˈbɑːnstɔːmɪŋ; *NAmE* ˈbɑːrnstɔːrmɪŋ/ *adj.* [only before noun] a **barnstorming** performance or show of skill in a sports game, etc. is one that people find very exciting to watch（演出、比賽等）令人興奮的，激烈的，精彩的

barn·yard /ˈbɑːnjɑːd; *NAmE* ˈbɑːrnjɑːrd/ *noun* an area on a farm that is surrounded by farm buildings 倉院（農場倉房圍着的空地）

bar·om·eter /bəˈrɒmɪtə(r); *NAmE* -ˈrɑːm-/ *noun* **1** an instrument for measuring air pressure to show when the weather will change 氣壓計；晴雨表：*The barometer is falling* (= showing that it will probably rain). 氣壓在下降（表示可能要下雨）。**2** something that shows the changes that are happening in an economic, social or political situation（顯示經濟、社會、政治變化的）晴雨表，標誌，指標：*Infant mortality is a reliable barometer of socio-economic conditions.* 嬰兒死亡率是社會經濟狀況的可靠指標。▸ **baro·metric** /ˌbærəˈmetrɪk/ *adj.*：*barometric pressure* 大氣壓

baron /ˈbærən/ *noun* **1** a NOBLEMAN of the lowest rank. In Britain, barons use the title *Lord*; in other countries they use the title *Baron*. 男爵（貴族中的最末一等。英國男爵頭銜為 Lord；其他國家為 Baron）**2** a person who owns or controls a large part of a particular industry 工商業鉅頭：*a press baron* 報業大王 ◇ *drug barons* 毒梟

bar·on·ess /ˈbærənəs; *NAmE* ˌbærəˈnes/ *noun* **1** a woman who has the same rank as a baron. In Britain, baronesses use the title *Lady* or *Baroness*. 女男爵（英國女男爵頭銜為 Lady 或 Baroness）：*Baroness Thatcher* 撒切爾女男爵 **2** the wife of a baron 男爵夫人

bar·onet /ˈbærənət/ *noun* (*abbr.* **Bart**, **Bt**) (in Britain) a man who has the lowest rank of honour that can be passed from a father to his son when he dies. Baronets use the title *Sir*. 準男爵（英國爵位的最低一級，稱號世襲。頭銜為 Sir）➲ compare KNIGHT *n.* (2)

bar·on·et·cy /ˈbærənətsi/ *noun* (*pl.* **-ies**) the rank or position of a baronet 準男爵爵位

bar·on·ial /bəˈrəʊniəl; *NAmE* -ˈroʊ-/ *adj.* [usually before noun] connected with or typical of a BARON 男爵的；有男爵特色的；豪華的：*a baronial hall* 豪華的大廳

bar·ony /ˈbærəni/ *noun* (*pl.* **-ies**) **1** the rank or position of a BARON 男爵爵位 **2** an area of land that is owned and controlled by a BARON 男爵領地

bar·oque /bəˈrɒk; *NAmE* bəˈroʊk/ (also **Baroque**) *adj.* [usually before noun] used to describe European ARCHITECTURE, art and music of the 17th and early 18th centuries that has a grand and highly decorated style 巴羅克風格的（17 至 18 世紀早期流行於歐洲，氣勢雄偉、裝飾華麗的特色反映在建築、繪畫和音樂等藝術上）：*baroque churches/music* 巴羅克風格教堂／音樂 ◇ *the baroque period* 巴羅克風格流行時期 ▸ **bar·oque** (also **Baroque**) *noun* [sing.]：*paintings representative of the baroque* 典型的巴羅克風格繪畫

barque /bɑːk; *NAmE* bɑːrk/ *noun* a sailing ship with three or more MASTS (= posts that support the sails) 三桅（或多桅）帆船

bar·rack /ˈbærək/ *verb* **1** [I, T] **~ (sb)** (*BrE*) to shout criticism at players in a game, speakers at a meeting, performers, etc. 喝倒彩；起鬨；發出噓聲 **2** [I, T] **~ (for) sb** (*AustralE, NZE*) to shout encouragement to a person or team that you support 給（所支持的人或隊）加油；喝彩助威 ▸ **bar·rack·ing** *noun* [U]

bar·racks /ˈbærəks/ *noun* [C+sing./pl. v.] (*pl.* **bar·racks**) **1** a large building or group of buildings for soldiers to live in 營房；兵營：*an army barracks* 一座兵營 ◇ *The troops were ordered* ***back to barracks***. 士兵們被命令返回營房。**2** any large ugly building or buildings（一所或一群）簡陋的大房子 ▸ **bar·rack** *adj.* [only before noun]：*a barrack unit* 一處兵營（單位）

bar·ra·cuda /ˌbærəˈkjuːdə; *NAmE* -ˈkuːdə/ *noun* a large aggressive fish with sharp teeth that lives in warm seas 魣，梭（子）魚（掠食性魚類，生活於溫暖海域）

bar·rage /ˈbærɑːʒ; *NAmE* bəˈrɑːʒ/ *noun* **1** [C, usually sing.] the continuous firing of a large number of guns in a particular direction, especially to protect soldiers while they are attacking or moving towards the enemy 火力網；彈幕射擊；（尤指）掩護炮火 **2** [sing.] **~ (of sth)** a large number of sth, such as questions or comments, that are directed at sb very quickly, one after the other, often in an aggressive way 接二連三的一大堆（質問或指責等）：*a* **barrage** *of questions/criticisms/ complaints* 連珠炮似的問題／批評／抱怨 **3** /*NAmE* ˈbɑːrɪdʒ/ [C] a wall or barrier built across a river to store water, prevent a flood, etc. 堰；水壩；攔河壩

ˈ**barrage balloon** *noun* a large BALLOON that floats in the air and is held in place by cables, used in the past to make the progress of enemy aircraft more difficult 阻攔氣球，阻塞氣球（舊時防空用）

bar·ra·mundi /ˌbærəˈmʌndi/ *noun* (*pl.* **bar·ra·mundi**) a large fish found in rivers in Australia and SE Asia 尖吻鱸（見於澳大利亞和東南亞河流）

bar·rel /ˈbærəl/ *noun, verb*

▪ ***noun*** **1** a large round container, usually made of wood or metal, with flat ends and, usually, curved sides 桶：*a* **beer/wine barrel** 啤酒／葡萄酒桶 **2** the contents of or the amount contained in a barrel; a unit of measurement in the oil industry equal to between 120 and 159 litres 一桶（的量）；桶（石油計量單位，相當於 120 到 159 升）：*They got through two barrels of beer.* 他們喝了兩桶啤酒。◇ *Oil prices fell to $9 a barrel.* 石油價格降到了每桶 9 元。 **3** the part of a gun like a tube through which the bullets are fired 槍管

IDM **a barrel of ˈlaughs** (often *ironic*) very amusing; a lot of fun 很有趣；開心；快樂：*Life hasn't exactly been a barrel of laughs lately.* 最近生活並不十分令人開心。 **(get/have sb) over a barrel** (*informal*) (to put/have sb) in a situation in which they must accept or do what you want （使某人）聽從擺佈，處於被動地位：*They've got us over a barrel. Either we agree to their terms or we lose the money.* 他們讓我們別無選擇。我們要麼答應他們的條件，要麼損失這筆錢。 ➲ more at LOCK *n.*, SCRAPE *v.*, SHOOT *v.*

▪ ***verb*** (**-ll-**) [I] **+ adv./prep.** (*NAmE, informal*) to move very fast in a particular direction, especially in a way that you cannot control （無法控制地）高速行進，飛馳：*He came barreling down the hill and smashed into a phone booth.* 他沿山坡飛馳下來，撞進了一個電話亭。

ˌ**barrel-ˈchested** *adj.* (of a man 男子) having a large rounded chest 胸肌發達的；胸圍寬大的

ˈ**barrel organ** *noun* a musical instrument that is played by turning a handle, usually played in the streets for money 手搖風琴（街頭賣藝常用）➲ see also ORGAN-GRINDER

bar·ren /ˈbærən/ *adj.* **1** (of land or soil 土地或土壤) not good enough for plants to grow on it 貧瘠的；不毛的：*a barren desert* 不毛的沙漠 ◇ *a barren landscape* (= one that is empty, with few plants) 寸草不生的荒涼景色 **2** (of plants or trees 花草樹木) not producing fruit or seeds 不結果實的 **SYN** **infertile** **3** (*old-fashioned* or *formal*) (of women or female animals 女人或雌性動物) not able to produce children or young animals 不育的；不孕的 **SYN** **infertile** **4** [usually before noun] not producing anything useful or successful 無益的；無效果的：*The team will come through this* ***barren patch*** *and start to win again.* 這個隊將會在經歷這段低潮時期之後再創佳績。 ▸ **bar·ren·ness** /ˈbærənnəs/ *noun* [U]

bar·rette /bæˈret/ (*NAmE*) (*BrE* **hair·slide, slide**) *noun* a small decorative piece of metal or plastic used by women for holding their hair in place （裝飾性）小髮夾

bar·ri·cade /ˌbærɪˈkeɪd/ *noun, verb*

▪ ***noun*** a line of objects placed across a road, etc. to stop people from getting past 路障；街壘：*The police stormed the barricades the demonstrators had put up.* 警察衝破了示威者築起的街壘。

▪ ***verb*** **~ sth** to defend or block sth by building a barricade 設路障防護；阻擋：*They barricaded all the doors and windows.* 他們用障礙物堵住了所有的門窗。

PHR V **barriˌcade yourself ˈin/inˈside (sth)** to build a barricade in front of you in order to prevent anyone from coming in 躲在…裏：*He had barricaded himself in his room.* 他把自己關在房間裏。

bar·rier 🔑 /ˈbæriə(r)/ *noun*

1 🔑 an object like a fence that prevents people from moving forward from one place to another 屏障；障礙物：*The crowd had to stand behind barriers.* 人群只好站在障礙物後面。◇ *Show your ticket at the barrier.* 請在驗票處出示車票。 ➲ see also CRASH BARRIER **2** 🔑 a problem, rule or situation that prevents sb from doing sth, or that makes sth impossible 障礙；阻力；關卡：*the removal of trade barriers* 貿易壁壘的消除 ◇ **~ to sth** *Lack of confidence is a psychological barrier to success.* 缺乏信心是阻礙成功的心理因素。 ➲ COLLOCATIONS at INTERNATIONAL **3** 🔑 something that exists between one thing or person and another and keeps them separate 分界線；隔閡；障礙：*The Yangtze river is a natural barrier to the north-east.* 長江是東北面的一道天然屏障。 ◇ *the* ***language barrier*** (= when people cannot communicate because they do not speak the same language) 語言隔閡（因語言不通而無法交流）◇ **~ between A and B** *There was no real barrier between reality and fantasy in his mind.* 在他的頭腦中，現實與幻想之間沒有真正的界線。◇ **~ against sth** *Ozone is the earth's barrier against ultra-violet radiation.* 臭氧是地球防止紫外線輻射的屏障。 **4** a particular amount, level or number that it is difficult to get past 難以逾越的數量（或水平、數目）；關口：*the first player whose earnings passed the $10 million barrier* 第一位收入超過 1 000 萬元大關的運動員

ˈ**barrier method** *noun* a method of avoiding becoming pregnant by stopping the SPERM from reaching the egg, for example by using a CONDOM 屏障避孕法（使用避孕套等）

ˌ**barrier ˈreef** *noun* a line of rock and CORAL in the sea, often not far from land 堡礁（近海岸的珊瑚礁）

bar·ring /ˈbɑːrɪŋ/ *prep.* except for; unless there is/are 除了；除非：*Barring accidents, we should arrive on time.* 除非有意外情況，我們應可按時到達。

bar·rio /ˈbæriəʊ; *NAmE* ˈbɑːrioʊ/ *noun* (from *Spanish*) (*pl.* **-os**) **1** a district of a city in Spain or in another Spanish-speaking country （西班牙或西班牙語國家的）區 **2** (*US*) a district of a city in the US where a lot of Spanish-speaking people live （美國城市中說西班牙語的人聚居的）西語區

bar·ris·ter /ˈbærɪstə(r)/ *noun* a lawyer in Britain who has the right to argue cases in the higher courts of law 大律師，出庭律師，辯護律師（在英國有資格出席高等法庭進行辯護）➲ note at LAWYER

bar·room /ˈbɑːruːm; -rʊm/ *noun* a room in which alcoholic drinks are served at a bar 酒吧間：*a topic much discussed in barrooms across the country* 全國各地酒吧間議論紛紛的話題 ◇ *a barroom brawl* 酒吧間的鬥毆

bar·row /ˈbærəʊ; *NAmE* -roʊ/ *noun* **1** (*BrE*) a small open vehicle with two wheels from which fruit, vegetables, etc. are sold in the street 兩輪流動售貨車（售賣水果、蔬菜等）**2** a large pile of earth built over a place where people were buried in ancient times 古墳；古塚 **3** = WHEELBARROW

ˈ**barrow boy** *noun* (*BrE*) a man or boy who sells things from a barrow in the street 街頭推車售貨男子（或男孩）；街頭推車小販

ˈ**bar stool** *noun* a tall seat for customers at a bar to sit on 酒吧高腳凳

Bart /bɑːt; *NAmE* bɑːrt/ *abbr.* BARONET

bar·tend·er /ˈbɑːtendə(r); *NAmE* ˈbɑːrt-/ *noun* (*especially NAmE*) **1** (*BrE* also **bar·maid**) a woman who works in a bar, serving drinks 酒吧女招待 **2** = BARMAN

bar·ter /ˈbɑːtə(r); *NAmE* ˈbɑːrt-/ *verb* [I, T] to exchange goods, property, services, etc. for other goods, etc. without using money （同某人）以物易物；以財產（或勞務等）作交換：**~ (with sb) (for sth)** *The prisoners tried to barter with the guards for items like writing paper and books.* 囚犯們試着從看守那裏換得信紙和書之類的東西。 ◇ **~ sth (for sth)** *The local people bartered wheat for*

B

tools. 當地人用小麥換取工具。 ▸ **bar·ter** *noun* [U]: *The islanders use a system of barter instead of money.* 島上的居民採用以物易物的交易方式，而不是用貨幣。

basal /ˈbeɪsl/ *adj.* (*technical* 術語) forming or belonging to a bottom layer or base 底層的；基部的；基底的：*basal cells of the skin* 皮膚基底細胞

bas·alt /ˈbæsɔːlt; *NAmE* bəˈsɔːlt/ *noun* [U] a type of dark rock that comes from VOLCANOES 玄武岩（深色的火山岩）

base 🔑 /beɪs/ *noun, verb, adj.*

■ ***noun***

▸ **LOWEST PART** 底部 **1** 🔑 [C, usually sing.] the lowest part of sth, especially the part or surface on which it rests or stands 根基；基底；底座：*the base of a column/glass* 柱基；玻璃杯底座 ◇ *a pain at the base of the spine* 脊柱末端的疼痛 ◇ *The lamp has a heavy base.* 這枱燈的底座很沉。➲ VISUAL VOCAB pages V14, V23 ➲ SYNONYMS at BOTTOM

▸ **ORIGINAL IDEA/SITUATION** 根源思想／狀況 **2** 🔑 [C] an idea, a fact, a situation, etc. from which sth is developed 根據；出發點 SYN **basis**: *She used her family's history as a base for her novel.* 她以她的家族史作為小說的素材。◇ *His arguments have a sound economic base.* 他的論點有充分的經濟上的根據。➲ SYNONYMS at BASIS

▸ **OF SUPPORT/INCOME/POWER** 支持；收入；力量 **3** [C, usually sing.] the people, activity, etc. from which sb/sth gets most of their support, income, power, etc.（支持、收入、力量等的）來源，源泉，基礎：*These policies have a broad base of support.* 這些政策受到廣泛支持。◇ *an economy with a solid* ***manufacturing base*** 以製造業為堅實基礎的經濟體 ➲ see also CUSTOMER BASE, POWER BASE **4** (*especially NAmE*) (*BrE* usually **basic**) **~ pay/salary/wage** the pay that you get before anything extra is added 基本工資：*All we got was base pay—we didn't reach profitability levels to award a bonus.* 我們只拿到了基本工資，因為沒有達到可發獎金的盈利水平。

▸ **FIRST/MAIN SUBSTANCE** 首要／主要材料 **5** [C, usually sing.] the first or main part of a substance to which other things are added 混合物的首要（或主要）成分：*a drink with a rum base* 主要成分為朗姆酒的飲料 ◇ *Put some moisturizer on as a base before applying your make-up.* 化妝前先搽些潤膚霜打底。

▸ **MAIN PLACE** 主要地方 **6** 🔑 [C] the main place where you live or stay or where a business operates from 據點；總部；大本營：*I spend a lot of time in Britain but Paris is still my base.* 我有很多時間在英國度過，但主要還是居住在巴黎。◇ *The town is an ideal base for touring the area.* 這個鎮子是在這一地區旅遊觀光的理想據點。◇ *The company has its base in New York, and branch offices all over the world.* 公司總部設在紐約，分支遍及全世界。

▸ **OF ARMY, NAVY, ETC.** 陸軍、海軍等 **7** 🔑 [C, U] a place where an army, a navy, etc. operates from 基地：*a* ***military/naval base*** 軍事／海軍基地 ◇ *an* ***air base*** 空軍基地 ◇ *After the attack, they returned to base.* 他們發動攻擊之後返回了基地。

▸ **CHEMISTRY** 化學 **8** [C] a chemical substance, for example an ALKALI, that can combine with an acid to form a salt 鹼；鹽基

▸ **MATHEMATICS** 數學 **9** [C, usually sing.] a number on which a system of counting and expressing numbers is built up, for example 10 in the DECIMAL system and 2 in the BINARY system 基數（如十進制的 10 和二進制的 2）

▸ **IN BASEBALL/ROUNDERS** 棒球；圓場棒球 **10** [C] one of the four positions that a player must reach in order to score points 壘 ➲ see also DATABASE

IDM **off base** (*NAmE, informal*) completely wrong about sth 完全錯誤：*If that's what you think, you're way off base.* 你如果那麼想就全錯了。➲ more at COVER *v.*, FIRST BASE, TOUCH *v.*

■ ***verb*** 🔑 [usually passive] **~ sb/sth/yourself in …** to use a particular city, town, etc. as the main place for a business, holiday/vacation, etc. 以…為據點（或大本營等）；把（總部等）設在：*They decided to base the new company in York.* 他們決定將新成立的公司總部設在約克。◇ *We're going to base ourselves in Tokyo and make trips from there.* 我們將以東京為據點到各地旅行。

PHR V **ˈbase sth on/upon sth** 🔑 to use an idea, a fact, a situation, etc. as the point from which sth can be developed 以…為基礎（或根據）：*What are you basing this theory on?* 你這理論的根據是什麼？➲ see also BASED

■ ***adj.*** (**baser**, **bas·est**) (*formal*) not having moral principles or rules 卑鄙的；不道德的：*He acted from base motives.* 他的行動動機卑鄙。▸ **base·ly** *adv.*

base·ball /ˈbeɪsbɔːl/ *noun* **1** [U] a game played especially in the US by two teams of nine players, using a BAT and ball. Each player tries to hit the ball and then run around four BASES before the other team can return the ball. 棒球運動：*a baseball bat/team/stadium* 棒球球棒／球隊／球場 ◇ *a pair of baseball boots* 一雙棒球靴 ➲ compare ROUNDERS ➲ VISUAL VOCAB page V44 **2** [C] the ball used in this game 棒球

ˈbaseball cap *noun* a cap with a long PEAK (= a curved part sticking out in front), originally worn by BASEBALL players 棒球帽（有長鴨舌）➲ VISUAL VOCAB page V65

base·board /ˈbeɪsbɔːd; *NAmE* -bɔːrd/ (*NAmE*) (*BrE* **ˈskirting board**, **skirt·ing**) *noun* a narrow piece of wood that is fixed along the bottom of the walls in a house 踢腳板；壁腳板

ˈbase camp *noun* a camp where people start their journey when climbing high mountains 登山大本營

based 🔑 /beɪst/ *adj.* [not before noun]

1 🔑 **~ (on sth)** if one thing is **based** on another, it uses it or is developed from it（以某事）為基礎（或根據）：*The movie is based on a real-life incident.* 這部電影以真實事件為藍本。◇ *The report is based on figures from six different European cities.* 報告的依據是歐洲六個不同城市的數據。 **2** 🔑 (also in compounds 亦構成複合詞) if a person or business is **based** in a particular place, that is where they live or work, or where the work of the business is done 在…居住（或工作）；基地（或總部）在…：*We're based in Chicago.* 我們住在芝加哥。◇ *a Chicago-based company* 總部設在芝加哥的公司 **3** 🔑 **-based** (in compounds 構成複合詞) containing sth as an important part or feature 以…為重要部份（或特徵）；以…為主：*lead-based paints* 鉛基塗料 ◇ *a class-based society* 以階級為特徵的社會 ➲ see also BROAD-BASED

ˈbase form *noun* (*grammar* 語法) the basic form of a word to which endings can usually be added, for example *wall* is the base form of *walls* and *walled*. The base form is the form in which words in the dictionary are usually shown.（詞的）基礎形式；派生詞基礎式

ˈbase jumping (also **BASE jumping**) *noun* [U] the sport of jumping with a PARACHUTE from a high place such as a building or a bridge 高處跳傘（從建築物、大橋等高處乘降落傘跳下）▸ **ˈbase jumper** *noun*

base·less /ˈbeɪsləs/ *adj.* (*formal*) not supported by good reasons or facts 無根據的；無緣無故的 SYN **unfounded**: *The rumours were completely baseless.* 那些謠傳毫無根據。

base·line /ˈbeɪslaɪn/ *noun* [usually sing.] **1** (*sport* 體) a line marking each end of the COURT in TENNIS or the edge of the area where a player can run in BASEBALL（網球場的）底線；（棒球場的）壘線 **2** (*technical* 術語) a line or measurement that is used as a starting point when comparing facts 基礎；起點：*The figures for 2009 were used as a baseline for the study.* 這項研究以 2009 年的數據為基礎。

base·man /ˈbeɪsmæn/ *noun* (*pl.* **-men** /-mən/) (in BASEBALL 棒球) a player who defends first, second or third base 守壘員；壘手

base·ment /ˈbeɪsmənt/ *noun* a room or rooms in a building, partly or completely below the level of the ground 地下室；地庫：*Kitchen goods are sold in the basement.* 廚房用具在地下室出售。◇ ***a basement flat/apartment*** 設在地下室的一套房間 ➲ VISUAL VOCAB page V17 ➲ see also BARGAIN BASEMENT

ˌbase ˈmetal *noun* a metal, for example iron or LEAD, that is not a PRECIOUS METAL such as gold 賤金屬

ˈbase rate *noun* (*finance* 財) a rate of interest, set by a central bank, that banks in Britain use when calculating the amount of interest that they charge on money they lend 基本利率（英國各銀行使用的貸款利率，由中央銀行規定）➲ compare PRIME RATE

bases 1 *pl.* of BASIS 2 *pl.* of BASE

bash /bæʃ/ *verb, noun*

■ *verb* (*informal*) **1** [T, I] to hit sb/sth very hard 猛擊；猛撞：**~ sb/sth** *He bashed her over the head with a hammer.* 他用錘子猛擊她的頭部。◇ **~ into sb/sth** *I braked too late and bashed into the car in front.* 我剎車太晚，撞上了前面的車。➲ SYNONYMS at HIT **2** [T] **~ sb/sth** to criticize sb/sth strongly 嚴厲批評：*Bashing politicians is normal practice in the press.* 嚴厲批判政治人物乃是新聞界常事。◇ *a liberal-bashing administration* 打擊自由主義者的政府 ➲ see also BASHING

PHR V **,bash a'way (on/at sth)** | **,bash 'on (with sth)** (*BrE*) to continue working hard at sth 持續努力；持之以恆：*He sat bashing away at his essay all day.* 他一整天都坐着不停地寫文章。◇ *We'll never get finished at this rate. We'd better bash on.* 以這種速度我們永遠也完成不了。我們最好加把勁。 **,bash sth↔'down/'in** to destroy sth by hitting it very hard and often 不斷猛擊使之毀壞：*The police bashed the door down.* 警察使勁把門撞倒了。◇ *I'll bash your head in if you do that again.* 如果你再那麼做，我就砸扁你的腦袋。 **,bash sth↔'out** (*informal*) to produce sth quickly and in large quantities, but not of very good quality 大量粗製濫造 **SYN** **knock out**：*She bashed out about four books a year.* 她一年大概炮製出四本書。 **,bash sb 'up** (*BrE, informal*) to attack sb violently 猛擊某人

■ *noun* (*informal*) **1** a hard hit 猛擊；重擊：*He gave Mike a bash on the nose.* 他衝着邁克的鼻子狠狠地打了一下。**2** a large party or celebration 盛大的聚會；盛典：*a birthday bash* 生日慶典

IDM **have a bash (at sth)** (*BrE, informal*) to try to do sth, especially when you are not sure if you will succeed 嘗試做（沒有把握的事）：*I'm not sure I'll be any good but I'll have a bash.* 我不敢保證我能幫上什麼忙，但我會試試。

bash·ful /'bæʃfl/ *adj.* shy and easily embarrassed 羞怯的；忸怩的 ▸ **bash·ful·ly** /-fəli/ *adv.*：*She smiled bashfully.* 她忸怩地笑了笑。 **bash·ful·ness** *noun* [U]

bash·ing /'bæʃɪŋ/ *noun* [U, C] (often in compounds 常構成複合詞) **1** (used especially in newspapers 尤用於報章) very strong criticism of a person or group 猛烈抨擊；嚴厲批評：*union-bashing* 對工會的猛烈抨擊 **2** a physical attack, or a series of attacks, on a person or group of people（對某人或群體的）毆打，接連打擊：*gay-bashing* (= attacking HOMOSEXUALS) 對同性戀者的攻擊 ◇ *to give sb a bashing* 痛打某人

basic 0-w /'beɪsɪk/ *adj.*

1 0-w forming the part of sth that is most necessary and from which other things develop 基本的；基礎的：*basic information/facts/ideas* 基本信息／事實／思想 ◇ *the basic principles of law* 法律的基本原則 ◇ **~ to sth** *Drums are basic to African music.* 鼓是非洲音樂的基本樂器。**2** 0-w of the simplest kind or at the simplest level 最簡單的；初級的；初步的：*The campsite provided only basic facilities.* 野營地只提供最基本的設施。◇ *My knowledge of French is pretty basic.* 我的法語學得很粗淺。**3** 0-w [only before noun] necessary and important to all people 必需的；基本需要的：*basic human rights* 基本人權 ◇ *the cost of basic foods* 基本食糧的費用 **4** (*especially BrE*) (*NAmE* usually **base**) before anything extra is added 基本的；沒有附加成分的：*The* ***basic pay*** *of the average worker has risen by 3 per cent.* 工人的平均基本工資上升了 3%。

BASIC /'beɪsɪk/ *noun* [U] a simple language, using familiar English words, for writing computer programs ＊BASIC 語言，初學者通用符號指令碼（一種使用一般英語詞彙的簡單計算機編程語言）

ba·sic·ally 0-w /'beɪsɪkli/ *adv.*

1 0-w in the most important ways, without considering things that are less important 大體上；基本上 **SYN** **essentially**：*Yes, that's basically correct.* 對，基本正確。◇ *The two approaches are basically very similar.* 兩種方法其實差不多。◇ *There have been some problems but basically it's a good system.* 雖然出現過一些問題，但這基本上仍不失為一個好系統。**2** 0-w used when you are giving your opinion or stating what is important about a situation 總的說來；從根本上說：*Basically, there's not a lot we can do about it.* 總的說來，我們對此做不了很多事。◇ *He basically just sits there and does nothing all day.* 他根本就是一天到晚坐在那兒無所事事。◇ *And that's it, basically.* 說穿了，就是這麼回事。

,Basic 'English *noun* [U] a set of 850 carefully chosen words of English, used for international communication 基本英語（簡化國際通用語，共有 850 個詞語）

basics /'beɪsɪks/ *noun* [pl.] **1 ~ (of sth)** the most important and necessary facts, skills, ideas, etc. from which other things develop 基本因素（或原理、原則、規律等）：*the basics of computer programming* 計算機編程概要 **2** the simplest and most important things that people need in a particular situation 基本設施；基本需要：*Some schools lack money for basics like books and pencils.* 有些學校缺少資金購買書本、鉛筆之類的基本工具。

IDM **go/get back to 'basics** to think about the simple or most important ideas within a subject or an activity instead of new ideas or complicated details 回歸本原；返璞歸真

basil /'bæzl; *NAmE* also 'beɪzl/ *noun* [U] a plant with shiny green leaves that smell sweet and are used in cooking as a HERB 羅勒（葉子碧綠芳香，用於烹調）➲ VISUAL VOCAB page V28

ba·sil·ica /bə'zɪlɪkə/ *noun* a large church or hall with a curved end and two rows of columns inside 大教堂，大殿，廊柱會堂（一端呈半圓形，內設兩排廊柱）

basi·lisk /'bæzɪlɪsk/ *noun* (in ancient stories) a creature like a snake, which can kill people by looking at them or breathing on them 蛇怪，巴茲里斯克蛇（古代傳說中目光或氣息可致人死亡的怪物）

basin /'beɪsn/ *noun* **1** (*especially BrE*) = WASHBASIN **2** a large round bowl for holding liquids or (in British English) for preparing foods in; the amount of liquid, etc. in a basin 盆；（英式英語）調菜盆；一盆（的量）：*a pudding basin* 布丁盆 **3** an area of land around a large river with streams running down into it 流域：*the Amazon Basin* 亞馬孫河流域 **4** (*technical* 術語) a place where the earth's surface is lower than in other areas of the world 盆地；凹地；海盆：*the Pacific Basin* 太平洋海盆 **5** a sheltered area of water providing a safe HARBOUR for boats 港池；內港；內灣；船塢：*a yacht basin* 停放遊艇的內港

basis 0-w /'beɪsɪs/ *noun* (*pl.* **bases** /'beɪsiːz/)

1 0-w [sing.] the reason why people take a particular action 原因；緣由：*She was chosen for the job* ***on the basis of*** *her qualifications.* 她因資歷適合而獲選中擔任這項工作。◇ *Some movies have been banned* ***on the basis that*** *they are too violent.* 有些影片因暴力鏡頭過多而被查禁。➲ SYNONYMS at REASON **2** 0-w [sing.] the way things are organized or arranged 基準；準則；方式：*on a* ***regular/permanent/part-time/temporary basis*** 以定期／永久／兼職／臨時性的方式 ◇ *on a* ***daily/day-to-day/weekly basis*** 按每天／每日／每週一次的標準 **3** 0-w [C, usually sing., U] the important facts, ideas or events that support sth and that it can develop from 基礎；要素；基點：*The basis of a good marriage is trust.* 美滿婚姻的基礎是信賴。◇ *This article will* ***form the basis*** *for our discussion.* 這篇文章將作為我們討論的基點。◇ *The theory seems to have no basis in fact.* 這一理論似乎沒有事實根據。➲ SYNONYMS at next page

bask /bɑːsk; *NAmE* bæsk/ *verb* [I] **~ (in sth)** to enjoy sitting or lying in the heat or light of sth, especially the sun 曬太陽；取暖：*We sat basking in the warm sunshine.* 我們坐着享受溫暖的陽光。

PHR V **'bask in sth** to enjoy the good feelings that you have when other people praise or admire you, or when they give you a lot of attention 沉浸，沐浴（在讚美、關注等中）：*He had always basked in his parents' attention.* 他一直沉浸在父母的呵護中。◇ *I never minded* ***basking in*** *my wife's* ***reflected glory*** (= enjoying the praise, attention, etc. she got). 妻子的榮耀惠及於我，我並不覺得有什麼不好意思。

B

Synonyms 同義詞辨析

basis

foundation • base

These are all words for the ideas or facts that sth is based on. 以上各詞均指基礎、根據。

basis [usually sing.] a principle, an idea or a fact that supports sth and that it can develop from 指基礎、要素、基點： *This article will form the basis for our discussion.* 這篇文章將作為我們討論的基點。

foundation [C, U] a principle, an idea or a fact that supports sth and that it develops from 指基本原理、基礎、根據： *Respect and friendship provide a solid foundation for marriage.* 尊重和伴侶關係是婚姻的牢固基礎。◇ *The rumour is totally without foundation* (= is not based on any facts). 這謠傳毫無事實根據。

BASIS OR FOUNDATION? 用 basis 還是 foundation？

Foundation is often used to talk about larger or more important things than **basis**. 與 basis 相比，foundation 常用以指更大、更重要的事物： *He laid the foundations of Japan's modern economy.* 他奠定了日本現代經濟的基礎。◇ *These figures formed the basis of their pay claim.* 這些數字是他們要求提高工資的根據。

base [usually sing.] an idea, a fact or a situation from which sth is developed 指根據、出發點： *His arguments have a sound economic base.* 他的論點在經濟上有充分的根據。

PATTERNS

- a/the basis/foundation/base **for/of** sth
- a **secure/solid/sound/strong/weak** basis/foundation/base
- to **form** the basis/foundation/base of sth
- to **be without** basis/foundation

bas·ket /ˈbɑːskɪt; *NAmE* ˈbæs-/ *noun* **1** a container for holding or carrying things. Baskets are made of thin strips of material that bends and twists easily, for example plastic, wire or WICKER. 籃；簍；筐： *a **shopping basket*** 購物籃 ◇ *a **picnic basket*** 野餐籃子 ◇ *a **clothes/laundry basket*** (= in which dirty clothes are put before being washed) （存放待洗衣服的）洗衣筐 ◇ *a **wicker/wire basket*** 柳條／鐵絲筐 ◇ *a **cat/dog basket*** (= in which a cat or dog sleeps or is carried around) 貓／狗籃 ➲ VISUAL VOCAB page V53 ➲ see also WASTE-PAPER BASKET **2** the amount contained in a basket 一籃，一筐，一簍（的量）： *a basket of fruit* 一筐水果 **3** the net and the metal ring it hangs from, high up at each end of a BASKETBALL COURT; a point that is scored by throwing the ball through this net （籃球運動的）籃；投籃得分： *to **make/shoot a basket*** 投球得分／入籃 ➲ VISUAL VOCAB page V44 **4** (*economics* 經) a number of different goods or CURRENCIES 一組（不同的物品或貨幣）： *the value of the rupee against a basket of currencies* 盧比對各種貨幣的比值 IDM see EGG *n.*

bas·ket·ball /ˈbɑːskɪtbɔːl; *NAmE* ˈbæs-/ *noun* **1** [U] a game played by two teams of five players, using a large ball which players try to throw into a high net hanging from a ring 籃球運動： *a **basketball game/coach/team*** 籃球比賽／教練／球隊 ➲ VISUAL VOCAB page V44 **2** [C] the ball used in this game 籃球

ˈ**basket case** *noun* (*informal*) **1** a country or an organization whose economic situation is very bad 經濟狀況極差的國家（或機構） **2** a person who is slightly crazy and who has problems dealing with situations 精神失常的人；無適應能力的人

bas·ket·work /ˈbɑːskɪtwɜːk; *NAmE* ˈbæskɪtwɜːrk/ *noun* [U] **1** material twisted together in the style of a basket 籃狀編製物 **2** the craft of making baskets, etc. 編籃工藝；編製工藝

bas·mati /bæsˈmæti; bæz-/ (also **bas,mati ˈrice**) *noun* [U] a type of rice with long grains and a delicate flavour 巴斯馬蒂香米；印度香米

bas mitzvah /ˌbæs ˈmɪtsvə/ *noun* = BAT MITZVAH

Basque /bɑːsk; bæsk; *NAmE* bæsk/ *noun, adj.*
■ ***noun*** **1** [C] a person who was born in the Basque country 巴斯克人 **2** [U] the language of the people living in the Basque country of France and Spain 巴斯克語（指法國和西班牙的巴斯克鄉村居民的語言）
■ ***adj.*** connected with these people or their language 巴斯克人的；巴斯克語的

basque /bɑːsk; bæsk; *NAmE* bæsk/ *noun* a piece of women's underwear that covers the body from just under the arms to the tops of the legs 巴斯克衫（自臂部以下至腿根處的女子內衣）

bas-relief /ˌbæs rɪˈliːf/ *noun* [U, C] a form of SCULPTURE in which the shapes are cut so that they are slightly raised from the background; a SCULPTURE made in this way 淺浮雕；淺浮雕品

bass¹ /beɪs/ *noun, adj.* ➲ see also BASS²
■ ***noun*** **1** [U] the lowest tone or part in music, for instruments or voices （音樂、樂器、聲樂等的）低音，低音部： *He always plays his stereo with the bass turned right up.* 他放立體聲音響時總把低音調得很大。◇ *He sings bass.* 他唱低音。◇ *a pounding bass line* 深沉有力的歌聲 ➲ compare TREBLE *n.* (1) ➲ see also DRUM AND BASS **2** [C] a man's singing voice with a low range; a man with a bass voice 男低音；男低音歌手 ➲ compare ALTO *n.* (1), BARITONE (1), TENOR *n.* (1) **3** [sing.] a musical part that is written for a bass voice （樂曲的）低音部 **4** (also ˌ**bass guiˈtar**) [C] an electric GUITAR that plays very low notes 低音電吉他： *a bass player* 低音電吉他手 ◇ *bass and drums* 低音電吉他和鼓的合奏 ◇ *Eilís Phillips on* (= playing) *bass* 由艾利斯 • 菲利普斯演奏低音電吉他 **5** [C] = DOUBLE BASS
■ ***adj.*** [only before noun] low in tone 低音的；低聲調的： *a bass voice* 低音部 ◇ *the **bass clef*** (= the symbol in music showing that the notes following it are low) 低音譜號 ➲ picture at MUSIC ➲ compare TREBLE *adj.*

bass² /bæs/ *noun* [C, U] (*pl.* **bass**) a sea or FRESHWATER fish that is used for food 鱸（包括多種食用海魚和淡水魚） ➲ see also BASS¹

ˌ**bass ˈdrum** *noun* a large drum that makes a very low sound, used in ORCHESTRAS （管弦樂隊用的）大鼓，低音鼓 ➲ VISUAL VOCAB page V35

baskets 籃；簍；筐

shopping basket 購物籃

washing basket 洗衣筐

clothes basket (*BrE*) hamper (*NAmE*) 髒衣籃

picnic basket (*BrE also* hamper) 野餐籃子

hanging basket 吊籃

waste-paper basket (*BrE*) wastebasket (*NAmE*) 廢紙簍

bas·set /ˈbæsɪt/ (also ˈ**basset hound**) *noun* a dog with short legs, a long body and long ears 短腿獵犬

bas·sinet /ˌbæsɪˈnet/ (*especially NAmE*) (*BrE* usually **Moses basket**) *noun* a small bed for a baby, that looks like a BASKET 嬰兒搖籃；搖籃式嬰兒牀

bass·ist /ˈbeɪsɪst/ *noun* a person who plays the BASS GUITAR or the DOUBLE BASS 低音電吉他手；低音提琴手

bas·soon /bəˈsuːn/ *noun* a musical instrument of the WOODWIND group. It is shaped like a large wooden tube with a double REED that you blow into, and produces notes with a low sound. 大管；巴松管 ➲ VISUAL VOCAB page V34

bas·soon·ist /bəˈsuːnɪst/ *noun* a person who plays the bassoon 大管演奏者；巴松管手

bas·tard /ˈbɑːstəd; ˈbæs-; *NAmE* ˈbæstərd/ *noun* **1** (*taboo, slang*) used to insult sb, especially a man, who has been rude, unpleasant or cruel 雜種；渾蛋；惡棍：*He's a real bastard.* 他是個十足的惡棍。◊ *You bastard! You've made her cry.* 你這個渾蛋！你把她弄哭了。**2** (*BrE, slang*) a word that some people use about or to sb, especially a man, who they feel very jealous of or sorry for（認為別人走運或不幸時說）傢伙，可憐蟲：*What a lucky bastard!* 真是個走運的傢伙！◊ *You poor bastard!* 你這個可憐蟲！**3** (*BrE, slang*) used about sth that causes difficulties or problems 討厭的事物；麻煩事：*It's a bastard of a problem.* 那是個挺麻煩的問題。**4** (*old-fashioned, disapproving*) a person whose parents were not married to each other when he or she was born 私生子

bas·tard·ize (*BrE* also **-ise**) /ˈbɑːstədaɪz; ˈbæs-; *NAmE* ˈbæstərd-/ *verb* **~ sth** (*formal*) to copy sth, but change parts of it so that it is not as good as the original 拙劣地仿造；假冒

baste /beɪst/ *verb* **1 ~ sth** to pour liquid fat or juices over meat, etc. while it is cooking（烹調時往肉等上）澆滷汁 **2 ~ sth** to sew pieces of cloth together temporarily with long loose STITCHES 用長針腳縫；絎縫；粗縫

ˈ**basting brush** *noun* a brush used for brushing liquid fat or juices over meat, etc. while it is cooking（烹調肉類等用的）滷汁刷，烤肉刷 ➲ VISUAL VOCAB page V26

bas·tion /ˈbæstiən/ *noun* **1** (*formal*) a group of people or a system that protects a way of life or a belief when it seems that it may disappear 堡壘；捍衞者：*a bastion of male privilege* 大男子主義的堡壘 ◊ *a bastion of freedom* 捍衞自由的堡壘 **2** a place that military forces are defending 堡壘；防禦工事

bat /bæt/ *noun, verb*

■ *noun* **1** a piece of wood with a handle, made in various shapes and sizes, and used for hitting the ball in games such as BASEBALL, CRICKET and TABLE TENNIS 球棒；球拍；球板：*a* ***baseball/cricket bat*** 棒球球棒；板球球板 ➲ VISUAL VOCAB pages V44, V45 ➲ compare RACKET (3) **2** an animal like a mouse with wings, that flies and feeds at night (= it is NOCTURNAL). There are many types of bat. 蝙蝠 ➲ VISUAL VOCAB page V12 ➲ see also FRUIT BAT, OLD BAT, VAMPIRE BAT

IDM **like a bat out of ˈhell** (*informal*) very fast 疾速地；迅速地 **off your own ˈbat** (*BrE, informal*) if you do sth **off your own bat**, it is your own idea and you do it without help or encouragement from anyone else 自覺地；主動地 ➲ more at BLIND *adj.*, RIGHT *adv.*

■ *verb* (**-tt-**) **1** [I, T] **~ (sth)** to hit a ball with a bat, especially in a game of CRICKET or BASEBALL 用球板擊球，用球棒擊球（尤指板球或棒球運動）：*He bats very well.* 他擅長擊球。◊ *Who's batting first for the Orioles?* 巴爾的摩金鶯隊誰第一個出場擊球？**2** [T] **~ sth + adv./prep.** to hit sth small that is flying through the air 揮打，拍打（空中飛舞的小東西）：*He batted the wasp away.* 他把那隻黃蜂趕跑了。

IDM ˌ**bat your ˈeyes/ˈeyelashes** to open and close your eyes quickly, in a way that is supposed to be attractive 眉目傳情；擠眉弄眼 **bat a ˈthousand** (*NAmE, informal*) to be very successful 非常成功；大獲全勝 **go to ˈbat for sb** (*NAmE, informal*) to give sb help and support 幫助（或支持）某人 **not bat an ˈeyelid** (*BrE*) (*NAmE* **not bat an ˈeye**) (*informal*) to show no surprise or embarrassment when sth unusual happens 不動聲色；面不改色；眼睛都不眨一下：*She didn't bat an eyelid when I told her my news.* 我把我最近的事告訴她時，她一點也不為所動。

PHR V ˌ**bat sth↔aˈround** (*informal*) to discuss whether an idea or a plan is good or not, before deciding what to do 詳細討論（想法、計劃等）的可行性：*It's just an idea we've been batting around.* 這只不過是我們一直在討論的一種想法。

batch /bætʃ/ *noun, verb*

■ *noun* **1** a number of people or things that are dealt with as a group 一批：*Each summer a new batch of students tries to find work.* 每年夏天都有一批新的學生要找工作。◊ *We deliver the goods* ***in batches.*** 我們分批交付貨物。**2** an amount of food, medicine, etc. produced at one time（食物、藥物等的）一批生產的量：*a batch of cookies* 一批曲奇餅 **3** (*computing* 計) a set of jobs that are processed together on a computer 成批作業：*to process a batch job* 處理一批作業 ◊ *a* ***batch file/program*** 批處理文件／程序

■ *verb* [T, I] **~ (sth)** to put things into groups in order to deal with them 分批處理：*The service will be improved by batching and sorting enquiries.* 分批及分類處理查詢將會提高服務質量。

batch·mate /ˈbætʃmeɪt/ *noun* (*IndE*) a person who is or was in the same year group as you at school or college 同年級同學（或同窗）；同批同學（或同窗）

ˌ**batch ˈprocessing** *noun* [U] (*computing* 計) a way of running a group of programs at the same time, usually automatically（自動）批處理，整批處理

bated /ˈbeɪtɪd/ *adj.*

IDM **with bated ˈbreath** (*formal*) feeling very anxious or excited 焦慮；興奮：*We waited with bated breath for the winner to be announced.* 我們屏住呼吸等待宣佈冠軍是誰。

Which Word? 詞語辨析

bath / bathe / swim / sunbathe

- When you wash yourself you can say that you **bath** (*BrE*) or **bathe** (*NAmE*), but it is much more common to say **have a bath** (*BrE*) or **take a bath** (*NAmE*). 自己洗澡可用 bath（英式英語）或 bathe（美式英語），但一般說 have a bath（英式英語）或 take a bath（美式英語）。
- You can also **bath** (*BrE*) or **bathe** (*NAmE*) another person, for example a baby. 給別人（如嬰兒）洗澡亦可用 bath（英式英語）或 bathe（美式英語）。
- You **bathe** a part of your body, especially to clean a wound. 洗身體某部位（尤指清洗傷口）用 bathe。
- When you go swimming it is old-fashioned to say that you **bathe**, and you cannot say that you *bath* or *take a bath*. It is more common to **swim**, **go for a swim**, **have a swim** or **go swimming**. 游泳舊時說 bathe，但不能說 bath 或 take a bath。較通用的說法為 swim、go for a swim、have a swim 或 go swimming：*Let's go for a quick swim in the pool.* 咱們去游泳池游會兒泳吧。◊ *She goes swimming every morning before breakfast.* 她每天早飯前去游泳。What you wear for this activity is usually called a **swimming costume** in *BrE* and a **bathing suit** in *NAmE*. 游泳衣在英式英語中通常叫做 swimming costume，在美式英語中叫做 bathing suit。
- When you lie in the sun in order to go brown you **sunbathe**. 沐日光浴為 sunbathe。

bath 🔑 /bɑːθ; *NAmE* bæθ/ *noun, verb*

■ *noun* (*pl.* **baths** /bɑːðz; *NAmE* bæðz/) **1** 🔑 [C] (*BrE*) (also **bath·tub**, *informal* **tub** *NAmE, BrE*) a large, long container that you put water in and then get into to wash your whole body 浴缸；浴盆 ➲ VISUAL VOCAB page V24 ➲ see also BIRD BATH **2** 🔑 [C] (*BrE*) the water in a bath/BATHTUB, ready to use 浴缸的水：*a long soak in a hot bath* 一次長時間的熱水浴 ◊ *Please* ***run a bath*** *for me* (= fill the bath with water). 請給我把浴缸放滿水。

B

3 🔑 [C] an act of washing your whole body by sitting or lying in water 洗澡；洗浴：*I think I'll **have a bath** and go to bed.* 我想洗個澡，然後睡覺。◇ (*especially NAmE*) *to **take a bath*** 洗澡 ➲ see also BUBBLE BATH **4 baths** [pl.] (*old-fashioned, BrE*) a public building where you can go to swim 游泳池 ➲ see also SWIMMING BATH, SWIMMING POOL **5** [C, usually pl.] a public place where people went in the past to wash or have a bath（舊時的）公共浴室，澡堂：*Roman villas and baths* 羅馬別墅和浴室 ➲ see also TURKISH BATH **6** [C] (*technical* 術語) a container with a liquid such as water or a DYE in it, in which sth is washed or placed for a period of time. Baths are used in industrial, chemical and medical processes. 浴器，浴鍋，染缸（工業、化學以及醫學加工處理用）➲ see also BLOODBATH

IDM **take a 'bath** (*NAmE*) to lose money on a business agreement（在交易中）蒙受經濟損失

■ *verb* (*BrE*) (*NAmE* **bathe**) **1** [T] **~ sb** to give a bath to sb 給…洗澡：*It's your turn to bath the baby.* 輪到你給嬰兒洗澡了。**2** [I] (*old-fashioned*) to have a bath 洗澡

ˌbath 'chair *noun* a special chair with wheels, used in the past for moving a person who was sick or old 巴斯輪椅（舊時用來推病人或老人）

bathe /beɪð/ *verb, noun*

■ *verb* **1** [T] **~ sth** to wash sth with water, especially a part of your body 用水清洗（尤指身體部位）：*Bathe the wound and apply a clean dressing.* 洗清傷口，再用潔淨敷料包紮。**2** [T, I] **~ (sb)** (*NAmE*) = BATH：*Have you bathed the baby yet?* 你給嬰兒洗澡了嗎？◇ *I bathe every day.* 我每天洗澡。➲ note at BATH **3** [I] (*old-fashioned*) to go swimming in the sea, a river, etc. for enjoyment（到海、河等中）游泳消遣 ➲ see also SUNBATHE **4** [T] **~ sth (in sth)** (*literary*) to fill or cover sth with light（以光線）撒滿，覆蓋；使沐浴在（光線）裏：*The moon bathed the countryside in a silver light.* 月光讓鄉村沐浴在一片銀輝之中。

■ *noun* [sing.] (*BrE, formal*) an act of swimming in the sea, a river, etc.（在海、河等中的）游泳：*to go for a bathe* 去游泳

bathed /beɪðd/ *adj.* **1 ~ in sth** (*literary*) covered with light 被（光線）覆蓋；沐浴着（光線）：*The castle was bathed in moonlight.* 城堡沐浴在月光裏。**2 ~ in sth** wet because covered with sweat or tears 汗流浹背；淚流滿面：*I was so nervous that I was bathed in perspiration.* 我緊張得渾身是汗。

bather /'beɪðə(r)/ *noun* **1** [C] (*BrE*) a person who is swimming in the sea, a river, etc.（在海、河等中）游泳的人 **2 bathers** [pl.] (*AustralE*) = SWIMMING COSTUME, SWIMMING TRUNKS

bath·house /'bɑːθhaʊs; *NAmE* 'bæθ-/ *noun* **1** a public building in which there are baths, steam rooms, etc. 澡堂；公共浴室 **2** (*NAmE*) a building in which you change your clothes for swimming（游泳處的）更衣室

bath·ing /'beɪðɪŋ/ *noun* [U] (*BrE*) the activity of going into the sea, a river, etc. to swim（到海、河等中）游泳，暢游：*facilities for bathing and boating* 游泳和划船設施 ◇ *a safe bathing beach* 一處可以安全游泳的海灘

'bathing cap (*especially NAmE*) (*BrE* also **'swimming cap, 'swimming hat**) *noun* a soft rubber or plastic cap that fits closely over your head to keep your hair dry while you are swimming 游泳帽

'bathing costume *noun* (*BrE, old-fashioned*) = SWIMMING COSTUME

'bathing machine *noun* a shelter with wheels that people in the past went into to put swimming clothes on, which was then pulled to the edge of the sea so they could swim from it 活動更衣室（舊時推到海邊）

'bathing suit *noun* (*NAmE* or *old-fashioned*) = SWIMSUIT

'bath mat *noun* **1** a piece of material that you put beside the bath/BATHTUB to stand on when you get out 浴室腳墊（放在浴缸旁）➲ VISUAL VOCAB page V24 **2** a piece of rubber that you put on the bottom of the bath/BATHTUB so that you do not slip 浴缸防滑墊（放在浴缸裏）

bathos /'beɪθɒs; *NAmE* -θɑːs/ *noun* [U] (*formal*) (in writing or speech 寫作或演講) a sudden change, that is not always intended, from a serious subject or feeling to sth that is silly or not important 突降（嚴肅的內容突然變得荒謬，常非出自本意）

bath·robe /'bɑːθrəʊb; *NAmE* 'bæθroʊb/ (also **robe**) *noun* **1** a loose piece of clothing worn before and after taking a bath 浴衣；浴袍 ➲ VISUAL VOCAB page V24 **2** (*NAmE*) (*BrE* **'dressing gown**) a long loose piece of clothing, usually with a belt, worn indoors over night clothes, for example when you first get out of bed 晨衣，晨袍（起牀後套於睡衣外在室內穿的寬鬆長罩衫，通常有束帶）➲ VISUAL VOCAB page V63

bath·room 🔑 /'bɑːθruːm; -rʊm; *NAmE* 'bæθ-/ *noun* **1** 🔑 a room in which there is a bath/BATHTUB, a WASHBASIN and often a toilet 浴室：*Go and wash your hands in the bathroom.* 到盥洗室洗手去。➲ VISUAL VOCAB page V24 **2** 🔑 (*NAmE*) a room in which there is a toilet, a SINK and sometimes a bath/BATHTUB or shower 洗手間；浴室：*I have to **go to the bathroom*** (= use the toilet). 我得上洗手間。◇ *Where's the bathroom?* (= for example in a restaurant) 衛生間在哪裏？➲ note at TOILET

bath·tub /'bɑːθtʌb; *NAmE* 'bæθ-/ (also *informal* **tub**) (both *especially NAmE*) (*BrE* also **bath**) *noun* a large, long container that you put water in and then get into to wash your whole body 浴缸；浴盆 ➲ VISUAL VOCAB page V24

bath·water /'bɑːθwɔːtə(r); *NAmE* 'bæθwɔːtər; -wɑːt-/ *noun* [U] water in a bath/BATHTUB 洗澡水 IDM see BABY *n.*

batik /bə'tiːk/ *noun* [U, C] a method of printing patterns on cloth using WAX (= a solid substance made from fat or oil) on the parts that will not have any colour; a piece of cloth printed in this way 巴蒂克印花法；蠟防印花法；蠟染；蠟防印花布

bat·man /'bætmən/ *noun* (*pl.* **-men** /-mən/) (*BrE*) the personal servant of an officer in the armed forces 勤務兵；傳令兵

bat mitzvah /ˌbæt 'mɪtsvə/ (also **ˌbas 'mitzvah**) *noun* **1** a ceremony and celebration that is held for a Jewish girl between the ages of 12 and 14 at which she accepts the religious responsibilities of an adult 受誡禮（為 12 至 14 歲的猶太女孩舉行的成人儀式）**2** the girl who is celebrating this occasion 行受誡禮的猶太女孩 ➲ compare BAR MITZVAH

baton /'bætɒn; -tõ; *NAmE* bə'tɑːn/ *noun* **1** (*especially BrE*) = TRUNCHEON：*a **baton charge*** (= one made by police carrying batons, to force a crowd back) 持警棍驅擊 **2** a thin light stick used by the person (called a CONDUCTOR) who is in control of an ORCHESTRA, etc.（樂隊）指揮棒 **3** a short light stick that one member of a team in a RELAY race passes to the next person to run 接力棒：*to **pass/hand over the baton*** 交接力棒 ◇ (*figurative*) *The President **handed over the baton*** (= passed responsibility) *to his successor.* 總統把權杖傳給了他的繼任者。**4** a long stick that is held and thrown in the air by a person marching in front of a band, or by a MAJORETTE（行進中軍樂隊隊長的）指揮杖

'baton round *noun* (*BrE*) a rubber or plastic bullet that is fired to control a crowd that has become violent 橡膠子彈，塑料子彈（鎮壓暴亂等用）

bats·man /'bætsmən/ *noun* (*pl.* **-men** /-mən/) (in CRICKET 板球) the player who is hitting the ball 擊球手 ➲ VISUAL VOCAB page V44

bat·tal·ion /bə'tæliən/ *noun* **1** (*BrE*) a large group of soldiers that form part of a BRIGADE（軍隊的）營 **2** (*formal*) a large group of people, especially an organized group with a particular purpose（有組織的）隊伍：*a battalion of supporters* 由支持者組成的隊伍

bat·ten /'bætn/ *noun, verb*

■ *noun* (*technical* 術語) a long strip of wood that is used to keep other building materials in place on a wall or roof 板條，壓條，掛瓦條（用於固定其他建築材料）

■ *verb*

IDM **ˌbatten down the 'hatches** **1** to prepare yourself for a period of difficulty or trouble 做好迎接困難的準備

2 (on a ship 船上) to firmly shut all the entrances to the lower part, especially because a storm is expected（風暴來臨前）封住底艙口

PHR V ˌbatten sth↔ˈdown to fix sth firmly in position with wooden boards 用木板固定某物：*He was busy battening down all the shutters and doors.* 他正忙着用板條釘牢所有的百葉窗和門。 **ˈbatten on sb** (*BrE, disapproving, formal*) to live well by using other people's money, etc. 靠（別人的錢等）享福；損人肥己

bat·ter /ˈbætə(r)/ *verb, noun*

■ *verb* [I, T, often passive] to hit sb/sth hard many times, especially in a way that causes serious damage 連續猛擊；毆打：**~ at/on sth** *She battered at the door with her fists.* 她用雙拳不斷地捶門。◇ **~ sb** *He had been badly battered about the head and face.* 他被打得鼻青臉腫。◇ *Her killer had* ***battered*** *her* ***to death.*** 殺害她的兇手把她毆打致死。◇ **~ sth** *Severe winds have been battering the north coast.* 狂風一直在北海岸肆虐。 ➲ SYNONYMS at BEAT

PHR V ˌbatter sth↔ˈdown to hit sth hard many times until it breaks or comes down（以連續重擊）砸毀，砸倒

■ *noun* **1** [U, C] a mixture of eggs, milk and flour used in cooking to cover food such as fish or chicken before you fry it, or to make PANCAKES 麪糊（煎料） **2** [U, C] (*NAmE*) a mixture of eggs, milk, flour, etc. used for making cakes 麪糊（用於做糕餅） **3** [C] (*NAmE*) (in BASEBALL 棒球) the player who is hitting the ball 擊球手；擊球員 ➲ VISUAL VOCAB page V44

bat·tered /ˈbætəd; *NAmE* -tərd/ *adj.* **1** old, used a lot, and not in very good condition 破舊不堪的：*a battered old car* 一輛破舊的老爺車 **2** [usually before noun] attacked violently and injured; attacked and badly damaged by weapons or by bad weather 受到嚴重虐待的；受到（武器、惡劣天氣）重創的：***battered women/children*** 受虐待的婦女／兒童 ◇ *The child had suffered what has become known as 'battered baby syndrome'.* 那孩子患的是後來人稱"受虐兒童綜合症"的疾病。◇ *Rockets and shells continued to hit the battered port.* 火箭和炮彈繼續襲擊已遭受重創的港口。

bat·ter·ing /ˈbætərɪŋ/ *noun* [U, sing.] a violent attack that injures or damages sb/sth 毆打；猛擊：*wife battering* 對妻子的暴力行為 ◇ (*figurative*) *The film* ***took a battering*** *from critics in the US.* 該影片在美國遭遇到批評家的猛烈抨擊。

ˈbattering ram *noun* a long, heavy piece of wood used in war in the past for breaking down doors and walls（舊時的圓木）攻城錘

bat·tery 0-w /ˈbætri; -təri/ *noun* (*pl.* **-ies**)

1 0-w [C] a device that is placed inside a car engine, clock, radio, etc. and that produces the electricity that makes it work 電池：*to replace the batteries* 更換電池 ◇ *a rechargeable battery* 充電電池 ◇ ***battery-powered/-operated*** 用電池供電的／發動的 ◇ *a car battery* 汽車蓄電池 ◇ *The battery is flat* (= it is no longer producing electricity). 電池沒電了。 **2** [C] **~ (of sth)** a large number of things or people of the same type 一系列；一批；一群：*He faced a battery of questions.* 他面臨一連串的問題。◇ *a battery of reporters* 一大批記者 **3** [C] (*technical* 術語) a number of large guns that are used together 排炮 **4** [C] (*BrE*) (often used as an adjective 常用作形容詞) a large number of small CAGES that are joined together and are used for keeping chickens, etc. in on a farm 層架式雞籠；層架式飼養籠：*a battery hen* 層架式養雞籠養的母雞 ◇ *battery eggs* 層架式養雞場所產的蛋 ➲ compare FREE-RANGE **5** [U] (*law* 律) the crime of attacking sb physically 毆打罪 ➲ see also ASSAULT AND BATTERY IDM see RECHARGE

ˈbattery farm *noun* (*BrE*) a farm where large numbers of chickens or other animals are kept in very small CAGES or crowded conditions 密集式養雞場（或牲畜動物飼養場） ➲ compare FACTORY FARM, FREE-RANGE ▸ **ˈbattery farming** *noun* [U]

bat·tle 0-w /ˈbætl/ *noun, verb*

■ *noun* **1** 0-w [C, U] a fight between armies, ships or planes, especially during a war; a violent fight between groups of people 戰役；戰鬥；搏鬥：*the battle of Waterloo* 滑鐵盧戰役 ◇ *to be killed* ***in battle*** 陣亡 ◇ *a gun battle* 槍戰 ➲ see also PITCHED BATTLE **2** 0-w [C] **~ (with sb) (for sth)** a competition, an argument or a struggle between people or groups of people trying to win power or control 較量；爭論；鬥爭：*a legal battle for compensation* 要求賠償的法律鬥爭 ◇ *a battle with an insurance company* 同一家保險公司的爭執 ◇ *a* ***battle of wits*** (= when each side uses their ability to think quickly to try to win) 智鬥 ◇ *a* ***battle of wills*** (= when each side is very determined to win) 意志的較量 ➲ SYNONYMS at CAMPAIGN **3** 0-w [C, usually sing.] a determined effort that sb makes to solve a difficult problem or succeed in a difficult situation 奮鬥；鬥爭：**~ (against sth)** *her long battle against cancer* 她同癌症的長期鬥爭 ◇ *to fight an uphill battle against prejudice* 同偏見作艱苦鬥爭 ◇ **~ (for sth)** *a battle for survival* 一場生死鬥 ◇ **~ (with sth)** *his battle with alcoholism* 他的反酗酒鬥爭

IDM **the battle lines are ˈdrawn** used to say that people or groups have shown which side they intend to support in an argument or contest that is going to begin 戰線已經劃清（指人或群體已表明打算支持爭論或比賽哪一方） **do ˈbattle (with sb) (over sth)** to fight or argue with sb（同某人就某事）進行鬥爭或辯論 **half the ˈbattle** the most important or difficult part of achieving sth（完成某事的）關鍵；最艱難的階段 ➲ more at FIGHT *v.*, JOIN *v.*

■ *verb* [I, T] to try very hard to achieve sth difficult or to deal with sth unpleasant or dangerous 搏鬥；奮鬥；鬥爭：*Both teams battled hard.* 兩隊拚得很厲害。◇ *I had to battle hard just to stay afloat.* 我得用力掙扎才能勉強浮住。◇ **~ with/against sb/sth (for sth)** *She's still battling with a knee injury.* 她還在同膝部的傷痛作鬥爭。◇ **~ for sth** *The two leaders are battling for control of the government.* 兩位領導人在為控制政府而鬥爭。◇ *The two sides will* ***battle it out*** *in the final next week.* 雙方將於下週決賽中決一勝負。◇ **~ sth** (*NAmE*) *He battled cancer for four years.* 他同癌症鬥爭了四年。

battle·axe (*BrE*) (*US* also **battle·ax**) /ˈbætlæks/ *noun* **1** (*informal, disapproving*) an aggressive and unpleasant older woman 悍婦；母老虎 **2** a heavy AXE with a long handle, used in the past as a weapon（舊時的）戰斧

battle·cruiser /ˈbætlkruːzə(r)/ *noun* a large fast ship used in war in the past, faster and lighter than a BATTLESHIP 戰列巡洋艦（舊時作戰用，比戰列艦快而輕）

ˈbattle cry *noun* **1** a shout that soldiers used to give in battle to encourage their own army or to frighten the enemy（戰鬥中的）吶喊助威，喊殺聲 **2** a word or phrase used by a group of people who work together for a particular purpose, especially a political one（尤指政治的）戰鬥口號，口號

battle·dress /ˈbætldres/ *noun* [U] (*BrE*) the uniform that soldiers wear for training and when they go to fight 戰地服裝

ˈbattle fatigue *noun* [U] = COMBAT FATIGUE

ˈbattle fatigues *noun* [pl.] = COMBAT FATIGUES

battle·field /ˈbætlfiːld/ (also **battle·ground** /ˈbætlɡraʊnd/) *noun* **1** a place where a battle is being fought or has been fought 戰場 **2** a subject that people feel strongly about and argue about 爭論主題；鬥爭領域

ˈbattle-hardened *adj.* (of soldiers 士兵) having experience of war and therefore effective at fighting battles 久經沙場的；身經百戰的

battle·ments /ˈbætlmənts/ *noun* [pl.] a low wall around the top of a castle with spaces in it that people inside could shoot through 城垛；雉堞 ➲ VISUAL VOCAB page V15

ˈbattle-scarred *adj.* a person or place that is **battle-scarred** has been in a war or fight and shows the signs of injury or damage 傷痕纍纍的；滿目瘡痍的

battle·ship /ˈbætlʃɪp/ *noun* a very large ship used in war, with big guns and heavy ARMOUR (= metal plates that cover the ship to protect it) 戰列艦

batty /ˈbæti/ *adj.* (*informal, especially BrE*) (of people or ideas 人或思想) slightly crazy, in a harmless way 瘋瘋癲癲的；古怪的 ➲ SYNONYMS at MAD

B

bau·ble /ˈbɔːbl/ *noun* **1** a piece of jewellery that is cheap and has little artistic value 低廉花哨的首飾 **2** (*BrE*) a decoration for a Christmas tree in the shape of a ball 聖誕樹裝飾球

baud /bɔːd/ *noun* (*computing* 計) a unit for measuring the speed at which electronic signals and information are sent from one computer to another 波特（信號、信息傳輸速率單位）

Bau·haus /ˈbaʊhaʊs/ *noun* [U] (from *German*) a style and movement in German ARCHITECTURE and design in the early 20th century that was influenced by the methods and materials used in industry and placed emphasis on how things would be used 包豪斯建築學派（20 世紀初的德國建築和設計的風格、流派，受工業界方法和材料的影響，強調實用功能）

baulk (*BrE*) (*NAmE* usually **balk**) /bɔːk/ *verb* **1** [I] **~ (at sth)** to be unwilling to do sth or become involved in sth because it is difficult, dangerous, etc. 畏縮；迴避：*Many parents may baulk at the idea of paying $100 for a pair of shoes.* 許多父母可能不願出 100 塊錢買一雙鞋。 **2** [I] **~ (at sth)** (of a horse 馬) to stop suddenly and refuse to jump a fence, etc. 逡巡不前；突然拒絕前行（如跳越障礙物等） **3** [T] **~ sb (of sth)** [usually passive] (*formal*) to prevent sb from getting sth or doing sth 阻止；阻礙：*She looked like a lion baulked of its prey.* 她看上去像一頭被奪走了獵物的獅子。

baux·ite /ˈbɔːksaɪt/ *noun* [U] a soft mineral from which ALUMINIUM/ALUMINUM is obtained 鋁土礦；鋁礬土

bawd /bɔːd/ *noun* (*old use*) a woman who was in charge of a BROTHEL (= a house where men pay to have sex) 妓院女老闆；鴇母

bawdy /ˈbɔːdi/ *adj.* (**bawd·ier**, **bawd·iest**) (*old-fashioned*) (of songs, plays, etc. 歌曲、戲劇等) loud, and dealing with sex in an amusing way 喧鬧並猥褻作樂的；說黃色笑話的

bawl /bɔːl/ *verb* **1** [I, T] to shout loudly, especially in an unpleasant or angry way 大喊；怒吼：**~ (at sb)** *She bawled at him in front of everyone.* 她當着大家的面衝他大喊大叫。◇ **~ (out) sth (at sb)** *He sat in his office bawling orders at his secretary.* 他坐在辦公室裏，對秘書厲聲發號施令。◇ **+ speech (+ out)** *'Get in here now!' she bawled out.* "馬上進來！"她嚷道。 **2** [I, T] **(+ speech)** to cry loudly, especially in an unpleasant and annoying way 號哭：*A child was bawling in the next room.* 隔壁有個孩子在大聲哭鬧。◇ *He was* ***bawling his eyes out*** (= crying very loudly). 他正號啕大哭。

PHR V **,bawl sb↔'out** (*informal*) to speak angrily to sb because they have done sth wrong 大聲訓斥：*The teacher bawled him out for being late.* 老師因他遲到而把他訓斥了一頓。

bay 0‑w /beɪ/ *noun, verb, adj.*

■ ***noun*** **1** 0‑w [C] a part of the sea, or of a large lake, partly surrounded by a wide curve of the land（海或湖的）灣：*the Bay of Bengal* 孟加拉灣 ◇ *Hudson Bay* 哈得孫灣 ◇ *a magnificent view across the bay* 海灣對面的壯觀景象 ➲ VISUAL VOCAB pages V4, V5 **2** [C] a marked section of ground either inside or outside a building, for example for a vehicle to park in, for storing things, etc. 分隔間（戶外或室內的，用以停放車輛、存放貨物等）：*a* ***parking/loading bay*** 停車位；裝貨區 ◇ *Put the equipment in No 3 bay.* 把設備放在 3 號倉房。➲ see also SICKBAY **3** [C] a curved area of a room or building that sticks out from the rest of the building（建築物的）突出結構 **4** [C] a horse of a dark brown colour 深棕色馬；栗色馬：*He was riding a big bay.* 他騎着一匹高大的栗色馬。 **5** [C] a deep noise, especially the noise made by dogs when hunting（尤指獵犬捕獵時的）低沉吠聲 **6** (also **ˈsweet bay**) [C] = BAY TREE **7** [U] a HERB used to give flavour to food, made of the leaves of the BAY TREE 月桂（用作香料）➲ VISUAL VOCAB page V32

IDM **at ˈbay** when an animal that is being hunted is **at bay**, it must turn and face the dogs and HUNTERS because it is impossible to escape from them（獵物）被圍困，被迫作困獸之鬥 **hold/keep sb/sth at ˈbay** to prevent an enemy from coming close or a problem from having a bad effect 不讓（敵人）接近；防止（問題）惡化 SYN **ward off**：*I'm trying to keep my creditors at bay.* 我在竭力避開債主。◇ *Charlotte bit her lip to hold the tears at bay.* 夏洛特咬住嘴唇不讓眼淚流出來。

■ ***verb*** **1** [I] (of a dog or WOLF 狗或狼) to make a long deep sound, especially while hunting（尤指捕獵時）發出長嗥，低沉地吠叫 SYN **howl**：*a pack of baying hounds* 一群不斷吠叫着的獵犬 **2** [I] **~ (for sth)** (usually used in the progressive tenses 通常用於進行時) to demand sth in a loud and angry way 厲聲強要：*The referee's decision left the crowd* ***baying for blood*** (= threatening violence towards him). 裁判的裁決引起群眾怒吼着要暴力相向。

■ ***adj.*** (of a horse 馬) dark brown in colour 深棕色的；栗色的：*a bay mare* 一匹栗色的母馬

ˈbay leaf *noun* the dried leaf of the BAY TREE that is used in cooking as a HERB 月桂葉（乾葉常作香料）

bay·onet *noun, verb*

■ ***noun*** /ˈbeɪənət/ a long, sharp knife that is fastened onto the end of a RIFLE and used as a weapon in battle 槍刺；刺刀

■ ***verb*** /ˈbeɪənət; ˌbeɪəˈnet/ **~ sb** to push a bayonet into sb in order to kill them 用刺刀刺；下刺刀

bayou /ˈbaɪuː/ *noun* a branch of a river in the southern US that moves very slowly and has many plants growing in it（美國南部水流緩慢、多水草的）河道支流

ˈbay tree (also **bay**) *noun* a small tree with dark green leaves with a sweet smell that are used in cooking 月桂樹，甜月桂（葉子可作香料）➲ see also BAY LEAF

ˌbay ˈwindow *noun* a large window, usually with glass on three sides, that sticks out from the outside wall of a house 凸窗 ➲ VISUAL VOCAB page V17

ba·zaar /bəˈzɑː(r)/ *noun* **1** (in some Eastern countries) a street or an area of a town where there are many small shops（某些東方國家的）集市 **2** (in Britain, the US, etc.) a sale of goods, often items made by hand, to raise money for a charity or for people who need help（英、美等國的）義賣

ba·zooka /bəˈzuːkə/ *noun* a long gun, shaped like a tube, which is held on the shoulder and used to fire ROCKETS at military vehicles（反坦克）火箭筒

ba·zoom /bəˈzuːm/ *noun* [usually pl.] (*informal, especially NAmE*) a woman's breast（女人的）乳房，奶子

BBC /ˌbiː biː ˈsiː/ *abbr.* British Broadcasting Corporation (a national organization which broadcasts television and radio programmes and which is paid for by the public and not by advertising) 英國廣播公司：*The news is on BBC One at 6.* 新聞在英國廣播公司電視一台 6 點鐘播出。◇ *BBC Radio 4* 英國廣播公司第 4 頻道

the ˌBBC World ˈService *noun* [sing.] a department of the BBC which broadcasts programmes, including news programmes, in English and many other languages to other countries 英國廣播公司環球廣播部

BBQ *abbr.* BARBECUE

BBS /ˌbiː ˌbiː ˈes/ *noun* [C, U] (*computing* 計) bulletin board system (a system which allows a group of people to leave messages which the others in the group can read and reply to) 留言板系統；公告板系統；電子佈告欄系統

BC (*BrE*) (*US* **B.C.**) /ˌbiː ˈsiː/ *abbr.* before Christ (used in the Christian CALENDAR to show a particular number of years before the year when Christ is believed to have been born) 公元前（基督教會曆法用）：*in (the year) 2 000 BC* 在公元前 2 000 年 ◇ *the third century BC* 公元前 3 世紀 ➲ compare AD, AH, BCE, CE

BCE /ˌbiː siː ˈiː/ (also **B.C.E.** especially in *NAmE*) *abbr.* before the Common Era (before the birth of Christ, when the Christian CALENDAR starts counting years. BCE can be used to give dates in the same way as BC) 公元前（用於表示年份，用法與 BC 同）：*in (the year) 2 000 BCE* 在公元前 2 000 年 ◇ *the third century BCE* 公元前 3 世紀 ➲ compare AD, BC, CE

be 0‑w /bi; *strong form* biː/ *verb, auxiliary verb*
➲ IRREGULAR VERBS at page R5

■ ***verb*** **1** 0‑w *linking verb* **there is/are + noun** to exist; to be present 有；存在：*Is there a God?* 上帝存在嗎？◇ *Once upon a time there was a princess …* 從前有一位公主…◇

I tried phoning but there was no answer. 我試打過電話，但沒人接。◇ *There's a bank down the road.* 沿馬路不遠有一家銀行。◇ *Was there a pool at the hotel?* 旅館裏有游泳池嗎？ **2** [I] **+ adv./prep.** to be located; to be in a place 位於；在（某處）: *The town is three miles away.* 鎮子距此地三英里遠。◇ *If you're looking for your file, it's on the table.* 你要找的文件在桌子上。◇ *Mary's upstairs.* 瑪麗在樓上。 **3** [I] **+ adv./prep.** to happen at a time or in a place（在某時或某地）發生: *The party is on Friday evening.* 聚會定於週五晚上舉行。◇ *The meetings are always in the main conference room.* 會議總是在主會議室進行。 **4** [I] **+ adv./prep.** to remain in a place 留在（某地）；逗留: *She has been in her room for hours.* 她已經在她的房間裏待了幾個小時了。◇ *They're here till Christmas.* 他們將在這裏一直住到聖誕節。 **5** [I] **+ adv./prep.** to attend an event; to be present in a place 出席；到場: *I'll be at the party.* 我將出席聚會。◇ *He'll be here soon* (= will arrive soon). 他很快就會到達。 **6** [I] (only used in the perfect tenses 僅用於完成時) **+ adv./prep.** to visit or call 前往；造訪；訪問: *I've never been to Spain.* 我從未去過西班牙。◇ *He had been abroad many times.* 他曾多次出國。◇ (*BrE*) *Has the postman been yet?* 郵遞員來過了嗎？ **HELP** In *NAmE*, **come** is used instead 在美式英語中用 come 代替: *Has the mailman come yet?* 郵遞員來過了嗎？ **7** [I] **~ from ...** used to say where sb was born or where their home is 出生於（某地）；來自…；是（某地的）人: *She's from Italy.* 她是意大利人。 **8** *linking verb* used when you are naming people or things, describing them or giving more information about them（提供名稱或信息時用）: **+ noun** *Today is Monday.* 今天是星期一。◇ *'Who is that?' 'It's my brother.'* "那個人是誰？" "是我哥哥。" ◇ *She's a great beauty.* 她是個大美人。◇ *Susan is a doctor.* 蘇珊是醫生。◇ *He wants to be* (= become) *a pilot when he grows up.* 他想在長大後當飛行員。◇ **+ adj.** *It's beautiful!* 美呀！◇ *Life is unfair.* 人生沒有公平。◇ *He is ten years old.* 他十歲了。◇ *'How are you?' 'I'm very well, thanks.'* "你好嗎？" "我很好，謝謝。" ◇ *Be quick!* 快點！◇ **~ (that) ...** ***The fact is*** (that) *we don't have enough money.* 事實是我們沒有那麼多錢。◇ **~ doing sth** *The problem is getting it all done in the time available.* 問題是要在現有的時間內把它全部完成。◇ **~ to do sth** *The problem is to get it all done in the time available.* 問題是要在現有的時間內把它全部完成。 **9** *linking verb* **it is/was** used when you are describing a situation or saying what you think about it（描述情況或表達想法時用）: **+ adj.** *It was really hot in the sauna.* 桑拿浴的確很熱。◇ *It's strange how she never comes to see us any more.* 奇怪，她怎麼再也不來看我們了。◇ *He thinks it's clever to make fun of people.* 他覺得拿別人開玩笑顯得聰明。◇ **+ noun** *It would be a shame if you lost it.* 你要是把它丢了就太可惜了。◇ *It's going to be a great match.* 這將是一場了不起的比賽。 **10** *linking verb* **it is/was** used to talk about time（用於表達時間）: **+ noun** *It's two thirty.* 現在是兩點三十。◇ **+ adj.** *It was late at night when we finally arrived.* 我們最後到達時已是深夜。 **11** *linking verb* **+ noun** used to say what sth is made of（表示所用的材料）: *Is your jacket real leather?* 你的夾克是真皮的嗎？ **12** *linking verb* [I] used to say who sth belongs to or who it is intended for（表示某物所屬）: **~ mine, yours, etc.** *The money's not yours, it's John's.* 這錢不是你的，是約翰的。◇ **~ for me, you, etc.** *This package is for you.* 這份包裹是給你的。 **13** *linking verb* **+ noun** to cost 花費；值: *'How much is that dress?' 'Eighty dollars.'* "那條連衣裙多少錢？" "八十塊錢。" **14** *linking verb* **+ noun** to be equal to 等於；等同: *Three and three is six.* 三加三等於六。◇ *How much is a thousand pounds in euros?* 一千英鎊合多少歐元？◇ *Let x be the sum of a and b.* 設 x 為 a 加 b 之和。◇ *London is not England* (= do not think that all of England is like London). 倫敦並不等於英格蘭（不要以為整個英格蘭都像倫敦）。 **15** *linking verb* **~ everything, nothing, etc. (to sb)** used to say how important sth is to sb（表示對某人的重要性）: *Money isn't everything* (= it is not the only important thing). 金錢不是一切（不是唯一重要的東西）。◇ *A thousand dollars is nothing to somebody as rich as he is.* 一千元對於像他這麼富有的人來說算不上什麼。

IDM Most idioms containing **be** are at the entries for the nouns and adjectives in the idioms, for example **be the death of sb** is at **death**. 大多數含 be 的習語，都可在該等習語中的名詞及形容詞相關詞條找到，如 be the death of sb 在詞條 death 下。 **the ˌbe-all and ˈend-all (of sth)** (*informal*) the most important part; all that matters 最重要的部份；最要緊的事: *Her career is the be-all and end-all of her existence.* 她的事業是她生活中至關重要的事。 **as/that was** as sb/sth used to be called 像以往所稱呼的；作為曾用名: *Jill Davis that was* (= before her marriage)（婚前）姓名為吉爾 • 戴維斯◇ *the Soviet Union, as was* 舊稱蘇聯 **(he, she, etc. has) been and ˈdone sth** (*BrE, informal*) used to show that you are surprised and annoyed by sth that sb has done（表示吃驚和惱怒）: *Someone's been and parked in front of the entrance!* 有人居然把車停在大門口前！ ➲ see also GO AND DO STH at GO *v.* **if it wasn't/weren't for ...** used to say that sb/sth stopped sb/sth from happening 若不是（某人／某事）；幸虧: *If it weren't for you, I wouldn't be alive today.* 如果不是你，我今天不會還活着。 **ˌleave/ˌlet sb/sth ˈbe** to leave sb/sth alone without disturbing them or it 隨…去；不打擾某人／某事: *Leave her be, she obviously doesn't want to talk about it.* 別煩她了，她顯然不想談論這事。◇ *Let the poor dog be* (= don't annoy it). 別逗弄那條可憐的狗了。 **-to-be** (in compounds 構成複合詞) future 將來: *his bride-to-be* 他的未婚妻 ◇ *mothers-to-be* (= pregnant women) 孕婦

■ ***auxiliary verb*** **1** used with a past participle to form the passive（與過去分詞連用構成被動語態）: *He was killed in the war.* 他死於這場戰爭。◇ *Where were they made?* 這些東西是在哪裏製造的？◇ *The house was still being built.* 房子還在建造中。◇ *You will be told what to do.* 會有人告訴你該幹什麼的。 **2** used with a present participle to form progressive tenses（與現在分詞連用構成進行時）: *I am studying Chinese.* 我正在學中文。◇ *I'll be seeing him soon.* 我很快就要見到他了。◇ *What have you been doing this week?* 你這個星期都在做些什麼？◇ *I'm always being criticized.* 我總是受到批評。 **3** used to make QUESTION TAGS (= short questions added to the end of statements)（用於反意疑問句）: *You're not hungry, are you?* 你不餓，對吧？◇ *Ben's coming, isn't he?* 本要來，是不是？◇ *The old theatre was pulled down, wasn't it?* 老戲院被拆了，對不？ **4** used to avoid repeating the full form of a verb in the passive or a progressive tense（在被動語態或進行時中代替重複的動詞完整形式）: *Karen wasn't beaten in any of her games, but all the others were.* 卡倫沒有輸掉任何一場比賽，但所有其他人都輸過。◇ *'Are you coming with us?' 'No, I'm not.'* "你和我們一起去嗎？" "不，我不了。" **5** **~ to do sth** used to say what must or should be done（表示必須或應該）: *I am to call them once I reach the airport.* 我一到機場就得給他們打電話。◇ *You are to report this to the police.* 這件事你應該報警。◇ *What is to be done about this problem?* 該如何處理這個問題？ **6** **~ to do sth** used to say what is arranged to happen（表示已安排好要做的事）: *They are to be married in June.* 他們計劃於六月份結婚。 **7** **~ to do sth** used to say what happened later（表示後來發生的事）: *He was to regret that decision for the rest of his life* (= he did regret it). 他終生都會後悔作出了那一決定。 **8** **~ not, never, etc. to be done** used to say what could not or did not happen（表示不會或沒有發生時用）: *Anna was nowhere to be found* (= we could not find her anywhere). 我們到處都找不到安娜。◇ *He was never to see his wife again* (= although he did not know it would be so at the time, he did not see her again). 他注定再也見不到他的妻子了。◇ *She wanted to write a successful novel, but* ***it was not to be*** (= it turned out never to happen). 她曾想寫一部成功的小說，但從未如願。 **9** **if sb/it were to do sth ...** | **were sb/it to do sth ...** (*formal*) used to express a condition（表述條件）: *If we were to offer you more money, would you stay?* 假如我們給你加錢，你願意留下嗎？◇ *Were we to offer you more money, would you stay?* 假如我們給你加錢，你願意留下嗎？

be- /bɪ-/ *prefix* **1** (in verbs 構成動詞) to make or treat sb/sth as 使…變成；把…當作: *Don't belittle his achievements* (= say they are not important). 不要貶低他的成就。◇ *An older girl befriended me.* 一個年紀大些

B

B

的女孩對我很友善。 **2** (in adjectives ending in *-ed* 構成以 -ed 結尾的形容詞) wearing or covered with 穿着；戴着；裹着： *heavily bejewelled fingers* 戴滿珠寶的手指 ◇ *bespattered with mud* 濺滿污泥 **3** (in verbs and adjectives ending in *-ed* 構成以 -ed 結尾的動詞和形容詞) to cause sth to be 使；使成為： *The ship was becalmed.* (= there was no wind so it could not move) 帆船因無風而停航。 ◇ *The rebels besieged the fort.* 叛亂者包圍了城堡。 **4** used to turn INTRANSITIVE verbs (= without an object) into TRANSITIVE verbs (= with an object)（與不及物動詞結合，構成及物動詞）： *She is always bemoaning her lot.* 她總是怪命不好。

beach 0ꟷ /biːtʃ/ *noun, verb*

■ **noun** 0ꟷ an area of sand or small stones (called SHINGLE), beside the sea or a lake 海灘；沙灘；海濱；湖濱： *tourists sunbathing on the beach* 在海灘上沐浴着陽光的遊客 ◇ *a **sandy/pebble/shingle beach*** 細沙 / 卵石 / 礫石海灘 ◇ *a beach bar* 海濱酒吧 ➲ SYNONYMS at COAST ➲ VISUAL VOCAB pages V4, V5

■ **verb** [T, I] ~ (sth) to come or bring sth out of the water and onto the beach（使）上岸；把…拖上岸： *He beached the boat and lifted the boy onto the shore.* 他把小船拖上岸，把男孩抱到海岸上。 ◇ *a beached whale* (= one that has become stuck on land and cannot get back into the water) 擱淺在海灘上的鯨

'beach ball *noun* a large, light, coloured plastic ball that people play games with on the beach 沙灘球

'beach buggy (also **'dune buggy**) *noun* a small car used for driving on sand 沙灘車

beach·comb·er /ˈbiːtʃkəʊmə(r); *NAmE* -koʊm-/ *noun* a person who walks along beaches collecting interesting or valuable things, either for pleasure or to sell 海灘拾荒者（或尋寶的人）

beach·front /ˈbiːtʃfrʌnt/ (often **the beachfront**) *noun* [sing.] (*especially NAmE*) the part of a town facing the beach 濱海區；濱河區；濱湖區；濱水區： *beachfront hotels/apartments* 海濱旅館 / 公寓

beach·head /ˈbiːtʃhed/ *noun* a strong position on a beach from which an army that has just landed prepares to go forward and attack（軍隊的）灘頭堡，灘頭陣地 ➲ see also BRIDGEHEAD

beach 'volleyball *noun* [U] a form of VOLLEYBALL played on sand by teams of two players 沙灘排球

beach·wear /ˈbiːtʃweə(r); *NAmE* -wer/ *noun* [U] (used especially in shops/stores 尤用於商店) clothes for wearing on the beach 沙灘服裝

bea·con /ˈbiːkən/ *noun* **1** a light that is placed somewhere to guide vehicles and warn them of danger（指引車船等的）燈標，燈塔；立標： *a navigation beacon* 航標燈 ◇ (*figurative*) *He was **a beacon of hope** for the younger generation.* 他是年輕一代的希望之燈。 ➲ see also BELISHA BEACON **2** a radio station whose signal helps ships and aircraft to find their position（導航）無線電信標台 **3** (in the past) a fire lit on top of a hill as a signal（舊時）烽火

Beacon 'Hill *noun* an old, fashionable area of Boston in the US, where many rich families and politicians live 燈塔山（美國波士頓一處古老的高級住宅區）

bead /biːd/ *noun* **1** [C] a small piece of glass, wood, etc. with a hole through it, that can be put on a string with others of the same type and worn as jewellery, etc.（有孔的）珠子： *a necklace of wooden beads* 一條木珠項鏈 ◇ *A bead curtain separated the two rooms.* 一掛珠簾子把兩個房間分開。 ➲ VISUAL VOCAB page V65 ➲ see also WORRY BEADS **2 beads** [pl.] a ROSARY（玫瑰）唸珠 **3** [C] a small drop of liquid（液體的）小滴： *There were beads of sweat on his forehead.* 他的額頭上掛滿汗珠。

IDM **draw/get a 'bead on sb/sth** (*especially NAmE*) to aim carefully at sb/sth before shooting a gun（射擊前）瞄準

bead·ed /ˈbiːdɪd/ *adj.* **1** decorated with beads 飾以珠子的： *a beaded dress* 綴着珠子的連衣裙 **2** ~ **with sth** with small drops of a liquid on it 帶着小滴液體的： *His face was beaded with sweat.* 他臉上掛着汗珠子。

bead·ing /ˈbiːdɪŋ/ *noun* [U] **1** a strip of wood, stone or plastic with a pattern on it, used for decorating walls, doors and furniture 串珠狀緣飾 **2** BEADS that are sewn together and used as a decoration on clothes（衣服上的）串珠飾

beady /ˈbiːdi/ *adj.* (of eyes 眼睛) small, round and bright; watching everything closely or with suspicion 小圓珠般而亮晶晶的；機警的： (*BrE*) *I shall certainly **keep a beady eye** on his behaviour.* 我一定會時刻睜大眼睛提防他的行為。

ˌbeady-'eyed *adj.* (*informal*) watching carefully and noticing every small detail 機警地盯着的；目光銳利的

bea·gle /ˈbiːɡl/ *noun* a small dog with short legs, used in hunting 小獵兔犬

beak 0ꟷ /biːk/ *noun*

1 0ꟷ the hard pointed or curved outer part of a bird's mouth 鳥喙 SYN **bill**： *The gull held the fish in its beak.* 海鷗嘴裏叼着魚。 ➲ VISUAL VOCAB page V12 **2** (*humorous*) a person's nose, especially when it is large and/or pointed 鷹鈎鼻；尖鼻；鼻子 **3** (*old-fashioned, BrE, slang*) a person in a position of authority, especially a judge 掌權者；（尤指）法官

beaked /biːkt/ *adj.* (usually in compounds 通常構成複合詞) having a beak, or the type of beak mentioned 有…喙的： *flat-beaked* 扁平喙的

bea·ker /ˈbiːkə(r)/ *noun* **1** (*BrE*) a plastic or paper cup, often without a handle, used for drinking from（常指無柄的）塑料杯，紙杯 ➲ VISUAL VOCAB pages V22, V24 **2** (*BrE*) the amount contained in a beaker 一杯（的量）： *a beaker of coffee* 一杯咖啡 **3** a glass cup with straight sides and a lip, used in chemistry, for example for measuring liquids 燒杯 ➲ VISUAL VOCAB page V70

beam /biːm/ *noun, verb*

■ **noun** **1** a line of light, electric waves or PARTICLES 光線；（電波的）波束；（粒子的）束： *narrow **beams of light/sunlight*** 一絲絲的光線 / 陽光 ◇ *the **beam of a torch/flashlight*** 手電筒光柱 ◇ *a **laser/electron beam*** 激光束；電子束 ◇ (*BrE*) *The car's headlights were on **full beam*** (= shining as brightly as possible and not directed downwards). 那輛汽車大開着前燈。 ◇ (*NAmE*) *a car with its **high beams** on* 前燈大開着的汽車 **2** a long piece of wood, metal, etc. used to support weight, especially as part of the roof in a building 梁： *The cottage had exposed oak beams.* 小屋的橡木梁裸露着。 **3** (*especially BrE*) (*NAmE* usually **'balance beam**) a wooden bar that is used in the sport of GYMNASTICS for people to move and balance on 平衡木 **4** a wide and happy smile 笑容；眉開眼笑： *a beam of satisfaction* 滿意的笑容

IDM **off 'beam** (*informal*) not correct; wrong 不正確；錯誤： *Your calculation is way off beam.* 你的計算完全錯誤。

■ **verb** **1** [I, T, no passive] to have a big happy smile on your face 笑容滿面；眉開眼笑： ~ **(at sb)** *He beamed at the journalists.* 他笑容滿面地面對記者。 ◇ ~ **(with sth)** *She was positively beaming with pleasure.* 她的確喜不自勝。 ◇ ~ **sth (at sb)** *The barman beamed a warm smile at her.* 酒吧侍者對她熱情地微笑。 ◇ *'I'd love to come,' she beamed* (= said with a large smile). "我很樂意來。" 她滿面笑容地說。 **2** [T] + **adv./prep.** to send radio or television signals over long distances using electronic equipment 發射（電波）；播送： *Live pictures of the ceremony were beamed around the world.* 典禮的實況經電視直播傳到世界各地。 **3** [I] + **adv./prep.** to produce a stream of light and/or heat 照射；發光；發熱： *The morning sun beamed down on us.* 早上的太陽照射着我們。 ◇ *Light beamed through a hole in the curtain.* 光線透過窗簾上的一個孔照射進來。 IDM see EAR

PHR V **ˌbeam sb 'down/'up** (in SCIENCE FICTION stories 科幻小說中) to transport sb to or from a SPACESHIP using special electronic equipment 用特殊的電子設備將人運送至太空飛船或從太空飛船運送至其他地方 ORIGIN From the American television series *Star Trek*. 源自美國電視連續劇《星際迷航》。

beamed /biːmd/ *adj.* having beams of wood 有木梁的： *a high beamed ceiling* 木梁高高支撐着的天花板

bean /biːn/ *noun, verb*

■ *noun* **1** a seed, or POD containing seeds, of a climbing plant, eaten as a vegetable. There are several types of bean and the plants that they grow on are also called beans. 豆；菜豆；豆莢；豆科植物：*broad beans* 蠶豆 ◇ *runner beans* 紅花菜豆 ◇ *beans* (= BAKED BEANS) *on toast* 麵包片加烘豆 ➲ VISUAL VOCAB page V31 **2** (usually in compounds 通常構成複合詞) a seed from a coffee plant, or some other plants（咖啡樹或其他某些植物的）籽實：*coffee/cocoa beans* 咖啡 / 可可豆 ➲ see also JELLY BEAN

IDM **full of 'beans/'life** (of a person 人) having a lot of energy 精力充沛 **not have a 'bean** (*BrE, informal*) to have no money 沒錢；不名一文 ➲ more at HILL, KNOW *v.*, SPILL *v.*

■ *verb* **~ sb** (*NAmE, informal*) to hit sb on the head 擊中（某人）頭部：*I got beaned by a rock someone threw.* 我的頭被扔出的石頭砸中了。

bean·bag /ˈbiːnbæg/ *noun* **1** a very large bag made of cloth and filled with small pieces of plastic, used for sitting on 豆袋坐墊（內填碎塑料）**2** a small bag made of cloth filled with BEANS or small pieces of plastic and used as a ball 豆子袋（內填豆粒或碎塑料的小布袋，當作球玩）

'bean counter *noun* (*informal, disapproving*) a person who works with money, for example as an ACCOUNTANT and who wants to keep strict control of how much money a company spends 精打細算的賬房先生；"鐵公雞"會計

'bean curd *noun* [U] = TOFU

bean·feast /ˈbiːnfiːst/ *noun* (*old-fashioned, BrE*) a party or celebration 聚會；喜慶

beanie /ˈbiːni/ *noun* a small, round close-fitting hat 無簷小便帽 ➲ VISUAL VOCAB page V65

beano /ˈbiːnəʊ; *NAmE* -noʊ/ *noun* (*pl.* **-os**) (*BrE, informal*) a party 招待會；聚會；宴會

bean·pole /ˈbiːnpəʊl; *NAmE* -poʊl/ *noun* (*informal*, usually *disapproving*) a tall thin person 瘦高個子

'bean sprouts *noun* [pl.] BEAN seeds that are just beginning to grow, often eaten raw 豆芽（常生食）➲ VISUAL VOCAB page V31

bean·stalk /ˈbiːnstɔːk/ *noun* the tall fast-growing STEM of a BEAN plant 豆莖

bear 0ᵒ /beə(r); *NAmE* ber/ *verb, noun*

■ *verb* (**bore** /bɔː(r)/, **borne** /bɔːn; *NAmE* bɔːrn/)

▸ ACCEPT/DEAL WITH 承受；應付 **1** 0ᵒ [T] (used with *can/could* in negative sentences and questions 在否定句和疑問句中與 can/could 連用) to be able to accept and deal with sth unpleasant 承受；忍受 SYN **stand**：**~ sth** *The pain was almost more than he could bear.* 這種痛苦幾乎使他無法忍受。◇ *She* ***couldn't bear the thought of*** *losing him.* 失去他的情況她想都不敢想。◇ **~ doing sth** *I can't bear having cats in the house.* 家裏有貓我可受不了。◇ *He can't bear being laughed at.* 他無法忍受遭人嘲笑。◇ **~ to do sth** *He can't bear to be laughed at.* 他無法忍受遭人嘲笑。◇ **~ sb doing sth** *I can't bear you doing that.* 我無法忍受你做那種事。➲ SYNONYMS at HATE

▸ NOT BE SUITABLE 不合適 **2** [T] **not ~** to not be suitable for sth 不適於某事（或做某事）：**~ sth** *Her later work* ***does not bear comparison*** *with her earlier novels* (= because it is not nearly as good). 她後期的作品比不上她早期的小說。◇ *The plan* ***won't bear*** *close* ***inspection*** (= it will be found to be unacceptable when carefully examined). 這項計劃經不起仔細檢查。◇ **~ doing sth** *The joke* ***doesn't bear repeating*** (= because it is not funny or may offend people). 這個笑話不可說第二遍（因為不好笑或可能得罪人）。◇ *His sufferings* ***don't bear thinking about*** (= because they are so terrible). 他遭受的苦難不堪回首。

▸ BE RESPONSIBLE FOR STH 負責 **3** 0ᵒ [T] **~ sth** (*formal*) to take responsibility for sth 承擔責任：*She* ***bore the responsibility*** *for most of the changes.* 她對大多數變革負責。◇ *Do parents have to* ***bear the*** *whole* ***cost*** *of tuition fees?* 父母是否應當負擔全部學費？◇ *You shouldn't have to* ***bear the blame*** *for other people's mistakes.* 你不應該非得代人受過。

▸ NEGATIVE FEELING 壞心情 **4** [T] to have a feeling, especially a negative feeling 心懷（感情，尤指壞心情）：**~ sth (against/towards sb)** *He* ***bears no resentment*** *towards them.* 他對他們毫無怨恨。◇ *He's* ***borne a grudge*** *against me ever since that day.* 從那一天起他便對我懷恨在心。◇ **~ sb sth** *He's* ***borne me a grudge*** *ever since that day.* 從那一天起他便對我懷恨在心。◇ *She* ***bore him no ill will.*** 她對他沒有惡意。

▸ SUPPORT WEIGHT 支撐重量 **5** 0ᵒ [T] **~ sth** to support the weight of sb/sth 支撐，承受（重量）：*The ice is too thin to bear your weight.* 冰太薄，承受不住你的重量。

▸ SHOW 顯示 **6** [T] **~ sth** (*formal*) to show sth; to carry sth so that it can be seen 顯示；帶有：*The document bore her signature.* 文件上有她的簽字。◇ *He was badly wounded in the war and still bears the scars.* 他在戰爭中負了重傷，現在還留有傷疤。◇ *She* ***bears little resemblance to*** (= is not much like) *her mother.* 她很不像她的母親。◇ *The title of the essay* ***bore little relation to*** (= was not much connected with) *the contents.* 這篇文章的題目與內容很不相符。

▸ NAME 名稱 **7** [T] **~ sth** (*formal*) to have a particular name 有（某個名稱）：*a family that bore an ancient and honoured name* 名門世家

▸ CARRY 攜帶 **8** [T] **~ sb/sth** (*old-fashioned* or *formal*) to carry sb/sth, especially while moving 攜帶：*three kings bearing gifts* 三個帶着禮品的國王

▸ YOURSELF 自身 **9** [T] **~ yourself well, etc.** (*formal*) to move, behave or act in a particular way 舉止；表現：*He bears himself* (= stands, walks, etc.) *proudly, like a soldier.* 他昂首闊步，像個軍人。◇ *She bore herself with dignity throughout the funeral.* 整個葬禮過程中她都保持着尊嚴。

▸ CHILD 孩子 **10** [T] (*formal*) to give birth to a child 生孩子：**~ sth** *She was not able to bear children.* 她不能生育。◇ **~ sb sth** *She had borne him six sons.* 她為他生了六個兒子。

▸ OF TREES/PLANTS 樹木花草 **11** [T] **~ sth** (*formal*) to produce flowers or fruit 開（花）；結（果實）

▸ TURN 轉向 **12** [I] **~ (to the) left, north, etc.** to go or turn in the direction mentioned 轉向（左或北等）：*When you get to the fork in the road, bear right.* 走到岔道時向右拐。

IDM **bear 'arms** (*old use*) to be a soldier; to fight 當兵；打仗 **bear 'fruit** to have a successful result 成功；取得成果 **bear 'hard, 'heavily, se'verely, etc. on sb** (*formal*) to be a cause of difficulty or suffering to sb 使為難；使受苦；壓迫：*Taxation bears heavily on us all.* 賦稅給我們大家帶來沉重的負擔。**be borne 'in on sb** (*formal, especially BrE*) to be realized by sb, especially after a period of time（逐漸）認識到：*It was gradually borne in on us that defeat was inevitable.* 我們逐漸認識到，失敗是不可避免的。**bring sth to bear (on sb/sth)** (*formal*) to use energy, pressure, influence, etc. to try to achieve sth or make sb do sth 把精力用於；對…施加壓力（或影響等）：*We must bring all our energies to bear upon the task.* 我們必須全力以赴不辱使命。◇ ***Pressure was brought to bear*** *on us to finish the work on time.* 我們得按時完成工作，沒有迴旋餘地。➲ more at BRUNT, CROSS *n.*, GRIN *v.*, MIND *n.*, WITNESS *n.*

PHR V **,bear 'down on sb/sth 1** (*especially BrE*) to move quickly towards sb/sth in a determined or threatening way 衝向；咄咄逼近 **2** (*especially NAmE*) to press on sb/sth 施加壓力於；壓住：*Bear down on it with all your strength so it doesn't move.* 用全力壓住它，別讓它動彈。

'bear on sth (*formal*) to relate to sth 和（某事物）有關；涉及 SYN **affect**：*These are matters that bear on the welfare of the community.* 這些是關係到整個社群的福祉的事情。**,bear sb/sth↔'out** (*especially BrE*) to show that sb is right or that sth is true 證實；為…作證：*The other witnesses will bear me out.* 其他證人將給我作證。◇ *The other witnesses will bear out what I say.* 其他證人將會證實我的話。**,bear 'up (against/under sth)** to remain as cheerful as possible during a difficult time 保持振作；承受；挺住：*He's bearing up well under the strain of losing his job.* 他堅強地頂住了失業的壓力。◇ *'How are you?' 'Bearing up.'* "你怎麼樣了？""還挺得住。"

'bear with sb/sth to be patient with sb/sth 耐心對待；容忍：*She's under a lot of strain. Just bear with her.* 她承受着很大的壓力。對她容忍一下。◇ *If you will bear with*

B

me (= be patient and listen to me) *a little longer, I'll answer your question.* 你如果能耐心點聽我把話說完，我會回答你的問題的。

■ **noun** **1** a heavy wild animal with thick fur and sharp CLAWS (= pointed parts on the ends of its feet). There are many types of bear. 熊：*a black bear* 黑熊 ➲ see also GRIZZLY BEAR, POLAR BEAR, TEDDY BEAR **2** (*finance* 財) a person who sells shares in a company, etc., hoping to buy them back later at a lower price （在證券市場等）賣空的人 ➲ compare BULL (3) ➲ see also BEARISH

IDM **like a bear with a sore 'head** (*informal*) bad-tempered or in a bad-tempered way 急性子；脾氣暴躁

bear·able /'beərəbl; NAmE 'ber-/ *adj.* a person or thing that is **bearable** can be accepted or dealt with 可忍受的；能應付的：*She was the only thing that made life bearable.* 只因有了她生活才可以過得下去。OPP **unbearable**

beard 0‑ /bɪəd; NAmE bɪrd/ *noun, verb*

■ **noun** 0‑ [C, U] hair that grows on the chin and cheeks of a man's face; similar hair that grows on some animals （人的）鬍鬚，絡腮鬍子；（動物的）頜毛，鬚：*He has decided to grow a beard and a moustache.* 他已經決定留起絡腮鬍子和髭。◇ *a week's growth of beard* 一星期未刮的鬍子 ◇ *a goat's beard* 山羊的鬍子 ➲ COLLOCATIONS at PHYSICAL ➲ VISUAL VOCAB page V60 ➲ compare MOUSTACHE ▸ **beard·ed** *adj.*：*a bearded face/man* 有鬍子的臉／男子

■ **verb**

IDM **to beard the lion in his 'den** to go to see an important or powerful person to tell them that you disagree with them, that you want sth, etc. 進獅穴捋獅鬚（敢於觸犯有權勢者）

beardie /'bɪədi; NAmE 'bɪrdi/ *noun* (*BrE, informal, disapproving*) a man with a beard 蓄鬚的男子；大鬍子

bear·er /'beərə(r); NAmE 'ber-/ *noun* **1** a person whose job is to carry sth, especially at a ceremony （尤指在禮儀中）持…者：*coffin bearers* 扶靈者 ➲ see also PALLBEARER, RING BEARER, STANDARD-BEARER, STRETCHER-BEARER **2** a person who brings a message, a letter, etc. 傳達消息者；送信人：*I'm sorry to be the bearer of bad news.* 很遺憾我帶來了壞消息。**3** (*formal*) a person who has sth with them or is the official owner of sth, such as a document 持有者；正式持有人；持票人：*A pass will allow the bearer to enter the building.* 持有通行證者方可進入這棟大樓。**4** a person who has knowledge of sth, such as an idea or a tradition, and makes sure that it is not forgotten, by teaching others about it （觀念、傳統等的）傳授者，傳播者

'bear hug *noun* an act of showing affection for sb by holding them very tightly and strongly in your arms 緊緊的（或熱烈的）擁抱

bear·ing /'beərɪŋ; NAmE 'ber-/ *noun* **1** [U] **~ on sth** the way in which sth is related to sth or influences it 關係；影響：*Recent events had no bearing on our decision.* 近期的事件與我們的決定沒有關係。◇ *Regular exercise has a direct bearing on fitness and health.* 經常性鍛煉對於身體健康有直接影響。**2** [sing.] the way in which you stand, walk or behave 姿態；舉止：*Her whole bearing was alert.* 她整個人保持着戒備狀態。**3** [C] (*technical* 術語) a direction measured from a fixed point using a COMPASS （用羅盤測定的）方位 **4** [C] (*technical* 術語) a part of a machine that supports a moving part, especially one that is turning （機器的）承座；（尤指）軸承 ➲ see also BALL BEARING

IDM **get/find/take your 'bearings** to make yourself familiar with your surroundings in order to find out where you are or to feel comfortable in a place 判明方位；弄清自己所處的地位；熟悉環境 **lose your 'bearings** to become lost or confused 迷失方向；陷入困惑

bear·ish /'beərɪʃ; NAmE 'ber-/ *adj.* (*finance* 財) showing or expecting a fall in the prices of shares 熊市的；（證券市場）看跌的：*a bearish market* 跌市 ◇ *Japanese banks remain bearish.* 日本銀行繼續看跌。➲ compare BULLISH (2)

'bear market *noun* (*finance* 財) a period during which people are selling shares, etc. rather than buying, because they expect the prices to fall 熊市（預期價格下跌而售出股票的一段時期）➲ compare BULL MARKET

bear·skin /'beəskɪn; NAmE 'bers-/ *noun* **1** the skin and fur of a BEAR 熊皮：*a bearskin rug* 熊皮地毯 **2** a tall hat of black fur worn for special ceremonies by some British soldiers 熊皮高帽；英國禁衞軍帽

beast /bi:st/ *noun* **1** (*old-fashioned* or *formal*) an animal, especially one that is large or dangerous, or one that is unusual （尤指大型或兇猛、獨特的）動物，獸：***wild/savage/ferocious beasts*** 野獸；猛獸；兇殘的動物 ◇ ***mythical beasts*** *such as unicorns and dragons* 獨角獸和龍之類的神異動物 **2** a person who is cruel and whose behaviour is uncontrolled 性情兇殘的人；行為粗暴的人 SYN **animal** **3** (*informal*, often *humorous*) an unpleasant person or thing 討厭的人（或事物）：*The maths exam was a real beast.* 數學考試實在令人憎惡。**4** (*informal*) a thing of a particular kind （某種）東西 SYN **animal**：*His new guitar is a very expensive beast.* 他的新吉他貴得嚇人。

beast·ly /'bi:stli/ *adj.* (*old-fashioned, BrE, informal*) unpleasant 惡劣的；討厭的；令人厭惡的 SYN **horrible, nasty** ▸ **beast·li·ness** *noun* [U]

Synonyms 同義詞辨析

beat

batter • pound • lash • hammer

These words all mean to hit sb/sth many times, especially hard. 以上各詞均含多次擊打之義，尤指用力打。

beat to hit sb/sth a lot of times, especially very hard 指反複敲打、使勁錘砸：*Someone was beating at the door.* 有人在打門。◇ *A young man was found beaten to death last night.* 昨天夜裏有人發現一名小伙子被打死了。◇ *At that time, children were often beaten for quite minor offences* (= as a punishment). 那時候孩子們常常因為很小的過錯而捱打。

batter to hit sb/sth hard a lot of times, especially in a way that causes serious damage 指連續猛擊，尤指造成傷害或破壞：*He had been badly battered around the head and face.* 他被打得鼻青臉腫。◇ *Severe winds have been battering the coast.* 狂風一直在海岸肆虐。

pound to hit sb/sth hard a lot of times, especially in a way that makes a lot of noise 指連續猛擊，尤指發出砰砰的撞擊聲：*Heavy rain pounded on the roof.* 暴雨砰砰地砸在屋頂上。

lash to hit sb/sth with a lot of force 指猛擊、狠打：*The rain lashed at the window.* 雨點猛烈地打在窗戶上。NOTE The subject of **lash** is often *rain, wind, hail, sea* or *waves.* * lash 的主語常為 rain、wind、hail、sea 或 waves。

hammer to hit sb/sth hard a lot of times, in a way that is noisy or violent 指大聲、猛烈地反複敲打、連續擊打：*He hammered the door with his fists.* 他不斷地用拳頭擂門。

POUND OR HAMMER? 用 pound 還是 hammer？

There is not much difference in meaning between these two, but to **pound** is sometimes a steadier action. To **hammer** can be more violent and it is often used figuratively. 這兩個詞意思差別不大，但 pound 有時指較勻速而穩定地擊打；hammer 更猛烈，且常用作比喻。

PATTERNS

- to beat/batter/pound/lash/hammer sb/sth **with** sth
- to beat/batter/pound/lash/hammer **against** sth
- to beat/batter/pound/hammer **on** sth
- to beat/batter/hammer sth **down**
- the **rain/wind/sea** beats/batters/pounds/lashes (at) sth

ˌ**beast of ˈburden** *noun* an animal used for heavy work such as carrying or pulling things 役畜；牲口；馱獸

beat 🔑 /biːt/ *verb, noun, adj.*

■ *verb* (**beat**, **beaten** /ˈbiːtn/)

▸ **IN GAME** 比賽 **1** 🔑 [T] **~ sb (at sth)** to defeat sb in a game or competition （在比賽或競爭中）贏，打敗（某人） **SYN** **defeat**： *He beat me at chess.* 他下棋贏了我。◇ *Their recent wins have proved they're still **the ones to beat*** (= the most difficult team to beat). 他們最近的勝利已證明，他們仍然是最難打敗的隊。

▸ **CONTROL** 控制 **2** 🔑 [T] **~ sth** (*informal*) to get control of sth 控制： *The government's main aim is to beat inflation.* 政府的主要目標是抑制通貨膨脹。

▸ **BE TOO DIFFICULT** 太難 **3** 🔑 [T] (*informal*) to be too difficult for sb 難倒 **SYN** **defeat**： **~ sb** *a problem that beats even the experts* 連專家都難以解決的問題 ◇ **~ sb why, how, etc. …** ***It beats me*** (= I don't know) *why he did it.* 我弄不懂他為什麼這樣做。◇ ***What beats me** is how it was done so quickly* (= I don't understand how). 使我困惑不解的是，這事怎麼這麼快就完成了。

▸ **BE BETTER** 更好 **4** 🔑 [T] **~ sth** (rather *informal*) to do or be better than sth 比…更好；賽過；勝過： ***Nothing beats** home cooking.* 什麼也比不上家裏做的好吃。◇ ***You can't beat** Italian shoes.* 意大利鞋是無與倫比的。◇ *They want to **beat the** speed **record*** (= go faster than anyone before). 他們想打破這一速度紀錄。

▸ **AVOID** 避免 **5** [T] **~ sth** (*informal*) to avoid sth 避免；逃避： *If we go early we should beat the traffic.* 我們早點出發應該就可以避開交通擁擠。◇ *We were up and off early to **beat the heat**.* 我們很早就起牀出發了，趁天還沒熱。

▸ **HIT** 擊打 **6** 🔑 [I, T] to hit sb/sth many times, usually very hard 敲打；錘砸： **+ adv./prep.** *Somebody was beating at the door.* 有人在打門。◇ *Hailstones beat against the window.* 冰雹不斷地砸在窗戶上。◇ **~ sth** *Someone was beating a drum.* 有人在敲鼓。◇ **~ sth + adv./prep.** *She was beating dust out of the carpet* (= removing dust from the carpet by beating it). 她正在拍掉地毯上的灰塵。◇ **~ sb** *At that time children were regularly beaten for quite minor offences* (= a punishment). 那時候孩子們常常因為很小的過錯而捱打。◇ **~ sb + adv./prep.** *An elderly man was found **beaten to death**.* 有人發現一名老翁被打死了。◇ **~ sb + adj.** *They beat him unconscious* (= hit him until he became unconscious). 他們把他打得不省人事。

▸ **OF HEART/DRUMS/WINGS** 心臟；鼓；翅膀 **7** 🔑 [I, T] to make, or cause sth to make, a regular sound or movement （使）規律作響，作節奏運動： *She's alive—her **heart is** still **beating**.* 她沒死 —— 她的心還在跳動。◇ *We heard the **drums beating**.* 我們聽到鼓聲。◇ *The bird was **beating its wings*** (= moving them up and down) *frantically.* 鳥兒沒命地撲着翅膀。

▸ **MIX** 攪拌 **8** 🔑 [T] to mix sth with short quick movements with a fork, etc. （用叉等）快速攪拌，打： **~ sth (up)** *Beat the eggs up to a frothy consistency.* 把雞蛋打成黏稠泡沫狀。◇ **~ A and B together** *Beat the flour and milk together.* 把麪粉和牛奶攪拌在一起。

▸ **SHAPE METAL** 使金屬成形 **9** [T] to change the shape of sth, especially metal, by hitting it with a hammer, etc. 把（金屬等）錘成；敲打（成…）： **~ sth (out) (into sth)** *beaten silver* 銀箔 ◇ *The gold is beaten out into thin strips.* 金子被錘成了薄薄的長條。◇ **~ sth + adj.** *The metal had been beaten flat.* 那塊金屬被錘薄了。

▸ **MAKE PATH** 開闢路徑 **10** [T] **~ sth (through, across, along, etc. sth)** to make a path, etc. by walking somewhere or by pressing branches down and walking over them 踏出，踩出（道路）： *a well-beaten track* (= one that has been worn hard by much use) 經過很多人踏出來的路 ◇ *The hunters beat a path through the undergrowth.* 獵人們在灌木叢中踩出了一條小徑。

IDM **beat about the ˈbush** (*BrE*) (*NAmE* **beat around the ˈbush**) to talk about sth for a long time without coming to the main point 拐彎抹角地講話；繞圈子： *Stop beating about the bush and tell me what you want.* 別繞來繞去了，告訴我你想要什麼吧。 **beat sb at their own ˈgame** to defeat or do better than sb in an activity which they have chosen or in which they think they are strong 贏某人的看家本領；打敗某人的強項 **beat your ˈbrains out** (*informal, especially NAmE*) to think very hard about sth for a long time 絞盡腦汁；反複推敲 **beat your ˈbreast** to show that you feel sorry about sth that you have done, especially in public and in an exaggerated way 捶胸頓足（尤指對自己的作為刻意表示悲傷或愧疚） **beat the ˈclock** to finish a task, race, etc. before a particular time 提前完成任務（或跑到終點等） **ˈbeat it** (*slang*) (usually used in orders 通常用於命令) to go away immediately 滾開；立即走開： *This is private land, so beat it!* 這裏是私人土地，滾開！ **beat a path to sb's ˈdoor** if a lot of people **beat a path to sb's door**, they are all interested in sth that person has to sell, or can do or tell them 使門庭若市；蜂擁而至；使成注意焦點： *Top theatrical agents are beating a path to the teenager's door.* 頂尖級戲劇演員代理人正紛紛把目光投向那個青少年。 **beat the ˈrap** (*NAmE, slang*) to escape without being punished 逃脱懲罰 **beat a (hasty) reˈtreat** to go away or back quickly, especially to avoid sth unpleasant （倉促）逃走；（慌忙）撤退 **beat ˈtime (to sth)** to mark or follow the rhythm of music, by waving a stick, tapping your foot, etc. （隨着音樂）打拍子： *She beat time with her fingers.* 她用手指打拍子。 **beat sb to the ˈpunch** (*informal*) to get or do sth before sb else can 搶先下手；搶在前面 **can you beat that/it!** (*informal*) used to express surprise or anger 難以置信；太不像話 **if you can't beat them, ˈjoin them** (*saying*) if you cannot defeat sb or be as successful as they are, then it is more sensible to join them in what they are doing and perhaps get some advantage for yourself by doing so 打不贏，就投靠 ˌ**off the ˌbeaten ˈtrack** far away from other people, houses, etc. 遠離鬧市；偏遠： *They live miles off the beaten track.* 他們住在偏遠地帶。 **a rod/stick to ˈbeat sb with** a fact, an argument, etc. that is used in order to blame or punish sb 用以責備或懲罰某人的事實依據（或把柄等） **take some ˈbeating** to be difficult to beat 難以超越： *That score is going to take some beating.* 那一得分將很難超過。◇ *For sheer luxury, this hotel takes some beating.* 單看豪華的程度，這家旅館是難以超越的。 ➲ more at BLACK *adj.*, DAYLIGHTS, DRUM *n.*, HELL

PHR V ˌ**beat sth↔ˈdown** to hit a door, etc. many times until it breaks open 砸開，砸破（門等） ˌ**beat ˈdown (on sb/sth)** if the sun **beats down** it shines with great heat （陽光）強烈照射，曝曬 ˌ**beat sb/sth ˈdown (to sth)** to persuade sb to reduce the price at which they are selling sth 說服某人降價；殺價： *He wanted $8 000 for the car but I beat him down to $6 000.* 他那輛汽車要價 8 000 元，但我壓到了 6 000 元。◇ *I beat down the price to $6 000.* 我把價殺到了 6 000 元。 ˌ**beat ˈoff** (*NAmE, taboo, slang*) to MASTURBATE 手淫 ˌ**beat sb/sth↔ˈoff** to force sb/sth back or away by fighting 擊退；驅走： *The attacker was beaten off.* 襲擊者被擊退了。◇ *She beat off a challenge to her leadership.* 她戰勝了對她的領導地位的挑戰。 ˈ**beat on sb** = BEAT UP ON SB ˌ**beat sth↔ˈout** **1** to produce a rhythm by hitting sth many times 敲打出節奏 **2** to put a fire out by beating 撲打滅（火）： *We beat the flames out.* 我們把火撲打滅了。 **3** to remove sth by hitting it with a HAMMER, etc. 敲掉；錘平： *They can beat out the dent in the car's wing.* 他們能把汽車擋泥板上的凹痕敲平。 ˌ**beat sth ˈout of sb** to hit sb until they tell you what you want to know 毆打某人逼其說出 ˈ**beat sb out of sth** (*NAmE, informal*) to cheat sb by taking sth from them （從某人）騙取，騙得： *Her brother beat her out of $200.* 她哥哥騙走了她 200 元。 ˈ**beat sb to sth/ …** | ˌ**beat sb ˈto it** to get somewhere or do sth before sb else 搶先；捷足先登： *She beat me to the top of the hill.* 她比我先到達山頂。◇ *I was about to take the last cake, but he beat me to it.* 我正要拿那最後一塊餅，卻給他搶先一步。 ˌ**beat sb↔ˈup** 🔑 to hit or kick sb hard, many times 痛毆；毒打： *He was badly beaten up by a gang of thugs.* 他被一幫暴徒打得遍體鱗傷。 ˌ**beat ˈup on sb** (also ˈ**beat on sb**) (*NAmE*) to blame sb too much for sth 過分責備： *Don't beat up on Paul, he tried his best.* 不要過分責備保羅，他已經盡力了。 ˌ**beat yourself ˈup (about/over sth)** (also ˌ**beat ˈup on yourself (about/over sth)**) (*NAmE, informal*) to blame yourself too much for sth （為某事）過分自責： *Look, there's no need to beat yourself up over this.* 聽我說，沒有必要為此過分自責。

B

■ *noun*
▸ OF DRUMS/HEART/WINGS 鼓；心臟；翅膀 **1** [C] a single blow to sth, such as a drum, or a movement of sth, such as your heart; the sound that this makes （鼓的）一擊；（翅的）一振；（心臟等的）跳動；擊鼓聲；振翅聲；跳動聲：*several loud beats on the drum* 幾下隆隆鼓聲 ◇ (*figurative*) *His heart missed a beat when he saw her.* 他在見到她的一剎那心跳頓了一下。 **2** [sing.] a series of regular blows to sth, such as a drum; the sound that this makes 有規律的敲擊（聲）：*the steady beat of the drums* 有節奏的敲鼓聲 ➲ see also HEARTBEAT
▸ RHYTHM 節奏 **3** [C] the main rhythm, or a unit of rhythm, in a piece of music, a poem, etc.（音樂、詩歌等的）主節奏，節拍：*This type of music has a strong beat to it.* 這種音樂節奏感很強。◇ *The piece has four beats to the bar.* 這首曲子每小節四拍。
▸ OF POLICE OFFICER 警察 **4** [C, usually sing.] the area that a police officer walks around regularly and which he or she is responsible for （警察）巡邏地段：*More police officers out* ***on the beat*** *may help to cut crime.* 增加巡邏的警察可能有助於減少罪行。 IDM see HEART, MARCH *v.*, WALK *v.*
■ *adj.* [not before noun] (*informal*) = DEAD BEAT

beat·box /ˈbiːtbɒks; *NAmE* -bɑːks/ *noun, verb*
■ *noun* **1** [C] (*informal*) an electronic machine that produces drum sounds 電子鼓 **2** [C] (*informal*) a radio, CD player, etc. that can be carried around and is used for playing loud music 播放重音樂的收音機（或 CD 播放機等）；重音樂播放機 **3** (also **beat·boxer**) [C] a person who uses the voice to make sounds in HIP HOP （嘻哈音樂的）節奏口技表演者，口技說唱者 **4** [U] music that is created using sounds made with the human voice 人聲敲擊樂；節奏口技
■ *verb* [I] to imitate the sound of a drum with the voice 人聲模仿鼓聲；表演節奏口技

beat·box·ing /ˈbiːtbɒksɪŋ; *NAmE* -bɑːks-/ *noun* [U] the use of the human voice to create the beat in HIP HOP （嘻哈音樂的）節奏口技：*an amazing beatboxing performance* 令人驚歎的節奏口技表演

ˌbeaten-ˈup *adj.* = BEAT-UP

beat·er /ˈbiːtə(r)/ *noun* **1** (often in compounds 常構成複合詞) a tool used for beating things 拍打器；攪拌器：*a carpet beater* 地毯拍子 ◇ *an egg beater* 打蛋器 **2** a person employed to drive birds and animals out of bushes, etc., into the open, so they can be shot for sport 驅獵物者（受雇將鳥獸從樹叢中趕到開闊地供人射獵） **3** **-beater** (in compounds 構成複合詞) a person who hits someone 打…的人：*a wife-beater* 毆打妻子的人 **4** (*NAmE*) (*BrE* **bang·er**) (*informal*) an old car that is in bad condition 破舊的汽車 ➲ see also WORLD-BEATER

the ˈbeat generation *noun* [sing.] a group of young people in the 1950s and early 1960s who rejected the way most people lived in society, wanted to express themselves freely, and liked modern JAZZ 垮掉的一代（指 20 世紀 50 年代和 60 年代初期拒絕主流生活方式、追求個性自我表現、欣賞現代爵士樂的一批年輕人）

bea·tif·ic /ˌbiːəˈtɪfɪk/ *adj.* (*formal*) showing great joy and peace 快樂安詳的；幸福的：***a beatific smile/expression*** 幸福的微笑／表情

be·atify /biˈætɪfaɪ/ *verb* (**be·ati·fies**, **be·ati·fy·ing**, **be·ati·fied**, **be·ati·fied**) **~ sb** (of the Pope 教宗) to give a dead person a special honour by stating officially that he/she is very holy 為（逝者）行宣福禮 ➲ compare BLESS, CANONIZE ▸ **be·ati·fi·ca·tion** /biˌætɪfɪˈkeɪʃn/ *noun* [C, U]

beat·ing /ˈbiːtɪŋ/ *noun* **1** [C] an act of hitting sb hard and repeatedly, as a punishment or in a fight 狠打；揍；笞打：*to give sb a beating* 把某人揍一頓 **2** [C] (*informal*) a very heavy defeat 慘敗；嚴重受挫：*The team has* ***taken*** *a few* ***beatings*** *this season.* 本賽季該隊已經幾次嚴重受挫。 **3** [U] a series of regular blows to sth such as a drum, or movements of sth, such as your heart; the sound that this makes 有規律的敲打（聲）；有節奏的運動（聲）：*He could hear the beating of his own heart.* 他聽得到自己的心跳。◇ *the* ***beating of drums/wings*** 敲鼓聲；翅膀的拍打聲
IDM **take some ˈbeating** (*BrE*) to be difficult to do or be better than 難以超越：*As a place to live, Oxford takes some beating.* 就居住環境而論，牛津市是個難得的好地方。

be·ati·tude /biˈætɪtjuːd; *NAmE* -tuːd/ *noun* **the Beati·tudes** [pl.] (in the Bible《聖經》) the eight statements made by Christ about people who are BLESSED 八福，真福八端（耶穌的山中聖訓）

beat·nik /ˈbiːtnɪk/ *noun* a young person in the 1950s and early 1960s who rejected the way of life of ordinary society and showed this by behaving and dressing in a different way from most people “垮掉的一代”的一員（20 世紀 50 年代及 60 年代初擯棄傳統生活與衣着的年輕人）

ˌbeat-ˈup (also **ˌbeaten-ˈup**) *adj.* [usually before noun] (*informal*) old and damaged 破舊的；破損的：*a beat-up old truck* 破舊的老卡車

beau /bəʊ; *NAmE* boʊ/ *noun* (*pl.* **beaux** or **beaus** /bəʊz; *NAmE* boʊz/) (*old-fashioned*) a woman's male lover or friend （女性的）男友，情郎

beau·coup /ˈbəʊkuː; *NAmE* ˈboʊ-/ *det.* (*US, informal*, from *French*) many or a lot 很多的：*You can spend beaucoup bucks* (= a lot of money) *on software.* 買軟件可能花掉很多錢。

the Beau·fort scale /ˈbəʊfət skeɪl; *NAmE* ˈboʊfərt/ *noun* [sing.] a range of numbers used for measuring how strongly the wind is blowing. The lowest number 0 means that there is no wind and the highest number 12 means that there is a HURRICANE (= a violent storm with very strong winds). 蒲福風級，蒲福風力等級（按風力大小分為 0 至 12 級）：*The storm measured 10 on* ***the Beaufort scale****.* 這次風暴按蒲福風級測量為 10 級。
ORIGIN From Sir Francis Beaufort, the English admiral who invented it. 源自發明此方法的英格蘭海軍上將弗朗西斯 • 蒲福爵士（Sir Francis Beaufort）。

Beau·jo·lais /ˈbəʊʒəleɪ; *NAmE* ˌboʊʒəˈleɪ/ *noun* (*pl.* **Beau·jo·lais**) [C, U] a light wine, usually red, from the Beaujolais district of France 博若萊葡萄酒（通常為紅色，醇度低，產於法國博若萊地區）

beaut /bjuːt/ *noun, adj., exclamation*
■ *noun* (*NAmE, AustralE, NZE, informal*) an excellent or beautiful person or thing 出眾的人（或事物）；美人；美好的東西
■ *adj., exclamation* (*AustralE, informal*) excellent; very good 極好的；很棒的

beaut·eous /ˈbjuːtiəs/ *adj.* (*literary*) beautiful 美麗的；美好的

beaut·ician /bjuːˈtɪʃn/ *noun* a person, usually a woman, whose job is to give beauty treatments to the face and body 美容師

beau·ti·ful /ˈbjuːtɪfl/ *adj.*
1 having beauty; pleasing to the senses or to the mind 美麗的；美好的：*a beautiful woman/face/baby/voice/poem/smell/evening* 漂亮的女人／面孔／嬰兒；美妙的聲音／詩歌／香味／夜晚 ◇ *beautiful countryside/weather/music* 美麗的鄉村；美好的天氣；美妙的音樂 **2** very good or skilful 很好的；出色的；巧妙的：*What beautiful timing!* 時間把握得正好！

beau·ti·ful·ly /ˈbjuːtɪfli/ *adv.*
1 in a beautiful way 美好地；美妙地；漂亮地：*She sings beautifully.* 她唱歌很動聽。◇ *a beautifully decorated house* 裝潢典雅的房子 **2** very well; in a pleasing way 很好；令人滿意地：*It's all working out beautifully.* 一切進展都很順利。

beaut·ify /ˈbjuːtɪfaɪ/ *verb* (**beau·ti·fies**, **beau·ti·fy·ing**, **beau·ti·fied**, **beau·ti·fied**) **~ sb/sth** to make sb/sth beautiful or more beautiful 美化；使更美麗

beauty /ˈbjuːti/ *noun* (*pl.* **-ies**)
1 [U] the quality of being pleasing to the senses or to the mind 美；美麗：*the* ***beauty of*** *the sunset/of poetry/of his singing* 落日／詩作／他的歌聲之美 ◇ *a woman of great beauty* 大美人 ◇ *The woods were designated an* ***area of outstanding natural beauty****.* 這片森林被劃定為超級自然美景區。◇ ***beauty products/treatment*** (= intended to make a person more beautiful) 美容產品；美容 **2** [C] a person or thing that is beautiful 美人；美好的

東西： *She had been a beauty in her day.* 她年輕時是個美人。 **3** [C] an excellent example of its type 極好的榜樣；典型的例子： *That last goal was a beauty!* 最後進的一球真絕！ **4** [C] a pleasing feature 好處；優點 SYN **advantage**： *One of the beauties of living here is that it's so peaceful.* 在這裏生活的好處之一是安寧。◇ *The project will require very little work to start up; **that's the beauty of it**.* 這項工程幾乎不需要啟動工作，好就好在這裏。

IDM **beauty is in the eye of the 'beholder** (*saying*) people all have different ideas about what is beautiful 情人眼裏出西施；對美的判別因人而異 **beauty is only skin-'deep** (*saying*) how a person looks is less important than their character 美貌不過一張皮；貌美不如心靈美

Synonyms 同義詞辨析

beautiful

pretty • handsome • attractive • lovely • good-looking • gorgeous

These words all describe people who are pleasant to look at. 以上各詞均形容人好看。

beautiful (especially of a woman or girl) very pleasant to look at（尤指女子或女孩）漂亮的，美麗的： *She looked stunningly beautiful that night.* 她那天晚上美極了。

pretty (especially of a girl or woman) pleasant to look at（尤指女孩或女子）漂亮的，俊俏的： *She's got a very pretty face.* 她有一張非常俏麗的臉。 NOTE **Pretty** is used most often to talk about girls. When it is used to talk about a woman, it usually suggests that she is like a girl, with small, delicate features. * pretty 多用以指女孩。如果用以指女子，通常表示這女子像女孩一樣小巧玲瓏。

handsome (of a man) pleasant to look at; (of a woman) pleasant to look at, with large strong features rather than small delicate ones 指（男子）英俊的，漂亮的；（女子）健美的： *He was described as **'tall, dark and handsome'**.* 他被描述為“高大黝黑、相貌堂堂”。

attractive (of a person) pleasant to look at, especially in a sexual way 指（人）性感的、嫵媚的、俊朗的、迷人的： *She's a very attractive woman.* 她是個非常迷人的女子。

lovely (of a person) beautiful; very attractive 指（人）美麗的、迷人的： *She looked particularly lovely that night.* 她那天晚上特別嫵媚動人。 NOTE When you describe sb as **lovely**, you are usually showing that you also have a strong feeling of affection for them. 用 lovely 形容人時，通常表示說話者很喜歡這個人。

good-looking (of a person) pleasant to look at, often in a sexual way 指（人）好看的、漂亮的、性感的： *She arrived with a very good-looking man.* 她和一個非常英俊的男人一起到來。

gorgeous (*informal*) (of a person) extremely attractive, especially in a sexual way 指（人）非常漂亮的、美麗動人的、性感的： *You look gorgeous!* 你美極了！

ATTRACTIVE OR GOOD-LOOKING? 用 attractive 還是 good-looking？

If you describe sb as **attractive** you often also mean that they have a pleasant personality as well as being pleasant to look at; **good-looking** just describes sb's physical appearance. 用 attractive 形容人時，常常還表示這人不僅長得漂亮，性格也很可愛，而 good-looking 只指人的長相好看。

PATTERNS

- a(n) beautiful/pretty/handsome/attractive/lovely/good-looking/gorgeous **girl/woman**
- a(n) beautiful/handsome/attractive/good-looking/gorgeous **boy/man**
- a(n) beautiful/pretty/handsome/attractive/lovely/good-looking **face**

,Beauty and the 'Beast *noun* **1** a traditional story about a young girl who saves a large ugly creature from a magic SPELL by her love. He becomes a HANDSOME prince and they get married. 美女與野獸（傳說中少女用愛拯救醜陋的野獸擺脫魔法，變成英俊王子，然後兩人結婚） **2** (*informal, humorous*) two people of whom one is much more attractive than the other 美女與野獸（指相貌差別很大的兩個人）

'beauty contest *noun* (*BrE*) **1** a competition to choose the most beautiful from a group of women 選美比賽 ➲ compare PAGEANT (2) **2** (*US* **,beauty pa'rade**) an occasion on which several competing companies or people try to persuade sb to use their services “選美式”競爭（指互相競爭的公司或個人為說服某人採用其服務而舉行的展示活動）

'beauty mark *noun* (*NAmE*) = BEAUTY SPOT

'beauty queen *noun* a woman who is judged to be the most beautiful in a BEAUTY CONTEST 選美比賽冠軍；選美王后

'beauty salon (also **'beauty parlour**) (*US* also **'beauty shop**) *noun* a place where you can pay for treatment to your face, hair, nails, etc., which is intended to make you more beautiful 美容院

'beauty school *noun* (*NAmE*) a place that trains people to cut hair, take care of nails, etc. as a job 美容學校

'beauty sleep *noun* [U] (*humorous*) enough sleep at night to make sure that you look and feel healthy and beautiful 美容覺（夜間睡足以保持健康美麗）

'beauty spot *noun* **1** (*BrE*) a place in the countryside which is famous because it is beautiful 風景點；名勝 **2** (*NAmE* also **'beauty mark**) a small dark spot on a woman's face, which used to be thought to make her more beautiful 美人痣；美人斑

beaux *pl.* of BEAU

bea·ver /'biːvə(r)/ *noun, verb*

■ *noun* **1** [C] an animal with a wide flat tail and strong teeth. Beavers live in water and on land and can build DAMS (= barriers across rivers) made of pieces of wood and mud. It is an official symbol of Canada. 河狸，海狸（生活在水邊，會築壩，是加拿大的象徵） ➲ **VISUAL VOCAB** page V12 ➲ see also EAGER BEAVER **2** [U] the fur of the beaver, used in making hats and clothes 海狸毛皮（用以製作衣帽） **3** [C] (*taboo, slang, especially NAmE*) the area around a woman's sex organs 女子陰部

■ *verb*

PHR V **,beaver a'way (at sth)** (*informal*) to work very hard at sth 忙於（某事）；勤奮工作： *He's been beavering away at the accounts all morning.* 他一上午都忙於做賬。

bebop /'biːbɒp; *NAmE* -bɑːp/ (also **bop**) *noun* [U] a type of JAZZ with complicated rhythms 比博普（一種節奏複雜的爵士樂）

BEC /bek/ *abbr.* Business English Certificate (British tests, set by the University of Cambridge, in English as a foreign language for students who are preparing for a career in business) 商務英語證書，商用英語認證（由英國劍橋大學命題、針對英語為外語而準備進入商界的學生設立的考試）

be·calmed /bɪ'kɑːmd/ *adj.* (of a ship with a sail 帆船) unable to move because there is no wind （因無風而）不能航行的

be·came *past tense* of BECOME

be·cause 0-w /bɪ'kɒz; -'kəz; *NAmE* -'kɔːz; -'kʌz/ *conj.* for the reason that 因為： *I did it because he told me to.* 是他吩咐我才做的。◇ *Just because I don't complain, people think I'm satisfied.* 就因為我不發牢騷，大家便以為我滿意了。 ▸ **because of** 0-w *prep.*： *They are here because of us.* 他們是因為我們來這裏的。◇ *He walked slowly because of his bad leg.* 他因為腿不方便而行走緩慢。◇ *Because of his wife('s) being there, I said nothing about it.* 他的妻子在場，我便沒提及這事。 ➲ **LANGUAGE BANK** at next page

B

Language Bank 用語庫

because of

Explaining reasons 解釋原因

- The number of people with diabetes is growing, partly **because of** an increase in levels of obesity. 患糖尿病的人數不斷上升，部份原因是肥胖人數增加。
- The number of overweight children has increased dramatically in recent years, largely **as a result of** changes in diet and lifestyle. 近年來肥胖兒童的數量急劇上升，很大程度上是由飲食和生活方式的改變引起的。
- The increase in childhood obesity is largely **due to/the result of** changes in lifestyle and diet over the last twenty years. 肥胖兒童人數的增多主要是過去二十年來飲食和生活方式的改變所致。
- Many obese children are bullied at school **on account of** their weight. 許多肥胖兒童因為其體重問題在學校受到欺負。
- Part of the problem with treating childhood obesity **stems from** the fact that parents do not always recognize that their children are obese. 治療肥胖兒童的困難部份源自父母有時並不認為自己的孩子肥胖。
- Childhood obesity may be **caused by** genetic factors, as well as environmental ones. 兒童肥胖既可能由環境因素引起，也可能是遺傳因素所致。

➲ Language Banks at CAUSE, CONSEQUENTLY, THEREFORE

béch·amel /ˈbeɪʃəmel/ (also **ˌbéchamel ˈsauce**) *noun* [U] a thick sauce made with milk, flour and butter 貝夏美調味白汁（用牛奶、麪粉和黃油調製而成）SYN **white sauce**

beck /bek/ *noun* (*BrE, dialect*) a small river 小溪 SYN **stream**

IDM **at sb's ˌbeck and ˈcall** always ready to obey sb's orders 隨時待命：*Don't expect to have me at your beck and call.* 休想隨意擺佈我。

beckon /ˈbekən/ *verb* **1** [I, T] to give sb a signal using your finger or hand, especially to tell them to move nearer or to follow you 招手示意；舉手召喚 SYN **signal**：**~ to sb (to do sth)** *He beckoned to the waiter to bring the bill.* 他招手示意服務生把賬單送過來。◇ **~ sb (+ adv./prep.)** *He beckoned her over with a wave.* 他揮手讓她過去。◇ *The boss beckoned him into her office.* 老闆招手示意他進她的辦公室。◇ **~ sb to do sth** *She beckoned him to come and join them.* 她打手勢要他來加入他們的活動。**2** [I, T] to appear very attractive to sb 吸引；誘惑：*The clear blue sea beckoned.* 清澈蔚藍的大海令人嚮往。◇ **~ sb** *The prospect of a month without work was beckoning her.* 一個月的閒暇時光令她神往。**3** [I] to be sth that is likely to happen or will possibly happen to sb in the future 很可能發生（或出現）：*For many kids leaving college the prospect of unemployment beckons.* 許多剛踏出大學校門的孩子可能會面臨失業。

be·come 🔑 /bɪˈkʌm/ *verb* (**be·came** /bɪˈkeɪm/, **be·come**) **1** 🔑 *linking verb* to start to be sth 開始變得；變成；成為：**+ adj.** *It was becoming more and more difficult to live on his salary.* 他越來越難以靠他的工資維持生計了。◇ *It soon became apparent that no one was going to come.* 很快就很清楚，沒人會來。◇ *She was becoming confused.* 她開始糊塗了。◇ **+ noun** *She became queen in 1952.* 她於 1952 年成為女王。◇ *The bill will become law next year.* 該議案將於明年成為法律。**2** [T, no passive] (not used in the progressive tenses 不用於進行時) **~ sb** (*formal*) to be suitable for sb 適合（某人）；（與…）相稱：*Such behaviour did not become her.* 這種舉止與她的身分不相稱。**3** [T, no passive] (not used in the progressive tenses 不用於進行時) **~ sb** (*formal*) to look attractive on sb 使（人）顯得漂亮；使好看 SYN **suit**：*Short hair really becomes you.* 你理短髮很好看。

IDM **what became, has become, will become of sb/sth?** used to ask what has happened or what will happen to sb/sth（遭遇）如何；（結果）怎麼樣：*What became of that student who used to live with you?* 以前和你住在一起的那個學生後來怎麼樣了？◇ *I dread to think what will become of them if they lose their home.* 我不敢設想他們如果無家可歸將會怎麼樣。

Synonyms 同義詞辨析

become / get / go / turn

These verbs are used frequently with the following adjectives. 這些動詞常與下列形容詞連用：

become ~	get ~	go ~	turn ~
involved	used to	wrong	blue
clear	better	right	sour
accustomed	worse	bad	bad
pregnant	pregnant	white	red
extinct	tired	crazy	cold
famous	angry	bald	
ill	dark	blind	

- **Become** is more formal than **get**. Both describe changes in people's emotional or physical state, or natural or social changes. * become 較 get 正式。兩者均指人的感情、身體狀況、自然或社會的變化。
- **Go** is usually used for negative changes. * go 常用於負面變化。
- **Go** and **turn** are both used for changes of colour. * go 和 turn 均用以指顏色的變化。
- **Turn** is also used for changes in the weather. * turn 亦用於天氣的變化。

be·com·ing /bɪˈkʌmɪŋ/ *adj.* (*formal*) **1** (of clothes, etc. 衣服等) making the person wearing them look more attractive 相配的；合身的 SYN **flattering** **2** suitable or appropriate for sb or their situation 合適的；與…相稱的 SYN **fitting**：*It was not very becoming behaviour for a teacher.* 這種舉止與一個教師的身分不太相稱。OPP **unbecoming**

bec·que·rel /ˈbekərel/ *noun* (*abbr.* **Bq**) (*physics* 物) a unit for measuring RADIOACTIVITY 貝可勒爾，貝可（放射性活度單位）

BEd (also **B.Ed.** especially in *NAmE*) /ˌbiː ˈed/ *noun* the abbreviation for 'Bachelor of Education' (a first university degree in education) 教育學士（全寫為 Bachelor of Education，大學教育學的初級學位）：(*BrE*) *Sarah Wells BEd* 教育學士薩拉 • 韋爾斯

bed 🔑 /bed/ *noun, verb*

■ *noun*

▸ FURNITURE 傢具 **1** 🔑 [C, U] a piece of furniture for sleeping on 牀：*a single/double bed* 一張單人／雙人牀 ◇ *She lay on the bed* (= on top of the covers). 她躺在牀上（指未掀被子）。◇ *He lay in bed* (= under the covers). 他躺在牀上（指蓋着被子）。◇ *I'm tired—I'm going to bed.* 我累了，我要睡覺了。◇ *It's time for bed* (= time to go to sleep). 該是睡覺的時候了。◇ *I'll just put the kids to bed.* 我這就安排孩子們去睡覺。◇ *He likes to have a mug of cocoa before bed* (= before going to bed). 他睡前喜歡喝一大杯可可。◇ *to get into/out of bed* 就寢；起牀 ◇ *to make the bed* (= arrange the covers in a tidy way) 鋪牀 ◇ *Could you give me a bed for the night* (= somewhere to sleep)? 今晚你能給我弄個睡的地方嗎？◇ *There's a shortage of hospital beds* (= not enough room for patients to be admitted). 醫院牀位短缺。◇ *He has been confined to bed with flu for the past couple of days.* 他因患流感，已經幾天未下牀了。➲ VISUAL VOCAB page V23 ➲ see also AIRBED, CAMP BED, SOFA BED, TWIN BED, WATERBED

▸ OF RIVER/LAKE/SEA 河；湖；海 **2** 🔑 [C] the bottom of a river, the sea, etc.（河）牀；（海等的）底：*the ocean* *bed* 海洋底 ◇ *oyster beds* (= an area in the sea where there are many OYSTERS) 牡蠣層

▸ FOR FLOWERS/VEGETABLES 花卉；蔬菜 **3** [C] an area of ground in a garden/yard or park for growing flowers, vegetables, etc. 花壇；苗圃；菜園：*flower beds* 花壇 ➲ see also SEEDBED (1)

▸ BOTTOM LAYER 底層 **4** [C] **~ of sth** a layer of sth that other things lie or rest on 底層；基；基座：*grilled chicken, served on a bed of rice* 烤雞蓋飯 ◇ *The blocks should be laid on a bed of concrete.* 石塊應該固定在混凝土基座上。

▸ GEOLOGY 地質學 **5** [C] a layer of CLAY, rock, etc. in the ground （地下由黏土、岩石等構成的）地層 ➲ see also BEDROCK (2)

IDM **(not) a bed of 'roses** (not) an easy or a pleasant situation （並非）輕鬆的境況，令人愉快的情況：*Their life together hasn't exactly been a bed of roses.* 他們在一起的生活並不十分幸福。 **get out of bed on the wrong side** (*BrE*) (*NAmE* **get up on the wrong side of the bed**) to be bad-tempered for the whole day for no particular reason （無緣由地）一起牀就整天情緒不好 **go to bed with sb** (*informal*) to have sex with sb 與（某人）發生性關係 **in bed** used to refer to sexual activity （指性行為）：*What's he like in bed?* 他的牀上功夫怎麼樣？ ◇ *I caught them in bed together* (= having sex). 我撞見他們睡在一起。 **you've made your bed and you must 'lie in/on it** (*saying*) you must accept the results of your actions 自己承擔後果 **take to your 'bed** to go to bed and stay there because you are ill/sick （因病）臥牀；臥病 ➲ more at DIE *v.*, WET *v.*

■ *verb* (-dd-) **1 ~ sth (in sth)** to fix sth firmly in sth 把…固定在：*The bricks were bedded in sand to improve drainage.* 沙裏埋入磚塊，以改進排水系統。◇ *Make sure that you bed the roots firmly in the soil.* 一定要使根部牢牢地扎在土壤裏。 **2 ~ sb** (*old-fashioned*) to have sex with sb 與（某人）發生性關係

PHR V **,bed 'down** to sleep in a place where you do not usually sleep 換個地方睡覺：*You have my room and I'll bed down in the living room.* 你用我的房間，我睡客廳。

,bed and 'board *noun* [U] (*BrE*) a room to sleep in and food 食宿；連吃帶住

,bed and 'breakfast *noun* (*abbr.* **B and B**, **B & B**) **1** [U] (*BrE*) a service that provides a room to sleep in and a meal the next morning in private houses and small hotels 住宿加（次日）早餐；牀位加早餐：*Do you do bed and breakfast?* 你們提供住宿加早餐的服務嗎？◇ *Bed and breakfast costs £50 a night.* 住宿加次日早餐每晚合共50英鎊。 ➲ compare EUROPEAN PLAN, FULL BOARD, HALF BOARD **2** [C] a place that provides this service 提供住宿加早餐的旅館：*There were several good bed and breakfasts in the area.* 這個地區有幾家不錯的提供住宿加早餐的旅館。

be·dazzle /bɪ'dæzl/ *verb* [usually passive] **~ sb** to impress sb very much with intelligence, beauty, etc. 深深打動；使着迷；使眼花繚亂：*He was so bedazzled by her looks that he couldn't speak.* 她的美貌令他驚訝得說不出話來。 ▸ **be·dazzle·ment** /bɪ'dæzlmənt/ *noun* [U]

bed·bug /'bedbʌg/ *noun* a small flat insect that lives especially in beds, where it bites people and sucks their blood 臭蟲；牀虱

bed·cham·ber /'bedtʃeɪmbə(r)/ *noun* (*old use*) a bedroom 臥室：*the royal bedchamber* 國王的臥室

bed·clothes /'bedkləʊðz; *NAmE* -kloʊðz/ (*BrE* also **bed·covers**) *noun* [pl.] the sheets and other covers that you put on a bed 牀上用品；寢具；鋪蓋

bed·cover /'bedkʌvə(r)/ *noun* (*BrE*) **1** = BEDSPREAD **2 bedcovers** = BEDCLOTHES

bed·ding /'bedɪŋ/ *noun* [U] **1** the sheets and covers that you put on a bed, often also the MATTRESS and the PILLOWS 寢具；鋪蓋 ➲ VISUAL VOCAB page V23 **2** STRAW, etc. for animals to sleep on （給動物歇息的）墊草

'bedding plant *noun* a plant that is planted out in a garden bed, usually just before it gets flowers. It usually grows and dies within one year. 開花前種在花壇裏的植物；花壇植物

beddy-byes /'bedi baɪz/ (*BrE*) (*NAmE* **'beddy-bye**) *noun* [U] a child's word for bed, used when talking about the time sb goes to bed （兒語）牀牀，睏睏牀：*Time for beddy-byes.* 該上牀牀睡覺了。

be·deck /bɪ'dek/ *verb* [usually passive] **~ sth/sb (with/in sth)** (*literary*) to decorate sth/sb with flowers, flags, PRECIOUS STONES, etc. （用花、旗子、珠寶等）裝飾，打扮

be·devil /bɪ'devl/ *verb* (-ll-, *especially US* -l-) **~ sb/sth** (*formal*) to cause a lot of problems for sb/sth over a long period of time 長期攪擾 SYN **beset**：*The expedition was bedevilled by bad weather.* 探險隊深受惡劣天氣的困擾。

bed·fel·low /'bedfeləʊ; *NAmE* -feloʊ/ *noun* a person or thing that is connected with or related to another, often in a way that you would not expect（常指意外的）夥伴，同伴，相伴之物：***strange/unlikely bedfellows*** 奇怪的夥伴；不大可能做夥伴的人

bed·head /'bedhed/ *noun* the part of the bed that is at the end, behind the head of the person sleeping on it 牀頭

bed·jacket /'beddʒækɪt/ *noun* a short jacket worn when sitting up in bed 牀上用短上衣（坐起時披）

bed·lam /'bedləm/ *noun* [U] a scene full of noise and confusion 混亂嘈雜的場面 SYN **chaos**：*It was bedlam at our house on the morning of the wedding.* 婚禮的那天早上，我們家鬧哄哄的。

bed·linen /'bedlɪnɪn/ *noun* [U] sheets and PILLOWCASES for a bed 牀單及枕套

Bed·ouin /'beduɪn/ *noun* (*pl.* **Bed·ouin**) a member of an Arab people that traditionally lives in tents in the desert 貝都因人（阿拉伯人，傳統上生活在沙漠裏，住帳篷）

bed·pan /'bedpæn/ *noun* a container used as a toilet by a person who is too ill/sick to get out of bed （臥牀病人用的）便盆

bed·post /'bedpəʊst; *NAmE* -poʊst/ *noun* one of the four vertical supports at the corners of a bed (especially an old type of bed with a wooden or metal frame) （四帷柱牀的）牀柱 ➲ VISUAL VOCAB page V23

be·drag·gled /bɪ'drægld/ *adj.* made wet, dirty or untidy by rain, mud, etc. 弄濕的；給泥水弄髒的；不整潔的：***bedraggled hair/clothes*** 濕漉漉的頭髮；滿是泥污的衣服

bed·rid·den /'bedrɪdn/ *adj.* having to stay in bed all the time because you are sick, injured or old 長期臥牀的

bed·rock /'bedrɒk; *NAmE* -rɑːk/ *noun* **1** [sing.] a strong base for sth, especially the facts or the principles on which it is based 牢固基礎；基本事實；基本原則：*The poor suburbs traditionally **formed the bedrock of** the party's support.* 貧窮的郊區在傳統上構成了支持該黨的牢固基礎。◇ *Honesty is the bedrock of any healthy relationship.* 誠實是維持一切良好關係的基本原則。 **2** [U] the solid rock in the ground below the loose soil and sand 基岩（鬆軟的沙、土層下的岩石）

bed·roll /'bedrəʊl; *NAmE* -roʊl/ *noun* (*especially NAmE*) a thick piece of material or a SLEEPING BAG that you can roll up for carrying and use for sleeping on or in, for example when you are camping 鋪蓋，睡袋（露營等用）

bed·room /'bedruːm; -rʊm/ *noun, adj.*

■ *noun* **1** a room for sleeping in 臥室：*the spare bedroom* 備用臥室 ◇ *a hotel with 20 bedrooms* 有 20 個房間的旅館 ◇ *This is the **master bedroom*** (= the main bedroom of the house). 這是主臥室。 **2 -bedroomed** having the number of bedrooms mentioned 有…個臥室的：*a three-bedroomed house* 有三個臥室的房子

■ *adj.* [only before noun] used as a way of referring to sexual activity 房事的；男女性愛的：*the bedroom scenes in the movie* 電影中的牀上戲

'bedroom community (also **'bedroom suburb**) (both *NAmE*) (*BrE* **'dormitory town**) *noun* a town that people live in and from where they travel to work in a bigger town or city 郊外住宅區

B

bed·side /ˈbedsaɪd/ *noun* [usually sing.] the area beside a bed 牀邊：*His mother has been **at his bedside** throughout his illness.* 在他生病期間，他母親一直守候在他牀邊。◇ *a bedside lamp* 牀頭燈

ˌbedside ˈmanner *noun* [sing.] the way in which a doctor or other person talks to sb who is ill/sick（醫護人員等）對待病人的態度

ˌbedside ˈtable (*especially BrE*) (*NAmE* usually **night-stand**, **ˈnight table**) *noun* a small table beside a bed 牀頭小几；牀頭櫃 ➲ VISUAL VOCAB page V23

bed·sit /ˈbedsɪt/ (also **bed·sit·ter** /ˈbedsɪtə(r)/) (also *formal* **ˌbedˈsitting room**) *noun* (all *BrE*) a room that a person rents and uses for both living and sleeping in 起居兼卧室兩用租間 ➲ COLLOCATIONS at HOUSE

bed·sore /ˈbedsɔː(r)/ *noun* a painful and sometimes infected place on a person's skin, caused by lying in bed for a long time 褥瘡

bed·spread /ˈbedspred/ (*BrE* also **bed·cover**) (*NAmE* also **spread**) *noun* an attractive cover put on top of all the sheets and covers on a bed 牀罩 ➲ VISUAL VOCAB page V23

bed·stead /ˈbedsted/ *noun* the wooden or metal frame of an old-fashioned type of bed（舊式）牀架

bed·time /ˈbedtaɪm/ *noun* [U, C] the time when sb usually goes to bed 就寢時間：*It's way past your bedtime.* 你早該睡覺了。◇ *Will you read me a bedtime story?* 給我讀個睡前故事好嗎？

ˈbed-wetting *noun* [U] the problem of URINATING in bed, usually by children while they are asleep 尿牀

bee /biː/ *noun* **1** a black and yellow flying insect that can sting. Bees live in large groups and make HONEY (= a sweet sticky substance that is good to eat). 蜜蜂：*a swarm of bees* 一群蜜蜂 ◇ *a bee sting* 蜜蜂蜇傷 ◇ *Bees were buzzing in the clover.* 蜜蜂在三葉草叢中嗡嗡作響。➲ see also BEEHIVE (2), BEESWAX, BUMBLEBEE, QUEEN BEE **2** (*NAmE*) a meeting in a group where people combine work, competition and pleasure（集工作、競賽、娛樂為一體的）聚會：*a sewing bee* 縫紉友誼賽 ➲ see also SPELLING BEE

IDM **the ˌbee's ˈknees** (*informal*) an excellent person or thing 出類拔萃的人（或物）：*She thinks she's the bee's knees* (= she has a very high opinion of herself). 她自以為很了不起。 **have a ˈbee in your bonnet (about sth)** (*informal*) to think or talk about sth all the time and to think that it is very important 一心想着；念念不忘；總認為很重要 ➲ more at BIRD *n.*, BUSY *adj.*

the Beeb /biːb/ *noun* [sing.] an informal name for the BBC 英國廣播公司（非正式名稱）

beech /biːtʃ/ *noun* **1** [U, C] (also **ˈbeech tree** [C]) a tall forest tree with smooth grey BARK, shiny leaves and small nuts 山毛櫸：*forests planted with beech* 山毛櫸林 ◇ *beech hedges* 山毛櫸樹籬 ◇ *The great beeches towered up towards the sky.* 一棵棵山毛櫸高聳入雲。➲ VISUAL VOCAB page V10 ➲ see also COPPER BEECH **2** (also **ˈbeech·wood** /ˈbiːtʃwʊd/) [U] the wood of the beech tree 山毛櫸木材

beef 0➔ /biːf/ *noun, verb*

■ ***noun*** **1** 0➔ [U] meat that comes from a cow 牛肉：***roast/minced beef*** 烤牛肉；碎牛肉 ◇ *beef and dairy cattle* 菜牛和奶牛 ➲ see also CORNED BEEF **2** [C] (*informal*) a complaint 抱怨；牢騷：*What's his latest beef?* 他最近在抱怨什麼？

■ ***verb*** [I] **~ (about sb/sth)** (*informal*) to complain a lot about sb/sth 老是抱怨；大發牢騷

PHR V **ˌbeef sth↔ˈup** (*informal*) to make sth bigger, better, more interesting, etc. 使更大（或更好、更有意思等）

beef·bur·ger /ˈbiːfbɜːɡə(r); *NAmE* -bɜːrɡ-/ *noun* (*BrE*) = HAMBURGER

beef·cake /ˈbiːfkeɪk/ *noun* [U] (*slang*) attractive men with big muscles, especially those that appear in magazines（尤指雜誌中健壯性感的）肌肉男

beef·eater /ˈbiːfiːtə(r)/ *noun* a guard who dresses in a traditional uniform at the Tower of London 倫敦塔衞兵（穿傳統制服）

beef·steak /ˈbiːfsteɪk/ *noun* [C, U] = STEAK

ˌbeef ˈtea *noun* [U] (*BrE*) a hot drink made by boiling beef in water. It used to be given to people who were sick. 牛肉茶，牛肉湯（舊時給病人喝）

ˌbeef toˈmato (also **ˌbeefsteak toˈmato** especially in *NAmE*) *noun* a type of large tomato 牛肉番茄，牛茄（一種大個番茄）

beefy /ˈbiːfi/ *adj.* (**beef·ier**, **beefi·est**) (*informal*) (of a person or their body 人或人體) big or fat 高大的；肥胖的：*beefy men/arms/thighs* 粗壯的人／胳膊／大腿

bee·hive /ˈbiːhaɪv/ *noun* **1** = HIVE (1) **2** a HAIRSTYLE for women, with the hair piled high on top of the head 蜂窩狀髮型

ˈbee-keeper *noun* a person who owns and takes care of BEES 養蜂人 ▶ **ˈbee-keeping** *noun* [U]

bee·line /ˈbiːlaɪn/ *noun*

IDM **make a ˈbeeline for sth/sb** (*informal*) to go straight towards sth/sb as quickly as you can 直奔某物；逕直奔向某人

Be·el·ze·bub /biˈelzɪbʌb/ *noun* a name for the DEVIL 別西卜，貝耳則步（魔鬼的名字）

been /biːn; bɪn; *NAmE* bɪn/ ➲ BE ➲ see also GO *v.*

ˈbeen-to *noun* (*WAfrE*) a person who returns to his or her home in Africa after studying, working, etc. in a foreign country. People are often identified as **been-tos** because they have a different accent.（非洲操異國口音的）學成歸來者，海歸人

beep /biːp/ *noun, verb*

■ ***noun*** a short high sound such as that made by a car horn or by electronic equipment（汽車喇叭或電子設備發出的）嘟嘟聲，嗶嗶聲

■ ***verb*** **1** [I] (of an electronic machine 電子機器) to make a short high sound 發出嗶嗶聲；發出嘟嘟聲：*The microwave beeps to let you know when it has finished.* 微波爐烹飪完畢時會發出嗶嗶聲提醒你。 **2** [I, T] when a car horn, etc. **beeps** or when you **beep** it, it makes a short noise（使汽車喇叭等）發出嘟嘟聲：*The car behind started beeping at us.* 後面的汽車開始對我們鳴喇叭。◇ **~ sth** *He beeped his horn at the cyclist.* 他對騎自行車的人按喇叭。 **3** (*NAmE*) (*BrE* **bleep**) [T] **~ sb** to call sb on their beeper 打（某人）的傳呼機；給（某人）打傳呼

beep·er /ˈbiːpə(r)/ *noun* (*especially NAmE*) = BLEEPER

beer 0➔ /bɪə(r); *NAmE* bɪr/ *noun*

1 0➔ [U, C] an alcoholic drink made from MALT and flavoured with HOPS. There are many types of beer. 啤酒：*a **barrel/bottle/glass of beer*** 一桶／一瓶／一杯啤酒 ◇ *beers brewed in Germany* 德國釀造的啤酒 ◇ *a beer glass* 啤酒杯 ◇ *Are you a beer drinker?* 你經常喝啤酒嗎？ **2** 0➔ [C] a glass, bottle or can of beer 一杯（或一瓶、一罐）啤酒：*Shall we have a beer?* 我們來杯啤酒吧？ ➲ see also GINGER BEER, GUEST BEER, KEG BEER, ROOT BEER, SMALL BEER

ˈbeer belly (also **ˈbeer gut**) *noun* (*informal*) a man's very fat stomach, caused by drinking a lot of beer over a long period 啤酒肚

ˈbeer cellar *noun* **1** a room for storing beer below a pub or bar（酒館的）酒窖 **2** a pub or bar that is underground or partly underground（半）地下酒館

ˈbeer garden *noun* an outdoor area at a pub or bar with tables and chairs 酒館的露天攤位

ˈbeer mat *noun* (*BrE*) a small piece of cardboard that you put under a glass, usually in a bar, etc. in order to protect the surface below 啤酒杯墊子

beery /ˈbɪəri; *NAmE* ˈbɪri/ *adj.* smelling of beer; influenced by the drinking of beer 啤酒味的；喝啤酒所致的

bees·wax /ˈbiːzwæks/ *noun* [U] a yellow sticky substance that is produced by BEES and is used especially for making CANDLES and polish for wood 蜂蠟；黃蠟

beet /biːt/ *noun* [C, U] **1** a plant with a root that is used as a vegetable, especially for feeding animals or making sugar 甜菜；糖蘿蔔 ➲ see also SUGAR BEET **2** (*NAmE*)

(*BrE* **beet·root**) a plant with a round dark red root that is cooked and eaten as a vegetable 甜菜；甜菜根 ➲ VISUAL VOCAB page V31

bee·tle /ˈbiːtl/ *noun, verb*

■ ***noun*** **1** an insect, often large and black, with a hard case on its back, covering its wings. There are several types of beetle. 甲蟲 ➲ VISUAL VOCAB page V13 ➲ see also DEATH-WATCH BEETLE **2 Beetle™** (*NAmE* also **bug**) the English names for the original Volkswagen small car with a round shape at the front and the back "甲殼蟲"（英國人用以指稱一款圓頭圓頂的原大眾牌的小汽車）

■ ***verb*** [I] + **adv./prep.** (*BrE*, *informal*) to move somewhere quickly 快速移動 SYN **scurry**：*I last saw him beetling off down the road.* 我上次見到他時，他正快步沿路而去。

beet·root /ˈbiːtruːt/ (*BrE*) (*NAmE* **beet**) *noun* [U, C] a plant with a round dark red root that is cooked and eaten as a vegetable 甜菜；甜菜根 ➲ VISUAL VOCAB page V31

be·fall /bɪˈfɔːl/ *verb* (**be·fell** /bɪˈfel/, **be·fallen** /bɪˈfɔːlən/) **~ sb** (used only in the third person 僅用於第三人稱) (*literary*) (of sth unpleasant 令人不快的事) to happen to sb 降臨到（某人）頭上；發生：*They were unaware of the fate that was to befall them.* 他們並不知道即將降臨到他們頭上的厄運。

befit /bɪˈfɪt/ *verb* (**-tt-**) (used only in the third person and in participles 僅用於第三人稱和分詞) **sth befits sb** (*formal*) to be suitable and good enough for sb/sth 適合；對…相稱：*It was a lavish reception **as befitted** a visitor of her status.* 這場鋪張的招待可算得正適合她這種身分的來訪者。◇ *He lived in the style befitting a gentleman.* 他過的是一種與紳士相稱的生活。

befog /bɪˈfɒg; *NAmE* -ˈfɑːg/ *verb* **~ sb** to make sb confused 使迷惑；使困惑：*Her brain was befogged by lack of sleep.* 她因缺乏睡眠而頭腦昏沉。

be·fore 🔑 /bɪˈfɔː(r)/ *prep., conj., adv.*

■ ***prep.*** **1** 🔑 earlier than sb/sth 在…以前：*before lunch* 午餐前 ◇ *the day before yesterday* 前天 ◇ *The year before last he won a gold medal, and the year before that he won a silver.* 他前年得了一枚金牌，大前年得了一枚銀牌。◇ *She's lived there since before the war.* 她從戰前起就一直住在那裏。◇ *He arrived before me.* 他比我先到。◇ *She became a lawyer as her father had before her.* 像她父親先前一樣，她成了一名律師。◇ *Leave your keys at reception before departure.* 離開前請把鑰匙留在服務枱。◇ *Something ought to have been done before now.* 先前就該採取措施了。◇ *We'll know **before long*** (= soon). 我們很快就會知道了。◇ *Turn left just before* (= before you reach) *the bank.* 在快到銀行時向左拐。 **2** (rather *formal*) used to say that sb/sth is in a position in front of sb/sth 在…面前（或前面）：*They knelt before the throne.* 他們跪在御座前。◇ *Before you is a list of the points we have to discuss.* 放在你面前的是一份我們所要討論的要點清單。 ➲ compare BEHIND *prep.* **3** 🔑 used to say that sb/sth is ahead of sb/sth in an order or arrangement（次序或排列）在前面：*Your name is before mine on the list.* 名單上你的名字在我之前。◇ *He puts his work before everything* (= regards it as more important than anything else). 他一切以工作為重。 **4** 🔑 used to say that sth is facing sb in the future（表示面臨或臨近）：*The task before us is a daunting one.* 我們所面臨的任務令人膽怯。◇ *The whole summer lay before me.* 整個夏季正等待着我。 **5** in the presence of sb who is listening, watching, etc. 當面：*He was brought before the judge.* 他被帶上法庭。◇ *She said it before witnesses.* 她當着證人的面講出這事。◇ *They had the advantage of playing before their home crowd.* 他們有在主場觀眾面前比賽的優勢。 **6** (*formal*) used to say how sb reacts when they have to face sb/sth（表示面對某人、某事時的反應）：*They retreated before the enemy.* 面對敵人，他們撤退了。

■ ***conj.*** **1** 🔑 earlier than the time when 在…以前：*Do it before you forget.* 儘早動手，免得忘了。◇ *Did she leave a message before she went?* 她走之前留言了嗎？ **2** 🔑 until 到…為止；到…之前：*It may be many years before the situation improves.* 這種狀況或許要過很多年才能得到改善。◇ *It was some time before I realized the truth.* 過了很長一段時間我才悟出真相。 **3** 🔑 used to warn or threaten sb that sth bad could happen 以免；不然：*Put that away before it gets broken.* 把它收好，免得砸碎了。 **4** (*formal*) rather than（寧可…而）不願：*I'd die before I apologized!* 我寧願死也不道歉！

■ ***adv.*** 🔑 at an earlier time; in the past; already 以前；過去；已經：*You should have told me so before.* 你早該告訴我的。◇ *It had been fine the week before* (= the previous week). 前一個星期天氣很好。◇ *That had happened long before* (= a long time earlier). 那是很早以前的事了。◇ *I think we've met before.* 我覺得我們以前見過面。

be·fore·hand /bɪˈfɔːhænd; *NAmE* -ˈfɔːrh-/ *adv.* earlier; before sth else happens or is done 預先；事先：*two weeks/three days/a few hours beforehand* 提前兩星期／三天／幾小時 ◇ *I wish we'd known about it beforehand.* 要是我們預先知道這事就好了。

be·friend /bɪˈfrend/ *verb* [usually passive] **~ sb** to become a friend of sb, especially sb who needs your help（尤指和需要幫助者）做朋友；友善相待：*Shortly after my arrival at the school, I was befriended by an older girl.* 我到學校後不久便得到了一位年齡較大的女孩友善對待。

be·fud·dled /bɪˈfʌdld/ *adj.* confused and unable to think normally 迷糊的；糊塗的：*He was befuddled by drink.* 他喝得迷迷糊糊的。

beg /beg/ *verb* (**-gg-**) **1** [I, T] to ask sb for sth especially in an anxious way because you want or need it very much 懇求；祈求；哀求：**~ (for sth)** *He wants to see them beg for mercy.* 他想親眼看着他們求饒。◇ **~ sb (for sth)** *They begged him for help.* 他們向他求援。◇ **~ sth (of/from sb)** *She begged permission to leave.* 她請求允許她離開。◇ *I managed to beg a lift from a passing motorist.* 我設法求得一位開車路過的人讓我搭車。◇ **~ (sb) + speech** *'Give me one more chance,' he begged (her).* "再給我一次機會吧。" 他懇求（她）道。◇ **~ sb to do sth** *She begged him not to go.* 她求他別離開。◇ **~ to do sth** *He begged to be told the truth.* 他請求把真相告訴他。◇ **~ that …** (*formal*) *She begged that she be allowed to go.* 她請求讓她離開。◇ (*BrE* also) *She begged that she should be allowed to go.* 她請求讓她離開。◇ **~ of sb** (*formal*) *Don't leave me here, I beg of you!* 別把我扔在這兒，求求你！ **2** [I, T] to ask sb for money, food, etc., especially in the street 乞討；行乞：*London is full of homeless people begging in the streets.* 倫敦的街頭到處都是無家可歸的乞丐。◇ *a begging letter* (= one that asks sb for money)（要錢的）求援信 ◇ **~ for sth (from sb)** *The children were begging for food.* 那些孩子在討飯。◇ **~ sth (from sb)** *We managed to beg a meal from the cafe owner.* 我們設法向咖啡館老闆討了一頓飯。 **3** [I] if a dog **begs**, it sits on its back legs with its front legs in the air, waiting to be given sth（狗蹲坐在後腿上將前腿抬起）等食物

IDM **beg ˈleave to do sth** (*formal*) to ask sb for permission to do sth 請求准許做某事 **be going ˈbegging** (*BrE*, *informal*) if sth **is going begging**, it is available because nobody else wants it 無人問津；沒人要 **beg sb's ˈpardon** (*formal, especially BrE*) to ask sb to forgive you for sth you have said or done 請人原諒；向人道歉 **beg the ˈquestion 1** to make sb want to ask a question that has not yet been answered 令人置疑；引起疑問：*All of which begs the question as to who will fund the project.* 所有這一切都令人想到究竟由誰來投資該工程的問題。 **2** to talk about sth as if it were definitely true, even though it might not be 想當然：*These assumptions beg the question that children learn languages more easily than adults.* 這些假設想當然地認為兒童比成年人學習語言容易。 **I beg to differ** used to say politely that you do not agree with sth that has just been said 很抱歉，我不敢苟同 **I beg your pardon 1** (*formal*) used to tell sb that you are sorry for sth you have said or done 請原諒；對不起：*I beg your pardon, I thought that was my coat.* 對不起，我還以為那是我的外衣呢。 **2** used to ask sb to repeat what they have just said because you did not hear（未聽清楚）請再說一遍：*'It's on Duke Street.' 'I beg your pardon.' 'Duke Street.'* "在公爵大街上。" "請再說一遍。" "公爵大街。" **3** (*especially BrE*) used to tell sb that you are offended by what they have just said or by the way that they have said it（感到被冒犯時說）：*'Just go away.' 'I beg your pardon!'* "走開。" "有你這樣說話的嗎！"

B

PHR V ˌ**beg ˈoff** to say that you are unable to do sth that you have agreed to do 推辭（已答應做的事）；反悔：*He's always begging off at the last minute.* 他總是在最後一分鐘反悔。

begad /bɪˈɡæd/ *exclamation* (*old use*) used to express surprise or for emphasis（表示驚奇或強調）天哪，的確呀

began *past tense of* BEGIN

beget /bɪˈɡet/ *verb* (**be·get·ting**, **begot**, **begot** /bɪˈɡɒt; *NAmE* -ˈɡɑːt/) **HELP** In sense 1 **begat** /bɪˈɡæt/ is used for the past tense, and **begotten** /bɪˈɡɒtn; *NAmE* -ˈɡɑːtn/ is used for the past participle. 第 1 義的過去時用 begat，過去分詞用 begotten。 **1** (old use, for example in the Bible 舊用法，如《聖經》中) **~ sb** to become the father of a child 成為…之父：*Isaac begat Jacob.* 以撒生了雅各。 **2 ~ sth** (*formal* or *old-fashioned*) to make sth happen 引發；導致：*Violence begets violence.* 暴力招致暴力。
▸ **be·get·ter** *noun*

beg·gar /ˈbeɡə(r)/ *noun, verb*

■ **noun 1** a person who lives by asking people for money or food 乞丐；叫花子 **2** (*BrE, informal*) used with an adjective to describe sb in a particular way（與形容詞連用）傢伙：*Aren't you dressed yet, you lazy beggar?* 你這個懶漢還沒穿好衣服嗎？

IDM ˌ**beggars can't be ˈchoosers** (*saying*) people say **beggars can't be choosers** when there is no choice and sb must be satisfied with what is available 要飯就不能嫌餿；給什麼就得要什麼 ➲ more at WISH *n.*

■ **verb ~ sb/sth/yourself** to make sb/sth very poor 使貧窮；使匱乏：*Why should I beggar myself for you?* 我為什麼要為你受窮？

IDM **beggar beˈlief/deˈscription** to be too extreme, shocking, etc. to believe/describe 難以相信；無法形容：*It beggars belief how things could have got this bad.* 真是難以置信，情況怎麼會惡化到這種地步。

beg·gar·ly /ˈbeɡəli; *NAmE* -ɡərli/ *adj.* (*literary*) very small in amount 微量的；少得可憐的

ˈ**begging bowl** *noun* a bowl held out by sb asking for food or money 討飯碗；討錢缽；乞缽：(*figurative*) *He is taking round the begging bowl on behalf of the party's campaign fund.* 他為籌集該黨的競選資金而四處求助。

begin 🔑 /bɪˈɡɪn/ *verb* (**be·gin·ning**, **began** /bɪˈɡæn/, **begun** /bɪˈɡʌn/)

1 🔑 [I, T] to start doing sth; to do the first part of sth 開始；啟動：*Shall I begin?* 我可以開始了嗎？◇ **~ at/with sth** *Let's begin at page 9.* 咱們從第 9 頁開始。◇ **~ by doing sth** *She began by thanking us all for coming.* 她首先對我們大家的到來表示感謝。◇ **~ sth** *We began work on the project in May.* 我們於五月份啟動這個項目。◇ *I began* (= started reading) *this novel last month and I still haven't finished it.* 我上月就開始讀這本小說，到現在還沒讀完。◇ **~ sth at/with sth** *He always begins his lessons with a warm-up exercise.* 他講課前總是先讓學生做預備練習題。◇ **~ sth as sth** *He began his political career as a student* (= when he was a student). 他從當學生時起就開始了他的政治生涯。◇ **~ to do sth** *I began to feel dizzy.* 我開始感到頭暈目眩。◇ *At last the guests began to arrive.* 客人們終於陸續到達了。◇ *She began to cry.* 她哭起來了。◇ *It was beginning to snow.* 開始下雪了。◇ *I was beginning to think you'd never come.* 我開始以為你是不會來了。◇ **~ doing sth** *Everyone began talking at once.* 大家同時開始講話。◇ *When will you begin recruiting?* 你們何時開始招募人員？ ➲ SYNONYMS at START ➲ LANGUAGE BANK at FIRST **2** 🔑 [I] to start to happen or exist, especially from a particular time 起始；開始存在（或進行）：*When does the concert begin?* 音樂會什麼時間開始？◇ *Work on the new bridge is due to begin in September.* 新橋定於九月份動工。◇ *The evening began well.* 晚會開始得很順利。 **3** 🔑 [I] **~ as sth** to be sth first, before becoming sth else 起初是；本來是：*He began as an actor, before starting to direct films.* 他先是當演員，後來開始執導影片。◇ *What began as a minor scuffle turned into a full-scale riot.* 最初的小衝突演變成了大規模的暴亂。 **4** 🔑 [I] to have sth as the first part or the point where sth starts（從…）開始；（以…）為起點：*Where does Europe end and Asia begin?* 歐洲和亞洲的交界處在哪裏？◇ **~ with sth** *Use 'an' before words beginning with a vowel.* 在以元音開始的詞之前用 an。◇ *'I'm thinking of a country in Asia.' 'What does it begin with* (= what is the first letter)?' "我在想一個亞洲國家。" "它的首字母是什麼？" ◇ *Each chapter begins with a quotation.* 每一章的開頭都有一條引語。◇ **~ at …** *The path begins at Livingston village.* 這條小路始於利文斯頓村。 **5** 🔑 [T] **+ speech** to start speaking 開始講話：*'Ladies and gentlemen,' he began, 'welcome to the Town Hall.'* 他開始講話："女士們、先生們，歡迎光臨市政廳。" **6** 🔑 [I, T] to start or make sth start for the first time 創始；創辦：*The school began in 1920, with only ten pupils.* 這所學校創建於 1920 年，當時只有十名學生。◇ **~ sth** *He began a new magazine on post-war architecture.* 他創辦了一份專論戰後建築的新雜誌。 **7** [T] **not ~ to do sth** to make no attempt to do sth or have no chance of doing sth 不想；絕不能：*I can't begin to thank you enough.* 我說不盡對你的感激。◇ *He didn't even begin to understand my problem.* 他完全沒有弄明白我的問題。

IDM **to beˈgin with 1** 🔑 at first 起初；開始：*I found it tiring to begin with but I soon got used to it.* 我起初覺得很累，但不久便適應了。◇ *We'll go slowly to begin with.* 我們開始時會慢慢來的。 **2** 🔑 used to introduce the first point you want to make 首先；第一點：*'What was it you didn't like?' 'Well, to begin with, our room was far too small.'* "你不喜歡的是什麼呢？" "唔，首先是，我們的屋子太小了。" ➲ more at CHARITY

Which Word? 詞語辨析

begin / start

- There is not much difference in meaning between **begin** and **start**, though **start** is more common in spoken English. * begin 和 start 的含義差別不大，不過 start 較常用於英語口語：*What time does the concert start/begin?* 音樂會什麼時候開場？◇ *She started/began working here three months ago.* 她三個月前開始在這里工作。 **Begin** is often used when you are describing a series of events. * begin 常用以指一系列事情的開始：*The story begins on the island of Corfu.* 故事從科孚島上開始。 **Start**, but not **begin**, can also mean 'to start a journey', 'to start something happening' or 'to start a machine working'. * start 亦含出發、使發生、使（機器）運轉之意，begin 不含此義：*We'll need to start at 7.00.* 我們需要在 7 點鐘出發。◇ *Who do you think started the fire?* 你看是誰點的火？◇ *The car won't start.* 汽車發動不起來。
- You can use either an infinitive or a form with *-ing* after **begin** and **start**, with no difference in meaning. * begin 和 start 之後接動詞不定式或 -ing 形式均可，在意義上無差別：*I didn't start worrying/to worry until she was 2 hours late.* 她晚了兩小時後我才開始擔憂起來。
- After the forms **beginning** and **starting**, the *-ing* form of the verb is not normally used. * beginning 和 starting 之後一般不用動詞的 -ing 形式：*It's starting/beginning to rain.* 開始下雨了。◇ ~~*It's starting/beginning raining.*~~

be·gin·ner /bɪˈɡɪnə(r)/ *noun* a person who is starting to learn sth and cannot do it very well yet 新手；初學者：*She's in the beginners' class.* 她在初級班。

beˌginner's ˈluck *noun* [U] good luck or unexpected success when you start to do sth new 新手的好運；生手的意外成功

be·gin·ning 🔑 /bɪˈɡɪnɪŋ/ *noun*

1 🔑 [C, usually sing.] **~ (of sth)** the time when sth starts; the first part of an event, a story, etc. 開頭；開端；開始部份：*We're going to Japan* ***at the beginning of*** *July.* 我們七月初要去日本。◇ *She's been working there* ***since the beginning of*** *last summer.* 她自從去年夏初起就一直在那裏工作。◇ *We missed the beginning of the movie.* 我們錯過了電影的開頭部份。◇ *Let's start again* ***from the beginning***. 讓我們再從頭開始。◇ *The birth of their first child* ***marked the beginning of*** *a new era in their* *married life.* 第一個孩子的出世使他們的婚姻生活開始了一個新階段。◇ *I've read the whole book* ***from beginning to end*** *and still can't understand it.* 我把整本書從頭到尾看了一遍，但還是沒看懂。**HELP** **At the beginning** (of) is used for the time and place when something begins. **In the beginning** = **at first** and suggests a contrast with a later situation. * at the beginning (of) 指開始的時間和起點。in the beginning 等於 at first，與後來相對。**2 beginnings** [pl.] the first or early ideas, signs or stages of sth 原始思想；前兆；初級階段：*Did democracy have its beginnings in ancient Greece?* 民主制度創始於古希臘嗎？◇ *He built up his multimillion-pound music business* ***from small beginnings.*** 他從小本生意起步，逐步建立起了數百萬英鎊的音樂企業。

IDM **the beginning of the 'end** the first sign of sth ending 結束的前兆；結局的開始

be·gone /bɪ'gɒn; *NAmE* -'gɔːn; -'gɑːn/ *exclamation* (*old use*) a way of telling sb to go away immediately 走開；滾開

be·go·nia /bɪ'gəʊniə; *NAmE* -'goʊ-/ *noun* a plant with large shiny flowers that may be pink, red, yellow or white, grown indoors or in a garden 秋海棠

be·gorra /bɪ'gɒrə; *NAmE* bɪ'gɔːrə; -'gɑːr-/ *exclamation* (*IrishE, old-fashioned*) used to express surprise （表示驚奇）天哪，哎呀

begot *past tense* of BEGET

be·got·ten *past part.* of BEGET

be·grudge /bɪ'grʌdʒ/ *verb* (often used in negative sentences 常用於否定句) **1** to feel unhappy that sb has sth because you do not think that they deserve it 嫉妒；對（某人所享有的）感到不滿：**~ sb sth** *You surely don't begrudge him his happiness.* 你肯定不是嫉妒他的幸福吧。◇ **~ sb doing sth** *I don't begrudge her being so successful.* 我並沒有因她如此成功而怏怏不樂。**2** to feel unhappy about having to do, pay or give sth 勉強做；不樂意地做（或付出）：**~ sth** *I begrudge every second I spent trying to help him.* 我為了幫助他而花掉的每一秒鐘都令我不痛快。◇ **~ doing sth** *They begrudge paying so much money for a second-rate service.* 花這麼多的錢，卻得到二流的服務，這使他們十分不快。

be·grudg·ing·ly /bɪ'grʌdʒɪŋli/ *adv.* = GRUDGINGLY

be·guile /bɪ'gaɪl/ *verb* (*formal*) **1 ~ sb (into doing sth)** to trick sb into doing sth, especially by being nice to them 哄騙（某人做某事）；誘騙：*She beguiled them into believing her version of events.* 她哄騙他們相信了她敘述的事情。**2 ~ sb** to attract or interest sb 吸引（某人）；使感興趣：*He was beguiled by her beauty.* 他為她的美麗所傾倒。

be·guil·ing /bɪ'gaɪlɪŋ/ *adj.* (*formal*) attractive and interesting but sometimes mysterious or trying to trick you 迷人的；誘人的；誘騙的；難以琢磨的：*beguiling advertisements* 富有誘惑力的廣告 ◇ *Her beauty was beguiling.* 她美得迷人。▸ **be·guil·ing·ly** *adv.*

begum /'beɪgəm/ *noun* a title of respect used for a Muslim woman of high rank and for a married Muslim woman（對穆斯林貴婦或已婚婦女的稱呼）貴夫人：*Begum Zia* 齊亞夫人

begun *past part.* of BEGIN

be·half 0┳ **AW** /bɪ'hɑːf; *NAmE* bɪ'hæf/ *noun*

IDM **in behalf of sb | in sb's behalf** 0┳ (*US*) in order to help sb 為幫助某人：*We collected money in behalf of the homeless.* 我們為幫助無家可歸者而募捐。**on behalf of sb | on sb's behalf** **1** 0┳ as the representative of sb or instead of them 代表（或代替）某人：*On behalf of the department I would like to thank you all.* 我謹代表全系感謝大家。◇ *Mr Knight cannot be here, so his wife will accept the prize on his behalf.* 奈特先生不能來，因此由他的夫人代他領獎。**2** 0┳ in order to help sb 為幫助某人：*They campaigned on behalf of asylum seekers.* 他們為政治難民發起運動。**3** because of sb; for sb 因為某人；為了某人：*Don't worry on my behalf.* 別為我擔心。

be·have 0┳ /bɪ'heɪv/ *verb*

1 0┳ [I] **+ adv./prep.** to do things in a particular way 表現 **SYN** **act**：*The doctor behaved very unprofessionally.* 那位醫生的做法違反專業道德。◇ *They behaved very badly towards their guests.* 他們對客人很不禮貌。◇ *He behaved like a true gentleman.* 他的行為像個真正的紳士。◇ *She behaved with great dignity.* 她顯得很尊貴。◇ *He* ***behaved as if/though*** *nothing had happened.* 他顯得像是什麼都沒發生過。◇ *They behave differently when you're not around.* 你不在時他們就是另一副面孔。**HELP** In spoken English people often use **like** instead of **as if** or **as though**, especially in *NAmE*. 英語口語中，尤其是美式英語，常用 like 代替 as if 或 as though：*He behaved like nothing had happened.* This is not considered correct in written *BrE*. 英式英語書面語中，此用法被視為不正確。**2** 0┳ [I, T] to do things in a way that people think is correct or polite 表現得體；有禮貌：*Will you kids just behave!* 孩子們，規矩點！◇ *She doesn't know how to behave in public.* 她在公共場合舉止無措。◇ **~ yourself** *I want you to behave yourselves while I'm away.* 我不在時你們要乖乖的。**OPP** **misbehave** **3** 0┳ **-behaved** (in adjectives 構成形容詞) behaving in the way mentioned 表現得…的：***well-/badly-behaved*** *children* 表現好／差的孩子 **4** [I] **+ adv./prep.** (*technical* 術語) to naturally react, move, etc. in a particular way 作某種自然反應（或變化等）：*a study of how metals behave under pressure* 對於金屬受壓反應的研究 **IDM** see OWN *v.*

be·hav·iour 0┳ (*especially US* **be·hav·ior**) /bɪ'heɪvjə(r)/ *noun*

1 0┳ [U] the way that sb behaves, especially towards other people 行為；舉止；態度：***good/bad behaviour*** 良好／惡劣行為 ◇ ***social/sexual/criminal behaviour*** 社會／性／犯罪行為 ◇ *His behaviour towards her was becoming more and more aggressive.* 他對待她的態度越來越蠻橫。**2** 0┳ [U, C] the way a person, an animal, a plant, a chemical, etc. behaves or functions in a particular situation（人、動植物、化學品等的）表現方式，活動方式：*the behaviour of dolphins/chromosomes* 海豚／染色體的習性 ◇ *studying human and animal behaviour* 研究人類和動物的行為模式 ◇ (*technical* 術語) *to study learned behaviours* 研究習得行為 ▸ **be·hav·iour·al** (*especially US* **be·hav·ior·al**) /-jərəl/ *adj.*：*children with behavioural difficulties* 有行為問題的兒童 ◇ *behavioural science* (= the study of human behaviour) 行為科學 **be·hav·iour·al·ly** (*especially US* **be·hav·ior·al·ly**) *adv.*

IDM **be on your best be'haviour** to behave in the most polite way you can 盡量表現得體

be·hav·iour·ism (*especially US* **be·hav·ior·ism**) /bɪ'heɪvjərɪzəm/ *noun* [U] (*psychology* 心) the theory that all human behaviour is learnt by adapting to outside conditions and that learning is not influenced by thoughts and feelings 行為主義 ▸ **be·hav·iour·ist** (*especially US* **be·hav·ior·ist**) /-jərɪst/ *noun*

be·head /bɪ'hed/ *verb* [usually passive] **~ sb** to cut off sb's head, especially as a punishment 斬首（尤指刑罰）**SYN** **decapitate**

be·held *past tense, past part.* of BEHOLD

be·he·moth /bɪ'hiːmɒθ; 'biːhɪmɒθ; *NAmE* -mɔːθ/ *noun* (*formal*) a very big and powerful company or organization 超級公司（或機構）

be·hest /bɪ'hest/ *noun* [sing.]

IDM **at sb's be'hest** (*old use* or *formal*) because sb has ordered or requested it 受某人的吩咐（或要求）

be·hind 0┳ /bɪ'haɪnd/ *prep., adv., noun*

■ *prep.* **1** 0┳ at or towards the back of sb/sth, and often hidden by it or them 在（或向）…的後面；在（或向）…的背面：*Who's the girl standing behind Jan?* 站在簡身後的女孩是誰？◇ *Stay close behind me.* 緊跟在我後面。◇ *a small street behind the station* 車站後面的小街 ◇ *She glanced behind her.* 她扭頭朝背後掃了一眼。◇ *Don't forget to lock the door behind you* (= when you leave). 出門時記着把門鎖上。◇ *The sun disappeared behind the clouds.* 太陽消失在雲層裏。➲ note at BACK ➲ compare IN FRONT OF at FRONT *n.* **2** 0┳ making less progress than sb/sth 落後於：*He's behind the rest of the class in reading.* 他的閱讀能力不及班上其他人。◇ *We're* ***behind schedule*** (= late). 我們的工作進度落後了。**3** 0┳ giving support to or approval of sb/sth 支持；贊成：*She knew that, whatever she decided, her family was right behind her.* 她知道，無論她做出什麼決定，她的家人肯定會支持她

的。 **4** responsible for starting or developing sth 是…產生（或發展）的原因： *What's behind that happy smile* (= what is causing it)? 為什麼會笑得那麼開心？◇ *He was the man behind the plan to build a new hospital.* 他就是策劃建立新醫院的人。 **5** used to say that sth is in sb's past 成為（某人的）過去： *The accident is behind you now, so try to forget it.* 這次意外已經過去了，把它忘掉吧。◇ *She has ten years' useful experience behind her.* 她有十年的經驗，能派上用場。

■ ***adv.*** **1** at or towards the back of sb/sth; further back 在（或向）後面；在後面較遠處： *She rode off down the road with the dog running behind.* 她騎車沿路而去，狗跟在後面奔跑着。◇ *The others are a long way behind.* 其餘的人遠遠地落在後面。◇ *He was shot from behind as he ran away.* 他逃跑時後背中了彈。◇ *I had fallen so far behind that it seemed pointless trying to catch up.* 我落後太多，似乎追趕下去也毫無意義。 **2** in the place where sb/sth is or was 留在原地： *I was told to* ***stay behind*** *after school* (= remain in school). 我被告知放學後留下。◇ *This bag was* ***left behind*** *after the class.* 這個書包是有人下課後落下的。 **3** late in paying money or completing work 拖欠；積壓（工作）： **~ (with sth)** *She's* ***fallen behind*** *with the payments.* 她尚未付款。◇ **~ (in sth)** *He was terribly behind in his work.* 他積壓了大量工作。

■ ***noun*** (*informal*) a person's bottom. People often say 'behind' to avoid saying 'bottom'. 屁股（義同 bottom，委婉說法） SYN **backside** ： *The dog bit him on his behind.* 狗咬了他的屁股。

be·hind·hand /bɪˈhaɪndhænd/ *adj.* [not before noun] **~ (with/in sth)** late in doing sth or in paying money that is owed 拖欠；拖拉： *They were behindhand in settling their debts.* 他們沒有及時還清債務。

be·hold /bɪˈhəʊld; *NAmE* bɪˈhoʊld/ *verb* (**be·held** /bɪˈheld/, **be·held**) **~ sb/sth** (*old use* or *literary*) to look at or see sb/sth 看；看見： *Her face was a joy to behold.* 她的容貌十分悅目。◇ *They beheld a bright star shining in the sky.* 他們看到了一顆明亮的星在天空中閃閃發光。

IDM see LO

be·holden /bɪˈhəʊldən; *NAmE* -ˈhoʊld-/ *adj.* **~ to sb (for sth)** (*formal*) owing sth to sb because of sth that they have done for you （因受恩惠而心存）感激，感謝；欠人情： *She didn't like to be beholden to anyone.* 她不願欠任何人的情。

be·hold·er /bɪˈhəʊldə(r); *NAmE* -ˈhoʊld-/ *noun* IDM see BEAUTY

be·hove /bɪˈhəʊv; *NAmE* bɪˈhoʊv/ (*BrE*) (*NAmE* **be·hoove** /bɪˈhuːv/) *verb*

IDM **it behoves sb to do sth** (*formal*) it is right or necessary for sb to do sth （對某人來說）理應，應當，有必要： *It behoves us to study these findings carefully.* 我們理應認真研究這些發現。

beige /beɪʒ/ *adj.* light yellowish-brown in colour 淺褐色的；米黃色的 ▸ **beige** *noun* [U]

being /ˈbiːɪŋ/ *noun* **1** [U] existence 存在；生存： *The Irish Free State* ***came into being*** *in 1922.* 愛爾蘭自由邦成立於 1922 年。◇ *A new era was* ***brought into being*** *by the war.* 那場戰爭帶來了一個新的時代。 ➲ see also WELL-BEING **2** [C] a living creature 生物： *human beings* 人 ◇ *a strange being from another planet* 來自另一星球的奇怪生物 **3** [U] (*formal*) your mind and all of your feelings 思想感情；身心： *I hated him with my whole being.* 我從心底憎恨他。 ➲ see also BE *v.*

be·jew·elled (*BrE*) (*US* **be·jew·eled**) /bɪˈdʒuːəld/ *adj.* (*literary*) decorated with PRECIOUS STONES; wearing jewellery 飾以珠寶的；佩戴珠寶的

bel /bel/ *noun* (*technical* 術語) a measurement of sound equal to 10 DECIBELS 貝，貝爾（聲音計量單位，等於 10 分貝）

be·la·bour (*especially US* **be·la·bor**) /bɪˈleɪbə(r)/ *verb*

IDM **belabour the ˈpoint** (*formal*) to repeat an idea, argument, etc. many times to emphasize it, especially when it has already been mentioned or understood 一再強調觀點（或論點等）

be·lated /bɪˈleɪtɪd/ *adj.* coming or happening late 遲來的；晚出現的： *a belated birthday present* 遲來的生日禮物 ▸ **be·lated·ly** *adv.*

belay /ˈbiːleɪ; bɪˈleɪ/ *verb* [I, T] **~ (sth/sb)** (*technical* 術語) (in climbing 攀緣) to attach a rope to a rock, etc.; to make a person safe while climbing by attaching a rope to the person and to a rock, etc. 把（繩索）固定在岩石等上；把（攀岩者）用繩索拴在岩石等上

bel canto /ˌbel ˈkæntəʊ; *NAmE* -toʊ/ *noun* [U] (*music* 音) a style of OPERA or opera singing in the 19th century in which producing a beautiful tone was considered very important 美聲唱法（19 世紀歌劇藝術或演唱風格）

belch /beltʃ/ *verb* **1** [I] to let air come up noisily from your stomach and out through your mouth 打嗝： *He wiped his hand across his mouth, then belched loudly.* 他用手抹了抹嘴，然後打了個響亮的飽嗝。 SYN **burp** **2** [I, T] **~ (out/forth) (sth)** to send out large amounts of smoke, flames, etc.; to come out of sth in large amounts （大量）噴出，吐出 SYN **spew out** ▸ **belch** *noun*： *He sat back and gave a loud belch.* 他靠到椅背上，大聲打了個嗝。

be·lea·guered /bɪˈliːɡəd; *NAmE* -ɡərd/ *adj.* **1** (*formal*) experiencing a lot of criticism and difficulties 飽受批評的；處於困境的： *The beleaguered party leader was forced to resign.* 那位飽受指責的黨領導人被迫辭職。 **2** surrounded by an enemy 受到圍困（或圍攻）的： *supplies for the beleaguered city* 給受圍困城市的補給品

bel·fry /ˈbelfri/ *noun* (*pl.* **-ies**) a tower in which bells hang, especially as part of a church （尤指教堂的）鐘樓，鐘塔

belie /bɪˈlaɪ/ *verb* (**be·lies**, **be·ly·ing**, **be·lied**, **be·lied**) (*formal*) **1 ~ sth** to give a false impression of sb/sth 掩飾；遮掩；給人以假象： *Her energy and youthful good looks belie her 65 years.* 她的活力與年輕美貌使人看不出她有 65 歲了。 **2 ~ sth** to show that sth cannot be true or correct 顯示（某事）不正確；證明（某事）錯誤： *Government claims that there is no poverty are belied by the number of homeless people on the streets.* 大街上那些無家可歸者證明政府所聲稱的沒有貧困的說法是謊言。

be·lief /bɪˈliːf/ *noun*

1 [U] **~ (in sth/sb)** a strong feeling that sth/sb exists or is true; confidence that sth/sb is good or right 相信；信心： *I admire his passionate belief in what he is doing.* 我佩服他對自己的工作所抱的堅定信心。◇ *belief in God/democracy* 對上帝／民主的篤信 **2** [sing., U] **~ (that ...)** an opinion about sth; sth that you think is true 看法；信念： *She acted* ***in the belief that*** *she was doing good.* 她這麼做是因為她認定自己是在做好事。◇ ***Contrary to popular belief*** (= in spite of what people may think), *he was not responsible for the tragedy.* 與大家的看法相反，他對這樁悲劇沒有責任。◇ *There is a general belief that things will soon get better.* 大家普遍認為情況很快就會好轉。 **3** [C, usually pl.] something that you believe, especially as part of your religion 信仰；宗教信仰： ***religious/political beliefs*** 宗教／政治信仰 ➲ compare DISBELIEF, UNBELIEF

IDM **beyond beˈlief** (in a way that is) too great, difficult, etc. to be believed 令人難以置信： *Dissatisfaction with the government has grown beyond belief.* 對政府的不滿已經達到令人難以置信的程度。◇ *icy air that was cold beyond belief* 冷得令人無法相信的冰冷空氣 ➲ more at BEGGAR *v.*, BEST *n.*

be·liev·able /bɪˈliːvəbl/ *adj.* that can be believed 可相信的；可信任的 SYN **plausible** ： *Her explanation certainly sounded believable.* 她的解釋聽起來的確可信。◇ *a play with believable characters* 劇中人物真實可信的戲劇 OPP **unbelievable**

be·lieve /bɪˈliːv/ *verb* (not used in the progressive tenses 不用於進行時)

▸ FEEL CERTAIN 相信 **1** [T] to feel certain that sth is true or that sb is telling you the truth 相信；認為真實： **~ sb** *I don't believe you!* 我不相信你的話！◇ *The man claimed to be a social worker and the old woman believed him.* 那個男人自稱是社會福利工作者，老婦人信以為真。◇ *Believe me, she's not right for you.* 相信我，她不適合你。◇ **~ sth** *I believed his lies for years.* 我很多年都對他的謊話信以為真。◇ *I find that* ***hard to believe.*** 我對此感到難

以相信。◇ ***Don't believe a word of it*** (= don't believe any part of what sb is saying). 一點也不要相信那些話。◇ **~ (that)** … *People used to believe (that) the earth was flat.* 人們一度認為地球是平的。◇ *He refused to believe (that) his son was involved in drugs.* 他不願相信他的兒子沾染毒品。◇ ***I do believe** you're right* (= I think sth is true, even though it is surprising). 我的確相信你是對的。

▸ THINK POSSIBLE 認為有可能 **2** [I, T] to think that sth is true or possible, although you are not completely certain 把（某事）當真；認為有可能：*'Where does she come from?' 'Spain, I believe.'* "她是哪裏人？" "我想是西班牙人。" ◇ *'Does he still work there?' 'I **believe so/not**.'* "他還在那裏工作嗎？" "我想是 / 不是。" ◇ **~ (that)** … *Police believe (that) the man may be armed.* 警方認為那個人可能攜有武器。◇ **it is believed (that)** … *It is believed that the couple have left the country.* 據信那對夫婦已經離開了這個國家。◇ **~ sb/sth to be, have, etc. sth** *The vases are believed to be worth over $20 000 each.* 那些花瓶據估計每個價值都超過 2 萬元。◇ **~ sb/sth + adj.** *Three sailors are missing, believed drowned.* 有三位船員失踪，相信是淹死了。➲ SYNONYMS at THINK

▸ HAVE OPINION 認定 **3** [T] **~ (that)** … to have the opinion that sth is right or true 認定；看作：*The party believes (that) education is the most important issue facing the government.* 該黨把教育視為政府面臨的最重要的問題。➲ LANGUAGE BANK at ACCORDING TO, OPINION

▸ BE SURPRISED/ANNOYED 吃驚；惱怒 **4** [T] **don't/can't ~** used to say that you are surprised or annoyed at sth（表示對某事吃驚或惱怒）：**~ (that)** … *She couldn't believe (that) it was all happening again.* 她簡直無法相信整件事又在重演。◇ **~ how, what, etc.** … *I can't believe how much better I feel.* 真想不到我覺得好多了。

▸ RELIGION 宗教 **5** [I] to have a religious faith 有宗教信仰：*The god appears only to those who believe.* 信神如神在。

IDM **believe it or 'not** (*informal*) used to introduce information that is true but that may surprise people 信不信由你：*Believe it or not, he asked me to marry him!* 信不信由你，他向我求婚了！**believe (you) 'me** (*informal*) used to emphasize that you strongly believe what you are saying 我敢保證：*You haven't heard the last of this, believe you me!* 我敢保證你沒聽說過最新的消息。**don't you be'lieve it!** (*informal*) used to tell sb that sth is definitely not true 絕對不正確（不可相信）**I don't be'lieve it!** (*informal*) used to say that you are surprised or annoyed about sth（表示吃驚或惱怒）我簡直無法相信：*I don't believe it! What are you doing here?* 我簡直無法相信！你在這裏幹什麼？**if you believe that, you'll believe 'anything** (*informal*) used to say that you think sb is stupid if they believe that sth is true 你要是連這都相信，還有什麼不信的 **make believe (that …)** to pretend that sth is true 假裝 ➲ related noun MAKE-BELIEVE **not believe your 'ears/'eyes** (*informal*) to be very surprised at sth you hear/see 不相信自己的耳朵（或眼睛）；對所聞（或所見）非常吃驚：*I couldn't believe my eyes when she walked in.* 她走進來時我簡直不相信自己的眼睛。**seeing is be'lieving** (*saying*) used to say that sb will have to believe that sth is true when they see it, although they do not think it is true now 眼見為實；百聞不如一見 **would you be'lieve (it)?** (*informal*) used to show that you are surprised and annoyed about sth（表示驚訝或氣憤）你能相信嗎：*And, would you believe, he didn't even apologize!* 而且，可氣的是，他連個道歉都沒有！**you/you'd better be'lieve it!** (*informal*) used to tell sb that sth is definitely true 當然沒錯；千真萬確 ➲ more at GIVE *v.*

PHR V **be'lieve in sb/sth** to feel certain that sb/sth exists 相信某人（或事物）的存在：*Do you believe in God?* 你相信有上帝嗎？**be'lieve in sb** to feel that you can trust sb and/or that they will be successful 信賴；信任；相信某人會成功：*They need a leader they can believe in.* 他們需要一個可以信賴的領導。➲ SYNONYMS at TRUST **be'lieve in sth** to think that sth is good, right or acceptable 認為某事好（或對、可接受）：**~ doing sth** *I don't believe in hitting children.* 我不贊成打孩子。**be'lieve sth of sb** to think that sb is capable of sth 相信某人能幹出某事：*Are you sure he was lying? I can't believe that of him.* 你確信他在說謊嗎？我不相信他會幹這種事。

be·liever /bɪˈliːvə(r)/ *noun* a person who believes in the existence or truth of sth, especially sb who believes in a god or religious faith 信徒 OPP **unbeliever**

IDM **be a (great/firm) believer in sth** to believe strongly that sth is good, important or valuable 堅信（或極力推崇）某事物的人

Be·li·sha bea·con /bəˌliːʃə ˈbiːkən/ *noun* (in Britain) a post with an orange flashing light on top marking a place where cars must stop to allow people to cross the road 人行橫道指示燈柱，行人穿越道指示燈（英國指示剎車的橘黃色閃光燈）

be·lit·tle /bɪˈlɪtl/ *verb* **~ sb/sth** to make sb or the things that sb does seem unimportant 貶低；小看：*She felt her husband constantly belittled her achievements.* 她覺得她的丈夫時常貶低她的成就。

bell /bel/ *noun*

1 a hollow metal object, often shaped like a cup, that makes a ringing sound when hit by a small piece of metal inside it; the sound that it makes 鈴（聲）；鐘（聲）：*A peal of church bells rang out in the distance.* 遠處響起了一陣教堂的鐘聲。◇ *a bicycle bell* 自行車鈴鐺 ◇ *His voice came down the line **as clear as a bell**.* 他的聲音如鈴聲般清脆地從聽筒裏傳出來。◇ *the bell of a trumpet* (= the bell-shaped part at the end of it) 小號的喇叭口 ◇ *a bell-shaped flower* 喇叭形花朵 ➲ VISUAL VOCAB page V34 **2** an electrical device which makes a ringing sound when a button on it is pushed; the sound that it makes, used as a signal or a warning 電鈴（聲）：***Ring the bell** to see if they're in.* 按按門鈴，看他們在不在家。◇ *The **bell's ringing**!* 打鈴了！◇ *The bell went for the end of the lesson.* 下課的鈴聲響了。◇ *An **alarm bell** went off.* 警鐘響了。◇ (*figurative*) ***Warning bells** started ringing in her head as she sensed that something was wrong.* 當她意識到有差錯時，頭腦中便敲了警鐘。

IDM **give sb a 'bell** (*BrE, informal*) to call sb by telephone 打電話給某人 ➲ more at ALARM *n.*, PULL *v.*, RING² *v.*, SOUND *adj.*

bella·donna /ˌbeləˈdɒnə; *NAmE* -ˈdɑːnə/ *noun* [U] **1** = DEADLY NIGHTSHADE **2** a poisonous drug made from DEADLY NIGHTSHADE 顛茄製劑

'bell-bottoms *noun* [pl.] trousers/pants with legs that become very wide below the knee 喇叭褲

bell·boy /ˈbelbɔɪ/ (*especially NAmE*) (*NAmE* also **bell·hop**) *noun* a person whose job is to carry people's cases to their rooms in a hotel（旅館的）行李員

'bell curve *noun* (*mathematics* 數) a line on a GRAPH that rises to a high round curve in the middle, showing NORMAL DISTRIBUTION 鐘形曲線

belle /bel/ *noun* (*old-fashioned*) a beautiful woman; the most beautiful woman in a particular place 美女；（某地）最美的女人

belles-lettres /ˌbel ˈletrə/ *noun* [U+sing./pl. v.] (from *French, old-fashioned*) studies or writings on the subject of literature or art, contrasted with those on technical or scientific subjects 純文學，美文學（指有別於科技題材的文學或藝術研究或作品）

bell·hop /ˈbelhɒp; *NAmE* -hɑːp/ *noun* (*NAmE*) = BELLBOY

bel·li·cose /ˈbelɪkəʊs; -kəʊz; *NAmE* -koʊs; -koʊz/ *adj.* (*formal*) having or showing a desire to argue or fight 好爭辯的；好鬥的；好戰的 SYN **aggressive, warlike** ▸ **bel·li·cos·ity** /ˌbelɪˈkɒsəti; *NAmE* -ˈkɑːs-/ *noun* [U]

-bellied ➲ BELLY

bel·liger·ent /bəˈlɪdʒərənt/ *adj., noun*

▪ ***adj.*** **1** unfriendly and aggressive 好鬥的；尋釁的；挑釁的 SYN **hostile**：*a belligerent attitude* 尋釁的態度 **2** [only before noun] (*formal*) (of a country 國家) fighting a war 參戰的；交戰的：*the **belligerent countries/states/nations*** 交戰各國 ▸ **bel·liger·ence** /-əns/ *noun* [U] **bel·liger·ent·ly** *adv.*

▪ ***noun*** (*formal*) a country or group that is fighting a war 交戰國；交戰團體

B

'bell jar *noun* a tall round glass cover, used by scientists 鐘形長玻璃罩（科學家使用）

bel·low /'beləʊ; *NAmE* -loʊ/ *verb* **1** [I, T] to shout in a loud deep voice, especially because you are angry 大聲吼叫；怒吼 SYN **yell** : ~ **(at sb)** *They bellowed at her to stop.* 他們吼叫着讓她停下。◇ ~ **sth (at sb)** *The coach bellowed instructions from the sidelines.* 教練在場邊大聲發號施令。◇ **+ speech** *'Get over here!' he bellowed.* "給我過來！" 他吼道。➲ SYNONYMS at SHOUT **2** [I] when a large animal such as a BULL **bellows**, it makes a loud deep sound（公牛等）吼叫 ▸ **bel·low** *noun* : *to let out a bellow of rage/pain* 發出怒吼；疼痛地叫喊

bellows 風箱

bel·lows /'beləʊz; *NAmE* -loʊz/ *noun* (*pl.* **bel·lows**) [C+sing./pl. v.] a piece of equipment for blowing air into or through sth. Bellows are used for making a fire burn better or for producing sound in some types of musical instruments. 風箱；吹風器 : *a pair of bellows* (= a small bellows with two handles to be pushed together) 手用吹風器（俗稱皮老虎）

'bell pepper (*NAmE*) (also **,sweet 'pepper** *BrE, NAmE*) (*BrE* **pep·per**) *noun* a hollow fruit, usually red, green or yellow, eaten as a vegetable either raw or cooked 甜椒；柿子椒；燈籠椒 ➲ VISUAL VOCAB page V31

'bell pull *noun* a rope or handle that you pull to make a bell ring, for example to make sb in another room hear you 拉鈴索；拉鈴手柄

'bell push *noun* (*BrE*) a button that you press to make an electric bell ring 電鈴按鈕

'bell-ringer (also **ringer**) *noun* a person who rings church bells as a hobby 教堂的業餘敲鐘人 ▸ **'bell-ringing** *noun* [U] ➲ see also CAMPANOLOGIST, CAMPANOLOGY

,bells and 'whistles *noun* [pl.] (*computing* 計) attractive extra features 華麗的點綴

bell·wether /'belweðə(r)/ *noun* [usually sing.] something that is used as a sign of what will happen in the future 徵兆；前導 : *University campuses are often the bellwether of change.* 大學校園往往引領變革的新潮。

belly /'beli/ *noun, verb*

■ ***noun*** (*pl.* **-ies**) **1** the part of the body below the chest 腹部；肚子 SYN **stomach, gut** : *They crawled along on their bellies.* 他們匍匐前進。➲ see also BEER BELLY, POT BELLY at POT-BELLIED **2** (*literary*) the round or curved part of an object（物體的）圓形或凸起部份 : *the belly of a ship* 船腹 ➲ VISUAL VOCAB page V34 **3 -bellied** (in adjectives 構成形容詞) having the type of belly mentioned 腹部…形的 : *swollen-bellied* 腹部腫脹的 ◇ *round-bellied* 肚子圓圓的

IDM **go belly 'up** (*informal*) to fail completely 徹底失敗；垮掉；完蛋 : *Last year the business went belly up after one of the partners resigned.* 去年一位合夥人退出後，這家企業就垮掉了。

■ ***verb*** (**bel·lies**, **belly·ing**, **bel·lied**, **bel·lied**) [I] ~ **(out)** (especially of sails 尤指船帆) to fill with air and become rounder 脹滿；鼓起

belly·ache /'belieɪk/ *noun, verb*

■ ***noun*** [C, U] (*informal*) a pain in the stomach 腹痛；肚子疼 : *I've got (a) bellyache.* 我肚子疼。

■ ***verb*** [I] (*informal*) to complain a lot about sth in an annoying or unreasonable way 無端地猛發牢騷

'belly button *noun* (*informal*) = NAVEL

'belly dance *noun* a dance, originally from the Middle East, in which a woman moves her belly and hips around 肚皮舞（起源於中東地區，跳舞女郎扭動肚皮和臀部）▸ **'belly dancer** *noun*

belly·flop /'beliflɒp; *NAmE* -flɑːp/ *noun* (*informal*) a bad DIVE into water, in which the front of the body hits the water flat 跳水時肚子先落水

belly·ful /'belifʊl/ *noun*

IDM **have had a 'bellyful of sb/sth** (*informal*) to have had more than enough of sb/sth, so that you cannot deal with any more 受夠了某人／某事物 : *I've had a bellyful of your moaning.* 我已經聽夠了你的抱怨了。

'belly laugh *noun* (*informal*) a deep loud laugh 捧腹大笑

be·long 0-w /bɪ'lɒŋ; *NAmE* -lɔːŋ/ *verb* (not used in the progressive tenses 不用於進行時)

1 0-w [I] **+ adv./prep.** to be in the right or suitable place 應在（某處）: *Where do these plates belong* (= where are they kept)? 這些盤子該放在哪裏？◇ *Are you sure these documents belong together?* 你肯定這些文件應放在一起嗎？ **2** 0-w [I] to feel comfortable and happy in a particular situation or with a particular group of people 適應；合得來 : *I don't feel as if I belong here.* 我在這裏感覺格格不入。▸ **be·long·ing** *noun* [U] : *to feel a sense of belonging* 有一種歸屬感

PHR V **be'long to sb 1** 0-w to be owned by sb 屬於某人；歸某人所有 : *Who does this watch belong to?* 這塊錶是誰的？◇ *The islands belong to Spain.* 這些島嶼隸屬西班牙。 **2** an event, a competition, etc. that **belongs to** sb is one in which they are the most successful or popular（事件、比賽等中某人）獲勝，最受歡迎 : *British actors did well at the award ceremony, but the evening belonged to the Americans.* 英國演員在頒獎儀式上表現很好，但整個晚上卻是美國人大出風頭。 **be'long to sth 1** 0-w to be a member of a club, an organization, etc. 是（俱樂部、組織等）的成員 : *Have you ever belonged to a political party?* 你加入過什麼政黨嗎？ **2** 0-w to be part of a particular group, type, or system 是（某族類或綱目）的一部份；屬於 : *Lions and tigers belong to the cat family.* 獅子和老虎屬於貓科。

be·long·ings /bɪ'lɒŋɪŋz; *NAmE* -'lɔːŋ-/ *noun* [pl.] the things that you own which can be moved, for example not land or buildings 動產；財物 SYN **possessions** : *insurance of property and personal belongings* 不動產和個人財物保險 ◇ *She packed her few belongings in a bag and left.* 她把她的幾件東西裝進包裹便離開了。➲ SYNONYMS at THING

be·loved *adj., noun*

■ ***adj.*** (*formal*) **1** /bɪ'lʌvd/ ~ **by/of sb** loved very much by sb; very popular with sb 鍾愛的；深受喜愛的 : *the deep purple flowers so beloved by artists* 受藝術家青睞的深紫色花 **2** /bɪ'lʌvɪd/ [only before noun] loved very much 深愛的；親愛的 : *in memory of our dearly beloved son, John* 為紀念我們的愛子，約翰

■ ***noun*** /bɪ'lʌvɪd/ (*old use* or *literary*) a person who is loved very much by sb 心愛的人 : *It was a gift from her beloved.* 那是她心愛的人送的禮物。

below 0-w /bɪ'ləʊ; *NAmE* bɪ'loʊ/ *prep., adv.*

■ ***prep.*** **1** 0-w at or to a lower level or position than sb/sth 在（或到）…下面 : *He dived below the surface of the water.* 他潛入了水中。◇ *Please do not write below this line.* 請不要在這條線下面書寫。◇ *Skirts will be worn below* (= long enough to cover) *the knee.* 穿裙子要過膝。 **2** 0-w of a lower amount or standard than sb/sth（數量）少於；（標準）低於 : *The temperatures remained below freezing all day.* 氣溫一整天都保持在冰點以下。◇ *Her work was well below average for the class.* 她的功課遠在班上的中等水平以下。 **3** 0-w of a lower rank or of less importance than sb/sth（級別、重要性）低於 : *A police sergeant is below an inspector.* 巡佐的級別低於巡官。

■ ***adv.*** **1** 0-w at or to a lower level, position or place 在（或到）下面 : *They live on the floor below.* 他們住在下一層樓。◇ *I could still see the airport buildings far below.* 我還能遠遠地看到下方的機場建築。◇ *See below* (= at the bottom of the page) *for references.* 見本頁末參考資料。◇ *The passengers who felt seasick stayed below* (= on a lower DECK). 暈船的乘客待在下層客艙。 **2** (of a temperature 溫度) lower than zero 零度以下： *The thermometer had dropped to a record 40 below* (= –40 degrees). 溫度計降到了零下 40 度的紀錄。 **3** at a lower rank 下級： *This ruling applies to the ranks of Inspector and below.* 這項規定適用於巡官及以下人員。

be,low-the-'fold *adj.* not in a position where it is seen first, for example on the bottom part of a newspaper page or web page （報紙版面、網頁等）居於下端的，位置不明顯的，第一眼看不到的： *below-the-fold links* 網頁下端的鏈接 ◇ *That story would have been better in a less prominent, below-the-fold position.* 那則報道如果刊登在不那麼醒目的頁底位置效果本可以更好。 ➲ compare ABOVE-THE-FOLD **IDM** see FOLD *n.*

belt 🗝 /belt/ *noun, verb*

■ ***noun*** **1** 🗝 a long narrow piece of leather, cloth, etc. that you wear around the waist 腰帶；皮帶： *to* ***do up/fasten/tighten a belt*** 繫上／紮牢／紮緊腰帶 ◇ *a belt buckle* 腰帶扣 ➲ VISUAL VOCAB page V63 ➲ see also BLACK BELT, LIFEBELT, SEAT BELT, SUSPENDER BELT **2** a continuous band of material that moves round and is used to carry things along or to drive machinery 傳送帶；傳動帶 ➲ see also CONVEYOR BELT, FAN BELT **3** an area with particular characteristics or where a particular group of people live 地帶；地區： *the country's* ***corn/industrial belt*** 這個國家的產糧區／工業區 ◇ *We live in the* ***commuter belt.*** 我們住在通勤者居住帶。 ◇ *a belt of rain moving across the country* 橫穿這個國家的降雨帶 ➲ see also GREEN BELT **4** (*informal*) an act of hitting sth/sb hard 狠打；猛擊： *She gave the ball a terrific belt.* 她猛擊了一下球。

IDM **below the 'belt** (of a remark 說話) unfair or cruel 不公正的；傷人的： *That was distinctly below the belt!* 那顯然是不公正的！ **,belt and 'braces** (*informal*) taking more actions than are really necessary to make sure that sth succeeds or works as it should 雙管齊下；多重保障： *a belt-and-braces policy* 穩妥可靠的政策 **have sth under your 'belt** (*informal*) to have already achieved or obtained sth 已經獲得某物： *She already has a couple of good wins under her belt.* 她已將兩項冠軍收入囊中。 ➲ more at TIGHTEN

■ ***verb*** **1 ~ sb/sth** (*informal*) to hit sb/sth hard 猛擊；狠打： *He belted the ball right out of the park.* 他用力一擊，球逕直飛出了球場外。 ◇ *I'll belt you if you do that again.* 你要是再這樣，我就揍你。 **2** [I] **+ adv./prep.** (*informal, especially BrE*) to move very fast 飛奔；飛馳 **SYN** **tear**： *A truck came belting up behind us.* 一輛貨車從我們後方飛馳而來。 **3** [T] **~ sth** to fasten a belt around sth 繞着繫上帶子： *The dress was belted at the waist.* 那件連衣裙的裙腰束着條帶子。

PHR V **,belt sth↔'out** (*informal*) to sing a song or play music loudly 高聲唱歌（或奏樂） **,belt 'up** (*BrE*) **1** (*NAmE* **,buckle 'up**) (*informal*) to fasten your SEAT BELT (= a belt worn by a passenger in a vehicle) 繫上安全帶 **2** (*informal*) used to tell sb rudely to be quiet 住口；閉嘴 **SYN** **shut up**： *Just belt up, will you!* 你安靜點行不行！

belt·ed /'beltɪd/ *adj.* with a belt around it 繫着帶子的： *a belted jacket* 有腰帶的夾克

belt·way /'beltweɪ/ *noun* (*US*) a RING ROAD, especially the one around Washington DC （尤指環繞華盛頓特區的）環行路，環路

be·luga /bə'lu:gə/ (*pl.* **be·luga** or **be·lugas**) *noun* **1** [C] a type of small WHALE 白鯨 **2** [C] a type of large fish that lives in rivers and lakes in eastern Europe 歐洲鰉，歐鰉（大型鱘魚） **3** (also **be,luga 'caviar**) [U] a type of CAVIAR (= fish eggs), from a beluga 鱘魚魚子醬

be·moan /bɪ'məʊn; *NAmE* bɪ'moʊn/ *verb* **~ sth** (*formal*) to complain or say that you are not happy about sth 哀怨；悲歎： *They sat bemoaning the fact that no one would give them a chance.* 他們坐着埋怨別人不肯給他們一個機會。

be·mused /bɪ'mju:zd/ *adj.* showing that you are confused and unable to think clearly 困惑的；茫然的 **SYN** **bewildered**： *a* ***bemused expression/smile*** 困惑不解的表情／微笑 ▸ **be·muse** *verb* **~ sb** **be·mus·ed·ly** /bɪ'mju:zɪdli/ *adv.*

bench /bentʃ/ *noun* **1** [C] a long seat for two or more people, usually made of wood （木製）長凳，長椅： *a park bench* 公園長椅 ➲ VISUAL VOCAB page V19 **2 the bench** [sing.] (*law* 律) a judge in court or the seat where he/she sits; the position of being a judge or MAGISTRATE 法官；法官席位；法官（或裁判官）的職位： *His lawyer turned to address the bench.* 他的律師轉身對法官講話。 ◇ *She has recently been appointed to the bench.* 她最近當上了法官。 **3** [C, usually pl.] (in the British Parliament) a seat where a particular group of politicians sit （英國議會的）議員席： *There was cheering from the Opposition benches.* 反對黨議員席那邊響起了歡呼聲。 ➲ see also BACK BENCH, THE FRONT BENCH **4 the bench** [sing.] (*sport* 體) the seats where players sit when they are not playing in the game 場邊的運動員休息區： *the substitutes' bench* 替補隊員席 **5** [C] = WORKBENCH： *a carpenter's bench* 木工的工作枱

bench·mark /'bentʃmɑ:k; *NAmE* -mɑ:rk/ *noun, verb*

■ ***noun*** something that can be measured and used as a standard that other things can be compared with 基準： *Tests at the age of seven provide a benchmark against which the child's progress at school can be measured.* 七歲時進行的測試為孩子在學校中的學習發展提供了一個測量基準。

■ ***verb*** **~ sth** (**against sth**) to judge the quality of sth in relation to that of other similar things 以（某事物）為標準評估（某事物）： *Projects are assessed and benchmarked against the targets.* 以這些目標作為對項目進行評估和檢測的基準。

'bench press *noun* an exercise in which you lie on a raised surface with your feet on the floor and raise a weight with both arms 仰卧推舉

bench·warm·er /'bentʃwɔ:mə(r); *NAmE* -wɔ:rm-/ *noun* (*NAmE, informal*) a sports player who is not chosen to play in a particular game, but is available if their team needs them （運動隊的）板凳隊員，替補隊員 **SYN** **substitute**

bend 🗝 /bend/ *verb, noun*

■ ***verb*** (**bent**, **bent** /bent/) **1** 🗝 [I, T] (especially of sb's body or head 尤指人的身體或頭部) to lean, or make sth lean, in a particular direction （使）傾斜，偏向： *He bent and kissed her.* 他低下頭吻了她。 ◇ **+ adv./prep.** *fields of poppies bending in the wind* 一畦畦隨風搖擺的罌粟 ◇ *His dark head bent over her.* 他對她低下他那黑髮的頭。 ◇ *She bent forward to pick up the newspaper.* 她彎腰去撿報紙。 ◇ *Slowly bend from the waist and bring your head down to your knees.* 慢慢彎下腰，把頭低垂到膝部。 ◇ **~ sth** (**+ adv./prep.**) *He bent his head and kissed her.* 他低下頭吻了她。 ◇ *She was bent over her desk writing a letter.* 她正伏案寫信。 **2** 🗝 [T, I] **~ (sth)** if you **bend** your arm, leg, etc. or if it **bends**, you move it so that it is no longer straight （使四肢等）彎曲： *Bend your knees, keeping your back straight.* 膝蓋彎曲，背部挺直。 ◇ *Lie flat and let your knees bend.* 平躺曲膝。 **3** 🗝 [T] **~ sth** to force sth that was straight into an angle or a curve 把…弄彎（或摺起）： *Mark the pipe where you want to bend it.* 在管子上把要弄彎的地方做個記號。 ◇ *The knives were bent out of shape.* 那些刀已經彎曲變形了。 ◇ *He bent the wire into the shape of a square.* 他把鐵絲折成正方形。 **4** 🗝 [I, T] to change direction to form a curve or an angle; to make sth change direction in this way （使）拐彎，彎曲： *The road bent sharply to the right.* 路向右急拐。 ◇ **~ sth** *Glass and water both bend light.* 玻璃和水都折光。

IDM **bend sb's 'ear** (**about sth**) (*informal*) to talk to sb a lot about sth, especially about a problem that you have 向某人嘮叨訴説（尤指自己的難處） **bend your 'mind/'efforts to sth** (*formal*) to think very hard about or put a lot of effort into one particular thing 致力於某事；專心致志 **bend the 'truth** to say sth that is not completely true 扭曲事理；歪曲事實 **on bended 'knee(s)** if you ask for sth **on bended knee(s)**, you ask for it in a very anxious and/or HUMBLE way 下跪（請求…）；央求；苦苦哀求 ➲ more at BACKWARDS, RULE *n.*

PHR V **'bend sb to sth** (*formal*) to force or persuade sb to do what you want or to accept your opinions 迫使；説服： *He manipulates people and tries to* ***bend them to***

B

his will (= make them do what he wants). 他能左右民眾，讓大家跟隨他的意志。

■ *noun* **1** [C] a curve or turn, especially in a road or river（尤指道路或河流的）拐彎，彎道： *a sharp bend in the road* 道路的急拐彎 ➲ see also HAIRPIN BEND **2 the bends** [pl.] severe pain and difficulty in breathing experienced by a DIVER who comes back to the surface of the water too quickly（潛水員過快浮出水面造成的）減壓病，潛涵病

IDM **round the bend/twist** (*informal, especially BrE*) crazy 瘋狂： *She's gone completely round the bend.* 她完全瘋了。◇ *The kids have been* ***driving me round the bend*** *today* (= annoying me very much). 孩子們今天快把我氣瘋了。

bend·er /ˈbendə(r)/ *noun* (*slang*) a period of drinking a lot of alcohol or taking a lot of drugs（一段時間）狂飲作樂，大量吸毒： *to go on a bender* 飲酒作樂

bendy /ˈbendi/ *adj.* (*BrE, informal*) **1** that can be bent easily 易彎曲的；易折的 SYN **flexible 2** with many bends 多彎道的： *a bendy road* 迂迴的道路

ˈbendy bus *noun* (*BrE, informal*) a long bus that bends in the middle so that it can turn corners more easily 鉸接式公共汽車；多節巴士

be·neath /bɪˈniːθ/ *prep.* (*formal*)
1 in or to a lower position than sb/sth; under sb/sth 在（或往）…下面；在（或往）…下方： *They found the body buried beneath a pile of leaves.* 他們發現屍體被埋在一堆樹葉下面。◇ *The boat sank beneath the waves.* 小船被大浪吞沒了。 **2** not good enough for sb（對某人來說）不夠好： *He considers such jobs beneath him.* 他覺得這些工作有失他的身分。◇ *They thought she had married beneath her* (= married a man of lower social status). 他們認為她下嫁了（嫁給了地位比她低的人）。 ▸ **be·neath** *adv.*： *Her careful make-up hid the signs of age beneath.* 她細膩的化妝掩蓋了她年齡的痕跡。

Bene·dic·tine /ˌbenɪˈdɪktɪn/ *noun* a member of a Christian group of MONKS or NUNS following the rules of St Benedict 本篤會修士（或修女） ▸ **Bene·dic·tine** *adj.*： *a Benedictine monastery* 本篤會隱修院

bene·dic·tion /ˌbenɪˈdɪkʃn/ *noun* [C, U] (*formal*) a Christian prayer of BLESSING（基督教的）祝福，祝禱

bene·fac·tion /ˌbenɪˈfækʃn/ *noun* (*formal*) a gift, usually of money, that is given to a person or an organization in order to do good 捐贈；捐款

bene·fac·tor /ˈbenɪfæktə(r)/ *noun* (*formal*) a person who gives money or other help to a person or an organization such as a school or charity 施主；捐款人；贊助人

bene·fice /ˈbenɪfɪs/ *noun* the paid position of a Christian priest in charge of a PARISH（教區牧師等的）有俸聖職

be·nefi·cent /bɪˈnefɪsnt/ *adj.* (*formal*) giving help; showing kindness 有幫助的；行善的；慈善的 SYN **generous** ▸ **be·nefi·cence** /bɪˈnefɪsns/ *noun* [U]

bene·fi·cial AW /ˌbenɪˈfɪʃl/ *adj.* ~ **(to sth/sb)** (*formal*) improving a situation; having a helpful or useful effect 有利的；有幫助的；有用的 SYN **advantageous, favourable**： *A good diet is beneficial to health.* 良好的飲食有益於健康。 OPP **detrimental**

bene·fi·ciary AW /ˌbenɪˈfɪʃəri; *NAmE* -ˈfɪʃieri/ *noun* (*pl.* **-ies**) **1** ~ **(of sth)** a person who gains as a result of sth 受益者；受惠人： *Who will be the main beneficiary of the cuts in income tax?* 削減所得稅的主要受益者將是誰？ **2** ~ **(of sth)** a person who receives money or property when sb dies 遺產繼承人

bene·fit AW /ˈbenɪfɪt/ *noun, verb*

■ *noun* **1** [U, C] an advantage that sth gives you; a helpful and useful effect that sth has 優勢；益處；成效： *I've* ***had the benefit of*** *a good education.* 我得益於受過良好教育。◇ *The new regulations will be* ***of benefit*** *to everyone concerned.* 新規章將使所有有關人員受益。◇ *It will be* ***to your benefit*** *to arrive early.* 早到將會對你有利。◇ *He couldn't see the benefit of arguing any longer.* 他看不出再爭論下去有什麼好處。◇ *the benefits of modern medicine* 現代醫學的助益 ◇ *It was good to see her finally* ***reaping the benefits*** (= enjoying the results) *of all her hard work.* 看到她終於得享辛勤勞動的成果令人欣慰。 ➲ see also COST-BENEFIT, FRINGE BENEFIT **2** [U, C] (*BrE*) money provided by the government to people who need financial help because they are unemployed, ill/sick, etc. 福利費（政府對失業者、病人等提供的補助金） ➲ see also CHILD BENEFIT, HOUSING BENEFIT, SICKNESS BENEFIT **3** [C, usually pl.] an advantage that you get from a company in addition to the money that you earn; money from an insurance company（公司發的）獎金，補貼；（保險公司發的）給付： *The insurance plan will provide substantial cash benefits to your family in case of your death.* 投保人一旦死亡，該項保險將支付給其家屬相當可觀的保險金。 ➲ see also FRINGE BENEFIT **4** [C] an event such as a performance, a dinner, etc., organized in order to raise money for a particular person or charity 慈善（或公益）活動： *a* ***benefit match/concert*** 義賽；慈善音樂會

IDM **for sb's benefit** especially in order to help or be useful to sb 為幫助某人；為某人的利益： *I have typed out some lecture notes for the benefit of those people who were absent last week.* 我幫上星期缺席的人打了些課堂筆記。◇ *Don't go to any trouble for my benefit!* 別為我費工夫！ **give sb the ˌbenefit of the ˈdoubt** to accept that sb has told the truth or has not done sth wrong because you cannot prove that they have not（在證據不足的情況下）假定某人說實話，假定某人沒有錯

■ *verb* (**-t-** or **-tt-**) **1** [T] ~ **sb** to be useful to sb or improve their life in some way 對（某人）有用；使受益： *We should spend the money on something that will benefit everyone.* 我們應該把這筆錢花在大家都能得益的事上。 **2** [I] ~ **(from/by sth)** to be in a better position because of sth 得益於；得利於： *Who exactly* ***stands to benefit*** *from these changes?* 到底是誰會從這些變革中直接獲益？

Bene·lux /ˈbenɪlʌks/ *noun* [U] a name for Belgium, the Netherlands and Luxembourg, when they are thought of as a group 比荷盧（比利時、荷蘭、盧森堡三國並提時的簡稱）

be·nevo·lent /bəˈnevələnt/ *adj.* **1** (*formal*) (especially of people in authority 尤指當權者) kind, helpful and generous 慈善的；行善的；樂善好施的： *a benevolent smile/attitude* 和藹的笑容 / 態度 ◇ *belief in the existence of a benevolent god* 對於存在仁慈的神的篤信 OPP **malevolent 2** used in the names of some organizations that give help and money to people in need（用於慈善機構名稱）： *the RAF Benevolent Fund* 英國皇家空軍慈善基金（組織） ▸ **be·nevo·lence** /bəˈnevələns/ *noun* [U] **be·nevo·lent·ly** *adv.*

Ben·gali /beŋˈɡɔːli; *NAmE* -ˈɡɑːli/ *noun* **1** [C] a person from Bangladesh or West Bengal in eastern India 孟加拉國人；（印度東部的）西孟加拉邦人 **2** [U] the language of people from Bangladesh or West Bengal in eastern India 孟加拉語 ▸ **Ben·gali** *adj.*

be·night·ed /bɪˈnaɪtɪd/ *adj.* (*old-fashioned*) **1** (of people 人) without understanding 愚昧無知的 **2** (of places 地方) without the benefits of modern life 落後的；未開發的

be·nign /bɪˈnaɪn/ *adj.* **1** (*formal*) (of people 人) kind and gentle; not hurting anybody 善良的；和善的；慈祥的 **2** (*medical* 醫) (of TUMOURS growing in the body 體內生長的腫瘤) not dangerous or likely to cause death 良性的 OPP **malignant** ▸ **be·nign·ly** *adv.*： *He smiled benignly.* 他露出了和藹的笑容。

bent /bent/ *adj., noun* ➲ see also BEND

■ *adj.* **1** not straight 彎曲的： *a piece of bent wire* 一段彎曲的金屬絲 ◇ *Do this exercise with your knees bent* (= not with your legs straight). 做這個動作要雙膝彎曲。 ➲ picture at CURVED **2** (of a person 人) not able to stand up straight, usually as a result of being old or ill/sick（因年老或生病）駝背的，彎腰的： *a small bent old woman* 一個矮小駝背的老太太 ◇ *He was* ***bent double*** *with laughter.* 他笑彎了腰。 **3** (*BrE, informal*) (of a person in authority 當權者) dishonest 不誠實的；不正派的

IDM **ˈbent on sth/on doing sth** determined to do sth (usually sth bad) 決心要做，一心想做（通常指壞事）： *She seems bent on making life difficult for me.* 她似乎專門和我過不去。 ➲ see also HELL-BENT **get bent out of**

'shape (about/over sth) (*NAmE, informal*) to become angry, anxious or upset（為某事）生氣，焦慮，煩躁：*Don't get bent out of shape about it. It was just a mistake!* 不要為這事煩惱了，那只是一個錯誤而已！
■ ***noun*** [usually sing.] **~ (for sth)** a natural skill or interest in sth（某方面的）天賦，愛好：*She has a bent for mathematics.* 她有數學天賦。

bent·wood /ˈbentwʊd/ *noun* [U] wood that is artificially shaped for making furniture 曲木（經處理用於做傢具）：*bentwood chairs* 曲木椅

ben·zene /ˈbenziːn/ *noun* [U] a clear liquid obtained from PETROLEUM and COAL TAR, used in making plastics and many chemical products 苯

be·queath /bɪˈkwiːð/ *verb* (*formal*) **1** to say in a WILL that you want sb to have your property, money, etc. after you die（在遺囑中）把…遺贈給 **SYN** **leave**：**~ sth (to sb)** *He bequeathed his entire estate (= all his money and property) to his daughter.* 他把全部財產遺贈給他的女兒。◇ **~ sb sth** *He bequeathed his daughter his entire estate.* 他把全部財產遺贈給他的女兒。 **2 ~ sth (to sb)** | **~ sb sth** to leave the results of your work, knowledge, etc. for other people to use or deal with, especially after you have died（尤指死後）將（工作成果、知識等）留下（給後人享用或處理）

be·quest /bɪˈkwest/ *noun* (*formal*) money or property that you ask to be given to a particular person when you die 遺產；遺贈：*He left a bequest to each of his grandchildren.* 他給他的孫子孫女每人留下一筆遺產。

be·rate /bɪˈreɪt/ *verb* **~ sb/yourself** (*formal*) to criticize or speak angrily to sb because you do not approve of sth they have done 痛斥；嚴厲指責

be·reave /bɪˈriːv/ *verb* **be bereaved** if sb **is bereaved**, a relative or close friend has just died 喪失（親友）：*The ceremony was an ordeal for those who had been recently bereaved.* 這個儀式對於那些新近喪失親友的人來說是一種折磨。

be·reaved /bɪˈriːvd/ *adj.* (*formal*) **1** having lost a relative or close friend who has recently died 喪失親友的：*recently bereaved families* 剛剛痛失親人的家庭 **2 the bereaved** *noun* (*pl.* **the bereaved**) a person who is bereaved 死者的親友：*an organization offering counselling for the bereaved* 為死者親友提供輔導的組織

be·reave·ment /bɪˈriːvmənt/ *noun* **1** [U] the state of having lost a relative or close friend because they have died 喪失親人；喪親之痛：*the pain of an emotional crisis such as divorce or bereavement* 諸如離婚或痛失親人等的情感危機的痛苦 **2** [C] the death of a relative or close friend 親友的喪亡：*A family bereavement meant that he could not attend the conference.* 他家裏有人去世了，所以不能出席會議。

be·reft /bɪˈreft/ *adj.* [not before noun] (*formal*) **1 ~ of sth** completely lacking sth; having lost sth 完全沒有，喪失，失去（某物）：*bereft of ideas/hope* 無計可施；失去希望 **2** (of a person 人) sad and lonely because you have lost sth 感到失落：*He was utterly bereft when his wife died.* 他的妻子去世時，他十分淒涼。

beret /ˈbereɪ; *NAmE* bəˈreɪ/ *noun* a round flat cap made out of soft cloth and with a tight band around the head 貝雷帽（扁圓無簷）➲ **VISUAL VOCAB** page V65

berg /bɜːɡ; *NAmE* bɜːrɡ/ *noun* (*SAfrE*) **1** a mountain or group of mountains 山；群山；山脈 **2 the Berg** [sing.] the Drakensberg, a group of tall mountains in South Africa（南非）德拉肯斯山脈

ber·ga·mot /ˈbɜːɡəmɒt; *NAmE* ˈbɜːrɡəmɑːt/ *noun* [U] **1** (also **'bergamot oil**) oil from the skin of a small orange 香檸檬精油 **2** a type of HERB 香檸檬香草；香檸檬草藥

berg·schrund /ˈbɜːɡʃrʊnd; *NAmE* ˈbɜːrkʃrʊnt/ *noun* (*geology* 地) a deep crack formed where a GLACIER (= a large moving mass of ice) meets the side of a mountain 冰後隙（山側面的冰河邊沿裂隙）

beri·beri /ˌberiˈberi/ *noun* [U] a disease that affects the nerves and heart, caused by a lack of VITAMIN B 腳氣病

berk /bɜːk; *NAmE* bɜːrk/ *noun* (*old-fashioned, BrE, slang*) a stupid person 傻瓜；蠢人 **SYN** **idiot**

ber·ke·lium /bɜːˈkiːliəm; ˈbɜːkliəm; *NAmE* ˈbɜːrkliəm/ *noun* [U] (*symb.* **Bk**) a chemical element. Berkelium is a RADIOACTIVE metal that is produced artificially from AMERICIUM and HELIUM. 錇（放射性化學元素）

Ber·lin·er /ˌbɜːˈlɪnə(r); *NAmE* ˌbɜːr-/ *adj.* (*BrE*) (of a newspaper 報紙) printed on pages measuring 470mm by 315mm, smaller than a BROADSHEET and larger than a TABLOID 柏林型版式的（紙張規格為 470 × 315 毫米）

berm /bɜːm; *NAmE* bɜːrm/ *noun* (*technical* 術語) **1** an area of ground at the side of a road; a raised area of ground at the side of a river or CANAL 路邊的狹長地帶；河邊護堤 **2** a narrow raised area of sand formed on a beach by the waves coming in from the sea 灘沿，後濱階地（海浪淘沙淤積而成）

Bermuda shorts /bəˌmjuːdə ˈʃɔːts; *NAmE* bərˌmjuːdə ˈʃɔːrts/ (also **Ber·mu·das** /bəˈmjuːdəz; *NAmE* bərˈm-/) *noun* [pl.] SHORTS (= short trousers/pants) that come down to just above the knee 百慕大短褲（長及膝部）：*a pair of Bermudas* 一條百慕大短褲

the Berˌmuda 'Triangle *noun* [sing.] an area in the Atlantic Ocean between Bermuda, Florida and Puerto Rico where a large number of ships and aircraft are believed to have disappeared in a mysterious way 百慕大三角（大西洋中位於百慕大、佛羅里達州和波多黎各之間的海域，已有許多船隻、飛機在此神秘地失踪）：*This area of town is known as the Bermuda Triangle because drinkers can disappear into the pubs and clubs and be lost to the world.* 城裏的這一地區稱作"百慕大三角"，因為酒徒進入這裏的酒吧和夜總會後就可能消失得無影無踪。

berry /ˈberi/ *noun* (*pl.* **-ies**) (often in compounds 常構成複合詞) a small fruit that grows on a bush. There are several types of berry, some of which can be eaten. 漿果；莓：*Birds feed on nuts and berries in the winter.* 鳥類靠堅果和漿果過冬。◇ *blackberries/raspberries* 黑莓；懸鈎子 ➲ **VISUAL VOCAB** pages V10, V30

ber·serk /bəˈzɜːk; -ˈsɜːk; *NAmE* bərˈzɜːrk; -ˈsɜːrk/ *adj.* [not usually before noun] (*informal*) **1** very angry, often in a violent or uncontrolled way 盛怒；暴跳如雷：*He **went berserk** when he found out where I'd been.* 他弄清楚我去過哪兒後勃然大怒。 **2** very excited 極為激動；興奮不已；發狂：*People were going berserk with excitement.* 人們興奮得發狂了。

berth /bɜːθ; *NAmE* bɜːrθ/ *noun, verb*
■ ***noun*** **1** a place to sleep on a ship or train, or in a CARAVAN/CAMPER（船或火車等的）臥鋪，艙位，鋪位 **SYN** **bunk** **2** a place where a ship or boat can stop and stay, usually in a HARBOUR（船的）泊位，錨地 **IDM** see WIDE *adj.*
■ ***verb*** [T, I] **~ (sth)** to put a ship in a berth or keep it there; to sail into a berth（使船）停泊：*The ship is berthed at Southampton.* 船停泊在南安普敦。

beryl /ˈberəl/ *noun* [U] a transparent pale green, blue or yellow SEMI-PRECIOUS STONE, used in making jewellery 綠柱石

beryl·lium /bəˈrɪliəm/ *noun* [U] (*symb.* **Be**) a chemical element. Beryllium is a hard grey metal found mainly in the mineral BERYL. 鈹

besan /ˈbeɪsʌn/ *noun* = GRAM FLOUR

be·seech /bɪˈsiːtʃ/ *verb* (**be·sought**, **be·sought** /bɪˈsɔːt/) or (**be·seeched**, **be·seeched**) **~ sb (to do sth)** (*formal*) to ask sb for sth in an anxious way because you want or need it very much 懇求；哀求；乞求 **SYN** **implore, beg**：*Let him go, I beseech you!* 求求你讓他走吧！

be·seech·ing /bɪˈsiːtʃɪŋ/ *adj.* [only before noun] (*formal*) (of a look, tone of voice, etc. 眼神、語調等) showing that you want sth very much 懇求的；哀求的；乞求的 ▸ **be·seech·ing·ly** *adv.*

beset /bɪˈset/ *verb* (**be·set·ting**, **beset**, **beset**) [usually passive] **~ sb/sth** (*formal*) to affect sb/sth in an unpleasant or harmful way 困擾；威脅：*The team was beset by injury all season.* 這個隊整個賽季都因隊員受傷而受困擾。◇ *It's one of the most difficult problems besetting* *our modern way of life.* 那是困擾我們現代生活方式的一個最棘手的問題。

B

be·side /bɪˈsaɪd/ *prep.*
1 next to or at the side of sb/sth 在旁邊（或附近）：*He sat beside her all night.* 整個晚上他都坐在她的身邊。◇ *a mill beside a stream* 小溪旁的磨房 **2** compared with sb/sth 與…相比：*My painting looks childish beside yours.* 同你的相比，我的畫顯得很幼稚。
IDM **be beside the ˈpoint** to not be important or closely related to the main thing you are talking about 無關緊要；離題；不相關：*Yes, I know it was an accident, but that's beside the point.* 是的，我知道那是個事故，可是這無關緊要。 **beˈside yourself (with sth)** unable to control yourself because of the strength of emotion you are feeling（情緒上）失去自制力；失常：*He was beside himself with rage when I told him what I had done.* 我告訴他我做了什麼事，他就情緒失控。

Which Word? 詞語辨析

beside / besides

- The preposition **beside** usually means 'next to something/somebody' or 'at the side of something/somebody'. 介詞 beside 通常表示靠近、在旁邊：*Sit here beside me.* 坐到我旁邊來。 **Besides** means 'in addition to something'. * besides 表示除…之外（還）：*What other sports do you play besides hockey?* 除了玩曲棍球你還做哪些運動？ Do not use **beside** with this meaning. 此義不用 beside。
- The adverb **besides** is not usually used on its own with the same meaning as the preposition. It is mainly used to give another reason or argument for something. * besides 作副詞單獨使用時通常與作介詞時的含義不同，主要用以提出另一理由或論據：*I don't think I'll come on Saturday. I have a lot of work to do. Besides, I don't really like parties.* 我想我星期六不會來。我有好多事要做。再說，我不太喜歡社交聚會。◇ ~~*She likes football. Besides, she likes tennis and basketball.*~~

be·sides /bɪˈsaɪdz/ *prep., adv.*
■ ***prep.*** in addition to sb/sth; apart from sb/sth 除…之外（還）：*We have lots of things in common besides music.* 除了音樂，我們還有很多共通點。◇ *Besides working as a doctor, he also writes novels in his spare time.* 除了當醫生之外，他在業餘時間還寫小說。◇ *I've got no family besides my parents.* 除了父母外，我沒有其他親人。➲ LANGUAGE BANK at EXCEPT ➲ note at BESIDE
■ ***adv.*** **1** used for making an extra comment that adds to what you have just said 而且；再說：*I don't really want to go. Besides, it's too late now.* 我並不真的想去，而且現在太晚了。➲ LANGUAGE BANK at ADDITION ➲ note at BESIDE **2** in addition; also 此外；以及；也：*discounts on televisions, stereos and much more besides* 對電視、立體聲音響設備以及很多其他貨品的折扣

Which Word? 詞語辨析

besides / apart from / except

- The preposition **besides** means 'in addition to'. * besides 作介詞表示除…之外（還）：*What other sports do you like besides football?* 除足球外你還喜歡哪些運動？ You use **except** when you mention the only thing that is not included in a statement. 指僅有某事物不包括在內用 except：*I like all sports except football.* 除足球外我喜歡所有的運動。 You can use **apart from** with both these meanings. 上述兩種含義均可用 apart from：*What other sports do you like apart from football?* 除足球外你還喜歡哪些運動？◇ *I like all sports apart from football.* 除足球外我喜歡所有的運動。

be·siege /bɪˈsiːdʒ/ *verb* **1 ~ sth** to surround a building, city, etc. with soldiers until the people inside are forced to let you in 圍困；包圍 SYN **lay siege to**：*Paris was besieged for four months and forced to surrender.* 巴黎被圍困了四個月後被迫投降。◇ (*figurative*) *Fans besieged the box office to try and get tickets for the concert.* 歌迷們圍着售票處，試圖買到音樂會的票。**2** [usually passive] **~ sb/sth** (especially of sth unpleasant or annoying 尤指令人不快或煩惱的事) to surround sb/sth in large numbers 團團圍住：*The actress was besieged by reporters at the airport.* 那位女演員在機場被記者團團圍住。 **3 ~ sb (with sth)** to send so many letters, ask so many questions, etc. that it is difficult for sb to deal with them all（用大量的信件、提問等）使某人應接不暇：*The radio station was besieged with calls from angry listeners.* 廣播電台疲於應付憤怒的聽眾打來的電話。

be·smirch /bɪˈsmɜːtʃ; *NAmE* bɪˈsmɜːrtʃ/ *verb* **~ sb/sth** (*formal*) to damage the opinion that people have of sb/sth 詆譭；敗壞…的名聲 SYN **sully**

besom /ˈbiːzəm/ *noun* a brush for sweeping floors, made from sticks tied onto a long handle（長柄）掃帚

be·sot·ted /bɪˈsɒtɪd; *NAmE* -ˈsɑːt-/ *adj.* **~ (by/with sb/sth)** loving sb/sth so much that you do not behave in a sensible way（對某人、某物）愛得發狂的，痴迷的：*He is completely besotted with his new girlfriend.* 他對他的新女友一片痴心。

be·sought *past tense, past part.* of BESEECH

be·spat·ter /bɪˈspætə(r)/ *verb* **~ sth** (*literary*) to accidentally cover sth with small drops of water 濺灑；濺污

be·speak /bɪˈspiːk/ *verb* (**be·spoke** /-ˈspəʊk; *NAmE* -ˈspoʊk/, **be·spoken** /-ˈspəʊkən; *NAmE* -ˈspoʊ-/) **~ sth** (*literary*) to show or suggest sth 展現；顯示：*His style of dressing bespoke great self-confidence.* 他的衣着風格顯得十分自信。

be·spec·tacled /bɪˈspektəkld/ *adj.* (*formal*) wearing SPECTACLES 戴眼鏡的

be·spoke /bɪˈspəʊk; *NAmE* bɪˈspoʊk/ *adj.* [usually before noun] (*especially BrE, formal*) **1** (*NAmE* usually ˌ**custom-ˈmade**) (of a product 產品) made specially, according to the needs of an individual customer 訂做的 SYN **tailor-made**：*bespoke software* 訂製的軟件 ◇ *a bespoke suit* 一套訂做的衣服 **2** making products specially, according to the needs of an individual customer 專做訂貨的：*a bespoke tailor* 做訂做衣服的裁縫

best /best/ *adj., adv., noun, verb*
■ ***adj.*** (superlative of *good* * good 的最高級) **1** of the most excellent type or quality 最好的；最出色的；最優秀的：*That's the best movie I've ever seen!* 那是我看過的最棒的電影！◇ *She was one of the best tennis players of her generation.* 她是同輩中最出色的網球運動員之一。◇ *Is that your best suit?* 那是你最漂亮的一套衣服嗎？◇ *They've been **best friends*** (= closest friends) *since they were children.* 他們從孩提時起就是最要好的朋友。◇ *the company's **best-ever** results* 公司有史以來最大的成就 ◇ *We want the kids to have the **best possible** education.* 我們想讓孩子們接受最好最好的教育。 **2** most enjoyable; happiest 最愉快的；最幸福的：*Those were the best years of my life.* 那些年是我一生最幸福的時光。 **3** most suitable or appropriate 最合適的；最恰當的：*What's the best way to cook steak?* 牛排怎麼做最好？◇ *The best thing to do would be to apologize.* 最恰當的做法應該是道歉。◇ *He's the best man for the job.* 他是擔任這項工作的最佳人選。◇ ***It's best** if you go now.* 你最好現在就走。◇ *I'm not in the best position to advise you.* 我並不十分應該給你提出建議。
IDM Idioms containing **best** *adj.* are at the entries for the nouns and verbs in the idioms, for example **on your best behaviour** is at **behaviour**. 含形容詞 best 的習語，都可在該等習語中的名詞及動詞相關詞條找到，如 on your best behaviour 在詞條 behaviour 下。
■ ***adv.*** (superlative of *well*, often used in adjectives * well 的最高級，常用於構成形容詞) **1** most; to the greatest extent 最；最高程度地：*Which one do you like best?* 你最喜歡哪一個？◇ *Well-drained soil suits the plant best.* 排水性好的土壤最適合於這種植物。◇ *her **best-known** poem* 她的最有名的詩 **2** in the most excellent way; to the highest standard 最出色地；最高標準地：*He works*

best in the mornings. 他早上工作效果最佳。◇ *Britain's* ***best-dressed*** *woman* 英國最佳穿戴女士 ◇ *The beaches are beautiful, but,* ***best of all****, there are very few tourists.* 這些海灘很美，尤其令人滿意的是遊客稀少。 **3** 🔑 in the most suitable or appropriate way 最適合地；最恰當地：*Painting is best done in daylight.* 作畫的最佳時間是白天。◇ *Do as you* ***think best*** (= what you think is the most suitable thing to do). 你覺得怎麼好，就怎麼辦吧。

IDM **as ˌbest you ˈcan** not perfectly but as well as you are able 盡可能；盡力：*We'll manage as best we can.* 我們將盡力處理。

■ ***noun*** [sing.] (usually **the best**) **1** 🔑 the most excellent thing or person 最好的事物（或人）：*We all want the best for our children.* 我們都想給孩子提供最好的條件。◇ *They only buy the best.* 他們只買最好的。◇ *They're all good players, but she's the best of all.* 他們都是優秀運動員，而她更是其中的佼佼者。◇ *We're* ***the best of friends*** (= very close friends). 我們是至交。 **2** 🔑 the highest standard that sb/sth can reach（人或事物所能達到的）最高標準：*She always brings out the best in people.* 她總是讓人表現出最優秀的品質。◇ *The town* ***looks its best*** (= is most attractive) *in the spring.* 這個小鎮在春天景色最美。◇ *Don't worry about the exam—just* ***do your best****.* 別擔心考試，盡你的最大努力吧。◇ *The roses are* ***past their best*** *now.* 這些玫瑰花已開敗了。◇ *I don't really feel* ***at my best*** *today.* 我今天狀態不佳。 **3** 🔑 something that is as close as possible to what you need or want 最合乎要求的事物：*Fifty pounds is the best I can offer you.* 我頂多出五十英鎊。◇ *The best we can hope for in the game is a draw.* 我們至多能希望比賽打成平局。 **4** the highest standard that a particular person has reached, especially in a sport（個人的）最高水平，最高紀錄：*She won the race with a* ***personal best*** *of 2 minutes 22.* 她以 2 分 22 秒的個人最好成績贏得了這項比賽。

IDM **all the ˈbest** (*informal*) used when you are saying goodbye to sb or ending a letter, to give sb your good wishes（告別用語或書信結語）祝一切順利，萬事如意 **at ˈbest** used for saying what is the best opinion you can have of sb/sth, or the best thing that can happen, when the situation is bad（表達最好的看法，或惡劣狀況下可能出現的最好轉機）充其量：*Their response to the proposal was, at best, cool.* 他們對提議的反應充其量只能說是漠然置之。◇ *We can't arrive before Friday at best.* 我們無論如何星期五之前也到不了。 **be (all) for the ˈbest** used to say that although sth appears bad or unpleasant now, it will be good in the end 結局總會好的：*I don't want you to leave, but perhaps it's for the best.* 我並不想讓你走，但也許還是走的好。 **the best of a bad ˈbunch** (*BrE* also **the best of a bad ˈlot**) (*informal*) a person or thing that is a little better than the rest of a group, although none are very good 一群（或堆）壞的裏較好者；矮子裏拔的將軍 **the best of ˈthree, ˈfive, etc.** (especially in games and sports 尤指遊戲和體育比賽) up to three, five, etc. games played to decide who wins, the winner being the person who wins most of them 三局兩勝（或五局三勝等） **the best that money can ˈbuy** the very best 佳品；精品；極品：*We make sure our clients get the best that money can buy.* 我們確保客戶買到最好的產品。 **do, mean, etc. sth for the ˈbest** to do or say sth in order to achieve a good result or to help sb 為美好的目的；出於好意：*I just don't know what to do for the best.* 我就是弄不清做什麼才好。◇ *I'm sorry if my advice offended you—I meant it for the best.* 如果我的建議冒犯了你，我很抱歉。但我原本是出於好意。 **have/get the ˈbest of sth** to gain more advantage from sth than sb else 獲勝；勝過；佔上風：*I thought you had the best of that discussion.* 我以為你在那場討論中佔了上風。 **make the best of sth/it | make the best of things | make the best of a bad job** to accept a bad or difficult situation and do as well as you can 盡力而為 **to the best of your ˈknowledge/beˈlief** as far as you know 據某人所知（或瞭解）：*He never made a will, to the best of my knowledge.* 據我所知，他從未立過遺囑。 **with the ˈbest (of them)** as well as anyone 不亞於任何人；不比任何人差：*He'll be out there, dancing with the best of them.* 他將出現在舞池中，跳得不亞於任何人。 ➲ more at BUNCH *n.*, HOPE *v.*, LUCK *n.*, SUNDAY

■ ***verb*** [usually passive] **~ sb** (*formal*) to defeat or be more successful than sb 打敗；勝過

ˌbest-beˈfore date *noun* (*BrE*) a date printed on a container or package, advising you to use food or drink before this date as it will not be of such good quality after that 最佳食用期限，最佳保質期，保存期限（見於食物或飲料包裝）

bes·tial /ˈbestiəl; *NAmE* ˈbestʃəl/ *adj.* (*formal*) cruel and disgusting; of or like a BEAST 兇殘的；野獸的；野獸般的；獸性的：***bestial acts/cruelty/noises*** 毫無人性的行為／殘忍；野獸般的喧鬧聲

bes·ti·al·ity /ˌbestiˈæləti; *NAmE* ˌbestʃi-/ *noun* [U] **1** (*technical* 術語) sexual activity between a human and an animal 人獸交合；獸姦 **2** (*formal*) cruel or disgusting behaviour 獸行

bes·tiary /ˈbestɪəri; *NAmE* -eri/ *noun* (*pl.* **-ies**) a collection of descriptions of, or stories about, various types of animal, especially one written in the Middle Ages（尤指中世紀的）動物寓言集

be·stir /bɪˈstɜː(r)/ *verb* (**-rr-**) **~ yourself** (*formal* or *humorous*) to start doing things after a period during which you have been doing nothing 發奮；振作起來 **SYN** **rouse**

ˌbest ˈman *noun* [sing.] a male friend or relative of the BRIDEGROOM at a wedding, who helps him during the wedding ceremony 男儐相；伴郎 ➲ compare BRIDESMAID

be·stow /bɪˈstəʊ; *NAmE* bɪˈstoʊ/ *verb* **~ sth (on/upon sb)** (*formal*) to give sth to sb, especially to show how much they are respected 給予；授予；獻給：*It was a title bestowed upon him by the king.* 那是國王賜給他的頭銜。

ˌbest ˈpractice *noun* [U, C] a way of doing sth that is seen as a very good example of how it should be done and can be copied by other companies or organizations（公司或機構的）典範實務，最佳做法

be·stride /bɪˈstraɪd/ *verb* **~ sth** (*literary*) to sit with one leg on either side of sth 跨坐；騎：*He bestrode his horse.* 他騎上馬。

ˌbest-ˈseller (also **best·seller**) /ˌbestˈselə(r)/ *noun* a product, usually a book, which is bought by large numbers of people 暢銷品；暢銷書：*the best-seller list* 暢銷書榜 ▸ **ˌbest-ˈselling** *adj.*：*a* ***best-selling novel/author*** 暢銷小說；暢銷書作者

be·suit·ed /bɪˈsuːtɪd; *BrE* also -sjuːt-/ *adj.* (*formal*) wearing a suit 身着套裝的：*besuited businessmen* 身着套裝的商界人員

bet 🔑 /bet/ *verb, noun*

■ ***verb*** (**bet·ting, bet, bet**) **1** 🔑 [I, T] to risk money on a race or an event by trying to predict the result 下賭注（於）；用…打賭：*You have to be over 16 to bet.* 賭博者年齡不得低於 16 歲。◇ **~ on/against sth** *I wouldn't bet on them winning the next election.* 下一次選舉我不會賭他們贏。◇ **~ sth (on sth)** *He bet $2 000 on the final score of the game.* 他下 2 000 元賭比賽的最後比分。◇ **~ (sb) (sth) (that …)** *She bet me £20 that I wouldn't do it.* 她和我打 20 英鎊的賭，說我不會那麼做。 ➲ see also BETTING, GAMBLE *v.* (1) **2** 🔑 [T] (*informal*) used to say that you are almost certain that sth is true or that sth will happen 敢說；八成兒：**~ (that)** … *I bet (that) we're too late.* 我們八成兒太晚了。◇ *You can bet (that) the moment I sit down, the phone will ring.* 幾乎可以肯定，我一坐下，電話鈴就會響起來。◇ **~ sb (that)** … *I'll bet you (that) he knows all about it.* 我敢說他瞭解一切。

IDM **I/I'll bet!** (*informal*) **1** used to show that you can understand what sb is feeling, describing, etc.（表示理解）有同感，當然：*'I nearly died when he told me.' 'I bet!'* "他告訴我時，我差一點死掉了。" "肯定是這樣！" **2** used to tell sb that you do not believe what they have just said（表示不相信對方的話）：*'I'm going to tell her what I think of her.' 'Yeah, I bet!'* "我要告訴她我對她的看法。" "量你不敢！" **I wouldn't ˈbet on it | don't ˈbet on it** (*informal*) used to say that you do not think that sth is very likely 不大可能：*'She'll soon get used to the idea.' 'I wouldn't bet on it.'* "她很快就會接受

B

這種看法的。" "很難說。" ,**you 'bet!** (*informal*) used instead of 'yes' to emphasize that sb has guessed sth correctly or made a good suggestion 的確；當然：*'Are you nervous?' 'You bet!'* "你緊張嗎？" "這還用說！"

you can bet your 'life/your bottom 'dollar (on sth/(that) ...) (*informal*) used to say that you are certain that sth will happen 肯定；毫無疑問：*You can bet your bottom dollar that he'll be late.* 他肯定會遲到。

■ ***noun*** **1** an arrangement to risk money, etc. on the result of a particular event; the money that you risk in this way 打賭；賭注：*to **win/lose a bet*** 贏／輸一場賭 ◇ **~ on sth** *We've got a bet on who's going to arrive first.* 我們打了個賭，看誰先到。◇ *He had a bet on the horses.* 他在那些馬上下了賭注。◇ *They all put a bet on the race.* 他們都對比賽下了賭注。◇ *I hear you're taking bets on whether she'll marry him.* 我聽說你在拿她是否會嫁給他的事和人打賭。◇ *I did it **for a bet*** (= because sb had agreed to pay me money if I did). 我是為了打賭才這麼幹的。◇ *'Liverpool are bound to win.' '**Do you want a bet?**'* (= I disagree with you, I don't think they will.) "利物浦必勝。" "你敢打賭嗎？" **2** (*informal*) an opinion about what is likely to happen or to have happened 預計；估計：*My bet is that they've been held up in traffic.* 我估計他們是堵車了。

IDM **all bets are 'off** used to say that if a particular event happens then your current forecast, agreement, etc. will no longer apply （某事發生則）結局難料：*We expect shares to rise unless the economy slows down again, in which case all bets are off.* 我們預計股票會漲，除非經濟再次下滑。如果真是那樣的話，結局就難料了。 **the/your best bet** (*informal*) used to tell sb what is the best action for them to take to get the result they want 最好的辦法：*If you want to get around London fast, the Underground is your best bet.* 如果你想在倫敦快速地到處去，最好是乘地鐵。 **a ,good/,safe 'bet** something that is likely to happen, to succeed or to be suitable 很可能發生的事；有望成功的事；合適的東西：*Clothes are a safe bet as a present for a teenager.* 衣服適合作為送給十幾歲孩子的禮物。➲ more at HEDGE *v.*

beta /ˈbiːtə; *NAmE* ˈbeɪtə/ *noun* the second letter of the Greek alphabet (Β, β) 希臘字母表的第 2 個字母

'beta blocker *noun* a drug used to control heart rhythm, treat severe chest pain and reduce high blood pressure * β 受體阻滯藥（用以控制心率、治療嚴重胸部疼痛和降低血壓）

,beta-'carotene *noun* [U] a substance found in carrots and other plants, which is needed by humans * β–胡蘿蔔素

'beta decay *noun* [sing.] (*physics* 物) the breaking up of an atom in which an ELECTRON is given off * β 衰變（指原子分裂並釋放出一個電子）

be·take /bɪˈteɪk/ *verb* (**be·took** /-ˈtʊk/, **be·taken** /-ˈteɪkən/) **~ yourself + adv./prep.** (*literary*) to go somewhere 前往，去（某處）：*He betook himself to his room.* 他進了自己的房間。

'beta particle (also **'beta ray**) *noun* (*physics* 物) a fast-moving ELECTRON that is produced when some RADIO-ACTIVE substances decay * β 粒子；貝塔粒子

'beta test *noun* a test on a new product, done by sb who does not work for the company that is developing the product * β 測試（外部對公司新產品的測試）➲ compare ALPHA TEST ▸ **'beta-test** *verb* **~ sth**

'beta version *noun* [usually sing.] the version of a new product, especially computer software, that is almost ready for the public to buy or use, but is given to a few customers to test first（計算機軟件等新產品上市前的）β 版，測試版

betel /ˈbiːtl/ *noun* [U] the leaves of a climbing plant, also called betel, chewed by people in Asia 檳榔葉

'betel nut *noun* the slightly bitter nut of a tropical Asian PALM, that is cut into small pieces, wrapped in betel leaves, and chewed 檳榔果

bête noire /ˌbet ˈnwɑː(r)/ *noun* (*pl.* **bêtes noires** /ˌbet ˈnwɑː(r); *NAmE* also ˈnwɑːrz/) (from *French*) a person or thing that particularly annoys you and that you do not like 特別討厭的人（或事物）

be·tide /bɪˈtaɪd/ *verb* IDM see WOE

be·token /bɪˈtəʊkən; *NAmE* -ˈtoʊ-/ *verb* **~ sth** (*literary*) to be a sign of sth 預示；表示：*a clear blue sky betokening a fine day* 預示着好天氣的晴朗藍天

be·tray /bɪˈtreɪ/ *verb* **1** to give information about sb/sth to an enemy 出賣；泄露（機密）：**~ sb/sth** *He was offered money to betray his colleagues.* 有人收買他出賣他的同事。◇ **~ sb/sth to sb** *For years they had been betraying state secrets to Russia.* 他們多年來一直向俄羅斯泄露國家機密。 **2 ~ sb/sth** to hurt sb who trusts you, especially by not being loyal or faithful to them 辜負；對…不忠：*She felt betrayed when she found out the truth about him.* 她發現他的真實情況時，感到受了欺騙。◇ *She **betrayed his trust** over and over again.* 她一次又一次地辜負了他的信任。◇ *I have never known her to **betray a confidence*** (= tell other people sth that should be kept secret). 我從未聽說過她泄露秘密。➲ SYNONYMS at CHEAT **3 ~ sth** to ignore your principles or beliefs in order to achieve sth or gain an advantage for yourself 背叛（原則或信仰）：*He has been accused of betraying his former socialist ideals.* 有人指責他背棄了他先前的社會主義理想。 **4** to tell sb or make them aware of a piece of information, a feeling, etc., usually without meaning to（無意中）泄露信息，流露情感 SYN **give away**：**~ sth** *His voice betrayed the worry he was trying to hide.* 他的聲音掩蓋不了內心的擔憂。◇ **~ yourself** *She was terrified of saying something that would make her betray herself* (= show her feelings or who she was). 她害怕說話時泄了自己的底。

be·tray·al /bɪˈtreɪəl/ *noun* [U, C] the act of betraying sb/sth or the fact of being betrayed（被）背叛，出賣：***a sense/a feeling/an act of betrayal*** 被出賣的感覺；背叛行為 ◇ *I saw her actions as a betrayal of my trust.* 我認為她的所作所為辜負了我的信任。◇ *the many disappointments and betrayals in his life* 他一生中遭受的諸多失望與背叛

be·troth·al /bɪˈtrəʊðl; *NAmE* -ˈtroʊ-/ *noun* **~ (to sb)** (*formal* or *old-fashioned*) an agreement to marry sb 婚約；訂婚 SYN **engagement**

be·trothed /bɪˈtrəʊðd; *NAmE* -ˈtroʊ-/ *adj.* (*formal* or *old-fashioned*) **1 ~ (to sb)** having promised to marry sb 訂了婚的 SYN **engaged** **2 sb's betrothed** *noun* [sing.] the person that sb has promised to marry 已訂婚的人；未婚妻（或夫）

bet·ter /ˈbetə(r)/ *adj., adv., noun, verb*

■ ***adj.*** (comparative of *good* * good 的比較級) **1** of a higher standard or less poor quality; not as bad as sth else 較好的；更好的：*We're hoping for better weather tomorrow.* 我們希望明天天氣轉好。◇ *Her work is getting **better and better**.* 她的工作幹得越來越好了。◇ *He is in a much better mood than usual.* 他的情緒比平時好多了。◇ *The meal couldn't have been better.* 這頓飯再好吃不過了。◇ *There's nothing better than a long soak in a hot bath.* 沒有什麼比好好地泡個熱水澡更舒服的了。◇ *If you can only exercise once a week, that's **better than nothing*** (= better than taking no exercise at all). 即便是一個星期鍛煉一次，也比完全不鍛煉好。 **2** more able or skilled 能力更強的；更熟練的：*She's far better at science than her brother.* 她在理科方面比她的弟弟強得多。 **3** more suitable or appropriate 更合適的；更恰當的：*Can you think of a better word than 'nice'?* 你能找到一個比 nice 更合適的字眼嗎？◇ *It would be better for him to talk to his parents about his problems.* 他把自己的問題同父母談談會比較好。◇ ***You'd be better** going by bus.* 你坐公共汽車去會更好些。 **4** less ill/sick or unhappy（病勢）好轉的，見輕的；舒暢些的：*She's a lot better today.* 她今天好多了。◇ *His leg was getting better.* 他的腿在漸漸恢復。◇ *You'll feel **all the better for** a good night's sleep.* 你晚上睡個好覺就會感覺好得多。 **5** fully recovered after an illness; in good health again 痊癒；恢復健康：*Don't go back to work until you are better.* 身體康復之前，不要回去工作。➲ see also WELL *adj.*

IDM Most idioms containing **better** are at the entries for the nouns and verbs in the idioms, for example **better luck next time** is at **luck**. 大多數含 better 的習語，都可在該等習語中的名詞及動詞相關詞條找到，如

better luck next time 在詞條 luck 下。**little/no better than** almost or just the same as; almost or just as bad as 同…（幾乎）一樣；和…（幾乎）一樣壞：*The path was no better than a sheep track.* 那條小路簡直就像是給羊群踏出來的。**that's (much) 'better 1** used to give support to sb who has been upset and is trying to become calmer（安慰他人時說）很好，這就對了：*Dry your eyes now. That's better.* 把眼淚擦乾。這就對了。**2** used to praise sb who has made an effort to improve（稱讚努力加以改進的人）很好：*That's much better—you played the right notes this time.* 很好，你這次把音彈準了。**the ˌbigger, ˌsmaller, ˌfaster, ˌslower, etc. the 'better** used to say that sth should be as big, small, etc. as possible 越大（或小、快、慢等）越好：*As far as the hard disk is concerned, the bigger the better.* 就硬盤而言，容量越大越好。➲ more at DISCRETION, HEAD *n.*, PART *n.*, PREVENTION

■ ***adv.*** (comparative of *well* * well 的比較級) **1** 🗝 in a more excellent or pleasant way; not as badly 更好；更愉快；不那麼差：*She sings much better than I do.* 她的歌唱得比我好得多。◇ *Sound travels better in water than in air.* 聲音在水中比在空氣中傳播得快。◇ *People are better educated now.* 現在人們教育程度更高了。 **2** 🗝 more; to a greater degree 更；較大程度地：*You'll like her when you know her better.* 你對她瞭解得多一點就會喜歡她。◇ *A cup of tea? There's nothing I'd like better!* 一杯茶嗎？那最好不過了！◇ *Fit people are better able to cope with stress.* 健康的人較能應付壓力。 **3** used to suggest that sth would be a suitable or appropriate thing to do 更妥；更恰當：*The money could be better spent on more urgent cases.* 這筆錢用於較緊迫的事情也許會好些。◇ *Some things are better left unsaid.* 有些事還是不提為好。◇ *You'd* ***do better to*** *tell her everything before she finds out from someone else.* 你把一切都告訴她才是上策，免得她從別人口中聽到。

IDM Most idioms containing **better** are at the entries for the nouns, adjectives and verbs in the idioms, for example **better the devil you know** is at **devil**. 大多數含 better 的習語，都可在該等習語中的名詞、形容詞及動詞相關詞條找到，如 better the devil you know 在詞條 devil 下。**be better 'off** 🗝 to have more money 有較多錢；比較寬裕：*Families will be better off under the new law.* 新法律會使家庭經濟寬裕一些。◇ *Her promotion means she's $100 a week better off.* 她的晉升意味着她每星期多掙 100 元。**OPP** **be worse off** **be better off (doing sth)** used to say that sb is/would be happier or more satisfied if they were in a particular position or did a particular thing（在某情況下或因做某事）更幸福，更滿意：*She's better off without him.* 沒有他，她活得更幸福。◇ *The weather was so bad we'd have been better off staying at home.* 天氣非常惡劣，我們還不如待在家裏舒服。**had better/best (do sth)** 🗝 used to tell sb what you think they should do（告訴別人應該做的事）應該，最好：*You'd better go to the doctor about your cough.* 你最好去找醫生看看你的咳嗽。◇ *We'd better leave now or we'll miss the bus.* 我們最好現在就走，不然就趕不上公共汽車了。◇ *You'd better not do that again.* 你最好別再這樣做了。◇ *'I'll give you back the money tomorrow.' 'You'd better!'* (= as a threat) "我明天會還你錢。" "那樣最好！" ➲ note at SHOULD

■ ***noun*** **1** 🗝 [sing., U] something that is better 更好的事物；較好者：*the better of the two books* 兩本書中較好的一本 ◇ *I expected better of him* (= I thought he would have behaved better). 我本以為他會表現得好一些。 **2 your betters** [pl.] (*old-fashioned*) people who are more intelligent or more important than you 更有才智者；更重要的人

IDM **for ˌbetter or (for) 'worse** used to say that sth cannot be changed, whether the result is good or bad 不論好壞；不管是福是禍；不管怎樣 **get the better of sb/sth** to defeat sb/sth or gain an advantage 挫敗…；佔上風：*No one can get the better of her in an argument.* 辯論起來沒人能辯過她。◇ *She always gets the better of an argument.* 她在爭辯中總是佔上風。◇ *His curiosity got the better of him* (= he didn't intend to ask questions, but he wanted to know so badly that he did). 好奇心使得他不禁要問。**so much the 'better/'worse** used to say that sth is even better/worse 那就更好了／更糟了：*We don't actually need it on Tuesday, but if it*

arrives by then, so much the better. 實際上我們星期二並不需要它，但如果那時能到就更好。➲ more at CHANGE *n.*, ELDER *n.*, THINK *v.*

■ ***verb*** **1** [often passive] **~ sth** to be better or do sth better than sb/sth else 勝過；超過：*The work he produced early in his career has never really been bettered.* 他後來沒出過什麼作品能真正比得上他的早期作品。 **2 ~ yourself** to improve your social position through education, a better job, etc.（通過教育、更好的工作等）改進社會地位，上進：*Thousands of Victorian workers joined educational associations in an attempt to better themselves.* 維多利亞時代成千上萬名工人加入了各種教育協會，以求上進。

ˌbetter 'half *noun* = OTHER HALF

bet·ter·ment /'betəmənt; *NAmE* 'betərm-/ *noun* [U] (*formal*) the process of becoming or making sth/sb better 改進；改善；改良 **SYN** **improvement**

bet·ting 🗝 /'betɪŋ/ *noun* [U] the act of risking money, etc. on the unknown result of an event 打賭；賭錢：*illegal betting* 非法賭博 ➲ see also SPREAD BETTING

IDM **what's the betting ...? | the betting is that ...** (*informal*) it seems likely that ... 很可能；大概會：*What's the betting that he gets his own way?* 你認為他可能會獨行其是嗎？◇ *The betting is that he'll get his own way.* 他很可能會獨行其是。

'betting shop *noun* (*BrE*) a shop where you can bet on horse races and other competitions 賭馬店；彩票經銷點

be·tween 🗝 /bɪ'twiːn/ *prep., adv.*

■ ***prep.*** **1** 🗝 in or into the space separating two or more points, objects, people, etc.（空間上）在…中間，介於…之間：*Q comes between P and R in the English alphabet.* 英語字母表中，Q 在 P 和 R 之間。◇ *I sat down between Jo and Diana.* 我在喬和黛安娜中間坐下。◇ *Switzerland lies between France, Germany, Austria and Italy.* 瑞士位於法國、德國、奧地利和意大利之間。◇ *The paper had fallen down between the desk and the wall.* 那張紙掉在桌子和牆壁之間的縫隙裏。◇ (*figurative*) *My job is somewhere between a secretary and a personal assistant.* 我的工作介於秘書和私人助理之間。 **2** 🗝 in the period of time that separates two days, years, events, etc.（時間上）在…之間，在…中間：*It's cheaper between 6 p.m. and 8 a.m.* 下午 6 點到早晨 8 點間價錢較便宜。◇ *Don't eat between meals.* 正餐之間不要吃零食。◇ *Children must attend school between the ages of 5 and 16.* * 5 到 16 歲的孩子必須上學。◇ *Many changes took place between the two world wars.* 兩次世界大戰之間發生了很多變化。 **3** 🗝 at some point along a scale from one amount, weight, distance, etc. to another（數量、重量、距離等）介於…之間：*It weighed between nine and ten kilos.* 重量在九到十公斤之間。◇ *The temperature remained between 25 °C and 30 °C all week.* 整個星期氣溫都保持在 25 到 30 攝氏度之間。 **4** 🗝 (of a line 界線) separating one place from another 分隔着；在…之間：*the border between Sweden and Norway* 瑞典和挪威之間的邊界 **5** 🗝 from one place to another 從（一地）到（另一地）；往返於：*We fly between Rome and Paris twice daily.* 我們每天有兩次航班穿梭於羅馬和巴黎之間。 **6** 🗝 used to show a connection or relationship（表示聯繫或關係）：*a difference/distinction/contrast between two things* 兩事物之間的差異／區別／對比 ◇ *a link between unemployment and crime* 失業與犯罪之間的關聯 ◇ *There's a lot of bad feeling between them.* 他們彼此間芥蒂頗多。◇ *I had to choose between the two jobs.* 我得在兩份工作之間作出選擇。 **7** 🗝 shared by two or more people or things 合用；共享：*We ate a pizza between us.* 我們合吃了一張比薩餅。◇ *This is just* ***between you and me/between ourselves*** (= it is a secret). 這事只限我們兩人知道。 **8** 🗝 by putting together the efforts or actions of two or more people or groups 通過共同努力；一起：*We ought to be able to manage it between us.* 我們齊心協力應該能把這事辦妥。 **9 ~ doing sth** used to show that several activities are involved（同時進行幾項活動時用）：*Between working full-time and taking care of the kids, he didn't have much time for hobbies.*

他一邊全職工作一邊又要照顧孩子，所以抽不出很多時間搞業餘愛好。

■ *adv.* (usually **in between**) in the space or period of time separating two or more points, objects, etc. or two dates, events, etc.（空間或時間上）在中間，當中：*The house was near a park but there was a road in between.* 房子在一處公園附近，但兩者之間隔着一條馬路。◇ *I see her most weekends but not very often in between.* 我週末大多都能見到她，但平時不常見到。IDM see BETWIXT

be·twixt /bɪ'twɪkst/ *adv., prep.* (*literary* or *old use*) between 在…之間（或中間）

IDM **be,twixt and be'tween** (*old-fashioned*) in a middle position; neither one thing nor the other 居中；非此非彼

bevel /'bevl/ *noun* **1** a sloping edge or surface, for example at the side of a picture frame or sheet of glass 斜邊；斜面 **2** a tool for making sloping edges on wood or stone 斜角規

bevelled
(*especially US* **beveled**)
斜面的

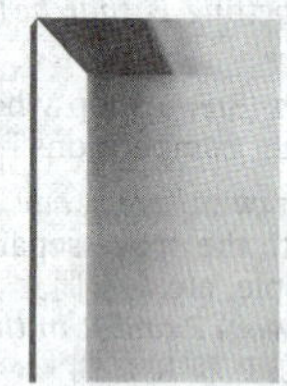

bev·elled (*especially US* **bev·eled**) /'bevld/ *adj.* [usually before noun] having a sloping edge or surface 斜邊的；斜面的

bev·er·age /'bevərɪdʒ/ *noun* (*formal*) any type of drink except water（除水以外的）飲料：*laws governing the sale of alcoholic beverages* 控制酒類銷售的法規

bevvy /'bevi/ *noun* (*pl.* **-ies**) (*BrE, informal*) an alcoholic drink, especially beer 酒；啤酒：*We went out for a few bevvies last night.* 我們昨晚出去喝了幾杯。

bevy /'bevi/ *noun* [sing.] (*informal*) a large group of people or things of the same kind（同類人或東西的）一群，一批，一堆：*a bevy of beauties* (= beautiful young women) 一群美麗的姑娘

be·wail /bɪ'weɪl/ *verb* **~ sth** (*formal* or *humorous*) to express great sadness about sth 悲悼；哀歎；為…感到悲慟

be·ware /bɪ'weə(r); *NAmE* -'wer/ *verb* [I, T] (used only in infinitives and in orders 僅用於不定式和命令) if you tell sb to **beware**, you are warning them that sb/sth is dangerous and that they should be careful 當心；小心；提防：**~ of sb/sth** *Motorists have been warned to beware of icy roads.* 已經提醒開車的人當心冰封的路面。◇ **~ (of) doing sth** *Beware of saying anything that might reveal where you live.* 說話時謹防透露你的住址。◇ **~ sb/sth** *It's a great place for swimming, but beware dangerous currents.* 那是個游泳的好去處，但要當心危險的水流。

be·wigged /bɪ'wɪgd/ *adj.* (*formal*) (of a person 人) wearing a WIG 戴假髮的

be·wil·der /bɪ'wɪldə(r)/ *verb* [usually passive] **~ sb** to confuse sb 使迷惑；使糊塗：*She was totally bewildered by his sudden change of mood.* 他的情緒突變搞得她全然不知所措。▸ **be·wil·dered** *adj.*：*He turned around, with a bewildered look on his face.* 他轉過身來，滿臉困惑。

be·wil·der·ing /bɪ'wɪldərɪŋ/ *adj.* making you feel confused because there are too many things to choose from or because sth is difficult to understand 令人困惑的；使人糊塗的 SYN **confusing**：*a bewildering array/range* 令人眼花繚亂的擺設／種類 ◇ *There is a bewildering variety of software available.* 各種可供挑選的軟件使人目不暇接。▸ **be·wil·der·ing·ly** *adv.*：*All the houses looked bewilderingly similar.* 所有的房屋都一樣，使人難以分辨。

be·wil·der·ment /bɪ'wɪldəmənt; *NAmE* -dərm-/ *noun* [U] a feeling of being completely confused 迷惘；困惑；迷亂 SYN **confusion**：*to look/stare in bewilderment* 迷惑地看着／盯着

be·witch /bɪ'wɪtʃ/ *verb* **1** [often passive] **~ sb** to attract or impress sb so much that they cannot think in a sensible way 迷住；迷惑：*He was completely bewitched by her beauty.* 他完全被她的美貌迷住了。**2 ~ sb** to put a magic SPELL on sb 施魔法於；使中魔法 SYN **enchant**

be·witch·ing /bɪ'wɪtʃɪŋ/ *adj.* so beautiful or interesting that you cannot think about anything else 迷人的；令人沉醉的：*a bewitching girl/smile* 迷人的女孩／微笑 ◇ *a bewitching performance* 令人陶醉的表演

be·yond 0‑m /bɪ'jɒnd; *NAmE* bɪ'jɑːnd/ *prep., adv.*

■ *prep.* **1** 0‑m on or to the further side of sth 在（或向）…較遠的一邊：*The road continues beyond the village up into the hills.* 那條路經過村子後又往上延伸到群山中。**2** 0‑m later than a particular time 晚於；遲於：*It won't go on beyond midnight.* 這事不會延續到午夜以後。◇ *I know what I'll be doing for the next three weeks but I haven't thought beyond that.* 我知道我未來三週要幹什麼，但再往後我還沒有想過。**3** 0‑m more than sth 超出；除…之外：*Our success was far beyond what we thought possible.* 我們的成功遠遠超出了我們的估計範圍。◇ *She's got nothing beyond her state pension.* 除了政府發的養老金外，她就什麼都沒有領取。**4** 0‑m used to say that sth is not possible（表示不可能）：*The bicycle was beyond repair* (= is too badly damaged to repair). 自行車已損壞得無法修理。◇ *The situation is beyond our control.* 我們已無法控制這一局面。**5** 0‑m too far or too advanced for sb/sth 超出…之外；非…所能及：*The handle was just beyond my reach.* 我差一點兒才夠得着把手。◇ *The exercise was beyond the abilities of most of the class.* 這個練習超出了班上大多數學生的能力。

IDM **be beyond sb** (*informal*) to be impossible for sb to imagine, understand or do 使人無法想像（或理解、做等）：*It's beyond me why she wants to marry Jeff.* 我無法理解她為什麼要嫁給傑夫。

■ *adv.* 0‑m on the other side; further on 在另一邊；在（或向）更遠處；以遠：*Snowdon and the mountains beyond were covered in snow.* 斯諾登山及其以遠的山脈都被積雪覆蓋着。◇ *The immediate future is clear, but it's hard to tell what lies beyond.* 不久的將來已經明朗，但更往後就很難說了。◇ *the year 2010 and beyond* * 2010 年及以後

IDM see BACK *n.*, DOUBT *n.*

bez·el /'bezl/ *noun* (*technical* 術語) a ring with a long narrow cut around the inside, used to hold sth in place, such as the cover of a watch or mobile/cell phone（手錶、手機等的）嵌玻璃凹槽

Bhag·wan /bʌg'wɑːn/ *noun* (*IndE*) **1** God 神：*'May Bhagwan bless you,' he said.* "願神保祐你。"他說。**2** a title for a GURU or a god in the form of a man 巴關（對古魯或神的化身的稱呼）：*Bhagwan Rajneesh* 拉吉尼希巴關大人

bhai /baɪ/ *noun* (*IndE*) **1** a brother 哥哥；弟弟 **2** used as a polite form of address to a man; in western India, often added to the first or last name 白（對男子的禮貌稱呼；在西印度，常綴於名或姓）：*Suresh Bhai* 蘇雷什 • 白 ◇ *Gandhi Bhai* 甘地 • 白

bhaji /'bɑːdʒi/ (also **bha·jia** /'bɑːdʒiə/) *noun* (*pl.* **bhajis, bha·jia**) **1** [C] a spicy S Asian food consisting of vegetables fried in BATTER (= a mixture of flour and liquid) 巴吉（南亞食品，將蔬菜放入麪糊後油炸而成）**2** [U] a S Asian dish of spicy fried vegetables 南亞油炸辣菜

bhang (also **bang**) /bæŋ/ *noun* [U] the leaves and flower tops of the CANNABIS plant, used as a drug 大麻的葉和花穗（用作麻醉品）

bhangra /'bɑːŋgrə/ *noun* [U] a type of dance music that combines traditional Punjabi music from India and Pakistan with Western pop music 彭戈拉（融合了印度和巴基斯坦的旁遮普音樂和西方流行樂的舞蹈音樂）

Bha·rata·na·tyam /ˌbʌrətəˈnɑːtjəm/ *noun* [U] a CLASSICAL dance form from southern India 婆羅多舞（一種印度南部的古典舞）

bha·van /ˈbʌvən/ *noun* (*IndE*) a building made or used for a special purpose, for example for meetings or concerts（用於集會、音樂會等的）廳，館，府

bhindi /ˈbɪndi/ *noun* (*pl.* **bhindi** or **bhindis**) [C, U] (*IndE*) = OKRA

bi /baɪ/ *adj.* (*informal*) = BISEXUAL

bi- /baɪ/ *combining form* (in nouns and adjectives 構成名詞和形容詞) two; twice; double 二；兩次；兩倍；雙：*bilingual* 雙語的 ◇ *bicentenary* 兩百週年 **HELP** **Bi-** with a period of time can mean either 'happening twice' in that period of time, or 'happening once in every two' periods. * bi- 和某個時期結合可表示在該時期內發生兩次，或每兩個時期發生一次。

bi·an·nual /baɪˈænjuəl/ *adj.* [only before noun] happening twice a year 一年兩度的 ➲ compare ANNUAL *adj.* ➲ see also BIENNIAL *adj.*

bias **AW** /ˈbaɪəs/ *noun, verb*

■ ***noun*** **1** [U, C, usually sing.] a strong feeling in favour of or against one group of people, or one side in an argument, often not based on fair judgement 偏見；偏心；偏向：*accusations of political bias in news programmes* (= that reports are unfair and show favour to one political party) 對新聞報道中政治偏袒的指責 ◇ *Employers must consider all candidates impartially and without bias.* 雇主必須公平而毫無成見地考慮所有求職者。◇ *Some institutions still have a strong bias against women.* 有些機構仍然對女性持有很大偏見。➲ COLLOCATIONS at RACE **2** [C, usually sing.] an interest in one thing more than others; a special ability 偏愛；特殊能力：*The course has a strong practical bias.* 這個課程偏重實用。 **3** [U, sing.] the **bias** of a piece of cloth is an edge cut DIAGONALLY across the threads 斜紋：*The skirt is cut on the bias.* 這條裙子是斜裁的。

■ ***verb*** (-s- or -ss-) **1 ~ sb/sth (toward(s)/against/in favour of sb/sth)** to unfairly influence sb's opinions or decisions 使有偏見；使偏心；使偏向 **SYN** **prejudice**：*The newspapers have biased people against her.* 報章使人們對她產生了偏見。 **2 ~ sth** to have an effect on the results of research or an experiment so that they do not show the real situation 影響（研究或實驗結果）以致產生偏差：*The experiment contained an error which could bias the results.* 這項實驗有一個錯誤，可能導致結果出現偏差。

ˈbias-cut *adj.* (of cloth or of an item of clothing 布料或衣物) cut across the natural direction of the lines in the cloth 斜（紋）裁的

biased **AW** (also **biassed**) /ˈbaɪəst/ *adj.* **1 ~ (toward(s)/against/in favour of sb/sth)** having a tendency to show favour towards or against one group of people or one opinion for personal reasons; making unfair judgements 有偏見的；傾向性的；片面的：*biased information/sources/press reports* 片面的信息／消息來源／新聞報道 ◇ *a biased jury/witness* 有成見的陪審團／證人 **OPP** **unbiased** **2 ~ toward(s) sth/sb** having a particular interest in one thing more than others 偏重；偏向：*a school biased towards music and art* 一所偏重音樂和藝術的學校

bi·ath·lon /baɪˈæθlən/ *noun* a sporting event that combines CROSS-COUNTRY SKIING and RIFLE shooting 兩項運動（越野滑雪和步槍射擊）➲ compare DECATHLON, HEPTATHLON, PENTATHLON, TRIATHLON

bib /bɪb/ *noun* **1** a piece of cloth or plastic that you put under a baby's chin to protect its clothes while it is eating 圍嘴；圍兜 **2** (*especially BrE*) a piece of cloth or plastic with a number or special colours on it that people wear on their chests and backs when they are taking part in a sport, so that people know who they are（運動員佩戴的）號碼布，彩色身分標記
IDM **your best bib and ˈtucker** (*humorous*) your best clothes that you only wear on special occasions（個人）最漂亮的衣服

bible /ˈbaɪbl/ *noun* **1 the Bible** [sing.] the holy book of the Christian religion, consisting of the Old Testament and the New Testament 基督教的《聖經》（包括《舊約》和《新約》） **2 the Bible** [sing.] the holy book of the Jewish religion, consisting of the Torah (or Law), the PROPHETS and the Writings 猶太教的《聖經》（包括《律法書》、《先知書》以及《聖錄》） **3** [C] a copy of the holy book of the Christian or Jewish religion 一冊（基督教或猶太教的）《聖經》 **4** [C] a book containing important information on a subject, that you refer to very often 權威著作（或參考書）：*the stamp-collector's bible* 集郵者的寶典

ˈBible-bashing (also **ˈBible-thumping**) *noun* [U] (*informal, disapproving*) the act of teaching or talking about the Bible in public in a very enthusiastic or aggressive way 對《聖經》的狂熱宣講 ▸ **ˈBible-basher**, **ˈBible-thumper** *noun*

the ˈBible Belt *noun* [sing.] an area of the southern and middle western US where people have strong and strict Christian beliefs（美國南部和中西部有着較強基督教信仰基礎的）《聖經》地帶

bib·lical /ˈbɪblɪkl/ (also **Biblical**) *adj.* **1** connected with the Bible; in the Bible 有關《聖經》的；《聖經》中的：***biblical scholarship/times/scenes*** 與《聖經》有關的研究／時代／場景 ◇ ***biblical stories/passages*** 《聖經》故事／章節 **2** very great; on a large scale 宏大的；大規模的：*a thunderstorm **of biblical proportions*** 特大雷暴
IDM **know sb in the ˈbiblical sense** (*humorous*) to have had sex with sb 與某人發生過性關係：*He had known her—but not in the biblical sense.* 他認識她，但未有過肌膚之親。

biblio- /ˈbɪbliəʊ; *NAmE* -lioʊ/ *combining form* (in nouns, adjectives and adverbs 構成名詞、形容詞和副詞) connected with books（有關）書的：*bibliophile* 愛書者

bibli·og·raphy /ˌbɪbliˈɒɡrəfi; *NAmE* -ˈɑːɡ-/ *noun* (*pl.* **-ies**) **1** [C] a list of books or articles about a particular subject or by a particular author; the list of books, etc. that have been used by sb writing an article, etc.（某一專題或作家的）書目，索引；參考書目 ➲ WRITING TUTOR page WT18 **2** [U] the study of the history of books and their production 目錄學；文獻學；書誌學 ▸ **bibli·og·raph·er** /-ˈɒɡrəfə(r); *NAmE* -ˈɑːɡ-/ *noun* **bib·lio·graph·ic·al** /ˌbɪbliəˈɡræfɪkl/ (also **bib·lio·graph·ic** /ˌbɪbliəˈɡræfɪk/) *adj.*

bib·lio·phile /ˈbɪbliəfaɪl/ *noun* (*formal*) a person who loves or collects books 愛書者；藏書家

ˈbib overalls *noun* [pl.] (*NAmE*) = OVERALLS at OVERALL *n.* (3)

bibu·lous /ˈbɪbjələs/ *adj.* (*old-fashioned* or *humorous*) liking to drink too much alcohol 愛喝酒的；嗜酒的

bi·cam·eral /ˌbaɪˈkæmərəl/ *adj.* (*technical* 術語) (of a parliament 議會) having two main parts, such as the Senate and the House of Representatives in the US, and the House of Commons and the House of Lords in Britain 兩院制的（如美國的參議院和眾議院，英國的下議院和上議院）

bi·carb /ˈbaɪkɑːb; *NAmE* -kɑːrb/ *noun* [U] (*informal*) = SODIUM BICARBONATE

bi·car·bon·ate /ˌbaɪˈkɑːbənət; *NAmE* -ˈkɑːrb-/ *noun* [U] (*chemistry* 化) a salt made from CARBONIC ACID containing CARBON, HYDROGEN and OXYGEN together with another element 碳酸氫鹽

biˌcarbonate of ˈsoda *noun* [U] = SODIUM BICARBONATE

bi·cen·ten·ary /ˌbaɪsenˈtiːnəri; *NAmE* -ˈten-/ *noun* (*pl.* **-ies**) (*BrE*) (*NAmE* **bi·cen·ten·nial**) the year, or the day, when you celebrate an important event that happened exactly 200 years earlier * 200 週年；200 週年紀念日 ▸ **bi·cen·ten·ary** *adj.* [only before noun]: *bicentenary celebrations* * 200 週年慶典

bi·cen·ten·nial /ˌbaɪsenˈteniəl/ (*NAmE*) (*BrE* **bi·cen·ten·ary**) *noun* the year, or the day, when you celebrate an important event that happened exactly 200 years earlier * 200 週年；200 週年紀念日 ▸ **bi·cen·ten·nial** *adj.* [only before noun] (*especially NAmE*) : *bicentennial celebrations* * 200 週年慶典

B

bi·ceps /ˈbaɪseps/ *noun* (*pl.* **bi·ceps**) the main muscle at the front of the top part of the arm 二頭肌（上臂前側的主要肌肉）➲ compare TRICEPS

bicker /ˈbɪkə(r)/ *verb* [I] **~ (about/over sth)** to argue about things that are not important（為小事）鬥嘴，爭吵 SYN **squabble**：*The children are always bickering about something or other.* 孩子們有事沒事總是在爭吵。 ▸ **bicker·ing** *noun* [U]

bicky (also **bikky**) /ˈbɪki/ *noun* (*pl.* **-ies**) (*informal*) a biscuit 餅乾

IDM **big ˈbickies** (*AustralE, NZE, informal*) a large sum of money 一大筆錢

bi·coast·al /ˌbaɪˈkəʊstl; *NAmE* -ˈkoʊstl/ *adj.* (*NAmE*) involving people and places on both the east and west coasts of the US（美國）東西海岸的

bi·cycle 0‑ /ˈbaɪsɪkl/ *noun, verb*

▪ ***noun*** 0‑ (also *informal* **bike**) a road vehicle with two wheels that you ride by pushing the PEDALS with your feet 自行車；腳踏車：*He got on his bicycle and rode off.* 他騎上自行車走了。◇ *We went for a* ***bicycle ride*** *on Sunday.* 我們星期天騎自行車兜風了。➲ VISUAL VOCAB pages V8, V51

▪ ***verb*** [I] (+ adv./prep.) (*old-fashioned*) to go somewhere on a bicycle 騎自行車 ➲ compare BIKE *v.*, CYCLE *v.*

ˈbicycle clip *noun* one of the two bands that people wear around their ankles when they are riding a bicycle to stop their trousers/pants getting caught in the chain 褲管夾（騎自行車時用）

ˈbicycle lane (also *informal* **ˈbike lane**) (both *NAmE*) (*BrE* **ˈcycle lane**) *noun* a part of a road that only bicycles are allowed to use 自行車車道 ➲ VISUAL VOCAB page V3

bi·cyc·list /ˈbaɪsɪklɪst/ *noun* (*old-fashioned* in British English, *formal* in North American English 英式英語中屬過時用語，美式英語中屬正式用語) a person who rides a bicycle 騎自行車者 ➲ compare CYCLIST

bid[1] 0‑ /bɪd/ *verb, noun* ➲ see also BID[2]

▪ ***verb*** (**bid·ding, bid, bid**) **1** 0‑ [I, T] to offer to pay a particular price for sth, especially at an AUCTION 出價；（尤指拍賣中）喊價：**~ (sth) (for sth)** *I bid £2 000 for the painting.* 我出 2 000 英鎊買這幅畫。◇ **~ (against sb)** *We wanted to buy the chairs but another couple were bidding against us.* 我們想買下那幾把椅子，但另一對夫婦在同我們較勁出價。 **2** 0‑ [I] **~ (for sth)** | (*NAmE* also) **~ (on sth)** | **~ (to do sth)** to offer to do work or provide a service for a particular price, in competition with other companies, etc. 投標 SYN **tender**：*A French firm will be bidding for the contract.* 一家法國公司將投標爭取這項合同。 **3** [T] **~ to do sth** (used especially in newspapers 尤用於報章) to try to do, get or achieve sth 努力爭取；企圖獲得 SYN **attempt**：*The team is bidding to retain its place in the league.* 這個隊正爭取保住它在聯賽中的位置。 **4** [T, I] **~ (sth)** (in some card games 某些牌戲中) to say how many points you expect to win 叫牌：*She bid four hearts.* 她叫 4 紅桃。

IDM **what am I ˈbid?** used by an AUCTIONEER when he or she is selling sth（拍賣人用語）諸位願出多少錢：*What am I bid for this vase?* 諸位願給這個花瓶出多少錢？

▪ ***noun*** **1** 0‑ **~ (for sth)** an offer by a person or a company to pay a particular amount of money for sth（買方的）出價：*Granada mounted a hostile* ***takeover bid*** *for Forte.* 格蘭納達公司向福特公司出價進行敵意收購。◇ *At the auction* (= a public sale where things are sold to the person who offers the most), *the highest bid for the picture was £200.* 拍賣會上，這幅畫的最高出價為 200 英鎊。◇ *Any more bids?* 還有誰出更高的價嗎？ **2** 0‑ **~ (for sth)** | (*NAmE* also) **~ (on sth)** an offer to do work or provide a service for a particular price, in competition with other companies, etc. 投標 SYN **tender**：*The company submitted a bid for the contract to clean the hospital.* 該公司投標承包這所醫院的清潔工作。 **3** (used especially in newspapers 尤用於報章) an effort to do sth or to obtain sth 努力爭取：**~ for sth** *a bid for power* 權力之爭◇ **~ to do sth** *a desperate bid to escape from his attackers* 竭力躲避攻擊他的人 **4** (in some card games 某些牌戲中) a statement of the number of points a player thinks he or she will win 叫牌；叫出的點數

bid[2] /bɪd/ *verb* ➲ see also BID[1] (**bid·ding, bade** /beɪd; bæd/, **bidden** /ˈbɪdn/ or **bid·ding, bid, bid**) **1 ~ (sb) good morning, farewell, etc.** (*formal*) to say 'good morning', etc. to sb 向（某人）問候（或道別等）：*I bade farewell to all the friends I had made in Paris.* 我告別了我在巴黎結交的所有朋友。◇ *I bade all my friends farewell.* 我告別了所有的朋友。 **2 ~ sb (do sth)** (*old use* or *literary*) to tell sb to do sth 告訴（某人做某事）；吩咐：*He bade me come closer.* 他讓我靠近些。

bid·dable /ˈbɪdəbl/ *adj.* (*formal, especially BrE*) (of people 人) willing to obey and to do what they are told to 順從的；聽話的

bid·der /ˈbɪdə(r)/ *noun* **1** a person or group that offers to pay an amount of money to buy sth 出價者：*It went to the highest bidder* (= the person who offered the most money). 這賣給了出價最高的人。 **2** a person or group that offers to do sth or to provide sth for a particular amount of money, in competition with others 投標者：*There were six bidders for the catering contract.* 投標承辦餐宴的有六家公司。

bid·ding /ˈbɪdɪŋ/ *noun* [U] **1** the act of offering prices, especially at an AUCTION（尤指拍賣中的）出價，喊價：*There was fast bidding between private collectors and dealers.* 私人收藏家和交易商急速競相喊價。◇ *Several companies remained* ***in the bidding***. 有幾家公司仍在競價。 **2** the act of offering to do sth or to provide sth for a particular price 投標：*competitive bidding for the contract* 這一合同的有競爭力的投標 **3** (in some card games 某些牌戲中) the process of stating the number of points that players think they will win 叫牌 **4** (*old-fashioned* or *formal*) what sb asks or orders you to do 請求；吩咐；命令：***to do sb's bidding*** (= to obey sb) 服從某人

biddy /ˈbɪdi/ *noun* (*pl.* **-ies**) (*informal, disapproving*) an old woman, especially an annoying one（尤指令人厭煩的）老太婆

bide /baɪd/ *verb* [I] (*old use*) = ABIDE

IDM **bide your ˈtime** to wait for the right time to do sth 等待時機

bidet /ˈbiːdeɪ; *NAmE* bɪˈdeɪ/ *noun* a low bowl in the bathroom, usually with taps/faucets, that you fill with water and sit on to wash your bottom 坐浴盆 ➲ VISUAL VOCAB page V24

bi·di·rec·tion·al /ˌbaɪdəˈrekʃənl; -dɪ-; -daɪ-/ *adj.* (*technical* 術語) functioning in two directions 雙向的

bi·en·nial /baɪˈeniəl/ *adj., noun*

▪ ***adj.*** [usually before noun] happening once every two years 兩年一次的：*a biennial convention* 兩年召開一次的大會 ▸ **bi·en·ni·al·ly** *adv.* ➲ see also ANNUAL, BIANNUAL

▪ ***noun*** any plant that lives for two years, producing flowers in the second year 兩年生植物（第二年開花）➲ compare ANNUAL, PERENNIAL

bier /bɪə(r); *NAmE* bɪr/ *noun* a frame on which the dead body or the COFFIN is placed or carried at a funeral 停屍架；棺材架

biff /bɪf/ *verb* **~ sb** (*old-fashioned, informal*) to hit sb hard with your FIST（用拳頭）狠打，猛擊：*He biffed me on the nose.* 他一拳砸在我鼻子上。 ▸ **biff** *noun*

bi·focals /ˌbaɪˈfəʊklz; *NAmE* -ˈfoʊ-/ *noun* [pl.] a pair of glasses with each LENS made in two parts. The upper part is for looking at things at a distance, and the lower part is for looking at things that are close to you. 雙光眼鏡（上半片為看遠，下半片為看近）➲ compare VARIFOCALS ▸ **bi·focal** *adj.*

bi·fur·cate /ˈbaɪfəkeɪt; *NAmE* -fərk-/ *verb* [I] (*formal*) (of roads, rivers, etc. 路、河等) to divide into two separate parts 分叉；分支 ▸ **bi·fur·ca·tion** /ˌbaɪfəˈkeɪʃn; *NAmE* -fərˈk-/ *noun* [C, U]

big 0‑ /bɪɡ/ *adj., adv., verb* ➲ see also BIGS *n.*

▪ ***adj.*** (**big·ger, big·gest**)

▸ LARGE 大 **1** 0‑ large in size, degree, amount, etc.（體積、程度、數量等）大的，巨大的：*a big man/house/increase* 高大的男人；大房子；大幅度增長◇ *This shirt isn't big enough.* 這件襯衣不夠大。◇ *It's the world's* biggest computer company. 它是全球最大的計算機公司。◇ (informal) He had this **great big** grin on his face. 他樂開了花。◇ They were earning big money. 他們在賺大錢。◇ The news came as a big blow. 那消息猶如晴天霹靂。

‣ OLDER 年齡較大 **2** (informal) older 年齡較大的：my big brother 我哥哥 ◇ You're a big girl now. 你現在已長成大姑娘了。

‣ IMPORTANT 重大 **3** [only before noun] (rather informal) important; serious 重大的；嚴重的：a big decision 重大決定 ◇ Tonight is the biggest match of his career. 今晚是他職業生涯中最重要的比賽。◇ You are making a big mistake. 你正在犯一個嚴重的錯誤。◇ She took the stage for her **big moment**. 她把這一階段視為她的重要歷程。◇ (informal) Do you really think we can take on the **big boys** (= compete with the most powerful people)? 你真的認為我們能與那些大人物抗衡？

‣ AMBITIOUS 有雄心 **4** (informal) (of a plan 計劃) needing a lot of effort, money or time to succeed 龐大的；宏大的：They're full of big ideas. 他們滿懷勃勃雄心。

‣ POPULAR 受歡迎 **5** (informal) popular with the public; successful 大受歡迎的；成功的：Orange is the big colour this year. 橘黃色是今年的流行色。◇ **~ in ...** The band's very big in Japan. 這個樂隊在日本很走紅。

‣ ENTHUSIASTIC 熱衷 **6** (informal) enthusiastic about sb/sth 熱衷於…的；狂熱的：I'm a big fan of hers. 我是她的狂熱追隨者。

‣ DOING STH A LOT 大量做 **7** doing sth often or to a large degree 經常（或大量）做某事的：a big eater/drinker/spender 食量大的／有酒量的／花錢手大的人

‣ GENEROUS 慷慨 **8** **~ of sb** (usually ironic) kind or generous 大方的；慷慨的：He gave me an extra five pounds for two hours' work. I thought 'That's big of you'. 我做兩小時的工作他多給我五英鎊。我心想"您真大方"。▸ **big·ness** noun [U]

IDM **be/get too big for your 'boots** to be/become too proud of yourself; to behave as if you are more important than you really are 自視過高 **a ˌbig 'cheese** (informal, humorous) an important and powerful person, especially in an organization 大人物；要員 **ˌbig 'deal!** (informal, ironic) used to say that you are not impressed by sth 沒什麼了不起：So he earns more than me. Big deal! 他不就是比我多賺點錢，有什麼了不起的！ **the big enchi'lada** (NAmE, informal, humorous) the most important person or thing 首要人物（或事物） **a big fish (in a small pond)** an important person (in a small community)（小圈子裏的）大人物 **a ˌbig girl's 'blouse** (BrE, informal) a weak man, who is not brave or confident 懦弱的男人；膽小沒自信的男人 **a big noise/shot/name** an important person 大人物；要人 **the big 'picture** (informal, especially NAmE) the situation as a whole 整個局面；大局：Right now forget the details and take a look at the big picture. 現在別管細節問題，先通觀全局。 **the big 'stick** (informal) the use or threat of force or power 大棒政策（以武力或權力相威脅）：The authorities used quiet persuasion instead of the big stick. 當權者平心靜氣地勸說，而不是施加壓力。 **the big three, four, etc.** the three, four, etc. most important countries, people, companies, etc. 三（或四等）強；前三個（或四個等）首要的國家（或人物、公司等）：She works for one of the Big Six. 她為六鉅頭之一工作。 **give sb/get a big 'hand** to show your approval of sb by clapping your hands; to be APPLAUDED in this way 給某人／受到鼓掌喝彩：Ladies and gentlemen, let's give a big hand to our special guests tonight. 女士們、先生們，讓我們熱烈鼓掌歡迎今晚的特邀嘉賓。 **have a big 'mouth** **1** to be bad at keeping secrets 嘴不嚴；愛泄露秘密 **2** to talk too much, especially about your own abilities and achievements 多嘴；吹牛；自吹自擂 **me and my big 'mouth** (informal) used when you realize that you have said sth that you should not have said 我真多嘴；真不該說出來 **no big 'deal** (informal) used to say that sth is not important or not a problem 沒什麼大不了；無所謂；沒關係：If I don't win it's no big deal. 我輸了也沒關係。 ➲ more at EYE n., FISH n., THING, WAY n.

■ **adv.** in an impressive way 大大；給人印象深地：We need to think big. 我們應該考慮幹一番大事。

IDM **go over 'big (with sb)** (informal) to make a good impression on sb; to be successful（給某人）留下好印象；成功：This story went over big with my kids. 這個故事我的孩子們非常喜歡。 **make it 'big** to be very successful 獲得成功：He's hoping to make it big on TV. 他正期待着在電視上幹出個名堂來。 ➲ more at HIT v.

■ **verb** (-gg-)

PHR V **ˌbig sb/sth↔'up** (BrE, slang) to praise or recommend sb/sth strongly 高度讚揚；極力推薦：He's been bigging up the CD on his radio show. 他在電台廣播節目中一直極力推薦這張 CD。

Synonyms 同義詞辨析

big / large / great

These adjectives are frequently used with the following nouns. 這些形容詞常與下列名詞連用：

big ~	large ~	great ~
man	numbers	success
house	part	majority
car	area	interest
boy	room	importance
dog	company	difficulty
smile	eyes	problem
problem	family	pleasure
surprise	volume	beauty
question	population	artist
difference	problem	surprise

- **Large** is more formal than **big** and should be used in writing unless it is in an informal style. It is not usually used to describe people, except to avoid saying 'fat'. * large 較 big 正式，應該用於書面語，但非正式語體除外。該詞通常不用以指人，除非是為了避免使用 fat（胖）。
- **Great** often suggests quality and not just size. * great 不僅指大，還常含偉大之意。Note also the phrases 另注意下列短語的用法：a large amount of 大量 ◇ a large number of 許多 ◇ a large quantity of 大量 ◇ a great deal of 大量 ◇ in great detail 非常詳細 ◇ a person of great age 年長者

bigam·ist /ˈbɪɡəmɪst/ noun a person who commits the crime of bigamy 犯重婚罪者

big·amy /ˈbɪɡəmi/ noun [U] the crime of marrying sb when you are still legally married to sb else 重婚罪 ➲ compare MONOGAMY (1), POLYGAMY ▸ **big·am·ous** /ˈbɪɡəməs/ adj.：a bigamous relationship 重婚關係

the ˌBig 'Apple noun [sing.] (informal) New York City 紐約市

the ˌBig Bad 'Wolf noun [sing.] (informal) a dangerous and frightening enemy "大壞狼"；兇險的敵人 **ORIGIN** From the wolf in several children's stories and the song Who's Afraid of the Big Bad Wolf? 源自幾個童話故事中的狼以及兒歌"誰怕大壞狼？"

'big band noun a large group of musicians playing JAZZ or dance music（演奏爵士樂或舞曲的）大樂隊：the big-band sound 大樂隊的風格

ˌBig 'Bang noun [sing.] (usually **the Big Bang**) the single large explosion that some scientists suggest created the universe（宇宙的）創世大爆炸

ˌbig 'box (also **ˌbig-box 'store**) noun (NAmE, informal) a very large shop/store, built on one level and located outside a town, which sells goods at low prices 大賣場（指位於市郊的全層大超市，貨品售價低廉）：When a big-box store opens, smaller retailers often go out of business. 大賣場一開業，往往使零售小店結業。◇ Efforts were made to limit big-box expansion. 人們努力限制大賣場的擴展。

ˌBig 'Brother noun [sing.] a leader, a person in authority or a government that tries to control people's behaviour and thoughts, but pretends to act for their benefit

B

老大哥（意欲控制人們思想行為的虛偽領導者）**ORIGIN** From George Orwell's novel *Nineteen Eighty-Four*, in which the leader of the government, **Big Brother**, had total control over the people. The slogan 'Big Brother is watching you' reminded people that he knew everything they did. 源自喬治•奧威爾的小說《一九八四》。書中的政府頭目"老大哥"（Big Brother）徹底控制着人民。"老大哥在看着你"這一標語提醒人們注意，他知道他們所做的一切。

ˌbig ˈbucks *noun* [pl.] (*NAmE, informal*) a large amount of money 一大筆錢

ˌbig ˈbusiness *noun* [U] **1** large companies that have a lot of power, considered as a group（統稱）大企業：*links between politics and big business* 政治和大企業之間的聯繫 **2** something that has become important because people are willing to spend a lot of money on it 大生意：*Health and fitness have become big business.* 保健已經成為大生意。

ˌbig ˈcat *noun* any large wild animal of the cat family. LIONS, TIGERS and LEOPARDS are all big cats. 大型貓科動物（如獅、虎和豹）

ˌBig ˈChief *noun* (*informal*) the person in charge of a business or other organization 總經理；主管；一把手

ˌbig ˈdipper *noun* **1** (*old-fashioned, BrE*) a small train at an AMUSEMENT PARK, which goes very quickly up and down a steep track and around bends（遊樂場的）雲霄飛車，過山車 ➲ see also ROLLER COASTER **2 the ˌBig ˈDipper** (*NAmE*) (*BrE* **the Plough**) [sing.] a group of seven bright stars that can only be seen from the northern half of the world 北斗七星；大熊星座

ˌbig ˈend *noun* (in a car engine) the end of a connecting ROD that fits around the CRANKSHAFT（汽車引擎中帶動曲軸的連桿）大端

Big·foot /ˈbɪgfʊt/ *noun* (*pl.* **Big·feet**) (also **Sas·quatch**) a large creature covered with hair like an APE, which some people believe lives in western N America（據信出沒於北美西部的）大腳野人，大腳怪

ˌbig ˈgame *noun* [U] large wild animals that people hunt for sport, for example ELEPHANTS and LIONS 大獵物（如大象和獅子）

big·gie /ˈbɪgi/ *noun* (*informal*) an important thing, person or event 重要的人（或事物）；大事；大人物

ˌbig ˈgovernment *noun* [U] (*disapproving*) a type of government that has a lot of control over people's lives and the economy（對人民生活、經濟等控制嚴厲的）大政府

ˌbig ˈgun *noun* (*informal*) a person who has a lot of power or influence 大人物；有影響力的人物

ˌbig ˈhair *noun* [U] hair in a style that makes a large shape around the head 蜂窩頭，爆炸頭（一種髮型）

ˌbig-ˈheaded *adj.* (*informal, disapproving*) having a very high opinion of how important and clever you are; too proud 自負的；傲慢的 ▸ **ˈbig-head** *noun*

ˌbig-ˈhearted *adj.* very kind; generous 善良的；慷慨的

ˌbig ˈhitter *noun* (*informal*) a person who is successful and has a lot of influence 大人物；大腕；大咖：*They've appointed one of the industry's big hitters to the board.* 他們委任了行內的一位大人物為董事會成員。

bight /baɪt/ *noun* a long curved part of a coast or river 海灣；河灣：*the Great Australian Bight* 大澳大利亞灣

ˈbig league *noun* (*NAmE*) **1** [C] a group of teams in a professional sport, especially BASEBALL, that play at the highest level 大聯盟（棒球等職業運動的一流水平運動隊組織）**2 the big league** [sing.] (*informal*) a very successful and important group 一流水平的團體；星級團體；佼佼者：*Over the past year, the company has joined the big league.* 過去一年中，公司已躋身一流之列。

ˈbig-league *adj.* (*NAmE*) **1** connected with sports teams that are in a big league 大聯盟運動隊的 **2** very important and successful 一流水平的；出色的

ˌBig Man on ˈCampus *noun* (*abbr.* **BMOC**) (*NAmE, informal*) a successful popular male student at a college or university 校園大人物（大學裏成功而受歡迎的男生）

ˈbig mouth *noun* (*informal*) a person who talks a lot, especially about him- or herself, and who cannot keep secrets 多嘴的人；自吹自擂的人；嘴不嚴的人 ▸ **ˈbig-mouthed** *adj.*

ˌBig ˈMuddy *noun* (*US, informal*) **1** the Mississippi River（多泥沙的）密西西比河 **2** a name for Vietnam used especially by US soldiers who fought there 大泥地（美國越戰士兵等對越南的別稱）

bigot /ˈbɪgət/ *noun* a person who has very strong, unreasonable beliefs or opinions about race, religion or politics and who will not listen to or accept the opinions of anyone who disagrees（種族、宗教或政治的）頑固盲從者，偏執者：*a* ***religious/racial bigot*** 宗教／種族的偏執者

big·ot·ed /ˈbɪgətɪd/ *adj.* showing strong, unreasonable beliefs or opinions and a refusal to change them 頑固盲從的；偏執的

big·ot·ry /ˈbɪgətri/ *noun* [U] the state of feeling, or the act of expressing, strong, unreasonable beliefs or opinions 頑固盲從；偏執

bigs /bɪgz/ *noun* [pl.] (*NAmE, informal*) **1 the bigs** the major league in a professional sport（職業體育運動）大聯盟 **2** large companies with a lot of money and influence 各大公司：*software bigs* 軟件業諸鉅頭 ◇ *the Internet travel bigs* 經營在線旅行服務的各大公司

the ˌbig ˈscreen *noun* [sing.] the cinema (when contrasted with television) 大銀幕；電影：*The movie hits the big screen in July.* 這部電影於七月份在影院上映。◇ *her first big-screen success* 她在影壇的初次成功

the ˌbig ˈsmoke *noun* (*BrE, informal*) London, or another large city 倫敦；大城市

ˌbig ˈtent *noun* a group or philosophy that accepts and includes individuals and organizations that have a wide variety of opinions or styles "大帳篷"（指兼容並蓄的團體或理念）**SYN** **broad church**：*The movement soon became a big tent under which many campaign groups gathered.* 這場運動很快便集結了五花八門的運動團體。

ˈbig-ticket *adj.* [only before noun] (*NAmE*) costing a lot of money 高價的：*big-ticket items* 高價項目

ˈbig time *noun, adv.* (*informal*)

■ ***noun* the big time** great success in a profession, especially the entertainment business（尤指在娛樂行業的）巨大成功，大紅大紫：*a bit-part actor who finally* ***made/hit the big time*** 一位終於走紅的小角色演員 ➲ compare SMALL-TIME

■ ***adv.*** on a large scale; to a great extent 大範圍地；很大程度地：*This time they've messed up big time!* 這一次他們把事情搞得糟透了！

ˌbig ˈtoe *noun* the largest toe on a person's foot 大腳趾 ➲ VISUAL VOCAB page V59

ˌbig ˈtop (usually **the big top**) *noun* the large tent in which a CIRCUS gives performances（馬戲團演出用的）大帳篷

ˌbig ˈwheel *noun* **1** (usually **the Big Wheel**) (*BrE*) (also **Fer·ris wheel** *NAmE, BrE*) a large wheel which stands in a vertical position at an AMUSEMENT PARK, with seats hanging at its edge for people to ride in（遊樂場的）大轉輪，摩天輪 **2** (*NAmE, informal*) an important person in a company or an organization 要人；大亨

big·wig /ˈbɪgwɪg/ *noun* (*informal*) an important person 要人；大人物：*She had to entertain some boring local bigwigs.* 她不得不款待當地一些無聊的大人物。

bijou /ˈbiːʒuː/ *adj.* [only before noun] (*BrE*, sometimes *ironic*) (of a building or a garden 建築或花園) small but attractive and fashionable 小巧玲瓏的；別致新穎的：*The house was terribly small and cramped, but the agent described it as a bijou residence.* 房子十分狹小擁擠，但經紀人卻把它說成是小巧別致的住宅。

bike 🔑 /baɪk/ *noun, verb*

■ ***noun*** (*informal*) **1** 🔑 a bicycle 自行車；腳踏車：*She got on her bike and rode off.* 她騎上自行車走了。◇ *I usually go to work* ***by bike***. 我通常騎自行車上班。➲ VISUAL

B

VOCAB page V51 ➲ see also MOUNTAIN BIKE, PUSHBIKE, QUAD BIKE **2** 🔑 a motorcycle 摩托車

IDM **on your bike!** (*BrE, informal*) a rude way of telling sb to go away 走開；滾開

■ *verb* **1** [I] (+ **adv./prep.**) (*informal*) to go somewhere on a bicycle or motorcycle 騎自行車（或摩托車）；騎車：*My dad bikes to work every day.* 我爸爸每天騎車上班。**2** [T] **~ sth** (+ **adv./prep.**) (*informal*) to send sth to sb by motorcycle 騎摩托車遞送：*I'll bike the contract over to you this afternoon.* 今天下午我騎摩托車把合同給你送過去。▸ **bik·ing** *noun* [U]：*The activities on offer include sailing and **mountain biking**.* 提供的活動項目有帆船運動和山地騎車。➲ compare BICYCLE, CYCLE

ˈbike lane *noun* (*NAmE, informal*) = BICYCLE LANE

biker /ˈbaɪkə(r)/ *noun* **1** a person who rides a motorcycle, usually as a member of a large group 騎摩托車的人（常為大團夥成員） **2** a person who rides a bicycle, especially a MOUNTAIN BIKE 騎自行車的人（尤指騎山地自行車者）

bikie /ˈbaɪki/ *noun* (*AustralE, NZE, informal*) a member of a group of people who ride motorcycles 摩托車隊成員

bi·kini /bɪˈkiːni/ *noun* a piece of clothing in two pieces that women wear for swimming and lying in the sun 比基尼泳裝

biˈkini line *noun* the area of skin around the bottom half of a BIKINI and the hair that grows there, which some women remove 比基尼線（指比基尼泳褲邊緣外露的一圈皮膚）；比基尼線體毛

bikky = BICKY

bi·la·bial /ˌbaɪˈleɪbiəl/ *noun* (*phonetics* 語音) a speech sound made by using both lips, such as /b/, /p/ and /m/ in *buy*, *pie* and *my* 雙唇音 ▸ **bi·la·bial** *adj.*

bi·lat·eral /ˌbaɪˈlætərəl/ *adj.* **1** involving two groups of people or two countries 雙方的；雙邊的：***bilateral relations/agreements/trade/talks*** 雙邊關係／協議／貿易／談判 **2** (*medical* 醫) involving both of two parts or sides of the body or brain （身體部位）兩側的，對稱的；（大腦）兩半球的 ▸ **bi·lat·eral·ly** *adv.* ➲ compare MULTILATERAL, TRILATERAL, UNILATERAL

bil·berry /ˈbɪlbəri; *NAmE* -beri/ (also **whortle·berry**) *noun* (*pl.* **-ies**) a small dark blue BERRY that grows on bushes on hills and in woods in northern Europe and can be eaten. The bush is also called a bilberry. 歐洲越橘（指植物或漿果，漿果深藍色，可食）➲ compare BLUEBERRY

bilby /ˈbɪlbi/ *noun* (*pl.* **-ies**) a small Australasian animal with a long nose, a long tail and big ears 兔耳袋狸（生活於澳大拉西亞）

bile /baɪl/ *noun* [U] **1** the greenish brown liquid with a bitter unpleasant taste that is produced by the LIVER to help the body to deal with the fats we eat, and that can come into your mouth when you VOMIT with an empty stomach 膽汁 **2** (*formal*) anger or hatred 憤怒；憎恨：*The critic's review of the play was just a paragraph of bile.* 那位批評家對這部戲劇的評論不過是在發泄怒氣。

ˈbile duct *noun* the tube that carries bile from the LIVER and the GALL BLADDER to the DUODENUM 膽管 ➲ VISUAL VOCAB page V59

bilge /bɪldʒ/ *noun* **1** [C] (also **bilges** [pl.]) the almost flat part of the bottom of a boat or a ship, inside or outside 底艙；船舭 **2** (also **ˈbilge water**) [U] dirty water that collects in a ship's bilge 底艙污水

bil·har·zia /bɪlˈhɑːtsiə; *NAmE* -ˈhɑːrt-/ *noun* [U] a serious disease, common in parts of Africa and S America, caused by small WORMS that get into the blood 裂體吸蟲病，血吸蟲病（常見於非洲和南美洲的某些地區）

bil·iary /ˈbɪliəri; *NAmE* -eri/ *adj.* (*medical* 醫) relating to BILE or to the BILE DUCT 膽汁的；膽管的

bi·lin·gual /ˌbaɪˈlɪŋgwəl/ *adj.* **1** able to speak two languages equally well 會說兩種語言的：*She is bilingual in English and Punjabi.* 她會說英語和旁遮普語。**2** using two languages; written in two languages 用兩種語言（寫）的：***bilingual education/communities*** 雙語教育／社群 ◇ *a bilingual dictionary* 雙語詞典 ▸ **bi·lin·gual** *noun*：*Welsh/English bilinguals* 會說威爾士語和英語的人 ➲ compare MONOLINGUAL, MULTILINGUAL

bili·ous /ˈbɪliəs/ *adj.* **1** feeling as if you might VOMIT soon 惡心的；想嘔吐的 **2** (of colours, usually green or yellow 顏色，通常指綠色或黃色) creating an unpleasant effect 刺眼的；花哨的；難看的：*a bilious green dress* 一條綠得扎眼的連衣裙 **3** (*formal*) bad-tempered; full of anger 脾氣壞的；易怒的

bili·ru·bin /ˌbɪlɪˈruːbɪn/ *noun* [U] (*medical* 醫) an orange substance produced in the LIVER 膽紅素

bilk /bɪlk/ *verb* (*informal, especially NAmE*) **~ sb** (**out of sth**) | **~ sth** (**from sb**) to cheat sb, especially by taking money from them 欺騙；詐騙（錢財）：*a con man who bilked investors out of millions of dollars* 詐取投資者幾百萬元的騙子

Synonyms 同義詞辨析

bill

account • invoice • check

These are all words for a record of how much you owe for goods or services you have bought or used. 以上各詞均指賬單、賬目。

- **bill** a list of goods that you have bought or services that you have used, showing how much you owe; the price or cost of sth 指賬單：*the gas bill* 煤氣費賬單
- **account** an arrangement with a shop/store or business to pay bills for goods or services at a later time, for example in regular amounts every month 指賒銷賬、賒欠賬、賒購：*Put it on my account please.* 請記在我的賒購賬上。
- **invoice** (*rather formal*) a bill for goods that sb has bought or work that has been done for sb 指發票、發貨或服務費用清單：*The builders sent an invoice for £250.* 營造商發出了一張 250 英鎊的發票。

BILL OR INVOICE? 用 bill 還是 invoice？

You would get a **bill** in a restaurant, bar or hotel; from a company that supplies you with gas, electricity, etc; or from sb whose property you have damaged. An **invoice** is for goods supplied or work done as agreed between a customer and supplier. * bill 指餐館、酒吧、旅館、煤氣公司、電力公司等開出的賬單或財產所有者開出的索賠清單。invoice 指客戶與供應商約定的供貨或服務費用清單。

- **check** (*NAmE*) a piece of paper that shows how much you have to pay for the food and drinks that you have had in a restaurant 指餐館的賬單：*Can I have the check, please?* 請給我結賬。**NOTE** In British English the usual word for this is **bill**. 此義英式英語常用 bill。

PATTERNS

- the bill/invoice/check **for** sth
- to **pay/settle** a(n) bill/account/invoice/check
- to **put sth on** the/sb's bill/account/invoice/check

bill 🔑 /bɪl/ *noun, verb*

■ *noun*

▸ **FOR PAYMENT 付款** **1** 🔑 a piece of paper that shows how much you owe sb for goods or services 賬單：*the **telephone/electricity/gas bill*** 電話費／電費／煤氣費賬單 ◇ *We **ran up a** massive hotel **bill**.* 我們累積了大筆的旅館費。◇ *She always **pays** her **bills** on time.* 她總是按時支付賬單。◇ *The bills are piling up* (= there are more and more that have still not been paid). 賬單越積越多。➲ COLLOCATIONS at FINANCE **2** 🔑 (*especially BrE*) (*NAmE* usually **check**) a piece of paper that shows how much you have to pay for the food and drinks that you have had in a restaurant （餐館的）賬單：*Let's ask for the bill.* 我們結賬吧。➲ COLLOCATIONS at RESTAURANT

▸ **MONEY 貨幣** **3** 🔑 (*NAmE*) = NOTE (6)：*a ten-dollar bill* 一張十元的鈔票

B

▸ **IN PARLIAMENT 議會 4** a written suggestion for a new law that is presented to a country's parliament so that its members can discuss it （提交議會討論的）議案，法案：*to **introduce/approve/reject a bill*** 提出／通過／否決一項議案 ◇ *the Education Reform Bill* 教育改革法案

▸ **AT THEATRE, ETC. 劇院等 5** a programme of entertainment at a theatre, etc. （劇院等的）節目單：*a horror **double bill*** (= two horror films/movies shown one after the other) 雙場恐怖片節目單 ◇ ***Topping the bill*** (= the most important performer) *is Paul Simon.* 領銜演出的是保羅・西蒙。

▸ **ADVERTISEMENT 廣告 6** a notice in a public place to advertise an event 海報；招貼；廣告 SYN **poster** ➲ see also HANDBILL

▸ **OF BIRDS 鳥 7** the hard pointed or curved outer part of a bird's mouth 鳥嘴；喙 SYN **beak** ➲ VISUAL VOCAB page V12 **8 -billed** (in adjectives 構成形容詞) having the type of bill mentioned 有…形喙的：*long-billed waders* 長嘴涉禽

▸ **ON HAT 帽子 9** (also **visor**) (both *NAmE*) (*BrE* **peak**) the stiff front part of a cap that sticks out above your eyes 帽舌；帽簷 ➲ VISUAL VOCAB page V65 ➲ see also OLD BILL

IDM **fill/fit the 'bill** to be what is needed in a particular situation or for a particular purpose 符合要求；合格：*On paper, several of the applicants fit the bill.* 從書面材料看，有幾位申請人符合條件。➲ more at CLEAN *adj.*, FOOT *v.*

■ *verb*

▸ **ASK FOR PAYMENT 要求付款 1 ~ sb (for sth)** to send sb a bill for sth 開賬單，發賬單（要求付款）：*Please bill me for the books.* 請就所購的書給我開列賬單。

▸ **ADVERTISE 做廣告 2** [usually passive] **~ sb/sth as sth** to advertise or describe sb/sth in a particular way 把（某人或事物）宣傳為…：*He was billed as the new Tom Cruise.* 他被宣傳為新湯姆・克魯斯。**3** [usually passive] **~ sb/sth to do sth** to advertise that sb/sth will do sth 宣佈…將做某事：*She was billed to speak on 'China—Yesterday and Today'.* 海報上說她要發表題為"中國——昨天和今天"的演講。

IDM **bill and 'coo** (*old-fashioned, informal*) if two people who are in love **bill and coo**, they kiss and speak in a loving way to each other 卿卿我我；情話綿綿

billa·bong /ˈbɪləbɒŋ; *NAmE* -bɔːŋ/ *noun* (in Australia) a lake that is formed when a river floods（澳大利亞河水泛濫形成的）死水潭

bill·board /ˈbɪlbɔːd; *NAmE* -bɔːrd/ (*especially NAmE*) (*BrE* also **hoard·ing**) *noun* a large board on the outside of a building or at the side of the road, used for putting advertisements on 大幅廣告牌 ➲ VISUAL VOCAB pages V2, V3

bil·let /ˈbɪlɪt/ *noun, verb*

■ *noun* a place, often in a private house, where soldiers live temporarily 部隊臨時營舍（常設在民宅裏）

■ *verb* [T, usually passive] **+ adv./prep.** to send soldiers to live somewhere temporarily, especially in private houses during a war 部隊臨時設營（常在民宅裏）

billet-doux /ˌbɪleɪ ˈduː/ *noun* (*pl.* **billets-doux** /ˌbɪleɪ ˈduːz/) (from *French*, *humorous* or *literary*) a love letter 情書

bill·fold /ˈbɪlfəʊld; *NAmE* -foʊld/ *noun* (*NAmE*) = WALLET

bill·hook /ˈbɪlhʊk/ *noun* a tool with a long handle and a curved blade, used for cutting the small branches off trees 長柄鈎鐮（修剪樹枝用）

bil·liards /ˈbɪliədz; *NAmE* ˈbɪljərdz/ *noun* [U] a game for two people played with CUES (= long sticks) and three balls on a long table covered with green cloth. Players try to hit the balls against each other and into pockets at the edge of the table. 枱球；撞球：*a game of billiards* 一局枱球賽 ➲ compare POOL, SNOOKER ▸ **bil·liard** *adj.* [only before noun]：*a billiard cue* 枱球球杆

bill·ing /ˈbɪlɪŋ/ *noun* **1** [U] the position, especially an important one, that sb is advertised or described as having in a show, etc. （演員表上的）排名；演員名次：*to have **top/star billing*** 有明星演員陣容 **2** [U] the act of preparing and sending bills to customers 開具賬單 **3** [C, usually pl.] the total amount of business that a company does in a particular period of time 營業額：*billings around $7 million* * 700 萬元左右的營業額

bil·lion /ˈbɪljən/ *number* (*plural verb* 複數動詞)

1 (*abbr.* **bn**) 1 000 000 000; one thousand million 十億：*Worldwide sales reached 2.5 billion.* 全球銷售額達到了 25 億。◇ *half a billion dollars* 五億元 ◇ *They have spent billions on the problem* (= billions of dollars, etc.). 他們花了幾十億元解決這個問題。HELP You say **a, one, two, several, etc. billion** without a final 's' on 'billion'. **Billions (of …)** can be used if there is no number or quantity before it. Always use a plural verb with **billion** or **billions**, except when an amount of money is mentioned. 說 a, one, two, several, etc. billion 時，billion 後面不加 s。若前面沒有數目或數量，可用 billions (of …)。除非指金額，billion 和 billions 均用複數動詞：*Two billion (people) worldwide are expected to watch the game.* 預計全世界將有 20 億人觀看這場比賽。◇ *Two billion (dollars) was withdrawn from the account.* 從該賬戶提取了 20 億元。There are more examples of how to use numbers at the entry for **hundred**. 更多數詞用法示例見 hundred 條。**2 a billion** or **billions (of …)** (*informal*) a very large amount 數以十億計；大量：*Our immune systems are killing billions of germs right now.* 我們的免疫系統正在殺死數以十億計的細菌。**3** (*old-fashioned, BrE*) 1 000 000 000 000; one million million 一萬億 SYN **trillion**

bil·lion·aire /ˌbɪljəˈneə(r); *NAmE* -ˈner/ *noun* an extremely rich person, who has at least a thousand million pounds, dollars, etc. in money or property 巨富；億萬富翁

ˌbill of 'costs *noun* (*BrE, law* 律) a list of the charges and expenses that sb must pay to a lawyer or to sb who has won a legal case 訴訟費清單

ˌbill of ex'change *noun* (*pl.* **bills of exchange**) (*business* 商) a written order to pay a sum of money to a particular person on a particular date 匯票

ˌbill of 'fare *noun* (*pl.* **bills of fare**) (*old-fashioned*) a list of the food that can be ordered in a restaurant（餐館的）菜單，菜譜 SYN **menu**

ˌbill of 'lad·ing /ˌbɪl əv ˈleɪdɪŋ/ *noun* (*pl.* **bills of lad·ing**) (*business* 商) a list giving details of the goods that a ship, etc. is carrying 提單；提貨單

ˌbill of 'rights *noun* [sing.] a written statement of the basic rights of the citizens of a country 權利宣言；人權宣言

ˌbill of 'sale *noun* (*pl.* **bills of sale**) (*business* 商) an official document showing that sth has been bought 轉讓契據；賣據

bil·low /ˈbɪləʊ; *NAmE* -loʊ/ *verb, noun*

■ *verb* **1** [I] (of a sail, skirt, etc. 船帆、裙子等) to fill with air and swell out 鼓起：*The curtains billowed in the breeze.* 微風吹得窗簾鼓了起來。**2** [I] if smoke, cloud, etc. **billows**, it rises and moves in a large mass（煙霧等）湧出，大量冒出：*A great cloud of smoke billowed out of the chimney.* 滾滾濃煙從煙囪中噴湧而出。

■ *noun* [usually pl.] a moving mass or cloud of smoke, steam, etc. like a wave 波濤般的濃煙（或蒸汽等）

billy /ˈbɪli/ *noun* (*pl.* **-ies**) (also **billy·can** /ˈbɪlikæn/) (both *BrE*) a metal can with a lid and a handle used for boiling water or for cooking when you are camping 帶蓋金屬罐（有柄，露營時燒水或煮東西用）

'billy club *noun* (*NAmE*) a short wooden stick used as a weapon by police officers（木製）警棍

'billy goat *noun* a male GOAT 公山羊 ➲ compare NANNY GOAT

billy-o /ˈbɪliəʊ; *NAmE* -oʊ/ *noun*

IDM **like 'billy-o** (*BrE, informal*) very hard or fast 猛烈地；迅雷似地：*I ran like billy-o.* 我飛快地跑着。

bil·tong /ˈbɪltɒŋ; ˈbəl-; *NAmE* ˈbɪltɔːŋ/ *noun* [U] (*SAfrE*) raw dry meat that is eaten in small pieces. Biltong is preserved by being treated with salt.（鹽滷）生肉乾，乾肉條

bimbo /ˈbɪmbəʊ; *NAmE* -boʊ/ *noun* (*pl.* **-os**) (*informal, disapproving*) a young person, usually a woman, who is sexually attractive but not very intelligent 傻乎乎的性

感青年（通常為女子）：*He's going out with an empty-headed bimbo half his age.* 他正在同一個年齡比他小一半的傻裏傻氣的性感女子來往。

bi·month·ly /ˌbaɪˈmʌnθli/ *adj., adv.* produced or happening every two months or twice each month 兩月一次（的）；一月兩次（的）

bin /bɪn/ *noun, verb*

■ ***noun*** **1** a container that you put waste in 垃圾箱：*a rubbish bin* 垃圾箱 ➲ see also DUSTBIN, WASTE BIN **2** a large container, usually with a lid, for storing things in（有蓋）大容器，箱，櫃：*a bread bin* 麪包箱

■ ***verb*** (-nn-) **~ sth** (*BrE, informal*) to throw sth away 扔掉；丟棄：*Do you need to keep these letters or shall we bin them?* 你需要保存這些信件嗎，還是乾脆把它們扔掉？

bin·ary /ˈbaɪnəri/ *adj.* **1** (*computing* 計, *mathematics* 數) using only 0 and 1 as a system of numbers 二進制的（用 0 和 1 記數）：*the* ***binary system*** 二進制 ◇ *binary arithmetic* 二進制算術 **2** (*technical* 術語) based on only two numbers; consisting of two parts 僅基於兩個數字的；二元的；由兩部份組成的：***binary code/numbers*** 二進制代碼／數字 ▶ **bin·ary** *noun* [U]：*The computer performs calculations in binary and converts the results to decimal.* 計算機以二進制數運算，然後把運算結果轉換為十進制數。

ˈbin bag *noun* (*BrE, informal*) a large plastic bag for putting rubbish/garbage in 塑料垃圾袋；塑膠垃圾袋

bind /baɪnd/ *verb, noun*

■ ***verb*** (**bound, bound** /baʊnd/)

▸ **TIE WITH ROPE/CLOTH** 綑綁 **1** [T] (*formal*) to tie sb/sth with rope, string, etc. so that they cannot move or are held together firmly 捆綁；繫：**~ sb/sth to sth** *She was bound to a chair.* 她被捆在一把椅子上。◇ **~ sb/sth together** *They bound his hands together.* 他們把他的雙手綁在一起。◇ **~ sb/sth** *He was left* ***bound and gagged*** (= tied up and with a piece of cloth tied over his mouth). 他被捆起來，用布封住嘴，扔在那兒了。**2** [T] **~ sth (up)** (*formal*) to tie a long thin piece of cloth around sth（用長布條）纏繞：*She bound up his wounds.* 她把他的傷口包紮好。

▸ **UNITE** 結合 **3** [T] to unite people, organizations, etc. so that they live or work together more happily or effectively（使）聯合在一起，結合：**~ A (and B) (together)** *Organizations such as schools and clubs bind a community together.* 諸如學校、俱樂部等機構使社區成為一個整體。◇ **~ A to B** *She thought that having his child would bind him to her forever.* 她以為生了他的孩子就會永遠把他留住。

▸ **MAKE SB DO STH** 驅使 **4** [T, usually passive] to force sb to do sth by making them promise to do it or by making it their duty to do it 約束；迫使：**~ sb (to sth)** *He had been bound to secrecy* (= made to promise not to tell people about sth). 他被迫保守秘密。◇ **~ sb to do sth** *The agreement binds her to repay the debt within six months.* 根據協議，她必須在六個月內還清債務。➲ see also BINDING *adj.*, BOUND *adj.* (2)

▸ **STICK TOGETHER** 粘合 **5** [I, T] to stick together or to make things stick together in a solid mass（使）粘合，凝結：**~ (together)** *Add an egg yolk to make the mixture bind.* 加個蛋黃使混合料凝結。◇ **~ sth (together)** *Add an egg yolk to bind the mixture together.* 加個蛋黃使混合料凝結在一起。

▸ **BOOK** 書籍 **6** [T, usually passive] **~ sth (in sth)** to fasten the pages of a book together and put them inside a cover 裝訂：*two volumes bound in leather* 兩卷皮面裝幀的書

▸ **SEW EDGE** 縫邊 **7** [T, often passive] **~ sth (with sth)** to sew a piece of material to the edge of sth to decorate it or to make it stronger 給…鑲邊；縫牢…的邊：*The blankets were bound with satin.* 那些毯子是用緞子包邊的。

IDM see HAND *n.*

PHR V **ˌbind sb ˈover** [usually passive] **1** (*NAmE, law* 律) to give sb BAIL while they are waiting to go to trial 允許某人保釋候審：*He was bound over for trial.* 他獲准了保釋候審。**2** (*BrE, law* 律) to give sb a formal warning that if they break the law again they will be punished 令某人具結保證（不再違法）：*She was* ***bound over to keep the peace*** *for a year.* 她被責令具保一年內不再鬧事。

■ ***noun*** [sing.] (*BrE, informal*) an annoying situation that is often difficult to avoid 窘境 ➲ see also DOUBLE BIND

IDM **in a ˈbind** (*NAmE*) in a difficult situation that you do not know how to get out of 陷於困境；進退維谷

bind·er /ˈbaɪndə(r)/ *noun* **1** [C] a hard cover for holding sheets of paper, magazines, etc. together 活頁夾：*a ring binder* 活頁夾 ➲ VISUAL VOCAB page V69 **2** [C] a person or machine that puts covers on books 裝訂工；裝訂機 **3** [C, U] a substance that makes things stick or mix together in a solid form 黏合劑；結合劑 **4** [C] a machine that fastens WHEAT into bunches after it has been cut（穀物）割捆機

bindi /ˈbɪndi/ *noun* a decorative mark worn in the middle of the FOREHEAD, usually by Hindu women（印度婦女等的）眉心紅點，眉心飾記

bind·ing /ˈbaɪndɪŋ/ *adj., noun*

■ ***adj.*** **~ (on/upon sb)** that must be obeyed because it is accepted in law 必須遵守的；有法律約束力的：*a* ***binding promise/agreement/contract*** 有約束力的承諾／協議／合同

■ ***noun*** **1** [C, U] the cover that holds the pages of a book together（書籍的）封皮 **2** [C, U] cloth that is fastened to the edge of sth to protect or decorate it 鑲邊；緄邊 **3** [C] a device on a SKI that holds the heel and toe of your boot in place and releases the boot automatically if you fall（滑雪板的）皮靴固定裝置 ➲ VISUAL VOCAB page V48

ˈbinding theory *noun* ➲ GOVERNMENT AND BINDING THEORY

bind·weed /ˈbaɪndwiːd/ *noun* [U] a wild plant that twists itself around other plants 旋花類植物

binge /bɪndʒ/ *noun, verb*

■ ***noun*** (*informal*) a short period of time when sb does too much of a particular activity, especially eating or drinking alcohol（短時間的）狂熱活動，尋歡作樂，大吃大喝：*to go on a binge* 飲酒作樂 ◇ *One of the symptoms is* ***binge eating.*** 症狀之一是飲食無度。

■ ***verb*** (**binge·ing** or **bin·ging, binged, binged**) [I] **~ (on sth)** to eat or drink too much, especially without being able to control yourself 大吃大喝；狂歡作樂：*When she's depressed she binges on chocolate.* 她心情不好的時候就大嚼巧克力。

bingo /ˈbɪŋɡəʊ; *NAmE* -ɡoʊ/ *noun, exclamation*

■ ***noun*** [U] a game in which each player has a card with numbers on. Numbers are called out in no particular order and the first player whose numbers are all called out, or who has a line of numbers called out, wins a prize. 賓戈遊戲（玩者均持有一張數字卡，第一個湊齊莊家喊出的全部或一組數字者勝出）：*to play bingo* 玩賓戈遊戲 ◇ *a bingo hall* 賓戈遊戲廳

■ ***exclamation*** used to express pleasure and/or surprise because you have found sth that you were looking for, or done sth that you were trying to do（事情如願時說）好，瞧：*The computer program searches, and bingo! We've got a match.* 電腦程序在搜索，瞧！找到匹配的了。

ˈbingo wings *noun* [pl.] (*BrE, informal, humorous*) long folds of loose skin and fat that hang down from the upper arms, especially of older people 賓果翼，蝴蝶臂，蝴蝶袖（尤指較年長的人上臂鬆弛下垂的部份）

ˈbin liner *noun* (*BrE*) a plastic bag that is placed inside a container for holding waste 垃圾箱襯袋

bin·man /ˈbɪnmæn/ *noun* (*pl.* **-men** /-men/) (*BrE, informal*) = DUSTMAN

bin·ocu·lar /bɪˈnɒkjələ(r); *NAmE* bɪˈnɑːkjələr/ *adj.* (*technical* 術語) using two eyes to see 雙目並用的；雙眼的：*binocular vision* 雙眼視覺

bin·ocu·lars /bɪˈnɒkjələz; *NAmE* bɪˈnɑːkjələrz/ (also **ˈfield glasses**) *noun* [pl.] an instrument, like two small TELESCOPES fixed together, that makes objects that are far away seem nearer when you look through it 雙筒望遠鏡：*a pair of binoculars* 一副雙筒望遠鏡 ◇ *We looked at the birds through binoculars.* 我們用雙筒望遠鏡觀鳥。➲ picture at next page

B

binoculars 雙筒望遠鏡

telescope 望遠鏡

bi·no·mial /baɪˈnəʊmiəl; *NAmE* -ˈnoʊ-/ *noun* **1** (*mathematics* 數) an expression that has two groups of numbers or letters, joined by the sign + or − 二項式 **2** (*linguistics* 語言) a pair of nouns joined by a word like 'and', where the order of the nouns is always the same, for example 'knife and fork' 雙名詞組（由 and 連接的一對名詞，兩個名詞的前後順序不變，如 knife and fork）▶ **bi·no·mial** *adj.*

bint /bɪnt/ *noun* (*BrE, slang*) an offensive way of referring to a woman（含冒犯意）娘們兒，雌兒：*a posh bint* 時髦娘們兒

bio- /ˈbaɪəʊ; *NAmE* ˈbaɪoʊ/ *combining form* (in nouns, adjectives and adverbs 構成名詞、形容詞和副詞) connected with living things or human life 生物的；人生的：*biodegradable* 可生物降解的 ◇ *biography* 傳記

bio·break /ˈbaɪəʊbreɪk; *NAmE* ˈbaɪoʊ-/ *noun* a short period of time when you leave your computer or a meeting in order to go to the toilet/bathroom 方便時間（離開電腦或會議去洗手間的時間）：*I need to take a biobreak.* 我得去方便一下。

bio·chem·ist /ˌbaɪəʊˈkemɪst; *NAmE* ˌbaɪoʊ-/ *noun* a scientist who studies biochemistry 生（物）化學家

bio·chem·is·try /ˌbaɪəʊˈkemɪstri; *NAmE* ˌbaɪoʊ-/ *noun* **1** [U] the scientific study of the chemistry of living things 生物化學 **2** [U, C] the chemical structure and behaviour of a living thing 生物的化學結構和特性 ▶ **bio·chem·ical** /ˌbaɪəʊˈkemɪkl; *NAmE* ˌbaɪoʊ-/ *adj.*

bio·data /ˈbaɪəʊdeɪtə; *NAmE* ˈbaɪoʊ-; -dætə/ *noun* [U, pl.] information about a person and about what they have done in their life 個人簡歷

bio·degrad·able /ˌbaɪəʊdɪˈɡreɪdəbl; *NAmE* ˌbaɪoʊ-/ *adj.* a substance or chemical that is **biodegradable** can be changed to a harmless natural state by the action of bacteria, and will therefore not damage the environment 可生物降解的 OPP **non-biodegradable** ➲ COLLOCATIONS at ENVIRONMENT

bio·de·grade /ˌbaɪəʊdɪˈɡreɪd; *NAmE* ˌbaɪoʊ-/ *verb* [I] (of a substance or chemical 物質或化學品) to change back to a harmless natural state by the action of bacteria 生物降解

bio·diesel /ˈbaɪəʊdiːzl; *NAmE* ˈbaɪoʊ-/ *noun* [U] a type of fuel made from plant or animal material and used in engines 生物柴油

bio·di·ver·sity /ˌbaɪəʊdaɪˈvɜːsəti; *NAmE* ˌbaɪoʊdaɪˈvɜːrs-/ (also *less frequent* **ˌbioˌlogical diˈversity**) *noun* [U] the existence of a large number of different kinds of animals and plants which make a balanced environment 生態多樣性（大量各種生物的共存以維持生態環境平衡）➲ COLLOCATIONS at ENVIRONMENT

bio·engin·eer·ing /ˌbaɪəʊˌendʒɪˈnɪərɪŋ; *NAmE* ˌbaɪoʊˌendʒɪˈnɪrɪŋ/ *noun* [U] the use of engineering methods to solve medical problems, for example the use of artificial arms and legs 生物工程（指利用工程方法解決醫學問題，如使用義肢等）

bio·eth·ics /ˌbaɪəʊˈeθɪks; *NAmE* ˌbaɪoʊ-/ *noun* [U] (*technical* 術語) the moral principles that influence research in medicine and biology 生物倫理學，生命倫理學（影響醫學和生物學研究的道德準則）

bio·feed·back /ˌbaɪəʊˈfiːdbæk; *NAmE* ˌbaɪoʊ-/ *noun* [U] (*technical* 術語) the use of electronic equipment to record and display activity in the body that is not usually under your conscious control, for example your heart rate, so that you can learn to control that activity 生物反饋（指利用電子儀器監測心跳等身體狀況，以便加以控制）

bio·fuel /ˈbaɪəʊfjuːəl; *NAmE* ˈbaɪoʊ-/ *noun* [C, U] fuel made from plant or animal sources and used in engines 生物燃料；生質燃料：*biofuels made from sugar cane and sugar beet* 用甘蔗和甜菜製成的生物燃料

bio·gas /ˈbaɪəʊɡæs; *NAmE* ˈbaɪoʊ-/ *noun* [U] gas, especially METHANE, that is produced by dead plants and that can be burned to produce heat 沼氣（由枯萎植物產生的甲烷等可燃氣體）

biog·raph·er /baɪˈɒɡrəfə(r); *NAmE* -ˈɑːɡ-/ *noun* a person who writes the story of another person's life 傳記作家

biog·raphy /baɪˈɒɡrəfi; *NAmE* -ˈɑːɡ-/ *noun* [C, U] (*pl.* **-ies**) the story of a person's life written by sb else; this type of writing 傳記；傳記作品：*Boswell's biography of Johnson* 博斯韋爾寫的約翰遜傳 ➲ compare AUTOBIOGRAPHY ▶ **bio·graph·ic·al** /ˌbaɪəˈɡræfɪkl/ *adj.*

bio·hazard /ˈbaɪəʊhæzəd; *NAmE* ˈbaɪoʊhæzərd/ *noun* a risk to human health or to the environment, from a BIOLOGICAL source（生物源對人體或環境造成的）生物危害

bio·logic·al /ˌbaɪəˈlɒdʒɪkl; *NAmE* -ˈlɑːdʒ-/ *adj.* **1** connected with the science of biology 生物學的：*the biological sciences* 生物科學 **2** connected with the processes that take place within living things 生物的；與生命過程有關的：*the biological effects of radiation* 輻射對生物體的影響 ◇ *the* ***biological control*** *of pests* (= using living ORGANISMS to destroy them, not chemicals) 對害蟲的生物防治（用生物天敵而非化學藥劑來消滅它們）◇ *a child's* ***biological parents*** (= natural parents, not the people who adopted him/her) 孩子的親生父母 **3** (of washing powder, etc. 洗衣粉等) using ENZYMES (= chemical substances that are found in plants and animals) to get clothes, etc. clean 加（生化）酶的：*biological and non-biological powders* 加酶和不加酶的洗衣粉 ▶ **bio·logic·al·ly** /-kli/ *adv.*

ˌbioˌlogical ˈclock *noun* (*technical* 術語) a natural system in living things that controls regular physical activities such as sleeping 生物鐘；生理鐘：(*figurative*) *At 35, Kate's biological clock was ticking* (= she was beginning to think that she would soon be too old to have children). 到 35 歲時，凱特的生物鐘開始滴答作響（她開始覺得她很快就會年齡大得不宜生育了）。

ˌbioˌlogical diˈversity *noun* = BIODIVERSITY

ˌbioˌlogical ˈwarfare (also **ˌgerm ˈwarfare**) *noun* [U] the use of harmful bacteria as weapons of war 生物戰；細菌戰

ˌbioˌlogical ˈweapon *noun* a weapon of war that uses harmful bacteria 生物武器 ➲ compare CHEMICAL WEAPON

biolo·gist /baɪˈɒlədʒɪst; *NAmE* -ˈɑːl-/ *noun* a scientist who studies biology 生物學家

biol·ogy 🔑 /baɪˈɒlədʒi; *NAmE* -ˈɑːl-/ *noun* [U] **1** 🔑 the scientific study of the life and structure of plants and animals 生物學：*a degree in biology* 生物學學位 ➲ compare BOTANY, ZOOLOGY **2** 🔑 the way in which the body and cells of a living thing behave 生理：*How far is human nature determined by biology?* 人性在多大程度上是由其生理因素決定的？◇ *the biology of marine animals* 海洋動物的生理習性

bio·lu·min·es·cence /ˌbaɪəʊluːmɪˈnesns; *NAmE* ˌbaɪoʊ-/ *noun* [U] (*biology* 生) the natural production of light by living creatures such as GLOW-WORMS 生物發光

bio·mass /ˈbaɪəʊmæs; *NAmE* ˈbaɪoʊ-/ *noun* [U, sing.] (*technical* 術語) **1** the total quantity or MASS (= weight) of plants and animals in a particular area or volume 生物量（特定生境面積或體積中所含有機體的質量）**2** natural materials from living or recently dead plants, trees and animals, used as fuel and in industrial production, especially in the generation of electricity 生物質（死去動植物的天然腐化物質，用於燃料或工業生產，尤其是發電）：*biomass crops* 生物質農作物 ➲ compare FOSSIL FUEL

biome /ˈbaɪəʊm; *NAmE* ˈbaɪoʊm/ *noun* (*biology* 生) the characteristic plants and animals that exist in a particular type of environment, for example in a forest or desert 生物群系（類似環境條件的植物和動物群落）

bio·mech·an·ics /ˌbaɪəʊməˈkænɪks; *NAmE* ˌbaɪoʊ-/ *noun* [U] the scientific study of the physical movement and structure of living creatures 生物力學

bio·med·ical /ˌbaɪəʊˈmedɪkl; *NAmE* ˌbaɪoʊ-/ *adj.* [usually before noun] relating to how biology affects medicine 生物醫學的

bio·metric /ˌbaɪəʊˈmetrɪk; *NAmE* ˌbaɪoʊ-/ *adj.* [usually before noun] using measurements of human features, such as fingers or eyes, in order to identify people 生物計量識別的

bi·onic /baɪˈɒnɪk; *NAmE* -ˈɑːnɪk/ *adj.* having parts of the body that are electronic, and therefore able to do things that are not possible for normal humans（因體內有電子裝置）能力超人的

bio·phys·ics /ˌbaɪəʊˈfɪzɪks; *NAmE* ˌbaɪoʊ-/ *noun* [U] the science that uses the laws and methods of physics to study biology 生物物理學

bio·pic /ˈbaɪəʊpɪk; *NAmE* ˈbaɪoʊ-/ *noun* a film/movie about the life of a particular person 傳記片

bi·opsy /ˈbaɪɒpsi; *NAmE* -ɑːpsi/ *noun* (*pl.* -ies) the removal and examination of TISSUE from the body of sb who is ill/sick, in order to find out more about their disease 活組織檢查（從身體取下細胞或組織進行檢驗）

bio·rhythm /ˈbaɪəʊrɪðəm; *NAmE* ˈbaɪoʊ-/ *noun* [usually pl.] the changing pattern of how physical processes happen in the body, that some people believe affects human behaviour 生物節律（指體內生物過程的變化模式，據信對行為有影響）

bio·sci·ence /ˌbaɪəʊˈsaɪəns; *NAmE* ˌbaɪoʊ-/ *noun* [C, U] any of the LIFE SCIENCES (= sciences concerned with studying humans, animals or plants) 生物科學；生命科學

bio·se·cur·ity /ˌbaɪəʊsɪˈkjʊərəti; *NAmE* ˌbaɪoʊsəˈkjʊr-/ *noun* [U] the activities involved in preventing the spread of animal and plant diseases from one area to another 生物安全保障；生物防疫

bio·sphere /ˈbaɪəʊsfɪə(r); *NAmE* ˈbaɪoʊsfɪr/ *noun* [sing.] (*technical* 術語) the part of the earth's surface and atmosphere in which plants and animals can live 生物圈

bio·tech·nol·ogy /ˌbaɪəʊtekˈnɒlədʒi; *NAmE* ˌbaɪoʊtekˈnɑːl-/ (also *informal* **bio·tech** /ˈbaɪəʊtek; *NAmE* ˈbaɪoʊ-/) *noun* [U] (*technical* 術語) the use of living cells and bacteria in industrial and scientific processes 生物技術 ▸ **bio·tech·no·logic·al** /ˌbaɪəʊteknəˈlɒdʒɪkl; *NAmE* ˌbaɪoʊteknəˈlɑːdʒɪkl/：*biotechnological research* 生物科技研究

bi·ot·ic /baɪˈɒtɪk; *NAmE* baɪˈɑːtɪk/ *adj.* (*biology* 生) of or related to living things 生物的；生命的

bio·type /ˈbaɪəʊtaɪp; *NAmE* ˈbaɪoʊ-/ *noun* (*biology* 生) a group of living things with exactly the same combination of GENES 生物型（基因組合完全相同的一組生物）

bi·par·tisan /ˌbaɪpɑːtɪˈzæn; *NAmE* ˌbaɪˈpɑːrtɪzn/ *adj.* involving two political parties 兩黨的；涉及兩黨的：*a bipartisan policy* 兩黨都支持的政策

bi·par·tite /baɪˈpɑːtaɪt; *NAmE* -ˈpɑːrt-/ *adj.* (*technical* 術語) involving or made up of two separate parts 有兩個部份的；兩部份組成的

biped /ˈbaɪped/ *noun* (*technical* 術語) any creature with two feet 兩足動物 ➲ compare QUADRUPED

bi·pedal /ˌbaɪˈpiːdl; *NAmE* also -ˈpedl/ *adj.* (*technical* 術語) (of animals 動物) using only two legs for walking 雙足行走的；兩腿行走的

Collocations 詞語搭配

Biotechnology 生物技術

GM crops: for 支持轉基因作物

- **face/suffer from/alleviate** food shortages 面臨／遭受／緩解食物短缺
- **begin/do/conduct** field trials of GM crops 開始／進行／實施轉基因作物的田間試驗
- **grow/develop** GM crops/seeds/plants/foods 種植／研發轉基因作物／種子／植物／食物
- **improve/increase** food security/crop yields 提高／增加食品安全／糧食產量
- **label** food that contains GMOs (= genetically modified organisms) 給含有轉基因生物的食物貼上標籤
- **fund/invest in** genetic engineering/research 資助／投資基因工程／研究
- **promote/support/be in favour of** GM food/GM crops/genetic engineering 推廣／支持／贊同轉基因食物／轉基因作物／基因工程
- **embrace** biotechnology/GM technology 欣然接受生物技術／轉基因技術

GM crops: against 反對轉基因作物

- **oppose/be against** GM technology/food/crops/trials 反對／不贊成轉基因技術／食品／作物／試驗
- **call for/introduce/impose** a ban on genetic modification/a moratorium on the release of GMOs 呼籲／開始實施／強行禁止基因改造／暫停轉基因生物上市
- **ban/prohibit/outlaw** the use of pesticides/chemical fertilizers/GMOs/so-called 'Frankenfoods' 明令禁止使用殺蟲劑／化肥／轉基因生物／所謂的"弗蘭肯斯坦食物"
- **stop/halt/wreck/destroy** GM crop trials 停止／中止／破壞轉基因作物試驗
- **promote/support/be in favour of** organic farming 促進／支持／贊成有機農業

Biotechnology in medicine: for 支持生物醫學技術

- **grow/obtain/harvest** human organs/stem cells from human embryos 從人類胚胎中培育／獲取／採集人類器官／幹細胞
- **transplant** organs/genes/tissue/cells (into mice/animals/embryos) 移植器官／基因／組織／細胞（給老鼠／動物／胚胎）
- **use** biotechnology/gene therapy to treat/repair/cure sth 應用生物技術／基因療法來治療／修復／治癒某種疾病
- **fund/invest in/promote/support/be in favour of** (embryonic) stem cell research 資助／投資於／促進／支持／贊同（胚胎）幹細胞研究
- **successfully clone/succeed in cloning** a sheep/a human embryo/a human being 成功克隆羊／人類胚胎／人

Biotechnology in medicine: against 反對生物醫學技術

- **create/produce** 'designer babies' 製造"訂製嬰兒"
- **consider/explore/address** the ethical issues raised by/related to/surrounding sth 研究／探究／論及由…引起／與…相關的道德問題
- **oppose/be against** human cloning/stem cell research 反對人體克隆／幹細胞研究
- **call for/introduce/impose** a ban on human cloning/a moratorium on xenotransplantation 呼籲／開始實施／強行禁止人類克隆／暫停異種移植
- **ban/prohibit/outlaw** human cloning/stem cell research/xenotransplantation 明令禁止人類克隆／幹細胞研究／異種移植

B

bi·plane /ˈbaɪpleɪn/ *noun* an early type of plane with two sets of wings, one above the other （早期的）雙翼飛機 ➲ VISUAL VOCAB page V53 ➲ compare MONOPLANE

bi·polar /ˌbaɪˈpəʊlə(r); *NAmE* -ˈpoʊlər/ (also ˌ**manic-deˈpressive**) *adj.* (*psychology* 心) suffering from or connected with bipolar disorder 雙相型障礙的；躁狂抑鬱性精神病的 ▸ **bi·polar** (also ˌ**manic-deˈpressive**) *noun*

ˌ**biˌpolar disˈorder** (also ˌ**biˌpolar afˌfective disˈorder**) *noun* [U, C] (also ˌ**manic deˈpression** [U]) (*psychology* 心) a mental illness causing sb to change suddenly from being extremely depressed to being extremely happy 雙相型障礙；躁狂抑鬱性精神病

bi·racial /ˌbaɪˈreɪʃl/ *adj.* (*NAmE*) (*especially BrE* **mixed race**) concerning or containing members of two different races 雙種族的

birch /bɜːtʃ; *NAmE* bɜːrtʃ/ *noun* **1** [C, U] (also ˈ**birch tree** [C]) a tree with smooth BARK and thin branches, that grows in northern countries 樺樹；白樺樹 ➲ see also SILVER BIRCH **2** (also **birch·wood** /ˈbɜːtʃwʊd; *NAmE* ˈbɜːrtʃ-/) [U] the hard pale wood of the birch tree 樺木 **3 the birch** [sing.] the practice of hitting sb with a bunch of birch sticks, as a punishment 用樺木條抽打（作為懲罰）

bird 🔑 /bɜːd; *NAmE* bɜːrd/ *noun, verb*

■ ***noun*** **1** 🔑 a creature that is covered with feathers and has two wings and two legs. Most birds can fly. 鳥；禽：*a bird's nest with two eggs in it* 內有兩隻鳥蛋的鳥窩 ◇ *a species of bird* 一種鳥 ◇ *The area has a wealth of bird life.* 這個地區棲息着大量的鳥。➲ COLLOCATIONS at LIFE ➲ VISUAL VOCAB page V12 ➲ see also GAME BIRD, SEABIRD, SONGBIRD, WATERBIRD **2** (*BrE, slang*, sometimes *offensive*) a way of referring to a young woman 姑娘；妞 ➲ see also DOLLY BIRD **3** (*informal*) a person of a particular type, especially sb who is strange or unusual in some way 某類人；（尤指）古怪的人，不尋常的人：*a wise old bird* 處世老練的人 ◇ *She is that rare bird: a politician with a social conscience.* 她是這麼一種少見的人：有社會良知的政治家。

IDM **be (strictly) for the birds** (*informal*) to not be important or practical 不重要；不實際 **the bird has ˈflown** the wanted person has escaped 要抓的人逃掉了 **a bird in the ˈhand is worth two in the ˈbush** (*saying*) it is better to keep sth that you already have than to risk losing it by trying to get much more 一鳥在手勝過雙鳥在林（滿足於現有的總比因過分追求而失去一切好）**the birds and the ˈbees** (*humorous*) the basic facts about sex, especially as told to children （尤指跟兒童講的）性的基本知識 **a ˌbird's-ˌeye ˈview (of sth)** a view of sth from a high position looking down 鳥瞰；俯視 **birds of a ˈfeather (flock toˈgether)** (*saying*) people of the same sort (are found together) 同類的人（聚在一起）；物以類聚 **give sb/get the ˈbird** (*informal*) **1** (*BrE*) to shout at sb as a sign of disapproval; to be shouted at （被）喝倒彩 **2** (*NAmE*) to make a rude sign at sb with your middle finger; to have this sign made at you 向某人豎起中指（表示侮辱）；受到豎中指的侮辱 ➲ more at EARLY *adj.*, KILL *v.*, LITTLE *adj.*

■ ***verb*** [I, T] (*NAmE, informal*) **~ (sth)** to go BIRDWATCHING 去觀鳥

ˈ**bird bath** *noun* a bowl filled with water for birds to wash in and drink from, usually in a garden/yard 鳥盆（通常置於園中，供鳥兒洗澡和飲水）

bird·brain /ˈbɜːdbreɪn; *NAmE* ˈbɜːrd-/ *noun* (*especially NAmE*) a stupid person 愚笨的人；傻瓜

bird·cage /ˈbɜːdkeɪdʒ; *NAmE* ˈbɜːrd-/ *noun* a CAGE in which birds are kept, usually one in a house 鳥籠

ˈ**bird dog** *noun* (*NAmE, informal*) **1** a dog used in hunting to bring back birds that have been shot 獵鳥犬（狩獵時用以撿回擊落的鳥）**2** a person whose job involves searching for good players for a sports team （運動隊的）星探

bird·er /ˈbɜːdə(r); *NAmE* ˈbɜːrdər/ (*informal*) = BIRDWATCHER ➲ compare ORNITHOLOGIST

ˈ**bird feeder** *noun* a container or platform in a garden in/on which people put food for birds（放在花園裏的）鳥食槽，鳥食盒

ˈ**bird flu** (also ˈ**chicken flu**) (also *formal* ˈ**avian flu**) *noun* [U] a serious illness that affects birds, especially chickens, that can be spread from birds to humans and that can cause death 禽流感（鳥類傳染病，可感染人類並導致死亡）：*Ten new cases of bird flu were reported yesterday.* 昨天新增十例禽流感病例報告。

bir·die /ˈbɜːdi; *NAmE* ˈbɜːrdi/ *noun* **1** (*informal*) a child's word for a little bird 小鳥（兒語）**2** (in GOLF 高爾夫球) a score of one stroke less than PAR (= the standard score for a hole) 小鳥擊（比標準杆少一杆入穴的得分）➲ compare BOGEY (4), EAGLE **3** (*NAmE*) = SHUTTLECOCK

bird·ing /ˈbɜːdɪŋ; *NAmE* ˈbɜːrd-/ (*informal*) = BIRDWATCHING

ˌ**bird of ˈparadise** *noun* (*pl.* **birds of paradise**) a bird with very bright feathers, found mainly in New Guinea 極樂鳥，風鳥，天堂鳥（羽毛鮮豔，主要分佈於新幾內亞）

ˌ**bird of ˈpassage** *noun* (*pl.* **birds of passage**) **1** a bird that travels regularly from one part of the world to another at different seasons of the year 候鳥 **2** a person who passes through a place without staying there long 過客

ˌ**bird of ˈprey** *noun* (*pl.* **birds of prey**) a bird that hunts and kills other creatures for food. EAGLES, HAWKS and OWLS are all birds of prey. 猛禽（捕食其他動物的鳥，如鷹、隼和貓頭鷹）➲ VISUAL VOCAB page V12

bird·seed /ˈbɜːdsiːd; *NAmE* ˈbɜːrd-/ *noun* [U] special seeds for feeding birds 鳥食種籽

bird·song /ˈbɜːdsɒŋ; *NAmE* ˈbɜːrdsɔːŋ/ *noun* [U] the musical sounds made by birds（婉轉動聽的）鳥鳴

ˈ**bird strike** *noun* an occasion when a bird hits an aircraft 鳥撞擊飛機事故；鳥擊

ˈ**bird table** *noun* (*BrE*) a wooden platform in a garden/yard on which people put food for birds 鳥食平台（花園中供人們投放鳥食的木板台）➲ VISUAL VOCAB page V19

bird·watch·er /ˈbɜːdwɒtʃə(r); *NAmE* ˈbɜːrdwɑːtʃər/ (also *informal* **birder**) *noun* a person who watches birds in their natural environment and identifies different breeds, as a hobby 觀鳥者（在自然環境中觀察並鑒定鳥類，作為一種愛好）➲ compare ORNITHOLOGIST ▸ **bird·watch·ing** (also *informal* **birding**) *noun* [U]

bi·retta /bɪˈretə/ *noun* a square cap worn by Roman Catholic priests（羅馬天主教神職人員所戴的）四角帽，禮節帽，方形帽

biri·ani = BIRYANI

Biro™ /ˈbaɪrəʊ; *NAmE* ˈbaɪroʊ/ *noun* (*pl.* **-os**) (*BrE*) a plastic pen with a metal ball at the top that rolls ink onto the paper 伯羅圓珠筆 ➲ VISUAL VOCAB page V69 ➲ compare BALLPOINT

birth 🔑 /bɜːθ; *NAmE* bɜːrθ/ *noun*

1 🔑 [U, C] the time when a baby is born; the process of being born 出生；誕生；分娩：*The baby weighed three kilos **at birth**.* 嬰兒出生時體重為三公斤。◇ *John was present at the birth of both his children.* 約翰的兩個孩子出生時他均在場。◇ *It was a difficult birth.* 那是一次難產。◇ *a **hospital/home birth*** 在醫院裏／家中的分娩 ◇ *Mark has been blind **from birth**.* 馬克先天失明。◇ *Please state your **date and place of birth**.* 請列明你的出生日期和地點。➲ COLLOCATIONS at CHILD **2** 🔑 [sing.] the beginning of a new situation, idea, place, etc. 創始；起源：*the birth of a new society in South Africa* 南非一個新社會的誕生 **3** 🔑 [U] a person's origin or the social position of their family 出身；門第：*Anne was French **by birth** but lived most of her life in Italy.* 安妮在血統上是法國人，但大部份時間住在意大利。◇ *a woman of noble birth* 出身貴族的女子

IDM **give ˈbirth (to sb/sth)** 🔑 to produce a baby or young animal 生孩子；產崽：*She died shortly after giving birth.* 她生下孩子後不久便死了。◇ *Mary gave birth to a healthy baby girl.* 瑪麗生了個健康的女嬰。◇ (*figurative*) *It was the study of history that gave birth to the social sciences.* 對歷史的研究孕育了社會科學。

ˈ**birth certificate** *noun* an official document that shows when and where a person was born 出生證明（書）

ˈ**birth control** *noun* [U] the practice of controlling the number of children a person has, using various methods of CONTRACEPTION 節育：*a reliable method of birth control* 可靠的節育措施

birth·day /ˈbɜːθdeɪ; *NAmE* ˈbɜːrθ-/ *noun* the day in each year which is the same date as the one on which you were born 生日：*Happy Birthday!* 生日快樂！◇ *Oliver's 13th birthday* 奧利弗的 13 歲生日 ◇ *a* ***birthday card/party/present*** 生日賀卡／聚會／禮物

IDM **in your ˈbirthday suit** (*humorous*) not wearing any clothes 光着身子；裸體

birth·ing /ˈbɜːθɪŋ; *NAmE* ˈbɜːrθ-/ *noun* [U] the action or process of giving birth 分娩；生產：*a birthing pool* 分娩池

birth·mark /ˈbɜːθmɑːk; *NAmE* ˈbɜːrθmɑːrk/ *noun* a red or brown mark on a person's skin that has been there since they were born 胎記；胎痣

ˈ**birth mother** *noun* the woman who gave birth to a child who has been adopted（被領養的孩子的）生母

ˈ**birth partner** *noun* a person whom a woman chooses to be with her when she is giving birth to a baby（產婦挑選的）分娩陪護，陪產者

birth·place /ˈbɜːθpleɪs; *NAmE* ˈbɜːrθ-/ *noun* **1** the house or area where a person was born, especially a famous person（尤指名人的）出生時的住宅，出生地 **2** the place where sth first happened 發源地；發祥地：*Hawaii was the birthplace of surfing.* 夏威夷是衝浪運動的發源地。

ˈ**birth rate** *noun* the number of births every year for every 1 000 people in the population of a place 出生率（某地區每年每 1 000 人中的出生數目）：*a* ***low/high birth rate*** 低／高出生率

birth·right /ˈbɜːθraɪt; *NAmE* ˈbɜːrθraɪt/ *noun* (*formal*) a thing that sb has a right to because of the family or country they were born in, or because it is a basic right of all humans 與生俱來的權利（或所有物）；基本人權：*The property is the birthright of the eldest child.* 長子享有財產的繼承權。◇ *Education is every child's birthright.* 接受教育是每個孩子的基本權利。

birth·stone /ˈbɜːθstəʊn; *NAmE* ˈbɜːrθstoʊn/ *noun* a SEMI-PRECIOUS STONE that is associated with the month of sb's birth or their sign of the ZODIAC 誕生石（表示出生月份或星座的半寶石）

birth·weight /ˈbɜːθweɪt; *NAmE* ˈbɜːrθ-/ *noun* [U, C] the recorded weight of a baby when it is born（嬰兒的）出生體重

biry·ani (also **biri·ani**, **biri·yani**) /ˌbɪriˈɑːni/ *noun* [U, C] a S Asian dish made from rice with meat, fish or vegetables 比爾亞尼飯（南亞的一種肉飯、魚肉飯或菜飯）：*chicken biryani* 比爾亞尼雞肉飯

bis /bɪs/ *adv.* (*music* 音) (used as an instruction 指示語) again 重複

bis·cuit /ˈbɪskɪt/ *noun*
1 [C] (*BrE*) a small flat dry cake for one person, usually sweet, and baked until crisp 餅乾：*a packet of chocolate biscuits* 一包巧克力餅乾 ◇ *a selection of cheese biscuits* 精選的乳酪餅乾 ➲ compare COOKIE (1) ➲ see also DIGESTIVE BISCUIT, DOG BISCUIT **2** [C] (*NAmE*) a soft bread roll, often eaten with GRAVY 鬆餅（食用時常佐以肉汁）**3** [U] a pale yellowish-brown colour 淡黃褐色

IDM **take the ˈbiscuit** (*BrE*) (also **take the ˈcake** *NAmE, BrE*) (*informal*) to be the most surprising, annoying, etc. thing that has happened or that sb has done 空前驚人；極其討厭：*You've done some stupid things before, but this really takes the biscuit!* 你以前確也幹過些蠢事，但這一次實在嚇人！

bi·sect /baɪˈsekt/ *verb* **~ sth** (*technical* 術語) to divide sth into two equal parts 對半分；二等分

bi·sex·ual /ˌbaɪˈsekʃuəl/ *adj., noun*
■ ***adj.*** **1** (also *informal* **bi**) sexually attracted to both men and women 雙性戀的 **2** (*biology* 生) having both male and female sexual organs 有兩性生殖器官的；兩性的；雌雄同體的 ▸ **bi·sexu·al·ity** /ˌbaɪˌsekʃuˈæləti/ *noun* [U]
■ ***noun*** a person who is bisexual 雙性戀者 ➲ compare HETEROSEXUAL, HOMOSEXUAL

bishop /ˈbɪʃəp/ *noun* **1** a senior priest in charge of the work of the Church in a city or district 主教：*the Bishop of Oxford* 牛津區主教 ◇ *Bishop Harries* 哈里斯主教 ➲ see also ARCHBISHOP **2** a piece used in the game of CHESS that is shaped like a bishop's hat and can move any number of squares in a DIAGONAL line（國際象棋中的）象；（西洋棋中的）主教 ➲ VISUAL VOCAB page V38

bish·op·ric /ˈbɪʃəprɪk/ *noun* **1** the position of a bishop 主教職位 **2** the district for which a bishop is responsible 主教的轄區 SYN **diocese**

bis·muth /ˈbɪzməθ/ *noun* [U] (*symb.* **Bi**) a chemical element. Bismuth is a reddish-white metal that breaks easily and is used in medicine. 鉍（用於醫學）

bison /ˈbaɪsn/ *noun* (*pl.* **bison**) a large wild animal of the cow family that is covered with hair. There are two types of bison, the N American (also called BUFFALO) and the European. 野牛（分北美野牛和歐洲野牛兩類）：*a herd of bison* 一群野牛

bisque /bɪsk; biːsk/ *noun* [U, C] a thick soup, especially one made from SHELLFISH（尤指貝類）濃湯：*lobster bisque* 龍蝦濃湯 ➲ see also CHOWDER

bis·tro /ˈbiːstrəʊ; *NAmE* -stroʊ/ *noun* (*pl.* **-os**) a small informal restaurant 小餐館；小酒館

bit /bɪt/ *noun*

▸ **SMALL AMOUNT** 小量 **1** **a bit** [sing.] (used as an adverb 用作副詞) (*especially BrE*) rather 有點兒；稍微 SYN **a little**：*These trousers are a bit tight.* 這條褲子有點緊。◇ *'Are you tired?' 'Yes, I am a bit.'* "你累了嗎？" "是的，有點。" ◇ *It costs a bit more than I wanted to spend.* 它比我預計的消費高了一點。◇ *I can lend you fifty pounds, if you want. That should help a bit.* 如果你需要，我可以借給你五十英鎊。那應該有些幫助。 **2** **a bit** [sing.] (*especially BrE*) a short time or distance 稍頃；短距離：*Wait a bit!* 等會兒！◇ *Can you move up a bit?* 你請挪過去點兒好嗎？◇ *Greg thought for a bit before answering.* 格雷格略微思考了一下才回答。 **3** [C] **~ of sth** (*especially BrE*) a small amount or piece of sth 小量；小塊：*some useful bits of information* 一些有用的零星信息 ◇ *With* ***a bit of luck***, *we'll be there by 12.* 如果順利點，我們將於 12 點鐘趕到那裏。◇ *I've got a bit of shopping to do.* 我要買點東西。◇ *a bit of cake* 一小塊餅 ◇ *bits of grass/paper* 些許的草；紙屑

▸ **PART OF STH** 部份 **4** [C] (*especially BrE*) a part of sth larger（事物的）一部份，一段：*The best bit of the holiday was seeing the Grand Canyon.* 假期中最精彩的片段是參觀大峽谷。◇ *The school play was a huge success—the audience roared with laughter at all the funny bits.* 學校的演出獲得了巨大成功，所有的滑稽片段都令觀眾哄堂大笑。

▸ **LARGE AMOUNT** 大量 **5** [sing.] **a ~ (of sth)** (*informal, especially BrE*) a large amount 大量：*'How much does he earn?'* ***'Quite a bit!'*** "他有多少收入？" "挺多的！" ◇ *The new system will* ***take a bit of*** *getting used to* (= it will take a long time to get used to). 適應新系統將需花很多時間。

▸ **COMPUTING** 計算機技術 **6** [C] the smallest unit of information used by a computer 比特，二進制位，位元（計算機的最小信息單位）

▸ **FOR HORSE** 馬 **7** [C] a metal bar that is put in a horse's mouth so that the rider can control it 嚼子

▸ **TOOL** 工具 **8** [C] a tool or part of a tool for DRILLING (= making) holes 鑽頭；刀頭；釺頭 ➲ VISUAL VOCAB page V20 ➲ see also DRILL

▸ **MONEY** 錢 **9** [C] (*NAmE, informal*) an amount of money equal to 12½ cents * 12.5 分；一角二分半

▸ **SEXUAL ORGANS** 生殖器官 **10** **bits** [pl.] (*BrE, informal*) a person's sexual organs（人的）生殖器 ➲ see also BITE, BIT, BITTEN *v.*

IDM **be in ˈbits** (*BrE, informal*) to be very sad or worried 非常難過（或焦慮）：*Inside I'm in bits because I miss*

B

him so much. 我內心非常難受，因為太想念他了。**the (whole)... bit** (*informal, disapproving*) behaviour or ideas that are typical of a particular group, type of person or activity（某團體、某類人或活動的）典型行為，特有觀念：*She couldn't accept the whole drug-culture bit.* 她無法接受這種典型的毒品文化。**bit by 'bit** a piece at a time; gradually 一點一點地；逐漸地：*He assembled the model aircraft bit by bit.* 他把飛機模型一點一點地組裝起來。◇ *Bit by bit memories of the night came back to me.* 我漸漸回憶起了那晚的點點滴滴。**a bit 'much** (*informal*) not fair or not reasonable 過分；不應當；不合理：*It's a bit much calling me at three in the morning.* 凌晨三點鐘打電話給我，太過分了。**a bit of a ...** (*informal, especially BrE*) used when talking about unpleasant or negative things or ideas, to mean 'rather a ...'（談及負面事情時用）相當，有點兒：*We may have a bit of a problem on our hands.* 我們手頭的問題可能有點棘手。◇ *The rail strike is a bit of a pain.* 這次鐵路罷工有點頭痛。**a bit of all 'right** (*BrE, slang*) a person that you think is sexually attractive 有魅力的人；性感的人 **a bit of 'rough** (*BrE, slang*) a person of a low social class who has a sexual relationship with sb of a higher class（與社會地位較高者有性關係的）草根情人 **a bit on the 'side** (*BrE, slang*) the boyfriend or girlfriend of sb who is already married or in a steady sexual relationship with sb else 婚外情人；第三者 **,bits and 'pieces/'bobs** (*BrE, informal*) small objects or items of various kinds 零七碎八；零星物品：*She stuffed all her bits and pieces into a bag and left.* 她把她零零碎碎的東西都塞進了一隻包裹就走了。**do your 'bit** (*informal*) to do your share of a task 幹分內的事：*We can finish this job on time if everyone does their bit.* 要是每個人都盡職，我們就能按時完成這項工作。**every bit as good, bad, etc. (as sb/sth)** just as good, bad, etc.; equally good, bad, etc.（和某人、某事物）同樣好、同樣壞等：*Rome is every bit as beautiful as Paris.* 羅馬和巴黎一樣美麗。**get the bit between your teeth** (*informal*) to become very enthusiastic about sth that you have started to do so that you are unlikely to stop until you have finished 果斷地做某事；義無反顧 **not a 'bit | not one (little) 'bit** not at all; not in any way 一點也不；毫不：*'Are you cold?' 'Not a bit.'* "你冷嗎？" "一點不冷。" ◇ *It's not a bit of use* (= there's no point in) *complaining.* 抱怨毫無意義。◇ *I don't like that idea one bit.* 我根本不喜歡那個主意。**not a 'bit of it!** (*informal, BrE*) used for saying that sth that you had expected to happen did not happen（預計要發生的事）根本不是那樣，壓根兒沒有發生：*You'd think she'd be tired after the journey but not a bit of it!* 你以為她旅行之後會疲勞，根本沒那回事！**to bits 1** into small pieces 成為碎片；變成小塊：*The book fell to bits in my hands.* 那本書在我手中成了碎頁。◇ *She took the engine to bits, then carefully put it together again.* 她把發動機拆開，又再仔細裝好。**2** (*informal*) very much 非常；十分：*I love my kids to bits.* 我非常愛我的孩子。◇ *She was **thrilled to bits** when I said I'd come.* 我說我會來，她就興奮不已。➲ more at BLIND *adj.*, CHAMP *v.*

British/American 英式/美式英語

a bit / a little

- In *BrE* it is common to use **a bit** to mean 'slightly' or 'to a small extent'. 英式英語常用 a bit 表示稍微、有點兒：*These shoes are a bit tight.* 這鞋有點兒緊。◇ *I'll be a bit later home tomorrow.* 明天我要晚點兒回家。◇ *Can you turn the volume up a bit?* 你能把音量開大點兒嗎？
- It is more common in *NAmE* to say **a little**, or (*informal*) **a little bit**. You can also use these phrases in *BrE*. 美式英語較常用 a little 或 a little bit（非正式），英式英語亦可以這樣說：*These shoes are a little bit too tight.* 這鞋有點兒緊。◇ *I'll be a little later home tomorrow.* 明天我要晚點兒回家。◇ *Can you turn the volume up a little bit?* 你能把音量開大點兒嗎？

bitch /bɪtʃ/ *noun, verb*

■ *noun* **1** [C] a female dog 母狗：*a greyhound bitch* 母靈猩 **2** [C] (*slang, disapproving*) an offensive way of referring to a woman, especially an unpleasant one 潑婦；討厭的女人：*You stupid little bitch!* 你這個愚蠢的小悍婦！◇ *She can be a real bitch.* 她撒起潑來可真不得了。**3** [sing.] (*slang*) a thing that causes problems or difficulties 棘手的事；難辦的事：***Life's a bitch.*** 人生真受罪。**4** [sing.] **~ (about sb/sth)** (*informal*) a complaint about sb/sth or a conversation in which you complain about them 怨言；牢騷：*We've been having a bitch about our boss.* 我們一直對老闆牢騷滿腹。➲ see also SON OF A BITCH

■ *verb* [I] **~ (about sb/sth)** (*informal*) to make unkind and critical remarks about sb/sth, especially when they are not there 挖苦；（尤指背後）說壞話

bitch·in' (also **bitch·ing**) /ˈbɪtʃɪn/ *adj.* (*slang, especially NAmE*) very good 很好的；很棒的

bitchy /ˈbɪtʃi/ *adj.* (*informal*) (**bitch·ier, bitchi·est**) saying unpleasant and unkind things about other people 說人壞話的；出言不遜的：*bitchy remarks* 刻薄的話 ▸ **bitchi·ness** *noun* [U]

bite 0̶ /baɪt/ *verb, noun*

■ *verb* (**bit** /bɪt/, **bit·ten** /ˈbɪtn/)

▸ **USE TEETH** 用牙齒 **1** 0̶ [I, T] to use your teeth to cut into or through sth 咬：*Does your dog bite?* 你的狗咬人嗎？◇ *Come here! I won't bite!* (= you don't need to be afraid) 過來吧！我不會咬人的！◇ **~ into/through sth** *She bit into a ripe juicy pear.* 她咬了一口熟透多汁的梨。◇ **~ sb/sth** *She was bitten by the family dog.* 她被家裏的狗咬傷了。◇ *Stop biting your nails!* 別咬指甲了！◇ **~ off sth/sth off** *He bit off a large chunk of bread/He bit a large chunk of bread off.* 他咬下了一大塊麪包。

▸ **OF INSECT/SNAKE** 昆蟲；蛇 **2** 0̶ [I, T] to wound sb by making a small hole or mark in their skin 叮；蜇；咬：*Most European spiders don't bite.* 大多數歐洲蜘蛛不咬人。◇ **~ sb** *We were badly bitten by mosquitoes.* 我們被蚊子叮得不行。

▸ **OF FISH** 魚 **3** [I] if a fish **bites**, it takes food from the hook of a FISHING LINE and may get caught 咬餌；上鉤

▸ **HAVE EFFECT** 產生影響 **4** [I] to have an unpleasant effect 產生不良影響：*The recession is beginning to bite.* 經濟衰退開始產生不良影響。

IDM **be bitten by sth** to develop a strong interest in or enthusiasm for sth 對某事物着迷；熱衷於某事物：*He's been **bitten by the travel bug**.* 他迷上了旅遊。**bite the 'bullet** (*informal*) to start to deal with an unpleasant or difficult situation which cannot be avoided 硬着頭皮對付不愉快的（或艱難的）情況；咬緊牙關應付 ORIGIN From the custom of giving soldiers a bullet to bite on during a medical operation without anaesthetic. 源自戰地手術習慣。戰士們在無麻醉劑的情況下咬住子彈接受手術。**bite the 'dust** (*informal*) **1** to fail, or to be defeated or destroyed 失敗；被打敗；被摧毀：*Thousands of small businesses bite the dust every year.* 每年有數以千計的小企業倒閉。**2** (*humorous*) to die 死 **bite the hand that 'feeds you** to harm sb who has helped you or supported you 傷害恩人；恩將仇報 **bite your 'lip** to stop yourself from saying sth or from showing an emotion 忍住話；抑制情感的流露 **bite off more than you can 'chew** to try to do too much, or sth that is too difficult 想一口吃成胖子；不自量力 **bite your 'tongue** to stop yourself from saying sth that might upset sb or cause an argument, although you want to speak 隱忍不言（避免禍從口出）：*I didn't believe her explanation but I bit my tongue.* 我不相信她的解釋，但我忍着沒有說出來。➲ more at HAIR, HEAD *n.*, ONCE *adv.*

PHR V **,bite 'back (at sb/sth)** to react angrily, especially when sb has criticized or harmed you 反擊；反駁 **,bite sth↔'back** to stop yourself from saying sth or from showing your feelings 忍住不說出某事；不流露情感：*She bit back her anger.* 她按捺住怒火。**,bite 'into sth** to cut into the surface of sth 咬（或切、陷等）入某物：*The horses' hooves bit deep into the soft earth.* 馬蹄深深地陷進了鬆軟的土裏。

■ *noun*

▸ **USING TEETH** 用牙齒 **1** 0̶ [C] an act of biting 咬：*The dog gave me a playful bite.* 狗鬧着玩地咬了我一下。◇ *He has* *to wear a brace to correct his bite* (= the way the upper and lower teeth fit together). 他得戴着牙箍矯正牙齒的咬合。

▸ **FOOD 食物 2** [C] a small piece of food that you can bite from a larger piece（咬下的）一口：*She took a couple of bites of the sandwich.* 她咬了兩口三明治。◇ *He didn't eat a bite of his dinner* (= he ate nothing). 他一口飯也沒吃。**3 a ~ (to eat)** [sing.] (*informal*) a small amount of food; a small meal 小量食物；簡單的一餐：*How about a bite of lunch?* 簡單吃點午飯好嗎？◇ *We just have time for* ***a bite to eat*** *before the movie.* 電影開演之前，我們只夠時間匆匆吃一點東西。

▸ **OF INSECT/ANIMAL 昆蟲；動物 4** [C] a wound made by an animal or insect 咬傷；叮傷；蜇傷：*Dog bites can get infected.* 狗咬的傷口會感染。◇ *a mosquito/snake bite* 蚊子叮傷；蛇咬傷

▸ **STRONG TASTE 濃郁的味道 5** [U] a pleasant strong taste 濃味：*Cheese will add extra bite to any pasta dish.* 乾酪會增加麵食的香味。

▸ **COLD 冷 6** [sing.] a sharp cold feeling 寒冷；凜冽：*There's a bite in the air tonight.* 今晚寒氣刺骨。

▸ **POWERFUL EFFECT 強烈影響 7** [U] a quality that makes sth effective or powerful 影響力；感染力：*The performance had no bite to it.* 這次演出毫無感染力。

▸ **OF FISH 魚 8** [C] the act of a fish biting food on a hook 咬餌；上鈎 ➲ see also FROSTBITE, LOVE BITE, SOUND BITE

IDM **a bite at/of the 'cherry** (*BrE*) an opportunity to do sth 做某事的機會（或時機）：*They were eager for a second bite of the cherry.* 他們渴望能得到第二次機會。➲ more at BARK *n.*

'bite-sized (also **'bite-size**) *adj.* [usually before noun] **1** small enough to put into the mouth and eat 一口能吃下的；小塊的：*Cut the meat into bite-sized pieces.* 把肉切成小塊。**2** (*informal*) very small or short 很小的；很短的：*The exams are taken in bite-size chunks over two years.* 這些考試零零碎碎，得兩年才考完。

bit·ing /ˈbaɪtɪŋ/ *adj.* **1** (of a wind 風) very cold and unpleasant 刺骨的；凜冽的 **2** (of remarks 說話) cruel and critical 刻薄的；辛辣的：***biting sarcasm/wit*** 尖酸刻薄的諷刺／俏皮話 ▸ **bit·ing·ly** *adv.*

bit·map /ˈbɪtmæp/ *noun* (*computing* 計) a way in which an image is stored with a fixed number of BITS (= units of information) for each unit of the image 位圖；位元圖 ▸ **bit·map** *verb* **(-pp-) ~ sth**

bi·tonal /ˌbaɪˈtəʊnl; *NAmE* -ˈtoʊ-/ *adj.* (*music* 音) having parts in two different KEYS sounding together 雙調性的；二重調性的 ▸ **bi·ton·al·ity** /ˌbaɪtəʊˈnæləti; *NAmE* -toʊ-/ *noun* [U]

'bit part *noun* a small part in a film/movie（電影中的）小角色

'bit player *noun* **1** an actor with a small part in a film/movie 小角色；小演員 **2** a person or an organization that is involved in a situation but does not have an important role and has little influence 無足輕重的人（或組織）

bit·stream /ˈbɪtstriːm/ *noun* (*computing* 計) a flow of data in BINARY form 位流；位元流

bit·ten *past part.* of BITE

bit·ter /ˈbɪtə(r)/ *adj., noun*

▪ *adj.* **HELP** **More bitter** and **most bitter** are the usual comparative and superlative forms, but **bitterest** can also be used. * more bitter 和 most bitter 是常用的比較級和最高級形式，但也可以用 bitterest。**1** (of arguments, disagreements, etc. 爭論、分歧等) very serious and unpleasant, with a lot of anger and hatred involved 激烈而不愉快的；充滿憤怒與仇恨的：*a long and bitter dispute* 漫長的激烈爭論 **2** (of people 人) feeling angry and unhappy because you feel that you have been treated unfairly 憤憤不平的：*She is very bitter about losing her job.* 她丟掉了工作，心裏很不服氣。**3** [usually before noun] making you feel very unhappy; caused by great unhappiness 令人不快的；使人悲痛的；由痛苦引起的：*to* ***weep/shed bitter tears*** 傷心落淚 ◇ *Losing the match was* ***a bitter disappointment*** *for the team.* 輸掉這場比賽對這個隊來說是一件傷心失望的事。◇ *I've learnt from* ***bitter experience*** *not to trust what he says.* 我已從痛苦的經驗中得到了教訓，不再相信他的話。**4** (of food, etc. 食物等) having a strong, unpleasant taste; not sweet 味苦的：*Black coffee leaves a bitter taste in the mouth.* 清咖啡在嘴裏留下苦味。➲ compare SWEET (1) **5** (of weather conditions 天氣) extremely cold and unpleasant 嚴寒的：*bitter cold* 嚴寒 ◇ *a bitter wind* 刺骨寒風 ◇ *It's really bitter out today.* 今天戶外的確很冷。▸ **bit·ter·ness** *noun* [U]：*The pay cut caused bitterness among the staff.* 降低工資使職員們十分憤懣。◇ *The flowers of the hop plant add bitterness to the beer.* 忽布花可增加啤酒的苦味。

IDM **a bitter 'pill (for sb) (to swallow)** a fact or an event that is unpleasant and difficult to accept 嚴酷的現實；（難以嚥下的）苦果 **to/until the bitter 'end** continuing until you have done everything you can, or until sth is completely finished, despite difficulties and problems（不怕艱苦）堅持到底，奮鬥到底：*They were prepared to fight to the bitter end for their rights.* 他們甘願為自己的權利鬥爭到底。

▪ *noun* (*BrE*) **1** [U, C] a type of beer with a dark colour and a strong bitter taste, that is very popular in Britain 苦啤酒（在英國很受歡迎）：*A pint of bitter, please.* 請來一品脫苦啤酒。➲ compare MILD *n.* **2 bitters** [U+sing./pl. v.] a strong bitter alcoholic liquid that is made from plants and added to other alcoholic drinks to give flavour 苦酒原汁（從植物中提取的苦酒精液體，可增加其他酒精飲料的味道）：*gin with a dash of bitters* 摻了少量苦酒汁的杜松子酒

ˌbitter 'lemon *noun* [U] (*BrE*) a FIZZY drink (= with bubbles) that tastes of lemon and is slightly bitter 苦檸檬（發泡飲料）

bit·ter·ly /ˈbɪtəli; *NAmE* -tərli/ *adv.*
1 in a way that shows feelings of sadness or anger 傷心地；憤怒地：*She wept bitterly.* 她哭得很傷心。◇ *They complained bitterly.* 他們氣憤地抱怨。◇ *The development was bitterly opposed by the local community.* 這一開發項目遭到了當地社區的憤怒抵制。**2** (describing unpleasant or sad feelings 形容不快或傷痛) extremely 極其；非常：***bitterly disappointed/ashamed*** 極其失望／羞愧 **3 ~ cold** very cold 非常寒冷；嚴寒

bit·tern /ˈbɪtən; *NAmE* -tərn/ *noun* a European bird of the HERON family, that lives on wet ground and has a loud call 麻鳽（沼澤鳥，鳴聲響亮）

ˌbitter-'sweet *adj.* (*BrE*) **1** bringing pleasure mixed with sadness 甜中有苦的；既有歡樂又有悲傷的：*bitter-sweet memories* 悲喜交集的回憶 **2** (of tastes or smells 味道或氣味) bitter and sweet at the same time 又苦又甜的

bitty /ˈbɪti/ *adj.* (*BrE, informal*) (**bit·tier**, **bit·ti·est**) made up of many small separate parts, which do not seem to fit together well 零散的；支離破碎的

bitu·men /ˈbɪtʃəmən; *NAmE* bəˈtuːmən; -ˈtjuː-/ *noun* [U] **1** a black sticky substance obtained from oil, used for covering roads or roofs 瀝青 **2** (*AustralE, informal*) the surface of a road that is covered with TAR 瀝青路面；柏油路面：*a kilometre and a half of bitumen* 一公里半的柏油路面

bi·tu·min·ous /bɪˈtjuːmɪnəs; *NAmE* bəˈtuː-/ *adj.* containing bitumen 含瀝青的；瀝青的

bit·zer /ˈbɪtsə(r)/ *noun* (*AustralE, NZE, informal*) **1** a thing that is made from parts that originally did not belong together 拼湊的東西；雜燴 **2** a dog that is a mixture of different breeds 雜種狗；混種狗 **SYN** **mongrel**

bi·valve /ˈbaɪvælv/ *noun* (*technical* 術語) any SHELLFISH with a shell in two parts, for example a MUSSEL 雙殼軟體動物（如貽貝）➲ compare MOLLUSC

biv·ouac /ˈbɪvuæk/ *noun, verb*

▪ *noun* a temporary camp or shelter, without using a tent, that is made and used especially by people climbing mountains or by soldiers 臨時露營，軍事野營（無帳篷）

▪ *verb* **(-ck-)** [I] to spend the night in a bivouac 臨時露營；野營

B

Synonyms 同義詞辨析

bitter

pungent • sour • acrid • sharp • acid

These words all describe a strong, unpleasant taste or smell. 以上各詞均形容味道或氣味強烈、令人不適。

bitter (of a taste or smell) strong and usually unpleasant; (of food or drink) having a bitter taste 指（味道或氣味）強烈的、令人不適的，（食物或飲料）味苦的

pungent (of a smell or taste) strong and usually unpleasant; (of food or smoke) having a pungent smell or taste 指（氣味或味道）強烈的、令人不適的，（食物）味苦的，（煙）嗆人的、刺鼻的： *the pungent smell of burning rubber* 燒橡膠的刺鼻氣味

sour (of a taste) bitter like the taste of a lemon or of fruit that is not ripe; (of food or drink) having a sour taste 指（味道）酸的，（食物或飲料）有酸味的： *Too much pulp produces a sour wine.* 過多的果肉會讓酒變酸。

acrid (of a smell or taste) strong and unpleasant; (of smoke) having an acrid smell 指（氣味或味道）刺激的、難聞的，（煙）嗆人的、刺鼻的： *acrid smoke from burning tyres* 燃燒輪胎產生的熏煙

sharp (of a taste or smell) strong and slightly bitter; (of food or drink) having a sharp taste 指（味道或氣味）強烈而略苦的、刺鼻的，（食物或飲料）味苦的、辛辣的： *The cheese has a distinctively sharp taste.* 這奶酪味道很衝。

acid (of a taste or smell) bitter, like the taste of a lemon or of fruit that is not ripe; (of food or drink) having an acid taste 指（味道）酸的，（氣味）有刺激性的，（食物或飲料）有酸味的

WHICH WORD? 詞語辨析

A **bitter** taste is usually unpleasant, but some people enjoy the bitter flavour of coffee or chocolate. No other word can describe this flavour. A **sharp** or **pungent** flavour is more strong than unpleasant, especially when describing cheese. **Sharp**, **sour** and **acid** all describe the taste of a lemon or a fruit that is not ripe. An **acrid** smell is strong and unpleasant, especially the smell of smoke or burning, but not the smell of food. * bitter 指味道通常為苦的、令人不快的，有人卻喜歡咖啡或巧克力的苦味。沒有其他詞可用來形容這種味道。sharp 或 pungent 主要強調味道強烈而非令人不快，在描述奶酪的味道時尤其如此。sharp、sour 和 acid 均形容檸檬或未熟水果的酸味。acrid 指氣味強烈而令人不快，尤指煙味或燃燒產生的氣味，但不用於指食物的氣味。

PATTERNS

- a(n) bitter/pungent/sour/acrid/sharp/acid **taste/flavour**
- a(n) bitter/pungent/acrid/sharp/acid **smell/odour**
- a(n) bitter/sour/sharp/acid **fruit**
- pungent/sharp **cheese**
- pungent/acrid **smoke**

bivvy /ˈbɪvi/ *noun, verb*
■ ***noun*** (*pl.* **biv·vies**) a tent or temporary shelter 帳篷；臨時遮蔽處
■ ***verb*** (*third person sing. pres. t.* **biv·vies** *pres. part.* **bivvy·ing** *pt, pp* **biv·vied**) [I] to sleep in a tent or temporary shelter 睡帳篷；睡在臨時遮蔽處

the biz /bɪz/ *noun* [sing.] (*informal*) a particular type of business, especially one connected with entertainment 生意；（尤指）娛樂業： *people in the music biz* 音樂圈的人
IDM **be the 'biz** (*informal*) to be very good 非常棒

bi·zarre /bɪˈzɑː(r)/ *adj.* very strange or unusual 極其怪誕的；異乎尋常的 **SYN** **weird** ： *a bizarre situation/incident/story* 稀奇古怪的局勢／事件／故事 ◇ *bizarre behaviour* 古怪的行為 ▶ **bi·zarre·ly** *adv.* ： *bizarrely dressed* 穿着奇裝異服

blab /blæb/ *verb* (**-bb-**) [I, T] **~ (to sb) (about sth)** | **~ (sth) (to sb)** (*informal*) to tell sb information that should be kept secret （向某人）透露秘密，告密： *Someone must have blabbed to the police.* 一定有人向警方告密了。

blab·ber /ˈblæbə(r)/ *verb* [I] **~ (on) (about sth)** (*informal*) to talk in a way that other people think is silly and annoying 說蠢話；胡扯；瞎說： *What was she blabbering on about this time?* 她這會兒又在瞎扯些什麼？

blab·ber·mouth /ˈblæbəmaʊθ; *NAmE* -bərm-/ *noun* (*informal, disapproving*) a person who tells secrets because they talk too much 多嘴多舌的人；碎嘴子

black 0➡ /blæk/ *adj., noun, verb*
■ ***adj.*** (**black·er, black·est**)
▸ **COLOUR 顏色** **1** 0➡ having the very darkest colour, like night or coal 黑的；黑色的： *a shiny black car* 發亮的黑汽車 ◇ *black storm clouds* 帶來暴風雨的烏雲
▸ **WITH NO LIGHT 無光線** **2** 0➡ without light; completely dark 黑暗的；漆黑的： *a black night* 漆黑的夜晚
▸ **PEOPLE 人** **3** 0➡ (also **Black**) belonging to a race of people who have dark skin; connected with black people 黑色人種的；黑人的：*a black woman writer* 一位黑人女作家 ◇ *black culture* 黑人文化 **HELP** **Black** is the word most widely used and generally accepted in Britain. In the US the currently accepted term is **African American**. * black 在英國最廣為使用和接受。在美國目前為人所接受的詞是 African American。
▸ **TEA/COFFEE 茶；咖啡** **4** 0➡ without milk 不加牛奶的： *Two black coffees, please.* 請來兩杯清咖啡。➲ compare WHITE (4)
▸ **DIRTY 骯髒** **5** 0➡ very dirty; covered with dirt 很髒的；佈滿污垢的： *chimneys black with smoke* 滿佈煙塵的煙囱 ◇ *Go and wash your hands; they're absolutely black!* 洗洗手去，你的手髒極了！
▸ **ANGRY 憤怒** **6** full of anger or hatred 憤怒的；仇恨的： *She's been in a really black mood all day.* 她一整天都心情很壞。◇ *Rory shot her a black look.* 羅里憤怒地瞪了她一眼。
▸ **DEPRESSING 令人沮喪** **7** without hope; very depressing 無希望的；令人沮喪的： *The future looks pretty black.* 前景看來很暗淡。◇ *It's been another black day for the north-east with the announcement of further job losses.* 東北部又經歷了一個黑色的日子，當地公佈的失業人數再度上升。
▸ **EVIL 邪惡** **8** (*literary*) evil or immoral 邪惡的；不道德的： *black deeds/lies* 邪惡行為；昧良心的謊言
▸ **HUMOUR 幽默** **9** dealing with unpleasant or terrible things, such as murder, in a humorous way 黑色的（以幽默的方式對待討厭的或可怕的事物，如兇殺）： *'Good place to bury the bodies,' she joked with* ***black humour***. "真是個掩埋屍體的風水寶地。" 她以黑色幽默打趣道。◇ *The play is a* ***black comedy***. 那是個黑色喜劇。➲ see also BLACKLY
▶ **black·ness** *noun* [U, sing.] ： *She peered out into the blackness of the night.* 她凝視着外面黑沉沉的夜色。
IDM **(beat sb) black and 'blue** (to hit sb until they are) covered with BRUISES (= blue, brown or purple marks on the body) （把某人打得）青一塊紫一塊，傷痕斑斑 **not as black as he/she/it is 'painted** not as bad as people say he/she/it is 不像別人說的那麼壞： *He's not very friendly, but he's not as black as he's painted.* 他不太友善，但也不像別人說的那麼壞。➲ more at POT *n.*
■ ***noun***
▸ **COLOUR 顏色** **1** 0➡ [U] the very darkest colour, like night or coal 黑色： *the black of the night sky* 夜空的漆黑 ◇ *Everyone at the funeral was dressed in black.* 參加葬禮的人都身着黑服。
▸ **PEOPLE 人** **2** 0➡ (also **Black**) [C, usually pl.] a member of a race of people who have dark skin 黑色人種的人；黑人 **HELP** In this meaning **black** is more common in the plural. It can sound offensive in the singular. Instead, you can use the adjective ('a black man/woman') or, in the US, **African American**. * black 在此義中常以複數形式出現。單數形式可能使人感到冒犯。但可用作形容詞 (a black man/woman)，或者，在美國可說 African American。

IDM **be in the 'black** to have money, for example in your bank account 有盈餘；有結餘 ➲ compare BE IN THE RED at RED *n.* **,black and 'white** having no colours except black, white and shades of grey (in photographs, on television, etc.) (照片、電視等) 黑白的：*a film made in black and white* 黑白電影 ◊ *black-and-white photos* 黑白照片 **in black and white** in writing or in print 白紙黑字；書寫的；印刷的：*I never thought they'd put it in black and white on the front page.* 我從未想到他們會在頭版把它登出來。 **(in) black and white** in a way that makes people or things seem completely bad or good, or completely right or wrong 黑白分明 (好壞、是非等清楚的)：*It's a complex issue, but he only sees it in black and white.* 那是個複雜的問題，但他卻只看到對與錯的分別。◊ *This is not a black-and-white decision* (= where the difference between two choices is completely clear). 這不是個非此即彼的決定。

■ *verb* **1 ~ sth/sb** (*BrE*) to refuse to deal with goods or to do business with sb as a political protest 抵制；拒絕處理 (貨物)；拒絕 (同某人) 做生意 **SYN** **boycott**：*The unions have blacked all imports from the country.* 工會拒絕處理從這個國家進口的所有貨物。 **2 ~ sth** to make sth black 使變黑；染黑；塗黑 **SYN** **blacken**

PHR V **,black 'out** to become unconscious for a short time 暫時失去知覺；昏厥 **SYN** **faint**：*The driver had probably blacked out at the wheel.* 司機很可能在開車時昏厥了。 ➲ related noun BLACKOUT **,black sth↔'out** **1** to make a place dark by turning off lights, covering windows, etc. 使 (某處) 變黑暗：*A power failure blacked out the city last night.* 昨晚停電造成整個城市一片漆黑。◊ *a house with blacked out windows* 窗戶被遮住不透光的房子 ➲ related noun BLACKOUT **2** to prevent sth such as a piece of writing or a television broadcast from being read or seen 塗掉 (文章)；截斷 (電視廣播)；封鎖 (新聞)：*Some lines of the document have been blacked out for security reasons.* 為安全起見，這份文件的一些句子被塗掉了。

black·amoor /ˈblækəmɔː(r)/ *noun* (*old use, taboo*) an offensive word for a black person (含冒犯意) 黑人；黑鬼

the ,black 'arts *noun* [pl.] = BLACK MAGIC

black·ball /ˈblækbɔːl/ *verb* **~ sb** to prevent sb from joining a club or a group by voting against them 投票反對 (某人加入俱樂部或團體)

,black 'belt *noun* **1** a belt that you can earn in a sport such as JUDO or KARATE which shows that you have reached a very high standard (柔道、空手道等運動中顯示已達到很高水平的) 黑腰帶 **2** a person who has gained a black belt 黑帶級選手

Black·Berry™ /ˈblækbəri; *NAmE* -beri/ *noun* (*pl.* **-ys**) a very small computer that you can hold in your hand and that you can use for storing information, sending and receiving emails and TEXT MESSAGES, making and receiving phone calls and looking at the Internet 黑莓手機 (具備多項電腦功能)：*Check your emails via your BlackBerry.* 用黑莓手機查收郵件。◊ *a BlackBerry handset* 黑莓手機

black·berry /ˈblækbəri; *NAmE* -beri/ (*pl.* **-ies**) (*BrE* also **bram·ble**) *noun* a small soft black fruit that grows on a bush with THORNS in gardens/yards or in the countryside. The bush is also called a blackberry/bramble. 黑莓 (漿果)；黑莓 (有刺灌木)：*blackberry and apple pie* 黑莓蘋果餡餅 ➲ VISUAL VOCAB page V30

black·berry·ing /ˈblækbəriŋ; *NAmE* -beriŋ/ *noun* [U] the act of picking blackberries 採集黑莓：*Shall we go blackberrying?* 我們去採黑莓好不好？

black·bird /ˈblækbɜːd; *NAmE* -bɜːrd/ *noun* **1** a European bird: the male is black with a yellow beak and the female is brown with a brown beak 烏鶇 (見於歐洲，雄鳥黑羽黃喙，雌鳥棕色) **2** a black N American bird, larger than the European blackbird, related to the STARLING 黑鸝 (見於北美洲)

black·board /ˈblækbɔːd; *NAmE* -bɔːrd/ (also **chalk·board** especially in *NAmE*) *noun* a large board with a smooth black or dark green surface that teachers write on with a piece of CHALK 黑板：*to write on the blackboard* 在黑板上寫字 ➲ compare WHITEBOARD

,black 'box *noun* **1** (also **'flight recorder**) a small machine in a plane that records all the details of each flight and is useful for finding out the cause of an accident 黑匣子；黑盒；飛行記錄儀 **2** [usually sing.] (*technical* 術語) a complicated piece of equipment, usually electronic, that you know produces particular results, but that you do not completely understand 未知框 (常為電子的複雜儀器，內部結構不詳)

,black 'cab *noun* (*BrE*) a traditional type of taxi in London and some other British cities. Its driver is licensed by the city to stop and pick up passengers in the street. 黑色出租車 (倫敦等英國城市的市區老牌出租車)：*a queue of black cabs at the station* 車站前的一溜老牌黑色出租車

the 'Black Country *noun* [sing.] an area in the West Midlands of England where there used to be a lot of heavy industry 黑鄉 (在英格蘭西米德蘭茲，原為重工業地帶)

black·cur·rant /ˌblækˈkʌrənt; ˈblækkʌrənt; *NAmE* -kɜːr-/ *noun* a small black BERRY that grows in bunches on a garden bush and can be eaten 黑茶藨子；黑加侖子：*blackcurrant jam* 黑茶藨子醬 ◊ *a blackcurrant bush* 黑茶藨子灌木

the ,Black 'Death *noun* [sing.] the name used for the very serious infectious disease (called BUBONIC PLAGUE), which killed millions of people in Europe and Asia in the 14th century 黑死病 (14 世紀蔓延於歐亞的鼠疫)

,black 'diamond *noun* **1** [C] (*BrE, informal*) a lump of coal 煤塊 **2** [U, C] a dark form of diamond 黑金剛石；黑鑽石 **3** [C] (*NAmE*) a slope that is difficult to SKI down 黑鑽石坡道 (難以下滑的陡坡)：*a black diamond run* 黑鑽石滑道

the ,black e'conomy (*BrE*) (*NAmE* **the ,under·ground e'conomy**) *noun* [sing.] business activity or work that is done without the knowledge of the government or other officials so that people avoid paying tax on the money they earn 黑市經濟；黑市經營；地下經濟活動

,black em'powerment (also **,black eco,nomic em'powerment**) *noun* [U] in southern Africa, a policy which aims to give black people the chance to earn more money, own more property, etc., and have a greater role in the economy than they did before 黑人賦權 (非洲南部政策，旨在給黑人提供機會增加收入並擁有財產等，以及參與更多經濟活動)

black·en /ˈblækən/ *verb* **1** [T, I] **~ (sth)** to make sth black; to become black (使) 變黑：*Their faces were blackened with soot.* 他們滿臉煤灰。◊ *Smoke had blackened the walls.* 煙把牆壁都熏黑了。 **2** [T] **~ sb's name/reputation/character** to say unpleasant things that give people a bad opinion of sb 抹黑；醜化；敗壞…的名譽：*He accused the newspaper of trying to blacken his name.* 他指責報紙企圖敗壞他的名聲。

,Black 'English *noun* [U] any of various forms of English spoken by black people, especially a form spoken in US cities 黑人英語

,black 'eye *noun* an area of dark skin (called a BRUISE), that can form around sb's eye when they receive a blow on it (被打成的) 青腫眼眶

black·face /ˈblækfeɪs/ *noun* **1** [C] a type of sheep with a black face 黑面羊；黑臉羊 **2** [U] a dark substance used by actors to make their skin look dark (演員用) 黑油彩，黑臉化妝品

,black 'flag *noun* **1** a black flag used in motor racing to stop a driver who has done sth wrong 黑旗 (賽車中用以示意犯規車手停車) **2** a flag with a SKULL AND CROSSBONES on it 海盜旗 (上有骷髏和交叉的股骨圖形)

black·fly /ˈblækflaɪ/ *noun* (*pl.* **black·fly** or **black·flies**) **1** a small black or dark green insect that damages plants 黑蚜蟲，深綠色蚜蟲 (侵害植物) **2** (also **'black fly**) a small black fly that sucks blood from humans and animals 蚋 (吸血)

B

Black·foot /ˈblækfʊt/ *noun* (*pl.* **Black·feet** /ˈblækfiːt/ or **Black·foot**) a member of a Native American people, many of whom live in the US state of Montana and in Alberta in Canada 黑腳族人，黑腳人（美洲土著，很多居於美國蒙大拿州和加拿大艾伯塔省）

ˌBlack Forest ˈgateau *noun* a type of chocolate cake with layers of CHERRIES and cream 黑森林巧克力蛋糕（有奶油櫻桃夾層）

ˌblack ˈgold *noun* [U] (*NAmE, informal*) oil 黑金子；石油

black·guard /ˈblæɡɑːd; *NAmE* -ɡɑːrd/ *noun* (*old-fashioned, BrE*) a man who is dishonest and has no sense of what is right and what is wrong 無賴；惡棍

black·head /ˈblækhed/ *noun* a small spot on the skin, often on the face, with a black top 黑頭粉刺（常長在面部）

ˌblack ˈhole *noun* an area in space that nothing, not even light, can escape from, because GRAVITY (= the force that pulls objects in space towards each other) is so strong there 黑洞（宇宙中包括光線在內的任何東西都無法逃逸的強引力區域）：(*figurative*) *The company viewed the venture as a financial black hole* (= it would use a lot of the company's money with no real result). 公司認為該項投資是財政上的一個大黑洞。

ˌblack ˈice *noun* [U] ice in a thin layer on the surface of a road 黑冰，薄冰（路面上很薄的冰層）

black·jack /ˈblækdʒæk/ *noun* **1** (*BrE* also **pon·toon**) [U] a card game in which players try to collect cards with a total value of 21 and no more * 21 點紙牌遊戲（玩者力爭取得 21 點的總點數）**2** [C] (*especially NAmE*) a type of CLUB used as a weapon, especially a metal pipe covered with leather（包革）金屬棍棒，金屬警棍

black·leg /ˈblækleg/ *noun* (*BrE, disapproving*) a person who continues to work when the people they work with are on strike; a person who is employed to work instead of those who are on strike 破壞罷工者，工賊（罷工時繼續工作或受雇頂替罷工者工作）➲ compare STRIKE-BREAKER ➲ see also SCAB (4)

ˌblack ˈlight *noun* [U] ULTRAVIOLET OR INFRARED RAYS, which cannot be seen 不可見光，黑光（指紫外線和紅外線）

black·list /ˈblæklɪst/ *noun, verb*

■ ***noun*** a list of the names of people, companies, products or countries that an organization or a government considers unacceptable and that must be avoided 黑名單

■ ***verb*** **~ sb/sth** to put the name of a person, a company, a product or a country on a blacklist 將…列入黑名單：*She was blacklisted by all the major Hollywood studios because of her political views.* 由於她的政見，所有好萊塢大製片公司都拒絕用她。

ˌblack ˈlung *noun* [U] (*NAmE*) a lung disease caused by breathing in coal dust over a long period of time 黑肺病，煤肺病，肺塵病（長期吸入煤塵引起）

black·ly /ˈblækli/ *adv.* **~ comic/funny/humorous/satirical** dealing with unpleasant or terrible things, such as murder, in a humorous way 以黑色幽默方式：*The movie takes a blackly humorous look at death.* 這影片以黑色幽默視角看待死亡。

ˌblack ˈmagic *noun* [U] (also **the black ˈarts**) a type of magic which is believed to use the power of the DEVIL in order to do evil 魔法；妖術；巫術

black·mail /ˈblækmeɪl/ *noun, verb*

■ ***noun*** [U] **1** the crime of demanding money from a person by threatening to tell sb else a secret about them 勒索；敲詐 **2** the act of putting pressure on a person or a group to do sth they do not want to do, for example by making threats or by making them feel guilty 脅迫；威脅；恐嚇：***emotional/moral blackmail*** 情感上／道德上脅迫

■ ***verb*** to force sb to give you money or do sth for you by threatening them, for example by saying you will tell people a secret about them 勒索；敲詐；要挾；脅迫：**~ sb** *She blackmailed him for years by threatening to tell the newspapers about their affair.* 她以向報界公開他們的戀情要挾了他很多年。◇ **~ sb into doing sth** *The President said he wouldn't be blackmailed into agreeing to the terrorists' demands.* 總統說他不會因受恐怖分子的威脅而答應他們的要求。

black·mail·er /ˈblækmeɪlə(r)/ *noun* a person who commits blackmail 勒索者；敲詐者

Black Maria /ˌblæk məˈraɪə/ *noun* (*old-fashioned, slang*) a police van that was used in the past for transporting prisoners in（舊時）囚車

ˌblack ˈmark *noun* (*BrE*) a note, either in writing on an official record, or in sb's mind, of sth you have done or said that makes people think badly of you（記錄在案的或留在別人印象中的）污點：*She earned a black mark for opposing company policy.* 她因反對公司政策而得到考績不良的評語。◇ *The public scandal was a black mark against him.* 那條盡人皆知的醜聞成了他的一個污點。

ˌblack ˈmarket *noun* [usually sing.] an illegal form of trade in which foreign money, or goods that are difficult to obtain, are bought and sold 黑市（交易）：*to buy or sell goods **on the black market*** 從事黑市買賣 ◇ *a flourishing black market in foreign currency* 猖獗的外幣黑市交易

ˌblack markeˈteer *noun* a person who sells goods on the black market 在黑市出售商品者；黑市商人

ˌblack ˈmass *noun* a ceremony in which people worship the DEVIL 黑彌撒（崇拜撒旦）

ˌBlack ˈMuslim *noun* a member of a group of black people, especially in the US, who follow the religion of Islam and want a separate black society 黑人穆斯林（尤指美國的黑人民權運動支持者）

black·out /ˈblækaʊt/ *noun* **1** a period when there is no light as a result of an electrical power failure 斷電；停電 **2** a situation when the government or the police will not allow any news or information on a particular subject to be given to the public 新聞封鎖 **3** [usually sing.] (*especially BrE*) a period of time during a war when all lights must be put out or covered at night, so that they cannot be seen by an enemy attacking by air 燈火管制（期）**4** [usually pl.] (*BrE*) a covering for windows that stops light being seen from outside, or light from outside from coming into a room 不透光窗罩（或窗簾）**5** a temporary loss of CONSCIOUSNESS, sight or memory 一時性黑蒙；眼前昏黑：*She had a blackout and couldn't remember anything about the accident.* 她眼前一黑，那場事故就怎麼也想不起來了。

ˌblack ˈpepper *noun* [U] a black powder made from dried BERRIES (called PEPPERCORNS), used to give a spicy flavour to food 黑胡椒粉：*salt and freshly ground black pepper* 鹽和新研磨的黑胡椒粉

ˌBlack ˈPower *noun* [U] a movement supporting rights and political power for black people 黑人民權運動

ˌblack ˈpudding (*BrE*) (*NAmE* **ˈblood sausage**) (also **ˌblood ˈpudding** *BrE, NAmE*) *noun* [U, C] a type of large dark SAUSAGE made from pig's blood, fat and grain 黑香腸（用豬血、乳脂以及穀粒製成）

ˌBlack ˈRod *noun* [U] an official who takes part in the opening ceremony of the British parliament（英國國會開幕儀式上的）黑杖侍衛，黑杖禮儀官

ˌblack ˈsheep *noun* [usually sing.] a person who is different from the rest of their family or another group, and who is considered bad or embarrassing 有辱家族的人；害群之馬：*the black sheep of the family* 家族敗類

black·shirt /ˈblækʃɜːt; *NAmE* -ʃɜːrt/ (also **Blackshirt**) *noun* a member of a FASCIST organization, especially in the 1920s and 30s 黑衫黨成員（尤指 19 世紀 20 和 30 年代的法西斯組織成員）

black·smith /ˈblæksmɪθ/ (also **smith**) *noun* a person whose job is to make and repair things made of iron, especially HORSESHOES 鐵匠（尤指打馬蹄鐵者）➲ compare FARRIER

ˌblack spot *noun* (*BrE*) a place, a situation or an event that is a problem or that causes a lot of problems 事故多發區；問題成堆的狀況；（問題）焦點：*an environmental black spot* 環境污染嚴重的地區 ◇ *That corner is a notorious accident black spot* (= a lot of accidents happen there). 那個拐彎處是有名的事故多發區。

black·thorn /ˈblækθɔːn; *NAmE* -θɔːrn/ *noun* [U] a bush with THORNS with black branches, white flowers and sour purple fruit called SLOES 黑刺李（多刺灌木，開白花，結紫色酸果）

ˌblack ˈtie *noun* a black BOW TIE worn with a DINNER JACKET（晚禮服佩戴的）黑領結 ▸ **ˌblack ˈtie** *adj.*: *The party is black tie* (= dinner jackets should be worn). 聚會要求穿禮服。◇ *a black-tie dinner* 要求穿晚禮服的宴會

black·top /ˈblæktɒp; *NAmE* -tɑːp/ *noun, verb* (*NAmE*) = TARMAC

ˌblack ˈwidow *noun* a poisonous American spider. The female black widow often eats the male. 黑寡婦毒蛛（美洲蜘蛛，雌蛛常吃掉雄蛛）

blad·der /ˈblædə(r)/ *noun* **1** an organ that is shaped like a bag in which liquid waste (= URINE) collects before it is passed out of the body 膀胱 ➲ see also GALL BLADDER ➲ VISUAL VOCAB page V59 **2** a bag made of rubber, leather, etc. that can be filled with air or liquid, such as the one inside a football 皮囊，氣囊（如球膽）

blad·dered /ˈblædəd; *NAmE* ˈblædərd/ *adj.* [not before noun] (*BrE, slang*) drunk 喝醉

blades 刀身；刀刃；刀片；槳葉；葉片

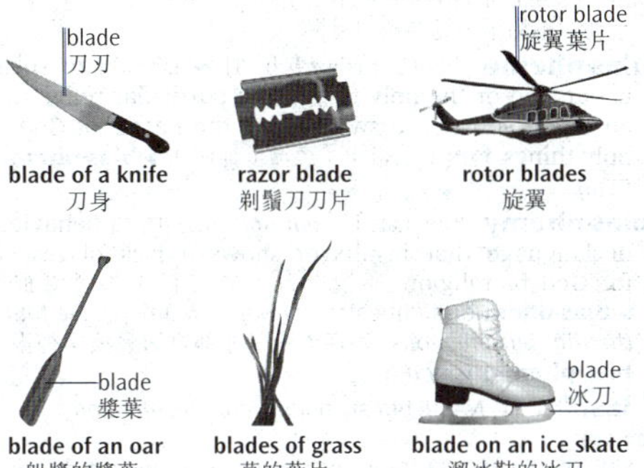

blade 🔑 /bleɪd/ *noun*
1 🔑 the flat part of a knife, tool or machine, which has a sharp edge or edges for cutting 刀身；刀片；刀刃 ➲ VISUAL VOCAB pages V20, V22, V24, V26 ➲ see also RAZOR BLADE, SWITCHBLADE **2** one of the flat parts that turn around in an engine or on a HELICOPTER（機器上旋轉的）葉片；槳葉：*the blades of a propeller* 螺旋槳葉 ◇ *rotor blades on a helicopter* 直升機的旋翼 ➲ VISUAL VOCAB page V53 **3** the flat wide part of an OAR (= one of the long poles that are used to ROW a boat) that goes in the water（船槳的）槳葉，槳身 ➲ VISUAL VOCAB page V55 **4** a single flat leaf of grass（草的）葉片 **5** the flat metal part on the bottom of an ICE SKATE（溜冰鞋的）冰刀 ➲ see also SHOULDER BLADE

blad·ing /ˈbleɪdɪŋ/ *noun* [U] the sport of moving on ROLLERBLADES 輪滑；直排輪溜冰運動；滾軸溜冰

blag /blæg/ *verb* (**-gg-**) **~ sth** (*BrE, informal*) to persuade sb to give you sth, or to let you do sth, by talking to them in a clever or amusing way 哄…；哄得：*I blagged some tickets for the game.* 我騙到了這場比賽的幾張門票。◇ *We* ***blagged our way*** *into the reception by saying that we were from the press.* 我們自稱記者混進了招待會。

blah /blɑː/ *noun, adj.*
▪ ***noun*** [U] (*informal*) people say **blah, blah, blah,** when they do not want to give the exact words that sb has said or written because they think they are not important or are boring（覺得厭煩不想重複別人的話時說）：*They said, 'Come in, sit down, blah, blah, blah, sign here'.* 他們說："進來，坐下，幹這個，幹那個，在這裏簽字。"
▪ ***adj.*** (*NAmE, informal*) **1** not interesting 乏味的：*The movie was pretty blah.* 那場電影真沒意思。 **2** not feeling well; feeling slightly unhappy 不舒服；悶悶不樂

blame 🔑 /bleɪm/ *verb, noun*
▪ ***verb*** 🔑 to think or say that sb/sth is responsible for sth bad 把…歸咎於；責怪；指責：**~ sb/sth (for sth)** *She doesn't blame anyone for her father's death.* 她沒把她父親的死歸罪於任何人。◇ *A dropped cigarette is being blamed for the fire.* 一根亂扔的煙被認為是引起這場火災的肇因。◇ **~ sth on sb/sth** *Police are blaming the accident on dangerous driving.* 警方把事故原因歸咎於危險駕駛。
IDM **be to blame (for sth)** 🔑 to be responsible for sth bad 對（壞事）負有責任：*If anyone's to blame, it's me.* 如果有人該承擔責任，那就是我。◇ *Which driver was to blame for the accident?* 哪個司機是此次事故的肇事者？ **don't blame ˈme** (*informal*) used to advise sb not to do sth, when you think they will do it despite your advice（勸阻別人時說）別怪我：*Call her if you like, but don't blame me if she's angry.* 你想給她打電話就打吧，不過要是她生氣就別怪我。 **I don't ˈblame you/her, etc. (for doing sth)** (*informal*) used to say that you think that what sb did was reasonable and the right thing to do 我不怪你（或她等）；你（或她等）的做法是可以理解的：*'I just slammed the phone down when he said that.' 'I don't blame you!'* "他一說那話我就啪地一下掛了電話。" "你做得對！" **only have yourself to ˈblame** used to say that you think sth is sb's own fault 只能怪你自己；是你自己的錯：*If you lose your job, you'll only have yourself to blame.* 如果你丟掉了工作，你只能責怪你自己。
▪ ***noun*** 🔑 [U] **~ (for sth)** responsibility for doing sth badly or wrongly; saying that sb is responsible for sth（壞事或錯事的）責任；責備；指責：*to* ***lay/put the blame*** *for sth on sb* 把某事歸咎於某人 ◇ *The government will have* ***to take the blame*** *for the riots.* 政府將不得不對騷亂承擔責任。◇ *Why do I always* ***get the blame*** *for everything that goes wrong?* 為什麼出了事總是讓我背黑鍋？ ➲ compare CREDIT *n.* (7)

blame·less /ˈbleɪmləs/ *adj.* doing no wrong; free from responsibility for doing sth bad 無過錯的；無可指責的 SYN **innocent**: *to lead a blameless life* 活得清白 ◇ *None of us is entirely blameless in this matter.* 在這件事上我們沒有一個人是完全沒有責任的。 ▸ **blame·less·ly** *adv.*

blame·worthy /ˈbleɪmwɜːði; *NAmE* -wɜːrði/ *adj.* (*formal*) deserving disapproval and criticism; responsible for doing sth wrong 該受指責的；（對壞事）負有責任的

blanch /blɑːntʃ; *NAmE* blæntʃ/ *verb* **1** [I] **~ (at sth)** (*formal*) to become pale because you are shocked or frightened（受驚嚇）臉發白 **2** [T] **~ sth** to prepare food, especially vegetables, by putting it into boiling water for a short time 焯（把蔬菜等放在沸水中略微一煮）

blanc·mange /bləˈmɒnʒ; *NAmE* -ˈmɑːnʒ/ *noun* [C, U] (*BrE*) a cold DESSERT (= a sweet dish) that looks like jelly, made with milk and flavoured with fruit 果味牛奶凍

bland /blænd/ *adj.* (**bland·er, bland·est**) **1** with little colour, excitement or interest; without anything to attract attention 平淡的；乏味的 SYN **nondescript**: *bland background music* 毫無情調的背景音樂 **2** not having a strong or interesting taste 清淡的；無滋味的：*a rather bland diet of soup, fish and bread* 一個淡而無味的湯、魚加麵包的食譜 **3** showing no strong emotions or excitement; not saying anything very interesting 沉穩的；無動於衷的；講話枯燥的：*a bland smile* 淡然一笑 ◇ *After the meeting, a bland statement was issued.* 會後發佈了一條乏味的聲明。 ▸ **bland·ly** *adv.* **bland·ness** *noun* [U]

bland·ish·ments /ˈblændɪʃmənts/ *noun* [pl.] (*formal*) pleasant things that you say to sb or do for them to try to persuade them to do sth（因有所求而）說的好話，討人歡心

blank 🔑 /blæŋk/ *adj., noun, verb*
▪ ***adj.*** **1** 🔑 empty, with nothing written, printed or recorded on it 空白的：*Sign your name in the blank space below.* 把名字簽在下面的空白處。◇ *a blank CD* 空白光盤 ◇ *Write on one side of the paper and leave the other side blank.* 寫在紙的一面，把另一面空出來。◇ *She turned to a blank page in her notebook.* 她翻開筆記本

B

的一張空白頁。 **2** (of a wall or screen 牆壁或屏幕) empty; with no pictures, marks or decoration 空的；無圖畫（或標記、裝飾）的：*blank whitewashed walls* 光禿禿的白灰牆 ◇ *Suddenly the screen* ***went blank****.* 屏幕突然變成一片空白。 **3** showing no feeling, understanding or interest 沒表情的；不理解的；不感興趣的：*She stared at me with a blank expression on her face.* 她一臉木然地盯着我。◇ *Steve* ***looked blank*** *and said he had no idea what I was talking about.* 史蒂夫顯得很迷惑，說他不知道我在說什麼。◇ *Suddenly* ***my mind went blank*** (= I could not remember anything). 我腦子裏突然一片空白。 **4** [only before noun] (of negative things 否定的事情) complete and total 完全的；徹底的：*a* ***blank refusal/denial*** 斷然拒絕／否認 ➲ see also POINT-BLANK ▸ **blank·ly** *adv.*：*She stared blankly into space, not knowing what to say next.* 她木然地凝視着，不知道下面該說什麼。 **blank·ness** *noun* [U]

■ ***noun*** **1** [C] an empty space on a printed form or document for you to write answers, information, etc. in（文件等的）空白處，空格：*Please* ***fill in the blanks****.* 請在空白處填寫。◇ *If you can't answer the question, leave a blank.* 如果回答不了問題，就空着它。 **2** [sing.] a state of not being able to remember anything（記憶中的）空白，遺忘：*My* ***mind was a blank*** *and I couldn't remember her name.* 我腦子裏一片空白，記不起她的名字了。 **3** [C] (also ˌ**blank ˈcartridge**) a CARTRIDGE in a gun that contains an EXPLOSIVE but no bullet 空彈：*The troops fired blanks in the air.* 部隊向空中放空彈。
IDM see DRAW *v.*

■ ***verb*** **1** [T] **~ sb** (*BrE, informal*) to ignore sb completely 毫不理睬（某人）：*I saw her on the bus this morning, but she totally blanked me.* 我今天早晨在公共汽車上見到她，但她連一眼都沒瞧我。 **2** [I] (*NAmE*) to be suddenly unable to remember or think of sth 突然忘掉；突然思路模糊：*I knew the answer, but I totally blanked during the test.* 我本來知道答案，但考試時我什麼都忘了。
PHR V ˌ**blank ˈout** to suddenly become empty 突然變空：*The screen blanked out.* 屏幕突然變成一片空白。 ˌ**blank sth↔ˈout 1** to cover sth completely so that it cannot be seen 掩蓋；遮蓋：*All the names in the letter had been blanked out.* 信中所有的名字都已塗掉。 **2** to deliberately forget sth unpleasant 刻意忘記；抹去記憶：*She had tried to blank out the whole experience.* 她曾試圖把全部經歷從記憶中抹去。

ˌ**blank ˈcheque** (*BrE*) (*NAmE* ˌ**blank ˈcheck**) *noun* **1** a cheque that is signed but which does not have the amount of money to be paid written on it 空白支票，空額支票（已簽名但未填金額） **2** permission or authority to do sth that is necessary in a particular situation（特定情況下的）自由行動權：*The President was* ***given a blank check*** *by Congress to continue the war.* 國會授予總統全權可繼續這場戰爭。

blan·ket /ˈblæŋkɪt/ *noun, adj., verb*
■ ***noun*** **1** a large cover, often made of wool, used especially on beds to help people keep warm 毯子；毛毯 ➲ VISUAL VOCAB page V23 ➲ see also ELECTRIC BLANKET **2** [usually sing.] **~ of sth** a thick layer or covering of sth 厚層；厚的覆蓋層：*a* ***blanket of fog/snow/cloud*** 厚厚的一層霧／雪／雲 ◇ (*figurative*) *The trial was conducted under a blanket of secrecy.* 審訊在高度保密下進行。➲ see also WET BLANKET
■ ***adj.*** [only before noun] including or affecting all possible cases, situations or people 包括所有情形（或人員）的；總括的；綜合的：*a* ***blanket ban*** *on tobacco advertising* 煙草廣告的全面取締 ◇ *a blanket refusal* 完全拒絕
■ ***verb*** [often passive] **~ sth** (*formal*) to cover sth completely with a thick layer 以厚層覆蓋：*Snow soon blanketed the frozen ground.* 凍土上很快就形成了一層厚厚的積雪。

ˈ**blanket bath** *noun* (*BrE*) an act of washing the whole of sb's body when they cannot get out of bed because they are sick, injured or old（為傷病或年老者所做的）臥牀浴，臥牀全身擦浴

blankety-blank /ˌblæŋkəti ˈblæŋk/ *adj.* [only before noun] (*informal*) used in place of a rude word that the speaker does not want to say（委婉語，義同該死）：*It's not my blankety-blank fault!* 這他媽不是我的錯！

ˌ**blank ˈverse** *noun* [U] (*technical* 術語) poetry that has a regular rhythm, usually with ten syllables and five stresses in each line, but which does not RHYME 無韻詩（不押韻的抑揚五音步詩行，常為每行十個音節） ➲ compare FREE VERSE

blare /bleə(r); *NAmE* bler/ *verb, noun*
■ ***verb*** [I, T] to make a loud unpleasant noise 發出響亮而刺耳的聲音：*police cars with lights flashing and sirens blaring* 警燈閃爍、警笛刺耳的警車 ◇ **~ out** *Music blared out from the open window.* 喧鬧的音樂從敞開的窗口傳出。◇ **~ sth (out)** *The radio was blaring (out) rock music.* 收音機在高聲播放着嘈雜的搖滾樂。
■ ***noun*** [sing.] a loud unpleasant noise 響亮刺耳的聲音：*the blare of car horns* 汽車喇叭的刺耳聲

blar·ney /ˈblɑːni; *NAmE* ˈblɑːrni/ *noun* [U] (*informal*) talk that is friendly and amusing but probably not true, and which may be used to persuade or trick you 花言巧語；諂媚 **ORIGIN** From **Blarney**, a castle in Ireland where there is a stone which is said to have magic powers: anyone who kisses the 'Blarney stone' is given the gift of speaking persuasively ('the gift of the gab'). 源自愛爾蘭的布拉尼城堡（Blarney），那裏有一塊布拉尼石。相傳此石具有魔力，吻了可變得能言善辯。

blasé /ˈblɑːzeɪ; *NAmE* blɑːˈzeɪ/ *adj.* **~ (about sth)** not impressed, excited or worried about sth, because you have seen or experienced it many times before（對某事物）不稀罕，認為司空見慣

blas·pheme /blæsˈfiːm/ *verb* [I, T] **~ (sb/sth)** to speak about God or the holy things of a particular religion in an offensive way; to swear using the names of God or holy things 褻瀆（上帝）；褻瀆（神明） ▸ **blas·phemer** *noun*

blas·phemy /ˈblæsfəmi/ *noun* (*pl.* **-ies**) [U, C] behaviour or language that insults or shows a lack of respect for God or religion 褻瀆上帝（的言行）；褻瀆神明 ▸ **blas·phem·ous** /ˈblæsfəməs/ *adj.*：*Many people found the film blasphemous.* 很多人覺得那部電影褻瀆了神靈。 **blas·phem·ous·ly** *adv.*

blast /blɑːst; *NAmE* blæst/ *noun, verb, exclamation*
■ ***noun***
▸ **EXPLOSION 爆炸 1** [C] an explosion or a powerful movement of air caused by an explosion 爆炸；（爆炸引起的）氣浪，衝擊波：*a bomb blast* 炸彈爆炸 ◇ *27 schoolchildren were injured in the blast.* * 27 名學齡兒童在爆炸中受了傷。
▸ **OF AIR 空氣 2** [C] a sudden strong movement of air 突如其來的強勁氣流：*A blast of hot air hit us as we stepped off the plane.* 我們下飛機時，一股熱浪向我們襲來。◇ *the wind's icy blasts* 狂風捲起的寒流
▸ **LOUD NOISE 大聲 3** [C] a sudden loud noise, especially one made by a musical instrument that you blow, or by a whistle or a car horn（吹奏樂器、哨子、汽車喇叭等突然發出的）響聲，吹奏聲，轟鳴：*three short blasts on the ship's siren* 船上三次短促的汽笛聲
▸ **CRITICISM 批評 4** [C] (used especially in newspapers 尤用於報章) strong criticism 嚴厲的批評；激烈的抨擊：*Blast for prison governors in judge's report* 法官報告中對典獄長猛烈抨擊
▸ **FUN 歡樂 5** [sing.] (*informal, especially NAmE*) a very enjoyable experience that is a lot of fun 熱鬧的聚會；狂歡：*The party was a blast.* 聚會非常熱鬧。◇ *We had a blast at the party.* 我們在聚會上玩得很開心。
▸ **EMAIL 電子郵件 6** [C] (*NAmE, informal*) advertising or information that is sent to a large number of people at the same time by email 群發的電子郵件廣告（或信息）
IDM **a** ˌ**blast from the ˈpast** (*informal*) a person or thing from your past that you see, hear, meet, etc. again in the present（現在又看見、聽到、遇到等的）故人，往事，舊物 **(at) full ˈblast** with the greatest possible volume or power 最大音量地；最大馬力地：*She had the car stereo on at full blast.* 她把汽車音響開到了最大音量。
■ ***verb***
▸ **EXPLODE 爆炸 1** [T, I] **~ (sth) (+ adv./prep.)** to violently destroy or break sth into pieces, using EXPLOSIVES（用炸藥）炸毀，把…炸成碎片；爆破：*They blasted a huge crater in the runway.* 他們在飛機跑道上炸了一個大坑。◇ *They had to blast a tunnel through the mountain.*

他們得炸出一條穿山隧道。◇ *All the windows were blasted inwards with the force of the explosion.* 爆炸的震動力把所有窗戶都震碎到屋裏。◇ *The jumbo jet was blasted out of the sky.* 那架巨型噴氣式飛機在空中被炸成碎片。◇ *Danger! Blasting in Progress!* 危險！爆破進行中！

▸ **MAKE LOUD NOISE 發出高聲** **2** [I, T] to make a loud unpleasant noise, especially music 發出刺耳的高音，轟鳴（尤指音樂）：**~ (out)** *Music suddenly blasted out from the speakers.* 喇叭中突然響起了轟鳴的音樂。◇ **~ sth (out)** *The radio blasted out rock music at full volume.* 收音機以最大音量播放搖滾樂。

▸ **CRITICIZE 批評** **3** [T] **~ sb/sth (for sth/for doing sth)** (*informal*) to criticize sb/sth severely 嚴厲批評；猛烈抨擊：*The movie was blasted by all the critics.* 這部影片受到了所有評論家的嚴厲抨擊。

▸ **HIT/KICK/SHOOT 打；踢；擊** **4** [T] **~ sb/sth (+ adv./prep.)** (*informal*) to hit, kick or shoot sb/sth with a lot of force 狠打；猛踢；猛擊：*He blasted the ball past the goalie.* 他飛腳將球踢過了守門員。◇ *He blasted (= shot) the policeman right between the eyes.* 他對着那個警察的鼻梁開了一槍。

▸ **AIR/WATER 空氣；水** **5** [T] **~ sb/sth (+ adv./prep.)** to direct air, water, etc. at sb/sth with a lot of force 向…猛吹；（用水）向…噴射：*Police blasted the demonstrators with water cannons.* 警察用高壓水炮噴射示威者。

▸ **DESTROY WITH DISEASE, ETC. 使毀於疾病等** **6** [T, usually passive] **~ sth** to destroy sth such as a plant with disease, cold, heat, etc. 使（植物等）毀於疾病（或寒冷、酷熱等）：*Their whole crop had been blasted by a late frost.* 一場晚霜把他們的莊稼全毀了。

PHR V **,blast a'way** if a gun or sb using a gun **blasts away**, the gun fires continuously and loudly 連續高聲地射擊 **,blast 'off** (of SPACECRAFT 宇宙飛船) to leave the ground 發射升空 **SYN** **lift off, take off** ➲ related noun BLAST-OFF

■ ***exclamation*** (*informal, especially BrE*) people sometimes say **Blast!** when they are annoyed about sth（惱怒時說）該死，倒霉：*Oh blast! The car won't start.* 真該死！車子就是發動不了。

blast·ed /'blɑːstɪd; *NAmE* 'blæs-/ *adj.* [only before noun] (*informal*) used when you are very annoyed about sth（十分惱火時說）該死的，可惡的：*Make your own blasted coffee!* 煮你自己的那該死的咖啡吧！

'blast furnace *noun* a large structure like an oven in which iron ORE (= rock containing iron) is melted in order to take out the metal（煉鐵的）高爐，鼓風爐

'blast-off *noun* [U] the moment when a SPACECRAFT leaves the ground（宇宙飛船的）發射，升空

bla·tant /'bleɪtnt/ *adj.* (*disapproving*) (of actions that are considered bad 壞的行為) done in an obvious and open way without caring if people are shocked 明目張膽的；公然的 **SYN** **flagrant**：*a blatant attempt to buy votes* 公然的賄選企圖 ◇ *It was a blatant lie.* 那是個赤裸裸的謊言。▸ **bla·tant·ly** *adv.*：*a blatantly unfair decision* 明顯不公正的裁決 ◇ *He just blatantly lied about it.* 他簡直是睜着眼睛說瞎話。

blather /'blæðə(r)/ (also **bleth·er**) *verb* [I] **~ (on) (about sth)** (*informal, especially BrE*) to talk continuously about things that are silly or unimportant 喋喋不休地胡說；嘮叨 ▸ **blather** (also **blether**) *noun* [U]

blax·ploit·ation /,blæksplɔɪ'teɪʃn/ *noun* [U] the use of black people in films/movies, especially in a way which shows them in fixed ways that are different from real life 黑人利用（尤指在電影中黑人形象模式化且脫離現實）

blaze /bleɪz/ *verb, noun*

■ ***verb*** **1** [I] to burn brightly and strongly 熊熊燃燒：*A huge fire was blazing in the fireplace.* 壁爐中火燒得正旺。◇ *Within minutes the whole building was blazing.* 不消幾分鐘整個大樓便成了一片火海。◇ *He rushed back into the blazing house.* 他又返回，衝進了燃燒着的房子。**2** [I] to shine brightly 閃耀；發亮光：*The sun blazed down from a clear blue sky.* 耀眼的陽光從清澈蔚藍的天空中照射下來。◇ *The garden blazed with colour.* 花園裏姹紫嫣紅。**3** [I] **~ (with sth)** (*formal*) if sb's eyes **blaze**, they look extremely angry 怒視；（怒火）燃燒：*Her eyes were blazing with fury.* 她的雙眼燃燒着怒火。**4** (also **blazon**) [T, usually passive] **~ sth (across/all over sth)** to make news or information widely known by telling people about it in a way they are sure to notice 大肆宣揚：*The story was blazed all over the daily papers.* 那個傳聞被各家報紙炒得沸沸揚揚。**5** [I] **~ (away)** if a gun or sb using a gun **blazes**, the gun fires continuously 連續射擊：*In the distance machine guns were blazing.* 機關槍在遠處不停地射擊。

IDM **blaze a 'trail** to be the first to do or to discover sth that others follow 作開路先鋒；領先：*The department is blazing a trail in the field of laser surgery.* 這個部門正在為激光外科學領域開闢一條新路。➲ compare TRAIL-BLAZER ➲ more at GUN *n.*

PHR V **,blaze 'up** **1** to suddenly start burning very strongly（突然）熊熊燃燒起來 **2** to suddenly become very angry 突然動怒

■ ***noun*** **1** [C] (used especially in newspapers 尤用於報章) a very large fire, especially a dangerous one 烈火；火災：*Five people died in the blaze.* 火災中有五人喪生。**2** [sing.] strong bright flames in a fire 火焰：*Dry wood makes a good blaze.* 乾木柴燒得旺。**3** [sing.] **a ~ of sth** a very bright show of lights or colour; an impressive or noticeable show of sth（光或色彩等的）展現：*The gardens are a blaze of colour.* 花園裏姹紫嫣紅。◇ *a blaze of lights in the city centre* 市中心通明的燈火 ◇ *the bright blaze of the sun* 太陽的光輝 ◇ *a blaze of glory* 榮耀 ◇ *They got married in a blaze of publicity.* 他們結婚的事受到了傳媒大力宣揚。**4** [sing.] **(a) ~ of sth** a sudden show of very strong feeling（感情）迸發；發泄：*a **blaze of anger/passion/hate*** 怒火／激情／仇恨的迸發 **5** [C, usually sing.] a white mark on an animal's face 動物面部的白斑

IDM **what/where/who the 'blazes ...?** (*old-fashioned, informal*) used to emphasize that you are annoyed and surprised, to avoid using the word 'hell'（委婉語，煩惱和驚奇時說，與 hell 同義）：*What the blazes have you done?* 你到底搞的什麼名堂？ **like blazes** (*old-fashioned, informal*) very hard; very fast 猛烈地；迅速地

blazer /'bleɪzə(r)/ *noun* a jacket, not worn with matching trousers/pants, often showing the colours or BADGE of a club, school, team, etc.（常帶有俱樂部、學校、運動隊等的顏色或徽章的）夾克

blaz·ing /'bleɪzɪŋ/ *adj.* [only before noun] **1** (also **,blazing 'hot**) extremely hot 酷熱的；熾熱的：*blazing heat* 十分炎熱 ◇ *a blazing hot day* 大熱天 **2** extremely angry or full of strong emotion 極其憤怒的；感情強烈的：*She had a **blazing row** with Eddie and stormed out of the house.* 她和埃迪大吵一架後怒氣沖沖地奪門而出。

blazon /'bleɪzn/ *verb* **1** [usually passive] **~ sth (on/across/over sth)** = EMBLAZON：*He had the word 'Cool' blazoned across his chest.* 他的胸前飾有 Cool 的字樣。**2** = BLAZE (4)

bleach /bliːtʃ/ *verb, noun*

■ ***verb*** [I, T] to become white or pale by a chemical process or by the effect of light from the sun; to make sth white or pale in this way（使）變白，漂白，曬白，褪色：*bones of animals bleaching in the sun* 在陽光中變白的動物骸骨 ◇ **~ sth** *His hair **was bleached by the sun**.* 他的頭髮被太陽曬得發白。◇ *bleached cotton/paper* 漂白棉／紙 ◇ **~ sth + adj.** *She bleached her hair blonde.* 她把頭髮染成了金黃色。

■ ***noun*** [U, C] a chemical that is used to make sth become white or pale and as a DISINFECTANT (= to prevent infection from spreading) 漂白劑

bleach·ers /'bliːtʃəz; *NAmE* -tʃərz/ *noun* [pl.] (*NAmE*) rows of seats at a sports ground（運動場的）露天看台 ▸ **bleach·er** *adj.* [only before noun]：*bleacher seats* 露天看台座位

bleak /bliːk/ *adj.* (**bleak·er**, **bleak·est**) **1** (of a situation 狀況) not encouraging or giving any reason to have hope 不樂觀的；無望的；暗淡的：*a **bleak outlook/prospect*** 暗淡的前景／前途 ◇ ***The future looks bleak** for the fishing industry.* 漁業前景暗淡。◇ *The medical prognosis was bleak.* 醫療預後不良。**2** (of the weather 天氣) cold and unpleasant 陰冷的：*a bleak winter's day* 一個陰冷的冬日 **3** (of a place 地方) exposed, empty, or with no pleasant features 無遮掩的；荒涼的；索然無味的：

B

B

a bleak landscape/hillside/moor 荒蕪的景色／山坡／野地 ◇ *bleak concrete housing* 索然乏味的混凝土住宅群 ▸ **bleak·ly** *adv.*：*'There seems no hope,' she said bleakly.* "好像沒希望了。" 她黯然地說。◇ *bleakly lit corridors* 光線很暗的走廊 **bleak·ness** *noun* [U]

blear·ily /ˈblɪərəli; *NAmE* ˈblɪr-/ *adv.* with bleary eyes; in a tired way 睡眼惺忪地；困乏地：*'I was asleep,' she explained blearily.* "我在睡覺。" 她懶洋洋地解釋說。

bleary /ˈblɪəri; *NAmE* ˈblɪri/ *adj.* (of eyes 眼睛) not able to see clearly, especially because you are tired（因疲倦等）視力模糊的，看不清的：*She had bleary red eyes from lack of sleep.* 她由於缺乏睡眠而雙眼昏花，佈滿血絲。

ˌbleary-ˈeyed *adj.* with bleary eyes and seeming tired 睏倦而視線模糊的：*He appeared at breakfast bleary-eyed and with a hangover.* 他吃早餐時兩眼迷糊，宿醉未醒。

bleat /bliːt/ *verb* **1** [I] to make the sound that sheep and GOATS make 咩咩叫 **2** [I, T] **~ (on) (about sth)** | **~ that …** | **+ speech** to speak in a weak or complaining voice 以微弱的聲音說話；抱怨：*'But I've only just got here,' he bleated feebly.* "可我剛剛才到這裏呢。" 他小聲抱怨說。▸ **bleat** *noun*：*The lamb gave a faint bleat.* 羊羔輕輕地咩了一聲。 **bleat·ing** *noun* [U, C]：*the distant bleating of sheep* 遠處的羊叫聲

bleed /bliːd/ *verb* (**bled**, **bled** /bled/) **1** [I] to lose blood, especially from a wound or an injury 流血；失血：*My finger's bleeding.* 我的手指出血了。◇ *She slowly* ***bled to death.*** 她慢慢地失血死去。◇ *He was bleeding from a gash on his head.* 他頭上的傷口在出血。 **2** [T] **~ sb** (in the past 舊時) to take blood from sb as a way of treating disease 給（某人）放血 **3** [T] **~ sb (for sth)** (*informal*) to force sb to pay a lot of money over a period of time 長期榨取（某人的錢）：*My ex-wife is bleeding me for every penny I have.* 我的前妻不斷地榨取我的每一分錢。 **4** [T] **~ sth** to remove air or liquid from sth so that it works correctly 放掉氣體或水（以使某物運行正常）；抽乾 **5** [I] **~ (into sth)** to spread from one area of sth to another area 散開；滲開：*Keep the paint fairly dry so that the colours don't bleed into each other.* 塗料盡量乾一些，以免顏色相互滲透。
IDM **bleed sb ˈdry** (*disapproving*) to take away all sb's money 榨取某人所有的錢；把某人榨乾：*The big corporations are bleeding some of these small countries dry.* 一些大企業正在把這些小國家榨乾。 ➲ more at HEART

bleed·er /ˈbliːdə(r)/ *noun* (*old-fashioned, BrE, informal*) a rude way of referring to a person 吸血鬼；渾蛋

bleed·ing /ˈbliːdɪŋ/ *adj., noun*
▪ **adj.** [only before noun] (*BrE, slang*) = BLOODY[1]
▪ **noun** [U] the process of losing blood from the body 流血；失血：*Press firmly on the wound to stop the bleeding.* 用力壓住傷口止血。

ˌbleeding ˈedge *noun* [sing.] **the ~ (of sth)** (*computing* 計) technology that is so advanced that there may be problems when you use it 有潛在問題的前沿技術：*They were working at the bleeding edge of chip design.* 他們正在研究芯片設計可能發生問題的方方面面。 ➲ compare CUTTING EDGE

ˌbleeding ˈheart *noun* (*disapproving*) a person who is too kind and sympathetic towards people that other people think do not deserve kindness 過於善良的人；濫好人：*a bleeding-heart liberal* 一個心腸太軟的自由主義者

bleep /bliːp/ *noun, verb*
▪ **noun** a short high sound made by a piece of electronic equipment（電子儀器發出的）短促響亮的聲音，嗶嗶聲
▪ **verb 1** [I] to make a short high electronic sound 發出短促響亮的聲音；發嗶嗶聲：*The microwave will bleep when your meal is ready.* 烹調結束時，微波爐會發出嗶嗶的聲音。 **2** (*BrE*) (*NAmE* **beep**) [T] **~ sb** to call sb on their bleeper 打（某人）的傳呼機；給（某人）打傳呼：*Please bleep the doctor on duty immediately.* 請立即打值班醫生的傳呼機。 **3** [T] **~ sth (out)** to broadcast a short high electronic sound in place of a SWEAR WORD on a television or radio show, so that people will not be offended（電視或廣播節目中）用嗶嗶聲覆蓋（髒話）

bleep·er /ˈbliːpə(r)/ (*NAmE* **beep·er**) *noun* a small electronic device that you carry around with you and that lets you know when sb is trying to contact you, by making a sound 無線電傳呼機；BP 機

blem·ish /ˈblemɪʃ/ *noun, verb*
▪ **noun** a mark on the skin or on an object that spoils it and makes it look less beautiful or perfect 斑點；疤痕；瑕疵：*make-up to cover blemishes* 遮蓋霜 ◇ (*figurative*) *His reputation is without a blemish.* 他的名譽可說是白璧無瑕。
▪ **verb** [usually passive] **~ sth** (*formal*) to spoil sth that is beautiful or perfect in all other ways 破壞…的完美；玷污

blench /blentʃ/ *verb* [I] (*BrE, formal*) to react to sth in a way that shows you are frightened（因驚嚇而）退縮；驚悸

blend /blend/ *verb, noun*
▪ **verb 1** [T] to mix two or more substances together 使混合；摻和：**~ A with B** *Blend the flour with the milk to make a smooth paste.* 把麵粉和牛奶調成均勻的麵糊。◇ **~ A and B (together)** ***Blend together*** *the eggs, sugar and flour.* 把雞蛋、糖和麵粉摻到一起。 ➲ SYNONYMS at MIX **2** [I] to form a mixture with sth（和某物）混合；融合：**~ with sth** *Oil does not blend with water.* 油不融於水。◇ **~ (together)** *Oil and water do not blend.* 油與水不相融。 **3** [I, T] to combine with sth in an attractive or effective way; to combine sth in this way（使）調和，協調，融合：**~ (sth) (together)** *The old and new buildings blend together perfectly.* 新舊建築物相映成趣。◇ **~ sth (and/with sth)** *Their music blends traditional and modern styles.* 他們的音樂融合了傳統和現代風格。 **4** [T, usually passive] **~ sth** to produce sth by mixing different types together 調製；配製：***blended whisky/tea*** 調配的威士忌；混合茶葉 IDM see WOODWORK
PHR V **ˌblend ˈin (with sth/sb)** if sth **blends in**, it is similar to its surroundings or matches its surroundings（與環境）和諧，協調：*Choose curtains that blend in with your decor.* 挑選和裝飾格調一致的窗簾。◇ *The thieves soon blended in with the crowd and got away.* 竊賊很快混入人群逃跑了。 **ˌblend sth↔ˈin** (in cooking 烹飪) to add another substance and mix it in with the others 調入：*Beat the butter and sugar; then blend in the egg.* 把黃油和糖打好，然後調入雞蛋。 **ˌblend ˈinto sth** to look so similar to the background that it is difficult for you to see it separately 融合到（背景）中：*He blended into the crowd.* 他消失在人群中。
▪ **noun 1** a mixture of different types of the same thing（同一事物中不同類型的）混合品，混合物：*a blend of tea* 混合茶葉 **2** [usually sing.] a pleasant or useful combination of different things（不同事物的）和諧結合，融合：*a blend of youth and experience* 年輕而且有經驗

ˌblended ˈfamily *noun* (*especially NAmE*) a family that consists of two people and their children from their own relationship and from previous ones 混合家庭（成員包括夫婦、其子女及其各自過去關係中所生的子女）

ˌblended ˈlearning *noun* [U] a way of studying a subject that combines being taught in class with the use of different technologies, including learning over the Internet 混合式學習（將課堂學習與互聯網學習等技術相結合）：*Blended learning is a cost-effective way of delivering training.* 混合式學習是一種划算的培訓方式。

blend·er /ˈblendə(r)/ (*BrE* also **li·quid·izer**) *noun* an electric machine for mixing soft food or liquid（電動）食物攪拌器 ➲ VISUAL VOCAB page V25

bless /bles/ *verb, exclamation*
▪ **verb** (**blessed**, **blessed** /blest/) **1 ~ sb/sth** to ask God to protect sb/sth 求上帝降福；祝福：*They brought the children to Jesus and he blessed them.* 他們把孩子帶到耶穌跟前，耶穌祝福了他們。◇ *God bless you!* 願上帝保祐你！ **2 ~ sth** to make sth holy by saying a prayer over it 祝聖：*The priest blessed the bread and wine.* 神父祝聖了麵餅和葡萄酒。 **3 ~ sb/sth** (*formal*) to call God holy; to praise God 稱頌上帝；讚美上帝：*We bless your holy name, O Lord.* 主啊，我們頌揚您的聖名。 **4 ~ sb/sth** (*old-fashioned, informal*) used to express surprise（表示驚奇）：*Bless my soul! Here comes Bill!* 我的天哪！比爾

來了！◇ *'Where's Joe?' 'I'm blessed if I know!'* (= I don't know) "喬在哪兒？" "我要是知道才怪呢！"

IDM be blessed with sth/sb to have sth good such as ability, great happiness, etc. 賦有（能力等）；享有（幸福等）：*She's blessed with excellent health.* 她身體很好，是一種福氣。◇ *We're blessed with five lovely grandchildren.* 我們很有福氣，有五個可愛的孫子孫女。**'bless you** said to sb after they have SNEEZED（別人打噴嚏時說）**'bless you, her, him, etc.** (*informal*) used to show that you are pleased with sb, especially because of sth they have done（表示滿意或感謝）：*Sarah, bless her, had made a cup of tea.* 真得感謝薩拉，她給沏了一杯茶。➲ more at GOD

■ ***exclamation*** (*BrE*, sometimes *humorous*) used to show affection towards sb because of sth they have done（對他人所做之事表示喜愛）哎呀，太好啦，太謝謝了：*'He bought us all a present.' 'Oh, bless!'* "他給我們都買了一件禮物。" "啊，太好了！"

blessed /ˈblesɪd/ *adj.* **1 Blessed** holy 神聖的：*the Blessed Virgin Mary* 榮福童貞瑪利亞 **2** (in religious language) lucky（宗教用語）有福的：*Blessed are the poor.* 神貧的人是有福的。**3** [only before noun] enjoyable in a way that gives you a sense of peace or a feeling of freedom from anxiety or pain 愉快安寧的；無憂無慮的：*a moment of blessed calm* 片刻愉快的寧靜 **4** [only before noun] (*old-fashioned, informal*) used to express mild anger（表示惱怒）：*I can't see a blessed thing without my glasses.* 我不戴眼鏡根本看不清什麼東西。▸ **bless·ed·ly** *adv.*：*The kitchen was warm and blessedly familiar.* 廚房又温暖又親切温馨。**bless·ed·ness** /ˈblesɪdnəs/ *noun* [U]

bless·ing /ˈblesɪŋ/ *noun* **1** [usually sing.] God's help and protection, or a prayer asking for this 上帝的恩寵；祝福；祝頌：*to pray for God's blessing* 祈求上帝降福◇ *The bishop said the blessing.* 主教祝福（會眾）。➲ COLLOCATIONS at RELIGION **2** [usually sing.] approval of or permission for sth 贊同；許可：*The government **gave its blessing** to the new plans.* 政府已批准這些新計劃。◇ *He went **with** his parents' **blessing**.* 他是得到父母的同意去的。**3** something that is good or helpful 好事；有益之事：*Lack of traffic is one of the blessings of country life.* 往來車輛少是鄉村生活的一大好處。◇ ***It's a blessing** that nobody was in the house at the time.* 幸好當時屋子裏沒人。➲ see also MIXED BLESSING

IDM a blessing in dis'guise something that seems to be a problem at first, but that has good results in the end 因禍得福；禍中有福 ➲ more at COUNT *v.*

blether /ˈbleðə(r)/ *verb, noun* = BLATHER

blew *past tense of* BLOW

blight /blaɪt/ *verb, noun*

■ ***verb* ~ sth** to spoil or damage sth, especially by causing a lot of problems 損害；妨害；貽害：*His career has been blighted by injuries.* 他的事業不斷受到傷病的困擾。◇ *an area blighted by unemployment* 飽受失業之苦的地區

■ ***noun* 1** [U, C] any disease that kills plants, especially crops（農作物等的）枯萎病，疫病：*potato blight* 馬鈴薯枯萎病 **2** [sing., U] **~ (on sb/sth)** something that has a bad effect on a situation, a person's life or the environment（對局勢、生活或環境）有害的事物，不利因素：*His death **cast a blight on** the whole of that year.* 他的死使那一整年都處在陰影之中。◇ ***urban blight*** (= areas in a city that are ugly or not cared for well) 城市裏環境髒、亂、差的地區

blight·er /ˈblaɪtə(r)/ *noun* (*old-fashioned, BrE, informal*) a way of referring to a person (usually a man) that you either find unpleasant or that you feel some sympathy for 討厭的（或可憐的）傢伙（通常指男性）

Blighty /ˈblaɪti/ *noun* [U] (*BrE*) a name for Britain or England, used especially by soldiers in the First and Second World Wars, and now sometimes used in a humorous way 英國，英格蘭（第一次和第二次世界大戰期間英國士兵用語，現含詼諧意味）

bli·mey /ˈblaɪmi/ (also **,cor 'bli·mey**) *exclamation* (*BrE, informal, slang*) used to express surprise or anger（表示驚奇或生氣）：*Blimey, it's hot today.* 哎呀，今天真熱。

blimp /blɪmp/ *noun* **1** (*especially NAmE*) a small AIRSHIP (= an aircraft without wings) 軟式飛艇 **2** (also **,Colonel 'Blimp**) (*old-fashioned, BrE, disapproving*) an older person, especially an old army officer, with very old-fashioned political opinions 政見保守的老人（尤指年長的軍官）▸ **blimp·ish** *adj.*

Which Word? 詞語辨析

blind / blindly

■ There are two adverbs that come from the adjective **blind**. **Blindly** means 'not being able to see what you are doing' or 'not thinking about something'. The adverb **blind** is mainly used in the context of flying and means 'without being able to see', 'using instruments only'. 形容詞 blind 有兩個副詞。blindly 表示沒有看清楚或盲目，副詞 blind 主要用於指飛行時的黑蒙、單憑儀器導航。

blind 🔑 /blaɪnd/ *adj., verb, noun, adv.*

■ ***adj.*** (**blind·er, blind·est**) **1** 🔑 not able to see 瞎的；失明的：*Doctors think he will **go blind**.* 醫生們認為他會失明。◇ *blind and partially sighted people* 盲人和弱視者 ◇ *One of her parents is blind.* 她的父母有一個是盲人。**2 the blind** *noun* [pl.] people who are blind 盲人：*recorded books for the blind* 為盲人製作的錄音書◇ *guide dogs for the blind* 導盲犬 **3 ~ (to sth)** not noticing or realizing sth（對某事）視而不見的，未察覺的：*She is blind to her husband's faults.* 她對丈夫的過錯毫無察覺。◇ *I must have been blind not to realize the danger we were in.* 當時我一定是眼瞎了，竟然沒有意識到我們所處的危險。**4** [usually before noun] (of strong feelings 強烈的感覺) seeming to be unreasonable, and accepted without question; seeming to be out of control 盲目接受的；不能自制的：***blind faith/obedience*** 盲目的信念；盲從◇ *It was a moment of **blind panic**.* 這是一陣莫名的驚慌。**5** [usually before noun] (of a situation or an event 局勢或事情) that cannot be controlled by reason 無理性的：*blind chance* 盲目的偶然性◇ *the blind force of nature* 無法抵擋的自然力 **6** that a driver in a car cannot see, or cannot see around 汽車司機看不見的；隱蔽的：*a blind driveway* 視線盲區內的車道◇ *a **blind bend/corner*** 隱蔽的彎道／拐角 ▸ **blind·ness** *noun* [U]：***total/temporary/partial blindness*** 全盲；暫時性失明；半盲 ➲ see also BLINDLY

IDM (as) blind as a 'bat (*humorous*) not able to see well 視力不佳 **the blind leading the 'blind** a situation in which people with almost no experience or knowledge give advice to others who also have no experience or knowledge 盲人教盲人；盲人引導瞎子 **not a blind bit/the blindest bit of …** (*BrE, informal*) not any 絲毫沒有：*He didn't **take a blind bit of notice** of me* (= he ignored me). 他壓根兒沒理睬我。◇ *It won't **make the blindest bit of difference*** (= it will make no difference at all). 那根本不會有什麼分別的。**turn a blind 'eye (to sth)** to pretend not to notice sth bad that is happening, so you do not have to do anything about it（對某事）佯裝不見，睜一隻眼閉一隻眼 ➲ more at LOVE *n.*

■ ***verb* 1 ~ sb** to permanently destroy sb's ability to see 使變瞎；使失明：*She was blinded in the explosion.* 她在那場爆炸中雙目失明了。**2 ~ sb/sth** to make it difficult for sb to see for a short time 使眼花；使目眩：*When she went outside she was temporarily blinded by the sun.* 走出戶外時，她一時被陽光照得眼睛昏花。**3 ~ sb (to sth)** to make sb no longer able to think clearly or behave in a sensible way 使思維混沌；使失去判斷力：*His sense of loyalty blinded him to the truth.* 他的赤誠忠心使他看不清真相。

IDM blind sb with science to confuse sb by using technical or complicated language that they do not understand 用術語（或深奧的言語）使某人困惑 ➲ more at EFF

■ ***noun* 1** (*NAmE* also **shade, 'window shade**) [C] a covering for a window, especially one made of a roll of cloth that is fixed at the top of the window and can be pulled up and down 窗簾；（尤指）捲簾 ➲ see also VENETIAN BLIND **2** [sing.] something people say or do to hide the truth about sth in order to trick other people 用以欺騙人的言行；藉口；託辭；幌子

■ ***adv.*** (in connection with flying 有關飛行) without being able to see; using instruments only 視線受阻地；僅靠儀表操縱地；盲目地

IDM **blind 'drunk** extremely drunk 爛醉如泥 ➲ more at ROB, SWEAR

ˌblind 'alley *noun* a way of doing sth that seems useful at first, but does not produce useful results, like following a path that suddenly stops 行不通的方法；死胡同

ˌblind 'date *noun* a meeting between two people who have not met each other before. The meeting is sometimes organized by their friends because they want them to develop a romantic relationship. （由第三方安排的）男女初次約會

blind·er /ˈblaɪndə(r)/ *noun* **1** [C, usually sing.] (*BrE, informal*) something which is excellent, especially in sport （尤指體育運動中的）出色之舉，精彩表現：*a blinder of a game* 比賽中的精彩表現 **2** **blinders** [pl.] (*NAmE*) = BLINKERS

blind·fold /ˈblaɪndfəʊld; *NAmE* -foʊld/ *noun, verb, adj., adv.*

■ ***noun*** something that is put over sb's eyes so they cannot see 障眼物；眼罩

■ ***verb*** **~ sb** to cover sb's eyes with a piece of cloth or other covering so that they cannot see （用布等）蒙住眼睛：*The hostages were tied up and blindfolded.* 人質被捆綁起來並蒙上了眼睛。

■ ***adj., adv.*** (*BrE*) (also **blind·fold·ed** *BrE, NAmE*) with the eyes covered 被蒙住眼睛：*The reporter was taken blindfold to a secret location.* 那位記者被蒙着眼睛帶到了一處秘密的地方。◇ *I knew the way home blindfold* (= because it was so familiar). 我蒙着眼都能走到家。◇ *I could do that blindfold* (= very easily, with no problems). 我做這事易如反掌。

blind·ing /ˈblaɪndɪŋ/ *adj.* [usually before noun] **1** very bright; so strong that you cannot see 雪亮的；刺眼的；使人視線模糊的：*a blinding flash of light* 令人目眩的閃光 ◇ (*figurative*) *a blinding* (= very bad) *headache* 使人兩眼昏花的頭痛 **2** (*BrE, informal*) very good or enjoyable 絕妙的；精彩的

blind·ing·ly /ˈblaɪndɪŋli/ *adv.* very; extremely 很；極其：*The reason is* ***blindingly obvious****.* 原因十分明顯。◇ *The latest computers can work at a* ***blindingly fast*** *speed.* 最新的計算機能達到極高的運行速度。

blind·ly /ˈblaɪndli/ *adv.* **1** without being able to see what you are doing 摸黑地；在黑暗中：*She groped blindly for the light switch in the dark room.* 她在黑暗的房間裏摸索電燈開關。**2** without thinking about what you are doing 不加思考地；盲目地：*He wanted to decide for himself instead of blindly following his parents' advice.* 他想自己拿主意，而不是盲目聽從他父母的意見。➲ note at BLIND

ˌblind man's 'buff (*BrE*) (*NAmE* **ˌblind man's 'bluff**) *noun* [U] a children's game in which a player whose eyes are covered with a piece of cloth tries to catch and identify the other players 捉迷藏（遊戲）

'blind side *noun* a direction in which sb cannot see very much, especially approaching danger （尤指接近危險時）看不清的一側，未加防備的一側

blind·side /ˈblaɪndsaɪd/ *verb* (*NAmE*) **1** **~ sb** to attack sb from the direction where they cannot see you coming 攻其不備；出其不意地襲擊 **2** [usually passive] **~ sb** to give sb an unpleasant surprise 使遭受意外的打擊：*Just when it seemed life was going well, she was blindsided by a devastating illness.* 正當生活似乎一帆風順的時候，她出人意料地得了一場重病。

'blind spot *noun* **1** an area that sb cannot see, especially an area of the road when they are driving a car 視線盲區（尤指車輛駕駛員看不見的路段）**2** if sb has a **blind spot** about sth, they ignore it or they are unwilling or unable to understand it 無視；沒有認識 **3** the part of the RETINA in the eye that is not sensitive to light（視網膜的）盲點 **4** an area where a radio signal cannot be received（無線電）靜區

ˌblind 'test *noun* a way of deciding which product out of a number of competing products is the best or most popular, or how a new product compares with others. People are asked to try the different products and to say which ones they prefer, but they are not told the names of the products. 盲測（比較產品質量或受歡迎程度，參加者不知道產品名稱）

ˌblind 'trust *noun* a type of TRUST that takes care of sb's investments, without the person knowing how their money is being invested. It is used by politicians, for example, so that their private business does not influence their political decisions. 盲目信託，全權信託，保密委託（信託人對投資方式不知情，如從政者為避免私人業務影響其政策決定而採用）

bling /blɪŋ/ (also **ˌbling-'bling**) *noun* [U] (*informal*) expensive shiny jewellery and bright fashionable clothes worn in order to attract attention to yourself 閃亮風潮的穿戴 ▸ **bling** (also **ˌbling-'bling**) *adj.*：*women with big hair and bling jewellery* 梳着爆炸頭、穿金戴銀的婦女 ◇ *bling culture/lifestyles* 穿戴奢華的文化／生活方式

blini /ˈblɪni; ˈbliːni/ (also **blinis**) *noun* [pl.] (*sing.* **blin**) small Russian PANCAKES (= thin flat round cakes), served with SOUR CREAM 俄式薄煎餅，蕎麥薄烤餅（佐以酸奶油）

blink /blɪŋk/ *verb, noun*

■ ***verb*** **1** [I, T] **~ (sth)** when you **blink** or **blink your eyes** or **your eyes blink**, you shut and open your eyes quickly 眨眼睛：*He blinked in the bright sunlight.* 他在強烈的陽光下直眨眼睛。◇ *I'll be back* ***before you can blink*** (= very quickly). 我眨眼工夫就回來。◇ *When I told him the news he* ***didn't even blink*** (= showed no surprise at all). 我把那個消息告訴他時，他眼都沒眨一下。➲ compare WINK *v.* (1) **2** [I] to shine with an unsteady light; to flash on and off 閃爍：*Suddenly a warning light blinked.* 突然有一盞警告燈開始閃亮。

PHR V **ˌblink sth↔a'way/'back** to try to control tears or clear your eyes by blinking 眨眼控制淚水（或擠掉髒東西）：*She bravely blinked back her tears.* 她勇敢地抑制住了淚水。

■ ***noun*** [usually sing.] the act of shutting and opening your eyes very quickly 眨眼睛

IDM **in the blink of an 'eye** very quickly; in a short time 眨眼的工夫；很快 **on the 'blink** (*informal*) (of a machine 機器) no longer working correctly 失靈；出毛病

blink·er /ˈblɪŋkə(r)/ *noun* **1** [C] (*informal*) = INDICATOR (3), TURN SIGNAL **2** **blinkers** (*NAmE* also **blind·ers**) [pl.] pieces of leather that are placed at the side of a horse's eyes to stop it from looking sideways 馬眼罩：(*figurative*) *We need to have a fresh look at the plan, without blinkers* (= we need to consider every aspect of it). 我們應該用新的眼光全面地考慮這個計劃。

blink·ered /ˈblɪŋkəd; *NAmE* -kərd/ *adj.* (*disapproving*) not aware of every aspect of a situation; not willing to accept different ideas about sth 目光狹窄的；心胸隘窄的 **SYN** **narrow-minded**：*a* ***blinkered policy/attitude/approach*** 褊狹的政策／態度／方法

blink·ing /ˈblɪŋkɪŋ/ *adj., adv.* (*BrE, old-fashioned, informal*) a mild swear word that some people use when they are annoyed, to avoid saying 'bloody'（委婉語，與 bloody 同義）討厭，可惡：*Shut the blinking door!* 關上那扇該死的門！

blip /blɪp/ *noun* **1** a change in a process or situation, usually when it gets worse for a short time before it gets better; a temporary problem 變故；暫時性問題：*a temporary blip* 暫時的麻煩 **2** a short high sound made by an electronic device（電子裝置發出的）短促尖聲 **3** a small flashing point of light on a RADAR screen, representing an object（雷達屏幕上代表物體的）光點

bliss /blɪs/ *noun, verb*

■ ***noun*** [U] extreme happiness 極樂：***married/wedded/domestic bliss*** 婚後的／家庭的幸福 ◇ *My idea of bliss is a month in the Bahamas.* 我理想中的極樂是在巴哈馬群島度假一個月。◇ *Swimming on a hot day is* ***sheer bliss****.* 熱天游泳是天大的樂事。**IDM** see IGNORANCE

B

■ *verb*
PHR V ˌ**bliss ˈout** (also **be ˌblissed ˈout**) (*especially BrE*) to reach a state of perfect happiness, when you are not aware of anything else 欣喜若狂；樂不可支

bliss·ful /ˈblɪsfl/ *adj.* extremely happy; showing happiness 極樂的；幸福的： *We spent three blissful weeks away from work.* 我們無憂無慮地度了三個星期的假。◇ *a blissful smile* 欣喜的笑容 ◇ *We preferred to remain in* ***blissful ignorance*** *of* (= not to know) *what was going on.* 我們樂得對正在發生的事情一無所知。➲ SYNONYMS at HAPPY ▸ **bliss·ful·ly** /-fəli/ *adv.*： *blissfully happy* 極其幸福 ◇ ***blissfully ignorant/unaware*** 樂得無知／不知情

ˈ**B-list** *adj.* [usually before noun] used to describe the group of people who are considered to be fairly famous, successful or important, but not as much as the A-LIST people 第二等的；比較出名（或成功、重要）的： *a TV chat show full of* ***B-list celebrities*** 由眾多二流人物參加的電視訪談節目

blis·ter /ˈblɪstə(r)/ *noun, verb*
■ *noun* **1** a swelling on the surface of the skin that is filled with liquid and is caused, for example, by rubbing or burning（皮膚上摩擦或燙起等的）水疱，疱 ➲ see also FEVER BLISTER **2** a similar swelling, filled with air or liquid, on metal, painted wood or another surface（金屬、油漆過的木頭或其他表面上的）泡，氣泡，水泡
■ *verb* **1** [I, T] to form blisters; to make sth form blisters（使）起水疱，起疱： *His skin was beginning to blister.* 他的皮膚開始起疱。◇ **~ sth** *Her face had been blistered by the sun.* 她的臉讓太陽曬起水疱了。 **2** [I, T] **~ (sth)** when a surface **blisters** or sth **blisters** it, it swells and cracks（使表皮等）漲破，爆裂 **3** [T] **~ sb** (*NAmE*) to criticize sb strongly 猛烈抨擊；嚴厲批評 ▸ **blis·tered** *adj.*： *cracked and blistered skin* 開裂起疱的皮膚 ◇ *blistered paintwork* 起泡的漆面

blis·ter·ing /ˈblɪstərɪŋ/ *adj.* [usually before noun] **1** (describing actions in sport) done very fast or with great energy（描述體育動作）迅速的，勁頭十足的： *The runners set off at a blistering pace.* 賽跑運動員如脫韁野馬般起跑了。 **2** extremely hot in a way that is uncomfortable 酷熱的 SYN **baking**： *a blistering July day* 七月的一個大熱天 ◇ *blistering heat* 酷熱 **3** very critical 言辭激烈的；尖刻的： *a blistering attack* 激烈的抨擊 ▸ **blis·ter·ing·ly** *adv.*

ˈ**blister pack** (also ˈ**bubble pack**) *noun* a pack in which small goods, such as tablets, are sold, with each individual item in its own separate plastic or FOIL section on a piece of card（藥片等的）吸塑包裝 ➲ VISUAL VOCAB page V33

blithe /blaɪð/ *adj.* [usually before noun] **1** (*disapproving*) showing you do not care or are not anxious about what you are doing 不在意的；漫不經心的： *He drove with blithe disregard for the rules of the road.* 他開車時全然不顧交通法規。 **2** (*literary*) happy; not anxious 快樂的；無憂無慮的： *a blithe and carefree girl* 快樂無憂的女孩 ▸ **blithe·ly** *adv.*： *He was blithely unaware of the trouble he'd caused.* 他漫不經心，絲毫沒有察覺他惹的麻煩。◇ *'It'll be easy,' she said blithely.* "那很容易。" 她不在乎地說。

blith·er·ing /ˈblɪðərɪŋ/ *adj.* [only before noun] (*old-fashioned, BrE, informal*) complete 完全的；全部的： *He was a* ***blithering idiot.*** 他是個十足的傻瓜。

BLitt (*NAmE* **B.Litt**) /ˌbiː ˈlɪt/ *noun* the abbreviation for 'Bachelor of Letters' or 'Bachelor of Literature' (a university degree in an ARTS subject that may be a first or second degree) 文學學士（全寫為 Bachelor of Letters 或 Bachelor of Literature，大學文科的初級或二級學位）

blitz /blɪts/ *noun, verb*
■ *noun* **1** [C, usually sing.] something which is done with a lot of energy 集中力量的行動；閃擊式行動： *an* ***advertising/a media blitz*** (= a lot of information about sth on television, in newspapers, etc.) 集中火力的廣告／媒體宣傳 **2** [C, usually sing.] a sudden attack 突襲；閃電戰： *Five shops were damaged in a firebomb blitz.* 在一次燃燒彈襲擊中有五家店鋪被燒燬。 **~ on sth** (*figurative*) *a blitz on passengers who avoid paying fares* 對逃票乘客的突襲檢查 ◇ (*figurative*) *I've had a blitz on the house* (= cleaned it very thoroughly). 我徹底打掃了房子。 **3 the Blitz** [sing.] the German air attacks on the United Kingdom in 1940–41 * 1940 至 1941 年德國對英國的空襲
■ *verb* **~ sth** to attack or damage a city by dropping a large number of bombs on it in a short time 用閃電戰空襲（或毀壞）

blitz·krieg /ˈblɪtskriːɡ/ *noun* (from *German*) a sudden military attack intended to win a quick victory 閃電戰；閃擊戰

bliz·zard /ˈblɪzəd; *NAmE* -zərd/ *noun* **1** a SNOWSTORM with very strong winds 暴風雪；雪暴： *blizzard conditions* 暴風雪天氣 ◇ *a* ***raging/howling blizzard*** 猛烈的／怒吼着的暴風雪 ➲ COLLOCATIONS at WEATHER **2** a large quantity of things that may seem to be attacking you 大批侵擾性的事物；大量的負擔： *a blizzard of documents* 一大堆棘手的文件

bloat /bləʊt; *NAmE* bloʊt/ *verb* [T, I] **~ sth** to swell or make sth swell, especially in an unpleasant way（使）膨脹，腫脹： *Her features had been bloated by years of drinking.* 她酗酒多年，已變得面部浮腫。

bloat·ed /ˈbləʊtɪd; *NAmE* ˈbloʊ-/ *adj.* **1** full of liquid or gas and therefore bigger than normal, in a way that is unpleasant 膨脹的；腫脹的；臃腫的： *a bloated body floating in the canal* 運河裏一具發脹的浮屍 ◇ (*figurative*) *a bloated organization* (= with too many people in it) 臃腫的機構 **2** full of food and feeling uncomfortable 飲食過度的；胃脹的： *I felt bloated after the huge meal they'd served.* 吃過他們提供的大餐後，我覺得肚子脹得很。

bloat·er /ˈbləʊtə(r); *NAmE* ˈbloʊ-/ *noun* (*BrE*) a HERRING (a type of fish) that has been left in salt water and then smoked 醃熏鯡魚

blob /blɒb; *NAmE* blɑːb/ *noun* a small amount or drop of sth, especially a liquid; a small area of colour（尤指液體的）一點，一滴；（顏色的）一小片，斑點： *a blob of ink* 一滴墨水 ◇ *a pink blob* 粉紅色斑點

bloc /blɒk; *NAmE* blɑːk/ *noun* a group of countries that work closely together because they have similar political interests（政治利益一致的）國家集團 ➲ COLLOCATIONS at INTERNATIONAL ➲ see also EN BLOC

block 0 /blɒk; *NAmE* blɑːk/ *noun, verb*
■ *noun*
▸ SOLID MATERIAL 固體 **1** 0 [C] a large piece of a solid material that is square in shape and usually has flat sides（方形平面）大塊；立方體： *a block of ice/concrete/stone* 一方冰／混凝土／石頭 ◇ *a chopping block* (= for cutting food on) 砧板 ➲ see also BREEZE BLOCK, BUILDING BLOCK, CINDER BLOCK
▸ BUILDING 建築 **2** 0 [C] (*BrE*) a tall building that contains flats or offices; buildings that form part of a school, hospital, etc. which are used for a particular purpose（公寓、辦公、教學、醫院等）大樓；（成組建築中的）一棟樓房： *a tower block* 高層建築 ◇ *a block of flats* 公寓大樓 ◇ *an office block* 辦公大樓 ◇ *the university's science block* 這所大學的理科大樓 ➲ VISUAL VOCAB page V16 ➲ SYNONYMS at BUILDING
▸ STREETS 街道 **3** 0 [C] a group of buildings with streets on all sides 四面臨街的一方塊樓群；街區： *She took the dog for a walk around the block.* 她帶着狗繞街區散步。 **4** 0 [C] (*NAmE*) the length of one side of a piece of land or group of buildings, from the place where one street crosses it to the next（兩條街道之間的）一段街區： *His apartment is three blocks away from the police station.* 他住在和警察局相隔三個街區的公寓裏。
▸ AREA OF LAND 一片土地 **5** [C] (*especially NAmE*) a large area of land 一大片土地 **6** [C] (*AustralE*) an area of land for building a house on 房基地；宅基地
▸ AMOUNT 數量 **7** [C] a quantity of sth or an amount of time that is considered as a single unit（東西的）一批，一組；（時間的）一段： *a block of shares* 一大宗股份 ◇ *a block of text in a document* 文件中的一段文字 ◇ (*BrE*) *The theatre gives discounts for* ***block bookings*** (= a large number of tickets bought at the same time). 該劇院給團體票打折。◇ *The three-hour class is divided into four*

B

blocks of 45 minutes each. 三小時的課分成四節，每節45分鐘。

▸ THAT STOPS PROGRESS 形成阻礙 **8** [C, usually sing.] something that makes movement or progress difficult or impossible 障礙物；阻礙；妨害 SYN **obstacle**: *Lack of training acts as a block to progress in a career.* 缺乏訓練會妨礙事業的發展。 ➲ see also ROADBLOCK, STUMBLING BLOCK, WRITER'S BLOCK

▸ IN SPORT 體育運動 **9** [C] a movement that stops another player from going forward 阻擋；攔截 **10 the blocks** [pl.] = STARTING BLOCKS

▸ FOR PUNISHMENT 刑罰 **11 the block** [sing.] (in the past) the piece of wood on which a person's head was cut off as a punishment（舊時斬首用的）墊頭木

IDM **go on the 'block** to be sold, especially at an AUCTION (= a sale in which items are sold to the person who offers the most money) 被拿去賣；推上拍賣場 **have been around the 'block (a few times)** (*informal*) to have a lot of experience 經驗豐富；見多識廣 **put/lay your head/neck on the block** to risk losing your job, damaging your reputation, etc. by doing or saying sth 冒（失業、損失名譽等）的險 ➲ more at CHIP *n.*, KNOCK *v.*, NEW

■ *verb* **1** ~ sth to stop sth from moving or flowing through a pipe, a passage, a road, etc. by putting sth in it or across it 堵塞；阻塞：*After today's heavy snow, many roads are still blocked.* 今天下過大雪，很多道路仍然堵塞。◇ *a blocked sink* 堵塞了的洗滌槽 **2** ~ **the/sb's way, exit, view, etc.** to stop sb from going somewhere or seeing sth by standing in front of them or in their way 堵住（某人的路等）；擋住（某人的視線等）：*One of the guards moved to block her path.* 一名守衛走過去擋住她的路。◇ *An ugly new building blocked the view from the window.* 一座難看的大樓把窗外的景物遮住了。**3** ~ **sth** to prevent sth from happening, developing or making progress 妨礙；阻礙：*The proposed merger has been blocked by the government.* 建議中的合併計劃遭到了政府的阻力。**4** ~ **sth** to stop a ball, blow, etc. from reaching somewhere by moving in front of it 攔截，擋住（球、打擊等）：*His shot was blocked by the goalie.* 他的射門被守門員攔住了。

PHR V ˌ**block sb/sth↔'in** to prevent a car from being able to be driven away by parking too close to it（緊挨着停靠車輛）把另一輛車堵住 ˌ**block sth↔'in** to draw or paint sth roughly, without showing any detail 畫（某物）的草圖：*I have blocked in the shapes of the larger buildings.* 我勾出了較大型建築的輪廓。ˌ**block sth↔'off** to close a road or an opening by placing a barrier at one end or in front of it（用路障）封鎖，堵住 ˌ**block sth↔'out 1** to stop light or noise from coming in 擋住，遮住（光線或聲音）：*Black clouds blocked out the sun.* 烏雲遮住了太陽。**2** to stop yourself from thinking about or remembering sth unpleasant 忘掉，抹去（不愉快的事）：*Over the years she had tried to block out that part of her life.* 多年來她努力想把她生命中的那一段經歷從記憶中抹去。ˌ**block sth↔'up** to completely fill a hole or an opening and so prevent anything from passing through it 塞住，封住（孔、洞）：*One door had been blocked up.* 一扇門被封死了。◇ *My nose is blocked up.* 我的鼻子塞了。

block·ade /blɒˈkeɪd; *NAmE* blɑːˈk-/ *noun, verb*

■ *noun* **1** the action of surrounding or closing a place, especially a port, in order to stop people or goods from coming in or out（尤指對港口的）包圍，封鎖：*a naval blockade* 海上封鎖 ◇ *to **impose/lift a blockade*** 實行／解除封鎖 ◇ *an economic blockade* (= stopping goods from entering or leaving a country) 經濟封鎖 **2** a barrier that stops people or vehicles from entering or leaving a place 障礙物；屏障：*The police set up blockades on highways leading out of the city.* 警察在出城的公路上設了路障。

■ *verb* ~ **sth** to surround a place, especially a port, in order to stop people or goods from coming in or out 包圍，封鎖（尤指港口）

block·age /ˈblɒkɪdʒ; *NAmE* ˈblɑːk-/ *noun* **1** a thing that blocks flow or movement, for example of a liquid in a narrow place 造成阻塞的東西；阻塞物 SYN **obstruction**: *a blockage in an artery/a pipe/a drain* 動脈／管道／排水溝堵塞物 **2** the state of being blocked 堵塞；阻塞：*to **cause/clear the blockage*** 引起／排除阻塞

block and tackle 滑輪組

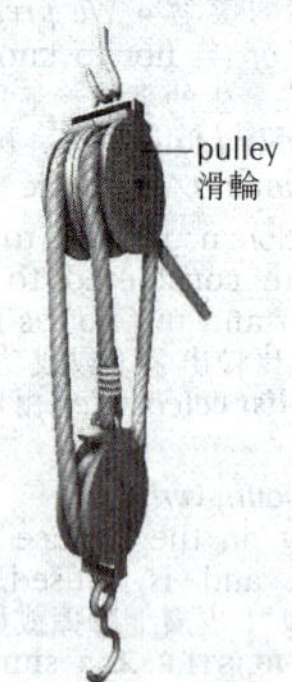

ˌ**block and 'tackle** *noun* [sing.] a piece of equipment for lifting heavy objects, which works by a system of ropes and PULLEYS (= small wheels around which the ropes are stretched) 滑輪組；滑車組

block·bust·er /ˈblɒkbʌstə(r); *NAmE* ˈblɑːk-/ *noun* (*informal*) something very successful, especially a very successful book or film/movie 一鳴驚人的事物；（尤指）非常成功的書（或電影）：*a Hollywood blockbuster* 一部好萊塢大片 ▸ **block·bust·ing** *adj.*: *a blockbusting performance* 引起轟動的演出

ˌ**block 'capitals** (also ˌ**block 'letters**) *noun* [pl.] separate capital letters 正楷大寫字母：*Please fill out the form in block capitals.* 請用正楷大寫字母填寫表格。

block·head /ˈblɒkhed; *NAmE* ˈblɑːk-/ *noun* (*informal*) a very stupid person 愚蠢的人；傻瓜

block·house /ˈblɒkhaʊs; *NAmE* ˈblɑːk-/ *noun* **1** a strong concrete shelter used by soldiers, for example during a battle 碉堡 **2** (*NAmE*) a house made of LOGS (= thick pieces of wood) 木屋

ˌ**block 'vote** *noun* a voting system in which each person who votes represents a number of people 集體投票（投票人代表着一批人的投票制度）

blog /blɒg; *NAmE* blɑːg/ *noun, verb*

■ *noun* (also **web·log**) a website where a person writes regularly about recent events or topics that interest them, usually with photos and links to other websites that they find interesting 網誌；博客；部落格 ➲ COLLOCATIONS at EMAIL

■ *verb* (-gg-) [I] to keep a blog 寫網誌；寫博客；寫部落格 ▸ **blog·ger** *noun* **blog·ging** *noun* [U]

blogo·sphere /ˈblɒgəsfɪə(r); *NAmE* ˈblɑːgəsfɪr/ *noun* (usually **the blogosphere**) [sing.] (*informal*) all the personal websites that exist on the Internet, viewed as a network of people communicating with each other 博客圈；博客世界；部落格空間：*It's one of the top stories in the blogosphere.* 那件事是博客圈熱門的話題之一。◇ *the growing influence of the political blogosphere* 政治博客世界與日俱增的影響力

blog·roll /ˈblɒgrəʊl; *NAmE* ˈblɑːgroʊl/ *noun* (*computing* 計) a list on a website of other linked websites that the website owner thinks are useful or interesting 博客鏈接；部落格清單

bloke /bləʊk; *NAmE* bloʊk/ *noun* (*BrE, informal*) a man 男人；傢伙：*He seemed like a nice bloke.* 他看上去像個好人。

bloke·ish (also **blok·ish**) /ˈbləʊkɪʃ; *NAmE* ˈbloʊk-/ *adj.* (*BrE, informal*) behaving in a way that is supposed to be typical of men, especially men enjoying themselves in a group（尤指成夥作樂的男子）舉止豪爽的，爺兒們般的

blonde 0-π /blɒnd; *NAmE* blɑːnd/ *adj., noun*

■ *adj.* (also **blond**) **HELP** In British English it is usual to spell this word **blonde** when writing about a woman or girl and **blond** when writing about a man or boy, although the spelling **blonde** is sometimes used for men and boys too. In American English the spelling **blond** is often preferred for either sex. **Blonde** may be used to describe a woman's hair, but it is sometimes considered offensive to refer to a woman as 'a blonde' because hair colour is not a whole person. 英式英語中通常用 blonde 描述女性，blond 描述男性，不過，blonde 有時也用於男性。美式英語中描述男女都傾向於用 blond。blonde 可用以描述女性的頭髮，但用 a blonde 來指代女性有時被認為是不禮貌的，因為頭髮顏色並不代表整個人。 **1** 0-π (of hair 頭髮) pale gold in colour 金黃色的 **2** 0-π (of a person 人) having blonde hair 頭髮金黃的： *a small, blond boy* 一個金髮小男孩

■ *noun* 0-π (sometimes *offensive*) a woman with hair that is pale gold in colour 金髮女郎： *Is she a natural blonde* (= Is her hair naturally blonde)? 她的頭髮原本就是金黃色嗎？ ➲ compare BRUNETTE, REDHEAD

blood 0-π /blʌd/ *noun, verb*

■ *noun* **1** 0-π [U] the red liquid that flows through the bodies of humans and animals 血： *He lost a lot of blood in the accident.* 他在那場事故中流了很多血。◇ *Blood was pouring out of a cut on her head.* 血不斷地從她頭上的傷口中湧出。◇ *to* ***give blood*** (= to have blood taken from you so that it can be used in the medical treatment of other people) 獻血 ◇ *to* ***draw blood*** (= to wound a person so that they lose blood) 放血（傷人以致流血）◇ *a* ***blood cell/sample*** 血細胞；血樣 **2** **-blooded** (in adjectives 構成形容詞) having the type of blood mentioned 有…類型的血的： *cold-blooded reptiles* 冷血爬行動物 ➲ see also BLUE-BLOODED, HOT-BLOODED, RED-BLOODED **3** [U] (*formal*) family origins 血統；家世： *She is of noble blood.* 她有貴族血統。 **4** [C] (*old-fashioned, BrE*) a rich and fashionable man 紈絝子弟；花花公子

IDM **bad 'blood (between A and B)** (*old-fashioned*) feelings of hatred or strong dislike（甲、乙之間的）仇恨，厭惡 **be after/out for sb's 'blood** (*informal*, often *humorous*) to be angry with sb and want to hurt or punish them 恨不得傷害（或懲罰）某人；恨不得放某人的血 **be/run in your 'blood** to be a natural part of your character and of the character of other members of your family 是與生俱來的（或遺傳的）特性 **blood is thicker than 'water** (*saying*) family relationships are stronger than any others 血濃於水；親屬關係最牢靠 **sb's 'blood is up** (*BrE*) somebody is very angry and ready to argue or fight 怒氣沖天；怒從心上來；怒不可遏 **blood, sweat and 'tears** very hard work; a lot of effort 血汗；艱苦奮鬥 **have sb's 'blood on your hands** to be responsible for sb's death 對某人的死亡罪責難逃： *a dictator with the blood of thousands on his hands* 手上沾滿千萬人鮮血的獨裁者 **like getting blood out of/from a 'stone** almost impossible to obtain 水中撈月；緣木求魚： *Getting an apology from him was like getting blood from a stone.* 讓他道歉幾乎是不可能的。 **make sb's 'blood boil** to make sb extremely angry 使某人怒不可遏 **make sb's blood run cold** to make sb very frightened or fill them with horror 使某人不寒而慄（或毛骨悚然） **new/fresh 'blood** new members or employees, especially young ones, with new ideas or ways of doing things 新成員（尤指年輕、有新思想或方法的）；新生力量；新鮮血液 ➲ more at COLD *adj.*, FLESH *n.*, FREEZE *v.*, SPILL *v.*, SPIT *v.*, STIR *v.*, SWEAT *v.*

■ *verb* **~ sb** (*especially BrE*) to give sb their first experience of an activity 讓新人初試做某事

'blood bank *noun* a place where blood is kept for use in hospitals, etc. 血庫

blood·bath /'blʌdbɑːθ; *NAmE* -bæθ/ *noun* [sing.] a situation in which many people are killed violently 大屠殺 **SYN** **massacre**

'blood brother *noun* a man who has promised to treat another man as his brother, usually in a ceremony in which their blood is mixed together（尤指歃血為盟的）結義兄弟；血盟兄弟

'blood clot (also **clot**) *noun* a lump that is formed when blood dries or becomes thicker 血凝塊；血塊： *a blood clot on the brain* 大腦中的血塊

'blood count *noun* the number of red and white cells in sb's blood; a medical test to count these 血細胞總數；血細胞計數

'blood-curdling *adj.* (of a sound or a story 聲音或故事) filling you with horror; extremely frightening 使人毛骨悚然的；極為可怕的： *a* ***blood-curdling scream/story*** 令人不寒而慄的尖叫／故事

'blood donor *noun* a person who gives some of his or her blood to be used in the medical treatment of other people 獻血者；捐血者

'blood group (also **'blood type** especially in *NAmE*) *noun* any of the different types that human blood is separated into for medical purposes 血型： (*BrE*) *What blood group are you?* 你是什麼血型？◇ (*NAmE*) *What blood type do you have?* 你是什麼血型？◇ *blood group/type O* * O 型血

'blood heat *noun* [U] the normal temperature of a human body 血溫；人體正常的溫度

blood·hound /'blʌdhaʊnd/ *noun* a large dog with a very good sense of smell, used to follow or look for people 大警犬（嗅覺十分靈敏，常用於追踪人）

blood·ied /'blʌdid/ *adj.* covered in blood 血染的；有血的： *his bruised and bloodied nose* 他沾滿血的青腫的鼻子

blood·less /'blʌdləs/ *adj.* **1** without any killing 不流血的；和平的： *a* ***bloodless coup/revolution*** 不流血的政變／革命 **2** (of a person or a part of the body 人或身體部位) very pale 蒼白的；無血色的： *bloodless lips* 沒有血色的雙唇 **3** lacking human emotion 無情的；冷酷的 **SYN** **cold, unemotional**

blood·let·ting /'blʌdletɪŋ/ *noun* [U] **1** (*formal*) the killing or wounding of people 殺戮；傷害 **SYN** **bloodshed** **2** a medical treatment used in the past in which some of a patient's blood was removed 放血療法

blood·line /'blʌdlaɪn/ *noun* (*technical* 術語) the set of ANCESTORS of a person or an animal 世系；血統；（動物的）種系

blood·lust /'blʌdlʌst/ *noun* [U] a strong desire to kill or be violent 殺戮慾；暴力慾

'blood money *noun* [U] (*disapproving*) **1** money paid to a person who is hired to murder sb（付給受雇殺人者的）血腥錢 **2** money paid to the family of a murdered person（付給被殺害者家屬的）贖罪金

'blood orange *noun* a type of orange with red flesh 血橙（果肉紅色）

'blood poisoning *noun* an illness where the blood becomes infected with harmful bacteria 敗血病

'blood pressure *noun* [U] the pressure of blood as it travels around the body 血壓： *to have* ***high/low blood pressure*** 血壓高／低 ◇ *to* ***take*** (= measure) ***sb's blood pressure*** 測量某人的血壓 ➲ COLLOCATIONS at DIET

,blood-'red *adj.* bright red in colour, like fresh blood 血紅色的；鮮紅色的

'blood relation (also **'blood relative**) *noun* a person related to sb by birth rather than by marriage 血親；骨肉

'blood sausage (*NAmE*) (*BrE* **,black 'pudding**) *noun* [U, C] a type of large dark SAUSAGE made from pig's blood, fat and grain 黑香腸（用豬血、乳脂和穀粒製成）

blood·shed /'blʌdʃed/ *noun* [U] the killing or wounding of people, usually during fighting or a war（戰鬥或戰爭中的）人員傷亡，流血事件： *The two sides called a truce to avoid further bloodshed.* 雙方宣佈休戰，以免再有人員傷亡。

blood·shot /'blʌdʃɒt; *NAmE* -ʃɑːt/ *adj.* (of eyes 眼睛) with the part that is usually white full of red lines because of lack of sleep, etc. 佈滿血絲的

'blood sport *noun* [usually pl.] a sport in which animals or birds are killed 獵殺動物（或飛禽）的運動

blood·stain /ˈblʌdsteɪn/ *noun* a mark or spot of blood on sth 血跡；血污 ▸ **blood·stained** *adj.*：*a bloodstained shirt* 血跡斑斑的襯衫

blood·stock /ˈblʌdstɒk; *NAmE* -stɑːk/ *noun* [U] horses of pure breed, bred especially for racing（為賽馬特地培育的）純種馬

blood·stream /ˈblʌdstriːm/ *noun* [sing.] the blood flowing through the body 體內循環的血液；血流：*They injected the drug directly into her bloodstream.* 他們把麻醉劑直接注射到她的血液裏。

blood·sucker /ˈblʌdsʌkə(r)/ *noun* **1** an animal or insect that sucks blood from people or animals 吸血動物（或昆蟲）**2** (*informal, disapproving*) a person who takes advantage of other people in order to gain financial benefit 敲詐勒索者；吸血鬼 ▸ **blood·suck·ing** /ˈblʌdsʌkɪŋ/ *adj.* [only before noun]：*bloodsucking insects* 吸血昆蟲 ◇ (*disapproving*)：*bloodsucking lawyers* 敲詐勒索的律師

ˌblood ˈsugar *noun* [U] the amount of GLUCOSE in your blood 血糖

ˈblood test *noun* an examination of a small amount of your blood by doctors in order to make judgements about your medical condition 驗血

blood·thirsty /ˈblʌdθɜːsti; *NAmE* -θɜːrsti/ *adj.* **1** wanting to kill or wound; enjoying seeing or hearing about killing and violence 嗜殺成性的；喜好看（或聽）兇殺與暴力的 **2** (of a book, film/movie, etc. 書、電影等) describing or showing killing and violence 描寫（或表現）兇殺與暴力的

ˈblood transfusion (also **transfusion**) *noun* [C, U] the process of putting new blood into the body of a person or an animal 輸血：*He was given a blood transfusion.* 他接受了輸血。

ˈblood type *noun* (*especially NAmE*) = BLOOD GROUP

ˈblood vessel *noun* any of the tubes through which blood flows through the body 血管 ➲ see also ARTERY (1), CAPILLARY, VEIN (1)

bloody¹ /ˈblʌdi/ *adj.* [only before noun], *adv.* ➲ see also BLOODY² (*BrE, taboo, slang*) a swear word that many people find offensive that is used to emphasize a comment or an angry statement（用以加強語氣；很多人認為含冒犯意）：*Don't be such a bloody fool.* 別像個大傻瓜似的。◇ *That was a bloody good meal!* 那頓飯真他媽豐盛！◇ *What bloody awful weather!* 多麼糟糕透頂的天氣！◇ *She did bloody well to win that race.* 她非常出色地贏得了那場賽跑。◇ *He doesn't bloody care about anybody else.* 他根本不關心別人。◇ *'Will you apologize?' 'Not bloody likely!'* (= Certainly not) "你會道歉嗎？" "沒門兒。"

IDM **bloody well** (*BrE, taboo*) used to emphasize an angry statement or an order（強調氣憤的話或命令）：*You can bloody well keep your job—I don't want it!* 你就留着你那份臭工作吧，我才不稀罕呢！

bloody² /ˈblʌdi/ *adj.* ➲ see also BLOODY¹ (**blood·ier**, **bloodi·est**) **1** involving a lot of violence and killing 嗜殺的；血腥的；殘暴的：*a bloody battle* 一場血戰 ◇ *The terrorists have halted their bloody campaign of violence.* 恐怖分子已經停止了他們兇殘的暴力活動。**2** covered with blood; BLEEDING 血淋淋的；流血的：*to give sb a bloody nose* (= in a fight) 把某人打得鼻孔流血 ▸ **blood·ily** *adv.* **IDM** see SCREAM *v.*

Bloody Mary /ˌblʌdi ˈmeəri; *NAmE* ˈmeri/ *noun* (*pl.* **Bloody Marys**) an alcoholic drink made by mixing VODKA with tomato juice 紅瑪麗雞尾酒，血腥瑪麗（用伏特加酒加番茄汁調製而成）

ˌbloody-ˈminded *adj.* (*BrE, informal*) behaving in a way that makes things difficult for other people; refusing to be helpful 和別人過不去的；故意不合作的 ▸ **ˌbloody-ˈminded·ness** *noun* [U]

bloom /bluːm/ *noun, verb*

■ ***noun*** (*formal* or *technical* 術語) **1** [C] a flower (usually one on a plant that people admire for its flowers)（常指供觀賞的）花：*the exotic blooms of the orchid* 奇異的蘭花 **2** [sing., U] a healthy fresh appearance 健康有精神的面貌：*the bloom in her cheeks* 她面頰上的紅潤光澤

IDM **in (full) bloom** (of trees, plants, gardens, etc. 樹木花草、花園等) with the flowers fully open 鮮花盛開

■ ***verb*** **1** [I] to produce flowers 開花 **SYN** **flower**：*Most roses will begin to bloom from late May.* 大多數玫瑰從五月末開始開花。**2** [I] to become healthy, happy or confident 變得健康（或快活、自信）**SYN** **blossom**：*The children had bloomed during their stay on the farm.* 孩子們在農場期間健康活潑有生氣。

bloom·er /ˈbluːmə(r)/ *noun* (*old-fashioned, BrE, informal*) a mistake 錯誤

bloom·ers /ˈbluːməz; *NAmE* -ərz/ *noun* [pl.] **1** (*informal*) an old-fashioned piece of women's underwear like long loose UNDERPANTS（舊時婦女穿的）寬鬆長內褲 **2** short loose trousers/pants that fit tightly at the knee, worn in the past by women for games, riding bicycles, etc.（舊時婦女騎自行車等穿的）短燈籠褲：*a pair of bloomers* 一條短燈籠褲

bloom·ing /ˈbluːmɪŋ; ˈblʊm-/ *adj.* [only before noun], *adv.* (*BrE, informal*) a mild swear word, used to emphasize a comment or a statement, especially an angry one（氣憤等時用以加強語氣）：*What blooming awful weather!* 多糟糕的天氣！

bloop /bluːp/ *verb* [I] (*NAmE, informal*) to make a mistake 出錯

bloop·er /ˈbluːpə(r)/ *noun* (*NAmE*) an embarrassing mistake that you make in public 當眾出的洋相；出醜

blos·som /ˈblɒsəm; *NAmE* ˈblɑːs-/ *noun, verb*

■ ***noun*** [C, U] a flower or a mass of flowers, especially on a fruit tree or bush（尤指果樹或灌木的）花朵，花簇：*cherry/orange/apple blossom* 櫻桃 / 橘子 / 蘋果花 ◇ *The trees are **in blossom**.* 樹上鮮花盛開。➲ VISUAL VOCAB page V10

■ ***verb*** **1** [I] (of a tree or bush 樹或灌木) to produce blossom 開花 **2** [I] to become more healthy, confident or successful 變得更加健康（或自信、成功）：*She has visibly blossomed over the last few months.* 她近幾個月以來身體明顯好多了。◇ **~ into sth** *Their friendship blossomed into love.* 他們的友誼發展成了愛情。

blot /blɒt; *NAmE* blɑːt/ *verb, noun*

■ ***verb*** (**-tt-**) **1 ~ sth (up)** to remove liquid from a surface by pressing soft paper or cloth on it（用軟紙或布）吸乾液體 **2 ~ sth** to make a spot or spots of ink fall on paper 把墨水濺到（紙上）

IDM **blot your ˈcopybook** (*old-fashioned, informal*) to do sth to spoil the opinion that other people have of you 做出有損形象的事；玷污名譽

PHR V **ˌblot sth↔ˈout** **1** to cover or hide sth completely 遮住；掩蓋；隱藏：*Clouds blotted out the sun.* 雲遮住了太陽。**2** to deliberately try to forget an unpleasant memory or thought 有意地忘記（不愉快的記憶或想法）；抹去：*He tried to blot out the image of Helen's sad face.* 他盡量不去想海倫的那張憂傷的臉。

■ ***noun*** **1** a spot or dirty mark on sth, made by ink, etc. 污點；墨漬 ➲ SYNONYMS at MARK **2 ~ (on sth)** something that spoils the opinion that other people have of you, or your happiness 有損形象（或幸福）的事情；污點：*Her involvement in the fraud has left a serious blot on her character.* 她捲入了這次欺詐案，在她的品格上留下了一個很大的污點。

IDM **a blot on the ˈlandscape** an object, especially an ugly building, that spoils the beauty of a place 影響景觀的物體（尤指醜陋建築物）

blotch /blɒtʃ; *NAmE* blɑːtʃ/ *noun* a mark, usually not regular in shape, on skin, plants, material, etc.（皮膚、植物、物體等上面不規則的）斑點，污點：*He had come out in* (= become covered in) *dark red blotches.* 他身上長出了一塊塊深紅色的斑。

blotchy /ˈblɒtʃi; *NAmE* ˈblɑː-/ (*BrE* also **blotched**) *adj.* covered in blotches 有斑點的；有污點的：*her blotchy and swollen face* 她的佈滿黑斑的浮腫的臉

blot·ter /ˈblɒtə(r); *NAmE* ˈblɑːt-/ *noun* **1** a large piece of blotting paper in a cover with a stiff back which is kept on a desk 吸墨紙板；吸墨用具 **2** (*NAmE*) the record of arrests in a police district（警察管區的）拘捕記錄

B

ˈ**blotting paper** *noun* [U] soft thick paper used for drying ink after you have written sth on a piece of paper 吸墨紙

blotto /ˈblɒtəʊ; *NAmE* ˈblɑːtoʊ/ *adj.* [not before noun] (*old-fashioned, informal*) very drunk 爛醉如泥

blouse /blaʊz; *NAmE* blaʊs/ *noun* a piece of clothing like a shirt, worn by women （女式）短上衣，襯衫 ➲ VISUAL VOCAB page V61 **IDM** see BIG *adj.*

blouson /ˈbluːzɒn; *NAmE* ˈblaʊsɑːn/ *noun* a short loose jacket that is gathered together at the waist 束腰短上衣

blo·vi·ate /ˈbləʊvieɪt; *NAmE* ˈbloʊ-/ [I] (*NAmE, informal, disapproving*) to talk or write in a way that shows that you think you know a lot and have sth important to say, when in fact you do not know much and have nothing important to say（空泛地）高談闊論；夸夸其談

blow 🔑 /bləʊ; *NAmE* bloʊ/ *verb, noun, exclamation*

■ *verb* (**blew** /bluː/, **blown** /bləʊn; *NAmE* bloʊn/) **HELP** In sense 14 **blowed** is used for the past participle. 作第 14 義時過去分詞用 blowed。

▸ **FROM MOUTH** 口 **1** 🔑 [I, T] to send out air from the mouth 吹：**+ adv./prep.** *You're not blowing hard enough!* 你沒有用勁吹！◇ *The policeman asked me to blow into the breathalyser.* 警察要我對着呼吸分析器吹氣。◇ **~ sth + adv./prep.** *He drew on his cigarette and blew out a stream of smoke.* 他含着煙捲吸了一口，接着吐出一股煙。

▸ **OF WIND** 風 **2** 🔑 [I, T] (+ **adv./prep.**) when the wind or a current of air **blows**, it is moving; when **it blows**, the wind is blowing 颳；吹：*A cold wind blew from the east.* 東邊吹來一股冷風。◇ *It was blowing hard.* 颳着大風。◇ *It was* **blowing a gale** (= there was a strong wind). 狂風大作。

▸ **MOVE WITH WIND/BREATH** 風／口吹動 **3** 🔑 [I, T] to be moved by the wind, sb's breath, etc.; to move sth in this way（被）颳動，吹動：**+ adv./prep.** *My hat blew off.* 我的帽子被風吹走了。◇ **+ adj.** *The door blew open.* 門被風吹開了。◇ **~ sth + adv./prep.** *I was almost blown over by the wind.* 我被風颳得快站不住了。◇ *She blew the dust off the book.* 她吹掉了書上的灰塵。◇ *The ship was blown onto the rocks.* 強風使船撞上了礁石。◇ **~ sth + adj.** *The wind blew the door shut.* 風把門吹關上了。

▸ **WHISTLE/INSTRUMENT** 哨子；樂器 **4** 🔑 [T, I] **~ (sth)** if you **blow** a whistle, musical instrument, etc. or if a whistle, etc. **blows**, you produce a sound by blowing into the whistle, etc. 吹，吹奏（哨子、樂器等）；（哨子、樂器等）吹奏出音：*The referee blew his whistle.* 裁判吹響了哨子。◇ *the sound of trumpets blowing* 吹喇叭的聲音

▸ **YOUR NOSE** 鼻 **5** 🔑 [T] **~ your nose** to clear your nose by blowing strongly through it into a TISSUE or HANDKERCHIEF 擤（鼻子）

▸ **A KISS** 吻 **6** [T] **~ (sb) a kiss** to kiss your hand and then pretend to blow the kiss towards sb（向某人）送飛吻

▸ **SHAPE STH** 使成形 **7** [T] **~ sth** to make or shape sth by blowing 吹出（某物）；把（某物）吹出形狀：*to blow smoke rings* 吐煙圈 ◇ *to* **blow bubbles** (= for example, by blowing onto a thin layer of water mixed with soap) 吹（肥皂等）泡泡 ◇ *to* **blow glass** (= to send a current of air into melted glass to shape it) 吹製玻璃器皿

▸ **ELECTRICITY** 電 **8** [I, T] **~ (sth)** if a FUSE **blows** or you **blow** a FUSE, the electricity stops flowing suddenly because the FUSE (= a thin wire) has melted because the current was too strong（使保險絲）熔化，燒斷

▸ **TYRE** 輪胎 **9** [I, T] to break open or apart, especially because of pressure from inside; to make a tyre break in this way 破裂；爆裂；爆胎：*The car spun out of control when a tyre blew.* 車胎爆了一個，車隨後失去了控制。◇ *The truck blew a tyre and lurched off the road.* 這輛卡車爆了一個胎，傾斜着衝出了公路。

▸ **WITH EXPLOSIVES** 炸藥 **10** [T] **~ sth** to break sth open with EXPLOSIVES 炸開：*The safe had been blown by the thieves.* 保險櫃被竊賊炸開了。

▸ **SECRET** 秘密 **11** [T] **~ sth** (*informal*) to make known sth that was secret 泄露；暴露：*One mistake could* **blow your cover** (= make your real name, job, intentions, etc. known). 一不小心就會讓你暴露身分。

▸ **MONEY** 錢 **12** [T] **~ sth (on sth)** (*informal*) to spend or waste a lot of money on sth（在某事物上）花大錢，揮霍：*He inherited over a million dollars and blew it all on drink and gambling.* 他繼承了一百多萬元，全部揮霍在飲酒和賭博上了。

▸ **OPPORTUNITY** 機會 **13** [T] **~ sth** (*informal*) to waste an opportunity 浪費（機會）：*She* **blew her chances** *by arriving late for the interview.* 她面試時遲到，結果錯過了機會。◇ *You had your chance and you* **blew it**. 你本來有機會，卻沒有抓住。

▸ **EXCLAMATION** 感歎 **14** [T] **~ sb/sth** (*BrE, informal*) used to show that you are annoyed, surprised or do not care about sth（表示生氣、吃驚或不在乎）：*Blow it! We've missed the bus.* 真該死！我們錯過了公交車。◇ *Well, blow me down! I never thought I'd see you again.* 啊，天哪！我以為再也見不到你了。◇ ***I'm blowed if*** *I'm going to* (= I certainly will not) *let him treat you like that.* 我絕不會允許他那麼對待你。◇ *Let's take a taxi and blow* (= never mind) *the expense.* 我們乘出租車吧，別在意費用。

▸ **LEAVE SUDDENLY** 突然離開 **15** [T, I] **~ (sth)** (*NAmE, slang*) to leave a place suddenly 突然離開（某地）：*Let's blow this joint.* 咱們馬上離開這家酒吧。

IDM **blow your/sb's ˈbrains out** to kill yourself/sb by shooting yourself/them in the head 槍擊頭部自殺／殺人 **blow ˈchunks** (*NAmE, slang*) to VOMIT 嘔；嘔吐 **blow a ˈfuse** (*informal*) to get very angry 大怒；暴跳如雷 **blow the ˈgaff (on sb/sth)** (*BrE, informal*) to tell sth secret, especially by mistake（尤指因大意）泄露秘密 **blow hot and ˈcold (about sth)** (*informal*) to change your opinion about sth often 拿不定主意；出爾反爾 **blow sb/sth out of the ˈwater** (*informal*) **1** to destroy sb/sth completely 徹底摧毀；毀滅 **2** to show that sb/sth is not good by being very much better than it/them（以更加優異者）表明…不好，顯得…差得多：*A DVD music system plays discs that look like CDs, but blows them out of the water.* * DVD 音樂播放機裏放的碟片看似 CD，卻要比 CD 強多了。**blow ˈsmoke (up sb's ass)** (*taboo, NAmE, slang*) to try to trick sb or lie to sb, particularly by saying sth is better than it really is 吹牛皮；説大話蒙人 **blow your ˈmind** (*informal*) to produce a very strong pleasant or shocking feeling 使某人興奮（或吃驚）：*Wait till you hear this. It'll blow your mind.* 等着聽聽這個吧。它會讓你大感意外的。➲ see also MIND-BLOWING **blow your own ˈtrumpet** (*especially BrE*) (*NAmE* usually **blow/toot your own ˈhorn**) (*informal*) to praise your own abilities and achievements 自吹自擂 **SYN** **boast** **ORIGIN** This phrase refers to the custom of announcing important guests by blowing a horn. 這個短語源自吹號宣佈貴賓到達的習俗。**blow your ˈtop** (*BrE*) (*NAmE* **blow your ˈstack**) (*informal*) to get very angry 大怒；暴跳如雷 **blow up in sb's ˈface** if a plan, etc. **blows up in your face**, it goes wrong in a way that causes you damage, embarrassment, etc. 事情失敗，害了自己 **blow the ˈwhistle on sb/sth** (*informal*) to tell sb in authority about sth wrong or illegal that sb is doing 告發 ➲ see also WHISTLE-BLOWER **IDM** see COBWEB, ILL *adj.*, KINGDOM, LARK *n.*, LID, PUFF *v.*, SOCK *n.*, WAY *n.*

PHR V ˌ**blow sth↔aˈpart** **1** to completely destroy sth in an explosion 炸毀；炸掉 **2** to show that an idea is completely false 推翻（觀點）；表明…是錯誤的：*What we discovered blew apart all our preconceptions about this fascinating species.* 我們的發現將我們對這一奇妙物種的先入之見全盤推翻了。ˌ**blow sb↔aˈway** (*informal, especially NAmE*) **1** to kill sb by shooting them 槍殺某人 **2** to impress sb a lot or to make them very happy 給某人留下深刻印象；使某人很高興 **3** to defeat sb easily 輕易擊敗某人 ˌ**blow ˈin** | ˌ**blow ˈinto sth** (*informal*) to arrive or enter a place suddenly 突然來到；突然進入：*Look who's just blown in!* 看，誰來了！◇ *Have you heard who's* **blown into town**? 你聽説誰突然進城來了嗎？ˌ**blow ˈoff** (*BrE, informal*) a rude way of saying 'BREAK WIND' (= release gas through your bottom)（粗俗語）放屁 ˌ**blow sb↔ˈoff** (*NAmE*) to deliberately not meet sb when you said you would; to end a romantic relationship with sb 失約；結束（戀愛關係）ˌ**blow sth↔ˈoff** (*NAmE*) to deliberately not do sth that you said you would（故意）推脱，逃避：*He looks for any excuse he can to blow off work.* 他尋找任何可能的藉口來逃避工作。ˌ**blow ˈout** **1** if a flame, etc. **blows out**, it is put out by the wind, etc. 被（風等）吹滅；熄滅：*Somebody*

B

opened the door and the candle blew out. 有人打開了門，蠟燭就被吹滅了。 **2** if an oil or gas WELL **blows out**, it sends out gas suddenly and with force（油井或氣井）噴氣；井噴 ➲ related noun BLOWOUT **,blow itself 'out** when a storm **blows itself out**, it finally loses its force（風暴等）平息，減弱 **,blow sb↔'out** (*NAmE, informal*) to defeat sb easily 輕易擊敗某人 **,blow sth↔'out** 🗝 to put out a flame, etc. by blowing 吹滅（火焰等） **,blow 'over** to go away without having a serious effect 颳過去了，平靜下來（未造成嚴重影響）: *The storm blew over in the night.* 風暴在夜間平息了。◇ *The scandal will soon blow over.* 流言蜚語很快就會煙消雲散的。 **,blow 'up 1** 🗝 to explode; to be destroyed by an explosion 爆炸；被炸毀： *The bomb blew up.* 炸彈爆炸了。◇ *A police officer was killed when his car blew up.* 一名警官在其汽車爆炸時遇難。 ➲ SYNONYMS at EXPLODE **2** to start suddenly and with force 爆發： *A storm was blowing up.* 狂風大作。◇ *A crisis has blown up over the President's latest speech.* 總統最近的講話引發了一場危機。 **,blow sth↔'up 1** to destroy sth by an explosion 炸毀： *The police station was blown up by terrorists.* 警察局被恐怖分子炸毀了。 ➲ SYNONYMS at EXPLODE **2** 🗝 to fill sth with air or gas so that it becomes firm 給（某物）充氣： *The tyres on my bike need blowing up.* 我的自行車該打氣了。 **3** to make a photograph bigger 放大（照片） SYN **enlarge** ➲ related noun BLOW-UP **4** to make sth seem more important, better, worse, etc. than it really is 誇大；誇張： *The whole affair was **blown up out of all proportion**.* 整個事件被渲染得太過了。 **,blow 'up (at sb)** (*informal*) to get angry with sb （對某人）發火，動怒 SYN **lose your temper**: *I'm sorry I blew up at you.* 對不起，我對你發脾氣了。 ➲ related noun BLOW-UP

■ ***noun* 1** 🗝 a hard hit with the hand, a weapon, etc. （用手、武器等的）猛擊： *She received a severe blow on the head.* 她頭上捱了重重的一擊。◇ *He was knocked out by a single blow to the head.* 他頭上只被打了一下便昏過去了。◇ *The two men were **exchanging blows**.* 那兩個人在相互廝打。◇ *He **landed a blow** on Hill's nose.* 他對着希爾的鼻子來了一拳。 **2** 🗝 **~ (to sb/sth)** a sudden event which has damaging effects on sb/sth, causing sadness or disappointment 打擊；挫折： *Losing his job **came as a** terrible **blow** to him.* 失業給他造成了沉重的打擊。◇ *It was a shattering blow to her pride.* 那事徹底摧毀了她的自尊心。 ➲ see also BODY BLOW **3** 🗝 the action of blowing 吹： *Give your nose a good blow* (= clear it completely). 把你的鼻子擤乾淨。

IDM **a ,blow-by-,blow ac'count, de'scription, etc. (of sth)** (*informal*) a description of an event which gives you all the details in the order in which they happen 順序的詳情、描述等 **come to 'blows (over sth)** to start fighting because of sth（因某事）動武，打起架來 **soften/cushion the 'blow** to make sth that is unpleasant seem less unpleasant and easier to accept 緩解；緩和 ➲ more at DEAL *v.*, STRIKE *v.*

■ ***exclamation*** (*old-fashioned, BrE*) used to show that you are annoyed about sth（表示厭煩）: *Blow! I completely forgot it.* 哎呀！我給忘得一乾二淨了。

blow·back /ˈbləʊbæk; *NAmE* ˈbloʊbæk/ *noun* [U, C] **1** a process in which gases expand or travel in a direction that is opposite to the usual one 反吹；回吹；逆吹： *blowback gas* 回膛氣體 ◇ *Blowback may be caused by a defective mechanism.* 氣體後泄可能是由機械結構缺陷引起的。 **2** (*especially NAmE*) the results of a political action or situation that are not what was intended or wanted 違背初衷的結果： *The policy has led to blowback.* 這項政策結果適得其反。◇ *The war created a ferocious blowback.* 這場戰爭激起了強烈的反沖效應。

'blow-dry *verb* **~ sth** to dry hair with a HAIRDRYER and shape it into a particular style 吹髮（用吹風機吹乾頭髮並使之成型） ▶ **'blow-dry** *noun*： *a cut and blow-dry* 修剪及吹髮

blow·er /ˈbləʊə(r); *NAmE* ˈbloʊ-/ *noun* **1** [C] a device that produces a current of air 吹風機；送風機： *a hot-air blower* 熱風機 **2 the blower** [sing.] (*old-fashioned, BrE, informal*) the telephone 電話 ➲ see also WHISTLE-BLOWER

blow·fly /ˈbləʊflaɪ; *NAmE* ˈbloʊ-/ *noun* (*pl.* **blow·flies**) a large fly that lays its eggs on meat and other food 麗蠅（在肉等食物上產卵）

blow·hard /ˈbləʊhɑːd; *NAmE* ˈbloʊhɑːrd/ *noun* (*NAmE, informal, disapproving*) a person who talks too proudly about sth they own or sth they have done 吹牛大王；自吹自擂的人

blow·hole /ˈbləʊhəʊl; *NAmE* ˈbloʊhoʊl/ *noun* **1** a hole in the top of a WHALE's head through which it breathes（鯨頭頂的）呼吸孔 ➲ VISUAL VOCAB page V12 **2** a hole in a large area of ice, through which SEALS, etc. breathe（供海豹等呼吸的）冰窟窿

blowie /ˈbləʊi; *NAmE* ˈbloʊi/ *noun* (*AustralE, NZE, informal*) a BLOWFLY 麗蠅

'blow-in *noun* (*AustralE, informal*) a person who has recently arrived somewhere 剛到的人；新來的人

'blow job *noun* (*taboo, slang*) the act of touching a man's PENIS with the tongue and lips to give sexual pleasure（對陰莖的）口淫，口交 SYN **fellatio**

blow·lamp /ˈbləʊlæmp; *NAmE* ˈbloʊ-/ (*BrE*) (*US* **'blow-torch, torch**) *noun* a tool for directing a very hot flame onto part of a surface, for example to remove paint 噴燈

blown *past part.* of BLOW

blow·out /ˈbləʊaʊt; *NAmE* ˈbloʊ-/ *noun* **1** an occasion when a tyre suddenly bursts on a vehicle while it is moving（機動車行駛過程中的）爆胎 SYN **puncture**: *to have a blowout* 車胎爆裂 **2** [usually sing.] (*informal*) a large meal at which people eat too much 大餐；盛宴： *a four-course blowout* 有四道菜的大餐 **3** (*NAmE, informal*) a large party or social occasion 盛大聚會；交誼會： *We're going to have a huge blowout for Valentine's Day.* 情人節時我們會舉辦一場盛大聚會。 **4** (*NAmE, informal*) an easy victory 輕易的勝利： *The game was a blowout, 8–1.* 這場比賽贏得易如反掌，結果是 8 比 1。 **5** a sudden escape of oil or gas from an OIL WELL 井噴

blow·pipe /ˈbləʊpaɪp; *NAmE* ˈbloʊ-/ *noun* **1** a weapon consisting of a long tube through which an arrow is blown 吹箭筒 **2** a long tube for blowing glass into a particular shape（吹製玻璃器皿的）吹管

blowsy (also **blowzy**) /ˈblaʊzi/ *adj.* (*BrE, informal, disapproving*) a woman who is **blowsy** is big and fat and looks untidy（女人）肥碩邋遢的

blow·torch /ˈbləʊtɔːtʃ; *NAmE* ˈbloʊtɔːrtʃ/ (also **torch**) (both *NAmE*) (*BrE* **blow·lamp**) *noun* a tool for directing a very hot flame onto part of a surface, for example to remove paint 噴燈

'blow-up *noun* **1** an ENLARGEMENT of a photograph, picture or design 照片（或圖畫、圖案等）的放大： *Can you do me a blow-up of his face?* 你能幫我把他的臉部放大嗎？ **2** (*NAmE*) an occasion when sb suddenly becomes angry 發脾氣；發怒

BLT /ˌbiː el ˈtiː/ *noun* the abbreviation for 'bacon, lettuce and tomato' (used to refer to a SANDWICH filled with this) 熏豬肉、生菜加番茄三明治（全寫為 bacon, lettuce and tomato）： *I'll have a BLT with extra mayonnaise.* 我要一個熏肉、生菜加番茄三明治，多加蛋黃醬。

blub /blʌb/ *verb* (**-bb-**) [I] (*BrE, informal*) to cry 哭

blub·ber /ˈblʌbə(r)/ *noun, verb*

■ ***noun*** [U] the fat of WHALES and other sea animals 鯨脂；海獸脂

■ ***verb*** [I, T] (**+ speech**) (*informal, disapproving*) to cry noisily 大聲哭： *There he sat, blubbering like a baby.* 他坐在那裏像個嬰兒似的啼哭。

bludge /blʌdʒ/ *verb, noun* (*AustralE, NZE, informal*)

■ ***verb* 1** [I] to not do any work and live from what other people give you 不勞動而靠別人維持生活；吃現成飯 **2** [T] **~ sth** to ask sb for sth especially because you cannot or do not want to pay for it yourself 乞討；討要 SYN **cadge**: *The girls bludged smokes.* 那些女孩子要煙抽。

■ ***noun*** an easy job 輕鬆的工作

bludg·eon /ˈblʌdʒən/ *verb* **1 ~ sb** to hit sb several times with a heavy object 用重器連擊（某人） **2 ~ sb (into sth/into doing sth)** to force sb to do sth, especially by arguing with them（尤指通過爭辯）迫使⋯： *They tried* *to bludgeon me into joining their protest.* 他們試圖強迫我和他們一同抗議。

bludger /ˈblʌdʒə(r)/ *noun* (*AustralE, NZE, informal*) **1** a lazy person 懶貨；懶骨頭 **2** a person who asks other people for sth because they cannot or do not want to pay for it 吃現成飯的人 SYN **scrounger**

blue /bluː/ *adj., noun*

■ ***adj.*** (**bluer**, **blu·est**) **1** having the colour of a clear sky or the sea/ocean on a clear day 藍色的；天藍色的；蔚藍色的：*piercing blue eyes* 銳利的藍眼睛 ◇ *a blue shirt* 藍色襯衫 **2** (of a person or part of the body 人或身體部位) looking slightly blue in colour because the person is cold or cannot breathe easily（由於冷或呼吸困難）發青的，青紫的：*Her hands were blue with cold.* 她的雙手凍得發青。 **3** (*informal*) sad 憂鬱的；悲傷的 SYN **depressed**：*He'd been feeling blue all week.* 他整個星期都鬱鬱不樂。 **4** films/movies, jokes or stories that are **blue** are about sex（電影、玩笑或故事）色情的，黃色的：*a blue movie* 色情片 **5** (*politics* 政) (of an area in the US) having more people who vote for the DEMOCRATIC candidate than the REPUBLICAN one（美國地區）藍色的（支持民主黨候選人多於支持共和黨候選人）：*blue states/counties* 藍州；藍縣 OPP **red** ➲ see also TRUE-BLUE ▸ **blue·ness** *noun* [U, sing.]：*the blueness of the water* 水的蔚藍色

IDM **do sth till you are blue in the ˈface** (*informal*) to try to do sth as hard and as long as you possibly can but without success 徒然拚命地幹；徒勞無功：*You can argue till you're blue in the face, but you won't change my mind.* 你可以費盡口舌，但改變不了我的主意。 ➲ more at BLACK *adj.*, DEVIL, ONCE *adv.*, SCREAM *v.*

■ ***noun*** ➲ see also BLUES **1** [C, U] the colour of a clear sky or the sea/ocean on a clear day 藍色；天藍色；蔚藍色：***bright/dark/light/pale blue*** 明亮的／深／淺／淡藍色 ◇ *The room was decorated in vibrant blues and yellows.* 房間內部以鮮明的藍色和黃色作為裝飾。◇ *She was dressed in blue.* 她身着藍色服裝。 **2** [C] (*BrE*) a person who has played a particular sport for Oxford or Cambridge University; a title given to them 藍色榮譽者（牛津或劍橋大學的校隊運動員）；藍色榮譽的頭銜 **3** [C] (*AustralE, NZE, informal*) a mistake 錯誤；失誤 **4** [C] (*AustralE, NZE, informal*) a name for a person with red hair 紅髮人 **5** [C] (*AustralE, NZE, informal*) a fight 打架；打鬥；鬥毆

IDM **out of the ˈblue** unexpectedly; without warning 出乎意料；突然；晴天霹靂：*The decision came out of the blue.* 這個決定來得很突然。 ➲ more at BOLT *n.*, BOY *n.*

ˌblue ˈbaby *noun* a baby whose skin is slightly blue at birth because there is sth wrong with its heart 青紫嬰兒（因先天性心臟損害而在出生時皮膚呈淡藍色）

blue·bell /ˈbluːbel/ *noun* **1** a garden or wild flower with a short STEM and small blue or white flowers shaped like bells 藍鐘花；風鈴草 ➲ **VISUAL VOCAB** page V11 **2** (*ScotE*) = HAREBELL

blue·berry /ˈbluːbəri; *NAmE* -beri/ *noun* (*pl.* **-ies**) a dark blue BERRY that grows on bushes in N America and can be eaten 越橘藍色漿果，藍莓（產於北美，可食） ➲ compare BILBERRY

blue·bird /ˈbluːbɜːd; *NAmE* -bɜːrd/ *noun* a small N American bird with blue feathers on its back or head 藍鴝（北美小鳥，背及頭有藍色羽毛）

ˌblue-ˈblooded *adj.* from a royal or NOBLE family 出身皇族（或貴族）的 ▸ **ˌblue ˈblood** *noun* [U]

ˈblue book *noun* **1** (*US*) a book with a blue cover used by students for writing the answers to examination questions（考試用）藍皮答題卷 **2** (*NAmE*) a book that lists the prices that people should expect to pay for used cars 二手車參考價目冊

blue·bot·tle /ˈbluːbɒtl; *NAmE* -bɑːtl/ *noun* a large fly with a blue body 青蠅；綠頭蠅

ˌblue ˈcheese *noun* [U, C] cheese with lines of blue MOULD in it 藍紋奶酪（有黴菌引起的斑紋）

ˌblue-ˈchip *adj.* [only before noun] (*finance* 財) a **blue-chip** investment is thought to be safe and likely to make a profit（投資）穩妥可靠的；藍籌的：*blue-chip companies* 藍籌公司

ˌblue-ˈcollar *adj.* [only before noun] connected with people who do physical work in industry 從事體力勞動的；藍領的：***blue-collar workers/voters/votes*** 藍領工人／選民／選票 ➲ compare PINK-COLLAR, WHITE-COLLAR

ˌblue ˈcrane *noun* a type of CRANE (= a large bird with long legs and a long neck) that has blue-grey feathers. It is the national bird of South Africa. 藍蓑羽鶴（南非國鳥）

ˌblue-eyed ˈboy *noun* [usually sing.] (*BrE, informal*, often *disapproving*) a person treated with special favour by sb 寵兒：*He's the manager's blue-eyed boy.* 他備受經理的青睞。

ˌblue ˈflag *noun* **1** (*BrE*) a blue flag used in motor racing to show that a driver who is much further ahead is trying to pass 藍旗（賽車中用以示意領先車手試圖超圈） **2** an award given to beaches in Europe that are clean and safe（為歐洲清潔安全的海灘頒發的）"藍旗"獎

ˌblue ˈfunk *noun* (*old-fashioned, informal*) = FUNK

blue·grass /ˈbluːgrɑːs; *NAmE* -græs/ *noun* [U] a type of traditional American country music played on GUITARS and BANJOS 藍草音樂（美國傳統鄉村音樂，用吉他和班卓琴演奏）

ˌblue ˈhelmet *noun* a member of a United Nations force that is trying to prevent war or violence in a place 藍盔；聯合國維和部隊成員

blue·jay /ˈbluːdʒeɪ/ *noun* a large N American bird with blue feathers on its back and a row of feathers (called a CREST) standing up on its head 藍松鴉，冠藍鴉（北美大鳥，背部羽毛藍色，頭部有羽冠）

ˈblue jeans *noun* [pl.] (*especially NAmE*) trousers/pants made of blue DENIM 藍色牛仔褲

ˈblue law *noun* [usually pl.] (in the US) a law that bans business and certain other activities, such as sports, on Sundays 藍色法規（美國法規，禁止星期天從事商業和體育運動等活動）

ˌblue-on-ˈblue *adj.* [only before noun] (*BrE*) in a war, used to describe an accident or attack in which people are hit by a bomb or weapon that is fired by their own side（戰爭中）誤傷己方的 ➲ compare FRIENDLY FIRE

ˌblue ˈpages *noun* [pl.] (in the US) the blue pages in a TELEPHONE DIRECTORY that give a list of government departments and their telephone numbers（美國列出政府部門及電話號碼的）電話藍頁

blue·print /ˈbluːprɪnt/ *noun* **1** a PHOTOGRAPHIC print of a plan for a building or a machine, with white lines on a blue background（建築、機器等的）藍圖 **2 ~ (for sth)** a plan which shows what can be achieved and how it can be achieved 行動方案；計劃藍圖：*a blueprint for the privatization of health care* 保健私有化方案 **3** (*technical* 術語) the pattern in every living cell, which decides how the plant, animal or person will develop and what it will look like（生物細胞的）模型，型板：*DNA carries the **genetic blueprint** which tells any organism how to build itself.* 脫氧核糖核酸帶有表明有機體形成方式的遺傳型板。

blue riband /ˌbluː ˈrɪbənd/ (*BrE*) (also **ˌblue ˈribbon** *NAmE, BrE*) *noun* an honour (sometimes in the form of a blue RIBBON) given to the winner of the first prize in a competition 冠軍榮譽，優勝者稱號（有時以藍綬帶形式授予冠軍得主）：*a blue-riband event* (= a very important one) 重大事件

blues /bluːz/ *noun* **1** (often **the blues**) [U] a type of slow sad music with strong rhythms, developed by African American musicians in the southern US 布魯斯音樂，藍調（源於美國南部黑人，節奏感強、緩慢憂鬱）：***a blues band/singer*** 布魯斯樂隊／歌手 **2** [C] (*pl.* **blues**) a blues song 布魯斯歌曲；藍調歌曲 **3 the blues** [pl.] (*informal*) feelings of sadness 憂鬱；悲傷；沮喪：*the Monday morning blues* 星期一早晨的鬱悶情緒 ➲ see also BABY BLUES

ˌblue-ˈsky *adj.* [only before noun] involving new and interesting ideas which are not yet possible or practical

B

新穎而未可行的；未能付諸實行的：*The government has been doing some* ***blue-sky thinking*** *on how to improve school standards.* 就如何提高學校的水平，政府仍然在作一些漫無邊際構想。

blue·stock·ing /ˈbluːstɒkɪŋ; *NAmE* -stɑːk-/ *noun* (*old-fashioned, BrE*, sometimes *disapproving*) a well-educated woman who is more interested in ideas and studying than in traditionally FEMININE things 才女（受過相當教育，不喜歡傳統女性生活）

bluesy /ˈbluːzi/ *adj.* having the slow strong rhythms and sad mood of blues music 布魯斯音樂的；有布魯斯音樂情調的；藍調的：*a* ***bluesy sound/voice*** 布魯斯音樂風格/歌聲

ˈblue tit *noun* a small European bird of the TIT family, with a blue head, wings and tail and yellow parts underneath 藍山雀（歐洲小山雀，頭頂藍色，胸腹部黃色）

Blue·tooth™ /ˈbluːtuːθ/ *noun* [U] a radio technology that makes it possible for mobile phones/cell phones, computers and other electronic devices to be linked over short distances, without needing to be connected by wires 藍牙（用於移動電話、計算機等電子設備的短距離無線連接技術）：*Bluetooth-enabled devices* 具有藍牙功能的設備

ˌblue ˈwhale *noun* a type of WHALE that is the largest known living animal 藍鯨（已知的最大動物）

bluff /blʌf/ *verb, noun, adj.*

■ ***verb*** [I, T] **~ (sth)** to try to make sb believe that you will do sth that you do not really intend to do, or that you know sth that you do not really know 虛張聲勢；唬人；吹牛：*I don't think he'll shoot—I think he's just bluffing.* 我認為他不會開槍，我想他不過是在嚇唬人。 **PHR V** **ˈbluff sb into doing sth** to make sb do sth by tricking them, especially by pretending you have more experience, knowledge, etc. than you really have 靠吹牛哄人… **ˌbluff it ˈout** to get out of a difficult situation by continuing to tell lies, especially when they suspect you are not being honest（受到懷疑後）繼續矇混過關，靠說謊擺脫困境 **ˌbluff your way ˈin/ˈout/ˈthrough** | **ˌbluff your way ˈinto/ˈout of/ˈthrough sth** to succeed in dealing with a difficult situation by making other people believe sth which is not true 矇混過關：*She successfully bluffed her way through the interview.* 她胡亂吹噓，成功地通過了面試。

■ ***noun*** **1** [U, C] an attempt to trick sb by making them believe that you will do sth when you really have no intention of doing it, or that you know sth when you do not, in fact, know it 虛張聲勢的做法；唬人：*It was just a game of bluff.* 那只不過是唬人的把戲。◇ *He said he would resign if he didn't get more money, but it was only a bluff.* 他說如果不給他加薪他就辭職，但那不過是虛張聲勢而已。 ➲ see also DOUBLE BLUFF **2** [C] a steep CLIFF or slope, especially by the sea or a river（尤指海邊或河邊的）峭壁，陡岸 **IDM** see CALL *v.*

■ ***adj.*** (of people or their manner 人或態度) very direct and cheerful, with good intentions, although not always very polite 直率豪爽的（儘管有時不夠禮貌）：*Beneath his bluff exterior he was a sensitive man.* 他外表大大咧咧，但其實是個敏感的人。

blu·ish /ˈbluːɪʃ/ *adj.* fairly blue in colour 帶藍色的；有點藍的：*a bluish-green carpet* 綠中帶藍的地毯

blun·der /ˈblʌndə(r)/ *noun, verb*

■ ***noun*** a stupid or careless mistake 愚蠢（或粗心）的錯誤：*to make a terrible blunder* 犯大錯 ◇ *a series of political blunders* 一連串政治失誤

■ ***verb*** [I] to make a stupid or careless mistake 犯愚蠢的（或粗心的）錯誤：*The government had blundered in its handling of the affair.* 政府在這件事的處理上犯了大錯。 **PHR V** **ˌblunder aˈbout, aˈround, etc.** to move around in an awkward way, knocking into things, as if you cannot see where you are going 跌跌撞撞 **ˌblunder ˈinto sth** **1** to knock into sth because you are awkward or are not able to see（因笨拙或看不見）撞上某物 **2** to find yourself in a difficult or unpleasant situation by accident 無意中陷入（困境）；偶然遇到（尷尬事） **ˌblunder ˈon** to continue doing sth in a careless or stupid way 一再粗心（或荒唐）地做某事；一錯再錯

blun·der·buss /ˈblʌndəbʌs; *NAmE* -dərb-/ *noun* an old type of gun with a wide end（老式）大口徑槍；喇叭槍

blunt /blʌnt/ *adj., verb*

■ ***adj.*** (**blunt·er**, **blunt·est**) **1** without a sharp edge or point 不鋒利的；鈍的：*a blunt knife* 鈍刀子 ◇ *This pencil's blunt!* 這支鉛筆不尖了！◇ *The police said he had been hit with a* ***blunt instrument***. 警方說他遭到了鈍器襲擊。 **OPP** **sharp** **2** (of a person or remark 人或說話) very direct; saying exactly what you think without trying to be polite 嘴直的；直言的：*She has a reputation for blunt speaking.* 她說話出了名地直截了當。◇ *To be blunt, your work is appalling.* 坦率地說，你的活幹得糟透了。 ➲ SYNONYMS at HONEST ▸ **blunt·ness** *noun* [U]

■ ***verb*** **1 ~ sth** to make sth weaker or less effective 使減弱；使降低效應：*Age hadn't blunted his passion for adventure.* 歲月沒有沖淡他的冒險激情。 **2 ~ sth** to make a point or an edge less sharp 使（尖端、刃）變鈍

blunt·ly /ˈblʌntli/ *adv.* in a very direct way, without trying to be polite or kind 直言地；單刀直入地：***To put it bluntly****, I want a divorce.* 坦白地說，我要離婚。◇ *'Is she dead?' he asked bluntly.* "她死了嗎？"他衝口而出。

blur /blɜː(r)/ *noun, verb*

■ ***noun*** [usually sing.] **1** a shape that you cannot see clearly, often because it is moving too fast（移動的）模糊形狀：*His arm was a rapid blur of movement as he struck.* 他出擊時胳膊快速一晃，令人眼花繚亂。◇ *Everything is a blur when I take my glasses off.* 我摘掉眼鏡什麼都變得模糊不清。 **2** something that you cannot remember clearly 模糊的記憶：*The events of that day were just a blur.* 那天發生的事只剩一片模糊的記憶。

■ ***verb*** (-rr-) **1** [I, T] if the shape or outline of sth **blurs**, or if sth **blurs** it, it becomes less clear and sharp（使）變得模糊不清：*The writing blurred and danced before his eyes.* 字跡變得一片模糊，在他眼前晃動。◇ **~ sth** *The mist blurred the edges of the buildings.* 建築群在薄霧中若隱若現。 **2** [T, I] **~ (sth)** if sth **blurs** your eyes or vision, or your eyes or vision **blur**, you cannot see things clearly（使）視線模糊；（使）看不清：*Tears blurred her eyes.* 淚水模糊了她的視線。 **3** [I, T] to become or make sth become difficult to distinguish clearly（使）難以區分：*The differences between art and life seem to have blurred.* 藝術和生活之間的差別似乎已變得模糊不清。◇ **~ sth** *She tends to* ***blur the distinction*** *between her friends and her colleagues.* 她往往將朋友和同事混淆起來。

Blu-ray /ˈbluː reɪ/ *noun* [U] technology that uses a blue LASER (= a very strong line of light) to record and play large amounts of high quality data on a type of CD 藍光（用藍色激光刻錄並播放大容量高品質資料的光盤技術）：*These high definition movies are all out on Blu-ray.* 這些高清晰度影片全部以藍光技術推出。

ˈBlu-ray Disc™ *noun* (*abbr.* **BD**, **BD-ROM**) a type of CD on which large amounts of data can be stored, used especially to play high quality video 藍光光盤，藍光光碟（尤用以播放高品質影像）

blurb /blɜːb; *NAmE* blɜːrb/ *noun* a short description of a book, a new product, etc., written by the people who have produced it, that is intended to attract your attention and make you want to buy it（書的）簡介；（生產商等的）產品推介

blurred /blɜːd; *NAmE* blɜːrd/ *adj.* **1** not clear; without a clear outline or shape 模糊不清的：*She suffered from dizziness and blurred vision.* 她飽受頭暈目眩之苦。◇ *a* ***blurred image/picture*** 模糊的圖像/照片 **2** difficult to remember clearly 記不清的：*blurred memories* 模糊的記憶 **3** difficult to distinguish, so that differences are not clear 難以區分的；模稜兩可的：***blurred distinctions/boundaries*** 含混不清的區別/界線

blurry /ˈblɜːri/ *adj.* (*informal*) without a clear outline; not clear 模糊不清的：*blurry, distorted photographs* 模糊走樣的照片 ◇ (*figurative*) *a blurry policy* 不明確的政策

blurt /blɜːt; *NAmE* blɜːrt/ *verb* **~ sth (out)** | **~ that …** | **~ what, how, etc. …** | **+ speech** to say sth suddenly

B

and without thinking carefully enough 脫口而出：*She blurted it out before I could stop her.* 我還沒來得及制止，她已脫口而出。➲ SYNONYMS at CALL

blush /blʌʃ/ *verb, noun*

▪ *verb* **1** [I] to become red in the face because you are embarrassed or ashamed（因尷尬或害羞）臉紅，漲紅了臉 SYN **go red**：**~ (with sth)** (**at sth**) *to blush with embarrassment/shame* 尷尬／羞愧得面頰緋紅 ◇ *She blushed furiously at the memory of the conversation.* 她一想起那次談話就氣得滿臉通紅。◇ **+ adj./noun** *He blushed scarlet at the thought.* 他想起那事便面紅耳赤。 **2** [T] **~ to do sth** to be ashamed or embarrassed about sth（因某事）羞愧，尷尬：*I blush to admit it, but I quite like her music.* 不好意思，但我得承認我很喜歡她的音樂。

▪ *noun* **1** [C] the red colour that spreads over your face when you are embarrassed or ashamed（因難堪、羞愧）面部泛起的紅暈：*She felt a warm blush rise to her cheeks.* 她感到雙頰熱辣辣的。◇ *He turned away to hide his blushes.* 他轉過身去，不讓人看見他臉紅。 **2** [U, C] (*NAmE*) = BLUSHER IDM see SPARE *v.*

blush·er /ˈblʌʃə(r)/ (*NAmE* also **blush**) *noun* [U, C] a coloured cream or powder that some people put on their cheeks to give them more colour 胭脂 ➲ VISUAL VOCAB page V60

blus·ter /ˈblʌstə(r)/ *verb* **1** [T, I] **~ (sth)** | **+ speech** to talk in an aggressive or threatening way, but with little effect 氣勢洶洶地說話，咄咄逼人，威嚇（但效果不大）：*'I don't know what you're talking about,' he blustered.* "我不知道你到底在說什麼！"他氣勢洶洶地說。◇ *a blustering bully* 咄咄逼人的惡霸 **2** [I] (of the wind 風) to blow violently 狂吹；咆哮 ▸ **blus·ter** *noun* [U]：*I wasn't frightened by what he said—it was all bluster.* 我沒有被他的話嚇倒——那不過是在嚇唬人。

blus·tery /ˈblʌstəri/ *adj.* (of weather 天氣) with strong winds 狂風大作的：***blustery winds/conditions*** 狂風；大風天氣 ◇ *The day was cold and blustery.* 日間天氣寒冷，狂風呼嘯。

Blu-tack™ /ˈbluː tæk/ *noun* [U] a blue sticky material used to attach paper to walls 寶貼萬用膠

Blvd. *abbr.* (used in written addresses 用於書寫地址) BOULEVARD 要道；大街

BMI /ˌbiː em ˈaɪ/ *abbr.* BODY MASS INDEX

BMOC /ˌbiː em əʊ ˈsiː; *NAmE* oʊ/ *abbr.* (*US*) BIG MAN ON CAMPUS

ˈB-movie (also **ˈB-picture**) *noun* a film/movie which is made cheaply and is not very good 二流電影；劣質電影：*a B-movie actress* 一個二流電影女演員

BMus (*NAmE* **B.Mus**) /ˌbiː ˈmʌz/ *noun* the abbreviation for 'Bachelor of Music' (a university degree in music that is usually a first degree) 音樂學士（全寫為 Bachelor of Music，通常為大學音樂專業的初級學位）

BMX /ˌbiː em ˈeks/ *noun* **1** [C] a strong bicycle which can be used for riding on rough ground 小輪車；越野自行車 **2** (also **BMXing**) [U] the sport of racing BMX bicycles on rough ground 小輪車越野賽

bn *abbr.* (*BrE*) (in writing) BILLION（書寫形式）十億

the BNP /ˌbiː en ˈpiː/ *abbr.* the British National Party (a small British political party on the extreme right) 英國國家黨（極右派小政黨）

BO /ˌbiː ˈəʊ; *NAmE* ˈoʊ/ *noun* [U] the abbreviation for 'body odour/odor' (an unpleasant smell from a person's body, especially of sweat) 汗臭，體臭（全寫為 body odour/odor）：*She's got BO.* 她有狐臭。

boa /ˈbəʊə; *NAmE* ˈboʊə/ *noun* **1** = BOA CONSTRICTOR **2** = FEATHER BOA

boa constrictor /ˈbəʊə kənstrɪktə(r); *NAmE* ˈboʊə/ (also **boa**) *noun* a large S American snake that kills animals for food by winding its long body around them and crushing them 巨蚺（南美蟒，捕食時把獵物縊死）

boar /bɔː(r)/ *noun* (*pl.* **boar** or **boars**) **1** (also **ˌwild ˈboar**) a wild pig 野豬 **2** a male pig that has not been CASTRATED 未閹的公豬 ➲ compare HOG, SOW

board 🔑 /bɔːd; *NAmE* bɔːrd/ *noun, verb*

▪ *noun*

▸ PIECE OF WOOD ETC. 木板等 **1** 🔑 [C, U] a long thin piece of strong hard material, especially wood, used, for example, for making floors, building walls and roofs and making boats 板；（尤指）木板：*He had ripped up the carpet, leaving only the bare boards.* 他用力扯去了地毯，只剩下裸露的地板。➲ see also CHIPBOARD, FLOORBOARD, HARDBOARD, SKIRTING BOARD **2** 🔑 [C] (especially in compounds 尤用於構成複合詞) a piece of wood, or other strong material, that is used for a special purpose …用木板（或板材）：*a blackboard* 黑板 ◇ *I'll write it up on the board.* 我會把它寫在黑板上。◇ (*BrE*) *a noticeboard* 佈告牌 ◇ (*NAmE*) *a bulletin board* 佈告牌 ◇ *The exam results went up on the board.* 考試成績張貼在佈告牌上。◇ *a diving board* 跳水板 ◇ *She jumped off the top board.* 她從高層跳板上跳了下來。◇ *a chessboard* 棋盤 ◇ *He removed the figure from the board.* 他從黑板上抹去了那個數字。➲ see also MESSAGE BOARD

▸ IN WATER SPORTS 水上運動 **3** [C] = BODYBOARD, SAILBOARD, SURFBOARD

▸ GROUP OF PEOPLE 班子 **4** 🔑 [C+sing./pl. v.] a group of people who have power to make decisions and control a company or other organization（公司或其他機構的）董事會，委員會，理事會：*She has a seat on the board of directors.* 她是董事會成員。◇ *The board is/are unhappy about falling sales.* 董事會對銷售額下降感到不滿。◇ *members of the board* 全體委員 ◇ *discussions at board level* 董事會討論 ◇ *the* ***academic board*** (= for example, of a British university) 高等學校教務委員會 ◇ (*NAmE*) *the* ***Board of Education*** (= a group of elected officials who are in charge of all the public schools in a particular area) 管理地方公立學校的教育委員會

▸ ORGANIZATION 機構 **5** [C] used in the name of some organizations（用於機構名稱）：*the Welsh Tourist Board* (= responsible for giving tourist information) 威爾士旅遊局

▸ MEALS 膳食 **6** [U] the meals that are provided when you stay in a hotel, GUEST HOUSE, etc.; what you pay for the meals（旅館、招待所等提供的）伙食，膳食；膳食費用：*He pays £90 a week board and lodging.* 他每週的膳宿花費為 90 英鎊。➲ see also BED AND BOARD, FULL BOARD, HALF BOARD

▸ EXAMS 考試 **7 boards** [pl.] (*old-fashioned, US*) exams that you take when you apply to go to college in the US（美國大學的）入學考試

▸ IN THEATRE 劇院 **8 the boards** [pl.] (*old-fashioned, informal*) the stage in a theatre 舞台：*His play is on the boards on Broadway.* 他的戲劇搬上了百老匯的舞台。◇ *She's treading the boards* (= working as an actress). 她當上了演員。

▸ ICE HOCKEY 冰球運動 **9 the boards** [pl.] (*NAmE*) the low wooden wall surrounding the area where a game of ICE HOCKEY is played（冰球場周圍的）界牆：*The puck went wide, hitting the boards.* 冰球去偏了，打在了界牆上。

HELP There are many other compounds ending in **board**. You will find them at their place in the alphabet. 以 board 結尾的複合詞還有很多，可在各字母中的適當位置查到。

IDM **aˌcross the ˈboard** involving everyone or everything in a company, an industry, etc. 全體；整體；全面：*The industry needs more investment across the board.* 這一行業需要全面增加投資。◇ *an across-the-board wage increase* 全體人員的加薪 **ˌgo by the ˈboard** (*BrE*) (of plans or principles 計劃或原則) to be rejected or ignored; to be no longer possible 被廢棄；被忽視：*All her efforts to be polite went by the board and she started to shout.* 她力圖保持和顏悅色的一切努力都白費了，於是她開始大喊大叫。 **on ˈboard** 🔑 **1** on or in a ship, an aircraft or a train 在船上（或飛機上、火車上）SYN **aboard**：*Have the passengers gone on board yet?* 乘客們登機了嗎？ **2** giving your support to an idea or a project 支持：*We must get more sponsors on board.* 我們必須得到更多贊助商的支持。◇ *You need to bring the whole staff on board.* 你需要取得全體員工的支持。 **take sth on ˈboard** to accept and understand an idea or a suggestion 採納，接納（主意、建議）：*I told her what I thought, but she didn't take my advice on board.* 我把我的想法告訴了她，可她沒有聽取我的建議。➲ more at SWEEP *v.*

B

■ *verb*
▸ GET ON PLANE/SHIP, ETC. 上飛機／船等 **1** [I, T] (*formal*) to get on a ship, train, plane, bus, etc. 上船（或火車、飛機、公共汽車等）: *Passengers are waiting to board.* 乘客們正在候機。◇ **~ sth** *The ship was boarded by customs officials.* 海關官員登上了這艘船。 **2** [I] **be boarding** when a plane or ship **is boarding**, it is ready for passengers to get on 讓乘客登機（或上船等）: *Flight BA193 for Paris is now boarding at Gate 37.* * BA193 次往巴黎航班的乘客現在可以在 37 號登機口登機。
▸ LIVE SOMEWHERE 住宿 **3** [I] **~ at .../with sb** to live and take meals in sb's home, in return for payment 付費（在某人家裏）膳宿: *She always had one or two students boarding with her.* 她的家總有一兩名寄宿學生。 **4** [I] to live at a school during the school year（在學校）寄宿
PHR V **,board sb 'out** (*BrE*) to arrange for sb to live somewhere away from their place of work, school, etc. in return for payment 把（某人）安排在外膳宿 **,board sth↔'up** to cover a window, door, etc. with wooden boards 用木板封住（窗門等）

board·er /ˈbɔːdə(r); *NAmE* ˈbɔːrd-/ *noun* (*especially BrE*) **1** a child who lives at school and goes home for the holidays 在學校寄宿的學生；寄宿生: *boarders and day pupils* 寄宿生和走讀生 **2** a person who pays money to live in a room in sb else's house 付費寄住者；寄膳宿者 SYN **lodger**

'board game *noun* any game played on a board, often using DICE and small pieces that are moved around 棋盤遊戲；圖版遊戲

board·ing /ˈbɔːdɪŋ; *NAmE* ˈbɔːrd-/ *noun* [U] **1** (*BrE*) long pieces of wood that are put together to make a wall, etc.（做牆等的）木板；板材 **2** the arrangement by which school students live at their school, going home during the holidays（學生的）寄宿: *boarding fees* 寄宿費用

'boarding card (*BrE*) (also **'boarding pass** *NAmE, BrE*) *noun* a card that you show before you get on a plane or boat 登機卡；登船卡

'boarding house *noun* a private house where people can pay for accommodation and meals 提供膳宿的私人住宅

'boarding kennel *noun* [usually pl.] (*BrE*) a place where people can leave their dogs to be taken care of when they go on holiday/vacation 狗的臨時寄養所 ➲ see also KENNEL (2)

'boarding school *noun* a school where children can live during the school year 寄宿學校 ➲ compare DAY SCHOOL (1)

board·room /ˈbɔːdruːm; -rʊm; *NAmE* ˈbɔːrd-/ *noun* a room in which the meetings of the board of a company (= the group of people who control it) are held 董事會會議室: *a boardroom row* 董事會會議上的爭吵

board·sail·ing /ˈbɔːdseɪlɪŋ; *NAmE* ˈbɔːrd-/ *noun* [U] = WINDSURFING

board·walk /ˈbɔːdwɔːk; *NAmE* ˈbɔːrd-/ *noun* (*especially NAmE*) a path made of wooden boards, especially on a beach or near water 木板人行道（尤指海灘或岸邊的）

boast /bəʊst; *NAmE* boʊst/ *verb, noun*
■ *verb* **1** [I, T] to talk with too much pride about sth that you have or can do 自誇；自吹自擂: *I don't want to boast, but I can actually speak six languages.* 我並不想吹噓，但我確實能講六種語言。◇ **~ about sth** *She is always boasting about how wonderful her children are.* 她總是誇耀她的孩子多麼出色。◇ **~ of sth** *He openly boasted of his skill as a burglar.* 他公然炫耀他的盜竊手法。◇ **~ that ...** *Sam boasted that she could beat anyone at poker.* 薩姆吹噓說打撲克牌誰都贏不了她。◇ **+ speech** *'I won!' she boasted.* "我贏了！" 她誇口道。 **2** [T] (not used in the progressive tenses 不用於進行時) **~ sth** to have sth that is impressive and that you can be proud of 有（值得自豪的東西）: *The hotel also boasts two swimming pools and a golf course.* 那家酒店還有兩個游泳池和一個高爾夫球場。
■ *noun* **~ (that ...)** (often *disapproving*) something that a person talks about in a very proud way, often to seem more important or clever 誇耀；誇口: *Despite his boasts that his children were brilliant, neither of them went to college.* 儘管他誇讚他的兩個孩子聰明，他們卻都沒唸上大學。◇ *It was her* **proud boast** *that she had never missed a day's work because of illness.* 她所引以自豪的是她從未因病而耽誤過一天工作。

boast·ful /ˈbəʊstfl; *NAmE* ˈboʊstfl/ *adj.* (*disapproving*) talking about yourself in a very proud way 自吹自擂的；自誇的: *I tried to emphasize my good points without sounding boastful.* 我在強調自己的優點時盡量不讓人覺得是在自我吹噓。

boat /bəʊt; *NAmE* boʊt/ *noun*
1 a vehicle (smaller than a ship) that travels on water, moved by OARS, sails or a motor 小船；汽艇；舟: *a* **rowing/sailing boat** 划艇；帆船 ◇ *a fishing boat* 漁船 ◇ *You can take a* **boat trip** *along the coast.* 你可以乘船沿海岸旅遊一趟。➲ see also CANAL BOAT, LIFEBOAT, MOTORBOAT, POWERBOAT, SPEEDBOAT, STEAMBOAT **2** any ship（泛指）船: *'How are you going to France?' 'We're going* **by boat** *(= by FERRY).'* "你們怎麼去法國？" "我們乘船去。" ➲ VISUAL VOCAB pages V54, V55, V56 ➲ see also GRAVY BOAT, SAUCE BOAT
IDM **be in the same 'boat** to be in the same difficult situation 處於同樣的困境 ➲ more at BURN *v.*, FLOAT *v.*, MISS *v.*, PUSH *v.*, ROCK *v.*

boat·er /ˈbəʊtə(r); *NAmE* ˈboʊt-/ *noun* a hard STRAW hat with a flat top 平頂硬草帽 ➲ VISUAL VOCAB page V65

boat·hook /ˈbəʊthʊk; *NAmE* ˈboʊt-/ *noun* a long pole with a hook at one end, used for pulling or pushing boats 撐篙（一端有鉤，用於推拉船隻）

boat·house /ˈbəʊthaʊs; *NAmE* ˈboʊt-/ *noun* a building beside a river or lake for keeping a boat in 船庫

boat·ing /ˈbəʊtɪŋ; *NAmE* ˈboʊtɪŋ/ *noun* [U] the activity of using a small boat for pleasure 划船（運動或消遣）: *to go boating* 去划船 ◇ *Local activities include walking, boating and golf.* 當地的活動包括散步、划船以及打高爾夫球。

boat·man /ˈbəʊtmən; *NAmE* ˈboʊt-/ *noun* (*pl.* **-men** /-mən/) a man who earns money from small boats, either by carrying passengers or goods on them, or by renting them out 靠小船營生的人；擺渡者；小船出租人

'boat people *noun* [pl.] people who escape from their own country in small boats to try to find safety in another country 船民（乘小船逃到他國的難民）

boat·swain /ˈbəʊsn; *NAmE* ˈboʊ-/ *noun* = BOSUN

'boat train *noun* a train that takes passengers to or from a place where a boat arrives or leaves 港口聯運列車；港口接駁列車

boat·yard /ˈbəʊtjɑːd; *NAmE* ˈboʊtjɑːrd/ *noun* a place where boats are built, repaired or kept 造船廠；修船廠；船塢

Bob /bɒb; *NAmE* bɑːb/ *noun*
IDM **Bob's your 'uncle** (*BrE, informal*) used to say how easy and quick it is to do a particular task 易如反掌: *Press here and Bob's your uncle! It's disappeared.* 按一下這裏就成了！消失了。

bob /bɒb; *NAmE* bɑːb/ *verb, noun*
■ *verb* (**-bb-**) **1** [I, T] to move or make sth move quickly up and down, especially in water（使在水中）上下快速移動，擺動: **~ up and down** *Tiny boats bobbed up and down in the harbour.* 一些小船在港灣中顛簸。◇ **~ sth (up and down)** *She bobbed her head nervously.* 她緊張地不斷點頭。 **2** [T] **~ sth** to cut sb's hair so that it is the same length all the way around 剪短（頭髮）
PHR V **,bob 'up** to come to the surface suddenly（突然）冒出: *The dark head of a seal bobbed up a few yards away.* 在幾碼遠處一隻海豹的黑腦袋猛地鑽出水面。
■ *noun* **1** a quick movement down and up of your head and body 快速的點頭（或鞠躬）: *a bob of the head* 點頭 **2** a style of a woman's hair in which it is cut the same length all the way around（女式）齊短髮型: *She wears her hair in a bob.* 她留齊短髮。➲ VISUAL VOCAB page V60 **3** (*pl.* **bob**) (*informal*) an old British coin, the SHILLING, worth 12 old pence 先令（英國舊制硬幣，等於 12 舊便士）: *That'll cost a few bob (= a lot of money).* 那東西很值錢。 **4** = BOBSLEIGH IDM see BIT

bobbed /bɒbd; *NAmE* bɑːbd/ *adj.* (of hair 頭髮) cut so that it hangs loosely to the level of the chin all around the back and sides 齊而短的

bob·ber /ˈbɒbə(r); *NAmE* ˈbɑːb-/ *noun* **1** a floating object used in fishing to hold the hook at the right depth（釣魚用的）浮子，浮標 **2** (*BrE*) a person who rides on a BOBSLEIGH 乘大雪橇的人

bob·bin /ˈbɒbɪn; *NAmE* ˈbɑːbɪn/ *noun* a small device on which you wind thread, used, for example, in a sewing machine 線軸；繞線筒

bob·ble /ˈbɒbl; *NAmE* ˈbɑːbl/ *noun, verb*

■ ***noun*** (*BrE*) a small, soft ball, usually made of wool, that is used especially for decorating clothes 小絨球，小羊毛球（尤用作衣服綴飾）**SYN** **pompom**：*a woolly hat with a bobble on top* 帽頂帶一隻小絨球的羊毛帽子 ➲ VISUAL VOCAB page V65

■ ***verb*** (*informal*) **1** [I] **+ adv./prep.** to move along the ground with small BOUNCES 彈跳着向前移動：*The ball somehow bobbled into the net.* 球不知怎麼在地上彈了幾下鑽入網窩。 **2** [T] **~ sth** (*NAmE*) to drop a ball or to fail to stop it 漏球；漏接球；沒有停住球：*She tried to catch the ball but bobbled it.* 她想要接球，但沒有接住。 **3** [I] (*BrE, informal*) (of a piece of clothing, especially one made of wool 衣服，尤指毛料的) to become covered in very small balls of FIBRE 起絨線球

bobby /ˈbɒbi; *NAmE* ˈbɑːbi/ *noun* (*pl.* **-ies**) (*old-fashioned, BrE, informal*) a police officer 警察 **ORIGIN** Named after Sir Robert Peel, the politician who created London's police force in the 19th century. **Bobby** is a familiar form of 'Robert'. 源自羅伯特 • 皮爾爵士的名字。他於 19 世紀創建了倫敦的警察隊伍。Bobby 是 Robert 的昵稱。

ˌbobby-ˈdazzler *noun* (*old-fashioned, BrE, informal*) an excellent or very special person or thing 出色的人（或事物）；與眾不同的人（或事物）

ˈbobby pin (*NAmE*) (*BrE* **hair·grip**, **grip**, **kirby grip**) *noun* a small thin piece of metal or plastic folded in the middle, used by women for holding their hair in place 髮夾 ➲ compare HAIRPIN (1)

ˈbobby socks *noun* [pl.] short white socks worn with a dress or skirt, especially by girls and young women in the US in the 1940s and 50s（20 世紀 40 和 50 年代美國少女和年輕婦女愛穿的）白色短襪

bob·cat /ˈbɒbkæt; *NAmE* ˈbɑːb-/ *noun* a N American wild cat 短尾貓，紅貓（北美野貓）

bobs /bɒbz; *NAmE* bɑːbz/ *noun* [pl.] **IDM** see BIT *n.*

bob·sleigh /ˈbɒbsleɪ; *NAmE* ˈbɑːb-/ (*BrE*) (*NAmE* **bob·sled** /ˈbɒbsled; *NAmE* ˈbɑːb-/) (also **bob**) *noun* a racing SLEDGE (= a vehicle for two or more people that slides over snow) 大雪橇（供兩人或以上比賽用）➲ VISUAL VOCAB page V48

bob·tail /ˈbɒbteɪl; *NAmE* ˈbɑːbteɪl/ *noun* **1** a dog, cat or horse with a tail that has been cut short 短尾狗（或貓、馬）**2** a tail that has been cut short 截短的尾巴；短尾

bod /bɒd; *NAmE* bɑːd/ *noun* (*informal*) **1** (*BrE*) a person 人：*She's a bit of an odd bod* (= rather strange). 她是個相當古怪的人。 **2** a person's body 人體；身體：*He's got a great bod.* 他是個大塊頭。

bo·da·cious /bəʊˈdeɪʃəs; *NAmE* boʊ-/ *adj.* (*informal, especially NAmE*) **1** excellent; extremely good 出色的；非凡的；非常棒的 **2** willing to take risks or to do sth shocking 敢於冒險的；大膽的 **SYN** **audacious**

bode /bəʊd; *NAmE* boʊd/ *verb*

IDM **bode ˈwell/ˈill (for sb/sth)** (*formal*) to be a good/bad sign for sb/sth（對某人／某事）是吉兆，是凶兆 **SYN** **augur**：*These figures do not bode well for the company's future.* 這些數據對於公司的前景不是個好兆頭。

bodge /bɒdʒ; *NAmE* bɑːdʒ/ *verb* **~ sth (up/together)** (*BrE, informal*) to make or repair sth in a way that is not as good as it should be 粗製濫造；拙劣地修補

Bodhi·sat·tva /ˌbɒdɪˈsɑːtvə; *NAmE* ˌboʊd-/ *noun* (in Mahayana Buddhism 大乘佛教) a person who is able to reach NIRVANA (= a state of peace and happiness) but who delays doing this because of the suffering of other humans 菩提薩埵；菩薩

bodh·rán /ˈbaʊrɑːn; *NAmE* ˈbɔːr-/ *noun* (*IrishE*) a shallow Irish drum that you hold sideways in your hand and play with a short wooden stick 寶蘭鼓（愛爾蘭小鼓）

bod·ice /ˈbɒdɪs; *NAmE* ˈbɑːdɪs/ *noun* the top part of a woman's dress, above the waist 連衣裙上身

ˈbodice-ripper *noun* (*informal*) a romantic novel or film/movie with a lot of sex in it, which is set in the past（以舊時生活為背景的）性愛小說（或電影）

bod·ily /ˈbɒdɪli; *NAmE* ˈbɑːd-/ *adj., adv.*

■ ***adj.*** [only before noun] connected with the human body 人體的；身體的：*bodily functions/changes/needs* 身體的機能／變化／需要 ◇ *bodily fluids* 體液 ◇ *bodily harm* (= physical injury) 對身體的傷害

■ ***adv.*** **1** by moving the whole of sb's body; by force 移動全身地；用力地：*The force of the blast hurled us bodily to the ground.* 爆炸的力量把我們震落在地上。◇ *He lifted her bodily into the air.* 他把她整個人舉到空中。 **2** in one piece; completely 整個地；完全地：*The monument was moved bodily to a new site.* 整個紀念碑被遷到了新的地點。

bod·kin /ˈbɒdkɪn; *NAmE* ˈbɑːd-/ *noun* a thick needle with no point 粗鈍的縫針；大眼粗針；錐子

body 🔑 /ˈbɒdi; *NAmE* ˈbɑːdi/ *noun* (*pl.* **-ies**)

▸ OF PERSON/ANIMAL 人；動物 **1** 🔑 [C] the whole physical structure of a human or an animal 身體；軀體：*a **human/female/male/naked body*** 人／女性／男性／赤裸的身體 ◇ *parts of the body* 身體的部位 ◇ *His whole body was trembling.* 他渾身發抖。◇ ***body fat/weight/temperature/size/heat*** 身體的脂肪；體重；體溫；身材；體熱 **2** 🔑 [C] the main part of a body not including the head, or not including the head, arms and legs 軀幹：*She had injuries to her head and body.* 她的頭上和身上都有傷。◇ *He has a large body, but thin legs.* 他身寬腿細。 **3** 🔑 [C] the body of a dead person or animal 屍體；死屍：*a dead body* 一具屍體 ◇ *The family of the missing girl has been called in by the police to identify the body.* 失踪女孩的家人已被警察叫來認屍。

▸ MAIN PART 主體 **4** [sing.] **the ~ of sth** the main part of sth, especially a building, a vehicle or a book, an article, etc.（尤指建築、車輛或書、文章等的）主體，主要部份：*the body of a plane* (= the central part where the seats are) 飛機機身 ◇ *the **main body** of the text* 課文的正文

▸ GROUP OF PEOPLE 集體 **5** 🔑 [C+sing./pl. v.] a group of people who work or act together, often for an official purpose, or who are connected in some other way 團體；社團；群體：*a **regulatory**/**an advisory**/**a review body*** 監管／咨詢／評審機構 ◇ *The governing body of the school is/are concerned about discipline.* 學校的管理部門很重視紀律問題。◇ *recognized professional bodies such as the Law Association* 諸如律師公會之類的獲得承認的專業團體 ◇ *An independent body has been set up to investigate the affair.* 已成立了一個獨立機構調查這件事。◇ *A large body of people will be affected by the tax cuts.* 將有一大批人受到減稅的影響。◇ *The protesters marched **in a body*** (= all together) *to the White House.* 抗議者集體遊行到白宮。◇ *a meeting of representatives of the student body and teaching staff* 全體學生和教師代表大會

▸ LARGE AMOUNT 大量 **6** [C] **~ of sth** a large amount or collection of sth 大量；大批；大堆：*a vast **body of evidence/information/research*** 大量證據／信息／研究 ◇ *large bodies of water* (= lakes or seas) 大片水域 ◇ *There is a powerful body of opinion against the ruling.* 裁決引起一片譁然。

▸ OBJECT 物體 **7** [C] (*formal*) an object 物體：***heavenly bodies*** (= stars, planets, etc.) 天體（恒星、行星等）◇ *an operation to remove a **foreign body*** (= sth that would not usually be there) *from a wound* 清除傷口異物的手術

▸ OF DRINK/HAIR 飲料；頭髮 **8** [U] the full strong flavour of alcoholic drinks or the thick healthy quality of sb's hair（酒的）濃香，香醇；（頭髮的）濃密：*a wine with plenty of body* 濃郁香醇的葡萄酒 ◇ *Regular use of conditioner is supposed to give your hair more body.* 經常使用護髮素能使頭髮更濃密。

B

▸ **-BODIED** 有…軀體，濃郁味道等 **9** (in adjectives 構成形容詞) having the type of body mentioned 有…的身體（或濃郁味道等）的：*full-bodied red wines* 醇厚的紅葡萄酒 ◇ *soft-bodied insects* 軟體昆蟲 ➲ see also ABLE-BODIED

▸ **CLOTHING** 衣服 **10** [C] (*BrE*) (*NAmE* **body·suit**) a piece of clothing which fits tightly over a woman's upper body and bottom, usually fastening between the legs 女緊身衣（通常扣於兩腿間）

IDM ▸ **body and 'soul** with all your energy 竭盡全力；全心全意：*She committed herself body and soul to fighting for the cause.* 她全心全意為這一事業而奮鬥。 **keep body and 'soul together** to stay alive with just enough of the food, clothing, etc. that you need 勉強餬口；生活拮据 **SYN** **survive**：*They barely have enough money to keep body and soul together.* 他們僅有活命的錢。 ➲ more at BONE *n.*, DEAD *adj.*, SELL *v.*

Vocabulary Building 詞彙擴充

Actions expressing emotions 表達情感的動作

Often parts of the body are closely linked to particular verbs. The combination of the verb and part of the body expresses an emotion or attitude. 身體部位常與某些動詞緊密相連，搭配運用可表達特定的情感或態度。

action	part of body	you are ...
bite	lips	nervous
clench	fist	angry, aggressive
click	fingers	trying to remember sth
click	tongue	annoyed
drum/tap	fingers	impatient
hang	head	ashamed
lick	lips	anticipating sth good, nervous
nod	head	agreeing
purse	lips	disapproving
raise	eyebrows	enquiring, surprised
scratch	head	puzzled
shake	head	disagreeing
shrug	shoulders	doubtful, indifferent
stamp	foot	angry
wrinkle	nose	feeling dislike or distaste
wrinkle	forehead	puzzled

For example 比如：*She bit her lip nervously.* 她緊張地咬嘴唇。◇ *He scratched his head and looked thoughtful.* 他撓着頭顯出一副深思的表情。◇ *I wrinkled my nose in disgust.* 我厭惡地皺起鼻子。◇ *She raised questioning eyebrows.* 她揚起眉毛表示懷疑。

'body armour (*especially US* **'body armor**) *noun* [U] clothing worn by the police, etc. to protect themselves 防彈服，胸甲，防彈背心（警察等穿）

'body bag *noun* a bag for carrying a dead body in, for example in a war 運屍袋

'body blow *noun* something which has damaging effects on sb/sth, creating problems or causing severe disappointment 嚴重打擊；挫折

body·board /ˈbɒdibɔːd; *NAmE* ˈbɑːdibɔːrd/ *noun* a short light type of SURFBOARD that you ride lying on your front 俯伏衝浪板；趴板 ▸ **body·board·ing** *noun* [U] ➲ VISUAL VOCAB page V50

body·build·ing /ˈbɒdibɪldɪŋ; *NAmE* ˈbɑːdi-/ *noun* [U] the activity of doing regular exercises in order to make your muscles bigger and stronger 健身 ▸ **body·build·er** *noun*

'body-check *noun* (in ICE HOCKEY 冰上曲棍球) an attempt to prevent a player's movement by blocking them with your shoulder or hip（用肩或臀的）身體阻截，身體阻擋

'body clock *noun* the natural tendency that your body has to sleep, eat, etc. at particular times of the day（人體）生物鐘

'body double *noun* a person who takes part in a film/movie in place of an actor when the scene involves being naked, or using special or dangerous skills 替身演員

body·guard /ˈbɒdigɑːd; *NAmE* ˈbɑːdigɑːrd/ *noun* [C+sing./pl. v.] a person or a group of people who are employed to protect sb 保鏢，警衛（隊）：*The President's bodyguard is/are armed.* 總統的護衛人員攜帶着武器。

'body language *noun* [U] the process of communicating what you are feeling or thinking by the way you place and move your body rather than by words 身勢語，肢體語言（通過姿勢等表露思想感情）

body mass index *noun* (*abbr.* **BMI**) an approximate measure of whether sb weighs too much or too little, calculated by dividing their weight in kilograms by their height in metres squared 體重指數；身體質量指數

'body odour (*especially US* **'body odor**) *noun* [U] (*abbr.* **BO**) an unpleasant smell from a person's body, especially of sweat 汗臭；體臭

'body piercing (also **pier·cing**) *noun* [U] the making of holes in parts of the body as a decoration 穿體裝飾：*tattooing and body piercing* 文身和穿體裝飾

the ˌbody 'politic *noun* [sing.] (*formal*) all the people of a particular nation considered as an organized political group 全體人民，國家（被視為政治集體）

'body-popping *noun* [U] a way of dancing in which you make stiff movements like a ROBOT 機械舞（動作如機器人般僵硬的舞蹈風格）

'body search *noun* a search of a person's body, for example by the police or by a customs official, for drugs, weapons, etc. 搜身

'body shop *noun* **1** the part of a car factory where the main bodies of the cars are made（汽車廠）車身製造車間 **2** a place where repairs are made to the main bodies of cars（汽車）車身維修廠

body·snatch·er /ˈbɒdisnætʃə(r); *NAmE* ˈbɑːdi-/ *noun* a person who stole bodies from GRAVEYARDS in the past, especially to sell for medical experiments（舊時為出售屍體供醫學實驗等的）墓地盜屍人

'body stocking *noun* a piece of clothing that fits closely over the whole body from the neck to the ankles, often including the arms, worn for example by dancers 連褲緊身衣（常有袖）

body·suit /ˈbɒdisuːt; *NAmE* ˈbɑːdisuːt; *BrE* also -sjuːt/ **1** (*NAmE*) (*BrE* **body**) *noun* a piece of clothing which fits tightly over a woman's upper body and bottom, usually fastening between the legs 女緊身衣（通常扣於兩腿間）**2** a piece of clothing that fits closely over the body, including the arms and legs, worn by men and women for sports（運動時穿的）緊身衣褲

'body swerve *noun* a sudden movement that you make to the side when running to avoid crashing into sb/sth（奔跑過程中為避免衝撞的）突然側身

'body warmer *noun* (*BrE*) a thick warm jacket without sleeves that you wear outdoors（戶外穿的）無袖厚夾克 ➲ VISUAL VOCAB page V61

body·work /ˈbɒdiwɜːk; *NAmE* ˈbɑːdiwɜːrk/ *noun* [U] the main outside structure of a vehicle, usually made of painted metal 車輛等的外殼，車身（通常為噴漆金屬）

Boer /bɔː(r)/ *noun* **1** a South African whose family originally came from the Netherlands 布爾人（即荷裔南非人）：*the Boer War* (= the war between the Boers and the British, 1899-1902) 布爾戰爭（1899 至 1902 年間布爾人與英國人的戰爭）➲ see also AFRIKANER **2 boer** (*SAfrE*) a farmer 農民；農夫 **3 boer** (*SAfrE, disapproving*) used to refer to a member of the police or the army, especially in the past（舊時用以指）警察，軍人

boere·wors /ˈbʊərəvɔːs; ˈbʊ-; *NAmE* -vɔːrs/ *noun* [U] (*SAfrE*) a spicy SAUSAGE that is prepared in a long piece and sold usually wound into a COIL (= a series of circles) 南非農夫香腸（盤起來出售的長條香腸）

bof·fin /ˈbɒfɪn; NAmE ˈbɑːfən/ *noun* (*BrE, informal*) a scientist, especially one doing research（尤指從事研究工作的）科學家，研究員

bog /bɒg; NAmE bɑːg; bɔːg/ *noun, verb*

■ ***noun*** **1** [C, U] (an area of) wet soft ground, formed of decaying plants 沼澤（地區）：*a peat bog* 泥炭沼 ➲ see also BOGGY **2** [C] (*BrE, slang*) a toilet/bathroom 廁所；浴室：*Have you got any **bog roll** (= toilet paper)?* 你帶衛生紙了嗎？

■ ***verb*** (**-gg-**)

PHR V **ˌbog sth/sb ˈdown (in sth)** [usually passive] **1** to make sth sink into mud or wet ground 使某人／某物陷進爛泥（或泥沼）：*The tank became bogged down in mud.* 坦克陷入了爛泥中。 **2** to prevent sb from making progress in an activity 妨礙；阻礙：*We mustn't get **bogged down** in details.* 我們一定不能因細節問題誤事。 **ˌbog ˈoff** (*BrE, taboo, slang*) only used in orders, to tell sb to go away（只用於命令）走開：*Bog off, I'm trying to sleep!* 走開，我要睡覺啦！

bogan /ˈbəʊgən; NAmE ˈboʊ-/ *noun* (*AustralE, NZE, informal*) a rude or socially unacceptable person 粗人；怪人

bogey /ˈbəʊgi; NAmE ˈboʊgi/ *noun* **1** (also **bogy**) a thing that causes fear, often without reason（無緣無故）使人害怕的事物 **2** (also **bogy**) (both *BrE*) (*NAmE* **boo·ger**) (*informal*) a piece of dried MUCUS from inside your nose（乾結的）鼻屎 **3** (also **bogy**) (*BrE*) = BOGEYMAN **4** (in GOLF 高爾夫球) a score of one stroke over PAR (= the standard score for a hole) 超一擊（超過擊入一洞的標準杆數一杆）➲ compare BIRDIE (2), EAGLE (2)

bo·gey·man (also **bogy·man**) /ˈbəʊgimæn; NAmE ˈboʊgi-/ *noun* (*BrE* also **bogey**, **bogy**) (*NAmE* usually **boo·gey·man**) (*pl.* **-men** /-men/) an imaginary evil spirit that is used to frighten children（用以嚇唬小孩的）鬼怪：*The bogeyman's coming!* 妖怪來了！

bog·gle /ˈbɒgl; NAmE ˈbɑːgl/ *verb* [I] **~ (at sth)** (*informal*) to be slow to do or accept sth because you are surprised or shocked by it（因吃驚而）不知所措，猶豫不決：*Even I boggle at the idea of spending so much money.* 一想到要花這麼多錢，連我都有點猶豫。

IDM **sth boggles the ˈmind** (also **the mind ˈboggles**) (*informal*) if sth **boggles the mind** or **the mind boggles** at it, it is so unusual that people find it hard to imagine or accept 使人無法想像；使人難以接受：*The vastness of space really boggles the mind.* 太空之遼闊的確使人難以想像。◇ *'He says he's married to his cats!' 'The mind boggles!'* "他說他和他的那些貓結婚了！" "難以置信！" ➲ compare MIND-BOGGLING

boggy /ˈbɒgi; NAmE ˈbɑːgi; ˈbɔːgi/ *adj.* (**bog·gier**, **bog·gi·est**) (of land 土地) soft and wet, like a BOG 鬆軟潮濕的；沼澤般的：*boggy ground* 鬆軟潮濕的地面

bogie /ˈbəʊgi; NAmE ˈboʊgi/ *noun* **1** (*especially BrE*) a frame with four or six wheels that forms part of a railway carriage/railroad car. The main body of the carriage/car usually rests on two bogies, one at each end.（軌道車輛）轉向架 **2** (*IndE*) a railway carriage/railroad car（火車的）客車廂

BOGOF /ˈbɒgɒf; NAmE ˈbɑːgɑːf/ *abbr.* (*BrE, informal*) buy one, get one free (a type of special offer used in shops/stores) 買一送一：*BOGOF offers and bargains* 買一送一的優惠與便宜貨

ˌbog-ˈstandard *adj.* (*BrE, informal*) ordinary; with no special features 普通的；一般的 **SYN** **average**

bogus /ˈbəʊgəs; NAmE ˈboʊ-/ *adj.* pretending to be real or genuine 假的；偽造的 **SYN** **false**：*a bogus doctor/contract* 冒牌醫生；偽造的合同 ◇ *bogus claims of injury by workers* 工人們對受傷情況的虛報

bogy, **bogy·man** = BOGEY, BOGEYMAN

bo·he·mian /bəʊˈhiːmiən; NAmE boʊˈh-/ *noun* a person, often sb who is involved with the arts, who lives in a very informal way without following accepted rules of behaviour 行為舉止不拘泥成規者；放蕩不羈的藝術家 ▸ **bo·he·mian** *adj.*：*a **bohemian** existence/lifestyle* 放蕩不羈的生活／生活方式

boho /ˈbəʊhəʊ; NAmE ˈboʊhoʊ/ (also **ˈboho chic**) *noun* [U] a style of women's fashion that was popular at the beginning of the 21st century. It included loose tops, long skirts, wide belts and boots. 波西米亞風格（流行於 21 世紀初的女性着裝風格，包括寬鬆上衣、長裙、寬腰帶和靴子）

boh·rium /ˈbɔːriəm/ *noun* [U] (*symb.* **Bh**) a RADIOACTIVE chemical element. Bohrium is produced when atoms COLLIDE (= crash into each other) 鈹（放射性化學元素）

boil 🔑 /bɔɪl/ *verb, noun*

■ ***verb*** **1** 🔑 [I, T] when a liquid **boils** or when you **boil** it, it is heated to the point where it forms bubbles and turns to steam or VAPOUR（使）沸騰；煮沸；燒開：*The water was bubbling and boiling away.* 水在咕嘟咕嘟地沸騰着。◇ **~ sth** *Boil plenty of salted water, then add the spaghetti.* 把足量的鹽水燒開，再放入意大利麪條。➲ VISUAL VOCAB page V27 **2** 🔑 [I, T] when a KETTLE, pan, etc. **boils** or when you **boil** a KETTLE, etc., it is heated until the water inside it **boils**（把壺、鍋等裏面的水）燒開：(*BrE*) *The kettle's boiling.* 壺開了。◇ **~ sth** *I'll boil the kettle and make some tea.* 我來燒壺開水泡點茶。◇ **+ adj.** *She left the gas on by mistake and the pan **boiled dry*** (= the water boiled until there was none left). 她忘了關煤氣，結果把鍋燒乾了。 **3** 🔑 [I, T] to cook or wash sth in boiling water; to be cooked or washed in boiling water 用沸水煮（或燙洗）；被煮（或燙洗）：*She put some potatoes on to boil.* 她煮了些土豆。◇ **~ sth** *boiled carrots/cabbage* 水煮胡蘿蔔／捲心菜 ◇ *to boil an egg for sb* 給某人煮個雞蛋 ◇ **~ sb sth** *to boil sb an egg* 給某人煮個雞蛋 ➲ COLLOCATIONS at COOKING **4** [I] **~ (with sth)** if you **boil** with anger, etc. or anger, etc. **boils** inside you, you are very angry 怒火中燒；異常氣憤：*He was boiling with rage.* 他怒不可遏。 **IDM** see BLOOD *n.*, WATCH *v.*

PHR V **ˌboil ˈdown** | **ˌboil sth↔ˈdown** to be reduced or to reduce sth by boiling（使）煮濃，熬濃 **ˌboil sth ˈdown (to sth)** to make sth, especially information, shorter by leaving out the parts that are not important 概括；歸納；壓縮：*The original speech I had written got boiled down to about ten minutes.* 我寫的演講原稿被壓縮到了大約十分鐘。 **ˌboil ˈdown to sth** (not used in the progressive tenses 不用於進行時) (of a situation, problem, etc. 局勢、問題等) to have sth as a main or basic part 歸結為；基本問題是：*In the end, **what it all boils down to** is money, or the lack of it.* 問題的癥結是錢，或者說是缺錢。 **ˌboil ˈover 1** (of liquid 液體) to boil and flow over the side of a pan, etc. 煮溢；漕出 **2** (*informal*) to become very angry 怒火中燒；大怒 **3** (of a situation, an emotion, etc. 局勢、情緒等) to change into sth more dangerous or violent 惡化；爆發 **SYN** **explode**：*Racial tension finally boiled over in the inner city riots.* 種族間的緊張狀態最終演化成了內城區的暴亂。 **ˌboil ˈup** if a situation or an emotion **boils up**, it becomes dangerous, worrying, etc.（局勢、情緒等）進入危急關頭，令人擔憂：*I could feel anger boiling up inside me.* 我感到怒火中燒。 **ˌboil sth↔ˈup** to heat a liquid or some food until it boils 把（液體或食物）燒開

■ ***noun*** **1** [sing.] a period of boiling; the point at which liquid boils 沸騰；沸點：(*BrE*) ***Bring** the soup **to the boil**, then allow it to simmer for five minutes.* 把湯煮開，然後文火煮五分鐘。◇ (*NAmE*) ***Bring** the soup **to a boil**.* 把湯煮開。 **2** [C] a painful infected swelling under the skin which is full of a thick yellow liquid (called PUS) 癤；皮下膿腫；黃水瘡

IDM **off the ˈboil** (*BrE*) less good than before 不如以前：*The second series of the show really went off the boil.* 節目的續集的確遜色一些。 **on the ˈboil** very active 十分活躍；如火如荼：*We have several projects all on the boil at once.* 我們熱火朝天地同時開展了幾個項目。

ˌboiled ˈsweet (*BrE*) (*NAmE* **ˌhard ˈcandy**) *noun* a hard sweet/candy made from boiled sugar, often with fruit flavours 硬糖（常加水果味）

boil·er /ˈbɔɪlə(r)/ (also **fur·nace** especially in *NAmE*) *noun* a container in which water is heated to provide hot water and heating in a building or to produce steam in an engine 鍋爐；汽鍋

B

boiler·maker /ˈbɔɪləmeɪkə(r); *NAmE* -lərm-/ *noun* **1** a person or company that makes boilers 鍋爐製造工（或公司） **2** (*NAmE*) a person who makes and repairs metal objects for industry 金屬製造維修工 **3** (*NAmE*) a drink of WHISKY followed immediately by a glass of beer 加啤威士忌（指飲下威士忌後立刻飲一杯啤酒）

boil·er·plate /ˈbɔɪləpleɪt; *NAmE* -lər-/ *noun* [C, U] (*NAmE*) a standard form of words that can be used as a model for writing parts of a business document, legal agreement, etc.（可供模仿的）樣板文件，文件範例

ˈboiler room *noun* **1** a room in a building or ship containing the boiler 鍋爐房；鍋爐間 **2** (*NAmE*) a room or office used by people using telephones to sell sth, especially shares, in an aggressive or a dishonest way 電話交易所，電話推銷室（以硬性或欺騙性手段推銷證券等的場所）

ˈboiler suit *noun* (*especially BrE*) (*NAmE* usually **cov·er·alls**) a piece of clothing like trousers/pants and a jacket in one piece, worn for doing dirty work 連衫褲工作服 ➲ compare OVERALLS *n.* (2)

boil·ing /ˈbɔɪlɪŋ/ (also **ˌboiling ˈhot**) *adj.* very hot 熾熱的；很熱的 **SYN** **baking**：*You must be boiling in that sweater!* 你穿着那件毛衣一定很熱！◇ *a boiling hot day* 酷熱的一天 **OPP** **freezing**

ˈboiling point *noun* [U, C] **1** the temperature at which a liquid starts to boil 沸點 **2** the point at which a person becomes very angry, or a situation is likely to become violent 極度憤怒；（某種狀態的）爆發點：*Racial tension has **reached boiling point**.* 種族間的緊張狀態已達到一觸即發的程度。

bois·ter·ous /ˈbɔɪstərəs/ *adj.* (of people, animals or behaviour 人、動物或行為) noisy and full of life and energy 熱鬧的；充滿活力的；活蹦亂跳的：*It was a challenge, keeping ten boisterous seven-year-olds amused.* 要逗着十個好動的七歲孩子玩真是一種挑戰。▶ **bois·ter·ous·ly** *adv.*

bok choy /ˌbɒk ˈtʃɔɪ; *NAmE* ˌbɑːk/ (*NAmE*) (*BrE* **pak choi**) *noun* [U] a type of CHINESE CABBAGE with long dark green leaves and thick white STEMS 白菜；小白菜

bold /bəʊld; *NAmE* boʊld/ *adj., noun*

■ ***adj.*** (**bold·er**, **bold·est**) **1** (of people or behaviour 人或舉止) brave and confident; not afraid to say what you feel or to take risks 大膽自信的；敢於表白情感的；敢於冒險的：*It was a bold move on their part to open a business in France.* 在法國開業是他們的一個大膽舉動。◇ *The wine made him bold enough to approach her.* 他趁着酒勁，鼓足勇氣上前和她說話。 **2** (of shape, colour, lines, etc. 形狀、顏色、線條等) that can be easily seen; having a strong clear appearance 明顯的；輪廓突出的：*the bold outline of a mountain against the sky* 天空映襯下的山的清晰輪廓 ◇ *She paints with bold strokes of the brush.* 她的繪畫筆鋒遒勁。 **3** (*technical* 術語) (of printed words or letters 印刷字或字符) in a thick, dark TYPE 粗體的；黑體的：*Highlight the important words in bold type.* 用黑體突出重要詞語。◇ *bold lettering* 黑字體 ▶ **bold·ly** *adv.* **bold·ness** *noun* [U]

IDM **be/make so bold (as to do sth)** (*formal*) used especially when politely asking a question or making a suggestion which you hope will not offend anyone (although it may criticize them slightly)（謙辭，表示自己輕率說話）不揣冒昧，恕我無禮；擅自；膽敢：*If I may be so bold as to suggest that he made a mistake in his calculations …* 恕我冒昧說，他的計算有個錯誤… **(as) bold as ˈbrass** (*BrE, informal*) without showing any respect, shame or fear 放肆的；厚顏無恥的；膽大妄為的

■ ***noun*** (also **bold·face**) /ˈbəʊldfeɪs; *NAmE* ˈboʊld-/) [U] (*technical* 術語) thick, dark TYPE used for printing words or letters 黑體；粗體：*Headwords are printed **in bold**.* 首詞用黑體印刷。

bole /bəʊl; *NAmE* boʊl/ *noun* the main STEM of a tree 樹幹 **SYN** **trunk**

bol·ero /bəˈleərəʊ; *NAmE* bəˈleroʊ/ *noun* (*pl.* **-os**) **1** a traditional Spanish dance; a piece of music for this dance 波列羅舞（一種傳統的西班牙舞）；波列羅舞曲 **2** /*BrE* also ˈbɒlərəʊ/ a women's short jacket that is not fastened at the front 波蕾若外套（前胸敞開的女短上衣）

bol·etus /bəˈliːtəs/ (also **bol·ete** /bəˈliːt/) *noun* [C, U] a MUSHROOM with small round holes under the top part. Some types of boletus can be eaten. 牛肝菌屬真菌（有些種類可食用）

boll /bəʊl; *NAmE* boʊl/ *noun* the part of the cotton plant that contains the seeds 棉鈴

bol·lard /ˈbɒlɑːd; *NAmE* ˈbɑːlərd/ *noun* **1** (*BrE*) a short thick post that is used to stop vehicles from going on to a road or part of a road（阻止車輛開到某段路上的）短柱，護柱 ➲ VISUAL VOCAB page V3 **2** a short thick post on a ship, or on land close to water, to which a ship's rope may be tied（甲板或岸邊的）繫纜柱

bol·lock·ing /ˈbɒləkɪŋ; *NAmE* ˈbɑːl-/ *noun* (*BrE, taboo*) an occasion when sb tells you that they are very angry with you, often by shouting at you 訓斥；臭罵：*to give sb a bollocking* 把某人臭罵一通 ◇ *to get a bollocking* 捱了一頓臭罵 **HELP** There are more polite ways to express this, for example **to give sb/to get a rocket**, or **to tear a strip off sb**. 較禮貌的說法有 to give sb/to get a rocket，或 to tear a strip off sb 等。

bol·locks /ˈbɒləks; *NAmE* ˈbɑːl-/ *noun* (*BrE, taboo, slang*) **1** [U] nonsense 胡說；廢話：*You're talking a load of bollocks!* 你這是一派胡言！ **2** [pl.] a man's TESTICLES 睾丸 **3 Bollocks!** *exclamation* used as a swear word when sb is disagreeing with sth, or when they are angry about sth（粗俗話，表示不贊同或氣憤）：*Bollocks! He never said that!* 胡說！他從沒那麼說過！

ˈboll weevil *noun* an insect that damages cotton plants 棉鈴象甲，棉鈴象鼻蟲（棉花害蟲）

Bol·ly·wood /ˈbɒliwʊd; *NAmE* ˈbɑːl-/ *noun* [U] (*informal*) used to refer to the Hindi film/movie industry, which mainly takes place in the Indian city of Mumbai (formerly called Bombay) 寶萊塢（指主要集中於孟買的印度電影業）

bol·ogna /bəˈləʊnjə; bəˈlɒnjə; *NAmE* -ˈloʊ-/ (also **ba·lo·ney**) *noun* [U] (*NAmE*) a type of SAUSAGE that is put in SANDWICHES, made of a mixture of meats 波倫亞大紅腸（用各種肉混合製成）

bolo tie /ˈbəʊləʊ taɪ; *NAmE* ˈboʊloʊ/ *noun* (*NAmE*) a string worn around the neck and fastened with a decorative CLASP or bar 波羅領帶（用飾物或搭扣繫的線編領帶） ➲ see also BOOTLACE

Bol·shevik /ˈbɒlʃəvɪk; *NAmE* ˈboʊl-/ *noun* a member of the group in Russia that took control after the 1917 Revolution 布爾什維克（1917 年大革命後掌權的俄國社會民主黨黨員） ▶ **Bol·shevik** *adj.* **Bol·shevism** /ˈbɒlʃəvɪzəm; *NAmE* ˈboʊl-/ *noun* [U]

bol·shie (also **bol·shy**) /ˈbɒlʃi; *NAmE* ˈboʊl-/ *adj.* (*BrE, informal, disapproving*) (of a person 人) creating difficulties or arguments deliberately, and refusing to be helpful 找茬的；不給人方便的

bol·ster /ˈbəʊlstə(r); *NAmE* ˈboʊl-/ *verb, noun*

■ ***verb*** to improve sth or make it stronger 改善；加強：**~ sth** *to bolster sb's **confidence/courage/morale*** 增加某人的信心／勇氣／士氣 ◇ **~ sth up** *Falling interest rates may help to bolster up the economy.* 利率下降可能有助於刺激經濟。

■ ***noun*** a long thick PILLOW that is placed across the top of a bed under the other pillows 墊枕（長而厚）

bolt /bəʊlt; *NAmE* boʊlt/ *noun, verb, adv.*

■ ***noun*** **1** a long, narrow piece of metal that you slide across the inside of a door or window in order to lock it（門窗的）閂，插銷 **2** a piece of metal like a screw without a point which is used with a circle of metal (= a NUT) to fasten things together 螺栓：*nuts and bolts* 螺帽和螺栓 ➲ VISUAL VOCAB page V20 **3 ~ of lightning** a sudden flash of LIGHTNING in the sky, appearing as a line 閃電 **4** a short heavy arrow shot from a CROSSBOW 弩箭 **5** a long piece of cloth wound in a roll around a piece of cardboard 一匹布

IDM **a ˌbolt from the ˈblue** an event or a piece of news which is sudden and unexpected; a complete surprise 突如其來的事件（或消息）；晴天霹靂：*Her dismissal came as a bolt from the blue.* 她的解雇簡直就是晴天

霹靂。 **make a 'bolt for sth | make a 'bolt for it** to run away very fast, in order to escape 迅速逃跑；溜走 ➲ more at NUT *n.*, SHOOT *v.*

■ *verb* **1** [T, I] **~ (sth)** to fasten sth such as a door or window by sliding a bolt across; to be able to be fastened in this way 用插銷閂上；能被閂上：*Don't forget to bolt the door.* 別忘了閂門。◇ *The gate bolts on the inside.* 大門在裏面上閂。 **2** [T] to fasten things together with a bolt 用螺栓（把甲和乙）固定在一起： **~ A to B** *The vice is bolted to the workbench.* 這虎鉗是用螺栓固定在工作枱上的。◇ **~ A and B together** *The various parts of the car are then bolted together.* 然後汽車的各種部件便用螺栓裝配在一起。 **3** [I] if an animal, especially a horse, **bolts**, it suddenly runs away because it is frightened （馬等受驚）脫繮 **4** [I] (**+ adv./prep.**) (of a person 人) to run away, especially in order to escape 跑開；（尤指）逃跑：*When he saw the police arrive, he bolted down an alley.* 他看見警察來了，便從小巷逃走了。 **5** [T] **~ sth (down)** to eat sth very quickly 狼吞虎嚥：*Don't bolt your food!* 吃飯不能狼吞虎嚥！ **6** (*NAmE*) [T, I] **~ (sth)** to stop supporting a particular group or political party 停止支持（某團體或政黨）：*Many Democrats bolted the party to vote Republican.* 很多民主黨人放棄本黨，轉而投共和黨的票。 **7** [I] (of a plant, especially a vegetable 植物，尤指蔬菜) to grow too quickly and start producing seeds and so become less good to eat 過早結實（因而食用價值降低） IDM see STABLE DOOR *n.*

■ *adv.*

IDM **sit/stand bolt 'upright** to sit or stand with your back straight 背部筆挺地坐 / 站；坐 / 站得筆直

bolts 插銷；螺栓；弩箭

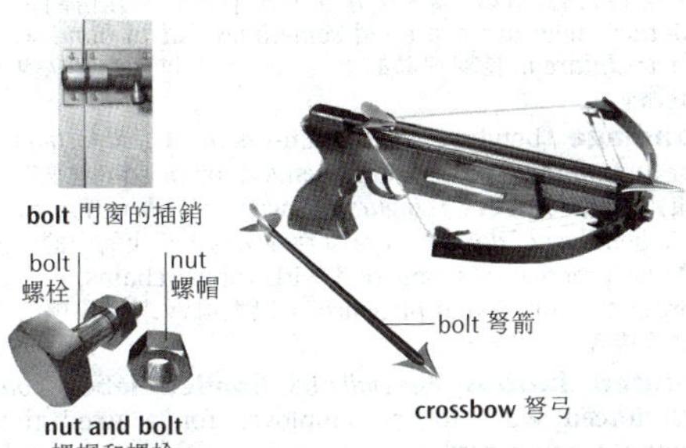

'bolt-action *adj.* (of a gun 槍) having a back part that is opened by turning a BOLT and sliding it back 手動栓式槍機的；用槍機的

'bolt-hole *noun* (*BrE*) a place that you can escape to, for example when you are in a difficult situation 匿身處；躲避困境之地

'bolt-on *adj.* [only before noun] able to be easily added to a machine, etc. to make it able to do sth new 易安裝的；貼附式的

bolus /ˈbəʊləs; *NAmE* ˈboʊləs/ *noun* **1** (*medical* 醫) a single amount of a drug that is given at one time（單次給藥的）劑量 SYN **dose 2** (*technical* 術語) a small round mass of substance, especially chewed food that is swallowed 小團；小丸；（尤指咀嚼後吞嚥的）食團

boma /ˈbəʊmə; *NAmE* ˈboʊ-/ *noun* (*EAfrE, SAfrE*) (in wild country) an area surrounded by a fence, often made of sticks, used to protect animals or people（野外的）圍欄防護場地

bomb 0- /bɒm; *NAmE* bɑːm/ *noun, verb*

■ *noun* **1** 0- [C] a weapon designed to explode at a particular time or when it is dropped or thrown 炸彈：*a* ***bomb attack/blast/explosion*** 轟炸；炸彈爆炸 ◇ *a* ***bomb goes off/explodes*** 炸彈爆炸 ◇ *extensive bomb damage* 轟炸造成的巨大破壞 ◇ *Hundreds of bombs were dropped on the city.* 幾百枚炸彈投到了這座城市。 ➲ see also DIRTY BOMB **2 the bomb** [sing.] nuclear weapons (ATOMIC or HYDROGEN bombs) 核武器；核彈：*countries which have the bomb* 擁有核武器的國家 **3 a bomb** [sing.] (*BrE, informal*) a lot of money 很多錢：*That dress must have cost a bomb!* 那條連衣裙所費不菲吧！ **4 a bomb** [sing.] (*NAmE, informal*) a complete failure 徹底的失敗：*The musical was a complete bomb on Broadway.* 那齣音樂劇在百老匯的演出完全失敗。 **5** [C] (*NAmE*) (in AMERICAN FOOTBALL 美式足球) a long forward throw of the ball 長傳 **6** [C] (*NAmE*) a container in which a liquid such as paint or insect poison is kept under pressure and released as a spray or as FOAM 氣溶膠彈式容器（油漆、殺蟲劑等液體加壓貯存可噴出）：*a bug bomb* (= used for killing insects) 殺蟲劑氣霧彈

IDM **be the 'bomb** (*NAmE*) to be very good; to be the best 很好；最佳：*Check out the new website. It's the bomb!* 看一看這新網站。簡直是太棒了！ **go down a 'bomb | go (like) a 'bomb** (*BrE*) to be very successful 十分成功：*Our performance went down a bomb.* 我們的演出獲得了巨大成功。◇ *The party was really going (like) a bomb.* 聚會辦得非常成功。 **go like a 'bomb** (*BrE*) (of a vehicle 車輛等) to go very fast 飛馳

■ *verb* **1** 0- [T] **~ sth** to attack sb/sth by leaving a bomb in a place or by dropping bombs from a plane 轟炸；對…投炸彈：*Terrorists bombed several army barracks.* 恐怖分子轟炸了幾處兵營。◇ *The city was heavily bombed in the war.* 這座城市在戰爭中遭到了猛烈轟炸。 **2** [I] **+ adv./prep.** (*BrE, informal*) to move very fast, especially in a vehicle, in a particular direction 快速移動，疾行（尤指乘車）：*They were bombing down the road at about 80 miles an hour.* 他們正以大約一小時 80 英里的速度沿路飛馳。 **3** [T, I] **~ (sth)** (*NAmE, informal*) to fail a test or an exam very badly （考試）慘敗：*The exam was impossible! I definitely bombed it.* 考試太難了！我肯定考砸了。 **4** [I] (*informal*) (of a play, show, etc. 戲劇、演出等) to fail very badly 大敗；票房極差；不賣座：*His latest musical bombed and lost thousands of dollars.* 他最近的一部音樂劇演砸了，賠了幾千元。

PHR V **be ˌbombed 'out (of sth)** **1** if you are **bombed out**, your home is destroyed by bombs （家園）被炸毀；被炸得無家可歸 **2** if a building is **bombed out**, it has been destroyed by bombs （建築）被炸毀

'bomb alert *noun* (*BrE*) = BOMB SCARE

bom·bard /bɒmˈbɑːd; *NAmE* bɑːmˈbɑːrd/ *verb* **1 ~ sb/sth (with sth)** to attack a place by firing large guns at it or dropping bombs on it continuously 轟炸；轟擊 **2 ~ sb/sth (with sth)** to attack sb with a lot of questions, criticisms, etc. or by giving them too much information 大量提問；大肆抨擊；提供過多信息：*We have been bombarded with letters of complaint.* 我們接二連三收到了大批的投訴信件。 ▸ **bom·bard·ment** *noun* [U, C]：*The city came under heavy bombardment.* 那座城市受到猛烈轟炸。

bom·bard·ier /ˌbɒmbəˈdɪə(r); *NAmE* ˌbɑːmbərˈdɪr/ *noun* **1** the person on a military plane in the US AIR FORCE who is responsible for aiming and dropping bombs （美國空軍的）投彈手 **2** a member of a low rank in the Royal Artillery (= a part of the British army that uses large guns) （英國皇家炮兵的）下士

bom·bast /ˈbɒmbæst; *NAmE* ˈbɑːm-/ *noun* [U] (*formal*) words which sound important but have little meaning, used to impress people 華而不實的言辭；大話 ▸ **bom·bas·tic** /bɒmˈbæstɪk; *NAmE* bɑːm-/ *adj.*：*a bombastic speaker* 大放厥詞的演說家

Bombay mix /ˌbɒmbeɪ ˈmɪks; *NAmE* ˌbɑːm-/ *noun* [U] an Indian food consisting of LENTILS, PEANUTS and spices, eaten as a SNACK 兵豆花生香味什錦（印度小吃）

'bomb bay *noun* a part of an aircraft in which bombs are held and from which they can be dropped （飛機的）炸彈艙

'bomb disposal *noun* [U] the job of removing or exploding bombs in order to make an area safe 未爆彈處理：*a* ***bomb disposal expert/squad/team*** 拆彈專家 / 小組

bombed /bɒmd; *NAmE* bɑːmd/ *adj.* [not before noun] (*informal*) extremely drunk 爛醉如泥

B

bomb·er /ˈbɒmə(r); *NAmE* ˈbɑːm-/ *noun* **1** a plane that carries and drops bombs 轟炸機 **2** a person who puts a bomb somewhere illegally 非法放置炸彈者

ˈbomber jacket *noun* a short jacket that fits tightly around the waist and fastens with a ZIP/ZIPPER 緊腰短夾克

bomb·ing /ˈbɒmɪŋ; *NAmE* ˈbɑːm-/ *noun* [C, U] an occasion when a bomb is dropped or left somewhere; the act of doing this 炸彈投擲（或安放）：*recent bombings in major cities* 近期發生在大城市的投放炸彈事件 ◇ *enemy bombing* 敵機轟炸

bom·bora /bɒmˈbɔːrə; *NAmE* bɑːm-/ *noun* (*AustralE*) **1** a wave which forms over an underwater rock, sometimes producing a dangerous area of broken water 潛浪（遇暗礁形成，可造成危險的碎浪水域） **2** an area of rock underwater 暗礁水域

bomb·proof /ˈbɒmpruːf; *NAmE* ˈbɑːm-/ *adj.* strong enough to give protection against an attack by a bomb 防炸彈的

ˈbomb scare (also **ˈbomb threat** especially in *NAmE*) (*BrE* also **ˈbomb alert**) *noun* an occasion when sb says that they have put a bomb somewhere and everyone has to leave the area 炸彈恐嚇（聲稱在某處放置炸彈，所有人都得撤離）

bomb·shell /ˈbɒmʃel; *NAmE* ˈbɑːm-/ *noun* [usually sing.] (*informal*) **1** an event or a piece of news which is unexpected and usually unpleasant 出乎意料的事情，意外消息（常指不幸）：*The news of his death came as a bombshell.* 他去世的消息令人震驚。◇ *She* ***dropped a bombshell*** *at the meeting and announced that she was leaving.* 她在會上宣佈了令人吃驚的消息，說她將要離開。 **2 a blond(e) bombshell** a very attractive woman with blonde hair 金髮美女

ˈbomb site *noun* an area where all the buildings have been destroyed by bombs 轟炸後的廢墟

bona fide /ˌbəʊnə ˈfaɪdi; *NAmE* ˌboʊnə/ *adj.* [usually before noun] (from *Latin*) genuine, real or legal; not false 真誠的；真實的；合法的：*a bona fide reason* 真正原因 ◇ *Is it a bona fide, reputable organization?* 這是不是個合法的、值得信賴的機構？

bona fides /ˌbəʊnə ˈfaɪdiːz; *NAmE* ˌboʊnə/ *noun* [pl.] (from *Latin*) evidence that sb is who they say that they are; evidence that sb/sth is honest 真誠；信譽

bon·anza /bəˈnænzə/ *noun* [sing.] **1** a situation in which people can make a lot of money or be very successful 發財（或成功）的機遇：*a cash bonanza for investors* 投資者的賺錢機會 ◇ *a bonanza year for the computer industry* 計算機業興旺發達的一年 **2** a situation where there is a large amount of sth pleasant 興盛；繁榮：*the usual bonanza of sport in the summer* 夏季體育運動的一貫熱潮

bon·bon /ˈbɒnbɒn; *NAmE* ˈbɑːnbɑːn/ *noun* a sweet/candy, especially one with a soft centre（尤指軟夾心的）糖果

bonce /bɒns; *NAmE* bɑːns/ *noun* (*BrE, informal*) a person's head 人頭

bond AW /bɒnd; *NAmE* bɑːnd/ *noun, verb*

▪ ***noun***

▸ STRONG CONNECTION 牢固的聯繫 **1** [C] **~ (between A and B)** something that forms a connection between people or groups, such as a feeling of friendship or shared ideas and experiences 紐帶；聯繫；關係；契合：*A bond of friendship had been forged between them.* 他們之間形成了一種友誼的紐帶。◇ *The agreement strengthened the bonds between the two countries.* 協議加強了兩國間的聯繫。◇ *the special bond between mother and child* 母子間的獨特關係

▸ MONEY 錢 **2** [C] an agreement by a government or a company to pay you interest on the money you have lent; a document containing this agreement 債券；公債 ➲ see also JUNK BOND **3** [U] (*law* 律) (*especially NAmE*) a sum of money that is paid as BAIL 保釋金：*He was released on $5 000 bond.* 他以 5 000 元取保釋放。 **4** [C] (also **ˈmortgage bond**) (*SAfrE*) a legal agreement by which a bank lends you money to buy a house, etc. which you pay back over many years; the sum of money that is lent 按揭貸款協議；按揭貸款：*to pay off a bond* 償清按揭貸款 ◇ *We had to take out a second bond on the property.* 我們得申請第二按揭以購買這個房產。◇ *bond rates* (= of interest) 按揭貸款利率

▸ ROPES/CHAINS 繩索；鏈條 **5 bonds** [pl.] (*formal*) the ropes or chains keeping sb prisoner; anything that stops you from being free to do what you want 捆綁犯人的繩索（或鐐銬）；羈絆；桎梏：*to release sb from their bonds* 給某人脫去枷鎖 ◇ *the* ***bonds of oppression/injustice*** 壓迫 / 不公正的枷鎖

▸ LEGAL AGREEMENT 法律協定 **6** [C] (*formal*) a legal written agreement or promise 書面的法律協定（或承諾）：*We entered into a solemn bond.* 我們締結了一項莊嚴的協定。

▸ JOIN 結合 **7** [C] the way in which two things are joined together 連接；結合：*a firm bond between the two surfaces* 兩個面之間的牢固接合

▸ CHEMISTRY 化學 **8** [C] the way in which atoms are held together in a chemical COMPOUND 鍵合；鍵 IDM see WORD *n.*

▪ ***verb***

▸ JOIN FIRMLY 牢固地結合 **1** [T, I] to join two things firmly together; to join firmly to sth else 使牢固結合；把…緊緊地連接到：**~ sth** *This new glue bonds a variety of surfaces in seconds.* 這種新型膠水可迅速粘牢各種材質的面板。◇ **~ (A) to B** *It cannot be used to bond wood to metal.* 這不能把木料粘貼在金屬上。◇ **~ (A and B) together** *The atoms bond together to form a molecule.* 原子結合形成分子。

▸ DEVELOP RELATIONSHIP 發展關係 **2** [I, T] **~ (with sb)** to develop or create a relationship of trust with sb 增強（與某人的）信任關係；建立（與某人的）互信關係：*Mothers who are depressed sometimes fail to bond with their children.* 長期抑鬱的母親有時無法和孩子建立親子關係。

bond·age /ˈbɒndɪdʒ; *NAmE* ˈbɑːn-/ *noun* **1** (*old-fashioned* or *formal*) the state of being a SLAVE or prisoner 奴役；束縛 SYN **slavery**：(*figurative*) *women's liberation from the bondage of domestic life* 女性從家庭生活束縛中的解脫 **2** the practice of being tied with ropes, chains, etc. in order to gain sexual pleasure（以捆綁尋求性快感的）性虐待癖

ˌbonded ˈlabour (*especially US* **ˌbonded ˈlabor**) *noun* [U] forced work for an employer for a fixed time without being paid, often as a way of paying a debt 債役勞動；抵押勞動：*Many of the immigrants are used as bonded labour.* 移民中有很多人被用作債役勞工。
▸ **ˌbonded ˈlabourer** (*especially US* **ˌbonded ˈlaborer**) *noun*

ˌbonded ˈwarehouse *noun* (*BrE*) a government building where imported goods are stored until tax has been paid on them 保稅倉庫

bond·ing AW /ˈbɒndɪŋ; *NAmE* ˈbɑːn-/ *noun* [U] **1** the process of forming a special relationship with sb or with a group of people 人與人之間的關係（或聯結）：*mother-child bonding* 母子親情 ◇ *male bonding* 男性的情誼 **2** (*chemistry* 化) the process of atoms joining together 原子的結合；鍵合：*hydrogen bonding* 氫鍵結合

bone 0-w /bəʊn; *NAmE* boʊn/ *noun, verb*

▪ ***noun*** **1** 0-w [C] any of the hard parts that form the SKELETON of the body of a human or an animal 骨頭；骨：*He survived the accident with no broken bones.* 他在事故中幸免於難，沒有骨折。◇ *This fish has a lot of bones in it.* 這種魚多刺。 **2** [U] the hard substance that bones are made of 骨質：*knives with bone handles* 有骨質手把的刀子 **3 -boned** (in adjectives 構成形容詞) having bones of the type mentioned 有…樣的骨頭的：*fine-boned* 骨質細密的

IDM **a bone of conˈtention** a subject which causes disagreement and arguments between people 爭執所在 **close to the ˈbone** (*BrE, informal*) (of a remark, joke, story, etc. 話語、玩笑、故事等) so honest or clearly expressed that it is likely to cause offence to some people 過於直率 **cut, pare, etc. sth to the ˈbone** to reduce sth, such as costs, as much as you possibly can 盡量削減（開支等） **have a ˈbone to pick with sb** (*informal*) to be angry with sb about sth and want to discuss it with them 對某人生氣，想與之解決；有理由反對（或惱恨）某人 **make no bones about (doing) sth** to be honest and open about sth; to not hesitate to do sth 開誠佈公；毫不猶疑：*She made no bones about telling him exactly what she thought of him.* 她毫無保留地把對他的看法照直告訴了他。 **not have a ... bone in your body** to have none of the quality mentioned 毫無…的素質：*She was honest and hard-working, and didn't have an unkind bone in her body.* 她誠實勤勞，身上沒有一點兒不好的氣質。 **throw sb a 'bone** to give sb a small part of what they want as a way of showing that you want to help them, without offering them the main thing they want 施以小惠（以示助人，卻不滿足主要的要求）；丟給某人一塊骨頭 **to the 'bone** affecting you very strongly 影響極強地；深刻地：*His threats chilled her to the bone.* 他的威脅使她不寒而慄。➲ more at BAG *n.*, BARE *adj.*, FEEL *v.*, FINGER *n.*, FLESH *n.*, SKIN *n.*

■ ***verb*** **~ sth** to take the bones out of fish or meat 挑魚刺；剔骨頭

PHR V **,bone 'up on sth** (*informal*) to try to learn about sth or to remind yourself of what you already know about it 鑽研學習；複習：*She had boned up on the city's history before the visit.* 她在前往這個城市之前先對它的歷史研究了一番。

,bone 'china *noun* [U] thin delicate CHINA made of CLAY mixed with crushed bone; cups, plates, etc. made of this 骨灰瓷，骨灰瓷器（用瓷土與骨灰混合燒製成）

,bone 'dry *adj.* [not usually before noun] completely dry 完全乾燥

bone·head /'bəʊnhed; *NAmE* 'boʊn-/ *noun* (*informal*) a stupid person 笨蛋；傻瓜

,bone 'idle *adj.* (*old-fashioned, BrE, informal*) very lazy 懶透了的

bone·less /'bəʊnləs; *NAmE* 'boʊn-/ *adj.* (of meat or fish 肉或魚) without any bones 無骨的；去骨的：*boneless chicken breasts* 去骨雞胸肉

'bone marrow (also **mar·row**) *noun* [U] a soft substance that fills the hollow parts of bones 骨髓：*a bone marrow transplant* 骨髓移植

bone·meal /'bəʊnmiːl; *NAmE* 'boʊn-/ *noun* [U] a substance made from crushed animal bones which is used to make soil richer（用作肥料的）骨粉

boner /'bəʊnə(r); *NAmE* 'boʊn-/ *noun* (*NAmE, informal*) **1** (*taboo*) an ERECTION of the PENIS（陰莖的）勃起 **2** an embarrassing mistake 令人尷尬的錯誤

bone·shaker /'bəʊnʃeɪkə(r); *NAmE* 'boʊn-/ *noun* (*BrE, informal*) **1** an old vehicle that is in bad condition 破舊的車 **2** an old type of bicycle without rubber tyres（舊時的）無胎自行車，硬輪自行車

bon·fire /'bɒnfaɪə(r); *NAmE* 'bɑːn-/ *noun* a large outdoor fire for burning waste or as part of a celebration（在室外為焚燒垃圾或為慶祝而燃起的）大火堆，篝火

'Bonfire Night (also **,Guy 'Fawkes night**) *noun* [U, C] the night of 5 November, when there is a tradition in Britain that people light bonfires and have FIREWORKS to celebrate the failure of the plan in 1605 to destroy the parliament buildings with EXPLOSIVES 篝火之夜（11 月 5 日夜晚，英國人藉以慶祝 1605 年炸毀議會大廈的陰謀失敗）

bong /bɒŋ; *NAmE* bɑːŋ/ *noun* **1** the sound made by a large bell（大鐘發出的）噹噹聲：*the bongs of Big Ben* 大本鐘的噹噹聲 **2** a long pipe for smoking CANNABIS and other drugs, which passes the smoke through a container of water 煙槍；水煙斗

bongo /'bɒŋgəʊ; *NAmE* 'bɑːŋgoʊ; 'bɔːŋgoʊ/ (*pl.* **-os**) (also **'bongo drum**) *noun* a small drum, usually one of a pair, that you play with your fingers 邦戈鼓（用手指扣擊的小手鼓，通常成對）

bon·homie /'bɒnəmi; *NAmE* ,bɑːnə'miː/ *noun* [U] (from *French, formal*) a feeling of cheerful friendship 歡快友好的感覺；歡樂的友情

bonk /bɒŋk; *NAmE* bɑːŋk/ *noun, verb*

■ ***noun*** (*BrE, informal*) **1** [sing.] an act of having sex with sb 性交 **2** [C] the act of hitting sb on the head or of hitting your head on sth 猛擊（某人頭部）；（頭部）受到撞擊

■ ***verb*** (*BrE, informal*) **1** [T, I] **~ (sb)** to have sex with sb（和某人）性交：*He's been bonking one of his students.* 他同他的一名學生一直有性關係。 **2** [T] **~ sth** to hit sb lightly on the head or to hit yourself by mistake 輕擊（或拍某人的頭）；（不小心）碰撞：*I bonked my head on the doorway.* 我沒留意在門口碰了一下頭。

bonk·buster /'bɒŋkbʌstə(r); *NAmE* 'bɑːŋk-/ *noun* (*BrE, informal*) a type of popular novel in which there is a lot of sex or romantic love 情色小說；言情小說

bonk·ers /'bɒŋkəz; *NAmE* 'bɑːŋkərz/ *adj.* [not before noun] (*informal*) completely crazy and silly 瘋狂；愚蠢透頂：*I'll **go bonkers** if I have to wait any longer.* 如果再等下去，我非發瘋不可。 **IDM** see RAVING *adv.*

bon mot /,bɒn 'məʊ; *NAmE* ,bɑːn 'moʊ; ,bɔːn 'moʊ/ *noun* (*pl.* **bons mots** /,bɒn 'məʊ; *NAmE* ,bɑːn 'moʊ; ,bɔːn 'moʊ/) (from *French, formal*) a funny and clever remark 妙語；詼諧的話

bon·net /'bɒnɪt; *NAmE* 'bɑːnət/ *noun* **1** a hat tied with strings under the chin, worn by babies and, especially in the past, by women（帶子繫於下巴的）童帽，舊式女帽 **2** (*BrE*) (*NAmE* **hood**) the metal part over the front of a vehicle, usually covering the engine（車輛的）引擎蓋 ➲ **COLLOCATIONS** at DRIVING ➲ **VISUAL VOCAB** page V52 **IDM** see BEE

bonny (also **bonnie**) /'bɒni; *NAmE* 'bɑːni/ *adj.* (**bon·nier**, **bon·ni·est**) (*dialect, especially ScotE*) very pretty; attractive 十分漂亮的；有魅力的：*a **bonny baby/lass*** 漂亮的嬰兒／姑娘

bonsai 盆景

bon·sai /'bɒnsaɪ; *NAmE* 'bɑːn-/ *noun* (*pl.* **bonsai**) **1** [C] a small tree that is grown in a pot and prevented from reaching its normal size 盆景 **2** [U] the Japanese art of growing bonsai 日本盆栽藝術

bon·sella /bɒn'selə; *NAmE* bɑːn-/ *noun* (*SAfrE, informal*) something that you receive as a present or reward, especially money 禮物；獎品；（尤指）禮金，獎金

bonus /'bəʊnəs; *NAmE* 'boʊ-/ *noun* (*pl.* **-es**) **1** an extra amount of money that is added to a payment, especially to sb's wages as a reward 津貼；獎金；紅利：*a £100 Christmas bonus* * 100 英鎊聖誕節獎金 ◇ *productivity bonuses* 生產獎金 **2** anything pleasant that is extra and more or better than you were expecting 意外收穫：*Being able to walk to work is an **added bonus** of the new job.* 能夠步行去上班是這份新工作額外的好處。➲ see also NO-CLAIMS BONUS

bon viv·ant /,bõ viː'vɒ̃; *NAmE* ,bɑːn viː'vɑːnt/ (also **bon viv·eur** /-'vɜː(r)/) *noun* (from *French*) a person who enjoys going out with friends and eating good food, drinking good wine, etc. 喜歡吃喝玩樂的人

bon voy·age /,bɒn vɔɪ'ɑːʒ; *NAmE* ,bɑːn/ *exclamation* (from *French*) said to sb who is leaving on a journey, to wish them a good journey 一路平安；旅途愉快

bony /'bəʊni; *NAmE* 'boʊni/ *adj.* (**boni·er**, **boni·est**) **1** (of a person or part of the body 人或人體部位) very thin so that the bones can be seen under the skin 瘦骨嶙峋的 **2** (of fish 魚) full of small bones 多刺的 **3** consisting of or like bone 由骨骼組成的；類似骨頭的

bon·zer /'bɒnzə(r); *NAmE* 'bɑːn-/ *adj.* (*AustralE, NZE, informal*) excellent 極好的；很棒的

B

boo /buː/ *exclamation, noun, verb*

■ ***exclamation, noun*** **1** a sound that people make to show that they do not like an actor, speaker, etc. （對演員、講話者等表示不滿）噓：*'Boo!' they shouted, 'Get off!'* "去！"他們大聲喊道，"滾下去！" ◇ *The speech was greeted with loud boos from the audience.* 演講引來觀眾一片噓聲。 **2** people shout **Boo!** when they want to surprise or frighten sb（驚嚇他人的聲音）乒 IDM see SAY *v.*

■ ***verb*** [I, T] to show that you do not like a person, performance, idea, etc. by shouting 'boo' 發噓聲；喝倒彩：*The audience booed as she started her speech.* 她一開始講話，聽眾便發出一陣噓聲。◇ **~ sb** *He was* ***booed off the stage.*** 他在一片倒彩聲中退下舞台。

boob /buːb/ *noun, verb*

■ ***noun*** **1** (*slang*) a woman's breast（女人的）乳房 **2** (*BrE, informal*) a stupid mistake 愚蠢的錯誤：*I made a bit of a boob throwing that file away.* 我犯了個愚蠢的錯誤，把那份文件扔掉了。 **3** (*NAmE*) a stupid person 傻瓜；蠢貨

■ ***verb*** [I] (*informal*) to make a stupid mistake 犯愚蠢的錯誤

'boo-boo *noun* **1** (*informal*) a stupid mistake 愚蠢的錯誤：*I think I've made a boo-boo.* 我想我犯了個愚蠢的錯誤。 **2** (*NAmE*) a child's word for a small cut or injury（兒童用語）小傷口，輕傷

'boob tube *noun* **1** (*BrE, informal*) (*NAmE* **'tube top**) a piece of women's clothing that is made of cloth that stretches and covers the chest（女人的）緊身平口胸衣 **2** (*NAmE, informal, disapproving*) the television 電視機

booby /ˈbuːbi/ *noun* (*pl.* **-ies**) **1** (*informal*) a stupid person 笨蛋；傻瓜：*Don't be such a booby!* 不要那麼傻！ **2** [usually pl.] (*informal*) a word for a woman's breast, used especially by children（女人的）乳房（多見於兒童用語） **3** a large tropical bird with brightly coloured feet that lives near the sea 鰹鳥（大型熱帶海鳥）

'booby prize *noun* a prize that is given as a joke to the person who is last in a competition 末名獎（作為玩笑贈予比賽中最後一名）

'booby trap *noun* **1** a hidden bomb that explodes when the object that it is connected to is touched 餌雷；詭雷 **2** a hidden device that is meant as a joke to surprise sb, for example an object placed above a door so that it will fall on the first person who opens the door（為開玩笑而設下的）陷阱

'booby-trap *verb* (**-pp-**) **~ sth** to place a booby trap in or on sth 設陷阱；佈置機關；設餌雷

boof·head /ˈbuːfhed/ *noun* (*AustralE, informal*) a stupid person 笨蛋；傻瓜

boo·ger /ˈbʊɡə(r)/ (*NAmE*) (*BrE* **bogey**, **bogy**) *noun* (*informal*) a piece of dried MUCUS from inside your nose 鼻屎

boo·gey·man /ˈbuːɡimæn/ *noun* (*NAmE*) = BOGEYMAN

boo·gie /ˈbuːɡi; *NAmE* ˈbʊɡi/ *noun, verb*

■ ***noun*** (also **ˌboogie-ˈwoogie** /-ˈwuːɡi; *NAmE* -ˈwʊɡi/) [U] a type of blues music played on the piano, with a fast strong rhythm 布吉樂（布魯斯鋼琴樂，節奏快而強）

■ ***verb*** [I] (*informal*) to dance to fast pop music 隨着快節奏的流行音樂跳舞

'boogie board *noun* a small board used for riding on waves in a lying position 趴板（卧式小型衝浪板）

boo·hoo /ˈbuːhuː; ˌbuːˈhuː/ *exclamation* used in written English to show the sound of sb crying（書面語，表示哭聲）嗚嗚

book ⁰ᵚ /bʊk/ *noun, verb*

■ ***noun***

▸ PRINTED WORK 印刷品 **1** ⁰ᵚ [C] a set of printed pages that are fastened inside a cover so that you can turn them and read them 書；書籍：*a pile of books* 一摞書 ◇ ***hardback/paperback books*** 精裝／平裝書 **2** ⁰ᵚ [C] a written work published in printed or electronic form 印刷（或電子）出版物；著作：*a book by Stephen King* 斯蒂芬•金寫的書 ◇ *a* ***book about/on*** *wildlife* 有關野生生物的書 ◇ ***reference/children's/library books*** 參考書；兒童讀物；館藏書籍 ➲ COLLOCATIONS at LITERATURE

▸ FOR WRITING IN 書寫用 **3** ⁰ᵚ [C] a set of sheets of paper that are fastened together inside a cover and used for writing in 本子；簿子：*an exercise book* 練習本 ◇ *a notebook* 筆記本 ➲ see also ADDRESS BOOK

▸ OF STAMPS/TICKETS/MATCHES, ETC. 郵票、票券、火柴等 **4** ⁰ᵚ [C] a set of things that are fastened together like a book 裝訂成冊的一套東西：*a* ***book of stamps/tickets/matches*** 一封郵票；一本票券；一紙板火柴 ◇ *a chequebook* 支票簿

▸ ACCOUNTS 賬目 **5 the books** [pl.] the written records of the financial affairs of a business（企業的）賬簿 SYN **accounts**：*to do the books* (= to check the accounts) 查賬

▸ SECTION OF BIBLE, ETC.《聖經》等的卷、部 **6** [C] a section of a large written work（長篇作品的）篇，卷，部：*the books of the Bible*《聖經》中各卷

▸ FOR BETTING 賭博用 **7** [C] (*BrE*) a record of bets made on whether sth will happen, sb will win a race, etc. 賭注記錄

IDM **be in sb's good/bad 'books** (*informal*) used to say that sb is pleased/annoyed with you 令某人喜歡／厭煩：*I'm in her good books at the moment because I cleared up the kitchen.* 她現在對我有好感，因為我把廚房清理乾淨了。 **bring sb to 'book (for sth)** (*formal, especially BrE*) to punish sb for doing sth wrong and make them explain their behaviour（為某事）懲罰某人並要求作出解釋 **by the 'book** following rules and instructions in a very strict way 循規蹈矩；嚴格遵守章法：*She always does everything by the book.* 她總是照章行事。 **in my 'book** (*informal*) used when you are giving your opinion（發表意見時說）：*That's cheating in my book.* 依我看那是欺騙。 **(be) on sb's 'books** (to be) on an organization's list, for example of people who are available for a particular type of work（在某機構）登記備用的：*We have very few nurses on our books at the moment.* 目前在我們這裏登記備用的護士很少。◇ *Most of the houses on our books are in the north of the city.* 我們手頭的房子大多數在城北。 **throw the 'book at sb** (*informal*) to punish sb who has committed an offence as severely as possible 從嚴懲處（罪犯） ➲ more at CLOSE[1] *v.*, CLOSED, COOK *v.*, HISTORY, JUDGE *v.*, LEAF *n.*, OPEN *adj.*, READ *v.*, SUIT *v.*, TRICK *n.*

■ ***verb*** **1** ⁰ᵚ [I, T] to arrange to have or use sth on a particular date in the future; to buy a ticket in advance 預約；預訂：*Book early to avoid disappointment.* 及早預約，以免向隅。◇ **~ sth** *She booked a flight to Chicago.* 她訂了張去芝加哥的機票。◇ *The performance is* ***booked up*** (= there are no more tickets available). 演出票被訂完了。◇ *I'm sorry—we're* ***fully booked.*** 對不起，客滿了。◇ (*BrE*) *I'd like to book a table for two for 8 o'clock tonight.* 我想訂一張今晚 8 點鐘的二人餐桌。 HELP In American English **book** is not used if you do not have to pay in advance; instead use **make a reservation**. 美式英語中，不必預付款時不用 book，而用 make a reservation：(*NAmE*) *I'd like to make a reservation for 8 o'clock tonight.* ➲ compare RESERVE *v.* (1) **2** ⁰ᵚ [T] to arrange for sb to have a seat on a plane, etc. 給（某人）預訂飛機等座位：**~ sb + adv./prep.** *I've booked you on the 10 o'clock flight.* 我給你訂了 10 點鐘的飛機票。◇ **~ sb sth (+ adv./prep.)** *I've booked you a room at the Park Hotel.* 我已在百樂酒店為你訂了一個房間。 **3** [T] **~ sb/sth (for sth)** to arrange for a singer, etc. to perform on a particular date 和（歌手等）預約演出日期：*We've booked a band for the wedding reception.* 我們已經為婚宴預約了樂隊。 **4** [T] **~ sb (for sth)** (*informal*) to write down sb's name and address because they have committed a crime or an offence 立案（控告某人）：*He was booked for possession of cocaine.* 他因藏有可卡因而被立案審查。 **5** [T] **~ sb** (*BrE, informal*) (of a REFEREE 裁判) to write down in an official book the name of a player who has broken the rules of the game 記名警告（犯規運動員）

PHR V **ˌbook ˈin/ˈinto sth** (*BrE*) to arrive at a hotel, etc. and arrange to stay there 到（旅館等）辦理入住手續：*I got in at ten and booked straight into a hotel.* 我十點鐘到達後直接到一家旅館辦理了住宿手續。 **ˌbook sb ˈin/ˈinto sth** to arrange for sb to have a room at a hotel, etc. 為某人預訂（旅館房間等）

B

book·able /ˈbʊkəbl/ *adj.* **1** tickets, etc. that are **bookable** can be ordered in advance 可預訂的 **2** (*BrE*) if an offence in football (SOCCER) is **bookable**, the name of the player responsible is written down in a book by the REFEREE as a punishment （足球隊員犯規）可記名警告的 **3** (*NAmE*) if a crime is a **bookable** offence, the person responsible can be arrested 夠拘捕條件的

book·bind·er /ˈbʊkbaɪndə(r)/ *noun* a person whose job is fastening the pages of books together and putting covers on them 裝訂工人 ▸ **book·bind·ing** *noun* [U]

book·case /ˈbʊkkeɪs/ *noun* a piece of furniture with shelves for keeping books on 書架；書櫃 ➲ VISUAL VOCAB page V21

ˈ**book club** *noun* **1** an organization that sells books cheaply to its members 讀書俱樂部（會員購書享受打折優惠） **2** = BOOK GROUP

book·cross·ing /ˈbʊkkrɒsɪŋ; *NAmE* -krɔːs-/ *noun* [U] the practice of leaving a book in a public place so that another person can find it, read it and then leave it where sb else will find it 圖書漂流（將書留在公共場所供後來者逐人繼續閱讀）

book·end /ˈbʊkend/ *noun* [usually pl.] one of a pair of objects used to keep a row of books standing up 書擋 ➲ VISUAL VOCAB page V21

ˈ**book group** (also ˈ**book club**, ˈ**reading group**) *noun* a group of people who meet together regularly to discuss a book they have all read 讀書小組；讀書會；讀書俱樂部

bookie /ˈbʊki/ *noun* (*informal*) = BOOKMAKER

book·ing /ˈbʊkɪŋ/ *noun* **1** [C, U] (*especially BrE*) an arrangement that you make in advance to buy a ticket to travel somewhere, go to the theatre, etc. 預訂：*a* ***booking form/hall/clerk*** 訂票表；售票廳／員 ◇ *Can I* ***make a booking*** *for Friday?* 我可以訂星期五的票嗎？ ◇ ***Early booking*** *is recommended.* 請提早訂票。◇ *No* ***advance booking*** *is necessary.* 無須提前訂票。◇ *We can't take any more bookings.* 我們不能再接受訂票了。➲ compare RESERVATION (1) **2** [C] an arrangement for sb to perform at a theatre, in a concert, etc. （演出等的）預約，約定 **3** [C] (*BrE*) (in football (SOCCER) 足球) an act of the REFEREE writing a player's name in a book, as a punishment because an offence has been committed （對犯規者的）記名警告

ˈ**booking office** *noun* (*BrE*) a place where you can buy tickets, at a train or bus station or at a theatre （車站、劇院等的）售票處

book·ish /ˈbʊkɪʃ/ *adj.* (often *disapproving*) interested in reading and studying, rather than in more active or practical things 書呆子氣的；學究似的

book·keep·er /ˈbʊkkiːpə(r)/ *noun* a person whose job is to keep an accurate record of the accounts of a business 簿記員 ▸ **book·keep·ing** *noun* [U]

ˈ**book learning** *noun* [U] knowledge from books or study rather than from experience 書本知識，學堂知識（有別於實踐經驗）

book·let /ˈbʊklət/ *noun* a small thin book with a paper cover that contains information about a particular subject 小冊子

book·maker /ˈbʊkmeɪkə(r)/ (also *informal* **bookie**) (also *BrE, formal* ˈ**turf accountant**) *noun* a person whose job is to take bets on the result of horse races, etc. and pay out money to people who win （賽馬等）賭注登記人 ▸ **book·mak·ing** *noun* [U]

book·mark /ˈbʊkmɑːk; *NAmE* -mɑːrk/ *noun* **1** a strip of paper, etc. that you put between the pages of a book when you finish reading so that you can easily find the place again 書籤 **2** (*computing* 計) a record of the address of a file, a page on the Internet, etc. that enables you to find it quickly 書籤（對文件或互聯網網頁地址的登記，有助於迅速查找） ▸ **book·mark** *verb* : **~ sth** *Do you want to bookmark this site?* 你想給這個站點做書籤嗎？

book·mobile /ˈbʊkməbiːl/ (*NAmE*) (*BrE* ˌ**mobile** ˈ**library**) *noun* a van/truck that contains a library and travels from place to place so that people in different places can borrow books 流動圖書館；圖書館車

book·plate /ˈbʊkpleɪt/ *noun* a decorative piece of paper that is stuck in a book to show the name of the person who owns it 藏書者標籤（貼在書中）

book·sel·ler /ˈbʊkselə(r)/ *noun* a person whose job is selling books 書商

book·shelf /ˈbʊkʃelf/ *noun* (*pl.* **book·shelves** /ˈbʊkʃelvz/) a shelf that you keep books on 書架

book·shop /ˈbʊkʃɒp; *NAmE* -ʃɑːp/ (*especially BrE*) (*NAmE* usually **book·store** /ˈbʊkstɔː(r)/) *noun* a shop/store that sells books 書店

ˈ**book-smart** *adj.* (*NAmE*, becoming *old-fashioned*, often *disapproving*) having a lot of academic knowledge learned from books and studying, but not necessarily knowing much about people and living in the real world 書本知識豐富的；書呆子的：*He's book-smart but he's got no common sense.* 他學究氣十足，但缺乏常識。 ➲ compare STREET-SMART

book·stall /ˈbʊkstɔːl/ (*especially BrE*) (*NAmE* usually **news-stand**) *noun* a small shop/store that is open at the front, where you can buy books, newspapers or magazines, for example at a station or an airport 書亭；書攤

ˈ**book token** *noun* (*BrE*) a card, usually given as a gift, that you can exchange for books of a particular value 購書禮券

book·worm /ˈbʊkwɜːm; *NAmE* -wɜːrm/ *noun* a person who likes reading very much 極愛讀書的人；書迷；書呆子

Bool·ean /ˈbuːliən/ *adj.* (*mathematics* 數, *computing* 計) connected with a system, used especially in COMPUTING and ELECTRONICS, that uses only the numbers 1 (to show sth is true) and 0 (to show sth is false) 布爾邏輯體系的（分別以 1 和 0 代指是和非）

ˌ**Boolean** ˈ**operator** *noun* (*computing* 計) a symbol or word such as 'or' or 'and', used in computer programs and searches to show what is or is not included 布爾運算符（計算機程序或搜索中 or 或 and 等表示“包括”或“排除”的符號或詞）

boom /buːm/ *noun, verb*

■ ***noun***

▸ IN BUSINESS/ECONOMY 商業；經濟 **1** a sudden increase in trade and economic activity; a period of wealth and success（貿易和經濟活動的）激增，繁榮：*Living standards improved rapidly during the post-war boom.* 在戰後那段繁榮昌盛的時期裏，生活水平得到了迅速提高。◇ **~ in sth** *a boom in car sales* 汽車銷售額的巨增 ◇ *a* ***boom year*** *(for trade, exports, etc.)*（貿易、出口等）興盛的一年 ◇ *a* ***property/housing boom*** 房地產／住房的迅速發展 ◇ *a chaotic period of* ***boom and bust*** 經濟繁榮與經濟蕭條交替出現的混亂時期 ➲ COLLOCATIONS at ECONOMY ➲ compare SLUMP *n.* ➲ see also BABY BOOM

▸ POPULAR PERIOD 風靡期 **2** [usually sing.] a period when sth such as a sport or a type of music suddenly becomes very popular and successful（某種體育運動、音樂等）突然風靡的時期：*The only way to satisfy the golf boom was to build more courses.* 滿足這場高爾夫球熱的唯一途徑是增建球場。

▸ ON BOAT 船 **3** a long pole that the bottom of a sail is attached to and that you move to change the position of the sail 帆桁 ➲ VISUAL VOCAB page V56

▸ SOUND 聲音 **4** [usually sing.] a loud deep sound 深沉的響聲：*the distant boom of the guns* 遠處隆隆的炮聲 ➲ see also SONIC BOOM

▸ IN RIVER/HARBOUR 河；港口 **5** a floating barrier that is placed across a river or the entrance to a HARBOUR to prevent ships or other objects from coming in or going out 水柵

▸ FOR MICROPHONE 麥克風 **6** a long pole that carries a MICROPHONE or other equipment 吊杆

■ ***verb***

▸ MAKE LOUD SOUND 發出巨響 **1** [I] to make a loud deep sound 轟鳴；轟響：*Outside, thunder boomed and crashed.* 外面雷聲隆隆，霹靂炸響。 **2** [T, I] to say sth in a loud deep voice 以低沉有力的聲音說話：**+ speech** *'Get*

B

out of my sight!' he boomed.“別讓我再見到你！”他低沉而有力地說。◇ ~ (**out**) *A voice boomed out from the darkness.* 黑暗中傳來低沉有力的噪音。◇ *He had a* ***booming** voice.* 他的嗓音低沉洪亮。

▸ OF BUSINESS/ECONOMY 商業；經濟 **3** [I] to have a period of rapid growth; to become bigger, more successful, etc. 迅速發展；激增；繁榮昌盛：*By the 1980s, the computer industry was booming.* 到 20 世紀 80 年代時，計算機行業迅猛發展。◇ *Business is booming!* 生意興隆！

'boom box *noun* (*especially NAmE*) = GHETTO BLASTER

boom·er /'bu:mə(r)/ *noun* **1** (*NAmE*) = BABY BOOMER **2** a large male KANGAROO 大雄袋鼠

boomerang 回力鏢

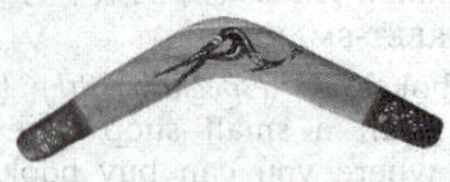

boom·er·ang /'bu:məræŋ/ *noun, verb*

▪ ***noun*** a curved flat piece of wood that you throw and that can fly in a circle and come back to you. Boomerangs were first used by Australian Aborigines as weapons when they were hunting. 回力鏢，飛去來器（澳大利亞土著人最先用於狩獵）

▪ ***verb*** [I] if a plan **boomerangs** on sb, it hurts them instead of the person it was intended to hurt 害人反害己；自食其果 SYN **backfire**

'boomerang kid (also **'boomerang child**) *noun* (*informal*) an adult child who returns home to live with his or her parents after being away for some time（成年子女離家一段時間後回家與父母同住的）還巢兒，回巢族

'boom town *noun* a town that has become rich and successful because trade and industry has developed there（由於發展貿易和工業而）發達的城市

boon /bu:n/ *noun* ~ (**to/for sb**) something that is very helpful and makes life easier for you 非常有用的東西；益處：*The new software will prove a boon to Internet users.* 這種新軟件將會對互聯網用戶大有益處。

,boon com'panion *noun* (*literary*) a very good friend 密友

boon·docks /'bu:ndɒks; *NAmE* -dɑ:ks/ (also **boon·ies**) *noun* [pl.] (*NAmE, informal, disapproving*) an area far away from cities or towns 偏僻地區

boon·dog·gle /'bu:ndɒgl; *NAmE* -dɑ:gl; -dɔ:gl/ *noun* (*NAmE, informal*) a piece of work that is unnecessary and that wastes time and/or money 毫無意義的工作（或事情）；浪費時間金錢的工作（或事情）

boor /bʊə(r); bɔ:(r); *NAmE* bʊr/ *noun* (*old-fashioned*) a rude unpleasant person 粗魯討厭的人；粗野的人

boor·ish /'bʊərɪʃ; 'bɔ:r-; *NAmE* 'bʊr-/ *adj.* (of people and their behaviour 人及行為) very unpleasant and rude 粗魯討厭的；粗野的

boost /bu:st/ *verb, noun*

▪ ***verb*** **1** ~ **sth** to make sth increase, or become better or more successful 使增長；使興旺：*to boost exports/profits* 增加出口；提高利潤 ◇ *The movie helped boost her screen career.* 那部電影有助於她的銀幕生涯的發展。◇ ***to boost sb's confidence/morale*** 增強某人的信心/士氣 ◇ *Getting that job did a lot to* ***boost his ego*** (= make him feel more confident). 得到那份工作使他信心倍增。**2** ~ **sth** (*NAmE, informal, becoming old-fashioned*) to steal sth 偷竊

▪ ***noun*** [usually sing.] **1** something that helps or encourages sb/sth 幫助；激勵：*a* ***great/tremendous/welcome boost*** 很大的／極大的／令人感激的激勵 ◇ *The tax cuts will give a much needed boost to the economy.* 減稅將給經濟帶來迫切需要的推動力。◇ *Winning the competition was a wonderful boost for her morale.* 贏得了那場比賽使她士氣大振。**2** an increase in sth 增長；提高：*a boost in car sales* 汽車銷售額的增長 **3** an increase in power in an engine or a piece of electrical equipment（發動機或電氣設備的）功率增大 **4** (*especially NAmE*) an act of pushing sb up from behind（從後面的）向上一推，一舉：*He gave her a boost over the fence.* 他推了她一把，幫她翻過圍牆。

boost·er /'bu:stə(r)/ *noun* **1** (also **'booster rocket**) a ROCKET that gives a SPACECRAFT extra power when it leaves the earth, or that makes a MISSILE go further 助推火箭 **2** a device that gives extra power to a piece of electrical equipment（電器的）增壓機，升壓器 **3** an extra small amount of a drug that is given to increase the effect of one given earlier, for example to protect you from a disease for longer 加強劑量：*a tetanus booster* 破傷風加強劑 **4** a thing that helps, encourages or improves sb/sth 幫助（或激勵、改善）…的事物：*a* ***morale/confidence booster*** 士氣／信心的激勵 **5** (*especially NAmE*) a person who gives their support to sb/sth, especially in politics（尤指政治上的）支持者，擁護者：*a meeting of Republican boosters* 共和黨支持者的會議

'booster seat *noun* a seat that you put on a car seat, or on a chair at a table, so that a small child can sit higher 幼兒加高座位（可放在車座或椅子上）

boot 0‑w /bu:t/ *noun, verb*

▪ ***noun*** **1** 0‑w a strong shoe that covers the foot and ankle and often the lower part of the leg 靴子：(*BrE*) *walking boots* 便靴 ◇ (*NAmE*) *hiking boots* 旅行靴 ◇ *a pair of black leather boots* 一雙黑皮靴 ◇ *cowboy boots* 牛仔靴 ➲ VISUAL VOCAB page V64 ➲ see also DESERT BOOT, FOOTBALL BOOT, WELLINGTON **2** (*BrE*) (*NAmE* **trunk**) the space at the back of a car that you put bags, cases, etc. in（汽車後部的）行李箱：*I'll put the luggage in the boot.* 我去把行李放進行李箱裏。➲ VISUAL VOCAB page V52 ➲ see also CAR BOOT SALE **3** [usually sing.] (*informal*) a quick hard kick 猛踢：*He gave the ball a tremendous boot.* 他抽起腳猛踢了一下球。**4** (*NAmE*) = DENVER BOOT

IDM **be given the 'boot** | **get the 'boot** (*informal*) to be told that you must leave your job or that a relationship you are having with sb is over 被解雇；被拋棄；（和某人的關係）被解除 **the boot is on the other 'foot** (*BrE*) (*NAmE* **the shoe is on the other 'foot**) used to say that a situation has changed so that sb now has power or authority over the person who used to have power or authority over them 情況正好相反；賓主易位 **put/stick the 'boot in** (*BrE, informal*) **1** to kick sb very hard, especially when they are on the ground 猛踢（倒地的人）**2** to attack sb by criticizing them when they are in a difficult situation 乘人之危抨擊某人 **to boot** (*old-fashioned* or *humorous*) used to add a comment to sth that you have said（用作附帶評述）而且，另外，加之：*He was a vegetarian, and a fussy one to boot.* 他是個素食主義者，而且過於講究。➲ more at BIG *adj.*, FILL *v.*, LICK *v.*, TOUGH *adj.*

▪ ***verb*** **1** [T] ~ **sth + adv./prep.** to kick sb/sth hard with your foot 猛踢：*He booted the ball clear of the goal.* 他一個大腳把球踢離了球門。**2** [I, T] ~ (**sth**) (**up**) (*computing* 計) to prepare a computer for use by loading its OPERATING SYSTEM; to be prepared in this way 裝入操作系統；啟動（計算機）**3** [T] **be/get booted** (*NAmE, informal*) if you or your car is **booted**, a piece of equipment is fixed to the car's wheel so that you cannot drive it away, usually because the car is illegally parked 在（通常為非法停放的汽車）車輪上裝制動裝置 ➲ see also CLAMP *v.* (3)

PHR V **,boot sb↔'out (of sth)** (*informal*) to force sb to leave a place or job 趕走；解雇 SYN **throw out**

boot·boy /'bu:tbɔɪ/ *noun* (*BrE*) **1** (*informal*) a violent young man, especially one with very short hair and big heavy boots（尤指蓄短髮穿厚重靴子的）兇暴小青年 **2** in the past, a boy employed to clean boots and shoes（舊時的）擦鞋男童

'boot camp *noun* **1** a training camp for new members of the armed forces, where they have to work hard 新兵訓練營 **2** a type of prison for young criminals where there is strict discipline（青少年犯的）勞教營

ˌ**boot-cut** *adj.* [usually before noun] **boot-cut** trousers/pants are slightly wider at the bottom of the legs where the material goes over the feet or shoes（褲子）褲腳套鞋面的，蓋沒腳面的

bootee (also **bootie**) /buːˈtiː/ *noun* **1** a baby's sock, worn instead of shoes 編織嬰兒鞋；編織嬰兒襪：*a pair of bootees* 一雙當鞋穿的編織嬰兒襪 **2** a woman's short boot 短筒女靴

booth /buːð; *NAmE* buːθ/ *noun* **1** a small confined place where you can do sth privately, for example make a telephone call, or vote 不受干擾的劃定空間（如電話亭、投票間等）：*a phone booth* 電話亭 ◇ *a polling/voting booth* 投票間 ➲ see also PHOTO BOOTH, TOLLBOOTH **2** a small tent or temporary structure at a market, an exhibition or a FAIRGROUND, where you can buy things, get information or watch sth 臨時貨攤（或放映棚等）**3** a place to sit in a restaurant which consists of two long seats with a table between them（餐館中的）火車座，卡座

ˌ**Boot ˈHill** *noun* [U] (*US, informal, humorous*) (in the Wild West) a place where people are buried 靴丘（美國西大荒地區的墳地）

boot·lace /ˈbuːtleɪs/ *noun* [usually pl.] a long thin piece of leather or string used to fasten boots or shoes 鞋帶

boot·leg /ˈbuːtleg/ *adj., verb*

▪ ***adj.*** [only before noun] made and sold illegally 非法製造販賣的：*a bootleg CD* (= for example, one recorded illegally at a concert) 一張非法錄製的 CD ➲ see also PIRATE ▸ **boot·leg** *noun*：*a bootleg of the concert* 非法錄製的音樂會唱片

▪ ***verb*** (-gg-) **~ sth** to make or sell goods, especially alcohol, illegally 非法生產或銷售（商品，尤指酒）▸ **boot·leg·ger** *noun* **boot·leg·ging** *noun* [U]

boot·lick·er /ˈbuːtlɪkə(r)/ *noun* (*informal, disapproving*) a person who is too friendly to sb in authority and is always ready to do what they want 馬屁精 ▸ **boot·lick·ing** /ˈbuːtlɪkɪŋ/ *noun* [U]

boot·strap /ˈbuːtstræp/ *noun*

IDM **pull/drag yourself up by your (own) ˈbootstraps** (*informal*) to improve your situation yourself, without help from other people 自力更生

booty /ˈbuːti/ (*pl.* -ies) *noun* **1** [U] valuable things that are stolen, especially by soldiers in a time of war 贓物；掠奪物；戰利品 SYN **loot** **2** [U] (*informal*) valuable things that sb wins, buys or obtains（贏得、購買、得到的）貴重物品：*When we got home from our day's shopping, we laid all our booty out on the floor.* 我們購物一天回到家裏，把搜羅到的好東西都攤開擺在地板上。**3** [C] (*informal, especially NAmE*) the part of the body that you sit on 屁股 SYN **buttocks**：*to shake your booty* (= to dance with great energy) 扭屁股（指用力跳舞）

boo·ty·li·cious /ˌbuːtɪˈlɪʃəs/ *adj.* (*informal, especially NAmE*) sexually attractive 性感的

booze /buːz/ *noun, verb*

▪ ***noun*** [U] (*informal*) alcoholic drink 酒精飲料

▪ ***verb*** [I] (*informal*) (usually used in the progressive tenses 通常用於進行時) to drink alcohol, especially in large quantities 喝酒；（尤指）狂飲：*He's out boozing with his mates.* 他和他的朋友們喝酒去了。

ˈ**booze cruise** *noun* (*informal, humorous*) **1** (*BrE*) a short trip by FERRY from Britain to France or Belgium in order to buy alcohol or cigarettes cheaply 煙酒掃貨遊（指從英國乘船去法國或比利時買便宜的煙酒）：*to go on a booze cruise* 作煙酒掃貨遊 **2** (*especially NAmE*) a social occasion when people travel on a ship or boat and enjoy themselves by drinking alcohol, eating and dancing 遊艇酒會遊

boozer /ˈbuːzə(r)/ *noun* (*informal*) **1** (*BrE*) a pub 酒吧 **2** a person who drinks a lot of alcohol 豪飲者；酒鬼

ˈ**booze-up** *noun* (*BrE, informal*) an occasion when people drink a lot of alcohol 狂飲作樂

boozy /ˈbuːzi/ *adj.* (*informal*) liking to drink a lot of alcohol; involving a lot of alcoholic drink 嗜酒的；豪飲的：*one of my boozy friends* 我的一位酒友 ◇ *a boozy lunch* 午間聚飲

bop /bɒp; *NAmE* bɑːp/ *noun, verb*

▪ ***noun*** **1** [C] (*BrE, informal*) a dance to pop music; a social event at which people dance to pop music 博普舞，博普舞會（伴以流行音樂）**2** [U] = BEBOP

▪ ***verb*** (-pp-) **1** [I] (*BrE, informal*) to dance to pop music 跳博普舞 **2** [T] **~ sb** to hit sb lightly 輕打（某人）

bor·age /ˈbɒrɪdʒ; *NAmE* ˈbɔːrɪdʒ; ˈbɑːrɪdʒ/ *noun* [U] a Mediterranean plant with blue flowers that are shaped like stars, and leaves covered with small hairs. Borage leaves are eaten raw as a salad vegetable. 玻璃苣（地中海植物，開星形藍花，葉子多絨毛，可作色拉菜生食）

borax /ˈbɔːræks/ *noun* [U] a white mineral, usually in powder form, used in making glass and as an ANTISEPTIC (= a substance that helps to prevent infection in wounds) 硼砂（作玻璃成分或用以給傷口消毒）

bor·dello /bɔːˈdeləʊ; *NAmE* bɔːrˈdeloʊ/ *noun* (*pl.* -os) (*especially NAmE*) = BROTHEL

bor·der 🔑 /ˈbɔːdə(r); *NAmE* ˈbɔːrd-/ *noun, verb*

▪ ***noun*** **1** 🔑 the line that divides two countries or areas; the land near this line 國界；邊界；邊疆；邊界地區：*a national park on the border between Kenya and Tanzania* 位於肯尼亞和坦桑尼亞邊界的國家公園 ◇ *Denmark's border with Germany* 丹麥和德國的國界線 ◇ *in the US, near the Canadian border* 在美國，接近加拿大邊界 ◇ *Nevada's northern border* 內華達州的北部邊界 ◇ *to cross the border* 穿越邊界 ◇ *to flee **across/over the border*** 穿越邊境逃亡 ◇ ***border guards/controls*** 邊防警衛；邊境管制 ◇ *a **border dispute/incident*** 邊界爭端／事件 ◇ *a **border town/state*** 位於邊疆的城鎮／州 ◇ (*figurative*) *It is difficult to define the border between love and friendship.* 愛情和友情之間的界線難以劃清。➲ **COLLOCATIONS** at INTERNATIONAL **2** 🔑 a strip around the edge of sth such as a picture or a piece of cloth 鑲邊；包邊：*a pillowcase with a lace border* 有花邊的枕套 ➲ picture at EDGE **3** (in a garden 花園) a strip of soil which is planted with flowers, along the edge of the grass（草坪邊等的）狹長花壇 ➲ **VISUAL VOCAB** page V19 ➲ **SYNONYMS** at next page

▪ ***verb*** **1 ~ sth** (of a country or an area 國家或地區) to share a border with another country or area 和…毗鄰；與…接壤：*the countries bordering the Baltic* 波羅的海沿岸國家 **2 ~ sth** to form a line along or around the edge of sth 沿…的邊；環繞…；給…鑲邊：*Meadows bordered the path to the woods.* 通往樹林的小徑兩邊都是草坪。◇ *The large garden is bordered by a stream.* 大花園緊臨着一條小溪。

PHR V ˈ**border on sth** **1** to come very close to being sth, especially a strong or unpleasant emotion or quality 瀕於；近乎：*She felt an anxiety bordering on hysteria.* 她感覺到一種近乎歇斯底里的焦慮。**2** to be next to sth 挨着；接壤：*areas bordering on the Black Sea* 黑海沿岸地區

ˌ**Border ˈcollie** *noun* a medium-sized black and white dog, often used as a SHEEPDOG 邊境科利狗（被毛黑白相間，常作牧羊狗）

bor·der·land /ˈbɔːdəlænd; *NAmE* ˈbɔːrdər-/ *noun* **1** [C] an area of land close to a border between two countries 邊疆；邊境 **2** [sing.] an area between two qualities, ideas or subjects that has features of both but is not clearly one or the other（介乎兩種品質、思想或學科等之間的）邊緣領域：*the murky borderland between history and myth* 歷史與神話之間的邊緣領域

bor·der·line /ˈbɔːdəlaɪn; *NAmE* ˈbɔːrdər-/ *adj., noun*

▪ ***adj.*** not clearly belonging to a particular condition or group; not clearly acceptable 所屬不清的；兩可之間的；臨界的：*In **borderline cases** teachers will take the final decision, based on the student's previous work.* 在難以定奪的情況下，教師將根據學生先前的作業作出最終評分。◇ *a **borderline pass/fail** in an exam* 考試得分剛剛在及格線上／下

▪ ***noun*** the division between two qualities or conditions 兩種品質（或狀況）之間的分界線：*This biography sometimes crosses the borderline between fact and fiction.* 這部傳記有時混淆了事實和虛構。

Synonyms 同義詞辨析

border

boundary • frontier

These are all words for a line that marks the edge of sth and separates it from other areas or things. 以上各詞均指邊界、分界線。

border the line that separates two countries or areas; the land near this line 指國界、邊界、邊疆、邊界地區：*a national park on the border between Kenya and Tanzania* 位於肯尼亞和坦桑尼亞邊界的國家公園

boundary a line that marks the edges of an area of land and separates it from other areas 指邊界、界限、分界線：*The fence marked the boundary between my property and hers.* 那道籬笆曾是我和她的房產之間的地界。

frontier (*BrE*) the line that separates two countries or areas; the land near this line 指國界、邊界、邊疆、邊境：*The river formed the frontier between the land of the Saxons and that of the Danes.* 這條河曾是撒克遜人與古斯堪的納維亞人土地的分界線。

WHICH WORD? 詞語辨析

The point where you cross from one country to another is usually called the **border**. In British English it can also be called the **frontier**, but this is often in a context of wildness, danger and uncertainty. 國界線通常叫 border；英式英語亦可叫 frontier，但 frontier 常與荒蕪、危險和不確定聯繫在一起：*The rebels control the frontier and the surrounding area.* 叛亂分子控制了邊疆地區。The line on a map that shows the border of a country can be called the **boundary** but 'boundary' is not used when you cross from one country to another. 地圖上標示的國界線可叫 boundary，但穿越國界不用 boundary：*After the war the national boundaries were redrawn.* 戰後重新劃定了國界。◇ ~~*Thousands of immigrants cross the boundary every day.*~~ **Boundary** can also be a physical line between two places, for example between property belonging to two different people, marked by a fence or wall. * boundary 亦可指兩地間的分界線，如用籬笆或牆隔開的分屬於不同的兩個人的土地分界線：*the boundary fence/wall between the properties* 分隔兩所房子的籬笆／牆

PATTERNS

- **across/along/on/over** a/the border/boundary/frontier
- **at** the boundary/frontier
- the border/boundary/frontier **with** a place
- the **northern/southern/eastern/western** border/boundary/frontier
- a **national/common/disputed** border/boundary/frontier

bore 0-π /bɔː(r)/ *verb, noun* ➲ see also BEAR, BORE, BORNE *v.*

■ ***verb* 1** 0-π [T] to make sb feel bored, especially by talking too much（尤指因嘮叨）使厭煩：**~ sb** *I'm not boring you, am I?* 我沒有讓你厭煩吧，是不是？◇ **~ sb with sth** *Has he been boring you with his stories about his trip?* 他是不是用他旅遊的見聞在煩你？ **2** [I, T] to make a long deep hole with a tool or by digging 鑽，鑿，挖（長而深的洞）：**~ into/through sth** *The drill is strong enough to bore through solid rock.* 這把鑽足以鑽透堅固的岩石。◇ **~ sth (in/through sth)** *to bore a hole in sth* 在某物體上挖個洞 **3** [I] **~ into sb/sth** (of eyes 眼睛) to stare in a way that makes sb feel uncomfortable 盯着看：*His blue eyes seemed to bore into her.* 他的一雙藍眼睛似乎要穿透她。

■ ***noun* 1** [C] a person who is very boring, usually because they talk too much（常因話多）令人厭煩的人 **2** [sing.] a situation or thing that is boring or that annoys you 煩人的狀況（或事情）：*It's such a bore having to stay late this evening.* 今天晚上非得熬夜，真是煩人。**3** [C] (also **gauge** especially in *NAmE*) the hollow inside of a tube, such as a pipe or a gun; the width of the hole（管道、槍炮等的）孔，內徑，口徑；膛徑：*a tube with a **wide/narrow bore*** 內徑寬／窄的管子◇ *a twelve-bore shotgun* 一支十二口徑獵槍 **4** [C] a strong, high wave that rushes along a river from the sea at particular times of the year（海水湧入江河的）湧潮，激潮 **5** [C] (also **bore-hole**) a deep hole made in the ground, especially to find water or oil（尤指找水或石油的）探孔，鑽孔 IDM see CRASH *v.*

bored 0-π /bɔːd; *NAmE* bɔːrd/ *adj.* feeling tired and impatient because you have lost interest in sb/sth or because you have nothing to do（對某人／事物）厭倦的；煩悶的：*There was a bored expression on her face.* 她臉上有一種厭倦的表情。◇ **~ with sb/sth** | **~ with doing sth** *The children quickly **got bored** with staying indoors.* 孩子們在屋子裏很快就待不住了。

IDM **bored 'stiff** | **bored to 'death/'tears** | **bored out of your 'mind** extremely bored 厭煩透了的；極其厭倦的 ➲ more at WITLESS

bore·dom /ˈbɔːdəm; *NAmE* ˈbɔːrdəm/ *noun* [U] the state of feeling bored; the quality of being very boring 厭煩；厭倦；無聊：*I started to eat too much out of sheer boredom.* 由於實在閒極無聊，我開始無節制地大吃起來。◇ *Television helps to relieve the boredom of the long winter evenings.* 電視有助於打發漫長無聊的冬天晚上。

bore·hole /ˈbɔːhəʊl; *NAmE* ˈbɔːrhoʊl/ *noun* = BORE (5)

bore·well /ˈbɔːwel; *NAmE* ˈbɔːrwel/ *noun* (*IndE*) a pipe that is put into a hole that has been BORED in the ground, and used with a PUMP in order to get water from under the ground 孔式水井；泵壓水井

bor·ing 0-π /ˈbɔːrɪŋ/ *adj.* not interesting; making you feel tired and impatient 沒趣的；令人厭倦（或厭煩）的：*a boring man* 惹人煩的人◇ *a boring job/book/evening* 無聊的工作／書／夜晚 ▸ **bor·ing·ly** *adv.*：*boringly normal* 平淡無味

Synonyms 同義詞辨析

boring

dull • tedious

These words all describe a subject, activity, person or place that is not interesting or exciting. 以上各詞均形容課題、活動、人或地方等沒意思、乏味。

boring not interesting; making you feel tired and impatient 指沒有趣味的、令人厭倦或厭煩的：*He's such a boring man!* 他那人無趣得很！◇ *She found her job very boring.* 她覺得自己的工作很無聊。

dull not interesting or exciting 指枯燥無味的、沉悶的：*Life in a small town could be deadly dull.* 小城鎮的生活可能會非常沒意思。

tedious lasting or taking too long and not interesting, so that you feel bored and impatient 指冗長的、單調乏味的、令人厭倦的：*The journey soon became tedious.* 那次旅行不久就變得乏味起來。

PATTERNS

- to be boring/dull/tedious **for** sb
- boring/dull/tedious **subjects/books**
- boring/dull/tedious **jobs/work/games**
- a boring/dull **place/man/woman/person**
- **deadly** boring/dull

born 0-π /bɔːn; *NAmE* bɔːrn/ *verb, adj.*

■ ***verb* be born** (used only in the passive, without *by* 僅用於被動語態，不用 by) **1** 0-π (*abbr.* **b.**) to come out of your mother's body at the beginning of your life 出生；出世：*I was born in 1976.* 我生於 1976 年。◇ *She was born with a weak heart.* 她生來就有一個衰弱的心臟。◇ **~ into sth** *She was born into a very musical family.* 她生於音樂之家。◇ **~ of/to sb** *He was born of/to German parents.* 他的生身父母是德國人。◇ **+ adj.** *Her brother was **born blind*** (= was blind when he was born). 她的哥

哥先天性失明。◇ + **noun** *John Wayne was born Marion Michael Morrison* (= that was his name at birth). 約翰 • 韋恩出生時取名馬里恩 • 邁克爾 • 莫里森。➲ COLLOCATIONS at AGE **2** 🔑 (of an idea, an organization, a feeling, etc. 思想、機構、感情等) to start to exist 出現；形成；成立：*the city where the protest movement was born* 抗議運動發源的城市 ◇ **~ (out) of sth** *She acted with a courage born (out) of desperation.* 絕望驅使她鼓起勇氣，作出行動。**3 -born** (in compounds 構成複合詞) born in the order, way, place, etc. mentioned 以…的順序（或方式、地點等）出生的：*firstborn* 第一個孩子 ◇ *nobly-born* 出身貴族 ◇ *French-born* 法國出生的 ➲ see also NEWBORN

IDM **be 'born to be/do sth** to have sth as your DESTINY (= what is certain to happen to you) from birth 注定會成為；注定要做：*He was born to be a great composer.* 他是個天生的偉大作曲家。**,born and 'bred** born and having grown up in a particular place with a particular background and education （在某地）出生長大；受過…薰陶：*He was born and bred in Boston.* 他生於波士頓，長於波士頓。◇ *I'm a Londoner, born and bred.* 我是個土生土長的倫敦人。**born with a silver 'spoon in your mouth** (*saying*) having rich parents 生於富裕之家；出身富裕 **in all my born 'days** (*old-fashioned, informal*) used when you are very surprised at sth you have never heard or seen before（表示驚訝）聞所未聞，見所未見：*I've never heard such nonsense in all my born days.* 我這輩子還從沒聽說過此等廢話呢。**not be born 'yesterday** (*informal*) used to say that you are not stupid enough to believe what sb is telling you（表示自己並不傻，不會輕信別人的話）：*Oh yeah? I wasn't born yesterday, you know.* 是嗎？我可不是三歲的小孩子，你知道的。**there's one born every 'minute** (*saying*) used to say that sb is very stupid 總有那種傻瓜 ➲ more at KNOW *v.*, MANNER, WAY *n.*

■ **adj.** [only before noun] having a natural ability or skill for a particular activity or job 天生（有某方面才能）的：*a* **born** *athlete/writer/leader* 天生的運動員／作家／領袖 ◇ *a* **born loser** (= a person who always loses or is unsuccessful) 永遠的失敗者

,born-a'gain *adj.* [usually before noun] having come to have a strong belief in a particular religion (especially EVANGELICAL Christianity) or idea, and wanting other people to have the same belief（宗教等信仰上）再生的；（尤指基督教徒）重生的：*a born-again Christian* 皈依基督教的人 ◇ *a born-again vegetarian* 開始信仰素食的人

borne /bɔːn; *NAmE* bɔːrn/ **1** *past part.* of BEAR **2 -borne** (in adjectives 構成形容詞) carried by 由…攜帶的：*waterborne diseases* 由水傳染的疾病

boron /'bɔːrɒn; *NAmE* -rɑːn/ *noun* [U] (*symb.* **B**) a chemical element. Boron is a solid substance used in making steel ALLOYS and parts for nuclear REACTORS. 硼

bor·ough /'bʌrə; *NAmE* 'bɜːroʊ/ *noun* a town or part of a city that has its own local government 自治鎮；（城市）行政區：*the London borough of Westminster* 倫敦的威斯敏斯特自治市 ◇ *The Bronx is one of the five boroughs of New York.* 布朗克斯是紐約市的五個行政區之一。◇ *a borough council* 自治鎮政務會

bor·row 🔑 /'bɒrəʊ; *NAmE* 'bɑːroʊ; 'bɔːr-/ *verb*

1 🔑 [T] to take and use sth that belongs to sb else, and return it to them at a later time 借；借用：**~ sth** *Can I borrow your umbrella?* 借你的傘用一下行嗎？◇ **~ sth from sb/sth** *Members can borrow up to ten books from the library at any one time.* 會員在圖書館每次最多可借十本書。◇ (*BrE, informal*) **~ sth off sb** *I borrowed the DVD off my brother.* 我從我哥哥那裏借了這張 DVD。➲ compare LEND (1) **2** 🔑 [T, I] to take money from a person or bank and agree to pay it back to them at a later time 借入（款項）；（向…）借貸：**~ sth (from sb/sth)** *She borrowed £2 000 from her parents.* 她向她的父母借了 2 000 英鎊。◇ **~ (from sb/sth)** *I don't like to borrow from friends.* 我不喜歡向朋友借錢。**~ sth off sb** (*informal*) *I had to borrow the money off a friend.* 我不得不向一個朋友開口借這筆錢。➲ compare LEND (3) **3** [I, T] to take words, ideas, etc. from another language, person, etc. and use them, as your own 引用，借用（思想、言語等）：**~ (from sb/sth)** *The author borrows heavily from Henry James.* 那位作家大量引用亨利 • 詹姆斯的作品。◇ **~ sth (from sb/sth)** *Some musical terms are borrowed from Italian.* 某些音樂術語是從意大利語引入的。

IDM **be (living) on borrowed 'time 1** to still be alive after the time when you were expected to die 活過壽限；大限已近 **2** to be doing sth that other people are likely to soon stop you from doing 做很快就會遭到制止的事；好景不長

Which Word? 詞語辨析

borrow / lend

■ These two words are often confused. You **borrow** something from someone else, while they **lend** it to you. 這兩個詞常被混淆，借入用 borrow，借出用 lend：*Can I borrow your pen?* 我可以借用你的鋼筆嗎？◇ *Can I borrow a pen from you?* 我可以借用你的鋼筆嗎？◇ *Here, I'll lend you my pen.* 喏，我把鋼筆借給你。

bor·row·er /'bɒrəʊə(r); *NAmE* 'bɑːroʊər; 'bɔːr-/ *noun* a person or an organization that borrows money, especially from a bank 借款人；借方 ➲ compare LENDER

bor·row·ing /'bɒrəʊɪŋ; *NAmE* 'bɑːroʊɪŋ; 'bɔːr-/ *noun* **1** [C, U] the money that a company, an organization or a person borrows; the act of borrowing money 借款；貸款；借貸：*an attempt to reduce bank borrowings* 減少向銀行借貸的努力 ◇ *High interest rates help to keep borrowing down.* 高利率有助於控制借貸。➲ COLLOCATIONS at ECONOMY **2** [C] a word, a phrase or an idea that sb has taken from another person's work or from another language and used in their own 借用的言語（或思想等）

borscht /bɔːʃt; *NAmE* bɔːrʃt/ (*BrE* also **borsch** /bɔːʃ; *NAmE* bɔːrʃ/) *noun* [U] a Russian or Polish soup made from BEETROOT (= a dark red root vegetable)（俄羅斯或波蘭）甜菜湯；羅宋湯

bor·stal /'bɔːstl; *NAmE* 'bɔːrstl/ *noun* [C, U] (in Britain in the past) a type of prison for young criminals（英國舊時的）青少年犯教養院 ➲ see also YOUTH CUSTODY

bor·zoi /'bɔːzɔɪ; *NAmE* 'bɔːr-/ *noun* a large Russian dog with soft white hair 俄羅斯靈猩

bos·ber·aad /'bɒsbərɑːt; 'bɔːs-; 'bɑːs-/ *noun* (*SAfrE*) a meeting of business leaders, politicians, etc. at a place that is a long way from a town, in order to discuss important matters（商界領袖、政治家等參加，遠離市區的）重大會議，戰略會議

bosom /'bʊzəm/ *noun* **1** [C] a woman's chest or breasts 女人的胸部（或乳房）：*her ample bosom* 她的豐滿的乳房 ◇ *She pressed him to her bosom.* 她緊緊地把他抱在胸前。**2** [C] the part of a piece of clothing that covers a woman's bosom 女衣胸部（或胸襟）：*a rose pinned to her bosom* 別在她胸襟上的一朵玫瑰 **3 the ~ of sth** [sing.] a situation in which you are with people who love and protect you 和愛護自己的人在一起的情形；在…的懷抱中：*to live in the bosom of your family* 生活在家庭的溫暖懷抱中

,bosom 'friend (*NAmE* also **,bosom 'buddy**) *noun* a very close friend 密友；知己

bos·omy /'bʊzəmi/ *adj.* (*old-fashioned, BrE, informal*) (of a woman 女人) having large breasts 乳房發達的；胸部豐滿的

boss 🔑 /bɒs; *NAmE* bɔːs; bɑːs/ *noun, verb, adj.*

■ **noun 1** 🔑 a person who is in charge of other people at work and tells them what to do 老闆；工頭；領班：*I'll ask my boss if I can have the day off.* 我要問一下老闆我能不能請一天假。◇ *I like being* **my own boss** (= working for myself and making my own decisions). 我喜歡自己做老闆，自己拿主意。◇ *Who's the boss* (= who's in control) *in this house?* 這個家裏誰說了算？**2** 🔑 (*informal*) a person who is in charge of a large organization 總經理；領導：*the new boss at IBM* 國際商用機器公司的新領導 ◇ *Hospital bosses protested at the decision.* 醫院領導們抗議這一決定。IDM see SHOW *v.*

■ ***verb*** **~ sb (about/around)** to tell sb what to do in an aggressive and/or annoying way 對（某人）發號施令：*I'm sick of you bossing me around!* 我討厭你對我指手畫腳。

■ ***adj.*** (*slang*) very good 很好的

bossa nova /ˌbɒsə ˈnəʊvə; *NAmE* ˌbɑːsə ˈnoʊvə; ˌbɔːsə ˈnoʊvə/ *noun* [U, C] a style of Brazilian popular music, popular in the 1960s 巴薩諾瓦（20 世紀 60 年代廣受歡迎的一種巴西流行樂）

bossy /ˈbɒsi; *NAmE* ˈbɔːsi; ˈbɑːsi/ *adj.* (*disapproving*) (**boss·ier**, **bossi·est**) always telling people what to do 好指揮人的；專橫的 ▸ **boss·ily** *adv.* **bossi·ness** *noun* [U]

bossy·boots /ˈbɒsibuːts; *NAmE* ˈbɔːs-/ *noun* (*pl.* **bossy·boots**) (*informal, disapproving*) a person who always tells people what they should do 愛支使人的人；頤指氣使的人

Boston baked ˈbeans (also **baked ˈbeans**) *noun* [pl.] (*NAmE*) small white beans baked with pork and brown sugar or MOLASSES (= a dark, sweet, thick liquid obtained from sugar)（加豬肉和紅糖或糖漿製的）波士頓烤豆

bo·sun (also **bo'sun**, **boat·swain**) /ˈbəʊsn; *NAmE* ˈboʊ-/ *noun* an officer on a ship whose job is to take care of the equipment and the people who work on the ship 水手長

bot /bɒt; *NAmE* bɑːt/ *noun* (*computing* 計) a computer program that performs a particular task again and again many times 自動程序；機器人程式

bo·tan·ic·al /bəˈtænɪkl/ *adj.* connected with the science of botany 植物學的

boˌtanical ˈgarden (also **boˌtanic ˈgarden**) *noun* [usually pl.] a park where plants, trees and flowers are grown for scientific study 植物園

bot·an·ist /ˈbɒtənɪst; *NAmE* ˈbɑːt-/ *noun* a scientist who studies botany 植物學家

bot·any /ˈbɒtəni; *NAmE* ˈbɑːt-/ *noun* [U] the scientific study of plants and their structure 植物學 ➲ compare BIOLOGY (1), ZOOLOGY

botch /bɒtʃ; *NAmE* bɑːtʃ/ *verb, noun*

■ ***verb*** **~ sth (up)** (*informal*) to spoil sth by doing it badly 笨拙地弄糟（某事物）：*He completely botched up the interview.* 他面試表現得糟透了。◇ *The work they did on the house was a botched job.* 他們整修房子做得一塌糊塗。

■ ***noun*** (also **ˈbotch-up**) (*BrE, informal*) a piece of work or a job that has been done badly 拙劣的工作；粗製濫造的活兒：*I've made a real botch of the decorating.* 我的裝潢工作做得實在是糟糕。

both 🗝 /bəʊθ; *NAmE* boʊθ/ *det., pron.*

1 🗝 used with plural nouns to mean 'the two' or 'the one as well as the other'（與複數名詞連用）兩個，兩個都：*Both women were French.* 兩名婦女都是法國人。◇ *Both the women were French.* 兩名婦女都是法國人。◇ *Both of the women were French.* 兩名婦女都是法國人。◇ *I talked to the women. Both of them were French/They were both French.* 我和兩位婦女交談了，她們都是法國人。◇ *I liked them both.* 他倆我都喜歡。◇ *We were both tired.* 咱倆都累了。◇ *Both of us were tired.* 咱倆都累了。◇ *We have both seen the movie.* 我們倆都看過這部電影。◇ *I have two sisters. Both of them live in London/They both live in London.* 我有兩個姐妹，她倆都住在倫敦。◇ *Both (my) sisters live in London.* 我的兩個姐妹都住在倫敦。**2** 🗝 **both ... and ...** not only ... but also ... 不僅…而且…；…和…都：*Both his mother and his father will be there.* 他父母二人都要去那裏。◇ *For this job you will need a good knowledge of both Italian and Spanish.* 擔任這項工作需要精通意大利語和西班牙語。➲ LANGUAGE BANK at SIMILARLY

bother 🗝 /ˈbɒðə(r); *NAmE* ˈbɑːð-/ *verb, noun, exclamation*

■ ***verb*** **1** 🗝 [I, T] (often used in negative sentences and questions 常用於否定句和疑問句) to spend time and/or energy doing sth 花費時間精力（做某事）：*'Shall I wait?' 'No, don't bother.'* "要我等一下嗎？" "不，別費事了。" ◇ *I don't know why I bother! Nobody ever listens!* 我不知道我幹嗎要浪費時間！根本沒人聽！◇ **~ with/about sth** *It's not worth bothering with* (= using) *an umbrella—the car's just outside.* 不必打傘，汽車就停在外面。◇ *I don't know why you bother with that crowd* (= why you spend time with them). 我弄不懂你為什麼和那夥人浪費時間。◇ **~ to do sth** *He didn't even bother to let me know he was coming.* 他甚至連通知都沒通知我他要來。◇ **~ doing sth** *Why bother asking if you're not really interested?* 如果你不是真的感興趣，幹嗎費口舌打聽呢？**2** 🗝 [T] to annoy, worry or upset sb; to cause sb trouble or pain 使（某人）煩惱（或擔憂、不安）；給（某人）造成麻煩（或痛苦）：**~ sb** *The thing that bothers me is ...* 讓我感到不安的是…◇ *That sprained ankle is still bothering her* (= hurting). 她那扭傷的腳踝還在隱隱作痛。◇ *'I'm sorry he was so rude to you.' 'It doesn't bother me.'* "對不起，他對你太沒禮貌。" "沒關係。" ◇ **~ sb with sth** *I don't want to bother her with my problems at the moment.* 我此刻不想讓她為我的事操心。◇ **be bothered about sth** *You don't sound too bothered about it.* 看來你並不十分擔心這事。◇ **~ sb that ...** *Does it bother you that she earns more than you?* 她比你掙的錢多，你是不是覺得不自在？◇ **it bothers sb to do sth** *It bothers me to think of her alone in that big house.* 想到她孤零零地待在那所大房子裏，我便坐立不安。**3** 🗝 [T] to interrupt sb; to talk to sb when they do not want to talk to you 打擾；搭話：**~ sb** *Stop bothering me when I'm working.* 我工作時別來煩我。◇ *Let me know if he bothers you again.* 他要是再攪擾你，就告訴我。◇ ***Sorry to bother you**, but there's a call for you on line two.* 很抱歉打擾你一下，二號線有你的電話。

IDM **be bothered (about sb/sth)** 🗝 (*informal, especially BrE*) to think that sb/sth is important 認為（某人或某事）重要；關心（某人或某事）：*I'm not bothered about what he thinks.* 我不在乎他怎麼想。◇ *'Where shall we eat?' 'I'm not bothered.'* (= I don't mind where we go). "我們去哪裏吃飯？" "隨便。" **can't be bothered (to do sth)** 🗝 used to say that you do not want to spend time and/or energy doing sth（表示不想花時間精力做某事）：*I should really do some work this weekend but I can't be bothered.* 我這個週末真該做點事了，可我懶得做。◇ *All this has happened because you couldn't be bothered to give me the message.* 就是因為你嫌麻煩沒通知我，才出了這事。**not bother yourself/your head with/about sth** (*especially BrE*) to not spend time/effort on sth, because it is not important or you are not interested in it 不為某事花費時間（或精力）；不操心 ➲ more at HOT *adj.*

■ ***noun*** **1** [U] trouble or difficulty 麻煩；困難：*You seem to have got yourself into a **spot of bother**.* 你似乎讓自己遇上了點麻煩。◇ *I don't want to **put you to any bother*** (= cause you any trouble). 我不想給你添亂子。◇ ***Don't go to the bother** of tidying up on my account* (= don't make the effort to do it). 別為了我費事整理一番。◇ *'Thanks for your help!' 'It was no bother.'* "多謝你的幫助！" "沒什麼。" ◇ *Call them and save yourself the bother of going round.* 給他們打個電話就免得你親自去了。**2 a bother** [sing.] (*BrE*) an annoying situation, thing or person 令人煩惱的情況（或事物、人）SYN **nuisance**：*I hope I haven't been a bother.* 希望我沒煩擾你。

■ ***exclamation*** (*BrE*) used to express the fact that you are annoyed about sth/sb（表示對某事或某人煩惱）：*Bother! I've left my wallet at home.* 真煩人！我把錢包留在家裏了。◇ *Oh, bother him! He's never around when you need him.* 哎呀，他可真討厭！需要他的時候從來都找不到他。

both·er·ation /ˌbɒðəˈreɪʃn; *NAmE* ˈbɑːð-/ *exclamation* (*old-fashioned*) a word that people use to show that they are annoyed 討厭；煩人

both·er·some /ˈbɒðəsəm; *NAmE* ˈbɑːðərsəm/ *adj.* (*old-fashioned*) causing trouble or difficulty 引起麻煩的；困擾人的 SYN **annoying**

bothy /ˈbɒθi; *NAmE* ˈbɔːθi/ *noun* (*pl.* **-ies**) a small building in Scotland for farm workers to live in or for people to shelter in（蘇格蘭供農場工人居住或供人棲身的）茅屋，棚屋

bot·net /ˈbɒtnet; *NAmE* ˈbɑːt-/ *noun* (*computing* 計) a group of computers that are controlled by MALWARE (= software such as a virus that the users do not know about or want) 僵屍網絡，僵屍網路（指受惡意軟件控制的計算機群）

Bo·tox™ /ˈbəʊtɒks; *NAmE* ˈboʊtɑːks/ *noun* [U] a substance that makes muscles relax. It is sometimes INJECTED into the skin around sb's eyes to remove lines and make the skin look younger. 保妥適注射液，肉毒桿菌素（可用於除皺）▸ **Bo·tox** *verb* **~ sb/sth** [usually passive]: *Do you think she's been Botoxed?* 你認為她曾用保妥適來除皺嗎？

bot·tle 🔑 /ˈbɒtl; *NAmE* ˈbɑːtl/ *noun, verb*

■ *noun* **1** 🔑 [C] a glass or plastic container, usually round with straight sides and a narrow neck, used especially for storing liquids（細頸）瓶子：*a* ***wine/beer/milk bottle*** 酒／啤酒／奶瓶 ◇ *Put the top back on the bottle.* 把瓶蓋蓋上。➲ VISUAL VOCAB page V33 **2** 🔑 [C] (also **bottle·ful** /-fʊl/) the amount contained in a bottle 一瓶（的量）：*He drank a whole bottle of wine.* 他喝了整整一瓶酒。 **3** **the bottle** [sing.] (*informal*) alcoholic drink 酒：*After his wife died, he really* ***hit the bottle*** (= started drinking heavily). 他妻子死後，他就酗酒了。**4** [C, usually sing.] a bottle used to give milk to a baby; the milk from such a bottle (used instead of mother's milk)（嬰兒）奶瓶；奶瓶裏的奶（非母乳）：*It's time for her bottle.* 她該喝奶了。 **5** [U] (*BrE, informal*) courage or confidence, for example to do sth that is dangerous or unpleasant 勇氣；信心 SYN **nerve**：*It took a lot of bottle to do that.* 那樣做需要很大的勇氣。

■ *verb* **1 ~ sth** to put a liquid into a bottle 把（液體）裝入瓶中：*The wines are bottled after three years.* 那些酒是在釀了三年之後裝瓶的。 **2 ~ sth** to put fruit or vegetables into glass containers in order to preserve them 把（水果或蔬菜等）裝入玻璃瓶 ▸ **bot·tled** *adj.*：***bottled beer/water/pickles*** 瓶裝啤酒／水／腌菜 ◇ ***bottled gas*** (= sold in metal containers for use in heating and cooking) 瓶裝液化氣

IDM **ˈbottle it** (*BrE, informal*) to not do sth, or not finish sth, because you are frightened 不敢做；（中途）放棄，退縮

PHR V **ˌbottle ˈout (of sth/doing sth)** (*BrE, informal*) to not do sth that you had intended to do because you are too frightened（因恐懼而）放棄原計劃 **ˌbottle sth↔ˈup** to not allow other people to see that you are unhappy, angry, etc., especially when this happens over a long period of time 長時間掩飾，遏制，隱瞞（不快等）：*Try not to bottle up your emotions.* 盡量不要壓抑自己的情感。

ˈbottle bank *noun* (*BrE*) a large container in a public place where people can leave their empty bottles so that the glass can be used again (= RECYCLED); a public place with several of these containers 玻璃瓶回收箱；玻璃瓶回收點 ➲ VISUAL VOCAB page V8

ˌbottle ˈblonde (also **ˌbottle ˈblond**) *adj.* (*disapproving*) (of hair 頭髮) artificially coloured blonde 染成金色的 ▸ **ˌbottle ˈblonde** *noun*

ˈbottle-feed *verb* [T, I] **~ (sb)** to feed a baby with artificial milk from a bottle 用奶瓶餵（嬰兒）➲ compare BREASTFEED

ˌbottle-ˈgreen *adj.* (*especially BrE*) dark green in colour 深綠色的：*a bottle-green coat* 一件深綠色的大衣 ▸ **ˌbottle ˈgreen** *noun* [U]

bottle·neck /ˈbɒtlnek; *NAmE* ˈbɑːtl-/ *noun* **1** a narrow or busy section of road where the traffic often gets slower and stops 瓶頸路段，狹窄街道（常引起交通阻塞） **2** anything that delays development or progress, particularly in business or industry（尤指工商業發展的）瓶頸，阻礙，障礙 SYN **logjam**

ˈbottle opener *noun* a small tool for opening bottles with metal tops, for example beer bottles 開瓶器 ➲ VISUAL VOCAB page V26

ˈbottle party *noun* (*BrE*) a party to which the people who have been invited are asked to bring a bottle, usually of wine 自帶酒水聚會

ˈbottle store (also **ˈbottle shop**) *noun* (*AustralE, NZE, SAfrE*) a shop/store that sells a variety of alcoholic drinks in bottles, cans, etc. to take away 瓶裝酒銷售店；酒鋪 ➲ compare OFF-LICENCE

bot·tom 🔑 /ˈbɒtəm; *NAmE* ˈbɑːtəm/ *noun, adj., verb*

■ *noun*

▸ LOWEST PART 底部 **1** 🔑 [C, usually sing.] **~ (of sth)** the lowest part of sth 底部；最下部：*Footnotes are given at the bottom of each page.* 腳註附於每頁的下端。◇ *I waited for them at the bottom of the hill.* 我在山腳下等候他們。◇ *The book I want is right at the bottom* (= of the pile). 我想要的書就壓在（那堆書的）最下面。OPP **top** **2** 🔑 [C, usually sing.] **~ (of sth)** the part of sth that faces downwards and is not usually seen（朝下的）底，底面：*The manufacturer's name is on the bottom of the plate.* 廠家的名稱在盤子底面。

▸ OF CONTAINER 容器 **3** 🔑 [C, usually sing.] **~ (of sth)** the lowest surface on the inside of a container（容器內的）底：*I found some coins at the bottom of my bag.* 我在我的手提包底找到了幾枚硬幣。

▸ OF RIVER/POOL 河；池 **4** 🔑 [sing.] the ground below the water in a lake, river, swimming pool, etc.（湖、河、游泳池等的）底；水底：*He dived in and hit his head on the bottom.* 他跳水時頭撞到了池底。

▸ END OF STH 尾端 **5** 🔑 **the ~ (of sth)** [sing.] (*especially BrE*) the part of sth that is furthest from you, your house, etc. …盡頭：*I went to the school at the bottom of our street.* 我在我們那條街尾上的學校上學。◇ *There was a stream at the bottom of the garden.* 花園盡頭有一條小溪。

▸ LOWEST POSITION 最末位置 **6** 🔑 [sing.] **~ (of sth)** the lowest position in a class, on a list, etc.; a person, team, etc. that is in this position（班級、名單等的）最末位置；排名最後的人（或團隊等）：*a battle between the teams at the bottom of the league* 聯盟排名最後的幾個隊之間的爭鬥 ◇ *You have to be prepared to start at the bottom and work your way up.* 你得準備好從最基層幹起，努力向上。◇ *I was always bottom of the class in math.* 我的數學成績總是班上最後一名。OPP **top**

▸ PART OF BODY 身體部位 **7** 🔑 [C] (*especially BrE*) the part of the body that you sit on 屁股；臀部 SYN **backside, behind**

▸ CLOTHING 衣服 **8** [C, usually pl.] the lower part of a set of clothes that consists of two pieces 套裝的裙（或褲）：*a bikini bottom* 比基尼泳裝的短褲 ◇ *a pair of pyjama/tracksuit bottoms* 一條睡褲／運動褲 ➲ compare TOP *n.* (6)

▸ OF SHIP 船 **9** [C] the lower part of a ship that is below the surface of the water（吃水線以下的）船底，船身 SYN **hull**

▸ -BOTTOMED 有…底 **10** (in adjectives 構成形容詞) having the type of bottom mentioned 有…底的：*a flat-bottomed boat* 平底船

IDM **at bottom** used to say what sb/sth is really like 歸根結底；本質上；實際上：*Their offer to help was at bottom self-centred.* 他們提出要幫忙，這其實還是他們為自己考慮。 **be/lie at the bottom of sth** to be the original cause of sth, especially sth unpleasant 是某事的根源（或起因、導火線） **the bottom drops/falls out (of sth)** people stop buying or using the products of a particular industry（某行業）產品滯銷；銷量暴跌：*The bottom has fallen out of the travel market.* 旅遊市場出現了蕭條局面。 **bottoms ˈup!** (*informal*) used to express good wishes when drinking alcohol, or to tell sb to finish their drink 乾杯 **get to the bottom of sth** to find out the real cause of sth, especially sth unpleasant 找到起因；挖出禍根 ➲ more at HEAP *n.*, HEART, PILE *n.*, SCRAPE *v.*, TOP *n.*, TOUCH *v.*

■ *adj.* 🔑 [only before noun] in the lowest, last or furthest place or position 底部的；最後的；盡頭的：*the bottom line (on a page)*（一頁的）最末一行 ◇ *your bottom lip* 下嘴唇 ◇ *the bottom step (of a flight of stairs)*（樓梯的）最低一級 ◇ *on the bottom shelf* 在架子底層 ◇ *Put your clothes in the bottom drawer.* 把你的衣服放在最下面的抽屜裏。◇ *Their house is at the bottom end of Bury Road* (= the end furthest from where you enter the road). 他們的房子位於貝里路的盡頭。◇ *in the bottom right-hand corner of the page* 在這一頁的右下角 ◇ *the bottom end of the price range* 最低價位 ◇ *to go up a hill in bottom gear* 用低擋爬山 ◇ *We **came bottom*** (= got the worst result) *with 12 points.* 我們以 12 分墊底兒。 IDM see BET *v.* ➲ see also ROCK-BOTTOM

■ ***verb***

PHR V ˌ**bottom ˈout** (of prices, a bad situation, etc. 價格、惡劣局勢等) to stop getting worse 降到最底點；停止惡化：*The recession is finally beginning to show signs of bottoming out.* 經濟衰退終於出現了走出谷底的跡象。

Synonyms 同義詞辨析

bottom

base • foundation • foot

These are all words for the lowest part of sth. 以上各詞均指底部、最下部。

bottom [usually sing.] the lowest part of sth 指底部、最下部：*Footnotes are given at the bottom of each page.* 腳註附於每頁的下端。◇ *I waited for them at the bottom of the hill.* 我在山腳下等他們。

base [usually sing.] the lowest part of sth, especially the part or surface on which it rests or stands 指根基、基底、底座：*The lamp has a heavy base.* 這枱燈的底座很沉。

foundation [usually pl.] a layer of bricks, concrete, etc. that forms the solid underground base of a building 指地基、房基、基礎：*to lay the foundations of the new school* 給新校舍打地基

foot [sing.] the lowest part of sth 指最下部、底部：*At the foot of the stairs she turned to face him.* 她在樓梯底轉過身來面對着他。

BOTTOM OR FOOT? 用 bottom 還是 foot？

Foot is used to talk about a limited number of things: it is used most often with *tree, hill/mountain, steps/stairs* and *page*. **Bottom** can be used to talk about a much wider range of things, including those mentioned above for **foot**. **Foot** is generally used in more literary contexts. * foot 用於有限的一些事物，最常與 tree、hill/mountain、steps/stairs 和 page 等連用。bottom 適用的範圍要廣得多，其中也包括上面提到的與 foot 搭配的詞。foot 一般用於文學性較強的語境中。

PATTERNS

- **at/near/towards** the bottom/base/foot of sth
- **on** the bottom/base of sth
- (a) **firm/solid/strong** base/foundation(s)

ˌ**bottom ˈdrawer** *noun* (*BrE*) items for the house collected by a woman, especially in the past, in preparation for her marriage (and often kept in a drawer)（尤指舊時）女子為結婚而存貯的物品，壓箱錢財 ➲ compare HOPE CHEST

ˈ**bottom feeder** *noun* **1** (*NAmE, informal*) a person who earns money by taking advantage of bad things that happen to other people or by using things that other people throw away 乘人之危謀利的人；利用他人丟棄物為生的人；拾荒者 **2** a fish that feeds at the bottom of a river, lake or the sea 底棲魚

bot·tom·less /ˈbɒtəmləs; *NAmE* ˈbɑːt-/ *adj.* (*formal*) very deep; seeming to have no bottom or limit 很深的；深不可測的；深不見底的

IDM **a bottomless ˈpit (of sth)** a thing or situation which seems to have no limits or seems never to end 無限度事物；無休止的狀況；無底洞：*There isn't a bottomless pit of money for public spending.* 公共開支並非用之不盡的。◇ *the bottomless pit of his sorrow* 他無盡的悲哀

ˌ**bottom ˈline** *noun* [sing.] **1 the bottom line** the most important thing that you have to consider or accept; the essential point in a discussion, etc. 要旨；基本論點；底線：*The bottom line is that we have to make a decision today.* 底線是，我們今天必須作出決定。 **2** (*business* 商) the amount of money that is a profit or a loss after everything has been calculated 最終贏利（或虧損）；損益表底線：*The bottom line for 2008 was a pre-tax profit of £85 million.* * 2008 年最終獲得稅前利潤 8 500 萬英鎊。**3** the lowest price that sb will accept 可接受的最低價格；底價：*Two thousand—and that's my bottom line!* 兩千塊，不能再低了！

ˌ**bottom-ˈup** *adj.* (of a plan, project, etc. 計劃、項目等) starting with details and then later moving on to more general principles 自下而上的；從點到面的：*a bottom-up approach to tackling the problem* 處理這個問題的自下而上的方法 ➲ compare TOP-DOWN (1)

botu·lin /ˈbɒtjulɪn; *NAmE* ˈbɑːtjə-/ *noun* [U] the poisonous substance in the bacteria that cause BOTULISM 肉毒桿菌毒素

botu·lism /ˈbɒtjulɪzəm; *NAmE* ˈbɑːtʃə-/ *noun* [U] a serious illness caused by bacteria in badly preserved food 肉毒中毒（由加工食品中的桿菌引起）

bou·doir /ˈbuːdwɑː(r)/ *noun* (*old-fashioned*) a woman's small private room or bedroom 閨房；女子臥室

bouf·fant /ˈbuːfɒ̃; *NAmE* buːˈfɑːnt/ *adj.* (of a person's hair 頭髮) in a style that raises it up and back from the head in a high round shape（往後梳）蓬鬆式的

bou·gain·vil·lea (also **bou·gain·vil·laea**) /ˌbuːɡənˈvɪliə/ *noun* a tropical climbing plant with red, purple, white or pink flowers 葉子花，九重葛（熱帶攀緣植物，開紅、紫、白或粉色花）

bough /baʊ/ *noun* (*formal* or *literary*) a large branch of a tree 大樹枝

bought *past tense, past part.* of BUY

bouil·la·baisse /ˈbuːjəbeɪs/ *noun* [U] (from *French*) a spicy fish soup from the south of France 普羅旺斯魚湯；法式魚羹

bouil·lon /ˈbuːjɒn; -jɒ̃; *NAmE* -jɑːn/ *noun* [U, C] a liquid made by boiling meat or vegetables in water, used for making clear soups or sauces（用作清湯或調味的）肉湯，菜湯

boul·der /ˈbəʊldə(r); *NAmE* ˈboʊl-/ *noun* a very large rock which has been shaped by water or the weather（受水或天氣侵蝕而成的）巨石；漂礫 ➲ VISUAL VOCAB pages V4, V5

boul·der·ing /ˈbəʊldərɪŋ; *NAmE* ˈboʊl-/ *noun* [U] the sport or activity of climbing on large rocks 攀岩（運動）

boule (also **boules**) /buːl/ *noun* [U] a French game in which players take turns to roll metal balls as near as possible to a small ball 法式滾球戲（遊戲者依次將金屬球滾至靠近靶球）

boule·vard /ˈbuːləvɑːd; *NAmE* ˈbʊləvɑːrd/ *noun* **1** (*BrE*) a wide city street, often with trees on either side（市區的）林蔭大道 **2** (*abbr.* **Blvd.**) (*NAmE*) a wide main road (often used in the names of streets)（常用作街道名稱）要道，大街：*Sunset Boulevard* 日落大道

bounce /baʊns/ *verb, noun*

■ ***verb***

▸ **MOVE OFF SURFACE 離開表面 1** [I, T] if sth **bounces** or you **bounce** it, it moves quickly away from a surface it has just hit or you make it do this（使）彈起，彈跳：*The ball bounced twice before he could reach it.* 球彈跳兩次他才接到。◇ **~ off sth** *Short sound waves bounce off even small objects.* 短聲波即使遇到小物體都會產生回音。◇ *The light bounced off the river and dazzled her.* 河面上銀波粼粼，令她目眩。◇ **~ sth (against/on/off sth)** *She bounced the ball against the wall.* 她對着牆打球。

▸ **MOVE UP AND DOWN 上下移動 2** [I] **~ (up and down) (on sth)** (of a person 人) to jump up and down on sth（在…上）跳動，蹦：*She bounced up and down excitedly on the bed.* 她興奮地在牀上蹦蹦跳跳。 **3** [T] **~ sb (up and down) (on sth)** to move a child up and down while he or she is sitting on your knee in order to entertain him or her 把小孩放在膝上顛着玩 **4** [I, T] **~ (sth) (up and down)** to move up and down; to move sth up and down（使）上下晃動：*Her hair bounced as she walked.* 她走起路來頭髮上下晃動。 **5** [I] **+ adv./prep.** to move up and down in a particular direction（朝某個方向）顛簸行進：*The bus bounced down the hill.* 公共汽車顛簸着開下山去。

▸ **MOVE WITH ENERGY** 有活力地走動 **6** [I] **+ adv./prep.** (of a person 人) to move somewhere in a lively and cheerful way 活潑興奮地走，蹦蹦跳跳地去（到某處）：*He bounced across the room to greet them.* 他興奮地衝過房間去迎接他們。

▸ **CHEQUE** 支票 **7** [I, T] **~ (sth)** (*informal*) if a cheque **bounces**, or a bank **bounces** it, the bank refuses to accept it because there is not enough money in the account 拒付，退回（支票等）

▸ **IDEAS** 主意 **8** [T] **~ ideas (off sb)/(around)** to tell sb your ideas in order to find out what they think about them（向某人）透露主意（以試探其反應）：*He bounced ideas off colleagues everywhere he went.* 他在同事中逢人便試探地大講他的想法。

▸ **COMPUTING** 計算機技術 **9** [I, T] **~ (sth) (back)** if an email **bounces** or the system **bounces** it, it returns to the person who sent it because the system cannot deliver it（電子郵件）彈回；退回（電子郵件）

▸ **MAKE SB LEAVE** 使離開 **10** [T] **~ sb (from sth)** (*informal, especially NAmE*) to force sb to leave a job, team, place, etc. 解雇；開除；攆走；逐出：*He was soon bounced from the post.* 他不久被解職。

IDM **be 'bouncing off the walls** (*informal*) to be so full of energy or so excited that you cannot keep still 精力充沛得待不住；激動得難以平靜

PHR V **,bounce 'back** to become healthy, successful or confident again after being ill/sick or having difficulties 恢復健康（或信心等）；重整旗鼓 **SYN** **recover**：*He's had a lot of problems, but he always seems to bounce back pretty quickly.* 他遭遇過很多挫折，但他似乎總能很快地振作起來。 **,bounce 'back | ,bounce sth↔ 'back** (*computing* 計) if an email **bounces back**, or the system **bounces** it **back**, it returns to the person who sent it because the system cannot deliver it（使郵件）退回 **,bounce 'back (from sth)** (*business* 商) (of prices, shares, etc. 價格、股票等) to return to their previous high level or value after a period of difficulty 回升；反彈；上揚：*The airline's shares have bounced back from two days of heavy losses.* 航空公司的股票狂跌兩天後已經反彈回來。 **,bounce sb 'into sth** (*BrE*) to make sb do sth without giving them enough time to think about it 追逼（或催逼）別人做某事

■ ***noun***

▸ **MOVEMENT** 動作 **1** [C] the action of bouncing 彈跳；跳動：*one bounce of the ball* 球的一次彈起 ◇ (*NAmE*) *a bounce* (= increase) *in popularity* 聲望的增加 **2** [U] the ability to bounce or to make sth bounce 彈性；反彈力：*There's not much bounce left in these balls.* 這些球已沒有多少彈性了。◇ *Players complained about the uneven bounce of the tennis court.* 運動員抱怨說網球場的反彈力不均勻。

▸ **ENERGY** 精力 **3** [U, C] the energy that a person has 活力；精力：*All her old bounce was back.* 她完全恢復了以往的活力。◇ *There was a bounce to his step.* 他的步伐矯健有力。

▸ **OF HAIR** 頭髮 **4** [U] the quality in a person's hair that shows that it is in good condition and means that it does not lie flat 富有彈性；蓬鬆：*thin fine hair, lacking in bounce* 沒有彈性、稀疏纖細的頭髮

IDM **on the 'bounce** (*BrE, informal*) one after the other, without anything else coming between 接連；連續；相繼：*We've won six matches on the bounce.* 我們已經六連勝。

bounce·back·abil·ity /ˌbaʊnsbækəˈbɪləti/ *noun* (*BrE*) [U] (*informal*) (especially in sport 尤用於體育運動) the ability to be successful again after playing or performing badly for a time 重整旗鼓的能力：*The team have shown great bouncebackability.* 這支隊伍表現出很強的東山再起的實力。◇ *This will be a test of their famous bouncebackability.* 這將是對他們眾所周知的逆轉能力的考驗。

boun·cer /ˈbaʊnsə(r)/ *noun* **1** a person employed to stand at the entrance to a club, pub, etc. to stop people who are not wanted from going in, and to throw out people who are causing trouble inside（俱樂部、酒店等的）門衛 **2** (in CRICKET 板球) a ball thrown very fast that rises high after it hits the ground 彈得很高的快球 **3** (also **in,flatable 'bouncer**) (both *NAmE*) (*BrE* **,bouncy 'castle**) a plastic castle or other shape which is filled with air and which children can jump and play on 充氣歡樂堡（兒童遊戲用的塑料城堡）

boun·cing /ˈbaʊnsɪŋ/ *adj.* **~ (with sth)** healthy and full of energy 健壯的；茁壯的：*a bouncing baby boy* 茁壯的男嬰

bouncy /ˈbaʊnsi/ *adj.* (**boun·cier**, **boun·ci·est**) **1** that bounces well or that has the ability to make sth bounce 彈性好的；有反彈力的：*a very bouncy ball* 彈性很好的球 ◇ *his bouncy blond curls* 他富有彈性的金色鬈髮 **2** lively and full of energy 生氣勃勃的；精神飽滿的

,bouncy 'castle (*BrE*) (*NAmE* **bouncer**, **in,flatable 'bouncer**) *noun* a plastic castle or other shape which is filled with air and which children can jump and play on（供兒童蹦跳玩樂的）充氣城堡

bound 🔑 /baʊnd/ *adj.*, *verb*, *noun* ➲ see also BIND *v.*

■ ***adj.*** [not before noun] **1** 🔑 **~ to do/be sth** certain or likely to happen, or to do or be sth 一定會；很可能會：*There are bound to be changes when the new system is introduced.* 引進新系統後一定會發生變化。◇ *It's bound to be sunny again tomorrow.* 明天肯定又是陽光燦爛。◇ *You've done so much work—you're bound to pass the exam.* 你下了這麼大工夫，考試準能及格。◇ *It was bound to happen sooner or later* (= we should have expected it). 這事遲早都是要發生的。◇ *You're bound to be nervous the first time* (= it's easy to understand). 第一次總是會緊張的。 ➲ **SYNONYMS** at CERTAIN **2** forced to do sth by law, duty or a particular situation 受（法律、義務或情況）約束（必須做某事）；有義務（做某事）：**~ by sth** *We are not bound by the decision.* 我們不受該決定的約束。◇ *You are bound by the contract to pay before the end of the month.* 按照合同規定，你必須在月底前付款。◇ **~ (by sth) to do sth** (*BrE, formal*) *I am* **bound to say** *I disagree with you on this point.* 我覺得有必要指出，在這一點上我不同意你的觀點。 **3** (in compounds 構成複合詞) prevented from going somewhere or from working normally by the conditions mentioned 因…受阻（或不能正常工作）：*Strike-bound travellers face long delays.* 因罷工滯留的旅客要耽擱很長時間。◇ *fogbound airports* 因霧不能正常作業的機場 **4** (also in compounds 亦構成複合詞) travelling, or ready to travel, in a particular direction or to a particular place 正旅行去（某地）；準備前往（某地）：*homeward bound* (= going home) 在回家途中 ◇ *Paris-bound* 前往巴黎的 ◇ ***northbound/southbound/eastbound/westbound*** 向北／向南／向東／向西行進的 ◇ **~ for …** *a plane bound for Dublin* 開往都柏林的飛機

IDM **be bound 'up in sth** very busy with sth; very interested or involved in sth 忙於某事；熱衷於某事：*He's too bound up in his work to have much time for his children.* 他工作太忙，沒有很多時間陪孩子們。 **bound and de'termined** (*NAmE*) very determined to do sth 矢志不渝；下定決心 **be bound to'gether by/in sth** to be closely connected 因…（或在…方面）密切聯繫：*communities bound together by customs and traditions* 因習俗和傳統而結合在一起的社區 **bound 'up with sth** closely connected with sth 和某事密切相關：*From that moment my life became inextricably bound up with hers.* 從那一刻起，我的一生就和她結下不解之緣。 **'I'll be bound** (*old-fashioned, BrE, informal*) I feel sure 我敢肯定 ➲ more at HONOUR *n.*

■ ***verb*** **1** [I] **+ adv./prep.** to run with long steps, especially in an enthusiastic way 跳躍着跑：*The dogs bounded ahead.* 那些狗在前面蹦蹦跳跳地跑。 **2** [T, usually passive] **~ sth** (*formal*) to form the edge or limit of an area 形成…的邊界（或界限）：*The field was bounded on the left by a wood.* 那片地左邊依傍着一片樹林。

B

■ **noun** (*formal*) a high or long jump 蹦跳；跳躍 ➲ see also BOUNDS **IDM** see LEAP *n.*

bound·ary /ˈbaʊndri/ *noun* (*pl.* **-ies**) **1** a real or imagined line that marks the limits or edges of sth and separates it from other things or places; a dividing line 邊界；界限；分界線：*national boundaries* 國界 ◇ (*BrE*) *county boundaries* 郡界 ◇ ***boundary changes/disputes*** 邊界變化 / 爭端 ◇ *The fence marks the boundary between my property and hers.* 那道籬笆是我和她的住宅之間的分界。◇ *Scientists continue to* ***push back the boundaries*** *of human knowledge.* 科學家不斷擴大人類知識的範圍。◇ *the boundary between acceptable and unacceptable behaviour* 可接受和不可接受的行為之間的分界線 ➲ SYNONYMS at BORDER **2** (in CRICKET 板球) a hit of the ball that crosses the boundary of the playing area and scores extra points 使球越過邊界線的擊球（得加分）

bound·en /ˈbaʊndən/ *adj.*
IDM **a/your bounden 'duty** (*old-fashioned, formal*) something that you feel you must do; a responsibility which cannot be ignored 應盡的義務；不可推卸的責任

bound·er /ˈbaʊndə(r)/ *noun* (*old-fashioned, BrE, informal*) a man who behaves badly and cannot be trusted 缺德的人；無賴

bound·less /ˈbaʊndləs/ *adj.* without limits; seeming to have no end 無限的；無止境的 **SYN** **infinite**

bounds /baʊndz/ *noun* [pl.] the accepted or furthest limits of sth 限制範圍；極限：***beyond/outside/within the bounds of*** *decency* 沒 / 有體統 ◇ *Public spending must be kept within reasonable bounds.* 公共開支必須控制在合理的範圍內。◇ *It was not* ***beyond the bounds of possibility*** *that they would meet again one day.* 他們有一天會再度相遇，這不是沒有可能。◇ *His enthusiasm* ***knew no bounds*** (= was very great). 他有無限熱情。
IDM **out of 'bounds 1** (in some sports 某些體育運動) outside the area of play which is allowed 出界；界外：*His shot went out of bounds.* 他的球出界了。**2** (*NAmE*) not reasonable or acceptable 不合理的；令人無法接受的：*His demands were out of bounds.* 他的要求不合理。 **out of 'bounds (to/for sb)** (*especially BrE*) if a place is **out of bounds**, people are not allowed to go there 不准進入；禁止入內 ➲ see also OFF-LIMITS ➲ more at LEAP *n.*

boun·teous /ˈbaʊntiəs/ *adj.* (*formal* or *literary*) giving very generously 十分慷慨的；非常大方的

boun·ti·ful /ˈbaʊntɪfl/ *adj.* (*formal* or *literary*) **1** in large quantities; large 大量的；巨大的：*a bountiful supply of food* 富足的食物供應 **2** giving generously 慷慨的；大方的 **SYN** **generous**：*belief in a bountiful god* 對寬宏的神的信仰

bounty /ˈbaʊnti/ *noun* (*pl.* **-ies**) **1** [U, C] (*literary*) generous actions; sth provided in large quantities 慷慨之舉；大量給予之物 **2** [C] money given as a reward 獎金；賞金：*a* ***bounty hunter*** (= sb who catches criminals or kills people for a reward) 為得到賞金而抓捕罪犯或去殺人的人

bou·quet /buˈkeɪ/ *noun* **1** [C] a bunch of flowers arranged in an attractive way so that it can be carried in a ceremony or presented as a gift 花束：*The little girl presented the princess with a large* ***bouquet of flowers.*** 那小女孩向公主獻上了一大束鮮花。**2** [C, U] the pleasant smell of a type of food or drink, especially of wine（尤指酒的）香味，芬芳

bou·quet garni /ˌbuːkeɪ ɡɑːˈniː; *NAmE* ɡɑːrˈniː; *NAmE* also boʊˌkeɪ/ *noun* (*pl.* **bou·quets gar·nis** /ˌbuːkeɪ ɡɑːˈniː; *NAmE* ɡɑːrˈniː; *NAmE* also boʊˌkeɪ/) (from *French*) a bunch of different HERBS in a small bag, used in cooking to give extra flavour to food 香料束，香料袋（有各種香草，用於烹調食物）

bour·bon /ˈbɜːbən; *NAmE* ˈbɜːrbən/ *noun* **1** [U, C] a type of American WHISKY made with CORN (MAIZE) and RYE 波旁威士忌酒（產於美國，用玉米和黑麥釀製）**2** [C] a glass of bourbon 一杯波旁威士忌

bour·geois /ˈbʊəʒwɑː; ˌbʊəˈʒwɑː; *NAmE* ˌbʊrˈʒ-; ˈbʊrʒ-/ *adj.* **1** belonging to the middle class 中產階級的：*a traditional bourgeois family* 一個傳統的中產階級家庭 ➲ see also PETIT BOURGEOIS **2** (*disapproving*) interested mainly in possessions and social status and supporting traditional values 追求名利且平庸的；世俗的：***bourgeois attitudes/tastes*** 世俗的態度 / 趣味 ◇ *They've become very bourgeois since they got married.* 他們結婚後變得十分庸俗。**3** (*politics* 政) supporting the interests of CAPITALISM 資產階級的；資本家的：*bourgeois ideology* 資產階級意識形態 ▸ **bour·geois** *noun* (*pl.* **bour·geois**)

bour·geoisie /ˌbʊəʒwɑːˈziː; *NAmE* ˌbʊrʒ-/ *noun* **the bourgeoisie** [sing.+sing./pl. v.] **1** the middle classes in society 中產階級：*the rise of the bourgeoisie in the nineteenth century* 十九世紀中產階級的興起 **2** (*politics* 政) the CAPITALIST class 資產階級；資本家階級：*the proletariat and the bourgeoisie* 無產階級和資產階級

Bourke /bɜːk; *NAmE* bɜːrk/ *noun*
IDM **back of Bourke** (*AustralE*) (in) the country, a long way from the coast and towns; in the OUTBACK（在）鄉村，遠離海濱和城鎮；在內地 **ORIGIN** From the name of the town in New South Wales. 源自新南威爾士伯克鎮。

bourse /bʊəs; *NAmE* bʊrs/ *noun* (from *French*) a STOCK EXCHANGE, especially the one in Paris（尤指巴黎的）證券交易所

bout /baʊt/ *noun* **1** a short period of great activity; a short period during which there is a lot of a particular thing, usually sth unpleasant 一陣；一場；（尤指壞事的）一通，一次：*a drinking bout* 狂飲一通 ◇ **~ of sth/of doing sth** *the latest bout of inflation* 最近一陣通貨膨脹 **2 ~ (of sth)** an attack or period of illness（疾病的）發作；發病期：*a severe bout of flu/coughing* 流感 / 咳嗽的猛烈發作 ◇ *He suffered occasional bouts of depression.* 他有時會犯抑鬱症。◇ (*NAmE*) *a bout with the flu* 流感發作期 **3** a BOXING or WRESTLING match 拳擊（或摔跤）比賽

bou·tique /buːˈtiːk/ *noun, adj.*
■ **noun** a small shop/store that sells fashionable clothes or expensive gifts 時裝店；精品店
■ **adj.** [only before noun] (of a business) small and offering products or services of a high quality to a small number of customers（商店）精品的，提供專門服務的（針對小量的顧客）：*a boutique hotel that offers an escape from the outside world* 讓人遠離塵世喧囂的精品酒店 ◇ *a boutique investment bank* 精品投資銀行

bou·ton·nière /ˌbuːtɒnˈjeə(r); *NAmE* ˌbuːtnˈɪr; -tənˈjer/ (*NAmE*, from *French*) (*BrE* **but·ton·hole**) *noun* a flower that is worn in the BUTTONHOLE of a coat or jacket 佩戴在扣眼上的花

bou·zou·ki /buˈzuːki/ *noun* a Greek musical instrument with strings that are played with the fingers 布祖基琴（希臘弦樂器）

bo·vine /ˈbəʊvaɪn; *NAmE* ˈboʊ-/ *adj.* [usually before noun] **1** (*technical* 術語) connected with cows 牛的；與牛有關的：*bovine diseases* 牛病 **2** (*disapproving*) (of a person 人) stupid and slow 愚笨的；反應遲鈍的

Bov·ril™ /ˈbɒvrɪl; *NAmE* ˈbɑːv-/ *noun* **1** [U] a dark substance made from beef, used in cooking and for making drinks 保衛爾牛肉汁（用牛肉製，用以調味或沖淡飲用）**2** [U, C] a hot drink made by mixing Bovril with water 保衛爾牛肉汁熱飲

bow 船頭；鞠躬

bow of a ship 船頭

take a bow 鞠躬答謝

bow¹ /baʊ/ *verb, noun* ➲ see also BOW²
■ **verb 1** [I] to move your head or the top half of your body forwards and downwards as a sign of respect or to say hello or goodbye 鞠躬；點頭：**~ (to/before**

sb/sth) *He bowed low to the assembled crowd.* 他向集結的人群深深地鞠了一躬。◇ **~ down (to/before sb/sth)** *The people all bowed down before the Emperor.* 全體給皇帝鞠躬。 **2** [T] **~ your head** to move your head forwards and downwards 低頭；垂首： *She bowed her head in shame.* 她羞愧地低下了頭。◇ *They stood in silence with their heads bowed.* 他們默默地垂頭而立。 **3** [I, T] to bend or make sth bend（使）彎曲：(**+ adv./prep.**) *The pines bowed in the wind.* 松樹被風吹彎了。◇ **~ sth (+ adv./prep.)** *Their backs were bowed under the weight of their packs.* 沉重的背包壓彎了他們的脊背。

IDM **,bow and 'scrape** (*disapproving*) to be too polite to an important person in order to gain their approval 卑躬屈膝；點頭哈腰

PHR V **,bow 'down to sb/sth** (*disapproving*) to allow sb to tell you what to do 屈從於人；聽任擺佈 **,bow 'out (of sth)** to stop taking part in an activity, especially one in which you have been successful in the past 退出，告別（尤指一度成功的事業）： *She has finally decided it's time to bow out of international tennis.* 她最終認定是退出世界網壇的時候了。 **'bow to sth** to agree unwillingly to do sth because other people want you to 勉強同意做（某事）；屈從於： *They finally bowed to pressure from the public.* 他們終於在公眾的壓力下讓步了。◇ *She* **bowed to the inevitable** (= accepted a situation in which she had no choice) *and resigned.* 她迫於無奈，只得辭職。

■ ***noun*** **1** the act of bending your head or the upper part of your body forward in order to say hello or goodbye to sb or to show respect 鞠躬；彎腰行禮 **2** (also **bows** [pl.]) the front part of a boat or ship 船頭；艏 ➲ **VISUAL VOCAB** page V54 ➲ compare STERN *n.*

IDM **take a/your 'bow** (of a performer 演員) to bow to the audience as they are APPLAUDING you 謝幕；鞠躬答謝 ➲ more at SHOT *n.*

bows 弓；蝴蝶結；琴弓

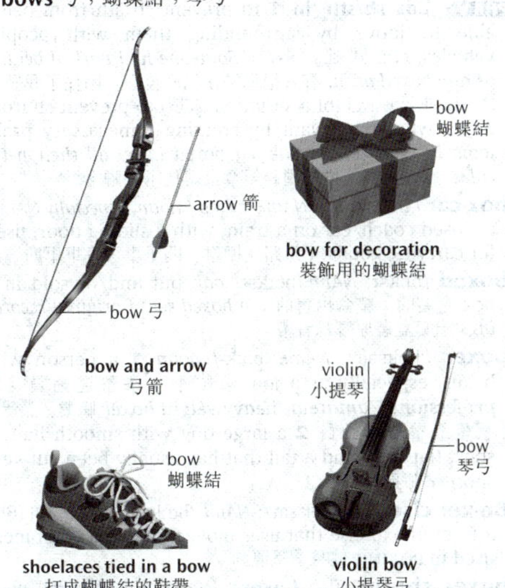

bow² /baʊ; *NAmE* boʊ/ *noun, verb* ➲ see also BOW¹

■ ***noun*** **1** a weapon used for shooting arrows, consisting of a long curved piece of wood with a tight string joining its ends 弓： *He was armed with a bow and arrow.* 他佩帶着弓箭。 ➲ **VISUAL VOCAB** page V40 **2** a knot with two LOOPS and two loose ends which is used for decoration on clothes, in hair, etc. or for tying shoes 蝴蝶結： *to tie your shoelaces in a bow* 把鞋帶打成蝴蝶結 ◇ *Her hair was tied back in a neat bow.* 她的頭髮紮在腦後打了個整齊的蝴蝶結。 ➲ picture at KNOT **3** a long thin piece of wood with thin string stretched along it, used for playing musical instruments such as the VIOLIN 琴弓 ➲ **VISUAL VOCAB** page V34 **IDM** see STRING *n.*

■ ***verb*** [I, T] **~ (sth)** to use a bow to play a musical instrument that has strings 用琴弓拉奏弦樂器

bowd·ler·ize (*BrE* also **-ise**) /ˈbaʊdləraɪz/ *verb* **~ sth** (usually *disapproving*) to remove the parts of a book, play, etc. that you think are likely to shock or offend people 刪改（認為書或戲劇等中有傷風化或有冒犯性的部份）；鮑德勒化 **SYN** **expurgate** **ORIGIN** Named after Dr Thomas **Bowdler**, who in 1818 produced a version of Shakespeare from which he had taken out all the material which he considered not suitable for family use. 源自托馬斯 • 鮑德勒博士（Dr Thomas Bowdler）的名字。他於 1818 年出版了莎士比亞戲劇的改寫本，刪掉了他認為不適合家庭閱讀的內容。

bowel /ˈbaʊəl/ *noun* **1** [C, usually pl.] the tube along which food passes after it has been through the stomach, especially the end where waste is collected before it is passed out of the body 腸：(*medical* 醫) *to* ***empty/move/open your bowels*** (= to pass solid waste out of the body) 解大便 ◇ *bowel cancer/cancer of the bowel* 腸癌 **2 the bowels of sth** [pl.] (*literary*) the part that is deepest inside sth 內部最深處： *A rumble came from* ***the bowels of the earth*** (= deep underground). 從地下深處傳來隆隆的響聲。

'bowel movement (also **movement**) *noun* (*medical* 醫) an act of emptying waste material from the bowels; the waste material that is emptied 解大便；糞便

bower /ˈbaʊə(r)/ *noun* (*literary*) a pleasant place in the shade under trees or climbing plants in a wood or garden/yard 樹蔭處；陰涼處

bower·bird /ˈbaʊəbɜːd; *NAmE* ˈbaʊərbɜːrd/ *noun* a bird found in Australia, the male of which decorates a place with shells, feathers, etc. to attract females 涼亭鳥，造園鳥（見於澳大利亞，雄鳥構築涼亭狀物求偶）

bow·fin /ˈbəʊfɪn; *NAmE* ˈboʊ-/ *noun* (*pl.* **bow·fin** or **bow·fins**) an American fish with a large head that can survive for a long time out of water 弓鰭魚（產於美洲，頭大，耐旱）

bow·ie knife /ˈbəʊi naɪf; *NAmE* ˈboʊi/ *noun* a large heavy knife with a long blade, used in hunting 長刃獵刀

bowl 🔑 /bəʊl; *NAmE* boʊl/ *noun, verb*

■ ***noun***

▸ CONTAINER 容器 **1** 🔑 [C] (especially in compounds 尤用於構成複合詞) a deep round dish with a wide open top, used especially for holding food or liquid 碗；鉢；盆： *a* ***salad/fruit/sugar, etc. bowl*** 色拉碗、水果盆、糖鉢等 ◇ *a* ***washing-up bowl*** 洗碗碟盆 ➲ **VISUAL VOCAB** page V22

▸ AMOUNT 量 **2** 🔑 [C] (also **bowl·ful** /-fʊl/) the amount contained in a bowl 一碗，一鉢，一盆（的量）： *a bowl of soup* 一碗湯

▸ SHAPE 形狀 **3** [C] the part of some objects that is shaped like a bowl 物體的碗狀部份： *the bowl of a spoon* 勺子頭 ◇ *a* ***toilet/lavatory bowl*** 馬桶 ➲ **VISUAL VOCAB** page V22

▸ THEATRE 劇場 **4** [C] (*especially NAmE*) (in names 構成名稱) a large round theatre without a roof, used for concerts, etc. outdoors 露天圓形劇場： *the Hollywood Bowl* 好萊塢露天劇場

▸ BALL 球 **5** [C] a heavy wooden ball that is used in the games of BOWLS and BOWLING（草地滾球和保齡球中用的）木球

▸ GAME 遊戲 **6 bowls** [U] (*NAmE* also **'lawn bowling**) a game played on an area of very smooth grass, in which players take turns to roll bowls as near as possible to a small ball 草地滾球 ➲ **VISUAL VOCAB** page V40

▸ FOOTBALL GAME 橄欖球比賽 **7** [C] (*NAmE*) (in names 構成名稱) a game of AMERICAN FOOTBALL played after the main season between the best teams（美式足球主要賽季後強隊之間的）季後賽： *the Super Bowl* 超級杯季後賽

■ ***verb***

▸ ROLL BALL 滾球 **1** [I, T] **~ (sth)** to roll a ball in the games of bowls and BOWLING（草地滾球或保齡球中）滾球，投球

▸ IN CRICKET 板球 **2** [I, T] **~ (sth)** to throw a ball to the BATSMAN (= the person who hits the ball) 把（球）投給擊球員 ➲ **SYNONYMS** at THROW **3** [T] **~ sb (out)** to make the BATSMAN have to leave the field by throwing a ball that hits the WICKET 擊中三柱門把（擊球員）殺出局

B

▸ **MOVE QUICKLY** 迅速移動 **4** [I] **+ adv./prep.** (*BrE*) to move quickly in a particular direction, especially in a vehicle（向某處）迅速移動；（尤指）快速行駛： *Soon we were bowling along the country roads.* 我們不久便在鄉村的公路上疾馳了。

PHR V **,bowl sb 'over** **1** to run into sb and knock them down 把某人撞倒 **2** to surprise or impress sb a lot 使某人驚歎；讓某人印象深刻

bow legs /ˌbəʊ ˈlegz; *NAmE* ˌboʊ/ *noun* [pl.] legs that curve out at the knees 弓形腿；羅圈腿 ▸ **bow-legged** /ˌbəʊ ˈlegɪd; *NAmE* ˌboʊ/ *adj.*

bowl·er /ˈbəʊlə(r); *NAmE* ˈboʊ-/ *noun* **1** (in CRICKET 板球) a player who throws the ball towards the BATSMAN 投球手 **2** (also **,bowler 'hat**) (both *especially BrE*) (*NAmE* usually **derby**) a hard black hat with a curved BRIM and round top, worn, for example, in the past by men in business in Britain 常禮帽（英國舊時商人常戴） ➲ VISUAL VOCAB page V65

bow·line¹ /ˈbaʊlaɪn/ *noun* a rope that attaches one side of a sail to the BOW of a boat 船頭帆繩

bow·line² /ˈbəʊlɪn; *NAmE* ˈboʊlən/ *noun* a type of knot, used for making a LOOP at the end of a rope 單套結；稱人結

bowl·ing /ˈbəʊlɪŋ; *NAmE* ˈboʊ-/ *noun* [U] a game in which players roll heavy balls (called BOWLS) along a special track towards a group of PINS (= bottle-shaped objects) and try to knock over as many of them as possible 保齡球 ➲ compare BOWLS at BOWL *n.* (6) ➲ VISUAL VOCAB page V40

'bowling alley *noun* a building or part of a building where people can go bowling 保齡球場

'bowling green *noun* an area of grass that has been cut short on which the game of BOWLS is played 草地滾球場 ➲ VISUAL VOCAB page V40

bow·man /ˈbəʊmən; *NAmE* ˈboʊ-/ *noun* (*pl.* **-men** /-mən/) (*old-fashioned*) = ARCHER

bow·ser™ /ˈbaʊzə(r)/ *noun* (*especially BrE*) a container, often on wheels, used for holding liquids such as water or fuel, often because the normal supply is not available（臨時）加水車；（應急）加油車

bow·sprit /ˈbəʊsprɪt; *NAmE* ˈboʊ-/ *noun* a thick pole that sticks forward at the front of a ship 船頭斜桁

bow·string /ˈbəʊstrɪŋ; *NAmE* ˈboʊ-/ *noun* the string on a BOW² which is pulled back to shoot arrows 弓弦

bow tie /ˌbəʊ ˈtaɪ; *NAmE* ˌboʊ/ *noun* a man's tie that is tied in the shape of a bow and that does not hang down 蝶形領結 ➲ VISUAL VOCAB page V61

bow-wow /ˈbaʊ waʊ/ *noun* a child's word for a dog 汪汪（兒語指狗）

box 🔑 /bɒks; *NAmE* bɑːks/ *noun, verb*

■ *noun*

▸ **CONTAINER** 容器 **1** 🔑 [C] (especially in compounds 尤用於構成複合詞) a container made of wood, cardboard, metal, etc. with a flat stiff base and sides and often a lid, used especially for holding solid things 盒；箱；匣： *She kept all the letters in a box.* 她把信件都保存在一個盒子裏。◇ *a money box* 錢匣 ◇ *cardboard boxes* 紙板箱 ◇ *a toolbox* 工具箱 ◇ *a matchbox* 火柴盒 ➲ VISUAL VOCAB page V33 **2** 🔑 [C] a box and its contents 一盒，一箱（東西）： ***a box of chocolates/matches*** 一盒巧克力／火柴 ➲ VISUAL VOCAB page V33

▸ **IN THEATRE/COURT** 劇院；法庭 **3** [C] a small area in a theatre or court separated off from where other people sit（劇院中的）包廂；（法庭中的）專席： *a box at the opera* 歌劇院的包廂 ◇ *the **witness/jury box*** 證人／陪審團席

▸ **SHELTER** 遮蔽處 **4** [C] a small shelter used for a particular purpose 小亭；崗亭： *a **sentry/signal box*** 崗亭；鐵路信號所 ◇ (*BrE*) *a telephone box* 電話亭 ◇ *I called him from the phone box on the corner.* 我在拐角處的電話亭打電話給他。

▸ **SHAPE** 形狀 **5** 🔑 [C] a small square or RECTANGLE drawn on a page for people to write information in 方框；長方格： *Put a cross in the appropriate box.* 在適當的方格裏打叉號。◇ ***to tick/check a box*** 在方格裏畫鉤

▸ **TELEVISION** 電視 **6 the box** [sing.] (*informal, especially BrE*) the television 電視： *What's on the box tonight?* 今晚有什麼電視節目？

▸ **ON ROAD** 道路 **7** [C] (*BrE*) = BOX JUNCTION： *Only traffic turning right may enter the box.* 只允許右拐的車輛進入交叉路口黃格區。

▸ **IN SPORT** 體育運動 **8** [C] an area on a sports field that is marked by lines and used for a particular purpose 運動場上以線標出的特定區域： (*BrE*) *He was fouled in the box* (= the penalty box). 有人在禁區對他犯規。

▸ **FOR MAIL** 郵遞 **9** [C] = BOX NUMBER ➲ see also PO BOX

▸ **PROTECTION** 保護 **10** [C] (*BrE*) a piece of plastic that a man wears over his sex organs to protect them while he is playing a sport, especially CRICKET（運動員的）下體護身

▸ **TREE/WOOD** 樹木 **11** [C, U] a small EVERGREEN tree or bush with thick dark leaves, used especially for garden HEDGES 黃楊（常綠，尤用作花園樹籬） **12** (also **box-wood**) [U] the hard wood of this bush 黃楊木

IDM **give sb a box on the 'ears** (*old-fashioned*) to hit sb with your hand on the side of their head as a punishment 打某人耳光 ➲ more at THINK *v.*, TICK *v.*, TRICK *n.*

■ *verb*

▸ **FIGHT** 擊打 **1** [I, T] **~ (sb)** to fight sb in the sport of BOXING（拳擊運動）擊打（某人）

▸ **PUT IN CONTAINER** 裝入容器 **2** [T] **~ sth (up)** to put sth in a box 把（某物）裝箱（或盒、匣）

IDM **box 'clever** (*BrE, informal*) to act in a clever way to get what you want, sometimes tricking sb 巧妙地得到想要的東西（有時矇騙人） **box sb's 'ears** (*old-fashioned*) to hit sb with your hand on the side of their head as a punishment 打某人耳光

PHR V **,box sb/sth 'in** **1** to prevent sb/sth from being able to move by surrounding them with people, vehicles, etc. 圍困；攔擋： *Someone had parked behind us and boxed us in.* 有人把車停在我們後面，困住了我們。 **2** [usually passive] (of a situation 處境) to prevent sb from doing what they want by creating unnecessary problems 阻擋；阻礙： *She felt boxed in by all their petty rules.* 她覺得被他們的瑣碎規章束縛住了手腳。

box·car /ˈbɒkskɑː(r); *NAmE* ˈbɑːks-/ *noun* (*especially NAmE*) a closed coach/car on a train, with a sliding door, used for carrying goods（鐵路）棚車，悶子車，貨車車廂

boxed /bɒkst; *NAmE* bɑːkst/ *adj.* put and/or sold in a box 盒裝的；整盒出售的： *a boxed set of original recordings* 一套盒裝原聲錄音帶

boxer /ˈbɒksə(r); *NAmE* ˈbɑːk-/ *noun* **1** a person who boxes, especially as a job 拳擊手；拳擊運動員： *a **professional/amateur/heavyweight boxer*** 職業／業餘／重量級拳擊運動員 **2** a large dog with smooth hair, a short flat nose and a tail that has usually been cut very short 拳師狗

Bo·xer·cise™ /ˈbɒksəsaɪz; *NAmE* ˈbɑːksər-/ *noun* [U] (*BrE*) a form of exercise that uses movements and equipment used in BOXING 健身拳擊運動

'boxer shorts (also **boxers**) (*NAmE* also **shorts**) *noun* [pl.] men's UNDERPANTS similar to the SHORTS worn by boxers 男用平腳短內褲（類似拳擊短褲）： *a pair of boxer shorts* 一條平腳短內褲

box·ful /ˈbɒksfʊl; *NAmE* ˈbɑːksfʊl/ *noun* a full box (of sth) 一盒，一箱（的量）

box·ing /ˈbɒksɪŋ; *NAmE* ˈbɑːks-/ *noun* [U] a sport in which two people fight each other with their hands, while wearing very large thick gloves (called **boxing gloves**) 拳擊（運動）： *a **boxing champion/match*** 拳擊冠軍／比賽 ◇ *heavyweight boxing* 重量級拳擊 ➲ VISUAL VOCAB page V47

'Box·ing Day *noun* [U, C] (*BrE*) the first day after Christmas Day that is not a Sunday. Boxing Day is an official holiday in Britain and some other countries. 節禮日（聖誕節後的第一個工作日，英國和其他一些國家定為假日）

ˈbox junction (also **box**) *noun* (*BrE*) a place where two roads cross or join, marked with a pattern of yellow lines to show that vehicles must not stop 交叉路口黃格區（車輛不得停留）

ˈbox kite *noun* a KITE in the shape of a long box which is open at both ends （兩端開口的）箱形風箏

ˈbox lunch *noun* (*NAmE*) a meal of SANDWICHES, fruit, etc. that you take to school, work, etc. in a box 自備的盒裝午餐；便當 ➲ compare BAG LUNCH, PACKED LUNCH

ˈbox number (also **box**) *noun* a number used as an address, especially one given in newspaper advertisements to which replies can be sent 信箱號碼（報章廣告常用）

ˈbox office *noun* the place at a theatre, cinema/movie theater, etc. where the tickets are sold 售票處；票房：*The movie has been a huge **box-office success*** (= many people have been to see it). 那部電影十分賣座。➲ COLLOCATIONS at CINEMA

ˈbox room *noun* (*BrE*) a small room in a house for storing things in 貯藏室

ˈbox score *noun* the results of a BASEBALL game or other sporting event shown in the form of rows and columns which include details of each player's performance （棒球等運動的）得分記錄表，個人技術統計表

ˈbox seat *noun*
IDM **in the ˈbox seat** (*AustralE, NZE, informal*) in a position in which you have an advantage 處於有利地位

box·wood /ˈbɒkswʊd; *NAmE* ˈbɑːks-/ *noun* [U] = BOX (12)

boxy /ˈbɒksi; *NAmE* ˈbɑːksi/ *adj.* having a square shape 箱狀的；四四方方的：*a boxy car* 廂式汽車

boy 0┳ /bɔɪ/ *noun, exclamation*
■ ***noun* 1** 0┳ [C] a male child or a young male person 男孩；男青年：***a little/small/young boy*** 小男孩；小伙子 ◇ *I used to play here as a boy.* 我小時候常在這裏玩。◇ *The older boys at school used to tease him.* 學校裏大一些的男生過去常常取笑他。◇ *Now she's a teenager, she's starting to be interested in boys.* 她現在已經是個十幾歲的姑娘了，開始對男孩子感興趣。➲ see also OLD BOY, TOY BOY **2** 0┳ [C] a young son 年少的兒子：*They have two boys and a girl.* 他們有兩個兒子和一個女兒。◇ *Her eldest boy is at college.* 她的長子在上大學。**3** [C] (in compounds; offensive when used of an older man 構成複合詞；用於年長的男子時含冒犯意) a boy or young man who does a particular job 做某工作的男孩（或小伙子）；夥計：*a delivery boy* 報童 ➲ see also BACK-ROOM BOYS, BARROW BOY **4** [C] a way of talking about sb who comes from a particular place, etc.（指稱某地等的人）：*He's a **local boy**.* 他是本地人。◇ *a **city/country boy*** 城裏／鄉下來的人 **5 the boys** [pl.] (*informal*) a group of male friends who often go out together 一幫男夥伴：*a night out with the boys* 和弟兄們一同消遣的一夜 **6 our boys** [pl.] a way of talking with affection about your country's soldiers（對本國士兵的昵稱）兵哥們，小伙子們 **7** [C] (*NAmE, taboo*) used as an offensive way of addressing a black man, especially in the past（尤為舊時不禮貌地稱呼黑人男子用）黑仔，小子
IDM **the boys in ˈblue** (*informal*) the police 警察 **ˌboys ˌwill be ˈboys** (*saying*) you should not be surprised when boys or men behave in a noisy or rough way as this is part of typical male behaviour 男孩子總歸是男孩子（不必為男孩或男子的吵鬧粗野大驚小怪）➲ more at JOB, MAN *n.*, WORK *n.*
■ ***exclamation*** (*informal, especially NAmE*) used to express feelings of surprise, pleasure, pain, etc.（表示驚奇、高興、痛苦等）：*Boy, it sure is hot!* 嗬，真夠辣的！◇ *Oh boy! That's great!* 哇！真了不起！

ˈboy band *noun* a group of attractive young men who sing pop music and dance, and who are especially popular with girls 男孩樂隊；男孩組合

boy·cott /ˈbɔɪkɒt; *NAmE* -kɑːt/ *verb, noun*
■ ***verb* ~ sth** to refuse to buy, use or take part in sth as a way of protesting 拒絕購買（或使用、參加）；抵制：*We are asking people to boycott goods from companies that use child labour.* 我們正呼籲大家抵制雇用童工的公司的產品。
■ ***noun*** an act of boycotting sb/sth （對某事物的）抵制：**~ (of sth)** *a trade boycott of British goods* 對英國貨品的貿易抵制 ◇ **~ (on sth)** *a boycott on the use of tropical wood* 拒絕使用熱帶木材

boyf /bɔɪf/ *noun* (*BrE, informal*) a boyfriend 男友

boy·friend 0┳ /ˈbɔɪfrend/ *noun*
a man or boy that sb has a romantic or sexual relationship with 男朋友

boy·hood /ˈbɔɪhʊd/ *noun* [U] (becoming *old-fashioned*) the time in a man's life when he is a boy（男子的）孩童期，青少年時代：***boyhood days/memories/friends*** 童年時代／回憶；兒時的朋友

boy·ish /ˈbɔɪɪʃ/ *adj.* (*approving*) looking or behaving like a boy, in a way that is attractive （長相或舉止）像男孩的，頑皮可愛的：***boyish charm/enthusiasm*** 男孩般的魅力／熱心 ◇ *her slim boyish figure* 她那男孩子般修長的體形 ▸ **boy·ish·ly** *adv.*

boyo /ˈbɔɪəʊ; *NAmE* ˈbɔɪoʊ/ *noun* (*informal*) used for addressing a boy or a man in Wales （在威爾士用以稱呼男孩或男子）小傢伙，小伙子

ˌboy ˈracer *noun* (*BrE, informal, disapproving*) a man, especially a young man, who drives his car too fast and without care 飆車者（尤指年輕男子）

ˌBoy ˈScout *noun* (*US* or *old-fashioned*) a boy who is a member of the SCOUTS 童子軍

boy·sen·berry /ˈbɔɪznbəri; *NAmE* -beri/ *noun* (*pl.* **-ies**) a large red fruit like a BLACKBERRY. The bush it grows on is also called a boysenberry. 博伊森莓，博伊森莓樹（果大，暗紅黑色）

ˈboy shorts *noun* [pl.] a piece of women's underwear that covers the body from the hips to the top of the legs 平腳女內褲；女用平口褲

ˈboy toy *noun* (*NAmE, informal*) **1** (*BrE* **ˈtoy boy**) (*humorous*) a woman's male lover who is much younger than she is （女子的）小男友，小狼狗 **2** (*disapproving*) a young woman who is happy to be considered only for her sexual attraction and not for her character or intelligence 女玩偶，花瓶（甘願以貌取悅男人）

ˌboy ˈwonder *noun* (*informal, humorous*) a boy or young man who is extremely good at sth （指男孩或年輕男子）神童，天才

bozo /ˈbəʊzəʊ; *NAmE* ˈboʊzoʊ/ *noun* (*pl.* **-os**) (*informal, especially NAmE*) a stupid person 傻瓜；笨蛋

BPhil (*NAmE* **B.Phil**) /ˌbiː ˈfɪl/ *noun* the abbreviation for 'Bachelor of Philosophy' (a university degree in philosophy that is usually a second degree) 哲學學士（全寫為 Bachelor of Philosophy，通常為大學哲學專業的二級學位）

bpi /ˌbiː piː ˈaɪ/ *abbr.* (*computing* 計) bits per inch (a measure of the amount of data that can fit onto a tape or disk) 每英寸位數，每英寸字節數，每英寸位元數（磁帶或磁盤的數據容量標準）

ˈB-picture = B-MOVIE

bps /ˌbiː piː ˈes/ *abbr.* (*computing* 計) bits per second (a measure of the speed at which data is sent or received) 每秒位數，位／秒，每秒位元數（數據收發速度的量度標準）

Bq *abbr.* = BECQUEREL

Br. *abbr.* (in writing) British （書寫形式）英國的

bra /brɑː/ *noun* **1** (also *formal* **brassière**) a piece of women's underwear worn to cover and support the breasts 胸罩；文胸 **2** (also **ˈcar bra**, **ˈauto bra**) a tightly fitting cover that is put over the front end of a car to protect it, sometimes made of a material that absorbs the waves from police RADAR equipment, so that it is more difficult to tell if a driver is going too fast （汽車前部的）活動罩，車頭罩

braai /braɪ/ *noun, verb* (*SAfrE*)
■ ***noun* 1** (also **braai·vleis**) a social event at which food is cooked outdoors over an open fire 露天燒烤餐會：*We're having a braai at our place next Saturday.* 下個星期六我們家要搞一場露天燒烤。◇ *a bring-and-braai*

B

(= everyone brings their own meat) 自帶肉食的露天燒烤餐會 **2** the surface or piece of equipment where the fire is made 燒烤位；燒烤爐

■ *verb* (**braais**, **braai·ing** or **braaing**, **braaied**) [T, I] **~ (sth)** to cook food over an open fire, especially as part of a social event 露天燒烤（聚會）➲ compare BARBECUE

braai·vleis /ˈbraɪfleɪs/ *noun* (*SAfrE*) **1** = BRAAI (1) **2** [U] meat that is cooked over an open fire（露天燒烤的）烤肉

brace /breɪs/ *noun, verb*

■ *noun* **1** [C] a device that holds things firmly together or holds and supports them in position 箍子；夾子；支架：*a neck brace* (= worn to support the neck after an injury) 矯治用的頸箍 **2** [C] (*NAmE* **braces** [pl.]) a metal device that children wear inside the mouth to help their teeth grow straight（兒童）牙箍 **3** **braces** (*BrE*) (*NAmE* **sus·pend·ers**) [pl.] long narrow pieces of cloth, leather, etc. for holding trousers/pants up. They are fastened to the top of the trousers/pants at the front and back and passed over the shoulders. 吊褲帶；背帶：*a pair of braces* 一副吊褲帶 ➲ VISUAL VOCAB page V61 **4** (*NAmE*) (*BrE* **cal·li·per**) [C, usually pl.] a metal support for weak or injured legs 雙腳規形夾（腿無力或受傷時使用的金屬支架）**5** [C] either of the two marks, { }, used to show that the words, etc. between them are connected 大括弧；大括號 ➲ compare BRACKET **6** [C] (*pl.* **brace**) a pair of birds or animals that have been killed in hunting 獵獲的一對鳥（或獸）IDM see BELT *n.*

■ *verb* **1 ~ sb/yourself (for sth)** | **~ sb/yourself (to do sth)** to prepare sb/yourself for sth difficult or unpleasant that is going to happen（為困難或壞事）做準備；防備：*UN troops are braced for more violence.* 聯合國部隊準備應付更多的暴行。◇ *They are bracing themselves for a long legal battle.* 他們在為漫長的法律訴訟做準備。**2 ~ sth/yourself (against sth)** to press your body or part of your body firmly against sth in order to stop yourself from falling 頂住，抵住（以免跌倒等）：*They braced themselves against the wind.* 他們頂着大風站穩。**3 ~ sth** to contract the muscles in your body or part of your body before doing sth that is physically difficult（做費勁的事之前）繃緊肌肉：*He stood with his legs and shoulders braced, ready to lift the weights.* 他繃緊腿和肩膀站着，準備舉起槓鈴。**4 ~ sth** (*technical* 術語) to make sth stronger or more solid by supporting it with sth 加強；加固：*The roof was braced by lengths of timber.* 屋頂用幾根木頭支撐固定住了。

brace·let /ˈbreɪslət/ *noun* a piece of jewellery worn around the wrist or arm 手鐲；手鏈；臂鐲 ➲ VISUAL VOCAB page V65

bracer /ˈbreɪsə(r)/ *noun* a drink, usually alcoholic, which is intended to give strength to the person who drinks it 用於提神（或壯膽）的飲料；晨酒

bra·chio·pod /ˈbrækiəpɒd; *NAmE* -pɑːd/ *noun* (*biology* 生) a shellfish that has two joined shells and uses small TENTACLES (= long thin parts) to find food 腕足動物

bra·chio·saurus /ˌbrækiəˈsɔːrəs/ *noun* a very large DINOSAUR whose front legs were much longer than its back legs 腕龍（大型恐龍，前肢長於後肢）

brac·ing /ˈbreɪsɪŋ/ *adj.* (especially of weather 尤指天氣) making you feel full of energy because it is cold 涼爽宜人的；令人精神煥發的：*bracing sea air* 清新宜人的海風

bracken /ˈbrækən/ *noun* [U] a wild plant with large leaves that grows thickly on hills and in woods and turns brown in the autumn/fall 歐洲蕨（葉大，秋季乾枯）

bracket /ˈbrækɪt/ *noun, verb*

■ *noun* **1** (also ˈ**round bracket**) (both *BrE*) (also **par·en·thesis** *NAmE* or *formal*) [usually pl.] either of a pair of marks, ( ) placed around extra information in a piece of writing or part of a problem in mathematics 括號：*Publication dates are given* ***in brackets*** *after each title.* 出版日期括於書名後面。◇ *Add the numbers in brackets first.* 先把括號裏的數字加起來。➲ see also ANGLE BRACKET ➲ compare BRACE *n.* (5) **2** (*NAmE*) (*BrE* ˌ**square** ˈ**bracket**) [usually pl.] either of a pair of marks, [ ], placed at the beginning and end of extra information in a text, especially comments made by an editor 方括號 **3** **price, age, income, etc. ~** prices, etc. within a particular range（價格、年齡、收入等的）組級，等級：*people in the lower income bracket* 低收入等級的人們 ◇ *Most of the houses are out of our price bracket.* 大多數房子都超出我們的價格範圍。◇ *the 30–34 age bracket* (= people aged between 30 and 34) * 30–34 歲的年齡組 **4** a piece of wood, metal or plastic fixed to the wall to support a shelf, lamp, etc.（固定在牆上的）托架，支架

■ *verb* **1 ~ sth** to put words, information, etc. between brackets 用括弧括上 **2 ~ A and B (together)** | **~ A (together) with B** [often passive] to consider people or things to be similar or connected in some way 把…等同考慮；把…相提並論：*It is unfair to bracket together those who cannot work with those who will not.* 把不能工作的人和不願工作的人等同看待是不公平的。

brack·ish /ˈbrækɪʃ/ *adj.* (of water 水) salty in an unpleasant way 鹹的；太鹹的：***brackish lakes/lagoons/marshes*** 鹹水湖／潟湖／沼澤

brad /bræd/ *noun* a small thin nail with a small head and a flat tip 角釘；平頭釘

brad·awl /ˈbrædɔːl/ *noun* a small pointed tool used for making holes 打眼鑽；錐鑽 ➲ VISUAL VOCAB page V20

brae /breɪ/ *noun* (*ScotE*) (often in place names 常用於地名) a steep slope or hill 陡坡

brag /bræɡ/ *verb, noun*

■ *verb* [I, T] (**-gg-**) **~ (to sb) (about/of sth)** | **~ that ...** | **+ speech** (*disapproving*) to talk too proudly about sth you own or sth you have done 吹噓；自吹自擂 SYN **boast**：*He bragged to his friends about the crime.* 他向朋友炫耀他的罪行。

■ *noun* [U] a card game which is a simple form of POKER 勃萊格牌戲（簡化的撲克牌戲）

brag·ga·docio /ˌbræɡəˈdəʊtʃiəʊ; *NAmE* -ˈdoʊtʃioʊ/ *noun* [U] (*literary*) behaviour that seems too proud or confident 傲慢；自負

brag·gart /ˈbræɡət; *NAmE* -ɡərt/ *noun* (*old-fashioned*) a person who brags 吹牛大王；自吹自擂者

Brah·man /ˈbrɑːmən/ (also **Brah·min**) *noun* a Hindu who belongs to the CASTE (= division of society) that is considered the highest, originally that of priests 婆羅門（印度教種姓制度中最高階層成員，原為僧侶級）

Brah·min /ˈbrɑːmɪn/ *noun* **1** = BRAHMAN **2** (*NAmE*) a person who is rich and has a lot of influence in society, especially sb from New England whose family belongs to the highest social class（尤指來自新英格蘭某些高貴家族的）要人，名士，鉅頭：*a Boston Brahmin* 波士頓的上層人物

braid /breɪd/ *noun, verb*

■ *noun* **1** [U] thin coloured rope that is used to decorate furniture and military uniforms（裝飾傢具和軍裝的）彩色穗帶：*The general's uniform was trimmed with gold braid.* 將軍的制服飾有金色穗帶。**2** (*especially NAmE*) (*BrE* also **plait**) [C] a long piece of sth, especially hair, that is divided into three parts and twisted together 辮狀物；髮辮；辮子：*She wears her hair in braids.* 她梳着髮辮。➲ VISUAL VOCAB page V60

■ *verb* **~ sth** (*especially NAmE*) (*BrE* also **plait**) to twist three or more long pieces of hair, rope, etc. together to make one long piece 將（頭髮、繩子等）編成辮：*She'd braided her hair.* 她梳着髮辮。

Braille /breɪl/ (also **braille**) *noun* [U] a system of printing for blind people in which the letters of the alphabet and the numbers are printed as raised dots that can be read by touching them 布拉耶盲文（凸點符號）

brain 0‑π /breɪn/ *noun, verb*

■ *noun*

▸ IN HEAD 頭 **1** 0‑π [C] the organ inside the head that controls movement, thought, memory and feeling 腦：*damage to the brain* 腦部損傷 ◇ *brain cells* 腦細胞 ◇ *She died of a brain tumour.* 她死於腦瘤。◇ *a device to measure brain activity during sleep* 檢測睡眠時腦部活動的儀器 ➲ VISUAL VOCAB page V59

▸ FOOD 食物 **2 brains** [pl.] the brain of an animal, eaten as food（供食用的）動物腦髓：*sheep's brains* 羊腦
▸ INTELLIGENCE 智力 **3** 🔑 [U, C, usually pl.] the ability to learn quickly and think about things in a logical and intelligent way 智力；腦力；邏輯思維能力：*It doesn't take much brain to work out that both stories can't be true.* 不必費多大腦筋就知道，兩種説法都不可能是真的。◇ *Teachers spotted that he had a good brain at an early age.* 老師們發現他小時候就很聰穎。◇ *You need brains as well as brawn* (= intelligence as well as strength) *to do this job.* 這項工作既需要腦力又需要體力。➲ see also NO-BRAINER
▸ INTELLIGENT PERSON 聰明人 **4** [C, usually pl.] (*informal*) an intelligent person 聰明的人；有智慧的人：*one of the best scientific brains in the country* 國家最優秀的科技人才之一 **5 the brains** [sing.] the most intelligent person in a particular group; the person who is responsible for thinking of and organizing sth（群體中）最聰明的人；策劃組織者：*He's always been the brains of the family.* 這家人數他聰明。◇ *The band's drummer is* ***the brains behind*** *their latest venture.* 這位樂隊鼓手是他們最近一次活動的策劃人。
IDM **have sth on the brain** (*informal*) to think about sth all the time, especially in a way that is annoying 某事縈繞心頭；過分熱衷：*He has sex on the brain.* 他腦子裏想的全是性。➲ more at BEAT *v.*, BLOW *v.*, CUDGEL *v.*, PICK *v.*, RACK *v.*
■ *verb* **~ sb/sth/yourself** (*informal*) to kill a person or an animal by hitting them very hard on the head 猛擊…的腦袋致死：*I nearly brained myself on that low beam.* 那根低橫梁差點兒把我撞死。

brain·box /ˈbreɪnbɒks; *NAmE* -bɑːks/ *noun* (*BrE, informal*) a person who is very intelligent 腦瓜靈的人

brain·child /ˈbreɪntʃaɪld/ *noun* [sing.] an idea or invention of one person or a small group of people（個人或小群體的）主意，發明

ˈ**brain damage** *noun* [U] permanent damage to the brain caused by illness or an accident（疾病、事故導致的）腦損傷 ▸ ˈ**brain-damaged** *adj.*

ˈ**brain-dead** *adj.* **1** suffering from serious damage to the brain and needing machines to stay alive 腦死亡的 **2** (*humorous*) very stupid and boring; not intelligent 愚笨的；愚不可耐的

ˈ**brain death** *noun* [U] very serious damage to the brain that cannot be cured. A person who is suffering from brain death needs machines to keep them alive, even though their heart is still beating. 腦死亡（腦功能永久喪失，儘管心臟仍然跳動）

ˈ**brain drain** *noun* [sing.] (*informal*) the movement of highly skilled and qualified people to a country where they can work in better conditions and earn more money（國家的）人才流失

brain·iac /ˈbreɪniæk/ *noun* (*NAmE, informal*) a very intelligent person 超天才 ORIGIN From the name of a character in the *Superman* stories. 源自“超人”系列故事中的人名。

brain·less /ˈbreɪnləs/ *adj.* stupid; not able to think or talk in an intelligent way 愚蠢的；無頭腦的

brain·power /ˈbreɪnpaʊə(r)/ *noun* [U] the ability to think; intelligence 智能；智力

brain·stem /ˈbreɪnstem/ *noun* (*anatomy* 解) the central part of the brain, which continues downwards to form the SPINAL CORD 腦幹

brain·storm /ˈbreɪnstɔːm; *NAmE* -stɔːrm/ *noun* [sing.] **1** (*BrE*) a sudden inability to think clearly which causes unusual behaviour 突然神志不清；腦猝病：*She had a brainstorm in the exam and didn't answer a single question.* 她考試時腦子裏突然一片混亂，一個題也沒答。**2** (*NAmE*) = BRAINWAVE

brain·storm·ing /ˈbreɪnstɔːmɪŋ; *NAmE* -stɔːrm-/ *noun* [U] a way of making a group of people all think about sth at the same time, often in order to solve a problem or to create good ideas 集思廣益：*a brainstorming session* 一個集思廣益的討論會 ▸ **brain·storm** *verb* [T, I]：**~ (sth)** *Brainstorm as many ideas as possible.* 大家盡量獻計。

ˈ**brain surgery** *noun* [U]
IDM **it's not ˈbrain surgery** (*informal*) used to emphasize that sth is easy to do or understand（強調容易完成或理解）這又不是大腦開刀 SYN **rocket science**：*Look, this isn't brain surgery we're doing here.* 聽着，我們在這兒做的事又不像大腦開刀那麼難。

ˈ**brain-teaser** *noun* a problem that is difficult but fun to solve 有趣的難題

brain·wash /ˈbreɪnwɒʃ; *NAmE* -wɔːʃ; -wɑːʃ/ *verb* to force sb to accept your ideas or beliefs, for example by repeating the same thing many times or by preventing the person from thinking clearly 給（某人）洗腦；強制説服：**~ sb** *The group is accused of brainwashing its young members.* 那個團體被指控對年輕成員洗腦。◇ **~ sb into doing sth** *Women have been brainwashed into thinking that they must go out to work in order to fulfil themselves.* 婦女們被反複灌輸的思想是：她們必須出去工作，才能實現自己的價值。▸ **brain·wash·ing** *noun* [U]：*the victims of brainwashing and torture* 飽受洗腦和肉體折磨的人

brain·wave /ˈbreɪnweɪv/ *noun* **1** (*NAmE* also **brain·storm**) a sudden good idea 靈感；妙計：*I've had a brainwave!* 我靈機一動，想出了個主意來。**2** an electrical signal in the brain 腦電波

brainy /ˈbreɪni/ *adj.* (*informal*) (**brain·ier**, **braini·est**) very intelligent 十分聰明的

braise /breɪz/ *verb* **~ sth** to cook meat or vegetables very slowly with a little liquid in a closed container 燉：*braising steak* (= that is suitable for braising) 供燉煮的肉排

brake /breɪk/ *noun, verb*
■ *noun* **1** a device for slowing or stopping a vehicle 刹車；制動器；車閘：*to* ***put/slam*** *on the* ***brakes*** 踩／猛踩刹車 ◇ *the brake pedal* 刹車踏板 ➲ COLLOCATIONS at DRIVING ➲ VISUAL VOCAB pages V51, V52 ➲ see also AIR BRAKE, DISC BRAKE, FOOTBRAKE, HANDBRAKE **2 ~ (on sth)** a thing that stops sth or makes it difficult 阻力；障礙：*High interest rates are a brake on the economy.* 高利率阻礙了經濟發展。IDM see JAM *v.*
■ *verb* [I, T] to go slower or make a vehicle go slower using the brake 用閘減速；刹（車）：*The car braked and swerved.* 那輛車減慢車速並來了個急轉彎。◇ *The truck* ***braked to a halt****.* 那輛卡車刹住了。◇ *You don't need to brake at every bend.* 沒必要一遇到拐彎就用車閘。◇ *She had to brake hard to avoid running into the car in front.* 她不得不猛踩刹車，以免撞上前面的車。◇ **~ sth** *He braked the car and pulled in to the side of the road.* 他減緩車速，然後開到路邊。

ˈ**brake fluid** *noun* [U] liquid used in BRAKES to make the different parts move smoothly 刹車油；制動液

ˈ**brake light** (*NAmE* also ˈ**stop light**) *noun* a red light on the back of a vehicle that comes on when the brakes are used 刹車指示燈，制動燈（在車尾）

ˈ**brake pad** *noun* a thin block that presses onto the disc in a DISC BRAKE in a vehicle, in order to stop the vehicle（汽車盤式制動器上的）制動墊塊

bram·ble /ˈbræmbl/ *noun* **1** (*especially BrE*) a wild bush with THORNS on which BLACKBERRIES grow 黑莓灌木 **2** (*BrE*) = BLACKBERRY

bran /bræn/ *noun* [U] the outer covering of grain which is left when the grain is made into flour 糠；麩皮

branch 🔑 /brɑːntʃ; *NAmE* bræntʃ/ *noun, verb*
■ *noun*
▸ OF TREE 樹 **1** 🔑 a part of a tree that grows out from the main STEM and on which leaves, flowers and fruit grow 樹枝 ➲ VISUAL VOCAB page V10
▸ OF COMPANY 公司 **2** 🔑 a local office or shop/store belonging to a large company or organization 分支；分部；分行；分店：*The bank has branches all over the country.* 那家銀行在全國各地設有分行。◇ *Our New York branch is dealing with the matter.* 我們的紐約分部正在處理這件事。

▸ **OF GOVERNMENT** 政府 **3** 🔑 a part of a government or other large organization that deals with one particular aspect of its work 政府部門；分支機構 **SYN** **department**：*the anti-terrorist branch* 反恐部門
▸ **OF KNOWLEDGE** 知識 **4** 🔑 a division of an area of knowledge or a group of languages（學科及語言的）分支：*the branch of computer science known as 'artificial intelligence'* 計算機科學中的所謂"人工智能"分科
▸ **OF RIVER/ROAD** 河；路 **5** a smaller or less important part of a river, road, railway/railroad, etc. that leads away from the main part 支流；支路；支線：*a branch of the Rhine* 萊茵河的支流 ◇ *a* ***branch line*** (= a small line off a main railway line, often in country areas) 鐵路支線
▸ **OF FAMILY** 家庭 **6** a group of members of a family who all have the same ANCESTORS 家族分支：*My uncle's branch of the family emigrated to Canada.* 我們家族中我叔父的這一支移居到了加拿大。**IDM** see ROOT *n.*
■ ***verb*** [I] to divide into two or more parts, especially smaller or less important parts 分開；分岔：*The accident happened where the road branches.* 事故發生在岔道處。
PHR V ˌ**branch 'off 1** (of a road or river 路或河) to be joined to another road or river but lead in a different direction 分岔：*Just after the lake, the path branches off to the right.* 小路在經過湖後右邊有一岔道。**2** (of a person 人) to leave a road or path and travel in a different direction 改道；轉道 ˌ**branch 'out (into sth)** to start to do an activity that you have not done before, especially in your work or business 涉足（新工作）；拓展（新業務）**SYN** **diversify**：*The company branched out into selling insurance.* 該公司開展了保險銷售業務。◇ *I decided to* ***branch out on my own.*** 我決定自己開業。

brand 🔑 /brænd/ *noun, verb*
■ ***noun*** **1** 🔑 a type of product made by a particular company 品牌：*Which brand of toothpaste do you use?* 你用什麼牌子的牙膏？◇ *(BrE) You pay less for the supermarket's* ***own brand.*** 超市自己品牌的東西要便宜些。◇ *(NAmE) You pay less for the* ***store brand.*** 商店品牌的東西要便宜些。◇ ***brand loyalty*** (= the tendency of customers to continue buying the same brand) 品牌忠誠（顧客購買同一牌子商品的傾向）◇ *Champagne houses owe their success to* ***brand image.*** 香檳公司的成功在於他們的品牌形象。◇ *the* ***leading brand*** *of detergent* 一流品牌的洗滌劑 ➲ see also OWN-BRAND **2** a particular type or kind of sth 類型：*an unorthodox brand of humour* 別具一格的幽默 **3** a mark made with a piece of hot metal, especially on farm animals to show who owns them 烙印（尤指農場牲畜身上表示所屬的印記）
■ ***verb*** [often passive] **1** to describe sb as being sth bad or unpleasant, especially unfairly（尤指不公正地）醜化（某人），敗壞（某人）名聲：**~ sb as sth** *They were branded as liars and cheats.* 他們被說成是說謊者和騙子。◇ **~ sb + noun/adj.** *The newspapers branded her a hypocrite.* 報章指她是偽君子。**2 ~ sth (with sth)** to mark an animal with a BRAND *n.* (3) to show who owns it 給（牲畜）打烙印

brand·ed /ˈbrændɪd/ *adj.* [only before noun] (of a product 產品) made by a well-known company and having that company's name on it 名牌的：***branded drugs/goods/products*** 名牌藥／商品／產品

brand·ing /ˈbrændɪŋ/ *noun* [U] the activity of giving a particular name and image to goods and services so that people will be attracted to them and want to buy them 品牌創建

ˈ**branding iron** *noun* a metal tool that is heated and used to BRAND farm animals（給農場牲畜打烙印的）烙鐵

bran·dish /ˈbrændɪʃ/ *verb* **~ sth** to hold or wave sth, especially a weapon, in an aggressive or excited way 挑釁地揮舞，激動地揮舞（尤指武器）

ˈ**brand name** (also ˈ**trade name**) *noun* the name given to a product by the company that produces it 品牌名稱

ˌ**brand 'new** *adj.* completely new 全新的；嶄新的：*a brand new computer* 全新的計算機 ◇ *She bought her car brand new.* 她買的汽車是全新的。

brandy /ˈbrændi/ *noun* (*pl.* **-ies**) **1** [U, C] a strong alcoholic drink made from wine 白蘭地（酒）**2** [C] a glass of brandy 一杯白蘭地

ˌ**brandy 'butter** *noun* [U] a very thick sweet sauce made with butter, sugar and brandy, often eaten with CHRISTMAS PUDDING 白蘭地黃油（用黃油、糖和白蘭地酒調製而成，常配聖誕布丁食用）

ˈ**brandy snap** *noun* (*especially BrE*) a thin crisp biscuit/cookie in the shape of a tube, flavoured with GINGER and often filled with cream 薑味薄脆捲心餅，白蘭地小脆餅（常帶奶油夾心）

ˈ**bran tub** *noun* (*BrE*) a container that holds prizes hidden in BRAN, paper, etc., which children have to find as a game 摸彩桶（內有藏在麩皮、紙等中的獎品，供兒童遊戲用）

brash /bræʃ/ *adj.* (*disapproving*) **1** confident in an aggressive way 盛氣凌人的；自以為是的：*Beneath his brash exterior, he's still a little boy inside.* 他外表盛氣凌人，內心裏還是個孩子。**2** (*BrE*) (of things and places 東西、地方) too bright or too noisy in a way that is not attractive 耀眼的；嘈雜的 ▸ **brash·ly** *adv.* **brash·ness** *noun* [U]

brass /brɑːs; *NAmE* bræs/ *noun*
▸ **METAL** 金屬 **1** [U] a bright yellow metal made by mixing COPPER and ZINC; objects made of brass 黃銅；黃銅製品：*solid* ***brass fittings/door*** *handles* 純黃銅裝置／門把手 ◇ *a* ***brass plate*** (= a sign outside a building giving the name and profession of the person who works there) 黃銅門牌（刻有姓名和職業）◇ *to* ***clean/polish the brass*** 擦淨／擦亮黃銅器
▸ **MUSICAL INSTRUMENTS** 樂器 **2** [U+sing./pl. v.] the musical instruments made of metal, such as TRUMPETS or FRENCH HORNS, that form a band or section of an ORCHESTRA; the people who play them（管弦樂團的）銅管樂器，銅管樂器組：*music for piano, strings and brass* 鋼琴、弦樂器和銅管樂器的合奏樂曲 ➲ compare PERCUSSION, STRINGS at STRING *n.* (6), WOODWIND, WIND INSTRUMENT ➲ **VISUAL VOCAB** page V34
▸ **FOR A HORSE** 馬用 **3** [C] (*BrE*) a decorated piece of brass used as a decorative object, especially a round flat piece attached to a horse's HARNESS 黃銅飾品（尤指馬挽具上的黃銅圓片）
▸ **IN CHURCH** 教堂 **4** [C] (*especially BrE*) a flat piece of brass with words or a picture on it, fixed to the floor or wall of a church in memory of sb who has died 黃銅紀念牌（釘在教堂的地上或牆上以紀念死者，上面刻有文字或雕像）
▸ **IMPORTANT PEOPLE** 要人 **5** (*especially NAmE*) (also *BrE, informal* ˌ**top 'brass**) [U+sing./pl. v.] the people who are in the most important positions in a company, an organization, etc.（公司、機構等的）最高負責人，要員
▸ **MONEY** 錢 **6** [U] (*old-fashioned, BrE, informal*) money 錢 ➲ see also BRASSY
IDM ˌ**brass 'monkeys** | ˌ**brass 'monkey weather** (*BrE, slang*) if you say that it is **brass monkeys** or **brass monkey weather**, you mean that it is very cold weather 極冷的天氣；天寒地凍 ˌ**brass 'neck/'nerve** (*BrE, informal*) a combination of confidence and lack of respect 自以為是；傲慢無理：*I didn't think she would have the brass neck to do that.* 我本以為她不會膽大妄為的。**the ˌbrass 'ring** (*NAmE, informal*) the opportunity to be successful; success that you have worked hard to get 成功機遇；獲勝良機；（來之不易的）成功：*The girls' outdoor track team has* ***grabbed the brass ring*** *seven times.* 女子室外徑賽運動隊已經七次奪冠。**ORIGIN** From the custom of giving a free ride to any child who grabbed one of the rings hanging around the side of a merry-go-round at a fairground. 源自一種習俗，孩子只要抓住露天遊樂場旋轉木馬邊懸掛的銅環，就可以免費騎木馬一次。**(get down to) brass 'tacks** (*informal*) (to start to consider) the basic facts or practical details of sth（開始考慮）基本事實，具體問題 ➲ more at BOLD *adj.*, MUCK *n.*

ˌ**brass 'band** *noun* [C+sing./pl. v.] a group of musicians who play brass instruments 銅管樂隊

ˌ**brassed 'off** *adj.* (*BrE, slang*) annoyed 惱怒的；厭煩的 **SYN** **fed up**

B

bras·serie /ˈbræsəri; *NAmE* ˌbræsəˈriː/ *noun* a type of restaurant, often one in a French style that is not very expensive 法式（廉價）餐館

bras·sica /ˈbræsɪkə/ *noun* a plant of a type that includes CABBAGE, RAPE and MUSTARD 芥屬植物（包括甘藍、油菜及芥菜類）

brass·ière /ˈbræziə(r); *NAmE* brəˈzɪr/ *noun* (*formal*) = BRA (1)

ˌbrass ˈknuckles *noun* [pl.] (*NAmE*) = KNUCKLEDUSTER

ˈbrass rubbing *noun* [U, C] the art of rubbing a soft pencil or CHALK on a piece of paper placed over a BRASS in a church; the pattern you get by doing this（在教堂黃銅紀念牌上拓印圖文的）拓印；拓印的圖文

brassy /ˈbrɑːsi; *NAmE* ˈbræsi/ *adj.* **1** (sometimes *disapproving*) (of music 音樂) loud and unpleasant 聲高刺耳的；喧鬧的；嘈雜的 **2** (*informal, disapproving*) (of a woman 女人) dressing in a way that makes her sexual attraction obvious, but without style 衣着花裏胡哨的：*the brassy blonde behind the bar* 酒吧櫃枱後面的花哨金髮女郎 **3** like BRASS (1) in colour; too yellow and bright 黃銅色的；黃得耀眼的 **4** (*NAmE, informal*) saying what you think, without caring about other people 直截了當的；過於直率的

brat /bræt/ *noun* (*informal, disapproving*) a person, especially a child, who behaves badly 沒有規矩的人；（尤指）頑童：*a* ***spoiled/spoilt brat*** 被寵壞了的頑皮孩子 ▸ **bratty** /ˈbræti/ *adj.*：*a bratty kid* 一個刁蠻小子

the ˈbrat pack *noun* [usually sing.] a group of famous young people, especially film/movie actors, who sometimes behave badly 新星幫（少年得志、有時行為不端的一夥電影明星等）

bra·vado /brəˈvɑːdəʊ; *NAmE* -doʊ/ *noun* [U] a confident way of behaving that is intended to impress people, sometimes as a way of hiding a lack of confidence 逞能；逞強；（有時）虛張聲勢：*an act of sheer bravado* 純屬逞能的舉動

brave 0→ /breɪv/ *adj., verb, noun*

■ ***adj.*** (**braver**, **brav·est**) **1** 0→ (of a person 人) willing to do things which are difficult, dangerous or painful; not afraid 勇敢的；無畏的 SYN **courageous**：*brave men and women* 英勇無畏的男女 ◇ *Be brave!* 勇敢一些！◇ *I wasn't brave enough to tell her what I thought of her.* 我當時沒有勇氣告訴她我對她的看法。 **2** 0→ (of an action 行為) requiring or showing courage 需要勇氣的；表現勇敢的：*a brave decision* 有勇氣的決定 ◇ *She died after a brave fight against cancer.* 她在同癌症進行了頑強的搏鬥之後死去了。◇ *He felt homesick, but made a brave attempt to appear cheerful.* 他很想家，但卻竭力表現得很高興。 **3 ~ new** (sometimes *ironic*) new in an impressive way 新穎的；嶄新的：*a vision of a brave new Britain* 令人歎為觀止的新英國遠景 ▸ **brave·ly** *adv.* **bravery** /ˈbreɪvəri/ *noun* [U] SYN **courage**：*an award for outstanding bravery* 傑出英勇獎 ◇ *acts of skill and bravery* 有勇有謀的行為

IDM **(a) ˌbrave new ˈworld** a situation or society that changes in a way that is meant to improve people's lives but is often a source of extra problems 美好的新世界（本欲改善人們的生活，實則帶來預料不到的問題）：*the brave new world of technology* 科技進步的美好新世界 **put on a brave ˈface | put a brave ˈface on sth** to pretend that you feel confident and happy when you do not 強裝自信快樂；佯裝滿不在乎

■ ***verb*** **~ sb/sth** to have to deal with sth difficult or unpleasant in order to achieve sth 勇敢面對；冒風險；經受困難：*He did not feel up to braving the journalists at the airport.* 他怯於在機場直接面對記者。◇ *Over a thousand people* ***braved the elements*** (= went outside in spite of the bad weather) *to attend the march.* 一千多人不顧天氣惡劣參加了遊行。

■ ***noun*** **1 the brave** [pl.] people who are brave 勇敢的人：*America, the land of the free and the home of the brave* 美國，自由者的土地、勇士的家園 **2** [C] (*old-fashioned*) a Native American WARRIOR 美洲印第安武士

bravo /ˌbrɑːˈvəʊ; *NAmE* -ˈvoʊ/ *exclamation* (becoming *old-fashioned*) people say **Bravo!** at the end of sth they have enjoyed, such as a play at the theatre（喝彩聲、叫好聲）好哇

bra·vura /brəˈvjʊərə; *NAmE* -ˈvjʊrə/ *noun* [U] (*formal*) great skill and enthusiasm in doing sth artistic 精湛技藝：*a bravura performance* 出色的演出

braw /brɔː/ *adj.* (*ScotE*) fine 好的；不錯的：*braw lads and bonny lasses* 俊男靚女 ◇ *It was a braw day.* 那天天氣挺好。

brawl /brɔːl/ *noun, verb*

■ ***noun*** a noisy and violent fight involving a group of people, usually in a public place 喧鬧；鬥毆；鬧事：*a drunken brawl* 酒後鬧事 ➲ SYNONYMS at FIGHT

■ ***verb*** [I] to take part in a noisy and violent fight, usually in a public place 打鬥；鬧事：*They were arrested for brawling in the street.* 他們因在街上打鬥而遭到拘捕。 ▸ **brawl·er** *noun*

brawn /brɔːn/ *noun* [U] **1** physical strength 體力：*In this job you need brains as well as brawn.* 這項工作耗神又耗力。 **2** (*BrE*) (*NAmE* **head·cheese**) meat made from the head of a pig or CALF that has been boiled and pressed into a container, served cold in thin slices（罐裝）豬頭肉，牛犢頭肉

brawny /ˈbrɔːni/ *adj.* (*informal*) having strong muscles 健壯的；肌肉發達的 SYN **burly**：*He was a great brawny brute of a man.* 他是個魁梧壯實、冷酷無情的人。

bray /breɪ/ *verb* **1** [I] when a DONKEY **brays**, it makes a loud unpleasant sound（驢子）嘶叫 **2** [I] (of a person 人) to talk or laugh in a loud unpleasant voice 以刺耳的高聲講話（或笑）：*He brayed with laughter.* 他刺耳地大笑。◇ *a braying voice* 刺耳的聲音 ▸ **bray** *noun*

bra·zen /ˈbreɪzn/ *adj., verb*

■ ***adj.*** **1** (*disapproving*) open and without shame, usually about sth that people find shocking 厚顏無恥的 SYN **shameless**：*She had become brazen about the whole affair.* 她對整件事已經不感到羞恥了。◇ *his brazen admission that he was cheating* 他恬不知恥地承認自己作弊 **2** made of, or the colour of, BRASS (1) 黃銅製的；黃銅色的 ▸ **brazen·ly** *adv.*：*She had brazenly admitted allowing him back into the house.* 她恬不知恥地承認了讓他回到屋裏的事。 **brazen·ness** *noun* [U]

■ ***verb***

PHR V **ˌbrazen it ˈout** to behave as if you are not ashamed or embarrassed about sth even though you should be 厚着臉皮：*Now that everyone knew the truth, the only thing to do was to brazen it out.* 既然大家都知道真相了，只好硬着頭皮撐過去。

bra·zier /ˈbreɪziə(r)/ *noun* a large metal container that holds a fire and is used to keep people warm when they are outside（金屬）火盆

bra·zil /brəˈzɪl/ (also **braˈzil nut**) *noun* the curved nut of a large S American tree. It has a hard shell with three sides. 巴西堅果 ➲ VISUAL VOCAB page V32

Bra·zil·ian /brəˈzɪliən/ *adj., noun*

■ ***adj.*** from or connected with Brazil 巴西的

■ ***noun*** a person from Brazil 巴西人

Braˌzilian ˈwax *noun* a style of removing a woman's PUBIC hair using WAX, in which almost all the hair is removed with only a very small central strip remaining 巴西蜜蠟脫毛（一種女子陰部脫毛方式）

breach /briːtʃ/ *noun, verb*

■ ***noun*** (*formal*) **1** [C, U] **~ of sth** a failure to do sth that must be done by law 違背，違犯（法規等）：***a breach of contract/copyright/warranty*** 違犯合同；侵犯版權；違反保證 ◇ *They are* ***in breach of*** *Article 119.* 他們違犯了第 119 條。◇ (*BrE*) *(a)* ***breach of the peace*** (= the crime of behaving in a noisy or violent way in public) 擾亂治安 **2** [C, U] **~ of sth** an action that breaks an agreement to behave in a particular way 破壞；辜負：***a breach of confidence/trust*** 泄密；背信 ◇ *a breach of security* (= when sth that is normally protected is no longer secure) 破壞安全 **3** [C] a break in a relationship between people or countries（關係）中斷，終止：*a breach in Franco-German relations* 法德關係的破裂 **4** [C] an opening that is created during a military attack or by strong winds or seas 突破口；缺口；窟窿：*They escaped through a breach in the wire fence.* 他們從鐵絲網上的一個缺口逃走了。 IDM see STEP *v.*

B

■ *verb* (*formal*) **1 ~ sth** to not keep to an agreement or not keep a promise 違反；違背 SYN **break**：*The government is accused of breaching the terms of the treaty.* 政府被控違反條約中的規定。 **2 ~ sth** to make a hole in a wall, fence, etc. so that sb/sth can go through it 在…上打開缺口：*The dam had been breached.* 大壩決口了。

bread /bred/ *noun* [U]
1 a type of food made from flour, water and usually YEAST mixed together and baked 麪包：*a **loaf/slice/piece of bread*** 一條／一片／一塊麪包 ◇ ***white/brown/wholemeal bread*** 白／黑／全麥麪包 ➲ see also CRISPBREAD, FRENCH BREAD, GINGERBREAD **2** (*old-fashioned, slang*) money 錢

IDM **take the bread out of sb's 'mouth** to take away sb's job so that they are no longer able to earn enough money to live 剝奪某人的生計；砸某人的飯碗 ➲ more at DAILY *adj.*, HALF *det.*, KNOW *v.*, SLICED

ˌbread and 'butter *noun* [U] **1** slices of bread that have been spread with butter 黃油麪包片：*a piece of bread and butter* 一塊黃油麪包 **2** (*informal*) a person or company's main source of income （某人或公司的）主要收入來源

ˌbread-and-'butter *adj.* [only before noun] basic; very important 基本的；很重要的：*Employment and taxation are the bread-and-butter issues of politics.* 就業和徵稅是很重要的政治問題。

ˌbread-and-butter 'pudding *noun* [U, C] a DESSERT (= sweet dish) consisting of layers of bread with butter on, cooked with dried fruit in a mixture of eggs and milk 麪包黃油布丁，麪包奶油布丁（黃油麪包層加乾果在雞蛋奶油中烘焙而成）

bread·bas·ket /ˈbredbɑːskɪt; *NAmE* -bæs-/ *noun* [sing.] (*especially NAmE*) the part of a country or region that produces large amounts of food, especially grain, for the rest of the country or region 糧倉（指一國或地區的糧食生產基地，尤指穀物生產基地）

'bread bin (*BrE*) (*NAmE* **bread·box** /ˈbredbɒks; *NAmE* -bɑːks/) *noun* a wooden, metal or plastic container for keeping bread in so that it stays fresh 麪包箱（存放麪包用）

bread·board /ˈbredbɔːd; *NAmE* -bɔːrd/ *noun* a flat board used for cutting bread on 切麪包板

bread·crumbs /ˈbredkrʌmz/ *noun* [pl.] very small pieces of bread that can be used in cooking 麪包屑

bread·ed /ˈbredɪd/ *adj.* covered in breadcrumbs 裹着麪包屑的

bread·fruit /ˈbredfruːt/ *noun* [C, U] (*pl.* **bread·fruit**) a large tropical fruit with a thick skin, that tastes and feels like bread when it is cooked. It grows on a tree which is called a **breadfruit tree**. 麪包果（皮厚個大，煮熟似麪包）

bread·line /ˈbredlaɪn/ *noun* **1** [sing.] the lowest level of income on which it is possible to live 只能勉強維持生計的收入水平；貧困線：*Many people without jobs are living **on the breadline*** (= are very poor). 很多沒工作的人生活十分貧苦。 **2** [C] (*NAmE*) (in the past) a line of people waiting to receive free food （舊時）等待領取救濟食品的隊伍

ˌbread 'roll *noun* = ROLL (3)

bread·stick /ˈbredstɪk/ *noun* **1** a long thin piece of bread, which is dry like a biscuit 棍子麪包；餅乾棒 **2** a piece of fresh bread, baked in the shape of a small stick 小棍狀烤麪包

breadth /bredθ/ *noun* [U, C] **1** the distance or measurement from one side to the other; how broad or wide sth is 寬度 SYN **width**：*She estimated the breadth of the lake to be 500 metres.* 她估計湖面大約有 500 米寬。 ➲ compare LENGTH (1) **2** a wide range (of knowledge, interests, etc.) （知識、興趣等的）廣泛：*He was surprised at her breadth of reading.* 他對於她的博覽群書感到驚訝。◇ *The curriculum needs breadth and balance.* 課程設置應該內容廣泛而且均衡。◇ *a new political leader whose **breadth of vision*** (= willingness to accept new ideas) *can persuade others to change* 一位憑遠見卓識說服他人改變舊思想的新政治領袖 IDM see LENGTH

'bread tree (also **'bread palm**) *noun* a large plant found in tropical and southern Africa whose thick main STEM can be made into a type of flour 麪包樹，麪包棕櫚（產於非洲南部，樹幹可製成麪粉）

bread·win·ner /ˈbredwɪnə(r)/ *noun* a person who supports their family with the money they earn 掙錢養家的人

Vocabulary Building 詞彙擴充

Words that mean 'break' 表示弄碎、破碎的詞

burst	*The balloon hit a tree and burst.* 氣球碰到樹上就爆了。
crack	*The ice started to crack.* 冰開始裂了。
crumble	*Crumble the cheese into a bowl.* 將乾酪弄碎放進碗裏。
cut	*Now cut the wire in two.* 現在將電線剪成兩段。
fracture	*He fell and fractured his hip.* 他跌了一跤摔裂了髖骨。
shatter	*The vase hit the floor and shattered.* 花瓶掉在地板上摔了個粉碎。
smash	*Vandals had smashed two windows.* 故意破壞公物者打碎了兩扇窗戶。
snap	*I snapped the pencil in half.* 我啪的一聲將鉛筆折成兩段。
split	*The bag had split open on the way home.* 在回家的路上袋子裂開了。
tear	*She tore the letter into pieces.* 她把信撕碎了。

All these verbs, except **cut**, can be used with or without an object. 除 cut 外，上述動詞帶不帶賓語均可。

break /breɪk/ *verb, noun*

■ *verb* (**broke** /brəʊk; *NAmE* broʊk/, **broken** /ˈbrəʊkən; *NAmE* ˈbroʊkən/)

▸ IN PIECES 破碎 **1** [I, T] to be damaged and separated into two or more parts , as a result of force; to damage sth in this way （使）破，裂，碎：*All the windows broke with the force of the blast.* 爆炸的巨大力量震碎了所有的窗戶。◇ **~ in/into sth** *She dropped the plate and it **broke into pieces**.* 她把盤子掉在地上打碎了。◇ **~ sth** *to break a cup/window* 打破杯子／窗戶 ◇ *She fell off a ladder and broke her arm.* 她從梯子上掉下來，摔斷了胳膊。◇ **~ sth in/into sth** *He **broke** the chocolate **in two**.* 他把那塊巧克力一分為二。 ➲ COLLOCATIONS at INJURY

▸ STOP WORKING 停止運轉 **2** [I, T] to stop working as a result of being damaged; to damage sth and stop it from working 弄壞；損壞；壞掉：*My watch has broken.* 我的錶壞了。◇ **~ sth** *I think I've broken the washing machine.* 我想我把洗衣機弄壞了。

▸ SKIN 皮膚 **3** [T] **~ sth** to cut the surface of the skin and make it BLEED 弄破；使流血：*The dog bit me but didn't break the skin.* 那條狗咬了我，但沒咬破皮膚。

▸ LAW/PROMISE 法律；承諾 **4** [T] **~ sth** to do sth that is against the law; to not keep a promise, etc. 違犯；背棄：*to break the law/rules/conditions* 違反法律／規章／所定條件 ◇ *to break an agreement/a contract/a promise/your word* 違反協議／合同／允諾；食言 ◇ *to break an appointment* (= not to come to it) 失約 ◇ *He was breaking the speed limit* (= travelling faster than the law allows). 他違章超速駕駛。

▸ STOP FOR SHORT TIME 暫停 **5** [I, T] to stop doing sth for a while, especially when it is time to eat or have a drink 稍停；暫停：**~ (for sth)** *Let's break for lunch.* 我們休息一會兒，吃午飯。◇ **~ sth** *a broken night's sleep* (= a night during which you often wake up) 夜間時時醒來不安穩的睡眠 ◇ (*especially BrE*) *We **broke our journey** in Oxford* (= stopped in Oxford on the way to the place we were going to). 我們途中在牛津停留了一下。

▸ END STH 中斷 **6** [T] **~ sth** to interrupt sth so that it ends suddenly 打斷；中斷：*She **broke the silence** by* coughing. 她的咳嗽聲打破了寂靜。◇ *A tree* **broke his fall** (= stopped him as he was falling). 他墜落時一棵樹擋住了他。◇ *The phone rang and broke my train of thought.* 電話鈴響起來，打斷了我的思路。 **7** [T] **~ sth** to make sth end by using force or strong action 強行終止；破壞：*an attempt to break the year-long siege* 企圖衝破長達一年的圍困 ◇ *Management has not succeeded in* **breaking the strike**. 資方未能使罷工中止。 **8** [T] **~ sth** to end a connection with sth or a relationship with sb 終止，斷絕（關係、聯繫）：*He broke all ties with his parents.* 他斷絕了與父母的一切關係。

▸ **ESCAPE** 逃跑 **9** [I] **~ free** (**from sb/sth**) (of a person or an object 人或物體) to get away from or out of a position in which they are stuck or trapped 逃脱；掙脱：*He finally managed to break free from his attacker.* 他終於設法逃脱了襲擊他的人。

▸ **DESTROY, BE DESTROYED** 毀壞；被毀壞 **10** [T, I] **~ (sb/sth)** to destroy sth or make sb/sth weaker; to become weak or be destroyed（被）摧毀，削弱：*to break sb's morale/resistance/resolve/spirit* 瓦解某人的士氣 / 抵抗 / 決心 / 精神 ◇ *The government was determined to break the power of the trade unions.* 政府決心削弱工會的力量。◇ *The scandal broke him* (= ruined his reputation and destroyed his confidence). 這樁醜聞把他毀了。◇ *She broke under questioning* (= was no longer able to bear it) *and confessed to everything.* 她經不住盤問，招認了一切。

▸ **MAKE SB FEEL BAD** 使難過 **11** [T] **~ sb** to make sb feel so sad, lonely, etc. that they cannot live a normal life 使心碎；使十分悲傷；使孤寂：*The death of his wife broke him completely.* 妻子的死使他悲痛欲絕。

▸ **OF WEATHER** 天氣 **12** [I] to change suddenly, usually after a period when it has been fine（常指好天氣）突變

▸ **SHOW OPENING** 露出縫隙 **13** [I] to show an opening 露出縫隙；散開：*The clouds broke and the sun came out.* 雲開日出。

▸ **OF DAY/DAWN/STORM** 白天；黎明；風暴 **14** [I] when the day or DAWN or a storm **breaks**, it begins 開始；（風暴）發作：*Dawn was breaking when they finally left.* 他們終於離開時正是破曉時分。➲ see also DAYBREAK

▸ **OF NEWS** 消息 **15** [I] if a piece of news **breaks**, it becomes known 透露；傳開：*There was a public outcry when the scandal broke.* 醜聞一傳開，輿論一片譁然。◇ ***breaking news*** (= news that is arriving about events that have just happened) 突發性新聞 **16** [T] **~ it/the news to sb** to be the first to tell sb some bad news（第一個將壞消息向某人）公佈，透露，說出：*Who's going to break it to her?* 由誰來把這事告訴她呢？◇ *I'm sorry to be the one to break the news to you.* 我很難過，這消息得由我來告訴你。

▸ **OF VOICE** 嗓音 **17** [I] if sb's voice **breaks**, it changes its tone because of emotion（因激動）變調：*Her voice broke as she told us the dreadful news.* 她告訴我們這可怕的消息時，聲音都變了。 **18** [I] when a boy's voice **breaks**, it becomes permanently deeper at about the age of 13 or 14（指男孩在 13 或 14 歲時嗓音）變粗，變粗渾

▸ **A RECORD** 紀錄 **19** 🗝 [T] **~ a record** to do sth better, faster, etc. than anyone has ever done it before 打破（紀錄）：*She had broken the world 100 metres record.* 她打破了 100 米世界紀錄。◇ *The movie broke all box-office records.* 這部影片打破了所有的票房紀錄。

▸ **OF WAVES** 波浪 **20** [I] when waves **break**, they fall and are dissolved into FOAM, usually near land 拍岸；迸濺：*the sound of waves breaking on the beach* 浪濤拍岸的聲音 ◇ *The sea was breaking over the wrecked ship.* 海浪沖刷着破船的殘骸。

▸ **STH SECRET** 秘密 **21** [T] **~ a code/cipher** to find the meaning of sth secret 破譯；破解：*to break a code* 破譯密碼

▸ **MONEY** 錢 **22** [T] **~ sth** (*especially NAmE*) to change a BANKNOTE for coins 換成零錢；找開：*Can you break a twenty-dollar bill?* 可以給我找開二十元的鈔票嗎？

IDM Idioms containing **break** are at the entries for the nouns and adjectives in the idioms, for example **break sb's heart** is at **heart**. 含 break 的習語，都可在該等習語中的名詞及形容詞相關詞條找到，如 break sb's heart 在詞條 heart 下。

PHR V **ˌbreak aˈway (from sb/sth)** **1** to escape suddenly from sb who is holding you or keeping you prisoner 突然掙脱；逃脱：*The prisoner broke away from his guards.* 犯人掙脱了看守。 **2** to leave a political party, state, etc., especially to form a new one 脱離，背叛（政黨、國家等，尤指再組建新的）：*The people of the province wished to break away and form a new state.* 該省人民希望分離成立一個新國家。➲ related noun BREAKAWAY (1) **3** to move away from a crowd or group, especially in a race（尤指賽跑）搶跑，甩掉：*She broke away from the pack and opened up a two-second lead.* 她甩開所有其他賽跑者，以兩秒領先。

ˌbreak ˈdown **1** 🗝 (of a machine or vehicle 機器或車輛) to stop working because of a fault 出故障；壞掉：*The telephone system has broken down.* 電話系統癱瘓了。◇ *We* (= the car) *broke down on the freeway.* 我們的車在高速公路上拋錨了。➲ related noun BREAKDOWN (1) **2** 🗝 to fail 失敗：*Negotiations between the two sides have broken down.* 雙方談判失敗了。➲ related noun BREAKDOWN (2) **3** to become very bad 被搞垮；垮掉：*Her health broke down under the pressure of work.* 她因工作壓力身體垮掉了。➲ see also NERVOUS BREAKDOWN **4** 🗝 to lose control of your feelings and start crying 情不自禁地哭起來：*He broke down and wept when he heard the news.* 聽到這個消息，他不禁失聲痛哭。 **5** to divide into parts to be analysed 劃分（以便分析）：*Expenditure on the project breaks down as follows: wages $10m, plant $4m, raw materials $5m.* 這項工程的支出費用分項列明如下：工資 1 000 萬元，設備 400 萬元，原料 500 萬元。➲ related noun BREAKDOWN (3) ➲ LANGUAGE BANK at ILLUSTRATE

ˌbreak sth↔ˈdown **1** 🗝 to make sth fall down, open, etc. by hitting it hard 打倒，砸破（某物）：*Firefighters had to break the door down to reach the people trapped inside.* 消防隊員不得不破門而入，解救困在裏面的人。 **2** to destroy sth or make it disappear, especially a particular feeling or attitude that sb has 破壞，消除（尤指某種感情或態度）：*to break down resistance/opposition* 瓦解抵抗 / 反對 ◇ *to break down sb's reserve/shyness* 驅除某人的矜持 / 膽怯 ◇ *Attempts must be made to break down the barriers of fear and hostility which divide the two communities.* 必須設法消除造成這兩個社區不和的恐懼和敵意。 **3** to divide sth into parts in order to analyse it or make it easier to do 把…分類；劃分：*Break your expenditure down into bills, food and other.* 把支出費用按賬單、食物及其他分類列明。◇ *Each lesson is broken down into several units.* 每一課都分成幾部份。➲ related noun BREAKDOWN (3) **4** to make a substance separate into parts or change into a different form in a chemical process 使分解（為）；使變化（成）：*Sugar and starch are broken down in the stomach.* 糖和澱粉在胃裏被分解。➲ related noun BREAKDOWN (4)

ˈbreak for sth to suddenly run towards sth when you are trying to escape（試圖逃脱）突然衝向；向…掙脱：*She had to hold him back as he tried to break for the door.* 他試圖向門口逃去，她只好拉住他。

ˌbreak ˈin 🗝 to enter a building by force 強行進入；破門而入：*Burglars had broken in while we were away.* 我們不在家時，竊賊闖進屋裏了。➲ related noun BREAK-IN

ˌbreak sb/sth ˈin **1** to train sb/sth in sth new that they must do 訓練某人 / 某物；培訓：*to break in new recruits* 訓練新兵 ◇ *The young horse was not yet broken in* (= trained to carry a rider). 那匹剛長成的馬還沒被馴服。 **2** to wear sth, especially new shoes, until they become comfortable 把…穿得合身，使舒適自如（尤指新鞋）

ˌbreak ˈin (on sth) to interrupt or disturb sth 打斷；攪擾：*She longed to break in on their conversation but didn't want to appear rude.* 她很想打斷他們的談話，但又不願顯得粗魯。◇ **+ speech** *'I didn't do it!' she broke in.* "不是我幹的！" 她插嘴說。

ˌbreak ˈinto sth **1** 🗝 to enter a building by force; to open a car, etc. by force 強行闖入；撬開（汽車等）：*We had our car broken into last week.* 我們的車上週被撬了。➲ related noun BREAK-IN **2** to begin laughing, singing, etc. suddenly 突然開始（笑、唱等）：*As the President's car drew up, the crowd broke into loud applause.* 總統的座駕停下時，人群中爆發出熱烈的掌聲。 **3** to suddenly start running; to start running faster than before 突然開始（跑）；開始快跑：*He broke into a* *run when he saw the police.* 他看見警察，撒腿就跑。◇ *Her horse broke into a trot.* 她的馬突然開始加速小跑。**4** (*BrE*) to use a BANKNOTE of high value to buy sth that costs less 找開（大面值鈔票買小額商品）：*I had to break into a £20 note to pay the bus fare.* 我只好找開一張 20 英鎊的鈔票買公交車票。 **5** to open and use sth that has been kept for an emergency 啟用（應急備用品）：*They had to break into the emergency food supplies.* 他們不得不動用應急食物。 **6** to be successful when you get involved in sth 成功參與；順利打入：*The company is having difficulty breaking into new markets.* 該公司在打入新市場時遇到困難。

ˌbreak ˈoff 1 🗝 to become separated from sth as a result of force 斷開；折斷：*The back section of the plane had broken off.* 飛機尾部脫落了。 **2** to stop speaking or stop doing sth for a time 停頓；中斷：*He broke off in the middle of a sentence.* 他一句話說了一半就停住口。 **ˌbreak sth↔ˈoff** 🗝 **1** to separate sth, using force 使折斷：*She broke off a piece of chocolate and gave it to me.* 她掰了一塊巧克力給我。 **2** 🗝 to end sth suddenly 突然終止：*Britain threatened to break off diplomatic relations.* 英國威脅說要斷絕外交關係。◇ *They've broken off their engagement.* 他們突然解除了婚約。

ˌbreak ˈout 🗝 (of war, fighting or other unpleasant events 戰爭、打鬥等不愉快事件) to start suddenly 突然開始；爆發：*They had escaped to America shortly before war broke out in 1939.* * 1939 年戰爭爆發前不久他們逃到了美國。◇ *Fighting had broken out between rival groups of fans.* 雙方球迷發生了打鬥。◇ *Fire broke out during the night.* 夜間突然發生了火災。➲ related noun OUTBREAK

ˌbreak ˈout (of sth) to escape from a place or situation 逃離（某地）；擺脫（某狀況）：*Several prisoners broke out of the jail.* 幾名囚犯越獄了。◇ *She needed to break out of her daily routine and do something exciting.* 她需要從日常事務中解脫出來，找點有意思的事做。➲ related noun BREAKOUT **ˌbreak ˈout in sth** to suddenly become covered in sth 突然佈滿某物：*Her face broke out in a rash.* 她臉上突然長出一片紅疹。◇ *He broke out in a cold sweat* (= for example, through fear). 他突然冒出一身冷汗。

ˌbreak ˈthrough to make new and important discoveries 作出新的重大發現；突破：*Scientists think they are beginning to break through in the fight against cancer.* 科學家認為他們在對抗癌症的研究中開始有所突破。➲ related noun BREAKTHROUGH **ˌbreak ˈthrough** | **ˌbreak ˈthrough sth 1** to make a way through sth using force 衝破；突破：*Demonstrators broke through the police cordon.* 示威群眾衝破了警方的警戒線。 **2** (of the sun or moon 太陽或月亮) to appear from behind clouds 從雲層後露出：*The sun broke through at last in the afternoon.* 下午太陽終於撥雲而出。 **ˌbreak ˈthrough sth** to succeed in dealing with an attitude that sb has and the difficulties it creates 克服；戰勝 SYN **overcome**：*He had finally managed to break through her reserve.* 他終於設法消除了她的拘謹。

ˌbreak ˈup 1 🗝 to separate into smaller pieces 粉碎；破碎：*The ship broke up on the rocks.* 船觸礁撞碎了。 **2** 🗝 to come to an end 結束：*Their marriage has broken up.* 他們的婚姻已經破裂。➲ related noun BREAK-UP **3** to go away in different directions 散開；解散：*The meeting broke up at eleven o'clock.* 會議在十一點散會。 **4** (*especially BrE*) to begin the holidays when school closes at the end of a term （學校）期終放假：*When do you break up for Christmas?* 你們什麼時候放假過聖誕？ **5** (*BrE*) to become very weak 變得虛弱；垮掉：*He was breaking up under the strain.* 過度的勞累使他快要垮了。**6** (*NAmE*) to laugh very hard 捧腹大笑：*Woody Allen makes me just break up.* 伍迪 • 艾倫令我幾乎笑破肚皮。 **7** when a person who is talking on a mobile/cell phone **breaks up**, you can no longer hear them clearly because the signal has been interrupted（打移動電話的人）聲音不清（因信號受干擾） **ˌbreak sth↔ˈup 1** 🗝 to make sth separate into smaller pieces; to divide sth into smaller parts 拆開；打散：*The ship was broken up for scrap metal.* 船被拆解成為廢鐵。◇ *Sentences can be broken up into clauses.* 句子可以分成從句。 **2** to end a relationship, a company, etc. 結束（關係）；關閉（公司）：*They decided to break up the partnership.* 他們決定拆夥。➲ related noun BREAK-UP **3** to make people leave sth or stop doing sth, especially by using force （尤指用武力）迫使放棄（某事）：*Police were called in to break up the fight.* 有人叫來了警察制止打鬥。 **ˌbreak ˈup (with sb)** 🗝 to end a relationship with sb （同某人）絕交：*She's just broken up with her boyfriend.* 她剛剛和男朋友分手。➲ related noun BREAK-UP

ˈbreak with sth to end a connection with sth 和某事終止關聯；破除：*to break with tradition/old habits/the past* 摒棄傳統 / 舊習慣 / 過去

■ ***noun***

▸ **SHORT STOP/PAUSE** 暫停；間歇 **1** 🗝 [C] a short period of time when you stop what you are doing and rest, eat, etc. 間歇；休息：*a **coffee/lunch/tea break*** 用咖啡 / 午飯 / 茶的休息時間 ◇ *Let's **take a break**.* 咱們休息會兒吧。◇ *a break for lunch* 午餐休息 ◇ *She worked all day without a break.* 她接連工作了一整天。➲ SYNONYMS at REST **2** (also **ˈbreak time**) (both *BrE*) (*NAmE* **reˑcess**) [U] a period of time between lessons at school 課間休息：*Come and see me at break.* 課間休息時來見我。 **3** 🗝 [C] a pause or period of time when sth stops before starting again 間歇；暫停：*a break in my daily routine* 我日常生活中的一段小插曲 ◇ *She wanted to take a **career break** in order to have children.* 她想暫時放下工作，去生孩子。 **4** 🗝 [C] a pause for advertisements in the middle of a television or radio programme （電視或電台節目的）插播廣告的間隙：*More news after the break.* 廣告後繼續報道新聞。

▸ **HOLIDAY/VACATION** 假期 **5** 🗝 [C] a short holiday/vacation 短期休假：*We had a weekend break in New York.* 我們在紐約度過了一個週末假日。◇ *a well-earned break* 應得的休假

▸ **CHANGE IN SITUATION** 狀況改變 **6** [sing.] the moment when a situation or a relationship that has existed for a time changes, ends or is interrupted （持續一段時間的狀況或關係的）改變，終止，中斷：**~ (with sb/sth)** *He needed to make a complete break with the past.* 他得與過去徹底告別。◇ *a **break with tradition/convention*** (= a change from what is accepted, in sth such as art, behaviour, etc.) 突破傳統；破除習俗 ◇ **~ (in sth)** *a **break in the weather*** (= a change from one type of weather to a different one) 天氣的轉變 ◇ *a break in diplomatic relations* 外交關係的中斷

▸ **OPENING/SPACE** 縫隙；空間 **7** [C] **~ (in sth)** a space or an opening between two or more things 間隔；縫隙：*We could see the moon through a break in the clouds.* 我們能從雲縫裏看到月亮。

▸ **OPPORTUNITY** 機遇 **8** [C] (*informal*) an opportunity to do sth, usually to get sth that you want or to achieve success 機會；機遇：*I got my **lucky break** when I won a 'Young Journalist of the Year' competition.* 我時來運轉，在"年度最佳青年記者"競賽中取勝。◇ *We've had a few **bad breaks*** (= pieces of bad luck) *along the way.* 我們一路上遭遇了幾次厄運。

▸ **OF BONE** 骨骼 **9** [C] a place where sth, especially a bone in your body, has broken 破裂；骨折：*The X-ray showed there was no break in his leg.* * X 光照片顯示他的腿沒有骨折。

▸ **IN TENNIS** 網球 **10** (also **break of ˈserve**) [C] a win in a game in which your opponent is SERVING 接發球得分：*It was her second break in the set.* 這是本盤比賽中她第二次接發球得分。◇ ***break point*** (= a situation in which, if you win the next point, you win the game) 破對方發球局的末點

▸ **IN BILLIARDS/SNOOKER** 枱球；斯諾克 **11** [C] a series of successful shots by one player; the number of points scored in a series of successful shots 接連擊中；接連擊中所得的分數：*He's put together a magnificent break.* 他連續得了很多分。◇ *a 147 break* (= the highest possible break in SNOOKER) 連得 147 分（斯諾克中的最高連續得分）

IDM **break of ˈday/ˈdawn** (*literary*) the moment in the early hours of the morning when it begins to get light 破曉；黎明 **give me a ˈbreak!** (*informal*) used when sb wants sb else to stop doing or saying sth that is annoying, or to stop saying sth that is not true 別煩我了；別胡說了 **give sb a ˈbreak** to give sb a chance; to not judge sb too severely 給某人一次機會；不苛求某人：*Give the lad a break—it's only his second day on the* *job.* 給這小伙子一次機會，他上工才第二天。 **make a 'break for sth/for it** to run towards sth in order to try and escape 向某處逃竄；試圖逃跑： *He suddenly leapt up and made a break for the door.* 他突然一躍而起，向門口逃竄。◇ *They decided to make a break for it* (= to try and escape) *that night.* 他們決定那天晚上逃跑。 ➲ more at CLEAN *adj.*

break·able /ˈbreɪkəbl/ *adj.* likely to break; easily broken 會碎的；易碎的

break·age /ˈbreɪkɪdʒ/ *noun* **1** [C, usually pl.] an object that has been broken 破碎物品： *The last time we moved house there were very few breakages.* 我們上次搬家時幾乎沒有什麼物品破損。 **2** [U, C] the act of breaking sth 毀壞；損壞： *Wrap it up carefully to protect against breakage.* 把它包好，以免破損。

break·away /ˈbreɪkəweɪ/ *adj., noun*

■ ***adj.*** [only before noun] (of a political group, an organization, or a part of a country 政治團體、組織、國家的一部份) having separated from a larger group or country 已分離的；已脱離的；已獨立的： *a **breakaway faction/group/section*** 脱離原組織的派系／集體／部份 ◇ *a breakaway republic* 一個已經獨立的共和國

■ ***noun*** [sing.] **1** an occasion when members of a political party or an organization leave it in order to form a new party, etc. 脱離；獨立 **2** a change from an accepted style 對（公認風格的）改變： *a breakaway from his earlier singing style* 對他以往演唱風格的改變

break·beat /ˈbreɪkbiːt/ *noun* **1** [C] a series of drum beats that are repeated to form the rhythm of a piece of dance music 碎拍（組成舞曲節奏的一系列鼓點） **2** [U] dance music, for example HIP HOP, that uses breakbeats 碎拍舞曲（如嘻哈音樂）

break·bone fever /ˈbreɪkbəʊn fiːvə(r); *NAmE* -boʊn/ *noun* [U] = DENGUE

'break-dancing *noun* [U] a style of dancing with ACROBATIC movements, often performed in the street 霹靂舞（摻入雜技動作，常在街頭表演） ▸ **'break-dance** *verb* [I] **'break-dancer** *noun*

break·down /ˈbreɪkdaʊn/ *noun* **1** [C] an occasion when a vehicle or machine stops working （車輛或機器的）故障，損壞： *a breakdown on the motorway* 在高速公路上出的故障 ◇ *a breakdown recovery service* 車輛搶修服務 **2** [C, U] a failure of a relationship, discussion or system （關係）破裂；（討論、系統）失敗： *the breakdown of a marriage* 婚姻破裂 ◇ *marriage breakdown* 婚姻破裂 ◇ *a breakdown in communications* 通信中斷 ◇ *The breakdown of the negotiations was not unexpected.* 談判的失敗是預料之中的事。◇ *the breakdown of law and order* 治安陷入癱瘓 **3** [C, usually sing.] detailed information that you get by studying a set of figures 數字細目；分類： *First, let's look at a breakdown of the costs.* 我們首先看一下成本的詳細數字。 **4** [U] (*technical* 術語) the breaking of a substance into the parts of which it is made 分解： *the breakdown of proteins in the digestive system* 蛋白質在消化系統中的分解 **5** [C] = NERVOUS BREAKDOWN： *She's still recovering from her breakdown.* 她精神崩潰後還在恢復中。

'breakdown lane (*US*) (*BrE* **ˌhard ˈshoulder**) *noun* a strip of ground with a hard surface beside a major road such as a MOTORWAY or INTERSTATE where vehicles can stop in an emergency 硬質路肩（在高速公路旁，可供緊急停車）

'breakdown truck (*BrE*) (also **'tow truck** *NAmE, BrE*) *noun* a truck that is used for taking cars away to be repaired when they have had a breakdown （把故障車輛送去修理的）救險車 ➲ **VISUAL VOCAB** page V57

break·er /ˈbreɪkə(r)/ *noun* a large wave covered with white bubbles that is moving towards land 拍岸的白浪 ➲ see also CIRCUIT-BREAKER, ICEBREAKER, HOUSEBREAKER at HOUSEBREAKING, LAWBREAKER, RECORD-BREAKER, STRIKE-BREAKER, TIEBREAKER

'break-even *noun* [U] (*business* 商) a time when a company or piece of business earns just enough money to pay for its costs 收支相抵： *The company expects to reach break-even next year.* 公司期待明年達到盈虧平衡。 ➲ see also EVEN *adj.*

break·fast 🔑 /ˈbrekfəst/ *noun, verb*

■ ***noun*** 🔑 [C, U] the first meal of the day 早餐；早飯： *a **big/hearty/light breakfast*** 量大的／豐盛的／量少的早餐 ◇ (*especially BrE*) *a cooked breakfast* 熱食早餐 ◇ *Do you want bacon and eggs **for breakfast**?* 你早飯要吃熏鹹肉和雞蛋嗎？◇ *They were having breakfast when I arrived.* 我到達時他們正在吃早飯。◇ *She doesn't eat much breakfast.* 她早飯吃得不多。 ➲ see also BED AND BREAKFAST, CONTINENTAL BREAKFAST, ENGLISH BREAKFAST, POWER BREAKFAST, WEDDING BREAKFAST **IDM** see DOG *n.*

■ ***verb*** [I] **~ (on sth)** (*formal*) to eat breakfast 吃早飯；用早餐

'break-in *noun* an entry into a building using force, usually to steal sth 破門而入；闖入；入室偷竊

ˌbreaking and ˈentering *noun* [U] (*NAmE* or *old-fashioned*) the crime of entering a building illegally and using force 破門侵入（罪）

'breaking point (also **'break point**) *noun* [U] the time when problems become so great that a person, an organization or a system can no longer deal with them （問題難以遏制的）頂點，極限；斷點： *to **be at/to reach breaking point*** 處於／達到極限 ◇ *to be stretched to breaking point* 已撐至極限

break·neck /ˈbreɪknek/ *adj.* [only before noun] very fast and dangerous 飛速驚險的： *to drive, etc. **at breakneck speed*** 亡命飛車等

break·out /ˈbreɪkaʊt/ *noun, adj.*

■ ***noun*** an escape from prison, usually by a group of prisoners （常指集體的）越獄： *a mass breakout from a top security prison* 從防守高度嚴密的監獄的集體越獄

■ ***adj.*** [only before noun] **1** (*NAmE, informal*) suddenly and extremely popular and successful; establishing sb's reputation 一炮走紅的；揚名的： *a breakout hit/movie* 一炮走紅的唱片／電影 **2** (*especially NAmE*) taking place separately from the main meeting with a smaller number of people 分組會議的： *a **breakout session** before the plenary* （全體會議前的）分組會議 ◇ *a **breakout group** on ethical issues* 討論道德問題的小組

'break point *noun* **1** the point where sth, especially a computer program, is interrupted （尤指計算機程序的）斷點，中斷點 **2 ˌbreak ˈpoint** (especially in TENNIS 尤指網球) a point that the person who is SERVING must win in order not to lose a game 破發點；破對方發球局的末點 **3** = BREAKING POINT

break·through /ˈbreɪkθruː/ *noun, adj.*

■ ***noun*** an important development that may lead to an agreement or achievement 重大進展；突破： *to **make/achieve a breakthrough*** 作出／取得突破性進展 ◇ *a significant breakthrough in negotiations* 談判中的重大突破 ◇ *a major breakthrough in cancer research* 癌症研究中的重要突破

■ ***adj.*** [only before noun] in which a performer or type of product is successful for the first time, when it is likely to be even more successful in the future 突破性的： *It was a breakthrough album for the band.* 這是該樂隊的成名專輯。◇ *breakthrough technology/products* 突破性技術／產品

'break time *noun* [U] (*BrE*) = BREAK (2)

'break-up *noun* **1** the ending of a relationship or an association （關係、聯繫、交往的）破裂，中斷： *the break-up of their marriage* 他們婚姻的破裂 ◇ *family break-ups* 家庭破裂 **2** the division of a large organization or country into smaller parts （組織、國家的）拆分，分裂，分離

break·water /ˈbreɪkwɔːtə(r)/ *noun* a wall built out into the sea to protect the SHORE or HARBOUR from the force of the waves 防波堤

bream /briːm/ *noun* (*pl.* **bream**) a FRESHWATER or sea fish that is used for food 歐鯿（食用淡水魚）；海鯛

breast 🔑 /brest/ *noun, verb*

■ ***noun***

▸ **PART OF BODY** 身體部位 **1** 🔑 [C] either of the two round soft parts at the front of a woman's body that produce

B

milk when she has had a baby（女子的）乳房：*She put the baby to her breast.* 她開始給嬰兒哺乳。◇ *breast cancer* 乳腺癌 ◇ *breast milk* 母乳 **2** [C] the similar, smaller part on a man's body, which does not produce milk（男子的）退化乳房 **3** [C] (*literary*) the top part of the front of your body, below your neck 胸部；胸脯 **SYN chest**：*He cradled the child against his breast.* 他把孩子抱在懷裏。

▸ **CLOTHING** 衣服 **4** [C] the part of a piece of clothing that covers your chest 前胸部份：*A row of medals was pinned to the breast of his coat.* 他的外套胸前別着一排勳章。

▸ **OF BIRD** 鳥 **5** [C] the front part of a bird's body（鳥的）胸部：*breast feathers* 胸部羽毛 ◇ *The robin has a red breast.* 知更鳥的胸部為紅色。

▸ **MEAT** 肉 **6** [C, U] meat from the front part of the body of a bird or an animal（鳥或動物的）胸脯肉：***chicken/turkey breasts*** 雞／火雞胸脯肉 ◇ *breast of lamb* 羊羔胸脯肉

▸ **-BREASTED** 有…胸脯 **7** (in adjectives 構成形容詞) having the type of chest or breasts mentioned 胸脯（或乳房）…的：*a **small-breasted/full-breasted** woman* 乳房小／豐滿的女子 ◇ *bare-breasted* 裸胸 ◇ *the yellow-breasted male of the species* 這個物種中有黃色胸部的雄性 ➲ see also DOUBLE-BREASTED, SINGLE-BREASTED

▸ **HEART** 心 **8** [C] (*literary*) the part of the body where the feelings and emotions are thought to be 心窩；情感：*a troubled breast* 憂慮的心情 ➲ see also CHIMNEY BREAST

IDM see BEAT *v.*, CLEAN *adj.*

■ ***verb*** (*formal*) **1 ~ sth** to reach the top of a hill, etc. 登上…的頂部：*As they breasted the ridge, they saw the valley and lake before them.* 他們到達山脊時山谷和湖泊盡收眼底。 **2 ~ sth** to push through sth, touching it with your chest 挺胸從…中擠過：*He strode into the ocean, breasting the waves.* 他挺胸頂着波浪大步走進海裏。

breast·bone /ˈbrestbəʊn; *NAmE* -boʊn/ *noun* the long flat bone in the chest that the seven top pairs of RIBS are connected to 胸骨 **SYN sternum** ➲ VISUAL VOCAB page V59

breast·feed /ˈbrestfiːd/ *verb* (**breast·fed**, **breast·fed** /-fed/) [I, T] **~ (sb)** when a woman **breastfeeds**, she feeds her baby with milk from her breasts. 用母乳餵養；哺乳 ➲ compare BOTTLE-FEED, NURSE *v.* (6)

breast·plate /ˈbrestpleɪt/ *noun* a piece of ARMOUR worn by soldiers in the past to protect the upper front part of the body（古時士兵護胸的）胸鎧

ˌbreast ˈpocket *noun* a pocket on a shirt, or on the outside or inside of the part of a jacket that covers the chest（衣服）胸部的口袋 ➲ VISUAL VOCAB page V63

ˈbreast pump *noun* a device for getting milk from a woman's breasts, so that her baby can be fed later from a bottle 吸奶器；吸乳器

breast·stroke /ˈbreststrəʊk; *NAmE* -stroʊk/ *noun* [U, sing.] a style of swimming that you do on your front, moving your arms and legs away from your body and then back towards it in a circle 蛙泳 ➲ VISUAL VOCAB page V45

breath 🔑 /breθ/ *noun*

1 🔑 [U] the air that you take into your lungs and send out again 呼吸的空氣：*His breath smelt of garlic.* 他呼出的氣中有大蒜味。◇ *bad breath* (= that smells bad) 口臭 ◇ *We had to stop for breath before we got to the top.* 我們不得不喘口氣，然後再登山頂。◇ *She was very **short of breath*** (= had difficulty breathing). 她呼吸很困難。 **2** 🔑 [C] an amount of air that enters the lungs at one time 一次吸入的空氣：*to take a deep breath* 深深吸一口氣 ◇ *He recited the whole poem in one breath.* 他一口氣背出了整篇詩。 **3** [sing.] **~ of sth** (*formal*) a small amount of sth; slight evidence of sth 微量；跡象：*a **breath of suspicion/scandal*** 一絲懷疑；醜聞的嫌疑 **4** [sing.] **a ~ of air/wind** (*literary*) a slight movement of air（空氣的）微微流動，拂動

IDM **a breath of (fresh) ˈair** clean air breathed in after being indoors or in a dirty atmosphere 新鮮空氣；透氣：*We'll get a breath of fresh air at lunchtime.* 我們午餐時出去透透氣。 **a breath of fresh ˈair** a person, thing or place that is new and different and therefore interesting and exciting 令人耳目一新的人（或事物、地方） **the breath of ˈlife to/for sb** (*literary*) an essential part of a person's existence 某人生存的必需品 **get your ˈbreath (again/back)** (*BrE*) (also **catch your ˈbreath** *NAmE, BrE*) to breathe normally again after running or doing some tiring exercise 恢復正常呼吸 **hold your ˈbreath** **1** to stop breathing for a short time 閉氣；屏氣：*Hold your breath and count to ten.* 屏住呼吸，數到十。 **2** to be anxious while you are waiting for sth that you are worried about 屏息以待；焦慮地等待：*He held his breath while the results were read out.* 宣讀結果時，他屏住了呼吸。 **3** (*informal*) people say **don't hold your breath!** to emphasize that sth will take a long time or may not happen 別眼巴巴等着；有你等的：*She said she'd do it this week, but don't hold your breath!* 她說她這個星期要幹，不過你可別因此眼巴巴乾等！ **in the same ˈbreath** immediately after saying sth that suggests the opposite intention or meaning 但緊接着，但同時（意味着與前一段意圖或意思相反）：*He praised my work and in the same breath told me I would have to leave.* 他稱讚了一番我的工作，但緊接着卻對我說不得不辭退我。 **his/her last/dying ˈbreath** the last moment of a person's life 最後一口氣；臨終；臨死 **out of ˈbreath** 🔑 having difficulty breathing after exercise（運動後）喘不上氣，透不過氣來：*We were out of breath after only five minutes.* 我們五分鐘後便氣喘吁吁了。 **say sth, speak, etc. under your ˈbreath** to say sth quietly so that people cannot hear 小聲地，輕聲地（說）：*'Rubbish!' he murmured under his breath.* "胡說！" 他悄悄地小聲說。 **take sb's ˈbreath away** to be very surprising or beautiful 令人驚歎；讓人歎絕：*My first view of the island from the air took my breath away.* 我第一次從空中看到這個島時，歎賞不已。➲ more at BATED, CATCH *v.*, DRAW *v.*, SAVE *v.*, WASTE *v.*

breath·able /ˈbriːðəbl/ *adj.* (*technical* 術語) (of material used in making clothes 衣料) allowing air to pass through 透氣的：*Breathable, waterproof clothing is essential for most outdoor sports.* 大多數戶外運動服必須透氣且防水。

breath·alyse (*BrE*) (*NAmE* **breath·alyze**) /ˈbreθəlaɪz/ *verb* [usually passive] **~ sb** to check how much alcohol a driver has drunk by making him or her breathe into a breathalyser（用呼吸分析器）測量（駕駛者）的呼氣酒精含量：*Both drivers were breathalysed at the scene of the accident.* 兩方司機均在事故現場接受了呼氣酒精檢測。

breath·alyser (*BrE*) (*NAmE* **Breath·alyzer™**) /ˈbreθəlaɪzə(r)/ *noun* a device used by the police to measure the amount of alcohol in a driver's breath（測量酒精含量的）呼吸分析器

breathe 🔑 /briːð/ *verb*

▸ **AIR/BREATH** 空氣；呼吸 **1** 🔑 [I, T] to take air into your lungs and send it out again through your nose or mouth 呼吸：*He breathed deeply before speaking again.* 他深深吸一口氣，然後繼續說下去。◇ *The air was so cold we could hardly breathe.* 空氣非常寒冷，我們難以呼吸。◇ *She was beginning to breathe more easily.* 她呼吸開始較為順暢了。◇ **~ sth** *Most people don't realize that they are breathing polluted air.* 大多數人沒有意識到自己正呼吸着污染了的空氣。 **2** [T] **~ sth (+ adv./prep.)** to send air, smoke or a particular smell out of your mouth 呼出：*He came up close, breathing alcohol fumes all over me.* 他走過來靠近我，噴得我滿身酒氣。

▸ **SAY QUIETLY** 低聲說 **3** [T] **~ sth | + speech** (*literary*) to say sth quietly 低聲說：*'I'm over here,' she breathed.* "我在這兒呢。" 她輕聲說。

▸ **OF WINE** 酒 **4** [I] if you allow wine to **breathe**, you open the bottle and let air get in before you drink it（打開瓶蓋，讓酒）通氣飄香

▸ **OF CLOTH/SKIN** 布料；皮膚 **5** [I] if cloth, leather, skin, etc. can **breathe**, air can move around or through it 透氣：*Cotton clothing allows your skin to breathe.* 棉織品能使皮膚透氣。

▸ **FEELING/QUALITY** 感覺；品質 **6** [T] **~ sth** (*formal*) to be full of a particular feeling or quality 充滿，散發（某種

感情或品質）：*Her performance breathed wit and charm.* 她的表演靈巧迷人。

IDM **breathe (easily/freely) again** to feel calm again after sth unpleasant or frightening has ended 平靜下來；鬆一口氣 **breathe down sb's 'neck** (*informal*) to watch closely what sb is doing in a way that makes them feel anxious and/or annoyed 緊盯着某人看；看得某人發毛（或心煩）；監視 **,breathe (new) 'life into sth** to improve sth by introducing new ideas and making people more interested in it（給某事物）帶來起色，注入活力 **breathe your 'last** (*literary*) to die 氣絕（身亡）；斷氣 ➲ more at EASY *adv.*, LIVE[1]

PHR V **,breathe 'in** 🔑 to take air into your lungs through your nose or mouth 吸氣 SYN **inhale** **,breathe sth↔'in** to take air, smoke, etc. into your lungs through your nose or mouth 吸入（氣體）：*His illness is a result of breathing in paint fumes over many years.* 他的病是多年吸入油漆氣體引起的。 **,breathe 'out** 🔑 to send air out of your lungs through your nose or mouth 呼氣 SYN **exhale** **,breathe sth↔'out** to send air, smoke, etc. out of your lungs through your nose or mouth 呼出（氣體）：*Humans take in oxygen and breathe out carbon dioxide.* 人吸入氧氣，呼出二氧化碳。

breather /ˈbriːðə(r)/ *noun* (*informal*) a short pause for rest or to relax 短暫的休息：*to* ***take/have a breather*** 歇一下 ◇ *Tell me when you need a breather.* 你需要休息時就告訴我。◇ *a five-minute breather* 休息五分鐘 ➲ see also HEAVY BREATHER

breath·ing 🔑 /ˈbriːðɪŋ/ *noun* [U] the action of taking air into the lungs and sending it out again 呼吸：*Her breathing became steady and she fell asleep.* 她的呼吸變得均勻，便睡着了。◇ *Deep breathing exercises will help you relax.* 深呼吸運動有助於放鬆自己。◇ *Heavy* (= loud) *breathing was all I could hear.* 我所能聽到的只有沉重的呼吸聲。

'breathing space *noun* [C, U] a short rest in the middle of a period of mental or physical effort 短暫休息；喘息時間 ➲ SYNONYMS at REST

breath·less /ˈbreθləs/ *adj.* **1** having difficulty in breathing; making it difficult for sb to breathe（使）氣喘吁吁的，上氣不接下氣的：*He arrived breathless at the top of the stairs.* 他爬上樓梯頂時氣喘吁吁的。◇ *They maintained a breathless* (= very fast) *pace for half an hour.* 他們用疾速的步伐走了半小時。**2** (*formal*) experiencing, or making sb experience, a strong emotional reaction（使）屏息，目瞪口呆：*the breathless excitement of seeing each other again* 再次相互見面時令人無比的興奮 ◇ **~ with sth** *breathless with terror* 嚇得目瞪口呆 **3** (*formal*) with no air or wind 令人窒息的；無風的：*the breathless heat of a summer afternoon* 夏日午後的悶熱 ▶ **breath·less·ly** *adv.* **breath·less·ness** *noun* [U]

breath·tak·ing /ˈbreθteɪkɪŋ/ *adj.* very exciting or impressive (usually in a pleasant way); very surprising 激動人心的；驚人的：*a breathtaking view of the mountains* 群山的壯麗景色 ◇ *The scene was one of breathtaking beauty.* 美妙的景色令人歎為觀止。◇ *He spoke with breathtaking arrogance.* 他說話時的傲慢態度令人咋舌。▶ **breath·tak·ing·ly** *adv.*：*a breathtakingly expensive diamond* 昂貴得驚人的鑽石

'breath test *noun* a test used by the police to show the amount of alcohol in a driver's breath（警察對駕駛者的）呼氣酒精含量測驗

breathy /ˈbreθi/ *adj.* speaking or singing with a noticeable sound of breathing（講話或唱歌時）帶呼吸聲的

bred *past tense, past part.* of BREED

breech /briːtʃ/ *noun* the part of a gun at the back where the bullets are loaded 槍炮的後膛

'breech birth (also **,breech de'livery**) *noun* a birth in which the baby's bottom or feet come out of the mother first 臀位分娩

breeches /ˈbrɪtʃɪz/ *noun* [pl.] short trousers/pants fastened just below the knee（褲腳束於膝下的）半長褲，馬褲：*a pair of breeches* 一條半長褲 ◇ *riding breeches* 馬褲

breed 🔑 /briːd/ *verb, noun*

■ ***verb*** (**bred**, **bred** /bred/) **1** 🔑 [I] (of animals 動物) to have sex and produce young 交配繁殖：*Many animals breed only at certain times of the year.* 很多動物只在一年的某個時候交配繁殖。➲ see also INTERBREED **2** 🔑 [T] **~ sth (for/as sth)** to keep animals or plants in order to produce young ones in a controlled way 飼養，培育（動植物）：*The rabbits are bred for their long coats.* 飼養兔子是為了獲取它們的長毛。➲ COLLOCATIONS at FARMING ➲ see also CROSS-BRED, PURE-BRED, THOROUGHBRED **3** [T] **~ sth** to be the cause of sth 孕育；導致：*Nothing breeds success like success.* 一事成功萬事亨通。**4** [T, usually passive] **~ sth into sb** to educate sb in a particular way as they are growing up 以…方式教育；使養成：*Fear of failure was bred into him at an early age.* 他從小就養成了對失敗的恐懼。➲ see also WELL BRED IDM see BORN *v.*, FAMILIARITY

■ ***noun*** **1** 🔑 a particular type of animal that has been developed by people in a controlled way, especially a type of dog, cat or farm animal 品種（尤指人工培育的狗、貓或牲畜）：*Labradors and other large breeds of dog* 拉布拉多犬及其他大型品種狗 ◇ ***a breed of cattle/sheep*** 某個品種的牛／羊 **2** [usually sing.] a type of person（人的）類型，種類：*He represents a new breed of politician.* 他代表着新一類的政治家。◇ *Players as skilful as this are* ***a rare breed***. 如此有技巧的演奏者很少見。

breed·er /ˈbriːdə(r)/ *noun* a person who breeds animals 飼養員：***a dog/horse/cattle, etc. breeder*** 飼養狗、馬、牛等的人

breed·ing /ˈbriːdɪŋ/ *noun* [U] **1** the keeping of animals in order to breed from them（為繁殖的）飼養：*the breeding of horses* 馬的飼養 **2** the producing of young animals, plants, etc.（動植物的）生育，繁殖：*the breeding season* 繁殖季節 **3** the family or social background that is thought to result in good manners 教養：*a sign of good breeding* 良好教養的體現

'breeding ground *noun* **1** [usually pl.] a place where wild animals go to produce their young（野生動物的）繁殖地 **2 ~ (for sth)** [usually sing.] a place where sth, especially sth bad, is able to develop（尤指壞事物的）滋生地：*This area of the city has become a breeding ground for violent crime.* 這個市區已成為暴力犯罪的滋生地。

breeze /briːz/ *noun, verb*

■ ***noun*** **1** [C] a light wind 微風；和風：*a sea breeze* 柔和的海風 ◇ *The flowers were gently swaying* ***in the breeze***. 花兒在微風中輕輕舞動。◇ *A light breeze was blowing.* 輕風習習。➲ COLLOCATIONS at WEATHER **2** [sing.] (*informal*) a thing that is easy to do 輕而易舉的事：*It was a breeze.* 這事不費吹灰之力。IDM see SHOOT *v.*

■ ***verb*** [I] **+ adv./prep.** to move in a cheerful and confident way in a particular direction 輕盈而自信地走：*She just breezed in and asked me to help.* 她一陣風似的飄然進來，要求我幫她。

PHR V **,breeze 'through sth** to do sth successfully and easily 輕易通過；輕鬆完成：*He breezed through the tests.* 他輕鬆順利地通過了這些測試。

'breeze block (*BrE*) (*NAmE* **'cinder block**) *noun* a light building block, made of sand, coal ASHES and CEMENT 煤渣砌塊，焦渣石（用沙、煤渣和水泥製成）

breeze·way /ˈbriːzweɪ/ *noun* (*NAmE*) an outside passage with a roof and open sides between two separate parts of a building（建築物兩部份之間的）有頂通道，有頂過道

breezy /ˈbriːzi/ *adj.* (**breez·ier**, **breezi·est**) **1** with the wind blowing quite strongly 通風良好的；有微風的：*It was a bright, breezy day.* 那天和風麗日。◇ *the breezy east coast* 微風吹拂的東海岸 **2** having or showing a cheerful and relaxed manner 輕鬆愉快的：*You're very bright and breezy today!* 你今天精神煥發！▶ **breez·ily** /ˈbriːzɪli/ *adv.*：*'Hi folks,' he said breezily.* "嗨，諸位。"他快活地說。**breezi·ness** /ˈbriːzinəs/ *noun* [U]

breth·ren /ˈbreðrən/ *noun* [pl.] (*old-fashioned*) **1** used to talk to people in church or to talk about the members

B

of a male religious group （稱呼教友或男修會等的成員）弟兄們：*Let us pray, brethren.* 請眾同禱。**2** people who are part of the same society as yourself 同一組織等的成員；同道；同仁：*We should do all we can to help our less fortunate brethren.* 我們應當盡力幫助那些不幸的兄弟姐妹。

Bre·ton /ˈbretən/ *noun, adj.*

■ **noun** **1** [U] the Celtic language of Brittany in NW France （法國西北部）布列塔尼語 **2** [C] a person who was born in Brittany or who lives in Brittany （法國）布列塔尼人

■ **adj.** connected with Brittany or its language or culture 布列塔尼（文化）的；布列塔尼語的

breve /briːv/ *noun* (*music* 音) a note that lasts as long as eight CROTCHETS/QUARTER NOTES, which is rarely used in modern music 二全音符（現已罕用）

brev·ity AW /ˈbrevəti/ *noun* [U] (*formal*) **1** the quality of using few words when speaking or writing 簡潔；簡煉 SYN **conciseness**：*The report is a masterpiece of brevity.* 那份報告是言簡意賅的典範。**2** the fact of lasting a short time 短暫：*the brevity of human life* 人生之短暫 ➲ see also BRIEF *adj.*

brew /bruː/ *verb, noun*

■ **verb** **1** [T, I] **~ sth** to make beer 釀製（啤酒）：*This beer is brewed in the Czech Republic.* 這種啤酒是在捷克共和國釀造的。**2** [T] **~ sth** to make a hot drink of tea or coffee 沏（茶）；煮（咖啡）：*freshly brewed coffee* 剛剛煮好的咖啡 **3** [I] (*especially BrE*) (of tea or coffee 茶或咖啡) to be mixed with hot water and become ready to drink 沖泡；沏：*Always let tea brew for a few minutes.* 每次都要讓茶泡上幾分鐘。**4** [I] **~ (up)** (usually used in the progressive tenses 通常用於進行時) if sth unpleasant **is brewing** or **brewing up**, it seems likely to happen soon （不愉快的事）即將來臨，醞釀

PHR V **ˌbrew ˈup** | **ˌbrew sth↔ˈup** (*BrE, informal*) to make a hot drink of tea or coffee 沏（茶）；煮（咖啡）：*Whose turn is it to brew up?* 該誰煮咖啡了？ ➲ related noun BREW-UP

■ **noun** **1** [C, U] a type of beer, especially one made in a particular place （尤指某地釀造的）啤酒：*I thought I'd try the local brew.* 我想我還是嚐嚐本地的啤酒。◇ *home brew* (= beer made at home) 家釀啤酒 **2** [C, usually sing.] (*BrE, informal*) an amount of tea made at one time （茶）一次的沖泡量：*I'll make a fresh brew.* 我來重新沏壺茶。◇ *Let's have a brew.* 我們來泡杯茶喝吧。**3** [C, usually sing.] a mixture of different ideas, events, etc. （不同思想、事件等的）交融，混合：*The movie is a potent brew of adventure, sex and comedy.* 這部影片將歷險、性愛和喜劇有機地揉和在一起。◇ *His music is a* ***heady brew*** (= a powerful mixture) *of heavy metal and punk.* 他的音樂是重金屬樂和朋客搖滾樂的強節奏混合體。

IDM **a witch's/an evil ˈbrew** (*BrE*) an unpleasant drink that is a mixture of different things 難喝的混合飲料

brew·er /ˈbruːə(r)/ *noun* a person or company that makes beer 釀造啤酒者；啤酒公司

brew·ery /ˈbruːəri/ *noun* (*pl.* **-ies**) a factory where beer is made; a company that makes beer 啤酒廠；啤酒公司

brew·house /ˈbruːhaʊs/ *noun* a factory where beer is made 啤酒廠 SYN **brewery**

ˈbrew-up *noun* (*BrE, informal*) an act of making tea 沏茶：*We always have a brew-up at 11 o'clock.* 我們總是在 11 點沏茶。

briar (also **brier**) /ˈbraɪə(r)/ *noun* **1** a wild bush with THORNS, especially a wild ROSE bush 多刺野灌木；（尤指）野薔薇叢 **2** a bush with a hard root that is used for making TOBACCO pipes; a tobacco pipe made from this root 歐石楠（其堅硬根部可製煙斗）；（用歐石楠根製的）煙斗

bribe /braɪb/ *noun, verb*

■ **noun** a sum of money or sth valuable that you give or offer to sb to persuade them to help you, especially by doing sth dishonest 賄賂：*It was alleged that he had* ***taken bribes*** *while in office.* 他被指稱在任時收受賄賂。◇ *She had been offered a $50 000 bribe to drop the charges.* 有人用 5 萬元賄賂她，要她撤回控告。➲ COLLOCATIONS at CRIME

■ **verb** to give sb money or sth valuable in order to persuade them to help you, especially by doing sth dishonest 向（某人）行賄；賄賂：**~ sb (with sth)** *They bribed the guards with cigarettes.* 他們用香煙賄賂看守。◇ **~ sb into doing sth** *She was bribed into handing over secret information.* 她被收買交出了機密。◇ **~ sb to do sth** *She bribed him to sign the certificate.* 她賄賂他簽署了這張證明。◇ **~ your way ...** *He managed to* ***bribe his way*** *onto the ship.* 他設法行賄混上了船。

brib·ery /ˈbraɪbəri/ *noun* [U] the giving or taking of bribes 行賄；受賄；賄賂：*She was arrested on bribery charges.* 她因被控賄賂罪而遭逮捕。◇ *allegations of bribery and corruption* 有關賄賂和貪污的指控

bric-a-brac /ˈbrɪk ə bræk/ *noun* [U] ORNAMENTS and other small decorative objects of little value （不值錢的）小裝飾品，小擺設：*market stalls selling cheap bric-a-brac* 出售廉價小擺設的攤販

brick 0→ /brɪk/ *noun, verb*

■ **noun** **1** 0→ [C, U] baked CLAY used for building walls, houses and other buildings; an individual block of this 磚；磚塊：*The school is built of brick.* 那所學校是用磚建造的。◇ *a pile of bricks* 一摞磚 ◇ *a brick wall* 磚牆 ➲ see also RED-BRICK ➲ VISUAL VOCAB page V17 **2** [C] a plastic or wooden block, used as a toy for young children to build things with 積木 **3** [C, usually sing.] (*old-fashioned, BrE, informal*) a friend that you can rely on when you need help 可靠的朋友

IDM **be up against a brick ˈwall** to be unable to make any progress because there is a difficulty that stops you 遇到難以逾越的障礙 **bricks and ˈmortar** buildings, when you are thinking of them in connection with how much they cost to build or how much they are worth 實體產業（借房產來指代具體規模）：*They put their money into bricks and mortar.* 他們把錢投資到了房產上。◇ (*business* 商) *a new Internet company without a lot of bricks-and-mortar businesses* (= businesses with buildings that customers go to) 一家沒有多少實體產業的新網絡公司 ◇ (*NAmE* also) *brick-and-mortar businesses* 實體企業 **make bricks without ˈstraw** (*BrE*) to try to work without the necessary material, money, information, etc. 作無米之炊 ➲ more at CAT *n.*, DROP *v.*, HEAD *n.*, TON *n.*

■ **verb**

PHR V **ˌbrick sth↔ˈin/ˈup** to fill an opening in a wall with bricks 用磚堵住牆上的洞：*The windows had been bricked up.* 那些窗戶用磚堵住了。

brick·bat /ˈbrɪkbæt/ *noun* [usually pl.] an insulting remark made in public 公開辱罵；當眾侮辱

brick·lay·er /ˈbrɪkleɪə(r)/ (also *BrE, informal* **brickie**) *noun* a person whose job is to build walls, etc. with bricks 砌磚工；瓦工 ▸ **brick·lay·ing** *noun* [U]

brick·work /ˈbrɪkwɜːk; *NAmE* -wɜːrk/ *noun* **1** [U] the bricks in a wall, building, etc. （建築物的）磚結構：*Plaster had fallen away in places, exposing the brickwork.* 有些地方的灰泥脱落了，露出了磚。**2 brick·works** [C] (*pl.* **brick·works**) (*BrE*) a place where bricks are made 磚廠；磚窰

bri·dal /ˈbraɪdl/ *adj.* [only before noun] connected with a bride or a wedding 新娘的；婚禮的：*a bridal gown* 新娘的禮服 ◇ *the* ***bridal party*** (= the bride and the bridegroom and the people helping them at their wedding, sometimes used to refer only to the bride and those helping her) 新人及協助其婚禮的人 ◇ *a* ***bridal suite*** (= a set of rooms in a hotel for a couple who have just got married) 賓館的新婚套間 ◇ (*NAmE*) *a* ***bridal shower*** (= a party for a woman who will get married soon) 女子新婚前的送禮會

bride /braɪd/ *noun* a woman on her wedding day, or just before or just after it 新娘；即將（或剛剛）結婚的女子：*a toast to the* ***bride and groom*** 向新娘新郎祝酒 ◇ *He introduced his new bride.* 他介紹了他的新娘。

bride·groom /ˈbraɪdɡruːm/ (also **groom**) *noun* a man on his wedding day, or just before or just after it 新郎；即將（或剛剛）結婚的男子

brides·maid /'braɪdzmeɪd/ *noun* a young woman or girl who helps a BRIDE before and during the marriage ceremony 女儐相；伴娘 ➲ compare BEST MAN, PAGEBOY (1)

bridges 橋；鼻梁；鼻梁架；琴馬

bridge 鼻梁

bridge over a river 河上的橋

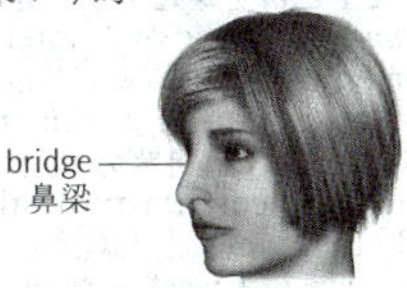

bridge of the nose 鼻梁

strings 弦

bridge 琴馬

bridge 鼻梁架

bridge of a pair of glasses 眼鏡的鼻梁架

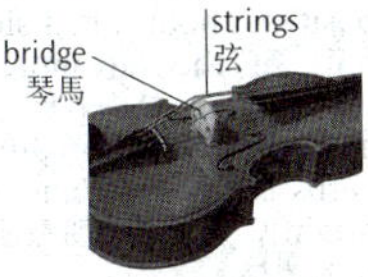

bridge of a violin 小提琴的琴馬

bridge 🔑 /brɪdʒ/ *noun*, *verb*

■ ***noun***

▸ **OVER ROAD/RIVER** 路／河上方 **1** 🔑 [C] a structure that is built over a road, railway/railroad, river, etc. so that people or vehicles can cross from one side to the other 橋：*We crossed the bridge over the river Windrush.* 我們穿過了溫德拉什河上的橋。➲ **VISUAL VOCAB** pages V3, V14 ➲ see also SUSPENSION BRIDGE, SWING BRIDGE

▸ **CONNECTION** 聯繫 **2** 🔑 [C] a thing that provides a connection or contact between two different things 起聯繫作用的東西；橋梁；紐帶：*Cultural exchanges are a way of **building bridges** between countries.* 文化交流是各國之間建立聯繫的紐帶。

▸ **OF SHIP** 船 **3** [C, usually sing.] (usually **the bridge**) the part of a ship where the captain and other officers stand when they are controlling and steering the ship（艦船的）駕駛台；船橋；艦橋 ➲ **VISUAL VOCAB** page V54

▸ **CARD GAME** 紙牌遊戲 **4** [U] a card game for two pairs of players who have to predict how many cards they will win. They score points if they succeed in winning that number of cards and lose points if they fail. 橋牌 ➲ see also CONTRACT BRIDGE

▸ **OF NOSE** 鼻 **5 the ~ of sb's nose** [sing.] the hard part at the top of the nose, between the eyes 鼻梁 ➲ **VISUAL VOCAB** page V59

▸ **OF GLASSES** 眼鏡 **6** [C] the part of a pair of glasses that rests on your nose 鼻梁架

▸ **OF GUITAR/VIOLIN** 吉他；小提琴 **7** [C] a small piece of wood on a GUITAR, VIOLIN, etc. over which the strings are stretched 琴馬 ➲ **VISUAL VOCAB** page V36

▸ **FALSE TEETH** 假牙 **8** [C] a false tooth or false teeth, held permanently in place by being fastened to natural teeth on either side（固定的）假牙；齒橋 **IDM** see BURN *v.*, CROSS *v.*, WATER *n.*

■ ***verb***

▸ **BUILD/FORM BRIDGE** 造橋 **~ sth** to build or form a bridge over sth 在…上架橋：*The valley was originally bridged by the Romans.* 那條峽谷上的橋最初是古羅馬人修建的。◇ *A plank of wood bridged the stream.* 溪上架了一條木板橋。

IDM **bridge the 'gap/'gulf/di'vide (between A and B)** to reduce or get rid of the differences that exist between two things or groups of people 消除（甲、乙間的）隔閡／鴻溝／分歧

'bridge-building *noun* [U] activities intended to make relations between two groups, countries, etc. friendlier 友好往來；友善活動

bridge·head /'brɪdʒhed/ *noun* **1** a strong position that an army has captured in enemy land, from which it can go forward or attack the enemy 橋頭堡（部隊在敵佔區內奪取的據點）**2** [usually sing.] a good position from which to make progress（進一步前進的）立足點，據點

bridge·work /'brɪdʒwɜːk; *NAmE* -wɜːrk/ *noun* [U] **1** artificial teeth and the parts that keep them in place in the mouth（假牙的）齒橋；橋托（牙）**2** the work of making these teeth or putting them in place 齒橋製作；鑲齒橋

'bridging loan (*BrE*) (*NAmE* **'bridge loan**) *noun* an amount of money that a bank lends you for a short time, especially so that you can buy a new house while you are waiting to sell your old one 過渡性貸款（常在賣掉舊房前作買新房之用）

bri·die /'braɪdi/ *noun* (*ScotE*) a small PIE containing meat 肉餡餅

bridle /'braɪdl/ *noun*, *verb*

■ ***noun*** a set of leather bands, attached to REINS, which is put around a horse's head and used for controlling it 馬勒；馬籠頭

■ ***verb*** **1** [T] **~ sth** to put a bridle on a horse 給（馬）套籠頭 **2** [I] **~ (at sth)** (*literary*) to show that you are annoyed and/or offended at sth, especially by moving your head up and backwards in a proud way（尤指傲慢地昂首對…）表示惱怒，表示不快：*She bridled at the suggestion that she was lying.* 她對暗示她在說謊的言論嗤之以鼻。

'bridle path (*BrE* also **bridle·way** /'braɪdlweɪ/) *noun* a rough path that is suitable for people riding horses or walking, but not for cars 馬道；步行道

Brie /briː/ *noun* [U, C] a type of soft French cheese 布里乾酪（一種鬆軟的法國奶酪）

brief 🔑 **AW** /briːf/ *adj.*, *noun*, *verb*

■ ***adj.*** (**brief·er**, **brief·est**) **1** 🔑 lasting only a short time; short 短時間的；短暫的：*a brief visit/meeting/conversation* 短時間的參觀／會議／交談 ◇ *a brief pause/silence* 暫時停頓／沉默 ◇ *Mozart's life was brief.* 莫扎特的一生很短暫。**2** 🔑 using few words 簡潔的；簡單的：*a brief description/summary/account* 簡明扼要的描述／總結／敘述 ◇ *Please **be brief*** (= say what you want to say quickly). 請簡明扼要。**3** (of clothes 衣服) short and not covering much of the body 過短的；暴露身體的：*a brief skirt* 超短裙 ➲ see also BREVITY, BRIEFLY

IDM **in brief** in a few words, without details 簡言之；一言以蔽之：*In brief, the meeting was a disaster.* 總之，那會議糟透了。◇ *Now the rest of the news in brief.* 現在簡要報道其他新聞。

■ ***noun*** ➲ see also BRIEFS **1** (*BrE*) the instructions that a person is given explaining what their job is and what their duties are 任務簡介；指示：*It wasn't part of his brief to speak to the press.* 交付他的任務不包括向新聞界發言。◇ *I was **given the brief** of reorganizing the department.* 我被分派去改組這個部門。◇ ***to stick to your brief*** (= to only do what you are asked to do) 僅做分內的事 ◇ *to **prepare/produce a brief** for sb* 給某人準備／制訂指示 **2** (*BrE*, *law* 律) a legal case that is given to a lawyer to argue in court; a piece of work for a BARRISTER（向辯護律師提供的）案情摘要；委託辯護 **3** (*NAmE*, *law* 律) a written summary of the facts that support one side of a legal case, that will be presented to a court 辯護狀 **4** (*BrE*, *informal*) a SOLICITOR or a defence lawyer 事務律師；辯護律師：*I want to see my brief.* 我想見我的律師。**5** (*especially NAmE*) = BRIEFING (2)：*Officials are pushing for this target to be included in the next presidential brief.* 官員正敦促在下一次總統的簡報中一定要包括這個目標。

IDM **hold no brief for sb/sth** (*BrE*, *formal*) to not support or be in favour of sb/sth 不支持，不贊成（某人或某事）；不為…辯護：*I hold no brief for either side in this war.* 這次戰爭的雙方我都不支持。

■ ***verb*** **1** to give sb information about sth so that they are prepared to deal with it 給（某人）指示；向（某人）介紹情況：**~ sb** *I expect to be kept fully briefed at all times.* 我希望隨時向我報告全面情況。◇ **~ sb on/about sth** *The officer briefed her on what to expect.* 軍官簡要向她說了一下可能遇到的情況。➲ compare DEBRIEF **2 ~ sb (to do sth)** (*BrE*, *law* 律) to give a lawyer, especially a

BARRISTER, the main facts of a legal case so that it can be argued in court 向（辯護律師）提供案情摘要

brief·case /ˈbriːfkeɪs/ *noun* a flat case used for carrying papers and documents 公文包；公事包 ➲ VISUAL VOCAB page V64 ➲ compare ATTACHÉ CASE

brief·ing AW /ˈbriːfɪŋ/ *noun* **1** [C] a meeting in which people are given instructions or information 傳達指示會；情況介紹會：*a press briefing* 新聞發佈會 ➲ compare DEBRIEFING at DEBRIEF **2** (also **brief** especially in *NAmE*) [C, U] the detailed instructions or information that are given at such a meeting 詳細指示；詳情介紹：*Captain Trent gave his men a full briefing.* 特倫特隊長給了他的部屬詳細的指示。◇ *a* ***briefing session/paper*** 任務發佈會 / 文件

brief·ly ⚷ AW /ˈbriːfli/ *adv.*
1 ⚷ for a short time 短暫地；暫時地：*He had spoken to Emma* ***only briefly****.* 他和埃瑪只講了短短的幾句話。**2** ⚷ in few words 簡短地；簡要地：*Briefly, the argument is as follows ...* 簡言之，理由如下…◇ *Let me tell you briefly what happened.* 我來大致給你講一下所發生的事情吧。

briefs /briːfs/ *noun* [pl.] men's UNDERPANTS or women's KNICKERS（男子或女子的）內褲：*a pair of briefs* 一條內褲

brier = BRIAR

brig /brɪɡ/ *noun* **1** a ship with two MASTS (= posts that support the sails) and square sails 橫帆雙桅船 **2** (*NAmE*) a prison, especially one on a WARSHIP（尤指軍艦上的）禁閉室

Brig. *abbr.* (in writing) BRIGADIER（書寫形式）陸軍准將

bri·gade /brɪˈɡeɪd/ *noun* **1** a large group of soldiers that forms a unit of an army 旅（陸軍編制單位）**2** [usually sing.] (often *disapproving*) used, always with a word or phrase in front of it, to describe a group of people who share the same opinions or are similar in some other way（主張相同或其他某方面相似的）夥，幫，派：*the anti-smoking brigade* 反吸煙派 ➲ see also FIRE BRIGADE
IDM see HEAVY *adj.*

briga·dier /ˌbrɪɡəˈdɪə(r); *NAmE* -ˈdɪr/ *noun* (*abbr.* **Brig.**) an officer of high rank in the British army（英國陸軍）准將，旅長：*Brigadier Michael Swift* 邁克爾 • 斯威夫特准將

ˌbrigadier ˈgeneral *noun* an officer of high rank in the US army, AIR FORCE or MARINES（美國陸軍、空軍或海軍陸戰隊）准將

brig·and /ˈbrɪɡənd/ *noun* (*old-fashioned*) a member of a group of criminals that steals from people, especially one that attacks travellers 盜賊；強盜 SYN **bandit**

bright ⚷ /braɪt/ *adj., adv., noun*
■ *adj.* (**bright·er**, **bright·est**) **1** ⚷ full of light; shining strongly 光線充足的；明亮的：***bright light/sunshine*** 明亮的光線；明媚的陽光 ◇ *a bright room* 明亮的屋子 ◇ *Her eyes were bright with tears.* 她的雙眼淚光閃閃。◇ *a bright morning* (= with the sun shining) 陽光燦爛的早晨 **2** ⚷ (of a colour 顏色) strong and easy to see 鮮豔奪目的：*I like bright colours.* 我喜歡豔麗的色彩。◇ *a bright yellow dress* 鮮黃色的連衣裙 ◇ *Jack's face turned* ***bright red****.* 傑克的臉變得通紅。**3** ⚷ cheerful and lively 快活而生氣勃勃的：*His eyes were bright and excited.* 他目光發亮，興奮不已。◇ *She gave me a bright smile.* 她對我粲然一笑。◇ *Why are you so* ***bright and cheerful*** *today?* 你今天怎麼這麼高興？◇ *His face was* ***bright with*** *excitement.* 他興奮得滿臉放光。**4** ⚷ intelligent; quick to learn 聰明的；悟性強的：*the brightest pupil in the class* 班裏最聰明的學生 ◇ *Do you have any* ***bright ideas*** (= clever ideas)? 你有何高見？ ➲ SYNONYMS at INTELLIGENT **5** giving reason to believe that good things will happen; likely to be successful 有希望的；大有可能成功的：*This young musician has* ***a bright future****.* 這位年輕的音樂家前途無量。◇ *Prospects for the coming year look bright.* 來年的前景一片光明。◇ *a bright start to the week* 本週的良好開端 ▸ **bright·ly** ⚷ *adv.*：*a brightly lit room* 亮堂的屋子 ◇ *'Hi!' she called brightly.* "嗨！" 她輕快地招呼道。 **bright·ness** *noun* [U]

IDM **bright and ˈearly** very early in the morning 大清早：*You're up bright and early today!* 你今天起得很早啊！ **(as) bright as a ˈbutton** (*BrE*) intelligent and quick to understand 機靈的；聰穎的 **the bright ˈlights** the excitement of city life 城市生活的多姿多彩：*Although he grew up in the country, he's always had a taste for the bright lights.* 儘管他是在農村長大的，他始終對城市的五光十色情有獨鍾。 **a bright ˈspark** (*BrE, informal*, often *ironic*) a lively and intelligent person, especially sb young 活潑機靈的人（尤指年輕人）：*Some bright spark* (= stupid person) *left the tap running all night.* 不知是哪個聰明人讓自來水流了一夜。 **a/the ˈbright spot** a good or pleasant part of sth that is unpleasant or bad in all other ways（不幸或逆境中的）可喜部份，閃光點：*The win last week was the only bright spot in their last ten games.* 上週的勝利是他們最近十場比賽中唯一振奮人心的一次。 **look on the ˈbright side** to be cheerful or positive about a bad situation, for example by thinking only of the advantages and not the disadvantages（對壞情況）持樂觀態度，看到光明的一面
■ *adv.* (**bright·er**, **bright·est**) (*literary*) (usually with the verbs *burn* and *shine* 通常與動詞 burn、shine 連用) brightly 光亮地；明亮地：*The stars were shining bright.* 星光閃爍。
■ *noun* **brights** [pl.] (*NAmE*) the HEADLIGHTS on a vehicle set to a position in which they are shining as brightly as possible and not directed downwards（車輛的）前大燈，頭燈

Synonyms 同義詞辨析

bright

brilliant • vivid • vibrant

These words all describe things that are shining or full of light or colours that are strong and easy to see. 以上各詞均形容事物明亮、光線充足、鮮豔奪目。

bright full of light; shining strongly; (of colours) strong and easy to see 指光線充足的、明亮的、色彩鮮明的：*a bright yellow dress* 鮮黃色的連衣裙

brilliant very bright 指明亮的、鮮豔的：*The sky was a brilliant blue.* 天空一片蔚藍。

vivid (*approving*) (of colours) bright and strong 指（顏色）耀眼的、鮮豔的、醒目的：*His eyes were a vivid green.* 他的眼睛碧綠。

vibrant (*approving*) (of colours) bright and strong 指（顏色）耀眼的、鮮豔的、醒目的：*The room was decorated in vibrant blues and greens.* 那房間以鮮豔的藍綠兩色裝飾。

VIVID OR VIBRANT? 用 vivid 還是 vibrant？

These two words are very similar, but **vivid** emphasizes how bright a colour is, while **vibrant** suggests a more lively and exciting colour or combination of colours. 這兩個詞非常相似，但 vivid 強調顏色鮮豔明亮，而 vibrant 則指色彩或顏色組合活潑而富生氣。

PATTERNS

- bright/brilliant/vivid/vibrant **colours**
- bright/brilliant **light/sunlight/sunshine/eyes**

bright·en /ˈbraɪtn/ *verb* **1** [I, T] to become or make sth lighter or brighter in colour（使）更明亮，色彩鮮豔：*In the distance, the sky was beginning to brighten.* 遠方的天空開始泛白。◇ **~ sth** *a shampoo to brighten and condition your hair* 增加光澤並保護頭髮的洗髮劑 **2** [I, T] to become, feel or look happier; to make sb look happier（使）快活起來：*Her eyes brightened.* 她的眼睛亮了起來。◇ **~ up** *He brightened up at their words of encouragement.* 聽到他們鼓勵的話，他高興起來。◇ **~ sth (up)** *A smile brightened her face.* 她的臉上露出了笑容。**3** [T, I] **~ (sth) (up)** to become or make sth become more pleasant or enjoyable; to bring hope（使）增添樂趣，有希望：*A personal letter will usually brighten up a person's day.* 一封私人來信往往就能使人一天心情愉快。**4** [T] **~ sth (up)** to make sth look more brightly coloured and attractive 使更豔麗；使更美麗： *Fresh flowers will brighten up any room in the house.* 鮮花會使屋裏的任何房間都亮麗生色。 **5** [I] **~ (up)** (of the weather 天氣) to improve and become brighter 放晴： *According to the forecast, it should brighten up later.* 根據天氣預報，晚一點天應該會轉晴。

ˌbright-ˈeyed (also **ˌbright-eyed and ˌbushy-ˈtailed**) *adj.* (of a person 人) full of interest and enthusiasm 興致勃勃的；精神奮發的

ˌbright young ˈthing *noun* an enthusiastic and intelligent young person who wants to be successful in their career 聰明的有志青年 **ORIGIN** From the name used in the 1920s for rich young people whose behaviour was considered shocking. 源自 20 世紀 20 年代對放蕩不羈的年輕富人的稱呼。

brill /brɪl/ *adj.* (*BrE, informal*) very good 很好的；很棒的

bril·liant 0-w /ˈbrɪliənt/ *adj.*
1 0-w extremely clever or impressive 巧妙的；使人印象深的： *What a brilliant idea!* 真是個絕妙的主意！◇ *a brilliant performance/invention* 出色的表演；傑出的發明 **2** 0-w very successful 很成功的： *a brilliant career* 一帆風順的事業◇ *The play was a brilliant success.* 那個劇獲得了巨大成功。 **3** 0-w very intelligent or skilful 聰穎的；技藝高的： *a brilliant young scientist* 一位才華橫溢的青年科學家 ◇ *She has one of the most brilliant minds in the country.* 她是全國最有才氣的人之一。 ➲ **SYNONYMS** at INTELLIGENT **4** 0-w (of light or colours 光線或色彩) very bright 明亮的；鮮豔的： *brilliant sunshine* 明媚的陽光◇ *brilliant blue eyes* 明亮的藍眼睛 ➲ **SYNONYMS** at BRIGHT **5** 0-w (*BrE, informal*) very good; excellent 很好的；傑出的： *'How was it?' 'Brilliant!'* "怎麼樣？" "棒極了！" ◇ *Thanks. You've been brilliant* (= very helpful). 多謝。你幫大忙了。➲ **SYNONYMS** at GREAT ▸ **bril·liance** /ˈbrɪliəns/ *noun* [U] **bril·li·ant·ly** *adv.*： *The plan worked brilliantly.* 計劃實施得十分順利。◇ *It was brilliantly sunny.* 陽光明媚。

bril·lian·tine /ˈbrɪliəntiːn/ *noun* [U] oil used in the past to make men's hair shiny （舊時）男用潤髮油

brim /brɪm/ *noun, verb*
■ *noun* **1** the top edge of a cup, bowl, glass, etc.（杯、碗等的）口，邊沿： *two wine glasses, **filled to the brim*** 兩隻斟滿的酒杯 **2** the flat edge around the bottom of a hat that sticks out 帽簷 ➲ **VISUAL VOCAB** page V65 **3 -brimmed** (in adjectives 構成形容詞) having the type of brim mentioned 有…邊的： *a wide-brimmed hat* 寬簷帽
■ *verb* (**-mm-**) [I] to be full of sth; to fill sth （使）滿，盛滿： *Tears brimmed in her eyes.* 她熱淚盈眶。◇ **~ with sth** *Her eyes brimmed with tears.* 她熱淚盈眶。◇ *The team were brimming with confidence before the game.* 該隊在賽前信心十足。
PHR V **ˌbrim ˈover (with sth)** (of a cup, container, etc. 杯、容器等) to be so full of a liquid that it flows over the edge 盛滿（…）；滿溢 **SYN** **overflow**： (*figurative*) *Her heart was brimming over with happiness.* 她心中洋溢着幸福。

brim·ful /ˈbrɪmfʊl/ *adj.* **~ of sth** completely full of sth 裝滿…的；充盈的： *She's certainly brimful of energy.* 她的確精力充沛。◇ *a jug brimful of cream* 一滿罐奶油

brim·stone /ˈbrɪmstəʊn; *NAmE* -stoʊn/ *noun* (*old use*) the chemical element SULPHUR 硫磺

brin·dle /ˈbrɪndl/ (also **brin·dled** /ˈbrɪndld/) *adj.* (of dogs, cats and cows 狗、貓、牛) brown with bands or marks of another colour 棕色間雜其他花紋（或斑點）的

brine /braɪn/ *noun* [U] very salty water, used especially for preserving food 鹽水（常用於醃製食物）➲ see also BRINY

bring 0-w /brɪŋ/ *verb* (**brought**, **brought** /brɔːt/)
▸ **COME WITH SB/STH** 帶來 **1** 0-w to come to a place with sb/sth 帶…到某處；帶來；取來： **~ sb/sth (with you)** *Don't forget to bring your books with you.* 別忘了把書帶來。◇ **~ sb/sth to sth** *She brought her boyfriend to the party.* 她帶着男朋友去參加聚會。◇ **~ sth for sb** *Bring a present for Helen.* 給海倫帶件禮物去。◇ **~ sb sth** *Bring Helen a present.* 給海倫帶件禮物去。
▸ **PROVIDE** 提供 **2** 0-w to provide sb/sth with sth 提供；供給： **~ sb/sth sth** *His writing brings him $10 000 a year.* 寫作每年為他賺 1 萬元。◇ **~ sth to sb/sth** *The team's new manager brings ten years' experience to the job.* 該隊的新經理到任時已有十年的相關經驗。
▸ **CAUSE** 導致 **3** 0-w **~ sth** to cause sth 導致；引起： *The revolution brought many changes.* 這場革命導致很多變化。◇ *The news **brought tears to his eyes*** (= made him cry). 這個消息使他不禁流下淚來。◇ *Retirement usually **brings with it** a massive drop in income.* 收入通常隨着退休而大大減少。 **4** 0-w **~ sb/sth + adv./prep.** to cause sb/sth to be in a particular condition or place 使處於某種狀況；使到某地： *to **bring** a meeting **to an end*** 結束會議◇ ***Bring** the water **to the boil**.* 把水燒開。◇ *The article brought her into conflict with the authorities.* 這篇文章使她與當局發生衝突。◇ *Hello Simon! What brings you here?* 你好，西蒙！什麼風把你吹來了？
▸ **MAKE SB/STH MOVE** 移動 **5** to make sb/sth move in a particular direction or way 使朝（某方向或按某方式）移動： **~ sb/sth + adv./prep.** *The judge brought his hammer down on the table.* 法官在桌子上敲下他的木槌。◇ **~ sb/sth running** *Her cries brought the neighbours running* (= made them run to her). 鄰居們聽到她的叫喊聲便紛紛趕來。
▸ **ACCUSATION** 指控 **6 ~ sth (against sb)** to officially accuse sb of a crime 起訴： ***to bring a charge/a legal action/an accusation** against sb* 控告某人；對某人起訴；控告某人
▸ **FORCE YOURSELF** 強迫自己 **7 ~ yourself to do sth** to force yourself to do sth 強迫自己做某事： *She could not bring herself to tell him the news.* 她難以開口把這個消息告訴他。
IDM Idioms containing **bring** are at the entries for the nouns and adjectives in the idioms, for example **bring sb/sth to heel** is at **heel**. 含 bring 的習語，都可在該等習語中的名詞及形容詞相關詞條找到，如 bring sb/sth to heel 在詞條 heel 下。
PHR V **ˌbring sth↔aˈbout** to make sth happen 導致；引起 **SYN** **cause**： *What brought about the change in his attitude?* 是什麼使他改變了態度？ ➲ **LANGUAGE BANK** at CAUSE
ˌbring sb aˈround (*NAmE*) = BRING SB ROUND **ˌbring sth aˈround to sth** (*NAmE*) = BRING STH ROUND TO STH
ˌbring sb/sth↔ˈback 0-w to return sb/sth 把…送回；歸還： *Please bring back all library books by the end of the week.* 請在週末前把圖書館的書全部歸還。◇ *He brought me back* (= gave me a ride home) *in his car.* 他用車把我送回家。 **ˌbring sth↔ˈback** **1** to make sb remember sth or think about it again 使回憶起；使想起： *The photographs brought back many pleasant memories.* 那些照片給人帶來很多美好的回憶。 **2** to make sth that existed before be introduced again 恢復；重新使用 **SYN** **reintroduce**： *Most people are against bringing back the death penalty.* 大多數人反對恢復死刑。 **ˌbring sb sth↔ˈback** | **ˌbring sth↔ˈback (for sb)** to return with sth for sb 給…帶回： *What did you bring the kids back from Italy?* 你從意大利給孩子們帶了什麼回來？◇ *I brought a T-shirt back for Mark.* 我給馬克帶回來一件 T 恤衫。
ˈbring sb/sth before sb (*formal*) to present sb/sth for discussion or judgement 將…提交討論（或審判等）： *The matter will be brought before the committee.* 這件事將交給委員會討論。◇ *He was brought before the court and found guilty.* 他被送交法庭審判，並被裁定有罪。
ˌbring sb↔ˈdown **1** to make sb lose power or be defeated 打垮；擊敗： *The scandal may bring down the government.* 那件醜聞可能使政府垮台。 **2** (in sports 體育運動) to make sb fall over 使跌倒： *He was brought down in the penalty area.* 他在罰球區被撞倒。 **ˌbring sth↔ˈdown** **1** 0-w to reduce sth 減少；降低： *We aim to bring down prices on all our computers.* 我們打算降低我們所有計算機的價格。 **2** to land an aircraft 使（飛機）着陸： *The pilot managed to bring the plane down in a field.* 飛行員設法將飛機降落在一處田裏。 **3** to make an aircraft fall out of the sky 擊落： *Twelve enemy fighters had been brought down.* 有十二架敵方的戰鬥機被擊落。 **4** to make an animal or a bird fall down or fall out of the sky by killing or wounding it 打倒（動物）；打落（鳥）： *He brought down the bear with a single shot.* 他一槍就撂倒了那頭熊。

B

ˌbring sb/sth↔ˈforth (*old use* or *formal*) to give birth to sb; to produce sth 生產；產出：*She brought forth a son.* 她生了個兒子。◇ *trees bringing forth fruit* 結果實的樹木

ˌbring sth↔ˈforward **1** 🗝 to move sth to an earlier date or time 將（…的日期或時間）提前：*The meeting has been brought forward from 10 May to 3 May.* 會議已由 5 月 10 號提前到 5 月 3 號。**2** to suggest sth for discussion 提議；提出討論：*Please bring the matter forward at the next meeting.* 請將這事在下次會議上提出。**3** to move a total sum from the bottom of one page or column of numbers to the top of the next 把賬目轉入次頁；承前頁：*A credit balance of $50 was brought forward from his September account.* * 50 元的貸方餘額是從他九月份的賬上轉來的。

ˌbring sb↔ˈin **1** to ask sb to do a particular job or to be involved in sth 請…做；讓…參與：*Local residents were angry at not being brought in on* (= asked for their opinion about) *the new housing proposal.* 新的住房方案未徵求當地居民的意見，對此他們感到憤怒。◇ **~ to do sth** *Experts were brought in to advise the government.* 政府請來專家們出謀劃策。**2** (of the police 警方) to bring sb to a police station in order to ask them questions or arrest them 將（某人）帶到警察局訊問；逮捕：*Two men were brought in for questioning.* 有兩名男子被帶到警察局進行訊問。**ˌbring sb/sth↔ˈin** **1** to introduce a new law 提出（新法案）：*They want to bring in a bill to limit arms exports.* 他們想提出一項限制武器出口的議案。**2** to attract sb/sth to a place or business 吸引；引入：*We need to bring in a lot more new business.* 我們需要帶來更多的新生意。**3** to give a decision in court 宣佈，作出（裁決）：*The jury brought in a verdict of guilty.* 陪審團作出裁決宣判有罪。**ˌbring sb ˈin sth** | **ˌbring ˈin sth** to make or earn a particular amount of money 賺得；掙：*His freelance work brings him in about $20 000 a year.* 他做特約工作每年大約賺 2 萬元。◇ *How much does she bring in now?* 她現在掙多少錢？

ˌbring sth↔ˈoff to succeed in doing sth difficult 完成，做完（艱難的工作）SYN **pull off**：*It was a difficult task but we brought it off.* 那是一項艱難的工作，但我們還是完成了。◇ *The goalie brought off a superb save.* 守門員撲出了一個高難度的險球。

ˌbring sb↔ˈon to help sb develop or improve while they are learning to do sth 幫助（學習者）進步；促使提高 **ˌbring sth↔ˈon** **1** to make sth develop, usually sth unpleasant 使發展，導致（通常指壞事）SYN **cause**：*He was suffering from stress brought on by overwork.* 他正苦於超負荷工作帶來的壓力。**2** to make crops, fruit, etc. grow well 促使（作物、水果等）成長 **ˈbring sth on yourself/sb** to be responsible for sth unpleasant that happens to you/sb 使（自己 / 他人）遭受…：*I have no sympathy—you brought it all on yourself.* 我根本不同情你——這都怪你自己。

ˌbring sb↔ˈout (*BrE*) to make people go on strike 使罷工 **ˌbring sb ˈout of himself, herself, etc.** to help sb to feel more confident 使更加自信：*She's a shy girl who needs friends to bring her out of herself.* 她是個靦腆的女孩，需要朋友幫助克服羞怯心理。**ˌbring sth↔ˈout** **1** 🗝 to make sth appear 使顯現；使表現出：*A crisis **brings out the best in her**.* 危機促使她表現得特別出色。**2** to make sth easy to see or understand 使顯出；闡明：*That dress really brings out the colour of your eyes.* 那件衣服果真能襯托出你眼睛的顏色。**3** 🗝 to produce sth; to publish sth 生產；出版：*The band have just brought out their second album.* 這個樂隊剛剛推出了他們的第二張專輯。**ˌbring sb ˈout in sth** to make sb's skin be covered in spots, etc. 使（皮膚）長出（斑點等）：*The heat brought him out in a rash.* 炎熱的天氣使他渾身長滿了痱子。

ˌbring sb ˈround (*BrE*) (*NAmE* **ˌbring sb aˈround**) (also **ˌbring sb ˈto**) to make sb who is unconscious become conscious again 使蘇醒 **ˌbring sb ˈround (to …)** (*BrE*) (*NAmE* **ˌbring sb aˈround**) to bring sb to sb's house 帶某人串門：*Bring the family round one evening. We'd love to meet them.* 哪天晚上帶全家人來坐坐吧，我們很想見見他們。**ˌbring sb ˈround (to sth)** (*BrE*) (*NAmE* **ˌbring sb aˈround**) to persuade sb to agree to sth 說服某人同意（某事）：*He didn't like the plan at first, but we managed to bring him round.* 他起初並不喜歡這個計劃，但我們終於使他回心轉意了。**ˌbring sth ˈround to sth** (*BrE*) (*NAmE* **ˌbring sth aˈround to sth**) to direct a conversation to a particular subject 將（話題）導向…

ˌbring sb ˈto = BRING SB ROUND

ˌbring A and B toˈgether to help two people or groups to end a disagreement 使雙方言和；使雙方和好：*The loss of their son brought the two of them together.* 喪子使他們兩人重歸於好。

ˌbring sb↔ˈup **1** 🗝 [often passive] to care for a child, teaching him or her how to behave, etc. 撫養；養育；教養 SYN **raise**：*She brought up five children.* 她撫育了五個孩子。◇ *He was brought up by his aunt.* 他是由姨媽帶大的。◇ *a **well/badly brought up** child* 有教養 / 缺乏教養的孩子 ◇ **~ to do sth** *They were brought up to* (= taught as children to) *respect authority.* 他們從小就被教導尊敬權威。◇ **+ noun** *I was brought up a Catholic.* 我從小就受教養成為天主教徒。➲ related noun UPBRINGING **2** (*law* 律) to make sb appear for trial 使出庭受審；傳訊：*He was brought up on a charge of drunken driving.* 他因酒後開車而受到傳訊。**ˌbring sth↔ˈup** **1** 🗝 to mention a subject or start to talk about it 提出（討論等）SYN **raise**：*Bring it up at the meeting.* 請將此事在會議上提出。**2** (*BrE*) to VOMIT 嘔吐：*to bring up your lunch* 把午飯吐出來 **3** to make sth appear on a computer screen 使顯示在計算機屏幕上；調出：*Click with the right mouse button to bring up a new menu.* 單擊鼠標的右鍵，調出一個新選單。**ˌbring sb ˈup against sth** to force sb to know about sth and have to deal with it （使）面臨，面對：*Working in the slums brought her up against the realities of poverty.* 在貧民窟工作使她直面瞭解貧困的現實。

ˌbring-and-ˈbuy sale *noun* (*BrE*) a sale, usually for charity, at which people bring things for sale and buy those brought by others（捐獻物品）義賣

brin·jal /ˈbrɪndʒl/ *noun* [C, U] (*IndE, SAfrE*) an AUBERGINE/EGGPLANT (= a vegetable with shiny dark purple skin and soft white flesh) 茄子

brink /brɪŋk/ *noun* [sing.] **1 the ~ (of sth)** if you are on the **brink** of sth, you are almost in a very new, dangerous or exciting situation（新的、危險的，或令人興奮的處境的）邊緣，初始狀態：*on the **brink of collapse/war/death/disaster*** 瀕於崩潰 / 戰爭 / 死亡 / 災難 ◇ *Scientists are on the brink of making a major new discovery.* 科學家很快就會有新的重大發現。◇ *He's pulled the company **back from the brink*** (= he has saved it from disaster). 他使公司起死回生。**2** (*literary*) the extreme edge of land, for example at the top of a CLIFF or by a river（峭壁、河岸等的）邊沿，邊緣：*the brink of the precipice* 懸崖邊緣 IDM see TEETER

brink·man·ship /ˈbrɪŋkmənʃɪp/ (*NAmE* also **brinks·man·ship** /ˈbrɪŋks-/) *noun* [U] the activity, especially in politics, of getting into a situation that could be very dangerous in order to frighten people and make them do what you want 邊緣政策（刻意進入極其危險的處境，以恐嚇並馴服人民）

briny /ˈbraɪni/ *adj.* (of water 水) containing a lot of salt 多鹽分的；很鹹的 SYN **salty** ➲ see also BRINE

brio /ˈbriːəʊ; *NAmE* ˈbriːoʊ/ *noun* [U] (*formal*) enthusiasm and individual style 熱情活潑

bri·oche /briˈɒʃ; *NAmE* briˈoʊʃ/ *noun* [C, U] a type of sweet bread made from flour, eggs and butter, usually in the shape of a small bread roll 黃油雞蛋圓麪包

bri·quette /brɪˈket/ *noun* a small hard block made from coal dust and used as fuel 煤磚；煤球；煤餅

brisk /brɪsk/ *adj.* (*comparative* **brisk·er**, no *superlative*) **1** quick; busy 快的；敏捷的；忙碌的：*a brisk walk* 輕盈的步履 ◇ *to set off at a brisk pace* 以輕快的步伐上路 ◇ *Ice-cream vendors were doing a brisk trade* (= selling a lot of ice cream). 冰淇淋小販的生意很紅火。**2** (of a person, their voice or manner 人、嗓音或舉止) practical and confident; showing a desire to get things done quickly 現實自信的；麻利的：*His tone became brisk and businesslike.* 他的語氣變得自信幹練而務實。**3** (of wind and the weather 風和天氣) cold but pleasantly fresh 涼爽的；清新的：***a brisk wind/breeze*** 涼爽的風；微風

▸ **brisk·ly** *adv.* **brisk·ness** *noun* [U]

bris·ket /ˈbrɪskɪt/ *noun* [U] meat that comes from the chest of an animal, especially a cow（牛等的）胸脯肉

bris·tle /ˈbrɪsl/ *noun, verb*

■ ***noun*** **1** a short stiff hair 短而硬的毛髮；剛毛：*the bristles on his chin* 他下巴上的鬍茬子 **2** one of the short stiff hairs or wires in a brush 刷子毛

■ ***verb*** **1** [I] **~ (with sth) (at sth)** to suddenly become very annoyed or offended at what sb says or does（對某人的言行）大為惱怒；被激怒：*His lies made her bristle with rage.* 他的謊話使她火冒三丈。**2** [I] (of an animal's fur 動物的毛) to stand up on the back and neck because the animal is frightened or angry（背部或頸部的毛因驚嚇或發怒）豎起，聳起

PHR V **ˈbristle with sth** to contain a large number of sth 裝滿；充斥着：*The whole subject bristles with problems.* 整個事情問題成堆。

brist·ly /ˈbrɪsli/ *adj.* like or full of bristles; rough 剛毛似的；佈滿剛毛的；粗糙的：***a bristly chin/moustache*** 長滿鬍茬子的下巴；短而硬的小鬍子

ˈBristol fashion *adj.* (*old-fashioned*) [not before noun] (*BrE, informal*) in good order or neat and clean 井然有序；整潔：*all shipshape and Bristol fashion* 一切都井井有條，準備就緒

bris·tols /ˈbrɪstlz/ *noun* [pl.] (*BrE, slang*) a woman's breasts（女人的）乳房，奶子

Brit /brɪt/ *noun* (*informal*) a person from Britain 英國人 ➲ note at BRITISH

Brit·ain /ˈbrɪtn/ *noun* [sing.] the island containing England, Scotland and Wales 不列顛（包括英格蘭、蘇格蘭及威爾士）➲ see also GREAT BRITAIN, UNITED KINGDOM

Bri·tan·nia /brɪˈtænjə/ *noun* [sing.] a figure of a woman used as a symbol of Britain. She is usually shown sitting down wearing a HELMET and holding a SHIELD and a TRIDENT (= a long weapon with three points). 不列顛尼亞（英國的擬人化稱呼，以頭戴鋼盔手持盾牌及三叉戟的女人為象徵）

Bri·tan·nic /brɪˈtænɪk/ *adj.* (*old-fashioned, formal*) (used mainly in names or titles 主要用於名稱或頭銜) relating to Britain or the British Empire 不列顛的；英國的；大英帝國的：*her Britannic Majesty* (= the Queen) 英國女王陛下

Brit·ish /ˈbrɪtɪʃ/ *adj.* **1** (*abbr.* **Br.**) connected with the United Kingdom of Great Britain and Northern Ireland or the people who live there（大不列顛及北愛爾蘭）聯合王國的；英國的；英國人的：*the British Government* 英國政府 ◇ *He was born in France but his parents are British.* 他生在法國，但父母是英國人。◇ *British-based/British-born/British-made* 以英國為基地的；英國出生的；英國製造的 **2 the British** *noun* [pl.] the people of the United Kingdom 聯合王國人民；（統稱）英國人 ▸ **Brit·ish·ness** *noun* [U]

More About 補充說明

the British

- There is no singular noun which is commonly used to refer to a person from Britain. Instead the adjective **British** is used. 英語中沒有指英國人的通用單數名詞，一般用形容詞 British：*She's British.* 她是英國人。◇ *The British have a very odd sense of humour.* 英國人的幽默感很奇特。The adjective **English** refers only to people from England, not the rest of the United Kingdom. 形容詞 English 只指英格蘭人，不包括英國其他地方的人。
- The noun **Briton** is used mainly in newspapers. 名詞 Briton 主要用於報刊：*The survivors of the avalanche included 12 Britons.* 雪崩的幸存者中有 12 名英國人。It also describes the early inhabitants of Britain. 該詞亦指英國早期居民：*the ancient Britons* 古代不列顛人 **Brit** is informal and can sound negative. **Britisher** is now very old-fashioned. * Brit 是非正式用語，可能含貶義。Britisher 現已過時。

➲ note at SCOTTISH

the ˌBritish ˈCouncil *noun* [sing.] an organization that represents British culture in other countries and develops closer cultural relations with them 英國文化協會（設立於其他國家，旨在加強文化交流）

ˌBritish ˈEnglish *noun* [U] the English language as spoken in Britain and certain other countries 英式英語

Brit·ish·er /ˈbrɪtɪʃə(r)/ *noun* (*old-fashioned, NAmE, informal*) a person from Britain 英國人

the ˌBritish ˈLions *noun* [pl.] a RUGBY team of the best players from England, Ireland, Scotland and Wales that plays abroad 英國雄獅隊（由英格蘭、愛爾蘭、蘇格蘭和威爾士的一流橄欖球員組成）

ˌBritish ˌoverseas ˈterritory *noun* (*BrE*) an island or group of islands in which the British government is responsible for defence and relations with other countries 英國海外領地

ˌBritish ˈSummer Time *noun* [U] (*abbr.* **BST**) the time used in the UK in summer that is one hour ahead of GMT 英國夏令時間（比格林尼治平時早一個小時）

Briton /ˈbrɪtn/ *noun* (*formal*) a person from Britain 英國人：*the ancient Britons* 古英國人 ◇ *the first Briton to climb Everest without oxygen* 第一個未借助氧氣設備登上珠穆朗瑪峰的英國人 ➲ note at BRITISH

brit·tle /ˈbrɪtl/ *adj.* **1** hard but easily broken 硬但易碎的；脆性的：***brittle bones/nails*** 易折的骨骼／指甲 **2** a **brittle** mood or state of mind is one that appears to be happy or strong but is actually nervous and easily damaged 脆弱的：*a brittle temperament* 脆弱的性情 **3** (of a sound 聲音) hard and sharp in an unpleasant way 尖利的；刺耳的：*a brittle laugh* 尖利的笑聲 ▸ **brittle·ness** *noun* [U]

ˌbrittle ˈbone disease *noun* [U] (*medical* 醫) **1** a rare disease in which sb's bones break extremely easily 骨質疏鬆症；脆骨病 **2** = OSTEOPOROSIS

bro /brəʊ; *NAmE* broʊ/ *noun* (*pl.* **bros**) (*informal*) **1** a brother 兄（或弟）**2** (*especially NAmE*) a friendly way of addressing a male person（對男子的友好稱呼）哥們兒，夥計：*Thanks, bro!* 謝謝你，老兄！

broach /brəʊtʃ; *NAmE* broʊtʃ/ *verb* **~ sth (to/with sb)** to begin talking about a subject that is difficult to discuss, especially because it is embarrassing or because people disagree about it 開始談論，引入（尤指令人尷尬或有異議的話題）：*She was dreading having to* ***broach the subject*** *of money to her father.* 她正在為不得不向父親提出錢的事犯愁。

ˈB-road *noun* (in Britain) a road that is less important than an A-ROAD and usually joins small towns and villages（英國）B 級公路（次於 A 級公路，通常連接小城鎮及村落）

broad 🔑 /brɔːd/ *adj., noun*

WORD FAMILY
broad *adj.*
broadly *adv.*
broaden *verb*
breadth *noun*

■ ***adj.*** (**broad·er, broad·est**)

▸ WIDE 寬闊 **1** 🔑 wide 寬闊的；廣闊的：*a broad street/avenue/river* 寬廣的街道／林蔭道／河流 ◇ *broad shoulders* 寬肩 ◇ *He is tall, broad and muscular.* 他身高體寬，肌肉發達。◇ *a* ***broad smile/grin*** (= one in which your mouth is stretched very wide because you are very pleased or amused) 咧嘴笑 OPP **narrow** (1) **2** used after a measurement of distance to show how wide sth is …寬（用於表示距離的量度之後）：*two metres broad and one metre high* 兩米寬，一米高

▸ WIDE RANGE 廣泛 **3** including a great variety of people or things 涉及各種各樣的人（或事物）的；廣泛的：*a broad range of products* 各種各樣的產品 ◇ *a broad spectrum of interests* 廣泛的興趣 ◇ *There is broad support for the government's policies.* 政府的政策得到了廣泛的支持。◇ *She* ***took a broad view*** *of the duties of being a teacher* (= she believed her duties included a wide range of things). 她認為教師的職責範圍很廣。OPP **narrow**

▸ GENERAL 概括 **4** 🔑 [only before noun] general; not detailed 概括的；一般的；不具體的：*the broad outline of a*

B

B

proposal 提案的綱要 ◇ *The negotiators were in broad agreement on the main issues.* 談判代表們在主要問題上的意見大致相同。◇ *She's a feminist, in the **broadest sense of the word**.* 廣義而言，她算是個女權主義者。◇ ***In broad terms**, the paper argues that each country should develop its own policy.* 從大體上説，這份報紙認為各國應該建立自己的政策。
▸ LAND/WATER 陸地；水 **5** 🗝 covering a wide area 開闊的；遼闊的：*a broad expanse of water* 一片遼闊的水域
▸ ACCENT 口音 **6** if sb has a **broad accent**, you can hear very easily which area they come from 口音重的；鄉音濃的 SYN **strong**
▸ HINT 暗示 **7** if sb gives a **broad hint**, they make it very clear what they are thinking or what they want 明確的；明顯的
▸ HUMOUR 幽默 **8** (*NAmE*) dealing with sex in an amusing way 粗俗滑稽的；以肉慾作笑料的：*The movie mixes broad humor with romance.* 那部電影把粗俗幽默和浪漫故事結合在一起。➲ note at WIDE
IDM **a broad 'church** (*BrE*) an organization that accepts a wide range of opinions 廣納眾議的機構 SYN **big tent** **(in) broad 'daylight** (in) the clear light of day, when it is easy to see 光天化日（之下）：*The robbery occurred in broad daylight, in a crowded street.* 搶劫就發生在光天化日之下的一條熙熙攘攘的街道上。 **it's as ˌbroad as it's 'long** (*BrE, informal*) it makes no real difference which of two possible choices you make 兩種選擇都一樣 ➲ more at PAINT *v.*
■ ***noun*** (*old-fashioned, NAmE, slang*) an offensive way of referring to a woman（對女人的粗俗稱呼）婆娘

broad·band /ˈbrɔːdbænd/ *noun* [U] **1** (*technical* 術語) signals that use a wide range of FREQUENCIES 寬頻帶；寬波段 ➲ compare NARROWBAND **2** a way of connecting a computer to the Internet, which allows you to receive information, including pictures, etc., very quickly（互聯網的）寬帶連接，寬頻連接：*We have broadband at home now.* 我們家裏現在裝了寬帶。➲ COLLOCATIONS at EMAIL

ˌbroad-ˈbased (also **ˌbroadly-ˈbased**) *adj.* based on a wide variety of people, things or ideas; not limited 有廣泛基礎的；無限制的

ˌbroad ˈbean (*BrE*) (*NAmE* **ˈfava bean**) *noun* a type of round, pale green BEAN. Several broad beans grow together inside a fat POD. 蠶豆

ˌbroad-ˈbrush *adj.* [only before noun] dealing with a subject or problem in a general way rather than considering details 粗線條的；不考慮細節的：*a broad-brush approach* 粗線條的處理方法

broad·cast 🗝 /ˈbrɔːdkɑːst; *NAmE* -kæst/ *verb, noun*
■ ***verb*** (**broad·cast, broad·cast** or **broad·cast, broad·casted**)
1 🗝 [T, I] **~ (sth)** to send out programmes on television or radio 播送（電視或無線電節目）；廣播：*The concert will be **broadcast live** (= at the same time as it takes place) tomorrow evening.* 明晚的音樂會將現場直播。◇ *They began broadcasting in 1922.* 他們於 1922 年開播。➲ COLLOCATIONS at TELEVISION **2** [T] **~ sth** to tell a lot of people about sth 散佈，傳播（信息等）：*I don't like to **broadcast the fact** that my father owns the company.* 我不想宣揚這家公司為我父親所有。
■ ***noun*** 🗝 a radio or television programme 廣播節目；電視節目：(*BrE*) *a party political broadcast* (= for example, before an election) 政黨政治廣播節目 ◇ *We watched a **live broadcast** of the speech* (= one shown at the same time as the speech was made). 我們觀看了那場演説的現場直播。

broad·cast·er /ˈbrɔːdkɑːstə(r); *NAmE* -kæst-/ *noun* **1** a person whose job is presenting or talking on television or radio programmes 廣播員；（電視或電台的）節目主持人 **2** a company that sends out television or radio programmes 電視台；廣播公司

broad·cast·ing /ˈbrɔːdkɑːstɪŋ; *NAmE* -kæst-/ *noun* [U] the business of making and sending out radio and television programmes（無線電和電視的）節目製作和播放；廣播：*to work in broadcasting* 從事廣播工作 ◇ *the British Broadcasting Corporation* (= the BBC) 英國廣播公司

broad·en /ˈbrɔːdn/ *verb* **1** [I] to become wider 變寬；變闊：*Her smile broadened.* 她笑得更加燦爛了。**2** [T, I] **~ (sth)** to affect or make sth affect more people or things（使）擴大影響：*a promise to broaden access to higher education* 拓寬高等教育渠道的承諾 ◇ *The party needs to broaden its appeal to voters.* 該黨需要進一步吸引選民。**3** [T] **~ sth** to increase your experience, knowledge, etc. 增長（經驗、知識等）：*Few would disagree that travel **broadens the mind*** (= helps you to understand other people's customs, etc.). 旅遊有助於開闊眼界，很少有人會不同意這一點。◇ *Spending a year working in the city helped to **broaden his horizons**.* 在城市工作的一年拓寬了他的視野。
PHR V **ˌbroaden ˈout** (of a road, river, etc. 路、河等) to become wider 變寬；變闊 SYN **widen out**

the ˈbroad ˈjump *noun* [sing.] (*NAmE*) = THE LONG JUMP

broad·leaved /ˈbrɔːdliːvd/ (also *less frequent* **broad·leaf** /ˈbrɔːdliːf/) *adj.* (*technical* 術語) (of plants 植物) having broad flat leaves 闊葉的

broad·ly 🗝 /ˈbrɔːdli/ *adv.*
1 🗝 generally, without considering details 大體上；基本上；不考慮細節地：***Broadly speaking**, I agree with you.* 我大體上贊同你的意見。◇ ***broadly similar/comparable/equivalent/consistent*** 大致相似／相當／相等／一致 **2** 🗝 if you smile **broadly**, you smile with your mouth stretched very wide because you are very pleased or amused 咧開嘴（笑）的；開心粲（笑）的

ˌbroad-ˈminded *adj.* willing to listen to other people's opinions and accept behaviour that is different from your own 願意聽取他人意見的；胸懷寬闊的；有氣量的 SYN **tolerant** OPP **narrow-minded** ▸ **ˌbroad-ˈminded·ness** *noun* [U]

Broad·moor /ˈbrɔːdmɔː(r)/ *noun* a special hospital in southern England for criminals who are mentally ill and considered very dangerous 布羅德穆爾醫院（位於英國南部，專門收治十分危險的精神病犯人）

broad·ness /ˈbrɔːdnəs/ *noun* [U] the quality of being broad 寬闊；寬廣；遼闊

broad·scale /ˈbrɔːdskeɪl/ *adj.* on a large scale 大規模的；大範圍的：*The broadscale cutting down of trees is damaging the environment.* 對樹木的大規模砍伐正在破壞環境。

broad·sheet /ˈbrɔːdʃiːt/ *noun* **1** a newspaper printed on a large size of paper, generally considered more serious than smaller newspapers 大幅報紙（一般比小幅報紙內容嚴肅）➲ compare TABLOID **2** a large piece of paper printed on one side only with information or an advertisement 單面全版大幅信息（或廣告）

broad·side /ˈbrɔːdsaɪd/ *noun, adv., verb*
■ ***noun*** an aggressive attack in words, whether written or spoken（書面或口頭的）猛烈抨擊：*The prime minister **fired a broadside** at his critics.* 首相對批評他的人進行了猛烈反擊。
■ ***adv.*** with one side facing sth 一側對着某物 SYN **sideways**：*The car skidded and crashed broadside into another car.* 汽車打滑，車身撞上了另一輛車。◇ (*BrE*) *The boat swung **broadside on** to the current of the river.* 小船打轉以舷側沖入河水的洪流。
■ ***verb*** **~ sth** (*NAmE*) to crash into the side of sth 撞上（某物的）側面：*The driver ran a stop light and broadsided the truck.* 司機闖紅燈，撞上了卡車的一側。

ˌbroad-ˈspectrum *adj.* [only before noun] (*technical* 術語) (of a drug or chemical 藥物或化學品) effective against a large variety of bacteria, insects, etc. 廣譜的；效用廣泛的

broad·sword /ˈbrɔːdsɔːd; *NAmE* -sɔːrd/ *noun* a large SWORD with a broad flat blade 大砍刀；闊劍

Broad·way /ˈbrɔːdweɪ/ *noun* [U] a street in New York City where there are many theatres, sometimes used to refer to the US theatre industry in general 百老匯（美國紐約市戲院集中的一條大街）；（美國的）戲劇業：*a Broadway musical* 百老匯音樂劇 ◇ *The play opened **on***

Broadway in 2008. 該劇於 2008 年在百老匯首演。➲ see also OFF-BROADWAY

bro·cade /brəˈkeɪd/ *noun* [U, C] a type of thick heavy cloth with a raised pattern made especially from gold or silver silk thread 織錦緞；（尤指用金銀線織出凸紋的）厚織物

bro·caded /brəˈkeɪdɪd/ *adj.* [usually before noun] made of or decorated with brocade 用錦緞製作（或裝飾）的；織錦緞的

Broca's area /ˈbrəʊkəz eəriə; *NAmE* ˈbroʊkəz eriə/ *noun* (*anatomy* 解) an area in the front part of the brain connected with speech 布羅卡區（大腦前部控制語言表達的區域）

broc·coli /ˈbrɒkəli; *NAmE* ˈbrɑːk-/ *noun* [U] a vegetable with a thick green STEM and several dark green or purple flower heads 綠菜花；西蘭花 ➲ VISUAL VOCAB page V31

bro·chette /brɒˈʃet; *NAmE* broʊ-/ *noun* (from *French*) **1** [C, U] a dish consisting of pieces of food cooked on a thin stick over a fire 串烤肉（用扦子明火烤製） **2** [C] one of the sticks used for cooking food in this way 烤肉扦

bro·chure /ˈbrəʊʃə(r); *NAmE* broʊˈʃʊr/ *noun* a small magazine or book containing pictures and information about sth or advertising sth 資料（或廣告）手冊：*a travel brochure* 旅遊手冊

bro·derie ang·laise /ˌbrəʊdəri ˈɒŋgleɪz; *NAmE* ˌbroʊdəri ˈɑːŋgleɪz/ *noun* [U] (from *French*) decoration with sewing on fine white cloth; the cloth decorated in this way 英格蘭刺繡；細白布繡飾；英格蘭刺繡品

broer /ˈbruːə(r)/ *noun* (*SAfrE, informal*) **1** a brother 哥哥；弟弟 **2** (used of a boy or man) a friend（稱男孩或男子）朋友，哥兒們 **3** a friendly form of address that is used by one boy or man to another 老兄；老弟：*How's it going, my broer?* 怎麼樣了，老兄？

brogue /brəʊg; *NAmE* broʊg/ *noun* **1** [usually pl.] a strong shoe which usually has a pattern in the leather（粗革）拷花皮鞋：*a pair of brogues* 一雙拷花皮鞋 ➲ VISUAL VOCAB page V64 **2** [usually sing.] the accent that sb has when they are speaking, especially the accent of Irish or Scottish speakers of English 口音；（尤指講英語的愛爾蘭或蘇格蘭人的）土腔

broil /brɔɪl/ *verb* **1** [T] **~ sth** (*NAmE*) to cook meat or fish under direct heat or over heat on metal bars 烤，焙（肉或魚）：*broiled chicken* 烤雞 ➲ compare BARBECUE *v.*, GRILL *v.* (1) **2** [I, T] **~ (sb)** to become or make sb become very hot （使）變得灼熱，受炙熱：*They lay broiling in the sun.* 他們躺在太陽底下幾乎要曬熟了。

broil·er /ˈbrɔɪlə(r)/ *noun* **1** (also **ˈbroiler chicken**) (*especially NAmE*) a young chicken suitable for broiling or ROASTING （適於烤焙的）嫩雞 **2** (*NAmE*) the part inside the oven of a cooker/stove that directs heat downwards to cook food that is placed underneath it 烤箱；烤爐；烤架 ➲ compare GRILL *n.* (1)

broke /brəʊk; *NAmE* broʊk/ *adj.* [not before noun] (*informal*) having no money 沒錢；囊中羞澀；破產：*I'm always broke by the end of the month.* 我總是一到月底就沒錢花了。◇ *During the recession thousands of small businesses* ***went broke*** (= had to stop doing business). 經濟衰退期間成千上萬家小企業被迫關門了。◇ ***flat/stony broke*** (= completely broke) 徹底破產 ➲ see also BREAK
IDM **go for ˈbroke** (*informal*) to risk everything in one determined effort to do sth 孤注一擲 ➲ more at AIN'T

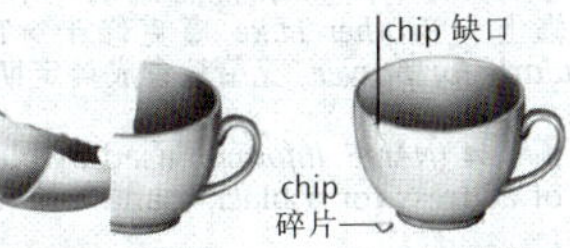
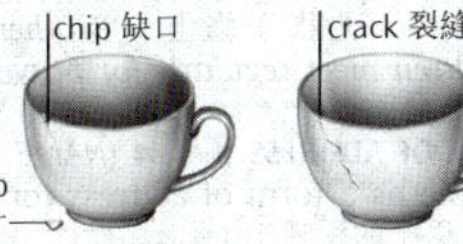

broken 破碎的 **chipped** 破損的 **cracked** 破裂的

broken 0‑ /ˈbrəʊkən; *NAmE* ˈbroʊ-/ *adj.*
▸ **DAMAGED** 受損 **1** 0‑ that has been damaged or injured; no longer whole or working correctly 破損的；傷殘的；殘缺的；出了毛病的：*a broken window/plate* 破碎的窗戶／盤子 ◇ *a broken leg/arm* 斷了的腿／臂 ◇ *pieces of broken glass* 破玻璃碎片 ◇ *How did this dish* ***get broken****?* 這個盤子是怎麼打破的？◇ *The TV's broken.* 電視機壞了。➲ see also BROKEN HEART
▸ **RELATIONSHIP** 關係 **2** 0‑ [usually before noun] ended or destroyed 中止了的；破壞了的：*a* ***broken marriage/engagement*** 破裂的婚姻；解除了的婚約 ➲ see also BROKEN HOME
▸ **PROMISE/AGREEMENT** 諾言；協定 **3** 0‑ [usually before noun] not kept 被違背的；未履行的
▸ **NOT CONTINUOUS** 不連續 **4** 0‑ [usually before noun] not continuous; disturbed or interrupted 不連續的；間斷的；被打擾的：*a night of broken sleep* 睡得不踏實的一夜 ◇ *a single broken white line across the road* 橫穿馬路的一條斷斷續續的白線
▸ **PERSON** 人 **5** [only before noun] made weak and tired by illness or difficulties 衰弱的；精疲力竭的：*He was a broken man after the failure of his business.* 生意失敗後他變得心灰意懶。
▸ **LANGUAGE** 語言 **6** [only before noun] (of a language that is not your own 非母語) spoken slowly and with a lot of mistakes; not FLUENT 說得結結巴巴的；不流利的：*to speak in broken English* 說着一口結結巴巴的英語
▸ **GROUND** 地面 **7** having a rough surface 凹凸不平的；坎坷的：*an area of broken, rocky ground* 崎嶇、多岩石的地區 ➲ see also BREAK, BROKE, BROKEN *v.*

ˌbroken-ˈdown *adj.* [usually before noun] in a very bad condition; not working correctly; very tired and sick 狀況很差的；出故障的；衰弱的：*a broken-down old car/horse* 出了毛病的舊車；衰老的馬

ˌbroken ˈheart *noun* a feeling of great sadness, especially when sb you love has died or left you 破碎的心；哀慟：*No one ever died of a broken heart.* 從來沒有人因為過度悲傷而死。▸ **ˌbroken-ˈhearted** *adj.*：*He was broken-hearted when his wife died.* 他的妻子去世，他傷心極了。➲ compare HEARTBROKEN

ˌbroken ˈhome *noun* a family in which the parents are divorced or separated 破裂的家庭；父母離異（或分居）的家庭：*She comes from a broken home.* 她生長於一個破碎的家庭。

broken·ly /ˈbrəʊkənli; *NAmE* ˈbroʊ-/ *adv.* (*formal*) (of sb's manner of speaking 講話方式) in phrases that are very short or not complete, with a lot of pauses; not FLUENTLY 結結巴巴地；不流利地

broker /ˈbrəʊkə(r); *NAmE* ˈbroʊ-/ *noun, verb*
■ ***noun*** **1** a person who buys and sells things for other people 經紀人；掮客：*an insurance broker* 保險經紀人 **2** = STOCKBROKER ➲ see also HONEST BROKER, PAWNBROKER, POWER BROKER
■ ***verb*** **~ sth** to arrange the details of an agreement, especially between different countries 安排，協商（協議的細節，尤指在兩國間）：*a peace plan brokered by the UN* 由聯合國出面協商的和平計劃

broker·age /ˈbrəʊkərɪdʒ; *NAmE* ˈbroʊ-/ *noun* [U] **1** the business of being a broker 經紀業務：*a* ***brokerage firm/house*** 經紀公司；經紀行 **2** an amount of money charged by a broker for work that he/she does 經紀人佣金（或回扣）

ˈbroker-dealer *noun* (*finance* 財) a person who works on the Stock Exchange buying shares from and selling shares to BROKERS and the public （證券交易所的）交易經紀人，證券商 ➲ compare JOBBER

brolly /ˈbrɒli; *NAmE* ˈbrɑːli/ *noun* (*pl.* **-ies**) (*BrE, informal*) = UMBRELLA (1)

brom·ide /ˈbrəʊmaɪd; *NAmE* ˈbroʊ-/ *noun* [C, U] a chemical which contains BROMINE, used, especially in the past, to make people feel calm 溴化物（舊時尤用作鎮靜劑）

brom·ine /ˈbrəʊmiːn; *NAmE* ˈbroʊ-/ *noun* [U] (*symb.* **Br**) a chemical element. Bromine is a dark red poisonous liquid and has a very strong unpleasant smell. It is mainly found in the form of salts in sea water. 溴（富集於海水）

B

bron·chial /ˈbrɒŋkiəl; *NAmE* ˈbrɑːŋ-/ *adj.* [usually before noun] (*medical* 醫) of or affecting the two main branches of the WINDPIPE (called **bronchial tubes**) leading to the lungs 支氣管的：*bronchial pneumonia* 支氣管肺炎 ➲ VISUAL VOCAB page V59

bron·chitis /brɒŋˈkaɪtɪs; *NAmE* brɑːŋ-/ *noun* [U] an illness that affects the bronchial tubes leading to the lungs 支氣管炎：*He was suffering from chronic bronchitis.* 他患有慢性支氣管炎。▶ **bron·chit·ic** /brɒŋˈkɪtɪk; *NAmE* brɑːŋ-/ *adj.*：*a bronchitic cough* 支氣管炎引起的咳嗽

bron·chus /ˈbrɒŋkəs; *NAmE* ˈbrɑːŋ-/ *noun* (*pl.* **bron·chi** /ˈbrɒŋkaɪ; *NAmE* ˈbrɑːŋ-/) (*anatomy* 解) any one of the system of tubes which make up the main branches of the WINDPIPE through which air passes in and out of the lungs 支氣管

bronco /ˈbrɒŋkəʊ; *NAmE* ˈbrɑːŋkoʊ/ *noun* (*pl.* **-os**) a wild horse of the western US 布朗科馬；北美野馬：*a bucking bronco in the rodeo* 牛仔競技表演中一匹弓背跳躍的野馬

bron·to·saurus /ˌbrɒntəˈsɔːrəs; *NAmE* ˌbrɑːn-/ *noun* = APATOSAURUS

Bronx cheer /ˌbrɒŋks ˈtʃɪə(r); *NAmE* ˌbrɑːŋks ˈtʃɪr/ *noun* (*NAmE, informal*) = RASPBERRY (2)

bronze /brɒnz; *NAmE* brɑːnz/ *noun, adj.*

■ ***noun*** **1** [U] a dark reddish-brown metal made by mixing COPPER and tin 青銅：*a bronze statue* 青銅像 ◇ *a figure cast in bronze* 一尊青銅鑄像 **2** [U] a dark reddish-brown colour, like bronze 深紅褐色；青銅色 **3** [C] a work of art made of bronze, for example a statue 青銅藝術品 **4** [C, U] = BRONZE MEDAL

■ ***adj.*** dark reddish-brown in colour 深紅棕色的；青銅色的：*bronze skin* 古銅色的皮膚

the ˈBronze Age *noun* [sing.] the period in history between the Stone Age and the Iron Age when people used tools and weapons made of bronze 青銅時代；青銅器時代

bronzed /brɒnzd; *NAmE* brɑːnzd/ *adj.* having skin that has been turned brown in an attractive way by the sun 古銅色的（太陽曬的健康膚色）SYN **tanned**

ˌbronze ˈmedal (also **bronze**) *noun* [C, U] a MEDAL given as third prize in a competition or race 銅牌；銅質獎章：*an Olympic bronze medal winner* 奧林匹克銅牌得主 ◇ *She won (a) bronze at the Olympics.* 她在奧林匹克運動會上贏得了一枚銅牌。➲ compare GOLD MEDAL, SILVER MEDAL ▶ **ˌbronze ˈmedallist** (*BrE*) (*NAmE* **ˌbronze ˈmedalist**) *noun*：*She's an Olympic bronze medallist.* 她是奧林匹克銅牌得主。

brooch /brəʊtʃ; *NAmE* broʊtʃ/ (*especially BrE*) (*NAmE* usually **pin**) *noun* a piece of jewellery with a pin on the back of it, that can be fastened to your clothes 飾針；胸針；領針 ➲ VISUAL VOCAB page V65

brood /bruːd/ *verb, noun*

■ ***verb*** **1** [I] **~ (over/on/about sth)** to think a lot about sth that makes you annoyed, anxious or upset 焦慮，憂思（使人厭煩、擔憂或不安的事）：*You're not still brooding over what he said, are you?* 你不是還在為他的話悶悶不樂吧？ **2** [I, T] **~ (sth)** if a bird **broods**, or **broods** its eggs, it sits on the eggs in order to HATCH them (= make the young come out of them) 孵（蛋）

■ ***noun*** [C+sing./pl. v.] **1** all the young birds or creatures that a mother produces at one time （一次孵或生的）一窩鳥，一窩動物 SYN **clutch** **2** (*humorous*) a large family of children 一大家孩子

brood·ing /ˈbruːdɪŋ/ *adj.* (*literary*) sad and mysterious or threatening 幽怨的；憂思的；森然的；險惡的：*dark, brooding eyes* 一雙烏黑憂思的眼睛 ◇ *a brooding silence* 森然的寂靜 ◇ *Ireland's brooding landscape* 愛爾蘭的險要地形

ˈbrood mare *noun* a female horse kept for breeding 傳種母馬

broody /ˈbruːdi/ *adj.* **1** (of a woman 女人) wanting very much to have a baby 急於生孩子的：*I reached the age of 27 and suddenly started to feel broody.* 到 27 歲時，我突然產生了很想要個孩子的念頭。 **2** (of a female bird 雌禽) wanting to lay eggs and sit on them 要抱窩的：*a broody hen* 要抱窩的母雞 **3** quiet and thinking about sth because you are unhappy or disappointed 悶悶不樂的；鬱鬱寡歡的 ▶ **broodi·ness** *noun* [U]

brook /brʊk/ *noun, verb*

■ ***noun*** a small river 溪；小河；小川

■ ***verb*** **not brook sth/not brook sb doing sth/brook no …** (*formal*) to not allow sth （不）允許（某事）：*The tone in his voice brooked no argument.* 他的聲音裏透露着一種不容爭辯的語調。

broom /bruːm/ *noun* **1** [C] a brush on the end of a long handle, used for sweeping floors 掃把；掃帚 ➲ VISUAL VOCAB page V20 ➲ see also NEW BROOM **2** [U] a wild bush with small yellow flowers 金雀花（野生，開小黃花）IDM see NEW

ˈbroom cupboard *noun* (*BrE*) **1** a large built-in cupboard used for keeping cleaning equipment, etc. in 清潔用具壁櫥 **2** (often *humorous*) a very small room 狹小的房間：*I couldn't afford more than a broom cupboard to set up office in.* 我的錢也就夠搞一間雞窩大的辦公室。

broom·stick /ˈbruːmstɪk/ *noun* a broom with a long handle and small thin sticks at the end, or the handle of a broom. In stories WITCHES (= women with evil magic powers) ride through the air on broomsticks. 長柄掃帚；掃帚柄（傳說中巫婆用以飛行）

Bros (also **Bros.** especially in *NAmE*) *abbr.* (used in the name of a company) Brothers （用於公司名稱）兄弟：*Warner Bros* 華納兄弟娛樂公司

broth /brɒθ; *NAmE* brɑːθ; brɔːθ/ *noun* [U, C] thick soup made by boiling meat or fish and vegetables in water （加入蔬菜的）肉湯，魚湯：*chicken broth* 雞湯 ➲ see also SCOTCH BROTH IDM see COOK *n.*

brothel /ˈbrɒθl; *NAmE* ˈbrɑːθl; ˈbrɔːθl/ (also **bor·dello** especially in *NAmE*) *noun* a house where people pay to have sex with PROSTITUTES 妓院

ˈbrothel creepers *noun* [pl.] (*BrE, informal*) SUEDE shoes with thick soft SOLES, popular in the 1950s （流行於 20 世紀 50 年代的）絨面革厚軟底鞋

brother 🔑 /ˈbrʌðə(r)/ *noun, exclamation*

■ ***noun***

▸ IN FAMILY 家庭 **1** 🔑 a boy or man who has the same mother and father as another person （同父母的）兄，弟：*We're brothers.* 我們是親兄弟。◇ *He's my brother.* 他是我哥哥（或弟弟）。◇ *an **older/younger brother*** 哥哥；弟弟 ◇ *a **twin brother*** 孿生哥哥（或弟弟）◇ *Does she have any **brothers and sisters**?* 她有兄弟姐妹嗎？◇ *Edward was the youngest of the Kennedy brothers.* 愛德華是肯尼迪弟兄中最小的一個。◇ *He was like a brother to me* (= very close). 他如同我的親兄弟一樣。➲ see also HALF-BROTHER, STEPBROTHER

▸ OTHER MEN 其他男性 **2** (*pl.* **brothers** or *old-fashioned* **brethren**) used for talking to or talking about other male members of an organization or other men who have the same ideas, purpose, etc. as yourself （稱男性的共事者或同道）同事，弟兄，夥伴：*We must work together, brothers!* 我們必須攜手工作，夥計們！◇ *He was greatly respected by his brother officers.* 他非常受軍官同僚的敬重。◇ *We must support our weaker brethren.* 我們必須支持弱勢的同胞。

▸ IN RELIGIOUS GROUP 宗教團體 **3** (also **Brother**) (*pl.* **brethren** or **brothers**) a male member of a religious group, especially a MONK （同一宗教團體的男性）教友；（尤指）修士：*Brother Luke* 盧克修士 ◇ *The Brethren meet regularly for prayer.* 兄弟教會成員定期聚集祈禱。

▸ FORM OF ADDRESS 稱呼 **4** (*NAmE, informal*) used by black people as a form of address for a black man （黑人對黑人男子的稱呼）

▸ AT COLLEGE/UNIVERSITY 大學 **5** (in the US) a member of a FRATERNITY (= a club for a group of male students at a college or university) （美國）大學生聯誼會成員

■ ***exclamation*** (*old-fashioned, especially NAmE*) used to express the fact that you are annoyed or surprised（表示生氣或吃驚）: *Oh brother!* 天哪！

brother·hood /ˈbrʌðəhʊd; *NAmE* -ðərh-/ *noun* **1** [U] friendship and understanding between people 友誼與諒解；手足情誼: *to live in peace and brotherhood* 生活在和平互愛中 **2** [C+sing./pl. v.] an organization formed for a particular purpose, especially a religious society or political organization 宗教（或政治等）組織 **3** [U] the relationship of brothers 兄弟關係: *the ties of brotherhood* 兄弟情義

ˈbrother-in-law (*pl.* **brothers-in-law**) *noun* the brother of your husband or wife; your sister's husband; the husband of your husband or wife's sister 大伯子；小叔子；內兄（或弟）；姐（或妹）夫；姑兄（或弟）；連襟 ➲ compare SISTER-IN-LAW

brother·ly /ˈbrʌðəli; *NAmE* -ðərli/ *adj.* [usually before noun] showing feelings of affection and kindness that you would expect a brother to show 兄弟的；兄弟般的；親切友好的: ***brotherly love/advice*** 兄弟間的愛；親切的勸告 ◇ *He gave her a brotherly kiss on the cheek.* 他像親兄弟一樣吻了她的面頰。

brougham /ˈbru:əm/ *noun* a type of CARRIAGE used in the past, which had a closed roof and four wheels and was pulled by one horse（舊時的）四輪單馬馬車

brought *past tense, past part.* of BRING **IDM** see LOW *adj.*

brou·haha /ˈbru:hɑ:hɑ:/ *noun* [U, sing.] (*old-fashioned, informal*) noisy excitement or complaints about sth 喧鬧；喧譁；起鬨

brow /braʊ/ *noun* **1** (*literary*) the part of the face above the eyes and below the hair 額頭 **SYN** **forehead**: *The nurse mopped his fevered brow.* 護士擦拭了他發燙的前額。◇ *Her* ***brow furrowed*** *in concentration.* 她眉頭緊鎖全神貫注。**2** [usually pl.] = EYEBROW: *One dark brow rose in surprise.* 一道烏黑的眉毛因驚奇而挑起。 **3** [usually sing.] the top part of a hill 山脊；坡頂: *The path disappeared over the brow of the hill.* 小徑過山頂後消失了。➲ see also HIGHBROW, MIDDLEBROW, LOWBROW **IDM** see KNIT *v.*

brow·beat /ˈbraʊbi:t/ *verb* (**brow·beat**, **brow·beat·en** /ˈbraʊbi:tn/) **~ sb (into doing sth)** to frighten or threaten sb in order to make them do sth 恫嚇；威逼 **SYN** **intimidate**: *They were browbeaten into accepting the offer.* 他們被威逼接受了提議。

brown 🔑 /braʊn/ *adj., noun, verb*

■ ***adj.*** (**brown·er**, **brown·est**) **1** 🔑 having the colour of earth or coffee 棕色的；褐色的: *brown eyes* 褐色的眼睛 ◇ *brown bread* 黑麵包 ◇ *dark brown shoe polish* 深棕色鞋油 ◇ *a package wrapped in brown paper* 用牛皮紙包紮的包裹 **2** 🔑 having skin that is naturally brown or has been made brown by the sun（皮膚）棕色的，被曬黑的: (*BrE*) *I don't go brown very easily.* 我不容易曬黑。◇ *After the summer in Spain, the children were* ***brown as berries.*** 在西班牙度過了一個夏天之後，孩子們被曬得黝黑。

IDM **in a brown ˈstudy** (*old-fashioned, BrE*) thinking deeply so that you do not notice what is happening around you 出神；沉思默想（以致沒注意到周圍情況）

■ ***noun*** 🔑 [U, C] the colour of earth or coffee 棕色；褐色: *leaves of various shades of brown* 深淺不一的棕色葉子 ◇ *Brown doesn't* (= brown clothes do not) *suit you.* 你不適合穿棕色衣服。

■ ***verb*** [I, T] to become brown; to make sth brown（使）變成棕色；成褐色: *Heat the butter until it browns.* 把黃油加熱，使之呈棕色。◇ *The grass was browning in patches.* 草地一片片地變成褐色。◇ **~ sth** *Brown the onions before adding the meat.* 把洋蔥炒成褐色，然後放進肉。

IDM **ˌbrowned ˈoff (with sb/sth)** (*BrE, informal*) bored, unhappy and/or annoyed（對某人）厭倦，不快，煩惱 **SYN** **fed up**: *By now the passengers were getting browned off with the delay.* 此時乘客們對延誤已開始感到不滿。

ˌbrown ˈale *noun* (*BrE*) **1** [U, C] a type of mild sweet dark beer sold in bottles 棕色淡啤酒（瓶裝出售） **2** [C] a bottle or glass of brown ale 一瓶（或一杯）棕色淡啤酒

ˈbrown-bag *verb* (**-gg-**) **~ sth** (*NAmE, informal*) to bring your lunch with you to work or school, usually in a brown paper bag 自帶午餐（常用棕色紙袋）: *My kids have been* ***brown-bagging it*** *this week.* 我幾個孩子這個星期都是自帶午餐上學。

ˌbrown ˈdwarf *noun* (*astronomy* 天) an object in space that is between a large planet and a small star in size, and produces heat 棕矮星（體積在大行星和小星體之間，產生熱）

brown·field /ˈbraʊnfi:ld/ *adj.* [only before noun] (*BrE*) used to describe an area of land in a city that was used by industry or for offices in the past and that may now be cleared for new building development 棕色地帶（待重新開發的城市用地）: *a brownfield site* 城市棕色地帶工地

ˈbrown goods *noun* [pl.] small electrical items such as televisions, radios, music and video equipment 棕色家電，小型家電（如電視、收音機、視頻設備等） ➲ compare WHITE GOODS

Brown·ian motion /ˈbraʊniən məʊʃn; *NAmE* moʊʃn/ *noun* [U] (*physics* 物) the movement without any regular pattern made by very small pieces of matter in a liquid or gas 布朗運動（流體中懸浮顆粒所作的不規則運動）

brownie /ˈbraʊni/ *noun* **1** [C] a thick soft flat cake made with chocolate and sometimes nuts and served in small squares 巧克力方塊蛋糕（有時放有堅果）: *a fudge brownie* 一塊巧克力軟糖糕 **2 the Brownies** [pl.] a branch of the SCOUT ASSOCIATION for girls between the ages of seven and ten or eleven 幼女童軍（由 7 到 10 或 11 歲的女孩組成）: *to join the Brownies* 加入幼女童軍 **3** [C] **Brownie** (*BrE* also **ˈBrownie Guide**) a member of the Brownies（一個）幼女童軍 ➲ compare CUB (3), GUIDE *n.* (6), SCOUT

ˈbrownie point *noun* [usually pl.] (*informal*) if sb does sth to earn **brownie points**, they do it to make sb in authority have a good opinion of them 討好上級所得的好印象；拍馬屁得分 **ORIGIN** The Brownies is a club for young girls who are not yet old enough to be Guides. They are awarded points for good behaviour and achievements. 源自布朗尼俱樂部（the Brownies）。該俱樂部是為年齡不夠參加女童子軍的女孩設立的，表現好或有成績的女孩獎以分數鼓勵。

brown·ish /ˈbraʊnɪʃ/ (also *less frequent* **browny** /ˈbraʊni/) *adj.* fairly brown in colour 帶棕色的；近棕色的: *You can't see in this light, but my new coat is a sort of brownish colour.* 這種光線下你看不清楚，其實我的新外衣帶棕色。

ˈbrown-nose *verb* [I] (*informal, disapproving*) to treat sb in authority with special respect in order to make them approve of you or treat you better 諂媚；拍馬屁

ˈbrown-out *noun* (*especially NAmE*) a period of time when the amount of electrical power that is supplied to an area is reduced 電力減弱；電壓降低

ˌbrown ˈrat (also **ˌcommon ˈrat**, **ˌNorway ˈrat**) *noun* a common type of RAT 褐鼠；家鼠

ˌbrown ˈrice *noun* [U] rice that is light brown because it has not had all of its outside part removed 糙米

ˌbrown ˈsauce *noun* [U] **1** (*BrE*) a sauce made with VINEGAR and spices, sold in bottles（用醋、調味品等製成、瓶裝出售的）棕色調味料 **2** (*NAmE*) a sauce made with fat and flour, cooked until it becomes brown（將脂油和麵粉煮至呈棕色後製成的）棕色沙司

brown·stone /ˈbraʊnstəʊn; *NAmE* -stoʊn/ *noun* (*NAmE*) a house built of, or with a front made of, a type of reddish-brown stone, which is also called brownstone 褐沙石房屋；外牆為褐沙石的房屋；褐沙石: *New York brownstones* 紐約的褐沙石房屋

ˌbrown ˈsugar *noun* [U] sugar that has a brown colour and has only been partly REFINED 紅糖；黃糖

ˌBrown v Board of Eduˈcation *noun* a law case in 1954 which led to a decision of the US Supreme Court that made separate education for black and white children illegal 布朗起訴教育局案（1954 年導致美國最高法院作出學校種族隔離制度為非法的裁決）

B

browse /braʊz/ *verb* **1** [I, T] to look at a lot of things in a shop/store rather than looking for one particular thing（在商店裏）隨便看看：*You are welcome to come in and browse.* 歡迎您光臨本店隨便看看。◇ **~ sth** *She browsed the shelves for something interesting to read.* 她瀏覽着書架，想找本有趣的書看。**2** [I, T] **~ (through) sth** to look through the pages of a book, newspaper, etc. without reading everything 瀏覽；翻閱：*I found the article while I was browsing through some old magazines.* 我在翻閱一些舊雜誌時找到了這篇文章。**3** [I, T] **~ (sth)** (*computing* 計) to look for information on a computer, especially on the Internet（在計算機，尤指互聯網上）搜尋信息，瀏覽信息 **4** [I] **~ (on sth)** (of cows, GOATS, etc. 牛、羊等) to eat leaves, etc. that are growing high up 吃（青草、綠葉等）▸ **browse** *noun* [sing.]：*The gift shop is well worth a browse.* 這家禮品店很值得一看。

browser /ˈbraʊzə(r)/ *noun* **1** (*computing* 計) a program that lets you look at or read documents on the Internet 瀏覽程序，瀏覽器（用於在互聯網上查閱信息）：*a Web browser* 互聯網瀏覽器 ➲ COLLOCATIONS at EMAIL ➲ VISUAL VOCAB page V68 **2** a person who looks through books, magazines, etc. or at things for sale, but may not seriously intend to buy anything 瀏覽圖書報刊者；逛商店的人

brrr /brrr/ *exclamation* a sound that people make to show that they are very cold（表示感覺寒冷）呵，哦：*Brrr, it's freezing here.* 呵，這兒真冷啊。

bru·cel·losis /ˌbruːsəˈləʊsɪs; *NAmE* -ˈloʊs-/ *noun* [U] a disease caused by bacteria that affects cows and that can cause fever in humans 布魯氏菌病，布氏桿菌病（由細菌引起的牛類疾病，人類感染可引起發燒）

bruise /bruːz/ *verb, noun*

■ ***verb*** **1** [I, T] to develop a bruise, or make a bruise or bruises appear on the skin of sb/sth（使）出現傷痕；撞傷；擦傷：*Strawberries bruise easily.* 草莓容易碰傷。◇ **~ sth** *She had slipped and badly bruised her face.* 她滑了一跤，摔得鼻青臉腫。➲ SYNONYMS at INJURE ➲ COLLOCATIONS at INJURY **2** [T, usually passive] **~ sb** to affect sb badly and make them feel unhappy and less confident 打擊；挫傷：*They had been badly bruised by the defeat.* 失敗使他們的自信心大為受挫。▸ **bruised** *adj.*：*He suffered badly bruised ribs in the crash.* 他在事故中肋骨被嚴重撞傷。◇ *bruised fruit* 碰傷的水果◇ *a bruised ego* 受傷的自尊心 **bruis·ing** *noun* [U]：*She suffered severe bruising, but no bones were broken.* 她挫傷嚴重，但骨骼完好。◇ *internal bruising* 內傷 ➲ see also BRUISING *adj.*

■ ***noun*** **1** a blue, brown or purple mark that appears on the skin after sb has fallen, been hit, etc. 青腫；瘀傷；碰傷：*to be covered in bruises* 渾身青腫◇ *cuts and bruises* 傷口和瘀傷 ➲ SYNONYMS at INJURE **2** a mark on a fruit or vegetable where it is damaged（水果或蔬菜的）碰傷，傷痕

bruiser /ˈbruːzə(r)/ *noun* (*informal*) a large strong aggressive man 好勇鬥狠的彪形大漢

bruis·ing /ˈbruːzɪŋ/ *adj.* difficult and unpleasant, making you feel tired or weak 艱難討厭的；繁重麻煩的：*a bruising meeting/experience* 令人厭煩的會議；艱辛的經歷

bruit /bruːt/ *verb* **~ sth (about)** (*formal*) to spread a piece of news widely 傳播，散播（信息）：*This rumour has been bruited about for years.* 這個謠言已傳播多年了。

Brum·mie /ˈbrʌmi/ *noun* (*BrE, informal*) a person from the city of Birmingham in England（英國）伯明翰人 ▸ **Brum·mie** *adj.*：*a Brummie accent* 伯明翰口音

brunch /brʌntʃ/ *noun* [C, U] a meal that you eat in the late morning as a combination of breakfast and lunch 早午餐（早午兩餐併作一餐）

bru·nette /bruːˈnet/ *noun* (sometimes *offensive*) a white-skinned woman with dark brown hair 深褐色頭髮的白人女子 ➲ compare BLONDE *n.*, REDHEAD

brunt /brʌnt/ *noun*

IDM **bear, take, etc. the ˈbrunt of sth** to receive the main force of sth unpleasant 承受某事的主要壓力；首當其衝：*Schools will bear the brunt of cuts in government spending.* 政府削減開支，學校將首當其衝受到影響。

brus·chetta /bruˈsketə/ *noun* [U] (from *Italian*) an Italian dish consisting of pieces of warm bread covered with oil and chopped raw tomatoes（意大利）番茄塗油麪包片：*a first course of bruschetta* 番茄塗油麪包片作為第一道菜

brush 🔑 /brʌʃ/ *noun, verb*

■ ***noun*** **1** 🔑 [C] an object made of short stiff hairs (called BRISTLES) or wires set in a block of wood or plastic, usually attached to a handle. Brushes are used for many different jobs, such as cleaning, painting and tidying your hair. 刷子；毛刷；畫筆：*a paintbrush* 畫筆 ◇ *a hairbrush* 髮刷 ◇ *a toothbrush* 牙刷 ◇ *brush strokes* (= the marks left by a brush when painting) 畫筆的筆觸 ◇ *a dustpan and brush* 簸箕和刷子◇ *Apply the paint with a fine brush.* 用細畫筆塗顏料。➲ VISUAL VOCAB pages V20, V60 **2** [sing.] an act of brushing 刷：*to give your teeth a good brush* 好好刷一刷牙 **3** [sing.] a light touch made in passing sth/sb 輕擦；掠過：*the brush of his lips on her cheek* 他的嘴唇在她臉上的輕輕一碰 **4** [C] **~ with sb/sth** a short unfriendly meeting with sb; an occasion when you nearly experience sth unpleasant 小衝突；稍有不快的場合：*She had a nasty brush with her boss this morning.* 她今天早晨和老闆鬧得挺彆扭的。◇ *In his job he's had frequent brushes with death.* 他在工作中常常與死神擦肩而過。◇ *a brush with the law* 輕微的觸犯法律 **5** [U] land covered by small trees or bushes 灌木叢：*a brush fire* 灌木叢火 **6** [C] the tail of a FOX 狐狸尾巴

IDM see DAFT *adj.*, PAINT *v.*, TAR *v.*

■ ***verb*** **1** 🔑 [T] to clean, polish, or make smooth with a brush（用刷子）刷淨，刷亮，刷平順：**~ sth** *to brush your hair/teeth/shoes* 刷頭髮／牙／鞋◇ **~ sth + adj.** *A tiled floor is easy to brush clean.* 瓷磚地板容易打掃乾淨。**2** [T] to put sth, for example oil, milk or egg, on sth using a brush（用刷子）抹，塗：**~ A with B** *Brush the pastry with beaten egg.* 用刷子把打勻的雞蛋抹在油酥麪糰上。◇ **~ B over A** *Brush beaten egg over the pastry.* 用刷子把打勻的雞蛋抹在油酥麪糰上。**3** 🔑 [T] **~ sth + adv./prep.** to remove sth from a surface with a brush or with your hand（用刷子或手）拂，撣，擦掉：*He brushed the dirt off his jacket.* 他拂掉衣服上的灰塵。◇ *She brushed the fly away.* 她揮手趕走了蒼蠅。**4** [I, T] to touch sb/sth lightly while moving close to them/it 輕擦，掠過（某人／某物）：**~ against/by/past sb/sth** *She brushed past him.* 她和他擦肩而過。◇ *His hand accidentally brushed against hers.* 他的手無意之中碰了一下她的手。◇ **~ sth** *The leaves brushed her cheek.* 葉子輕拂着她的面頰。◇ **~ sth with sth** *He brushed her lips with his.* 他輕輕地吻了一下她的嘴唇。

PHR V **ˌbrush sb/sth↔aˈside** to ignore sb/sth; to treat sb/sth as unimportant 不理會某人／某物；漠視 SYN **dismiss**：*He brushed aside my fears.* 他不理會我的恐懼。**ˌbrush sb/yourself ˈdown** (*BrE*) = BRUSH SB/YOURSELF OFF **ˌbrush sth↔ˈdown** to clean sth by brushing it 刷乾淨：*to brush a coat/horse down* 把外套／馬刷乾淨 **ˌbrush ˈoff** to be removed by brushing 被刷掉；被拂去：*Mud brushes off easily when it is dry.* 泥巴乾了容易刷掉。**ˌbrush sb↔ˈoff** to rudely ignore sb or refuse to listen to them 不理睬某人；打發：*She brushed him off impatiently.* 她不耐煩地把他打發走了。➲ related noun BRUSH-OFF **ˌbrush sb/yourself ˈoff** (*BrE* **ˌbrush sb/yourself ˈdown**) to make sb/yourself tidy, especially after you have fallen, by brushing your clothes, etc. with your hands 撣淨某人／自己，拂去衣服上的灰塵（尤指跌到後）**ˌbrush sth↔ˈup** | **ˌbrush ˈup on sth** to quickly improve a skill, especially when you have not used it for a time 奮起直追（重溫生疏了的技術等）：*I must brush up on my Spanish before I go to Seville.* 我去塞維利亞之前一定得好好溫習我的西班牙語。

ˈbrush-off *noun* [sing.] (*informal*) rude or unfriendly behaviour that shows that a person is not interested in sb 漠視；不理睬：*Paul asked Tara out to dinner but she*

B

gave him the brush-off. 保羅邀請塔拉外出吃飯，但遭到拒絕。

brush·wood /ˈbrʌʃwʊd/ *noun* [U] small broken or dead branches of trees, often used to make fires（常指當柴火用的）斷樹枝，枯樹枝

brush·work /ˈbrʌʃwɜːk; *NAmE* -wɜːrk/ *noun* [U] the particular way in which an artist uses a brush to paint（畫家的）筆觸，畫法 ➲ COLLOCATIONS at ART

brusque /bruːsk; brʊsk; *NAmE* brʌsk/ *adj.* using very few words and sounding rude 寡言而無禮的 **SYN** **abrupt**, **curt**：*The doctor spoke in a brusque tone.* 醫生不客氣地簡單說了幾個字。▸ **brusque·ly** *adv.*：*'What's your name?' he asked brusquely.* "你叫什麼名字？"他唐突地問道。**brusque·ness** *noun* [U]

Brus·sels sprout /ˌbrʌslz ˈspraʊt/ (also **Brussel sprout**, **sprout**) *noun* a small round green vegetable like a very small CABBAGE 湯菜；抱子甘藍 ➲ VISUAL VOCAB page V31

bru·tal /ˈbruːtl/ *adj.* **1** violent and cruel 殘暴的；獸性的：*a brutal attack/murder/rape/killing* 野蠻的攻擊／謀殺／強姦／殺害 **2** direct and clear about sth unpleasant; not thinking of people's feelings 直截了當的；冷酷的：*With brutal honesty she told him she did not love him.* 她冷酷地直接告訴他，她不愛他。▸ **bru·tal·ity** /bruːˈtæləti/ *noun* [U, C] (*pl.* **-ies**)：*police brutality* 警察的粗暴 ◇ *the brutalities of war* 戰爭的殘酷 **bru·tal·ly** /-təli/ *adv.*：*He was brutally assaulted.* 他遭到毒打。◇ *Let me be brutally frank about this.* 讓我把這件事無情地挑明說吧。

bru·tal·ism /ˈbruːtəlɪzəm/ *noun* [U] (*architecture* 建) (sometimes *disapproving*) a style of architecture used especially in the 1950s and 60s which uses large concrete blocks, steel, etc., and is sometimes considered ugly and unpleasant 粗野主義，野性主義，粗獷主義（尤見於 20 世紀 50 和 60 年代的建築風格，採用大塊混凝土板、鋼筋等，有時被認為粗陋欠雅）▸ **bru·tal·ist** /ˈbruːtəlɪst/ *adj.*, *noun*

bru·tal·ize (*BrE* also **-ise**) /ˈbruːtəlaɪz/ *verb* **1** [usually passive] **~ sb** to make sb unable to feel normal human emotions such as pity 使喪失人類情感；使變殘忍：*soldiers brutalized by war* 在戰爭中變得殘酷無情的士兵 **2 ~ sb** to treat sb in a cruel or violent way 殘酷對待

brute /bruːt/ *noun*, *adj.*

■ *noun* **1** (sometimes *humorous*) a man who treats people in an unkind, cruel way 殘酷的人；暴君：*His father was a drunken brute.* 他父親是個蠻橫的醉鬼。◇ *You've forgotten my birthday again, you brute!* 你又忘了我的生日了，你這個沒良心的！ **2** a large strong animal 大野獸；牲畜 **3** a thing which is awkward and unpleasant 突兀難看的東西；麻煩事

■ *adj.* [only before noun] **1** involving physical strength only and not thought or intelligence 蠻幹不動腦筋的：***brute force/strength*** 暴力；蠻勁 **2** basic and unpleasant 根本而令人不快的；赤裸裸的：*the brute facts of inequality* 赤裸裸的不平等事實

bru·tish /ˈbruːtɪʃ/ *adj.* unkind and violent and not showing thought or intelligence 殘忍的；粗野的；蠻橫的 ▸ **bru·tish·ness** *noun* [U]

BS (*NAmE* also **B.S.**) /ˌbiː ˈes/ *abbr.* **1** (*NAmE*) = BSc **2** (*BrE*) Bachelor of Surgery (a university degree in medicine) 外科學士（大學醫學學位） **3** British Standard (used on labels, etc. showing a number given by the British Standards Institution which controls the quality of products) 英國標準（寫在商品標籤上，表明英國標準協會的規格編號）：*produced to BS4353* 按英國標準規格編號 4353 生產的 **4** (*US*, *taboo*, *slang*) BULLSHIT 胡說；狗屁：*That guy's full of BS.* 那傢伙滿嘴噴糞。

BSc /ˌbiː es ˈsiː/ (*BrE*) (*NAmE* **B.S.**, **BS**) *noun* the abbreviation for 'Bachelor of Science' (a first university degree in science) 理學士（全寫為 Bachelor of Science，大學理科初級學位）：(*BrE*) *to* ***be/have/do a BSc*** *in Zoology* 是／有／攻讀動物學理學士（學位）◇ (*BrE*) *Jill Ayres BSc* 理學士吉爾 • 艾爾斯

BSE /ˌbiː es ˈiː/ (also *informal* **ˌmad ˈcow disease**) *noun* [U] the abbreviation for 'bovine spongiform encephalopathy' (a brain disease of cows that causes death) 瘋牛病（全寫為 bovine spongiform encephalopathy，導致牛死亡的腦病）

BSI /ˌbiː es ˈaɪ/ *abbr.* the British Standards Institution (the organization that decides the standard sizes for goods produced in Britain, and tests the safety of electrical goods, children's toys, etc.) 英國標準協會（負責制訂英國國內產品的規格標準並檢測電器商品、兒童玩具等的安全）

ˈB-side *noun* the side of a pop record that was considered less likely to be successful（唱片的）B 面（一般認為較平庸）➲ compare A-SIDE

BST /ˌbiː es ˈtiː/ *abbr.* BRITISH SUMMER TIME 英國夏令時間（全寫為 British Summer Time）

BTEC /ˈbiːtek/ *noun* used to refer to any of a large group of British qualifications that can be taken in many different subjects at several levels (the abbreviation for 'Business and Technology Education Council') 商業與技術教育委員會（全寫為 Business and Technology Education Council，BTEC 在英國代表多個學科的不同程度資格）：*a BTEC Higher National Diploma in Public Service Studies* * BTEC 公共服務科高等國家證書

BTW *abbr.* used in writing to mean 'by the way'（書寫形式）順便提一句

bub·ble 0━ /ˈbʌbl/ *noun*, *verb*

■ *noun* **1** 0━ a ball of air or gas in a liquid, or a ball of air inside a solid substance such as glass 泡；氣泡：*champagne bubbles* 香檳酒的泡沫 ◇ *a bubble of oxygen* 氧氣泡 ◇ *blowing bubbles into water through a straw* 用麥管在水裏吹泡泡 ➲ picture at FROTH ➲ see also SPEECH BUBBLE **2** 0━ a round ball of liquid, containing air, produced by soap and water 肥皂泡：*The children like to have bubbles in their bath.* 孩子們喜歡浴盆裏有肥皂泡。 **3** a small amount of a feeling that sb wants to express（欲表達的）一點感情：*a* ***bubble of laughter/hope/enthusiasm*** 一點笑聲／希望／熱心 **4** a good or lucky situation that is unlikely to last long（很可能持續不長的）好景，好運；泡沫：*At the time the telecoms bubble was at its height.* 當時電信業的泡沫正處於極度膨脹時期。

IDM **the bubble ˈbursts** there is a sudden end to a good or lucky situation（好事或好運）突然告吹，成為泡影；泡沫破滅：*When the bubble finally burst, hundreds of people lost their jobs.* 當泡沫最終破滅時，有幾百人丟了飯碗。➲ more at BURST *v.*

■ *verb* **1** [I] to form bubbles 起泡；冒泡：*The water in the pan was beginning to bubble.* 鍋裏的水開始冒泡。◇ *Add the white wine and let it* ***bubble up***. 加入白葡萄酒，讓它產生泡沫。 **2** [I] (**+ adv./prep.**) to make a bubbling sound, especially when moving in the direction mentioned（移動時）發出冒泡的聲音：*I could hear the soup bubbling away.* 我聽到湯在咕嘟咕嘟地響。◇ *A stream came bubbling between the stones.* 一條小溪沿着石縫汩汩地流過來。 **3** [I] **~ (over) with sth** to be full of a particular feeling 洋溢着（某種感情）：*She was bubbling over with excitement.* 她興奮不已。 **4** [I] **+ adv./prep.** (of a feeling 感情) to be felt strongly by a person; to be present in a situation 強烈感受；充溢；存在：*Laughter bubbled up inside him.* 他忍不住心中竊笑。◇ *the anger that bubbled beneath the surface* 內心潛湧着的憤怒

PHR V **ˌbubble ˈunder** (*especially BrE*) (*NAmE* usually **ˌbubble under the ˈradar**) (*informal*) to be likely to be very successful or popular soon 即將成功；快要出名：*Here are two records that are bubbling under.* 這兩張唱片將會走紅。

ˌbubble and ˈsqueak *noun* [U] a type of British food made from cold cooked potatoes and CABBAGE that are mixed together and fried 捲心菜煎土豆（英國菜）

ˈbubble bath *noun* **1** [U] a liquid soap that smells pleasant and makes a lot of bubbles when it is added to bath water 泡沫浴液 **2** [C] a bath with bubble bath in the water 泡沫浴

bubble·gum /ˈbʌblgʌm/ *noun*, *adj.*

■ *noun* [U] a type of CHEWING GUM that can be blown into bubbles 泡泡糖

B

■ *adj.* [only before noun] simple in style, not serious and liked mainly by young people "泡泡糖"的（簡單隨意，主要為年輕人所喜歡）: *This CD is pure bubblegum pop.* 這張 CD 純粹是"泡泡糖"流行音樂。

bubble·jet printer /ˈbʌbldʒet prɪntə(r)/ *noun* a type of printer that uses bubbles of air to blow small dots of ink in order to form letters, numbers, etc. on paper 噴墨打印機

ˈ**bubble pack** *noun* = BLISTER PACK

ˈ**bubble wrap** (*BrE*) (*NAmE* ˈ**Bubble Wrap™**) *noun* [U] a sheet of plastic which has lots of small raised parts filled with air, used for protecting things that are being carried or sent by post/mail 氣泡膜包裝；泡塑包裝；氣泡墊

bubb·ly /ˈbʌbli/ *adj.* (**bub·blier**, **bub·bli·est**) *noun*
■ *adj.* **1** full of bubbles 充滿氣泡的；多泡沫的 **2** (*informal*) (of a person 人) always cheerful, friendly and enthusiastic 快活熱情的
■ *noun* [U] (*informal*) = CHAMPAGNE

bu·bon·ic plague /bjuːˌbɒnɪk ˈpleɪɡ; *NAmE* -ˌbɑːnɪk/ (also **the plague**) *noun* [U] a disease spread by RATS that causes fever, swellings on the body and usually death 腺鼠疫；腹股溝淋巴結鼠疫

buc·can·eer /ˌbʌkəˈnɪə(r); *NAmE* -ˈnɪr/ *noun* **1** (in the past) a sailor who attacked ships at sea and stole from them（舊時）海盜 SYN **pirate** **2** (especially in business 尤指商業) a person who achieves success in a skilful but not always honest way 投機取巧者

bucc·an·eer·ing /ˌbʌkəˈnɪərɪŋ; *NAmE* -ˈnɪrɪŋ/ *adj.* enjoying taking risks, especially in business 愛冒險的，大膽的（尤指經商方面）: *Virgin's buccaneering founder, Richard Branson* 維珍公司富有冒險精神的創始人里查德 • 布蘭森

buck /bʌk/ *noun, verb*
■ *noun* **1** [C] (*informal*) a US, Australian or New Zealand dollar; a South African RAND; an Indian RUPEE（一）美元；（一）澳元；（一）新西蘭元；（一）南非蘭特；（一）印度盧比: *They cost ten bucks.* 這些值十元錢。◇ *We're talking **big bucks*** (= a lot of money) *here.* 我們這當兒談的可是大買賣。 **2** [C] a male DEER, HARE or RABBIT (also called a **buck rabbit**) 雄鹿；公兔 ➲ compare DOE, HART, STAG **3** [C] (*pl.* **buck**) (*SAfrE*) a DEER, whether male or female 鹿（不論雌雄）: *a herd of buck* 一群鹿 **4** [C] (*old-fashioned, informal*) a young man 小伙子 **5 the buck** [sing.] used in some expressions to refer to the responsibility or blame for sth（用於某些表達方式）責任，過失: *It was my decision. **The buck stops here*** (= nobody else can be blamed). 那是我的決定，不要追究別人了。◇ *I was tempted to **pass the buck*** (= make sb else responsible). 我很想把責任推給別人。 ORIGIN From **buck**, an object which in a poker game is placed in front of the player whose turn it is to deal. 源自 buck（培克），撲克牌遊戲中的莊家標誌。
IDM **make a fast/quick buck** (*informal, often disapproving*) to earn money quickly and easily 輕易地賺錢 ➲ more at BANG *n.*, MILLION
■ *verb* **1** [I] (of a horse 馬) to jump with the two back feet or all four feet off the ground 尥起後蹄跳躍；弓背四蹄跳起 **2** [I] to move up and down suddenly or in a way that is not controlled 猛然震盪；猛烈顛簸: *The boat bucked and heaved beneath them.* 小船在他們腳下猛烈顛簸着。 **3** [T] **~ sth** (*informal*) to resist or oppose sth 抵制；反抗: *One or two companies have managed to **buck the trend** of the recession.* 有一兩家公司頂住了經濟滑坡的勢頭。◇ *He admired her willingness to **buck the system*** (= oppose authority or rules). 他讚賞她反抗現存體制的主動性。
IDM **buck your ˈideas up** (*BrE, informal*) to start behaving in a more acceptable way, so that work gets done better, etc. 振作起來
PHR V ˌ**buck ˈup** (*informal*) **1** (often in orders 常用於命令) to become more cheerful 振作 SYN **cheer up**: *Buck up, kid! It's not the end of the game.* 年輕人，振作起來！比賽還未結束呢。 **2 buck up!** (*old-fashioned*) used to tell sb to hurry 快點；趕快 SYN **hurry up** ˌ**buck sb ˈup** (*BrE, informal*) to make sb more cheerful 使某人振作 SYN **cheer up**: *The good news bucked us all up.* 好消息使我們全都為之振奮。

bucket /ˈbʌkɪt/ *noun, verb*
■ *noun* **1** (*NAmE* also **pail**) [C] an open container with a handle, used for carrying or holding liquids, sand, etc.（有提梁的）桶: *a plastic bucket* 塑料桶 ◇ (*BrE*) *They were playing on the beach with their **buckets and spades**.* 他們帶着桶和鏟子在沙灘上玩。 ➲ VISUAL VOCAB page V20 **2** [C] a large container that is part of a CRANE or DIGGER and is used for lifting things 大桶狀物；（起重機的）吊斗；（挖土機的）鏟斗 ➲ VISUAL VOCAB page V58 **3** (also **bucket·ful** /-fʊl/) (*NAmE* also **pail**, **pail·ful**) [C] the amount contained in a bucket 一桶（的量）: *two buckets/bucketfuls of water* 兩桶水 ◇ *They used to drink tea **by the bucket/bucketful*** (= in large quantities). 他們過去喝很多茶。 **4 buckets** [pl.] (*informal*) a large amount 大量: *To succeed in show business, you need buckets of confidence.* 要想在演藝界幹出名堂，就得有十足的信心。◇ *We **wept buckets**.* 我們淚如泉湧。◇ *He was **sweating buckets** by the end of the race.* 跑到終點時他汗流浹背。◇ *The rain was coming down **in buckets*** (= it was raining very heavily). 下着瓢潑大雨。
IDM see DROP *n.*, KICK *v.*
■ *verb*
PHR V ˈ**bucket down** (*BrE, informal*) to rain heavily 下大雨 SYN **pour**: *It's bucketing down.* 大雨傾盆。

ˈ**bucket seat** *noun* a seat with a curved back for one person, especially in a car（尤指汽車上的）凹背單人座位

ˈ**bucket shop** *noun* (*informal, especially BrE*) a place that sells cheap plane tickets 廉價機票店

buck·eye /ˈbʌkaɪ/ *noun* **1** a N American tree that has bright red or white flowers and produces nuts 鹿眼樹，七葉樹（產於北美洲） **2** an orange and brown BUTTERFLY with large spots on its wings that look like eyes（橙棕雜色的）眼形斑翅蝴蝶 **3 Buckeye** (*US, informal*) a person from the US state of Ohio 俄亥俄州人

ˌ**Buck ˈHouse** *noun* (*BrE*, often *ironic*) an informal name for Buckingham Palace 白金漢宮（非正式名稱）: *We stayed at Tom's place. It isn't exactly Buck House, but it's comfortable enough.* 我們待在湯姆那裏。那並不是白金漢宮，但足夠舒適了。

Buck·ing·ham Pal·ace /ˌbʌkɪŋəm ˈpæləs/ *noun* **1** the official home of the British royal family in London 白金漢宮（在倫敦的英國王室官邸） **2** the British royal family or the people who advise them 英國王室；英國王室幕僚: *Buckingham Palace refused to comment.* 英國王室拒絕發表評論。

buckle /ˈbʌkl/ *verb, noun*
■ *verb* **1** [T, I] to fasten sth or be fastened with a buckle（使）搭扣扣住: **~ (sth)** *She buckled her belt.* 她扣上了腰帶。◇ **~ (sth on/up)** *He buckled on his sword.* 他把劍扣好。◇ *These shoes buckle at the side.* 這雙鞋從旁邊上扣。 **2** [I, T] to become crushed or bent under a weight or force; to crush or bend sth in this way（被）壓垮，壓彎: *The steel frames began to buckle under the strain.* 鋼架在重壓下開始變形。◇ (*figurative*) *A weaker man would have buckled under the pressure.* 意志薄弱的人在這種壓力下可能就垮了。◇ **~ sth** *The crash buckled the front of my car.* 我的汽車前部被撞扁了。 **3** [I] when your knees or legs **buckle** or when you **buckle** at the knees, your knees become weak and you start to fall 雙腿發軟
PHR V ˌ**buckle ˈdown (to sth)** (*informal*) to start to do sth seriously 開始認真做；努力幹: *I'd better buckle down to those reports.* 我最好認真靜下來努力完成那些報告。 ˌ**buckle ˈup** (*NAmE*) (*BrE* ˌ**belt ˈup**) (*informal*) to fasten your SEAT BELT (= a belt worn by a passenger in a vehicle) 繫上安全帶
■ *noun* a piece of metal or plastic used for joining the ends of a belt or for fastening a part of a bag, shoe, etc.（皮帶等的）搭扣，鎖扣 ➲ VISUAL VOCAB pages V63, V64

Buck·ley's /ˈbʌkliz/ *noun*
IDM **not have Buckley's (chance)** (*AustralE, NZE, informal*) used to suggest that sb has little or no hope of achieving a particular aim 希望（或機會）渺茫

buck 'naked *adj.* (*NAmE, informal*) (of a person 人) not wearing any clothes at all 一絲不掛的；赤裸裸的

buck·ram /ˈbʌkrəm/ *noun* [U] a type of stiff cloth made especially from cotton or LINEN, used in the past for covering books and for making clothes stiffer （舊時用作書皮或衣服襯裏的）硬棉布，硬麻布，硬襯布

,Buck's 'Fizz (*BrE*) (*NAmE* **mi·mosa**) *noun* [U, C] an alcoholic drink made by mixing SPARKLING white wine (= with bubbles) with orange juice 巴克泡騰酒（發泡白葡萄酒與橙汁混合而成）

buck·shot /ˈbʌkʃɒt; *NAmE* -ʃɑːt/ *noun* [U] balls of LEAD that are fired from a SHOTGUN （獵槍用的）鉛彈

buck·skin /ˈbʌkskɪn/ *noun* [U] soft leather made from the skin of DEER or GOATS, used for making gloves, bags, etc. 鹿皮革；羊皮革

,buck 'teeth *noun* [pl.] top teeth that stick forward 齙牙 ▸ **,buck-'toothed** *adj.*

buck·wheat /ˈbʌkwiːt/ *noun* [U] small dark grain that is grown as food for animals and for making flour 蕎麥

bu·col·ic /bjuːˈkɒlɪk; *NAmE* -ˈkɑːlɪk/ *adj.* (*literary*) connected with the countryside or country life 鄉村的；鄉村生活的；田園的

bud /bʌd/ *noun, verb*

■ *noun* **1** a small lump that grows on a plant and from which a flower, leaf or STEM develops 芽；苞；花蕾：*the first buds appearing in spring* 春天的初芽 ◇ *The tree is **in bud** already.* 樹已長出花蕾。➲ COLLOCATIONS at LIFE ➲ VISUAL VOCAB page V10 **2** a flower or leaf that is not fully open 半開的花；未長大的葉 ➲ VISUAL VOCAB page V11 **3** (*NAmE, informal*) = BUDDY：*Listen, bud, enough of the wisecracks, OK?* 聽着，老兄，別再說俏皮話了行不行？➲ see also COTTON BUD, ROSEBUD, TASTE BUD
IDM see NIP *v.*

■ *verb* [I] to produce buds 發芽

Bud·dha /ˈbʊdə/ *noun* **1** (also **the Buddha**) [sing.] the person on whose teachings the Buddhist religion is based 佛陀（佛教創始人） **2** [C] a statue or picture of the Buddha 佛像 **3** [C] a person who has achieved ENLIGHTENMENT (= spiritual knowledge) in Buddhism 佛，覺者，知者（佛教中覺行圓滿的人）

Bud·dhism /ˈbʊdɪzəm/ *noun* [U] an Asian religion based on the teaching of Siddhartha Gautama (or Buddha) 佛教 ▸ **Bud·dhist** /ˈbʊdɪst/ *noun*：*a devout Buddhist* 虔誠的佛教徒 **Bud·dhist** /ˈbʊdɪst/ *adj.* [usually before noun]：*a **Buddhist monk/temple*** 佛教僧侶／寺廟

bud·ding /ˈbʌdɪŋ/ *adj.* [only before noun] beginning to develop or become successful 開始發展的；嶄露頭角的：*a **budding artist/writer*** 一位藝術界／文壇新秀 ◇ *our budding romance* 我們剛剛發展起來的戀愛關係

bud·dleia /ˈbʌdliə/ *noun* [C, U] a bush with purple or white flowers that grow in groups 醉魚草屬植物

buddy /ˈbʌdi/ *noun, verb*

■ *noun* (*pl.* **-ies**) **1** (*NAmE* also **bud**) (*informal*) a friend 朋友；同伴：*an old college buddy of mine* 我的一位老校友 **2** (also **bud**) (both *NAmE, informal*) used to speak to a man you do not know （稱呼不認識的男子）老兄，喂：*'Where to, buddy?' the driver asked.* "去哪兒，老兄？"司機問道。 **3** (*especially NAmE*) a partner who does an activity with you so that you can help each other 搭檔；夥伴：*The school uses a **buddy system** to pair newcomers with older students.* 學校採用結伴制讓每個新生跟一較大的學生結伴以獲得照顧。

■ *verb* (**bud·dies, buddy·ing, bud·died, bud·died**)
PHR V **,buddy 'up (to/with sb)** (*NAmE*) **1** (*BrE* **,pal 'up (with sb)**) (*informal*) to become friendly with sb 成為（某人的）朋友：*You and your neighbour might want to buddy up to make the trip more enjoyable.* 你同你的鄰居或許想結伴旅遊，熱鬧一點。 **2** to become friendly with sb in order to get an advantage for yourself （為謀私利）親近（某人），（和某人）結交

'buddy movie *noun* (*informal*) a film/movie in which there is a close friendship between two people 夥伴電影（兩角色之間關係密切）

budge /bʌdʒ/ *verb* (usually used in negative sentences 通常用於否定句) (rather *informal*) **1** [I, T] to move slightly; to make sth/sb move slightly （使）輕微移動，挪動：*She pushed at the door but it wouldn't budge.* 她推了推門，門卻一動不動。◇ *The dog refused to budge.* 狗不肯動彈。◇ **~ sth** *I heaved with all my might but still couldn't budge it.* 我用盡全力也沒把它拽動。 **2** [I, T] to change your opinion about sth; to make sb change their opinion （使）改變主意，改變觀點：*He **won't budge an inch** on the issue.* 在這一點上他絲毫不肯讓步。◇ **~ sb** *He was not to be budged on the issue.* 在這一點上他不會讓步。
PHR V **,budge 'up** (*BrE, informal*) to move, so that there is room for other people 讓開；挪開 SYN **move up**：*Budge up a bit!* 閃開點！

budg·eri·gar /ˈbʌdʒərigɑː(r)/ *noun* (also *informal* **budgie**) (both *BrE*) a small bird of the PARROT family, often kept in a CAGE as a pet 虎皮鸚鵡

budget 🔑 /ˈbʌdʒɪt/ *noun, verb, adj.*

■ *noun* **1** 🔑 [C, U] the money that is available to a person or an organization and a plan of how it will be spent over a period of time 預算：*a **monthly/an annual/a family budget*** 每月／年度／家庭預算 ◇ *the **education/defence budget*** (= the amount of money that can be spent on this) 教育／國防預算 ◇ *an advertising budget of $2 million* 預計 200 萬元的廣告費 ◇ *a big-budget movie* 一部巨額預算的電影 ◇ *We decorated the house **on a tight budget*** (= without much money to spend). 我們儉省地裝修了房子。◇ *The work was finished on time and **within budget*** (= did not cost more money than was planned). 工作按時完成且未超出預算。◇ *They went **over budget*** (= spent too much money). 他們超出了預算。◇ *budget cuts* 預算削減 ➲ COLLOCATIONS at BUSINESS, FINANCE **2** (*BrE* also **Budget**) [C, usually sing.] an official statement by the government of a country's income from taxes, etc. and how it will be spent 政府的年度預算：*tax cuts in this year's budget* 本年度政府預算中的稅收削減 ◇ *a budget deficit* (= when the government spends more money than it earns) 政府預算赤字 ➲ COLLOCATIONS at ECONOMY

■ *verb* [I, T] to be careful about the amount of money you spend; to plan to spend an amount of money for a particular purpose 謹慎花錢；把…編入預算：*If we budget carefully we'll be able to afford the trip.* 我們精打細算一點，就能夠負擔這次旅行。◇ **~ for sth** *I've budgeted for two new members of staff.* 我已經把兩名新職員名額編入預算。◇ **~ sth (for sth)** *Ten million francs has been budgeted for the project.* 為該工程已編制了一千萬法郎的預算。◇ **~ sth (at sth)** *The project has been budgeted at ten million francs.* 該工程已制訂一千萬法郎的預算。➲ SYNONYMS at SAVE ▸ **budget·ing** *noun* [U]

■ *adj.* [only before noun] (used in advertising, etc. 用於廣告等) low in price 價格低廉的；花錢少的：*a **budget flight/hotel*** 便宜的航班／旅館 ➲ SYNONYMS at CHEAP

'budget account *noun* (*BrE*) an arrangement with a shop/store or company to pay your bills in fixed regular amounts and not as one large payment 預算賬戶（作定期付賬之用）

budget·ary /ˈbʌdʒɪtəri; *NAmE* -teri/ *adj.* connected with a budget 預算的：*budgetary control/policies/reform* 預算控制／政策／改革 ➲ SYNONYMS at ECONOMIC

budgie /ˈbʌdʒi/ *noun* (*BrE, informal*) = BUDGERIGAR

buff /bʌf/ *noun, adj., verb*

■ *noun* **1** [C] (used in compounds 用於構成複合詞) a person who is very interested in a particular subject or activity and knows a lot about it 愛好者；行家裏手：*an opera buff* 歌劇愛好者 **2** [U] a pale yellow-brown colour 米色；淺黃褐色 SYN **beige** **3** [U] soft strong yellowish-brown leather 堅韌的黃褐色軟皮革 ➲ see also BLIND MAN'S BUFF
IDM **in the 'buff** (*informal*) wearing no clothes 一絲不掛；赤裸 SYN **naked**

■ *adj.* **1** pale yellow-brown in colour 淺黃褐色的 SYN **beige**：*a buff envelope* 淺黃褐色信封 **2** (*slang*) physically fit and attractive with big muscles 健美（或健壯）而肌肉發達的

■ *verb* **~ sth (up)** to polish sth with a soft cloth 用軟布擦亮
PHR V **,buff 'up | ,buff yourself 'up** (*slang*) to make yourself more attractive, especially by exercising in

B

order to make your muscles bigger 練健美；使更健美：*He buffed up to take the role of the commando captain.* 他為飾演這個突擊隊隊長的角色練出了一身肌肉。**ˌbuff sb/sth ˈup** (*informal*) to work on sb/sth to make them/it seem more attractive or impressive 提升…的形象：*The team will have to buff up their tarnished image.* 這支隊伍必須改善其受損的形象。

buf·falo /ˈbʌfələʊ; *NAmE* -loʊ/ *noun* (*pl.* **buf·falo** or **buf·faloes**) **1** a large animal of the cow family. There are two types of buffalo, the African and the Asian, which has wide, curved horns. 水牛（分非洲水牛和亞洲水牛兩種）➲ see also WATER BUFFALO **2** = BISON

buf·fer /ˈbʌfə(r)/ *noun, verb*

■ ***noun*** **1** a thing or person that reduces a shock or protects sb/sth against difficulties 緩衝物；起緩衝作用的人：**~ (against sth)** *Support from family and friends acts as a buffer against stress.* 家庭和朋友的支持有助於減緩壓力。◇ **~ (between sth and sth)** *She often had to act as a buffer between father and son.* 她常常不得不在父子之間扮演調解人角色。◇ *a* ***buffer state*** (= a small country between two powerful states that helps keep peace between them) 緩衝國（兩敵對大國之間有助於維持和平的小國家）◇ *a* ***buffer zone*** (= an area of land between two opposing armies or countries) 緩衝區（兩敵對軍隊或國家之間的地區）**2** (*BrE*) one of two round metal devices on the front or end of a train, or at the end of a railway/railroad track, that reduce the shock if the train hits sth（火車頭尾或軌道末端的）減震器，緩衝器 **3** (*computing* 計) an area in a computer's memory where data can be stored for a short time 緩存區；緩衝存貯區；緩衝存貯器 **4** (also **old ˈbuffer**) (*old-fashioned, BrE*) a silly old man 愚蠢老頭 **IDM** see HIT *v.*

■ ***verb*** **1 ~ sth** to reduce the harmful effects of sth 減少，減緩（傷害）：*to buffer the effects of stress on health* 減少壓力對健康的影響 **2 ~ sb (against sth)** to protect sb from sth 保護；使不受…的侵害：*They tried to buffer themselves against problems and uncertainties.* 他們盡力保護自己免受困難和不確定因素的影響。**3 ~ sth** (*computing* 計) (of a computer 計算機) to hold data for a short time before using it 緩衝存貯；緩存

buf·fet¹ /ˈbʊfeɪ; ˈbʌfeɪ; *NAmE* bəˈfeɪ/ *noun* ➲ see also BUFFET² **1** a meal at which people serve themselves from a table and then stand or sit somewhere else to eat 自助餐：*a* ***buffet lunch/supper*** 自助午餐／晚餐◇ *Dinner will be a cold buffet, not a sit-down meal.* 主餐是自助冷食，不是坐着等服務員送來的那種。**2** a place, for example in a train or bus station, where you can buy food and drinks to eat or drink there, or to take away（火車）飲食櫃枱；（車站）快餐部 **3** (*BrE*) = BUFFET CAR **4** (*especially NAmE*) = SIDEBOARD (1)

buf·fet² /ˈbʌfɪt/ ➲ see also BUFFET¹ *verb* [often passive] **~ sb/sth** to knock or push sb/sth roughly from side to side 打來打去；推來搡去：*to be buffeted by the wind* 被風吹得左右搖擺◇ (*figurative, formal*) *The nation had been buffeted by a wave of strikes.* 罷工浪潮使這個國家受到了重創。▸ **buf·fet·ing** *noun* [U, C, usually sing.]

buffet car /ˈbʊfeɪ kɑː(r); ˈbʌfeɪ; *NAmE* bəˈfeɪ/ (also **buffet**) *noun* (*BrE*) the part of a train where you can buy sth to eat and drink（火車）餐車

buf·foon /bəˈfuːn/ *noun* (*old-fashioned*) a person who does silly but amusing things 小丑；滑稽可笑的人 ▸ **buf·foon·ery** /-əri/ *noun* [U]

bug /bʌg/ *noun, verb*

■ ***noun*** **1** [C] (*especially NAmE*) any small insect 小昆蟲；蟲子 **2** [C] (*informal*) an infectious illness that is usually fairly mild 輕微的傳染病；小病：*a flu bug* 流感◇ *There's a stomach* ***bug going round*** (= people are catching it from each other). 現在流行一種腸胃傳染病。◇ *I picked up a bug in the office.* 我在辦公室被傳染了疾病。➲ **SYNONYMS** at DISEASE ➲ **COLLOCATIONS** at ILL **3** (usually **the … bug**) [sing.] (*informal*) an enthusiastic interest in sth such as a sport or a hobby 熱衷；着迷：*the travel bug* 旅遊狂熱◇ *She was never interested in fitness before but now* ***she's been bitten by the bug.*** 她以前從來不在乎健身，現在她卻着了迷。**4** [C] (*informal*) a small hidden device for listening to other people's conversations 竊聽器 **5** [C] a fault in a machine, especially in a computer system or program（機器，尤指計算機的）故障，程序錯誤，缺陷 **6** [C] (*NAmE*) = BEETLE at BEETLE *n.* (2)

■ ***verb*** (-gg-) **1 ~ sth** to put a special device (= a bug) somewhere in order to listen secretly to other people's conversations 裝竊聽器：*They bugged her hotel room.* 他們在她的旅館房間裏裝了竊聽器。◇ *They were bugging his telephone conversations.* 他們在竊聽他的電話交談。◇ *a bugging device* 竊聽器 **2 ~ sb** (*informal*) to annoy or irritate sb 使煩惱；使惱怒：*Stop bugging me!* 別煩我了！◇ *It's something that's been bugging me a lot recently.* 那事使我最近一直大傷腦筋。

IDM **ˌbug the ˈhell/ˈcrap/ˈshit out of sb** (*taboo, slang*) to annoy sb very much 使十分煩惱；使惱怒：*The song just bugs the hell out of me.* 這首歌真他媽的煩死我了。

PHR V **bug ˈoff!** (*NAmE, informal*) a rude way of telling sb to go away 滾開 **ˌbug ˈout** (*informal*) **1** (*NAmE*) (especially of sb's eyes) to be wide open and stick out（尤指眼睛）圓瞪着：*Their eyes were bugging out of their heads when they saw it.* 他們看到它時眼珠都瞪掉了。**2** (*NAmE, AustralE*) to leave a place or situation, especially because it is becoming dangerous（尤指危險來臨之時）撤離，逃生：*We should bug out now before it's too late.* 我們現在就應該撤離，以免為時太晚。**3** (*NAmE*) to become too frightened to do sth 驚呆了：*Susan started to bug out when she heard a noise in the bushes.* 蘇珊聽到灌木叢中的聲音時嚇呆了。

bug·a·boo /ˈbʌgəbuː/ *noun* (*NAmE, informal*) a thing that people are afraid of 恐怖的東西

bug·bear /ˈbʌgbeə(r); *NAmE* -ber/ *noun* (*especially BrE*) a thing that annoys people and that they worry about 使人煩惱擔憂的事；牽掛：*Inflation is the government's main bugbear.* 通貨膨脹是政府最頭痛的問題。

ˈbug-eyed *adj.* (*informal*) having eyes that stick out 眼睛凸出的

bug·ger /ˈbʌgə(r)/ *noun, verb*

■ ***noun*** (*BrE, taboo, slang*) **1** an offensive word used to insult sb, especially a man, and to show anger or dislike（侮辱性稱呼，尤用於男子）傢伙；渾蛋；壞蛋：*Come here, you little bugger!* 過來，你這個小渾蛋！◇ *You stupid bugger! You could have run me over!* 蠢貨！你差點兒碾死我！**2** used to refer to a person, especially a man, that you like or feel sympathy for（表示親昵或同情，尤用於男子）小伙子；老頭兒；漢子：*Poor bugger! His wife left him last week.* 可憐的傢伙！他妻子上週離開了他。◇ *He's a tough old bugger.* 他是個鐵漢子。**3** [usually sing.] a thing that is difficult or causes problems 難題；麻煩的事：*This door's a bugger to open.* 這扇門很難打開。◇ *Question 6 is a real bugger.* 第 6 題真難。**IDM** see SILLY *adj.*

■ ***verb*** **1** [I, T] (*BrE, taboo, slang*) used as a swear word when sb is annoyed about sth or to show that they do not care about sth at all（生氣或不在乎時說）該死，媽的，去它的：*Bugger! I've left my keys at home.* 媽的！我把鑰匙忘在家裏了。◇ **~ sth** *Bugger it! I've burnt the toast.* 該死！我把麪包烤煳了。◇ *Oh, bugger the cost! Let's get it anyway.* 嗨，管它多貴！咱們還是買了吧。**2** [T] **~ sth** (*BrE, taboo, slang*) to break or ruin sth 毀壞：*I think I've buggered the computer.* 我想我把計算機搞壞了。**3** [T] **~ sb** (*taboo* or *law* 律) to have ANAL sex with sb 雞姦（某人）

IDM **ˌbugger ˈme** (*BrE, taboo, slang*) used to express surprise（表示驚奇）好傢伙；哎呀：*Bugger me! Did you see that?* 好傢伙！你看見了嗎？

PHR V **ˌbugger aˈbout/aˈround** (*BrE, taboo, slang*) to waste time by behaving in a silly way or with no clear purpose 閒混；胡鬧：*Stop buggering about and get back to work.* 別瞎混了，回去幹活吧。**HELP** A more polite, informal way of saying this is **mess about** (*BrE*) or **mess around** (*NAmE, BrE*). 較禮貌和非正式的說法是 mess about（英式英語）或 mess around（美式、英式英語）。**ˌbugger sb aˈbout/aˈround** (*BrE, taboo, slang*) to treat sb in a way that is deliberately not helpful to them or wastes their time 難為某人；故意浪費某人的時間：*I'm sick of being buggered about by the company.* 那家公司就跟我拖着，我真是受夠了。**HELP** A more polite, informal way of saying this is **mess sb about/around**.

較禮貌和非正式的說法是 mess sb about/around。**ˌbugger ˈoff** (*BrE, taboo, slang*) (often used in orders 常用於命令) to go away 走開：*Bugger off and leave me alone.* 走開，別管我。◇ *Where is everyone? They've all buggered off.* 大家都在哪兒呀？他們都走了。**ˌbugger sth↔ˈup** (*BrE, taboo, slang*) to do sth badly or spoil sth 弄糟；破壞；糟蹋：*I buggered up the exam.* 我考試考砸了。◇ *Sorry for buggering up your plans.* 對不起，打亂了你的計劃。**HELP** A more polite, informal way of saying this is **foul sth up**, **mess sth up** or **bungle sth**. 較禮貌和非正式的說法是 foul sth up、mess sth up 或 bungle sth。

ˌbugger ˈall *noun* [U] (*BrE, taboo, slang*) nothing at all; none at all 什麼也沒有；屁都沒有：*There's bugger all on TV tonight.* 今晚電視屁也沒有。◇ *Well, she was bugger all help* (= no help at all). 咳，她幫個屁忙。

bug·gered /ˈbʌɡəd; *NAmE* -ɡərd/ *adj.* [not before noun] (*BrE, taboo, slang*) **1** very tired 累得要死；筋疲力盡 **2** broken or ruined 毀壞；壞掉：*Oh no, the TV's buggered.* 哎呀！電視機壞了。

IDM **I'll be buggered** (*BrE, taboo, slang*) used to express great surprise（表示吃驚）：*Well, I'll be buggered! Look who's here.* 嘀，老天爺！看是誰在這兒。**I'm ˈbuggered if ...** (*BrE, taboo, slang*) used to say that you do not know sth or to refuse to do sth（表示不知道或拒絕做某事）：*'What's this meeting all about?' 'I'm buggered if I know.'* "這次開的是什麼會？" "我要是知道才怪呢。" ◇ *Well I'm buggered if I'm going to help her after what she said to me.* 哼，她對我說那種話，我再也不會幫她了。

bug·gery /ˈbʌɡəri/ *noun* [U] (*BrE, taboo, slang* or *law* 律) ANAL sex 雞姦

Bug·gins' turn /ˈbʌɡɪnz tɜːn; ˈbʌɡɪnzɪz; *NAmE* tɜːrn/ *noun* [U] (*BrE, informal*) used to refer to the way in which it sometimes seems that people get jobs or are promoted not because they are good at what they do, but because they have been doing it for longer than anybody else 論資排輩；輪流坐莊

Synonyms 同義詞辨析

build

construct • assemble • erect • put sth up

These words all mean to make sth, especially by putting different parts together. 以上各詞均含製造、建造之意。

build to make sth, especially a building, by putting parts together 指製造、建造、修建（尤指房屋）：*a house built of stone* 用石頭建造的房子 ◇ *They're going to build on the site of the old power station.* 他們要在老發電站那裏蓋房子。

construct [often passive] (*rather formal*) to build sth such as a road, building or machine 指修建、建造（公路、房屋、機器等）

assemble (*rather formal*) to fit together all the separate parts of sth such as a piece of furniture or a machine 指裝配、組裝（傢具、機器等）：*The cupboard is easy to assemble.* 這個櫥櫃容易組裝。

erect (*formal*) to build sth; to put sth in position and make it stand upright 指建立、建造、安裝、豎立、搭起：*Police had to erect barriers to keep crowds back.* 警察只得設立路障來阻截人群。

put sth up to build sth or place sth somewhere 指搭建、建立、設立、設置：*They're putting up new hotels in order to boost tourism in the area.* 他們正在蓋新旅館以促進該地區的旅遊業。

PATTERNS

- to build/construct/erect/put up a **house/wall**
- to build/construct/erect/put up some **shelves**
- to build/construct/erect/put up a **barrier/fence/shelter**
- to build/construct/assemble a(n) **engine/machine**
- to build/construct a **road/railway/railroad/tunnel**
- to erect/put up a **tent/statue/monument**

buggy /ˈbʌɡi/ *noun* (*pl.* **-ies**) **1** (*BrE*) (*NAmE* **cart**) a small car, often without a roof or doors, used for a particular purpose（常指無頂無門的）專用小汽車：*a garden/golf buggy* 花園／高爾夫球場小汽車 ➲ see also BEACH BUGGY **2** (also **ˈBaby Buggy™**) (both *BrE*) (*NAmE* **stroll·er**) a type of light folding chair on wheels in which a baby or small child is pushed along 嬰兒車；童車 ➲ compare PUSHCHAIR **3** a light CARRIAGE for one or two people, pulled by one horse（由一匹馬拉的單座或雙座）輕便馬車

bugle /ˈbjuːɡl/ *noun* a musical instrument like a small TRUMPET, used in the army for giving signals 軍號

bu·gler /ˈbjuːɡlə(r)/ *noun* a person who plays the bugle 司號兵；號手

bui·bui /ˈbʊibʊi/ *noun* (*EAfrE*) an item of clothing worn by some Muslim women, consisting of a long black dress and piece of black cloth that covers the head showing only the face or eyes 布依布依（一些穆斯林婦女穿戴的黑長袍頭巾）

build 🔑 /bɪld/ *verb, noun*

■ *verb* (**built**, **built** /bɪlt/) **1** 🔑 [T, I] to make sth, especially a building, by putting parts together 建築；建造：**~ (sth)** *They have permission to build 200 new houses.* 他們得到建 200 座新房的許可。◇ *Robins build nests almost anywhere.* 知更鳥幾乎可隨處築巢。◇ *They're going to build on the site of the old power station.* 他們要在老發電站那裏蓋房子。◇ **~ sth of/in/from sth** *a house built of stone* 用石頭建造的房子 ◇ **~ sth for sb** *They had a house built for them.* 他們讓人給他們建了一棟房子。◇ **~ sb sth** *David built us a shed in the back yard.* 戴維幫我們在後院搭了個棚子。**2** 🔑 [T] **~ sth** to create or develop sth 創建；開發：*She's built a new career for herself.* 她為自己開闢了一條新的謀生之路。◇ *We want to build a better life.* 我們想創造更美好的生活。◇ *This information will help us build a picture of his attacker.* 這條信息將有助於描畫出襲擊他的人的相貌。**3** [I] (of a feeling 感覺) to become gradually stronger 逐漸增強：*The tension and excitement built gradually all day.* 那一整天裏緊張與興奮的氣氛越來越濃。**IDM** see CASTLE, ROME

PHR V **ˌbuild sth aˈround sth** [usually passive] to create sth, using sth else as a basis 在…基礎上創作：*The story is built around a group of high school dropouts.* 故事圍繞着一群輟學的中學生展開。**ˌbuild sth↔ˈin** | **ˌbuild sth ˈinto sth** [often passive] **1** to make sth a permanent part of a larger structure 把…建造在（較大的建築物）裏；使…固定於：*We're having new wardrobes built in.* 我們的新衣櫥是嵌入式的。◇ *The pipes were built into the concrete.* 管子已固定在混凝土裏。**2** to make sth a permanent part of a system, plan, etc. 使…成為（體系、計劃等的）組成部份：*A certain amount of flexibility is built into the system.* 該體系加入了一定的靈活性。➲ see also BUILT-IN **ˈbuild on sth** to use sth as a basis for further progress 在…的基礎上發展：*This study builds on earlier work.* 這項研究是在以往工作的基礎上進行的。**ˈbuild sth on sth** [usually passive] to base sth on sth 把…作為…的基礎：*an argument built on sound logic* 建立在邏輯基礎上的站得住腳的論點 **ˌbuild sth↔ˈon** | **ˌbuild sth ˈonto sth** to add sth (for example, an extra room) to an existing structure by building 在（已有建築物上）增建某物：*They've built an extension on.* 他們進行了一項擴建。◇ *The new wing was built onto the hospital last year.* 醫院的新翼樓是去年增建的。**ˌbuild ˈup (to sth)** 🔑 to become greater, more powerful or larger in number 加大；加強；增多：*All the pressure built up and he was off work for weeks with stress.* 各方面的壓力越來越大，他因負荷太重有好幾個星期沒上班。◇ *The music builds up to a rousing climax.* 音樂逐漸達到了令人振奮的高潮。➲ related noun BUILD-UP (1) **ˌbuild ˈup to sth** | **ˌbuild yourself ˈup to sth** to prepare for a particular moment or event 為…作準備：*Build yourself up to peak performance on the day of the exam.* 好好準備在考試那天發揮出最高水平。➲ related noun BUILD-UP (2) **ˌbuild sb/sth ˈup** [usually passive] to give a very positive and enthusiastic description of sb/sth, often exaggerating your claims 吹捧；鼓吹：*The play*

B

was built up to be a masterpiece but I found it very disappointing. 那部戲被捧為傑作，可我卻大失所望。➲ related noun BUILD-UP (3) **ˌbuild sb/yourself↔ˈup** to make sb/yourself healthier or stronger 增強…的體質；使更加強壯：*You need more protein to build you up.* 你得多吃蛋白質以增強體質。**ˌbuild sth↔ˈup 1** 🔑 to create or develop sth 創建；開發：*She's built up a very successful business.* 她創辦的生意很紅火。◇ *These finds help us **build up a picture** of life in the Middle Ages.* 這些發現有助於建構中世紀的生活畫面。◇ *I am anxious not to **build up false hopes*** (= to encourage people to hope for too much). 我非常着意不要讓大家期望過高。**2** to make sth higher or stronger than it was before 增高；加強

■ ***noun*** [U, C, usually sing.] the shape and size of the human body 體形；體格；身材：*a man of average build* 中等身材的人

build·er /ˈbɪldə(r)/ *noun* **1** a person or company whose job is to build or repair houses or other buildings 建築工人；建築公司；營造商 **2** (usually in compounds 通常構成複合詞) a person or thing that builds, creates or develops sth 建築者；創建者；開發者：*a shipbuilder* 造船工人 ◇ *a confidence builder* 令人增強信心的事物 ➲ see also BODYBUILDER at BODYBUILDING

ˈbuilders' merchant *noun* a person or shop that supplies materials to the building trade 建材商；建材商店

Synonyms 同義詞辨析

building

property • premises • complex • structure • block

These are all words for a structure such as a house, office block or factory that has a roof and four walls 以上各詞均指建築物、房屋、樓房。

building a structure such as a house, office block or factory that has a roof and four walls 指建築物、房屋、樓房

property a building or buildings and the surrounding land; land and buildings 指房屋及院落、莊園、房地產：*We have a buyer who would like to view the property.* 我們有一買主想看這房產。◇ *The price of property has risen enormously.* 房地產的價格大幅上升了。NOTE This word is often used when talking about buying/selling houses or other buildings and land. 談及買賣房屋或房地產時常用該詞。

premises [pl.] the building or buildings and surrounding land that a business owns or uses 指企業擁有或使用的建築及附屬場地、營業場所：*The company is looking for larger premises.* 這家公司正在尋找更大的營業場所。

complex a group of buildings of a similar type together in one place 指類型相似的建築群：*a leisure complex* 休閒活動中心

structure a thing that is made of several parts, especially a building 指結構體、建築物：*The pier is a wooden structure.* 這個碼頭是木結構建築。

block (*BrE*) a tall building that contains flats or offices; a building that forms part of a school, hospital, etc. and is used for a particular purpose 指公寓、辦公大樓或學校、醫院等作特定用途的大樓：*a block of flats* 公寓大樓 ◇ *the school's science block* 這所學校的理科大樓

PATTERNS

- a(n) **commercial/industrial/residential** building/property/premises/complex/block
- an **apartment** building/complex/block
- a/the **school** building/premises
- to **build** a property/complex/structure/block
- to **put up** a building/property/structure/block
- to **demolish/pull down** a building/property/complex/structure/block

build·ing 🔑 /ˈbɪldɪŋ/ *noun*
1 🔑 [C] a structure such as a house or school that has a roof and walls 建築物；房子；樓房：*tall/old/historic buildings* 高大／老／有歷史意義的建築物 ➲ COLLOCATIONS at DECORATE ➲ VISUAL VOCAB page V15 **2** 🔑 [U] the process and work of building 建築；建築業：*the building of the school* 學校的修建 ◇ *There's building work going on next door.* 鄰居正大興土木。◇ *the building trade* 建築業 ◇ ***building materials/costs/regulations*** 建築材料／費用／規章

ˈbuilding block *noun* **1** [C] a piece of wood or plastic used as a toy for children to build things with 積木；塑料積木 ➲ VISUAL VOCAB page V37 **2 building blocks** [pl.] parts that are joined together in order to make a large thing exist 組成部份；構成要素：*Single words are the building blocks of language.* 單詞是語言結構的基本單位。

ˈbuilding site (*especially BrE*) (*NAmE* usually **conˈstruction site**) *noun* an area of land where sth is being built 建築工地

ˈbuilding society *noun* (*BrE*) (*US* **ˌsavings and ˈloan association**) an organization like a bank that lends money to people who want to buy a house. People also save money with a building society. 房屋互助協會（提供住房貸款及儲蓄服務）

ˈbuild-up *noun* **1** [sing., U] an increase in the amount of sth over a period of time 逐步的增長：*a steady build-up of traffic in the evenings* 晚間逐漸繁忙的交通 **2** [C, usually sing.] **~ (to sth)** the time before an important event, when people are preparing for it （重要事情的）準備期，準備過程：*the build-up to the President's visit* 總統訪問前的準備工作 **3** [C, usually sing.] a very positive and enthusiastic description of sth that is going to happen, that is intended to make people excited about it 宣揚；鼓吹：*The media have given the show a huge build-up.* 傳媒為這次演出大力造勢。

built /bɪlt/ *combining form* (after adverbs and in compound adjectives 用於副詞後，或構成複合形容詞) made in the particular way that is mentioned …建成的；…造的：*a newly built station* 新建的車站 ◇ *American-built cars* 美國製造的汽車 ➲ see also PURPOSE-BUILT, WELL BUILT

ˌbuilt-ˈin (also *less frequent* **ˌin-ˈbuilt**) *adj.* [only before noun] included as part of sth and not separate from it 是…的組成部份的；嵌入式的；內置的：*built-in cupboards* 壁櫥 ➲ compare INBUILT

ˌbuilt-ˈup *adj.* [usually before noun] (*especially BrE*) (of an area of land 地區) covered in buildings, roads, etc. 建築物密集的：*to reduce the speed limit in built-up areas* 在樓房林立的地區降低最高車速限制

bulb /bʌlb/ *noun* **1** (also **ˈlight bulb**) the glass part that fits into an electric lamp, etc. to give light when it is switched on 電燈泡：*a 60-watt bulb* * 60 瓦的燈泡 ◇ *a room lit by bare bulbs* (= with no decorative cover) 只有光禿禿的電燈泡照明的屋子（無燈罩、燈飾）➲ VISUAL VOCAB page V21 **2** the round underground part of some plants, shaped like an onion , that grows into a new plant every year （植物）鱗莖 ➲ VISUAL VOCAB page V11 **3** an object shaped like a bulb, for example the end of a THERMOMETER 鱗莖狀物（如溫度計的球部）

bulb·ous /ˈbʌlbəs/ *adj.* shaped like a bulb; round and fat in an ugly way 鱗莖狀的；圓胖難看的：*a bulbous red nose* 蒜頭紅鼻子

bul·gar (also **bul·gur**) /ˈbʌlgə(r)/ (also **ˈbulgar wheat**) *noun* [U] a type of food consisting of grains of WHEAT that are boiled then dried 乾小麥，蒸穀麥（將小麥煮後烘乾）

bulge /bʌldʒ/ *verb, noun*

■ ***verb*** **1** [I] **~ (with sth)** (usually used in the progressive tenses 通常用於進行時) to be completely full (of sth) 充滿，塞滿（某物）：*Her pockets were bulging with presents.* 她的口袋裏裝滿了禮物。◇ *a bulging briefcase* 鼓鼓囊囊的公文包 **2** [I] to stick out from sth in a round shape 凸出；鼓脹：*His eyes bulged.* 他雙眼凸出。

IDM see SEAM

■ ***noun*** **1** a lump that sticks out from sth in a round shape 鼓起；凸起：*the bulge of a gun in his pocket* 他衣

袋裏鼓起一把槍的模樣 **2** (*informal*) fat on the body that sticks out in a round shape （身體的）肥胖部位：*That skirt's too tight. It shows all your bulges.* 那條裙子太緊了，把你的發胖部位全顯出來了。 **3** a sudden temporary increase in the amount of sth 一時的激增；暴漲：*After the war there was a bulge in the birth rate.* 戰後出生率激增。

bul·ging /ˈbʌldʒɪŋ/ *adj.* that sticks out from sth in a round shape 鼓起的；隆起的：*bulging eyes* 凸出的眼睛

bu·limia /buˈlɪmiə; bju-; -ˈliːmiə/ (also **bulimia nervosa** /buˌlɪmiə nɜːˈvəʊsə; *NAmE* nɜːrˈvoʊsə/) *noun* [U] an emotional DISORDER in which a person repeatedly eats too much and then forces him- or herself to VOMIT 貪食症；食慾過盛 ➲ **COLLOCATIONS** at DIET ➲ compare ANOREXIA ▸ **bu·lim·ic** /buˈlɪmɪk; bju-; -ˈliːmɪk/ *adj.*, *noun*

bulk AW /bʌlk/ *noun*, *verb*

■ ***noun*** **1** [sing.] **the ~** (**of sth**) the main part of sth; most of sth 主體；大部份：*The bulk of the population lives in cities.* 大多數人口居住在城市裏。 **2** [U] the (large) size or quantity of sth （大）體積；大（量）：*Despite its bulk and weight, the car is extremely fast.* 儘管這輛車大而且重，速度卻非常快。◇ *a* ***bulk order*** (= one for a large number of similar items) 一份大批量的訂單 ◇ ***bulk buying*** (= buying in large amounts, often at a reduced price) （常指以低價）大量購買 ◇ *It's cheaper to buy* ***in bulk***. 大批購買便宜些。 **3** [sing.] the weight or shape of sb/sth large 巨大的體重（或重量、形狀、身體等）：*She heaved her bulk out of the chair.* 她挪動龐大的軀體，費力地從椅子裏站起來。

■ ***verb***

IDM **bulk ˈlarge** (*BrE*, *formal*) to be the most important part of sth 是…的最重要部份

PHR V **ˌbulk sth↔ˈout/ˈup** to make sth bigger, thicker or heavier 使某物加大（或加厚、加重）

bulk·head /ˈbʌlkhed/ *noun* (*technical* 術語) a wall that divides a ship or an aircraft into separate parts （船的）艙壁；（飛機的）隔板

bulky AW /ˈbʌlki/ *adj.* (**bulk·ier**, **bulki·est**) **1** (of a thing 東西) large and difficult to move or carry 龐大的；笨重的：*Bulky items will be collected separately.* 大件物品將分開收集。 **2** (of a person 人) tall and heavy 大塊頭的；高大肥胖的：*The bulky figure of Inspector Jones appeared at the door.* 瓊斯督察的壯碩身軀出現在門口。

bull /bʊl/ *noun* **1** [C] the male of any animal in the cow family 公牛：*a bull neck* (= a short thick neck like a bull's) （公牛般的）短粗脖子 ➲ compare BULLOCK, COW *n.* (1), OX, STEER *n.* (2) **2** [C] the male of the ELEPHANT, WHALE and some other large animals （象、鯨等動物的）雄獸 ➲ compare COW *n.* (2) **3** [C] (*finance* 財) a person who buys shares in a company, hoping to sell them soon afterwards at a higher price （預期證券價格上升的）買空者，多頭 ➲ compare BEAR *n.* (2) **4** [C] an official order or statement from the POPE (= the head of the Roman Catholic Church) 教宗詔書；教宗訓諭：*a papal bull* 教宗訓諭 **5** [U] (*slang*) = BULLSHIT：*That's a load of bull!* 那是胡說八道！ **6** [C] = BULLSEYE ➲ see also COCK AND BULL STORY

IDM **a bull in a ˈchina shop** a person who is careless, or who moves or acts in a rough or awkward way, in a place or situation where skill and care are needed （不顧環境）笨拙莽撞的人，冒失鬼 **take the bull by the ˈhorns** to face a difficult or dangerous situation directly and with courage 勇敢面對困境（或險境） ➲ more at RED *adj.*, SHOOT *v.*

ˈbull bars *noun* [pl.] (*BrE*) a set of strong metal bars fixed to the front of a large vehicle to protect it from damage （大汽車前端的）保險槓

bull·dog /ˈbʊldɒɡ; *NAmE* -dɔːɡ/ *noun* a short strong dog with a large head, a short flat nose and a short thick neck 鬥牛狗，牛頭犬（頭大鼻短平、脖子短粗）

ˈBulldog clip™ *noun* (*BrE*) a metal device for holding papers together 布爾多戈牌金屬紙夾 ➲ **VISUAL VOCAB** page V69

bull·doze /ˈbʊldəʊz; *NAmE* -doʊz/ *verb* **1** [T] **~ sth** to destroy buildings, trees, etc. with a bulldozer （用推土機）推倒，鏟平：*The trees are being bulldozed to make way for a new superstore.* 那片樹正被推土機鏟除，以興建一家新超市。 **2** [I, T] to force your way somewhere; to force sth somewhere （使）強行通過：**+ adv./prep.** *Rooney bulldozed through to score.* 魯尼強攻突破得分。◇ **~ sth + adv./prep.** *They bulldozed the tax through Parliament.* 他們強行使稅收提案在議會通過。◇ *He* ***bulldozed his way*** *to victory.* 他一路上過關斬將，取得了最後勝利。 **3** [T] **~ sb** (**into doing sth**) to force sb to do sth 強迫（某人做某事） SYN **railroad**：*They bulldozed him into selling.* 他們脅迫他賣出。

B

bull·dozer /ˈbʊldəʊzə(r); *NAmE* -doʊz-/ *noun* a powerful vehicle with a broad steel blade in front, used for moving earth or knocking down buildings 推土機 ➲ **VISUAL VOCAB** page V58

bull·dyke (also **bull·dike**) /ˈbʊldaɪk/ *noun* (*offensive*) a LESBIAN who is thought to look very male or to act in a typically male way 女公牛（指女子同性戀中充當男角者）

bul·let 🔑 /ˈbʊlɪt/ *noun*
a small metal object that is fired from a gun 子彈；彈丸：*bullet wounds* 槍傷 ◇ *There were bullet holes in the door.* 門上有彈孔。◇ *He was killed by a bullet in the head.* 他頭部中彈死亡。 ➲ see also MAGIC BULLET, PLASTIC BULLET, RUBBER BULLET IDM see BITE *v.*

bul·letin /ˈbʊlətɪn/ *noun* **1** a short news report on the radio or television （電台或電視台的）新聞簡報 **2** an official statement about sth important 公告；佈告：*a bulletin on the President's health* 關於總統健康的公告 **3** a printed report that gives news about an organization or a group （機構或組織的）簡報

ˈbulletin board *noun* **1** (*NAmE*) (*BrE* **no·tice·board**) (also **board** *BrE*, *NAmE*) a board for putting notices on 告示牌；佈告板 ➲ **VISUAL VOCAB** page V69 **2** (*computing* 計) a place in a computer system where any user can write or read messages 公告牌；佈告欄

ˈbullet point *noun* an item in a list in a document, that is printed with a square, diamond or circle in front of it in order to show that it is important. The square, etc. is also called a bullet point. 點句重要項目（文件中列舉時用正方形、菱形等點句符開始）；點句符；項目符號

bul·let·proof /ˈbʊlɪtpruːf/ *adj.* that can stop bullets from passing through it 防彈的：*a bulletproof vest* 防彈背心

ˈbullet train *noun* (*informal*) a Japanese train that carries passengers at high speeds （日本載客的）高速列車，子彈列車

bull·fight /ˈbʊlfaɪt/ *noun* a traditional public entertainment, popular especially in Spain, in which BULLS are fought and usually killed （尤指盛行於西班牙的）鬥牛表演 ▸ **bull·fight·er** *noun* **bull·fight·ing** *noun* [U] ➲ see also MATADOR

bull·finch /ˈbʊlfɪntʃ/ *noun* a small European bird of the FINCH family, with a strong curved beak and a pink breast 紅腹灰雀

bull·frog /ˈbʊlfrɒɡ; *NAmE* -frɔːɡ; -frɑːɡ/ *noun* a large American FROG with a loud CROAK （美洲）牛蛙

bull·head·ed /ˌbʊlˈhedɪd/ *adj.* (*NAmE*) unwilling to change your opinion about sth, in a way that other people think is annoying and unreasonable 固執的；死心眼兒的 SYN **obstinate, stubborn** ▸ **bull·head·ed·ness** *noun* [U]

bull·horn /ˈbʊlhɔːn; *NAmE* -hɔːrn/ (*NAmE*) (*BrE* **loud·hail·er**) *noun* an electronic device, shaped like a horn, with a MICROPHONE at one end, that you speak into in order to make your voice louder so that it can be heard at a distance 電子喇叭；擴音器 ➲ compare MEGAPHONE

bul·lion /ˈbʊliən/ *noun* [U] gold or silver in large amounts or in the form of bars 大量的金（或銀）；金（或銀）條：*gold bullion* 金條

bull·ish /ˈbʊlɪʃ/ *adj.* **1** feeling confident and positive about the future 對未來有信心的；積極樂觀的：*in a bullish mood* 滿懷希望 **2** (*finance* 財) causing, or connected with, an increase in the price of shares

(對股票價格)看漲的；牛市的：*a bullish market* 牛市 ➲ compare BEARISH

B

'bull market *noun* (*finance* 財) a period during which share prices are rising and people are buying shares 牛市（股票價格上升、股民紛紛購買股票的時期）➲ compare BEAR MARKET

ˌbull 'mastiff *noun* a large strong dog with short smooth hair 鬥牛獒

bul·lock /'bʊlək/ *noun* a young BULL (= a male cow) that has been CASTRATED (= had part of its sex organs removed) 閹小公牛 ➲ compare OX (1), STEER *n.* (2)

bull·pen /'bʊlpen/ *noun* (*NAmE*) **1** the part of a BASEBALL field where players practise PITCHING (= throwing) before the game（棒球場中的）賽前投手練習區 **2** extra PITCHERS (= players who throw the ball) in a BASEBALL team who are used, if necessary, to replace the usual pitchers 全體候補投手：*The team's bullpen is solid this year.* 今年該隊的候補投手實力不錯。 **3** a type of large office which is OPEN-PLAN (= it does not have walls dividing the office area) 敞開式辦公室 **4** a room where prisoners wait before they go into the court for their trial（嫌犯）候審室

bull·ring /'bʊlrɪŋ/ *noun* the large round area, like an outdoor theatre, where BULLFIGHTS take place 鬥牛場

bull·rush = BULRUSH

'bull session *noun* (*NAmE, informal*) an occasion when people meet and talk in an informal way 閒談；聊天

bulls·eye /'bʊlzaɪ/ (also **bull**) *noun* [usually sing.] the centre of the target that you shoot or throw at in shooting, ARCHERY or DARTS; a shot or throw that hits this 靶心；鵠的；命中靶心：*He scored a bullseye.* 他命中了靶心。➲ VISUAL VOCAB page V40

bull·shit /'bʊlʃɪt/ *noun, verb*

■ ***noun*** [U] (*taboo, slang*) (also *informal* **bull**) (*abbr.* **BS**) nonsense 胡說；狗屁：*That's just bullshit.* 那純粹是胡說。

■ ***verb*** (**-tt-**) [I, T] (*taboo, slang*) to say things that are not true, especially in order to trick sb 胡說（尤指哄騙）：*She's just bullshitting.* 她不過是在瞎扯。◇ **~ sb** *Don't try to bullshit me!* 休想哄我！▸ **bull·shit·ter** *noun*

ˌbull 'terrier *noun* a strong dog with short hair, a thick neck and a long nose 鬥牛㹴狗（毛短脖子粗、身體壯實）➲ see also PIT BULL TERRIER

bully /'bʊli/ *noun, verb, exclamation*

■ ***noun*** (*pl.* **-ies**) a person who uses their strength or power to frighten or hurt weaker people 仗勢欺人者；橫行霸道者：*the school bully* 學校裏的惡霸學生

■ ***verb*** (**bul·lies, bully·ing, bul·lied, bul·lied**) to frighten or hurt a weaker person; to use your strength or power to make sb do sth 恐嚇；傷害；脅迫：**~ sb** *My son is being bullied at school.* 我兒子在學校裏受欺負。◇ **~ sb into sth/into doing sth** *I won't be bullied into signing anything.* 我絕不會屈服於壓力簽署任何東西。▸ **bully·ing** *noun* [U]：*Bullying is a problem in many schools.* 很多學校都出現學生仗勢作惡的問題。◇ *He refused to give in to bullying and threats.* 他拒不向恐嚇威逼勢力讓步。◇ ***bullying behaviour/tactics*** 霸道行為／手段 ➲ COLLOCATIONS at EDUCATION

■ ***exclamation***

IDM **bully for you, etc.** (*informal*) used to show that you do not think that what sb has said or done is very impressive 沒什麼了不起：*He's got a job in New York? Well, bully for him!* 他在紐約找到了份工作？哼，那沒什麼了不起！

'bully boy *noun* (*BrE, informal*) an aggressive violent man 流氓；惡霸：*The group have frequently used bully-boy tactics.* 那個團夥常常要流氓。

'bully pulpit *noun* [sing.] (*NAmE*) a position of authority that gives sb the opportunity to speak in public about an issue 名望講壇（能提供機會闡明自己觀點的重要公職）

bul·rush (also **bull·rush**) /'bʊlrʌʃ/ *noun* a tall plant with long narrow leaves and a long brown head of flowers, that grows in or near water 藨草；寬葉香蒲；燈芯草 ➲ VISUAL VOCAB page V11

bul·wark /'bʊlwək; *NAmE* -wɜːrk/ *noun* **1** [usually sing.] **~ (against sth)** (*formal*) a person or thing that protects or defends sth 保護者，防禦者（指人或事物）：*a bulwark against extremism* 堅決反對極端主義的人 **2** [C] a wall built as a defence 堡壘；防禦工事 **3** [usually pl.] the part of a ship's side that is above the level of the DECK（船的）舷牆

bum /bʌm/ *noun, verb, adj.*

■ ***noun*** (*informal*) **1** (*BrE*) the part of the body that you sit on 屁股 SYN **backside, behind, bottom** **2** (*especially NAmE*) a person who has no home or job and who asks other people for money or food 流浪乞丐；無業遊民：*a beach bum* (= sb who spends all their time on the beach, without having a job) 海濱流浪漢 **3** a lazy person who does nothing for other people or for society 懶漢；遊手好閒者：*He's nothing but a no-good bum!* 他不過是個沒用的懶漢。

IDM **bums on 'seats** (*BrE, informal*) used to refer to the number of people who attend a show, talk, etc., especially when emphasizing the need or desire to attract a large number 觀眾（或聽眾）的數量大（尤用於強調吸引大量觀眾的需要或願望）：*They're not bothered about attracting the right audience—they just want bums on seats.* 他們不在乎觀眾是什麼樣的人，只求賣座。 **give sb/get the ˌbum's 'rush** (*informal, especially NAmE*) to force sb/be forced to leave a place quickly 趕走某人；被攆走：*He was soon given the bum's rush from the club.* 他很快從俱樂部裏被攆了出來。

■ ***verb*** (**-mm-**) **1 ~ sth (off sb)** (*informal*) to get sth from sb by asking 提出要；乞討 SYN **cadge**：*Can I bum a cigarette off you?* 給我一根煙好嗎？ **2 ~ sb (out)** (*NAmE, informal*) to make sb feel upset or disappointed 使不安；使灰心

PHR V **ˌbum a'round/a'bout** (*informal*) to travel around or spend your time with no particular plans（漫無目的地）閒蕩，漫遊：*He bummed around the world for a year.* 他在世界各地漫遊了一年。

■ ***adj.*** [only before noun] (*informal*) of bad quality; wrong or useless 劣質的；錯誤的；沒用的：*He didn't play one bum note.* 他一個音也沒奏錯。◇ ***a bum deal*** (= a situation where you do not get what you deserve or have paid for) 不合算的交易

bum·bag /'bʌmbæg/ (*BrE*) (*NAmE* **'fanny pack**) *noun* (*informal*) a small bag attached to a belt and worn around the waist, to keep money, etc. in（圍在腰間，放錢物的）腰包 ➲ VISUAL VOCAB page V64

bum·ble /'bʌmbl/ *verb* [I] **+ adv./prep.** to act or move in an awkward or confused way 笨手笨腳；跌跌撞撞：*I could hear him bumbling around in the kitchen.* 我聽得見他在廚房裏瞎折騰。

bumble·bee /'bʌmblbiː/ *noun* a large BEE covered with small hairs that makes a loud noise as it flies 熊蜂；大黃蜂 ➲ VISUAL VOCAB page V13

bum·bling /'bʌmblɪŋ/ *adj.* [only before noun] behaving in an awkward confused way, often making careless mistakes 笨手笨腳的（常馬虎出錯）

bumf (also **bumph**) /bʌmf/ *noun* [U] (*BrE, informal*) written information, especially advertisements, official documents, forms, etc., that seem boring or unnecessary 乏味（或多餘）的書面材料（尤指廣告、公文、表格等）：*He threw away my letter, thinking it was just more election bumf.* 他扔掉我的信，以為那不過又是些選舉傳單。

bum·fluff /'bʌmflʌf/ *noun* [U] (*informal*) the soft hair that grows on the upper lip and chin of a boy, as his beard begins to grow（男孩開始長鬍子時上唇的）茸毛，小鬍子

bum·mer /'bʌmə(r)/ *noun* **a bummer** [sing.] (*informal*) a disappointing or unpleasant situation 失望（或不愉快）的局面：*It's a real bummer that she can't come.* 她不能來，實在令人失望。

bump /bʌmp/ *verb, noun*

■ ***verb*** **1** [I] to hit sb/sth by accident（無意地）碰，撞：**~ into sb/sth** *In the dark I bumped into a chair.* 我在黑暗中撞上了一把椅子。◇ **~ against sb/sth** *The car bumped* *against the kerb.* 汽車撞上了路緣。➲ SYNONYMS at HIT **2** [T] **~ sth (against/on sth)** to hit sth, especially a part of your body, against or on sth（尤指身體部位）碰上，撞上：*Be careful not to bump your head on the beam when you stand up.* 當心站起來時頭別撞了橫梁。 **3** [I, T] to move across a rough surface 顛簸行進： **+ adv./prep.** *The jeep bumped along the dirt track.* 吉普車在土路上顛簸着行駛。◇ **~ sth + adv./prep.** *The car* ***bumped its way*** *slowly down the drive.* 汽車沿車道緩慢地顛簸行進。 **4** [T] **~ sb + adv./prep.** to move sb from one group or position to another; to remove sb from a group 把（某人）掉換到（另一群體或位置）；調出，開除出（某群體）：*The airline apologized and bumped us up to first class.* 航空公司道歉後把我們掉換到頭等艙。◇ *If you are bumped off an airline because of overbooking, you are entitled to compensation.* 假如機票超售而不能登機，你有權獲得賠償。◇ *The coach told him he had been bumped from the crew.* 教練通知他已被調出賽艇隊。

PHR V **ˌbump ˈinto sb** (*informal*) to meet sb by chance 碰見；偶然遇見 **ˌbump sb↔ˈoff** (*informal*) to murder sb 謀殺；殺害 **ˌbump sth↔ˈup** (*informal*) to increase or raise sth 增加；提高 **ˌbump ˈup against sth** to experience a problem or factor that you did not expect 突然碰到；遭遇到：*We kept bumping up against inflexible regulations.* 我們不斷遭遇到僵化的管理條例。

■ ***noun*** **1** [C] the action or sound of sth hitting a hard surface 碰撞（聲）；撞擊（聲）：*He fell to the ground* ***with a bump.*** 他砰的一聲摔倒在地上。◇ *We could hear loud bumps from upstairs where the children were playing.* 我們聽到孩子們在樓上嬉戲的乒乓聲。 **2** [C] a swelling on the body, often caused by a blow 腫塊（常因擊打所致）SYN **lump**：*She was covered in bumps and bruises.* 她全身青腫，傷痕纍纍。◇ *How did you get that bump on your forehead?* 你額頭上怎麼起了個包？ **3** [C] a part of a flat surface that is not even, but raised above the rest of it 隆起；凸塊：*a bump in the road* 路面上的凸塊 ➲ see also BUMPY (1) **4** [C] a slight accident in which your vehicle hits sth 輕微撞車事故 **5 the bumps** [pl.] (*BrE*) (on a child's birthday) the act of lifting the child in the air and then putting them down on the ground, once for every year of their age 生日舉放儀式（在孩子生日時將其舉高後再放在地上的儀式，舉放次數與年齡相等）：*We gave her the bumps.* 我們給她舉行了生日舉放儀式。IDM see EARTH *n.*, THING

bump·er /ˈbʌmpə(r)/ *noun, adj.*

■ ***noun*** a bar fixed to the front and back of a car, etc. to reduce the effect if it hits anything（汽車頭尾的）保險槓：*a* ***bumper sticker*** (= a sign that people stick on the bumperof their cars with a message on it) 貼在保險槓上的小標語◇ *The cars were* ***bumper to bumper*** *on the road to the coast* (= so close that their bumpers were nearly touching). 車輛一輛緊接一輛把通往海岸的馬路擠得水泄不通。➲ VISUAL VOCAB page V52

■ ***adj.*** [only before noun] (*approving*) unusually large; producing an unusually large amount 異常大的；豐盛的：*a bumper issue* (= of a magazine, etc.)（期刊的）特大號◇ *a* ***bumper crop/harvest/season/year*** 豐收；豐收季節；豐收年

ˈbumper car (*especially NAmE*) (*BrE* also **dodgem**, **ˈdodgem car**) *noun* one of the small electric cars that you drive in the dodgems 碰碰車

bumph = BUMF

bump·kin /ˈbʌmpkɪn/ *noun* = COUNTRY BUMPKIN

bump·tious /ˈbʌmpʃəs/ *adj.* (*disapproving*) showing that you think that you are very important; often giving your opinions in a loud, confident and annoying way 傲慢的；自以為了不起的；驕橫的

bumpy /ˈbʌmpi/ *adj.* (**bump·ier**, **bumpi·est**) **1** (of a surface 平面) not even; with a lot of bumps 不平的；多凸塊的：*a bumpy road/track* 崎嶇不平的道路／小道◇ *bumpy ground* 坑坑窪窪的地面 **2** (of a journey 旅途) uncomfortable with a lot of sudden unpleasant movements caused by the road surface, weather conditions, etc. 顛簸的：*a* ***bumpy ride/flight*** 顛簸的行車／飛行

IDM **have/give sb a bumpy ˈride** to have a difficult time; to make a situation difficult for sb（使）處境艱難

bun /bʌn/ *noun* **1** [C] (*BrE*) a small round sweet cake 小圓甜蛋糕；小圓甜餅：*an iced bun* 加糖霜的小圓蛋糕 ➲ see also HOT CROSS BUN **2** [C] (*BrE* also **bap**) a small round flat bread roll 圓麵包：*a hamburger bun* 一個用來夾漢堡餅的麵包 ➲ compare ROLL *n.* (3) **3** [C] long hair that has been twisted into a round shape and is worn on top or at the back of the head 圓髮髻：*She wore her hair in a bun.* 她盤了個髮髻。➲ VISUAL VOCAB page V60 **4 buns** [pl.] (*slang, especially NAmE*) the two sides of a person's bottom 屁股

IDM **have a ˈbun in the oven** (*informal, humorous*) to be pregnant 大肚子；懷孕

bunch 0‑w /bʌntʃ/ *noun, verb*

■ ***noun*** **1** 0‑w [C] **~ of sth** a number of things of the same type which are growing or fastened together 串；束；紮：*a bunch of bananas/grapes, etc.* 一把香蕉、葡萄等◇ *a bunch of keys* 一串鑰匙◇ *She picked me a* ***bunch of flowers.*** 她給我採了一束鮮花。➲ VISUAL VOCAB page V30 **2** [sing.] **a ~ (of sth)** (*informal, especially NAmE*) a large amount of sth; a large number of things or people 大量；大批：*I have* ***a whole bunch of*** *stuff to do this morning.* 我今天上午有一大堆活兒。 **3** [sing.] (*informal*) a group of people 群體：*The people that I work with are a great bunch.* 和我一起工作的那些人很不錯。 **4 bunches** [pl.] (*BrE*) long hair that is divided in two and tied at each side of the head（紮在頭兩側的）髮辮：*She wore her hair in bunches.* 她梳着兩條辮子。➲ VISUAL VOCAB page V60

IDM **the best/pick of the ˈbunch** the best out of a group of people or things 出類拔萃的人（或事物）；精英；精品 ➲ more at BEST *n.*

■ ***verb*** [I, T] to become tight or to form tight folds; to make sth do this（使）變緊，成皺褶：*His muscles bunched under his shirt.* 他襯衫下面的肌肉緊繃繃的。◇ **~ (sth) up** *Her skirt had bunched up round her waist.* 她的裙子在腰際成皺褶收攏。◇ **~ sth** *His forehead was bunched in a frown.* 他皺緊眉頭。

PHR V **ˌbunch ˈup/toˈgether** | **ˌbunch sb/sth ˈup/toˈgether** to move closer and form into a group; to make people or things do this（使）集中，聚攏：*The sheep bunched together as soon as they saw the dog.* 那些綿羊一見到狗就擠作一團。

bun·dle /ˈbʌndl/ *noun, verb*

■ ***noun*** **1** [C] a number of things tied or wrapped together; sth that is wrapped up（一）捆，包，紮：*a* ***bundle of rags/papers/firewood*** 一捆碎布／報紙／木柴◇ *She held her little bundle* (= her baby) *tightly in her arms.* 她懷中緊緊地抱着襁褓中的嬰兒。 **2** [C] a number of things that belong, or are sold together 一批（同類事物或出售的貨品）：*a bundle of ideas* 一套想法◇ *a bundle of graphics packages for your PC* 一批個人電腦圖形軟件包 **3** [sing.] **a ~ of laughs, fun, etc.** (*informal*) a person or thing that makes you laugh 風趣的人；笑料：*He wasn't exactly a bundle of laughs* (= a happy person to be with) *last night.* 他昨晚有點讓人掃興。➲ see also BUNDLE OF JOY **4 a bundle** [sing.] (*informal*) a large amount of money 一大筆錢：*That car must have cost a bundle.* 那部車一定所費不菲。

IDM **not go a bundle on sb/sth** (*BrE, informal*) to not like sb/sth very much 不十分喜歡某人／某事物 ➲ more at DROP *v.*, NERVE *n.*

■ ***verb*** **1** [T] **~ sb + adv./prep.** to push or send sb somewhere quickly and not carefully 匆匆送走；推搡；趕：*They bundled her into the back of a car.* 他們把她塞進了車後座。◇ *He was bundled off to boarding school.* 他被匆匆送到了寄宿學校。 **2** [I] **+ adv./prep.** to move somewhere quickly in a group（成群地）匆忙趕往：*We bundled out onto the street.* 我們大夥急忙跑到街上。 **3** [T] **~ sth (with sth)** to supply extra equipment, especially software when selling a new computer, at no extra cost 額外免費提供（設備等）；（尤指出售計算機時）贈送軟件：*A further nine applications are bundled with the system.* 該系統免費附送九套應用軟件。

PHR V **ˌbundle sth↔ˈup** | **ˌbundle sth↔toˈgether** to make or tie sth into a bundle 捆紮；把…打包：*He bundled up the dirty clothes and stuffed them into the bag.* 他把髒衣服捆起來塞進袋子。◇ *The papers were all bundled together, ready to be thrown out.* 報紙全部捆

好，準備扔掉。**,bundle sb 'up (in sth)** to put warm clothes or coverings on sb 使穿暖和（或蓋被子等）: *I bundled her up in a blanket and gave her a hot drink.* 我給她裹了條毯子，又給了她一杯熱飲。

,bun·dle of 'joy *noun (informal, humorous, sometimes ironic)* a baby son or daughter 幸福襁褓（指嬰兒）: *Here are the latest pictures of our little bundle of joy.* 這些是我們的小淘氣包的最新照片。

bun·fight /ˈbʌnfaɪt/ *noun (BrE, informal)* **1** an impressive or important party or other social event 隆重的聚會；重要聚會；重大場合 **2** an angry argument or discussion 爭吵；爭論

bung /bʌŋ/ *verb, noun, adj.*

▪ *verb* **~ sth + adv./prep.** *(BrE, informal)* to put or throw sth somewhere, carelessly and quickly 扔；丟: *Bung this in the bin, can you?* 你可以把它扔進垃圾箱裏嗎？

PHR V **,bung sth 'up (with sth)** [usually passive] to block sth 堵塞；塞住: *My nose is all bunged up.* 我的鼻子全堵了。◇ *The drains are bunged up with dead leaves.* 排水溝被枯樹葉堵住了。

▪ *noun* **1** a round piece of wood, rubber, etc. used for closing the hole in a container such as a BARREL or JAR（桶、罐、廣口瓶的）塞子，蓋子 **2** *(BrE, informal)* an amount of money that is given to sb to persuade them to do sth illegal 賄款；賄金；賄賂

▪ *adj. (AustralE, NZE, informal)* broken 破損的；破壞了的

bun·ga·low /ˈbʌŋɡələʊ; *NAmE* -loʊ/ *noun* **1** *(BrE)* a house built all on one level, without stairs 平房 ➲ VISUAL VOCAB page V16 ➲ compare RANCH HOUSE (2) **2** (in some Asian countries) a large house, sometimes on more than one level, that is not joined to another house on either side（某些亞洲國家的）平房，獨座房屋

bun·gee /ˈbʌndʒi/ *noun* **1** a long rope which can stretch, that people tie to their feet when they do bungee jumping 蹦極索；高空彈跳繩索 ➲ VISUAL VOCAB page V50 **2** *(NAmE)* a thick ELASTIC rope with a hook at each end that can be used to hold packages together, keep things in position, etc.（兩端帶鉤子的）彈力繩索

bun·gee jump·ing *noun* [U] a sport in which a person jumps from a high place, such as a bridge or a CLIFF, with a bungee tied to their feet 蹦極跳，高空彈跳（體育運動，用彈力長繩捆腳從高空跳下）: *to go bungee jumping* 去蹦極 ➲ VISUAL VOCAB page V50 ▸ **bun·gee jump** *noun*: *to do a bungee jump* 玩蹦極跳

bun·gle /ˈbʌŋɡl/ *verb, noun*

▪ *verb* [T, I] **~ (sth)** to do sth badly or without skill; to fail at sth 笨拙地做；失敗 SYN **botch**: *They bungled the job.* 他們把活兒搞糟了。◇ *a bungled robbery/raid/attempt* 未遂的搶劫／襲擊／嘗試 ▸ **bun·gler** /ˈbʌŋɡlə(r)/ *noun* **bun·gling** *adj.*: *bungling incompetence* 笨拙無能

▪ *noun* [usually sing.] something that is done badly and that causes problems 搞糟了的事情；失誤: *Their pay was late because of a computer bungle.* 由於計算機出錯，他們的工資晚發了。

bun·ion /ˈbʌnjən/ *noun* a painful swelling on the foot, usually on the big toe 腳部的腫塊；（通常指）拇囊炎

bunk /bʌŋk/ *noun, verb*

▪ *noun* **1** [C] a narrow bed that is fixed to a wall, especially on a ship or train（尤指船或火車的）臥鋪 **2** [C] (also **'bunk bed**) one of two beds that are fixed together, one above the other, especially for children（尤指兒童的）雙層牀，架子牀；上鋪；下鋪 ➲ VISUAL VOCAB page V23 **3** [U] *(old-fashioned, informal)* nonsense 瞎話；胡話 SYN **bunkum**

IDM **do a 'bunk** *(BrE, informal)* to run away from a place without telling anyone 溜走；悄悄離開

▪ *verb*

PHR V **,bunk 'off | ,bunk off 'school/'work** *(BrE, informal)* to stay away from school or work when you should be there; to leave school or work early 逃學；曠工；早退 SYN **skive, play truant**

bun·ker /ˈbʌŋkə(r)/ *noun, verb*

▪ *noun* **1** a strongly built shelter for soldiers or guns, usually underground 地堡；掩體: *a concrete/underground/secret bunker* 混凝土／地下／秘密掩體 **2** a container for storing coal, especially on a ship or outside a house 煤艙；煤箱: *a coal bunker* 煤箱 **3** *(NAmE* also **'sand trap, trap)** a small area filled with sand on a GOLF COURSE（高爾夫球場上的）沙坑 ➲ VISUAL VOCAB page V40

▪ *verb* **be bunkered** (in GOLF 高爾夫球) to have hit your ball into a bunker (and therefore to be in a difficult position) 把球擊入了沙坑（因而處境艱難）

bunk·house /ˈbʌŋkhaʊs/ *noun* a building for workers to sleep in 工棚；工寮；簡易工人宿舍

bun·kum /ˈbʌŋkəm/ *noun* [U] *(old-fashioned, informal)* nonsense 廢話；瞎話 SYN **bunk**

bunny /ˈbʌni/ *noun (pl.* **-ies)** (also **'bunny rabbit**) a child's word for a RABBIT（兒語）兔子 IDM see HAPPY *adj.*

'bunny-hop *noun* a small jump forward in a CROUCHING position 兔子跳；蹲跳 ▸ **'bunny-hop** *verb* **(-pp-)** [I]

'bunny slope *(NAmE) (BrE* **'nursery slope)** *noun* a slope that is not very steep and is used by people who are learning to SKI（初學滑雪者使用的）平緩坡地

Bun·sen burn·er /ˌbʌnsn ˈbɜːnə(r); *NAmE* ˈbɜːrn-/ *noun* an instrument used in scientific work that produces a hot gas flame 本生燈（科學實驗用煤氣燈）➲ VISUAL VOCAB page V70

bunt /bʌnt/ *verb* [T, I] **~ (sth)** *(NAmE)* (in BASEBALL 棒球) to deliberately hit the ball only a short distance 短打；觸擊 ▸ **bunt** *noun*

bunt·ing /ˈbʌntɪŋ/ *noun* **1** [U] coloured flags or paper used for decorating streets and buildings in celebrations（裝飾街道、房屋等的）彩旗，彩紙 **2** [C] a small bird related to the FINCH and SPARROW families. There are several types of bunting. 鵐: *a corn/reed/snow bunting* 黍鵐；蘆鵐；雪鵐

bun·yip /ˈbʌnjɪp/ *noun (AustralE)* (in stories) a MONSTER that lives in or near water 本耶普（傳說中的沼澤湖泊地區怪獸）

buoy /bɔɪ; *NAmE* also ˈbuːi/ *noun, verb*

▪ *noun* an object which floats on the sea or a river to mark the places where it is dangerous and where it is safe for boats to go 浮標；航標 ➲ see also LIFEBUOY

▪ *verb* [usually passive] **1 ~ sb (up)** to make sb feel cheerful or confident 鼓舞；鼓勵: *Buoyed by their win yesterday the team feel confident of further success.* 在昨天的勝利鼓舞下，該隊有信心再次獲勝。 **2 ~ sb/sth (up)** to keep sb/sth floating on water 使漂浮；使浮起 **3 ~ sth (up)** to keep prices at a high or acceptable level 使保持高價；使價格維持於較高水平

buoy·ant /ˈbɔɪənt; *NAmE* ˈbuːjənt/ *adj.* **1** (of prices, business activity, etc. 價格、商業活動等) tending to increase or stay at a high level, usually showing financial success 看漲的；保持高價的；繁榮的: *a buoyant economy/market* 繁榮的經濟／市場 ◇ *buoyant sales/prices* 上升的銷售額／價格 ◇ *a buoyant demand for homes* 越來越大的住房需求 **2** cheerful and feeling sure that things will be successful 愉快而充滿信心的；樂觀的: *They were all in buoyant mood.* 他們都很樂觀。 **3** floating, able to float or able to keep things floating 漂浮的；能夠漂起的；有浮力的: *The boat bobbed like a cork on the waves: light and buoyant.* 小船在大浪中猶如軟木塞：輕輕漂來漂去。◇ *Salt water is more buoyant than fresh water.* 鹽水比淡水浮力大。 ▸ **buoy·ancy** /-ənsi/ *noun* [U]: *the buoyancy of the market* 市場的活躍 ◇ *a mood of buoyancy* 輕鬆愉快的心情 ◇ *a buoyancy aid* (= sth to help you float) 助浮物

bup·pie (also **buppy**) /ˈbʌpi/ *(pl.* **-ies)** *noun (SAfrE, informal)* a black person who is a YUPPIE 黑人雅皮士；黑人雅痞

bur = BURR (3)

Bur·berry™ /ˈbɜːbəri; *NAmE* ˈbɜːrberi/ *noun (pl.* **-ies)** a type of RAINCOAT 巴寶利雨衣

bur·ble /ˈbɜːbl; *NAmE* ˈbɜːrbl/ *verb* **1** [I, T] **~ (on) (about sth) | + speech** *(BrE, disapproving)* to speak in a confused or silly way that is difficult to hear or understand 語無倫次地講；說蠢話: *What's he burbling* *about?* 他在嘟囔些啥？ **2** [I] to make the gentle sound of a stream flowing over stones 汩汩作響

burbs /bɜːbz; *NAmE* bɜːrbz/ *noun* **the burbs** [pl.] (*NAmE, informal*) = SUBURBS

bur·den /ˈbɜːdn; *NAmE* ˈbɜːrdn/ *noun, verb*

■ *noun* **1 the ~ (of sth)** | **a ~ (on/to sb)** a duty, responsibility, etc. that causes worry, difficulty or hard work（義務、責任等的）重擔，負擔：*to bear/carry/ease/reduce/share the burden* 承受／擔負／減輕／減少／分擔重擔 ◇ *The main burden of caring for old people falls on the state.* 國家擔負起了照料老人的大部份責任。◇ *the heavy tax burden on working people* 加在勞動者頭上的重稅 ◇ *I don't want to become a burden to my children when I'm old.* 我不想在年老的時候成為孩子們的累贅。 **2** (*formal*) a heavy load that is difficult to carry 重擔；重負 ➲ see also BEAST OF BURDEN

■ *verb* **1 ~ sb/yourself (with sth)** to give sb a duty, responsibility, etc. that causes worry, difficulty or hard work（使）擔負（沉重或艱難的任務、職責等）：*They have burdened themselves with a high mortgage.* 他們負擔了一筆很高的按揭借款。◇ *I don't want to burden you with my worries.* 我不想讓你為我的煩惱操心。◇ *to be burdened by high taxation* 不堪重稅負荷 **OPP unburden** **2 be burdened with sth** to be carrying sth heavy 負重：*She got off the bus, burdened with two heavy suitcases.* 她提着兩個沉重的手提箱下了公共汽車。

the ˌburden of ˈproof *noun* [sing.] (*law* 律) the task or responsibility of proving that sth is true 舉證責任

bur·den·some /ˈbɜːdnsəm; *NAmE* ˈbɜːrd-/ *adj.* (*formal*) causing worry, difficulty or hard work 負擔沉重的；難以承擔的；繁重的 **SYN onerous**

bur·dock /ˈbɜːdɒk; *NAmE* ˈbɜːrdɑːk/ *noun* [U] a plant with flowers that become PRICKLY and stick to passing animals 牛蒡（植物）

bur·eau /ˈbjʊərəʊ; *NAmE* ˈbjʊroʊ/ *noun* (*pl.* **bur·eaux** or **bur·eaus** /-rəʊz; *NAmE* -roʊz/) **1** (*BrE*) a desk with drawers and usually a top that opens down to make a table to write on（附抽屜及活動寫字枱的）書桌 **2** (*NAmE*) = CHEST OF DRAWERS **3** an office or organization that provides information on a particular subject（提供某方面信息的）辦事處，辦公室，機構：*an employment bureau* 職業介紹所 **4** (in the US) a government department or part of a government department（美國政府部門）局，處，科：*the Federal Bureau of Investigation* 聯邦調查局

bur·eau·cracy /bjʊəˈrɒkrəsi; *NAmE* bjʊˈrɑːk-/ *noun* (*pl.* **-ies**) **1** [U] (often *disapproving*) the system of official rules and ways of doing things that a government or an organization has, especially when these seem to be too complicated 官僚主義；官僚作風：***unnecessary/excessive bureaucracy*** 不必要的官僚式繁文縟節；過分的官僚作風 **2** [U, C] a system of government in which there are a large number of state officials who are not elected; a country with such a system 官僚體制；實行官僚體制的國家：*the power of the state bureaucracy* 國家官僚體制的權力 ◇ *living in a modern bureaucracy* 生活在一個現代官僚體制中

bur·eau·crat /ˈbjʊərəkræt; *NAmE* ˈbjʊr-/ *noun* (often *disapproving*) an official working in an organization or a government department, especially one who follows the rules of the department too strictly 官僚主義者；官僚

bur·eau·crat·ic /ˌbjʊərəˈkrætɪk; *NAmE* ˌbjʊr-/ *adj.* (often *disapproving*) connected with a bureaucracy or bureaucrats and involving complicated official rules which may seem unnecessary 官僚的；官僚主義的：***bureaucratic power/control/procedures/organizations*** 官僚權力／管理／程序／組織 ◇ *The report revealed a great deal of bureaucratic inefficiency.* 報道大量揭示了官僚體制的無能。 ▸ **bur·eau·crat·ic·al·ly** /-ɪkli/ *adv.*

bur·eau de change /ˌbjʊərəʊ də ˈʃɑːnʒ; *NAmE* ˌbjʊroʊ/ *noun* (*pl.* **bur·eaux de change** /ˌbjʊərəʊ; *NAmE* ˌbjʊroʊ/) (from *French*) an office at a hotel, in an airport, etc., where you can exchange money from one country for that from another 外幣兌換處；外幣兌換所

bur·ette (*US* also **buret**) /bjuˈret/ *noun* a glass tube with measurements on it and a tap/faucet at one end, used, for example, in chemical experiments for measuring out amounts of a liquid 滴定管；量管 ➲ VISUAL VOCAB page V70

burg /bɜːg; *NAmE* bɜːrg/ *noun* (*NAmE, informal*) a town or city 鎮；市；城

bur·geon /ˈbɜːdʒən; *NAmE* ˈbɜːrdʒən/ *verb* [I] (*formal*) to begin to grow or develop rapidly 激增；迅速發展 ▸ **bur·geon·ing** *adj.*：*a burgeoning population* 急劇增長的人口 ◇ *burgeoning demand* 迅速增加的需求

bur·ger /ˈbɜːgə(r); *NAmE* ˈbɜːrg-/ *noun* **1** = HAMBURGER **2 -bur·ger** (in compounds 構成複合詞) finely chopped fish, vegetables, nuts, etc. made into flat round shapes like HAMBURGERS（漢堡牛肉式的）魚鬆餅，菜末餅，果仁餅：*a spicy beanburger* 香辣豆蓉餅 ➲ see also CHEESEBURGER, VEGGIE BURGER

burgh /ˈbʌrə/ *noun* (*old-fashioned* or *ScotE*) a town or part of a city that has its own local government 自治市；（城市的）自治區

bur·gher /ˈbɜːgə(r); *NAmE* ˈbɜːrg-/ *noun* (*old use* or *humorous*) a citizen of a particular town（某市的）市民

burg·lar /ˈbɜːglə(r); *NAmE* ˈbɜːrg-/ *noun* a person who enters a building illegally in order to steal 破門盜賊；入室竊賊

ˈburglar alarm *noun* an electronic device, often fixed to a wall, that rings a loud bell if sb tries to enter a building by force 防盜鈴 ➲ VISUAL VOCAB page V17

burg·lary /ˈbɜːgləri; *NAmE* ˈbɜːrg-/ *noun* [U, C] (*pl.* **-ies**) the crime of entering a building illegally and stealing things from it 入室偷盜罪 **SYN housebreaking**：*The youth was charged with three counts of burglary.* 那個年輕人被控犯有三次入室盜竊罪。◇ *a rise in the number of burglaries committed in the area* 該地區盜竊案例數目的上升 ➲ compare ROBBERY, THEFT

bur·gle /ˈbɜːgl; *NAmE* ˈbɜːrgl/ (*BrE*) (*NAmE* **burg·lar·ize** /ˈbɜːgləraɪz; *NAmE* ˈbɜːrg-/) *verb* **~ sb/sth** to enter a building illegally, usually using force, and steal from it 入室盜竊：*We were burgled while we were away* (= our house was burgled). 我們外出時家裏失竊了。◇ *The house next door was burgled.* 鄰居家被盜了。 ➲ COLLOCATIONS at CRIME

bur·goo /bɜːˈguː; *NAmE* bɜːrˈguː/ *noun* (*pl.* **-oos**) (*NAmE*) **1** [U] a type of thick soup, especially one eaten outdoors（常在野宴時喝的）雜燴湯 **2** [C] an event at which burgoo is eaten outdoors 雜燴湯野宴

bur·gundy /ˈbɜːgəndi; *NAmE* ˈbɜːrg-/ *noun* **1 Burgundy** [U, C] (*pl.* **-ies**) a red or white wine from the Burgundy area of eastern France 勃艮第葡萄酒（產於法國東部的勃艮第地區，有紅葡萄酒和白葡萄酒） **2** [U] a dark red colour 深紅色 ▸ **bur·gundy** *adj.*：*a burgundy leather briefcase* 深紅色的皮革公文包

bur·ial /ˈberiəl/ *noun* [U, C] the act or ceremony of burying a dead body 埋葬；葬禮：***a burial place/mound/site*** 安葬地；墳頭；墳地 ◇ *Her body was sent home for burial.* 她的屍骨已運回家鄉安葬。◇ *His family insisted he should be given a proper burial.* 他的家人堅持應該為他舉行適當的葬禮。

ˈburial ground *noun* a place where dead bodies are buried, especially an ancient place（尤指古老的）墓地，墳地

burka (also **burkha**) /ˈbʊəkə; ˈbɜːkə; *NAmE* ˈbɜːrkə/ *noun* a long loose piece of clothing that covers the whole body, including the head and face, worn in public by Muslim women in some countries 布爾卡（一些國家中穆斯林女子在公共場所穿戴的面紗女袍）

bur·lap /ˈbɜːlæp; *NAmE* ˈbɜːrl-/ *noun* [U] (*NAmE*) = HESSIAN

bur·lesque /bɜːˈlesk; *NAmE* bɜːrˈl-/ *noun* **1** [C] a performance or piece of writing which tries to make sth look ridiculous by representing it in a humorous way 滑稽諷刺表演（或作品） **SYN parody**：*a burlesque of literary life* 對文學生活的戲謔 **2** [U] (*NAmE*) a type of entertainment, popular in the past in the US, involving humorous acts, singing, dancing, etc. and often

B

including STRIPTEASE 滑稽娛樂（曾經風靡美國，常伴有脫衣舞）▸ **bur·lesque** *adj.* [usually before noun]

burly /ˈbɜːli; *NAmE* ˈbɜːrli/ *adj.* (**bur·lier**, **bur·li·est**) (of a man or a man's body 男人或男人身體) big, strong and heavy 高大強壯的；魁梧的 SYN **brawny**

burn /bɜːn; *NAmE* bɜːrn/ *verb, noun*

■ *verb* (**burnt**, **burnt** /bɜːnt; *NAmE* bɜːrnt/ or **burned**, **burned** /bɜːnd; *NAmE* bɜːrnd/)

▸ FIRE 火 **1** [I] to produce flames and heat 燃燒；燒：*A welcoming fire was burning in the fireplace.* 壁爐裏燃燒着暖融融的爐火。◇ *Fires were burning all over the city.* 全城處處燃燒着大火。 **2** [I] (used especially in the progressive tenses 尤用於進行時) to be on fire 着火；燒着：*By nightfall the whole city was burning.* 到黃昏時，全城已是一片火海。◇ *Two children were rescued from the burning car.* 兩名兒童從燃燒着的車中被救了出來。◇ *The smell of burning rubber filled the air.* 空氣中瀰漫着橡膠燃燒的氣味。 **3** [T, I] to destroy, damage, injure or kill sb/sth by fire; to be destroyed, etc. by fire（使）燒燬，燒壞，燒傷，燒死：**~ (sb/sth)** *to burn waste paper/dead leaves* 焚燒廢紙／枯樹葉 ◇ *All his belongings were burnt in the fire.* 他所有的財物都在大火中付之一炬。◇ *The cigarette burned a hole in the carpet.* 香煙把地毯燒了個洞。◇ *The house was* **burnt to the ground** (= completely destroyed). 那座房子徹底焚燬了。◇ *The house* **burned to the ground.** 房子被大火夷為平地。◇ *Ten people* **burned to death** *in the hotel fire.* 旅館火災中有十人被燒死。◇ **~ sb/sth + adj.** *His greatest fear is of being* **burnt alive.** 他最怕的是被活活燒死。

▸ FUEL 燃料 **4** [T, I] **~ (sth)** if you **burn** a fuel, or a fuel **burns**, it produces heat, light or energy（使燃料）燃燒：*a furnace that burns gas/oil/coke* 煤氣／煤油／焦炭熔爐 ◇ (*figurative*) *Some people burn calories* (= use food to produce energy) *faster than others.* 有些人熱量消耗得比其他人快。◇ *Which fuel burns most efficiently?* 哪種燃料燃燒效果最佳？

▸ FOOD 食物 **5** [I, T] if food **burns**, or if you **burn** it, it is spoiled because it gets too hot（使）燒焦，燒煳：*I can smell something burning in the kitchen.* 我聞到廚房裏有東西燒焦了。◇ **~ sth** *Sorry—I burnt the toast.* 抱歉，我把麪包烤煳了。

▸ SUN/HEAT/ACID 太陽；熱；酸 **6** [I, T] to be damaged or injured by the sun, heat, acid, etc.; to damage or injure sb/sth in this way（使）曬傷，燙傷，燒傷：*My skin burns easily* (= in the sun). 我的皮膚容易曬傷。◇ **~ sb** *I got badly burned by the sun yesterday.* 我昨天嚴重曬傷。◇ **~ sth** *The soup's hot. Don't burn your mouth.* 湯很熱，別燙了嘴。◇ **~ yourself** *I burned myself on the stove.* 我被爐子燙了。

▸ OF PART OF BODY 身體部位 **7** [I] if part of your body **burns** or **is burning**, it feels very hot and painful 火辣辣地痛；發燙：*Your forehead's burning. Have you got a fever?* 你的前額很燙，你發燒了嗎？◇ *Her cheeks burned with embarrassment.* 她羞得面頰發燙。➲ SYNONYMS at HURT

▸ OF A LIGHT 燈 **8** [I] to produce light 發光；發亮：*Lights were burning upstairs, but no one answered the door.* 樓上亮着燈，但叫門沒人回應。

▸ FEEL EMOTION/DESIRE 有情感／熱望 **9** [I, T] (*literary*) to feel a very strong emotion or desire 有強烈的情感；渴望：**~ with sth** *to be burning with rage/ambition/love* 滿懷強烈的仇恨／遠大的抱負／熾熱的愛 ◇ **~ to do sth** *He was burning to go climbing again.* 他渴望再去爬山。

▸ GO FAST 走得快 **10** [I] **+ adv./prep.** (*informal*) to move very fast in a particular direction 向…迅速移動：*The car was burning down the road.* 汽車沿着公路疾馳而去。

▸ MAKE ANGRY 使生氣 **11** [T] **~ sb** (*NAmE, informal*) to make sb very angry 激怒；使大怒：*So you did it just to burn me?* 這麼說，你那樣做只是為了氣我？

▸ CD, ETC. 光盤等 **12** [T, I] **~ (sth) (to sth)** to put information onto a CD, etc. 刻錄（光盤等）

IDM **burn your ˈbridges** (*BrE* also **burn your ˈboats**) to do sth that makes it impossible to return to the previous situation later 不留退路；破釜沉舟；背水而戰：*Think carefully before you resign—you don't want to burn your bridges.* 辭職前要三思，你得給自己留條退路。 **burn the candle at both ˈends** to become very tired by trying to do too many things and going to bed late and getting up early 過度勞累；起早貪黑而疲憊不堪 **burn your ˈfingers | get your ˈfingers burnt** to suffer as a result of doing sth without realizing the possible bad results, especially in business（尤指生意上）沒有先見之明而蒙受損失，因不慎而吃虧：*He got his fingers badly burnt dabbling in the stock market.* 他糊裏糊塗地進入股票市場，結果賠了老本。 **burn a ˈhole in your pocket** if money **burns a hole in your pocket**, you want to spend it as soon as you have it 一有（錢）就想花；花錢沒有節制 **burn the midnight ˈoil** to study or work until late at night 挑燈夜戰；熬夜 **burn ˈrubber** (*informal*) to drive very fast 飛車 **burn sth to a ˈcinder/ˈcrisp** to cook sth for too long or with too much heat, so that it becomes badly burnt 把某物燒焦（或燒煳） ➲ more at EAR, FEEL *v.*, MONEY

PHR V **ˌburn aˈway | ˌburn sth↔aˈway** to disappear as a result of burning; to make sth do this（使）燒掉，燒光：*Half the candle had burnt away.* 那根蠟燭燒掉了一半。◇ *The clothing on his back got burnt away in the fire.* 他穿的衣服背部在大火中燒掉了。 **ˌburn ˈdown** if a fire **burns down**, it becomes weaker and has smaller flames（火勢）減弱 **ˌburn ˈdown | ˌburn sth↔ˈdown** to be destroyed, or to destroy sth, by fire（被）焚燬：*The house burned down in 1895.* 那房子在1895年燒燬了。 **ˌburn sth↔ˈoff 1** to remove sth by burning 燒掉；燒除：*Burn off the old paint before repainting the door.* 先把門上的舊漆燒掉，再刷新油漆。 **2** to use energy by doing exercise（通過鍛煉等）消耗能量：*This workout helps you to burn off fat and tone muscles.* 這項鍛煉有助於消耗脂肪，使肌肉強健。 **ˌburn ˈout | ˌburn itself ˈout** (of a fire 火) to stop burning because there is nothing more to burn 燒盡；熄滅：*The fire had burnt (itself) out before the fire engines arrived.* 救火車到達之前火就熄滅了。 **ˌburn ˈout | ˌburn sth↔ˈout** to stop working or to make sth stop working because it gets too hot or is used too much（因過熱或使用過多）出故障：*The clutch has burnt out.* 離合器因過熱而失靈了。 **ˌburn ˈout | ˌburn yourself/sb ˈout** to become extremely tired or sick by working too hard over a period of time 耗盡體力；積勞成疾；累垮：*If he doesn't stop working so hard, he'll burn himself out.* 他要是繼續這樣拚命工作，就會把自己累垮。◇ *By the age of 25 she was completely burned out and retired from the sport.* 她到25歲時就已體力耗盡，退出了體壇。➲ related noun BURNOUT **ˌburn sth ˈout** [usually passive] to destroy sth completely by fire so that only the outer frame remains 把…燒成空架子：*The hotel was completely burnt out.* 旅館被燒得只剩一片廢墟。◇ *the burnt-out wreck of a car* 汽車燒燬後的殘骸 **ˌburn ˈup 1** to be destroyed by heat 被燒燬；被燒掉：*The spacecraft burned up as it entered the earth's atmosphere.* 宇宙飛船進入地球大氣層時被燒燬。 **2** (usually used in the progressive tenses 通常用於進行時) (*informal*) to have a high temperature 發燒；體溫高：*You're burning up—have you seen a doctor?* 你發燒了，你看過醫生嗎？ **3** (of a fire 火) to burn more strongly and with larger flames 燒得更旺；火勢加大 **ˌburn sb ˈup** (*NAmE, informal*) to make sb very angry 激怒；使大怒：*The way he treats me really burns me up.* 他這樣對待我真使我惱火。 **ˌburn sth↔ˈup 1** to get rid of or destroy sth by burning 焚燬；燒掉：*The fire burned up 1 500 acres of farmland.* 大火燒掉了1 500英畝農田。 **2** to use CALORIES or energy by doing exercise（通過鍛煉）消耗熱能：*Which burns up more calories—swimming or cycling?* 游泳和騎車，哪種運動消耗熱量大？

■ *noun*

▸ INJURY 傷 **1** [C] an injury or a mark caused by fire, heat or acid 燒傷；燙傷；灼傷；燒（或燙、灼）的痕跡：***minor/severe/third-degree burns*** 輕度／重度／三度燒傷 ◇ *cigarette burns on the furniture* 煙頭在傢具上燙出的痕跡 ◇ *burn marks* 烙印 ◇ *a specialist burns unit in a hospital* 醫院的燒傷專科

▸ IN MUSCLES 肌肉 **2 the burn** [sing.] the feeling that you get in your muscles when you have done a lot of exercise 疲痛感

▸ RIVER 河流 **3** [C] (*ScotE*) a small river 小河；溪流 SYN **stream** IDM see SLOW *adj.*

B

Synonyms 同義詞辨析

burn

char • scald • scorch • singe

These words all mean to damage, injure, destroy or kill sb/sth with heat or fire. 以上各詞均含因高溫或火導致損壞、損傷、毀滅之意。

burn to damage, injure, destroy or kill sb/sth with fire, heat or acid; to be damaged, etc. by fire, heat or acid 指燒（或灼）壞、燒（或灼）傷、燒（或灼）死： *She burned all his letters.* 她把他的信全部付之一炬。◇ *The house **burned down** in 1995.* 那所房子在 1995 年燒燬了。

char [usually passive] to make sth black by burning it; to become black by burning 指（使）燒黑、燒焦： *The bodies had been charred beyond recognition.* 這些屍體已燒焦，無法辨認。

scald to burn part of your body with very hot liquid or steam 指被高溫液體或氣體燙傷

scorch to burn and slightly damage a surface by making it too hot 指把物體表面燙壞、燒煳、烤焦： *I scorched my dress when I was ironing it.* 我把自己的連衣裙熨焦了。

singe to burn the surface of sth slightly, usually by mistake; to be burnt in this way 尤指不小心把物體表面烤焦、燙煳： *He singed his hair as he tried to light his cigarette.* 他點煙時把頭髮給燎了。

SCORCH OR SINGE? 用 scorch 還是 singe？

Things are **scorched** by heat or fire. Things can only be **singed** by fire or a flame. * scorched 指被高溫燙壞或被火燒煳； singed 只用於被火或火舌燒焦。

PATTERNS

- to burn/scald **yourself/your hand**
- to burn/scorch/singe your **hair/clothes**
- burned out/charred/scorched **remains/ruins/buildings**

burn·er /ˈbɜːnə(r); *NAmE* ˈbɜːrn-/ *noun* **1** the part of a cooker/stove, etc. that produces a flame 煤氣頭；煤氣灶火圈；爐膛 ➲ **VISUAL VOCAB** page V25 **2** a large, solid, metal piece of equipment for burning wood or coal, used for heating a room （取暖用的）爐子： *a wood burner* 燒木柴的爐子 ➲ see also BUNSEN BURNER **IDM** see BACK *adj.*, FRONT *adj.*

burn·ing /ˈbɜːnɪŋ; *NAmE* ˈbɜːrn-/ *adj., adv.*
■ ***adj.*** [only before noun] **1** (of feelings, etc. 感情等) very strong; extreme 強烈的；極度的： *a **burning desire** to win* 取勝的迫切願望 ◇ *He's always had a **burning ambition** to start his own business.* 他總是雄心勃勃地想自己創業。**2 a ~ issue/question** a very important and urgent problem 重大迫切的問題；當務之急 **3** (of pain, etc. 疼痛等) very strong and giving a feeling of burning 強烈的；火辣辣的 ➲ **SYNONYMS** at PAINFUL **4** very hot; looking and feeling very hot 熾熱的；（看似或感覺）熱辣辣的： *the burning sun* 灼熱的太陽 ◇ *her burning face* 她的熱辣辣的臉 **5 ~ eyes** (*literary*) eyes that seem to be staring at you very hard 緊盯着看的眼睛；熱切的目光
■ ***adv.*** **burning hot** very hot 灼熱地

bur·nish /ˈbɜːnɪʃ; *NAmE* ˈbɜːrnɪʃ/ *verb* **~ sth** (*formal*) to polish metal until it is smooth and shiny 磨光，擦亮（金屬）▸ **bur·nished** *adj.* [usually before noun]： ***burnished gold/copper*** 擦得鋥亮的金器／銅器

bur·nous (*NAmE* usually **bur·noose**) /bɜːˈnuːs; *NAmE* bɜːrˈn-/ *noun* a long loose item of outer clothing with a HOOD (= covering for the head), worn by Arabs 布爾努斯袍（阿拉伯人穿的帶風帽長外衣）

burn·out /ˈbɜːnaʊt; *NAmE* ˈbɜːrn-/ *noun* [C, U] **1** the state of being extremely tired or ill, either physically or mentally, because you have worked too hard 精疲力竭；過度勞累 **2** the point at which a ROCKET has used all of its fuel and has no more power （火箭）熄火點，燃燒終止

ˈ**Burns Night** *noun* [U, C] the evening of 25 January when Scottish people celebrate the birthday of the Scottish POET, Robert Burns, with traditional Scottish music, WHISKY and dishes such as HAGGIS 彭斯之夜（元月 25 日，蘇格蘭人民紀念蘇格蘭詩人羅伯特•彭斯誕辰的節日）

burnt 0➛ /bɜːnt; *NAmE* bɜːrnt/ *adj.*
damaged or injured by burning 燒壞的；燒傷的；燙傷的；灼傷的： *burnt toast* 烤焦了的麪包片 ◇ *Your hand looks badly burnt.* 你的手似乎燒傷很重。

ˌ**burnt ˈochre** *noun* [U] **1** a deep yellow-brown colour 焦赭色；赤土色 **2** a yellow-brown PIGMENT, used in art 燒赭石（顏料）

ˌ**burnt ˈoffering** *noun* **1** something (usually an animal) that is burnt in a religious ceremony as a gift offered to a god 燔祭品（宗教儀式上焚燒祭神的動物等） **2** (*BrE, humorous*) food that has been badly burnt by accident 燒焦的食物

ˌ**burnt-ˈout** (*NAmE* ˌ**burned-ˈout**) *adj.* **1** destroyed or badly damaged by fire 燒燬的；燒壞的： *a burnt-out car* 燒燬的汽車 **2** feeling as if you have done sth for too long and need to have a rest 精疲力竭的；疲乏的： *I'm feeling burnt-out at work—I need a holiday.* 我覺得工作得太累了 —— 我需要休假。

burnt sienna /ˌbɜːnt siˈenə; *NAmE* ˌbɜːrnt/ *noun* [U] **1** a deep red-brown colour 熟褐色；赭褐色 **2** a deep red-brown PIGMENT, used in art 煅黃土（顏料）

burnt umber /ˌbɜːnt ˈʌmbə(r); *NAmE* ˌbɜːrnt/ *noun* [U] **1** a dark brown colour 深赭色；深褐色 **2** a dark brown PIGMENT, used in art 燒棕土（顏料）

burp /bɜːp; *NAmE* bɜːrp/ *verb* (*informal*) **1** [I] to let out air from the stomach through the mouth, making a noise 打嗝 **SYN** **belch 2** [T] **~ sb** to make a baby bring up air from the stomach, especially by rubbing or PATTING its back 使（嬰兒）打嗝（尤指通過撫摩或輕拍背部）▸ **burp** *noun*

burr /bɜː(r)/ *noun* **1** [usually sing.] a strong pronunciation of the 'r' sound, typical of some accents in English; an accent with this type of pronunciation 小舌 r 音，顫音 r，帶濃重 r 音的口音（某些英語方言中的典型發音）： *She speaks with a soft West Country burr.* 她說話帶有一種西部地區濃重 r 音的口音。 **2** [usually sing.] the soft regular noise made by parts of a machine moving quickly （機器部件快速運轉時有規律的）呼呼聲 **SYN** **whirr 3** (also **bur**) [C] the seed container of some plants which is covered in very small hooks that stick to clothes or fur （某些植物）帶芒刺的小果實

bur·rito /bʊˈriːtəʊ; *NAmE* -toʊ/ *noun* (*pl.* **-os**) (from *Spanish*) a Mexican dish consisting of a TORTILLA filled with meat or BEANS （墨西哥）肉餡（或豆餡）玉米粉圓餅

burro /ˈbʊrəʊ; *NAmE* ˈbɜːroʊ/ *noun* (*pl.* **-os**) (*NAmE*, from *Spanish*) a small DONKEY 小驢

bur·row /ˈbʌrəʊ; *NAmE* ˈbɜːroʊ/ *verb, noun*
■ ***verb*** **1** [I, T] to make a hole or a tunnel in the ground by digging 挖掘（洞或隧道）；挖洞 **SYN** **dig** ： (**+ adv./prep.**) *Earthworms burrow deep into the soil.* 蚯蚓鑽土很深。◇ **~ sth + adv./prep.** *The rodent **burrowed its way** into the sand.* 這隻鼠掘洞鑽進沙裏。 **2** [I, T] to press yourself close to sb or under sth 偎依；鑽到…下面： **+ adv./prep.** *He burrowed down beneath the blankets.* 他鑽到毯子下面。◇ **~ sth + adv./prep.** *She burrowed her face into his chest.* 她把臉埋進他的懷裏。 **3** [I] **+ adv./prep.** to search for sth under or among things （在…裏）搜尋： *She burrowed in the drawer for a pair of socks.* 她在抽屜裏翻找一雙襪子。◇ *He was afraid that they would burrow into his past.* 他擔心他們會追查他的過去。
■ ***noun*** a hole or tunnel in the ground made by animals such as RABBITS for them to live in （動物的）洞穴，地道

bursa /ˈbɜːsə; *NAmE* ˈbɜːrsə/ *noun* (*pl.* **bur·sae** /-siː/ or **bur·sas**) (*anatomy* 解) a part inside the body like a bag or sleeve, which is filled with liquid, especially around a joint so that it can work smoothly 囊；黏液囊

bur·sar /ˈbɜːsə(r); NAmE ˈbɜːrs-/ *noun* (*especially BrE*) a person whose job is to manage the financial affairs of a school or college（學校或大學的）財務主管

bur·sary /ˈbɜːsəri; NAmE ˈbɜːrs-/ *noun* (*pl.* **-ies**) (*especially BrE*) an amount of money that is given to sb so that they can study, usually at a college or university（通常指大學的）獎學金 SYN **grant, scholarship**

bur·sitis /ˌbɜːˈsaɪtɪs; NAmE ˌbɜːr-/ *noun* [U] (*medical* 醫) a condition in which a bursa becomes swollen and sore 滑囊炎；黏液囊炎

burst /bɜːst; NAmE bɜːrst/ *verb, noun*

■ *verb* (**burst**, **burst**) **1** [I, T] to break open or apart, especially because of pressure from inside; to make sth break in this way（使）爆裂，脹開：*That balloon will burst if you blow it up any more.* 你再給氣球充氣，它就要爆了。◇ *The dam burst under the weight of water.* 大壩在水的巨大壓力下潰決了。◇ *Shells were bursting* (= exploding) *all around us.* 炮彈在我們四周爆炸。◇ (*figurative*) *He felt he would burst with anger and shame.* 他惱羞成怒，都要氣炸了。◇ *a burst pipe* 爆裂的管子 ◇ **~ sth** *Don't burst that balloon!* 別把氣球弄炸了！◇ *The river* **burst its banks** *and flooded nearby towns.* 那條河決堤淹沒了附近的城鎮。➲ SYNONYMS at EXPLODE **2** [I] **+ adv./prep.** to go or move somewhere suddenly with great force; to come from somewhere suddenly 猛衝；突然出現：*He burst into the room without knocking.* 他沒敲門就闖進了屋子。◇ *The sun burst through the clouds.* 太陽破雲而出。◇ *The words burst from her in an angry rush.* 她破口說出了那一大堆氣話。 **3** [I] **be bursting (with sth)** to be very full of sth; to be very full and almost breaking open 爆滿；漲滿：*The roads are bursting with cars.* 車輛把那些道路擠滿了。◇ *to be* **bursting with ideas/enthusiasm/pride** 滿懷想法 / 熱情 / 驕傲 ◇ *The hall was filled to* **bursting point**. 大廳裏擠滿了人。◇ *The hall was* **full to bursting**. 大廳裏擠滿了人。◇ (*informal*) ***I'm bursting*** (*for a pee*)! (= I need to use the toilet right now). 我（被尿）憋壞了！

IDM **be bursting to do sth** to want to do sth so much that you can hardly stop yourself 急於（或迫切想）做某事：*She was bursting to tell him the good news.* 她急不可待要把好消息告訴他。 **ˌburst sb's ˈbubble** to bring an end to sb's hopes, happiness, etc. 使某人希望破滅；毀掉某人的幸福 **ˌburst ˈopen | ˌburst (sth) ˈopen** to open suddenly or violently; to make sth open in this way（使）猛然打開：*The door burst open.* 門突然開了。◇ *Firefighters burst the door open and rescued them.* 消防隊員撞開門，把他們救了出來。➲ more at BUBBLE *n.*, SEAM

PHR V **ˌburst ˈin | ˌburst into a ˈroom, ˈbuilding, etc.** to enter a room or building suddenly and noisily 闖進；突然破門而入 **ˌburst ˈin on sb/sth** to interrupt sb/sth by entering a place suddenly and noisily（突然闖進而）打斷，擾亂：*He burst in on the meeting.* 他闖進來打斷了會議。 **ˈburst into sth** to start producing sth suddenly and with great force 突然爆發：*The aircraft crashed and* **burst into flames** (= suddenly began to burn). 飛機墜毀後猛烈燃燒起來。◇ *She* **burst into tears** (= suddenly began to cry). 她突然大哭起來。 **ˈburst on/onto sth** to appear somewhere suddenly in a way that is very noticeable 突然在…出現；突然顯現：*A major new talent has* **burst onto the literary scene**. 文壇突然冒出一位重要的新秀。 **ˌburst ˈout 1** to speak suddenly, loudly and with strong feeling 突然激動地喊叫：**+ speech** *'For heavens' sake!' he burst out.* "天哪！" 他大叫一聲。➲ related noun OUTBURST ➲ SYNONYMS at CALL **2** to begin doing sth suddenly 突然開始（做某事）：**~ doing sth** *Karen* **burst out laughing**. 卡倫突然大笑起來。

■ *noun* **1** a short period of a particular activity or strong emotion that often starts suddenly 突發；猝發；迸發；爆破：*a sudden* ***burst of activity/energy/anger/enthusiasm*** 活動 / 能量 / 怒火 / 熱情的迸發 ◇ *Her breath was coming* **in short bursts**. 她的呼吸急迫短促。◇ *I tend to work* **in bursts**. 我的工作勁頭往往是一陣一陣的。◇ *spontaneous bursts of applause* 自發的陣陣掌聲 **2** an occasion when sth bursts; the hole left where sth has burst 爆裂；裂口：*a burst in a water pipe* 水管上的裂縫 **3** a short series of shots from a gun 一陣短促的射擊：*frequent bursts of machine-gun fire* 機槍的頻頻掃射

bursty /ˈbɜːsti; NAmE ˈbɜːrsti/ *adj.* (**burst·ier**, **bursti·est**) **1** (*technical* 術語) used to describe data that is sent in small, sudden groups of signals 突發式數據的；集送數據的；脈衝數據的：*a bursty connection* 突發式連接 ◇ *bursty Internet traffic* 突發性網絡擁塞 **2** (*informal*) occurring at intervals, for short periods of time 陣發性的；間歇的

bur·ton /ˈbɜːtn; NAmE ˈbɜːrtn/ *noun*

IDM **gone for a ˈburton** (*old-fashioned, BrE, informal*) lost or destroyed 失蹤；毀壞了

bury /ˈberi/ *verb* (**bur·ies**, **bury·ing**, **bur·ied**, **bur·ied**)

▸ DEAD PERSON 死人 **1 ~ sb/sth** to place a dead body in a grave 埋葬；安葬：*He was buried in Highgate Cemetery.* 他被安葬在海格特墓地。◇ (*figurative*) *Their ambitions were finally* **dead and buried**. 他們的雄心壯志最終給埋葬了。 **2 ~ sb** (*old-fashioned*) to lose sb by death 喪失（某人）：*She's 85 and has buried three husbands.* 她 85 歲了，三度喪夫。

▸ HIDE IN GROUND 埋藏 **3 ~ sth** to hide sth in the ground 把（某物）掩藏在地下；埋藏：*buried treasure* 埋藏的財寶 ◇ *The dog had buried its bone in the garden.* 狗把骨頭埋在花園裏。

▸ COVER 覆蓋 **4** [often passive] to cover sb/sth with soil, rocks, leaves, etc.（以土、石、樹葉等）覆蓋：**~ sb/sth** *The house was buried under ten feet of snow.* 房子被埋在十英尺厚的積雪中。◇ **~ sb/sth + adj.** *The miners were* **buried alive** *when the tunnel collapsed.* 坑道塌方，礦工都被活埋。 **5 ~ sth** to cover sth so that it cannot be seen 遮蓋；掩蓋：*Your letter got buried under a pile of papers.* 你的信被壓在一堆文件底下。◇ *He buried his face in his hands and wept.* 他雙手掩面而泣。

▸ HIDE FEELING 掩藏感情 **6 ~ sth** to ignore or hide a feeling, a mistake, etc. 不顧，掩藏（感情、錯誤等）：*She had learnt to bury her feelings.* 她已經學會了感情不外露。

▸ PUT DEEPLY INTO STH 插入 **7 ~ sth (in sth)** to put sth deeply into sth else 使陷入，把…插入（某物）：*He walked slowly, his hands buried in his pockets.* 他雙手插在口袋裏緩步而行。◇ *She always has her head buried in a book.* 她總是埋頭讀書。

IDM **ˌbury the ˈhatchet | ˌbury your ˈdifferences** to stop being unfriendly and become friends again 消除隔閡（重歸於好）➲ more at HEAD *n.*

PHR V **ˈbury yourself in sth 1** to give all your attention to sth 專心致志於某事：*Since she left, he's buried himself in his work.* 自從她走後，他全心撲在工作上。 **2** to go to or be in a place where you will not meet many people 隱居：*She buried herself in the country to write a book.* 她隱居鄉間寫書。

bus /bʌs/ *noun, verb*

■ *noun* (*pl.* **buses**, *US* also **busses**) **1** a large road vehicle that carries passengers, especially one that travels along a fixed route and stops regularly to let people get on and off 公共汽車；巴士：*Shall we walk or go* **by bus**? 我們步行呢，還是坐公共汽車？◇ *A regular bus service connects the train station with the town centre.* 火車站和市中心之間有定時班車。◇ *a* **bus company/driver** 公共汽車公司 / 司機 ◇ *a school bus* 校車 ➲ VISUAL VOCAB page V57 ➲ compare COACH *n.* (4), (5), (6) ➲ see also BUS LANE, BUS SHELTER, BUS STATION, BUS STOP, MINIBUS, TROLLEYBUS **2** (*computing* 計) a set of wires that carries information from one part of a computer system to another（計算機系統的）總線

■ *verb* (**-s-** or **-ss-**) **1 ~ sb (from/to ...)** to transport sb by bus 用公共汽車運送：*We were bussed from the airport to our hotel.* 公共汽車把我們從機場送到旅館。 **2 ~ sb** (*NAmE*) to transport young people by bus to another area so that students of different races can be educated together 用校車送（學生往外區就讀，使不同種族的學生一起受教育） **3 ~ sth** (*NAmE*) to take the dirty plates, etc. off the tables in a restaurant, as a job（在餐廳裏）收盤子，打雜

B

bus·boy /ˈbʌsbɔɪ/ *noun* (*NAmE*) a person who works in a restaurant and whose job is to clear the dirty dishes, etc. 餐廳勤雜工（負責收餐具、抹桌等）

busby /ˈbʌzbi/ *noun* (*pl.* **-ies**) a tall fur hat worn by some British soldiers for special ceremonies （英國士兵在特別場合戴的）毛皮高頂帽

bush /bʊʃ/ *noun*
1 [C] a plant that grows thickly with several hard STEMS coming up from the root 灌木： *a rose bush* 玫瑰叢 ◇ *holly bushes* 冬青樹叢 ➲ compare TREE **2** [C] a thing that looks like a bush, especially an area of thick hair or fur 類似灌木的東西（尤指濃密的毛髮或皮毛）**3** (often **the bush**) [U] an area of wild land that has not been cleared, especially in Africa and Australia; in New Zealand an area where the forest has not been cleared （尤指非洲和澳大利亞的）荒野；（新西蘭未被砍伐的）林區 **IDM** see BEAT *v.*, BIRD *n.*

bush·baby /ˈbʊʃbeɪbi/ *noun* (*pl.* **-ies**) a small African animal with large eyes, which lives in trees 灌叢嬰猴（生活於非洲叢林）

bushed /bʊʃt/ *adj.* [not before noun] (*informal*) very tired 疲乏不堪 **SYN** **exhausted**

bushel /ˈbʊʃl/ *noun* **1** [C] a unit for measuring grain and fruit (equal in volume to 8 gallons) 蒲式耳（穀物和水果的容量單位，相當於 8 加侖）**2** **bushels** [pl.] **~ (of sth)** (*NAmE, informal*) a large amount of sth 大量；很多 **IDM** see HIDE *v.*

ˈbush fire *noun* a fire in a large area of rough open ground, especially one that spreads quickly 野火；山林大火

bush·fowl /ˈbʊʃfaʊl/ *noun* [C, U] (**bush·fowl** or **bush·fowls**) (*WAfrE*) a bird with a large body and brown and white feathers that walks a lot on the ground and is often used for food 鷓鴣（常食用）

bu·shido /ˈbʊʃiːdəʊ; bʊˈʃiːdəʊ; *NAmE* -doʊ/ *noun* [U] (from *Japanese*) the system of honour and morals of the Japanese SAMURAI 武士道

ˈbush-league *adj.* (*NAmE, informal*) of very low quality 質量低劣的；次等的

Bush·man /ˈbʊʃmən/ *noun* (*pl.* **-men** /-mən/) **1** a member of one of the races of people from southern Africa who live and hunt in the African BUSH 布須曼人（非洲南部土著民族）**2** **bushman** a person who lives, works or travels in the Australian BUSH 布須曼人（在澳大利亞灌木地帶流寓、工作的人）

bush·meat /ˈbʊʃmiːt/ *noun* [U] the meat of wild animals used as food, for example African animals 野味

bush·ran·ger /ˈbʊʃreɪndʒə(r)/ *noun* (*AustralE, NZE*) (in the past) an OUTLAW (= a person who has done sth illegal and is hiding to avoid being caught) who lives in the bush (= areas of wild land far away from large towns) 綠林好漢（舊時的叢林逃犯）

ˈbush rat *noun* [C, U] (*pl.* **bush rat** or **bush rats**) (in W Africa) a type of large RODENT similar to a RAT that is found in wild areas and used for food 蹊鼠（產於西非，可食用）

ˌbush ˈtelegraph *noun* [U, sing.] (*informal, humorous*) the process by which information and news are passed quickly from person to person （信息等的）迅速傳播，迅速散播

bush·whack /ˈbʊʃwæk/ *verb* **1** [I] to live or travel in wild country 在野外生活（或旅行）**2** [I] **+ adv./prep.** to cut your way through bushes, plants, etc. in wild country 在叢林（或植物叢等）中開路： *We had to bush-whack through undergrowth.* 我們只好在灌木叢中劈開一條路。 **3** [T] **~ sb** to attack sb very suddenly from a hidden position 伏擊 **SYN** **ambush** **4** [I] to fight as a GUERRILLA 游擊作戰；打游擊戰 ▶ **bush·whacking** *noun* [U]

bush·whack·er /ˈbʊʃwækə(r)/ *noun* **1** a person who lives or travels in an area of wild country 荒野居民；荒野旅行者 **2** a person who fights in a GUERRILLA war 游擊隊員

bushy /ˈbʊʃi/ *adj.* (**bush·ier**, **bushi·est**) **1** (of hair or fur 毛髮或毛皮) growing thickly 濃密的： *a bushy beard/tail* 密匝匝的鬍子；毛茸茸的尾巴 ◇ *bushy eyebrows* 濃密的眉毛 **2** (of plants 植物) growing thickly, with a lot of leaves 茂密的；多葉的

ˌbushy-ˈtailed *adj.* ➲ BRIGHT-EYED

busily ➲ BUSY

busi·ness /ˈbɪznəs/ *noun*
▸ **TRADE** 貿易 **1** [U] the activity of making, buying, selling or supplying goods or services for money 商業；買賣；生意 **SYN** **commerce, trade**： *business contacts/affairs/interests* 商業聯繫／事務／利益 ◇ *a business investment* 商業投資 ◇ *It's been a pleasure to* ***do business with*** *you.* 和你做買賣很愉快。◇ *She has set up* ***in business*** *as a hairdresser.* 她已經開店當理髮師。◇ *When he left school, he* ***went into business*** *with his brother.* 他畢業後和他哥哥去經商了。◇ *She works in the computer business.* 她從事電腦業。 ➲ see also AGRIBUSINESS, BIG BUSINESS, SHOW BUSINESS
▸ **WORK** 工作 **2** [U] work that is part of your job 商務；公事： *Is the trip to Rome* ***business or pleasure****?* 這次去羅馬是公幹還是遊玩？◇ *a business lunch* 商務午餐 ◇ *He's away* ***on business****.* 他出差去了。 **3** [U] the amount of work done by a company, etc.; the rate or quality of this work 營業額；貿易額： *Business was bad.* 生意不景氣。◇ *Business was booming.* 生意興隆。◇ *Her job was to drum up* (= increase) *business.* 她的工作是提高營業額。◇ *How's business?* 生意如何？
▸ **COMPANY** 公司 **4** [C] a commercial organization such as a company, shop/store or factory 商業機構；企業；公司；商店；工廠： *to* ***have/start/run a business*** 擁有／開辦／經營企業 ◇ *business premises* 商務場址 ◇ *She works in the family business.* 她在家族的企業工作。◇ *They've got a small catering business.* 他們從事小規模的餐宴承辦業務。
▸ **RESPONSIBILITY** 職責 **5** [U] something that concerns a particular person or organization 歸（某人或某機構）管的事；職責： *It is the business of the police to protect the community.* 警察的職責是保護社會。◇ *I shall* ***make it my business*** *to find out who is responsible.* 我要親自查出是誰的責任。◇ *My private life is* ***none of your business*** (= does not concern you). 我的私生活與你無關。◇ *It's* ***no business of yours*** *who I invite to the party.* 你無權過問我邀請誰參加聚會。
▸ **IMPORTANT MATTERS** 要事 **6** [U] important matters that need to be dealt with or discussed （需要處理或討論的）重要事情，要點： *the main business of the meeting* 會議的主要議題 ◇ *He has some* ***unfinished business*** *to deal with.* 他還要處理一些尚未了結的事務。
▸ **EVENT** 事情 **7** [sing.] (usually with an adjective 通常與形容詞連用) a matter, an event or a situation 事情；事件；狀況： *That plane crash was a terrible business.* 那次飛機墜毀是十分可怕的事。◇ *I found the whole business very depressing.* 我覺得整件事令人沮喪。◇ *The business of the missing tickets hasn't been sorted out.* 遺失票這件事還沒解決呢。
▸ **BEING A CUSTOMER** 消費 **8** (*especially NAmE*) (also *BrE, formal* **cus·tom**) [U] the fact of a person or people buying goods or services at a shop/store or business （顧客對商店的）惠顧，光顧： *We're grateful for your business.* 感謝您光顧本店。

IDM **any other ˈbusiness** the things that are discussed at the end of an official meeting that do not appear on the AGENDA （會議結束前）議程以外的議題： *I think we've finished item four. Now is there any other business?* 我想我們已經討論完第四項。還有其他要討論的嗎？ ➲ see also AOB **be in ˈbusiness** (*informal*) to have everything that you need in order to be able to start sth immediately 準備就緒： *All we need is a car and we'll be in business.* 我們所需要的只是一輛車，然後我們就準備就緒了。 **be the ˈbusiness** (*informal*) to be very good 很好 **business as ˈusual** a way of saying that things will continue as normal despite a difficult situation （儘管處境困難）一切照常，不受干擾 **ˌbusiness is ˈbusiness** a way of saying that financial and commercial matters are the important things to consider and you should not be influenced by friendship, etc. 公事公辦 **get down to ˈbusiness** to start dealing with the matter that needs to be dealt with, or doing the work that needs to be done 着手處理正事；開始認真工作 **go about your 'business** to do the things that you normally do 忙自己的事；做通常做的事：*streets filled with people going about their daily business* 擠滿為日常工作奔忙的人的街道 **have no business doing sth | have no business to do sth** to have no right to do sth 無權做某事：*You have no business being here.* 你無權待在這裏。**like 'nobody's business** (*BrE, informal*) very much, very fast, very well, etc. 非常；很多；很快；很好：*I've been working like nobody's business to get it finished in time.* 為按時完成任務，我一直在快馬加鞭地工作。**not be in the business of doing sth** not intending to do sth (which it would be surprising for you to do) 無意做某事：*I'm not in the business of getting other people to do my work for me.* 我無意讓別人替我工作。**out of 'business** having stopped operating as a business because there is no more money or work available 停業；歇業：*The new regulations will put many small businesses* ***out of business.*** 新法規將使很多小企業關閉。◇ *Some travel companies will probably* ***go out of business*** *this summer.* 今年夏天一些旅遊公司很可能歇業。➲ more at MEAN *v.*, MIND *v.*, PLY *v.*

'business administration *noun* [U] the study of how to manage a business 工商管理學：*a master's degree in business administration* (= an MBA) 工商管理學碩士學位

'business card (also **card**) *noun* a small card printed with sb's name and details of their job and company （業務）名片 ➲ compare VISITING CARD

'business class (*BrE* also **'club class**) *noun* [U] the part of a plane where passengers have a high level of comfort and service, designed for people travelling on business, and less expensive than first class （飛機上的）公務艙，商務艙 ▶ **'business class** (*BrE* also **'club class**) *adv.*：*I always fly business class.* 我總是乘坐商務艙旅行。

the 'business end *noun* [sing.] **~ (of sth)** (*informal*) the end of a tool or weapon which performs its main function （工具或武器）行使主要功能的一端，使用的一頭

Collocations 詞語搭配

Business 商業

Running a business 經營企業

- **buy/acquire/own/sell** a company/firm/franchise 收購／獲得／擁有／出售公司／商行／特許經銷權
- **set up/establish/ start/start up/launch** a business/company 創辦企業／公司
- **run/operate** a business/company/franchise 經營企業／公司／專賣店
- **head/run** a firm/department/team 管理公司／部門／團隊
- **make/secure/win/block** a deal 達成／阻止一筆交易
- **expand/grow/build** the business 擴展業務
- **boost/increase** investment/spending/sales/turnover/earnings/exports/trade 增加投資／支出／銷售量／營業額／收入／出口／貿易
- **increase/expand** production/output/sales 增加產量／輸出量／銷售量
- **boost/maximize** production/productivity/efficiency/income/revenue/profit/profitability 使產量／生產力／效率／收入／收益／利潤／收益增加／最大化
- **achieve/maintain/sustain** growth/profitability 實現／維持／保持增長／收益
- **cut/reduce/bring down/lower/slash** costs/prices 削減成本／價格
- **announce/impose/make** cuts/cutbacks 宣佈／強制實行／實施削減

Sales and marketing 銷售和市場營銷

- **break into/enter/capture/dominate** the market 打入／進入／佔領／控制市場
- **gain/grab/take/win/boost/lose** market share 取得／奪取／得到／贏得／增加／丟失市場份額
- **find/build/create** a market for sth 為某物找到／建立／開創市場
- **start/launch** an advertising/a marketing campaign 發起廣告／營銷宣傳活動
- **develop/launch/promote** a product/website 開發／推出／推銷產品／網站
- **create/generate** demand for your product 為產品創造需求
- **attract/get/retain/help** customers/clients 吸引／贏得／留住／幫助顧客／客戶
- **drive/generate/boost/increase** demand/sales 刺激／創造／提高／增加需求／銷售量
- **beat/keep ahead of/out-think/outperform** the competition 打敗／領先於／智勝／勝過競爭對手
- **meet/reach/exceed/miss** sales targets 完成／達到／超過／未達到銷售目標

Finance 財務

- **draw up/set/present/agree/approve** a budget 起草／制訂／提出／同意／批准預算
- **keep to/balance/cut/reduce/slash** the budget 執行／平衡／削減／大幅削減預算
- **be/come in below/under/over/within** budget 未超出／超出預算；在預算之內
- **generate** income/revenue/profit/funds/business 產生收益／利潤／資金／營業額
- **fund/finance** a campaign/a venture/an expansion/spending/a deficit 為活動／商業項目／擴張／開支／赤字提供資金
- **provide/raise/allocate** capital/funds 提供／籌集／分配資金
- **attract/encourage** investment/investors 吸引／鼓勵投資／投資者
- **recover/recoup** costs/losses/an investment 收回成本／虧損／投資
- **get/obtain/offer sb/grant sb** credit/a loan 獲得／為某人提供／准予某人貸款
- **apply for/raise/secure/arrange/provide** finance 申請／籌集／獲得／安排／提供資金

Failure 失敗；不成功

- **lose** business/trade/customers/sales/revenue 失去生意／買賣／顧客／銷量／收益
- **accumulate/accrue/incur/run up** debts 累積／積累／招致／積欠債務
- **suffer/sustain** enormous/heavy/serious losses 蒙受慘重損失
- **face** cuts/a deficit/redundancy/bankruptcy 面臨削減／赤字／裁員／破產
- **file for/** (*NAmE*) **enter/avoid/escape** bankruptcy 申請／避免／幸免破產
- (*BrE*) **go into** administration/liquidation 進入行政接管／清算
- **liquidate/wind up** a company 清算／關閉公司
- **survive/weather** a recession/downturn 艱難度過蕭條期／衰退期
- **propose/seek/block/oppose** a merger 提出／尋求／阻止／反對合併
- **launch/make/accept/defeat** a takeover bid 發起／進行／接受／阻止收購投標

'business hours *noun* [pl.] the hours in a day that a shop/store or company is open 營業時間；辦公時間

busi·ness·like /'bɪznəslaɪk/ *adj.* (of a person 人) working in an efficient and organized way and not wasting time or thinking about personal things 效率高的；井然有序的；工作認真而有條理的：*She adopted a brisk businesslike tone.* 她用一種公務口吻，說話乾脆利落。

busi·ness·man 0‒ /'bɪznəsmæn; -mən/, **busi·ness·woman** /'bɪznəswʊmən/ *noun* (*pl.* **-men** /-men; -mən/, **-women** /-wɪmɪn/)
1 0‒ a person who works in business, especially at a high level（尤指上層）商界人員；企業家 **2** 0‒ a person who is skilful in business and financial matters 商界能手；善做生意的人：*I should have got a better price for the car, but I'm not much of a businessman.* 那輛車我本應賣個更好的價錢，但我不大會做生意。➲ note at GENDER

'business park *noun* an area of land that is specially designed for offices and small factories 工商業園區

'business person *noun* a person who works in business, especially at a high level（尤指高層的）商界人士；實業家

'business school *noun* a part of a college or university that teaches business, often to GRADUATES (= people who already have a first degree)（大學裏針對畢業生的）工商學院

'business studies *noun* [U+sing./pl. v.] the study of subjects connected with money and managing a business 企業管理研究；商學：*a degree in business studies* 企業管理學位

,business-to-'business *adj.* [usually before noun] (*abbr.* **B2B**) done between one business and another rather than between a business and its ordinary customers 企業對企業的

bus·ing (*NAmE*) = BUSSING

busk /bʌsk/ *verb* [I] to perform music in a public place and ask for money from people passing by 街頭賣藝 ▸ **busk·er** *noun* ➲ VISUAL VOCAB pages V2, V3 **busk·ing** *noun* [U]

'bus lane *noun* a part of a road that only buses are allowed to use 公共汽車專用道

bus·load /'bʌsləʊd; *NAmE* -loʊd/ *noun* (*especially NAmE*) a large group of people on a bus 公共汽車上一大車的人

,bus·man's 'holi·day *noun* [sing.] a holiday that is spent doing the same thing that you do at work 做日常工作的假日

'bus pass *noun* **1** a ticket that allows you to travel on any bus within a particular area for a fixed period of time 公車月票（憑此票可在特定時間內在某一地區乘坐任何公共汽車） **2** a ticket that allows people from particular groups (for example, students or old people) to travel free or at a reduced cost 免費巴士票，乘車優惠票（為學生、老人等而設）：(*BrE, humorous*) *I'm not old enough for my bus pass yet!* 我還不到領取免費乘車票的年齡。

'bus shelter *noun* a structure with a roof where people can stand while they are waiting for a bus 公共汽車候車亭

buss·ing (also *NAmE* **bus·ing**) /'bʌsɪŋ/ *noun* [U] (in the US) a system of transporting young people by bus to another area so that students of different races can be educated together（美國）校車接送制度（用校車接送學生去其他校區上學，讓不同種族的學生一同受教育）

'bus station *noun* the place in a town or city where buses (especially to or from other towns) leave and arrive 公共汽車站；（尤指）長途汽車站

'bus stop *noun* a place at the side of a road that is marked with a sign, where buses stop 公共汽車停靠站 ➲ VISUAL VOCAB page V3

bust /bʌst/ *verb, noun, adj.*
■ *verb* (**bust, bust**) or (**bust·ed, bust·ed**) (*informal*) **1 ~ sth** to break sth 打破；摔碎：*I bust my camera.* 我把照相機摔壞了。◇ *The lights are busted.* 燈泡被砸碎了。◇ *Come out, or I'll bust the door down!* 出來，不然我就砸門了！ **2 ~ sb/sth (for sth)** (of the police 警方) to suddenly enter a place and search it or arrest sb 突擊搜查（或搜捕）：*He's been busted for drugs.* 他因涉嫌毒品而遭到拘捕。 **3 ~ sb** (*especially NAmE*) to make sb lower in military rank as a punishment（使）降級，降低軍階 SYN **demote**
IDM **bust a 'gut (doing sth/to do sth)** (*informal*) to make a great effort to do sth 努力（做某事）… **or 'bust** (*informal*) used to say that you will try very hard to get somewhere or achieve sth（表示將全力以赴）：*For him it's the Olympics or bust.* 他將竭盡全力參加奧運會。
PHR V **,bust 'up** (*informal*) (of a couple, friends, partners, etc. 夫妻、朋友、合夥人等) to have an argument and separate 吵翻；分手 SYN **break up**：*They bust up after five years of marriage.* 他們結婚五年後離異了。➲ related noun BUST-UP **,bust sth↔'up** (*informal*) to make sth end by disturbing or ruining it 斷送；毀滅 SYN **break sth up**：*It was his drinking that bust up his marriage.* 是他的酗酒葬送了他的婚姻。
■ *noun* **1** a stone or metal model of a person's head, shoulders and chest（石或金屬的）半身像 **2** (used especially when talking about clothes or measurements) a woman's breasts or the measurement around the breasts and back（尤指衣服或尺寸）女子的胸部，胸圍：*What is your bust measurement, Madam?* 您的胸圍是多少，太太？ **3** (*informal*) an unexpected visit made by the police in order to arrest people for doing sth illegal（警方的）突擊搜捕，突擊搜查：*a drug bust* 突擊搜查毒品 **4** (*NAmE*) a thing that is not good 蹩腳的東西；沒價值的事物：*As a show it was a bust.* 作為一場演出，那可不怎麼樣。
■ *adj.* [not usually before noun] (*informal*) **1** (*BrE*) broken 破碎；毀壞：*My watch is bust.* 我的錶壞了。 **2** (of a person or business 個人或企業) failed because of a lack of money 破產 SYN **bankrupt**：*We're bust!* 我們破產了！◇ *We lost our money when the travel company **went bust**.* 旅行社破產，我們的錢都賠了進去。

bus·tard /'bʌstəd; *NAmE* 'bʌstərd/ *noun* a large European bird that can run fast 鴇（見於歐洲，奔跑速度快）

busted /'bʌstɪd/ *adj.* [not before noun] (*NAmE, informal*) caught in the act of doing sth wrong and likely to be punished 被當場逮住：*You are so busted!* 你被當場逮住了！

bus·ter /'bʌstə(r)/ *noun* **1** (*NAmE, informal*) used to speak to a man you do not like（稱呼不喜歡的男子）：*Get lost, buster!* 走開，小子！ **2** (usually in compounds; often used in newspapers 通常構成複合詞；常用於報章) a person or thing that stops or gets rid of sth 遏制者；破壞者：*crime-busters* 打擊犯罪活動的人

bus·tier /'bʌstieɪ/ *noun* a woman's tight top which does not cover the arms or shoulders（露臂肩的）緊身女胸衣

bus·tle /'bʌsl/ *verb, noun*
■ *verb* [I, T] to move around in a busy way or to hurry sb in a particular direction 四下忙碌；催促（某人向某方向）：**+ adv./prep.** *She bustled around in the kitchen.* 她在廚房裏忙得團團轉。◇ **~ sb + adv./prep.** *The nurse bustled us out of the room.* 護士催促我們離開房間。
■ *noun* **1** [U] busy and noisy activity 忙亂嘈雜；喧鬧：*the **hustle and bustle** of city life* 都市生活的喧鬧繁忙 **2** [C] a frame that was worn under a skirt by women in the past in order to hold the skirt out at the back（舊時女子用的）裙撐

bust·ling /'bʌslɪŋ/ *adj.* full of people moving about in a busy way 繁忙的；熙熙攘攘的：*a bustling city* 熙熙攘攘的城市 ◇ **~ with sth** *The market was bustling with life.* 市場一片蓬勃。

'bust-up *noun* (*informal, especially BrE*) **1** a bad argument or very angry disagreement 激烈的爭吵；憤怒的爭執 SYN **row**：*Sue and Tony had a bust-up and aren't speaking to each other.* 蘇和托尼大吵了一架，現在誰也不理誰。 **2** the end of a relationship 關係的結束；破裂 SYN **break-up**：*the final bust-up of their marriage* 他們的婚姻的最終破裂

busty /'bʌsti/ *adj.* (*informal*) (of a woman 女子) having large breasts 胸部豐滿的

bus·way /ˈbʌsweɪ/ *noun* (*BrE*) a road or section of a road that can only be used by buses, especially one with special tracks for guiding the buses 公共汽車專用路；公交專用道

busy 🔑 /ˈbɪzi/ *adj., verb*

■ ***adj.*** (**busier**, **busi·est**)

▸ **DOING STH** 做事情 **1** 🔑 having a lot to do; perhaps not free to do sth else because you are working on sth 忙碌的；無暇的：*Are you busy tonight?* 你今晚忙嗎？◇ *I'm afraid the doctor is busy at the moment. Can he call you back?* 恐怕醫生現在沒空。讓他給你回話行嗎？◇ *I'll be too busy to come to the meeting.* 我會很忙，不能到會。◇ *The principal is a very busy woman.* 校長是個大忙人。◇ *She was always too busy to listen.* 她總是很忙，無暇聽我說話。◇ *a very busy life* 繁忙的生活 ◇ **~ with sth/sb** *Kate's busy with her homework.* 凱特正忙着做家庭作業。 **2** 🔑 **~ (doing sth)** spending a lot of time on sth 忙於（做某事）：*James is busy practising for the school concert.* 詹姆斯正忙着為學校音樂會排練。◇ *Let's get busy with the clearing up.* 我們開始清理吧。

▸ **PLACE** 地方 **3** 🔑 full of people, activity, vehicles, etc. 人來車往的；熙熙攘攘的：*a busy main road* 熙熙攘攘的大街 ◇ *Victoria is one of London's busiest stations.* 維多利亞站是倫敦最繁忙的車站之一。

▸ **PERIOD OF TIME** 一段時間 **4** 🔑 full of work and activity 工作忙的；充滿活動的：*Have you had a busy day?* 你今天忙了一天嗎？◇ *This is one of the busiest times of the year for the department.* 這是部門裏一年中最忙的時間。

▸ **TELEPHONE** 電話 **5** 🔑 (*especially NAmE*) being used 正被佔用的；佔線的 **SYN** **engaged**：*The line is busy—I'll try again later.* 電話佔線，我過會兒再打。◇ *the busy signal* 忙音 ➲ COLLOCATIONS at PHONE

▸ **PATTERN/DESIGN** 圖案；圖樣 **6** too full of small details 雜亂的；紛繁的；令人眼花繚亂的 ▸ **busily** *adv.*：*He was busily engaged repairing his bike.* 他正忙着修他的自行車。

IDM **as busy as a ˈbee** very busy 忙得不可開交 **keep yourself ˈbusy** to find enough things to do 不讓自己閒着：*Since she retired she's kept herself very busy.* 自從退休後，她一直沒閒着。

■ ***verb*** (**busies**, **busy·ing**, **busied**, **busied**) to fill your time doing an activity or a task 忙着做某事：**~ yourself (with sth)** *She busied herself with the preparations for the party.* 她忙於準備晚會。◇ **~ yourself (in/with) doing sth** *While we talked, Bill busied himself fixing lunch.* 我們談話時，比爾忙着做午飯。

busy·body /ˈbɪzibɒdi; *NAmE* -bɑːdi/ *noun* (*pl.* **-ies**) (*disapproving*) a person who is too interested in what other people are doing 好事的人：*He's an interfering old busybody!* 他老愛管閒事！

busy Lizzie /ˌbɪzi ˈlɪzi/ *noun* a small plant with a lot of red, pink or white flowers, often grown indoors or in gardens 非洲鳳仙花

busy·work /ˈbɪziwɜːk; *NAmE* -wɜːrk/ *noun* [U] (*NAmE*) work that is given to sb to keep them busy, without really being useful 消磨時間的工作

but 🔑 /bət; *strong form* bʌt/ *conj., prep., adv., noun*

■ ***conj.*** **1** 🔑 used to introduce a word or phrase that contrasts with what was said before 而；相反：*I got it wrong. It wasn't the red one but the blue one.* 我弄錯了。不是紅的那個，是藍的那個。◇ *His mother won't be there, but his father might.* 他母親不會去那裏，但他父親也許會去。◇ *It isn't that he lied exactly, but he did tend to exaggerate.* 他不見得是真的說謊，但他的確是有意誇大。 **2** 🔑 however; despite this 然而；儘管如此：*I'd asked everybody but only two people came.* 每個人我都請了，卻只來了兩個人。◇ *By the end of the day we were tired but happy.* 一天結束時，我們很累，但很高興。➲ LANGUAGE BANK at NEVERTHELESS **3** 🔑 used when you are saying sorry about sth（表示歉意時說）：*I'm sorry but I can't stay any longer.* 很抱歉，我不能再待下去了。 **4** 🔑 used to introduce a statement that shows that you are surprised or annoyed, or that you disagree（引出下文，表示吃驚、生氣或不同意）：*But that's not possible!* 但那是不可能的！◇ *'Here's the money I owe you.' 'But that's not right—it was only £10.'* "這是我欠你的錢。" "但這不對呀，我只借了 10 英鎊給你。" **5** except 除⋯外；只有：*I had no choice but to sign the contract.* 我別無選擇，只好簽了合同。 **6** used before repeating a word in order to emphasize it（重複字詞前用，加強語氣）：*Nothing, but nothing would make him change his mind.* 沒有什麼，絕對沒有什麼會使他改變主意。 **7** (*literary*) used to emphasize that sth is always true（強調一貫真實）：*She never passed her old home but she thought of the happy years she had spent there* (= she always thought of them). 她從沒有經過自己的舊居，但會想起在那裏度過的幸福歲月。

IDM **but for** **1** if it were not for 倘若沒有；若非；要不是：*He would have played but for a knee injury.* 他要不是膝部有傷的話，就上場了。 **2** except for（表示不包括在內）除了⋯外：*The square was empty but for a couple of cabs.* 除了幾輛出租汽車外，廣場上空空如也。 **but then (again)** **1** however; on the other hand 然而；另一方面：*He might agree. But then again he might have a completely different opinion.* 他可能同意，但也可能會意見完全相反。 **2** used before a statement that explains or gives a reason for what has just been said（引出解釋或原因）：*She speaks very good Italian. But then she did live in Rome for a year* (= so it's not surprising). 她的意大利語講得很流利。不過她畢竟在羅馬生活過一年。 **you cannot/could not but ...** (*formal*) used to show that everything else is impossible except the thing that you are saying 只有；除⋯之外別無可能：*What could he do but forgive her?* (= that was the only thing possible) 他不原諒她又能怎麼辦？

■ ***prep.*** except; apart from 除了；除⋯之外：*We've had nothing but trouble with this car.* 我們這輛車淨出毛病。◇ *The problem is anything but easy.* 這個問題一點也不簡單。◇ *Who but Rosa could think of something like that?* 除了羅莎，誰會想得到那種事？◇ *Everyone was there but him.* 除他之外，大家都在。◇ *I came* ***last but one*** *in the race* (= I wasn't last but next to last). 我賽跑得了倒數第二名。◇ *Take the first turning but one* (= not the first one but the one after it). 在第二個拐彎處轉彎。

■ ***adv.*** only 只有；僅僅：*I don't think we'll manage it. Still, we can but try.* 我想我們應付不了這事。但不妨試試。◇ *There were a lot of famous people there: Tom Hanks and Julia Roberts, to name but two.* 那裏有很多名人：只提兩個名字吧，有湯姆•漢克斯和朱莉婭•羅伯茨。

■ ***noun*** /bʌt/ [usually pl.] a reason that sb gives for not doing sth or not agreeing 藉口；託辭：*'Let us have no buts,' he said firmly. 'You are coming.'* "別找藉口了。" 他堅定地說，"你得來。" ◇ *With so many* ***ifs and buts****, it is easier to wait and see.* 有這麼多託辭，還是靜觀其變吧。

bu·tane /ˈbjuːteɪn/ *noun* [U] a gas produced from PETROLEUM, used in liquid form as a fuel for cooking etc. 丁烷

butch /bʊtʃ/ *adj.* (*informal*) **1** (of a woman 女子) behaving or dressing like a man（舉止或衣着）男子般的，男性化的 ➲ compare FEMME **2** (of a man 男子) big, and often behaving in an aggressive way 高大的；（常指）雄赳赳氣昂昂的

butcher /ˈbʊtʃə(r)/ *noun, verb*

■ ***noun*** **1** a person whose job is cutting up and selling meat in a shop/store or killing animals for this purpose 屠夫；肉販 **2** **butcher's** (*pl.* **butchers**) a shop/store that sells meat 肉店；肉鋪：*He owns the butcher's in the main street.* 他在大街上開了一家肉鋪。 **3** a person who kills people in a cruel and violent way 劊子手

IDM **have/take a ˈbutcher's** (*BrE, slang*) to have a look at sth 觀看 **ORIGIN** From rhyming slang, in which **butcher's hook** stands for 'look'. 源自同韻俚語，其中的 butcher's hook 代表 look。

■ ***verb*** **1 ~ sb** to kill people in a very cruel and violent way 屠殺；殺戮 **2 ~ sth** to kill animals and cut them up for use as meat 屠宰；宰殺 **3 ~ sth** (*especially NAmE*) to spoil sth by doing it very badly 弄砸；糟蹋：*The script was good, but those guys butchered it.* 劇本很好，但讓那幫傢伙演砸了。

ˈbutcher block *noun* [U] (*NAmE*) a material used for surfaces in kitchens, especially those that you work on 廚房面板；（尤指）案板，砧板

ˈbutcher's block *noun* a thick block of wood on which a butcher cuts meat, also used in kitchens as a surface for cutting food on （肉販的）砧板，肉墩子；（廚房）案板，砧板

butch·ery /ˈbʊtʃəri/ *noun* [U] **1** cruel, violent and unnecessary killing 殘殺；殺戮 **2** the work of preparing meat to be sold 屠宰工作

but·ler /ˈbʌtlə(r)/ *noun* the main male servant in a large house 男管家

butt /bʌt/ *verb, noun*

■ ***verb* 1 ~ sb/sth** to hit or push sb/sth hard with your head （人）用頭頂撞 **2 ~ sb/sth** if an animal **butts** sb/sth, it hits them or it hard with its horns and head （動物）用頭（或角）頂

PHR V **ˌbutt ˈin (on sb/sth)** **1** to interrupt a conversation rudely 插嘴；打斷說話：*How can I explain if you keep butting in?* 你一直插嘴，我還怎麼解釋？◇ **+ speech** *'Is that normal?' Josie butted in.* "那是正常的嗎？"喬西插了一句。 **2** (*informal*) to become involved in a situation that does not concern you 插手；干涉 **SYN** **interfere (in)**: *I didn't ask you to butt in on my private business.* 我沒請你干預我的私事。 **ˌbutt ˈout** (*informal, especially NAmE*) used to tell sb rudely to go away or to stop INTERFERING in sth that does not concern them 走開；別管閒事：*Butt out, Neil! This is none of your business.* 不許插手，尼爾！這不關你的事。

■ ***noun* 1** the thick end of a weapon or tool （武器或工具的）粗大的一端：*a rifle butt* 步槍的槍托 **2** the part of a cigarette or CIGAR that is left after it has been smoked 煙蒂；煙頭 **3** (*BrE*) a large round container for storing or collecting liquids （盛液體的）大桶：*a water butt* 集雨桶 **4** (*informal, especially NAmE*) the part of the body that you sit on 屁股 **SYN** **buttocks**: *Get off your butt and do some work!* 起來幹點活兒吧！◇ *Get your butt over here!* (= Come here!) 過來！ **5** the act of hitting sb with your head （頭的）頂撞：*a butt from his head* 被他的頭撞的一下 ➲ see also HEADBUTT

IDM **be the butt of sth** to be the person or thing that other people often joke about or criticize 受到嘲諷（或批評）；是笑柄（或話柄等） **SYN** **target**: *She was the butt of some very unkind jokes.* 她受到了刻薄的嘲弄。 ➲ more at PAIN *n.*

butte /bjuːt/ *noun* (*especially NAmE*) a hill that is flat on top and is separate from other high ground 地垛（頂部平坦的小丘、高地）

but·ter 🔑 /ˈbʌtə(r)/ *noun, verb*

■ ***noun*** 🔑 [U] a soft yellow food made from cream, used in cooking and for spreading on bread 黃油；奶油：*Fry the onions in butter.* 用黃油炒洋蔥。 ➲ see also BREAD AND BUTTER (1), PEANUT BUTTER

IDM **butter wouldn't melt (in sb's ˈmouth)** (*informal*) used to say that sb seems to be innocent, kind, etc. when they are not really 假裝一副老實樣；裝作天真無邪 ➲ more at KNIFE *n.*

■ ***verb* ~ sth** to spread butter on sth 塗黃油：*She buttered four thick slices of bread.* 她用黃油塗了四片厚麵包。

IDM see KNOW *v.*

PHR V **ˌbutter sb↔ˈup** (*informal*) to say nice things to sb so that they will help you or give you sth 以甜言蜜語巴結某人；奉承；拍馬屁

ˈbutter bean *noun* a large pale yellow BEAN. Butter beans are often sold dried. 利馬豆

but·ter·cream /ˈbʌtəkriːm; *NAmE* -tərk-/ *noun* [U] a soft mixture of butter and sugar, used inside and on top of cakes 黃油乳脂（用黃油和糖調製而成，用於糕點）

but·ter·cup /ˈbʌtəkʌp; *NAmE* -tərk-/ *noun* a wild plant with small shiny yellow flowers that are shaped like cups 毛茛（野生植物，開杯狀有光澤的小黃花） ➲ VISUAL VOCAB page V11

but·ter·fat /ˈbʌtəfæt; *NAmE* ˈbʌtər-/ *noun* [U] the natural fat contained in milk and milk products 乳脂

but·ter·fin·gers /ˈbʌtəfɪŋɡəz; *NAmE* ˈbʌtərfɪŋɡərz/ *noun* [sing.] (*informal*) a person who often drops things 常掉落東西的人

but·ter·fly /ˈbʌtəflaɪ; *NAmE* -tərf-/ *noun* (*pl.* **-ies**) **1** [C] a flying insect with a long thin body and four large, usually brightly coloured, wings 蝴蝶：*butterflies and moths* 蝴蝶和蛾 ◇ *She's like a butterfly. She flits in and out of people's lives.* 她像一隻蝴蝶，每天在人前人後飛來飛去。 ➲ VISUAL VOCAB page V13 **2** [U] a swimming stroke in which you swim on your front and lift both arms forward at the same time while your legs move up and down together 蝶泳：*She was third in the 200m butterfly* (= a swimming race). 她得了 200 米蝶泳比賽的第三名。 ➲ VISUAL VOCAB page V45

IDM **have ˈbutterflies (in your stomach)** (*informal*) to have a nervous feeling in your stomach before doing sth （做某事前）心慌，緊張

ˈbutter knife *noun* a knife that has a flat blade with a round end, used for spreading butter on bread 黃油刀 ➲ VISUAL VOCAB page V22

but·ter·milk /ˈbʌtəmɪlk; *NAmE* -tərm-/ *noun* [U] the liquid that remains after butter has been separated from milk, used in cooking or as a drink 脫脂乳；白脫牛奶

but·ter·nut /ˈbʌtənʌt; *NAmE* ˈbʌtər-/ *noun* a N American tree grown as a decoration and for its wood 灰胡桃樹（北美觀賞樹，木材可用）

but·ter·nut squash *noun* [C, U] a long vegetable that grows on the ground, has a hard yellow skin and orange flesh and is fatter at one end than the other 冬南瓜

but·ter·scotch /ˈbʌtəskɒtʃ; *NAmE* ˈbʌtərskɑːtʃ/ *noun* [U] **1** a type of hard pale brown sweet/candy made by boiling butter and brown sugar together 奶油硬糖（用奶油和黃糖熬製） **2** (*especially NAmE*) a sauce flavoured with butterscotch, used for pouring on ice cream, etc. 奶油硬糖汁（用於澆在冰淇淋等上）

but·tery /ˈbʌtəri/ *adj.* like, containing or covered with butter 黃油般的；含黃油的；以黃油覆蓋的

but·tock /ˈbʌtək/ *noun* [usually pl.] either of the two round soft parts at the top of a person's legs 屁股的一邊；臀部 ➲ VISUAL VOCAB page V59

but·ton 🔑 /ˈbʌtn/ *noun, verb*

■ ***noun* 1** 🔑 a small round piece of metal, plastic, etc. that is sewn onto a piece of clothing and used for fastening two parts together 鈕扣；扣子：(*BrE*) *to* ***do up/undo your buttons*** 繫上／解開扣子 ◇ (*NAmE*) *to* ***button/unbutton your buttons*** 繫上／解開扣子 ◇ *to sew on a button* 縫上扣子 ◇ *shirt buttons* 襯衫的鈕扣 ➲ VISUAL VOCAB page V63 **2** 🔑 a small part of a machine that you press to make it work （機器的）按鈕：*the* ***play/stop/rewind button*** 播放鍵；停止鍵；倒帶鍵 ◇ *Adam pressed a button and waited for the lift.* 亞當按了一個按鈕，然後等着乘坐電梯。 ◇ *Choose 'printer' from the menu and click with the right mouse button.* 從選單上選取"打印機"，然後點擊鼠標右鍵。 ◇ *The windows slide down* ***at the touch of a button.*** 按一下開關，窗戶便落下來。 ➲ picture at HANDLE ➲ see also PUSH-BUTTON **3** a small area on a computer screen that you click on to make it do sth （電腦屏幕上的）按鍵：*Click on the back button to go back to the previous screen.* 點擊返回鍵，回到上一屏幕。 **4** (*especially NAmE*) a BADGE, especially one with a message printed on it （尤指印有信息的）徽章 ➲ VISUAL VOCAB page V65 ➲ see also BELLY BUTTON

IDM **on the ˈbutton** (*informal, especially NAmE*) **1** at exactly the right time or at the exact time mentioned 準時；正好：*We arrived at 4 o'clock on the button.* 我們在 4 點鐘準時到達。 **2** exactly right 精確；準確；確切：*You're on the button there!* 那讓你說準了！ **ˌpush all the (right) ˈbuttons** (also **ˌpress all the (right) ˈbuttons** especially in *BrE*) (*informal*) to do exactly the right things to please sb 做得面面俱到以討好人：*a new satirical comedy show that pushes all the right buttons* 一齣新的極盡搞笑之能事的諷刺喜劇 **ˌpush sb's ˈbuttons** (also **ˌpress sb's ˈbuttons** especially in *BrE*) (*informal*) to make sb react in either a positive or a negative way 使有所反應（無論是積極或消極的）：*I've known him for years, but I still don't know what pushes his buttons.* 我已認識他多年，可還是摸不透他的脾氣。 ➲ more at BRIGHT *adj.*

■ ***verb* 1** [T] **~ sth (up)** to fasten sth with buttons 扣…的鈕扣：*She hurriedly buttoned (up) her blouse.* 她急忙扣

好襯衫。 **2** [I] **~ (up)** to be fastened with buttons 用鈕扣扣上： *The dress buttons (up) at the back.* 這件連衣裙是從後背繫扣的。

IDM **'button it!** (*BrE, informal*) used to tell sb rudely to be quiet 閉嘴；住口

,button-'down *adj.* a **button-down** COLLAR, shirt, etc. has the ends of the COLLAR fastened to the shirt with buttons （領尖）用鈕扣繫（在襯衫上）的 ➲ VISUAL VOCAB page V63

,buttoned-'up *adj.* (*informal, especially BrE*) not expressing your emotions openly 沉默寡言的；嘴緊的

but·ton·hole /ˈbʌtnhəʊl; *NAmE* -hoʊl/ *noun, verb*

■ ***noun*** **1** a hole on a piece of clothing for a button to be put through 鈕扣孔；扣眼 ➲ VISUAL VOCAB page V63 **2** (*BrE*) (*NAmE* **bou·ton·nière**) a flower that is worn in the buttonhole of a coat or jacket 佩帶在扣眼上的花

■ ***verb*** **~ sb** (*informal*) to make sb stop and listen to you, especially when they do not want to 勉強（某人）停下來聽

'button lift (*BrE*) (also **Poma™**) *noun* a machine with poles which pulls people up the mountain on their SKIS 上山牽引機（用吊杆拉滑雪者上山）

,button 'mushroom *noun* a small young MUSHROOM used in cooking （食用）小蘑菇

but·tress /ˈbʌtrəs/ *noun, verb*

■ ***noun*** a stone or brick structure that supports a wall 扶壁；支墩

■ ***verb*** **~ sb/sth** (*formal*) to support or give strength to sb/sth 支持；給…以力量： *The sharp increase in crime seems to buttress the argument for more police officers on the street.* 犯罪率急劇上升似乎支持了增加巡警的論點。

butty /ˈbʌti/ *noun* (*pl.* **-ies**) **1** (*BrE, informal*) a SANDWICH 三明治： *a jam butty* 果醬麪包 **2** (*WelshE, informal*) a friend; a person that you work with 朋友；夥伴

buxom /ˈbʌksəm/ *adj.* (of a woman 女子) large in an attractive way, and with large breasts 豐盈的；乳房豐滿的

buy 0-w /baɪ/ *verb, noun*

■ ***verb*** (**bought**, **bought** /bɔːt/)

▸ **WITH MONEY** 用錢 **1** 0-w [T, I] to obtain sth by paying money for it 買；購買： **~ (sth)** *Where did you buy that dress?* 那件連衣裙你是在哪裏買的？◇ *If you're thinking of getting a new car, now is a good time to buy.* 你要是想買輛新車的話，現在正是時候。◇ **~ sth from sb** *I bought it from a friend for £10.* 我從朋友那裏花 10 英鎊買來的。◇ **~ sb sth** *He bought me a new coat.* 他給我買了一件新外套。◇ **~ sth for sb** *He bought a new coat for me.* 他給我買了一件新外套。◇ **~ sth + adj.** *I bought my car second-hand.* 我買了一輛二手車。 **OPP** **sell** **2** [T] **~ sth** (of money 錢) to be enough to pay for sth 夠支付： *He gave his children the best education that money can buy.* 他讓孩子們接受花錢能買到的最好的教育。◇ *Five pounds doesn't buy much nowadays.* 如今五英鎊買不到多少東西了。 **3** [T] **~ sb** to persuade sb to do sth dishonest in return for money 買通；收買；賄賂 **SYN** **bribe** : *He can't be bought* (= he's too honest to accept money in this way). 他是收買不了的。

▸ **OBTAIN** 獲得 **4** [T, usually passive] **~ sth** to obtain sth by losing sth else of great value 以…為代價： *Her fame was bought at the expense of her marriage.* 她出了名，卻犧牲了她的婚姻。

▸ **BELIEVE** 相信 **5** [T] **~ sth** (*informal*) to believe that sth is true, especially sth that is not very likely 相信（尤指不大可能的事）： *You could say you were ill but I don't think they'd* **buy it** (= accept the explanation). 你可以稱病，但我想他們不會相信的。

IDM (**have**) **'bought it** (*informal*) to be killed, especially in an accident or a war 被殺死；（尤指）在事故中喪生，陣亡 **buy the 'farm** (*NAmE, informal*) to die 死；死亡 **buy 'time** to do sth in order to delay an event, a decision, etc. 拖延時間 ➲ more at BEST *n.*, PIG *n.*, PUP

PHR V **,buy sth↔'in** (*BrE*) to buy sth in large quantities 大量購買 **,buy 'into sth** **1** to buy shares in a company, especially in order to gain some control over it 購買公司股份（尤指為取得部份控制權） **2** (*informal*) to believe sth, especially an idea that many other people believe in 信從（尤指隨大溜）： *She had never bought into the idea that to be attractive you have to be thin.* 她從不隨大溜認為要想有魅力，就得瘦身。 ➲ related noun BUY-IN **,buy sb↔'off** to pay sb money, especially dishonestly, to prevent them from doing sth you do not want them to do 收買，賄賂（某人不幹某事） **,buy sb↔'out** **1** to pay sb for their share in a business, usually in order to get total control of it for yourself 買斷…的股份；買下…的全部股權 ➲ related noun BUYOUT **2** to pay money so that sb can leave an organization, especially the army, before the end of an agreed period 付給補償金，付遣散費（為使某人提前退役、離職等） **,buy sth↔'up** to buy all or as much as possible of sth 全部（或盡量）買下某物；收購： *Developers are buying up all the land on the island.* 開發商們正在收購島上的全部土地。

■ ***noun***

▸ **STH BOUGHT** 購買的東西 **1** **a good, better, etc. ~** a thing that is worth the money that you pay for it 合算的商品： *That jacket was a really good buy.* 那件夾克確實買得很划算。◇ *Best buys this week are carrots and cabbages.* 這個星期最便宜的是胡蘿蔔和捲心菜。 **2** something that is bought or that is for sale; the act of buying sth 買進（或出售）的東西；購買： *Computer games are a popular buy this Christmas.* 這個聖誕節電腦遊戲很暢銷。

buyer 0-w /ˈbaɪə(r)/ *noun*

1 0-w a person who buys sth, especially sth expensive （尤指貴重物品的）買主；買方： *Have you found a buyer for your house?* 你的房子找到買主了嗎？ ➲ compare PURCHASER **OPP** **seller, vendor** **2** a person whose job is to choose goods that will be sold in a large shop/store 採購員

IDM **a ,buyer's 'market** a situation in which there is a lot of a particular item for sale, so that prices are low and people buying have a choice 買方市場

,buyer's re'morse *noun* [U] (*NAmE*) the feeling of disappointment sb has after they have bought sth when they think they have made a mistake 買主的懊悔（認為自己買錯東西）

'buy-in *noun* [U] (*business* 商) the fact of accepting a policy or change because you agree with it （對政策或變更的）認可，接受： *If you want to make major changes you need buy-in from everyone in the organization.* 如果想進行重大變革，就需要得到機構中所有人的認可。◇ *You need to win people's buy-in.* 你需要贏得人們的支持。 ➲ see also BUY *v.*

buy·out /ˈbaɪaʊt/ *noun* a situation in which a person or group gains control of a company by buying all or most of its shares 控制股權收購： *a management buyout* 管理層購買控制性股權

buzz /bʌz/ *verb, noun*

■ ***verb*** **1** [I] (of a BEE 蜜蜂) to make a continuous low sound 發出嗡嗡聲： *Bees buzzed lazily among the flowers.* 蜜蜂在花叢中懶洋洋地嗡嗡叫着。 **2** [I] to make a sound like a BEE buzzing 發出蜂鳴聲： *The doorbell buzzed loudly.* 門鈴蜂鳴聲大作。◇ *My ears were buzzing* (= were filled with a continuous sound). 我耳鳴了。 **3** [I] to be full of excitement, activity, etc. 充滿興奮（或活動等）： *New York buzzes from dawn to dusk.* 紐約從早到晚都熙熙攘攘的。◇ *My head was still buzzing after the day's events.* 一天的活動結束後，我頭腦中還是鬧哄哄的。◇ **~ with sth** *The place was buzzing with journalists.* 那個地方被記者搞得鬧哄哄的。 **4** [I, T] **~ (sth) (for sb/sth)** to call sb to come by pressing a BUZZER 用蜂鳴器（發信號）： *The doctor buzzed for the next patient to come in.* 醫生按蜂鳴器叫下一個病人進來。 **5** [T] **~ sb/sth** (*informal*) to fly very close to sb/sth, especially as a warning or threat 飛近（尤指作為警告或威脅）

PHR V **,buzz a'bout/a'round** to move around quickly, especially because you are very busy （忙得）團團轉： *I've been buzzing around town all day sorting out my trip.* 我一整天都在城裏轉來轉去，安排旅行的事情。 **,buzz 'off** (*informal*) used to tell sb rudely to go away 走開： *Just buzz off and let me get on with my work.* 走開，我得繼續幹活了。

■ ***noun*** **1** [C, usually sing.] (also **buzz·ing** [U, sing.]) a continuous sound like the one that a BEE, a BUZZER or other electronic device makes 嗡嗡聲；蜂鳴聲： *the buzz of bees hunting nectar* 尋找花蜜的蜜蜂的嗡嗡聲 ◇ *The buzz of the Entryphone interrupted our conversation.* 大門口對話機的蜂響聲打斷了我們的談話。◇ *hums and buzzes from the amplifier* 揚聲器發出的嗡嗡聲 **2** [sing.] the sound of people talking, especially in an excited way 唧唧喳喳的談話聲： *The buzz of conversation suddenly stopped when she came into the room.* 她一踏進屋子裏，熱烈的談話便戛然而止。 **3** [sing.] (*informal*) a strong feeling of pleasure, excitement or achievement（愉快、興奮或成就的）強烈情感： *a **buzz of excitement/expectation*** 十分興奮 / 期待 ◇ *She **gets a buzz** out of her work.* 她從工作中得到了很大樂趣。◇ *Flying **gives me a real buzz**.* 飛行真讓我興奮。◇ *You can sense the creative buzz in the city.* 在城市裏可以感覺到創造的熱情。 **4 the buzz** [sing.] (*informal*) news that people tell each other that may or may not be true 傳聞；謠傳 SYN **rumour**

IDM **give sb a 'buzz** (*informal*) to telephone sb 給某人打電話： *I'll give you a buzz on Monday, OK?* 我星期一給你打電話行嗎？

buz·zard /'bʌzəd; NAmE -zərd/ *noun* **1** (*BrE*) a large European BIRD OF PREY (= a bird that kills other creatures for food) of the HAWK family 鵟（歐洲猛禽） **2** (*NAmE*) a large American bird like a VULTURE that eats the flesh of animals that are already dead 禿鷲（食腐鳥類，尤指紅頭美洲鷲）

'buzz cut *noun* a style of cutting the hair in which all the hair is cut very short, close to the skin of the head 寸頭髮型（頭髮理得很短，貼近頭皮）

buzz·er /'bʌzə(r)/ *noun* an electrical device that produces a BUZZING sound as a signal 蜂鳴器

IDM **at the 'buzzer** (*NAmE*) at the end of a game or period of play 比賽結束；遊戲結束： *He missed a three-point attempt at the buzzer.* 終場哨響時，他投三分球未中。

'buzz group *noun* one of the small groups of people that a large group can be divided into in order to discuss and give their opinions about a particular subject. The information obtained is used by people doing MARKET RESEARCH. 蜂議小組，大家說小組（由大團體劃分而成，組員討論某一問題並各抒己見，意見用於市場研究）

'buzz saw *noun* (*NAmE*) = CIRCULAR SAW

buzz·word /'bʌzwɜːd; NAmE -wɜːrd/ *noun* a word or phrase, especially one connected with a particular subject, that has become fashionable and popular and is used a lot in newspapers, etc.（報刊等的）時髦術語，流行行話

b/w *abbr.* (in writing 書寫形式) black and white 黑白

bwana /'bwɑːnə/ *noun* a word used in parts of E Africa to address a man who has authority over you, for example your employer（東非部份地區用以稱呼上司）主人，老闆

by 🔑 /baɪ/ *prep., adv.*

■ *prep.* **1** 🔑 near sb/sth; at the side of sb/sth; beside sb/sth 靠近；在…旁邊： *a house by the river* 河邊的一所房子 ◇ *The telephone is by the window.* 電話在窗戶旁邊。◇ *Come and sit by me.* 過來挨着我坐。 **2** 🔑 used, usually after a passive verb, to show who or what does, creates or causes sth（常置於表示被動的動詞後，表示施事者）： *He was knocked down by a bus.* 他被公共汽車撞倒了。◇ *a play by Ibsen* 易卜生寫的劇本 ◇ *Who's that book by?* 誰是那本書的作者？◇ *I was frightened by the noise.* 我被那響聲嚇壞了。 **3** 🔑 used for showing how or in what way sth is done（表示方式）： *The house is heated by gas.* 這房子是煤氣供暖的。◇ *May I pay by cheque?* 我能用支票付款嗎？◇ *I will contact you by letter.* 我會給你寫信聯繫的。◇ *to travel **by boat/bus/car/plane*** 乘船 / 公共汽車 / 轎車 / 飛機 ◇ *to travel **by air/land/sea*** 坐飛機；經陸路 / 海路 ◇ *Switch it on by pressing this button.* 按下這個開關啟動它。 **4** 🔑 used before particular nouns without *the*, to say that sth happens as a result of sth（置於不帶 the 的名詞前，表示原因）由於： *They met by chance.* 他們不期而遇。◇ *I did it by mistake.* 我誤做了這事。◇ *The coroner's verdict was 'death by misadventure'.* 驗屍官判定是"意外致死"。 **5** 🔑 not later than the time mentioned; before 不遲於；在…之前： *Can you finish the work by five o'clock?* 你五點鐘前能完成工作嗎？◇ *I'll have it done by tomorrow.* 我會在明天之前完成這件事。◇ *By this time next week we'll be in New York.* 下星期的這個時候我們將在紐約。◇ *He ought to have arrived **by now/by this time**.* 他現在應該已經到了。◇ ***By the time** (**that**) this letter reaches you I will have left the country.* 你收到這封信時，我已離開這個國家了。 **6** 🔑 past sb/sth 經過： *He walked by me without speaking.* 他一言不發地從我身邊走過。 **7** 🔑 during sth; in a particular situation 在…期間；處於某種狀況： *to travel **by day/night*** 白天 / 夜間旅行 ◇ *We had to work by candlelight.* 我們不得不借助燭光工作。 **8** 🔑 used to show the degree or amount of sth（表示程度、數量）： *The bullet missed him by two inches.* 子彈只差兩英寸就擊中他了。◇ *House prices went up by 10%.* 房價上漲了 10%。◇ *It would be better by far* (= much better) *to ...* 那比…好得多。 **9** 🔑 from what sth shows or says; according to sth 從…看；依；按照： *By my watch it is two o'clock.* 我的錶是兩點鐘。◇ *I could tell by the look on her face that something terrible had happened.* 從她的臉色我可以看出，發生了可怕的事情。◇ *By law, you are a child until you are 18.* 按照法律規定，18 歲之前是未成年人。 **10** 🔑 used to show the part of sb/sth that sb touches, holds, etc.（表示觸及或抓住的人或物的部份）： *I took him by the hand.* 我拉着他的手。◇ *She seized her by the hair.* 她揪住她的頭髮。◇ *Pick it up by the handle!* 抓着手柄把它提起來！ **11** 🔑 used with *the* to show the period or quantity used for buying, selling or measuring sth（與 the 連用，表示時間或量度單位）： *We rented the car by the day.* 我們按日租用汽車。◇ *They're paid by the hour.* 他們的報酬是按小時計算的。◇ *We only sell it by the metre.* 我們只按米出售。 **12** 🔑 used to state the rate at which sth happens（表示速率）： *They're improving day by day.* 他們在一天天地改進。◇ *We'll do it bit by bit.* 我們會一點一點地做。◇ *It was getting worse by the minute* (= very fast). 情況急速惡化。◇ *The children came in two by two* (= in groups of two). 孩子們一對一對地走了進來。 **13** 🔑 used to show the measurements of sth（表示尺寸時用）： *The room measures fifteen feet by twenty feet.* 房間 15 英尺寬 20 英尺長。 **14** 🔑 used when multiplying or dividing（用於乘除運算）： *6 multiplied by 2 equals 12.* * 6 乘以 2 等於 12。◇ *6 divided by 2 equals 3.* * 6 除以 2 等於 3。 **15** used for giving more information about where sb comes from, what sb does, etc.（補充有關出生地、職業等的信息）： *He's German by birth.* 他是德國血統的。◇ *They're both doctors by profession.* 他們兩人的職業都是醫生。 **16** used when swearing to mean 'in the name of'（起誓時用）以…的名義： *I swear by Almighty God ...* 我以全能上帝之名發誓…

IDM **by the 'by/'bye** = BY THE WAY at WAY *n.*

■ *adv.* **1** 🔑 past 經過： *Just drive by. Don't stop.* 直接開過去。別停車。◇ *He hurried by without speaking to me.* 他沒和我說話就匆匆過去了。◇ *Excuse me, I can't get by.* 勞駕，請讓開點路。◇ *Time goes by so quickly.* 時光飛逝。 **2** used to say that sth is saved so that it can be used in the future（表示保留或保存時用）： *I've put some money by for college fees.* 我已經存了些錢作大學學費。 **3** in order to visit sb for a short time 短暫拜訪： *I'll come by this evening and pick up the books.* 我今晚過來取書。

IDM **by and 'by** (*old-fashioned*) before long; soon 不久；很快： *By and by she met an old man with a beard.* 她不久就碰到了一個大鬍子老頭。

by- (also **bye-**) /baɪ/ *prefix* (in nouns and verbs 構成名詞和動詞) **1** less important 次要的： *a by-product* 副產品 **2** near 附近： *a bystander* 旁觀者

by·catch /'baɪkætʃ/ *noun* [U] fish that are caught by ships by accident when other types of fish are being caught 誤捕的魚（捕撈其他種類的魚時意外捕獲）： *Thousands of small fish are thrown back into the sea as bycatch.* 成千上萬誤捕的魚扔回大海中去了。

bye 🔑 /baɪ/ *exclamation, noun*

■ *exclamation* 🔑 (also **,bye-'bye**, **'bye-bye**) (*informal*) goodbye 再見；再會： *Bye! See you next week.* 再見！下星

B

期再會。◇ *She waved bye-bye and got into the car.* 她揮手道別後就鑽進了汽車。◇ *Bye for now Dad!* 再見了老爸！

■ ***noun*** (*sport* 體) a situation in which a player or team does not have an opponent in one part of the competition and continues to the next part as if they had won 輪空（參賽者無對手而自動進入下一輪比賽）IDM see BY *prep.*

ˈbye-byes *noun*

IDM **go (to) ˈbye-byes** (*BrE, informal*) used by small children or to small children, to mean 'go to sleep'（兒童用語）去睡覺

ˈbye-law = BY-LAW

ˈby-election *noun* (*BrE*) an election of a new Member of Parliament to replace sb who has died or left parliament（議員等的）補缺選舉，補選 ➲ compare GENERAL ELECTION

by·gone /ˈbaɪɡɒn; *NAmE* -ɡɔːn/ *adj.* [only before noun] happening or existing a long time ago 很久以前的；以往的：***a bygone age/era*** 一個過去的時代／歷史時期

by·gones /ˈbaɪɡɒnz; *NAmE* -ɡɔːnz/ *noun* [pl.]

IDM **let ˌbygones be ˈbygones** to decide to forget about disagreements that happened in the past 過去的事就讓它過去吧

ˈby-law (also **ˈbye-law**) *noun* **1** (*BrE*) a law that is made by a local authority and that applies only to that area 地方法規 **2** (*NAmE*) a law or rule of a club or company（俱樂部或公司的）規章制度

by·line /ˈbaɪlaɪn/ *noun* a line at the beginning or end of a piece of writing in a newspaper or magazine that gives the writer's name（報刊文章的）署名行

by·name /ˈbaɪneɪm/ *noun* a name given to sb who has the same first name as sb else, so that it is clear who is being referred to（為區分同名者而起的）別名

by·pass /ˈbaɪpɑːs/ *noun, verb*

■ ***noun*** **1** (*especially BrE*) a road that passes around a town or city rather than through the centre（繞過城市的）旁路，旁道 **2** a medical operation on the heart in which blood is directed along a different route so that it does not flow through a part that is damaged or blocked; the new route that the blood takes（給心臟接旁通管的）分流術，搭橋術；旁通管：*heart bypass surgery* 心臟搭橋手術 ◇ *a triple bypass operation* 接三通管的手術

■ ***verb*** **1 ~ sth** to go around or avoid a place 繞過；避開：*A new road now bypasses the town.* 一條新路繞城鎮而過。 **2 ~ sth** to ignore a rule, an official system or sb in authority, especially in order to get sth done quickly 不顧（規章制度）；不請示

ˈby-product *noun* **1** a substance that is produced during the process of making or destroying sth else 副產品：*When burnt, plastic produces dangerous by-products.* 塑料燃燒時產生出危險的副產品。 **2** a thing that happens, often unexpectedly, as the result of sth else 意外結果；副作用：*One of the by-products of unemployment is an increase in crime.* 失業帶來的一大惡果是犯罪率上升。

byre /ˈbaɪə(r)/ *noun* (*old-fashioned, BrE*) a farm building in which cows are kept 牛棚 SYN **cowshed**

by·road /ˈbaɪrəʊd; *NAmE* -roʊd/ *noun* a minor road 小路；支路

by·stand·er /ˈbaɪstændə(r)/ *noun* a person who sees sth that is happening but is not involved 旁觀者 SYN **onlooker**：***innocent bystanders*** *at the scene of the accident* 事故現場的無辜旁觀者 ➲ SYNONYMS at WITNESS

byte /baɪt/ *noun* a unit of information stored in a computer, equal to 8 BITS. A computer's memory is measured in bytes. 字節；位組；位元組

byway /ˈbaɪweɪ/ *noun* **1** [C] a small road that is not used very much 偏僻小路 **2 byways** [pl.] the less important areas of a subject（學科的）次要領域，冷僻部份

by·word /ˈbaɪwɜːd; *NAmE* -wɜːrd/ *noun* [usually sing.] **1 a ~ for sth** a person or thing that is a well-known or typical example of a particular quality（某種品質或特徵的）代表人，代表事物，典範：*The name Chanel became a byword for elegance.* 香奈兒這個名字成了優雅的代名詞。 **2** (*especially NAmE*) a word or phrase that is well known or often used 諺語；俗語

By·zan·tine /baɪˈzæntaɪn; bɪ-; -tiːn; *NAmE* ˈbɪzəntiːn/ *adj.* [usually before noun] **1** connected with Byzantium or the Eastern Roman Empire 拜占庭帝國的；東羅馬帝國的 **2** used to describe ARCHITECTURE of the 5th to the 15th centuries in the Byzantine Empire, especially churches with high central DOMES and MOSAICS 拜占庭建築風格的（尤指有高穹頂和馬賽克裝飾的教堂） **3** (also **byzantine**) (*formal*) (of an idea, a system, etc. 思想、制度等) complicated, secret and difficult to change 複雜神秘而死板的：*an organization of byzantine complexity* 拜占庭式複雜詭秘死板的機構

Cc

C /siː/ *noun, abbr., symbol*

■ ***noun*** (also **c**) [C, U] (*pl.* **Cs, C's, c's** /siːz/) **1** the third letter of the English alphabet 英語字母表的第 3 個字母：*'Cat' begins with (a) C/'C'.* * cat 一詞以字母 c 開頭。**2 C** (*music* 音) the first note in the SCALE of C MAJOR * C 音（C 大調的第 1 音或音符）➲ see also MIDDLE C **3 C** the third highest mark/grade that a student can get for a piece of work（學業成績）第三等，中：*She got (a) C/'C' in/for Physics.* 她物理成績得中。

■ ***abbr.*** **1 C.** CAPE 海角；岬：*C. Horn* (= for example, on a map) 合恩角（例如地圖標示）**2** CELSIUS, CENTIGRADE 攝氏度：*Water freezes at 0°C.* 水在零攝氏度時結冰。**3** (also ©) (*NAmE* also **C.**) COPYRIGHT 版權；著作權：*© Oxford University Press 2010* 版權所有，牛津大學出版社 2010 ➲ see also C OF E, C & W

■ ***symbol*** **1** (also **c**) the number 100 in ROMAN NUMERALS（羅馬數字）100 **2** the symbol for the chemical element CARBON（化學元素）碳

c (*BrE*) (also **c.** *NAmE, BrE*) *abbr.* **1** (in writing) CENT(S)（書寫形式）分（幣）**2** (also **C**) (in writing) century（書寫形式）世紀：*in the 19th c* 在 19 世紀 ◇ (*NAmE*) *a C19th church* 一座 19 世紀的教堂 ➲ see also CENT. **3** (also **ca**) (especially before dates 尤用於日期前) about; approximately (from Latin *circa*) 大約，約（源自拉丁語 circa）：*c1890* 約在 1890 年 **4** (*NAmE*) (in cooking) cup（用於烹飪）杯：*add 2c. flour* 加入兩杯麪粉

cab /kæb/ *noun* **1** a taxi 出租汽車；計程車；的士 ➲ VISUAL VOCAB page V58 **2** the place where the driver sits in a bus, train or lorry/truck（公共汽車、火車、卡車的）駕駛室 ➲ VISUAL VOCAB page V57

cabal /kəˈbæl; *NAmE* also -ˈbɑːl/ *noun* (*formal*, usually *disapproving*) a small group of people who are involved in secret plans to get political power 政治陰謀小集團

Ca·bala = KABBALAH

caba·ret /ˈkæbəreɪ; *NAmE* ˌkæbəˈreɪ/ *noun* **1** [C, U] entertainment with singing and dancing that is performed in restaurants or clubs in the evenings 卡巴萊（餐館或夜總會於晚間提供的歌舞表演）：*a cabaret act/singer/band* 卡巴萊表演／歌手／樂隊 **2** [C] a restaurant or club where cabaret entertainment is performed（有歌舞表演的）卡巴萊餐館，夜總會

cab·bage /ˈkæbɪdʒ/ *noun* **1** [U, C] a round vegetable with large green, purplish-red or white leaves that can be eaten raw or cooked 甘藍；捲心菜；洋白菜：*Do you like cabbage?* 你喜歡捲心菜嗎？◇ *two cabbages* 兩棵洋白菜 ◇ ***white/red cabbage*** 白色的／紅色的洋白菜 ➲ see also CHINESE CABBAGE, PAK CHOI ➲ VISUAL VOCAB page V31 **2** [C] (*BrE*) = VEGETABLE (2)

cab·bal·is·tic /ˌkæbəˈlɪstɪk/ *adj.* relating to secret or MYSTICAL beliefs 神秘信仰的；神秘論的

cabby (also **cab·bie**) /ˈkæbi/ *noun* (*pl.* **-ies**) (*informal*) a person who drives a taxi 出租汽車司機；計程車司機

caber /ˈkeɪbə(r)/ *noun* a long heavy wooden pole that is thrown into the air as a test of strength in the traditional Scottish sport of **tossing the caber**（在蘇格蘭傳統的投擲比賽運動中使用的）長而重的木杆，長木柱

cabin /ˈkæbɪn/ *noun* **1** a small room on a ship in which you live or sleep（輪船上生活或睡覺的）隔間 **2** one of the areas for passengers to sit in a plane（飛機的）座艙 ➲ VISUAL VOCAB page V53 **3** a small house or shelter, usually made of wood（通常為木製的）小屋，小棚屋：*a log cabin* 原木小屋 ➲ VISUAL VOCAB page V15

ˈcabin boy *noun* a boy or young man who works as a servant on a ship（船上的）男服務員

ˈcabin crew *noun* [C+sing./pl. v.] the people whose job is to take care of passengers on a plane（飛機上的）全體乘務員

ˈcabin cruiser *noun* = CRUISER (2)

cab·inet 🔑 /ˈkæbɪnət/ *noun*

1 🔑 (usually **the Cabinet**) [C+sing./pl. v.] a group of chosen members of a government, which is responsible for advising and deciding on government policy 內閣：*a cabinet meeting* 內閣會議 ◇ (*BrE*) *a cabinet minister* 內閣閣員 ◇ (*BrE*) *the shadow Cabinet* (= the most important members of the opposition party) 影子內閣（反對黨中最重要的成員）**2** 🔑 [C] a piece of furniture with doors, drawers and/or shelves, that is used for storing or showing things 貯藏櫃；陳列櫃：*kitchen cabinets* 櫥櫃 ◇ *a medicine cabinet* 藥櫃 ◇ *The china was displayed in a glass cabinet.* 瓷器陳列在玻璃櫃裏。➲ see also FILING CABINET ➲ VISUAL VOCAB page V24

cab·inet·maker /ˈkæbɪnətmeɪkə(r)/ *noun* a person who makes fine wooden furniture, especially as a job（尤指專業的）傢具木工，細木工

the ˈCabinet Office *noun* [sing.] (in Britain) a government department that is responsible for the work of the Cabinet and the CIVIL SERVICE 內閣辦公室（英國政府部門，負責內閣和文職部門的工作）

cab·in·et·ry /ˈkæbɪnətri/ *noun* [U] (*NAmE*) CABINETS (= cupboards, especially fitted in a kitchen) 貯藏櫃；（尤指）櫥櫃

cable 🔑 /ˈkeɪbl/ *noun, verb*

■ ***noun*** **1** 🔑 [U, C] thick strong metal rope used on ships, for supporting bridges, etc.（繫船用的）纜繩；（支撐橋梁等用的）鋼索 ➲ picture at CORD **2** 🔑 [C, U] a set of wires, covered in plastic or rubber, that carries electricity, telephone signals, etc. 電纜：***overhead/underground cables*** 高架／地下電纜 ◇ *a 10 000 volt cable* * 1 萬伏特高壓電纜 ◇ *fibre-optic cable* 光纜 **3** [U] = CABLE TELEVISION：*We can receive up to 500 cable channels.* 我們可以接收多達 500 個有線電視頻道。**4** [C] (*old-fashioned*) a message sent by electrical signals and printed out 電報

■ ***verb*** [T, I] **~ (sb)** (*old-fashioned*) to send sb a CABLE *n.* (4)（給…）發電報

ˈcable car *noun* **1** a vehicle that hangs from and is pulled by a moving cable and that carries passengers up and down a mountain（懸空的）纜車，索車 **2** (*especially NAmE*) a vehicle that runs on tracks and is pulled by a moving cable 有軌纜車 ➲ VISUAL VOCAB page V58

ˌcable ˈtelevision (also **cable**, **ˌcable TˈV**) *noun* [U] a system of broadcasting television programmes along wires rather than by radio waves 有線電視

cab·ling /ˈkeɪblɪŋ/ *noun* [U] all the cables that are required for particular equipment or a particular system（統稱）纜索

ca·boo·dle /kəˈbuːdl/ *noun*

IDM **the whole (kit and) caˈboodle** (*informal*) everything 全部；全體：*I had new clothes, a new hairstyle—the whole caboodle.* 我身着新衣服，頭理新髮型，上下一身新。

ca·boose /kəˈbuːs/ *noun* (*NAmE*) the part at the back of a train where the person who is in charge of the train rides 守車（列車末尾供列車職工使用的車廂）

cab·ri·olet /ˈkæbriəʊleɪ; *NAmE* -əʊleɪ/ *noun* a car with a roof that can be folded down or removed（車頂可摺疊或拆除的）敞篷車 SYN **convertible** ➲ compare SOFT TOP

ca·cao /kəˈkaʊ/ *noun* [U] a tropical tree with seeds that are used to make chocolate and COCOA; the seeds from this tree 可可（種子用以製作巧克力和可可粉）；可可豆

cache /kæʃ/ *noun, verb*

■ ***noun*** **1** a hidden store of things such as weapons 隱藏物（如武器）；（秘密）貯存物：*an arms cache* 隱藏的武器 **2** (*computing* 計) a part of a computer's memory that stores copies of data that is often needed while a program is running. This data can be accessed very quickly. 高速緩衝存貯器；快取記憶體

■ ***verb*** **1 ~ sth** to store things in a secret place, especially weapons 匿藏，隱藏（尤指武器）**2 ~ sth** (*computing* 計) to store data in a cache 把（數據）存入高速緩衝存貯器；高速緩存：*This page is cached.* 這一頁存入高速緩衝存貯器了。

C

cachet /ˈkæʃeɪ; NAmE kæˈʃeɪ/ *noun* [U, sing.] (*formal*) if sth has **cachet**, it has a special quality that people admire and approve of 威信；聲望 SYN **prestige**

cack /kæk/ *noun* [U] (*BrE, slang*) solid waste matter that is passed from the body through the BOWELS 屎

cack-handed /ˌkæk ˈhændɪd/ *adj.* (*BrE, informal, disapproving*) a **cack-handed** person often drops or breaks things or does things badly 笨手笨腳的；笨拙的 SYN **clumsy**

cackle /ˈkækl/ *verb, noun*

■ *verb* **1** [I] (of a chicken 雞) to make a loud unpleasant noise 咯咯叫 **2** [I, T] (+ **speech**) to laugh in a loud unpleasant way 嘎嘎地笑：*They all cackled with delight.* 他們都高興得嘎嘎地笑。

■ *noun* **1** the loud noise that a HEN makes（母雞的）咯咯叫聲 **2** a loud unpleasant laugh（難聽的）大笑聲；嘎嘎的笑聲

cac·oph·ony /kəˈkɒfəni; NAmE -ˈkɑːf-/ *noun* [U, sing.] (*formal*) a mixture of loud unpleasant sounds 刺耳的嘈雜聲 ▸ **cac·oph·on·ous** /-nəs/ *adj.*

cac·tus /ˈkæktəs/ *noun* (*pl.* **cac·tuses** or **cacti** /ˈkæktaɪ/) a plant that grows in hot dry regions, especially one with thick STEMS covered in SPINES but without leaves. There are many different types of cactus. 仙人掌科植物；仙人掌 ⊃ VISUAL VOCAB page V11

CAD /kæd; ˌsiː eɪ ˈdiː/ *noun* [U] the abbreviation for 'computer-aided design' (the use of computers to design machines, buildings, vehicles, etc.) 計算機輔助設計，電腦輔助設計（全寫為 computer-aided design）

cad /kæd/ *noun* (*old-fashioned*) a man who behaves in a dishonest or unfair way 卑鄙的人；粗鄙的人；無賴

ca·da·ver /kəˈdævə(r)/ *noun* (*technical* 術語) a dead human body 死屍；屍體 SYN **corpse**

ca·da·ver·ous /kəˈdævərəs/ *adj.* (*literary*) (of a person 人) extremely pale, thin and looking ill/sick 慘白的；形容枯槁的

cad·die (also **caddy**) /ˈkædi/ *noun, verb*

■ *noun* (*pl.* **-ies**) (in GOLF 高爾夫球) a person who helps a player by carrying his or her CLUBS and equipment during a game 球童（比賽時替運動員背球棒、拿器具等）

■ *verb* (**cad·dies**, **caddy·ing**, **cad·died**, **cad·died**) [I] to act as a caddie in the game of GOLF（為高爾夫球手）當球童

cad·dis /ˈkædɪs/ (also **ˈcaddis fly**) *noun* a small insect. The young forms, called **caddis worms**, are often used for catching fish. 石蛾（幼蟲常用作魚餌）

caddy /ˈkædi/ *noun* (*pl.* **-ies**) **1** (*especially BrE*) = TEA CADDY **2** (*NAmE*) a small bag for storing or carrying small objects（裝小件物品的）小包：*a sewing/make-up caddy* 針線／化妝包 **3** = CADDIE

ca·dence /ˈkeɪdns/ *noun* **1** (*formal*) the rise and fall of the voice in speaking（說話時語調的）抑揚頓挫，起落：*He delivered his words in slow, measured cadences.* 他講話緩慢而抑揚頓挫、把握有度。 **2** the end of a musical phrase（樂段或樂句的）收束，靜止

ca·denza /kəˈdenzə/ *noun* **1** (*music* 音) a short passage, usually near the end of a piece of CLASSICAL music, which is played or sung by the SOLOIST alone, and intended to show the performer's skill 華彩段，華彩樂段（通常在古典樂曲結尾，以突顯獨唱或獨奏演員的技巧） **2** (*SAfrE*) if sb has a **cadenza**, they react suddenly and angrily to sth, especially in a way that seems unreasonable or humorous（尤指無端的或滑稽的）暴怒，大發雷霆

cadet /kəˈdet/ *noun* a young person who is training to become an officer in the police or armed forces 警官（或軍官）學員；警官（或軍官）候補生

cadge /kædʒ/ *verb* [T, I] **~ (sth) (from/off sb)** (*BrE, informal*) to ask sb for food, money, etc. especially because you cannot or do not want to pay for sth yourself 乞討；乞得；索取：*I managed to cadge some money off my dad.* 我設法從我父親那裏要了一些錢。 ▸ **cadger** *noun*

Cad·il·lac™ /ˈkædɪlæk/ *noun* **1** a large and expensive US make of car 凱迪拉克轎車（美國豪華轎車） **2 the ~ of sth** (*NAmE*) something that is thought of as an example of the highest quality of a type of thing 典範；典型：*This is the Cadillac of watches.* 這款手錶堪稱極品。

cad·mium /ˈkædmiəm/ *noun* [U] (*symb.* **Cd**) a chemical element. Cadmium is a soft, poisonous, bluish-white metal that is used in batteries and nuclear REACTORS. 鎘

cadre /ˈkɑːdə(r); NAmE ˈkædri/ *noun* (*formal*) **1** [C+sing./pl. v.] a small group of people who are specially chosen and trained for a particular purpose 骨幹（隊伍） **2** [C] a member of this kind of group 幹部

CAE /ˌsiː eɪ ˈiː/ *noun* [U] the abbreviation for 'Certificate in Advanced English' (a British test that measures a person's ability to speak and write English as a foreign language at an advanced level) 高級英語證書考試，劍橋高級英語認證（全寫為 Certificate in Advanced English，英國考試，檢測英語作為外語的高級口語和寫作能力）

cae·cum (*BrE*) (*NAmE* **cecum**) /ˈsiːkəm/ *noun* (*pl.* **cae·ca**, **ceca** /ˈsiːkə/) a small bag which is part of the INTESTINE, between the small and the large intestine 盲腸

Cae·sar·ean /sɪˈzeəriən; NAmE -ˈzer-/ (also **Cae·sar·ian**, **Caeˌsarean ˈsection**, **Caeˌsarian ˈsection**) (*US* also **ce·sar·ean**, **ce·sar·ian**, **ˈC-section**) *noun* [C, U] a medical operation in which an opening is cut in a woman's body in order to take out a baby 剖宮產，剖腹產（手術）：*an emergency Caesarean* 緊急剖宮產手術 ◇ *The baby was born by Caesarean section.* 那嬰兒是施行剖宮產手術出生的。◇ *She had to have a Caesarean.* 她不得不接受剖宮產手術。

Caesar salad /ˌsiːzə ˈsæləd; NAmE ˌsiːzər/ *noun* [U, C] a salad of LETTUCE and CROUTONS served with a mixture of oil, lemon juice, egg, etc. 凱撒色拉，凱撒沙拉（用生菜和油炸小麪包塊等製成）

cae·sium (*BrE*) (*NAmE* **ces·ium**) /ˈsiːziəm/ *noun* [U] (*symb.* **Cs**) a chemical element. Caesium is a soft silver-white metal that reacts strongly in water, used in PHOTOELECTRIC CELLS. 銫

caes·ura /sɪˈzjʊərə; NAmE sɪˈzjʊrə/ *noun* (*technical* 術語) a pause near the middle of a line of poetry 音頓（詩行中間的停頓） ⊃ compare ENJAMBEMENT

cafe (also **café**) /ˈkæfeɪ; NAmE kæˈfeɪ/ *noun* **1** a place where you can buy drinks and simple meals. Alcohol is not usually served in British or American cafes. 咖啡館，小餐館（供應飲料和便餐，在英美國家通常不供應酒類） ⊃ compare RESTAURANT ⊃ VISUAL VOCAB pages V2, V3 **2** (*SAfrE*) a small shop/store that sells sweets, newspapers, food, etc. and usually stays open later than other shops/stores 便利商店（出售糖果，報紙，食物等，通常比其他商店晚一些關門）

cafe·teria /ˌkæfəˈtɪəriə; NAmE -ˈtɪr-/ *noun* a restaurant where you choose and pay for your meal at a counter and carry it to a table. Cafeterias are often found in factories, colleges, hospitals, etc. 自助餐廳；自助食堂

cafe·tière /ˌkæfəˈtjeə(r); NAmE -ˈtjer/ (*BrE*) (*NAmE* **ˌFrench ˈpress**) *noun* a special glass container for making coffee with a metal FILTER that you push down 法式咖啡壺（有活動金屬過濾網） ⊃ VISUAL VOCAB page V25

caff /kæf/ *noun* (*BrE, informal*) a CAFE serving simple, basic food（供應便餐的）小餐館：*a transport caff* 公路邊小餐館

caf·fein·ated /ˈkæfɪneɪtɪd/ *adj.* (of coffee or tea 咖啡或茶) containing caffeine 含有咖啡因的 ⊃ compare DECAFFEINATED

caf·feine /ˈkæfiːn/ *noun* [U] a drug found in coffee and tea that makes you feel more active 咖啡因；咖啡鹼 ⊃ COLLOCATIONS at DIET ⊃ see also DECAFFEINATED

caffè latte /ˌkæfeɪ ˈlɑːteɪ/ (also **latte**) *noun* (from *Italian*) a drink made by adding a small amount of strong coffee to a glass or cup of FROTHY steamed milk 熱奶沫咖啡；拿鐵咖啡

caf·tan *noun* = KAFTAN

cage /keɪdʒ/ *noun, verb*

■ *noun* a structure made of metal bars or wire in which

animals or birds are kept 籠子：*a birdcage* 鳥籠 ➲ see also RIBCAGE IDM see RATTLE *v.*

■ ***verb*** [usually passive] **~ sth (up)** to put or keep an animal in a cage 把（動物）關在籠中：*The dogs are caged (up) at night.* 晚上狗被關進籠裏。▸ **caged** *adj.*：*He paced the room like a **caged animal**.* 他像籠中的動物一樣在房間裏踱來踱去。

cagey /ˈkeɪdʒi/ *adj.* (**cagi·er**, **cagi·est**) **~ (about sth)** (*informal*) not wanting to give sb information 守口如瓶的；諱莫如深的 SYN **evasive, secretive**：*Tony is very cagey about his family.* 托尼對自己家的事諱莫如深。▸ **cagi·ly** *adv.*

ca·goule (also **ka·goul**) /kəˈɡuːl/ *noun* (*BrE*) a long light jacket with a HOOD, worn to give protection from wind and rain 連帽式輕便長風雨衣

ca·hoots /kəˈhuːts/ *noun*

IDM **be in cahoots (with sb)** (*informal*) to be planning or doing sth dishonest with sb else 與…結夥；共謀；勾結（…做壞事）SYN **be in collusion**

cai·man (also **cay·man**) /ˈkeɪmən/ *noun* (*pl.* **-mans**) a N and S American REPTILE similar to an ALLIGATOR 凱門鱷

cairn /keən; *NAmE* kern/ *noun* a pile of stones which mark a special place such as the top of a mountain or a place where sb is buried 堆石標（以石堆標示山頂或某人埋葬的地點等）

ca·jole /kəˈdʒəʊl; *NAmE* kəˈdʒoʊl/ *verb* [T, I] to make sb do sth by talking to them and being very nice to them 勸誘；哄騙；誘騙 SYN **coax**：**~ sb (into sth/into doing sth)** *He cajoled me into agreeing to do the work.* 他誘騙我同意幹那件活兒。◇ **~ sth out of sb** *I managed to cajole his address out of them.* 我設法從他們那裏套出了他的地址。◇ **(+ speech)** *'Please say yes,' she cajoled.* "就同意了吧。" 她哄騙道。

Cajun /ˈkeɪdʒn/ *noun, adj.*

■ ***noun*** **1** [C] a person of French origin from Louisiana who speaks an old form of French, also called Cajun 卡津人（法裔路易斯安那州人，講舊式法語）**2** [U] a type of music originally played by Cajuns, that is a mixture of BLUES and FOLK MUSIC 卡津音樂（一種法裔路易斯安那州人的音樂，布魯斯歌曲混合民樂）

■ ***adj.*** connected with the Cajuns, their language, music or spicy cooking 卡津人（或語言、音樂、多香料烹飪）的：*Cajun chicken/cuisine* 卡津香味雞／烹飪

cake 🔑 /keɪk/ *noun, verb*

■ ***noun*** **1** 🔑 [C, U] a sweet food made from a mixture of flour, eggs, butter, sugar, etc. that is baked in an oven. Cakes are made in various shapes and sizes and are often decorated, for example with cream or ICING. 糕餅；蛋糕：*a **piece/slice of cake*** 一塊／一片蛋糕 ◇ *to **make/bake a cake*** 做／烘烤蛋糕 ◇ *a chocolate cake* 巧克力蛋糕 ◇ *a birthday cake* 生日蛋糕 ◇ (*BrE*) *a cake tin* (= for cooking a cake in) 蛋糕烤盤 ◇ (*NAmE*) *a cake pan* 蛋糕烤盤 ➲ see also ANGEL FOOD CAKE, CHRISTMAS CAKE, FRUIT CAKE, SPONGE CAKE, WEDDING CAKE **2** [C] a food mixture that is cooked in a round flat shape 餅狀食物；餅：*potato cakes* 土豆餅 ➲ see also FISHCAKE

IDM **have your cake and 'eat it** (*BrE*) (also **have your cake and eat it too** *NAmE, BrE*) to have the advantages of sth without its disadvantages; to have both things that are available 得其利而無其弊；兩者兼得 **a slice/share of the 'cake** (*BrE*) (*NAmE* **a piece/slice/share of the 'pie**) a share of the available money or benefits that you believe you have a right to 應分得的一份錢財（或利益）**take the 'cake** (*especially NAmE*) (*BrE* also **take the 'biscuit**) (*informal*) to be the most surprising, annoying, etc. thing that has happened or that sb has done 空前驚人；極其討厭 ➲ more at HOT *adj.*, ICING, PIECE *n.*

■ ***verb*** **1** [T, usually passive] **~ sth (in/with sth)** to cover sth with a thick layer of sth soft that becomes hard when it dries（厚厚一層乾後即變硬的軟東西）覆蓋：*Her shoes were caked with mud.* 她的鞋上粘着污泥。**2** [I] if a substance **cakes**, it becomes hard when it dries（乾後）結成硬塊；膠凝 ▸ **caked** *adj.*：*caked blood* 凝結了的血

cake·walk /ˈkeɪkwɔːk/ *noun* [sing.] (*informal*) something that is extremely easy to do 易如反掌的事

CAL /kæl/ *abbr.* computer assisted learning 計算機輔助學習；電腦輔助學習 ➲ compare CALL

cala·bash /ˈkæləbæʃ/ *noun* **1** a container made from the hard covering of a fruit or vegetable; the fruit or vegetable from which a calabash is made 葫蘆瓢；葫蘆果製的容器；葫蘆果 ➲ see also GOURD **2** (also **'cala·bash tree**) a tropical tree that produces a large round fruit with very hard skin, also called calabash 葫蘆瓢樹；蒲瓜樹

cala·brese /ˈkæləbriːs; ˌkæləˈbriːs/ *noun* [U] a type of BROCCOLI (= a vegetable with a thick green STEM and green or purple flower heads) 青花菜

cala·mine /ˈkæləmaɪn/ (also **'calamine lotion**) *noun* [U] a pink liquid that you put on burnt or sore skin to make it less painful 爐甘石（治療皮膚灼傷或疼痛的一種粉紅色水劑）

ca·lami·t·ous /kəˈlæmɪtəs/ *adj.* (*formal*) causing great damage to people's lives, property, etc.（對人命、財產等）引起災難的，災難性的 SYN **disastrous**

ca·lam·ity /kəˈlæməti/ *noun* [C, U] (*pl.* **-ies**) an event that causes great damage to people's lives, property, etc. 災難；災禍 SYN **disaster**

cal·cify /ˈkælsɪfaɪ/ *verb* (**cal·ci·fies**, **cal·ci·fy·ing**, **cal·ci·fied**, **cal·ci·fied**) [I, T] **~ (sth)** (*technical* 術語) to become hard or make sth hard by adding CALCIUM salts（使）鈣化，骨化 ▸ **cal·ci·fi·ca·tion** /ˌkælsɪfɪˈkeɪʃn/ *noun* [U]

cal·cite /ˈkælsaɪt/ *noun* [U] (*chemistry* 化) a white or clear mineral consisting of CALCIUM CARBONATE. It forms a major part of rocks such as LIMESTONE, MARBLE and CHALK. 方解石

cal·cium /ˈkælsiəm/ *noun* [U] (*symb.* **Ca**) a chemical element. Calcium is a soft silver-white metal that is found in bones, teeth and CHALK. 鈣

ˌcalcium 'carbonate *noun* [U] (*symb.* $CaCO_3$) (*chemistry* 化) a white solid substance that exists naturally as CHALK, LIMESTONE and MARBLE 碳酸鈣

cal·cul·able /ˈkælkjələbl/ *adj.* that can be calculated 可計算的；可估計的：*a calculable risk* 可預計的風險 ➲ compare INCALCULABLE

cal·cu·late 🔑 /ˈkælkjuleɪt/ *verb*

1 🔑 to use numbers to find out a total number, amount, distance, etc. 計算；核算 SYN **work out**：**~ sth** *Use the formula to calculate the volume of the container.* 用公式計算容器的容積。◇ *Benefit is calculated on the basis of average weekly earnings.* 補助金按平均週收入計算。◇ **~ how much, what, etc.** *You'll need to calculate how much time the assignment will take.* 你需要算一算要花多少時間才能完成分配的任務。◇ **it is calculated that …** *It has been calculated that at least 47 000 jobs were lost last year.* 據估算，去年至少喪失了 47 000 個工作。**2** 🔑 to guess sth or form an opinion by using all the information available 預測；推測 SYN **estimate**：**~ that …** *Conservationists calculate that hundreds of species could be lost in this area.* 自然資源保護主義者預測，數以百計的物種可能會從這個地區消失。◇ **~ how much, what, etc.** *It is impossible to calculate what influence he had on her life.* 無法估計他對她的生活產生過多大影響。

cal·cu·lated /ˈkælkjuleɪtɪd/ *adj.* [usually before noun] carefully planned to get what you want 精心策劃的；蓄意的：*a calculated insult* 蓄意的侮辱 ◇ *He took **a calculated risk*** (= a risk that you decide is worth taking even though you know it might have bad results). 他甘冒風險，因為他覺得值。

IDM **be calculated to do sth** to be intended to do sth; to be likely to do sth 打算做；故意做；可能做：*Her latest play is calculated to shock.* 她最新推出的劇本故意要聳人聽聞。◇ *This sort of life is not calculated to appeal to a young man of 20.* 這種生活對於一個 20 歲的年輕小伙子不大可能有吸引力。

cal·cu·lat·ing /ˈkælkjuleɪtɪŋ/ *adj.* (*disapproving*) good at planning things so that you have an advantage, without caring about other people 精明的；精於算計的：*a cold and calculating killer* 一個工於心計的冷酷殺手 ◇ *I never* *realized you could be so calculating.* 我真沒有想到你會這樣有心計。

cal·cu·la·tion /ˌkælkjuˈleɪʃn/ *noun* **1** [C, U] the act or process of using numbers to find out an amount 計算：*Cathy did a rough calculation.* 卡西作了一個粗略的計算。◇ *By my calculation(s), we made a profit of £20 000 last year.* 我算了一下，我們去年贏利 2 萬英鎊。◇ *Our guess was confirmed by calculation.* 我們的猜測通過計算得到證實。➲ COLLOCATIONS at SCIENTIFIC **2** [C, U] the process of using your judgement to decide what the results would be of doing sth 估計；預測；推測 **3** [U] (*disapproving*) careful planning for yourself without caring about other people 算計；自私的打算：*an act of cold calculation* 冷酷無情的算計

cal·cu·la·tor /ˈkælkjuleɪtə(r)/ *noun* a small electronic device for calculating with numbers 計算器：*a pocket calculator* 袖珍計算器 ➲ VISUAL VOCAB page V69

cal·cu·lus /ˈkælkjələs/ *noun* [U] the type of mathematics that deals with rates of change, for example in the slope of a curve or the speed of a falling object 微積分

cal·dera /kɒlˈdeərə; *NAmE* kɔːlˈdɪrə; -ˈderə; -ˈdɪrə/ *noun* (*technical* 術語) a very large hole in the top of a VOLCANO, usually caused by an ERUPTION 破火山口（巨大碗口形火山凹地）

cal·dron (*US*) = CAULDRON

Cale·do·nian /ˌkælɪˈdəʊniən; *NAmE* -ˈdoʊ-/ *adj.* connected with Scotland 蘇格蘭的

cal·en·dar /ˈkælɪndə(r)/ *noun* **1** a page or series of pages showing the days, weeks and months of a particular year, especially one that you hang on a wall 日曆；掛曆：*a calendar for 2010* * 2010 年日曆 ➲ VISUAL VOCAB page V69 ➲ see also ADVENT CALENDAR **2** (*NAmE*) a record of what you have to do each day; the book in which you write this down 日程表；記事本 **3** [usually sing.] a list of important events or dates of a particular type during the year（一年之中的）重大事件（或重要日期）一覽表：*This is one of the biggest weeks in the racing calendar.* 這是全年賽馬日程表中最重要的幾個星期之一。**4** a system by which time is divided into fixed periods, showing the beginning and end of a year 曆法：*the Islamic calendar* 伊斯蘭教曆

ˌcalendar ˈmonth *noun* (*technical* 術語) **1** one of the twelve months of the year 日曆月（一年十二個月中的一個月）➲ compare LUNAR MONTH **2** a period of time from a particular date in one month to the same date in the next one 一整月的時間（即從某月某日到下月同一日的期間）

ˌcalendar ˈyear *noun* (*technical* 術語) the period of time from 1 January to 31 December in the same year 日曆年（公曆 1 月 1 日至 12 月 31 日）

calf /kɑːf; *NAmE* kæf/ *noun* (*pl.* **calves** /kɑːvz; *NAmE* kævz/) **1** [C] the back part of the leg between the ankle and the knee 腓；小腿肚：*I've torn a calf muscle.* 我拉傷了小腿肌肉。➲ VISUAL VOCAB page V59 **2** [C] a young cow 小牛；牛犢 **3** [C] a young animal of some other type such as a young ELEPHANT or WHALE（象、鯨等的）崽，幼獸 **4** [U] = CALFSKIN

IDM **in/with ˈcalf** (of a cow 母牛) pregnant 懷崽的

calf·skin /ˈkɑːfskɪn; *NAmE* ˈkæf-/ (also **calf**) *noun* [U] soft thin leather made from the skin of calves, used especially for making shoes and clothing 小牛皮，小牛皮革（尤用於製作皮鞋和皮衣）

cali·brate /ˈkælɪbreɪt/ *verb* **~ sth** (*technical* 術語) to mark units of measurement on an instrument such as a THERMOMETER so that it can be used for measuring sth accurately 標定，校準（刻度，以使測量準確）

cali·bra·tion /ˌkælɪˈbreɪʃn/ *noun* (*technical* 術語) **1** [U] the act of calibrating 標定；校準：*a calibration error* 校準誤差 **2** [C] the units of measurement marked on a THERMOMETER or other instrument（溫度計或其他儀表上的）刻度

cali·bre (*especially US* **cali·ber**) /ˈkælɪbə(r)/ *noun* **1** [U] the quality of sth, especially a person's ability 質量；（尤指人的）能力 SYN **standard**：*He was impressed by the **high calibre of** applicants for the job.* 求職人員出色的能力給他留下了深刻印象。◇ *The firm needs more people of your calibre.* 公司需要更多像你這樣有才幹的人。**2** [C] the width of the inside of a tube or gun; the width of a bullet（管子、槍炮的）口徑，內徑；（子彈的）直徑，彈徑

cal·ico /ˈkælɪkəʊ; *NAmE* -koʊ/ *noun* [U] **1** (*especially BrE*) a type of heavy cotton cloth that is usually plain white（本色白）厚棉布 **2** (*especially NAmE*) a type of rough cotton cloth that has a pattern printed on it 印花厚布

ˈcalico cat *noun* (*NAmE*) = TORTOISESHELL (2)

cali·for·nium /ˌkælɪˈfɔːniəm; *NAmE* -ˈfɔːrn-/ *noun* [U] (*symb.* **Cf**) a chemical element. Californium is a RADIOACTIVE metal produced artificially with CURIUM or AMERICIUM. 鐦（人工合成放射性化學元素）

cali·per (*especially NAmE*) = CALLIPER

ca·liph /ˈkeɪlɪf/ *noun* a title used by Muslim rulers, especially in the past 哈里發（尤為舊時穆斯林國家統治者的稱號）

ca·liph·ate /ˈkælɪfeɪt; ˈkeɪl-; *NAmE* ˈkeɪl-/ *noun* **1** the position of a caliph 哈里發的職位 **2** an area of land that is ruled over by a caliph 哈里發的轄地

cal·is·then·ics *noun* (*NAmE*) = CALLISTHENICS

CALL /kɔːl/ *abbr.* computer assisted language learning 計算機輔助語言學習；電腦輔助語言學習 ➲ compare CAL

call /kɔːl/ *verb, noun*

■ *verb*

▸ GIVE NAME 命名 **1** [T] to give sb/sth a particular name; to use a particular name or title when you are talking to sb 給…命名；稱呼；把…叫做：**~ sb/sth + noun** *They decided to call the baby Mark.* 他們決定給嬰兒取名馬克。◇ *His name's Hiroshi but everyone calls him Hiro.* 他名叫廣志，但人人都稱他廣。◇ *What do they call that new fabric?* 他們把那種新織品叫做什麼？◇ **~ sb** *They called their first daughter after her grandmother.* 他們給大女兒取了祖母的名字。◇ *We call each other by our first names here.* 我們這兒彼此直呼其名。➲ see also CALLED

▸ DESCRIBE 看作 **2** [T] to describe sb/sth in a particular way; to consider sb/sth to be sth 認為…是；把…看作：**~ sb/sth + noun** *I wouldn't call German an easy language.* 我並不認為德語是一門容易學的語言。◇ *Are you calling me a liar?* 你是說我撒謊？◇ *He was in the front room, or the lounge or whatever you want to call it.* 他當時在客廳，或者說是在起居室，或者在叫什麼都行的房間裏。◇ *I make it ten pounds forty-three you owe me. Let's call it ten pounds.* 我算下來你欠我十英鎊四十三便士。就算作十英鎊吧。◇ **~ sb/sth + adj.** *Would you call it blue or green?* 你認為它是藍色還是綠色？➲ SYNONYMS at REGARD **3** [T] **~ yourself + noun** to claim that you are a particular type of person, especially when other people question whether this is true 把自己稱為；自詡：*Call yourself a friend? So why won't you help me, then?* 你說你夠朋友？夠朋友怎麼不肯幫我？◇ *She's no right to call herself a feminist.* 她無權以女權主義者身分自居。

▸ SHOUT 喊叫 **4** [I, T] to shout or say sth loudly to attract sb's attention 大聲呼叫，大聲說（以吸引注意力）：*I thought I heard somebody calling.* 我彷彿聽見有人在呼喊。◇ **~ (out) to sb (for sth)** *She called out to her father for help.* 她向父親大聲呼救。◇ **~ (sth) out** *He called out a warning from the kitchen.* 他在廚房裏大聲發出警告。◇ **~ sth** *Did somebody call my name?* 有人叫我的名字嗎？◇ **+ speech** *'See you later!' she called.* "再見！"她叫道。**5** [T, I] **~ (sb)** to ask sb to come by shouting or speaking loudly 召喚；呼喚：*Will you call the kids in for lunch?* 把孩子們叫進來吃午飯好嗎？◇ *Did you call?* 你叫我？

▸ TELEPHONE 電話 **6** [T] to ask sb/sth to come quickly to a particular place by telephoning 打電話叫：**~ sb/sth** *to call the fire department/the police/a doctor/an ambulance* 打電話叫消防署／警察／醫生／救護車 ◇ *The doctor has been called to an urgent case.* 醫生接到電話去看急症。◇ *I'll call a taxi for you.* 我來打電話給你叫輛出租車。◇ **~ sb sth** *I'll call you a taxi.* 我來打電話給你叫輛出租車。**7** [I, T] to telephone sb（給…）打電話：*I'll call again later.* 我以後再打電話來。◇ **~ sb/sth** *I called the office to* *tell them I'd be late.* 我給辦公室打電話説我可能晚到一會兒。◊ *My brother called me from Spain last night.* 我弟弟昨晚從西班牙給我打電話來了。➲ note at PHONE

▸ **ORDER SB TO COME** 召見 **8** [T, usually passive] **+ adv./prep.** (*formal*) to order sb to come to a place 命令，召（至某處）：*Several candidates were called for a second interview.* 幾個候選人被通知去參加第二次面試。◊ *The ambassador was called back to London by the prime minister.* 大使被首相召回倫敦。◊ *He felt called to the priesthood* (= had a strong feeling that he must become a priest). 他感受到要成為司鐸的召喚。

▸ **VISIT** 拜訪 **9** 🔑 [I] (*especially BrE*) to make a short visit to a person or place（短暫地）訪問：*I'll call round and see you on my way home.* 我想在回家的路上去看看你。◊ **~ on sb** *Let's call on John.* 咱們去看看約翰吧。◊ **~ to do sth** *He was out when I called to see him.* 我去拜訪時，他不在家。

▸ **MEETING/STRIKE, ETC.** 集會、罷工等 **10** 🔑 [T] **~ sth** to order sth to happen; to announce that sth will happen 下令舉行；宣佈進行：*to* ***call a meeting/an election/a strike*** 舉行會議／選舉／罷工

▸ **OF BIRD/ANIMAL** 禽；獸 **11** [I] to make the cry that is typical for it 啼；鳴叫

▸ **IN GAMES** 比賽 **12** [T, I] **~ (sth)** to say which side of a coin you think will face upwards after it is thrown 拋硬幣説正反面：*to* ***call heads/tails*** 要硬幣的正面／反面

IDM **call sb's 'bluff** to tell sb to do what they are threatening to do, because you believe that they will not be cruel or brave enough to do it 要求…攤牌，要求…兑現其恫嚇（因相信對方不至於或不敢這樣做）**call sth into 'play** (*formal*) to make use of sth 利用；使用：*Chess is a game that calls into play all your powers of concentration.* 國際象棋是一項需要全神貫注的活動。 **call sth into 'question** to doubt sth or make others doubt sth 懷疑；引起懷疑 **SYN** **question**：*His honesty has never been called into question.* 他的誠實從未受到過懷疑。 **call it a 'day** (*informal*) to decide or agree to stop doing sth 結束一天的工作；到此為止；停止：*After forty years in politics I think it's time for me to call it a day* (= to retire). 從政四十年，我想現在也該退休了。 **call it 'quits** (*informal*) **1** to agree to end a contest, disagreement, etc. because both sides seem equal（因勢均力敵）同意停止比賽（或爭論等）**2** to decide to stop doing sth 決定停止 **call sb 'names** to use insulting words about sb 辱罵；謾罵 **call the 'shots/'tune** (*informal*) to be the person who controls a situation 控制；操縱 **call a spade a 'spade** to say exactly what you think without trying to hide your opinion 是啥説啥；直言不諱 **call 'time (on sth)** (*BrE*) to say or decide that it is time for sth to finish 宣佈結束；決定結束 **call sb to ac'count (for/over sth)** to make sb explain a mistake, etc. because they are responsible for it 責成…作出解釋；責問 **call sb/sth to 'order** to ask people in a meeting to be quiet so that the meeting can start or continue 要求保持安靜（以便開始或繼續會議）；要求遵守會議秩序 ➲ more at CARPET *n.*, MIND *n.*, PAY *v.*, POT *n.*, WHAT

PHR V **'call at ...** (*BrE*) (of a train, etc. 火車等) to stop at a place for a short time 停靠；（短時間）停留：*This train calls at Didcot and Reading.* 這趟列車在迪德科特和雷丁停車。 **,call sb a'way** to ask sb to stop what they are doing and to go somewhere else 叫走；把…叫到別處去：*She was called away from the meeting to take an urgent phone call.* 她被叫出會場去接一個緊急電話。 **,call 'back | ,call sb 'back** 🔑 to telephone sb again or to telephone sb who telephoned you earlier 再打電話；回電話：*She said she'd call back.* 她説她會再打電話來。◊ *I'm waiting for someone to call me back with a price.* 我在等人回電話報價。 **'call for sb** (*especially BrE*) to collect sb in order to go somewhere（去）接：*I'll call for you at 7 o'clock.* 我 7 點鐘來接你。 **'call for sth 1** to need sth 需要：*The situation calls for prompt action.* 目前的形勢需要立即採取行動。◊ *'I've been promoted.' 'This calls for a celebration!'* "我升職了。" "那得慶祝一下！" ➲ see also UNCALLED FOR **2** 🔑 to publicly ask for sth to happen（公開）要求：*They called for the immediate release of the hostages.* 他們要求立即釋放人質。◊ *The opposition have called for him to resign.* 反對派已要求他辭職。 **,call sth↔'forth** (*formal*) to produce a particular reaction 引起；使產生：*His speech called forth an angry response.* 他的發言引起了一陣憤怒。 **,call 'in** to telephone a place, especially the place where you work 打電話來（工作單位等）：*Several people have* ***called in sick*** *today.* 今天有幾個人打電話請病假。 **,call sb↔'in** to ask for the services of sb 召來，叫來（服務）：*to call in a doctor/the police* 請醫生／叫警察來 **,call sth↔'in** to order or ask for the return of sth 下令收回；要求退回：*Cars with serious faults have been called in by the manufacturers.* 有嚴重缺陷的汽車已被製造商召回。 **,call sb/sth↔'off** to order a dog or a person to stop attacking, searching, etc. 把（人）叫走（不再搜查等）；把（狗）叫開（不讓它咬人等） **,call sth↔'off** 🔑 to cancel sth; to decide that sth will not happen 取消；停止進行：*to call off a deal/trip/strike* 取消交易／旅行／罷工 ◊ *They have called off their engagement* (= decided not to get married). 他們已經解除婚約。◊ *The game was called off because of bad weather.* 比賽因天氣惡劣被取消。 **'call on/upon sb** (*formal*) **1** to formally invite or ask sb to speak, etc. 邀請，要求（某人講話等）；恭請：*I now call upon the chairman to address the meeting.* 現在請主席向大會致辭。 **2** to ask or demand that sb do sth 請求，要求，要（某人做某事）：*I feel called upon* (= feel that I ought) *to warn you that ...* 我覺得我應該警告你… **,call sb 'out 1** to ask sb to come, especially to an emergency 要求某人來，召喚出動（尤指處理緊急情況）：*to call out an engineer/a plumber/the troops* 召來工程師／管道工；出動軍隊 **2** to order or advise workers to stop work as a protest 下令罷工；通知罷工 ➲ related noun CALL-OUT **,call sb↔'up 1** 🔑 (*especially NAmE*) to make a telephone call to sb（給某人）打電話 **2** to make sb do their training in the army, etc. or fight in a war 徵召（服役）；徵召入伍 **SYN** **conscript, draft 3** to give sb the opportunity to play in a sports team, especially for their country 選入，徵調（運動員為國參賽）➲ related noun CALL-UP **,call sth↔'up 1** to bring sth back to your mind 使回憶起；使想起 **SYN** **recall**：*The smell of the sea called up memories of her childhood.* 大海的氣息勾起了她對童年的回憶。 **2** to use sth that is stored or kept available 調用貯存；調出備用：*I called his address up on the computer.* 我在計算機上調出了他的地址。◊ *She called up her last reserves of strength.* 她使盡了最後一點力氣。

■ ***noun***

▸ **ON TELEPHONE** 電話 **1** 🔑 [C] (also **'phone call**) the act of speaking to sb on the telephone 打電話；通話：*to* ***get/have/receive a call*** *from sb* 接到某人的電話 ◊ *to* ***give sb/to make a call*** 給某人打電話 ◊ *Were there any calls for me while I was out?* 我不在時有電話找我嗎？◊ *I'll* ***take*** (= answer) ***the call*** *upstairs.* 我會上樓接電話。◊ *I left a message but he didn't* ***return my call.*** 我留了口信，但他沒有回電話。◊ *a* ***local call*** 本地電話 ◊ *a* ***long-distance call*** 長途電話 ➲ note at PHONE ➲ see also WAKE-UP CALL

▸ **LOUD SOUND** 響亮的聲音 **2** 🔑 [C] a loud sound made by a bird or an animal, or by a person to attract attention（禽、獸的）叫聲；（喚起注意的）喊聲：*the distinctive call of the cuckoo* 布穀鳥獨特的叫聲 ◊ *a call for help* 呼救聲

▸ **VISIT** 拜訪 **3** [C] a short visit to sb's house 短暫拜訪：*The doctor has five calls to make this morning.* 醫生今天上午要出診五次。◊ (*old-fashioned*) ***to pay a call*** *on an old friend* 拜訪一位老朋友

▸ **REQUEST/DEMAND** 請求；要求 **4** [C] **~ (for sth)** a request, an order or a demand for sb to do sth or to go somewhere 要求；請求；呼籲：*calls for the minister to resign* 要部長辭職的要求 ◊ *calls for national unity* 國家統一的呼聲 ◊ *This is the last call for passengers travelling on British Airways flight 199 to Rome.* 乘坐英國航空公司 199 次班機飛往羅馬的乘客，這是最後一次通知登機。◊ (*formal*) *a* ***call to arms*** (= a strong request to fight in the army, etc.) 戰鬥號召 ➲ see also CURTAIN CALL **5** [U] **no ~ for sth | no ~ (for sb) to do sth** no demand for sth; no reason for sb's behaviour 沒有需要；沒有理由（做…）：*There isn't a lot of call for small specialist shops nowadays.* 如今對小型專賣店已沒有多大需求了。 **6** [C] **~ on sb/sth** a demand or pressure placed on sb/sth（對某人或某事物的）需求，壓力：*She is a busy woman* *with many calls on her time.* 她是個大忙人，有很多事等着她去辦。

‣ **OF A PLACE** 地方 **7** [sing.] **~ (of sth)** (*literary*) a strong feeling of attraction that a particular place has for you （某地的）吸引力，誘惑力：*the call of the sea/your homeland* 大海的 / 家鄉的魅力

‣ **TO A PARTICULAR JOB** 職業 **8** [sing.] **~ (to do sth)** a strong feeling that you want to do sth, especially a particular job 召喚；呼喚；使命感

‣ **DECISION** 決定 **9** [C] (*informal*) a decision 決定：*It's your call!* 那是你的決定！◇ *a good/bad call* 正確的 / 不恰當的決定 ◇ *That's a tough call.* 那是個艱難的決定。

‣ **IN TENNIS** 網球 **10** [C] a decision made by the UMPIRE （裁判員的）判決：*There was a disputed call in the second set.* 第二盤比賽有一個有爭議的判決。

‣ **IN CARD GAMES** 紙牌遊戲 **11** [C] a player's BID or turn to BID 叫牌；吊牌

IDM **the call of 'nature** (*humorous*) the need to go to the toilet 生理需要（指上廁所） **have first 'call (on sb/sth)** to be the most important person or thing competing for sb's time, money, etc. and to be dealt with or paid for before other people or things 優先佔用（時間、金錢等）；優先得到照顧（或支付）：*The children always have first call on her time.* 她的時間總是先花在孩子們身上。 **(be) on 'call** (of a doctor, police officer, etc. 醫生、警察等) available for work if necessary, especially in an emergency （尤指緊急情況下）隨叫隨到：*I'll be on call the night of the party.* 在聚會的晚上我將隨時聽憑召喚。 ➲ see also ON-CALL *adj.* ➲ more at BECK, CLOSE[2] *adj.*

Synonyms 同義詞辨析

call

cry out • exclaim • blurt • burst out

These words all mean to shout or say sth loudly or suddenly. 以上各詞均含突然大聲喊叫、説話之義。

call to shout or say sth loudly to attract sb's attention 指大聲呼叫或説話以吸引注意：*I thought I heard someone calling.* 我彷彿聽見有人在呼喊。

cry out (sth) to shout sth loudly, especially when you need help or are in trouble 尤指需要幫助或陷入困境時大聲呼喊：*She cried out for help.* 她大聲呼救。◇ *I cried out his name.* 我大聲呼喚他的名字。

exclaim to say sth suddenly and loudly, especially because of a strong emotion 尤指因強烈的情感而突然大聲說話：*'It isn't fair!' he exclaimed angrily.* "這不公平！"他氣憤地喊道。

blurt to say sth suddenly and without thinking carefully enough 指脱口而出：*He **blurted out** the answer without thinking.* 他不假思索脱口説出了答案。

burst out to say sth suddenly and loudly, especially with a lot of emotion 尤指突然激動地大聲喊叫：*'He's a bully!' the little boy burst out.* "他仗勢欺人！"小男孩突然大叫。

PATTERNS

- to call/cry out/exclaim/blurt out (sth) **to** sb
- to call/cry out **for** sth
- to cry out/exclaim/blurt out/burst out **in/with** sth
- to call/cry out/exclaim/blurt out/burst out **suddenly**
- to call/cry out/exclaim/burst out **loudly**

call·back /ˈkɔːlbæk/ *noun* **1** [C] a telephone call which you make to sb who has just called you 回撥的電話；打回的電話 **2 Callback™** [U, C] = RINGBACK **3** [U, C] (*computing* 計) a process by which the user of a computer or telephone system proves their identity by contacting a computer, which then contacts them 回叫（指計算機或電話系統用戶通過連接某台計算機證實自己的身分，然後該系統對之進行回調）**4** [C] (*especially NAmE*) an occasion when you are asked to return somewhere, for example for a second interview when you are trying to get a job （對求職者等的）召回 **5** [C] an occasion when people are asked to return goods that they have bought, usually because they are not safe 商品召回（因有安全隱患等）；回收瑕疵品

'call box *noun* **1** (*BrE*) = PHONE BOX **2** (*NAmE*) a small box beside a road, with a telephone in it, to call for help after an accident, etc. （路邊供求救等用的）電話亭

'call centre (*BrE*) (*NAmE* **'call center**) *noun* an office in which a large number of people work using telephones, for example arranging insurance for people, or taking customers' orders and answering questions 電話服務中心（安排保險、接受訂單、解答問題等）

called /kɔːld/ *adj.* [not before noun] having a particular name 叫做；稱作：*What's their son called?* 他們的兒子叫什麼名字？◇ *I don't know anyone called Scott.* 我不認識叫斯科特的人。◇ *I've forgotten what the firm he works for is called.* 我已經忘記他工作的公司名稱。◇ *What's it called again? Yeah, that's right. A modem.* 再説一遍它叫什麼？好的，對，調制解調器。 ➲ see also SO-CALLED

call·er /ˈkɔːlə(r)/ *noun* **1** a person who is making a telephone call 打電話者：*The caller hung up.* 打電話的人掛斷了電話。◇ *an anonymous caller* 打匿名電話的人 **2** a person who goes to a house or a building 訪問者；來訪者 **3** a person who shouts out the steps for people performing a SQUARE DANCE or COUNTRY DANCE （方形舞或土風舞中）喊出舞步的指揮

'caller ID *noun* [U] a system that uses a device on your telephone to identify and display the telephone number of the person who is calling you （電話的）來電顯示系統

'call girl *noun* a PROSTITUTE who makes her arrangements by telephone （電話）應召女郎

cal·lig·raphy /kəˈlɪɡrəfi/ *noun* [U] beautiful HANDWRITING that you do with a special pen or brush; the art of producing this 書法；書法藝術 ‣ **cal·lig·raph·er** *noun*

'call-in (*NAmE*) (*BrE* **'phone-in**) *noun* a radio or television programme in which people can telephone and make comments or ask questions about a particular subject （廣播或電視的）觀眾熱線節目，聽眾來電直播節目

call·ing /ˈkɔːlɪŋ/ *noun* **1** a strong desire or feeling of duty to do a particular job, especially one in which you help other people 使命感；（尤指想幫助他人的）強烈願望，責任感 **SYN** **vocation**：*He realized that his calling was to preach the gospel.* 他體悟到宣講福音是他的使命。 **2** (*formal*) a profession or career 職業；事業

'calling card *noun* (*NAmE*) **1** (*BrE* **'visiting card**) (also **card** *BrE, NAmE*) (especially in the past) a small card with your name on it which you leave with sb after, or instead of, a formal visit （尤指舊時訪客留下或其他人用以表示到訪的）名片，拜帖 **2** = PHONECARD

cal·li·per *noun* (*BrE*) (also **cali·per** *NAmE, BrE*) /ˈkælɪpə(r)/ **1** **callipers** [pl.] an instrument with two long thin parts joined at one end, used for measuring the DIAMETER of tubes and round objects (= the distance across them) 測徑規，兩腳規，卡鉗，卡尺（用於測量管子、圓形物體的直徑）：*a pair of callipers* 一把測徑規 **2** (*BrE*) (*NAmE* **brace**) [C, usually pl.] a metal support for weak or injured legs 雙腳規形夾（支撐無力或受傷的腿的金屬支架）

cal·lis·then·ics (*BrE*) (*NAmE* **cal·is·then·ics**) /ˌkælɪsˈθenɪks/ *noun* [U+sing./pl. v.] physical exercises intended to develop a strong and attractive body 健美操；健身操

'call letters *noun* [pl.] (*NAmE*) the letters that are used to identify a radio or television station （電台、電視台的）代號字母，呼號：*the call letters WNBC* 台號字母 WNBC

cal·lous /ˈkæləs/ *adj.* not caring about other people's feelings or suffering 冷酷無情的；無同情心的；冷漠的 **SYN** **cruel, unfeeling**：*a callous killer/attitude/act* 冷血殺手；漠不關心的態度；冷酷的行為 ◇ *a **callous disregard** for the feelings of others* 對他人感情的漠視 ‣ **cal·lous·ly** *adv.* **cal·lous·ness** *noun* [U]

cal·loused (also **cal·lused**) /'kæləst/ *adj.* (of the skin 皮膚) made rough and hard, usually by hard work 粗糙的；粗硬的；起老繭的： *calloused hands* 有老繭的雙手

'call-out *noun* an occasion when sb is called to do repairs, rescue sb, etc. 應召出勤；上門服務： *a call-out charge* 上門服務費 ◇ *ambulance call-outs* 救護車出車

cal·low /'kæləʊ; *NAmE* -loʊ/ *adj.* (*formal, disapproving*) young and without experience 幼稚無經驗的；未諳世事的 SYN **inexperienced**： *a callow youth* 乳臭未乾的年輕人

'call sign *noun* the letters and numbers used in radio communication to identify the person who is sending a message（無線電通訊的）呼叫信號，呼號

'call-up (*BrE*) *noun* **1** [U, C, usually sing.] an order to join the armed forces（服兵役的）徵召令，徵集令 SYN **conscription, the draft**： *to receive your* ***call-up papers*** 收到徵召入伍的通知 **2** [C] the opportunity to play in a sports team, especially for your country（尤指國家隊運動員的）選調，徵調： *His recent form has earned him a call-up to the England squad.* 他最近的表現使他得以入選英格蘭代表隊。

cal·lus /'kæləs/ *noun* an area of thick hard skin on a hand or foot, usually caused by rubbing 胼胝，老繭（手、足上的硬皮）

cal·lused = CALLOUSED

'call waiting *noun* [U] a telephone service that tells you if sb is trying to call you when you are using the telephone 來電等待服務，插撥服務（通話時提醒用戶有人正在打進電話）

Which Word? 詞語辨析

calm / calmness

- The noun **calm** is usually used to talk about a peaceful time or situation. 名詞 calm 通常指平靜的時期或形勢： *There was a short period of uneasy calm after the riot.* 動亂之後是令人不安的短暫平靜。 It can also be used to describe a person's manner. 該詞亦可指人的態度： *She spoke with icy calm.* 她說話時一副冷漠若無其事的樣子。 **Calmness** is usually used to talk about a person. * calmness 通常用以形容人鎮定、鎮靜： *We admired his calmness under pressure.* 我們佩服他在壓力下的鎮靜。

calm 🔑 /kɑːm/ *adj., verb, noun*

■ ***adj.*** (**calm·er, calm·est**) **1** 🔑 not excited, nervous or upset 鎮靜的；沉着的： *It is important to* ***keep calm*** *in an emergency.* 情況緊急的時候，保持鎮靜是重要的。◇ *Try to* ***remain calm.*** 盡量保持冷靜。◇ *Her voice was surprisingly calm.* 她的聲音出人意料地平靜。◇ *The city is calm again* (= free from trouble and fighting) *after yesterday's riots.* 昨天的騷亂過後，城裏又恢復了平靜。 **2** 🔑 (of the sea 海洋) without large waves 風平浪靜的 **3** 🔑 (of the weather 天氣) without wind 無風的： *a calm, cloudless day* 晴朗無風的一天 ▶ **calm·ly** 🔑 *adv.*： *'I'll call the doctor,' he said calmly.* "我去請醫生。" 他鎮定地說。 **calm·ness** *noun* [U]

■ ***verb*** 🔑 **~ sb/sth** to make sb/sth become quiet and more relaxed, especially after strong emotion or excitement 使平靜；使鎮靜： *Have some tea; it'll calm your nerves.* 喝點茶吧，這會使你緊張的神經鬆弛下來。◇ *His presence had* ***a calming influence.*** 有他在場對大家的情緒起到了穩定作用。 ➲ see also TRAFFIC CALMING

PHR V **,calm 'down | ,calm sb/sth↔'down** 🔑 to become or make sb become calm（使）平靜，鎮靜，安靜： *Look, calm down! We'll find her.* 喂，鎮靜一點！我們會找到她的。◇ *We waited inside until things calmed down.* 我們待在室內，直到一切都恢復了平靜。◇ *He took a few deep breaths to calm himself down.* 他深深地吸了幾口氣，使自己平靜下來。

■ ***noun*** [C, U] **1** 🔑 a quiet and peaceful time or situation 平靜的時期；寧靜的狀態： *the calm of a summer evening* 夏日夜晚的寧靜 ◇ *The police* ***appealed for calm.*** 警察要求大家保持安靜。 **2** a quiet and relaxed manner 泰然自若： *Her previous calm gave way to terror.* 她先前的泰然自若已變為驚恐。

IDM **the calm before the storm** a calm time immediately before an expected period of violent activity or argument 暴風雨（或大動盪、激烈辯論）前的平靜

Calor gas™ /'kælə gæs; *NAmE* 'kælər/ (*BrE*) (*US* **'cooking gas**) *noun* [U] a type of gas stored as a liquid under pressure in metal containers and used for heating and cooking in places where there is no gas supply 罐裝液化氣（用於取暖和做飯）

C

cal·orie /'kæləri/ *noun* **1** a unit for measuring how much energy food will produce 大卡，千卡，卡路里（測量食物含多少熱量的單位）： *No sugar for me, thanks—I'm* ***counting my calories.*** 我不要糖，謝謝。我在控制攝取的熱量。◇ *a* ***low-calorie drink/diet*** 低熱量的飲料／飲食 ➲ COLLOCATIONS at DIET **2** (*technical* 術語) a unit for measuring a quantity of heat; the amount of heat needed to raise the temperature of a gram of water by one degree Celsius 卡，卡路里（熱量單位，或 1 克水升高 1 攝氏度時所需要的熱量）

cal·or·if·ic /,kælə'rɪfɪk/ *adj.* [usually before noun] **1** (*technical* 術語) relating to the amount of energy contained in food or fuel（熱）卡的；產生熱量的： *the calorific value of food* (= the quantity of heat or energy produced by a particular amount of food) 食物的熱值（即某一數量的食物所產生的熱量或能量） **2** (of food and drink 飲食) containing a lot of calories and likely to make you fat 高卡（路里）的；高熱量的： *calorific chocolate cake* 高卡巧克力蛋糕

cal·or·im·eter /,kælə'rɪmɪtə(r)/ *noun* (*technical* 術語) a device which measures the amount of heat in a chemical reaction 熱量計；量熱儀

calque /kælk/ (also **'loan translation**) *noun* (*linguistics* 語言) a word or expression in a language that is a translation of a word or expression in another language 仿造詞，借譯詞語（外國詞語的直譯詞）： *'Traffic calming' is a calque of the German 'Verkehrsberuhigung'.* * traffic calming 是由德語 Verkehrsberuhigung 直譯過來的。

cal·umny /'kæləmni/ *noun* (*pl.* **-ies**) (*formal*) **1** [C] a false statement about a person that is made to damage their reputation 誣衊，誹謗（的言論） **2** [U] the act of making such a statement 誣衊，誹謗（的行為） SYN **slander**

Cal·va·dos /'kælvədɒs; *NAmE* ,kælvə'doʊs/ *noun* [U] a French drink made by DISTILLING apple juice（法國）蘋果白蘭地

calve /kɑːv; *NAmE* kæv/ *verb* [I] (of a cow 母牛) to give birth to a CALF 生小牛；產犢

calves *pl.* of CALF

Cal·vin·ist /'kælvɪnɪst/ (also **Cal·vin·is·tic**) *adj.* **1** connected with a Church that follows the teachings of the French Protestant, John Calvin 加爾文宗的，加爾文派的（與信奉法國新教教徒約翰 • 加爾文教義的教派有關的） **2** having very strict moral attitudes 嚴守道德的 ▶ **Cal·vin·ism** *noun* [U] **Cal·vin·ist** *noun*

ca·lypso /kə'lɪpsəʊ; *NAmE* -soʊ/ *noun* [C, U] (*pl.* **-os**) a Caribbean song about a subject of current interest; this type of music 卡利普索民歌（以時事為主題，流行於加勒比海地區）

calyx /'keɪlɪks/ *noun* (*pl.* **ca·lyxes** or **ca·ly·ces** /'keɪlɪsiːz/) (*technical* 術語) the ring of small green leaves (called SEPALS) that protect a flower before it opens 花萼

CAM /kæm/ *abbr.* computer aided manufacturing 計算機輔助製造；電腦輔助製造

cam /kæm/ *noun* a part on a wheel that sticks out and changes the CIRCULAR movement of the wheel into up-and-down or backwards-and-forwards movement 凸輪（把圓周運動轉變為上下或前後運動的機械部件）

cama·rad·erie /,kæmə'rɑːdəri; *NAmE* ,kɑːmə'rɑːdəri/ *noun* [U] a feeling of friendship and trust among people who work or spend a lot of time together 同志情誼；友情

cam·ber /'kæmbə(r)/ *noun* a slight downward curve from the middle of a road to each side 拱曲度（路面中間微拱的曲面）

cam·bric /ˈkæmbrɪk/ *noun* [U] a type of thin white cloth made from cotton or LINEN 細棉布；細亞麻布

cam·cord·er /ˈkæmkɔːdə(r); *NAmE* -kɔːrd-/ *noun* a video camera that records pictures and sound and that can be carried around（便攜式）攝像機，攝錄影機

came *past tense* of COME

camel /ˈkæml/ *noun* **1** [C] an animal with a long neck and one or two HUMPS on its back, used in desert countries for riding on or for carrying goods 駱駝 ➲ compare DROMEDARY **2** [U] = CAMEL HAIR：*a camel coat* 駝毛外衣 **IDM** see STRAW

ˈcamel hair *noun* [U] (also **camel**) a type of thick soft pale brown cloth made from camel's hair or a mixture of camel's hair and wool, used especially for making coats 駝毛，駝絨（尤用以製外衣）：*a camel-hair coat* 駝絨外衣

cam·el·lia /kəˈmiːliə/ *noun* a bush with shiny leaves and white, red or pink flowers that look like ROSES and are also called camellias 山茶；山茶花

Cam·em·bert /ˈkæməmbeə(r); *NAmE* -ber/ *noun* [U, C] a type of soft French cheese with a strong flavour 卡芒貝爾奶酪（法國軟乾酪，味濃）

cameo /ˈkæmiəʊ; *NAmE* -mioʊ/ *noun* (*pl.* **-os**) **1** a small part in a film/movie or play for a famous actor（電影、戲劇中）名演員演的配角：*a* ***cameo role/appearance*** 小配角；配角登台 **2** a short piece of writing that gives a good description of sb/sth 小品文 **3** a piece of jewellery that consists of a raised design, often of a head, on a background of a different colour 浮雕珠寶飾物：*a* ***cameo brooch/ring*** 浮雕針飾／戒指

cam·era 🔑 /ˈkæmərə/ *noun*
a piece of equipment for taking photographs, moving pictures or television pictures 照相機；（電影）攝影機；（電視）攝像機：*Just point the camera and press the button.* 只要把照相機對準，然後按動快門就可以了。◇ *Cameras started clicking as soon as she stepped out of the car.* 她一跨出汽車，照相機就開始咔嚓咔嚓地響成一片。◇ *a* ***TV/video camera*** 電視攝像機；攝像機 ◇ *a camera crew* 攝製組
IDM **in ˈcamera** (*law* 律) in a judge's private room, without the press or the public being present 在法官的私室裏；秘密地；不公開地：*The trial was held in camera.* 審判秘密進行。 **on ˈcamera** being filmed or shown on television 在攝製中；在電視上播放：*Are you prepared to tell your story on camera?* 你願意在電視上講述你的經歷嗎？

cam·era·man /ˈkæmrəmæn/, **came·ra·woman** /ˈkæmrəwʊmən/ *noun* (*pl.* **-men** /-men/, **-women** /-wɪmɪn/) a person whose job is operating a camera for making films/movies or television programmes（電影、電視節目的）攝影師，攝像師 ➲ note at GENDER

camera obscura /ˌkæmərə əbˈskjʊərə; *NAmE* -skjʊrə/ *noun* an early form of camera consisting of a dark box with a tiny hole or LENS in the front and a small screen inside, on which the image appears 暗箱（早期的照相機）

ˈcamera operator *noun* (also **ˈcamera person** *pl.* **ˈcamera people**) a person whose job is operating a camera for making films/movies or television programmes（電影、電視節目的）攝影師，攝像師

cam·era·work /ˈkæmrəwɜːk; *NAmE* -wɜːrk/ *noun* [U] the style in which sb takes photographs or uses a film/movie camera 拍攝風格

cami·sole /ˈkæmɪsəʊl; *NAmE* -soʊl/ *noun* a short piece of women's underwear that is worn on the top half of the body and is held up with narrow strips of material over the shoulders（背心式）女內衣

camo·mile (*especially BrE*) (also **chamo·mile** especially in *NAmE*) /ˈkæməmaɪl/ *noun* [U] a plant with a sweet smell and small white and yellow flowers. Its dried leaves and flowers are used to make tea, medicine, etc. 蘋果菊，黃春菊，甘菊（花及葉可製茶、藥等）：*camomile tea* 蘋果菊花茶

cam·ou·flage /ˈkæməflɑːʒ/ *noun, verb*
■ ***noun*** **1** [U] a way of hiding soldiers and military equipment, using paint, leaves or nets, so that they look like part of their surroundings（軍事上的）偽裝，隱蔽：*a camouflage jacket* (= covered with green and brown marks and worn by soldiers) 迷彩夾克衫 ◇ *troops dressed in camouflage* 穿迷彩服的軍隊 **2** [U, sing.] the way in which an animal's colour or shape matches its surroundings and makes it difficult to see（動物的）保護色，保護形狀 **3** [U, sing.] behaviour that is deliberately meant to hide the truth 隱瞞：*Her angry words were camouflage for the way she felt.* 她以氣憤的言辭掩蓋自己的真實感情。
■ ***verb*** **~ sth** (**with sth**) to hide sb/sth by making them or it look like the things around, or like sth else 偽裝；掩飾：*The soldiers camouflaged themselves with leaves.* 士兵用樹葉來偽裝自己。◇ *Her size was camouflaged by the long loose dress she wore.* 她穿的那件寬鬆長裙遮掩了她身材的大小。 ➲ SYNONYMS at HIDE

camp 🔑 /kæmp/ *noun, verb, adj.*
■ ***noun***
▸ **IN TENTS** 帳篷 **1** 🔑 [C, U] a place where people live temporarily in tents or temporary buildings 營地：*Let's return to camp.* 咱們回營地吧。◇ *to* ***pitch/make camp*** (= put up tents) 紮營；搭帳篷 ◇ *to break camp* (= to take down tents) 拔營 ➲ see also HOLIDAY CAMP
▸ **HOLIDAY/VACATION** 度假 **2** 🔑 [C, U] a place where young people go on holiday/vacation and take part in various activities or a particular activity 度假營：*a tennis camp* 網球度假營 ◇ *He spent two weeks at camp this summer.* 他今年夏天在度假營玩了兩個星期。◇ *summer camp* 夏令營 ➲ see also FAT CAMP
▸ **PRISON, ETC.** 拘留營等 **3** 🔑 [C] (used in compounds 用於構成複合詞) a place where people are kept in temporary buildings or tents, especially by a government and often for long periods（尤指民政府讓人長時間住宿的）營房，營帳：*a refugee camp* 難民營 ◇ *a camp guard* 拘留營看守 ➲ see also CONCENTRATION CAMP, PRISON CAMP, TRANSIT CAMP
▸ **ARMY** 軍隊 **4** [C, U] a place where soldiers live while they are training or fighting 兵營：*an army camp* 軍營
▸ **GROUP OF PEOPLE** 群體 **5** [C] a group of people who have the same ideas about sth and oppose people with other ideas 陣營（指觀點相同且與持不同觀點者對立的集團）：*the socialist camp* 社會主義陣營 ◇ *We were in opposing camps.* 我們屬於彼此對立的陣營。 **6** [C] one of the sides in a competition and the people connected with it 陣營（比賽的一方及其支持者）：*There was an air of confidence in the England camp.* 英格蘭隊陣營信心十足。
IDM see FOOT *n.*
■ ***verb***
▸ **LIVE IN TENT** 住帳篷 **1** 🔑 [I] to put up a tent and live in it for a short time 宿營；露營：*I camped overnight in a field.* 我在田野裏露營過夜。 **2** 🔑 [I] **go camping** to stay in a tent, especially while you are on holiday/vacation（尤指在假日）野營：*They go camping in France every year.* 他們每年去法國野營度假。
▸ **STAY FOR SHORT TIME** 暫住 **3** [I] **~** (**out**) to live in sb's house for a short time, especially when you do not have a bed there 借住；借宿；暫住：*I'm camping out at a friend's apartment at the moment.* 我目前暫時寄宿在朋友的住處。
PHR V **ˌcamp ˈout** to live outside for a short time 露宿：*Dozens of reporters camped out on her doorstep.* 許多記者在她家門口露宿。 **ˌcamp it ˈup** (*BrE, informal*) to behave in a very exaggerated manner, especially to attract attention to yourself or to make people laugh 裝腔作勢，裝模作樣（尤指想引人注意或令人發笑）
■ ***adj.*** **1** (of a man or his manner 男人或其舉止) deliberately behaving in a way that some people think is typical of a HOMOSEXUAL 故意帶女子氣的，女性化的（被某些人認為是典型同性戀的特徵）**SYN** **effeminate** **2** exaggerated in style, especially in a deliberately amusing way 誇張的，滑稽可笑的（尤指故意逗笑）；做作的：*The movie is a camp celebration of the fashion industry.* 這部電影誇張地頌揚時裝行業。

cam·paign 🔑 /kæmˈpeɪn/ *noun, verb*
■ ***noun*** **1** 🔑 **~** (**against/for sth**) a series of planned activities that are intended to achieve a particular social,

commercial or political aim 運動（為社會、商業或政治目的而進行的一系列有計劃的活動）：*to* **conduct** *a* **campaign** 領導一場運動 ◇ *a campaign against ageism in the workplace* 反對在工作場所實行年齡歧視的運動 ◇ *the campaign for parliamentary reform* 要求議會進行改革的運動 ◇ *an anti-smoking campaign* 反對吸煙的運動 ◇ *Today police* **launched** (= began) **a campaign** *to reduce road accidents.* 警方今天已開展了一場減少道路交通事故的運動。◇ *an advertising campaign* 一場廣告宣傳運動 ◇ *an election campaign* 競選運動 ◇ *the President's* **campaign team/manager** 總統的競選班子／主管 ➲ COLLOCATIONS at VOTE **2** a series of attacks and battles that are intended to achieve a particular military aim during a war 戰役

■ *verb* [I, T] to take part in or lead a campaign, for example to achieve political change or in order to win an election 參加運動，領導運動（如為實現政治變革或贏得競選勝利）：*The party* **campaigned vigorously** *in the north of the country.* 該黨在本國北部展開了強有力的競選運動。◇ **~ for/against sb/sth** *We have campaigned against whaling for the last 15 years.* 我們過去 15 年一直參加反對捕鯨的運動。◇ **~ to do sth** *They are campaigning to save the area from building development.* 他們正開展一場反對在這個地區進行房地產開發的運動。▶ **cam·paign·ing** *noun* [U]

cam·paign·er /kæmˈpeɪnə(r)/ *noun* a person who leads or takes part in a campaign, especially one for political or social change（尤指政治或社會變革的）運動領導者，運動參加者：*a leading human rights campaigner* 人權運動的主要領導人 ◇ *a campaigner on environmental issues* 環保問題的活動家 ◇ *a campaigner for women priests* 主張女性也可擔任司祭的倡導者 ◇ *an* **old/veteran/seasoned campaigner** (= a person with a lot of experience of a particular activity) 老練／資深／經驗豐富的活動家 ◇ (*especially NAmE*) *Obama campaigners* (= people working for Obama in a campaign) 奧巴馬競選班子

cam·pa·nile /ˌkæmpəˈniːli/ *noun* a tower that contains a bell, especially one that is not part of another building（尤指獨立的）鐘樓

cam·pan·ology /ˌkæmpəˈnɒlədʒi; *NAmE* -ˈnɑːl-/ *noun* [U] (*formal*) the study of bells and the art of ringing bells 鐘學；鳴鐘術 ▶ **cam·pan·olo·gist** /-ədʒɪst/ *noun* ➲ see also BELL-RINGER

ˌcamp ˈbed (*BrE*) (*NAmE* **cot**) *noun* a light narrow bed that you can fold up and carry easily 摺疊牀；行軍牀 ➲ VISUAL VOCAB page V23

camp·er /ˈkæmpə(r)/ *noun* **1** a person who spends a holiday/vacation living in a tent or at a holiday camp 野營者；露營者；度假營營員 **2** (also **ˈcamper van**) (both *BrE*) (*NAmE* **RV**, **recreˌational ˈvehicle**) (also **motor·home** *NAmE*, *BrE*) a large vehicle designed for people to live and sleep in when they are travelling 野營車（供旅行時居住）➲ VISUAL VOCAB page V58 **3** (*NAmE*) (*BrE* **cara·van**) a road vehicle without an engine that is pulled by a car, designed for people to live and sleep in, especially when they are on holiday/vacation 旅行拖車，宿營拖車（無發動機，由其他車拖動，多供度假時住宿用）➲ VISUAL VOCAB page V58 IDM see HAPPY *adj.*

camp·fire /ˈkæmpfaɪə(r)/ *noun* an outdoor fire made by people who are sleeping outside or living in a tent 營火；篝火

ˌcamp ˈfollower *noun* **1** a person who supports a particular group or political party but is not a member of it（支持某一團體或政黨但並非其正式成員的）追隨者

Synonyms 同義詞辨析

campaign

battle • struggle • drive • war • fight

These are all words for an effort made to achieve or prevent sth. 以上各詞均指為達到某目的或為阻止某事而作出的努力。

campaign a series of planned activities that are intended to achieve a particular social, commercial or political aim 指為社會、商業或政治目的而進行的一系列有計劃的活動或運動：*the campaign for parliamentary reform* 要求議會改革的運動 ◇ *an advertising campaign* 廣告宣傳計劃

battle a competition or argument between people or groups of people trying to win power or control 指個人或集體為贏得權力或控制權而進行的較量、爭論或鬥爭：*She finally won the legal battle for compensation.* 她終於贏得了這場要求賠償的法律鬥爭。◇ *the endless battle between man and nature* 人與大自然永無休止的鬥爭

struggle a competition or argument between people or groups of people trying to win power or control 指個人或集體為贏得權力或控制權而進行的較量、爭論或鬥爭：*the struggle for independence* 為獨立的鬥爭 ◇ *the struggle between good and evil* 正邪之爭

BATTLE OR STRUGGLE? 用 battle 還是 struggle？

A **struggle** is always about things that seem absolutely necessary, such as life and death or freedom. A **battle** can also be about things that are not absolutely necessary, just desirable, or about the pleasure of winning. * struggle 總是用於似乎絕對必要的鬥爭，如關乎生死、自由等。battle 還可用於並非絕對必要的鬥爭，如僅僅是想得到或者為了獲得勝利的滿足感：*the battle/struggle between good and evil* 正邪之爭 ◇ ~~*a legal struggle for compensation*~~ ◇ ~~*a struggle of wills/wits*~~

drive an organized effort by a group of people to achieve sth 指團體為達到目的而作出的有組織的努力：*the drive for greater efficiency* 為提高效率而作出的努力 ◇ *a drive to reduce energy consumption* 為減少能源消耗而發起的運動

CAMPAIGN OR DRIVE? 用 campaign 還是 drive？

A **campaign** is usually aimed at getting other people to do sth; a **drive** may be an attempt by people to get themselves to do sth. * campaign 通常為發動別人參加的運動；drive 可指讓自己作出努力：*From today, we're going on an* **economy drive** (= we must spend less). 從今天起，我們要展開厲行節約運動。A **campaign** may be larger, more formal and more organized than a **drive**. * campaign 所指的運動可能比 drive 更大規模、更正式和更有組織。

war [sing.] an effort over a long period of time to get rid of or stop sth bad 指為消滅或阻止有害事物而進行的長期鬥爭：*the war against crime* 撲滅罪行的鬥爭

fight [sing.] the work of trying to stop or prevent sth bad or achieve sth good; an act of competing, especially in a sport 指為制止或防止壞事物或為達到好目的而進行的鬥爭，或指競賽，尤指體育競賽：*Workers won their fight to stop compulsory redundancies.* 工人贏得了阻止強制裁員的鬥爭。

WAR OR FIGHT? 用 war 還是 fight？

A **war** is about stopping things, like drugs and crime, that everyone agrees are bad. A **fight** can be about achieving justice for yourself. * war 用於制止人人摒棄的事物（如毒品和犯罪）而進行的鬥爭；fight 可用於為自己伸張正義而進行的鬥爭。

PATTERNS

- a campaign/battle/struggle/drive/war/fight **against** sth
- a campaign/battle/struggle/drive/fight **for** sth
- a **one-man/one-woman/personal** campaign/battle/struggle/war
- a **bitter** campaign/battle/struggle/drive/war/fight
- to **launch/embark on** a campaign/battle/drive
- to **lead/continue** the campaign/battle/struggle/drive/fight
- to **win/lose** a battle/struggle/war/fight

C

2 (in the past) a person who was not a soldier but followed an army from place to place to sell goods or services（舊時的）隨軍商販，隨軍雜役

camp·ground /ˈkæmpɡraʊnd/ (*NAmE*) (*BrE* **camp·site**, **ˈcamping site**) *noun* a place where people on holiday/vacation can put up their tents, park their CARAVAN/CAMPER, etc., often with toilets, water, etc. 野營地；度假營地

cam·phor /ˈkæmfə(r)/ *noun* [U] a white substance with a strong smell, used in medicine, for making plastics and to keep insects away from clothes 樟腦

camp·ing ⊶ /ˈkæmpɪŋ/ *noun* [U] living in a tent, etc. on holiday/vacation 野營度假：*Do you go* ***camping***? 你去野營度假嗎？◇ *a camping trip* 野營旅行

camp·site /ˈkæmpsaɪt/ *noun* **1** (also **ˈcamping site**) (both *BrE*) (*NAmE* **ˈcamp·ground**) a place where people on holiday/vacation can put up their tents, park their CARAVAN/CAMPER, etc., often with toilets, water, etc. 野營地；度假營地 **2** (*NAmE*) a place in a CAMPGROUND where you can put up one tent or park one CAMPER, etc. 露營帳篷位；野營車位

cam·pus /ˈkæmpəs/ *noun* the buildings of a university or college and the land around them（大學、學院的）校園，校區：*She lives* ***on campus*** (= within the main university area). 她住在大學校園區內。◇ *campus life* 大學校園生活

cam·shaft /ˈkæmʃɑːft; *NAmE* -ʃæft/ *noun* a long straight piece of metal with a CAM on it joining parts of machinery, especially in a vehicle 凸輪軸

can[1] ⊶ /kən; *strong form* kæn/ *modal verb* ➲ see also CAN² (*negative* **can·not** /ˈkænɒt; *NAmE* -nɑːt/, *short form* **can't** /kɑːnt; *NAmE* kænt/, *pt* **could** /kəd; *strong form* kʊd/, *negative* **could not**, *short form* **couldn't** /ˈkʊdnt/) **1** ⊶ used to say that it is possible for sb/sth to do sth, or for sth to happen（表示有能力做或能夠發生）能，會：*I can run fast.* 我能跑得快。◇ *Can you call back tomorrow?* 明天你能回電話嗎？◇ *He couldn't answer the question.* 他不能回答那個問題。◇ *The stadium can be emptied in four minutes.* 這個體育場能在四分鐘以內讓觀眾全部散場。◇ *I can't promise anything, but I'll do what I can.* 我不能許諾什麼，但會盡力而為。◇ *Please let us know if you cannot attend the meeting.* 你若不能參加會議，請通知我們。 **2** ⊶ used to say that sb knows how to do sth（表示知道如何做）懂得，會：*She can speak Spanish.* 她會講西班牙語。◇ *Can he cook?* 他會做飯嗎？◇ *I could drive a car before I left school.* 我在中學畢業前就會開車了。 **3** ⊶ used with the verbs 'feel', 'hear', 'see', 'smell', 'taste'（與動詞 feel、hear、see、smell、taste 連用）：*She could feel a lump in her breast.* 她摸到自己的乳房上有一個腫塊。◇ *I can hear music.* 我聽見有音樂聲。 **4** ⊶ used to show that sb is allowed to do sth（表示允許）可以：*You can take the car, if you want.* 如果想用那輛車，你就儘管用吧。◇ *We can't wear jeans at work.* 我們工作時不准穿牛仔褲。 **5** ⊶ (*informal*) used to ask permission to do sth（請求允許）可以：*Can I read your newspaper?* 我可以看一下你的報紙嗎？◇ *Can I take you home?* 我送你回家好嗎？ **6** ⊶ (*informal*) used to ask sb to help you（請求幫助）能：*Can you help me with this box?* 你能幫我搬這個箱子嗎？◇ *Can you feed the cat, please?* 請你餵一下貓好嗎？ **7** ⊶ used in the negative for saying that you are sure sth is not true（用於否定句，表示某事肯定不真實）：*That can't be Mary—she's in New York.* 那不可能是瑪麗——她在紐約呢。◇ *He can't have slept through all that noise.* 他不可能在那種鬧哄哄的環境裏睡好覺。 **8** ⊶ used to express doubt or surprise（表示疑惑或驚訝）究竟能，難道會，到底是：*What can they be doing?* 他們究竟在幹些什麼呢？◇ *Can he be serious?* 他難道會當真麼？◇ *Where can she have put it?* 她到底把它放哪兒了呢？ **9** ⊶ used to say what sb/sth is often like（表示常有的行為和情形）有時會，時而可能：*He can be very tactless sometimes.* 他有時太莽撞。◇ *It can be quite cold here in winter.* 這裏的冬天有時還真夠冷的。 **10** ⊶ used to make suggestions（提出建議）可以：*We can eat in a restaurant, if you like.* 如果你願意，我們可以去餐館吃飯。◇ *I can take the car if necessary.* 如果必要的話，我可以乘汽車去。 **11** (*informal*) used to say that sb must do sth, usually when you are angry（表示對方必須做，常指說話人在生氣時）必須，得：*You can shut up or get out!* 你給我閉嘴，要不然就滾出去！➲ note at MODAL

IDM **can't be doing with sb/sth/sb doing sth** (*informal*) used to say that you do not like sth and are unwilling to accept it（表示因不喜歡而不願接受）無法接受…：*I can't be doing with people who complain all the time.* 我無法忍受那些整天發牢騷的人。 **no can ˈdo** (*informal*) used to say that you are not able or willing to do sth 幹不了；不行；不成：*Sorry, no can do. I just don't have the time.* 對不起，不行。我就是沒有時間。

Grammar Point 語法說明

can / could / be able to / manage

- **Can** is used to say that somebody knows how to do something. * can 表示懂得做：*Can you play the piano?* 你會彈鋼琴嗎？It is also used with verbs of seeing, noticing, etc. 該詞亦與表示看見、注意到等動詞連用：*I can hear someone calling.* 我聽見有人在呼叫。and with passive infinitives. 並與不定式的被動形式連用：*The DVD can be rented from your local store.* 這 DVD 可在你們區內的商店租借。
- **Can** or **be able to** are used to say that something is possible or that somebody has the opportunity to do something. * can 或 be able to 表示某事情有可能或某人有機會做某事：*Can you/are you able to come on Saturday?* 你星期六能來嗎？
- You use **be able to** to form the future and perfect tenses and the infinitive. 用 be able to 構成將來時、完成時和動詞不定式：*You'll be able to get a taxi outside the station.* 在車站外可搭乘出租車。◇ *I haven't been able to get much work done today.* 我今天未能幹多少工作。◇ *She'd love to be able to play the piano.* 她很希望能彈鋼琴。
- **Could** is used to talk about what someone was generally able to do in the past. * could 表示過去通常能做：*Our daughter could walk when she was nine months old.* 我們的女兒九個月大就會走路了。
- You use **was/were able to** or **manage** (but not **could**) when you are saying that something was possible on a particular occasion in the past. 關於在過去特定情況下可能的事用 was/were able to 或 manage，但不用 could：*I was able to/managed to find some useful books in the library.* 我總算在圖書館找到了一些有用的書。◇ ~~*I could find some useful books in the library.*~~ In negative sentences, **could not** can also be used. 否定句也可用 could not：*We weren't able to/didn't manage to/couldn't get there in time.* 我們未能及時趕到那兒。**Could** is also used with this meaning with verbs of seeing, noticing, understanding, etc. 亦可用 could 加表示看見、注意到、明白等動詞表示此義：*I could see there was something wrong.* 我發覺出事了。
- **Could have** is used when you are saying that it was possible for somebody to do something in the past but they did not try. 表示過去有可能做某事但沒有做，用 could have：*I could have won the game but decided to let her win.* 我本可以贏得那場比賽，但還是決定讓她贏了。

can[2] ⊶ /kæn/ *noun, verb* ➲ see also CAN¹

■ ***noun*** **1** ⊶ (*BrE* also **tin**) [C] a metal container in which food and drink is sold（盛食品或飲料的）金屬罐：*a can of beans* 豆罐頭 ◇ *a beer/paint can* 啤酒罐；漆筒 ➲ **VISUAL VOCAB** page V33 **HELP** In *NAmE* **can** is the usual word used for both food and drink. In *BrE* **can** is always used for drink, but **tin** or **can** can be used for food, paint, etc. 美式英語中，can 一詞通常用於食品和飲料。英式英語中，can 一詞總是用於飲料，而 tin 或 can 可用於食品、塗料等。 **2** ⊶ [C] the amount contained in a can 一罐（的量）：*We drank a can of Coke each.* 我們每人喝了一罐可樂。 **3** [C] a metal or plastic container for holding or carrying liquids（裝運液體用的）金屬容器，塑料容器：*an oil can* 油罐 ◇ *a watering can* 灑水壺 **4** [C] a metal container in which liquids are kept under pressure and let out in a fine spray when you press a button on the lid 噴霧器：*a can of hairspray* 一瓶噴髮定型劑 ➲ **VISUAL VOCAB** page V33 **5 the can** [sing.] (*NAmE, slang*) prison 班房；監獄；牢房 **6 the can** [sing.] (*NAmE, slang*) the toilet 茅房；廁所

IDM **a can of 'worms** (*informal*) if you open up **a can of worms**, you start doing sth that will cause a lot of problems and be very difficult 棘手的問題；難題；麻煩事 **be in the 'can** (*informal*) (especially of filmed or recorded material 尤指影片、錄像資料) to be completed and ready for use 已拍攝好；錄製完畢 ➲ more at CARRY

■ *verb* (**-nn-**) **1 ~ sth** (*especially NAmE*) to preserve food by putting it in a can 把（食品）裝罐保存 **2 ~ sb** (*NAmE, informal*) to dismiss sb from their job 讓…捲鋪蓋走人；炒…的魷魚 **SYN** **fire, sack**

Which Word? 詞語辨析

can / may

■ **Can** and **cannot** (or **can't**) are the most common words used for asking for, giving or refusing permission. * can 和 cannot（或 can't）是表示請求、給予或拒絕許可的最通用詞：*Can I borrow your calculator?* 我可以借用你的計算器嗎？◇ *You can come with us if you want to.* 如果你願意可以跟我們一起來。◇ *You can't park your car there.* 你不能在那兒停車。

■ **May** (negative **may not**) is used as a polite and fairly formal way to ask for or give permission. * may（否定式 may not）用以表示禮貌的正式請求或給予許可：*May I borrow your newspaper?* 把你的報紙借我看行嗎？◇ *You may come if you wish.* 你想來的話可以來。It is often used in official signs and rules. 該詞常用於正式標誌和規定：*Visitors may use the swimming pool between 7 a.m. and 7 p.m.* 訪客從早上 7:00 到下午 7:00 可在游泳池游泳。◇ *Students may not use the college car park.* 學生不得在學院停車場停車。The form **mayn't** is hardly ever used in modern English. 現代英語幾乎不用 mayn't。

'Canada Day *noun* (in Canada) a national holiday held on 1 July to celebrate the original joining together of PROVINCES to form Canada in 1867 加拿大獨立日，加拿大國慶日（7 月 1 日，紀念 1867 年加拿大的成立）

ˌCanada 'goose *noun* a common N American GOOSE with a black head and neck 加拿大雁，黑額黑雁（繁殖於北美）

Can·adian /kəˈneɪdiən/ *adj., noun*
■ *adj.* from or connected with Canada 加拿大的
■ *noun* a person from Canada 加拿大人

canal /kəˈnæl/ *noun* **1** a long straight passage dug in the ground and filled with water for boats and ships to travel along; a smaller passage used for carrying water to fields, crops, etc. 運河；灌溉渠：*the Panama/Suez Canal* 巴拿馬 / 蘇伊士運河 ◇ *an irrigation canal* 一條灌溉渠 **2** a tube inside the body through which liquid, food or air can pass 食道；氣管 ➲ see also ALIMENTARY CANAL

ca'nal boat *noun* a long narrow boat used on canals 運河船（船體狹長）➲ **VISUAL VOCAB** page V54

can·al·ize (*BrE* also **-ise**) /ˈkænəlaɪz/ *verb* **1 ~ sth** (*technical* 術語) to make a river wider, deeper or straighter; to make a river into a canal 把（河道）加寬，加深，變直；把（河流）改建成運河 **2 ~ sth** (*formal*) to control an emotion, activity, etc. so that it is aimed at a particular purpose 把（情緒、行為等）引向某一渠道 **SYN** **channel** ▸ **can·al·iza·tion, -isa·tion** /ˌkænəlaɪˈzeɪʃn; *NAmE* -nələˈz-/ *noun* [U]

can·apé /ˈkænəpeɪ; *NAmE* ˌkænəˈpeɪ/ *noun* [usually pl.] a small biscuit or piece of bread with cheese, meat, fish, etc. on it, usually served with drinks at a party 小餅乾，麵包片，開胃餅（上面附有奶酪、肉、魚等，通常在聚會上與飲料一起提供）

can·ard /kæˈnɑːd; ˈkænɑːd; *NAmE* kəˈnɑːrd; ˈkænɑːrd/ *noun* (*formal*) a false report or piece of news 虛假的報道；假新聞

can·ary /kəˈneəri; *NAmE* -ˈneri/ *noun* (*pl.* **-ies**) a small yellow bird with a beautiful song, often kept in a CAGE as a pet 金絲雀 **IDM** see CAT

can·asta /kəˈnæstə/ *noun* [U] a card game played with two packs of cards, in which players try to collect sets of cards 卡納斯塔紙牌戲（用兩副紙牌，參與者盡量組成牌組）

can·can /ˈkænkæn/ *noun* (often **the cancan**) [sing.] a fast dance in which a line of women kick their legs high in the air 康康舞，坎坎舞（女子排成隊、高高踢腿）

can·cel 🔑 /ˈkænsl/ *verb* (**-ll-**, *US* **-l-**)
1 🔑 [T] **~ sth** to decide that sth that has been arranged will not now take place 取消；撤銷；終止：*All flights have been cancelled because of bad weather.* 因天氣惡劣，所有航班均已取消。◇ *Don't forget to cancel the newspaper* (= arrange for it not to be delivered) *before going away.* 外出前，別忘了停訂報紙。➲ compare POSTPONE **2** 🔑 [T, I] **~ (sth)** to say that you no longer want to continue with an agreement, especially one that has been legally arranged 撤銷，取消，廢除（具有法律效力的協議）：*to cancel a policy/subscription* 取消保單；停止訂閱 ◇ *Is it too late to cancel my order?* 我現在取消訂單是不是太晚了？◇ *The US has agreed to cancel debts* (= say that they no longer need to be paid) *totalling $10 million.* 美國已同意免除總額為 1 000 萬元的債務。◇ *No charge will be made if you cancel within 10 days.* 如果在 10 天以內取消，不收費用。**3** [T] **~ sth** to mark a ticket or stamp so that it cannot be used again 蓋銷，註銷（票或郵票）

PHR V **ˌcancel 'out | ˌcancel sth↔'out** if two or more things **cancel out** or one **cancels out** the other, they are equally important but have an opposite effect on a situation so that the situation does not change 抵消；對消：*Recent losses have cancelled out any profits made at the start of the year.* 最近的虧損與年初的盈利相抵消。◇ *The advantages and disadvantages would appear to* ***cancel each other out***. 看來是利弊參半。

can·cel·la·tion /ˌkænsəˈleɪʃn/ (*US* **can·cel·ation**) *noun* **1** [U, C] a decision to stop sth that has already been arranged from happening; a statement that sth will not happen 取消；撤銷：*We need at least 24 hours' notice of cancellation.* 如欲取消，請至少提前 24 小時告知。◇ *a cancellation fee* 註銷費 ◇ *Heavy seas can cause cancellation of ferry services.* 海上起風浪會導致渡輪航班取消。◇ *Cancellations must be made in writing.* 撤銷必須有書面通知。**2** [C] something that has been cancelled 被取消了的事物：*Are there any cancellations for this evening's performance?* (= tickets that have been returned) 今晚的演出有退票嗎？**3** [U] the fact of making sth no longer valid 作廢；廢除；取消；中止：*the cancellation of the contract* 合同的取消

Can·cer /ˈkænsə(r)/ *noun* **1** [U] the fourth sign of the ZODIAC, the CRAB 黃道第四宮；巨蟹宮；巨蟹（星）座 **2** [sing.] a person born when the sun is in this sign, that is between 22 June and 22 July, approximately 屬巨蟹座的人（約出生於 6 月 22 日至 7 月 22 日）▸ **Can·cer·ian** /kænˈsɪəriən; *NAmE* -ˈsɪr-/ *noun, adj.*

can·cer 🔑 /ˈkænsə(r)/ *noun*
1 🔑 [U, C] a serious disease in which GROWTHS of cells, also called cancers, form in the body and kill normal body cells. The disease often causes death. 癌；癌症：*lung/breast cancer* 肺癌；乳腺癌 ◇ *cancer of the bowel/stomach* 腸癌；胃癌 ◇ *Most skin cancers are completely curable.* 大多數的皮膚癌是可以完全治癒的。◇ *The cancer has spread to his stomach.* 癌已擴散到他的胃部。◇ *cancer patients* 癌症病人 ◇ *cancer research* 癌症研究 ➲ **COLLOCATIONS** at ILL **2** [C] (*literary*) an evil or dangerous thing that spreads quickly（迅速蔓延的）邪惡；（社會）毒瘤：*Violence is a cancer in our society.* 暴力行為是我們社會的毒瘤。▸ **can·cer·ous** /ˈkænsərəs/ *adj.*：*to become*

C

cancerous 發生癌變 ◇ ***cancerous cells/growths/tumours*** 癌細胞；癌性腫瘤；癌腫瘤

can·dela /kæn'delə; -'diːlə; 'kændɪlə/ *noun* (*physics* 物) (*abbr.* **cd**) a unit for measuring the amount of light that shines in a particular direction 坎，坎德拉，燭光（光強度單位）

can·de·la·bra /ˌkændə'lɑːbrə/ (also *less frequent* **can·de·la·brum** /ˌkændə'lɑːbrəm/) *noun* (*pl.* **can·de·la·bra**, **can·de·la·bras**, *US* also **can·de·la·brums**) an object with several branches for holding CANDLES or lights 枝狀大燭台（或燈台）

can·did /'kændɪd/ *adj.* **1** saying what you think openly and honestly; not hiding your thoughts 坦率的；坦誠的；直言不諱的： *a candid statement/interview* 坦率的陳述／會談 ➲ see also CANDOUR **2** a **candid** photograph is one that is taken without the person in it knowing that they are being photographed （照片）搶拍的，偷拍的 ▸ **can·did·ly** *adv.*

can·dida /'kændɪdə/ *noun* [U] (*medical* 醫) the FUNGUS that can cause an infection of THRUSH 唸珠菌（可導致感染鵝口瘡）

can·di·dacy /'kændɪdəsi/ *noun* [C, U] (*pl.* **-ies**) (also **can·di·da·ture** especially in *BrE*) the fact of being a candidate in an election 候選人的資格（或身分）： *to* ***announce/declare/withdraw your candidacy*** *for the post* 宣佈／宣告／撤銷你的職位候選人資格

can·di·date 0▬ /'kændɪdət; -deɪt/ *noun*
1 0▬ **~ (for sth)** a person who is trying to be elected or is applying for a job （競選或求職的）候選人，申請人： *one of the leading candidates for the presidency* 總統職位的主要候選人之一 ◇ *a presidential candidate* 總統候選人 ◇ (*BrE*) *He stood as a candidate in the local elections.* 他作為候選人參加地方選舉。◇ *There were a large number of candidates for the job.* 有許多求職者申請這份工作。 ➲ COLLOCATIONS at VOTE **2** 0▬ (*BrE*) a person taking an exam 投考者；應試者；參加考試的人： *a candidate for the degree of MPhil* 攻讀哲學碩士學位者 **3 ~ (for sth)** a person or group that is considered suitable for sth or that is likely to get sth or to be sth 被認定適合者；被認定有某種結局者： *Our team is a* ***prime candidate for*** *relegation this year.* 今年我們隊最有可能降級。◇ *Your father is an obvious candidate for a heart attack.* 你父親顯然是容易患心臟病的人。

can·di·da·ture /'kændɪdətʃə(r)/ *noun* (*especially BrE*) = CANDIDACY

can·died /'kændid/ *adj.* [only before noun] (of fruit or other food 水果或其他食物) preserved by boiling in sugar; cooked in sugar 蜜餞的；糖煮的；糖製的： *candied fruit* 果脯

can·dle /'kændl/ *noun* a round stick of WAX with a piece of string (called a WICK) through the middle which is lit to give light as it burns 蠟燭 ➲ VISUAL VOCAB page V22

IDM **cannot hold a candle to sb/sth** is not as good as sb or sth else 不如…好；比不上…；無法與…媲美： *His singing can't hold a candle to Bocelli's.* 他的演唱無法與波切利媲美。 ➲ more at BURN *v.*, WORTH *adj.*

candle·light /'kændllaɪt/ *noun* [U] the light that a candle produces 燭光： *to read by candlelight* 在燭光下閱讀

candle·lit /'kændllɪt/ *adj.* [only before noun] lit by candles 燭光照亮的： *a romantic candlelit dinner* 浪漫的燭光晚餐

candle·stick /'kændlstɪk/ *noun* an object for holding a candle 蠟燭台（或架） ➲ VISUAL VOCAB page V22

candle·wick /'kændlwɪk/ *noun* [U] a type of soft cotton cloth with a raised pattern of threads, used especially for making BEDSPREADS 燭芯紗（有凸起花紋，尤用於製作牀罩）

ˌcan-'do *adj.* [only before noun] (*informal*) willing to try new things and expecting that they will be successful 勇於嘗試的；積極的： ***a can-do attitude/spirit*** 樂觀態度／精神

cand·our (*especially US* **can·dor**) /'kændə(r)/ *noun* [U] the quality of saying what you think openly and honestly 真誠；誠懇；坦率 SYN **frankness**： *'I don't trust him,' he said in a rare moment of candour.* "我信不過他。"他以難得的坦率說道。 ➲ see also CANDID *adj.* (1)

C & W *abbr.* COUNTRY AND WESTERN

candy 0▬ /'kændi/ *noun* [U, C] (*pl.* **-ies**) (*NAmE*) sweet food made of sugar and/or chocolate, eaten between meals; a piece of this 糖果；巧克力；一塊糖（或巧克力） SYN **sweet**： *a box of candy* 一盒糖果 ◇ *a candy store* 糖果店 ◇ *a candy bar* 一條巧克力 ◇ *Who wants the last piece of candy?* 誰想要這最後一塊糖？ ➲ see also ARM CANDY, EYE CANDY

IDM **be like taking ˌcandy from a 'baby** (*informal*) used to emphasize how easy it is to do sth 像從娃娃手裏搶糖吃；手到擒來；輕而易舉

'candy apple (*NAmE*) (*BrE* **'toffee apple**) *noun* an apple covered with a thin layer of hard toffee and fixed on a stick 太妃蘋果（外塗奶油乳脂，用籤子插起）

candy·floss /'kændiflɒs; *NAmE* -flɔːs; -flɑːs/ (*BrE*) (*NAmE* **ˌcotton 'candy**) *noun* [U] a type of sweet/candy in the form of a mass of sticky threads made from melted sugar and served on a stick, especially at FAIRGROUNDS （尤指遊樂場出售的）棉花糖

candy·man /'kændimæn/ *noun* (*US, slang*) a person who sells illegal drugs 毒品販子

'candy-striped *adj.* (of cloth or clothes 布料或衣服) with a pattern of stripes in white and another colour, especially pink 有兩色條紋圖案的（通常為粉白相間）

cane /keɪn/ *noun, verb*

■ ***noun*** **1** [C] the hard hollow STEM of some plants, for example BAMBOO or sugar （某些植物，如竹或甘蔗的）莖 ➲ VISUAL VOCAB page V19 **2** [U] these STEMS used as a material for making furniture, etc. （用於製作傢具等的）竹竿，藤條： *a cane chair* 藤椅 **3** [C] a piece of cane or a thin stick, used as a support for plants （用於支撐植物的）藤條，細竿 **4** [C] a piece of cane or a thin stick, used to help sb to walk 竹杖；藤杖；手杖 ➲ see also WALKING STICK **5** [C] a piece of cane or a thin stick, used in the past in some schools for beating children as a punishment （舊時學校用於懲罰學童的）竹杖，藤條： *to get the cane* (= be punished with a cane) 受藤條鞭罰

■ ***verb* ~ sb** to hit a child with a cane as a punishment 用藤條鞭打，用藤杖打，鞭笞（作為懲罰） ▸ **can·ing** *noun* [U, C]： *the abolition of caning in schools* 學校中鞭笞體罰的廢除

'cane rat *noun* a type of large RODENT found in wild areas of Africa, which can be used for food 蔗鼠（分佈於非洲荒野，其肉可食） ➲ see also CUTTING GRASS

'cane sugar *noun* [U] sugar obtained from the juice of SUGAR CANE 蔗糖

ca·nine /'keɪnaɪn/ *adj., noun*

■ ***adj.*** connected with dogs 犬的；似犬的

■ ***noun*** **1** (also **'canine tooth**) one of the four pointed teeth in the front of a human's or animal's mouth（人或動物的）犬齒 ➲ compare INCISOR, MOLAR **2** (*formal*) a dog 犬

can·is·ter /'kænɪstə(r)/ *noun* **1** a container with a lid for holding tea, coffee, etc. （裝茶葉，咖啡等有蓋的）小罐 **2** a strong metal container containing gas or a chemical substance, especially one that bursts when it is fired from a gun or thrown 霰彈筒： *tear-gas canisters* 催淚彈 **3** a flat round metal container used for storing film （用以放置膠片的）扁平圓金屬盒： *a film canister* 膠片盒

can·ker /'kæŋkə(r)/ *noun* **1** [U] a disease that destroys the wood of plants and trees （植物和樹木的）潰瘍病，枝枯病 **2** [U] a disease that causes sore areas in the ears of animals, especially dogs and cats （尤指貓狗耳部的）潰瘍，癰，瘡 **3** [C] (*literary*) an evil or dangerous influence that spreads and affects people's behaviour （蔓延並影響人的行為的）邪惡，禍害，禍患，腐敗

'canker sore (*NAmE*) (*BrE* **'mouth ulcer**) *noun* a small sore area in the mouth 口腔潰瘍

can·na·bis /'kænəbɪs/ *noun* [U] a drug made from the dried leaves and flowers or RESIN of the HEMP plant, which is smoked or eaten and which gives the user a feeling of being relaxed. Use of the drug is illegal in many countries. 大麻毒品

canned /kænd/ *adj.* **1** (*BrE* also **tinned**) (of food 食品) preserved in a can 罐裝的；聽裝的：*canned food/soup* 罐裝食品 / 湯羹 **2 ~ laughter/music** the sound of people laughing or music that has been previously recorded and used in television and radio programmes （電視和電台節目中）預先錄製的笑聲（或音樂）

can·nel·loni /ˌkænəˈləʊni; *NAmE* -ˈloʊni/ *noun* [U] (from *Italian*) large tubes of PASTA that are served filled with meat or cheese 捲子，麵捲（包裹肉餡或奶酪）

can·nery /ˈkænəri/ *noun* (*pl.* **-ies**) a factory where food is put into cans 罐頭食品廠

can·ni·bal /ˈkænɪbl/ *noun* **1** a person who eats human flesh 食人肉者：*a tribe of cannibals* 食人部落 **2** an animal that eats the flesh of other animals of the same kind 同類相食的動物 ▸ **can·ni·bal·ism** /ˈkænɪbəlɪzəm/ *noun* [U]：*to practise cannibalism* 噬食同類 **can·ni·bal·is·tic** /ˌkænɪbəˈlɪstɪk/ *adj.*

can·ni·bal·ize (*BrE* also **-ise**) /ˈkænɪbəlaɪz/ *verb* **1 ~ sth** to take the parts of a machine, vehicle, etc. and use them to repair or build another 拆用（舊零件修理或裝配另一部機器或車） **2 ~ sth** (*business* 商) (of a company 公司) to reduce the sales of one of its products by introducing a similar new product 同類相食（以推出一種類似新產品來減少某種產品的銷售） ▸ **can·ni·bal·iza·tion, -isa·tion** /ˌkænɪbəlaɪˈzeɪʃn; *NAmE* -ləˈz-/ *noun* [U]

can·non /ˈkænən/ *noun, verb*

▪ ***noun*** (*pl.* **can·non** or **can·nons**) **1** an old type of large heavy gun, usually on wheels, that fires solid metal or stone balls （通常裝有輪子並發射鐵彈或石彈的舊式）大炮 ➲ see also LOOSE CANNON, WATER CANNON **2** an automatic gun that is fired from an aircraft （飛機上的）自動機關炮

▪ ***verb*** [I] **+ adv./prep.** to hit sb/sth with a lot of force while you are moving 猛撞；碰撞：*He ran around the corner, cannoning into a group of kids.* 他跑過拐角時與一群小孩相撞。

can·non·ade /ˌkænəˈneɪd/ *noun* a continuous firing of large guns 連續炮轟

can·non·ball /ˈkænənbɔːl/ *noun* a large metal or stone ball that is fired from a CANNON （用舊式大炮發射的）鐵彈，石彈

ˈcannon fodder *noun* [U] soldiers who are thought of not as people whose lives are important, but as material to be used up in war 炮灰

can·not 0-w /ˈkænɒt; *NAmE* -nɑːt/ = CAN NOT：*I cannot believe the price of the tickets!* 我簡直無法相信竟有這樣的票價！

can·nula /ˈkænjʊlə/ *noun* (*pl.* **can·nulae** /-liː/ or **can·nulas**) (*medical* 醫) a thin tube that is put into a VEIN or other part of the body, for example to give sb medicine （輸藥等的）套管，插管

canny /ˈkæni/ *adj.* intelligent, careful and showing good judgement, especially in business or politics （尤指在商業或政治方面）精明謹慎的，老謀深算的：*a canny politician* 老謀深算的政治家 ◇ *a canny move* 一步妙棋 ▸ **can·nily** *adv.*

canoe /kəˈnuː/ *noun, verb*

▪ ***noun*** a light narrow boat which you move along in the water with a PADDLE 獨木舟；小划子 ➲ VISUAL VOCAB page V55 ➲ see also KAYAK

▪ ***verb*** (**ca·noe·ing, ca·noed, ca·noed**) [I] (often **go canoeing**) to travel in a canoe 划（或乘）獨木舟

ca·noe·ing /kəˈnuːɪŋ/ *noun* [U] the sport of travelling in or racing a CANOE 划獨木舟運動（或比賽）：*to go canoeing* 去划獨木舟

ca·noe·ist /kəˈnuːɪst/ *noun* a person travelling in a canoe 划獨木舟的人

can·ola /kəˈnəʊlə; *NAmE* -ˈnoʊ-/ *noun* [U] a type of cooking oil made from a variety of RAPESEED that was developed in Canada and is grown widely in N America. The plant is also referred to as **canola**. 芥花籽油；菜籽油；芥花籽油作物

canon /ˈkænən/ *noun* **1** a Christian priest with special duties in a CATHEDRAL （主教座堂的）詠禮司鐸，法政會長 **2** (*formal*) a generally accepted rule, standard or principle by which sth is judged 原則；準則；標準 **3** a list of the books or other works that are generally accepted as the genuine work of a particular writer or as being important （某作家的）真作，精品：*the Shakespeare canon* 莎士比亞的精品 ◇ *'Wuthering Heights' is a central book in the canon of English literature.*《呼嘯山莊》是英國文學原著經典中非常重要的一部作品。**4** a piece of music in which singers or instruments take it in turns to repeat the MELODY (= tune) 兩重輪唱（或演奏）；卡農曲

ca·non·ic·al /kəˈnɒnɪkl; *NAmE* -ˈnɑːn-/ (also **ca·non·ic**) *adj.* **1** included in a list of holy books that are accepted as genuine; connected with works of literature that are highly respected 被收入真經篇目的；經典的 **2** according to the law of the Christian Church 按照基督教教會法規的 **3** (*technical* 術語) in the simplest accepted form in mathematics （數學表達式）最簡潔的

caˌnonical ˈform *noun* (*linguistics* 語言) the most basic form of a GRAMMATICAL structure or expression, for example the infinitive in the case of a verb （語法結構或表達的）標準形式，最基本形式（如動詞的不定式）

can·on·ize (*BrE* also **-ise**) /ˈkænənaɪz/ *verb* [usually passive] **~ sb** (of the POPE 教宗) to state officially that sb is now a SAINT 正式宣佈（某人）為聖徒；宣聖；列入聖品 ➲ compare BEATIFY ▸ **can·on·iza·tion, -isa·tion** /ˌkænənaɪˈzeɪʃn; *NAmE* -nəˈz-/ *noun* [C, U]

ˌcanon ˈlaw *noun* [U] the law of the Christian church 基督教教會法規

ca·noo·dle /kəˈnuːdl/ *verb* [I] (*BrE, old-fashioned, informal*) (of two people 兩人) to kiss and touch each other in a sexual way 親吻愛撫

ˈcan opener (*especially NAmE*) (*BrE* also **ˈtin opener**) *noun* a kitchen UTENSIL (= a tool) for opening cans of food 開罐器 ➲ VISUAL VOCAB page V26

can·opy /ˈkænəpi/ *noun* (*pl.* **-ies**) **1** a cover that is fixed or hangs above a bed, seat, etc. as a shelter or decoration （牀、座位等上面的）罩篷，遮篷，罩蓋 ➲ VISUAL VOCAB page V23 ➲ picture at PUSHCHAIR **2** a layer of sth that spreads over an area like a roof, especially branches of trees in a forest 頂篷；天篷；（尤指森林裏）天篷似的樹蔭 **3** (*especially NAmE*) a roof that is supported on posts and is sometimes also attached at one side to a building （有時與建築的一側相連的）天篷，遮篷：*a new steel entrance canopy for the building* 大樓入口的新式鋼製遮篷 ◇ *a fabric canopy to provide shade in the backyard* 後院遮陽用的編織天篷 **4** a cover for the COCKPIT of an aircraft （飛機的）座艙蓋

canst /kænst/ *verb* **thou canst** (*old use*) used to mean 'you can', when talking to one person （對某人說話時表示 you can）

cant /kænt/ *noun, verb*

▪ ***noun*** [U] statements, especially about moral or religious issues, that are not sincere and that you cannot trust （尤指有關道德或宗教問題的）偽善言辭，虛假的話，空話 **SYN** **hypocrisy**

▪ ***verb*** [I, T] **~ (sth)** (*formal*) to be or put sth in a sloping position （使）傾斜

can't /kɑːnt; *NAmE* kænt/ *short form* cannot

Cantab /ˈkæntæb/ *abbr.* (used after degree titles) of Cambridge University （用於學位名稱後）劍橋大學的：*James Cox MA (Cantab)* 文科碩士詹姆斯 • 考克斯（劍橋大學）

Can·ta·bri·gian /ˌkæntəˈbrɪdʒiən/ *adj.* (*formal* or *humorous*) relating to Cambridge in England, or to Cambridge University （英格蘭）劍橋的；劍橋大學的

can·ta·loupe /ˈkæntəluːp/ *noun* a MELON (= a type of fruit) with a green skin and orange flesh 甜瓜；哈蜜瓜

can·tan·ker·ous /kænˈtæŋkərəs/ *adj.* bad-tempered and always complaining 脾氣壞且抱怨不休的：*a cantankerous old man* 愛抱怨的倔老頭

有能力命令沖向陸地的海水回頭；這個故事常被改編，表示克努特實際上以為他能夠令海水回頭。

can·tata /kænˈtɑːtə/ *noun* a short musical work, often on a religious subject, sung by SOLO singers, often with a CHOIR and ORCHESTRA 康塔塔（常為宗教題材的短小音樂作品，由獨唱演員演唱，常有合唱和管弦樂隊伴奏）➲ compare MOTET, ORATORIO

C

can·teen /kænˈtiːn/ *noun* **1** (*especially BrE*) a place where food and drink are served in a factory, a school, etc. 食堂；餐廳 **2** a small container used by soldiers, travellers, etc. for carrying water or other liquid （士兵、旅遊者等用的）水壺 **3 ~ of cutlery** (*BrE*) a box containing a set of knives, forks and spoons （裝有一套刀、叉和勺的）餐具盒

canˈteen culture *noun* [U] (*BrE, disapproving*) a set of old-fashioned and unfair attitudes that are said to exist among police officers （警隊內部的）陳舊不公正態度

can·ter /ˈkæntə(r)/ *noun, verb*

■ ***noun*** [usually sing.] a movement of a horse at a speed that is fairly fast but not very fast; a ride on a horse moving at this speed （馬的）慢跑，小跑；騎馬慢跑：*She set off at a canter.* 她騎着馬慢跑出發。

■ ***verb*** [I, T] **~ (sth)** (of a horse or rider 馬或騎手) to move or make a horse move at a canter 慢跑；使馬慢跑：*We cantered along the beach.* 我們騎着馬沿海灘慢跑。➲ compare GALLOP *v.* (1), (2), TROT *v.* (1), (3)

can·ticle /ˈkæntɪkl/ *noun* a religious song with words taken from the Bible 聖歌，頌歌，讚美詩（歌詞取自《聖經》）

can·ti·lever /ˈkæntɪliːvə(r)/ *noun* a long piece of metal or wood that sticks out from a wall to support the end of a bridge or other structure （橋梁或其他構架的）懸臂，懸桁，伸臂：*a cantilever bridge* 懸臂橋 ➲ VISUAL VOCAB page V14

canto /ˈkæntəʊ; *NAmE* -toʊ/ *noun* (*pl.* **-os**) one of the sections of a long poem （長詩的）篇，章

can·ton /ˈkæntɒn; *NAmE* -tən; -tɑːn/ *noun* one of the official regions which some countries, such as Switzerland, are divided into （瑞士等國的）行政區，州

Can·ton·ese /ˌkæntəˈniːz/ *noun, adj.*

■ ***noun* 1** (also **Yue**) [U] a form of Chinese spoken mainly in southern China, including Hong Kong 粵語；廣東話 **2** [C] (*pl.* **Can·ton·ese**) a person whose first language is Cantonese 說粵語的人；廣東人

■ ***adj.*** of or relating to people who speak Cantonese, or their language or culture 說粵語的人的；粵語的；廣東人（或文化）的：*Cantonese cooking* 粵菜

can·ton·ment /kænˈtɒnmənt; -ˈtuːn-; *NAmE* kænˈtɑːn-/ *noun* a military camp, especially a permanent British military camp in India in the past 軍隊駐地；軍隊營房；（尤指舊時英軍駐印度的）永久性兵站

Can·to·pop /ˈkæntəʊpɒp; *NAmE* ˈkæntoʊpɑːp/ *noun* [U] (*SEAsianE*) a type of pop music that combines Cantonese words and Western pop music 粵語流行歌曲（粵語填詞，西方流行樂為曲）

can·tor /ˈkæntɔː(r)/ *noun* the person who leads the singing in a SYNAGOGUE or in a church CHOIR （猶太教會堂和教堂唱詩班的）領唱

Ca·nuck /kəˈnʌk/ *noun* (*NAmE, informal*) a person from Canada, especially sb whose first language is French. In the US this term is often offensive. （尤指第一語言為法語的）加拿大人（此稱呼在美國常含冒犯意）

Ca·nute /kəˈnjuːt; *NAmE* -ˈnuːt/ *noun* used to describe a person who tries to stop sth from happening but will never succeed 克努特式的人；妄想阻擋某事的人：*His efforts to stem the tide of violent crime have been as effective as Canute's.* 他阻止暴力犯罪增長的努力一直是螳臂擋車。**ORIGIN** From the story of a Danish king of England who was said to have stood in front of the sea and shown people that he was not able to order the water that was moving in towards the land to turn back. The story is often changed to suggest that Canute really thought that he could turn back the sea. 源自英格蘭丹麥裔國王的故事，據說他臨海而立，向民眾顯示他沒

can·vas /ˈkænvəs/ *noun* **1** [U] a strong heavy rough material used for making tents, sails, etc. and by artists for painting on 帆布 ➲ COLLOCATIONS at ART **2** [C] a piece of canvas used for painting on; a painting done on a piece of canvas, using oil paints （帆布）畫布；油畫：*a sale of the artist's early canvases* 那位畫家早期油畫的拍賣 ➲ VISUAL VOCAB page V41
IDM **under ˈcanvas** in a tent 在帳篷裏

can·vass /ˈkænvəs/ *verb* **1** [I, T] to ask sb to support a particular person, political party, etc., especially by going around an area and talking to people 遊說；拉選票：**~ (for sth)** *He spent the whole month canvassing for votes.* 他花了整整一個月四處游說拉選票。◇ **~ sb (for sth)** *Party workers are busy canvassing local residents.* 黨務工作者正忙於游說當地居民。**2** [T] to ask people about sth in order to find out what they think about it 調查（民意）；徵求（意見）：**~ sth** *He has been canvassing opinion on the issue.* 他一直在徵求對這個問題的意見。◇ **~ sb** *People are being canvassed for their views on the proposed new road.* 正在就計劃修建的新道路徵求人們的意見。**3** [T] **~ support** to try and get support from a group of people 努力爭取支持 **SYN** **drum up** **4** [T] **~ sth** to discuss an idea thoroughly 詳細（或徹底）討論：*The proposal is currently being canvassed.* 目前人們正在詳細討論這個提案。▸ **can·vass** *noun*：*to carry out a canvass* 拉選票 **can·vass·er** *noun*

can·yon /ˈkænjən/ *noun* a deep valley with steep sides of rock （周圍有懸崖峭壁的）峽谷 **SYN** **gorge** ➲ VISUAL VOCAB pages V4, V5

can·yon·ing /ˈkænjənɪŋ/ *noun* [U] a sport in which you jump into a mountain stream and allow yourself to be carried down at high speed 懸崖跳水運動

CAP /ˌsiː eɪ ˈpiː/ *abbr.* Common Agricultural Policy (of the European Union)（歐盟的）共同農業政策

cap 0→ /kæp/ *noun, verb*

■ ***noun***

▸ HAT 帽子 **1** 0→ a type of soft flat hat with a PEAK (= a hard curved part sticking out in front). Caps are worn especially by men and boys, often as part of a uniform. （尤指男用有帽舌的）便帽，制服帽：*a school cap* 學生帽 ➲ see also BASEBALL CAP, CLOTH CAP, MOB CAP ➲ VISUAL VOCAB page V65 **2** 0→ (usually in compounds 通常構成複合詞) a soft hat that fits closely and is worn for a particular purpose 軟帽：*a shower cap* 浴帽 **3** a soft hat with a square flat top worn by some university teachers and students at special ceremonies （大學師生在特別場合戴的）方帽 ➲ compare MORTAR BOARD

▸ IN SPORT 體育運動 **4** (*BrE*) a cap given to sb who is chosen to play for a school, country, etc.; a player chosen to play for their country, etc. （校隊、國家隊等的）隊員帽；（被選入國家隊等的）運動員：*He won his first cap* (= was first chosen to play) *for England against France.* 他首次被選為英格蘭隊的隊員與法國隊比賽。◇ *There are three new caps in the side.* 這一方有三名新隊員。

▸ ON PEN/BOTTLE 鋼筆；瓶子 **5** a cover or top for a pen, bottle, etc.（鋼筆、瓶子等的）帽，蓋：*a lens cap* 鏡頭蓋 ➲ VISUAL VOCAB page V33 ➲ see also FILLER CAP, HUBCAP ➲ SYNONYMS at LID

▸ LIMIT ON MONEY 資金限額 **6** an upper limit on an amount of money that can be spent or borrowed by a particular institution or in a particular situation （可用或可借資金的）最高限額：*The government has placed a cap on local council spending.* 政府給地方議會的經費支出規定了最高限額。

▸ IN TOY GUNS 玩具槍 **7** a small paper container with EXPLOSIVE powder inside it, used especially in toy guns （尤用於玩具槍的）火藥帽，火藥紙

▸ FOR WOMAN 婦女 **8** (*BrE*) = DIAPHRAGM (2) ➲ see also ICE CAP, THINKING CAP

IDM **go cap in ˈhand (to sb)** (*BrE*) (*US* **go hat in ˈhand**) to ask sb for sth, especially money, in a very polite way that makes you seem less important 謙卑地要，恭敬地討（尤指錢） **if the cap fits (, wear it)** (*BrE*) (*NAmE* **if the shoe fits (, wear it)**) (*informal*) if you feel that a remark applies to you, you should accept it and take it as a warning or criticism 有則改之：*I didn't actually say that you were lazy, but if the cap fits ...* 我並沒有真的說你懶，但有則改之… ➲ more at FEATHER *n.*

■ ***verb*** (-pp-)

▸ **COVER TOP** 覆蓋頂部 **1** [usually passive] **~ sth (with sth)** to cover the top or end of sth with sth 用…覆蓋頂部（或端部）：*mountains capped with snow* 積雪皚皚的山峰 ◇ *snow-capped mountains* 頂端積雪的群山

▸ **LIMIT MONEY** 限定金額 **2** [often passive] **~ sth** (*especially BrE*) to limit the amount of money that can be charged for sth or spent on sth 限額收取（或支出）：*a capped mortgage* 限額按揭

▸ **BEAT** 超越 **3 ~ sth** (*especially BrE*) to say or do sth that is funnier, more impressive, etc. than sth that has been said or done before 勝過；超過；比…更…：*What an amazing story. Can anyone cap that?* 這真是個精彩的故事！還有人能講得更精彩嗎？

▸ **TOOTH** 牙齒 **4** [usually passive] **~ sth** to put an artificial covering on a tooth to make it look more attractive 包（牙） **SYN** **crown**：*He's had his front teeth capped.* 他包了門牙。

▸ **IN SPORT** 體育運動 **5** [usually passive] **~ sb** (*BrE*) to choose sb to play in their country's national team for a particular sport 選入（某項體育運動的國家隊）：*He has been capped more than 30 times for Wales.* 他已 30 多次入選威爾士隊參加比賽。

IDM **to cap/top it 'all** (*informal*) used to introduce the final piece of information that is worse than the other bad things that you have just mentioned 最糟糕的是；最倒霉的是

cap·abil·ity **AW** /ˌkeɪpəˈbɪləti/ *noun* [C, U] (*pl.* **-ies**) **1 ~ (to do sth/of doing sth)** the ability or qualities necessary to do sth 能力；才能：*Animals in the zoo have lost the capability to catch/of catching food for themselves.* 動物園的動物已經喪失自己捕食的能力。◇ ***beyond/within the capabilities*** *of current technology* 超出了當前技術能力的範圍；在當前技術能力的範圍以內 ◇ *Age affects the range of a person's capabilities.* 年齡影響着一個人能力的大小。 **2** the power or weapons that a country has for war or for military action（國家的）軍事力量，軍事武器：*Britain's* ***nuclear/military capability*** 英國的核力量／軍事力量

cap·able 🔑 **AW** /ˈkeɪpəbl/ *adj.*
1 🔑 having the ability or qualities necessary for doing sth 有能力；有才能：**~ of sth** *You are capable of better work than this.* 你有能力做得比這更好。◇ **~ of doing sth** *He's quite capable of lying to get out of trouble.* 他頗有能耐靠撒謊渡過難關。◇ *I'm perfectly capable of doing it myself, thank you.* 謝謝，我完全有能力自己做這項工作。 **2** 🔑 having the ability to do things well 能力強的；足以勝任的 **SYN** **skilled, competent**：*She's a very capable teacher.* 她是一位能力很強的教師 ◇ *I'll leave the organization in your capable hands.* 我要把組織工作交給你這位能手。 **OPP** **incapable** ▸ **cap·ably** *adv.*

cap·acious /kəˈpeɪʃəs/ *adj.* (*formal*) having a lot of space to put things in 容量大的；容積大的；寬敞的 **SYN** **roomy**：*capacious pockets* 能裝許多東西的大口袋

cap·aci·tance /kəˈpæsɪtəns/ *noun* [U] (*physics* 物) **1** the ability of a system to store an electrical charge 電容，電容量（系統貯存電荷的能力） **2** a comparison between change in electrical charge and change in electrical POTENTIAL 電容率（電荷和電位變化之比值）

cap·aci·tor /kəˈpæsɪtə(r)/ *noun* (*physics* 物) a device used to store an electrical charge 電容器

cap·acity 🔑 **AW** /kəˈpæsəti/ *noun* (*pl.* **-ies**)

▸ **OF CONTAINER** 容器 **1** 🔑 [U, C, usually sing.] the number of things or people that a container or space can hold 容量；容積；容納能力：*The theatre has a seating capacity of 2 000.* 那座劇院能容納 2 000 名觀眾。◇ *a fuel tank with a capacity of 50 litres* 可裝 50 升油的油箱 ◇ *The hall was filled* ***to capacity*** (= was completely full). 大廳內座無虛席。◇ *They played to a* ***capacity crowd*** (= one that filled all the space or seats). 他們給人山人海的觀眾表演。

▸ **ABILITY** 能力 **2** 🔑 [C, usually sing., U] the ability to understand or to do sth 領悟（或理解、辦事）能力：*intellectual capacity* 智能 ◇ **~ for sth** *She has an enormous capacity for hard work.* 她特別能吃苦耐勞。◇ **~ for doing sth** *Limited resources are restricting our capacity for developing new products.* 有限的資源正制約着我們開發新產品的能力。◇ **~ to do sth** *your capacity to enjoy life* 你那享受生活樂趣的能力

▸ **ROLE** 職責 **3** [C, usually sing.] the official position or function that sb has 職位；職責 **SYN** **role**：*acting* ***in her capacity as*** *manager* 以她作為經理的身分行事 ◇ *We are simply involved in an* ***advisory capacity*** *on the project.* 我們只不過是以顧問身分參與這個項目。

▸ **OF FACTORY/MACHINE** 工廠；機器 **4** [sing., U] the quantity that a factory, machine, etc. can produce 生產量；生產能力：*The factory is working at full capacity.* 這家工廠在開足馬力生產。

▸ **OF ENGINE** 發動機 **5** [C, U] the size or power of a piece of equipment, especially the engine of a vehicle（尤指車輛發動機的）容積，功率：*an engine with a capacity of 1 600 cc* 排量為 1.6 升的發動機

ca·pari·soned /kəˈpærɪsnd/ *adj.* in the past a **caparisoned** horse or other animal was one covered with a decorated cloth（馬等）披掛裝飾的；披掛馬衣的

cape /keɪp/ *noun* **1** a loose outer piece of clothing that has no sleeves, fastens at the neck and hangs from the shoulders, like a CLOAK but shorter 披肩；披風；短斗篷：*a bullfighter's cape* 鬥牛士的披風 **2** (*abbr.* **C.**) (often in place names 常用於地名) a piece of high land that sticks out into the sea 海角；岬：*Cape Horn* 合恩角

caped /keɪpt/ *adj.* wearing a cape 穿披肩的；披斗篷的

caper /ˈkeɪpə(r)/ *noun, verb*

■ ***noun*** **1** [usually pl.] the small green flower BUD of a Mediterranean bush, preserved in VINEGAR and used to flavour dishes and sauces 刺山柑花蕾（產於地中海，醃泡於醋中用作調味料） **2** (*informal*) an activity, especially one that is illegal or dangerous 活動；（尤指）不法活動，危險活動：*A call to the police should put an end to their little caper.* 給警察打個電話應該就能制止他們的胡鬧。 **3** an amusing film/movie that contains a lot of action 驚險喜劇片：*a British spy caper* 英國間諜喜劇片 **4** a short jumping or dancing movement 跳躍；雀躍；蹦蹦跳跳：*He* ***cut a*** *little celebratory* ***caper*** (= jumped or danced a few steps) *in the middle of the road.* 他高興得在路中央又蹦又跳的。

■ ***verb*** [I] (+ **adv./prep.**) (*formal*) to run or jump around in a happy and excited way 雀躍；歡躍

cap·er·cail·lie /ˌkæpəˈkeɪli; *NAmE* ˌkæpər-/ *noun* a large GROUSE (= a type of large bird) similar to a TURKEY, the male of which spreads out his tail feathers to attract females 大松雞

ca·pil·lary /kəˈpɪləri; *NAmE* ˈkæpəleri/ *noun* (*pl.* **-ies**) (*anatomy* 解) any of the smallest tubes in the body that carry blood 毛細血管 ➲ **VISUAL VOCAB** page V59

ca'pillary action *noun* [U] (*technical* 術語) the force that makes a liquid move up a narrow tube 毛細作用；毛細引力（或吸力）

cap·ital 🔑 /ˈkæpɪtl/ *noun, adj.*

■ ***noun***

▸ **CITY** 城市 **1** 🔑 (also **ˌcapital ˈcity**) [C] the most important town or city of a country, usually where the central government operates from 首都；國都：*Cairo is the capital of Egypt.* 開羅是埃及的首都。◇ (*figurative*) *Paris, the fashion capital of the world* 巴黎，世界時裝的中心之都

▸ **MONEY** 金錢 **2** 🔑 [sing.] a large amount of money that is invested or is used to start a business 資本；資金；啟動資金：*to set up a business with a* ***starting capital*** *of £100 000* 以 10 萬英鎊為啟動資金創辦一個企業 **3** [U] wealth or property that is owned by a business or a person 財富；財產：*capital assets* 資本資產 ◇ *capital expenditure* (= money that an organization spends on buildings, equipment, etc.) 資本投資 **4** [U] (*technical* 術語) people who use their money to start businesses, considered as a group 資方：*capital and labour* 資方與勞方

▸ **LETTER** 字母 **5** 🔑 (also **ˌcapital ˈletter**) [C] a letter of the form and size that is used at the beginning of a sentence or a name (= A,B,C rather than a,b,c) 大寫字母：*Use*

C

block capitals (= separate capital letters). 使用大寫字母。◇ *Please write* ***in capitals/in capital letters.*** 請用大寫字母書寫。

▸ **ARCHITECTURE** 建築 **6** the top part of a column 柱頂；柱頭 ➲ VISUAL VOCAB page V14

IDM **make capital (out) of sth** to use a situation for your own advantage 從…中撈取好處；利用…謀求私利：*The opposition parties are making political capital out of the government's problems.* 各反對黨都在利用政府面臨的問題撈取政治資本。

■ ***adj.***

▸ **PUNISHMENT** 懲罰 **1** [only before noun] involving punishment by death 死刑的：*a capital offence* 死罪

▸ **LETTER** 字母 **2** [only before noun] (of letters of the alphabet 字母表字母) having the form and size used at the beginning of a sentence or a name 大寫的：*English is written with a capital 'E'.* * English 一詞中字母 E 大寫。 ➲ compare LOWER CASE

▸ **EXCELLENT** 優秀 **3** (*old-fashioned, BrE*) excellent 頂好的；極好的

IDM **with a capital A, B, etc.** used to emphasize that a word has a stronger meaning than usual in a particular situation（強調有特別含義的字眼）真正地，名副其實地，不折不扣地：*He was romantic with a capital R.* 他純屬浪漫派。

ˌcapital ˈgains *noun* [pl.] profits that you make from selling sth, especially property（尤指出售固定資產所得的）資本收益：*to pay* ***capital gains tax*** 繳納資本收益稅

ˈcapital goods *noun* [pl.] (*business* 商) goods such as factory machines that are used for producing other goods 資本財貨（如工廠用於生產其他貨物的機器）➲ compare CONSUMER GOODS

ˌcapital-inˈtensive *adj.* (of a business, an industry, etc. 企業、行業等) needing large amounts of money in order to operate well 資本密集的 ➲ compare LABOUR-INTENSIVE

cap·it·al·ism /ˈkæpɪtəlɪzəm/ *noun* [U] an economic system in which a country's businesses and industry are controlled and run for profit by private owners rather than by the government 資本主義 ➲ compare SOCIALISM

cap·it·al·ist /ˈkæpɪtəlɪst/ *noun, adj.*

■ ***noun*** **1** a person who supports capitalism 資本主義者 **2** a person who owns or controls a lot of wealth and uses it to produce more wealth 資本家

■ ***adj.*** (also *less frequent* **cap·it·al·is·tic** /ˌkæpɪtəˈlɪstɪk/) based on the principles of capitalism 資本主義的：*a* ***capitalist society/system/economy*** 資本主義社會／體制／經濟

cap·it·al·ize (*BrE* also **-ise**) /ˈkæpɪtəlaɪz/ *verb* **1** ~ **sth** to write or print a letter of the alphabet as a capital; to begin a word with a capital letter 用大寫字母書寫（或印刷）；把…首字母大寫 **2** ~ **sth** (*business* 商) to sell possessions in order to change them into money 變賣資產；變現 **3** [usually passive] ~ **sth** (*business* 商) to provide a company etc. with the money it needs to function 為…提供運營資本（或資金）▸ **cap·it·al·iza·tion, -isa·tion** /ˌkæpɪtəlaɪˈzeɪʃn; *NAmE* -ləˈz-/ *noun* [U, sing.]

PHR V **ˈcapitalize on/upon sth** to gain a further advantage for yourself from a situation 充分利用；從…中獲得更多的好處 **SYN** **take advantage of sth**：*The team failed to capitalize on their early lead.* 這個隊未能充分利用開場初期領先的優勢。

ˌcapital ˈletter *noun* = CAPITAL *n.* (5)

ˌcapital ˈpunishment *noun* [U] punishment by death 死刑；極刑

ˌcapital ˈsum *noun* a single payment of money that is made to sb, for example by an insurance company 整筆應付款額（如由保險公司支付的賠償金）

capi·ta·tion /ˌkæpɪˈteɪʃn/ *noun* [C, U] (*technical* 術語) a tax or payment of an equal amount for each person; the system of payments of this kind 人頭稅；按人攤派的費用；按人付費制度：*a capitation fee for each pupil* 按每個小學生的收費

cap·itol /ˈkæpɪtl/ *noun* **1** (usually **the Capitol**) [sing.] the building in Washington DC where the US Congress (= the national parliament) meets to work on new laws（美國）國會大廈 **2** [usually sing.] a building in each US state where politicians meet to work on new laws（美國）州議會大廈：*the California state capitol* 加利福尼亞州議會大廈

ˌCapitol ˈHill (also *informal* **the Hill**) *noun* [sing.] used to refer to the US Capitol and the activities that take place there 國會山，國會山莊（指美國國會）

ca·pitu·late /kəˈpɪtʃuleɪt/ *verb* **1** [I] ~ **(to sb/sth)** to agree to do sth that you have been refusing to do for a long time 屈服；屈從 **SYN** **give in, yield**：*They were finally forced to capitulate to the terrorists' demands.* 他們最後被迫屈從恐怖分子的要求。 **2** [I] ~ **(to sb/sth)** to stop resisting an enemy and accept that you are defeated 投降 **SYN** **surrender**：*The town capitulated after a three-week siege.* 這座城鎮被圍困三個星期後投降了。 ▸ **ca·pitu·la·tion** /kəˌpɪtʃuˈleɪʃn/ *noun* [C, U]

Cap·let™ /ˈkæplət/ *noun* a long narrow tablet of medicine, with rounded ends, that you swallow 囊片；膠囊

capo·eira /ˌkæpuˈeɪrə/ *noun* [U] a Brazilian system of movements which is similar to dance and MARTIAL ARTS 卡波埃拉（一種巴西運動，類似於舞蹈和武術）

capon /ˈkeɪpɒn; ˈkeɪpən; *NAmE* -pɑːn/ *noun* a male chicken that has been CASTRATED (= had part of its sex organs removed) and made fat for eating 閹雞（育肥以供食用）

cap·pella ➲ A CAPPELLA

cap·puc·cino /ˌkæpuˈtʃiːnəʊ; *NAmE* -noʊ/ *noun* (*pl.* **-os**) **1** [U] a type of coffee made with hot FROTHY milk and sometimes with chocolate powder on the top 卡普契諾咖啡，卡布奇諾咖啡（加熱奶，有時上面撒有巧克力粉） **2** [C] a cup of cappuccino 一杯卡普契諾咖啡

ca·price /kəˈpriːs/ *noun* (*formal*) **1** [C] a sudden change in attitude or behaviour for no obvious reason（態度或行為的）無緣無故突變，反覆無常；任性 **SYN** **whim** **2** [U] the tendency to change your mind suddenly or behave unexpectedly 反覆無常；善變

ca·pri·cious /kəˈprɪʃəs/ *adj.* (*formal*) **1** showing sudden changes in attitude or behaviour（態度或行為）反覆無常的；任性的 **SYN** **unpredictable** **2** changing suddenly and quickly 變化無常的；變幻莫測的；多變的 **SYN** **changeable**：*a capricious climate* 變化無常的氣候 ▸ **ca·pri·cious·ly** *adv.* **ca·pri·cious·ness** *noun* [U]

Cap·ri·corn /ˈkæprɪkɔːn; *NAmE* -kɔːrn/ *noun* **1** [U] the 10th sign of the ZODIAC, the Goat 黃道第十宮；摩羯宮；摩羯（星）座 **2** [C] a person born when the sun is in this sign, that is between 21 December and 20 January, approximately 屬摩羯座的人（約出生於 12 月 21 日至 1 月 20 日）

caˈpri pants /kəˈpriː pænts/ (also **ca·pris**) *noun* [pl.] a type of trousers/pants for women ending between the knee and the foot 卡普里褲，七分褲（長及小腿的女褲）

caps /kæps/ *noun* [pl.] (*technical* 術語) capital letters 大寫字母：*a title printed in bold caps* 以粗體大寫字母印刷的題目

cap·sicum /ˈkæpsɪkəm/ *noun* (*technical* 術語) a type of plant which has hollow fruits. Some types of these are eaten as vegetables, either raw or cooked, for example SWEET PEPPERS or CHILLIES. 辣椒

cap·size /kæpˈsaɪz; *NAmE* ˈkæpsaɪz/ *verb* [I, T] ~ **(sth)** if a boat **capsizes** or sth **capsizes** it, it turns over in the water（船）翻，傾覆

cap·stan /ˈkæpstən/ *noun* a thick CYLINDER that winds up a rope, used for lifting heavy objects such as an ANCHOR on a ship 起錨機；絞盤

cap·stone /ˈkæpstəʊn; *NAmE* -stoʊn/ *noun* **1** a stone placed at the top of a building or wall 拱頂石；壓頂石 **2** (*especially NAmE*) the best and final thing that sb achieves, thought of as making their career or life complete（使事業等臻於圓滿的）頂點

cap·sule /ˈkæpsjuːl; *NAmE* also ˈkæpsl/ *noun* **1** a small container which has a measured amount of a medicine inside and which dissolves when you swallow it（裝藥

物的）膠囊 **2** a small plastic container with a substance or liquid inside（裝物或裝液體的）小塑料容器 **3** the part of a SPACECRAFT in which people travel and that often separates from the main ROCKET 太空艙；航天艙 **4** (*technical* 術語) a shell or container for seeds or eggs in some plants and animals（植物的）莢，蒴果；（動物的）囊，被膜 ➲ see also TIME CAPSULE

Capt. *abbr.* captain 船長；艦長；（陸軍）上尉；（海軍）上校；機長

cap·tain 🔑 /ˈkæptɪn/ *noun, verb*

■ ***noun*** **1** 🔑 the person in charge of a ship or commercial aircraft 船長；機長：*Captain Cook* 庫克船長 ◇ *The captain gave the order to abandon ship.* 船長下令棄船。 **2** 🔑 an officer of fairly high rank in the navy, the army and the US AIR FORCE（海軍）上校；（陸軍或美國空軍的）上尉：*Captain Lance Price* 蘭斯•普賴斯上尉 ➲ see also GROUP CAPTAIN **3** 🔑 the leader of a group of people, especially a sports team 首領；領導者；（尤指運動隊的）隊長：*She was captain of the hockey team at school.* 她過去是學校曲棍球隊的隊長。 **4** an officer of high rank in a US police or fire department（美國警察局的）副巡長；（美國消防署的）中隊長

■ ***verb*** **~ sth** to be a captain of a sports team or a ship 擔任運動隊隊長（或船長）

cap·tain·cy /ˈkæptənsi/ *noun* [C, usually sing., U] (*pl.* **-ies**) the position of captain of a team; the period during which sb is captain 隊長職位（或任期）

ˌcaptain of ˈindustry *noun* (*pl.* **captains of industry**) used in newspapers, etc. to describe a person who manages a large business company（報章等用語）業界鉅頭

cap·tion /ˈkæpʃn/ *noun, verb*

■ ***noun*** words that are printed underneath a picture, CARTOON, etc. that explain or describe it（圖片、漫畫等的）説明文字 ➲ see also CLOSED-CAPTIONED

■ ***verb*** [usually passive] **~ sth** to write a caption for a picture, photograph, etc. 給（圖片、照片等）加説明文字

cap·tiv·ate /ˈkæptɪveɪt/ *verb* [often passive] **~ sb** to keep sb's attention by being interesting, attractive, etc. 迷住；使着迷 SYN **enchant**：*The children were captivated by her stories.* 孩子們被她的故事迷住了。

cap·tiv·at·ing /ˈkæptɪveɪtɪŋ/ *adj.* taking all your attention; very attractive and interesting 迷人的；有魅力的；有吸引力的 SYN **enchanting**：*He found her captivating.* 他發覺她很迷人。

cap·tive /ˈkæptɪv/ *adj., noun*

■ ***adj.*** **1** kept as a prisoner or in a confined space; unable to escape 被監禁的；被關起來的；被困住的：*captive animals* 關在籠子裏的動物 ◇ *They were **taken captive** by masked gunmen.* 他們被蒙面的持槍歹徒劫持了。◇ *captive breeding* (= the catching and breeding of wild animals) 野生動物的人工捕獲飼養 **2** [only before noun] not free to leave a particular place or to choose what you want to do 人身自由受限制的；受控制的；無權選擇的：*A salesman loves to have a **captive audience*** (= listening because they have no choice). 推銷員喜歡不得不聽的聽眾。

■ ***noun*** a person who is kept as a prisoner, especially in a war 囚徒；俘虜；戰俘

cap·tiv·ity /kæpˈtɪvəti/ *noun* [U] the state of being kept as a prisoner or in a confined space 監禁；關押；困住：*He was held **in captivity** for three years.* 他被監禁了三年。◇ *The bird had escaped from captivity.* 那隻鳥已經逃離樊籠。

cap·tor /ˈkæptə(r)/ *noun* (*formal*) a person who captures a person or an animal and keeps them as a prisoner 捕獲…者；捕捉者；劫持者

cap·ture 🔑 /ˈkæptʃə(r)/ *verb, noun*

■ ***verb***

▸ **CATCH** 抓住 **1** 🔑 to catch a person or an animal and keep them as a prisoner or in a confined space 俘虜；俘獲；捕獲：**~ sb** *Allied troops captured over 300 enemy soldiers.* 盟軍俘虜了 300 多名敵方士兵。◇ **~ sth** *The animals are captured in nets and sold to local zoos.* 那些動物用網捕獲後被賣到當地的動物園。

▸ **TAKE CONTROL** 控制 **2** 🔑 **~ sth** to take control of a place, building, etc. using force 用武力奪取；攻取；攻佔：*The city was captured in 1941.* 這座城市於 1941 年被攻佔。

▸ **3** 🔑 **~ sth** to succeed in getting control of sth that other people are also trying to control 奪得；贏得；爭得：*The company has captured 90% of the market.* 這家公司已取得九成的市場份額。

▸ **MAKE SB INTERESTED** 使感興趣 **4** **~ sb's attention/imagination/interest** to make sb interested in sth 引起（注意、想像、興趣）：*They use puppets to capture the imagination of younger audiences.* 他們用木偶來啟發小觀眾的想像力。

▸ **FEELING/ATMOSPHERE** 感覺；氣氛 **5** **~ sth** to succeed in accurately expressing a feeling, an atmosphere, etc. in a picture, piece of writing, film/movie, etc.（用圖畫、文章、電影等準確地）表達，刻畫，描述 SYN **catch**：*The article captured the mood of the nation.* 這篇文章把國民的情緒表達得淋漓盡致。

▸ **FILM/RECORD/PAINT** 電影；唱片；繪畫 **6** [often passive] **~ sb/sth on film/tape/canvas, etc.** to film/record/paint, etc. sb/sth 拍攝；錄製；繪製：*The attack was captured on film by security cameras.* 襲擊事件已被保安攝像機拍攝下來。

▸ **SB'S HEART** 某人的心 **7** **~ sb's heart** to make sb love you 使…愛上（或傾心於）

▸ **COMPUTING** 計算機技術 **8** **~ sth** to put sth into a computer in a form it can use 把…輸入計算機；採集

■ ***noun*** 🔑 [U] the act of capturing sb/sth or of being captured（被）捕獲；（被）俘獲：*the capture of enemy territory* 佔領敵方領土 ◇ *He evaded capture for three days.* 他逃避緝捕已經三天了。◇ *data capture* 數據採集

capy·bara /ˌkæpɪˈbɑːrə; *NAmE* ˌkæpəˈberə/ *noun* (*pl.* **capy·bara** or **capy·baras**) an animal like a very large RABBIT with thick legs and small ears, which lives near water in S and Central America 水豚（生活於南美和中美洲水濱，形似大兔子）

car 🔑 /kɑː(r)/ *noun*

1 🔑 (also *BrE formal* **ˈmotor car**) (*NAmE* also **auto·mo·bile**) a road vehicle with an engine and four wheels that can carry a small number of passengers 小汽車；轎車：*Paula got into the car and drove off.* 葆拉鑽進汽車後駕車而去。◇ *'How did you come?' '**By car.**'* "你怎麼來的？""開車來的。" ◇ *Are you going **in the car**?* 你要開車去嗎？◇ *a **car driver/manufacturer/dealer*** 汽車司機／製造商／經銷商 ◇ *a **car accident/crash*** 汽車事故；撞車 ◇ *Where can I park the car?* 我可以在哪裏停車呀？ ➲ **COLLOCATIONS** at DRIVING ➲ **VISUAL VOCAB** page V52 ➲ see also COMPANY CAR **2** 🔑 (also **rail·car** both *NAmE*) a separate section of a train 火車車廂：*Several cars went off the rails.* 有幾節火車車廂出軌了。 ➲ **VISUAL VOCAB** page V58 **3** (*BrE*) (in compounds 構成複合詞) a coach/car on a train of a particular type （某種類型的）火車車廂：*a **sleeping/dining car*** 卧鋪車廂；餐車

ca·rafe /kəˈræf/ *noun* a glass container with a wide neck in which wine or water is served at meals; the amount contained in a carafe（餐桌上盛酒或水的）喇叭口玻璃瓶，飲料瓶；一瓶（的量） ➲ **VISUAL VOCAB** page V22

cara·mel /ˈkærəmel/ *noun* **1** [U, C] a type of hard sticky sweet/candy made from butter, sugar and milk; a small piece of this 黃油奶糖 **2** [U] burnt sugar used for adding colour and flavour to food 焦糖（用於食品着色和調味） ➲ see also CRÈME CARAMEL **3** [U] a light brown colour 焦糖色；淺褐色

cara·mel·ize (*BrE* also **-ise**) /ˈkærəməlaɪz/ *verb* **1** [I] (of sugar 糖) to turn into caramel 變成焦糖 **2** [T] **~ sth** to cook sth, especially fruit, with sugar so that it is covered with caramel（尤指把水果）炒上一層焦糖

cara·pace /ˈkærəpeɪs/ *noun* (*technical* 術語) the hard shell on the back of some animals such as CRABS, that protects them（某些動物，如蟹的）甲殼，背甲，外殼

carat /ˈkærət/ *noun* (*abbr.* **ct**) **1** a unit for measuring the weight of diamonds and other PRECIOUS STONES, equal to 200 milligrams 克拉（鑽石或其他寶石的重量單位，等於 200 毫克） **2** (*especially BrE*) (*NAmE* usually **karat**) a unit for measuring how pure gold is. The purest gold is 24 carats. 開（黃金成色單位，純金為 24 開）：*an 18-carat gold ring* * 18 開的金戒指

C

cara·van /ˈkærəvæn/ *noun* **1** (*BrE*) (*NAmE* **camp·er**) a road vehicle without an engine that is pulled by a car, designed for people to live and sleep in, especially when they are on holiday/vacation 旅行拖車，宿營拖車（無發動機，由其他車拖動，多供度假時住宿用）：*a caravan site/park* 旅行拖車停車場 ➲ VISUAL VOCAB page V58 **2** (*BrE*) a covered vehicle that is pulled by a horse and used for living in （供居住用的）有篷馬車，大篷車：*a Gypsy caravan* 吉卜賽人的大篷車 **3** a group of people with vehicles or animals who are travelling together, especially across the desert （尤指穿越沙漠的）旅行隊，車隊

cara·van·ning /ˈkærəvænɪŋ/ *noun* [U] (*BrE*) the activity of spending a holiday/vacation in a caravan 乘旅行拖車度假

cara·van·serai /ˌkærəˈvænsəraɪ; -ri/ (*especially US* **cara·van·sary** /ˌkærəˈvænsəri/ *pl.* **-ies**) *noun* **1** in the past, a place where travellers could stay in desert areas of Asia and N Africa （舊時亞洲和北非沙漠地區的）商隊客店 **2** (*formal*) a group of people travelling together 旅行隊

cara·way /ˈkærəweɪ/ *noun* [U] the dried seeds of the caraway plant, used to give flavour to food 葛縷子乾籽（用於食物調味）：*caraway seeds* 葛縷子籽

carb /kɑːb; *NAmE* kɑːrb/ *noun* = CARBOHYDRATE

car·bine /ˈkɑːbaɪn; *NAmE* ˈkɑːrb-/ *noun* a short light RIFLE 卡賓槍

carbo·hy·drate /ˌkɑːbəʊˈhaɪdreɪt; *NAmE* ˌkɑːrboʊ-/ *noun* **1** (also *informal* **carb**) [C, U] a substance such as sugar or STARCH that consists of CARBON, HYDROGEN and OXYGEN. Carbohydrates in food provide the body with energy and heat. 碳水化合物；糖類 **2** **carbohydrates** (also *informal* **carbs**) [pl.] foods such as bread, potatoes and rice that contain a lot of carbohydrate 含碳水化合物的食物；澱粉質食物

car·bol·ic /kɑːˈbɒlɪk; *NAmE* kɑːrˈbɑːlɪk/ (also **carˌbolic ˈacid**) *noun* [U] a chemical that kills bacteria, used as an ANTISEPTIC and as a DISINFECTANT (= to prevent infection from spreading) 石碳酸，（苯）酚（用作消毒劑）：*carbolic soap* 石碳酸皂

ˈcar bomb *noun* a bomb hidden inside or under a car 汽車炸彈

car·bon /ˈkɑːbən; *NAmE* ˈkɑːrb-/ *noun* **1** [U] (*symb.* **C**) a chemical element. Carbon is found in all living things, existing in a pure state as diamond and GRAPHITE and BUCKMINSTERFULLERENE. 碳：*carbon fibre* 碳纖維 **2** [U] used when referring to the gas CARBON DIOXIDE in terms of the effect it has on the earth's climate in causing GLOBAL WARMING 碳（指導致全球變暖的二氧化碳氣體）：*carbon emissions/levels/taxes* 碳排放；碳水平；碳稅 ◇ (*BrE*) *How do we move to a low carbon economy?* 我們如何轉向低碳經濟？ **3** [C] = CARBON COPY **4** [C] a piece of CARBON PAPER 複寫紙

car·bon·ate /ˈkɑːbəneɪt; *NAmE* ˈkɑːrbənət/ *noun* (*chemistry* 化) a salt that contains CARBON and OXYGEN together with another chemical 碳酸鹽

car·bon·ated /ˈkɑːbəneɪtɪd; *NAmE* ˈkɑːrb-/ *adj.* (*technical* 術語) (of a drink 飲料) containing small bubbles of CARBON DIOXIDE 含二氧化碳的；起泡的 SYN **fizzy**

ˌcarbon ˈcopy (also **car·bon**) *noun* **1** a copy of a document, letter, etc. made with CARBON PAPER （文件、信等的）複寫本 ➲ see also CC **2** a person or thing that is very similar to sb/sth else 極相像的人；極類似的事：*She is a carbon copy of her sister.* 她跟她姐姐長得一模一樣。

ˈcarbon credit *noun* **1** a key element in the system of national and international CARBON TRADING. A country or organization has the right to produce a particular amount of CARBON DIOXIDE and other gases that cause GLOBAL WARMING, which is expressed in terms of **carbon credits**, which may be traded between countries or organizations. 碳信用額（指有權擁有且可交易的溫室氣體排放量）：*The sale of carbon credits can finance renewable energy projects.* 碳信用額的銷售可為可再生能源項目提供資金。 **2** a CARBON OFFSET, which a person or company may choose to buy as a way of reducing the level of CARBON DIOXIDE for which they are responsible 碳補償信用額（購入後用以抵消自身碳排放量）：*Wind energy companies sell carbon credits to consumers.* 風能公司向消費者出售碳補償信用額。

ˈcarbon cycle *noun* [C, U] the processes by which carbon is changed from one form to another within the environment, for example in plants and when wood or oil is burned 碳循環（指碳在自然環境中的形式變化過程）

ˌcarbon ˈdating (also *formal* **ˌradiocarbon ˈdating**) *noun* [U] a method of calculating the age of very old objects by measuring the amounts of different forms of carbon in them 碳定年法（根據測定古物不同形態的碳含量以計算年代）

ˌcarbon diˈoxide *noun* [U] (*symb.* CO_2) a gas breathed out by people and animals from the lungs or produced by burning CARBON 二氧化碳

ˌcarbon ˈfootprint *noun* a measure of the amount of carbon dioxide that is produced by the daily activities of a person or company 碳足跡（日常活動所產生的碳排放量的量度方式）：*Flying is the biggest contribution to my carbon footprint.* 乘坐飛機在我的碳足跡中佔有的比例最大。 ➲ COLLOCATIONS at ENVIRONMENT

car·bon·ic acid /kɑːˌbɒnɪk ˈæsɪd; *NAmE* kɑːrˌbɑːnɪk/ *noun* [U] (*chemistry* 化) a very weak acid that is formed when carbon dioxide is dissolved in water 碳酸

car·bon·ifer·ous /ˌkɑːbəˈnɪfərəs; *NAmE* ˌkɑːrb-/ *adj.* (*geology* 地) **1** producing or containing coal 產煤（或炭）的；含煤（或炭）的 **2** **Carboniferous** of the period in the earth's history when layers of coal were formed underground 石炭紀的

car·bon·ize (*BrE* also **-ise**) /ˈkɑːbənaɪz; *NAmE* ˈkɑːrb-/ *verb* **1** [I, T] **~ (sth)** to become CARBON, or to make sth become carbon （使）碳化；（使）焦化 **2** [T] **~ sth** to cover sth with CARBON 給…塗碳 ▸ **car·bon·iza·tion, -isa·tion** /ˌkɑːbənaɪˈzeɪʃn; *NAmE* ˈkɑːrb-/ *noun* [U]

ˌcarbon monˈoxide /ˌkɑːbən mənˈɒksaɪd; *NAmE* ˌkɑːrbən mənˈɑːksaɪd/ *noun* [U] (*symb.* **CO**) a poisonous gas formed when CARBON burns partly but not completely. It is produced when petrol/gas is burnt in car engines. 一氧化碳

ˌcarbon ˈneu·tral *adj.* in which the amount of CARBON DIOXIDE produced has been reduced to nothing or is balanced by actions that protect the environment 碳中和的，碳平衡的（指碳排放量減低為零，或通過環保措施抵消排放）SYN **zero-carbon**：*All of these fuels are renewable and carbon neutral.* 所有這些燃料都可再生並達至碳中和。

ˌcarbon ˈoffset *noun* [C, U] a way for a company or person to reduce the level of CARBON DIOXIDE for which they are responsible by paying money to a company that works to reduce the total amount produced in the world, for example by planting trees 碳補償，碳抵消（出錢給從事全球減碳的公司，以降低自身碳排放水平）：*carbon offset initiatives for air travellers* 供航空旅客採用的碳補償倡議 ➲ compare CARBON CREDIT

ˈcarbon paper *noun* thin paper with a dark substance on one side, that is used between two sheets of paper for making copies of written or typed documents 複寫紙

ˈcarbon trading (also **eˈmissions trading**) *noun* [U] a system that gives countries and organizations the right to produce a particular amount of CARBON DIOXIDE and other gases that cause GLOBAL WARMING, and allows them to sell this right 碳排放權交易；碳交易

ˌcar ˈboot sale *noun* (*BrE*) an outdoor sale where people sell things that they no longer want, using tables or the backs of their cars to put the goods on （於戶外擺放在桌子上或車尾箱裏的）舊貨銷售，舊貨市場

Car·bor·un·dum™ /ˌkɑːbəˈrʌndəm; *NAmE* ˌkɑːrb-/ *noun* [U] (*chemistry* 化) a very hard black solid substance, used as an ABRASIVE 金剛砂

car·boy /ˈkɑːbɔɪ; *NAmE* ˈkɑːrbɔɪ/ *noun* a large round bottle, usually protected by an outer frame of wood and used for storing and transporting dangerous liquids 大瓶，大罐（通常有木架保護，用於貯藏和運輸危險液體）

ˈcar bra *noun* = BRA (2)

car·bun·cle /ˈkɑːbʌŋkl; *NAmE* ˈkɑːrb-/ *noun* **1** a large painful swelling under the skin 癰；疔 **2** a bright red JEWEL, usually cut into a round shape 紅榴石；紅寶石；紅玉

car·bur·et·tor (*BrE*) (*NAmE* **car·bur·etor**) /ˌkɑːbəˈretə(r); *NAmE* ˈkɑːrbəreɪtər/ *noun* the part of an engine, for example in a car, where petrol/gas and air are mixed together 汽化器，化油器（汽車發動機部件）

car·cass (*BrE* also *less frequent* **car·case**) /ˈkɑːkəs; *NAmE* ˈkɑːrkəs/ *noun* the dead body of an animal, especially of a large one or of one that is ready for cutting up as meat 動物屍體；（尤指供食用的）畜體

car·cino·gen /kɑːˈsɪnədʒən; *NAmE* kɑːrˈs-/ *noun* a substance that can cause cancer 致癌物

car·cino·gen·ic /ˌkɑːsɪnəˈdʒenɪk; *NAmE* ˌkɑːrs-/ *adj.* likely to cause cancer 致癌的

car·cin·oma /ˌkɑːsɪˈnəʊmə; *NAmE* ˌkɑːrsɪˈnoʊmə/ *noun* (*medical* 醫) a cancer that affects the top layer of the skin or the LINING of the body's internal organs 癌（影響上皮組織或腹腔器官內膜的惡性腫瘤）

card 🔑 /kɑːd; *NAmE* kɑːrd/ *noun, verb*

■ ***noun***

▸ PAPER 紙 **1** 🔑 [U] (*BrE*) thick stiff paper 卡片紙；厚紙片；薄紙板：*a piece of card* 一張卡片紙 ◇ *The model of the building was made of card.* 建築物的模型是用厚紙片製造的。

▸ WITH INFORMATION 資料 **2** 🔑 [C] a small piece of stiff paper or plastic with information on it, especially information about sb's identity （尤指顯示個人資料的）卡片：*a membership card* 會員卡 ◇ *an appointment card* 預約卡 ➲ see also GREEN CARD, IDENTITY CARD, LOYALTY CARD, RED CARD, REPORT CARD at REPORT *n.* (5), YELLOW CARD **3** [C] = BUSINESS CARD：*Here's my card if you need to contact me again.* 如果你需要再和我聯繫，這是我的名片。 **4** [C] = VISITING CARD

▸ FOR MONEY 代替貨幣 **5** 🔑 [C] a small piece of plastic, especially one given by a bank or shop/store, used for buying things or obtaining money 信用卡；現金卡；儲值卡：*I put the meal on* (= paid for it using) *my card.* 我用信用卡支付餐費。 ➲ see also CASH CARD, CHARGE CARD, CHEQUE CARD, CHIP CARD, CREDIT CARD, DEBIT CARD, PHONECARD, SIM CARD, SMART CARD, SWIPE CARD

▸ WITH A MESSAGE 信息 **6** 🔑 [C] a piece of stiff paper that is folded in the middle and has a picture on the front of it, used for sending sb a message with your good wishes, an invitation, etc. 賀卡；慰問卡；請柬：*a **birthday/get-well/good luck card*** 生日賀卡；祝願康復卡；幸運賀卡 ➲ see also CHRISTMAS CARD, GREETINGS CARD **7** [C] = POSTCARD：*Did you get my card from Italy?* 你收到我從意大利寄出的明信片了嗎？

▸ IN GAMES 遊戲 **8** 🔑 [C] = PLAYING CARD：(*BrE*) *a pack of cards* 一副紙牌 ◇ (*NAmE*) *a deck of cards* 一副紙牌 ➲ VISUAL VOCAB page V37 ➲ see also TRUMP CARD, WILD CARD **9** 🔑 **cards** [pl.] a game or games in which PLAYING CARDS are used 紙牌遊戲：*Who wants to play cards?* 誰想玩牌？◇ *I've never been very good at cards.* 我打牌的技術向來不高。◇ *Let's have a game of cards.* 咱們來玩紙牌吧。◇ *She won £20 at cards.* 她打牌贏了20英鎊。

▸ COMPUTING 計算機技術 **10** [C] a small device containing an electronic CIRCUIT that is part of a computer or added to it, enabling it to perform particular functions 電路板卡；插件：*a printed circuit card* 印刷電路卡 ◇ *a **graphics/network/sound card*** 圖形卡；網卡；聲卡 ➲ see also EXPANSION CARD

▸ PERSON 人 **11** [C] (*old-fashioned, informal*) an unusual or amusing person 怪人；引人發笑的人；活寶

▸ HORSE RACES 賽馬 **12** [C] a list of all the races at a particular RACE MEETING (= a series of horse races) （賽馬大會的）賽事一覽表

▸ FOR WOOL/COTTON 毛；棉 **13** [C] (*technical* 術語) a machine or tool used for cleaning and COMBING wool or cotton before it is spun 梳理機；梳理工具

IDM **sb's best/strongest/winning ˈcard** something that gives sb an advantage over other people in a particular situation 某人的王牌；最強有力的一招；制勝的絕招 **get your ˈcards** (*BrE, informal*) to be told to leave a job 被解雇；被炒魷魚 **give sb their ˈcards** (*BrE, informal*) to make sb leave their job 解雇；開除；炒…的魷魚 **have a card up your ˈsleeve** to have an idea, a plan, etc. that will give you an advantage in a particular situation and that you keep secret until it is needed 有錦囊妙計；留有一招 **hold all the ˈcards** (*informal*) to be able to control a particular situation because you have an advantage over other people 能控制局勢；應付自如；佔上風 **hold/keep/play your cards close to your ˈchest** to keep your ideas, plans, etc. secret 守口如瓶；秘而不宣 **lay/put your cards on the ˈtable** to tell sb honestly what your plans, ideas, etc. are 攤牌；（把計劃或想法等）和盤托出 **on the ˈcards** (*BrE*) (*NAmE* **in the ˈcards**) (*informal*) likely to happen 可能發生的；可能的：*The merger has been on the cards for some time now.* 合併的事情已經醞釀了一段時間。 **play the … card** to mention a particular subject, idea or quality in order to gain an advantage 打…牌；出…招：*He accused his opponent of playing the immigration card during the campaign.* 他指責對手在競選活動中打移民牌。➲ see also RACE CARD **play your ˈcards right** to deal successfully with a particular situation so that you achieve some advantage or sth that you want 辦事精明；做事有盤算；處理得當 ➲ more at SHOW *v.*, STACKED

■ ***verb*** **1 ~ sth** (*technical* 術語) to clean wool using a wire instrument （用鋼絲刷）梳理 **2 ~ sb** (*NAmE, informal*) to ask a person to show their identity card as a means of checking how old they are, for example if they want to buy alcohol 要求出示身分證（以確認年齡，如購酒時）

car·da·mom /ˈkɑːdəməm; *NAmE* ˈkɑːrd-/ *noun* [U] the dried seeds of a SE Asian plant, used in cooking as a spice 豆蔻乾籽（用作調味料） ➲ VISUAL VOCAB page V32

card·board 🔑 /ˈkɑːdbɔːd; *NAmE* ˈkɑːrdbɔːrd/ *noun, adj.*

■ ***noun*** 🔑 [U] stiff material like very thick paper, often used for making boxes 硬紙板，卡紙板（常用於製造盒子）：*a cardboard box* 紙板盒 ◇ *a piece of cardboard* 一張硬紙板

■ ***adj.*** [only before noun] not seeming real or genuine 不真實的；虛假的：*a novel with superficial cardboard characters* 人物不真實而又缺乏深度的小說

ˌcardboard ˈcity *noun* an area of a city where people who have nowhere to live sleep outside, protected only by cardboard boxes （城市中無家可歸者聚集過夜的）紙箱街區

ˈcard-carrying *adj.* [only before noun] known to be an official and usually active member of a political organization （政治組織）正式成員的：*a card-carrying member of the Conservative party* 保守黨正式黨員

ˈcard catalog (*NAmE*) (*BrE* **ˈcard index, index**) *noun* a box of cards with information on them, arranged in alphabetical order 卡片目錄（或索引） ➲ VISUAL VOCAB page V69

ˈcard game *noun* a game in which playing cards are used 紙牌遊戲

card·hold·er /ˈkɑːdhəʊldə(r); *NAmE* ˈkɑːrdhoʊl-/ *noun* a person who has a credit card from a bank, etc. 持有信用卡的人；持卡人

car·diac /ˈkɑːdiæk; *NAmE* ˈkɑːrd-/ *adj.* [only before noun] (*medical* 醫) connected with the heart or heart disease 心臟的；心臟病的：***cardiac disease/failure/surgery*** 心臟病；心力衰竭；心臟手術 ◇ ***to suffer cardiac arrest*** (= an occasion when a person's heart stops temporarily or permanently) 心臟停搏

car·di·gan /ˈkɑːdɪgən; *NAmE* ˈkɑːrd-/ (*NAmE* also **ˌcardigan ˈsweater**) *noun* a knitted jacket made of wool, usually with no COLLAR and fastened with

C

buttons at the front（無領）開襟毛衣 ➲ VISUAL VOCAB page V63

car·din·al /ˈkɑːdɪnl; NAmE ˈkɑːrd-/ *noun, adj.*

■ ***noun*** **1** a priest of the highest rank in the Roman Catholic Church. Cardinals elect and advise the POPE. 樞機；樞機主教：*Cardinal Brady* 布雷迪樞機主教 **2** (also ˌ**cardinal ˈnumber**) a number, such as 1, 2 and 3, used to show quantity rather than order 基數；純數 ➲ compare ORDINAL **3** a N American bird. The male cardinal is bright red. 紅衣鳳頭鳥（見於北美，雄鳥為鮮紅色）

■ ***adj.*** [only before noun] (*formal*) most important; having other things based on it 最重要的；基本的：*Respect for life is a cardinal principle of English law.* 尊重生命是英國法律最重要的原則。

ˌ**cardinal ˈpoints** *noun* [pl.] (*technical* 術語) the four main points (North, South, East and West) of the COMPASS 基本方位（羅盤上的東、西、南、北）

ˌ**cardinal ˈsin** *noun* **1** (sometimes *humorous*) an action that is a serious mistake or that other people disapprove of 嚴重過失；過錯：*He committed the cardinal sin of criticizing his teammates.* 他犯了指責隊友的大錯。 **2** a serious SIN in the Christian Church（基督教中嚴重的）罪，罪孽

ˈ**card index** (also **index**) (both *BrE*) (*NAmE* ˈ**card catalog**) *noun* a box of cards with information on them, arranged in alphabetical order 卡片目錄（或索引） ➲ VISUAL VOCAB page V69

cardio /ˈkɑːdiəʊ; NAmE ˈkɑːrdioʊ/ *noun* [U] (*informal*) exercises to make your heart work harder, that you do to keep yourself fit 健心運動：*Cardio is the answer if you want to lose weight.* 想減肥就得做健心運動。◇ *cardio exercise/workouts* 健心體操 / 鍛煉 ➲ see also CARDIOVASCULAR

cardio- /ˈkɑːdiəʊ; NAmE ˈkɑːrdioʊ/ *combining form* (in nouns, adjectives and adverbs 構成名詞、形容詞和副詞) connected with the heart 心臟的：*cardiogram* 心電圖

car·di·olo·gist /ˌkɑːdiˈɒlədʒɪst; NAmE ˌkɑːrdiˈɑːl-/ *noun* a doctor who studies and treats heart diseases 心臟病醫生；心臟病學家 ▸ **car·di·ology** /-dʒi/ *noun* [U]

car·dio·vas·cu·lar /ˌkɑːdiəʊˈvæskjələ(r); NAmE ˌkɑːrdioʊ-/ *adj.* (*medical* 醫) connected with the heart and the BLOOD VESSELS (= the tubes that carry blood around the body) 心血管的

card·phone /ˈkɑːdfəʊn; NAmE ˈkɑːrdfoʊn/ *noun* (*BrE*) a public telephone in which you use a plastic card (= a PHONECARD) instead of money 磁卡電話

ˈ**card sharp** *noun* a person who cheats in games of cards in order to make money（玩紙牌時）作弊贏錢的人，耍老千的人

ˈ**card swipe** *noun* an electronic device through which you pass a credit card, etc. in order to record the information on it, open a door, etc. 讀卡機；磁卡識別機

ˈ**card table** *noun* a small table for playing card games on, especially one that you can fold（摺疊式）牌桌

care 🔑 /keə(r); NAmE ker/ *noun, verb*

> **WORD FAMILY**
> **care** *noun, verb*
> **careful** *adj.* (≠ careless)
> **carefully** *adv.* (≠ carelessly)
> **caring** *adj.* (≠ uncaring)

■ ***noun*** **1** 🔑 [U] the process of caring for sb/sth and providing what they need for their health or protection 照料；照顧；照看；護理：*medical/patient care* 醫療保健；病人護理 ◇ *How much do men share housework and the care of the children?* 男人分擔多少家務和照看小孩的工作？◇ *the provision of care for the elderly* 為老人提供的護理 ◇ ***skin/hair care** products* 護膚 / 護髮品 ➲ see also COMMUNITY CARE, DAY CARE, EASY-CARE, HEALTH CARE, INTENSIVE CARE **2** 🔑 [U] attention or thought that you give to sth that you are doing so that you will do it well and avoid mistakes or damage 小心；謹慎：*She chose her words **with care**.* 她措辭謹慎。◇ *Great care is needed when choosing a used car.* 選購舊車時要特別小心。◇ *Fragile—handle with care* (= written on a container holding sth which is easily broken or damaged) 易碎物品 — 小心輕放 **3** [C, usually pl., U] (*formal*) a feeling of worry or anxiety; something that causes problems or anxiety 憂慮；焦慮；引起煩惱的事；令人焦慮的事：*I felt free from the cares of the day as soon as I left the building.* 我一離開那棟大樓便覺得輕鬆自在，不再為那天的事煩心了。◇ *Sam looked as if he **didn't have a care in the world**.* 薩姆看上去好像什麼事都不操心似的。

IDM ˈ**care of sb** (*NAmE* also **in ˈcare of sb**) (*abbr.* **c/o**) used when writing to sb at another person's address（以別人的地址給某人寫信時用）由某人轉交：*Write to him care of his lawyer.* 寫給他的信由他的律師轉交。 **in ˈcare** (*BrE*) (of children 兒童) living in an institution run by the local authority rather than with their parents 由福利院收養：*The two girls were **taken into care** after their parents were killed.* 兩個女孩在父母遇害後由福利院收養。 **in the care of sb/in sb's care** being cared for by sb 由…照管：*The child was left in the care of friends.* 小孩被留下由朋友照管。 **take ˈcare** (*informal*) used when saying goodbye（告別用語）走好，保重：*Bye! Take care!* 再見！多保重！ **take care (that .../to do sth)** to be careful 小心；當心：*Take care (that) you don't drink too much!* 當心別喝得太多！◇ *Care should be taken to close the lid securely.* 容器蓋應小心扣緊。 **take care of sb/sth/yourself** **1** 🔑 to care for sb/sth/yourself; to be careful about sth 照顧；照料；愛護；小心：*Who's taking care of the children while you're away?* 你外出時誰來照料這些孩子？◇ *She takes great care of her clothes.* 她非常愛惜自己的衣服。◇ *He's old enough to take care of himself.* 他已經不小了，能照顧自己了。 **2** 🔑 to be responsible for or to deal with a situation or task 負責；處理：*Don't worry about the travel arrangements. They're all being taken care of.* 別擔心旅行安排，一切都會有人照管的。◇ *Celia takes care of the marketing side of things.* 西莉亞負責產品營銷方面的事宜。 **under the care of sb** receiving medical care from sb 接受某人的治療：*He's under the care of Dr Parks.* 他在接受帕克斯醫生的治療。

■ ***verb*** (not used in the progressive tenses 不用於進行時) **1** 🔑 [I, T] to feel that sth is important and worth worrying about 關注；在意；擔憂：***I don't care*** (= I will not be upset) *if I never see him again!* 即使我永遠再也見不到他，我也不在乎！◇ *He threatened to fire me, **as if I cared!*** 他威脅要解雇我，好像我多在乎似的！◇ **~ about sth** *She cares deeply about environmental issues.* 她對環境問題深感擔憂。◇ **~ what/whether, etc.** *I don't care what he thinks.* 我才不管他怎麼想呢。◇ **~ that ...** *She doesn't seem to care that he's been married four times before.* 她似乎不介意他以前結過四次婚。 **2** 🔑 [I] **~ (about sb)** to like or love sb and worry about what happens to them 關心；關懷：*He genuinely cares about his employees.* 他真誠地關心他的雇員。 **3** [T] **~ to do sth** to make the effort to do sth 努力做：*I've done this job more times than I care to remember.* 這事我都記不清做了多少遍了。

IDM **couldn't care ˈless** (*informal*) used to say, often rudely, that you do not think that sb/sth is important or worth worrying about（常用於無禮地表示）不在乎，不在意：*Quite honestly, I couldn't care less what they do.* 說實在的，我才不在乎他們做什麼。 **for all you, I, they, etc. care** (*informal*) used to say that a person is not worried about or interested in what happens to sb/sth 漠不關心；無動於衷；全然不在乎：*I could be dead for all he cares!* 我是死是活，他才不關心呢！ **who ˈcares?** | **What do I, you, etc. care?** (*informal*) used to say, often rudely, that you do not think that sth is important or interesting（常用於無禮地表示）管它呢，誰管呢：*Who cares what she thinks?* 誰管她怎麼想呢！ **Would you care for sth?** | **Would you care to do sth?** (*formal*) used to ask sb politely if they would like sth or would like to do sth, or if they would be willing to do sth（禮貌問語）您想要，您喜歡，您願意：*Would you care for another drink?* 您再來一杯好嗎？◇ *If you'd care to follow me, I'll show you where his office is.* 如果您願意跟我走，我會把您領到他的辦公室去。 ➲ note at WANT ➲ more at DAMN *n.*, FIG, HOOT *n.*, TUPPENCE

PHR V ˈ**care for sb** **1** 🔑 to look after sb who is sick, very old, very young, etc. 照顧，照料（病、老、幼者等） **SYN** **take care of**：*She moved back home to care for*

her elderly parents. 她搬回家住，好照料年邁的雙親。➲ see also UNCARED FOR **2** to love or like sb very much 深深地愛；非常喜歡： *He cared for her more than she realized.* 她不知道他是多麼在乎她。➲ SYNONYMS at LOVE **not 'care for sb/sth** (*formal*) to not like sb/sth 不喜歡： *He didn't much care for her friends.* 他不太喜歡她的朋友。

Synonyms 同義詞辨析

care

caution • prudence

These are all words for attention or thought that you give to sth in order to avoid mistakes or accidents. 以上各詞均指小心、謹慎。

care attention or thought that you give to sth that you are doing so that you will do it well and avoid mistakes or damage 指小心、謹慎以做好某事，同時避免出現錯誤或損失： *She chose her words with care.* 她措辭謹慎。

caution care that you take in order to avoid danger or mistakes; not taking any risks 指小心、謹慎，以免發生危險或錯誤： *The utmost caution must be exercised when handling explosives.* 處理爆炸品一定要慎之又慎。

prudence (*rather formal*) being sensible and careful when you make judgements and decisions; avoiding unnecessary risks 指判斷和決策時謹慎、慎重，處事時避免不必要的風險： *As a matter of prudence, keep a record of all your financial transactions.* 為慎重起見，請記下你所有的財務往來。NOTE **Prudence** is used particularly in financial contexts. * prudence 尤用於金融、財務方面。

PATTERNS

- to do sth **with** care/caution/prudence
- **great/extreme** care/caution/prudence
- to **use/exercise** care/caution/prudence
- to **proceed with** care/caution

'care assistant *noun* (*BrE*) = CARE WORKER

ca·reen /kəˈriːn/ *verb* [I] **+ adv./prep.** (*especially NAmE*) (of a person or vehicle 人或車輛) to move forward very quickly especially in a way that is dangerous or uncontrolled（尤指危險或失控地）猛衝，疾駛 SYN **hurtle**

ca·reer 🔑 /kəˈrɪə(r); *NAmE* kəˈrɪr/ *noun, verb*

■ *noun* **1** 🔑 the series of jobs that a person has in a particular area of work, usually involving more responsibility as time passes 生涯；職業： *a* ***career in*** *politics* 從政生涯 ◇ *a teaching career* 教學生涯 ◇ *What made you decide on a* ***career as*** *a vet?* 是什麼驅使你選擇獸醫這門職業的？◇ *She has been concentrating on her career.* 她一直專心致志於她的本職工作。◇ *a change of career* 改換職業 ◇ *That will be a good* ***career move*** (= something that will help your career). 那將是事業發展上明智的一步。◇ *a* ***career soldier/diplomat*** (= a professional one) 職業軍人；外交人員 ◇ (*BrE*) *a* ***careers adviser/officer*** (= a person whose job is to give people advice and information about jobs) 指導選擇職業的顧問 / 官員 ➲ SYNONYMS at WORK ➲ COLLOCATIONS at JOB **2** 🔑 the period of time that you spend in your life working or doing a particular thing 經歷；事業： *She started her career as an English teacher.* 她以當英語教師開始了她的職業生涯。◇ *He is playing the best tennis of his career.* 他正處於他網球事業的巔峰時期。◇ *My school career was not very impressive.* 我的學業成績並不很出色。

■ *verb* [I] **+ adv./prep.** (of a person or vehicle 人或車輛) to move forward very quickly, especially in an uncontrolled way （尤指失控地）猛衝，疾馳，飛奔 SYN **hurtle**： *The vehicle careered across the road and hit a cyclist.* 那輛車橫衝過馬路，撞上了一個騎自行車的人。

ca'reer break *noun* a period of time when you do not do your usual job, for example because you have children to care for 離職期（如因照料小孩之需）

Which Word? 詞語辨析

take care of / look after / care for

- You can **take care of** or, especially in *BrE*, **look after** someone who is very young, very old, or sick, or something that needs keeping in good condition. 照看小孩、老人、病人或物品可用 take care of，英式英語尤用 look after： *We've asked my mother to take care of/look after the kids while we're away.* 我們已請我母親在我們外出時照看孩子。◇ *You can borrow my camera if you promise to take care of/look after it.* 只要你答應把我的照相機保管好就可以借去用。
- In more formal language you can also **care for** someone. 在較正式用語中，照看或照顧某人亦可用 care for： *She does some voluntary work, caring for the elderly.* 她幹一些照顧老人的義務工作。But **care for** is more commonly used to mean 'like'. 但 care for 較常用於表示喜歡： *I don't really care for spicy food.* 我其實不喜歡吃辛辣食物。

car·eer·ist /kəˈrɪərɪst; *NAmE* -ˈrɪr-/ *noun* (often *disapproving*) a person whose career is more important to them than anything else 視事業重於一切的人；事業狂 ▸ **car·eer·ism** *noun* [U]

ca'reer woman *noun* a woman whose career is more important to her than getting married and having children 職業婦女，職業女性（視事業比結婚生孩子更重要的女人）

care·free /ˈkeəfriː; *NAmE* ˈkerf-/ *adj.* having no worries or responsibilities 無憂無慮的；無牽掛的；無責任的： *He looked happy and carefree.* 他看起來輕鬆愉快。◇ *a* ***carefree attitude/life*** 輕鬆自在的態度；無憂無慮的生活

care·ful 🔑 /ˈkeəfl; *NAmE* ˈkerfl/ *adj.*

1 🔑 [not before noun] giving attention or thought to what you are doing so that you avoid hurting yourself, damaging sth or doing sth wrong 小心；注意；謹慎： *Be careful!* 小心！◇ **~ to do sth** *He was careful to keep out of sight.* 他小心翼翼地躲開別人的視線。◇ **~ not to do sth** *Be careful not to wake the baby.* 注意別吵醒了寶寶。◇ **~ when/what/how, etc.** *You must be careful when handling chemicals.* 搬運化學品必須小心謹慎。◇ **~ of/about/with sth** *Be careful of the traffic.* 注意交通安全。◇ *Please be careful with my glasses* (= Don't break them). 請當心別打碎我的眼鏡。◇ **~ (that) …** *Be careful you don't bump your head.* 留神別撞了你的頭。**2** 🔑 giving a lot of attention to details 細緻的；精心的；慎重的： *a careful piece of work* 精雕細琢的作品 ◇ *a careful examination of the facts* 對事實的仔細調查 ◇ *After careful consideration we have decided to offer you the job.* 經過慎重考慮後，我們決定給你這份工作。OPP **careless** ▸ **care·ful·ly** 🔑 /ˈkeəfəli; *NAmE* ˈker-/ *adv.*： *Please listen carefully.* 請仔細地聽。◇ *She put the glass down carefully.* 她小心翼翼地放下玻璃杯。◇ *Drive carefully.* 小心開車。OPP **carelessly** ▸ **care·ful·ness** *noun* [U]

IDM **you can't be too 'careful** used to warn sb that they should take care to avoid danger or problems 無論怎樣小心也不會過分；越小心越好： *Don't stay out in the sun for too long—you can't be too careful.* 別在太陽底下待得太久，你得盡量小心。**careful with money** not spending money on unimportant things 花錢精打細算；不亂花錢

care·giver /ˈkeəɡɪvə(r); *NAmE* ˈkerɡ-/ (*NAmE*) (*BrE* **carer**) *noun* a person who takes care of a sick or old person at home 照料家居老弱病患者的人；家庭護理員

'care home *noun* (*BrE*) a place where people live and are cared for when they cannot live at home or look after themselves 護理院；照護所： *a care home for the elderly* 養老院

ˌcare in the comˈmunity *noun* [U] = COMMUNITY CARE

ˈcare label *noun* a label attached to the inside of a piece of clothing, giving instructions about how it should be washed and ironed（衣服的）熨洗須知標籤

care·less 🔑 /ˈkeələs; *NAmE* ˈkerləs/ *adj.*

1 🔑 not giving enough attention and thought to what you are doing, so that you make mistakes 不小心的；不仔細的；粗心的：*It was careless of me to leave the door open.* 怪我粗心忘了關門。◇ *Don't be so **careless about/with** spelling.* 別那麼粗心大意地犯拼寫錯誤。◇ *a careless worker/driver* 粗心大意的工人／司機 OPP **careful** **2** 🔑 resulting from a lack of attention and thought 粗心造成的；疏忽引起的：*a **careless mistake/error*** 疏忽造成的錯誤／差錯 **3 ~ of sth** (*formal*) not at all worried about sth 不擔憂的；無憂無慮的：*He seemed careless of his own safety.* 他彷彿已把自己的安危置之度外。**4** not showing interest or effort 淡漠的；不關心的；漫不經心的 SYN **casual**：*She gave a careless shrug.* 她漠然地聳了聳肩。◇ *a **careless laugh/smile*** 淡然的一笑 ▸ **care·less·ly** 🔑 *adv.*：*Someone had carelessly left a window open.* 有人粗心大意忘了關一扇窗。◇ *She threw her coat carelessly onto the chair.* 她把外套隨手扔在了椅子上。◇ *'I don't mind,' he said carelessly.* "我無所謂。" 他滿不在乎地說。**care·less·ness** *noun* [U]：*a moment of carelessness* 一時的疏忽大意

care·line /ˈkeəlaɪn; *NAmE* ˈkerl-/ *noun* a telephone service that you can call to get advice or information on a company's products（公司的）產品咨詢熱線，服務熱線，客服熱線：*Call our customer careline for advice.* 請撥打我們的客戶服務熱線咨詢。

carer /ˈkeərə(r); *NAmE* ˈker-/ (*BrE*) (*NAmE* **care·giver**) *noun* a person who takes care of a sick or old person at home 照料家居老弱病患者的人；家庭護理員

ca·ress /kəˈres/ *verb, noun*

■ ***verb*** **~ sb/sth** to touch sb/sth gently, especially in a sexual way or in a way that shows affection 撫摩；愛撫：*His fingers caressed the back of her neck.* 他的手指撫摩着她的脖頸。

■ ***noun*** a gentle touch or kiss to show you love sb 撫摩；愛撫；親吻

caret /ˈkærət/ *noun* a mark (^) placed below a line of printed or written text to show that words or letters should be added at that place in the text 脫字號；補註號

care·taker /ˈkeəteɪkə(r); *NAmE* ˈkert-/ *noun, adj.*

■ ***noun*** **1** (*BrE*) (*NAmE, ScotE* **jani·tor**) (*NAmE* also **cus·to·dian**) a person whose job is to take care of a building such as a school or a block of flats or an apartment building（建築物的）管理員，看管人，看門人 **2** (*especially NAmE*) a person who takes care of a house or land while the owner is away（主人外出時房地產的）看管人，代管人 **3** (*especially NAmE*) a person such as a teacher, parent, nurse, etc., who takes care of other people 照看人；監護人；護理人員

■ ***adj.*** [only before noun] in charge for a short time, until a new leader or government is chosen 臨時代理的；暫時主管的：*a **caretaker manager/government*** 代經理；看守政府

ˈcare worker (also **ˈcare assistant**) (both *BrE*) *noun* a person whose job is to help and take care of people who are mentally ill, sick or disabled, especially those who live in special homes or hospitals（精神病人、殘疾人、尤指住院治療者的）護理員

care·worn /ˈkeəwɔːn; *NAmE* ˈkerwɔːrn/ *adj.* looking tired because you have a lot of worries 憂慮憔悴的

cargo /ˈkɑːɡəʊ; *NAmE* ˈkɑːrɡoʊ/ *noun* [C, U] (*pl.* **-oes**, *NAmE* also **-os**) the goods carried in a ship or plane（船或飛機裝載的）貨物：*The tanker began to spill its cargo of oil.* 油輪已開始漏油。◇ *a cargo ship* 貨船

ˈcargo pants (also **car·goes**) (*BrE* also **com·bats**, **ˈcombat trousers**) *noun* [pl.] loose trousers that have pockets in various places, for example on the side of the leg above the knee 工裝褲（多口袋、寬鬆）➲ VISUAL VOCAB page V63

Carib·bean /ˌkærɪˈbiːən; kəˈrɪbiən/ *noun, adj.*

■ ***noun* the Caribbean** the region consisting of the Caribbean Sea and its islands, including the West Indies, and the coasts which surround it 加勒比海地區（指加勒比海及其島嶼，包括西印度群島及其周圍海岸）

■ ***adj.*** connected with the Caribbean 加勒比海地區的；加勒比海諸島的

cari·bou /ˈkærɪbuː/ *noun* (*pl.* **cari·bou**) a N American REINDEER 北美馴鹿

cari·ca·ture /ˈkærɪkətʃʊə(r); *NAmE* -tʃər; -tʃʊr/ *noun, verb*

■ ***noun*** **1** [C] a funny drawing or picture of sb that exaggerates some of their features 人物漫畫 **2** [C] a description of a person or thing that makes them seem ridiculous by exaggerating some of their characteristics 誇張的描述：*He had unfairly presented a caricature of my views.* 他歪曲了我的觀點。**3** [U] the art of drawing or writing caricatures 漫畫藝術；漫畫手法 ▸ **cari·ca·tur·ist** *noun*

■ ***verb*** [often passive] **~ sb/sth** (**as sth**) to produce a caricature of sb; to describe or present sb as a type of person you would laugh at or not respect 把…畫成漫畫；滑稽地描述：*She was unfairly caricatured as a dumb blonde.* 她被不公正地醜化成了一個傻頭傻腦的金髮女郎。

car·ies /ˈkeəriːz; *NAmE* ˈker-/ *noun* [U] (*medical* 醫) decay in teeth or bones 齲齒；骨瘍；骨疽：*dental caries* 齲齒

car·il·lon /kəˈrɪljən; *NAmE* ˈkærəlɑːn/ *noun* **1** a set of bells on which tunes can be played, sometimes using a keyboard 組鐘；大鐘琴 **2** a tune played on bells 編鐘樂曲；鐘樂

car·ing /ˈkeərɪŋ; *NAmE* ˈker-/ *adj.* [usually before noun] kind, helpful and showing that you care about other people 樂於助人的；關心他人的；體貼人的：*He's a very caring person.* 他是個非常體貼別人的人。◇ *Children need a caring environment.* 兒童需要一個充滿關懷的環境。◇ (*BrE*) *a **caring profession*** (= a job that involves looking after or helping other people) 護理職業

car·jack·ing /ˈkɑːdʒækɪŋ; *NAmE* ˈkɑːrdʒ-/ *noun* [U, C] the crime of forcing the driver of a car to take you somewhere or give you their car, using threats and violence 劫持汽車（罪）；劫車（罪）➲ compare HIJACKING at HIJACK ▸ **car·jack** *verb* **~ sth** **car·jack·er** *noun*

car·load /ˈkɑːləʊd; *NAmE* ˈkɑːrloʊd/ *noun* the number of people or things that a car is carrying or is able to carry 汽車荷載量

car·mine /ˈkɑːmaɪn; *NAmE* ˈkɑːrm-/ *adj.* (*formal*) dark red in colour 深紅色的；暗紅色的 ▸ **car·mine** *noun* [U]

carn·age /ˈkɑːnɪdʒ; *NAmE* ˈkɑːrn-/ *noun* [U] the violent killing of a large number of people 大屠殺 SYN **slaughter**：*a scene of carnage* 大屠殺的場面

car·nal /ˈkɑːnl; *NAmE* ˈkɑːrnl/ *adj.* [usually before noun] (*formal* or *law* 律) connected with the body or with sex 肉體的；肉慾的；性慾的：***carnal desires/appetites*** 肉慾 ▸ **car·nal·ly** /ˈkɑːnəli; *NAmE* ˈkɑːrn-/ *adv.*

ˌcarnal ˈknowledge *noun* [U] (*old-fashioned* or *law* 律) = SEXUAL INTERCOURSE

car·na·tion /kɑːˈneɪʃn; *NAmE* kɑːrˈn-/ *noun* a white, pink, red or yellow flower, often worn as a decoration on formal occasions 香石竹；康乃馨：*He was wearing a carnation in his buttonhole.* 他在鈕扣眼裏插了一朵康乃馨。➲ VISUAL VOCAB page V11

car·ne·lian /kɑːˈniːliən; *NAmE* kɑːrˈn-/ (also **cor·nel·ian**) *noun* [C, U] a red, brown or white stone, used in jewellery 光玉髓（寶石）

car·ni·val /ˈkɑːnɪvl; *NAmE* ˈkɑːrn-/ *noun* **1** [C, U] a public festival, usually one that happens at a regular time each year, that involves music and dancing in the streets, for which people wear brightly coloured clothes 狂歡節；嘉年華：*There is a local carnival every year.* 當地每年都舉行狂歡節。◇ *the carnival in Rio* 里約熱內盧的狂歡節 ◇ *a carnival atmosphere* 狂歡節的氣氛 **2** [C] (*NAmE*) = FAIR *n.* (1) **3** (*NAmE*) (*BrE* **fete**, **fair**) [C] an outdoor entertainment at which people can play games to win prizes, buy food and drink, etc., usually arranged to make money for a special purpose 露天遊樂會；義賣遊樂會 **4** [sing.] **~ of sth** (*formal*) an exciting or brightly coloured mixture of things 激動人心的事物組合；五彩

繽紛的事物組合：*this summer's carnival of sport* 今年夏季的體育盛會

car·ni·vore /ˈkɑːnɪvɔː(r); *NAmE* ˈkɑːrn-/ *noun* any animal that eats meat 食肉動物 ➲ compare HERBIVORE, INSECTIVORE, OMNIVORE ▸ **car·ni·vor·ous** /kɑːˈnɪvərəs; *NAmE* kɑːrˈn-/ *adj.*：*a carnivorous diet* 多肉的飲食 ➲ compare OMNIVOROUS

carob /ˈkærəb/ (also ˈ**carob tree**) *noun* a southern European tree with dark brown fruit that can be made into a powder that tastes like chocolate 角豆樹（產於南歐，果實可製粉，味道似巧克力）

carol /ˈkærəl/ *noun, verb*
■ *noun* (also ˌ**Christmas** ˈ**carol**) a Christian religious song sung at Christmas 聖誕頌歌
■ *verb* (-ll-, *US* -l-) [I, T] ~ (**sth**) | + **speech** to sing sth in a cheerful way 歡樂地唱

ˈ**carol singing** *noun* [U] the singing of Christmas carols especially in a church or outdoors, often to collect money for charity 聖誕報佳音（尤指在教堂或戶外唱聖誕頌歌）▸ ˈ**carol singer** *noun*

carom /ˈkærəm/ *verb* [I] (*especially NAmE*) to hit a surface and come off it fast at a different angle 撞擊後彈開

car·ot·ene /ˈkærətiːn/ *noun* [U] a red or orange substance found in carrots and other plants 胡蘿蔔素 ➲ see also BETA-CAROTENE

ca·rotid ar·tery /kəˈrɒtɪd ɑːtəri; *NAmE* -ˈrɑːt- ɑːrt-/ *noun* (*anatomy* 解) either of the two large ARTERIES in the neck that carry blood to the head 頸動脈

ca·rouse /kəˈraʊz/ *verb* [I] (*literary*) to spend time drinking alcohol, laughing and enjoying yourself in a noisy way with other people 痛飲狂歡；狂飲作樂

car·ou·sel /ˌkærəˈsel/ *noun* **1** (*especially NAmE*) = MERRY-GO-ROUND (1) ➲ picture at ROUNDABOUT **2** a moving belt from which you collect your bags at an airport（機場的）行李傳送帶

carp /kɑːp; *NAmE* kɑːrp/ *noun, verb*
■ *noun* [C, U] (*pl.* **carp**) a large FRESHWATER fish that is used for food 鯉魚
■ *verb* [I] ~ (**at sb**) (**about sth**) to keep complaining about sb/sth in an annoying way 不停地抱怨；嘮叨

car·pal /ˈkɑːpl; *NAmE* ˈkɑːrpl/ *noun* (*anatomy* 解) any of the eight small bones that form the wrist 腕骨

car·pal tun·nel syn·drome /ˌkɑːpl ˈtʌnl sɪndrəʊm; *NAmE* ˌkɑːrpl ˈtʌnl sɪndroʊm/ *noun* [U] (*medical* 醫) a painful condition of the hand and fingers caused by pressure on a nerve because of repeated movements over a long period 腕管綜合症（手腕長期受力壓迫神經引起手和手指疼痛）

ˈ**car park** *noun* (*BrE*) an area or a building where people can leave their cars 停車場；停車房 ➲ see also GARAGE (1), MULTI-STOREY CAR PARK ➲ compare PARKING LOT

carpe diem /ˌkɑːpeɪ ˈdiːem; ˈdaɪem; *NAmE* ˌkɑːrpeɪ/ *exclamation* (from *Latin*) an expression used when you want to say that sb should not wait, but should take an opportunity as soon as it appears 抓住機遇；把握時機

car·pel /ˈkɑːpl; *NAmE* ˈkɑːrpl/ *noun* (*biology* 生) the part of a plant in which seeds are produced 心皮（植物長出子實的部份）➲ VISUAL VOCAB page V11

car·pen·ter /ˈkɑːpəntə(r); *NAmE* ˈkɑːrp-/ *noun* a person whose job is making and repairing wooden objects and structures 木工；木匠 ➲ compare JOINER (1)

car·pen·try /ˈkɑːpəntri; *NAmE* ˈkɑːrp-/ *noun* [U] **1** the work of a carpenter 木工；木工工藝；木匠活 **2** things made by a carpenter 木工製品；木器；木作

car·pet 🔑 /ˈkɑːpɪt; *NAmE* ˈkɑːrpɪt/ *noun, verb*
■ *noun* **1** 🔑 [U] a thick WOVEN material made of wool, etc. for covering floors or stairs 地毯：*a roll of carpet* 一捲地毯 **2** 🔑 [C] a piece of carpet used as a floor covering, especially when shaped to fit a room（尤指鋪滿房間的一塊）地毯：*to lay a carpet* 鋪地毯 ◇ *a bedroom carpet* 臥室地毯 ◇ (*BrE*) *We have* ***fitted carpets*** (= carpets from wall to wall) *in our house.* 我們家的地上都鋪了地毯。➲ VISUAL VOCAB page V23 ➲ see also CARPETING (1), RED CARPET, RUG (1) **3** [C] ~ (**of sth**) (*literary*) a thick layer of sth on the ground 覆蓋地面的一層厚東西：*a carpet of snow* 一層厚厚的雪
IDM (**be/get called**) **on the** ˈ**carpet** (*informal, especially NAmE*) called to see sb in authority because you have done sth wrong（因做錯事）被上司叫去訓斥：*I got called on the carpet for being late.* 我因為遲到被叫去訓了一頓。➲ more at SWEEP *v.*
■ *verb* [usually passive] **1** ~ **sth** to cover the floor of a room with a carpet 用地毯鋪（房間的）地板：*The hall was carpeted in blue.* 大廳鋪上了藍色的地毯。 **2** ~ **sth** (**with/in sth**) (*literary*) to cover sth with a thick layer of sth 把…厚厚地覆蓋；厚厚地鋪上：*The forest floor was carpeted with wild flowers.* 森林的地面上開滿了野花。 **3** ~ **sb** (*informal, especially BrE*) to speak angrily to sb because they have done sth wrong 訓斥；斥責 **SYN** **reprimand**

ˈ**carpet bag** *noun* a bag used in the past for carrying your things when travelling（舊時的）毛氈旅行包

car·pet·bag·ger /ˈkɑːpɪtbægə(r); *NAmE* ˈkɑːrp-/ *noun* **1** (*disapproving*) a politician who tries to be elected in an area where he or she is not known and is therefore not welcome（在知名度不高的地區參加競選因而不受當地歡迎的）外來政客 **2** a person from the northern states of the US who went to the South after the Civil War in order to make money or get political power（美國內戰後去南方）投機鑽營的北方人

ˈ**carpet-bomb** *verb* **1** ~ **sth** to drop a large number of bombs onto every part of an area 實行地毯式轟炸 **2** ~ **sb** (*business* 商) to send an advertisement to a very large number of people, especially by email（尤指通過電子郵件）廣泛散發廣告 ▸ ˈ**carpet-bombing** *noun* [U]

car·pet·ing /ˈkɑːpɪtɪŋ; *NAmE* ˈkɑːrp-/ *noun* **1** [U] carpets in general or the material used for carpets（統稱）地毯；地毯織料：*new offices with wall-to-wall carpeting* 房內鋪滿地毯的新辦公室 ◇ (*NAmE*) *We need new carpeting* (= a new carpet) *in the living room.* 我們的起居室需要鋪新地毯了。 **2** [C] (*BrE, informal*) an act of speaking angrily to sb because they have done sth wrong 訓斥；斥責

ˈ**carpet slipper** *noun* [usually pl.] (*old-fashioned, BrE*) a type of SLIPPER (= a shoe that you wear in the house), with the upper part made of cloth（布面）室內拖鞋；軟拖鞋

ˈ**carpet sweeper** *noun* a simple machine for cleaning carpets, with a long handle and brushes that go around 地毯清掃器

ˈ**car phone** *noun* a radio telephone for use in a car 車載電話

ˈ**car pool** *noun* **1** a group of car owners who take turns to drive everyone in the group to work, so that only one car is used at a time 合夥用車的一夥人（一群各自都有汽車的人每次輪流開一輛車送大家上班） **2** (*BrE*) (also ˈ**motor pool** *US, BrE*) a group of cars owned by a company or an organization, that its staff can use（公司或機構的）公用車隊

car·pool /ˈkɑːpuːl; *NAmE* ˈkɑːr-/ *verb* [I] if a group of people **carpool**, they travel to work together in one car and divide the cost between them 合夥用車；拼車

car·port /ˈkɑːpɔːt; *NAmE* ˈkɑːrpɔːrt/ *noun* a shelter for a car, usually built beside a house and consisting of a roof supported by posts（沿房搭建的）汽車棚

car·rel /ˈkærəl/ *noun* a small area with a desk, separated from other desks by a dividing wall or screen, where one person can work in a library（圖書館內備有書桌供單人工作用的）研習間

car·riage /ˈkærɪdʒ/ *noun* **1** (also **coach**) (both *BrE*) (*NAmE* **car**) [C] a separate section of a train for carrying passengers（火車的）客車廂：*a railway carriage* 鐵路客車廂 ➲ VISUAL VOCAB page V58 **2** [C] a road vehicle, usually with four wheels, that is pulled by one or more horses and was used in the past to carry people（舊時載客的）四輪馬車：*a horse-drawn carriage* 四輪馬車 **3** (*BrE*) (also **hand·ling** *NAmE, BrE*) [U] (*formal*) the act or cost of transporting goods from one place to another

運輸；運費：*£16.95 including VAT and carriage* * 16.95 英鎊，包含增值稅和運費 **4** [C] a moving part of a machine that supports or moves another part, for example on a TYPEWRITER （打字機等機器上的）滑動托架：*a carriage return* (= the act of starting a new line when typing) 回車 **5** [sing.] (*old-fashioned*) the way in which sb holds and moves their head and body 儀態；舉止 SYN **bearing** ➲ see also BABY CARRIAGE, UNDERCARRIAGE

ˈcarriage clock *noun* a small clock inside a case with a handle on top 帶提手的鐘

ˈcarriage house (*US*) (*BrE* **ˈmews house**) *noun* a house in a row of houses converted from stables (= buildings used to keep horses in) 馬廄改建的房屋

car·riage·way /ˈkærɪdʒweɪ/ *noun* (*BrE*) **1** one of the two sides of a MOTORWAY or other large road, used by traffic moving in the same direction （高速公路等的）車道：*the eastbound carriageway of the M50* * 50 號高速公路的東行車道 ➲ see also DUAL CARRIAGEWAY **2** the part of a road intended for vehicles, not people walking, etc. 車行道；行車道

car·rier /ˈkæriə(r)/ *noun* **1** a company that carries goods or passengers from one place to another, especially by air （尤指經營空運的）運輸公司 **2** a military vehicle or ship that carries soldiers or equipment from one place to another 軍輸車；運輸艦；航空母艦：*an armoured personnel carrier* 裝甲運兵車 ➲ see also AIRCRAFT CARRIER, PEOPLE CARRIER **3** a person or animal that passes a disease to other people or animals but does not suffer from it 帶菌者，病原攜帶者（自身不受感染而傳播疾病的人或動物） **4** a metal frame that is fixed to a bicycle and used for carrying bags （自行車的）載物架 **5** a person or thing that carries sth 搬運人；運送人；運輸工具：*Aquarius, the Water Carrier* 寶瓶座 ◇ *a baby carrier* (= for carrying a baby on your back or in front of you) （用於前胸或後背的）嬰兒背帶 **6** (*BrE*) = CARRIER BAG **7** a company that provides a telephone or Internet service 電話公司；互聯網公司；通信公司：*a telecoms carrier* 通信公司

ˈcarrier bag (also **car·rier**) (both *BrE*) (*NAmE* **ˈshopping bag**) *noun* a paper or plastic bag for carrying shopping （紙或塑料的）購物袋，手提袋 ➲ VISUAL VOCAB page V33

ˈcarrier pigeon *noun* a PIGEON (= a type of bird) that has been trained to carry messages 信鴿

car·rion /ˈkæriən/ *noun* [U] the decaying flesh of dead animals （死動物的）腐肉：*crows feeding on carrion* 以腐肉為食的烏鴉 ➲ VISUAL VOCAB page V12

ˈcarrion crow *noun* a type of medium-sized CROW 小嘴烏鴉

car·rot 🔑 /ˈkærət/ *noun* **1** 🔑 [U, C] a long pointed orange root vegetable 胡蘿蔔：*grated carrot* 擦成絲的胡蘿蔔 ◇ *a pound of carrots* 一磅胡蘿蔔 ➲ VISUAL VOCAB page V31 **2** [C] a reward promised to sb in order to persuade them to do sth （為說服人做事所許諾的）酬報，好處 SYN **incentive**：*They are holding out a carrot of $120 million in economic aid.* 他們許諾給予 1.2 億元的經濟援助。

IDM **the carrot and (the) stick (approach)** if you use **the carrot and stick approach**, you persuade sb to try harder by offering them a reward if they do, or a punishment if they do not 胡蘿蔔加大棒；威逼利誘

car·roty /ˈkærəti/ *adj.* (sometimes *disapproving*) (of hair 頭髮) orange in colour 胡蘿蔔色的；橘紅色的

carry 🔑 /ˈkæri/ *verb* (**car·ries**, **carry·ing**, **car·ried**, **car·ried**)

▸ **TAKE WITH YOU** 帶走 **1** 🔑 [T] **~ sb/sth** to support the weight of sb/sth and take them or it from place to place; to take sb/sth from one place to another 拿；提；搬；扛；背；抱；運送：*He was carrying a suitcase.* 他提着一個手提箱。◇ *She carried her baby in her arms.* 她懷裏抱着她的嬰兒。◇ *The injured were carried away on stretchers.* 傷員用擔架抬走了。◇ *a train carrying commuters to work* 載送人們上班的列車 **2** 🔑 [T] **~ sth** to have sth with you and take it wherever you go 攜帶；佩戴：*Police in many countries carry guns.* 許多國家的警察都帶槍。◇ *I never carry much money on me.* 我身上從不多帶錢。

▸ **OF PIPES/WIRES** 管道；線路 **3** 🔑 [T] **~ sth** to contain and direct the flow of water, electricity, etc. 輸送，傳輸，傳送（水、電等）：*a pipeline carrying oil* 輸油管道 ◇ *The veins carry blood to the heart.* 靜脈把血液輸送到心臟。

▸ **DISEASE** 疾病 **4** [T] **~ sth** if a person, an insect, etc. **carries** a disease, they are infected with it and might spread it to others although they might not become sick themselves 傳播；傳染：*Ticks can carry a nasty disease which affects humans.* 壁虱可傳播危害人類的嚴重疾病。

▸ **REMEMBER** 記憶 **5** [T] **~ sth in your head/mind** to be able to remember sth 能記住；能回想起

▸ **SUPPORT WEIGHT** 承重 **6** [T] **~ sth** to support the weight of sth 支撐；承載：*A road bridge has to carry a lot of traffic.* 公路橋必須承載很多來往車輛。

▸ **RESPONSIBILITY** 責任 **7** [T] **~ sth** to accept responsibility for sth; to suffer the results of sth 承擔（責任）；承受（結果）：*He is carrying the department* (= it is only working because of his efforts). 他維持着這個部門的工作。◇ *Their group was targeted to* ***carry the burden*** *of job losses.* 他們那個小組被選中成為裁員的目標。

▸ **HAVE AS QUALITY/FEATURE** 具有品質／特點 **8** [T] **~ sth** to have sth as a quality or feature 具有（某品質或特點）：*Her speech carried the ring of authority.* 她的講話帶着權威的口吻。◇ *My views don't* ***carry much weight*** *with* (= have much influence on) *the boss.* 我的意見對老闆起不了多少作用。◇ *Each bike carries a ten-year guarantee.* 每輛自行車保修十年。 **9** [T] **~ sth** to have sth as a result 帶有，帶來（某種結果或後果）：*Crimes of violence carry heavy penalties.* 暴力犯罪要受到嚴懲。◇ *Being a combat sport, karate* ***carries with it*** *the risk of injury.* 作為一項格鬥運動，空手道有受傷的風險。

▸ **OF THROW/KICK** 扔；踢 **10** [I] **+ noun + adv./prep.** if sth that is thrown, kicked, etc. **carries** a particular distance, it travels that distance before stopping 扔（或踢等）到…距離：*The fullback's kick carried 50 metres into the crowd.* 後衛一腳把球踢出 50 米遠，落入人群中。

▸ **OF SOUND** 聲音 **11** [I] **(+ adv./prep.)** if a sound **carries**, it can be heard a long distance away 傳得很遠

▸ **TAKE TO PLACE/POSITION** 帶到…地方／位置 **12** [T] **~ sth/sb to/into sth** to take sth/sb to a particular point or in a particular direction 向…前進；推進到：*The war was carried into enemy territory.* 戰爭已推進到敵方境內。◇ *Her abilities carried her to the top of her profession.* 她的才能使她在其從事的行業中出類拔萃。

▸ **APPROVAL/SUPPORT** 贊成；支持 **13** [T, usually passive] **~ sth** to approve of sth by more people voting for it than against it （以多數票）獲得通過：*The resolution was carried by 340 votes to 210.* 這項決議以 340 票對 210 票獲得通過。 **14** [T] to win the support or sympathy of sb; to persuade people to accept your argument 贏得…支持（或同情）；勸說…接受論點：**~ sb** *His moving speech was enough to carry the audience.* 他感人的演講足以贏得聽眾的支持。◇ **~ sth** *She nodded in agreement, and he saw he had carried his point.* 她同意地點點頭，他明白他的話已收到效果。

▸ **HAVE LABEL** 有標籤 **15** [T] **~ sth** to have a particular label or piece of information attached 貼有（標籤）；附有（信息）：*Cigarettes carry a health warning.* 香煙上標註着有害健康的警告。

▸ **NEWS STORY** 新聞報道 **16** [T] **~ sth** if a newspaper or broadcast **carries** a particular story, it publishes or broadcasts it 刊登；登載；播出；報道

▸ **ITEM IN STORE** 商店商品 **17** [T] **~ sth** if a shop/store **carries** a particular item, it has it for sale 銷售；出售：*We* ***carry a range*** *of educational software.* 我們出售各種教育軟件。

▸ **BABY** 嬰兒 **18** [T] **be carrying sb** to be pregnant with sb 懷孕；懷胎：*She was carrying twins.* 她懷上了雙胞胎。

▸ **YOURSELF** 自己 **19** [T] **~ yourself + adv./prep.** to hold or move your head or body in a particular way 保持姿態；做姿勢：*to carry yourself well* 姿勢正確

▸ **ADDING NUMBERS** 加法 **20** [T] **~ sth** to add a number to the next column on the left when adding up numbers, for example when the numbers add up to more than ten 進位

IDM **be/get carried a'way** to get very excited or lose control of your feelings 變得很激動；失去自制力：*I got carried away and started shouting at the television.* 我激動得不能自持，衝着電視機大叫起來。 **carry all/everything be'fore you** to be completely successful 全勝；大獲成功 **carry the 'ball** (*US, informal*) to take responsibility for getting sth done 承擔責任：*My co-worker was sick, so I had to carry the ball.* 我的搭檔病了，所以我得負起全責。 **carry the 'can (for sb/sth)** (*BrE, informal*) to accept the blame for sth, especially when it is not your fault 承受責難；（尤指）代人受過，背黑鍋 **carry a torch for sb** to be in love with sb, especially sb who does not love you in return 愛上；（尤指）單相思，痴戀 ➲ more at DAY, FAR *adv.*, FAST *adv.*, FETCH

PHR V **,carry sb 'back (to sth)** to make sb remember a time in the past 使回想起；使回憶：*The smell of the sea carried her back to her childhood.* 大海的氣息勾起了她童年的回憶。 **,carry sth↔'forward** (also **,carry sth↔'over**) to move a total amount from one column or page to the next 把總金額轉入次欄（或次頁）；過賬；結轉 **,carry sth↔'off 1** to win sth 贏得；獲得：*He carried off most of the prizes.* 他贏得了大多數的獎項。 **2** to succeed in doing sth that most people would find difficult 成功地對付，不費勁地處理（大多數人認為難以應付的事）：*She's had her hair cut really short, but she can* ***carry it off****.* 她把頭髮剪得非常短，但她還是能撐得起這種髮型。 **,carry 'on 1** 🔑 (*especially BrE*) to continue moving 繼續移動：*Carry on until you get to the junction, then turn left.* 繼續往前走到交叉路口，然後向左轉。 **2** (*informal*) to argue or complain noisily 爭吵；吵鬧；吵鬧地抱怨：*He was shouting and carrying on.* 他在大吵大鬧。 ➲ related noun CARRY-ON **,carry 'on (with sth) | ,carry sth↔'on** 🔑 to continue doing sth 繼續做；堅持幹：*Carry on with your work while I'm away.* 我不在時你要接着幹。◇ *After he left I just tried to carry on as normal* (= do the things I usually do). 他離開後，我只管盡力像往常一樣繼續幹。◇ *Carry on the good work!* 幹得不錯，繼續努力吧！◇ **~ doing sth** *He carried on peeling the potatoes.* 他不停地削土豆皮。 **,carry 'on (with sb)** (*old-fashioned*) to have a sexual relationship with sb when you should not （與…）有不正當的男女關係：*His wife found out he'd been carrying on with another woman.* 他的妻子發現他和另一個女人勾勾搭搭。 **,carry sth↔'out 1** 🔑 to do sth that you have said you will do or have been asked to do 履行；實施；執行；落實：*to carry out a promise/a threat/a plan/an order* 把承諾／威脅／計劃／命令付諸行動 **2** 🔑 to do and complete a task 完成（任務）：*to carry out an inquiry/an investigation/a survey* 進行查詢／調查／考察 ◇ *Extensive tests have been carried out on the patient.* 已對患者進行了全面檢查。 **,carry 'over** to continue to exist in a different situation （在不同情況下）繼續存在，保持下去：*Attitudes learned at home carry over into the playground.* 家裏養成的作風會表現在學校的運動場上。 **,carry sth↔'over 1** to keep sth from one situation and use it or deal with it in a different situation 運用；應用 **2** to delay sth until a later time 延遲；延期：*The match had to be carried over until Sunday.* 比賽不得不推遲到星期天。 **3** = CARRY STH FORWARD **,carry sb 'through | ,carry sb 'through sth** to help sb to survive a difficult period 幫助…渡過難關：*His determination carried him through the ordeal.* 他靠堅強的信心渡過了難關。 **,carry sth 'through** to complete sth successfully 成功完成；順利實現：*It's a difficult job but she's the person to carry it through.* 這是一項艱巨的工作，但她這個人是能夠順利完成的。 **,carry 'through (on/with sth)** (*NAmE*) to do what you have said you will do 履行（承諾）：*He has proved he can carry through on his promises.* 他已證明他能履行自己的諾言。

carry·cot /ˈkærikɒt; *NAmE* -kɑːt/ *noun* (*BrE*) a small bed for a baby, with handles at the sides so you can carry it 手提式嬰兒牀 ➲ picture at PUSHCHAIR

'carry-on *noun* **1** [usually sing.] (*BrE, informal*) a display of excitement, anger or silly behaviour over sth unimportant （對小事的）大驚小怪，歇斯底里發作，愚蠢的舉動：*What a carry-on!* 真是大驚小怪！ **2** (*NAmE*) a small bag or case that you carry onto a plane with you （可隨身攜帶上飛機的）小包，小行李箱：*Only one carry-on is allowed.* 隨身只能攜帶一個小包。◇ *carry-on baggage* 隨身攜帶的行李

'carry-out *noun* (*US, ScotE*) = TAKEAWAY：*Let's get a carry-out.* 咱們叫份外賣吧。◇ *carry-out coffees* 外賣咖啡

'carry-over *noun* **1** [usually sing.] something that remains or results from a situation in the past 保存的事物；遺留下的東西；影響；結果：*His neatness is a carry-over from his army days.* 他愛整潔的習慣是他當兵時養成的。 **2** an amount of money that has not been used and so can be used later 結轉下期的款項：*The £20 million included a £7 million carry-over from last year's underspend.* 這筆 2 000 萬英鎊的款項包括了去年結轉的 700 萬英鎊。

'car seat *noun* **1** (also **'child seat**) a special safety seat for a child, that can be fitted into a car （可安裝在汽車上的）兒童安全座椅 **2** a seat in a car 汽車座位

car·sick /ˈkɑːsɪk; *NAmE* ˈkɑːrsɪk/ *adj.* [not usually before noun] feeling ill/sick because you are travelling in a car 暈車：*Do you get carsick?* 你暈車嗎？ ▶ **car·sick·ness** *noun* [U]

cart /kɑːt; *NAmE* kɑːrt/ *noun, verb*

■ *noun* **1** a vehicle with two or four wheels that is pulled by a horse and used for carrying loads （兩輪或四輪）運貨馬車：*a horse and cart* 一套馬車 **2** (also **hand·cart**) a light vehicle with wheels that you pull or push by hand 手推車；手拉車 **3** (*NAmE*) (*BrE* **trol·ley**) a small vehicle with wheels that can be pushed or pulled along and is used for carrying things 手推車；手拉車：*a* ***shopping/baggage cart*** 購物車；行李車◇ *a serving cart* 上菜手推車 **4** (*NAmE*) (*BrE* **buggy**) a small car, often without a roof or doors, used for a particular purpose （常指無頂無門的）專用小汽車：*a golf cart* 高爾夫球車

IDM **put the ,cart before the 'horse** to put or do things in the wrong order 本末倒置；因果倒置

■ *verb* **1 ~ sth (+ adv./prep.)** to carry sth in a cart or other vehicle 用馬車運送；用車裝運：*The rubbish is then carted away for recycling.* 垃圾接着被運去作回收處理。 **2 ~ sth + adv./prep.** (*informal*) to carry sth that is large, heavy or awkward in your hands 用手提（笨重物品）：*We had to cart our luggage up six flights of stairs.* 我們得把行李提着上六段樓梯。 **3 ~ sb + adv./prep.** (*informal*) to take sb somewhere, especially with difficulty 強行帶走；抓走：*The demonstrators were carted off to the local police station.* 示威遊行者被強行帶到當地的警察局。

carte blanche /ˌkɑːt ˈblɑːnʃ; *NAmE* ˌkɑːrt/ *noun* [U] (from *French*) **~ (to do sth)** the complete freedom or authority to do whatever you like 自由行使權；全權

car·tel /kɑːˈtel; *NAmE* kɑːrˈtel/ *noun* [C+sing./pl. v.] a group of separate companies that agree to increase profits by fixing prices and not competing with each other 卡特爾，企業聯盟（通過統一價格、防止競爭來增加共同利潤）

Car·te·sian /kɑːˈtiːziən; -ʒən; *NAmE* kɑːrˈt-/ *adj.* connected with the French PHILOSOPHER Descartes and his ideas about philosophy and mathematics （法國哲學家和數學家）笛卡兒的；笛卡兒主義的

cart·horse /ˈkɑːthɔːs; *NAmE* ˈkɑːrthɔːrs/ *noun* a large strong horse used especially in the past for heavy work on farms （尤指舊時在農場幹重活的）強壯高大的馬

car·til·age /ˈkɑːtɪlɪdʒ; *NAmE* ˈkɑːrt-/ *noun* [U, C] the strong white TISSUE that is important in support and especially in joints to prevent the bones rubbing against each other 軟骨 ➲ VISUAL VOCAB page V59

car·ti·la·gin·ous /ˌkɑːtɪˈlædʒɪnəs; *NAmE* ˌkɑːrt-/ *adj.* (*anatomy* 解) made of cartilage 軟骨的；軟骨性的

cart·load /ˈkɑːtləʊd; *NAmE* ˈkɑːrtloʊd/ *noun* **1** the amount of sth that fills a CART 一大車的裝載量 **2** [usually pl.] (*informal*) a large amount of sth 大量；大批

car·tog·raph·er /kɑːˈtɒɡrəfə(r); *NAmE* kɑːrˈtɑːɡ-/ *noun* a person who draws or makes maps 製圖員；地圖繪製員

C

car·tog·raphy /kɑːˈtɒɡrəfi; *NAmE* kɑːrˈtɑːɡ-/ *noun* [U] the art or process of drawing or making maps 製圖學；地圖繪製 ▸ **carto·graph·ic** /ˌkɑːtəˈɡræfɪk; *NAmE* ˌkɑːrt-/ *adj.*

car·ton /ˈkɑːtn; *NAmE* ˈkɑːrtn/ *noun* **1** a light cardboard or plastic box or pot for holding goods, especially food or liquid; the contents of a carton （尤指裝食品或液體的）硬紙盒，塑料盒，塑料罐；硬紙盒（或塑料盒）所裝物品：*a milk carton/a carton of milk* 牛奶盒；一盒牛奶 ➲ VISUAL VOCAB page V33 **2** (*NAmE*) a large container in which goods are packed in smaller containers （內裝小盒的）大包裝盒：*a carton of cigarettes* 一條香煙 ➲ VISUAL VOCAB page V33

car·toon /kɑːˈtuːn; *NAmE* kɑːrˈt-/ *noun* **1** an amusing drawing in a newspaper or magazine, especially one about politics or events in the news（報刊中尤與政治或時事有關的）漫畫，諷刺畫 ➲ WRITING TUTOR page WT34 **2** = COMIC STRIP **3** (also ˌ**animated carˈtoon**) a film/movie made by photographing a series of gradually changing drawings or models, so that they look as if they are moving 動畫片；卡通片：*a Walt Disney cartoon* 迪斯尼動畫片 ◇ *a cartoon character* 動畫片人物 **4** (*technical* 術語) a drawing made by an artist as a preparation for a painting 草圖；底圖

car·toon·ist /kɑːˈtuːnɪst; *NAmE* kɑːrˈt-/ *noun* a person who draws cartoons 漫畫家；動畫片畫家

car·touche /kɑːˈtuːʃ; *NAmE* kɑːr-/ *noun* an OBLONG or OVAL shape which contains a set of ancient Egyptian HIEROGLYPHS, often representing the name and title of a king or queen（常印有古埃及國王或王后名號的）象形文字長方形（或橢圓）圖形

cart·ridge /ˈkɑːtrɪdʒ; *NAmE* ˈkɑːrt-/ *noun* **1** (*NAmE* also **shell**) a tube or case containing EXPLOSIVE and a bullet or SHOT, for shooting from a gun 彈藥筒；彈夾 **2** a case containing sth that is used in a machine, for example film for a camera, ink for a printer, etc. Cartridges are put into the machine and can be removed and replaced when they are finished or empty. 膠片盒；暗盒；墨盒 **3** a thin tube containing ink which you put inside a pen （鋼筆的）筆芯，墨水囊

ˈ**cartridge paper** *noun* [U] (*BrE*) thick strong paper for drawing on 繪畫紙；圖畫紙

ˈ**cart track** *noun* (*BrE*) a rough track that is not suitable for ordinary cars, etc. （崎嶇不平的）馬車道，大車道

cart·wheel /ˈkɑːtwiːl; *NAmE* ˈkɑːrt-/ *noun* **1** a fast physical movement in which you turn in a circle sideways by putting your hands on the ground and bringing your legs, one at a time, over your head 側手翻；側身筋斗：*to* **do/turn cartwheels** 做側手翻 **2** the wheel of a CART （馬車或手推車）車輪 ▸ **cart·wheel** *verb* [I]

carve /kɑːv; *NAmE* kɑːrv/ *verb* **1** [T, I] to make objects, patterns, etc. by cutting away material from wood or stone 雕刻：**~ sth** *a carved doorway* 雕花的門道 ◇ **~ sth from/out of sth** *The statue was carved out of a single piece of stone.* 這座雕像是用整塊石料雕成的。◇ **~ sth into/in sth** *The wood had been carved into the shape of a flower.* 木頭雕成了花朵狀。◇ **~ in sth** *She carves in both stone and wood.* 她既做石雕也做木雕。➲ COLLOCATIONS at ART **2** [T] **~ sth** (**on sth**) to write sth on a surface by cutting into it 刻：*They carved their initials on the desk.* 他們把自己姓名的首字母刻在書桌上。 **3** [T, I] **~ (sth)** | **~ (sb) sth** to cut a large piece of cooked meat into smaller pieces for eating 把（熟肉）切成塊：*Who's going to carve the turkey?* 誰來把火雞切成小塊？ **4** [T, no passive] to work hard in order to have a successful career, reputation, etc. 艱苦創業；奮鬥取得（事業、名聲等）：**~ sth (out)** *He succeeded in carving out a career in the media.* 他在傳媒界闖出了一片天地。◇ **~ sth (out) for yourself** *She has carved a place for herself in the fashion world.* 她已在時裝界謀得一席之地。 IDM see STONE *n.*

PHR V ˌ**carve sth↔ˈup** (*disapproving*) to divide a company, an area of land, etc. into smaller parts in order to share it between people 劃分；瓜分

car·very /ˈkɑːvəri; *NAmE* ˈkɑːrv-/ *noun* (*pl.* **-ies**) (*BrE*) a restaurant that serves ROAST meat 烤肉餐館

ˈ**carve-up** *noun* [sing.] (*BrE, informal*) the dividing of sth such as a company or a country into separate parts 劃分；瓜分

carv·ing /ˈkɑːvɪŋ; *NAmE* ˈkɑːrvɪŋ/ *noun* **1** [C, U] an object or a pattern made by cutting away material from wood or stone 雕刻品；雕刻圖案；雕像 **2** [U] the art of making objects in this way 雕刻術 ➲ VISUAL VOCAB page V41

ˈ**carving knife** *noun* a large sharp knife for cutting cooked meat 切（熟）肉刀 ➲ VISUAL VOCAB page V26

ˈ**car wash** *noun* a place with special equipment, where you can pay to have your car washed 洗車處；洗車場

cary·atid /ˌkæriˈætɪd/ *noun* (*architecture* 建) a statue of a female figure used as a supporting PILLAR in a building 女像柱

Casa·nova /ˌkæsəˈnəʊvə; ˌkæzə-; *NAmE* -ˈnoʊvə/ *noun* a man who has sex with a lot of women 浪蕩公子；風流浪子 ORIGIN From Giovanni Jacopo Casanova, an Italian man in the 18th century who was famous for having sex with many women. 源自卡薩諾瓦（Giovanni Jacopo Casanova）。這名 18 世紀的意大利人以放蕩不羈的生活而聞名。

cas·bah = KASBAH

cas·cade /kæˈskeɪd/ *noun, verb*

▪ ***noun*** **1** a small WATERFALL, especially one of several falling down a steep slope with rocks 小瀑布（尤指一連串瀑布中的一支） **2** a large amount of water falling or pouring down 傾瀉；流注：*a cascade of rainwater* 如注的雨水 **3** (*formal*) a large amount of sth hanging down 大簇的下垂物：*Her hair tumbled in a cascade down her back.* 她的長髮瀑布般地傾瀉在後背上。 **4** (*formal*) a large number of things falling or coming quickly at the same time 傾瀉（或湧出）的東西：*He crashed to the ground in a cascade of oil cans.* 他隨着一連串的油桶跌落墜地。

▪ ***verb*** **1** [I] **+ adv./prep.** to flow downwards in large amounts 傾瀉；流注：*Water cascaded down the mountainside.* 水從山腰傾瀉而下。 **2** [I] **+ adv./prep.** (*formal*) to fall or hang in large amounts 大量落下；大量垂懸：*Blonde hair cascaded over her shoulders.* 她的金髮像瀑布似的披落在肩頭。

case 0➡ /keɪs/ *noun, verb*

▪ ***noun***

▸ SITUATION 情況 **1** 0➡ [C] a particular situation or a situation of a particular type 具體情況；事例；實例：*In some cases people have had to wait several weeks for an appointment.* 在某些情況下，人們必須等上好幾週才能得到約見。◇ *The company only dismisses its employees in cases of gross misconduct.* 這家公司只有在雇員嚴重瀆職時才予以解聘。◇ *It's a* ***classic case*** (= a very typical case) *of bad planning.* 這是計劃不當的一個典型事例。➲ see also WORST-CASE ➲ SYNONYMS at EXAMPLE **2** 0➡ **the case** [sing.] **~ (that ...)** the true situation 實情；事實：*If that is the case* (= if the situation described is true), *we need more staff.* 如果真是那樣，那我們就需要更多的員工了。◇ *It is simply not the case that prison conditions are improving.* 監獄條件得到改善的情況絕非事實。➲ SYNONYMS at SITUATION **3** 0➡ [C, usually sing.] a situation that relates to a particular person or thing 特殊情況：*In your case, we are prepared to be lenient.* 根據你的情況，我們可以從寬處理。◇ *I cannot make an exception in your case* (= for you and not for others). 我不能對你破例。◇ *Every application will be decided* ***on a case-by-case basis*** (= each one will be considered separately). 各項申請將根據情況逐一審定。➲ SYNONYMS at EXAMPLE

▸ POLICE INVESTIGATION 警方調查 **4** 0➡ [C] a matter that is being officially investigated, especially by the police （尤指警方）偵查的案情，調查的案件：*a murder case* 謀殺案 ◇ *a case of theft* 盜竊案 ➲ COLLOCATIONS at CRIME

▸ IN COURT 法院 **5** 0➡ [C] a question to be decided in court 待裁決的案件：*The case will be heard next week.* 此案下週審理。◇ *a court case* 訴訟案件 ◇ *to* ***win/lose a case*** 勝 / 敗訴 ➲ see also TEST CASE

▸ ARGUMENTS 論據 **6** 0➡ [C, usually sing.] **~ (for/against sth)** a set of facts or arguments that support one side in a trial, a discussion, etc. （在審判、討論等中支持一方的）論據，理由：*the case for the defence/prosecution* 有利

於被告／原告的論據◇ *Our lawyer didn't think we* **had a case** (= had enough good arguments to win in a court of law). 我們的律師認為我們論據不足，無法贏得官司。◇ *the* **case for/against** *private education* 贊成／反對實行私立學校教育的理由◇ *The report* **makes out a** *strong* **case** (= gives good arguments) *for spending more money on hospitals.* 報告充分闡明了增加醫院經費的理由。◇ *You will each be given the chance to* **state** *your* **case**. 你們每人都有機會陳述理由。

▸ **CONTAINER 容器** **7** 🔑 [C] (often in compounds 常構成複合詞) a container or covering used to protect or store things; a container with its contents or the amount that it contains 容器；箱；盒；套；罩；容器及內裝物；（容器的）容量： *a pencil case* 鉛筆盒◇ *a jewellery case* 首飾盒◇ *a packing case* (= a large wooden box for packing things in) 包裝箱◇ *The museum was full of stuffed animals in glass cases.* 博物館的玻璃櫃裏擺滿了動物標本。◇ *a case* (= 12 bottles) *of champagne* 一箱（12 瓶）香檳酒 ➲ picture at CLOCK ➲ see also VANITY CASE **8** 🔑 [C] = SUITCASE： *Let me carry your case for you.* 我來幫你提箱子吧。

▸ **OF DISEASE 疾病** **9** 🔑 [C] the fact of sb having a disease or an injury; a person suffering from a disease or an injury 病例；病案；病人；傷員： *a severe case of typhoid* 傷寒重病例◇ *The most serious cases were treated at the scene of the accident.* 受傷最嚴重的人在事故現場就得到了救治。

▸ **PERSON 人** **10** [C] a person who needs, or is thought to need, special treatment or attention （需特別對待或注意的）人： *He's a hopeless case.* 他是無可救藥了。

▸ **GRAMMAR 語法** **11** [C, U] the form of a noun, an adjective or a pronoun in some languages, that shows its relationship to another word 格（某些語言中表示名詞、形容詞或代詞與另一詞關係的形式）： *the* **nominative/accusative/genitive case** 主格；賓格；所有格◇ *Latin nouns have case, number and gender.* 拉丁語名詞有格、數和性。

IDM **as the ˌcase may ˈbe** used to say that one of two or more possibilities is true, but which one is true depends on the circumstances 根據具體情況；視情況而定： *There may be an announcement about this tomorrow—or not, as the case may be.* 這件事明天可能有個聲明，也可能沒有，那要看情況了。 **be on sb's ˈcase** (*informal*) to criticize sb all the time 不停地指責某人： *She's always on my case about cleaning my room.* 她老是對我的房間需要打掃的事指責個沒完。 **be on the ˈcase** to be dealing with a particular matter, especially a criminal investigation 處理事件（尤指刑事偵查）： *We have two agents on the case.* 我們有兩名探員在偵察此案。 **get off my ˈcase** (*informal*) used to tell sb to stop criticizing you 別再批評我 **a case in ˈpoint** a clear example of the problem, situation, etc. that is being discussed 明證；恰當的例證 ➲ LANGUAGE BANK at E.G. **in ˈany case** 🔑 whatever happens or may have happened 無論如何；不管怎樣： *There's no point complaining now—we're leaving tomorrow in any case.* 現在抱怨毫無意義，反正我們明天就要離開了。 **(just) in case (...)** 🔑 because of the possibility of sth happening 以防；以防萬一： *You'd better take the keys in case I'm out.* 你最好帶上鑰匙以防我不在家。◇ *You probably won't need to call—but take my number, just in case.* 你很可能無需打電話，不過還是記下我的電話號碼吧，以防萬一。◇ *In case* (= if it is true that) *you're wondering why Jo's here—let me explain ...* 我來解釋一下吧，免得你奇怪喬為什麼在這兒。 **in case of sth** 🔑 (often on official notices 常用於正式通知) if sth happens 如果；假使： *In case of fire, ring the alarm bell.* 如遇火警，即按警鈴。 **in ˈthat case** 🔑 if that happens or has happened; if that is the situation 既然那樣；假使那樣的話： *'I've made up my mind.' 'In that case, there's no point discussing it.'* "我已經拿定主意。""既然如此，討論這件事就毫無意義了。" ➲ more at DOG *n.*, REST *v.*

■ ***verb***

IDM **case the joint** (*informal*) to look carefully around a building so that you can plan how to steal things from it at a later time （為日後行竊）踩點，踩道，探路

case·book /ˈkeɪsbʊk/ *noun* a written record kept by doctors, lawyers, etc. of cases they have dealt with （醫生、律師等保存的）書面記錄，病歷，案卷

cased /keɪst/ *adj.* **~ in sth** completely covered with a particular material 用…完全覆蓋的： *The towers are made of steel cased in granite.* 這些塔樓是鋼結構，花崗岩貼面。 ➲ see also CASING

ˌcase ˈhistory *noun* a record of a person's background, past illnesses, etc. that a doctor or SOCIAL WORKER studies （醫生用的）病歷；（社會工作者用的）個案史

ˈcase law *noun* [U] (*law* 律) law based on decisions made by judges in earlier cases 判例法，案例法（以已往的判例為依據的法律） ➲ compare COMMON LAW, STATUTE LAW ➲ see also TEST CASE

case·load /ˈkeɪsləʊd; *NAmE* -loʊd/ *noun* all the people that a doctor, SOCIAL WORKER, etc. is responsible for at one time （醫生、社會工作者等的）個案總量，工作量： *a heavy caseload* (= a large number of people) 龐大的個案量

case·ment /ˈkeɪsmənt/ (also **ˌcasement ˈwindow**) *noun* a window that opens on HINGES like a door 平開窗；豎鉸鏈窗；門式窗 ➲ VISUAL VOCAB page V17

ˌcase-ˈsensitive *adj.* (*computing* 計) a program which is **case-sensitive** recognizes the difference between capital letters and small letters （程序）能識別大小寫字母的，區分大小寫的

ˈcase study *noun* a detailed account of the development of a person, a group of people or a situation over a period of time 個案研究；專題研究；案例研究

case·work /ˈkeɪswɜːk; *NAmE* -wɜːrk/ *noun* [U] social work (= work done to help people in the community with special needs) involving the study of a particular person's family and background 社會工作（指幫助社區特殊困難者）

case·work·er /ˈkeɪswɜːkə(r); *NAmE* -wɜːrk-/ *noun* (*especially NAmE*) a SOCIAL WORKER who helps a particular person or family in the community with special needs 社會工作者（幫助社區特殊困難者）

cash 🔑 /kæʃ/ *noun, verb*

■ ***noun*** [U] **1** 🔑 money in the form of coins or notes/bills 現金： *How much cash do you have on you?* 你身上帶着多少現金？◇ *Payments can be made by cheque or* **in cash**. 支票或現金付款均可。◇ *Customers are offered a 10% discount if they* **pay cash**. 顧客若付現金，可獲九折優惠。◇ *The thieves stole £500* **in cash**. 小偷盜走 500 英鎊現金。 ➲ COLLOCATIONS at FINANCE ➲ picture at MONEY ➲ see also HARD CASH, PETTY CASH ➲ SYNONYMS at MONEY **2** 🔑 (*informal*) money in any form（任何形式的）金錢，資金： *The museum needs to find ways of raising cash.* 博物館需要找到募集資金的途徑。◇ *I'm short of cash right now.* 我眼下正缺錢。◇ *I'm constantly* **strapped for cash** (= without enough money). 我總是缺錢。

IDM **cash ˈdown** (*BrE*) (also **ˌcash up ˈfront** *NAmE, BrE*) with immediate payment of cash 即付現款；即期付款： *to pay for sth cash down* 用現款支付 **ˌcash in ˈhand** (*BrE, informal*) if you pay for goods and services **cash in hand**, you pay in cash, especially so that the person being paid can avoid paying tax on the amount 現金支付（尤指受款人可避税） **ˌcash on deˈlivery** (*abbr.* **COD**) a system of paying for goods when they are delivered 貨到付款；交貨付現

■ ***verb*** **~ a cheque/check** to exchange a cheque/check for the amount of money that it is worth 兑現支票

IDM **cash in your ˈchips** (*informal*) to die 死

PHR V **ˌcash ˈin (on sth)** (*disapproving*) to gain an advantage for yourself from a situation, especially in a way that other people think is wrong or immoral 從中牟利；撈到好處： *The film studio is being accused of cashing in on the singer's death.* 那家電影製片廠被指責利用這位歌手的死來賺錢。 **ˌcash sth↔ˈin** to exchange sth, such as an insurance policy, for money before the date on which it would normally end 把（保險單等）提前兑成現金 **ˌcash ˈup** (*BrE*) (*NAmE* **ˌcash ˈout**) to add up the amount of money that has been received in a shop/store, club, etc., especially at the end of the day（商店、俱樂部等在每天營業結束時）結算當日進款

C

ˌcash and ˈcarry *noun* [C, U] a large WHOLESALE shop/store that sells goods in large quantities at low prices to customers from other businesses who pay in cash and take the goods away themselves; the system of buying and selling goods in this way 現款自運批發商店；付現自運批發

cash·back (*BrE*) (*US* **cash-back**) /ˈkæʃbæk/ *noun* **1** [U] if you ask for **cashback** when you are paying for goods in a shop/store with a DEBIT CARD (= a plastic card that takes money directly from your bank account), you get a sum of money in cash, that is added to your bill 現金提取（指借記卡持有者可在商店刷卡付賬時提取小額現金，此現金附加在購物賬單上）**2** [U, C] a sum of money that is offered to people who buy particular products or services （購買某些特定商品或支付某些特定服務費時的）現金返還，現金折扣：*There's £200 cashback on this computer if you buy before January 31.* 在 1 月 31 日前購買這台電腦可獲得 200 英鎊的現金返還。

ˈcash bar *noun* a bar at a wedding, party, etc., at which the guests have to pay for their own drinks rather than getting them free （婚禮、聚會等場合的）售飲料櫃枱

ˈcash box *noun* a box with a lock for keeping money in, usually made of metal 錢箱；銀箱

ˈcash card *noun* (*BrE*) (*US* **ATˈM card**) a plastic card used to get money from a CASH MACHINE (= a machine in or outside a bank) 現金卡；自動取款卡 ➲ compare CHEQUE CARD, CREDIT CARD, DEBIT CARD

ˈcash cow *noun* (*business* 商) the part of a business that always makes a profit and that provides money for the rest of the business 金牛（指持續獲得利潤，為其他業務提供資金的業務或產品）

ˈcash crop *noun* a crop grown for selling, rather than for use by the person who grows it 商品作物；經濟作物 ➲ compare SUBSISTENCE

ˈcash desk *noun* (*BrE*) the place in a shop/store where you pay for goods that you have bought 收款處；收銀枱

ˈcash dispenser *noun* (*BrE*) = CASH MACHINE

ˌcashed ˈup *adj.* (*informal*, *especially AustralE*) very rich 有大把錢的；富得流油的：*Mark was cashed up that night, so he got the drinks.* 馬克那天晚上有一大筆錢，所以酒都歸他買了。◇ *support from cashed-up investors* 腰纏萬貫的投資者的資助

cashew /ˈkæʃuː; kæˈʃuː/ (also **ˈcashew nut**) *noun* the small curved nut of the tropical American **cashew tree**, used in cooking and often eaten salted with alcoholic drinks 腰果（產於美洲熱帶，用於烹飪，常鹽漬後佐酒）➲ VISUAL VOCAB page V32

ˈcash flow *noun* [C, U] the movement of money into and out of a business as goods are bought and sold （隨貨物買賣而產生的）現金流，資金流動：*a healthy cash flow* (= having enough money to make payments when necessary) 良好的資金週轉狀況 ◇ *cash-flow problems* 資金週轉問題

cash·ier /kæˈʃɪə(r); *NAmE* -ˈʃɪr/ *noun*, *verb*

■ ***noun*** a person whose job is to receive and pay out money in a bank, shop/store, hotel, etc. 出納員

■ ***verb*** [usually passive] **~ sb** to make sb leave the army, navy, etc. because they have done sth wrong 開除…的軍職

cash·less /ˈkæʃləs/ *adj.* done or working without using cash 不用現金的：*We are moving towards the cashless society.* 我們正在向不用現鈔的社會發展。

ˈcash machine (*BrE* also **ˈcash dispenser**, **ˈcash-point™**) (also **ATM** *NAmE*, *BrE*) (also **ABM** *CanE*) *noun* a machine in or outside a bank, etc., from which you can get money from your bank account using a special plastic card 自動取款機 ➲ COLLOCATIONS at FINANCE

cash·mere /ˈkæʃmɪə(r); ˌkæʃˈm-; *NAmE* ˈkæʒmɪr; ˈkæʃ-/ *noun* [U] fine soft wool made from the long hair of a type of GOAT, used especially for making expensive clothes （山羊絨）開司米；山羊絨；喀什米爾羊毛

ˈcash register (*BrE* also **till**) (*NAmE* also **regis·ter**) *noun* a machine used in shops/stores, restaurants, etc. that has a drawer for keeping money in, and that shows and records the amount of money received for each thing that is sold 現金收入記錄機；現金出納機

ˈcash-starved *adj.* [only before noun] without enough money, usually because another organization, such as the government, has failed to provide it 資金不足的（尤指因政府等未能提供資金）：*cash-starved public services* 資金匱乏的公共事業

ˈcash-strapped *adj.* [only before noun] without enough money 資金短缺的：***cash-strapped governments/shoppers*** 缺資金的政府；缺錢的購物者

cas·ing /ˈkeɪsɪŋ/ *noun* [C, U] a covering that protects sth 箱；盒；套；罩

ca·sino /kəˈsiːnəʊ; *NAmE* -noʊ/ *noun* (*pl.* **-os**) a public building or room where people play gambling games for money 賭場

cask /kɑːsk; *NAmE* kæsk/ *noun* a small wooden BARREL used for storing liquids, especially alcoholic drinks; the amount contained in a cask 小木桶；酒桶；一桶（的量）：*a wine cask/a cask of wine* 酒桶；一桶酒

cas·ket /ˈkɑːskɪt; *NAmE* ˈkæs-/ *noun* **1** a small decorated box for holding jewellery or other valuable things, especially in the past （尤指舊時放珠寶等貴重物品的）精緻小盒，裝飾精美的小箱 **2** (*NAmE*) (also **coffin** especially in *BrE*) a box in which a dead body is buried or CREMATED 棺材；棺槨；棺木；靈柩

Cas·san·dra /kəˈsændrə/ *noun* a person who predicts that sth bad will happen, especially a person who is not believed （尤指無人相信的）凶事預言者 **ORIGIN** From the name of a princess in ancient Greek stories to whom Apollo gave the ability to predict the future. After she tricked him, he stopped people from believing her. 源自古希臘神話中一位公主的名字，阿波羅神給她預言能力，她違背諾言後阿波羅神使人不信她的預言。

cas·sava /kəˈsɑːvə/ (also **man·ioc**) *noun* [U] **1** a tropical plant with many branches and long roots that you can eat 木薯（熱帶植物，多枝長根，可食用）**2** the roots of this plant, which can be boiled, fried, ROASTED or made into flour 木薯塊根（可製成木薯粉）

cas·ser·ole /ˈkæsərəʊl; *NAmE* -roʊl/ *noun* **1** [C, U] a hot dish made with meat, vegetables, etc. that are cooked slowly in liquid in an oven 燉燒菜，燉鍋菜（有肉、蔬菜等）：*a chicken casserole* 燉雞 ◇ *Is there any casserole left?* 還剩有燉鍋菜嗎？ **2** [C] (also **ˈcasserole dish**) a container with a lid used for cooking meat, etc. in liquid in an oven 燉鍋；砂鍋 ➲ VISUAL VOCAB page V27

▸ **cas·ser·ole** *verb* **~ sth**

cas·sette /kəˈset/ *noun* **1** a small flat plastic case containing tape for playing or recording music or sound 磁帶盒；盒式磁帶；卡式磁帶：***a cassette recorder/player*** 盒式磁帶錄音機／放音機 ◇ *available* ***on cassette*** 已錄製成磁帶 ◇ *a video cassette* (= for recording sound and pictures) 盒式錄像帶 **2** a plastic case containing film that can be put into a camera 膠片盒

cas·sock /ˈkæsək/ *noun* a long piece of clothing, usually black or red, worn by some Christian priests and other people with special duties in a church （基督教會教士等穿的黑或紅色的）長袍

cas·sou·let /ˈkæsʊleɪ/ *noun* [U] (from *French*) a dish consisting of meat and BEANS cooked slowly in liquid 法式鍋菜（有鮮肉和白扁豆）

cas·so·wary /ˈkæsəwəri; -weəri; *NAmE* -weri/ *noun* (*pl.* **-ies**) a very large bird related to the EMU, that does not fly. It is found mainly in New Guinea. 鶴鴕（主要生長於新幾內亞）

cast 🔑 /kɑːst; *NAmE* kæst/ *verb*, *noun*

■ ***verb*** (**cast**, **cast**)

▸ **A LOOK/GLANCE/SMILE** 瞧；瞥；笑 **1** [T] **~ (sb) sth** to look, smile, etc. in a particular direction 向…投以（視線、笑容等）：*She cast a welcoming smile in his direction.* 她向他微笑以示歡迎。

▸ **LIGHT/A SHADOW** 光；影子 **2** [T] **~ sth (over sth)** to make light, a shadow, etc. appear in a particular place 投射（光、影子等）：*The setting sun cast an orange glow over the mountains.* 橘紅色的夕陽輝映着群山。◇ (*figurative*)

The sad news cast a shadow over the proceedings (= made people feel unhappy). 這個壞消息給事件的進程蒙上了一層陰影。

▸ DOUBT 懷疑 **3** [T] **~ doubt/aspersions (on/upon sth)** to say, do or suggest sth that makes people doubt sth or think that sb is less honest, good, etc. 使人懷疑；造謠中傷：*This latest evidence casts serious doubt on his version of events.* 最新的證據使人們十分懷疑他對事件的說法。

▸ FISHING LINE 釣魚線 **4** [I, T] **~ (sth)** to throw one end of a FISHING LINE into a river, etc. 投（釣線）；拋（釣鉤）

▸ THROW 投；擲 **5** [T] **~ sb/sth** (*literary*) to throw sb/sth somewhere, especially using force 扔；擲；拋：*The priceless treasures had been cast into the Nile.* 價值連城的珍寶被扔進了尼羅河。◇ *They cast anchor at nightfall.* 他們傍晚拋錨停泊。

▸ SKIN 皮 **6** [T] **~ sth** when a snake **casts** its skin, the skin comes off as part of a natural process （蛇）蛻（皮） **SYN** **shed**

▸ SHOE 蹄鐵 **7** [T] **~ sth** if a horse **casts** a shoe, the shoe comes off by accident （馬）踢落（蹄鐵）

▸ ACTORS 演員 **8** [T] to choose actors to play the different parts in a film/movie, play, etc.; to choose an actor to play a particular role 分配角色；選派角色： **~ sth** *The play is being cast in both the US and Britain.* 目前正在英美兩國挑選這部戲劇的演員。◇ **~ sb (as sb)** *He has cast her as an ambitious lawyer in his latest movie.* 他選定她在他最近的一部影片裏扮演一名雄心勃勃的律師。

▸ DESCRIBE 描寫 **9** [T] to describe or present sb/yourself in a particular way 把某人描寫成；把某人表現為： **~ sb/yourself (as sth)** *He cast himself as the innocent victim of a hate campaign.* 他把自己說成是一場詆譭聲譽運動的無辜犧牲品。◇ **~ sb/yourself (in sth)** *The press were quick to cast her in the role of 'the other woman'.* 新聞界很快把她描述成"第三者"。

▸ VOTE 表決 **10** [T] **~ a/your vote/ballot (for sb/sth)** to vote for sb/sth 投票

▸ SHAPE METAL 模鑄金屬 **11** [T] **~ sth (in sth)** to shape hot liquid metal, etc. by pouring it into a hollow container (called a MOULD) 澆鑄；鑄造：*a statue cast in bronze* 青銅鑄像 ◇ (*figurative*) *an artist* ***cast in the mould of*** (= very similar to) *Miró* 風格酷似米羅的一名藝術家

IDM **cast your mind back (to sth)** to make yourself think about sth that happened in the past 回顧；回想：*I want you to cast your minds back to the first time you met.* 我要你們回憶初次見面的情景。 **cast your net wide** to consider a lot of different people, activities, possibilities, etc. when you are looking for sth 撒開大網（搜尋時考慮面要寬） **cast a 'spell (on sb/sth)** to use words that are thought to be magic and have the power to change or influence sb/sth （對…）施魔法，唸咒語 ➲ more at ADRIFT, CAUTION *n.*, DIE *n.*, EYE *n.*, LIGHT *n.*, LOT *n.*

PHR V **,cast a'bout/a'round for sth** to try hard to think of or find sth, especially when this is difficult 苦苦思索；四處尋找：*She cast around desperately for a safe topic of conversation.* 她絞盡腦汁尋找穩妥的話題。 **,cast sb/sth↔a'side** (*formal*) to get rid of sb/sth because you no longer want or need them 拋棄；丟棄 **SYN** **discard** **be ,cast a'way** to be left somewhere after a SHIPWRECK （船遇難後幸存者）流落某處 ➲ related noun CASTAWAY **be ,cast 'down (by sth)** (*literary*) to be sad or unhappy about sth （因某事）沮喪，不愉快 ➲ see also DOWNCAST **,cast 'off | ,cast sth↔'off** **1** to undo the ropes that are holding a boat in a fixed position, in order to sail away 解纜；解（船）；解纜出航 **2** (in knitting 編織) to remove STITCHES from the needles in a way that forms an edge that will not come undone 收針 **,cast sth↔'off** (*formal*) to get rid of sth because you no longer want or need it 拋棄；丟棄：*The town is still trying to cast off its dull image.* 該鎮仍在努力擺脫自己沉悶無趣的形象。 **,cast 'on | ,cast sth↔'on** (in knitting 編織) to put the first row of STITCHES on a needle 起針；放針 **,cast sb/sth↔'out** (*literary*) to get rid of sb/sth, especially by using force 驅逐；趕走：*He claimed to have the power to cast out demons.* 他宣稱有驅魔的神力。➲ related noun OUTCAST

■ ***noun***

▸ ACTORS 演員 **1** 🔑 [C+sing./pl. v.] all the people who act in a play or film/movie （一齣戲劇或一部電影的）全體演員：*The whole cast performs/perform brilliantly.* 全體演員都表現出色。◇ *members of the cast* 劇組成員 ◇ *an* ***all-star cast*** (= including many well-known actors) 明星雲集的演員陣容 ◇ *the* ***supporting cast*** (= not the main actors, but the others) 配角演員 ◇ *a cast list* 演員表

▸ IN SHAPING METAL 模鑄金屬 **2** [C] an object that is made by pouring hot liquid metal, etc. into a MOULD (= a specially shaped container) 鑄件；鑄造品 **3** [C] a shaped container used to make an object 模子；鑄模 **SYN** **mould**

▸ APPEARANCE 外表 **4** [sing.] (*BrE, formal*) the way that a person or thing is or appears 特性；特徵；外表；外貌：*He has an unusual* ***cast of mind***. 他的思想與眾不同。◇ *I disliked the arrogant cast to her mouth.* 我不喜歡她傲慢的口吻。

▸ THROW 投 **5** [C] an act of throwing sth, especially a fishing line 投，擲，拋（釣線）

▸ ON ARM/LEG 手臂；腿 **6** [C] = PLASTER CAST (1)：*Her leg's* ***in a cast***. 她的一條腿打上了石膏。➲ see also OPENCAST

cas·ta·nets /ˌkæstəˈnets/ *noun* [pl.] a musical instrument that consists of two small round pieces of wood that you hold in the hand and hit together with the fingers to make a noise. Castanets are used especially by Spanish dancers. 響板（西班牙人跳舞時常用的伴奏樂器） ➲ VISUAL VOCAB page V35

cast·away /ˈkɑːstəweɪ; *NAmE* ˈkæst-/ *noun* a person whose ship has sunk (= who has been SHIPWRECKED) and who has had to swim to a lonely place, usually an island （沉船後）游泳逃生到孤島等荒僻處的人

caste /kɑːst; *NAmE* kæst/ *noun* **1** [C] any of the four main divisions of Hindu society, originally those made according to functions in society （印度教的四大）種姓：*the caste system* 種姓制度 ◇ *high-caste Brahmins* 最高種姓婆羅門 **2** [C] a social class, especially one whose members do not allow others to join it （尤指禁止其他等級成員進入的）社會階層，社會等級：*the ruling caste* 統治階層 **3** [U] the system of dividing society into classes based on differences in family origin, rank or wealth 社會等級制度

cas·tel·lated /ˈkæstəleɪtɪd/ *adj.* (*architecture* 建) built in the style of a castle with BATTLEMENTS 像城堡的；有城垛的；有雉堞的

cas·tel·la·tions /ˌkæstəˈleɪʃnz/ *noun* [pl.] the top edge of a castle wall, that has regular spaces along it 城堡雉堞

cas·ter (*NAmE*) (*BrE* **cas·tor**) /ˈkɑːstə(r); *NAmE* ˈkæs-/ *noun* one of the small wheels fixed to the bottom of a piece of furniture so that it can be moved easily （傢具底部的）小腳輪，萬向輪

,caster 'sugar (also **,castor 'sugar**) *noun* [U] (*BrE*) white sugar in the form of very fine grains, used in cooking 精白砂糖

cas·ti·gate /ˈkæstɪɡeɪt/ *verb* **~ sb/sth/yourself (for sth)** (*formal*) to criticize sb/sth severely 嚴厲批評；申斥：*He castigated himself for being so stupid.* 他責怪自己太笨。 ▸ **cas·ti·ga·tion** /ˌkæstɪˈɡeɪʃn/ *noun* [U]

cast·ing /ˈkɑːstɪŋ; *NAmE* ˈkæst-/ *noun* **1** [U] the process of choosing actors for a play or film/movie 角色分配；演員挑選 **2** [C] an object made by pouring hot liquid metal, etc. into a MOULD (= a specially shaped container) 鑄件；鑄造品

'casting couch *noun* used to refer to a process in which actors are chosen for a film/movie, etc. if they have sex with the person in charge of choosing the actors 牀笫選角（為爭演角色與負責選派角色者發生性關係）

,casting 'vote *noun* [usually sing.] the vote given by the person in charge of an official meeting to decide an issue when votes on each side are equal （會議主席在贊成票和反對票票數相等時所投的）決定票

,cast 'iron *noun* [U] a hard type of iron that does not bend easily and is shaped by pouring the hot liquid metal into a MOULD (= a specially shaped container) 鑄鐵

ˌcast-ˈiron *adj.* **1** made of cast iron 鑄鐵製的：*a cast-iron bridge* 鑄鐵橋 **2** (*BrE*) very strong or certain; that cannot be broken or fail 有力的；確實的；堅定不移的：*a cast-iron guarantee/promise* 永不反悔的保證；鐵誓 ◇ *a cast-iron excuse/alibi* 有說服力的辯解；不在犯罪現場的確鑿證據 ➲ compare IRONCLAD

cas·tle 0➡ /ˈkɑːsl; *NAmE* ˈkæsl/ *noun*
1 0➡ a large strong building with thick high walls and towers, built in the past by kings or queens, or other important people, to defend themselves against attack 城堡；堡壘 ➲ VISUAL VOCAB page V15 ➲ see also SANDCASTLE **2** (also **rook**) (in CHESS 國際象棋) any of the four pieces placed in the corner squares of the board at the start of the game, usually made to look like a castle 車；城堡 ➲ VISUAL VOCAB page V38
IDM **(build) castles in the ˈair** (*BrE*) (to have) plans or dreams that are not likely to happen or come true（建）空中樓閣；幻想；空想 ➲ more at ENGLISHMAN

ˈcast-off (*especially BrE*) (also **ˈhand-me-down** especially in *NAmE*) *noun* [usually pl.] a piece of clothing that the original owner no longer wants to wear 被拋棄的衣物 ▸ **ˈcast-off** (also **ˈhand-me-down**) *adj.*：*a cast-off overcoat* 被丟棄的大衣

cas·tor (*BrE*) (*NAmE* **cas·ter**) /ˈkɑːstə(r); *NAmE* ˈkæs-/ *noun* one of the small wheels fixed to the bottom of a piece of furniture so that it can be moved easily（傢具底部的）小腳輪，萬向輪 ➲ VISUAL VOCAB page V69

ˌcastor ˈoil *noun* [U] a thick yellow oil obtained from a tropical plant and used in the past as a type of medicine, usually as a LAXATIVE 蓖麻油

ˌcastor ˈsugar *noun* [U] = CASTER SUGAR

cas·trate /kæˈstreɪt; *NAmE* ˈkæstreɪt/ *verb* **~ sb/sth** to remove the TESTICLES of a male animal or person 割除（男子或雄性動物的）睾丸；閹割 ▸ **cas·tra·tion** /kæˈstreɪʃn/ *noun* [U, C]

cas·ual /ˈkæʒuəl/ *adj., noun*
■ *adj.*
▸ WITHOUT CARE/ATTENTION 不介意；不注意 **1** [usually before noun] not showing much care or thought; seeming not to be worried; not wanting to show that sth is important to you 不經意的；無憂無慮的；漫不經心的；不在乎的：*a casual manner* 漫不經心的樣子 ◇ *It was just a casual remark—I wasn't really serious.* 我只是隨便說說，並不當真。◇ *He tried to sound casual, but I knew he was worried.* 他講話時試圖顯得不在乎，但我知道他心裏着急。◇ *They have a casual attitude towards safety* (= they don't care enough). 他們對安全問題採取無所謂的態度。**2** [usually before noun] without paying attention to detail 馬虎的；疏忽的：*a casual glance* 隨便掃一眼 ◇ *It's obvious even to the casual observer.* 即便再馬虎的人也能一眼看明白是怎麼回事。
▸ NOT FORMAL 非正式 **3** not formal 非正式的；隨便的：*casual clothes* (= comfortable clothes that you choose to wear in your free time) 便裝 ◇ *family parties and other casual occasions* 家庭聚會和其他非正式場合
▸ WORK 工作 **4** [usually before noun] (*BrE*) not permanent; not done, or doing sth regularly 臨時的；不定期的：*casual workers/labour* 臨時工 ◇ *Students sometimes do casual work in the tourist trade.* 學生有時做些旅遊方面的零工。◇ *They are employed* **on a casual basis** (= they do not have a permanent job with the company). 他們被雇為臨時工。
▸ RELATIONSHIP 關係 **5** [usually before noun] without deep affection 感情不深的；疏遠的：*a casual acquaintance* 泛泛之交 ◇ *a casual friendship* 一般的友誼 ◇ *to have casual sex* (= to have sex without having a steady relationship with that partner) 做露水鴛鴦
▸ BY CHANCE 偶然 **6** [only before noun] happening by chance; doing sth by chance 偶然的；碰巧的：*a casual encounter/meeting* 不期而遇 ◇ *a casual passer-by* 碰巧過路的人 ◇ *The exhibition is interesting to both the enthusiast and the casual visitor.* 這方面的愛好者和碰巧來參觀的人都認為這個展覽有意思。◇ *The disease is not spread by casual contact.* 此病不會通過偶然接觸傳染。▸ **cas·ual·ly** *adv.*：*'What did he say about me?' she asked as casually as she could.* "他說了我什麼？" 她盡量裝着不在意地問。◇ *They chatted casually on the phone.* 他們在電話上閒聊。◇ *dressed casually in jeans and T-shirt* 隨便穿着牛仔褲和 T 恤衫 **cas·ual·ness** *noun* [U]：*He was sure that the casualness of the gesture was deliberate.* 他確信那似乎漫不經心的姿態是有意裝出來的。
■ *noun* (*BrE*)
▸ CLOTHES 服裝 **1** **casuals** [pl.] informal clothes or shoes 便裝；便鞋：*dressed in casuals* 穿着便裝
▸ WORKER 工人 **2** [C] a casual worker (= one who does not work permanently for a company) 臨時工

casu·al·iza·tion /ˌkæʒuəlaɪˈzeɪʃn/ *noun* [U] the practice of employing temporary staff for short periods instead of permanent staff, in order to save costs 雇用臨時工制（以節省開支）

casu·alty /ˈkæʒuəlti/ *noun* (*pl.* **-ies**) **1** [C] a person who is killed or injured in war or in an accident（戰爭或事故的）傷員，亡者，遇難者：*road casualties* 交通事故傷亡人員 ◇ *Both sides had suffered* **heavy casualties** (= many people had been killed). 雙方都傷亡慘重。➲ COLLOCATIONS at WAR **2** [C] a person that suffers or a thing that is destroyed when sth else takes place 受害者；毀壞物；損壞物 **SYN** **victim**：*She became a casualty of the reduction in part-time work* (= she lost her job). 她成了減兼職工作的受害人。◇ *Small shops have been a casualty of the recession.* 小商店在經濟蕭條中深受其害。**3** [U] (also **ˈcasualty department**, **ˌaccident and eˈmergency**) (all *BrE*) (*NAmE* **eˈmergency room**) the part of a hospital where people who need urgent treatment are taken 急診室：*The victims were rushed to casualty.* 受傷者被迅速送往急救室。

casu·is·try /ˈkæʒuɪstri/ *noun* [U] (*formal, disapproving*) a way of solving moral or legal problems by using clever arguments that may be false 詭辯（指用似是而非的論點解決倫理或法律問題）

casus belli /ˌkeɪsəs ˈbelaɪ; ˌkɑːsʊs ˈbeliː/ *noun* (*pl.* **casus belli**) (*formal*) an act or situation that is used to justify a war 交戰理由；開戰藉口

cat 0➡ /kæt/ *noun*
1 0➡ a small animal with soft fur that people often keep as a pet. Cats catch and kill birds and mice. 貓：*cat food* 貓食品 ➲ see also KITTEN, TOMCAT **2** a wild animal of the cat family 貓科動物：*the big cats* (= LIONS, TIGERS, etc.) 大型貓科動物（獅、虎等）➲ see also FAT CAT, WILDCAT *n.*
IDM **be the cat's ˈwhiskers/pyˈjamas** (*informal*) to be the best thing, person, idea, etc. 最棒的東西（或人、主意等）：*He thinks he's the cat's whiskers* (= he has a high opinion of himself). 他自以為了不起。**let the ˈcat out of the bag** to tell a secret carelessly or by mistake（無意中）泄露秘密：*I wanted it to be a surprise, but my sister let the cat out of the bag.* 我想給大家來個驚喜，可我妹妹卻先說漏了嘴。**like a ˌcat on hot ˈbricks** (*BrE*) very nervous 局促不安；如坐針氈；像熱鍋上的螞蟻：*She was like a cat on hot bricks before her driving test.* 她考駕駛執照前十分緊張不安。**like a cat that's got the ˈcream** (*BrE*) (*US* **like the cat that got/ate/swallowed the canˈary**) very pleased with yourself 揚揚得意；躊躇滿志 **SYN** **smug** **look like sth the ˈcat brought/dragged in** (*informal*) (of a person 人) to look dirty and untidy 穿着邋遢；衣衫襤褸；不修邊幅 **not have/stand a cat in ˈhell's chance (of doing sth)** to have no chance at all 毫無機會 **play (a game of) ˌcat and ˈmouse with sb | play a ˌcat-and-ˈmouse game with sb** to play a cruel game with sb in your power by changing your behaviour very often, so that they become nervous and do not know what to expect 和某人玩起貓捉老鼠的遊戲；耍弄 **put/set the cat among the ˈpigeons** (*BrE*) to say or do sth that is likely to cause trouble 引起麻煩；招惹是非 **when the cat's aˈway the mice will ˈplay** (*saying*) people enjoy themselves more and behave with greater freedom when the person in charge of them is not there 貓兒不在，老鼠玩得自在（指管事的不在，下面的玩個痛快）➲ more at CURIOSITY, RAIN *v.*, ROOM *n.*, WAY *n.*

ca·tab·ol·ism (also **ka·tab·ol·ism**) /kəˈtæbəlɪzəm/ *noun* [U] (*biology* 生) the process by which chemical structures are broken down and energy is released 分解代謝

cata·clysm /ˈkætəklɪzəm/ *noun* (*formal*) a sudden disaster or a violent event that causes change, for example a flood or a war（突然降臨的）大災難，大災變，大動亂 ▸ **cata·clys·mic** /ˌkætəˈklɪzmɪk/ *adj.* [usually before noun]

cata·combs /ˈkætəkuːmz; *NAmE* -koʊmz/ *noun* [pl.] a series of underground tunnels used for burying dead people, especially in ancient times（尤指古代縱橫交錯的）地下墓穴

cata·falque /ˈkætəfælk/ *noun* a decorated platform on which the dead body of a famous person is placed before a funeral 靈柩台

Cata·lan /ˈkætəlæn/ *noun, adj.*

■ ***noun*** **1** [U] a language spoken in Catalonia, Andorra, the Balearic Islands and parts of southern France 加泰羅尼亞語（通行於西班牙加泰羅尼亞、安道爾、巴利阿里群島和法國南部一些地區） **2** [C] a person who was born in or who lives in Catalonia 加泰羅尼亞人

■ ***adj.*** connected with Catalonia, its people, its language, or its culture 加泰羅尼亞的；加泰羅尼亞人（或語言、文化）的

cata·lepsy /ˈkætəlepsi/ *noun* [U] (*medical* 醫) a condition in which sb's body becomes stiff and they temporarily become unconscious 全身僵硬症；僵住症；強直性昏厥；僵強症 ▸ **cata·lep·tic** /ˌkætəˈleptɪk/ *adj.*

cata·logue (*NAmE* also **cata·log**) /ˈkætəlɒg; *NAmE* -lɔːg; -lɑːg/ *noun, verb*

■ ***noun*** **1** a complete list of items, for example of things that people can look at or buy 目錄；目錄簿：*a mail-order catalogue* (= a book showing goods for sale to be sent to people's homes) 郵購商品目錄 ◊ *to consult the library catalogue* 查看圖書館目錄 ◊ *An illustrated catalogue accompanies the exhibition.* 展覽會有插圖目錄。◊ *an online catalogue* 在線檢索目錄 **2** a long series of things that happen (usually bad things) 一連串（糟糕）事：*a **catalogue of** disasters/errors/misfortunes* 接二連三的災難 / 錯誤 / 不幸

■ ***verb*** **1 ~ sth** to arrange a list of things in order in a catalogue; to record sth in a catalogue 列入目錄；編入目錄 **2 ~ sth** to give a list of things connected with a particular person, event, etc. 記載，登記（某人、某事等的詳情）：*Interviews with the refugees catalogue a history of discrimination and violence.* 對難民的採訪記錄下了一部歧視和暴力的歷史。

cata·lyse (*BrE*) (*NAmE* **cata·lyze**) /ˈkætəlaɪz/ *verb* **~ sth** (*chemistry* 化) to make a chemical reaction happen faster 催化

cata·lyst /ˈkætəlɪst/ *noun* **1** (*chemistry* 化) a substance that makes a chemical reaction happen faster without being changed itself 催化劑 **2 ~ (for sth)** a person or thing that causes a change 促使變化的人；引發變化的因素：*I see my role as being a catalyst for change.* 我認為我的角色是促成變革。

cata·lyt·ic con·vert·er /ˌkætəˌlɪtɪk kənˈvɜːtə(r); *NAmE* -ˈvɜːrt-/ *noun* a device used in the EXHAUST system of vehicles to reduce the damage caused to the environment 催化轉化器，催化式排氣淨化器（用以淨化機動車廢氣）

cata·ma·ran /ˌkætəməˈræn/ *noun* a fast sailing boat with two HULLS 雙體船 ➲ VISUAL VOCAB page V54 ➲ compare TRIMARAN

cata·mite /ˈkætəmaɪt/ *noun* (*old use*) a boy kept as a SLAVE for a man to have sex with 孌童；當性奴的男童

cata·pult /ˈkætəpʌlt/ *noun, verb*

■ ***noun*** **1** (*BrE*) (*NAmE* **sling·shot**) a stick shaped like a Y with a rubber band attached to it, used by children for shooting stones 彈弓 **2** a weapon used in the past to throw heavy stones（舊時的）石弩，弩炮 **3** a machine used for sending planes up into the air from a ship 彈射器（用以從艦船上彈射飛機升空）

■ ***verb*** [T, I] to throw sb/sth or be thrown suddenly and violently through the air（被）猛擲，猛扔：**~ (sb/sth) + adv./prep.** *She was catapulted out of the car as it hit the wall.* 汽車撞牆時，她被甩出車外。◊ (*figurative*) *The movie catapulted him to international stardom.* 這部電影使他一躍成為國際明星。

catapult (*BrE*)
slingshot (*NAmE*)
彈弓

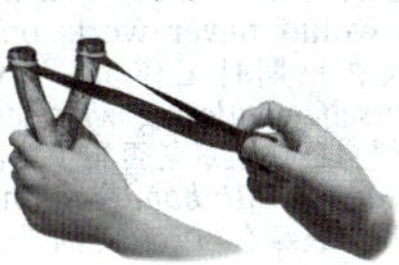

cat·ar·act /ˈkætərækt/ *noun* **1** a medical condition that affects the LENS of the eye and causes a gradual loss of sight 內障；白內障 **2** (*literary*) a large steep WATERFALL 大瀑布

ca·tarrh /kəˈtɑː(r)/ *noun* [U] thick liquid (called PHLEGM) that you have in your nose and throat because, for example, you have a cold（鼻喉黏膜炎引起的）黏液，痰

ca·tas·trophe /kəˈtæstrəfi/ *noun* **1** a sudden event that causes many people to suffer 災難；災禍；橫禍 SYN **disaster**：*Early warnings of rising water levels prevented another major catastrophe.* 提前發出的洪水水位上漲警報防止了又一次的重大災害。 **2** an event that causes one person or a group of people personal suffering, or that makes difficulties 不幸事件；困難：*The attempt to expand the business was a catastrophe for the firm.* 擴展業務的嘗試使這家公司陷入困境。◊ *We've had a few catastrophes with the food for the party.* 我們為聚會準備食物時遇到了一些困難。 ▸ **cata·stroph·ic** /ˌkætəˈstrɒfɪk; *NAmE* -ˈstrɑː-/ SYN **disastrous** *adj.*：*catastrophic effects/losses/results* 災難性的影響 / 損失 / 結果 ◊ (*US*) *a catastrophic illness* (= one that costs a very large amount to treat) 要花費巨資治療的疾病 **cata·stroph·ic·al·ly** /-kli/ *adv.*

cata·to·nia /ˌkætəˈtəʊniə; *NAmE* -ˈtoʊ-/ *noun* [U] (*medical* 醫) a condition resulting from a mental illness, especially SCHIZOPHRENIA, in which a person does not move for long periods 緊張症；緊張型精神分裂症

cata·ton·ic /ˌkætəˈtɒnɪk; *NAmE* -ˈtɑːnɪk/ *adj.* (*medical* 醫) not able to move or show any reaction to things because of illness, shock, etc. 緊張型的；緊張性的

cat·bird seat /ˈkætbɜːd siːt; *NAmE* -bɜːrd/ *noun*

IDM **be in the ˈcatbird seat** (*NAmE*) to have an advantage over other people or be in control of a situation 處於有利地位；控制着局勢

ˈcat burglar *noun* a thief who climbs up the outside of a building in order to enter it and steal sth 翻牆入室的竊賊；飛賊

cat·call /ˈkætkɔːl/ *noun* [usually pl.] a noise or shout expressing anger at or disapproval of sb who is speaking or performing in public（表示憤怒或反對的）噓聲，不滿之聲

catch 🔑 /kætʃ/ *verb, noun*

■ ***verb*** (**caught**, **caught** /kɔːt/)

▸ HOLD 接住 **1** 🔑 [T] **~ sth** to stop and hold a moving object, especially in your hands 接住；截住；攔住：*She managed to catch the keys as they fell.* 她接住了落下的鑰匙。◊ *'Throw me over that towel, will you?' 'OK. Catch!'* "請你把毛巾扔過來好嗎？" "好，接住！" ◊ *The dog caught the stick in its mouth.* 狗銜住了木棍。 **2** 🔑 [T] **~ sth** to hold a liquid when it falls 接（落下的液體）：*The roof was leaking and I had to use a bucket to catch the drips.* 屋頂漏雨，我不得不用桶來接。 **3** 🔑 [T] **~ sb/sth (+ adv./prep.)** to take hold of sb/sth 抓住；握住：*He **caught hold of** her arm as she tried to push past him.* 她試圖從他身邊擠過去時，他一把抓住了她的手臂。

▸ CAPTURE 捉住 **4** 🔑 [T] **~ sb/sth** to capture a person or an animal that tries or would try to escape 逮住；捕捉；捕獲：*The murderer was never caught.* 這個殺人犯一直未抓到。◊ *Our cat is hopeless at catching mice.* 我們的貓絕對捉不到老鼠。◊ *How many fish did you catch?* 你捕到幾條魚？

C

▸ **SB DOING STH 某人正做某事 5** [T] to find or discover sb doing sth, especially sth wrong 當場發現（或發覺）: **~ sb doing sth** *I caught her smoking in the bathroom.* 我撞見她在盥洗室裏抽煙。◇ ***You wouldn't catch me working*** (= I would never work) *on a Sunday!* 你絕對不會看到我在星期日工作！◇ **~ yourself doing sth** *She caught herself wondering whether she had made a mistake.* 她發覺自己在懷疑是否犯了錯誤。◇ **~ sb + adv./prep.** *He was caught with bomb-making equipment in his home.* 他被發現家裏藏有製造炸彈的設備。◇ *Mark walked in and **caught them at it*** (= in the act of doing sth wrong). 馬克走了進去，當場發現他們正在幹壞事。◇ *thieves **caught in the act*** 偷竊時被當場抓住的竊賊 ◇ *You've caught me at a bad time* (= at a time when I am busy). 你現在來找我可不是時候。

▸ **BUS/TRAIN/PLANE 公共汽車；火車；飛機 6** [T] **~ sth** to be in time for a bus, train, plane, etc. and get on it 趕上（公共汽車、火車、飛機等）: *We caught the 12.15 from Oxford.* 我們趕上了 12:15 從牛津發出的火車。◇ *I must go—I have a train to catch.* 我得走了，我要趕火車。

▸ **BE IN TIME 及時 7** [T] **~ sb/sth** to be in time to do sth, talk to sb, etc. 及時做（或談等）: *I caught him just as he was leaving the building.* 他正要離開大樓時，我追上了他。◇ *I was hoping to catch you at home* (= to telephone you at home when you were there). 我本希望趕上你在家的時候給你打電話。◇ *The illness can be treated provided it's caught* (= discovered) *early enough.* 此病若及早發現是可醫治的。◇ (*BrE*) *to **catch the post*** (= post letters before the box is emptied)（寄信）趕上郵局的收信時刻 ◇ (*BrE, informal*) *Bye for now! I'll **catch you later*** (= speak to you again later). 再見！下次再談。

▸ **SEE/HEAR 看見；聽到 8** [T] **~ sth** (*informal, especially NAmE*) to see or hear sth; to attend sth 看見；聽到；出席；參加: *Let's eat now and maybe we could catch a movie later.* 咱們現在就吃吧，也許還能趕上一場電影。➲ SYNONYMS at SEE

▸ **HAPPEN UNEXPECTEDLY 意外地發生 9** [T] **~ sb** to happen unexpectedly and put sb in a difficult situation 突然遭受: *His arrival **caught** me **by surprise**.* 他的到來讓我感到意外。◇ *She **got caught in** a thunderstorm.* 她遇上了雷雨。

▸ **ILLNESS 疾病 10** [T] to get an illness 得病；染疾: **~ sth** *to catch measles* 染上麻疹 ◇ **~ sth from sb** *I think I must have caught this cold from you.* 我的感冒想必是你傳染的。

▸ **BECOME STUCK 被纏住 11** [I, T] to become stuck in or on sth; to make sth become stuck （被）鈎住，夾住，絆住: **~ (in/on sth)** *Her dress caught on a nail.* 她的連衣裙被釘子鈎住了。◇ **~ sth (in/on sth)** *He caught his thumb in the door.* 他的拇指被門夾住了。

▸ **HIT 打 12** [T] to hit sb/sth 擊中；打: **~ sb/sth + adv./prep.** *The stone caught him on the side of the head.* 他頭的側面被石頭擊中。◇ **~ sb sth + adv./prep.** *She caught him a blow on the chin.* 她一拳打在他下巴上。

▸ **NOTICE 注意到 13** [T] **~ sth** to notice sth only for a moment 察覺；瞥見: *She **caught sight** of a car in the distance.* 她瞥見遠處有一輛車。◇ *He **caught a glimpse** of himself in the mirror.* 他看了一眼鏡子中的自己。◇ *I caught a look of surprise on her face.* 我發現她面露驚奇。◇ *He **caught a whiff** of her perfume.* 他聞到一股她身上的香水味。

▸ **HEAR/UNDERSTAND 聽見；理解 14** [T] **~ sth** to hear or understand sth 聽清楚；領會: *Sorry, I didn't quite catch what you said.* 對不起，我沒聽清楚你的話。

▸ **INTEREST 興趣 15** [T] **~ sb's interest, imagination, attention, etc.** if sth **catches** your interest, etc., you notice it and feel interested in it 引起，激發（興趣、想像、注意等）

▸ **SHOW ACCURATELY 逼真地顯示 16** [T] **~ sth** to show or describe sth accurately 逼真再現；準確描繪 **SYN** **capture** *The artist has caught her smile perfectly.* 藝術家維妙維肖地畫出了她的微笑。

▸ **LIGHT 光 17** [T] **~ sth** if sth **catches** the light or the light **catches** it, the light shines on it and makes it shine too （光）照射；受到（光的）照射: *The knife gleamed as it **caught the light**.* 刀在光照下閃閃發亮。

▸ **THE SUN 太陽 18** [T] **~ the sun** (*informal*) if you **catch the sun**, you become red or brown because of spending time in the sun 曬黑；曬紅；曬成棕色

▸ **BURN 燃燒 19** [T, I] **~ (fire)** to begin to burn 燒着；着（火）: *The wooden rafters caught fire.* 木椽子着火了。◇ *These logs are wet: they won't catch.* 這些木柴是濕的，燒不着。

▸ **IN CRICKET 板球 20** [T] **~ sb** to make a player unable to continue BATTING by catching the ball they have hit before it touches the ground （在球落地前）接住球

IDM **catch your 'breath 1** to stop breathing for a moment because of fear, shock, etc. （由於恐懼、震驚等）屏息，屏氣 **2** to breathe normally again after running or doing some tiring exercise （跑或激烈運動後）喘口氣 **catch your 'death (of 'cold)** (*old-fashioned, informal*) to catch a very bad cold 患重感冒 **catch sb's 'eye** to attract sb's attention 引起某人注意；惹人注目: *Can you catch the waiter's eye?* 你能引起服務員的注意嗎？ **'catch it** (*BrE*) (*NAmE* **catch 'hell**, **'get it**) (*informal*) to be punished or spoken to angrily about sth 受罰；受斥責: *If your dad finds out you'll really catch it!* 要是你老爸知道了，你非捱罵不可！ **catch sb 'napping** (*BrE*) to get an advantage over sb by doing sth when they are not expecting it and not ready for it 使人措手不及；乘其不備 **catch sb on the 'hop** (*informal*) to surprise sb by doing sth when they are not expecting it and not ready for it 使某人措手不及 **catch sb red-'handed** to catch sb in the act of doing sth wrong or committing a crime 當場抓住；現場捕獲 **catch sb with their 'pants down** (*BrE* also **catch sb with their 'trousers down**) (*informal*) to arrive or do sth when sb is not expecting it and not ready, especially when they are in an embarrassing situation 使突陷窘境；乘人措手不及；出其不意；冷不防 ➲ more at BALANCE *n.*, CLEFT *adj.*, EARLY *adj.*, FANCY *n.*, RAW *n.*, ROCK *n.*, SHORT *adv.*

PHR V **'catch at sth** = CLUTCH AT STH **,catch 'on** to become popular or fashionable 受歡迎；流行起來；變得時髦: *He invented a new game, but it never really caught on.* 他發明了一種新的遊戲，但從未真正流行起來。 **,catch 'on (to sth)** (*informal*) to understand sth 理解: *He is very quick to catch on to things.* 他領悟能力很強。 **,catch sb 'out 1** to surprise sb and put them in a difficult position 使突陷困境: *Many investors were caught out by the fall in share prices.* 許多投資者由於股價下跌而突然陷入困境。 **2** to show that sb does not know much or is doing sth wrong 抓住某人的短處；指出無知；指出過失: *They tried to catch her out with a difficult question.* 他們試圖用一道難題去難倒她。 **,catch 'up on sth 1** to spend extra time doing sth because you have not done it earlier 補做（未做的事）；趕做；補上: *I have a lot of work to catch up on.* 我有許多工作要補做。 **2** to find out about things that have happened 瞭解（已發生的事情）: *We spent the evening catching up on each other's news.* 我們那一晚上都一直在彼此通報情況。 **be/get ,caught 'up in sth** to become involved in sth, especially when you do not want to be 被捲入；陷入: *Innocent passers-by got caught up in the riots.* 無辜的過路人被捲入了那場暴亂。 **,catch 'up (with sb)** (*BrE* also **,catch sb 'up**) **1** to reach sb who is ahead by going faster 趕上，追上（某人）: *Go on ahead. I'll catch up with you.* 你先走，我隨後趕上你。◇ *I'll catch you up.* 我會追上你的。 **2** to reach the same level or standard as sb who was better or more advanced 趕上，達到（某水平）: *After missing a term through illness he had to work hard to catch up with the others.* 他因病休學一學期，不得不努力學習好趕上別的同學。 **,catch 'up with sb 1** to finally start to cause problems for sb after they have managed to avoid this for some time 產生（曾設法避免的）問題: *She was terrified that one day her past problems would catch up with her.* 她十分害怕過去的問題總有一天又會來困擾她。 **2** if the police or authorities **catch up with** sb, they find and punish them after some time 終於查到某人頭上: *The law caught up with him years later when he had moved to Spain.* 多年後當他已移居西班牙時最終還是受到法律的制裁。

■ ***noun***

▸ **OF BALL 球 1** [C] an act of catching sth, for example a ball 接（球等）: *to make a catch* 接球

▸ **AMOUNT CAUGHT 捕獲量 2** [C] the total amount of things

that are caught 總捕獲量： *a huge catch of fish* 捕獲大量的魚

▸ **FASTENING** 固着裝置 **3** [C] a device used for fastening sth 扣拴物；扣件： *a catch on the door* 門閂 ◇ *safety catches for the windows* 安全窗鈎

▸ **DIFFICULTY** 困難 **4** [C, usually sing.] (*informal*) a hidden difficulty or disadvantage 隱藏的困難；暗藏的不利因素：*All that money for two hours' work—what's the catch?* 幹了兩小時的活就給那麼多錢，這裏面有什麼鬼？

▸ **CHILD'S GAME** 兒童遊戲 **5** [U] a child's game in which two people throw a ball to each other （兒童）傳接球遊戲

▸ **PERSON** 人 **6** [sing.] (*old-fashioned*) a person that other people see as a good person to marry, employ, etc. 理想的對象；意中人；雇用的好對象；看中的人

IDM **(a) catch-22** | **a catch-22 situation** (*informal*) a difficult situation from which there is no escape because you need to do one thing before doing a second, but you need to do the second thing before you can do the first 進退維谷的局面： *I can't get a job because I haven't got anywhere to live but I can't afford a place to live until I get a job—it's a catch-22 situation.* 我沒有住所就找不到工作，但是沒有工作就沒錢租房子，這真是左右為難。

'catch-all *noun* **1** (*especially NAmE*) a thing for holding many small objects 裝雜物的容器；放雜物的東西 **2** a group or description that includes different things and that does not state clearly what is included or not 籠統的一類（或描述） ▸ **'catch-all** *adj.* [only before noun]： *a* **catch-all** *phrase/term* 涵義甚廣的短語／術語

catch·er /ˈkætʃə(r)/ *noun* **1** (in BASEBALL 棒球) the player who stands behind the BATTER and catches the ball if he or she does not hit it 接球手 ➲ VISUAL VOCAB page V44 **2** (usually in compounds 通常構成複合詞) a person or thing that catches sth 捕捉者；捕捉器： *a rat catcher* 捕鼠器

catch·ing /ˈkætʃɪŋ/ *adj.* [not before noun] **1** (of a disease 疾病) easily caught by one person from another 有傳染性 **SYN** **infectious** **2** (of an emotion or a mood 情感或情緒) passing quickly from one person to another 有感染力 **SYN** **infectious**： *Try to be as enthusiastic as possible (enthusiasm is catching)!* 盡量表現出熱情（熱情具有感染力）！

catch·line /ˈkætʃlaɪn/ *noun* **1** (*technical* 術語) a short line of text which can be easily noticed, for example at the top of a page （頁面頂端等處）引人注目的語句，醒目的字行 **2** a phrase used in an advertisement 廣告語

catch·ment area /ˈkætʃmənt eəriə; *NAmE* eriə/ *noun* **1** (*BrE*) the area from which a school takes its students, a hospital its patients, etc. （學校的）招生地區；（醫院等的）服務地區 **2** (also **catch·ment**) (*technical* 術語) the area from which rain flows into a particular river or lake 流域；匯流面積

catch·penny /ˈkætʃpeni/ *adj.* (*old-fashioned*) (of a product or service 產品或服務) produced or provided just to make money, without being of good quality （劣質）只求賺錢的

catch·phrase /ˈkætʃfreɪz/ *noun* a popular phrase that is connected with the politician or entertainer who used it and made it famous 名言；流行辭令；時行的話

'catch-up *noun* **1** [U] the act of trying to reach the same level or standard as sb who is ahead of you （向別人水平的）追趕： *It was a month of catch-up for them.* 他們那個月急起直追。 **2** [C, sing.] an occasion when two or more people meet to discuss what has happened since the last time they met 敍舊： *We must get together for a catch-up.* 我們得聚在一起敍敍舊。

IDM **play 'catch-up** to try to equal sb that you are competing against in a sport or game （在體育運動或比賽中）拚命趕超： *After our bad start to the season we were always playing catch-up.* 我們在賽季開始時受挫之後一直在努力追趕。

catchy /ˈkætʃi/ *adj.* (*informal*) (**catch·ier**, **catchi·est**) (of music or the words of an advertisement 音樂或廣告詞) pleasing and easily remembered 悅耳易記的： *a catchy* **tune/slogan** 容易上口的樂曲／口號

'cat door (*NAmE*) (*BrE* **'cat flap**) *noun* a hole cut in the bottom of the door to a house, covered by a piece of plastic that swings, so a pet cat can go in and out（門下供家貓進出的）活動板貓洞

cat·ech·ism /ˈkætəkɪzəm/ *noun* [usually sing.] a set of questions and answers that are used for teaching people about the beliefs of the Christian religion（基督教的）教理問答

cat·egor·ic·al /ˌkætəˈɡɒrɪkl; *NAmE* -ˈɡɔːr-/ *adj.* [usually before noun] (*formal*) expressed clearly and in a way that shows that you are very sure about what you are saying 明確的；絕對的： *to make a categorical statement* 發表明確聲明 ◇ *to give a categorical assurance* 提供絕對保證 ▸ **cat·egor·ic·al·ly** /-kli/ *adv.*： *He categorically rejected our offer.* 他斷然拒絕我們的提議。

cat·egor·ize (*BrE* also **-ise**) **AW** /ˈkætəɡəraɪz/ *verb* to put people or things into groups according to what type they are 將…分類；把…加以歸類 **SYN** **classify**： **~ sb/sth** *Participants were categorized according to age.* 參加者按年齡分組。◇ **~ sb/sth as sth** *His latest work cannot be categorized as either a novel or an autobiography.* 他最近的作品既不屬於小說也不屬於自傳。 ▸ **cat·egor·iza·tion, -isa·tion** **AW** /ˌkætəɡəraɪˈzeɪʃn/ *noun* [U, C]

cat·egory 🔑 **AW** /ˈkætəɡəri; *NAmE* -ɡɔːri/ *noun* (*pl.* **-ies**) a group of people or things with particular features in common （人或事物的）類別，種類 **SYN** **class**： *Students over 25* **fall into a** *different* **category**. * 25 歲以上的學生屬另一類。◇ *The results can be divided into three* **main categories**. 結果可分為三大類。

cater /ˈkeɪtə(r)/ *verb* [I, T] to provide food and drinks for a social event （為社交活動）提供飲食，承辦餐宴：(*BrE*) **~ for sb/sth** *Most of our work now involves catering for weddings.* 我們現在的工作多半是承辦婚宴。◇ (*NAmE*) **~ sth** *Who will be catering the wedding?* 誰來承辦婚宴？

PHR V **'cater for sb/sth** to provide the things that a particular person or situation needs or wants 滿足需要；適合： *The class caters for all ability ranges.* 這個班對各種不同水平的人都適合。 **'cater to sb/sth** to provide the things that a particular type of person wants, especially things that you do not approve of 滿足需要；迎合： *They only publish novels which cater to the mass market.* 他們只出版適銷大眾市場的小說。

cater·er /ˈkeɪtərə(r)/ *noun* a person or company whose job is to provide food and drinks at a business meeting or for a special occasion such as a wedding （商務會議或婚禮等的）餐宴承辦商，飲食服務公司

cater·ing /ˈkeɪtərɪŋ/ *noun* [U] the work of providing food and drinks for meetings or social events （會議或社交活動的）飲食服務，餐宴承辦： *Who did the catering for your son's wedding?* 你兒子的婚宴是由誰承辦的？

cat·er·pil·lar /ˈkætəpɪlə(r); *NAmE* -tərp-/ *noun* a small creature like a WORM with legs, that develops into a BUTTERFLY or MOTH (= flying insects with large, sometimes brightly coloured, wings). Caterpillars eat the leaves of plants. 毛蟲，蠋（蝴蝶或蛾的幼蟲） ➲ VISUAL VOCAB page V13

'Caterpillar track™ (*especially BrE*) (also **'tank tread** especially in *NAmE*) *noun* a metal belt fastened around the wheels of a heavy vehicle, used for travelling over rough or soft ground 卡特彼勒履帶（重型車輛使用） ➲ VISUAL VOCAB page V58

cat·er·waul /ˈkætəwɔːl; *NAmE* ˈkætər-/ *verb* [I] to make the loud unpleasant noise that is typical of a cat （貓）號叫

cat·fight /ˈkætfaɪt/ *noun* (*informal*) a fight between women 女鬥（指女人之間的打鬥）

cat·fish /ˈkætfɪʃ/ *noun* (*pl.* **cat·fish**) a large fish with long stiff hairs, like a cat's WHISKERS, around its mouth. There are several types of catfish, most of which are FRESHWATER fish. 鯰魚，鮎魚（多為淡水魚）

'cat flap (*BrE*) (*NAmE* **'cat door**) *noun* a hole cut in the bottom of the door to a house, covered by a piece of plastic that swings, so a pet cat can go in and out（門下供家貓進出的）活動板貓洞

C

C

cat·gut /ˈkætɡʌt/ (also **gut**) *noun* [U] thin strong string made from animals' INTESTINES and used in making musical instruments 腸線（用於製樂器的弦）

cath·ar·sis /kəˈθɑːsɪs; *NAmE* -ˈθɑːrs-/ *noun* [U, C] (*pl.* **cath·arses** /-siːz/) (*technical* 術語) the process of releasing strong feelings, for example through plays or other artistic activities, as a way of providing relief from anger, suffering, etc. 情感宣泄，精神淨化（如通過戲劇或其他藝術活動）▸ **cath·ar·tic** /kəˈθɑːtɪk; *NAmE* -ˈθɑːrt-/ *adj.*：*It was a cathartic experience.* 那是一次情感宣泄的體驗。

cath·edral /kəˈθiːdrəl/ *noun* the main church of a district, under the care of a BISHOP (= a priest of high rank) 主教座堂；教區總教堂：*St Paul's Cathedral* 聖保羅大教堂 ◇ (*BrE*) *a cathedral city* 有主教座堂的城市

Cath·er·ine wheel /ˈkæθrɪn wiːl/ (*especially BrE*) (*NAmE* usually **pin·wheel**) *noun* a round flat FIREWORK that spins around when lit 凱瑟琳車輪式焰火；轉輪煙火

cath·eter /ˈkæθɪtə(r)/ *noun* a thin tube that is put into the body in order to remove liquid such as URINE 導管（如導尿管）

cath·ode /ˈkæθəʊd; *NAmE* -oʊd/ *noun* (*technical* 術語) the ELECTRODE in an electrical device where REDUCTION occurs; the negative electrode in an ELECTROLYTIC cell and the positive electrode in a battery 陰極；負極 ➲ compare ANODE

ˌcathode ˈray tube *noun* a VACUUM tube inside a television or computer screen, etc. from which a stream of ELECTRONS produces images on the screen 陰極射線管

Cath·olic /ˈkæθlɪk/ *noun* = ROMAN CATHOLIC：*They're Catholics.* 他們是天主教徒。▸ **Cath·oli·cism** /kəˈθɒləsɪzəm; *NAmE* -ˈθɑːlə-/ *noun* [U] = ROMAN CATHOLICISM

cath·olic /ˈkæθlɪk/ *adj.* **1 Catholic** = ROMAN CATHOLIC：*Are they Catholic or Protestant?* 他們是天主教徒還是新教徒？◇ *a Catholic church* 天主教教堂 **2** (often **Catholic**) (*technical* 術語) connected with all Christians or the whole Christian Church 全體基督教徒的；基督教會的 **3** (*formal*) including many or most things 包羅萬象的；廣泛的：*to have catholic tastes* (= to like many different things) 愛好廣泛的

cat·ion /ˈkætaɪən/ *noun* (*chemistry* 化, *physics* 物) an ION with a positive electrical CHARGE 正離子；陽離子 ➲ compare ANION

cat·kin /ˈkætkɪn/ *noun* a long thin hanging bunch, or short standing group, of soft flowers on the branches of trees such as the WILLOW 柔荑花序 ➲ VISUAL VOCAB page V10

cat·mint /ˈkætmɪnt/ (*BrE*) (also **cat·nip** /ˈkætnɪp/*NAmE*, *BrE*) *noun* [U] a plant that has white flowers with purple spots, leaves covered with small hairs and a smell that is attractive to cats 假荊芥；貓薄荷

cat·nap /ˈkætnæp/ *noun* a short sleep 小睡；打盹兒；瞌睡 ▸ **cat·nap** *verb* (-pp-) [I]

cat-o'-nine-tails /ˌkæt ə ˈnaɪn teɪlz/ *noun* [sing.] a WHIP made of nine strings with knots in them, that was used to punish prisoners in the past 九尾鞭（用九條帶結的細繩編成，舊時鞭打囚犯用）

CAT scan /ˈkæt skæn/ (also **ˌCT scan**) *noun* a medical examination that uses a computer to produce an image of the inside of sb's body from X-RAY or ULTRASOUND pictures 計算機層析成像掃描

cat's cradle 翻線戲

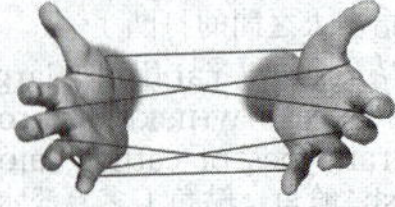

ˌcat's ˈcradle *noun* **1** [U] a game in which you wrap string around the fingers of both hands to make different patterns 翻線戲，翻繩兒，挑綳子（遊戲）**2** [C] a pattern made with string in a game of cat's cradle 翻線戲花樣

Cats·eye™ /ˈkætsaɪ/ *noun* (*BrE*) one of a line of small objects that are fixed into a road and that reflect a car's lights in order to guide traffic at night 貓眼（固定安裝在道路上的夜間反光路標）

cat·suit /ˈkætsuːt; *BrE* also -sjuːt/ *noun* a piece of women's clothing that fits closely and covers the body and legs 女式緊身連衣褲

cat·tery /ˈkætəri/ *noun* (*pl.* **-ies**) (*BrE*) a place where people can pay to leave their cats to be cared for while they are away 貓代養所

cat·tle /ˈkætl/ *noun* [pl.] cows and BULLS that are kept as farm animals for their milk or meat 牛：*a herd of cattle* 一群牛 ◇ *twenty **head of cattle*** (= twenty cows) 二十頭牛 ◇ ***dairy/beef cattle*** 乳 / 菜牛 ➲ COLLOCATIONS at FARMING ➲ VISUAL VOCAB page V6

cat·tle duff·ing /ˈkætl dʌfɪŋ/ *noun* (*AustralE*) the stealing of cows 偷牛；盜牛

ˈcattle grid (*BrE*) (*NAmE* **ˈcattle guard**) *noun* metal bars that are placed over a hole that has been made in the road. Cars can pass over the metal bars but animals such as sheep and cows cannot. 攔畜溝柵（鋪在公路坑上的金屬架，車輛可通過，但牛羊過不去）

catty /ˈkæti/ *adj.* (*informal*) (**cat·tier**, **cat·ti·est**) (of a woman 女人) saying unkind things about other people 散佈流言蜚語的；刁鑽刻薄的；搬弄是非的 SYN **bitchy, spiteful**：*a catty comment* 尖酸刻薄的話 ▸ **cat·ti·ness** *noun* [U]

ˌcatty-ˈcorner(ed) (also **ˌkitty-ˈcorner(ed)**) *adj.*, *adv.* (*NAmE*, *informal*) opposite and at a DIAGONAL angle from sth/sb 成對角線（的）；斜對面（的）：*a restaurant catty-corner from the theater* 斜對着劇院的餐館 ◇ *Motorcyclists cut catty-cornered across his yard.* 騎摩托車的人斜穿過他的院子。

cat·walk /ˈkætwɔːk/ *noun* **1** (*NAmE* also **run·way**) the long stage that models walk on during a fashion show（時裝表演時供模特兒用的）狹長表演台，T 形台 ➲ COLLOCATIONS at FASHION **2** a narrow platform for people to walk on, for example along the outside of a building or a bridge（樓房旁、橋面等處的）狹窄人行通道

Cau·ca·sian /kɔːˈkeɪziən; kɔːˈkeɪʒn/ *noun* a member of any of the races of people who have pale skin 白種人；高加索人 ▸ **Cau·ca·sian** *adj.*

cau·cus /ˈkɔːkəs/ *noun*, *verb*

■ ***noun*** (*especially NAmE*) **1** a meeting of the members or leaders of a political party to choose candidates or to decide policy; the members or leaders of a political party as a group（領導人或一般成員為挑選候選人或制訂政策而舉行的）政黨會議；（政黨的）全體成員，領導班子 **2** a group of people with similar interests, often within a larger organization or political party（常指較大組織或政黨內部志趣相投的）派別，小集團，小組：*the Congressional Black Caucus* 美國國會內部提倡黑人民權的核心小組

■ ***verb*** [I, T] (*NAmE*) **~ (sb)** to meet in a caucus or other group to discuss sth 開領導班子會；開小組會議

caught *past tense*, *past part.* of CATCH

caul·dron (*US* also **cal·dron**) /ˈkɔːldrən/ *noun* a large deep pot for boiling liquids or cooking food over a fire 大鍋：*a witch's cauldron* 女巫的大鍋 ◇ (*figurative*) *The stadium was a seething cauldron of emotion.* 體育場內群情沸騰。

cauli·flower /ˈkɒliflaʊə(r); *NAmE* ˈkɔːli-; ˈkɑːli-/ *noun* [U, C] a vegetable with green leaves around a large hard white head of flowers 花椰菜；菜花：*Do you like cauliflower?* 你喜歡菜花嗎？◇ *two cauliflowers* 兩個花椰菜 ➲ VISUAL VOCAB page V31

ˌcauliflower ˈcheese (*BrE*) (*NAmE* **ˌcauliflower with ˈcheese**) *noun* [U] a hot dish of cauliflower cooked and served in a cheese sauce 奶酪菜花

ˌcauliflower ˈear *noun* an ear that is permanently swollen because it has been hit many times（因多次遭毆打而永久腫脹的）菜花耳，開花耳朵

caulk /kɔːk/ *verb* **~ sth** to fill the holes or cracks in sth, especially a ship, with a substance that keeps out water 補（船的）漏洞；填（船）縫

causal /ˈkɔːzl/ *adj.* **1** (*formal*) connected with the relationship between two things, where one causes the other to happen 因果關係的；前因後果的；原因的：*the causal relationship between poverty and disease* 貧窮與疾病的因果關係 **2 ~ conjunction/connective** (*grammar* 語法) a word such as *because* that introduces a statement about the cause of sth 表示因果關係的（連接詞，如 because）▸ **caus·al·ly** *adv.*：*Are the two factors causally connected?* 這兩個因素有因果關係嗎？

caus·al·ity /kɔːˈzæləti/ (also **caus·ation**) *noun* [U] (*formal*) the relationship between sth that happens and the reason for it happening; the principle that nothing can happen without a cause 因果關係；因果律（或性）

caus·ation /kɔːˈzeɪʃn/ *noun* [U] (*formal*) **1** the process of one event causing or producing another event 誘因；起因；原因 **2** = CAUSALITY

causa·tive /ˈkɔːzətɪv/ *adj.* **1** (*formal*) acting as the cause of sth 成為原因的；起因的：*Smoking is a causative factor in several major diseases.* 抽煙是引起幾種主要疾病的病因。 **2** (*grammar* 語法) a **causative verb** expresses a cause, for example *blacken* which means 'to cause to become black' 使役的（動詞，如 blacken）➲ compare ERGATIVE, INCHOATIVE

Language Bank 用語庫

cause

X causes Y * X 導致 Y

- Childhood obesity can **cause/lead to** long-term health problems. 兒童肥胖可能導致長期的健康問題。
- Changes in lifestyle and diet over the last twenty years have **caused/led to/resulted in** a sharp increase in childhood obesity. 過去二十年生活方式及飲食的變化導致肥胖兒童數量急劇上升。
- Several factors, including changes in diet and lifestyle, **have contributed to** the increase in childhood obesity. 包括飲食及生活方式變化在內的多個因素促使肥胖兒童數量增加。
- Research suggests that fast food and soft drinks directly **contribute to** childhood obesity. 研究表明快餐和軟飲料會直接導致兒童肥胖。
- Genetics, lifestyle and diet **are** all important **factors** in cases of childhood obesity. 基因、生活方式和飲食都是造成兒童肥胖的重要因素。
- Even small changes in lifestyle and diet can **bring about** significant weight loss. 甚至生活方式及飲食的細微變化都可能帶來明顯的體重下降。

➲ Language Banks at BECAUSE OF, CONSEQUENTLY, THEREFORE

cause 🗝 /kɔːz/ *noun, verb*

■ ***noun*** **1** 🗝 [C] the person or thing that makes sth happen 原因；起因：*Unemployment is a major cause of poverty.* 失業是貧困的主要原因。◇ *There was discussion about the fire and its likely cause.* 對那場火災及其可能的起因進行了討論。◇ *Drinking and driving is one of the most common causes of traffic accidents.* 酒後駕車是導致交通事故最常見的原因之一。 **2** 🗝 [U] **~ (for sth)** a reason for having particular feelings or behaving in a particular way 理由；動機；緣故：*There is no* ***cause for concern.*** 沒有理由擔憂。◇ *The food was excellent—I had no* ***cause for complaint.*** 飯菜好極了，我沒理由抱怨。◇ ***with/without good cause*** (= with/without a good reason) 理由充分；無緣無故 **3** 🗝 [C] an organization or idea that people support or fight for（支持或為之奮鬥的）事業，目標，思想：*Animal welfare campaigners raised £70 000 for their cause last year.* 動物保護主義者去年為保護動物募集了 7 萬英鎊。◇ *a* ***good cause*** (= an organization that does good work, such as a charity) 崇高的事業 ◇ *fighting for the Republican cause* 為共和黨的事業而奮鬥 ➲ see also LOST CAUSE **4** [C] (*law* 律) a case that goes to court 訴訟案

IDM **be for/in a good ˈcause** worth doing, because it is helping other people 做好事；行善 ➲ more at COMMON *adj.*

■ ***verb*** 🗝 to make sth happen, especially sth bad or unpleasant 使發生；造成；引起；導致：**~ sth** *Do they know what caused the fire?* 他們知道引起這場火災的原因嗎？◇ *Are you* ***causing trouble*** *again?* 你還要惹麻煩嗎？◇ *deaths caused by dangerous driving* 危險駕駛造成的死亡 ◇ **~ sth for sb** *The bad weather is causing problems for many farmers.* 惡劣的天氣正給許多農民造成困難。◇ **~ sb sth** *The project is still causing him a lot of problems.* 這項工程現在仍然給他帶來許多的麻煩。◇ **~ sth to do sth** *The poor harvest caused prices to rise sharply.* 收成不好導致物價急劇上漲。

ˈcause *conj.* = COS[1]

cause célèbre /ˌkɔːz seˈlebrə/ *noun* (from *French*) (*pl.* **causes célèbres** /ˌkɔːz seˈlebrə/) an issue that attracts a lot of attention and is supported by a lot of people 廣受關注的問題；公眾支持的事物

cause·way /ˈkɔːzweɪ/ *noun* a raised road or path across water or wet ground（穿越水面或濕地的）堤道

caus·tic /ˈkɔːstɪk/ *adj.* **1** (of a chemical substance 化學物質) able to destroy or dissolve other substances 腐蝕性的；苛性的 **SYN** **corrosive** **2** critical in a bitter or SARCASTIC way 尖酸刻薄的；挖苦的；譏諷的 **SYN** **scathing**：***caustic comments/wit*** 刻薄話；長於諷刺 ▸ **caus·tic·al·ly** /-kli/ *adv.*

caustic ˈsoda *noun* [U] a chemical used in making paper and soap 苛性鈉；燒鹼；氫氧化鈉

caut·er·ize (*BrE* also **-ise**) /ˈkɔːtəraɪz/ *verb* **~ sth** (*medical* 醫) to burn a wound, using a chemical or heat, in order to stop the loss of blood or to prevent infection 燒灼，烙（用化學藥劑或高溫燒灼傷口以止血或消毒）

cau·tion /ˈkɔːʃn/ *noun, verb*

■ ***noun*** **1** [U] care that you take in order to avoid danger or mistakes; not taking any risks 謹慎；小心；慎重：***extreme/great caution*** 特別謹慎；小心翼翼 ◇ *Statistics should be treated* ***with caution.*** 對待統計數字要小心。➲ SYNONYMS at CARE **2** [C] (*BrE*) a warning that is given by the police to sb who has committed a crime that is not too serious（警察向犯輕罪的人發出的）警告：*As a first offender, she got off with a caution.* 她由於是初犯而獲從輕發落，只受到了警告。 **3** [U, C] (*formal*) a warning or a piece of advice about a possible danger or risk（對危險或風險的）警告，告誡：*a* ***word/note of caution*** 忠告；警告的提示 ◇ *Some cautions must be mentioned—for example good tools are essential to do the job well.* 有些警句必須提及，如：工欲善其事，必先利其器。

IDM **throw/cast caution to the ˈwind(s)** to stop caring about how dangerous sth might be; to start taking risks 不顧危險；魯莽行事；冒險

■ ***verb*** **1** [I, T] to warn sb about the possible dangers or problems of sth 警告；告誡；提醒：**~ against sth** *I would caution against getting too involved.* 我要提出警告，別陷得太深。◇ **~ sb against/about sth** *Sam cautioned him against making a hasty decision.* 薩姆告誡他不要草率作出決定。◇ **~ (sb) that …** *The government cautioned that pay increases could lead to job losses.* 政府警告說增加工資會導致失業。◇ **~ sb to do sth** *Employees were cautioned to be careful about what they said to people outside the company.* 員工受到告誡，對公司外的人說話要小心謹慎。◇ **~ (sb) + speech** *'I'd take care if I were you,' she cautioned (him).* "我要是你，我會當心的。" 她提醒（他）道。 **2** [T] **~ sb** (*BrE, law* 律) to warn sb officially that anything they say may be used as evidence against them in court 警告，提醒（某人說的任何話都可能在法庭上被當作對其不利的證據）：*Suspects must be cautioned before any questions are asked.* 嫌疑犯在回答問題前必須得到提醒。 **3** [T, usually passive] **~ sb (for sth)** (*BrE, law* 律) to warn sb officially that they will be punished if they do sth wrong or illegal again 警告（某人不得再做錯事或非法的事）：*She wasn't sent to the* *juvenile court; instead she was cautioned.* 她未被送上少年法庭，而是受到了警告。

cau·tion·ary /ˈkɔːʃənəri; *NAmE* -neri/ *adj.* giving advice or a warning 勸告的；告誡的；警告的：*a **cautionary tale** about the problems of buying a computer* 有關購買計算機時可能遇到種種問題的告誡 ◇ *In her conclusion, the author sounds a **cautionary note**.* 作者在結尾時敲響了警鐘。

cau·tious /ˈkɔːʃəs/ *adj.* being careful about what you say or do, especially to avoid danger or mistakes; not taking any risks 小心的；謹慎的：*The government has been cautious in its response to the report.* 政府對此報道反應謹慎。◇ *They've taken a very **cautious approach**.* 他們採取了十分謹慎的態度。◇ *They expressed cautious optimism about a solution to the crisis.* 他們對解決危機持謹慎的樂觀態度。◇ **~ about sb/sth** | **~ about doing sth** *He was very cautious about committing himself to anything.* 他謹小慎微，從不輕易作出承諾。▶ **cau·tious·ly** *adv.*：*She looked cautiously around and then walked away from the house.* 她先小心地環顧了一下四周，然後才離開了房子。◇ *I'm cautiously optimistic.* 我持謹慎的樂觀態度。**cau·tious·ness** *noun* [U]

Which Word? 詞語辨析

cautious / careful

- A **cautious** person is nervous that something may be dangerous or unwise, so they only do it very slowly or after a lot of thought. (opposite= **rash**) * cautious 指人因擔心某事危險或不明智而緩慢行事或深思熟慮。（反義詞為 rash）
- A **careful** person is not nervous but does take extra care to make sure that everything is correct or nothing goes wrong. (opposite= **careless**) * careful 指人並非擔心害怕，但為確保萬無一失而做事小心仔細。（反義詞為 careless）
- Notice also 還要注意：

***Be careful/Take care** when you drive on icy roads.* 在冰霜覆蓋的道路上駕駛時要小心。

***Caution/Warning**—thin ice.* 小心／警告 —— 冰薄勿踏。

cava /ˈkɑːvə/ *noun* [U, C] a type of SPARKLING white wine (= with bubbles) from Spain 卡瓦酒（西班牙發泡白葡萄酒）

cav·al·cade /ˌkævlˈkeɪd/ *noun* a line of people on horses or in vehicles forming part of a ceremony（參加典禮的）騎馬隊列，車隊

Cava·lier /ˌkævəˈlɪə(r); *NAmE* -ˈlɪr/ *noun* a supporter of the King in the English Civil War (1642-49) 騎士（英國內戰中支持國王者）➲ compare ROUNDHEAD

cava·lier /ˌkævəˈlɪə(r); *NAmE* -ˈlɪr/ *adj.* [usually before noun] not caring enough about sth important or about the feelings of other people 漫不經心的；不在乎的：*The government takes a **cavalier attitude** to the problems of prison overcrowding.* 政府對監獄擁擠不堪的問題不聞不問。▶ **cava·lier·ly** *adv.*

cav·alry /ˈkævlri/ *noun* (usually **the cavalry**) [sing.+sing./pl. v.] (in the past) the part of the army that fought on horses; the part of the modern army that uses ARMOURED vehicles（舊時的）騎兵；裝甲兵

cave /keɪv/ *noun, verb*

■ ***noun*** a large hole in the side of a hill or under the ground 山洞；洞穴：*the mouth* (= the entrance) *of the cave* 洞口 ◇ *a **cave-dweller*** (= a person who lives in a cave) 穴居人 ➲ VISUAL VOCAB pages V4, V5

■ ***verb***

PHR V **ˌcave ˈin (on sb/sth)** (of a roof, wall, etc. 房頂、牆等) to fall down and towards the centre 塌落；塌陷；坍塌：*The ceiling suddenly caved in on top of them.* 天花板突然塌落在他們身上。➲ related noun CAVE-IN **ˌcave ˈin (to sth)** to finally do what sb wants after you have been strongly opposing them 讓步；屈服；屈從：*The President is unlikely to cave in to demands for a public inquiry.* 總統未必會同意進行公開調查。➲ see also CAVING

cav·eat /ˈkæviæt/ *noun* (*formal*, from *Latin*) a warning that particular things need to be considered before sth can be done 警告；告誡

cav·eat emp·tor /ˌkæviæt ˈemptɔː(r)/ *noun* (from *Latin*) the principle that a person who buys sth is responsible for finding any faults in the thing they buy 買主購物自行小心（買主購物時有責任檢查所購貨物是否有問題）

ˈcave-in *noun* the fact of sth suddenly collapsing（突然的）塌陷，坍塌，倒塌

cave·man /ˈkeɪvmæn/ *noun* (*pl.* **-men** /-men/) **1** a person who lived in a CAVE thousands of years ago（數千年前的）穴居人 **2** (*informal*) a man who behaves in an aggressive way 野蠻的人；粗野的人

ˈcave painting *noun* a PREHISTORIC painting on the walls of a CAVE, often showing animals and hunting scenes（史前期畫有動物和狩獵場面的）洞穴壁畫

caver /ˈkeɪvə(r)/ (also **pot·holer**) (both *BrE*) (*NAmE* **spe·lunk·er**) *noun* a person who goes into CAVES under the ground as a sport or hobby 探察洞穴者（以此為體育運動或業餘愛好）➲ compare SPELEOLOGIST

cav·ern /ˈkævən; *NAmE* -vərn/ *noun* a CAVE, especially a large one 大洞穴；大山洞

cav·ern·ous /ˈkævənəs; *NAmE* -vərn-/ *adj.* (*formal*) (of a room or space 房間或空間) very large and often empty and/or dark; like a CAVE 大而空的；又黑又深的；像洞穴的

cav·iar (also **cavi·are**) /ˈkæviɑː(r)/ *noun* [U] the eggs of some types of fish, especially the STURGEON, that are preserved using salt and eaten as a very special and expensive type of food（尤指用鱘魚子醃製的）魚子醬

cavil /ˈkævl/ *verb* (**-ll-**, *especially US* **-l-**) [I] **~ (at sth)** (*formal*) to make unnecessary complaints about sth 無端抱怨；挑剔；吹毛求疵 **SYN** **quibble**

cav·ing /ˈkeɪvɪŋ/ (also **pot·hol·ing**) (both *BrE*) (*NAmE* **spe·lunk·ing**) *noun* [U] the sport or activity of going into CAVES under the ground 洞穴探察：*He had always wanted to **go caving**.* 他過去一直想探索洞穴。➲ VISUAL VOCAB page V40

cav·ity /ˈkævəti/ *noun* (*pl.* **-ies**) (*formal* or *technical* 術語) **1** a hole or empty space inside sth solid 洞；孔；窟窿；腔：*the abdominal cavity* 腹腔 **2** a hole in a tooth（齲齒的）洞

ˌcavity ˈwall *noun* a wall consisting of two walls with a space between them, designed to prevent heat from escaping（有保暖作用的）空心牆，夾壁牆：*cavity wall insulation* 空心牆隔熱

ca·vort /kəˈvɔːt; *NAmE* kəˈvɔːrt/ *verb* [I] **+ adv./prep.** to jump or move around in a noisy, excited and often sexual way 歡躍；歡蹦亂跳；嬉戲；放蕩地玩樂：*The photos showed her cavorting on the beach with her new lover.* 這些照片展現了她和新情人在海灘上放蕩嬉戲的情景。

caw /kɔː/ *noun* the loud, unpleasant sound that is made by birds such as CROWS and ROOKS 鴉叫聲；聒耳的叫聲 ▶ **caw** *verb* [I]

cay·enne /keɪˈen/ (also **ˌcayenne ˈpepper**) *noun* [U] a type of red pepper used in cooking to give a hot flavour to food 紅辣椒

cay·man = CAIMAN

CB /ˌsiː ˈbiː/ *noun* [U] the abbreviation for 'Citizens' Band' (a range of waves on a radio on which people can talk to each other over short distances, especially when driving) 民用波段，民用電台頻帶（全寫為 Citizens' Band，在短距離內，尤指駕車時可通話的無線電波段）：*A truck driver used his CB radio to call for help.* 卡車司機用民用波段無線電呼救。

CBE /ˌsiː biː ˈiː/ *noun* the abbreviation for 'Commander (of the Order) of the British Empire' (an award given in Britain to some people for a special achievement) 英帝國高級勳位獲得者，英帝國司令勳銜獲得者（全寫為 Commander (of the Order) of the British Empire，英國

授予有特殊功績的人的獎勵）：*He was made a CBE in 2006.* 他在 2006 年獲授予英帝國高級勳位。◇ *Shami Chakrabarti CBE* 英帝國高級勳爵沙米 • 查克拉巴提

CBI /ˌsiː biː ˈaɪ/ *abbr.* Confederation of British Industry (an important organization to which businesses and industries belong) 英國產業聯合會

CBS /ˌsiː biː ˈes/ *abbr.* Columbia Broadcasting System (an American recording and broadcasting company that produces records, television programmes, etc.)（美國）哥倫比亞廣播公司

cc /ˌsiː ˈsiː/ *abbr.*, *verb*

■ ***abbr.*** **1** carbon copy (to) (used on business letters and emails to show that a copy is being sent to another person) 副本，抄送（用於商務書信和電子郵件，表示副本同時發送給另一人）：*to Luke Peters, cc Janet Gold* 寄盧克 • 彼得斯，抄送珍妮特 • 戈爾德 **2** cubic centimetre(s) 立方厘米：*an 850cc engine* * 0.85 升發動機

■ ***verb*** (**cc's**, **cc'ing**, **cc'ed**, **cc'ed** /ˌsiː ˈsiːd/) **~ sth (to sb)** | **~ sb sth** (*informal*) to send sb a copy of a letter or email message that you are sending to sb else 抄送（將信函或電郵同時發送給收信人以外的人）：*Her message was sent to the company president and cc'ed to us.* 她的郵件發給了公司總裁，同時抄送我們了。

CCRA /ˌsiː siː ɑːr ˈeɪ/ *abbr.* Canada Customs and Revenue Agency (the department of the Canadian government that deals with personal income tax, and with taxes on goods that are bought and sold) 加拿大海關與稅務局

CCTV /ˌsiː siː tiː ˈviː/ *abbr.* CLOSED-CIRCUIT TELEVISION 閉路電視

CD 0‑π /ˌsiː ˈdiː/ (also **disc**) *noun* the abbreviation for 'compact disc' (a small disc on which sound or information is recorded. CDs are played on a special machine called a **CD player**) 光盤，激光唱片，光碟（全寫為 compact disc）：*His albums are available* ***on CD*** *and online.* 他的專輯可以通過購買 CD 或在線獲得。➲ **COLLOCATIONS** at MUSIC

ˌC'D burn·er (also **ˌC'D writer**) *noun* a piece of equipment used for copying sound or information from a computer onto a CD 光盤刻錄機；光碟燒錄機

CD-I (*US* **CDI™**) /ˌsiː diː ˈaɪ/ *noun* **1** [U] the abbreviation for 'compact disc interactive' (a MULTIMEDIA system which uses CDs that can react to instructions given by the user) 交互式光盤系統（全寫為 compact disc interactive，一種受使用者指令控制的多媒體光盤系統）**2** [C] the type of CD that this type of system uses 交互式光盤

CD-R™ /ˌsiː diː ˈɑː(r)/ *noun* [C, U] the abbreviation for 'compact disc recordable' (a CD on which information, sound and pictures can be recorded once only) 一次寫入式光盤，可錄光盤（全寫為 compact disc recordable，可作一次性刻錄）

Cdr (also **Cdr.** especially in *US*) *abbr.* (in writing) COMMANDER（書寫形式）海軍中校，高級警官：*Cdr (John) Stone*（約翰 •）斯通警官

CD-ROM /ˌsiː diː ˈrɒm; *NAmE* ˈrɑːm/ *noun* [C, U] the abbreviation for 'compact disc read-only memory' (a CD on which large amounts of information, sound and pictures can be stored, for use on a computer) 只讀光盤，唯讀光碟（全寫為 compact disc read-only memory）：*The software package contains 5 CD-ROMs.* 這個軟件包含 5 片光盤。◇ *The encyclopedia is available on CD-ROM.* 百科全書備有光盤形式。◇ *a CD-ROM drive* (= in a computer) 只讀光盤驅動器 ➲ **VISUAL VOCAB** page V66 ➲ compare ROM

CD-RW /ˌsiː diː ɑː ˈdʌbljuː; *NAmE* ɑːr/ *noun* [C, U] the abbreviation for 'compact disc rewritable' (a CD on which information, sound and pictures can be recorded and removed more than once) 可重寫光盤（全寫為 compact disc rewritable）

CDT /ˌsiː diː ˈtiː/ *abbr.* **1** (*BrE*) Craft, Design and Technology (taught as a subject in schools) 工藝、設計與技術（學校科目）**2** CENTRAL DAYLIGHT TIME

ˌC'D writer *noun* = CD BURNER

CE /ˌsiː ˈiː/ *abbr.* **1** (in Britain) Church of England 英國國教會；英格蘭聖公會 **2** (also **C.E.** especially in *NAmE*) Common Era (the period since the birth of Christ when the Christian CALENDAR starts counting years). CE can be used to give dates in the same way as AD. 基督紀元，公元（用於表示日期，用法同 AD）➲ compare AD, BC, BCE

C

cease 0‑π **AW** /siːs/ *verb* [I, T] (*formal*) to stop happening or existing; to stop sth from happening or existing（使）停止，終止，結束：*Welfare payments cease as soon as an individual starts a job.* 一旦就業，即停發福利救濟。◇ **~ to do sth** *You never cease to amaze me!* 你總能讓我感到驚奇！◇ **~ sth** *They voted to cease strike action immediately.* 他們投票決定立即停止罷工。◇ *He ordered his men to cease fire* (= stop shooting). 他命令手下停止射擊。◇ **~ doing sth** *The company ceased trading in June.* 這家公司已於六月停業。➲ see also CESSATION **IDM** see WONDER *n.*

cease·fire /ˈsiːsfaɪə(r)/ *noun* a time when enemies agree to stop fighting, usually while a way is found to end the fighting permanently（通常指永久性的）停火，停戰 **SYN** **truce**：*a call for an immediate ceasefire* 要求立即停火的呼籲 ◇ *Observers have reported serious violations of the ceasefire.* 觀察員報告說停火協議遭到嚴重破壞。➲ **COLLOCATIONS** at WAR

cease·less **AW** /ˈsiːsləs/ *adj.* (*formal*) not stopping; seeming to have no end 不停的；（好像）無休止的，不斷的 **SYN** **constant, interminable** ▸ **cease·less·ly** *adv.*

cecum (*NAmE*) (*BrE* **cae·cum**) /ˈsiːkəm/ *noun* (*pl.* **ceca** /ˈsiːkə/) a small bag which is part of the INTESTINE, between the small and the large intestine 盲腸

cedar /ˈsiːdə(r)/ *noun* **1** (also **ˈcedar tree**) [C] a tall EVERGREEN tree with wide spreading branches 雪松 **2** (also **cedar·wood**) [U] the hard red wood of the cedar tree, which has a sweet smell 雪松木

cede /siːd/ *verb* **~ sth (to sb)** (*formal*) to give sb control of sth or give them power, a right, etc., especially unwillingly 割讓；讓給；轉讓：*Cuba was ceded by Spain to the US in 1898.* 古巴在 1898 年被西班牙割讓給美國。➲ see also CESSION

ce·dilla /sɪˈdɪlə/ *noun* the mark placed under the letter *c* in French, Portuguese, etc. to show that it is pronounced like an *s* rather than a *k*, as in *français*; a similar mark under *s* in Turkish and some other languages 下加符，下加變音符（法語、葡萄牙語等 c 字母下面加的符號，表示發音像 s 而不像 k，如 français；土耳其語和其他一些語言中 s 字母下有類似的符號）

cei·lidh /ˈkeɪli/ *noun* a social occasion with music and dancing, especially in Scotland and Ireland（蘇格蘭、愛爾蘭有音樂舞蹈的）同樂會，社交集會

ceil·ing 0‑π /ˈsiːlɪŋ/ *noun*

1 0‑π the top inside surface of a room 天花板；頂棚：*She lay on her back staring up at the ceiling.* 她仰臥着凝視天花板。◇ *a large room with a high ceiling* 屋頂很高的大房間 **2** the highest limit or amount of sth 最高限度；上限；最大限量：*price ceilings* 最高價 ➲ compare FLOOR *n.* (7) **3** (*technical* 術語) the greatest height at which a particular aircraft is able to fly 最高飛行限度；升限 ➲ see also GLASS CEILING **IDM** see HIT *v.*

ˈceiling rose (also **rose**) *noun* (*technical* 術語) a round object that is fixed to the ceiling of a room for the wires of an electric light to go through（天花板或頂棚的）接線盒

celeb /səˈleb/ *noun* (*informal*) = CELEBRITY (1)

cele·brant /ˈselɪbrənt/ *noun* **1** a priest who leads a church service, especially the COMMUNION service; a person who attends a service 宗教禮儀主持人；聖餐主持者（或參加者）**2** (*NAmE*) a person who is celebrating sth, for example at a party 參加聚會（或慶典）的人

cele·brate 0‑π /ˈselɪbreɪt/ *verb*

1 0‑π [I, T] to show that a day or an event is important by doing sth special on it 慶祝；慶賀：*Jake's passed his exams. We're going out to celebrate.* 傑克已通過考試，我們要外出慶祝一下。◇ **~ sth** *We celebrated our 25th wedding anniversary in Florence.* 我們在佛羅倫薩慶祝結婚 25 週年。◇ *How do people celebrate New Year in your* country? 你們國家的人怎樣慶賀新年？ **2** [T] **~ sth** to perform a religious ceremony, especially the Christian COMMUNION service 主持宗教儀式（尤指聖餐） **3** [T] **~ sb/sth** (*formal*) to praise sb/sth 讚美；頌揚；歌頌：*a movie celebrating the life and work of Martin Luther King* 頌揚馬丁•路德•金生平事跡的影片

C

cele·brated /ˈselɪbreɪtɪd/ *adj.* famous for having good qualities 著名的；聞名的；馳名的：*a celebrated painter* 著名的畫家

cele·bra·tion 0→ /ˌselɪˈbreɪʃn/ *noun*
1 0→ [C] a special event that people organize in order to celebrate sth 慶典；慶祝活動：*birthday/wedding celebrations* 生日/結婚慶典 **2** 0→ [U, C] the act of celebrating sth 慶祝；頌揚：*Her triumph was a* ***cause for celebration****.* 她的勝利是慶祝的理由。◇ *a party* ***in celebration of*** *their fiftieth wedding anniversary* 慶祝他們金婚紀念的聚會 ◇ *The service was a celebration of his life* (= praised what he had done in his life). 舉行的宗教禮儀頌揚了他的一生。

cele·bra·tory /ˌseləˈbreɪtəri; *NAmE* ˈseləbrətɔːri/ *adj.* celebrating sth or marking a special occasion 慶祝的；慶典的：*a* ***celebratory drink/dinner*** 喜慶酒/宴會

ce·leb·rity /səˈlebrəti/ *noun* (*pl.* **-ies**) **1** (also *informal* **celeb**) [C] a famous person 名人；名流：*TV celebrities* 電視名人 **2** [U] the state of being famous 名望；名譽；著名 SYN **fame**：*Does he find his new celebrity intruding on his private life?* 他是否感覺到他最近的成名侵擾了他的私生活？

cel·eri·ac /səˈleriæk/ *noun* [U] a large white root vegetable which is a type of CELERY and which is eaten raw or cooked 塊根芹；根芹菜

cel·ery /ˈseləri/ *noun* [U] a vegetable with long crisp light green STEMS that are often eaten raw 芹菜：(*BrE*) *a stick of celery* 一根芹菜 ◇ (*NAmE*) *a stalk of celery* 一根芹菜 ➲ VISUAL VOCAB page V31

cel·esta /səˈlestə/ (also **ce·leste** /səˈlest/) *noun* a small musical instrument with a keyboard, that produces a sound like bells 鋼片琴

ce·les·tial /səˈlestiəl; *NAmE* -tʃl/ *adj.* [usually before noun] (*formal* or *literary*) of the sky or of heaven 天空的；天上的：***celestial bodies*** (= the sun, moon, stars, etc.) 天體（太陽、月球、恒星等）◇ *celestial light/music* 天體光；美妙仙樂 ➲ compare TERRESTRIAL (2)

ce·liac dis·ease (*NAmE*) (*BrE* **coel·iac disease**) /ˈsiːliæk dɪziːz/ a disease in which sb cannot DIGEST food (= break it down in their body) because their body is very sensitive to GLUTEN (= a PROTEIN that is found in WHEAT) 乳糜瀉（因麩膠過敏引起的消化不良）

celi·bate /ˈselɪbət/ *adj., noun*
■ ***adj.*** **1** not married and not having sex, especially for religious reasons（尤指因宗教原因）獨身的，不結婚的，沒有性生活的：*celibate priests* 獨身的教士 **2** not having sex 無性生活的；禁慾的：*I've been celibate for the past six months.* 我已禁慾六個月。 ▸ **celi·bacy** /ˈselɪbəsi/ *noun* [U]：*a vow of celibacy* 獨身誓言
■ ***noun*** (*formal*) a person who has chosen not to marry; a person who never has sex 獨身主義者；禁慾者；從不過性生活的人

cell 0→ /sel/ *noun*
1 0→ a room for one or more prisoners in a prison or police station 單間牢房；牢房 ➲ see also PADDED CELL **2** a small room without much furniture in which a MONK or NUN lives（修道士或修女住的）小房間 **3** 0→ the smallest unit of living matter that can exist on its own. All plants and animals are made up of cells. 細胞：*blood cells* 血細胞 ◇ *the nucleus of a cell* 細胞核 ➲ see also STEM CELL **4** each of the small sections that together form a larger structure, for example a HONEYCOMB（大結構中的）小隔室（如蜂房巢室） **5** a device for producing an electric current, for example by the action of chemicals or light 電池：*a photoelectric cell* 光電池 **6** a small group of people who work as part of a larger political organization, especially secretly（尤指秘密的）政治小組，基層組織：*a terrorist cell* 恐怖分子小組 **7** one of the small squares in a SPREADSHEET computer program in which you enter a single piece of data（計算機電子表格的）單元格 **8** (*informal, especially NAmE*) = CELL PHONE

cel·lar /ˈselə(r)/ *noun* **1** an underground room often used for storing things 地窖；地下室：*a coal cellar* 貯煤地窖 **2** = WINE CELLAR ➲ see also SALT CELLAR

cell·ist /ˈtʃelɪst/ *noun* a person who plays the CELLO 大提琴手；大提琴演奏者

cell·mate /ˈselmeɪt/ *noun* a prisoner with whom another prisoner shares a cell 同牢難友

cello /ˈtʃeləʊ; *NAmE* -loʊ/ (also *formal* **vio·lon·cello**) *noun* (*pl.* **-os**) a musical instrument with strings, shaped like a large VIOLIN. The player sits down and holds the cello between his or her knees. 大提琴 ➲ VISUAL VOCAB page V34

Cel·lo·phane™ /ˈseləfeɪn/ *noun* [U] a thin transparent plastic material used for wrapping things 賽璐玢（用於包裝的玻璃紙）

ˈcell phone 0→ (also ˌ**cellular** ˈ**phone**, *informal* **cell**) (*especially NAmE*) (*BrE* usually ˌ**mobile** ˈ**phone**, **mo·bile**) *noun* a telephone that does not have wires and works by radio, that you can carry with you and use anywhere 手機：*cell phone users* 手機用戶 ◇ *I talked to her on my cell phone.* 我用手機跟她通話。◇ *The use of cellular phones is not permitted on most aircraft.* 大多數飛機上禁止使用手機。➲ COLLOCATIONS at PHONE

cel·lu·lar /ˈseljələ(r)/ *adj.* **1** connected with or consisting of the cells of plants or animals 細胞的；由細胞組成的：***cellular structure/processes*** 細胞結構/變化過程 **2** connected with a telephone system that works by radio instead of wires（無線電話）蜂窩狀的：*a cellular network* 蜂窩式網絡系統 ◇ *cellular radio* 蜂窩式無線傳輸系統 **3** (*BrE*) (of cloth 布料) loosely WOVEN for extra warmth 網狀的；網眼的：*cellular blankets* 網眼毯

cel·lu·lite /ˈseljulaɪt/ *noun* [U] a type of fat that some people get below their skin, which stops the surface of the skin looking smooth 皮下脂肪團

cel·lu·loid /ˈseljulɔɪd/ *noun* [U] **1** a thin transparent plastic material made in sheets, used in the past for cinema film（舊時攝影用的）膠片，賽璐珞片 **2** (*old-fashioned*) used as a way of referring to films/movies 電影

cel·lu·lose /ˈseljuləʊs; *NAmE* -loʊs/ *noun* [U] **1** a natural substance that forms the cell walls of all plants and trees and is used in making plastics, paper, etc. 纖維素 **2** any COMPOUND of cellulose used in making paint, LACQUER, etc.（用於製作塗料、漆等的）纖維素化合物

Cel·sius /ˈselsiəs/ (also **centi·grade**) *adj.* (*abbr.* **C**) of or using a scale of temperature in which water freezes at 0° and boils at 100° 攝氏的：*It will be a mild night, around nine degrees Celsius.* 晚間天氣溫和，溫度約九攝氏度。◇ *the Celsius Scale* 攝氏溫標 ▸ **Cel·sius** *noun* [U]：*temperatures in Celsius and Fahrenheit* 攝氏和華氏溫度

Celt /kelt/ *noun* **1** a member of a race of people from western Europe who settled in ancient Britain before the Romans came 凱爾特人（在羅馬人之前定居不列顛的西歐人） **2** a person whose ANCESTORS were Celts, especially one from Ireland, Wales, Scotland, Cornwall or Brittany（尤指來自愛爾蘭、威爾士、蘇格蘭、康沃爾或布列塔尼的）凱爾特人後裔

CELTA /ˈseltə/ *noun* [U] the abbreviation for 'Certificate in English Language Teaching to Adults' (a British qualification from the University of Cambridge for teachers with little or no experience of teaching English as a foreign language) 成人英語教學證書（全寫為 Certificate in English Language Teaching to Adults，英國劍橋大學為不具備英語作為外語教學經驗的教師頒發的資格證書）

Cel·tic /ˈkeltɪk/ *adj.* connected with the Celts or their language 凱爾特人的；凱爾特語的：*Celtic history* 凱爾特人的歷史

ˌ**Celtic** ˈ**cross** *noun* a cross with the vertical part longer than the horizontal part and a circle round the centre 凱爾特十字（垂直線比水平線長，中間有圓環）

the ˌCeltic ˈfringe *noun* [sing.] (*BrE*) the people in Ireland and western parts of Britain whose ANCESTORS were CELTS, often used to refer to Ireland, Scotland and Wales 凱爾特外緣（祖先為凱爾特人的愛爾蘭和英國西部的人，常用以指愛爾蘭、蘇格蘭和威爾士）

ce·ment /sɪˈment/ *noun, verb*

■ ***noun*** [U] **1** a grey powder made by burning CLAY and LIME that sets hard when it is mixed with water. Cement is used in building to stick bricks together and to make very hard surfaces. 水泥 **2** the hard substance that is formed when cement becomes dry and hard（乾燥後硬化的）水泥：*a floor of cement* 水泥地板 ◇ *a cement floor* 水泥地板 ➲ see also CONCRETE *n.*, MORTAR *n.* (1) **3** a soft substance that becomes hard when dry and is used for sticking things together or filling in holes 膠合劑；膠接劑；粘固粉：*dental cement* (= for filling holes in teeth) 補牙用的粘固粉 **4** (*formal*) something that unites people in a common interest（使有共同利益者聯合起來的）紐帶，凝聚力：*values which are the cement of society* 使社會具有凝聚力的價值觀念

■ ***verb*** **1** [often passive] **~ A and B (together)** to join two things together using cement, glue, etc.（用水泥、膠等）粘結，膠合 **2 ~ sth** to make a relationship, an agreement, etc. stronger 加強，鞏固（關係、協定等）**SYN strengthen**：*The President's visit was intended to cement the alliance between the two countries.* 總統的訪問是為了加強兩國的聯盟。

cemen·ta·tion /ˌsiːmenˈteɪʃn/ *noun* [U] **1** (*chemistry* 化) the process of changing a metal by heating it together with a powder（金屬的）滲碳處理 **2** (*geology* 地) the process of grains of sand, etc. sticking together to form SEDIMENTARY rocks（沙粒等的）膠結，膠結作用

ceˈment mixer (also **ˈconcrete mixer**) *noun* a machine with a drum that holds sand, water and cement and turns to mix them together 混凝土攪拌機 ➲ **VISUAL VOCAB** page V58

cem·et·ery /ˈsemətri; *NAmE* -teri/ *noun* (*pl.* **-ies**) an area of land used for burying dead people, especially one that is not beside a church（尤指不靠近教堂的）墓地，墳地，公墓 ➲ compare CHURCHYARD, GRAVEYARD (1)

ceno·taph /ˈsenətɑːf; *NAmE* -tæf/ *noun* a MONUMENT built in memory of soldiers killed in war who are buried somewhere else（為葬於他處的陣亡士兵建立的）紀念碑

cen·ser /ˈsensə(r)/ *noun* a container for holding and burning INCENSE (= a substance that produces a pleasant smell), used especially during religious ceremonies（尤用於宗教儀式的）香爐

cen·sor /ˈsensə(r)/ *noun, verb*

■ ***noun*** a person whose job is to examine books, films/movies, etc. and remove parts which are considered to be offensive, immoral or a political threat（書籍、電影等的）審查員，審查官

■ ***verb*** **~ sth** to remove the parts of a book, film/movie, etc. that are considered to be offensive, immoral or a political threat 刪剪（書籍、電影等中被認為犯忌、違反道德或政治上危險的內容）：*The news reports had been **heavily censored**.* 這些新聞報道已被大肆刪剪。

cen·sori·ous /senˈsɔːriəs/ *adj.* (*formal*) tending to criticize people or things a lot 愛挑剔的；吹毛求疵的 **SYN critical**

cen·sor·ship /ˈsensəʃɪp; *NAmE* -sərʃ-/ *noun* [U] the act or policy of CENSORING books, etc. 審查；檢查；審查制度：*press censorship* 新聞審查制度 ◇ *The decree imposed strict censorship of the media.* 這個法令強制實行嚴格的媒體審查制度。

cen·sure /ˈsenʃə(r)/ *noun, verb*

■ ***noun*** [U] (*formal*) strong criticism 嚴厲的批評；斥責；譴責：*a vote of censure on the government's foreign policy* 投票表決譴責政府的外交政策

■ ***verb*** **~ sb (for sth)** (*formal*) to criticize sb severely, and often publicly, because of sth they have done（公開地）嚴厲斥責，譴責 **SYN rebuke**：*He was censured for leaking information to the press.* 他因泄露消息給新聞界而受到譴責。

cen·sus /ˈsensəs/ *noun* (*pl.* **cen·suses**) the process of officially counting sth, especially a country's population, and recording various facts（官方的）統計；人口普查；人口調查

cent 0➡ /sent/ *noun* (*abbr.* **c**, **ct**)
a coin and unit of money worth 1% of the main unit of money in many countries, for example of the US dollar or of the euro 分（輔幣單位，相當於許多國家主幣面值的 1%，如美元或歐元的 1%）；分幣 ➲ see also PER CENT, RED CENT

IDM put in your two ˈcents' worth (*NAmE*) (*BrE* **put in your two ˈpennyworth, put in your two ˈpenn'orth**) (*informal*) to give your opinion about sth, even if other people do not want to hear it 發表意見（即使別人不想聽）

cent. *abbr.* century 世紀：*in the 20th cent.* 在 20 世紀

cen·taur /ˈsentɔː(r)/ *noun* (in ancient Greek stories) a creature with a man's head, arms and upper body on a horse's body and legs（古希臘神話中的）半人半馬怪

cen·ten·ar·ian /ˌsentɪˈneəriən; *NAmE* -ˈner-/ *noun* a person who is 100 years old or more 人瑞；百歲人瑞

cen·ten·ary /senˈtiːnəri; *NAmE* -ˈtenəri/ (*pl.* **-ies**) (*BrE*) (also **cen·ten·nial** *NAmE, BrE*) *noun* the 100th anniversary of an event * 100 週年紀念：*The club will celebrate its centenary next year.* 俱樂部明年要慶祝成立一百週年。◇ *the centenary year* 一百週年紀念年 ➲ see also BICENTENARY, TERCENTENARY

cen·ten·nial /senˈteniəl/ (*especially NAmE*) (*BrE* also **cen·ten·ary**) *noun* the 100th anniversary of an event * 100 週年紀念：*The year 1889 was the centennial of the inauguration of George Washington.* * 1889 年是喬治 • 華盛頓就職一百週年紀念。➲ see also BICENTENNIAL

cen·ter (*US*) = CENTRE

cen·ter·board, **cen·tered**, **cen·ter·fold**, **cen·ter·piece** (*US*) = CENTREBOARD, CENTRED, CENTREFOLD, CENTREPIECE

centi- /ˈsentɪ-/ *combining form* (in nouns 構成名詞) **1** hundred 一百：*centipede* 蜈蚣 **2** (often used in units of measurement 常用於計量單位) one hundredth 百分之一：*centimetre* 厘米

centi·grade /ˈsentɪgreɪd/ *adj.* = CELSIUS：*a temperature of 40 degrees centigrade* * 40 攝氏度的溫度 ▸ **centi·grade** *noun* [U]：*temperatures in centigrade and Fahrenheit* 攝氏和華氏溫度

centi·gram (also **centi·gramme**) /ˈsentɪgræm/ *noun* a unit for measuring weight. There are 100 centigrams in a gram. 厘克；公毫

centi·litre (*especially US* **centi·liter**) /ˈsentɪliːtə(r)/ *noun* (*abbr.* **cl**) a unit for measuring liquids. There are 100 centilitres in a litre. 厘升；公勺

centi·metre 0➡ (*especially US* **centi·meter**) /ˈsentɪmiːtə(r)/ *noun* (*abbr.* **cm**)
a unit for measuring length. There are 100 centimetres in a metre. 厘米；公分

centi·pede /ˈsentɪpiːd/ *noun* a small creature like an insect, with a long thin body and many legs 蜈蚣

cen·tral 0➡ /ˈsentrəl/ *adj.*
1 0➡ most important 最重要的；首要的；主要的：*The central issue is that of widespread racism.* 最重要的問題是種族主義到處泛濫。◇ *She has been a central figure in the campaign.* 她一直是這場運動的主要人物。◇ *Prevention also plays a central role in traditional medicine.* 預防在傳統醫學中也起着主導作用。◇ *Reducing inflation is **central to*** (= is an important part of) *the government's economic policy.* 減少通貨膨脹是政府經濟政策最重要的一環。➲ **SYNONYMS** at MAIN **2** 0➡ having power or control over other parts 起支配作用的；有控制力的：*the central committee* (= of a political party)（政黨的）中央委員會 ◇ *The organization has a central office in York.* 該組織在約克設有總部。 **3** 0➡ in the centre of an area or object 在中心的；中央的：*central London* 倫敦中心區 ◇ *Central America/Europe/Asia* 中美洲；中歐；中亞 ◇ *the central area of the brain* 大腦中樞 **4** 0➡ easily reached from many areas 容易到達的；交通方便的；四通八達的：*The flat is very central—just five*

C

minutes from Princes Street. 這座公寓位於市中心，離王子街只需要五分鐘。◇ *a central location* 中心位置 **5** (*phonetics* 語音) (of a vowel 元音) produced with the centre of the tongue in a higher position than the front or the back, for example /ɜː/ in *bird* 中央的（發音時舌高點在口腔中間位置）➲ compare BACK (4), FRONT (2) ▸ **cen·tral·ity** /senˈtræləti/ *noun* [U]：(*formal*) *the centrality of the family as a social institution* 家庭作為一種社會機構的重要性 **cen·tral·ly** /ˈsentrəli/ *adv.*：*The hotel is centrally located for all major attractions.* 這家旅館位於中心地帶，前往所有主要景點都很方便。◇ *a centrally planned economy* 中央計劃經濟 ◇ *Is the house centrally heated* (= does it have central heating)? 這房子有中央供暖嗎？

ˌCentral Aˈmerica *noun* [U] the part of N America that consists of Guatemala, Belize, Honduras, El Salvador, Nicaragua, Costa Rica and Panama 中美洲（包括危地馬拉、伯利茲、洪都拉斯、薩爾瓦多、尼加拉瓜、哥斯達黎加以及巴拿馬）▸ **ˌCentral Aˈmerican** *adj.*, *noun*

ˌcentral ˈbank *noun* a national bank that does business with the government and other banks, and issues the country's coins and paper money 中央銀行

ˌCentral ˈDaylight Time *noun* [U] (*abbr.* **CDT**) the time used in summer in the central US and Canada, which is five hours earlier than GMT 中部日光節約時間，中部夏令時間（美國中部和加拿大中部的夏季時間，比格林尼治平時早五小時）

ˌCentral Euroˈpean Time *noun* [U] (*abbr.* **CET**) the time used in central and part of western Europe, which is one hour later than GMT in winter, and two hours later in summer 歐洲中部時間（歐洲中部和西歐部份地區的時間，冬季時比格林尼治平時晚一小時，夏季時比格林尼治平時晚兩小時）

ˌcentral ˈgovernment *noun* [U, C] the government of a whole country, rather than LOCAL GOVERNMENT which is concerned with smaller areas 中央政府

ˌcentral ˈheating *noun* [U] a system for heating a building from one source which then sends the hot water or hot air around the building through pipes 集中供熱；中央供暖（系統）➲ **COLLOCATIONS** at DECORATE

the ˌCentral Inˈtelligence Agency *noun* [sing.] = CIA

cen·tral·ism /ˈsentrəlɪzəm/ *noun* [U] a way of organizing sth, such as government or education, that involves one central group of people controlling the whole system 中央集權制（或主義）；集中制 ▸ **cen·tral·ist** *adj.*：*centralist control of schools* 學校的集中控制

cen·tral·ize (*BrE* also **-ise**) /ˈsentrəlaɪz/ *verb* **~ sth** to give the control of a country or an organization to a group of people in one particular place 集權控制；實行集中：*a highly centralized system of government* 高度中央集權的政府體制 ▸ **cen·tral·iza·tion, -isa·tion** /ˌsentrəlaɪˈzeɪʃn; *NAmE* -ləˈz-/ *noun* [U]：*the centralization of political power* 政治權力的集中

ˌcentral ˈlocking *noun* [U] a system for locking a car in which all the doors can be locked or opened at the same time（汽車的）中央門鎖系統，中央控制門鎖

ˌcentral ˈnervous system *noun* (*anatomy* 解) the part of the system of nerves in the body that consists of the brain and the SPINAL CORD 中樞神經系統 ➲ see also NERVOUS SYSTEM

ˌcentral ˈprocessing unit *noun* (*computing* 計) (*abbr.* **CPU**) the part of a computer that controls all the other parts of the system 中央處理器；中央處理機

ˌcentral reserˈvation (*BrE*) (*NAmE* **me·dian**, **ˈmedian strip**) *noun* a narrow strip of land that separates the two sides of a major road such as a MOTORWAY or INTERSTATE（高速公路、州際公路等的）中央隔離帶

ˌCentral ˈStandard Time *noun* [U] (*abbr.* **CST**) the time used in winter in the central US and Canada, which is six hours earlier than GMT 中部標準時間（美國中部和加拿大中部的冬季時間，比格林尼治平時早六小時）

ˈCentral time *noun* [U] the time at the line of LONGITUDE 90°W, which is the standard time in the central US and Canada 中部時間（指西經 90 度的時間，是美國中部和加拿大中部的標準時間）

centre 🔑 (*especially US* **cen·ter**) /ˈsentə(r)/ *noun, verb*

■ ***noun***

▸ **MIDDLE** 中間 **1** 🔑 [C] the middle point or part of sth 中心點；中心；正中；中央：*the centre of a circle* 圓心 ◇ *a long table in the centre of the room* 房間中央的長桌 ◇ *chocolates with soft centres* 軟心巧克力糖 ➲ **VISUAL VOCAB** page V71

▸ **TOWN/CITY** 城鎮；城市 **2** 🔑 [C] (*especially BrE*) (*NAmE* usually **down·town** [usually sing.]) the main part of a town or city where there are a lot of shops/stores and offices（市鎮的）中心區：*in the* ***town/city centre*** 在鎮／市中心區 ◇ *the centre of town* 市中心 ◇ *a town-centre car park* 市中心停車場 **3** 🔑 [C] a place or an area where a lot of people live; a place where a lot of business or cultural activity takes place 人口集中的地區；商業中心區；文化中心區：*major urban/industrial centres* 主要城市／工業中心 ◇ *a centre of population* 人口密集區 ◇ *Small towns in South India serve as economic and cultural centres for the surrounding villages.* 印度南部的小城鎮是周圍村莊的經濟文化中心。

▸ **BUILDING** 建築物 **4** 🔑 [C] a building or place used for a particular purpose or activity 中心；活動中心：*a* ***shopping/sports/leisure/community centre*** 購物／運動／休閒／社區中心 ◇ *the Centre for Policy Studies* 政策研究中心

▸ **OF EXCELLENCE** 優秀 **5** [C] **~ of excellence** a place where a particular kind of work is done extremely well 居領先地位的中心；（某領域中成績突出的）中心

▸ **OF ATTENTION** 注意 **6** [C, usually sing.] the point towards which people direct their attention 中心；聚集點：*Children like to be the* ***centre of attention****.* 小孩子喜歡受到大家的關注。◇ *The prime minister is* ***at the centre of*** *a political row over leaked Cabinet documents.* 首相成了內閣文件泄秘政治風波的中心人物。

▸ **-CENTRED** 以…為中心 **7** (in adjectives 構成形容詞) having the thing mentioned as the most important feature or centre of attention 有…最重要特徵的；有…中心的；以…為中心的：*a child-centred approach to teaching* 以兒童為中心的教學法 ➲ see also SELF-CENTRED

▸ **IN POLITICS** 政治 **8** (usually **the centre**) [sing.] a MODERATE (= middle) political position or party, between the extremes of LEFT-WING and RIGHT-WING parties 中間派；中間黨：*a party of the centre* 中間黨派

▸ **IN SPORT** 體育運動 **9** [C] (in some team sports 用於某些團體運動) a player or position in the middle of the pitch/field, court, etc. 中鋒；中鋒位置 **IDM** see FRONT *n.*, LEFT *adv.*

■ ***verb*** **~ sth** to move sth so that it is in the centre of sth else 把…放在中央：*Carefully centre the photograph on the page and stick it in place.* 把照片小心地放在頁面中央並粘貼好。

PHR V **ˈcentre around/on/round/upon sb/sth** | **ˈcentre sth around/on/round/upon sb/sth** to be or make sb/sth become the person or thing around which most activity, etc. takes place 把…當作中心；（使）成為中心：*State occasions always centred around the king.* 國家慶典總是以國王為中心。◇ *Discussions were centred on developments in Eastern Europe.* 討論圍繞着東歐的發展這一中心議題進行。 **ˈcentre sth in …** [usually passive] to make somewhere the place where an activity or event takes place 使活動等集中於…：*Most of the fighting was centred in the north of the capital.* 戰鬥大多集中在首都北部。

ˌcentre ˈback (*especially US* **ˌcenter ˈback**) (also **ˌcentre ˈhalf** *especially US* **ˌcenter ˈhalf**) *noun* (in football (SOCCER) and some other sports 足球及其他一些體育運動) a player or position in the middle of the back line of players 中後衛；中後衛位置

centre·board (*especially US* **cen·ter·board**) /ˈsentəbɔːd; *NAmE* ˈsentərbɔːrd/ *noun* a board that can be passed through a hole in the bottom of a sailing boat to keep it steady when sailing（帆船的）穩向板龍骨

cen·tred (*especially US* **cen·tered**) /ˈsentəd; *NAmE* -ərd/ *adj.* (*especially NAmE*) calm, sensible and emotionally in control 冷靜的；理智的：*My family helps to keep me centred.* 家人幫助我保持冷靜。 ➲ see also CENTRE (7)

centre·fold (*especially US* **cen·ter·fold**) /ˈsentəfəʊld; *NAmE* -tərfoʊld/ *noun* **1** a large picture, often of a young woman with few or no clothes on, folded to form the middle pages of a magazine（雜誌內常刊登性感女郎照片的）中間插頁 **2** a person whose picture is the centrefold of a magazine 中間插頁圖片上的人

ˌcentre ˈforward (*especially US* **ˌcenter ˈforward**) *noun* (in football (SOCCER) and some other sports 足球及其他一些體育運動) a player or position in the middle of the front line of players 中鋒；中鋒位置

ˌcentre ˈhalf (*especially US* **ˌcenter ˈhalf**) *noun* = CENTRE BACK

ˌcentre-ˈleft (*especially US* **ˌcenter-ˈleft**) (*BrE* also **ˌleft-of-ˈcentre** *US* also **ˌleft-of-ˈcenter**) *adj.* (*politics* 政) supporting both CAPITALISM and gradual social change 中左的（指支持資本主義和漸進式社會改革的）：*a centre-left coalition government* 中間靠左的聯合政府 ▸ **ˌcentre-ˈleft** (*especially US* **ˌcenter-ˈleft**) *noun* [sing.]：*Most of the centre-left will give their support.* 大多數中左派將給予支持。

ˌcentre of ˈgravity *noun* (*pl.* **centres of gravity**) the point in an object at which its weight is considered to act（物體的）重心

centre·piece (*especially US* **cen·ter·piece**) /ˈsentəpiːs; *NAmE* -tərp-/ *noun* **1** [sing.] the most important item 最重要的項目（或物品）：*This treaty is the centrepiece of the government's foreign policy.* 這個條約是政府外交政策最重要的一環。 **2** a decoration for the centre of a table 桌子中央的裝飾品

ˌcentre-ˈright (*especially US* **ˌcenter-ˈright**) (also **ˌright-of-ˈcentre** *especially US* **ˌright-of-ˈcenter**) *adj.* (*politics* 政) supporting CAPITALISM and accepting some social change 中右的（指支持資本主義並接受某些社會改革的）：*Europe's centre-right parties* 歐洲的中右黨派 ▸ **ˌcentre-ˈright** (*BrE*) (*US* **ˌcenter-ˈright**) *noun* [sing.]：*a politician of the centre-right* 中右派從政者

ˌcentre ˈspread (*especially US* **ˌcenter ˈspread**) *noun* the two facing middle pages of a newspaper or magazine（報紙或雜誌的）中間跨頁

ˌcentre ˈstage (*especially US* **ˌcenter ˈstage**) *noun* [U] an important position where sb/sth can easily get people's attention 重要位置；中心；核心：*Education is **taking centre stage** in the government's plans.* 教育正在成為政府計劃的核心。◇ *This region continues to **occupy centre stage** in world affairs.* 這個地區繼續在國際舞台上佔主導地位。 ▸ **ˌcentre ˈstage** *adv.*：*The minister said, 'We are putting full employment centre stage'.* 部長說："我們正在把充分就業放到首要位置。"

-centric /ˈsentrɪk/ *suffix* **1** having a particular centre 以…為中心；有…中心：*geocentric* 以地球為中心的 **2** (often *disapproving*) based on a particular way of thinking 基於…思路；以…想法為出發點：*Eurocentric* 歐洲中心主義的◇ *ethnocentric* 種族中心主義的

cen·tri·fu·gal /ˌsentrɪˈfjuːɡl; senˈtrɪfjəɡl/ *adj.* (*technical* 術語) moving or tending to move away from a centre 離心的

ˌcentriˌfugal ˈforce (also **cenˈtrifugal force**) *noun* (*physics* 物) a force that appears to cause an object travelling around a centre to fly away from the centre and off its CIRCULAR path 離心力

cen·tri·fuge /ˈsentrɪfjuːdʒ/ *noun* a machine with a part that spins around to separate substances, for example liquids from solids, by forcing the heavier substance to the outer edge 離心機；離心分離機；離心過濾機

cen·tri·pet·al /senˈtrɪpɪtl; ˌsentrɪˈpiːtl/ *adj.* (*technical* 術語) moving or tending to move towards a centre 向心的

cen·trist /ˈsentrɪst/ *noun* a person with political views that are not extreme（政治上的）中間派，溫和派 SYN **moderate** ▸ **cen·trist** *adj.*

cen·tur·ion /senˈtjʊəriən; *NAmE* -ˈtʃʊr-/ *noun* (in ancient Rome) an army officer who commanded 100 soldiers 百夫長（古羅馬軍隊中管理 100 名士兵的軍官）

cen·tury 0‑w /ˈsentʃəri/ *noun* (*pl.* **-ies**)
1 0‑w a period of 100 years * 100 年；百年 **2** 0‑w (*abbr.* **c**, **cent.**) any of the periods of 100 years before or after the birth of Christ 世紀：*the 20th century* (= AD 1901–2000 or 1900–1999) * 20 世紀 ◇ *eighteenth-century writers* * 18 世紀的作家 **3** (in CRICKET 板球) a score of 100 RUNS by one player（一個運動員所得的）100 分 IDM see TURN *n.*

CEO /ˌsiː iː ˈəʊ; *NAmE* ˈoʊ/ *abbr.* chief executive officer (the person with the highest rank in a business company) 行政總裁；首席執行官

cep /sep/ *noun* a type of MUSHROOM which many people consider to be one of the best to eat 牛肝菌（一種可食用的蘑菇）

ceph·al·ic /sɪˈfælɪk; *BrE* also keˈfælɪk/ *adj.* (*anatomy* 解) in or related to the head 頭的；（頭）顱的

ceph·alo·pod /ˈsefələpɒd; *NAmE* -pɑːd/ *noun* (*biology* 生) a type of MOLLUSC with a combined head and body and large eyes. Cephalopods have arms and/or TENTACLES (= long thin parts like arms), which may have SUCKERS (= round parts that suck) on them. OCTOPUS and SQUID are cephalopods. 頭足動物（如章魚和烏賊） ➲ VISUAL VOCAB page V13

cer·am·ic /səˈræmɪk/ *noun* **1** [C, usually pl.] a pot or other object made of CLAY that has been made permanently hard by heat 陶瓷製品；陶瓷器：*an exhibition of ceramics by Picasso* 畢加索陶瓷作品展 **2** **ceramics** [U] the art of making and decorating ceramics 製陶藝術；陶瓷裝潢藝術 ▸ **cer·am·ic** *adj.*：*ceramic tiles* 瓷磚

cer·eal /ˈsɪəriəl; *NAmE* ˈsɪr-/ *noun* **1** [C] one of various types of grass that produce grains that can be eaten or are used to make flour or bread. WHEAT, BARLEY and RYE are all cereals. 穀類植物：*cereal crops* 穀類作物 ➲ VISUAL VOCAB page V32 **2** [U] the grain produced by cereal crops 穀物 **3** [C, U] food made from the grain of cereals, often eaten for breakfast with milk（常加牛奶作早餐用的）穀類食物：*breakfast cereals* 穀類早餐食物 ◇ *a bowl of cereal* 一碗麥片粥

ce·re·bel·lum /ˌserəˈbeləm/ *noun* (*pl.* **ce·re·bel·lums** or **cere·bella** /-ˈbelə/) (*anatomy* 解) the part of the brain at the back of the head that controls the activity of the muscles 小腦

cere·bral /ˈserəbrəl; *NAmE* səˈriːbrəl/ *adj.* **1** relating to the brain 大腦的；腦的：*a cerebral haemorrhage* 腦出血 **2** (*formal*) relating to the mind rather than the feelings 理智的；智力的 SYN **intellectual**：*His poetry is very cerebral.* 他的詩富於理性。

ˌcerebral ˈpalsy *noun* [U] a medical condition usually caused by brain damage before or at birth that causes the loss of control of movement in the arms and legs 大腦性癱瘓

cere·brum /səˈriːbrəm; ˈserəbrəm/ *noun* (*pl.* **ce·re·bra** /-brə/) (*anatomy* 解) the front part of the brain, responsible for thoughts, emotions and personality 大腦

cere·mo·nial /ˌserɪˈməʊniəl; *NAmE* -ˈmoʊ-/ *adj.*, *noun*
■ ***adj.*** relating to or used in a ceremony 禮儀的；禮節的；用於禮儀的：*ceremonial occasions* 禮儀場合 ◇ *a ceremonial sword* 禮儀佩劍 ▸ **cere·mo·ni·al·ly** /-niəli/ *adv.*
■ ***noun*** [U, C] the system of rules and traditions that states how things should be done at a ceremony or formal occasion 禮儀；禮節：*The visit was conducted with all due ceremonial.* 訪問按照一切應有的禮儀進行。

cere·mo·ni·ous /ˌserəˈməʊniəs; *NAmE* -ˈmoʊ-/ *adj.* (*formal*) behaving or performed in an extremely formal way 講究禮儀的 OPP **unceremonious** ▸ **cere·mo·ni·ous·ly** *adv.*

cere·mony 0‑w /ˈserəməni; *NAmE* -moʊni/ *noun* (*pl.* **-ies**)
1 0‑w [C] a public or religious occasion that includes a series of formal or traditional actions 典禮；儀式：*an awards/opening ceremony* 頒獎 / 開幕儀式 ◇ *a wedding/marriage ceremony* 婚禮 ➲ COLLOCATIONS at MARRIAGE

C

2 [U] formal behaviour; traditional actions and words used on particular formal occasions 禮節；禮儀；禮貌 IDM **stand on 'ceremony** (*BrE*) to behave formally 講究客套；拘於禮節：*Please don't stand on ceremony* (= Please be natural and relaxed) *with me.* 請別跟我講客套。 **without 'ceremony** in a very rough or informal way 粗魯無禮；不拘禮節；隨便：*He found himself pushed without ceremony out of the house and the door slammed in his face.* 他被毫不客氣地推出了房子，門砰的一聲當着他的面關上了。 ➲ see also MASTER OF CEREMONIES

ce·rise /səˈriːz; səˈriːs/ *adj.* pinkish-red in colour 鮮紅色的；櫻桃色的 ▸ **ce·rise** *noun* [U]

ce·rium /ˈsɪəriəm; *NAmE* ˈsɪr-/ *noun* [U] (*symb.* **Ce**) a chemical element. Cerium is a silver-white metal used in the production of glass and CERAMICS. 鈰

cert /sɜːt; *NAmE* sɜːrt/ *noun* (*BrE, informal*) a thing that is sure to happen or be successful 必然發生的事；確定無疑的事；有把握成功的事 SYN **certainty**：*That horse is a* **dead cert** *for* (= is sure to win) *the next race.* 那匹馬下一場比賽準贏。

cert. *abbr.* **1** CERTIFICATE **2** CERTIFIED

cer·tain 🔑 /ˈsɜːtn; *NAmE* ˈsɜːrtn/ *adj., pron.*

■ *adj.* **1** 🔑 that you can rely on to happen or to be true 確實；確定；肯定：*The climbers face certain death if the rescue today is unsuccessful.* 救援行動如果今天不能成功，登山隊員必死無疑。◇ **~ (that)** ... *It is certain that they will agree.* 他們一定會同意。◇ **~ to do sth** *She looks certain to win an Oscar.* 看來奧斯卡金像獎非她莫屬。◇ *They are certain to agree.* 他們一定會同意。◇ **~ of sth/of doing sth** *If you want to be certain of getting a ticket, book now.* 要想有把握買到票，現在就得預訂。➲ SYNONYMS at SURE **2** 🔑 firmly believing sth; having no doubts 確信；確定；無疑：**~ (that)** ... *She wasn't certain (that) he had seen her.* 她不敢肯定他見過她。◇ **~ of/about sth** *Are you absolutely certain about this?* 你對這事絕對確信無疑嗎？◇ **~ who/where, etc.** ... *I'm not certain who was there.* 我無法確定誰當時在場。◇ *To my certain knowledge he was somewhere else at the time* (= I am sure about it). 我敢肯定他當時不在現場。 **3** 🔑 used to mention a particular thing, person or group without giving any more details about it or them（不提及細節時用）某事，某人，某種：*For certain personal reasons I shall not be able to attend.* 由於某種個人原因，我將不能出席。◇ *Certain people might disagree with this.* 某些人對這事可能不會贊同。◇ *They refused to release their hostages unless certain conditions were met.* 除非某些條件得到滿足，否則他們不會釋放人質。 **4** (*formal*) used with a person's name to show that the speaker does not know the person（與人名連用，表示說話者不識其人）某某，某位，一位叫…的：*It was a certain Dr Davis who performed the operation.* 是一位叫戴維斯的醫生做的手術。 **5** 🔑 slight; noticeable, but difficult to describe 輕微的；微小的；顯而易見卻難以描述的：*That's true,* **to a certain extent**. 在一定程度上的確如此。◇ *I felt there was a certain coldness in her manner.* 我覺得她的態度有點冷淡。

IDM **for 'certain** 🔑 without doubt 肯定；確定；無疑：*I can't say for certain when we'll arrive.* 我說不準我們什麼時候能到。 **make certain (that ...)** 🔑 to find out whether sth is definitely true 弄確實；弄清楚；弄明白：*I think there's a bus at 8 but you'd better call to make certain.* 好像 8 點有一班公共汽車，不過你最好打電話弄清楚。 **make certain of sth/of doing sth** to do sth in order to be sure that sth else will happen 確保（做某事）：*You'll have to leave soon to make certain of getting there on time.* 你得快點出發，好確保準時到達那裏。 **of a certain 'age** if you talk about a person being **of a certain age**, you mean that they are no longer young but not yet old 不算年輕的；年紀不輕的；中年的：*The show appeals to an audience of a certain age.* 這個節目中年觀眾感興趣。

■ *pron.* **certain of ...** (*formal*) used for talking about some members of a group of people or things without giving their names（不提及人或事物的名稱時用）某些：*Certain of those present were unwilling to discuss the matter further.* 某些出席會議的人不願意進一步討論這個問題。

Synonyms 同義詞辨析

certain

bound • sure • definite • guaranteed

These are all words describing sth that will definitely happen or is definitely true. 以上各詞均指某事肯定、必定會發生或屬實。

certain that you can rely on to happen or be true 指確實、確定、肯定（會發生或是事實）：*It's certain that they will agree.* 他們肯定會同意。◇ *They are certain to agree.* 他們肯定會同意。

bound [not before noun] certain to happen, or to do or be sth 指肯定會、一定會 NOTE **Bound** is only used in the phrase *bound to do/be, etc.* * bound 只用於 bound to do/be 等短語中：*There are bound to be changes when the new system is introduced.* 新系統引進後肯定會有變化。◇ *You've done so much work—you're bound to pass the exam.* 你下了這麼大工夫，一定能通過考試。

sure certain to happen or be true; that can be trusted or relied on 指必定、無疑（會發生或是事實）或不容置疑、確切、可靠：*She's sure to be picked for the team.* 她肯定會入選該隊。◇ *It's sure to rain.* 一準會下雨。

definite (*rather informal*) certain to happen; that is not going to change 指必將發生、不會改變：*Is it definite that he's leaving?* 他肯定要離開嗎？

guaranteed certain to have a particular result 指肯定會、必定會（有特定結果）：*That kind of behaviour is guaranteed to make him angry.* 那樣的行為肯定會讓他生氣。

PATTERNS

- certain/sure **of** sth
- certain/bound/sure/guaranteed **to do sth**
- certain/definite **that** ...
- I couldn't say **for** certain/sure/definite.

cer·tain·ly 🔑 /ˈsɜːtnli; *NAmE* ˈsɜːrtnli/ *adv.*

1 🔑 without doubt 無疑；確定；肯定 SYN **definitely**：*Without treatment, she will almost certainly die.* 要是不治療，她十有八九會死。◇ *Certainly, the early years are crucial to a child's development.* 毫無疑問，幼年對兒童的發展至關重要。◇ *I'm certainly never going there again.* 我肯定不會再去那裏了。➲ note at SURELY ➲ LANGUAGE BANK at NEVERTHELESS **2** 🔑 (used in answer to questions 用於回答問題) of course 當然；行：*'May I see your passport, Mr Scott?' 'Certainly.'* "斯科特先生，請出示您的護照好嗎？" "當然可以。" ◇ *'Do you think all this money will change your life?' 'Certainly not.'* "你認為這些錢會改變你的生活嗎？" "當然不會。"

cer·tainty /ˈsɜːtnti; *NAmE* ˈsɜːrtnti/ *noun* (*pl.* **-ies**) **1** [C] a thing that is certain 確實的事；必然的事：*political/moral certainties* 政治上／道德上確定無疑的事 ◇ *Her return to the team now seems a certainty.* 她的歸隊現在似乎已成定局。 **2** [U] the state of being certain 確信；確實；確定性：*There is no certainty that the president's removal would end the civil war.* 總統下台是否會結束內戰現在還很難說。◇ *I can't say* **with** *any* **certainty** *where I'll be next week.* 我不能說準我下週會在什麼地方。

cer·ti·fi·able /ˈsɜːtɪfaɪəbl; *NAmE* ˈsɜːrt-/ *adj.* **1** a person who is **certifiable** can or should be officially stated to be INSANE 可證明患有精神病的；應被證明為精神病患者的：(*informal*) *He's certifiable* (= he's crazy). 他腦子有問題。 **2** (*especially NAmE*) good enough to be officially accepted or recommended 可接納的；可推薦的 ▸ **cer·ti·fi·ably** *adv.*：*certifiably insane* 確認患有精神病的

cer·tifi·cate 🔑 *noun, verb*

■ *noun* /səˈtɪfɪkət; *NAmE* sərˈt-/ (*abbr.* **cert.**) **1** 🔑 an official document that may be used to prove that the facts it states are true 證明；證明書：*a birth/marriage/death certificate* 出生／結婚／死亡證明 **2** an official document proving that you have completed a course of study or passed an exam; a qualification obtained after a course of study or an exam 文憑；結業證書；合格證書：*a Postgraduate Certificate in Education* (= a British qualification for teachers) 教育學研究生證書（英國教師資格證書）

■ ***verb*** /səˈtɪfɪkeɪt; *NAmE* sərˈt-/ **~ sb (to do sth)** (*BrE*) to give sb an official document proving that they have successfully completed a training course, especially for a particular profession 發給結業證書；（尤指）發給職業培訓證書

cer·tifi·cated /səˈtɪfɪkeɪtɪd; *NAmE* sərˈt-/ *adj.* (*BrE*) having the certificate which shows that the necessary training for a particular job has been done 持有職業培訓證書的；有執業資格的

cer·ti·fi·ca·tion /ˌsɜːtɪfɪˈkeɪʃn; *NAmE* ˌsɜːrt-/ *noun* [U] (*technical* 術語) **1** the act of CERTIFYING sth 證明；鑒定：*the medical certification of the cause of death* 為死因出具醫學鑒定書 **2** the process of giving certificates for a course of education 出具課程結業證書：*the certification of the exam modules* 出具考試課程結業證書

ˌcertified ˈcheque (*BrE*) (*NAmE* **ˌcertified ˈcheck**) *noun* a cheque that a bank guarantees 保付支票；保兑支票

ˌcertified ˈmail (*NAmE*) (*BrE* **reˌcorded deˈlivery**) *noun* [U] a method of sending a letter or package in which the person sending it gets an official note to say it has been posted and the person receiving it must sign a form when it is delivered 掛號郵寄 ➲ compare REGISTERED MAIL

ˌcertified ˌpublic acˈcountant (*NAmE*) (*BrE* **ˌchartered acˈcountant**) *noun* a fully trained and qualified ACCOUNTANT 註冊會計師；特許會計師

cer·tify /ˈsɜːtɪfaɪ; *NAmE* ˈsɜːrt-/ *verb* (**cer·ti·fies**, **cer·ti·fy·ing**, **cer·ti·fied**, **cer·ti·fied**) **1** (*formal*) to state officially, especially in writing, that sth is true（尤指書面）證明，證實：**~ (that)** … *He handed her a piece of paper certifying (that) she was in good health.* 他遞給她一份她的健康證明書。◇ *This* (= this document) *is to certify that* … 茲證明…◇ **~ sb/sth + adj.** *He was certified dead on arrival.* 他送達時被證實已死亡。◇ **~ sb/sth (as) sth** *The accounts were certified (as) correct by the finance department.* 賬目經財務部門證實無誤。◇ **~ sb/sth to be/do sth** *The plants must be certified to be virus free.* 這些植物必須具備無病毒證明。 **2** [usually passive] **~ sb (as sth)** to give sb an official document proving that they are qualified to work in a particular profession 頒發（或授予）專業合格證書 **3** [usually passive] **~ sb (+ adj.)** (*BrE, law* 律) to officially state that sb is mentally ill, so that they can be given medical treatment 證明（某人）患有精神病：*Patients must be certified before they can be admitted to the hospital.* 精神病院只接納經證明患有精神病的人。

cer·ti·tude /ˈsɜːtɪtjuːd; *NAmE* ˈsɜːrtɪtuːd/ *noun* [U, C] (*formal*) a feeling of being certain; a thing about which you are certain 確信；確定；確實的事：*'You will like Rome,' he said, with absolute certitude.* "你會喜歡羅馬的。"他深信不疑地說道。◇ *the collapse of moral certitudes* 道德信念的崩潰

cer·ul·ean /sɪˈruːliən/ *adj.* (*literary*) deep blue in colour 深藍色的；蔚藍色的

ceru·men /sɪˈruːmən/ *noun* [U] (*technical* 術語) a substance like WAX which is produced in the ear 耵聹；耳垢 SYN **earwax**

cer·vical /ˈsɜːvɪkl; səˈvaɪkl; *NAmE* ˈsɜːrvɪkl/ *adj.* [only before noun] (*anatomy* 解) **1** connected with the cervix 子宮頸的：*cervical cancer* 宮頸癌 **2** connected with the neck 頸的：*the cervical spine* 頸椎

ˌcervical ˈsmear *noun* (*BrE*) = SMEAR TEST

cer·vix /ˈsɜːvɪks; *NAmE* ˈsɜːrv-/ *noun* (*pl.* **cer·vi·ces** /-vɪsiːz/ or **cer·vi·xes** /-vɪksɪz/) (*anatomy* 解) the narrow passage at the opening of a woman's WOMB 子宮頸

ce·sar·ean, ce·sar·ian (*US*) = CAESAREAN

ces·ium (*NAmE*) (*BrE* **cae·sium**) /ˈsiːziəm/ *noun* [U] (*symb.* **Cs**) a chemical element. Cesium is a soft silver-white metal that reacts strongly in water, used in PHOTOELECTRIC CELLS. 銫

ces·sa·tion /seˈseɪʃn/ *noun* [U, C] (*formal*) the stopping of sth; a pause in sth 停止；終止；中斷；暫停：*Mexico called for an immediate cessation of hostilities.* 墨西哥要求立即停止敵對行動。

ces·sion /ˈseʃn/ *noun* [U, C] (*formal*) the act of giving up land or rights, especially to another country after a war（尤指戰爭結束後領土或權利的）割讓 ➲ see also CEDE

cess·pit /ˈsespɪt/ (also **cess·pool** /ˈsespuːl/) *noun* **1** a covered hole or container in the ground for collecting waste from a building, especially from the toilets（覆蓋的）糞池，污水坑，垃圾坑 **2** a place where dishonest or immoral people gather 藏污納垢的場所：*a cesspit of corruption* 墮落腐化的淵藪

CET /ˌsiː iː ˈtiː/ *abbr.* CENTRAL EUROPEAN TIME

cet·acean /sɪˈteɪʃn/ *adj., noun* (*biology* 生)

■ ***adj.*** (also **cet·aceous** /sɪˈteɪʃəs/) connected with the group of creatures that includes WHALES and DOLPHINS 鯨目動物的；鯨類的

■ ***noun*** a WHALE, DOLPHIN, or other sea creature that belongs to the same group 鯨類 ➲ **VISUAL VOCAB** page V12

cf. *abbr.* (in writing) compare （書寫形式）比較

CFC /ˌsiː ef ˈsiː/ *noun* [C, U] the abbreviation for 'chlorofluorocarbon' (a type of gas used especially in AEROSOLS (= types of container that release liquid in the form of a spray). CFCs are harmful to the earth's OZONE LAYER.) 氯氟化碳，含氯氟烴，氯氟代烴（全寫為 chlorofluorocarbon，尤用於噴霧劑，有害於臭氧層）

CFL /ˌsiː ef ˈel/ *abbr.* Canadian Football League (the organization of professional football teams in Canada) 加拿大（職業）橄欖球聯合會；加拿大橄欖球聯盟

CGI /ˌsiː dʒiː ˈaɪ/ *abbr.* computer-generated imagery 計算機生成影像：*The movie 'Dinosaur' combines CGI animation with live-action location shots.* 《恐龍》這部電影結合了計算機成像動畫和實地拍攝的畫面。

chaat /tʃɑːt/ *noun* [U] a S Asian dish consisting of fruit or vegetables with spices 南亞香料水果（或煮蔬菜）

Chab·lis /ˈʃæbliː; *NAmE* ʃæˈbliː/ *noun* [U, C] a type of dry white French wine （法國）沙布利乾白葡萄酒

cha·cha /ˈtʃɑːtʃɑː/ *noun* (*IndE*) **1** an uncle 叔叔；舅舅；伯父；姑丈；姨丈 **2** a male cousin of your parents 表（或堂）叔；表（或堂）伯；表（或堂）舅 **3** a male friend of your family （一家人的）男性朋友

cha-cha /ˈtʃɑː tʃɑː/ (also **ˈcha-cha-cha**) *noun* a S American dance with small fast steps 恰恰舞（南美洲小快步舞）：*to* ***dance/do the cha-cha*** 跳恰恰舞

cha-ching /tʃəˈtʃɪŋ/ *exclamation* (*NAmE, informal*) = KA-CHING

chad /tʃæd/ *noun* the small piece that is removed when a hole is made in a piece of card, etc. （在卡片等上打孔時打出的）孔屑

cha·dor /ˈtʃɑːdɔː(r)/ *noun* a large piece of cloth that covers a woman's head and upper body so that only the face can be seen, worn by some Muslim women （一些穆斯林婦女用以遮蓋頭部和上身的）罩袍

chafe /tʃeɪf/ *verb* **1** [I, T] if skin **chafes**, or if sth **chafes** it, it becomes sore because the thing is rubbing against it 擦痛；擦得紅腫：*Her wrists chafed where the rope had been.* 她的手腕上給繩子勒過的地方都磨紅了。◇ **~ sth** *The collar was far too tight and chafed her neck.* 衣領特別緊，把她脖子擦痛了。 **2** [I] **~ (at/under sth)** (*formal*) to feel annoyed and impatient about sth, especially because it limits what you can do （尤指因受限制而）惱怒，煩惱，焦躁：*He soon chafed at the restrictions of his situation.* 他很快便因為處處受到限制而感到惱火。

chaff /tʃɑːf; *NAmE* tʃæf/ *noun, verb*

■ ***noun*** [U] **1** the outer covering of the seeds of grain such as WHEAT, which is separated from the grain before it is eaten 穀殼；糠 **2** STRAW (= dried STEMS of WHEAT) and HAY (= dried grass) cut up as food for cows （作為牛飼料的）麥稭，乾草 IDM see WHEAT

■ *verb* ~ **sb** (*old-fashioned* or *formal*) to make jokes about sb in a friendly way （友善地）開玩笑，取笑，打趣 SYN tease

chaf·finch /ˈtʃæfɪntʃ/ *noun* a small European bird of the FINCH family 蒼頭燕雀（見於歐洲）

C

ˈ**chafing dish** *noun* a metal pan used for keeping food warm at the table 火鍋

chag·rin /ˈʃæɡrɪn; *NAmE* ʃəˈɡrɪn/ *noun* [U] (*formal*) a feeling of being disappointed or annoyed 失望；惱怒；煩惱；懊惱 ▸ **chag·rined** *adj.*

chai /tʃaɪ/ *noun* [U] (*IndE, informal*) tea 茶

chain 0━ /tʃeɪn/ *noun, verb*

■ ***noun***

▸ **METAL RINGS** 金屬鏈 **1** 0━ [C, U] a series of connected metal rings, used for pulling or fastening things; a length of chain used for a particular purpose 鏈子；鏈條；鎖鏈：*a short length of chain* 一截短鏈條 ◇ *She wore a heavy gold chain around her neck.* 她戴着一條粗實的金項鏈。◇ *The mayor wore his chain of office.* 市長佩戴着標誌他職務的鏈飾。◇ *a bicycle chain* 自行車鏈條 ◇ *The prisoners were kept* ***in chains*** (= with chains around their arms and legs, to prevent them from escaping). 囚犯帶着鐐銬。➲ picture at ROPE ➲ VISUAL VOCAB pages V51, V65

▸ **CONNECTED THINGS** 相關連的事 **2** 0━ [C] a series of connected things or people 一系列，一連串（人或事）：*to set in motion a* ***chain of events*** 觸發一連串的事件 ◇ *a* ***chain of command*** (= a system in an organization by which instructions are passed from one person to another) 指揮系統 ◇ ***mountain/island chains*** 山脈；島群 ◇ *Volunteers formed a* ***human chain*** *to rescue precious items from the burning house.* 志願者排成一條長龍，從着火的房子裏手傳手把貴重物品搶救出來。➲ see also FOOD CHAIN

▸ **OF SHOPS/HOTELS** 商店；旅館 **3** 0━ [C] a group of shops/stores or hotels owned by the same company 連鎖商店（或旅館）：*a chain of supermarkets/a supermarket chain* 連鎖超市

▸ **RESTRICTION** 限制 **4** [C, usually pl.] (*formal* or *literary*) a thing that restricts sb's freedom or ability to do sth 約束；束縛：*the chains of fear/misery* 恐懼的桎梏；苦難的枷鎖

▸ **IN HOUSE BUYING** 購房 **5** [C, usually sing.] (*BrE*) a situation in which a number of people selling and buying houses must each complete the sale of their house before buying from the next person 連環式（指一群房主先售後購的置屋方式）IDM see BALL *n.*, LINK *n.*, WEAK

■ ***verb*** 0━ [often passive] to fasten sth with a chain; to fasten sb/sth to another person or thing with a chain, so that they do not escape or get stolen 用鎖鏈拴住（或束縛、固定）：**~ sb/sth** *The doors were always locked and chained.* 那些門總是上着鎖鏈。◇ **~ sb/sth up** *The dog was chained up for the night.* 夜間那條狗用鏈子拴起來。◇ **~ sb/sth to sb/sth** *She chained her bicycle to the gate.* 她用鏈子把自行車鎖在大門上。◇ (*figurative*) *I've been chained to my desk all week* (= because there was so much work). 我整個星期都在伏案工作，脱不開身。

ˈ**chain gang** *noun* a group of prisoners chained together and forced to work 一群被鏈子拴在一起服勞役的囚犯

ˈ**chain letter** *noun* a letter sent to several people asking them to make copies of the letter and send them on to more people 連鎖信（收信人複印多份寄出）

ˌ**chain-ˌlink ˈfence** *noun* a fence made of wire in a diamond pattern 鋼絲網眼柵欄

ˈ**chain mail** (also **mail**) *noun* [U] ARMOUR (= covering to protect the body when fighting) made of small metal rings linked together 鎖子甲（護身鎧甲）

ˌ**chain reˈaction** *noun* **1** (*chemistry* 化, *physics* 物) a chemical or nuclear change that forms products which themselves cause more changes and new products 鏈式反應 **2** a series of events, each of which causes the next（事情的）連鎖反應：*It set off a chain reaction in the international money markets.* 這一事件在國際金融市場上引起了連鎖反應。

chain·saw /ˈtʃeɪnsɔː/ *noun* a tool made of a chain with sharp teeth set in it, that is driven by a motor and used for cutting wood 鏈鋸

ˈ**chain-smoke** *verb* [I, T] **~ (sth)** to smoke cigarettes continuously, lighting the next one from the one you have just smoked 一支接一支地吸（煙）▸ ˈ**chain-smoker** *noun*

ˈ**chain store** (*BrE* also **mul·tiple**, ˌ**multiple ˈstore**) *noun* a shop/store that is one of a series of similar shops/stores owned by the same company 連鎖商店

chair 0━ /tʃeə(r); *NAmE* tʃer/ *noun, verb*

■ ***noun*** **1** 0━ [C] a piece of furniture for one person to sit on, with a back, a seat and four legs 椅子：*a table and chairs* 一套桌椅 ◇ *Sit on your chair!* 坐在你的椅子上！◇ *an old man asleep in a chair* (= an ARMCHAIR) 在扶手椅裏睡着了的老人 ➲ VISUAL VOCAB pages V21,V22 ➲ see also ARMCHAIR, DECKCHAIR, EASY CHAIR, HIGH CHAIR, MUSICAL CHAIRS, ROCKING CHAIR, WHEELCHAIR **2** **the chair** [sing.] the position of being in charge of a meeting or committee; the person who holds this position（主持會議或委員會的）主席席位；委員長職位；（會議或委員會的）主席；委員長：*She takes the chair in all our meetings.* 她主持我們所有的會議。◇ *Who is in the chair today?* 今天誰主持？◇ *He was elected chair of the city council.* 他當選為市議會主席。**3** [C] the position of being in charge of a department in a university（大學的）系主任：*He holds the chair of philosophy at Oxford.* 他是牛津大學哲學系的系主任。**4** **the chair** [sing.] (*US, informal*) = THE ELECTRIC CHAIR

■ ***verb*** **~ sth** to act as the chairman or chairwoman of a meeting, discussion, etc. 擔任（會議、討論等的）主席；主持（會議、討論等）：*Who's chairing the meeting?* 誰主持這次會議？

chair·lift /ˈtʃeəlɪft; *NAmE* ˈtʃer-/ *noun* a series of chairs hanging from a moving cable, for carrying people up and down a mountain（統稱）登山吊椅

chair·man 0━ /ˈtʃeəmən; *NAmE* ˈtʃer-/ *noun* (*pl.* **-men** /-mən/)
1 0━ the person in charge of a meeting, who tells people when they can speak, etc.（會議的）主席，主持人 **2** 0━ the person in charge of a committee, a company, etc.（委員會的）委員長，主席；（公司等的）董事長：*the chairman of the board of governors* (= of a school) 校董會主席 ◇ *The chairman of the company presented the annual report.* 公司董事長提交了年度報告。➲ note at GENDER

chair·man·ship /ˈtʃeəmənʃɪp; *NAmE* ˈtʃer-/ *noun* **1** [C] the position of a chairman or chairwoman（男或女）主席職位：*the chairmanship of the committee* 委員會的主席職位 **2** [U] the state of being a chairman or chairwoman（男或女）主席的任職：*under her skilful chairmanship* 在她這位主席的英明領導下

chair·per·son /ˈtʃeəpɜːsn; *NAmE* ˈtʃerpɜːrsn/ *noun* (*pl.* **-per·sons**) a chairman or chairwoman（男或女）主席，主持人，委員長，董事長 ➲ see also CHAIR (2)

chair·woman 0━ /ˈtʃeəwʊmən; *NAmE* ˈtʃer-/ *noun* (*pl.* **-women** /-wɪmɪn/)
a woman in charge of a meeting, a committee or an organization（會議、委員會或機構的）女主席，女主持人，女委員長，女董事長 ➲ note at GENDER

chaise /ʃeɪz/ *noun* a CARRIAGE pulled by a horse or horses, used in the past（舊時的）馬車

chaise longue /ˌʃeɪz ˈlɒŋ; *NAmE* ˈlɔːŋ/ *noun* (*pl.* **chaises longues** /ˌʃeɪz ˈlɒŋ; *NAmE* ˈlɔːŋ/) (from *French*) **1** a long low seat with a back and one arm, on which the person sitting can stretch out their legs 躺椅 **2** (*NAmE*) (also *informal* **chaise lounge**) a long chair with a back that can be vertical for sitting on or flat for lying on outdoors 活動睡椅（可在戶外豎起當座椅或平放當躺椅）➲ VISUAL VOCAB page V21

chakra /ˈtʃʌkrə/ *noun* (in YOGA 瑜伽) each of the main centres of spiritual power in the human body 輪（人體精神集中點之一）

cha·let /ˈʃæleɪ; *NAmE* ʃæˈleɪ/ *noun* **1** a wooden house with a roof that slopes steeply down over the sides, usually built in mountain areas, especially in

Switzerland（尤指瑞士山區的）小木屋 **2** (*BrE*) a small house or HUT, especially one used by people on holiday/vacation at the sea（尤指海邊度假用的）小屋，棚屋

chal·ice /ˈtʃælɪs/ *noun* a large cup for holding wine, especially one from which wine is drunk in the Christian COMMUNION service 大酒杯；（尤指基督教的）聖爵 IDM see POISON *v.*

chalk /tʃɔːk/ *noun, verb*

■ ***noun*** **1** [U] a type of soft white stone 白堊：*the chalk cliffs of southern England* 英格蘭南部的白堊質峭壁 **2** [U, C] a substance similar to chalk made into white or coloured sticks for writing or drawing（白色或彩色的）粉筆：*a **piece/stick of chalk*** 一支粉筆 ◇ *drawing diagrams with chalk on the blackboard* 用粉筆在黑板上畫圖表 ◇ *a box of coloured chalks* 一盒彩色粉筆

IDM **ˌchalk and ˈcheese** (*BrE*) if two people or things are like **chalk and cheese** or as different as **chalk and cheese**, they are completely different from each other 截然不同；天淵之別 ➲ more at LONG *adj.*

■ ***verb*** **~ sth (up) (on sth)** to write or draw sth with chalk 用粉筆寫（或畫）：*She chalked (up) the day's menu on the board.* 她把當天的菜單用粉筆寫在黑板上。

PHR V **ˌchalk ˈup sth** (*informal*) to achieve or record a success, points in a game, etc. 獲得，取得（成功）；記下，記錄（成就、比賽得分等）：*The team chalked up their tenth win this season.* 這支隊本賽季已赢了十場比賽。 **ˌchalk sth ˈup to sth** (*NAmE, informal*) to consider that sth is caused by sth 把某事歸因於：*We can chalk that win up to a lot of luck.* 我們可以把那次勝利歸因於好運十足。 IDM see EXPERIENCE *n.*

chalk·board /ˈtʃɔːkbɔːd; *NAmE* -bɔːrd/ *noun* (*especially NAmE*) = BLACKBOARD

chalky /ˈtʃɔːki/ *adj.* containing chalk or like chalk 含（或似）白堊的；含（或似）粉筆的

chal·lenge 0→ AW /ˈtʃælɪndʒ/ *noun, verb*

■ ***noun*** **1** 0→ a new or difficult task that tests sb's ability and skill 挑戰；艱巨任務：*an **exciting/interesting challenge*** 刺激的／富趣味的挑戰 ◇ *The role will be the biggest challenge of his acting career.* 扮演這個角色將是他演藝生涯中最大的挑戰。 ◇ *to **face a challenge*** (= to have to deal with one) 面臨挑戰 ◇ *Destruction of the environment is one of the most **serious challenges** we face.* 環境的破壞是我們所面臨的最嚴峻的挑戰之一。 ◇ *Schools must **meet the challenge of** new technology* (= deal with it successfully). 學校必須迎接新技術的挑戰。 **2** 0→ an invitation or a suggestion to sb that they should enter a competition, fight, etc. 挑戰書；（比賽、打鬥等的）邀請，提議：*to **accept/take up a challenge*** 接受挑戰 ◇ *to **mount a challenge*** 發起挑戰 **3** 0→ **~ (to sth)** a statement or an action that shows that sb refuses to accept sth and questions whether it is right, legal, etc. 質詢；質疑；提出異議：*It was a direct challenge to the president's authority.* 這是對主席權威的直接質疑。 ◇ *Their legal challenge was unsuccessful.* 他們在法律上的挑戰未能成功。

■ ***verb*** **1** 0→ **~ sth** to question whether a statement or an action is right, legal, etc.; to refuse to accept sth 對…懷疑（或質疑）；拒絕接受 SYN **dispute**：*The story was completely untrue and was successfully challenged in court.* 此案情純屬捏造，已在法庭上被揭穿。 ◇ *She does not like anyone challenging her authority.* 她不喜歡任何人挑戰她的權威。 ◇ *This discovery challenges traditional beliefs.* 這項發現是對傳統信念的衝擊。 ➲ LANGUAGE BANK at ARGUE **2** 0→ to invite sb to enter a competition, fight, etc.; to suggest strongly that sb should do sth (especially when you think that they might be unwilling to do it) 向（某人）挑戰；（尤指在對方不情願時）強烈建議（某人做某事）：**~ sb (to sth)** *Mike challenged me to a game of chess.* 邁克硬逼着要和我下一盤棋。 ◇ **~ sb to do sth** *The opposition leader challenged the prime minister to call an election.* 反對黨領袖要求首相宣佈進行大選。 **3** 0→ **~ sb** to test sb's ability and skills, especially in an interesting way 考查，考驗（能力和技巧）：*The job doesn't really challenge her.* 這項工作不能真正考驗出她的能力。 **4 ~ sb** to order sb to stop and say who they are or what they are doing 盤問；查問：*We were challenged by police at the border.* 我們在邊境受到警察盤問。

chal·lenged AW /ˈtʃælɪndʒd/ *adj.* (*especially NAmE*) (used with an adverb 與副詞連用) a polite way of referring to sb who has a DISABILITY of some sort（委婉說法）傷殘的，有殘疾的：*a competition for physically challenged athletes* 殘疾運動員的比賽 ◇ (*humorous*) *I'm financially challenged at the moment* (= I have no money). 我眼下身無分文。

chal·len·ger AW /ˈtʃælɪndʒə(r)/ *noun* a person who competes with sb else in sport or in politics for an important position that the other person already holds（體育運動或政治的）挑戰者：*the official challenger for the world championship title* 世界冠軍頭銜的正式挑戰者

chal·len·ging AW /ˈtʃælɪndʒɪŋ/ *adj.* **1** 0→ difficult in an interesting way that tests your ability 挑戰性的；考驗能力的：*challenging work/questions/problems* 具有挑戰性的工作／提問／問題 ◇ *a challenging and rewarding career as a teacher* 富有挑戰性且有意義的教師職業 ➲ SYNONYMS at DIFFICULT **2** done in a way that invites people to disagree or argue with you, or shows that you disagree with them 挑起爭論的；不贊同的：*She gave him a challenging look. 'Are you really sure?' she demanded.* 她用挑釁的眼光看了他一眼。"你敢肯定嗎？"她問道。

cham·ber 0→ /ˈtʃeɪmbə(r)/ *noun*

1 0→ [C] a hall in a public building that is used for formal meetings 會議廳：*The members left the council chamber.* 議員離開了會議廳。 ◇ *the **Senate/House chamber*** 參議院／眾議院會議廳 ➲ see also CHAMBER OF COMMERCE **2** [C+sing./pl. v.] one of the parts of a parliament（議會的）議院：*the **Lower/Upper Chamber*** (= in Britain, the House of Commons/House of Lords) 下／上議院 ◇ *the Chamber of Deputies in the Italian parliament* 意大利國會的眾議院 ◇ *Under Senate rules, the chamber must vote on the bill by this Friday.* 根據規定，參議院必須在本星期五以前投票表決此項議案。 **3** 0→ [C] (in compounds 構成複合詞) a room used for the particular purpose that is mentioned（作特定用途的）房間，室：*a burial chamber* 墓室 ◇ *Divers transfer from the water to a decompression chamber.* 潛水員從水裏轉入減壓艙。 ➲ see also GAS CHAMBER **4** [C] a space in the body, in a plant or in a machine, which is separated from the rest（人體、植物或機器內的）腔，室：*the chambers of the heart* 心腔 ◇ *the rocket's combustion chamber* 火箭燃燒室 ◇ *the chamber of a gun* (= the part that holds the bullets) 槍膛 **5** [C] a space under the ground which is almost completely closed on all sides 洞穴：*They found themselves in a vast underground chamber.* 他們發現身處一個地下大洞穴。 **6** [C] (*old use*) a bedroom or private room 卧室；寢室；私人房間

cham·ber·lain /ˈtʃeɪmbəlɪn; *NAmE* -bərlɪn/ *noun* an official who managed the home and servants of a king, queen or important family in past centuries（國王或女王的）內侍；（舊時貴族的）管家

cham·ber·maid /ˈtʃeɪmbəmeɪd; *NAmE* -bərm-/ *noun* a woman whose job is to clean bedrooms, usually in a hotel（通常指旅館內）打掃房間的女工

ˈchamber music *noun* [U] CLASSICAL music written for a small group of instruments 室內樂（為小型樂隊譜寫的古典樂曲）

ˌChamber of ˈCommerce *noun* a group of local business people who work together to help business and trade in a particular town 商會

ˌchamber of ˈhorrors *noun* [sing.] a part of a museum displaying objects used to kill people in a cruel and painful way or scenes showing how they died（博物館中的）恐怖物像陳列室

ˈchamber orchestra *noun* a small group of musicians who play CLASSICAL music together 室內樂隊（演奏古典樂曲的小型樂隊）

ˈchamber pot (also *slang, offensive* **piss·pot**) *noun* a round container that people in the past had in the bedroom and used for URINATING in at night（舊時的）夜壺，尿壺 ➲ compare POTTY

cha·meleon /kə'miːliən/ *noun* **1** a small LIZARD (= a type of REPTILE) that can change colour according to its surroundings 避役；變色蜥蜴；變色龍 **2** (often *disapproving*) a person who changes their behaviour or opinions according to the situation 見風使舵的人；善變的人

cham·fer /'tʃæmfə(r)/ *noun* (*technical* 術語) a cut made along an edge or on a corner so that it slopes rather than being at 90° 斜切面；削角

cham·ois *noun* (*pl.* **cham·ois**) **1** /'ʃæmwɑː; *NAmE* 'ʃæmi/ [C] an animal like a small DEER, that lives in the mountains of Europe and Asia （歐亞山區的）岩羚羊 **2** /'ʃæmi/ (also **sham·my**) (*BrE* also ˌ**chamois 'leather**, ˌ**shammy 'leather**) [U, C] a type of soft leather, made from the skin of GOATS, sheep, etc.; a piece of this, used especially for cleaning windows （由山羊、綿羊等的皮製成的）麂皮；（尤指）擦窗用的軟皮革；擦拭用的軟皮 **3** /'ʃæmi/ [U] (*NAmE*) a type of soft thick cotton cloth, used especially for making shirts （尤指製襯衣用的）厚軟棉織物

chamo·mile (*especially NAmE*) (also **camo·mile** especially in *BrE*) /'kæməmaɪl/ *noun* [U] a plant with a sweet smell and small white and yellow flowers. Its dried leaves and flowers are used to make tea, medicine, etc. 蘋果菊，春黃菊，甘菊（花及葉可製茶、藥等）：*chamomile tea* 蘋果菊花茶

champ /tʃæmp/ *verb, noun*

■ **verb** [I, T] **~ (sth)** (especially of horses 尤指馬) to bite or eat sth noisily 大聲地咬（或咀嚼）

IDM ˌ**champing at the 'bit** (*informal*) impatient to do or start doing sth 迫不及待；急不可耐

■ **noun** an informal way of referring to a champion, often used in newspapers （常用於報章，champion 的非正式寫法）冠軍：*Scottish champs celebrate victory!* 蘇格蘭的冠軍慶祝勝利！

cham·pagne /ʃæm'peɪn/ *noun* [U, C] a French SPARKLING white wine (= one with bubbles) that is drunk on special occasions 香檳酒：*a glass of champagne* 一杯香檳酒

ˌ**champagne 'socialist** *noun* (*BrE, disapproving*) a person who has SOCIALIST ideas but is rich or has social advantages 香檳酒社會主義者（有社會主義思想但享有社會特權的富人）

cham·pers /'ʃæmpəz; *NAmE* -pərz/ *noun* [U] (*BrE, informal*) = CHAMPAGNE

cham·pion /'tʃæmpiən/ *noun, verb*

■ **noun 1** a person, team, etc. that has won a competition, especially in a sport 冠軍；第一名；優勝者：*the world basketball champions* 世界籃球冠軍 ◇ *a* ***champion jockey/boxer/swimmer*** 獲得冠軍的賽馬騎師／拳擊手／游泳運動員 ◇ *the reigning champion* (= the person who is champion now) 本屆冠軍 **2 ~ (of sth)** a person who fights for, or speaks in support of, a group of people or a belief 鬥爭者；捍衛者；聲援者；擁護者：*She was a champion of the poor all her life.* 她終身都是窮苦人的衛士。

■ **verb ~ sth** to fight for or speak in support of a group of people or a belief 為…而鬥爭；捍衛；聲援：*He has always championed the cause of gay rights.* 他一直在為爭取同性戀者的權利而鬥爭。

cham·pion·ship /'tʃæmpiənʃɪp/ *noun* **1** (also **champion·ships** [pl.]) a competition to find the best player or team in a particular sport 錦標賽：*the National Basketball Association Championship* * NBA 大賽 ◇ *He won a silver medal at the European Championships.* 他獲得了歐洲錦標賽的銀牌。**2** the position of being a champion 冠軍地位：*They've held the championship for the past two years.* 他們在過去的兩年裏一直保持着冠軍地位。

chance 0-ᴡ /tʃɑːns; *NAmE* tʃæns/ *noun, verb, adj.*

■ **noun 1** 0-ᴡ [C, U] a possibility of sth happening, especially sth that you want （尤指希望發生的事的）可能性：**~ of doing sth** *Is there any chance of getting tickets for tonight?* 有可能弄到今晚的票嗎？◇ *She has only* ***a slim chance*** *of passing the exam.* 她通過考試的希望很渺茫。◇ **~ that** … *There's a* ***slight chance*** *that he'll be back in time.* 他及時趕回來的可能性不大。◇ *There is* ***no chance*** *that he will change his mind.* 他不可能改變主意。◇ **~ of sth happening** *What chance is there of anybody being found alive?* 找到生還者的希望有多大？◇ **~ of sth** *Nowadays a premature baby* ***has a very good chance*** *of survival.* 如今早產兒存活的希望非常大。◇ *The operation has a* ***fifty-fifty chance*** *of success.* 這次手術成功和失敗的可能性各佔一半。◇ *an* ***outside chance*** (= a very small one) 非常小的可能性 ◇ *The chances are a million to one against being struck by lightning.* 遭雷擊的可能性是微乎其微的。**2** 0-ᴡ [C] a suitable time or situation when you have the opportunity to do sth 機會；機遇；時機：*It was the chance she had been waiting for.* 那正是她一直等待的機會。◇ *Jeff deceived me once already—I won't give him* ***a second chance.*** 傑夫已騙過我一次，我不會再給他機會。◇ *This is your* ***big chance*** (= opportunity for success). 這是你成功的大好機會。◇ **~ of sth** *We won't get* ***another chance*** *of a holiday this year.* 我們今年不會再有機會度假了。◇ **~ to do sth** *Please* ***give me a chance*** *to explain.* 請給我一個解釋的機會。◇ *Tonight is your* ***last chance*** *to catch the play at your local theatre.* 今晚是你在本地劇院看這齣戲的最後一次機會。◇ **~ for sb to do sth** *There will be a chance for parents to look around the school.* 家長將有機會參觀學校。**3** 0-ᴡ [C] an unpleasant or dangerous possibility 風險；冒險：*When installing electrical equipment don't* ***take any chances.*** *A mistake could kill.* 安裝電器設備時千萬不要冒險，弄錯了有可能出人命的。**4** 0-ᴡ [U] the way that some things happen without any cause that you can see or understand 偶然；碰巧；意外：*I met her* ***by chance*** (= without planning to) *at the airport.* 我碰巧在機場遇見她。◇ *Chess is not a* ***game of chance.*** 國際象棋不是靠運氣取勝的。◇ *It was* ***pure chance*** *that we were both there.* 我們倆當時都在場純屬巧合。◇ *We'll plan everything very carefully and* ***leave nothing to chance.*** 我們將非常周密地籌劃一切，決不留任何紕漏。➲ SYNONYMS at LUCK

IDM as ˌ**chance would 'have it** happening in a way that was lucky, although it was not planned 湊巧；碰巧：*As chance would have it, John was going to London too, so I went with him.* 趕巧約翰也去倫敦，所以我跟他一塊兒去了。**be** ˌ**in with a 'chance (of doing sth)** (*BrE, informal*) to have the possibility of succeeding or achieving sth 有可能成功；有機會獲得：*'Do you think we'll win?' 'I think we're in with a chance.'* "你認為我們會獲勝嗎？" "我覺得有可能。" ◇ *He's in with a good chance of passing the exam.* 他大有可能考試合格。**by 'any chance** used especially in questions, to ask whether sth is true, possible, etc. （尤用於問句，詢問是否真實、可能等）或許，可能：*Are you in love with him, by any chance?* 或許你愛上他了？**the chances 'are (that)** … (*informal*) it is likely that … 可能…：*The chances are you won't have to pay.* 你可能不用付錢。**'chance would be a fine thing** (*BrE, informal*) people say **chance would be a fine thing** to show that they would like to do or have the thing that sb has mentioned, but that they do not think that it is very likely 苦於沒有機會 **give sb/sth half a 'chance** to give sb/sth some opportunity to do sth 給…一些機會：*That dog will give you a nasty bite, given half a chance.* 只要一有機會，那條狗就會狠咬你一口。**'no chance** (*informal*) there is no possibility 不可能：*'Do you think he'll do it?' 'No chance.'* "你認為他會做這事嗎？" "不可能。" **on the 'off chance (that)** because of the possibility of sth happening, although it is unlikely 抱（一線）希望；碰碰運氣：*I didn't think you'd be at home but I just called by on the off chance.* 我想你不會在家，只是碰碰運氣順路來看一下。**stand a 'chance (of doing sth)** to have the possibility of succeeding or achieving sth 有可能成功；有機會獲得：*The driver didn't stand a chance of stopping in time.* 司機沒有來得及剎車。**take a 'chance (on sth)** to decide to do sth, knowing that it might be the wrong choice 冒險：*We took a chance on the weather and planned to have the party outside.* 我們懷着天氣可能會好的僥幸心理籌劃到戶外聚會。**take your 'chances** to take a risk or to use the opportunities that you have and hope that things will happen in the way that you want 碰運氣：*He took his chances and jumped* *into the water.* 他冒險跳進水裏。➲ more at CAT, DOG *n.*, EVEN *adj.*, EYE *n.*, FAT *adj.*, FIGHT *v.*, SNOWBALL *n.*, SPORTING

■ *verb* **1** [T] (*informal*) to risk sth, although you know the result may not be successful 冒險；拿…去冒風險：**~ sth** *She was* **chancing her luck** *driving without a licence.* 她無照駕車，完全是在冒險。◇ *'Take an umbrella.' 'No, I'll* **chance it** *'* (= take the risk that it may rain). "帶上傘吧。" "不帶了，我就冒冒險吧。" ◇ **~ doing sth** *I stayed hidden; I couldn't chance coming out.* 我躲了起來，不能冒險出去。 **2** *linking verb* (*formal*) to happen or to do sth by chance 偶然發生；碰巧：**~ to do sth** *If I do chance to find out where she is, I'll inform you immediately.* 要是我真的碰巧發現她的行踪，會立即通知你的。◇ *They chanced to be staying at the same hotel.* 他們碰巧住在同一家旅館。◇ **it chanced (that)** … *It chanced (that) they were staying at the same hotel.* 碰巧他們住在同一家旅館。

IDM **ˌchance your ˈarm** (*BrE, informal*) to take a risk although you will probably fail 冒險一試；碰碰運氣

PHR V **ˈchance on/upon sb/sth** (*formal*) to find or meet sb/sth unexpectedly or by chance 偶然發現；碰巧遇到：*One day he chanced upon Emma's diary and began reading it.* 有一天他偶然發現了埃瑪的日記，便開始讀了起來。

■ *adj.* [only before noun] not planned 意外的；偶然的；碰巧的 SYN **unplanned**：*a chance meeting/encounter* 邂逅

chan·cel /ˈtʃɑːnsl; *NAmE* ˈtʃænsl/ *noun* the part of a church near the ALTAR, where the priests and the CHOIR (= singers) sit during services （教堂的）祭壇，聖所

chan·cel·lery /ˈtʃɑːnsələri; *NAmE* ˈtʃæn-/ *noun* (*pl.* **-ies**) **1** [C, usually sing.] the place where a chancellor has his or her office 大臣（或大法官等）的官署 **2** [sing.+sing./pl. v.] the staff in the department of a chancellor 大臣（或大法官等）官署的全體工作人員

chan·cel·lor /ˈtʃɑːnsələ(r); *NAmE* ˈtʃæns-/ (also **Chan·cellor**) *noun* (often used in a title 常用於頭銜) **1** the head of government in Germany or Austria （德國或奧地利的）總理：*Chancellor Adenauer* 阿登納總理 **2** (*BrE*) = CHANCELLOR OF THE EXCHEQUER：*MPs waited for the chancellor's announcement.* 議員們等待着財政大臣發佈公告。 **3** the official head of a university in Britain. Chancellor is an HONORARY title. （英國大學的）名譽校長 ➲ compare VICE CHANCELLOR **4** the head of some American universities （某些美國大學的）校長 **5** used in the titles of some senior state officials in Britain （用於英國某些高級政府官員的頭銜）：*the Lord Chancellor* (= a senior law official) 大法官

ˌChancellor of the Exˈchequer *noun* (in Britain) the government minister who is responsible for financial affairs （英國）財政大臣

chan·cer /ˈtʃɑːnsə(r); *NAmE* ˈtʃænsər/ *noun* (*BrE, informal*) a person who is always looking for opportunities to gain an advantage, even when they do not deserve to do so 投機者；鑽門子的人

chan·cery /ˈtʃɑːnsəri; *NAmE* ˈtʃæns-/ *noun* [sing.] **1 Chancery** (*law* 律) a division of the High Court in Britain （英國）高等法院的大法官法庭 **2** (*especially BrE*) an office where public records are kept 公共檔案館；公共檔案室 **3** (also **ˈchancery court**) a court in the US that decides legal cases based on the principle of EQUITY （美國）衡平法院 **4** the offices where the official representative of a country works, in another country 大使館（或領事館）辦公處

chancy /ˈtʃɑːnsi; *NAmE* ˈtʃænsi/ *adj.* (*informal*) involving risks and UNCERTAINTY 有風險的；不確定的 SYN **risky**

chan·de·lier /ˌʃændəˈlɪə(r); *NAmE* -ˈlɪr/ *noun* a large round frame with branches that hold lights or CANDLES. Chandeliers are decorated with many small pieces of glass and hang from the ceiling. 枝形吊燈

chand·ler /ˈtʃɑːndlə(r); *NAmE* ˈtʃænd-/ (also **ˈship's chandler**) *noun* a person or shop/store that sells equipment for ships 船用雜貨商（或雜貨店）

change ⚷ /tʃeɪndʒ/ *verb, noun*

■ *verb*

▸ **BECOME/MAKE DIFFERENT** （使）變化 **1** ⚷ [I] to become different 改變；變化：*Rick hasn't changed. He looks exactly the same as he did at school.* 里克一點兒沒變，他和上學時一模一樣。◇ *changing attitudes towards education* 不斷變化的對教育的看法 ◇ *Her life changed completely when she won the lottery.* 買彩票中獎後她的生活完全變了。 **2** ⚷ [T] **~ sb/sth** to make sb/sth different 使不同：*Fame hasn't really changed him.* 名聲並沒有使他有絲毫改變。◇ *Computers have changed the way people work.* 計算機已改變了人的工作方式。 **3** ⚷ [I, T] to pass or make sb/sth pass from one state or form into another （使）變換，改換，變成：*Wait for the traffic lights to change.* 等待交通燈變換顏色。◇ **~ (from A) to/into B** *The lights changed from red to green.* 交通燈已由紅變綠。◇ *Caterpillars change into butterflies.* 毛蟲變成蝴蝶。◇ **~ sb/sth (from A) to/into B** *With a wave of her magic wand, she changed the frog into a handsome prince.* 她魔杖一揮，把青蛙變成了英俊的王子。 **4** ⚷ [T] **~ sth** to stop having one state, position or direction and start having another 轉換；變更：*Leaves change colour in autumn.* 樹葉在秋天改變顏色。◇ *The wind has changed direction.* 風向已經變了。◇ *Our ship changed course.* 我們的船改變了航向。

▸ **REPLACE** 代替 **5** ⚷ [T] to replace one thing, person, service, etc. with sth new or different 替代；替換；更換：**~ sb/sth** *I want to change my doctor.* 我想另找一位醫生看病。◇ *That back tyre needs changing.* 那個後輪胎需要更換。◇ **~ sb/sth (for sb/sth)** *We change our car every two years.* 我們的車每兩年更換一次。◇ *We changed the car for a bigger one.* 我們換了一輛較大的車。◇ **~ sth (to sth)** *Marie changed her name when she got married.* 瑪麗婚後改了姓。◇ *She changed her name to his.* 她改用了他的姓氏。

▸ **EXCHANGE** 交換 **6** ⚷ [T] (used with a plural object 與複數賓語連用) to exchange positions, places, etc. with sb else, so that you have what they have, and they have what you have 互換；交換：**~ sth** *At half-time the teams change ends.* 球隊在半場時交換場地。◇ *Can we change seats?* 咱們可以交換一下座位嗎？◇ **~ sth with sb** *Can I change seats with you?* 我可以和您換一下座位嗎？

▸ **CLOTHES** 衣物 **7** ⚷ [I, T] to put on different or clean clothes 換衣服；更衣：*I went into the bedroom to change.* 我走進卧室更衣。◇ **~ into sth** *She changed into her swimsuit.* 她換上了游泳衣。◇ **~ out of sth** *You need to change out of those wet things.* 你該把那些濕衣服換掉。 **~ sth** (*especially NAmE*) *I didn't have time to* **change clothes** *before the party.* 我沒時間在聚會前更換衣服。◇ (*especially BrE*) *I didn't have time to* **get changed** *before the party* (= to put different clothes on). 我沒時間在聚會前更換衣服。

▸ **BABY** 嬰兒 **8** [T] **~ sb/sth** to put clean clothes or a clean NAPPY/DIAPER on a baby 更換（衣服或尿布）：*She can't even change a nappy.* 她連換尿布都不會。◇ *The baby needs changing.* 該給嬰兒換尿布了。◇ *There are baby changing facilities in all our stores.* 我們所有的商店都有供顧客給嬰兒換尿布的地方。

▸ **BED** 牀 **9** [T] **~ sth** to put clean sheets, etc. on a bed 換（牀單等）：*to change the sheets* 換牀單 ◇ *Could you help me change the bed?* 你幫我換一下牀單好嗎？

▸ **MONEY** 錢 **10** ⚷ [T] to exchange money into the money of another country 把（貨幣）兑換（成另一種貨幣）：**~ sth** *Where can I change my traveller's cheques?* 哪裏可以兑換旅行支票？◇ **~ sth into sth** *to change dollars into yen* 把美元兑換成日元 **11** ⚷ [T] to exchange money for the same amount in different coins or notes 換零錢：**~ sth** *Can you change a £20 note?* 你能把一張 20 英鎊的鈔票換成零錢嗎？◇ **~ sth for/into sth** *to change a dollar bill for four quarters* 把一元美鈔換為四個二十五分幣

▸ **GOODS** 貨品 **12** ⚷ [T] **~ sth (for sth)** (*BrE*) to exchange sth that you have bought for sth else, especially because there is sth wrong with it; to give a customer a new item because there is sth wrong with the one they have bought 退換；掉換：*This shirt I bought's too small—I'll have to change it for a bigger one.* 我買的這件襯衫太小，得換件大一點的。◇ *Of course we'll change it for a larger size, Madam.* 夫人，我們當然會給您掉換件大號的。

C

▸ BUS/TRAIN/PLANE 公共汽車；火車；飛機 **13** [I, T] to go from one bus, train, etc. to another in order to continue a journey 換乘；轉乘：*Where do I have to change?* 我該在哪兒換車？◇ *Change at Reading (for London).* 在雷丁換車（去倫敦）。◇ **~ sth** *I stopped in Moscow only to change planes.* 我為了轉機才在莫斯科停留。➲ see also UNCHANGING

IDM **change 'hands** to pass to a different owner 換主人；易主；轉手：*The house has changed hands several times.* 這房子已幾易其主。 **change horses in mid-'stream** to change to a different or new activity while you are in the middle of sth else; to change from supporting one person or thing to another 中流換馬；中途變卦；中途支持另外的人（或事） **change your/sb's 'mind** to change a decision or an opinion 改變決定（或看法、主意）：*Nothing will make me change my mind.* 什麼都不能讓我改變主意。 **change your 'tune** (*informal*) to express a different opinion or behave in a different way when your situation changes 改變口風；轉變態度；變卦：*Wait until it happens to him—he'll soon change his tune.* 等着瞧吧，到他遇上這事時，他很快就會改變看法了。 **change your 'ways** to start to live or behave in a different way from before 開始過另一種生活；換個活法 ➲ more at CHOP *v.*, LEOPARD, PLACE *n.*

PHR V **,change sth↔a'round/'round** to move things or people into different positions 改變…的位置：*You've changed all the furniture around.* 你改變了所有傢具的位置。**,change 'back (into sb/sth)** to return to a previous situation, form, etc. 恢復原狀；還原；復原 **,change 'back (into sth)** to take off your clothes and put on what you were wearing earlier 換上（原來穿的衣服）：*She changed back into her work clothes.* 她又換上了工作服。**,change sth 'back (into sth)** to exchange an amount of money into the CURRENCY that it was in before 把（錢）換成（原貨幣）：*You can change back unused dollars into pounds at the bank.* 你可以到銀行把沒有用掉的美元兌換回英鎊。 **,change 'down** (*BrE*) to start using a lower gear when you are driving a car, etc.（開車等）換低一擋，換成低速擋，減速：*Change down into second.* 把車速調低到第二擋。 **,change 'over (from sth) (to sth)** to change from one system or position to another 改變系統（或位置）：*The farm has changed over to organic methods.* 農場已改用有機耕作方法。➲ related noun CHANGEOVER **,change 'up** (*BrE*) to start using a higher gear when driving a car, etc.（開車等）換高一擋，換成高速擋，加速：*Change up into fifth.* 把車速調高到第五擋。

■ *noun*

▸ DIFFERENCE 差別 **1** [C, U] **~ (in/to sth)** the act or result of sth becoming different 改變；變化；變更；變革：*a change in the weather* 天氣的變化 ◇ *important changes to the tax system* 稅收制度的重大變革 ◇ *There was* **no change** *in the patient's condition overnight.* 病人整夜病情穩定。◇ *She is someone who hates change.* 她是十分討厭變革的那種人。◇ *social/political/economic change* 社會／政治／經濟變革

▸ STH NEW AND INTERESTING 新奇有趣的事 **2** **a change** [sing.] **~ (from sth)** the fact of a situation, a place or an experience being different from what is usual and therefore likely to be interesting, enjoyable, etc.（會令人感興趣或可喜的）變化，變更：*Finishing early was* **a welcome change.** 能早日結束是個可喜的變化。◇ *Let's stay in tonight* **for a change.** 咱們今晚換換口味，就待在家裏吧。◇ *Can you just listen* **for a change?** 你就當一回聽眾，好嗎？◇ *It* **makes a change** *to read some good news for once.* 破例讀到點好消息，真讓人高興。

▸ REPLACING STH 代替 **3** [C] **~ (of sth)** | **~ (from sth to sth)** the process of replacing sth with sth new or different; a thing that is used to replace sth 替代；更換；替代物：*a change of address* 地址的變更 ◇ *a change of government* 政府的更迭 ◇ *a change from agriculture to industry* 從農業向工業轉換 ◇ *There will be a crew change when we land at Dubai.* 我們在迪拜着陸後將更換機組人員。◇ (*BrE*) *Let's get away for the weekend. A* **change of scene** (= time in a different place) *will do you good.* 咱們出去度週末吧，換換環境會對你有好處的。

▸ OF CLOTHES 衣物 **4** **~ of clothes, etc.** [C] an extra set of clothes, etc. 額外一套衣物（等）：*She packed a change of clothes for the weekend.* 她已收拾好度週末的一套換洗衣物。◇ *I keep a change of shoes in the car.* 我在車裏放有一雙供替換的鞋。

▸ MONEY 錢 **5** [U] the money that you get back when you have paid for sth giving more money than the amount it costs 找給的零錢；找頭：*Don't forget your change!* 別忘了找給你的零錢！◇ *That's 40p change.* 這是找給您的 40 便士。◇ *The ticket machine gives change.* 自動售票機可以找零。 **6** [U] coins rather than paper money 輔幣；硬幣；分幣：*Do you have any change for the phone?* 你有打電話的硬幣嗎？◇ *a dollar* **in change** (= coins that together are worth one dollar) 總值一元錢的硬幣 ◇ *I didn't have any* **small change** (= coins of low value) *to leave as a tip.* 我沒有零錢留下來付小費。◇ *He puts his* **loose change** *in a money box for the children.* 他把身上的零錢放進了給孩子的錢箱。◇ *Could you give me* **change for** *a ten pound note* (= coins or notes that are worth this amount)? 你能換給我十英鎊的零錢嗎？➲ SYNONYMS at MONEY

▸ OF BUS/TRAIN/PLANE 公共汽車；火車；飛機 **7** [C] an occasion when you go from one bus, train or plane to another during a journey 換車；轉車；換機：*The journey involved three changes.* 這趟旅行中轉乘過三次。

IDM **a change for the 'better/'worse** a person, thing, situation, etc. that is better/worse than the previous or present one 變好（或壞） **a ,change of 'heart** if you have **a change of heart**, your attitude towards sth changes, usually making you feel more friendly, helpful, etc. 改變態度，改變看法（通常指變得更友好、有益等） **a ,change of 'mind** an act of changing what you think about a situation, etc. 改變看法；改變主意 **get no change out of sb** (*BrE, informal*) to get no help or information from sb（從某人處）得不到幫助，打聽不到消息 ➲ more at RING² *v.*, WIND¹ *n.*

change·able /ˈtʃeɪndʒəbl/ *adj.* likely to change; often changing 可能變化的；易變的；常變的 **SYN** **unpredictable**：*The weather is very changeable at this time of year.* 年年在這個時候天氣都變化無常。➲ compare UNCHANGEABLE ▸ **change·abil·ity** /ˌtʃeɪndʒəˈbɪləti/ *noun* [U]

changed /tʃeɪndʒd/ *adj.* [only before noun] (of people or situations 人或情況) very different from what they were before 與以前截然不同的；變化大的；已變的：*She's a* **changed woman** *since she got that job.* 她自從得到了那份工作，變得判若兩人。◇ *This will not be possible in the changed economic climate.* 這在經濟氣候已經改變的條件下是不可能的。**OPP** **unchanged**

change·less /ˈtʃeɪndʒləs/ *adj.* (*formal*) never changing 永遠不變的；永恆的

change·ling /ˈtʃeɪndʒlɪŋ/ *noun* (*literary*) a child who is believed to have been secretly left in exchange for another, especially (in stories) by FAIRIES（尤指童話中被仙女）偷換後留下的孩童

the ,change of 'life *noun* [sing.] (*informal*) = MENOPAUSE

change·over /ˈtʃeɪndʒəʊvə(r); *NAmE* -oʊv-/ *noun* a change from one system, or method of working to another（系統或工作方法的）改變，轉變，更換 **SYN** **switch**：*the changeover from a manual to a computerized system* 由手工操作向計算機化系統的轉換 ◇ *a changeover period* 轉變時期

'change purse *noun* (*NAmE*) a small bag made of leather, plastic, etc. for carrying coins（裝硬幣的）零錢包 ➲ VISUAL VOCAB page V64 ➲ compare PURSE (1)

chan·ger /ˈtʃeɪndʒə(r)/ *noun* (often in compounds 常構成複合詞) **1** a piece of equipment that holds several discs, etc. and is able to switch between them（光盤等的）換片裝置；光盤轉換器；光碟更換器：*The car comes with white leather seats and a 6-CD changer.* 這輛車配置了白色皮座椅和一台 6 碟光盤換片裝置。 **2** a person or thing that changes sth, usually in order to improve it 改變者；改進者：*The whole experience was a life changer for me.* 這整個經歷改變了我的一生。

'changing room *noun* (*especially BrE*) a room for changing clothes in, especially before playing sports（尤指做運動前使用的）更衣室 ➲ compare LOCKER ROOM ➲ see also FITTING ROOM

chan·nel 0-ᴡ AW /ˈtʃænl/ *noun, verb*

■ *noun*

▸ ON TELEVISION/RADIO 電視；無線電 **1** 0-ᴡ [C] a television station 電視台：*What's on Channel 4 tonight?* 電視四台今晚有什麼節目？◇ *a* ***movie/sports channel*** 電影台；體育台 ◇ *to* ***change/switch channels*** 換頻道 ➲ COLLOCATIONS at TELEVISION **2** 0-ᴡ [C] a band of radio waves used for broadcasting television or radio programmes 頻道；波段：***terrestrial/satellite channels*** 地面／衛星頻道

▸ FOR COMMUNICATING 交流 **3** 0-ᴡ [C] (also **channels** [pl.]) a method or system that people use to get information, to communicate, or to send sth somewhere 途徑；渠道；系統：*Complaints must be made* ***through the proper channels****.* 投訴必須通過正當途徑進行。◇ *The newsletter is a useful* ***channel of communication*** *between teacher and students.* 簡訊是有助於師生溝通的渠道。◇ *The company has worldwide distribution channels.* 這家公司擁有遍佈全世界的銷售網絡。

▸ FOR IDEAS/FEELINGS 思想感情 **4** [C] a way of expressing ideas and feelings（表達的）方式，方法，手段：*The campaign provided a channel for protest against the war.* 這場運動是反對戰爭的一種方式。◇ *Music is a great channel for releasing your emotions.* 欣賞音樂是宣泄情感的好方法。

▸ WATER 水 **5** [C] a passage that water can flow along, especially in the ground, on the bottom of a river, etc. 水渠；溝渠；河槽：*drainage channels in the rice fields* 稻田的排水溝 **6** [C] a deep passage of water in a river or near the coast that can be used as route for ships 水道；航道 **7** [C] a passage of water that connects two areas of water, especially two seas 海峽：*the Bristol Channel* 布里斯托爾海峽 **8 the Channel** [sing.] the area of sea between England and France, also known as **the English Channel** 英吉利海峽：*the Channel Tunnel* 英吉利海峽隧道 ◇ *cross-Channel ferries* 橫渡英吉利海峽的渡船 ◇ *news from* ***across the Channel*** (= from France) 來自英吉利海峽對岸（指法國）的消息

■ *verb* (-ll-, *especially US* -l-)

▸ IDEAS/FEELINGS 思想感情 **1** ~ **sth** (**into sth**) to direct money, feelings, ideas, etc. towards a particular thing or purpose 為…引資；引導；貫注：*He channels his aggression into sport.* 他把他的好鬥勁傾注於體育比賽之中。

▸ MONEY/HELP 金錢；幫助 **2** ~ **sth** (**through sth**) to send money, help, etc. using a particular route（利用某途徑）輸送資金，提供幫助：*Money for the project will be channelled through local government.* 這個項目的資金將由地方政府提供。

▸ WATER/LIGHT 水；光 **3** ~ **sth** to carry or send water, light, etc. through a passage（經過通道）輸送，傳送：*A sensor channels the light signal along an optical fibre.* 傳感器沿光導纖維輸送光信號。

ˈchannel-hop *verb* (-pp-) (also **ˈchannel-surf**) [I] to repeatedly switch from one television channel to another 不斷地轉換電視頻道

the ˈChannel Islands *noun* [pl.] a group of islands near the north-western coast of France that belong to Britain but have their own parliaments and laws 海峽群島（位於法國西北海岸附近，隸屬英國，但有自己的議會和法律）

chant /tʃɑːnt; *NAmE* tʃænt/ *noun, verb*

■ *noun* **1** [C] words or phrases that a group of people shout or sing again and again 反複呼喊的話語；重複唱的歌詞：*The crowd broke into chants of 'Out! Out!'* 人群爆發出一陣陣"下台！下台！"的呼喊聲。◇ *football chants* 此起彼伏的足球助威聲 **2** [C, U] a religious song or prayer or a way of singing, using only a few notes that are repeated many times 聖歌；反複吟詠的禱文；單調的吟唱：*a Buddhist chant* 佛經誦唸 ➲ see also GREGORIAN CHANT

■ *verb* **1** [I, T] to sing or shout the same words or phrases many times 反複唱；反複呼喊：*A group of protesters, chanting and carrying placards, waited outside.* 一群抗議者等候在外面，舉着標語牌不停地喊着口號。◇ ~ **sth** *The crowd chanted their hero's name.* 人群不斷地呼喚着自己英雄的名字。◇ *'Resign! Resign!' they chanted.* "辭職！辭職！"他們反複喊叫着。**2** [I, T] ~ (**sth**) to sing or say a religious song or prayer using only a few notes that are repeated many times 唱聖歌；反複地吟詠禱文；單調重複地唱 ▸ **chant·ing** *noun* [U]：*The chanting rose in volume.* 聖歌的聲音漸漸響亮起來。

chant·er /ˈtʃɑːntə(r); *NAmE* ˈtʃæntər/ *noun* (*music* 音) the part of a set of BAGPIPES that is like a pipe with finger holes, on which the music is played（風笛的）曲調管

chan·ter·elle /ˈʃɑːntərel; ˌʃɑːntəˈrel/ *noun* a yellowish MUSHROOM that grows in woods and has a hollow part in the centre 雞油菌（食用蘑菇）

chant·euse /ʃɑːnˈtɜːz/ *noun* (from *French*) a female singer of popular songs, especially in a NIGHTCLUB（尤指夜總會的）流行歌曲女歌手

chan·try /ˈtʃɑːntri; *NAmE* ˈtʃæntri/ *noun* (*pl.* -**ies**) (also **ˌchantry ˈchapel**) a small church or part of a church paid for by sb, so that priests could say prayers for them there after their death（由某人捐款建造並為之做追思彌撒用的）小教堂，祭壇，追思彌撒堂

chanty *noun* (*pl.* -**ies**) (also **chantey**) (both *US*) /ˈʃænti/ (*BrE*, *CanE* **shanty**, **ˈsea shanty**) a song that sailors traditionally used to sing while pulling ropes, etc. 水手號子（舊時水手邊拉繩索等邊唱的歌）

Cha·nuk·kah, **Cha·nu·kah** = HANUKKAH

chaos /ˈkeɪɒs; *NAmE* ˈkeɪɑːs/ *noun* [U] a state of complete confusion and lack of order 混亂；雜亂；紊亂：*economic/political/domestic chaos* 經濟／政治／國內的混亂 ◇ *Heavy snow has caused* ***total chaos*** *on the roads.* 大雪導致道路上交通一片混亂。◇ *The house was* ***in chaos*** *after the party.* 聚會後，房子裏一片狼藉。

ˈchaos theory *noun* [U] (*mathematics* 數) the study of a group of connected things that are very sensitive so that small changes in conditions affect them very much 混沌理論

cha·ot·ic /keɪˈɒtɪk; *NAmE* -ˈɑːtɪk/ *adj.* in a state of complete confusion and lack of order 混亂的；雜亂的；紊亂的：*The traffic in the city is chaotic in the rush hour.* 在上下班高峰時間，城市的交通混亂不堪。▸ **cha·ot·ic·al·ly** /keɪˈɒtɪkli; *NAmE* -ˈɑːtɪk-/ *adv.*

chap /tʃæp/ *noun* (*BrE*, *informal*, becoming *old-fashioned*) used to talk about a man in a friendly way（對男子的友好稱呼）傢伙，夥計：*He isn't such a bad chap really.* 他這個傢伙並不真的這麼壞。

chap. *abbr.* (in writing) chapter（書寫形式）章，篇，回

chap·ar·ral /ˌʃæpəˈræl/ *noun* [U] (*NAmE*) an area of dry land that is covered with small bushes 濃密常綠闊葉灌叢；灌木叢

cha·patti (also **cha·pati**) /tʃəˈpæti; -ˈpɑːti/ *noun* a type of flat round S Asian bread（南亞）薄餅

chapel /ˈtʃæpl/ *noun* **1** [C] a small building or room used for Christian worship in a school, prison, large private house, etc.（學校、監獄、私人宅院等基督教徒禮拜用的）小教堂：*a college chapel* 學院的小教堂 **2** [C] a separate part of a church or CATHEDRAL, with its own ALTAR, used for some services and private prayer（教堂內的）分堂，小教堂 **3** [C, U] the word for a church used in some Christian DENOMINATIONS, for example by Nonconformists in Britain（基督教某些教派如英國的非國教教徒做禮拜的）教堂：*a Methodist chapel* 衛理公會教堂 ◇ *a Mormon chapel* 摩門教教堂 ◇ *She always went to chapel on Sundays.* 她總是在星期天去教堂做禮拜。**4** [C] a small building or room used for funeral services, especially at a CEMETERY or CREMATORIUM（尤指墓地或火葬場的）葬禮祈禱間，祈禱室 **5** [C+sing./pl. v.] (*BrE*) a branch of a TRADE/LABOR UNION in a newspaper office or printing house; the members of the branch（報館或印刷所的）工會分會，工會分會會員

ˌchapel of ˈrest *noun* (*BrE*) a room at an UNDERTAKER'S where dead bodies are kept before the funeral（殯儀館的）停屍間，停屍室

chap·er·one (*BrE* also **chap·eron**) /ˈʃæpərəʊn; *NAmE* -oʊn/ *noun, verb*

■ *noun* **1** (in the past) an older woman who, on social occasions, took care of a young woman who was not married（舊時照顧未婚少女的）年長女伴 **2** a person who takes care of children in public, especially when they are working, for example as actors（尤指兒童表演時的）在場監護人 **3** (*NAmE*) a person, such as a parent or a teacher, who goes with a group of young people on a trip or to a dance to encourage good behaviour（未成年人集體旅行的）保護人，監護人；（未成年人舞會上的）行為監督人

C

■ ***verb*** **~ sb** to act as a chaperone for sb, especially a woman 當女子陪伴人；作監護人

chap·kan /ˈtʃæpkən/ *noun* a long coat worn by men, especially in northern India and Pakistan 查普坎（尤指印度北方和巴基斯坦等地男子穿的長外套）

chap·lain /ˈtʃæplɪn/ *noun* a priest or other Christian minister who is responsible for the religious needs of people in a prison, hospital, etc. or in the armed forces（監獄、醫院、軍隊等的）教士，牧師，神父；牧靈司鐸 ➲ compare PADRE, PRIEST

chap·lain·cy /ˈtʃæplənsi/ *noun* (*pl.* **-ies**) the position or work of a chaplain; the place where a chaplain works 牧靈司鐸的職位（或職責）；牧靈司鐸工作的地方

chap·let /ˈtʃæplət/ *noun* a circle of leaves, flowers or JEWELS worn on the head（用葉、花或珠寶做成的）花冠

chapped /tʃæpt/ *adj.* (of the skin or lips 皮膚或唇) rough, dry and sore, especially because of wind or cold weather（尤指因風吹或天冷而）皸裂的，開裂的

chaps /tʃæps/ *noun* [pl.] leather coverings worn as protection over trousers/pants by COWBOYS, etc. when riding a horse（牛仔等騎馬時穿的）皮護腿套褲，皮套褲：*a pair of chaps* 一條皮套褲

chap·ter 🔑 AW /ˈtʃæptə(r)/ *noun*
1 🔑 (*abbr.* **chap.**) [C] a separate section of a book, usually with a number or title（書的）章，篇，回：*I've just finished Chapter 3.* 我剛完成第 3 章。◇ *in the* ***previous/next/last chapter*** 在前 / 下 / 最後一章 ◇ *Have you read the chapter on the legal system?* 你讀過論述法律制度的那一章嗎？ **2** [C] a period of time in a person's life or in history（人生或歷史的）時期，時代，篇章：*a difficult chapter in our country's history* 我們國家歷史上的一段困難時期 **3** [C+sing./pl. v.] all the priests of a CATHEDRAL or members of a religious community 主教座堂全體教士；宗教團體的全體成員：*a meeting of the dean and chapter* 總鐸和全體教士的會議 **4** [C] (*especially NAmE*) a local branch of a society, club, etc.（社團、俱樂部等的）地方分會：*the local chapter of the Rotary club* 扶輪社的地方分會

IDM **ˌchapter and ˈverse** the exact details of sth, especially the exact place where particular information may be found 準確細節；（尤指信息的）確切出處：*I can't give chapter and verse, but that's the rough outline of our legal position.* 我無法提供準確細節，但那是我們所處法律地位的大致情況。 **a ˌchapter of ˈaccidents** (*BrE*) a series of unfortunate events 接二連三的不幸事故；接踵而來的災禍

ˌChapter ˈ11 *noun* [U] (*law* 律) in the US, a section of the law dealing with BANKRUPTCY (= being unable to pay debts), that allows companies to stop paying their debts in the normal way while they try to find a solution to their financial problems 破產保護（美國破產法的一章，允許公司在解決財務問題期間停止償還債務）：*The company has* ***filed for Chapter 11*** *bankruptcy protection.* 公司已經申請破產保護。➲ compare ADMINISTRATION (6)

ˌChapter ˈ7 *noun* [U] (*law* 律) in the US, a section of the law dealing with BANKRUPTCY (= being unable to pay debts), that allows a court to take property belonging to a company or person which is then sold to pay their debts 破產（美國破產法的一章，允許法院清算變賣財產以償還債務）➲ compare LIQUIDATION (1)

ˈchapter house *noun* a building where all the priests of a CATHEDRAL or members of a religious community meet 座堂會議廳；宗教團體會議廳

char /tʃɑː(r)/ *verb, noun*

■ ***verb*** (**-rr-**) **1** [I, T] **~ (sth)** to become black by burning; to make sth black by burning it（使）燒黑，燒焦 ➲ see also CHARRED ➲ SYNONYMS at BURN **2** [I] (*old-fashioned, BrE*) to work as a cleaner in a house 當家庭清潔工

■ ***noun*** (*old-fashioned, BrE*) **1** [C] = CHARWOMAN **2** [U] (*informal*) tea 茶：*a cup of char* 一杯茶

chara·banc /ˈʃærəbæŋ/ *noun* (*old-fashioned, BrE*) an early type of bus, used in the past especially for pleasure trips（舊時尤用於遊覽的）旅遊車，遊覽車

char·ac·ter 🔑 /ˈkærəktə(r)/ *noun*

▸ QUALITIES/FEATURES 品質；特點 **1** 🔑 [C, usually sing.] all the qualities and features that make a person, groups of people, and places different from others（人、集體的）品質，性格；（地方的）特點，特性：*to have a* ***strong/weak character*** 個性強 / 不強 ◇ ***character traits/defects*** 性格特點 / 弱點 ◇ *The book gives a fascinating insight into Mrs Obama's character.* 這部書對奧巴馬夫人的性格作了生動的剖析。◇ *Generosity is part of the American character.* 慷慨是美國人性格的一部份。◇ *The character of the neighbourhood hasn't changed at all.* 這片住宅區的風貌依舊。 **2** 🔑 [C, usually sing., U] the way that sth is, or a particular quality or feature that a thing, an event or a place has（事物、事件或地方的）特點，特徵，特色 SYN **nature**：*the delicate character of the light in the evening* 夜間燈火所具有的那種柔和的特點 ◇ *buildings that are very simple* ***in character*** 造型很簡潔的建築物 **3** 🔑 [U] (*approving*) strong personal qualities such as the ability to deal with difficult or dangerous situations 勇氣；毅力：*Everyone admires her strength of character and determination.* 每一個人都欽佩她堅強的性格和決心。◇ *He showed great character returning to the sport after his accident.* 他在出了事故後仍能重返體壇表現出他頑強的毅力。◇ *Adventure camps are considered to be* ***character-building*** (= meant to improve sb's strong qualities). 冒險野營生活被認為能磨練意志。 **4** 🔑 [U] (usually *approving*) the interesting or unusual quality that a place or a person has（地方或人的）與眾不同之處，特色：*The modern hotels here have no real character.* 此處的現代化旅館其實毫無特色。◇ *a face with a lot of character* 與眾不同的面孔

▸ STRANGE/INTERESTING PERSON 古怪的 / 有趣的人 **5** [C] (*informal*) (used with an adjective 與形容詞連用) a person, particularly an unpleasant or strange one（令人討厭的或古怪的）人：*There were some really strange characters hanging around the bar.* 有些不三不四的人在酒吧周圍遊蕩。 **6** [C] (*informal*) an interesting or unusual person（有趣的或不同尋常的）人：*She's a character!* 她真是個有趣的人！

▸ REPUTATION 名譽 **7** [C, U] (*formal*) the opinion that people have of you, particularly of whether you can be trusted or relied on 名譽；聲望；名氣：*She was a victim of* ***character assassination*** (= an unfair attack on the good opinion people had of her). 她是誹謗行為的受害者。◇ *a* ***slur/attack on his character*** 對他名譽的詆譭 / 攻擊 ◇ *My teacher agreed to be a* ***character witness*** *for me in court.* 我的老師同意出庭做我的品德信譽見證人。◇ *a* ***character reference*** (= a letter that a person who knows you well writes to an employer to tell them about your good qualities) 品德證明書

▸ IN BOOK/PLAY/MOVIE 書；戲劇；電影 **8** 🔑 [C] a person or an animal in a book, play or film/movie（書籍、戲劇或電影中的）人物，角色：*a* ***major/minor character*** *in the book* 書中的主要 / 次要人物 ◇ *cartoon characters* 動畫片中的角色 ➲ COLLOCATIONS at LITERATURE

▸ SYMBOL/LETTER 符號；字母 **9** [C] a letter, sign, mark or symbol used in writing, printing or on computers（書寫、印刷或計算機上的）文字，字母，符號：*Chinese characters* 漢字 ◇ *a line 30 characters long* 長達 30 字符的一行 ➲ picture at IDEOGRAM

IDM **ˌin ˈcharacter | ˌout of ˈcharacter** typical/not typical of a person's character 符合（或不符合）某人的性格：*Her behaviour last night was completely out of character.* 她昨晚的舉止與她的性格截然不符。 **ˌin ˈcharacter (with sth)** in the same style as sth（與…）風格相同：*The new wing of the museum was not really in character with the rest of the building.* 博物館新建的側翼樓與大樓其他部份的風格有些不一樣。

ˈcharacter actor *noun* an actor who always takes the parts of interesting or unusual people 性格演員

char·ac·ter·ful /ˈkærəktəfl; *NAmE* -tərfl/ *adj.* very interesting and unusual 很有趣且富有特色的

char·ac·ter·is·tic 0-w /ˌkærəktəˈrɪstɪk/ *adj., noun*

■ *adj.* 0-w ~ (of sth/sb) very typical of sth or of sb's character 典型的；獨特的；特有的：*She spoke with characteristic enthusiasm.* 她說話帶着特有的熱情。OPP **uncharacteristic** ▸ **char·ac·ter·is·tic·al·ly** *adv.*：*Characteristically, Helen paid for everyone.* 一如既往，海倫為每一個人付了費。

■ *noun* 0-w ~ (of sth/sb) a typical feature or quality that sth/sb has 特徵；特點；品質：*The need to communicate is a key characteristic of human society.* 需要交流是人類社會最重要的一個特徵。◇ *The two groups of children have quite different characteristics.* 這兩組兒童具有截然不同的特點。◇ *Personal characteristics, such as age and sex are taken into account.* 個人的特徵，如年齡和性別等，都要考慮進去。◇ *genetic characteristics* 遺傳特徵

char·ac·ter·iza·tion (*BrE* also **-isa·tion**) /ˌkærəktəraɪˈzeɪʃn/ *noun* [U, C] **1** the way that a writer makes characters in a book or play seem real（對書或戲劇中人物的）刻畫，描繪，塑造 **2** (*formal*) the way in which sb/sth is described or defined 描述方法；界定方法 SYN **portrayal**：*This is an unfair characterization of the Prime Minister.* 這是對首相不公正的描述。

char·ac·ter·ize (*BrE* also **-ise**) /ˈkærəktəraɪz/ *verb* (*formal*) **1 ~ sb/sth** to be typical of a person, place or thing 是…的特徵；以…為典型：*the rolling hills that characterize this part of England* 成為英格蘭這一地區特徵的綿延起伏的丘陵地 **2 ~ sb/sth** [often passive] to give sb/sth its typical or most noticeable qualities or features 使…具有特點（或最引人注目的特徵）：*The city is characterized by tall modern buildings in steel and glass.* 這座城市的特點是鋼鐵和玻璃建造的現代化高樓大廈林立。 **3 ~ sb/sth (as sth)** to describe or show the qualities of sb/sth in a particular way 描述，刻畫，表現（…的特徵、特點）：*activities that are characterized as 'male' or 'female' work* 被描述為"男性"或"女性"工作的各種活動

char·ac·ter·less /ˈkærəktələs; *NAmE* -tərləs/ *adj.* having no interesting qualities 無特徵的；無個性的；平凡的

ˈcharacter recognition *noun* [U] the ability of a computer to read numbers or letters that are printed or written by hand 字符識別，字元識別（計算機讀取印刷或手寫數字或字母的能力）

cha·rade /ʃəˈrɑːd; *NAmE* ʃəˈreɪd/ *noun* **1** [C] a situation in which people pretend that sth is true when it clearly is not 明顯的偽裝；做戲；裝模作樣 SYN **pretence**：*Their whole marriage had been a charade—they had never loved each other.* 他們的整個婚姻都是在做戲，他們從未相愛過。 **2 charades** [U] a game in which one player acts out the syllables of a word or title and the other players try to guess what it is 打啞謎猜字遊戲：*Let's play charades.* 咱們來玩打啞謎猜字遊戲吧。

char·broil /ˈtʃɑːbrɔɪl; *NAmE* ˈtʃɑːr-/ *verb* **~ sth** to cook meat or other food over CHARCOAL 炭烤，炭炙（肉等食物）

char·coal /ˈtʃɑːkəʊl; *NAmE* ˈtʃɑːrkoʊl/ *noun* [U] **1** a black substance made by burning wood slowly in an oven with little air. Charcoal is used as a fuel or for drawing. 炭，木炭（可作燃料或供作畫）：*charcoal grilled steaks* 用木炭烤製的牛排 ◇ *a charcoal drawing* 炭筆畫 **2** (also ˌ**charcoal ˈgrey**) a very dark grey colour 深灰色

chard /tʃɑːd; *NAmE* tʃɑːrd/ (also ˌ**Swiss ˈchard**) *noun* [U] a vegetable with large leaves and thick white, yellow or red STEMS 莙薘菜；牛皮菜；葉甜菜

Char·don·nay /ˈʃɑːdəneɪ; *NAmE* ˈʃɑːrd-/ *noun* [U, C] a type of white wine, or the type of GRAPE from which it is made 霞多麗白葡萄酒；霞多麗葡萄

charge 0-w /tʃɑːdʒ; *NAmE* tʃɑːrdʒ/ *noun, verb*

■ *noun*

▸ MONEY 錢 **1** 0-w [C, U] **~ (for sth)** the amount of money that sb asks for goods and services（商品和服務所需的）要價，收費：*We have to make a small charge for refreshments.* 我們得收取少量茶點費。◇ *admission charges* 入場費 ◇ *Delivery is* **free of charge**. 免費送貨。➲ SYNONYMS at RATE **2** [C, U] (*NAmE, informal*) = ACCOUNT (3), CHARGE ACCOUNT, CREDIT ACCOUNT：*Would you like to put that on your charge?* 你願意把這筆費用記在你的賬上嗎？◇ *'Are you paying cash?' 'No, it'll be a charge.'* "你用現金支付嗎？" "不，記賬吧。"

▸ OF CRIME/STH WRONG 罪行；過失 **3** 0-w [C, U] an official claim made by the police that sb has committed a crime 指控；控告：*criminal charges* 刑事指控 ◇ *a murder/an assault charge* 謀殺罪的／侵犯人身罪的指控 ◇ *He will be sent back to England* **to face a charge of** (= to be on trial for) *armed robbery.* 他將被遣返回英國面臨持械搶劫罪的指控。◇ *They decided to* **drop the charges** *against the newspaper and settle out of court.* 他們已決定撤銷對那家報紙的指控，在庭外和解。◇ *After being questioned by the police, she was released* **without charge**. 她被警察傳訊後無罪釋放。➲ COLLOCATIONS at JUSTICE **4** 0-w [C] a statement accusing sb of doing sth wrong or bad 指責；譴責 SYN **allegation**：*She rejected the charge that the story was untrue.* 她否認了說她編造事實的指責。◇ *Be careful you don't* **leave yourself open to charges** *of political bias.* 你要小心別留下把柄，讓人家指責你帶有政治偏見。

▸ RESPONSIBILITY 職責 **5** 0-w [U] a position of having control over sb/sth; responsibility for sb/sth 主管；掌管；照管；職責；責任：*She has charge of the day-to-day running of the business.* 她負責掌管日常業務。◇ *They left the au pair* **in charge of** *the children for a week.* 他們把孩子留給做換工的照料一週。◇ *He* **took charge of** *the farm after his father's death.* 他在父親去世後掌管了農場。◇ *I'm leaving the school in your charge.* 我這就把學校交給你掌管。 **6** [C] (*formal* or *humorous*) a person that you have responsibility for and care for 被照管的人；受照料者

▸ ELECTRICITY 電 **7** [C, U] the amount of electricity that is put into a battery or carried by a substance（電池或帶電物質的）充電量，電荷：*a* **positive/negative charge** 正／負電荷

▸ RUSH/ATTACK 猛衝；攻擊 **8** [C] a sudden rush or violent attack, for example by soldiers, wild animals or players in some sports 突然猛衝；猛攻；衝鋒：*He led the charge down the field.* 他帶頭沿着球場衝殺過去。

▸ EXPLOSIVE 炸藥 **9** [C] the amount of EXPLOSIVE needed to fire a gun or make an explosion（射擊或爆炸需要的）炸藥量 ➲ see also DEPTH CHARGE

▸ STRONG FEELING 強烈感情 **10** [sing.] the power to cause strong feelings 感染力；震撼力：*the emotional charge of the piano piece* 那首鋼琴曲扣人心弦的感染力

▸ TASK 任務 **11** [sing.] (*formal*) a task or duty 任務；責任：*His charge was to obtain specific information.* 他的任務是收集具體的信息。

IDM **bring/press/prefer ˈcharges against sb** (*law* 律) to accuse sb formally of a crime so that there can be a trial in court 起訴；控告 **get a ˈcharge out of sth** (*NAmE*) to get a strong feeling of excitement or pleasure from sth 從…中得到快感（或快樂、樂趣）

■ *verb*

▸ MONEY 錢 **1** 0-w [T, I] to ask an amount of money for goods or a service 收費；要價：**~ sth for sth** *What did they charge for the repairs?* 他們收了多少修理費？◇ *The restaurant charged £20 for dinner.* 這家餐館收了 20 英鎊的餐費。◇ **~ sb for sth** *We won't charge you for delivery.* 我們送貨不收費。◇ **~ sth at sth** *Calls are charged at 36p per minute.* 電話費按每分鐘 36 便士收取。◇ **~ sb sth (for sth)** *He only charged me half price.* 他只收我半價。◇ **~ for sth** *Do you think museums should charge for admission?* 你認為博物館應該收入場費嗎？◇ **~ (sb) to do sth** *The bank doesn't charge to stop a payment.* 銀行不收取停止付款的手續費。 **2** 0-w [T] to record the cost of sth as an amount that sb has to pay 把…記在賬上；在某人賬上記入：**~ sth to sth** *They charge the calls to their credit-card account.* 他們用信用卡賬戶支付電話費。◇ (*NAmE*) **~ sth** *Don't worry. I'll* **charge it** (= pay by credit card). 別擔心，我會用信用卡付款的。

▸ WITH CRIME/STH WRONG 犯罪；過失 **3** 0-w [T] to accuse sb formally of a crime so that there can be a trial in court 控告；起訴：**~ sb** *Several people were arrested but nobody was charged.* 有數人被捕，但均未受到起訴。◇ **~ sb with sth/with doing sth** *He was charged with murder.* 他被指控犯有謀殺罪。 **4** [T] **~ sb (with sth/with**

C

C

doing sth) (*formal*) to accuse sb publicly of doing sth wrong or bad 指責；譴責：*Opposition MPs charged the minister with neglecting her duty.* 反對黨議員指責這名女部長玩忽職守。

▸ **RUSH/ATTACK 猛衝；攻擊 5** [I, T] to rush forward and attack sb/sth 猛衝；猛攻；衝鋒：*The bull put its head down and charged.* 公牛低下頭猛衝過來。◇ **~ (at) sb/sth** *We charged at the enemy.* 我們向敵人發起衝鋒。 **6** 🔑 [I] **+ adv./prep.** to rush in a particular direction 向…方向衝去：*The children charged down the stairs.* 孩子們衝下了樓梯。◇ *He came charging into my room and demanded to know what was going on.* 他衝進我的房間，要求知道發生了什麼事。

▸ **WITH ELECTRICITY 電 7** 🔑 [T] to pass electricity through sth so that it is stored there 充電：**~ sth** *Before use, the battery must be charged.* 電池使用前必須充電。◇ **~ sth up** *The shaver can be charged up and used when travelling.* 這種電動剃鬚刀可充電供旅行使用。

▸ **WITH RESPONSIBILITY/TASK 職責；任務 8** [T] (usually passive 通常用於被動語態) (*formal*) to give sb a responsibility or task 賦予…職責（或任務）；使…承擔責任（或任務）：**~ sb with sth** *The committee has been charged with the development of sport in the region.* 委員會已被賦予在該地區發展體育運動的職責。◇ **~ sb with doing sth** *The governing body is charged with managing the school within its budget.* 學校管理部門負有在預算範圍內管理好學校的職責。

▸ **WITH STRONG FEELING 強烈感情 9** [T] (usually passive 通常用於被動語態) **~ sth (with sth)** (*literary*) to fill sb with an emotion 使充滿（…情緒）：*The room was charged with hatred.* 這個房間裏充滿了敵意。◇ *a* ***highly charged*** *atmosphere* 一觸即發的緊張氣氛

▸ **GLASS 玻璃杯 10** [T] **~ sth** (*BrE, formal*) to fill a glass 注滿（玻璃杯）：*Please charge your glasses and drink a toast to the bride and groom!* 請各位斟滿酒杯向新娘、新郎敬酒！

▸ **GUN 槍 11** [T] **~ sth** (*old use*) to load a gun 裝（彈藥）

charge·able /ˈtʃɑːdʒəbl; *NAmE* ˈtʃɑːrdʒ-/ *adj.* **~ (to sb/sth) 1** (of a sum of money 一筆錢) that must be paid by sb 應支付的；應償付的：*Any expenses you may incur will be chargeable to the company.* 你的所有開銷均由本公司支付。 **2** (of income or other money that you earn 正常收入或其他所得) that you must pay tax on 應徵稅的：***chargeable earnings/income*** 應徵稅的工資／收入

ˈcharge account *noun* (*NAmE*) = ACCOUNT *n* (3)

ˈcharge capping *noun* [U] (*BrE*) the act of setting a limit on the amount of money that the local government of an area can charge people in order to pay for public services（地方政府為公共服務向公眾收取的）收費限額

ˈcharge card *noun* a small plastic card provided by a shop/store which you use to buy goods there, paying for them later（購物的）賒購卡，記賬卡 ➲ see also CREDIT CARD

charged /tʃɑːdʒd; *NAmE* tʃɑːrdʒd/ *adj.* **~ (with sth)** full of or causing strong feelings or opinions 充滿（某種情緒或想法）的；緊張的：*a highly charged atmosphere* 一觸即發的緊張氣氛 ◇ *a politically charged issue* 極具政治敏感的問題 ◇ *The dialogue is charged with menace.* 對話充滿威脅。

chargé d'af·faires /ˌʃɑːʒeɪ dæˈfeə(r); *NAmE* ˌʃɑːrʒeɪ dæˈfer/ *noun* (*pl.* **chargés d'af·faires** /ˌʃɑːʒeɪ dæˈfeə(r); *NAmE* ˌʃɑːrʒeɪ dæˈfer/) (from *French*) **1** an official who takes the place of an AMBASSADOR in a foreign country when he or she is away 臨時代辦（大使不在時代行其職責） **2** an official below the rank of AMBASSADOR who acts as the senior representative of his or her country in a foreign country where there is no AMBASSADOR 代辦（出使沒有派駐大使的國家，其級別低於大使的外交代表）

charge·hand /ˈtʃɑːdʒhænd; *NAmE* ˈtʃɑːrdʒ-/ *noun* (*BrE*) a worker in charge of others on a particular job, but below the rank of a FOREMAN 副領班；副組長

ˈcharge nurse *noun* (*BrE*) a nurse, especially a man, who is in charge of a hospital WARD 主管護士，護士長（多為男性）

char·ger /ˈtʃɑːdʒə(r); *NAmE* ˈtʃɑːrdʒ-/ *noun* **1** a piece of equipment for loading a battery with electricity 充電器 **2** (*old use*) a horse that a soldier rode in battle in the past（舊時的）軍馬，戰馬

ˈcharge sheet *noun* (*BrE*) a record kept in a police station of the names of people that the police have stated to be guilty of a crime (= that they have charged)（警察局的）被起訴者名錄

charge·sheet /ˈtʃɑːdʒʃiːt; *NAmE* ˈtʃɑːrdʒ-/ *verb* [T] **~ sb (for sth)** (*IndE*) to accuse sb formally of committing an offence and to ask for an official reply or defence（因某事）起訴，控告（某人）

char·grill /ˈtʃɑːɡrɪl; *NAmE* ˈtʃɑːr-/ *verb* **~ sth** [usually passive] to cook meat, fish, or vegetables over a very high heat so that the outside is slightly burnt 高温烤炙，高温燒烤（至表皮焦黃）

char·iot /ˈtʃæriət/ *noun* an open vehicle with two wheels, pulled by horses, used in ancient times in battle and for racing（古代用於戰鬥或比賽的）雙輪敞篷馬車

char·iot·eer /ˌtʃæriəˈtɪə(r); *NAmE* -ˈtɪr/ *noun* the driver of a chariot 駕雙輪馬車的人

cha·risma /kəˈrɪzmə/ *noun* [U] the powerful personal quality that some people have to attract and impress other people 超凡的個人魅力；感召力；號召力：*The President has great personal charisma.* 總統具有超凡的個人魅力。◇ *a lack of charisma* 缺乏個人魅力

cha·ris·mat·ic /ˌkærɪzˈmætɪk/ *adj., noun*
■ ***adj.*** **1** having charisma 有超凡魅力的；有號召力（或感召力）的：*a charismatic leader* 魅力超凡的領袖 **OPP uncharismatic 2** (of a Christian religious group 基督教宗教團體) believing in special gifts from God; worshipping in a very enthusiastic way 蒙受神恩的；有特恩的；虔誠崇拜的 ▸ **cha·ris·mat·ic·al·ly** /-kli/ *adv.*
■ ***noun*** (often **Charismatic**) a charismatic Christian 有特恩的基督徒

char·it·able /ˈtʃærətəbl/ *adj.* **1** connected with a charity or charities 慈善團體的；慈善事業的：*a* ***charitable institution/foundation/trust*** 慈善機構／基金會／信託 ◇ *a* ***charitable donation/gift*** 慈善捐贈／贈品 ◇ (*BrE*) *to have* ***charitable status*** (= to be an official charity) 是認可的慈善機構 **2** helping people who are poor or in need 慈善的；行善的；布施的：*His later years were devoted largely to* ***charitable work.*** 他晚年主要致力於慈善工作。 **3** kind in your attitude to other people, especially when you are judging them 仁愛的；寬厚的；寬容的：*Let's be charitable and assume she just made a mistake.* 咱們寬容些吧，就當她只是犯了個錯誤。 **OPP uncharitable** ▸ **char·it·ably** /-bli/ *adv.*：*Try to think about him a little more charitably.* 看待他這個人盡量大度一點吧。

char·ity 🔑 /ˈtʃærəti/ *noun* (*pl.* **-ies**)
1 🔑 [C] an organization for helping people in need 慈善機構（或組織）：*Many charities sent money to help the victims of the famine.* 許多慈善機構捐款賑濟饑民。◇ *The concert will raise money for local charities.* 這場音樂會將為當地慈善機構募捐。 **2** 🔑 [U] the aim of giving money, food, help, etc. to people who are in need 慈善；賑濟；施捨：*Most of the runners in the London Marathon are* ***raising money for charity.*** 大多數人參加倫敦馬拉松賽跑是為慈善事業募集資金。◇ *Do you give much to charity?* 慈善捐助你捐得多嗎？◇ *a charity concert* (= organized to get money for charity) 慈善音樂會 ◇ *to* ***live on/off charity*** (= to live on money which other people give you because you are poor) 靠賑濟生活 **3** [U] (*formal*) kindness and sympathy towards other people, especially when you are judging them 仁愛；寬容；寬厚：*Her article showed no charity towards her former friends.* 她的文章對她以前的朋友毫不寬容。
IDM charity begins at ˈhome (*saying*) you should help and care for your own family, etc. before you start helping other people 博愛始於自家

ˈcharity shop (*BrE*) (*NAmE* **ˈthrift shop/store**) *noun* a shop/store that sells clothes and other goods given by people to raise money for a charity 慈善商店（通過出售捐贈的衣物等募集慈善資金）

char·lady /ˈtʃɑːleɪdi; *NAmE* ˈtʃɑːr-/ *noun* (*pl.* **-ies**) (*old-fashioned, BrE*) = CHARWOMAN

char·la·tan /ˈʃɑːlətən; *NAmE* ˈʃɑːrl-/ *noun* a person who claims to have knowledge or skills that they do not really have 假充內行的人；騙子

charles·ton /ˈtʃɑːlstən; *NAmE* ˈtʃɑːrl-/ *noun* (usually **the charleston**) [sing.] a fast dance that was popular in the 1920s 查爾斯頓舞（流行於 20 世紀 20 年代的快步舞）

char·ley horse /ˈtʃɑːli hɔːs; *NAmE* ˈtʃɑːrli hɔːrs/ *noun* [usually sing.] (*NAmE, informal*) = CRAMP (1)：*Ow! I just got a charley horse in my leg.* 哎唷！我的腿抽筋了。

char·lie /ˈtʃɑːli; *NAmE* ˈtʃɑːrli/ *noun* (*old-fashioned, BrE, informal*) a silly person 蠢人；傻瓜；笨蛋：*You must have felt a proper charlie!* 你一定覺得自己是個十足的笨蛋！

charm /tʃɑːm; *NAmE* tʃɑːrm/ *noun, verb*

■ ***noun*** **1** [U] the power of pleasing or attracting people 魅力；魔力；吸引力：*a man of great charm* 富有魅力的男人 ◇ *The hotel is full of charm and character.* 這家旅館風格獨特，極具吸引力。 **2** [C] a feature or quality that is pleasing or attractive 迷人的特徵；吸引人的特性；嫵媚：*her physical charms* (= her beauty) 她那嫵媚的外貌 **3** [C] a small object worn on a chain or BRACELET, that is believed to bring good luck （鏈或手鐲上的）吉祥小飾物：*a lucky charm* 吉祥飾物 ◇ *a charm bracelet* 帶有吉祥飾物的手鐲 ➲ **VISUAL VOCAB** page V65 **4** [C] an act or words believed to have magic power 魔法；咒語；符咒 **SYN** **spell**

IDM ˌ**work like a** ˈ**charm** to be immediately and completely successful 立見功效；效驗如神 ➲ more at THIRD

■ ***verb*** **1** [T, I] **~ (sb)** to please or attract sb in order to make them like you or do what you want 吸引；迷住：*He was charmed by her beauty and wit.* 他被她的才貌迷住了。◇ *Her words had lost their power to charm.* 她的話再也沒有吸引力了。 **2** [T] **~ sb/sth** to control or protect sb/sth using magic, or as if using magic （以魔法或似有魔法）控制，保護：*He has led **a charmed life*** (= he has been lucky even in dangerous or difficult situations). 他的日子過得如有神祐（即使遇到艱險都能逢凶化吉）。

PHR V ˌ**charm sth** ˈ**out of sb** to obtain sth such as information, money, etc. from sb by using charm 利用魅力從…獲取

ˌ**charmed** ˈ**circle** *noun* [sing.] a group of people who have special influence 有特別影響力的一群人

charm·er /ˈtʃɑːmə(r); *NAmE* ˈtʃɑːrm-/ *noun* a person who acts in a way that makes them attractive to other people, sometimes using this to influence others 使人着迷的人；有吸引力的人；施展魅力的人 ➲ see also SNAKE CHARMER

charm·ing /ˈtʃɑːmɪŋ; *NAmE* ˈtʃɑːrmɪŋ/ *adj.* **1** very pleasant or attractive 令人着迷的；迷人的；吸引人的：*The cottage is tiny, but it's charming.* 這間村舍雖小，卻十分迷人。◇ *She's a charming person.* 她是個有魅力的人。 **2** (*ironic, informal*) used to show that you have a low opinion of sb's behaviour （表示對某人的行為評價不高）真是太好了：*They left me to tidy it all up myself. Charming, wasn't it?* 他們留下我一個人來收拾這一切。真是照顧我啲，不是嗎？ ▸ **charm·ing·ly** *adv.*

charm·less /ˈtʃɑːmləs; *NAmE* ˈtʃɑːrm-/ *adj.* (*formal*) not at all pleasant or interesting 無魅力的；無吸引力的；無趣的：*a charmless industrial town* 一座毫無吸引力的工業城鎮

ˈ**charm offensive** *noun* a situation in which a person, for example a politician, is especially friendly and pleasant in order to get other people to like them and to support their opinions 魅力攻勢（如政客為拉攏民眾所採取的）

ˈ**charm school** *noun* a school where young people are taught to behave in a polite way （青少年）禮儀學校

char·nel house /ˈtʃɑːnl haʊs; *NAmE* ˈtʃɑːrnl/ *noun* a place used in the past for keeping dead human bodies or bones （舊時）存放屍骨的地方

charred /tʃɑːd; *NAmE* tʃɑːrd/ *adj.* [usually before noun] burnt and black 燒焦的；燒黑的：*the charred remains of a burnt-out car* 被燒焦的轎車殘骸

charts 圖表

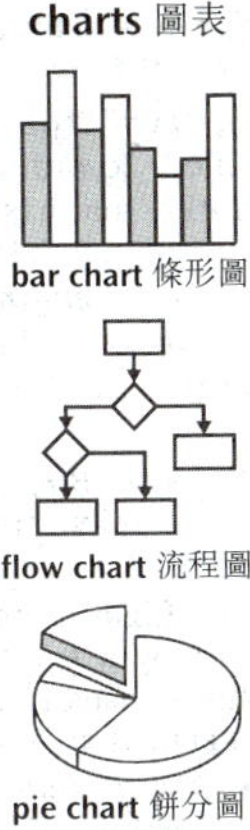

bar chart 條形圖

flow chart 流程圖

pie chart 餅分圖

chart 🔑 **AW** /tʃɑːt; *NAmE* tʃɑːrt/ *noun, verb*

■ ***noun*** **1** 🔑 [C] a page or sheet of information in the form of diagrams, lists of figures, etc. 圖表：*a weather chart* 天氣圖 ◇ *a sales chart* (= showing the level of a company's sales) 銷售圖表 ➲ **LANGUAGE BANK** at ILLUSTRATE ➲ **WRITING TUTOR** page WT25 ➲ see also BAR CHART, FLOW CHART, PIE CHART **2** [C] a detailed map of the sea 海圖：*a naval chart* 海軍航圖 **3 the charts** [pl.] (*especially BrE*) a list, produced each week, of the songs or albums that have sold the most copies or been DOWNLOADED the most （歌曲或唱片每週銷售或下載數量）排行榜：*The album went straight into the charts at number 1.* 這張專輯一進入流行唱片排行榜便佔首位。◇ *to top the charts* (= to be the song or album that has sold more copies than all the others) 位居排行榜之首

IDM ˌ**off the** ˈ**charts** (*informal, especially NAmE*) extremely high in level 高得離譜；高極了：*World demand for the product is off the charts.* 此產品的世界需求量高極了。

■ ***verb*** **1** 🔑 **~ sth** to record or follow the progress or development of sb/sth 記錄，跟踪（進展或發展）：*The exhibition **charts the history of** the palace.* 展覽記載了這座王宮的歷史。 **2 ~ sth** to plan a course of action 計劃行動步驟；制訂計劃：*She had carefully charted her route to the top of her profession.* 她周密地制訂了達到她職業巔峰的行動計劃。 **3 ~ sth** to make a map of an area 繪製區域地圖 **SYN** **map**：*Cook charted the coast of New Zealand in 1768.* 庫克於 1768 年繪製了新西蘭的海岸圖。

char·ter /ˈtʃɑːtə(r); *NAmE* ˈtʃɑːrt-/ *noun, verb*

■ ***noun*** **1** [C] a written statement describing the rights that a particular group of people should have （說明某部份民眾應有權利的）憲章：*the European Union's Social Charter of workers' rights* 保障工人權利的歐盟社會憲章 **2** [C] a written statement of the principles and aims of an organization（表明某一組織之宗旨和原則的）憲章，章程 **SYN** **constitution**：*the United Nations Charter* 聯合國憲章 **3** [C] an official document stating that a ruler or government allows a new organization, town or university to be established and gives it particular rights （統治者或政府准許成立新的組織、城鎮、大學等並授予某種權利的）特許狀，許可證，憑照：*The Royal College received its charter as a university in 1967.* 皇家學院於 1967 年獲得升格為大學的特許狀。 **4** [sing.] **~ (for sth)** (*BrE*) a law or policy that seems likely to help people do sth bad （法律或政策的）不完善，漏洞，缺陷：*The new law will be a charter for unscrupulous financial advisers.* 新的法律會使不誠實的金融顧問有機可乘。◇ *a blackmailer's charter* 敲詐者可鑽的法律空子 **5** [U] the

C

hiring of a plane, boat, etc. （飛機、船等的）租賃：*a yacht available for charter* 可供租賃的遊艇

■ ***verb*** **1 ~ sth** to hire/rent a plane, boat, etc. for your own use 包租（飛機、船等）：*a chartered plane* 包機 **2 ~ sth** to state officially that a new organization, town or university has been established and has special rights 特許設立；給予…特權；發給許可證（或憑照）

char·tered /ˈtʃɑːtəd; *NAmE* ˈtʃɑːrtərd/ *adj.* [only before noun] **1** (*BrE*) qualified according to the rules of a professional organization that has a royal charter（持有皇家特許狀的專業組織認定為）合格的，特許的：*a chartered accountant/surveyor/engineer* 特許會計師／測量師／工程師 **2** (of an aircraft, a ship or a boat 飛機或船) hired for a particular purpose 包租的；租賃的：*a chartered plane* 包機

ˌchartered acˈcountant (*BrE*) (*US* **ˌcertified public acˈcountant**) *noun* a fully trained and qualified ACCOUNTANT 特許會計師

ˈcharter flight *noun* a flight in an aircraft in which all the seats are paid for by a travel company and then sold to their customers, usually at a lower cost than that of a SCHEDULED FLIGHT 包機；包機航班

ˌcharter ˈmember (*NAmE*) (*BrE* **ˌfounder ˈmember**) *noun* one of the first members of a society, an organization, etc., especially one who helped start it（社團、組織等的）創始人，發起人，創建人

char·treuse /ʃɑːˈtrɜːz; *NAmE* ʃɑːrˈtruːz/ *noun* [U] **1** a green or yellow LIQUEUR (= a strong sweet alcoholic drink) 察吐士酒，蕁麻酒（一種烈性甜酒，呈綠色或黃色）**2** a pale yellow or pale green colour 淺黃色；淺綠色

ˈchart-topping *adj.* [only before noun] (of a CD, singer, etc. 唱片、歌手等) having reached the highest position in the music CHARTS 位居流行音樂排行榜榜首的：*his latest chart-topping hit* 他大受歡迎、佔據排行榜首位的新作 ▸ **ˈchart-topper** *noun*

char·woman /ˈtʃɑːwʊmən; *NAmE* ˈtʃɑːr-/ *noun* (*pl.* **-women** /-wɪmɪn/) (also **char**, **char·lady**) (all *BrE*, *old-fashioned*) a woman whose job is to clean a house, an office building, etc. 女清潔工

chary /ˈtʃeəri; *NAmE* ˈtʃeri/ *adj.* **~ of sth/of doing sth** not willing to risk doing sth; fearing possible problems if you do sth 不願冒風險的；小心謹慎的；謹小慎微的 **SYN** wary

chase 0→ /tʃeɪs/ *verb, noun*

■ ***verb***

▸ **RUN/DRIVE AFTER** 追趕；追逐 **1** 0→ [T, I] to run, drive, etc. after sb/sth in order to catch them 追趕；追逐；追捕：**~ sb/sth** *My dog likes chasing rabbits.* 我的狗喜歡追捕兔子。◇ *The kids* ***chased each other*** *around the kitchen table.* 孩子們圍着廚房的桌子相互追逐嬉戲。◇ **~ after sb/sth** *He chased after the burglar but couldn't catch him.* 他追趕那個盜賊卻沒有抓住他。

▸ **MONEY/WORK/SUCCESS** 錢；工作；成功 **2** [T] **~ sth** to try to obtain or achieve sth, for example money, work or success 努力獲得；爭取得到：*Too many people are chasing too few jobs nowadays.* 如今有太多的人在角逐寥寥無幾的工作職位。◇ *The team is chasing its first win in five games.* 這支隊伍正全力爭取五場比賽的首場勝利。

▸ **MAN/WOMAN** 男女 **3** [I, T] (*informal*) to try to persuade sb to have a sexual relationship with you 追求；求愛：**~ after sb** *Kevin's been chasing after Joan for months.* 凱文幾個月來一直在追求瓊。◇ **~ sb** *Girls are always chasing him.* 姑娘們總是在追求他。

▸ **REMIND SB** 提醒 **4** [T] **~ sb** (*informal*) to persuade sb to do sth that they should have done already 催促：*I need to chase him about organizing the meeting.* 我得催他有關籌辦會議的事。

▸ **RUSH** 急奔 **5** [I] **+ adv./prep.** (*informal*) to rush or hurry somewhere 急奔；急趕；匆忙地走：*I've been* ***chasing around*** *town all morning looking for a present for Sharon.* 為了送給沙倫一件禮物，我一上午都在滿城奔走尋覓。

▸ **METAL** 金屬 **6** [T] **~ sth** (*technical* 術語) to cut patterns or designs on metal 鏤刻；雕刻：*chased silver* 雕花銀器

IDM **chase your (own) ˈtail** (*informal*) to be very busy but in fact achieve very little 瞎忙活；徒勞無功

PHR V **ˌchase sb/sth↔aˈway, ˈoff, ˈout, etc.** 0→ to force sb/sth to run away 驅逐；趕走 **ˌchase sb↔ˈup** to contact sb in order to remind them to do sth that they should have done already 催促：*We need to chase up all members who have not yet paid.* 我們得催促所有未付費的成員交費。**ˌchase sth↔ˈup** (*BrE*) (*NAmE* **ˌchase sth↔ˈdown**) to find sth that is needed; to deal with sth that has been forgotten 找尋（所需的東西）；催辦：*My job was to chase up late replies.* 我的工作是催促遲遲未答覆者。

■ ***noun***

▸ **RUNNING/DRIVING AFTER** 追趕；追逐 **1** 0→ [C] (often used with *the* 常與 the 連用) an act of running or driving after sb/sth in order to catch them 追趕；追捕；追逐：*The thieves were caught by police after a short chase.* 經過短暫追捕，小偷被警察擒獲。◇ *a high-speed car chase* 一場汽車的高速角逐 ◇ *We lost him in the narrow streets and had to* ***give up the chase*** (= stop chasing him). 我們在狹窄的街道上被他甩掉，不得不放棄對他的追捕。◇ *to* ***take up the chase*** (= start chasing sb) 開始追捕行動

▸ **FOR SUCCESS/MONEY/WORK** 成功；錢；工作 **2** [sing.] a process of trying hard to get sth 努力獲得；爭取：*Three teams are involved in the chase for the championship.* 有三支隊伍角逐冠軍的寶座。

▸ **IN SPORT** 體育運動 **3 the chase** [sing.] hunting animals as a sport 打獵 **4** [C] = STEEPLECHASE ➲ see also WILD GOOSE CHASE

IDM **cut to the ˈchase** (*informal*) to stop wasting time and start talking about the most important thing 不繞圈子直截了當地說；開門見山：*Right, let's cut to the chase. How much is it going to cost?* 對啦，咱們開門見山吧。這要多少錢？ **give ˈchase** to run after sb/sth in order to catch them 追逐；追趕；追捕：*We gave chase along the footpath.* 我們開始沿小路追趕。

chaser /ˈtʃeɪsə(r)/ *noun* **1** a drink that you have after another of a different kind, for example a stronger alcoholic drink after a weak one（飲淡酒後喝的）烈性酒：*a beer with a whisky chaser* 喝啤酒後接着喝威士忌酒 **2** a horse for STEEPLECHASE racing (= in which horses must jump over a series of fences)（參加障礙賽的）馬

Chas·id·ism /ˈxæsɪdɪzəm/ *noun* [U] = HASIDISM

chasm /ˈkæzəm/ *noun* **1** [C] (*literary*) a deep crack or opening in the ground（地上的）深裂口，裂隙，深坑 **2** [sing.] **~ (between A and B)** (*formal*) a very big difference between two people or groups, for example because they have different attitudes（兩個人或團體之間的）巨大分歧，顯著差別 **SYN** **gulf**

chas·sis /ˈʃæsi/ *noun* (*pl.* **chas·sis** /-siz/) the frame that a vehicle is built on（車輛的）底盤，底座，底架

chaste /tʃeɪst/ *adj.* **1** (*old-fashioned*) not having sex with anyone; only having sex with the person that you are married to 貞潔的；忠貞的：*to remain chaste* 保持貞潔 **2** (*formal*) not expressing sexual feelings 不含有性意味的；純潔的：*a* ***chaste kiss*** *on the cheek* 在面頰上純潔的一吻 **3** (*formal*) simple and plain in style; not decorated（風格）簡樸的，樸實的；不修飾的：*the cool, chaste interior of the hall* 清爽樸實的大廳內部 ▸ **chaste·ly** *adv.*：*He kissed her chastely on the cheek.* 他在她的臉上留下了純潔的一吻。

chas·ten /ˈtʃeɪsn/ *verb* [often passive] **~ sb** (*formal*) to make sb feel sorry for sth they have done 使內疚；使懊悔：*He felt* ***suitably chastened*** *and apologized.* 他恰當地感到內疚並表示歉意。◇ *She gave them a chastening lecture.* 她給他們做了一次令他們深感汗顏的演講。◇ *It was a* ***chastening experience****.* 那是一次讓人接受磨練的經歷。

chas·tise /tʃæˈstaɪz/ *verb* **1 ~ sb (for sth/for doing sth)** (*formal*) to criticize sb for doing sth wrong 批評；指責；責備：*He chastised the team for their lack of commitment.* 他指責隊伍未竭盡全力。**2 ~ sb** (*old-fashioned*) to punish sb physically 體罰 **SYN** **beat** ▸ **chas·tise·ment** /tʃæˈstaɪzmənt; ˈtʃæstɪzmənt/ *noun* [U]

chas·tity /ˈtʃæstəti/ *noun* [U] the state of not having sex with anyone or only having sex with the person you are married to; being CHASTE（性方面的）忠貞；貞潔；貞操： *vows of chastity* (= those taken by some priests)（神父的）忠貞誓言

'chastity belt *noun* a device worn by some women in the past to prevent them from being able to have sex（舊時防止婦女私通的）貞操帶

chat /tʃæt/ *verb, noun*

■ ***verb*** (-tt-) **1** [I] to talk in a friendly informal way to sb 閒聊；閒談；聊天： **~ (to/with sb)** *My kids spend hours chatting on the phone to their friends.* 我的幾個孩子在電話上和朋友聊天一聊就是幾個小時。◇ **~ away (to/with sb)** *Within minutes of being introduced they were chatting away like old friends.* 他們經人介紹認識才幾分鐘，便一見如故地聊個沒完。◇ **~ about sth/sb** *What were you chatting about?* 你們聊了些什麼？ **2** [I] **~ (away) (to/with sb)** | **~ (about sth/sb)** to exchange messages with other people on the Internet, especially in a CHAT ROOM（尤指在網上聊天室的）閒聊，聊天，交談： *He's been on the computer all morning, chatting with his friends.* 他整個上午都在上網和朋友聊天。

PHR V **,chat sb↔'up** (*BrE, informal*) to talk in a friendly way to sb you are sexually attracted to（受異性吸引而）親昵地攀談，與某人搭訕： *She went straight over and tried to chat him up.* 她逕直走了過去試圖同他搭訕。

■ ***noun*** **1** [C] (*especially BrE*) a friendly informal conversation 閒聊；閒談；聊天： *I just called in for a chat.* 我只是來聊聊天。◇ *I had a long chat with her.* 我和她閒聊了很久。 ➲ SYNONYMS at DISCUSSION **2** [U] talking, especially informal conversation（尤指非正式的）談話，講話： *That's enough chat from me—on with the music!* 我不再多講了，繼續欣賞音樂吧！ ➲ SYNONYMS at DISCUSSION **3** [U, C] communication between people on the Internet 網上聊天： *chat software* 聊天軟件◇ *Internet chat services* 互聯網聊天服務◇ *Fans are invited to an online chat.* 愛好者獲邀參與網上聊天。

cha·teau (also **châ·teau**) /'ʃætəʊ; *NAmE* ʃæ'toʊ/ *noun* (*pl.* **cha·teaux**, **châ·teaux** or **cha·teaus**, **châ·teaus** /-təʊz; *NAmE* -'toʊz/) (from *French*) a castle or large country house in France（法國的）城堡，鄉間別墅

chat·line /'tʃætlaɪn/ *noun* **1** a telephone service which allows a number of people who call in separately to have a conversation, especially for fun（消遣性的）熱線電話交談服務 **2** a telephone service which people can call to talk to sb about sex in order to feel sexually excited 熱線電話色情交談服務

'chat room *noun* an area on the Internet where people can communicate with each other, usually about one particular topic（互聯網上的）聊天室 ➲ COLLOCATIONS at EMAIL

'chat show (*BrE*) (also **'talk show** *NAmE, BrE*) *noun* a television or radio programme in which famous people are asked questions and talk in an informal way about their work and opinions on various topics（電視或電台的）訪談節目： *a chat-show host* 訪談節目主持人

chat·tel /'tʃætl/ *noun* [C, U] (*law* 律 or *old-fashioned*) something that belongs to you（個人的）財產，動產 ➲ see also GOODS AND CHATTELS

chat·ter /'tʃætə(r)/ *verb, noun*

■ ***verb*** **1** [I] **~ (away/on) (to sb) (about sth)** to talk quickly and continuously, especially about things that are not important 喋喋不休；嘮叨；饒舌： *They chattered away happily for a while.* 他們高興地閒扯了一會兒。◇ *The children chattered to each other excitedly about the next day's events.* 孩子們很興奮，沒完沒了地談論着第二天的活動。 **2** [I] (of teeth 牙齒) to knock together continuously because you are cold or frightened（因冷或害怕）打顫 **3** [I] (of birds or MONKEYS 禽或猴) to make a series of short high sounds 鳴叫；啼囀；啁啾；唧唧叫；吱吱叫

IDM **the 'chattering classes** (*BrE*, usually *disapproving*) the people in society who like to give their opinions on political or social issues 喜歡（對政治或社會問題）發表意見的人

■ ***noun*** [U] **1** continuous rapid talk about things that are not important 嘮叨的話；喋喋不休： *Jane's constant chatter was beginning to annoy him.* 簡無休止的嘮叨開始使他心煩。◇ *idle chatter* 無聊的嘮叨 **2** a series of quick short high sounds that some animals make 鳴叫聲；啼囀聲；吱吱叫聲： *the chatter of monkeys* 猴子的吱吱叫聲 **3** a series of short sounds made by things knocking together 碰擊聲；咯咯聲；打顫聲： *the chatter of teeth* 牙齒打顫的咯咯聲

chat·ter·box /'tʃætəbɒks; *NAmE* 'tʃætərbɑːks/ *noun* (*informal*) a person who talks a lot, especially a child 話多的人，話匣子（尤指小孩）

chatty /'tʃæti/ *adj.* (**chat·tier**, **chat·ti·est**) (*informal, especially BrE*) **1** talking a lot in a friendly way 愛說話的；愛閒聊的；健談的： *You're very chatty today, Alice.* 艾麗斯，你今天很健談。 **2** having a friendly informal style 閒聊式的： *a chatty letter* 一封聊天式的信

'chat-up *noun* [C, U] an occasion when a person is talking to sb in a way that shows they are interested in them sexually 親昵攀談；搭訕： *Is that your best **chat-up line**?* 那是你最拿手的調情話嗎？

chauf·feur /'ʃəʊfə(r); *NAmE* ʃoʊ'fɜːr/ *noun, verb*

■ ***noun*** a person whose job is to drive a car, especially for sb rich or important（尤指富人或要人的）司機

■ ***verb*** **~ sb** to drive sb in a car, usually as your job 為某人開車；當司機： *He was chauffeured to all his meetings.* 他由司機開車送去參加所有的會議。◇ *a chauffeured limousine* 有專職司機駕駛的豪華轎車

chau·vin·ism /'ʃəʊvɪnɪzəm; *NAmE* 'ʃoʊ-/ *noun* [U] (*disapproving*) **1** an aggressive and unreasonable belief that your own country is better than all others 沙文主義 **2** = MALE CHAUVINISM

chau·vin·ist /'ʃəʊvɪnɪst; *NAmE* 'ʃoʊ-/ *noun* **1** = MALE CHAUVINIST **2** a person who has an aggressive and unreasonable belief that their own country is better than all others 沙文主義者 ▶ **chau·vin·is·tic** /,ʃəʊvɪ'nɪstɪk; *NAmE* ,ʃoʊ-/ (also *less frequent* **chau·vin·ist**) *adj.* **chau·vin·is·tic·al·ly** /-kli/ *adv.*

chav /tʃæv/ *noun* (*BrE, slang*) a young person, often without a high level of education, who follows a particular fashion 趕浪頭的年輕人

ChB /,siː eɪtʃ 'biː/ *abbr.* (*BrE*) Bachelor of Surgery 外科醫學士

cheap /tʃiːp/ *adj., adv.*

■ ***adj.*** (**cheap·er**, **cheap·est**)

▸ LOW PRICE 低價 **1** costing little money or less money than you expected 花錢少的；便宜的；廉價的 SYN **inexpensive**： *cheap fares* 便宜的票價◇ *Personal computers are cheap and getting cheaper.* 個人電腦現在價格便宜，以後還會越來越便宜。◇ *Cycling is a cheap way to get around.* 騎自行車是一種省錢的旅遊方式。◇ *The printer isn't exactly cheap at £200.* 價格為 200 英鎊的打印機並不是很便宜。◇ *immigrant workers, used as a source of **cheap labour*** (= workers who are paid very little, especially unfairly) 作為廉價勞動力來源的移民工人 ➲ see also DIRT CHEAP OPP **expensive** **2** charging low prices 收費低廉的： *a cheap restaurant/hotel* 收費低廉的餐館／旅館◇ (*BrE*) *We found a **cheap and cheerful** cafe* (= one that is simple and charges low prices but is pleasant). 我們找到了一家價格低廉環境宜人的咖啡館。 OPP **expensive**

▸ POOR QUALITY 劣質 **3** (*disapproving*) low in price and quality 價低質劣的：*cheap perfume/jewellery/shoes* 低價劣質香水／珠寶／鞋◇ (*BrE*) *a **cheap and nasty** bottle of wine* 一瓶便宜的劣質葡萄酒

▸ UNKIND 不友好 **4** unpleasant or unkind and rather obvious 令人討厭的；明顯不友好的；不和善的： *I was tired of his cheap jokes at my expense.* 我討厭他拿我開低級庸俗的玩笑。

▸ LOW STATUS 地位低下 **5** (*disapproving*) having a low status and therefore not deserving respect 卑微的；卑賤的；可鄙的： *He's just a cheap crook.* 他簡直是個卑鄙的騙子。◇ *His treatment of her made her **feel cheap*** (= ashamed, because she had lost her respect for herself). 他那樣對待她使她感到很丟臉。

▸ NOT GENEROUS 不大方 **6** (*NAmE*) (*BrE* **mean**) (*informal, disapproving*) not liking to spend money 小氣的；摳門兒的： *Don't be so cheap!* 別這麼小氣！ ▶ **cheap·ness** *noun* [U]

C

C

IDM **cheap at the 'price** (also **cheap at 'twice the price**) (*BrE* also **cheap at 'half the price**) so good or useful that the cost does not seem too much 價錢雖高但還合算 **on the 'cheap** spending less money than you usually need to spend to do sth 低廉地；廉價地：*a guide to decorating your house on the cheap* 房屋廉價裝潢指南 ➲ more at LIFE

■ ***adv.*** (*comparative* **cheap·er**, no *superlative*) (*informal*) for a low price 低價地；廉價地；便宜地：*I got this dress cheap in a sale.* 這件衣服是我在大減價時便宜買的。

IDM **be ,going 'cheap** to be offered for sale at a lower price than usual 降價出售；廉價銷售 **sth does not come 'cheap** something is expensive 昂貴；不便宜：*Violins like this don't come cheap.* 像這樣的小提琴不會便宜。

Synonyms 同義詞辨析

cheap

competitive • budget • affordable • reasonable • inexpensive

These words all describe a product or service that costs little money or less money than you expected. 以上各詞均指產品或服務花錢少或低於預期。

cheap costing little money or less money than you expected; charging low prices 指花錢少、便宜、收費低廉 **NOTE** **Cheap** can also be used in a disapproving way to suggest that sth is poor quality as well as low in price. * cheap 亦可作貶義，指價低質劣：*a bottle of cheap perfume* 一瓶低價劣質香水

competitive (of prices, goods or services) as cheap as or cheaper than those offered by other companies; able to offer goods or services at competitive prices 指價格、產品或服務收費方面具有競爭力

budget [only before noun] (used especially in advertising) cheap because it offers only a basic level of service （尤用於廣告）指僅提供基本服務因而價格低廉

affordable cheap enough for most people to afford 指多數人買得起或負擔得來的

reasonable (of prices) not too expensive 指價格不太高、公道的

inexpensive (*rather formal*) cheap 指不昂貴 **NOTE** **Inexpensive** is often used to mean that sth is good value for its price. It is sometimes used instead of **cheap**, because **cheap** can suggest that sth is poor quality. inexpensive 常含物有所值之意，有時用以代替 cheap，因為 cheap 可有質量低劣的含義。

PATTERNS

- cheap/competitive/budget/affordable/reasonable **prices/fares/rates**
- cheap/competitive/budget/affordable/inexpensive **products/services**

cheap·en /'tʃiːpən/ *verb* **1 ~ sb/yourself** to make sb lose respect for himself or herself 使喪失威信；使貶低 **SYN** **degrade**：*She never cheapened herself by lowering her standards.* 她從不降低標準來貶低自己。 **2 ~ sth** to make sth lower in price 降低…的價格：*to cheapen the cost of raw materials* 降低原材料的成本 **3 ~ sth** to make sth appear to have less value 使貶值；貶低：*The movie was accused of cheapening human life.* 有人指責這部電影貶低了人的生命價值。

cheap·ly 🔑 /'tʃiːpli/ *adv.* without spending or costing much money 便宜地；廉價地；低廉地：*I'm sure I could buy this more cheaply somewhere else.* 我相信我能在別的地方更便宜地買到這種物品。◇ *a cheaply made movie* 一部低成本電影

cheapo /'tʃiːpəʊ; *NAmE* -poʊ/ *adj.* [only before noun] (*informal, disapproving*) cheap and often of poor quality 價廉質劣的

cheap·skate /'tʃiːpskeɪt/ *noun* (*informal, disapproving*) a person who does not like to spend money 小氣鬼；守財奴

cheat 🔑 /tʃiːt/ *verb, noun*

■ ***verb*** **1** 🔑 [T] **~ sb/sth** to trick sb or make them believe sth which is not true 欺騙；矇騙：*She is accused of attempting to cheat the taxman.* 她被指控企圖矇騙稅務員。◇ *Many people **feel cheated** by the government's refusal to hold a referendum.* 由於政府拒絕舉行公民投票表決，許多人都覺得上當受騙。◇ *He **cheated his way** into the job.* 他騙取了這份工作。 **2** 🔑 [I] **~ (at sth)** to act in a dishonest way in order to gain an advantage, especially in a game, a competition, an exam, etc. （尤指在遊戲、比賽、考試等中）作弊，舞弊：*He cheats at cards.* 他玩牌愛作弊。◇ *You're not allowed to look at the answers— **that's cheating**.* 你們不許看答案，那是作弊。 **3** [I] **~ (on sb)** (of sb who is married or who has a regular sexual partner 已婚或有固定性伴侶的人) to have a secret sexual relationship with sb else 與他人有秘密性關係；對某人不忠（或不貞）

IDM **cheat 'death** (often used in newspapers 常用於報章) to survive in a situation where you could have died 死裏逃生；幸免於難

PHR V **'cheat sb ('out) of sth** 🔑 to prevent sb from having sth, especially in a way that is not honest or fair （尤指用不誠實或不正當的手段）阻止某人得到某物：*They cheated him out of his share of the profits.* 他們施展伎倆，不讓他獲得他的那份利潤。

■ ***noun*** (*especially BrE*) **1** 🔑 (also **cheat·er** especially in *NAmE*) [C] a person who cheats, especially in a game （尤指遊戲中的）作弊者，騙子：*You little cheat!* 你這小滑頭！ **2** [sing.] something that seems unfair or dishonest, for example a way of doing sth with less effort than it usually needs 欺騙手段；欺詐行為：*It's really a cheat, but you can use ready-made pastry if you want.* 這樣做其實是騙人，但如果你願意的話，可以用現成的油酥麵糰。 **3** [C] (*computing* 計) a program you can use to move immediately to the next stage of a computer game without needing to play the game （電腦遊戲的）秘技，欺騙程序，作弊軟件：*There's a cheat you can use to get to the next level.* 有種秘技，你可以用來到達下一關。

'cheat sheet *noun* (*informal*) a set of notes to help you remember important information, especially one taken secretly into an exam room 備忘紙條；（尤指考試用的）作弊紙條

check 🔑 /tʃek/ *verb, noun, exclamation*

■ ***verb***

▸ **EXAMINE** 檢查 **1** 🔑 [T] **~ sth (for sth)** to examine sth to see if it is correct, safe or acceptable 檢查；審查；核查；檢驗：*Check the container for cracks or leaks.* 檢驗容器是否有裂縫或者漏洞。◇ *She gave me the minutes of the meeting to read and check.* 她把會議記錄交給我審閱。◇ *Check the oil and water before setting off.* 出發前應查看一下油和水。◇ *Check your work before handing it in.* 交作業前先檢查一遍。

▸ **MAKE SURE** 確定 **2** 🔑 [I, T] to find out if sth/sb is present, correct or true or if sth is how you think it is 查明；查看；核實；弄確實：*'Is Mary in the office?' 'Just a moment. I'll go and check.'* "瑪麗在辦公室嗎？""請稍等，我去看看。"◇ **~ sth** *Hang on—I just need to check my email.* 稍等，我得查看一下我的電郵。◇ **~ (that)** … *Go and check (that) I've locked the windows.* 去查看一下我是不是把窗戶鎖上了。◇ **~ (with sb) (what/whether, etc. …)** *You'd better check with Jane what time she's expecting us tonight.* 你最好向簡核實一下她今晚要見我們的時間。➲ see also CROSS-CHECK, DOUBLE-CHECK

▸ **CONTROL** 控制 **3** [T] **~ sth** to control sth; to stop sth from increasing or getting worse 控制；抑制；阻止：*The government is determined to check the growth of public spending.* 政府決心要控制公共開支的增長。 **4** [T] to stop yourself from saying or doing sth or from showing a particular emotion 克制，抑制（做某事或表露感情）：**~ sth** *to check your anger/laughter/tears* 忍住怒火／笑／眼淚 ◇ **~ yourself** *She wanted to tell him the whole truth but she checked herself—it wasn't the right moment.* 她本想告訴他全部真相，但是又忍住了，當時還不是時候。

▸ COATS/BAGS/CASES 外套；包；箱子 **5** [T] **~ sth** (*NAmE*) to leave coats, bags, etc. in an official place (called a CHECKROOM) while you are visiting a club, restaurant, etc. 存放；寄放： *Do you want to check your coats?* 你們要寄放外套嗎？ **6** [T] **~ sth** (*NAmE*) to leave bags or cases with an official so that they can be put on a plane or train 託運（行李）

▸ MAKE MARK 標上符號 **7** [T] **~ sth** (*NAmE*) (*BrE* **tick**) to put a mark (✓) next to an item on a list, an answer, etc. 標記號；打上鉤；打對號： *Check the box next to the right answer.* 在正確答案旁邊的方框中打鉤。

PHR V ˌ**check 'in** (**at** …) to go to a desk in a hotel, an airport, etc. and tell an official there that you have arrived（在旅館、機場等）登記，報到： *Please check in at least an hour before departure.* 請至少在飛機起飛前一小時辦理登機手續。◇ *We've checked in at the hotel.* 我們已經在旅館登記入住。➲ related noun CHECK-IN ˌ**check sth↔'in** to leave bags or cases with an official to be put on a plane or train 託運（行李）： *We checked in our luggage and went through to the departure lounge.* 我們託運行李後直接進入候機室。➲ related noun CHECK-IN '**check into** … to arrive at a hotel or private hospital to begin your stay there 登記入住（旅館或私立醫院）： *He checked into a top London clinic yesterday for an operation on his knee.* 他昨天住進了倫敦一家最高級的診所，準備做膝部手術。ˌ**check sb/sth ↔'off** (*NAmE*) (*BrE* ˌ**tick sb/sth 'off**) to put a mark (✓) beside a name or an item on a list to show that sth has been dealt with 給…畫上鉤；給…打核對號： *Check the names off as the guests arrive.* 客人到來時在其姓名上打鉤。'**check on sb/sth** to make sure that there is nothing wrong with sb/sth 核實，檢查（是否一切正常）： *I'll just go and check on the children.* 我去看看孩子們。ˌ**check 'out** to be found to be true or acceptable after being examined（經檢查）得到證實，獲得證明： *The local police found her story didn't check out.* 當地警方證實她的說法不成立。ˌ**check 'out** (**of** …) to pay your bill and leave a hotel, etc. 結賬離開（旅館等）： *Guests should check out of their rooms by noon.* 客人必須在中午以前辦理退房手續。➲ related noun CHECKOUT (2) ˌ**check sb/sth↔'out 1** to find out if sth is correct, or if sb is acceptable 調查；查證；核實： *The police are checking out his alibi.* 警察在查證他不在案發現場的證據。◇ *We'll have to check him out before we employ him.* 我們得先調查一下才雇用他。 **2** (*informal*) to look at or examine a person or thing that seems interesting or attractive 察看，觀察（有趣或有吸引力的人或事物）： *Check out the prices at our new store!* 看一看我們新商店的價格吧！◇ *Hey, check out that car!* 嘿，看看那輛車！ ˌ**check sth↔'out** to borrow sth from an official place, for example a book from a library（從圖書館等）借出： *The book has been checked out in your name.* 這本書已用你的名字從圖書館借出。ˌ**check 'over/'through↔sth** to examine sth carefully to make sure that it is correct or acceptable 仔細檢查；核對；核查： *Check over your work for mistakes.* 仔細檢查你的作業以防有錯。ˌ**check 'up on sb** to make sure that sb is doing what they should be doing 監督；督促： *My parents are always checking up on me.* 我父母總是督促我。ˌ**check 'up on sth** to find out if sth is true or correct 查證；核實： *I need to check up on a few things before I can decide.* 我得核實幾件事情才能作決定。

■ ***noun***

▸ EXAMINATION 檢查 **1** [C] **~** (**for/on sth**) an act of making sure that sth is safe, correct or in good condition by examining it 檢查，查看（是否安全、正確、狀況良好）： *Could you give the tyres a check?* 你能檢查一下輪胎嗎？◇ *a health check* 體格檢查 ◇ *The drugs were found in their car during a routine check by police.* 警方作例行檢查時在他們的車裏搜出了毒品。◇ *a check for spelling mistakes* 檢查有無拼寫錯誤 ◇ *I'll just have a quick check to see if the letter's arrived yet.* 我要快速查看一下，

Synonyms 同義詞辨析

cheat

fool • deceive • betray • take in • trick • con

These words all mean to make sb believe sth that is not true, especially in order to get what you want. 以上各詞均含使人誤信之意，尤指有目的地這樣做。

cheat to make sb believe sth that is not true, in order to get money or sth else from them 指為得到錢財或其他東西而欺騙、欺詐： *She is accused of attempting to cheat the taxman.* 她被指控企圖矇騙稅務員。◇ *He cheated his way into the job.* 他騙取了這份工作。 **NOTE** **Cheat** also means to act in a dishonest way in order to gain an advantage, especially in a game, competition or exam. * cheat 亦指在遊戲、競賽或考試中作弊、舞弊： *You're not allowed to look at the answers—**that's cheating**.* 你們不許看答案，那是作弊。

fool to make sb believe sth that is not true, especially in order to laugh at them or to get what you want 指矇騙、愚弄： *Just don't be fooled into investing any money with them.* 別上當受騙，同他們一起搞什麼投資。

deceive to make sb believe sth that is not true, especially sb who trusts you, in order to get what you want 尤指利用別人的信任欺騙、矇騙、誆騙： *She deceived him into handing over all his savings.* 她把他所有的積蓄都騙取了。

betray to hurt sb who trusts you, especially by deceiving them or not being loyal to them 指辜負別人的信任、出賣： *She felt betrayed when she found out the truth about him.* 她發現他的真實情況時，感到受了欺騙。

take sb in [often passive] to deceive sb, usually in order to get what you want 指為個人目的而欺騙、矇騙： *I was taken in by her story.* 我被她的花言巧語矇騙了。

trick to deceive sb, especially in a clever way, in order to get what you want 尤指以巧妙的方式欺騙、欺詐

con (*informal*) to deceive sb, especially in order to get money from them or get them to do sth for you 尤指為獲取錢財或使人為自己做事而欺騙、哄騙、詐騙： *They had been conned out of £100 000.* 他們被騙走了10萬英鎊。

WHICH WORD? 詞語辨析

Many of these words involve making sb believe sth that is not true, but some of them are more disapproving than others. **Deceive** is probably the worst because people typically deceive friends, relations and others who know and trust them. People may *feel cheated/betrayed* by sb in authority who they trusted to look after their interests. If sb **takes you in**, they may do it by acting a part and using words and charm effectively. If sb **cheats/fools/tricks/cons** you, they may get sth from you and make you feel stupid. However, sb might **fool** you just as a joke; and to **trick** sb is sometimes seen as a clever thing to do, if the person being tricked is seen as a bad person who deserves it. 以上各詞多含使人將假話信以為真之義，但其中有些詞貶義較另一些詞強。deceive 大概貶義最強，主要指欺騙朋友、親戚和其他認識和信任自己的人。相信掌權者能夠顧全自己利益卻遭欺騙可用 feel cheated/betrayed。通過裝腔作勢或花言巧語等騙人用 take sb in。哄騙、愚弄他人用 cheat/fool/trick/con。只為開玩笑可用 fool。如果被戲弄者是應該受到懲罰的壞人，可用 trick，表示計謀巧妙。

PATTERNS

- to cheat/fool/trick/con sb **out of** sth
- to cheat/fool/deceive/betray/trick/con sb **into doing** sth
- to **feel** cheated/fooled/deceived/betrayed/tricked/conned
- to fool/deceive **yourself**
- to cheat/trick/con **your way** into sth

看看那封信是否已經寄到。◇ *It is vital to* **keep a check on** *your speed* (= look at it regularly in order to control it). 經常檢查並控制你的車速是至關重要的。➲ see also REALITY CHECK
▸ **INVESTIGATION** 調查 **2** [C] ~ **(on sb/sth)** an investigation to find out more information about sth 調查；審查：*The police* **ran a check** *on the registration number of the car.* 警方對那輛車的牌照號碼進行了調查。◇ *Was any check made on Mr Morris when he applied for the post?* 莫里斯先生申請這個職位時對他進行調查了嗎？
▸ **CONTROL** 控制 **3** [C] ~ **(on/to sth)** *(formal)* something that delays the progress of sth else or stops it from getting worse 阻礙進程的事物；阻止惡化的事物：*A cold spring will provide a natural check on the number of insects.* 寒冷的春季會自然控制昆蟲的數量。**4 checks** [pl.] *(formal)* rules that are designed to control the amount of power, especially political power, that one person or group has（對政治等權力的）規定，條令，約束 ➲ see also CHECKS AND BALANCES
▸ **PATTERN** 圖案 **5** [C, U] a pattern of squares, usually of two colours（通常指雙色的）方格圖案，方格，格子：*Do you prefer checks or stripes?* 你喜歡方格還是條紋？◇ *a check shirt/suit* 格子襯衫／西服 ◇ *a yellow and red check skirt* 紅黃色相間的方格裙子 ➲ see also CHECKED
▸ **MONEY** 錢 **6** [C] *(US)* = CHEQUE **7** [C] *(NAmE)* = BILL：*Can I have the check, please?* 請給我結賬。➲ SYNONYMS at BILL
▸ **FOR COATS/BAGS** 外套；包 **8** [C] *(NAmE)* **coat ~** a place in a club, restaurant, etc. where you can leave your coat or bag（俱樂部、餐館等外套、包的）寄存處，存放處 **9** [C] *(NAmE)* a ticket that you get when you leave your coat, bag, etc. in, for example, a restaurant or theatre（餐館或劇院等的）存物牌，存放證
▸ **IN GAME** 競技活動 **10** [U] (in CHESS 國際象棋) a position in which a player's king (= the most important piece) can be directly attacked by the other player's pieces 被將軍的局面：*There, you're in check.* 瞧，將你一軍。➲ see also CHECKMATE
▸ **MARK** 符號 **11** (also **'check mark**) (both *NAmE*) (*BrE* **tick**) [C] a mark (✓) put beside a sum or an item on a list, usually to show that it has been checked or done or is correct 核對號；對號；鈎號 ➲ compare CROSS *n.* (1), X (4)
IDM **hold/keep sth in 'check** to keep sth under control so that it does not spread or get worse 控制；制止 ➲ more at RAIN CHECK
■ ***exclamation*** used to show that you agree with sb or that sth on a list has been dealt with 行；已經辦好：*'Do you have your tickets?' 'Check.' 'Passport?' 'Check.'* "你有票嗎？" "有。" "護照呢？" "有。"

check·book *noun (US)* = CHEQUEBOOK

check·box /ˈtʃekbɒks; *NAmE* -bɑːks/ (*BrE* also **tick·box**) *noun* a small square on a computer screen that you click on with the mouse to choose whether a particular function is switched on or off（計算機屏幕上的）複選框

checked /tʃekt/ *adj.* having a pattern of squares, usually of two colours 有方格圖案的（常為雙色）：*checked material* 印有方格圖案的布料 ➲ see also CHECK *n.* (5)

check·er /ˈtʃekə(r)/ *noun* ➲ see also CHECKERS **1** (*especially US*) a person who works at the CHECKOUT in a supermarket（超級市場的）收款員，收銀員 **2** (in compounds 構成複合詞) a computer program that you use to check sth, for example the spelling and grammar of sth you have written（計算機的）檢查程序，檢查程式：*a* ***spelling/grammar/virus checker*** 拼寫／語法／病毒檢查程序 **3** a person who checks things 檢驗員；審核員：*a quality control checker* 質量控制檢驗員

check·er·board /ˈtʃekəbɔːd; *NAmE* ˈtʃekərbɔːrd/ *(NAmE)* (*BrE* **draught·board**) *noun* a board with black and white squares, used for playing DRAUGHTS/CHECKERS 國際跳棋棋盤；西洋跳棋棋盤

check·ered *adj.* (*especially NAmE*) = CHEQUERED

Synonyms 同義詞辨析

check

examine • inspect • go over sth

These words all mean to look closely to make sure that everything is correct, in good condition, or acceptable. 以上各詞均含仔細檢查、審查之義。

check to look at sth closely to make sure that everything is correct, in good condition, safe or satisfactory 指檢查、審查、核查，以確保完好、正常和安全：*Check your work before handing it in.* 交作業前先檢查一遍。

examine to look at sb/sth closely to see if there is anything wrong or to find the cause of a problem 指仔細檢查或檢驗人或事物，以確認有無問題或找出問題所在：*The goods were examined for damage on arrival.* 貨物到達時已檢查是否有破損。

inspect to look at sb/sth closely to make sure that everything is satisfactory; to officially visit a school, factory, etc. in order to check that rules are being obeyed and that standards are acceptable 指檢查、查看、審視，以確保一切妥當；視察（學校、工廠等）：*Make sure you inspect the goods before signing for them.* 要確保在簽收貨物之前進行檢驗。◇ *The Tourist Board inspects all recommended hotels at least once a year.* 旅遊局至少每年視察一次所有舉薦的旅館。

CHECK, EXAMINE OR INSPECT? 用 check、examine 還是 inspect？

All these words can be used when you are looking for possible problems, but only **check** is used for mistakes. 以上各詞均可用於檢查可能出現的問題，但檢查錯誤只用 check：~~Examine/Inspect your work before handing it in.~~ Only **examine** is used when looking for the cause of a problem. 查找問題的原因只用 examine：~~The doctor checked/inspected her but could find nothing wrong.~~ **Examine** is used more often about a professional person. * examine 較常用於專業人員所做的檢查：*The surveyor examined the walls for signs of damp.* 房屋鑒定人檢查了牆壁，看是否有水漬。**Inspect** is used more often about an official. * inspect 較常用於官方檢查：*Public health officials were called in to inspect the restaurant.* 公共衞生官員奉召來視察了這家餐館。

go over sth to check sth carefully for mistakes, damage or anything dangerous 指仔細檢查是否有錯誤、損壞或危險：*Go over your work for spelling mistakes before you hand it in.* 交作業前仔細檢查一下拼寫錯誤。

PATTERNS

- to check/examine/inspect/go over (sth) **for** sth
- to check/examine/inspect/go over sth **to see if/whether** ...
- to check/examine/inspect/go over sth **carefully/thoroughly**

check·ers /ˈtʃekəz; *NAmE* -ərz/ *(NAmE)* (*BrE* **draughts**) *noun* [U] a game for two players using 24 round pieces on a board marked with black and white squares 國際跳棋；西洋跳棋

'check-in *noun* **1** [C, U] the place where you go first when you arrive at an airport, to show your ticket, etc.（機場的）登機手續辦理處 **2** [U] the act of showing your ticket, etc. when you arrive at an airport（機場的）辦理登機手續：*Do you know your check-in time?* 你知道辦理登機手續的時間嗎？◇ (*BrE*) *the check-in desk* 辦理登機手續的服務枱 ◇ (*NAmE*) *the check-in counter* 辦理登機手續的服務枱

'checking account *(US)* (*BrE* **'current account**) (*CanE* **'chequing account**) *noun* a type of bank account that you can take money out of at any time, and that provides you with a CHEQUEBOOK and CASH CARD 活期存款賬戶；往來賬戶 ➲ compare DEPOSIT ACCOUNT

check·list /ˈtʃeklɪst/ *noun* a list of the things that you must remember to do, to take with you or to find out （記事）清單，一覽表

check·mate /ˌtʃekˈmeɪt; ˈtʃekmeɪt/ (also **mate**) *noun* [U] **1** (in CHESS 國際象棋) a position in which one player cannot prevent his or her king (= the most important piece) being captured and therefore loses the game 將死；輸棋 ➲ see also CHECK *n.* (10) ➲ compare STALEMATE (2) **2** a situation in which sb has been completely defeated 敗局；敗北；徹底戰敗 ▸ **check·mate** (also **mate**) *verb* ：**~ sb/sth** *His king had been checkmated.* 他的王棋已被將死。◇ *She hoped the plan would checkmate her opponents.* 她希望這一計劃能徹底戰勝對手。

check·out /ˈtʃekaʊt/ *noun* **1** [C] the place where you pay for the things that you are buying in a supermarket （超級市場的）付款枱，付款處：*a* ***checkout assistant/operator*** 付款枱助手／收銀員 **2** [U] the time when you leave a hotel at the end of your stay （在旅館）結賬離開的時間：*At checkout, your bill will be printed for you.* 結賬時，旅館會把你的賬單打印給你。

check·point /ˈtʃekpɔɪnt/ *noun* a place, especially on a border between two countries, where people have to stop so their vehicles and documents can be checked （邊防）檢查站；邊防關卡

check·room /ˈtʃekruːm; -rʊm/ *noun* (*NAmE*) = CLOAKROOM (1)

ˌchecks and ˈbalances *noun* [pl.] **1** influences in an organization or political system which help to keep it fair and stop a small group from keeping all the power 制約與平衡（為保持機構或政體內的公正並防止權力集中於小團體） **2** (in the US) the principle of government by which the President, Congress and the Supreme Court each have some control over the others 三權分立（美國政府中總統、國會以及最高法院之間相互制約的政體原則） ➲ compare SEPARATION OF POWERS

check·sum /ˈtʃeksʌm/ *noun* (*computing* 計) the total of the numbers in a piece of DIGITAL data, used to check that the data is correct 檢查和（用以校驗數據項的和）

ˈcheck-up *noun* an examination of sth, especially a medical one to make sure that you are healthy 檢查；（尤指）體格檢查：*to* ***go for/to have a check-up*** 去做體檢 ◇ *a* ***medical/dental/routine/thorough check-up*** 體格／牙科／常規／全面檢查

Ched·dar /ˈtʃedə(r)/ (also **ˌCheddar ˈcheese**) *noun* [U] a type of hard yellow cheese 切德乾酪（一種黃色硬奶酪）

cheek 🔑 /tʃiːk/ *noun, verb*

■ ***noun*** **1** 🔑 [C] either side of the face below the eyes 面頰；臉頰：***chubby/rosy/pink cheeks*** 豐滿的／紅潤的／粉紅的臉頰 ◇ *He kissed her on both cheeks.* 他親吻了一下她的雙頰。◇ *Couples were dancing* ***cheek to cheek***. 成雙成對的舞伴在跳貼面舞。➲ COLLOCATIONS at PHYSICAL ➲ VISUAL VOCAB page V59 **2** **-cheeked** (in adjectives 構成形容詞) having the type of cheeks mentioned 有…面頰的；面頰…的：***chubby-cheeked/rosy-cheeked/hollow-cheeked*** 雙頰豐滿／紅潤／瘦削 **3** [C] (*informal*) either of the BUTTOCKS 半邊屁股 **4** [U, sing.] (*BrE*) talk or behaviour that people think is annoying, rude or lacking in respect 令人討厭（或粗魯、無禮）的話（或行為） SYN **nerve**：*What a cheek!* 真不要臉！◇ *He* ***had the cheek*** *to ask his ex-girlfriend to babysit for them.* 他竟厚着臉皮要他以前的女朋友為他們臨時照看小孩。◇ *I think they've* ***got a cheek*** *making you pay to park the car.* 我想不到他們居然有臉要你付停車費。

IDM **ˌcheek by ˈjowl (with sb/sth)** very close to sb/sth （和…）緊靠着，緊挨着 **turn the other ˈcheek** to make a deliberate decision to remain calm and not to act in an aggressive way when sb has hurt you or made you angry （受到傷害或被激怒時）甘心容忍，不予回擊 ➲ more at ROSE *n.*, TONGUE *n.*

■ ***verb*** **~ sb** (*BrE, informal*) to speak to sb in a rude way that shows a lack of respect 對…粗魯無禮地說

cheek·bone /ˈtʃiːkbəʊn; *NAmE* -boʊn/ *noun* the bone below the eye 顴骨 ➲ VISUAL VOCAB page V59

cheeky /ˈtʃiːki/ *adj.* (**cheek·ier**, **cheeki·est**) (*BrE, informal*) rude in an amusing or an annoying way 厚臉皮的；魯莽的；放肆的：*You cheeky monkey!* 你這厚臉皮的猴崽子！◇ *a cheeky grin* 厚顏無恥的齜牙一笑 ◇ *You're getting far too cheeky!* 你太放肆了！➲ SYNONYMS at RUDE ▸ **cheek·ily** *adv.* **cheeki·ness** *noun* [U]

cheep /tʃiːp/ *verb* [I] (of young birds 雛鳥) to make short high sounds 唧唧叫；吱吱叫 ▸ **cheep** *noun*

cheer /tʃɪə(r); *NAmE* tʃɪr/ *noun, verb*

■ ***noun*** ➲ see also CHEERS **1** [C] a shout of joy, support or praise 歡呼聲；喝彩聲：*A great* ***cheer went up*** *from the crowd.* 觀眾爆發出一陣熱烈的歡呼聲。◇ *cheers of encouragement* 鼓勵的喝彩聲 ◇ ***Three cheers for*** *the winners!* (= used when you are asking a group of people to cheer three times, in order to CONGRATULATE sb, etc.) 為優勝者歡呼三次吧！ OPP **boo** **2** [C] (*NAmE*) a special song or poem used by CHEERLEADERS （拉拉隊的）加油歌，加油詩 **3** [U] (*formal* or *literary*) an atmosphere of happiness 歡樂（或幸福）的氣氛

■ ***verb*** **1** [I, T] to shout loudly, to show support or praise for sb, or to give them encouragement 歡呼；喝彩；加油：*We all cheered as the team came on to the field.* 球隊入場時我們都為之歡呼。◇ *Cheering crowds greeted their arrival.* 歡呼的人群歡迎他們的到來。◇ **~ sb** *The crowd cheered the President as he drove slowly by.* 當總統的車緩緩經過時，群眾向他歡呼致意。➲ SYNONYMS at SHOUT OPP **boo** **2** [T] **~ sb** [usually passive] to give hope, comfort or encouragement to sb 鼓勵；鼓舞：*She was cheered by the news from home.* 來自家裏的消息使她受到鼓舞。▸ **cheer·ing** *noun* [U]：*He came on stage amid clapping and cheering.* 他在掌聲和歡呼聲中走上舞台。 **cheer·ing** *adj.*：*The results of the test were very cheering.* 化驗結果令人歡欣鼓舞。

PHR V **ˌcheer sb↔ˈon** to give shouts of encouragement to sb in a race, competition, etc. （賽跑、比賽等中）以喝彩聲鼓勵，為（某人）加油 **ˌcheer ˈup | ˌcheer sb/sth↔ˈup** to become more cheerful; to make sb/sth more cheerful （使）變得更高興，振奮起來：*Oh, come on—cheer up!* 噢，得了，高興起來吧！◇ *Give Mary a call; she needs cheering up.* 給瑪麗打個電話，她需要人安慰。◇ *Bright curtains can cheer up a dull room.* 色彩鮮豔的窗簾可以讓單調的房間變得亮麗起來。

cheer·ful 🔑 /ˈtʃɪəfl; *NAmE* ˈtʃɪrfl/ *adj.*

1 🔑 happy, and showing it by the way that you behave 快樂的；高興的；興高采烈的：*You're not your usual cheerful self today.* 你今天不像往常那麼快快樂樂的。◇ *a cheerful, hard-working employee* 快快樂樂勤奮工作的雇員 ◇ *a cheerful smile/voice* 歡快的微笑／說話聲 **2** 🔑 giving you a feeling of happiness 令人愉快的：*a bright, cheerful restaurant* 明亮宜人的餐館 ◇ *walls painted in cheerful* (= light and bright) *colours* 用亮麗色彩塗飾一新的牆壁 ◇ *a chatty, cheerful letter* 一封令人愉快的拉家常的信 ▸ **cheer·ful·ly** 🔑 /-fəli/ *adv.*：*to* ***laugh/nod/whistle cheerfully*** 歡快地笑／點頭／吹口哨 ◇ *I could cheerfully have killed him when he said that* (= I would have liked to). 他說那話時我真想把他宰了。◇ *She cheerfully admitted that she had no experience at all* (= she wasn't afraid to do so). 她坦然承認她毫無經驗。 **cheer·ful·ness** *noun* [U]

cheerio /ˌtʃɪəriˈəʊ; *NAmE* ˌtʃɪriˈoʊ/ *exclamation* (*BrE, informal*) goodbye 再見：*Cheerio! I'll see you later.* 再見！回頭見。

cheer·lead·er /ˈtʃɪəliːdə(r); *NAmE* ˈtʃɪrl-/ *noun* **1** (in the US) one of the members of a group of young people (usually women) wearing special uniforms, who encourage the crowd to CHEER for their team at a sports event 拉拉隊隊員（美國體育比賽時鼓動觀眾為本隊加油，通常為女性） **2** a person who supports a particular politician, idea, or way of doing sth （某一政治家、某種觀點或做法等的）支持者，搖旗吶喊者 ▸ **cheer·leading** /ˈtʃɪəliːdɪŋ/ *noun* [U]：*a* ***cheerleading squad/team*** 拉拉隊 ◇ *the President's continued cheerleading for the 'strong dollar'* 總統為"強勢美元"的持續搖旗吶喊

cheer·less /ˈtʃɪələs; *NAmE* ˈtʃɪrl-/ *adj.* (*formal*) (of a place, etc. 地方等) without warmth or colour so it makes you feel depressed 陰冷的；陰暗的；陰鬱的

SYN gloomy：*a dark and cheerless room* 黑暗陰森的房間

cheers /tʃɪəz; *NAmE* tʃɪrz/ *exclamation* **1** a word that people say to each other as they lift up their glasses to drink （用於祝酒）乾杯 **2** (*BrE, informal*) thank you 謝謝：*'Have another biscuit.' 'Cheers.'* "再來一塊餅乾。""謝謝。" **3** (*BrE, informal*) goodbye 再見：*Cheers then. See you later.* 告辭了。再見。

cheery /ˈtʃɪəri; *NAmE* ˈtʃɪri/ *adj.* (**cheer·ier**, **cheeri·est**) (*informal*) (of a person or their behaviour 人或行為) happy and cheerful 高興的；興高采烈的：*a cheery remark/smile/wave* 開心的話 / 微笑 / 揮手 ◊ *He left with a cheery 'See you again soon'.* 他高興地說了聲"希望早日再見到你"就離開了。▸ **cheer·ily** *adv.*

cheese 0-w /tʃiːz/ *noun*

1 0-w [U, C] a type of food made from milk that can be either soft or hard and is usually white or yellow in colour; a particular type of this food 乾酪；奶酪：*Cheddar cheese* 切德乾酪 ◊ *goat's cheese* (= made from the milk of a GOAT) 山羊奶酪（由山羊奶製成）◊ *a cheese sandwich/salad* 奶酪三明治 / 色拉 ◊ *a chunk/piece/slice of cheese* 一厚塊 / 碎塊 / 薄片奶酪 ◊ *a selection of French cheeses* 精選的法國奶酪 ◊ *a cheese knife* (= a knife with a special curved blade with two points on the end, used for cutting and picking up pieces of cheese) 乾酪切刀 ➲ VISUAL VOCAB page V22 ➲ see also AMERICAN CHEESE, BLUE CHEESE, CAULIFLOWER CHEESE, COTTAGE CHEESE, CREAM CHEESE, MACARONI CHEESE **2** **cheese!** what you ask sb to say before you take their photograph "茄子"（要求照相的人說的口形詞）IDM see BIG *adj.*, CHALK *n.*, HARD *adj.*

cheese·board /ˈtʃiːzbɔːd; *NAmE* -bɔːrd/ *noun* **1** a board that is used to cut cheese on 乾酪切板 ➲ VISUAL VOCAB page V22 **2** a variety of cheeses that are served at the end of a meal （一餐飯結束前上的）乾酪拼盤 ➲ VISUAL VOCAB page V22

cheese·bur·ger /ˈtʃiːzbɜːɡə(r); *NAmE* -bɜːrg-/ *noun* a HAMBURGER with a slice of cheese on top of the meat 乾酪漢堡包

cheese·cake /ˈtʃiːzkeɪk/ *noun* [C, U] a cold DESSERT (= a sweet dish) made from a soft mixture of CREAM CHEESE, sugar, eggs, etc. on a base of cake or crushed biscuits/cookies, sometimes with fruit on top 奶酪蛋糕（冷甜食）：*a strawberry cheesecake* 草莓奶酪蛋糕 ◊ *Is there any cheesecake left?* 還有剩下的奶酪蛋糕嗎？

cheese·cloth /ˈtʃiːzklɒθ; *NAmE* -klɔːθ/ *noun* [U] a type of loose cotton cloth used especially for making shirts （尤指製襯衣用的）薄紗棉布

ˌcheesed ˈoff *adj.* [not before noun] ~ (**with/about sb/sth**) (*BrE, informal*) annoyed or bored 厭煩；厭倦；煩惱

ˈcheese-paring *adj.* (*disapproving*) not liking to spend money 吝嗇的；吝惜金錢的 SYN **mean** ▸ **ˈcheese-paring** *noun* [U]

ˌcheese ˈstraw *noun* (*BrE*) a stick of PASTRY with cheese in it, eaten as a SNACK 乾酪酥條；乳酪酥條

cheesy /ˈtʃiːzi/ *adj.* (**chees·ier**, **cheesi·est**) **1** (*informal*) not very good or original, and without style, in a way that is embarrassing but amusing 拙劣可笑的；令人尷尬發笑的：*a cheesy horror movie* 拙劣可笑的恐怖片 **2** (*informal*) too emotional or romantic, in a way that is embarrassing 過於多愁善感的：*a cheesy love song* 傷感的情歌 **3** (of a smile 笑容) done in an exaggerated and probably not sincere way 刻意的；做作的：*She had a cheesy grin on her face.* 她勉強齜牙笑了一笑。**4** smelling or tasting of cheese 乾酪氣味的；乾酪味道的

chee·tah /ˈtʃiːtə/ *noun* a wild animal of the cat family, with black spots, that runs very fast 獵豹

chef /ʃef/ *noun* a professional cook, especially the most senior cook in a restaurant, hotel, etc. 廚師；（尤指餐館、旅館等的）主廚，廚師長

chef-d'oeuvre /ˌʃeɪ ˈdɜːvrə; *NAmE* also ˈduːvrə/ *noun* (*pl.* **chefs-d'oeuvre** /ˌʃeɪ ˈdɜːvrə; *NAmE* also ˈduːvrə/) (from French, *formal*) a very good piece of work, especially the best work by a particular artist, writer, etc. （尤指某一藝術家、作家等的）傑作，代表作 SYN **masterpiece**

ˌchef's ˈsalad (also **ˌchef ˈsalad**) *noun* (*NAmE*) a large salad consisting of LETTUCE, tomato and other vegetables with slices of cheese and meat such as chicken or HAM on top 大廚色拉，大廚沙拉（用萵苣、番茄等蔬菜製作而成，上面配有乾酪片和肉片）

ˌChelsea ˈbun *noun* (*BrE*) a small round cake containing dried fruit 切爾西果乾圓蛋糕

ˌChelsea ˈtractor *noun* (*BrE, informal, disapproving*) a large vehicle such as an SUV that is designed to be used in the country but is used in towns and cities instead of a normal car 切爾西拖拉機（指在城鎮中使用的越野車之類的大車）：*the environmental cost of driving a Chelsea tractor* 駕駛切爾西拖拉機所產生的環境污染成本

chem·ical 0-w AW /ˈkemɪkl/ *adj., noun*

■ *adj.* **1** 0-w connected with chemistry 與化學有關的；化學的：*a chemical element* 化學元素 ◊ *the chemical industry* 化學工業 **2** 0-w produced by or using processes which involve changes to atoms or MOLECULES 用化學方法製造的；化學作用的：*chemical reactions/processes* 化學反應 / 過程 ▸ **chem·ic·al·ly** AW /-kli/ *adv.*：*The raw sewage is chemically treated.* 未經處理的污水要進行化學處理。

■ *noun* 0-w a substance obtained by or used in a chemical process 化學製品；化學品

ˌchemical engiˈneering *noun* [U] the study of the design and use of machines in industrial chemical processes 化學工程 ▸ **ˌchemical engiˈneer** *noun*

ˌchemical ˈwarfare *noun* [U] the use of poisonous gases and chemicals as weapons in a war 化學戰

ˌchemical ˈweapon *noun* a weapon that uses poisonous gases and chemicals to kill and injure people 化學武器 ➲ compare BIOLOGICAL WEAPON

che·mise /ʃəˈmiːz/ *noun* a piece of women's underwear or a NIGHTDRESS 女式內衣；女式睡衣

chem·ist 0-w /ˈkemɪst/ *noun*

1 (also **disˈpensing chemist**) (both *BrE*) (*NAmE* **drug·gist**) a person whose job is to prepare and sell medicines, and who works in a shop 藥劑師；藥商 ➲ compare PHARMACIST (1) **2** 0-w **chemist's** (*pl.* **chem·ists**) (*BrE*) a shop/store that sells medicines and usually also soap, make-up, etc. 藥房；（通常也出售肥皂、化妝品等的）藥店：*You can obtain the product from all good chemists.* 你可從各大藥房買到這種產品。◊ *Take this prescription to the chemist's.* 帶着這張藥方到藥房去。◊ *I'll get it at the chemist's.* 我要去藥房買。◊ *a chemist's/chemist shop* 藥房 ➲ see also DRUGSTORE ➲ compare PHARMACY (1) **3** 0-w a scientist who studies chemistry 化學家：*a research chemist* 從事研究工作的化學家

chem·is·try 0-w /ˈkemɪstri/ *noun* [U]

1 0-w the scientific study of the structure of substances, how they react when combined or in contact with one another, and how they behave under different conditions 化學：*a degree in chemistry* 化學學位 ◊ *the university's chemistry department* 那所大學的化學系 ◊ *inorganic/organic chemistry* 無機 / 有機化學 ➲ see also BIOCHEMISTRY **2** (*technical* 術語) the chemical structure and behaviour of a particular substance 物質的化學組成（或性質）：*the chemistry of copper* 銅的化學性質 ◊ *The patient's blood chemistry was monitored regularly.* 那名患者的血液化學成分受到了定時的監測。**3** the relationship between two people, usually a strong sexual attraction （常指有強烈性吸引力的）兩人間的關係：*sexual chemistry* 相互吸引的兩性關係 ◊ *The chemistry just wasn't right.* 他倆就是擦不出火花。

chemo /ˈkiːməʊ; *NAmE* -moʊ/ *noun* [U] (*informal*) = CHEMOTHERAPY

chemo·recep·tor /ˈkiːməʊrɪseptə(r); *NAmE* ˈkiːmoʊ-/ *noun* (*biology* 生) a cell or sense organ that is sensitive to chemical STIMULI, making a response possible 化學感受器（對化學刺激敏感的細胞或感覺器官）

chemo·ther·apy /ˌkiːməʊˈθerəpi; *NAmE* -moʊ-/ (also *informal* **chemo**) *noun* [U] the treatment of disease, especially cancer, with the use of chemical substances （尤指對癌的）化學治療，化學療法，化療 ➲ compare RADIATION (3), RADIOTHERAPY

che·nille /ʃə'niːl/ *noun* [U] a type of thick, soft thread; cloth made from this 繩絨線；雪尼爾花線；繩絨織物：*a chenille sweater* 雪尼爾絨套頭衫

cheong·sam /tʃɒŋ'sæm; *NAmE* 'tʃɑːŋsæm/ *noun* (from *Chinese*) a straight, tightly fitting silk dress with a high neck and short sleeves and an opening at the bottom on each side, worn by women from China and Indonesia 旗袍

cheque 0-ᵚ (*BrE*) (*US* **check**) /tʃek/ *noun* a printed form that you can write on and sign as a way of paying for sth instead of using money 支票：*a cheque for £50* 一張 50 英鎊的支票 ◊ *to write a cheque* 開支票 ◊ *to make a cheque out to sb* 給某人開出一張支票 ◊ *to pay by cheque* 用支票支付 ◊ *to cash a cheque* (= to get or give money for a cheque) 兌現支票 ➲ COLLOCATIONS at FINANCE ➲ picture at MONEY ➲ see also BLANK CHEQUE, TRAVELLER'S CHEQUE

cheque·book (*BrE*) (*US* **check·book**) /'tʃekbʊk/ *noun* a book of printed cheques 支票簿 ➲ picture at MONEY

ˌchequebook 'journalism *noun* [U] (*BrE, disapproving*) the practice of journalists paying people large amounts of money to give them personal or private information for a newspaper story 支票新聞（記者花大筆錢獲得個人隱私信息在報紙上報道）

'cheque card (also **ˌcheque guaran'tee card**) *noun* (both *BrE*) a card that you must show when you pay by cheque to prove that the bank you have an account with will pay the money on the cheque 支票（保付）卡（用支票付款時出示，證明本人的開戶銀行會支付該支票）➲ compare CASH CARD

che·quered (*BrE*) (also **check·ered** *NAmE, BrE*) /'tʃekəd; *NAmE* -kərd/ *adj.* **1 ~ past/history/career** a person's past, etc. that contains both successful and not successful periods 成功與失敗並存的（過去、歷史、事業） **2** having a pattern of squares of different colours 有不同顏色方格圖案的

the ˌchequered 'flag (*BrE*) (also **check·ered flag** *NAmE, BrE*) *noun* a flag with black and white squares that is waved when a driver has finished a motor race （賽車到達終點時揮動的）黑白方格旗

'chequing account *noun* (*CanE*) = CURRENT ACCOUNT

cher·ish /'tʃerɪʃ/ *verb* (*formal*) **1 ~ sb/sth** to love sb/sth very much and want to protect them or it 珍愛；鍾愛；愛護：*Children need to be cherished.* 兒童需要無微不至的愛護。◊ *her **most cherished possession*** 她最珍愛的物品 **2 ~ sth** to keep an idea, a hope or a pleasant feeling in your mind for a long time 抱有（信念、希望）；懷有（好感）；懷念：***Cherish the memory** of those days in Paris.* 懷念在巴黎的歲月。

Chero·kee /'tʃerəkiː/ *noun* (*pl.* **Chero·kee** or **Chero·kees**) a member of a Native American people, many of whom now live in the US states of Oklahoma and North Carolina 切羅基人（美洲土著居民，很多現居於美國俄克拉何馬州和北卡羅來納州）

che·root /ʃə'ruːt/ *noun* a type of CIGAR with two open ends （兩端開口的）雪茄煙

cherry /'tʃeri/ *noun, adj.*

▪ *noun* (*pl.* **-ies**) **1** [C] a small soft round fruit with shiny red or black skin and a large seed inside 櫻桃 ➲ VISUAL VOCAB page V30 **2** (also **'cherry tree**) [C] a tree on which cherries grow, or a similar tree, grown for its flowers 櫻桃樹；櫻花樹：*cherry blossom* 櫻花 ◊ *a winter-flowering cherry* 冬季開花的櫻桃樹 **3** (also **cherry·wood** /'tʃeriwʊd/) [U] the wood of the cherry tree 櫻桃木 **4** (also **ˌcherry 'red**) [U] a bright red colour 櫻桃色；鮮紅色 IDM see BITE *n.*

▪ *adj.* (also **ˌcherry 'red**) bright red in colour 櫻桃色的；鮮紅色的：*cherry lips* 櫻唇

'cherry-pick *verb* [T, I] **~ (sb/sth)** to choose the best people or things from a group and leave those which are not so good 篩選；精選

'cherry picker *noun* **1** a type of tall CRANE which lifts people up so that they can work in very high places 櫻桃夾式升降台；車載升降台 **2** a person who picks CHERRIES 摘櫻桃的人

'cherry tomato *noun* a type of very small tomato 櫻桃番茄

cherub /'tʃerəb/ *noun* **1** (*pl.* **cher·ubs** or **cher·ubim** /-bɪm/) (in art 藝術) a type of ANGEL, shown as a small, fat, usually male, child with wings 小天使（常被繪為有翅膀的胖男孩）➲ compare SERAPH **2** (*pl.* **cher·ubs**) (*informal*) a pretty child; a child who behaves well 可愛的小孩；乖小孩 ▸ **cher·ub·ic** /tʃə'ruːbɪk/ *adj.*：(*formal*) *a cherubic face* (= looking round and innocent, like a small child's) 胖乎乎、天真無邪的娃娃臉

cher·vil /'tʃɜːvɪl; *NAmE* 'tʃɜːrvɪl/ *noun* [U] a plant with leaves that are used in cooking as a HERB 細葉芹，有喙歐芹（葉用作調料）

chess /tʃes/ *noun* [U] a game for two people played on a board marked with black and white squares on which each playing piece (representing a king, queen, castle, etc.) is moved according to special rules. The aim is to put the other player's king in a position from which it cannot escape (= to CHECKMATE it). 國際象棋；西洋棋 ➲ VISUAL VOCAB page V38

chess·board /'tʃesbɔːd; *NAmE* -bɔːrd/ *noun* a board with 64 black and white squares that chess is played on 國際象棋棋盤；西洋棋棋盤 ➲ VISUAL VOCAB page V38

chess·man /'tʃesmæn/ *noun* (*pl.* **-men** /-men/) any of the 32 pieces used in the game of chess 國際象棋棋子；西洋棋棋子

chest 0-ᵚ /tʃest/ *noun*

1 0-ᵚ the top part of the front of the body, between the neck and the stomach 胸部；胸膛：*The bullet hit him in the chest.* 子彈擊中了他的胸部。◊ *She gasped for breath, her chest heaving.* 她喘着氣，胸部不停地起伏。◊ *a chest infection* 胸部感染 ◊ *chest pains* 胸部疼痛 ◊ *a hairy chest* 毛茸茸的胸部 ➲ COLLOCATIONS at PHYSICAL ➲ VISUAL VOCAB page V59 **2 -chested** (in adjectives 構成形容詞) having the type of chest mentioned 有…胸的；胸部…的：*flat-chested* 胸部扁平的 ◊ *broad-chested* 胸部寬闊的 **3** a large strong box, usually made of wood, used for storing things in and/or moving them from one place to another（常為木製的）大箱子：*a medicine chest* 藥箱 ◊ *a treasure chest* 財寶箱 ➲ see also HOPE CHEST, TEA CHEST, WAR CHEST

IDM **ˌget sth off your 'chest** to talk about sth that has been worrying you for a long time so that you feel less anxious 傾吐心裏的煩惱；吐出心事；一吐為快 ➲ more at CARD *n.*

ches·ter·field /'tʃestəfiːld; *NAmE* 'tʃestərf-/ *noun* **1** a type of SOFA that has arms and a back that are all the same height 切斯特菲爾德長沙發（扶手和靠背同高） **2** (*CanE*) any type of SOFA 長沙發

chest·nut /'tʃesnʌt/ *noun, adj.*

▪ *noun* **1** (also **'chestnut tree**) [C] a large tree with spreading branches, that produces smooth brown nuts inside cases which are covered with SPIKES. There are several types of chestnut tree. 栗樹 ➲ see also HORSE CHESTNUT (1) **2** [C] a smooth brown nut of a chestnut tree, some types of which can be eaten 栗子；板栗：*roast chestnuts* 炒板栗 ➲ VISUAL VOCAB page V32 ➲ see also WATER CHESTNUT ➲ compare CONKER (1) **3** [U] a deep reddish-brown colour 栗色；深紅棕色 **4** [C] a horse of a reddish-brown colour 栗色馬；紅棕馬 **5 old chestnut** [C] (*informal*) an old joke or story that has been told so many times that it is no longer amusing or interesting 陳腐的笑話；老掉牙的故事

▪ *adj.* reddish-brown in colour 栗色的；紅棕色的

ˌchest of 'drawers *noun* (*pl.* **chests of drawers**) (*NAmE* also **bur·eau**, **dresser**) a piece of furniture with drawers for keeping clothes in 五斗櫥；（有抽屜的）衣櫥 ➲ VISUAL VOCAB page V23

chesty /'tʃesti/ *adj.* (*informal, especially BrE*) suffering from or showing signs of chest disease 患胸部疾病的；有胸部疾病徵兆的

C

chev·ron /ˈʃevrən/ *noun* **1** a line or pattern in the shape of a V * V 形線條；V 形圖案 **2** a piece of cloth in the shape of a V which soldiers and police officers wear on their uniforms to show their rank（軍人、警察制服上表示軍銜或警銜的）V 形標誌

chew /tʃuː/ *verb, noun*

■ ***verb*** **1** [I, T] to bite food into small pieces in your mouth with your teeth to make it easier to swallow 咀嚼；嚼碎：**~ (at/on/through sth)** *After the operation you may find it difficult to chew and swallow.* 手術後你咀嚼和吞嚥可能會感到困難。◇ **~ sth (up)** *teeth designed for chewing meat* 用於咀嚼肉食的牙齒 ◇ *He is always chewing gum.* 他總是在嚼口香糖。**2** [I, T] to bite sth continuously, for example because you are nervous or to taste it（因為緊張等）咬住，不停地啃；（為嚐味道）不停地咀嚼：**~ on sth** *Rosa chewed on her lip and stared at the floor.* 羅莎咬着嘴唇，眼睛盯着地板。◇ *The dog was chewing on a bone.* 那隻狗在一個勁兒地啃骨頭。◇ **~ sth** *to chew your nails* 啃指甲

IDM ˌ**chew the ˈfat** (*informal*) to have a long friendly talk with sb about sth（長時間）閒聊，閒扯 ➲ more at BITE *v.*

PHR V ˌ**chew sb ˈout** (*NAmE, informal*) to tell sb angrily that you do not approve of their actions 氣憤地罵（某人）：*He got chewed out by the boss for lying.* 他因說謊遭到老闆的痛罵。ˌ**chew sth↔ˈover** to think about or discuss sth slowly and carefully 仔細考慮；深思熟慮；詳細討論

■ ***noun*** **1** an act of chewing sth 咀嚼 **2** a type of sweet/candy that you chew 口香糖 **3** a piece of TOBACCO that you chew 供嚼用的煙草

ˈ**chewing gum** (also **gum**) *noun* [U] a sweet/candy that you chew but do not swallow 口香糖

ˈ**chewing-stick** *noun* a stick made from the STEM or root of particular plants that you chew at one end and then use to clean your teeth (used in some parts of Africa and Asia) 咀嚼潔齒棒（用於非洲和亞洲的一些地區，取材於植物根莖）

chewy /ˈtʃuːi/ *adj.* (**chew·ier**, **chewi·est**) (of food 食物) needing to be chewed a lot before it can be swallowed 需要多嚼的；不易嚼爛的；耐嚼的

Chey·enne /ʃaɪˈen/ *noun* (*pl.* **Chey·enne** or **Chey·ennes**) a member of a Native American people, many of whom now live in the US states of Oklahoma and Montana 夏延人（美洲土著居民，很多現居於美國俄克拉何馬州和蒙大拿州）

chez /ʃeɪ/ *prep.* (from *French*) at the home of 在…家：*I spent a pleasant evening chez the Stewarts.* 我在斯圖爾特家度過了一個愉快的夜晚。

chi /kaɪ/ *noun* the 22nd letter of the Greek alphabet (Χ, χ) 希臘字母表的第 22 個字母

Chi·anti /kiˈænti/ *noun* [U, C] a dry red wine from the region of Tuscany in Italy 基安蒂乾紅葡萄酒（產於意大利托斯卡納區）

chiaro·scuro /kiˌɑːrəˈskʊərəʊ; *NAmE* -ˈskʊroʊ/ *noun* [U] (*art* 美術) the way light and shade are shown; the contrast between light and shade 明暗對比法；明暗對比

chi·as·mus /kaɪˈæzməs; *NAmE* krˈæz-/ *noun* [U, C] (*pl.* **chi·as·mi** /kaɪˈæzmi; krˈæz-/) (*technical* 術語) a technique used in writing or in speeches, in which words, ideas, etc. are repeated in reverse order 交錯配列（對詞、思想等的倒序重複排列）

chic /ʃiːk/ *adj.* very fashionable and elegant 時髦的；優雅的；雅致的 SYN **stylish**：*She is always so chic, so elegant.* 她總是那麼時髦，那麼優雅。◇ *a chic new restaurant* 雅致的新餐館 ▸ **chic** *noun* [U]：*a perfectly dressed woman with an air of chic that was unmistakably French* 一位衣着講究、明顯地流露出法國式優雅姿態的女士

chi·ca /ˈtʃiːkə/ *noun* (*US*, from *Spanish, informal*) a girl or young woman 小妞；姑娘

Chi·cana /tʃɪˈkɑːnə; ʃɪ-; -ˈkem-; *NAmE* tʃɪˈkɑːnə; ʃɪ-/ *noun* (*especially US*, from *Spanish*) a girl or woman living in the US whose family came from Mexico 女奇卡諾人（墨西哥裔美國女孩或婦女）➲ compare CHICANO, HISPANIC *n.*, LATINO

chi·cane /ʃɪˈkem/ *noun* (*BrE*) a sharp double bend, either on a track where cars race, or on an ordinary road to stop vehicles from going too fast（賽車或一般車道上防止車速過快的）雙急轉彎

chi·can·ery /ʃɪˈkemərі/ *noun* [U] (*formal*) the use of complicated plans and clever talk in order to trick people 欺詐；詐騙；欺騙

Chi·cano /tʃɪˈkɑːnəʊ; ʃɪ-; *NAmE* -noʊ; *BrE* also -ˈkem-/ *noun* (*pl.* **-os**) (*especially US*, from *Spanish*) a person living in the US whose family came from Mexico 奇卡諾人（墨西哥裔美國人）➲ compare CHICANA, HISPANIC *n.*, LATINO

chi·chi /ˈʃiːʃiː/ *adj.* used to describe a style of decoration that contains too many details and lacks taste（裝飾）華麗而俗氣的，過分豔麗的

chick /tʃɪk/ *noun* **1** a baby bird, especially a baby chicken 雛鳥；（尤指）雛雞，小雞 **2** (*old-fashioned*, sometimes *offensive*) a way of referring to a young woman 少女；少婦；小妞兒

chicka·dee /ˈtʃɪkədiː; ˌtʃɪkəˈdiː/ *noun* a small N American bird of the TIT family. There are many types of chickadee. 北美山雀

chick·en /ˈtʃɪkɪn/ *noun, verb, adj.*

■ ***noun*** **1** [C] a large bird that is often kept for its eggs or meat 雞：*They keep chickens in the back yard.* 他們在後院養雞。◇ *free-range chickens* 自由放養的雞 ➲ compare COCK, HEN ➲ VISUAL VOCAB page V12 **2** [U] meat from a chicken 雞肉：***fried/roast chicken*** 炸／燒雞 ◇ ***chicken stock/soup*** 原汁雞湯；雞湯 ◇ ***chicken breasts/livers/thighs*** 雞胸脯肉／肝／大腿 ◇ *chicken and chips* 炸雞塊配炸薯條 ➲ see also SPRING CHICKEN

IDM **a ˌchicken-and-ˈegg situation, problem, etc.** a situation in which it is difficult to tell which one of two things was the cause of the other 雞與蛋孰先難定的情況；因果難定的問題 **play ˈchicken** to play a game in which people do sth dangerous for as long as they can to show how brave they are. The person who stops first has lost the game. 比試膽量 ➲ more at COUNT *v.*, HEADLESS, HOME *adv.*

■ ***verb***

PHR V ˌ**chicken ˈout (of sth/of doing sth)** (*informal*) to decide not to do sth because you are afraid 因害怕而放棄；臨陣退縮；膽怯

■ ***adj.*** [not before noun] (*informal*) not brave; afraid to do sth 膽怯；懦弱；怯懦 SYN **cowardly**

ˈ**chicken feed** *noun* [U] (*informal*) an amount of money that is not large enough to be important 一筆微不足道的錢；一筆錢

ˈ**chicken flu** *noun* [U] = BIRD FLU

chick·en·pox /ˈtʃɪkɪnpɒks; *NAmE* -pɑːks/ *noun* [U] a disease, especially of children, that causes a slight fever and many spots on the skin 水痘：*to **catch/get/have chickenpox*** 染上／患上／得了水痘

ˈ**chicken run** *noun* an area surrounded by a fence in which chickens are kept 養雞場

chick·en·shit /ˈtʃɪkɪnʃɪt/ *noun, adj.*

■ ***noun*** [U] (*NAmE, slang*) nonsense 廢話；瞎說；胡說八道

■ ***adj.*** (*NAmE, slang*) (of a person 人) not brave 膽怯的；懦弱的；怯懦的 SYN **cowardly**

ˈ**chicken wire** *noun* [U] thin wire made into sheets like nets with a pattern of shapes with six sides 六角形網眼鐵絲網

ˈ**chick flick** *noun* (*informal*) a film/movie that is intended especially for women 女性電影（旨在迎合女性口味的電影）

ˈ**chick lit** *noun* [U] (*informal*) novels that are intended especially for women, often with a young, single woman as the main character 小妞文學（旨在迎合女性口味、主角常為單身少女的小說）

chick·pea /ˈtʃɪkpiː/ *noun* (*especially BrE*) (*NAmE* usually **gar·banzo**, **garˈbanzo bean**) a hard round seed, like a light brown PEA, that is cooked and eaten as a vegetable 鷹嘴豆（淺棕色的硬圓豆，可烹食）➲ VISUAL VOCAB page V31

ˈchickpea flour *noun* = GRAM FLOUR

chick·weed /ˈtʃɪkwiːd/ *noun* [U] a small plant with white flowers that often grows as a WEED over a wide area 繁縷（雜草，花白色）

chi·co /ˈtʃiːkəʊ; *NAmE* -koʊ/ *noun* (*pl.* **-os**) (*US*, from *Spanish*, *informal*) a boy or young man 小傢伙；小伙子

chic·ory /ˈtʃɪkəri/ *noun* [U] **1** (*BrE*) (*NAmE* **en·dive**) [C, U] a small pale green plant with bitter leaves that are eaten raw or cooked as a vegetable. The root can be dried and used with or instead of coffee. 菊苣（根乾燥後可與咖啡同用或作其替代品）**2** (*NAmE*) (*BrE* **en·dive**) (*NAmE* also **ˌcurly ˈendive, fri·sée**) a plant with green curly leaves that are eaten raw as a vegetable（捲葉）歐洲菊苣

chide /tʃaɪd/ *verb* (*formal*) to criticize or blame sb because they have done sth wrong 批評；指責；責備 SYN **rebuke**：**~ sb/yourself (for sth/for doing sth)** *She chided herself for being so impatient with the children.* 她責怪自己對孩子不夠耐心。◇ **~ (sb) + speech** *'Isn't that a bit selfish?' he chided.* "那不有點自私嗎？"他責備道。

chief 🔑 /tʃiːf/ *adj.*, *noun*

■ ***adj.*** [only before noun] **1** 🔑 most important 最重要的；首要的；主要的：*the chief cause/problem/reason* 主要原因／問題／理由 ◇ *one of the President's chief rivals* 總統的主要政敵之一 ➲ SYNONYMS at MAIN **2** 🔑 (often **Chief**) highest in rank 最高級別的；為首的；首席的：*the Chief Education Officer* 首席教育官 ◇ *the chief financial officer of the company* 公司的首席財務官 ◇ *Detective Chief Inspector Williams* 探長威廉斯 **3 -in-ˈchief** (in nouns 構成名詞) of the highest rank 最高級別的；為首的：*commander-in-chief* 總司令 ➲ see also CHIEFLY

■ ***noun*** **1** 🔑 a person with a high rank or the highest rank in a company or an organization（公司或機構的）首領，頭目，最高領導人：***army/industry/police chiefs*** 部隊首長；行業巨擘；警察局長 **2** (often as a title 常用作頭銜) a leader or ruler of a people or community 首領；酋長；族長：*Chief Buthelezi* 布特萊齊酋長 ◇ *Chief Crazy Horse* "瘋馬"酋長

IDM **too many ˌchiefs and not enough ˈIndians** (*BrE*, *informal*) used to describe a situation in which there are too many people telling other people what to do, and not enough people to do the work 將多兵少；官多兵少

ˌchief ˈconstable *noun* (in Britain) a senior police officer who is in charge of the police force in a particular area（英國）地區警察局長：*Chief Constable Brian Turner* 地區警察局長布賴恩 • 特納

ˌchief eˈxecutive *noun* **1** the person with the highest rank in a company or an organization（公司或機構的）總經理，總裁 **2 Chief Executive** the President of the US 美國總統

ˌchief eˈxecutive officer *noun* (*abbr.* **CEO**) the person in a company who has the most power and authority 總裁；首席執行官

ˌchief inˈspector *noun* (in Britain) a police officer above the rank of an INSPECTOR（英國警察的）總巡官，總督察

ˌchief ˈjustice (also **Chief Justice**) *noun* the most important judge in a court, especially the US Supreme Court 首席法官；（尤指）美國最高法院首席法官

chief·ly /ˈtʃiːfli/ *adv.* not completely, but as a most important part 主要地；首要地 SYN **primarily, mainly**：*We are chiefly concerned with improving educational standards.* 我們主要關心的是提高教育水平。◇ *He's travelled widely, chiefly in Africa and Asia.* 他遊歷了許多地方，主要在非洲和亞洲。

ˌchief of ˈstaff *noun* (*pl.* **ˌchiefs of ˈstaff**) an officer of very high rank, responsible for advising the person who commands each of the armed forces 總參謀長；參謀總長 ➲ see also JOINT CHIEFS OF STAFF

ˌchief superinˈtendent *noun* (in Britain) a police officer above the rank of SUPERINTENDENT（英國警察的）總警司，警務長

chief·tain /ˈtʃiːftən/ *noun* the leader of a people or a CLAN in Scotland 首領；酋長；（蘇格蘭的）族長

chif·fon /ˈʃɪfɒn; *NAmE* ʃɪˈfɑːn/ *noun* [U] a type of fine transparent cloth made from silk or NYLON, used especially for making clothes 雪紡綢，薄綢，尼龍綢（尤用於製衣）➲ VISUAL VOCAB page V65

chig·ger /ˈtʃɪɡə(r)/ (also **jig·ger**) *noun* a small FLEA that lives in tropical regions and lays eggs under a person's or animal's skin, causing painful areas on the skin 恙蟎

chi·gnon /ˈʃiːnjɒn; *NAmE* -jɑːn/ *noun* (from *French*) a style for women's hair in which the hair is pulled back and twisted into a smooth knot at the back（女人的）髮髻 ➲ VISUAL VOCAB page V60

chi·hua·hua /tʃɪˈwɑːwə; *NAmE* -ˈwɑːwɑː/ *noun* a very small dog with smooth hair 奇瓦瓦狗（體型小，毛平滑）

chi·kun·gun·ya /ˌtʃɪkənˈɡʌnjə/ *noun* [U] a disease similar to DENGUE caused by a virus, found in E Africa and parts of Asia and carried by MOSQUITOES 奇昆古尼亞熱病（東非和亞洲部份地區的一種類似登革熱的病毒性傳染病，由蚊子傳播）

chil·blain /ˈtʃɪlbleɪn/ *noun* [usually pl.] a painful red swelling on the hands or feet that is caused by cold or bad CIRCULATION of the blood 凍瘡

child 🔑 /tʃaɪld/ *noun* (*pl.* **chil·dren** /ˈtʃɪldrən/)

1 🔑 a young human who is not yet an adult 兒童；小孩：*a child of three/a three-year-old child* 三歲小孩 ◇ *men, women and children* 男人、女人及兒童 ◇ *an unborn child* 胎兒 ◇ *not suitable for young children* 不適於幼兒 ◇ *I lived in London as a child.* 我小時候住在倫敦。◇ *a child star* 童星 ➲ see also BRAINCHILD, LATCHKEY CHILD, POSTER CHILD, SCHOOLCHILD **2** 🔑 a son or daughter of any age 兒子；女兒：*They have three grown-up children.* 他們有三個成年的孩子。◇ *a support group for adult children of alcoholics* 幫助酗酒者成年子女的小組 ◇ *They can't* ***have children.*** 他們不能生孩子。➲ see also GODCHILD, GRANDCHILD, LOVE CHILD, ONLY CHILD, STEPCHILD ➲ compare KID *n.* (1) **3** a person who is strongly influenced by the ideas and attitudes of a particular time or person 深受…影響的人：*a child of the 90s* 屬於 20 世紀 90 年代的人 **4** (*disapproving*) an adult who behaves like a child and is not MATURE or responsible 孩子氣的人；幼稚的人；不負責任的人 ➲ COLLOCATIONS at next page

IDM **be with ˈchild** (*old-fashioned*) to be pregnant 懷孕；有喜 **be ˈchild's play** (*informal*) to be very easy to do, so not even a child would find it difficult 極容易做；輕而易舉

ˈchild abuse *noun* [U] the crime of harming a child in a physical, sexual or emotional way 摧殘兒童；虐待兒童：*victims of child abuse* 受虐待的兒童

child·bear·ing /ˈtʃaɪldbeərɪŋ; *NAmE* -ber-/ *noun* [U] the process of giving birth to children 分娩；生孩子：*women* ***of childbearing age*** 育齡婦女

ˌchild ˈbenefit *noun* [U] (in Britain) money that the government regularly pays to parents of children up to a particular age 兒童補助金（由英國政府定期發給兒童的父母，直至兒童長到某一年齡為止）

child·birth /ˈtʃaɪldbɜːθ; *NAmE* -bɜːrθ/ *noun* [U] the process of giving birth to a baby 分娩；生孩子：*pregnancy and childbirth* 懷孕及分娩 ◇ *His wife died* ***in childbirth.*** 他妻子生孩子的時候死了。

child·care /ˈtʃaɪldkeə(r); *NAmE* -ker/ *noun* [U] the care of children, especially while parents are at work（尤指父母上班時的）兒童保育，兒童照管：*childcare facilities for working parents* 為職業父母提供的照管兒童的設施 ➲ COLLOCATIONS at CHILD

child·hood /ˈtʃaɪldhʊd/ *noun* [U, C] the period of sb's life when they are a child 童年；幼年；孩童時期：*childhood, adolescence and adulthood* 童年、青少年及成年 ◇ *in early childhood* 在嬰幼兒時期 ◇ ***childhood memories/experiences*** 童年的回憶／經歷 ◇ *She had a happy childhood.* 她有一個幸福的童年。◇ *childhood cancer* 兒童癌症 ➲ COLLOCATIONS at AGE

IDM **a/sb's second ˈchildhood** a time in the life of an adult person when they behave like a child again 老小孩時期；行為像小孩的晚年時期

C

Collocations 詞語搭配

Children 孩子

Having a baby/child 懷孕

- **want** a baby/a child/kids 想要孩子
- **start** a family 生孩子
- **conceive/be expecting/be going to have** a baby/child 懷孕
- **miss** your period 月經未按期來
- **become/get/ be/find out that you are** pregnant 懷孕了；發現懷孕了
- **have** a baby/a child/kids/a son/a daughter/twins/a family 有一個寶寶 / 一個孩子 / 孩子 / 一個兒子 / 一個女兒 / 一對雙胞胎 / 家室
- **have** a normal/a difficult/an unwanted pregnancy; an easy/a difficult/a home birth 正常 / 歷經艱難 / 意外懷孕；順產；難產；在家中分娩
- **be in/go into/induce** labour/(*especially US*) labor 分娩；催產
- **have/suffer/cause** a miscarriage 流產；引起流產
- **give birth** to a child/baby/daughter/son/twins 生了一個孩子 / 一個寶寶 / 一個女兒 / 一個兒子 / 一對雙胞胎

Parenting 養育；撫養；教養

- **bring up**/(*especially NAmE*) **raise** a child/family 撫養孩子；養家
- **care for**/(*especially BrE*) **look after** a baby/child/kid 照看 / 照顧小孩
- **change** (*BrE*) a nappy/(*NAmE*) a diaper/a baby 換尿布；給嬰兒換尿布
- **feed/breastfeed/bottle-feed** a baby 餵孩子；給孩子哺乳；用奶瓶餵養孩子
- **be entitled to/go on** maternity/paternity leave 有權利休 / 正在休產假 / 陪產假
- **go back/return to work** after maternity leave 產假後回到工作崗位
- **need/find/get** a babysitter/good quality affordable childcare 需要 / 找到一個臨時保母 / 負擔得起的高質量兒童保育
- **balance/combine work and** childcare/child-rearing/family life 平衡 / 兼顧工作與照顧小孩 / 撫養小孩 / 家庭生活
- **educate/teach/home-school** a child/kid 教育孩子；給孩子家庭教育
- **punish/discipline/spoil** a child/kid 懲罰 / 管教 / 嬌慣孩子
- **adopt** a baby/child/kid 收養小孩
- **offer a baby for/put a baby up for** adoption 把小孩給人收養
- (*especially BrE*) **foster** a child/kid 代養小孩
- **be placed with/be raised by** foster parents 被交給寄養父母；由寄養父母撫養

child·ish /ˈtʃaɪldɪʃ/ *adj.* **1** connected with or typical of a child 孩子的；孩子氣的；稚嫩的： *childish handwriting* 稚嫩的筆跡 **2** (*disapproving*) (of an adult 成人) behaving in a stupid or silly way 幼稚的；天真的 SYN **immature**： *Don't be so childish!* 別那麼幼稚！ OPP **mature** ➲ compare CHILDLIKE ▸ **child·ish·ly** *adv.*： *to behave childishly* 舉止幼稚 **child·ish·ness** *noun* [U]

child·less /ˈtʃaɪldləs/ *adj.* having no children 無子女的；無後代的： *a* ***childless couple/marriage*** 無子女的夫婦 / 婚姻生活

child·like /ˈtʃaɪldlaɪk/ *adj.* (usually *approving*) having the qualities that children usually have, especially INNOCENCE 孩子般的；童稚的；單純的；（尤指）天真無邪的： ***childlike enthusiasm/simplicity/delight*** 孩子般的熱情 / 淳樸 / 興高采烈 ➲ compare CHILDISH

child·mind·er /ˈtʃaɪldmaɪndə(r)/ *noun* (*BrE*) a person who is paid to care for children while their parents are at work. A childminder usually does this in his or her own home.（通常指在自己家中）受雇照看孩子者 ➲ see also BABYSITTER

child·proof /ˈtʃaɪldpruːf/ *adj.* designed so that young children cannot open, use, or damage it 防孩童開啟（或使用、損壞）的；對孩童安全的： *childproof containers for medicines* 防孩童開啟的藥瓶

ˈchild restraint *noun* a belt, or small seat with a belt, that is used in a car to control and protect a child（汽車的）兒童安全帶，兒童安全座椅

ˈchild seat *noun* = CAR SEAT (1)

chili /ˈtʃɪli/ (*NAmE*) **1** [C] = CHILLI **2** [U] = CHILLI CON CARNE

chill /tʃɪl/ *noun, verb, adj.*

■ ***noun*** **1** [sing.] a feeling of being cold 寒冷；寒意；涼意： *There's a chill in the air this morning.* 今天早晨寒氣襲人。◇ *A small fire was burning to* ***take the chill off*** *the room.* 房間裏生着小火爐驅寒。 **2** [C] an illness caused by being cold and wet, causing fever and SHIVERING (= shaking of the body) 着涼；受寒 **3** [sing.] a feeling of fear 害怕的感覺： *a* ***chill of fear/apprehension*** 一陣害怕 / 恐懼 ◇ *His words* ***sent a chill down her spine.*** 他的話讓她覺得毛骨悚然。

■ ***verb*** **1** [T, usually passive] **~ sb** to make sb very cold 使很冷；使冰冷： *They were chilled by the icy wind.* 凜冽的寒風吹得他們遍體冰涼。◇ *Let's go home, I'm* ***chilled to the bone*** (= very cold). 咱們回家吧，我感到寒氣刺骨。 **2** [I, T] when food or a drink **chills** or when sb **chills** it, it is made very cold but it does not freeze （使）冷卻；（被）冷藏： *Let the pudding chill for an hour until set.* 把布丁冷卻一小時直至凝固成形。◇ **~ sth** *This wine is best served chilled.* 這種葡萄酒冰鎮後飲用最佳。◇ *chilled foods* (= for example in a supermarket) 冷藏食物 **3** [T] **~ sb/sth** (*literary*) to frighten sb 使恐懼；恐嚇；嚇唬： *His words chilled her.* 他的話使她不寒而慄。◇ *What he saw* ***chilled his blood/chilled him to the bone.*** 他看到的情景使他毛骨悚然。 **4** [I] (also ˌ**chill ˈout**) (*informal*) = CHILL OUT： *We went home and chilled in front of the TV.* 我們回家坐在電視機前放鬆了一下。◇ *Just chill, Mum, everything's going to be OK.* 媽媽，放鬆些，一切都會沒事的。

PHR V ˌ**chill ˈout** (*informal*) to spend time relaxing; to relax and stop feeling angry or nervous about sth 放鬆；冷靜；鎮靜： *They sometimes meet up to chill out and watch a movie.* 他們有時聚在一起，看場電影放鬆一下。◇ *Sit down and chill out!* 坐下來冷靜一下！

■ ***adj.*** (*formal*) (especially of weather and the wind 尤指天氣和風) cold, in an unpleasant way 寒冷的；冷颼颼的；陰冷的： *the chill grey dawn* 寒冷陰沉的拂曉 ◇ *a chill wind* 寒風

chill·ax /tʃɪˈlæks/ *verb* [I] (*slang*) to relax and stop feeling angry or nervous about sth 冷靜；放鬆： *Chillax, dude—I'm on your team.* 別緊張，哥們，我和你一夥的。

ˌ**chilled-ˈout** (also **chilled**) *adj.* (*informal*) very relaxed 十分放鬆的；休閒舒適的： *a chilled-out atmosphere* 輕鬆的氣氛 ◇ *He felt totally chilled.* 他感覺完全放鬆了下來。

ˈchill factor *noun* the extent to which the wind makes the air feel colder; a number which represents this 風寒效應；風寒指數

chilli (*BrE*) (*NAmE* **chili**) /ˈtʃɪli/ *noun* (*pl.* **chil·lies**, *NAmE* **chilies**) **1** (*NAmE* also **ˈchili pepper**) [C, U] the small green or red fruit of a type of pepper plant that is used in cooking to give a hot taste to food, often dried or made into powder, also called chilli or **chilli powder** 辣椒（經常在乾後製成辣椒粉）➲ VISUAL VOCAB page V31 **2** [U] = CHILLI CON CARNE

chilli con carne /ˌtʃɪli kɒn ˈkɑːni; *NAmE* kɑːn ˈkɑːrni/ (*especially BrE*) (*BrE* also **chilli**) (*NAmE* also **chili**) *noun* [U] a hot spicy Mexican dish made with meat, BEANS and chillies 辣味肉豆（墨西哥菜肴）

chill·ing /ˈtʃɪlɪŋ/ *adj.* frightening, usually because it is connected with sth violent or cruel（常與殘暴有關）令人恐懼的，令人害怕的： *a chilling story* 令人毛骨悚然的故事 ◇ *The film evokes chilling reminders of the war.* 這部電影使人回憶起戰爭的可怕場景。

chill·out /ˈtʃɪlaʊt/ *noun* [U] a style of electronic music that is not fast or lively and is intended to make you relaxed and calm 舒放音樂（節奏平緩、讓人放鬆的電子音樂）

chilly /ˈtʃɪli/ *adj.* (**chill·ier**, **chilli·est**) **1** (especially of the weather or a place, but also of people 尤指天氣或地方，亦指人) too cold to be comfortable 寒冷的；陰冷的： *It's chilly today.* 今天很寒冷。◇ *I was feeling chilly.* 我感到冷得難受。➲ SYNONYMS at COLD **2** not friendly 不友好的；冷淡的；冷漠的： *The visitors got a chilly reception.* 客人遭到了冷遇。▸ **chil·li·ness** *noun* [U]

chime /tʃaɪm/ *verb, noun*

■ ***verb*** [I, T] (of a bell or a clock 鈴或鐘) to ring; to show the time by making a ringing sound 鳴響；敲響；報時： *I heard the clock chime.* 我聽見鐘響報時。◇ *Eight o'clock had already chimed.* 已敲過八點鐘了。◇ **~ sth** *The clock chimed midday.* 時鐘響過正午十二點。

PHR V **ˌchime ˈin (with sth)** to join or interrupt a conversation 插嘴；打斷談話： *He kept chiming in with his own opinions.* 他不斷插話發表自己的意見。◇ **+ speech** *'And me!' she chimed in.* "還有我！"她插嘴道。 **chime (in) with sth** (of plans, ideas, etc. 計劃、主意等) to agree with sth; to be similar to sth 與…相一致（或相似）： *His opinions chimed in with the mood of the nation.* 他的主張與國民的心態相吻合。

■ ***noun*** a ringing sound, especially one that is made by a bell 鈴聲；鐘聲： *door chimes* 門鈴聲 ➲ see also WIND CHIMES

chi·mera (also **chi·maera**) /kaɪˈmɪərə; *NAmE* -ˈmɪrə/ *noun* **1** (in ancient Greek stories) a creature with a LION's head, a GOAT's body and a snake's tail, that can breathe out fire 喀邁拉（古希臘故事中獅頭、羊身、蛇尾的吐火怪物） **2** (*formal*) an impossible idea or hope 妄想；幻想；空想

chim·ney /ˈtʃɪmni/ *noun* **1** a structure through which smoke or steam is carried up away from a fire, etc. and through the roof of a building; the part of this that is above the roof 煙囱；煙道；（屋頂上的）煙囱管： *He threw a bit of paper onto the fire and it flew up the chimney.* 他把一些紙屑扔進火裏，紙飄進了煙道。◇ *the factory chimneys of an industrial landscape* 工廠煙囱林立的工業區景觀 ➲ VISUAL VOCAB page V17 **2** (*technical* 術語) a narrow opening in an area of rock that a person can climb up（岩石間可供攀登的）狹孔，狹縫

ˈchim·ney breast *noun* (*BrE*) the wall around the bottom part of a chimney, above a FIREPLACE 壁爐腔

ˈchim·ney piece *noun* (*BrE*) a brick or stone structure that is built over a FIREPLACE 壁爐台

ˈchim·ney pot *noun* (*BrE*) a short wide pipe that is placed on top of a chimney 煙囱管帽 ➲ VISUAL VOCAB page V17

ˈchim·ney stack *noun* (*BrE*) **1** the part of the chimney that is above the roof of a building（屋頂上的）煙囱體 **2** (*NAmE* **smoke·stack**) a very tall chimney, especially one in a factory（尤指工廠的）高煙囱

ˈchimney sweep (also **sweep**) *noun* a person whose job is to clean the inside of chimneys 煙囱清掃工

chim·pan·zee /ˌtʃɪmpænˈziː/ (also *informal* **chimp**) *noun* a small intelligent African APE (= an animal like a large MONKEY without a tail) 黑猩猩 ➲ VISUAL VOCAB page V12

chin 0‑ᴡ /tʃɪn/ *noun*

the part of the face below the mouth and above the neck 頦；下巴 ➲ COLLOCATIONS at PHYSICAL ➲ VISUAL VOCAB page V59 ➲ see also DOUBLE CHIN

IDM **(keep your) ˈchin up** (*informal*) used to tell sb to try to stay cheerful even though they are in a difficult or unpleasant situation 振作起來；不氣餒；不灰心： *Chin up! Only two exams left.* 別泄氣！只剩下兩門考試了。 **take sth on the ˈchin** (*informal*) **1** to accept a difficult or unpleasant situation without complaining, trying to make excuses, etc.（無怨無悔地）承受某事 **2** (*NAmE*) to be damaged or badly affected by something 受損；受到嚴重影響 ➲ more at CHUCK *v.*

china /ˈtʃaɪnə/ *noun* [U] **1** white CLAY which is baked and used for making delicate cups, plates, etc. 瓷；瓷料： *a china vase* 瓷花瓶 ➲ see also BONE CHINA **2** cups, plates, etc. that are made of china 瓷製品；瓷器： *She got out the best china.* 她造出最好的瓷器。 IDM see BULL, TEA

ˌchina-ˈblue *adj.* pale greyish-blue in colour 中國瓷藍的；淺灰藍的 ▸ **ˌchina ˈblue** *noun* [U]

ˌchina ˈclay *noun* [U] = KAOLIN

China·town /ˈtʃaɪnətaʊn/ *noun* [U, C] the area of a city where many Chinese people live and there are Chinese shops/stores and restaurants 中國城；唐人街

chin·chilla /tʃɪnˈtʃɪlə/ *noun* **1** [C] an animal like a RABBIT with soft silver-grey fur. Chinchillas are often kept on farms for their fur. 毛絲鼠，南美栗鼠（似兔，皮毛銀灰色，常養殖以獲取毛皮） **2** [U] the skin and fur of the chinchilla, used for making expensive coats, etc. 毛絲鼠毛皮，栗鼠毛皮（用以製作名貴大衣等）

Chi·nese /ˌtʃaɪˈniːz/ *adj., noun* (*pl.* **Chi·nese**)

■ ***adj.*** from or connected with China 中國的

■ ***noun*** **1** [C] a person from China, or whose family was originally from China 中國人；華裔；華人 **2** [U] the language of China 中國話；漢語；中文

ˌChinese ˈcabbage *noun* [U] (*BrE* also **ˌChinese ˈleaves** [pl.], **ˌChinese ˈleaf** [U]) a type of vegetable that is eaten cooked or in salads. There are two types of Chinese cabbage, one with long light-green leaves and thick white STEMS which is similar to LETTUCE and one with darker green leaves and thicker white STEMS. The first type is usually called 'Chinese leaves' in British English and the second type is called 'pak choi' (*BrE*) or 'bok choy' (*NAmE*). 白菜；大白菜

ˌChinese ˈchequers (*BrE*) (*NAmE* **ˌChinese ˈcheckers**) *noun* [U] a game for two to six players who try to move the playing pieces from one corner to the opposite corner of the board, which is shaped like a star（彈子）跳棋 ➲ VISUAL VOCAB page V38

ˌChinese ˈlantern *noun* **1** a lamp that is inside a paper case, with a handle to carry it 燈籠 **2** a plant with white flowers and round orange fruits inside a material like paper 酸漿

ˌChinese ˈwhispers *noun* [U] (*BrE*) the situation when information is passed from one person to another and gets slightly changed each time 消息從一個人向另一個人傳播時每次都發生一些變化

Ching·lish /ˈtʃɪŋglɪʃ/ *noun* [U] (*informal*) language which is a mixture of ENGLISH and CHINESE, especially a type of English that includes many Chinese words and/or follows Chinese grammar rules 中國式英語

Chink /tʃɪŋk/ *noun* (*taboo, slang*) a very offensive word for a Chinese person（對中國人的蔑稱）中國佬

chink /tʃɪŋk/ *noun, verb*

■ ***noun*** **1** a narrow opening in sth, especially one that lets light through（尤指光線可進入的）裂口，縫隙，裂縫： *a chink in the curtains* 窗簾上的縫隙 **2 ~ of light** a small area of light shining through a narrow opening 一縷，一束，一線（從縫隙間射入的光） **3** [usually sing.] the light ringing sound that is made when glass objects or coins touch（玻璃物品或硬幣的）輕微碰撞聲，叮噹聲： *the chink of glasses* 玻璃杯相碰的叮噹聲

IDM **a chink in sb's ˈarmour** a weak point in sb's argument, character, etc., that can be used in an attack（論點、性格等易受攻擊的）弱點，缺陷，薄弱環節

■ ***verb*** [I, T] when glasses, coins or other glass or metal objects **chink** or when you **chink** them, they make a light ringing sound（使）叮噹響 SYN **clink**： *the sound of bottles chinking* 瓶子叮噹的碰撞聲 ◇ **~ sth** *We chinked glasses and drank to each other's health.* 我們互相碰杯，祝對方身體健康。

chin·less /'tʃɪnləs/ *adj.* (of a man 男子) having a very small chin (often thought of as a sign of a weak character) 下巴短小的（常被認為性格軟弱）

IDM **a chinless 'wonder** (*BrE, humorous, disapproving*) a young, upper-class man who is weak and stupid 上流膿包；上流青年懦夫

C

chi·nois·erie /ʃɪn'wɑːzəri/ *noun* [U] (*art* 美術) the use of Chinese images, designs and techniques in Western art, furniture and ARCHITECTURE 中國式風格，中國藝術風格（見於西方藝術、傢具、建築）

chi·nook /tʃɪ'nuːk; ʃɪ-/ *noun* **1** (also **chi,nook 'wind**) a warm dry wind that blows down the east side of the Rocky Mountains at the end of winter 奇努克風（冬末從落基山脈東側吹下來的乾燥暖風） **2** (also **chi,nook 'salmon**) a large N Pacific SALMON which is eaten as food 奇努克鮭，王鮭，大鱗大麻哈魚，大鱗鮭魚（產於北太平洋的食用魚）

chinos /'tʃiːnəʊz; *NAmE* -noʊz/ *noun* [pl.] informal trousers/pants made from strong cotton 斜紋布褲：*a pair of chinos* 一條斜紋布褲

chintz /tʃɪnts/ *noun* [U, C] a type of shiny cotton cloth with a printed design, especially of flowers, used for making curtains, covering furniture, etc. 軋光印花棉布（用於製作窗簾、傢具套等）

chintzy /'tʃɪntsi/ *adj.* **1** (*BrE*) covered in or decorated with chintz 用磨擦軋光印花棉布覆蓋（或裝飾）的 **2** (*NAmE, informal*) cheap and not attractive 便宜而俗氣的；廉價的 **3** (*NAmE, humorous*) not willing to spend money 吝嗇的；小氣的 SYN **cheap, stingy**

'chin-up *noun* (*especially NAmE*) = PULL-UP

chin·wag /'tʃɪnwæɡ/ *noun* [sing.] (*BrE, informal*) a friendly, informal conversation with sb that you know well（與熟人的）閒談，閒聊 SYN **chat**

chips (*BrE*)
(*also* **French fries** *NAmE, BrE*)
炸薯條

crisps (*BrE*)
chips (*NAmE*)
炸薯片

chip 0‐ /tʃɪp/ *noun, verb*

■ *noun* **1** 0‐ the place from which a small piece of wood, glass, etc. has broken from an object（木頭、玻璃等的）缺口，缺損處：*This mug has a chip in it.* 這缸子有個豁口。➲ picture at BROKEN **2** 0‐ a small piece of wood, glass, etc. that has broken or been broken off an object（木頭、玻璃等破損後留下的）碎屑，碎片，碎渣：*chips of wood* 碎木屑 ◇ *chocolate chip cookies* (= biscuits containing small pieces of chocolate) 碎粒巧克力餅乾 **3** 0‐ (*BrE*) (also **,French 'fry**, **fry** *NAmE, BrE*) [usually pl.] a long thin piece of potato fried in oil or fat 油炸土豆條；炸薯條：*All main courses are served with chips or baked potato.* 所有的主菜都配有炸土豆條或烤土豆。➲ see also FISH AND CHIPS **4** (also **po'tato chip**) (both *NAmE*) (*BrE* **crisp**, **po,tato 'crisp**) a thin round slice of potato that is fried until hard then dried and eaten cold. Chips are sold in bags and have many different flavours. 油炸土豆片；炸薯片 **5** = TORTILLA CHIP **6** = MICROCHIP *n.*：*chip technology* 芯片科技 ➲ see also V-CHIP **7** a small flat piece of plastic used to represent a particular amount of money in some types of gambling（作賭注用的）籌碼：(*figurative*) *The release of prisoners was used as a **bargaining chip**.* 釋放戰俘被用作討價還價的籌碼。 **8** (also **'chip shot**) (in GOLF, football (SOCCER), etc. 高爾夫球、足球等) an act of hitting or kicking a ball high in the air so that it lands within a short distance（高爾夫球）近穴球；（足球）高球 ➲ see also BLUE-CHIP

IDM **a ,chip off the old 'block** (*informal*) a person who is very similar to their mother or father in the way that they look or behave（相貌或性格）酷似父親或母親的人 **have a 'chip on your shoulder (about sth)** (*informal*) to be sensitive about sth that happened in the past and become easily offended if it is mentioned because you think that you were treated unfairly（因受過委屈而變得）敏感，好生氣 **have had your 'chips** (*BrE, informal*) to be in a situation in which you are certain to be defeated or killed 注定要失敗（或完蛋） **when the chips are 'down** (*informal*) used to refer to a difficult situation in which you are forced to decide what is important to you 在危急關頭；在關鍵時刻：*I'm not sure what I'll do when the chips are down.* 我拿不準到了關鍵時刻我會幹出些什麼事來。➲ more at CASH *v.*

■ *verb* (-pp-) **1** [T, I] **~ (sth)** to damage sth by breaking a small piece off it; to become damaged in this way 打破；弄缺；被損壞：*a badly chipped saucer* 破損厲害的碟子 ◇ *She chipped one of her front teeth.* 她銹了一顆門牙。◇ *These plates chip easily.* 這些盤子容易破損。➲ picture at BROKEN **2** [T] **~ sth + adv./prep.** to cut or break small pieces off sth with a tool 切下，削下，鑿下（碎片、屑片）：*Chip away the damaged area.* 把損壞的部份鑿掉。◇ *The fossils had been chipped out of the rock.* 那些化石已從岩石上被鑿了下來。 **3** [T, I] **~ (sth)** (especially in GOLF and football (SOCCER) 尤指高爾夫球和足球) to hit or kick the ball so that it goes high in the air and then lands within a short distance 打（或踢）高球；近穴擊球 **4** [T] **~ potatoes** (*BrE*) to cut potatoes into long thin pieces and fry them in deep oil 將（土豆）切條油炸 **5** [T] **~ sth** to put a MICROCHIP under the skin of a dog or other animal so that it can be identified if it is lost or stolen（為辨認而在狗或其他動物的皮下）植入微芯片

PHR V **,chip a'way at sth** to keep breaking small pieces off sth 不停地削（或鑿）：*He was chipping away at the stone.* 他不停地鑿那塊石頭。◇ (*figurative*) *They chipped away at the power of the government* (= gradually made it weaker). 他們不斷削弱政府的權力。 **,chip 'in (with sth)** (*informal*) **1** to join in or interrupt a conversation; to add sth to a conversation or discussion 插話；插嘴；（對談話或討論）作補充：*Pete and Anne chipped in with suggestions.* 皮特和安妮插話提出了建議。◇ **+ speech** *'That's different,' she chipped in.* "那可不一樣。"她插嘴說道。 **2** (also **,chip 'in sth**) to give some money so that a group of people can buy sth together 湊份子 SYN **contribute**：*If everyone chips in we'll be able to buy her a really nice present.* 如果大家都湊錢，我們就能給她買件很好的禮物。◇ *We each chipped in (with) £5.* 我們每人湊了 5 英鎊。 **,chip 'off | ,chip sth↔'off** to damage sth by breaking a small piece off it; to be damaged in this way（小塊地）損壞，毀壞，剝落，被損壞，被毀壞：*He chipped off a piece of his tooth.* 他銹缺了一點牙齒。◇ *The paint had chipped off.* 油漆已經剝落。

,chip and 'PIN (also **chip and pin**) *noun* [U] a system of paying for sth with a credit card or DEBIT CARD in which the card has information stored on it in the form of a MICROCHIP and you prove your identity by typing a number (your PIN) rather than by signing your name 芯片卡付款系統，智能卡付款系統（信用卡或借記卡上帶有貯存信息的微型芯片，付款時輸入密碼即可）：*Chip and PIN is designed to combat credit card fraud.* 智能卡系統是專為防止信用卡詐騙設計的。

chip·board /'tʃɪpbɔːd; *NAmE* -bɔːrd/ *noun* [U] a type of board that is used for building, made of small pieces of wood that are pressed together and stuck with glue 刨花板；碎木膠合板

'chip card *noun* a plastic card on which information is stored in the form of a MICROCHIP 芯片卡；智能卡：

Chip cards will be the money of the future. 智能卡將是未來的貨幣。

chip·munk /ˈtʃɪpmʌŋk/ *noun* a small N American animal of the SQUIRREL family, with light and dark marks on its back 花鼠，金花鼠，花栗鼠（棲於北美，屬松鼠科）

chipo·lata /ˌtʃɪpəˈlɑːtə/ *noun* (*especially BrE*) a small thin SAUSAGE 契普拉塔小香腸

chip·per /ˈtʃɪpə(r)/ *adj., noun*

▪ *adj.* (*informal*) cheerful and lively 生氣勃勃的

▪ *noun* **1** a machine which cuts wood into very small pieces 木材削片機 **2** a device which cuts potatoes into chips/fries 土豆條機；薯條機 **3** (*ScotE, IrishE, informal*) a chip shop 薯條店

chip·pings /ˈtʃɪpɪŋz/ *noun* [pl.] (*BrE*) small pieces of stone or wood 碎石；木屑

chippy /ˈtʃɪpi/ *noun, adj.*

▪ *noun* (also **chip·pie**) (*pl.* **-ies**) (*BrE, informal*) **1** = CHIP SHOP **2** = CARPENTER

▪ *adj.* (*informal*) (of a person 人) getting annoyed or offended easily 易怒的；易生氣的

ˈchip shop (also *informal* **chip·py**, **chip·pie**) *noun* (in Britain) a shop that cooks and sells fish and chips and other fried food for people to take home and eat（在英國以炸魚薯條為主的）油炸食品外賣店

ˈchip shot *noun* = CHIP (8)

chiro·mancy /ˈkaɪrəʊmænsi; *NAmE* ˈkaɪroʊ-/ *noun* [U] the practice of telling what will happen in the future by looking at the lines on sb's PALMS 手相術 **SYN** **palm·istry** ▸ **chiro·man·cer** /ˈkaɪrəʊmænsə(r); *NAmE* ˈkaɪroʊ-/ *noun*

chir·opo·dist /kɪˈrɒpədɪst; *NAmE* kɪˈrɑːp-/ (*especially BrE*) (*NAmE* usually **po·dia·trist**) *noun* a person whose job is the care and treatment of people's feet 足病診療師；足部護理師

chir·opody /kɪˈrɒpədi; *NAmE* kɪˈrɑːp-/ (*especially BrE*) (*NAmE* usually **po·dia·try**) *noun* [U] the work of a chiropodist 足病治療

chiro·prac·tic /ˌkaɪərəʊˈpræktɪk; *NAmE* -roʊ-/ *noun* [U] the medical profession which involves treating some diseases and physical problems by pressing and moving the bones in a person's SPINE or joints; the work of a chiropractor 手療法；脊骨神經治療

chiro·prac·tor /ˈkaɪərəʊpræktə(r); *NAmE* -roʊ-/ *noun* a person whose job involves treating some diseases and physical problems by pressing and moving the bones in a person's SPINE or joints 手療法醫師；脊骨神經科醫生 ➲ compare OSTEOPATH

chirp /tʃɜːp; *NAmE* tʃɜːrp/ (also **chir·rup**) *verb* **1** [I] (of small birds and some insects 小鳥或某些昆蟲) to make short high sounds 吱喳叫；唧唧叫；發啁啾聲 **2** [I, T] to speak in a lively and cheerful way 輕鬆愉快地講（話）；喊喊喳喳地說 ▸ **chirp** (also **chir·rup**) *noun*

chirpy /ˈtʃɜːpi; *NAmE* ˈtʃɜːrpi/ *adj.* (*informal*) lively and cheerful; in a good mood 活潑快活的；輕鬆愉快的；心情好的 ▸ **chirp·ily** *adv.* **chirpi·ness** *noun* [U]

chir·rup /ˈtʃɪrəp/ *verb, noun* = CHIRP

chisel /ˈtʃɪzl/ *noun, verb*

▪ *noun* a tool with a sharp flat edge at the end, used for shaping wood, stone or metal 鑿子；錾子 ➲ VISUAL VOCAB pages V20, V41

▪ *verb* (**-ll-**, *especially US* **-l-**) **1** [T, I] **~ (sth) (+ adv./prep.)** to cut or shape wood or stone with a chisel（用鑿子）鑿，刻，雕：*A name was chiselled into the stone.* 石頭上刻着一個人名。◇ *She was chiselling some marble.* 她在雕刻大理石。 **2** [T] **~ sb (out of sth)** (*informal, especially NAmE*) to get money or some advantage from sb by cheating them 欺騙；欺詐；宰（人）：*They chiseled him out of hundreds of dollars.* 他們騙了他幾百元錢。 ▸ **chisel·ler** (*especially US* **chisel·er**) /ˈtʃɪzlə(r)/ *noun*

chis·elled (*BrE*) (*especially US* **chis·eled**) /ˈtʃɪzld/ *adj.* (of a person's face 人的臉部) having clear strong features 輪廓鮮明的

chi-square test /ˌkaɪ ˈskweə test; *NAmE* ˈskwer/ *noun* (*statistics* 統計) a calculation that is used to test how well a set of data fits the results that were expected according to a theory * X^2 檢驗；卡方檢驗

chit /tʃɪt/ *noun* (*BrE*) **1** a short written note, signed by sb, showing an amount of money that is owed, or giving sb permission to do sth 欠賬字據；欠條；（允許某人去做某事的）便條 **2** (*old-fashioned, disapproving*) a young woman or girl, especially one who is thought to have no respect for older people（尤指對長輩無禮的）毛丫頭；不知禮的年輕女子

C

ˈchit-chat *noun* [U] (*informal*) conversation about things that are not important 閒聊；聊天；閒談 **SYN** **chat**

chit·ter·lings /ˈtʃɪtəlɪŋz; *NAmE* ˈtʃɪtər-/ *noun* [pl.] pig's INTESTINES, eaten as food（食用）豬小腸

chiv·al·rous /ˈʃɪvəlrəs/ *adj.* (of men 男人) polite, kind and behaving with honour, especially towards women（尤指對女人）彬彬有禮的，殷勤的，體貼的 **SYN** **gallant** ▸ **chiv·al·rous·ly** *adv.*

chiv·alry /ˈʃɪvəlri/ *noun* [U] **1** polite and kind behaviour that shows a sense of honour, especially by men towards women（尤指男人對女人的）彬彬有禮，殷勤，體貼 **2** (in the Middle Ages) the religious and moral system of behaviour which the perfect KNIGHT was expected to follow（中世紀的）騎士制度

chives /tʃaɪvz/ *noun* [pl.] the long thin leaves of a plant with purple flowers. Chives taste like onions and are used to give flavour to food. 細香蔥，四季蔥（長細葉，開紫色花，味似洋蔥）➲ VISUAL VOCAB page V32 ▸ **chive** *adj.* [only before noun]：*a chive and garlic dressing* 細香蔥蒜泥調料

chivvy /ˈtʃɪvi/ *verb* (**chiv·vies**, **chivvy·ing**, **chiv·vied**, **chiv·vied**) **~ sb (into sth/along)** | **~ sb to do sth** (*BrE*) to try and make sb hurry or do sth quickly, especially when they do not want to do it 強求；催促：*He chivvied them into the car.* 他催促他們上車。

chla·mydia /kləˈmɪdiə/ *noun* [U] (*medical* 醫) a disease caused by bacteria, which is caught by having sex with an infected person 衣原體病（通過與病患者性交傳染）

chlor·ide /ˈklɔːraɪd/ *noun* [U, C] (*chemistry* 化) a COMPOUND of CHLORINE and another chemical element 氯化物 ➲ see also SODIUM CHLORIDE

chlor·in·ate /ˈklɔːrɪneɪt/ *verb* **~ sth** to put chlorine in sth, especially water（尤指在水中）加氯消毒 ▸ **chlor·in·ation** /ˌklɔːrɪˈneɪʃn/ *noun* [U]：*a chlorination plant* 氯氣消毒廠

chlor·ine /ˈklɔːriːn/ *noun* [U] (*symb.* **Cl**) a chemical element. Chlorine is a poisonous greenish gas with a strong smell. It is often used in swimming pools to keep the water clean. 氯；氯氣

chloro·fluoro·car·bon /ˌklɔːrəʊˈflʊərəʊkɑːbən; *NAmE* ˌklɔːroʊˈflʊroʊkɑːrbən/ *noun* (*chemistry* 化) a CFC; a COMPOUND containing CARBON FLUORINE and CHLORINE that is harmful to the OZONE LAYER 氯氟化碳，含氯氟烴（有害於臭氧層）

chloro·form /ˈklɒrəfɔːm; *NAmE* ˈklɔːrəfɔːrm/ *noun* [U] (*symb.* $CHCl_3$) a clear liquid used in the past in medicine, etc. to make people unconscious, for example before an operation 氯仿，三氯甲烷（舊時醫用麻醉劑）

chloro·phyll /ˈklɒrəfɪl; *NAmE* ˈklɔːr-/ *noun* [U] the green substance in plants that absorbs light from the sun to help them grow 葉綠素 ➲ see also PHOTOSYNTHESIS

chloro·plast /ˈklɒrəplɑːst; *NAmE* ˈklɔːrəplæst/ *noun* (*biology* 生) the structure in plant cells that contains CHLOROPHYLL and in which PHOTOSYNTHESIS takes place 葉綠體

choc /tʃɒk; *NAmE* tʃɑːk/ *noun* (*BrE, informal*) a chocolate 巧克力；朱古力：*a box of chocs* 一盒巧克力糖

choca·hol·ic = CHOCOHOLIC

choccy /ˈtʃɒki; *NAmE* ˈtʃɑːki/ *noun* (*pl.* **-ies**) [U, C] (*BrE, informal*) chocolate; a sweet/candy made of chocolate 巧克力；巧克力糖果：*a box of choccies* 一盒巧克力糖果

ˈchoc ice *noun* (*BrE*) a small block of ice cream covered with chocolate 巧克力脆皮冰淇淋；紫雪糕

C

chock-a-block /ˌtʃɒk ə ˈblɒk; *NAmE* ˌtʃɑːk ə ˈblɑːk/ (also **chocka** /ˈtʃɒkə; *NAmE* ˈtʃɑːkə/) *adj.* [not before noun] **~ (with sth/sb)** (*BrE, informal*) very full of things or people pressed close together 充滿；擠滿；塞滿：*The shelves were chock-a-block with ornaments.* 架子上堆滿了裝飾品。◇ *It was chock-a-block in town today* (= full of people). 今天城裏人多得不得了。

chock-full /ˌtʃɒk ˈfʊl; *NAmE* ˌtʃɑːk/ *adj.* [not before noun] **~ (of sth/sb)** (*informal*) completely full 塞滿；擠滿；充滿

choco·hol·ic (also **choca·hol·ic**) /ˌtʃɒkəˈhɒlɪk; *NAmE* ˌtʃɑːkəˈhɑːlɪk; -ˈhɔːlɪk/ *noun* (*informal*) a person who likes chocolate very much and eats a lot of it 嗜食巧克力的人

choc·olate 0ᵐ /ˈtʃɒklət; *NAmE* ˈtʃɑːk-; ˈtʃɔːk-/ *noun* **1** 0ᵐ [U] a hard brown sweet food made from COCOA BEANS, used in cooking to add flavour to cakes, etc. or eaten as a sweet/candy 巧克力；朱古力：*a **bar/piece of chocolate*** 一條／一塊巧克力 ◇ *a chocolate cake* 巧克力蛋糕 ◇ *a chocolate factory* 巧克力製造廠 ➲ see also MILK CHOCOLATE, PLAIN CHOCOLATE **2** 0ᵐ [C] a sweet/candy that is made of or covered with chocolate 巧克力糖；夾心巧克力糖：*a box of chocolates* 一盒巧克力糖 **3** [U, C] (*BrE*) = HOT CHOCOLATE：*a mug of drinking chocolate* 一杯巧克力飲料 ➲ compare COCOA **4** [U] a dark brown colour 深褐色；巧克力色

ˈ**chocolate-box** *adj.* [only before noun] (*BrE*) (especially of places 尤指地方) very pretty, but in a way that does not seem real 如糖罐上描繪的；華麗但不真實的；花裏胡哨的：*a chocolate-box village* 裝飾得花裏胡哨的村莊

choice 0ᵐ /tʃɔɪs/ *noun, adj.*

■ ***noun*** **1** 0ᵐ [C] **~ (between A and B)** an act of choosing between two or more possibilities; something that you can choose 選擇；挑選；抉擇：*women forced to make a choice between family and career* 被迫在家庭和事業之間作出抉擇的婦女 ◇ *We are faced with a difficult choice.* 我們面臨着困難的抉擇。◇ *We aim to help students make more informed career choices.* 我們旨在幫助學生作出更有依據的職業抉擇。◇ *There is a wide range of choices open to you.* 你有很多選擇。➲ SYNONYMS at OPTION **2** 0ᵐ [U, sing.] the right to choose or the possibility of choosing 選擇權；選擇的可能性：*If I had the choice, I would stop working tomorrow.* 如果讓我選擇，我明天就停止工作。◇ *He **had no choice** but to leave* (= this was the only thing he could do). 除了離去，他別無選擇。◇ *She's going to do it. She doesn't have **much choice**, really, does she?* 她就要做那件事了。她真的沒有多少選擇的餘地了，不是嗎？◇ *This government is committed to extending parental choice in education.* 本屆政府承諾擴大父母在教育方面的選擇權。**3** 0ᵐ [C] a person or thing that is chosen 入選者；被選中的東西：*She's the obvious choice for the job.* 她是這個職位最合適的人選。◇ *Hawaii remains a popular choice for winter vacation travel.* 夏威夷一直是深受人們青睞的冬季假日旅遊勝地。◇ *This colour wasn't my first choice.* 這種顏色並非我的首選。◇ *She wouldn't be my choice as manager.* 我不會選中她做經理。**4** 0ᵐ [sing., U] the number or range of different things from which to choose 供選擇的品種；可選的範圍：*The menu has a good choice of desserts.* 菜單上有多種甜食可供選擇。◇ *There wasn't **much choice** of colour.* 可供選擇的顏色不多。➲ see also HOBSON'S CHOICE, MULTIPLE-CHOICE

IDM **by ˈchoice** because you have chosen 出於自己的選擇：*I wouldn't go there by choice.* 讓我選擇，我不會去那裏。**of ˈchoice (for sb/sth)** (used after a noun 用於名詞後) that is chosen by a particular group of people or for a particular purpose 精選的；特選的：*It's the software of choice for business use.* 這是商務專用軟件。**of your ˈchoice** that you choose yourself 自己選擇（或選定）的：*First prize will be a meal for two at the restaurant of your choice.* 頭等獎是一頓雙人餐，餐館任選。➲ more at PAY *v.*, SPOILT

■ ***adj.*** (**choicer**, **choicest**) [only before noun] **1** (especially of food 尤指食物) of very good quality 優質的；上等的；優選的 **2** (*NAmE*) (of meat 肉) of very good, but not the highest, quality（質量）中上級的 **3 ~ words/phrases** carefully chosen words or phrases 字斟句酌的；仔細推敲過的：*She summed up the situation in a few choice phrases.* 她簡明扼要地總結了情況。◇ (*humorous*) *He used some pretty choice* (= rude or offensive) *language.* 他出言不遜。

Synonyms 同義詞辨析

choice

favourite • preference • selection • pick

These are all words for a person or thing that is chosen, or that is liked more than others. 以上各詞均指選中或特別喜愛的人或事物。

choice a person or thing that is chosen 指入選者、選中的東西：*She's the obvious choice for the job.* 她是這個職位最合適的人選。

favourite/favorite a person or thing that you like more than the others of the same type 指同類人或事物中最喜歡的一個：*Which one's your favourite?* 你最喜歡哪一個？

preference a thing that is liked better or best 指偏愛的或最喜愛的事物：*Tastes and preferences vary from individual to individual.* 人的愛好和選擇各不相同。

FAVOURITE OR PREFERENCE? 用 favourite 還是 preference？

Your **favourites** are the things you like best, and that you have, do, listen to, etc. often; your **preferences** are the things that you would rather have or do if you can choose. * favourite 指最喜歡因而常有、常做或常聽等的事物；preference 指在可以選擇的情況下會較喜歡有或做的事物。

selection a number of people or things that have been chosen from a larger group 指從大類別中選出來的人或事物：*A selection of reader's comments are published below.* 下面選登了部份讀者的評論。

pick (*rather informal, especially NAmE*) a person or thing that is chosen 指選中的人或事物：*She was his pick for best actress.* 她是他認為最好的女演員。

PATTERNS

- sb's choice/favourite/pick **for** sth
- sb's choice/selection/pick **as** sth
- an **obvious** choice/favourite/selection
- a(n) **excellent/good/popular/fine** choice/selection

choir /ˈkwaɪə(r)/ *noun* **1** [C+sing./pl. v.] a group of people who sing together, for example in church services or public performances（教堂的）唱詩班；（公開演出的）合唱團，歌唱隊：*She sings in the school choir.* 她是校合唱隊的成員。➲ COLLOCATIONS at MUSIC **2** [C] the part of a church where the choir sits during services（教堂）唱經樓，唱詩席

choir·boy /ˈkwaɪəbɔɪ; *NAmE* ˈkwaɪərbɔɪ/, **choir·girl** /ˈkwaɪəgɜːl; *NAmE* ˈkwaɪərgɜːrl/ *noun* a boy or girl who sings in the choir of a church 唱詩班的男童（或女童）➲ see also CHORISTER

choir·mas·ter /ˈkwaɪəmɑːstə(r); *NAmE* ˈkwaɪərmæstər/ *noun* a person who trains a CHOIR to sing 唱詩班指揮；合唱團指揮

choke /tʃəʊk; *NAmE* tʃoʊk/ *verb, noun*

■ ***verb*** **1** [I, T] to be unable to breathe because the passage to your lungs is blocked or you cannot get enough air; to make sb unable to breathe（使）窒息，哽噎：*She almost **choked to death** in the thick fumes.* 她幾乎被濃煙嗆死。◇ **~ on sth** *He was choking on a piece of toast.* 他被一塊烤麵包噎得透不過氣來。◇ **~ sb** *Very small toys can choke a baby.* 很小的玩具也能使嬰兒窒息。**2** [T] **~ sb** to make sb stop breathing by squeezing their throat（掐住喉嚨）使停止呼吸，使窒息 **SYN** **strangle**：*He may have been choked or poisoned.* 他可能是被掐死或毒死的。**3** [I, T] to be unable to speak normally especially because of strong emotion; to make sb feel too emotional to speak normally（尤指感情激

動而）説不出話來；使哽咽：**~ (with sth)** *His voice was choking with rage.* 他氣得聲音哽咽。◇ **~ sth** *Despair choked her words.* 她絕望得説不出話來。◇ *'I can't bear it,' he said in a choked voice.* "我實在忍不下去了。"他聲音哽咽地説道。➲ see also CHOKED **4** [T] to block or fill a passage, space, etc. so that movement is difficult 阻塞，塞滿，堵塞（通道、空間等）：**~ sth (with sth)** *The pond was choked with rotten leaves.* 池塘被腐爛的葉子塞滿了。◇ **~ sth up (with sth)** *The roads are choked up with traffic.* 幾條馬路都在塞車。**5** [I] (*NAmE, informal*) to fail at sth, for example because you are nervous（因緊張等而）失敗，失靈，失去作用

PHR V **ˌchoke sth↔ˈback** to try hard to prevent your feelings from showing 強忍住；抑制；克制：*to choke back* **tears/anger/sobs** 強忍住眼淚／憤怒／哭泣 **ˌchoke sth↔ˈdown** to swallow sth with difficulty 硬嚥；硬吞 **ˌchoke sth↔ˈoff 1** to prevent or limit sth 阻止；制止；限制：*High prices have choked off demand.* 高昂的價格制約了需求。**2** to interrupt sth; to stop sth 打斷；停止；終止：*Her screams were suddenly choked off.* 她的尖叫聲戛然而止。**ˌchoke ˈout | choke out sth** to say sth with great difficulty because you feel a strong emotion（因感情激動而）哽咽着説，哽咽地説出某事：*He choked out a reply.* 他哽咽着回答。◇ **+ speech** *'I hate you!' she choked out.* "我恨你！"她哽咽着説道。**ˌchoke ˈup** (*NAmE*) to find it difficult to speak, because of the strong emotion that you are feeling（因感情激動而）哽咽：*She choked up when she began to talk about her mother.* 她開始談起母親時，便哽咽着説不出話來。

■ ***noun* 1** a device that controls the amount of air flowing into the engine of a vehicle（車輛發動機的）阻風門，阻塞門 **2** an act or the sound of choking 窒息；哽噎；哽噎聲；嗆住的聲音

choked /tʃəʊkt; *NAmE* tʃoʊkt/ *adj.* [not before noun] **~ up (about sth)** (*BrE* also, *informal*) **~ (about sth)** upset or angry about sth, so that you find it difficult to speak 心煩意亂，憤怒，生氣（而難以説出話來）

choker /ˈtʃəʊkə(r); *NAmE* ˈtʃoʊ-/ *noun* a piece of jewellery or narrow band of cloth worn closely around the neck 貼頸項鏈；項圈

chola /ˈtʃəʊlə; *NAmE* ˈtʃoʊlə/ *noun* (from *Spanish*) a woman from Latin America who has both Spanish and Native American ANCESTORS 拉美混血女子（西班牙人與美洲土著的混血女性後裔）➲ compare CHOLO

chol·era /ˈkɒlərə; *NAmE* ˈkɑːl-/ *noun* [U] a disease caught from infected water that causes severe DIARRHOEA and VOMITING and often causes death 霍亂

chol·er·ic /ˈkɒlərɪk; *NAmE* ˈkɑːl-/ *adj.* (*formal*) easily made angry 易怒的；暴躁的；動輒發怒的 SYN **bad-tempered**

chol·es·terol /kəˈlestərɒl; *NAmE* -rɔːl/ *noun* [U] a substance found in blood, fat and most TISSUES of the body. Too much cholesterol can cause heart disease. 膽固醇 ➲ COLLOCATIONS at DIET

cholo /ˈtʃəʊləʊ; *NAmE* ˈtʃoʊloʊ/ *noun* (*pl.* **-os**) a person from Latin America who has both Spanish and Native American ANCESTORS 拉美混血兒（西班牙人與美洲土著的混血後裔）➲ compare CHOLA

chomp /tʃɒmp; *NAmE* tʃɑːmp; tʃɔːmp/ *verb* [I, T] to eat or bite food noisily 大聲地吃（或咬、咀嚼食物）SYN **munch**：**~ (away) (on/through sth)** *She was chomping away on a bagel.* 她在嘎嘣嘎嘣地啃着一個硬麪包圈。◇ **~ sth** *He* **chomped his way** *through two hot dogs.* 他呼哧呼哧地吃掉了兩個熱狗。

choo-choo /ˈtʃuːtʃuː/ *noun* (*pl.* **choo-choos**) a child's word for a train（兒語）火車

chook /tʃʊk/ *noun* (*AustralE, NZE, informal*) **1** a chicken 雞 **2** an offensive word for an older woman（含冒犯意）老太婆

choose 0-w /tʃuːz/ *verb* (**chose** /tʃəʊz; *NAmE* tʃoʊz/, **chosen** /ˈtʃəʊzn; *NAmE* ˈtʃoʊzn/)

1 0-w [I, T] to decide which thing or person you want out of the ones that are available 選擇；挑選；選取：*You choose, I can't decide.* 你來選吧，我拿不定主意。◇ *There are plenty of restaurants to choose from.* 有許多餐館可供選擇。◇ **~ between A and/or B** *She had to choose between staying in the UK or going home.* 她不得不在留在英國和回國之間作出選擇。◇ **~ sth** *Sarah chose her words carefully.* 薩拉措辭謹慎。◇ *This site has been chosen for the new school.* 這塊場地已被選作新學校的校址。◇ **~ A from B** *We have to choose a new manager from a shortlist of five candidates.* 我們得從最終人選名單上的五位候選人中選出一個新經理。◇ **~ sb/sth as/for sth** *He chose banking as a career.* 他選中銀行業為職業。◇ *We chose Phil McSweeney as/for chairperson.* 我們選菲爾•麥克斯威尼當主席。◇ **~ whether, what, etc. …** *You'll have to choose whether to buy it or not.* 買還是不買，你得作出選擇。◇ **~ to do sth** *We chose to go by train.* 我們選擇乘火車去。◇ **~ sb to be/do sth** *We chose Phil McSweeney to be chairperson.* 我們選菲爾•麥克斯威尼當主席。**2** 0-w [I, T] to prefer or decide to do sth 寧願；情願；決定：*Employees can retire at 60 if they choose.* 如果雇員願意的話，可在 60 歲退休。◇ **~ to do sth** *Many people choose not to marry.* 許多人情願不結婚。➲ see also CHOICE *n.*

IDM **there is nothing/not much/little to choose between A and B** there is very little difference between two or more things or people 不相上下；難分高低；相差無幾 ➲ more at PICK *v.* ➲ SYNONYMS at next page

chooser /ˈtʃuːzə(r)/ *noun* IDM see BEGGAR *n.*

choosy /ˈtʃuːzi/ *adj.* (**choos·ier**, **choosi·est**) (*informal*) careful in choosing; difficult to please 精挑細選的；愛挑剔的；難以取悦的 SYN **fussy, picky**：*I'm very choosy about my clothes.* 我對自己的衣着很講究。

chop 0-w /tʃɒp; *NAmE* tʃɑːp/ *verb, noun*

■ ***verb* (-pp-) 1** 0-w to cut sth into pieces with a sharp tool such as a knife 切碎；剁碎；砍；劈：**~ sth** *He was chopping logs for firewood.* 他在把原木劈成木柴。◇ *Add the finely chopped onions.* 加入切碎的洋葱。◇ **~ sth (up) (into sth)** *Chop the carrots up into small pieces.* 把胡蘿蔔切成小塊。◇ (*figurative*) *The country was chopped up into small administrative areas.* 這個國家被劃分為若干小的行政區。➲ COLLOCATIONS at COOKING ➲ VISUAL VOCAB page V28 **2** [usually passive] **~ sth (from sth) (to sth)** (*informal*) to reduce sth by a large amount; to stop sth（大幅度地）削減，降低；取消；終止 SYN **cut**：*The share price was chopped from 50 pence to 20 pence.* 股價由每股 50 便士猛降至 20 便士。**3 ~ sb/sth** to hit sb/sth with a short downward stroke or blow 向下猛擊

IDM **ˌchop and ˈchange** (*BrE, informal*) to keep changing your mind or what you are doing 變化無常；反覆變換

PHR V **ˈchop (away) at sth** to aim blows at sth with a heavy sharp tool such as an AXE 對準…砍去（或猛擊）**ˌchop sth↔ˈdown** 0-w to make sth, such as a tree, fall by cutting it at the base with a sharp tool 砍伐，伐倒（如樹木）**ˌchop sth↔ˈoff (sth)** 0-w to remove sth by cutting it with a sharp tool 砍掉；砍下；砍斷：*He chopped a branch off the tree.* 他從那棵樹上砍下一根樹枝。◇ (*informal*) *Anne Boleyn had her head chopped off.* 安妮•博林被斬首。

■ ***noun* 1** [C] a thick slice of meat with a bone attached to it, especially from a pig or sheep 豬（或羊等）排：*a* **pork/lamb chop** 豬排；羊排 **2** [C] an act of cutting sth with a quick downward movement using an AXE or a knife 砍；劈；剁 **3** [C] an act of hitting sb/sth with the side of your hand in a quick downward movement 掌劈：*a karate chop* 空手道中的掌劈 **4 chops** [pl.] (*informal*) the part of a person's or an animal's face around the mouth（人或動物的）嘴周圍的地方：*The dog sat licking its chops.* 那隻狗坐着在舔嘴。

IDM **get/be given the ˈchop** (*BrE, informal*) **1** (of a person 人) to be dismissed from a job 被解雇；被撤職：*The whole department has been given the chop.* 整個部門的員工都已被解雇。**2** (of a plan, project, etc. 計劃、工程等) to be stopped or ended 被取消；被終止：*Three more schemes have got the chop.* 又有三個方案遭斧削了。**be for the ˈchop** (*BrE, informal*) **1** (of a person 人) to be likely to be dismissed from a job 可能遭裁員：*Who's next for the chop?* 下一個輪到誰被裁員？**2** (of a plan, project, etc. 計劃、工程等) to be likely to be stopped or ended 可能被取消（或終止）**not much**

C

'chop (*AustralE, NZE, informal*) not very good or useful 不算好的；不太有用的

,chop-'chop *exclamation* (*BrE, informal*) hurry up! 快，趕快：*Chop-chop! We haven't got all day!* 快！快！我們的時間不多！ **ORIGIN** From pidgin English based on a Chinese word for 'quick'. 源自漢語"快"字的洋涇浜英語。

chop·per /'tʃɒpə(r); *NAmE* 'tʃɑːp-/ *noun* **1** [C] (*informal*) = HELICOPTER **2** [C] a large heavy knife or small AXE 大砍刀；小斧頭 **3** [C] (*NAmE*) a type of motorcycle with a very long piece of metal connecting the front wheel to the HANDLEBARS 長前叉摩托車 **4 choppers** [pl.] (*informal*) teeth 牙齒

'chopping board (*BrE*) (*NAmE* **'cutting board**) *noun* a board made of wood or plastic used for cutting meat or vegetables on 砧板；切菜板 ➲ **VISUAL VOCAB** page V26

Synonyms 同義詞辨析

choose

select • pick • decide • opt • go for

These words all mean to decide which thing or person you want out of the ones that are available. 以上各詞均含選擇、挑選人或物之意。

choose to decide which thing or person you want out of the ones that are available 指選擇、選取人或物：*You choose—I can't decide.* 你來選吧，我拿不定主意。

select [often passive] to choose sb/sth, usually carefully, from a group of people or things 指仔細選擇、挑選：*He was selected for the team.* 他已入選進隊了。◇ *a randomly selected sample of 23 schools* 隨機抽選的 23 所學校

pick (*rather informal*) to choose sb/sth from a group of people or things 指選擇、挑選：*She picked the best cake for herself.* 她為自己挑了一塊最好的蛋糕。

CHOOSE, SELECT OR PICK? 用 choose、select 還是 pick？

Choose is the most general of these words and the only one that can be used without an object. When you **select** sth, you choose it carefully, unless you actually say that it is *selected randomly/at random*. **Pick** is a more informal word and often a less careful action, used especially when the choice being made is not very important. * choose 是以上各詞中最通用的詞，也是唯一可以不帶賓語的詞。select 表示仔細挑選，除非表明 select randomly/at random（隨機選取）。pick 較非正式，常指隨意挑選，尤用於所作選擇不甚重要的事情。

decide to choose between two or more possibilities 指在兩個或更多可能的情況中作出抉擇、決定、選擇：*We're still trying to* ***decide on*** *a venue.* 我們仍在設法選定一個聚會地點。

opt to choose to take or not to take a particular course of action 指選擇是否採取某種行動：*After graduating she opted for a career in music.* 畢業後她選擇了從事音樂工作。◇ *After a lot of thought, I* ***opted against*** *buying a motorbike.* 經過反複考慮，我決定不買摩托車。

go for sth (*rather informal*) to choose sth 指選擇某物：*I think I'll go for the fruit salad.* 我想要水果色拉。

PATTERNS

- to choose/select/pick/decide **between** A and/or B
- to choose/select/pick A **from** B
- to opt/go **for** sb/sth
- to choose/decide/opt **to do sth**
- to choose/select/pick sb/sth **carefully/at random**
- **randomly** chosen/selected/picked

choppy /'tʃɒpi; *NAmE* 'tʃɑːpi/ *adj.* (**chop·pier, chop·pi·est**) **1** (of the sea, etc. 海洋等) with a lot of small waves; not calm 波浪起伏的；不平靜的：*choppy waters* 波浪起伏的水面 **2** (*NAmE, disapproving*) (of a style of writing 寫作文體) containing a lot of short sentences and changing topics too often 不連貫的；支離破碎的

chop·stick /'tʃɒpstɪk; *NAmE* 'tʃɑːp-/ *noun* [usually pl.] either of a pair of thin sticks that are used for eating with, especially in some Asian countries 筷子 ➲ **VISUAL VOCAB** page V22 ➲ picture at STICK

chop suey /,tʃɒp 'suːi; *NAmE* ,tʃɑːp/ *noun* [U] a Chinese-style dish of small pieces of meat fried with vegetables and served with rice 炒雜碎（中式菜，碎肉和蔬菜一起炒後配米飯吃）

choral /'kɔːrəl/ *adj.* connected with, written for or sung by a CHOIR (= a group of singers) 唱詩班的；為唱詩班譜寫的；由唱詩班演唱的；合唱的：*choral music* 合唱音樂

chor·ale /kɒ'rɑːl; *NAmE* kə'ræl; -'rɑːl/ *noun* **1** a piece of church music sung by a group of singers 眾讚歌 **2** (*especially NAmE*) a group of singers; a CHOIR 合唱隊；唱詩班

chord /kɔːd; *NAmE* kɔːrd/ *noun* **1** (*music* 音) two or more notes played together 和弦；和音 **2** (*mathematics* 數) a straight line that joins two points on a curve 弦 ➲ **VISUAL VOCAB** page V71 ➲ see also VOCAL CORDS
IDM **strike/touch a 'chord (with sb)** to say or do sth that makes people feel sympathy or enthusiasm 引起同情（或共鳴）：*The speaker had obviously struck a chord with his audience.* 講演者顯然已引起了聽眾的共鳴。

chore /tʃɔː(r)/ *noun* **1** a task that you do regularly 日常事務；例行工作：*doing the* ***household/domestic chores*** 幹家務雜活 ➲ **SYNONYMS** at TASK **2** an unpleasant or boring task 令人厭煩的任務；乏味無聊的工作：*Shopping's a real chore for me.* 對我來說，購物真是件苦差事。

cho·rea /kə'rɪə/ *noun* [U] (*medical* 醫) a condition in which parts of the body make quick sudden movements that cannot be controlled 舞蹈症（身體部位不自主地抽動）

choreo·graph /'kɒriəgrɑːf; -græf; *NAmE* 'kɔːriəgræf/ *verb* **~ sth** to design and arrange the steps and movements for dancers in a BALLET or a show （為芭蕾舞或表演）設計舞蹈動作，編舞：(*figurative*) *There was some carefully choreographed flag-waving as the President drove by.* 總統的車經過時，人們按精心編排的動作揮舞着旗幟。

chore·og·raphy /,kɒri'ɒgrəfi; *NAmE* ,kɔːri'ɑːg-/ *noun* [U] the art of designing and arranging the steps and movements in dances, especially in BALLET; the steps and movements in a particular ballet or show （尤指芭蕾舞的）編舞藝術，舞蹈設計 ▶ **chore·og·raph·er** /,kɒri'ɒgrəfə(r); *NAmE* ,kɔːri'ɑːg-/ *noun* **choreo·graph·ic** /,kɒriə'græfɪk; *NAmE* ,kɔːriə-/ *adj.*

chor·ic /'kɔːrɪk; *BrE* also 'kɒrɪk/ *adj.* (*technical* 術語) relating to a CHORUS that is spoken in a play, etc. 合唱的；合唱曲的

chor·is·ter /'kɒrɪstə(r); *NAmE* 'kɔːr-; 'kɑːr-/ *noun* a person, especially a boy, who sings in the CHOIR of a church 唱詩班的成員（尤指男童）

chor·izo /tʃə'riːzəʊ; *NAmE* -zoʊ/ *noun* [U, C] (*pl.* **-os**) (from *Spanish*) a spicy Spanish or Latin American SAUSAGE 西班牙（或拉美）辣味香腸

chor·tle /'tʃɔːtl; *NAmE* 'tʃɔːrtl/ *verb* [I, T] to laugh loudly with pleasure or because you are amused 開懷大笑；高興地咯咯笑；哈哈大笑：*Gill chortled with delight.* 吉爾高興得哈哈大笑。▶ **chor·tle** *noun*

chorus /'kɔːrəs/ *noun, verb*
■ *noun* **1** [C] part of a song that is sung after each VERSE 副歌 **SYN** **refrain**：*Everyone joined in the chorus.* 唱到副歌時，大家都跟着齊唱起來。**2** [C] a piece of music, usually part of a larger work, that is written for a CHOIR (= a group of singers) 合唱曲：*the Hallelujah Chorus* 哈利路亞合唱曲 **3** [C+sing./pl. v.] (often in names 常用於名稱) a large group of singers 合唱團；歌詠隊 **SYN** **choir**：*the Bath Festival Chorus* 巴斯音樂節大合唱團 **4** [C+sing./pl. v.] a group of performers who sing

and dance in a musical show 歌舞隊： *the chorus line* (= a line of singers and dancers performing together) 排成一排同台表演的歌舞演員 **5 a ~ of sth** [sing.] the sound of a lot of people expressing approval or disapproval at the same time 齊聲，異口同聲（表示同意或不同意）：*a **chorus of praise/complaint*** 一片讚揚聲／抱怨聲 ◇ *a chorus of voices calling for her resignation* 異口同聲要求她辭職 ➲ see also DAWN CHORUS **6** [sing.+sing./pl. v.] (in ancient Greek drama 古希臘戲劇) a group of performers who comment together on the events of the play 歌隊，合唱隊（對劇情加以評論） **7** [sing.] (especially in 16th century drama 尤指在 16 世紀的戲劇中) an actor who speaks the opening and closing words of the play 開場白和收場白的朗誦演員

IDM **in chorus** all together 一起；一齊；同時 SYN **in unison**：*'Thank you,' they said in chorus.* “謝謝。”他們齊聲説道。

■ ***verb* ~ sth** to sing or say sth all together 合唱；齊聲説；異口同聲地説：*'Hello, Paul,' they chorused.* “你好，保羅。”他們齊聲問候道。

'chorus girl *noun* a girl or young woman who is a member of the chorus in a musical show, etc. 合唱團女成員

chose *past tense* of CHOOSE

chosen *past part.* of CHOOSE

chough /tʃʌf/ *noun* a bird of the CROW family, with blue-black feathers and red legs 山鴉

choux pastry /ˌʃuː ˈpeɪstri/ *noun* [U] a type of very light PASTRY made with eggs 泡夫酥麵

chow /tʃaʊ/ *noun* **1** [U] (*slang*) food 吃的東西 **2** (also **'chow chow**) [C] a dog with long thick hair, a curled tail and a blue-black tongue, originally from China 雄獅狗（原產中國，毛厚長，尾捲曲，舌藍黑色）

chow·der /ˈtʃaʊdə(r)/ *noun* [U] a thick soup made with fish and vegetables 雜燴羹湯（用魚加蔬菜烹製）：*clam chowder* 蛤肉菜湯 ➲ see also BISQUE

chowk /tʃaʊk/ *noun* (*IndE*) an open area with a market at a place where two roads meet in a city （城市交叉路口處的）集市廣場：*Chandni Chowk* 昌德尼集市

chow mein /ˌtʃaʊ ˈmeɪn/ *noun* [U] a Chinese-style dish of fried NOODLES served with small pieces of meat and vegetables （中國）炒麵：*chicken chow mein* 雞肉炒麵

Chrimbo (also **Crimbo**) /ˈkrɪmbəʊ; *NAmE* -boʊ/ *noun* [U] (*BrE, informal*) Christmas 聖誕節

Chris·sake /ˈkraɪseɪk/ (also **Chris·sakes** /-seɪks/) *noun* [U] (*taboo, informal*)

IDM **for 'Chrissake** a swear word that many people find offensive, used to show that you are angry, annoyed or surprised （很多人認為含冒犯意，表示生氣、惱火或吃驚）天哪，上帝：*For Chrissake, listen!* 天哪，聽！

Christ /kraɪst/ (also **Jesus**, **ˌJesus 'Christ**) *noun, exclamation*

■ ***noun*** the man that Christians believe is the son of God and on whose teachings the Christian religion is based 基督；耶穌基督

■ ***exclamation*** (*taboo, informal*) a swear word that many people find offensive, used to show that you are angry, annoyed or surprised （很多人認為含冒犯意，表示憤怒、煩惱或驚訝）天哪：*Christ! Look at the time—I'm late!* 天哪！看看時間，我遲到了！

chris·ten /ˈkrɪsn/ *verb* **1** to give a name to a baby at his or her baptism to welcome him or her into the Christian Church （施洗時）為…命名；給…施洗：**~ sb + noun** *The child was christened Mary.* 這孩子受洗時取名瑪麗。◇ **~ sb** *Did you have your children christened?* 你的孩子都受洗了嗎？ **2 ~ sb/sth (+ noun)** to give a name to sb/sth 給…取名（或命名）：*This area has been christened 'Britain's last wilderness'.* 這個地區被命名為“英國最後的荒野”。◇ *They christened the boat 'Oceania'.* 他們把這條船命名為“大洋洲號”。 **3 ~ sth** (*informal*) to use sth for the first time 首次使用

Chris·ten·dom /ˈkrɪsndəm/ *noun* [U] (*old-fashioned*) all the Christian people and countries of the world （全世界的）基督教徒，信奉基督教的國家

chris·ten·ing /ˈkrɪsnɪŋ/ *noun* a Christian ceremony in which a baby is officially named and welcomed into the Christian Church （基督教的）洗禮 ➲ compare BAPTISM

Chris·tian /ˈkrɪstʃən/ *adj., noun*

■ ***adj.* 1** based on or believing the teachings of Jesus Christ 基督教的；信奉基督教的：*the **Christian Church/faith/religion*** 基督教會；基督教的信仰；基督教 ◇ *She had a Christian upbringing.* 她從小接受基督教教育。◇ *a Christian country* 信奉基督教的國家 **2** connected with Christians 基督教徒的：*the Christian sector of the city* 城市的基督教徒區 **3** (also **christian**) showing the qualities that are thought of as typical of a Christian; good and kind 有基督教徒品行的；慈善的；仁慈的；友愛的

■ ***noun*** a person who believes in the teachings of Jesus Christ or has been BAPTIZED in a Christian church 基督徒；基督教徒：*Only 10% of the population are now practising Christians.* 現在僅有 10% 的人口是熱心基督教教徒。

the 'Christian era *noun* [sing.] the period of time that begins with the birth of Christ 基督紀元；公元

Chris·tian·ity /ˌkrɪstiˈænəti/ *noun* [U] the religion that is based on the teachings of Jesus Christ and the belief that he was the son of God 基督教

'Christian name *noun* (*BrE*) (in Western countries) a name given to sb when they are born or when they are CHRISTENED; a personal name, not a family name （西方人的）聖名，教名，洗禮名：*We're all on Christian name terms here.* 我們這裏所有的人都用教名相互稱呼。

ˌChristian 'Science *noun* [U] the beliefs of a religious group called **the Church of Christ, Scientist**, which include the belief that the physical world is not real and that you can cure illness only by prayer 基督教科學（基督教科學派的信仰，認為客觀世界是不真實的，只有通過祈禱才能治癒疾病） ▸ **ˌChristian 'Scientist** *noun*

Christ·mas /ˈkrɪsməs/ *noun* [U, C] **1** (also **ˌChristmas 'Day**) 25 December, the day when Christians celebrate the birth of Christ 聖誕節（12 月 25 日）：***Christmas dinner/presents*** 聖誕大餐／禮物 ➲ see also BOXING DAY **2** (also **Christ·mas·time**) the period that includes Christmas Day and the days close to it 聖誕節期間：*the **Christmas holidays/vacation*** 聖誕節假期 ◇ *Are you spending Christmas with your family?* 你和家人共度聖誕節假日嗎？◇ *Happy Christmas!* 聖誕快樂！◇ *Merry Christmas and a Happy New Year!* 聖誕快樂並恭賀新禧！ ➲ see also WHITE CHRISTMAS

'Christmas box *noun* (*BrE, old-fashioned*) a small gift, usually of money, given at Christmas to sb who provides a service during the year, for example a POSTMAN （給郵差等服務人員的）聖誕節禮品，聖誕禮金

'Christmas cake *noun* [C, U] a fruit cake covered with MARZIPAN and ICING, traditionally eaten in Britain and some other countries at Christmas （英國和其他一些國家傳統的）聖誕蛋糕（上面覆有杏仁蛋白糊和糖霜）

'Christmas card *noun* a card with a picture on it that you send to friends and relatives at Christmas with your good wishes 聖誕賀卡

ˌChristmas 'carol *noun* = CAROL

ˌChristmas 'cracker *noun* = CRACKER (2)

ˌChristmas 'Eve *noun* [U, C] the day before Christmas Day, 24 December; the evening of this day 聖誕節前一天（12 月 24 日）；聖誕夜，平安夜（12 月 24 日晚）

ˌChristmas 'pudding *noun* [C, U] a hot PUDDING (= a sweet dish) like a dark fruit cake, traditionally eaten in Britain at Christmas （英國傳統的）聖誕布丁

ˌChristmas 'stocking (also **stock·ing**) *noun* a long sock which children leave out when they go to bed on Christmas Eve so that it can be filled with presents 聖誕襪（聖誕夜小孩睡前留在外邊供裝聖誕禮物的長襪）

Christ·massy /ˈkrɪsməsi/ *adj.* (*informal*) typical of Christmas 具有聖誕節特徵的：*We put up the decorations and the tree and started to feel Christmassy at last.* 我們

C

佈置好了裝飾品和聖誕樹，這才開始感受到聖誕節的氣氛。

Christ·mas·time /ˈkrɪsməstaɪm/ *noun* [U, C] = CHRISTMAS (2)

ˈ**Christmas tree** *noun* an EVERGREEN tree, or an artificial tree that looks similar, that people cover with decorations and coloured lights and have in their homes or outside at Christmas 聖誕樹

chroma /ˈkrəʊmə; *NAmE* ˈkroʊmə/ *noun* [U] (*technical* 術語) the degree to which a colour is pure or strong, or the fact that it is pure or strong 色品（度）；色品飽和度

chro·mat·ic /krəˈmætɪk/ *adj.* (*music* 音) of the **chromatic scale**, a series of musical notes that rise and fall in SEMITONES/HALF TONES 半音（階）的 ➲ compare DIATONIC

chro·ma·tog·raphy /ˌkrəʊməˈtɒɡrəfi; *NAmE* ˌkroʊməˈtɑːɡ-/ *noun* [U] (*chemistry* 化) the separation of a mixture by passing it through a material through which some parts of the mixture travel further than others 色譜法，色層分析法，層析法（利用混合物各部份在介質中的通透距離差異而將其分離的方法）▸ **chro·ma·to·graph·ic** /ˌkrəʊˌmætəˈɡræfɪk; *NAmE* ˌkroʊ-/ *adj.*

chrome /krəʊm; *NAmE* kroʊm/ *noun* [U] a hard shiny metal used especially as a covering which protects another metal; chromium or an ALLOY of chromium and other metals 鉻；鉻合金

ˌ**chrome ˈsteel** (also ˌ**chromium ˈsteel**) *noun* [U] a hard steel containing CHROMIUM that is used for making tools 鉻鋼（用以製作工具）

chro·mium /ˈkrəʊmiəm; *NAmE* ˈkroʊ-/ *noun* [U] (*symb.* **Cr**) a chemical element. Chromium is a hard grey metal that shines brightly when polished and is often used to cover other metals in order to prevent them from RUSTING. 鉻：*chromium-plated steel* 鍍鉻的鋼

ˌ**chromium ˈsteel** *noun* [U] = CHROME STEEL

chromo·some /ˈkrəʊməsəʊm; *NAmE* ˈkroʊməsoʊm/ *noun* (*biology* 生) one of the very small structures like threads in the NUCLEI (= central parts) of animal and plant cells, that carry the GENES 染色體 ➲ see also SEX CHROMOSOME, X CHROMOSOME, Y CHROMOSOME ▸ **chromo·somal** /ˌkrəʊməˈsəʊməl; *NAmE* ˌkroʊməˈsoʊməl/ *adj.*：*chromosomal abnormalities* 染色體畸形

chron·ic /ˈkrɒnɪk; *NAmE* ˈkrɑːn-/ *adj.* **1** (especially of a disease 尤指疾病) lasting for a long time; difficult to cure or get rid of 長期的；慢性的；難以治癒（或根除）的：*chronic bronchitis/arthritis/asthma* 慢性支氣管炎／關節炎／哮喘 ◇ *the country's chronic unemployment problem* 該國長期存在的失業問題 ◇ *a chronic shortage of housing in rural areas* 農村地區住房的長期匱乏 **OPP** **acute** **2** having had a disease for a long time 長期患病的：*a* ***chronic alcoholic/depressive*** 慢性酒精中毒者；長期抑鬱症患者 **3** (*BrE, informal*) very bad 糟透的；拙劣的：*The film was just chronic.* 這部電影簡直糟透了。▸ **chron·ic·al·ly** /ˈkrɒnɪkli; *NAmE* ˈkrɑːn-/ *adv.*：*a hospital for the chronically ill* 慢性病醫院

ˌ**chronic faˈtigue syndrome** (*BrE* also **ME**, **my·al·gic en·ceph·alo·my·eli·tis**) *noun* [U] an illness that makes people feel extremely weak and tired and that can last a long time 慢性疲勞綜合症

chron·icle /ˈkrɒnɪkl; *NAmE* ˈkrɑːn-/ *noun, verb*

▪ ***noun*** a written record of events in the order in which they happened 編年史；歷史：*the Anglo-Saxon Chronicle* 《盎格魯—撒克遜人編年史》◇ *Her latest novel is a chronicle of life in a Devon village.* 她的最近一部小說是德文郡一個小村莊的生活記事。

▪ ***verb*** **~ sth** (*formal*) to record events in the order in which they happened 把…載入編年史；按事件順序記載：*Her achievements are chronicled in a new biography out this week.* 她的成就已載入本週出版的一本新傳記中。▸ **chron·ic·ler** /ˈkrɒnɪklə(r); *NAmE* ˈkrɑːn-/ *noun*

chrono- /ˈkrɒnəʊ; *NAmE* ˈkrɑːnoʊ/ *combining form* (in nouns, adjectives and adverbs 構成名詞、形容詞和副詞) connected with time 與時間有關的：*chronological* 按時間順序排列的

chrono·graph /ˈkrɒnəɡrɑːf; *NAmE* ˈkrɑːnəɡræf/ *noun* **1** a device for recording time extremely accurately 精密時計 **2** a STOPWATCH 秒錶；碼錶

chrono·logic·al /ˌkrɒnəˈlɒdʒɪkl; *NAmE* ˌkrɑːnəˈlɑːdʒ-/ *adj.* **1** (of a number of events 許多事件) arranged in the order in which they happened 按發生時間順序排列的：*The facts should be presented* ***in chronological order.*** 這些事實應按時間先後順序陳述。 **2 ~ age** (*formal*) the number of years a person has lived as opposed to their level of physical, mental or emotional development 按時間計算的（年齡）（相對於身體、智力或情感方面的發展而言）➲ compare MENTAL AGE ▸ **chrono·logic·al·ly** /-kli/ *adv.*

chron·ology /krəˈnɒlədʒi; *NAmE* -ˈnɑːl-/ *noun* (*pl.* **-ies**) [U, C] the order in which a series of events happened; a list of these events in order 按事件發生的年代排列的順序；年表：*Historians seem to have confused the chronology of these events.* 歷史學家好像把這些事件發生的年代順序攪混了。◇ *a chronology of Mozart's life* 莫扎特生平年表

chron·om·eter /krəˈnɒmɪtə(r); *NAmE* -ˈnɑːm-/ *noun* a very accurate clock, especially one used at sea 精密時計（尤用於航海）

chrys·alis /ˈkrɪsəlɪs/ *noun* (also **chrys·alid**) the form of an insect, especially a BUTTERFLY or MOTH, while it is changing into an adult inside a hard case, also called a chrysalis （尤指蝴蝶或蛾的）蛹，蛹殼 ➲ VISUAL VOCAB page V13 ➲ compare PUPA

chrys·an·the·mum /krɪˈsænθəməm; -ˈzæn-/ *noun* a large, brightly coloured garden flower that is shaped like a ball and made up of many long narrow PETALS 菊花 ➲ VISUAL VOCAB page V11

chub /tʃʌb/ *noun* (*pl.* **chub**) a FRESHWATER fish with a thick body 查布魚；圓鰭雅羅魚；白鮭；雪鰷

chubby /ˈtʃʌbi/ *adj.* (**chub·bier**, **chub·bi·est**) slightly fat in a way that people usually find attractive 胖乎乎的；圓胖的；豐滿的：***chubby cheeks/fingers/hands*** 胖乎乎的臉頰／手指／手 ▸ **chub·bi·ness** *noun* [U]

chuck /tʃʌk/ *verb, noun*

▪ ***verb*** **1** (*informal, especially BrE*) to throw sth carelessly or without much thought （隨便或貿然地）扔，拋：**~ sth (+ adv./prep.)** *He chucked the paper in a drawer.* 他把那份報紙順手丟進了抽屜。◇ **~ sb sth** *Chuck me the newspaper, would you?* 請你把報紙扔給我好嗎？➲ SYNONYMS at THROW **2** (*informal*) to give up or stop doing sth 放棄；停止；終止：**~ sth** *You haven't chucked your job!* 你還沒有辭掉你的工作！◇ **~ sth in/up** *I'm going to* ***chuck it all in*** (= give up my job) *and go abroad.* 我要離職出國。 **3 ~ sb** (*BrE, informal*) to leave your boyfriend or girlfriend and stop having a relationship with him or her 終止（或斷絕）戀愛關係：*Has he chucked her?* 他把她甩了嗎？ **4 ~ sth** (*informal*) to throw sth away 扔掉；丟棄；拋棄：*That's no good—just chuck it.* 那東西毫無用處，扔掉好啦。

IDM **chuck sb under the chin** (*old-fashioned, BrE*) to touch sb gently under the chin in a friendly way 輕撫某人的下巴 **it's ˈchucking it down** (*BrE, informal*) it's raining heavily 下著傾盆大雨；大雨滂沱

PHR V ˌ**chuck sth↔aˈway** | ˌ**chuck sth↔ˈout** (*informal*) to throw sth away 扔掉；丟棄；拋棄：*Those old clothes can be chucked out.* 那些舊衣服可以扔掉了。 ˌ**chuck sb ˈoff (sth)** | ˌ**chuck sb ˈout (of sth)** (*informal*) to force sb to leave a place or a job 攆走；解雇：*They got chucked off the bus.* 他們被趕下了公共汽車。◇ *You can't just chuck him out.* 你不能只把他解雇了事。

▪ ***noun*** **1** [C] a part of a tool such as a DRILL that can be adjusted to hold sth tightly （固定鑽頭等用的）夾盤，卡盤，夾頭 ➲ VISUAL VOCAB page V20 **2** [sing.] (*NEngE, informal*) a friendly way of addressing sb （熟人之間友好的稱呼）小親親：*What's up with you, chuck?* 你怎麼了，親愛的？ **3** (also ˌ**chuck ˈsteak**) [U] meat from the shoulder of a cow 牛肩胛肉

ˌ**chucker ˈout** *noun* (*BrE, informal*) a person employed to make people leave a social event if they have not been invited or if they cause trouble （在社交場合攆走無關人員或鬧事者的）護衛，護場員

chuckle /ˈtʃʌkl/ *verb* [I] ~ **(at/about sth)** to laugh quietly 低聲輕笑；輕聲地笑：*She chuckled at the memory.* 想起這件事她就暗自發笑。▸ **chuckle** *noun*：*She gave a chuckle of delight.* 她高興得輕聲笑了出來。

chuffed /tʃʌft/ *adj.* [not before noun] ~ **(about sth)** (*BrE, informal*) very pleased 很愉快；很高興；很滿意

chuff·ing /ˈtʃʌfɪŋ/ *adj.* (*NEngE, slang*) a mild swear word that some people use when they are annoyed, to avoid saying 'fucking' 昏了頭的，不像話的（用以替代 fucking）：*The whole chuffing world's gone mad.* 全世界的人都他媽的瘋了。

chug /tʃʌg/ *verb, noun*

■ ***verb*** (-gg-) **1** [I] (+ **adv./prep.**) to move making the sound of an engine running slowly（發動機緩慢運轉時）發出突突聲：*The boat chugged down the river.* 小船突突地沿江而下。 **2** [T] ~ **sth** (*NAmE, slang*) to drink all of sth quickly without stopping 一飲而盡；一口氣喝完

■ ***noun*** the sound made by a chugging engine（發動機的）突突聲

chukka /ˈtʃʌkə/ *noun* one of the periods of 7½ minutes into which a game of POLO is divided（馬球比賽的）一局（7 分半鐘）

chum /tʃʌm/ *noun* (*old-fashioned, informal*) a friend 朋友；友人；夥伴：*an old school chum* 老校友

chummy /ˈtʃʌmi/ *adj.* (*old-fashioned, informal*) very friendly 非常友好的；親切的 ▸ **chum·mily** *adv.* **chum·mi·ness** *noun* [U]

chump /tʃʌmp/ *noun* (*old-fashioned, informal*) a stupid person 笨蛋；傻瓜；蠢貨：*Don't be such a chump!* 別這麼蠢！

chun·der /ˈtʃʌndə(r)/ *verb* [I] (*BrE, informal*) to VOMIT 嘔吐；嘔出 ▸ **chun·der** *noun* [U]

chunk /tʃʌŋk/ *noun* **1** a thick solid piece that has been cut or broken off sth 厚塊；厚片；大塊：*a chunk of cheese/masonry* 一塊厚厚的奶酪／磚石 **2** (*informal*) a fairly large amount of sth 相當大的量：*I've already written a fair chunk of the article.* 我已寫出文章的大部份。 **3** (*linguistics* 語言) a phrase or group of words which can be learnt as a unit by sb who is learning a language. Examples of chunks are 'Can I have the bill, please?' and 'Pleased to meet you'. 話語組成部份；組塊 IDM see BLOW *v.*

chunk·ing /ˈtʃʌŋkɪŋ/ *noun* [U] (*linguistics* 語言) the use of chunks (3) in language 組塊；斷句；分拆；劃分話語成分

chunky /ˈtʃʌŋki/ *adj.* (**chunki·er**, **chunki·est**) **1** thick and heavy 粗重的；厚實的；結實的：*a chunky gold bracelet* 沉甸甸的金手鐲 ◇ (*BrE*) *a chunky sweater* 厚實的套頭毛衣 **2** having a short strong body 敦實的；矮胖的：*a squat chunky man* 矮胖敦實的男人 **3** (of food 食品) containing thick pieces（含有）厚片的，大塊的：*chunky marmalade* 橙塊果醬

chun·ter /ˈtʃʌntə(r)/ *verb* [I] ~ **(on)** (**about sth**) (*BrE, informal*) to talk or complain about sth in a way that other people think is boring or annoying 咕噥；抱怨 SYN witter

church 🔑 /tʃɜːtʃ; *NAmE* tʃɜːrtʃ/ *noun*

1 🔑 [C] a building where Christians go to worship（基督教的）教堂，禮拜堂：*a church tower* 教堂塔樓 ◇ *The procession moved into the church.* 人們排着隊走進教堂。◇ *church services* 教堂禮拜儀式 **2** 🔑 [U] a service or services in a church 禮拜；禮拜儀式：*How often do you go to church?* 你多久去教堂做一次禮拜？◇ (*BrE*) *They're at church* (= attending a church service). 他們在做禮拜。◇ (*NAmE*) *They're* **in church**. 他們在做禮拜。◇ *Church is at 9 o'clock.* 禮拜儀式 9 點鐘開始。➲ COLLOCATIONS at RELIGION ➲ note at SCHOOL **3** 🔑 **Church** [C] a particular group of Christians 基督教教派：*the Anglican Church* 聖公會 ◇ *the Catholic Church* 天主教會 ◇ *the Free Churches* 自由教會 ➲ see also DENOMINATION (1) **4** 🔑 **(the) Church** [sing.] the ministers of the Christian religion; the institution of the Christian religion 基督教牧師；基督教機構：*The Church has a duty to condemn violence.* 基督教會有義務譴責暴力。◇ *the conflict between Church and State* 教會與政府的衝突 ◇ *to go into the Church* (= to become a Christian minister) 成為基督教牧師 IDM see BROAD *adj.*

church·goer /ˈtʃɜːtʃɡəʊə(r); *NAmE* ˈtʃɜːrtʃɡoʊər/ *noun* a person who goes to church services regularly 按時去教堂做禮拜的人 ▸ **church·going** *noun* [U]

church·man /ˈtʃɜːtʃmən; *NAmE* ˈtʃɜːrtʃ-/, **church·woman** /ˈtʃɜːtʃwʊmən; *NAmE* ˈtʃɜːrtʃ-/ *noun* (*pl.* **-men** /-mən/, **-women** /-wɪmɪn/) = CLERGYMAN, CLERGYWOMAN

C

the ˌChurch of ˈEngland *noun* (*abbr.* **CE**, **C of E**) [sing.] the official Church in England, whose leader is the Queen or King 英國國教會；英格蘭聖公會

the ˌChurch of ˈScotland *noun* [sing.] the official (Presbyterian) Church in Scotland 蘇格蘭長老會

church·war·den /ˌtʃɜːtʃˈwɔːdn; *NAmE* ˌtʃɜːrtʃˈwɔːrdn/ *noun* (in the Anglican Church 聖公會) a person who is chosen by the members of a church to take care of church property and money 堂會理事（管理教會財務）

churchy /ˈtʃɜːtʃi; *NAmE* ˈtʃɜːr-/ *adj.* (**church·ier**, **churchi·est**) (*disapproving*) (of a person 人) religious in a way that involves going to church, PRAYING, etc. a lot, but often not accepting other people's views 表現得熱衷教會活動的；恪守教會儀式的

church·yard /ˈtʃɜːtʃjɑːd; *NAmE* ˈtʃɜːrtʃjɑːrd/ *noun* an area of land around a church, often used for burying people in 教堂庭院（常用作墓地）➲ compare CEMETERY, GRAVEYARD (1)

churi·dar /ˈtʃʊrɪdɑː(r)/ *noun* tight trousers worn with a KAMEEZ or KURTA（配克米茲長袍或柯泰衫穿的）緊身長褲

churl /tʃɜːl; *NAmE* tʃɜːrl/ *noun* (*old-fashioned*) a rude unpleasant person 粗魯無禮的人；粗野的人

churl·ish /ˈtʃɜːlɪʃ; *NAmE* ˈtʃɜːrlɪʃ/ *adj.* (*formal*) rude or bad-tempered 粗魯無禮的；粗野的；脾氣壞的：*It would be churlish to refuse such a generous offer.* 拒絕這樣一個慷慨的提議未免失禮。▸ **churl·ish·ly** *adv.* **churl·ish·ness** *noun* [U]

churn /tʃɜːn; *NAmE* tʃɜːrn/ *verb, noun*

■ ***verb*** **1** [I, T] if water, mud, etc. **churns**, or if sth **churns it (up)**, it moves or is moved around violently 劇烈攪動；猛烈翻騰：~ **(up)** *The water churned beneath the huge ship.* 水在巨輪下面劇烈翻滾。◇ ~ **sth (up)** *Vast crowds had churned the field into a sea of mud.* 大批大批的人把場地踩得一片泥濘。**2** [I, T] ~ **(sth)** if your stomach **churns** or if sth **churns** your stomach, you feel a strong, unpleasant feeling of worry, disgust or fear 反胃，惡心（憂慮、厭惡或恐懼的強烈感覺）：*My stomach churned as the names were read out.* 名單一宣佈，我就覺得胃裏翻騰得難受。 **3** [I, T] ~ **(sb)** (**up**) to feel or to make sb feel upset or emotionally confused（使）感到不安，心煩意亂：*Conflicting emotions churned inside him.* 相互矛盾的情緒使他感到心煩意亂。 **4** [T] ~ **sth** to turn and stir milk in a special container in order to make butter 用攪乳器攪乳（製作黃油）

PHR V **ˌchurn sth↔ˈout** (*informal*, often *disapproving*) to produce sth quickly and in large amounts（粗製濫造地）大量生產，大量炮製

■ ***noun*** **1** a machine in which milk or cream is shaken to make butter（製作黃油的）攪乳器 **2** (*BrE*) a large metal container in which milk was carried from a farm in the past（舊時）盛奶大罐，奶桶

ˈchurn rate *noun* (*business* 商) the number of people who stop using a product and change to another or who leave the company they work for and go to another 客戶流失率；員工流失率

chute /ʃuːt/ *noun* **1** a tube or passage down which people or things can slide（人或物可順勢滑下的）斜槽，溜道：***a water chute*** (= at a swimming pool) 滑水槽 ◇ *a* ***laundry/rubbish/garbage chute*** (= from the upper floors of a high building) 洗衣槽；垃圾道（高層建築上面各層用的） **2** (*informal*) = PARACHUTE

ˌChutes and ˈLadders™ *noun* [U] (*US*) a children's game played on a special board with pictures of chutes and ladders on it. Players move their pieces up the ladders to go forward and down the chutes to go back. 滑道梯子棋（兒童遊戲，棋盤上有滑道和梯子的圖案，棋子遇梯子往前走，遇滑道則往回走）➲ see also SNAKES AND LADDERS

C

chut·ney /ˈtʃʌtni/ *noun* [U] a cold thick sauce made from fruit, sugar, spices, and VINEGAR, eaten with cold meat, cheese, etc. 酸辣醬

chutz·pah /ˈxʊtspə; ˈhʊ-/ *noun* [U] (often *approving*) behaviour, or a person's attitude, that is rude or shocking but so confident that people may feel forced to admire it 無所顧忌；敢作敢為 **SYN** **nerve**

Ci *abbr.* CURIE(s) 居里（放射性活度單位）

CIA /ˌsiː aɪ ˈeɪ/ *abbr.* Central Intelligence Agency (a department of the US government which collects information about other countries, often secretly)（美國）中央情報局

cia·batta /tʃəˈbætə; -ˈbɑːtə/ *noun* [U, C] (from *Italian*) a type of Italian bread made in a long flat shape; a SANDWICH made with this type of bread 拖鞋麵包（一種意大利扁平長麵包）；拖鞋三明治

ciao /tʃaʊ/ *exclamation* (from *Italian, informal*) goodbye 再見

ci·cada /sɪˈkɑːdə; *NAmE* sɪˈkeɪdə/ *noun* a large insect with transparent wings, common in hot countries. The male makes a continuous high sound after dark by making two MEMBRANES (= pieces of thin skin) on its body VIBRATE (= move very fast). 蟬；知了

CID /ˌsiː aɪ ˈdiː/ *abbr.* Criminal Investigation Department (the department of the British police force that is responsible for solving crimes)（英國警察）刑事調查部

-cide *combining form* (in nouns 構成名詞) **1** the act of killing 殺死；毀滅：*suicide* 自殺 ◇ *genocide* 種族滅絕 **2** a person or thing that kills 殺手；殺滅劑：*insecticide* 殺蟲劑 ▸ **-cidal** (in adjectives 構成形容詞)：*homicidal* 有殺人傾向的

cider /ˈsaɪdə(r)/ *noun* **1** (*BrE*) (*NAmE* **ˈhard cider**) [U, C] an alcoholic drink made from the juice of apples 蘋果酒：***dry/sweet cider*** 乾／甜蘋果酒 ◇ *cider apples* 釀造果酒的蘋果 ◇ *a cider press* (= for squeezing the juice from apples) 蘋果榨汁器 **2** (*NAmE*) [U, C] a drink made from the juice of apples that does not contain alcohol 蘋果汁 **3** [C] a glass of cider 一杯蘋果酒（或蘋果汁）➲ compare PERRY

cigar /sɪˈɡɑː(r)/ *noun* a roll of dried TOBACCO leaves that people smoke, like a cigarette but bigger and without paper around it 雪茄煙：*cigar smoke* 雪茄煙霧 **IDM** see CLOSE[2] *adj.*

cig·ar·ette 🔑 /ˌsɪɡəˈret; *NAmE* ˈsɪɡəret/ *noun* a thin tube of paper filled with TOBACCO, for smoking 香煙；紙煙；捲煙：*a **packet/pack of cigarettes*** 一包香煙 ◇ *to light a cigarette* 點燃一支香煙

cigaˈrette end (*BrE*) (also **cigaˈrette butt** *NAmE, BrE*) *noun* the part of a cigarette that is left when sb has finished smoking it 香煙頭；煙蒂

cigaˈrette holder *noun* a narrow tube for holding a cigarette in while you are smoking 香煙煙嘴

cigaˈrette lighter *noun* = LIGHTER (1)

cigaˈrette paper *noun* a thin piece of paper in which people roll TOBACCO to make their own cigarettes 捲煙紙

cig·ar·illo /ˌsɪɡəˈrɪləʊ; *NAmE* -loʊ/ *noun* (*pl.* **-os**) a small CIGAR 小雪茄

ciggy /ˈsɪɡi/ *noun* (*pl.* **-ies**) (*informal*) a cigarette 香煙

ci·lan·tro /sɪˈlæntrəʊ; *NAmE* -troʊ/ *noun* [U] (*NAmE*) the leaves of the CORIANDER plant, used in cooking as a HERB 芫荽葉，香菜葉（用作調味）➲ VISUAL VOCAB page V32

cil·iary muscle /ˈsɪliəri mʌsl/ *noun* (*anatomy* 解) a muscle in the eye that controls how much the LENS curves 睫狀肌（控制眼睛晶狀體彎曲度）➲ VISUAL VOCAB page V59

C.-in-C. /ˌsiː ɪn ˈsiː/ *abbr.* COMMANDER-IN-CHIEF

cinch /sɪntʃ/ *noun, verb*

■ ***noun*** [sing.] (*informal*) **1** something that is very easy 很容易的事；小菜 **SYN** **doddle**：*The first question is a cinch.* 第一個問題是小菜一碟。 **2** (*especially NAmE*) a thing that is certain to happen; a person who is certain to do sth 必然發生的事；必能做某事的人：*He's a cinch to win the race.* 這場比賽他必贏無疑。

■ ***verb*** **1 ~ sth** (*especially NAmE*) to fasten sth tightly around your waist; to be fastened around sb's waist（使）緊縛在腰上 **2 ~ sth** (*NAmE*) to fasten a GIRTH around a horse（給馬）繫上肚帶 **3 ~ sth** (*NAmE, informal*) to make sth certain 弄確實；弄清楚；確保

cin·der /ˈsɪndə(r)/ *noun* [usually pl.] a small piece of ASH or partly burnt coal, wood, etc. that is no longer burning but may still be hot 灰燼；餘燼：*a cinder track* (= a track for runners made with finely crushed cinders) 用細煤渣鋪成的跑道 **IDM** see BURN *v.*

ˈcinder block (*NAmE*) (*BrE* **ˈbreeze block**) *noun* a light building block, made of sand, coal ASHES and CEMENT 煤渣砌塊，煤渣磚（用沙、煤渣和水泥製成）

Cin·der·ella /ˌsɪndəˈrelə/ *noun* [usually sing.] a person or thing that has been ignored and deserves to receive more attention 灰姑娘；未得到應有注意的人（或事物）：*For years radio has been the Cinderella of the media world.* 多年來電台廣播在傳媒界中一直不受重視。

ORIGIN From the European fairy tale about a beautiful girl, **Cinderella**, who was treated in a cruel way by her two ugly sisters. She had to do all the work and received no reward or thanks until she met and married Prince Charming. 源自歐洲童話，美麗的灰姑娘（Cinderella）受兩個醜陋的姐姐虐待，被迫幹所有的活兒，直至後來遇上了白馬王子並與之締結良緣。

cine /ˈsɪni/ *adj.* [only before noun] (*BrE*) connected with films/movies and the film/movie industry 電影的；電影業的：***a cine camera/film/photographer*** 電影攝影機／膠片／攝影師

cine·aste (also **cine·ast**) /ˈsɪniæst/ *noun* (from *French*) a person who knows a lot about films/movies and is very enthusiastic about them 電影愛好者；電影迷

cin·ema 🔑 /ˈsɪnəmə/ *noun*

1 🔑 (*BrE*) (*NAmE* **ˈmovie theater**, **theater**) [C] a building in which films/movies are shown 電影院：*the local cinema* 當地的電影院 ➲ VISUAL VOCAB page V3 **2** 🔑 **the cinema** [sing.] (*BrE*) (*NAmE* **the movies**) when you go to **the cinema** or to **the movies**, you go to a cinema/movie theater to see a film/movie（去電影院）看電影：*I used to go to the cinema every week.* 我過去每週都去看電影。 **3** 🔑 [U, sing.] (*especially BrE*) (*NAmE* usually **the movies**) films/movies as an art or an industry 電影藝術；電影製片業：*one of the great successes of British cinema* 英國電影藝術的巨大成就之一

ˈcinema-goer *noun* (*BrE*) = FILM-GOER

Cinema·Scope™ /ˈsɪnəməskəʊp; *NAmE* -skoʊp/ *noun* a method of showing films/movies which makes the picture on the screen very wide 西尼瑪斯柯普寬銀幕技術

cine·mat·ic /ˌsɪnəˈmætɪk/ *adj.* (*technical* 術語) connected with films/movies and how they are made 電影的；電影製作的：***cinematic effects/techniques*** 電影製作效果／技術

cine·ma·tog·raphy /ˌsɪnəməˈtɒɡrəfi; *NAmE* -ˈtɑːɡ-/ *noun* [U] (*technical* 術語) the art or process of making films/movies 電影攝製藝術；電影製作方法 ▸ **cine·ma·tog·raph·er** /ˌsɪnəməˈtɒɡrəfə(r); *NAmE* -ˈtɑːɡ-/ *noun* **cine·ma·tog·raph·ic** /ˌsɪnəmætəˈɡræfɪk/ *adj.*

cine·phile /ˈsɪnifaɪl/ *noun* a person who is very interested in films/movies 電影愛好者；電影迷

cinna·bar /ˈsɪnəbɑː(r)/ *noun* [U] **1** a bright red mineral that is sometimes used to give colour to things 辰砂，朱砂（可用作顏料） **2** the bright red colour of cinnabar 朱紅色

cin·na·mon /ˈsɪnəmən/ *noun* [U] the inner BARK of a SE Asian tree, used in cooking as a spice, especially to give flavour to sweet foods 肉桂皮，桂皮香料（東南亞一種樹的內層樹皮，尤用於甜食調味）➲ VISUAL VOCAB page V32

ci·pher (also **cy·pher**) /ˈsaɪfə(r)/ *noun* **1** [U, C] a secret way of writing, especially one in which a set of letters or symbols is used to represent others 密碼；暗號 **SYN** **code**：*a message in cipher* 密碼信 ➲ see also DECIPHER **2** [C] (*formal, disapproving*) a person or thing of no importance 無足輕重的人；無關緊要的東西 **3** (*BrE*) the first letters of sb's name combined in a design and used to mark things（姓名首字母的）拼合字，花押

circa /ˈsɜːkə; *NAmE* ˈsɜːrkə/ *prep.* (from *Latin*) (*abbr.* c) (used with dates 與日期連用) about 大約：*born circa 150 BC* 生於約公元前 150 年

cir·ca·dian /sɜːˈkeɪdiən; *NAmE* sɜːrˈk-/ *adj.* [only before noun] (*technical* 術語) connected with the changes in the bodies of people or animals over each period of 24 hours（每 24 小時人或動物體內變化）晝夜節律的，生理節奏的

cir·cle 0‑w /ˈsɜːkl; *NAmE* ˈsɜːrkl/ *noun, verb*

■ *noun* **1** 0‑w a completely round flat shape 圓；圓形：*Cut out two circles of paper.* 剪出兩個圓形紙塊。➲ VISUAL VOCAB page V71 ➲ see also SEMICIRCLE **2** 0‑w the line that forms the edge of a circle 圓周；圓圈：*Draw a circle.* 畫一個圓圈。◇ *She walked the horse round **in a circle**.* 她牽着馬遛圈子。➲ see also ANTARCTIC CIRCLE, ARCTIC CIRCLE, TURNING CIRCLE **3** 0‑w a thing or a group of people or things shaped like a circle 圓形物；環狀物；圈；環：*a circle of trees/chairs* 一圈樹／椅子 ◇ *The children stood in a circle.* 孩子們站成一圈。➲ see also CORN CIRCLE, CROP CIRCLE **4** (*BrE*) (also **bal·cony** *NAmE, BrE*) an upper floor of a theatre or cinema/movie theater where the seats are arranged in curved rows（劇院或電影院的）弧形樓座：*We had seats in the circle.* 我們坐的是樓座座位。➲ see also DRESS CIRCLE **5** a group of people who are connected because they have the same interests, jobs, etc.（相同興趣、職業等的人形成的）圈子，階層，界：*the family circle* 家庭圈子 ◇ *She's well known in theatrical circles.* 她在戲劇界赫赫有名。◇ *a large **circle of friends*** 一大群朋友 ➲ see also CHARMED CIRCLE, INNER CIRCLE, VICIOUS CIRCLE

IDM **come, turn, etc. full ˈcircle** to return to the situation in which you started, after a series of events or experiences（事情或經歷）兜了一圈回到原處 **go round in ˈcircles** to work hard at sth or discuss sth without making any progress 在原地繞圈子；總是回到同一個問題 **run round in ˈcircles** (*informal*) to be busy doing sth without achieving anything important or making progress 徒勞無功；瞎忙；空忙

■ *verb* **1** [I, T] to move in a circle, especially in the air（尤指在空中）盤旋，環行，轉圈：**~ (around) (above/over sb/sth)** *Seagulls circled around above his head.* 海鷗在他的頭頂上盤旋。◇ **~ sth** *The plane circled the airport to burn up excess fuel.* 飛機在機場上空盤旋以耗掉多餘的燃料。**2** [T] **~ sth** to draw a circle around sth 圍繞…畫圈；圈出；圈起：*Spelling mistakes are circled in red ink.* 拼寫錯誤都用紅筆圈了出來。

IDM **circle the ˈwagons** (*NAmE*) to join together with people who have the same ideas and beliefs as you, and avoid contact with those who do not, who may threaten or attack you（聯合理念相同者）結成統一戰線：*When your way of life is threatened you have to circle the wagons and defend yourself.* 當你的生活方式受到威脅時，你必須與他人結盟保護自己。**ORIGIN** From

Collocations 詞語搭配

Cinema/the movies 電影

Watching 觀看

- **go to/take sb to (see)** a film/movie 去／帶某人去看電影
- **go to/sit in** (*BrE*) the cinema/(*NAmE*) the (movie) theater 去／在看電影
- **rent** a film/movie/DVD 租借影片／DVD 光碟
- **download** a film/movie/video 下載電影／視頻
- **burn/copy/rip** a DVD 燒錄／複製／抄錄一張 DVD 碟片
- **see/watch** a film/movie/DVD/video/preview/trailer 觀看電影／DVD 碟片／視頻／預映／預告片

Showing 放映；播放

- **show/screen** a film/movie 放映電影
- **promote/distribute/review** a film/movie 宣傳／發行／評論電影
- (*BrE*) **be on at** the cinema 在電影院上映
- **be released on/come out on/be out on** DVD 發行 DVD
- **captivate/delight/grip/thrill** the audience 使觀眾着迷／高興／感興趣／激動
- **do well/badly** at the box office 票房好／不好
- **get a lot of/live up to the** hype 受到大肆炒作；與天花亂墜的廣告宣傳相符

Film-making 電影製作

- **write/co-write** a film/movie/script/screenplay 寫／合寫一部電影劇本
- **direct/produce/make/shoot/edit** a film/movie/sequel/video 導演／製作／拍攝／編輯電影／續集／視頻
- **make** a romantic comedy/a thriller/an action movie 拍攝一部浪漫喜劇／恐怖片／動作片
- **do/work on** a sequel/remake 拍攝續集；重拍
- **film/shoot** the opening scene/an action sequence/footage (of sth) 拍攝（…的）開場戲／一套動作／連續鏡頭
- **compose/create/do/write** the soundtrack 製作電影聲帶
- **cut/edit (out)** a scene/sequence 剪輯掉一個鏡頭／一組鏡頭

Acting 表演

- **have/get/do** an audition 試演
- **get/have/play** a leading/starring/supporting role 得以飾演／飾演主角／配角
- **play** a character/James Bond/the bad guy 飾演一個人物／詹姆斯 • 邦德／反面角色
- **act in/appear in/star in** a film/movie/remake 出演／主演一部影片／翻拍電影
- **do/perform/attempt** a stunt 做／嘗試特技表演
- **work in/make it big in** Hollywood 在好萊塢工作／取得成功
- **forge/carve/make/pursue** a career in Hollywood 在好萊塢闖出／追求一番事業

Describing films 描述電影

- the camera **pulls back/pans over sth/zooms in (on sth)** 攝影機拉回／追拍／推近…
- the camera **focuses on sth/lingers on sth** 攝影機聚焦於／長時間拍攝某物
- **shoot sb/show sb** in extreme close-up 用特寫鏡頭拍攝／表現某人
- **use odd/unusual camera angles** 採用奇特的／不同尋常的攝影機角度
- **be filmed/shot** on location/in a studio 在外景地／攝影棚拍攝
- **be set/take place** in London/in the '60s 以倫敦／60 年代為背景
- **have** a happy ending/plot twist 有美滿的結局／出人意料的情節轉折

the practice of arranging a WAGON TRAIN in a circle to defend against attack. 源自將馬拉篷車隊圍成一圈以抵禦進攻的做法。

circ·let /ˈsɜːklət; NAmE ˈsɜːrk-/ *noun* a round band made of PRECIOUS METAL, flowers, etc., worn around the head for decoration 圓箍飾環，環形飾物（用貴重金屬、花等製作，戴在頭上）

cir·cuit /ˈsɜːkɪt; NAmE ˈsɜːrkɪt/ *noun* **1** a line, route, or journey around a place 環行；環行路線：*The race ended with eight laps of a city centre circuit.* 比賽以環繞城中心跑八圈結束。◇ *The earth takes a year to make a circuit of* (= go around) *the sun.* 地球繞太陽運行一週需要一年的時間。**2** the complete path of wires and equipment along which an electric current flows 電路；線路：*an electrical circuit* 電路 ◇ *a circuit diagram* (= one showing all the connections in the different parts of the circuit) 電路圖 ➲ see also INTEGRATED CIRCUIT, PRINTED CIRCUIT, SHORT CIRCUIT **3** (in sport 體育運動) a series of games or matches in which the same players regularly take part 巡迴賽：*the women's tennis circuit* 女子網球巡迴賽 **4** a track for cars or motorcycles to race around 賽車道 **5** a series of places or events of a particular kind at which the same people appear or take part 巡迴；巡遊：*the **lecture/cabaret circuit*** 巡迴講學；卡巴萊歌舞巡迴表演 ➲ see also CLOSED-CIRCUIT TELEVISION **6** a regular journey made by a judge to hear court cases in each of the courts of law in a particular area（法官的）巡迴審判：*a circuit court/judge* 巡迴法院／法官

ˈcircuit board *noun* a board that holds electrical circuits inside a piece of electrical equipment 電路板；線路板

ˈcircuit-breaker *noun* a device that can automatically stop an electric current if it becomes dangerous（自動斷電的）斷路器

cir·cu·it·ous /səˈkjuːɪtəs; NAmE sərˈk-/ *adj.* (*formal*) (of a route or journey 路線或旅程) long and not direct 迂迴的；繞道的；曲折的 SYN **roundabout** ▸ **cir·cu·it·ous·ly** *adv.*

cir·cuit·ry /ˈsɜːkɪtri; NAmE ˈsɜːrk-/ *noun* [U] a system of electrical CIRCUITS or the equipment that forms this 電路系統；電路；電路裝置

ˈcircuit training *noun* [U] a type of training in sport in which different exercises are each done for a short time 循環訓練（輪番做不同的體育運動，每種只做很短時間）

cir·cu·lar /ˈsɜːkjələ(r); NAmE ˈsɜːrk-/ *adj.*, *noun*

■ ***adj.*** **1** shaped like a circle; round 圓形的；環形的；圓的：*a circular building* 圓形建築物 **2** moving around in a circle 環行的；繞圈的：*a circular tour of the city* 環城遊覽 **3** (of an argument or a theory 論點或理論) using an idea or a statement to prove sth which is then used to prove the idea or statement at the beginning 循環論證的（以一種觀點證明另一觀點，接着再用後一種觀點反過來去證明前一觀點）**4** (of a letter 信函) sent to a large number of people 大量送發的；傳閱的 ▸ **cir·cu·lar·ity** /ˌsɜːkjəˈlærəti; NAmE ˌsɜːrk-/ *noun* [U]：*There is a dangerous circularity about this argument.* 這個論點存在着危險的循環論證。

■ ***noun*** a printed letter, notice or advertisement that is sent to a large number of people at the same time（同時送達很多人的）印刷信函（或通知、廣告）

ˌcircular ˈsaw (*NAmE* also **ˈbuzz saw**) *noun* a SAW in the form of a metal disc that turns quickly, driven by a motor, and is used for cutting wood, etc. 圓鋸

cir·cu·late /ˈsɜːkjəleɪt; NAmE ˈsɜːrk-/ *verb* **1** [I, T] when a liquid, gas, or air **circulates** or **is circulated**, it moves continuously around a place or system（液體或氣體）環流，循環：*The condition prevents the blood from circulating freely.* 這種病會阻礙血液的暢通循環。◇ **~ sth** *Cooled air is circulated throughout the building.* 冷氣在整座大樓循環。**2** [I, T] **~ (sth)** if a story, an idea, information, etc. **circulates** or if you **circulate** it, it spreads or it is passed from one person to another 傳播；流傳；散佈：*Rumours began to circulate about his financial problems.* 有關他財務困難的謠言開始流傳開來。**3** [T] **~ sth (to sb)** to send goods or information to all the people in a group 傳送；傳遞；傳閱：*The document will be circulated to all members.* 這份文件將在所有成員間傳閱。**4** [I] to move around a group, especially at a party, talking to different people（尤指在聚會上）往來應酬，周旋

cir·cu·la·tion /ˌsɜːkjəˈleɪʃn; NAmE ˌsɜːrk-/ *noun* **1** [U] the movement of blood around the body 血液循環：*Regular exercise will improve blood circulation.* 經常鍛煉會促進血液循環。◇ *to have **good/bad circulation*** 血液循環良好／不暢 **2** [U] the passing or spreading of sth from one person or place to another 傳遞；流傳；流通：*the **circulation of money/information/ideas*** 貨幣的流通；消息的傳播；觀念的流行 ◇ *A number of forged tickets are **in circulation**.* 有一些假入場券在流通。◇ *The coins were **taken out of circulation**.* 這種硬幣已停止流通。◇ *Copies of the magazine were **withdrawn from circulation**.* 這期雜誌有不少已從市場上收回。**3** [U] the fact that sb takes part in social activities at a particular time（某段時間的）社交活動，交際：*Anne has been ill but now she's back **in circulation**.* 安妮一直生病，但現在又回來參加社交活動了。◇ *I was **out of circulation** for months after the baby was born.* 孩子出生後我有幾個月都沒有參加社交活動。**4** [C, usually sing.] the usual number of copies of a newspaper or magazine that are sold each day, week, etc.（報刊）發行量，銷售量：*a daily circulation of more than one million* 日發行量超過一百萬份 **5** [U, C] the movement of sth (for example air, water, gas, etc.) around an area or inside a system or machine（氣、水等的）環流，迴流，循環

cir·cu·la·tory /ˌsɜːkjəˈleɪtəri; NAmE ˈsɜːrkjələtɔːri/ *adj.* relating to the circulation of the blood 血液循環的

cir·cum·cise /ˈsɜːkəmsaɪz; NAmE ˈsɜːrk-/ *verb* **1 ~ sb** to remove the FORESKIN of a boy or man for religious or medical reasons（因宗教或醫學）對（男子）行割禮，環割（男子的）包皮 **2 ~ sb** to cut off part of the sex organs of a girl or woman 割除（女子的）陰蒂

cir·cum·ci·sion /ˌsɜːkəmˈsɪʒn; NAmE ˌsɜːrk-/ *noun* [U, C] the act of circumcising sb; the religious ceremony when sb, especially a baby, is circumcised 包皮環割術；陰蒂切除術；（宗教儀式尤指為嬰孩施行的）割禮

cir·cum·fer·ence /səˈkʌmfərəns; NAmE sərˈk-/ *noun* [C, U] a line that goes around a circle or any other curved shape; the length of this line 圓周；圓周長：*the circumference of the earth* 地球的周長 ◇ *The earth is almost 25 000 miles **in circumference**.* 地球的周長大約為25 000英里。➲ VISUAL VOCAB page V71 ➲ compare PERIMETER

cir·cum·flex /ˈsɜːkəmfleks; NAmE ˈsɜːrk-/ (also **ˌcircum·flex ˈaccent**) *noun* the mark placed over a vowel in some languages to show how it should be pronounced, as over the *o* in *rôle* 音調符號（標在元音字母上表發音，如 rôle 一詞中 o 字母上的符號）➲ compare ACUTE ACCENT, GRAVE², TILDE, UMLAUT

cir·cum·lo·cu·tion /ˌsɜːkəmləˈkjuːʃn; NAmE ˌsɜːrk-/ *noun* [U, C] (*formal*) using more words than are necessary, instead of speaking or writing in a clear, direct way 迂迴曲折的說法；遁詞 ▸ **cir·cum·lo·cu·tory** /ˌsɜːkəmˈlɒkjʊtəri; ˌsɜːkəmləˈkjuːtəri; NAmE ˌsɜːrkəmˈlɑːkjətɔːri/ *adj.*

cir·cum·navi·gate /ˌsɜːkəmˈnævɪɡeɪt; NAmE ˌsɜːrk-/ *verb* **~ sth** (*formal*) to sail all the way around sth, especially all the way around the world 環繞…航行；（尤指）環繞地球航行 ▸ **cir·cum·navi·ga·tion** /ˌsɜːkəmˌnævɪˈɡeɪʃn; NAmE ˌsɜːrk-/ *noun* [U]

cir·cum·scribe /ˈsɜːkəmskraɪb; NAmE ˈsɜːrk-/ *verb* **1** [often passive] **~ sth** (*formal*) to limit sb/sth's freedom, rights, power, etc. 限制，約束（自由、權利、權力等）SYN **restrict**：*The power of the monarchy was circumscribed by the new law.* 君主統治的權力受到了新法律的制約。**2 ~ sth** (*technical* 術語) to draw a circle around another shape 畫…的外接圓 ▸ **cir·cum·scrip·tion** /ˌsɜːkəmˈskrɪpʃn; NAmE ˌsɜːrk-/ *noun* [U]

cir·cum·spect /ˈsɜːkəmspekt; NAmE ˈsɜːrk-/ *adj.* (*formal*) thinking very carefully about sth before doing it, because there may be risks involved 小心謹慎的；考慮

周密的；慎重的 SYN **cautious** ▸ **cir·cum·spec·tion** /ˌsɜːkəmˈspekʃn; *NAmE* ˌsɜːrk-/ *noun* [U] **cir·cum·spect·ly** *adv.*

cir·cum·stance 0➡ AW /ˈsɜːkəmstəns; -stɑːns; -stæns; *NAmE* ˈsɜːrkəmstæns/ *noun* **1** 0➡ [C, usually pl.] the conditions and facts that are connected with and affect a situation, an event or an action 條件；環境；狀況：*The company reserves the right to cancel this agreement in certain circumstances.* 本公司保留在一定條件下取消這項協議的權利。◇ *changing social and political circumstances* 正在變化的社會和政治環境 ◇ *I know I can trust her in any circumstance.* 我知道我在任何情況下都能信任她。◇ *Police said there were no **suspicious circumstances** surrounding the boy's death.* 警方說關於男孩死亡一事沒有發現可疑的情況。◇ *The ship sank in mysterious circumstances.* 那艘船神秘地沉沒了。◇ *She never discovered the true circumstances of her birth.* 她從未弄清她身世的真相。➲ SYNONYMS at SITUATION **2** 0➡ **circumstances** [pl.] the conditions of a person's life, especially the money they have 境況；境遇；（尤指）經濟狀況：*Grants are awarded according to your **financial circumstances**.* 補助金根據經濟狀況發給。◇ ***family/domestic/personal circumstances*** 家庭／個人經濟狀況 **3** [U] (*formal*) situations and events that affect and influence your life and that are not in your control 命運；客觀環境：*a **victim of circumstance*** (= a person who has suffered because of a situation that they cannot control) 客觀環境的犧牲品 ◇ *He had to leave the country through **force of circumstance*** (= events made it necessary). 為勢所迫，他不得不離開這個國家。

IDM **in/under the ˈcircumstances** used before or after a statement to show that you have thought about the conditions that affect a situation before making a decision or a statement 在這種情況下；既然如此：*Under the circumstances, it seemed better not to tell him about the accident.* 在這種情況下，不告訴他有關這次事故的情況似乎更好。◇ *She did the job very well in the circumstances.* 她在那種情況下仍把工作幹得很出色。**in/under no circumstances** used to emphasize that sth should never happen or be allowed 決不；無論如何不：*Under no circumstances should you lend Paul any money.* 你無論如何都不能借錢給保羅。◇ *Don't open the door, in any circumstances.* 在任何情況下都不要開門。➲ more at POMP, REDUCE

cir·cum·stan·tial /ˌsɜːkəmˈstænʃl; *NAmE* ˌsɜːrk-/ *adj.* **1** (*law* 律) containing information and details that strongly suggest that sth is true but do not prove it 按情況推測的；視情況而定的；間接的：*circumstantial evidence* 情況證據 ◇ *The case against him was largely circumstantial.* 對他不利的案情大多為間接推測的。**2** (*formal*) connected with particular circumstances 與特定條件（或環境、情況）有關的：*Their problems were circumstantial rather than personal.* 他們的困難是環境而非個人所致。

cir·cum·vent /ˌsɜːkəmˈvent; *NAmE* ˌsɜːrk-/ *verb* (*formal*) **1 ~ sth** to find a way of avoiding a difficulty or a rule 設法迴避；規避：*They found a way of circumventing the law.* 他們找到了規避法律的途徑。**2 ~ sth** to go or travel around sth that is blocking your way 繞過；繞行；繞道旅行 ▸ **cir·cum·ven·tion** /ˌsɜːkəmˈvenʃn; *NAmE* ˌsɜːrk-/ *noun* [U]

cir·cus /ˈsɜːkəs; *NAmE* ˈsɜːrkəs/ *noun* **1** [C] a group of entertainers, sometimes with trained animals, who perform skilful or amusing acts in a show that travels around to different places 馬戲團 **2 the circus** [sing.] a show performed by circus entertainers, usually in a large tent called a BIG TOP 馬戲表演（常在大帳篷裏進行）：*We took the children to the circus.* 我們帶孩子去看了馬戲表演。**3** [sing.] (*informal, disapproving*) a group of people or an event that attracts a lot of attention 引人注意的人（或事）；熱鬧場面：*A media circus surrounded the royal couple wherever they went.* 無論王室夫婦走到何處，他們的身後都會跟着一大群媒體記者。◇ *the American electoral circus* 美國選舉的熱鬧場面 **4** [C] (*BrE*) (used in some place names 用於一些地名) a round open area in a town where several streets meet 圓形廣場；環形交叉路口：*Piccadilly Circus* 皮卡迪利廣場 **5** [C] (in ancient Rome 古羅馬) a place like a big round outdoor theatre for public games, races, etc. 露天圓形競技場

cirque /sɜːk; *NAmE* sɜːrk/ *noun* (*geology* 地) = CORRIE

cir·rho·sis /səˈrəʊsɪs; *NAmE* -ˈroʊ-/ *noun* [U] a serious disease of the LIVER, caused especially by drinking too much alcohol 肝硬化；肝硬變

cir·rus /ˈsɪrəs/ *noun* [U] (*technical* 術語) a type of light cloud that forms high in the sky 捲雲

CIS /ˌsiː aɪ ˈes/ *abbr.* Commonwealth of Independent States (a group of independent countries that were part of the Soviet Union until 1991) 獨立國家聯合體，獨聯體，獨立國家國協（1991 年之前的蘇聯主權國家組成）

cissy (*BrE*) = SISSY

cis·tern /ˈsɪstən; *NAmE* -tərn/ *noun* (*BrE*) a container in which water is stored in a building, especially one in the roof or connected to a toilet（屋頂上的）蓄水箱，貯水箱；（抽水馬桶的）水箱 ➲ VISUAL VOCAB page V24

cita·del /ˈsɪtədəl; -del/ *noun* (in the past) a castle on high ground in or near a city where people could go when the city was being attacked（舊時的）城堡，要塞，堡壘：(*figurative*) *citadels of private economic power* 私人經濟力量的堡壘

cit·ation AW /saɪˈteɪʃn/ *noun* (*formal*) **1** [C] words or lines taken from a book or a speech 引語；引文；引述 SYN **quotation** **2** [C] an official statement about sth special that sb has done, especially about acts of courage in a war 表彰；表揚；（尤指對戰爭中英勇表現的）嘉獎令：*a citation for bravery* 因勇敢而受到的嘉獎 **3** [U] an act of citing or being cited（被）引用，引證：*Space does not permit the citation of the examples.* 篇幅有限，示例從略。**4** [C] (*NAmE*) = SUMMONS (1)：*The judge issued a contempt citation against the woman for violating a previous court order.* 法官對上一次拒不遵守庭諭的那名婦女發出了藐視法庭的傳訊。

cite AW /saɪt/ *verb* (*formal*) **1 ~ sth (as sth)** to mention sth as a reason or an example, or in order to support what you are saying 提及（原因）；舉出（示例）；列舉：*He cited his heavy workload as the reason for his breakdown.* 他提到繁重的工作負荷是導致他累垮的原因。➲ SYNONYMS at MENTION **2 ~ sth** to speak or write the exact words from a book, an author, etc. 引用；引述；援引 SYN **quote** **3 ~ sb (for sth)** (*law* 律) to order sb to appear in court; to name sb officially in a legal case 傳喚；傳訊：*She was cited in the divorce proceedings.* 她在離婚訴訟中被傳喚。**4 ~ sb (for sth)** to mention sb officially or publicly because they deserve special praise 嘉獎；表彰；表揚：*He was cited for bravery.* 他因表現勇敢而得到嘉獎。

citi·fied /ˈsɪtɪfaɪd/ *adj.* (usually *disapproving*) characteristic of a city 有城市特徵的；城市氣的：*his citified surroundings* 他那充滿市井氣息的環境

citi·zen 0➡ /ˈsɪtɪzn/ *noun* **1** 0➡ a person who has the legal right to belong to a particular country 公民：*She's Italian by birth but is now an Australian citizen.* 她生於意大利，但現在是澳大利亞公民。◇ *British citizens living in other parts of the European Union* 居住在歐盟其他地區的英國公民 **2** 0➡ a person who lives in a particular place 居民；市民：*the citizens of Budapest* 布達佩斯市民 ◇ *When you're old, people treat you like a **second-class citizen**.* 當你年邁時，人們會把你當成二等公民對待。➲ see also SENIOR CITIZEN ➲ compare SUBJECT *n.* (6)

ˌcitizen ˈjournalism *noun* [U] reports and pictures of events recorded by ordinary people and shown on the Internet 公民新聞；網民新聞：*citizen journalism websites* 公民新聞網站 ▸ **ˌcitizen ˈjournalist** *noun*

citi·zen·ry /ˈsɪtɪzənri/ *noun* [sing.+sing./pl. v.] (*formal*) (less *formal* in *NAmE*) all the citizens of a particular town, country, etc. 全體市民（或公民）

ˌcitizen's arˈrest *noun* an arrest made by a member of the public, not by the police 公民拘捕（由公民而非警察實行）

ˈCitizens' Band *noun* [U] = CB

C

citi·zen·ship /ˈsɪtɪzənʃɪp/ *noun* [U] **1** the legal right to belong to a particular country 公民權利（或資格）：*French citizenship* 法國國籍 ◇ *You can apply for citizenship after five years' residency.* 居住五年後可申請公民資格。➲ COLLOCATIONS at RACE **2** the state of being a citizen and accepting the responsibilities of it 公民身分（或義務）：*an education that prepares young people for citizenship* 培養年輕人履行公民義務的教育

cit·ric /ˈsɪtrɪk/ *adj.* relating to fruit such as lemons, oranges and LIMES 檸檬的；酸橙的；柑橘類水果的：*a citric flavour* 檸檬味

cit·ric acid /ˌsɪtrɪk ˈæsɪd/ *noun* [U] a weak acid found in the juice of lemons and other sour fruits 檸檬酸

cit·ron /ˈsɪtrən/ *noun* [C, U] a yellow fruit like a large lemon 枸櫞；香櫞

cit·ron·ella /ˌsɪtrəˈnelə/ *noun* [U] a type of grass from which an oil used in PERFUMES and soap is obtained 香茅（香茅油用於香水和肥皂）

cit·rus /ˈsɪtrəs/ *noun* [U] fruit belonging to the group of fruit that includes oranges, lemons, LIMES and GRAPEFRUIT 柑橘類果實：***citrus fruit/trees/growers*** 柑橘果實／果樹／種植者 ◇ *fabric in bright citrus shades* (= orange, yellow or green) 色調鮮豔的橙黃色布料 ➲ VISUAL VOCAB page V30

city 🔑 /ˈsɪti/ *noun* (*pl.* **-ies**)
1 🔑 [C] a large and important town 都市；城市：*the city centre* 市中心 ◇ *one of the world's most beautiful cities* 世界上最優美的城市之一 ◇ *a major city* 大城市 ◇ *the country's* ***capital city*** 這個國家的首都 ◇ *Mexico City* 墨西哥城 ➲ COLLOCATIONS at TOWN ➲ VISUAL VOCAB pages V2, V3 ➲ see also INNER CITY **2** [C] (*BrE*) a town that has been given special rights by a king or queen, usually one that has a CATHEDRAL（由國王或女王授予特權，通常有大教堂的）特許市：*the city of York* 約克特許市 **3** [C] (*NAmE*) a town that has been given special rights by the state government（由政府授予特權的）特權市 **4** 🔑 [sing.+sing./pl. v.] all the people who live in a city 全市居民：*The city turned out to welcome the victorious team home.* 全市居民傾城而出歡迎凱旋歸來的隊伍。 **5 the City** [sing.] (*BrE*) Britain's financial and business centre, in the oldest part of London 倫敦商業區，倫敦城（倫敦最古老的金融商務中心）：*a City stockbroker* 倫敦商業區的證券經紀人 ◇ *What is the City's reaction to the cut in interest rates?* 倫敦金融界對削減利率的反應如何？ **6** [U] (*informal*) used after other nouns to say that a place is full of a particular thing（用於其他名詞之後）充滿…的地方：*It's not exactly fun city here, is it?* 這裏並不是好玩的地方，對吧？ IDM see FREEDOM

the ˌCity and ˈGuilds Institute *noun* [sing.] (in Britain) an organization that gives qualifications in technical subjects and practical skills 英國倫敦城市行業協會（頒發職業技能證書的機構）

ˈcity desk *noun* **1** (*BrE*) the department of a newspaper that deals with financial news（報社的）財經新聞部 **2** (*NAmE*) the department of a newspaper that deals with local news（報社的）地方新聞部

ˈcity editor *noun* **1** (*BrE*) a journalist who is responsible for financial news in a newspaper or magazine（報刊的）財經新聞編輯 **2** (*NAmE*) a journalist who is responsible for local news in a newspaper or magazine（報刊的）地方新聞編輯

ˌcity ˈfather *noun* [usually pl.] a person with experience of governing a city 城市元老（有城市管理經驗者）

ˌcity ˈgent *noun* (*BrE, informal*) a business person, especially a man who works in the financial area of London（尤指在倫敦金融區工作的）商人

ˌcity ˈhall *noun* [C, U] (*NAmE*) the local government of a city and the offices it uses 市政府；市政廳

city·scape /ˈsɪtiskeɪp/ *noun* the appearance of a city or urban area, especially in a picture; a picture of a city（尤指圖畫中的）城市景象，城市風光；城市風光畫（或照片）

ˌcity ˈslicker *noun* (*informal, often disapproving*) a person who behaves in a way that is typical of people who live in big cities 油頭滑腦的城裏人；城裏老油子；城裏滑頭

ˌcity ˈstate *noun* (especially in the past) an independent state consisting of a city and the area around it (for example, Athens in ancient times)（尤指舊時的）城邦（如古代雅典）

civet /ˈsɪvɪt/ *noun* **1** [C] a wild animal like a cat, that lives in central Africa and Asia 靈貓，麝貓（分佈於中非和亞洲） **2** [U] a substance with a strong smell, obtained from a civet, and used in making PERFUME 麝貓香，靈貓香（用於製作香水）

civic /ˈsɪvɪk/ *adj.* [usually before noun] **1** officially connected with a town or city 市政的；城市的；城鎮的：***civic buildings/leaders*** 市政建築物／領導人 **2** connected with the people who live in a town or city 市民的；城鎮居民的：*a sense of* ***civic pride*** (= pride that people feel for their town or city) 作為某市市民的自豪感 ◇ ***civic duties/responsibilities*** 市民的義務／職責

ˌcivic ˈcentre *noun* **1** (*BrE*) the area where the public buildings are, in a town 市中心 **2 civic center** (*NAmE*) a large building where public entertainments and meetings are held 市政大廈；市政中心：*Atlanta Civic Center* 亞特蘭大市政大廈

ˌcivic ˈholiday *noun* (*CanE*) a holiday that is taken on the first Monday in August in all of Canada apart from Quebec, Alberta and Prince Edward Island 市政日（八月的第一個星期一，除魁北克、艾伯塔和愛德華王子島省之外加拿大各地的假日）

civ·ics /ˈsɪvɪks/ *noun* [U] (*especially NAmE*) the school subject which studies the way government works and deals with the rights and duties that you have as a citizen and a member of a particular society 公民學；市政學

civil 🔑 AW /ˈsɪvl/ *adj.*
1 🔑 [only before noun] connected with the people who live in a country 國民的；平民的：*civil unrest* (= that is caused by groups of people within a country) 民眾的騷亂 ➲ see also CIVIL WAR **2** 🔑 [only before noun] connected with the state rather than with religion or with the armed forces 國家的，政府的（非宗教或軍事的）：*a civil marriage ceremony* 非宗教儀式的結婚典禮 **3** [only before noun] involving personal legal matters and not criminal law 民事的（非刑事的）：*a civil court* 民事法庭 ➲ compare CRIMINAL *adj.* (2) ➲ see also CIVIL LAW **4** polite in a formal way but possibly not friendly 有禮貌的；客氣的 OPP **uncivil** ▸ **civ·il·ly** /ˈsɪvəli/ *adv.*：*She greeted him civilly but with no sign of affection.* 她禮貌地向他打招呼，但沒有一絲愛意。

ˌcivil deˈfence (*especially US* **ˌcivil deˈfense**) *noun* [U] the organization and training of ordinary people to protect themselves from attack during a war or, in the US, from natural disasters such as HURRICANES 民防

ˌcivil disoˈbedience *noun* [U] refusal by a large group of people to obey particular laws or pay taxes, usually as a form of peaceful political protest 非暴力反抗；溫和抵抗；不合作主義

ˌcivil engiˈneering *noun* [U] the design, building and repair of roads, bridges, CANALS, etc.; the study of this as a subject 土木工程；土木工程學 ▸ **ˌcivil engiˈneer** *noun*

ci·vil·ian /səˈvɪliən/ *noun* a person who is not a member of the armed forces or the police 平民；老百姓；庶民 ➲ COLLOCATIONS at WAR ▸ **ci·vil·ian** *adj.* [usually before noun]：*He left the army and returned to civilian life.* 他從軍隊退了役，重新過上平民百姓的生活。➲ compare MILITARY

ci·vil·ity /səˈvɪləti/ *noun* (*formal*) **1** [U] polite behaviour 彬彬有禮的行為；禮貌；客氣：*Staff members are trained to treat customers with civility at all times.* 員工經過培訓，要做到任何時候都以禮待客。 **2 civilities** [pl.] remarks that are said only in order to be polite 客套話；客氣話

civ·il·iza·tion (*BrE* also **-isa·tion**) /ˌsɪvəlaɪˈzeɪʃn; *NAmE* -ləˈz-/ *noun* **1** [U] a state of human society that is very developed and organized 文明：*the technology of modern civilization* 現代文明的技術 ◇ *The Victorians regarded the railways as bringing progress and civilization.* 維多利亞時代的人認為鐵路帶來了進步和文明。**2** [U, C] a society, its culture and its way of life during a particular period of time or in a particular part of the world（特定時期和地區的）社會文明：*the civilizations of ancient Greece and Rome* 古希臘和古羅馬的社會文明 ◇ *diseases that are common in Western civilization* 西方文明社會的常見弊病 **3** [U] all the people in the world and the societies they live in, considered as a whole 文明世界；文明社會：*Environmental damage threatens the whole of civilization.* 環境的破壞威脅着整個文明世界。**4** [U] (often *humorous*) a place that offers you the comfortable way of life of a modern society 人類文明的生活：*It's good to be back in civilization after two weeks in a tent!* 在帳篷裏住了兩個星期後又回到人類文明的生活可真好呀！

civ·il·ize (*BrE* also **-ise**) /ˈsɪvəlaɪz/ *verb* **~ sb/sth** to educate and improve a person or a society; to make sb's behaviour or manners better 教化；開化；使文明；使有教養：*The girls in a class tend to have a civilizing influence on the boys.* 班上的女生往往能讓男生文雅起來。

civ·il·ized (*BrE* also **-ised**) /ˈsɪvəlaɪzd/ *adj.* **1** well-organized socially with a very developed culture and way of life 文明的；開化的：*the civilized world* 文明世界 ◇ *rising crime in our so-called civilized societies* 在我們所謂文明社會中日益增多的犯罪行為 ◇ *civilized peoples* 文明的民族 **2** having laws and customs that are fair and morally acceptable 有法制倫理的；有道德的：*No civilized country should allow such terrible injustices.* 凡有法制倫理的國家都不該允許這種可怕的不公正行為。**3** having or showing polite and reasonable behaviour 有禮貌的；有教養的；舉止得體的：*We couldn't even have a civilized conversation any more.* 我們之間甚至連禮貌的寒暄都沒有了。**4** typical of a comfortable and pleasant way of life（生活）愜意的，愉快舒適的：*Breakfast on the terrace—how civilized!* 在陽台上用早餐，真是愜意無比！**OPP** **uncivilized**

ˌcivil ˈlaw *noun* [U] law that deals with the rights of private citizens rather than with crime 民法

ˌcivil ˈliberty *noun* [C, usually pl., U] the right of people to be free to say or do what they want while respecting others and staying within the law 公民自由

the ˈCivil List *noun* [sing.] a sum of money that is given to the British royal family each year by Parliament（英國議會每年提供的）王室年俸

ˌcivil ˈmarriage *noun* a marriage with no religious ceremony 民事婚姻，世俗結婚（不採用宗教儀式）

ˌcivil ˈpartnership *noun* a relationship between two people of the same sex, recognized as having the same legal status as a marriage between a man and a woman 民事伴侶關係（同性伴侶得到認可享有與男女婚姻同等的法律地位）

ˌcivil ˈrights *noun* [pl.] the rights that every person in a society has, for example to be treated equally, to be able to vote, work, etc. whatever their sex, race or religion 公民權：*the civil rights leader Martin Luther King* 民權領袖馬丁•路德•金

the ˌcivil ˈrights movement *noun* [sing.] (in the US) the campaign in the 1950s and 1960s to change the laws so that African Americans have the same rights as others（美國）民權運動（20 世紀 50 年代和 60 年代非裔美國人爭取平等權利的運動）➲ COLLOCATIONS at RACE

ˌcivil ˈservant *noun* a person who works in the civil service（政府的）公務員，文職人員

the ˌcivil ˈservice *noun* [sing.] the government departments in a country, except the armed forces, and the people who work for them（政府的）文職部門，行政部門；（統稱）政府工作人員，公務員

ˌcivil ˈwar *noun* **1** [C, U] a war between groups of people in the same country 內戰：*the Spanish Civil War* 西班牙內戰 ◇ *30 years of bitter civil war* * 30 年慘烈的內戰 ➲ COLLOCATIONS at WAR **2 the Civil War** the war fought in the US between the northern and the southern states in the years 1861 to 1865 美國內戰，美國南北戰爭（1861–1865）

civ·vies /ˈsɪviz/ *noun* [pl.] (*slang*) (used by people in the armed forces) ordinary clothes, not military uniform（軍人穿的）便服

Civvy Street /ˈsɪvi striːt/ *noun* [U] (*old-fashioned, BrE, slang*) ordinary life outside the armed forces（非軍隊的）平民生活，老百姓生活

CJD /ˌsiː dʒeɪ ˈdiː/ *abbr.* CREUTZFELDT-JAKOB DISEASE 克 — 雅氏病；克羅伊茨費爾特 — 雅各布病 ➲ see also NEW VARIANT CJD

cl *abbr.* (*pl.* **cl** or **cls**) CENTILITRE：*75cl* * 75 厘升

clack /klæk/ *verb* [I] if two hard objects **clack**, they make a short loud sound when they hit each other 發出啪嗒聲；劈啪作響；使咔嗒地響：*Her heels clacked on the marble floor.* 她的鞋後跟在大理石地面上發出咔嗒咔嗒的響聲。► **clack** *noun* [sing.]：*the clack of high heels on the floor* 高跟鞋在地板上發出的咔咔聲 ◇ *the clack of her knitting needles* 她的織針發出的啪嗒啪嗒聲

clad /klæd/ *adj.* (usually *formal*) **1 ~ (in sth)** (often used after an adverb or in compounds 常用於副詞後或構成複合詞) wearing a particular type of clothing 穿…衣服的 **SYN** **dressed**：*She was clad in blue velvet.* 她身着藍色的天鵝絨服裝。◇ ***warmly/scantily clad*** 衣着暖和／單薄 ◇ *leather-clad motorcyclists* 穿皮外套的摩托車手 **2 -clad** (in compounds 構成複合詞) covered in a particular thing …覆蓋的：*snow-clad hills* 白雪覆蓋的山巒

clad·ding /ˈklædɪŋ/ *noun* [U] a covering of a hard material, used as protection 鍍層；保護層

claim 🔑 /kleɪm/ *verb, noun*

■ *verb*

► SAY STH IS TRUE 表示真實性 **1** 🔑 [T] to say that sth is true although it has not been proved and other people may not believe it 宣稱；聲稱；斷言：**~ (that)** … *He claims (that) he was not given a fair hearing.* 他聲稱他未得到公正的申述機會。◇ **~ (sb/sth) to be/do sth** *I don't claim to be an expert.* 我不敢自稱為專家。◇ **~ sth** *Scientists are claiming a major breakthrough in the fight against cancer.* 科學家們宣稱攻克癌症已有重大的突破。◇ **it is claimed that** … *It was claimed that some doctors were working 80 hours a week.* 據説有些醫生每週工作 80 小時。➲ LANGUAGE BANK at ARGUE

► DEMAND LEGAL RIGHT 要求合法權利 **2** 🔑 [T] **~ sth** to demand or ask for sth because you believe it is your legal right to own or to have it 要求（擁有）；索取；認領：*A lot of lost property is never claimed.* 許多失物從未被認領。◇ *He claimed political asylum.* 他要求政治避難。

► MONEY 金錢 **3** 🔑 [T, I] to ask for money from the government or a company because you have a right to it 索要；索取：**~ sth** *He's not entitled to claim unemployment benefit.* 他無權要求領取失業救濟金。◇ **~ sth from sth** *She claimed damages from the company for the injury she had suffered.* 她因受傷向公司要求獲得損害賠償金。◇ *You could have claimed the cost of the hotel room from your insurance.* 你本可以從你的保險中索取旅館住房費。◇ **~ (on sth) (for sth)** *You can claim on your insurance for that coat you left on the train.* 你可按你的保險索賠你遺忘在火車上的大衣。

► ATTENTION/THOUGHT 注意；思考 **4** [T] **~ sth** to get or take sb's attention 引起注意：*A most unwelcome event claimed his attention.* 一件非常討厭的事情需要他去考慮。

► GAIN/WIN 獲得；贏得 **5** [T] **~ sth** to gain, win or achieve sth 獲得；贏得；取得：*She has finally claimed a place on the team.* 她終於成了那支隊的隊員。

► CAUSE DEATH 導致死亡 **6** [T] **~ sth** (of a disaster, an accident, etc. 災難、事故等) to cause sb's death 奪走，奪去（生命）：*The car crash claimed three lives.* 那次撞車事故導致三人死亡。

PHR V **ˌclaim sth↔ˈback** to ask or demand to have sth returned because you have a right to it 索回；要回：*You can claim back the tax on your purchases.* 你可以要求退回購物時繳納的稅款。

■ *noun*

► SAYING STH IS TRUE 表示真實 **1** 🔑 [C] **~ (that …)** a statement that sth is true although it has not been proved and other people may not agree with or believe it

聲明；宣稱；斷言：*The singer has denied the magazine's claim that she is leaving the band.* 這名歌手已否認那家雜誌有關她要離開樂隊的說法。
▸ **LEGAL RIGHT** 合法權利 **2** [C, U] **~ (on/to sth)** a right that sb believes they have to sth, especially property, land, etc. (尤指對財產、土地等要求擁有的) 所有權：*They had no claim on the land.* 他們無權索要那塊土地。◇ *She has more claim to the book's success than anybody* (= she deserves to be praised for it). 她為這本書的成功立了頭功。
▸ **FOR MONEY** 錢款 **3** [C] **~ (for sth)** a request for a sum of money that you believe you have a right to, especially from a company, the government, etc. (尤指向公司、政府等) 索款，索賠：*You can **make a claim** on your insurance policy.* 你可按保險單索賠。◇ *to **put in a claim** for an allowance* 提出領取津貼的要求 ◇ *a claim for £2 000* 要求 2 000 英鎊的索賠 ◇ *Make sure your claims for expenses are submitted by the end of the month.* 你的費用一定要在月底以前辦理報銷。◇ *a three per cent **pay claim*** 提高工資 3% 的要求 ◇ *Complete a **claim form*** (= an official document which you must use in order to request money from an organization). 填寫索賠表格。
IDM **ˌclaim to ˈfame** (often *humorous*) one thing that makes a person or place important or interesting 一舉出名的事；成名的一件事：*His main claim to fame is that he went to school with the Prime Minister.* 他出名主要是因為他曾經是首相的同學。 **have a claim on sb** to have the right to demand time, attention, etc. from sb 對某人有…的要求權 **lay claim to sth** to state that you have a right to own sth 聲稱對…的擁有權；提出對…的所有權 **make no claim** used when you are saying that you cannot do sth (表示不能做某事) 自認為不：*I make no claim to understand modern art.* 我自認為不懂現代藝術。➲ more at STAKE *v.*

Synonyms 同義詞辨析

claim

allegation • assertion

These are all words for a statement that sth is true, although it has not been proved. 以上各詞均表示未經證實的說法。

claim a statement that sth is true, although it has not been proved 指聲明、宣稱、斷言

allegation (*rather formal*) a public statement that is made without giving proof, accusing sb of doing sth that is wrong or illegal 指無證據的說法、指控

assertion (*rather formal*) a statement of sth that you strongly believe to be true, although it has not been proved 指明確肯定、斷言

CLAIM OR ASSERTION? 用 claim 還是 assertion？

When the point in doubt is a matter of opinion, not fact, use **assertion**. 如果對所談問題存疑是因為看法不同，而非因與事實不符，用 assertion：~~*She made sweeping claims about the role of women in society.*~~
When you are talking about a matter of fact you can use either word; an **assertion** may be slightly stronger than a **claim** and it is a more formal word. 如果所談問題是事實，用任何一詞均可。assertion 比 claim 語氣稍強，且更正式。

PATTERNS

- a(n) claim/allegation/assertion **that** ...
- a(n) claim/allegation/assertion **about/of** sth
- **false/unfounded/conflicting** claims/allegations/assertions
- to **make/deny** a(n) claim/allegation/assertion
- to **withdraw** a(n) claim/allegation

claim·ant /ˈkleɪmənt/ *noun* **1** a person who claims sth because they believe they have a right to it 要求者；索要者 **2** (*BrE*) a person who is receiving money from the state because they are unemployed, etc. (因失業等) 領取救濟金者

clair·voy·ance /kleəˈvɔɪəns; *NAmE* klerˈv-/ *noun* [U] the power that some people are believed to have to be able to see future events or to communicate with people who are dead or far away 預見力；洞察力；神視力 ▸ **clair·voy·ant** /kleəˈvɔɪənt; *NAmE* klerˈv-/ *noun*：*to consult a clairvoyant* 咨詢先知 **clair·voy·ant** *adj.*

clam /klæm/ *noun, verb*
■ ***noun*** a SHELLFISH that can be eaten. It has a shell in two parts that can open and close. 蛤；蛤蜊；蚌：***clam chowder/soup*** 蛤蜊雜燴湯；蛤蜊湯 ➲ picture at SHELLFISH
■ ***verb*** **(-mm-)**
PHR V **ˌclam ˈup (on sb)** (*informal*) to refuse to speak, especially when sb asks you about sth (尤指被詢問時) 拒絕說話，拒不開口，閉口不言

clam·bake /ˈklæmbeɪk/ *noun* (*NAmE*) an outdoor party, especially for eating clams and other SEAFOOD 野餐會；(尤指) 烤蛤及海鮮野餐會

clam·ber /ˈklæmbə(r)/ *verb* [I] **+ adv./prep.** to climb or move with difficulty or a lot of effort, using your hands and feet (吃力地) 攀登，攀爬 **SYN** **scramble**：*The children clambered up the steep bank.* 孩子們攀登上了陡峭的河岸。

clammy /ˈklæmi/ *adj.* (**clam·mier, clam·mi·est**) damp in an unpleasant way 濕乎乎的；濕漉漉的：*His skin felt cold and clammy.* 他的皮膚摸上去冷冰冰濕乎乎的。◇ *clammy hands* 又濕又黏的雙手

clam·our (*especially US* **clamor**) /ˈklæmə(r)/ *verb, noun*
■ ***verb*** **1** [I, T] (*formal*) to demand sth loudly 大聲 (或吵鬧) 地要求：**~ (for sth)** *People began to clamour for his resignation.* 人們開始大聲疾呼要求他辭職。◇ **~ to do sth** *Everyone was clamouring to know how much they would get.* 大家都吵鬧着想知道他們能得到多少。◇ **+ speech** *'Play with us!' the children clamoured.* "跟我們一起玩吧！"孩子們吵吵嚷嚷地要求道。 **2** [I] (of many people 許多人) to shout loudly, especially in a confused way (尤指亂哄哄地) 大聲地喊叫，呼叫
■ ***noun*** [sing., U] (*formal*) **1** a loud noise especially one that is made by a lot of people or animals 喧鬧聲；嘈雜聲；吵鬧：*the clamour of the market* 市場上鼎沸的人聲 **2 ~ (for sth)** a demand for sth made by a lot of people 民眾的要求：*The clamour for her resignation grew louder.* 民眾要求她辭職的呼聲越來越高。 ▸ **clam·or·ous** /ˈklæmərəs/ *adj.*

clamp /klæmp/ *verb, noun*
■ ***verb*** **1** [T] to hold sth tightly, or fasten two things together, with a clamp (用夾具) 夾緊，夾住，固定：**~ A to B** *Clamp one end of the plank to the edge of the table.* 把厚木板的一端用夾具固定在桌子的邊上。◇ **~ A and B (together)** *Clamp the two halves together until the glue dries.* 用夾具把兩半物品緊夾在一起，待膠乾後再鬆開。 **2** [T, I] to hold or fasten sth very tightly so that it does not move; to be held tightly 緊緊抓住；緊夾住；被抓住；被夾緊：**~ sth + adv./prep.** *He had a cigar clamped between his teeth.* 他嘴裏叼着一根雪茄。◇ *She clamped a pair of headphones over her ears.* 她把一副耳機戴在兩邊耳朵上。◇ **+ adv./prep.** *Her lips clamped tightly together.* 她的雙唇緊閉。◇ **~ (sth) + adj.** *He clamped his mouth shut.* 他緊閉着嘴。 **3** [T, often passive] **~ sth/sb** (*BrE*) to fix a clamp to a car's wheel so that the car cannot be driven away 用夾鎖鎖住 (車輪)
PHR V **ˌclamp ˈdown (on sb/sth)** to take strict action in order to prevent sth, especially crime 嚴厲打擊 (犯罪等)：*a campaign by police to clamp down on street crime* 警方嚴厲打擊街頭犯罪的運動 ➲ related noun CLAMPDOWN **ˈclamp sth on sb** (*especially NAmE*) to force sb to accept sth such as a restriction or law 強制…接受 (限制或法律等)：*The army **clamped a curfew on** the city.* 軍隊對這座城市實行了宵禁。
■ ***noun*** **1** a tool for holding things tightly together, usually by means of a screw 夾具；夾子；夾鉗 ➲ VISUAL VOCAB page V70 **2** (also **ˈwheel clamp**) (both *BrE*) (*US* **ˌDenver ˈboot, boot**) a device that is attached to the wheel of a car that has been parked illegally, so that it

cannot be driven away 車輪鎖，車輪夾鎖（用於鎖住違章停放的車輛）

clamp·down /ˈklæmpdaʊn/ *noun* [usually sing.] sudden action that is taken in order to stop an illegal activity 嚴禁，制止，取締（非法活動）: *a clampdown on drinking and driving* 嚴禁酒後駕車

clam·shell /ˈklæmʃel/ *adj.* [only before noun] having a lid or other part that opens and shuts like the shell of a CLAM 蛤殼式的；掀蓋式的：*a* ***clamshell phone*** 翻蓋式手機 ▶ **clam·shell** *noun*

clan /klæn/ *noun* [C+sing./pl. v.] **1** a group of families who are related to each other, especially in Scotland（尤指蘇格蘭的）宗族，氏族，家族：*the Macleod clan* 麥克勞德氏族 ◇ *clan warfare* 宗族衝突 **2** (*informal*, *sometimes humorous*) a very large family, or a group of people who are connected because of a particular thing 龐大的家族；宗派；幫派；小集團：*one of a growing clan of stars who have left Hollywood* 脱離了好萊塢的那幫人數日益增多的明星中的一員

clan·des·tine /klænˈdestɪn; ˈklændəstaɪn/ *adj.* (*formal*) done secretly or kept secret 暗中從事的；保密的；秘密的：*a* ***clandestine meeting/relationship*** 秘密會議 / 關係

clang /klæŋ/ *verb* [I, T] to make a loud ringing sound like that of metal being hit; to cause sth to make this sound（使）叮噹作響，鏗鏘作響 SYN **clank**：*Bells were clanging in the tower.* 塔樓上的鐘噹噹地敲響了。◇ **+ adj.** *The gates* ***clanged shut***. 大門咣地一聲合上了。◇ **~ sth + adv./prep.** *The trams clanged their way along the streets.* 有軌電車哐啷哐啷沿街駛過。◇ *He clanged a spoon against a glass.* 他用勺子叮叮噹噹地敲玻璃杯。▶ **clang** (also **clang·ing**) *noun* [usually sing.]

clang·er /ˈklæŋə(r)/ *noun* (*BrE*, *informal*) an obvious and embarrassing mistake 明顯且令人難堪的錯誤；大錯：*Mentioning her ex-husband was a bit of a clanger.* 提及她的前夫是有點令人難堪的失言。◇ *He was always* ***dropping clangers*** (= making embarrassing mistakes or remarks). 他總是出岔子，令人十分尷尬。

clang·our (*especially US* **clangor**) /ˈklæŋgə(r)/ *noun* (*formal*) a continuous loud crashing or ringing sound（持續的）鏗鏘聲，叮噹聲 ▶ **clang·or·ous** /ˈklæŋgərəs/ *adj.*

clank /klæŋk/ *verb* [I, T] to make a loud sound like pieces of metal hitting each other; to cause sth to make this sound（使）發出叮噹聲，發出噹啷聲：*clanking chains* 叮噹作響的鐐銬 ◇ **+ adj.** *I heard a door clank shut.* 我聽見門咣地一聲關上了。◇ **~ sth** *The guard clanked his heavy ring of keys.* 看守把他的那串沉甸甸的鑰匙弄得叮噹響。▶ **clank** (also **clank·ing**) *noun* [usually sing.]

clan·nish /ˈklænɪʃ/ *adj.* (often *disapproving*) (of members of a group 集團成員) not showing interest in people who are not in the group 小集團的；宗派的；排他的

clans·man /ˈklænzmən/ *noun* (*pl.* **-men** /-mən/) a member of a CLAN 氏族（或宗族）成員；宗派（或小集團）的成員

clap 🔑 /klæp/ *verb*, *noun*

■ *verb* (**-pp-**) **1** 🔑 [I, T] to hit your open hands together several times to show that you approve of or have enjoyed sth 鼓掌，拍手（表示讚許或欣賞）：*The audience cheered and clapped.* 觀眾又是喝彩又是鼓掌。◇ **~ sb/sth** *Everyone clapped us when we went up to get our prize.* 我們上前領獎時，大家都為我們鼓掌。 **2** 🔑 [I, T] to hit your open hands together 拍手；擊掌：*Everyone clapped in time to the music.* 大家合着音樂的節奏拍手。◇ **~ your hands** *She clapped her hands in delight.* 她高興地拍起手來。◇ *He clapped his hands for silence.* 他拍手要大家安靜下來。 **3** [T] **~ sb on the back/shoulder** to lightly hit sb with your open hand, usually in a friendly way（常指友好地）輕拍某人的背（或肩） **4** [T] **~ sth + adv./prep.** to put sth/sb somewhere quickly and suddenly 急速放置：*'Oh dear!' she cried,* ***clapping a hand*** *over her mouth.* "哎呀！"她叫道，急急用手捂住了嘴。◇ *to* ***clap sb in irons/jail/prison*** 迅速把某人關進監獄 ▶ **clap·ping** *noun* [U]：*I could hear the sound of clapping from the other room.* 我聽得見另一個房間裏傳來的鼓掌聲。 IDM see EYE *n.*

■ *noun* **1** 🔑 [sing.] an act of clapping the hands; the sound this makes 鼓掌；拍手；掌聲；拍手聲：*Give him a clap!* (= to praise sb at the end of a performance) 為他鼓掌吧！ **2** [C] a sudden loud noise 砰然巨響；霹靂聲：*a clap of thunder* 一聲霹靂 **3** (also **the clap**) [U] (*informal*) a disease of the sexual organs, caught by having sex with an infected person 淋病 SYN **gonorrhoea**

clap·board /ˈklæpbɔːd; *NAmE* ˈklæbərd/ *noun* [U] (*especially NAmE*) = WEATHERBOARD

Clap·ham omni·bus /ˌklæpəm ˈɒmnɪbəs; *NAmE* ˈɑːmnɪbəs/ *noun* (*BrE*)

IDM **the man on the ˌClapham ˈomnibus** (*BrE*, *informal*) an ordinary person who is typical of many others 普通人；正常人：*Can you persuade the man on the Clapham omnibus that it is useful?* 你能讓普通人相信這個有用嗎？

ˌclapped ˈout *adj.* (*BrE*, *informal*) (of a car or machine 汽車或機器) old and in bad condition 破舊的；殘破的；破爛的：*The van's totally clapped out.* 那輛貨車已破得不成樣子。◇ *a clapped-out old Mini* 又舊又破的迷你牌汽車

clap·per /ˈklæpə(r)/ *noun* the piece of metal inside a bell that hits the sides and makes the bell ring 鐘錘；鐘舌；鈴舌

IDM **like the ˈclappers** (*BrE*, *informal*) extremely fast 特別快；飛快；疾速：*to* ***run/ride/drive like the clappers*** 飛快地奔跑；騎馬飛奔；駕車疾馳

clap·per·board /ˈklæpəbɔːd; *NAmE* ˈklæpərbɔːrd/ *noun* a device that is used when making films/movies. It consists of two connected boards that are hit together at the start of a scene, and its purpose is to help to match the pictures with the sound.（拍攝電影用的）場記板，拍板

clap·trap /ˈklæptræp/ *noun* [U] (*informal*) stupid talk that has no value 無聊的蠢話；廢話

claque /klæk/ *noun* a group of people who are paid to clap or BOO a performer or public speaker 受雇喝（倒）彩的一夥人；職業觀眾

claret /ˈklærət/ *noun* **1** [U, C] a dry red wine, especially from the Bordeaux area of France. There are several types of claret.（尤指產於法國波爾多地區的）乾紅葡萄酒 **2** [U] a dark red colour 深紅色；暗紅色

clar·ify AW /ˈklærəfaɪ/ *verb* (**clari·fies**, **clari·fy·ing**, **clari·fied**, **clari·fied**) **1** (*formal*) to make sth clearer or easier to understand 使更清晰易懂；闡明；澄清：**~ sth** *to* ***clarify a situation/problem/issue*** 澄清情況 / 問題 ◇ *I hope this* ***clarifies my position***. 我希望這能闡明我的立場。◇ **~ what/how, etc. …** *She asked him to clarify what he meant.* 她要他説清楚他是什麼意思。 ➲ LANGUAGE BANK at DEFINE **2 ~ sth** to make sth, especially butter, pure by heating it（尤指通過加熱使黃油）純淨，淨化：*clarified butter* 已淨化的黃油 ▶ **clari·fi·ca·tion** AW /ˌklærəfɪˈkeɪʃn/ *noun* [U, C]：*I am* ***seeking clarification*** *of the regulations.* 我正在努力弄清楚這些規則。

clari·net /ˌklærəˈnet/ *noun* a musical instrument of the WOODWIND group. It is shaped like a pipe and has a REED and a MOUTHPIECE at the top that you blow into. 單簧管；黑管 ➲ VISUAL VOCAB page V34

cla·ri·net·tist (*NAmE* **cla·ri·net·ist**) /ˌklærəˈnetɪst/ *noun* a person who plays the clarinet 單簧管（或黑管）演奏者

clar·ion call /ˈklæriən kɔːl/ *noun* [sing.] (*formal*) a clear message or request for people to do sth 口號；號召；召喚

clar·ity AW /ˈklærəti/ *noun* [U] **1** the quality of being expressed clearly 清晰；清楚；明確：*a lack of clarity in the law* 法律上不明確 **2** the ability to think about or understand sth clearly 清晰的思維（或理解）能力：***clarity of thought/purpose/vision*** 思路清楚；目的明確；視野清晰 **3** if a picture, substance or sound has **clarity**, you can see or hear it very clearly, or see through it easily（畫、物質或聲音的）清晰，清楚，清澈：*the clarity of sound on a CD* 激光唱片的清晰音質

clash /klæʃ/ *noun*, *verb*

■ *noun*

▸ FIGHT 打鬥 **1 ~ (with sb)** | **~ (between A and B)** a short fight between two groups of people（兩群人之間的）打鬥，打架，衝突：*Clashes broke out between police and demonstrators.* 警方與示威者發生了衝突。➲ SYNONYMS at FIGHT

▸ **ARGUMENT** 爭論 **2 ~ (with sb) (over sth) | ~ (between A and B) (over sth)** an argument between two people or groups of people who have different beliefs and ideas 爭論；辯論；爭執 **SYN conflict**：*a head-on clash between the two leaders over education policy* 兩位領導人就教育政策進行的針鋒相對的爭論

▸ **DIFFERENCE** 差異 **3** the difference that exists between two things that are opposed to each other 差別；差異；分歧 **SYN conflict**：*a **clash of interests/opinions/cultures*** 利益衝突；意見分歧；文化差異 ◇ *a **personality clash** with the boss* 與老闆的個性不合

▸ **OF TWO EVENTS** 兩件事 **4** a situation in which two events happen at the same time so that you cannot go to or see them both（時間上的）衝突，矛盾：*a clash in the timetable/schedule* 與時間安排有衝突

▸ **OF COLOURS** 顏色 **5** the situation when two colours, designs, etc. look ugly when they are put together 不協調；不和諧；搭配不當

▸ **LOUD NOISE** 大聲 **6** a loud noise made by two metal objects being hit together（金屬的）撞擊聲：*a **clash of cymbals/swords*** 鐃鈸的敲擊聲；劍的撞擊聲

▸ **IN SPORT** 體育運動 **7** (used in newspapers, about sports 用於報章中有關體育運動的報道) an occasion when two teams or players compete against each other 交鋒；交戰；比賽：*Bayern's clash with Roma in the Champions League* 拜仁隊在歐洲冠軍聯賽中與羅馬隊的交鋒

■ ***verb***

▸ **FIGHT/COMPETE** 打鬥；比賽 **1** [I] **~ (with sb)** to come together and fight or compete in a contest 打鬥；衝突；比賽：*The two sets of supporters clashed outside the stadium.* 雙方的支持者在體育場外打了起來。◇ *The two teams clash in tomorrow's final.* 這兩支隊將在明天的決賽中廝殺。

▸ **ARGUE** 爭論 **2** [I] **~ (with sb) (over/on sth)** to argue or disagree seriously with sb about sth, and to show this in public（公開地）爭論，辯論，爭辯：*The leaders and members clashed on the issue.* 領袖和下屬的成員在這個問題上產生了分歧。◇ *The leaders clashed with party members on the issue.* 政黨領袖與該黨黨員在這個問題上產生了分歧。

▸ **BE DIFFERENT** 差異 **3** [I] **~ (with sth)** (of beliefs, ideas or personalities 信念、思想或個性) to be very different and opposed to each other 迥然不同；不相容；抵觸：*His left-wing views clashed with his father's politics.* 他的左翼觀點與他父親的政見分歧很大。◇ *His views and his father's clashed.* 他的觀點與他父親的觀點相抵觸。◇ *They have clashing personalities.* 他們的個性迥然相異。

▸ **OF TWO EVENTS** 兩件事 **4** [I] **~ (with sth)** (of events 活動) to happen at the same time so that you cannot go to or see them both（時間上）相衝突，相矛盾：*Unfortunately your party clashes with a wedding I'm going to.* 不巧得很，你的聚會和我要參加的婚禮在時間上有衝突。◇ *There are two good movies on TV tonight, but they clash.* 今晚電視有兩部好電影，但播出時間有衝突。

▸ **OF COLOURS** 顏色 **5** [I] **~ (with sth)** (of colours, patterns or styles 顏色、圖案或風格) to look ugly when put together 不協調；不和諧；搭配不當：*The wallpaper clashes with the carpet.* 牆紙與地毯的色彩不協調。◇ *The wallpaper and the carpet clash.* 牆紙和地毯的色彩不相配。

▸ **MAKE LOUD NOISE** 發出大聲 **6** [I, T] to hit together and make a loud ringing noise; to make two metal objects do this 撞擊出巨大的響聲；使噹啷作響：**~ (together)** *The long blades clashed together.* 長刀相擊鏗然作響。◇ **~ sth (together)** *She clashed the cymbals.* 她噹啷一聲敲響鐃鈸。

clasp /klɑːsp; *NAmE* klæsp/ *verb, noun*

■ ***verb* 1 ~ sth** to hold sth tightly in your hand 握緊；攥緊；抓緊：*He leaned forward, his **hands clasped** tightly together.* 他俯身向前，雙手十字交錯地緊握着。◇ *They clasped hands* (= held each other's hands). 他們相互緊握着對方的手。◇ *I stood there, clasping the door handle.* 我站在那裏，緊攥着門把手。➲ SYNONYMS at HOLD **2 ~ sb/sth** to hold sb/sth tightly with your arms around them 抱緊；緊緊擁抱：*She clasped the children in her arms.* 她把孩子緊緊地摟抱在懷裏。◇ *He **clasped** her **to him**.* 他緊緊地擁抱着她。 **3 ~ sth (+ adv./prep.)** to fasten sth with a clasp 扣緊；扣住；扣牢：*She clasped the bracelet around her wrist.* 她把手鐲戴上手腕扣牢。

■ ***noun* 1** [C] a device that fastens sth, such as a bag or the ends of a belt or a piece of jewellery（包、皮帶或首飾的）扣子，扣環：*the clasp of a necklace/handbag* 項鏈扣環；手提包扣 ➲ VISUAL VOCAB page V65 **2** [sing.] a tight hold with your hand or in your arms 緊握；緊攥；緊抱：*He took her hand in his firm warm clasp.* 他用温暖結實的手緊緊握住她的手。

class 0➔ /klɑːs; *NAmE* klæs/ *noun, verb, adj.*

■ ***noun***

▸ **IN EDUCATION** 教育 **1** 0➔ [C+sing./pl. v.] a group of students who are taught together 班；班級：*We were in the same class at school.* 我們在上學時同過班。◇ *She is the youngest in her class.* 她在班裏年齡最小。◇ *He came **top of the class**.* 他在全班名列前茅。◇ *The whole class was/were told to stay behind after school.* 全班收到通知放學後留下。 **2** 0➔ [C, U] an occasion when a group of students meet to be taught 課；上課 **SYN lesson**：*I was late for a class.* 我上課遲到了。◇ *See me after class.* 下課後來見我。◇ *She works hard **in class*** (= during the class). 她在課堂上學習用功。◇ *I have a history class at 9 o'clock.* 我 9 點鐘有歷史課。➲ COLLOCATIONS at EDUCATION **3** 0➔ [C] (also **classes** [pl.]) a series of classes on a particular subject（某科目的）系列課程 **SYN course**：*I've been **taking classes** in pottery.* 我一直在上課學習陶器製作。◇ *Are you still doing your French evening class?* 你還在上夜校法語課程嗎？ **4** [C+sing./pl. v.] (*especially NAmE*) a group of students who finish their studies at school, college or university in a particular year 同屆畢業生：*the class of 2008* * 2008 年畢業生

▸ **IN SOCIETY** 社會 **5** 0➔ [C+sing./pl. v.] one of the groups of people in a society that are thought of as being at the same social or economic level 階級；階層：*the **working/middle/upper class*** 工人／中產／上層階級 ◇ *The party tries to appeal to all classes of society.* 這個政黨盡力吸引社會各階層人士。◇ *the professional classes* 專業階層 **6** 0➔ [U] the way that people are divided into different social and economic groups 社會等級：*differences of class, race or gender* 社會等級、種族或性別差異 ◇ *the class system* 社會等級制度 ◇ *a society in which class is more important than ability* 一個社會等級比能力更為重要的社會

▸ **GROUP OF PEOPLE/ANIMALS** 人／動物群體 **7** 0➔ [C] a group of people, animals or things that have similar characteristics or qualities 種類；類別；等級：*It was good accommodation for a hotel of this class.* 就這種檔次的旅館來說，住宿條件算是不錯了。◇ *different classes of drugs* 不同種類的毒品 ◇ *Dickens was **in a different class** from* (= was much better than) *most of his contemporaries.* 與大多數的同代作家相比，狄更斯更為出類拔萃。◇ *As a jazz singer she's **in a class of her own*** (= better than most others). 作為爵士樂歌手，她比大多數同行都要出色。➲ see also FIRST-CLASS, HIGH-CLASS, LOW-CLASS, SECOND-CLASS

▸ **SKILL/STYLE** 技巧；風格 **8** 0➔ [U] an elegant quality or a high level of skill that is impressive 優雅；典雅；高超：*She **has class** all right—she looks like a model.* 她的確手姿嫺雅，看上去像模特兒一樣。◇ *There's a real touch of class about this team.* 這支隊確實技藝超群。

▸ **IN TRAIN/PLANE** 火車；飛機 **9** 0➔ [C] (especially in compounds 尤用於構成複合詞) each of several different levels of comfort that are available to travellers in a plane, etc. 等級；艙位等級：*He always travels business class.* 他總是坐公務艙旅行。◇ *The first-class compartment is situated at the front of the train.* 頭等車廂位於火車的前部。➲ see also BUSINESS CLASS, ECONOMY CLASS SYNDROME, FIRST CLASS, SECOND CLASS, THIRD CLASS, TOURIST CLASS

▸ **OF UNIVERSITY DEGREE** 大學學位 **10** [C] (especially in compounds 尤用於構成複合詞) one of the levels of achievement in a British university degree exam（英國學位考試的）等級：*a **first-/second-/third-class** degree* 一級優等／二級優等／第三等學位

C

▸ BIOLOGY 生物學 **11** [C] a group into which animals, plants, etc. that have similar characteristics are divided, below a PHYLUM （動植物等分類的）綱 ➲ compare FAMILY (5), GENUS, SPECIES **IDM** see CHATTER *v.*
▪ *verb* [often passive] **~ sb/sth (as sth)** to think or decide that sb/sth is a particular type of person or thing 把…看作（或分類、歸類） **SYN** **classify**：*Immigrant workers were classed as aliens.* 移民勞工被歸為外僑類。
▪ *adj.* [only before noun] (*informal*) very good 很好的；優秀的；出色的：*a **class player/performer*** 優秀的選手／表演者 ◇ *She's a real **class act**.* 她真是魅力非凡。

ˌclass ˈaction *noun* (*NAmE*) a type of LAWSUIT that is started by a group of people who have the same problem 集體訴訟

ˈclass-conscious *adj.* very aware of belonging to a particular social class and of the differences between social classes 有階級意識的；有社會階層意識的 ▸ **ˈclass-conscious·ness** *noun* [U]

Synonyms 同義詞辨析

classic / classical

These adjectives are frequently used with the following nouns. 以上形容詞常與下列名詞連用：

classic ~	classical ~
example	music
case	ballet
novel	architecture
work	scholar
car	period

- **Classic** describes something that is accepted as being of very high quality and one of the best of its kind. * classic 指經典的、優秀的、一流的：*a classic movie/work* 經典影片／作品 It is also used to describe a typical example of something 該詞亦可表示典型的：*a classic example/mistake* 典型的例子／錯誤 or something elegant but simple and traditional. 或表示古典的、典雅的：*classic design* 典雅的設計
- **Classical** describes a form of traditional Western music and other things that are traditional in style. * classical 表示西方古典音樂及其他傳統的事物：*a classical composer* 古典派作曲家 ◇ *a classical theory* 古典學說 It is also used to talk about things that are connected with the culture of Ancient Greece and Rome. 該詞亦用於指與古希臘和古羅馬文化有關的事物：*a classical scholar* 古典學者 ◇ *classical mythology* 古典神話

clas·sic 🔑 **AW** /ˈklæsɪk/ *adj., noun*
▪ *adj.* [usually before noun] **1** 🔑 accepted or deserving to be accepted as one of the best or most important of its kind 最優秀的；第一流的：*a classic novel/study/goal* 最佳小說／研究／進球 **2** 🔑 (also **clas·sic·al**) with all the features you would expect to find; very typical 有特點的；有代表性的；典型的：*a **classic example** of poor communication* 缺乏溝通的典型實例 ◇ *She displayed the classic symptoms of depression.* 她顯現出了抑鬱症的典型症狀。◇ *I made the classic mistake of clapping in a pause in the music!* 我在樂曲演奏暫停的間歇鼓起掌來，真是大錯特錯！ **3** 🔑 elegant, but simple and traditional in style or design; not affected by changes in fashion （風格或設計）典雅的，古樸的；傳統的：*a classic grey suit* 一套典雅的灰色服裝 ◇ *classic design* 古樸典雅的設計 ◇ ***classic cars*** (= cars which are no longer made, but which are still popular) 古典雅致的老式車 **4** (*informal*) people say **That's classic!** when they find sth very amusing, when they think sb has been very stupid or when sth annoying, but not surprising, happens 惹笑的；愚蠢（或令人討厭）而又不足為奇的：*She's not going to help? Oh, that's classic!* 她不來幫忙？哦，那不足為奇！
▪ *noun* **1** 🔑 [C] a book, film/movie or song which is well known and considered to be of very high quality, setting standards for other books, etc. （書、電影或歌曲的）經典作品，名著，傑作：*English classics such as 'Alice in Wonderland'* 英語經典作品如《艾麗絲漫遊奇境記》◇ *The novel may become a modern classic.* 這部小說可能會成為現代名著。 **2** 🔑 [C] a thing that is an excellent example of its kind 優秀的典範：*That match was a classic.* 那場比賽堪稱經典。 **3** **Classics** [U] the study of ancient Greek and Roman culture, especially their languages and literature 古希臘與古羅馬的文化研究（尤指對其語言與文學的研究）：*a degree in Classics* 古希臘與古羅馬文化研究的學位

clas·sic·al **AW** /ˈklæsɪkl/ *adj.* [usually before noun] **1** widely accepted and used for a long time; traditional in style or idea 古典的；經典的；傳統的：*the classical economics of Smith and Ricardo* 亞當 • 斯密與李嘉圖的古典經濟學 ◇ *the classical theory of unemployment* 傳統的失業理論 ◇ *classical and modern ballet* 古典與現代芭蕾舞 **2** connected with or influenced by the culture of ancient Greece and Rome 和古希臘與古羅馬文化相關的；受古希臘與古羅馬的文化影響的：*classical studies* 古希臘與古羅馬的文化研究 ◇ *a classical scholar* (= an expert in Latin and Greek) 研究拉丁文與希臘文的學者 **3** (of music 音樂) written in a Western musical tradition, usually using an established form (for example a SYMPHONY) and not played on electronic instruments. Classical music is generally considered to be serious and to have a lasting value. 古典的：*He plays classical music, as well as pop and jazz.* 他既演奏古典音樂，也演奏流行音樂和爵士樂。◇ *a **classical composer/violinist*** 古典音樂作曲家／小提琴手 ➲ **COLLOCATIONS** at MUSIC **4** = CLASSIC *adj.* (2)：*These are classical examples of food allergy.* 這些是食物過敏的典型病例。 **5** (of a language 語言) ancient in its form and no longer used in a spoken form 古文的；文言的：*classical Arabic* 古阿拉伯語 **6** simple and attractive 簡潔優美的；樸實美觀的：*the classical elegance of the design* 設計簡潔典雅 ▸ **clas·sic·al·ly** /ˈklæsɪkli/ *adv.*：*Her face is classically beautiful.* 她的臉質樸秀麗。◇ *a **classically trained** singer* 受過古典派訓練的歌手

clas·si·cism /ˈklæsɪsɪzəm/ *noun* [U] **1** a style of art and literature that is simple and elegant and is based on the styles of ancient Greece and Rome. Classicism was popular in Europe in the 18th century. 古典主義（基於古希臘與古羅馬風格，18 世紀盛行於歐洲） **2** a style or form that has simple, natural qualities and pleasing combinations of parts 古典風格

clas·si·cist /ˈklæsɪsɪst/ *noun* **1** a person who studies ancient Greek or Latin 古希臘文研究者；拉丁文研究者；古典學者 **2** a person who follows classicism in art or literature （藝術或文學上的）古典主義者

clas·si·fi·able /ˈklæsɪfaɪəbl/ *adj.* that you can or should CLASSIFY 可分類（或級別）的；應分類（或級別）的：*The information was not easily classifiable.* 此信息不易分類。◇ *top-secret or classifiable information* 絕密或機密信息

clas·si·fi·ca·tion /ˌklæsɪfɪˈkeɪʃn/ *noun* **1** [U] the act or process of putting people or things into a group or class (= of CLASSIFYING them) 分類；歸類；分級：*a style of music that defies classification* (= is like no other) 獨特的音樂風格 **2** [C] a group, class, division, etc. into which sb or sth is put 類別；等級；門類 **3** [U] (*biology* 生) the act of putting animals, plants, etc. into groups, classes or divisions according to their characteristics （動植物等的）分類學，分類法 **4** [C] (*technical* 術語) a system of arranging books, tapes, magazines, etc. in a library into groups according to their subject （圖書館的書、磁帶、雜誌等的）分類系統，編目

clas·si·fied /ˈklæsɪfaɪd/ *adj.* [usually before noun] **1** (of information 信息) officially secret and available only to particular people 機密的；保密的：***classified information/documents/material*** 機密信息／文件／材料 **OPP** **unclassified** **2** with information arranged in groups according to subjects 分類的；歸類的：*a classified catalogue* 分類目錄 **3** **classifieds** *noun* [pl.] = CLASSIFIED ADVERTISEMENTS

C

ˌ**classified adˈvertisements** (also ˌ**classified ˈads**, ˈ**classifieds**) (*BrE* also ˈ**small ads**) (*NAmE* also ˈ**want ads**) *noun* [pl.] the section in a newspaper with small advertisements arranged in groups according to their subject, that are placed by people or small companies who want to buy or sell sth, find or offer a job, etc.（報章上的）分類廣告

clas·si·fier /ˈklæsɪfaɪə(r)/ *noun* (*grammar* 語法) an AFFIX or word which shows that a word belongs to a group of words with similar meanings. For example the prefix 'un' is a classifier that shows the word is negative. 分類成分，分類詞（能顯示同義所屬關係，如前綴 un 是表示反義的分類成分）

clas·sify /ˈklæsɪfaɪ/ *verb* (**clas·si·fies**, **clas·si·fy·ing**, **clas·si·fied**, **clas·si·fied**) **1** **~ sth** to arrange sth in groups according to features that they have in common 分類；歸類：*The books in the library **are classified according to** subject.* 圖書館的書按學科分類。◇ *Patients **are classified into** three categories.* 病人被歸為三種類型。**2** **~ sb/sth as sth** to decide which type or group sb/sth belongs to 劃分；區分；界定：*Only eleven of these accidents were classified as major.* 這些事故中只有十一例被判定為重大事故。

class·less /ˈklɑːsləs; *NAmE* ˈklæs-/ *adj.* **1** (*approving*) with no divisions into social classes 無階級的：*Will Britain ever become a classless society?* 英國會有可能成為無階級的社會嗎？**2** not clearly belonging to a particular social class 不明顯屬於社會某階級（或階層）的：*a classless accent* 不帶社會階層特徵的口音 ▸ **class·less·ness** *noun* [U]

class·mate /ˈklɑːsmeɪt; *NAmE* ˈklæs-/ *noun* a person who is or was in the same class as you at school or college 同班同學

class·room 🔑 /ˈklɑːsruːm; -rʊm; *NAmE* ˈklæs-/ *noun* a room where a class of children or students is taught 教室；課堂：*classroom activities* 課堂活動 ◇ *the use of computers in the classroom* 在課堂使用計算機 ➲ VISUAL VOCAB page V70

ˌ**class ˈstruggle** (also ˌ**class ˈwar**) *noun* [U, sing.] (*politics* 政) opposition between the different social classes in society, especially that described in Marxist theory（尤指馬克思主義理論描述的）階級鬥爭

classy /ˈklɑːsi; *NAmE* ˈklæsi/ *adj.* (**class·ier**, **classi·est**) (*informal*) of high quality; expensive and/or fashionable 上等的；豪華的；時髦的：*a classy player* 優秀選手 ◇ *a classy hotel/restaurant* 豪華的旅館/餐館

clat·ter /ˈklætə(r)/ *verb* **1** [I] if hard objects **clatter**, they knock together and make a loud noise（硬物相碰）發出響亮的撞擊聲：*He dropped the knife and it clattered on the stone floor.* 他一失手，刀子噹啷一聲掉到石頭地面上。◇ *Her cup clattered in the saucer.* 她的杯子把茶碟碰得叮噹響。**2** [I] **+ adv./prep.** to move making a loud noise like hard objects knocking together 移動發出（像硬物碰撞）的響聲：*The cart clattered over the cobbles.* 大車哐噹哐噹地行駛在卵石路上。◇ *She heard him clattering around downstairs.* 她聽到他在樓下咔嗞咔嗞地走來走去。▸ **clat·ter** (also **clat·ter·ing**) *noun* [sing.]：*the clatter of horses' hoofs* 嗒嗒的馬蹄聲

clause AW /klɔːz/ *noun* **1** (*grammar* 語法) a group of words that includes a subject and a verb, and forms a sentence or part of a sentence 從句；分句；子句：*In the sentence 'They often go to Italy because they love the food', 'They often go to Italy' is the main clause and 'because they love the food' is a subordinate clause.* 在 They often go to Italy because they love the food 這個句子裏，They often go to Italy 是主句，because they love the food 是從句。**2** an item in a legal document that says that a particular thing must or must not be done（法律文件的）條款

claus·tro·pho·bia /ˌklɔːstrəˈfəʊbiə; *NAmE* -ˈfoʊ-/ *noun* [U] an extreme fear of being in a small confined place; the unpleasant feeling that a person gets in a situation which restricts them 幽閉恐怖（症）；因受限制而產生的不適感：*to suffer from claustrophobia* 患幽閉恐怖症 ◇ *She felt she had to escape from the claustrophobia of family life.* 她感到她得擺脫家庭生活的那種幽閉感覺了。➲ compare AGORAPHOBIA

claus·tro·pho·bic /ˌklɔːstrəˈfəʊbɪk; *NAmE* -ˈfoʊ-/ *adj.* giving you claustrophobia; suffering from claustrophobia 引起幽閉恐怖的；患幽閉恐怖症的：*the claustrophobic atmosphere of the room* 房間裏的幽閉恐怖氣氛 ◇ *to feel claustrophobic* 感到幽閉恐怖 ▸ **claus·tro·pho·bic** *noun*

clave /kleɪv; ˈklɑːveɪ/ *noun* **1** one of a pair of wooden sticks that are hit together to make a sound 克拉維棍（打擊樂器，成雙）**2** a rhythm that forms the basis of Latin music 敲擊節奏（拉丁音樂的一個基本節奏）

clavi·chord /ˈklævɪkɔːd; *NAmE* -kɔːrd/ *noun* an early type of musical instrument, like a piano with a very soft tone 古鋼琴；擊弦鍵琴

clav·icle /ˈklævɪkl/ *noun* (*anatomy* 解) the COLLARBONE 鎖骨 ➲ VISUAL VOCAB page V59

claw /klɔː/ *noun, verb*

■ ***noun*** **1** one of the sharp curved nails on the end of an animal's or a bird's foot（動物或禽類的）爪，腳爪 ➲ VISUAL VOCAB page V12 **2** a long, sharp curved part of the body of some types of SHELLFISH, used for catching and holding things（水生有殼動物的）螯，鉗：*the claws of a crab* 螃蟹的螯 ➲ picture at SHELLFISH ➲ VISUAL VOCAB page V13 **3** part of a tool or machine, like a claw, used for holding, pulling or lifting things 爪形夾具；（機械的）爪 ➲ VISUAL VOCAB page V20 ➲ see also CLAW HAMMER

IDM **get your claws into sb** **1** (*disapproving*) if a woman **gets her claws** into a man, she tries hard to make him marry her or to have a relationship with her（女人）死死纏住（男人）**2** to criticize sb severely 嚴厲批評：*Wait until the media gets its claws into her.* 等着媒體來嚴厲批駁她吧。➲ more at RED *adj.*

■ ***verb*** [I, T] to scratch or tear sb/sth with claws or with your nails（用爪子或手指甲）抓，撕，撓：**~ at sb/sth** *The cat was clawing at the leg of the chair.* 那隻貓在抓撓椅子腿。◇ **~ sb/sth** *She had clawed Stephen across the face.* 她抓過斯蒂芬的臉。◇ (*figurative*) *His hands clawed the air.* 他的雙手在空中亂抓。

IDM **claw your way back, into sth, out of sth, to sth, etc.** to gradually achieve sth or move somewhere by using a lot of determination and effort 努力逐步獲得；艱難地移動：*She clawed her way to the top of her profession.* 她努力不懈，終於爬到了職業的頂峰。◇ *Slowly, he clawed his way out from under the collapsed building.* 他艱難地從倒塌的大樓廢墟底下慢慢爬了出來。

PHR V ˌ**claw sth↔ˈback** **1** to get sth back that you have lost, usually by using a lot of effort 設法撈回；費力地挽回 **2** (of a government 政府) to get back money that has been paid to people, usually by taxing them（常通過稅收手段）收回（已支付給民眾的錢款）➲ related noun CLAWBACK

claw·back /ˈklɔːbæk/ *noun* (*BrE, business* 商) the act of getting money back from people it has been paid to; the money that is paid back 已支付給民眾錢款的收回；回收款

ˈ**claw hammer** *noun* a hammer with one split, curved side that is used for pulling out nails 魚尾錘；拔釘錘；羊角榔頭

clay /kleɪ/ *noun* [U] a type of heavy, sticky earth that becomes hard when it is baked and is used to make things such as pots and bricks 黏土；陶土 ➲ SYNONYMS at SOIL IDM see FOOT *n.*

ˈ**clay court** *noun* a TENNIS COURT that has a surface made of clay 紅土網球場；沙地網球場

clayey /kleɪi/ *adj.* containing clay; like clay 含黏土的；黏土質的；似黏土的：*clayey soil* 黏性土壤

clay·more /ˈkleɪmɔː(r)/ *noun* a large SWORD with a broad blade with two sharp edges that was used in Scotland in the past（舊時蘇格蘭的）雙刃大刀

ˌ**clay ˈpigeon shooting** (*BrE*) (*NAmE* ˈ**skeet shooting**) *noun* a sport in which a disc of baked clay (called a **clay pigeon**) is thrown into the air for people to shoot at 泥鴿飛靶射擊運動

C

Synonyms 同義詞辨析

clean

wash • rinse • cleanse • dry-clean

These words all mean to remove dirt from sth, especially by using water and/or soap. 以上各詞均含打掃、洗淨之意，尤指用水、肥皂等。

clean to remove dirt or dust from sth, especially by using water or chemicals 指除去灰塵、打掃，尤指用水或化學品洗淨、擦淨：*The villa is cleaned twice a week.* 這棟別墅一週打掃兩次。◇ *Have you cleaned your teeth?* 你刷牙了嗎？◇ *This coat is filthy. I'll have it cleaned* (= dry-cleaned). 這件大衣髒了，我得送去乾洗。

wash to remove dirt from sth using water and usually soap 指洗、洗滌：*He quickly washed his hands and face.* 他很快把手和臉洗了。◇ *These jeans need washing.* 這條牛仔褲該洗了。

rinse to remove dirt, etc. from sth using clean water only, not soap; to remove the soap from sth with clean water after washing it 指用清水沖洗、清洗、沖掉皂液：*Make sure you rinse all the soap out.* 一定要把皂液沖洗乾淨。

cleanse to clean your skin or a wound 指清潔（皮膚）、清洗（傷口）

dry-clean to clean clothes using chemicals instead of water 指乾洗

PATTERNS

- to clean/wash/rinse/cleanse sth **in/with** sth
- to clean/wash/rinse sth **from** sth
- to clean/wash/cleanse a **wound**
- to clean/wash the **car/floor**
- to wash/rinse your **hair**
- to **have sth** cleaned/washed/dry-cleaned

clean 🔑 /kliːn/ *adj.*, *verb*, *adv.*, *noun*

■ ***adj.*** (**clean·er**, **clean·est**)

▸ **NOT DIRTY 清潔 1** 🔑 not dirty 潔淨的；乾淨的：*Are your hands clean?* 你的手乾淨嗎？◇ *to **wipe sth clean*** 把某物擦乾淨 ◇ *The hotel was **spotlessly*** (= extremely) ***clean***. 這家旅館乾淨得一塵不染。◇ (*BrE*) *It is your responsibility to **keep** the room **clean and tidy**.* 保持房間整潔是你的職責。◇ (*NAmE*) ***Keep** your room **neat and clean**.* 保持房間整潔。◇ *I can't find a clean shirt* (= one I haven't worn since it was washed). 我找不到一件乾淨的襯衫。 **2** 🔑 having a clean appearance and clean surroundings 愛乾淨的；愛整潔的：*Cats are very clean animals.* 貓是很愛乾淨的動物。

▸ **NOT HARMFUL 無害 3** 🔑 free from harmful or unpleasant substances 無有害物的；無污染的：*clean drinking water* 潔淨的飲用水 ◇ *clean air* 清潔的空氣 ◇ *cleaner cars* (= not producing so many harmful substances) 環保型汽車

▸ **PAPER 紙 4** 🔑 [usually before noun] with nothing written on it 空白的；未寫過的：*a clean sheet of paper* 一張空白紙

▸ **NOT OFFENSIVE 文明 5** 🔑 not offensive or referring to sex; not doing anything that is considered immoral or bad 文明的；無色情的；正派的：*The entertainment was **good clean fun** for the whole family.* 這種娛樂正派有趣，對全家老少都適合。◇ *Keep the jokes clean please!* 開玩笑請文明點！◇ *The sport has a very clean image.* 這項運動享有很文明的聲譽。

▸ **NOT ILLEGAL 合法 6** 🔑 not showing or having any record of doing sth that is against the law 無犯罪記錄的；守法的；清白的：*a **clean driving licence/driver's license*** 無違章記錄的駕駛執照 ◇ *a clean police record* 無違警記錄 **7** (*informal*) not owning or carrying anything illegal such as drugs or weapons 沒有私藏（或攜帶）違禁品（如毒品、武器等）的：*The police searched her but she was clean.* 警察搜了她的身，但未發現她攜帶任何違禁品。

▸ **FAIR 公正 8** played or done in a fair way and within the rules 公平的；守規則的；不違例的：*It was a tough but clean game.* 這是一場打得艱苦但卻是規規矩矩的比賽。

▸ **SMOOTH/SIMPLE 平整；簡潔 9** having a smooth edge, surface or shape; simple and regular 邊緣平整的；表面平滑的；簡潔規則的：*A sharp knife makes a clean cut.* 快刀切得整齊。◇ *a modern design with clean lines and a bright appearance* 線條流暢、外觀明快的現代設計

▸ **ACCURATE 準確 10** done in a skilful and accurate way 動作熟練而準確的；乾淨利落的：*The plane made a clean take-off.* 飛機起飛得乾淨利落。

▸ **TASTE/SMELL 味道；氣味 11** tasting, smelling or looking pleasant and fresh 清醇的；清新的：*The wine has a clean taste and a lovely golden colour.* 這葡萄酒味道清醇，色澤金黃。 ➲ compare UNCLEAN

IDM **as clean as a 'whistle** (*informal*) very clean 乾乾淨淨 **a clean bill of 'health** a report that says sb is healthy or that sth is in good condition 健康證明；合格證明 **a clean 'break 1** a complete separation from a person, an organization, a way of life, etc. （與人、組織、生活方式等的）徹底決裂：*She wanted to make a clean break with the past.* 她想與過去完全斷絕。 **2** a break in a bone in one place 一處骨折 **a clean 'sheet/'slate** a record of your work or behaviour that does not show any mistakes or bad things that you have done 無過錯記錄；清白的歷史：*No government operates with a completely clean sheet.* 沒有任何政府執政一點也不失誤。◇ *They kept a clean sheet in the match* (= no goals were scored against them). 他們在比賽中保持了未失一分的紀錄。 **make a clean 'breast of sth** to tell the truth about sth so that you no longer feel guilty 徹底坦白；如實供認；把…和盤托出 **make a clean sweep (of sth) 1** to remove all the people or things from an organization that are thought to be unnecessary or need changing 全部撤換；徹底清除 **2** to win all the prizes or parts of a game or competition; to win an election completely （比賽或競賽中）大獲全勝，包攬（所有獎項）；獲得選舉全勝：*China made a clean sweep of the medals in the gymnastics events.* 中國隊在體操比賽中包攬了所有的獎牌。◇ *The opinion poll suggests a clean sweep for the Democrats.* 民意測驗表明民主黨有可能大獲全勝。 ➲ more at NOSE *n.*, WIPE *v.*

■ ***verb* 1** 🔑 [T, I] **~ (sth)** to make sth free from dirt or dust by washing or rubbing it 除去…的灰塵；使…乾淨；打掃：*to clean the windows/bath/floor* 擦窗戶／浴缸／地板 ◇ *to clean a wound* 洗淨傷口 ◇ *Have you **cleaned your teeth**?* 你刷牙了嗎？◇ *The villa is cleaned twice a week.* 這棟別墅一週打掃兩次。◇ *I spent all day cooking and cleaning.* 我一整天都忙着做飯和打掃清潔。 ➲ see also DRY-CLEAN, SPRING-CLEAN **2** [I] to become clean 變乾淨：*This oven cleans easily* (= is easy to clean). 這烤箱容易擦洗。 **3** [T] **~ sth** = DRY-CLEAN：*This coat is filthy. I'll **have it cleaned**.* 這件大衣髒了，我得送去乾洗。 **4** [T] **~ sth** to remove the inside parts of a fish, chicken, etc. before you cook it （烹調前給魚、雞等）清除內臟

IDM **clean 'house** (*NAmE*) **1** to remove people or things that are not necessary or wanted 清除不必要的人（或事物）；裁減：*The new manager said he wanted to clean house.* 新上任的經理說他要裁員。 **2** to make your house clean 打掃房屋 **clean up your 'act** (*informal*) to start behaving in a moral or responsible way 改邪歸正；重新做人：*He cleaned up his act and came off drugs.* 他已改邪歸正戒掉了毒品。

PHR V **,clean sth↔'down** to clean sth thoroughly 徹底打掃；使…徹底乾淨：*All the equipment should be cleaned down regularly.* 所有設備都應該定期徹底打掃。 **'clean sth off/from sth | ,clean sth↔'off** to remove sth from sth by brushing, rubbing, etc. 把…刷（或擦）掉：*I cleaned the mud off my shoes.* 我刷掉了鞋子上的泥土。 **,clean sth↔'out** to clean the inside of sth thoroughly 把（某物）內部徹底打掃乾淨：*I must clean the fish tank out.* 我必須把養魚缸徹底清洗乾淨。 **,clean sb 'out** (*informal*) to use all of sb's money 耗盡（某人的）錢；用光（某人的）錢：*Paying for all those drinks has cleaned me out.* 購買那些飲料把我的錢花得一乾二淨。 **,clean sb/sth 'out** (*informal*) to steal everything from a person or place 洗劫：*The burglars totally cleaned her out.* 竊賊把她洗劫一空。 **,clean 'up** (*informal*) to win or make a lot of money 贏錢；賺大錢；發財：*This film should clean up at the box offices.* 這部電影在票房收入上應該能賺大錢。 **,clean (yourself) 'up** 🔑 (*informal*) to make yourself clean, usually by washing 把（身體）洗乾淨：*I need to change and clean up.* 我需要換洗一下。◇ *Go and clean yourself up.* 去梳洗乾淨吧。◇ *You'd better* ***get cleaned up***. 你最好去梳洗一下。➲ related noun CLEAN-UP **ˌclean ˈup | ˌclean sth↔ˈup** to remove dirt, etc. from somewhere 打掃（或清除）乾淨：*He always expected other people to* ***clean up after*** *him* (= when he had made the place dirty or untidy). 他總是指望別人來打掃他弄髒了的地方。◇ *Who's going to clean up this mess?* 這麼又髒又亂的，誰來清理？◇ *to clean up beaches after an oil spillage* 清理石油泄漏後被污染的海灘 ➲ related noun CLEAN-UP **ˌclean sth↔ˈup** to remove crime and immoral behaviour from a place or an activity 清除（某地或某活動中的）犯罪及不道德行為；清理；整頓：*The new mayor is determined to clean up the city.* 新上任的市長決心要整治好這座城市。◇ *Soccer needs to* ***clean up its image***. 足球界的形象需要改善。➲ related noun CLEAN-UP

▪ ***adv.*** (*informal*) used to emphasize that an action takes place completely （行動）徹底地，完全地：*The thief got clean away.* 那小偷已逃之夭夭。◇ *I clean forgot about calling him.* 我把給他打電話的事忘得一乾二淨。

IDM **come clean (with sb) (about sth)** to admit and explain sth that you have kept as a secret 全盤招供；和盤托出：*Isn't it time the government came clean about their plans for education?* 這難道不是政府徹底說明教育計劃的時候了嗎？

▪ ***noun*** [sing.] the act or process of cleaning sth 打掃；清掃：*The house needed a good clean.* 這房子需要徹底打掃。

ˌclean and ˈjerk *noun* an exercise in WEIGHTLIFTING in which a bar with weights is lifted to the shoulder, and then raised above the head （舉重）挺舉

ˌclean-ˈcut *adj.* (especially of a young man 尤指年輕男子) looking neat and clean and therefore socially acceptable 外表整潔的：*Simon's clean-cut good looks* 西蒙整潔英俊的外表

clean·er /ˈkliːnə(r)/ *noun* **1** a person whose job is to clean other people's houses or offices, etc. 清潔工：*an office cleaner* 辦公室清潔工 **2** a machine or substance that is used for cleaning 吸塵器；清潔劑；去污劑：*a vacuum cleaner* 真空吸塵器 ◇ *a bottle of kitchen cleaner* 一瓶廚房清潔劑 **3 cleaner's** (*pl.* **cleaners**) (also **ˌdry-ˈcleaner's**) a shop/store where clothes, curtains, etc. are cleaned, especially with chemicals 乾洗店：*Can you pick up my suit from the cleaner's?* 你能幫我從乾洗店取回我的西服嗎？

IDM **take sb to the ˈcleaners** (*informal*) **1** to steal all of sb's money, etc., or to get it using a trick 將某人洗劫一空；搶光（或騙盡）某人的錢財 **2** to defeat sb completely 徹底打敗某人：*Our team got taken to the cleaners.* 我們隊被打得一敗塗地。

clean·ing /ˈkliːnɪŋ/ *noun* [U] the work of making the inside of a house, etc. clean 打掃；掃除；清潔：*They pay someone to* ***do the cleaning***. 他們花錢雇人打掃。➲ VISUAL VOCAB page V20

ˈcleaning lady (also **ˈcleaning woman**) *noun* a woman whose job is to clean the rooms and furniture in an office, a house, etc. （辦公室、房屋等的）清潔女工

ˌclean-ˈlimbed *adj.* (of a person 人) thin and with a good shape 體形修長優美的；苗條的：*a clean-limbed model* 身材苗條的模特兒

clean·li·ness /ˈklenlinəs/ *noun* [U] the state of being clean or the habit of keeping things clean 清潔；乾淨；愛乾淨的習慣：*Some people are obsessive about cleanliness.* 有些人有潔癖。

ˌclean-ˈliving *adj.* (of a person 人) living a healthy life, by not drinking alcohol, not having sex with a lot of different people, etc. 生活健康正派的

clean·ly /ˈkliːnli/ *adv.* **1** easily and smoothly in one movement 乾淨利落地；利索地：*The boat moved cleanly through the water.* 小船在水面上輕快地行進。**2** in a clean way 清潔地；乾淨地：*fuel that burns cleanly* 環保型的燃料

cleanse /klenz/ *verb* **1** [T, I] **~ (sth)** to clean your skin or a wound 清潔（皮膚）；清洗（傷口）：*a cleansing cream* 潔膚霜 ➲ SYNONYMS at CLEAN **2** [T] **~ sb (of/from sth)** (*literary*) to take away sb's guilty feelings or SIN 使免除（罪過）；使淨化 ➲ see also ETHNIC CLEANSING

cleans·er /ˈklenzə(r)/ *noun* **1** a liquid or cream for cleaning your face, especially for removing make-up （尤指用於清除臉上化妝的）潔膚液，潔膚霜 **2** a substance that contains chemicals and is used for cleaning things 清潔劑

ˌclean-ˈshaven *adj.* a man who is **clean-shaven** does not have a beard or MOUSTACHE (= hair that has been allowed to grow on the face) 鬍子刮淨的；刮過臉的

ˈclean-up *noun* [usually sing.] the process of removing dirt, pollution, or things that are considered bad or immoral from a place 清掃；清除（污染物）；清理；整頓：*the clean-up of the river* 河流清理 ◇ *a clean-up campaign* 整頓運動

clear 0-w /klɪə(r); *NAmE* klɪr/ *adj., verb, adv., noun*

> **WORD FAMILY**
> **clear** *adj.* (≠ unclear)
> **clearly** *adv.*
> **clarity** *noun*
> **clarify** *verb*

▪ ***adj.*** (**clear·er, clear·est**)

▸ **WITHOUT CONFUSION/DOUBT 清晰；無疑問** **1** 0-w easy to understand and not causing any confusion 清晰易懂的；明白清楚的；不含混的：*She gave me clear and precise directions.* 她給了我清晰而準確的指示。◇ *Are these instructions clear enough?* 這些說明夠清楚了嗎？◇ *You'll do as you're told, is that clear?* 叫你做什麼你就去做什麼，明白嗎？◇ *This behaviour must stop—do I* ***make myself clear*** (= express myself clearly so there is no doubt about what I mean)? 這種行為必須停止。我講清楚了吧？◇ *I hope I* ***made it clear*** *to him that he was no longer welcome here.* 我希望我已經給他講清楚他在這裏不再受歡迎。**2** 0-w obvious and leaving no doubt at all 明顯的；顯然的；明確的：*This is a clear case of fraud.* 這無疑是一樁詐騙案。◇ *She won the election by a clear majority.* 她以明顯的多數贏得選舉。◇ *His height gives him a clear advantage.* 他的身高使他具有明顯的優勢。◇ **~ (to sb) (that) ...** ***It was*** *quite* ***clear*** *to me* ***that*** *she was lying.* 我十分清楚她在撒謊。◇ **~ what, how, whether, etc. ...** *It is not clear what they want us to do.* 我們不肯定他們要我們做什麼。➲ LANGUAGE BANK at EVIDENCE, IMPERSONAL **3** 0-w having or feeling no doubt or confusion 無疑的；清楚的；明白的：**~ about/on sth** *Are you clear about the arrangements for tomorrow?* 你清楚明天的安排嗎？◇ *My memory is not clear on that point.* 那一點我記不清了。◇ **~ what, how, whether, etc. ...** *I'm still not clear what the job involves.* 我仍然不明白這項工作包括哪些內容。◇ *We need a* ***clear understanding*** *of the problems involved.* 我們需要瞭解清楚所涉及的各種問題。➲ SYNONYMS at SURE

▸ **MIND 頭腦** **4** 0-w thinking in a sensible and logical way, especially in a difficult situation （尤指在困境中）思維敏銳而有邏輯的，頭腦清醒的：*a clear thinker* 思維清晰的人 ◇ *You'll need to* ***keep a clear head*** *for your interview.* 你面試時須要保持清醒的頭腦。

▸ **EASY TO SEE/HEAR 容易看見／聽到** **5** 0-w easy to see or hear 容易看見的；聽得清的：*The photo wasn't very clear.* 這張照片不太清晰。◇ *The voice on the phone was clear and strong.* 電話上的聲音清晰洪亮。◇ *She was in Australia but I could hear her voice* ***as clear as a bell***. 她雖然在澳大利亞，但我卻能非常清楚地聽到她的聲音。

▸ **TRANSPARENT 透明** **6** 0-w that you can see through 透明的；清澈的：*The water was so clear we could see the bottom of the lake.* 湖水清澈見底。◇ *clear glass* 透明的玻璃 ◇ *a clear colourless liquid* 透明的無色液體

▸ **SKY/WEATHER 天空；天氣** **7** 0-w without cloud or MIST 無雲（或霧）的；晴朗的：*a clear blue sky* 晴朗的碧空 ◇ *On a clear day you can see France.* 天氣晴朗時你可以看見法國。

▸ **SKIN 皮膚** **8** without spots or marks 無斑（或疤痕）的：*clear skin* 沒有絲毫斑點的皮膚 ◇ *a clear complexion* 無瑕的面龐

▸ **EYES 眼睛** **9** bright and lively 明亮有神的

▸ **NOT BLOCKED 無阻礙** **10 ~ (of sth)** free from things that are blocking the way or covering the surface of sth

暢通無阻的；無障礙的；（表面）收拾乾淨的：*The road was clear and I ran over.* 路上沒有東西擋着，我就跑了過來。◇ *All exits must be kept clear of baggage.* 所有出口必須保持通暢，不得堆放行李。◇ *You won't get a clear view of the stage from here.* 從這裏看舞台，你的視野會受到遮擋。◇ *I always leave a clear desk at the end of the day.* 每天工作結束時，我總是把桌面收拾乾淨。

▸ **CONSCIENCE 良心 11** if you have a **clear** CONSCIENCE or your CONSCIENCE is **clear**, you do not feel guilty 無罪的；清白的；問心無愧的

▸ **FREE FROM STH BAD 與壞事不沾邊 12 ~ of sth** free from sth that is unpleasant 擺脱掉（不愉快事物）的：*They were still not clear of all suspicion.* 他們仍未解除所有的嫌疑。◇ *We are finally clear of debt.* 我們終於償清了債務。

▸ **NOT TOUCHING/NEAR 不接觸；不靠近 13** [not before noun] **~ (of sb/sth)** not touching sth; a distance away from sth 不接觸；遠離：*The plane climbed until it was clear of the clouds.* 飛機爬升直至穿出了雲層。◇ *Make sure you park your car clear of the entrance.* 切莫把車停在入口處。

▸ **PERIOD OF TIME 一段時間 14** [only before noun] whole or complete 全部的；整體的；完整的：*Allow three clear days for the letter to arrive.* 信要整整三天才能寄到。

▸ **SUM OF MONEY 款項 15** [only before noun] remaining when taxes, costs, etc. have been taken away（扣除稅項、成本等後）淨的，純的 **SYN net**：*They had made a clear profit of £2 000.* 他們已賺得 2 000 英鎊的淨利。

▸ **PHONETICS 語音學 16** (of a speech sound 語音) produced with the central part of the tongue close to the top of the mouth. In many accents of English, clear /l/ is used before a vowel, as in *leave*. 清晰的 **OPP dark**

IDM be clear 'sailing (*US*) = BE PLAIN SAILING at PLAIN *adj.* **(as) clear as 'day** easy to see or understand 顯而易見；容易理解 **(as) clear as 'mud** (*informal, humorous*) not clear at all; not easy to understand 一點不清楚；難懂：*Oh well, that's all as clear as mud, then.* 哎呀，那麼一來這真是成了一本糊塗賬了。➲ more at COAST *n.*, FIELD *n.*, HEAD *n.*, LOUD *adv.*

■ ***verb***

▸ **REMOVE STH/SB 移動某物；使某人離去 1** 🔑 [T] to remove sth that is not wanted or needed from a place 移走，搬走，清除（不需要的東西）：**~ sth/sb** *I had cleared my desk before I left.* 離開前我清理乾淨了辦公桌。◇ *It was several hours before the road was cleared after the accident.* 事故過去幾小時後這條道路才被疏通。◇ *It's your turn to **clear the table*** (= to take away the dirty plates, etc. after a meal). 該輪到你收拾餐桌了。◇ *She **cleared a space** on the sofa for him to sit down.* 她在沙發上清出一個空位讓他坐下。◇ **~ A (of B)** *I cleared my desk of papers.* 我清理好了寫字枱上的文件。◇ *The streets had been cleared of snow.* 街道上的積雪已被清除乾淨。◇ **~ B (from/off A)** *Clear all those papers off the desk.* 把桌子上所有那些文件都拿走。◇ *The remains of the snow had been cleared from the streets.* 街道上的殘雪已被清掃乾淨。➲ see also CLEAR AWAY at CLEAR *v.* **2** 🔑 [T] **~ sth** to make people leave a place 使人離開：*After the bomb warning, police cleared the streets.* 接到有炸彈的警告後，警察疏散了街上的行人。

▸ **NOT BE BLOCKED 不受阻礙 3** 🔑 [I] to move freely again; to no longer be blocked 恢復暢通；不再受阻：*The traffic took a long time to clear after the accident.* 事故後很久交通才恢復暢通。◇ *The boy's lungs cleared and he began to breathe more easily.* 男孩的肺部恢復通暢後，呼吸開始比較輕鬆。

▸ **OF LIQUID 液體 4** 🔑 [I] when a liquid **clears**, it becomes transparent and you can see through it 變透明；變清澈：*The muddy water slowly cleared.* 渾濁的水慢慢變得清澈起來。

▸ **OF SMOKE, ETC. 煙等 5** 🔑 [I] **~ (away)** when smoke, FOG, etc. **clears**, it disappears so that it is easier to see things（煙、霧等）消散，散去，消失：*The mist will clear by mid-morning.* 霧將在上午十時左右消散。

▸ **OF SKY/WEATHER 天空；天氣 6** [I] when the sky or the weather **clears**, it becomes brighter and free of cloud or rain 變明朗；轉晴；放晴：*The sky cleared after the storm.* 暴風雨過後，天轉晴了。◇ *The rain is clearing slowly.* 雨漸漸停下來。

▸ **YOUR HEAD/MIND 頭腦；思路 7** [I, T] if your head or mind **clears**, or you **clear** it, you become free of

thoughts that worry or confuse you or the effects of alcohol, a blow, etc. and you are able to think clearly（使）變清醒，變清晰：*As her mind cleared, she remembered what had happened.* 頭腦清醒之後，她想起了所發生的一切。◇ **~ sth** *I went for a walk to clear my head.* 我去散一會兒步好清醒清醒頭腦。

▸ **OF FACE/EXPRESSION 臉色；表情 8** [I] if your face or expression **clears**, you stop looking angry or worried 變平靜；變開朗

▸ **PROVE SB INNOCENT 證明無罪 9** [T] **~ sb (of sth)** to prove that sb is innocent 證明無罪（或無辜）：*She was cleared of all charges against her.* 對她的所有指控均已撤銷。◇ *Throughout his years in prison, he fought to **clear his name**.* 在整個服刑期間，他奮力證明自己名譽的清白。

▸ **GIVE OFFICIAL PERMISSION 正式批准 10** [T] to give or get official approval for sth to be done 批准；准許；得到許可：**~ sth** *His appointment had been cleared by the board.* 他的任命已由董事會批准。◇ **~ sth with sb/sth** *I'll have to **clear it** with the manager.* 這事我須要獲得經理的准許。 **11** [T] **~ sth** to give official permission for a person, a ship, a plane or goods to leave or enter a place 批准（人、船隻、飛機或貨物）離境（或入境）；使通過（海關）：*The plane had been cleared for take-off.* 飛機已獲准起飛。◇ *to clear goods through customs* 給貨物結關 **12** [T] **~ sb** to decide officially, after finding out information about sb, that they can be given special work or allowed to see secret papers（經審查後）正式批准（某人）做機密工作（或閱讀機密文件）：*She hasn't been cleared by security.* 她未獲保安部門批准做機要工作。

▸ **MONEY 款項 13** [I, T] **~ (sth)** if a cheque that you pay into your bank account **clears**, or a bank **clears** it, the money is available for you to use 兑現（支票）：*Cheques usually take three working days to clear.* 兑現支票通常需要三個工作日。 **14** [T] **~ sth** to gain or earn a sum of money as profit 獲利；淨賺：*She cleared £1 000 on the deal.* 她在那筆交易中淨賺 1 000 英鎊。 **15** [T] **~ sth** if you **clear** a debt or a loan, you pay all the money back 償清，還清（債務或貸款）

▸ **GET OVER/PAST 越過；通過 16** [T] **~ sth** to jump over or get past sth without touching it（無接觸地）躍過，越過，通過：*The horse cleared the fence easily.* 那匹馬輕鬆地躍過了柵欄。◇ *The car only just cleared* (= avoided hitting) *the gatepost.* 那輛汽車通過時險些撞上門柱。

▸ **IN SPORT 體育運動 17** [T, I] **~ (sth)** (in football (SOCCER) and some other sports 足球及其他一些體育運動) if you **clear** a ball, or a ball **clears**, it is kicked or hit away from the area near your own goal 將（球）擊出己方球門區；（球）滾出己方球門區

IDM clear the 'air to improve a difficult or TENSE situation by talking about worries, doubts, etc.（通過傾訴）改變困境，緩解緊張狀態，改善氣氛 **clear the 'decks** (*informal*) to prepare for an activity, event, etc. by removing anything that is not essential to it 清除障礙準備行動 **clear your 'throat** to cough so that you can speak clearly 清喉嚨；清嗓子 **clear the way (for sth/for sth to happen)** to remove things that are stopping the progress or movement of sth（為…）清除障礙，掃清道路：*The ruling could clear the way for extradition proceedings.* 這項裁決也許能為引渡程序鋪平道路。➲ more at COBWEB

PHR V ˌclear a'way | ˌclear sth↔a'way to remove sth because it is not wanted or needed, or in order to leave a clear space 把…清除掉（以留出空間）：*He cleared away and made coffee.* 他把東西收拾好以後煮了咖啡。◇ *It's time your toys were cleared away.* 現在該收走你的玩具了。 **ˌclear 'off** (*informal*) to go or run away 離開；逃離；逃跑：*He cleared off when he heard the police siren.* 他聽到警笛便逃之夭夭。◇ *You've no right to be here. Clear off!* 你無權在這裏，走開！ **ˌclear 'out (of ...)** (*informal*) to leave a place quickly 迅速離開：*He cleared out with all the money and left her with the kids.* 他捲款而逃，把孩子丟給她。 **ˌclear 'out | ˌclear sth↔'out** 🔑 to make sth empty and clean by removing things or throwing things away 把…清空；清理；丟掉：*to clear out a drawer/room* 把抽屜／房間騰空 ◇ *We cleared out*

C

all our old clothes. 我們扔掉了所有的舊衣服。◇ *I found the letters when I was clearing out after my father died.* 我在父親去世後清理遺物時發現了這些信件。➲ related noun CLEAR-OUT ˌ**clear ˈup 1** (of the weather 天氣) to become fine or bright 轉晴；放晴；變晴朗：*I hope it clears up this afternoon.* 我希望今天下午天氣放晴。**2** (of an illness, infection, etc. 疾病、感染等) to disappear 痊癒；治癒；消失：*Has your rash cleared up yet?* 你的皮疹消失了嗎？ˌ**clear ˈup** | ˌ**clear sth↔ˈup** to make sth clean and neat 使整潔；清理：*It's time to clear up.* 該打掃了。◇ *I'm fed up with* ***clearing up after you!*** 你弄髒了的地方總是要我來打掃，我受夠了！◇ *Clear up your own mess!* 看你把這裏弄得又髒又亂的，你自己來收拾吧！ˌ**clear sth↔ˈup** to solve or explain sth 解決；解答；解釋：*to* ***clear up a mystery/difficulty/misunderstanding*** 揭開謎團；解決困難；消除誤會

■ ***adv.***

▸ **NOT NEAR/TOUCHING** 不靠近；不觸及 **1** ~ (of sth) away from sth; not near or touching sth 遠離；不靠近；不接觸：*Stand clear of the train doors.* 不要靠近列車門站立。◇ *He injured his arm as he jumped clear of the car.* 他跳離汽車時手臂受了傷。◇ *By lap two Walker was two metres clear of the rest of the runners.* 跑第二圈時，沃克已領先了其他賽跑者兩米。

▸ **ALL THE WAY** 一直 **2** (*especially NAmE*) all the way to sth that is far away 一直（到遠處）：*She could see clear down the highway into the town.* 她順着公路一直望去，能看到遠處的那座城鎮。

IDM **keep/stay/steer clear (of sb/sth)** to avoid a person or thing because it may cause problems 避開；迴避；躲避 ➲ more at WAY *n.*

■ ***noun***

IDM **in the ˈclear** (*informal*) no longer in danger or thought to be guilty of sth 不再有危險；不再被認為有罪：*It seems that the original suspect is in the clear.* 好像原先的嫌疑犯已被認定無罪。

clear·ance /ˈklɪərəns; *NAmE* ˈklɪr-/ *noun* **1** [C, U] the removal of things that are not wanted 清除；排除；清理：*forest clearances* 伐空的林地 ◇ *slum clearance* (= the removal of houses that are in very bad condition in an area of a town) 拆除貧民窟 ◇ *a clearance sale* (= in a shop/store, when goods are sold cheaply to get rid of them quickly) 清倉大甩賣 **2** [U, C] the amount of space or distance that is needed between two objects so that they do not touch each other 淨空；間距；間隙：*There is not much clearance for vehicles passing under this bridge.* 車輛在這座橋下通過時沒有多少餘隙。◇ *a clearance of one metre* 一米的間距 **3** [U, C] official permission that is given to sb before they can work somewhere, have particular information, or do sth they want to do（錄用或准許接觸機密以前的）審查許可，審核批准：*I'm waiting for clearance from headquarters.* 我在等待總部的錄用審查許可。◇ *All employees at the submarine base require security clearance.* 所有潛水艇基地的雇員必須得到安全部門的審查許可方可錄用。**4** [U] official permission for a person or vehicle to enter or leave an airport or a country（人、交通工具進出機場或出入境的）許可，准許：*The pilot was waiting for clearance for take-off.* 飛行員在等待起飛的許可。**5** [U, C] the process of a cheque being paid by a bank（支票的）兑現 **6** [C] a **clearance** in football (SOCCER) and some other sports is when a player kicks or hits the ball away from the goal of his or her own team（足球及其他一些體育運動中的）解圍

ˌ**clear-ˈcut** *adj.* definite and easy to see or identify 明確的；明顯的；易辨認的：*There is no clear-cut answer to this question.* 這個問題沒有確切的答案。

ˌ**clear-ˈheaded** *adj.* able to think in a clear and sensible way, especially in a difficult situation（尤指在困境中）頭腦清醒的，明白事理的

clear·ing /ˈklɪərɪŋ; *NAmE* ˈklɪrɪŋ/ *noun* **1** [C] an open space in a forest where there are no trees 林中空地 **SYN** glade ➲ VISUAL VOCAB pages V4, V5 **2** [U] (in Britain) the system used by universities to find students for the places on their courses that have not been filled shortly before the beginning of the academic year（英國大學的）補錄（學年開始前補招學生填補空缺名額）：*She got into university through clearing.* 她通過補錄上了大學。◇ *You can apply for a place through the clearing system.* 你可以通過補錄系統申請一個名額。◇ *The university has a limited number of clearing places this year.* 今年這所大學的補錄名額有限。

ˈ**clearing bank** *noun* (in Britain) a bank that uses a clearing house when dealing with other banks（英國）清算銀行，票據交換銀行

ˈ**clearing house** *noun* **1** a central office that banks use in order to pay each other money and exchange cheques, etc.（銀行）票據交換所，清算中心，結算所 **2** an organization that collects and exchanges information on behalf of people or other organizations 信息交換機構；信息交流所

Synonyms 同義詞辨析

clear

obvious • apparent • evident • plain

These words all describe sth that is easy to see or understand and leaves no doubts or confusion. 以上各詞均形容事物顯而易見、明白易懂、清楚、明確。

clear easy to see or understand and leaving no doubts 指顯而易見的、明白易懂的、清楚的、明確的：*It was quite clear to me that she was lying.* 我十分清楚她在撒謊。

obvious easy to see or understand 指明顯的、顯然的、易理解的：*It's obvious from what he said that something is wrong.* 根據他所説的，顯然是出問題了。

apparent [not usually before noun] (*rather formal*) easy to see or understand 指顯而易見、明白易懂、顯然：*It was apparent from her face that she was really upset.* 從面容上一眼就可以看出她確實心緒煩亂。

evident (*rather formal*) easy to see or understand 指清楚的、明白的、顯然的：*The orchestra played with evident enjoyment.* 管弦樂隊演奏得興致勃勃。

plain easy to see or understand 指清楚的、明顯的、淺白的：*He* ***made it*** *very* ***plain*** *that he wanted us to leave.* 他明確表示要我們離開。

WHICH WORD? 詞語辨析

These words all have almost exactly the same meaning. There are slight differences in register and patterns of use. If you *make sth clear/plain*, you do so deliberately because you want people to understand sth; if you *make sth obvious*, you usually do it without meaning to. 以上各詞意思幾乎相同，只是在語體風格和句型使用上稍有區別。make sth clear/plain 表示刻意為使別人明白；make sth obvious 通常並非刻意：~~*I hope I make myself obvious.*~~ ◇ ~~*Try not to make it so clear/plain.*~~ In the expressions *clear majority, for obvious reasons, for no apparent reason* and *plain to see*, none of the other words can be used instead. You can have *a clear/an obvious/a plain case of sth* but not ~~*an evident case of sth.*~~ 在 clear majority（明顯多數）、for obvious reasons（因為顯而易見的原因）、for no apparent reason（沒有明顯的原因）和 plain to see（顯而易見）中，不能用其他詞語替換。可以用 clear/obvious/plain case of sth（明顯的情況），但不能用 an evident case of sth。

PATTERNS

- clear/obvious/apparent/evident/plain **to** sb/sth
- clear/obvious/apparent/evident/plain **that/what/who/how/where/why** ...
- to **seem/become/make sth** clear/obvious/apparent/evident/plain
- **perfectly/quite/very** clear/obvious/apparent/evident/plain

clear·ly 0-w /ˈklɪəli; NAmE ˈklɪrli/ *adv.*
1 0-w in a way that is easy to see or hear 清楚地；清晰地：*Please speak clearly after the tone.* 請聽到信號後清楚地講話。 **2** 0-w in a way that is sensible and easy to understand 明白地；易懂地：*She explained everything very clearly.* 她把一切都解釋得很明白。 **3** 0-w used to emphasize that what you are saying is obvious and true 明顯地；顯然地 SYN **obviously**：*Clearly, this will cost a lot more than we realized.* 顯而易見，這將比我們所以為的花費要多得多。

clear·ness /ˈklɪənəs; NAmE ˈklɪrnəs/ *noun* [U] (much less frequent than *clarity* 不及 clarity 一詞用得頻繁) the state of being clear 清楚；清晰；明確

ˈclear-out *noun* [usually sing.] (*informal, especially BrE*) a process of getting rid of things or people that you no longer want 清理；清除：*have a clear-out* 清理一下

ˌclear-ˈsighted *adj.* understanding or thinking clearly; able to make good decisions and judgements 明智的；頭腦清楚的；有眼光的

ˈclear-up *noun* (*BrE*) the process of removing rubbish and tidying things 打掃清理：*a massive clear-up operation* 大掃除活動

clear·way /ˈklɪəweɪ; NAmE ˈklɪrweɪ/ *noun* (in Britain) a road on which vehicles must not stop （英國）禁停公路

cleat /kliːt/ *noun* **1** [C] a small wooden or metal bar fastened to sth, on which ropes may be fastened by winding （可繞繩索的）小木樁，金屬樁 **2** [C] a piece of rubber on the bottom of a shoe, etc. to stop it from slipping （鞋底等的）防滑釘 **3 cleats** [pl.] (*NAmE*) shoes with cleats, often worn for playing sports 防滑（運動）鞋 ➲ compare FOOTBALL BOOT, SPIKE *n.* (2), STUD (3)

cleav·age /ˈkliːvɪdʒ/ *noun* **1** [C, U] the space between a woman's breasts that can be seen above a dress that does not completely cover them （婦女穿低胸服時露出的）乳溝 **2** [C] (*formal*) a difference or division between people or groups （個人或集團之間的）差異，差別，分歧

cleave /kliːv/ *verb* (**cleaved**, **cleaved**) HELP Less commonly, **cleft** /kleft/ and **clove** /kləʊv/ /kloʊv/ are used for the past tense, and **cleft** and **cloven** /ˈkləʊvn/ /ˈkloʊvn/ for the past participle. 過去式 cleft 或 clove 以及過去分詞 cleft 或 cloven 比較不常用。 **1** [T] **~ sth** (*old-fashioned* or *literary*) to split or cut sth in two using sth sharp and heavy 劈開；砍開；剁開：*She cleaved his skull (in two) with an axe.* 她用斧頭把他的顱骨劈成兩半。◇ (*figurative*) *His skin was cleft with deep lines.* 他的皮膚佈滿深深的皺紋。 **2** [I, T] (*old-fashioned* or *literary*) to move quickly through sth 迅速穿過；迅速穿越：**~ through sth** *a ship cleaving through the water* 破浪前進的船 ◇ **~ sth** *The huge boat cleaved the darkness.* 那艘巨輪在黑暗中破浪前行。 **3** [I] **~ to sth/sb** (*literary*) to stick close to sth/sb 緊貼；緊挨：*Her tongue clove to the roof of her mouth.* 她的舌頭緊緊地貼着上腭。 **4** (**cleaved**, **cleaved**) [I] **~ to sth** (*formal*) to continue to believe in or be loyal to sth 堅信；信守；忠於：*to* ***cleave to a belief/idea*** 堅守信仰／信念 IDM see CLEFT *adj.*

cleav·er /ˈkliːvə(r)/ *noun* a heavy knife with a broad blade, used for cutting large pieces of meat 砍肉刀；剁肉刀 ➲ VISUAL VOCAB page V26

clef /klef/ *noun* (*music* 音) a symbol at the beginning of a line of printed music (called a STAVE or STAFF) that shows the PITCH of the notes on it 譜號：*the treble/bass clef* 高音／低音譜號 ➲ picture at MUSIC

cleft /kleft/ *noun, adj.* ➲ see also CLEAVE *v.*
■ *noun* a natural opening or crack, for example in the ground or in rock, or in a person's chin （自然的）裂口，裂縫：*a cleft in the rocks* 岩石的裂縫
■ *adj.*
IDM **be (caught) in a cleft ˈstick** to be in a difficult situation when any action you take will have bad results 進退維谷；陷入困境

ˌcleft ˈlip *noun* a condition in which sb is born with their upper lip split 唇裂；兔唇

ˌcleft ˈpalate *noun* a condition in which sb is born with the roof of their mouth split, making them unable to speak clearly 腭裂

ˌcleft ˈsentence *noun* (*grammar* 語法) a sentence that begins with 'it' or 'that' and has a following clause, for example, 'it is you that I love', or 'that is my mother you're insulting' 分裂句（以 it 或 that 開始，後接從句）

cle·ma·tis /ˈklemətɪs; kləˈmeɪtɪs/ *noun* [C, U] a climbing plant with large white, purple or pink flowers 鐵線蓮，轉子蓮（開白、紫或粉紅色花的攀緣植物）

clem·ency /ˈklemənsi/ *noun* [U] (*formal*) kindness shown to sb when they are being punished; willingness not to punish sb so severely （對受懲罰的人表現出的）仁慈，慈悲；寬恕；寬容 SYN **mercy**：*a plea for clemency* 乞求開恩

clem·ent /ˈklemənt/ *adj.* (*formal*) **1** (especially of weather 尤指天氣) mild and pleasant 溫和的；溫暖的 OPP **inclement** **2** showing kindness and MERCY to sb who is being punished （對受懲罰的人）仁慈的，寬恕的，寬容的

clem·en·tine /ˈklementiːn/ *noun* a fruit like a small orange 小柑橘

clench /klentʃ/ *verb* **1** [T, I] **~ (sth)** when you **clench** your hands, teeth, etc., or when they **clench**, you press or squeeze them together tightly, usually showing that you are angry, determined or upset（通常表示憤怒、決心或不安時）捏緊，攥緊（拳頭等），咬緊（牙齒等）：*He* ***clenched his fists*** *in anger.* 他憤怒地攥緊了拳頭。◇ *Through* ***clenched teeth*** *she told him to leave.* 她咬牙切齒地叫他離開。◇ *His fists clenched slowly until his knuckles were white.* 他的拳頭慢慢地捏緊，直捏得指關節都發白了。 **2** [T] **~ sth (in/between sth)** to hold sth tightly and firmly 握緊；抓牢；攥住：*Her pen was clenched between her teeth.* 她咬着筆。

clere·story /ˈklɪəstɔːri; NAmE ˈklɪrs-/ *noun* (*pl.* **-ies**) (*architecture* 建) the upper part of a wall in a large church, with a row of windows in it, above the level of the lower roofs （大教堂中在高於周圍屋頂的牆壁上開的）天窗，高側窗

clergy /ˈklɜːdʒi; NAmE ˈklɜːrdʒi/ (often **the clergy**) *noun* [pl.] the priests or ministers of a religion, especially of the Christian Church （統稱）聖職人員，神職人員：*All the local clergy were asked to attend the ceremony.* 所有當地的聖職人員都獲邀參加這項儀式。◇ *The new proposals affect both clergy and laity.* 新的提案使神職人員和平信徒都會受到影響。 ➲ COLLOCATIONS at RELIGION ➲ compare LAITY

cler·gy·man /ˈklɜːdʒimən; NAmE ˈklɜːrdʒ-/ (also **church·man**) *noun* (*pl.* **-men** /-mən/) a male priest or minister in the Christian Church （男）聖職人員，神職人員 ➲ compare PRIEST

cler·gy·wo·man /ˈklɜːdʒiwʊmən; NAmE ˈklɜːrdʒ-/ (also **church·wo·man**) *noun* (*pl.* **-women** /-wɪmɪn/) a female priest or minister in the Christian Church （女）聖職人員，神職人員

cler·ic /ˈklerɪk/ *noun* **1** (*old-fashioned* or *formal*) a member of the clergy 聖職人員；神職人員 **2** a religious leader in any religion 宗教領袖；宗教領導人：*Muslim clerics* 穆斯林神職領導人

cler·ic·al /ˈklerɪkl/ *adj.* **1** connected with office work 辦公室工作的：***clerical workers/staff/assistants*** 辦公室工作人員；全體辦事員；文書助理 ◇ *a clerical error* (= one made in copying or calculating sth) 筆誤（謄寫或計算中的錯誤） **2** connected with the CLERGY (= priests) 聖職人員的；神職人員的：***a clerical collar*** (= one that fastens at the back, worn by some priests) 聖職人員白領

clerk 0-w /klɑːk; NAmE klɜːrk/ *noun, verb*
■ *noun* **1** 0-w a person whose job is to keep the records or accounts in an office, shop/store, etc. 職員；簿記員；文書：*an office clerk* 辦公室職員 ➲ see also FILING CLERK **2** 0-w an official in charge of the records of a council, court, etc. （議會、法院等的）書記員：*the Town Clerk* 市政府書記員 ◇ *the Clerk of the Court* 法院書記員 ➲ see also CLERK OF WORKS, COUNTY CLERK, PARISH CLERK **3** 0-w (*NAmE*) = SALES CLERK：*The clerk*

at the counter gave me too little change. 櫃枱的售貨員給我少找了零錢。 **4** (also **'desk clerk**) (both *NAmE*) a person whose job is dealing with people arriving at or leaving a hotel 旅館服務枱接待員 SYN **receptionist**

C

■ ***verb*** [I] (*NAmE*) to work as a clerk 當職員（或文書、書記員）：*a clerking job* 職員工作

,clerk of 'works *noun* (*BrE*) a person whose job is to be in charge of repairs to buildings or of building works, for an organization or institution 物業維修（或建築工程）管理人員

clever /ˈklevə(r)/ *adj.* (**clever·er**, **clever·est**) HELP You can also use **more clever** and **most clever**. 亦可用 more clever 和 most clever。

1 (*especially BrE*) quick at learning and understanding things 聰明的；聰穎的 SYN **intelligent**：*a clever child* 聰明伶俐的孩子 ◇ *Clever girl!* 多麼聰慧的女孩！◇ *How clever of you to work it out!* 你解決了這個問題真是太聰明了！◇ *He's **too clever by half**, if you ask me* (= it annoys me or makes me suspicious). 恕我直言，他未免聰明過頭了。➲ SYNONYMS at INTELLIGENT **2** ~ (**at sth**) (*especially BrE*) skilful 熟練的；靈巧的：*She's clever at getting what she wants.* 她想把什麼東西弄到手的時候總是很精的。◇ *He's clever with his hands.* 他的手很靈巧。**3** showing intelligence or skill, for example in the design of an object, in an idea or sb's actions 精巧的；精明的：*a clever little gadget* 精巧的小器具 ◇ *What a clever idea!* 多麼精明的主意！◇ *That* (= what you just did) *wasn't very clever, was it?* (= it wasn't sensible) 那樣做很不明智，是不是？ **4** (*BrE, informal, disapproving*) quick with words in a way that annoys people or does not show respect 油腔滑調的：*Don't you get clever with me!* 別跟我油嘴滑舌的！ ▶ **clev·er·ly** *adv.* **clev·er·ness** *noun* [U] IDM see BOX *v.*

'clever Dick (also **'clever clogs**) *noun* (both *BrE, informal, disapproving*) a person who thinks they are always right or that they know everything 自以為總是對（或無所不知）的人；自以為是的人

cli·ché (also **cliche**) /ˈkliːʃeɪ; *NAmE* kliːˈʃeɪ/ *noun* (*disapproving*) **1** [C] a phrase or an idea that has been used so often that it no longer has much meaning and is not interesting 陳詞濫調；陳腐的套語：*She trotted out the old cliché that 'a trouble shared is a trouble halved.'* 她又重複了"與人說愁愁減半"的陳詞濫調。**2** [U] the use of clichés in writing or speaking 使用陳詞濫調 ▶ **cli·chéd** *adj.*：*a clichéd view of upper-class life* 對上層社會的生活所持的陳腐看法

click /klɪk/ *verb, noun*

■ ***verb*** **1** [I, T] to make or cause sth to make a short sharp sound （使）發出咔嗒聲，咔嗒（或咔嚓）響：(**+ adv./prep.**) *The cameras clicked away.* 照相機咔嚓咔嚓地不停拍照。◇ *The bolt clicked into place.* 門閂咔嗒一聲插上了。◇ **+ adj.** *The door **clicked shut**.* 門咔嗒一聲關上了。◇ **~ sth** *He **clicked his fingers** at the waiter.* 他衝服務員打了個響指。◇ *Polly **clicked her tongue** in annoyance.* 波利氣得舌頭發出嘖嘖聲。**2** [T, I] to choose a particular function or item on a computer screen, etc., by pressing one of the buttons on a mouse or TOUCH PAD （用鼠標或在觸控板上）點擊，單擊：**~ sth** *Click the OK button to start.* 單擊 OK 按鈕啟動。◇ **~ (on sth)** *I clicked on the link to the next page of the website.* 我單擊鏈接好翻到網站的下一頁。◇ *To run a window, just double-click on the icon.* 要運行視窗，只需雙擊圖標即可。➲ see also DOUBLE-CLICK **3** [I] (*informal*) to suddenly become clear or understood 突然明白；恍然大悟；茅塞頓開：*Suddenly **it clicked**—we'd been talking about different people.* 我們突然領悟到原來我們談論的不是同一個人。◇ *It all **clicked into place**.* 一切都豁然開朗。**4** [I] (*informal*) to become friends with sb at once; to become popular with sb （與某人）頃刻成為朋友；受（某人）的歡迎：*We met at a party and clicked immediately.* 我們在聚會上相識，一見如故。◇ **~ with sb** *He's never really clicked with his students.* 他從未真正受到過他的學生的歡迎。**5** [I] (*informal*) to work well together 配合默契；運作協調：*The team don't seem to have clicked yet.* 這支隊伍好像還沒有配合默契。

PHR V **,click 'through** (**to sth**) to visit a website by clicking on an electronic link or advertisement on another web page 點擊，點進，點通（網站）

■ ***noun*** **1** a short sharp sound 短而尖的聲音；咔嗒（或咔嚓）聲：*The door closed with a click.* 門咔嗒一聲關上了。**2** the act of pressing the button on a computer mouse or TOUCH PAD （對計算機鼠標或觸控板的）點擊，單擊 **3** (*phonetics* 語音) a speech sound made by pressing the tongue against the top of the mouth or the part of the mouth behind the upper front teeth, then releasing it quickly, causing air to be sucked in. Clicks are found especially in southern African languages. （尤見於非洲南部某些語言的）吸氣音：*click languages* 有吸氣音的語言 **4** = KLICK

click·able /ˈklɪkəbl/ *adj.* (*computing* 計) if text or an image is **clickable**, you can click on it with the mouse or TOUCH PAD in order to make sth happen （文本或圖像）可點擊的

click·stream /ˈklɪkstriːm/ *noun* a record of all the websites a person visits when spending time on the Internet 點擊流路徑（個人瀏覽網站的記錄）

cli·ent /ˈklaɪənt/ *noun*

1 a person who uses the services or advice of a professional person or organization 委託人；當事人；客戶：*a lawyer with many famous clients* 接受許多名人委託的律師 ◇ *to act on behalf of a client* 代表當事人 ◇ *Social workers must always consider the best interests of their clients.* 社會工作者必須時刻考慮其當事人的最佳利益。**2** (*computing* 計) a computer that is linked to a SERVER （連接在服務器上的）客戶機

cli·en·tele /ˌkliːənˈtel; *NAmE* ˌklaɪənˈtel/ *noun* [sing.+sing./pl. v.] all the customers or clients of a shop/store, restaurant, organization, etc. （統稱）顧客，主顧，客戶：*an international clientele* 國際客戶網

,client-'server *adj.* [only before noun] (*computing* 計) (of a computer system 計算機系統) in which a central SERVER provides data to a number of computers connected together in a network 客戶服務器的；客戶伺服器的 ➲ see also PEER-TO-PEER

,client 'state *noun* a country which depends on a larger and more powerful country for support and protection （依賴強國的）附庸國

cliff /klɪf/ *noun* a high area of rock with a very steep side, often at the edge of the sea or ocean （常指海洋邊的）懸崖，峭壁：*the **cliff edge/top*** 懸崖邊緣 / 頂端 ◇ *the chalk cliffs of southern England* 英格蘭南部的白堊質峭壁 ◇ *a castle perched high on the cliffs above the river* 高高聳立在臨河峭壁上的城堡 ➲ VISUAL VOCAB page V5

cliff·hang·er /ˈklɪfhæŋə(r)/ *noun* a situation in a story, film/movie, competition, etc. that is very exciting because you cannot guess what will happen next, or you do not find out immediately what happens next （故事、電影、競賽等扣人心弦的）懸念：*The first part of the serial ended with a real cliffhanger.* 這部連續劇的第一集以扣人心弦的懸念告終。▶ **cliff·hang·ing** *adj.*

cliff·top /ˈklɪftɒp; *NAmE* -tɑːp/ *noun* the area of land at the top of a cliff 懸崖頂 ➲ VISUAL VOCAB page V5

cli·mac·tic /klaɪˈmæktɪk/ *adj.* (*formal*) (of an event or a point in time 事情或時刻) very exciting, most important 非常激動人心的；高潮的；最重要的

cli·mate /ˈklaɪmət/ *noun*

1 [C, U] the regular pattern of weather conditions of a particular place 氣候：*a **mild/temperate/warm/wet climate*** 温和的 / 暖和的 / 温暖的 / 潮濕的氣候 ◇ *the harsh climate of the Arctic regions* 北極地區的惡劣氣候 **2** [C] an area with particular weather conditions 氣候區：*They wanted to move to a warmer climate.* 他們想遷移到氣候較温暖的地區。**3** [C] a general attitude or feeling; an atmosphere or a situation which exists in a particular place 傾向；思潮；風氣；環境氣氛：*the present political climate* 當前的政治氣候 ◇ *the current **climate of opinion*** (= what people generally are thinking about a particular issue) 目前的輿論傾向 ◇ ***a climate of suspicion/violence*** 懷疑 / 暴力的風氣 ◇ *We need to create a climate in which business can prosper.* 我們需要創造一個有利於商業繁榮的環境。

'climate change *noun* [U] changes in the earth's weather, including changes in temperature, wind patterns and RAINFALL, especially the increase in the temperature of the earth's atmosphere that is caused by the increase of particular gases, especially CARBON DIOXIDE 氣候變化： *the threat of global climate change* 全球氣候變化的威脅 ➲ COLLOCATIONS at ENVIRONMENT ➲ compare GLOBAL WARMING

cli·mat·ic /klaɪˈmætɪk/ *adj.* [only before noun] connected with the climate of a particular area 與某一地區氣候有關的： ***climatic changes/conditions*** 氣候變化／條件 ▶ **cli·mat·ic·al·ly** /-kli/ *adv.*

cli·mat·ology /ˌklaɪməˈtɒlədʒi; *NAmE* -ˈtɑːl-/ *noun* [U] the scientific study of climate 氣候學 ▶ **cli·ma·to·logic·al** /ˌklaɪmətəˈlɒdʒɪkl; *NAmE* -ˈlɑːdʒ-/ *adj.* **cli·mat·olo·gist** /ˌklaɪməˈtɒlədʒɪst; *NAmE* -ˈtɑːl-/ *noun*

cli·max /ˈklaɪmæks/ *noun, verb*

■ *noun* **1** the most exciting or important event or point in time（重要事情或時刻的）高潮，極點，頂點： ***to come to/reach a climax*** 達到極點 ◇ *the climax of his political career* 他政治生涯的巔峰 **2** the most exciting part of a play, piece of music, etc. that usually happens near the end（戲劇、音樂等通常接近結束時出現的）高潮 **3** the highest point of sexual pleasure 性高潮 SYN **orgasm** ➲ compare ANTICLIMAX

■ *verb* **1** [I, T] to come to or form the best, most exciting, or most important point in sth 達成（或形成）極點（或頂點、高潮）： **~ with/in sth** *The festival will climax on Sunday with a gala concert.* 星期天的音樂盛會將把這個節日推向高潮。◇ **~ sth** (*especially NAmE*) *The sensational verdict climaxed a six-month trial.* 那項引起轟動的裁決使長達六個月的審判達到了高潮。 **2** [I] to have an ORGASM 達到性高潮

climb 🔑 /klaɪm/ *verb, noun*

■ *verb*

▸ GO UP 上去 **1** 🔑 [T, I] **~ (up) (sth)** to go up sth towards the top 攀登；爬： *to climb a mountain/hill/tree/wall* 爬山；爬樹；爬牆 ◇ *She climbed up the stairs.* 她爬上了樓梯。◇ *The car slowly climbed the hill.* 汽車緩慢地爬上了山坡。◇ *As they climbed higher, the air became cooler.* 他們攀登得越高，空氣就變得越涼爽。

▸ GO THROUGH/DOWN/OVER 通過；下去；越過 **2** 🔑 [I] **+ adv./prep.** to move somewhere, especially with difficulty or effort（尤指吃力地向某處）爬： *I climbed through the window.* 我從窗口爬了出來。◇ *Sue climbed into bed.* 蘇吃力地爬上牀。◇ *Can you climb down?* 你能爬下去嗎？◇ *The boys climbed over the wall.* 那些男孩翻過了那堵牆。

▸ MOUNTAIN/ROCK, ETC. 山、岩石等 **3** 🔑 **go climbing** to go up mountains or climb rocks as a hobby or sport 登山，攀岩（作為業餘愛好或運動）： *He likes to go climbing most weekends.* 在多數週末他都喜歡去登山。

▸ AIRCRAFT/SUN, ETC. 飛機、太陽等 **4** 🔑 [I] to go higher in the sky 爬升；上升： *The plane climbed to 33 000 feet.* 飛機爬升到 33 000 英尺。

▸ SLOPE UP 傾斜着上升 **5** 🔑 [I] to slope upwards 傾斜上升： *From here the path climbs steeply to the summit.* 這條小路從這裏突然變陡，直上山頂。

▸ OF PLANTS 植物 **6** [I] to grow up a wall or frame（沿牆或構架）攀緣生長： *a climbing rose* 攀緣生長的玫瑰

▸ INCREASE 增加 **7** 🔑 [I] (of temperature, a country's money, etc. 溫度、國家的貨幣等) to increase in value or amount 上升；增值；升值： *The dollar has been climbing all week.* 整個星期美元一直在升值。◇ *The paper's circulation continues to climb.* 這份報紙的發行量持續增長。

▸ IMPROVE POSITION/STATUS 提高身分／地位 **8** [I] **~ (to sth)** to move to a higher position or social rank by your own effort（靠自己的努力）晉升，提高社會地位： *In a few years he had climbed to the top of his profession.* 他在幾年內攀上了職業的巔峰。◇ *The team has now climbed to fourth in the league.* 這支隊現已上升到聯賽的第四名。

IDM see BANDWAGON

PHR V **ˌclimb ˈdown (over sth)** to admit that you have made a mistake or that you were wrong 承認做錯事；認錯 ➲ related noun CLIMBDOWN

■ *noun*

▸ MOUNTAIN/STEPS 山；台階 **1** an act of climbing up a mountain, rock or large number of steps; a period of time spent climbing 攀登；攀緣；爬階梯；攀登用的時間： *an exhausting climb* 令人精疲力竭的攀登 ◇ *It's an hour's climb to the summit.* 爬到頂峰需要一小時。 **2** a mountain or rock which people climb up for sport（登山或攀岩運動的）山，岩： *Titan's Wall is the mountain's hardest rock climb.* "巨人牆"是這座山最難攀登的一段山岩。

▸ INCREASE 增加 **3** [usually sing.] an increase in value or amount 增值；升值；增加： *the dollar's climb against the euro* 美元對歐元的升值

▸ TO A HIGHER POSITION OR STATUS 提高身分／地位 **4** [usually sing.] progress to a higher status, standard or position（地位、標準、身分的）躍升，提高，晉升： *a rapid climb to stardom* 一躍而成為明星 ◇ *the long slow climb out of the recession* 經濟衰退期後長時間的緩慢復蘇

climb·down /ˈklaɪmdaʊn/ *noun* (*BrE*) an act of admitting that you were wrong, or of changing your position in an argument 認錯；（爭論中）改變立場，讓步： *The Chancellor was forced into a humiliating climbdown on his economic policies.* 財政大臣被迫狼狽地承認他的經濟政策存在失誤。

climb·er /ˈklaɪmə(r)/ *noun* **1** a person who climbs (especially mountains) or an animal that climbs 攀登者；登山者；攀爬的動物： *climbers and hill walkers* 登山者和山地徒步旅行者 ◇ *Monkeys are efficient climbers.* 猴子的攀緣能力很強。 **2** a climbing plant 攀緣植物 ➲ VISUAL VOCAB page V19 ➲ see also SOCIAL CLIMBER

climb·ing 🔑 /ˈklaɪmɪŋ/ *noun* [U] the sport or activity of climbing rocks or mountains 登山運動；攀岩活動： *to **go climbing*** 去登山 ◇ *a climbing accident* 登山事故

ˈclimbing frame (*BrE*) (*NAmE* **ˈjungle gym**) *noun* a structure made of metal bars joined together for children to climb and play on 攀爬架（遊樂設施）➲ picture at FRAME ➲ VISUAL VOCAB page V37

ˈclimbing wall *noun* a wall with parts to hold onto, usually inside a building, for people to practise climbing on（室內供練習用的）攀登牆，攀岩牆

clime /klaɪm/ *noun* [usually pl.] (*literary* or *humorous*) a country with a particular kind of climate（具有某種氣候的）地區，地帶；氣候帶： *I'm heading for sunnier climes next month.* 我下個月要去陽光比較明媚的地區。

clinch /klɪntʃ/ *verb, noun*

■ *verb* (*informal*) **1 ~ sth** to succeed in achieving or winning sth 成功取得；贏得： ***to clinch an argument/a deal/a victory*** 贏得辯論；成交；贏得勝利 **2 ~ sth** to provide the answer to sth; to settle sth that was not certain 提供解決辦法；解決；確定： *'I'll pay your airfare.' 'Okay, **that clinches it**—I'll come with you.'* "我會幫你付飛機票。""好，就這麼說定，我跟你一起去。" ◇ *a clinching argument* 讓人折服的論證

■ *noun* **1** (*informal*) a position in which two lovers hold each other tightly（戀人相互的）摟抱，擁抱 SYN **embrace** **2** a position in a fight in which two opponents hold each other tightly（格鬥中對手的）互相扭抱

clinch·er /ˈklɪntʃə(r)/ *noun* [usually sing.] (*informal*) a fact, a remark or an event that settles an argument, a decision or a competition 起決定性作用的事實（或話語、事情）

cline /klaɪn/ *noun* a series of similar items in which each is almost the same as the ones next to it, but the last is very different from the first 漸變群（群體中相鄰的兩個成員相差無幾，但第一個和最後一個之間差異極明顯）SYN **continuum**

cling /klɪŋ/ *verb* (**clung**, **clung** /klʌŋ/) **1** [I] to hold on tightly to sb/sth 抓緊；緊握；緊抱： **~ to sb/sth** *survivors clinging to a raft* 緊緊抓住救生筏的幸存者 ◇ **~ on to sb/sth** *She clung on to her baby.* 她緊緊抱住她的嬰兒。◇ **~ on** *Cling on tight!* 緊緊抓住！◇ **~ together** *They clung together, shivering with cold.* 他們緊緊地抱在一起，冷得直發抖。➲ SYNONYMS at HOLD **2** [I] to stick to sth 粘住；附着： *a dress that clings* (= fits closely and shows the shape of your body) 緊身連衣裙 ◇ **~ to sth** *The wet shirt clung to his chest.* 濕襯衫緊貼在他的胸部。◇ *The smell of smoke still clung to her clothes.* 煙味仍附着在她的衣服上不散。**3** [I] **~ (to sb)** (usually *disapproving*) to stay close to sb, especially because you need them emotionally（尤指因感情需要而）依戀，依附：*After her mother's death, Sara clung to her aunt more than ever.* 薩拉在母親去世後比以往任何時候都更依附於她的姨媽。

PHR V **ˈcling to sth | ˌcling ˈon to sth** to be unwilling to get rid of sth, or stop doing sth 不願放棄；堅持：*Throughout the trial she had clung to the belief that he was innocent.* 在整個審判中，她都堅信他是清白的。◇ *He had one last hope to cling on to.* 他還抱着最後的一線希望。◇ *She managed to cling on to life for another couple of years.* 她頑強地又活了幾年。

ˈcling film (*BrE*) (*NAmE* **ˈplastic wrap, Saˈran Wrap™**) *noun* [U] a thin transparent plastic material that sticks to a surface and to itself, used especially for wrapping food（尤指包裝食物的）透明薄膜，保鮮塑料薄膜

cling·ing /ˈklɪŋɪŋ/ (also **clingy** /ˈklɪŋi/) *adj.* **1** (of clothes or material 衣服或衣料) sticking to the body and showing its shape 緊身的；貼身的 **2** (usually *disapproving*) needing another person too much（對別人）依賴性強的，離不開的：*a clinging child* 纏人的孩子

clin·ic /ˈklɪnɪk/ *noun* **1** a building or part of a hospital where people can go for special medical treatment or advice 診所；（醫院的）門診部：*the local family planning clinic* 當地的計劃生育診所 **2** (*especially BrE*) a period of time during which doctors give special medical treatment or advice 門診時間；會診時間：*The antenatal clinic is on Wednesdays.* 產前檢查時間為星期三。**3** (*especially BrE*) a private hospital or one that treats health problems of a particular kind 私人診所；專科醫院：*He is being treated at the London clinic.* 他正在倫敦一家私人診所接受治療。◇ *a rehabilitation clinic for alcoholics* 戒酒康復專科診所 **4** (*NAmE*) a building where visiting patients can get medical treatment; a building shared by a group of doctors who work together 門診治療部；醫療中心 **5** an occasion in a hospital when medical students learn by watching a specialist examine and treat patients 臨牀實習；臨牀教學 **6** an occasion at which a professional person, especially a SPORTSMAN or SPORTSWOMAN gives advice and training（尤指運動員舉辦的）講習班，培訓班，研習班：*a coaching clinic for young tennis players* 為年輕網球運動員舉辦的研習班

clin·ic·al /ˈklɪnɪkl/ *adj.* **1** [only before noun] relating to the examination and treatment of patients and their illnesses 臨牀的；臨牀診斷的：*clinical research* (= done on patients, not just considering theory) 臨牀研究 ◇ *clinical training* (= the part of a doctor's training done in a hospital) 臨牀培訓 ◇ *clinical trials of a drug* 藥物的臨牀試驗 **2** (*disapproving*) cold and calm and without feeling or sympathy 冷淡的；無動於衷的；無同情心的：*He watched her suffering with clinical detachment.* 他無動於衷地看着她受苦。**3** (*disapproving*) (of a room, building, etc. 房間、建築物等) very plain; without decoration 簡陋的；無裝飾的 ▸ **clin·ic·al·ly** /-kli/ *adv.*: *clinically dead* (= judged to be dead from the condition of the body) 臨牀死亡的（從身體的狀況判斷為死亡的）◇ *clinically depressed* 臨牀診斷為抑鬱症的

clin·ician /klɪˈnɪʃn/ *noun* a doctor, PSYCHOLOGIST, etc. who has direct contact with patients 臨牀醫師

clink /klɪŋk/ *verb, noun*

■ ***verb*** [I, T] to make or cause sth to make a sharp ringing sound, like that of glasses being hit against each other（使）發出叮噹聲，叮噹作響 **SYN** **chink**：*clinking coins* 叮噹響的硬幣 ◇ **~ sth** *They clinked glasses and drank to each other's health.* 他們碰杯互祝身體健康。

■ ***noun*** [sing.] **1** (also **clink·ing**) a sharp ringing sound like the sound made by glasses being hit against each other 叮噹聲 **2** (*old-fashioned, slang*) prison 班房；牢房

clink·er /ˈklɪŋkə(r)/ *noun* **1** [U, C] the hard rough substance left after coal has burnt at a high temperature; a piece of this substance 煤渣；爐渣；煤渣塊 **2** [sing.] (*NAmE*) a wrong musical note 錯誤的音符：*The singer hit a clinker.* 那名歌手唱錯了一個音符。

clip /klɪp/ *noun, verb*

■ ***noun*** **1** [C] (often in compounds 常構成複合詞) a small metal or plastic object used for holding things together or in place（金屬或塑料的）夾子，迴形針：*a hair clip* 髮夾 ◇ *toe clips on a bicycle* 自行車上的踏腳夾套 ➲ **VISUAL VOCAB** page V69 ➲ see also BICYCLE CLIP, BULLDOG CLIP, PAPER CLIP **2** [C] a piece of jewellery that fastens to your clothes 首飾別針：*a diamond clip* 鑽石別針 **3** [sing.] the act of cutting sth to make it shorter 剪短；修剪：*He gave the hedge a clip.* 他把樹籬修剪了一下。**4** [C] a short part of a film/movie that is shown separately 電影片段：*Here is a clip from her latest movie.* 這是她最近一部電影的片段。**5** [C] (*BrE, informal*) a quick hit with your hand（用手）猛擊，抽打：*She gave him **a clip round the ear** for being cheeky.* 她因他放肆給了他一記耳光。**6** [C] a set of bullets in a metal container that is placed in or attached to a gun for firing 子彈夾；彈匣

IDM **at a fast, good, steady, etc. ˈclip** (*especially NAmE*) quickly 迅速；很快地

■ ***verb*** (-pp-) **1** [T, I] to fasten sth to sth else with a clip; to be fastened with a clip 夾住；別住；被夾住：**~ sth + adv./prep.** *He **clipped** the microphone (**on**) **to** his collar.* 他把麥克風別在衣領上。◇ ***Clip** the pages **together**.* 把這些散頁夾在一起。◇ **+ adv./prep.** *Do those earrings clip on?* 那些耳環是夾戴的嗎？**2** [T] to cut sth with scissors or SHEARS, in order to make it shorter or neater; to remove sth from somewhere by cutting it off 剪（掉）；修剪：**~ sth** *to clip a hedge* 修剪樹籬 ◇ **~ sth from sth/off (sth)** *He clipped off a length of wire.* 他剪掉了一段金屬線。**3** [T] to hit the edge or side of sth 碰撞（某物的邊緣或側面）：**~ sth** *The car clipped the kerb as it turned.* 汽車轉彎時撞上了馬路牙子。◇ **~ sth + adv./prep.** *She clipped the ball into the net.* 她把球斜劈入球網。**4** [T] **~ sth (out of/from sth)** to cut sth out of sth else using scissors 從…剪下：*to clip a coupon (out of the paper)*（從報紙上）剪下贈券

IDM **clip sb's ˈwings** to restrict a person's freedom or power 限制某人的自由（或權力）

PHR V **ˌclip sth ˈoff sth** (*informal*) to reduce the time that it takes to do sth by a particular length of time 縮短，削減（做某事的時間）：*She clipped two seconds off her previous best time.* 她把自己之前的最佳紀錄縮短了兩秒。

ˈclip art *noun* [U] (*computing* 計) pictures and symbols that are stored in computer programs or on websites for computer users to copy and add to their own documents 剪貼畫（計算機程序或網站中供用戶複製自用的圖像和符號）

clip·board /ˈklɪpbɔːd; *NAmE* -bɔːrd/ *noun* **1** a small board with a clip at the top for holding papers, used by sb who wants to write while standing or moving around 寫字夾板；帶夾寫字板 ➲ **VISUAL VOCAB** page V69 **2** (*computing* 計) a place where information from a computer file is stored for a time until it is added to another file（歸檔前臨時貯存信息的）剪貼板

clip-clop /ˈklɪp klɒp; *NAmE* klɑːp/ *noun* a sound like the sound of a horse's HOOFS on a hard surface（像馬蹄踏在硬路面上發出的）嗒嗒聲，得得聲

ˈclip joint *noun* (*informal, disapproving*) a NIGHTCLUB which charges prices that are too high（收費太高的）宰客夜總會

ˈclip-on *adj.* [only before noun] fastened to sth with a CLIP 用夾子夾住的；用別針別牢的：*clip-on earrings* 夾式耳環 ➲ **VISUAL VOCAB** page V65

clipped /klɪpt/ *adj.* (of a person's way of speaking 說話方式) clear and fast but not very friendly 清脆快速但不太友好的：*his clipped military tones* 他那短促的軍人語調

clip·per /ˈklɪpə(r)/ *noun* **1** **clippers** [pl.] a tool for cutting small pieces off things 剪具：*a pair of clippers* 一把剪子 ➲ see also NAIL CLIPPERS **2** a fast sailing ship, used in the past（舊時的）快速帆船

clip·ping /ˈklɪpɪŋ/ *noun* **1** [usually pl.] a piece cut off sth 剪下物：***hedge/nail clippings*** 剪下的樹籬／指甲 **2** (*especially NAmE*) (also **ˈpress clipping** *BrE, NAmE*) (*BrE* also **cut·ting**, **ˈpress cutting**) an article or a story that you cut from a newspaper or magazine and keep 剪報；雜誌剪輯資料

clique /kliːk/ *noun* [C+sing./pl. v.] (*often disapproving*) a small group of people who spend their time together and do not allow others to join them 派系；私黨；小集團；小圈子

cliquey /ˈkliːki/ (also **cliqu·ish** /ˈkliːkɪʃ/) *adj.* (*disapproving*) tending to form a clique; controlled by cliques 有派系傾向的；有結成小集團傾向的；派系控制的：*He found the school very cliquey and elitist.* 他發現這所學校很排外並以精英自居。

clit·oris /ˈklɪtərɪs/ *noun* the small sensitive organ just above the opening of a woman's VAGINA which becomes larger when she is sexually excited 陰蒂；陰核 ▸ **clit·or·al** /ˈklɪtərəl/ *adj.* [only before noun]

Cllr *abbr.* (*BrE*) (used before names in writing 寫在姓名前) COUNCILLOR 市議員；政務委員會委員：*Cllr Michael Booth* 市議員邁克爾 • 布思

cloak /kləʊk; *NAmE* kloʊk/ *noun, verb*

■ *noun* **1** [C] a type of coat that has no sleeves, fastens at the neck and hangs loosely from the shoulders, worn especially in the past（尤指舊時的）披風，斗篷 **2** [sing.] (*literary*) a thing that hides or covers sb/sth 遮蓋物：*They left under the cloak of darkness.* 他們在黑暗的掩護下離開了。

■ *verb* **~ sth (in sth)** [often passive] (*literary*) to cover or hide sth 遮蓋；掩蓋：*The hills were cloaked in thick mist.* 大霧籠罩着群山。◇ *The meeting was* ***cloaked in mystery***. 會議籠罩着神秘的氣氛。▸ **cloaked** *adj.*：*a tall cloaked figure* (= a person wearing a cloak) 一個穿着披風、身材很高的人

ˌcloak-and-ˈdagger *adj.* [only before noun] **cloak-and-dagger** activities are secret and mysterious, sometimes in a way that people think is unnecessary or ridiculous 秘密的，神秘兮兮的（有時被認為不必要或荒謬）

cloak·room /ˈkləʊkruːm; -rʊm; *NAmE* ˈkloʊk-/ *noun* **1** (*especially BrE*) (*NAmE* usually **check·room**, **ˈcoat check**, **coat·room**) a room in a public building where people can leave coats, bags, etc. for a time 衣帽間；衣帽寄放處 **2** (*BrE*) a room that contains a toilet or toilets 廁所；衛生間；洗手間 ➲ note at TOILET

clob·ber /ˈklɒbə(r); *NAmE* ˈklɑːb-/ *verb, noun*

■ *verb* (*informal*) **1 ~ sb** to hit sb very hard 狠擊；狠揍；猛打 **2** [often passive] **~ sb/sth** to affect sb badly or to punish them, especially by making them lose money 極大地打擊；懲罰；使受到（嚴重經濟損失）：*The paper got clobbered with libel damages of half a million pounds.* 該報被罰以五十萬英鎊的誹謗損害賠償金。**3** [usually passive] **~ sb/sth** to defeat sb completely 徹底戰勝（或擊敗）：*We got clobbered in the game on Saturday.* 我們在星期六的比賽中一敗塗地。

■ *noun* [U] (*BrE, informal*) a person's clothes or equipment 衣服；隨身物品 SYN **stuff**

clocks and watches 鐘錶

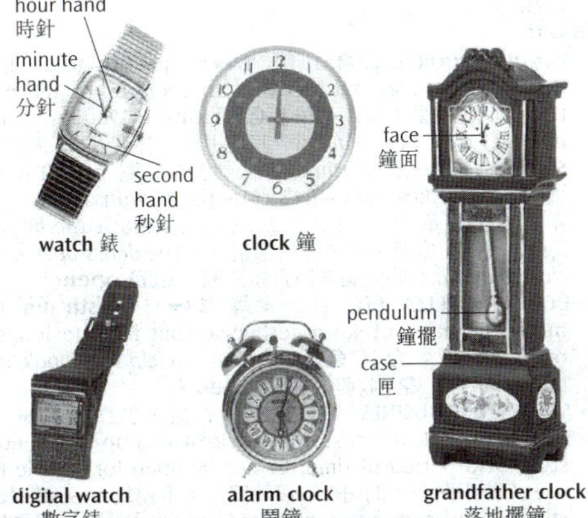

cloche /klɒʃ; *NAmE* kloʊʃ/ *noun* **1** (also **ˌcloche ˈhat**) a woman's hat, shaped like a bell, and fitting close to the head, worn especially in the 1920s（尤指 20 世紀 20 年代的）鐘形女帽 **2** a glass or plastic cover placed over young plants to protect them from cold weather（保護植物幼苗不受凍的）玻璃罩，塑料罩 ➲ VISUAL VOCAB page V19

clock 🔑 /klɒk; *NAmE* klɑːk/ *noun, verb*

■ *noun* **1** 🔑 [C] an instrument for measuring and showing time, in a room or on the wall of a building (not worn or carried like a watch) 時鐘；鐘：*It was ten past six by the kitchen clock.* 廚房的鐘六點十分了。◇ *The clock* ***struck*** *twelve/midnight.* 時鐘已敲響十二點／午夜十二點。◇ *The clock is* ***fast/slow***. 這鐘走得快了／慢了。◇ *The clock has stopped.* 鐘停了。◇ *the* ***clock face*** (= the front part of a clock with the numbers on) 鐘面 ◇ *The* ***hands of the clock*** *crept slowly around.* 鐘的時針在緩慢地走着。◇ *Ellen heard the loud* ***ticking of the clock*** *in the hall.* 埃倫聽見大廳的鐘滴答滴答地大聲走着。➲ see also ALARM CLOCK, BIOLOGICAL CLOCK, BODY CLOCK, CARRIAGE CLOCK, CUCKOO CLOCK, GRANDFATHER CLOCK, O'CLOCK, TIME CLOCK **2 the clock** [sing.] (*informal*) = MILOMETER：*a used car with 20 000 miles on the clock* 一輛計程器上累計行程為 2 萬英里的舊汽車

IDM **against the ˈclock** if you do sth **against the clock**, you do it fast in order to finish before a particular time 搶時間；爭分奪秒 **around/round the ˈclock** all day and all night without stopping 日夜不停；夜以繼日 **put the clocks forward/back** (*BrE*) (*NAmE* **set/move the clocks ahead/back**) to change the time shown by clocks, usually by one hour, when the time changes officially, for example at the beginning and end of summer（夏時制開始和結束時）把時鐘撥快／撥回（一般為一個小時） **put/turn the ˈclock back 1** to return to a situation that existed in the past; to remember a past age 倒退；復舊；懷舊：*I wish we could turn the clock back two years and give the marriage another chance.* 我但願時光能倒退兩年，再給我們的婚姻一次機會。**2** (*disapproving*) to return to old-fashioned methods or ideas 開倒車：*The new censorship law will turn the clock back 50 years.* 新的審查制度將使社會倒退回 50 年前的狀態。 **run down/out the ˈclock** (*US*) if a sports team tries to **run down/out the clock** at the end of a game, it stops trying to score and just tries to keep hold of the ball to stop the other team from scoring 消耗掉剩餘的比賽時間（比賽接近結束時，球隊只設法控制住球，以阻止對方進球得分）➲ compare TIME-WASTING (2) **the clocks go forward/back** the time changes officially, for example at the beginning and end of summer（夏時制）時鐘被撥快／撥回 ➲ more at BEAT *v.*, RACE *n.*, STOP *v.*, WATCH *v.*

■ *verb* **1 ~ sth** to reach a particular time or speed 達到（某時間或速度）：*He clocked 10.09 seconds in the 100 metres final.* 他 100 米決賽跑出了 10.09 秒的速度。**2** to measure the speed at which sb/sth is travelling 測…的速度：**~ sb doing sth** *The police clocked her doing over 100 miles an hour.* 警察測出她的車速每小時超過 100 英里。◇ **~ sb/sth (at sth)** *Wind gusts at 80 m.p.h. were clocked at Rapid City.* 據測拉皮德城的狂風速度為每小時 80 英里。**3 ~ sb** | **~ that …** | **~ what/where, etc. …** (*BrE, informal*) to notice or recognize sb 注意到；認出：*I clocked her in the driving mirror.* 我從汽車後視鏡裏注意到她。**4 ~ sth** (*BrE, informal*) to illegally reduce the number of miles shown on a vehicle's MILOMETER (= instrument that measures the number of miles it has travelled) in order to make the vehicle appear to have travelled fewer miles than it really has 非法減少（車輛）計程器上的里程數；回撥（車輛）里程表作弊

PHR V **ˌclock ˈin/ˈon** (*BrE*) (*NAmE* **ˌpunch ˈin**) to record the time at which you arrive at work, especially by putting a card into a machine（尤指用機器）記錄上班時間，上班打卡 **ˌclock ˈout/ˈoff** (*BrE*) (*NAmE* **ˌpunch ˈout**) to record the time at which you leave work, especially by putting a card into a machine（尤指用機器）記錄下班時間，下班打卡 **ˌclock ˈup sth** to reach a particular amount or number 達到（某一數量或數目）：

C

On the trip we clocked up over 1 800 miles. 這次旅行我們的行程超過了 1 800 英里。◇ *He has clocked up more than 25 years on the committee.* 他擔任委員會的委員已超過 25 年。

C

clock·er /ˈklɒkə(r); *NAmE* ˈklɑːk-/ *noun* (*informal*) **1** (*BrE*) a person who illegally changes a car's MILOMETER so that the car seems to have travelled fewer miles than it really has 倒撥里程表的人；里程表作弊者 **2** (*NAmE*) a person who sells illegal drugs, especially COCAINE or CRACK（可卡因等的）毒品販子

ˌclock ˈradio *noun* a clock combined with a radio that can be set to come on at a particular time in order to wake sb up 收音機鬧鐘 ➲ **VISUAL VOCAB** page V23

ˈclock speed *noun* [U] (*computing* 計) the speed at which a computer operates 時鐘頻率（計算機的運行速度）：*This machine has a clock speed of 1.6GHz.* 這台機器的時鐘頻率為 1.6 千兆赫。

ˈclock tower *noun* a tall tower, usually part of another building, with a clock at the top 鐘樓 ➲ **VISUAL VOCAB** pages V2, V3

ˈclock-watcher *noun* (*disapproving*) a worker who is always checking the time to make sure that they do not work longer than they need to 老是看時間等下班的人

clock·wise /ˈklɒkwaɪz; *NAmE* ˈklɑːk-/ *adv., adj.* moving around in the same direction as the hands of a clock 順時針方向（的）：*Turn the key clockwise.* 把鑰匙按順時針方向扭動。◇ *a clockwise direction* 順時針方向 **OPP** **anticlockwise, counterclockwise**

clock·work /ˈklɒkwɜːk; *NAmE* ˈklɑːkwɜːrk/ *noun* [U] machinery with wheels and SPRINGS like that inside a clock（有類似時鐘齒輪和發條裝置的）機械；齒輪發條裝置：*clockwork toys* (= toys that you wind up with a key) 有齒輪發條裝置的玩具

IDM **go/run like ˈclockwork** to happen according to plan; to happen without difficulties or problems 按計劃進行；進展順利 ➲ more at REGULAR *adj.*

clod /klɒd; *NAmE* klɑːd/ *noun* **1** [usually pl.] a lump of earth or CLAY 泥塊；土塊 **2** (*informal*) a stupid person 笨蛋；蠢人；傻瓜

clod·hop·per /ˈklɒdhɒpə(r); *NAmE* ˈklɑːdhɑːp-/ *noun* (*informal*) **1** [usually pl.] a large heavy shoe 笨重的大鞋子 **2** (*disapproving*) an awkward or CLUMSY person 笨拙的人；笨蛋

clog /klɒɡ; *NAmE* klɑːɡ; klɔːɡ/ *verb, noun*

■ *verb* (-gg-) [T, often passive, I] to block sth or to become blocked（使）阻塞，堵塞：**~ sth (up) (with sth)** *The narrow streets were clogged with traffic.* 狹窄的街道上交通堵塞。◇ *Tears clogged her throat.* 她哽咽了。◇ **~ (up) (with sth)** *Within a few years the pipes began to clog up.* 沒有幾年管子就開始堵塞了。

■ *noun* a shoe that is completely made of wood or one that has a thick wooden SOLE and a leather top 木底鞋；木鞋；木屐 ➲ **VISUAL VOCAB** page V64 **IDM** see POP *v.*

ˈclog dance *noun* a dance that is performed by people wearing clogs 木底鞋舞

clois·ter /ˈklɔɪstə(r)/ *noun* **1** [C, usually pl.] a covered passage with ARCHES around a square garden, usually forming part of a CATHEDRAL, CONVENT or MONASTERY（常為教堂、修院或寺院的）迴廊；修院（或聖堂）禁地 ➲ **VISUAL VOCAB** page V14 **2** [sing.] life in a CONVENT or MONASTERY 修院（或寺院）的生活

clois·tered /ˈklɔɪstəd; *NAmE* -tərd/ *adj.* (*formal*) protected from the problems and dangers of normal life 隱居的；躲開塵世紛爭的：*a cloistered life* 隱居的生活 ◇ *the cloistered world of the university* 與世隔絕的大學

clone /kləʊn; *NAmE* kloʊn/ *noun, verb*

■ *noun* **1** (*biology* 生) a plant or an animal that is produced naturally or artificially from the cells of another plant or animal and is therefore exactly the same as it 克隆動物（或植物）；無性繁殖動物（或植物）；複製動物（或植物）**2** (sometimes *disapproving*) a person or thing that seems to be an exact copy of another 好像一模一樣的人；複製品；仿造品；翻版 **3** (*computing* 計) a computer designed to work in exactly the same way as another, usually one made by a different company and more expensive 複製器；仿製機

■ *verb* **1 ~ sth** to produce an exact copy of an animal or a plant from its cells 以無性繁殖技術複製；克隆：*A team from the UK were the first to successfully clone an animal.* 英國的一個小組率先克隆動物成功。◇ *Dolly, the cloned sheep* 複製羊多利 **2 ~ sth** to illegally make an electronic copy of stored information from a person's credit card or mobile/cell phone so that you can make payments or phone calls but the owner of the card or phone receives the bill 非法複製，克隆（複製他人信用卡或手機的貯存信息，從而使卡主或機主付費）

clonk /klɒŋk; *NAmE* klɑːŋk/ *noun* (*BrE, informal*) a short loud sound of heavy things hitting each other（重物的）碰擊聲，哐噹聲 ▸ **clonk** *verb* [I, T] **~ (sth)**

Which Word? 詞語辨析

close / shut

You can **close** and **shut** doors, windows, your eyes, mouth, etc. 關門、關窗、閉眼、閉嘴等用 close 或 shut 均可。

- **Shut** can suggest more noise and is often found in phrases such as *slammed shut, banged shut, snapped shut.* * shut 可含發出較大聲音之意，常見於 slammed shut、banged shut、snapped shut（砰的一聲關上）等短語中。
- **Shut** is also usually used for containers such as boxes, suitcases, etc. 關上盒子、手提箱等亦常用 shut。
- To talk about the time when shops, offices, etc. are not open, use **close** or **shut**. 商店、辦事處等停業或不辦公用 close 或 shut 均可：*What time do the banks close/shut?* 銀行什麼時候關門？◇ *A strike has shut the factory.* 罷工使工廠停業。 You can also use **closed** or **shut** (*NAmE* usually **closed**). 亦可用 closed 或 shut（美式英語常用 closed）表示：*The store is closed/shut today.* 這家商店今天不營業。 Especially in *NAmE*, **shut** can sound less polite. 尤其在美式英語中，shut 聽起來欠禮貌。
- **Closed** is used in front of a noun, but **shut** is not. * closed 可用於名詞前，shut 則不能：*a closed window* 關着的窗戶
- We usually use **closed** about roads, airports, etc. 道路封閉、機場關閉等常用 closed：*The road is closed because of the snow.* 這條路因下雪而封閉。
- **Close** is also used in formal English to talk about ending a meeting or conversation. * close 亦用於正式英語中，表示結束會議或談話。

close¹ 0→ /kləʊz; *NAmE* kloʊz/ *verb, noun* ➲ see also CLOSE²

■ *verb*

▸ **WINDOW/DOOR, ETC.** 窗、門等 **1** 0→ [T, I] **~ (sth)** to put sth into a position so that it covers an opening; to get into this position 關；關閉；閉上 **SYN** **shut**：*Would anyone mind if I closed the window?* 我關上窗戶會有人介意嗎？◇ *She closed the gate behind her.* 她隨手關上了身後的大門。◇ *It's dark now—let's close the curtains.* 天黑了，咱們拉上窗簾吧。◇ *I closed my eyes against the bright light.* 我閉上眼睛以防強光的照射。◇ *The doors open and close automatically.* 這些門自動開關。**OPP** **open**

▸ **BOOK/UMBRELLA, ETC.** 書、傘等 **2** 0→ [T] **~ sth (up)** to move the parts of sth together so that it is no longer open 合上；合攏 **SYN** **shut**：*to close a book/an umbrella* 合上書；收起傘 **OPP** **open**

▸ **SHOP/STORE/BUSINESS, ETC.** 店鋪、商店、生意等 **3** 0→ [T, often passive, I] to make the work of a shop/store, etc. stop for a period of time; to not be open for people to use（使）關門，關閉（一段時間）；不開放：**~ sth (for sth)** *The museum has been closed for renovation.* 博物館已閉館整修。◇ **~ sth (to sb/sth)** *The road was closed to* *traffic for two days.* 這條路已經封閉兩天了。◇ **~ (for sth)** *What time does the bank close?* 那家銀行什麼時候關門？◇ *We close for lunch between twelve and two.* 十二點至兩點是我們的午餐打烊時間。**OPP open 4** 🔑 [T, I] **~ (sth)** (also **ˌclose ˈdown, ˌclose sth↔ˈdown**) if a company, shop/store, etc. **closes**, or if you **close** it, it stops operating as a business 停業；關閉；歇業；倒閉：*The club was closed by the police.* 那家夜總會被警察查封了。◇ *The hospital closed at the end of last year.* 這所醫院去年年底關閉。◇ *The play closed after just three nights.* 這部劇僅上演了三個晚上就停演了。**OPP open**

▸ **END** 結束 **5** 🔑 [T, I] to end or make sth end（使）結束，終止：*The meeting will close at 10.00 p.m.* 會議將在晚上 10 點結束。◇ *The offer closes at the end of the week.* 優惠將在本週末截止。◇ **~ sth** *to close a meeting/debate* 結束會議 / 辯論 ◇ *to close a case/an investigation* 結案；結束調查 ◇ *to close an account* (= to stop keeping money in a bank account) 註銷賬戶 ◇ *The subject is now closed* (= we will not discuss it again). 這個話題的討論現在已告結束。**OPP open**

▸ **FINANCE** 金融 **6** [I] **~ (at sth)** to be worth a particular amount at the end of the day's business 收盤：*Shares in the company closed at 265p.* 這家公司的股票收盤價為 265 便士。◇ *closing prices* 收盤價

▸ **DISTANCE/DIFFERENCE** 距離；差別 **7** [T, I] **~ (sth)** to make the distance or difference between two people or things smaller; to become smaller or narrower（使）縮小，接近；變小；變窄：*These measures are aimed at* ***closing the gap*** *between rich and poor.* 這些措施旨在縮小貧富差距。◇ *The gap between the two top teams is closing all the time.* 兩支頂尖球隊的差距一直在縮小。

▸ **HOLD FIRMLY** 牢牢抓住 **8** [T, I] **~ (sth) about/around/over sb/sth** to hold sth/sb firmly 把…牢牢抱住（或抓住、握住）：*She closed her hand over his.* 她牢牢抓住他的手不放。◇ *Her hand closed over his.* 她牢牢抓住他的手不放。

IDM close the book on sth to stop doing sth because you no longer believe you will be successful or will find a solution（因相信不會成功或沒有結論而）放棄：*The police have closed the book on the case* (= they have stopped trying to solve it). 警方已經放棄偵破此案。**close its doors** (of a business, etc. 企業等) to stop trading 停業；歇業；關閉：*The factory closed its doors for the last time in 2009.* 這家工廠最後於 2009 年關閉。**close your ˈmind to sth** to refuse to think about sth as a possibility 對…拒不考慮（或置之不理、置若罔聞）**close ˈranks 1** if a group of people **close ranks**, they work closely together to defend themselves, especially when they are being criticized（尤指受到批評時）抱團，攜手合作：*It's not unusual for the police to close ranks when one of their officers is being investigated.* 在一位警員受到調查時，警察抱團的事並不罕見。**2** if soldiers **close ranks**, they move closer together in order to defend themselves（士兵）成密集隊形，相互靠攏 ➲ more at DOOR, EAR, EYE *n.*

PHR V ˌclose ˈdown (*BrE*) when a radio or television station **closes down**, it stops broadcasting at the end of the day（電台或電視台在一天的播送後）結束播放，停止播音 ➲ related noun CLOSE-DOWN **ˌclose ˈdown | ˌclose sth↔ˈdown** = CLOSE[1] (4)：*All the steelworks around here were closed down in the 1980s.* 這一帶的所有鋼鐵廠都在 20 世紀 80 年代倒閉了。➲ related noun CLOSE-DOWN **OPP open up ˌclose ˈin 1** when the days **close in**, they become gradually shorter during the autumn/fall（秋季白天）逐漸變短 **2** if the weather **closes in**, it gets worse（天氣）變壞 **3** when the night **closes in**, it gets darker（夜色）加濃；（夜幕）降臨：*They huddled around the fire as the night closed in.* 夜幕降臨的時候，他們聚攏在爐火旁。**ˌclose ˈin (on sb/sth)** to move nearer to sb/sth, especially in order to attack them（尤指為了進攻）逼近，靠近：*The lions closed in on their prey.* 獅子逼近它們的獵物。**ˌclose sth↔ˈoff** to separate sth from other parts so that people cannot use it 隔離；封鎖：*The entrance to the train station was closed off following the explosion.* 爆炸發生後隨即封鎖了火車站入口。**ˌclose ˈout sth** (*NAmE*) **1** to sell goods very cheaply in order to get rid of them quickly 削價銷售；清倉處理；大甩賣 ➲ related noun CLOSEOUT **2** to finish or settle sth 結束；了結：*A rock concert closed out the festivities.* 一場搖滾音樂會為慶典活動畫下句點。**ˌclose ˈover sb/sth** to surround and cover sb/sth 環繞；遮蓋；淹沒：*The water closed over his head.* 水沒過他的頭頂。**ˌclose ˈup 1** when a wound **closes up**, it heals（傷口）痛合 **2** to hide your thoughts or emotions 隱瞞，掩飾（思想感情）：*She closed up when I asked about her family.* 我問起她的家人時她避而不談。**ˌclose ˈup | ˌclose sth↔ˈup 1** to shut and lock sth such as a shop/store or a building, especially for a short period of time（尤指臨時）關門停業，鎖上門：*Why don't we close up and go out for lunch?* 我們何不關上門出去吃頓午飯？◇ *Can the last one out close up the office?* 最後離開的人把辦公室鎖上好嗎？**OPP open up 2** to come closer together; to bring people or things closer together（使）靠攏，靠緊：*Traffic was heavy and cars were closing up behind each other.* 交通擁擠不堪，汽車一輛緊挨一輛地前行。**3** to become narrower and less open 變狹窄：*Every time he tried to speak, his throat closed up with fear.* 每當他試圖講話時，他都害怕得喉嚨發緊說不出話來。**OPP open up**

■ ***noun*** [sing.] (*formal*) the end of a period of time or an activity（一段時間或活動的）結束，終結，終了：*at the close of the 17th century* 在 17 世紀末 ◇ *His life was* ***drawing to a close***. 他的生命正走向終點。◇ *Can we* ***bring*** *this meeting* ***to a close***? 我們可以結束會議了嗎？

close[2] 🔑 /kləʊs; *NAmE* kloʊs/ *adj., adv., noun* ➲ see also CLOSE[1]

■ ***adj.*** (**closer, clos·est**)

▸ **NEAR** 接近 **1** 🔑 [not usually before noun] **~ (to sb/sth) | ~ (together)** near in space or time（在空間、時間上）接近：*Our new house is close to the school.* 我們的新房子離學校很近。◇ *I had no idea the beach was so close.* 我不知道海灘會這麼近。◇ *The two buildings are* ***close together***. 兩座建築物相距很近。◇ *This is the closest we can get to the beach by car.* 開車去海灘到了這兒就再也不能往前走了。◇ *We all have to work* ***in close proximity*** (= near each other). 我們都不得不緊挨在一起工作。◇ *The President was shot* ***at close range*** (= from a short distance away). 總統遭到了近距離的槍擊。◇ *The children are close to each other in age.* 這些兒童彼此的年齡很接近。◇ *Their birthdays are very* ***close together***. 他們的生日挨得很近。➲ note at NEAR

▸ **ALMOST/LIKELY** 幾乎；可能 **2** 🔑 [not before noun] **~ to sth | ~ to doing sth** almost in a particular state; likely to do sth soon 幾乎（處於某種狀態）；可能（快要做某事）：*He was close to tears.* 他幾乎掉眼淚了。◇ *The new library is close to completion.* 新圖書館快要竣工了。◇ *She knew she was close to death.* 她知道自己已命不久矣。◇ *We are close to signing the agreement.* 我們可能很快要簽訂協議。

▸ **RELATIONSHIP** 關係 **3** 🔑 **~ (to sb)** knowing sb very well and liking them very much 親密的；密切的：*Jo is a very* ***close friend***. 喬是一位很親密的朋友。◇ *She is very close to her father.* 她和父親的關係很親密。◇ *She and her father are very close.* 她和她父親很親。◇ *We're a very close family.* 我們全家彼此親密無間。**4** 🔑 near in family relationship（家庭關係）親近的：*close relatives, such as your mother and father, and brothers and sisters* 近親，如父母和兄弟姊妹 **OPP distant 5** 🔑 very involved in the work or activities of sb else, usually seeing and talking to them regularly（與某人的工作或活動）緊密相關的，密切的：*He is one of the prime minister's closest advisers.* 他是首相最親信的顧問之一。◇ *The college has close links with many other institutions.* 這所學院與其他許多的機構有着緊密的聯繫。◇ *She has kept in* ***close contact*** *with the victims' families.* 她與受害者的家人一直保持着密切的聯繫。◇ *We keep in* ***close touch*** *with the police.* 我們與警方保持着密切聯繫。

▸ **CAREFUL** 仔細 **6** 🔑 [only before noun] careful and thorough 細緻的；嚴密的；周密的：*Take a* ***close look*** *at this photograph.* 仔細看看這張照片。◇ ***On closer examination*** *the painting proved to be a fake.* 經過更加仔細的查看，那幅畫被證實是件贗品。◇ *Pay* ***close attention*** *to what I am telling you.* 要認真聽我給你講的話。

▸ **SIMILAR** 相似 **7** 🔑 **~ (to sth)** very similar to sth else or to an amount 酷似的；幾乎相等的：*There's a close resemblance* (= they look very similar). 彼此間有酷似之處。◇ *His feeling for her was close to hatred.* 他對她的感情近乎

仇恨。◇ *The total was close to 20% of the workforce.* 總數接近勞動力的 20%。◇ *We tried to match the colours, but this is the closest we could get.* 我們盡量使顏色搭配協調，但最好也只能做到這樣了。

‣ **COMPETITION/ELECTION, ETC.** 競爭、選舉等 **8** won by only a small amount or distance 實力相差無幾的；僅以些微之差獲勝的： *a **close** contest/match/election* 雙方實力很接近的競賽／比賽；勝負雙方差距很小的選舉◇ *It was a very **close finish**.* 比賽結果的勝負雙方差距極小。◇ *I think it's going to be close.* 我認為這將是一場勢均力敵的角逐。◇ *Our team came a **close second*** (= nearly won). 我們隊的得分與第一名相差很小，屈居第二。◇ *The game was closer than the score suggests.* 雙方實力比得分所顯示的要更接近。◇ *The result is going to be **too close to call*** (= either side may win). 雙方實力非常接近，因此結果無法預料。

‣ **ALMOST BAD RESULT** 近乎於不好的結果 **9** used to describe sth, usually a dangerous or unpleasant situation, that nearly happens（通常指危險或不愉快的情況幾乎發生）差一點兒，險些： *Phew! That was close—that car nearly hit us.* 啊！好險！那輛車差點兒撞上我們。◇ *We caught the bus in the end but it was close* (= we nearly missed it). 雖然我們最後總算趕上了那趟公共汽車，但也是夠懸的。

‣ **WITHOUT SPACE** 無空間 **10** with little or no space in between 空隙極小的；無空隙的；密集的；緊湊的： *over 1 000 pages of close print* * 1 000 多頁字體密集的印刷品 ◇ *The soldiers advanced in close formation.* 士兵排着密集的隊形前進。

‣ **CUT SHORT** 剪短 **11** cut very short, near to the skin 剪到齊根的；剪得很短的： *a **close** haircut/shave* 剪到齊根的頭髮；刮剃乾淨

‣ **GUARDED** 戒備 **12** [only before noun] carefully guarded 嚴加戒備的；守衛嚴密的： *The donor's identity is a **close secret**.* 捐贈人的身分是保密的。◇ *She was kept under **close arrest**.* 她被嚴密監禁。

‣ **WEATHER/ROOM** 天氣；房間 **13** warm in an uncomfortable way because there does not seem to be enough fresh air 悶熱的；不通風的 **SYN** **stuffy**

‣ **PRIVATE** 私人 **14** [not before noun] **~ (about sth)** not willing to give personal information about yourself（對自己的個人信息）守口如瓶： *He was close about his past.* 他對他的過去守口如瓶。

‣ **MEAN** 吝嗇 **15** [not before noun] (*BrE*) not liking to spend money 吝嗇；小氣： *She's always been very close with her money.* 她用錢總是很吝嗇。

‣ **PHONETICS** 語音學 **16** (also **high**) (of a vowel 元音) produced with the mouth in a relatively closed position 閉塞音的，閉的（發音時口形相對閉合的）➲ compare OPEN *adj.* (19)

▸ **close·ly** adv. : *I sat and watched everyone very closely* (= carefully). 我坐着仔細觀察每一個人。◇ *He walked into the room, closely followed by the rest of the family.* 他走進房間，後面緊跟着他的家人。◇ *a closely contested election* 實力相差無幾的競選◇ *She closely resembled her mother at the same age.* 她與她母親在相同的年齡時長相酷似。◇ *The two events are closely connected.* 兩起事件之間有密切的聯繫。 **close·ness** *noun* [U]

IDM **at/from ˌclose ˈquarters** very near 很近；非常靠近： *fighting at close quarters* 近距離作戰 **close, but no ciˈgar** (*informal, especially NAmE*) used to tell sb that their attempt or guess was almost but not quite successful 很接近，但還是錯了；猜得差不多，但不完全對 **a ˌclose ˈcall/ˈshave** (*informal*) a situation in which you only just manage to avoid an accident, etc. 僥幸避免事故；僥幸脫險；幸免於難 **a close ˈthing** a situation in which success or failure is equally possible 成敗機會各半： *We got him out in the end, but it was a close thing.* 我們最後總算把他救了出來，可那是真險啊。 **close to ˈhome** if a remark or topic of discussion is **close to home**, it is accurate or connected with you in a way that makes you uncomfortable or embarrassed（話語或討論的話題）因點中要害而使人局促不安（或尷尬）： *Her remarks about me were embarrassingly close to home.* 她說我的那些話使我尷尬不已。 **keep a close ˈeye/ˈwatch on sb/sth** to watch sb/sth carefully 密切注視；嚴密監視： *Over the next few months we will keep a close eye on sales.* 在今後的幾個月裏我們將密切關注銷售情況。➲ more at HAND *n.*, HEART

■ ***adv.*** (**closer**, **clos·est**) near; not far away 接近；靠近；緊挨着；不遠地： *They sat **close together**.* 他們緊挨着坐在一起。◇ *Don't **come** too **close**!* 別靠得太近！◇ *She **held** Tom **close** and pressed her cheek to his.* 她緊緊地抱着湯姆，並把臉緊貼在他的臉上。◇ *I couldn't **get close** enough to see.* 我無法靠得很近去看清楚。◇ *A second police car followed **close behind**.* 第二輛警車緊緊跟在後面。

IDM **close at ˈhand** near; in a place where sb/sth can be reached easily 在附近；在觸手可及的地方： *There are good cafes and a restaurant close at hand.* 附近有幾家挺不錯的咖啡館和一家餐館。 **close ˈby (sb/sth)** at a short distance (from sb/sth)（離…）不遠；在不遠處；在近旁： *Our friends live close by.* 我們的朋友住得不遠。◇ *The route passes close by the town.* 這條路離那座城鎮不遠。 **close on | close to** almost; nearly 幾乎；接近；差不多： *She is close on sixty.* 她快滿六十歲了。◇ *It is close on midnight.* 時近午夜。◇ *a profit close to £200 million* 接近 2 億英鎊的利潤 **a close run ˈthing** a situation in which sb only just wins or loses, for example in a competition or an election（比賽或選舉等中的）險勝，差距很小的敗北 **close ˈto | close ˈup** in a position very near to sth 在很近處；很近地： *The picture looks very different when you see it close to.* 這幅畫貼近看時就很不一樣。 **close up to sb/sth** very near in space to sb/sth（在空間上）離…很近： *She snuggled close up to him.* 她緊緊地依偎着他。 **come close (to sth/to doing sth)** to almost reach or do sth 幾乎達到；差不多： *He'd come close to death.* 他曾與死神擦肩而過。◇ *We didn't win but we came close.* 我們輸了，但離贏只差了那麼一小點兒。 **run sb/sth ˈclose** (*BrE*) to be nearly as good, fast, successful, etc. as sb/sth else 與…不相上下；可與…媲美： *Germany ran Argentina very close in the final.* 在決賽中，德國隊發揮得幾乎和阿根廷隊一樣出色。➲ more at CARD *n.*, MARK *n.*, SAIL *v.*

■ ***noun*** **1** (*BrE*) (especially in street names 尤用於街道名稱) a street that is closed at one end 一端不通的街道；死胡同；死巷道： *Brookside Close* 布魯克賽德巷 **2** the grounds and buildings that surround and belong to a CATHEDRAL 大教堂所屬的周圍場地及建築物

close-cropped /ˌkləʊs ˈkrɒpt; *NAmE* ˌkloʊs ˈkrɑːpt/ *adj.* (of hair, grass, etc. 頭髮、草等) cut very short 剪得很短的

closed /kləʊzd; *NAmE* kloʊzd/ *adj.*
1 shut 關閉；封閉： *Keep the door closed.* 讓門關着吧。 **2** [not before noun] shut, especially of a shop/store or public building that is not open for a period of time 關閉；（尤指一段時間）停止營業，不開放： *The museum is closed on Mondays.* 博物館每逢星期一閉館。◇ *This road is closed to traffic.* 這條道路暫停通行。 **3** not willing to accept outside influences or new ideas 封閉的；閉關自守的；不願接受新思想的： *a closed society* 閉關自守的社會◇ *He has a closed mind.* 他思想僵化守舊。 **4** [usually before noun] limited to a particular group of people; not open to everyone 只限於某些人的；僅為少數人的；不向公眾開放的： *a closed membership* 只限於少數人的成員資格 **OPP** **open** ➲ note at CLOSE[1]

IDM **behind closed ˈdoors** without the public being allowed to attend or know what is happening; in private 與外界隔絕；秘密地；暗地裏 **a closed ˈbook (to sb)** a subject or person that you know nothing about 一竅不通的事物；不瞭解的人

ˌclosed-ˈcaptioned *adj.* (*NAmE*) (of a TV programme 電視節目) having CAPTIONS that can only be read if you have a special machine (= a DECODER) 閉路字幕的（用解碼器才能閱讀）

ˌclosed-ˌcircuit ˈtelevision *noun* [U] (*abbr.* **CCTV**) a television system that works within a limited area, for example a public building, to protect it from crime 閉路電視

close-down /ˈkləʊz daʊn; *NAmE* ˈkloʊz/ *noun* [U, sing.] the stopping of work, especially permanently, in an office, a factory, etc.（尤指永久的）停工，停業；倒閉

ˈclosed season *noun* [sing.] = CLOSE SEASON (1)

ˌ**closed ˈshop** *noun* a factory, business, etc. in which employees must all be members of a particular TRADE/LABOR UNION 只雇用工會會員的工廠（或企業等）

ˈ**closed syllable** *noun* (*phonetics* 語音) a syllable which ends with a consonant, for example *sit* 閉音節（以輔音結束的音節，如 sit）

close-fitting /ˌkləʊs ˈfɪtɪŋ; *NAmE* ˌkloʊs/ *adj.* (of clothes 衣服) fitting tightly, showing the shape of the body 緊身的

close harmony /ˌkləʊs ˈhɑːməni; *NAmE* ˌkloʊs ˈhɑːrməni/ *noun* [U] (*music* 音) a style of singing in HARMONY in which the different notes are close together 密集和聲（聲部緊靠在一起）

close-knit /ˌkləʊs ˈnɪt; *NAmE* ˌkloʊs/ (also *less frequent* ˌ**closely-ˈknit**) *adj.* (of a group of people 一群人) having strong relationships with each other and taking a close, friendly interest in each other's activities and problems 緊密結合在一起的；志同道合的；意氣相投的：*the close-knit community of a small village* 小村莊裏親密結合在一起的村民

close-mouthed /ˌkləʊs ˈmaʊðd; *NAmE* ˌkloʊs/ *adj.* [not usually before noun] not willing to say much about sth because you want to keep a secret 守口如瓶；口緊；緘口不言

close·out /ˈkləʊzaʊt; *NAmE* ˈkloʊz-/ *noun* (*NAmE*) an occasion when goods are sold cheaply in order to get rid of them quickly 削價銷售；清倉處理；大甩賣

close-range /ˌkləʊs ˈreɪndʒ; *NAmE* ˌkloʊs/ *adj.* [only before noun] at or from a short distance 近距離的：*The close-range shot was blocked by the goalkeeper.* 那次近距離的射門被守門員截住了。

close-run /ˌkləʊs ˈrʌn; *NAmE* ˌkloʊs/ *adj.* [usually before noun] (of a race or competition 比賽或競爭) won by a very small amount or distance 險勝的：*The election was a close-run thing.* 這次選舉是一次險勝。

close season /ˈkləʊz siːzn; *NAmE* ˈkloʊz/ *noun* [sing.] (*BrE*) **1** (also ˈ**closed season** *NAmE*, *BrE*) the time of year when it is illegal to kill particular kinds of animal, bird and fish because they are breeding 禁獵期；禁漁期 **OPP** **open season** **2** (*NAmE* ˈ**off season**) (in sport 體育運動) the time during the summer when teams do not play important games（夏季的）比賽淡季

close-set /ˌkləʊs ˈset; *NAmE* ˌkloʊs/ *adj.* very close together 緊靠在一起的；很近的：*close-set eyes* 長得距離很近的眼睛

closet 🔑 /ˈklɒzɪt; *NAmE* ˈklɑːzət/ *noun, adj., verb*

■ ***noun*** 🔑 (*especially NAmE*) a small room or a space in a wall with a door that reaches the floor, used for storing things 貯藏室；壁櫥：*a walk-in closet* 步入式衣帽間 ➲ **VISUAL VOCAB** page V23 ➲ compare CUPBOARD (2), WARDROBE (1) ➲ see also WATER CLOSET

IDM **come out of the ˈcloset** to admit sth openly that you kept secret before, especially because of shame or embarrassment 公開承認秘密（尤指因恥辱或尷尬而一直保守着的秘密）；"出櫃"：*Homosexuals in public life are now coming out of the closet.* 公眾人物中的同性戀者如今逐漸公開自己的性取向。➲ see also COME OUT (10) at COME *v.* **IDM** see SKELETON

■ ***adj.*** [only before noun] used to describe people who want to keep some fact about themselves secret 隱藏（身分）的；不公開（個人信息）的：*closet gays* 不公開表明的同性戀者 ◇ *I suspect he's a closet fascist.* 我懷疑他是秘密的法西斯分子。

■ ***verb*** **~ sb/yourself + adv./prep.** to put sb in a room away from other people, especially so that they can talk privately with sb, or so that they can be alone 把…關在房間裏（尤指為了私下會談或避免他人打擾）：*He was closeted with the President for much of the day.* 他與總統閉門進行了幾乎一整天的密談。◇ *She had closeted herself away in her room.* 她把自己關在房間裏不見任何人。

close-up /ˈkləʊs ʌp; *NAmE* ˈkloʊs/ *noun* [C, U] a photograph, or picture in a film/movie, taken very close to sb/sth so that it shows a lot of detail（照片、電影畫面的）特寫，特寫鏡頭：*a close-up of a human eye* 呈現人眼睛的特寫鏡頭 ◇ *It was strange to see her own face in close-up on the screen.* 在屏幕上看見她自己的臉部特寫使她感到新奇。◇ *close-up pictures of the planet* 這顆行星的特寫照片

clos·ing /ˈkləʊzɪŋ; *NAmE* ˈkloʊzɪŋ/ *adj., noun*

■ ***adj.*** [only before noun] coming at the end of a speech, a period of time or an activity（講話、時段或活動）接近尾聲的，結尾的，結束的：*his closing remarks* 他的結束語 ◇ *the closing stages of the game* 比賽的尾段 **OPP** **opening**

■ ***noun*** [U] the act of shutting sth such as a factory, hospital, school, etc. permanently（永久的）停業，關閉；倒閉：*the closing of the local school* 當地學校的關閉 **OPP** **opening**

ˈ**closing date** *noun* the last date by which sth must be done, such as applying for a job or entering a competition 截止日期

ˈ**closing time** *noun* [C, U] the time when a pub, shop/store, bar, etc. ends business for the day and people have to leave（酒館、商店等的）打烊時間

clos·ure /ˈkləʊʒə(r); *NAmE* ˈkloʊ-/ *noun* **1** [C, U] the situation when a factory, school, hospital, etc. shuts permanently（永久的）停業，關閉，倒閉：*factory closures* 工廠倒閉 ◇ *The hospital has been threatened with closure.* 這家醫院面臨着關閉的威脅。**2** [C, U] the temporary closing of a road or bridge（路或橋的）暫時封閉 **3** [U] the feeling that a difficult or an unpleasant experience has come to an end or been dealt with in an acceptable way（因困境結束或事情得到妥善處理等的）寬慰；如釋重負：*The conviction of their son's murderer helped to give them a sense of closure.* 謀殺兒子的兇手被判罪，讓他們得到了一些安慰。

clot /klɒt; *NAmE* klɑːt/ *noun, verb*

■ ***noun*** **1** = BLOOD CLOT：*They removed a clot from his brain.* 他們從他的大腦裏取出了血塊。**2** (*old-fashioned, BrE, informal*) a stupid person 蠢人；笨蛋；傻瓜

■ ***verb*** (**-tt-**) [I, T] **~ (sth)** when blood or cream **clots** or when sth **clots** it, it forms thick lumps or clots（使血或乳脂）凝結成塊：*a drug that stops blood from clotting during operations* 手術時防止血液凝結成塊的藥物 ◇ *the blood clotting agent, Factor 8* 凝血因子 VIII

cloth 🔑 /klɒθ; *NAmE* klɔːθ/ *noun* (*pl.* **cloths** /klɒθs; *NAmE* klɔːðz/)

1 🔑 [U] material made by WEAVING or knitting cotton, wool, silk, etc. 布；布料：***woollen/cotton cloth*** 毛料；棉布料 ◇ *bandages made from strips of cloth* 用布條做的繃帶 ◇ *the **cloth industry/trade*** 織布業；布業貿易 ◇ *a cloth bag* 布袋 ➲ **SYNONYMS** at FABRIC **2** 🔑 [C] (often in compounds 常構成複合詞) a piece of cloth, often used for a special purpose, especially cleaning things or covering a table 一塊布；（尤指）一塊抹布，一塊桌布：*Wipe the surface with a damp cloth.* 用濕布擦拭表面。➲ see also DISHCLOTH, DROP CLOTH, FLOORCLOTH, TABLECLOTH **3** **the cloth** [sing.] (*literary*) used to refer to Christian priests as a group（統稱）牧師，神父：*a man of the cloth* 一位牧師 **IDM** see COAT *n.*

ˌ**cloth ˈcap** (also ˌ**flat ˈcap**) (both *BrE*) *noun* a soft cap, normally made of wool, traditionally a symbol of working men 布帽，羊毛軟帽（傳統上為勞工的象徵）：*The party has shed its cloth cap image* (= it is not just a working-class party any more). 這個政黨已經擺脱工人階級的形象。➲ **VISUAL VOCAB** page V65

clothe /kləʊð; *NAmE* kloʊð/ *verb* **1 ~ sb/yourself (in sth)** (*formal*) to dress sb/yourself 給…穿衣：*They clothe their children in the latest fashions.* 他們給他們的孩子穿最時髦的服裝。◇ (*figurative*) *Climbing plants clothed the courtyard walls.* 攀緣植物給院牆披上了綠裝。**2 ~ sb** to provide clothes for sb to wear 為（某人）提供衣服：*the costs of feeding and clothing a family* 一家人的衣食費用

ˈ**cloth-eared** *adj.* (*BrE, informal, disapproving*) (of a person 人) unable to hear or understand things clearly 耳背的；呆頭呆腦的

clothed /kləʊðd; *NAmE* kloʊðd/ *adj.* [not usually before noun] **~ (in sth)** dressed in a particular way 衣着…；穿…衣服：*a man clothed in black* 黑衣男子 ◇ *She*

C

jumped **fully clothed** into the water. 她沒有脫衣服就跳進了水裏。◇ (*figurative*) *The valley was clothed in trees and shrubs.* 樹林和灌木叢覆蓋着山谷。

C

Synonyms 同義詞辨析

clothes

clothing • garment • dress • wear • gear

These are all words for the things that you wear, such as shirts, jackets, dresses and trousers. 以上各詞均指衣服、服裝。

clothes [pl.] the things that you wear, such as shirts, jackets, dresses and trousers 指衣服、服裝

clothing [U] (*rather formal*) clothes, especially a particular type of clothes 指衣服，尤指某種類型的服裝：*warm clothing* 保暖服

CLOTHES OR CLOTHING? 用 clothes 還是 clothing？

Clothing is more formal than **clothes** and is used especially to mean 'a particular type of clothes'. There is no singular form of **clothes** or **clothing**: *a piece/an item/an article of clothing* is used to talk about one thing that you wear such as a dress or shirt. * clothing 較 clothes 更正式，尤用以指某種類型的服裝。clothes 或 clothing 無單數形式，指一件衣服用 a piece/an item/an article of clothing。

garment (*formal*) a piece of clothing 指一件衣服：*He was wearing a strange shapeless garment.* 他穿着一件不成形的奇怪衣服。NOTE **Garment** should only be used in formal or literary contexts; in everyday contexts use *a piece of clothing.* * garment 只用於正式場合或文學語境，在日常生活中，一件衣服用 a piece of clothing。

dress [U] clothes, especially when worn in a particular style or for a particular occasion 指着裝、衣着，尤指某種樣式或某種場合穿的衣服：*We were allowed to wear casual dress on Fridays.* 我們在星期五可以穿便服。

wear [U] (usually in compounds) clothes for a particular purpose or occasion, especially when it is being sold in shops/stores（通常構成複合詞）指為特定用途或場合穿的衣服，尤指商店中售賣的衣服：*the children's wear department* 童裝部

gear [U] (*informal*) clothes 指衣服、服裝：*Her friends were all wearing the latest gear* (= fashionable clothes). 她的朋友都穿着最新款的衣服。

PATTERNS

- **casual** clothes/clothing/dress/wear/gear
- **evening/formal** clothes/dress/wear
- **designer/sports** clothes/clothing/garments/wear/gear
- **children's/men's/women's** clothes/clothing/garments/wear
- to **have on/be in/wear** … clothes/garments/dress/gear

clothes 🔑 /kləʊðz; kləʊz; *NAmE* kloʊðz; kloʊz/ *noun* [pl.]
the things that you wear, such as trousers/pants, dresses and jackets 衣服；服裝：*I bought some new clothes for the trip.* 我為這次旅行買了一些新衣服。◇ *to* ***put on/take off your clothes*** 穿上/脫下衣服 ◇ *Bring* ***a change of clothes*** *with you.* 你要帶上一套換洗衣服。◇ *She has no* ***clothes sense*** (= she does not know what clothes look attractive). 她不懂穿着打扮。➲ COLLOCATIONS at FASHION ➲ VISUAL VOCAB pages V61, V62, V63 IDM see EMPEROR

'clothes hanger *noun* = HANGER

'clothes horse *noun* **1** (*BrE*) a wooden or plastic folding frame that you put clothes on to dry after you have washed them 晾衣架；曬衣架 **2** (*disapproving*) a person, especially a woman, who is too interested in fashionable clothes 講究衣着的人，追求時裝的人（尤指婦女）

'clothes line (*BrE*) (also **line** *NAmE, BrE*) (*BrE* also **'washing line**) *noun* a piece of thin rope or wire, attached to posts, that you hang clothes on to dry outside after you have washed them 曬衣繩

'clothes peg (*BrE*) (*NAmE* **'clothes·pin**) *noun* = PEG (3) ➲ picture at PEG

clo·thier /ˈkləʊðiə(r); *NAmE* ˈkloʊ-/ *noun* (*formal*) a person or company that makes or sells clothes or cloth 服裝製造（或銷售）商；衣料商

cloth·ing 🔑 /ˈkləʊðɪŋ; *NAmE* ˈkloʊðɪŋ/ *noun* [U]
clothes, especially a particular type of clothes 衣服；（尤指某種）服裝：*protective clothing* 防護服 ◇ *the high cost of food and clothing* 衣食的昂貴費用 ◇ *an* ***item/article of clothing*** 一件衣服 ➲ SYNONYMS at CLOTHES IDM see WOLF *n.*

,clot·ted 'cream *noun* [U] a very thick type of cream made by slowly heating milk, and eaten especially in Britain（尤指在英國用文火加熱牛奶製作的）凝脂奶油：*scones and jam with clotted cream* 夾有凝脂奶油和果醬的烤餅

'clotting factor *noun* [C, U] (*biology* 生) any of the substances in the blood which help it to CLOT (= become thick and form lumps) 凝血因子

cloud 🔑 /klaʊd/ *noun, verb*

■ ***noun* 1** 🔑 [C, U] a grey or white mass made of very small drops of water, that floats in the sky 雲；雲朵：*The sun went behind a cloud.* 太陽躲在了一朵雲的後面。◇ *The plane was flying in cloud most of the way.* 飛機一路大多在雲層裏飛行。➲ COLLOCATIONS at WEATHER ➲ see also STORM CLOUD, THUNDERCLOUD **2** 🔑 [C] a large mass of sth in the air, for example dust or smoke, or a number of insects flying all together 雲狀物（如塵霧、煙霧、一群飛行的昆蟲）**3** [C] something that makes you feel sad or anxious 陰影；憂鬱；焦慮；令人憂慮的事：*Her father's illness* ***cast a cloud over*** *her wedding day.* 她父親的病給她的結婚喜慶日蒙上了一層陰影。◇ *The only dark* ***cloud on the horizon*** *was that they might have to move house.* 唯一的憂慮是他們可能要搬家。◇ *He still has* ***a cloud*** *of suspicion* ***hanging over him.*** 他的心頭仍有一團疑雲。

IDM **every cloud has a silver 'lining** (*saying*) every sad or difficult situation has a positive side 黑暗中總有一線光明；朵朵烏雲襯銀邊，處處黑暗透光明 **on cloud 'nine** (*old-fashioned, informal*) extremely happy 極其快樂；樂不可支 **under a 'cloud** if sb is **under a cloud**, other people think that they have done sth wrong and are suspicious of them 有嫌疑；被懷疑 ➲ more at HEAD *n.*

■ ***verb* 1** [T] **~ sth** if sth **clouds** your judgement, memory, etc., it makes it difficult for you to understand or remember sth clearly 使難以理解；使記不清楚；使模糊：*Doubts were beginning to cloud my mind.* 種種疑問開始使我的思路變模糊了。◇ *His judgement was clouded by jealousy.* 妒忌心蒙蔽了他的判斷力。**2** [I, T] (*formal*) (of sb's face 臉色) to show sadness, fear, anger, etc.; to make sb look sad, afraid, angry, etc. 顯得陰沉（或恐懼、憤怒等）；看起來憂愁（或害怕、憤怒等）：**~ (over)** *Her face clouded over with anger.* 她滿面怒容。◇ **~ sth** *Suspicion clouded his face.* 他狐疑滿面。**3** [T] **~ the issue** to make sth you are discussing or considering less clear, especially by introducing subjects that are not connected with it（尤指用無關的話題來）混淆，攪混（問題）**4** [I] **~ (over)** (of the sky 天空) to fill with clouds 佈滿雲：*It was beginning to cloud over.* 天空開始陰雲密佈。**5** [T] **~ sth** to make sth less pleasant or enjoyable 使減少樂趣；使不快：*His last years were clouded by financial worries.* 由於經濟窘困，他的晚年生活過得悶悶不樂。**6** [I, T] if glass, water, etc. **clouds**, or if sth **clouds** it, it becomes less transparent 使不透明；使模糊：**~ (with sth)** *Her eyes clouded with tears.* 淚水模糊了她的眼睛。◇ **~ sth** *Steam had clouded the mirror.* 水蒸氣使鏡子變得模糊不清。

cloud·burst /ˈklaʊdbɜːst; *NAmE* -bɜːrst/ *noun* a sudden very heavy fall of rain（驟然降下的）大暴雨，傾盆大雨

ˈcloud computing *noun* [U] a way of using computers in which data and software are stored mainly on a central computer, to which users have access over the Internet 雲計算，雲端運算（用戶通過互聯網調用主要貯存於中央計算機的數據和軟件的方式）

ˌcloud ˈcuckoo land (*BrE*) (*NAmE* **cloud·land**, **ˈla-la land**) *noun* [U] (*informal, disapproving*) if you say that sb is living **in cloud cuckoo land**, you mean that they do not understand what a situation is really like, but think it is much better than it is 幻想世界；脱離現實的幻境

ˈcloud forest *noun* [C, U] a forest in tropical or SUBTROPICAL parts of the world that usually has thick cloud at the level of the tops of the trees（熱帶或亞熱帶的）雲霧林 ➲ compare RAINFOREST

cloud·less /ˈklaʊdləs/ *adj.* clear; with no clouds 晴朗的；無雲的：*a cloudless sky* 晴朗的天空

cloudy /ˈklaʊdi/ *adj.* (**cloud·ier**, **cloudi·est**) **1** (of the sky or the weather 天空或天氣) covered with clouds; with a lot of clouds 被雲遮住的；陰雲密佈的；陰天的；多雲的 OPP **clear**：*a grey, cloudy day* 灰暗多雲的一天 **2** (of liquids 液體) not clear or transparent 不清澈的；不透明的；渾濁的 ▸ **cloudi·ness** *noun* [U]

clout /klaʊt/ *noun, verb*

■ **noun** **1** [U] power and influence 影響力；勢力：***political/financial clout*** 政治／經濟勢力 ◇ *I knew his opinion carried a lot of clout with them.* 我知道他的觀點對他們很有影響力。 **2** [C, usually sing.] (*informal*) a blow with the hand or a hard object（用手或硬物的）擊，打

■ **verb ~ sb** (*informal*) to hit sb hard, especially with your hand（尤指用手）猛擊，重打

clove /kləʊv; *NAmE* kloʊv/ *noun* **1** [C, U] the dried flower of a tropical tree, used in cooking as a spice, especially to give flavour to sweet foods. Cloves look like small nails. 丁香（熱帶樹木的乾花，形似小釘子，用於烹飪調味，尤用作甜食的香料）➲ VISUAL VOCAB page V32 **2** [C] **a garlic ~** | **a ~ of garlic** one of the small separate sections of a BULB (= the round underground part) of GARLIC 蒜瓣 ➲ VISUAL VOCAB page V31 ➲ see also CLEAVE *v.*

ˌcloven ˈhoof *noun* the foot of an animal such as a cow, a sheep, or a GOAT, that is divided into two parts（牛、羊等的）偶蹄，分趾蹄

clo·ver /ˈkləʊvə(r); *NAmE* ˈkloʊ-/ *noun* [U] a small wild plant that usually has three leaves on each STEM and purple, pink or white flowers that are shaped like balls 三葉草；車軸草：*a four-leaf clover* (= one with four leaves instead of three, thought to bring good luck) 四葉車軸草（一般為三葉，故被認為可帶來好運）

IDM **be/live in clover** (*informal*) to have enough money to be able to live a very comfortable life 過舒適優裕的生活

clover·leaf /ˈkləʊvəliːf; *NAmE* ˈkloʊvər-/ *noun* (*NAmE*) a place where a number of main roads meet at different levels, with curved sections that form the pattern of a four-leaf clover 四葉苜蓿葉形立交路口；葉形交流道

clown /klaʊn/ *noun, verb*

■ **noun** **1** an entertainer who wears funny clothes and a large red nose and does silly things to make people laugh 丑角；小丑：(*figurative*) *Robert was always the class clown* (= he did silly things to make the other students laugh). 那時候羅伯特總是班裏的活寶。 **2** (*disapproving*) a person that you disapprove of because they act in a stupid way 蠢貨；笨蛋：*What do those clowns in the government think they are doing?* 政府裏的那些蠢貨自以為他們在做什麼呢？

■ **verb** [I] **~ (around)** (often *disapproving*) to behave in a silly way, especially in order to make other people laugh（尤指為逗人笑而故意）做出蠢相

clown·ish /ˈklaʊnɪʃ/ *adj.* like a clown; silly 小丑似的；滑稽的；愚蠢的；傻的

cloy /klɔɪ/ *verb* [I] (of sth pleasant or sweet 美好事物或香甜的東西) to start to become slightly disgusting or annoying, because there is too much of it 讓人膩煩：*After a while, the rich sauce begins to cloy.* 過了一會兒，濃味醬汁開始顯得油膩了。

cloy·ing /ˈklɔɪɪŋ/ *adj.* (*formal*) **1** (of food, a smell, etc. 食物、氣味等) so sweet that it is unpleasant 甜得發膩的；使人膩煩的 **2** using emotion in a very obvious way, so that the result is unpleasant（感情過於外露而）令人膩煩的：*the cloying sentimentality of her novels* 她的小説過度傷感的情調 ▸ **cloy·ing·ly** *adv.*

cloze test /ˈkləʊz test; *NAmE* ˈkloʊz/ *noun* a type of test in which you have to put suitable words in spaces in a text where words have been left out 填空測驗

club 🔑 /klʌb/ *noun, verb*

■ **noun**

▸ FOR ACTIVITY/SPORT 活動；體育運動 **1** 🔑 [C+sing./pl. v.] (especially in compounds 尤用於構成複合詞) a group of people who meet together regularly, for a particular activity, sport, etc. 俱樂部；社團；會：***a golf/tennis, etc. club*** 高爾夫球、網球等俱樂部 ◇ ***a chess/film/movie, etc. club*** 國際象棋、電影等俱樂部 ◇ ***to join/belong to a club*** 加入俱樂部；屬於某俱樂部 ◇ *The club has/have voted to admit new members.* 俱樂部通過投票同意接納新成員。 ➲ see also FAN CLUB, YOUTH CLUB **2** 🔑 [C] the building or rooms that a particular club uses（俱樂部使用的）建築設施，活動室：*We had lunch at the golf club.* 我們在高爾夫球俱樂部吃了午飯。 ◇ *the club bar* 俱樂部酒吧 ➲ see also COUNTRY CLUB, HEALTH CLUB **3** 🔑 [C+sing./pl. v.] (*BrE*) a professional sports organization that includes the players, managers, owners and members 職業運動俱樂部：*Manchester United Football Club* 曼聯職業足球俱樂部

▸ MUSIC/DANCING 音樂；舞蹈 **4** 🔑 [C] a place where people, especially young people, go and listen to music, dance, etc.（尤指年輕人聽音樂、跳舞等的）俱樂部，夜總會：*a jazz club* 爵士樂夜總會 ◇ *the club scene in Newcastle* 紐卡斯爾的夜總會場景 ➲ see also CLUBBING, NIGHTCLUB, STRIP CLUB

▸ SOCIAL 社交 **5** [C+sing./pl. v.] (especially in Britain) an organization and a place where people, usually men only, can meet together socially or stay（尤指英國）男性俱樂部：*He's a member of several London clubs.* 他是倫敦幾個男性俱樂部的會員。

▸ SELLING BOOKS/CDS 銷售書／激光唱片 **6** [C] an organization that sells books, CDs, etc. cheaply to its members（以優惠價出售圖書、激光唱片等給成員的）讀者俱樂部，聽眾俱樂部，…會：*a music club* 音樂聽眾俱樂部 ➲ see also BOOK CLUB

▸ WEAPON 武器 **7** [C] a heavy stick with one end thicker than the other, that is used as a weapon 擊棍（一頭粗一頭細）➲ see also BILLY CLUB

▸ IN GOLF 高爾夫球 **8** [C] = GOLF CLUB (1)

▸ IN CARD GAMES 紙牌遊戲 **9 clubs** [pl., U] one of the four sets of cards (called SUITS) in a PACK/DECK of cards. The clubs have a black design shaped like three black leaves on a short STEM. 梅花：*the five/queen/ace of clubs* 梅花五／Q／A ➲ VISUAL VOCAB page V37 **10** [C] one card from the SUIT called clubs 梅花牌：*I played a club.* 我出梅花。

IDM **be in the club** (*BrE, informal*) to be pregnant 懷孕；肚子大了 ➲ more at JOIN *v.*

■ **verb** (**-bb-**) **1** [T] **~ sb/sth** to hit a person or an animal with a heavy stick or similar object 用棍棒（或類似棍棒之物）打：*The victim was* ***clubbed to death*** *with a baseball bat.* 受害者被人用棒球球棒毆打致死。 **2** [I] **go clubbing** (*BrE, informal*) to spend time dancing and drinking in NIGHTCLUBS 泡夜總會

PHR V **ˌclub toˈgether** (*BrE*) if two or more people **club together**, they each give an amount of money and the total is used to pay for sth 湊份子；分擔費用：*We clubbed together to buy them a new television.* 我們湊錢給他們買了一台新電視機。

club·bing /ˈklʌbɪŋ/ *noun* [U] the activity of going to NIGHTCLUBS regularly 泡夜總會：*They* ***go clubbing*** *most weekends.* 他們大多數的週末都去泡夜總會。 ▸ **club·ber** *noun*：*The venue was packed with 3 000 clubbers.* 夜總會場地擠滿了 3 000 人。

ˈclub car *noun* (*NAmE*) a coach/car on a train with comfortable chairs and tables, where you can buy sth to eat or drink（火車的）休閒車廂（設有舒適桌椅，並出售食品飲料）

ˈclub class *noun* [U] (*BrE*) = BUSINESS CLASS

ˌclub ˈfoot *noun* [C, U] a foot that has been DEFORMED (= badly shaped) since birth （先天性的）畸形足 ▸ **ˌclub-ˈfooted** *adj.*

club·house /ˈklʌbhaʊs/ *noun* the building used by a club, especially a sports club（尤指體育）俱樂部會所

club·land /ˈklʌblænd/ *noun* [U] (*BrE*) popular NIGHTCLUBS in general and the people who go to them; an area of a town where there are a lot of NIGHTCLUBS 受歡迎的夜總會及其顧客；夜總會區：*modern clubland* 現代夜總會區◇*London's clubland* 倫敦的夜總會區

ˌclub ˈsandwich *noun* a SANDWICH consisting of three slices of bread with two layers of food between them 總會三明治（三片麵包，兩層夾餡）

cluck /klʌk/ *verb, noun*

▪ *verb* **1** [I] when a chicken **clucks**, it makes a series of short low sounds（雞）咯咯地叫，發出咯咯聲 **2** [I] to make a short low sound with your tongue to show that you feel sorry for sb or that you disapprove of sth（表示遺憾或不贊成）發出嘖嘖聲：*The teacher clucked sympathetically at the child's story.* 對那小孩講述的遭遇，老師嘖嘖地表示同情。

▪ *noun* the low, short sounds that a chicken makes（雞的）格格聲：(*figurative*) *a* ***cluck of impatience/annoyance*** 不耐煩 / 氣惱的嘖嘖聲

clucky /ˈklʌki/ *adj.* (*AustralE, NZE, informal*) **1** (of a HEN 母雞) sitting or ready to sit on eggs（準備）孵蛋的 SYN **broody** **2** (of a woman 女人) wanting to have a baby 想生孩子的 SYN **broody**

clue /kluː/ *noun, verb*

▪ *noun* **1** ~ **(to sth)** an object, a piece of evidence or some information that helps the police solve a crime（幫助警方破案的）線索，跡象：*The police think the videotape may hold some vital clues to the identity of the killer.* 警方認為那盤錄像帶可能錄有能確認兇手身分的一些重要線索。 **2** ~ **(to sth)** a fact or a piece of evidence that helps you discover the answer to a problem（問題答案的）線索，提示：*Diet may hold the clue to the causes of migraine.* 從飲食習慣有可能找出偏頭痛的原因。 **3** some words or a piece of information that helps you find the answers to a CROSSWORD, a game or a question（縱橫填字謎、遊戲或問題的）提示詞語，解答提示：*'You'll never guess who I saw today!' 'Give me a clue.'* "你絕對猜不着我今天見到誰了！" "給我提示一下吧。"

IDM **not have a ˈclue** (*informal*) **1** to know nothing about sth or about how to do sth 一無所知；不知怎麼做：*I don't have a clue where she lives.* 我完全不知道她住在哪裏。 **2** (*disapproving*) to be very stupid 很愚蠢；很笨拙：*Don't ask him to do it—he doesn't have a clue!* 這事別叫他做，他笨極了。

▪ *verb*

PHR V **ˌclue sb ˈin (on sth)** (*informal*) to give sb the most recent information about sth 給（某人）提供最新信息：*He's just clued me in on the latest developments.* 他剛給我提供了最新的進展情況。

ˌclued-ˈup (*BrE*) (*NAmE* **ˌclued-ˈin**) *adj.* ~ **(on sth)** (*informal*) knowing a lot about sth; having a lot of information about sth（對某事）很熟悉，所知甚多

clue·less /ˈkluːləs/ *adj.* (*informal, disapproving*) very stupid; not able to understand or to do sth 很愚蠢的；（對某事）不懂的，無能的：*He's completely clueless about computers.* 他對計算機一竅不通。

clump /klʌmp/ *noun, verb*

▪ *noun* **1** a small group of things or people very close together, especially trees or plants; a bunch of sth such as grass or hair（尤指樹或植物的）叢，簇，束，串；（人的）群，組；（草的）堆；（毛髮的）縷：*a clump of trees/bushes* 樹 / 灌木叢 **2** the sound made by sb putting their feet down very heavily 沉重的腳步聲

▪ *verb* **1** [I] + **adv./prep.** (*especially BrE*) to put your feet down noisily and heavily as you walk 以沉重的腳步行走：*The children clumped down the stairs.* 孩子們腳步嗵嗵地走下了樓梯。 **2** [I, T] ~ **(together)** | ~ **A and B (together)** to come together or be brought together to form a tight group 聚集；被聚集成群：*Galaxies tend to clump together in clusters.* 星系往往聚集形成星團。

clumpy /ˈklʌmpi/ *adj.* (*BrE*) (of shoes and boots 鞋和靴) big, thick and heavy 大而厚重的

clumsy /ˈklʌmzi/ *adj.* (**clum·sier**, **clum·si·est**) **1** (of people and animals 人和動物) moving or doing things in a very awkward way 笨拙的；不靈巧的：*I spilt your coffee. Sorry—that was clumsy of me.* 我弄灑了你的咖啡。對不起，我真是笨手笨腳的。◇ *His clumsy fingers couldn't untie the knot.* 他的手很笨拙，無法解開這個結。 **2** (of actions and statements 行動和陳述) done without skill or in a way that offends people 無技巧的；冒犯人的；不得體的：*She made* ***a clumsy attempt*** *to apologize.* 她本想道歉，但措詞生硬。 **3** (of objects 物體) difficult to move or use easily; not well designed 難以移動的；難用的；設計欠佳的 **4** (of processes 程序) awkward; too complicated to understand or use easily 難處理的；複雜難懂的；使用不便的：*The complaints procedure is clumsy and time-consuming.* 申訴程序複雜耗時。 ▸ **clum·si·ly** /-ɪli/ *adv.* **clum·si·ness** *noun* [U]

clung *past tense, past part.* of CLING

clunk /klʌŋk/ *noun* a dull sound made by two heavy objects hitting each other（重物的）碰撞聲，哐啷聲 ▸ **clunk** *verb* [I]

clunk·er /ˈklʌŋkə(r)/ *noun* (*NAmE, informal*) **1** an old car in bad condition 破舊不堪的汽車 **2** a serious mistake 嚴重的錯誤；大錯

clunky /ˈklʌŋki/ *adj.* (*informal, especially NAmE*) heavy and awkward 笨重的：*clunky leather shoes* 笨重的皮鞋◇ (*figurative*) *The movie is ruined by wooden acting and clunky dialogue.* 這部電影被木訥的表演和笨拙的對白給毀了。

clus·ter /ˈklʌstə(r)/ *noun, verb*

▪ *noun* **1** a group of things of the same type that grow or appear close together（同類物叢生或聚集的）簇，團，束，串：*a cluster of stars* 星團 ◇ *The plant bears its flowers in clusters.* 這種植物開花成簇。◇ *a leukaemia cluster* (= an area where there are more cases of the disease than you would expect) 白血病高發區 **2** a group of people, animals or things close together（人或動物的）群，團，組；（物品的）堆，批：*a cluster of spectators* 一群觀眾◇ *a little cluster of houses* 擠在一起的幾處房屋 **3** (*phonetics* 語音) a group of consonants which come together in a word or phrase, for example /str/ at the beginning of *string* 輔音叢；輔音連綴：*a consonant cluster* 輔音叢

▪ *verb* [I] to come together in a small group or groups 群聚；聚集：**~ together** *The children clustered together in the corner of the room.* 孩子們聚集在房間的角落裏。◇ **~ around/round sb/sth** *The doctors* ***clustered*** *anxiously* ***around*** *his bed.* 醫生焦急地圍在他的牀邊。

ˈcluster bomb *noun* a type of bomb that throws out smaller bombs when it explodes 榴霰彈；集束炸彈；子母彈

clutch /klʌtʃ/ *verb, noun*

▪ *verb* **1** [T, I] to hold sb/sth tightly 緊握；抱緊；抓緊 SYN **grip** : **~ sth (+ adv./prep.)** *He clutched the child to him.* 他緊緊地抱住小孩。◇ *She stood there, the flowers still clutched in her hand.* 她站在那裏，手裏仍然緊握着花束。◇ **+ adv./prep.** *I clutched on to the chair for support.* 我緊緊抓住椅子撐着身體。 ➲ **SYNONYMS** at HOLD **2** [T, I] to take hold of sth suddenly, because you are afraid or in pain（因害怕或痛苦）突然抓住：**~ sth** *He gasped and clutched his stomach.* 他喘着氣突然按住自己的胃部。◇ **~ at sb/sth** (*figurative*) *Fear clutched at her heart.* 她突然感到一陣恐懼襲上心頭。 IDM see STRAW ➲ **SYNONYMS** at HOLD

PHR V **ˈclutch/ˈcatch at sth/sb** to try to quickly get hold of sth/sb 試圖一把抓住 SYN **grab at**

▪ *noun* **1** [C] the PEDAL in a car or other vehicle that you press with your foot so that you can change gear（汽車等起換擋功能的）離合器踏板：*Put your foot on the clutch.* 把你的腳放在離合器踏板上。 ➲ **COLLOCATIONS** at DRIVING ➲ **VISUAL VOCAB** page V52 **2** [C] a device in a machine that connects and DISCONNECTS working parts, especially the engine and the gears（尤指發動機和排擋的）離合器：*The car needs a new clutch.* 這輛車需要換一個新的離合器了。**3 a ~ of sth** [sing.] (*BrE*) a group of people, animals or things 一群（人或動物）；一批（物品）：*He's won a whole clutch of awards.* 他獲得一大堆獎品。**4 clutches** [pl.] (*informal*) power or control 勢力範圍；控制；掌管：*He managed to escape from their* ***clutches***. 他設法擺脱了他們的控制。◇ *Now that she had him* ***in*** *her* ***clutches***, *she wasn't going to let go.* 她既然已經把他控制在自己手裏，就不打算讓他脱身。**5** [C, usually sing.] a tight hold on sb/sth 攫住；緊緊抓住 SYN **grip**：(*figurative*) *She felt the sudden clutch of fear.* 她突然感到一陣恐懼。**6** [C] a group of eggs that a bird lays at one time; the young birds that come out of a group of eggs at the same time（一次下的）一窩蛋；（同時孵出的）一窩小鳥 **7** [C] (*NAmE*) = CLUTCH BAG

'clutch bag (*NAmE* also **clutch**) *noun* a small, flat bag that women carry in their hands, especially on formal occasions（尤指出席正式場合時用的）女式小手提包 ➲ VISUAL VOCAB page V64

clut·ter /'klʌtə(r)/ *verb, noun*

■ ***verb*** **~ sth (up) (with sth/sb)** to fill a place with too many things, so that it is untidy 凌亂地塞滿；亂堆放：*Don't clutter the page with too many diagrams.* 別用太多的圖表來堆砌版面。◇ *I don't want all these files cluttering up my desk.* 我不想看到所有這些文檔亂堆在我的桌子上。◇ (*figurative*) *Try not to clutter your head with trivia.* 盡量別滿腦子都想些雞毛蒜皮的事。

■ ***noun*** [U, sing.] (*disapproving*) a lot of things in an untidy state, especially things that are not necessary or are not being used; a state of confusion 雜亂的東西（尤指不需要的或無用的）；雜亂 SYN **mess**：*There's always so much clutter on your desk!* 你桌子上總有那麼多亂七八糟的東西！◇ *There was a clutter of bottles and tubes on the shelf.* 架子上胡亂堆滿了瓶子和管子。

clut·tered /'klʌtəd; *NAmE* -tərd/ *adj.* **~ (up) (with sb/sth)** covered with, or full of, a lot of things or people, in a way that is untidy 雜亂的；淩亂的；擠滿的：*a* ***cluttered room/desk*** 亂七八糟的房間／桌面 ◇ (*figurative*) *a cluttered mind* 雜亂無序的思路 OPP **uncluttered**

CM *abbr.* COMMAND MODULE

cm *abbr.* (*pl.* **cm** or **cms**) CENTIMETRE

CND /ˌsiː en 'diː/ *abbr.* Campaign for Nuclear Disarmament (a British organization whose aim is to persuade countries to get rid of their nuclear weapons) 核裁軍運動（英國反核運動組織）

CNN /ˌsiː en 'en/ *abbr.* Cable News Network (an American broadcasting company that sends television news programmes all over the world) 有線電視新聞網（美國廣播公司，向全世界播送新聞節目）

CO /ˌsiː 'əʊ; *NAmE* 'oʊ/ *abbr.* Commanding Officer (an officer who commands a group of soldiers, sailors, etc.) 指揮官；指揮長

Co. /kəʊ; *NAmE* koʊ/ *abbr.* **1** (*business* 商) company 公司；商號；商行：*Pitt, Briggs & Co.* 皮特 — 布里格斯公司 **2** (in writing 書寫形式) county 郡；縣 **3 and co.** (*BrE, informal*) and other members of a group of people 及其他成員；及其一夥：*Were Jane and co. at the party?* 簡那幾個人都參加聚會了嗎？

co- /kəʊ; *NAmE* koʊ/ *prefix* (used in adjectives, adverbs, nouns and verbs 構成形容詞、副詞、名詞和動詞) together with 和…一起；共同；聯合：*co-produced* 合作生產的 ◇ *cooperatively* 合作地 ◇ *co-author* 合著者 ◇ *coexist* 共存

c/o /ˌsiː 'əʊ; *NAmE* 'oʊ/ *abbr.* (used on letters to a person staying at sb else's house) care of（用於投遞給寄居人的信件上）由…轉交：*Mr P Brown, c/o Ms M Jones* * M•瓊斯女士轉交 P•布朗先生

coach 🔑 /kəʊtʃ; *NAmE* koʊtʃ/ *noun, verb*

■ ***noun*** **1** 🔑 [C] a person who trains a person or team in sport（體育運動的）教練：*a* ***basketball/football/tennis, etc. coach*** 籃球、足球、網球等教練 ◇ *Italy's national coach* 意大利國家隊教練 **2** [C] (*BrE*) a person who gives private lessons to sb, often to prepare them for an exam 私人教師；（多指）考前輔導教師：*a maths coach* 數學應試輔導教師 **3** [C] = LIFE COACH **4** 🔑 [C] (*BrE*) a comfortable bus for carrying passengers over long distances 長途汽車；長途客車：*They went to Italy on a* ***coach tour***. 他們乘長途客車去意大利旅遊。◇ *Travel is* ***by coach*** *overnight to Berlin.* 旅程為乘一夜長途汽車去柏林。◇ *a* ***coach station*** (= where coaches start and end their journey) 長途汽車總站 ◇ *a coach party* (= a group of people travelling together on a coach) 乘坐長途客車的旅遊團 ➲ VISUAL VOCAB page V57 **5** 🔑 [C] (*BrE*) = CARRIAGE (1)：*a railway coach* 火車車廂 **6** [C] a large closed vehicle with four wheels, pulled by horses, used in the past for carrying passengers（舊時載客的）四輪大馬車 ➲ see also STAGECOACH **7** [U] (*NAmE*) the cheapest seats in a plane（客機的）經濟艙：*to fly coach* 坐飛機經濟艙 ◇ ***coach fares/passengers/seats*** 飛機經濟艙票價／乘客／座位 IDM see DRIVE *v.*

■ ***verb*** **1** to train sb to play a sport, to do a job better, or to improve a skill（對體育運動、工作或技能進行）訓練，培訓，指導：**~ sb (in/for sth)** *Her father coached her for the Olympics.* 她的父親訓練她準備參加奧林匹克運動會。◇ **~ sb (to do sth)** *She has coached hundreds of young singers.* 她培養了許許多多的青年歌手。◇ **~ sth** *He coaches basketball and soccer.* 他執教籃球和足球。**2 ~ sb (in/for sth)** (*especially BrE*) to give a student extra teaching in a particular subject especially so that they will pass an exam 輔導（尤指為讓學員通過考試）**3 ~ sb (in/on sth)** | **~ sb (to do sth)** to give sb special instructions for what they should do or say in a particular situation 指示；特殊指導；專門傳授：*They believed the witnesses had been coached on what to say.* 他們認為證人所作的證詞是別人教他們那樣說的。

'coach house *noun* a building where CARRIAGES pulled by horses are or were kept 馬車房

coach·ing /'kəʊtʃɪŋ; *NAmE* 'koʊtʃ-/ *noun* [U] **1** the process of training sb to play a sport, to do a job better or to improve a skill（體育運動、工作或技能的）訓練，培訓，指導：*a coaching session* 集訓期 **2** (*especially BrE*) the process of giving a student extra teaching in a particular subject（某科目上的）輔導

'coaching inn *noun* in the past, an INN along a route used by horses, at which horses could be changed 驛馬旅館，驛站（舊時可掉換驛馬的旅館）

coach·load /'kəʊtʃləʊd; *NAmE* 'koʊtʃloʊd/ *noun* (*BrE*) a group of people travelling together in a coach（乘同一長途客車旅遊的）團體旅客：*Tourists were arriving* ***by the coachload***. 整團整團的遊客乘着大巴到達。

coach·man /'kəʊtʃmən; *NAmE* 'koʊtʃ-/ *noun* (*pl.* **-men** /-mən/) (in the past) a man who drove a COACH pulled by horses（舊時）馬車夫

coach·work /'kəʊtʃwɜːk; *NAmE* 'koʊtʃwɜːrk/ *noun* [U] (*BrE*) the metal outer part of a road or railway/railroad vehicle 汽車（或火車）車身

co·agu·late /kəʊ'ægjuleɪt; *NAmE* koʊ-/ *verb* [I, T] **~ (sth)** if a liquid **coagulates** or sth **coagulates** it, it becomes thick and partly solid 凝固；使凝結 SYN **congeal**：*Blood began to coagulate around the edges of the wound.* 血液開始在傷口的邊緣凝固。▸ **co·agu·la·tion** /kəʊˌægju'leɪʃn; *NAmE* koʊ-/ *noun* [U]

coal 🔑 /kəʊl; *NAmE* koʊl/ *noun*

1 🔑 [U] a hard black mineral that is found below the ground and burnt to produce heat 煤：*I put more coal on the fire.* 我往火裏再加了些煤。◇ *a lump of coal* 一塊煤 ◇ *a coal fire* 煤火 ◇ *a coal mine* 煤礦 ◇ *the coal industry* 煤炭工業 **2** [C] a piece of coal, especially one that is burning（尤指燃燒着的）煤塊：*A hot coal fell out of the fire and burnt the carpet.* 一塊燃燒着的煤塊從火爐裏掉出來把地毯燒了。

IDM **carry, take, etc. coals to 'Newcastle** (*BrE*) to take goods to a place where there are already plenty of them; to supply sth where it is not needed 多此一舉 ORIGIN Newcastle-upon-Tyne, in the north of England, was once an important coal-mining centre. 英格蘭北部泰恩河畔紐卡斯爾曾是重要的煤礦開採中心。➲ more at HAUL *v.*, RAKE *v.*

ˌcoal-'black *adj.* very dark in colour 烏黑的；漆黑的：*coal-black eyes* 烏黑的眼睛

C

co·alesce /ˌkəʊəˈles; *NAmE* ˌkoʊə-/ *verb* [I] **~ (into/with sth)** (*formal*) to come together to form one larger group, substance, etc. 合併；聯合；結合 **SYN** **amalgamate**：*The puddles had coalesced into a small stream.* 地面上水窪子裏的水匯流成了一條小溪。▶ **co·ales·cence** /ˌkəʊəˈlesns; *NAmE* ˌkoʊə-/ *noun* [U]

coal·face /ˈkəʊlfeɪs; *NAmE* ˈkoʊl-/ (also **face**) *noun* the place deep inside a mine where the coal is cut out of the rock（煤礦井裏的）採煤工作面，採掘面
IDM **at the ˈcoalface** (*BrE*) where the real work is done, not just where people talk about it 在工作現場；在工作第一線：*Many of the best ideas come from doctors at the coalface.* 許多最好的意見都來自臨牀醫師。

coal·field /ˈkəʊlfiːld; *NAmE* ˈkoʊl-/ *noun* a large area where there is a lot of coal under the ground 煤田

ˌcoal-ˈfired *adj.* using coal as fuel 用煤作燃料的；燒煤的：*a coal-fired power station* 一座燃煤火力發電站

ˈcoal gas *noun* [U] a mixture of gases produced from coal, that can be used for electricity and heating 煤氣

coal·house /ˈkəʊlhaʊs; *NAmE* ˈkoʊl-/ *noun* a small building for storing coal, especially in sb's garden in the past（尤指舊時家中花園的）煤庫，煤屋

co·ali·tion /ˌkəʊəˈlɪʃn; *NAmE* ˌkoʊə-/ *noun* **1** [C+sing./pl. v.] a government formed by two or more political parties working together（兩黨或多黨）聯合政府：*to form a coalition* 組成聯合政府 ◇ *a two-party coalition* 兩黨聯合的政府 ◇ *a coalition government* 聯合政府 **2** [C+sing./pl. v.] a group formed by people from several different groups, especially political ones, agreeing to work together for a particular purpose（尤指多個政治團體的）聯合體，聯盟：*a coalition of environmental and consumer groups* 環境保護和消費者團體的聯盟 **3** [U] the act of two or more groups joining together 聯合；結合；聯盟：*They didn't rule out coalition with the Social Democrats.* 他們不排除與社會民主黨人結盟的可能性。

coal·man /ˈkəʊlmən; *NAmE* ˈkoʊl-/ *noun* (*pl.* **-men** /-mən/) a man whose job is to deliver coal to people's houses 送煤工

ˈcoal mine (also **pit**) *noun* a place underground where coal is dug 煤礦

ˈcoal miner *noun* a person whose job is digging coal in a coal mine 煤礦工人

ˈcoal scuttle (also **scuttle**) *noun* a container with a handle, used for carrying coal and usually kept beside the FIREPLACE（通常置於壁爐邊的）煤斗，煤筐，煤桶 ➲ **VISUAL VOCAB** page V21

ˈcoal tar *noun* [U] a thick black sticky substance produced when gas is made from coal（製作煤氣時產生的）煤焦油

coarse /kɔːs; *NAmE* kɔːrs/ *adj.* (**coars·er**, **coars·est**) **1** (of skin or cloth 皮膚或布料) rough 粗糙的；粗織的：*coarse hands/linen* 粗糙的手；粗亞麻布 **OPP** **smooth**, **soft** **2** consisting of relatively large pieces 粗的；大顆粒的：*coarse sand/salt/hair* 粗沙／鹽；粗硬的毛髮 **OPP** **fine** **3** rude and offensive, especially about sex 粗魯無禮的，粗俗的（尤指涉及性的）**SYN** **vulgar**：*coarse manners/laughter* 粗俗的舉止／笑聲 ▶ **coarse·ly** *adv.*：*coarsely chopped onions* (= cut into large pieces) 剁成大塊的洋葱 ◇ *He laughed coarsely at her.* 他粗魯無禮地嘲笑她。 **coarse·ness** *noun* [U]

ˌcoarse ˈfish *noun* (*pl.* **coarse fish**) (*BrE*) any fish, except SALMON and TROUT, that lives in rivers and lakes rather than in the sea 粗魚，雜魚（指肉質粗糙的淡水魚，不包括鮭和鱒魚）

ˌcoarse ˈfishing *noun* [U] (*BrE*) the sport of catching coarse fish 捕捉雜魚運動：*to go coarse fishing* 去捕捉雜魚

coars·en /ˈkɔːsn; *NAmE* ˈkɔːrsn/ *verb* **1** [I, T] to become or make sth become thicker and/or rougher（使）變厚，變粗糙：*Her hair gradually coarsened as she grew older.* 隨着年齡的增長，她的頭髮逐漸變粗糙了。◇ **~ sth** *His features had been coarsened by the weather.* 氣候使他的容貌變得粗糙。 **2** to become or make sb become less polite and often offensive in the way they behave（使）變得粗魯無禮：[T, I] **~ (sb)** *The six long years in prison had coarsened him.* 六年漫長的監獄生活使他變得粗魯無禮。

Synonyms 同義詞辨析

coast

beach • seaside • coastline • sand • seashore

These are all words for the land beside or near to the sea, a river or a lake. 以上各詞均指海岸、河岸或湖畔。

coast the land beside or near to the sea or ocean 指海岸、海濱：*a town on the south coast of England* 英格蘭南海岸的一座城鎮 ◇ *The coast road is closed due to bad weather.* 由於天氣惡劣，濱海公路暫時封閉。**NOTE** It is nearly always **the coast**, except when it is uncountable. 除用作不可數名詞外，coast 幾乎總是與 the 連用：*That's a pretty stretch of coast.* 那是一段美麗的海岸線。

beach an area of sand, or small stones, beside the sea or a lake 指有沙石的海灘、海濱或湖濱：*She took the kids to the beach for the day.* 她帶了孩子去海灘玩一天。◇ *sandy beaches* 沙灘

seaside (*especially BrE*) an area that is by the sea, especially one where people go for a day or a holiday 尤指人們遊玩、度假的海邊、海濱：*a trip to the seaside* 去海濱旅行 **NOTE** It is always **the seaside**, except when it is used before a noun. 除用於名詞前外，seaside 總是與 the 連用：*a seaside resort* 海濱勝地 **The seaside** is British English; in American English **seaside** is only used before a noun. * the seaside 為英式英語，在美式英語中，seaside 只用於名詞前。

coastline the land along a coast, especially when you are thinking of its shape or appearance 指沿海地帶，尤其是海岸線、海岸地形或輪廓：*California's rugged coastline* 加利福尼亞州崎嶇的海岸線

sand a large area of sand on a beach 指沙灘：*We went for a walk along the sand.* 我們去沙灘上散了散步。◇ *a resort with miles of golden sands* 綿延數英里金色沙灘的度假勝地

the seashore the land along the edge of the sea or ocean, usually where there is sand and rocks 通常指有沙石的海岸、海濱：*He liked to look for shells on the seashore.* 他喜歡在海濱撿貝殼。

BEACH OR SEASHORE? 用 beach 還是 seashore？

Beach is usually used to talk about a sandy area next to the sea where people lie in the sun or play, for example when they are on holiday/vacation. **Seashore** is used more to talk about the area by the sea in terms of things such as waves, seashells, rocks, etc., especially where people walk for pleasure. * beach 通常指海邊的沙灘，人們度假時可以躺着沐浴陽光或玩樂；seashore 多指有海浪、貝殼、岩石等的海岸，尤指人們散步消遣的海濱。

PATTERNS

- **along** the coast/beach/coastline/seashore
- **on** the coast/beach/coastline/sands/seashore
- **at** the coast/beach/seaside/seashore
- **by** the coast/seaside/seashore
- a(n) **rocky/unspoiled** coast/beach/coastline
- to **go to** the coast/beach/seaside/seashore

coast 0→ /kəʊst; *NAmE* koʊst/ *noun, verb*
■ *noun* 0→ [C, U] the land beside or near to the sea or ocean 海岸；海濱：*a town on the south coast of England* 英格蘭南海岸的一座城鎮 ◇ *islands off the west coast of Ireland* 愛爾蘭西海岸的島嶼 ◇ *a trip to the coast* 海濱旅遊 ◇ *We walked along the coast for five miles.* 我們沿着海岸步行了五英里。◇ *the Welsh coast* 威爾士海岸 ◇ *a pretty stretch of coast* 一段美麗的海岸線 ◇ *the coast road* 濱海道路 ➲ **VISUAL VOCAB** pages V4, V5

IDM **the ˌcoast is ˈclear** (*informal*) there is no danger of being seen or caught 沒有被發現（或抓住）的危險：*As soon as the coast was clear he climbed in through the window.* 等到四下無人，他便從窗戶爬了進去。

■ ***verb*** **1** [I] (+ **adv./prep.**) (of a car or a bicycle 汽車或自行車) to move, especially down a hill, without using any power（尤指不用動力向山坡下）滑行，慣性滑行：*The car coasted along until it stopped.* 汽車隨慣性而下直至滑行停止。◇ *She took her feet off the pedals and coasted downhill.* 她從自行車的踏板上鬆開腳，沿山坡滑行而下。**2** [I] (+ **adv./prep.**) (of a vehicle 交通工具) to move quickly and smoothly, without using much power（不用多少動力）快速平穩地移動：*The plane coasted down the runway.* 飛機順着跑道平穩滑行。**3** [I] ~ (**through/to sth**) to be successful at sth without having to try hard 不費力地取得成功：*He coasted through his final exams.* 他毫不費勁地通過了期終考試。**4** [I] ~ (**along**) (*disapproving*) to put very little effort into sth（做事）不出力：*You're just coasting—it's time to work hard now.* 你根本是在躲懶，現在該努力幹了。**5** [I] (of a ship 船) to stay close to land while sailing around the coast 沿海岸航行

coast·al /ˈkəʊstl; *NAmE* ˈkoʊstl/ *adj.* [usually before noun] of or near a coast 沿海的；靠近海岸的：***coastal waters/resorts/scenery*** 沿海水域；海濱勝地／風景 ◇ ***a coastal path*** (= one that follows the line of the coast) 濱海小道 ➲ **VISUAL VOCAB** pages V4, V5 ➲ compare INLAND

coast·eer·ing /ˌkəʊstˈɪərɪŋ; *NAmE* ˌkoʊstˈɪrɪŋ/ *noun* [U] the sport of following a route around a coast by climbing, jumping off CLIFFS and swimming 海岸攀岩（沿着海岸路線攀爬、跳下懸崖和游泳的運動）

coast·er /ˈkəʊstə(r); *NAmE* ˈkoʊst-/ *noun* **1** a small flat object which you put under a glass to protect the top of a table 玻璃杯墊 ➲ **VISUAL VOCAB** page V21 **2** a ship that sails from port to port along a coast 航行於沿海港口間的輪船 ➲ see also ROLLER COASTER

coast·guard /ˈkəʊstgɑːd; *NAmE* ˈkoʊstgɑːrd/ *noun* **1** (usually **the coastguard**) [sing.] an official organization (in the US a branch of the armed forces) whose job is to watch the sea near a coast in order to help ships and people in trouble, and to stop people from breaking the law 海岸警衞隊（在美國隸屬於軍隊）：*The coastguard was alerted.* 海岸警衞隊已進入戒備狀態。◇ *They radioed Dover Coastguard.* 他們用無線電和多佛海岸警衞隊聯絡。◇ *a coastguard station* 海岸警衞隊駐地 **2** [C] (*especially BrE*) (*US* usually **coast·guards·man** /ˈkəʊstgɑːdzmən; *NAmE* ˈkoʊstgɑːrd-/ *pl.* **-men** /-mən/) a member of this organization 海岸警衞隊隊員

coast·line /ˈkəʊstlaɪn; *NAmE* ˈkoʊst-/ *noun* the land along a coast, especially when you are thinking of its shape or appearance 海岸線；海岸地形（或輪廓）；沿海地帶：*a **rugged/rocky/beautiful coastline*** 崎嶇的／多岩石的／美麗的海岸線 ◇ *to protect the coastline from oil spillage* 保護海岸線不受石油泄漏的污染 ➲ **SYNONYMS** at COAST

coat 🔑 /kəʊt; *NAmE* koʊt/ *noun, verb*

■ ***noun*** **1** 🔑 a piece of outdoor clothing that is worn over other clothes to keep warm or dry. Coats have sleeves and may be long or short. 外套；外衣；大衣：*a fur/leather coat* 毛皮／皮大衣 ◇ *a long winter coat* 冬天穿的長大衣 ◇ *to **put on/take off your coat*** 穿上／脫下外套 ➲ **VISUAL VOCAB** page V61 ➲ see also DUFFEL COAT, GREATCOAT, HOUSECOAT, OVERCOAT, PETTICOAT, RAINCOAT, TRENCH COAT **2** (*NAmE*) (*old-fashioned* in *BrE*) a jacket that is worn as part of a suit（套裝的）外套 ➲ see also FROCK COAT, MORNING COAT, TAILCOAT, WAISTCOAT **3** 🔑 the fur, hair or wool that covers an animal's body 動物皮毛：*a dog with a **smooth/shaggy coat*** 皮毛光滑的／蓬亂的狗 ➲ **VISUAL VOCAB** page V12 **4** 🔑 a layer of paint or some other substance that covers a surface 塗料層；覆蓋層：*to give the walls a second coat of paint* 給牆刷上第二層塗料 ➲ see also TOPCOAT, UNDERCOAT

IDM **ˌcut your ˈcoat acˌcording to your ˈcloth** (*saying*) to do only what you have enough money to do and no more 量入為出

■ ***verb*** [often passive] ~ **sth** (**with/in sth**) to cover sth with a layer of a substance 給…塗上一層；用…覆蓋：*cookies thickly coated with chocolate* 外面塗有厚厚一層巧克力的曲奇 ◇ *A film of dust coated the table.* 桌上覆蓋着一層灰塵。➲ see also SUGAR-COATED (1)

ˈcoat check *noun* (*NAmE*) = CLOAKROOM (1)

ˈcoat hanger *noun* = HANGER

coati /kəʊˈɑːti; *NAmE* koʊ-/ (also **co·ati·mundi** /kəʊˌɑːtiˈmʌndi; *NAmE* koʊ-/) *noun* a small animal with a long nose and a long tail with lines across it, which lives mainly in Central and S America 南美浣熊（主要生活於中美和南美）

coat·ing /ˈkəʊtɪŋ; *NAmE* ˈkoʊt-/ *noun* a thin layer of a substance covering a surface（薄的）覆蓋層，塗層：*a thin coating of chocolate* 薄薄一層巧克力 ◇ *magnetic coating on a floppy disk* 軟盤上的磁層

ˌcoat of ˈarms *noun* (*pl.* **coats of arms**) (also **arms**) a design or a SHIELD that is a special symbol of a family, city or other organization 盾形紋章；盾徽：*the royal coat of arms* 皇家盾徽

coat·room /ˈkəʊtruːm; -rʊm; *NAmE* ˈkoʊt-/ *noun* (*NAmE*) = CLOAKROOM (1)

ˈcoat stand *noun* a stand with hooks for hanging coats and hats on 衣帽架

ˈcoat-tails *noun* [pl.]

IDM **on sb's coat-tails** using the success and influence of another person to help yourself become successful 利用他人的成就和聲望（幫助自己成功）：*She got where she is today on her brother's coat-tails.* 她倚仗她哥哥的聲望爬上了今天的位置。

ˌco-ˈauthor *noun* a person who writes a book or an article with sb else（書或文章的）合著者 ▶ **ˌco-ˈauthor** *verb* [T] ~ **sth ˌco-ˈauthor·ship** *noun* [U]

coax /kəʊks; *NAmE* koʊks/ *verb* to persuade sb to do sth by talking to them in a kind and gentle way 哄勸；勸誘 SYN **cajole**：~ **sb/sth** (**into doing sth**) *She coaxed the horse into coming a little closer.* 她哄着那匹馬讓它再靠近了一點。◇ ~ **sb/sth** (**into/out of sth**) *He was coaxed out of retirement to help the failing company.* 他退休之後又被力勸出山幫助瀕臨破產的公司。◇ ~ **sb/sth** (+ **adv./prep.**) *She had to coax the car along.* 她得耐着性子發動汽車往前開。◇ ~ (**sb/sth**) + **speech** *'Nearly there,' she coaxed.* "快要到啦。" 她哄着說。

PHR V **coax sth out of/from sb** to gently persuade sb to do sth or give you sth 哄勸；哄誘得到：*The director coaxed a brilliant performance out of the cast.* 導演花言巧語地說服演員組做了一場精彩的表演。

coax·ing /ˈkəʊksɪŋ; *NAmE* ˈkoʊ-/ *noun* [U] gentle attempts to persuade sb to do sth or to get a machine to start 試圖勸誘；耐心地發動（機器）：*No amount of coaxing will make me change my mind.* 任你費盡口舌也不會說服我改變主意。▶ **coax·ing** *adj.* **coax·ing·ly** *adv.*

cob /kɒb; *NAmE* kɑːb/ *noun* **1** = CORNCOB：*corn on the cob* 玉米棒子 **2** a strong horse with short legs 短腿壯馬 **3** (*BrE*) a round LOAF of bread 圓麪包：*a crusty cob* 有硬皮的圓麪包

co·balt /ˈkəʊbɔːlt; *NAmE* ˈkoʊ-/ *noun* [U] **1** (*symb.* **Co**) a chemical element. Cobalt is a hard silver-white metal, often mixed with other metals and used to give a deep blue-green colour to glass. 鈷 **2** (also **ˌcobalt ˈblue**) a deep blue-green colour 深藍色；鈷藍

cob·ber /ˈkɒbə(r); *NAmE* ˈkɑːb-/ *noun* (*AustralE, NZE, informal*) (used especially by a man addressing another man 尤用作男子間的稱呼) a friend 夥計；老兄；兄弟

cob·ble /ˈkɒbl; *NAmE* ˈkɑːbl/ *verb* ~ **sth** (*old-fashioned*) to make or repair shoes 製（鞋）；修補（鞋）

PHR V **ˌcobble sth↔toˈgether** to produce sth quickly and without great care or effort, so that it can be used but is not perfect 草率匆忙地製作；胡亂拼湊；粗製濫造：*The essay was cobbled together from some old notes.* 這篇文章是用以前的一些筆記胡亂拼湊而成的。

cob·bled /ˈkɒbld; *NAmE* ˈkɑːbld/ *adj.* (of streets and roads 街道和道路) having a surface that is made of COBBLES 鋪有鵝卵石的

cob·bler /ˈkɒblə(r); NAmE ˈkɑːb-/ *noun* **1** [C] a type of fruit or meat PIE with a thick bread-like layer on top 厚皮水果餡餅（或肉餅）: *peach cobbler* 桃子餡餅 **2** [C] (*old-fashioned*) a person who repairs shoes 修鞋匠 ➲ compare SHOEMAKER **3** [U] **cobblers** (*BrE, informal*) nonsense 胡說；廢話: *He said it was all a load of cobblers.* 他說那完全是一派胡言。

cob·bles /ˈkɒblz; NAmE ˈkɑːblz/ (also **cobble·stones**) *noun* [pl.] small stones used to make the surfaces of roads, especially in the past（尤指舊時鋪路面用的）小石頭，鵝卵石

cobble·stones /ˈkɒblstəʊnz; NAmE ˈkɑːblstoʊnz/ *noun* [pl.] = COBBLES ▸ **cobble·stone** *adj.*

COBOL /ˈkəʊbɒl; NAmE ˈkoʊbɔːl/ *noun* [U] an early computer language used in business programs * COBOL 語言（早期的一種商用計算機程序語言）

cobra /ˈkəʊbrə; NAmE ˈkoʊ-/ *noun* a poisonous snake that can spread the skin at the back of its neck to make itself look bigger. Cobras live in Asia and Africa. 眼鏡蛇（毒蛇，分佈於亞洲和非洲）➲ VISUAL VOCAB page V13

cob·web /ˈkɒbweb; NAmE ˈkɑːb-/ *noun* a fine net of threads made by a spider to catch insects; a single thread of this net (usually used when it is old and covered with dirt) 蜘蛛網，蜘蛛絲（常指落滿灰塵的舊蜘蛛網）: *Thick cobwebs hung in the dusty corners.* 積有灰塵的角落掛着厚厚的蜘蛛網。◇ *He brushed a cobweb out of his hair.* 他拂去了頭髮上的蜘蛛絲。➲ see also WEB (1), SPIDER'S WEB ▸ **cob·webbed** /ˈkɒbwebd; NAmE ˈkɑːb-/ *adj.*: *cobwebbed corners* 佈滿蜘蛛網的角落

IDM **blow/clear the ˈcobwebs away** to help sb start sth in a fresh, lively state of mind 使頭腦清醒；使振作精神: *A brisk walk should blow the cobwebs away.* 輕快的散步可以使人頭腦清醒。

coca /ˈkəʊkə; NAmE ˈkoʊ-/ *noun* [U] a tropical bush whose leaves are used to make the drug COCAINE 古柯（熱帶灌木，葉子用於製作可卡因）

Coca-Cola™ /ˌkəʊkə ˈkəʊlə; NAmE ˌkoʊkə ˈkoʊlə/ (also *informal* **Coke™**) *noun* **1** [U, C] a popular type of COLA drink 可口可樂（飲料） **2** [C] a glass, bottle or can of Coca-Cola 一杯（或一瓶、一罐）可口可樂

co·caine /kəʊˈkeɪn; NAmE koʊ-/ (also *informal* **coke**) *noun* [U] a powerful drug that some people take illegally for pleasure and can become ADDICTED to. Doctors sometimes use it as an ANAESTHETIC. 可卡因；古柯鹼

coc·cyx /ˈkɒksɪks; NAmE ˈkɑːk-/ *noun* (*pl.* **coc·cyxes** or **coc·cy·ges** /ˈkɒksɪdʒiːz; NAmE ˈkɑːk-/) (*anatomy* 解) the small bone at the bottom of the SPINE 尾骨 **SYN** **tailbone** ➲ VISUAL VOCAB page V59

coch·in·eal /ˌkɒtʃɪˈniːl; NAmE ˈkɑːtʃəniːl/ *noun* [U] a bright red substance used to give colour to food 胭脂蟲紅顏料（用於食物）

coch·lea /ˈkɒkliə; NAmE ˈkoʊk-; ˈkɑːk-/ *noun* (*pl.* **coch·leae** /-klii:/) (*anatomy* 解) a small curved tube inside the ear, which contains a small part that sends nerve signals to the brain when sounds cause it to VIBRATE 耳蝸

cock /kɒk; NAmE kɑːk/ *noun, verb*

■ *noun* **1** (*BrE*) (also **roost·er** *NAmE, BrE*) [C] an adult male chicken 公雞；雄雞: *The cock crowed.* 公雞啼叫。➲ compare HEN (1) **2** [C] (especially in compounds 尤用於構成複合詞) a male of any other bird 雄禽: *a cock pheasant* 雄雉 ➲ see also PEACOCK **3** [C] (*taboo, slang*) a PENIS 雞巴 **4** [C] = STOPCOCK ➲ see also BALLCOCK **5** [sing.] (*old-fashioned, BrE, slang*) used as a friendly form of address between men（男子間友好的稱呼）老兄，傢伙，夥計 ➲ see also HALF-COCK

■ *verb* **1** ~ **sth** to raise a part of your body so that it is vertical or at an angle 立起，豎起，翹起（身體部位）: *The dog cocked its leg by every tree on our route* (= in order to URINATE). 這狗在我們一路上走過每棵樹時都抬起一條腿（撒尿）。◇ *He cocked an inquisitive eyebrow at her.* 他揚眉向她投以疑問的目光。◇ *She cocked her head to one side and looked at me.* 她抬起頭側向一邊看着我。◇ *The dog stood listening, its ears cocked.* 那狗站着，豎起耳朵聽靜。 **2** ~ **a gun/pistol/rifle** to raise the HAMMER on a gun so that it is ready to fire 扣（或扳）上扳機準備射擊

IDM **cock an ear/eye at sth/sb** to look at or listen to sth/sb carefully and with a lot of attention 側耳傾聽；凝神細看 **cock a snook at sb/sth** (*BrE*) to say or do sth that clearly shows you do not respect sb/sth（說話或做事）明顯地表示蔑視；輕蔑；不屑一顧: *to cock a snook at authority* 蔑視權威

PHR V **ˌcock sth↔ˈup** (*BrE, slang*) to ruin sth by doing it badly, or by making a careless or stupid mistake 把…搞糟（或弄得一塌糊塗）**SYN** **bungle**: *I really cocked that exam up!* 我那次考試考得真糟糕！◇ *She cocked up all the arrangements for the party.* 她把聚會的安排搞得一塌糊塗。➲ related noun COCK-UP

cock·ade /kɒˈkeɪd; NAmE kɑː-/ *noun* a decorated BADGE or an arrangement of RIBBONS, feathers, etc. that is worn in a hat to show military rank, membership of a political party, etc. 帽章，帽花結（顯示軍銜、政黨身分等）

cock-a-doodle-doo /ˌkɒk ə ˌduːdl ˈduː; NAmE ˌkɑːk/ *noun* the word for the sound that a COCK/ROOSTER makes（公雞的啼聲）喔喔喔

ˌcock-a-ˈhoop *adj.* [not usually before noun] ~ (**about/at/over sth**) (*informal*) very pleased and excited, especially about achieving sth 得意揚揚

cock-a-leekie /ˌkɒk ə ˈliːki; NAmE ˌkɑːk/ (also **ˌcock-a-leekie ˈsoup**) *noun* [U] a type of Scottish soup, made with chicken and LEEKS (= long vegetables that taste like onions)（蘇格蘭）雞肉韭菜湯

cock·ama·mie (also **cock·ama·my**) /ˈkɒkəmeɪmi; NAmE ˈkɑːk-/ *adj.* (*NAmE, informal*) (of an idea, a story, etc. 主意、故事等) silly; not to be believed 荒誕可笑的；不可信的

ˌcock and ˈbull story *noun* a story that is unlikely to be true but is used as an explanation or excuse 荒唐的解釋；荒誕的藉口

cocka·tiel /ˌkɒkəˈtiːl; NAmE ˌkɑːk-/ *noun* an Australian PARROT with a grey body and a yellow and orange face 雞尾鸚鵡，玄鳳（產於澳大利亞，毛灰色，面部黃色帶橙斑）

cocka·too /ˌkɒkəˈtuː; NAmE ˈkɑːkətuː/ *noun* (*pl.* **-oos**) an Australian bird of the PARROT family, with a large row of feathers (called a CREST) standing up on its head 鳳頭鸚鵡，葵花鸚鵡（見於澳大利亞）

cock·cha·fer /ˈkɒktʃeɪfə(r); NAmE ˈkɑːk-/ (also **ˈMay bug**) *noun* a large brown insect that flies and makes a loud noise in early evening in summer 西方五月鰓角金龜；五月甲蟲；大栗鰓角金龜

cock·crow /ˈkɒkkrəʊ; NAmE ˈkɑːkkroʊ/ *noun* [U] (*literary*) the time of the day when it is becoming light 黎明；拂曉 **SYN** **dawn**

ˌcocked ˈhat *noun* **IDM** see KNOCK *v.*

cock·er /ˈkɒkə(r); NAmE ˈkɑːk-/ (also **ˌcocker ˈspaniel**) *noun* a small SPANIEL (= type of dog) with soft hair 可卡犬（小型軟毛獵犬）

cock·erel /ˈkɒkərəl; NAmE ˈkɑːk-/ *noun* a young male chicken 小公雞

cock·eyed /ˈkɒkaɪd; NAmE ˈkɑːk-/ *adj.* (*informal*) **1** not level or straight 傾斜的；歪斜的 **SYN** **crooked**: *Doesn't that picture look cockeyed to you?* 你不覺得那張畫掛歪了嗎？ **2** not practical; not likely to succeed 不切實際的；不大可能成功的: *a cockeyed scheme to make people use less water* 讓大眾少用水的不切實際的計劃

cock·fight /ˈkɒkfaɪt; NAmE ˈkɑːk-/ *noun* a fight between two adult male chickens, watched as a sport and illegal in many countries 鬥雞 ▸ **cock·fight·ing** *noun* [U]

cockle /ˈkɒkl; NAmE ˈkɑːkl/ *noun* a small SHELLFISH that can be eaten 鳥蛤（可食用的有殼小水生動物）**IDM** see WARM *v.*

cockle·shell /ˈkɒklʃel; NAmE ˈkɑːkl-/ *noun* **1** the shell of a cockle 鳥蛤殼 **2** a small light boat 輕舟；小舟

cock·ney /ˈkɒkni; NAmE ˈkɑːkni/ *noun* **1** [C] a person from the East End of London 倫敦東區的人 **2** [U] the way of speaking that is typical of cockneys 倫敦東區的口音（或土腔）： *a cockney accent* 倫敦東區口音

cock·pit /ˈkɒkpɪt; *NAmE* ˈkɑːk-/ *noun* the area in a plane, boat or racing car where the pilot or driver sits（飛機、船或賽車的）駕駛艙，駕駛座 ➲ VISUAL VOCAB pages V53, V56

cock·roach /ˈkɒkrəʊtʃ; *NAmE* ˈkɑːkroʊtʃ/ (also *NAmE informal* **roach**) *noun* a large brown insect with wings, that lives in houses, especially where there is dirt 蟑螂

cock·sucker /ˈkɒksʌkə(r); *NAmE* ˈkɑːk-/ *noun* (*taboo, slang*) an offensive word used to insult sb, usually a man 狗雜種，渾蛋（通常指男人）

cock·sure /ˌkɒkˈʃʊə(r); -ˈʃɔː(r); *NAmE* ˌkɑːkˈʃʊr/ *adj.* (*old-fashioned, informal*) confident in a way that is annoying to other people and that they might find offensive 過分自信的；自高自大的；自以為是的

cock·tail /ˈkɒkteɪl; *NAmE* ˈkɑːk-/ *noun* **1** [C] a drink usually made from a mixture of one or more SPIRITS (= strong alcoholic drinks) and fruit juice. It can also be made without alcohol. 雞尾酒：*a* ***cocktail bar/cabinet/lounge*** 雞尾酒酒吧／陳列櫃／酒吧間 **2** [C, U] a dish of small pieces of food, usually served cold 涼菜；冷盤：*a prawn/shrimp cocktail* 大蝦／小蝦冷盤 ◇ *fruit cocktail* 什錦水果丁 **3** [C] a mixture of different substances, usually ones that do not mix together well（常指摻合不太相容的）混合物：*a lethal cocktail of drugs* 致命的混合藥物 ➲ see also MOLOTOV COCKTAIL

ˈ**cocktail dress** *noun* a dress that is suitable for formal social occasions（正式社交場合穿的）短裙

ˈ**cocktail party** *noun* a formal social occasion, usually in the early evening, when people drink COCKTAILS or other alcoholic drinks 雞尾酒會

ˈ**cocktail stick** *noun* (*BrE*) a small, sharp piece of wood on which small pieces of food are placed, for guests to eat at parties（聚會用的）取食籤

ˈ**cock-teaser** (also ˈ**cock-tease**, ˈ**prick-teaser**, ˈ**prick-tease**) *noun* (*taboo, slang*) an offensive word used to describe a woman who makes a man think she will have sex with him when she will not 煽情騷貨（含冒犯意，指激起男人性慾而不與之性交的女人）

ˈ**cock-up** *noun* (*BrE, informal*) a mistake that spoils people's arrangements; sth that has been spoilt because it was badly organized（打亂了原先所作安排的）差錯；（因組織不當而造成的）混亂，一團糟：*There's been a bit of a cock-up over the travel arrangements.* 旅行安排出了點兒岔子。

cocky /ˈkɒki; *NAmE* ˈkɑːki/ *adj.* (**cock·ier**, **cocki·est**) (*informal*) too confident about yourself in a way that annoys other people 過分自信的；自以為是的 ▸ **cocki·ness** *noun* [U]

cocoa /ˈkəʊkəʊ; *NAmE* ˈkoʊkoʊ/ *noun* **1** [U] dark brown powder made from the crushed seeds (called **cocoa beans**) of a tropical tree 可可粉 **2** [U] a hot drink made by mixing cocoa powder with milk and/or water and usually sugar 熱可可（飲料）：*a mug of cocoa* 一大杯熱可可飲料 **3** [C] a cup of cocoa 一杯熱可可飲料 ➲ compare CHOCOLATE (3), DRINKING CHOCOLATE

ˈ**cocoa butter** *noun* [U] fat that is obtained from cocoa BEANS and used in making chocolate and COSMETICS 可可油，可可脂（用於製作巧克力和化妝品）

co·co·nut /ˈkəʊkənʌt; *NAmE* ˈkoʊ-/ *noun* **1** [C] the large nut of a tropical tree called a **coconut palm**. It grows inside a hard shell and contains a soft white substance that can be eaten and juice that can be drunk. 椰子 ➲ VISUAL VOCAB page V30 **2** [U] the soft white substance inside a coconut, used in cooking（用於烹調的）椰子肉，椰蓉：*desiccated coconut* 椰子乾 ◇ *coconut biscuits/cookies* 椰蓉餅乾 ◇ *coconut oil* 椰子油

ˈ**coconut butter** *noun* [U] a solid substance inside COCONUTS that is used to make soap, CANDLES, etc. 椰子油（用以製作肥皂、蠟燭等）

ˌ**coconut** ˈ**matting** *noun* [U] (*BrE*) a material used to cover floors that is made from the hair inside the outer shell of coconuts 製地墊椰衣

ˈ**coconut shy** *noun* (*pl.* **coconut shies**) (*BrE*) an outdoor entertainment in which people try to knock coconuts off stands by throwing balls at them 打椰子遊戲（擲球把椰子從支架上擊落）

co·coon /kəˈkuːn/ *noun, verb*

■ ***noun*** **1** a covering of silk threads that some insects make to protect themselves before they become adults 繭 **2** a soft covering that wraps all around a person or thing and forms a protection 保護膜；防護層；軟罩：(*figurative*) *the cocoon of a caring family* 家庭中相互關愛所形成的保護

■ ***verb*** [usually passive] **~ sb/sth (in sth)** to protect sb/sth by surrounding them or it completely with sth 把…包圍起來保護；用…完全保護起來：*We were warm and safe, cocooned in our sleeping bags.* 我們在睡袋裏睡覺，暖和又安全。

co·coon·ing /kəˈkuːnɪŋ/ *noun* [U] the habit of spending more of your free time at home and less time going out and doing things with other people 蠶繭式生活；宅在家（指業餘時間大多待在家裏而很少外出交往）

coco·yam /ˈkəʊkəʊjæm; *NAmE* ˈkoʊkoʊ-/ *noun* [C, U] (*WAfrE*) a plant whose roots can be cooked and eaten or made into flour 芋頭：*roasted cocoyam* 烤芋頭 ➲ see also FUFU

COD /ˌsiː əʊ ˈdiː; *NAmE* oʊ/ *abbr.* cash on delivery or (in American English) collect on delivery (payment for goods will be made when the goods are delivered) 貨到付款；交貨付現

cod /kɒd; *NAmE* kɑːd/ *noun, adj.*

■ ***noun*** [C, U] (*pl.* **cod**) a large sea fish with white flesh that is used for food 鱈魚：*fishing for cod* 捕鱈魚 ◇ *cod fillets* 鱈魚魚片

■ ***adj.*** [only before noun] (*BrE, informal*) not genuine or real 假的；偽的；不真實的：*a cod American accent* 假裝的美國口音 ◇ *cod psychology* 偽心理學

coda /ˈkəʊdə; *NAmE* ˈkoʊdə/ *noun* the final passage of a piece of music（樂曲的）後奏，尾聲；結尾樂段：(*figurative*) *The final two months were a miserable coda to the President's first period in office.* 總統首屆任期的最後兩個月非常糟糕。

cod·dle /ˈkɒdl; *NAmE* ˈkɑːdl/ *verb* **1 ~ sb** (often *disapproving*) to treat sb with too much care and attention 嬌慣；嬌養；溺愛 ➲ compare MOLLYCODDLE **2 ~ sth** to cook eggs in water slightly below boiling point（在略低於沸點的水裏）煮（蛋）

code 🔑 AW /kəʊd; *NAmE* koʊd/ *noun, verb*

■ ***noun*** **1** 🔑 [C, U] (often in compounds 常構成複合詞) a system of words, letters, numbers or symbols that represent a message or record information secretly or in a shorter form 密碼；暗碼；電碼；代碼：*to* ***break/crack a code*** (= to understand and read the message) 破譯密碼 ◇ *It's written* ***in code***. 那是用密碼寫的。◇ *Tap your* ***code number*** *into the machine.* 把你的密碼數字輸入機器。◇ *In the event of the machine not operating correctly, an* ***error code*** *will appear.* 如果機器運轉不正常，就會出現錯誤代碼。➲ see also AREA CODE, BARCODE, MORSE CODE, POSTCODE, SORT CODE, ZIP CODE **2** 🔑 [C] = DIALLING CODE：*There are three codes for London.* 倫敦有三個電話區號。 **3** [U] (*computing* 計) a system of computer programming instructions 編碼 ➲ see also MACHINE CODE, SOURCE CODE **4** [C] a set of moral principles or rules of behaviour that are generally accepted by society or a social group 道德準則；行為規範：*a strict code of conduct* 嚴格的行為準則 **5** [C] a system of laws or written rules that state how people in an institution or a country should behave 法典；法規：*the penal code* 刑法典 ➲ see also DRESS CODE, HIGHWAY CODE

■ ***verb*** **1 ~ sth** to write or print words, letters, numbers, etc. on sth so that you know what it is, what group it belongs to, etc. 為…編碼：*Each order is coded separately.* 每份訂單都單獨編號。 **2 ~ sth** to put a message into code so that it can only be understood by a few people 把…譯成密碼 **3 ~ sth** (*computing* 計) to write a computer program by putting one system of numbers, words and symbols into another system 編程序；編碼 SYN **encode**

C

coded /ˈkəʊdɪd; *NAmE* ˈkoʊ-/ *adj.* **1** [only before noun] a **coded** message or **coded** information is written or sent using a special system of words, letters, numbers, etc. that can only be understood by a few other people or by a computer 密碼的；暗碼的；編碼的：*a coded warning of a bomb at the airport* 告知機場有炸彈的密碼警報 **2** expressed in an indirect way 間接表達的：*There was coded criticism of the government from some party members.* 一些黨員對政府進行了間接的批評。

co·deine /ˈkəʊdiːn; *NAmE* ˈkoʊ-/ *noun* [U] a drug used to reduce pain 可待因（用於減輕疼痛）

ˈcode name *noun* a name used for a person or thing in order to keep the real name secret 代號 ▸ **ˈcode-named** *adj.* [not before noun]：*a drug investigation, code-named Snoopy* 代號為史努比的一次毒品調查行動

ˌcode of ˈpractice *noun* (*pl.* **codes of practice**) a set of standards that members of a particular profession agree to follow in their work 行業規則；職業準則

co·depend·ency /ˌkəʊdɪˈpendənsi; *NAmE* koʊ-/ *noun* [U] (*psychology* 心) a situation in which two people have a close relationship in which they rely too much on each other emotionally, especially when one person is caring for the other one（兩人在感情等方面的）互為依賴 ▸ **co·depend·ent** *adj.*, *noun*

CODESA /kəʊˈdesə; *NAmE* koʊ-/ *abbr.* Convention for a Democratic South Africa (in the past, the group of politicians who discussed how South Africa would become a DEMOCRACY) 民主南非大會（舊時主張南非成為民主國家的政治組織）

ˈcode-sharing *noun* [U] (*technical* 術語) an agreement between two or more AIRLINES to carry each other's passengers and use their own set of letters and numbers for flights provided by another airline 代碼共享協議（航空公司之間可相互運送乘客並互用航班號）

ˈcode switching *noun* [U] (*linguistics* 語言) the practice of changing between languages when you are speaking 語碼切換（說話中不同語言間的變換）

codex /ˈkəʊdeks; *NAmE* ˈkoʊ-/ *noun* (*pl.* **co·di·ces** /ˈkəʊdɪsiːz; ˈkɒd-; *NAmE* ˈkoʊ-; ˈkɑːd-/ or **codexes**) **1** an ancient text in the form of a book 古書手抄本 **2** an official list of medicines or chemicals 藥典

cod·ger /ˈkɒdʒə(r); *NAmE* ˈkɑːdʒ-/ *noun* (*informal*) **old ~** an informal way of referring to an old man that shows that you do not respect him 老傢伙；老頭兒

co·di·cil /ˈkəʊdɪsɪl; *NAmE* ˈkɑːdəsl/ *noun* (*law* 律) an instruction that is added later to a WILL, usually to change a part of it 遺囑修改附錄

co·dify /ˈkəʊdɪfaɪ; *NAmE* ˈkɑːd-/ *verb* (**co·di·fies, co·di·fy·ing, co·di·fied, co·di·fied**) **~ sth** (*technical* 術語) to arrange laws, rules, etc. into a system 把…編成法典 ▸ **co·difi·ca·tion** /ˌkəʊdɪfɪˈkeɪʃn; *NAmE* ˌkɑːd-/ *noun* [U]

ˌcod liver ˈoil *noun* [U] a thick yellow oil from the LIVER of COD (= a type of fish), containing a lot of VITAMINS A and D and often given as a medicine 魚肝油

cod·piece /ˈkɒdpiːs; *NAmE* ˈkɑːd-/ *noun* a piece of cloth, especially a decorative one, attached to a man's lower clothing and covering his GENITALS, worn in Europe in the 15th and 16th centuries 遮陰布（15、16 世紀歐洲男子加貼在緊身褲中，常帶裝飾）

cods·wal·lop /ˈkɒdzwɒləp; *NAmE* ˈkɑːdzwɑːləp/ *noun* [U] (*old-fashioned, BrE, informal*) nonsense 廢話；胡言亂語：*I've never heard such a load of old codswallop in my life.* 我一輩子也沒有聽到過這麼一大堆胡說八道。

coed /ˌkəʊˈed; *NAmE* ˌkoʊ-/ *noun* (*old-fashioned, NAmE*) a female student at a co-educational school or college（男女同校的）女生

ˌco-eduˈcation·al (also *informal* **coed**) *adj.* (of a school or an EDUCATIONAL system 學校或教育體制) where girls and boys are taught together 男女同校的 ▸ **ˌco-eduˈcation** *noun* [U]

co·ef·fi·cient /ˌkəʊɪˈfɪʃnt; *NAmE* ˌkoʊ-/ *noun* **1** (*mathematics* 數) a number which is placed before another quantity and which multiplies it, for example 3 in the quantity 3x 係數 **2** (*physics* 物) a number that measures a particular property (= characteristic) of a substance（測定物質某種特性的）係數：*the coefficient of friction* 摩擦係數

coela·canth /ˈsiːləkænθ/ *noun* a large fish found mainly in the seas near Madagascar. It was thought to be EXTINCT until one was discovered in 1938. 腔棘魚，矛尾魚（產於馬達加斯加附近海域，1938 年發現之前被認為已滅絕）

coel·iac disease (*BrE*) (*NAmE* **celiac disease**) /ˈsiːliæk dɪziːz/ *noun* [U] a disease in which sb cannot DIGEST food (= break it down in their body) because their body is very sensitive to GLUTEN (= a substance that is found in flour, especially WHEAT flour) 乳糜瀉（因麩膠過敏引起的消化不良）

co·erce /kəʊˈɜːs; *NAmE* koʊˈɜːrs/ *verb* **~ sb (into sth/into doing sth)** | **~ sb (to do sth)** (*formal*) to force sb to do sth by using threats 強迫；脅迫；迫使：*They were coerced into negotiating a settlement.* 他們被迫通過談判解決。

co·er·cion /kəʊˈɜːʃn; *NAmE* koʊˈɜːrʒn/ *noun* [U] (*formal*) the action of making sb do sth that they do not want to do, using force or threatening to use force 強迫；脅迫：*He claimed he had only acted under coercion.* 他聲稱他只是被迫採取行動。

co·er·cive /kəʊˈɜːsɪv; *NAmE* koʊˈɜːrsɪv/ *adj.* (*formal*) using force or the threat of force 用武力的；強制的；脅迫的：***coercive measures/powers*** 強制的措施／力量

co·eval /kəʊˈiːvl; *NAmE* koʊ-/ *adj.* (*formal*) **~ (with sth)** (of two or more things 兩個或以上的事物) having the same age or date of origin（與…）同齡，同時代，同時期出現：*The industry is coeval with the construction of the first railways.* 這一產業和初期鐵路的建造相伴而生。

co·ex·ist /ˌkəʊɪɡˈzɪst; *NAmE* ˌkoʊ-/ *verb* [I] **~ (with sb/sth)** (*formal*) to exist together in the same place or at the same time, especially in a peaceful way 共存；（尤指）和平共處：*The illness frequently coexists with other chronic diseases.* 這種病往往與其他慢性病同時存在。◇ *English speakers now coexist peacefully with their Spanish-speaking neighbours.* 講英語的人現在與他們講西班牙語的鄰居和睦相處。◇ *Different traditions coexist successfully side by side.* 不同的傳統和諧地共存着。

co·ex·ist·ence /ˌkəʊɪɡˈzɪstəns; *NAmE* ˌkoʊ-/ *noun* [U] the state of being together in the same place at the same time 共處；共存：*to live in **uneasy/peaceful coexistence** within one nation* 在一個國家內難以／和平共存

C of E /ˌsiː əv ˈiː/ *abbr.* Church of England 英國國教會；英格蘭聖公會 ➲ see also CE

cof·fee 🔑 /ˈkɒfi; *NAmE* ˈkɔː-; ˈkɑː-/ *noun*
1 🔑 [U, C] the ROASTED seeds (called **coffee beans**) of a tropical bush; a powder made from them（烘烤過的）咖啡豆；咖啡粉：***decaffeinated/instant coffee*** 不含咖啡因的／速溶咖啡 ◇ ***ground/real coffee*** 現磨現喝的咖啡；鮮咖啡 ◇ *a jar of coffee* 一罐咖啡 ◇ *a blend of Brazilian and Colombian coffees* 巴西和哥倫比亞的混合咖啡 ◇ *coffee ice cream* 咖啡冰淇淋 **2** 🔑 [U] a hot drink made from coffee powder and boiling water. It may be drunk with milk and/or sugar added. 咖啡（熱飲料）：***black/white coffee*** (= without/with milk) 不加奶的／加奶的咖啡 ◇ *Tea or coffee?* 要茶還是要咖啡？◇ *I'll just make the coffee.* 我就來煮咖啡。◇ *Let's talk over coffee* (= while drinking coffee). 咱們邊喝咖啡邊聊吧。**3** 🔑 [C] a cup of coffee 一杯咖啡：*Two strong black coffees, please.* 請來兩杯不加奶的濃咖啡。**4** [U] the colour of coffee mixed with milk; light brown 咖啡色；淺褐色；淺棕色 **IDM** see WAKE *v.*

ˈcoffee bar *noun* **1** (*BrE*) (also **ˈcoffee shop** *NAmE, BrE*) a place, sometimes in a store, train station, etc., where you can buy coffee, tea, other drinks without alcohol and sometimes simple meals 小咖啡廳（有時設在商店、火車站等內，供應咖啡、茶、其他無酒精飲料及便餐）**2** (*NAmE*) a small restaurant that sells special sorts of coffee and cakes 小咖啡館（專賣咖啡和糕點）

ˈcoffee break *noun* a short period of rest when you stop working and drink coffee 工間喝咖啡休息時間：*to have a coffee break* 工間喝咖啡休息

'coffee cake *noun* (*NAmE*) a small cake with melted sugar on top that people eat with coffee 咖啡糕（覆蓋糖漿的小蛋糕，飲咖啡時吃）

'coffee house *noun* **1** a restaurant serving coffee, etc., especially one of a type popular in Britain in the 18th century or one in a city in Central Europe（尤指流行於英國 18 世紀或中歐城市裏的）咖啡館：*the coffee houses of Vienna* 維也納的咖啡館 **2** (*NAmE*) a restaurant serving coffee, etc. where people go to listen to music, poetry, etc.（可聽音樂、詩歌等的）咖啡館

'coffee machine *noun* **1** = COFFEE MAKER **2** a machine that you put coins in to get a cup of coffee 投幣咖啡機

'coffee maker (also **'coffee machine**) *noun* a small machine for making cups of coffee 煮咖啡機 ➲ **VISUAL VOCAB** page V25

'coffee morning *noun* (*BrE*) a social event held in the morning, often at a person's house, where money is usually given to help a charity 咖啡早茶會（通常在某人家裏為慈善募款而舉行）

'coffee shop *noun* a small restaurant, often in a store, hotel, etc., where coffee, tea, other drinks without alcohol and simple food are served 小咖啡廳（常設在商店、旅館等內，供應咖啡、茶、其他無酒精飲料及小吃）

'coffee table *noun* a small low table for putting magazines, cups, etc. on, usually in front of a SOFA 咖啡桌；茶几 ➲ **VISUAL VOCAB** page V21

'coffee-table book *noun* a large expensive book containing many pictures or photographs, that is designed for people to look through rather than to read carefully 咖啡桌圖書（多供瀏覽，開本大，插圖豐富，較昂貴）

cof·fer /ˈkɒfə(r); *NAmE* ˈkɔːf-; ˈkɑːf-/ *noun* **1** [C] a large strong box, used in the past for storing money or valuable objects（舊時的）保險櫃，貴重物品箱 **2** (also **coffers** [pl.]) a way of referring to the money that a government, an organization, etc. has available to spend（政府、機構等的）金庫，資金：*The nation's coffers are empty.* 國庫空虛。

cof·fin /ˈkɒfɪn; *NAmE* ˈkɔːfɪn; ˈkɑːfɪn/ (*especially BrE*) (*NAmE* usually **cas·ket**) *noun* a box in which a dead body is buried or CREMATED 棺材；棺槨；棺木；靈柩 **IDM** see NAIL *n.*

cog /kɒg; *NAmE* kɑːg/ *noun* **1** one of a series of teeth on the edge of a wheel that fit between the teeth on the next wheel and cause it to move（齒輪的）輪牙，輪齒，嵌齒 ➲ picture at COGWHEEL **2** = COGWHEEL
IDM **a cog in the ma'chine/'wheel** (*informal*) a person who is a small part of a large organization（大機構中的）小職員，小成員

co·gent /ˈkəʊdʒənt; *NAmE* ˈkoʊ-/ *adj.* (*formal*) strongly and clearly expressed in a way that influences what people believe 有說服力的；令人信服的 **SYN** **convincing**：*She put forward some cogent reasons for abandoning the plan.* 她為放棄這個計劃提出了一些具有說服力的理由。▶ **co·gency** /ˈkəʊdʒənsi; *NAmE* ˈkoʊ-/ *noun* [U] **co·gent·ly** *adv.*

cogi·tate /ˈkɒdʒɪteɪt; *NAmE* ˈkɑːdʒ-/ *verb* [I] **~ (about/on sth)** (*formal*) to think carefully about sth 仔細思考；慎重考慮；深思熟慮 ▶ **cogi·ta·tion** /ˌkɒdʒɪˈteɪʃn; *NAmE* ˌkɑːdʒ-/ *noun* [U, C]

co·gnac /ˈkɒnjæk; *NAmE* ˈkoʊn-/ *noun* **1** [U, C] a type of fine BRANDY made in western France 科尼亞克白蘭地酒，干邑（產於法國西部）**2** [C] a glass of cognac 一杯科尼亞克白蘭地酒

cog·nate /ˈkɒgneɪt; *NAmE* ˈkɑːg-/ *adj.*, *noun*
■ *adj.* **1** (*linguistics* 語言) having the same origin as another word or language（詞或語言）同源的，同族的，同語系的：*'Haus' in German is cognate with 'house' in English.* 德語中的 haus 一詞與英語中的 house 同源。◇ *German and Dutch are cognate languages.* 德語和荷蘭語是同源語言。 **2** (*formal*) related in some way and therefore similar 相關的；類似的：*a cognate development* 相關的發展
■ *noun* (*linguistics* 語言) a word that has the same origin as another 同源詞：*'Haus' and 'house' are cognates.* * haus 和 house 是同源詞。

cog·ni·tion /kɒgˈnɪʃn; *NAmE* kɑːg-/ *noun* [U] (*psychology* 心) the process by which knowledge and understanding is developed in the mind 認知；感知；認識

cog·ni·tive /ˈkɒgnətɪv; *NAmE* ˈkɑːg-/ *adj.* [usually before noun] connected with mental processes of understanding 認知的；感知的；認識的：*a child's cognitive development* 兒童的認知發展 ◇ *cognitive psychology* 認知心理學

cog·ni·zance (*BrE* also **-i·sance**) /ˈkɒgnɪzəns; *NAmE* ˈkɑːg-/ *noun* [U] (*formal*) knowledge or understanding of sth 認識；獲知；領悟 ▶ **cog·ni·zant**, **-i·sant** *adj.* [not before noun]：*cognizant of the importance of the case* 認識到這個論據的重要性
IDM **take cognizance of sth** (*law* 律) to understand or consider sth; to take notice of sth 獲知；察知；考慮到；注意到

co·gnos·centi /ˌkɒnjəˈʃenti; *NAmE* ˌkɑːn-/ *noun* [pl.] **the cognoscenti** (from *Italian*, *formal*) people with a lot of knowledge about a particular subject 專家；行家

cogwheel 齒輪

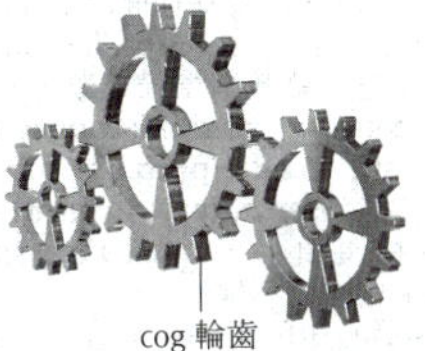

cog·wheel /ˈkɒgwiːl; *NAmE* ˈkɑːg-/ (also **cog**) *noun* a wheel with a series of teeth on the edge that fit between the teeth on the next wheel and cause it to move 齒輪

co·habit /kəʊˈhæbɪt; *NAmE* koʊ-/ *verb* [I] **~ (with sb)** (*formal*) (usually of a man and a woman 通常指男女) to live together and have a sexual relationship without being married（無婚姻關係）同居 ▶ **co·hab·it·ation** /ˌkəʊˌhæbɪˈteɪʃn; *NAmE* ˌkoʊ-/ *noun* [U]

co·here /kəʊˈhɪə(r); *NAmE* koʊˈhɪr/ *verb* (*formal*) **1** [I] **~ (with sth)** (of different ideas, arguments, sentences, etc. 不同的看法、論點、句子等) to have a clear logical connection so that together they make a whole 連貫；一致：*This view does not cohere with their other beliefs.* 這個觀點與他們的其他看法不一致。 **2** [I] (of people 人) to work closely together 齊心協力；團結一致：*It can be difficult to get a group of people to cohere.* 要使一群人做到彼此一條心有時候很困難。

co·her·ence **AW** /kəʊˈhɪərəns; *NAmE* koʊˈhɪr-/ *noun* [U] (*formal*) the situation in which all the parts of sth fit together well 連貫性；條理性：*The points you make are fine, but the whole essay lacks coherence.* 你提出的論點很好，但整篇文章缺乏呼應連貫。 **OPP** **incoherence**

co·her·ent **AW** /kəʊˈhɪərənt; *NAmE* koʊˈhɪr-/ *adj.* **1** (of ideas, thoughts, arguments, etc. 看法、思想、論點等) logical and well organized; easy to understand and clear 合乎邏輯的；有條理的；清楚易懂的：*a **coherent narrative/account/explanation*** 條理清楚的敘述／描述／闡述 ◇ *a coherent policy for the transport system* 運輸系統方面的一個前後一致的政策 **2** (of a person 人) able to talk and express yourself clearly 有表達能力的；能把自己的意思說清楚的：*She only became coherent again two hours after the attack.* 她受襲兩小時之後才恢復了清楚說話的能力。 **OPP** **incoherent** ▶ **co·her·ent·ly** **AW** *adv.*

co·he·sion /kəʊˈhiːʒn; *NAmE* koʊ-/ *noun* [U] **1** (*formal*) the act or state of keeping together 粘合；結合；凝聚性 **SYN** **unity**：*the cohesion of the nuclear family* 核心家庭的內聚性 ◇ ***social/political/economic cohesion*** 社會／政治／經濟凝聚性 **2** (*physics* 物, *chemistry* 化) the force causing MOLECULES of the same substance to stick together 內聚力

co·he·sive /kəʊˈhiːsɪv; *NAmE* koʊ-/ *adj.* (*formal*) **1** forming a united whole 結成一個整體的：*a cohesive group* 一個緊密團結的群體 **2** causing people or things to become united 使結合的；使凝結的；使內聚的：*the cohesive power of shared suffering* 共患難的內聚力 ◇ *well-structured sentences illustrating the use of cohesive markers such as 'nevertheless' and 'however'* 能夠表明像 nevertheless 和 however 這類連詞用法的結構嚴謹的句子 ▶ **co·he·sive·ness** *noun* [U]

co·hort /ˈkəʊhɔːt; *NAmE* ˈkoʊhɔːrt/ *noun* [C+sing./pl. v.] **1** (*technical* 術語) a group of people who share a common feature or aspect of behaviour（有共同特點或舉止類同的）一群人，一批人：*the 1999 birth cohort* (= all those born in 1999) * 1999 年出生的同齡人口 **2** (*disapproving*) a member of a group of people who support another person 同夥；支持者：*Robinson and his cohorts were soon ejected from the hall.* 魯濱遜及其同夥很快被趕出了大廳。

coif·fure /kwɑːˈfjʊə(r); *NAmE* -ˈfjʊr/ *noun* (from *French*, *formal* or *humorous*) the way in which a person's hair is arranged 髮式；髮型 SYN **hairstyle**

coil /kɔɪl/ *verb, noun*

■ ***verb*** [I, T] to wind into a series of circles; to make sth do this（使）纏繞，盤繞：**~ up** *The snake coiled up, ready to strike.* 那條蛇盤繞起來準備攻擊。◇ **~ round, around, etc. sth** *Mist coiled around the tops of the hills.* 薄霧盤繞着山巔。◇ **~ sth (+ adv./prep.)** *to coil a rope into a loop* 把繩索盤繞成圈 ◇ *Her hair was coiled on top of her head.* 她把頭髮盤在頭頂上。◇ *a coiled spring* 螺旋狀彈簧 ➲ picture at KNOT

■ ***noun*** **1** a series of circles formed by winding up a length of rope, wire, etc.（繩索、金屬線等的）圈，捲，盤：*a coil of wire* 一圈金屬線 **2** one circle of rope, wire, etc. in a series 一圈（繩索、金屬線等）：*Shake the rope and let the coils unwind.* 抖動繩索把繩圈展開。◇ *a snake's coils* 蛇的盤圈 **3** a length of wire, wound into circles, that can carry electricity 線圈；繞組 **4** = IUD

coin 0⊸ /kɔɪn/ *noun, verb*

■ ***noun*** **1** 0⊸ [C] a small flat piece of metal used as money（一枚）硬幣；金屬貨幣：*a euro coin* 歐元硬幣 ➲ picture at MONEY **2** [U] money made of metal（統稱）硬幣：*notes and coin* 紙幣和硬幣 IDM see SIDE *n.*, TWO

■ ***verb*** **1 ~ sth** to invent a new word or phrase that other people then begin to use 創造（新詞語）：*The term 'cardboard city' was coined to describe communities of homeless people living in cardboard boxes.* 人們創造了 cardboard city 一詞，用來指居住在紙板屋棚裏無家可歸者所聚集的地區。 **2 ~ sth** to make coins out of metal（用金屬）鑄幣，造硬幣

IDM **be ˈcoining it (in)** | **be ˌcoining ˈmoney** (*BrE, informal*) to earn a lot of money quickly or easily 暴富；賺大錢；發大財 SYN **rake in** **to coin a ˈphrase** **1** used to introduce a well-known expression that you have changed slightly in order to be funny 引出名言（為逗趣而稍加改動）**2** used to show that you are aware that you are using an expression that is not new 套用一句老話；用老話來說：*Oh well, no news is good news, to coin a phrase.* 噢，常言道，沒有消息就是好消息。

coin·age /ˈkɔɪnɪdʒ/ *noun* **1** [U] the coins used in a particular place or at a particular time; coins of a particular type（統稱某地或某時期的）金屬貨幣；（某種）硬幣：*Roman coinage* 古羅馬時期的硬幣 ◇ ***gold/silver/bronze coinage*** 金幣；銀幣；銅幣 **2** [U] the system of money used in a particular country（國家的）貨幣制度：*decimal coinage* 十進位貨幣制 **3** [C, U] a word or phrase that has been invented recently; the process of inventing a word or phrase 新創的詞語；新詞語的創造：*new coinages* 新創的詞語

ˈcoin box *noun* (*BrE, old-fashioned*) a public telephone that you put coins in to operate 投幣式公用電話

co·in·cide AW /ˌkəʊɪnˈsaɪd; *NAmE* ˌkoʊ-/ *verb* **1** [I] (of two or more events 兩件或更多的事情) to take place at the same time 同時發生：*It's a pity our trips to New York don't coincide.* 真遺憾我們不能同一時間去紐約。◇ **~ with sth** *The strike was timed to coincide with the party conference.* 那次罷工選擇在召開政黨大會的同一時間舉行。 **2** [I] (*formal*) (of ideas, opinions, etc. 想法、意見等) to be the same or very similar 相同；相符；極為類似：*The interests of employers and employees do not always coincide.* 雇主和雇員的利益並不總是一致的。◇ **~ with sth** *Her story coincided exactly with her brother's.* 她和她弟弟所講的完全一致。 **3** [I] (*formal*) (of objects or places 物品或地方) to meet; to share the same space 相接；相交；同位；位置重合；重疊：*At this point the two paths coincide briefly.* 兩條小路在這個地方有一小段交接了。◇ **~ with sth** *The present position of the house coincides with that of an earlier dwelling.* 這棟房子現在的位置恰與原住宅的位置一致。

co·in·ci·dence AW /kəʊˈɪnsɪdəns; *NAmE* koʊ-/ *noun* **1** [C, U] the fact of two things happening at the same time by chance, in a surprising way（令人吃驚的）巧合，巧事：***a strange/an extraordinary/a remarkable coincidence*** 奇怪的／意外的／不尋常的巧合 ◇ ***What a coincidence!*** *I wasn't expecting to see you here.* 真巧！我沒料到會在這裏見到你。◇ *It's* ***not a coincidence that*** *none of the directors are women* (= it did not happen by chance). 沒有一位董事是女性，這並非偶然。◇ ***By*** (***sheer***) ***coincidence,*** *I met the person we'd been discussing the next day.* 真是巧了，我在第二天就遇見了我們一直在談論的那個人。➲ **SYNONYMS** at LUCK **2** [sing.] (*formal*) the fact of things being present at the same time 同時存在；並存：*the coincidence of inflation and unemployment* 通貨膨脹與失業的並存 **3** [sing.] (*formal*) the fact of two or more opinions, etc. being the same（意見等的）相同，相符，一致：*a coincidence of interests between the two partners* 兩個合夥人之間利益的一致

co·in·ci·dent AW /kəʊˈɪnsɪdənt; *NAmE* koʊ-/ *adj.* **~ (with sth)** (*formal*) happening in the same place or at the same time 在同一地方發生的；同時發生的

co·in·ci·dent·al AW /kəʊˌɪnsɪˈdentl; *NAmE* koʊ-/ *adj.* [not usually before noun] happening by chance; not planned 巧合；碰巧；非計劃之中：*suppose your presence here today is not* ***entirely coincidental.*** 我認為你今天來這裏不完全是碰巧。◇ *It's* ***purely coincidental that*** *we both chose to call our daughters Emma.* 我們倆都給自己的女兒取名叫埃瑪，這完全是巧合。▶ **co·in·ci·den·tal·ly** /-təli/ *adv.*：*Coincidentally, they had both studied in Paris.* 碰巧的是，他們倆都在巴黎學習過。

coir /ˈkɔɪə(r)/ *noun* [U] rough material made from the shells of COCONUTS, used for making ropes, for covering floors, etc. 椰子殼粗纖維（用於製作繩索、地板墊等）

co·itus /ˈkɔɪtəs; ˈkəʊɪtəs; *NAmE* ˈkoʊ-/ *noun* [U] (*medical* 醫 or *formal*) = SEXUAL INTERCOURSE

coitus interruptus /ˌkɔɪtəs ɪntəˈrʌptəs; ˌkəʊɪtəs; *NAmE* ˌkoʊ-/ *noun* [U] an act of SEXUAL INTERCOURSE in which the man removes his PENIS from the woman's body before he EJACULATES, in order to prevent the woman from becoming pregnant（防止受孕的）體外射精，性交中斷

Coke™ /kəʊk; *NAmE* koʊk/ *noun* [C, U] (*informal*) = COCA-COLA：*Can I have a Diet Coke?* 能給我來一罐低熱量可樂嗎？

coke /kəʊk; *NAmE* koʊk/ *noun* [U] **1** (*informal*) = COCAINE **2** a black substance that is produced from coal and burnt to provide heat 焦炭

Col. *abbr.* (in writing) COLONEL（書寫形式）上校：*Col. Stewart* 斯圖爾特上校

col /kɒl; *NAmE* kɑːl/ *noun* (*technical* 術語) a low point between two higher points in a mountain range（山脈中兩個山峰之間的）山口 SYN **pass**

col. *abbr.* (in writing) COLUMN（書寫形式）欄

cola /ˈkəʊlə; *NAmE* ˈkoʊlə/ *noun* **1** [U, C] a sweet brown, FIZZY drink (= with bubbles) that does not contain alcohol. Its flavour comes from the seeds of a W African tree and other substances. 可樂飲料 **2** [C] a glass, can or bottle of cola 一杯（或一罐、一瓶）可樂 ➲ see also COCA-COLA, COKE

col·an·der /ˈkʌləndə(r); *NAmE* ˈkɑːl-/ *noun* a metal or plastic bowl with a lot of small holes in it, used for DRAINING water from vegetables, etc. after washing or cooking 濾器；濾鍋 ➲ **VISUAL VOCAB** page V26

ˈ**cola nut** (also ˈ**kola nut**) *noun* the seed of the cola tree, that can be chewed or made into a drink 可樂果樹籽（可咀嚼或製作飲料）

cold 🔑 /kəʊld; *NAmE* koʊld/ *adj., noun, adv.*

■ ***adj.*** (**cold·er**, **cold·est**)

▸ **LOW TEMPERATURE** 低氣溫 **1** 🔑 having a lower than usual temperature; having a temperature lower than the human body 寒冷的；冷的：*I'm cold. Turn the heating up.* 我覺得冷，把暖氣溫度調高一點。◇ *to* ***feel/look cold*** 感覺／看起來冷 ◇ *cold hands and feet* 冷手涼腳 ◇ *a cold room/house* 寒冷的房間／屋子 ◇ *hot and cold water in every room* 每個房間都供給的冷熱水 ◇ *Isn't it cold today?* 今天真冷，是不是？◇ *It's* ***freezing cold.*** 天氣寒冷徹骨。◇ *to* ***get/turn colder*** 變得更冷 ◇ ***bitterly cold*** *weather* 嚴寒的天氣 ◇ *the coldest May on record* 有記載以來最冷的五月 ◇ (*BrE*) *The water has gone cold.* 水已變涼。

▸ **FOOD/DRINK** 食物；飲料 **2** 🔑 not heated; cooled after being cooked 未熱過的；已涼的；冷卻的：*a cold drink* 冷飲 ◇ *Hot and cold food is available in the cafeteria.* 自助餐廳有冷熱食物供應。◇ *cold chicken for lunch* 午餐的雞肉冷盤

▸ **UNFRIENDLY** 不友好 **3** 🔑 (of a person 人) without emotion; unfriendly 冷漠的；不友好的：*to give sb a* ***cold look/stare/welcome*** 冷冷地看某人一眼／瞪着某人／歡迎某人 ◇ *Her manner was* ***cold and distant.*** 她的態度冷漠而疏遠。◇ *He was staring at her with* ***cold eyes.*** 他用冷漠的眼光盯着她。

▸ **LIGHT/COLOURS** 光線；顏色 **4** 🔑 seeming to lack warmth, in an unpleasant way 冷的；冷色的；寒色的：*clear cold light* 清寒的光 ◇ *cold grey skies* 冷灰色的天空

▸ **ROUTE** 路徑 **5** not easy to find 不易發現的：*The police followed the robbers to the airport but then the* ***trail went cold.*** 警察追踪搶劫犯到了機場，但是後來卻失去了他們的踪跡。

▸ **IN GAMES** 遊戲 **6** used in children's games to say that the person playing is not close to finding a person or thing, or to guessing the correct answer（兒童遊戲中）離目標遠的，未猜中的

▸ **UNCONSCIOUS** 失去知覺 **7** **out ~** [not before noun] (*informal*) unconscious 失去知覺：*He was knocked out cold in the second round.* 他在第二輪中被擊倒，失去了知覺。

▸ **FACTS** 事實 **8** **the ~ facts/truth** facts with nothing added to make them more interesting or pleasant 真實的；客觀的 ➲ see also COLDLY, COLDNESS

IDM **a cold ˈfish** a person who seems unfriendly and without strong emotions 冷漠無情的人 **get/have cold ˈfeet** (*informal*) to suddenly become nervous about doing sth that you had planned to do 臨陣膽怯；畏縮：*He was going to ask her but he got cold feet and said nothing.* 他本來是想問她的，可事到臨頭他卻膽怯得什麼也沒有說。**give sb the cold ˈshoulder** (*informal*) to treat sb in an unfriendly way 冷漠對待；使受到冷遇 ➲ see also COLD-SHOULDER **in cold ˈblood** acting in a way that is deliberately cruel; with no pity 殘忍地；蓄意地；冷酷地；無情地：*to kill sb in cold blood* 殘忍地殺害某人 **in the cold light of day** when you have had time to think calmly about sth; in the morning when things are clearer 有時間冷靜考慮時；在頭腦更清醒些的第二天早晨：*These things always look different in the cold light of day.* 這些事情在冷靜地考慮後總會顯得不同。**leave sb ˈcold** to fail to affect or interest sb 未打動某人；無法引起某人的興趣：*Most modern art leaves me cold.* 大多數的現代藝術引不起我的興趣。**pour/throw cold ˈwater on sth** to give reasons for not being in favour of sth; to criticize sth 潑冷水；批評；責備 ➲ more at BLOOD *n.*, BLOW *v.*, HOT *adj.*

■ ***noun***

▸ **LOW TEMPERATURE** 低氣溫 **1** 🔑 [U] a lack of heat or warmth; a low temperature, especially in the atmosphere 冷；寒冷；（尤指）低氣溫：*He shivered with cold.* 他凍得發抖。◇ *Don't stand outside* ***in the cold.*** 別站在外面凍着。◇ *She doesn't seem to* ***feel the cold.*** 她好像不覺得冷。◇ *You'll* ***catch your death of cold*** (= used to warn sb they could become ill if they do not keep warm in cold weather). 你會凍出病的。

▸ **ILLNESS** 疾病 **2** 🔑 [C] (also *less frequent* **the ˌcommon ˈcold**) a common illness that affects the nose and/or throat, making you cough, SNEEZE, etc. 感冒；傷風；着涼：*I've got a cold.* 我感冒了。◇ *a* ***bad/heavy/slight cold*** 嚴重／重／輕微感冒 ◇ *to* ***catch a cold*** 患感冒 ➲ COLLOCATIONS at ILL

IDM **come in from the ˈcold** to become accepted or included in a group, etc. after a period of being outside it 不再受冷落（或排斥）**leave sb ˌout in the ˈcold** to not include sb in a group or an activity 冷落；排斥 ➲ more at CATCH *v.*

■ ***adv.*** **1** (*NAmE*) suddenly and completely 突然；完全：*His final request stopped her cold.* 他最後的請求突然阻止了她。**2** without preparing 毫無準備地：*I can't just walk in there cold and give a speech.* 我不能什麼準備都沒有，進去就發表演講。

Synonyms 同義詞辨析

cold

cool • freezing • chilly • lukewarm • tepid

These words all describe sb/sth that has a low temperature. 以上各詞均表示溫度低。

cold having a temperature that is lower than usual or lower than the human body; (of food or drink) not heated; cooled after being cooked 指寒冷的、冷的，（食物、飲料）涼的、冷的：*I'm cold. Turn the heating up.* 我覺得冷，把暖氣溫度調高一點。◇ *Outside it was bitterly cold.* 外面非常寒冷。◇ *a cold wind* 寒風 ◇ *hot and cold water* 冷熱水 ◇ *It's cold chicken for lunch.* 午餐有雞肉冷盤。

cool (*often approving*) fairly cold, especially in a pleasant way 指涼爽的、涼快的：*a long cool drink* 一大口冷飲 ◇ *We found a cool place to sit.* 我們找了一個涼快的地方坐下來。

freezing extremely cold; having a temperature below 0° Celsius 指極冷的、冰凍的、冰點以下的：*It's absolutely freezing outside.* 外面冷得不得了。◇ *I'm freezing!* 我要凍僵了！

chilly (*rather informal*) too cold to be comfortable 指寒冷的、陰冷的：*Bring a coat. It might turn chilly later.* 帶件大衣，過一會兒天氣可能會變冷。

lukewarm (*often disapproving*) slightly warm, sometimes in an unpleasant way 指微温的、不冷不熱的、温吞的：*Her coffee was now lukewarm.* 她的咖啡變得微温。

tepid (*often disapproving*) slightly warm, sometimes in an unpleasant way 指微温的、不冷不熱的、温吞的：*a jug of tepid water* 一壺温水

LUKEWARM OR TEPID? 用 lukewarm 還是 tepid？

There is really no difference in meaning or use between these words. 以上兩詞在含義和用法上無實際區別。

PATTERNS

- to **feel/get** cold/cool/chilly
- cold/cool/freezing/chilly **air/weather**
- a cold/cool/freezing/chilly **wind**
- cold/cool/freezing/lukewarm/tepid **water**
- a cold/cool/lukewarm/tepid **shower/bath**
- cold/lukewarm/tepid **tea/coffee/food**
- a cold/cool **drink**
- **It's** cold/chilly/freezing outside.

ˌ**cold-ˈblooded** *adj.* **1** (of people and their actions 人及其行為) showing no feelings or pity for other people 冷酷的；無情的；殘酷的：*a cold-blooded killer* 冷酷無情的殺手 **2** (*biology* 生) (of animals, for example fish or snakes 動物，如魚或蛇) having a body temperature that depends on the temperature of the surrounding air or water 冷血的 ➲ compare WARM-BLOODED ▸ ˌ**cold-ˈblooded·ly** *adv.*

C

ˌ**cold-ˈcalling** *noun* [U] the practice of telephoning sb that you do not know, in order to sell them sth 銷售商品的電話 ▸ ˌ**cold ˈcall** *noun*

ˌ**cold ˈcash** (*NAmE*) (*BrE* ˌ**hard ˈcash**) *noun* [U] money, especially in the form of coins and notes, that you can spend 現金（尤指硬幣和紙幣）

ˌ**cold ˈcomfort** *noun* [U] the fact that sth that would normally be good does not make you happy because the whole situation is bad 於事無補的安慰；不起作用的慰藉：*A small drop in the inflation rate was cold comfort for the millions without a job.* 對數百萬失業者來說，一點點通貨膨脹率的下降是不起什麼作用的安慰。

ˈ**cold cream** *noun* [U] a thick white cream that people use for cleaning their face or making their skin soft 潔面乳；潤膚膏

ˈ**cold cuts** *noun* [pl.] (*especially NAmE*) slices of cooked meat that are served cold 冷盤肉片

ˈ**cold frame** (also **frame**) *noun* a small wooden or metal frame covered with glass that you grow seeds or small plants in to protect them from cold weather 冷牀，陽畦（保護育種或幼苗抗寒的牀框）➲ picture at FRAME ➲ **VISUAL VOCAB page V19**

ˌ**cold ˈfusion** *noun* [U] (*physics* 物) NUCLEAR FUSION that takes place at or near room temperature 冷核聚變

ˌ**cold-ˈhearted** *adj.* not showing any love or sympathy for other people; unkind 冷酷無情的；無同情心的；不仁慈的 ➲ compare WARM-HEARTED

coldie /ˈkəʊldi; *NAmE* ˈkoʊl-/ *noun* (*AustralE, informal*) a cold can or bottle of beer 一罐（或一瓶）冰鎮啤酒

cold·ly 🗝 /ˈkəʊldli; *NAmE* ˈkoʊld-/ *adv.* without any emotion or warm feelings; in an unfriendly way 冷淡地；冷漠地；不友好地

cold·ness /ˈkəʊldnəs; *NAmE* ˈkoʊld-/ *noun* [U] **1** the lack of warm feelings; unfriendly behaviour 冷淡；冷漠；不友好的舉止：*She was hurt by the coldness in his voice.* 他說話的冷漠語氣讓她很傷心。**2** the state of being cold 冷；寒冷：*the icy coldness of the water* 冰冷徹骨的水 **OPP** **warmth**

ˌ**cold-ˈshoulder** *verb* **~ sb** to treat sb in an unfriendly way 冷待；冷落；慢待 ➲ see also GIVE SB THE COLD SHOULDER at COLD *adj.*

ˈ**cold snap** *noun* (*informal*) a sudden short period of very cold weather（短時間的）驟冷期

ˈ**cold sore** (*NAmE* also ˈ**fever blister**) *noun* a small painful spot on the lips or inside the mouth that is caused by a virus 唇疱疹；嘴邊疱疹

ˈ**cold spell** *noun* a period when the weather is colder than usual 寒冷期

ˌ**cold ˈstorage** *noun* [U] a place where food, etc. can be kept fresh or frozen until it is needed; the storing of sth in such a place 冷藏庫；冷藏：(*figurative*) *I've had to* ***put*** *my plans* ***into cold storage*** (= I've decided not to carry them out immediately but to keep them for later). 我不得不把我的計劃暫時擱置起來。

ˈ**cold store** *noun* a room where food, etc. can be kept at a low temperature in order to keep it in good condition 冷藏室；冷藏庫

ˌ**cold ˈsweat** *noun* [usually sing.] a state when you have sweat on your face or body but still feel cold, usually because you are very frightened or anxious（通常因恐懼或焦急而出的）冷汗：*to break out into a cold sweat* 出了一身冷汗 ◇ *I woke up in a cold sweat about the interview.* 夢中的面試情景嚇得我在一身冷汗中驚醒。

ˌ**cold ˈturkey** *noun* [U] the unpleasant state that drug ADDICTS experience when they suddenly stop taking a drug; a way of treating drug ADDICTS that makes them experience this state（吸毒成癮者）突然戒毒時的痛苦；（治療吸毒成癮者的）突然戒毒方法 ▸ ˌ**cold ˈturkey** *adv.*：*I quit smoking cold turkey.* 我用突然戒煙法戒了煙。

ˌ**cold ˈwar** *noun* [sing., U] (often **Cold War**) a very unfriendly relationship between two countries who are not actually fighting each other, usually used about the situation between the US and the Soviet Union after the Second World War 冷戰（通常指第二次世界大戰後美國與蘇聯之間的對峙局面）

cole·slaw /ˈkəʊlslɔː; *NAmE* ˈkoʊl-/ *noun* [U] pieces of raw CABBAGE, carrot, onion, etc., mixed with MAYONNAISE and eaten with meat or salads 涼拌菜絲（用生圓白菜、胡蘿蔔、洋蔥等切絲與蛋黃醬攪拌而成）

coley /ˈkəʊli; *NAmE* ˈkoʊli/ *noun* [C, U] (*pl.* **coley** or **coleys**) a N Atlantic fish that is used for food 綠青鱈（產於北大西洋）

colic /ˈkɒlɪk; *NAmE* ˈkɑːlɪk/ *noun* [U] severe pain in the stomach and BOWELS, suffered especially by babies（尤指嬰兒的）急性腹痛，腹絞痛 ▸ **col·icky** *adj.*

col·itis /kəˈlaɪtɪs/ *noun* [U] (*medical* 醫) a disease that causes pain and swelling in the COLON (= part of the BOWELS) 結腸炎

col·lab·or·ate /kəˈlæbəreɪt/ *verb* **1** [I] to work together with sb in order to produce or achieve sth 合作；協作：*Researchers around the world are collaborating to develop a new vaccine.* 世界各地的研究人員正在合作培育一種新的疫苗。◇ **~ (with sb) (on sth)** *We have collaborated on many projects over the years.* 這些年來我們合作搞了許多項目。◇ **~ (with sb) (in sth/in doing sth)** *She agreed to collaborate with him in writing her biography.* 她同意與他合作撰寫她的傳記。**2** [I] **~ (with sb)** (*disapproving*) to help the enemy who has taken control of your country during a war 通敵；勾結敵人

col·lab·or·ation /kəˌlæbəˈreɪʃn/ *noun* **1** [U, C] the act of working with another person or group of people to create or produce sth 合作；協作：*It was a collaboration that produced extremely useful results.* 這是一次帶來豐碩成果的合作。◇ **~ (with sb) (on sth)** *She wrote the book* ***in collaboration*** *with one of her students.* 她和她的一個學生合寫了這本書。◇ *The government worked in close collaboration with teachers on the new curriculum.* 政府和教師就新的課程進行了緊密協作。◇ **~ (between A and B)** *collaboration between the teachers and the government* 教師和政府間的合作 **2** [C] a piece of work produced by two or more people or groups of people working together 合作成果（或作品）**3** [U] (*disapproving*) the act of helping the enemy during a war when they have taken control of your country 通敵；勾結敵人

col·lab·ora·tive /kəˈlæbərətɪv; *NAmE* -reɪtɪv/ *adj.* [only before noun] (*formal*) involving, or done by, several people or groups of people working together 合作的；協作的；協力的：***collaborative projects/studies/research*** 合作項目／研究 ◇ ***a collaborative effort/venture*** 共同的努力；合作企業 ▸ **col·lab·ora·tive·ly** *adv.*

col·lab·or·ator /kəˈlæbəreɪtə(r)/ *noun* **1** a person who works with another person to create or produce sth such as a book 合作者；協作者；合著者 **2** (*disapproving*) a person who helps the enemy in a war, when they have taken control of the person's country 通敵者

col·lage /ˈkɒlɑːʒ; *NAmE* kəˈlɑːʒ/ *noun* **1** [U, C] the art of making a picture by sticking pieces of coloured paper, cloth, or photographs onto a surface; a picture that you make by doing this 拼貼藝術；拼貼畫 **2** [C] a collection of things, which may be similar or different 收集品；收藏品：*an interesting collage of 1960s songs* 有趣的 20 世紀 60 年代歌曲的收藏集

col·lagen /ˈkɒlədʒən; *NAmE* ˈkɑːl-/ *noun* [U] a PROTEIN found in skin and bone, sometimes INJECTED into the body, especially the face, to improve its appearance 膠原蛋白，膠原（存在於皮膚和骨骼的蛋白質，可通過注射來美容等）：*collagen injections* 膠原蛋白注射劑

col·lapse 🗝 **AW** /kəˈlæps/ *verb, noun*

■ *verb*

▸ **OF BUILDING** 建築物 **1** 🗝 [I] to fall down or fall in suddenly, often after breaking apart（突然）倒塌，坍塌 **SYN** **give way**：*The roof collapsed under the weight of snow.* 房頂在雪的重壓下突然坍塌下來。

▸ **OF SICK PERSON** 病人 **2** 🗝 [I] to fall down (and usually become unconscious), especially because you are very ill/sick（尤指因病重而）倒下，昏倒，暈倒：*He collapsed in the street and died two hours later.* 他昏倒在大街上，兩小時後便去世了。

▸ **RELAX** 放鬆 **3** [I] (*informal*) to sit or lie down and relax, especially after working hard（尤指工作勞累後）坐下，躺下放鬆：*When I get home I like to collapse on the sofa and listen to music.* 回到家時，我喜歡倒在沙發上聽音樂。

▸ **FAIL** 失敗 **4** [I] to fail suddenly or completely 突然失敗；崩潰；瓦解 SYN **break down**：*Talks between management and unions have collapsed.* 資方與工會的談判已告破裂。◇ *All opposition to the plan has collapsed.* 所有反對此計劃的力量均已消除。

▸ **OF PRICES/CURRENCIES** 價格；貨幣 **5** [I] to decrease suddenly in amount or value（突然）降價，貶值；暴跌：*Share prices collapsed after news of poor trading figures.* 在交易數額不佳的消息公佈後，股票價格暴跌。

▸ **FOLD** 摺疊 **6** [I, T] **~ (sth)** to fold sth into a shape that uses less space; to be able to be folded in this way 摺疊；套縮；可摺疊（或套縮）SYN **fold up**：*The table collapses for easy storage.* 這桌子可摺疊起來方便存放。

▸ **MEDICAL** 醫學 **7** [I, T] **~ (sth)** if a lung or BLOOD VESSEL **collapses** or **is collapsed**, it falls in and becomes flat and empty（肺或血管）萎陷

▸ **col·lapsed** AW *adj.*：*collapsed buildings* 坍塌的建築物 ◇ *a collapsed investment bank* 破產的投資銀行 ◇ *a collapsed lung* 萎陷的肺

■ ***noun***

▸ **FAILURE** 失敗 **1** [C, usually sing., U] a sudden failure of sth, such as an institution, a business or a course of action（機構、生意、行動等的）突然失敗，倒閉，崩潰：*the collapse of law and order in the area* 該地區治安的癱瘓 ◇ *The peace talks were* ***on the verge of collapse.*** 和平談判瀕於破裂。

▸ **OF BUILDING** 建築物 **2** [U] the action of a building suddenly falling（突然的）倒塌，塌陷，垮掉：*The walls were strengthened to protect them from collapse.* 圍牆已加固以防倒塌。

▸ **ILLNESS** 疾病 **3** [U, C, usually sing.] a medical condition when a person suddenly becomes very ill/sick, or when sb falls because they are ill/sick or weak 病倒；（因病或體弱的）昏倒，暈倒：*a state of* ***mental/nervous collapse*** 精神／神經的崩潰狀態 ◇ *She was taken to hospital after her collapse at work.* 她在工作時暈倒後被送進了醫院。

▸ **OF PRICES/CURRENCIES** 價格；貨幣 **4** [C, usually sing.] a sudden fall in value 突然降價；突然貶值；暴跌：*the collapse of share prices/the dollar/the market* 股票價格／美元／市場價格暴跌

col·laps·ible AW /kəˈlæpsəbl/ *adj.* that can be folded flat or made into a smaller shape that uses less space 可摺疊的；可套縮的：*a* ***collapsible chair/boat/bicycle*** 摺疊式椅子／小船／自行車

col·lar /ˈkɒlə(r); NAmE ˈkɑːl-/ *noun, verb*

■ ***noun*** **1** the part around the neck of a shirt, jacket or coat that usually folds down 衣領；領子：*a coat with a fur collar* 毛皮領大衣 ◇ *I turned up my collar against the wind* (= to keep warm). 我把衣領豎起來擋風。◇ *He always wears* ***a collar and tie*** *for work.* 他上班總是繫着領帶。➲ VISUAL VOCAB page V63 ➲ see also BLUE-COLLAR, DOG COLLAR, WHITE-COLLAR, WING COLLAR **2** a band of leather or plastic put around the neck of an animal, especially a dog（動物，尤指狗的）頸圈：*a* ***collar and lead/leash*** 頸圈和繫帶 **3** (*technical* 術語) a band made of a strong material that is put round sth, such as a pipe or a piece of machinery, to make it stronger or to join two parts together（管子或機器部件的）圈，箍 IDM see HOT *adj.*

■ ***verb*** (*informal*) **1 ~ sb** to capture sb and hold them tightly so that they cannot escape from you 抓住；捉住；揪住；逮住：*Police collared the culprit as he was leaving the premises.* 罪犯正離開現場時，警察逮住了他。**2 ~ sb** to stop sb in order to talk to them 攔住（某人要與其）談話：*I was collared in the street by a woman doing a survey.* 我在大街上給一個做民意調查的女人攔住問話。

col·lar·bone /ˈkɒləbəʊn; NAmE ˈkɑːlərboʊn/ *noun* either of the two bones that go from the base of the neck to the shoulders 鎖骨 SYN **clavicle** ➲ VISUAL VOCAB page V59

col·lard greens /ˈkɒlɑːd griːnz; NAmE ˈkɑːlərd/ *noun* [pl.] (*NAmE*) = KALE

col·lar·less /ˈkɒlələs; NAmE ˈkɑːlərləs/ *adj.* with no collar 無領的：*a collarless shirt* 無領襯衫

col·late /kəˈleɪt/ *verb* **1 ~ sth** to collect information together from different sources in order to examine and compare it 核對，校勘，對照（不同來源的信息）：*to* ***collate data/information/figures*** 核對資料／信息／數字 **2 ~ sth** to collect pieces of paper or the pages of a book, etc. and arrange them in the correct order 整理（文件或書等）▸ **col·la·tion** /kəˈleɪʃn/ *noun* [U]：*the collation of information* 信息的整理

col·lat·eral /kəˈlætərəl/ *noun, adj.*

■ ***noun*** [U] (*finance* 財) property or sth valuable that you promise to give to sb if you cannot pay back money that you borrow 抵押物；擔保品

■ ***adj.*** (*formal*) connected with sth else, but in addition to it and less important 附屬的；附加的；附帶的：*collateral benefits* 附加津貼 ◇ *The government denied that there had been any* ***collateral damage*** (= injury to ordinary people or buildings) *during the bombing raid.* 政府否認空襲期間有任何附帶性的破壞（即對平民或建築物的損害）。

col·league AW /ˈkɒliːg; NAmE ˈkɑː-/ *noun* a person that you work with, especially in a profession or a business 同事；同僚；同仁：*a colleague of mine from the office* 我辦公室的一位同事 ◇ *We were friends and colleagues for more than 20 years.* * 20 多年來我們既是朋友又是同事。◇ *the Prime Minister and his Cabinet colleagues* 首相及其內閣同僚

col·lect /kəˈlekt/ *verb, adj., adv.*

■ ***verb***

▸ **BRING TOGETHER** 彙集 **1** [T] to bring things together from different people or places 收集；採集 SYN **gather**：**~ sth** *to* ***collect data/evidence/information*** 收集資料／證據／信息 ◇ *We're collecting signatures for a petition.* 我們在為請願書收集簽名。◇ **~ sth from sb/sth** *Samples were collected from over 200 patients.* 已從 200 多名病人取樣。

▸ **AS HOBBY** 業餘愛好 **2** [T] **~ sth** to buy or find things of a particular type and keep them as a hobby 收藏；搜集；收集：*to* ***collect stamps/postcards, etc.*** 集郵、收藏明信片等 ➲ see also STAMP COLLECTING ➲ VISUAL VOCAB page V41

▸ **OF PEOPLE** 人 **3** [I] to come together in one place to form a larger group 聚集；集合；彙集 SYN **gather**：*A crowd began to collect in front of the embassy.* 人群開始聚集在大使館的前面。

▸ **INCREASE IN AMOUNT** 數量增加 **4** [I, T] to gradually increase in amount in a place; to gradually obtain more and more of sth in a place 聚積；積聚；積累 SYN **accumulate**：*Dirt had collected in the corners of the room.* 房間的角落裏積滿了灰塵。◇ **~ sth** *We seem to have collected an enormous number of boxes* (= without intending to). 我們似乎無意中積存了大量的盒子。◇ *That guitar's been sitting* ***collecting dust*** (= not being used) *for years now.* 那把吉他至今已塵封多年。

▸ **TAKE AWAY** 取走 **5** [T] to go somewhere in order to take sb/sth away 領取；收走；接走：**~ sth (from ...)** *What day do they collect the rubbish/garbage?* 他們哪天收運垃圾？◇ *The package is waiting to be collected.* 這包裹在等待人領取。◇ (*BrE*) **~ sb (from ...)** *She's gone to collect her son from school.* 她到學校接她兒子去了。

▸ **MONEY** 金錢 **6** [I, T] to ask people to give you money for a particular purpose 募捐；募集：**~ (for sth)** *We're collecting for local charities.* 我們正在為當地慈善機構募捐。◇ **~ sth (for sth)** *We collected over £300 for the appeal.* 我們為募捐籌集了 300 多英鎊。**7** [T] **~ sth** to obtain the money, etc. that sb owes, for example by going to their house to get it 收（欠款）；（上門）收（賬）：*to* ***collect rent/debts/tax*** 收租金；討債；徵稅

▸ **RECEIVE/WIN** 收到；贏得 **8** [T, I] **~ (sth)** to receive sth; to win sth 收到；贏得；獲得：*She collected £25 000 in compensation.* 她得到了 25 000 英鎊賠償金。◇ *to collect a prize/a medal* 獲獎；贏得獎牌

IDM ***collect yourself/your thoughts*** **1** to try to control your emotions and become calm（盡力）鎮定下來，斂

神專注：*I'm fine—I just need a minute to collect myself.* 我沒事，只是需要稍稍鎮定一下。**2** to prepare yourself mentally for sth 為…做好精神準備：*She paused to collect her thoughts before entering the interview room.* 她停下來定了定神，才走進面試室。

C

PHR V **col,lect sth↔'up** to bring together things that are no longer being used 把某物收起擱置：*Would somebody collect up all the dirty glasses?* 誰來把這些髒玻璃杯收拾一下好嗎？

■ *adj.* (*NAmE*) (of a telephone call 電話) paid for by the person who receives the call 由受話人付費的：*to make a collect call* 打對方付費電話 ➲ see also REVERSE *v.* (7)
▸ **col·lect** *adv.*：*to call sb collect* 給某人打由受話人付費的電話

Synonyms 同義詞辨析

collect

gather • accumulate • amass

These words all mean to get more of sth over a period of time, or to increase in quantity over a period of time. 以上各詞均含收集、聚積、積累之意。

collect to bring things or information together from different people or places; to gradually increase in amount in a place 指收集、採集、聚積、積累：*We've been collecting data from various sources.* 我們一直從各種渠道收集資料。◇ *Dirt had collected in the corners of the room.* 房間的角落裏積滿了灰塵。
NOTE People sometimes **collect** things of a particular type as a hobby. 收藏物品作為愛好用 collect：*to collect stamps* 集郵

gather to bring things together that have been spread around; to collect information from different sources 指收攏、歸攏（分散的東西），搜集、收集（情報）：*I waited while he* ***gathered up*** *his papers.* 他整理文件時我就在一旁等待。◇ *Detectives have spent months gathering evidence.* 偵探花了數月時間搜集證據。

COLLECT OR GATHER? 用 collect 還是 gather？

Both **collect** and **gather** can be used in the same way to talk about bringing together data, information or evidence. When talking about things, **gather** is used with words like *things, belongings* or *papers* when the things are spread around within a short distance. **Collect** is used for getting examples of sth from different people or places that are physically separated. * collect 和 gather 均可指收集資料、情報或證據。將分散在附近的東西、財物或文件收攏用 gather；從不同的人或分散的地方收集樣品用 collect。

accumulate (*rather formal*) to gradually get more and more of sth over a period of time; to gradually increase in number or quantity over a period of time 指積累、聚積，（數量）逐漸增加：*I seem to have accumulated a lot of books.* 我好像已經積存了很多書。◇ *Debts began to accumulate.* 債務開始增加。

amass (*rather formal*) to collect sth in large quantities, especially money, debts or information 指大量積累、積聚（尤指金錢、債務或情報）：*He amassed a fortune from silver mining.* 他靠開採銀礦積累了一筆財富。

PATTERNS

- to collect/gather/accumulate/amass **data/evidence/information**
- to accumulate/amass **a fortune/debts**
- **dirt/dust/debris** collects/accumulates
- to **gradually/slowly** collect/gather/accumulate (sth)

col·lect·able (also **col·lect·ible**) /kəˈlektəbl/ *adj.* worth collecting because it is beautiful or may become valuable 值得收藏（或收集、採集）的 ▸ **col·lect·able** (also **col·lect·ible**) *noun* [usually pl.]

col·lect·ed /kəˈlektɪd/ *adj.* **1** [not before noun] very calm and in control of yourself 鎮靜；冷靜；泰然：*She always stays* ***cool, calm and collected*** *in a crisis.* 她在危急關頭總是很冷靜鎮定，處之泰然。**2 ~ works, papers, poems, etc.** all the books, etc. written by one author, published in one book or in a set 收成全集的

col·lec·tion 🔑 /kəˈlekʃn/ *noun*
▸ **GROUP OF OBJECTS/PEOPLE** 一批物品；一群人 **1** 🔑 [C] a group of objects, often of the same sort, that have been collected（常指同類的）收集物，收藏品：*a* ***stamp/coin, etc. collection*** 郵票、硬幣等收藏品 ◇ *The painting comes from his private collection.* 這幅畫來自他的私人收藏。**2** [C] a group of objects or people 一批物品；一群人：*There was a collection of books and shoes on the floor.* 地板上有成堆的書和鞋。◇ *There is always a strange collection of runners in the London Marathon.* 每次總會有一批稀奇古怪的選手參加倫敦馬拉松比賽。
▸ **TAKING AWAY/BRINGING TOGETHER** 取走；聚集 **3** 🔑 [C, U] an act of taking sth away from a place; an act of bringing things together into one place 取走；拿走；聚集；聚積：***refuse/garbage collection*** 廢物／垃圾的收運 ◇ *The last collection from this postbox is at 5.15.* 這郵筒最後一次收信的時間是 5:15。◇ *Your suit will be ready for collection on Tuesday.* 你的西服可在星期二領取。◇ *The first stage in research is data collection.* 研究工作的第一步是收集資料。➲ compare PICKUP *n.* (4)
▸ **POEMS/STORIES/MUSIC** 詩歌；故事；音樂 **4** [C] a group of poems, stories or pieces of music published together as one book or disc 作品集：*a collection of stories by women writers* 女作家故事集
▸ **MONEY** 金錢 **5** [C] an act of collecting money to help a charity or during a church service; the money collected（為慈善機構或做禮拜時的）募捐，募集；募集的錢：*a house-to-house collection for Cancer Research* 為資助癌症研究進行挨門逐戶的募捐 ◇ *The total collection last week amounted to £250.* 上週的募捐總額達 250 英鎊。
▸ **NEW CLOTHES** 新衣服 **6** [C] a range of new clothes or items for the home that are designed, made and offered for sale, often for a particular season（常為季節性推出的）系列時裝（或家用品）：*Armani's stunning new autumn collection* 款式新穎靚麗的阿瑪尼秋裝系列
➲ COLLOCATIONS at FASHION

col·lect·ive /kəˈlektɪv/ *adj., noun*
■ *adj.* [usually before noun] **1** done or shared by all members of a group of people; involving a whole group or society 集體的；共有的；共同的：***collective leadership/decision-making/responsibility*** 集體領導／決策；共同責任 ◇ *collective memory* (= things that a group of people or a community know or remember, that are often passed from parents to children) 集體記憶 **2** used to refer to all members of a group 全體成員的；總體的：*The collective name for mast, boom and sails on a boat is the 'rig'.* 船的桅杆、帆桁和帆總稱為"索具"。▸ **col·lect·ive·ly** *adv.*：*the collectively agreed rate* 共同商定的費率 ◇ *We have had a successful year, both collectively and individually.* 我們這一年幹得不錯，無論是整體還是個人都取得了成功。◇ *rain, snow and hail, collectively known as 'precipitation'* (= as a group) 總稱為"降水"的雨、雪和冰雹
■ *noun* a group of people who own a business or a farm and run it together; the business that they run 企業集團；合作農場；集體企業：*an independent collective making films for television* 為電視製作影片的獨立集體企業

col,lective 'bargaining *noun* [U] discussions between a TRADE/LABOR UNION and an employer about the pay and working conditions of the union members（勞資雙方就工資和工作條件進行的）集體談判

col,lective 'farm *noun* a large farm, or a group of farms, owned by the government and run by a group of people 集體農場

col,lective 'noun *noun* (*grammar* 語法) a singular noun, such as *committee* or *team*, that refers to a group of people, animals or things and, in British English, can be used with either a singular or a plural verb. In American English it must be used with a singular verb.

集合名詞（如 committee 或 team，在英式英語中既可用單數也可用複數動詞；在美式英語中必須用單數動詞）

col,lective un'conscious *noun* [sing.] (*psychology* 心) the part of the unconscious mind that is thought to be shared with other humans because it is passed from generation to generation 集體無意識（普遍存在於人類，成因是遺傳）

col·lect·iv·ism /kə'lektɪvɪzəm/ *noun* [U] the political system in which all farms, businesses and industries are owned by the government or by all the people 集體主義；（一切農場、工商企業都歸政府或全民所有的）公有制 ▸ **col·lect·iv·ist** *adj.*

col·lect·iv·ize (*BrE* also **-ise**) /kə'lektɪvaɪz/ *verb* [often passive] **~ sth** to join several private farms, industries, etc. together so that they are controlled by the community or by the government 使公有化，使集體化（將若干私營農場、工業企業等合併，使之歸集體或政府所有）▸ **col·lect·iv·iza·tion, -isa·tion** /kə,lektɪvaɪ'zeɪʃn; *NAmE* -və'z-/ *noun* [U]

col·lect·or /kə'lektə(r)/ *noun* **1** (especially in compounds 尤用於構成複合詞) a person who collects things, either as a hobby or as a job 收集者；收藏家：*a stamp collector* 集郵者 ◇ ***ticket/tax/debt collectors*** 收票員；收稅員；討債人 **2** the chief officer of a district in some S Asian countries（南亞某些國家的）地方行政長官

col·lect·or·ate /kə'lektərət/ *noun* **1** (in some S Asian countries) the area under the authority of a COLLECTOR（一些南亞國家的）地方行政長官轄區，行政區 **2** the office in which a COLLECTOR is based 地方行政長官辦公室

col'lector's item *noun* a thing that is valued because it is very old or rare, or because it has some special interest 收藏家的珍藏；珍藏品；珍品

col·leen /kɒ'liːn; *NAmE* kɑː'l-/ *noun* **1** (*IrishE*) a girl or young woman 女孩；少婦 **2** (*old-fashioned* or *humorous*) a girl or young woman from Ireland 愛爾蘭女孩；愛爾蘭少婦

col·lege 🗝 /'kɒlɪdʒ; *NAmE* 'kɑːl-/ *noun* **1** 🗝 [C, U] (often in names 常用於名稱) (in Britain) a place where students go to study or to receive training after they have left school（英國）學院，職業學校，技術學校：*a college of further education* (= providing education and training for people over 16) 進修學院 ◇ *a secretarial college* 文秘職業學校 ◇ *the Royal College of Art* 皇家藝術學院 ◇ *a **college course/library/student*** 學院的課程／圖書館／學生 ◇ *She's **at college**.* 她在學院讀書。➲ see also COMMUNITY COLLEGE (1), SIXTH-FORM COLLEGE **2** 🗝 [C, U] (often in names 常用於名稱) (in the US) a university where students can study for a degree after they have left school（美國）大學：*Carleton College* 卡爾頓大學 ◇ *a **college campus/student*** 大學校園／學生 ◇ *a private college* 私立大學 ◇ *He got interested in politics when he was **in college**.* 他在上大學時就開始對政治感興趣了。◇ *She's away **at college** in California.* 她去加利福尼亞州上大學了。◇ *He's hoping to **go to college** next year.* 他希望明年上大學。➲ **COLLOCATIONS** at EDUCATION ➲ see also COMMUNITY COLLEGE (2) **3** [C, U] (*CanE*) a place where you can study for higher or more specialist qualifications after you finish high school 高等專科學校；高等職業學院 **4** [C, U] one of the separate institutions that some British universities, such as Oxford and Cambridge, are divided into（英國大學如牛津和劍橋中獨立的）學院：*King's College, Cambridge* 劍橋大學的國王學院 ◇ *a tour of Oxford colleges* 參觀牛津大學的各學院 ◇ *Most students live in college.* 大多數學生住在學院裏。 **5** (in the US) one of the main divisions of some large universities（美國一些規模大的大學的）學院：*The history department is part of the College of Arts and Sciences.* 歷史系是文理學院的一部份。 **6** [C+sing./pl. v.] the teachers and/or students of a college（學院的）師生，教師，學生 **7** [C] (especially in names, in Britain and some other countries 在英國和其他國家尤用於名稱) a SECONDARY SCHOOL, especially one where you must pay（尤指必須交費的）中學，公學：*Eton College* 伊頓公學 **8** [C] (usually in names 通常用於名稱) an organized group of professional people with special interests, duties or powers 學會；協會；社團：*the Royal College of Physicians* 皇家醫師協會 ◇ *the American College of Cardiology* 美國心臟病研究學會 ➲ see also ELECTORAL COLLEGE

British/American 英式／美式英語

college / university

- In both *BrE* and *NAmE* a **college** is a place where you can go to study after you leave secondary school. In Britain you can go to a **college** to study or to receive training in a particular skill. In the US you can study for your first degree at a **college**. A **university** offers more advanced degrees in addition to first degrees. 在英式英語和美式英語中，college 均指中學畢業後的學習場所。在英國，college 開設初級學位課高等或職業教育。在美國，college 開設初級學位課程。university 除開設初級學位課程外還有更高學位的課程。
- In *NAmE* **college** is often used to mean a **university**, especially when talking about people who are studying for their first degree. **The** is not used when you are talking about someone studying there. 在美式英語中，college 常指大學（university），尤其談及學士學位。表示上大學不用定冠詞 the：*My son has gone away to college.* 我兒子上大學去了。◇ *'Where did you go to college?' 'Ohio State University.'* "你在什麼地方上的大學？" "俄亥俄州立大學"
- In *BrE* you can say 英式英語可以說：*My daughter is at university.* 我女兒在上大學。In *NAmE* you cannot use **university** or **college** in this way. You use it with **a** or **the** to mean a particular university or college. 在美式英語中，university 和 college 不能這樣用，表示上某所大學，應在 university 或 college 之前加 a 或 the：*I didn't want to go to a large university.* 我當時不想去大的綜合性大學讀書。

col·le·gi·ate /kə'liːdʒiət/ *adj.* **1** relating to a college or its students 大學的；學院的；大學生的：*collegiate life* 大學生活 **2** (*BrE*) divided into a number of colleges 分為學院的：*a collegiate university* 設有若干學院的大學

col,legiate 'institute *noun* (in some parts of Canada) a public high school（加拿大某些地區的）公立高中

col·lide /kə'laɪd/ *verb* **1** [I] if two people, vehicles, etc. **collide**, they crash into each other; if a person, vehicle, etc. **collides** with another, or with sth that is not moving, they crash into it 碰撞；相撞：*The car and the van collided head-on in thick fog.* 那輛小轎車和貨車在濃霧中迎面相撞。◇ **~ with sth/sb** *The car collided head-on with the van.* 那輛小轎車與貨車迎面相撞。◇ *As he fell, his head collided with the table.* 他跌倒時頭部撞上了桌子。➲ **SYNONYMS** at CRASH **2** [I] **~ (with sb) (over sth)** (*formal*) (of people, their opinions, etc. 人、意見等) to disagree strongly 嚴重不一致；衝突；抵觸：*They regularly collide over policy decisions.* 他們經常在政策決策上發生衝突。➲ see also COLLISION

col·lider /kə'laɪdə(r)/ *noun* (*physics* 物) a machine for making two streams of PARTICLES move at high speed and crash into each other 對撞機（產生兩股高速運動的粒子相互衝撞）

col·lie /'kɒli; *NAmE* 'kɑːli/ *noun* a dog of which there are several types. Those with long pointed noses and long thick hair are popular as pets. Smaller collies with shorter hair are often trained to help control sheep on a farm. 科利牧羊狗

col·lier /'kɒliə(r); *NAmE* 'kɑːl-/ *noun* **1** (*old-fashioned, especially BrE*) = COAL MINER **2** a ship that carries coal 運煤船

col·liery /'kɒliəri; *NAmE* 'kɑːl-/ *noun* (*pl.* **-ies**) (*BrE*) a coal mine with its buildings and equipment 煤礦（包括建築物和設備在內）

col·li·gate /'kɒlɪgeɪt; *NAmE* 'kɑːl-/ *verb* [I, T] **~ (with sth)** | **~ sth (with sth) 1** (*formal*) if two ideas, facts, etc. **colligate**, or **are colligated**, they are linked together by a single explanation or theory（使）發生緊密聯繫

C

2 (*linguistics* 語言) if two words **colligate**, or **are colligated**, they occur together and are linked by grammar （使）結成類聯結

col·li·sion /kəˈlɪʒn/ *noun* [C, U] **~ (with sb/sth)** | **~ (between/of A and B)** **1** an accident in which two vehicles or people crash into each other 碰撞（或相撞）事故： *a collision between two trains* 兩列火車相撞事故 ◇ *Stewart was injured in a collision with another player.* 斯圖爾特與另一選手相撞受了傷。◇ *a **head-on collision*** (= between two vehicles that are moving towards each other) （車輛的）迎頭相撞 ◇ *a mid-air collision* (= between two aircraft while they are flying) （兩架飛機的）空中相撞 ◇ *His car was **in collision with** a motorbike.* 他的車和一輛摩托車撞上了。**2** (*formal*) a strong disagreement between two people or between opposing ideas, opinions, etc.; the meeting of two things that are very different （兩人之間或對立意見、看法等之間的）衝突，抵觸： *a collision between two opposing points of view* 兩種對立觀點的衝突 ◇ *In his work we see the collision of two different traditions.* 在他的作品中我們看到兩種不同傳統的衝突。

IDM **be on a colˈlision course (with sb/sth)** **1** to be in a situation which is almost certain to cause a disagreement or argument 幾乎發生衝突（或爭端、糾紛）： *I was on a collision course with my boss over the sales figures.* 我和我的老闆在銷售數字問題上差點發生爭執。**2** to be moving in a direction in which it is likely that you will crash into sb/sth 朝着可能會碰撞的方向移動；有可能相撞的趨勢： *A giant iceberg was on a collision course with the ship.* 巨大的冰山朝着可能與船發生相撞的方向漂移。

col·lo·cate /ˈkɒləkeɪt; *NAmE* ˈkɑːl-/ *verb* [I] (*linguistics* 語言) **~ (with sth)** (of words 詞語) to be often used together in a language 搭配；連用： *'Bitter' collocates with 'tears' but 'sour' does not.* * bitter 可與 tears 搭配，而 sour 則不可。◇ *'Bitter' and 'tears' collocate.* * bitter 和 tears 可搭配使用。▸ **col·lo·cate** /ˈkɒləkət; *NAmE* ˈkɑː-/ *noun*： *'Bitter' and 'tears' are collocates.* * bitter 和 tears 可搭配使用。

col·lo·ca·tion /ˌkɒləˈkeɪʃn; *NAmE* ˌkɑːl-/ *noun* (*linguistics* 語言) **1** [C] a combination of words in a language, that happens very often and more frequently than would happen by chance 詞組；組合： *'Resounding success' and 'crying shame' are English collocations.* * resounding success 和 crying shame 是英語裏的兩個搭配詞組。**2** [U] the fact of two or more words often being used together, in a way that happens more frequently than would happen by chance （詞語的）搭配，連用： *Advanced students need to be aware of the importance of collocation.* 層次較高的學生需要意識到詞語搭配的重要性。

col·lo·quial /kəˈləʊkwiəl; *NAmE* -ˈloʊ-/ *adj.* (of words and language 詞語和語言) used in conversation but not in formal speech or writing 會話的；口語的 **SYN** **informal** ▸ **col·lo·qui·al·ly** /-kwiəli/ *adv.*

col·lo·qui·al·ism /kəˈləʊkwiəlɪzəm; *NAmE* -ˈloʊ-/ *noun* a word or phrase that is used in conversation but not in formal speech or writing 口語；口語體；俗語

col·lo·quium /kəˈləʊkwiəm; *NAmE* -ˈloʊ-/ *noun* (*pl.* **col·lo·quia** /kəˈləʊkwiə; *NAmE* -ˈloʊ-/) a formal academic SEMINAR or conference 學術研討會；學術會議

col·lo·quy /ˈkɒləkwi; *NAmE* ˈkɑːl-/ *noun* (*pl.* **-ies**) (*formal*) a conversation 談話；會談

col·lude /kəˈluːd/ *verb* [I] (*formal, disapproving*) to work together secretly or illegally in order to trick other people 密謀；勾結；串通： **~ (with sb) (in sth/in doing sth)** *Several people had colluded in the murder.* 這起謀殺案是幾個人串通策劃的。◇ **~ (with sb) (to do sth)** *They colluded with terrorists to overthrow the government.* 他們與恐怖分子密謀推翻政府。

col·lu·sion /kəˈluːʒn/ *noun* [U] (*formal, disapproving*) secret agreement especially in order to do sth dishonest or to trick people 密謀；勾結；串通： *The police were corrupt and were operating **in collusion with** the drug dealers.* 警察腐敗，與毒品販子內外勾結。◇ *There was collusion between the two witnesses* (= they gave the same false evidence). 兩個證人串通作偽證。▸ **col·lu·sive** /kəˈluːsɪv/ *adj.*

colly·wob·bles /ˈkɒliwɒblz; *NAmE* ˈkɑːliwɑː-/ *noun* [pl.] (*old-fashioned, BrE, informal*) **1** a nervous feeling of fear and worry 緊張；擔心 **2** a pain in the stomach 肚子痛

colo·bus /ˈkɒləbəs; *NAmE* ˈkɑːl-/ (also **ˈcolobus monkey**) *noun* a small African MONKEY with a long tail, that eats leaves （非洲）疣猴

co·logne /kəˈləʊn; *NAmE* kəˈloʊn/ (also **eau de cologne**) *noun* [U] a type of light PERFUME 科隆香水；古龍香水

colon /ˈkəʊlən; *NAmE* ˈkoʊ-/ *noun* **1** the mark (:) used to introduce a list, a summary, an explanation, etc. or before reporting what sb has said 冒號 ➲ compare SEMICOLON **2** (*anatomy* 解) the main part of the large INTESTINE (= part of the BOWELS) 結腸 ➲ **VISUAL VOCAB** page V59

col·onel /ˈkɜːnl; *NAmE* ˈkɜːrnl/ *noun* (*abbr.* **Col.**) an officer of high rank in the army, the MARINES, or the US AIR FORCE （陸軍、海軍陸戰隊或美國空軍）上校： *Colonel Jim Edge* 吉姆 • 埃奇上校

Colonel ˈBlimp *noun* = BLIMP (2)

co·lo·nial /kəˈləʊniəl; *NAmE* -ˈloʊ-/ *adj.*, *noun*

■ ***adj.*** **1** connected with or belonging to a country that controls another country 殖民的；殖民國家的： *a colonial power* 佔有殖民地的強國 ◇ *Tunisia achieved independence from French colonial rule in 1956.* 突尼斯於 1956 年從法國的殖民統治下獲得獨立。◇ *Western colonial attitudes* 西方的殖民主義態度 ➲ see also COLONY (1), (2), (3) **2** (often **Colonial**) typical of or connected with the US at the time when it was still a British COLONY （美國）具有英屬殖民地時期特色的，英屬殖民地時期的： *life in colonial times* 英屬殖民地時期的美國生活

■ ***noun*** a person who lives in a COLONY and who comes from the country that controls it 生活在殖民地的宗主國居民： *British colonials in India* 生活在印度這塊殖民地上的英國人

co·lo·ni·al·ism /kəˈləʊniəlɪzəm; *NAmE* -ˈloʊ-/ *noun* [U] the practice by which a powerful country controls another country or other countries 殖民主義： *European colonialism* 歐洲殖民主義 ▸ **co·lo·ni·al·ist** *adj.*, *noun*： *colonialist laws* 殖民主義的法律

co·lo·nic /kəˈlɒnɪk; *NAmE* -ˈlɑːn-/ *adj.* (*anatomy* 解) connected with the COLON (= part of the BOWELS) 結腸的： ***colonic irrigation*** (= the process of washing out the COLON with water) 灌腸

col·on·ist /ˈkɒlənɪst; *NAmE* ˈkɑːl-/ *noun* a person who settles in an area that has become a COLONY 殖民地定居者

col·on·ize (*BrE* also **-ise**) /ˈkɒlənaɪz; *NAmE* ˈkɑː-/ *verb* **1 ~ sth** to take control of an area or a country that is not your own, especially using force, and send people from your own country to live there 在（某國家或地區）建立殖民地；移民於殖民地： *The area was colonized by the Vikings.* 這一地區曾淪為維京人的殖民地。**2 ~ sth** (*biology* 生) (of animals or plants 動物或植物) to live or grow in large numbers in a particular area （在某一地區）聚居，大批生長： *The slopes are colonized by flowering plants.* 坡地上長滿了開花植物。◇ *Bats had colonized the ruins.* 蝙蝠聚居在這片廢墟上。▸ **col·on·iza·tion**, **-isa·tion** /ˌkɒlənaɪˈzeɪʃn; *NAmE* ˌkɑːlənəˈz-/ *noun* [U]： *the colonization of the 'New World'* "新大陸" 的殖民 ◇ *plant colonization* 植物的移植 **col·on·izer**, **-iser** *noun*

col·on·nade /ˌkɒləˈneɪd; *NAmE* ˌkɑːl-/ *noun* a row of stone columns with equal spaces between them, usually supporting a roof 列柱；柱廊 ➲ **VISUAL VOCAB** page V14 ▸ **col·on·naded** /ˌkɒləˈneɪdɪd; *NAmE* ˌkɑːl-/ *adj.*

col·ony /ˈkɒləni; *NAmE* ˈkɑːl-/ *noun* (*pl.* **-ies**) **1** [C] a country or an area that is governed by people from another, more powerful, country 殖民地： *former British colonies* 前英國殖民地 **2** [sing.+sing./pl. v.] a group of people who go to live permanently in a colony 殖民地定居者群體 **3** [C+sing./pl. v.] a group of people from the same place or with the same work or interests who live in a particular city or country or who live together

（來自同一地方，職業或興趣相同的）聚居人群：*the American colony in Paris* 聚居巴黎的美國僑民 ◇ *an artists' colony* 聚居的藝術家 **4** [C] (*IndE*) a small town set up by an employer or an organization for its workers（雇主或機構設立的）職工城，職工居住區 **5** [C+sing./pl. v.] (*biology* 生) a group of plants or animals that live together or grow in the same place（同地生長的植物或動物）群，群體，集落：*a colony of ants* 蟻群 ◇ *a bird colony* 鳥群

color (*especially US*) = COLOUR **HELP** You will find most words formed with **color** at the spelling **colour**. 大多數由 color 構成的詞都可在拼寫為 colour 的詞條下找到。

col·or·ant (*especially US*) = COLOURANT

col·or·ation (*BrE* also **col·our·ation**) /ˌkʌləˈreɪʃn/ *noun* [U] (*technical* 術語) the natural colours and patterns on a plant or an animal（植物或動物的）自然色彩，自然花紋

col·ora·tura /ˌkɒlərəˈtʊərə; *NAmE* ˌkʌlərəˈtʊrə/ *noun* [U] (*music* 音) complicated passages for a singer, for example in OPERA 花腔：*a coloratura soprano* (= one who often sings coloratura passages) 花腔女高音歌手

ˈcolor bar (*especially US*) = COLOUR BAR

ˈcolor-blind (*especially US*) = COLOUR-BLIND

ˈcolor code (*especially US*) = COLOUR CODE

col·ored (*especially US*) = COLOURED

color·fast (*especially US*) = COLOUR FAST

col·or·ful (*especially US*) = COLOURFUL

ˈcolor guard *noun* (*US*) a small group of people who carry official flags in a ceremony 掌旗儀仗隊

col·or·ing (*especially US*) = COLOURING

Synonyms 同義詞辨析

colour

shade • hue • tint • tinge

These words all describe the appearance of things, resulting from the way in which they reflect light. 以上各詞均涉及顏色、色彩。

colour/color the appearance that things have, resulting from the way in which they reflect light. Red, green and blue are colours. 指顏色、色彩（如紅色、綠色、藍色）：*What's your favourite colour?* 你最喜歡的顏色是什麼？◇ *bright/dark/light colours* 鮮豔的／深／淺顏色

shade a particular form of a colour, especially when describing how light or dark it is. Sky blue is a shade of blue. 指色彩的濃淡深淺、色度（如天藍是藍色的一種）

hue (*literary* or *technical*) a colour or a particular shade of a colour 指顏色、色度、色調：*His face took on an unhealthy, whitish hue.* 他的臉上透出一絲病態的蒼白。

tint a shade or small amount of a particular colour; a faint colour covering a surface 指色調、淡色彩、一層淡色：*leaves with red and gold autumn tints* 金秋時節略呈紅黃色的樹葉

tinge a small amount of a colour 指微量、少許顏色：*There was a pink tinge to the sky.* 天空略帶一點淡淡的粉紅色。

TINT OR TINGE? 用 tint 還是 tinge？

You can say 可以說：*a reddish tint/tinge* or 或：*a tinge of red* 略帶一點淡紅色 but not 但不說：~~*a tint of red*~~ **Tint** is often used in the plural, but **tinge** is almost always singular. * tint 常用複數，但 tinge 幾乎總是用單數。

PATTERNS

- a **warm/rich** colour/shade/hue/tint
- a **bright/vivid/vibrant/dark/deep** colour/shade/hue
- a **pale/pastel/soft/subtle/delicate** colour/shade/hue
- a **light/strong/neutral/natural** colour/shade

col·or·ist, **col·or·istic** (*especially US*) = COLOURIST, COLOURISTIC

col·or·ize (*BrE* also **col·our·ize**) /ˈkʌləraɪz/ *verb* **~ sth** (*technical* 術語) to add colour to a black and white film/movie, using a computer process（借助計算機）給（黑白影片）着色

col·or·less (*especially US*) = COLOURLESS

ˈcolor line (also **ˈcolor bar**) (both *US*) (*BrE* **ˈcolour bar**) *noun* [usually sing.] a social system which does not allow black people the same rights as white people 膚色障礙；種族歧視；種族障礙

ˈcolor scheme (*especially US*) = COLOUR SCHEME

ˈcolor separation (*especially US*) = COLOUR SEPARATION

col·os·sal /kəˈlɒsl; *NAmE* kəˈlɑːsl/ *adj.* extremely large 巨大的；龐大的：*a colossal statue* 巨大的雕像 ◇ *The singer earns a colossal amount of money.* 那歌手現在可賺大錢了。

col·os·sus /kəˈlɒsəs; *NAmE* -ˈlɑːs-/ *noun* **1** [sing.] (*formal*) a person or thing that is extremely important or large in size 巨人；巨物 **2** [C] (*pl.* **co·lossi** /kəˈlɒsaɪ; *NAmE* -ˈlɑːs-/) an extremely large statue 巨型雕像

col·os·tomy /kəˈlɒstəmi; *NAmE* kəˈlɑːs-/ *noun* (*pl.* **-ies**) (*medical* 醫) an operation in which part of a person's COLON (= the lower part of the BOWELS) is removed and an opening is made in the ABDOMEN through which the person can get rid of waste matter from the body 結腸造口術

col·os·trum /kəˈlɒstrəm; *NAmE* -ˈlɑːs-/ *noun* [U] the substance produced in the breasts of a new mother, which has a lot of ANTIBODIES which help her baby to resist disease 初乳（含豐富的抗體，有助於嬰兒免疫）

col·our 🔑 (*especially US* **color**) /ˈkʌlə(r)/ *noun, verb*

■ ***noun***

▸ **RED, GREEN, ETC.** 顏色 **1** 🔑 [C, U] the appearance that things have that results from the way in which they reflect light. Red, orange and green are colours. 顏色；色彩：*What's your favourite colour?* 你最喜歡的顏色是什麼？◇ ***bright/dark/light colours*** 鮮豔的／深／淺顏色 ◇ *available in 12 different colours* 有 12 種不同的顏色可供挑選 ◇ *the colour of the sky* 天空的顏色 ◇ *Her hair is a reddish-brown colour.* 她的頭髮是棕紅色的。◇ *Foods which go through a factory process lose much of their colour, flavour and texture.* 經過工廠加工的食品會失去許多色澤、味道和質地。◇ *The garden was a mass of colour.* 花園裏五彩繽紛。 **2** 🔑 [U] (usually before another noun 通常用於另一名詞前) the use of all the colours, not only black and white 彩色：*a colour TV* 彩色電視機 ◇ ***colour photography/printing*** 彩色攝影／印刷 ◇ *a full-colour brochure* 彩色小冊子 ◇ *Do you dream **in colour**?* 你的夢是彩色的嗎？

▸ **OF SKIN** 皮膚 **3** 🔑 [U, C] the colour of a person's skin, when it shows the race they belong to（人種的）膚色：*discrimination on the grounds of race, colour or religion* 以種族、膚色或宗教信仰為理由的歧視 ◇ (*especially NAmE*) ***a person/man/woman of colour*** (= who is not white) 有色人種的人／男子／女子

▸ **OF FACE** 面孔 **4** [U] a red or pink colour in sb's face, especially when it shows that they look healthy or that they are embarrassed（尤指臉色的）紅潤，粉紅；（尷尬時的）臉紅：*The fresh air brought colour to their cheeks.* 新鮮空氣使他們的臉頰紅潤。◇ *Colour flooded her face when she thought of what had happened.* 她想起所發生的事情，臉漲得通紅。◇ *His face was drained of colour* (= he looked pale and ill). 他臉色蒼白。

▸ **SUBSTANCE** 物質 **5** [C, U] a substance that is used to give colour to sth 顏料；染料：*a semi-permanent hair colour that lasts six to eight washes* 經得起連續洗滌六至八次的非永久性染髮劑 ➲ see also WATERCOLOUR

▸ **INTERESTING DETAILS** 有趣的細節 **6** [U] interesting and exciting details or qualities 趣味；樂趣：*The old town is full of colour and attractions.* 這座古城姿采紛呈，引人入勝。◇ *Her acting added warmth and colour to the production.* 她的表演給這齣戲增添了生氣和趣味。◇ *to* *add/give/lend colour* to sth (= make it brighter, more interesting, etc.) 給某物增色 ➲ see also LOCAL COLOUR

▸ OF TEAM/COUNTRY, ETC. 隊、國家等 **7 colours** [pl.] the particular colours that are used on clothes, flags, etc. to represent a team, school, political party or country（用於服裝、旗幟等代表團隊、學校、政黨或國家的）色彩：*Red and white are the team colours.* 紅白兩色是這支隊的隊服色。◇ *Spain's national colours* 西班牙國旗的顏色 ◇ (*figurative*) *There are people of different political colours on the committee.* 委員會由來自不同政黨的成員組成。**8 colours** [pl.] (*especially BrE*) a flag, BADGE, etc. that represents a team, country, ship, etc.（代表團隊、國家、船等的）旗幟，徽章：*Most buildings had a flagpole with the national colours flying.* 大多數的建築物都有懸掛着國旗的旗杆。◇ *sailing under the French colours* 掛法國國旗航行

IDM **see the colour of sb's 'money** (*informal*) to make sure that sb has enough money to pay for sth 確定某人有支付能力 ➲ more at FLYING *adj.*, LEND, NAIL *v.*, TRUE *adj.* ➲ see also OFF COLOUR

■ *verb*

▸ PUT COLOUR ON STH 着色 **1** 🔑 [I, T] to put colour on sth using paint, coloured pencils, etc.（用顏料、彩色筆等）為…着色：*The children love to draw and colour.* 兒童喜歡畫畫和塗顏色。◇ *a colouring book* (= with pictures that you can add colour to) 塗色畫冊 ◇ **~ sth** *How long have you been colouring* (= DYEING) *your hair?* 你染髮有多長時間了？◇ **~ sth + adj.** *He drew a monster and coloured it green.* 他畫了一個怪物，把它塗成綠色。

▸ OF FACE 面孔 **2** [I] **~ (at sth)** (of a person or their face 人或其面孔) to become red with embarrassment（因尷尬而）臉紅 SYN **blush**：*She coloured at his remarks.* 她聽到他的話臉紅了。

▸ AFFECT 影響 **3** [T] **~ sth** to affect sth, especially in a negative way（尤指負面地）影響：*This incident coloured her whole life.* 這事件影響了她的一生。◇ *Don't let your judgement be coloured by personal feelings.* 不要讓你的判斷受到個人感情的影響。

PHR V **,colour sth↔'in** to put colour inside a particular area, shape, etc. using coloured pencils, CRAYONS, etc.（用彩色筆、蠟筆等）給…塗色，給…着色：*I'll draw a tree and you can colour it in.* 我來畫一棵樹，你給它塗上顏色。

col·our·ant /ˈkʌlərənt/ (*especially US* **col·or·ant**) *noun* a substance that is used to put colour in sth, especially a person's hair 着色劑；染色劑（尤指染髮劑）

col·our·ation (*BrE*) = COLORATION

'colour bar (*especially US* **'color bar, color line**) *noun* [usually sing.] a social system which does not allow black people the same rights as white people 膚色障礙；種族歧視；種族障礙

'colour-blind (*especially US* **'color-blind**) *adj.* **1** unable to see the difference between some colours, especially red and green 色盲的 **2** treating people with different coloured skin in exactly the same way（對待不同膚色的人）一視同仁的，無種族歧視的 ▸ **'colour-blindness** (*especially US* **'color-blindness**) *noun* [U]

'colour code (*especially US* **'color code**) *noun* a system of marking things with different colours so that you can easily identify them 色標，色碼（用不同顏色表示識別標記）▸ **'colour-coded** (*especially US* **'color-coded**) *adj.*：*The files have labels that are colour-coded according to subject.* 這些檔案按主題內容貼有色標。

col·oured 🔑 (*especially US* **col·ored**) /ˈkʌləd; *NAmE* -ərd/ *adj.*, *noun*

■ *adj.* **1** 🔑 (often in compounds 常構成複合詞) having a particular colour or different colours 有…色的；色彩…的：*brightly coloured balloons* 色彩鮮豔的氣球 ◇ *coloured lights* 彩燈 ◇ *She was wearing a cream-coloured suit.* 她穿着一身米色套裝。**2** (*old-fashioned* or *offensive*) (of a person 人) from a race that does not have white skin 有色人種的 **3 Coloured** (in South Africa) having parents who are of different races（南非）混血種的

■ *noun* **1** (*old-fashioned* or *offensive*) a person who does not have white skin 有色人種的人 **2 Coloured** (in South Africa) a person whose parents are of different races（南非）混血種的人

'colour fast (*especially US* **'color·fast**) *adj.* cloth that is **colour fast** will not lose colour when it is washed（織物）不褪色的，不變色的，不掉色的

col·our·ful (*especially US* **col·or·ful**) /ˈkʌləfl; *NAmE* -ərfl/ *adj.* **1** full of bright colours or having a lot of different colours 顏色鮮豔的；五彩繽紛的：*colourful shop windows* 五彩繽紛的商店櫥窗 ◇ *The male birds are more colourful than the females.* 這種鳥雄性比雌性更加色彩豔麗。**2** interesting or exciting; full of variety, sometimes in a way that is slightly shocking 有趣的；令人激動的；豐富多彩的（有時令人有少許震驚）：*a* ***colourful history/past/career*** 豐富多彩的歷史／過去／事業 ◇ *one of the book's most colourful characters* 這部書中最有趣的人物之一

col·our·ing (*especially US* **col·or·ing**) /ˈkʌlərɪŋ/ *noun* **1** [U, C] a substance that is used to give a particular colour to food（食物的）着色劑，色素：*red food* ***colouring*** 紅色食物着色劑 **2** [U] the colour of a person's skin, eyes and hair（皮膚、眼睛和頭髮的）顏色：*Blue suited her fair colouring.* 藍色適合於她白皙的膚色。**3** [U] the colours that exist in sth, especially a plant or an animal（尤指動植物的）天然色，色彩：*insects with vivid yellow and black colouring* 軀體帶有鮮黃色和黑色的昆蟲

col·our·ist (*especially US* **col·or·ist**) /ˈkʌlərɪst/ *noun* a person who uses colour, especially an artist or a hairdresser 用色彩者；（尤指）畫家，着色師，染髮師

col·our·istic (also **col·or·istic**) /ˌkʌləˈrɪstɪk/ *adj.* (*technical* 術語) showing or relating to a special use of colour 着色的；用色的：*colouristic effects* 着色效果

col·our·ize (*BrE*) = COLORIZE

col·our·less (*especially US* **col·or·less**) /ˈkʌlələs; *NAmE* -lərl-/ *adj.* **1** without colour or very pale 無色的；蒼白的：*a colourless liquid like water* 像水一樣無色的液體 ◇ *colourless lips* 蒼白的嘴唇 **2** not interesting 無趣的；枯燥的 SYN **dull**：*a colourless personality* 乏味的個性

'colour scheme (*especially US* **'color scheme**) *noun* the way in which colours are arranged, especially in the furniture and decoration of a room（尤指房間傢具和裝飾的）色彩設計，色彩搭配

'colour separation (*especially US* **'color separation**) *noun* (*technical* 術語) **1** [C] one of four images of sth made using only the colours CYAN, MAGENTA, yellow, or black. The four images containing these colours are then used together to print an image in full colour. 分色製版圖片（用青藍、洋紅、黃、黑製成的四張製版用單色圖片之一）**2** [U] the process that is used to do this 分色製版

'colour supplement *noun* (*BrE*) a magazine printed in colour and forming an extra part of a newspaper, particularly on Saturdays or Sundays（尤指星期六或星期日報紙的）彩色增刊

col·our·way /ˈkʌləweɪ; *NAmE* -lərw-/ *noun* (*BrE*) a colour or combination of colours which a piece of clothing, etc. is available in（衣料等可供挑選的）色彩設計，顏色搭配，配色：*The designs are available in two colourways: red/grey or blue/grey.* 這些式樣有兩組配色：紅灰色或藍灰色。

colt /kəʊlt; *NAmE* koʊlt/ *noun* **1** a young male horse up to the age of four or five（四或五歲以下的）雄馬駒 ➲ compare FILLY, STALLION **2** (*BrE*) a member of a sports team consisting of young players（運動隊的）年輕隊員，新手 **3 Colt™** a type of small gun 科耳特左輪手槍

colt·ish /ˈkəʊltɪʃ; *NAmE* ˈkoʊlt-/ *adj.* (of a person 人) moving with a lot of energy but in an awkward way 活躍但笨拙的

col·um·bine /ˈkɒləmbaɪn; *NAmE* ˈkɑːl-/ *noun* **1** [C, U] a garden plant with delicate leaves and pointed blue flowers that hang down 耬斗菜；藍花耬斗菜 **2 Col·um·bine** [sing.] a female character in traditional Italian theatre 科隆比納（意大利傳統戲劇中的女角）

Col·um·bus Day /kəˈlʌmbəs deɪ/ *noun* [U, C] a national holiday in the US on the second Monday in October when people celebrate the arrival of Christopher Columbus in America in 1492 哥倫布紀念日（美國國定假日，在 10 月第二個星期一，紀念哥倫布 1492 年到達美洲大陸）

col·umn /ˈkɒləm; *NAmE* ˈkɑːləm/ *noun*
1 a tall, solid, vertical post, usually round and made of stone, which supports or decorates a building or stands alone as a MONUMENT 柱；（通常為）圓形石柱；紀念柱：*The temple is supported by marble columns.* 這座廟宇由大理石柱支撐。◇ *Nelson's Column in London* 倫敦的納爾遜紀念碑 ➲ VISUAL VOCAB page V14 **2** a thing shaped like a column 圓柱狀物；柱形物：*a column of smoke* (= smoke rising straight up) 煙柱 ➲ see also SPINAL COLUMN, STEERING COLUMN **3** (*abbr.* **col.**) one of the vertical sections into which the printed page of a book, newspaper, etc. is divided （書、報紙等印刷頁上的）欄：*a column of text* 一欄正文 ◇ *a dictionary with two columns per page* 每頁有兩欄正文的字典 ◇ *Put a mark in the appropriate column.* 在適當的欄裏標上記號。◇ *Their divorce filled a lot of* ***column inches*** *in the national papers* (= got a lot of attention). 他們的離婚引起了多家全國性報紙的關注。 **4** a part of a newspaper or magazine which appears regularly and deals with a particular subject or is written by a particular writer （報刊的）專欄，欄目：*the gossip/financial column* 漫談 / 財經專欄 ◇ *I always read her column in the local paper.* 我一直讀她在當地報紙上的專欄文章。➲ see also AGONY COLUMN, PERSONAL COLUMN **5** a series of numbers or words arranged one under the other down a page 縱行（數字或字）：*to add up a column of figures* 把縱行數字相加 **6** a long, moving line of people or vehicles （人或車輛排成行移動的）長列，縱隊：*a long column of troops and tanks* 部隊和坦克的長列縱隊 ➲ see also FIFTH COLUMN

col·um·nist /ˈkɒləmnɪst; *NAmE* ˈkɑːl-/ *noun* a journalist who writes regular articles for a newspaper or magazine 專欄作家

coma /ˈkəʊmə; *NAmE* ˈkoʊmə/ *noun* a deep unconscious state, usually lasting a long time and caused by serious illness or injury 昏迷：*to* ***go into/be in a coma*** 陷入 / 處於昏迷狀態

Com·an·che /kəˈmæntʃi/ *noun* (*pl.* **Com·an·che** or **Com·an·ches**) a member of a Native American people, many of whom live in the US state of Oklahoma 科曼切人（美洲土著，很多居於美國俄克拉何馬州）

co·ma·tose /ˈkəʊmətəʊs; *NAmE* ˈkoʊmətoʊs/ *adj.* **1** (*medical* 醫) deeply unconscious; in a coma 不省人事的；昏迷的 **2** (*humorous*) extremely tired and lacking in energy; sleeping deeply 困乏的；無精打采的；酣睡的

comb /kəʊm; *NAmE* koʊm/ *noun, verb*
■ ***noun*** **1** [C] a flat piece of plastic or metal with a row of thin teeth along one side, used for making your hair neat; a smaller version of this worn by women in their hair to hold it in place or as a decoration 梳子；篦子；壓髮梳 ➲ VISUAL VOCAB page V24 **2** [C, usually sing.] the act of using a comb on your hair 梳理（頭髮）：*Your hair needs a good comb.* 你的頭髮得好好梳理一下。 **3** [C, U] = HONEYCOMB **4** [C] the soft, red piece of flesh on the head of a male chicken （公雞的）雞冠 IDM see FINE-TOOTH COMB
■ ***verb*** **1** [T] **~ sth** to pull a comb through your hair in order to make it neat 梳，梳理（頭髮）：*Don't forget to comb your hair!* 別忘了梳一下頭髮！◇ *Her hair was neatly combed back.* 她的頭髮整齊地梳到後面。 **2** [T, I] to search sth carefully in order to find sb/sth 仔細搜索；搜尋 SYN **scour**：**~ sth** *I combed the shops looking for something to wear.* 我跑遍商店尋找可穿的東西。◇ **~ sth for sb/sth** *The police combed the area for clues.* 警察徹底搜索了那個地區以尋找線索。◇ **~ through sth (for sb/sth)** *They combed through the files for evidence of fraud.* 他們查遍檔案搜尋欺詐的證據。 **3** [T] **~ sth** (*technical* 術語) to make wool, cotton, etc. clean and straight using a special comb so that it can be used to make cloth 梳理（羊毛、棉花等）
PHR V **ˌcomb sth↔ˈout** to pull a comb through hair in order to make it neat or to remove knots from it 梳整；梳去（髮結）

com·bat /ˈkɒmbæt; *NAmE* ˈkɑːm-/ *noun, verb*
■ ***noun*** [U, C] fighting or a fight, especially during a time of war 搏鬥；打仗；戰鬥：*He was killed* ***in combat.*** 他在戰鬥中陣亡。◇ ***armed/unarmed combat*** (= with/without weapons) 武裝 / 非武裝對抗 ◇ *combat troops* 作戰部隊 ◇ *combat boots* 軍靴 ➲ see also SINGLE COMBAT
■ ***verb*** (**-t-** or **-tt-**) **1 ~ sth** to stop sth unpleasant or harmful from happening or from getting worse 防止；減輕：*measures to* ***combat crime/inflation/unemployment/disease*** 防止犯罪 / 通貨膨脹 / 失業 / 疾病的措施 **2 ~ sb** (*formal*) to fight against an enemy 戰鬥；與…搏鬥

com·bat·ant /ˈkɒmbətənt; *NAmE* ˈkɑːm-/ *noun* a person or group involved in fighting in a war or battle 參戰者；戰鬥人員；戰士 ➲ compare NON-COMBATANT

ˈcombat fatigue (also **ˈbattle fatigue**) *noun* [U] mental problems caused by being in a war for a long period of time 戰鬥疲勞

ˈcombat fatigues (also **ˈbattle fatigues**) *noun* [pl.] clothes that soldiers wear for fighting that are covered in brown and green marks to make them difficult to see （士兵穿的）戰鬥服，迷彩服

com·bat·ive /ˈkɒmbətɪv; *NAmE* kəmˈbætɪv/ *adj.* ready and willing to fight or argue 好戰的；好鬥的；好爭論的：*in a* ***combative mood/spirit*** 鬥志昂揚；銳氣旺盛

com·bats /ˈkɒmbæts; *NAmE* ˈkɑːm-/ (also **ˈcombat trousers**) *noun* [pl.] (*BrE*) = CARGO PANTS

combi = KOMBI

com·bin·ation /ˌkɒmbɪˈneɪʃn; *NAmE* ˌkɑːm-/ *noun*
1 [C] two or more things joined or mixed together to form a single unit 結合體；聯合體；混合體：*His treatment was a combination of surgery, radiation and drugs.* 對他的治療是把手術、放射和藥物結合起來。◇ *What an unusual combination of flavours!* 多麼與眾不同的混合風味啊！◇ *Technology and good management. That's a* ***winning combination*** (= one that will certainly be successful). 技術加良好的管理，這是取勝的組合。 **2** [U] the act of joining or mixing together two or more things to form a single unit 結合；聯合；混合：*The firm is working on a new product* ***in combination with*** *several overseas partners.* 這家公司與幾家海外合夥人在聯合開發新產品。◇ *These paints can be used individually or* ***in combination.*** 這些塗料可單獨或混合使用。 **3** [C] a series of numbers or letters used to open a combination lock （用於開密碼鎖的）數字或字母組合，字碼組合：*I can't remember the combination.* 我不記得密碼鎖的密碼了。 **4 combinations** (*BrE*) [pl.] a piece of underwear covering the body and legs, worn in the past（舊時的）連褲內衣

combiˈnation lock *noun* a type of lock which can only be opened by using a particular series of numbers or letters 密碼鎖；暗碼鎖；轉字鎖

com·bine *verb, noun*
■ ***verb*** /kəmˈbaɪn/ **1** [I, T] to come together to form a single thing or group; to join two or more things or groups together to form a single one （使）結合，組合，聯合，混合：*Hydrogen and oxygen combine to form water.* 氫與氧化合成水。◇ **~ with sth** *Hydrogen combines with oxygen to form water.* 氫與氧化合成水。◇ **~ to do sth** *Several factors had combined to ruin our plans.* 幾種因素加在一起毀了我們的計劃。◇ **~ sth** *Combine all the ingredients in a bowl.* 把所有的配料放在碗裏拌勻。◇ **~ sth with sth** *Combine the eggs with a little flour.* 把雞蛋和少量的麪粉攪勻。◇ **~ A and B (together)** *Combine the eggs and the flour.* 把雞蛋和麪粉攪勻。◇ *The German team scored a* ***combined total*** *of 652 points.* 德國隊綜合得分為 652 分。 **2** [T] to have two or more different features or characteristics; to put two or more different things, features or qualities together 兼有；兼備；使融合（或並存）：**~ sth** *We are still looking for someone who combines all the necessary qualities.* 我們仍在尋覓兼備所有必要才能的人選。◇ **~ A and/with B** *The hotel combines comfort with convenience.* 這家旅館既舒適又方

便。◇ *This model combines a telephone and fax machine.* 這種型號同時具備電話機和傳真機的功能。◇ *They have successfully combined the old with the new in this room.* 他們在這個房間裏成功地把古老和現代的風格融為一體。◇ *a kitchen and dining-room combined* 廚房兼飯廳 **3** 🗝 [T] **~ A and/with B** to do two or more things at the same time 同時做（兩件或以上的事）；兼做；兼辦：*The trip will combine business with pleasure.* 此次旅行將把公幹和遊玩結合起來。◇ *She has successfully combined a career and bringing up a family.* 她成功地兼顧了事業和撫養子女。 **4** [I, T] to come together in order to work or act together; to put two things or groups together so that they work or act together 合併；協力：*They combined against a common enemy.* 他們聯手對付共同的敵人。◇ **~ sth** (**with sth**) *the combined effects of the two drugs* 兩種藥物的複合療效 ◇ *You should try to combine exercise with a healthy diet.* 你應該把鍛煉和健康飲食結合起來。◇ *It took the* **combined efforts** *of both the press and the public to bring about a change in the law.* 這項法律的變更來自媒體和公眾的通力合作。**IDM** see FORCE *n.*

■ **noun** /ˈkɒmbaɪn; *NAmE* ˈkɑːm-/ **1** (*BrE* also **ˌcombine ˈharvester**) a large farm machine which cuts a crop and separates the grains from the rest of the plant 聯合收割機 **2** a group of people or organizations acting together in business 集團；聯合企業

comˈbining form *noun* (*grammar* 語法) a form of a word that can combine with another word or another combining form to make a new word, for example *techno-* and *-phobe* in *technophobe* 構詞成分，組合形式（能與另一詞或另一構詞成分構成新詞，如 technophobe 一詞中的 techno- 和 -phobe）

combo /ˈkɒmbəʊ; *NAmE* ˈkɑːmboʊ/ *noun* (*pl.* **-os**) **1** a small band that plays JAZZ or dance music 小型爵士樂隊；小型伴舞樂隊 **2** (*informal, especially NAmE*) a number of different things combined together, especially different types of food 混合物；（尤指食物的）雜燴，組合餐：*I'll have the steak and chicken combo platter.* 我要牛排和雞組合餐。

com·bust /kəmˈbʌst/ *verb* [I, T] **~** (**sth**) to start to burn; to start to burn sth 開始燃燒；開始燒

com·bust·ible /kəmˈbʌstəbl/ *adj.* able to begin burning easily 易燃的；可燃的 **SYN** **flammable**：***combustible material/gases*** 易燃材料／氣體

com·bus·tion /kəmˈbʌstʃən/ *noun* [U] **1** the process of burning 燃燒 **2** (*technical* 術語) a chemical process in which substances combine with the OXYGEN in the air to produce heat and light 燃燒過程

comˈbustion chamber *noun* a space in which combustion takes place, for example in an engine（發動機等的）燃燒室

come 🗝 /kʌm/ *verb, prep., exclamation, noun*

■ **verb** (**came** /keɪm/, **come**)

▸ **TO A PLACE** 地方 **1** 🗝 [I] to move to or towards a person or place 來：(**+ adv./prep.**) *He came into the room and shut the door.* 他進了房間，把門關上。◇ *She comes to work by bus.* 她乘公共汽車來上班。◇ *My son is coming home soon.* 我兒子很快就要回家了。◇ *Come here!* 到這兒來！◇ *Come and see us soon!* 快點來看我們吧！◇ ***Here comes*** *Jo!* (= Jo is coming) 喬來啦！◇ *There's a storm coming.* 暴風雨就要來了。◇ **~ to do sth** *They're coming to stay for a week.* 他們要來待上一星期。**HELP** In spoken English **come** can be used with **and** plus another verb, instead of with **to** and the infinitive, to show purpose or to tell sb what to do. 在英語口語中表示目的或告訴某人如何做時，come 可與 and 加上另一動詞使用，而不用 to 和動詞不定式：*When did she last come and see you?* ◇ *Come and have your dinner.* The **and** is sometimes left out, especially in *NAmE*. * and 有時被省掉，尤其在美式英語中：*Come* ***have*** *your dinner.* **2** 🗝 [I] **~** (**to …**) to arrive at or reach a place 來到；到達，抵達（某地）：*They continued until they came to a river.* 他們繼續往前一直來到河邊。◇ *What time did you come* (= to my house)? 你什麼時候到（我家）的？◇ *Spring came late this year.* 今年春天來得晚。◇ *Your breakfast is coming soon.* 你的早餐很快就到。◇ *Have any letters come for me?* 有給我的來信嗎？◇ *Help came at last.* 救援終於到了。◇ *The CD* ***comes complete*** *with all the words of the songs.* 這張唱片配有歌曲的全部歌詞。◇ *The time has come* (= now is the moment) *to act.* 採取行動的時機到了。 **3** 🗝 [I] to arrive somewhere in order to do sth or get sth 來做；來取；來拿：**~ for sth** *I've come for my book.* 我來拿我的書。◇ **~ about sth** *I've come about my book.* 我來拿我的書。◇ **~ to do sth** *I've come to get my book.* 我來拿我的書。◇ **~ doing sth** *He came looking for me.* 他來找我。 **4** 🗝 [I] to move or travel, especially with sb else, to a particular place or in order to be present at an event 來（尤指相聚、往某地或出席活動）：*I've only come for an hour.* 我來了才一個小時。◇ *Thanks for coming* (= to my house, party, etc.). 謝謝光臨。◇ **~** (**to sth**) (**with sb**) *Are you coming to the club with us tonight?* 你今晚和我們一起去俱樂部嗎？◇ **~ doing sth** *Why don't you come skating tonight?* 今晚來溜冰好嗎？

▸ **RUNNING/HURRYING ETC.** 奔跑、匆忙等 **5** 🗝 [I] **~ doing sth** (**+ adv./prep.**) to move in a particular way or while doing sth else（以某種方式）來；邊…邊來：*The children came running into the room.* 孩子們跑着進了房間。

▸ **TRAVEL** 行進 **6** 🗝 [I] **+ noun** to travel a particular distance 行進（某段距離）：*We've come 50 miles this morning.* 我們今天上午走了 50 英里。◇ (*figurative*) *The company has* ***come a long way*** (= made lot of progress) *in the last 5 years.* 公司在過去的 5 年裏取得了巨大進步。

▸ **HAPPEN** 發生 **7** 🗝 [I] to happen 發生：*The agreement came after several hours of negotiations.* 協議經過幾小時的談判後才達成。◇ *The rains came too late to do any good.* 這場雨來得太晚，什麼用也沒有。◇ **~ as sth** *Her death came as a terrible shock to us.* 她的死使我們極為震驚。◇ *His resignation came as no surprise.* 他的辭職毫不令人驚訝。 **8** [T] **~ to do sth** used in questions to talk about how or why sth happened（用於疑問句，表示怎麼或為什麼）：*How did he come to break his leg?* 他怎麼把腿弄斷的？◇ *How do you come to be so late?* 你怎麼這麼晚才來？ ➲ see also HOW COME?

▸ **TO A POSITION/STATE** 位置；狀態 **9** 🗝 [I] **+ adv./prep.** (not used in the progressive tenses 不用於進行時) to have a particular position 位於，處於（某位置）：*That comes a long way down my list of priorities.* 在我非做不可的事情當中，那事較不重要。◇ *His family comes first* (= is the most important thing in his life). 他把家庭放在首位。◇ *She came second* (= received the second highest score) *in the exam.* 她這次考試名列第二。 **10** 🗝 [I] **~ to/into sth** used in many expressions to show that sth has reached a particular state（用於許多詞組）達到，進入（某種狀態）：*At last winter* ***came to an end.*** 冬天終於結束了。◇ *He* ***came to power*** *in 2006.* 他於 2006 年上台執政。◇ *When will they* ***come to a decision?*** 他們何時會作出決定？◇ *The trees are coming into leaf.* 樹開始長葉子了。 **11** 🗝 [I] (not used in the progressive tenses 不用於進行時) (of goods, products, etc. 貨品、產品等) to be available or to exist in a particular way 可提供；有（貨）：**~ in sth** *This dress comes in black and red.* 這款連衣裙有黑、紅兩種顏色。◇ **+ adj.** (*informal*) *New cars don't* ***come cheap*** (= they are expensive). 新汽車沒有便宜的。 **12** 🗝 [I, T] to become 成為；變成；變得：**+ adj.** *The buttons had come undone.* 鈕釦都鬆開了。◇ *The handle came loose.* 這把手鬆了。◇ *Everything will* ***come right*** *in the end.* 一切到最後都會好起來的。◇ **~ to do sth** *This design came to be known as the Oriental style.* 這種設計後來被稱為東方風格。 **13** [T] **~ to do sth** to reach a point where you realize, understand or believe sth 達到（認識、理解或相信的程度）：*In time she came to love him.* 她終於愛上了他。◇ *She had come to see the problem in a new light.* 她開始用新的角度來看待這個問題。◇ *I've come to expect this kind of behaviour from him.* 對於他的這種舉止我漸漸不感到意外了。

▸ **SEX** 性 **14** [I] (*slang*) to have an ORGASM 達到性高潮

IDM Most idioms containing **come** are at the entries for the nouns or adjectives in the idioms, for example **come a cropper** is at **cropper**. 大多數含 come 的習語，都可在該等習語中的名詞或形容詞相關詞條找到，如 come a cropper 在詞條 cropper 下。 **be as ˌclever, ˌstupid, etc. as they ˈcome** (*informal*) to be very clever, stupid, etc. 非常聰明（或愚蠢等） **ˌcome aˈgain?** (*informal*) used to ask sb to repeat sth（要求重複）再說一遍，你說什麼來着：*'She's an entomologist.' 'Come again?' 'An* *entomologist—she studies insects.'* "她是昆蟲學家。" "請再說一遍？" "昆蟲學家 —— 她是研究昆蟲的。" **ˌcome and ˈgo 1** to arrive and leave; to move freely 來去；來往；自由走動：*They had a party next door—we heard people **coming and going** all night.* 他們在隔壁聚會，我們整夜都聽見有人來來往往的聲音。 **2** to be present for a short time and then go away 時來時去；忽隱忽現：*The pain in my leg comes and goes.* 我的腿時而疼時而不疼。 **ˌcome ˈeasily, ˈnaturally, etc. to sb** (of an activity, a skill, etc. 活動、技能等) to be easy, natural, etc. for sb to do（對某人而言）輕而易舉（或生來就會等）：*Acting comes naturally to her.* 她天生就會表演。 **ˌcome over (all) ˈfaint, ˈdizzy, ˈgiddy, etc.** (*old-fashioned, BrE, informal*) to suddenly feel ill/sick or faint 突然感到昏眩（或眩暈、頭暈等） **come to ˈnothing | not ˈcome to anything** to be unsuccessful; to have no successful result 不成功；失敗；毫無成果：*How sad that all his hard work should come to nothing.* 他的所有辛勤勞動竟全部付諸東流，太讓人傷心了。◇ *Her plans didn't come to anything.* 她的計劃全落空了。 **come to ˈthat | if it comes to ˈthat** (*informal, especially BrE*) used to introduce sth extra that is connected with what has just been said（引出與剛提及的事物相關的事）說起…來，既然如此，假如那樣的話：*I don't really trust him—nor his wife, come to that.* 我並不真的信任他。說起信任，我也不信任他的妻子。 **ˌcome what ˈmay** despite any problems or difficulties you may have 不管出現什麼問題；無論有什麼困難；不管怎樣：*He promised to support her come what may.* 他答應不管出現什麼問題都支持她。 **how come (…)?** 🔑 used to say you do not understand how sth can happen and would like an explanation（用以表示不理解情況是如何發生的，希望得到解釋）怎麼回事，怎麼發生的，怎樣解釋：*If she spent five years in Paris, how come her French is so bad?* 既然她在巴黎待了五年，她的法語怎麼還會這樣糟糕？ **not ˈcome to much** to not be important or successful 不重要；無關緊要；不成功 **to ˈcome** (used after a noun 用於名詞後) in the future 將來；未來的：*They may well regret the decision **in years to come**.* 他們很可能在以後的年月裏會為這個決定而後悔。◇ *This will be a problem **for some time to come*** (= for a period of time in the future). 這將是未來一段時期裏的一個問題。 **when it comes to sth/to doing sth** 🔑 when it is a question of sth 當涉及某事（或做某事）時：*When it comes to getting things done, he's useless.* 一涉及做事，他便不中用了。 **where sb is ˈcoming from** (*informal*) somebody's ideas, beliefs, personality, etc. that makes them say what they have said（決定某人言論的）某人的全部背景：*I see where you're coming from* (= I understand what you mean). 我明白你究竟是什麼意思。

PHR V **ˌcome aˈbout (that …)** to happen 發生：*Can you tell me how the accident came about?* 你能告訴我事故是怎樣發生的嗎？

ˌcome aˈcross (also **ˌcome ˈover**) **1** to be understood 被理解；被弄懂：*He spoke for a long time but his meaning didn't really come across.* 他講了很久，但並沒有人真正理解他的意思。 **2** to make a particular impression 給人以…印象；使產生…印象：*She comes across well in interviews.* 她在面試中常給人留下很好的印象。◇ *He came over as a sympathetic person.* 他給人的印象是一個富有同情心的人。 **ˈcome across sb/sth** 🔑 [no passive] to meet or find sb/sth by chance（偶然）遇見，碰見，發現：*I came across children sleeping under bridges.* 我偶然發現睡在橋下的孩子。◇ *She came across some old photographs in a drawer.* 她在抽屜裏偶然發現了一些舊照片。 **ˌcome aˈcross (with sth)** [no passive] to provide or supply sth when you need it（需要時）提供，供給，給予：*I hoped she'd come across with some more information.* 我希望她能再提供更多的信息。

ˌcome ˈafter sb [no passive] to chase or follow sb 追趕；追逐；追隨

ˌcome aˈlong 1 to arrive; to appear 到達；抵達；出現：*When the right opportunity comes along, she'll take it.* 適當的機會來臨時，她會抓住的。 **2** to go somewhere with sb 跟隨；跟着來：*I'm glad you came along.* 有你跟我一起來，我很高興。 **3** (*informal*) to improve or develop in the way that you want 進步；進展 **SYN** **progress**：*Your French has come along a lot recently.* 你的法語最近進步很大。 **4** used in orders to tell sb to hurry, or to try harder（用於命令）趕快，加把勁：*Come along! We're late.* 快點！我們遲到了。◇ *Come along! It's easy!* 再加把勁！這很容易！

ˌcome aˈpart to break into pieces 破碎；破裂：*The book just came apart in my hands.* 這本書就在我手中散開了。◇ (*figurative*) *My whole life had **come apart at the seams**.* 我的整個生活都崩潰了。

ˌcome aˈround/ˈround 1 🔑 (also **ˌcome ˈto**) to become conscious again 恢復知覺；蘇醒：*Your mother hasn't yet come round from the anaesthetic.* 你的母親麻醉後還沒有蘇醒過來。 **2** (of a date or a regular event 日期或有規律的事) to happen again 再度發生；再次出現：*My birthday seems to come around quicker every year.* 我的生日似乎一年比一年來得快。 **ˌcome aˈround/ˈround (to …)** 🔑 to come to a place, especially sb's house, to visit for a short time 短暫訪問（尤指某人的家）：*Do come around and see us some time.* 務必抽空來看看我們。 **ˌcome aˈround/ˈround (to sth)** to change your mood or your opinion 改變心態；改變觀點：*He'll never come round to our way of thinking.* 他絕不會改變觀點與我們的想法一致。

ˈcome at sb [no passive] to move towards sb as though you are going to attack them 撲向（某人）：*She came at me with a knife.* 她拿着刀子向我撲過來。◇ (*figurative*) *The noise came at us from all sides.* 噪音從四面八方向我們襲來。 **ˈcome at sth** to think about a problem, question, etc. in a particular way（用某方法）考慮，思考 **SYN** **approach**：*We're getting nowhere—let's come at it from another angle.* 我們這樣會毫無進展，還是換個角度考慮一下吧。

ˌcome aˈway (from sth) to become separated from sth 分離；脫離：*The plaster had started to come away from the wall.* 灰泥已開始從牆上脫落。 **ˌcome aˈway with sth** [no passive] to leave a place with a particular feeling or impression（帶着某種感覺或印象）離開：*We came away with the impression that all was not well with their marriage.* 我們離開時有一種印象：他們的婚姻並不十分美滿。

ˌcome ˈback 1 to return 回來；返回：*You came back* (= came home) *very late last night.* 你昨晚回來得很晚。◇ *The colour was coming back to her cheeks.* 她的雙頰又泛起了紅暈。◇ (*figurative*) *United came back from being two goals down to win 3–2.* 聯隊在先失兩球的情況下將比分扳回，最終以 3:2 取勝。 ➲ SYNONYMS at RETURN **2** to become popular or successful again 再度流行；再次成功：*Long hair for men seems to be coming back in.* 男子留長髮好像又在流行了。 ➲ related noun COMEBACK (2) **ˌcome ˈback (at sb) (with sth)** to reply to sb angrily or with force 回嘴；頂嘴；反駁：*She came back at the speaker with some sharp questions.* 她用一些尖銳的提問來反駁講者。 ➲ related noun COMEBACK (3) **ˌcome ˈback (to sb)** to return to sb's memory 恢復記憶；回想起：*It's all coming back to me now.* 現在我全都回想起來了。◇ *Once you've been in France a few days, your French will soon come back.* 只要在法國待上幾天，你的法語很快又會變得流利起來。 **ˌcome ˈback to sth** [no passive] to return to a subject, an idea, etc. 回到（主題、想法等）上來：*Let's come back to the point at issue.* 咱們還是回到問題的焦點吧。◇ *It all comes back to a question of money.* 一切又回到錢的問題上來了。

ˈcome before sb/sth [no passive] (*formal*) to be presented to sb/sth for discussion or a decision 被提交給…討論（或作決定）：*The case comes before the court next week.* 這案件在下週提交給法庭審理。

ˌcome beˈtween sb and sb [no passive] to damage a relationship between two people 損害…之間的關係；離間：*I'd hate anything to come between us.* 我不喜歡任何有損我們之間關係的事情。

ˌcome ˈby (*NAmE*) to make a short visit to a place, in order to see sb（為看望某人）作短暫拜訪：*She came by the house.* 她來家裏看了一下。 **ˈcome by sth 1** to manage to get sth 設法得到（或獲得）：*Jobs are hard to come by these days.* 如今找工作很難。 **2** to receive sth 收到；得到：*How did you come by that scratch on your cheek?* 你臉頰上的抓傷是怎麼來的？

ˌcome ˈdown 1 to break and fall to the ground 崩塌；坍塌：*The ceiling came down with a terrific crash.* 隨着一

C

C

聲可怕的巨響，天花板塌了下來。**2** (of rain, snow, etc. 雨、雪等) to fall 落下；降落：*The rain came down in torrents.* 大雨滂沱。**3** (of an aircraft 飛機) to land or fall from the sky 着陸；降落；從空中墜落：*We were forced to come down in a field.* 我們被迫降落在田野裏。**4** ⊶ if a price, a temperature, a rate, etc. **comes down**, it gets lower（價格、溫度、比率等）下降，降低：*The price of gas is coming down.* 煤氣價格在下跌。◇ *Gas is coming down in price.* 煤氣價格在下跌。**5** to decide and say publicly that you support or oppose sb 決定並宣佈（支持或反對）：*The committee came down in support of his application.* 委員會決定並宣佈支持他的申請。**6** ⊶ to reach as far down as a particular point 下垂，向下延伸（到某一點）：*Her hair comes down to her waist.* 她的頭髮垂至腰部。**ˌcome ˈdown (from …)** (*BrE, formal*) to leave a university, especially Oxford or Cambridge, at the end of a term or after finishing your studies（尤指在牛津或劍橋期末或學業結束後）離開大學，大學畢業 OPP **come up (to …)** **ˌcome ˈdown (from …) (to …)** to come from one place to another, usually from the north of a country to the south, or from a larger place to a smaller one 從…到…（通常指從一國的北部到南部，或從大地方到小地方）**ˌcome ˈdown on sb** [no passive] (*informal*) to criticize sb severely or punish sb 斥責；訓斥；懲罰：*Don't come down too hard on her.* 不要太嚴厲地責備她。◇ *The courts are coming down heavily on young offenders.* 法庭對年輕罪犯實行嚴懲。**ˌcome ˈdown (to sb)** to have come from a long time in the past（從很久以前）流傳下來：*The name has come down from the last century.* 這名稱是從上個世紀流傳下來的。**ˌcome ˈdown to sth** [no passive] to be able to be explained by a single important point 可歸結為；可歸納為：*What **it comes down to** is, either I get more money or I leave.* 歸結起來就是：不給我加薪，我就辭職。**ˌcome ˈdown with sth** [no passive] to get an illness that is not very serious 患，得，染上（小病）：*I think I'm coming down with flu.* 我想我得了流感。

ˌcome ˈforward to offer your help, services, etc. 主動提供（幫助或服務等）：*Several people came forward with information.* 有幾個人自動站出來提供了信息。◇ *Police have asked witnesses of the accident to come forward.* 警方呼籲事故的目擊者出來提供線索。

ˈcome from … ⊶ (not used in the progressive tenses 不用於進行時) to have as your place of birth or the place where you live 出生於；來自：*She comes from London.* 她是倫敦人。◇ *Where do you come from?* 你是什麼地方的人？**ˈcome from sth 1** ⊶ to start in a particular place or be produced from a particular thing 始於；產自；來自：*Much of our butter comes from New Zealand.* 我們的黃油大多產自新西蘭。◇ *This wool comes from goats, not sheep.* 這種羊毛是山羊毛，不是綿羊毛。◇ *This poem comes from his new book.* 這首詩出自他的新書。◇ *Where does her attitude come from?* 她的態度因何而起？◇ *Where's that smell coming from?* 那種氣味是哪裏來的？◇ *He comes from a family of actors.* 他出身於演員世家。◇ *'She doesn't try hard enough.' 'That's rich, **coming from you*** (= you do not try hard either).' "她沒有竭盡全力。""你自己也沒盡力，還說別人。" **2** = COME OF STH

ˌcome ˈin 1 when the TIDE **comes in**, it moves towards the land（潮水）上漲；漲潮 OPP **go out 2** to finish a race in a particular position（賽跑比賽中）取得（某名次）：*My horse came in last.* 我的馬跑了最後一名。**3** to become fashionable 變時髦；時興；流行：*Long hair for men came in in the sixties.* 男子留長髮在 60 年代流行開來。OPP **go out 4** to become available 可提供；可利用：*We're still waiting for copies of the book to come in.* 我們仍然在等這本書進貨。**5** to have a part in sth 在…中起作用；參與：*I understand the plan perfectly, but I can't see where I come in.* 我完全瞭解這項計劃，可是不明白我能起什麼作用。**6** ⊶ to arrive somewhere; to be received 到達；被收到：*The train is coming in now.* 火車現正進站。◇ *News is coming in of a serious plane crash in France.* 剛收到的消息說法國發生了一起嚴重的飛機失事事故。◇ *She has over a thousand pounds a month coming in from her investments.* 她每月從自己的投資中得到超過一千英鎊的收入。**7** to take part in a discussion 參加討論：*Would you like to come in at this point, Susan?* 蘇珊，你願意在此刻發表意見嗎？**8** (of a law or rule 法律或規則) to be introduced; to begin to be used 被推行；開始被採用 **ˌcome ˈin for sth** [no passive] to receive sth, especially sth unpleasant 遭到；受到：*The government's economic policies have come in for a lot of criticism.* 政府的經濟政策遭到了很多批評。**ˌcome ˈin (on sth)** to become involved in sth 捲入；陷入：*If you want to come in on the deal, you need to decide now.* 如果你要做這筆交易，你得現在作出決定。

ˌcome ˈinto sth [no passive] **1** to be left money by sb who has died 繼承，得到（遺產）：*She came into a fortune when her uncle died.* 她在叔叔去世後繼承了一大筆財產。**2** to be important in a particular situation（在某種情形下）是重要的：*I've worked very hard to pass this exam—luck doesn't come into it.* 我為通過這次考試下了很大的苦功，不是靠運氣。

ˈcome of/from sth to be the result of sth 是…的結果：*I made a few enquiries, but nothing **came of it** in the end.* 我做過一些查詢，但到頭來卻毫無結果。◇ **~ doing sth** *That comes of eating too much!* 那是吃得太多的結果！

ˌcome ˈoff 1 ⊶ to be able to be removed 能被去掉（或除去）：*Does this hood come off?* 這風帽能卸下來嗎？◇ *That mark won't come off.* 那污點去不掉。**2** (*informal*) to take place; to happen 舉行；發生：*Did the trip to Rome ever come off?* 去羅馬的事最後成了嗎？**3** (*informal*) (of a plan, etc. 計劃等) to be successful; to have the intended effect or result 成功；達到預期效果（或結果）：*They had wanted it to be a surprise but the plan didn't come off.* 他們本想一鳴驚人，然而計劃卻流產了。**4 ~ well, badly, etc.** (*informal*) to be successful/not successful in a fight, contest, etc.（搏鬥、比賽等）成功，不成功：*I thought they came off very well in the debate.* 我認為他們在辯論中表現非常出色。**ˌcome ˈoff (sth) 1** to fall from sth 從…掉下（或落下）：*to come off your bicycle/horse* 從自行車／馬上跌下 **2** ⊶ to become separated from sth 與…分離（或分開）：*When I tried to lift the jug, the handle came off in my hand.* 我剛想提起水壺，壺把子就掉在我的手中了。◇ *A button had come off my coat.* 我的外套掉了一顆鈕扣。**ˌcome ˈoff it** (*informal*) used to disagree with sb rudely（粗魯地表示不同意）別胡扯，別胡說，住口：*Come off it! We don't have a chance.* 別胡扯了！我們沒機會。**ˌcome ˈoff sth** [no passive] to stop taking medicine, a drug, alcohol, etc. 停止（服藥、吸毒、飲酒等）：*I've tried to get him to come off the tranquillizers.* 我試圖說服他停止服用鎮靜劑。

ˌcome ˈon 1 (of an actor 演員) to walk onto the stage 登台；出場；上場 **2** (of a player 運動員) to join a team during a game（比賽中）上場：*Owen came on for Brown ten minutes before the end of the game.* 終場前十分鐘，歐文上場替換了布朗。**3** ⊶ (*informal*) to improve or develop in the way you want 改進；改善；發展；完善：*The project is coming on fine.* 這項工程進展順利。**4** ⊶ used in orders to tell sb to hurry or to try harder（用於命令）趕快，加把勁：*Come on! We don't have much time.* 快點！我們時間不多了。◇ *Come on! Try once more.* 加把勁！再試一次。**5** ⊶ used to show that you know what sb has said is not correct（表示知道某人所說的話不正確）得了吧：*Oh, come on—you know that isn't true!* 咳，得了吧，你知道那不是真的！**6** (usually used in the progressive tenses 通常用於進行時) (of an illness or a mood 疾病或心情) to begin 開始：*I can feel a cold coming on.* 我覺得要感冒了。◇ *I think there's rain coming on.* 我看要下雨了。◇ **~ to do sth** *It came on to rain.* 天下起雨來了。**7** (of a TV programme, etc. 電視節目等) to start 開始：*What time does the news come on?* 新聞報道什麼時候開始？**8** ⊶ to begin to operate 開始運轉（或運行）：*Set the oven to come on at six.* 把烤箱設定在六點鐘開始烘烤。◇ *When does the heating come on?* 什麼時間來暖氣？**ˈcome on/upon sb/sth** [no passive] (*formal*) to meet or find sb/sth by chance 偶然遇見；偶然發現 **ˌcome ˈon to sb** (*informal*) to behave in a way that shows sb that you want to have a sexual relationship with them 勾引，勾搭（想與某人發生性關係）➲ related noun COME-ON **ˌcome ˈon to sth** [no passive] to start talking about a subject 開始討論（某一主題）：*I'd like to come on to that question later.* 我想稍後再討論那個問題。

ˌcome ˈout 1 when the sun, moon or stars **come out**, they appear（太陽、月亮或星星）出現，露出：*The rain stopped and the sun came out.* 雨停後太陽出來了。**2** (of flowers 花朵) to open 盛開；開花：*The daffodils came out early this year.* 水仙花今年開得早。**3** to be produced or published 出版；發行；發表：*When is her new novel coming out?* 她的新小說何時出版？**4** (of news, the truth, etc. 消息、真相等) to become known 被獲知；為人所知：*The full story came out at the trial.* 案情始末在審判時真相大白。◇ **it comes out that …** *It came out that he'd been telling lies.* 後來才知道他一直在說謊。**5** if a photograph **comes out**, it is a clear picture when it is developed and printed（照片）沖洗（或洗印）清楚：*The photos from our trip didn't come out.* 我們旅行的照片沖洗的效果不好。**6** to be shown clearly 顯示；顯出：*Her best qualities come out in a crisis.* 她的優秀品質在危難之中顯示了出來。**7** when words **come out**, they are spoken 說出；講出：*I tried to say 'I love you,' but the words wouldn't come out.* 我想說"我愛你"，但這話怎麼也說不出口。**8** to say publicly whether you agree or disagree with sth 公開表明（同意或不同意）：*He came out against the plan.* 他公開表示反對這個計劃。◇ *In her speech, the senator came out in favour of a change in the law.* 這位參議員在她的講話中公開贊成修改法律。**9** (*BrE*) to stop work and go on strike 罷工 **10** to no longer hide the fact that you are HOMOSEXUAL 不再隱瞞自己是同性戀者的事實；公開表明自己是同性戀者 **11** (of a young UPPER-CLASS girl, especially in the past 尤指舊時上層社會的少女) to be formally introduced into society（經正式介紹）初入社交界 **ˌcome ˈout (of sth) 1** (of an object 物體) to be removed from a place where it is fixed（從固定處）除掉，去掉：*This nail won't come out.* 這顆釘子拔不出來。**2** (of dirt, a mark, etc. 污垢、污跡等) to be removed from sth by washing or cleaning 洗掉；清除：*These ink stains won't come out of my dress.* 我衣服上的這些墨水斑點洗不掉。◇ *Will the colour come out* (= become faint or disappear) *if I wash it?* 我若用水洗，它會掉色嗎？**ˌcome ˈout at sth** [no passive] to add up to a particular cost or sum 總共；共計：*The total bill comes out at £500.* 賬單金額總計為 500 英鎊。**ˌcome ˈout in sth** [no passive] (of a person 人) to become covered in spots, etc. on the skin（皮膚上）佈滿（斑點等）：*Hot weather makes her come out in a rash.* 炎熱的天氣使她起了皮疹。**ˌcome ˈout of yourself** to relax and become more confident and friendly with other people 精神放鬆、更加自信和友好地與他人交往：*It was when she started drama classes that she really came out of herself.* 她是在開始學習戲劇課程時才真正不再害羞。**ˌcome ˈout of sth** [no passive] to develop from sth 由…產生（或形成）：*The book came out of his experiences in India.* 這本書取材於他在印度的經歷。◇ *Rock music came out of the blues.* 搖滾樂起源於布魯斯音樂。**ˌcome ˈout with sth** [no passive] to say sth, especially sth surprising or rude 說出（尤指令人吃驚或粗魯的話）：*He came out with a stream of abuse.* 他講了一連串的髒話。◇ *She sometimes comes out with the most extraordinary remarks.* 她有時說起話來語驚四座。

ˌcome ˈover 1 (*BrE, informal*) to suddenly feel sth 突然感到：**+ adj.** *to come over funny/dizzy/faint* 突然感到可笑／昏眩／眩暈 ◇ *I come over all shy whenever I see her.* 我每次看到她時都會突然感到很害羞。**2** = COME ACROSS：*He came over well in the interview.* 他在面試中給人留下了很好的印象。**ˌcome ˈover (to …)** to come to a place, especially sb's house, to visit for a short time（尤指到某人家中）短暫造訪 **ˌcome ˈover (to …) (from …)** to travel from one place to another, usually over a long distance（通常遠距離地）從…到，從…來：*Why don't you come over to England in the summer?* 你為何不在夏天來英格蘭呢？◇ *Her grandparents came over from Ireland during the famine.* 她的祖父母是在饑荒時期從愛爾蘭遷移過來的。**ˌcome ˈover (to sth)** to change from one side, opinion, etc. to another 改變立場（或看法等）**ˌcome ˈover sb** [no passive] to affect sb 影響某人：*A fit of dizziness came over her.* 她感到一陣頭暈目眩。◇ ***I can't think what came over me*** (= I do not know what caused me to behave in that way). 我不知道我是怎麼了。

ˌcome ˈround | ˌcome ˈround (to sth) (*BrE*) = COME AROUND

ˌcome ˈthrough (of news or a message 消息或信息) to arrive by telephone, radio, etc. or through an official organization（用電話、無線電等或由官方機構）傳來：*A message is just coming through.* 有消息剛傳來。**ˌcome ˈthrough (sth)** to get better after a serious illness or to avoid serious injury（重病後）康復；避免受嚴重傷害 **SYN** **survive**：*With such a weak heart she was lucky to come through the operation.* 她的心臟很弱，手術後能活下來真是幸運。**ˌcome ˈthrough (with sth)** to successfully do or complete sth that you have promised to do 履行諾言；實現諾言：*We were worried she wouldn't be able to handle it, but she came through in the end.* 我們擔心她沒有能力處理那件事，然而她最終說到做到了。◇ *The bank finally came through with the money.* 這家銀行終於兌現了那筆錢。

ˌcome ˈto = COME AROUND (1) **ˌcome to yourˈself** (*old-fashioned*) to return to your normal state 恢復常態 **ˈcome to sb** [no passive] (of an idea 主意) to enter your mind 被想出：*The idea came to me in the bath.* 我洗澡時想出了這個主意。◇ **~ that …** *It suddenly came to her that she had been wrong all along.* 她突然想到她一開始就錯了。**ˈcome to sth** [no passive] **1** to add up to sth 合計；共計；總共：*The bill came to $30.* 賬單金額總計為 30 元。◇ *I never expected those few items to come to so much.* 我根本沒想到就那麼幾件東西合計起來竟要花這麼多錢。**2** to reach a particular situation, especially a bad one 達到（某狀況，尤指壞的局面）：*The doctors will operate if necessary—but it may not come to that.* 必要時醫生會施行手術，但也許還不至於此。◇ *Who'd have thought things would come to this* (= become so bad)? 誰會想到事情竟會變成這個樣子？

ˌcome toˈgether if two or more different people or things **come together**, they form a united group 合成一體；結合；聯合：*Three colleges have come together to create a new university.* 三所學院合併成了一所新的大學。◇ *Bits and pieces of things he'd read and heard were coming together, and he began to understand.* 他把讀到和聽到的零碎片段綜合起來，便逐漸明白了。

ˈcome under sth [no passive] **1** to be included in a particular group 歸入；歸類：*What heading does this come under?* 這該歸入哪一個類目？**2** to be a person that others are attacking or criticizing 成為（攻擊或批評的）目標：*The head teacher came under a lot of criticism from the parents.* 校長受到了家長的很多批評。**3** to be controlled or influenced by sth 被…控制；受…影響：*All her students came under her spell.* 她所有的學生都被她迷住了。

ˌcome ˈup 1 (of plants 植物) to appear above the soil 長出地面；破土而出：*The daffodils are just beginning to come up.* 那些水仙花剛開始破土發芽。**2** (of the sun 太陽) to rise 升起：*We watched the sun come up.* 我們觀看了日出。**3** to happen 發生：*I'm afraid something urgent has come up.* 恐怕有緊急事情發生。◇ *We'll let you know if any vacancies come up.* 一有空缺，我們就會通知你。**4** to be mentioned or discussed 被提及；被討論：*The subject came up in conversation.* 談話中提到了這個話題。◇ *The question is bound to come up at the meeting.* 會上一定會討論這個問題。**5** (of an event or a time 事情或時間) to be going to happen very soon 即將發生（或出現、到來）：*Her birthday is coming up soon.* 她的生日就到了。**6** to be dealt with by a court（由法院）審理：*Her divorce case comes up next month.* 她的離婚案在下月審理。**7** if your number, name, ticket, etc. **comes up** in a betting game, it is chosen and you win sth（在博彩遊戲中指號碼、名字、獎券等）被抽中，中獎 **8** (*informal*) (usually used in the progressive tenses 通常用於進行時) to arrive; to be ready soon 來到；馬上備妥：*'Is lunch ready?' 'Coming up!'* "午餐準備好了嗎？""馬上就好！" **ˌcome ˈup (to …)** (*BrE, formal*) to arrive at a university, especially Oxford or Cambridge, at the beginning of a term or in order to begin your studies（尤指在牛津或劍橋學期開學時）到校上學 **OPP** **come down (from …)** **ˌcome ˈup (to …) (from …)** to come from one place to another, especially from the south of a country to the north or from a smaller place to a larger one 從…到…（通常指從一國的南部到北部，或從小地方到大地方）：*Why don't you come up to Scotland* for a few days? 你為何不上蘇格蘭來住幾天？ ˌ**come ˈup (to sb)** 🔑 to move towards sb, in order to talk to them（為攀談而）走到跟前，走近：*He came up to me and asked me the way to the station.* 他走到我跟前打聽去車站的路。 ˌ**come ˈup against sb/sth** [no passive] to be faced with or opposed by sb/sth 面對；遭到…的反對：*We expect to come up against a lot of opposition to the plan.* 我們預料這個計劃會遭到很多人的反對。 ˌ**come ˈup for sth** [no passive] **1** to be considered for a job, an important position, etc. 被考慮為…的候選人：*She comes up for re-election next year.* 她明年將再度參加競選。 **2** to be reaching the time when sth must be done 接近（期限）：*His contract is coming up for renewal.* 他的合同快到續訂期了。 ˌ**come ˈup to sth** [no passive] **1** 🔑 to reach as far as a particular point 達到（某點）：*The water came up to my neck.* 水淹到了我的脖子。 **2** 🔑 to reach an acceptable level or standard 達到（認可的水平或標準）：*His performance didn't really come up to his usual high standard.* 他的表現沒有真正達到他往常的高水平。◇ *Their trip to France didn't come up to expectations.* 他們的法國之行未盡如人意。 ˌ**come ˈup with sth** [no passive] to find or produce an answer, a sum of money, etc. 找到（答案等）；拿出（一筆錢等）：*She came up with a new idea for increasing sales.* 她想出了增加銷售量的新主意。◇ *How soon can you come up with the money?* 你什麼時候能拿出這筆錢？ ˈ**come upon sb/sth** = COME ON SB/STH

■ ***prep.*** (*old-fashioned, informal*) when the time mentioned comes（提及的時間）到來：*They would have been married forty years come this June.* 到今年六月他們結婚就有四十年了。

■ ***exclamation*** (*old-fashioned*) used when encouraging sb to be sensible or reasonable, or when showing slight disapproval（鼓勵某人要有理智或通情達理，或表示不太贊同）嗨，得啦，好啦：*Oh come now, things aren't as bad as all that.* 哦，好啦，情況並不是那麼糟。◇ *Come, come, Miss Jones, you know perfectly well what I mean.* 得啦，得啦，瓊斯小姐，你完全知道我的意思。

■ ***noun*** [U] (*slang*) SEMEN 精液；精子

come·back /ˈkʌmbæk/ *noun* **1** [usually sing.] if a person in public life makes a **comeback**, they start doing sth again which they had stopped doing, or they become popular again 復出；重返；再度受歡迎：*an ageing pop star trying to stage a comeback* 試圖重返歌壇的已經上了年紀的流行音樂歌星 **2** if a thing makes a **comeback**, it becomes popular and fashionable or successful again 再度流行並變得時髦；再度獲得成功 **3** (*informal*) a quick reply to a critical remark（對批評迅速作出的）反駁，回應 SYN **retort** **4** a way of holding sb responsible for sth wrong which has been done to you 可因自身受到傷害而追究某人的責任：*You agreed to the contract, so now you have no comeback.* 你同意了這份合同，所以現在你不能追究他人的責任了。

com·edian /kəˈmiːdiən/ *noun* an entertainer who makes people laugh by telling jokes or funny stories 滑稽演員；喜劇演員

com·edi·enne /kəˌmiːdiˈen/ *noun* (*old-fashioned*) a female entertainer who makes people laugh by telling jokes or funny stories 女滑稽演員；女喜劇演員

come·down /ˈkʌmdaʊn/ *noun* [usually sing.] (*informal*) a situation in which a person is not as important as before, or does not get as much respect from other people 失勢；落泊；潦倒

com·edy 🔑 /ˈkɒmədi; *NAmE* ˈkɑːm-/ *noun* (*pl.* **-ies**) **1** 🔑 [C, U] a play or film/movie that is intended to be funny, usually with a happy ending; plays and films/movies of this type 喜劇；喜劇片：*a romantic comedy* 浪漫喜劇 ◇ *slapstick comedy* 打鬧劇 ➲ see also BLACK *adj.* (9) ➲ compare TRAGEDY (2) ➲ see also SITUATION COMEDY **2** 🔑 [U] an amusing aspect of sth 滑稽；幽默；詼諧 SYN **humour**：*He didn't appreciate the comedy of the situation.* 他未領略到這種局面的滑稽可笑之處。

ˌ**comedy of ˈmanners** *noun* an amusing play, film/movie, or book that shows the silly behaviour of a particular group of people 風俗喜劇，風尚喜劇（諷刺某群體行為的戲劇、電影或書籍）

ˌ**come-ˈhither** *adj.* [only before noun] (of sb's expression 表情) appearing to be trying to attract sb sexually 勾引的；調情的：*a come-hither look* 挑逗的眼神

come·ly /ˈkʌmli/ *adj.* (*literary*) (especially of a woman 尤指女子) pleasant to look at 標致的；秀麗的 SYN **attractive**

ˈ**come-on** *noun* [usually sing.] (*informal*) an object or action which is intended to attract sb or to persuade them to do sth 引誘；誘惑；勸誘：*She was definitely giving him the come-on* (= trying to attract him sexually). 她肯定是在勾引他。

comer /ˈkʌmə(r)/ *noun* **1 all comers** [pl.] anyone who is interested in, or comes forward for, sth, especially a competition（尤指對比賽）感興趣的人，到場者，參加者：*The event is open to all comers.* 所有人均可參加這項比賽。 **2** (with adjectives 與形容詞連用) a person who arrives somewhere 到達者 ➲ see also LATECOMER, NEWCOMER **3** (*NAmE, informal*) a person who is likely to be successful 可能成功者

com·est·ible /kəˈmestɪbl/ *adj., noun* (*formal*)

■ ***adj.*** that can be eaten 可食用的 SYN **edible**

■ ***noun*** [usually pl.] an item of food 食物

comet /ˈkɒmɪt; *NAmE* ˈkɑːmət/ *noun* a mass of ice and dust that moves around the sun and looks like a bright star with a tail 彗星；掃帚星

come·up·pance /kʌmˈʌpəns/ *noun* [sing.] (*informal*) a punishment for sth bad that you have done, that other people feel you really deserve 報應；應得的懲罰：*I was glad to see that the bad guy **got his comeuppance** at the end of the movie.* 我很高興看到那個壞蛋在電影的結尾受到了應有的懲罰。

com·fit /ˈkʌmfɪt/ *noun* (*old-fashioned*) a sweet/candy consisting of a nut, seed or fruit covered with sugar 果仁糖果；蜜餞

com·fort 🔑 /ˈkʌmfət; *NAmE* -fərt/ *noun, verb*

> **WORD FAMILY**
> **comfort** *noun, verb*
> **comfortable** *adj.* (≠ uncomfortable)
> **comfortably** *adv.* (≠ uncomfortably)
> **comforting** *adj.*

■ ***noun*** **1** 🔑 [U] the state of being physically relaxed and free from pain; the state of having a pleasant life, with everything that you need 舒服；安逸；舒適：*These tennis shoes are designed **for comfort** and performance.* 這些網球鞋的設計以舒適為本，打起球來發揮更出色。◇ *With DVD, you can watch the latest movies **in the comfort of** your own home.* 有了 DVD，你就可以在自己家裏舒舒服服地看最新的電影。◇ *The hotel offers a high standard of comfort and service.* 這家旅館提供高標準的舒適享受和優質服務。◇ *They had enough money to live **in comfort** in their old age.* 他們有足夠的錢舒舒服服地安度晚年。 **2** 🔑 [U] a feeling of not suffering or worrying so much; a feeling of being less unhappy 安慰；慰藉；寬慰 SYN **consolation**：*to **take/draw comfort from** sb's words* 從某人的話中得到安慰 ◇ *I tried to offer a few **words of comfort**.* 我試圖說上幾句安慰的話。◇ *The sound of gunfire was **too close for comfort**.* 炮火聲太近，讓人恐慌不安。◇ ***If it's any comfort** to you, I'm in the same situation.* 就當是一句安慰的話，我的情況也跟你一樣。◇ *His words were **of little comfort** in the circumstances.* 在這種情況下，他的話起不了什麼安慰作用。◇ ***comfort food*** (= food that makes you feel better) 安慰性食品 **3** 🔑 [sing.] a person or thing that helps you when you are suffering, worried or unhappy 令人感到安慰的人（或事物）：*The children have **been a great comfort to** me through all of this.* 在我度過這一切的日子裏，孩子們一直是我的莫大安慰。◇ *It's a comfort to know that she is safe.* 知道她安然無恙是令人寬慰的事。 ➲ see also COLD COMFORT **4** 🔑 [C, usually pl.] a thing that makes your life easier or more comfortable 舒適的設施（或條件）：*The hotel has all modern comforts/every modern comfort.* 這家旅館擁有各種現代化的舒適設施。◇ *material comforts* (= money and possessions) 物質上的舒適條件（錢財） ➲ see also CREATURE COMFORTS

■ ***verb*** to make sb who is worried or unhappy feel better by being kind and sympathetic towards them 安慰；撫慰；寬慰： **~ sb** *The victim's widow was today being comforted by family and friends.* 受害人的遺孀今天正受到親屬和朋友的安慰。◇ *She comforted herself with the thought that it would soon be spring.* 她想到春天很快就要來臨，以此來寬慰自己。◇ **it comforts sb to do sth** *It comforted her to feel his arms around her.* 感受到他的擁抱使她得到安慰。

com·fort·able 0━ /ˈkʌmftəbl; *BrE* also -fət-; *NAmE* also -fərt-/ *adj.*

▸ **CLOTHES/FURNITURE** 衣服；傢具 **1** 0━ (of clothes, furniture, etc. 衣服、傢具等) making you feel physically relaxed; pleasant to wear, sit on, etc. 使人舒服的；舒適的： *It's such a comfortable bed.* 這牀真舒服。◇ *These new shoes are not very comfortable.* 這雙新鞋穿起來不太舒服。◇ *a warm comfortable house* 溫暖舒適的房子 OPP **uncomfortable**

▸ **PHYSICALLY RELAXED** 輕鬆 **2** 0━ feeling physically relaxed in a pleasant way; warm enough, without pain, etc. 閒適的；舒服的；安逸的： *Are you comfortable?* 你感覺舒服嗎？◇ *She shifted into a more comfortable position on the chair.* 她換了一個更舒適的姿勢坐在椅子上。◇ *Please* ***make yourself comfortable*** *while I get some coffee.* 我去沖咖啡，您別拘束。◇ *The patient is comfortable* (= not in pain) *after his operation.* 病人手術後感覺良好。 OPP **uncomfortable**

▸ **CONFIDENT** 有信心 **3** 0━ confident and not worried or afraid 自信而無憂慮的；自在的： *He's more comfortable with computers than with people.* 比起與人相處，他和電腦打交道更能應付自如。 OPP **uncomfortable**

▸ **HAVING MONEY** 有錢 **4** 0━ having enough money to buy what you want without worrying about the cost 富裕的；寬裕的： *They're not millionaires, but they're certainly very comfortable.* 他們不是百萬富翁，但也很富裕。 ➲ SYNONYMS at RICH

▸ **VICTORY** 勝利 **5** quite large; allowing you to win easily 相當大的；易取勝的： *The party won with a comfortable majority.* 該政黨以明顯的多數票獲勝。◇ *a comfortable 2–0 win* 以 2:0 輕取

com·fort·ably 0━ /ˈkʌmftəbli; *BrE* also -fət-; *NAmE* also -fərt-/ *adv.*

1 0━ in a comfortable way 舒服地；舒適地；安逸地： *All the rooms were comfortably furnished.* 所有的房間都配置了舒適的傢具。◇ *If you're all sitting comfortably, then I'll begin.* 要是你們都坐好了，那麼我就開始。 **2** with no problem 沒問題；容易地 SYN **easily**： *He can comfortably afford the extra expense.* 他支付這些額外的費用毫無問題。◇ *They are comfortably ahead in the opinion polls.* 他們在民意測驗中遙遙領先。

IDM ˌ**comfortably ˈoff** having enough money to buy what you want without worrying too much about the cost 生活富裕；豐衣富食

com·fort·er /ˈkʌmfətə(r); *NAmE* -fərt-/ *noun* **1** a person or thing that makes you feel calmer or less worried 令人感到安慰（或慰藉）的人（或事物） **2** (*NAmE*) a type of thick cover for a bed 加襯芯牀罩 ➲ compare QUILT

com·fort·ing /ˈkʌmfətɪŋ; *NAmE* -fərt-/ *adj.* making you feel calmer and less worried or unhappy 令人安慰的： *her comforting words* 她說的那些令人安慰的話 ◇ *It's comforting to know that you'll be there.* 知道你要去那裏令人感到欣慰。 ▸ **com·fort·ing·ly** *adv.*

com·fort·less /ˈkʌmfətləs; *NAmE* -fərt-/ *adj.* (*formal*) without anything to make a place more comfortable 沒有舒適設施的

ˈ**comfort** ˌ**station** *noun* (*NAmE*) a room with a toilet in a public place, for example for people who are travelling 公共廁所

ˈ**comfort zone** *noun* **1** (sometimes *disapproving*) a place or situation in which you feel safe or comfortable, especially when you choose to stay in this situation instead of trying to work harder or achieve more 舒適區，放鬆區，安樂窩（尤指自我放鬆、不追求更高成就的狀態）： *Stepping outside your comfort zone and trying new things can be a great experience.* 走出你的安樂窩去嘗試一下新事物會是個很棒的經歷。◇ *We cannot afford to have anyone operating in a comfort zone.* 我們可用不起工作中貪圖安逸不求上進的人。 **2** (*approving*) (especially in sport 尤用於體育運動) a state in which you feel confident and are performing at your best 最佳狀態： *I knew if I could find my comfort zone I would be difficult to beat.* 我知道如果我能達到自己的最佳狀態就難以被打敗。

com·frey /ˈkʌmfri/ *noun* [U, C] a plant with large leaves covered with small hairs and small bell-shaped flowers 聚合草（長細絨大葉，開鈴狀小花）

comfy /ˈkʌmfi/ *adj.* (**com·fier**, **com·fi·est**) (*informal*) comfortable 舒服的；舒適的： *a comfy armchair/bed* 舒適的扶手椅／牀 HELP **More comfy** is also common as a comparative. 比較級 more comfy 也常用。

comic /ˈkɒmɪk; *NAmE* ˈkɑːmɪk/ *adj.*, *noun*

■ ***adj.*** **1** amusing and making you laugh 滑稽的；使人發笑的： *a comic monologue/story* 滑稽的長篇獨白／故事 ◇ *The play is both comic and tragic.* 這部劇既滑稽又悲慘。◇ *She can always be relied on to provide* ***comic relief*** (= sth to make you laugh) *at a boring party.* 在沉悶的聚會上，她總是能搞些笑料調劑氣氛。 ➲ SYNONYMS at FUNNY **2** [only before noun] connected with comedy (= entertainment that is funny and that makes people laugh) 喜劇的： *a comic opera* 滑稽歌劇 ◇ *a comic actor* 喜劇演員

■ ***noun*** **1** an entertainer who makes people laugh by telling jokes or funny stories 喜劇演員 SYN **comedian** **2** (*NAmE* also ˈ**comic book**) a magazine, especially for children, that tells stories through pictures （尤指兒童看的）連環畫雜誌 **3** **the comics** [pl.] (*NAmE*) the section of a newspaper that contains COMIC STRIPS （報章上的）連環漫畫欄

com·ic·al /ˈkɒmɪkl; *NAmE* ˈkɑːm-/ *adj.* funny or amusing because of being strange or unusual 可笑的；滑稽的；有趣的 ▸ **com·ic·al·ly** /-kli/ *adv.*

ˈ**comic strip** (also **car·toon**) (*BrE* also ˌ**strip carˈtoon**) (*NAmE* also **strip**) *noun* a series of drawings inside boxes that tell a story and are often printed in newspapers （常登載於報紙上的）連環漫畫

com·ing /ˈkʌmɪŋ/ *noun*, *adj.*

■ ***noun*** [sing.] **the ~ of sth** the time when sth new begins （新事物的）到來，來臨： *With the coming of modern technology, many jobs were lost.* 隨着現代技術的到來，許多工作崗位不復存在。

IDM ˌ**comings and ˈgoings** (*informal*) the movement of people arriving at and leaving a particular place 來來往往： *It's hard to keep track of the children's comings and goings.* 這些孩子來來往往，很難跟得上他們的行蹤。

■ ***adj.*** [only before noun] happening soon; next 即將發生的；下一個的： *in the coming months* 在隨後的幾個月裏 ◇ *This coming Sunday is her birthday.* 下個星期天是她的生日。

ˌ**coming of ˈage** *noun* [sing.] the time when a person reaches the age at which they have an adult's legal rights and responsibilities 成年；成人年齡

comma /ˈkɒmə; *NAmE* ˈkɑːmə/ *noun* the mark (,) used to separate the items in a list or to show where there is a slight pause in a sentence 逗號 ➲ see also INVERTED COMMAS

com·mand 0━ /kəˈmɑːnd; *NAmE* kəˈmænd/ *noun*, *verb*

■ ***noun***

▸ **ORDER** 命令 **1** 0━ [C] an order given to a person or an animal （給人或動物的）命令： *Begin when I give the command.* 我發出命令時開始。◇ *You must obey the captain's commands.* 你必須服從船長的命令。

▸ **FOR COMPUTER** 計算機 **2** 0━ [C] an instruction given to a computer 指令；命令

▸ **CONTROL** 控制 **3** 0━ [U] control and authority over a situation or a group of people 控制；管轄；指揮： *He has 1 200 men under his command.* 他掌管着 1 200 人。◇ *He* ***has command*** *of 1 200 men.* 有 1 200 人由他管轄。◇ *The police arrived and* ***took command of*** *the situation.* 警察到達後就控制了場面。◇ *For the first time in years, she felt* ***in command of*** *her life.* 多少年來第一次，她覺得生活掌握在自己的手裏。◇ *He looked relaxed and totally* ***in command of himself.*** 他看起來很輕鬆，有絕對的自信

C

完全能控制住自己。◇ *Who is* **in command** *here?* 這裏誰負責？ ➲ see also SECOND IN COMMAND

▸ **IN ARMY** 軍隊 **4 Command** [C] a part of an army, AIR FORCE, etc. that is organized and controlled separately; a group of officers who give orders（陸軍、空軍等的）兵團，軍區，指揮部，司令部：*Bomber Command* 轟炸機組的指揮部

▸ **KNOWLEDGE** 知識 **5** [U, sing.] **~ (of sth)** your knowledge of sth; your ability to do or use sth, especially a language 知識；（尤指對語言的）掌握，運用能力：*Applicants will be expected to have (a) good command of English.* 申請人必須精通英語。

IDM **at your com'mand** if you have a skill or an amount of sth **at your command**, you are able to use it well and completely 可自由使用；可支配 **be at sb's com'mand** (*formal*) to be ready to obey sb 聽候某人的吩咐；服從某人的支配：*I'm at your command—what would you like me to do?* 我聽從您的吩咐，您要我做什麼？ ➲ more at WISH *n.*

■ ***verb***

▸ **ORDER** 命令 **1** 🔑 [T] (of sb in a position of authority 掌權者) to tell sb to do sth 命令 **SYN** **order**：**~ sb to do sth** *He commanded his men to retreat.* 他命令手下撤退。◇ **~ sth** *She commanded the release of the prisoners.* 她下令釋放囚犯。◇ **+ speech** *'Come here!' he commanded (them).* "過來！"他命令（他們）道。◇ **~ that ...** (*formal*) *The commission intervened and commanded that work on the building cease.* 委員會進行了干預，下令那棟大樓必須停建。◇ (*BrE* also) *The commission commanded that work on the building should cease.* 委員會下令那棟大樓必須停建。

▸ **IN ARMY** 軍隊 **2** 🔑 [T, I] **~ (sb/sth)** to be in charge of a group of people in the army, navy, etc. 指揮，統率（陸軍、海軍等）：*The troops were commanded by General Haig.* 這些部隊由黑格將軍統率。

▸ **DESERVE AND GET** 應得 **3** [T, no passive] (not used in the progressive tenses 不用於進行時) **~ sth** to deserve and get sth because of the special qualities you have 應得；博得；值得：*to command sympathy/support* 值得同情 / 支持 ◇ *She was able to command the respect of the class.* 她贏得了全班的尊敬。◇ *The headlines commanded her attention.* 那些標題引起了她的注意。◇ *As a top lawyer, he can expect to command a six-figure salary.* 作為首屈一指的律師，他可望拿到六位數的薪資。

▸ **VIEW** 視野 **4** [T, no passive] (not used in the progressive tenses 不用於進行時) **~ sth** (*formal*) to be in a position from where you can see or control sth 居高臨下；俯瞰：*The hotel commands a fine view of the valley.* 從這家旅館俯瞰下面的峽谷一覽無餘。

▸ **CONTROL** 控制 **5** [T, no passive] (not used in the progressive tenses 不用於進行時) **~ sth** (*formal*) to have control of sth; to have sth available for use 控制；擁有…可供使用；掌管：*The party was no longer able to command a majority in Parliament.* 該黨已不能在國會中再佔有多數。◇ *the power and finances commanded by the police* 警方掌握的權力和資金

com·mand·ant /ˈkɒməndænt; *NAmE* ˈkɑːm-/ *noun* the officer in charge of a particular military group or institution 司令；指揮官

com,mand e'conomy *noun* = PLANNED ECONOMY

com·man·deer /ˌkɒmənˈdɪə(r); *NAmE* ˌkɑːmənˈdɪr/ *verb* **~ sth** to take control of a building, a vehicle, etc. for military purposes during a war, or by force for your own use（戰爭期間為軍事目的而）強徵，徵用；強佔 **SYN** **requisition**

com·mand·er /kəˈmɑːndə(r); *NAmE* -ˈmæn-/ *noun* **1** a person who is in charge of sth, especially an officer in charge of a particular group of soldiers or a military operation 負責人；（尤指）司令官，指揮官：*military/allied/field/flight commanders* 軍事 / 盟軍 / 戰地 / 飛行指揮官 ◇ *the commander of the expedition* 探險隊隊長 **2** (*abbr.* **Cdr**) an officer of fairly high rank in the British or American navy（英國或美國）海軍中校 **3** (*abbr.* **Cdr**) (in Britain) a London police officer of high rank（英國）倫敦高級警官

com,mander-in-'chief (*abbr.* **C.-in-C.**) *noun* (*pl.* **commanders-in-chief**) the officer who commands all the armed forces of a country or all its forces in a particular area 總司令；最高統帥

com·mand·ing /kəˈmɑːndɪŋ; *NAmE* -ˈmæn-/ *adj.* **1** [only before noun] in a position of authority that allows you to give formal orders 指揮的；統帥的：*Who is your commanding officer?* 誰是你們的指揮官？ **2** [usually before noun] if you are in a **commanding position** or have a **commanding lead**, you are likely to win a race or competition（賽跑或比賽）居領先位置的，遙遙領先的 **3** [usually before noun] powerful and making people admire and obey you 權威的；威嚴的：*a commanding figure/presence/voice* 威嚴的人物 / 氣派 / 說話聲 **4** [only before noun] if a building is in a **commanding position** or has a **commanding view**, you can see the area around very well from it 居高臨下的；視野寬闊的：*The castle occupies a commanding position on a hill.* 城堡佔據着山上居高臨下的位置。

com·mand·ment /kəˈmɑːndmənt; *NAmE* -ˈmæn-/ *noun* a law given by God, especially any of **the Ten Commandments** given to the Jews in the Bible 誡條（尤指《聖經》中上帝給猶太人的十誡之一） ➲ COLLOCATIONS at RELIGION

com'mand module *noun* (*abbr.* **CM**) the part of a SPACECRAFT that remains after the rest has separated from it, where the controls and the people that operate them are located（航天器中載人和控制儀器的）指揮艙，指令艙

com·mando /kəˈmɑːndəʊ; *NAmE* kəˈmændoʊ/ *noun* (*pl.* **-os**) a soldier or a group of soldiers who are trained to make quick attacks in enemy areas 突擊手；突擊隊；突擊隊員

IDM **go com'mando** (*informal, humorous*) to not wear underwear under your clothes 不穿內衣；空身穿外衣

com,mand per'formance *noun* [usually sing.] a special performance, for example at a theatre, that is given for a head of state（為國家元首舉行的）專場演出，御前演出

com·media dell'arte /kɒˌmeɪdɪə del ˈɑːteɪ; *NAmE* kəˌmeɪdɪə del ˈɑːrteɪ/ *noun* [U] (from *Italian*) traditional Italian theatre in which the same characters appeared in different plays 即興喜劇，假面喜劇（意大利的一種傳統戲劇，相同的角色出現在不同的戲劇中）

com·mem·or·ate /kəˈmeməreɪt/ *verb* **~ sth/sb** to remind people of an important person or event from the past with a special action or object; to exist to remind people of a person or an event from the past（用…）紀念；作為…的紀念：*A series of movies will be shown to commemorate the 30th anniversary of his death.* 為紀念他逝世 30 週年，有一系列的電影將要上映。◇ *A plaque commemorates the battle.* 設了一塊牌匾來紀念那次戰役。

com·mem·or·ation /kəˌmeməˈreɪʃn/ *noun* [U, C] an action, or a ceremony, etc. that makes people remember and show respect for an important person or event in the past 紀念；紀念儀式：*a commemoration service* 紀念儀式 ◇ *a statue* **in commemoration of** *a national hero* 紀念民族英雄的雕像

com·mem·ora·tive /kəˈmemərətɪv; *NAmE* -əreɪt-/ *adj.* intended to help people remember and respect an important person or event in the past 紀念的：*commemorative stamps* 紀念郵票

com·mence **AW** /kəˈmens/ *verb* [I, T] (*formal*) to begin to happen; to begin sth 開始發生；開始；着手：*The meeting is scheduled to commence at noon.* 會議定於午間召開。◇ *I will be on leave during the week commencing 15 February.* 我將從 2 月 15 日開始一週的休假。◇ **~ with sth** *The day commenced with a welcome from the principal.* 那天由校長致歡迎詞開始。◇ **~ sth** *She commenced her medical career in 1956.* 她於 1956 年開始行醫。◇ **~ doing sth** *We commence building next week.* 我們下週破土動工。◇ **~ to do sth** *Operators commenced to build pipelines in 1862.* 運營商於 1862 年開始興建管道。 ➲ SYNONYMS at START

com·mence·ment **AW** /kəˈmensmənt/ *noun* [U, C, usually sing.] **1** (*formal*) beginning 開始；開端：*the* commencement of the financial year 財政年度的開始 **2** (*NAmE*) a ceremony at which students receive their academic degrees or DIPLOMAS 學位授予典禮；畢業典禮 **SYN** **graduation**

com·mend /kə'mend/ *verb* **1 ~ sb (for sth/for doing sth) | ~ sb (on sth/on doing sth)** to praise sb/sth, especially publicly（尤指公開地）讚揚，稱讚，表揚：*She was commended on her handling of the situation.* 她因妥善處理了那個局面而受到表揚。◊ *His designs were* ***highly commended*** *by the judges* (= they did not get a prize but they were especially praised). 他的設計受到了評委的高度讚揚。 **2 ~ sb/sth (to sb)** (*formal*) to recommend sb/sth to sb 推薦；舉薦：*She is an excellent worker and I commend her to you without reservation.* 她工作出色，我毫無保留地把她推薦給你。◊ *The movie* ***has little to commend it*** (= it has few good qualities). 這部電影乏善可陳。 **3 ~ itself to sb** (*formal*) if sth **commends** itself to sb, they approve of it 受到贊同；得到認可：*His outspoken behaviour did not commend itself to his colleagues.* 他直言不諱的行為不受他同事的歡迎。 **4 ~ sb/sth to sb** (*formal*) to give sb/sth to sb in order to be taken care of 把…託付給（或委託於）：*We commend her soul to God.* 我們把她的靈魂託付給上帝。

com·mend·able /kə'mendəbl/ *adj.* (*formal*) deserving praise and approval 值得讚揚（或嘉許）的：*commendable honesty* 值得稱讚的誠實 ▸ **com·mend·ably** /-əbli/ *adv.*

com·men·da·tion /ˌkɒmen'deɪʃn; *NAmE* ˌkɑːm-/ *noun* **1** [U] (*formal*) praise; approval 讚揚；稱讚；贊成；嘉許 **2** [C] **~ (for sth)** an award or official statement giving public praise for sb/sth 獎品；獎勵；表揚：*a commendation for bravery* 因勇敢而受到的嘉獎

com·men·sal /kə'mensl/ *adj.* (*biology* 生) living on another animal or plant and getting food from the situation, but doing no harm 共生的；共棲的：*commensal organisms* 共棲體 ▸ **com·men·sal·ism** /kə'menslɪzəm/ *noun* [U]

com·men·sur·ate /kə'menʃərət/ *adj.* **~ (with sth)** (*formal*) matching sth in size, importance, quality, etc.（在大小、重要性、質量等方面）相稱的，相當的：*Salary will be commensurate with experience.* 薪金將會與資歷相稱。 **OPP** **incommensurate** ▸ **com·men·sur·ate·ly** *adv.*

com·ment 🔑 **AW** /'kɒment; *NAmE* 'kɑːm-/ *noun*, *verb*

■ ***noun*** **1** 🔑 [C, U] **~ (about/on sth)** something that you say or write which gives an opinion on or explains sb/sth 議論；評論；解釋：*Have you any comment to make about the cause of the disaster?* 你對發生災難的原因有何評論？◊ *She* ***made*** *helpful* ***comments*** *on my work.* 她對我的工作提出了有益的意見。◊ *The director was not available for comment.* 經理抽不出時間來發表評論。◊ *He handed me the document without comment.* 他未作任何解釋就把文件交給了我。◊ (*especially BrE*) *What she said was* ***fair comment*** (= a reasonable criticism). 她所講的是合乎情理的批評。 ➲ **SYNONYMS** at STATEMENT **2** [sing., U] criticism that shows the faults of sth 批評；指責：*The results are a clear comment on government education policy.* 這些結果是對政府教育政策明顯的批評。◊ *There was a lot of comment about his behaviour.* 對他的行為舉止有很多的議論。

IDM ˌ**no** ˈ**comment** (said in reply to a question, usually from a journalist 通常用於回答記者的問題) I have nothing to say about that 無可奉告：*'Will you resign, sir?' 'No comment!'* "先生，你會辭職嗎？" "無可奉告！"

■ ***verb*** 🔑 [I, T] **~ (on/upon sth)** to express an opinion about sth 表達意見：*I don't feel I can comment on their decision.* 我覺得我無法對他們的決定作出評論。◊ *He refused to comment until after the trial.* 他拒絕在審判前作任何評論。◊ **~ that …** *A spokesperson commented that levels of carbon dioxide were very high.* 發言人稱二氧化碳的含量很高。◊ **+ speech** *'Not his best performance,' she commented to the woman sitting next to her.* "這不是他的最佳表現。" 她對坐在她旁邊的女士議論道。

com·men·tary **AW** /'kɒməntri; *NAmE* 'kɑːmənteri/ *noun* (*pl.* **-ies**) **~ (on sth)** **1** [C, U] a spoken description of an event that is given while it is happening, especially on the radio or television（尤指電台或電視台所作的）實況報道，現場解說：*a sports commentary* 體育實況報道 ◊ *Our reporters will give* ***a running commentary*** (= a continuous one) *on the election results as they are announced.* 我們的記者將對選舉的公佈結果作實況追踪報道。◊ *He kept up* ***a running commentary*** *on everyone who came in or went out.* 他不斷地對上下場的每一名隊員進行解說。 **2** [C] a written explanation or discussion of sth such as a book or a play 註釋；解釋；評註；評論：*a critical commentary on the final speech of the play* 對這劇本結尾的台詞所作的批判性評論 **3** [C, U] a criticism or discussion of sth 批評；議論：*The petty quarrels were a sad commentary on the state of the government.* 這些雞毛蒜皮的爭吵說明了政府的狀況很糟糕。◊ *political commentary* 政治評論

com·men·tate /'kɒmənteɪt; *NAmE* 'kɑːm-/ *verb* [I] **~ (on sth)** to give a spoken description of an event as it happens, especially on television or radio（尤指在電視台或電台上）作實況報道，作現場解說：*Who will be commentating on the game?* 誰來對這場比賽作現場解說？

com·men·ta·tor **AW** /'kɒmənteɪtə(r); *NAmE* 'kɑːm-/ *noun* **~ (on sth)** **1** a person who is an expert on a particular subject and talks or writes about it on television or radio, or in a newspaper（電視台、電台或報章的）評論員：*a political commentator* 政治評論員 **2** a person who describes an event while it is happening, especially on television or radio（尤指電視台或電台的）現場解說員，實況播音員：***a television/sports commentator*** 電視台／體育運動實況解說員

Synonyms 同義詞辨析

comment

note • remark • observe

These words all mean to say or write a fact or opinion. 以上各詞均指口頭或書面說明事實或發表意見。

comment to express an opinion or give facts about sth 指發表意見或說明事實：*He refused to comment until after the trial.* 他拒絕在審判前作任何評論。

note (*rather formal*) to mention sth because it is important or interesting 指特別提到或指出：*He noted in passing that the company's record on safety issues was not good.* 他順便提到該公司在安全方面的記錄不好。

remark to say or write what you have noticed about a situation 指說起、談論、評論：*Critics remarked that the play was not original.* 評論家指出這部戲劇缺乏創意。

observe (*formal*) to say or write what you have noticed about a situation 指說起、談論、評論：*She observed that it was getting late.* 她說天色晚了。

COMMENT, REMARK OR OBSERVE? 用 comment、remark 還是 observe？

If you **comment on** sth you say sth about it; if you **remark on** sth or **observe** sth, you say sth about it that you have noticed: there is often not much difference between the three. However, while you can *refuse to comment* (without *on*), you cannot 'refuse to remark' or 'refuse to observe' (without *on*). * comment on 表示談論某事，remark on 或 observe 表示談論或評論注意到的事物。以上三詞通常無大的區別，但拒絕評論可說 refuse to comment（不帶 on），不能說 refuse to remark 或 refuse to observe（不帶 on）：~~*He refused to remark/observe until after the trial.*~~

PATTERNS

- to comment/note/remark/observe **that** …
- to comment on/note/remark/observe **how** …
- to comment/remark **on** sth
- to comment/remark/observe **to** sb
- **'It's long,'** he commented/noted/remarked/observed.

C

com·merce /ˈkɒmɜːs; *NAmE* ˈkɑːmɜːrs/ *noun* [U] trade, especially between countries; the buying and selling of goods and services（尤指國際間的）貿易；商業；商務：*leaders of industry and commerce* 工商界領導人 ➲ see also CHAMBER OF COMMERCE

com·mer·cial 🔑 /kəˈmɜːʃl; *NAmE* kəˈmɜːrʃl/ *adj.*, *noun*

▪ *adj.* **1** 🔑 [usually before noun] connected with the buying and selling of goods and services 貿易的；商業的：*the commercial heart of the city* 城市的商業中心 ◇ *a commercial vehicle* (= one that is used for carrying goods or passengers who pay) 商用車輛 ➲ SYNONYMS at ECONOMIC **2** 🔑 [only before noun] making or intended to make a profit 營利的；以獲利為目的的：*The movie was not a commercial success* (= did not make money). 這部電影票房收入不佳。◇ *commercial baby foods* 市面上的嬰兒食品 ◇ *the first commercial flights across the Atlantic* 頭幾次橫跨大西洋的商業飛行 ➲ SYNONYMS at SUCCESSFUL **3** (*disapproving*) more concerned with profit and being popular than with quality 偏重利潤和聲望的；商業化的：*Their more recent music is far too commercial.* 他們最近的音樂過分商業化了。**4** (of television or radio 電視或電台) paid for by the money charged for broadcasting advertisements 由廣告收入支付的；商業性的：*a commercial radio station/TV channel* 商業電台／電視頻道 ▸ **com·mer·cial·ly** /-ʃəli/ *adv.*：*commercially produced/grown/developed* 商業化生產的／種植的／開發的 ◇ *The product is not yet commercially available.* 這種產品還沒有上市。◇ *His invention was not commercially successful.* 他的發明從營利角度看並不成功。

▪ *noun* an advertisement on the radio or on television（電台或電視播放的）廣告 ➲ SYNONYMS at ADVERTISEMENT ➲ COLLOCATIONS at TELEVISION

com·mer·cial·ism /kəˈmɜːʃəlɪzəm; *NAmE* -ˈmɜːrʃl-/ *noun* [U] (*disapproving*) the fact of being more interested in making money than in the value or quality of things 商業主義；營利主義

com·mer·cial·ize (*BrE* also **-ise**) /kəˈmɜːʃəlaɪz; *NAmE* -ˈmɜːrʃl-/ *verb* [often passive] **~ sth** to use sth to try to make a profit, especially in a way that other people do not approve of（尤指不擇手段地）利用…牟利；商業化：*Their music has become very commercialized in recent years.* 他們的音樂近幾年非常商業化了。▸ **com·mer·cial·iza·tion, -isa·tion** /kəˌmɜːʃəlaɪˈzeɪʃn; *NAmE* -ˌmɜːrʃləˈz-/ *noun* [U]

comˌmercial ˈtraveller *noun* (*old-fashioned*, *BrE*) = SALES REPRESENTATIVE

com·mie /ˈkɒmi; *NAmE* ˈkɑːmi/ *noun* (*especially NAmE*) an insulting way of referring to sb that you think has ideas similar to those of COMMUNISTS or SOCIALISTS, or who is a member of a COMMUNIST or SOCIALIST party（侮辱性用語）有共產思想的人，共黨成員

com·mingle /kəˈmɪŋgl/ *verb* [I, T] (*formal* or *technical* 術語) to mix two or more things together or to be mixed, when it is impossible for the things to be separated afterwards 混合；摻和：**~ (with sth)** *The fluid must be prevented from commingling with other fluids.* 一定要避免將這種液體與其他液體混合。◇ **~ sth (with sth)** (*finance* 財) *Campaign funds must not be commingled with other money.* 競選經費切忌與其他款項合併。

com·mis·er·ate /kəˈmɪzəreɪt/ *verb* [I, T] **~ (with sb) (on/about/for/over sth)** | **+ speech** to show sb sympathy when they are upset or disappointed about sth 同情；憐憫：*She commiserated with the losers on their defeat.* 她對失敗的一方表示同情。

com·mis·er·ation /kəˌmɪzəˈreɪʃn/ *noun* [U, C] (*formal*) an expression of sympathy for sb who has had sth unpleasant happen to them, especially not winning a competition（尤指對某人未贏得比賽而表示的）同情：*I offered him my commiseration.* 我對他表示同情。◇ *Commiserations to the losing team!* 落敗的隊伍太可惜了！

com·mis·sar /ˌkɒmɪˈsɑː(r); *NAmE* ˌkɑːm-/ *noun* an officer of the Communist Party, especially in the past in the Soviet Union（尤指舊時蘇聯的）共產黨政治委員，共產黨政委

com·mis·sar·iat /ˌkɒmɪˈseəriət; *NAmE* ˌkɑːmɪˈser-/ *noun* **1** a department of the army that is responsible for food supplies 軍需處 **2** a government department in the Soviet Union before 1946（1946 年前蘇聯的）人民委員部

com·mis·sary /ˈkɒmɪsəri; *NAmE* ˈkɑːmɪseri/ *noun* (*pl.* **-ies**) (*NAmE*) **1** a shop/store that sells food, etc. in a military base, a prison, etc.（軍事基地、監獄等處出售食品等的）雜貨商店 **2** a restaurant for people working in a large organization, especially a film studio（大型機構，尤指電影製片廠的）員工餐廳

com·mis·sion 🔑 AW /kəˈmɪʃn/ *noun*, *verb*

▪ *noun*

▸ **OFFICIAL GROUP 官方團體** **1** 🔑 (often **Commission**) [C] an official group of people who have been given responsibility to control sth, or to find out about sth, usually for the government（通常為政府管控或調查某事的）委員會：*the European Commission* 歐洲委員會 ◇ (*BrE*) *The government has set up a* ***commission of inquiry*** *into the disturbances at the prison.* 政府成立了一個委員會來調查監獄騷亂事件。◇ *a commission on human rights* 人權委員會

▸ **MONEY 金錢** **2** 🔑 [U, C] an amount of money that is paid to sb for selling goods and which increases with the amount of goods that are sold 佣金；回扣：*You get a 10% commission on everything you sell.* 你可從你售出的每件商品中獲得 10% 的佣金。◇ *He earned £2 000 in commission last month.* 他上個月掙了 2 000 英鎊的佣金。◇ *In this job you work* ***on commission*** (= are paid according to the amount you sell). 你做這份工作按銷售額提成。**3** 🔑 [U] an amount of money that is charged by a bank, etc. for providing a particular service（銀行等的）手續費：*1% commission is charged for cashing traveller's cheques.* 兌現旅行支票收取 1% 的手續費。

▸ **FOR ART/MUSIC, ETC. 藝術、音樂等** **4** 🔑 [C] a formal request to sb to design or make a piece of work such as a building or a painting（請某人作建築設計或作一幅畫等的）正式委託

▸ **IN ARMED FORCES 軍隊** **5** [C] an officer's position in the armed forces 軍官職務

▸ **OF CRIME 犯罪** **6** [U] (*formal*) the act of doing sth wrong or illegal 做錯事；犯罪：*the commission of a crime* 犯罪

IDM **in/out of comˈmission** available/not available to be used 可／不可使用：*Several of the airline's planes are temporarily out of commission and undergoing safety checks.* 這家航空公司有幾架飛機暫時不能使用，正在接受安全檢查。

▪ *verb*

▸ **PIECE OF ART/MUSIC, ETC. 藝術、音樂等作品** **1** 🔑 to officially ask sb to write, make or create sth or to do a task for you 正式委託（譜寫、製作、創作或完成）：**~ sb to do sth** *She has been commissioned to write a new national anthem.* 她已受委託譜寫新國歌。◇ **~ sth** *Publishers have commissioned a French translation of the book.* 出版商已委託人把這本書譯成法語。

▸ **IN ARMED FORCES 軍隊** **2** [usually passive] to choose sb as an officer in one of the armed forces 任命…為軍官：**~ sb** *She was commissioned in 2007.* 她於 2007 年獲任命為軍官。◇ **~ sb (as) sth** *He has just been commissioned (as a) pilot officer.* 他剛被任命為空軍少尉。

com·mis·sion·aire /kəˌmɪʃəˈneə(r); *NAmE* -ˈner/ *noun* (*BrE*, becoming *old-fashioned*) a person in uniform whose job is to stand at the entrance to a hotel, etc. and open the door for visitors, find them taxis, etc.（在旅館等門口為來賓開門、叫出租車等的）穿制服的看門人，門童 ➲ see also DOORMAN

comˌmissioned ˈofficer *noun* an officer in the armed forces who has a higher rank, such as a captain or a GENERAL 軍官（如上尉或將軍）➲ compare NON-COMMISSIONED OFFICER

com·mis·sion·er AW /kəˈmɪʃənə(r)/ *noun* **1** (usually **Commissioner**) a member of a COMMISSION (= an official group of people who are responsible for controlling sth or finding out about sth)（委員會的）委員，專員，特派員：*the Church Commissioners* (= the group of people responsible for controlling the financial affairs of the Church of England) 英國國教會財政管理委員會委員 ◇ *European Commissioners* 歐洲委員會委員 **2** (also **po'lice commissioner** especially in *NAmE*) the head of a particular police force in some countries 警察局長；警長 **3** the head of a government department in some countries（政府部門的）首長，長官：*the **agriculture/health, etc. commissioner*** 農業、衛生等部門首長 ◇ *Commissioner Rhodes was unavailable for comment.* 羅茲局長無暇評論。➲ see also HIGH COMMISSIONER **4** (in the US) an official chosen by a sports association to control it（美國體育協會的）總幹事，主管人：*the baseball commissioner* 棒球協會總幹事

com,missioner for 'oaths *noun* (*BrE*) a lawyer who has official authority to be present when sb makes a formal promise that a written statement that they will use as evidence in court is true 監誓官（得到正式任命在法庭上主持宣誓的律師）

the Com,mission on Civil 'Rights *noun* [sing.] (in the US) a government organization that works for equal rights for all Americans 民權委員會（美國政府機構，宗旨是爭取全體美國人的平等權利）

com·mit 🔑 AW /kə'mɪt/ *verb* (-tt-)

▸ CRIME 犯罪 **1** 🔑 [T] **~ a crime, etc.** to do sth wrong or illegal 做出（錯事）；犯（罪）：*to **commit murder/adultery*** 犯兇殺罪／通姦罪 ◇ *Most crimes are committed by young men.* 多數罪行都是年輕人犯下的。◇ *appalling crimes committed against innocent children* 對無辜兒童犯下的駭人聽聞的罪行

▸ SUICIDE 自殺 **2** 🔑 [T] **~ suicide** to kill yourself deliberately 自殺

▸ PROMISE/SAY DEFINITELY 承諾；肯定地說 **3** 🔑 [T, often passive] to promise sincerely that you will definitely do sth, keep to an agreement or arrangement, etc. 承諾，保證（做某事、遵守協議或遵從安排等）：**~ sb/yourself (to sth/to doing sth)** *The President is committed to reforming health care.* 總統承諾要改革衛生保健制度。◇ *Borrowers should think carefully before committing themselves to taking out a loan.* 借款人應當慎重考慮之後再行借貸。◇ **~ sb/yourself to do sth** *Both sides committed themselves to settle the dispute peacefully.* 雙方承諾和平解決爭端。 **4** [T] **~ yourself (to sth)** to give an opinion or make a decision openly so that it is then difficult to change it（公開地）表達意見，作出決定（以致日後難以更改）：*You don't have to commit yourself now, just think about it.* 你不必現在表態，只需考慮一下這件事。➲ see also NON-COMMITTAL

▸ BE LOYAL 忠誠 **5** [I] **~ (to sb/sth)** to be completely loyal to one person, organization, etc. or give all your time and effort to your work, an activity, etc. 忠於（某個人、機構等）；全心全意投入（工作、活動等）：*Why are so many men scared to commit?* (= say they will be loyal to one person) 為什麼有這麼多的男人害怕許諾忠誠於人？➲ see also COMMITTED

▸ MONEY/TIME 金錢；時間 **6** [T] **~ sth** to spend money or time on sth/sb 花（錢或時間）：*The council has committed large amounts of money to housing projects.* 市政會在住宅項目上投入了大量資金。

▸ TO HOSPITAL/PRISON 醫院；監獄 **7** [T, often passive] **~ sb to sth** to order sb to be sent to a hospital, prison, etc.（下令）把（某人）送進（醫院或監獄等）：*She was committed to a psychiatric hospital.* 她被送進了精神病院。

▸ SB FOR TRIAL 某人受審 **8** [T] **~ sb** to send sb for trial in court 把（某人）送交法庭受審

▸ STH TO MEMORY 記住 **9** [T] **~ sth to memory** to learn sth well enough to remember it exactly 把…學好記牢：*She committed the instructions to memory.* 她把指令記得很牢。

▸ STH TO PAPER/WRITING 用紙記下；書寫 **10** [T] **~ sth to paper/writing** to write sth down 把…記（或寫）下來

com·mit·ment 🔑 AW /kə'mɪtmənt/ *noun*
1 🔑 [C, U] a promise to do sth or to behave in a particular way; a promise to support sb/sth; the fact of committing yourself 承諾；許諾；允諾承擔；保證：**~ (to sb/sth)** *She doesn't want to **make a** big emotional **commitment** to Steve at the moment.* 她不想在此刻對史蒂夫在感情上作出重大的承諾。◇ *the government's commitment to public services* 政府對公共服務作出的承諾 ◇ **~ to do/doing sth** *The company's commitment to providing quality at a reasonable price has been vital to its success.* 這家公司保證供貨質優價廉的承諾對它的成功起了決定性的作用。 **2** 🔑 [U] **~ (to sb/sth)** the willingness to work hard and give your energy and time to a job or an activity（對工作或活動的）獻身，奉獻，投入：*A career as an actor requires one hundred per cent commitment.* 幹演員這一行需要百分之百的投入。 **3** 🔑 [C] a thing that you have promised or agreed to do, or that you have to do 已承諾（或同意）的事；不得不做的事：*He's busy for the next month with filming commitments.* 他正忙於準備已經承諾下個月接拍的電影工作。◇ *Women very often have to juggle work with their family commitments.* 婦女經常得兩頭兼顧，既要工作又要照管家庭。 **4** [U, C] **~ (of sth) (to sth)** agreeing to use money, time or people in order to achieve sth 花費，使用（資金、時間、人力）：*the commitment of resources to education* 對教育的資源投入 ◇ *Achieving success at this level requires a commitment of time and energy.* 取得這種水平的成就需要花費時間和精力。

com·mit·tal /kə'mɪtl/ *noun* [U] (*technical* 術語) the official process of sending sb to prison or to a mental hospital 收監；拘押；送入（精神病院）：*He was released on bail pending committal proceedings.* 他交保獲釋正在候審。

com·mit·ted AW /kə'mɪtɪd/ *adj.* (*approving*) willing to work hard and give your time and energy to sth; believing strongly in sth 盡心盡力的；堅信的；堅定的：*a committed member of the team* 忠於職守的隊員 ◇ *They are committed socialists.* 他們是堅定的社會主義者。 OPP **uncommitted**

com·mit·tee 🔑 /kə'mɪti/ *noun* [C+sing./pl. v.] a group of people who are chosen, usually by a larger group, to make decisions or to deal with a particular subject 委員會：*She's on the management committee.* 她任管理委員會委員。◇ *The committee has/have decided to close the restaurant.* 委員會已決定關閉這家餐館。◇ *a committee member/a member of the committee* 委員會的委員 ◇ *a committee meeting* 委員會的會議

com·mode /kə'məʊd; *NAmE* kə'moʊd/ *noun* **1** a piece of furniture that looks like a chair but has a toilet under the seat 座椅式便桶 **2** a piece of furniture, especially an old or ANTIQUE one, with drawers for storing things in（尤指舊式或古董）有抽屜的櫃櫥，五斗櫥

com·modi·ous /kə'məʊdiəs; *NAmE* -'moʊ-/ *adj.* (*formal*) having a lot of space 寬敞的

com·mod·ity AW /kə'mɒdəti; *NAmE* -'mɑːd-/ *noun* (*pl.* **-ies**) **1** (*economics* 經) a product or a raw material that can be bought and sold 商品：*rice, flour and other basic commodities* 稻米、麵粉和其他基本商品 ◇ *a drop in commodity prices* 商品價格的下跌 ◇ *Crude oil is the world's most important commodity.* 原油是世界上最重要的商品。➲ **SYNONYMS** at PRODUCT **2** (*formal*) a thing that is useful or has a useful quality 有用的東西；有使用價值的事物：*Water is a precious commodity that is often taken for granted in the West.* 水很寶貴，但在西方國家人們往往意識不到這一點。

com·mo·dore /'kɒmədɔː(r); *NAmE* 'kɑːm-/ *noun* (*abbr.* **Cdre**) an officer of high rank in the navy 海軍准將：*Commodore John Barry* 約翰 • 巴里海軍准將

com·mon 🔑 /'kɒmən; *NAmE* 'kɑːmən/ *adj., noun*
■ *adj.* (**com·mon·er, com·mon·est**) HELP **More common** and **most common** are more frequent. * more common 和 most common 更為常見。 **1** 🔑 happening often; existing in large numbers or in many places 常見的；通常的；普遍的：*Jackson is a common English name.* 傑克遜是常見的英語人名。◇ *Breast cancer is the most common form of cancer among women in this country.* 乳腺癌是這個國家婦女中最常見的一種癌症。◇ *Some birds which were once **a common sight** are now becoming rare.* 有些曾經隨處可見的鳥類現在日益稀少。◇ *a common spelling mistake* 常犯的拼寫錯誤 OPP **uncommon** **2** 🔑 [usually before noun] **~ (to sb/sth)** shared by or belonging to two

or more people or by the people in a group 共有的；共享的；共同的：*They share a common interest in photography.* 他們在攝影方面興趣相投。◇ *basic features which are common to all human languages* 所有人類語言共有的基本特徵 ◇ *We are working together for a common purpose.* 我們在為一個共同的目標一起工作。◇ *common ownership of the land* 土地的共同所有權 ◇ *This decision was taken for the* ***common good*** (= the advantage of everyone). 作出這個決定是為了共同的利益。◇ *It is, by* ***common consent***, *Scotland's prettiest coast* (= everyone agrees that it is). 這是蘇格蘭公認的最美麗的海岸。 **3** [only before noun] ordinary; not unusual or special 普通的；平常的；尋常的；平凡的：*the common garden frog* 園地裏常見的青蛙 ◇ *Shakespeare's work was popular among* ***the common people*** *in his day.* 莎士比亞的作品在他那個年代很受平民百姓的歡迎。◇ *In most people's eyes she was nothing more than a* ***common criminal***. 在多數人的眼裏她只不過是個普通的罪犯。◇ *You'd think he'd have the* ***common courtesy*** *to apologize* (= this would be the polite behaviour that people would expect). 你還以為他會懂得起碼的禮貌去道個歉呢。◇ *It's only* ***common decency*** *to let her know what's happening* (= people would expect it). 出於禮貌，該讓她知道正在發生的事。 **4** (*BrE, disapproving*) typical of sb from a low social class and not having good manners 粗俗的；庸俗的：*She thought he was very common and uneducated.* 她認為他很粗俗且無教養。

IDM **common or 'garden** (*BrE*) (*NAmE* **'garden-variety**) (*informal*) ordinary; with no special features 普通的；平常的；一般的 **the common 'touch** the ability of a powerful or famous person to talk to and understand ordinary people（有權勢者或名人的）平易近人的品質，親民作風 **make common 'cause with sb** (*formal*) to be united with sb about sth that you both agree on, believe in or wish to achieve 與某人聯合起來，與某人合作（以達到共同的目的）➲ more at KNOWLEDGE

■ *noun* **1** [C] an area of open land in a town or village that anyone may use 公共用地；公地：*We went for a walk on the common.* 我們在公地上散步。◇ *Wimbledon Common* 溫布爾登公地 **2 commons** [sing.] (*US*) a large room where students can eat in a school, college, etc.（學校、大學等的）學生公共食堂：*The commons is next to the gym.* 學生公共食堂在體育館的旁邊。➲ see also COMMONS

IDM **have sth in common (with sb)** (of people 人) to have the same interests, ideas, etc. as sb else（興趣、想法等方面）相同：*Tim and I have nothing in common./ I have nothing in common with Tim.* 我和蒂姆毫無共同之處。 **have sth in common (with sth)** (of things, places, etc. 東西、地方等) to have the same features, characteristics, etc. 有相同的特徵（或特點等）：*The two cultures have a lot in common.* 這兩種文化具有許多相同之處。 **in common** (*technical* 術語) by everyone in a group 共有；公有：*They hold the property as tenants in common.* 作為共同租賃人，他們共同佔用這份房地產。 **in common with sb/sth** (*formal*) in the same way as sb/sth 與…相同：*Britain, in common with many other industrialized countries, has experienced major changes over the last 100 years.* 與許多其他工業化國家一樣，英國在過去 100 年裏經歷了重大的變化。

the ˌcommon 'cold *noun* [sing.] = COLD *n.* (2)

ˌcommon de'nominator *noun* **1** (*mathematics* 數) a number that can be divided exactly by all the numbers below the line in a set of FRACTIONS 公分母 ➲ compare DENOMINATOR **2** an idea, attitude or experience that is shared by all the members of a group（想法、態度或經驗的）共同點 ➲ see also LOWEST COMMON DENOMINATOR

com·mon·er /ˈkɒmənə(r); *NAmE* ˈkɑːm-/ *noun* a person who does not come from a royal or NOBLE family 平民 ➲ compare ARISTOCRAT

ˌCommon 'Era *noun* [sing.] (*abbr.* **CE**) the period since the birth of Christ when the Christian CALENDAR starts counting years 基督紀元；公元：*1890 CE* 公元 1890 年

ˌcommon 'ground *noun* [U] opinions, interests and aims that you share with sb, although you may not agree with them about other things（觀點、利益和目標的）共同基礎，共同點，一致點：*Despite our disagreements, we have been able to find some common ground.* 儘管我們存在分歧，但仍能找到一些共同點。

com·mon·hold /ˈkɒmənhəʊld; *NAmE* ˈkɑːmənhoʊld/ *noun* [U] (*BrE, law* 律) a system in which each person owns their flat/apartment in a building but the building and shared areas are owned by everyone together 公寓樓共有制度（住戶共同擁有樓房及公用區域）

'common land *noun* [U] (*BrE*) land that belongs to or may be used by the local community 公共用地；公地

ˌcommon 'law *noun* [U] (in England) a system of laws that have been developed from customs and from decisions made by judges, not created by Parliament（英格蘭）普通法，習慣法，判例法 ➲ compare CASE LAW, STATUTE LAW

ˌcommon-law 'husband, ˌcommon-law 'wife *noun* a person that a woman or man has lived with for a long time and who is recognized as a husband or wife, without a formal marriage ceremony（未舉行結婚儀式的）事實婚姻的男方，事實婚姻的女方

com·mon·ly /ˈkɒmənli; *NAmE* ˈkɑːm-/ *adv.* usually; very often; by most people 通常；常常；大多數人地：*Christopher is commonly known as Kit.* 克里斯托弗通常被稱為基特。◇ *commonly held opinions* 多數人持有的觀點 ◇ *This is one of the most commonly used methods.* 這是最常採用的方法之一。

ˌcommon 'market *noun* **1** [C, usually sing.] a group of countries that have agreed on low taxes on goods traded between countries in the group, and higher fixed taxes on goods imported from countries outside the group 共同市場（成員國之間實行低關稅貿易，對從成員國之外的國家進口的商品規定較高關稅） **2 the Common Market** [sing.] a former name of the European Union 歐洲共同市場（歐洲聯盟舊稱）

ˌcommon 'noun *noun* (*grammar* 語法) a word such as *table*, *cat*, or *sea*, that refers to an object or a thing but is not the name of a particular person, place or thing 普通名詞（如 table、cat 或 sea）➲ compare ABSTRACT NOUN, PROPER NOUN

com·mon·place /ˈkɒmənpleɪs; *NAmE* ˈkɑːm-/ *adj., noun*
■ *adj.* done very often, or existing in many places, and therefore not unusual 平凡的；普通的；普遍的：*Computers are now commonplace in primary classrooms.* 計算機如今在小學教室裏很普遍。
■ *noun* (*formal*) **1** [usually sing.] an event, etc. that happens very often and is not unusual 常見的事；平常的事 **2** a remark, etc. that is not new or interesting 平淡無奇的言語等；老生常談

'commonplace book *noun* (especially in the past) a book into which you copy parts of other books, poems, etc. and add your own comments（尤指舊時的）摘錄本，摘記簿

ˌcommon 'rat *noun* = BROWN RAT

'common room *noun* (*especially BrE*) a room used by the teachers or students of a school, college, etc. when they are not teaching or studying（學校、學院等的）公共休息室

Com·mons /ˈkɒmənz; *NAmE* ˈkɑːm-/ *noun* **the Commons** [pl.] = THE HOUSE OF COMMONS ➲ compare THE LORDS at LORD *n.* (8)

ˌcommon 'sense *noun* [U] the ability to think about things in a practical way and make sensible decisions 常識：*For goodness' sake, just use your common sense!* 我的老天，你也憑常識想想！◇ *a common-sense approach to a problem* 按常理解決問題的方法

com·mon·wealth /ˈkɒmənwelθ; *NAmE* ˈkɑːm-/ *noun* [sing.] **1 the Commonwealth** an organization consisting of the United Kingdom and other countries, including most of the countries that used to be part of the British Empire 英聯邦（由英國和其他大多數曾經隸屬於大英帝國的國家組成）：*a member of the Commonwealth* 英聯邦成員國 ◇ *Commonwealth countries* 英聯邦國家 **2** (usually

the Commonwealth) used in the official names of, and to refer to, some states of the US (Kentucky, Massachusetts, Pennsylvania and Virginia)（用於美國肯塔基、馬薩諸塞、賓夕法尼亞和弗吉尼亞四州的正式名稱中）州：*the Commonwealth of Virginia* 弗吉尼亞州 ◇ *The city and the Commonwealth have lost a great leader.* 這座城市和這個州失去了一位偉大的領袖。 **3** (*NAmE*) an independent country that is strongly connected to the US（與美國聯繫緊密的）自治政區：*Puerto Rico remains a US commonwealth, not a state.* 波多黎各至今仍然是美國的一個自治政區，而不是一個州。 **4** (usually **Commonwealth**) used in the names of some groups of countries or states that have chosen to be politically linked with each other（用於某些政治上相互有聯繫的國家集團的名稱）聯合體：*the Commonwealth of Independent States (CIS)* 獨立國家聯合體（獨聯體）

com·mo·tion /kəˈməʊʃn; *NAmE* -ˈmoʊ-/ *noun* [C, usually sing., U] sudden noisy confusion or excitement（突然發生的）喧鬧，騷亂，騷動：*I heard a commotion and went to see what was happening.* 我聽到一陣喧鬧便去看看發生了什麼事情。◇ *The crowd waiting outside was causing a commotion.* 在外面等待的人群眼看就要發生騷亂。

com·mu·nal /kəˈmjuːnl; *BrE* also ˈkɒmjənl/ *adj.* **1** shared by, or for the use of, a number of people, especially people who live together（尤指居住在一起的人）共享的，共有的，共用的 SYN **shared**：*a **communal kitchen/garden, etc.*** 共用的廚房、花園等 ◇ *As a student he tried communal living for a few years.* 當學生時他嘗試過幾年集體生活。**2** involving different groups of people in a community（集體中）不同群體的，各團體的：*communal violence between religious groups* 不同教派之間的暴力衝突 ▶ **com·mu·nal·ly** *adv.*：*The property was owned communally.* 這財產屬集體所有。

com·mu·nal·ism /kəˈmjuːnəlɪzəm; ˈkɒmjənəl-; *NAmE* ˈkɑːm-/ *noun* [U] **1** the fact of living together and sharing possessions and responsibilities 公社生活 **2** (*IndE*) a strong sense of belonging to a particular, especially religious, community, which can lead to extreme behaviour or violence towards others 集團主義（可能排外）

com·mune *noun, verb*

■ ***noun*** /ˈkɒmjuːn; *NAmE* ˈkɑːm-/ [C+sing./pl. v.] **1** a group of people who live together and share responsibilities, possessions, etc.（共同生活、分擔責任、共享財產等的）群體，公社：*a 1970s hippy commune* * 20 世紀 70 年代的嬉皮士群體 **2** the smallest division of local government in France and some other countries（法國及其他一些國家的最小的）行政區

■ ***verb*** /kəˈmjuːn/

PHR V **comˈmune with sb/sth** (*formal*) to share your emotions and feelings with sb/sth without speaking 與…默默分享情感（或溝通、交融）：*He spent much of this time **communing with nature**.* 他這個時期的許多時間都沉浸在大自然中。

com·mu·nic·able AW /kəˈmjuːnɪkəbl/ *adj.* (*formal*) that sb can pass on to other people or communicate to sb else 可傳染的；可傳送的：*communicable diseases* 傳染性疾病

com·mu·ni·cant /kəˈmjuːnɪkənt/ *noun* a person who receives COMMUNION in a Christian church service 領受聖餐（或聖體）者

com·mu·ni·cate 🔑 AW /kəˈmjuːnɪkeɪt/ *verb*

▸ EXCHANGE INFORMATION 交流信息 **1** 🔑 [I, T] to exchange information, news, ideas, etc. with sb（與某人）交流信息（或消息、意見等）；溝通：*We only communicate by email.* 我們只是互通電郵。◇ *They communicated in sign language.* 他們用手語溝通。◇ **~ with sb/sth** *Dolphins use sound to communicate with each other.* 海豚用聲音相互溝通。◇ **~ sth** (**to sb**) *to communicate information/a message to sb* 把情報／信息傳遞給某人 ➲ SYNONYMS at TALK

▸ SHARE IDEAS/FEELINGS 分享想法／感情 **2** 🔑 [I, T] to make your ideas, feelings, thoughts, etc. known to other people so that they understand them 傳達，傳遞（想法、感情、思想等）：*Candidates must be able to communicate effectively.* 候選人必須善於有效地表達自己。◇ **~ sth** (**to sb**) *He was eager to communicate his ideas to the group.* 他急於把他的想法傳達給小組。◇ *Her nervousness was communicating itself to the children.* 她緊張不安的情緒傳遞給了孩子們。◇ **~ how/what, etc. …** *They failed to communicate what was happening and why.* 他們沒說清楚當時發生了什麼以及起因是什麼。 **3** 🔑 [I] **~ (with sb)** to have a good relationship because you are able to understand and talk about your own and other people's thoughts, feelings, etc. 溝通：*The novel is about a family who can't communicate with each other.* 這部小說寫的是一個彼此無法溝通的家庭。

▸ DISEASE 疾病 **4** [T, usually passive] **~ sth** to pass a disease from one person, animal, etc. to another 傳染；傳播：*The disease is communicated through dirty drinking water.* 這種疾病通過不乾淨的飲用水傳播。

▸ OF TWO ROOMS 兩個房間 **5** [I] if two rooms **communicate**, they are next to each other and you can get from one to the other 相通；相連：*a **communicating door*** (= one that connects two rooms) 連通門

com·mu·ni·ca·tion 🔑 AW /kəˌmjuːnɪˈkeɪʃn/ *noun*

1 🔑 [U] the activity or process of expressing ideas and feelings or of giving people information 表達；交流；交際；傳遞：*Speech is the fastest method of communication between people.* 說話是人與人之間最快捷的溝通方法。◇ *All channels of communication need to be kept open.* 所有溝通渠道都得保持暢通無阻。◇ *Doctors do not always have good **communication skills**.* 醫生不一定都具備良好的交際能力。◇ *non-verbal communication* 非言語交際 ◇ *We are in regular communication by email.* 我們定期通過電子郵件聯繫。 **2** 🔑 [U] (also **communications** [pl.]) methods of sending information, especially telephones, radio, computers, etc. or roads and railways 通信；交通聯繫：***communication systems/links/technology*** 通信系統／線路／技術 ◇ *The new airport will improve communications between the islands.* 新機場將改善島嶼間的交通聯繫。◇ *Snow has prevented communication with the outside world for three days.* 大雪使得與外界的通信聯繫中斷了三天。 **3** [C] (*formal*) a message, letter or telephone call 信息；書信；電話：*a communication from the leader of the party* 來自政黨領袖的信息

com·mu·ni·ca·tive AW /kəˈmjuːnɪkətɪv; *NAmE* -keɪtɪv/ *adj.* **1** willing to talk and give information to other people 樂意溝通的：*I don't find him very communicative.* 我發覺他不太愛說話。 OPP **uncommunicative** **2** connected with the ability to communicate in a language, especially a foreign language 語言交際能力的（尤指用外語）：*communicative skills* 語言交際能力

the comˈmunicative approach *noun* [sing.] (also **comˌmunicative ˈlanguage teaching** [U]) a method of teaching a foreign language which stresses the importance of learning to communicate information and ideas in the language 交際法（外語教學中強調語言交際作用）

comˌmunicative ˈcompetence *noun* [U] (*linguistics* 語言) a person's ability to communicate information and ideas in a foreign language（外語）交際能力

com·mu·ni·ca·tor /kəˈmjuːnɪkeɪtə(r)/ *noun* a person who communicates sth to others 溝通的人；交流者：*an effective/skilled/successful communicator* 有效的／熟練的／成功的交際者 ◇ *a poor communicator* 不善於交流的人 ➲ SYNONYMS at SPEAKER

com·mu·nion /kəˈmjuːniən/ *noun* **1** (also **Communion**, **ˌHoly Comˈmunion**) [U] a ceremony in the Christian Church during which people eat bread and drink wine in memory of the last meal that Christ had with his DISCIPLES（基督教教會的）聖餐儀式，領受聖體：*to go to Communion* (= attend church for this celebration) 去參加聖餐儀式 ◇ *to **take/receive communion*** (= receive the bread and wine) 領受聖餐 ➲ see also EUCHARIST, MASS **2** [U] **~ (with sb/sth)** (*formal*) the state of sharing or exchanging thoughts and feelings; the feeling of being part of sth（思想感情的）交流，交融：*poets living in communion with nature* 與大自然情感交融的詩人 **3** [C] (*technical* 術語) a group of people with the same religious beliefs 教派；教會；宗教團體：*the Anglican communion* 聖公會

C

com·mu·ni·qué /kəˈmjuːnɪkeɪ; *NAmE* kəˌmjuːnəˈkeɪ/ *noun* an official statement or report, especially to newspapers（尤指對報界發佈的）公報

com·mun·ism /ˈkɒmjunɪzəm; *NAmE* ˈkɑːm-/ *noun* [U] **1** a political movement that believes in an economic system in which the state controls the means of producing everything on behalf of the people. It aims to create a society in which everyone is treated equally. 共產主義 **2 Communism** the system of government by a ruling Communist Party, such as in the former Soviet Union 共產主義制度 ➲ compare CAPITALISM

com·mun·ist /ˈkɒmjənɪst; *NAmE* ˈkɑːm-/ *noun* **1** a person who believes in or supports communism 共產主義者；共產主義的支持者 **2 Communist** a member of a Communist Party 共產黨黨員 ▶ **com·mun·ist** (also **Communist**) *adj.*：*communist ideology* 共產主義的思想體系 ◇ *a Communist country/government/leader* 共產主義的國家／政府／領袖

the ˈCommunist Party *noun* a political party that supports COMMUNISM or rules in a COMMUNIST country 共產黨

com·mu·nity 🔑 AW /kəˈmjuːnəti/ *noun* (*pl.* **-ies**) **1** 🔑 [sing.] all the people who live in a particular area, country, etc. when talked about as a group 社區；社會：*The* ***local community*** *was shocked by the murders.* 當地社會對這些謀殺案感到震驚。◇ *health workers based in the community* (= working with people in a local area) 以社區為基地的保健工作人員 ◇ ***the international community*** (= the countries of the world as a group) 國際社會 ◇ *good community relations with the police* 社區與警方之間的良好關係 ◇ (*NAmE*) ***community parks/libraries*** (= paid for by the local town/city) 社區公園／圖書館 **2** 🔑 [C+sing./pl. v.] a group of people who share the same religion, race, job, etc. 團體；社團；界：*the Polish community in London* 在倫敦的波蘭僑民團體 ◇ *ethnic communities* 種族團體 ◇ *the farming community* 農業界 **3** 🔑 [U] the feeling of sharing things and belonging to a group in the place where you live 共享；共有：*There is a strong sense of community in this town.* 這個鎮上有一種強烈的社區意識。◇ *community spirit* 團體精神 ➲ COLLOCATIONS at TOWN **4** [C] (*biology* 生) a group of plants and animals growing or living in the same place or environment（動植物的）群落

comˌmunity ˈcare (also **ˌcare in the comˈmunity**) *noun* [U] (*BrE*) medical and other care for people who need help over a long period, which allows them to live at home rather than in a hospital 社區護理服務（讓長期需要幫助者在家中接受醫療等）

comˈmunity centre (*BrE*) (*NAmE* **comˈmunity center**) *noun* a place where people from the same area can meet for social events or sports or to take classes 社區活動中心

comˈmunity college *noun* **1** (also **comˈmunity school**) (in Britain) a SECONDARY SCHOOL that is open to adults from the local community as well as to its own students 社區中學（在英國除接收本校學生外亦向當地社區成人開放）**2** (in the US) a college that is mainly for students from the local community and that offers programmes that are two years long, including programmes in practical skills 社區學院（美國為社區成員提供兩年制課程，包括職業技術訓練）

comˌmunity ˈlanguage learning *noun* [U] a method of teaching a foreign language that uses small groups and other ways of reducing students' anxiety 團體語言教學法

comˌmunity ˈproperty *noun* [U] (*NAmE*, *law* 律) property that is considered to belong equally to a married couple（夫妻的）共同財產，共有財產

comˌmunity ˈservice *noun* [U] work helping people in the local community that sb does without being paid, either because they want to, or because they have been ordered to by a court as a punishment 社區服務（自願或因受法庭懲罰的無償勞動）

com·mut·able /kəˈmjuːtəbl/ *adj.* **1** (of a place or a distance 地方或距離) close enough or short enough to make travelling to work every day a possibility 上下班方便的；近的 **2** (*law* 律) a **commutable** punishment can be made less severe（刑罰）可減輕的 **3** (*formal*) able to be changed 可改變的；可變換的

com·mu·ta·tion /ˌkɒmjuˈteɪʃn; *NAmE* ˌkɑːm-/ *noun* [C, U] **1** (*law* 律) the act of making a punishment less severe 減刑：*a commutation of the death sentence to life imprisonment* 由死刑減為終身監禁 **2** (*finance* 財) the act of replacing one method of payment with another; a payment that is replaced with another 代償；折合償付；代償金

com·mu·ta·tive /kəˈmjuːtətɪv/ *adj.* (*mathematics* 數) (of a calculation 計算) giving the same result whatever the order in which the quantities are shown 交換的（排列次序不影響結果）

com·mu·ta·tor /ˈkɒmjuteɪtə(r); *NAmE* ˈkɑːm-/ *noun* (*physics* 物) **1** a device that connects a motor to the electricity supply（馬達）轉換開關，轉換器 **2** a device for changing the direction in which electricity flows（電流）換向器；整流子

com·mute /kəˈmjuːt/ *verb*, *noun*

■ ***verb*** **1** [I, T] to travel regularly by bus, train, car, etc. between your place of work and your home（乘公共汽車、火車、汽車等）上下班往返，經常往返（於兩地）：**~ (from A) (to B)** *She commutes from Oxford to London every day.* 她每天上下班往返於牛津與倫敦之間。◇ **~ between A and B** *He spent that year commuting between New York and Chicago.* 那年他穿梭來往於紐約與芝加哥之間。◇ *I live* ***within commuting distance of*** *Dublin.* 我住在離都柏林上下班可乘公交車往返的地方。◇ **~ sth** *People are prepared to commute long distances if they are desperate for work.* 極需得到工作的人會願意長途乘車往返上下班。**2** [T] **~ sth (to sth)** (*law* 律) to replace one punishment with another that is less severe 減刑 **3** [T] **~ sth (for/into sth)** (*finance* 財) to exchange one form of payment, for sth else 代償

■ ***noun*** the journey that a person makes when they commute to work 上下班路程：*a two-hour commute into downtown Washington* 去華盛頓中心區兩小時的上下班路程 ◇ *I have only a short commute to work.* 我上班的路程很短。

com·muter /kəˈmjuːtə(r)/ *noun* a person who travels into a city to work each day, usually from quite far away（通常指遠距離）上下班往返的人：(*BrE*) *the* ***commuter belt*** (= the area around a city where people live and from which they travel to work in the city) 上班族居住地帶

comp /kɒmp; *NAmE* kɑːmp/ *noun* (*informal*) **1** [C] (*BrE*) = COMPREHENSIVE *n.*：*Her children go to the local comp.* 她的孩子們上當地的綜合中學。**2** [C] (*BrE*) = COMPETITION **3** [C] (*NAmE*) a COMPLIMENTARY ticket, meal, etc. (= one that you do not have to pay for) 贈品（如入場券、膳食等）**4** [U] (*NAmE*) = COMPENSATION：***comp time*** (= time off work given for working extra hours)（加班後的）補休時間

com·pact *adj.*, *noun*, *verb*

■ ***adj.*** /kəmˈpækt; ˈkɒmpækt; *NAmE* ˈkɑːm-/ **1** smaller than is usual for things of the same kind 小型的；袖珍的：*a compact camera* 袖珍照相機 **2** using or filling only a small amount of space 緊湊的；體積小的：*The kitchen was compact but well equipped.* 這間廚房雖然空間小但設備齊全。**3** closely and firmly packed together 緊密的；堅實的：*a compact mass of earth* 一堆壓得很結實的泥土 **4** (of a person or an animal 人或動物) small and strong 矮小而健壯的：*He had a compact and muscular body.* 他個子矮小健壯。▶ **com·pact·ly** *adv.* **com·pact·ness** *noun* [U]

■ ***noun*** /ˈkɒmpækt; *NAmE* ˈkɑːm-/ **1** (*NAmE*) a small car 小汽車 ➲ compare SUBCOMPACT **2** a small flat box with a mirror, containing powder that women use on their faces 帶鏡小粉盒 ➲ VISUAL VOCAB page V60 **3** (*formal*) a formal agreement between two or more people or countries 協定；協議；契約；合約

■ ***verb*** /kəmˈpækt/ [usually passive] **~ sth** to press sth together firmly 把…緊壓在一起（或壓實）：*a layer of compacted snow* 壓緊的一層雪

ˌcompact ˈdisc *noun* = CD

com·padre /kɒmˈpɑːdreɪ; *NAmE* kəm-/ *noun* (*NAmE, informal*, from *Spanish*) used as a friendly way of addressing sb（用作友好的稱呼）朋友，老兄

com·pan·ion /kəmˈpæniən/ *noun* **1** a person or an animal that travels with you or spends a lot of time with you 旅伴；伴侶；陪伴：*travelling companions* 旅伴 ◇ (*figurative*) *Fear was the hostages' constant companion.* 人質一直都感到恐懼不安。 **2** a person who has similar tastes, interests, etc. to your own and whose company you enjoy（愛好、志趣等相投的）夥伴，同伴：*She was a charming dinner companion.* 與她同桌進餐使人感到十分高興。◇ *His younger brother is not much of a companion for him.* 他的弟弟和他志趣不太相投。◇ *They're drinking companions* (= they go out drinking together). 他們是酒友。 **3** a person who shares in your work, pleasures, sadness, etc. 同甘共苦的夥伴：*We became companions in misfortune.* 我們成了患難之交。 **4** a person, usually a woman, employed to live with and help sb, especially sb old or ill/sick 陪護（通常受雇照料老人或病人） **5** one of a pair of things that go together or can be used together 成對的物品之一；一副物品中的一個：*A companion volume is soon to be published.* 這卷書的姊妹篇即將問世。 **6** used in book titles to describe a book giving useful facts and information on a particular subject（用於書名）指南，手冊：*A Companion to French Literature*《法國文學指南》➲ see also BOON COMPANION

com·pan·ion·able /kəmˈpæniənəbl/ *adj.* friendly 朋友般的；友好的；友善的 ▸ **com·pan·ion·ably** /-əbli/ *adv.*

com·pan·ion·ship /kəmˈpæniənʃɪp/ *noun* [U] the pleasant feeling that you have when you have a friendly relationship with sb and are not alone 友情；交誼；友誼：*They meet at the club for companionship and advice.* 他們在俱樂部相會是為了聯誼和尋求建議。◇ *She had only her cat for companionship.* 她只有貓兒作伴。

com·pan·ion·way /kəmˈpæniənweɪ/ *noun* (*technical* 術語) a set of stairs on a ship（船上的）升降口扶梯

com·pany 0▬ /ˈkʌmpəni/ *noun* (*pl.* **-ies**)

▸ BUSINESS 商業 **1** 0▬ [C+sing./pl. v.] (*abbr.* **Co.**) (often in names 常用於名稱) a business organization that makes money by producing or selling goods or services 公司；商號；商行：*the largest computer company in the world* 全球最大的計算機公司 ◇ *the National Bus Company* 全國公共汽車公司 ◇ *She joined the company in 2009.* 她於 2009 年加入這家公司。◇ *Company profits were 5% lower than last year.* 公司的利潤比去年降低了 5%。 ➲ COLLOCATIONS at BUSINESS

▸ THEATRE/DANCE 戲劇；舞蹈 **2** 0▬ [C+sing./pl. v.] (often in names 常用於名稱) a group of people who work or perform together 劇團；演出團：*a* ***theatre/dance, etc. company*** 劇團、舞蹈團等 ◇ *the Royal Shakespeare Company* 皇家莎士比亞戲劇團

▸ BEING WITH SB 與某人在一起 **3** 0▬ [U] the fact of being with sb else and not alone 陪伴；做伴：*I enjoy Jo's company* (= I enjoy being with her). 我喜歡和喬在一起。◇ *She enjoys her own company* (= being by herself) *when she is travelling.* 她喜愛獨自旅行。◇ *The children are very* ***good company*** (= pleasant to be with) *at this age.* 和這個年齡的孩子在一起很開心。◇ *a pleasant evening in the company of friends* 與朋友一起度過的愉快夜晚 ◇ *He's coming with me* ***for company***. 他要陪伴我一起來。

▸ GUESTS 賓客 **4** [U] (*formal*) guests in your house 賓客；來賓：*I didn't realize you* ***had company***. 我不知道你有客人。

▸ GROUP OF PEOPLE 一群人 **5** [U] (*formal*) a group of people together 在一起的一群人：*She told the assembled company what had happened.* 她把發生的事告訴了聚會的人。◇ *It is bad manners to whisper* ***in company*** (= in a group of people). 在眾人面前竊竊私語是不禮貌的行為。

▸ SOLDIERS 士兵 **6** [C+sing./pl. v.] a group of soldiers that is part of a BATTALION 連隊

IDM **the ˈcompany sb keeps** the people that sb spends time with 某人所交往的人；夥伴；與之為伍的人：*Judging by the company he kept, Mark must have been a wealthy man.* 根據馬克所交往的人來判斷，他一定是位富翁。 **get into/keep bad ˈcompany** to be friends with people that others disapprove of 與壞人交往 **in ˈcompany with sb/sth** (*formal*) together with or at the same time as sb/sth 與…一起；與…同時：*She arrived in company with the ship's captain.* 她與船長一起到達。◇ *The US dollar went through a difficult time, in company with the oil market.* 美元與石油市場同時經歷了艱難時期。 **in good ˈcompany** if you say that sb is **in good company**, you mean that they should not worry about a mistake, etc. because sb else, especially sb more important, has done the same thing 無傷大雅（表示不必為錯誤等擔憂，因為他人，尤其是更重要的人也犯過同樣的錯誤） **keep sb ˈcompany** to stay with sb so that they are not alone 做伴；陪伴：*I'll keep you company while you're waiting.* 你等待時我會陪伴你。 **two's ˈcompany (, three's a ˈcrowd)** (*saying*) used to suggest that it is better to be in a group of only two people than have a third person with you as well 兩人成伴（三人太多） ➲ more at PART *v.*, PRESENT *adj.*

company ˈcar *noun* a car which is provided by the company that you work for（為工作人員提供的）公司車

com·par·able /ˈkɒmpərəbl; *NAmE* ˈkɑːm-/ *adj.* **~ (to/with sb/sth)** similar to sb/sth else and able to be compared 類似的；可比較的：*A comparable house in the south of the city would cost twice as much.* 一棟類似的房子位於城南部就要貴一倍的價錢。◇ *The situation in the US is not directly comparable to that in the UK.* 美國的情況與英國的不能直接相比。◇ *Inflation is now at a rate comparable with that in other European countries.* 現在通貨膨脹率已經和歐洲其他國家的差不多了。 ▸ **com·par·abil·ity** /ˌkɒmpərəˈbɪləti; *NAmE* ˌkɑːm-/ *noun* [U]: *Each group will have the same set of questions, in order to ensure comparability.* 為確保可比性，每一組將得到一套同樣的問題。

com·para·tive /kəmˈpærətɪv/ *adj., noun*

■ ***adj.*** **1** connected with studying things to find out how similar or different they are 比較的；相比的：*a comparative study of the educational systems of two countries* 兩國教育制度的比較研究 ◇ *comparative linguistics* 比較語言學 **2** measured or judged by how similar or different it is to sth else 比較而言的；相對的 SYN **relative**：*Then he was living in comparative comfort* (= compared with others or with his own life at a previous time). 他那時生活比較舒適。◇ *The company is a comparative newcomer to the software market* (= other companies have been in business much longer). 就軟件市場來說，這家公司相對而言就是新手了。 **3** (*grammar* 語法) relating to adjectives or adverbs that express more in amount, degree or quality, for example *better, worse, slower* and *more difficult*（形容詞或副詞）比較級的（如 better、worse、slower 和 more difficult） ➲ compare SUPERLATIVE

■ ***noun*** (*grammar* 語法) the form of an adjective or adverb that expresses more in amount, degree or quality（形容詞或副詞的）比較級形式：*'Better' is the comparative of 'good' and 'more difficult' is the comparative of 'difficult'.* * better 是 good 的比較級；more difficult 是 difficult 的比較級。 ➲ compare SUPERLATIVE

com·para·tive·ly /kəmˈpærətɪvli/ *adv.* as compared to sth/sb else 比較上；相對地 SYN **relatively**：*The unit is comparatively easy to install and cheap to operate.* 這種設備安裝比較容易且用起來便宜。◇ *He died comparatively young* (= at a younger age than most people die). 他死時年紀並不大。◇ *comparatively few/low/rare/recent* 比較少 / 低 / 罕見；時間上相對較近的

com·pare 0▬ /kəmˈpeə(r); *NAmE* -ˈper/ *verb, noun*

■ ***verb*** **1** 0▬ (*abbr.* **cf., cp.**) [T] to examine people or things to see how they are similar and how they are different 比較；對比：**~ A and B** *It is interesting to compare their situation and ours.* 把他們的狀況與我們的相比很有意思。◇ *We compared the two reports carefully.* 我們仔細地比較了兩個報告。◇ **~ A with/to B** *We carefully compared the first report with the second.* 我們仔細比較了第一份報告和第二份報告。◇ *My own problems seem insignificant* ***compared with*** *other people's.* 與別人的問題相比，我自己的問題算不得什麼。◇ *I've had some*

C

C

difficulties, but they were ***nothing compared to*** *yours* (= they were not nearly as bad as yours). 我遇到了一些困難，但與你的困難比起來就算不上什麼了。◇ *Standards in health care have improved enormously compared to 40 years ago.* 與 40 年前相比，衞生保健的水平提高了不少。 ➲ LANGUAGE BANK at CONTRAST, ILLUSTRATE **2** [I] **~ with sb/sth** to be similar to sb/sth else, either better or worse 與…類似（或相似）：*This school compares with the best in the country* (= it is as good as them). 這所學校可與全國最好的學校媲美。◇ *This house doesn't compare with our previous one* (= it is not as good). 這房子比不上我們以前的。◇ *Their prices* ***compare favourably*** *with those of their competitors.* 他們的價格比競爭者的要優惠。 **3** [T] **~ A to B** to show or state that sb/sth is similar to sb/sth else 表明…與…相似；將…比作：*The critics compared his work to that of Martin Amis.* 評論家把他的作品和馬丁•埃米斯的相提並論。

IDM **compare 'notes (with sb)** if two or more people **compare notes**, they each say what they think about the same event, situation, etc.（與…）交換看法（或意見等）**you can't compare ˌapples and 'oranges** (*NAmE*) it is impossible to say that one thing is better than another if the two are completely different（因兩樣事物完全不同）不具可比性，不能相提並論：*They are both great but you can't compare apples and oranges.* 他們兩個都很不錯，但是不可相提並論。

■ *noun*

IDM **beyond/without com'pare** (*literary*) better than anything else of the same kind 無與倫比；舉世無雙

com·pari·son /kəm'pærɪsn/ *noun*

1 [U] **~ (with sb/sth)** the process of comparing two or more people or things 比較：*Comparison with other oil-producing countries is extremely interesting.* 與其他石油生產國作一比較是很有意思的。◇ *I enclose the two plans* ***for comparison.*** 茲附上兩份計劃以供比較。◇ *The education system* ***bears/stands no comparison with*** (= is not as good as) *that in many Asian countries.* 這種教育制度比不上許多亞洲國家的教育制度。 **2** [C] an occasion when two or more people or things are compared 對比；相比：**~ of A and B** *a comparison of the rail systems in Britain and France* 英國和法國鐵路系統的比較 ◇ **~ of A with B** *a comparison of men's salaries with those of women* 男女薪酬的比較 ◇ **~ between A and B** *comparisons between Britain and the rest of Europe* 英國與歐洲其他國家之間的各種比較 ◇ **~ of A to B** *a comparison of the brain to a computer* (= showing what is similar) 將大腦比作計算機 ◇ **~ (with sth)** *It is difficult to* ***make a comparison*** *with her previous book—they are completely different.* 這很難與她以前的書相比，兩者是截然不同的。◇ *You can* ***draw comparisons*** *with the situation in Ireland* (= say how the two situations are similar). 這種情形可與愛爾蘭的相比。 ➲ LANGUAGE BANK at SIMILARLY ➲ WRITING TUTOR page WT10

IDM **by comparison** used especially at the beginning of a sentence when the next thing that is mentioned is compared with sth in the previous sentence（尤用於句首）比較起來，較之：*By comparison, expenditure on education increased last year.* 相比之下，去年教育經費增加了。 **by/in comparison (with sb/sth)** when compared with sb/sth（與…）相比較：*The second half of the game was dull by comparison with the first.* 與上半場相比，比賽的下半場有些沉悶。◇ *The tallest buildings in London are small in comparison with New York's skyscrapers.* 倫敦最高的建築物與紐約的摩天大廈一比就相形見絀。 **there's no com'parison** used to emphasize the difference between two people or things that are being compared（強調比較之下的差別）無法相比，根本不能相提並論：*In terms of price there's no comparison* (= one thing is much more expensive than the other). 在價格方面無法相比。 ➲ more at PALE *v.*

com·part·ment /kəm'pɑːtmənt; *NAmE* -'pɑːrt-/ *noun*

1 one of the separate sections which a coach/car on a train is divided into（鐵路客車車廂分隔成的）隔間 **2** one of the separate sections that sth such as a piece of furniture or equipment has for keeping things in（傢具或設備等的）分隔間，隔層：*The desk has a secret compartment.* 這書桌有一個秘密隔層。◇ *There is a handy storage compartment beneath the oven.* 在烤箱的下面有一個便利的櫥櫃。 ➲ see also GLOVE COMPARTMENT

com·part·men·tal·ize (*BrE* also **-ise**) /ˌkɒmpɑːt'mentəlaɪz; *NAmE* kəmˌpɑːrt-/ *verb* **~ sth (into sth)** to divide sth into separate sections, especially so that one thing does not affect the other 分隔；隔開；劃分：*Life today is rigidly compartmentalized into work and leisure.* 當今的生活被嚴格劃分為工作和休閒兩部份。

compasses 指南針；圓規

compass 指南針

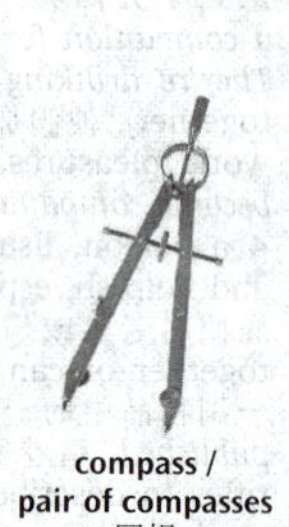
compass / pair of compasses 圓規

com·pass /'kʌmpəs/ *noun* **1** (also **magˌnetic 'compass**) [C] an instrument for finding direction, with a needle that always points to the north 羅盤；羅經；指南針；羅盤儀：*a map and compass* 地圖和指南針 ◇ *the* ***points of the compass*** (= N, S, E, W, etc.) 羅經方位點（東、南、西、北等） ➲ VISUAL VOCAB page V40 **2** [C] (also **compasses** [pl.]) an instrument with two long thin parts joined together at the top, used for drawing circles and measuring distances on a map 圓規；兩腳規：*a pair of compasses* 一副圓規 **3** [sing.] (*formal*) a range or an extent, especially of what can be achieved in a particular situation 範圍；範疇；界限：*the compass of a singer's voice* (= the range from the lowest to the highest note that he or she can sing) 歌手的音域

com·pas·sion /kəm'pæʃn/ *noun* [U] **~ (for sb)** a strong feeling of sympathy for people who are suffering and a desire to help them 同情；憐憫：*to* ***feel/show compassion*** 感到 / 表示同情

com·pas·sion·ate /kəm'pæʃənət/ *adj.* feeling or showing sympathy for people who are suffering 有同情心的；表示憐憫的：*He was allowed to go home on compassionate grounds* (= because he was suffering). 他因為得到同情而獲准回家。 ▸ **com·pas·sion·ate·ly** *adv.*

comˌpassionate 'leave *noun* [U] (*BrE*) time that you are allowed to be away from work because sb in your family is ill/sick or has died 恩恤休假；恩假（因家人生病或去世而准許的休假）

com·pati·bil·ity AW /kəmˌpætə'bɪləti/ *noun* [U] **~ (with sb/sth)** | **~ (between A and B)** **1** the ability of people or things to live or exist together without problems 和睦相處；並存；相容 **2** the ability of machines, especially computers, and computer programs to be used together（尤指計算機及程序的）兼容性，相容性

com·pat·ible AW /kəm'pætəbl/ *adj.* **1 ~ (with sth)** (of machines, especially computers 機器，尤指計算機) able to be used together 可共用的；兼容的：*compatible software* 可兼容的軟件 ◇ *The new system will be compatible with existing equipment.* 新的系統將與現有的設備相互兼容。 **2 ~ (with sth)** (of ideas, methods or things 想法、方法或事物) able to exist or be used together without causing problems 可共存的；可共用的；兼容的：*Are measures to protect the environment compatible with economic growth?* 保護環境的措施與經濟的增長協調嗎？◇ *compatible blood groups* 相容的血型 **3 ~ (with sb)** if two people are **compatible**, they can have a good relationship because they have similar ideas, interests, etc.（因思想、志趣等相投而）關係好的，和睦相處的 OPP **incompatible** ▸ **com·pat·ibly** /-əbli/ *adv.*

com·pat·riot /kəm'pætriət; *NAmE* -'peɪt-/ *noun* a person who was born in, or is a citizen of, the same country as sb else 同胞；同國人 **SYN** **countryman**：*He played against one of his compatriots in the semi-final.* 他在半決賽中與他的一位同胞選手對壘。

com·pel /kəm'pel/ *verb* (-ll-) (*formal*) **1** to force sb to do sth; to make sth necessary 強迫；迫使；使必須：**~ sb to do sth** *The law can compel fathers to make regular payments for their children.* 這項法律可強制父親定期支付子女的費用。◇ *I **feel compelled to** write and tell you how much I enjoyed your book.* 我覺得必須寫信告訴你我是多麼欣賞你的書。◇ **~ sth** *Last year ill health compelled his retirement.* 去年他因身體不好被迫退休了。**2 ~ sth** (not used in the progressive tenses 不用於進行時) to cause a particular reaction 引起反應：*He spoke with an authority that compelled the attention of the whole crowd.* 他用權威的口氣講話，引起了整個人群的注意。➲ see also COMPULSION

com·pel·ling /kəm'pelɪŋ/ *adj.* **1** that makes you pay attention to it because it is so interesting and exciting 引人入勝的；扣人心弦的：*Her latest book makes compelling reading.* 她新出的書讀起來扣人心弦。➲ SYNONYMS at INTERESTING **2** so strong that you must do sth about it 非常強烈的；不可抗拒的：*a **compelling need/desire*** 非常強烈的需要／慾望 **3** that makes you think it is true 令人信服的：*There is no compelling reason to believe him.* 沒有令人信服的理由讓人相信他。◇ *compelling evidence* 有說服力的證據 ▸ **com·pel·ling·ly** *adv.*：*compellingly attractive* 具有無法抗拒的魅力

com·pen·dious /kəm'pendiəs/ *adj.* (*formal*) containing all the necessary facts about sth 簡明扼要的；概括的：*a compendious description* 簡要說明

com·pen·dium /kəm'pendiəm/ *noun* (*pl.* **com·pen·dia** /-diə/ or **com·pen·diums**) a collection of facts, drawings and photographs on a particular subject, especially in a book（尤指書中某題材事實、圖畫及照片的）彙編，概要

com·pen·sate **AW** /'kɒmpenseɪt; *NAmE* 'kɑːm-/ *verb* **1** [I] **~ (for sth)** to provide sth good to balance or reduce the bad effects of damage, loss, etc. 補償；彌補 **SYN** **make up for**：*Nothing can compensate for the loss of a loved one.* 失去心愛的人是無法補償的。**2** [T] **~ sb (for sth)** to pay sb money because they have suffered some damage, loss, injury, etc. 給（某人）賠償（或賠款）：*Her lawyers say she should be compensated for the suffering she had been caused.* 她的律師說她應該為所遭受的痛苦得到賠償。▸ **com·pen·sa·tory** **AW** /ˌkɒmpen'seɪtəri; *NAmE* kəm'pensətɔːri/ *adj.*：*He received a compensatory payment of $20 000.* 他獲得了 2 萬元的賠償金。

com·pen·sa·tion **AW** /ˌkɒmpen'seɪʃn; *NAmE* ˌkɑːm-/ *noun* **1** [U, C] **~ (for sth)** something, especially money, that sb gives you because they have hurt you, or damaged sth that you own; the act of giving this to sb 補償（或賠償）物；（尤指）賠償金，補償金；賠償：*to **claim/award/receive compensation*** 要求／判給／得到賠償金 ◇ *to pay compensation for injuries at work* 支付工傷賠償金 ◇ *to receive £10 000 **in compensation**.* 得到賠償金 1 萬英鎊 **2** [C, usually pl.] **~ (for sth)** things that make a bad situation better 彌補的事物；（對不利局面的）補償：*I wish I were young again, but getting older has its compensations.* 我要是能再次年輕就好了，但上了年紀也有上了年紀的好處。

com·père /'kɒmpeə(r); *NAmE* 'kɑːmper/ *noun, verb*
■ ***noun*** (*BrE*) a person who introduces the people who perform in a television programme, show in a theatre, etc.（電視節目等的）主持人；（劇院等的）報幕員 **SYN** **emcee**：*to act as (a) compère* 當節目主持人
■ ***verb*** [T, I] **~ (sth)** (*BrE*) to act as a compère for a show 做（演出）主持人；做報幕員

com·pete 🔑 /kəm'piːt/ *verb* **1** 🔑 [I] to try to be more successful or better than sb else who is trying to do the same as you 競爭；對抗：**~ (with/against sb) (for sth)** *Several companies are competing for the contract.* 為得到那項合同，幾家公司正在競爭。◇ *We can't compete with them on price.* 我們在價格上無法與他們競爭。◇ *Young children will usually compete for their mother's attention.* 小孩子通常都會在母親面前爭寵。◇ *Small traders cannot compete in the face of cheap foreign imports.* 面對廉價的外國進口商品，經營規模小的商人無法與之抗衡。◇ **~ to do sth** *There are too many magazines competing to attract readers.* 競相吸引讀者的雜誌太多了。**2** 🔑 [I] **~ (in sth) (against sb)** to take part in a contest or game 參加比賽（或競賽）：*He's hoping to compete in the London marathon.* 他期盼着參加倫敦馬拉松比賽。

com·pe·tence /'kɒmpɪtəns; *NAmE* 'kɑːm-/ *noun* **1** (also *less frequent* **com·pe·ten·cy**) [U, C] **~ (in sth) | ~ (in doing sth)** the ability to do sth well 能力；勝任：*to gain a high level of competence in English* 獲得高水平的英語能力 ◇ *professional/technical competence* 專業／技術能力 **OPP** **incompetence** **2** [U] (*law* 律) the power that a court, an organization or a person has to deal with sth（法庭、機構或人的）權限，管轄權：*The judge has to act within the competence of the court.* 法官必須在法庭的權限範圍內行使權力。◇ *outside sb's area of competence* 超出某人的權限範圍 **3** [C] (also *less frequent* **com·pe·ten·cy**) (*technical* 術語) a skill that you need in a particular job or for a particular task 技能；本領：*The syllabus lists the knowledge and competences required at this level.* 教學大綱列出了這一級水平要求掌握的知識技能。

com·pe·tency /'kɒmpɪtənsi; *NAmE* 'kɑːm-/ *noun* (*pl.* **-ies**) = COMPETENCE

com·pe·tent /'kɒmpɪtənt; *NAmE* 'kɑːm-/ *adj.* **~ (to do sth)** **1** having enough skill or knowledge to do sth well or to the necessary standard 足以勝任的；有能力的；稱職的：*Make sure the firm is competent to carry out the work.* 要確保這家公司有能力完成這項工作。◇ *He's very competent in his work.* 他工作十分稱職。**OPP** **incompetent** **2** of a good standard but not very good 合格的；不錯的；尚好的 **3** having the power to decide sth 有決定權的：*The case was referred to a competent authority.* 事情已交給有關當局處理。▸ **com·pe·tent·ly** *adv.*：*to perform competently* 出色地完成

com·pe·ti·tion 🔑 /ˌkɒmpə'tɪʃn; *NAmE* ˌkɑːm-/ *noun* **1** 🔑 [U] **~ (between/with sb) (for sth)** a situation in which people or organizations compete with each other for sth that not everyone can have 競爭；角逐：*There is now intense competition between schools to attract students.* 現在學校之間為了招攬學生展開了激烈競爭。◇ *We are **in competition with** four other companies for the contract.* 我們在與其他四家公司競爭這項合同。◇ *We won the contract in the face of **stiff competition**.* 面對激烈的競爭，我們贏得了這份合同。**2** 🔑 [C] an event in which people compete with each other to find out who is the best at sth 比賽；競賽：*a **music/photo, etc. competition*** 音樂、攝影等比賽 ◇ *to **enter/win/lose a competition*** 參加／贏得／輸掉比賽 **3 the competition** [sing.+sing./pl. v.] the people who are competing against sb 競爭者；對手：*We'll be able to assess the competition at the conference.* 我們可以在會上對競爭對手進行估量。

com·peti·tive 🔑 /kəm'petətɪv/ *adj.* **1** 🔑 used to describe a situation in which people or organizations compete against each other 競爭的：***competitive games/sports*** 競技性的比賽／體育運動 ◇ *Graduates have to fight for jobs in a **highly competitive** market.* 畢業生不得不在競爭激烈的市場上奮力爭取工作。**2** 🔑 **~ (with sb/sth)** as good as or better than others（與…）一樣好的；（比…）更好的；有競爭力的：*a shop selling clothes at competitive prices* (= as low as any other shop) 在服裝價格上有競爭力的商店 ◇ *We need to work harder to remain competitive with other companies.* 我們需要更加努力工作以保持對其他公司具有競爭力。◇ *to gain a **competitive advantage** over rival companies* 佔有超越對手公司的競爭優勢 ➲ SYNONYMS at CHEAP **3** 🔑 (of a person 人) trying very hard to be better than others 努力競爭的；一心求勝的：*You have to be highly competitive to do well in sport these days.* 如今你必須有強烈的競爭意識才能在體育運動中取得好成績。**OPP** **uncompetitive** ▸ **com·peti·tive·ly** *adv.*：*competitively priced goods* 價格上具有競爭力的商品 **com·peti·tive·ness** *noun*：*the competitiveness of British industry* 英國工業的競爭力

com·peti·tor /kəmˈpetɪtə(r)/ *noun* **1** a person or an organization that competes against others, especially in business（尤指商業方面的）競爭者，對手：*our **main/major competitor*** 我們主要的競爭對手 **2** a person who takes part in a competition 參賽者；競賽者：*Over 200 competitors entered the race.* * 200 多名選手參加了賽跑。

com·pil·ation AW /ˌkɒmpɪˈleɪʃn; *NAmE* ˌkɑːm-/ *noun* **1** [C] a collection of items, especially pieces of music or writing, taken from different places and put together 收集；選編；選輯：*Her latest CD is a compilation of all her best singles.* 她最新的激光唱片收錄了她的所有最佳單曲。◇ *a compilation album* 一張選輯 **2** [U] the process of compiling sth 編纂；編著；編寫：*the compilation of a dictionary* 詞典的編纂

com·pile AW /kəmˈpaɪl/ *verb* **1 ~ sth** to produce a book, list, report, etc. by bringing together different items, articles, songs, etc. 編寫（書、列表、報告等）；編纂：*We are trying to compile a list of suitable people for the job.* 我們在努力編製一份適合做這項工作的人員的名單。◇ *The album was compiled from live recordings from last year's tour.* 這張選輯由去年巡迴演出的實況錄音彙編而成。 **2 ~ sth** (*computing* 計) to translate instructions from one computer language into another so that a particular computer can understand them 編譯

com·piler /kəmˈpaɪlə(r)/ *noun* **1** a person who compiles sth 編纂者；彙編者；編著者 **2** (*computing* 計) a program that translates instructions from one computer language into another for a computer to understand 編譯程序

com·pla·cency /kəmˈpleɪsnsi/ *noun* [U] (usually *disapproving*) a feeling of satisfaction with yourself or with a situation, so that you do not think any change is necessary; the state of being complacent 自滿；自得；自鳴得意：*Despite signs of an improvement in the economy, there is no room for complacency.* 儘管在經濟方面有改善的跡象，但仍不容自滿。

com·pla·cent /kəmˈpleɪsnt/ *adj.* **~ (about sb/sth)** (usually *disapproving*) too satisfied with yourself or with a situation, so that you do not feel that any change is necessary; showing or feeling complacency 自滿的；自鳴得意的；表現出自滿的：*a dangerously complacent attitude to the increase in unemployment* 對失業增加抱滿不在乎的危險態度 ◇ *We must not become complacent about progress.* 我們決不能因進步變得自滿。 ▸ **com·pla·cent·ly** *adv.*

com·plain 0-w /kəmˈpleɪn/ *verb* [I, T] to say that you are annoyed, unhappy or not satisfied about sb/sth 抱怨；埋怨；投訴；發牢騷：**~ (to sb) (about/of sth)** *I'm going to complain to the manager about this.* 我要就這件事向經理投訴。◇ *The defendant complained of intimidation during the investigation.* 被告申訴在調查期間受到了恐嚇。◇ *She never complains, but she's obviously exhausted.* 她雖然從不抱怨，但顯然已疲憊不堪。◇ (*informal*) *'How are you?' 'Oh, I can't complain* (= I'm all right).' "你好嗎？" "啊，沒得抱怨的。" ◇ **~ (that)** ... *He **complained bitterly** that he had been unfairly treated.* 他憤懣地訴說他所受到的不公平待遇。◇ **+ speech** *'It's not fair,' she complained.* "這不公平。" 她抱怨道。

PHR V **comˈplain of sth** to say that you feel ill/sick or are suffering from a pain 訴說（病情或痛苦）：*She left early, complaining of a headache.* 她說自己頭疼，很早就離開了。

com·plain·ant *noun* (*BrE, law* 律) = PLAINTIFF

com·plaint 0-w /kəmˈpleɪnt/ *noun* **1** 0-w [C] a reason for not being satisfied; a statement that sb makes saying that they are not satisfied 不滿的原因；抱怨；埋怨；投訴；控告：**~ (about sb/sth)** *The most common complaint is about poor service.* 最常見的投訴與服務差有關。◇ *We received a number of complaints from customers about the lack of parking facilities.* 我們收到了來自顧客的許多投訴，抱怨缺乏停車設施。◇ *I'd like to **make a complaint** about the noise.* 我要就噪音問題提出投訴。◇ **~ (against sb/sth)** *I believe you have a complaint against one of our nurses.* 我認為你對我們的一位護士有怨言。◇ **~ (that ...)** *a **complaint that** he had been unfairly treated* 對他受到了不公正待遇的投訴 ◇ *a **formal complaint*** 正式控告 ◇ (*formal*) *to **file/lodge** (= make) **a complaint*** 提出控告 ➲ WRITING TUTOR page WT37 **2** 0-w [U] the act of complaining 抱怨；埋怨；投訴：*I can see no **grounds for complaint**.* 我看沒理由抱怨。◇ *a letter of complaint* 投訴信 **3** [C] an illness, especially one that is not serious, and often one that affects a particular part of the body（尤指不嚴重、常影響身體某部位的）疾病：*a skin complaint* 皮膚病

Synonyms 同義詞辨析

complain

protest • object • grumble • moan • whine

These words all mean to say that you are annoyed, unhappy or not satisfied about sb/sth. 以上各詞均含對人或事物感到惱怒、不高興或不滿之意。

complain to say that you are annoyed, unhappy or not satisfied about sb/sth 指抱怨、埋怨、投訴、發牢騷：*I'm going to complain to the manager about this.* 我要就這件事向經理投訴。

protest to say or do sth to show that you disagree with or disapprove of sth, especially publicly; to give sth as a reason for protesting 指公開反對、抗議或申辯：*Students took to the streets to **protest against** the decision.* 學生走上街頭抗議這項決定。

object to say that you disagree with or disapprove of sth; to give sth as a reason for objecting 指不同意、不贊成、反對或抗辯：*If nobody objects, we'll postpone the meeting till next week.* 如果沒有人反對，我們就把會議推遲到下週。◇ *He objected that the police had arrested him without sufficient evidence.* 他抗辯說警察沒有充分證據就逮捕了他。

grumble (*rather informal, disapproving*) to complain about sb/sth in a bad-tempered way 指咕噥、嘟囔、發牢騷：*They kept grumbling that they were cold.* 他們不停地嘟囔着說冷。

moan (*BrE, rather informal, disapproving*) to complain about sb/sth in an annoying way 指抱怨、埋怨：*What are you moaning on about now?* 你在抱怨什麼呢？

whine (*rather informal, disapproving*) to complain in an annoying, crying voice 指哭哭啼啼或哭嚷着訴說：*Stop whining!* 別哭哭啼啼的！◇ *'I want to go home,' whined Toby.* "我要回家。" 托比哼哼唧唧地說。 NOTE **Whine** is often used to talk about the way that young children complain. * whine 通常用於小孩子抱怨。

PATTERNS

- to complain/protest/grumble/moan/whine **about** sth
- to complain/protest/grumble/moan **at** sth
- to complain/protest/object/grumble/moan/whine **to** sb
- to complain/protest/object/grumble/moan/whine **that** ...

com·plai·sant /kəmˈpleɪzənt/ *adj.* (*old-fashioned*) ready to accept other people's actions and opinions and to do what other people want 順從的；殷勤的 ▸ **com·plai·sance** /kəmˈpleɪzəns/ *noun* [U]

com·plect·ed /kəmˈplektɪd/ *adj.* (*NAmE, informal*) (used with adjectives 與形容詞連用) with skin and a COMPLEXION of the type mentioned 膚色…的：*fair/dark complected* 膚色白皙 / 黝黑

com·ple·ment AW *verb, noun*

■ *verb* /ˈkɒmplɪment; *NAmE* ˈkɑːm-/ **~ sth** to add to sth in a way that improves it or makes it more attractive 補充；補足；使完美；使更具吸引力：*The excellent menu is complemented by a good wine list.* 佳肴佐以美酒，堪稱完美無缺。◇ *The team needs players who **complement each other**.* 球隊需要能夠相互取長補短的隊員。 ➲ note at COMPLIMENT

C

■ **noun** /ˈkɒmplɪmənt; *NAmE* ˈkɑːm-/ **1 ~ (to sth)** a thing that adds new qualities to sth in a way that improves it or makes it more attractive 補充物；補足物 **2** the complete number or quantity needed or allowed 足數；足額：*We've taken our full complement of trainees this year.* 我們今年接收的實習生已滿員。**3** (*grammar* 語法) a word or phrase, especially an adjective or a noun, that is used after linking verbs such as *be* and *become*, and describes the subject of the verb. In some descriptions of grammar it is used to refer to any word or phrase which is GOVERNED by a verb and usually comes after the verb in a sentence. 補足語；補語：*In the sentences 'I'm angry' and 'He became a politician', 'angry' and 'politician' are complements.* 在句子 I'm angry 和 He became a politician 中，angry 和 politician 為補語。

com·ple·men·tary **AW** /ˌkɒmplɪˈmentri; *NAmE* ˌkɑːm-/ *adj.* **~ (to sth)** two people or things that are **complementary** are different but together form a useful or attractive combination of skills, qualities or physical features 互補的；補充的；相互補足的：*The school's approach must be complementary to that of the parents.* 學校與家長的教育方法必須相輔相成。➲ note at COMPLIMENT

ˌcomplementary ˈangle *noun* (*geometry* 幾何) either of two angles which together make 90° 餘角 ➲ compare SUPPLEMENTARY ANGLE

ˌcomplementary ˈcolour (*especially US* **ˌcomplementary ˈcolor**) *noun* (*technical* 術語) **1** a colour that, when mixed with another colour, gives black or white 互補色，補色（與另外一種顏色混合成為黑色或白色的顏色）**2** a colour that gives the greatest contrast when combined with a particular colour 對比色（與某特定顏色形成最大色差的顏色）：*The designer has chosen the complementary colours blue and orange.* 設計師選取了藍和橙黃兩種對比色。

ˌcomplementary ˈmedicine *noun* [U] (*BrE*) medical treatment that is not part of the usual scientific treatment used in Western countries, for example ACUPUNCTURE 輔助性醫療（不屬於西方國家通常採用的科學療法，如針灸）

com·ple·men·ta·tion /ˌkɒmplɪmenˈteɪʃn; *NAmE* ˌkɑːm-/ *noun* [U] **1** the fact of complementing sth 補充 **2** (*grammar* 語法) the complements of a verb in a clause（動詞的）補足語，補語

com·ple·men·tizer (*BrE* also **-iser**) /ˈkɒmplɪməntaɪzə(r); *NAmE* ˈkɑːm-/ *noun* (*grammar* 語法) a word or part of a word that shows a clause is being used as a complement 補語化成分

com·plete 🔑 /kəmˈpliːt/ *adj., verb*

■ **adj. 1** 🔑 [usually before noun] used when you are emphasizing sth, to mean 'to the greatest degree possible'（用以強調）完全的，徹底的 **SYN** **total**：*We were in complete agreement.* 我們意見完全一致。◇ *a complete change* 徹底的變化 ◇ *in complete silence* 萬籟俱寂 ◇ *a complete stranger* 素不相識的人 ◇ *It came as a complete surprise.* 這事來得十分意外。◇ *I felt a complete idiot.* 我覺得自己是個十足的笨蛋。**2** 🔑 including all the parts, etc. that are necessary; whole 全部的；完整的；整個的：*I've collected the complete set.* 我收集了全套。◇ *a complete guide to events in Oxford* 牛津全部大事的手冊 ◇ *the* **complete works** *of Tolstoy* 托爾斯泰全集 ◇ *You will receive payment for each complete day that you work.* 你將按你每一整天的工作領取報酬。**OPP** **incomplete** **3 ~ with sth** [not before noun] including sth as an extra part or feature 包括，含有（額外部份或特徵）：*The furniture comes complete with tools and instructions for assembly.* 這件傢具備有組裝工具和說明書。◇ *The book, complete with CD, costs £35.* 此書包括光盤，售價 35 英鎊。**4** 🔑 [not before noun] finished 完成；結束：*Work on the office building will be complete at the end of the year.* 辦公大樓工程將於年底竣工。**OPP** **incomplete**

▶ **com·plete·ness** *noun* [U]：*the accuracy and completeness of the information* 信息的準確完整性 ◇ *For the sake of completeness, all names are given in full.* 為完整起見，所有名稱均用全名。

■ **verb 1** 🔑 [often passive] **~ sth** to finish making or doing sth 完成；結束：*She's just completed a master's degree in Law.* 她剛讀完法律碩士學位。◇ *The project should be completed within a year.* 這項工程必須在一年之內完成。**2** 🔑 **~ sth** to write all the information you are asked for on a form 填寫（表格）**SYN** **fill in/out**：*2 000 shoppers completed our questionnaire.* * 2 000 名顧客填寫了我們的調查表。**3** 🔑 **~ sth** to make sth whole or perfect 使完整；使完美：*I only need one more card to complete the set.* 我只差一張卡片就配齊全套了。

com·plete·ly 🔑 /kəmˈpliːtli/ *adv.* (used to emphasize the following word or phrase 用於強調緊跟其後的詞或短語) in every way possible 徹底地；完全地；完整地 **SYN** **totally**：*completely different* 截然不同 ◇ *completely and utterly broke* 徹底破產 ◇ *I've completely forgotten her name.* 我完全把她的名字給忘了。◇ *The explosion completely destroyed the building.* 爆炸完全毀掉了那棟大樓。

com·ple·tion /kəmˈpliːʃn/ *noun* **1** [U] the act or process of finishing sth; the state of being finished and complete 完成；結束：*the completion of the new hospital building* 新醫院大樓的竣工 ◇ *Satisfactory completion of the course does not ensure you a job.* 圓滿完成課程並不能保證你能得到工作。◇ *The project is* **due for completion** *in the spring.* 這項工程預定在明年春季竣工。◇ *The road is* **nearing completion** (= it is nearly finished). 這條道路快要完工了。◇ *the date of completion/the completion date* 竣工日期 **2** [U, C] (*BrE*) the formal act of completing the sale of property, for example the sale of a house（房地產等的）完成交易，完成交割

com·plex 🔑 **AW** *adj., noun*

■ **adj.** /ˈkɒmpleks; *NAmE* kəmˈpleks; ˈkɑːm-/ **1** 🔑 made of many different things or parts that are connected; difficult to understand 複雜的；難懂的；費解的 **SYN** **complicated**：*complex machinery* 結構複雜的機器 ◇ *the complex structure of the human brain* 錯綜複雜的人腦構造 ◇ *a complex argument/problem/subject* 複雜難懂的論證／問題／科目 **2** (*grammar* 語法) (of a word or sentence 單詞或句子) containing one main part (= the ROOT of a word or MAIN CLAUSE of a sentence) and one or more other parts (called AFFIXES or SUBORDINATE CLAUSES) 複合的（指詞根加有詞綴或主句含有從句）➲ compare COMPOUND *adj.*

■ **noun** /ˈkɒmpleks; *NAmE* ˈkɑːm-/ **1** a group of buildings of a similar type together in one place（類型相似的）建築群：*a sports complex* 綜合體育場 ◇ *an industrial complex* (= a site with many factories) 工業建築群 ➲ **SYNONYMS** at BUILDING **2** a group of things that are connected 相關聯的一組事物：*This is just one of a whole complex of issues.* 這僅僅是所有相關的問題之一。**3** (especially in compounds 尤用於構成複合詞) a mental state that is not normal 不正常的精神狀態；情結：*to suffer from a guilt complex* 蒙受負罪感之苦 ➲ see also INFERIORITY COMPLEX, OEDIPUS COMPLEX, PERSECUTION COMPLEX **4** if sb has a **complex** about sth, they are worried about it in way that is not normal（對某事）不正常的憂慮

com·plex·ion /kəmˈplekʃn/ *noun* **1** the natural colour and condition of the skin on a person's face 面色；膚色；氣色：*a pale/bad complexion* 蒼白的／病態的臉色 ➲ **COLLOCATIONS** at PHYSICAL **2** [usually sing.] the general character of sth（事物的）性質，特性：*a move which changed the political complexion of the country* 改變國家政局的舉措

IDM **put a new/different comˈplexion on sth** to change the way that a situation appears 使形勢改觀

com·plex·ity **AW** /kəmˈpleksəti/ *noun* **1** [U] the state of being formed of many parts; the state of being difficult to understand 複雜性；難懂：*the increasing complexity of modern telecommunication systems* 日益複雜的現代電信系統 ◇ *I was astonished by the size and complexity of the problem.* 這個問題的複雜性和涉及面之廣使我感到驚訝。**2** **complexities** [pl.] the features of a problem or situation that are difficult to understand 難題；難以理解的局勢：*the complexities of the system* 這一系統的複雜之處

C

ˌcomplex ˈnumber *noun* (*mathematics* 數) a number containing both a REAL NUMBER and an IMAGINARY NUMBER 複數

com·pli·ance /kəm'plaɪəns/ *noun* [U] **~ (with sth)** the practice of obeying rules or requests made by people in authority 服從；順從；遵從：*procedures that must be followed to ensure full compliance with the law* 為確保嚴格遵守法律所必須遵行的程序 ◇ *Safety measures were carried out* ***in compliance with*** *paragraph 6 of the building regulations.* 遵照建築規程的第 6 條實施了安全措施。**OPP** **non-compliance** ➲ see also COMPLY

com·pli·ant /kəm'plaɪənt/ *adj.* **1** (usually *disapproving*) too willing to agree with other people or to obey rules 順從的；百依百順的；俯首帖耳的：*By then, Henry seemed less compliant with his wife's wishes than he had six months before.* 與六個月以前相比，亨利當時對他妻子的意願似乎已不那麼百依百順了。◇ *We should not be producing compliant students who do not dare to criticize.* 我們不應當把學生培養成不敢批評的唯唯諾諾的人。**2** in agreement with a set of rules（與一系列規則）符合的，一致的：*This site is HTML compliant.* 這個網站支持 HTML 語言。➲ see also COMPLY

com·pli·cate 🔑 /'kɒmplɪkeɪt; *NAmE* 'kɑːm-/ *verb* **~ sth** to make sth more difficult to do, understand or deal with 使複雜化：*I do not wish to complicate the task more than is necessary.* 我不想使這項任務不必要地複雜化。◇ ***To complicate matters*** *further, there will be no transport available till 8 o'clock.* 使事情更難辦的是 8 點鐘之前不會有交通工具。◇ *The issue* ***is complicated by the fact that*** *a vital document is missing.* 一份重要文件的丟失使這個問題複雜化了。

com·pli·cated 🔑 /'kɒmplɪkeɪtɪd; *NAmE* 'kɑːm-/ *adj.* made of many different things or parts that are connected; difficult to understand 複雜的；難懂的 **SYN** **complex**：*a complicated system* 複雜的系統 ◇ *The instructions look very complicated.* 這說明書看起來很難懂。◇ *It's all very complicated—but I'll try and explain.* 儘管這一切都很難理解，但我會盡力解釋。

com·pli·ca·tion /ˌkɒmplɪ'keɪʃn; *NAmE* ˌkɑːm-/ *noun* **1** [C, U] a thing that makes a situation more complicated or difficult 使更複雜化（或更困難）的事物：*The bad weather added a further complication to our journey.* 惡劣的天氣給我們的旅行增加了更多的困難。**2** [C, usually pl.] (*medical* 醫) a new problem or illness that makes treatment of a previous one more complicated or difficult 併發症：*She developed complications after the surgery.* 她手術後出現了併發症。

com·pli·cit /kəm'plɪsɪt/ *adj.* **~ (in/with sb/sth)** involved with other people in sth wrong or illegal（與某人在某事上）同謀的，串通的：*Several officers were complicit in the cover-up.* 幾名軍官串通一氣隱瞞真相。

com·pli·city /kəm'plɪsəti/ *noun* [U] **~ (in sth)** (*formal*) the act of taking part with another person in a crime 同謀；共犯；勾結 **SYN** **collusion**：*to be guilty of complicity in the murder* 犯兇殺同謀罪 ◇ *evident complicity between the two brothers* 兩兄弟間明顯的串通一氣

com·pli·ment *noun, verb*

■ ***noun*** /'kɒmplɪmənt; *NAmE* 'kɑːm-/ **1** [C] a remark that expresses praise or admiration of sb 讚揚；稱讚：***to pay sb a compliment*** (= to praise them for sth) 對某人表示讚揚 ◇ *'You understand the problem because you're so much older.' 'I'll* ***take that as a compliment****!'* "您能理解這個問題，因為您是長者。" "過獎了。" ◇ *It's a* ***great compliment*** *to be asked to do the job.* 獲聘請做這項工作是一項極大的榮譽。◇ *to* ***return the compliment*** (= to treat sb in the same way as they have treated you) 照樣回敬 **2 compliments** [pl.] (*formal*) polite words or good wishes, especially when used to express praise and admiration 致意；問候；祝賀：*My compliments to the chef!* 請向廚師代為致意！◇ (*BrE*) *Compliments of the season!* (= for Christmas or the New Year) 謹致節日的祝賀！（聖誕節或新年時的賀辭）◇ *Please accept these flowers* ***with the compliments of*** (= as a gift from) *the manager.* 請接受經理送的鮮花。**IDM** see BACKHANDED

■ ***verb*** /'kɒmplɪment; *NAmE* 'kɑːm-/ **~ sb (on sth)** to tell sb that you like or admire sth they have done, their appearance, etc. 讚美；稱讚；欽佩：*She complimented him on his excellent German.* 她誇獎他德語棒極了。

Which Word? 詞語辨析

compliment / complement

- These words have similar spellings but completely different meanings. If you **compliment** someone, you say something very nice to them. 這兩個詞拼寫相似，但意義完全不同。compliment 指讚美、稱讚：*She complimented me on my English.* 她誇獎我的英語好。If one thing **complements** another, the two things work or look better because they are together. * complement 表示相輔相成、相配合：*The different flavours complement each other perfectly.* 不同的味道搭配在一起，可口極了。
- The adjectives are also often confused. 上述詞的形容詞亦常混淆。**Complimentary:** *She made some very complimentary remarks about my English.* 她對我的英語讚賞有加。It can also mean 'free'. 該詞亦含免費贈送之意：*There was a complimentary basket of fruit in our room.* 我們房間裏有一籃免費贈送的水果。**Complementary**：*The team members have different but complementary skills.* 隊員技術不同但能互補。

com·pli·men·tary /ˌkɒmplɪ'mentri; *NAmE* ˌkɑːm-/ *adj.* **1** given free 免費的；贈送的：*complimentary tickets for the show* 演出贈券 **2 ~ (about sth)** expressing admiration, praise, etc. 表示欽佩的；讚美的：*a complimentary remark* 讚美的言辭 ◇ *She was extremely complimentary about his work.* 她對他的工作給予了高度評價。**OPP** **uncomplimentary** ➲ note at COMPLIMENT

ˈcompliments slip *noun* (*BrE*) a small piece of paper printed with the name of a company, that is sent out together with information, goods, etc.（附在信息、貨物等上印有公司名稱的）贈禮便條，禮帖

com·ply /kəm'plaɪ/ *verb* (**com·plies**, **com·ply·ing**, **com·plied**, **com·plied**) [I] **~ (with sth)** to obey a rule, an order, etc. 遵從；服從；順從：*They refused to comply with the UN resolution.* 他們拒絕遵守聯合國的決議。➲ see also COMPLIANCE

compo /'kɒmpəʊ; *NAmE* 'kɑːmpoʊ/ *noun* [U] (*AustralE, NZE, informal*) money that is paid to a worker if he/she gets injured at work 工傷賠償費 **SYN** **compensation**

com·pon·ent **AW** /kəm'pəʊnənt; *NAmE* -'poʊ-/ *noun* one of several parts of which sth is made 組成部份；成分；部件：*the components of a machine* 機器部件 ◇ *the car component industry* 汽車零部件製造業 ◇ ***Key components*** *of the government's plan are ...* 政府計劃的主要組成部份是… ◇ *Trust is a* ***vital component*** *in any relationship.* 在任何關係中，信任都是一個至關重要的因素。▶ **com·pon·ent** *adj.* [only before noun]：*Break the problem down into its* ***component parts****.* 把這個問題分解成若干組成部份。

com·pon·en·tial an·aly·sis /ˌkɒmpəˌnenʃl ə'næləsɪs; *NAmE* kɑːm-/ *noun* [U] (*linguistics* 語言) the study of meaning by analysing the different parts of words（語義的）成分分析

com·port /kəm'pɔːt; *NAmE* -'pɔːrt/ *verb* **~ yourself + adv./prep.** (*formal*) to behave in a particular way 行為表現；舉止：*She always comports herself with great dignity.* 她的舉止總是很端莊。

com·port·ment /kəm'pɔːtmənt; *NAmE* -'pɔːrt-/ *noun* [U] (*formal*) the way in which sb/sth behaves 行為；舉止；表現：*She won admiration for her comportment during the trial.* 她在選拔賽中的表現得到了讚賞。

com·pose /kəm'pəʊz; *NAmE* -'poʊz/ *verb* **1** [T] (not used in the progressive tenses 不用於進行時) **~ sth** (*formal*) to combine together to form a whole 組成，構成（一個整體）**SYN** **make up**：*Ten men compose the committee.* 委員會由十人組成。➲ see also COMPOSED (1) **2** [T, I] **~ (sth)** to write music 作曲；創作（音樂）：*Mozart* *composed his last opera shortly before he died.* 莫扎特在創作出他最後一部歌劇後不久便去世了。 **3** [T] **~ a letter/speech/poem** to write a letter, etc. usually with a lot of care and thought 撰寫（信函、講稿、詩歌等）： *She composed a letter of protest.* 她寫了一封抗議信。 **4** [T, no passive] (*formal*) to manage to control your feelings or expression 使鎮靜；使平靜： **~ yourself** *Emma frowned, making an effort to compose herself.* 埃瑪皺起了眉頭，努力使自己鎮定下來。◇ **~ sth** *I was so confused that I could hardly compose my thoughts.* 我心煩意亂難以鎮定思緒。 ➲ see also COMPOSURE

com·posed /kəm'pəʊzd; *NAmE* -'poʊzd/ *adj.* **1** **be composed of sth** (*formal*) to be made or formed from several parts, things or people 由…組成（或構成）的： *The committee is composed mainly of lawyers.* 委員會主要由律師組成。 ➲ SYNONYMS at CONSIST OF **2** [not usually before noun] calm and in control of your feelings 鎮靜；鎮定；平靜： *She seemed outwardly composed.* 她表面上好像很鎮靜。

com·poser /kəm'pəʊzə(r); *NAmE* -'poʊz-/ *noun* a person who writes music, especially CLASSICAL music （尤指古典音樂的）創作者；作曲者；作曲家

com·pos·ite /'kɒmpəzɪt; *NAmE* kəm'pɑːzət/ *adj., noun*

■ ***adj.*** [only before noun] made of different parts or materials 合成的；混成的；複合的： *a composite picture* (= one made from several pictures) 拼圖

■ ***noun*** **1** something made by putting together different parts or materials 合成物；混合物；複合材料： *The document was a composite of information from various sources.* 這份文件是不同來源信息的綜合。 **2** (also **com'posite sketch**) (both *US*) (*BrE* **Iden·ti·kit™**) a set of drawings of different features that can be put together to form the face of a person, especially sb wanted by the police, using descriptions given by people who saw the person; a picture made in this way 容貌拼圖（根據目擊者描述拼製出的面部畫像，尤用於警方要捉拿的人）

com·pos·ition /ˌkɒmpə'zɪʃn; *NAmE* ˌkɑːm-/ *noun* **1** [U] the different parts which sth is made of; the way in which the different parts are organized 成分；構成；組合方式： *the chemical composition of the soil* 土壤的化學成分◇ *the composition of the board of directors* 董事會的組成 ➲ SYNONYMS at STRUCTURE **2** [C] (*formal*) a piece of music or art, or a poem （音樂、藝術、詩歌的）作品： *one of Beethoven's finest compositions* 貝多芬最優美的音樂作品之一 **3** [U] the act of COMPOSING sth 作曲；創作： *pieces performed in the order of their composition* 按作曲順序表演的作品 **4** [U] the art of writing music 作曲藝術： *to study composition* 學習作曲藝術 **5** [C] a short text that is written as a school exercise; a short essay 作文；小論文 **6** [U] (*art* 美術) the arrangement of people or objects in a painting or photograph （繪畫、攝影的）構圖

com·posi·tor /kəm'pɒzɪtə(r); *NAmE* -'pɑːz-/ *noun* a person who arranges text on a page before printing 排版人員

com·pos men·tis /ˌkɒmpəs 'mentɪs; *NAmE* ˌkɑːm-/ *adj.* [not before noun] (from *Latin*, *formal* or *humorous*) having full control of your mind 能完全控制神志；心智健全 **OPP** **non compos mentis**

com·post /'kɒmpɒst; *NAmE* 'kɑːmpoʊst/ *noun, verb*

■ ***noun*** [U, C] a mixture of decayed plants, food, etc. that can be added to soil to help plants grow 混合肥料；堆肥： ***potting compost*** (= a mixture of soil and compost that you can buy to grow new plants in) 盆栽混合肥料 ➲ VISUAL VOCAB page V8

■ ***verb*** **1 ~ sth** to make sth into compost 把…製成堆肥 **2 ~ sth** to put compost on or in sth 施堆肥於

'compost bin *noun* a container in the garden where leaves, plants, etc. are put, to make compost （花園裏的）堆肥桶；落葉垃圾桶 ➲ VISUAL VOCAB pages V8, V19

'compost heap (*especially BrE*) (*NAmE* usually **'compost pile**) *noun* a place in the garden where leaves, plants, etc. are piled, to make compost （花園裏的）堆肥處；園中落葉堆

com·pos·ure /kəm'pəʊʒə(r); *NAmE* -'poʊ-/ *noun* [U] the state of being calm and in control of your feelings or behaviour 沉着；鎮靜；鎮定： *to* ***keep/lose/recover/regain your composure*** 保持 / 失去 / 恢復鎮靜

com·pote /'kɒmpɒt; *NAmE* 'kɑːmpoʊt/ *noun* [C, U] a cold DESSERT (= a sweet dish) made of fruit that has been cooked slowly with sugar （加糖慢火煮過後冷卻的）糖漬水果，蜜餞

com·pound **AW** *noun, adj., verb*

■ ***noun*** /'kɒmpaʊnd; *NAmE* 'kɑːm-/ **1** a thing consisting of two or more separate things combined together 複合物；混合物 **2** (*chemistry* 化) a substance formed by a chemical reaction of two or more elements in fixed amounts relative to each other 化合物： *Common salt is a compound of sodium and chlorine.* 普通食鹽是鈉和氯的化合物。 ➲ compare ELEMENT (4), MIXTURE (3) **3** (*grammar* 語法) a noun, an adjective or a verb made of two or more words or parts of words, written as one or more words, or joined by a hyphen. *Travel agent*, *dark-haired* and *bathroom* are all compounds. 複合詞 **4** an area surrounded by a fence or wall in which a factory or other group of buildings stands 有圍欄（或圍牆）的場地（內有工廠或其他建築群）： *a prison compound* 監獄場地

■ ***adj.*** /'kɒmpaʊnd; *NAmE* 'kɑːm-/ [only before noun] (*technical* 術語) formed of two or more parts 複合的： *a compound adjective, such as fair-skinned* 複合形容詞，如 fair-skinned◇ *A compound sentence contains two or more clauses.* 複合句包含兩個或多個從句。

■ ***verb*** /kəm'paʊnd/ **1** [often passive] **~ sth** to make sth bad become even worse by causing further damage or problems 使加重；使惡化： *The problems were compounded by severe food shortages.* 嚴重的食物短缺使問題進一步惡化。 **2** **be compounded of/from sth** (*formal*) to be formed from sth 由…構成（或形成）： *The DNA molecule is compounded from many smaller molecules.* 脱氧核糖核酸分子是由許多更小的分子組成的。 **3** [often passive] **~ sth** (**with sth**) (*formal* or *technical* 術語) to mix sth together 混合；摻和；拌和： *liquid soaps compounded with disinfectant* 用消毒劑混合製成的皂液 **4 ~ sth** (*finance* 財) to pay or charge interest on an amount of money that includes any interest already earned or charged 支付，收取（複利）

ˌcompound 'eye *noun* (*biology* 生) an eye like that of most insects, made up of several parts that work separately 複眼

ˌcompound 'fracture *noun* an injury in which a bone in the body is broken and part of the bone comes through the skin 開放性骨折 ➲ compare SIMPLE FRACTURE

ˌcompound 'interest *noun* [U] interest that is paid both on the original amount of money saved and on the interest that has been added to it 複利 ➲ compare SIMPLE INTEREST

com·pre·hend /ˌkɒmprɪ'hend; *NAmE* ˌkɑːm-/ *verb* [I, T] (often used in negative sentences 常用於否定句) (*formal*) to understand sth fully 理解；領悟；懂： *He stood staring at the dead body, unable to comprehend.* 他站在那裏，盯着那具屍體，弄不明白是怎麼回事。◇ **~ sth** *The infinite distances of space are too great for the human mind to comprehend.* 太空的廣闊無垠是人類無法理解的。◇ **~ how/why, etc. …** *She could not comprehend how someone would risk people's lives in that way.* 她不明白怎麼會有人竟拿人民的生命那樣去冒險。◇ **~ that …** *He simply could not comprehend that she could be guilty.* 他就是搞不懂她怎麼會有罪。 ➲ SYNONYMS at UNDERSTAND

com·pre·hen·sible /ˌkɒmprɪ'hensəbl; *NAmE* ˌkɑːm-/ *adj.* **~** (**to sb**) (*formal*) that can be understood by sb 可理解的；能懂的： ***easily/readily comprehensible*** *to the average reader* 一般讀者容易懂的 **OPP** **incomprehensible** ► **com·pre·hen·sib·il·ity** /ˌkɒmprɪˌhensə'bɪləti; *NAmE* ˌkɑːm-/ *noun* [U]

com·pre·hen·sion /ˌkɒmprɪ'henʃn; *NAmE* ˌkɑːm-/ *noun* **1** [U] the ability to understand 理解力；領悟能力： *speech and comprehension* 說話能力和理解力◇ *His behaviour was completely* ***beyond comprehension*** (= impossible to understand). 他的舉止完全令人費解。◇ *She had* no comprehension of what was involved. 她不明白所涉及的事情。 **2** [U, C] an exercise that trains students to understand a language （語言學習中的）理解練習（或訓練）: *listening comprehension* 聽力練習 ◇ *a reading comprehension* 閱讀理解練習

C

com·pre·hen·sive AW /ˌkɒmprɪˈhensɪv; *NAmE* ˌkɑːm-/ *adj., noun*

▪ **adj. 1** including all, or almost all, the items, details, facts, information, etc., that may be concerned 全部的；所有的；（幾乎）無所不包的；詳盡的 SYN **complete, full**: *a comprehensive list of addresses* 詳盡的地址目錄 ◇ *a comprehensive study* 全面的研究 ◇ *comprehensive insurance* (= covering all risks) 綜合保險 **2** (*BrE*) (of education 教育) designed for students of all abilities in the same school 綜合性的（接收各種資質的學生） ▸ **com·pre·hen·sive·ness** *noun* [U]

▪ **noun** (also **compreˈhensive school**) (also *informal* **comp**) (in Britain) a SECONDARY SCHOOL for young people of all levels of ability（英國為各種資質的學生設立的）綜合中學

com·pre·hen·sive·ly AW /ˌkɒmprɪˈhensɪvli; *NAmE* ˌkɑːm-/ *adv.* completely; thoroughly 完全地；徹底地: *They were comprehensively beaten in the final.* 他們在決賽中一敗塗地。

com·press *verb, noun*

▪ **verb** /kəmˈpres/ **1** [T, I] to press or squeeze sth together or into a smaller space; to be pressed or squeezed in this way （被）壓緊；壓縮: **~ sth (into sth)** *compressed air/gas* 壓縮空氣／氣體 ◇ **~ (into sth)** *Her lips compressed into a thin line.* 她的雙唇抿成了一道縫。 **2** [T] **~ sth (into sth)** to reduce sth and fit it into a smaller space or amount of time 精簡；濃縮；壓縮 SYN **condense**: *The main arguments were compressed into one chapter.* 主要的論證被精簡為一個章節。 **3** [T] **~ sth** (*computing* 計) to make computer files, etc. smaller so that they use less space on a disk, etc. 壓縮（文件等） OPP **decompress** ▸ **com·pres·sion** /kəmˈpreʃn/ *noun* [U]: *the compression of air* 空氣的壓縮 ◇ *data compression* 數據壓縮

▪ **noun** /ˈkɒmpres; *NAmE* ˈkɑːm-/ a cloth that is pressed onto a part of the body to stop the loss of blood, reduce pain, etc.（止血、減痛等的）敷布，壓布

com·pres·sor /kəmˈpresə(r)/ *noun* a machine that compresses air or other gases 壓氣機；壓縮機

com·prise AW /kəmˈpraɪz/ *verb* (not used in the progressive tenses 不用於進行時) (*formal*) **1** (also **be comprised of**) **~ sth** to have sb/sth as parts or members 包括；包含；由…組成 SYN **consist of**: *The collection comprises 327 paintings.* 這部畫冊收有 327 幅畫。◇ *The committee is comprised of representatives from both the public and private sectors.* 委員會由政府和私人部門的雙方代表組成。 **2 ~ sth** to be the parts or members that form sth 是（某事物的）組成部份；組成；構成 SYN **make sth up**: *Older people comprise a large proportion of those living in poverty.* 在那些生活貧困的人中，老年人佔有很大的比例。 ➲ SYNONYMS at CONSIST OF ➲ LANGUAGE BANK at PROPORTION

com·prom·ise /ˈkɒmprəmaɪz; *NAmE* ˈkɑːm-/ *noun, verb*

▪ **noun 1** [C] an agreement made between two people or groups in which each side gives up some of the things they want so that both sides are happy at the end 妥協；折衷；互讓；和解: *After lengthy talks the two sides finally* ***reached a compromise.*** 雙方經過長期的商談終於達成了妥協。◇ *In any relationship, you have to* ***make compromises.*** 在任何關係當中，人們都得作出讓步。◇ *a* ***compromise solution/agreement/candidate*** 折衷的解決方案／協議／候選人 **2** [C] **~ (between A and B)** a solution to a problem in which two or more things cannot exist together as they are, in which each thing is reduced or changed slightly so that they can exist together 妥協（或折衷）方案: *This model represents the best compromise between price and quality.* 這種型號是價格和質量間的最佳折衷方案。 **3** [U] the act of reaching a compromise 達成妥協（或和解）: *Compromise is an inevitable part of life.* 妥協是生活不可避免的一部份。◇ *There is no prospect of compromise in sight.* 目前還沒有和解的希望。

▪ **verb 1** [I] to give up some of your demands after a disagreement with sb, in order to reach an agreement （為達成協議而）妥協，折衷，讓步: *Neither side is prepared to compromise.* 雙方都不願意妥協。◇ **~ (with sb) (on sth)** *After much argument, the judges finally compromised on* (= agreed to give the prize to) *the 18-year old pianist.* 經過激烈爭論，評委終於同意把個 18 歲的鋼琴手獲獎。◇ *They were unwilling to compromise with the terrorists.* 他們不願與恐怖分子妥協。 **2** [T, I] to do sth that is against your principles or does not reach standards that you have set 違背（原則）；達不到（標準）: **~ sth** *I refuse to compromise my principles.* 我拒絕在原則問題上妥協。◇ **~ (on sth)** *We are not prepared to compromise on safety standards.* 我們不願在安全標準問題上放鬆。 **3** [T] **~ sb/sth/yourself** to bring sb/sth/yourself into danger or under suspicion, especially by acting in a way that is not very sensible （尤指因行為不很明智）使陷入危險，使受到懷疑: *She had already compromised herself by accepting his invitation.* 她接受了他的邀請，這件事已經使她的聲譽受到了損害。◇ *Defeat at this stage would* ***compromise their chances*** (= reduce their chances) *of reaching the finals of the competition.* 在這個階段的失敗會減少他們進入決賽的機會。

com·prom·is·ing /ˈkɒmprəmaɪzɪŋ; *NAmE* ˈkɑːm-/ *adj.* if sth is **compromising**, it shows or tells people sth that you want to keep secret, because it is wrong or embarrassing 有失體面的；不宜泄露的；不宜公開的: *compromising photos* 不宜公開的照片 ◇ *They were discovered together in a* ***compromising situation.*** 他們被人發現在一起，場面有傷風化。

comp·trol·ler /kənˈtrəʊlə(r); *NAmE* -ˈtroʊ-/ *noun* = CONTROLLER (3)

com·pul·sion /kəmˈpʌlʃn/ *noun* **1** [U, C] (*formal*) strong pressure that makes sb do sth that they do not want to do 強迫；強制: **~ (to do sth)** *You are under no compulsion to pay immediately.* 沒有人強迫你立刻付款。◇ **~ (on sb) to do sth** *There are no compulsions on students to attend classes.* 沒有強求學生上課。 **2** [C] **~ (to do sth)** a strong desire to do sth, especially sth that is wrong, silly or dangerous （尤指做不正確、愚蠢或危險事的）強烈慾望，衝動 SYN **urge**: *He felt a great compulsion to tell her everything.* 他感到一陣強烈的衝動，想要把一切都告訴她。 ➲ see also COMPEL

com·pul·sive /kəmˈpʌlsɪv/ *adj.* **1** (of behaviour 行為) that is difficult to stop or control 難以制止的；難控制的: ***compulsive eating/spending/gambling*** 強迫性進食／消費；上癮的賭博 **2** (of people 人) not being able to control their behaviour 無法控制行為的；禁不住的: *a* ***compulsive drinker/gambler/liar*** 酗酒成性的酒徒；嗜賭成癖的賭徒；說謊成性的人 **3** that makes you pay attention to it because it is so interesting and exciting 引人入勝的: *The programme made compulsive viewing.* 這節目引人入勝，收看起來欲罷不能。 ▸ **com·pul·sive·ly** *adv.*: *She watched him compulsively.* 她情不自禁地注視着他。◇ *a compulsively readable book* 引人入勝、非讀不可的書

com·pul·sory /kəmˈpʌlsəri/ *adj.* that must be done because of a law or a rule （因法律或規則而）必須做的，強制的，強迫的 SYN **mandatory**: ***It is compulsory for*** *all motorcyclists to wear helmets.* 所有騎摩托車的人都必須戴頭盔，這是強制性的。◇ *English is a* ***compulsory subject*** *at this level.* 英語在這一級次是必修科目。◇ ***compulsory education/schooling*** 義務教育 ◇ *compulsory redundancies* 強制裁員 OPP **voluntary** ▸ **com·pul·sor·ily** /kəmˈpʌlsərəli/ *adv.*: *Over 600 workers were made compulsorily redundant.* * 600 多名工人遭到強制性裁員。

comˌpulsory ˈpurchase *noun* [U, C] (*BrE*) an occasion when sb is officially ordered to sell land or property to the government or other authority（政府等對土地或財產的）強制徵購，強制性購買: *a compulsory purchase order* 強制徵購令

com·punc·tion /kəmˈpʌŋkʃn/ *noun* [U] (also [C] in *NAmE* 美式英語亦作可數名詞) **~ (about doing sth)** (*formal*) a guilty feeling about doing sth 內疚；愧疚: *She felt no compunction about leaving her job.* 她對自己的辭職一點兒也不感到愧疚。◇ *He had lied to her without compunction.* 他向她撒了謊卻毫無愧疚。◇ (*US*) *She has no* *compunctions about rejecting the plan.* 她對拒絕那個計劃絲毫也不後悔。

com·pu·ta·tion AW /ˌkɒmpjuˈteɪʃn; NAmE ˌkɑːm-/ *noun* [C, U] (*formal*) an act or the process of calculating sth 計算；計算過程：*All the statistical computations were performed by the new software system.* 所有的統計計算均由新的軟件系統完成。◇ *an error in the computation* 計算錯誤

com·pu·ta·tion·al AW /ˌkɒmpjuˈteɪʃənl; NAmE ˌkɑːm-/ *adj.* [usually before noun] using or connected with computers 使用計算機的；與計算機有關的：*computational methods* 用計算機做的方法 ◇ *a computational approach* 通過計算機進行

compuˌtational linˈguistics *noun* [U] the study of language and speech using computers 計算語言學（用計算機進行語言分析）

com·pute AW /kəmˈpjuːt/ *verb* **~ sth** (*formal*) to calculate sth 計算；估算：*The losses were computed at £5 million.* 損失估算為 500 萬英鎊。▸ **com·put·able** AW *adj.*

com·puter 0‑ AW /kəmˈpjuːtə(r)/ *noun* an electronic machine that can store, organize and find information, do calculations and control other machines 計算機；電腦：*a personal computer* 個人電腦 ◇ *Our sales information is processed by computer.* 我們的銷售信息是用計算機處理的。◇ *a computer program* 計算機程序 ◇ ***computer software/hardware/graphics*** 計算機軟件／硬件／製圖 ◇ *a computer error* 計算機錯誤 ◇ *computer-aided design* 計算機輔助設計 ➲ VISUAL VOCAB page V66 ➲ see also DESKTOP COMPUTER, MICROCOMPUTER, PERSONAL COMPUTER, SUPERCOMPUTER

comˈputer game *noun* a game played on a computer 電腦遊戲

com·pu·ter·ize (BrE also **-ise**) /kəmˈpjuːtəraɪz/ *verb* **1 ~ sth** to provide a computer or computers to do the work of sth 用計算機做；使計算機化；使電腦化：*The factory has been fully computerized.* 這家工廠已完全計算機化了。 **2 ~ sth** to store information on a computer 用計算機貯存，用電腦貯存（信息）：*computerized databases* 計算機化數據庫 ◇ *The firm has computerized its records.* 那家公司已把記錄存入計算機。▸ **com·pu·ter·iza·tion, -isa·tion** /kəmˌpjuːtəraɪˈzeɪʃn; NAmE -rəˈz-/ *noun* [U]

comˌputer-ˈliterate (also **com·puter·ate**) *adj.* able to use computers well 能熟練使用計算機的；會用電腦的 ▸ **comˌputer ˈliteracy** *noun* [U]

comˌputer ˈscience *noun* [U] the study of computers and how they can be used 計算機科學；電腦科學：*a degree in computer science* 計算機科學學位 ▸ **comˌputer ˈscientist** *noun*

com·put·ing AW /kəmˈpjuːtɪŋ/ *noun* [U] the fact of using computers 計算；計算機技術；信息處理技術：*to work in computing* 從事信息處理 ◇ *to study computing* 從事數據處理研究 ◇ ***educational/network/scientific computing*** 教育／網絡／科學信息處理技術 ◇ ***computing power/services/skills/systems*** 數據處理能力／服務／技術／系統 ➲ VISUAL VOCAB pages V66, V67, V68

com·rade /ˈkɒmreɪd; NAmE ˈkɑːmræd/ *noun* **1** a person who is a member of the same COMMUNIST or SOCIALIST political party as the person speaking（共產黨或社會主義政黨的）同志 **2** (BrE also **ˌcomrade-in-ˈarms**) (*old-fashioned*) a friend or other person that you work with, especially as soldiers during a war 朋友；同事；（尤指戰爭期間的）戰友：*They were old army comrades.* 他們是部隊的老戰友。▸ **com·rade·ly** /ˈkɒmreɪdli; NAmE ˈkɑːmrædli/ *adj.* **com·rade·ship** /ˈkɒmreɪdʃɪp; NAmE ˈkɑːmræd-/ *noun* [U]：(*formal*) *There was a sense of comradeship between them.* 他們之間存在着一種同志情誼。

Con. *abbr.* (in British politics) CONSERVATIVE（英國政治）保守黨（的）

con /kɒn; NAmE kɑːn/ *noun, verb*

■ ***noun*** (*informal*) **1** [sing.] (also BrE *formal* **ˈconfidence trick**) (also NAmE *formal* **ˈconfidence game**) a trick; an act of cheating sb 詭計；騙局；欺騙：*The so-called bargain was just a big con!* 這種所謂的減價優惠只不過是個大騙局！◇ (BrE) *a con trick* 騙人的花招 ◇ (NAmE) *a con game* 騙人的花招 ◇ *He's a real **con artist*** (= a person who regularly cheats others). 他真是個行騙老手。➲ see also CON MAN, MOD CONS **2** [C] = CONVICT IDM see PRO *n.*

■ ***verb*** (-nn-) (*informal*) to trick sb, especially in order to get money from them or persuade them to do sth for you（尤指為錢財或使人為自己做某事而）欺騙，哄騙，詐騙：**~ sb (into doing sth)** *I was conned into buying a useless car.* 我上當受騙買了輛不能用的汽車。◇ **~ sb (out of sth)** *They had been conned out of £100 000.* 他們被騙走了 10 萬英鎊。◇ **~ your way into sth** *He conned his way into the job using false references.* 他用假的推薦信騙取了那份工作。➲ SYNONYMS at CHEAT

con·ation /kəˈneɪʃn/ *noun* [U] (*philosophy* 哲, *psychology* 心) a mental process that makes you want to do sth or decide to do sth 意動；意圖 ▸ **cona·tive** /ˈkɒnətɪv; NAmE ˈkɑːn-/ *adj.*

con·cat·en·ation /kənˌkætəˈneɪʃn/ *noun* (*formal*) a series of things or events that are linked together 一系列相關聯的事物（或事件）：*a strange **concatenation of events*** 一連串奇怪的事

con·cave /kɒnˈkeɪv; NAmE kɑːnˈk-; ˈkɑːn-/ *adj.* (of an outline or a surface 輪廓或表面) curving in 凹的；凹面的：*a **concave lens/mirror*** 凹透鏡；凹鏡 OPP **convex**

con·cav·ity /ˌkɒnˈkævəti; NAmE kɑːn-/ *noun* (pl. **-ies**) (*technical* 術語) **1** [U] the quality of being concave (= curving in) 凹；凹陷 **2** [C] a shape or place that curves in 凹形；凹狀；凹陷處

con·ceal /kənˈsiːl/ *verb* (*formal*) to hide sb/sth 隱藏；隱瞞；掩蓋：**~ sb/sth** *The paintings were concealed beneath a thick layer of plaster.* 那些畫被隱藏在厚厚的灰泥層下面。◇ *Tim could barely conceal his disappointment.* 蒂姆幾乎掩飾不住自己的失望。◇ *She sat down to **conceal the fact that** she was trembling.* 她坐下來以不讓人看出她在發抖。◇ **~ sb/sth from sb/sth** *For a long time his death was concealed from her.* 他的死瞞了很長時間都沒告訴她。➲ SYNONYMS at HIDE ➲ see also ILL-CONCEALED

con·ceal·er /kənˈsiːlə(r)/ ***noun*** [U, C] a skin-coloured cream or powder used to cover spots or marks on the skin or dark circles under the eyes 遮瑕膏；遮瑕粉；美容劑 ➲ VISUAL VOCAB page V60

con·ceal·ment /kənˈsiːlmənt/ *noun* [U] (*formal*) the act of hiding sth; the state of being hidden 隱藏；隱瞞；掩蓋：*the concealment of crime* 對罪行的隱瞞 ◇ *Many animals rely on concealment for protection.* 許多動物靠藏匿自己來自保。

con·cede /kənˈsiːd/ *verb* **1** [T] to admit that sth is true, logical, etc. 承認（某事屬實、合乎邏輯等）：**+ speech** *'Not bad,' she conceded grudgingly.* "不錯。" 她勉強承認道。◇ **~ (that) …** *He was forced to concede (that) there might be difficulties.* 他被迫承認可能有困難。◇ **~ sth** *I had to concede the logic of this.* 我得承認這件事情有它的邏輯。◇ **~ sth to sb** *He reluctantly **conceded the point** to me.* 他不情願地向我承認了這一點。◇ **~ sb sth** *He reluctantly conceded me the point.* 他不情願地向我承認了這一點。◇ **it is conceded that …** ***It must be conceded that*** *different judges have different approaches to these cases.* 必須承認不同的法官會採用不同的方法來判定這些案件。➲ SYNONYMS at ADMIT **2** [T] to give sth away, especially unwillingly; to allow sb to have sth（尤指勉強地）讓與，讓步；允許：**~ sth (to sb)** *The President was obliged to concede power to the army.* 總統被迫把權力讓給軍隊。◇ *England conceded a goal immediately after half-time.* 英格蘭隊在下半場一開始就被攻入一球。◇ **~ sb sth** *Women were only conceded full voting rights in the 1950s.* 婦女在 20 世紀 50 年代才被容許完全享有選舉權。 **3** [I, T] **~ (defeat)** to admit that you have lost a game, an election, etc. 承認（比賽、選舉等失敗）：*After losing this decisive battle, the general was forced to concede.* 輸掉了這場決定性的戰役後，那位將軍不得不承認失敗。◇ *Injury forced Hicks to concede defeat.* 受傷後，希克斯被迫認輸。➲ see also CONCESSION

C

C

con·ceit /kən'siːt/ *noun* **1** [U] (*disapproving*) too much pride in yourself and what you do 自負；驕傲自大 **2** [C] (*formal*) an artistic effect or device, especially one that is very clever or tries to be very clever but does not succeed 別出心裁但不實用的效果；巧妙但不實用的東西：*The ill-advised conceit of the guardian angel dooms the film from the start.* 對守護天使的蹩腳設計弄巧成拙，從一開始就注定這部電影要失敗。 **3** (*technical* 術語) a clever expression in writing or speech that involves a comparison between two things 巧妙的言辭；別出心裁的比喻 SYN **metaphor**：*The idea of the wind singing is a romantic conceit.* 風兒在唱歌這一巧妙的比喻很有浪漫色彩。

con·ceit·ed /kən'siːtɪd/ *adj.* (*disapproving*) having too much pride in yourself and what you do 自負的；驕傲自大的：*a very conceited person* 極其自命不凡的人 ◇ *It's very conceited of you to assume that your work is always the best.* 你認為你的工作總是最好的，真是太自大了。 ▸ **con·ceit·ed·ly** *adv.*

con·ceiv·able AW /kən'siːvəbl/ *adj.* that you can imagine or believe 可想像的；可信的 SYN **possible**：*It is conceivable that I'll see her tomorrow.* 我可能明天會見到她。◇ *a beautiful city with buildings of every conceivable age and style* 擁有各個時代和各種風格建築物的美麗城市 OPP **inconceivable** ▸ **con·ceiv·ably** AW /-əbli/ *adv.*：*The disease could conceivably be transferred to humans.* 這種疾病可能會傳染給人類。

con·ceive AW /kən'siːv/ *verb* **1** [T] (*formal*) to form an idea, a plan, etc. in your mind; to imagine sth 想出（主意、計劃等）；想像；構想；設想：**~ sth** *He conceived the idea of transforming the old power station into an arts centre.* 他想出了把舊發電站改造為藝術中心的主意。◇ **~ of sth (as sth)** *God is often conceived of as male.* 上帝常常被想像為男性。◇ **~ (that)** … *I cannot conceive* (= I do not believe) *(that) he would wish to harm us.* 我無法想像他會存心傷害我們。◇ **~ what/how, etc.** … *I cannot conceive what it must be like.* 我想像不出它會是什麼樣子。 **2** [I, T] when a woman **conceives** or **conceives a child**, she becomes pregnant 懷孕；懷胎：*She is unable to conceive.* 她不能懷孕。◇ **~ sth** *Their first child was conceived on their wedding night.* 他們的第一個小孩是在新婚之夜懷上的。 ➲ see also CONCEPTION

> **WORD FAMILY**
> **conceive** *verb*
> **conceivable** *adj.*
> (≠ inconceivable)
> **conceivably** *adv.*
> **concept** *noun*
> **conception** *noun*
> **conceptual** *adj.*

con·cen·trate 🔑 AW /'kɒnsntreɪt; *NAmE* 'kɑːn-/ *verb, noun*

■ *verb* **1** 🔑 [I, T] to give all your attention to sth and not think about anything else 集中（注意力）；聚精會神：**~ (on sth/on doing sth)** *I can't concentrate with all that noise going on.* 吵鬧聲不絕於耳，我無法集中精神。◇ **~ sth** *Nothing* ***concentrates the mind*** *better than the knowledge that you could die tomorrow* (= it makes you think very clearly). 沒有什麼比知道自己明天就可能會死去更能讓人定下心來去思考種種問題的了。◇ **~ sth (on sth/on doing sth)** *I decided to* ***concentrate all my efforts*** *on finding somewhere to live.* 我決定全力以赴找個住的地方。 **2** [T] **~ sth + adv./prep.** to bring sth together in one place 使…集中（或集合、聚集）：*Power is largely concentrated in the hands of a small elite.* 權力主要集中在少數精英人物的手裏。◇ *We need to concentrate resources on the most run-down areas.* 我們需要把資源集中用於最衰敗的地區。◇ *Fighting was concentrated around the towns to the north.* 戰鬥集中在北方諸城鎮的周圍進行。 **3** [T] **~ sth** (*technical* 術語) to increase the strength of a substance by reducing its volume, for example by boiling it （使）濃縮 SYN **reduce**

PHR V **'concentrate on sth** 🔑 to spend more time doing one particular thing than others 集中時間做某事：*In this lecture I shall concentrate on the early years of Charles's reign.* 這一節課我將着重講查理王朝的早期統治時期。

■ *noun* [C, U] a substance that is made stronger because water or other substances have been removed 濃縮物：*mineral concentrates found at the bottom of rivers* 在河底發現的精礦 ◇ *jams made with fruit juice concentrate* 用濃縮果汁做的果醬

con·cen·trated AW /'kɒnsntreɪtɪd; *NAmE* 'kɑːn-/ *adj.* **1** showing determination to do sth 決心要做的；全力以赴的：*He made a concentrated effort to finish the work on time.* 他全力以赴以按時完成這項工作。 **2** (of a substance 物質) made stronger because water or other substances have been removed 濃縮的：*concentrated orange juice* 濃縮橙汁 ◇ *a concentrated solution of salt in water* 濃縮鹽水溶液 **3** if sth exists or happens in a **concentrated** way, there is a lot of it in one place or at one time 密集的；集中的：*concentrated gunfire* 密集的炮火

con·cen·tra·tion 🔑 AW /ˌkɒnsn'treɪʃn; *NAmE* ˌkɑːn-/ *noun*

1 🔑 [U] the ability to direct all your effort and attention on one thing, without thinking of other things 專心；專注：*This book requires a great deal of concentration.* 這本書需要全神貫注才能讀懂。◇ *Tiredness affects your powers of concentration.* 疲勞影響注意力的集中。 **2** [U] **~ (on sth)** the process of people directing effort and attention on a particular thing 關注；重視：*a need for greater concentration on environmental issues* 更加關注環境問題的必要性 **3** [C] **~ (of sth)** a lot of sth in one place 集中；聚集：*a concentration of industry in the north of the country* 該國北部的工業集中地 **4** [C, U] the amount of a substance in a liquid or in another substance 濃度；含量：*glucose concentrations in the blood* 血液中的葡萄糖含量

concen'tration camp *noun* a type of prison, often consisting of a number of buildings inside a fence, where political prisoners, etc. are kept in extremely bad conditions 集中營：*a Nazi concentration camp* 納粹集中營

concentric circles 同心圓

con·cen·tric /kən'sentrɪk/ *adj.* (*geometry* 幾何) (of circles 圓) having the same centre 同心的：*concentric rings* 同心環

con·cept 🔑 AW /'kɒnsept; *NAmE* 'kɑːn-/ *noun* an idea or a principle that is connected with sth ABSTRACT 概念；觀念：**~ (of sth)** *the concept of social class* 社會等級的概念 ◇ *concepts such as 'civilization' and 'government'* 諸如"文明"和"政府"的概念 ◇ *He can't grasp the basic concepts of mathematics.* 他無法掌握數學的基本概念。◇ **~ (that …)** *the concept that everyone should have equality of opportunity* 人人應當機會均等的觀念

'concept album *noun* a collection of pieces of popular music, all having the same theme and recorded on one CD, etc. 概念專輯，主題唱片（有同一主題的流行音樂）

con·cep·tion AW /kən'sepʃn/ *noun* **1** [U] the process of forming an idea or a plan 構思；構想；設想：*The plan was brilliant in its conception but failed because of lack of money.* 儘管這計劃構想絕妙，但終因資金不足而告流產。 **2** [C, U] **~ (of sth)** | **~ (that …)** an understanding or a belief of what sth is or what sth should be 理解（認為某事怎樣或應該怎樣）：*Marx's conception of social justice* 馬克思對社會公平概念的理解 ◇ *He has* ***no conception of*** *how difficult life is if you're unemployed.* 他不懂得失業後生活會是怎樣的艱難。 **3** [U, C] the process of an egg being FERTILIZED inside a woman's body so that she becomes pregnant 懷孕；受孕：*the moment of conception* 受孕的一刻 ➲ see also CONCEIVE

con·cep·tual AW /kən'septʃuəl/ *adj.* (*formal*) related to or based on ideas 概念（上）的；觀念（上）的：*a* *conceptual framework within which children's needs are assessed* 對兒童需求進行評估的概念框架 ◇ *a conceptual model* 概念模式 ▸ **con·cep·tu·al·ly** AW *adv.* : *conceptually similar/distinct* 概念上相似 / 不同

con,ceptual 'art *noun* [U] art in which the idea which the work of art represents is considered to be the most important thing about it 概念藝術，觀念藝術（將藝術品的思想作為精髓）

con·cep·tual·ism /kənˈseptʃuəlɪzəm/ *noun* [U] (*philosophy* 哲) the theory that general ideas such as 'beauty' and 'red' exist only as ideas in the mind 概念論（認為"美"、"紅"等籠統概念只存在於頭腦中）▸ **con·cep·tual·ist** /kənˈseptʃuəlɪst/ *noun*

con·cep·tu·al·ize (*BrE* also **-ise**) AW /kənˈseptʃuəlaɪz/ *verb* **~ sth (as sth)** (*formal*) to form an idea of sth in your mind 構思；使形成觀念；將…概念化（為…）

con·cern 0‑ /kənˈsɜːn; *NAmE* -ˈsɜːrn/ *verb, noun*

■ *verb*

▸ **AFFECT/INVOLVE** 影響；涉及 **1** 0‑ [often passive] **~ sb/sth** to affect sb/sth; to involve sb/sth 影響；涉及；牽涉：*Don't interfere in what doesn't concern you.* 不要管與自己無關的事。◇ *The loss was a tragedy for* ***all concerned*** (= all those affected by it). 這損失對有關各方來說都是極大的不幸。◇ *Where our children's education is concerned, no compromise is acceptable.* 在事關我們的孩子的教育問題上，那是毫無妥協餘地的。◇ *The individuals concerned have some explaining to do.* 涉及到的每個人都要作出一些解釋。◇ ***To whom it may concern*** ... (= used for example, at the beginning of a public notice or of a job reference about sb's character and ability) 敬啟者…（如用於公告或求職推薦信的開頭）◇ *Everyone who* ***was*** *directly* ***concerned in*** (= had some responsibility for) *the incident has now resigned.* 所有與該事件有直接牽連的人現在均已辭職。

▸ **BE ABOUT** 關於 **2** 0‑ **~ sth** (also **be concerned with sth**) to be about sth 與…有關；涉及：*The story concerns the prince's efforts to rescue Pamina.* 這故事講的是王子奮力解救帕米娜。◇ *The book is primarily concerned with Soviet-American relations during the Cold War.* 這部書主要講的是冷戰時期的蘇美關係。◇ *This chapter concerns itself with the historical background.* 本章旨在講述歷史背景。◇ *One major difference between these computers* ***concerns the way*** *in which they store information.* 這些計算機彼此之間的一個主要差異涉及其貯存信息的方式。

▸ **WORRY SB** 使某人擔心 **3** 0‑ to worry sb 讓（某人）擔憂：**~ sb** *What concerns me is our lack of preparation for the change.* 讓我擔心的是我們對事態的變化缺乏準備。◇ **~ sb that** ... *It concerns me that you no longer seem to care.* 你似乎不再在乎，這令我擔憂。➲ see also CONCERNED (1)

▸ **TAKE AN INTEREST** 感興趣 **4** **~ yourself with/about sth** to take an interest in sth（對…）感興趣：*He didn't concern himself with the details.* 他對細節不感興趣。

▸ **CONSIDER IMPORTANT** 認為重要 **5** **be concerned to do sth** (*formal*) to think it is important to do sth 認為（做某事）重要：*She was concerned to write about situations that everybody could identify with.* 她認為應該寫關於大家都能產生共鳴的情境。IDM see FAR *adv.*

■ *noun*

▸ **WORRY** 擔憂 **1** 0‑ [U, C] a feeling of worry, especially one that is shared by many people（尤指許多人共同的）擔心，憂慮：**~ (about sth/sb)** *There is growing concern about violence on television.* 人們對電視上充斥暴力內容的憂慮日益加重。◇ *In the meeting, voters raised concerns about health care.* 選民在會上提出了對衞生保健狀況的擔憂。◇ **~ (for sth/sb)** *She hasn't been seen for four days and there is concern for her safety.* 她已四天不見踪影，大家對她的安全很擔心。◇ **~ (over sth/sb)** *The report expressed concern over continuing high unemployment.* 報告表達了對失業率居高不下的憂慮。◇ **~ (that ...)** *There is widespread concern that new houses will be built on protected land.* 人們普遍對在保護區建新的房屋感到憂慮。◇ *Stress at work is* ***a matter of concern to*** *staff and management.* 工作壓力是一件讓員工和管理人員都關切的事。◇ *The President's health was giving serious* ***cause for concern.*** 總統的健康正令公眾極為關注。➲ compare UNCONCERN

▸ **DESIRE TO PROTECT** 保護的願望 **2** 0‑ [U] a desire to protect and help sb/sth 關愛；關心：*parents' concern for their children* 父母對子女的關愛

▸ **STH IMPORTANT** 重要的事 **3** 0‑ [C] something that is important to a person, an organization, etc.（對人、組織等）重要的事情：*What are your main concerns as a writer?* 作為一名作家，你主要關注的是哪些問題？◇ *The government's primary concern is to reduce crime.* 政府的頭等大事是減少犯罪。

▸ **RESPONSIBILITY** 責任 **4** [C, usually sing.] (*formal*) something that is your responsibility or that you have a right to know about（某人）負責的事，有權知道的事：*This matter is their concern.* 這件事由他們負責。◇ *How much money I make is none of your concern.* 我賺多少錢沒有必要告訴你。

▸ **COMPANY** 公司 **5** [C] a company or business 公司；商行；企業 SYN **firm**：*a major publishing concern* 一家大出版公司 IDM see GOING *adj.*

con·cerned 0‑ /kənˈsɜːnd; *NAmE* -ˈsɜːrnd/ *adj.*

1 0‑ worried and feeling concern about sth 擔心的；憂慮的：*Concerned parents held a meeting.* 憂心忡忡的家長們開了一次會。◇ **~ about/for sth** *The President is deeply concerned about this issue.* 總統對這個問題深感擔憂。◇ **~ for sth** *He didn't seem in the least concerned for her safety.* 對她的安全他似乎一點都不擔心。◇ **~ (that)** ... *She was concerned that she might miss the turning and get lost.* 她擔心自己會錯過轉彎的地方而迷路。➲ SYNONYMS at WORRIED **2** 0‑ **~ (about/with sth)** interested in sth 感興趣的；關切的；關注的：*They were more concerned with how the other women had dressed than with what the speaker was saying.* 他們對其他女人的衣着打扮比對演講者的講話更加感興趣。OPP **unconcerned** ➲ LANGUAGE BANK at ABOUT IDM see FAR *adv.*

con·cern·ing 0‑ /kənˈsɜːnɪŋ; *NAmE* -ˈsɜːrn-/ *prep.* (*formal*)

about sth; involving sb/sth 關於；涉及：*He asked several questions concerning the future of the company.* 他問了幾個有關公司前途的問題。◇ *All cases concerning children are dealt with in a special children's court.* 所有涉及兒童的案件均由兒童特別法庭審理。

con·cert 0‑ /ˈkɒnsət; *NAmE* ˈkɑːnsərt/ *noun* a public performance of music 音樂會；演奏會：*a concert of music by Bach* 巴赫作品音樂會 ◇ *a* ***classical/rock/pop concert*** 古典 / 搖滾 / 流行音樂會 ◇ *They're* ***in concert*** *at Wembley Arena.* 他們在文布利運動場舉行音樂會。◇ *a* ***concert hall/pianist*** 音樂廳；在音樂會上演奏的鋼琴家 ➲ COLLOCATIONS at MUSIC

IDM **in concert with sb/sth** (*formal*) working together with sb/sth 與…合作（或同心協力）

con·cer·tante /ˌkɒntʃəˈtænteɪ; -ti; *NAmE* ˌkɑːn-/ *adj.* [only before noun] (*music* 音) (from *Italian*) related to a piece of music which contains an important part for a SOLO singer or player and which is similar to a CONCERTO in character 復協奏性的；復協奏類型的

'concert band *noun* a large group of people who play wind instruments together, and who perform in a concert hall 管樂團 ➲ compare MILITARY BAND

con·cert·ed /kənˈsɜːtɪd; *NAmE* -ˈsɜːrt-/ *adj.* [only before noun] done in a planned and determined way, especially by more than one person, government, country, etc. 努力的；共同籌劃決定的；同心協力的：*a* ***concerted approach/attack/campaign*** 商定的方法；聯合攻擊；協同運動 ◇ *She has begun to* ***make a concerted effort to*** *find a job.* 她開始盡全力尋找工作。

con·cert·goer /ˈkɒnsətgəʊə(r); *NAmE* ˈkɑːnsərtgoʊər/ *noun* a person who regularly goes to concerts, especially of CLASSICAL music 常去聽音樂會的人（尤指古典音樂會）

,concert 'grand *noun* a piano of the largest size, used especially for concerts 大型三角鋼琴；音樂會大鋼琴

con·cer·tina /ˌkɒnsəˈtiːnə; *NAmE* ˌkɑːnsərˈt-/ *noun, verb*

■ *noun* a musical instrument like a small ACCORDION, that you hold in both hands. You press the ends together and pull them apart to produce sounds. 六角手風琴 ➲ picture at ACCORDION

C

■ *verb* (**con·cer·tina·ing, con·cer·tinaed, con·cer·tinaed**) [I] (*BrE*) to fold up like a concertina（像六角手風琴一樣）摺起，摺疊：*The truck crashed into the tree and concertinaed.* 貨車撞在樹上撞扁了。

con·cert·mas·ter /ˈkɒnsətmɑːstə(r); *NAmE* ˈkɑːnsərtmæs-/ (*especially NAmE*) (*BrE* also **lead·er**) *noun* the most important VIOLIN player in an ORCHESTRA（管弦樂隊的）首席小提琴手

con·certo /kənˈtʃɜːtəʊ; *NAmE* -ˈtʃɜːrtoʊ/ *noun* (*pl.* **-os**) a piece of music for one or more SOLO instruments playing with an ORCHESTRA 協奏曲：*a piano concerto* 鋼琴協奏曲 ◇ *a concerto for flute and harp* 長笛與豎琴協奏曲

con·ces·sion /kənˈseʃn/ *noun* **1** [C, U] something that you allow or do, or allow sb to have, in order to end an argument or to make a situation less difficult 讓步；妥協：*The firm will be forced to* **make concessions** *if it wants to avoid a strike.* 要想避免罷工，公司將不得不作出一些讓步。◇ *to win a concession from sb* 取得某人的讓步 ◇ ***a major/an important concession*** 重大的讓步 ◇ *She* **made no concession** *to his age; she expected him to work as hard as she did.* 她絲毫也不體諒他的年齡，要求他幹得像她一樣賣力。➲ see also CONCEDE (3) **2** [U] the act of giving sth or allowing sth; the act of CONCEDING 承認；給予；許可；讓步：*the concession of university status to some colleges* 對某些學院升為大學的許可 ◇ (*especially NAmE*) *McCain's concession speech* (= when he admitted that he had lost the election) 麥凱恩承認競選失敗的講話 **3** [C, usually pl.] (*BrE*) a reduction in an amount of money that has to be paid; a ticket that is sold at a reduced price to a particular group of people 減價；（對某類人的）減價票：*tax concessions* 稅收減免 ◇ *Tickets are £3; there is a £1 concession for students.* 票價為 3 英鎊，學生票減免 1 英鎊。◇ *Adults £2.50, concessions £2, family £5* 成人、優惠、家庭票價分別為 2.50 英鎊、2 英鎊、5 英鎊。**4** [C] a right or an advantage that is given to a group of people, an organization, etc., especially by a government or an employer（尤指由政府或雇主給予的）特許權，優惠：*The Bolivian government has granted logging concessions covering 22 million hectares.* 玻利維亞政府批准了在 2 200 萬公頃土地上的伐木特許權。**5** [C] the right to sell sth in a particular place; the place where you sell it, sometimes an area which is part of a larger building or store（在某地的）特許經營權；（有時為大型建築物或商場中的）銷售場地，攤位：*the burger concessions at the stadium* 體育場內的漢堡包小吃攤

con·ces·sion·aire /kənˌseʃəˈneə(r); *NAmE* -ˈner/ *noun* (*especially BrE*) a person or a business that has been given a concession to sell sth（銷售）特許權獲得者；特許經銷商

con·ces·sion·ary /kənˈseʃənəri; *NAmE* -neri/ *adj.* [usually before noun] (*BrE*) costing less money for people in particular situations; given as a CONCESSION (3)（在某種情況下）花費少的；優惠的；減價的：***concessionary rates/fares/travel*** 優惠費率／票價／旅行

con·ces·sive /kənˈsesɪv/ *adj.* (*grammar* 語法) (of a preposition or conjunction 介詞或連詞) used at the beginning of a clause to say that the action of the main clause is in fact true or possible, despite the situation. 'Despite' and 'although' are concessive words. 表示讓步的

conch /kɒntʃ; *NAmE* kɑːntʃ/ *noun* the shell of a sea creature which is also called a conch 海螺殼；海螺

con·chie (also **con·chy**) /ˈkɒntʃi; *NAmE* ˈkɑːn-/ *noun* (*pl.* **-ies**) (*BrE, informal, old-fashioned*) a CONSCIENTIOUS OBJECTOR 出於道義原因而拒服兵役者

con·cierge /ˈkɒnsieəʒ; *NAmE* kɔːnˈsjerʒ; kɑːnˈsjerʒ/ *noun* (from *French*) **1** a person, especially in France, who takes care of a building containing flats/apartments and checks people entering and leaving the building（尤指法國公寓等處的）看門人，司閽 **2** (*especially NAmE*) a person in a hotel whose job is to help guests by giving them information, arranging theatre tickets, etc.（旅館中負責提供信息、訂票等的）服務枱職員

con·cili·ate /kənˈsɪlieɪt/ *verb* **~ sb** (*formal*) to make sb less angry or more friendly, especially by being kind and pleasant or by giving them sth（尤指通過和藹友善或送給某物來）平息…的怒火，撫慰，安撫 SYN **pacify** ▸ **con·cili·ation** /kənˌsɪliˈeɪʃn/ *noun* [U]：*A conciliation service helps to settle disputes between employers and workers.* 調解機構幫助解決勞資糾紛。

con·cili·ator /kənˈsɪlieɪtə(r)/ *noun* a person or an organization that tries to make angry people calm so that they can discuss or solve their problems successfully 調解者；撫慰者；調解機構

con·cili·atory /kənˈsɪliətəri; *NAmE* -tɔːri/ *adj.* having the intention or effect of making angry people calm 調解的；撫慰的；意在和解的；和解的：***a conciliatory approach/attitude/gesture/move*** 調解的方法；和解的態度／姿態／行動

con·cise /kənˈsaɪs/ *adj.* **1** giving only the information that is necessary and important, using few words 簡明的；簡練的；簡潔的：*a concise summary* 簡明扼要的總結 ◇ *clear concise instructions* 言簡意賅的說明 **2** [only before noun] (of a book 書) shorter than the original book, on which it was based 簡略的；簡縮的；簡明的：*a concise dictionary* 簡明詞典 ▸ **con·cise·ly** *adv.* **con·cise·ness** (also *less frequent* **con·ci·sion** /kənˈsɪʒn/) *noun* [U]

con·clave /ˈkɒŋkleɪv; *NAmE* ˈkɑːŋ-/ *noun* (*formal*) a meeting to discuss sth in private; the people at this meeting 秘密會議；秘密會議與會者

con·clude 0-w AW /kənˈkluːd/ *verb*
1 0-w [T] (not used in the progressive tenses 不用於進行時) to decide or believe sth as a result of what you have heard or seen 斷定；推斷出；作出結論：**~ sth (from sth)** *What do you conclude from that?* 你從那件事中得出什麼結論？◇ **~ (that) ...** *The report concluded (that) the cheapest option was to close the laboratory.* 這份報告認為代價最低廉的選擇是關閉實驗室。◇ **~ from sth that ...** *He concluded from their remarks that they were not in favour of the plan.* 他從他們的話語中推斷出他們不贊同此項計劃。◇ **it is concluded that ...** *It was concluded that the level of change necessary would be low.* 結論是需要作出的變更程度很低。◇ **+ speech** *'So it should be safe to continue,' he concluded.* "那麼繼續下去應該是安全的。"他推斷說。➲ LANGUAGE BANK at CONCLUSION **2** 0-w [I, T] (*formal*) to come to an end; to bring sth to an end （使）結束，終止：*Let me make just a few concluding remarks.* 我來講幾句話作為結束語。◇ **~ with sth** *The programme concluded with Stravinsky's 'Rite of Spring'.* 演出節目以斯特拉文斯基的《春之祭》結束。◇ **~ by doing sth** *He concluded by wishing everyone a safe trip home.* 他講話結束時祝願大家回家一路平安。◇ **~ sth (with sth)** *The commission concluded its investigation last month.* 委員會在上個月終止了調查。◇ **+ speech** *'Anyway, she should be back soon,' he concluded.* "不管怎樣，她很快會回來。"他最後說道。**3** [T] **~ sth (with sb)** (*formal*) to arrange and settle an agreement with sb formally and finally 達成，訂立，締結（協定）：*They concluded a treaty with Turkey.* 他們同土耳其締結了一項條約。◇ *A trade agreement was concluded between the two countries.* 兩國之間簽署了貿易協定。

con·clu·sion 0-w AW /kənˈkluːʒn/ *noun*
1 0-w [C] something that you decide when you have thought about all the information connected with the situation 結論；推論：*I've* **come to the conclusion** *that he's not the right person for the job.* 我斷定他不適合做這項工作。◇ *It took the jury some time to* **reach the conclusion** *that she was guilty.* 陪審團花了很長時間才得出結論認為她有罪。◇ *New evidence might* **lead to the conclusion** *that we are wrong.* 根據新的證據可能會推斷出我們是錯的。◇ *We can safely* **draw some conclusions** *from our discussion.* 從討論中我們可以有把握地得出一些結論。➲ COLLOCATIONS at SCIENTIFIC **2** 0-w [C, usually sing.] the end of sth such as a speech or a piece of writing 結束；結果；結尾；結局：*The conclusion of the book was disappointing.* 這部書的結尾令人失望。◇ **In conclusion** (= finally), *I would like to thank ...* 最後，我想感謝… ◇ *If we took this argument to its* **logical conclusion** ... 假如我們把這個論點歸結到合乎其邏輯的

結論… **3** [U] the formal and final arrangement of sth official 簽訂；達成；締結 **SYN** **completion**：*the successful conclusion of a trade treaty* 貿易條約的成功簽署

IDM **jump/leap to con'clusions | jump/leap to the con'clusion that …** to make a decision about sb/sth too quickly, before you know or have thought about all the facts 匆忙下結論；貿然斷定：*There I go again—jumping to conclusions.* 我又犯老毛病了，匆忙草率地下結論。➲ more at FOREGONE

Language Bank 用語庫

conclusion

Summing up an argument 總結論點

- **In conclusion**, the study has provided useful insights into the issues relating to people's perception of crime. 綜上所述，本研究為人們對犯罪活動的認識問題提供了有益的見解。
- Based on this study, **it can be concluded that** the introduction of new street lighting did not reduce reported crime. 基於這項研究可以得出這樣的結論：增加街道照明設備並沒有使犯罪案件報案數量減少。
- **To sum up**, no evidence can be found to support the view that improved street lighting reduces reported crime. 總而言之，沒有證據表明街道照明的改進能使犯罪案件報案數量減少。
- The available evidence clearly **leads to the conclusion that** the media do have an influence on the public perception of crime. 現有證據顯然可以得出這一結論：公眾對犯罪活動的認識確實受到媒體的影響。
- **The main conclusion to be drawn from** this study is that public perception of crime is significantly influenced by crime news reporting. 本研究可以得出的一個主要結論是：公眾對犯罪活動的認識受到犯罪新聞報道的很大影響。
- **This study has shown that** people's fear of crime is out of all proportion to crime itself. 本研究表明，人們對犯罪活動的恐懼與犯罪活動本身並不相稱。
- Fear of crime is out of all proportion to the actual level of crime, and the reasons for this **can be summarized as follows**. First … 對犯罪活動的恐懼與實際犯罪水平並不相稱，其原因可歸結為以下幾點。第一，…
- **Overall/In general**, women are more likely than men to feel insecure walking alone after dark. 一般情況下，天黑後獨自行走，女人比男人更容易感到不安全。

➲ Language Banks at EMPHASIS, FIRST, GENERALLY

con·clu·sive **AW** /kən'kluːsɪv/ *adj.* proving sth, and allowing no doubt or confusion 結論性的；不容置疑的；確鑿的：*conclusive evidence/proof/results* 確鑿的證據；不容置疑的結果 **OPP** **inconclusive** ▸ **con·clu·sive·ly** **AW** *adv.*：*to prove sth conclusively* 確鑿地證明某事

con·coct /kən'kɒkt; *NAmE* -'kɑːkt/ *verb* **1 ~ sth** to make sth, especially food or drink, by mixing different things 調製，調合，配製（尤指食物或飲料）：*The soup was concocted from up to a dozen different kinds of fish.* 這種湯是用多達十幾種不同的魚熬製而成的。 **2 ~ sth** to invent a story, an excuse, etc. 虛構，杜撰，編造（故事、藉口等）**SYN** **cook up, make up**：*She concocted some elaborate story to explain her absence.* 她精心編造了解釋她不在現場的一些謊言。

con·coc·tion /kən'kɒkʃn; *NAmE* -'kɑːkʃn/ *noun* a strange or unusual mixture of things, especially drinks or medicines（古怪或少見的）混合物，調合物，調配品（尤指飲料或藥物）：*a concoction of cream and rum* 奶油和朗姆酒調製的怪味飲料

con·comi·tant /kən'kɒmɪtənt; *NAmE* -'kɑːm-/ *adj., noun*
▪ *adj.* (*formal*) happening at the same time as sth else, especially because one thing is related to or causes the other（尤指相關聯的或有因果關係的事）同時發生的，伴隨的，相伴的
▪ *noun* (*formal*) a thing that happens at the same time as sth else 同時發生的事；伴隨（或相伴）的事物

con·cord /'kɒŋkɔːd; *NAmE* 'kɑːŋkɔːrd/ *noun* [U] **1 ~ (with sb)** (*formal*) peace and agreement 和諧；和睦；協調 **SYN** **harmony**：*living in concord with neighbouring states* 與鄰國和睦相處 **OPP** **discord** **2** [U] **~ (with sth)** (*grammar* 語法) (of words in a phrase 短語中的單詞) the fact of having the same NUMBER, GENDER or PERSON（數、性或人稱的）一致 **SYN** **agreement**

con·cord·ance /kən'kɔːdəns; *NAmE* -'kɔːrd-/ *noun* **1** [C] an alphabetical list of the words used in a book, etc. showing where and how often they are used（書籍等中按字母順序排列的）詞語索引：*a Bible concordance*《聖經》用語索引 **2** [C] a list produced by a computer that shows all the examples of an individual word in a book, etc.（計算機顯示的）語彙索引 **3** [U] (*technical* 術語) the state of being similar to sth or CONSISTENT with it 相似；一致；協調：*There is reasonable concordance between the two sets of results.* 兩組結果之間有着合理的一致。

con·cordat /kən'kɔːdæt; *NAmE* -'kɔːrd-; *BrE* also kɒn-/ *noun* an agreement, especially between the Roman Catholic Church and the state（尤指羅馬教廷與各國政府訂立的）政教協定，政教條約

con·course /'kɒŋkɔːs; *NAmE* 'kɑːŋkɔːrs/ *noun* a large, open part of a public building, especially an airport or a train station（尤指機場或火車站的）大廳，廣場：*the station concourse* 車站大廳

con·crete 🔑 /'kɒŋkriːt; *NAmE* 'kɑːŋ-/ *adj., noun, verb*
▪ *adj.* **1** 🔑 made of concrete 混凝土製的：*a concrete floor* 混凝土地面 **2** 🔑 based on facts, not on ideas or guesses 確實的，具體的（而非想像或猜測的）：***concrete evidence/proposals/proof*** 確鑿的證據；具體的建議；確實的證明 ◇ *'It's only a suspicion,' she said, 'nothing concrete.'* "那只是懷疑，" 她說，"沒有任何確實的依據。" ◇ *It is easier to think **in concrete terms** rather than in the abstract.* 結合具體的事物來思考要比抽象思考容易些。➲ compare ABSTRACT *adj.* (1) **3** **a concrete** object is one that you can see and feel 有形的；實在的 ▸ **con·crete·ly** *adv.*
▪ *noun* 🔑 [U] building material that is made by mixing together CEMENT, sand, small stones and water 混凝土：*a slab of concrete* 混凝土板
▪ *verb* **~ sth (over)** to cover sth with concrete 用混凝土覆蓋：*The garden had been concreted over.* 花園裏鋪設了混凝土。

ˌconcrete 'jungle *noun* [usually sing.] a way of describing a city or an area that is unpleasant because it has many large modern buildings and no trees or parks 混凝土叢林（指高樓林立、無樹木無公園因而單調沉悶的現代化城市或地區）

'concrete mixer *noun* = CEMENT MIXER

ˌconcrete 'poetry *noun* [U] poetry in which the meaning or effect is communicated partly by using patterns of words or letters that are visible on the page 實體詩歌（部份借助於字詞或字母組合的視象方法表達）

con·cu·bine /'kɒŋkjubaɪn; *NAmE* 'kɑːŋ-/ *noun* (especially in some societies in the past) a woman who lives with a man, often in addition to his wife or wives, but who is less important than they are（尤指舊時某些社會裏的）妾，姨太太，小老婆

con·cu·pis·cence /kən'kjuːpɪsns/ *noun* [U] (*formal*, often *disapproving*) strong sexual desire 強烈的性慾；淫慾 **SYN** **lust**

con·cur /kən'kɜː(r)/ *verb* (-rr-) [I, T] **~ (with sb) (in sth) | ~ (with sth) | ~ (that …) | (+ speech)** (*formal*) to agree 同意；贊同：*Historians have concurred with each other in this view.* 歷史學家在這個觀點上已取得一致意見。◇ *The coroner concurred with this assessment.* 驗屍官同意這個鑒定。

C

con·cur·rence /kən'kʌrəns; *NAmE* -'kɜːr-/ *noun* (*formal*) **1** [U, sing.] agreement 同意；一致： *The doctor may seek the concurrence of a relative before carrying out the procedure.* 醫生可能會徵得親屬的同意後再施行此項手術。 **2** [sing.] an example of two or more things happening at the same time 同時發生；同時出現： *an unfortunate concurrence of events* 幾件事情不幸同時發生

con·cur·rent AW /kən'kʌrənt; *NAmE* -'kɜːr-/ *adj.* **~ (with sth)** existing or happening at the same time 並存的；同時發生的： *He was imprisoned for two concurrent terms of 30 months and 18 months.* 他被判處 30 個月和 18 個月的監禁，合併執行。 ▸ **con·cur·rent·ly** AW *adv.*： *The prison sentences will run concurrently.* 所判的幾個刑期合併執行。

con·cuss /kən'kʌs/ *verb* **~ sb** to hit sb on the head, making them become unconscious or confused for a short time 使腦部受到震盪 ▸ **con·cussed** *adj.*： *She was concussed after the fall.* 她跌倒造成了腦震盪。

con·cus·sion /kən'kʌʃn/ *noun* [U] (This word is only [C] in *NAmE*. 在美式英語中只作可數名詞) a temporary loss of CONSCIOUSNESS caused by a blow to the head; the effects of a severe blow to the head such as confusion and temporary loss of physical and mental abilities 腦震盪： (*BrE*) *He was taken to hospital with concussion.* 他因腦震盪被送進醫院。◇ (*NAmE*) *He was taken to the hospital with a concussion.* 他因腦震盪被送進醫院。

con·demn /kən'dem/ *verb*

▸ **EXPRESS DISAPPROVAL** 表示不贊成 **1 ~ sb/sth (for/as sth)** to express very strong disapproval of sb/sth, usually for moral reasons （通常因道義上的原因而）譴責，指責： *The government issued a statement condemning the killings.* 政府發表聲明譴責這些兇殺事件。◇ *The editor of the newspaper was condemned as lacking integrity.* 這家報紙的編輯被指責為缺乏操守。

▸ **SB TO PUNISHMENT** 處以刑罰 **2** [usually passive] to say what sb's punishment will be 宣判；判處（某人某種刑罰） SYN **sentence**： **~ sb (to sth)** *He was condemned to death for murder and later hanged.* 他因謀殺罪被判處死刑後被絞死了。◇ **~ sb to do sth** *She was condemned to hang for killing her husband.* 她因殺害親夫被處以絞刑。

▸ **SB TO DIFFICULT SITUATION** 把某人置於困境 **3** [usually passive] **~ sb to sth** to force sb to accept a difficult or unpleasant situation 迫使…接受困境（或不愉快的狀況） SYN **doom**： *He was condemned to a life of hardship.* 他不得不過苦日子。◇ *They were condemned to spend every holiday on a rainy campsite.* 他們得在陰雨連綿的野營地度過每一個假日，徒嘆奈何。

▸ **STH DANGEROUS** 危險的事物 **4** [usually passive] **~ sth (as sth)** to say officially that sth is not safe enough to be used 宣告使用…不安全： *a condemned building* 一座已宣告不能居住的危樓◇ *The meat was condemned as unfit to eat.* 這種肉被宣告不宜食用。

▸ **SHOW GUILT** 表明有罪 **5 ~ sb** to show or suggest that sb is guilty of sth 證明（或表明）有罪： *She is condemned out of her own mouth* (= her own words show that she is guilty). 她自己說的話顯示她有罪責。

con·dem·na·tion /ˌkɒndem'neɪʃn; *NAmE* ˌkɑːn-/ *noun* [U, C] **~ (of sb/sth)** an expression of very strong disapproval 譴責；指責： *There was widespread condemnation of the invasion.* 那次侵略遭到了人們普遍的譴責。

conˌdemned 'cell *noun* (*BrE*) a prison cell where a person who is going to be punished by death is kept 死囚牢房

con·den·sa·tion /ˌkɒnden'seɪʃn; *NAmE* ˌkɑːn-/ *noun* **1** [U] drops of water that form on a cold surface when warm water VAPOUR becomes cool 凝結的水珠 **2** [U] the process of a gas changing to a liquid （氣體）冷凝，凝結 **3** [C, usually sing., U] (*formal*) the process of making a book, etc. shorter by taking out anything that is not necessary （書等的）簡縮

con·dense /kən'dens/ *verb* **1** [I, T] to change from a gas into a liquid; to make a gas change into a liquid （由氣體）冷凝；（使氣體）凝結： **~ (into sth)** *Steam condenses into water when it cools.* 蒸汽冷卻時凝結為水。◇ **~ sth (into sth)** *The steam was condensed rapidly by injecting cold water into the cylinder.* 由於氣缸中注入了冷水，蒸汽迅速凝結了。 **2** [I, T] **~ (sth)** if a liquid **condenses** or you **condense** it, it becomes thicker and stronger because it has lost some of its water （使）濃縮，變濃，變稠 SYN **reduce**： *Condense the soup by boiling it for several minutes.* 煮幾分鐘把湯熬濃。 **3** [T] **~ sth (into sth)** to put sth such as a piece of writing into fewer words; to put a lot of information into a small space 簡縮；壓縮（文字、信息等）： *The article was condensed into just two pages.* 這篇文章被簡縮成僅兩頁。◇ *The author has condensed a great deal of material into just 100 pages.* 作者在短短 100 頁中濃縮了大量信息。

conˌdensed 'milk *noun* [U] a type of thick sweet milk that is sold in cans 煉乳

con·dens·er /kən'densə(r)/ *noun* **1** a device that cools gas in order to change it into a liquid 冷凝器 **2** a device that receives or stores electricity, especially in a car engine （尤指汽車發動機內的）電容器

con·des·cend /ˌkɒndɪ'send; *NAmE* ˌkɑːn-/ *verb* **1** [T] **~ to do sth** (often *disapproving*) to do sth that you think it is below your social or professional position to do 屈尊；俯就 SYN **deign**： *We had to wait almost an hour before he condescended to see us.* 我們等了幾乎一小時他才屈尊大駕來見我們。 **2** [I] **~ to sb** to behave towards sb as though you are more important and more intelligent than they are （對某人）表現出優越感： *When giving a talk, be careful not to condescend to your audience.* 發表講話時，注意別對聽眾表現出高人一等的樣子。 ▸ **con·des·cen·sion** /ˌkɒndɪ'senʃn; *NAmE* ˌkɑːn-/ *noun* [U]： *Her smile was a mixture of pity and condescension.* 她的微笑中夾雜着憐憫與傲慢。

con·des·cend·ing /ˌkɒndɪ'sendɪŋ; *NAmE* ˌkɑːn-/ *adj.* behaving as though you are more important and more intelligent than other people 表現出優越感的；居高臨下的： *He has a condescending attitude towards women.* 他對女性總是居高臨下。 ▸ **con·des·cend·ing·ly** *adv.*

con·dign /kən'daɪn/ *adj.* (*formal*) (of a punishment 懲罰) appropriate to the crime 適當的；應得的

con·di·ment /'kɒndɪmənt; *NAmE* 'kɑːn-/ *noun* [usually pl.] **1** (*BrE*) a substance such as salt or pepper that is used to give flavour to food 調味料；作料 **2** (*especially NAmE*) a sauce, etc. that is used to give flavour to food, or that is eaten with food 調味汁（或醬等）；醬料

con·di·tion 🔑 /kən'dɪʃn/ *noun, verb*

■ ***noun***

▸ **STATE OF STH** 事物的狀態 **1** 🔑 [U, sing.] the state that sth is in 狀態；狀況： *to be **in bad/good/excellent condition*** 處於糟糕的／良好的／極佳的狀態◇ *a used car in perfect condition* 車況完好的舊車

▸ **MEDICAL** 醫學上 **2** 🔑 [U, sing.] the state of sb's health or how fit they are 健康狀況： *He is overweight and **out of condition*** (= not physically fit). 他體重超重，健康狀況不佳。◇ *You are **in no condition*** (= too ill/sick, etc.) *to go anywhere.* 你的身體太差，哪兒都不宜去。◇ *The motorcyclist was in a **critical condition** in hospital last night.* 那位摩托車手昨晚在醫院生命垂危。 **3** 🔑 [C] an illness or a medical problem that you have for a long time because it is not possible to cure it （因不可能治癒而長期患有的）疾病： *a medical condition* 內科疾病◇ *He suffers from a serious **heart condition**.* 他患有嚴重的心臟病。 ➲ SYNONYMS at DISEASE

▸ **CIRCUMSTANCES** 環境 **4** 🔑 **conditions** [pl.] the circumstances or situation in which people live, work or do things （居住、工作或做事情的）環境，境況，條件： ***living/housing/working conditions*** 生活／住房／工作條件◇ *changing economic conditions* 不斷變化的經濟狀況◇ *neglected children living **under** the most appalling **conditions*** 生活在最惡劣環境下的無人關注的兒童◇ *a strike to improve **pay and conditions*** 要求提高工資和改善工作條件的罷工 ➲ SYNONYMS at SITUATION **5** 🔑 **conditions** [pl.] the physical situation that affects how sth happens （影響某事發生的）物質環境，狀態，條件： *The plants grow best in cool, damp conditions.* 這種植物最適合在陰涼、潮濕的環境下生長。◇ ***freezing/icy/humid, etc. conditions*** 冰凍、結冰、潮濕等的氣候條件

◇ *Conditions are ideal* (= the weather is very good) *for sailing today.* 今天是揚帆出海的理想天氣。◇ *treacherous* ***driving conditions*** 危險的行車環境

▸ **RULE 規則 6** 🔑 [C] a rule or decision that you must agree to, sometimes forming part of a contract or an official agreement 條件；條款；要件：*the* ***terms and conditions*** *of employment* 雇用的條款 ◇ *The offer is* ***subject to certain conditions.*** 此項優惠受制於某些條件。◇ *They agreed to lend us the car* ***on condition that*** (= only if) *we returned it before the weekend.* 他們同意借車給我們，條件是週末以前歸還。◇ *They will give us the money* ***on one condition****—that we pay it back within six months.* 他們給我們提供資金有一個條件，即我們在六個月以內償還。◇ (*especially NAmE*) *They agreed* ***under the condition that*** *the matter be dealt with promptly.* 他們同意了，前提是要迅速處理這件事。◇ *Congress can* ***impose strict conditions*** *on the bank.* 國會可能會迫使這家銀行接受苛刻的條件。◇ *They have agreed to the cease-fire provided their* ***conditions are met.*** 他們已經同意停火，只要他們提出的條件得到滿足。

▸ **NECESSARY SITUATION 必要的條件 7** 🔑 [C] a situation that must exist in order for sth else to happen（先決）條件；前提：*a necessary condition for economic growth* 經濟增長的必要條件 ◇ *A good training programme is one of the conditions for successful industry.* 良好的培訓計劃是企業成功的先決條件。

▸ **STATE OF GROUP 群體狀況 8** [sing.] (*formal*) the state of a particular group of people because of their situation in life, their problems, etc.（某群體的）生存狀態，處境：*He spoke angrily about the condition of the urban poor.* 他憤怒地談論城市貧民的處境。◇ *Work is basic to* ***the human condition*** (= the fact of being alive). 勞動是人類生存的基本條件。

IDM **on 'no condition** (*US* also **under 'no condition**) (*formal*) not in any situation; never 無論如何都不；決不：*You must on no condition tell them what happened.* 你決不能告訴他們所發生的事。➲ more at MINT *n.*

■ ***verb*** **1** [usually passive] to train sb/sth to behave in a particular way or to become used to a particular situation 訓練；使習慣於；使適應：**~ sb/sth (to sth)** *the difference between inborn and* ***conditioned reflexes*** (= reactions that are learned/not natural) 先天反應與條件反射的差異 ◇ *Patients can become conditioned to particular forms of treatment.* 病人會習慣某些治療方式。◇ **~ sb/sth to do sth** *The rats had been conditioned to ring a bell when they wanted food.* 這些老鼠已經過訓練，想吃食物時就會按鈴。 **2 ~ sb/sth** to have an important effect on sb/sth; to influence the way that sth happens 對…具有重要影響；影響（某事發生的方式）：*Gender roles are often conditioned by cultural factors.* 文化因素常常對性別的角色有着重要的影響。 **3 ~ sth** to keep sth such as your hair or skin healthy 保持（頭髮或皮膚等的）健康；養護：*a shampoo that cleans and conditions hair* 可清潔並養護頭髮的洗髮劑 ◇ *a polish for conditioning leather* 皮革護理油

con·di·tion·al /kən'dɪʃənl/ *adj.*, *noun*

■ ***adj.*** **1 ~ (on/upon sth)** depending on sth 附帶條件的；依…而定的：***conditional approval/acceptance*** 有條件的批准／接受 ◇ *Payment is conditional upon delivery of the goods* (= if the goods are not delivered the money will not be paid). 貨到方付款。◇ *He was found guilty and given a* ***conditional discharge*** (= allowed to go free on particular conditions). 他被判定有罪並被判處有條件的釋放。◇ *a conditional offer* (= that depends on particular conditions being met) 有條件的要約 **OPP** **unconditional** **2** [only before noun] (*grammar* 語法) expressing sth that must happen or be true if another thing is to happen or be true 條件的：*a* ***conditional sentence/clause*** 條件句／從句 ▸ **con·di·tion·al·ly** /-ʃənəli/ *adv.*：*The offer was made conditionally.* 這個報價附有條件。

■ ***noun*** (*grammar* 語法) **1** [C] a sentence or clause that begins with *if* or *unless* and expresses a condition 條件句，條件從句（由 if 或 unless 引導的） **2 the conditional** [sing.] the form of a verb that expresses a conditional action, for example *should* in *If I should die ...* 動詞的條件式（如 should 用在 If I should die...）：*the* ***present/past/perfect conditional*** 現在／過去／完成條件式 ◇ *the* ***first/second/third conditional*** 第一／第二／第三條件式

Synonyms 同義詞辨析

condition / state

The following adjectives are frequently used with these nouns. 下列形容詞常與這兩個名詞連用：

~ condition	~ state
good	present
excellent	current
physical	mental
poor	solid
human	no
perfect	emotional
no	physical
better	natural

■ **State** is a more general word than **condition** and is used for the condition that something is in at a particular time. It can be used without an adjective. * state 較 condition 通用，指特定時間的狀況，可不加形容詞：*the present state of medical knowledge* 目前醫學知識的狀況 ◇ *We're worried about his mental state.* 我們擔心他的精神狀況。◇ *What a state this room is in* (= very bad). 這房間真糟糕。

■ **Condition** is used with an adjective and refers especially to the appearance, quality or working order of somebody or something. * condition 與形容詞連用，尤指人或事物的外觀、品質或工作狀況：*The car is in excellent condition.* 這輛汽車狀態好極了。

con·di·tion·er /kən'dɪʃənə(r)/ *noun* [C, U] **1** a liquid that makes hair soft and shiny after washing 護髮劑；護髮素：*shampoo and conditioner* 洗髮劑與護髮素 **2** a liquid, used after washing clothes, that makes them softer（洗衣後用的）柔順劑：*fabric conditioner* 織物柔順劑

con·di·tion·ing /kən'dɪʃənɪŋ/ *noun* [U] the training or experience that an animal or a person has that makes them behave in a particular way in a particular situation 訓練；薰陶；條件作用：*Is personality the result of conditioning from parents and society, or are we born with it?* 個性是受父母和社會薰陶的結果，還是我們生而有之？ ➲ see also AIR CONDITIONING

condo /'kɒndəʊ; *NAmE* 'kɑːndoʊ/ *noun* (*pl.* **-os**) (*NAmE*, *informal*) = CONDOMINIUM

con·dol·ence /kən'dəʊləns; *NAmE* -'doʊ-/ *noun* [C, usually pl., U] sympathy that you feel for sb when a person in their family or that they know well has died; an expression of this sympathy 弔唁；慰唁：*to* ***give/offer/express*** *your* ***condolences*** 表示慰唁 ◇ *Our condolences go to his wife and family.* 向他的妻子和家人謹致弔慰之意。◇ *a letter of condolence* 弔唁信

con·dom /'kɒndɒm; *NAmE* 'kɑːndəm/ *noun* **1** (*BrE* also **sheath**) (also *NAmE formal* or *technical* 術語 **prophy·lac·tic**) a thin rubber covering that a man wears over his PENIS during sex to stop a woman from becoming pregnant or to protect against disease（男用）避孕套，保險套，安全套，陰莖套 **2 female condom** a thin rubber device that a woman wears inside her VAGINA during sex to prevent herself from becoming pregnant（女用）避孕套

con·do·min·ium /ˌkɒndə'mɪniəm; *NAmE* ˌkɑːn-/ (also *informal* **condo**) *noun* (*especially NAmE*) an apartment building or group of houses in which each flat/apartment/house is owned by the person living in it but the shared areas are owned by everyone together; a flat/apartment/house in such a building or group of houses 公寓（套房私有，其他地方屬業主共有）；公寓的套房；公寓的單元

con·done /kən'dəʊn; *NAmE* -'doʊn/ *verb* **~ sth** | **~ (sb) doing sth** to accept behaviour that is morally wrong or to treat it as if it were not serious 寬恕；饒恕；縱容：*Terrorism can never be condoned.* 決不能容忍恐怖主義。

con·dor /ˈkɒndɔː(r); *NAmE* ˈkɑːn-/ *noun* a large bird of the VULTURE family, that lives mainly in S America 神鷹，大禿鷹（主要棲居在南美洲）

con·du·cive /kənˈdjuːsɪv; *NAmE* -ˈduːs-/ *adj.* **~ to sth** making it easy, possible or likely for sth to happen 使容易（或有可能）發生的：*Chairs in rows are not as conducive to discussion as chairs arranged in a circle.* 椅子成排擺放不如成圈擺放便於討論。

con·duct 🔑 AW *verb, noun*

■ *verb* /kənˈdʌkt/ **1** 🔑 [T] **~ sth** (*formal*) to organize and/or do a particular activity 組織；安排；實施；執行：*to **conduct an experiment/an inquiry/a survey*** 進行實驗／詢問／調查 ◇ *The negotiations have been conducted in a positive manner.* 已積極進行過談判。**2** 🔑 [T, I] **~ (sth)** to direct a group of people who are singing or playing music 指揮（歌唱或音樂演奏）：*a concert by the Philharmonic Orchestra, conducted by Sir Colin Davis* 由科林 • 戴維斯爵士指揮、愛樂交響樂團演出的音樂會 **3** [T] **~ sb/sth + adv./prep.** (*formal*) to lead or guide sb through or around a place 帶領；引導；為（某人）導遊：*a **conducted tour** of Athens* (= one with a guide, giving information about it) 有導遊陪同的雅典之行 ◇ *The guide conducted us around the ruins of the ancient city.* 導遊帶領我們遊覽了古城遺跡。**4** [T] **~ yourself + adv./prep.** (*formal*) to behave in a particular way 舉止；表現：*He conducted himself far better than expected.* 他表現得比預料的要好得多。**5** [T] **~ sth** (*technical* 術語) (of a substance 物質) to allow heat or electricity to pass along or through it 傳導（熱或電等能量）：*Copper conducts electricity well.* 銅的導電性能好。

■ *noun* /ˈkɒndʌkt; *NAmE* ˈkɑːn-/ [U] (*formal*) **1** 🔑 a person's behaviour in a particular place or in a particular situation（人在某地或某種情況下的）行為，舉止：*The sport has a strict code of conduct.* 這種體育運動有嚴格的行為規範。**2 ~ of sth** the way in which a business or an activity is organized and managed 經營方式；管理方法；實施辦法：*There was growing criticism of the government's conduct of the war.* 政府對戰爭的指揮方式受到越來越多的指責。➲ see also SAFE CONDUCT

con·duct·ance /kənˈdʌktəns/ *noun* [U] (*physics* 物) the degree to which an object allows electricity or heat to pass through it 電導（率）；（熱）傳導性

con·duc·tion /kənˈdʌkʃn/ *noun* [U] (*physics* 物) the process by which heat or electricity passes through a material（熱或電等能量的）傳導

con·duct·ive /kənˈdʌktɪv/ *adj.* (*physics* 物) able to CONDUCT electricity, heat, etc. 導電（或熱等）的；能傳導（電、熱等）的 ▸ **con·duct·iv·ity** /ˌkɒndʌkˈtɪvəti; *NAmE* ˌkɑːn-/ *noun* [U]

conˌductive eduˈcation *noun* [U] a treatment for people with CEREBRAL PALSY that was developed in Hungary and that involves special physical exercises and learning methods 引導式教育（匈牙利為腦癱患者開發的療法，包括特定的動作訓練和學習方法）

con·duct·or /kənˈdʌktə(r)/ *noun* **1** a person who stands in front of an ORCHESTRA, a group of singers etc., and directs their performance, especially sb who does this as a profession（管弦樂隊、合唱隊等的）指揮；職業指揮 **2** (*BrE* also **guard**) a person who is in charge of a train and travels with it, but does not drive it 列車長 **3** (*BrE*) a person whose job is to collect money from passengers on a bus or check their tickets（公共汽車的）售票員：*a bus conductor* 公共汽車售票員 **4** (*physics* 物) a substance that allows electricity or heat to pass along it or through it 導體（導電或導熱等的物質）：*Wood is a poor conductor.* 木頭不是良好的導體。➲ see also LIGHTNING CONDUCTOR

con·duc·tress /kənˈdʌktrəs/ *noun* (*BrE, old-fashioned*) a woman who collects money from passengers on a bus or checks their tickets（公共汽車的）女售票員

con·duit /ˈkɒndjuɪt; *NAmE* ˈkɑːnduɪt/ *noun* **1** (*technical* 術語) a pipe, channel or tube which liquid, gas or electrical wire can pass through（液體、氣體或電線的）管道，導管 **2** (*formal*) a person, an organization or a country that is used to pass things or information to other people or places 中轉人；中轉機構；中轉國：*The organization had acted as a conduit for money from the arms industry.* 那家機構充當了從軍火工業向他處中轉資金的渠道。

cone /kəʊn; *NAmE* koʊn/ *noun, verb*

■ *noun* **1** a solid or hollow object with a round flat base and sides that slope up to a point（實心或空心的）圓錐體 ➲ VISUAL VOCAB page V71 ➲ see also CONIC, CONICAL **2** a solid or hollow object that is shaped like a cone（實心或空心的）圓錐形物：*a paper cone full of popcorn* 裝滿爆玉米花的錐形紙筒 ◇ *the cone of a volcano* 火山錐 ➲ see also NOSE CONE **3** (also **ˈtraffic cone**) a plastic object shaped like a cone and often red and white, or yellow, in colour, used on roads to show where vehicles are not allowed to go, for example while repairs are being done 錐形警告路標（常為紅白色或紅黃色的塑料錐形物，表示在維修道路等時禁止車輛通行）**4** (also *old-fashioned* **cornet**) a piece of thin crisp biscuit shaped like a cone, which you can put ice cream in to eat it（盛冰淇淋的）錐形蛋捲筒 **5** the hard dry fruit of a PINE or FIR tree（松樹或冷杉的）球果：*a pine cone* 松樹球果 ➲ VISUAL VOCAB page V10 ➲ see also FIR CONE

■ *verb*

PHR V **ˌcone sth↔ˈoff** to close a road or part of a road by putting a line of cones across it 用錐形警告路標關閉（道路或道路的一部份）

con·fab /ˈkɒnfæb; *NAmE* ˈkɑːn-/ *noun* (*informal*) **1** an informal private discussion or conversation 私人談話；閒談 **2** (*NAmE*) a meeting or conference of the members of a profession or group（行業或團體）會議：*the annual movie confab in Cannes* 在戛納舉行的電影年會

con·fabu·la·tion /kənˌfæbjəˈleɪʃn/ *noun* [C, U] (*formal*) **1** a story that sb has invented in their mind; the act of inventing a story in your mind 虛構的故事；虛構 **2** a conversation; the activity of having a conversation 談話；閒談

con·fec·tion /kənˈfekʃn/ *noun* **1** (*formal*) a cake or other sweet food that looks very attractive（精美誘人的）甜點，甜食 **2** a thing such as a building or piece of clothing, that is made in a skilful or complicated way 精工製作的物品（如建築物或衣物）

con·fec·tion·er /kənˈfekʃənə(r)/ *noun* a person or a business that makes or sells cakes and sweets/candy（製作或銷售糕餅和糖果的）甜食商，甜食業

conˈfectioner's sugar (also **ˈpowdered sugar**) (both *US*) (*BrE* **ˈicing sugar**) *noun* [U] fine white powder made from sugar, that is mixed with water to make icing（製糖霜用的）糖粉

con·fec·tion·ery /kənˈfekʃənəri; *NAmE* -ʃəneri/ *noun* [U] sweets/candy, chocolate, etc. 甜食（糖果、巧克力等）

con·fed·er·acy /kənˈfedərəsi/ *noun* **1** [C] a union of states, groups of people or political parties with the same aim 聯盟；同盟；聯邦 **2 the Confederacy** [sing.] = THE CONFEDERATE STATES

con·fed·er·ate /kənˈfedərət/ *noun, adj.*

■ *noun* a person who helps sb, especially to do sth illegal or secret 同謀；同夥；從犯；共犯 SYN **accomplice**

■ *adj.* belonging to a confederacy 聯盟的；同盟的；聯邦的

the Conˌfederate ˈStates *noun* [pl.] (also **the Confederacy**) the eleven southern states of the US which left the United States in 1860-1, starting the American Civil War（美國）南部邦聯（1860–1861 年脫離合眾國從而引發南北戰爭的美國南部 11 州）

con·fed·er·ation /kənˌfedəˈreɪʃn/ *noun* **1** an organization consisting of countries, businesses, etc. that have joined together in order to help each other 聯盟；聯合體：*the Confederation of British Industry* 英國工業聯合會 **2 Confederation** (in Canada) the joining together of PROVINCES and TERRITORIES forming Canada, which began 1 July, 1867 加拿大聯邦（從 1867 年 7 月 1 日起由若干省和地方組成加拿大）

con·fer AW /kənˈfɜː(r)/ *verb* (**-rr-**) (*formal*) **1** [I] **~ (with sb) (on/about sth)** to discuss sth with sb, in order to exchange opinions or get advice 商討；協商；交換意見：*He wanted to confer with his colleagues before reaching a decision.* 他想與他的同事先商議一下再作出決定。**2** [T] **~ sth (on/upon sb)** to give sb an award, a university degree or a particular honour or right 授予，頒發（獎項、學位、榮譽或權利）：*An honorary degree was conferred on him by Oxford University in 2009.* 牛津大學於 2009 年授予他榮譽學位。

con·fer·ence 🔑 AW /ˈkɒnfərəns; *NAmE* ˈkɑːn-/ *noun* **1** 🔑 a large official meeting, usually lasting for a few days, at which people with the same work or interests come together to discuss their views（通常持續幾天的大型正式）會議，研討會：*The hotel is used for exhibitions, conferences and social events.* 這家旅館用於舉行展覽、大型會議和社交活動。◇ *a* **conference room/centre/hall** 會議室／中心／廳 ◇ *She is attending a three-day conference on AIDS education.* 她正在出席一個為期三天的有關艾滋病教育的會議。◇ *The conference will be held in Glasgow.* 會議將在格拉斯哥舉行。◇ *delegates to the Labour Party's annual conference* 參加工黨年會的代表 **2** 🔑 a meeting at which people have formal discussions（正式）討論會，商討會：*Ministers from all four countries involved will meet at the* **conference table** *this week.* 有關四國將各派部長於本週開會協商。◇ *He was* **in conference** *with his lawyers all day.* 他與他的律師們商討了一整天。➲ see also PRESS CONFERENCE **3** (*especially NAmE*) a group of sports teams that play against each other in a league 體育協會（或聯合會）：*Southeast Conference football champions* 東南部聯盟的橄欖球聯賽

ˈ**conference call** *noun* a telephone call in which three or more people take part 電話會議

con·fer·en·cing /ˈkɒnfərənsɪŋ; *NAmE* ˈkɑːn-/ *noun* the activity of organizing or taking part in meetings, especially when people are in different places and use telephones, computers, or video to communicate 召集（或參加）會議（尤指電話、網絡或視頻會議）：*video conferencing* 召開視頻會議

con·fer·ment /kənˈfɜːmənt; *NAmE* -ˈfɜːrm-/ *noun* [U, C] (*formal*) the action of giving sb an award, a university degree or a particular honour or right（獎項、學位、榮譽或權利的）授予，頒發

con·fess /kənˈfes/ *verb* **1** [I, T] to admit, especially formally or to the police, that you have done sth wrong or illegal 供認，坦白，承認（錯誤或罪行）：*After hours of questioning, the suspect confessed.* 經過數小時的審問後，嫌疑犯終於招供。◇ **~ to sth/to doing sth** *She confessed to the murder.* 她供認犯了謀殺罪。◇ **~ (that)** ... *He confessed that he had stolen the money.* 他承認他偷了那筆錢。◇ **~ sth** *We persuaded her to confess her crime.* 我們說服她坦白她的罪行。**2** [I, T] to admit sth that you feel ashamed or embarrassed about 承認（自己感到羞愧或尷尬的事）：**~ sth** *She was reluctant to confess her ignorance.* 她不願承認她的無知。◇ **~ to sth/to doing sth** ***I must confess** to knowing nothing about computers.* 我得承認對電腦一竅不通。◇ **~ (that)** ... *I confess (that) I know nothing about computers.* 我承認我對電腦一竅不通。◇ **+ speech** *'I know nothing about them,' he confessed.* "我對他們一無所知。" 他承認道。◇ **~ yourself + adj.** (*formal*) *I confess myself bewildered by their explanation.* 我承認他們的解釋使我感到困惑。➲ see also SELF-CONFESSED ➲ **SYNONYMS** at ADMIT **3** [I, T] **~ (sth) (to sb)** (especially in the Roman Catholic Church 尤指羅馬天主教會) to tell God or a priest about the bad things you have done so that you can say that you are sorry and be forgiven 懺悔；悔過；告罪；告解 **4** [T] **~ sb** (of a priest 神父) to hear sb confess their SINS (= the bad things they have done) 聆聽（某人的）懺悔（或告罪、告解）

con·fes·sion /kənˈfeʃn/ *noun* **1** [C, U] a statement that a person makes, admitting that they are guilty of a crime; the act of making such a statement 供詞；供狀；認罪；供認；坦白：*After hours of questioning by police, she made a full confession.* 經過警察數小時的審問，她才供認了全部罪行。**2** [C, U] a statement admitting sth that you are ashamed or embarrassed about; the act of making such a statement（對使自己羞愧或尷尬的事的）表白，承認 SYN **admission**：*I've a confession to make—I lied about my age.* 我有錯要承認 —— 我謊報了年齡。**3** [U, C] (especially in the Roman Catholic Church 尤指羅馬天主教會) a private statement to a priest about the bad things that you have done（向神父作的）告罪，告解：*to go to confession* 去告解 ◇ *to hear sb's confession* 聽某人告解 **4** [C] (*formal*) a statement of your religious beliefs, principles, etc.（宗教的）信仰表白：*a confession of faith* 宗教信仰表白

con·fes·sion·al /kənˈfeʃənl/ *noun* a private place in a church where a priest listens to people making confessions（教堂內的）告解室，告解亭，懺悔室

con·fes·sor /kənˈfesə(r)/ *noun* a Roman Catholic priest who listens to sb's CONFESSION (3) 聽告解神父

con·fetti /kənˈfeti/ *noun* [U] small pieces of coloured paper that people often throw at weddings over people who have just been married, or (in the US) at other special events（在婚禮或美國其他特殊活動中撒的）五彩紙屑

con·fi·dant (*feminine also* **con·fi·dante**) /ˈkɒnfɪdænt; ˌkɒnfɪˈdɑːnt; *NAmE* ˈkɑːnfɪdænt/ *noun* a person that you trust and who you talk to about private or secret things（可吐露秘密的）知己，密友：*a* ***close/trusted confidant*** *of the President* 總統的密友／親信

con·fide /kənˈfaɪd/ *verb* to tell sb secrets and personal information that you do not want other people to know（向某人）吐露（秘密、隱私等）：**~ sth (to sb)** *She confided all her secrets to her best friend.* 她向她最要好的朋友傾吐了自己所有的秘密。◇ **~ (to sb) that** ... *He confided to me that he had applied for another job.* 他向我透露他已申請另一份工作。◇ **+ speech** *'It was a lie,' he confided.* "這是謊言。" 他透露說。

PHR V **conˈfide in sb** to tell sb secrets and personal information because you feel you can trust them 向（認為可信賴的人）透露秘密（或隱私）：*It is important to have someone you can confide in.* 有一位心腹知己很重要。

con·fi·dence 🔑 /ˈkɒnfɪdəns; *NAmE* ˈkɑːn-/ *noun*

▸ **BELIEF IN OTHERS** 對他人的信心 **1** 🔑 [U] **~ (in sb/sth)** the feeling that you can trust, believe in and be sure about the abilities or good qualities of sb/sth 信心；信任；信賴：*The players all* **have confidence in** *their manager.* 隊員都信賴他們的經理。◇ *A fall in unemployment will help to restore consumer confidence.* 失業人數的下降會有助於恢復消費者的信心。◇ *a lack of confidence in the government* 對政府缺乏信任 ◇ *The new contracts have undermined the confidence of employees.* 新的合同動搖了雇員們的信心。◇ *She has every confidence in her students' abilities.* 她完全相信她學生的能力。➲ see also VOTE OF CONFIDENCE, VOTE OF NO CONFIDENCE

▸ **BELIEF IN YOURSELF** 對自己的信心 **2** 🔑 [U] a belief in your own ability to do things and be successful 自信心：*He answered the questions* **with confidence**. 他有信心地回答了那些問題。◇ *People often* **lose confidence** *when they are criticized.* 人受到批評時經常會失去信心。◇ *He* **gained confidence** *when he went to college.* 他在走進大學門時增強了自信。◇ *She suffers from a* **lack of confidence**. 她深受缺乏自信心之苦。◇ *While girls* **lack confidence**, *boys often overestimate their abilities.* 女孩通常缺乏自信，而男孩則往往會高估自己的能力。◇ *I didn't have any confidence in myself at school.* 我在學校時對自己毫無信心。

▸ **FEELING CERTAIN** 感到有把握 **3** 🔑 [U] the feeling that you are certain about sth 把握；肯定：*They could not say* **with confidence** *that he would be able to walk again after the accident.* 他們不能肯定他經過那場事故後還能行走。◇ *He expressed his* **confidence that** *they would win.* 他表示了自己的信心：他們必定取勝。

▸ **TRUST** 信任 **4** [U] a feeling of trust that sb will keep information private（對某人會保守秘密的）信任，信賴：*Eva told me about their relationship* **in confidence**. 伊娃對我透露了他們倆的關係這個秘密。◇ *This is in the* **strictest confidence**. 這事切勿外傳。◇ *It took a long time to gain her confidence* (= make her feel she could trust me). 我花了很長的時間才贏得她的信任。

▸ **A SECRET** 秘密 **5** [C] (*formal*) a secret that you tell sb（向某人透露的）秘密，機密：*The girls exchanged*

C

confidences. 女孩子們相互吐露自己的心事。◇ *I could never forgive Mike for betraying a confidence.* 邁克泄露了秘密，我決不會原諒他。

IDM **be in sb's confidence** to be trusted with sb's secrets 受某人信任；是某人的心腹：*He is said to be very much in the President's confidence.* 據說他深受總統的信任。**take sb into your confidence** to tell sb secrets and personal information about yourself 向某人吐露內心秘密（或隱私）：*She took me into her confidence and told me about the problems she was facing.* 她把我當成知己，把她面臨的種種難題都向我和盤托出。

'confidence trick (*BrE*) (*NAmE* **'confidence game**) *noun* (*formal*) = CON *n.* (1)

'confidence trickster *noun* (*BrE, formal*) a person who tricks others into giving him or her money, etc. 行騙者；騙子

con·fi·dent /ˈkɒnfɪdənt; *NAmE* ˈkɑːn-/ *adj.* **1** feeling sure about your own ability to do things and be successful 自信的；有自信心的：*She was in a relaxed, confident mood.* 她的心態從容而自信。◇ *The teacher wants the children to feel confident about asking questions when they don't understand.* 教師要孩子們遇到不懂的問題就大膽提問。➲ see also SELF-CONFIDENT **2** feeling certain that sth will happen in the way that you want or expect 肯定的；確信的；有把握的：**~ of sth/doing sth** *The team feels confident of winning.* 這個隊覺得有把握取勝。◇ **~ that …** *I'm confident that you will get the job.* 我肯定你能得到那份工作。➲ SYNONYMS at SURE ▸ **con·fi·dent·ly** *adv.*

con·fi·den·tial /ˌkɒnfɪˈdenʃl; *NAmE* ˌkɑːn-/ *adj.* **1** meant to be kept secret and not told to or shared with other people 機密的；保密的；秘密的：***confidential information/documents*** 機密情報 / 文件 ◇ *Your medical records are **strictly confidential*** (= completely secret). 你的病歷是絕對保密的。**2** (of a way of speaking 說話的方式) showing that what you are saying is private or secret 隱密的；秘密的：*He spoke in a confidential tone, his voice low.* 他低聲用隱密的語氣說話。**3** [only before noun] trusted with private or secret information 受信任的；委以機密的：*a confidential secretary* 機要秘書 ▸ **con·fi·den·tial·ly** /-ʃəli/ *adv.*：*She told me confidentially that she is going to retire early.* 她私下告訴我她要提早退休。

con·fi·den·tial·ity /ˌkɒnfɪˌdenʃiˈæləti; *NAmE* ˌkɑːn-/ *noun* [U] a situation in which you expect sb to keep information secret 保密性；機密性：*They signed a confidentiality agreement.* 他們簽署了一份保守機密的協議。◇ *All letters will be treated with complete confidentiality.* 所有信件將按絕密處置。

con·fid·ing /kənˈfaɪdɪŋ/ *adj.* [usually before noun] showing trust; showing that you want to tell sb a secret 信任的；推心置腹的：*a confiding relationship* 可以推心置腹的關係 ▸ **con·fid·ing·ly** *adv.*

con·fig·ur·ation /kənˌfɪɡəˈreɪʃn; *NAmE* -ˌfɪɡjəˈr-/ *noun* **1** (*formal* or *technical* 術語) an arrangement of the parts of sth or a group of things; the form or shape that this arrangement produces 佈局；結構；構造；格局；形狀 **2** (*computing* 計) the equipment and programs that form a computer system and the way that these are set up to run（計算機的）配置

con·fig·ure /kənˈfɪɡə(r); *NAmE* -ˈfɪɡjər/ *verb* [usually passive] **~ sth** (*technical* 術語) to arrange sth in a particular way, especially computer equipment; to make equipment or software work in the way that the user prefers（尤指對計算機設備進行）配置；對（設備或軟件進行）設定

con·fine AW /kənˈfaɪn/ *verb* **1** **~ sb/sth to sth** [often passive] to keep sb/sth inside the limits of a particular activity, subject, area, etc. 限制；限定 SYN **restrict**：*The work will not be confined to the Glasgow area.* 此項工作不會局限於格拉斯哥地區。◇ *I will **confine myself** to looking at the period from 1900 to 1916.* 我將把自己考察的範圍限定在 1900 年至 1916 年這段時間以內。**2** **~ sb/sth (in sth)** [usually passive] to keep a person or an animal in a small or closed space 監禁；禁閉：*Keep the dog confined in a suitable travelling cage.* 把狗關進適於旅行的籠子裏。◇ *Here the river is confined in a narrow channel.* 這條河在這裏流入狹窄的河槽。◇ *The soldiers concerned were **confined to barracks*** (= had to stay in the BARRACKS, as a punishment). 有關的士兵已受到禁閉在營房的處分。**3 be confined to bed, a wheelchair, etc.** to have to stay in bed, in a WHEELCHAIR, etc. 使離不開（或受困於牀、輪椅等）：*She was confined to bed with the flu.* 她因患流感臥病在牀。◇ *He was confined to a wheelchair after the accident.* 經過那場事故後他就離不開輪椅了。

con·fined AW /kənˈfaɪnd/ *adj.* [usually before noun] (of a space or an area 空間或地區) small and surrounded by walls or sides 狹窄而圍起來的：*It is cruel to keep animals in confined spaces.* 把動物關在狹小的空間裏是殘酷的。

con·fine·ment /kənˈfaɪnmənt/ *noun* **1** [U] the state of being forced to stay in a closed space, prison, etc., the act of putting sb there 禁閉；監禁；關押：*her confinement to a wheelchair* 半步離不開輪椅對她的束縛 ◇ *years of confinement as a political prisoner* 作為政治犯被監禁的歲月 ➲ see also SOLITARY CONFINEMENT **2** [U, C] (*formal* or *old-fashioned*) the time when a woman gives birth to a baby 分娩；產期：*the expected date of confinement* 預產期 ◇ *a **hospital/home confinement*** 在醫院 / 家中分娩

con·fines /ˈkɒnfaɪnz; *NAmE* ˈkɑːn-/ *noun* [pl.] (*formal*) limits or borders 範圍；界限；邊界：*It is beyond the confines of human knowledge.* 這超出了人類的知識範圍。◇ *the confines of family life* 家庭生活的範圍

con·firm AW /kənˈfɜːm; *NAmE* -ˈfɜːrm/ *verb* **1** to state or show that sth is definitely true or correct, especially by providing evidence（尤指提供證據來）證實，證明，確認：**~ sth** *Rumours of job losses were later confirmed.* 裁員的傳言後來得到了證實。◇ *His guilty expression confirmed my suspicions.* 他內疚的表情證實了我的猜疑。◇ *Please write to confirm your reservation* (= say that it is definite). 預訂後請來函確認。◇ **~ (that) …** *Has everyone confirmed (that) they're coming?* 他們是不是每個人都確定了一定會來？◇ **~ what/when, etc. …** *Can you confirm what happened?* 你能證實一下發生了什麼事嗎？◇ **it is confirmed that …** *It has been confirmed that the meeting will take place next week.* 已經確定會議將於下個星期舉行。**2** **~ sth | ~ sb (in sth)** to make sb feel or believe sth even more strongly 使感覺更強烈；使確信：*The walk in the mountains confirmed his fear of heights.* 在山裏步行使他更加確信自己有恐高症。**3** to make a position, an agreement, etc. more definite or official; to establish sb/sth firmly 批准（職位、協議等）；確認；認可：**~ sth** *After a six-month probationary period, her position was confirmed.* 經過六個月的試用期後，她獲准正式擔任該職。◇ **~ sb as sth** *He was confirmed as captain for the rest of the season.* 他被正式任命在這個賽季剩下的一段時間內擔任隊長。◇ **~ sb in sth** *I'm very happy to confirm you in your post.* 我很高興確認你擔任此職位。**4** [usually passive] **~ sb** to make sb a full member of the Christian Church（給某人）施放堅振，施堅信禮：*She was baptized when she was a month old and confirmed when she was thirteen.* 她出生一個月時受洗禮，十三歲時受堅信禮。

con·firm·ation AW /ˌkɒnfəˈmeɪʃn; *NAmE* ˌkɑːnfərˈm-/ *noun* [U, C] **1** a statement, letter, etc. that shows that sth is true, correct or definite 證實；確認書；證明書：*I'm still waiting for confirmation of the test results.* 我仍在等待考試結果的通知書。**2** a ceremony at which a person becomes a full member of the Christian Church 堅振；堅振禮；堅信禮 **3** a Jewish ceremony similar to a BAR MITZVAH or BAT MITZVAH but usually for young people over the age of 16 受戒禮（通常為 16 歲以上猶太年輕人舉行的儀式）

con·firmed /kənˈfɜːmd; *NAmE* -ˈfɜːrmd/ *adj.* [only before noun] having a particular habit or way of life and not likely to change 成習慣的；根深蒂固的：*a **confirmed bachelor*** (= a man who is not likely to get married, often used in newspapers to refer to a HOMOSEXUAL man) 抱定獨身主義的男子（報章常用以指同性戀者）

con·fis·cate /ˈkɒnfɪskeɪt; *NAmE* ˈkɑːn-/ *verb* **~ sth** to officially take sth away from sb, especially as a punishment（尤指作為懲罰）沒收，把…充公：*Their land was confiscated after the war.* 他們的土地在戰後被沒收。◇ *The teacher threatened to confiscate their phones if they kept using them in class.* 老師警告說，如果他們上課時繼續使用手機就予以沒收。▸ **con·fis·ca·tion** /ˌkɒnfɪˈskeɪʃn; *NAmE* ˌkɑːn-/ *noun* [U, C]

con·flag·ra·tion /ˌkɒnfləˈɡreɪʃn; *NAmE* ˌkɑːn-/ *noun* (*formal*) a very large fire that destroys a lot of land or buildings 大火災；大火

con·flate /kənˈfleɪt/ *verb* **~ A and/with B** (*formal*) to put two or more things together to make one new thing 合併；合成；混合 ▸ **con·fla·tion** /kənˈfleɪʃn/ *noun* [U, C]

con·flict 0-w AW *noun, verb*

▪ *noun* /ˈkɒnflɪkt; *NAmE* ˈkɑːn-/ [C, U] **~ (between A and B)** | **~ (over sth)** **1** 0-w a situation in which people, groups or countries are involved in a serious disagreement or argument 衝突；爭執；爭論：*a conflict between two cultures* 兩種文化的衝突 ◇ *The violence was the result of political and ethnic conflicts.* 那次暴動是政治與種族衝突的結果。◇ *She found herself* ***in conflict with*** *her parents over her future career.* 她發現自己在將來擇業的問題上與父母出現分歧。◇ *John often* ***comes into conflict*** *with his boss.* 約翰經常和他的老闆發生爭執。◇ *The government has done nothing to* ***resolve the conflict*** *over nurses' pay.* 政府未採取任何措施來解決護士工資問題引發的衝突。 **2** 0-w a violent situation or period of fighting between two countries（軍事）衝突；戰鬥：***armed/military conflict*** 武裝 / 軍事衝突 ➲ COLLOCATIONS at WAR **3** 0-w a situation in which there are opposing ideas, opinions, feelings or wishes; a situation in which it is difficult to choose 抵觸；矛盾；不一致：*The story tells of a classic conflict between love and duty.* 這故事講的是典型的愛情與責任之間的矛盾。◇ *Her diary was a record of her inner conflict.* 她的日記記錄了她內心的矛盾。◇ *Many of these ideas appear to be* ***in conflict with*** *each other.* 這些觀念中有許多看上去似乎相互矛盾。

IDM **conflict of ˈinterest(s)** a situation in which sb has two jobs, aims, roles, etc. and cannot treat both of them equally and fairly at the same time 利益（或利害）衝突：*There was a conflict of interest between his business dealings and his political activities.* 他的商業活動與政治活動之間出現利益衝突。

▪ *verb* 0-w /kənˈflɪkt/ [I] **~ (with sth)** if two ideas, beliefs, stories, etc. **conflict**, it is not possible for them to exist together or for them both to be true（兩種思想、信仰、說法等）衝突，抵觸 SYN **clash**：***conflicting emotions/interests/loyalties*** 相互矛盾的感情 / 利益 / 忠誠 ◇ *These results conflict with earlier findings.* 這些結果與早期的發現相矛盾。◇ *Reports conflicted on how much of the aid was reaching the famine victims.* 對於究竟有多少援助到了饑民手裏，這些報告的說法彼此矛盾。

con·flict·ed /kənˈflɪktɪd/ *adj.* (*especially NAmE*) confused about what to do or choose because you have strong but opposing feelings 因心理衝突而不知所措的

con·flu·ence /ˈkɒnfluəns; *NAmE* ˈkɑːn-/ *noun* [usually sing.] **1** (*technical* 術語) the place where two rivers flow together and become one （河流的）匯合處，匯流處，交匯處 **2** (*formal*) the fact of two or more things becoming one （事物的）匯合，匯聚，彙集：*a confluence of social factors* 多種社會因素的彙集

con·form AW /kənˈfɔːm; *NAmE* -ˈfɔːrm/ *verb* **1** [I] to behave and think in the same way as most other people in a group or society 順從，順應（大多數人或社會）；隨潮流：*There is considerable pressure on teenagers to conform.* 青少年承受着相當大的社會壓力。◇ **~ to sth** *He refused to conform to the local customs.* 他拒絕遵從當地的風俗習慣。 **2** [I] **~ to/with sth** to obey a rule, law, etc. 遵守，遵從，服從（規則、法律等）SYN **comply**：*The building does not conform with safety regulations.* 這座建築物不符合安全條例。 **3** [I] **~ to sth** to agree with or match sth 相一致；相符合；相吻合：*It did not conform to the usual stereotype of an industrial city.* 這和工業城市那種千篇一律的格局不一樣。

con·form·able AW /kənˈfɔːməbl; *NAmE* -ˈfɔːrm-/ *adj.* **~ to/with sth** (*formal*) similar in form or nature to sth; in agreement with sth （與…）相似的，相配的 SYN **consistent**：*What happens in cases where common law is not conformable to the constitution?* 普通法與憲法相抵牾時該怎麼辦？▸ **con·form·abil·ity** AW /kənˌfɔːməˈbɪləti; *NAmE* -ˈfɔːrm-/ *noun* [U]

con·form·ance AW /kənˈfɔːməns; *NAmE* -ˈfɔːrm-/ *noun* [U] **~ (to/with sth)** (*formal*) the fact of following the rules or standards of sth 遵從；恪守：*You need to ensure conformance to strict quality guidelines.* 你得保證遵守嚴格的質量基準。SYN **conformity**

con·form·ation AW /ˌkɒnfɔːˈmeɪʃn; *NAmE* ˌkɑːnfɔːrˈm-/ *noun* [U, C] (*formal*) the way in which sth is formed; the structure of sth, especially an animal 構造；結構；形態；（尤指動物的）身體構造

con·form·ist AW /kənˈfɔːmɪst; *NAmE* -ˈfɔːrm-/ *noun* (often *disapproving*) a person who behaves and thinks in the same way as most other people and who does not want to be different 順從者；隨波逐流者；循規蹈矩的人 ▸ **con·form·ist** *adj.* ➲ see also NONCONFORMIST

con·form·ity AW /kənˈfɔːməti; *NAmE* -ˈfɔːrm-/ *noun* [U] **~ (to/with sth)** (*formal*) behaviour or actions that follow the accepted rules of society （對社會規則的）遵從，遵守

IDM **in conˈformity with sth** following the rules of sth; conforming to sth 遵循（規則）；與…相符合（或一致）：*regulations that are in conformity with European law* 符合歐洲法律的條例

con·found /kənˈfaʊnd/ *verb* (*formal*) **1 ~ sb** to confuse and surprise sb 使困惑驚訝；使驚疑 SYN **baffle**：*The sudden rise in share prices has confounded economists.* 股價的突然上漲使經濟學家大惑不解。 **2 ~ sb/sth** to prove sb/sth wrong 證明…有錯：*to confound expectations* 證明期望有誤 ◇ *She confounded her critics and proved she could do the job.* 她駁倒了批評者的看法，證明自己能夠勝任那項工作。 **3 ~ sb** (*old-fashioned*) to defeat an enemy 擊敗，戰勝（敵人）

IDM **conˈfound it/you!** (*old-fashioned*) used to show that you are angry about sth/with sb （表示憤怒）真討厭，去你的

con·found·ed /kənˈfaʊndɪd/ *adj.* [only before noun] (*old-fashioned*) used when describing sth to show that you are annoyed （表示某事令人厭煩）討厭的，該死的

con·fra·ter·nity /ˌkɒnfrəˈtɜːnɪti; *NAmE* ˌkɑːn-/ *noun* (*pl.* **-ies**) (*formal*) a group of people who join together especially for a religious purpose or to help other people （尤指宗教、慈善事業的）團體，協會

con·front 0-w /kənˈfrʌnt/ *verb*

1 0-w **~ sb/sth** (of problems or a difficult situation 問題或困境) to appear and need to be dealt with by sb 使…無法迴避；降臨於：*the economic problems confronting the country* 這個國家所面臨的經濟問題 ◇ *The government found itself confronted by massive opposition.* 政府發現自己遭到了強烈的反對。 **2** 0-w **~ sth** to deal with a problem or difficult situation 處理，解決（問題或困境）SYN **face up to**：*She knew that she had to confront her fears.* 她心裏明白自己必須克服恐懼心理。 **3** 0-w **~ sb** to face sb so that they cannot avoid seeing and hearing you, especially in an unfriendly or dangerous situation 面對；對抗；與（某人）對峙：*This was the first time he had confronted an armed robber.* 這是他第一次面對一個持械劫匪。 **4** 0-w **~ sb with sb/sth** to make sb face or deal with an unpleasant or difficult person or situation 使面對，使面臨，使對付（令人不快或難處的人、場合）：*He confronted her with a choice between her career or their relationship.* 他要她在事業和他們兩人關係之間作出抉擇。 **5 be confronted with sth** to have sth in front of you that you have to deal with or react to 面對（某事物）：*Most people when confronted with a horse will pat it.* 大多數人遇見馬時都會輕輕地拍拍它。

con·fron·ta·tion /ˌkɒnfrʌnˈteɪʃn; *NAmE* ˌkɑːnfrən-/ *noun* [U, C] **~ (with sb)** | **~ (between A and B)** a situation in which there is an angry disagreement between people or groups who have different opinions 對抗；對峙；衝突：*She wanted to avoid another confrontation*

C

with her father. 她想避免和父親再次發生衝突。◇ *confrontation between employers and unions* 資方與工會之間的對峙

con·fron·ta·tion·al /ˌkɒnfrʌnˈteɪʃnl; NAmE ˌkɑːnfrən-/ *adj.* tending to deal with people in an aggressive way that is likely to cause arguments, rather than discussing things with them 對抗性的；挑起衝突的

Con·fu·cian /kənˈfjuːʃən/ *adj.* [usually before noun] based on or believing the teachings of the Chinese PHILOSOPHER Confucius 儒家的；儒學的；孔子學說的 ▸ **Con·fu·cian** *noun* **Con·fu·cian·ism** *noun* [U]

con·fus·able /kənˈfjuːzəbl/ *adj.* if two things are **confusable**, it is easy to confuse them 易混淆的：*'Historic' and 'historical' are easily confusable.* * historic 和 historical 容易攪混。◇ *The various types of owl are easily confusable with one another.* 各種貓頭鷹之間很容易弄混。 ▸ **con·fus·able** *noun* : *confusables such as 'principle' and 'principal'* * principle 和 principal 之類容易混淆的詞

con·fuse /kənˈfjuːz/ *verb*
1 ~ **sb** to make sb unable to think clearly or understand sth 使糊塗；使迷惑：*They confused me with conflicting accounts of what happened.* 他們對發生的事所作的陳述自相矛盾，使我迷惑不解。**2** ~ **A and/with B** to think wrongly that sb/sth is sb/sth else （將…）混淆，混同 SYN **mix up**：*People often confuse me and my twin sister.* 人們常常把我和我的孿生妹妹搞錯。◇ *Be careful not to confuse quantity with quality.* 注意不要把數量與質量混淆了。**3** ~ **sth** to make a subject more difficult to understand 使更難於理解：*His comments only served to confuse the issue further.* 他的評論只是把問題弄得更加複雜。

con·fused /kənˈfjuːzd/ *adj.*
1 unable to think clearly or to understand what is happening or what sb is saying 糊塗的；迷惑的：*People are confused about all the different labels on food these days.* 人們如今被那些五花八門的食物標籤搞得稀裏糊塗。◇ *He was depressed and in a confused state of mind.* 他感到沮喪，心裏充滿了迷惑。◇ *I'm confused—say all that again.* 我被搞糊塗了，把那件事從頭到尾再說一遍吧。**2** not clear or easy to understand 不清楚的；混亂的；難懂的：*The children gave a confused account of what had happened.* 孩子們把發生的事敍述得顛三倒四。▸ **con·fused·ly** /-ədli/ *adv.*

con·fus·ing /kənˈfjuːzɪŋ/ *adj.*
difficult to understand; not clear 難以理解的；不清楚的：*The instructions on the box are very confusing.* 盒子上的使用說明令人費解。◇ *a very confusing experience* 讓人莫名其妙的經歷 ▸ **con·fus·ing·ly** *adv.*

con·fu·sion /kənˈfjuːʒn/ *noun*
1 [U, C] ~ **(about/over sth)** | ~ **(as to sth)** a state of not being certain about what is happening, what you should do, what sth means, etc. 不確定；困惑：*There is some confusion about what the correct procedure should be.* 對於什麼是正確的處理程序還是有些不清楚。◇ *a confusion as to what to do next* 不清楚下一步該怎麼辦 **2** [U, C] ~ **(between A and B)** the fact of making a mistake about who sb is or what sth is 混淆；混同：*To avoid confusion, please write the children's names clearly on all their school clothes.* 為避免搞錯，請在孩子所有的校服上寫清楚他們各自的姓名。◇ *confusion between letters of the alphabet like 'o' or 'a'* 像 o 或 a 這類字母之間的易於混淆 **3** [U] a feeling of embarrassment when you do not understand sth and are not sure what to do in a situation 困窘；尷尬；局促不安：*He looked at me **in confusion** and did not answer the question.* 他困窘地看着我，沒有回答問題。**4** [U] a confused situation in which people do not know what action to take （讓人不知所措的）混亂局面，亂成一團：*Fighting had broken out and all was chaos and confusion.* 戰鬥爆發了，一切都陷入了混亂不堪的狀態。◇ *Her unexpected arrival threw us into total confusion.* 她的突然到來使得我們不知所措，亂成一團。

con·fute /kənˈfjuːt/ *verb* ~ **sb/sth** (*formal*) to prove a person or an argument to be wrong 駁倒；駁斥

conga /ˈkɒŋgə; NAmE ˈkɑːŋgə/ *noun* **1** a fast dance in which the dancers follow a leader in a long winding line, with each person holding on to the person in front; a piece of music for this dance 康茄舞；康茄舞樂曲 **2** (also **ˈconga drum**) a tall narrow drum that you play with your hands 康茄鼓（用手擊打的狹長鼓）➲ VISUAL VOCAB page V35

con·geal /kənˈdʒiːl/ *verb* [I] (of blood, fat, etc. 血液、脂肪等) to become thick or solid 變稠；凝結：*congealed blood* 凝固了的血 ◇ *The cold remains of supper had congealed on the plate.* 晚餐剩下的冷飯菜已經凝結在盤子上了。◇ (*figurative*) *The bitterness and tears had congealed into hatred.* 苦難與眼淚凝結成了仇恨。

con·gen·ial /kənˈdʒiːniəl/ *adj.* (*formal*) **1** (of a person 人) pleasant to spend time with because their interests and character are similar to your own 意氣相投的；志趣相投的；合得來的：*a congenial colleague* 意氣相投的同事 **2** ~ **(to sb)** (of a place, job, etc. 地方、工作等) pleasant because it suits your character 相宜的；合意的；適宜的：*a congenial working environment* 宜人的工作環境 **3** ~ **(to sth)** (*formal*) suitable for sth 適合的；適當的：*a situation that was congenial to the expression of nationalist opinions* 適於表達民族主義者意見的場合

con·geni·tal /kənˈdʒenɪtl/ *adj.* **1** (of a disease or medical condition 疾病或病理狀況) existing since or before birth 先天的；天生的：*congenital abnormalities* 先天畸形 **2** [only before noun] existing as part of a person's character and not likely to change 生性的；生就的：*a congenital inability to tell the truth* 生就的不會說實話 **3** [only before noun] (of a person 人) born with a particular illness 生來有病的：(*figurative*) *a congenital liar* (= one who will not change) 生性好說謊的人 ▸ **con·geni·tal·ly** /-təli/ *adv.*

con·ger /ˈkɒŋgə(r); NAmE ˈkɑːŋ-/ (also ˌ**conger ˈeel**) *noun* a large EEL (= a long thin fish) that lives in the sea 康吉鰻（海產鰻類）

con·gest·ed /kənˈdʒestɪd/ *adj.* **1** ~ **(with sth)** crowded; full of traffic 擁擠的；擠滿的；（交通）堵塞的：*congested city streets* 交通擁塞的城市街道 ◇ *Many of Europe's airports are heavily congested.* 歐洲許多機場都十分擁擠。**2** (*medical* 醫) (of a part of the body 身體部位) blocked with blood or MUCUS 充血的；黏液阻塞的

con·ges·tion /kənˈdʒestʃən/ *noun* [U] **1** the state of being crowded and full of traffic （交通）擁塞；塞車：*traffic congestion and pollution* 交通擁塞和污染 ➲ COLLOCATIONS at TOWN **2** (*medical* 醫) the state of part of the body being blocked with blood or MUCUS 充血；瘀血；黏液阻塞：*congestion of the lungs* 肺瘀血 ◇ *medicine to relieve nasal congestion* 治療鼻塞的藥

conˈgestion charge *noun* (*BrE*) an amount of money that people have to pay for driving their cars into the centre of some cities as a way of stopping the city centre from becoming too full of traffic 交通擁塞費，進城費（為緩解市中心塞車狀況而收取）▸ **conˈgestion charging** *noun* [U]

con·glom·er·ate /kənˈglɒmərət; NAmE -ˈglɑːm-/ *noun* **1** [C] (*business* 商) a large company formed by joining together different firms 聯合大公司；企業集團：*a media conglomerate* 大眾傳媒聯合體 **2** [sing.] (*formal*) a number of things or parts that are put together to form a whole 合成物；組合物；聚合物 **3** [U] (*geology* 地) a type of rock made of small stones held together by dried CLAY 礫岩

con·glom·er·ation /kənˌglɒməˈreɪʃn; NAmE -ˌglɑːm-/ *noun* **1** [C, usually sing.] **a** ~ **(of sth)** (*formal*) a mixture of different things that are found all together 混合物；聚集物：*a conglomeration of buildings of different sizes and styles* 大小和風格各異的建築樓群 **2** [U] the process of forming a conglomerate or the state of being a conglomerate 聚集過程；聚集狀態

con·grats /kənˈgræts/ *noun* [pl.] (*informal*) = CONGRATULATIONS

con·gratu·late /kənˈgrætʃuleɪt/ *verb*
1 ~ **sb (on sth)** to tell sb that you are pleased about their success or achievements 向（某人）道賀；祝賀：

I congratulated them all on their results. 我為他們取得的成就向他們所有人表示祝賀。◇ *The authors are to be congratulated on producing such a clear and authoritative work.* 向創作出這樣一部具有權威性又清晰易懂的作品的作者們祝賀。 **2 ~ yourself** (**on sth**) to feel pleased and proud because you have achieved sth or been successful at sth （為成就或成功）感到高興，感到自豪：*You can congratulate yourself on having done an excellent job.* 你應該為你出色的工作感到自豪。

con·gratu·la·tion 🔑 /kənˌɡrætʃuˈleɪʃn/ *noun* **1** 🔑 **congratulations** [pl.] a message congratulating sb (= saying that you are happy about their good luck or success) 祝賀；恭賀；賀辭：*to* ***offer/send*** *your* ***congratulations*** *to sb* 向某人致以祝賀 **2** 🔑 **Congratulations!** used when you want to congratulate sb （用以向人祝賀）祝賀，恭喜：*'We're getting married!' 'Congratulations!'* "我們要結婚了！" "恭喜恭喜！" ◇ *Congratulations on your exam results!* 祝賀你考出了好成績！ **3** 🔑 [U] the act of congratulating sb 祝賀：*a letter of congratulation* 賀信

con·gratu·la·tory /kənˌɡrætʃuˈleɪtəri; *NAmE* kənˈɡrætʃələtɔːri/ *adj.* expressing congratulations 祝賀的；恭賀的：*a congratulatory message* 賀辭

con·gre·gate /ˈkɒŋɡrɪɡeɪt; *NAmE* ˈkɑːŋ-/ *verb* [I] to come together in a group 群集；聚集；集合：*Young people often congregate in the main square in the evenings.* 年輕人傍晚時經常聚集在大廣場上。

con·gre·ga·tion /ˌkɒŋɡrɪˈɡeɪʃn; *NAmE* ˌkɑːŋ-/ *noun* [C+sing./pl. v.] **1** a group of people who are gathered together in a church to worship God, not including the priest and CHOIR （教堂的）會眾：*The congregation stood to sing the hymn.* 會眾站起來唱聖歌。➲ **COLLOCATIONS** at RELIGION **2** the group of people who belong to a particular church and go there regularly to worship （從屬某教堂並定期做禮拜的）教堂會眾 ▸ **con·gre·ga·tion·al** /-ʃənl/ *adj.*

Con·gre·ga·tion·al·ism /ˌkɒŋɡrɪˈɡeɪʃnəlɪzəm; *NAmE* ˌkɑːŋ-/ *noun* [U] a type of Christianity in which the congregation of each church is responsible for its own affairs 公理制，公理主義（主張各地方教會獨立行事） ▸ **Con·gre·ga·tion·al** *adj.* **Con·gre·ga·tion·al·ist** *noun*

con·gress 🔑 /ˈkɒŋɡres; *NAmE* ˈkɑːŋɡrəs/ *noun* **1** 🔑 [C] a large formal meeting or series of meetings where representatives from different groups discuss ideas, make decisions, etc. 代表大會：*an international congress of trades unions* 工會國際代表大會 **2** 🔑 [C+sing./pl. v.] **Congress** (in the US and some other countries 美國及一些其他國家) the name of the group of people who are elected to make laws, in the US consisting of the Senate and the HOUSE OF REPRESENTATIVES 國會；議會：*Congress will vote on the proposals tomorrow.* 國會明天將對提案進行投票表決。➲ **COLLOCATIONS** at POLITICS **3** [C+sing./pl. v.] used in the names of political parties in some countries （用於某些國家的政黨名稱）國民大會：*the African National Congress* 非洲國民大會

con·gres·sion·al /kənˈɡreʃənl/ *adj.* [only before noun] related to or belonging to a congress or the Congress in the US 代表大會的；（美國）國會的：*a* ***congressional committee/bill*** 代表委員會；國會議案 ◇ *the midterm Congressional elections* 國會的中期選舉

con·gress·man /ˈkɒŋɡresmən; *NAmE* ˈkɑːŋɡrəs-/, **con·gress·woman** /ˈkɒŋɡreswʊmən; *NAmE* ˈkɑːŋɡrəs-/ *noun* (often **Congressman, Congresswoman**) (*pl.* **-men** /-mən/, **-women** /-wɪmɪn/) (also **con·gress·person** /-pɜːsn; *NAmE* -pɜːrsn/) a member of Congress in the US, especially the House of Representatives （尤指美國眾議院的）國會議員；眾議員

con·gru·ent /ˈkɒŋɡruənt; *NAmE* ˈkɑːŋ-/ *adj.* **1** (*geometry* 幾何) having the same size and shape 全等的；疊合的：*congruent triangles* 全等三角形 **2 ~** (**with sth**) (*formal*) suitable for sth; appropriate in a particular situation 適合的；適當的；恰當的；相稱的 ▸ **con·gru·ence** /ˈkɒŋɡruəns; *NAmE* ˈkɑːŋ-/ *noun* [U]

conic /ˈkɒnɪk; *NAmE* ˈkɑːnɪk/ *adj., noun* (*geometry* 幾何)
■ ***adj.*** of or related to a CONE 圓錐（體）的
■ ***noun*** = CONIC SECTION

con·ic·al /ˈkɒnɪkl; *NAmE* ˈkɑːn-/ *adj.* shaped like a CONE 圓錐形的；圓錐的

ˌ**conic** ˈ**section** (also **conic**) *noun* (*geometry* 幾何) a shape formed when a flat surface meets a CONE with a round base 圓錐截線；二次曲線 ➲ **VISUAL VOCAB** page V71

con·ifer /ˈkɒnɪfə(r); ˈkəʊn-; *NAmE* ˈkɑːn-; ˈkoʊn-/ *noun* any tree that produces hard dry fruit called CONES. Most conifers are EVERGREEN (= have leaves that stay on the tree all year). 針葉樹 ➲ **VISUAL VOCAB** pages V4, V5 ▸ **con·ifer·ous** /kəˈnɪfərəs/ *adj.*：***coniferous trees/forests*** 針葉樹／林

con·jec·ture /kənˈdʒektʃə(r)/ *noun, verb*
■ ***noun*** (*formal*) **1** [C] an opinion or idea that is not based on definite knowledge and is formed by guessing 猜測；推測 **SYN** **guess**：*The truth of his conjecture was confirmed by the newspaper report.* 新聞報道證明了他的推測果然不假。 **2** [U] the forming of an opinion or idea that is not based on definite knowledge 揣測；臆測：*What was going through the killer's mind is a matter for conjecture.* 兇手作案時心裏是怎樣想的，這個問題只能由人們去推測了。➲ see also GUESSWORK ▸ **con·jec·tural** /kənˈdʒektʃərəl/ *adj.*
■ ***verb*** [I, T] (*formal*) to form an opinion about sth even though you do not have much information on it 猜測；推測 **SYN** **guess**：**~** (**about sth**) *We can only conjecture about what was in the killer's mind.* 我們只能猜測當時兇手心裏想的是什麼。◇ **~ what/how, etc.** … *We can only conjecture what was in the killer's mind.* 我們只能猜測當時兇手心裏想的是什麼。◇ **~ that** … *He conjectured that the population might double in ten years.* 他推測人口在十年後可能會增加一倍。◇ **~ sth** *She conjectured the existence of a completely new species.* 她推測有一個全新物種存在。◇ **~ sth to do sth** *The remains are conjectured to be thousands of years old.* 據推測，這些古跡有幾千年的歷史。

con·join /kənˈdʒɔɪn/ *verb* [I, T] **~** (**sth**) (*formal*) to join together; to join two or more things together 結合；連接；把…結成一體

conˌjoined ˈ**twin** *noun* (*technical* 術語) (also ˌ**Siamese** ˈ**twin**) one of two people who are born with their bodies joined together in some way, sometimes sharing the same organs 聯體雙胎

con·joint /kənˈdʒɔɪnt/ *adj.* [usually before noun] (*formal*) combining all or both the people or things involved 聯合的；共同的；協同的 ▸ **con·joint·ly** *adv.*

con·ju·gal /ˈkɒndʒəɡl; *NAmE* ˈkɑːn-/ *adj.* [only before noun] (*formal*) connected with marriage and the sexual relationship between a husband and wife 婚姻的；夫妻間的：*conjugal love* 夫妻間的恩愛

ˌ**conjugal** ˈ**rights** *noun* [pl.] the rights that a husband and wife each has in a marriage, especially the right to have sex with their partner 夫妻婚姻權；（尤指）夫妻同居權

con·ju·gate /ˈkɒndʒəɡeɪt; *NAmE* ˈkɑːn-/ *verb* (*grammar* 語法) **1** [T] **~ sth** to give the different forms of a verb, as they vary according to NUMBER, PERSON, tense, etc. （根據數、人稱、時態等）列舉動詞的變化形式 **2** [I] (of a verb 動詞) to have different forms, showing NUMBER, PERSON, tense, etc. （表示數、人稱、時態等）有詞形變化形式：*How does this verb conjugate?* 這個動詞有哪些詞形變化？➲ compare DECLINE *v.* (3)

con·ju·ga·tion /ˌkɒndʒuˈɡeɪʃn; *NAmE* ˌkɑːndʒə-/ *noun* (*grammar* 語法) **1** [C, U] the way in which a verb conjugates 動詞的變化形式：*a verb with an irregular conjugation* 不規則動詞 **2** [C] a group of verbs that conjugate in the same way 詞形變化相同的一類動詞：*Latin verbs of the second conjugation* 屬於第二種詞形變化的拉丁語動詞

con·junc·tion /kənˈdʒʌŋkʃn/ *noun* **1** [C] (*grammar* 語法) a word that joins words, phrases or sentences, for example 'and', 'but', 'or' 連詞，連接詞（如 and、but、or） **2** [C] (*formal*) a combination of events, etc., that causes a particular result （引起某種結果的事物等的）

結合，同時發生：*The conjunction of low inflation and low unemployment came as a very pleasant surprise.* 低通貨膨脹與低失業的同時出現是一大驚喜。**3** [C, U] (*astronomy* 天) the fact of stars, planets, etc. passing close together as seen from the earth（恒星、行星等的）合

C

IDM **in con'junction with** (*formal*) together with 與…一起：*The police are working in conjunction with tax officers on the investigation.* 警方正和稅務官員協同進行調查。◇ *The system is designed to be used in conjunction with a word processing program.* 本系統是為與文字處理程序配合使用而設計的。

con·junc·tiv·itis /kənˌdʒʌŋktɪ'vaɪtɪs/ *noun* [U] an infectious eye disease that causes pain and swelling in part of the eye 結膜炎

con·jure /'kʌndʒə(r)/ *verb* [I, T] to do clever tricks such as making things seem to appear or disappear as if by magic 變魔術；變戲法；使…變戲法般地出現（或消失）：*Her grandfather taught her to conjure.* 她的祖父教她變魔術。◇ **~ sth + adv./prep.** *He could conjure coins from behind people's ears.* 他可以從人們的耳朵後面變出硬幣來。**IDM** see NAME *n.*

PHR V **ˌconjure sth↔'up** **1** to make sth appear as a picture in your mind 使…呈現於腦際；使想起 **SYN** **evoke**：*That smell always conjures up memories of holidays in France.* 那種氣味總是令人勾起在法國度假那段日子的回憶。**2** to make sb/sth appear by using special magic words 用咒語使…出現 **conjure sth from/out of sth** to create sth or make sth appear in a surprising or unexpected way 令人驚訝地創造出；使意外地出現：*He conjured a delicious meal out of a few leftovers.* 他居然用幾樣吃剩的東西做出了可口的一餐。

con·jur·ing /'kʌndʒərɪŋ/ *noun* [U] entertainment in the form of magic tricks, especially ones which seem to make things appear or disappear 變魔術；變戲法：*a conjuring trick* 魔術

con·juror (also **con·jurer**) /'kʌndʒərə(r)/ *noun* a person who performs conjuring tricks 魔術師；變戲法的人

conk /kɒŋk; *NAmE* kɑːŋk; kɔːŋk/ *verb, noun*

■ *verb* **~ sb** (*informal, especially NAmE*) to hit sb hard on their head 重擊（某人的）頭部

PHR V **ˌconk 'out** (*informal*) **1** (of a machine, etc. 機器等) to stop working 停止運轉；失靈：*The car conked out halfway up the hill.* 汽車在上坡時半途拋錨了。**2** (of a person 人) to go to sleep 入睡；睡着

■ *noun* (*BrE, informal*) a person's nose 人的鼻子

conk·er /'kɒŋkə(r); *NAmE* 'kɑːŋ-/ *noun* (*informal, especially BrE*) **1** [C] the smooth shiny brown nut of the HORSE CHESTNUT tree 七葉樹果 ➲ **VISUAL VOCAB** page V10 ➲ compare CHESTNUT *n.* (2), HORSE CHESTNUT (2) **2 conkers** [U] a children's game played with conkers on strings, in which two players take turns to try to hit and break each other's conker 康克戲（兒童遊戲，雙方用繫在繩上的七葉果輪流互擊，以擊破對方的七葉果）

'con man *noun* (*informal*) a man who tricks others into giving him money, etc. 騙子；欺詐者

con·nect 🔑 /kə'nekt/ *verb*

▸ **JOIN** 連接 **1** 🔑 [T, I] **~ (A to/with/and B)** to join together two or more things; to be joined together（使）連接；聯結：*The towns are connected by train and bus services.* 這些城鎮由火車和公共汽車連接起來。◇ *The canal was built to connect Sheffield with the Humber estuary.* 修建這條運河是為了將設菲爾德和亨伯河河口連接起來。◇ *a connecting door* (= one that connects two rooms) 連通兩間房的門 ◇ *The rooms on this floor connect.* 這層樓的房間是相通的。

▸ **ELECTRICITY/GAS/WATER** 電；煤氣；水 **2** 🔑 [T] **~ sth (to sth)** to join sth to the main supply of electricity, gas, water, etc. or to another piece of equipment 使…連接；接通：*First connect the printer to the computer.* 首先把打印機與計算機接通。◇ *We're waiting for the telephone to be connected.* 我們等待着接通電話。**OPP** **disconnect**

▸ **INTERNET** 互聯網 **3** 🔑 [I, T] **~ (sb) (to sth)** to join a computer to the Internet or a computer network 使（計算機）連接（到互聯網或計算機網絡）：*Click 'Continue' to connect to the Internet.* 點擊 Continue 連接到互聯網。**OPP** **disconnect**

▸ **LINK** 聯繫 **4** 🔑 [T] **~ sb/sth (with sb/sth)** to notice or make a link between people, things, events, etc. 注意到…有關聯；把…聯繫起來 **SYN** **associate**：*There was nothing to connect him with the crime.* 他與那起犯罪毫無關聯。◇ *I was surprised to hear them mentioned together: I had never connected them before.* 聽到有人把他們牽扯在一起讓我很吃驚；我以前從未把他們聯繫起來想過。

▸ **OF TRAIN/BUS/PLANE** 火車；公共汽車；飛機 **5** [I] **~ (with sth)** to arrive just before another one leaves so that passengers can change from one to the other 銜接；聯運：*His flight to Amsterdam connects with an afternoon flight to New York.* 他飛往阿姆斯特丹的班機與下午飛往紐約的一趟航班銜接。◇ *There's a connecting flight at noon.* 中午有一趟相銜接的航班。

▸ **TELEPHONE LINES** 電話線 **6** [T] **~ sb** to join telephone lines so that people can speak to each other 為（某人）接通電話；連接 **SYN** **put through**：*Hold on please, I'm trying to connect you.* 請別掛電話，我在試着給您接通。**OPP** **disconnect**

▸ **FORM RELATIONSHIP** 建立關係 **7** [I] **~ (with sb)** (*especially NAmE*) to form a good relationship with sb so that you like and understand each other（與某人）建立良好關係，溝通：*They met a couple of times but they didn't really connect.* 儘管他們見了幾次面，但仍未真正建立起良好的關係。

▸ **HIT** 擊 **8** [I] (*especially NAmE*) **~ (with sb/sth)** (*informal*) to hit sb/sth 打（某人）；擊中（某物）：*The blow connected and she felt a surge of pain.* 她遭到沉重的一擊，感到一陣疼痛。

PHR V **conˌnect sth↔'up (to sth)** | **conˌnect 'up (to sth)** to join sth to a supply of electricity, gas, etc. or to another piece of equipment; to be joined in this way 將…（與電源、煤氣、設備等）連接起來，接通：*She connected up the two computers.* 她把兩台計算機連接起來。**OPP** **disconnect**

con·nect·ed 🔑 /kə'nektɪd/ *adj.*

~ (with sb/sth) (of two or more things or people 兩個或以上的事物或人) having a link between them 有聯繫的；相關的：*market prices and other connected matters* 市場價格及其他相關事宜 ◇ *They are connected by marriage.* 他們是姻親。◇ *jobs connected with the environment* 與環境有關的工作 ◇ *The two issues are* ***closely connected***. 這兩個問題緊密相關。**OPP** **unconnected** ➲ see also WELL CONNECTED

con·nect·ed·ness /kə'nektɪdnəs/ *noun* [U] **~ (to/with sb/sth)** a feeling that you have a link with sb/sth or are part of a group 相關感；歸屬感：*the benefits of helping students feel a sense of connectedness to their school* 幫助學生感到自己是學校一分子的益處

con·nec·tion 🔑 (*BrE* also *old-fashioned* **con·nex·ion**) /kə'nekʃn/ *noun*

▸ **LINK** 聯繫 **1** 🔑 [C] something that connects two facts, ideas, etc.（兩種事實、想法等的）聯繫，關聯 **SYN** **link**：**~ (between A and B)** *Scientists have established a connection between cholesterol levels and heart disease.* 科學家已證實膽固醇含量與心臟病之間有關聯。◇ **~ (with sth)** *a* ***direct/close/strong connection*** *with sth* 與某事有直接的／密切的／牢固的聯繫 ◇ *How did you* ***make the connection*** (= realize that there was a connection between two facts that did not seem to be related)? 你怎麼看出來有這種關係的？

▸ **BEING CONNECTED** 連接 **2** 🔑 [U, C] **~ (to sth)** the act of connecting or the state of being connected 聯結；接通；連接：*Connection to the gas supply was delayed for three days.* 接通煤氣延遲了三天。◇ *I'm having problems with my Internet connection.* 我的互聯網連接有問題。

▸ **IN ELECTRICAL SYSTEM** 電力系統 **3** 🔑 [C] a point, especially in an electrical system, where two parts connect 連接點；（尤指電力系統的）接頭：*A faulty connection caused the machine to stop.* 線路接錯導致機器停止運轉。

▸ **TRAIN/BUS/PLANE** 火車；公共汽車；飛機 **4** 🔑 [C] a train, bus or plane at a station or an airport that a passenger can take soon after getting off another in order to continue their journey 轉車；轉機；聯運：*We arrived in good time for the connection to Paris.* 我們到達時有充分的時間接上去巴黎的聯運。**5** [C, usually pl.] a means of travelling to another place 旅行交通工具：*There are good bus and train connections between the resort and major cities.* 在度假勝地與主要城市之間有着便利的公車和火車運輸。 ▸ PERSON/ORGANIZATION 人；機構 **6** [C, usually pl.] a person or an organization that you know and that can help or advise you in your social or professional life 有社交或業務關係的人（或機構） SYN **contact**：*One of my business connections gave them my name.* 我生意上的一個關係戶向他們提供了我的名字。 ▸ DISTANT RELATIVES 遠親 **7 connections** [pl.] people who are your relatives, but not members of your close family 親戚；旁系親屬：*She is British but also has German connections.* 她是英國人，但也有德國親戚。

IDM **in connection with sb/sth** for reasons connected with sb/sth 與…有關（或相關）：*A man has been arrested in connection with the murder of the teenager.* 一名男子因與該謀殺少年案有關而被捕。◇ *I am writing to you in connection with your recent job application.* 我寫此信與你最近求職一事有關。 **in this/that connection** (*formal*) for reasons connected with sth recently mentioned 由於這（或那）事；為此

con·nect·ive /kəˈnektɪv/ *adj.*, *noun*

■ ***adj.*** (*medical* 醫) that connects things 連接的；聯結的：*connective tissue* 結締組織

■ ***noun*** (*grammar* 語法) a word that connects two parts of a sentence 連接詞；關聯詞：*Don't overuse a causal connective like 'because'.* 不要過多地使用像 because 這樣表示原因的連接詞。

con·nec·tiv·ity /ˌkɒnekˈtɪvɪti; *NAmE* ˌkɑːn-/ *noun* [U] (*technical* 術語) the state of being connected or the degree to which two things are connected 連接（度）；連結（度）：*ISDN connectivity allows computers to communicate over a network.* 綜合業務數字網連接實現了計算機網絡通訊。

con·nec·tor /kəˈnektə(r)/ *noun* a thing that links two or more things together 連接物；連接器；連線：*a cable connector* 電纜連接器

con·ning tower /ˈkɒnɪŋ taʊə(r); *NAmE* ˈkɑːnɪŋ/ *noun* a raised structure on a SUBMARINE containing the PERISCOPE（潛水艇的）指揮塔

con·nip·tion /kəˈnɪpʃn/ (also **conˈniption fit**) *noun* (*old-fashioned, NAmE*) a sudden attack of anger or fear 激怒；一陣驚恐：*He had a conniption when he heard the news.* 他聽到消息後大發雷霆。

con·niv·ance /kəˈnaɪvəns/ *noun* [U] (*disapproving*) help in doing sth wrong; the failure to stop sth wrong from happening 共謀；縱容；默許：*The crime was committed with the connivance of a police officer.* 這項罪行是在警察的縱容下發生的。

con·nive /kəˈnaɪv/ *verb* (*formal, disapproving*) **1** [I] **~ at/in sth** to seem to allow sth wrong to happen 縱容；默許；放任：*She knew that if she said nothing she would be conniving in an injustice.* 她知道她如果什麼也不說就是在縱容不公正的行為。 **2** [I] **~ (with sb) (to do sth)** to work together with sb to do sth wrong or illegal 共謀；狼狽為奸；同流合污 SYN **conspire**：*The government was accused of having connived with the security forces to permit murder.* 政府被指控與安全部隊狼狽為奸允許謀殺。

con·niv·ing /kəˈnaɪvɪŋ/ *adj.* (*disapproving*) behaving in a way that secretly hurts others or deliberately fails to prevent others from being hurt 暗算他人的；故意縱容的

con·nois·seur /ˌkɒnəˈsɜː(r); *NAmE* ˌkɑːnəˈsɜːr; -ˈsʊr/ *noun* an expert on matters involving the judgement of beauty, quality or skill in art, food or music 鑒賞家；鑒定家；行家：*a connoisseur of Italian painting* 意大利繪畫鑒賞家 ◇ *a wine connoisseur* 葡萄酒鑒定家

con·no·ta·tion /ˌkɒnəˈteɪʃn; *NAmE* ˌkɑːn-/ *noun* an idea suggested by a word in addition to its main meaning 含義；隱含意義：*The word 'professional' has connotations of skill and excellence.* * professional 這個詞隱含着技藝和專長的意思。◇ *negative connotations* 貶義 ➲ compare DENOTATION

con·note /kəˈnəʊt; *NAmE* kəˈnoʊt/ *verb* **~ sth** (*formal*) (of a word 詞) to suggest a feeling, an idea, etc. as well as the main meaning 意味着；暗示；隱含 ➲ compare DENOTE

con·nub·ial /kəˈnjuːbiəl; *NAmE* -ˈnuː-/ *adj.* (*literary*) related to marriage, or the relationship between husband and wife 婚姻的；夫妻（關係）的

C

con·quer /ˈkɒŋkə(r); *NAmE* ˈkɑːŋ-/ *verb* **1 ~ sb/sth** to take control of a country or city and its people by force 佔領；攻克；征服：*The Normans conquered England in 1066.* 諾曼人於 1066 年征服了英格蘭。◇ ***conquered peoples/races/territories*** 被征服的民族 / 種族；被佔領的領土 **2 ~ sb** to defeat sb, especially in a competition, race, etc.（尤指比賽、賽跑等中）擊敗，戰勝：*The world champion conquered yet another challenger last night.* 昨晚這位世界冠軍又戰勝了一名挑戰者。 **3 ~ sth** to succeed in dealing with or controlling sth（成功地）對付，克服，控制：*The only way to conquer a fear is to face it.* 克服恐懼的唯一方法是正視恐懼。◇ *Mount Everest was conquered* (= successfully climbed) *in 1953.* 珠穆朗瑪峰於 1953 年被征服。 **4 ~ sth** to become very popular or successful in a place 在（某地）很受歡迎；在（某地）成功：*The band is now setting out to conquer the world.* 這支樂隊現在要出發去征服世界。

con·queror /ˈkɒŋkərə(r); *NAmE* ˈkɑːŋ-/ *noun* a person who conquers 征服者；佔領者；勝利者：*William the Conqueror* (= King William I of England) 征服者威廉（英國國王威廉一世）

con·quest /ˈkɒŋkwest; *NAmE* ˈkɑːŋ-/ *noun* **1** [sing., U] the act of taking control of a country, city, etc. by force 征服；佔領：*the Norman Conquest* (= of England in 1066) 諾曼征服（即 1066 年諾曼人征服英格蘭） **2** [C] an area of land taken by force 佔領（或征服）的地區：*the Spanish conquests in South America* 西班牙人在南美洲的佔領地 **3** [C] (usually *humorous*) a person that sb has persuaded to love them or to have sex with them（愛情或性方面）被俘虜的人：*I'm just one of his many conquests.* 我僅僅是他的眾多俘虜之一。 **4** [U] the act of gaining control over sth that is difficult or dangerous（對困難、危險等的）控制：*the conquest of inflation* 對通貨膨脹的控制

con·quis·ta·dor /kɒnˈkwɪstədɔː(r); -ˈkɪst-; *NAmE* kɑːn-/ *noun* (*pl.* **con·quis·ta·dores** /kɒnˌkwɪstəˈdɔːreɪz; -ˌkɪstə-; *NAmE* kɑːn-/ or **con·quis·ta·dors**) (from *Spanish*) one of the Spanish people who took control of Mexico and Peru by force in the 16th century（16 世紀侵佔墨西哥和秘魯的）西班牙征服者

con·san·guin·ity /ˌkɒnsæŋˈgwɪnəti; *NAmE* ˌkɑːn-/ *noun* [U] (*formal*) relationship by birth in the same family 同宗；血緣；血親關係

con·science /ˈkɒnʃəns; *NAmE* ˈkɑːn-/ *noun* **1** [C, U] the part of your mind that tells you whether your actions are right or wrong 良心；良知：*to have a* ***clear/guilty conscience*** (= to feel that you have done right/wrong) 問心無愧 / 有愧 ◇ *This is a* ***matter of*** *individual* ***conscience*** (= everyone must make their own judgement about it). 這關係到個人的良知。◇ *He won't let it trouble his conscience.* 他不會讓這件事搞得自己良心不安的。 ➲ see also SOCIAL CONSCIENCE **2** [U, C] a guilty feeling about sth you have done or failed to do 內疚；愧疚：*She was seized by a sudden pang of conscience.* 她突然感到一陣內疚。◇ *I have a terrible conscience about it.* 我對此事深感愧疚。 **3** [U] the fact of behaving in a way that you feel is right even though this may cause problems 憑良心：*freedom of conscience* (= the freedom to do what you believe to be right) 憑良心行事的自由 ◇ *Emilia is the voice of conscience in the play.* 伊米莉亞在這齣戲劇中代表良知的一面。 ➲ see also PRISONER OF CONSCIENCE

IDM **in (all/good) conscience** (*formal*) believing your actions to be fair（認為行為）公正地，公平地，憑良心 SYN **honestly**：*We cannot in all conscience refuse to help.* 憑良心我們不能拒絕去幫助別人。 **on your ˈconscience** making you feel guilty for doing or failing to do sth 使人內疚；良心不安：*I'll write and apologize. I've had it on my conscience for weeks.* 我要寫信賠禮道歉。幾個星期以來我都為此而良心不安。 ➲ more at PRICK *v.*

C

ˌconscience-stricken *adj.* feeling guilty about sth you have done or failed to do 内疚的；不安的；受良心責備的

con·scien·tious /ˌkɒnʃiˈenʃəs; *NAmE* ˌkɑːn-/ *adj.* taking care to do things carefully and correctly 勤勉認真的；一絲不苟的：*a conscientious student/teacher/worker* 勤勉認真的學生；一絲不苟的老師；認真負責的工人 ▶ **con·scien·tious·ly** *adv.*：*She performed all her duties conscientiously.* 她認真負責地履行自己的所有職責。**con·scien·tious·ness** *noun* [U]

ˌconscientious obˈjector *noun* a person who refuses to serve in the armed forces for moral reasons 出於道義原因而拒服兵役者 ➲ compare DRAFT DODGER, PACIFIST

con·scien·tize (*BrE* also **-ise**) /ˈkɒnʃəntaɪz; *NAmE* ˈkɑːn-/ *verb* **~ sb/yourself** (*SAfrE*) to make sb/yourself aware of important social or political issues 使意識到（重大社會或政治問題）；使覺悟：*People need to be conscientized about their rights.* 需要讓人們明白自己的權利。

con·scious 🔑 /ˈkɒnʃəs; *NAmE* ˈkɑːn-/ *adj.*
1 🔑 [not before noun] aware of sth; noticing sth 意識到；注意到：**~ of sth** *She's very conscious of the problems involved.* 她完全意識到了所涉及的問題。◇ **~ of doing sth** *He became acutely conscious of having failed his parents.* 他深深感到自己辜負了父母的期望。◇ **~ that ...** *I was vaguely conscious that I was being watched.* 我隱隱約約地覺察到有人在監視我。**OPP** **unconscious** ➲ see also SELF-CONSCIOUS **2** 🔑 able to use your senses and mental powers to understand what is happening 神志清醒的；有知覺的；有意識的：*A patient who is not fully conscious should never be left alone.* 神志並非完全清醒的病人必須時刻有人照料。**OPP** **unconscious** **3** 🔑 (of actions, feelings, etc. 行為、感情等) deliberate or controlled 慎重的；有意的；刻意的：*to make a **conscious decision*** 作出慎重的決定 ◇ *I made a **conscious effort** to get there on time.* 我刻意約束自己準時到達那裏。◇ *a conscious act of cruelty* 蓄意的殘暴行徑 **OPP** **unconscious** ➲ compare SUBCONSCIOUS **4** 🔑 being particularly interested in sth 特別感興趣的；關注的：*environmentally conscious* 有環保意識的 ◇ *They have become increasingly health-conscious.* 他們的健康意識越來越強。▶ **con·scious·ly** *adv.*：*Consciously or unconsciously, you made a choice.* 不管是有意還是無意，你已作出了選擇。

con·scious·ness /ˈkɒnʃəsnəs; *NAmE* ˈkɑːn-/ *noun* [U]
1 the state of being able to use your senses and mental powers to understand what is happening 清醒狀態；知覺：*I can't remember any more—I must have **lost consciousness**.* 我什麼都想不起來了 —— 我當時一定是失去了知覺。◇ *She did not **regain consciousness** and died the next day.* 她再也沒有蘇醒過來，第二天便去世了。**2** the state of being aware of sth 覺察；感覺；意識 **SYN** **awareness**：*his consciousness of the challenge facing him* 他對所面臨的挑戰的清醒意識 ◇ ***class-consciousness*** (= consciousness of different classes in society) 階級意識 **3** the ideas and opinions of a person or group 觀念；看法：*her newly-developed political consciousness* 她最近形成的政治觀念 ➲ see also STREAM OF CONSCIOUSNESS

ˈconsciousness-raising *noun* [U] the process of making people aware of important social and political issues（對重大社會或政治問題的）覺悟提高，意識加強

con·script *verb, noun*
■ *verb* /kənˈskrɪpt/ (*especially BrE*) (*NAmE* usually **draft**) [usually passive] **~ sb (into sth)** to make sb join the armed forces 徵募；徵召 **SYN** **call up**：*He was conscripted into the army in 1939.* 他於 1939 年應徵入伍。
■ *noun* /ˈkɒnskrɪpt; *NAmE* ˈkɑːn-/ (*especially BrE*) (*US* usually **draft·ee**) a person who has been conscripted to join the armed forces 應徵入伍者：*young army conscripts* 年輕的應徵士兵 ◇ *conscript soldiers/armies* 應徵入伍的士兵；由應徵入伍者組成的部隊 ➲ compare VOLUNTEER

con·scrip·tion /kənˈskrɪpʃn/ *noun* [U] (*especially BrE*) (*US* usually **the draft**) the practice of ordering people by law to serve in the armed forces 徵募；徵兵 **SYN** **call-up**

con·se·crate /ˈkɒnsɪkreɪt; *NAmE* ˈkɑːn-/ *verb* **1 ~ sth** to state officially in a religious ceremony that sth is holy and can be used for religious purposes 祝聖；聖化；奉獻：*The church was consecrated in 1853.* 這座教堂於 1853 年祝聖。◇ *consecrated ground* 經祝聖的地方 **2 ~ sth** (in Christian belief 基督教信仰) to make bread and wine into the body and blood of Christ 祝聖餅酒；成聖體 **3 ~ sb (as) (sth)** to state officially in a religious ceremony that sb is now a priest, etc. 祝聖神職人員：*He was consecrated (as) bishop last year.* 他於去年被祝聖為主教。**4 ~ sth/sb/yourself to sth** (*formal*) to give sth/sb/yourself to a special purpose, especially a religious one（尤指為宗教而）奉獻，獻身 ▶ **con·se·cra·tion** /ˌkɒnsɪˈkreɪʃn; *NAmE* ˌkɑːn-/ *noun* [C, U]：*the consecration of a church/bishop* 教堂 / 主教祝聖禮

con·secu·tive /kənˈsekjətɪv/ *adj.* [usually before noun] following one after another in a series, without interruption 連續不斷的：*She was absent for nine consecutive days.* 她一連缺席了九天。◇ *He is beginning his fourth consecutive term of office.* 他將要開始第四屆任期。▶ **con·secu·tive·ly** *adv.*

con·sen·su·al /kənˈsenʃuəl/ *adj.* (*formal*) **1** which people in general agree with 一致同意的：*a consensual approach* 一致贊成的方法 **2** (of an activity 活動) which the people taking part have agreed to（參與者）同意的，贊同的：*consensual sex* 兩廂情願的性行為

con·sen·sus **AW** /kənˈsensəs/ *noun* [sing., U] an opinion that all members of a group agree with 一致的意見；共識：**~ (about/on sth)** *She is skilled at achieving consensus on sensitive issues.* 她擅長就敏感問題進行斡旋，從而達成共識。◇ *There is a growing **consensus of opinion** on this issue.* 對這個問題的看法日趨一致。◇ *an attempt to **reach a consensus*** 達成共識的嘗試 ◇ **~ (among sb) (about/on sth)** *There is a general consensus among teachers about the need for greater security in schools.* 教師們對必須加強學校的保安有普遍的共識。◇ **~ (that ...)** *There seems to be a consensus that the plan should be rejected.* 看來人們一致同意放棄這一計劃。

con·sent **AW** /kənˈsent/ *noun, verb*
■ *noun* **1** [U] **~ (to sth)** permission to do sth, especially given by sb in authority 同意；准許；允許：*Children under 16 cannot **give consent** to medical treatment.* * 16 歲以下的兒童不得自行同意接受治療。◇ *The written consent of a parent is required.* 要求有家長的書面同意。◇ *to **refuse/withhold** your **consent*** 拒不同意 ◇ *He is charged with taking a car **without** the owner's **consent**.* 他因未徵得車主的同意自行開走車而受到指控。➲ see also AGE OF CONSENT **2** [U] agreement about sth 同意；贊同：*She was chosen as leader **by common consent*** (= everyone agreed to the choice). 大家一致同意選她為領導人。◇ ***By mutual consent** they didn't go out* (= they both agreed not to). 按照雙方同意，他們沒有約會。**3** [C] an official document giving permission for sth 正式批准文件；批文
■ *verb* [I] (rather *formal*) to agree to sth or give your permission for sth 同意；准許；允許：*When she told them what she intended they readily consented.* 她告訴他們她的打算時，他們欣然同意。◇ **~ to sth** *He reluctantly consented to his daughter's marriage.* 他勉強同意了女兒的婚事。◇ **~ to do sth** *She finally consented to answer our questions.* 她最終同意回答我們的問題。➲ SYNONYMS at AGREE

conˌsenting ˈadult *noun* a person who is considered old enough, by law, to decide whether they should agree to have sex; a person who has agreed to have sex 到達法定性成熟年齡的已成年人；同意發生性行為的已成年人

con·se·quence 🔑 **AW** /ˈkɒnsɪkwəns; *NAmE* ˈkɑːnsəkwens/ *noun*
1 🔑 [C] **~ (of sth) (for sb/sth)** a result of sth that has happened 結果；後果：*This decision could have **serious consequences** for the industry.* 這項決定可能對該行業造成嚴重後果。◇ *Two hundred people lost their jobs **as a direct consequence** of the merger.* 合併一事直接導致二百人失去了工作。◇ *He drove too fast with tragic consequences.* 他開車太快，結果釀成慘劇。◇ *to **suffer/face/***

take the consequences of your actions 自食其果；面對／承擔自己行動的後果 ➲ SYNONYMS at RESULT ➲ LANGUAGE BANK at CONSEQUENTLY **2** [U] (*formal*) importance 重要性：*Don't worry. It's **of no consequence**.* 別擔心，這無關緊要。

IDM **in consequence (of sth)** (*formal*) as a result of sth 由於；作為…的結果：*The child was born deformed in consequence of an injury to its mother.* 由於母親受過傷，這小孩生下來是畸形。

con·se·quent **AW** /ˈkɒnsɪkwənt; *NAmE* ˈkɑːnsəkwənt/ *adj.* (*formal*) happening as a result of sth 隨之發生的；作為結果的 **SYN** **resultant**：*the lowering of taxes and the consequent increase in spending* 稅收降低與隨之引起的消費增長 ◇ **~ on/upon sth** *the responsibilities consequent upon the arrival of a new child* 新生兒出世後隨之而來的職責

con·se·quen·tial /ˌkɒnsɪˈkwenʃl; *NAmE* ˌkɑːnsəˈk-/ *adj.* (*formal*) **1** happening as a result or an effect of sth 隨之而來的；相應發生的；作為結果的 **SYN** **resultant**：*retirement and the consequential reduction in income* 退休與隨之而來的收入減少 **2** important; that will have important results 重要的；將產生重大結果的：*The report discusses a number of consequential matters that are yet to be decided.* 這份報告討論了許多有待決定的重大問題。**OPP** **inconsequential** ▸ **con·se·quen·tial·ly** /-ʃəli/ *adv.*

con·se·quent·ly **AW** /ˈkɒnsɪkwəntli; *NAmE* ˈkɑːnsəkwentli/ *adv.* as a result; therefore 因此；所以：*This poses a threat to agriculture and the food chain, and consequently to human health.* 這會對農業和食物鏈造成威脅，由此而危及人的健康。

Language Bank 用語庫

consequently

Describing the effect of something 描述某事的影響

- **One consequence of** changes in diet over recent years has been a dramatic increase in cases of childhood obesity. 近年來飲食變化帶來的一個結果是兒童肥胖人數急劇上升。
- Many parents today do not have time to cook healthy meals for their children. **Consequently/As a consequence**, many children grow up eating too much junk food. 現在許多家長沒有時間給孩子做健康的飯菜，結果造成許多孩子在成長過程中吃過多的垃圾食品。
- Many children spend their free time watching TV instead of playing outside. **As a result**, more and more of them are becoming overweight. 許多孩子把他們的閒暇時間都花在看電視上，而不是進行戶外活動，從而導致越來越多的孩子變得肥胖。
- Last year junk food was banned in schools. **The effect of this** has been to create a black market in the playground, with pupils bringing sweets from home to sell to other pupils. 去年學校禁售垃圾食品，結果是學校操場上出現了垃圾食品的黑市交易，有的學生把從家裏帶來的甜食賣給其他學生。

➲ Language Banks at BECAUSE OF, CAUSE, THEREFORE

con·ser·vancy /kənˈsɜːvənsi; *NAmE* -ˈsɜːrv-/ *noun* **1** **Conservancy** [sing.+sing./pl. v.] a group of officials who control the use of a port, a river, an area of land, etc. （港口、河流、地區等的）管理機構：*the Thames Conservancy* 泰晤士河管理委員會 ◇ *Texas Nature Conservancy* 得克薩斯州自然資源管理委員會 **2** [U] (*formal*) the protection of the natural environment（對自然環境的）保護 **SYN** **conservation**：*nature conservancy* 自然環境的保護

con·ser·va·tion /ˌkɒnsəˈveɪʃn; *NAmE* ˌkɑːnsərˈv-/ *noun* [U] **1** the protection of the natural environment（對自然環境的）保護 **SYN** **conservancy**：*to be interested in wildlife conservation* 對野生動物保護感興趣 ➲ LANGUAGE BANK at IMPERSONAL **2** the official protection of buildings that have historical or artistic importance（官方對歷史或藝術建築的）保護；文物保護 **3** the act of preventing sth from being lost, wasted, damaged or destroyed 防止流失（或浪費、損害、毀壞）；保存；保護：*to encourage the **conservation of water/fuel*** 鼓勵節約用水／燃料 ◇ *energy conservation* 能源的節約 ➲ see also CONSERVE

conser'vation area *noun* (in the UK) an area where the natural environment or the buildings are protected by law from being damaged or changed（英國自然環境或建築物的）保護區

con·ser·va·tion·ist /ˌkɒnsəˈveɪʃənɪst; *NAmE* ˌkɑːnsərˈv-/ *noun* a person who takes an active part in the protection of the environment 自然環境保護主義者：*a meeting of local conservationists* 當地自然環境保護主義者的會議

con·ser·va·tism /kənˈsɜːvətɪzəm; *NAmE* -ˈsɜːrv-/ *noun* [U] **1** the tendency to resist great or sudden change 保守；守舊：*the innate conservatism of older people* 老年人固有的保守性 **2** (also **Conservatism**) the political belief that society should change as little as possible 保守主義：*an examination of the political theories of conservatism and liberalism* 對保守主義和自由主義政治理論的審視 **3** (usually **Conservatism**) the principles of the Conservative Party in British politics（英國）保守黨的原則

con·ser·va·tive 🔑 /kənˈsɜːvətɪv; *NAmE* -ˈsɜːrv-/ *adj.*, *noun*

▪ ***adj.*** **1** 🔑 opposed to great or sudden social change; showing that you prefer traditional styles and values 保守的；守舊的：*the conservative views of his parents* 他父母的保守觀念 ◇ *Her style of dress was never conservative.* 她的服裝式樣一點兒也不保守。 **2** (usually **Conservative**) connected with the British Conservative Party（英國）保守黨的：*Conservative members/supporters* 保守黨的黨員／支持者 **3** 🔑 (of an estimate 估計) lower than what is probably the real amount or number 低於實際數量的；保守的：***At a conservative estimate**, he'll be earning £50 000.* 按照保守的估計，他會賺到 5 萬英鎊。 ▸ **con·ser·va·tive·ly** *adv.*

▪ ***noun*** **1** (usually **Conservative**) (*abbr.* **Con.**) a member or supporter of the British Conservative Party（英國）保守黨黨員，保守黨支持者 **2** a conservative person 保守者；因循守舊者

the Con'servative Party *noun* [sing.+sing./pl. v.] one of the main British political parties, on the political right, which especially believes in FREE ENTERPRISE and that industry should be privately owned 保守黨（英國主要政黨之一，尤其信奉自由企業制度及產業私有化）

con·ser·va·toire /kənˈsɜːvətwɑː(r); *NAmE* -ˈsɜːrv-/ (*BrE*) (*NAmE* **con·ser·va·tory**) *noun* a school or college at which people are trained in music and theatre 音樂（或戲劇）專科學校（或學院）

con·ser·va·tor /kənˈsɜːvətə(r); *NAmE* -ˈsɜːrv-/ *noun* a person who is responsible for repairing and preserving works of art, buildings and other things of cultural interest 文物修復員；文物保護員

con·ser·va·tory /kənˈsɜːvətri; *NAmE* -ˈsɜːrvətɔːri/ *noun* (*pl.* **-ies**) **1** (*BrE*) a room with glass walls and a glass roof that is built on the side of a house. Conservatories are used for sitting in to enjoy the sun, and to protect plants from cold weather.（靠房屋一側用玻璃建造的）溫室，暖房 ➲ VISUAL VOCAB page V19 **2** (*NAmE*) (*BrE* **con·ser·va·toire**) a school or college at which people are trained in music and theatre 音樂（或戲劇）專科學校（或學院）

con·serve *verb*, *noun*

▪ ***verb*** /kənˈsɜːv; *NAmE* -ˈsɜːrv/ **1 ~ sth** to use as little of sth as possible so that it lasts a long time 節省；節約：*Help to conserve energy by insulating your home.* 對房屋做隔熱處理來幫助節約能源。 **2 ~ sth** to protect sth and prevent it from being changed or destroyed 保護；保存；保藏：*new laws to conserve wildlife in the area* 保護該地區野生動物的新法令 ➲ see also CONSERVATION

C

■ *noun* /ˈkɒnsɜːv; *NAmE* ˈkɑːnsɜːrv/ [C, U] jam containing large or whole pieces of fruit（含有大塊或整塊水果的）果醬，蜜餞

con·sider /kənˈsɪdə(r)/ *verb*
1 [I, T] to think about sth carefully, especially in order to make a decision（尤指為作出決定而）仔細考慮，細想：*I'd like some time to consider.* 我希望有些時間考慮一下。◇ **~ sth** *She considered her options.* 她仔細考慮了自己的各種選擇。◇ *a* **carefully considered** *response* 經過仔細考慮的回覆 ◇ *The company is being actively considered as a potential partner* (= it is thought possible that it could become one). 這家公司正在被積極考慮為可能的合作夥伴。◇ **~ doing sth** *We're considering buying a new car.* 我們在考慮買一輛新車。◇ **~ how/what, etc. …** *We need to consider how the law might be reformed.* 我們得斟酌法律應如何修訂。◇ *He was considering what to do next.* 他在考慮下一步怎麼辦。➲ LANGUAGE BANK at ABOUT **2** [T] to think of sb/sth in a particular way 認為；以為；覺得：**~ sb/sth + noun** | **~ sb/sth (to be) sth** | **~ sb/sth (as) sth** *He considers himself an expert on the subject.* 他認為自己是這門學科的專家。◇ *This award is considered (to be) a great honour.* 這項獎被視為極大的榮譽。◇ *These workers are considered (as) a high-risk group.* 這些工人被視為屬高風險人群。◇ **~ sb/sth + adj.** | **~ sb/sth (to be) sth** *Consider yourself lucky you weren't fired.* 你沒被解雇，算是萬幸。◇ *Who do you consider (to be) responsible for the accident?* 你認為誰對這起事故負有責任？◇ **~ sb/sth to do sth** *He's generally considered to have the finest tenor voice in the country.* 普遍認為他是全國最佳男高音歌手。◇ **~ (that) …** *She considers that it is too early to form a definite conclusion.* 她認為現在下確切的結論還為時過早。◇ **it is considered that …** *It is considered that the proposed development would create much-needed jobs.* 人們認為所提出的發展計劃將創造急需的就業機會。➲ SYNONYMS at REGARD **3** [T] **~ sb/sth** to think about sth, especially the feelings of other people, and be influenced by it when making a decision, etc. 體諒；考慮到；顧及：*You should consider other people before you act.* 你在行動之前應當考慮到別人。**4** [T] **~ sb/sth** (*formal*) to look carefully at sb/sth 端詳；注視：*He stood there, considering the painting.* 他站在那裏，凝視着那幅畫。

IDM **all things conˈsidered** thinking carefully about all the facts, especially the problems or difficulties, of a situation 從各方面看來；考慮到所有情況；總而言之：*She's had a lot of problems since her husband died but she seems quite cheerful, all things considered.* 自從丈夫死後，她面臨很多困難，但總的來說她看上去情緒還是滿樂觀的。**your conˌsidered oˈpinion** your opinion that is the result of careful thought 成熟的意見；經過深思熟慮的意見

con·sid·er·able AW /kənˈsɪdərəbl/ *adj.* (rather *formal*)
great in amount, size, importance, etc. 相當多（或大、重要等）的 SYN **significant**：*The project wasted a considerable amount of time and money.* 那項工程耗費了相當多的時間和資金。◇ *Damage to the building was considerable.* 對這棟建築物的損壞相當嚴重。

con·sid·er·ably AW /kənˈsɪdərəbli/ *adv.* (*formal*)
much; a lot 非常；很；相當多地 SYN **significantly**：*The need for sleep varies considerably from person to person.* 不同的人對睡眠的需要差異相當大。

con·sid·er·ate /kənˈsɪdərət/ *adj.* always thinking of other people's wishes and feelings; careful not to hurt or upset others 考慮周到的；為（他人）着想的；體諒的；體貼的 SYN **thoughtful**：*She is always polite and considerate towards her employees.* 她對待雇員總是客客氣氣，關心體諒。◇ *It was very considerate of him to wait.* 他一直在等候着，真是體貼。OPP **inconsiderate**
▸ **con·sid·er·ate·ly** *adv.*

con·sid·er·ation /kənˌsɪdəˈreɪʃn/ *noun*
1 [U, C] (*formal*) the act of thinking carefully about sth 仔細考慮；深思；斟酌：*Careful consideration should be given to issues of health and safety.* 健康與安全的問題應該認真予以考慮。◇ *The proposals are currently* **under consideration** (= being discussed). 那些提案目前正在審議中。◇ *After a few moments' consideration, he began to speak.* 他想了片刻後開始講話。◇ *a consideration of the legal issues involved* 對有關法律問題的考慮 **2** [C] something that must be thought about when you are planning or deciding sth（作計劃或決定時）必須考慮的事（或因素、原因）：**economic/commercial/environmental/practical considerations** 需要考慮的經濟／商業／環境／實際因素 ◇ *Time is another important consideration.* 時間是另一個需要考慮的重要因素。**3** [U] **~ (for sb/sth)** the quality of being sensitive towards others and thinking about their wishes and feelings（對他人的）考慮周到，體諒，顧及：*They showed no consideration whatsoever for my feelings.* 他們根本不體諒我的感受。◇ *Journalists stayed away from the funeral* **out of consideration for** *the bereaved family.* 出於對喪失親人家屬着想，新聞記者沒有到葬禮現場。**4** [C] (*formal*) a reward or payment for a service 報酬；酬金；支付款

IDM **in consideration of sth** (*formal*) as payment for sth 作為…的報酬（或酬勞）：*a small sum in consideration of your services* 酬謝你服務的小費 **take sth into consideration** to think about and include a particular thing or fact when you are forming an opinion or making a decision 考慮到；顧及：*The candidates' experience and qualifications will be taken into consideration when the decision is made.* 作決定時要考慮候選人的經驗和資格。◇ *Taking everything into consideration, the event was a great success.* 總的說來，這項活動取得了極大的成功。➲ more at MATURE *adj.*

con·sider·ing /kənˈsɪdərɪŋ/ *prep., conj., adv.* used to show that you are thinking about a particular fact, and are influenced by it, when you make a statement about sth 考慮到；就…而言；鑒於：*She's very active, considering her age.* 就她的年齡來說，她是十分活躍的。◇ *Considering he's only just started, he knows quite a lot about it.* 鑒於他才剛剛開始，他懂得的已經不少了。◇ (*informal*) *You've done very well, considering* (= in the difficult circumstances). 考慮到處境的艱難，你已經做得相當不錯了。

con·sign /kənˈsaɪn/ *verb* (*formal*) **1 ~ sb/sth to sth** to put sb/sth somewhere in order to get rid of them/it（為擺脫而）把…置於，把…交付給：*I consigned her letter to the wastebasket.* 我把她的信丟進了廢紙簍。◇ *What I didn't want was to see my mother consigned to an old people's home.* 我所不願意的是看到我母親被送進養老院。**2 ~ sb/sth to sth** to put sb/sth in an unpleasant situation 把…置於（令人不快的境地）；打發；發落：*The decision to close the factory has* **consigned** *6 000 people* **to the scrapheap**. 關閉那家工廠的決定使 6 000 人遭到了遺棄。◇ *A car accident consigned him to a wheelchair for the rest of his life.* 一次車禍使他落得在輪椅上度過餘生。**3 ~ sth to sb** to give or send sth to sb 交給；交付；寄送

con·sign·ment /kənˈsaɪnmənt/ *noun* **1** [C] a quantity of goods that are sent or delivered somewhere 裝運的貨物；運送物：*a consignment of medicines* 運送的一批藥物 **2** [U] the act of sending or delivering sb/sth 發送；投遞；遞送

conˈsignment store *noun* (*NAmE*) a shop/store where people take their old clothes, etc. to be sold to sb else. The consignment store keeps part of the money after an item is sold and gives the other part to the person who brought it in. 委託商行；寄售店

con·sist AW /kənˈsɪst/ *verb*
(not used in the progressive tenses 不用於進行時)

PHR V **conˈsist in sth** (*formal*) to have sth as the main or only part or feature 存在於；在於：*The beauty of the city consists in its magnificent buildings.* 這座城市的美就在於它那些宏偉的建築。◇ **~ doing sth** *True education does not consist in simply being taught facts.* 真正的教育並不在於僅僅講授事實。**conˈsist of sb/sth** to be formed from the things or people mentioned 由…組成（或構成）：*The committee consists of ten members.* 委員會由十人組成。◇ *Their diet consisted largely of vegetables.* 他們的日常飲食以蔬菜為主。◇ **~ doing sth** *Most of the fieldwork consisted of making tape recordings.* 現場工作多半為進行磁帶錄音。

Synonyms 同義詞辨析

consist of sb/sth

comprise • make up sth • constitute • be composed of sb/sth

These words all mean to be formed from the things or people mentioned, or to be the parts that form sth. 以上各詞均表示由某些人或事物組成、構成。

consist of sb/sth to be formed from the things, people or activities mentioned 指由事物、人或活動組成、構成：*Their diet consists largely of vegetables.* 他們的日常飲食以蔬菜為主。

comprise (*rather formal*) to be formed from the things or people mentioned 指由…組成、構成：*The collection comprises 327 paintings.* 這部畫冊收有 327 幅畫。 NOTE **Comprise** can also be used to refer to the parts or members of sth. * comprise 亦可指組成、構成：*Older people comprise a large proportion of those living in poverty.* 貧困的人口中，老年人佔很大的比例。 However, this is less frequent. 不過這種用法不常見。

make up sth (*rather informal*) to be the parts or people that form sth 指組成、構成：*Women make up 56% of the student numbers.* 女生佔學生人數的 56%。

constitute to be the parts or people that form sth 指組成、構成：*People under the age of 40 constitute the majority of the labour force.* * 40 歲以下的人佔勞動力的大多數。

be composed of sb/sth (*rather formal*) to be formed from the things or people mentioned 指由…組成、構成：*Around 15% of our diet is composed of protein.* 我們的飲食中大約 15% 是蛋白質。

WHICH WORD? 詞語辨析

Consist of sb/sth is the most general of these words and the only one that can be used for activities with the *-ing* form of a verb. * consist of 是這組詞中最通用、也是唯一可與動詞 -ing 形式連用、表示包含…活動的詞：*My work at that time just consisted of typing letters.* 我那時的工作就是打字。 The other main difference is between those verbs that take the whole as the subject and the parts as the object 另一主要區別在於有些詞是將整體作為主語，部份作為賓語：*The group consists of/comprises/is made up of/is composed of ten people.* 這個小組由十個人組成。 and those that take the parts as the subject and the whole as the object. 另一些詞則是將部份作為主語，整體作為賓語：*Ten people make up/constitute/comprise the group.* 這個小組由十個人組成。 It is not correct to use 'comprises of' or 'is composed by/from'. 用 comprise of 或 be composed by/from 均不正確。

con·sist·ency AW /kənˈsɪstənsi/ *noun* (*pl.* **-ies**) **1** [U] (*approving*) the quality of always behaving in the same way or of having the same opinions, standard, etc.; the quality of being consistent 一致性；連貫性：*She has played with great consistency all season.* 她整個賽季表現相當穩定。◇ *We need to ensure the consistency of service to our customers.* 我們對客戶要確保服務的連貫性。 OPP **inconsistency** **2** [C, U] the **consistency** of a mixture or a liquid substance is how thick, smooth, etc. it is 黏稠度；密實度；平滑度；堅實度：*Beat the ingredients together to a creamy consistency.* 把配料攪拌成乳脂狀。◇ *The cement should have the consistency of wet sand.* 水泥應當具有濕沙的堅實度。

con·sist·ent AW /kənˈsɪstənt/ *adj.* **1** (*approving*) always behaving in the same way, or having the same opinions, standards, etc. 一致的；始終如一的：*She's not very consistent in the way she treats her children.* 她對待孩子反覆無常。◇ *He has been Milan's most consistent* (= most consistently good) *player this season.* 他是米蘭隊這個賽季狀態最穩定的隊員。◇ *We must be consistent in applying the rules.* 我們在實施這些規則時必須保持一致。◇ *a consistent approach to the problem* 解決問題的一貫方法 **2** happening in the same way and continuing for a period of time 連續的；持續的：*the party's consistent failure to come up with any new policies* 這個政黨長時期提不出任何新政策 ◇ *a pattern of consistent growth in the economy* 經濟持續增長的模式 **3 ~ with sth** in agreement with sth; not CONTRADICTING sth 與…一致的；相符的；符合的；不矛盾的：*The results are entirely consistent with our earlier research.* 這些結果與我們早些時候的研究完全吻合。◇ *injuries consistent with a fall from an upper storey* (= similar to those such a fall would have caused) 和從樓上摔下來的情形相符合的傷處 **4** (of an argument or a set of ideas 論點或一系列的觀點) having different parts that all agree with each other 相互連貫的：*a well-thought-out and consistent argument* 經過深思熟慮的、相互連貫的論點 OPP **inconsistent** ▸ **con·sist·ent·ly** AW *adv.*：*Her work has been of a consistently high standard.* 她的工作一直是高水準的。◇ *We have argued consistently for a change in the law.* 我們一直堅持不懈地鼓吹要更改法律。

con·sola·tion /ˌkɒnsəˈleɪʃn; *NAmE* ˌkɑːn-/ *noun* [U, C] a thing or person that makes you feel better when you are unhappy or disappointed 使感到安慰的人（或物）；安慰；慰藉 SYN **comfort**：*a few words of consolation* 幾句安慰的話 ◇ *If it's any consolation, she didn't get the job, either.* 不知道這算不算得上安慰，但她也沒有得到那份工作。◇ *The children were a great consolation to him when his wife died.* 他妻子去世後，幾個孩子就是他極大的安慰。

conso'lation prize *noun* a small prize given to sb who has not won a competition 安慰獎；鼓勵獎

con·sola·tory /kənˈsɒlətəri; *NAmE* kənˈsoʊlətɔːri; -ˈsɑːlə-/ *adj.* (*formal*) intended to make sb who is unhappy or disappointed feel better 安慰的；慰藉的

con·sole[1] /kənˈsəʊl; *NAmE* -ˈsoʊl/ *verb* to give comfort or sympathy to sb who is unhappy or disappointed 安慰；撫慰；慰藉 SYN **comfort**：**~ sb/yourself** *Nothing could console him when his wife died.* 他妻子去世後，什麼事情也不能使他感到寬慰。◇ *She put a consoling arm around his shoulders.* 她摟住他肩膀以示安慰。◇ **~ sb/yourself with sth** *Console yourself with the thought that you did your best.* 你可以安慰自己的是你已經盡了最大的努力。◇ **~ sb/yourself that …** *I didn't like lying but I consoled myself that it was for a good cause.* 我不願意撒謊，但我安慰自己那是出於好意。◇ **~ sb + speech** *'Never mind,' Anne consoled her.* "沒關係。" 安妮安慰她說。

con·sole[2] /ˈkɒnsəʊl; *NAmE* ˈkɑːnsoʊl/ *noun* a flat surface which contains all the controls and switches for a machine, a piece of electronic equipment, etc.（機器、電子設備等的）控制台，操縱台，儀表板

con·soli·date /kənˈsɒlɪdeɪt; *NAmE* -ˈsɑːl-/ *verb* **1** [T, I] **~ (sth)** to make a position of power or success stronger so that it is more likely to continue 使加強；使鞏固：*With this new movie he has* **consolidated** *his* **position** *as the country's leading director.* 他新執導的影片鞏固了他作為全國最佳導演的地位。◇ *Italy consolidated their lead with a second goal.* 意大利隊的第二個進球鞏固了其領先的地位。 **2** [T, I] **~ (sth)** (*technical* 術語) to join things together into one; to be joined into one （使）結成一體，合併：*All the debts have been consolidated.* 所有債項均已合併。◇ *consolidated accounts* 合併賬目 ◇ *The two companies consolidated for greater efficiency.* 為提高效率，這兩家公司已合併。 ▸ **con·soli·da·tion** /kənˌsɒlɪˈdeɪʃn; *NAmE* -ˌsɑːl-/ *noun* [U]：*the consolidation of power* 權力的鞏固 ◇ *the consolidation of Japan's banking industry* 日本銀行業的合併

con·sommé /kənˈsɒmeɪ; *NAmE* ˌkɑːnsəˈmeɪ/ *noun* [U] a clear soup made with the juices from meat 清燉肉湯

con·son·ance /ˈkɒnsənəns; *NAmE* ˈkɑːn-/ *noun* **1** [U] **~ (with sth)** (*formal*) agreement 一致；協調：*a policy that is popular because of its consonance with traditional party doctrine* 因與傳統的政黨宗旨一致而受歡迎的政策 **2** [U, C] (*music* 音) a combination of musical notes that sound pleasing together 協和 OPP **dissonance**

C

con·son·ant /ˈkɒnsənənt; NAmE ˈkɑːn-/ *noun, adj.*
■ ***noun*** **1** (*phonetics* 語音) a speech sound made by completely or partly stopping the flow of air being breathed out through the mouth 輔音；子音 **2** a letter of the alphabet that represents a consonant sound, for example 'b', 'c', 'd', 'f', etc. 輔音字母，子音字母（如 b、c、d、f 等）➲ compare VOWEL
■ ***adj.*** **~ with sth** (*formal*) agreeing with or being the same as sth else（與…）一致的，符合的，相同的，和諧的

con·son·ant·al /ˌkɒnsəˈnæntl; NAmE ˌkɑːn-/ *adj.* (*phonetics* 語音) relating to or consisting of a consonant or consonants 輔音的；輔音組成的 ➲ compare VOCALIC

con·sort *noun, verb*
■ ***noun*** /ˈkɒnsɔːt; NAmE ˈkɑːnsɔːrt/ **1** the husband or wife of a ruler（統治者的）配偶：*the prince consort* (= the queen's husband) 親王（女王的丈夫）**2** a group of old-fashioned musical instruments, or a group of musicians who play music from several centuries ago 一組古樂器；（演奏幾世紀前音樂的）一組樂師
■ ***verb*** /kənˈsɔːt; NAmE -ˈsɔːrt/ [I] **~ with sb** (*formal*) to spend time with sb that other people do not approve of 廝混；鬼混：*He is known to have consorted with prostitutes.* 眾所周知他曾與妓女廝混在一起。

con·sor·tium /kənˈsɔːtiəm; NAmE -ˈsɔːrt-/ *noun* (*pl.* **con·sor·tiums** or **con·sor·tia** /-tiə; BrE also -ˈsɔːʃə; NAmE also -ˈsɔːrʃə/) a group of people, countries, companies, etc. who are working together on a particular project（合作進行某項工程的）財團，銀團，聯營企業：*the Anglo-French consortium that built the Channel Tunnel* 修建英吉利海峽隧道的英法財團

con·spicu·ous /kənˈspɪkjuəs/ *adj.* easy to see or notice; likely to attract attention 易見的；明顯的；惹人注意的：*Mary's red hair always made her conspicuous at school.* 瑪麗的紅頭髮在學校裏總是很惹眼。◇ *I felt very conspicuous in my new car.* 坐在我的新車裏，我感到十分惹人注目。◇ *The advertisements were all posted in a conspicuous place.* 廣告都貼在了顯眼的地方。◇ *The event was a conspicuous success* (= a very great one). 這項活動至為成功。**OPP** **inconspicuous** ► **con·spicu·ous·ly** *adv.*：*Women were conspicuously absent from* (= there were surprisingly few women on) *the planning committee.* 規劃委員會裏沒有女性委員，惹人注意。**con·spicu·ous·ness** *noun* [U]
IDM **conˌspicuous by your ˈabsence** not present in a situation or place, when it is obvious that you should be there（本應在場）因缺席而招人注意：*When it came to cleaning up afterwards, Anne was conspicuous by her absence.* 後來到打掃時，本應在場的安妮卻因為不在而引起了注意。

conˌspicuous conˈsumption *noun* [U] the buying of expensive goods in order to impress people and show them how rich you are 誇耀性消費；炫耀性購買

con·spir·acy /kənˈspɪrəsi/ *noun* [C, U] (*pl.* **-ies**) a secret plan by a group of people to do sth harmful or illegal 密謀策劃；陰謀：**~ (to do sth)** *a conspiracy to overthrow the government* 顛覆政府的陰謀 ◇ **~ (against sb/sth)** *conspiracies against the president* 反對總統的陰謀詭計 ◇ **~ (to sth)** *They were charged with conspiracy to murder.* 他們被指控密謀策劃謀殺。◇ *a **conspiracy of silence*** (= an agreement not to talk publicly about sth which should be made public) 保持緘默的密約（對該公開的事情不公開談論的約定）◇ *a **conspiracy theory*** (= the belief that a secret conspiracy is responsible for a particular event) 陰謀論（認為某事件背後有陰謀）

con·spir·ator /kənˈspɪrətə(r)/ *noun* a person who is involved in a conspiracy 共謀者；搞陰謀的人

con·spira·tor·ial /kənˌspɪrəˈtɔːriəl/ *adj.* **1** connected with, or like, a conspiracy 陰謀的；密謀的；似陰謀的 **2** (of a person's behaviour 個人的舉止) suggesting that a secret is being shared 會意的；心照不宣的：*'I know you understand,' he said and gave a conspiratorial wink.* "我知道你明白。" 他說道，會意地眨一眨眼。► **con·spira·tori·al·ly** *adv.*

con·spire /kənˈspaɪə(r)/ *verb* (*formal*) **1** [I] to secretly plan with other people to do sth illegal or harmful 密謀；圖謀；合謀：**~ (with sb) (against sb)** *They were accused of conspiring against the king.* 他們被指控密謀反對國王。◇ **~ (together) (to do sth)** *They deny conspiring together to smuggle drugs.* 他們否認共謀走私毒品。◇ **~ (with sb) (to do sth)** *She admitted conspiring with her lover to murder her husband.* 她承認與情夫密謀殺害親夫。**2** [I] (of events 事件) to seem to work together to make sth bad happen 似乎共同導致（不良後果）：**~ against sb/sth** ***Circumstances had conspired against*** *them.* 各種情況都湊在一起和他們作對。◇ **~ to do sth** *Everything conspired to make her life a misery.* 她命運多舛，生活悲慘。

con·stable /ˈkʌnstəbl; NAmE ˈkɑːn-/ *noun* **1** (*BrE*) (used especially when talking to a police officer of the lowest rank 尤與最低級別的警察談話時用) = POLICE CONSTABLE：*Have you finished your report, Constable?* 警察先生，你的報告完成了嗎？➲ see also CHIEF CONSTABLE **2** (in the US 美國) a peace officer with some of the powers of a police officer, typically in a small town（通常指小城鎮的）警員，治安官

con·stabu·lary /kənˈstæbjələri; NAmE -leri/ *noun* [C+sing./pl. v.] (*pl.* **-ies**) (in Britain) the police force of a particular area or town（英國某地區或城鎮的）警察部隊

con·stancy **AW** /ˈkɒnstənsi; NAmE ˈkɑːn-/ *noun* [U] (*formal*) **1** the quality of staying the same and not changing 穩定性；持久不變；始終如一 **2** (*approving*) the quality of being faithful 忠誠；忠實；忠貞 **SYN** **fidelity**：*He admired her courage and constancy.* 他欽佩她的勇氣和忠貞。

con·stant 🔑 **AW** /ˈkɒnstənt; NAmE ˈkɑːn-/ *adj., noun*
■ ***adj.*** **1** 🔑 [usually before noun] happening all the time or repeatedly 連續發生的；不斷的；重複的：*constant interruptions* 無休止的干擾 ◇ *a constant stream of visitors all day* 整天絡繹不絕的遊客 ◇ *Babies need constant attention.* 嬰兒一刻也離不開人。◇ *This entrance is in constant use.* 此入口經常使用。**2** 🔑 that does not change 不變的；固定的；恒定的 **SYN** **fixed**：*travelling at a constant speed of 50 m.p.h.* 以每小時 50 英里的恒定速度行駛
■ ***noun*** (*technical* 術語) a number or quantity that does not vary 常數；常量 **OPP** **variable**

con·stant·ly 🔑 **AW** /ˈkɒnstəntli; NAmE ˈkɑːn-/ *adv.* all the time; repeatedly 始終；一直；重複不斷地：*Fashion is constantly changing.* 時尚總是日新月異。◇ *Heat the sauce, stirring constantly.* 加熱調味汁並不停地攪動。

con·sta·tive /ˈkɒnstətɪv; NAmE ˈkɑːn-, kənˈsteɪtɪv/ *adj.* (*grammar* 語法) stating that sth is real or true 描寫陳述的（陳述真實的事物）➲ see also PERFORMATIVE

con·stel·la·tion /ˌkɒnstəˈleɪʃn; NAmE ˌkɑːn-/ *noun* **1** a group of stars that forms a shape in the sky and has a name 星座 **2** (*formal*) a group of related ideas, things or people 一系列（相關的想法、事物）；一群（相關的人）：*a constellation of Hollywood talent* 一群好萊塢天才

con·ster·na·tion /ˌkɒnstəˈneɪʃn; NAmE ˌkɑːnstərˈn-/ *noun* [U] (*formal*) a worried, sad feeling after you have received an unpleasant surprise 驚愕；驚恐 **SYN** **dismay**：*The announcement of her retirement caused consternation among tennis fans.* 她宣佈掛拍告退的消息引起了網球迷的震驚。

con·sti·pated /ˈkɒnstɪpeɪtɪd; NAmE ˈkɑːn-/ *adj.* unable to get rid of waste material from the BOWELS easily 便秘的

con·sti·pa·tion /ˌkɒnstɪˈpeɪʃn; NAmE ˌkɑːn-/ *noun* [U] the condition of being unable to get rid of waste material from the BOWELS easily (= being constipated) 便秘

con·stitu·ency **AW** /kənˈstɪtjuənsi; NAmE -tʃu-/ (*pl.* **-ies**) *noun* **1** (*especially BrE*) [C] a district that elects its own representative to parliament（選舉議會議員的）選區：*Unemployment is high in her constituency.* 她的選區的失業人數居高不下。◇ *He owns a house in his Darlington constituency.* 他在自己的選區達靈頓擁有一座房子。**2** [C+sing./pl. v.] the people who live in and vote in a particular district 選區選民： *constituency opinion* 選區選民的意見 **3** [C+sing./pl. v.] a particular group of people in society who are likely to support a person, an idea or a product （統稱）支持者

con·stitu·ent AW /kən'stɪtjuənt; *NAmE* -tʃu-/ *noun, adj.*

■ ***noun*** **1** a person who lives, and can vote in a constituency （選區的）選民，選舉人： *She has the full support of her constituents.* 她得到本區選民的全力支持。 **2** one of the parts of sth that combine to form the whole 成分；構成要素

■ ***adj.*** [only before noun] (*formal*) forming or helping to make a whole 組成的；構成的： *to break something up into its **constituent parts/elements*** 把某物分離為各個組成部份 / 要素

con,stituent as'sembly *noun* [C+sing./pl. v.] a group of elected representatives with the power to make or change a country's CONSTITUTION 立憲議會（有權制訂或修改國家憲法）

con·sti·tute AW /'kɒnstɪtjuːt; *NAmE* 'kɑːnstətuːt/ *verb* (*formal*) **1** *linking verb* **+ noun** (not used in the progressive tenses 不用於進行時) to be considered to be sth （被認為或看作）是；被算作： *Does such an activity constitute a criminal offence?* 這樣的活動也算刑事犯罪嗎？◇ *The increase in racial tension constitutes a threat to our society.* 種族間緊張狀態的升級是對我們社會的一種威脅。 **2** *linking verb* **+ noun** (not used in the progressive tenses 不用於進行時) to be the parts that together form sth 組成；構成 SYN **make up**： *Female workers constitute the majority of the labour force.* 女性雇員佔勞動力的多數。 ➲ SYNONYMS at CONSIST OF **3** [T, usually passive] **~ sth** to form a group legally or officially （合法或正式地）成立，設立 SYN **establish, set up**： *The committee was constituted in 1974 by an Act of Parliament.* 該委員會是根據議會法案於 1974 年設立的。

con·sti·tu·tion AW /ˌkɒnstɪ'tjuːʃn; *NAmE* ˌkɑːnstə'tuːʃn/ *noun* **1** [C] the system of laws and basic principles that a state, a country or an organization is governed by 憲法；章程： *your right to vote under the constitution* 根據憲法所擁有的選舉權 ◇ *According to the constitution ...* 依照憲法…◇ *to propose a new amendment to the Constitution* 提出一項新的憲法修正案 ◇ *the South African Constitution* 南非憲法 **2** [C] the condition of a person's body and how healthy it is 身體素質；體質；體格： *to have a **healthy/strong/weak constitution*** 體質健康 / 強壯 / 虛弱 **3** [U, C] (*formal*) the way sth is formed or organized 構成；構造 SYN **structure**： *the genetic constitution of cells* 細胞的基因構造 **4** [U] (*formal*) the act of forming sth 組成；形成 SYN **establishment, setting up**： *He recommended the constitution of a review committee.* 他建議設立審查委員會。

con·sti·tu·tion·al AW /ˌkɒnstɪ'tjuːʃənl; *NAmE* ˌkɑːnstə'tuː-/ *adj., noun*

■ ***adj.*** **1** [only before noun] connected with the constitution of a country or an organization 憲法的；章程的： ***constitutional government/reform*** 立憲政體；憲法的修改 ◇ *a constitutional amendment* 憲法修正案 **2** allowed or limited by the constitution of a country or an organization 憲法准許的；受憲法限制的；受章程限制的： *They can't pass this law. It's not constitutional.* 他們無法通過這項法律，它不符合憲法。◇ ***constitutional rights*** 憲法規定的權利 ◇ *a **constitutional monarchy*** (= a country with a king or queen whose power is controlled by a set of laws and basic principles) 君主立憲制（國家） OPP **unconstitutional** **3** [usually before noun] related to the body's ability to stay healthy, be strong and fight illness 身體素質的；體質的；體格的： *constitutional remedies* 順勢療法 ▸ **con·sti·tu·tion·al·ly** AW /-ʃənəli/ *adv.*： *constitutionally guaranteed rights* 受到憲法保障的權利 ◇ *He was much weakened constitutionally by the disease.* 他讓疾病鬧得身體非常虛弱。

■ ***noun*** (*old-fashioned* or *humorous*) a short walk that people take because it is good for their health 保健散步

Cons,titutional 'Court *noun* [sing.] in South Africa, the highest court dealing with cases related to the constitution 憲法法院（南非處理與憲法相關案件的最高法院）

con·sti·tu·tion·al·ism /ˌkɒnstɪ'tjuːʃənəlɪzəm; *NAmE* ˌkɑːnstə'tuː-/ *noun* [U] a belief in constitutional government 立憲主義

con·sti·tu·tion·al·ity /ˌkɒnstɪˌtjuːʃə'næləti; *NAmE* ˌkɑːnstəˌtuː-/ *noun* [U] (*technical* 術語) the fact that sth is acceptable according to a CONSTITUTION 符合憲法： *They questioned the constitutionality of the law.* 他們質疑這項法律是否符合憲法。

con·sti·tu·tive AW /ˌkɒnstɪ'tjuːtɪv; *NAmE* ˌkɑːnstə'tuːtɪv/ *adj.* (*formal*) **~** (**of sth**) forming a part, often an essential part, of sth 組成部份的；本質的；基本的： *Memory is constitutive of identity.* 記憶是身分的一個重要構成部份。

con·strain AW /kən'streɪn/ *verb* (*formal*) **1** [usually passive] **~ sb to do sth** to force sb to do sth or behave in a particular way 強迫；強制；迫使： *The evidence was so compelling that he **felt constrained to** accept it.* 證據是那樣的令人折服，他覺得不得不接受。 **2** [often passive] to restrict or limit sb/sth 限制；限定；約束： **~ sth** *Research has been constrained by a lack of funds.* 研究工作因經費不足而受限制。◇ **~ sb** (**from doing sth**) *She felt constrained from continuing by the threat of losing her job.* 由於受到失去工作的威脅，她感到很難再堅持下去。 ➲ see also UNCONSTRAINED

con·strained /kən'streɪnd/ *adj.* (*formal*) not natural; forced or too controlled 不自然的；強迫的；過於受約束的： *constrained emotions* 受壓抑的情感

con·straint AW /kən'streɪnt/ *noun* **1** [C] a thing that limits or restricts sth, or your freedom to do sth 限制；限定；約束 SYN **restriction**： ***constraints of time/money/space*** 時間 / 資金 / 空間的限制 ◇ ***financial/economic/legal/political constraints*** 財政 / 經濟 / 法律 / 政治約束 ◇ **~ on sth** *This decision will impose serious constraints on all schools.* 這項決定將使所有的學校受到各種嚴格的限制。 ➲ SYNONYMS at LIMIT **2** [U] strict control over the way that you behave or are allowed to behave 約束；嚴管： *At last we could relax and talk without constraint.* 我們終於可以放鬆下來，無拘無束地談話了。

con·strict /kən'strɪkt/ *verb* **1** [I, T] to become tighter or narrower; to make sth tighter or narrower （使）緊縮，縮窄： *Her **throat constricted** and she swallowed hard.* 她喉嚨發緊，使勁地嚥了一下唾沫。◇ **~ sth** *a drug that constricts the blood vessels* 收縮血管的藥 **2 ~ sb** to limit or restrict what sb is able to do 限制；限定；抑制；約束： *Film-makers of the time were constricted by the censors.* 那時的電影製作人受到了審查官的限制。◇ *constricting rules and regulations* 具有約束性的規章制度 ▸ **con·strict·ed** *adj.*： *Her throat felt dry and constricted.* 她感到喉嚨發乾發緊。◇ *a constricted vision of the world* 受到局限的對世界的認識 **con·stric·tion** /kən'strɪkʃn/ *noun* [U, C]： *a feeling of constriction in the chest* 胸部的壓迫感 ◇ *political constrictions* 政治上的約束

con·struct O-w AW *verb, noun*

■ ***verb*** /kən'strʌkt/ **1** O-w [often passive] to build or make sth such as a road, building or machine 建築；修建；建造： **~ sth** *When was the bridge constructed?* 那座橋是何時修建的？◇ **~ sth from/out of/of sth** *They constructed a shelter out of fallen branches.* 他們用落下的枯樹枝搭了個窩棚。 ➲ SYNONYMS at BUILD **2** O-w **~ sth** to form sth by putting different things together 組成；創建 SYN **put together**： *You must learn how to construct a logical argument.* 你必須學會怎樣確立合乎邏輯的論點。◇ *to construct a theory* 創立一種理論 ◇ *a well-constructed novel* 構思巧妙的小說 **3 ~ sth** (*geometry* 幾何) to draw a line or shape according to the rules of mathematics （按照數學規則）編製，繪製： *to construct a triangle* 畫一個三角形

■ ***noun*** /'kɒnstrʌkt; *NAmE* 'kɑːn-/ (*formal*) **1** an idea or a belief that is based on various pieces of evidence which are not always true （根據不總是真實的各種證據得出的）構想，觀念，概念： *a contrast between lived reality and the construct held in the mind* 現實生活與頭腦所持概念之間的明顯差別 **2** (*linguistics* 語言) a group of words that form a phrase （短語的）結構成分，結構體 **3** a thing that is built or made 建造物；構築物；製成物

con·struc·tion 🔑 AW /kənˈstrʌkʃn/ *noun*
‣ OF ROADS/BUILDINGS 道路；建築物 **1** 🔑 [U] the process or method of building or making sth, especially roads, buildings, bridges, etc. 建築；建造；施工：*the construction industry* 建築業 ◇ *road construction* 道路的施工 ◇ *Work has begun on the construction of the new airport.* 新機場的修建已經開工。◇ *Our new offices are still* ***under construction*** (= being built). 我們的新辦公樓尚在修建中。◇ *the construction of a new database* 新數據庫的建立 **2** 🔑 [U] the way that sth has been built or made 建造（或構造）的方式：*strong in construction* 結構堅固 ◇ *ships of steel construction* 鋼結構船 ➲ **SYNONYMS** at STRUCTURE
‣ BUILDING/STRUCTURE 建築；結構 **3** [C] (*formal*) a thing that has been built or made 建造物；構築物；製成物：*The summer house was a simple wooden construction.* 那座避暑別墅是簡單的木結構建築。
‣ GRAMMAR 語法 **4** [C] the way in which words are used together and arranged to form a sentence, phrase, etc. （句子、短語等的）結構：*grammatical constructions* 語法結構
‣ OF THEORY, ETC. 理論等 **5** [U, C] the creating of sth from ideas, opinions and knowledge（理念、觀點和知識的）創造，創立，建立：*the construction of a new theory* 新理論的創立
‣ MEANING 含義 **6** [C] (*formal*) the way in which words, actions, statements, etc. are understood by sb（對詞語、行為、陳述等的）解釋，說明，理解 SYN **interpretation**：*What construction do you put on this letter* (= what do you think it means)? 你對這封信如何理解？

con·struc·tion·al /kənˈstrʌkʃənl/ *adj.* connected with the making or building of things 建造的；構造的；建築的

conˈstruction paper *noun* [U] (*NAmE*) thick coloured paper that people cut out to make designs, models, etc.（做設計、模型等的）彩色美術紙

conˈstruction site *noun* (*especially NAmE*) = BUILDING SITE

con·struct·ive AW /kənˈstrʌktɪv/ *adj.* having a useful and helpful effect rather than being negative or with no purpose 建設性的；有助益的；積極的：***constructive criticism/suggestions/advice*** 建設性的批評／提議／忠告 ◇ *His work involved helping hyperactive children to use their energy in a constructive way.* 他的工作包括幫助患有多動症的兒童往好的方面利用他們的精力。◇ *The government is encouraging all parties to play a constructive role in the reform process.* 政府鼓勵所有的政黨在改革過程中發揮建設性的作用。➲ compare DESTRUCTIVE ▸ **con·struct·ive·ly** *adv.*

conˌstructive disˈmissal *noun* [U] (*BrE, law* 律) a situation in which you are forced to leave your job because it is changed in a way that makes it impossible for you to continue doing it 推定解雇，變工解雇（指通過改變工作條件而迫使雇員自動離職）

con·struct·or /kənˈstrʌktə(r)/ *noun* a person or company that builds things, especially cars or aircraft（尤指汽車或飛機的）建造者，製造者，建造商

con·strue /kənˈstruː/ *verb* [usually passive] (*formal*) to understand the meaning of a word, a sentence, or an action in a particular way 理解；領會 SYN **interpret**：**~ sth** *He considered how the remark was to be construed.* 他考慮這話該如何理解。◇ **~ sth as sth** *Her words could hardly be construed as an apology.* 她的話怎麼想都不像是道歉。

con·sul /ˈkɒnsl; *NAmE* ˈkɑːnsl/ *noun* a government official who is the representative of his or her country in a foreign city 領事：*the British consul in Miami* 英國駐邁阿密領事 ▸ **con·su·lar** /ˈkɒnsjələ(r); *NAmE* ˈkɑːnsəl-/ *adj.*：*consular officials* 領事

con·sul·ate /ˈkɒnsjələt; *NAmE* ˈkɑːnsəl-/ *noun* the building where a consul works 領事館 ➲ compare EMBASSY (2)

con·sult 🔑 AW /kənˈsʌlt/ *verb*
1 🔑 [T, I] to go to sb for information or advice 咨詢；請教：**~ sb** *If the pain continues, consult your doctor.* 如果疼痛持續不消退，要請醫生診治。◇ **~ sb about sth** *Have you consulted your lawyer about this?* 你就此事咨詢過你的律師嗎？◇ *a consulting engineer* (= one who has expert knowledge and gives advice) 顧問工程師 ◇ (*NAmE*) **~ with sb (about/on sth)** *Consult with your physician about possible treatments.* 向你的醫生咨詢可行的治療方案。**2** 🔑 [T, I] to discuss sth with sb to get their permission for sth, or to help you make a decision（與某人）商議，商量（以得到許可或幫助決策）：**~ sb** *You shouldn't have done it without consulting me.* 你不該不和我商量就做了這件事。◇ **~ sb about/on sth** *I expect to be consulted about major issues.* 我認為重大問題必須找我商量。◇ **~ with sb (about/on sth)** *I need to consult with my colleagues on the proposals.* 我需要和我的同事商討這些建議。➲ **SYNONYMS** at TALK **3** 🔑 [T] **~ sth** to look in or at sth to get information 查閱；查詢；參看 SYN **refer to**：*He consulted the manual.* 他查閱了使用說明書。

con·sult·ancy AW /kənˈsʌltənsi/ *noun* (*pl.* **-ies**) **1** [C] a company that gives expert advice on a particular subject to other companies or organizations 咨詢公司：*a* ***management/design/computer, etc. consultancy*** 管理／設計／計算機等咨詢公司 **2** [U] expert advice that a company or person is paid to provide on a particular subject 專家咨詢：*consultancy fees* 咨詢費

con·sult·ant AW /kənˈsʌltənt/ *noun* **1** a person who knows a lot about a particular subject and is employed to give advice about it to other people 顧問：*a firm of management consultants* 管理咨詢公司 ◇ **~ on sth** *the President's consultant on economic affairs* 總統的經濟事務顧問 **2** (*BrE*) a hospital doctor of the highest rank who is a specialist in a particular area of medicine 高級顧問醫師；會診醫師：*a consultant in obstetrics* 產科顧問醫師 ◇ *a consultant surgeon* 外科顧問醫師 ➲ compare REGISTRAR (3)

con·sult·ation AW /ˌkɒnslˈteɪʃn; *NAmE* ˌkɑːn-/ *noun* **1** [U] the act of discussing sth with sb or with a group of people before making a decision about it 咨詢；商討；磋商：*a* ***consultation document/paper/period/process*** 咨詢文件／論文／時間／過程 ◇ *acting* ***in consultation with*** *all the departments involved* 和所有有關部門磋商後行事 ◇ *The decision was taken after close consultation with local residents.* 這項決定是在與當地居民仔細磋商後作出的。➲ **SYNONYMS** at DISCUSSION **2** [C] a formal meeting to discuss sth 商討會；協商會：*extensive consultations between the two countries* 兩國之間的廣泛磋商 ➲ **SYNONYMS** at DISCUSSION **3** [C] a meeting with an expert, especially a doctor, to get advice or treatment（向專家請教的）咨詢會；（尤指）就診 ➲ **SYNONYMS** at INTERVIEW **4** [U] the act of looking for information in a book, etc. 查找；查閱；查看：*There is a large collection of texts available for consultation on-screen.* 有大量的文本可通過電腦查閱。

con·sulta·tive AW /kənˈsʌltətɪv/ *adj.* giving advice or making suggestions 咨詢的；顧問的 SYN **advisory**：*a* ***consultative committee/body/document*** 咨詢委員會／機構／文件

conˈsulting room *noun* a room where a doctor talks to and examines patients 診療室

con·sum·able /kənˈsjuːməbl; *NAmE* -ˈsuːm-/ *adj., noun* (*business* 商)
■ *adj.* intended to be bought, used and then replaced 可消耗的；會用盡的：*consumable electronic goods* 電子消費品
■ *noun* **con·sum·ables** [pl.] goods that are intended to be used fairly quickly and then replaced 消耗品：*computer consumables such as CD-Rs and printer cartridges* 可錄光盤、打印機墨盒之類的電腦耗材

con·sume AW /kənˈsjuːm; *NAmE* -ˈsuːm/ *verb* (*formal*)
1 ~ sth to use sth, especially fuel, energy or time 消耗，耗費（尤指燃料、能量或時間）：*The electricity industry consumes large amounts of fossil fuels.* 電力工業消耗大量的礦物燃料。**2 ~ sth** to eat or drink sth 吃；喝；飲：*Before he died he had consumed a large quantity of alcohol.* 他死亡前喝了大量的酒。**3 ~ sb (with sth)** [usually passive] to fill sb with a strong feeling 使充滿（強烈的感情）：*Carolyn was consumed with guilt.* 卡羅琳深感

內疚。◇ *Rage consumed him.* 他無比憤怒。 **4 ~ sth** (of fire 火) to completely destroy sth 燒燬；毀滅：*The hotel was quickly consumed by fire.* 那座旅館很快被大火吞噬。 ➲ see also ALL-CONSUMING, CONSUMING, CONSUMPTION, TIME-CONSUMING

con·sumer 🔑 AW /kən'sjuːmə(r); *NAmE* -'suː-/ *noun* a person who buys goods or uses services 消費者；顧客；用戶：*consumer demand/choice/rights* 消費者的需求 / 選擇 / 權利 ◇ *Health-conscious consumers want more information about the food they buy.* 注重身體健康的消費者想得到更多有關他們所購買的食物的信息。◇ *a consumer society* (= one where buying and selling is considered to be very important) 消費社會 ◇ *Tax cuts will boost consumer confidence after the recession.* 減稅將增強消費者在經濟衰退後的信心。 ➲ compare PRODUCER (1)

con,sumer 'durables (*BrE*) (*NAmE* **'durable goods**) *noun* [pl.] (*business* 商) goods which are expected to last for a long time after they have been bought, such as cars, televisions, etc. 耐用消費品（如汽車、電視機等）

con'sumer goods *noun* [pl.] goods such as food, clothing, etc. bought by individual customers 消費品 ➲ compare CAPITAL GOODS

con·sumer·ism /kən'sjuːmərɪzəm; *NAmE* -'suː-/ *noun* [U] (sometimes *disapproving*) the buying and using of goods and services; the belief that it is good for a society or an individual person to buy and use a large quantity of goods and services 消費；消費主義（認為高消費對社會和個人有利）▸ **con·sumer·ist** *adj.*：*consumerist values* 消費主義的價值觀

con,sumer 'price index (*BrE* also **con,sumer 'prices index**) *noun* [sing.] (*abbr.* **CPI**) a list of the prices of some ordinary goods and services which shows how much these prices change each month 居民消費價格指數；消費價格指數 ➲ see also RETAIL PRICE INDEX

con·sum·ing /kən'sjuːmɪŋ; *NAmE* -'suː-/ *adj.* [only before noun] (of a feeling, an interest, etc. 感情、興趣等) so strong or important that it takes up all your time and energy 強烈的；重要的；令人着迷的：*Basketball is his consuming passion.* 籃球令他着迷。 ➲ see also ALL-CONSUMING, TIME-CONSUMING

con·sum·mate¹ /kən'sʌmət; 'kɒnsəmət; *NAmE* 'kɑːn-/ *adj.* [usually before noun] (*formal*) extremely skilled; perfect 技藝高超的；完美的：*She was a consummate performer.* 她是個技藝非凡的表演者。◇ *He played the shot with consummate skill.* 他以高超的技巧投球進籃。◇ (*disapproving*) *a consummate liar* 撒謊高手 ▸ **con·sum·mate·ly** *adv.*

con·sum·mate² /'kɒnsəmeɪt; *NAmE* 'kɑːn-/ *verb* (*formal*) **1 ~ sth** to make a marriage or a relationship complete by having sex（初次）行房；通過性交使（婚姻或兩人的關係）圓滿：*The marriage lasted only a week and was never consummated.* 那段婚姻僅維持了一星期，期間從未行房。**2 ~ sth** to make sth complete or perfect 使完整；使完美

con·sum·ma·tion /,kɒnsə'meɪʃn; *NAmE* ,kɑːn-/ *noun* [C, U] **1** the act of making a marriage or relationship complete by having sex（初次）行房；通過性交使婚姻或兩人關係圓滿 **2** the fact of making sth complete or perfect 完整；完美：*The paintings are the consummation of his life's work.* 這些畫是他畢生努力的完美結晶。

con·sump·tion AW /kən'sʌmpʃn/ *noun* [U] **1** the act of using energy, food or materials; the amount used（能量、食物或材料的）消耗，消耗量：*the production of fuel for* ***domestic consumption*** (= to be used in the country where it is produced) 供國內消耗的燃料生產 ◇ *Gas and oil consumption always increases in cold weather.* 燃氣和燃油的消耗量在天冷時總會增加。◇ *The meat was declared unfit for* ***human consumption***. 這種肉被宣佈不適於人食用。◇ *He was advised to reduce his alcohol consumption.* 他被勸告減少飲酒。◇ *Her speech to party members was not intended for* ***public consumption*** (= to be heard by the public). 她對黨員發表的講話並不打算公諸大眾。 ➲ see also CONSUME **2** the act of buying and using products 消費：*Consumption rather than saving has become the central feature of contemporary societies.* 現代社會的主要特徵是消費而不是儲蓄。 ➲ see also CONSPICUOUS CONSUMPTION, CONSUME **3** (*old-fashioned*) a serious infectious disease of the lungs 肺病；肺癆；肺結核 SYN **tuberculosis**

con·sump·tive /kən'sʌmptɪv/ *noun* (*old-fashioned*) a person who suffers from consumption (= a disease of the lungs) 肺癆（或肺結核）患者 ▸ **con·sump·tive** *adj.*

cont. (also **contd**) *abbr.* continued 繼續的；連續的：*cont. on p74* 下接第 74 頁

con·tact 🔑 AW /'kɒntækt; *NAmE* 'kɑːn-/ *noun, verb*

■ ***noun***

▸ **ACT OF COMMUNICATING** 聯繫 **1** 🔑 [U] **~ (with sb)** | **~ (between A and B)** the act of communicating with sb, especially regularly（尤指經常的）聯繫，聯絡：*I don't have much contact with my uncle.* 我和叔父甚少聯繫。◇ *There is little contact between the two organizations.* 這兩個機構相互之間沒有什麼聯繫。◇ *Have you kept* ***in contact with*** *any of your friends from college* (= do you still see them or speak or write to them)? 你和你大學裏的朋友還保持聯繫嗎？◇ *She's* ***lost contact with*** (= no longer sees or writes to) *her son.* 她和兒子失去了聯繫。◇ *I finally* ***made contact with*** (= succeeded in speaking to or meeting) *her in Paris.* 我最終在巴黎與她取得了聯繫。◇ *The organization* ***put me in contact with*** *other people in a similar position* (= gave me their addresses or telephone numbers). 這家機構為我提供了其他和我職務相若的人的聯繫方法。◇ *two people avoiding* ***eye contact*** (= avoiding looking directly at each other) 避免目光相遇的兩個人 ◇ *Here's my* ***contact number*** (= temporary telephone number) *while I'm away.* 這是我外出時的聯繫電話。◇ *I'll give you my* ***contact details*** (= telephone number, email address, etc.). 我會給你我的具體聯繫方式。

▸ **TOUCHING SB/STH** 接觸 **2** 🔑 [U] the state of touching sth 觸摸；接觸：*His fingers were briefly* ***in contact with*** *the ball.* 他的手指稍稍地碰了一下球。◇ *This substance should not* ***come into contact with*** *food.* 這種物質切莫與食物接觸。◇ *a fear of physical contact* 對身體接觸的恐懼感 ◇ *This pesticide kills insects* ***on contact*** (= as soon as it touches them). 這種殺蟲劑昆蟲一觸即死。

▸ **MEETING SB/STH** 遇到某人 / 事物 **3** 🔑 [U] the state of meeting sb or having to deal with sth 遇見（某人）；碰上（要處理的事）：*In her job she often* ***comes into contact with*** (= meets) *lawyers.* 她在工作中常與律師接觸。◇ *Children should be* ***brought into contact with*** *poetry at an early age.* 兒童應該在幼年接觸詩歌。

▸ **RELATIONSHIP** 關係 **4** 🔑 [C, usually pl.] an occasion on which you meet or communicate with sb; a relationship with sb 會見；交往；人際關係：*We have good contacts with the local community.* 我們與當地社區關係甚好。◇ *The company has maintained trade contacts with India.* 這家公司和印度一直保持着貿易往來。

▸ **PERSON** 人 **5** 🔑 [C] a person that you know, especially sb who can be helpful to you in your work 熟人；（尤指）社會關係：***social/personal contacts*** 社會上的 / 私下的熟人 ◇ *I've made some useful contacts in journalism.* 我在新聞界結交了一些有用的人。

▸ **ELECTRICAL** 電 **6** [C] an electrical connection（電流的）接觸，接通；接觸器：*The switches close the contacts and complete the circuit.* 這些開關可接通形成閉合電路。

▸ **FOR EYES** 眼睛 **7 contacts** [pl.] (*informal*) = CONTACT LENSES ➲ see also CONTACT LENS

▸ **MEDICAL** 醫學 **8** [C] a person who may be infectious because he or she has recently been near to sb with a CONTAGIOUS disease（與傳染病患者的）接觸者 IDM see POINT *n.*

■ ***verb*** 🔑 **~ sb** to communicate with sb, for example by telephone or letter 聯繫，聯絡（如用電話或信件）：*I've been trying to contact you all day.* 我整天一直在設法與你聯繫。▸ **con·tact·able** AW *adj.*：*I'll be contactable on this number: …* 這個號碼可以聯繫到我：…

'contact lens (also *informal* **con·tact, lens**) *noun* [usually pl.] a small round piece of thin plastic that you put on your eye to help you see better 隱形眼鏡片：*to* ***wear contact lenses*** 戴隱形眼鏡

C

C

ˈcontact sport *noun* a sport in which players have physical contact with each other 接觸式運動（運動員之間有身體接觸） OPP **non-contact sport**

con·ta·gion /kənˈteɪdʒən/ *noun* **1** [U] the spreading of a disease by people touching each other 接觸傳染：*There is no risk of contagion.* 沒有接觸傳染的風險。 **2** [C] (*old use*) a disease that can be spread by people touching each other 接觸性傳染病 **3** [C] (*formal*) something bad that spreads quickly by being passed from person to person（不良事物的快速）傳播，蔓延，擴散 ➲ compare INFECTION

con·ta·gious /kənˈteɪdʒəs/ *adj.* **1** a **contagious** disease spreads by people touching each other（疾病）接觸傳染的：*Scarlet fever is highly contagious.* 猩紅熱的接觸傳染性很強。◇ (*figurative*) *His enthusiasm was contagious* (= spread quickly to other people). 他的熱情富有感染力。◇ *a contagious laugh* 有感染力的笑聲 **2** [not usually before noun] if a person is **contagious**, they have a disease that can be spread to other people by touch 患接觸性傳染病 ➲ compare INFECTIOUS ▶ **con·ta·gious·ly** *adv.*

con·tain 0-w /kənˈteɪn/ *verb* (not used in the progressive tenses 不用於進行時) **1** 0-w **~ sth** if sth **contains** sth else, it has that thing inside it or as part of it 包含；含有；容納：*This drink doesn't contain any alcohol.* 這種飲料不含任何酒精。◇ *Her statement contained one or two inaccuracies.* 她的陳述有一兩處不準確。◇ *a brown envelope containing dollar bills* 裝有鈔票的棕色信封 ◇ *The bottle contains* (= can hold) *two litres.* 此瓶容量為兩升。 **2** to keep your feelings under control 控制，克制，抑制（感情） SYN **restrain**：**~ sth** *She was unable to contain her excitement.* 她無法抑制內心的激動。◇ **~ yourself** *I was so furious I just couldn't* ***contain myself*** (= I had to express my feelings). 我氣憤極了，簡直無法克制自己。 **3 ~ sth** to prevent sth harmful from spreading or getting worse 防止…蔓延（或惡化）：*to contain an epidemic* 防止流行病的蔓延 ◇ *Government forces have failed to contain the rebellion.* 政府軍未能遏止叛亂。

con·tain·er 0-w /kənˈteɪnə(r)/ *noun* **1** 0-w a box, bottle, etc. in which sth can be stored or transported 容器：*Food will last longer if kept in an airtight container.* 如果貯藏在密封的容器裏，食物能保存比較久的時間。 **2** a large metal or wooden box of a standard size in which goods are packed so that they can easily be lifted onto a ship, train, etc. to be transported 集裝箱；貨櫃：*a container ship* (= one designed to transport such containers) 集裝箱船 ➲ VISUAL VOCAB page V54

con·tain·er·ized /kənˈteɪnəraɪzd/ *adj.* packed and transported in CONTAINERS (2) 集裝箱裝運的；貨櫃裝運的：*containerized cargo* 集裝箱載運的貨物 ▶ **con·tain·er·iz·ation** /kənˌteɪnəraɪˈzeɪʃn/ *noun* [U]

con·tain·ment /kənˈteɪnmənt/ *noun* [U] (*formal*) **1** the act of keeping sth under control so that it cannot spread in a harmful way 控制；抑制：*the containment of the epidemic* 對流行病的控制 **2** the act of keeping another country's power within limits so that it does not become too powerful（對另一個國家力量的）遏制：*a policy of containment* 遏制政策

con·tam·in·ant /kənˈtæmɪnənt/ *noun* (*technical* 術語) a substance that makes sth IMPURE 致污物；污染物：*Filters do not remove all contaminants from water.* 過濾器無法過濾掉水中的所有污染物。

con·tam·in·ate /kənˈtæmɪneɪt/ *verb* **1 ~ sth** (**with sth**) to make a substance or place dirty or no longer pure by adding a substance that is dangerous or carries disease 污染；弄髒 SYN **adulterate**：*The drinking water has become contaminated with lead.* 飲用水被鉛污染了。◇ ***contaminated blood/food/soil*** 受到污染的血液／食物／土壤 **2 ~ sth** (*formal*) to influence people's ideas or attitudes in a bad way 玷污，毒害，腐蝕（人的思想或品德）：*They were accused of contaminating the minds of our young people.* 他們被指控毒害我們青少年的心靈。 ➲ see also UNCONTAMINATED ▶ **con·tam·in·ation** /kənˌtæmɪˈneɪʃn/ *noun* [U]：*radioactive contamination* 放射性污染 ➲ see also CROSS-CONTAMINATION

contd *abbr.* = CONT.

con·tem·plate /ˈkɒntəmpleɪt; *NAmE* ˈkɑːn-/ *verb* **1** [T] to think about whether you should do sth, or how you should do sth 考慮；思量；思忖 SYN **consider, think about/of**：**~ sth** *You're too young to be contemplating retirement.* 你考慮退休還太年輕。◇ **~ doing sth** *I have never contemplated living abroad.* 我從未考慮過去國外居住。◇ **~ how/what, etc. …** *He continued while she contemplated how to answer.* 她還在考慮如何回答時，他就繼續往下說了。 **2** [T] to think carefully about and accept the possibility of sth happening 考慮接受（發生某事的可能性）：**~ sth** *The thought of war is too awful to contemplate.* 戰爭太可怕了，真不敢去想。◇ **~ how/what, etc. …** *I can't contemplate what it would be like to be alone.* 我不能想像獨自一人會是個什麼樣子。◇ **~ that …** *She contemplated that things might get even worse.* 她想到事情可能會變得更糟。 **3** [T, I] **~ (sth)** (*formal*) to think deeply about sth for a long time 深思熟慮；沉思；苦思冥想：*to contemplate your future* 仔細盤算未來 ◇ *She lay in bed, contemplating.* 她躺在牀上冥思苦想。 **4** [T] **~ sb/sth** (*formal*) to look at sb/sth in a careful way for a long time 端詳；打量 SYN **stare at**：*She contemplated him in silence.* 她默默地注視着他。

con·tem·pla·tion /ˌkɒntəmˈpleɪʃn; *NAmE* ˌkɑːn-/ *noun* [U] (*formal*) **1** the act of thinking deeply about sth 深思；沉思：*He sat there deep in contemplation.* 他坐在那裏沉思着。◇ *a few moments of quiet contemplation* 默默沉思的片刻 ◇ *a life of prayer and contemplation* 祈禱與冥思的生活 **2** the act of looking at sth in a calm and careful way 凝視；默默注視：*She turned from her contemplation of the photograph.* 她從凝視着的那張照片上移開目光。

IDM **in contemˈplation** (*formal*) being considered 考慮中：*By 1613 even more desperate measures were in contemplation.* 到 1613 年，甚至考慮要採取更為孤注一擲的措施。

con·tem·pla·tive /kənˈtemplətɪv/ *adj.* (*formal*) **1** thinking quietly and seriously about sth 沉思默想的；深思熟慮的：*She was in contemplative mood.* 她陷入沉思之中。 **2** spending time thinking deeply about religious matters（對宗教問題）冥想的，斂心默禱的：*the contemplative life* (= life in a religious community) 宗教上的默觀生活

con·tem·por·an·eous /kənˌtempəˈreɪniəs/ *adj.* **~ (with sb/sth)** (*formal*) happening or existing at the same time 同時發生（或存在）的；同時期的；同時代的 SYN **contemporary**：*How do we know that the signature is contemporaneous with the document?* 我們怎樣才能知道這個簽字和文件是同一個時間的呢？◇ ***contemporaneous events/accounts*** 同一時期的事情／記述 ▶ **con·tem·por·an·eous·ly** *adv.*

con·tem·por·ary 0-w AW /kənˈtemprəri; *NAmE* -pəreri/ *adj.*, *noun*

■ *adj.* **1** 0-w **~ (with sb/sth)** belonging to the same time 屬同時期的；同一時代的：*We have no contemporary account of the battle* (= written near the time that it happened). 我們沒有當時人們對這一戰役的記載。◇ *He was contemporary with the dramatist Congreve.* 他與劇作家康格里夫屬於同一時代。 **2** 0-w belonging to the present time 當代的；現代的 SYN **modern**：*life in contemporary Britain* 當代英國的生活 ◇ ***contemporary fiction/music/dance*** 當代小說／音樂／舞蹈

■ *noun* (*pl.* **-ies**) a person who lives or lived at the same time as sb else, especially sb who is about the same age 同代人；同輩人；同齡人：*She and I were contemporaries at college.* 她和我在大學是同學。◇ *He was a contemporary of Freud and may have known him.* 他是弗洛伊德的同代人，可能認識弗洛伊德。

con·tempt /kənˈtempt/ *noun* [U, sing.] **1** the feeling that sb/sth is without value and deserves no respect at all 蔑視；輕蔑；鄙視：*She looked at him* ***with contempt.*** 她輕蔑地看着他。◇ *I shall treat that suggestion with the contempt it deserves.* 我對那項建議當然會不屑一顧。◇ *His treatment of his children is* ***beneath contempt*** (= so unacceptable that it is not even worth feeling contempt for). 他對待自己子女的那種行徑為人所不齒。◇ *Politicians* seem to be generally **held in contempt** by ordinary people. 一般百姓似乎普遍看不起從政者。◇ **~ for sb/sth** *They had shown a contempt for the values she thought important.* 他們對她所認為重要的價值表示蔑視。 **2 ~ for sth** a lack of worry or fear about rules, danger, etc. （對規則、危險等的）藐視，不顧：*The firefighters showed a contempt for their own safety.* 那些消防隊員已把他們自己的安全置之度外。◇ *His remarks betray a staggering contempt for the truth* (= are completely false). 他的話表明他完全無視事情的真相。 **3** = CONTEMPT OF COURT：*He could be jailed for two years for contempt.* 他由於藐視法庭可能被監禁兩年。◇ *She was held **in contempt** for refusing to testify.* 她因拒絕作證而被判藐視法庭罪。 IDM see FAMILIARITY

con·tempt·ible /kən'temptəbl/ *adj.* (*formal*) not deserving any respect at all 可輕蔑的；可鄙的；卑劣的 SYN **despicable**：*contemptible behaviour* 卑劣的行為

con,tempt of 'court (also **con·tempt**) *noun* [U] the crime of refusing to obey an order made by a court; not showing respect for a court or judge 藐視法庭（罪）：*Any person who disregards this order will be in contempt of court.* 凡漠視本法令者將被判藐視法庭罪。

con·temp·tu·ous /kən'temptʃuəs/ *adj.* feeling or showing that you have no respect for sb/sth 蔑視的；鄙視的；表示輕蔑的 SYN **scornful**：*She gave him a contemptuous look.* 她鄙夷地看了他一眼。◇ **~ of sb/sth** *He was contemptuous of everything I did.* 他看不起我做的一切。 ▸ **con·temp·tu·ous·ly** *adv.*：*to laugh contemptuously* 輕蔑地大笑

con·tend /kən'tend/ *verb* **1** [T] **~ that ...** (*formal*) to say that sth is true, especially in an argument（尤指在爭論中）聲稱，主張，認為 SYN **maintain**：*I would contend that the minister's thinking is flawed on this point.* 我倒認為部長的想法在這一點上有漏洞。 **2** [I] **~ (for sth)** to compete against sb in order to gain sth 競爭；爭奪：*Three armed groups were contending for power.* 三個武裝集團在爭奪權力。

PHR V **con'tend with sth/sb** to have to deal with a problem or with a difficult situation or person（不得不）應付，處理，對付：*Nurses often have to contend with violent or drunken patients.* 護士經常不得不應付粗暴的或喝醉酒的病人。

con·tend·er /kən'tendə(r)/ *noun* a person who takes part in a competition or tries to win sth 競爭者；角逐者；爭奪者：*a contender for a gold medal in the Olympics* 奧運金牌的爭奪者 ◇ *a **leading/serious/strong contender** for the party leadership* 該黨領導權最重要的／強勁的／有實力的角逐者

con·tent¹ 🔑 /'kɒntent; *NAmE* 'kɑːn-/ *noun* ➲ see also CONTENT² **1** 🔑 **contents** [pl.] the things that are contained in sth 所容納之物；所含之物；內容：*He tipped the contents of the bag onto the table.* 他把提包裏的東西倒在桌子上。◇ *Fire has caused severe damage to the contents of the building.* 大火導致那棟大樓裏的東西嚴重損毀。◇ *She hadn't read the letter and so was unaware of its contents.* 她沒有看過那封信，所以對其內容一無所知。 **2** 🔑 **contents** [pl.] the different sections that are contained in a book（書的）目錄，目次：*a table of contents* (= the list at the front of a book) 目錄 ◇ *a contents page* 目錄頁 **3** 🔑 [sing.] the subject matter of a book, speech, programme, etc.（書、講話、節目等的）主題，主要內容：*Your tone of voice is as important as the content of what you have to say.* 你的講話聲調和你要講的內容同樣重要。◇ *The content of the course depends on what the students would like to study.* 課程的內容取決於學生願意學什麼。◇ *Her poetry has a good deal of political content.* 她的詩歌包含大量的政治內容。 **4** 🔑 [sing.] (following a noun 用於名詞後) the amount of a substance that is contained in sth else 含量；容量：*food with a high fat content* 脂肪含量高的食物 ◇ *the alcohol content of a drink* 飲料的酒精含量 **5** [U] (*computing* 計) the information or other material contained on a website or CD-ROM（網站或只讀光盤上的）內容，目錄：*online content providers* 網絡內容提供商

con·tent² /kən'tent/ *adj.*, *verb*, *noun* ➲ see also CONTENT¹

■ ***adj.*** [not before noun] **1 ~ (with sth)** happy and satisfied with what you have 滿意；滿足：*Not content with stealing my boyfriend* (= not thinking that this was enough), *she has turned all my friends against me.* 她奪走了我的男朋友還不滿足，又挑起我所有的朋友和我作對。◇ *He seemed more content, less bitter.* 他看起來比較滿意，不那麼失望。◇ *He had to be content with third place.* 他只好屈居第三名。 ➲ SYNONYMS at HAPPY **2 ~ to do sth** willing to do sth 願意：*I was content to wait.* 我願意等候。 ➲ compare CONTENTED

■ ***verb* 1 ~ yourself with sth** to accept and be satisfied with sth and not try to have or do sth better 滿足；滿意；知足：*Martina contented herself with a bowl of soup.* 馬蒂娜喝了一碗湯就心滿意足了。 **2 ~ sb** (*formal*) to make sb feel happy or satisfied 使滿意；使滿足：*My apology seemed to content him.* 我的道歉好像使他感到滿意。

■ ***noun*** = CONTENTMENT IDM see HEART

con·tent·ed /kən'tentɪd/ *adj.* [usually before noun] showing or feeling happiness or satisfaction, especially because your life is good（尤指因生活好而）滿意的，愜意的，滿足的：*a contented smile* 愜意的微笑 ◇ *He was a contented man.* 他是個心滿意足的人。 ➲ compare CONTENT² *adj.* OPP **discontented** ➲ SYNONYMS at HAPPY ▸ **con·tent·ed·ly** *adv.*：*She smiled contentedly.* 她心滿意足地笑了。

con·ten·tion /kən'tenʃn/ *noun* (*formal*) **1** [U] angry disagreement between people 爭吵；爭執；爭論 SYN **dispute**：*One area of contention is the availability of nursery care.* 爭論的一個方面是提供幼兒保育的可能性。◇ *a point of contention* 爭論點 **2** [C] **~ (that ...)** a belief or an opinion that you express, especially in an argument（尤指爭論時的）看法，觀點：*It is our client's contention that the fire was an accident.* 我們當事人的看法是這場火災屬於事故。◇ *I would reject that contention.* 我不會同意那種觀點。

IDM **in con'tention (for sth)** with a chance of winning sth 有機會贏得：*Only three teams are now in contention for the title.* 現在只有三個隊有機會奪冠。 **out of con'tention (for sth)** without a chance of winning sth 沒有機會贏得 ➲ more at BONE *n.*

con·ten·tious /kən'tenʃəs/ *adj.* (*formal*) **1** likely to cause disagreement between people 可能引起爭論的：*a **contentious issue/topic/subject*** 有爭議的問題／話題／主題 ◇ *Both views are highly contentious.* 兩種觀點都很有爭議。 OPP **uncontentious 2** liking to argue; involving a lot of arguing 愛爭論的；好爭吵的：*a contentious meeting* 爭論不休的會議

con·tent·ment /kən'tentmənt/ (also *less frequent* **con·tent**) *noun* [U] a feeling of happiness or satisfaction 滿意；滿足：*He has found contentment at last.* 他最終得到了滿足。◇ *a sigh of contentment* 滿足地舒一口氣 ➲ compare DISCONTENT ➲ SYNONYMS at SATISFACTION

'content word *noun* (*linguistics* 語言) a noun, verb, adjective or adverb whose main function is to express meaning 實義詞；實詞 ➲ compare FUNCTION WORD

con·test 🔑 *noun*, *verb*

■ ***noun*** /'kɒntest; *NAmE* 'kɑːn-/ **1** 🔑 a competition in which people try to win sth 比賽；競賽：*a singing contest* 歌詠比賽 ◇ *a talent contest* 新秀大獎賽 ◇ *to **enter/win/lose a contest*** 參加／贏得競賽；競賽失敗 ➲ see also BEAUTY CONTEST **2** 🔑 **~ (for sth)** a struggle to gain control or power（控制權或權力的）爭奪，競爭：*a contest for the leadership of the party* 爭奪政黨的領導權

IDM **be ,no 'contest** used to say that one side in a competition is so much stronger or better than the other that it is sure to win easily（表示競爭中的一方過於強大或出色）完全不是對手，毫無競爭可言

■ ***verb*** /kən'test/ **1 ~ sth** to take part in a competition, election, etc. and try to win it 爭取贏得（比賽、選舉等）：*Three candidates contested the leadership.* 有三位候選人角逐領導權。◇ *a **hotly/fiercely/keenly contested** game* (= one in which the players try very hard to win and the scores are close) 競爭十分激烈的比賽 **2 ~ sth** to formally oppose a decision or statement because you think it is wrong 爭辯；提出異議：*to contest a will* (= try to show that it was not correctly made in law)

C

對遺囑提出質疑 ◇ *The divorce was not contested.* 這樁離婚案沒有人提出異議。

con·test·ant /kən'testənt/ *noun* a person who takes part in a contest 參賽者；競爭者：*Please welcome our next contestant.* 請歡迎我們的下一位競賽選手。

con·text 0━ AW /'kɒntekst; *NAmE* 'kɑːn-/ *noun* [C, U] **1** 0━ the situation in which sth happens and that helps you to understand it （事情發生的）背景，環境，來龍去脈：*This speech needs to be set* ***in the context of*** *Britain in the 1960s.* 這篇演說需要放到 20 世紀 60 年代的英國這一背景之下來看待。◇ *His decision can only be understood* ***in context.*** 只有瞭解來龍去脈才能明白他的決定。 **2** 0━ the words that come just before and after a word, phrase or statement and help you to understand its meaning 上下文；語境：*You should be able to guess the meaning of the word from the context.* 你應該能從上下文猜出這個詞的含義。◇ *This quotation has been taken* ***out of context*** (= repeated without giving the circumstances in which it was said). 這段引語是斷章取義。

con·text·ual AW /kən'tekstʃuəl/ *adj.* (*formal*) connected with a particular context 上下文的；與上下文有關的；與語境相關的：*contextual information* 與上下文有關的信息 ◇ *contextual clues to the meaning* 對理解此義的上下文線索 ▸ **con·text·ual·ly** *adv.*

con·text·ual·ize (*BrE* also **-ise**) AW /kən'tekstʃuəlaɪz/ *verb* **~ sth** (*formal*) to consider sth in relation to the situation in which it happens or exists 將…置於背景中考慮；將…置於上下文中理解 ▸ **con·text·ual·iza·tion**, **-isa·tion** /kən,tekstʃuəlaɪ'zeɪʃn/ *noun* [U]

con·tigu·ous /kən'tɪgjuəs/ *adj.* (*formal* or *technical* 術語) touching or next to sth 相接的；相鄰的：*The countries are contiguous.* 這些國家互相接壤。◇ **~ with/to sth** *The bruising was not contiguous to the wound.* 這青腫塊不在傷口邊上。 ▸ **con·tigu·ity** /,kɒntɪ'gjuːəti; *NAmE* ,kɑːn-/ *noun* [U]

con·tin·ence /'kɒntɪnəns; *NAmE* 'kɑːn-/ *noun* [U] **1** (*formal*) the control of your feelings, especially your desire to have sex（感情的）節制，自制；（尤指）性慾的節制 **2** the ability to control the BLADDER and BOWELS（大小便的）自控能力，節制力 OPP **incontinence** ▸ **con·tin·ent** /'kɒntɪnənt; *NAmE* 'kɑːn-/ *adj.* OPP **incontinent**

con·tin·ent 0━ /'kɒntɪnənt; *NAmE* 'kɑːn-/ *noun* **1** 0━ [C] one of the large land masses of the earth such as Europe, Asia or Africa 大陸；陸地；洲：*the continent of Africa* 非洲大陸 ◇ *the African continent* 非洲大陸 **2 the Continent** [sing.] (*BrE*) the main part of the continent of Europe, not including Britain or Ireland 歐洲大陸（不包括英國和愛爾蘭）：*We're going to spend a weekend on the Continent.* 我們要去歐洲大陸度週末。

con·tin·en·tal /,kɒntɪ'nentl; *NAmE* ,kɑːn-/ *adj., noun*
■ *adj.* **1** (also **Continental**) [only before noun] (*BrE*) of or in the continent of Europe, not including Britain and Ireland 歐洲大陸的（不包括英國和愛爾蘭）：*a popular continental holiday resort* 受歡迎的歐洲大陸度假勝地 ◇ *Britain's continental neighbours* 英國的歐洲大陸鄰國 **2** (*BrE*) following the customs of countries in western and southern Europe 隨（西、南歐國家）大陸風俗的：*a continental lifestyle* 西、南歐大陸的生活方式 ◇ *The shutters and the balconies make the street look almost continental.* 活動護窗和陽台使這條街看起來頗具歐洲大陸風格。 **3** [only before noun] connected with the main part of the N American continent 北美大陸的：*Prices are often higher in Hawaii than in the continental United States.* 夏威夷的物價常常比美國大陸高。 **4** forming part of, or typical of, any of the seven main land masses of the earth 大洲的；大陸的：*continental Antarctica/Asia/Europe* 南極洲／亞洲／歐洲大陸 ◇ *to study continental geography* 研究大陸地理學
■ *noun* (*BrE, old-fashioned*, often *disapproving*) a person who lives in the continent of Europe（歐洲）大陸人：*The continentals have never understood our preference for warm beer.* 歐洲大陸人根本不理解我們為什麼喜歡喝溫啤酒。

,continental 'breakfast *noun* a light breakfast, usually consisting of coffee and bread rolls with butter and jam 歐陸式早餐，簡易早餐（通常包括咖啡和黃油果醬圓麵包）➲ compare ENGLISH BREAKFAST

,continental 'climate *noun* a fairly dry pattern of weather with very hot summers and very cold winters, that is typical of the central regions of the US, Canada and Russia, for example 大陸（性）氣候

,continental 'drift *noun* [U] (*geology* 地) the slow movement of the continents towards and away from each other during the history of the earth 大陸漂移 ➲ see also PLATE TECTONICS

,continental 'quilt *noun* (*BrE*) = DUVET

,continental 'shelf *noun* [usually sing.] (*geology* 地) the area of land on the edge of a continent that slopes into the ocean 大陸架；大陸棚

,continental 'slope *noun* [sing.] (*geology* 地) the steep surface that goes down from the outer edge of the continental shelf to the ocean floor 大陸坡

con·tin·gency /kən'tɪndʒənsi/ *noun* (*pl.* **-ies**) an event that may or may not happen 可能發生的事；偶發（或不測、意外）事件 SYN **possibility**：*We must consider all possible contingencies.* 我們必須考慮一切可能發生的事。◇ *to make* ***contingency plans*** (= plans for what to do if a particular event happens or does not happen) 擬訂應變計劃 ◇ *a* ***contingency fund*** (= to pay for sth that might happen in the future) 意外開支準備金

con'tingency fee *noun* (in the US) an amount of money that is paid to a lawyer only if the person he or she is advising wins in court（美國）成功酬金（勝訴才付給律師）

con·tin·gent /kən'tɪndʒənt/ *noun, adj.*
■ *noun* [C+sing./pl. v.] **1** a group of people at a meeting or an event who have sth in common, especially the place they come from, that is not shared by other people at the event（志趣相投、尤指來自同一地方的）一組與會者，代表團：*The largest contingent was from the United States.* 最大的會議代表團來自美國。◇ *A strong contingent of local residents were there to block the proposal.* 由當地居民組成的強大的代表團在那裏阻止通過這項提案。 **2** a group of soldiers that are part of a larger force（軍隊的）分遣隊，小分隊：*the French contingent in the UN peacekeeping force* 聯合國維和部隊的法國分隊
■ *adj.* **1 ~ (on/upon sth)** (*formal*) depending on sth that may or may not happen 依情況而定的：*All payments are contingent upon satisfactory completion dates.* 所有的付款須視乎是否如期完成。 **2 ~ worker/work/job** (*business* 商) a person, or work done by a person, who does not have a permanent contract with a company 臨時工；臨時工作：*the spread of contingent work throughout the economy* 臨時工作在整個經濟領域的擴展 ▸ **con·tin·gent·ly** *adv.*

con·tin·ual /kən'tɪnjuəl/ *adj.* [only before noun] **1** repeated many times in a way that is annoying（令人厭煩地）多次重複的，頻繁的：***continual complaints/interruptions*** 不停的抱怨／打擾 **2** continuing without interruption 接連不斷的；連續的；頻頻的 SYN **continuous**：*He was in a continual process of rewriting his material.* 他一直在不斷地改寫他的材料。◇ *We lived in continual fear of being discovered.* 我們長期生活在害怕被發現的恐懼中。◇ *Her daughter was a continual source of delight to her.* 她的女兒是她無限快樂的源泉。➲ note at CONTINUOUS ▸ **con·tinu·al·ly** /-juəli/ *adv.*：*They argue continually about money.* 他們沒完沒了地為錢爭吵。◇ *the need to adapt to new and continually changing circumstances* 需要適應又新又不斷變化的情況 ◇ *New products are continually being developed.* 新產品正源源不斷地開發出來。

con·tinu·ance /kən'tɪnjuəns/ *noun* **1** [U] (*formal*) the state of continuing to exist or function 繼續；持續：*We can no longer support the President's continuance in office.* 我們不能再支持總統繼續任職。 **2** [C] (*NAmE, law* 律) a decision that a court case should be heard later 延期審理：*The judge refused his motion for a continuance.* 法官拒絕他要求延期審理的動議。

con·tinu·ant /kən'tɪnjuənt/ *noun* (*phonetics* 語音) a consonant that is pronounced with the breath passing through the throat, so that the sound can be continued. /f/, /l/ and /m/ are examples of continuants. 延續音 ▶ **con·tinu·ant** *adj.* [only before noun] : *continuant consonants* 延續輔音

con·tinu·ation /kənˌtɪnjuˈeɪʃn/ *noun* **1** [U, sing.] an act or the state of continuing 繼續；連續；持續： *They are anxious to ensure the continuation of the economic reform programme.* 他們渴望經濟改革計劃一定要持續下去。◇ **~ in sth** *This year saw a continuation in the upward trend in sales.* 今年銷售呈持續增長的趨勢。 **2** [C] something that continues or follows sth else 延續部份；續篇： *Her new book is a continuation of her autobiography.* 她的新書是她自傳的續篇。 **3** [C] something that is joined on to sth else and forms a part of it 附加物；延續物： *There are plans to build a continuation of the bypass next year.* 已有計劃明年修建這條支路的延伸線。

con·tinue /kənˈtɪnjuː/ *verb*
1 [I, T] to keep existing or happening without stopping 持續；繼續存在；不斷發生： *The exhibition continues until 25 July.* 展覽舉行至 7 月 25 日為止。◇ *The trial is expected to continue for three months.* 預計審判要持續三個月。◇ **~ to do sth** *The rain continued to fall all afternoon.* 這場雨整整一下午都下個不停。◇ **~ doing sth** *The rain continued falling all afternoon.* 這場雨整整一下午都下個不停。 **2** [I, T] to keep doing sth without stopping 繼續做；不停地幹： **~ doing sth** *She wanted to continue working until she was 60.* 她想要繼續工作到 60 歲。◇ **~ to do sth** *He continued to ignore everything I was saying.* 他仍對我所說的一切置若罔聞。◇ **~ (with sth)** *Are you going to continue with the project?* 你要繼續做這個項目嗎？◇ **~ sth** *The board of inquiry is continuing its investigations.* 調查委員會在繼續做調查。 **3** [I] (+ **adv./prep.**) to go or move further in the same direction （朝相同方向）走，移動；延伸： *The path continued over rough, rocky ground.* 這條小路穿過了崎嶇不平的石頭地。◇ *He continued on his way.* 他繼續走他的路。 **4** [I] **~ (as sth)** to remain in a particular job or condition 留任；維持原狀： *I want you to continue as project manager.* 我要你留任項目經理。◇ *She will continue in her present job until a replacement can be found.* 在找到替換人員以前，她將繼續做她目前的工作。 **5** [I, T] to start or start sth again after stopping for a time （停頓後）繼續，再開始 SYN **resume**： *The story continues in our next issue.* 這篇故事我們將在下一期裏繼續刊載。◇ **~ sth** *The story will be continued in our next issue.* 這篇故事我們將在下一期裏繼續刊載。 **6** [I, T] to start speaking again after stopping （停頓後）繼續說，接着說： *Please continue—I didn't mean to interrupt.* 請繼續往下說，我並非有意打斷你的話。◇ **+ speech** *'In fact,' he continued, 'I'd like to congratulate you.'* "其實，" 他接着說， "我想向你表示祝賀。"

con·tinued /kənˈtɪnjuːd/ (also **con·tinu·ing** /kənˈtɪnjuɪŋ/) *adj.* [only before noun] existing in the same state without change or interruption 繼續不變的；連續不斷的： *We are grateful for your* ***continued/continuing support.*** 我們對你們始終不渝的支持不勝感激。◇ *continued interest* 持久的興趣 ◇ *continuing involvement* 不斷的參與

conˌtinuing eduˈcation *noun* [U] = ADULT EDUCATION

con·tinu·ity /ˌkɒntɪˈnjuːəti; *NAmE* ˌkɑːntəˈnuː-/ *noun* (*pl.* **-ies**) **1** [U] the fact of not stopping or not changing 連續性；持續性：*to* ***ensure/provide/maintain continuity*** *of fuel supplies* 確保 / 提供 / 保持燃料供給的連續性 OPP **discontinuity** **2** [U, C] a logical connection between the parts of sth, or between two things （邏輯上的）連接，聯結： *The novel fails to achieve narrative continuity.* 這部小說敍述不連貫。◇ *There are obvious continuities between diet and health.* 日常飲食與健康之間有着明顯的邏輯關聯。 OPP **discontinuity** **3** [U] (*technical* 術語) the organization of a film/movie or television programme, especially making sure that people's clothes, objects, etc. are the same from one scene to the next （電影或電視節目場景中服裝、物體等的）一致性，銜接

con·tinuo /kənˈtɪnjuəʊ; *NAmE* -juoʊ/ *noun* [U] (*music* 音) (from *Italian*) a musical part played to accompany another instrument, in which a line of low notes is shown with figures to represent the higher notes to be played above them 數字低音；通奏低音： *a trio for two violins and continuo* 兩小提琴與通奏低音三重奏

con·tinu·ous /kənˈtɪnjuəs/ *adj.*
1 happening or existing for a period of time without interruption 不斷的；持續的；連續的： *She was in continuous employment until the age of sixty-five.* 她連續不斷地受雇於人，一直工作到 65 歲。◇ *The rain has been continuous since this morning.* 從早上到現在這雨就沒停過。 **2** spreading in a line or over an area without any spaces 延伸的；遍佈的： *a continuous line of traffic* 絡繹不絕的車輛 **3** (*informal*) repeated many times 反複的；頻繁的 SYN **continual**： *For four days the town suffered continuous attacks.* 那座市鎮連續四天遭到了襲擊。 HELP **Continual** is much more frequent in this meaning. 此義更多用 continual。 **4** (*grammar* 語法) = PROGRESSIVE *adj.* (3)：*the continuous tenses* 進行時態 ▶ **con·tinu·ous·ly** *adv.*： *He has lived and worked in France almost continuously since 1990.* 自從 1990 年以來，他差不多一直在法國居住和工作。

Synonyms 同義詞辨析

continuous / continual

These adjectives are frequently used with the following nouns. 這兩個形容詞常與下列名詞連用：

continuous ~	**continual ~**
process	change
employment	problems
flow	updating
line	questions
speech	pain
supply	fear

- **Continuous** describes something that continues without stopping. * continuous 指持續的、不間斷的。
- **Continual** usually describes an action that is repeated again and again. * continual 通常指一再重複。
- The difference between these two words is now disappearing. In particular, **continual** can also mean the same as **continuous** and is used especially about undesirable things. 上述兩詞的差異正逐漸消失，特別是 continual 亦含有與 continuous 相同的意義，尤指不希望發生的事： *Life was a continual struggle for them.* 生活對他們來說就是不斷的掙扎。 However, **continuous** is much more frequent in this sense. 不過，用 continuous 表達此義常見得多。

conˌtinuous asˈsessment *noun* [U] (*BrE*) a system of giving a student a final mark/grade based on work done during a course of study rather than on one exam 連續性評定（學生的最後成績不只根據一次考試而且根據課程作業）

con·tinuum /kənˈtɪnjuəm/ *noun* (*pl.* **con·tinua** /-juə/) a series of similar items in which each is almost the same as the ones next to it but the last is very different from the first （相鄰兩者相似但起首與末尾截然不同的）連續體 SYN **cline**： *It is impossible to say at what point along the continuum a dialect becomes a separate language.* 要說出同一語言的方言差異到什麼程度才成為一種別的語言是不可能的。

con·tort /kənˈtɔːt; *NAmE* -ˈtɔːrt/ *verb* [I, T] to become twisted or make sth twisted out of its natural or normal shape （使）扭曲，走樣： *His face contorted with anger.* 他臉都氣歪了。◇ **~ sth** *Her mouth was contorted in a snarl.* 她齜牙咧嘴地怒吼着。 ▶ **con·tort·ed** *adj.*： ***contorted limbs/bodies*** 扭曲的四肢 / 軀體 ◇ (*figurative*) *It was a contorted version of the truth.* 這是對事實的歪曲。

C

con·tor·tion /kən'tɔːʃn; *NAmE* -'tɔːrʃn/ *noun* **1** [U] the state of the face or body being twisted out of its natural shape（臉部或軀體的）扭曲，變形，走樣：*Their bodies had suffered contortion as a result of malnutrition.* 由於營養不良他們的軀體都變了形。**2** [C] a movement which twists the body out of its natural shape 扭曲的動作（或姿勢）：*His facial contortions amused the audience of schoolchildren.* 他扮鬼臉逗得小學生觀眾都笑起來了。◇ (*figurative*) *We had to go through all the usual contortions* (= a difficult series of actions) *to get a ticket.* 我們照例得費盡心機才能弄到一張票。

con·tor·tion·ist /kən'tɔːʃənɪst; *NAmE* -'tɔːrʃ-/ *noun* a performer who does contortions of their body to entertain others 柔體雜技演員

con·tour /'kɒntʊə(r); *NAmE* 'kɑːntʊr/ *noun* **1** the outer edges of sth; the outline of its shape or form 外形；輪廓：*The road follows the natural contours of the coastline.* 這條路沿着海岸線的自然輪廓延伸。◇ *She traced the contours of his face with her finger.* 她用手指摸遍了他臉部的輪廓。**2** (also **'contour line**) a line on a map that joins points that are the same height above sea level（地圖上連接相同海拔各點的）等高線：*a contour map* (= a map that includes these lines) 等高線地圖

con·toured /'kɒntʊəd; *NAmE* 'kɑːntʊrd/ *adj.* **1** with a specially designed outline that makes sth attractive or comfortable 外形設計獨特的：*It is smoothly contoured to look like a racing car.* 這輛車外形設計流暢，看起來像賽車。**2** having or showing contours (2) 標示等高線的：**contoured hills/maps** 標有等高線的山巒／地圖

contra- /'kɒntrə; *NAmE* 'kɑːntrə/ *combining form* **1** (in nouns, verbs and adjectives 構成名詞、動詞和形容詞) against; opposite 反對；相反：*contraflow* 一側雙向行駛 ◇ *contradict* 反駁 **2** (in nouns 構成名詞) (*music* 音) having a PITCH an OCTAVE below 聲音低八度的：*a contrabassoon* 低音大管

con·tra·band /'kɒntrəbænd; *NAmE* 'kɑːn-/ *noun* [U] goods that are illegally taken into or out of a country（非法帶入或帶出國境的）禁運品，走私貨：*contraband goods* 違禁貨物 ◇ *to smuggle contraband* 走私違禁品

con·tra·cep·tion /ˌkɒntrə'sepʃn; *NAmE* ˌkɑːn-/ *noun* [U] the practice of preventing a woman from becoming pregnant; the methods of doing this 避孕（法）；節育（法）**SYN** **birth control**：*to give advice about contraception* 就避孕方法提供咨詢

con·tra·cep·tive /ˌkɒntrə'septɪv; *NAmE* ˌkɑːn-/ *noun* a drug, device or practice used to prevent a woman becoming pregnant 避孕藥；避孕用具；避孕措施：*oral contraceptives* 口服避孕藥 ▸ **con·tra·cep·tive** *adj.* [only before noun]：*a contraceptive pill* 避孕藥丸 ◇ *contraceptive advice/precautions/methods* 避孕咨詢／措施／方法

con·tract 0-w **AW** *noun, verb*

▪ **noun** /'kɒntrækt; *NAmE* 'kɑːn-/ **1** 0-w an official written agreement 合同；合約；契約：*a contract of employment* 雇用合同 ◇ *a research contract* 從事研究的合同 ◇ **~ with sb** *to* **enter into/make/sign a contract** *with the supplier* 與供應商簽訂合同 ◇ **~ between A and B** *These clauses form part of the contract between buyer and seller.* 這些條款構成買賣雙方所簽合同的一部份。◇ **~ for sth** *a contract for the supply of vehicles* 提供車輛的合約 ◇ **~ to do sth** *to* **win/be awarded a contract** *to build a new school* 獲得承建一所新學校的合同 ◇ *a* **contract worker** (= one employed on a contract for a fixed period of time) 合同工 ◇ *I was* **on a** *three-year* **contract** *that expired last week.* 我簽訂的三年期合同已於上週期滿。◇ **Under the terms of the contract** *the job should have been finished yesterday.* 根據合同的條款，這項工作本應於昨天完成。◇ *She is* **under contract to** (= has a contract to work for) *a major American computer firm.* 她已簽約為一家大型美國計算機公司工作。◇ *The offer has been accepted,* **subject to contract** (= the agreement is not official until the contract is signed). 此報價已獲接受，尚須以簽約為準。◇ *They were sued for* **breach of contract** (= not keeping to a contract). 他們被指控違約。**2 ~ (on sb)** (*informal*) an agreement to kill sb for money（雇用殺人的）協議，合同：*to take out a contract on sb* 雇兇手殺害某人

▪ **verb** /kən'trækt/ **1** 0-w [I, T] to become less or smaller; to make sth become less or smaller（使）收縮，縮小：*Glass contracts as it cools.* 玻璃遇冷收縮。◇ *a contracting market* 萎縮的市場 ◇ *The heart muscles contract to expel the blood.* 心臟肌肉收縮以擠壓出血液。◇ **~ sth** *The exercise consists of stretching and contracting the leg muscles.* 此項訓練包括伸展和收縮腿部肌肉。◇ **~ sth to sth** *'I will' and 'I shall' are usually contracted to 'I'll'* (= made shorter). * I will 和 I shall 通常縮約為 I'll。**OPP** **expand** **2** [T] **~ sth** (*formal* or *medical* 醫) to get an illness 感染（疾病）；得（病）：*to contract AIDS/a virus/a disease* 感染艾滋病／病毒／疾病 **3** [T] to make a legal agreement with sb for them to work for you or provide you with a service 與…訂立合同（或契約）：**~ sb to do sth** *The player is contracted to play until August.* 這位選手簽約參加比賽到八月份。◇ **~ sb (to sth)** *Several computer engineers have been contracted to the finance department.* 有幾位計算機工程師與財務部門簽訂了合同。**4** [I] **~ to do sth** to make a legal agreement to work for sb or provide them with a service 訂立…的合同（或契約）：*She has contracted to work 20 hours a week.* 她已簽訂每週工作 20 小時的合同。**5** [T] **~ a marriage/an alliance (with sb)** (*formal*) to formally agree to marry sb/form an ALLIANCE with sb（與…）訂立（婚約）；（與…）締結（同盟）

PHR V **conˌtract 'in (to sth)** (*BrE*) to formally agree that you will take part in sth 訂約參與 **conˌtract 'out (of sth)** (*BrE*) to formally agree that you will not take part in sth 訂約不參與；退出（或不參加）…合約：*Many employees contracted out of the pension plan.* 許多雇員退出了養老金計劃的合約。**conˌtract sth↔'out (to sb)** to arrange for work to be done by another company rather than your own 訂約把…承包出去

ˌcontract 'bridge *noun* [U] the standard form of the card game BRIDGE, in which points are given only for sets of cards that are BID and won 定約橋牌（橋牌遊戲的標準形式，只能按叫到的定約取得成局獎分）

con·tract·ile /kən'træktaɪl/ *adj.* (*biology* 生) (of living TISSUE, organs, etc. 活組織、器官等) able to contract or, of an opening or tube, become narrower 可收縮的；（開口或管）可變窄的

con·trac·tion /kən'trækʃn/ *noun* **1** [U] the process of becoming smaller 收縮；縮小：*the expansion and contraction of the metal* 金屬的膨脹與收縮 ◇ *The sudden contraction of the markets left them with a lot of unwanted stock.* 股票市場驟然收縮，讓他們剩下了許多無人要的股票。**OPP** **expansion** **2** [C, U] a sudden and painful contracting of muscles, especially of the muscles around a woman's WOMB, that happens when she is giving birth to a child（肌肉的）收縮，攣縮；（尤指分娩時的）子宮收縮：*The contractions started coming every five minutes.* 子宮開始每隔五分鐘收縮一次。**3** [C] (*linguistics* 語言) a short form of a word 詞的縮約形式：*'He's' may be a contraction of 'he is' or 'he has'.* * he's 可以是 he is 或 he has 的縮約形式。

con·tract·or **AW** /kən'træktə(r)/ *noun* a person or company that has a contract to do work or provide goods or services for another company 承包人；承包商；承包公司：*a* **building/haulage, etc. contractor** 建築、貨運等承包商 ◇ *to employ an outside contractor* 雇用外來承包商

con·tract·ual /kən'træktʃuəl/ *adj.* connected with the conditions of a legal written agreement; agreed in a contract 合同的；契約的；按合同（或契約）規定的 ▸ **con·trac·tu·al·ly** *adv.*

con·tra·dict **AW** /ˌkɒntrə'dɪkt; *NAmE* ˌkɑːn-/ *verb* **1** to say that sth that sb else has said is wrong, and that the opposite is true 反駁；駁斥；批駁：**~ sth** *All evening her husband contradicted everything she said.* 整個晚上她說什麼丈夫都跟她拌嘴。◇ **~ sb/yourself** *You've just* **contradicted yourself** (= said the opposite of what you said before). 你恰好與你剛才說的自相矛盾。◇ **~ (sb) + speech** *'No, it's not,' she contradicted (him).* "不，不是的。" 她反駁（他）說。**2 ~ sth | ~ each other** (of statements or pieces of evidence 陳述或證據) to be so different from each other that one of them must be wrong 相抵觸；相矛盾；相反： *The two stories contradict each other.* 這兩種說法相互抵觸。 ➲ LANGUAGE BANK at EVIDENCE

con·tra·dic·tion AW /ˌkɒntrəˈdɪkʃn; *NAmE* ˌkɑːn-/ *noun* **1** [C, U] ~ (**between A and B**) a lack of agreement between facts, opinions, actions, etc.（事實、看法、行動等的）不一致，矛盾，對立： *There is a contradiction between the two sets of figures.* 這兩組數據相互矛盾。◇ *His public speeches are* ***in direct contradiction to*** *his personal lifestyle.* 他的公開言論與他本人的生活方式恰恰相反。◇ *How can we resolve this apparent contradiction?* 我們怎樣才能解決這個明顯的矛盾呢？ **2** [U, C] the act of saying that sth that sb else has said is wrong or not true; an example of this 反駁；駁斥： *I think I can say,* ***without fear of contradiction****, that …* 就算有人反駁，我也膽敢說…◇ *Now you say you both left at ten—that's a contradiction of your last statement.* 你現在說你們倆是十點鐘離開的，這可和你上次的說法不一致。
IDM **a ˌcontradiction in ˈterms** a statement containing two words that contradict each other's meaning 自相矛盾的說法： *A 'nomad settlement' is a contradiction in terms.* "遊牧者的定居"是用詞上的自相矛盾。

con·tra·dict·ory AW /ˌkɒntrəˈdɪktəri; *NAmE* ˌkɑːn-/ *adj.* containing or showing a contradiction 相互矛盾的；對立的；不一致的 SYN **conflicting**： *We are faced with two apparently contradictory statements.* 我們面前這兩種說法顯然是矛盾的。◇ *The advice I received was often contradictory.* 我所得到的建議常常是相互矛盾的。

con·tra·dis·tinc·tion /ˌkɒntrədɪˈstɪŋkʃn; *NAmE* ˌkɑːn-/ *noun*
IDM **in contradistinction to sth/sb** (*formal*) in contrast with sth/sb 與…相對比（或截然不同）

con·tra·flow /ˈkɒntrəfləʊ; *NAmE* ˈkɑːntrəfloʊ/ *noun* (*BrE*) a system that is used when one half of a large road is closed for repairs, and the traffic going in both directions has to use the other half（道路一側關閉維修時實行的）一側雙向行駛： *A contraflow system is in operation on this section of the motorway.* 這段高速公路的一側正在實行雙向行駛。

con·tra·indi·cate /ˌkɒntrəˈɪndɪkeɪt; *NAmE* ˌkɑːn-/ *verb* ~ **sth** (*medical* 醫) if a drug or treatment is **contraindicated**, there is a medical reason why it should not be used in a particular situation 禁忌使用（某物藥物或療法）： *This drug is contraindicated in patients with asthma.* 這種藥哮喘病人禁用。

con·tra·indi·ca·tion /ˌkɒntrəˌɪndɪˈkeɪʃn; *NAmE* ˌkɑːn-/ *noun* (*medical* 醫) a possible reason for not giving sb a particular drug or medical treatment（對某種藥物或療法的）禁忌

con·tralto /kənˈtræltəʊ; *NAmE* -toʊ/ *noun* (*pl.* **-os**) = ALTO *n.* (1)

con·trap·tion /kənˈtræpʃn/ *noun* a machine or piece of equipment that looks strange 奇異的機械；奇特的裝置： *She showed us a strange contraption that looked like a satellite dish.* 她給我們看了一個奇怪的玩意兒，樣子像碟形衛星信號接收器。

con·tra·pun·tal /ˌkɒntrəˈpʌntl; *NAmE* ˌkɑːn-/ *adj.* (*music* 音) having two or more tunes played together to form a whole 多曲調演奏的；複調音樂的 ➲ see also COUNTERPOINT *n.* (1)

con·trari·wise /kənˈtreəriwaɪz; *NAmE* -ˈtrer-/ *adv.* (*formal*) **1** used at the beginning of a sentence or clause to introduce a contrast（用於句首或從句的開頭以引出對比）相反，在另一方面 **2** in the opposite way 以相反的方式： *It worked contrariwise—first you dialled the number, then you put the money in.* 這部電話的操作方式相反，要先撥號碼，然後投入錢幣。

con·trary[1] AW /ˈkɒntrəri; *NAmE* ˈkɑːntreri/ *adj., noun* ➲ see also CONTRARY[2]
■ *adj.* **1** ~ **to sth** different from sth; against sth 與之相異的；相對立的；相反的： ***Contrary to popular belief****, many cats dislike milk.* 與普遍的看法相反，許多貓不喜歡牛奶。◇ *The government has decided that the publication of the report would be 'contrary to the public interest'.* 政府認為發表這份報告將會"違背公眾的利益"。 **2** [only before noun] completely different in nature or direction（在性質或方向上）截然不同的，完全相反的 SYN **opposite**： ***contrary advice/opinions/arguments*** 完全相反的建議／觀點／論點◇ *The contrary view is that prison provides an excellent education—in crime.* 截然不同的看法是監獄在犯罪方面提供極好的教育。
■ ***noun* the contrary** [sing.] the opposite fact, event or situation 相反的事實（或事情、情況）： *In the end the contrary was proved true: he was innocent and she was guilty.* 最後證明事實正好相反：他是無辜的，而她則有罪。
IDM **on the ˈcontrary** used to introduce a statement that says the opposite of the last one 與此相反；恰恰相反： *'It must have been terrible.' 'On the contrary, I enjoyed every minute.'* "那一定是很糟糕。" "恰恰相反，我非常喜歡。" **ˌquite the ˈcontrary** used to emphasize that the opposite of what has been said is true 恰恰相反；正相反： *I don't find him funny at all. Quite the contrary.* 正相反，我覺得他一點兒也不可笑。 **to the ˈcontrary** showing or proving the opposite 相反的；相反地： *Show me some evidence to the contrary* (= proving that sth is not true). 給我看看有什麼相反的證據吧。◇ *I will expect to see you on Sunday unless I hear anything to the contrary* (= that you are not coming). 我星期天等你，除非你說不來了。

con·trary[2] AW /kənˈtreəri; *NAmE* -ˈtreri/ *adj.* (*formal, disapproving*) (usually of children 通常指小孩) behaving badly; choosing to do or say the opposite of what is expected 乖戾的；好與人作對的；逆反的；犟的： *She was such a contrary child—it was impossible to please her.* 這孩子老跟人作對，沒法讓她高興。 ➲ see also CONTRARY[1] ▸ **con·trar·ily** AW *adv.* **con·trari·ness** *noun* [U]

con·trast 🔑 AW *noun, verb*
■ ***noun*** /ˈkɒntrɑːst; *NAmE* ˈkɑːntræst/ **1** 🔑 [C, U] a difference between two or more people or things that you can see clearly when they are compared or put close together; the fact of comparing two or more things in order to show the differences between them 明顯的差異；對比；對照： ~ (**between A and B**) *There is an obvious contrast between the cultures of East and West.* 東西方文化之間有明顯的差異。◇ ~ (**to sb/sth**) *The company lost $7 million this quarter* ***in contrast to*** *a profit of $6.2 million a year earlier.* 這家公司本季度虧損了 700 萬元，與去年同期 620 萬元的盈利形成了對照。◇ *The situation when we arrived was in* ***marked contrast*** *to the news reports.* 我們到達時的局勢與新聞報道的截然不同。◇ *The poverty of her childhood* ***stands in*** *total* ***contrast to*** *her life in Hollywood.* 她孩提時的貧困處境與她在好萊塢的生活有着天壤之別。◇ ~ (**with sb/sth**) *to show a* ***sharp/stark/striking contrast*** *with sth* 與某事物形成鮮明／明顯／顯著的對比◇ ~ (**in sth**) *A wool jacket complements the silk trousers and provides an interesting contrast in texture.* 毛料上衣配真絲長褲，質地上的差異非常有趣。◇ *When you look at their new system, ours seems very old-fashioned* ***by contrast****.* 看一看他們的新系統，就顯得我們的系統陳舊過時了。◇ ~ (**of sth**) *Careful contrast of the two plans shows some important differences.* 把兩個計劃仔細地加以對比就可看出一些重要的差異。 **2** [C, usually sing.] ~ (**to sb/sth**) a person or thing that is clearly different from sb/sth else 明顯不同的人（或事物）： *The work you did today is quite a contrast to* (= very much better/worse than) *what you did last week.* 你今天的表現與上週截然不同。 **3** [U] differences in colour or in light and dark, used in photographs and paintings to create a special effect（攝影或繪畫中的）顏色反差，明暗對比： *The artist's use of contrast is masterly.* 這位藝術家嫻熟地運用了明暗對比。 **4** [U] the amount of difference between light and dark in a photograph or the picture on a television screen（照片或電視圖像的）明暗對比度，反差： *Use this button to adjust the contrast.* 用此按鈕調節圖像明暗的對比度。
■ ***verb*** /kənˈtrɑːst; *NAmE* -ˈtræst/ **1** 🔑 [T] ~ (**A and/with B**) to compare two things in order to show the differences between them 對比；對照： *It is interesting to contrast the British legal system with the American one.* 把英國的法制與美國的加以對比很有意思。◇ *The poem contrasts*

youth and age. 這首詩對比了青春與老年。**2** [I] **~ (with sth)** to show a clear difference when close together or when compared（靠近或作比較時）顯出明顯的差異，形成對比：*Her actions* ***contrasted sharply*** *with her promises.* 她的行動與她的諾言相差甚遠。◇ *Her actions and her promises contrasted sharply.* 她的行動與她的諾言相差甚遠。

C

Language Bank 用語庫

contrast

Highlighting differences 突出差異／不同

- This survey **highlights a number of differences in** the way that teenage boys and girls in the UK spend their free time. 這項民意測驗凸顯出英國十幾歲的男孩和女孩在打發閒暇時間上的諸多不同。
- **One of the main differences between** the girls **and** the boys who took part in the research was the way in which they use the Internet. 參與了這項研究的女生和男生之間的主要差異之一在於他們使用互聯網的方式。
- **Unlike** the girls, who use the Internet mainly to keep in touch with friends, the boys questioned in this survey tend to use the Internet for playing computer games. 女生使用互聯網主要是和朋友聯繫，這一點和男生不同，參與調查的男生往往是使用互聯網來玩電腦遊戲。
- The girls **differ from** the boys **in that** they tend to spend more time keeping in touch with friends on the telephone or on social networking websites. 與男生不同的是，女生往往花更多的時間通過電話或社交網站與朋友保持聯繫。
- **Compared to** the boys, the girls spend much more time chatting to friends on the telephone. 與男生相比，女生花在與朋友電話聊天上的時間要多得多。
- On average the girls spend four hours a week chatting to friends on the phone. **In contrast**, very few of the boys spend more than five minutes a day talking to their friends in this way. 女生平均每週花四個小時與朋友電話聊天。相比之下，很少有男生每天以這種方式與朋友聊天五分鐘以上。
- The boys prefer competitive sports and computer games, **whereas/while** the girls seem to enjoy more cooperative activities, such as shopping with friends. 男生更喜歡競技性體育運動和電腦遊戲，而女生似乎更喜歡合作性活動，比如與朋友一起購物。
- When the girls go shopping, they mainly buy clothes and cosmetics. The boys, **on the other hand**, tend to purchase computer games or gadgets. 女生購物時主要買衣服和化妝品，而男生往往會買電腦遊戲或小器具。

➲ Language Banks at GENERALLY, ILLUSTRATE, PROPORTION, SIMILARLY, SURPRISING

con·trast·ing AW /kən'trɑːstɪŋ; *NAmE* -'træs-/ *adj.* [usually before noun] very different in style, colour or attitude（在式樣、顏色或態度上）極不相同的，差異大的：*bright, contrasting colours* 鮮豔斑斕的色彩 ◇ *The book explores contrasting views of the poet's early work.* 此書探討了人們對這位詩人早期作品截然不同的觀點。

con·trast·ive AW /kən'trɑːstɪv; *NAmE* -'træst-/ *adj.* (*linguistics* 語言) showing the differences between languages 作對比研究的：*a contrastive analysis of British and Australian English* 對英式英語和澳大利亞英語的對比分析

con·tra·vene /ˌkɒntrə'viːn; *NAmE* ˌkɑːn-/ *verb* **~ sth** (*formal*) to do sth that is not allowed by a law or rule 違犯，違反（法律或規則）SYN **infringe**：*The company was found guilty of contravening safety regulations.* 那家公司被判違反了安全條例。▸ **con·tra·ven·tion** /ˌkɒntrə'venʃn; *NAmE* ˌkɑːn-/ *noun* [U, C] SYN **infringement**：*These actions are* ***in contravention of*** *European law.* 這些行動違反了歐洲的法律。

con·tre·temps /'kɒntrətɒ̃; *NAmE* 'kɑːntrətɑ̃ː; 'kɔːntrətɑ̃ː/ *noun* (*pl.* **con·tre·temps**) (from *French, formal* or *humorous*) an unfortunate event or embarrassing disagreement with another person 不幸事情；令人難堪的齟齬

con·trib·ute AW /kən'trɪbjuːt; *BrE* also 'kɒntrɪbjuːt/ *verb* **1** [T, I] to give sth, especially money or goods, to help sb/sth 捐獻，捐贈（尤指金錢或物品）；捐助：**~ sth (to/towards sth)** *We contributed £5 000 to the earthquake fund.* 我們向地震基金捐贈了 5 000 英鎊。◇ **~ (to/towards sth)** *Would you like to contribute to our collection?* 你願意給我們的募捐捐款嗎？◇ *Do you wish to contribute?* 你想捐助嗎？**2** [I] **~ (to sth)** to be one of the causes of sth 是…的原因之一：*Medical negligence was said to have contributed to her death.* 據說醫務人員的玩忽職守是她死亡的原因之一。◇ *Human error may have been a* ***contributing factor***. 人為的失誤可能是一個起作用的因素。➲ LANGUAGE BANK at CAUSE **3** [I, T] to increase, improve or add to sth 增加；增進；添加（到某物）：**~ to sth** *Immigrants have contributed to British culture in many ways.* 移民在許多方面都對英國文化有所貢獻。◇ **~ sth to sth** *This book contributes little to our understanding of the subject.* 此書對我們瞭解這門學科助益甚少。**4** [T, I] to write things for a newspaper, magazine, or a radio or television programme; to speak during a meeting or conversation, especially to give your opinion（為報紙、雜誌、電台或電視節目）撰稿；（在會議或會談期間）講話，（尤指）發表意見：**~ sth (to sth)** *She contributed a number of articles to the magazine.* 她給這家雜誌撰寫了一些稿件。◇ **~ (to sth)** *He contributes regularly to the magazine 'New Scientist'.* 他定期給《新科學家》雜誌撰稿。◇ *We hope everyone will contribute to the discussion.* 我們希望大家都能參與討論。

con·tri·bu·tion AW /ˌkɒntrɪ'bjuːʃn; *NAmE* ˌkɑːn-/ *noun* **1** [C] a sum of money that is given to a person or an organization in order to help pay for sth 捐款；捐資 SYN **donation**：**~ (to sth)** *to* ***make a contribution*** *to charity* 給慈善事業捐款 ◇ *a substantial contribution* 一筆數額相當大的捐款 ◇ *All contributions will be gratefully received.* 我們對所有捐資表示感謝。◇ **~ (toward(s) sth/doing sth)** *valuable contributions towards the upkeep of the cathedral* 對維修大教堂很重要的捐資 **2** [C] **~ (to sth)** a sum of money that you pay regularly to your employer or the government in order to pay for benefits such as health insurance, a pension, etc.（給雇主或政府用作醫療保險、養老金等津貼的）定期繳款：*monthly contributions to the pension scheme* 養老金計劃的每月分攤款額 ➲ SYNONYMS at PAYMENT **3** [C, usually sing.] an action or a service that helps to cause or increase sth 貢獻；促成作用：**~ (to sth)** *He* ***made a*** *very positive* ***contribution*** *to the success of the project.* 他對項目的成功貢獻良多。◇ *the car's contribution to the greenhouse effect* 汽車對加劇溫室效應所起的作用 ◇ **~ (toward(s) sth/doing sth)** *These measures would make a valuable contribution towards reducing industrial accidents.* 這些措施將會對減少工業事故起重要的作用。**4** [C] **~ (to sth)** an item that forms part of a book, magazine, broadcast, discussion, etc.（書、雜誌、廣播、討論等部份內容的）一則，一條，稿件：*an important contribution to the debate* 這次辯論一項重要的內容 ◇ *All contributions for the May issue must be received by Friday.* 所有要在五月這一期發表的稿件必須在星期五以前寄到。**5** [U] **~ (to sth)** the act of giving sth, especially money, to help a person or an organization 捐贈；捐助；（尤指）捐款：*We rely entirely on voluntary contribution.* 我們全靠自願捐贈。

con·tribu·tor AW /kən'trɪbjətə(r)/ *noun* **1 ~ (to sth)** a person who writes articles for a magazine or a book, or who talks on a radio or television programme or at a meeting（雜誌或書的）撰稿人，投稿人；（電台、電視節目中的）嘉賓；（會議的）發言人 **2 ~ (to sth)** a person or thing that provides money to help pay for sth, or support sth 捐款者；捐贈者；作出貢獻者：*Older people* *are important contributors to the economy.* 老一輩人為發展經濟作出了重要貢獻。 **3** **~** (**to sth**) something that helps to cause sth 促成物： *Sulphur dioxide is a pollutant and a major contributor to acid rain.* 二氧化硫是一種污染物，並且是形成酸雨的主要因素。

con·tribu·tory /kən'trɪbjətəri; *NAmE* -tɔːri/ *adj.* [usually before noun] **1** helping to cause sth 促成的；促進的；起作用的： *Alcohol is a* ***contributory factor*** *in 10% of all road accidents.* 所有交通事故中有 10% 是酒後駕車造成的。 **2** involving payments from the people who will benefit 需要受益人付錢的： *a* ***contributory pension scheme/plan*** (= paid for by both employers and employees) 由雇主與雇員共同出資的養老金計劃 OPP **non-contributory**

con·trite /kən'traɪt; *BrE* also 'kɒntraɪt/ *adj.* (*formal*) very sorry for sth bad that you have done 深感懊悔的；痛悔的 ▸ **con·trite·ly** *adv.* **con·tri·tion** /kən'trɪʃn/ *noun* [U]： *a look of contrition* 追悔莫及的神色

con·triv·ance /kən'traɪvəns/ *noun* (*formal*) **1** [C, U] (usually *disapproving*) something that sb has done or written that does not seem natural; the fact of seeming artificial 非自然之物；人工產物；矯揉造作： *The film is spoilt by unrealistic contrivances of plot.* 這部電影被不實際的牽強情節給毀了。◇ *The story is told with a complete absence of contrivance.* 這故事講得毫不矯揉造作。 **2** [C] a clever or complicated device or tool made for a particular purpose 精巧（或複雜）的裝置；專用工具 **3** [C, U] a clever plan or trick; the act of using a clever plan or trick 計謀；圈套；採用計謀（或圈套）： *an ingenious contrivance to get her to sign the document without reading it* 使她未經過目就簽署文件的妙計

con·trive /kən'traɪv/ *verb* (*formal*) **1** **~ to do sth** to manage to do sth despite difficulties（不顧困難而）設法做到： *She contrived to spend a couple of hours with him every Sunday evening.* 每週星期日晚上她都設法與他待上幾個小時。 **2** **~ sth** to succeed in making sth happen despite difficulties（克服困難）促成某事： *I decided to contrive a meeting between the two of them.* 我決定設法讓他們雙方見上一面。 **3** **~ sth** to think of or make sth, for example a plan or a machine, in a clever way 巧妙地策劃；精巧地製造（如機器）： *They contrived a plan to defraud the company.* 他們精心策劃要欺詐那家公司。

con·trived /kən'traɪvd/ *adj.* (*disapproving*) planned in advance and not natural or genuine; written or arranged in a way that is not natural or realistic 預謀的；不自然的；人為的；矯揉造作的；做作的： *a contrived situation* 人為的狀況 ◇ *The book's happy ending seemed contrived.* 這部書大團圓的結局讀來讓人感到不真實。

con·trol 0-w /kən'trəʊl; *NAmE* -'troʊl/ *noun, verb*

■ ***noun***

▸ **POWER** 權力 **1** 0-w [U] **~** (**of/over sb/sth**) the power to make decisions about how a country, an area, an organization, etc. is run（對國家、地區、機構等的）管理權，控制權，支配權： *The party is expecting to* ***gain control of*** *the council in the next election.* 該黨期待着在下次選舉中獲得對地方議會的控制權。◇ *The Democrats will probably* ***lose control of*** *Congress.* 民主黨很可能失去對國會的控制。◇ *A military junta* ***took control of the country.*** 政變上台的軍政府接管了這個國家。◇ *The city is* ***in the control of*** *enemy forces.* 那座城市現處於敵軍的控制之下。◇ *The city is* ***under enemy control.*** 那座城市現處於敵人的控制之下。 **2** 0-w [U] **~** (**of/over sb/sth**) the ability to make sb/sth do what you want 控制（或操縱）能力： *The teacher* ***had no control*** *over the children.* 那位老師管不住學生。◇ *She struggled to* ***keep control of*** *her voice.* 她竭力控制住自己的聲音。◇ *She* ***lost control*** *of her car on the ice.* 她在冰上開車失去了控制。◇ *He got so angry he* ***lost control*** (= shouted and said or did things he would not normally do). 他氣得失去了自制。◇ *Owing to* ***circumstances beyond our control,*** *the flight to Rome has been cancelled.* 由於出現了我們無法控制的情況，飛往羅馬的航班已被取消。◇ *The coach made the team work hard on ball control* (= in a ball game). 教練讓全隊努力練習控球。 ➲ see also SELF-CONTROL

▸ **LIMITING/MANAGING** 限制；管理 **3** 0-w [U, C] **~** (**of/on sth**) (often in compounds 常構成複合詞) the act of restricting, limiting or managing sth; a method of doing this 限制；限定；約束；管理；管制： *traffic control* 交通管制 ◇ *talks on arms control* 軍備控制談判 ◇ *government controls on trade and industry* 政府對工商業的管理 ◇ *A new advance has been made in the control of malaria.* 在控制瘧疾方面已取得新的進展。◇ *Price controls on food were ended.* 對食物價格的控制已告結束。◇ *a pest control officer* 蟲害防治員 ➲ see also BIRTH CONTROL, QUALITY CONTROL ➲ **SYNONYMS** at LIMIT

▸ **IN MACHINE** 機器 **4** 0-w [C, usually pl.] the switches and buttons, etc. that you use to operate a machine or a vehicle（機器或車輛的）操縱裝置，開關，按鈕： *the controls of an aircraft* 飛機的操縱裝置 ◇ *the control panel* 控制面板 ◇ *the volume control of a CD player* 激光唱片機的音量調節器 ◇ *The co-pilot was* ***at the controls*** *when the plane landed.* 副駕駛員操縱着飛機着陸。 ➲ see also REMOTE CONTROL

▸ **IN EXPERIMENT** 實驗 **5** [C] (*technical* 術語) a person, thing or group used as a standard of comparison for checking the results of a scientific experiment; an experiment whose result is known, used for checking working methods 對照標準；（檢驗工作方法的）參照實驗： *One group was treated with the new drug, and the* ***control group*** *was given a sugar pill.* 一組採用新藥治療，而對照檢驗組服用的則是糖丸。

▸ **PLACE** 地點 **6** [sing.] a place where orders are given or where checks are made; the people who work in this place 指揮（或檢查、控制）站；指揮（或檢查、控制）人員： *air traffic control* 空中交通管制中心 ◇ *We went through passport control and into the departure lounge.* 我們通過護照檢查站進入了候機大廳。◇ *This is Mission Control calling the space shuttle Discovery.* 地面指揮中心現在呼叫航天飛機“發現號”。

▸ **ON COMPUTER** 計算機 **7** [U] (also **con'trol key** [sing.]) (on a computer keyboard) a key that you press when you want to perform a particular operation（鍵盤上的）控制鍵

IDM **be in control** (**of sth**) **1** 0-w to direct or manage an organization, an area or a situation 掌管，管理，控制，操縱（某機構、地區或局勢）： *He's reached retiring age, but he's still firmly in control.* 他雖然已到退休年齡，但仍大權在握。◇ *There has been some violence after the match, but the police are now in control of the situation.* 比賽後發生了一些暴力事件，但是現在警方已控制了局勢。 **2** 0-w to be able to organize your life well and keep calm 處之泰然；安之若素： *In spite of all her family problems, she's really in control.* 她雖然家庭問題重重，卻能完全處之泰然。 **be/get/run/etc. out of con'trol** 0-w to be or become impossible to manage or to control 無法管理；失去控制： *The children are completely out of control since their father left.* 這些孩子自他們的父親離開後就無法無天了。◇ *A truck ran out of control on the hill.* 一輛卡車在山上失去了控制。 **be under con'trol** 0-w to be being dealt with successfully 被控制住；處於控制之下： *Don't worry—everything's under control!* 別擔心，一切都控制住了！ **bring/get/keep sth under con'trol** 0-w to succeed in dealing with sth so that it does not cause any damage or hurt anyone 控制得住，抑制得住（從而不造成損害）： *It took two hours to bring the fire under control.* 花了兩個小時才控制住火勢。◇ *Please keep your dog under control!* 請管好你的狗！

■ ***verb*** (**-ll-**)

▸ **HAVE POWER** 擁有權力 **1** 0-w **~ sb/sth** to have power over a person, company, country, etc. so that you are able to decide what they must do or how it is run 指揮；控制；掌管；支配： *By the age of 21 he controlled the company.* 他 21 歲就掌管了公司。◇ *The whole territory is now controlled by the army.* 現在全境都在軍隊的控制之下。◇ *Can't you control your children?* 你就不能管管你這些孩子？

▸ **LIMIT/MANAGE** 限制；管理 **2** 0-w to limit sth or make it happen in a particular way 限制；限定： **~ sth** *government attempts to control immigration* 政府試圖限制移民的措施 ◇ *Many biological processes are controlled by hormones.* 許多生物變化過程都是由激素控制的。◇ **~ what/how, etc. …** *Parents should control what their kids watch on television.* 父母應該限定孩子看什麼樣的電視節目。 **3** 0-w **~ sth** to stop sth from spreading or

C

getting worse 阻止蔓延（或惡化）：*Firefighters are still trying to control the blaze.* 消防隊員仍在盡力控制火勢的蔓延。◇ *She was given drugs to control the pain.* 給她服用了鎮痛藥。

▸ MACHINE 機器 **4** ~ **sth** to make sth, such as a machine or system, work in the way that you want it to 操縱，控制（機器或系統等）：*This knob controls the volume.* 此旋鈕調節音量。◇ *The traffic lights are controlled by a central computer.* 交通信號燈由中心計算機控制。

▸ STAY CALM 保持鎮靜 **5** to manage to make yourself remain calm, even though you are upset or angry 抑制；克制：~ **yourself** *I was so furious I couldn't control myself and I hit him.* 我氣得無法自制，就打了他。◇ ~ **sth** *He was finding it difficult to control his feelings.* 他覺得很難克制住自己的感情。

con'trol freak *noun* (*informal, disapproving*) a person who always wants to be in control of their own and others' lives, and to organize how things are done 好多管事的人；愛指揮別人的人

con·trol·lable /kən'trəʊləbl; *NAmE* -'troʊ-/ *adj.* that can be controlled 可控制（或管理、操縱、支配）的

con·trolled /kən'trəʊld; *NAmE* -'troʊld/ *adj.* **1** done or arranged in a very careful way 十分小心完成的；精心安排的：*a controlled explosion* 控制爆破 ◇ *a controlled environment* 受到控制的生態環境 **2** limited, or managed by law or by rules（受法律或規則）限制的，控制的，管制的：*controlled airspace* 管制空域 **3 -controlled** (in compounds 構成複合詞) managed by a particular group, or in a particular way（受某團體或用某種方式）管理的，控制的，操縱的：*a British-controlled company* 英資公司 ◇ *computer-controlled systems* 用計算機控制的系統 **4** remaining calm and not getting angry or upset 保持冷靜的；克制的：*She remained quiet and controlled.* 她沉默不語保持克制。➲ compare UNCONTROLLED

con,trolled e'conomy *noun* (*economics* 經) a type of economic system in which a government controls its country's industries and decides what goods should be produced and in what amounts 管制經濟（由政府控制國家工業並決定產品的種類與數量）

con,trolled 'substance *noun* (*technical* 術語) an illegal drug 受管制藥品；毒品：*to be arrested for possession of a controlled substance* 因藏有毒品而被捕

con·trol·ler /kən'trəʊlə(r); *NAmE* -'troʊ-/ *noun* **1** a person who manages or directs sth, especially a large organization or part of an organization（尤指大型機構或部門的）管理者，控制者，指揮者 ➲ see also AIR TRAFFIC CONTROLLER **2** (*technical* 術語) a device that controls or REGULATES a machine or part of a machine（機器或部件的）控制器，調節器：*a temperature controller* 溫控器 **3** (also **comp·trol·ler**) a person who is in charge of the financial accounts of a business company（公司的）財務總管，主計長

con,trolling 'interest *noun* [usually sing.] the fact of owning enough shares in a company to be able to make decisions about what the company should do 控制股權

con'trol tower *noun* a building at an airport from which the movements of aircraft are controlled（機場的）指揮塔台，控制塔，指揮調度台

con·tro·ver·sial AW /,kɒntrə'vɜːʃl; *NAmE* ,kɑːntrə'vɜːrʃl/ *adj.* causing a lot of angry public discussion and disagreement 引起爭論的；有爭議的：*a **highly controversial** topic* 頗有爭議的話題 ◇ *a controversial plan to build a new road* 有爭議的修建新道路計劃 ◇ *Winston Churchill and Richard Nixon were both controversial figures.* 溫斯頓•丘吉爾和理查德•尼克松都是有爭議的人物。OPP **non-controversial, uncontroversial** ▸ **con·tro·ver·sial·ly** AW /-ʃəli/ *adv.*

con·tro·versy AW /'kɒntrəvɜːsi; *NAmE* 'kɑːntrəvɜːrsi; *BrE* also kən'trɒvəsi/ *noun* [U, C] (*pl.* **-ies**) ~ (**over/about/surrounding sb/sth**) public discussion and argument about sth that many people strongly disagree about, disapprove of, or are shocked by（公開的）爭論，爭議，論戰：*to **arouse/cause controversy*** 引起爭論 ◇ *a bitter **controversy over/about** the site of the new airport* 有關新機場選址的激烈爭論 ◇ *the controversy surrounding his latest movie* 圍繞他最近一部電影的爭論 ◇ *The President resigned amid considerable controversy.* 總統在一片爭論聲中辭職。

con·tro·vert /,kɒntrə'vɜːt; *NAmE* 'kɑːntrəvɜːrt/ *verb* ~ **sth** (*formal*) to say or prove that sth is not true 駁斥；反駁 SYN **refute** ➲ see also INCONTROVERTIBLE

con·tu·ma·cious /,kɒntju'meɪʃəs; *NAmE* ,kɑːntu-/ *adj.* (*old use* or *law* 律) lacking respect for authority 藐視權威的；違抗的；不服從的

con·tu·sion /kən'tjuːʒn; *NAmE* -'tuː-/ *noun* [C, U] (*medical* 醫) an injury to part of the body that does not break the skin 挫傷 SYN **bruise**

con·un·drum /kə'nʌndrəm/ *noun* **1** a confusing problem or question that is very difficult to solve 令人迷惑的難題；複雜難解的問題 **2** a question, usually involving a trick with words, that you ask for fun 謎語 SYN **riddle**

con·ur·ba·tion /,kɒnɜː'beɪʃn; *NAmE* ,kɑːnɜːr'b-/ *noun* (*formal*) a large area where towns have grown and joined together, often around a city（有衞星城鎮的）大都市，集合城市

con·va·lesce /,kɒnvə'les; *NAmE* ,kɑːn-/ *verb* [I] (*formal*) to spend time getting your health and strength back after an illness 逐步康復；（身體）恢復 SYN **recuperate**：*She is convalescing at home after her operation.* 手術後她正在家休養康復。

con·va·les·cence /,kɒnvə'lesns; *NAmE* ,kɑːn-/ *noun* [sing., U] a period of time when you get well again after an illness or a medical operation; the process of getting well 康復期；恢復期；康復：*You need four to six weeks' convalescence.* 你需要四至六個星期的康復期。

con·va·les·cent /,kɒnvə'lesnt; *NAmE* ,kɑːn-/ *adj.* connected with convalescence; in the process of convalescence 康復期的；正在康復的；漸痛的：*a convalescent home* (= a type of hospital where people go to get well after an illness) 康復醫院 ◇ *a convalescent child* 逐漸康復的小孩 ▸ **con·va·les·cent** *noun*：*I treated him as a convalescent, not as a sick man.* 我把他當作正在康復的人，而不是病人。

con·vec·tion /kən'vekʃn/ *noun* [U] (*technical* 術語) the process in which heat moves through a gas or a liquid as the hotter part rises and the cooler, heavier part sinks（熱通過氣體或液體的）運流，對流

con·vect·or /kən'vektə(r)/ (also **con,vector 'heater**) *noun* a device for heating the air in a room using convection 對流加熱器；換流器

con·vene AW /kən'viːn/ *verb* (*formal*) **1** [T] ~ **sth** to arrange for people to come together for a formal meeting 召集，召開（正式會議）：*to convene a meeting* 召開會議 ◇ *A Board of Inquiry was convened immediately after the accident.* 事故後調查委員會立即召開了會議。**2** [I] to come together for a formal meeting（為正式會議而）聚集，集合：*The committee will convene at 11.30 next Thursday.* 委員會將在下星期四上午 11:30 開會。

con·vener (also **con·venor**) /kən'viːnə(r)/ *noun* **1** a person who arranges meetings of groups or committees 會議召集人 **2** (*BrE*) a senior official of a TRADE/LABOR UNION at a factory or other place of work（工廠或基層單位的）資深工會領導人

con·veni·ence /kən'viːniəns/ *noun* **1** [U] the quality of being useful, easy or suitable for sb 方便；適宜；便利：*We have provided seats **for the convenience** of our customers.* 為方便顧客我們備有座位。◇ ***For** (**the sake of**) **convenience**, the two groups have been treated as one in this report.* 為方便起見，這兩個組在本報告中被視為一組。◇ *In this resort you can enjoy all the **comfort and convenience** of modern tourism.* 在這個度假勝地你可享受所有現代旅遊的舒適與便利。➲ compare INCONVENIENCE ➲ see also FLAG OF CONVENIENCE, MARRIAGE OF CONVENIENCE **2** [C] something that is useful and can make things easier or quicker to do, or more comfortable 便利的事物（或設施）；方便的用具：*It was a great convenience to have the school so near.* 學校這麼近真是

太方便了。◇ *The house had all the modern conveniences* (= central heating, etc.) *that were unusual at that time.* 這座房子擁有在當時並不常見的所有現代化設施。➲ see also PUBLIC CONVENIENCE

IDM **at sb's con'venience** (*formal*) at a time or a place which is suitable for sb 在（某人）方便時；在（某人）適宜的地點：*Can you telephone me at your convenience to arrange a meeting?* 你能不能在你方便時給我來個電話，安排見一次面？➲ more at EARLY *adj.*

con'venience food *noun* [C, U] food that you buy frozen or in a box or can, that you can prepare and cook very quickly and easily 方便食品；便利食品

con'venience store *noun* (*especially NAmE*) a shop/store that sells food, newspapers, etc. and often stays open 24 hours a day 便利店（常為 24 小時營業）

con·veni·ent 🔑 /kən'viːniənt/ *adj.*
1 🔑 **~ (for sb/sth)** useful, easy or quick to do; not causing problems 實用的；便利的；方便的；省事的：*It is very convenient to pay by credit card.* 用信用卡付款非常方便。◇ *You'll find these meals quick and convenient to prepare.* 你會發現準備這樣的飯既快又省事。◇ *Fruit is a convenient source of vitamins and energy.* 水果是維生素和能量的便利來源。◇ *A bicycle is often more convenient than a car in towns.* 在城鎮騎自行車常常比開車更方便。◇ *I can't see him now—it isn't convenient.* 我現在不便見他。◇ *I'll call back at a more convenient time.* 在比較方便的時候我會回電話的。◇ (*disapproving*) *He used his wife's birthday as a convenient excuse for not going to the meeting.* 他說要給妻子過生日，利用這個藉口，就不去參加會議了。 **2** 🔑 near to a particular place; easy to get to 附近的；近便的；容易到達的：(*BrE*) **~ (for sth)** *The house is very convenient for several schools.* 這座房子離幾所學校很近。◇ (*NAmE*) **~ (to sth)** *The hotel is convenient to downtown.* 這家旅館離市中心很近。**OPP** **inconvenient** ▸ **con·veni·ent·ly** *adv.*：*The report can be conveniently divided into three main sections.* 這份報告不用費事就可劃分為三個主要部份。◇ *The hotel is conveniently situated close to the beach.* 那家旅館坐落在海灘附近，非常方便。◇ *She conveniently forgot to mention that her husband would be at the party, too* (= because it suited her not to say). 她沒有提她丈夫也要參加聚會，她覺得還是不提為好。

con·venor = CONVENER

con·vent /'kɒnvənt; *NAmE* 'kɑːnvent; -vənt/ *noun*
1 a building in which NUNS (= members of a female religious community) live together 女隱修院；女修道院 ➲ COLLOCATIONS at RELIGION **2** (also **'convent school**) a school run by NUNS 女修會開辦的學校

con·ven·tion 🔑 **AW** /kən'venʃn/ *noun*
1 🔑 [C, U] the way in which sth is done that most people in a society expect and consider to be polite or the right way to do it 習俗；常規；慣例：*social conventions* 社會習俗 ◇ ***By convention** the deputy leader was always a woman.* 按慣例，這一領導職務的副職總是由女性擔任。◇ *She is a young woman who enjoys flouting conventions.* 她是一位喜歡無視傳統習俗的年輕女子。
2 🔑 [C] a large meeting of the members of a profession, a political party, etc.（某職業、政黨等成員的）大會，集會 **SYN** **conference**：*to hold a convention* 召開大會 ◇ *the Democratic Party Convention* (= to elect a candidate for president) 民主黨代表大會（選出總統候選人）
3 🔑 [C] an official agreement between countries or leaders（國家或首腦間的）公約，協定，協議：*the Geneva convention* 日內瓦公約 ◇ *the United Nations convention on the rights of the child* 聯合國兒童權利公約
4 [C, U] a traditional method or style in literature, art or the theatre（文學、藝術或戲劇的）傳統手法，傳統風格：*the conventions of Greek tragedy* 希臘悲劇的傳統手法

con·ven·tion·al 🔑 **AW** /kən'venʃənl/ *adj.*
1 🔑 (often *disapproving*) tending to follow what is done or considered acceptable by society in general; normal and ordinary, and perhaps not very interesting 依照慣例的；遵循習俗的；墨守成規的；普通平凡的：***conventional behaviour/morality*** 循規蹈矩的行為；傳統的道德規範 ◇ *She's very conventional in her views.* 她的觀點很守舊。**OPP** **unconventional** **2** 🔑 [usually before noun] following what is traditional or the way sth has been done for a long time 傳統的；習慣的：***conventional methods/approaches*** 傳統方法 ◇ ***conventional medicine*** 傳統醫學 ◇ *It's not a hotel, in the conventional sense, but rather a whole village turned into a hotel.* 這不是一家傳統意義上的旅館，而是由整個村莊變身而成的度假村。◇ *You can use a microwave or cook it in a conventional oven.* 你可以用微波爐或傳統烤箱烹製。**OPP** **unconventional** **3** [usually before noun] (especially of weapons 尤指武器) not nuclear 非核的；常規的：***conventional forces/weapons*** 常規部隊／武器 ◇ *a conventional power station* (= using oil or coal as fuel, rather than nuclear power) 非核動力發電站 ▸ **con·ven·tion·al·ity** /kənˌvenʃə'næləti/ *noun* [U] **con·ven·tion·al·ly** **AW** /-ʃənəli/ *adv.*：*conventionally dressed* 衣着傳統的 ◇ *conventionally grown food* (= grown according to conventional methods) 用傳統方法種植的糧食 **IDM** see WISDOM

con·ven·tion·eer /kənˌvenʃə'nɪə(r); *NAmE* -'nɪr/ *noun* (*NAmE*) a person who is attending a convention 與會者；大會代表

con·verge /kən'vɜːdʒ; *NAmE* -'vɜːrdʒ/ *verb* **1** [I] **~ (on …)** (of people or vehicles 人或車輛) to move towards a place from different directions and meet 匯集；聚集；集中：*Thousands of supporters converged on London for the rally.* 成千上萬的支持者從四面八方匯聚倫敦舉行集會。 **2** [I] (of two or more lines, paths, etc. 多條線、小路等) to move towards each other and meet at a point（向某一點）相交，會合：*There was a signpost where the two paths converged.* 兩條小路的相交處有一路標。 **3** [I] if ideas, policies, aims, etc. **converge**, they become very similar or the same（思想、政策、目標等）十分相似，相同 **OPP** **diverge** ▸ **con·ver·gent** /-dʒənt/ *adj.*：***convergent lines/opinions*** 相交的線條；趨於一致的意見 **con·ver·gence** *noun* [U]

con·ver·sant /kən'vɜːsnt; *NAmE* -'vɜːrs-/ *adj.* **~ with sth** (*formal*) knowing about sth; familiar with sth 通曉的；熟悉的：*You need to become fully conversant with the company's procedures.* 你得對公司的程序瞭如指掌。

con·ver·sa·tion 🔑 /ˌkɒnvə'seɪʃn; *NAmE* ˌkɑːnvər's-/ *noun* [C, U] **~ (with sb) (about sth)** an informal talk involving a small group of people or only two; the activity of talking in this way（非正式）交談，談話：*a telephone conversation* 電話交談 ◇ *I had a long conversation with her the other day.* 前幾天我與她作了一次長談。◇ *The main **topic of conversation** was the likely outcome of the election.* 談話的主題是選舉可能產生的結果。◇ *Don was **deep in conversation** with the girl on his right.* 唐與他右邊的女孩在專心交談。◇ (*BrE*) *to **get into conversation** with sb* 開始與某人攀談 ◇ (*NAmE*) *to **get into a conversation** with sb* 開始與某人攀談 ◇ *The conversation turned to gardening.* 話題轉到了園藝上。◇ *I tried to **make conversation*** (= to speak in order to appear polite). 我設法找些話題。➲ SYNONYMS at DISCUSSION

con·ver·sa·tion·al /ˌkɒnvə'seɪʃənl; *NAmE* ˌkɑːnvər's-/ *adj.* **1** not formal; as used in conversation 非正式的；用於交談的；口語的 **SYN** **colloquial**：*a casual and conversational tone* 不拘禮節的談話語氣 ◇ *I learnt conversational Spanish at evening classes.* 我在夜校班學過西班牙語會話。 **2** [only before noun] connected with conversation 交談的；談話的；會話的：*Men have a more direct conversational style.* 男人交談比較直截了當。▸ **con·ver·sa·tion·al·ly** *adv.*：*'Have you been here long?' he asked conversationally.* "你來這裏很久了嗎？" 他攀談着問道。

con·ver·sa·tion·al·ist /ˌkɒnvə'seɪʃənəlɪst; *NAmE* ˌkɑːnvər's-/ *noun* a person who is good at talking to others, especially in an informal way 健談的人；能聊的人

conver'sation piece *noun* **1** an object that is talked about a lot because it is unusual（因不尋常而成為）話題；談資 **2** (*art* 美術) a type of painting in which a group of people are shown in the countryside or in a home 人物風俗畫；鄉村（或室內）風情畫

C

conver'sation stopper *noun* (*informal*) an unexpected or shocking remark, which people do not know how to reply to 噎人的話；令人瞠目結舌的話

con·verse¹ /kən'vɜːs; *NAmE* -'vɜːrs/ *verb* [I] **~ (with sb)** (*formal*) to have a conversation with sb 交談；談話

con·verse² AW /'kɒnvɜːs; *NAmE* 'kɑːnvɜːrs/ *noun* **the converse** [sing.] (*formal*) the opposite or reverse of a fact or statement 相反的事物；（事實或陳述的）反面：*Building new roads increases traffic and the converse is equally true: reducing the number and size of roads means less traffic.* 修築新的道路會增加交通流量，反過來也是同樣的道理：減少道路的數量和規模就意味着減少交通流量。 ▸ **con·verse** *adj.*：*the converse effect* 相反的效果

con·verse·ly AW /'kɒnvɜːsli; *NAmE* 'kɑːnvɜːrs-/ *adv.* (*formal*) in a way that is the opposite or reverse of sth 相反地；反過來：*You can add the fluid to the powder, or, conversely, the powder to the fluid.* 可把液體加入粉末，或者相反，把粉末加入液體。

con·ver·sion AW /kən'vɜːʃn; *NAmE* -'vɜːrʒn; -ʃn/ *noun* **1** [U, C] **~ (from sth) (into/to sth)** the act or process of changing sth from one form, use or system to another 轉變；轉換；轉化：*the conversion of farm buildings into family homes* 農場建築物改建為家庭住宅 ◇ *No conversion from analogue to digital data is needed.* 沒有必要把模擬轉換為數字數據。◇ *a metric conversion table* (= showing how to change METRIC amounts into or out of another system) 公制換算表 ◇ *a firm which specializes in house conversions* (= turning large houses into several smaller flats/apartments) 專營房屋改建的公司 **2** [U, C] **~ (from sth) (to sth)** the process or experience of changing your religion or beliefs（宗教或信仰的）改變；皈依；歸附：*the conversion of the Anglo-Saxons by Christian missionaries* 基督教傳教士使盎格魯一撒克遜人的信仰改變 ◇ *his conversion from Judaism to Christianity* 他由猶太教改信基督教 **3** [C] (in RUGBY and AMERICAN FOOTBALL 橄欖球和美式足球) a way of scoring extra points after scoring a TRY or a TOUCHDOWN（持球觸地或持球越過對方球門線後的）附加得分 **4** [C] **barn/loft ~** a building or room that has been changed so that it can be used for a different purpose, especially for living in（尤指為居住而）改建的房屋

con'version van (also **'van conversion**) *noun* (*US*) a vehicle in which the back part behind the driver has been arranged as a living space 改裝旅行車

con·vert 🔑 AW *verb, noun*

■ **verb** /kən'vɜːt; *NAmE* -'vɜːrt/ **1** 🔑 [T, I] to change or make sth change from one form, purpose, system, etc. to another（使）轉變，轉換，轉化：**~ sth (into sth)** *The hotel is going to be converted into a nursing home.* 那家旅館將被改建成私人療養院。◇ *What rate will I get if I convert my dollars into euros?* 如果我把美元兌換成歐元，匯率是多少？◇ **~ (from sth) (into/to sth)** *We've converted from oil to gas central heating.* 我們已經把中央供熱系統由燃油改成了燃氣。 **2** 🔑 [I] **~ into/to sth** to be able to be changed from one form, purpose, or system to another 可轉變為；可變換成：*a sofa that converts into a bed* 可改作牀用的沙發 **3** 🔑 [I, T] to change or make sb change their religion or beliefs（使）改變（宗教或信仰）；（使）皈依，歸附：**~ (from sth) (to sth)** *He converted from Christianity to Islam.* 他由基督教改信伊斯蘭教。◇ **~ sb (from sth) (to sth)** *She was soon converted to the socialist cause.* 她不久便轉而獻身於社會主義事業了。 **4** [I, T] to change an opinion, a habit, etc. 改變（觀點、習慣等）：**~ (from sth) to sth** *I've converted to organic food.* 我改吃有機食物了。◇ **~ sb (from sth) (to sth)** *I didn't use to like opera but my husband has converted me.* 我過去不喜歡歌劇，但我丈夫改變了我。 **5** [T] **~ sth** (in RUGBY and AMERICAN FOOTBALL 橄欖球和美式足球) to score extra points after a TRY or a TOUCHDOWN（在持球觸地或持球越過對方球門線得分後）獲得附加分 IDM see PREACH

■ **noun** /'kɒnvɜːt; *NAmE* 'kɑːnvɜːrt/ **~ (from sth) (to sth)** a person who has changed their religion, beliefs or opinions 改變宗教（或信仰、觀點）的人；皈依者：*a convert to Islam* 改信伊斯蘭教的人 ◇ *converts from other faiths* 來自其他宗教信仰的皈依者 ◇ ***a convert to the cause*** 一個轉而支持這項事業的人

con·vert·er (also **con·ver·tor**) /kən'vɜːtə(r); *NAmE* -'vɜːrt-/ *noun* **1** a person or thing that converts sth 使發生轉化的人（或物）；轉換器：*a catalytic converter* 催化轉換器 **2** (*physics* 物) a device for converting ALTERNATING CURRENT into DIRECT CURRENT or the other way around 整流器；變流器 **3** (*physics* 物) a device for converting a radio signal from one FREQUENCY to another（改變無線電信號的）變頻器

con·vert·ible AW /kən'vɜːtəbl; *NAmE* -'vɜːrt-/ *adj., noun*

■ **adj.** that can be changed to a different form or use 可改變的；可轉換的；可兌換的：*a convertible sofa* (= one that can be used as a bed) 可當作牀用的沙發 ◇ *convertible currencies* (= ones that can be exchanged for those of other countries) 可兌換的貨幣 ◇ **~ into/to sth** *The bonds are convertible into ordinary shares.* 債券可兌換為普通股。 ▸ **con·vert·ibil·ity** /kən,vɜːtə'bɪləti; *NAmE* -,vɜːrt-/ *noun* [U]

■ **noun** a car with a roof that can be folded down or taken off 活動頂篷式汽車 ➲ VISUAL VOCAB page V52

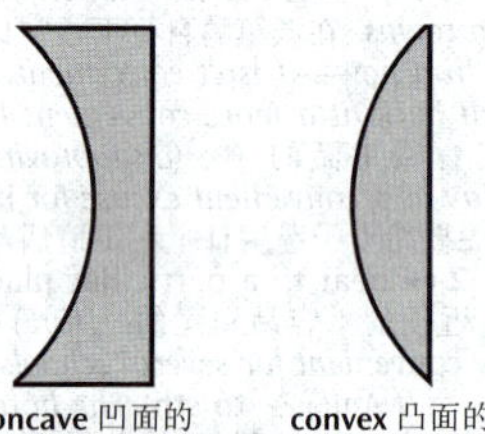

con·vex /'kɒnveks; *NAmE* 'kɑːn-/ *adj.* (of an outline or a surface 外形或表面) curving out 凸出的；凸面的：*a **convex lens/mirror*** 凸透鏡；凸鏡 OPP concave ▸ **con·vex·ity** /kɒn'veksəti; *NAmE* kɑːn'v-/ *noun* [U]

con·vey /kən'veɪ/ *verb* **1** to make ideas, feelings, etc. known to sb 表達，傳遞（思想、感情等） SYN **communicate**：**~ sth** *Colours like red convey a sense of energy and strength.* 紅色之類的顏色可給人以充滿活力與力量的感覺。◇ **~ sth to sb** (*formal*) *Please convey my apologies to your wife.* 請向你的妻子轉達我的歉意。◇ **~ how, what, etc. ...** *He tried desperately to convey how urgent the situation was.* 他不顧一切地試圖說明情況是多麼緊急。◇ **~ that ...** *She did not wish to convey that they were all at fault.* 她不願表示出他們人人都有錯。 **2 ~ sb/sth (from ...) (to ...)** (*formal*) to take, carry or transport sb/sth from one place to another 傳送；運送；輸送：*Pipes convey hot water from the boiler to the radiators.* 管道把熱水從鍋爐輸送到暖氣片。

con·vey·ance /kən'veɪəns/ *noun* **1** [U] (*formal*) the process of taking sb/sth from one place to another 傳送；運送；輸送：*the conveyance of goods by rail* 由火車運輸貨物 **2** [C] (*formal*) a vehicle 運載（或交通）工具；車輛：*horse-drawn conveyances* 馬拉車 **3** [C] (*law* 律) a legal document that moves property from one owner to another 產權轉讓證書

con·vey·an·cer /kən'veɪənsə(r)/ *noun* a lawyer who is an expert in conveyancing 承辦產權轉讓事務的律師

con·vey·an·cing /kən'veɪənsɪŋ/ *noun* [U] (*law* 律) the branch of law concerned with moving property from one owner to another 產權轉讓

con·vey·or /kən'veɪə(r)/ *noun* **1** = CONVEYOR BELT **2** (also **con·vey·er**) (*formal*) a person or thing that carries sth or makes sth known 運送者；傳送者；傳播者；傳達者

con'veyor belt (also **con·vey·or**) *noun* a continuous moving band used for transporting goods from one part of a building to another, for example products in a factory or suitcases in an airport 傳送帶，輸送帶（如輸送工廠的產品或機場的行李）

con·vict *verb, noun*

■ **verb** /kən'vɪkt/ [often passive] **~ sb (of sth)** to decide and state officially in court that sb is guilty of a crime 定罪；宣判⋯有罪： *a convicted murderer* 已定罪的謀殺犯 ◇ *He was convicted of fraud.* 他被判犯有詐騙罪。 **OPP** **acquit** ➲ COLLOCATIONS at JUSTICE

■ ***noun*** /ˈkɒnvɪkt; *NAmE* ˈkɑːn-/ (also *informal* **con**) a person who has been found guilty of a crime and sent to prison 已決犯；服刑囚犯： *an escaped convict* 越獄犯

con·vic·tion /kənˈvɪkʃn/ *noun* **1** [C, U] **~ (for sth)** the act of finding sb guilty of a crime in court; the fact of having been found guilty 判罪；定罪；證明有罪： *She has six previous convictions for theft.* 她有六次盜竊前科。 ◇ *He plans to appeal against his conviction.* 他不服判決，準備上訴。◇ *an offence which carries, on conviction, a sentence of not more than five years' imprisonment* 定罪後可判處五年或以下監禁的罪行 **OPP** **acquittal** ➲ COLLOCATIONS at JUSTICE **2** [C, U] **~ (that …)** a strong opinion or belief 堅定的看法（或信念）： *strong* ***political/moral convictions*** 堅定不移的政治／道德信念 ◇ *She was motivated by deep religious conviction.* 她的行動是出於虔誠的宗教信仰。◇ *a conviction that all would be well in the end* 最終一切都會好起來的堅定信念 **3** [U] the feeling or appearance of believing sth strongly and of being sure about it 深信；堅信；堅定；肯定： *'Not true!' she said with conviction.* "不真實！" 她肯定地說道。◇ *He said he agreed but his voice lacked conviction.* 他說他贊同，但語氣不堅定。◇ *The leader's speech in defence of the policy didn't* ***carry much conviction.*** 那位領導人為政策辯護的講話不是很有說服力。 **IDM** see COURAGE

con·vince 🔑 **AW** /kənˈvɪns/ *verb* **1** 🔑 to make sb/yourself believe that sth is true 使確信；使相信；使信服： **~ sb/yourself (of sth)** *You'll need to convince them of your enthusiasm for the job.* 你要使他們相信你殷切希望得到這份工作。◇ **~ sb/yourself (that)** … *I'd convinced myself (that) I was right.* 我確信自己是正確的。 **2** 🔑 **~ sb to do sth** to persuade sb to do sth 說服，勸說（某人做某事）： *I've been trying to convince him to see a doctor.* 我一直勸他去看病。 ➲ note at PERSUADE

con·vinced **AW** /kənˈvɪnst/ *adj.* **1** [not before noun] completely sure about sth 堅信；深信；確信： *Sam nodded but he didn't look convinced.* 薩姆點了點頭，可他看起來並沒有信服。◇ **~ of sth** *I am convinced of her innocence.* 我堅信她是清白無辜的。◇ **~ that** … *I am convinced that she is innocent.* 我堅信她是清白無辜的。 **OPP** **unconvinced** ➲ SYNONYMS at SURE **2** [only before noun] believing strongly in a particular religion or set of political ideas 堅信不移的；有堅定宗教信仰（或政治信念）的： *a convinced Christian* 虔誠的基督徒

con·vin·cing **AW** /kənˈvɪnsɪŋ/ *adj.* that makes sb believe that sth is true 令人信服的；有說服力的： *a* ***convincing argument/explanation/case*** 有說服力的論點／解釋／事例 ◇ *She sounded very convincing to me* (= I believed what she said). 我覺得她的話很有說服力。◇ *a* ***convincing victory/win*** (= an easy one) 令人折服的勝利 **OPP** **unconvincing** ▶ **con·vin·cing·ly** **AW** *adv.* : *Her case was convincingly argued.* 她的辯詞很有說服力。◇ *They won convincingly.* 他們贏得令人信服。

con·viv·ial /kənˈvɪviəl/ *adj.* cheerful and friendly in atmosphere or character （氣氛或性格）歡快友好的 **SYN** **sociable** : *a convivial evening/atmosphere* 歡樂的夜晚／氣氛 ◇ *convivial company* 快樂的夥伴 ▶ **con·vivi·al·ity** /kənˌvɪviˈæləti/ *noun* [U]

con·vo·ca·tion /ˌkɒnvəˈkeɪʃn; *NAmE* ˌkɑːn-/ *noun* (*formal*) **1** [C] a large formal meeting, especially of Church officials or members of a university （尤指教會或大學的）大型正式會議 **2** [U] the act of calling together a convocation 召集會議 **3** [C] (*NAmE*) a ceremony held in a university or college when students receive their degrees （大學的）學位授予典禮，畢業典禮

con·voke /kənˈvəʊk; *NAmE* -ˈvoʊk/ *verb* **~ sb/sth** (*formal*) to gather together a group of people for a formal meeting 召集，召開（會議） **SYN** **convene**

con·vo·luted /ˈkɒnvəluːtɪd; *NAmE* ˈkɑːn-/ *adj.* **1** extremely complicated and difficult to follow 錯綜複雜的；晦澀難懂的： *a* ***convoluted argument/explanation*** 晦澀費解的論證／闡述 ◇ *a book with a convoluted plot* 情節錯綜複雜的書 **2** (*formal*) having many twists or curves 盤繞的；彎曲的： *a convoluted coastline* 蜿蜒的海岸線

con·vo·lu·tion /ˌkɒnvəˈluːʃn; *NAmE* ˌkɑːn-/ *noun* [usually pl.] (*formal*) **1** a thing that is very complicated and difficult to follow 錯綜複雜的東西；晦澀費解的事： *the bizarre convolutions of the story* 那故事錯綜複雜的離奇情節 **2** a twist or curve, especially one of many （尤指其中之一的）盤繞，彎曲： *the convolutions of the brain* 腦迴

con·vol·vu·lus /kənˈvɒlvjələs; *NAmE* -ˈvɑːlv-/ *noun* [C, U] a wild plant with TRIANGULAR leaves and flowers that are shaped like TRUMPETS. It climbs up walls, fences, etc. and twists itself around other plants. 旋花科植物

con·voy /ˈkɒnvɔɪ; *NAmE* ˈkɑːn-/ *noun* a group of vehicles or ships travelling together, especially when soldiers or other vehicles travel with them for protection （尤指有士兵護送的）車隊，船隊： *a* ***convoy of trucks/lorries/freighters*** 被護送的卡車／貨船隊 ◇ *A United Nations* ***aid convoy*** *loaded with food and medicine finally got through to the besieged town.* 一支聯合國援助車隊載着食物和藥物終於抵達了被圍困的市鎮。

IDM **in ˈconvoy** (of travelling vehicles 行駛中的車輛) as a group; together 結隊；組隊： *We drove in convoy because I didn't know the route.* 因為我不熟悉路線，所以我們結隊行駛。

con·vulse /kənˈvʌls/ *verb* **1** [T, I] **~ (sb) (with sth)** (rather *formal*) to cause a sudden shaking movement in sb's body; to make this movement 使痙攣（或抽筋）；（身體）震動（或抖動）：*A violent shiver convulsed him.* 劇烈的顫抖使他抽搐不已。◇ *His whole body convulsed.* 他全身痙攣。 **2** [T] **be convulsed with laughter, anger, etc.** to be laughing so much, so angry, etc. that you cannot control your movements （因笑、生氣等）全身抖動

con·vul·sion /kənˈvʌlʃn/ *noun* [usually pl.] (rather *formal*) **1** a sudden shaking movement of the body that cannot be controlled 痙攣；抽搐： *The child went into convulsions.* 那孩子全身抽搐起來。 **SYN** **fit** **2** a sudden important change that happens to a country or an organization 動亂；騷動 **SYN** **upheaval**

con·vul·sive /kənˈvʌlsɪv/ *adj.* (of movements or actions 動作或行動) sudden and impossible to control 突然而無法控制的；痙攣的；抽搐的： *a* ***convulsive movement/attack/fit*** 痙攣的動作／發作 ◇ *Her breath came in convulsive gasps.* 她的呼吸突然變得喘不過氣來。 ▶ **con·vul·sive·ly** *adv.* : *weeping convulsively* 抽泣

coo /kuː/ *verb, exclamation*

■ ***verb*** (**coo·ing**, **cooed**, **cooed**) **1** [I] when a DOVE or a PIGEON **coos**, it makes a soft low sound （鴿子）咕咕地叫 **2** [I, T] **(+ speech)** to say sth in a soft quiet voice, especially to sb you love （尤指對所愛的人）輕柔低語，柔情地說 **IDM** see BILL *v.* ▶ **coo** *noun*

■ ***exclamation*** (*BrE, informal*) used to show that you are surprised （表示驚訝）唔，呣： *Coo, look at him!* 唔，看看他！

ˌco-ocˈcur *verb* [I] to occur together or at the same time 同現；共現： *The words 'heavy' and 'rain' co-occur frequently.* * heavy 和 rain 兩詞頻繁同現。 ▶ **co-ocˈcurrence** *noun* [U]

cooee /ˈkuːiː/ *exclamation* (*old-fashioned, BrE, informal*) used as a way of attracting sb's attention （用以引起注意）喂，嗨

IDM **within ˈcooee (of)** (*AustralE, NZE*) not far (from) （離⋯）不遠；（在⋯）附近： *There's loads of cheap accommodation within cooee of the airport.* 機場附近有很多便宜住處。

cook 🔑 /kʊk/ *verb, noun*

■ ***verb*** **1** 🔑 [I, T] to prepare food by heating it, for example by boiling, baking or frying it 烹飪；烹調： *Where did you learn to cook?* 你在哪裏學的烹調？◇ **~ sth** *What's the best way to cook trout?* 鱒魚怎麼做最好吃？◇ *Who's going to cook supper?* 誰來做晚飯？◇ *He cooked lunch for me.* 他給我做了午餐。◇ **~ sb sth** *He cooked me lunch.* 他給我做了午餐。 ➲ COLLOCATIONS at COOKING

C

➲ VISUAL VOCAB pages V27, V28 **2** 🔑 [I] (of food 食物) to be prepared by boiling, baking, frying, etc. 煮（或烘烤、煎炸等）：*While the pasta is cooking, prepare the sauce.* 煮意大利麪的時候，準備醬汁。 **3** [I] **be cooking** (*informal*) to be planned secretly 密謀；秘密策劃：*Everyone is being very secretive—there's something cooking.* 人人都神秘兮兮的，準是在搞什麼鬼把戲。

IDM **be cooking with 'gas** (*NAmE, informal*) to be doing sth very well and successfully 如火如荼地進行；做得起勁 **ˌcook the 'books** (*informal*) to change facts or figures dishonestly or illegally 篡改；杜撰；捏造：*His accountant had been cooking the books for years.* 多年來他的會計師一直在做假賬。 **cook sb's 'goose** (*informal*) to ruin sb's chances of success 毀掉某人成功的機會

PHR V **ˌcook sth↔'up** (*informal*) to invent sth, especially in order to trick sb 捏造；偽造；編造 SYN **concoct**：*to cook up a story* 編造故事

■ ***noun*** 🔑 a person who cooks food or whose job is cooking 做飯的人；炊事員；廚師：*John is a very good cook* (= he cooks well). 約翰很會做菜。◇ *Who was the cook* (= who cooked the food)? 誰做的飯菜？◇ *She was employed as a cook in a hotel.* 她受雇在一家旅館做廚師。➲ compare CHEF

IDM **too many cooks spoil the 'broth** (*saying*) if too many people are involved in doing sth, it will not be done well 廚師多了燒壞湯；人多手雜反壞事；人多添亂

cook·book /ˈkʊkbʊk/ (*BrE* also **ˈcookery book**) *noun* a book that gives instructions on cooking and how to cook individual dishes 烹飪書；烹飪菜譜；食譜

ˈcook-chill *adj.* [only before noun] (*BrE*) food prepared by the **cook-chill** method is cooked, kept at a low temperature and then heated again（食品）速凍的

cook·er 🔑 /ˈkʊkə(r)/ (*BrE*) (*NAmE* **range**) (also **stove** *NAmE, BrE*) *noun* a large piece of equipment for cooking food, containing an oven and gas or electric rings on top（帶烤箱、燃氣爐或電爐的）廚灶，爐具：*a gas cooker* 燃氣廚灶 ◇ *an electric cooker* 電灶 ➲ see also PRESSURE COOKER

cook·ery /ˈkʊkəri/ *noun* [U] (*especially BrE*) the art or activity of preparing and cooking food 烹飪術；烹飪；烹調：*a cookery course* 烹飪課程 ◇ *Italian cookery* 意大利烹飪

ˈcookery book *noun* (*BrE*) = COOKBOOK

cook·house /ˈkʊkhaʊs/ *noun* an outdoor kitchen, for example in a military camp（如軍營中的）戶外廚房，露天廚房

cookie 🔑 /ˈkʊki/ *noun* (*pl.* **-ies**) **1** 🔑 (*especially NAmE*) a small flat sweet cake for one person, usually baked until crisp 曲奇餅：*chocolate chip cookies* 巧克力碎片曲奇 ◇ *a cookie jar* 餅乾罐 ➲ compare BISCUIT (1), CRACKER (1) ➲ see also FORTUNE COOKIE **2** **smart/tough ~** (*NAmE, informal*) a smart/tough person 精明強幹的人；堅強的人 **3** (*computing* 計) a computer file with information in it that is sent to the central SERVER each time a particular person uses a NETWORK or the Internet 網絡餅乾（在用戶每次使用網絡或互聯網時發給中央服務器信息的計算機文件） ➲ COLLOCATIONS at EMAIL IDM see WAY *n.*

ˈcookie cutter *noun, adj.*

■ ***noun*** (*NAmE*) an object used for cutting biscuits in a particular shape 餅乾成型切割刀

■ ***adj.*** **ˈcookie-cutter** [only before noun] (*NAmE, disapproving*) having no special characteristics; not original in any way 千篇一律的；俗套的：*Handmade goods appeal to those who are tired of cookie-cutter products.* 手工製品受到那些已厭倦劃一產品的人的歡迎。

ˈcookie jar *noun* (*NAmE*) a container for biscuits 餅乾罐

IDM **get caught/found with your hand in the ˈcookie jar** (*informal*) to be discovered when doing sth that is illegal or dishonest 當場就擒；當場被發現

ˈcookie sheet (*NAmE*) (*BrE* **ˈbaking sheet**, **ˈbaking tray**) *noun* a small sheet of metal used for baking food on（小片）烘烤板（或盤）

cook·ing 🔑 /ˈkʊkɪŋ/ *noun, adj.*

■ ***noun*** [U] **1** 🔑 the process of preparing food 烹飪；烹調：*My husband does all the cooking.* 我丈夫把做飯全包了下來。◇ *a book on Indian cooking* 一本關於印度烹飪的書 ➲ VISUAL VOCAB pages V27, V28 **2** food that has been prepared in a particular way（用某種方法烹製的）食物，飯菜：*The restaurant offers traditional home cooking* (= food similar to that cooked at home). 這家餐館供應傳統的家常菜。◇ *They serve good French cooking.* 他們供應美味的法國菜。

■ ***adj.*** suitable for cooking rather than eating raw or drinking 適於烹飪的（不宜於生吃或直接飲用的）：*cooking sherry* 烹飪用的雪利酒

ˈcooking apple *noun* (*BrE*) any type of apple that is suitable for cooking, rather than eating raw 烹調用的蘋果 ➲ compare EATING APPLE

ˈcooking gas (*US*) (*BrE* **Calor gas™**) *noun* [U] a type of gas stored as a liquid under pressure in metal containers and used for heating and cooking in places where there is no gas supply 灌裝液化氣（用於取暖和做飯）

cook·out /ˈkʊkaʊt/ *noun* (*NAmE, informal*) a meal or party when food is cooked over an open fire outdoors, for example at a beach 露天燒烤餐；野外燒烤宴會 ➲ compare BARBECUE *n.* (2)

cook·shop /ˈkʊkʃɒp; *NAmE* -ʃɑːp/ *noun* (*BrE*) a shop/store where equipment for cooking with is sold 炊具店；廚具店

cook·ware /ˈkʊkweə(r); *NAmE* -wer/ *noun* [U] pots and containers used in cooking 炊具；烹飪用具

cool 🔑 /kuːl/ *adj., verb, noun*

■ ***adj.*** (**cool·er**, **cool·est**)

▸ FAIRLY COLD 涼爽 **1** 🔑 fairly cold; not hot or warm 涼的；涼爽的；涼快的：*a cool breeze/drink/climate* 涼爽的微風；清涼的飲料；涼快的氣候 ◇ *Cooler weather is forecast for the weekend.* 預報本週末天氣較涼。◇ *Let's sit in the shade and keep cool.* 咱們坐在陰涼處乘涼吧。◇ *Store lemons in a cool dry place.* 把檸檬貯存在乾燥涼爽的地方。 ➲ SYNONYMS at COLD

▸ COLOURS 顏色 **2** making you feel pleasantly cool 使人感到涼爽的；冷色的：*a room painted in cool greens and blues* 塗成令人感到涼爽的綠色和藍色的房間

▸ CALM 冷靜 **3** 🔑 calm; not excited, angry or emotional 冷靜的；鎮靜的；平靜的：*Keep cool!* 保持冷靜！◇ *She tried to remain **cool, calm and collected*** (= calm). 她試圖保持冷靜、沉着、鎮定。◇ *He has a **cool head*** (= he stays calm in an emergency). 他頭腦冷靜。

▸ NOT FRIENDLY/ENTHUSIASTIC 不友好／熱情 **4** 🔑 not friendly, interested or enthusiastic 不友好的；冷淡的；冷漠的：*She was decidedly cool about the proposal.* 她對這個提議顯然十分冷淡。◇ *They gave the Prime Minister **a cool reception**.* 他們對首相報以冷淡的反應。

▸ APPROVING 讚許 **5** (*informal*) used to show that you admire or approve of sth because it is fashionable, attractive and often different（因時髦、漂亮且與眾不同而）令人欽佩的，絕妙的，酷的：*You look pretty cool with that new haircut.* 你新剪的髮型真酷。◇ *It's a cool movie.* 那部電影真棒。 ➲ SYNONYMS at GREAT **6** (*informal*) people say **Cool!** or **That's cool** to show that they approve of sth or agree to a suggestion（表示滿意或贊同）妙極的，酷的：*'We're meeting Jake for lunch and we can go on the yacht in the afternoon.' 'Cool!'* "我們和傑克一起吃午飯，下午乘遊艇玩去。" "棒極了！" ◇ *'Can you come at 10.30 tomorrow?' 'That's cool.'* "你明天 10:30 能來嗎？" "沒問題。" ◇ *I was surprised that she got the job, but **I'm cool with it*** (= it's not a problem for me). 我對於她得到這份工作感到驚訝，但覺得還可以接受。

▸ CONFIDENT 自信 **7** (*informal*) calm and confident in a way that lacks respect for other people, but makes people admire you as well as disapprove 孤傲冷漠的；滿不在乎的：*She just took his keys and walked out with them, cool as you please.* 她拿了他的鑰匙就跟他們走了，你看多有性格。

▸ MONEY 金錢 **8** [only before noun] (*informal*) used about a sum of money to emphasize how large it is（強調金額之大）整整的，足足的：*The car cost a cool thirty thousand.* 那輛車花了整整三萬。 ➲ see also COOLLY, COOLNESS

IDM (as) ˌ**cool as a** ˈ**cucumber** very calm and controlled, especially in a difficult situation（尤指在困難情況下）非常冷靜，泰然自若 **play it** ˈ**cool** (*informal*) to deal with a situation in a calm way and not show what you are really feeling 沉着應付；冷靜處理；不動聲色 ➲ more at LONG *adj.*

■ *verb*

▸ BECOME COLDER 變涼 **1** [I, T] to become or to make sb/sth become cool or cooler（使）變涼，冷卻：*Glass contracts as it cools.* 玻璃遇冷收縮。◇ **~ sth** *The cylinder is cooled by a jet of water.* 氣缸可用噴水冷卻。

▸ BECOME CALMER 變得冷靜 **2** [I] to become calmer, less excited or less enthusiastic 冷靜下來；鎮靜下來；冷淡下來：*I think we should wait until tempers have cooled.* 我認為我們應該等到怒火平息下來再說。◇ *Relations between them have definitely cooled* (= they are not as friendly with each other as they were). 他們之間的關係已明顯地冷下來。

IDM ˈ**cool it!** (*informal*) used to tell sb to be calmer and less excited or angry（用於勸說）冷靜下來，沉住氣，別激動，息怒 ˌ**cool your** ˈ**heels** (*informal*) to have to wait for sb/sth 不得不等待；久等

PHR V ˌ**cool** ˈ**down**/ˈ**off 1** to become cool or cooler 變涼；冷卻下來：*We cooled off with a swim in the lake.* 在湖裏游泳後我們感到涼快了。 **2** to become calm, less excited or less enthusiastic 鎮靜下來；變冷淡；不再那麼激動：*I think you should wait until she's cooled down a little.* 我覺得你應該等她鎮靜一點再說。 ˌ**cool sb**↔ˈ**down**/ˈ**off 1** to make sb feel cooler 使感到涼快（或涼爽）：*Drink plenty of cold water to cool yourself down.* 多喝點涼水，讓自己涼快涼快。 **2** to make sb calm, less excited or less enthusiastic 使冷靜；使平靜；使冷淡：*A few hours in a police cell should cool him off.* 在警察局班房裏關上幾個小時就會使他平靜下來。 ˌ**cool sth**↔ˈ**down**/ˈ**off** to make sth cool or cooler 使（某物）變涼；使冷卻下來 ˌ**cool** ˈ**out** (*informal*) to relax and become calm after a period of activity or stress 放鬆下來；鎮靜下來：*It's a wonderful place to cool out with a glass of beer.* 這兒真是個不錯的地方，可以喝杯啤酒放鬆一下。◇ *It sounds like he needs some time to cool out.* 聽起來，他還需要一段時間鎮靜下來。

■ *noun* **the cool** [sing.] cool air or a cool place 涼氣；涼快的地方：*the cool of the evening* 夜晚的涼爽

IDM **keep your cool** (*informal*) to remain calm in a difficult situation（在困難的情況下）保持冷靜，沉着 **lose your cool** (*informal*) to become angry or excited 火冒三丈；失去冷靜

coola·bah *noun* = COOLIBAH

Collocations 詞語搭配

Cooking 烹飪

Preparing 準備

- **prepare** a dish/a meal/a menu/dinner/the fish 準備一道菜／一頓飯／一份菜單／正餐／魚
- **weigh out** 100g/4oz of sugar/the ingredients 稱出 100 克／4 盎司的糖／食材
- **wash/rinse** the lettuce/spinach/watercress 洗生菜／菠菜／西洋菜
- **chop/slice/dice** the carrots/onions/potatoes 把胡蘿蔔／洋葱／土豆切碎／切成片／切成丁
- **peel** the carrots/onion/potatoes/garlic/orange 給胡蘿蔔／洋葱／土豆／大蒜／橘子去皮
- **grate** a carrot/the cheese/some nutmeg 將胡蘿蔔／乾酪／一些肉豆蔻磨碎
- **remove/discard** the bones/seeds/skin 去骨；去籽；去皮
- **blend/combine/mix (together)** the flour and water/all the ingredients 把麪粉和水／所有的食材和在一起
- **beat/whisk** the cream/eggs/egg whites 攪打奶油／雞蛋／雞蛋清
- **knead/shape/roll (out)** the dough 揉捏／定型／擀平麪糰

Cooking 烹飪；烹調

- **heat** the oil in a frying pan 在平底煎鍋裏將油燒熱
- **preheat/heat** the oven/(*BrE*) the grill/(*NAmE*) the broiler 將烤箱／烤架預熱／加熱
- **bring to** (*BrE*) the boil/(*NAmE*) a boil 使沸騰
- **stir** constantly/gently with a wooden spoon 用木勺子不停地／輕輕地攪拌
- **reduce** the heat 把溫度調低
- **simmer** gently for 20 minutes/until reduced by half 用文火燉 20 分鐘／燉到量減少一半
- **melt** the butter/chocolate/cheese/sugar 使黃油／巧克力／奶酪／糖融化
- **brown** the meat for 8-20 minutes 把肉加熱 8 至 20 分鐘使之成棕色
- **drain** the pasta/the water from the pot/in a colander 把意大利麪濾乾；把水從鍋裏濾出來／濾到濾器裏
- **mash** the potatoes/banana/avocado 把土豆／香蕉／油梨搗碎

Ways of cooking 烹飪方式

- **cook** food/fish/meat/rice/pasta/a Persian dish 烹飪食物／魚／肉／米飯／意大利麪食／波斯菜
- **bake** (a loaf of) bread/a cake/(*especially NAmE*) cookies/(*BrE*) biscuits/a pie/potatoes/fish/scones/muffins 烤（一條）麪包／一塊蛋糕／曲奇餅／小甜餅／餡餅／土豆／魚／司康餅／小鬆糕
- **boil** cabbage/potatoes/an egg/water 煮洋白菜／土豆／雞蛋；燒開水
- **fry/deep-fry/stir-fry** the chicken/vegetables 煎／油炸／炒雞肉／蔬菜
- **grill** meat/steak/chicken/sausages/a hot dog 燒烤肉／牛排／雞肉／香腸／熱狗
- **roast** potatoes/peppers/meat/chicken/lamb 烘烤土豆／甜椒／肉／雞肉／羊羔肉
- **sauté** garlic/mushrooms/onions/potatoes/vegetables 炒大蒜／蘑菇／洋葱／土豆／蔬菜
- **steam** rice/vegetables/spinach/asparagus/dumplings 蒸米飯／蔬菜／菠菜／蘆筍／餃子
- **toast** bread/nuts 烤麪包／堅果
- **microwave** food/popcorn/(*BrE*) a ready meal 用微波爐烹調（或加熱）食物／爆米花／預製餐

Serving 上菜

- **serve** in a glass/on a bed of rice/with potatoes 盛在玻璃杯裏上；上蓋飯；和土豆一起上
- **arrange** the slices on a plate/in a layer 把切片在盤子裏擺好／鋪成一層
- **carve** the meat/lamb/chicken/turkey 把肉／羊羔肉／雞肉／火雞切成塊
- **dress/toss** a salad 給色拉加調味醬；拌色拉
- **dress with/drizzle with** olive oil/vinaigrette 澆上橄欖油／色拉調味汁
- **top with** a slice of lemon/a scoop of ice cream/whipped cream/syrup 上面放一片檸檬／一勺冰淇淋／攪打好的奶油／糖漿
- **garnish with** a sprig of parsley/fresh basil leaves/lemon wedges/a slice of lime/a twist of orange 用一小枝歐芹／新鮮的羅勒葉／檸檬角／一片酸橙／一捲橘子皮做飾菜
- **sprinkle with** salt/sugar/herbs/parsley/freshly ground black pepper 灑上鹽／糖／香草／歐芹／剛磨碎的黑胡椒

C

cool·ant /ˈkuːlənt/ *noun* [C, U] a liquid that is used for cooling an engine, a nuclear REACTOR, etc. 冷卻劑（用於發動機、核反應堆等）

ˈcool bag, ˈcool box *noun* (*BrE*) a bag or box which keeps food or drinks cold and which can be used for a PICNIC 冰袋，冰盒（用於保存野餐食物或飲料）➲ see also COOLER (1)

cool·drink /ˈkuːldrɪŋk/ *noun* (*SAfrE*) = SOFT DRINK

cool·er /ˈkuːlə(r)/ *noun* **1** [C] a container or machine which cools things, especially drinks, or keeps them cold 冷卻器；冷藏器：*the office water cooler* 辦公室的飲水冷卻器 ◇ (*especially NAmE*) *They took a cooler full of drinks to the beach.* 他們把冷藏器裝滿飲料帶到了海灘。➲ VISUAL VOCAB page V69 **2** [C] (*NAmE*) a drink with ice and usually wine in it（通常有冰和酒的）清涼飲料：*a wine cooler* 含酒的清涼飲料

ˌcool-ˈheaded *adj.* calm; not showing excitement or nerves 頭腦冷靜的；沉着的：*a cool-headed assessment of the situation* 對局勢頭腦冷靜的估計

coo·li·bah /ˈkuːlɪbɑː/ (also **coola·bah**) *noun* an Australian tree that produces a strong hard wood 澳洲膠樹

coolie /ˈkuːli/ *noun* (*old-fashioned, taboo*) an offensive word for a worker in Eastern countries with no special skills or training 苦力（含冒犯意，指東方國家裏沒有專門技能或未受過訓練的工人）

ˌcooling-ˈoff period *noun* **1** a period of time during which two sides in a disagreement try to reach an agreement before taking further action, for example by going on strike（爭執雙方試圖達成協議的）冷卻期，冷靜期 **2** a period of time after sb has agreed to buy sth, such as an insurance plan, during which they can change their mind（在同意購買某物如保險計劃後可改變主意的）可變更期，等待期

ˈcooling tower *noun* a large high round building used in industry for cooling water before it is used again 冷卻塔

cool·ly /ˈkuːlli/ *adv.* **1** in a way that is not friendly or enthusiastic 冷漠地；冷淡地：*'We're just good friends,' she said coolly.* "我們僅僅是好朋友而已。"她冷冷地説道。◇ *He received my suggestion coolly.* 他對我的建議反應冷淡。 **2** in a calm way 冷靜地；沉着地

cool·ness /ˈkuːlnəs/ *noun* [U] the quality of being cool 涼；涼爽；涼快；冷靜；冷漠：*the delicious coolness of the water* 清涼爽口的水 ◇ *I admire her coolness under pressure.* 我佩服她在壓力下能保持冷靜。◇ *I noticed a certain coolness* (= lack of friendly feeling) *between them.* 我覺察到他們之間有些冷淡。

coon /kuːn/ *noun* (*taboo, slang*) a very offensive word for a black person（冒犯語，指黑人）黑鬼

coop /kuːp/ *noun, verb*

■ ***noun*** a CAGE for chickens, etc.（關雞等的）籠子 IDM see FLY *v.*

■ ***verb***

PHR V **ˌcoop sb/sth ˈup** [usually passive] to keep a person or an animal inside a building or in a small space 把…關（或禁錮）起來；拘禁

ˈco-op *noun* (*informal*) a COOPERATIVE shop/store, society or business 合作商店；合作社；合作性商業機構：*a housing co-op* 住房合作社

coop·er /ˈkuːpə(r)/ *noun* a person who makes BARRELS 製桶工人；箍桶匠

co·oper·ate AW (*BrE* also **co-operate**) /kəʊˈɒpəreɪt; *NAmE* koʊˈɑːp-/ *verb* **1** [I] **~ (with sb) (in/on sth)** to work together with sb else in order to achieve sth 合作；協作：*The two groups agreed to cooperate with each other.* 這兩個組同意相互協作。◇ *They had cooperated closely in the planning of the project.* 他們曾密切合作，共同規劃這一項目。 **2** [I] **~ (with sb) (in/on sth)** to be helpful by doing what sb asks you to do 協助；配合：*Their captors told them they would be killed unless they cooperated.* 抓住他們的人説如果他們不配合就殺掉他們。

co·oper·ation AW (*BrE* also **co-operation**) /kəʊˌɒpəˈreɪʃn; *NAmE* koʊˌɑːp-/ *noun* [U] **1** the fact of doing sth together or of working together towards a shared aim 合作；協作：**~ (with sb) (in doing sth)** *a report produced by the government in cooperation with the chemical industry* 政府與化工行業合作提出的一份報告 ◇ **~ (between A and B)** *We would like to see closer cooperation between parents and schools.* 我們希望家長和學校有更加緊密的合作。 **2 ~ (in doing sth)** willingness to be helpful and do as you are asked 協助；配合：*We would be grateful for your cooperation in clearing the hall as quickly as possible.* 你們若大力協助儘快把大廳騰空，我們將不勝感激。

co·opera·tive AW (*BrE* also **co-operative**) /kəʊˈɒpərətɪv; *NAmE* koʊˈɑːp-/ *adj., noun*

■ ***adj.*** **1** [usually before noun] involving doing sth together or working together with others towards a shared aim 合作的；協作的；同心協力的：*Cooperative activity is essential to effective community work.* 要把社區工作做好，協作活動是必不可少的。 **2** helpful by doing what you are asked to do 協助的；配合的：*Employees will generally be more cooperative if their views are taken seriously.* 如果雇員的意見得到認真對待，他們一般都會更加配合。 OPP **uncooperative** **3** [usually before noun] (*business* 商) owned and run by the people involved, with the profits shared by them 共同擁有共同經營利益共享的；合作的：*a cooperative farm* 合作農場 ▶ **co·opera·tive·ly** AW (*BrE* also **co-operatively**) *adv.*

■ ***noun*** a cooperative business or other organization 合作企業；合作社組織：*agricultural cooperatives in India* 印度的農業合作社 ◇ *The factory is now a workers' cooperative.* 這家工廠現為工人合作企業。

ˌco-ˈopt *verb* **1 ~ sb (onto/into sth)** to make sb a member of a group, committee, etc. by the agreement of all the other members（經所有成員同意）增選（某人）為委員：*She was co-opted onto the board.* 她獲增選為董事會成員。 **2 ~ sb (onto/into sth)** to include sb in sth, often when they do not want to be part of it 拉攏；籠絡

co·ord·in·ate AW (*BrE* also **co-ordinate**) *verb, noun*

■ ***verb*** /kəʊˈɔːdɪneɪt; *NAmE* koʊˈɔːrd-/ **1** [T] **~ sth** to organize the different parts of an activity and the people involved in it so that it works well 使協調；使相配合：*They appointed a new manager to coordinate the work of the team.* 為協調這個隊的工作，他們任用了一位新經理。◇ *We need to develop a coordinated approach to the problem.* 我們需要制訂一個協調一致的方式來解決這個問題。 **2** [T] **~ sth** to make the different parts of your body work well together 使（身體各部位）動作協調；協同動作 ➲ see also UNCOORDINATED **3** [I, T] **~ (sth) (with sth)** (rather *formal*) if you **coordinate** clothes, furniture, etc. or if they **coordinate**, they look nice together（使衣服、傢具等）搭配，協調：*This shade coordinates with a wide range of other colours.* 這種深淺的顏色可與很多顏色搭配。 ▶ **co·ord·in·ator** (*BrE* also **co-ordinator**) *noun*：*The campaign needs an effective coordinator.* 這場運動需要一個能幹的協調人。

■ ***noun*** /kəʊˈɔːdɪnət; *NAmE* koʊˈɔːrd-/ **1** [C] either of two numbers or letters used to fix the position of a point on a map or GRAPH 坐標：*the x, y coordinates of any point on a line* 一條線上任意一點的 x、y 坐標 **2 coordinates** [pl.] (used in shops/stores etc. 商店等用) pieces of clothing that can be worn together because, for example, the colours look good together（顏色協調的）配套服裝，套裝

coordinate clause /kəʊˌɔːdɪnət ˈklɔːz; *NAmE* koʊˌɔːrd-/ *noun* (*grammar* 語法) each of two or more parts of a sentence, often joined by *and, or, but*, etc., that make separate statements that each have an equal importance 並列分句，並列子句（常由 and、or、but 等連接）➲ compare SUBORDINATE CLAUSE

coˌordinating conˈjunction *noun* (*grammar* 語法) a word such as *or, and* or *but*, that connects clauses or sentences of equal importance 並列連詞 ➲ compare SUBORDINATING CONJUNCTION

co·ord·in·ation AW (*BrE* also **co-ordination**) /kəʊˌɔːdɪˈneɪʃn; *NAmE* koʊˌɔːrd-/ *noun* [U] **1** the act of making parts of sth, groups of people, etc. work together in an efficient and organized way 協作；協調；配合：*a need for greater coordination between departments* 各部門間加強配合的必要 ◇ *a lack of coordination in conservation* *policy* 環保政策的不協調 ◇ *a pamphlet produced by the government* ***in coordination with*** (= working together with) *the Sports Council* 政府與體育委員會合作發行的小冊子 ◇ *advice on colour coordination* (= choosing colours that look nice together, for example in clothes or furniture) 對顏色搭配的建議 **2** the ability to control your movements well 協調動作的能力： *You need good hand-eye coordination to play ball games.* 玩球類遊戲，手和眼的動作要協調好。

coot /kuːt/ *noun* **1** a black bird with a white FOREHEAD and beak that lives on or near water 蹼雞（黑色水鳥，額和喙為白色） **2 old ~** (*NAmE, informal*) a stupid person 笨蛋；傻瓜 IDM see BALD

cop /kɒp; *NAmE* kɑːp/ *noun, verb*

■ ***noun*** (*informal*) a police officer 警察： *Somebody call the cops!* 去個人報警啊！ ◇ *children playing* ***cops and robbers*** 在玩警察抓壞蛋遊戲的孩子們 ◇ *a TV cop show* 電視警察節目

IDM **not much 'cop** (*BrE, slang*) not very good 不太好；不怎麼樣： *He's not much cop as a singer.* 他的歌唱得不怎麼樣。 ➲ more at FAIR *adj.*

■ ***verb*** (**-pp-**) (*informal*) **1 ~ sth** to receive or suffer sth unpleasant 遭受；忍受： *He copped all the hassle after the accident.* 他在事故發生後各種的麻煩都受了。 **2 ~ sth** to notice sth 注意到： ***Cop a load of this!*** (= Listen to this) 聽聽這一大套！

IDM **cop hold of sth** (*BrE, informal*) to take hold of sth 抓住，握住（某物） **cop a 'plea** (*NAmE, informal*) to admit in court to being guilty of a small crime in the hope of receiving less severe punishment for a more serious crime 避重就輕地認罪（以求輕判） ➲ compare PLEA-BARGAINING **'cop it** (*BrE, slang*) **1** to be punished 被罰；受罰 **2** to be killed 被殺

PHR V **,cop 'off (with sb)** (*BrE, slang*) to start a sexual or romantic experience with sb （與某人）開始發生性關係，調情： *Who did he cop off with at the party?* 他在聚會上與誰調情？ **,cop 'out (of sth)** (*informal*) to avoid or stop doing sth that you should do because you are afraid, lazy, etc. （因害怕、懶惰等而）逃避，迴避： *You're not going to cop out at the last minute, are you?* 你不是打算臨陣脫逃吧？ ➲ related noun COP-OUT

cope 🔑 /kəʊp; *NAmE* koʊp/ *verb, noun*

■ ***verb*** 🔑 [I] to deal successfully with sth difficult （成功地）對付，處理 SYN **manage**： *I got to the stage where I wasn't coping any more.* 到了這個階段，我已經無法應付了。 ◇ **~ with sth** *He wasn't able to cope with the stresses and strains of the job.* 對付這項工作的緊張與壓力，他無能為力。 ◇ *Desert plants are adapted to cope with extreme heat.* 沙漠植物適於耐酷熱。

■ ***noun*** a long loose piece of clothing worn by priests on special occasions （聖職人員在特定禮儀中穿的）斗篷式祭衣，大圓衣

copier /'kɒpiə(r); *NAmE* 'kɑːp-/ *noun* (*especially NAmE*) = PHOTOCOPIER

'co-pilot *noun* a second pilot who helps the main pilot in an aircraft （飛機的）副駕駛員

cop·ing /'kəʊpɪŋ; *NAmE* 'koʊpɪŋ/ *noun* (*architecture* 建) the top row of bricks or stones, usually sloping, on a wall 牆壓頂

co·pi·ous /'kəʊpiəs; *NAmE* 'koʊ-/ *adj.* in large amounts 大量的；充裕的；豐富的 SYN **abundant**： *copious* (= large) *amounts of water* 大量的水 ◇ *I took copious notes.* 我做了詳盡的筆記。 ◇ *She supports her theory with copious evidence.* 她以大量的論據來支持自己的理論。 ▸ **co·pi·ous·ly** *adv.*： *bleeding copiously* 大量出血

'cop-out *noun* (*informal, disapproving*) a way of avoiding doing sth that you should do, or an excuse for not doing it 逃避（或躲避）的方法；（不做某事的）藉口： *Not turning up was just a cop-out.* 不露面只不過是在逃避而已。

cop·per /'kɒpə(r); *NAmE* 'kɑːp-/ *noun* **1** [U] (*symb.* **Cu**) a chemical element. Copper is a soft reddish-brown metal used for making electric wires, pipes and coins. 銅： *a copper mine* 銅礦 ◇ *copper pipes* 銅管 ◇ *copper-coloured hair* 紅棕色的頭髮 **2 coppers** [pl.] (*BrE*) brown coins that do not have much value 銅幣： *I only paid a few coppers for it.* 我只花了幾個銅板買下這東西。 **3** [C] (*BrE, informal*) a police officer 警察

,copper 'beech *noun* a tall type of BEECH tree with smooth BARK and reddish-brown leaves 紫葉山毛櫸

,copper-'bottomed *adj.* (*BrE*) that you can trust or rely on completely 完全可靠的；穩妥的： *a copper-bottomed guarantee* 完全可信的保證

cop·per·head /'kɒpəhed; *NAmE* 'kɑːpər-/ *noun* one of several types of poisonous snake that are a brownish colour 銅頭蛇

cop·per·plate /'kɒpəpleɪt; *NAmE* 'kɑːpər-/ *noun* [U] a neat old-fashioned way of writing with sloping letters joined together 銅版體（老式書寫體，筆畫工整傾斜、相互連接）；工整的手寫體

cop·pery /'kɒpəri; *NAmE* 'kɑːp-/ *adj.* similar to or having the colour of COPPER 似銅的；紫銅色的： *coppery hair* 紅棕色的頭髮

cop·pice /'kɒpɪs; *NAmE* 'kɑːp-/ *verb, noun*

■ ***verb*** [T, I] **~ (sth)** (*technical* 術語) to cut back young trees in order to make them grow faster 修剪（小樹）以助長

■ ***noun*** = COPSE

copra /'kɒprə; *NAmE* 'kɑːprə/ *noun* [U] the dried white flesh of COCONUTS 椰仁乾

copse /kɒps; *NAmE* kɑːps/ (also **cop·pice**) *noun* a small area of trees or bushes growing together 矮林；萌生林 ➲ VISUAL VOCAB pages V2, V3

'cop shop *noun* (*informal*) a police station 警察局；局子

cop·ter /'kɒptə(r); *NAmE* 'kɑːp-/ *noun* (*informal*) = HELICOPTER

cop·ula /'kɒpjələ; *NAmE* 'kɑːp-/ *noun* (*grammar* 語法) = LINKING VERB

copu·late /'kɒpjuleɪt; *NAmE* 'kɑːp-/ *verb* [I] **~ (with sb/sth)** (*technical* 術語) to have sex 性交；交媾；交配；交尾 ▸ **copu·la·tion** /ˌkɒpju'leɪʃn; *NAmE* ˌkɑːp-/ *noun* [U]

copy 🔑 /'kɒpi; *NAmE* 'kɑːpi/ *noun, verb*

■ ***noun*** (*pl.* **-ies**) **1** 🔑 [C] **~ (of sth)** a thing that is made to be the same as sth else, especially a document or a work of art （尤指文件或藝術品的）複印件，副本，複製品： *I will send you a copy of the report.* 我會把這個報告的複印本寄給你。 ◇ *The thieves replaced the original painting with a copy.* 盜賊們用摹本換走了原畫。 ◇ *You should* ***make a copy*** *of the disk as a backup.* 你應該將磁盤複製一個備份。 ➲ see also HARD COPY **2** 🔑 [C] a single example of a book, newspaper, etc. of which many have been made （書、報紙等的）一本，一冊，一份： *a copy of 'The Times'* 一份《泰晤士報》 ◇ *The book sold 20 000 copies within two weeks.* 這本書在兩週內銷售了2萬冊。 ➲ see also BACK COPY **3** [U] written material that is to be printed in a newspaper, magazine, etc.; news or information that can be used in a newspaper article or advertisement （報刊等的）稿件；（可用於報紙文章或廣告的）消息，信息： *The subeditors prepare the reporters' copy for the paper and write the headlines.* 助理編輯處理記者為報紙寫的稿件並加標題。 ◇ *This will make great copy for the advertisement.* 這可當作這則廣告的絕妙廣告詞。 **4** [C] = PHOTOCOPY： *Could I have ten copies of this page, please?* 請把這一頁給我複印十份好嗎？ **5** [C] (*IndE*) a book used by students for writing exercises, etc. in 作業本；練習本

■ ***verb*** (**cop·ies**, **copy·ing**, **cop·ied**, **cop·ied**) **1** 🔑 [T] **~ sth** to make sth that is exactly like sth else 複製；複印；仿造；臨摹： *They copied the designs from those on Greek vases.* 他們臨摹希臘花瓶上的圖案。 ◇ *Everything in the computer's memory can be copied onto DVDs.* 計算機內存裏的所有資料都可以複製到 DVD 光盤上。 **2** 🔑 [T] to write sth exactly as it is written somewhere else 抄寫；謄寫： **~ sth (from sth) (into/onto sth)** *She copied the phone number into her address book.* 她把那個電話號碼抄寫在自己的通訊錄上。 ◇ **~ sth (down/out)** *I copied out several poems.* 我抄錄了幾首詩歌。 **3** 🔑 [T] **~ sb/sth** to behave or do sth in the same way as sb else 模仿；效法；仿效 SYN **imitate**： *She copies everything her sister does.* 她一切都效仿她的姐姐。 ◇ *Their tactics have been*

C

copied by other terrorist organizations. 他們的手段已被其他恐怖組織效仿。 **4** [I] ~ **(from/off sb)** to cheat in an exam, school work, etc. by writing what sb else has written and pretending it is your own work 作弊；抄襲 **5** [T] ~ **sth** (*especially NAmE*) = PHOTOCOPY

PHR V **,copy sb 'in (on sth)** to send sb a copy of a letter, email message, etc. that you are sending to sb else 把（信件、電子郵件等）抄送某人；給某人寄…的副本：*Can you copy me in on your report?* 你的報告給我抄送一份好嗎？

copy·book /ˈkɒpibʊk; *NAmE* ˈkɑːp-/ *noun, adj.*

■ ***noun*** a book, used in the past by children in school, containing examples of writing which school students had to copy（舊時有書法範例的）習字帖，練字本 IDM see BLOT *v.*

■ ***adj.*** [only before noun] (*BrE*) done exactly how it should be done（做得）精確的，準確的：*It was a copybook operation by the police.* 警方的這一行動非常出色。

copy·cat /ˈkɒpikæt; *NAmE* ˈkɑːp-/ *noun, adj.*

■ ***noun*** (*informal, disapproving*) used especially by children about and to a person who copies what sb else does because they have no ideas of their own（尤為兒童用語，指無主見的）模仿者，抄襲者，好跟人學的人

■ ***adj.*** [only before noun] (of crimes 罪行) similar to and seen as copying an earlier well-known crime 模仿犯罪的

ˈcopy editor *noun* a person whose job is to correct and prepare a text for printing 文字編輯 ▸ **ˈcopy-edit** *verb* [T, I]

copy·ist /ˈkɒpiɪst; *NAmE* ˈkɑːp-/ *noun* a person who makes copies of written documents or works of art 繕寫員；謄寫員；抄寫員；臨摹者

copy·right /ˈkɒpiraɪt; *NAmE* ˈkɑːp-/ *noun, adj., verb*

■ ***noun*** [U, C] ~ **(in/on sth)** if a person or an organization holds the **copyright** on a piece of writing, music, etc., they are the only people who have the legal right to publish, broadcast, perform it, etc., and other people must ask their permission to use it or any part of it 版權；著作權：*Who owns the copyright on this song?* 誰擁有這首歌曲的版權？◇ *Copyright expires seventy years after the death of the author.* 版權在作者去世七十年後期滿無效。◇ *They were sued for* ***breach/infringement*** *of copyright.* 他們被指控侵犯版權。

■ ***adj.*** (*abbr.* ©) protected by copyright; not allowed to be copied without permission 受版權保護的；未經准許不得複製的：*copyright material* 版權資料

■ ***verb*** ~ **sth** to get the copyright for sth 獲得…的版權

ˈcopyright library *noun* in the UK and Ireland, a library that must receive a copy of every book that is published in the country 版本圖書館（在英國和愛爾蘭，國內出版的每一種圖書都必須收藏一冊）

ˈcopy typist *noun* (*BrE*) a person whose job is to type things that they copy from written documents（文件的）打字員

copy·writer /ˈkɒpiraɪtə(r); *NAmE* ˈkɑːp-/ *noun* a person whose job is to write the words for advertising material 廣告文字撰寫人；撰稿人

coq au vin /ˌkɒk əʊ ˈvæ̃; *NAmE* ˌkoʊk oʊ; ˌkɑːk/ *noun* [U] (from *French*) a dish of chicken cooked in wine 紅酒燜雞

co·quet·ry /ˈkɒkɪtri; *NAmE* ˈkoʊk-/ *noun* [U] (*literary*) behaviour that is typical of a coquette 賣弄風情；賣俏；媚態

co·quette /kɒˈket; *NAmE* koʊˈket/ *noun* (*literary, often disapproving*) a woman who behaves in a way that is intended to attract men 賣弄風情的女人 SYN **flirt** ▸ **co·quet·tish** /kɒˈketɪʃ; *NAmE* koʊˈk-/ *adj.*: *a coquettish smile* 賣弄風騷的微笑 **co·quet·tish·ly** *adv.*

cor /kɔː(r)/ (also **ˌcor ˈbli·mey**) *exclamation* (*BrE, informal*) used when you are surprised, pleased or impressed by sth（驚訝、欣喜或感動時說）啊呀，天哪：*Cor! Look at that!* 啊呀！看看那個！

cor·acle /ˈkɒrəkl; *NAmE* ˈkɔːr-; ˈkɑːr-/ *noun* a small round boat with a wooden frame, used in Wales and Ireland 科拉科爾小艇（威爾士和愛爾蘭用的木結構圓形小船）

coral /ˈkɒrəl; *NAmE* ˈkɔːrəl; ˈkɑːrəl/ *noun, adj.*

■ ***noun*** **1** [U] a hard substance that is red, pink or white in colour, and that forms on the bottom of the sea from the bones of very small creatures. Coral is often used in jewellery. 珊瑚：***coral reefs/islands*** 珊瑚礁／島 ◇ *a coral necklace* 珊瑚項鏈 **2** [C] a creature that produces coral 珊瑚蟲

■ ***adj.*** pink or red in colour, like coral 珊瑚色的；紅色的；粉紅的：*coral lipstick* 珊瑚色的唇膏

cor ang·lais /ˌkɔːr ˈɒŋgleɪ; *NAmE* ɔːŋˈgleɪ/ *noun* (*pl.* **cors anglais** /ˌkɔːr ˈɒŋgleɪ; *NAmE* ɔːŋˈgleɪ/) (*especially BrE*) (also **ˌEnglish ˈhorn** especially in *NAmE*) a musical instrument of the WOODWIND group, like an OBOE but larger and playing lower notes 英國管；次中音雙簧管

cor·bel /ˈkɔːbl; *NAmE* ˈkɔːrbl/ *noun* (*architecture* 建) a piece of stone or wood that sticks out from a wall to support sth, for example an ARCH（牆壁上的）托臂，梁托

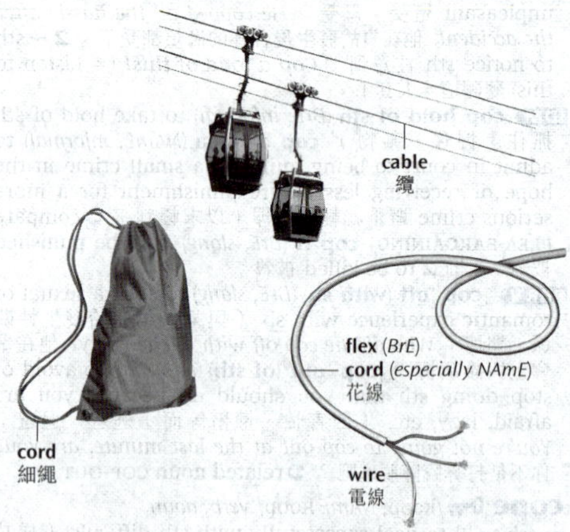

cord /kɔːd; *NAmE* kɔːrd/ *noun* **1** [U, C] strong thick string or thin rope; a piece of this（結實的）粗線，細繩；一根粗線（或細繩）：*a* ***piece/length of cord*** 一根／一段粗線 ◇ *picture cord* (= used for hanging pictures) 畫的掛繩 ◇ *a silk bag tied with a gold cord* 用金線捆紮的絲綢包 **2** (*especially NAmE*) (*BrE* also **flex**) [C, U] a piece of wire that is covered with plastic, used for carrying electricity to a piece of equipment 花線；皮線：*an electrical cord* 電線 ◇ *telephone cord* 電話線 ➲ see also CORDLESS **3** [U] = CORDUROY (1)：*a cord jacket* 燈芯絨夾克 **4 cords** (also *old-fashioned* **corduroys**) [pl.] trousers/pants made of CORDUROY 燈芯絨褲子：*a pair of cords* 一條燈芯絨褲子 ➲ see also SPINAL CORD, UMBILICAL CORD, VOCAL CORDS

cord·ed /ˈkɔːdɪd; *NAmE* ˈkɔːrd-/ *adj.* **1** (of cloth 布料) having raised lines 有凸紋的；有棱的 SYN **ribbed** **2** (of a muscle 肌肉) TENSE and standing out so that it looks like a piece of cord 繃緊鼓起的 **3** that has a cord attached 繫（或附）有繩（或線）的：*a corded phone* 有線電話 OPP **cordless**

cor·dial /ˈkɔːdiəl; *NAmE* ˈkɔːrdʒəl/ *adj., noun*

■ ***adj.*** (*formal*) pleasant and friendly 熱情友好的；和藹可親的：*a* ***cordial atmosphere/meeting/relationship*** 親切友好的氣氛／會議／關係 ▸ **cor·di·al·ity** /ˌkɔːdiˈæləti; *NAmE* ˌkɔːrdʒi-/ *noun* [U]: *I was greeted with a show of cordiality.* 我受到了熱情友好的接待。

■ ***noun*** **1** (*BrE*) [U, C] a sweet drink that does not contain alcohol, made from fruit juice. It is drunk with water added.（不含酒精、加水飲用的）甜果汁飲料：*blackcurrant cordial* 黑醋栗果汁飲料 **2** [U, C] (*NAmE*) = LIQUEUR **3** [C] a glass of cordial 一杯甜果汁飲料

cor·di·al·ly /ˈkɔːdiəli; *NAmE* ˈkɔːrdʒəli/ *adv.* (*formal*) **1** in a pleasant and friendly manner 熱情友好地；和藹

可親地：*You are cordially invited to a celebration for Mr Michael Brown on his retirement.* 熱誠邀請您參加為邁克爾•布朗先生退休舉行的慶祝會。 **2** (used with verbs showing dislike 與動詞連用表示厭惡) very much 非常；十分；很：*They cordially detest each other.* 他們對對方都深惡痛絕。

cord·ite /ˈkɔːdaɪt; *NAmE* ˈkɔːrd-/ *noun* [U] an EXPLOSIVE used in bullets, bombs, etc. 無煙線狀火藥

cord·less /ˈkɔːdləs; *NAmE* ˈkɔːrd-/ *adj.* (of a telephone or an electrical tool 電話或電動工具) not connected to its power supply by wires 不用電線與電源相連的；無電線的；無塞繩式的：*a* ***cordless phone/drill*** 無線電話；無塞繩式電鑽 OPP **corded**

cor·don /ˈkɔːdn; *NAmE* ˈkɔːrdn/ *noun, verb*

■ ***noun*** a line or ring of police officers, soldiers, etc. guarding sth or stopping people from entering or leaving a place（由警察、士兵等組成的）警戒線，封鎖線：*Demonstrators broke through the police cordon.* 示威者衝破了警方的警戒線。

■ ***verb***

PHR V **ˌcordon sth↔ˈoff** to stop people from getting into an area by surrounding it with police, soldiers, etc.（由警察、士兵等）包圍，警戒，封鎖：*Police cordoned off the area until the bomb was made safe.* 警方封鎖了這個地區直到炸彈被安全拆除為止。

cor·don bleu /ˌkɔːdɒ̃ ˈblɜː; *NAmE* ˌkɔːrdɔ̃ː/ *adj.* [usually before noun] (from *French*) of the highest standard of skill in cooking 烹飪手藝高超的：*a cordon bleu chef* 烹飪大師 ◇ *cordon bleu cuisine* 名廚師烹製的菜肴

cor·du·roy /ˈkɔːdərɔɪ; *NAmE* ˈkɔːrd-/ *noun* **1** (also **cord**) [U] a type of strong soft cotton cloth with a pattern of raised parallel lines on it, used for making clothes 燈芯絨：*a corduroy jacket* 燈芯絨夾克 **2** **cor·du·roys** [pl.] (*old-fashioned*) = CORDS at CORD (4)

core 🔑 AW /kɔː(r)/ *noun, adj., verb*

■ ***noun*** **1** 🔑 the hard central part of a fruit such as an apple, that contains the seeds（水果的）果心，核兒 ➲ **VISUAL VOCAB** page V30 **2** 🔑 the central part of an object（物體的）中心部份：*the earth's core* 地核 ◇ *the core of a nuclear reactor* 核反應堆的活性區 **3** 🔑 the most important or central part of sth 最重要的部份；核心；要點；精髓：*the core of the argument* 爭論的核心 ◇ *Concern for the environment is* ***at the core*** *of our policies.* 對環境的關注是我們政策的核心。 **4** a small group of people who take part in a particular activity（參加某項活動的）一小群人：*He gathered a small core of advisers around him.* 他的周圍聚集了一幫謀士。 ➲ see also HARD CORE

IDM **to the ˈcore** so that the whole of a thing or a person is affected 直至核心；十足；透頂：*She was shaken to the core by the news.* 這消息使她大為震驚。◇ *He's a politician to the core* (= in all his attitudes and actions). 他是個十足的政客。

■ ***adj.*** **1** most important; main or essential 最重要的；主要的；基本的：*core subjects* (= subjects that all the students have to study) *such as English and mathematics* 諸如英語和數學等核心科目 ◇ *the core curriculum* 核心課程 ◇ *We need to concentrate on our* ***core business****.* 我們需要集中在核心業務上。◇ *The use of new technology is core to our strategy.* 運用新技術是我們策略的關鍵。 **2 ~ beliefs, values, principles, etc.** the most important or central beliefs, etc. of a person or group 核心信念；核心價值；核心原則：*The party is losing touch with its core values.* 這個黨正在逐漸偏離其核心價值觀。 **3** used to describe the most important members of a group 核心成員的；骨幹的：*The team is built around a core group of players.* 這個隊是以幾名骨幹隊員為核心構建的。

■ ***verb*** **~ sth** to take out the core of a fruit 去掉果心；去核兒

co·referen·tial /ˌkəʊrefəˈrenʃl; *NAmE* ˌkoʊ-/ *adj.* (*linguistics* 語言) if two words or expressions are **coreferential**, they refer to the same thing. For example, in the sentence 'I had a camera but I lost it', 'a camera' and 'it' are coreferential. 同指的（兩個詞或表達方式所指稱的對象相同）

ˌco-reˈspond·ent *noun* (*law* 律) a person who is said to have committed ADULTERY with the husband or wife of sb who is trying to get divorced（通姦引起的離婚訴訟中的）共同被告

corgi /ˈkɔːɡi; *NAmE* ˈkɔːrɡi/ *noun* a small dog with short legs and a pointed nose 柯吉犬（短腿尖鼻）

cori·an·der /ˌkɒriˈændə(r); *NAmE* ˌkɔːr-/ *noun* [U] a plant whose leaves are used in cooking as a HERB and whose seeds are used in cooking as a spice 芫荽；香菜 ➲ compare CILANTRO ➲ **VISUAL VOCAB** page V32

Cor·inth·ian /kəˈrɪnθiən/ *adj.* [usually before noun] (*architecture* 建) used to describe a style of ARCHITECTURE in ancient Greece that has thin columns with decorations of leaves at the top 科林斯式的（古希臘建築風格，採用頂部雕刻葉子的細圓柱）：***Corinthian columns/capitals*** 科林斯式柱／柱頭

cork /kɔːk; *NAmE* kɔːrk/ *noun, verb*

■ ***noun*** **1** [U] a light, soft material that is the thick BARK of a type of Mediterranean OAK tree 木栓，軟木（一種地中海橡樹皮）：*a cork mat* 軟木墊 ◇ *cork tiles* 軟木薄砌塊 **2** [C] a small round object made of cork or plastic, that is used for closing bottles, especially wine bottles（尤指酒瓶的）軟木塞，塑料塞 ➲ **VISUAL VOCAB** page V33 ➲ **SYNONYMS** at LID

■ ***verb*** **~ sth** to close a bottle with a cork 用軟木塞封（瓶） OPP **uncork**

cork·age /ˈkɔːkɪdʒ; *NAmE* ˈkɔːrk-/ *noun* [U] the money that a restaurant charges if you want to drink wine there that you have bought somewhere else（餐館對顧客自備酒水所收取的）開瓶費

corked /kɔːkt; *NAmE* kɔːrkt/ *adj.* (of wine 酒) with a bad taste because the cork has decayed（因軟木塞腐朽而）味道不佳的，帶瓶塞異味的

cork·er /ˈkɔːkə(r); *NAmE* ˈkɔːrk-/ *noun* [usually sing.] (*old-fashioned, BrE, informal*) a person or thing that is extremely good, beautiful or amusing 傑出（或非凡）的人；絕色佳麗；趣味無窮的事

cork·screw /ˈkɔːkskruː; *NAmE* ˈkɔːrk-/ *noun, verb*

■ ***noun*** a tool for pulling CORKS from bottles. Most corkscrews have a handle and a long twisted piece of metal for pushing into the cork. 瓶塞鑽；螺旋開瓶起子 ➲ **VISUAL VOCAB** page V26

■ ***verb*** [I] (+ **adv./prep.**) to move in a particular direction while turning in circles（順某方向）旋轉

corm /kɔːm; *NAmE* kɔːrm/ *noun* the small round underground part of some plants, from which the new plant grows every year（植物的）球莖

cor·mor·ant /ˈkɔːmərənt; *NAmE* ˈkɔːrm-/ *noun* a large black bird with a long neck that lives near the sea or other areas of water 鸕鷀

corn /kɔːn; *NAmE* kɔːrn/ *noun* **1** (*BrE*) [U] any plant that is grown for its grain, such as WHEAT; the grain of these plants（小麥等）穀物；穀粒：*a field of corn* 一片莊稼 ◇ ***ears/sheaves of corn*** 穀穗；一捆捆的穀物 ◇ *corn-fed chicken* 用穀物飼養的雞 ➲ **COLLOCATIONS** at FARMING **2** (*NAmE*) (*BrE* **maize**) [U] a tall plant grown for its large yellow grains that are used for making flour or eaten as a vegetable; the grains of this plant 玉蜀黍；玉米 ➲ **VISUAL VOCAB** page V32 ➲ see also CORNCOB, CORN ON THE COB **3** (*NAmE*) (*BrE* **sweet·corn**) [U] the yellow seeds of a type of corn (MAIZE) plant, also called corn, which grow on thick STEMS and are cooked and eaten as a vegetable 玉米 ➲ **VISUAL VOCAB** page V31 **4** [C] a small area of hard skin on the foot, especially the toe, that is sometimes painful（尤指腳趾上的）釘胼，雞眼

ˌcorn ˈbeef *noun* [U] = CORNED BEEF

the ˈCorn Belt *noun* the US states of the Midwest where CORN (MAIZE) is an important crop 玉米地帶（美國中西部盛產玉米的幾個州）

corn·bread /ˈkɔːnbred; *NAmE* ˈkɔːrn-/ *noun* [U] (*NAmE*) a kind of flat bread made with CORN (MAIZE) flour 玉米麪包；玉米粉糕

ˈcorn chip *noun* (*NAmE*) a thin, crisp piece of food made from crushed CORN (MAIZE) that has been fried 炸玉米片

C

'corn circle *noun* = CROP CIRCLE

corn·cob /'kɔːnkɒb; *NAmE* 'kɔːrnkɑːb/ (*especially BrE*) (also **cob** *NAmE, BrE*) *noun* the long hard part of the MAIZE (CORN) plant that the rows of yellow grains grow on 玉米芯；玉米穗軸

cor·nea /'kɔːniə; *NAmE* 'kɔːrniə/ *noun* (*anatomy* 解) the transparent layer which covers and protects the outer part of the eye 角膜 ➲ **VISUAL VOCAB** page V59 ▸ **cor·neal** /'kɔːniəl; *NAmE* 'kɔːrn-/ *adj.* [only before noun]：*a corneal transplant* 角膜移植

corned beef /ˌkɔːnd 'biːf; *NAmE* ˌkɔːrnd/ (also ˌ**corn 'beef**) *noun* [U] beef that has been cooked and preserved using salt, often sold in cans（常為罐裝的）鹹牛肉

cor·ne·lian /kɔː'niːliən; *NAmE* kɔːr'n-/ *noun* = CARNELIAN

cor·ner 🔑 /'kɔːnə(r); *NAmE* 'kɔːrn-/ *noun, verb*

■ *noun*

▸ **OF BUILDING/OBJECT/SHAPE** 建築物；物體；形狀 **1** 🔑 a part of sth where two or more sides, lines or edges join 角：*the four corners of a square* 正方形的四個角 ◇ *Write your address in the top right-hand corner of the letter.* 把你的地址寫在信的右上角。◇ *I hit my knee on the corner of the table.* 我的膝蓋撞到桌子角上了。◇ *A smile lifted the corner of his mouth.* 他的嘴角掛着微笑。◇ *a speck of dirt in the corner of her eye* 她眼角裏的一點灰塵

▸ **-CORNERED** 有…角 **2** (in adjectives 構成形容詞) with the number of corners mentioned; involving the number of groups mentioned 有…角的；涉及…群體的：*a three-cornered hat* 三角帽 ◇ *a three-cornered fight* 三方爭鬥

▸ **OF ROOM/BOX** 房間；箱子 **3** 🔑 the place inside a room or a box where two sides join; the area around this place 角；牆角；壁角：*There was a television in the far corner of the room.* 房間那一頭的牆角裏擺着一台電視機。◇ *a* ***corner table/seat/cupboard*** 靠牆角的桌子／座位／櫥櫃

▸ **OF ROADS** 道路 **4** 🔑 a place where two streets join 街角；拐角：*There was a group of youths standing on the* ***street corner***. 有一群年輕人站在街角。◇ *Turn right at the corner of Sunset and Crescent Heights Boulevards.* 在夕陽街和新月山莊大街路口向右轉。◇ *There's a hotel* ***on/at the corner*** *of my street.* 我住的那條街拐角上有一家旅館。◇ *The wind hit him as he* ***turned the corner***. 他在街角一拐彎，狂風就向他襲來。 **5** 🔑 a sharp bend in a road（道路的）急轉彎：*The car was taking the corners too fast.* 那車急轉彎時開得太快。

▸ **AREA/REGION** 地區；區域 **6** a region or an area of a place (sometimes used for one that is far away or difficult to reach)（有時指偏僻或難以到達的）區域，地區：*She lives in a quiet corner of rural Yorkshire.* 她居住在約克郡鄉間一個僻靜的地方。◇ *Students come here* ***from the four corners*** *of the world.* 學生從世界各地來到這裏。◇ *He knew every corner of the old town.* 他熟悉這座古鎮的每個角落。

▸ **DIFFICULT SITUATION** 困境 **7** [usually sing.] a difficult situation 困境；窘境：*to* ***back/drive/force sb into a corner*** 把某人逼入困境 ◇ *They had got her in a corner, and there wasn't much she could do about it.* 他們把她逼得走投無路，而且她也沒有什麼辦法脫身。◇ *He was used to talking his way out of* ***tight corners***. 他慣於憑藉口才擺脫困境。

▸ **IN SPORT** 體育運動 **8** (in sports such as football (SOCCER) and HOCKEY 足球、曲棍球等) a free kick or hit that you take from the corner of your opponent's end of the field 角球：*to take a corner* 開角球 ◇ *The referee awarded a corner.* 裁判員判給了一次角球。 ➲ see also CORNER KICK **9** (in boxing and WRESTLING 拳擊運動和摔跤) any of the four corners of a RING; the supporters who help in the corner 場角；（場角處的）輔助人員

IDM **(just) around/round the 'corner** very near 很近；在附近：*Her house is just around the corner.* 她的房子就在附近。◇ (*figurative*) *There were good times around the corner* (= they would soon come). 好時光很快就會來臨。 **cut 'corners** (*disapproving*) to do sth in the easiest, cheapest or quickest way, often by ignoring rules or leaving sth out（常不按規則或省略地）用最簡捷經濟的方式做事，圖省事；（做事）走捷徑 **cut the 'corner** (also **cut off the 'corner** especially in *BrE*) to go across the corner of an area and not around the sides of it, because it is quicker 走捷徑；抄近道 **see sth out of the corner of your 'eye** to see sth by accident or not very clearly because you see it from the side of your eye and are not looking straight at it 偶然瞟見；睨視：*Out of the corner of her eye, she saw him coming closer.* 她用眼一瞟，見他正向她走過來。 **turn the 'corner** to pass a very important point in an illness or a difficult situation and begin to improve（患病時期）轉危為安，脫離危險，好轉；渡過難關；脫離困境 ➲ more at FIGHT *v.*, TIGHT *adj.*

■ *verb*

▸ **TRAP SB** 使落入圈套 **1** [T, often passive] **~ sb/sth** to get a person or an animal into a place or situation from which they cannot escape 使落入圈套（或陷阱）：*The man was finally cornered by police in a garage.* 那人最終被警方逼到了車庫裏。◇ *If cornered, the snake will defend itself.* 蛇在被逼得走投無路時會自衛。 **2** [T] **~ sb** to go towards sb in a determined way, because you want to speak to them 硬要走近想與（某人）說話：*I found myself cornered by her on the stairs.* 我發覺自己被她在樓梯上硬逼着說話。

▸ **THE MARKET** 市場 **3** [T] **~ the market** (**in sth**) to get control of the trade in a particular type of goods 壟斷（某種貨品的交易）：*They've cornered the market in silver.* 他們壟斷了白銀市場。

▸ **OF VEHICLE/DRIVER** 車輛；司機 **4** [I] (*BrE*) to go around a corner 轉彎；拐彎：*The car has excellent cornering* (= it is easy to steer around corners). 這汽車的轉彎性能極佳。

cor·ner·back /'kɔːnəbæk; *NAmE* 'kɔːrnər-/ *noun* (in AMERICAN FOOTBALL 美式足球) a defending player whose position is outside and behind the LINEBACKERS（在中後衛後外圍的）角衛

'corner kick (also **cor·ner**) *noun* (in football (SOCCER) 足球) a free kick that you take from the corner of your opponent's end of the field 角球；踢角球

'corner shop *noun* (*BrE*) a small shop that sells food, newspapers, cigarettes, etc., especially one near people's houses（尤指住宅區附近的）小商店，街頭小店

cor·ner·stone /'kɔːnəstəʊn; *NAmE* 'kɔːrnərstoʊn/ *noun* **1** (*especially NAmE*) a stone at the corner of the base of a building, often laid in a special ceremony 基石；奠基石 **2** the most important part of sth that the rest depends on 最重要部份；基礎；柱石：*This study is the cornerstone of the whole research programme.* 此項研究是整個研究計劃的基礎。

cor·net /'kɔːnɪt; *NAmE* 'kɔːrnɪt/ *noun* **1** a BRASS musical instrument like a small TRUMPET 短號 **2** (*BrE, old-fashioned*) = CONE (4)：*an ice-cream cornet* 蛋捲冰淇淋

cor·netto /kɔː'netəʊ; *NAmE* kɔːr'netoʊ/ *noun* (*pl.* **cor·netti**) (from *Italian*) an early musical instrument consisting of a curved tube with holes in that you cover with your fingers while blowing into the end 木管號，科爾內管（早期樂器）

'corn exchange *noun* (*BrE*) a building where grain used to be bought and sold（舊時）穀物市場

corn·field /'kɔːnfiːld; *NAmE* 'kɔːrn-/ *noun* a field in which CORN is grown 小麥田；玉米田

corn·flakes /'kɔːnfleɪks; *NAmE* 'kɔːrn-/ *noun* [pl.] small crisp yellow pieces of crushed MAIZE (CORN), usually eaten with milk and sugar for breakfast 脆玉米片（通常加牛奶和糖作早餐）

corn·flour /'kɔːnflaʊə(r); *NAmE* 'kɔːrn-/ (*BrE*) (*NAmE* **corn·starch**) *noun* [U] fine white flour made from MAIZE (CORN), used especially for making sauces thicker（精製）玉米粉；（尤指）玉米澱粉

corn·flower /'kɔːnflaʊə(r); *NAmE* 'kɔːrn-/ *noun* a small wild plant with blue flowers 矢車菊

cor·nice /'kɔːnɪs; *NAmE* 'kɔːrnɪs/ *noun* (*architecture* 建) a decorative border around the top of the walls in a room or on the outside walls of a building 簷口；楣；簷板；飛簷

Corn·ish /ˈkɔːnɪʃ; *NAmE* ˈkɔːrnɪʃ/ *noun, adj.*
■ ***noun*** [U] the Celtic language that was spoken in Cornwall in England. Nobody now uses Cornish as a first language. 康沃爾語（從前通行於英格蘭康沃爾地區）
■ ***adj.*** connected with Cornwall, or its people, language or culture 康沃爾的；康沃爾人（或語言、文化）的

ˌCornish ˈCream *noun* [U] CLOTTED CREAM (= a very thick type of cream) from Cornwall 康沃爾濃縮奶油

Cornish pasty /ˌkɔːnɪʃ ˈpæsti; *NAmE* ˌkɔːrnɪʃ/ *noun* (*BrE*) a small PIE in the shape of a half circle, containing meat and vegetables 康沃爾菜肉餡餅

corn·meal /ˈkɔːnmiːl; *NAmE* ˈkɔːrn-/ *noun* [U] flour made from MAIZE (CORN) 玉米粉

ˌcorn on the ˈcob *noun* [U] MAIZE (CORN) that is cooked with all the grains still attached to the inner part and eaten as a vegetable 玉米棒子 ➲ VISUAL VOCAB page V31

ˈcorn pone (also **pone**) (both *US*) *noun* [U] a type of bread made from CORN (MAIZE) and water 玉米麵包；玉米餅

corn·rows /ˈkɔːnrəʊz; *NAmE* ˈkɔːrnroʊz/ *noun* [pl.] a HAIRSTYLE worn especially by black women, in which the hair is put into lines of PLAITS along the head（尤指黑人婦女梳的）玉米壟髮式 ➲ VISUAL VOCAB page V60

corn·starch /ˈkɔːnstɑːtʃ; *NAmE* ˈkɔːrnstɑːrtʃ/ (*NAmE*) (*BrE* **corn·flour**) *noun* [U] fine white flour made from CORN (MAIZE), used especially for making sauces thicker（精製）玉米粉；（尤指）玉米澱粉

ˌcorn ˈsyrup *noun* [U] a thick sweet liquid made from CORN (MAIZE) and used in cooking 玉米糖漿

cor·nu·co·pia /ˌkɔːnjuˈkəʊpiə; *NAmE* ˌkɔːrnjuˈkoʊpiə/ *noun* **1** (also **ˌhorn of ˈplenty**) a decorative object shaped like an animal's horn, shown in art as full of fruit and flowers 豐饒角，豐饒角飾（藝術作品中裝滿水果和鮮花、形似動物角的裝飾物） **2** (*formal*) something that is or contains a large supply of good things 豐盛；豐富；豐饒： *The book is a cornucopia of good ideas.* 這部書裏有無數好主意。

corny /ˈkɔːni; *NAmE* ˈkɔːrni/ *adj.* (**corn·ier**, **corni·est**) (*informal*) not original; used too often to be interesting or to sound sincere 陳舊的；過時的；陳詞濫調的；老生常談的： *a* ***corny joke/song*** 老掉牙的笑話 / 歌曲 ◇ *I know it sounds corny, but it really was love at first sight!* 我知道這聽起來像陳詞濫調，然而的確是一見鍾情啊！

cor·olla /kəˈrɒlə; *NAmE* -ˈrɑːlə; -ˈroʊlə/ *noun* (*biology* 生) the ring of PETALS around the central part of a flower 花冠

cor·ol·lary /kəˈrɒləri; *NAmE* ˈkɔːrəleri; ˈkɑːr-/ *noun* (*pl.* **-ies**) **~ (of/to sth)** (*formal* or *technical* 術語) a situation, an argument or a fact that is the natural and direct result of another one 必然的結果（或結論）

cor·ona /kəˈrəʊnə; *NAmE* -ˈroʊ-/ *noun* (*pl.* **co·ro·nae** /-niː/) (*astronomy* 天) (also *informal* **halo**) a ring of light seen around the sun or moon, especially during an ECLIPSE（尤指在日蝕或月蝕期間的）日冕，日華，月華

cor·on·ary /ˈkɒrənri; *NAmE* ˈkɔːrəneri; ˈkɑːrəneri/ *adj.* (*medical* 醫) connected with the heart, particularly the ARTERIES that take blood to the heart 冠狀動脈的： *coronary (heart) disease* 冠狀動脈（心臟）病 ◇ *a coronary patient* (= sb suffering from coronary disease) 冠狀動脈疾病患者

ˌcoronary ˈartery *noun* (*anatomy* 解) either of the two ARTERIES that supply blood to the heart 冠狀動脈

ˌcoronary thromˈbosis (also *informal* **cor·on·ary**) *noun* [C, U] (*medical* 醫) a blocking of the flow of blood by a blood CLOT in an ARTERY supplying blood to the heart 冠狀動脈血栓形成 ➲ compare HEART ATTACK

cor·on·ation /ˌkɒrəˈneɪʃn; *NAmE* ˌkɔːr-; ˌkɑːr-/ *noun* a ceremony at which a crown is formally placed on the head of a new king or queen 加冕；加冕典禮

cor·on·er /ˈkɒrənə(r); *NAmE* ˈkɔːr-; ˈkɑːr-/ *noun* an official whose job is to discover the cause of any sudden, violent or suspicious death by holding an INQUEST 驗屍官

cor·onet /ˈkɒrənet; *NAmE* ˌkɔːrəˈnet; ˌkɑːr-/ *noun* **1** a small crown worn on formal occasions by princes, princesses, lords, etc.（王子、公主、貴族等戴的）冠冕 **2** a round decoration for the head, especially one made of flowers（尤指用花製作的）冠狀頭飾；花冠

Corp. *abbr.* CORPORATION (1)

cor·pora *pl.* of CORPUS

cor·poral /ˈkɔːpərəl; *NAmE* ˈkɔːrp-/ *noun* (*abbr.* **Cpl**) a member of one of the lower ranks in the army, the MARINES or the British AIR FORCE（陸軍、海軍陸戰隊或英國空軍的）下士： *Corporal Smith* 史密斯下士

ˌcorporal ˈpunishment *noun* [U] the physical punishment of people, especially by hitting them 體罰；肉刑

cor·por·ate **AW** /ˈkɔːpərət; *NAmE* ˈkɔːrp-/ *adj.* [only before noun] **1** connected with a corporation 公司的： ***corporate finance/planning/strategy*** 公司的財務 / 計劃 / 策略 ◇ ***corporate identity*** (= the image of a company, that all its members share) 公司形象 ◇ ***corporate hospitality*** (= when companies entertain customers to help develop good business relationships) 公司對顧客的熱情招待 **2** (*technical* 術語) forming a CORPORATION 組成公司（或團體）的；法人的： *The BBC is a* ***corporate body****.* 英國廣播公司為法人團體。◇ *The law applies to both individuals and corporate bodies.* 本法律既適用於個人也適用於法人團體。 **3** involving or shared by all the members of a group 社團的；全體的；共同的： *corporate responsibility* 共同的責任

ˌcorporate ˈraider *noun* (*business* 商) a person or company that regularly buys large numbers of shares in other companies against their wishes, either to control them or to sell them again for a large profit 公司掠奪者（經常強行大量購買其他公司股份的個人或公司，以對其加以控制或高價出售贏利）

cor·por·ation **AW** /ˌkɔːpəˈreɪʃn; *NAmE* ˌkɔːrp-/ *noun* **1** (*abbr.* **Corp.**) a large business company （大）公司： *multinational corporations* 跨國公司 ◇ *the Chrysler corporation* 克萊斯勒公司 **2** an organization or a group of organizations that is recognized by law as a single unit 法人；法人團體： *urban development corporations* 城市開發集團公司 **3** (*BrE*) a group of people elected to govern a large town or city and provide public services 市政委員會

ˌcorpoˈration tax *noun* [U] (*BrE*) a tax that companies pay on their profits 公司稅

cor·por·at·ism /ˈkɔːpərətɪzəm; *NAmE* ˈkɔːrp-/ *noun* [U] the control of a country, etc. by large groups, especially businesses 社團主義（以產業社團等作為政治代表機關支配人民的活動）

cor·por·at·or /ˈkɔːpəreɪtə(r); *NAmE* ˈkɔːrp-/ *noun* (*IndE*) an elected member of the government of a town or city 市政當局成員

cor·por·eal /kɔːˈpɔːriəl; *NAmE* kɔːrˈp-/ *adj.* (*formal*) **1** that can be touched; physical rather than spiritual 物質的；有形的；實體的： *his corporeal presence* 他的大駕親臨 **2** of or for the body 身體的；肉體的；身體所需的： *corporeal needs* 身體的需要

corps /kɔː(r)/ *noun* (*pl.* **corps** /kɔːz; *NAmE* kɔːrz/) [C+sing./pl. v.] **1** a large unit of an army, consisting of two or more DIVISIONS（由兩個或以上師組成的）軍，兵團： *the commander of the third army corps* 陸軍第三軍團的指揮官 **2** one of the groups of an army with a special responsibility（陸軍）特種部隊： *the Royal Army Medical Corps* 英國皇家陸軍醫療部 **3** a group of people involved in a particular job or activity（從事某工作或活動的）一群人，一組人： *a corps of trained and experienced doctors* 一隊訓練有素並富有經驗的醫生 ➲ see also DIPLOMATIC CORPS, PRESS CORPS

corps de bal·let /ˌkɔː də ˈbæleɪ; *NAmE* ˌkɔːr də bæˈleɪ/ *noun* [C+sing./pl. v.] (from *French*) dancers in a BALLET company who dance together as a group（芭蕾舞團的）群舞演員

C

corpse /kɔːps; *NAmE* kɔːrps/ *noun* a dead body, especially of a human 屍體；（尤指人的）死屍，屍首

cor·pu·lent /ˈkɔːpjələnt; *NAmE* ˈkɔːrp-/ *adj.* (*formal*) (of a person 人) fat. People say 'corpulent' to avoid saying 'fat'. 發福的，福態的（委婉說法，與 fat 同義）▸ **cor·pu·lence** *noun* [U]

cor·pus /ˈkɔːpəs; *NAmE* ˈkɔːrpəs/ *noun* (*pl.* **cor·pora** /ˈkɔːpərə; *NAmE* ˈkɔːrp-/ or **cor·puses** /-sɪz/) (*technical* 術語) a collection of written or spoken texts（書面或口語的）文集，文獻，彙編；語料庫：*a corpus of 100 million words of spoken English* 含有 1 億單詞的英語口語語料庫 ◇ *the whole corpus of Renaissance poetry* 文藝復興時期詩歌的總彙 ➲ see also HABEAS CORPUS

cor·puscle /ˈkɔːpʌsl; *NAmE* ˈkɔːrp-/ *noun* (*anatomy* 解) any of the red or white cells found in blood（紅或白）血球，血細胞：***red/white corpuscles*** 紅/白血球

cor·ral /kəˈrɑːl; *NAmE* -ˈræl/ *noun, verb*

■ ***noun*** (in N America) a fenced area for horses, cows, etc. on a farm or RANCH（北美農牧場的）畜欄，圍欄：*They drove the ponies into a corral.* 他們把矮種馬趕進了畜欄。

■ ***verb*** (-ll-, *US* also -l-) **1 ~ sth** to force horses or cows into a corral 把（馬或牛）趕入圍欄（或關進畜欄）**2 ~ sb** to gather a group of people together and keep them in a particular place 把（一群人）集中起來關在一起

cor·rect 🔑 /kəˈrekt/ *adj., verb*

■ ***adj.*** **1** 🔑 accurate or true, without any mistakes 準確無誤的；精確的；正確的 **SYN** **right**：*Do you have the correct time?* 你的錶走得準嗎？◇ *the correct answer* 正確答案 ◇ *Please check that these details are correct.* 請檢查這些細節是否準確無誤。◇ *'Are you in charge here?' 'That's correct.'* "你是這裏的負責人嗎？" "是的。" ◇ *Am I correct in saying that you know a lot about wine?* 你對酒瞭解頗深，我說得對吧？**OPP** **incorrect** ➲ SYNONYMS at TRUE **2** 🔑 right and suitable, so that sth is done as it should be done 恰當的；合適的：*Do you know the correct way to shut the machine down?* 你知道這台機器該怎麼關嗎？◇ *I think you've made the correct decision.* 我認為你的決定是正確的。➲ SYNONYMS at RIGHT **3** taking care to speak or behave in a way that follows the accepted standards or rules（舉止言談）符合公認準則的，得體的：*a correct young lady* 舉止得體的年輕女士 ◇ *He is always very correct in his speech.* 他說話總是很有分寸。**OPP** **incorrect** ➲ see also POLITICALLY CORRECT ▸ **cor·rect·ly** 🔑 *adv.*：*Have you spelled it correctly?* 你把它拼寫對了嗎？◇ *They reasoned, correctly, that she was away for the weekend.* 他們的推斷沒錯，她出去度週末了。◇ *He was looking correctly grave.* 他表情嚴肅得體。**cor·rect·ness** *noun* [U]：*The correctness of this decision may be doubted.* 此項決定是否正確值得懷疑。➲ see also POLITICAL CORRECTNESS **IDM** see PRESENT *adj.*

■ ***verb*** **1** 🔑 **~ sth** to make sth right or accurate, for example by changing it or removing mistakes 改正；糾正；修正：*Read through your work and correct any mistakes that you find.* 從頭至尾看一遍你們的作業，發現的錯誤都要改正過來。◇ *Their eyesight can be corrected in just a few minutes by the use of a laser.* 他們的視力用激光只要幾分鐘就可矯正。◇ *They issued a statement correcting the one they had made earlier.* 他們發表了一份聲明，更正早先聲明中的錯誤。**2** 🔑 **~ sth** (of a teacher 教師) to mark the mistakes in a piece of work (and sometimes give a mark/grade to the work) 批改；改：*I spent all evening correcting essays.* 我整個晚上都在批改論文。**3** to tell sb that they have made a mistake 指出錯誤：**~ sb** *Correct me if I'm wrong, but isn't this last year's brochure?* 這不是去年的小冊子嗎？若是我說錯了就請指出。◇ *Yes, you're right—**I stand corrected*** (= I accept that I made a mistake). 是的，你說得對。承蒙你指正。◇ **~ (sb) + speech** *'It's Yates, not Wates,' she corrected him.* "那是 Yates 而不是 Wates。" 她糾正他道。

cor·rec·tion /kəˈrekʃn/ *noun, exclamation*

■ ***noun*** **1** [C] a change that makes sth more accurate than it was before 改正；糾正；修正：*I've made a few small corrections to your report.* 我對你的報告作了幾處小的修改。◇ *The paper had to publish a correction to the story.* 這家報紙不得不對這則新聞報道發一個更正。**2** [U] the act or process of correcting sth 改正的行動（或過程）：*There are some programming errors that need correction.* 有一些程序錯誤需要改正。**3** [U] (*old-fashioned*) punishment 懲罰；處罰；懲治：*the correction of young offenders* 對失足青少年的管教

■ ***exclamation*** (*informal*) used when you want to correct sth that you have just said（想糾正剛說過的話時用）改正，更正：*I don't know. Correction—I do know, but I'm not going to tell you.* 我不知道。不，我知道不假，但不打算告訴你。

cor·rec·tion·al /kəˈrekʃənl/ *adj.* [only before noun] (*especially NAmE*) concerned with improving the behaviour of criminals, usually by punishing them 改造的：***a correctional center/institution/facility*** (= a prison) 監獄

corˈrection fluid *noun* [U] a white liquid that you use to cover mistakes that you make when you are writing or typing, and that you can write on top of 塗改液；修正液 ➲ VISUAL VOCAB page V69 ➲ see also TIPP-EX, WITEOUT

cor·rect·ive /kəˈrektɪv/ *adj., noun*

■ ***adj.*** (*formal*) designed to make sth right that was wrong before 改正的；糾正的；矯正的：*We need to take **corrective action** to halt this country's decline.* 我們得採取糾偏行動來阻止這個國家的衰落。◇ ***corrective measures*** 糾偏措施 ◇ ***corrective surgery/glasses*** 矯正外科/眼鏡

■ ***noun*** **~ (to sth)** (*formal*) something that helps to give a more accurate or fairer view of sb/sth 起糾正作用的東西；修改；糾正：*I should like to add a corrective to what I have written previously.* 我想對我先前寫的內容進行補充修改。

cor·rel·ate /ˈkɒrəleɪt; *NAmE* ˈkɔːr-; ˈkɑːr-/ *verb* (*formal*) **1** [I] if two or more facts, figures, etc. **correlate** or if a fact, figure, etc. **correlates** with another, the facts are closely connected and affect or depend on each other 相互關聯影響；相互依賴：*The figures do not seem to correlate.* 這些數字似乎毫不相干。◇ **~ with sth** *A high-fat diet correlates with a greater risk of heart disease.* 高脂肪飲食與增加心臟病發作的風險密切相關。**2** [T] **~ sth** to show that there is a close connection between two or more facts, figures, etc. 顯示緊密聯繫：*Researchers are trying to correlate the two sets of figures.* 研究人員正試圖展示這兩組數字的相關性。▸ **cor·rel·ate** /ˈkɒrələt; *NAmE* ˈkɔːr-; ˈkɑːr-/ *noun*

cor·rel·ation /ˌkɒrəˈleɪʃn; *NAmE* ˌkɔːr-/ *noun* [C, U] a connection between two things in which one thing changes as the other does 相互關係；相關；關聯：**~ (between A and B)** *There is a direct correlation between exposure to sun and skin cancer.* 暴露在太陽下與皮膚癌直接相關。◇ **~ (of A with B)** *the correlation of social power with wealth* 社會權力與財富的相關性

cor·rela·tive /kəˈrelətɪv/ *noun* (*formal*) a fact or an idea that is closely related to or depends on another fact or idea 緊密相關的；相互關聯的 ▸ **cor·rela·tive** *adj.*

cor·res·pond **AW** /ˌkɒrəˈspɒnd; *NAmE* ˌkɔːrəˈspɑːnd; ˌkɑː-/ *verb* **1** [I] to be the same as or match sth 相一致；符合 **SYN** **agree, tally**：*Your account and hers do not correspond.* 你說的情況與她說的不相符。◇ **~ with sth** *Your account of events does not correspond with hers.* 你對事情的陳述與她說的不相符。◇ **~ to sth** *The written record of the conversation doesn't correspond to* (= is different from) *what was actually said.* 那次談話的文字記錄與原話不符。**2** [I] **~ (to sth)** to be similar to or the same as sth else 類似於；相當於：*The British job of Lecturer corresponds roughly to the US Associate Professor.* 英國的講師職位大致相當於美國的副教授。**3** [I] **~ (with sb)** (*formal*) to write letters to sb and receive letters from them 通信

cor·res·pond·ence **AW** /ˌkɒrəˈspɒndəns; *NAmE* ˌkɔːrəˈspɑːn-; ˌkɑː-/ *noun* (*formal*) **1** [U] **~ (with sb)** the letters a person sends and receives 來往信件；往來書信：***personal/private correspondence*** 私人來往信件 ◇ *The editor welcomes correspondence from readers on any subject.* 編輯歡迎讀者有關任何問題的來信。◇ ***the correspondence column/page*** (= in a newspaper) 讀者來信專欄/版頁 **2** [U, C] **~ (with sb)** the activity of writing letters 通信；通信聯繫：*I refused to enter into any correspondence* (= to exchange letters) *with him about it.* 我拒絕就此問題與他通信聯繫。◇ *We have been* ***in correspondence*** *for months.* 我們通信幾個月了。◇ *We kept up a correspondence for many years.* 我們保持了很多年的通信聯繫。 **3** [C, U] **~ (between A and B)** a connection between two things; the fact of two things being similar 相關；相似：*There is a close correspondence between the two extracts.* 這兩段摘錄如出一轍。

corre'spondence course *noun* a course of study that you do at home, using books and exercises sent to you by post/mail or by email 函授課程

cor·res·pond·ent /ˌkɒrəˈspɒndənt; *NAmE* ˌkɔːrəˈspɑːn-; ˌkɑː-/ *noun* **1** a person who reports news from a particular country or on a particular subject for a newspaper or a television or radio station 記者；通訊員：*the BBC's political correspondent* 英國廣播公司的政治新聞記者 ◇ *a* ***foreign/war/sports, etc. correspondent*** 駐外、戰地、體育等記者 ◇ *our Delhi correspondent* 我們駐德里的通訊員 **2** (used with an adjective 與形容詞連用) a person who writes letters to another person 通信者：*She's a poor correspondent* (= she does not write regularly). 她是個懶於寫信的人。

cor·res·pond·ing **AW** /ˌkɒrəˈspɒndɪŋ; *NAmE* ˌkɔːrəˈspɑːn-; ˌkɑː-/ *adj.* matching or connected with sth that you have just mentioned 符合的；相應的；相關的 **SYN** **equivalent**：*A change in the money supply brings a corresponding change in expenditure.* 貨幣供應量的改變隨即引起支出的相應改變。◇ *Profits have risen by 15 per cent compared with the corresponding period last year.* 與去年同期相比利潤增長了 15%。◇ *The Redskins lost to the Cowboys in the corresponding game last year.* 在去年兩隊的交鋒中，紅皮隊輸給了牛仔隊。◇ **~ to sth** *Give each picture a number corresponding to its position on the page.* 按所在頁面位置給每一幅畫編上相對應的號碼。 ▸ **cor·res·pond·ing·ly** **AW** *adv.*：*a period of high demand and correspondingly high prices* 需求大、價格相應較高的時期

corres'ponding angles (also **'F angles**) *noun* (*geometry* 幾何) equal angles formed on the same side of a line that crosses two parallel lines 同位角；對應角 ➲ **VISUAL VOCAB** page V71 ➲ compare ALTERNATE ANGLES

cor·ri·dor /ˈkɒrɪdɔː(r); *NAmE* ˈkɔːr-; ˈkɑːr-/ *noun* **1** (*NAmE* also **hall·way**) a long narrow passage in a building, with doors that open into rooms on either side（建築物內的）走廊，過道，通道：*His room is along the corridor.* 他的房間就在走廊邊。➲ **VISUAL VOCAB** page V70 **2** a passage on a train（火車上的）走道，過道，通道 **3** a long narrow strip of land belonging to one country that passes through the land of another country; a part of the sky over a country that planes, for example from another country, can fly through 走廊（一國領土通過他國境內的狹長地帶）；空中走廊（一國領空中允許他國飛機經過的區域）➲ see also AIR CORRIDOR **4** a long narrow strip of land that follows the course of an important road or river（沿着重要道路或河道的）狹長地帶：*the electronics industry in the M4 corridor* * 4 號高速公路沿線一帶的電子工業區

IDM **the corridors of 'power** (sometimes *humorous*) the higher levels of government, where important decisions are made 權力走廊（高層政治決策機構）

cor·rie /ˈkɒri; *NAmE* ˈkɔːri; ˈkɑːri/ (also **cirque**, **cwm**) *noun* (*geology* 地) a round hollow area in the side of a mountain 山側圓形凹地

cor·rob·or·ate /kəˈrɒbəreɪt; *NAmE* -ˈrɑːb-/ [I, T, often passive] **~ (sth)** (*formal*) to provide evidence or information that supports a statement, theory, etc. 證實，確證（陳述、理論等）**SYN** **confirm**：*The evidence was corroborated by two independent witnesses.* 此證據由兩名獨立證人提供。◇ *corroborating evidence* 確鑿的證據 ▸ **cor·rob·or·ation** /kəˌrɒbəˈreɪʃn; *NAmE* -ˌrɑːbə-/ *noun* [U]

cor·rob·ora·tive /kəˈrɒbərətɪv; *NAmE* kəˈrɑːbəreɪtɪv/ *adj.* (*formal*) [usually before noun] giving support to a statement or theory（對陳述或理論）提供支持的；使確鑿的：*Is there any* ***corroborative evidence*** *for this theory?* 是否有進一步說明問題的論據來支持這個理論？

cor·rode /kəˈrəʊd; *NAmE* kəˈroʊd/ *verb* [T, I] **~ (sth)** to destroy sth slowly, especially by chemical action; to be destroyed in this way 腐蝕；侵蝕：*Acid corrodes metal.* 酸腐蝕金屬。◇ (*figurative*) *Corruption corrodes public confidence in a political system.* 腐敗可削弱公眾對政治制度的信心。◇ *The copper pipework has corroded in places.* 銅管有幾處受到了腐蝕。 ▸ **cor·ro·sion** /kəˈrəʊʒn; *NAmE* -ˈroʊ-/ *noun* [U]：*Look for signs of corrosion.* 尋找腐蝕的痕跡。◇ *Clean off any corrosion before applying the paint.* 先把銹跡清除乾淨再塗油漆。➲ **VISUAL VOCAB** page V6

cor·ro·sive /kəˈrəʊsɪv; *NAmE* -ˈroʊ-/ *adj.* **1** tending to destroy sth slowly by chemical action 腐蝕性的；侵蝕性的：*the corrosive effects of salt water* 鹽水的腐蝕作用 ◇ *corrosive acid* 具有腐蝕作用的酸 **2** (*formal*) tending to damage sth gradually 損害性的；逐漸起破壞作用的：*Unemployment is having a corrosive effect on our economy.* 失業對我國的經濟起着破壞作用。

corrugated 波紋形的

corrugated iron roof
波紋鐵屋頂

cor·ru·gated /ˈkɒrəɡeɪtɪd; *NAmE* ˈkɔːr-; ˈkɑːr-/ *adj.* shaped into a series of regular folds that look like waves 起皺的；起波紋的：*a* ***corrugated iron*** *roof* 波紋鐵屋頂 ◇ *corrugated cardboard* 瓦楞紙板

cor·rupt /kəˈrʌpt/ *adj.*, *verb*

▪ ***adj.*** **1** (of people 人) willing to use their power to do dishonest or illegal things in return for money or to get an advantage 貪污的；受賄的；腐敗的；營私舞弊的：*a corrupt regime* 貪污腐敗的政權 ◇ *corrupt officials accepting bribes* 接受賄賂的貪官污吏 **2** (of behaviour 行為) dishonest or immoral 不誠實的；不道德的：*corrupt practices* 徇私舞弊 ◇ *The whole system is inefficient and corrupt.* 整個體系都效率低下並且腐敗墮落。 **3** (*computing* 計) containing changes or faults, and no longer in the original state 已變換的；有缺陷的；有錯誤的：*corrupt software* 已受損的軟件 ◇ *The text on the disk seems to be corrupt.* 這張磁盤上的文本好像有錯誤。 ▸ **cor·rupt·ly** *adv.*

▪ ***verb*** **1** [T] **~ sb** to have a bad effect on sb and make them behave in an immoral or dishonest way 使腐化；使墮落：*He was corrupted by power and ambition.* 權力與野心使他腐化墮落。◇ *the corrupting effects of great wealth* 巨大財富的腐蝕作用 **2** [T, often passive] **~ sth** to change the original form of sth, so that it is damaged or spoiled in some way 破壞；損壞：*a corrupted form of Buddhism* 一種蛻變了的佛教 **3** [T, I] **~ (sth)** (*computing* 計) to cause mistakes to appear in a computer file, etc. with the result that the information in it is no longer correct 引起（計算機文件等的）錯誤；破壞：*The program has somehow corrupted the system files.* 這程序莫名其妙地導致系統文件出錯了。◇ *corrupted data* 被破壞數據 ◇ *The disk will corrupt if it is overloaded.* 磁盤如果過載，數據就會出錯。

cor·rupt·ible /kəˈrʌptəbl/ *adj.* that can be corrupted 易腐蝕的；易腐敗的；可收買的 **OPP** **incorruptible**

cor·rup·tion /kəˈrʌpʃn/ *noun* **1** [U] dishonest or illegal behaviour, especially of people in authority 腐敗；貪污；賄賂；受賄：*allegations of* ***bribery and corruption*** 對賄賂與貪污的指控 ◇ *The new district attorney has promised to fight police corruption.* 新上任的地方檢察官承諾要打擊警察腐敗的局面。➲ **COLLOCATIONS** at CRIME **2** [U] the act or effect of making sb change from moral to immoral standards of behaviour 墮落；腐蝕：*He claimed that sex and violence on TV led to the corruption of young people.* 他斷言電視中所宣揚的色情與暴力誘使青少年墮落。 **3** [C, usually sing.] the form of a word or phrase that has become changed from its original form in some way（單詞或短語的）變體：*The word 'holiday' is a corruption of 'holy day'.* 單詞 holiday 是 holy day 的變體。

cor·sage /kɔː'sɑːʒ; *NAmE* kɔːr'sɑːʒ/ *noun* a small bunch of flowers that is worn on a woman's dress, for example at a wedding（婚禮等女服上佩戴的）小花束

cor·set /'kɔːsɪt; *NAmE* 'kɔːrsɪt/ *noun* a piece of women's underwear, fitting the body tightly, worn especially in the past to make the waist look smaller（尤指舊時婦女束腰的）緊身內衣

cor·tège (also **cor·tege** especially in *US*) /kɔː'teʒ; -'teɪʒ; *NAmE* kɔːr'teʒ/ *noun* a line of cars or people moving along slowly at a funeral 送葬車隊（或行列、隊伍）**SYN** **funeral procession**

cor·tex /'kɔːteks; *NAmE* 'kɔːrt-/ *noun* (*pl.* **cor·ti·ces** /'kɔːtɪsiːz; *NAmE* 'kɔːrt-/) (*anatomy* 解) the outer layer of an organ in the body, especially the brain 皮層；皮質；（尤指）大腦皮層：*the* ***cerebral/renal cortex*** (= around the brain/KIDNEY) 大腦／腎皮層 ▶ **cor·tic·al** /'kɔːtɪkl; *NAmE* 'kɔːrt-/ *adj.*

cor·ti·sone /'kɔːtɪzəʊn; -səʊn; *NAmE* 'kɔːrtəsoʊn; -zoʊn/ *noun* [U] (*medical* 醫) a HORMONE used in the treatment of diseases such as ARTHRITIS, to reduce swelling 可的松，可體松（用於治療關節炎等緩解腫脹的激素）

cor·us·cate /'kɒrəskeɪt; *NAmE* 'kɔːr-; 'kɑːr-/ *verb* (*literary*) **1** [I] (of light 光) to flash 閃耀；閃爍 **2** [I] (of a person 人) to be full of life, enthusiasm or humour 充滿活力；朝氣蓬勃；幽默風趣 ▶ **cor·us·cat·ing** /'kɒrəskeɪtɪŋ; *NAmE* 'kɔːr-/ *adj.*：*coruscating wit* 敏捷的才思 **cor·us·cat·ing·ly** *adv.*：*coruscatingly brilliant* 熠熠生輝

cor·vette /kɔː'vet; *NAmE* kɔːr'vet/ *noun* a small fast ship used in war to protect other ships from attack 小型護衛艦

cos[1] (also **'cos**, **'cause**, **coz**) /kəz; *BrE* also kɒz/ *conj.* (*BrE, informal*) because 因為：*I can't see her at all, cos it's too dark.* 天太黑，我根本看不見她。

cos[2] *abbr.* (in writing) COSINE（書寫形式）餘弦

COSATU /kəʊ'sɑːtuː; *NAmE* 'koʊ-/ *abbr.* the Congress of South African Trade Unions (= a political organization in South Africa that represents many unions) 南非工會聯盟；南非總工會

cosh /kɒʃ; *NAmE* kɑːʃ/ *noun, verb*

■ ***noun*** (*especially BrE*) a short thick heavy stick, for example a piece of metal or solid rubber, that is used as a weapon（用作武器的）金屬短棍，實心橡膠棒

IDM **under the 'cosh** (*BrE, informal*) experiencing a lot of pressure 壓力沉重：*Our side was under the cosh for most of the second half.* 我方在下半場的大部份時間裏經受着很大的壓力。

■ ***verb*** **~ sb** (*especially BrE*) to hit sb hard with a cosh or sth similar 用短棒打；用短棒之類的東西打

,co-'signatory *noun* one of two or more people who sign a formal document（正式文件的）連署人：***co-signatories of/to*** *the treaty* 條約的連署人

co·sine /'kəʊsaɪn; *NAmE* 'koʊ-/ *noun* (*abbr.* **cos**) (*mathematics* 數) the RATIO of the length of the side next to an ACUTE ANGLE in a RIGHT-ANGLED triangle to the length of the longest side (= the HYPOTENUSE) 餘弦 ➲ compare SINE, TANGENT (2)

cos lettuce /,kɒs 'letɪs; ,kɒz; *NAmE* ,kɑːs; ,kɔːs/ (*BrE*) (*NAmE* **ro·maine**) *noun* [C, U] a type of LETTUCE with long crisp leaves 直立萵苣；長葉生菜

cos·met·ic /kɒz'metɪk; *NAmE* kɑːz-/ *noun, adj.*

■ ***noun*** [usually pl.] a substance that you put on your face or body to make it more attractive 化妝品；美容品：*the cosmetics industry* 化妝品行業 ◇ *a cosmetic company* 化妝品公司 ◇ *cosmetic products* 化妝產品 ➲ **COLLOCATIONS** at FASHION

■ ***adj.*** **1** improving only the outside appearance of sth and not its basic character 裝門面的；表面的：*These reforms are not merely cosmetic.* 這些改革不僅僅是裝點門面的。◇ *She dismissed the plan as a cosmetic exercise to win votes.* 她認為這項計劃是為了贏得選票所做的表面文章，因而不予考慮。 **2** connected with medical treatment that is intended to improve a person's appearance 整容的：*cosmetic surgery* 整容外科 ◇ *cosmetic dental work* 牙齒整形 ▶ **cos·met·ic·al·ly** /-kli/ *adv.*

cos·mic /'kɒzmɪk; *NAmE* 'kɑːz-/ *adj.* [usually before noun] **1** connected with the whole universe 宇宙的：*Do you believe in a cosmic plan?* 你相信冥冥中的安排嗎？ **2** very great and important 巨大且重要的：*This was disaster on a cosmic scale.* 這是塌天大禍。

,cosmic 'dust *noun* [U] (*astronomy* 天) very small pieces of matter floating in space 宇宙塵

,cosmic 'rays *noun* [pl.] RAYS that reach the earth from outer space 宇宙線

cos·mol·ogy /kɒz'mɒlədʒi; *NAmE* kɑːz'mɑːl-/ *noun* [U] the scientific study of the universe and its origin and development 宇宙學 ▶ **cosmo·logic·al** /,kɒzmə'lɒdʒɪkl; *NAmE* ,kɑːzmə'lɑːdʒ-/ *adj.* **cos·molo·gist** /kɒz'mɒlədʒɪst; *NAmE* kɑːz'mɑːl-/ *noun*

Synonyms 同義詞辨析

costs

spending • expenditure • expenses • overheads • outlay

These are all words for money spent by a government, an organization or a person. 以上各詞均指政府、機構或個人的開支、支出、花費。

costs the total amount of money that needs to be spent by a business 指成本：*labour/production costs* 人工／生產成本 ◇ *rising costs* 正在上漲的成本

spending the amount of money that is spent, especially by a government or an organization 尤指政府或機構的開支、支出、花銷：*public spending* 公共開支 ◇ *More spending on health was promised.* 已承諾增加醫療開支。

expenditure (*rather formal*) an amount of money spent by a government, an organization or a person 指政府、機構或個人的開支、支出、花費：*expenditure on education* 教育費用

expenses money that has to be spent by a person or an organization; money that you spend while you are working which your employer will pay back to you later 指個人或機構必需的開支、花費或報銷的費用：*legal expenses* 律師費 ◇ *travel expenses* 差旅費

overhead(s) the regular costs of running a business or organization, such as rent, electricity and wages 指經費、運營費用、經常性開支：*High overheads mean small profit margins.* 經費開銷大意味着利潤低。

outlay the money that you have to spend in order to start a new business or project, or in order to save yourself money or time later 指啟動新業務或項目所必要的開支、費用或省下的經費：*The best equipment is costly but is well worth the outlay.* 最好的設備花費大，但這種開支很值得。

PATTERNS

- spending/expenditure/outlay **on** sth
- **high/low** costs/spending/expenditure/expenses/overheads
- **total** costs/spending/expenditure/expenses/overheads/outlay
- **capital** costs/spending/expenditure/expenses/outlay
- **household** costs/spending/expenditure/expenses
- **government/public/education/health** costs/spending/expenditure
- to **increase/reduce** costs/spending/expenditure/expenses/overheads/the outlay

cosmo·naut /ˈkɒzmənɔːt; *NAmE* ˈkɑːz-/ *noun* an ASTRONAUT from the former Soviet Union （前蘇聯的）宇航員，航天員，太空人

cosmo·pol·itan /ˌkɒzməˈpɒlɪtən; *NAmE* ˌkɑːzməˈpɑːl-/ *adj.*, *noun*

■ ***adj.*** (*approving*) **1** containing people of different types or from different countries, and influenced by their culture 世界性的；全球各國的；有各國人的；受各國文化影響的：*a* ***cosmopolitan city/resort*** 國際性的都市／度假勝地 ◇ *The club has a cosmopolitan atmosphere.* 這個俱樂部具有世界文化的氣氛。 **2** having or showing a wide experience of people and things from many different countries 接觸過許多國家的人（或事物）的；見過世面的；見識廣的：*people with a truly cosmopolitan outlook* 真正具有世界眼光的人 ◇ *cosmopolitan young people* 見多識廣的年輕人

■ ***noun*** a person who has experience of many different parts of the world 周遊世界的人：*She's a real cosmopolitan.* 她是個真正的四海為家的人。

cos·mos /ˈkɒzmɒs; *NAmE* ˈkɑːzmoʊs; -məs/ **the cosmos** *noun* [sing.] the universe, especially when it is thought of as an ordered system（尤指被視為有序體系時的）宇宙：*the structure of the cosmos* 宇宙的結構 ◇ *our place in the cosmos* 我們在宇宙中的位置

cos·set /ˈkɒsɪt; *NAmE* ˈkɑːs-/ *verb* **~ sb** (often *disapproving*) to treat sb with a lot of care and give them a lot of attention, sometimes too much 寵愛；溺愛；嬌慣 SYN **pamper**

cost 0 /kɒst; *NAmE* kɔːst/ *noun*, *verb*

■ ***noun*** **1** 0 [C, U] the amount of money that you need in order to buy, make or do sth 費用；花費；價錢：*the* ***high/low cost*** *of housing* 住宅的高昂／低廉費用 ◇ *A new computer system has been installed* ***at a cost of*** *£80 000.* 新的計算機系統已安裝，費用為 8 萬英鎊。◇ *The plan had to be abandoned on grounds of cost.* 由於經費的原因此項計劃被迫放棄。◇ *We did not even make enough money to* ***cover the cost*** *of the food.* 我們掙的錢甚至無法餬口。◇ *Consumers will have to* ***bear the*** *full* ***cost*** *of these pay increases.* 消費者將不得不承擔增加工資所需的全部費用。◇ *The total cost to you* (= the amount you have to pay) *is £3 000.* 你總共要支付 3 000 英鎊。➲ SYNONYMS at PRICE **2** 0 **costs** [pl.] the total amount of money that needs to be spent by a business 成本：*The use of cheap labour helped to keep costs down.* 使用廉價勞動力有助於降低成本。◇ *to* ***cut/reduce costs*** 降低成本 ◇ ***running/operating/labour costs*** 營運／經營／人工成本 ◇ *We have had to raise our prices because of rising costs.* 因為成本日益上漲，我們不得不提高價格。➲ COLLOCATIONS at BUSINESS **3** 0 [U, sing.] the effort, loss or damage that is involved in order to do or achieve sth（為做某事涉及的）努力，代價，損失：*the terrible cost of the war in death and suffering* 這場戰爭造成的死亡與苦難的慘重代價 ◇ *the environmental cost of nuclear power* 核能對環境的破壞 ◇ *She saved him from the fire but* ***at the cost of*** *her own life* (= she died). 她從火中把他救了出來，卻犧牲了自己的生命。◇ *He worked non-stop for three months,* ***at*** *considerable* ***cost to*** *his health.* 他連續不斷地工作了三個月，大大損害了自己的身體健康。◇ *I felt a need to please people, whatever the* ***cost in*** *time and energy.* 我感到一定要使人們滿意，耗費多少時間和精力都在所不惜。 **4 costs** (*NAmE* also **ˈcourt costs**) [pl.] the sum of money that sb is ordered to pay for lawyers, etc. in a legal case 訴訟費用：*He was ordered to pay £2 000 costs.* 他被責令繳納 2 000 英鎊訴訟費。

IDM **at ˈall cost/costs** whatever is needed to achieve sth 不惜任何代價：*You must stop the press from finding out at all costs.* 你必須不惜一切代價阻止媒體查明真相。 **at ˈany cost** under any circumstances 在任何情況下；無論如何：*He is determined to win at any cost.* 他決心無論如何要爭取勝利。 **at ˈcost** for only the amount of money that is needed to make or get sth, without any profit being added on 按成本；按成本價格：*goods sold at cost* 按成本價銷售的商品 **know/learn/find sth to your ˈcost** to know sth because of sth unpleasant that has happened to you 付出過代價（或吃了苦頭）才知道：*He's a ruthless businessman, as I know to my cost.* 我吃了苦頭後才知道他是個無情的商人。➲ more at COUNT *v.*

■ ***verb*** (**cost**, **cost**) HELP In sense 4 **costed** is used for the past tense and past participle. 作第 4 義時過去時和過去分詞用 costed。 **1** 0 if sth **costs** a particular amount of money, you need to pay that amount in order to buy, make or do it 需付費；價錢為：**~ sth** *How much did it cost?* 這東西要多少錢？◇ *I didn't get it because it cost too much.* 因為那東西太昂貴我沒買。◇ *Tickets cost ten dollars each.* 每張票價為十元。◇ *Calls to the helpline cost 38p per minute.* 打服務熱線每分鐘為 38 便士。◇ *Don't use too much of it—it* ***cost a lot of money.*** 這東西很貴，不要用得太多。◇ *All these reforms will* ***cost money*** (= be expensive). 所有這些改革都要花很多錢。◇ *Good food need not* ***cost a fortune*** (= cost a lot of money). 好食物不一定要花很多的錢。◇ **~ sb sth** *The meal cost us about £40.* 這頓飯花了我們約 40 英鎊。◇ *This is costing the taxpayer £10 billion a year.* 這要花費納稅人每年 100 億英鎊。◇ **~ sth to do sth** *The hospital will cost an estimated £2 million to build.* 修建這座醫院估計要耗費 200 萬英鎊。◇ *It costs a fortune to fly first class.* 乘坐飛機頭等艙要花一大筆錢。 **2** 0 to cause the loss of sth 使喪失；使損失：**~ sb sth** *That one mistake almost cost him his life.* 那一個差錯幾乎使他喪命。◇ *A late penalty cost United the game* (= meant that they did not win the game). 臨近終場的罰球得分使得聯隊輸掉那場比賽。◇ **~ sth** *The closure of the factory is likely to cost 1 000 jobs.* 那家工廠一關閉，很可能 1 000 個工作崗位就沒有了。 **3 ~ sb sth** to involve you in making an effort or doing sth unpleasant 使付出努力；使做不愉快的事：*The accident cost me a visit to the doctor.* 那事故害得我去看了一趟醫生。◇ *Financial worries cost her many sleepless nights.* 她為錢發愁，許多夜晚無法入睡。 **4** (**costed**, **costed**) [usually passive] to estimate how much money will be needed for sth or the price that should be charged for sth 估算成本；估價：**~ sth** *The project needs to be costed in detail.* 這項工程需要作詳細的成本估算。◇ *Their accountants have costed the project at $8.1 million.* 他們的會計師估算此項工程成本為 810 萬元。◇ **~ sth out** *Have you costed out these proposals yet?* 你估算過這些提案所涉及的費用嗎？➲ see also COSTING

IDM **cost sb ˈdear** to make sb suffer a lot 使飽嚐苦頭；使付出沉重的代價：*That one mistake has cost him dear over the years.* 那一個差錯使他多年來付出了沉重的代價。 **it will ˈcost you** (*informal*) used to say that sth will be expensive 貴得很；要花很多錢：*There is a de luxe model available, but it'll cost you.* 有豪華型的，但貴得很。➲ more at ARM *n.*

ˈcost accounting *noun* [U] (*business* 商) the process of recording and analysing the costs involved in running a business 成本會計

cos·tal /ˈkɒstl; *NAmE* ˈkɑːstl/ *adj.* (*anatomy* 解) connected with the RIBS 肋骨的；肋部的

ˈco-star *noun*, *verb*

■ ***noun*** one of two or more famous actors who appear together in a film/movie or play（電影或戲劇中的）聯袂主演明星

■ ***verb*** (**-rr-**) **1** [I] **~ (with sb)** to appear as one of the main actors with sb in a play or film/movie（在電影或戲劇中）與其他明星聯合主演：*a new movie in which Russell Crowe co-stars with Cate Blanchett* 由羅素・克勞和凱特・布蘭切特聯袂主演的一部新電影 **2** [T] **~ sb** (of a film/movie or play 電影或戲劇) to have two or more famous actors acting in it（由明星演員）聯袂主演，合演：*a new movie co-starring Russell Crowe and Cate Blanchett* 由羅素・克勞和凱特・布蘭切特聯袂主演的一部新電影

ˈcost-benefit *noun* [U] (*economics* 經) the relationship between the cost of doing sth and the value of the benefit that results from it 成本效益：*cost-benefit analysis* 成本效益分析

ˈcost-cutting *noun* [U] the reduction of the amount of money spent on sth, especially because of financial difficulty（尤指因財政困難的）成本削減：*Deliveries of mail could be delayed because of cost-cutting.* 由於削減成本，郵件的遞送可能會延遲。◇ *a* ***cost-cutting exercise/measure/programme*** 成本削減的實施／措施／計劃

ˌcost-efˈfective *adj.* giving the best possible profit or benefits in comparison with the money that is spent 有最佳利潤的；有成本效益的；划算的 ▶ **ˌcost-efˈfect-ive·ness** *noun* [U]

C

cos·ter·mon·ger /ˈkɒstəmʌŋɡə(r); *NAmE* ˈkɑːstərm-/ *noun* (*BrE*) (in the past) a person who sold fruit and vegetables in the street （舊時的）水果蔬菜小販

cost·ing /ˈkɒstɪŋ; *NAmE* ˈkɔːst-/ *noun* an estimate of how much money will be needed for sth 成本估算：*Here is a detailed costing of our proposals.* 這是我們的方案的詳細成本估算。◇ *You'd better do some costings.* 你最好作一些成本估算。

cost·ly /ˈkɒstli; *NAmE* ˈkɔːst-/ *adj.* (**cost·lier**, **cost·li·est**) **HELP** You can also use **more costly** and **most costly**. 亦可用 more costly 和 most costly。 **1** costing a lot of money, especially more than you want to pay 花錢多的；昂貴的；價錢高的 **SYN** **expensive**：*Buying new furniture may prove too costly.* 購買新傢具可能會花錢太多。➲ SYNONYMS at EXPENSIVE **2** causing problems or the loss of sth 引起困難的；造成損失的 **SYN** **expensive**：*a costly mistake/failure* 造成重大損失的錯誤 / 失敗 ◇ *Mining can be costly in terms of lives* (= too many people can die). 採礦有時會造成重大的生命損失。▶ **cost·li·ness** *noun* [U]

the ˌcost of ˈliving *noun* [sing.] the amount of money that people need to pay for food, clothing and somewhere to live 生活費用：*a steady rise in the cost of living* 生活費用的持續上升 ◇ *the high cost of living in London* 倫敦昂貴的生活費用

ˌcost ˈprice *noun* [U] the cost of producing sth or the price at which it is sold without profit 成本價：*Copies of the CD can be purchased at cost price.* 這光盤可按成本價購買。➲ compare SELLING PRICE

cos·tume /ˈkɒstjuːm; *NAmE* ˈkɑːstuːm/ *noun* **1** [C, U] the clothes worn by people from a particular place or during a particular historical period （某地或某歷史時期的）服裝，裝束 ➲ see also NATIONAL COSTUME **2** [C, U] the clothes worn by actors in a play or film/movie, or worn by sb to make them look like sth else （戲劇或電影的）戲裝，服裝：*The actors were still in costume and make-up.* 這些演員仍是戲裝打扮。◇ *She has four costume changes during the play.* 她在這齣戲裏要換四次服裝。◇ *He went to the party in a giant chicken costume.* 他是打扮成一隻大雞去參加聚會的。◇ *a costume designer* 戲裝設計師 **3** [C] (*BrE, informal*) = SWIMMING COSTUME

cos·tumed /ˈkɒstjuːmd; *NAmE* ˈkɑːstuːmd/ *adj.* [usually before noun] wearing a costume 着戲裝的

ˈcostume drama *noun* [C, U] a play or film/movie set in the past 古裝戲；古裝電影

ˈcostume jewellery *noun* [U] large heavy jewellery that can look expensive but is made with cheap materials （廉價）人造珠寶飾物

ˈcostume party *noun* (*NAmE*) a party where all the guests wear special clothes, in order to look like a different person, an animal, etc. 化裝舞會

cos·tu·mier /kɒsˈtjuːmiə(r); *NAmE* kɑːsˈtuːmieɪ/ (*BrE*) (*NAmE* **ˈcos·tu·mer**) *noun* a person or company that makes COSTUMES or has COSTUMES to hire, especially for the theatre （尤指戲劇演出的）戲裝製作人，服裝公司，戲裝出租商：*a firm of theatrical costumiers* 戲劇服裝出租公司

cosy (*BrE*) (*NAmE* **cozy**) /ˈkəʊzi; *NAmE* ˈkoʊzi/ *adj.*, *verb*

■ *adj.* (**cosi·er**, **cosi·est**, **cozi·er**, **cozi·est**) **1** warm, comfortable and safe, especially because of being small or confined 溫暖舒適的（尤指細小的室內地方） **SYN** **snug**：*a cosy little room* 溫暖舒適的小房間 ◇ *a cosy feeling* 愜意的感覺 ◇ *I felt warm and cosy sitting by the fire.* 坐在爐火旁，我感到又暖和又舒服。 **2** friendly and private 親密無間的；密切的：*a cosy chat with a friend* 與朋友親切的閒聊 **3** (often *disapproving*) easy and convenient, but not always honest or right 輕易得到的，輕鬆的（但不一定是誠實或恰當的）：*The firm has a cosy relationship with the Ministry of Defence.* 這家公司與國防部關係密切。◇ *The danger is that things get too cosy.* 危險在於一切都來得太容易。▶ **cosi·ly** (*BrE*) (*NAmE* **cozi·ly**) *adv.*：*sitting cosily by the fire* 暖融融地坐在爐火旁 **cosi·ness** (*BrE*) (*NAmE* **cozi·ness**) *noun* [U]：*the warmth and cosiness of the kitchen* 廚房的溫暖與舒適

■ *verb* (**cosies**, **cosy·ing**, **cosied**, **cosied**)

PHR V **ˌcosy ˈup to sb** (*BrE*) (*NAmE* **ˌcozy ˈup to sb**) (*informal*) to act in a friendly way towards sb, especially sb who will be useful to you 獻殷勤；取悅

cot /kɒt; *NAmE* kɑːt/ *noun* **1** (*BrE*) (*NAmE* **crib**) a small bed with high sides for a baby or young child （有圍欄的）幼兒牀：*a travel cot* (= one that can be moved around easily, used when travelling) 旅行幼兒牀 ➲ VISUAL VOCAB page V23 ➲ see also CARRYCOT **2** (*NAmE*) (*BrE* **ˌcamp ˈbed**) a light narrow bed that you can fold up and carry easily 摺疊牀；行軍牀 ➲ VISUAL VOCAB page V23

ˈcot death (*BrE*) (*NAmE* **ˈcrib death**) *noun* [U, C] the sudden death while sleeping of a baby that appears to be healthy 嬰兒猝死

co·terie /ˈkəʊtəri; *NAmE* ˈkoʊ-/ *noun* [C+sing./pl. v.] (*formal*, often *disapproving*) a small group of people who have the same interests and do things together but do not like to include others （志趣相同、合夥幹事而排外的）小圈子，小集團

co·ter·min·ous /kəʊˈtɜːmɪnəs; *NAmE* koʊˈtɜːrm-/ *adj.* [not usually before noun] (*formal*) **1 ~ (with sth)** (of countries or areas 國家或地區) sharing a border 享有共同邊界；毗連；接壤 **2 ~ (with sth)** (of things or ideas 事物或看法) having so much in common that they are almost the same as each other 幾乎一致；差不多相同

cot·tage 0‑ /ˈkɒtɪdʒ; *NAmE* ˈkɑːt-/ *noun* a small house, especially in the country 小屋；（尤指）村舍，小別墅：*a charming country cottage with roses around the door* 門口四周開着玫瑰花的迷人的鄉村小屋 ◇ (*BrE*) *a holiday cottage* 度假小別墅 ➲ VISUAL VOCAB page V16

ˌcottage ˈcheese *noun* [U] soft white cheese with small lumps in it 農家乾酪（含小塊的白色軟乾酪）

ˌcottage ˈhospital *noun* (*BrE*) a small hospital in a country area 鄉村小醫院；鄉間診療所

ˌcot·tage ˈin·dus·try *noun* a small business in which the work is done by people in their homes 家庭手工業：*Weaving and knitting are traditional cottage industries.* 編織和針織是傳統的家庭手工業。

ˌcottage ˈloaf *noun* (*BrE*) a LOAF of bread consisting of a large round piece with a smaller round piece on top 農家麪包（用大、小兩個圓麪包疊在一起）

ˌcottage ˈpie *noun* [C, U] = SHEPHERD'S PIE

cot·tager /ˈkɒtɪdʒə(r); *NAmE* ˈkɑːt-/ *noun* (*BrE*) (especially in the past) a person who lives in a small house or cottage in the country （尤指舊時的）住農舍者，村民

cot·ta·ging /ˈkɒtɪdʒɪŋ; *NAmE* ˈkɑːt-/ *noun* [U] (*BrE, slang*) the practice of HOMOSEXUAL men looking for sexual partners in a public toilet/bathroom （男性同性戀者）在公共衞生間尋找性伴侶

cot·ton 0‑ /ˈkɒtn; *NAmE* ˈkɑːtn/ *noun*, *verb*

■ *noun* [U] **1** 0‑ a plant grown in warm countries for the soft white hairs around its seeds that are used to make cloth and thread 棉花植株：***cotton fields/plants*** 棉田 / 株 ◇ *bales of cotton* 大包的棉花 **2** 0‑ the cloth made from the cotton plant 棉織物；棉布：*The sheets are 100% pure cotton.* 這些被單是 100% 的純棉。◇ *a cotton shirt/skirt* 棉布襯衫 / 裙子 ◇ *printed cotton cloth* 印花棉布 ◇ *the cotton industry* 棉紡織業 ◇ *a cotton mill* 棉紡廠 **3** (*especially BrE*) thread that is used for sewing 棉線；棉紗：*sewing cotton* 縫紉用棉線 ◇ *a cotton reel* 棉線軸 ➲ VISUAL VOCAB page V41 **4** (*NAmE*) (*US* also **abˌsorbent ˈcotton**) (*BrE* **ˌcotton ˈwool**) a soft mass of white material that is used for cleaning the skin or a wound 藥棉；脫脂棉：*Use a cotton ball to apply the lotion.* 用棉球塗護膚液。

■ *verb*

PHR V **ˌcotton ˈon (to sth)** (*informal*) to begin to understand or realize sth without being told 明白；領悟；意識到：*I suddenly cottoned on to what he was doing.* 我突然明白了他在做什麼。 **ˈcotton (up) to sb/sth** (*NAmE*, informal) to make an attempt to be friendly to sb 向…討好；巴結；與…套近乎

the 'Cotton Belt *noun* the states in the southern US where cotton was the main crop 棉花地帶（美國南部盛產棉花的幾個州）

,cotton 'bud (*BrE*) (also **Q-tip™** *NAmE, BrE*) *noun* a small stick with COTTON WOOL at each end, used for cleaning inside the ears, etc.（用於清潔耳朵內部等的）棉籤

,cotton 'candy (*NAmE*) (*BrE* **candy·floss**) *noun* [U] a type of sweet/candy in the form of a mass of sticky threads made from melted sugar and served on a stick, especially at FAIRGROUNDS（尤指遊樂場出售的）棉花糖

'cotton gin (also **gin**) *noun* a machine for separating the seeds of a cotton plant from the cotton 軋棉機；軋花機

cotton·mouth /ˈkɒtnmaʊθ; *NAmE* ˈkɑːtn-/ (also **,cottonmouth 'moccasin**, **,water 'moccasin**) *noun* a poisonous snake which lives near water in the US 棉口蛇，水蝮蛇（毒蛇，生活於美國水濱）

cot·ton·wood /ˈkɒtnwʊd; *NAmE* ˈkɑːtn-/ (also **'cotton-wood tree**) *noun* a type of N American POPLAR tree, with seeds that are covered in hairs that look like white cotton 棉白楊，三角葉楊（產於北美）

,cotton 'wool (*BrE*) (*US* **,ab,sorbent 'cotton**) *noun* [U] a soft mass of white material that is used for cleaning the skin or a wound 藥棉；脱脂棉：*cotton wool balls* 藥用棉球

couch /kaʊtʃ/ *noun, verb*

■ ***noun*** **1** a long comfortable seat for two or more people to sit on 長沙發；長榻 SYN **settee, sofa** ➲ VISUAL VOCAB page V21 **2** a long piece of furniture like a bed, especially in a doctor's office（尤指診室內的）診察榻：*on the psychiatrist's couch* 在精神病醫生的診察榻上

■ ***verb*** [usually passive] **~ sth (in sth)** (*formal*) to say or write words in a particular style or manner（用某種文體或方式）表達，措辭：*The letter was deliberately **couched in** very vague **terms**.* 這封信故意寫得含糊其詞。

couch·ette /kuːˈʃet/ *noun* a narrow bed on a train, that folds down from the wall（列車上的）摺疊式卧鋪

'couch potato *noun* (*informal, disapproving*) a person who spends a lot of time sitting and watching television 老泡在電視機前的人

cou·gar /ˈkuːɡə(r)/ *noun* (*especially NAmE*) = PUMA

cough 🔑 /kɒf; *NAmE* kɔːf/ *verb, noun*

■ ***verb*** **1** 🔑 [I] to force out air suddenly and noisily through your throat, for example when you have a cold 咳嗽：*I couldn't stop coughing.* 我咳嗽不止。◊ *to **cough nervously/politely/discreetly*** 緊張地／斯文地／小心翼翼地咳嗽 **2** [T] **~ sth (up)** to force sth out of your throat or lungs by coughing（從喉嚨或肺中）咳出：*Sometimes she coughed (up) blood.* 她有時咯血。 **3** [I] (of an engine 發動機) to make a sudden unpleasant noise 發出刺耳的聲音

PHR V **,cough 'up | ,cough sth↔'up** (*informal*) to give sth, especially money, unwillingly 勉強給（尤指錢）：*Steve finally coughed up the money he owed us.* 史蒂夫最終勉強歸還了他欠我們的錢。

■ ***noun*** **1** 🔑 an act or a sound of coughing 咳嗽；咳嗽聲：*She gave a little cough to attract my attention.* 她輕輕地咳了一聲以引起我的注意。 **2** 🔑 an illness or infection that makes you cough often 咳嗽病：*to have a **dry/persistent/hacking cough*** 乾咳；頑固的咳嗽；頻咳 ◊ *My cold's better, but I can't seem to shake off this cough.* 我感冒好些了，但這咳嗽好像老也不好。➲ see also WHOOPING COUGH

cough·ing 🔑 /ˈkɒfɪŋ; *NAmE* ˈkɔːfɪŋ/ *noun* [U] the action of coughing 咳嗽：*Another fit of coughing seized him.* 他那咳嗽又一次發作了。

'cough mixture (*BrE*) (also **'cough syrup**, **'cough medicine** *BrE, NAmE*) *noun* [U] liquid medicine that you take for a cough 止咳藥水；止咳合劑

could 🔑 /kəd; *strong form* kʊd/ *modal verb* (*negative* **could not**, *short form* **couldn't** /ˈkʊdnt/)

1 🔑 used as the past tense of 'can'（用於 can 的過去時）：*She said that she couldn't come.* 她説她來不了。◊ *I couldn't hear what they were saying.* 我聽不見他們在説些什麼。◊ *Sorry, I couldn't get any more.* 對不起，我無法弄到更多了。➲ note at CAN[1] **2** 🔑 used to ask if you can do sth（詢問是否可做某事）能，可以：*Could I use your phone, please?* 請讓我用一下你的電話可以嗎？◊ *Could we stop by next week?* 我們下週能過來一下嗎？ **3** 🔑 used to politely ask sb to do sth for you（禮貌地請求別人做事）能，可以：*Could you babysit for us on Friday?* 你星期五幫我們看一下孩子好嗎？ **4** 🔑 used to show that sth is or might be possible（表示可能）可能：*I could do it now, if you like.* 如果你願意的話，我現在就可以做這事。◊ *Don't worry—they could have just forgotten to call.* 別擔心，他們可能只是忘了打電話。◊ *You couldn't have left it on the bus, could you?* 你不可能把它落在公共汽車上了吧？◊ *'Have some more cake.' 'Oh, I couldn't, thank you* (= I'm too full).' "再來點蛋糕吧。" "謝謝你，吃不下了。" **5** 🔑 used to suggest sth（用於建議）可以：*We could write a letter to the director.* 我們不妨給主管寫封信。◊ *You could always try his home number.* 你總可以試着給他往家裏打電話呀。 **6** 🔑 used to show that you are annoyed that sb did not do sth（對某人未做某事表示惱怒）本來可以：*They could have let me know they were going to be late!* 他們要晚來，也該早告訴我一聲呀！ **7** (*informal*) used to emphasize how strongly you want to express your feelings（強調感覺）真想：*I'm so fed up I could scream!* 我煩透了，非大喊大叫不可！➲ note at MODAL

IDM **could do with sth** (*informal*) used to say that you need or would like to have sth（表示需要或希望有）想要：*I could do with a drink!* 我真想喝一杯！◊ *Her hair could have done with a wash.* 她的頭髮該洗一洗了。

cou·lis /ˈkuːli; *NAmE* kuːˈliː/ *noun* (*pl.* **cou·lis**) (from *French*) a thin fruit sauce 稀果醬

cou·lomb /ˈkuːlɒm; *NAmE* -lɑːm; -lɔːm/ *noun* (*abbr.* **C**) (*physics* 物) a unit for measuring electric charge 庫侖（電量單位）

coun·cil 🔑 /ˈkaʊnsl/ *noun* [C+sing./pl. v.]

1 🔑 a group of people who are elected to govern an area such as a city or county（市、郡等的）政務委員會，地方議會：*a **city/county/borough/district council*** 市／郡／自治市／區政務委員會 ◊ *She's on the local council.* 她是地方議會的議員。◊ *a **council member/meeting*** 政務委員會委員／會議 **2** 🔑 (*BrE*) the organization that provides services in a city or county, for example education, houses, libraries, etc. 市政（或地方管理）服務機構：***council workers/services*** 市政工作人員／部門 **3** a group of people chosen to give advice, make rules, do research, provide money, etc.（顧問、立法、研究、基金等）委員會：*the Medical Research Council* 醫學研究會 ◊ *In Britain, the Arts Council gives grants to theatres.* 英國的藝術委員會向劇院提供資金。 **4** (*formal*) (especially in the past) a formal meeting to discuss what action to take in a particular situation（尤指舊時討論特定步驟的）協商會議：*The King held a council at Nottingham from 14 to 19 October 1330.* 國王於 1330 年 10 月 14 日至 19 日在諾丁漢召集協商會議。➲ see also PRIVY COUNCIL

'council chamber *noun* (*BrE*) a large room in which a council meets 會議廳；會議室；議事室

'council estate *noun* (*BrE*) a large group of houses built by a local council 地方當局所屬地產；地方政府建的住宅群

'council house, **'council flat** *noun* (*BrE*) a house or flat rented from the local council 地方政府出租住房（或公寓）

coun·cil·lor (*NAmE* also **coun·cil·or**) /ˈkaʊnsələ(r)/ *noun* (*abbr.* **Cllr**) a member of a council 市議員；政務委員會委員：*Councillor Ann Jones* 安•瓊斯委員 ◊ *Talk to your local councillor about the problem.* 關於這個問題可與你當地的市議員談一談。➲ see also COUNCILMAN, COUNCILWOMAN

coun·cil·man /ˈkaʊnslmən/ *noun* (*pl.* **-men** /-mən/) (*US*) = COUNCILLOR

ˌcouncil of ˈwar *noun* (*pl.* **councils of war**) (*BrE*) a meeting to discuss how to deal with an urgent and difficult situation（為處理緊急和困難局勢而召開的）緊急會議

C

ˈcouncil tax *noun* (often **the council tax**) [sing., U] (in Britain) a tax charged by local councils, based on the value of a person's home（英國根據個人住房的價值而收取的）市政稅

coun·cil·woman /ˈkaʊnslwʊmən/ *noun* (*pl.* **-women** /-wɪmɪn/) (*US*) = COUNCILLOR

coun·sel /ˈkaʊnsl/ *noun, verb*

■ **noun** [U, C] **1** (*formal*) advice, especially given by older people or experts; a piece of advice（尤指年長者或專家的）勸告，忠告，建議：*Listen to the counsel of your elders.* 要聽從長輩的忠告。◇ *In the end, wiser counsels prevailed.* 高明的建議最終佔了上風。**2** (*law* 律) a lawyer or group of lawyers representing sb in court 辯護律師：*to be represented by counsel* 由律師代表 ◇ *the* ***counsel for the defence/prosecution*** 被告 / 原告的律師 ◇ ***defence/prosecuting counsel*** 被告 / 原告的律師 ◇ *The court then heard counsel for the dead woman's father.* 法庭接着聽取了已死女人的父親所請律師的陳述。➲ COLLOCATIONS at JUSTICE ➲ see also KING'S/QUEEN'S COUNSEL ➲ note at LAWYER

IDM **a counsel of desˈpair** (*formal*) advice not to try to do sth because it is too difficult 知難而退的建議 **a counsel of perˈfection** (*formal*) advice that is good but that is difficult or impossible to follow 聽上去完美卻難以實行的建議 **keep your own ˈcounsel** (*formal*) to keep your opinions, plans, etc. secret 將自己意見（或計劃等）保密；不暴露自己的意圖

■ **verb** (**-ll-**, *especially US* **-l-**) **1** **~ sb** to listen to and give support or professional advice to sb who needs help 提供專業咨詢：*Therapists were brought in to counsel the bereaved.* 請了治療專家來勸慰死者的親屬。**2** (*formal*) to advise sb to do sth 建議，勸告（做某事）：**~ sth** *Most experts counsel caution in such cases.* 大多數專家建議在這樣的情況下要謹慎從事。◇ **~ sb to do sth** *He counselled them to give up the plan.* 他建議他們放棄此項計劃。

coun·sel·ling (*especially US* **coun·sel·ing**) /ˈkaʊnsəlɪŋ/ *noun* [U] professional advice about a problem 咨詢；輔導：*marriage guidance counselling* 婚姻指導咨詢 ◇ *a student counselling service* 學生輔導服務

coun·sel·lor (*especially US* **coun·sel·or**) /ˈkaʊnsələ(r)/ *noun* **1** a person who has been trained to advise people with problems, especially personal problems（尤指針對私人問題的）顧問；輔導顧問：*a marriage guidance counsellor* 婚姻指導顧問 **2** (*NAmE, IrishE*) a lawyer 律師 **3** (*NAmE*) a person who is in charge of young people at a summer camp 夏令營負責人

count 🔑 /kaʊnt/ *verb, noun*

■ **verb**

▸ SAY NUMBERS 數數 **1** 🔑 [I] to say numbers in the correct order（按順序）數數：*Billy can't count yet.* 比利還不會數數。◇ **~ to/up to sth** *She can count up to 10 in Italian.* 她可以用意大利語數到 10。◇ **~ (from sth) to/up to sth** *to count from 1 to 10* 從 1 數到 10

▸ FIND TOTAL 得到總數 **2** 🔑 [T, I] to calculate the total number of people, things, etc. in a particular group 計算（或清點）總數：**~ sth (up)** *The diet is based on counting calories.* 這個飲食安排以計算熱量為根據。◇ **~ (up) how many ...** *She began to count up how many guests they had to invite.* 她開始計算他們得邀請多少位客人。◇ **~ from ...** *There are 12 weeks to go, counting from today.* 從今天算起還有 12 個星期。

▸ INCLUDE 包括 **3** 🔑 [T] **~ sb/sth** to include sb/sth when you calculate a total 把…算入；包括：*We have invited 50 people,* ***not counting*** *the children.* 不算小孩，我們邀請了 50 人。

▸ MATTER 有重要性 **4** 🔑 [I] (not used in the progressive tenses 不用於進行時) to be important 重要 **SYN** **matter**：*Every point in this game counts.* 這場比賽每一分都很重要。◇ ***It's the thought that counts*** (= used about a small but kind action or gift). 貴在心意。◇ **~ for sth** *The fact that she had apologized counted for nothing with him.* 她已道歉，但他認為這沒有用。

▸ ACCEPT OFFICIALLY 正式接納 **5** 🔑 [I, T] to be officially accepted; to accept sth officially（被）正式接納，正式認可：*Don't go over that line or your throw won't count.* 別越過那條線，否則你的投擲就會被判無效。◇ **~ sth** *Applications received after 1 July will not be counted.* *7 月 1 日以後收到的申請書將不予受理。

▸ CONSIDER 認為 **6** [I, T] **~ as sb/sth** | **~ sb/sth (as) sb/sth** to consider sb/sth in a particular way; to be considered in a particular way 認為；看作；算作；被視為：**~ (sb/sth) as sb/sth** *For tax purposes that money counts/is counted as income.* 那筆錢算作收入，需要納稅。◇ **~ sb/sth/yourself + adv./prep.** *I count him among my closest friends.* 我把他看作我最親密的朋友之一。◇ **~ sb/sth/yourself + adj.** *I* ***count myself lucky*** *to have known him.* 和他相識，我覺得很幸運。◇ **~ sb/sth/yourself + noun** *She counts herself one of the lucky ones.* 她認為自己是一個幸運兒。

IDM **be able to count sb/sth on (the fingers of) one ˈhand** used to say that the total number of sb/sth is very small 屈指可數；寥寥無幾 **... and ˈcounting** used to say that a total is continuing to increase（總數）仍在繼續增加：*The movie's ticket sales add up to $39 million, and counting.* 這部電影的票房共 3 900 萬元，還在繼續上升。**count your ˈblessings** to be grateful for the good things in your life 知足 **don't count your ˈchickens (before they are ˈhatched)** (*saying*) you should not be too confident that sth will be successful, because sth may still go wrong 不要蛋未孵化先數小雞；別過早打如意算盤 **count the cost (of sth)** to feel the bad effects of a mistake, an accident, etc. 感受（錯誤、事故等造成的）不利後果：*The town is now counting the cost of its failure to provide adequate flood protection.* 這個鎮未採取充分的防洪措施，現在嚐到苦頭了。**count ˈsheep** to imagine that sheep are jumping over a fence and to count them, as a way of getting to sleep 數（假想中跳出柵欄的）羊以求入睡 **stand up and be ˈcounted** to say publicly that you support sb or you agree with sth 公開表示支持（或贊同）**who's ˈcounting?** (*informal*) used to say that you do not care how many times sth happens（表示不管發生多少次）誰在乎呢，管它呢

PHR V **ˌcount aˈgainst sb** | **ˌcount sth aˈgainst sb** to be considered or to consider sth to be a disadvantage in sb（被）認為對某人不利：*For that job her lack of experience may count against her.* 她缺乏經驗可能對她申請那份工作不利。**ˌcount ˈdown (to sth)** to think about a future event with pleasure or excitement and count the minutes, days, etc. until it happens 倒計時：*She's already counting down to the big day.* 她已經在對這一重大日子倒計時了。➲ related noun COUNTDOWN **ˌcount sb ˈin** to include sb in an activity 把某人算入；包括：*I hear you're organizing a trip to the game next week? Count me in!* 我聽說你們將在下週組織旅行去看比賽？把我也算上！**ˈcount on sb/sth** 🔑 to trust sb to do sth or to be sure that sth will happen 依賴，依靠，指望（某人做某事）；確信（某事會發生）**SYN** **bank on sth**：*'I'm sure he'll help.'* ***'Don't count on it.'*** "我肯定他會幫忙的。" "那可靠不住。" ◇ **~ sb/sth to do sth** *I'm counting on you to help me.* 我就靠你幫我啦。◇ **~ doing sth** *Few people can count on having a job for life.* 很少人會指望一輩子都幹一個工作。◇ **~ sb/sth doing sth** *We can't count on this warm weather lasting.* 我們不能指望這暖和的天氣會持久。➲ SYNONYMS at TRUST **ˌcount sb/sth↔ˈout** to count things one after the other as you put them somewhere 邊放置邊數；逐一地數出：*She counted out $70 in $10 bills.* 她數出了 70 元錢，都是 10 元一張的。**ˌcount sb ˈout** to not include sb in an activity 不把某人算入；不包括：*If you're going out tonight you'll have to count me out.* 假如你們今晚要出去，就別把我算在內。**ˌcount toˈwards/toˈward sth** to be included as part of sth that you hope to achieve in the future 被包括在內（成為將來所得的一部份）：*Students gain college credits which count towards their degree.* 學生獲得的學分將計入其學位積分。

■ **noun**

▸ TOTAL 總數 **1** [usually sing.] an act of counting to find the total number of sth; the total number that you find

數出總數；總數：*The bus driver did a quick count of the empty seats.* 公共汽車司機很快地數了數空位。◇ *If the election result is close, there will be a second count.* 如果選舉結果很接近，將進行第二次計票。◇ *The body count (= the total number of people who have died) stands at 24.* 死亡人數總計為 24 人。➲ see also HEADCOUNT

▸ **SAYING NUMBERS** 數數 **2** [usually sing.] an act of saying numbers in order beginning with 1 （按順序的）數數，點數：*Raise your leg and hold for a count of ten.* 抬起一條腿，保持這一姿勢，直至數到十。◇ *He was knocked to the ground and stayed down for a count of eight (= in boxing).* 他被擊倒在地，躺在地上直至數到八（拳擊用語）。

▸ **MEASUREMENT** 度量 **3** [usually sing.] (*technical* 術語) a measurement of the amount of sth contained in a particular substance or area （某物在某物質或面積中）量的計數：*a raised white blood cell count* 升高了的白血球數 ➲ see also BLOOD COUNT, POLLEN COUNT

▸ **CRIME** 罪行 **4** (*law* 律) a crime that sb is accused of committing （被指控的）罪狀，事項：*They were found guilty on all counts.* 他們被判各項罪名成立。◇ *She appeared in court on three counts of fraud.* 她因三項詐騙罪而出庭受審。

▸ **IN DISCUSSION/ARGUMENT** 討論；爭論 **5** [usually pl.] a point made during a discussion or an argument （討論或爭論的）論點，觀點，問題，事項：*I disagree with you on both counts.* 我對你的兩個觀點均不敢苟同。

▸ **RANK/TITLE** 等級；頭銜 **6** (in some European countries) a NOBLEMAN of high rank, similar to an EARL in Britain 伯爵（歐洲一些國家相當於英國 earl 的貴族封號）：*Count Tolstoy* 托爾斯泰伯爵 ➲ see also COUNTESS

IDM **at the last 'count** according to the latest information about the numbers of sth 根據有關…數字的最新消息：*She'd applied for 30 jobs at the last count.* 根據有關的最新消息她申請過 30 個職位。 **keep (a) count (of sth)** to remember or keep a record of numbers or amounts of sth over a period of time （在一段時期內）記得數目，數得清，記錄：*Keep a count of your calorie intake for one week.* 把你一星期的熱卡攝入量記錄下來。 **lose count (of sth)** to forget the total of sth before you have finished counting it 數不清：*I lost count and had to start again.* 我數着數着忘了，不得不又從頭開始數。◇ *She had lost count of the number of times she'd told him to be careful (= she could not remember because there were so many).* 她不知多少次告訴過他要小心。 **,out for the 'count** (*BrE*) (*NAmE* **,down for the 'count**) **1** (of a BOXER 拳擊手) unable to get up again within ten seconds after being knocked down （被擊倒後的十秒鐘以內）無法再站立起來 **2** in a deep sleep 熟睡；酣睡

count·able /'kaʊntəbl/ *adj.* (*grammar* 語法) a noun that is **countable** can be used in the plural or with *a* or *an*, for example *table*, *cat* and *idea* （名詞）可數的 **OPP** **uncountable**

count·down /'kaʊntdaʊn/ *noun* **~ (to sth)** **1** [sing., U] the action of counting seconds backwards to zero, for example before a SPACECRAFT is launched 倒數讀秒，倒計時（如發射宇宙飛船時） **2** [sing.] the period of time just before sth important happens 大事臨近的時期：*the countdown to the wedding* 婚禮的臨近

coun·ten·ance /'kaʊntənəns/ *noun, verb*

▪ ***noun*** (*formal* or *literary*) a person's face or their expression 面容；臉色；面部表情

▪ ***verb*** **~ sth | ~ (sb) doing sth** (*formal*) to support sth or agree to sth happening 支持；贊成；同意 **SYN** **consent to**：*The committee refused to countenance his proposals.* 委員會拒不同意他的方案。

coun·ter 🔑 /'kaʊntə(r)/ *noun, verb, adv.*

▪ ***noun*** **1** 🔑 a long flat surface over which goods are sold or business is done in a shop/store, bank, etc. （商店、銀行等的）櫃枱：*I asked the woman **behind the counter** if they had any postcards.* 我問櫃枱後面的女售貨員是否有明信片。 **2** (also **counter·top**) (both *NAmE*) (*BrE* **work·top**, **'work surface**) a flat surface in a kitchen for preparing food on （廚房的）操作枱，料理枱 ➲ VISUAL VOCAB page V25 **3** a small disc used for playing or scoring in some board games （某些棋盤遊戲的）籌碼 ➲ VISUAL VOCAB page V38 ➲ see also BARGAINING COUNTER at BARGAINING CHIP **4** (especially in compounds 尤用於構成複合詞) an electronic device for counting sth（電子）計數器，計算器：*The needle on the rev counter soared.* 轉速計的指針猛升。➲ VISUAL VOCAB page V52 ➲ see also GEIGER COUNTER ➲ compare BEAN COUNTER **5** [usually sing.] **~ (to sb/sth)** (*formal*) a response to sb/sth that opposes their ideas, position, etc.（對意見、態度等的）反對，反駁：*The employers' association was seen as a counter to union power.* 雇主協會被看作是工會權力的對頭。

IDM **over the 'counter** goods, especially medicines, for sale **over the counter** can be bought without a PRESCRIPTION (= written permission from a doctor to buy a medicine) or special licence （尤指購藥）不憑處方：*These tablets are available over the counter.* 這些藥片不用處方就可買到。 ➲ see also OVER-THE-COUNTER (1) **under the 'counter** goods that are bought or sold **under the counter** are sold secretly and sometimes illegally （商品銷售）秘密地，暗地裏，非法地

▪ ***verb*** **1** [T, I] **~ (sb/sth) (with sth)** to reply to sb by trying to prove that what they said is not true 反駁；駁斥：**~ sb/sth** *Such arguments are not easily countered.* 這種論點不易反駁。◇ **~ that …** *I tried to argue but he countered that the plans were not yet finished.* 我試圖爭辯，但他卻申辯説各項計劃尚未完成。◇ **~ (sb) + speech** *'But I was standing right here!' he countered.* "但我那時就站在這！"他反駁道。◇ **~ with sth** *Butler has countered with a lawsuit against the firm.* 巴特勒反訴了這家公司。 **2** [T] **~ sth** to do sth to reduce or prevent the bad effects of sth 抵制；抵消 **SYN** **counteract**：*Businesses would like to see new laws to counter late payments of debts.* 商界希望見到對付債務逾期不還的新法律出台。

▪ ***adv.*** **~ to sth** in the opposite direction to sth; in opposition to sth 逆向地；相反地；反對地：*The government's plans **run counter** to agreed European policy on this issue.* 政府的計劃違反了有關這個問題已協商好的歐洲政策。

counter- /'kaʊntə(r)/ *combining form* (in nouns, verbs, adjectives and adverbs 構成名詞、動詞、形容詞和副詞) **1** against; opposite 逆；反對；相反；對立：*counter-terrorism* 反恐怖主義◇ *counter-argument* 相對立的論點 **2** CORRESPONDING 相應；對應：*counterpart* 對方職位相當的人

coun·ter·act /,kaʊntər'ækt/ *verb* **~ sth** to do sth to reduce or prevent the bad or harmful effects of sth 抵制；抵消；抵抗 **SYN** **counter**：*These exercises aim to counteract the effects of stress and tension.* 這些運動旨在抵消壓力與緊張的影響。

'counter-attack *noun, verb*

▪ ***noun*** an attack made in response to the attack of an enemy or opponent in war, sport or an argument （戰爭、體育運動或爭論中的）反攻，反擊

▪ ***verb*** [I, T] **~ (sb)** to make an attack in response to the attack of an enemy or opponent in war, sport or an argument （在戰爭、體育運動或爭論中）反攻，反擊 **SYN** **retaliate**

coun·ter·bal·ance *verb, noun*

▪ ***verb*** /,kaʊntə'bæləns; *NAmE* ,kaʊntər'b-/ **~ sth** (*formal*) to have an equal but opposite effect to sth else 抗衡；抵消；對…起平衡作用 **SYN** **offset**：*Parents' natural desire to protect their children should be counterbalanced by the child's need for independence.* 父母保護孩子的本能願望應當與孩子獨立的需要相平衡。

▪ ***noun*** /'kaʊntəbæləns; *NAmE* 'kaʊntərb-/ (also **coun·ter·weight**) [usually sing.] **~ (to sth)** a thing that has an equal but opposite effect to sth else and can be used to limit the bad effects of sth 平衡抵消物；平衡重（或塊、錘）：*The accused's right to silence was a vital counterbalance to the powers of the police.* 被告人的沉默權對警方的權力是一種至關重要的抗衡。

coun·ter·blast /'kaʊntəblɑːst; *NAmE* 'kaʊntərblæst/ *noun* **~ (to sth)** a very strong spoken or written reply to sth that has been said or written （對某事的口頭或書面的）強硬駁斥

C

coun·ter·claim /ˈkaʊntəkleɪm; *NAmE* -tərk-/ *noun* a claim made in reply to another claim and different from it 反要求；反索賠；反訴

coun·ter·clock·wise /ˌkaʊntəˈklɒkwaɪz; *NAmE* -tərˈklɑːk-/ (*NAmE*) (*BrE* **anti·clock·wise**) *adv.*, *adj.* in the opposite direction to the movement of the hands of a clock 逆時針方向（的） OPP **clockwise**

coun·ter·cul·ture /ˈkaʊntəkʌltʃə(r); *NAmE* -tərk-/ *noun* [C, U] a way of life and set of ideas that are opposed to those accepted by most of society; a group of people who share such a way of life and such ideas 反主流文化；反正統文化；反主流文化的群體

ˌcounter-ˈespion·age *noun* [U] secret action taken by a country to prevent an enemy country from finding out its secrets 反間諜活動

coun·ter·fac·tual /ˌkaʊntəˈfæktʃuəl; *NAmE* -tər-/ *adj.* (*formal*) connected with what did not happen or what is not the case 反事實的；虛擬的：*counterfactual questions such as 'What if the President had not been assassinated?'* "假如總統不曾遇刺會怎麼樣？"之類的反事實問題 ◇ *an interesting exercise in counterfactual history* 違反史實的一個有趣活動 ► **coun·ter·fac·tual** *noun*: *'What if' questions involving counterfactuals are familiar in historical speculations.* "若非如此，將會怎樣？"這樣的反事實假設在歷史思考中很常見。

coun·ter·feit /ˈkaʊntəfɪt; *NAmE* -tərf-/ *adj.*, *verb*

■ ***adj.*** (*formal*) (of money and goods for sale 錢幣及商品) made to look exactly like sth in order to trick people into thinking that they are getting the real thing 偽造的；仿造的；假冒的 SYN **fake**: *counterfeit watches* 冒牌手錶 ◇ *Are you aware these notes are counterfeit?* 你覺察到這些鈔票是偽造的嗎？ OPP **genuine** ► **coun·ter·feit** *noun* ➲ compare FORGERY

■ ***verb*** **~ sth** (*formal*) to make an exact copy of sth in order to trick people into thinking that it is the real thing 偽造；仿造；製假 ➲ compare FORGE *v.* (2) ► **coun·ter·feit·ing** *noun* [U]

coun·ter·feit·er /ˈkaʊntəfɪtə(r); *NAmE* -tərf-/ *noun* a person who counterfeits money or goods 偽造者；仿造者；製假者 ➲ compare FORGER

coun·ter·foil /ˈkaʊntəfɔɪl; *NAmE* -tərfɔɪl/ *noun* (*BrE*) the part of a cheque, ticket, etc. that you keep when you give the other part to sb else（支票、票據等的）存根，票根 SYN **stub**

ˌcounter-inˈsurgency *noun* [U] action taken against a group of people who are trying to take control of a country by force 反叛亂；反暴動

ˌcounter-inˈtelli·gence *noun* [U] secret action taken by a country to prevent an enemy country from finding out its secrets, for example by giving them false information; the department of a government, etc. that is responsible for this 反情報秘密行動；反情報政府部門

ˌcounter-inˈtuitive *adj.* the opposite of what you would expect or what seems to be obvious 反直覺的；與正常預期相反的：*These results seem counter-intuitive.* 這些結果似乎與預料的相反。► **ˌcounter-inˈtuitive·ly** *adv.*

coun·ter·mand /ˌkaʊntəˈmɑːnd; *NAmE* ˈkaʊntərmænd/ *verb* **~ sth** (*formal*) to cancel an order that has been given, especially by giving a different order 取消，撤銷（尤指代以不同的新命令或訂單）

coun·ter·meas·ure /ˈkaʊntəmeʒə(r); *NAmE* -tərm-/ *noun* a course of action taken to protect against sth that is considered bad or dangerous 對策；對抗手段；反措施

coun·ter·of·fen·sive /ˈkaʊntərəfensɪv/ *noun* an attack made in order to defend against enemy attacks 反攻；反擊

coun·ter·pane /ˈkaʊntəpeɪn; *NAmE* -tərp-/ *noun* (*old-fashioned*, *BrE*) = BEDSPREAD

coun·ter·part /ˈkaʊntəpɑːt; *NAmE* -tərpɑːrt/ *noun* a person or thing that has the same position or function as sb/sth else in a different place or situation 職位（或作用）相當的人；對應的事物 SYN **opposite number**: *The Foreign Minister held talks with his Chinese counterpart.* 外交部長與中國外交部長舉行了會談。◇ *The women's shoe, like its male counterpart, is specifically designed for the serious tennis player.* 像同類的男款鞋一樣，這款女鞋是專為認真從事網球運動的人設計的。

coun·ter·point /ˈkaʊntəpɔɪnt; *NAmE* -tərp-/ *noun*, *verb*

■ ***noun*** **1** [U] (*music* 音) the combination of two or more tunes played together to form a single piece of music 對位法，對位（各聲部互相結合） SYN **polyphony**: *The two melodies are played in counterpoint.* 用對位法來演奏這兩首曲調。➲ see also CONTRAPUNTAL **2** [C] **~ (to sth)** (*music* 音) a tune played in combination with another one 複調 **3** [U, C] (*formal*) a pleasing or interesting contrast 愜意（或有趣）的對比：*This work is in austere counterpoint to that of Gaudi.* 這件作品的質樸風格與高迪的形成了有趣的對比。

■ ***verb*** **~ sth (with/against sth)** (*formal*) to contrast sth with sth else; to form a contrast with sth 用…作對比；與…形成對比

coun·ter·pro·duct·ive /ˌkaʊntəprəˈdʌktɪv; *NAmE* -tərp-/ *adj.* [not usually before noun] having the opposite effect to the one which was intended 產生相反效果；事與願違；適得其反 ➲ compare PRODUCTIVE (2)

ˌcounter-ˌrevoˈlu·tion *noun* [C, U] opposition to or violent action against a government that came to power as a result of a revolution, in order to destroy and replace it 反革命；反革命活動

ˌcounter-ˌrevoˈlu·tion·ary *noun* a person involved in a counter-revolution 反革命分子 ► **ˌcounter-ˌrevoˈlu·tion·ary** *adj.*

coun·ter·sign /ˈkaʊntəsaɪn; *NAmE* -tərs-/ *verb* **~ sth** (*technical* 術語) to sign a document that has already been signed by another person, especially in order to show that it is valid 連署，副署，會簽（文件）

coun·ter·tenor /ˌkaʊntəˈtenə(r); *NAmE* ˌkaʊntər-/ *noun* a man who is trained to sing with a very high voice; a male ALTO 高男高音；假聲男高音 ➲ compare ALTO

counter·terror·ism /ˌkaʊntəˈterərɪzəm; *NAmE* ˌkaʊntər-/ *noun* [U] action taken to prevent the activities of political groups who use violence to try to achieve their aims 反恐怖主義 ► **counter·terror·ist** /ˌkaʊntəˈterərɪst; *NAmE* ˌkaʊntər-/ *adj.*

coun·ter·top /ˈkaʊntətɒp; *NAmE* ˈkaʊntərtɑːp/ *noun* (*NAmE*) = COUNTER *n.* (2)

coun·ter·vail·ing /ˈkaʊntəveɪlɪŋ; *NAmE* -tərv-/ *adj.* [only before noun] (*formal*) having an equal but opposite effect 抗衡的；抵消的

coun·ter·weight /ˈkaʊntəweɪt; *NAmE* -tərw-/ *noun* [usually sing.] = COUNTERBALANCE

count·ess /ˈkaʊntəs; -es/ *noun* **1** a woman who has the rank of a COUNT or an EARL 女伯爵 **2** the wife of a COUNT or an EARL 伯爵夫人：*the Earl and Countess of Rosebery* 羅斯伯里伯爵及夫人

count·less /ˈkaʊntləs/ *adj.* [usually before noun] very many; too many to be counted or mentioned 無數的；數不勝數的；數不盡的：*I've warned her countless times.* 我警告過她無數次了。◇ *The new treatment could save Emma's life and the lives of countless others.* 新的療法可拯救埃瑪的生命以及無數其他人的生命。➲ compare UNCOUNTABLE

ˈcount noun *noun* (*grammar* 語法) a countable noun 具數名詞；可數名詞 OPP **uncount noun**

coun·tri·fied /ˈkʌntrifaɪd/ *adj.* (often *disapproving*) like the countryside or the people who live there 像鄉下的；像鄉下人的；鄉土氣的；土裏土氣的

coun·try 🔑 /ˈkʌntri/ *noun* (*pl.* -ies)

1 🔑 [C] an area of land that has or used to have its own government and laws 國；國家：*European countries* 歐洲國家 ◇ *leading industrial countries* 最重要的工業國家 ◇ *She didn't know what life in a **foreign country** would be like.* 她不知道外國的生活會是什麼樣。◇ *It's good to meet people from **different parts of the country**.* 結識來自這個國家不同地區的人是有益的。**2** 🔑 [U] (often following an adjective 常置於形容詞後) an area of land, especially with particular physical features, suitable for a particular purpose or connected with a particular person or people（尤指具有某種自然特徵、適於某目的或與某種人有關的）地區，區域：*open/wooded, etc.* **country** 空曠、樹木繁茂等的地區 ◇ *superb* **walking country** 極佳的徒步旅行區域 ◇ *Explore Thomas Hardy country.* 踏訪托馬斯・哈代小說描寫的地區。➲ see also BACKCOUNTRY **3** **the country** [sing.] the people of a country; the nation as a whole 全國人民；國民；全民：*They have the support of most of the country.* 他們有大多數國民的支持。◇ *The rich benefited from the reforms, not the* **country as a whole**. 富人而不是全體國民得益於這些改革。➲ see also MOTHER COUNTRY, THE OLD COUNTRY, UP-COUNTRY **4** **the country** [sing.] any area outside towns and cities, with fields, woods, farms, etc. 鄉下；鄉村：*to live* **in the country** 住在鄉下 ◇ *We spent a pleasant day in the country.* 我們在鄉下度過了愉快的一天。◇ *a country lane* 鄉間小路 ➲ COLLOCATIONS at TOWN **5** [U] = COUNTRY AND WESTERN：*pop, folk and country* 流行、民間和鄉村音樂

IDM **across 'country** directly across fields, etc.; not by a main road（直接）穿越田野；不走大路：*riding across country* 騎馬穿過田野 ➲ see also CROSS-COUNTRY **go to the 'country** (*BrE*) (of a government 政府) to hold an election to choose a new parliament 舉行大選（以組成新的議會）➲ more at FREE *adj.*

Which Word? 詞語辨析

country / state

- **Country** is the most usual, neutral word for a geographical area that has or used to have its own government. * country 是指國家的最普通的中性詞。
- **State** emphasizes the political organization of an area under an independent government. Especially in *BrE*, it can also mean the government. * state 側重指獨立政府統治下的政權機構，尤其在英式英語中，該詞亦可指政府：*the member states of the EU* 歐盟成員國 ◇ *The state provides free education.* 政府提供免費教育。In *NAmE* **the state** usually refers to one of the 50 states of the US, not to the government of the country as a whole. 在美式英語中，the state 通常指美國 50 個州中的一個州，而非指作為一個整體的國家政府。

ˌcountry and 'western (*abbr.* **C & W**) (also **'country music, country**) *noun* [U] a type of music in the style of the traditional music of the southern and western US（美國的）鄉村與西部音樂：*a country and western singer* 鄉村與西部音樂歌手

ˌcountry 'bumpkin (also **bump·kin**) *noun* (*disapproving*) a person from the countryside who seems stupid 鄉巴佬；土包子

'country club *noun* a club in the country, or on the edge of a town, where people can play sports and go to social events（體育運動和社交的）鄉村俱樂部

ˌcountry 'cousin *noun* a person from the country who does not know much about life in the city, and who dresses or behaves in a way that shows this 鄉下人

ˌcountry 'dance *noun* (*BrE*) a type of traditional dance, especially one in which couples dance in long lines or circles 鄉村舞，土風舞（尤為長排對舞或圓圈舞）▸ **ˌcountry 'dancing** *noun* [U]

ˌcountry 'house *noun* (*BrE*) a large house in the country, especially one that belongs or used to belong to a rich important family（尤指有地位富人家庭的）鄉間宅第，別墅

coun·try·made /ˈkʌntrimeɪd/ *adj.* (*IndE*) not made by a professional person 非專業製作的；土造的：*a country-made pistol* 土製手槍

coun·try·man /ˈkʌntrimən/ *noun* (*pl.* **-men** /-mən/) **1** a person born in or living in the same country as sb else 同國人；同胞；同鄉 SYN **compatriot**：*The champion looks set to play his* **fellow countryman** *in the final.* 看來這位冠軍在決賽中會遇上他的同胞。**2** a man living or born in the country, not in the town 鄉下人；農村人

ˌcountry 'mile *noun* (becoming *old-fashioned, especially BrE*) a long distance 遠程；長距離；長途：*He won the race by a country mile.* 他遙遙領先贏了比賽。

'country music *noun* [U] = COUNTRY AND WESTERN

ˌcountry 'seat *noun* (*BrE*) = SEAT (7)

coun·try·side 🔑 /ˈkʌntrisaɪd/ *noun* [U] land outside towns and cities, with fields, woods, etc. 鄉村；農村：*The surrounding countryside is windswept and rocky.* 這周圍的鄉村風多石頭多。◇ *magnificent views over open countryside* 開闊鄉村的壯麗景色 ◇ *Everyone should enjoy the right of access to the countryside.* 人人都應享有進入鄉村的權利。➲ SYNONYMS at COUNTRY ➲ COLLOCATIONS at TOWN ➲ VISUAL VOCAB pages V2, V3

coun·try·wide /ˌkʌntriˈwaɪd/ *adj.* over the whole of a country 遍及全國的；全國性的 SYN **nationwide**：*a countrywide mail-order service* 全國性的郵購服務 ▸ **coun·try·wide** *adv.*：*The film will be released in London in March and countrywide in May.* 這部電影將於三月在倫敦發行，五月在全國發行。

Synonyms 同義詞辨析

country

landscape • countryside • terrain • land • scenery

These are all words for areas away from towns and cities, with fields, woods and farms. 以上各詞均指遠離城鎮，有田野、樹林和農場的地區。

country (often **the country**) an area that is away from towns and cities, especially one with particular natural features（常作 the country）尤指具有自然特徵的鄉下、鄉村：*She lives in the country.* 她住在鄉下。◇ *an area of wooded country* 樹木覆蓋的鄉村地區

landscape everything that you can see when you look across a large area of land, especially in the country 尤指鄉村的風景或景色：*This pattern of woods and fields is typical of the English landscape.* 這種林地與田野的格局是典型的英格蘭鄉村景色。

countryside land outside towns and cities, with fields, woods and farms 指鄉村、農村 NOTE **Countryside** is usually used when you are talking about the beauty or peacefulness of a country area. * countryside 通常用於強調鄉村地區的美麗或寧靜：*a little village in the French countryside* 法國鄉間的小村莊

terrain (*formal*) land 指地帶、土地 NOTE **Terrain** is used when you are describing the natural features of an area, for example if it is rough, flat, etc. * terrain 用於描述某地區的地形或地勢：*The truck bumped its way over the rough terrain.* 卡車在崎嶇不平的地面上顛簸行進。

land (usually **the land**) the countryside; the way people live in the country as opposed to in towns and cities（通常作 the land）指與城鎮相對的農村、農村生活方式：*Many younger people are leaving the land to find work in the cities.* 許多較年輕的人陸續離開農村到城市去找工作。

scenery the natural features of an area, such as mountains, valleys, rivers and forests, especially when these are attractive to look at 指自然風景、景色、風光：*We stopped on the mountain pass to admire the scenery.* 我們在山口停下來欣賞風景。

PATTERNS

- **mountainous/mountain/wild/rugged** country/landscape/countryside/terrain/scenery
- **beautiful/glorious/dramatic** country/landscape/countryside/scenery
- **open** country/landscape/countryside/terrain/land
- **rolling** country/landscape/countryside
- to **protect** the landscape/countryside/land

C

coun·try·woman /ˈkʌntriwʊmən/ *noun* (*pl.* **-women** /-wɪmɪn/) **1** a woman living or born in the country, not the town 農村女人；鄉下女人 **2** a woman born or living in the same country as sb else 女同胞

county 🔑 /ˈkaʊnti/ *noun, adj.*
■ ***noun*** 🔑 (*pl.* **-ies**) (*abbr.* **Co.**) an area of Britain, Ireland or the US that has its own government（英國、愛爾蘭的）郡；（美國的）縣：*the southern counties* 南部各郡 ◇ *county boundaries* 郡分界線 ◇ *Orange County* 奧蘭治縣 ➲ see also THE HOME COUNTIES
■ ***adj.*** (*BrE*, usually *disapproving*) typical of English upper-class people 典型英國上流社會人物的；世家子弟的

ˌcounty ˈclerk *noun* (in the US) an elected county official who is responsible for elections and who keeps records of who owns buildings in the county, etc.（美國負責選舉及房產登記等的）縣政官員

ˌcounty ˈcouncil *noun* [C+sing./pl. v.] (in Britain) a group of people elected to the local government of a county（英國的）郡政務委員會，郡議會：*a member of Lancashire County Council* 蘭開夏郡政務委員會委員 ▸ **ˌcounty ˈcouncillor** *noun*

ˌcounty ˈcourt *noun* a local court. In Britain county courts only deal with private disagreements but in the US they also deal with criminal cases. 郡法院（在英國受理私人糾紛）；縣法院（在美國受理私人糾紛和刑事案件）➲ compare CROWN COURT

ˌcounty ˈtown (*BrE*) (*NAmE* **ˌcounty ˈseat**) *noun* the main town of a county, where its government is 郡（或縣）首府；郡（或縣）城

coun·ty·wide /ˌkaʊntiˈwaɪd/ *adj.* over the whole of a county 遍及全郡（或縣）的；全郡（或縣）的 ▸ **coun·ty·wide** *adv.*

coup /kuː/ *noun* (*pl.* **coups** /kuːz/) **1** (also **coup d'état**) a sudden change of government that is illegal and often violent 政變：*He seized power in a military coup in 2008.* 他在 2008 年的軍事政變中奪取了政權。◇ *to* ***stage/mount a coup*** 發動政變 ◇ *an attempted coup* 政變未遂 ◇ ***a failed/an abortive coup*** 失敗的／流產的政變 ◇ *She lost her position in a boardroom coup* (= a sudden change of power among senior managers in a company). 她在董事會的人事突變中失去了職位。**2** the fact of achieving sth that was difficult to do 努力辦到難辦的事：*Getting this contract has been quite a coup for us.* 把這份合同爭取到手讓我們費了很大力氣。

coup de grâce /ˌkuː də ˈɡrɑːs/ *noun* [sing.] (from *French*, *formal*) **1** an action or event that finally ends sth that has been getting weaker or worse 最後的一擊：*My disastrous exam results dealt the coup de grâce to my university career.* 我考試考得一塌糊塗，這就斷送了我的大學生涯。**2** a hit or shot that finally kills a person or an animal, especially to put an end to their suffering（尤指解除痛苦的）致命的一擊 **SYN** **death blow**

coup d'état /ˌkuː deɪˈtɑː/ *noun* (*pl.* **coups d'état** /ˌkuː deɪˈtɑː/) = COUP (1)

coup de théâtre /ˌkuː də teɪˈɑːtrə/ *noun* (*pl.* **coups de théâtre** /ˌkuː də teɪˈɑːtrə/) (from *French*) **1** something very dramatic and surprising that happens, especially in a play（尤指戲劇中）劇情的突變 **2** a play, show, etc. which is very successful 非常成功的戲劇（或演出等）

coupé /ˈkuːpeɪ; *NAmE* kuːˈpeɪ/ (*NAmE* also **coupe** /kuːp/) *noun* a car with two doors and usually a sloping back（通常斜背的）雙門小汽車

couple 🔑 **AW** /ˈkʌpl/ *noun, verb*
■ ***noun*** **HELP** In *BrE* a plural verb is usually used in all 3 senses. 在英式英語中 3 義均常用複數動詞。**1** 🔑 [sing.+sing./pl. v.] **~ (of sth)** two people or things 兩人；兩件事物：*I saw a couple of men get out.* 我看見有兩個男人出去了。**2** 🔑 [sing.+sing./pl. v.] **~ (of sth)** a small number of people or things 幾個人；幾件事物 **SYN** **a few**：*a couple of minutes* 幾分鐘 ◇ *We went there a couple of years ago.* 我們幾年前去過那裏。◇ *I've seen her a couple of times before.* 我以前見過她幾次。◇ *I'll be with you in a minute. There are a couple of things I have to do first.* 我一會兒就到你那裏去。我有幾件事情得先處理一下。◇ *There are a couple more files to read first.* 還有幾份檔案要先看一看。◇ *We can do it in the* ***next couple of*** *weeks.* 我們可在今後幾個星期裏完成這件事。◇ *The* ***last couple of*** *years have been difficult.* 最近的幾年一直是困難重重。**3** 🔑 [C+sing./pl. v.] two people who are seen together, especially if they are married or in a romantic or sexual relationship（人）一對；（尤指）夫妻，情侶：*married couples* 幾對夫婦 ◇ *a young/an elderly couple* 年輕／老年夫婦 ◇ *Several couples were on the dance floor.* 有幾對情侶在跳舞。◇ *The couple was/were married in 2006.* 這對夫婦於 2006 年結婚。➲ COLLOCATIONS at MARRIAGE **IDM** see SHAKE *n.* ▸ **a couple** 🔑 *pron.*：*Do you need any more glasses? I've got a couple I can lend you.* 你還需要玻璃杯嗎？我有幾個可以借給你。**couple** *det.*：(*NAmE*) *It's only a couple blocks away.* 那地方離這裏只有幾個街區。
■ ***verb*** **1** [T, usually passive] to join together two parts of sth, for example two vehicles or pieces of equipment（把車輛或設備等）連接，結合：**~ A and B together** *The two train cars had been coupled together.* 兩節火車車廂已經掛上鈎了。◇ **~ A (to B)** *CDTV uses a CD-ROM system that is coupled to a powerful computer.* 動態視頻系統使用的是與大功率計算機相連的只讀光盤系統。**2** [I] (*formal*) (of two people or animals 兩人或兩動物) to have sex 性交；交配
PHR V **ˈcouple sb/sth with sb/sth** [usually passive] to link one thing, situation, etc. to another 把…與…連接起來 **SYN** **combine with**：*Overproduction, coupled with falling sales, has led to huge losses for the company.* 生產過剩加上銷售下降使這家公司遭受巨大損失。

coup·let /ˈkʌplət/ *noun* two lines of poetry of equal length one after the other 對句（相連的兩行長度相等的詩句）；對聯：*a poem written in rhyming couplets* 用押韻對句寫成的詩 ➲ see also HEROIC COUPLET

coup·ling **AW** /ˈkʌplɪŋ/ *noun* **1** [usually sing.] an action of joining or combining two things 連接；結合；聯結：*a coupling of Mozart's Prague Symphony and Schubert's Unfinished Symphony* (= for example, on the same CD) 編排在一起的莫扎特的《布拉格交響曲》與舒伯特的《未完成交響曲》（如在同一張光盤上）**2** (*formal*) an act of having sex 性交：*illicit couplings* 不正當的性交 **3** (*technical* 術語) a thing that joins together two parts of sth, two vehicles or two pieces of equipment 耦接頭；聯軸器；（連接車輛的）車鈎

cou·pon /ˈkuːpɒn; *NAmE* -pɑːn; ˈkjuː-/ *noun* **1** a small piece of printed paper that you can exchange for sth or that gives you the right to buy sth at a cheaper price than normal 配給券；（購物）票證，優惠券：*money-off coupons* 優惠券 ◇ *clothing coupons* 服裝票 ◇ *an international reply coupon* 國際通用預付回信郵資券 **2** a printed form, often cut out from a newspaper, that is used to enter a competition, order goods, etc.（常為剪自報章的）參賽表，訂貨單：*Fill in and return the attached coupon.* 填寫所附上的參賽表並寄回。

cour·age 🔑 /ˈkʌrɪdʒ; *NAmE* ˈkɜːr-/ *noun* [U] the ability to do sth dangerous, or to face pain or opposition, without showing fear 勇氣；勇敢；無畏；膽量 **SYN** **bravery**：*He showed great courage and determination.* 他表現得十分勇敢和果斷。◇ *I haven't yet* ***plucked up the courage*** *to ask her.* 我還鼓不起勇氣去問她。◇ ***moral/physical courage*** 堅持正義的勇氣；勇敢無畏的膽量 ◇ *courage in the face of danger* 面對危險時的膽量 ➲ see also DUTCH COURAGE
IDM **have/lack the courage of your conˈvictions** to be/not be brave enough to do what you feel to be right 有／沒有勇氣做自己認為正確的事 **take courage (from sth)** to begin to feel happier and more confident because of sth （因某事而）鼓起勇氣 **take your ˌcourage in both ˈhands** to make yourself do sth that you are afraid of 鼓起勇氣（做自己害怕做的事）；敢作敢為：*Taking her courage in both hands, she opened the door and walked in.* 她壯着膽打開門，走了進去。➲ more at SCREW *v.*

cour·age·ous /kəˈreɪdʒəs/ *adj.* showing courage 勇敢的；無畏的 **SYN** **brave**：*a very courageous decision* 十分勇敢的決定 ◇ *I hope people will be courageous enough to speak out against this injustice.* 我希望人們能敢於大

膽說出來，反對這種不公。OPP cowardly ▸ **cour·age·ous·ly** *adv.*

cour·gette /kʊə'ʒet; kɔː'ʒet; *NAmE* kʊr'ʒet/ (*BrE*) (*NAmE* **zuc·chini**) *noun* a long vegetable with dark green skin and white flesh（深綠皮）密生西葫蘆，小胡瓜 ➲ VISUAL VOCAB page V31

cour·ier /'kʊriə(r)/ *noun* **1** a person or company whose job is to take packages or important papers somewhere（遞送包裹或重要文件的）信使，通訊員，專遞公司：*We sent the documents by courier.* 我們派了信使送交這些文件。 **2** (*BrE*) a person who is employed by a travel company to give advice and help to a group of tourists on holiday（旅遊公司的）導遊 ▸ **cour·ier** *verb*： **~ sth** *Courier that letter—it needs to get there today* (= send it by courier). 那封信必須今天到達，用專遞寄吧。

British/American 英式 / 美式英語

course / program

- In *BrE* **course** is used for a series of lessons or lectures on a particular subject. 在英式英語中，course 指某學科的系列課程或講座：*a physics course* 物理課程 ◇ *a course of ten lectures* 有十次講座的課程 In *NAmE* you would say 美式英語說：*a physics course/program* 物理課程 ◇ *a program of ten lectures* 有十次講座的課程
- In *NAmE* a **course** is usually an individual unit that forms part of a longer period of study 在美式英語中，course 通常指較長學習階段中的一個獨立單元：*I have to take a physics course/class.* 我得參加一個物理課程。 This is called a **module** in Britain, especially in a college or university. 在英國，尤其是高等院校，這種獨立單元叫 module。
- In *BrE* **course** can also mean a period of study at a college or university. 英式英語的 course 亦可指高等教育的一個階段：*a two-year college course* 兩年的大學課程 In *NAmE* you would say 美式英語說：*a two-year college program* 兩年的大學課程

course 0-w /kɔːs; *NAmE* kɔːrs/ *noun, verb*

■ *noun*

▸ EDUCATION 教育 **1** 0-w [C] **~ (in/on sth)** a series of lessons or lectures on a particular subject（有關某學科的系列）課程，講座：*a* ***French/chemistry, etc. course*** 法語、化學等課程 ◇ *to* ***take/do a course*** *in art and design* 攻讀美術與設計課程 ◇ *to* ***go on a*** *management training* ***course*** 去參加管理培訓講座 ◇ *The college* ***runs*** *specialist language* ***courses.*** 這所學院開設有專門語言課程。 ➲ COLLOCATIONS at EDUCATION ➲ see also CORRESPONDENCE COURSE, CRASH *adj.*, FOUNDATION COURSE, INDUCTION COURSE, REFRESHER COURSE, SANDWICH COURSE **2** 0-w [C] (*especially BrE*) a period of study at a college or university that leads to an exam or a qualification（學院或大學中要進行考試或取得資格的）課程：*a degree course* 學位課程 ◇ *a two-year postgraduate course leading to a master's degree* 兩年制碩士研究生課程 ➲ compare PROGRAMME *n.* (5)

▸ DIRECTION 方向 **3** [U, C, usually sing.] a direction or route followed by a ship or an aircraft（船或飛機的）航向，航線：*The plane was* ***on/off course*** (= going/not going in the right direction). 飛機航向正確 / 偏離。◇ *He radioed the pilot to* ***change course.*** 他用無線電通知飛行員改變航向。◇ *They* ***set a course*** *for the islands.* 他們確定了去群島的航線。 **4** [C, usually sing.] the general direction in which sb's ideas or actions are moving 方針；行動方向：*The president appears likely to* ***change course*** *on some key issues.* 總統看起來可能要在某些重要問題上改變方針。◇ *Politicians are often obliged to steer a course between incompatible interests.* 政治家常常被迫在互不相容的利益集團之間開闢航道。

▸ ACTION 行動 **5** (also ,**course of 'action**) [C] a way of acting in or dealing with a particular situation 行動方式；處理方法：*There are various courses open to us.* 我們有多種處理方法可採取。◇ *What course of action would you recommend?* 你想推薦什麼辦法呢？◇ *The wisest course would be to say nothing.* 最明智的對策是緘口不語。

▸ DEVELOPMENT 發展 **6** [sing.] **~ of sth** the way sth develops or should develop 進展；進程：*an event that changed the* ***course of history*** 改變了歷史進程的事件◇ *The unexpected* ***course of events*** *aroused considerable alarm.* 意外的事態發展引起了相當大的恐慌。

▸ PART OF MEAL 菜肴 **7** [C] any of the separate parts of a meal 一道菜：*a four-course dinner* 有四道菜的正餐◇ *The main course was roast duck.* 主菜是烤鴨。 ➲ COLLOCATIONS at RESTAURANT

▸ FOR GOLF 高爾夫球 **8** [C] = GOLF COURSE：*He set a new course record.* 他創下了高爾夫球的新紀錄。

▸ FOR RACES 比賽 **9** 0-w [C] an area of land or water where races are held 比賽場地；跑道；賽船水道；泳道：*She was overtaken on the last stretch of the course.* 她在最後的直線跑道上被超過。 ➲ see also ASSAULT COURSE, RACECOURSE

▸ OF RIVER 江河 **10** [C, usually sing.] the direction a river moves in 江河流向：*The path follows the course of the river.* 小路沿河道延伸。

▸ MEDICAL TREATMENT 醫療 **11** [C] **~ (of sth)** a series of medical treatments, pills, etc.（醫療、服藥等的）療程：*to prescribe a course of antibiotics* 開一個抗生素療程的處方

▸ IN WALL 牆壁 **12** [C] a continuous layer of bricks, stone, etc. in a wall（磚、石等牆的）層：*A new damp-proof course could cost £1 000 or more.* 新的防潮層可花掉 1 000 英鎊以上。

IDM **in course of sth** (*formal*) going through a particular process 在…的過程中：*The new textbook is in course of preparation.* 新的教科書正在準備之中。 **in/over the course of ...** (used with expressions for periods of time 與表示時間段的詞組連用) during 在…期間；在…的時候：*He's seen many changes in the course of his long life.* 他在漫長的一生中目睹了許許多多的變化。◇ *The company faces major challenges over the course of the next few years.* 這家公司今後幾年將面臨重大的挑戰。 **in the course of 'time** when enough time has passed 總有一天；最後；終於 SYN **eventually**：*It is possible that in the course of time a cure for cancer will be found.* 治療癌症的方法終有一天能找到。 **in the ordinary, normal, etc. course of events, things, etc.** as things usually happen 按通常情況；在一般情況下；通常 SYN **normally**：*In the normal course of things we would not treat her disappearance as suspicious.* 在一般情況下，她不露面，我們也不會覺得有什麼可疑之處。 **of course 1** 0-w (also **course**) (*informal*) used to emphasize that what you are saying is true or correct（強調所說的話屬實或正確）當然：*'Don't you like my mother?' 'Of course I do!'* "難道你不喜歡我母親？" "當然喜歡！" ◇ *'Will you be there?' 'Course I will.'* "你會去那裏嗎？" "當然會。" **2** 0-w (also **course**) (*informal*) used as a polite way of giving sb permission to do sth（允許某人做某事的客氣說法）當然：*'Can I come, too?' 'Course you can.'* "我也可以來嗎？" "當然可以。" ◇ *'Can I have one of those pens?' 'Of course—help yourself.'* "我能在那些筆中拿一支嗎？" "當然，自己拿吧。" **3** 0-w (*informal*) used as a polite way of agreeing with what sb has just said（禮貌地同意某人剛說的話）當然：*'I did all I could to help.' 'Of course,' he murmured gently.* "我盡全力幫忙了。" "當然。" 他輕聲低語道。 **4** 0-w used to show that what you are saying is not surprising or is generally known or accepted（表示所說的事不令人驚訝或具有普遍性）當然，自然：*Ben, of course, was the last to arrive.* 本當然是最後一個到的。◇ *Of course, there are other ways of doing this.* 當然還有別的方法做這件事。 ➲ LANGUAGE BANK at NEVERTHELESS **of 'course not** 0-w (also **'course not**) used to emphasize the fact that you are saying 'no'（強調不同意）當然不：*'Are you going?' 'Of course not.'* "你要去嗎？" "當然不去。" ◇ *'Do you mind?' 'No, of course not.'* "你介意嗎？" "不，當然不介意。" **on 'course for sth/to do sth** likely to achieve or do sth because you have already started to do it（因為已開始做而）很可能做成（或做）：*The American economy is on course for higher inflation than Britain by the end of the year.* 美國經濟很可能在今年年底前出現比英國高的通貨膨脹。 **run/take its 'course** to develop in the usual way and come to the usual end 任其發展；

聽其自然： *When her tears had run their course, she felt calmer and more in control.* 等她哭夠了，她就比較鎮靜，比較克制了。◇ *With minor ailments the best thing is often to let nature take its course.* 對於小病，往往最好是聽其自然。➲ more at COLLISION, DUE *adj.*, HORSE *n.*, MATTER *n.*, MIDDLE *adj.*, PAR, PERVERT *v.*, STAY *v.*

■ **verb** [I] + **adv./prep.** (*literary*) (of liquid 液體) to move or flow quickly 快速地流動；奔流

More About 補充說明

of course

- **Of course** is often used to show that what you are saying is not surprising or is generally known or accepted. For this reason, and because it can be difficult to get the right intonation, you may not sound polite if you use **of course** or **of course not** when you answer a request for information or permission. It can be safer to use a different word or phrase. * of course 常用以表示所說的事不足為奇或理所當然。與此同時，由於可能不容易掌握恰當的語調，用 of course 或 of course not 回答詢問或請求時可能顯得不禮貌。因此，用其他詞語或短語可能更穩妥。
- *'Is this the right room for the English class?' 'Yes, it is.'* "這是上英語課的教室嗎？" "是的。" ◇ ~~*'Of course.'*~~ or ~~*'Of course it is.'*~~
- *'Can I borrow your dictionary?' 'Certainly.'* (*formal*) "我可以借用一下你的詞典嗎？" "當然可以。"（正式）◇ *'Sure.'* (*informal*) "當然可以。"（非正式）
- *'Do you mind if I borrow your dictionary?' 'Not at all.'* "我借用一下你的詞典行嗎？" "沒問題。" ◇ *'Go ahead.'* (*informal*) "拿吧。"（非正式）
- If you say **of course/of course not** it may sound as though you think the answer to the question is obvious and that the person should not ask. In the same way, **of course** should not be used as a reply to a statement of fact or when someone expresses an opinion. 如果用 of course/of course not 回答，聽起來就好像是說答案太明顯，用不着問。同樣，of course 不宜用於回應別人對事實的陳述或意見的表達： *'It's a lovely day.' 'It certainly is.'/'Yes it is.'* "天氣真好。" "確實真好。"/ "是的，真好。" ◇ ~~*'Of course it is.'*~~ ◇ *'I think you'll enjoy that play.' 'I'm sure I will.'/'Yes, it sounds really good.'* "我想你會喜歡那齣戲的。" "我肯定會的。"/ "是的，這齣戲看來真棒。" ◇ ~~*'Of course.'*~~

course·book /ˈkɔːsbʊk; *NAmE* ˈkɔːrs-/ *noun* (*BrE*) a book for studying from, used regularly in class 教科書；課本

ˌcourse of ˈaction *noun* (*pl.* **ˌcourses of ˈaction**) = COURSE (5)

course·ware /ˈkɔːsweə(r); *NAmE* ˈkɔːrswer/ *noun* [U] (*computing* 計) computer programs that are designed to be used to teach a subject 課件；教學軟件；教學軟體

course·work /ˈkɔːswɜːk; *NAmE* ˈkɔːrswɜːrk/ *noun* [U] work that students do during a course of study, not in exams, that is included in their final mark/grade（計入最終成績的）課程作業： *Coursework accounts for 40% of the final marks.* 課程作業佔最後總成績的 40%。

cours·ing /ˈkɔːsɪŋ; *NAmE* ˈkɔːr-/ *noun* [U] the sport of hunting animals with dogs, using sight rather than smell 追蹤狩獵（用獵狗憑視力而不是嗅覺追捕獵物）： *hare coursing* 追蹤野兔

court 0→ /kɔːt; *NAmE* kɔːrt/ *noun, verb*

■ **noun**

▸ **LAW** 法律 **1** 0→ [C, U] the place where legal trials take place and where crimes, etc. are judged 法院；法庭；審判庭： *the* ***civil/criminal courts*** 民事 / 刑事法庭 ◇ *Her lawyer made a statement outside the court.* 她的律師在法庭外面發表了一份聲明。◇ *She will appear* ***in court*** *tomorrow.* 她明天出庭。◇ *They* ***took*** *their landlord* ***to court*** *for breaking the contract.* 因為房東毀約，他們把他告上了法庭。◇ *The case took five years to* ***come to court*** (= to be heard by the court). 那案件歷時五年才被法庭受理。◇ *There wasn't enough evidence to* ***bring the case to court*** (= start a trial). 沒有足夠的證據可把此案提交法庭。◇ *He won the* ***court case*** *and was awarded damages.* 他勝訴得到了賠償金。◇ *She can't pay her tax and is facing* ***court action.*** 她繳不起稅，將面臨法庭訴訟。◇ *The case was* ***settled out of court*** (= a decision was reached without a trial). 這案件已庭外和解。➲ **COLLOCATIONS** at JUSTICE ➲ note at SCHOOL ➲ see also COURTHOUSE (1), COURTROOM **2** 0→ **the court** [sing.] the people in a court, especially those who make the decisions, such as the judge and JURY 全體出庭人員；（尤指）全體審判人員： *Please tell the court what happened.* 請向法庭陳述事情的經過。➲ see also CONTEMPT OF COURT, COUNTY COURT, CROWN COURT, HIGH COURT, JUVENILE COURT, SUPREME COURT

▸ **FOR SPORT** 體育運動 **3** [C] a place where games such as TENNIS are played（網球等的）球場： *a* ***tennis/squash/badminton court*** 網球場；壁球場；羽毛球場 ◇ *He won after only 52 minutes* ***on court.*** 他上場僅 52 分鐘就贏得了勝利。➲ **VISUAL VOCAB** pages V44, V45 ➲ see also CLAY COURT, GRASS COURT

▸ **KINGS/QUEENS** 國王；女王 **4** [C, U] the official place where kings and queens live 王宮；宮殿；宮廷： *the court of Queen Victoria* 維多利亞女王的宮廷 **5 the court** [sing.] the king or queen, their family, and the people who work for them and/or give advice to them 王室人員；王宮人員

▸ **BUILDINGS** 建築物 **6** [C] = COURTYARD **7** (*abbr.* **Ct**) [C] used in the names of blocks of flats or apartment buildings, or of some short streets; (in Britain) used in the name of some large houses（用於套房、公寓或某些短街區的名稱）公寓大樓，短街；（英國用於某些大型宅第的名稱）宅第，邸宅 **8** [C] a large open section of a building, often with a glass roof 建築物的開闊部份（常有玻璃房頂）；大廳；館： *the food court at the shopping mall* 大型購物中心的食品區

IDM **hold ˈcourt (with sb)** to entertain people by telling them interesting or funny things（講趣聞或笑話）使人快樂，逗人樂 **rule/throw sth out of ˈcourt** to say that sth is completely wrong or not worth considering, especially in a trial（尤指在法庭上）指明完全錯誤，不予考慮，不予受理： *The charges were thrown out of court.* 這些指控未予受理。◇ *Well that's my theory ruled out of court.* 唉，那就是我遭到摒棄的意見。➲ more at BALL *n.*, LAUGH *v.*, PAY *v.*

■ **verb**

▸ **TRY TO PLEASE** 試圖取悅 **1** [T] **~ sb** to try to please sb in order to get sth you want, especially the support of a person, an organization, etc.（為有所求，尤指尋求支持而）試圖取悅，討好，爭取 **SYN** **cultivate**： *Both candidates have spent the last month courting the media.* 兩位候選人在過去的一個月裏都在取悅媒體。

▸ **TRY TO GET** 試圖得到 **2** [T] **~ sth** (*formal*) to try to obtain sth 試圖獲得；博得： *He has never courted popularity.* 他從不追求名望。

▸ **INVITE STH BAD** 招致災禍 **3** [T] **~ sth** (*formal*) to do sth that might result in sth unpleasant happening 招致，釀成，導致（不愉快的事）： *to* ***court danger/death/disaster*** 招致危險 / 死亡 / 災難 ◇ *As a politician he has often courted controversy.* 作為政治人物，他常常招致爭議。

▸ **HAVE RELATIONSHIP** 建立感情 **4** [T] **~ sb** (*old-fashioned*) if a man **courts** a woman, he spends time with her and tries to make her love him, so that they can get married（向女子）求愛，求婚 **5 be courting** [I] (*old-fashioned*) (of a man and a woman 男女) to have a romantic relationship before getting married 戀愛： *At that time they had been courting for several years.* 當時他們已經談了好幾年的戀愛了。➲ see also COURTSHIP

ˈcourt card (*BrE*) (also **ˈface card** *NAmE, BrE*) *noun* a PLAYING CARD with a picture of a king, queen or JACK on it 人頭牌，花牌（紙牌的 K、Q 或 J）➲ **VISUAL VOCAB** page V37

ˈcourt costs *noun* [pl.] (*NAmE*) = COSTS at COST *n.* (4)

Which Word? 詞語辨析

court / law court / court of law

- All these words can be used to refer to a place where legal trials take place. **Court** and (*formal*) **court of law** usually refer to the actual room where cases are judged. **Courtroom** is also used for this. **Law court** (*BrE*) is more often used to refer to the building. 以上各詞均可指法庭或法院。court 和 court of law（正式說法）通常指法庭、審判室，courtroom 亦用於此義。law court（英式英語）多指法院這座建築物：*The prison is opposite the law court.* 監獄在法院對面。**Courthouse** is used for this in *NAmE*. 美式英語用 courthouse 表達此義。

cour·te·ous /ˈkɜːtiəs; *NAmE* ˈkɜːrt-/ *adj.* polite, especially in a way that shows respect 有禮貌的；客氣的；（尤指）恭敬的，謙恭的：*a courteous young man* 彬彬有禮的年輕人 ◇ *The hotel staff are friendly and courteous.* 旅館服務人員友好而有禮貌。**OPP** **discourteous** ▸ **cour·te·ous·ly** *adv.*

cour·tesan /ˌkɔːtɪˈzæn; *NAmE* ˈkɔːrtɪzn/ *noun* (in the past) a PROSTITUTE, especially one with rich customers（舊時尤指伺候富豪的）高級妓女

cour·tesy /ˈkɜːtəsi; *NAmE* ˈkɜːrt-/ *noun, adj.*
- ***noun*** (*pl.* **-ies**) **1** [U] polite behaviour that shows respect for other people 禮貌；謙恭；彬彬有禮 **SYN** **politeness**：*I was treated with the utmost courtesy by the staff.* 我受到了工作人員極有禮貌的接待。◇ *It's only **common courtesy** to tell the neighbours that we'll be having a party* (= the sort of behaviour that people would expect). 告訴鄰居我們要舉行聚會，這是起碼的禮貌。**2** [C, usually pl.] (*formal*) a polite thing that you say or do when you meet people in formal situations（正式場合見面時的）客氣話，禮貌：*an exchange of courtesies before the meeting* 會議開始前互致問候

IDM **courtesy of sb/sth** **1** (also **by courtesy of sb/sth**) with the official permission of sb/sth and as a favour 承蒙…的允許（或好意）：*The pictures have been reproduced by courtesy of the British Museum.* 承蒙大英博物館惠允，複製了這些畫。**2** given as a prize or provided free by a person or an organization 蒙…提供；贊助；贈送：*Win a weekend in Rome, courtesy of Fiat.* 贏了就可以獲得菲亞特公司提供的到羅馬度週末的機會。**3** as the result of a particular thing or situation 作為…的結果：*Viewers can see the stadium from the air, courtesy of a camera fastened to the plane.* 由於飛機上安裝有攝像機，電視觀眾可從空中鳥瞰體育場。**do sb the courtesy of doing sth** to be polite by doing the thing that is mentioned（做提及的事）對某人表示禮貌：*Please do me the courtesy of listening to what I'm saying.* 請耐心聽一聽我的話。**have the courtesy to do sth** to know when you should do sth in order to be polite 知道何時該做…（以示禮貌）：*You think he'd at least have the courtesy to call to say he'd be late.* 誰都會覺得他至少應該懂得打個電話說一聲他要晚來。
- ***adj.*** [only before noun] (of a bus, car, etc. 公共汽車、小轎車等) provided free, at no cost to the person using it 免費乘坐（或使用）的：*A **courtesy bus** operates between the hotel and the town centre.* 有免費接送的公共汽車往返於旅館和市中心之間。◇ *The dealer will provide you with a **courtesy car** while your vehicle is being repaired.* 車輛維修期間，經銷商會提供免費使用的汽車。

ˈcourtesy call *noun* **1** (also **ˈcourtesy visit**) a formal or official visit, usually by one important person to another, just to be polite, not to discuss important business（正式或官方的）禮節性拜訪 **2** a telephone call from a company to one of its customers, for example to see if they are satisfied with the company's service 禮節性徵詢電話（如公司徵詢顧客對服務是否滿意）

ˈcourtesy light *noun* a small light inside a car which is automatically switched on when sb opens the door（汽車內的）門控照明燈

ˈcourtesy title *noun* a title that sb is allowed to use but which has no legal status（無法律實效的）尊稱

court·house /ˈkɔːthaʊs; *NAmE* ˈkɔːrt-/ *noun* **1** (*especially NAmE*) a building containing courts of law 法院大樓 ➲ note at COURT **2** (in the US) a building containing the offices of a county government（美國）縣政府大樓

court·ier /ˈkɔːtiə(r); *NAmE* ˈkɔːrt-/ *noun* (especially in the past) a person who is part of the COURT of a king or queen（尤指舊時的）侍臣，侍從，廷臣

court·ly /ˈkɔːtli; *NAmE* ˈkɔːrt-/ *adj.* (*formal* or *literary*) extremely polite and full of respect, especially in an old-fashioned way（尤指老式）極其恭敬有禮的，溫文爾雅的

ˌcourtly ˈlove *noun* [U] a tradition in literature, especially in Medieval times, involving the faithful love of a KNIGHT for his married LADY, with whom he can never have a relationship 典雅愛情（尤指中世紀的一種文學傳統，指騎士對貴婦人的忠貞但無結果的愛情）

ˌcourt ˈmartial *noun* [C, U] (*pl.* **courts martial**) a military court that deals with members of the armed forces who break military law; a trial at such a court 軍事法庭；軍事法庭的審判；軍法審判：*He was convicted at a court martial.* 他在軍事法庭上被判有罪。◇ *All the men now face court martial.* 現在所有這些軍人都面臨軍事法庭的審判。

ˌcourt-ˈmar·tial *verb* (**-ll-**, *US* **-l-**) [often passive] **~ sb** to hold a trial of sb in a military court（在軍事法庭上）舉行審判；以軍法審判：*He was court-martialled for desertion.* 他因擅離職守受到了軍法審判。

ˌcourt of apˈpeal *noun* **1** (*pl.* **courts of appeal**) a court that people can go to in order to try and change decisions that have been made by a lower court 上訴法院 ➲ see also APPELLATE COURT **2** **ˌCourt of Apˈpeal** [sing.] (*BrE*) the highest court in Britain (apart from the Supreme Court), that can change decisions made by a lower court（英國）上訴法院（僅次於最高法院的司法機構）**3** **ˌCourt of Apˈpeals** [C] (*US*) one of the courts in the US that can change decisions made by a lower court（美國）上訴法院

ˌcourt of ˈclaims *noun* (*US*) a court in the US that hears claims made against the government（美國）申訴法院（負責審理對政府的申訴案件）

ˌcourt of inˈquiry (also **ˌcourt of enˈquiry**) *noun* (*pl.* **courts of inquiry/enquiry**) (*BrE*) a special official group of people that investigates a particular problem 調查庭

ˌcourt of ˈlaw *noun* (*pl.* **courts of law**) (*formal*) (also **law court**) a room or building where legal cases are judged 法庭；法院 ➲ note at COURT

ˌCourt of ˈSession *noun* in Scotland, the highest court that deals with CIVIL cases (= not criminal cases)（蘇格蘭）最高民事法院

ˌcourt ˈorder *noun* a decision that is made in court about what must happen in a particular situation 法庭命令（或指令、庭諭）

court·room /ˈkɔːtruːm; -rʊm; *NAmE* ˈkɔːrt-/ *noun* a room in which trials or other legal cases are held 法庭；審判室 ➲ note at COURT

court·ship /ˈkɔːtʃɪp; *NAmE* ˈkɔːrt-/ *noun* **1** [C, U] (*old-fashioned*) the time when two people have a romantic relationship before they get married; the process of developing this relationship 求愛期；求愛；追求：*They married after a short courtship.* 他們戀愛不久便結婚了。◇ *Mr Elton's courtship of Harriet* 埃爾頓先生對哈麗雅特的追求 **2** [U] the special way animals behave in order to attract a mate for producing young animals（動物的）求偶：*courtship displays* 求偶的炫耀行為 **3 ~ (of sb/sth)** (*formal*) the process or act of attracting a business partner, etc. 招商：*the company's courtship by the government* 政府向公司獻殷勤

ˈcourt shoe (*BrE*) (*NAmE* **pump**) *noun* a woman's formal shoe that is plain and does not cover the top part of the foot 半高跟鞋（正式場合穿的樸素女鞋）➲ VISUAL VOCAB page V64

ˌcourt ˈtennis (*NAmE*) (*BrE* **ˈreal tennis**) (*AustralE* **ˈroyal tennis**) *noun* [U] an old form of tennis played

C

inside a building with a hard ball 庭院網球（使用硬球的舊式室內網球運動）

court·yard /ˈkɔːtjɑːd; *NAmE* ˈkɔːrtjɑːrd/ (also **court**) *noun* an open space that is partly or completely surrounded by buildings and is usually part of a castle, a large house, etc.（通常為城堡、大宅第等的）庭院，院子，天井：*the **central/inner courtyard*** 中心／內庭院

cous·cous /ˈkʊskʊs; ˈkuːskuːs/ *noun* [U] a type of N African food made from crushed WHEAT; a dish of meat and/or vegetables with couscous（北非的）蒸粗麥粉食物

cousin 0-w /ˈkʌzn/ *noun*
1 0-w (also ˌ**first** ˈ**cousin**) a child of your aunt or uncle 同輩表親（或堂親）；堂兄（或弟、姊、妹）；表兄（或弟、姊、妹）：*She's my cousin.* 她是我的表妹。◇ *We're cousins.* 我們是表親。➲ see also COUNTRY COUSIN, SECOND COUSIN **2** 0-w a person who is in your wider family but who is not closely related to you 遠房親戚；遠親：*He's a distant cousin of mine.* 他是我遠房的一個表親。**3** [usually pl.] a way of describing people from another country who are similar in some way to people in your own country 兄弟的…國人民（對與本民族有某些類似的另一國家人民的說法）：*our American cousins* 我們兄弟的美國人民 **4** [usually pl.] a way of describing things that are similar or related in some way 同族；同類：*Asian elephants are smaller than their African cousins.* 亞洲象比它們的非洲同類小些。

ˈ**cousin brother** *noun* (*IndE, informal*) a male cousin of your own generation 堂（或表）兄；堂（或表）弟

ˈ**cousin sister** *noun* (*IndE, informal*) a female cousin of your own generation 堂（或表）姐；堂（或表）妹

cou·ture /kuˈtjʊə(r); *NAmE* -ˈtʊr/ *noun* [U] (from *French*) the design and production of expensive and fashionable clothes; these clothes 時裝設計製作；時裝：*a couture evening dress* 昂貴時髦的晚禮服 ➲ see also HAUTE COUTURE

cou·tur·ier /kuˈtjʊəriei; *NAmE* -ˈtʊr-/ *noun* (from *French*) a person who designs, makes and sells expensive, fashionable clothes, especially for women（尤指）女裝設計師；時裝裁縫；女裝商人 SYN **fashion designer**

co·va·lent /ˌkəʊˈveilənt; *NAmE* ˌkoʊ-/ *adj.* (*chemistry* 化) (of a chemical BOND 化學鍵) sharing a pair of ELECTRONS 共價的 ➲ compare IONIC (2)

cove /kəʊv; *NAmE* koʊv/ *noun* **1** a small bay (= an area of sea that is partly surrounded by land) 小海灣：*a secluded cove* 僻靜的小海灣 ➲ VISUAL VOCAB page V5 **2** (*old-fashioned, BrE, informal*) a man 傢伙；漢子；小子

coven /ˈkʌvn/ *noun* a group or meeting of WITCHES 女巫團；女巫的聚會

cov·en·ant /ˈkʌvənənt/ *noun* a promise to sb, or a legal agreement, especially one to pay a regular amount of money to sb/sth 承諾；合同；協約；（尤指定期付款的）契約：*God's covenant with Abraham* 上帝與亞伯拉罕的立約 ◇ *a covenant to a charity* 向慈善機構定期捐款的契約
▸ **cov·en·ant** *verb*：**~ sth** *All profits are covenanted to medical charities.* 已立約把所有收益捐給醫療慈善機構。

Cov·en·try /ˈkʌvəntri; *BrE* also ˈkɒv-; *NAmE* also ˈkɑːv-/ *noun*
IDM **send sb to** ˈ**Coventry** (*BrE*) to refuse to speak to sb, as a way of punishing them for sth that they have done 拒絕與某人交談（作為懲罰）

cover 0-w /ˈkʌvə(r)/ *verb, noun*
■ *verb*
▸ **HIDE/PROTECT** 隱藏；保護 **1** 0-w [T] **~ sth** (**with sth**) to place sth over or in front of sth in order to hide or protect it 掩蔽；遮蓋：*Cover the chicken loosely with foil.* 用錫箔把雞肉鬆鬆地蓋起來。◇ *She covered her face with her hands.* 她雙手掩面。◇ (*figurative*) *He laughed to cover* (= hide) *his nervousness.* 他哈哈大笑以掩飾他緊張的心情。➲ SYNONYMS at HIDE
▸ **SPREAD OVER SURFACE** 覆蓋 **2** 0-w [T] **~ sth** to lie or spread over the surface of sth 蓋；覆蓋：*Snow covered the ground.* 大雪覆蓋了大地。◇ *Much of the country is covered by forest.* 森林覆蓋着這個國家的大片土地。 **3** 0-w [T] to put or spread a layer of liquid, dust, etc. on sb/sth 撒上，灑上，濺上（一層液體、塵土等）：**~ sb/sth in sth** *The players were soon covered in mud.* 那些運動員很快就渾身濺滿了泥。◇ **~ sb/sth with sth** *The wind blew in from the desert and covered everything with sand.* 風從沙漠那邊吹來把一切都蒙上了一層沙子。
▸ **INCLUDE** 包括 **4** 0-w [T] **~ sth** to include sth; to deal with sth 包括；包含；涉及；處理：*The survey covers all aspects of the business.* 調查包括這家企業的各個方面。◇ *The lectures **covered a lot of ground*** (= a lot of material, subjects, etc.). 這些講座涉及的內容極為廣泛豐富。◇ *the sales team covering the northern part of the country* (= selling to people in that area) 負責這個國家北部地區的銷售隊伍 ◇ *Do the rules cover* (= do they apply to) *a case like this?* 這些規則適用於這樣的情況嗎？
▸ **MONEY** 款項 **5** 0-w [T] **~ sth** to be or provide enough money for sth 足以支付；夠付：*$100 should cover your expenses.* * 100 元該足夠支付你的費用了。◇ *Your parents will have to cover your tuition fees.* 你的父母得支付你的學費。◇ *The show barely **covered its costs**.* 這場演出勉強夠本。
▸ **DISTANCE/AREA** 距離；面積 **6** [T] **~ sth** to travel the distance mentioned 行走（一段路程）：*By sunset we had covered thirty miles.* 到日落時我們已走了三十英里。◇ *They walked for a long time and **covered** a good deal of **ground**.* 他們步行了很長時間，走遍一大段路。**7** [T] **~ sth** to spread over the area mentioned 佔（一片面積）：*The reserve covers an area of some 1 140 square kilometres.* 保護區佔地面積大約 1 140 平方公里。
▸ **REPORT NEWS** 報道新聞 **8** [T] **~ sth** to report on an event for television, a newspaper, etc.; to show an event on television 報道；電視報道：*She's covering the party's annual conference.* 她正在報道這個政黨的年會新聞。◇ *The BBC will cover all the major games of the tournament.* 英國廣播公司將報道這次錦標賽的所有重要賽事。
▸ **FOR SB** 代替某人 **9** [I] **~ for sb** to do sb's work or duties while they are away 代替，頂替，替補（某人工作或履行職責）：*I'm covering for Jane while she's on leave.* 簡休假時我來頂替她工作。**10** [I] **~ for sb** to invent a lie or an excuse that will stop sb from getting into trouble（為免他人陷入麻煩而用謊話或藉口）遮掩，掩蓋，敷衍：*I have to go out for a minute—will you cover for me if anyone asks where I am?* 我得出去一會兒，假如有人問起我在哪裏你能為我搪塞一下嗎？
▸ **WITH INSURANCE** 保險 **11** [T] to protect sb against loss, injury, etc. by insurance 給…保險：**~ sb/sth** (**against/for sth**) *Are you fully covered for fire and theft?* 你是否充分地保了火險和盜竊險？◇ **~ sb/sth to do sth** *Does this policy cover my husband to drive?* 這份保險單是否保我丈夫的駕車險？
▸ **AGAINST BLAME** 防遭指責 **12** [T] **~ yourself** (**against sth**) to take action in order to protect yourself against being blamed for sth 採取行動（以使自己免遭責備）：*One reason doctors take temperatures is to cover themselves against negligence claims.* 醫生測量體温的一個原因是免得因玩忽職守而遭受索賠。
▸ **WITH GUN** 用槍 **13** [T] **~ sb** to protect sb by threatening to shoot at anyone who tries to attack them 掩護：*Cover me while I move forward.* 掩護我前進。**14** [T] **~ sb/sth** to aim a gun at a place or person so that nobody can escape or shoot 用槍瞄準（以致無人可逃跑或開槍）：*The police covered the exits to the building.* 警方用槍封鎖了那棟大樓的出口。◇ *Don't move—we've **got you covered**!* 不許動！我們的槍口正對着你們！
▸ **SONG** 歌曲 **15** [T] **~ sth** to record a new version of a song that was originally recorded by another band or singer 翻唱（原來由另一樂隊或歌手演唱的歌曲）：*They've covered an old Rolling Stones number.* 他們翻唱了滾石樂隊的一首老歌。
IDM **cover all the** ˈ**bases** to consider and deal with all the things that could happen or could be needed when you are arranging sth 考慮周全；面面俱到 **cover your** ˈ**back** (*informal*) (*NAmE* also **cover your** ˈ**ass**, *taboo, slang*) to realize that you may be blamed or criticized for sth later and take action to avoid this 粉飾污點；防止可預見的指摘：*Get everything in writing in order to cover your back.* 一切都要立字為據，以絕後患。**cover your** ˈ**tracks** to try and hide what you have done, because you do not want other people to find out

about it 掩蓋自己的行徑：*He had attempted to cover his tracks by making her death appear like suicide.* 他使她的死亡看起來像是自殺，企圖以此掩蓋自己的罪行。➲ more at MULTITUDE

PHR V **ˌcover sth↔ˈin** to put a covering or roof over an open space（給露天場地）裝頂蓋，加頂 **ˌcover sth↔ˈover** to cover sth completely so that it cannot be seen（完全）蓋住，遮住 **SYN** **conceal**：*The Roman remains are now covered over by office buildings.* 這些羅馬時代的遺址現已被棟棟辦公大樓完全遮住。**ˌcover ˈup | ˌcover yourself ˈup** to put on more clothes 加（或多）穿衣服；穿暖和 **ˌcover sth↔ˈup** 🔑 **1** to cover sth completely so that it cannot be seen（完全）蓋住，遮住：*He covered up the body with a sheet.* 他用一條布單把屍體蓋上了。**2** (*disapproving*) to try to stop people from knowing the truth about a mistake, a crime, etc. 掩蓋（錯誤、罪行等的）真相 ➲ related noun COVER-UP

■ ***noun***

▸ **PROTECTION/SHELTER** 保護；遮蔽物 **1** 🔑 [C] a thing that is put over or on another thing, usually to protect it or to decorate it 覆蓋物；掩蔽物；套子；罩子：*a cushion cover* 靠墊套 ◇ *a plastic waterproof cover for the stroller* 手推童車的塑料防水篷 ➲ VISUAL VOCAB page V70 ➲ see also DUST COVER, LOOSE COVER **2** [U] a place that provides shelter from bad weather or protection from an attack 躲避處；避難所；庇護所：*Everyone ran **for cover** when it started to rain.* 雨下起來時，大家都跑着找地方避雨。◇ *The climbers **took cover** from the storm in a cave.* 登山者在山洞裏躲避暴風雨。◇ *After the explosion the street was full of people **running for cover**.* 爆炸發生以後，滿街的人都奔跑躲避。

▸ **OF BOOK** 書 **3** 🔑 [C] the outside of a book or a magazine（書刊的）封面，封皮：*the **front/back cover*** 封面／底 ◇ *Her face was **on the cover*** (= the front cover) *of every magazine.* 各種雜誌的封面都有她的頭像。◇ *He always reads the paper **from cover to cover*** (= everything in it). 他總是把報紙從頭到尾全看一遍。

▸ **INSURANCE** 保險 **4** (*BrE*) (*NAmE* **cov·er·age**) [U] **~ (against sth)** protection that an insurance company provides by promising to pay you money if a particular event happens（保險公司的）保險：*accident cover* 事故保險 ◇ *cover against accidental damage* 意外損害保險

▸ **WITH WEAPONS** 武器 **5** [U] support and protection that is provided when sb is attacking or in danger of being attacked 掩護；防護：*The ships needed air cover* (= protection by military planes) *once they reached enemy waters.* 一到達敵方的水域，船隻就需要空中掩護。

▸ **TREES/PLANTS** 樹木；植物 **6** [U] trees and plants that grow on an area of land（生長在一個地區的）樹木植物，自然植被：*The total forest cover of the earth is decreasing.* 地球上森林覆蓋的總面積正在減少。

▸ **CLOUD/SNOW** 雲；雪 **7** [U] the fact of the sky being covered with cloud or the ground with snow（雲層的）遮蓋；（雪的）覆蓋：*Fog and low cloud cover are expected this afternoon.* 預計今天下午有霧和低空雲層。◇ *In this area there is snow cover for six months of the year.* 這個地區一年中有六個月被積雪覆蓋。

▸ **ON BED** 牀上 **8 the covers** [pl.] the sheets, BLANKETS, etc. on a bed 牀單；牀罩；毯子；被子：*She threw back the covers and leapt out of bed.* 她掀開被子跳下牀來。

▸ **SONG** 歌曲 **9** [C] = COVER VERSION

▸ **HIDING STH** 隱藏 **10** [C, usually sing.] **~ (for sth)** activities or behaviour that seem honest or true but that hide sb's real identity or feelings, or that hide sth illegal（對身分、感情或違法事情的）掩蓋，掩飾：*His work as a civil servant was a cover for his activities as a spy.* 他以公務員的工作來掩護他搞間諜活動。◇ *Her over-confident attitude was a cover for her nervousness.* 她以過分自信的態度來掩飾她緊張的心情。◇ *It would only take one phone call to **blow their cover*** (= make known their true identities and what they were really doing). 只要撥打一個電話就可揭穿他們的偽裝。

▸ **FOR SB'S WORK** 代替某人工作 **11** [U] the fact of sb doing another person's job when they are away or when there are not enough staff 代替工作；代勞；替補：*It's the manager's job to organize cover for staff who are absent.* 安排他人頂替缺席的員工是經理的工作。◇ *Ambulance drivers provided only emergency cover during the dispute.* 糾紛期間救護車司機只提供急救替班。

IDM **break ˈcover** to leave a place that you have been hiding in, usually at a high speed 匆匆離開隱蔽處；衝出躲藏處 **under ˈcover 1** pretending to be sb else in order to do sth secretly（為秘密活動）偽裝着，裝扮着，冒名頂替：*a police officer working under cover* 做隱蔽工作的警察 **2** under a structure that gives protection from the weather 在遮擋物下（避風雨） **under (the) cover of sth** hidden or protected by sth 在…的掩護（或保護）下：*Later, under cover of darkness, they crept into the house.* 後來他們在夜幕的掩護下溜進了房子。**under separate ˈcover** (*business* 商) in a separate envelope 另函：*The information you requested is being forwarded to you under separate cover.* 現另函寄上所要資料。➲ more at JUDGE *v.*

cov·er·age /ˈkʌvərɪdʒ/ *noun* [U] **1** the reporting of news and sport in newspapers and on the radio and television 新聞報道：***media/newspaper/press coverage*** 媒體／報紙／報刊的報道 ◇ *tonight's **live coverage** of the hockey game* 今晚曲棍球比賽的現場直播 **2** the range or quality of information that is included in a book or course of study, on television, etc.（書、課程學習、電視等的）信息範圍，信息質量：*magazines with extensive coverage of diet and health topics* 包含大量飲食與健康話題的雜誌 **3** the amount of sth that sth provides; the amount or way that sth covers an area 提供的數量；覆蓋範圍（或方式）：*Immunization coverage against fatal diseases has increased to 99% in some countries.* 在一些國家致命疾病免疫注射的覆蓋面已達到 99%。**4** (*NAmE*) (*BrE* **cover**) protection that an insurance company provides by promising to pay you money if a particular event happens（保險公司的）保險：*insurance coverage* 保險範圍 ◇ *Medicaid health coverage for low-income families* 對低收入家庭的醫療保險

cov·er·alls /ˈkʌvərɔːlz/ (*NAmE*) (*BrE* **overalls**) *noun* [pl.] a loose piece of clothing like a shirt and trousers/pants in one piece, made of heavy cloth and usually worn over other clothing by workers doing dirty work 工裝連衣褲；工裝服 ➲ picture at OVERALL

ˈcover charge *noun* [usually sing.] an amount of money that you pay in some restaurants or clubs in addition to the cost of the food and drink（餐館或俱樂部中飲食之外的）服務費

covered 🔑 /ˈkʌvəd; *NAmE* -vərd/ *adj.*
1 🔑 [not before noun] **~ in/with sth** having a layer or amount of sth on it 蓋着一層；蓋滿：*His face was covered in blood.* 他滿臉是血。◇ *The walls were covered with pictures.* 這些牆上掛滿了畫。**2** 🔑 having a roof over it 有頂的：*a covered area of the stadium with seats* 體育場有頂的座席區域

ˌcovered ˈwagon *noun* a large wooden vehicle with a curved roof made of cloth, that is pulled by horses, used especially in the past in N America by people travelling across the land to the west（尤指舊時用於橫跨北美大陸到西部的）有篷大馬車

ˈcover girl *noun* a young woman whose photograph is on the front of a magazine（雜誌的）封面女郎

cov·er·ing 🔑 /ˈkʌvərɪŋ/ *noun*
1 🔑 a layer of sth that covers sth else（一層）覆蓋層，遮蓋物：*a thick covering of snow on the ground* 地上厚厚的一層積雪 **2** 🔑 a layer of material such as carpet or WALLPAPER, used to cover, decorate and protect floors, walls, etc. 裝飾（或保護）性覆蓋物：***floor/wall coverings*** 地板／牆壁覆蓋物 **3** 🔑 a piece of material that covers sth 覆蓋某物的一塊（或一片）材料：*He pulled the plastic covering off the dead body.* 他拉掉了蓋在屍體上的塑料布。

ˌcovering ˈletter (*BrE*) (*NAmE* **ˈcover letter**) *noun* a letter containing extra information that you send with sth 附信（與某物一起寄出）➲ WRITING TUTOR page WT49

cov·er·let /ˈkʌvələt; *NAmE* -vərl-/ *noun* (*old-fashioned*) a type of BEDSPREAD to cover a bed 牀罩

ˈcover story *noun* **1** the main story in a magazine, that goes with the picture shown on the front cover 封面故

事（雜誌中與封面圖片有關的內容） **2** a story that is invented in order to hide sth, especially a person's identity or their reasons for doing sth （尤指掩飾身分或做某事原因的）託辭，藉口

C

cov·ert *adj., noun*

▪ ***adj.*** /ˈkʌvət; ˈkəʊvɜːt; *NAmE* ˈkoʊvɜːrt/ (*formal*) secret or hidden, making it difficult to notice 秘密的；隱蔽的；暗中的：*covert operations/surveillance* 暗中活動／監視 ◇ *He stole a covert glance at her across the table.* 他朝桌子對面偷偷地瞥了她一眼。➲ compare OVERT ▸ **cov·ert·ly** *adv.*：*She watched him covertly in the mirror.* 她從鏡子裏偷偷地望着他。

▪ ***noun*** /ˈkʌvət; *NAmE* -vərt/ an area of thick low bushes and trees where animals can hide（動物可藏身的）矮樹叢，灌木林

ˈcover-up *noun* [usually sing.] action that is taken to hide a mistake or illegal activity from the public 掩蓋；掩飾：*Government sources denied there had been a deliberate cover-up.* 政府方面否認了有故意掩飾的行為。

ˈcover version (also **cover**) *noun* a new recording of an old song by a different band or singer （不同樂隊或歌手演唱舊歌的）翻唱版本

covet /ˈkʌvət/ *verb* **~ sth** (*formal*) to want sth very much, especially sth that belongs to sb else 渴望；貪求（尤指別人的東西）；覬覦：*He had long coveted the chance to work with a famous musician.* 他一直渴望有機會與著名音樂家一起工作。◇ *They are this year's winners of the coveted trophy* (= that everyone would like to win). 他們是人人嚮往的本年度獲獎者。

cov·et·ous /ˈkʌvətəs/ *adj.* (*formal*) having a strong desire for the things that other people have 貪求的；垂涎的 ▸ **cov·et·ous·ness** *noun* [U]

cow 0- /kaʊ/ *noun, verb*

▪ ***noun*** **1** 0- a large animal kept on farms to produce milk or beef 母牛；奶牛；菜牛；肉牛：*cow's milk* 牛奶◇ *a herd of dairy cows* (= cows kept for their milk) 一群奶牛 ➲ compare BULL (1), CALF (2), HEIFER ➲ see also CATTLE **2** the female of the ELEPHANT, WHALE and some other large animals 雌象；雌鯨；某些大型雌性動物 ➲ compare BULL (2) **3** (*slang, disapproving*) an offensive word for a woman 婆娘；娘兒們：*You stupid cow!* 你這蠢婆娘！ **4** (*AustralE, NZE*) an unpleasant person, thing or situation 討厭的人（或事物、情況）➲ see also CASH COW, SACRED COW

IDM **have a ˈcow** (*NAmE, informal*) to become very angry or anxious about sth 暴跳如雷；焦慮不安：*Don't have a cow—it's no big deal.* 別發火，沒什麼大不了。 **till the ˈcows come home** (*informal*) for a very long time; for ever 很長時間；永遠

▪ ***verb*** [usually passive] **~ sb** to frighten sb in order to make them obey you 恐嚇；嚇唬；威脅；脅迫 SYN **intimidate**：*She was easily cowed by people in authority.* 她很容易被有權勢的人嚇住。

cow·ard /ˈkaʊəd; *NAmE* -ərd/ *noun* (*disapproving*) a person who is not brave or who does not have the courage to do things that other people do not think are especially difficult 膽小鬼；懦夫；膽怯者：*You coward! What are you afraid of?* 你這膽小鬼！你怕什麼呢？◇ *I'm a real coward when it comes to going to the dentist.* 我一去看牙醫就膽戰心驚。▸ **cow·ard·ly** *adj.*：*a cowardly attack on a defenceless man* 欺負一個沒有自衛能力的人的不光彩行為

cow·ard·ice /ˈkaʊədɪs; *NAmE* -ərd-/ *noun* [U] fear or lack of courage 懼怕；膽小；懦弱 OPP **bravery, courage**

cow·bell /ˈkaʊbel/ *noun* a bell that is put around a cow's neck so that the cow can easily be found 牛頸鈴

cow·boy /ˈkaʊbɔɪ/ *noun* **1** a man who rides a horse and whose job is to take care of CATTLE in the western parts of the US （美國西部的）牛仔，騎馬牧人：*cowboy boots* 牛仔靴 ➲ VISUAL VOCAB page V64 **2** a man like this as a character in a film/movie about the American West （美國西部影片中的）牛仔：*children playing a game of cowboys and Indians* 玩美國西部牛仔與印第安人遊戲的孩子們 **3** (*BrE, informal, disapproving*) a dishonest person in business, especially sb who produces work of bad quality or charges too high a price （尤指產品質量差或索價太高的）奸商

ˈcowboy hat *noun* a hat with a wide BRIM, worn by American cowboys （美國牛仔戴的）牛仔帽 ➲ VISUAL VOCAB page V65

cow·catch·er /ˈkaʊkætʃə(r)/ *noun* (*NAmE*) a pointed metal structure at the front of a train that is used for pushing things off the track （火車機車前的）排障器

ˈcow chip *noun* (*US*) a very hard COWPAT 硬牛糞團

cowed /kaʊd/ *adj.* made to feel afraid and that you are not as good as sb else 使感到膽怯的；自慚形穢的 ➲ see also COW *v.*

cower /ˈkaʊə(r)/ *verb* [I] to bend low and/or move backwards because you are frightened （因恐懼而）蜷縮，畏縮，退縮：*A gun went off and people cowered behind walls and under tables.* 一聲槍響，人們縮到牆後或桌子底下躲起來。

cow·girl /ˈkaʊɡɜːl; *NAmE* -ɡɜːrl/ *noun* a female COWBOY in the American West （美國西部的）女牛仔，女牧工，女牧童

cow·hand /ˈkaʊhænd/ *noun* a person whose job is taking care of cows 牧牛工；放牛人

cow·hide /ˈkaʊhaɪd/ *noun* [U] strong leather made from the skin of a cow （母）牛皮革

cowl /kaʊl/ *noun* **1** a large loose covering for the head, worn especially by MONKS （尤指修道士戴的）大兜帽，大風帽 **2** a cover for a CHIMNEY, etc., usually made of metal. Cowls often turn with the wind and are designed to improve the flow of air or smoke. 煙囱罩，通風帽（常可隨風轉動以利通風或排煙）

cow·lick /ˈkaʊlɪk/ *noun* a piece of hair that grows in a different direction from the rest of your hair and is difficult to make lie flat 翹起的一綹頭髮

cowl·ing /ˈkaʊlɪŋ/ *noun* (*technical* 術語) a metal cover for an engine, especially on an aircraft 整流罩；（尤指）飛機引擎罩 ➲ VISUAL VOCAB page V53

ˈcowl neck *noun* a COLLAR on a woman's sweater that hangs in several folds （女性套衫的）重褶領

ˈco-worker *noun* a person that sb works with, doing the same kind of job 共同工作者；合作者；同事；同僚 SYN **colleague**

ˈcow parsley *noun* [U] a European wild plant with a lot of very small white flowers that look like LACE 飾帶花（原産歐洲，開小白花）

cow·pat /ˈkaʊpæt/ (*BrE*) *noun* a round flat piece of solid waste from a cow 牛糞團

cow·pea /ˈkaʊpiː/ *noun* a type of BEAN that is white with a black spot and is grown for food 豇豆，黑眼豆（供食用）：*Cowpeas are an important crop in many African countries.* 黑眼豆是很多非洲國家的重要作物。

cow·poke /ˈkaʊpəʊk; *NAmE* -poʊk/ *noun* (*NAmE, old-fashioned* or *humorous*) = COWBOY

cow·rie /ˈkaʊri/ *noun* a small shiny shell that was used as money in the past in parts of Africa and Asia 寶貝貝殼（舊時亞非部份地區用作貨幣的小貝殼）

cow·shed /ˈkaʊʃed/ *noun* (*BrE*) a farm building in which cows are kept 牛棚；牛舍

cow·slip /ˈkaʊslɪp/ *noun* a small wild plant with yellow flowers with a sweet smell 櫻草；歐洲櫻草；黃花九輪草；野生報春花

cox /kɒks; *NAmE* kɑːks/ *noun, verb*

▪ ***noun*** (also **cox·swain**) the person who controls the direction of a ROWING BOAT while other people are ROWING （划艇的）舵手

▪ ***verb*** [T, I] **~ (sth)** to control the direction of a ROWING BOAT while other people are ROWING; to act as a cox （為划艇）掌舵；當（划艇的）舵手

cox·swain /ˈkɒksn; *NAmE* ˈkɑːksn/ *noun* **1** the person who is in charge of a LIFEBOAT and who controls its direction （救生艇的）艇長，舵手 **2** = COX

coy /kɔɪ/ *adj.* **1** shy or pretending to be shy and innocent, especially about love or sex, and sometimes in order to make people more interested in you （尤指對

愛情或性愛）羞羞答答的，假裝害羞無知的，故作忸怩的：*She gave me a coy smile.* 她羞答答地對我笑了笑。**2 ~** (**about sth**) not willing to give information about sth, or answer questions that tell people too much about you 不願提供信息的；不肯作答的；含糊其詞的 SYN **reticent**：*She was a little coy about how much her dress cost.* 她對她那條連衣裙花了多少錢有點吞吞吐吐。▶ **coyly** *adv.* **coy·ness** *noun* [U]

coy·ote /kaɪˈəʊti; *NAmE* -ˈoʊti; *BrE* also kɔɪ-; *NAmE* also ˈkaɪoʊt/ (also **ˈprairie wolf**) *noun* a N American wild animal of the dog family 叢林狼，草原狼（犬科動物，分佈於北美）

coy·pu /ˈkɔɪpuː/ *noun* a large S American animal, like a BEAVER, that lives near water 河狸鼠（南美洲動物）

coz *conj.* = COS[1]

cozy (*NAmE*) (*BrE* **cosy**) /ˈkəʊzi; *NAmE* ˈkoʊzi/ *adj., verb*

■ ***adj.*** (**cozi·er**, **cozi·est**, **cosi·er**, **cosi·est**) **1** warm, comfortable and safe, especially because of being small or confined 溫暖舒適的（尤指細小的室內地方）SYN **snug**：*a cozy little room* 溫暖舒適的小房間 ◇ *a cozy feeling* 愜意的感覺 ◇ *I felt warm and cozy sitting by the fire.* 坐在爐火旁，我感到又暖和又舒服。**2** friendly and private 親密無間的；密切的：*a cozy chat with a friend* 與朋友親切的閒聊 **3** (often *disapproving*) easy and convenient, but not always honest or right 輕易得到的，輕鬆的（但不一定是誠實或恰當的）：*The firm has a cozy relationship with the Department of Defense.* 這家公司與國防部關係密切。◇ *The danger is that things get too cozy.* 危險在於一切都來得太容易。▶ **cozi·ly** (*NAmE*) (*BrE* **cosi·ly**) *adv.*：*sitting cozily by the fire* 暖融融地坐在爐火旁 **cozi·ness** (*NAmE*) (*BrE* **cosi·ness**) *noun* [U]：*the warmth and coziness of the kitchen* 廚房的溫暖與舒適

■ ***verb*** (**cozies**, **cozy·ing**, **cozied**, **cozied**)

PHR V **ˌcozy ˈup to sb** (*NAmE*) (*BrE* **ˌcosy ˈup to sb**) (*informal*) to act in a friendly way towards sb, especially sb who will be useful to you 獻殷勤；取悅

cp. *abbr.* (in writing) compare（書寫形式）比較

CPE /ˌsiː piː ˈiː/ *noun* [U] the abbreviation for 'Certificate of Proficiency in English' (a British test, set by the University of Cambridge, that measures a person's ability to speak and write English at a very advanced level) 熟練英語證書考試，劍橋最高級英語認證（全寫為 Certificate of Proficiency in English）

CPI /ˌsiː piː ˈaɪ/ *abbr.* CONSUMER PRICE INDEX 居民消費價格指數；消費價格指數

Cpl (*BrE*) (*NAmE* **Cpl.**) *abbr.* (in writing) CORPORAL（書寫形式）下士

CPR /ˌsiː piː ˈɑː(r)/ *noun* [U] the abbreviation for 'cardiopulmonary resuscitation' (breathing air into the mouth of an unconscious person and pressing on their chest to keep them alive by sending air around their body) 心肺復蘇（全寫為 cardiopulmonary resuscitation，包括進行人工呼吸和體外心臟按摩）

CPU /ˌsiː piː ˈjuː/ *abbr.* (*computing* 計) central processing unit (the part of a computer that controls all the other parts of the system) 中央處理器

crab /kræb/ *noun* **1** [C] a sea creature with a hard shell, eight legs and two PINCERS (= curved and pointed arms for catching and holding things). Crabs move sideways on land. 蟹；螃蟹 ➲ VISUAL VOCAB page V13 ➲ see also HERMIT CRAB **2** [U] meat from a crab, used for food 蟹肉：*dressed crab* 經加工的螃蟹 **3 crabs** (*informal*) the condition caused by having LICE (called **crab lice**) in the hair around the GENITALS 陰虱寄生病

ˈcrab apple *noun* a tree that produces fruit like small hard sour apples, also called crab apples 酸蘋果樹；花紅樹；沙果樹

crabbed /ˈkræbɪd; kræbd/ *adj.* **1** (*literary*) (of sb's writing 筆跡) small and difficult to read 小而難辨認的 **2** (*old-fashioned*) = CRABBY

crabby /ˈkræbi/ *adj.* (*informal*) (of people 人) bad-tempered and unpleasant 脾氣乖戾的；易怒的

crab·grass /ˈkræbgrɑːs; *NAmE* -græs/ *noun* [U] (*especially NAmE*) a type of grass that grows where it is not wanted, spreads quickly and is hard to get rid of 馬唐，指草（多為雜草，難以根除）

ˈcrab stick *noun* a small pink stick made from pressed pieces of fish that have been flavoured to taste like CRAB 蟹肉棒，蟹肉條（用魚肉糜加香料製成）

crab·wise /ˈkræbwaɪz/ *adv.* (of a movement 移動) in a sideways direction, like a CRAB 向一邊地；橫向似螃蟹地

C

crack 🔑 /kræk/ *verb, noun, adj.*

■ ***verb***

▸ **BREAK** 破裂 **1** 🔑 [I, T] to break without dividing into separate parts; to break sth in this way 破裂；裂開；斷裂：*The ice cracked as I stepped onto it.* 我一踩冰就裂了。◇ **~ sth** *He has cracked a bone in his arm.* 他的手臂有一處骨裂。◇ *Her lips were dry and cracked.* 她的嘴唇乾裂了。**2** 🔑 [I, T] to break open or into pieces; to break sth in this way 砸開；破開；砸碎；打碎：**+ adv./prep.** *A chunk of the cliff had cracked off in a storm.* 懸崖上的一塊石頭在暴風雨中崩塌下來。◇ (*figurative*) *His face cracked into a smile.* 他臉上綻放了微笑。◇ **~ sth** *to crack a nut* 把堅果砸開 ◇ **~ sth + adv./prep.** *She cracked an egg into the pan.* 她往鍋裏打了一個雞蛋。

▸ **HIT** 擊中 **3** [T] **~ sth/sb** (**on/against sth**) to hit sth/sb with a short hard blow 重擊；猛擊：*I cracked my head on the low ceiling.* 我的頭撞上了低矮的天花板。◇ *He cracked me on the head with a ruler.* 他用尺子猛擊我的頭部。

▸ **MAKE SOUND** 發出聲音 **4** [I, T] to make a sharp sound; to make sth do this（使）發出爆裂聲，劈啪作響：*A shot cracked across the ridge.* 一顆炮彈飛過山脊爆炸了。◇ [no passive] **~** sth *He* ***cracked his whip*** *and galloped away.* 他抽響鞭子策馬飛奔而去。

▸ **OF VOICE** 嗓音 **5** [I] if your voice **cracks**, it changes in depth, volume, etc. suddenly and in a way that you cannot control（突然）變嘶啞，變沙啞：*In a voice cracking with emotion, he told us of his son's death.* 他悲慟失聲地告訴我們他兒子去世的消息。

▸ **UNDER PRESSURE** 在壓力下 **6** [I] to no longer be able to function normally because of pressure（因壓力而）吃不消，崩潰，瓦解：*Things are terrible at work and people are cracking under the strain.* 工作情況很糟糕，人們因過度緊張越來越吃不消了。◇ *They questioned him for days before he cracked.* 他們審訊他多日後他就垮掉了。◇ *The old institutions are cracking.* 舊的制度正在瓦解。

▸ **FIND SOLUTION** 找到解決方法 **7** [T] **~ sth** to find the solution to a problem, etc.; to find the way to do sth difficult 找到解決（難題等的）方法：*to crack the enemy's code* 破譯敵人的密碼 ◇ (*informal*) *After a year in this job I think* ***I've got it cracked!*** 幹了一年後，我覺得我已知道怎樣做好這項工作了！

▸ **STOP SB/STH** 阻止 **8** [T] **~ sth** to find a way of stopping or defeating a criminal or an enemy 阻止，打擊，擊敗，戰勝（罪犯或敵人）：*Police have cracked a major drugs ring.* 警方破獲了一個重大的販毒集團。

▸ **OPEN BOTTLE** 開瓶 **9** [T] **~** (**open**) **a bottle** (*informal*) to open a bottle, especially of wine, and drink it 開瓶；（尤指）開瓶飲酒

▸ **A JOKE** 玩笑 **10** [T] **~ a joke** (*informal*) to tell a joke 說（笑話）；開（玩笑）

IDM **get ˈcracking** (*informal*) to begin immediately and work quickly 立即大幹起來 SYN **get going**：*There's a lot to be done, so let's get cracking.* 要做的工作很多，咱們馬上就幹吧。 **not all, everything, etc. sb's cracked ˈup to be** (*informal*) not as good as people say 不像人們說的那麼好：*He's not nearly such a good writer as he's cracked up to be.* 他遠不是人們所說的那種優秀作家。 **crack the ˈwhip** to use your authority or power to make sb work very hard, usually by treating them in a strict way 極度役使 ➲ more at NUT *n.*, SLEDGEHAMMER

PHR V **ˌcrack ˈdown** (**on sb/sth**) to try harder to prevent an illegal activity and deal more severely with those who are caught doing it 竭力取締；嚴厲打擊；鎮壓：*Police are cracking down on drug dealers.* 警方正在嚴厲打擊毒品販子。➲ related noun CRACKDOWN **ˌcrack ˈon** (**with sth**) (*BrE, informal*) to work hard at sth so that you finish it quickly; to pass or continue quickly（為儘快完成而）努力幹；（急速）經過，穿過；快速繼續下去：*If we crack on with the painting we should finish it today.* 只要我們拚命幹，今天應該就能刷完漆。◇ *Time was cracking on and we were nowhere near finished.* 時間飛

逝，可我們卻遠遠沒有完成。 **ˌcrack ˈup** (*informal*) **1** to become ill, either physically or mentally, because of pressure（因壓力造成身體或精神）垮掉，崩潰：*You'll crack up if you carry on working like this.* 你再這樣幹下去，身體會垮掉的。 **2** to start laughing a lot 開始大笑起來：*He walked in and everyone just cracked up.* 他一進來，人人都捧腹大笑起來。 **ˌcrack sb ˈup** (*informal*) to make sb laugh a lot 使大笑起來： *Gill's so funny, she just cracks me up.* 吉爾滑稽極了，逗得我哈哈大笑。

■ ***noun***

▸ **BREAK 裂縫** **1** [C] **~ (in sth)** a line on the surface of sth where it has broken but not split into separate parts 裂紋；裂縫：*This cup has a crack in it.* 這杯子有一道裂痕。◇ *Cracks began to appear in the walls.* 牆壁開始出現裂縫了。◇ (*figurative*) *The cracks* (= faults) *in the government's economic policy are already beginning to show.* 政府經濟政策中的失誤已開始顯露出來。➲ picture at BROKEN

▸ **NARROW OPENING 縫隙** **2** [C] a narrow space or opening 縫隙；狹縫；窄縫：*She peeped through the crack in the curtains.* 她透過窗簾的隙縫窺視。◇ *The door opened a crack* (= a small amount). 那門開了一條縫。

▸ **SOUND 聲響** **3** [C] a sudden loud noise（突然的）爆裂聲，劈啪聲：*a crack of thunder* 一聲霹靂 ◇ *the sharp crack of a rifle shot* 尖利的步槍聲

▸ **HIT 擊中** **4** [C] **~ (on sth)** a sharp blow that can be heard（可聽到響聲的）重擊，猛擊：*She fell over and got a nasty crack on the head.* 她跌倒了，腦袋重重地磕了一下。

▸ **ATTEMPT 嘗試** **5** [C] **~ (at sth) | ~ (at doing sth)** (*informal*) an occasion when you try to do sth 嘗試；試做 **SYN** **attempt**：*She hopes to have another crack at the world record this year.* 她希望今年再一次衝擊世界紀錄。

▸ **DRUG 毒品** **6** (also **ˌcrack coˈcaine**) [U] a powerful, illegal drug that is a form of COCAINE 強效可卡因；強力古柯鹼：*a crack addict* 吸強效可卡因成癮的人

▸ **JOKE 玩笑** **7** [C] (*informal*) a joke, especially a critical one（尤指挖苦人的）玩笑，俏皮話：*He made a very unfair crack about her looks.* 他開玩笑地損了一下她的長相，言語很是刻薄。

▸ **CONVERSATION 交談** **8** (also **craic**) [U, sing.] (*IrishE, informal*) a good time; friendly, enjoyable talk 好時光；友好愉快的交談：*Where's the crack tonight?* 今晚去哪裏逍遙？◇ *He's a person who enjoys a drink and a bit of crack.* 他是個喜歡喝兩杯又愛聊天的人。

IDM **at the crack of ˈdawn** (*informal*) very early in the morning 黎明；破曉；清晨 ➲ more at FAIR *adj.*

■ ***adj.*** [only before noun] expert and highly trained; excellent at sth 訓練有素的；技藝高超的；優秀的；一流的：*crack troops* 精鋭部隊 ◇ *He's a crack shot* (= accurate and skilled at shooting). 他是個神槍手。

crack·brained /ˈkrækbreɪnd/ *adj.* (*informal*) crazy and unlikely to succeed 瘋狂而難以成功的：*a crackbrained idea* 異想天開的想法

crack·down /ˈkrækdaʊn/ *noun* **~ (on sb/sth)** severe action taken to restrict the activities of criminals or of people opposed to the government or sb in authority 嚴厲的打擊；鎮壓：*a military crackdown on student protesters* 對抗議的學生實行的軍事鎮壓 ◇ *a crackdown on crime* 對犯罪的嚴厲打擊

cracked 🔑 /krækt/ *adj.*

1 🔑 damaged with lines in its surface but not completely broken 破裂的；有裂紋的：*a cracked mirror/mug* 破裂的鏡子／杯子 ◇ *He suffered cracked ribs and bruising.* 他斷了肋骨還有挫傷。◇ *She passed her tongue over her cracked lips and tried to speak.* 她用舌頭舔了一下乾裂的嘴唇，試圖要説話。➲ picture at BROKEN **2** (of sb's voice 嗓音) sounding rough with sudden changes in how loud or high it is, because the person is upset（因心煩意亂而突然）粗聲的，沙啞的：*'I'm just fine,' she said in a cracked voice.* "我真的挺好。" 她聲音沙啞地説道。 **3** [not before noun] (*informal*) crazy 瘋狂；發瘋：*I think he must be cracked, don't you?* 我認為他一定是瘋了，你説是不是？

Christmas cracker 彩包爆竹

crack·er /ˈkrækə(r)/ *noun* **1** a thin dry biscuit that is often salty and usually eaten with cheese 薄脆餅乾（多為鹹味，常與乾酪一起食用）➲ see also CREAM CRACKER, GRAHAM CRACKER **2** (also **ˌChristmas ˈcracker**) a tube of coloured paper that makes a loud EXPLOSIVE sound when it is pulled open by two people. Crackers usually contain a paper hat, a small present and a joke, and are used in Britain at Christmas parties and meals. 彩包爆竹，彩色拉炮（在英國用於聖誕聚會和聚餐，通常裝有紙帽、小禮品及笑話紙條）：*Who wants to pull this cracker with me?* 誰跟我拉響這個彩炮？➲ see also FIRECRACKER **3** (*BrE, informal*) something that you think is very good, funny, etc.（認為）十分愉快的事，滑稽可笑的事：*It was a cracker of a goal.* 這球進得真精彩。◇ *I've got a joke for you. It's a real cracker!* 我給你講個笑話。好笑死了！ **4** (*NAmE, slang*) an offensive word for a poor white person with little education from the southern US（對幾乎未受過教育的美國南方貧苦白人的輕蔑語）車把式 **5** (*informal*) a person who illegally finds a way of looking at or stealing information on sb else's computer system 快客，破密高手（非法瀏覽或竊取他人的計算機系統上的信息） **6** (*old-fashioned, BrE, informal*) an attractive woman 有魅力的女人；迷人的女子

crack·er·jack /ˈkrækədʒæk; *NAmE* -kərdʒæk/ *noun* (*NAmE, informal*) an excellent person or thing 出色的人；優質的東西 ▸ **crack·er·jack** *adj.*

crack·ers /ˈkrækəz; *NAmE* -kərz/ *adj.* [not before noun] (*BrE, informal*) crazy 瘋狂；發狂：*That noise is driving me crackers.* 那噪聲鬧得我簡直要瘋了。

crack·head /ˈkrækhed/ *noun* (*slang*) a person who uses the illegal drug CRACK 強效可卡因癮君子；強力古柯鹼癮君子

ˈcrack house *noun* a place where people sell CRACK (= a type of illegal drug) 強效可卡因毒品站；強力古柯鹼毒品站

crack·ing /ˈkrækɪŋ/ *noun, adj.*

■ ***noun*** [U] **1** lines on a surface where it is damaged or beginning to break 裂紋；裂縫；裂痕：*All planes are being inspected for possible cracking and corrosion.* 所有的飛機都在接受檢查，看是否有裂紋和腐蝕現象。 **2** the sound of sth cracking 爆裂聲；劈啪聲：*the cracking of thunder/twigs* 霹靂聲；細枝發出的劈啪聲

■ ***adj.*** [usually before noun] (*BrE, informal*) excellent 優秀的；出色的；極好的；頂呱呱的：*That was a cracking goal.* 這球進得真精彩。◇ *She's in cracking form at the moment.* 她這會兒狀態好極了。◇ *We set off* ***at a cracking pace*** (= very quickly). 我們迅速地出發了。 ▸ **crack·ing** *adv.*：*a cracking good* (= extremely good) *dinner* 一頓佳肴美餐

crackle /ˈkrækl/ *verb, noun*

■ ***verb*** [I] to make short sharp sounds like sth that is burning in a fire（像東西在火裏燃燒一樣）發爆裂聲，劈啪作響：*A log fire crackled in the hearth.* 爐中的木柴燒得劈啪作響。◇ *The radio crackled into life.* 收音機嘎嘎地響了起來。◇ (*figurative*) *The atmosphere crackled with tension.* 氣氛頓時緊張了起來。

■ ***noun*** [U, C] a series of short sharp sounds（一連串的）劈啪聲；劈里啪啦的響聲：*the distant crackle of machine-gun fire* 遠處機槍掃射的劈啪聲 ▸ **crack·ly** /ˈkrækli/ *adj.*：*She picked up the phone and heard a crackly voice saying: 'Sue here.'* 她拿起電話，聽到一個刺耳的聲音在説："我是蘇。"

crack·ling /ˈkræklɪŋ/ *noun* **1** [U, sing.] a series of sharp sounds（一連串的）爆裂聲，劈啪聲：*He could hear the crackling of burning trees.* 他可以聽見樹木燃燒發出的劈啪聲。 **2** [U] (*BrE*) (*US* **crack·lings** [pl.]) the hard skin of PORK (= meat from a pig) that has been cooked in the oven（烤豬肉的）脆皮

crack·pot /ˈkrækpɒt; *NAmE* -pɑːt/ *noun* (*informal*) a person with strange or crazy ideas 有古怪想法的人；怪人 ▶ **crack·pot** *adj.* [only before noun]：***crackpot ideas/theories*** 離奇古怪的想法 / 理論

-cracy *combining form* (in nouns 構成名詞) the government or rule of …的政府；…的統治：*democracy* 民主政體 ◇ *bureaucracy* 官僚體制

cra·dle /ˈkreɪdl/ *noun, verb*

■ *noun* **1** a small bed for a baby which can be pushed gently from side to side 搖籃：*She rocked the baby to sleep in its cradle.* 她搖動搖籃哄嬰兒入睡。➲ VISUAL VOCAB page V23 **2** [usually sing.] **~ of sth** the place where sth important began 策源地；發源地；發祥地：*Greece, the cradle of Western civilization* 希臘，西方文明的搖籃 **3** (*BrE*) a small platform that can be moved up and down the outside of a high building, used by people cleaning windows, etc. （高樓外供清潔窗戶等用的）吊架，托架，吊籃 **4** the part of a telephone on which the RECEIVER rests （電話機的）聽筒架，叉托支架

IDM **from the ˌcradle to the ˈgrave** a way of referring to the whole of a person's life, from birth until death 一生；一世；從生到死 ➲ more at ROB

■ *verb* **~ sb/sth** to hold sb/sth gently in your arms or hands 輕輕抱着：*The old man cradled the tiny baby in his arms.* 老漢把幼小的嬰兒輕輕抱在懷裏。

ˈcradle cap *noun* [U] a skin condition that causes dry rough yellow areas on top of a baby's head 乳痂

ˈcradle-snatcher (*BrE*) (*NAmE* **ˈcradle-robber**) *noun* (*disapproving*) a person who has a sexual relationship with a much younger person 與比自己年輕得多的人發生性關係者 ▶ **ˈcradle-snatch** (*BrE*) (*NAmE* **ˈcradle-rob**) *verb* [I]

craft 0┳ /krɑːft; *NAmE* kræft/ *noun, verb*

■ *noun* **1** 0┳ [C, U] an activity involving a special skill at making things with your hands 手藝；工藝：*traditional crafts like basket-weaving* 像編籃子之類的傳統工藝 ◇ *a **craft fair/workshop*** 手工藝品交易會 / 製作坊 ◇ *Craft, Design and Technology* (= a subject in some British schools) 工藝、設計與技術（英國某些學校中的科目）➲ see also ARTS AND CRAFTS **2** 0┳ [sing.] all the skills needed for a particular activity 技巧；技能；技藝：*chefs who learned their craft in top hotels* 在高級旅館學過烹調技藝的廚師 ◇ *the writer's craft* 寫作技巧 **3** [U] (*formal, disapproving*) skill in making people believe what you want them to believe 詭計；手腕；騙術：*He knew how to win by craft and diplomacy what he could not gain by force.* 他擅長於通過計謀和外交手腕贏得他用武力無法得到的東西。 **4** [C] (*pl.* **craft**) (*formal*) a boat or ship 小船；船：*Hundreds of small craft bobbed around the liner as it steamed into the harbour.* 班輪駛進港口時，周圍的許多小船顛簸起來。◇ *a **landing/pleasure craft*** 登陸艇；遊艇 **5** [C] (*pl.* **craft**) an aircraft or SPACECRAFT 飛行器；飛機；航天器；宇宙飛船；航天飛機

■ *verb* [usually passive] **~ sth** to make sth using special skills, especially with your hands （尤指用手工）精心製作 SYN **fashion**：*All the furniture is crafted from natural materials.* 所有的傢具均採用天然材料精心製作而成。◇ *a carefully crafted speech* 精心準備的講話 ➲ see also HANDCRAFTED

ˈcraft knife *noun* (*BrE*) a very sharp knife used for cutting paper or thin pieces of wood 裁紙刀；削木刀

crafts·man /ˈkrɑːftsmən; *NAmE* ˈkræf-/ (also **crafts·person**) *noun* (*pl.* **-men** /-mən/) a skilled person, especially one who makes beautiful things by hand 工匠；手藝人；工藝師：*rugs handmade by local craftsmen* 由當地工藝師手工製作的小地毯 ◇ *It is clearly the work of a master craftsman.* 很明顯這是工藝大師的作品。➲ see also CRAFTSWOMAN

crafts·man·ship /ˈkrɑːftsmənʃɪp; *NAmE* ˈkræf-/ *noun* [U] **1** the level of skill shown by sb in making sth beautiful with their hands 手藝；技藝：*The whole house is a monument to her craftsmanship.* 那整座房子是她技藝的一座豐碑。 **2** the quality of design and work shown by sth that has been made by hand 精工細作：*the superb craftsmanship of the carvings* 這些雕刻品的一流工藝

crafts·person /ˈkrɑːftspɜːsn; *NAmE* ˈkræftspɜːrsn/ *noun* (*pl.* **-people** /-piːpl/) = CRAFTSMAN

crafts·woman /ˈkrɑːftswʊmən; *NAmE* ˈkræf-/ *noun* (*pl.* **-women** /-wɪmɪn/) a skilled woman, especially one who makes beautiful things by hand 女工匠；女手藝人；女巧匠；女工藝師 ➲ note at GENDER

craft·work /ˈkrɑːftwɜːk; *NAmE* ˈkræftwɜːrk/ *noun* [U] work done by a CRAFTSMAN 工藝品

crafty /ˈkrɑːfti; *NAmE* ˈkræfti/ *adj.* (**craft·ier**, **crafti·est**) (usually *disapproving*) clever at getting what you want, especially by indirect or dishonest methods 巧妙的；（尤指）狡詐的，詭計多端的 SYN **cunning, wily**：*He's a crafty old devil.* 他是個奸詐狡猾的老傢伙。◇ *one of the party's craftiest political strategists* 這個政黨最精明的政治策略家之一 ▶ **craft·ily** *adv.* **crafti·ness** *noun* [U]

crag /kræg/ *noun* a high steep rough mass of rock 懸崖；峭壁；絕壁：*a castle set on a crag above the village* 位於村子上方懸崖上的城堡

craggy /ˈkrægi/ *adj.* **1** having many crags 多峭壁的；峻峭的：*a craggy coastline* 陡峭的海岸 **2** (usually *approving*) (of a man's face 男人的臉) having strong features and deep lines 輪廓分明有皺紋的

craic *noun* = CRACK (8)

cram /kræm/ *verb* (**-mm-**) **1** [T, I] to push or force sb/sth into a small space; to move into a small space with the result that it is full 把…塞進；擠滿；塞滿：**~ sb/sth into/onto sth** *He crammed eight people into his car.* 他往他的車裏硬塞進八個人。◇ **~ sth in** *I could never cram in all that she does in a day.* 我可做不了她在一天之內所做的事情。◇ **~ sth + adv./prep.** *I managed to cram down a few mouthfuls of food.* 我好歹狼吞虎嚥地吃了幾口東西。◇ **~ sth** *Supporters crammed the streets.* 街上擠滿了支持者。◇ **~ sth full** *I bought a large basket and crammed it full of presents.* 我買了個大籃子，然後把它裝滿禮物。◇ **~ into/onto sth** *We all managed to cram into his car.* 我們大家好歹都擠進了他的車。 **2** [I] **~ (for sth)** (*NAmE, informal* or rather *old-fashioned, BrE*) to learn a lot of things in a short time, in preparation for an exam （為應考）臨時死記硬背 SYN **swot**：*He's been cramming for his exams all week.* 他整個星期都一直在拚命準備應考。

crammed /kræmd/ *adj.* **1 ~ (with sb/sth)** full of things or people 塞滿的；擠滿的 SYN **packed**：*All the shelves were crammed with books.* 所有的架子上都堆滿了書。◇ *The room was **crammed full** of people.* 房間裏擠滿了人。◇ *The article was **crammed full** of ideas.* 這篇文章包含着許多想法。 **2** [not before noun] **~ (with sb/sth)** if people are **crammed** into a place, there is not much room for them in it 擁擠不堪 SYN **packed**：*We were crammed four to an office.* 我們四個人擠在一間辦公室裏。

cram·mer /ˈkræmə(r)/ *noun* (*BrE*) a school or book that prepares people quickly for exams （應付考試的）強化訓練補習學校；（為應付考試而編寫的）強化訓練用書

cramp /kræmp/ *noun, verb*

■ *noun* **1** [U, C] (*NAmE* also **ˈcharley horse**) a sudden pain that you get when the muscles in a particular part of your body contract, usually caused by cold or too much exercise 痛性痙攣；抽筋：(*BrE*) *to get cramp in your leg* 腿部抽筋 ◇ (*NAmE*) *to get a cramp in your leg* 腿部抽筋 ➲ see also WRITER'S CRAMP **2 cramps** [pl.] severe pain in the stomach （腹部）絞痛

■ *verb* **~ sth** to prevent the development or progress of sb/sth 阻礙，阻止（發展或進步）SYN **restrict**：*Tighter trade restrictions might cramp economic growth.* 較嚴格的貿易限制會妨礙經濟的增長。

IDM **cramp sb's ˈstyle** (*informal*) to stop sb from behaving in the way they want to 束縛…的手腳；使不能放開手腳（或施展才能）

cramped /kræmpt/ *adj.* **1** a **cramped** room, etc. does not have enough space for the people in it 狹窄的；狹小的：*working in cramped conditions* 在擁擠的環境裏工作 **2** (of people 人) not having room to move freely 擁擠的；缺少自由活動空間的 **3** (of sb's writing 字跡) with small letters close together and therefore difficult to read 密小難認的；密密麻麻的

C

cram·pon /'kræmpɒn; *NAmE* -pɑːn/ *noun* [usually pl.] a metal plate with pointed pieces of metal underneath, worn on sb's shoes when they are walking or climbing on ice and snow 帶釘鐵鞋底（用以在冰雪上行走或攀登）

cran·berry /'krænbəri; *NAmE* -beri/ *noun* (*pl.* **-ies**) a small sour red BERRY that grows on a small bush and is used in cooking 越橘，小紅莓（用於烹飪）: *cranberry sauce* 越橘調味汁

crane /kreɪn/ *noun, verb*

■ *noun* **1** a tall machine with a long arm, used to lift and move building materials and other heavy objects 起重機；吊車 ➲ VISUAL VOCAB pages V2, V3 **2** a large bird with long legs and a long neck 鶴 ➲ see also BLUE CRANE

■ *verb* [I, T] to lean or stretch over sth in order to see sth better; to stretch your neck（為看得更清楚而）探着身子；伸長（脖子）: (+ **adv./prep.**) *People were craning out of the windows and waving.* 人們把頭探出窗外揮手致意。◇ **~ sth** *She **craned her neck** to get a better view of the stage.* 她伸長了脖子看舞台，好看清楚些。

'crane fly (also *informal* **,daddy-'long-legs**) *noun* a flying insect with very long legs 大蚊（腿長）

cra·nium /'kreɪniəm/ *noun* (*pl.* **cra·ni·ums** or **cra·nia** /'kreɪniə/) (*anatomy* 解) the bone structure that forms the head and surrounds and protects the brain 顱骨；頭蓋骨 SYN **skull** ➲ VISUAL VOCAB page V59 ▸ **cra·nial** /'kreɪniəl/ *adj.* [only before noun]: *cranial nerves/injuries* 顱神經／外傷

crank /kræŋk/ *noun, verb*

■ *noun* **1** (*disapproving*) a person with ideas that other people find strange（想法）古怪的人 SYN **eccentric**: *Vegetarians are no longer dismissed as cranks.* 素食者不再被視為有怪癖的人。**2** (*NAmE*) a person who easily gets angry or annoyed 脾氣壞的人；容易惱怒的人 **3** a bar and handle in the shape of an L that you pull or turn to produce movement in a machine, etc.（L字形）曲柄，曲軸 ➲ VISUAL VOCAB page V51

■ *verb* **~ sth (up)** to make sth turn or move by using a crank 用曲柄轉動（或啟動）: *to crank an engine* 用曲柄發動引擎 ◇ (*figurative*) *He has a limited time to crank the reforms into action.* 他推動各項改革的時間很有限。

PHR V **,crank sth↔'out** (*informal*) to produce a lot of sth quickly, especially things of low quality 快速地大量製造；（尤指）粗製濫造 SYN **turn out** **,crank sth↔'up** (*informal*) **1** to make a machine, etc. work or work at a higher level 使機器運轉；使…提高效率 **2** to make music, etc. louder（把音樂等的音量）開大，調高 SYN **turn up**: *Crank up the volume!* 把音量放大些！

crank·shaft /'kræŋkʃɑːft; *NAmE* -ʃæft/ *noun* (*technical* 術語) a long piece of metal in a vehicle that connects the engine to the wheels and helps turn the engine's power into movement 曲軸；曲柄軸

cranky /'kræŋki/ *adj.* (*informal*) **1** (*BrE*) strange 古怪的；怪異的 SYN **eccentric**: ***cranky ideas/schemes*** 離奇古怪的想法／計劃 **2** (*especially NAmE*) bad-tempered 脾氣壞的: *The kids were getting tired and a little cranky.* 孩子們越來越累，脾氣也有些變壞了。

cranny /'kræni/ *noun* (*pl.* **-ies**) a very small hole or opening, especially in a wall（尤指牆上的）小孔，縫隙，裂縫 IDM see NOOK

crap /kræp/ *noun, adj., verb*

■ *noun* (*taboo, slang*) **1** [U] nonsense 廢話；胡說；胡扯: *He's so full of crap.* 他淨胡說八道。◇ *Let's **cut the crap** and get down to business.* 咱們別說廢話了，開始幹正事吧。◇ (*BrE*) *You're talking a **load of crap**!* 你這是一派胡言！◇ (*NAmE*) *What a **bunch of crap**!* 真是廢話連篇！**2** [U] something of bad quality 質量差的東西；蹩腳貨: *This work is complete crap.* 這件作品蹩腳透頂。◇ (*BrE*) *Her latest film is a **load of crap**.* 她最近的一部電影很糟糕。◇ (*NAmE*) *Her latest movie is a **bunch of crap**.* 她最近的一部電影很糟糕。HELP More acceptable words are **rubbish**, **garbage**, **trash** or **junk**. 更常用的詞有 rubbish、garbage、trash 或 junk。**3** [U] criticism or unfair treatment 批評；非難；不公正的待遇: *I'm not going to take this crap any more.* 我再也不受這種委屈了。**4** [U] solid waste matter from the BOWELS 屎 SYN **excrement** **5** [sing.] an act of emptying solid waste matter from the BOWELS 拉屎: *to have a crap* 拉屎 IDM see BUG *v.*

■ *adj.* (*BrE, taboo, slang*) bad; of very bad quality 壞的；糟糕的；劣質的: *a crap band* 很差勁的樂隊 ◇ *The concert was crap.* 那場音樂會演得很差。▸ **crap** *adv.*: *The team played crap yesterday.* 這個隊昨天的表現很差勁。

■ *verb* (**-pp-**) [I] (*taboo, slang*) to empty solid waste from the BOWELS 拉屎 SYN **defecate** HELP A more polite way of expressing this is 'to go to the toilet/lavatory' (*BrE*), 'to go to the bathroom' (*NAmE*), or 'to go'. A more formal expression is 'to empty the bowels'. 比較有禮貌的表達方式為 to go to the toilet/lavatory（英式英語）、to go to the bathroom（美式英語）或 to go。比較正式的表達方式為 to empty the bowels。

crappy /'kræpi/ *adj.* (**crap·pier**, **crap·pi·est**) [usually before noun] (*slang*) of very bad quality 劣質的；蹩腳的: *a crappy novel* 粗製濫造的小說

craps /kræps/ *noun* [U] (*NAmE*) a gambling game played with two DICE 雙骰子賭博戲: *to **shoot craps*** (= play this game) 擲雙骰子賭博 ▸ **crap** *adj.* [only before noun]: *a crap game* 擲雙骰子的賭博

crap·shoot /'kræpʃuːt/ *noun* (*NAmE*) **1** a game of CRAPS 雙骰子賭博戲 **2** (*informal*) a situation whose success or result is based on luck rather than on effort or careful organization 碰運氣的事

crash 0-w /kræʃ/ *noun, verb, adj.*

■ *noun*

▸ VEHICLE ACCIDENT 交通事故 **1** 0-w (*NAmE* also **wreck**) an accident in which a vehicle hits sth, for example another vehicle, usually causing damage and often injuring or killing the passengers 撞車；碰撞；相撞: *A girl was killed yesterday in a crash involving a stolen car.* 昨天有個女孩在一樁涉及竊車撞車的事故中喪生。◇ *a car/plane crash* 汽車撞車事故；飛機失事 ➲ COLLOCATIONS at DRIVING

▸ LOUD NOISE 巨響 **2** 0-w [usually sing.] a sudden loud noise made, for example, by sth falling or breaking（倒下、破碎等突然的）碰撞聲，破裂聲，碎裂聲: *The tree fell with a great crash.* 那棵樹嘩啦一聲倒了。◇ *The first distant crash of thunder shook the air.* 遠處的第一聲霹靂震撼了天空。

▸ IN FINANCE/BUSINESS 金融；商業 **3** 0-w a sudden serious fall in the price or value of sth; the occasion when a business, etc. fails 暴跌；倒閉；破產；失敗 SYN **collapse**: *the 1987 stock market crash* * 1987 年的股票市場暴跌

▸ COMPUTING 計算機技術 **4** 0-w a sudden failure of a machine or system, especially of a computer or computer system（機器或系統，尤指計算機或計算機系統的）崩潰

■ *verb*

▸ OF VEHICLE 交通工具 **1** 0-w [I, T] if a vehicle **crashes** or the driver **crashes** it, it hits an object or another vehicle, causing damage 碰撞；撞擊: *I was terrified that the plane would crash.* 飛機會失事把我嚇壞了。◇ *We're going to crash, aren't we?* 我們要墜毀了，是不是？◇ **~ into sth** *A truck went out of control and crashed into the back of a bus.* 貨車失控撞上了一輛公共汽車的尾部。◇ **~ sth (into sth)** *He crashed his car into a wall.* 他的汽車撞到了牆上。

▸ HIT HARD/LOUD NOISE 猛撞；巨響 **2** 0-w [I, T] to hit sth hard while moving, causing noise and/or damage; to make sth hit sb/sth in this way（使）猛撞，碰撞: **+ adv./prep.** *A brick crashed through the window.* 磚塊嘩啦一聲砸入了窗戶。◇ *With a sweep of his hand he sent the glasses crashing to the floor.* 他一揮手把眼鏡摔到地上摔碎了。◇ **+ adj.** *The door crashed open.* 那門砰的一聲給砸開了。◇ **~ sth + adj.** *She stormed out of the room and crashed the door shut behind her.* 她憤怒地衝出房間並隨手把門砰的一聲關上。**3** 0-w [I] to make a loud noise 使發出巨響: *Thunder crashed overhead.* 頭頂上雷聲隆隆。

▸ IN FINANCE/BUSINESS 金融；商業 **4** 0-w [I] (of prices, a business, shares, etc. 價格、業務、股票等) to lose value or fail suddenly and quickly（突然）贬值，倒闭，失败；暴跌： *Share prices crashed to an all-time low yesterday.* 昨天股票價格暴跌到了前所未有的最低紀錄。◇ *The company crashed with debts of £50 million.* 那家公司由於負債 5 000 萬英鎊而告破產。

▸ COMPUTING 計算機技術 **5** [I, T] ~ (sth) if a computer **crashes** or you **crash** a computer, it stops working suddenly 崩潰： *Files can be lost if the system suddenly crashes.* 要是計算機系統突然崩潰，文件就可能丟失。

▸ PARTY 聚會 **6** [T] ~ sth (*informal*) = GATECRASH

▸ IN SPORT 體育運動 **7** [I] (+ adv./prep) (*especially BrE*) to lose very badly in a sports game（比賽中）潰敗，慘敗： *The team crashed to their worst defeat this season.* 那支隊在這個賽季中輸得最慘。

▸ SLEEP 睡覺 **8** [I] ~ (out) (*informal*) to fall asleep; to sleep somewhere you do not usually sleep 入睡；（在不常睡覺的地方）睡覺： *I was so tired I crashed out on the sofa.* 我累極了，在沙發上就睡着了。◇ *I've come to crash on your floor for a couple of nights.* 我來你家打幾個晚上的地鋪。

▸ MEDICAL 醫學 **9** [I] if sb **crashes**, their heart stops beating 心臟停止跳動

IDM **a crashing 'bore** (*old-fashioned, BrE*) a very boring person 討厭透頂的人

PHR V **,crash 'out (of sth)** (*sport* 體) (*BrE*) to lose a game with the result that you have to stop playing in a competition 被淘汰： *They crashed out of the World Cup after a 2-1 defeat to Brazil.* 他們以 1:2 輸給巴西隊之後在世界杯賽中淘汰出局。

■ *adj.* [only before noun] involving hard work or a lot of effort over a short period of time in order to achieve quick results 應急的；速成的： *a crash course in computer programming* 計算機編程速成課程 ◇ *a crash diet* 快速減肥規定飲食

'crash barrier (*BrE*) (*NAmE* **'guard rail**) *noun* a strong low fence or wall at the side of a road or between the two halves of a major road such as a MOTORWAY or INTERSTATE（高速公路或州際公路上的）防撞護欄，防撞牆

'crash helmet *noun* a hat made of very strong material and worn when riding a motorcycle to protect the head（騎摩托車的）防護頭盔，安全帽 ➲ VISUAL VOCAB page V65

'crash-land *verb* [I, T] ~ (sth) if a plane **crash-lands** or a pilot **crash-lands** it, the pilot lands it roughly in an emergency, usually because it is damaged and cannot land normally 緊急降落；強行着陸 ▸ **,crash 'landing** *noun*： *to make a crash landing* 實施緊急着陸

'crash-test *verb* ~ sth to deliberately crash a new vehicle under controlled conditions in order to test how it reacts or to improve its safety 撞擊試驗（檢驗新車反應或改進安全性能）▸ **'crash test** *noun*

,crash-test 'dummy *noun* a model of a person used in crash tests to see what would happen to a driver or passenger in a real crash 撞擊試驗假人（當作駕駛者或乘客）

crass /kræs/ *adj.* very stupid and showing no sympathy or understanding 愚蠢而無同情心的 SYN **insensitive**： *the crass questions all disabled people get asked* 所有殘疾人都會碰到的愚蠢而缺乏同情心的提問 ◇ *an act of crass* (= great) *stupidity* 愚不可及的行為 ▸ **crass·ly** *adv.* **crass·ness** *noun* [U]

-crat *combining form* (in nouns 構成名詞) a member or supporter of a particular type of government or system（某政體或體制的）成員，支持者： *democrat* 民主主義者 ◇ *bureaucrat* 官僚主義者 ▸ **-cratic** (in adjectives 構成形容詞)： *aristocratic* 貴族的

crate /kreɪt/ *noun, verb*

■ *noun* **1** a large wooden container for transporting goods 大木箱，板條箱（運貨用）： *a crate of bananas* 一箱香蕉 **2** a container made of plastic or metal divided into small sections, for transporting or storing bottles 塑料分格箱，金屬分格箱（運送或存放瓶子用）： *a beer crate* 啤酒箱 **3** the amount of sth contained in a crate 一箱（的量）： *They drank two crates of beer.* 他們喝了兩箱啤酒。

■ *verb* ~ sth (up) to pack sth in a crate 把…裝入大木箱（或板條箱、分格箱）

Synonyms 同義詞辨析

crash

slam • collide • smash • wreck

These are all words that can be used when sth, especially a vehicle, hits sth else very hard and is damaged or destroyed. 以上各詞均含碰撞、撞擊之意，尤指撞車。

crash (*rather informal*) to hit an object or another vehicle, causing damage; to make a vehicle do this 指（使）物體或交通工具碰撞或撞擊： *I was terrified that the plane would crash.* 我很害怕飛機會失事。

slam (sth) into/against sb/sth to crash into sth with a lot of force; to make sth do this 指（使）重重地撞上： *The car skidded and slammed into a tree.* 汽車打滑，嘭的一聲撞到樹上。

collide (*rather formal*) (of two vehicles or people) to crash into each other; (of a vehicle or person) to crash into sb/sth else 指交通工具或人碰撞、相撞或撞上： *The car and the van collided head-on in thick fog.* 那輛小轎車和貨車在濃霧中迎面相撞。

smash (*rather informal*) to crash into sth with a lot of force; to make sth do this; to crash a car 指（使）猛烈撞擊、猛烈碰撞或撞車： *Ramraiders smashed a stolen car through the shop window.* 飆車搶劫者駕着偷來的汽車撞破商店櫥窗。

CRASH, SLAM OR SMASH? 用 crash、slam 還是 smash？

Crash is used especially to talk about vehicles and can be used without a preposition. * crash 尤指車輛碰撞，可不與介詞連用： *We're going to crash, aren't we?* 我們要墜毀了，是不是？ In this meaning **slam** and **smash** always take a preposition. * slam 和 smash 表示此義時總是與介詞連用： ~~*We're going to slam/smash, aren't we?*~~ They are used for a much wider range of things than just vehicles. **Crash** can also be used for other things, if used with a preposition. 兩詞均可用於除交通工具外的範圍更廣的事物。crash 與介詞連用也可用於其他事物： *He crashed down the telephone receiver.* 他砰的一聲將電話聽筒摔下來。

wreck to crash a vehicle and damage it so badly that it is not worth repairing 指使交通工具徹底毀壞

PATTERNS

- **two vehicles** crash/collide
- **two vehicles** crash/slam/smash **into each other**
- to crash/smash/wreck **a car**

crater /'kreɪtə(r)/ *noun* **1** a large hole in the top of a VOLCANO 火山口 **2** a large hole in the ground caused by the explosion of a bomb or by sth large hitting it（由炸彈爆炸或巨物撞擊形成的）坑： *a meteorite crater* 隕石坑

cra·vat /krə'væt/ (*NAmE* also **ascot**) *noun* a short wide strip of silk, etc. worn by men around the neck, folded inside the COLLAR of a shirt（男用）闊領帶

crave /kreɪv/ *verb* **1** [T, I] ~ (for) sth | ~ to do sth to have a very strong desire for sth 渴望；熱望 SYN **long for**： *She has always craved excitement.* 她總盼望得到刺激。 **2** [T] ~ sth (*BrE, old use*) to ask for sth seriously 懇求；請求： *I must crave your pardon.* 我必須懇求您原諒。

cra·ven /'kreɪvn/ *adj.* (*formal, disapproving*) lacking courage 膽小的；膽怯的；怯懦的 SYN **cowardly** OPP **brave** ▸ **craven·ly** *adv.*

crav·ing /'kreɪvɪŋ/ *noun* a strong desire for sth 強烈的願望；渴望；熱望： ~ (for sth) *a craving for chocolate* 非常想吃巧克力 ◇ ~ (to do sth) *a desperate craving to be loved* 對被愛的極度渴望

craw /krɔː/ *noun* the part of a bird's throat where food is kept（禽的）嗉囊，嗉子 IDM see STICK *v.*

C

craw·fish /ˈkrɔːfɪʃ/ *noun* (*especially NAmE*) = CRAYFISH

crawl /krɔːl/ *verb, noun*

■ *verb* **1** [I] (+ **adv./prep.**) to move forward on your hands and knees, with your body close to the ground 爬；爬行；匍匐行進：*Our baby is just starting to crawl.* 我們的寶寶剛開始會爬。◇ *A man was crawling away from the burning wreckage.* 一個男人正從燃燒着的殘骸爬着往外逃。**2** [I] (+ **adv./prep.**) when an insect **crawls**, it moves forward on its legs （昆蟲）爬行：*There's a spider crawling up your leg.* 有隻蜘蛛正順着你的腿往上爬。**3** [I] (+ **adv./prep.**) to move forward very slowly 緩慢行進：*The traffic was crawling along.* 來往車輛緩緩而行。◇ *The weeks crawled by.* 幾個星期慢慢地過去了。**4** [I] **~ (to sb)** (*informal, disapproving*) to be too friendly or helpful to sb in authority, in a way that is not sincere, especially in order to get an advantage from them 卑躬屈膝；諂媚；巴結；拍馬屁：*She's always crawling to the boss.* 她對老闆總是諂媚奉承。IDM see SKIN *n.*, WOODWORK

PHR V **be 'crawling with sth** (*informal*) to be full of or completely covered with people, insects or animals, in a way that is unpleasant 擠滿；爬滿：*The place was crawling with journalists.* 這地方擠滿了記者。◇ *Her hair was crawling with lice.* 她的頭髮上爬滿了虱子。

■ *noun* **1** [sing.] a very slow speed 緩慢的速度：*The traffic slowed to a crawl.* 來往的車輛放緩速度慢慢前行。➲ see also PUB CRAWL **2** (often **the crawl**) [sing., U] a fast swimming stroke that you do lying on your front moving one arm over your head, and then the other, while kicking with your feet 爬泳；自由泳：*a swimmer doing the crawl* 游自由泳的運動員 ➲ VISUAL VOCAB page V45

crawl·er /ˈkrɔːlə(r)/ *noun* (*informal*) **1** (*BrE, disapproving*) a person who tries to get sb's favour by praising them, doing what will please them, etc. 奴顏婢膝的人；馬屁精 **2** a thing or person that crawls, such as a vehicle, an insect or a baby 爬行物（如車輛、昆蟲等）；爬行的人（如嬰兒等）➲ see also KERB-CRAWLER

cray·fish /ˈkreɪfɪʃ/ (*especially BrE*) (also **craw·fish** *NAmE, BrE*) *noun* [C, U] (*pl.* **cray·fish**, **craw·fish**) an animal like a small LOBSTER, that lives in rivers and lakes and can be eaten, or one like a large lobster, that lives in the sea and can be eaten 淡水螯蝦；海水大龍蝦

crayon /ˈkreɪən/ *noun* a coloured pencil or stick of soft coloured CHALK or WAX, used for drawing 彩色鉛筆（或粉筆、蠟筆）▸ **crayon** *verb* [I, T] **~ (sth)**

craze /kreɪz/ *noun* **~ (for sth)** an enthusiastic interest in sth that is shared by many people but that usually does not last very long; a thing that people have a craze for （通常為一時的）狂熱，瘋狂；風行一時的東西 SYN **fad**：*the latest fitness craze to sweep the country* 最近風靡全國的健身熱

crazed /kreɪzd/ *adj.* **~ (with sth)** (*formal*) full of strong feelings and lacking control 瘋狂的；發狂的：***crazed with fear/grief/jealousy*** 害怕／傷心／嫉妒得發瘋 ◇ *a **crazed killer** roaming the streets* 在街上遊蕩的喪心病狂的殺手

crazy 0- /ˈkreɪzi/ *adj., noun*

■ *adj.* (**cra·zier**, **crazi·est**) (*informal*) **1** 0- (*especially NAmE*) not sensible; stupid 不理智的；瘋狂的；愚蠢的；傻的：*Are you crazy? We could get killed doing that.* 你瘋了？我們那樣做會喪命的。◇ *She must be crazy to lend him money.* 她把錢借給他，一定是瘋了。◇ *He drove like an idiot, passing in the craziest places.* 他像白痴一樣淨把車往最不可思議的地方開。◇ *What a crazy idea!* 這個想法真荒唐！◇ *I know it sounds crazy but it just might work.* 我知道這事聽起來很蠢，然而也許就會奏效。**2** 0- very angry 非常氣憤：*That noise is **driving me crazy**.* 那噪聲吵得我快發瘋了。◇ *Marie says he **went crazy**, and smashed the room up.* 瑪麗說他氣得發瘋，把房間裏的東西都砸碎了。**3** 0- **~ (about sth)** (often in compounds 常構成複合詞) very enthusiastic or excited about sth 熱衷的；狂熱的：*Rick is crazy about football.* 里克對足球着了迷。◇ *He's football-crazy.* 他是個足球迷。◇ *I'm not crazy about Chinese food* (= I don't like it very much). 我並不十分熱衷於中國菜。◇ *The crowd **went crazy** when the band came on stage.* 樂隊出場時，觀眾欣喜若狂。◇ *You're so beautiful you're **driving me crazy**.* 你真美，弄得我神魂顛倒了。**4** 0- **~ about sb** liking sb very much; in love with sb 迷戀的；愛上的：*I've been crazy about him since the first time I saw him.* 我從第一次見面就愛上他了。**5** 0- (*especially NAmE*) mentally ill; INSANE 患精神病的；精神失常（或錯亂）的：*She's crazy—she ought to be locked up.* 她瘋了，應該把她關起來。➲ SYNONYMS at MAD ▸ **crazi·ly** *adv.* **cra·zi·ness** *noun* [U]

IDM **like 'crazy/'mad** (*informal*) very fast, hard, much, etc. 非常快地；拚命地；瘋狂地：*We worked like crazy to get it done on time.* 我們拚命地幹，好按時完成這項工作。

■ *noun* (*pl.* **-ies**) (*informal, especially NAmE*) a crazy person 瘋子

ˌcrazy ˈgolf *noun* [U] (*BrE*) = MINIGOLF

ˌcrazy ˈpaving *noun* [U] (*BrE*) pieces of stone of different shapes and sizes, fitted together on the ground to make a path or PATIO 用不規則形狀的石塊拼鋪的小路（或露台、天井、庭院）

ˌcrazy ˈquilt *noun* (*NAmE*) a type of QUILT in which small pieces of cloth of different shape, colour, design and size are sewn together 百衲被 ➲ compare PATCHWORK

CRE /ˌsiː ɑːr ˈiː/ *abbr.* Commission for Racial Equality (a government organization in Britain that protects the rights of people of all races) 種族平等委員會（英國維護各族人民權益的政府機構）

creak /kriːk/ *verb, noun*

■ *verb* [I] to make the sound that a door sometimes makes when you open it or that a wooden floor sometimes makes when you step on it 嘎吱作響（開門或踩上木地板等時發出的聲音）：*She heard a floorboard creak upstairs.* 她聽見樓上的地板發出嘎吱嘎吱的響聲。◇ *a creaking **bed/gate/stair*** 嘎吱作響的牀／大門／樓梯 ◇ *The table creaked and groaned under the weight.* 那張桌子在重壓下嘎吱嘎吱作響。◇ **+ adj.** *The door creaked open.* 門嘎吱一聲開了。

IDM **ˌcreak under the ˈstrain** if a system or service **creaks under the strain**, it cannot deal effectively with all the things it is expected to do or provide 因負擔過重而效率低下；由於壓力過大而運轉不靈

■ *noun* [C] (also **creak·ing** [U, C]) a sound, for example that sometimes made by a door when it opens or shuts, or by a wooden floor when you step on it 嘎吱聲：*the creak/creaking of the door* 門的嘎吱聲 ◇ *Distant creaks and groans echoed eerily along the dark corridors.* 遠處嘎吱嘎吱的聲音回響在漆黑的走廊裏，怪可怕的。

creaky /ˈkriːki/ *adj.* **1** making creaks 嘎吱作響的：*a creaky old chair* 嘎吱作響的舊椅子 **2** old and not in good condition 老朽的；破舊的；搖搖欲墜的：*the country's creaky legal machinery* 這個國家搖搖欲墜的司法機構

cream 0- /kriːm/ *noun, adj., verb*

■ *noun* **1** 0- [U] the thick pale yellowish-white FATTY liquid that rises to the top of milk, used in cooking or as a type of sauce to put on fruit, etc. 奶油；乳脂：*strawberries and cream* 加奶油的草莓 ◇ *Would you like milk or cream in your coffee?* 你的咖啡裏要牛奶還是奶油？◇ ***fresh/whipped cream*** 新鮮的／攪打過的奶油 ◇ (*BrE*) *cream cakes* (= containing cream) 奶油蛋糕 ◇ (*BrE*) ***double/single cream*** (= thick/thin cream) 濃／稀奶油 ➲ see also CLOTTED CREAM, ICE CREAM, SALAD CREAM, SOUR CREAM, WHIPPING CREAM **2** [C] (in compounds 構成複合詞) a sweet/candy that has a soft substance like cream inside 奶油夾心糖：*a **chocolate/peppermint cream*** 巧克力／薄荷奶油夾心糖 **3** 0- [U, C] a soft substance or thick liquid used on your skin to protect it or make it feel soft; a similar substance used for cleaning things 護膚霜；潔淨劑；清洗液：*hand/moisturizing cream* 護手霜；潤膚霜 ◇ *antiseptic cream* 抗菌藥膏 ◇ *a cream cleaner* 乳液清潔劑 ➲ see also COLD CREAM, FACE CREAM, SHAVING CREAM **4** 0- [U] a pale yellowish-white colour 奶油色；淡黃色；米色 **5 the ~ of sth** the best people or things in a particular group 精英；精華；精髓：*the cream of New York society* 紐約社會的精英 ◇ ***the cream of the crop** of this season's movies* 本季電影的最佳影片 IDM see CAT

■ *adj.* 🔑 pale yellowish-white in colour 奶油色的；淡黃色的；米色的： *a cream linen suit* 米色的亞麻布套裝

■ *verb* **1 ~ sth (together)** to mix things together into a soft smooth mixture 把…攪成糊狀（或奶油狀）混合物： *Cream the butter and sugar together.* 把黃油和糖攪成糊狀。 **2 ~ sb** (*NAmE, informal*) to completely defeat sb 徹底打敗；狠揍： *We got creamed in the first round.* 我們在第一輪就被徹底打敗了。

PHR V **ˌcream sb/sth↔ˈoff** to take sth away, usually the best people or things or an amount of money, in order to get an advantage for yourself 提取（精華）；選取（最好的人或物）；取走（某數額的金錢）： *The best students were creamed off by the grammar schools.* 最好的學生都已被文法學校錄取。

ˌcream ˈcheese *noun* [U, C] soft white cheese containing a lot of cream 奶油乾酪

ˌcream ˈcracker *noun* (*BrE*) a dry biscuit, often eaten with cheese 奶油餅乾（常與奶酪一起食用）

cream·er /ˈkriːmə(r)/ *noun* **1** [U] a liquid or powder that you can put in coffee, etc. instead of cream or milk （替代奶油或牛奶的可放入咖啡等中的）拌末，植脂末，咖啡伴侶： *non-dairy creamer* 不含奶的植脂末 **2** [C] (*NAmE*) a small container for holding and pouring cream 小奶油壺；小奶油罐；小奶油瓶

cream·ery /ˈkriːməri/ *noun* (*pl.* **-ies**) a place where milk and cream are made into butter and cheese 乳品廠

ˌcream ˈpuff *noun* (*NAmE*) **1** = PROFITEROLE **2** (*slang, disapproving*) a person who is not strong or brave 弱者；懦夫 **SYN** **wimp**

ˌcream ˈsoda *noun* [U, C] (*especially NAmE*) a FIZZY drink (= one with bubbles) that tastes of VANILLA 奶油蘇打水

ˌcream ˈtea *noun* (*BrE*) a special meal eaten in the afternoon, consisting of tea with SCONES, jam and thick cream （下午進食的）奶油茶點

creamy /ˈkriːmi/ *adj.* (**cream·ier**, **creami·est**) **1** thick and smooth like cream; containing a lot of cream 像奶油的；光滑細膩的；含乳脂的： *a* ***creamy sauce/soup*** 奶油沙司／湯羹 **2** pale yellowish-white in colour 奶油色的；淡黃色的；米色的： *creamy skin* 淡黃色的皮膚

crease /kriːs/ *noun, verb*

■ *noun* **1** an untidy line that is made in cloth or paper when it is pressed or crushed 褶痕；皺痕： *She smoothed the creases out of her skirt.* 她把裙子上的皺褶弄平。◇ *a shirt made of crease-resistant material* 用防皺布料製造的襯衫 **2** a neat line that you make in sth, for example when you fold it 褶縫；褶線： *trousers with a sharp crease in the legs* 褲線筆挺的褲子 ➲ VISUAL VOCAB page V61 **3** a line in the skin, especially on the face （皮膚上，尤指臉上的）皺紋： *creases around the eyes* 眼睛周圍的皺紋 **4** (in CRICKET 板球) a white line on the ground near each WICKET that marks the position of the BOWLER and the BATSMAN （投球手和擊球手的）位置線，區域線，擊球線

■ *verb* **1** [T, I] **~ (sth)** to make lines on cloth or paper by folding or crushing it; to develop lines in this way 弄皺；壓褶；（使）起褶子： *Pack your suit carefully so that you don't crease it.* 把你的西裝小心裝好以免弄皺。 **2** [T, I] **~ (sth)** to make lines in the skin; to develop lines in the skin （皮膚）皺起；使起皺紋： *A frown creased her forehead.* 她一皺眉，額頭顯出了皺紋。◇ *Her face creased into a smile.* 她的臉上露出了微笑。 ▸ **creased** *adj.*： *I can't wear this blouse. It's creased.* 我不能穿這件襯衫，它皺了。

PHR V **ˌcrease ˈup** | **ˌcrease sb ˈup** (*BrE, informal*) to start laughing or make sb start laughing （使）大笑起來 **SYN** **crack (sb) up**： *Ed creased up laughing.* 埃德哈哈大笑起來。◇ *Her jokes really creased me up.* 她的笑話真讓我笑死了。

cre·ate 🔑 **AW** /kriˈeɪt/ *verb*

1 🔑 **~ sth** to make sth happen or exist 創造；創作；創建： *Scientists disagree about how the universe was created.* 科學家對宇宙是怎樣形成的有分歧。◇ *The main purpose of industry is to create wealth.* 工業的主要宗旨是創造財富。◇ *The government plans to create more jobs for young people.* 政府計劃為年輕人創造更多的就業機會。◇ *Create a new directory and put all your files into it.* 創建一個新的目錄，然後把你所有的文件都放進去。◇ *Try this new dish, created by our head chef.* 品嚐一下這道新菜吧，是我們廚師長首創的。 ➲ SYNONYMS at MAKE **2** 🔑 **~ sth** to produce a particular feeling or impression 造成，引起，產生（感覺或印象）： *The company is trying to create a young energetic image.* 這家公司正試圖塑造一個充滿活力的年輕形象。◇ *The announcement only succeeded in creating confusion.* 那通告反而引起了混亂。◇ *They've painted it red to create a feeling of warmth.* 他們把它刷成紅色以造成一種溫暖的感覺。 **3** to give sb a particular rank or title 授予；冊封： **~ sth** *The government has created eight new peers.* 政府新封了八個貴族。◇ **~ sth + noun** *He was created a baronet in 1715.* 他於 1715 年被封為準男爵。

C

cre·ation **AW** /kriˈeɪʃn/ *noun* **1** [U] the act or process of making sth that is new, or of causing sth to exist that did not exist before 創造；創建： *the process of database creation* 數據庫的創建過程◇ *wealth creation* 財富的創造◇ *He had been with the company since its creation in 1989.* 他從 1989 年公司成立以來就一直在那裏工作。 ➲ see also JOB CREATION **2** [C] (often *humorous*) a thing that sb has made, especially sth that shows ability or imagination 作品；創作： *a literary creation* 文學作品◇ *The cake was a delicious creation of sponge, cream and fruit.* 這蛋糕是用鬆糕、奶油和水果製作的，又好吃，又好看。 **3** (usually **the Creation**) [sing.] the making of the world, especially by God as described in the Bible （尤指《聖經》所述由上帝）創造天地 **4** (often **Creation**) [U] the world and all the living things in it 世界；天地萬物

cre·ation·ism /kriˈeɪʃənɪzəm/ *noun* [U] the belief that the universe was made by God exactly as described in the Bible 創造論（按《聖經》所述認為萬物皆由上帝創造） ▸ **cre·ation·ist** *adj., noun*

creˈation science *noun* [U] science that tries to find proof that God created the world 創造科學（旨在找到上帝創造世界的證據）

cre·ative **AW** /kriˈeɪtɪv/ *adj., noun*

■ *adj.* **1** [only before noun] involving the use of skill and the imagination to produce sth new or a work of art 創造（性）的；創作的： *a course on* ***creative writing*** (= writing stories, plays and poems) 創作課程◇ *the creative and performing arts* 創作與表演藝術◇ ***creative thinking*** (= thinking about problems in a new way or thinking of new ideas) 創造性思維◇ *the company's creative team* 公司的創新組◇ *the creative process* 創作的過程 **2** having the skill and ability to produce sth new, especially a work of art; showing this ability 有創造力的；（尤指藝術作品）創作的；表現創造力的： *She's very creative—she writes poetry and paints.* 她極富創造力，既賦詩又作畫。◇ *Do you have any ideas? You're the creative one.* 你有何高見？你是有創見的人。 ▸ **cre·ative·ly** **AW** *adv.* **cre·ativ·ity** **AW** /ˌkriːeɪˈtɪvəti/ *noun* [U]： *Creativity and originality are more important than technical skill.* 創意和原創性比專門技術更為重要。

■ *noun* **1** [C] a person who is creative 富於創造力的人；搞創作的人： *The exhibition features the paintings of local creatives.* 這個展覽會展出的是當地畫家的作品。 **2** [U] creative ideas or material 創意；創作素材： *We need to produce better creative if we want to attract big clients.* 要吸引大客戶，我們就得拿出更好的創意。

creˌative acˈcounting *noun* [U] (*disapproving*) a way of doing or presenting the accounts of a business that might not show what the true situation really is 創造性做賬（指用取巧的方法入賬）

cre·ator **AW** /kriˈeɪtə(r)/ *noun* **1** [C] a person who has made or invented a particular thing 創造者；創作者；發明者： *Walt Disney, the creator of Mickey Mouse* 沃爾特 • 迪斯尼 —— 米老鼠的創作者 **2** **the Creator** [sing.] God 造物主；上帝；天主

crea·ture 🔑 /ˈkriːtʃə(r)/ *noun*

1 🔑 a living thing, real or imaginary, that can move around, such as an animal 生物；動物： *The dormouse is a shy, nocturnal creature.* 榛睡鼠是一種在夜間活動的膽小動物。◇ *respect for all* ***living creatures*** 對所有生命的尊重◇ *strange creatures from outer space* 來自外太空的怪物 **2** (especially following an adjective 尤置於形容

C

詞後) a person, considered in a particular way（具有某種特徵的）人：*You pathetic creature!* 你這可憐的傢伙！◇ *She was an exotic creature with long red hair and brilliant green eyes.* 她長着紅色長髮、明亮碧眼，是個少見的大美人。◇ *He always goes to bed at ten—he's **a creature of habit*** (= he likes to do the same things at the same time every day). 他總在十點鐘上牀睡覺，是個嚴守生活習慣的人。

IDM **a/the creature of sb | sb's creature** (*formal, disapproving*) a person or thing that depends completely on sb else and is controlled by them 傀儡

ˌcreature 'comforts *noun* [pl.] all the things that make life, or a particular place, comfortable, such as good food, comfortable furniture or modern equipment 使人舒適的所有東西（如食物、傢具或現代化設備）；物質享受

crèche (also **creche**) /kreʃ/ *noun* **1** (*BrE*) a place where babies and small children are taken care of while their parents are working, studying, shopping, etc. 日託託兒所 ➲ compare DAY NURSERY **2** (*NAmE*) (*BrE* **crib**) a model of the scene of Jesus Christ's birth, placed in churches and homes at Christmas 聖誕馬槽（復現耶穌誕生的情景）

cred /kred/ *noun* [U] = STREET CRED

cre·dence /ˈkriːdns/ *noun* [U] (*formal*) **1** a quality that an idea or a story has that makes you believe it is true 可信性；真實性：*Historical evidence **lends credence to** his theory.* 史學根據使他的理論更為可信。**2** belief in sth as true 信任；信念：*They could **give** no **credence** to the findings of the survey.* 他們可能不相信這次調查的結果。◇ *Alternative medicine has been **gaining credence*** (= becoming more widely accepted) *recently.* 近來非傳統醫學越來越得到大眾的認可。

cre·den·tial /krəˈdenʃl/ *verb* **~ sb** (*NAmE*) to provide sb with credentials 提供證明書（或證件）

cre·den·tials /krəˈdenʃlz/ *noun* [pl.] **1 ~ (as/for sth)** the qualities, training or experience that make you suitable to do sth 資格；資歷：*He has all the credentials for the job.* 他做這項工作完全夠格。◇ *She will first have to establish her leadership credentials.* 她得首先證明她有擔任領導的資格。**2** documents such as letters that prove that you are who you claim to be, and can therefore be trusted 資格證書；證明書；證件

cred·ibil·ity /ˌkredəˈbɪləti/ *noun* [U] the quality that sb/sth has that makes people believe or trust them 可信性；可靠性：*to **gain/lack/lose credibility*** 獲取／缺乏／失去信任 ◇ *The prosecution did its best to **undermine the credibility** of the witness.* 原告竭力削弱證人的可信性。◇ *Newspapers were talking of a **credibility gap** between what he said and what he did.* 各家報紙都在議論他言行不一。➲ see also STREET CRED

cred·ible /ˈkredəbl/ *adj.* **1** that can be believed or trusted 可信的；可靠的 SYN **convincing**：*a **credible explanation/witness*** 可信的解釋／證人 ◇ *It is just not credible that she would cheat.* 她會行騙簡直難以置信。**2** that can be accepted, because it seems possible that it could be successful（因看似可能成功而）可接受的 SYN **viable**：*Community service is seen as the only credible alternative to imprisonment.* 除監禁外，社區勞動被看作是唯一可接受的選擇。▸ **cred·ibly** /-əbli/ *adv.*：*We can credibly describe the band's latest album as their best yet.* 我們完全可以說，這支樂隊的最新專輯是他們迄今的最佳作品。

credit 🔑 AW /ˈkredɪt/ *noun, verb*

■ ***noun***

▸ **BUY NOW–PAY LATER** 賒購 **1** 🔑 [U] an arrangement that you make, with a shop/store for example, to pay later for sth you buy 賒購；賒欠：*to **get/refuse credit*** 允許／拒絕賒購 ◇ *We bought the dishwasher **on credit**.* 我們賒購了一台洗碗機。◇ *to offer **interest-free credit*** (= allow sb to pay later, without any extra charge) 提供免息賒購 ◇ *a credit agreement* 信貸協定 ◇ ***credit facilities/terms*** 信貸業務；賒欠期 ◇ *Your **credit limit** is now £2 000.* 你的信用額度現在為 2 000 英鎊。◇ *He's a bad **credit risk*** (= he is unlikely to pay the money later). 他有欠賬不還的危險。➲ compare HIRE PURCHASE

▸ **MONEY BORROWED** 借款 **2** 🔑 [U, C] money that you borrow from a bank; a loan（從銀行借的）借款；貸款：*The bank refused further credit to the company.* 銀行拒絕再給那家公司提供貸款。➲ COLLOCATIONS at FINANCE **3** [U] the status of being trusted to pay back money to sb who lends it to you（借錢償還的）信譽，信用：*Her credit isn't good anywhere now.* 她借錢不還，弄得聲名狼藉。

▸ **MONEY IN BANK** 銀行存款 **4** 🔑 [U] if you or your bank account are **in credit**, there is money in the account 結餘 **5** [C, U] a sum of money paid into a bank account; a record of the payment（付入銀行賬戶的）存款金額，貸記：*a credit of £50* * 50 英鎊的貸記 ◇ *You'll be paid by direct credit into your bank account.* 給你的付款將直接存入你的銀行賬戶。OPP **debit**

▸ **MONEY BACK** 返回的錢 **6** [C, U] (*technical* 術語) a payment that sb has a right to for a particular reason 有權索要的款項：*a tax credit* 課稅扣除

▸ **PRAISE** 讚揚 **7** 🔑 [U] **~ (for sth)** praise or approval because you are responsible for sth good that has happened 讚揚；稱讚；認可：*He's a player who rarely seems to get the credit he deserves.* 他這個選手好像很少得到應得的讚揚。◇ *I can't take all the credit for the show's success—it was a team effort.* 演出成功不能都算成我一個人的功勞，這是集體努力的結果。◇ *We did all the work and she gets all the credit!* 工作都是我們幹的，而功勞卻都歸了她！◇ *Credit will be given in the exam for good spelling and grammar.* 考試中拼寫和語法出色者將受到表揚。◇ *At least give him credit for trying* (= praise him because he tried, even if he did not succeed). 至少該表揚他嘗試過。➲ compare BLAME *n.*, DISCREDIT *n.* **8** [sing.] **~ to sb/sth** a person or thing whose qualities or achievements are praised and who therefore earns respect for sb/sth else 為…贏得榮譽的人（或事物）；因…受到尊重的人（或事物）：*She is a credit to the school.* 她為學校贏得了榮譽。

▸ **ON MOVIE/TV PROGRAMME** 電影；電視節目 **9** [C, usually pl.] the act of mentioning sb who worked on a project such as a film/movie or a television programme（電影或電視節目演職人員的）片頭字幕，片尾字幕：*She was given a programme credit for her work on the costumes for the play.* 她為這齣戲準備服裝，被列入劇目製作人員名單。◇ ***The credits*** (= the list of all the people involved) *seemed to last almost as long as the film!* 演職人員字幕持續的時間幾乎與這部電影一樣長！

▸ **UNIT OF STUDY** 學習單元 **10** [C] a unit of study at a college or university (in the US, also at a school); the fact of having successfully completed a unit of study（學院或大學，以及美國中小學的）學習單元，學分：*My math class is worth three credits.* 我的數學課為三個學分。

IDM **do sb credit | do credit to sb/sth** if sth **does credit** to a person or an organization, they deserve to be praised for it 使值得讚揚（或表揚）：*Your honesty does you great credit.* 你的誠實值得大大表揚。**have sth to your credit** to have achieved sth 完成；取得：*He's only 30, and he already has four novels to his credit.* 他年僅 30 歲，卻已著有四部小說。**on the 'credit side** used to introduce the good points about sb/sth, especially after the bad points have been mentioned（尤用於提及缺點之後）就優點方面而言 **to sb's credit** making sb deserve praise or respect 使值得讚揚；使受尊重：*To his credit, Jack never told anyone exactly what had happened.* 傑克對所發生的事守口如瓶，值得讚揚。

■ ***verb***

▸ **PUT MONEY IN BANK** 往銀行存錢 **1** to add an amount of money to sb's bank account（給銀行賬戶）存入金額；把…記入貸方；貸記（銀行賬戶）：**~ A (with B)** *Your account has been credited with $50 000.* 已把 5 萬元存入你的賬戶。◇ **~ B (to A)** *$50 000 has been credited to your account.* 已把 5 萬元存入你的賬戶。OPP **debit**

▸ **WITH ACHIEVEMENT** 成就 **2** [usually passive] to believe or say that sb is responsible for doing sth, especially sth good 認為是…的功勞；把…歸於：**~ sb** *All the contributors are credited on the title page.* 所有撰稿人的姓名均刊登在扉頁上。◇ **~ A with B** *The company is credited with inventing the industrial robot.* 發明工業機器人是那家公司的功勞。◇ **~ B to A** *The invention of the industrial* *robot is credited to the company.* 工業機器人的發明應歸功於那家公司。

▸ **WITH QUALITY** 品質 **3 ~ A with B** to believe that sb/sth has a particular good quality or feature 認為…有（良好的品質或特點）: *I credited you with a little more sense.* 我認為你更有見識。 **4** [usually passive] **~ sb/sth as sth** to believe that sb/sth is of a particular type or quality 認為…屬（某種類或性質）: *The cheetah is generally credited as the world's fastest animal.* 普遍認為獵豹是世界上跑得最快的動物。

▸ **BELIEVE** 相信 **5 ~ sth | ~ what, how, etc. … | ~ that …** (*BrE*) (used mainly in questions and negative sentences 主要用於疑問句和否定句) to believe sth, especially sth surprising or unexpected 相信（尤指令人驚奇或意外的事物）: *He's been promoted—would you credit it?* 他被擢升了，你相信嗎？

cred·it·able /ˈkredɪtəbl/ *adj.* (*formal*) **1** of a quite good standard and deserving praise or approval 值得讚揚的；應當認可的 **SYN** **praiseworthy**: *It was a very creditable result for the team.* 對這支隊來說，這比賽結果是十分值得稱道的。 **2** morally good 道德上好的；高尚的 **SYN** **admirable**: *There was nothing very creditable in what he did.* 他這事做得可實在不怎麼樣。 ▸ **cred·it·ably** /ˈkredɪtəbli/ *adv.*

ˈcredit account *noun* (*BrE*) = ACCOUNT (3)

ˈcredit card 0ᵚ *noun* a small plastic card that you can use to buy goods and services and pay for them later 信用卡: *All major credit cards are accepted at our hotels.* 我們的旅館接受所有主要的信用卡。 ➲ picture at MONEY ➲ see also CHARGE CARD, CHEQUE CARD, DEBIT CARD, STORE CARD

ˈcredit crunch *noun* [usually sing.] (*economics* 經) an economic condition in which it suddenly becomes difficult and expensive to borrow money 信貸緊縮

ˈcredit note *noun* (*BrE*) a letter that a shop/store gives you when you have returned sth and that allows you to have goods of the same value in exchange 貸項憑單（退貨時發給的憑證，可換取等值的商品）

cred·it·or **AW** /ˈkredɪtə(r)/ *noun* a person, company, etc. that sb owes money to 債權人；債主；貸方 ➲ compare DEBTOR

ˈcredit rating *noun* a judgement made by a bank, etc. about how likely sb is to pay back money that they borrow, and how safe it is to lend money to them（銀行等作出的）信用等級評定

ˈcredit transfer *noun* (*BrE*) the process of sending money from one person's bank account to another's 銀行轉賬

ˈcredit union *noun* an organization that lends money to its members at low rates of interest 互助儲金會，信用合作社（向會員提供低息貸款）

credit·worthy /ˈkredɪtwɜːði; *NAmE* -wɜːrði/ *adj.* able to be trusted to pay back money that is owed; safe to lend money to 可信賴償還借貸的；信譽好的；信用可靠的；借貸安全的 ▸ **credit·worthi·ness** *noun* [U]

credo /ˈkriːdəʊ; ˈkreɪdəʊ; *NAmE* -doʊ/ *noun* (*pl.* **-os**) (*formal*) a set of beliefs 信條 **SYN** **creed**

cre·du·lity /krɪˈdjuːləti; *NAmE* -ˈduː-/ *noun* [U] (*formal*) the ability or willingness to believe that sth is real or true 輕信: *The plot of the novel stretches credulity to the limit* (= it is almost impossible to believe). 這部小說的情節牽強得幾乎令人無法相信。

credu·lous /ˈkredjələs; *NAmE* -dʒə-/ *adj.* (*formal*) too ready to believe things and therefore easy to trick 輕信的；易受騙的 **SYN** **gullible** ➲ compare INCREDULOUS

Cree /kriː/ *noun* (*pl.* **Cree** or **Crees**) a member of a Native American people, many of whom live in central Canada 克里人（美洲土著，很多居於加拿大中部）

creed /kriːd/ *noun* **1** a set of principles or religious beliefs 信念；原則；綱領；宗教信仰: *people of all races, colours and creeds* 各種種族、膚色和宗教信仰的人 ◇ *What is his political creed?* 他的政治信仰是什麼？ **2** **the Creed** [sing.] a statement of Christian belief that is spoken as part of some church services（基督教）信經

Creek /kriːk/ *noun* (*pl.* **Creek** or **Creeks**) a member of a Native American people, many of whom now live in the US state of Oklahoma 克里克人（美洲土著，很多現居於美國俄克拉何馬州）

creek /kriːk/ *noun* **1** (*BrE*) a narrow area of water where the sea flows into the land 小海灣；小港灣 **SYN** **inlet** **2** (*NAmE, AustralE, NZE*) a small river or stream 小河；小溪

IDM **up the ˈcreek (without a ˈpaddle)** (*informal*) in a difficult or bad situation 處於困境（或窘境）: *I was really up the creek without my car.* 我沒了我的車真是不方便。

creel /kriːl/ *noun* a BASKET for holding fish that have just been caught（釣魚用的）魚簍

creep /kriːp/ *verb, noun*

▪ *verb* (**crept**, **crept** /krept/) **HELP** In the phrasal verb **creep sb out**, **creeped** is used for the past simple and past participle. 在短語動詞 creep sb out 中，creep 的過去時和過去分詞均為 creeped。 **1** [I] (**+ adv./prep.**) (of people or animals 人或動物) to move slowly, quietly and carefully, because you do not want to be seen or heard 悄悄地緩慢行進；躡手躡腳地移動: *I crept up the stairs, trying not to wake my parents.* 為了盡量不吵醒父母，我躡手躡腳地上了樓。 **2** [I] (**+ adv./prep.**) (*NAmE*) to move with your body close to the ground; to move slowly on your hands and knees 匍匐行進；爬行 **SYN** **crawl** **3** [I] (**+ adv./prep.**) to move or develop very slowly 非常緩慢地行進；不知不覺產生；漸漸出現: *Her arms crept around his neck.* 她的雙臂慢慢地摟住了他的脖子。◇ *A slight feeling of suspicion crept over me.* 我漸漸地產生了一絲疑慮。 **4** [I] (**+ adv./prep.**) (of plants 植物) to grow along the ground or up walls using long STEMS or roots 蔓生；蔓延 ➲ see also CREEPER **5** [I] **~ (to sb)** (*BrE, informal, disapproving*) to be too friendly or helpful to sb in authority in a way that is not sincere, especially in order to get an advantage from them 諂媚；巴結；拍馬屁 **IDM** see FLESH *n.*

PHR V **ˌcreep ˈin/ˈinto sth** to begin to happen or affect sth 開始發生（或影響）: *As she became more tired, errors began to creep into her work.* 由於越來越疲勞，她的工作開始出現差錯。 **ˌcreep sb ˈout** (**creeped**, **creeped**) (*NAmE, informal*) to make sb feel afraid, uncomfortable or disgusted 使人感到害怕（或不舒服、噁心）: *He said the empty streets creeped him out.* 他說空曠的街道令他毛骨悚然。 **ˌcreep ˈup** to gradually increase in amount, price, etc.（數量、價格等）逐漸增長: *House prices are creeping up again.* 住房價格又在漸漸上漲。 **ˌcreep ˈup on sb** **1** to move slowly nearer to sb, usually from behind, without being seen or heard（通常從後面）緩慢地悄悄靠近: *Don't creep up on me like that!* 別那樣躡手躡腳地靠近我！ **2** to begin to affect sb, especially before they realize it（尤指不知不覺地）開始影響（某人）: *Tiredness can easily creep up on you while you're driving.* 開車時會很容易不知不覺地就累了。

▪ *noun* **1** [C] (*informal*) a person that you dislike very much and find very unpleasant 討厭鬼: *He's a nasty little creep!* 他這小子真讓人討厭！ **2** [C] (*BrE, informal*) a person who is not sincere but tries to win your approval by being nice to you 討好賣乖的人；諂媚奉承的人；馬屁精 **3** [U] (in compounds 構成複合詞) (often *disapproving*) the development of a project beyond the goal that was originally agreed（對既定目標的）偏離: *The World Bank has been accused of* ***mission creep*** *when seeking to address these concerns.* 世界銀行被指控在尋求處理這些重大事務時偏離使命。◇ *The inclusion of health data on identity cards was condemned as* ***function creep.*** 在身分證中包含健康資料被譴責為超出功能範圍。

IDM **give sb the ˈcreeps** (*informal*) to make sb feel nervous and slightly frightened, especially because sb/sth is unpleasant or strange 嚇人；使驚慌；使心裏發毛

creep·er /ˈkriːpə(r)/ *noun* a plant that grows along the ground, up walls, etc., often winding itself around other plants 蔓生植物；攀緣植物 ➲ see also VIRGINIA CREEPER

C

creep·ing /'kriːpɪŋ/ *adj.* [only before noun] (of sth bad 壞事) happening or moving gradually and not easily noticed （不知不覺地）逐漸發生的，緩慢行進的：*creeping inflation* 慢慢加劇的通貨膨脹

C

creepy /'kriːpi/ *adj.* (**creep·ier**, **creepi·est**) (*informal*) **1** causing an unpleasant feeling of fear or slight horror 令人毛骨悚然的；令人不寒而慄的 **SYN** **scary**：*a creepy ghost story* 令人毛骨悚然的鬼故事 ◇ *It's kind of creepy down in the cellar!* 地窖裏真令人有點不寒而慄！**2** strange in a way that makes you feel nervous 怪異的，離奇的（使人感到緊張）：*What a creepy coincidence.* 多麼離奇的巧合。**SYN** **spooky**

creepy-crawly /ˌkriːpi 'krɔːli/ *noun* (*pl.* **-ies**) (*informal*) an insect, a WORM, etc. when you think of it as unpleasant（使人厭惡的）爬蟲，蠕蟲

cre·mains /krɪ'meɪnz/ *noun* [pl.] (*NAmE*) the powder that is left after a dead person's body has been CREMATED (= burned) 骨灰 **SYN** **ashes**

cre·mate /krə'meɪt/ *verb* [often passive] **~ sb/sth** to burn a dead body, especially as part of a funeral ceremony 焚燒，火化（屍體）；（尤指）火葬

cre·ma·tion /krə'meɪʃn/ *noun* **1** [U] the act of cremating sb 火化 **2** [C] a funeral at which the dead person is cremated 火葬；火化儀式

crema·tor·ium /ˌkremə'tɔːriəm/ *noun* (*pl.* **crema·toria** /-'tɔːriə/ or **crema·tor·iums**) (*NAmE* also **crema·tory** /'kriːmətɔːri; 'krem-/ *pl.* **-ies**) a building in which the bodies of dead people are burned 火葬場

crème brûlée /ˌkrem bruː'leɪ/ *noun* [C, U] (*pl.* **crèmes brûlées** /ˌkrem bruː'leɪ/) (from *French*) a cold DESSERT (= a sweet dish) made from cream, with burnt sugar on top 焦糖奶油（冷甜點）

crème caramel /ˌkrem 'kærəmel/ *noun* [C, U] (*pl.* **crèmes caramels** /ˌkrem 'kærəmel/) (*BrE*, from *French*) (*NAmE* **flan**) a cold DESSERT (= a sweet dish) made from milk, eggs and sugar 焦糖蛋奶（冷甜點）

crème de la crème /ˌkrem də lɑː 'krem/ *noun* [sing.] (from *French*, *formal* or *humorous*) the best people or things of their kind 精英；精華；精髓：*This school takes only the crème de la crème.* 這所學校只招收高材生。

crème de menthe /ˌkrem də 'mɒnθ; *NAmE* 'menθ/ *noun* [U, C] (*pl.* **crèmes de menthe** /ˌkrem də 'mɒnθ; *NAmE* 'menθ/) (from *French*) a strong sweet alcoholic drink made with MINT 薄荷烈性甜酒

crème fraiche /ˌkrem 'freʃ/ *noun* [U] (from *French*) thick cream with a slightly sour taste 鮮濃奶油，生奶油（略帶酸味）

cren·el·lated (*US* also **cren·el·ated**) /'krenəleɪtɪd/ *adj.* (*technical* 術語) (of a tower, castle, etc. 塔樓、城堡等) having BATTLEMENTS 有雉堞的

Cre·ole /'kriːəʊl; *NAmE* -oʊl/ (also **creole**) *noun* **1** [C] a person of mixed European and African race, especially one who lives in the West Indies 克里奧爾人（尤指居住在西印度群島的歐洲人和非洲人的混血兒）**2** [C] a person whose ANCESTORS were among the first Europeans who settled in the West Indies or S America, or one of the French or Spanish people who settled in the southern states of the US 克里奧爾人（指首批定居在西印度群島或南美的歐洲人的後裔，或定居在美國南部諸州的法國人和西班牙人的後裔）：*Creole cookery* 克里奧爾式烹飪方法 **3** [U] a language formed when a mixture of a European language with a local language (especially an African language spoken by SLAVES in the West Indies) is spoken as a first language 克里奧爾語（歐洲語言和當地語言的混合語，尤指與西印度群島奴隸講的非洲語言混合）➲ compare PIDGIN

cre·ol·ize (*BrE* also **-ise**) /'kriːəlaɪz; *BrE* also 'krɪə-/ *verb* **~ sth** (*linguistics* 語言) to change a language by combining it with a language from another place 使（語言）克里奧爾語化；使混合化：*Creolized forms of Latin were spoken in various parts of Europe.* 以前歐洲各地區都講克里奧爾語形式的拉丁語。▸ **cre·ol·iza·tion**, **-isa·tion** /ˌkriːəlaɪ'zeɪʃn; *BrE* also ˌkrɪəlaɪzeɪʃn/ *noun* [U, C]

creo·sote /'kriːəsəʊt; *NAmE* -soʊt/ *noun*, *verb*

■ ***noun*** [U] a thick brown liquid that is made from COAL TAR, used to preserve wood 雜酚油，木餾油（用於木材防腐）

■ ***verb*** **~ sth** to paint or preserve sth with creosote 用雜酚油塗抹（或防腐）

crêpe (also **crepe**) /kreɪp/ *noun* **1** [U] a type of light thin cloth, made especially from cotton or silk, with a surface that is covered in lines and folds（尤指用棉和絲織的）縐布，縐綢，縐織物：*a black crêpe dress* 黑色縐綢連衣裙 ◇ *a crêpe bandage* 彈力繃帶 **2** [U] a type of strong rubber with a rough surface, used for making the SOLES of shoes 縐膠（製鞋底用）：*crêpe-soled shoes* 縐膠底鞋 **3** [C] a thin PANCAKE 薄煎餅

ˈcrêpe paper *noun* [U] a type of thin brightly coloured paper that stretches and has a surface covered in lines and folds, used especially for making decorations（尤用於裝飾的）彩色皺紋紙

crept *past tense, past part.* of CREEP

cre·pus·cul·ar /krɪ'pʌskjələ(r)/ *adj.* (*literary*) related to the period of the evening when the sun has just gone down but there is still some light in the sky 黃昏的

cres·cendo /krə'ʃendəʊ; *NAmE* -doʊ/ *noun* (*pl.* **-os**) [C, U] **1** (*music* 音) a gradual increase in how loudly a piece of music is played or sung（音樂的）漸強 **OPP** **diminuendo** **2** a gradual increase in noise; the loudest point of a period of continuous noise 逐漸增強的喧鬧聲；持續噪聲的最高點 **SYN** **swell**：*Voices rose in a crescendo and drowned him out.* 人們講話的聲音越來越大，蓋過了他的聲音。◇ (*figurative*) *The advertising campaign reached a crescendo just before Christmas.* 聖誕節前夕，廣告攻勢達到了高潮。

cres·cent /'kresnt; *BrE* also 'kreznt/ *noun* **1** [C] a curved shape that is wide in the middle and pointed at each end 新月形；月牙形：*a crescent moon* 新月 **2** [C] (often used in street names 常用於街道名稱) a curved street with a row of houses on it 新月形街區（一排房屋）：*I live at 7 Park Crescent.* 我住在帕克新月街 7 號。**3 the Crescent** [sing.] the curved shape that is used as a symbol of Islam 新月（伊斯蘭教的象徵）➲ see also THE RED CRESCENT

cress /kres/ *noun* [U] a small plant with thin STEMS and very small leaves, often eaten in salads and SANDWICHES 水芹（常放在色拉和三明治中食用）➲ see also WATERCRESS

crest /krest/ *noun*, *verb*

■ ***noun*** **1** [usually sing.] **~ (of sth)** the top part of a hill or wave 山頂；頂峰；波峰；浪尖：*surfers riding the crest of the wave* 正在浪峰上衝浪的運動員 ➲ VISUAL VOCAB pages V4, V5 **2** a design used as the symbol of a particular family, organization, etc., especially one that has a long history（尤指象徵歷史悠久的家族、機構等的）飾章，紋章：*the university crest* 大學的紋章 **3** a group of feathers that stand up on top of a bird's head 鳥冠；羽冠 ➲ VISUAL VOCAB page V12

IDM **the crest of a/the ˈwave** a situation in which sb is very successful, happy, etc. 頂峰時期；極其成功；春風得意 ➲ more at RIDE *v.*

■ ***verb*** **1** [T] **~ sth** (*formal*) to reach the top of a hill, mountain or wave 到達山頂（或浪峰）：*He slowed the pace as they crested the ridge.* 當他們到達山脊時，他放慢了步伐。**2** [I] (*NAmE*) (of a flood, wave, etc. 洪水、波浪等) to reach its highest level before it falls again 到達洪峰；達到頂點：(*figurative*) *The level of debt crested at a massive $290 billion in 2009.* * 2009 年的巨額債務高達 2 900 億元。

crest·ed /'krestɪd/ *adj.* **1** marked with a crest 有飾章的：*crested notepaper* 有飾章的信箋 **2** used especially in names of birds or animals which have a crest（尤用於鳥獸名稱）有鳥冠的，有羽冠的：*crested newts* 冠歐螈

crest·fall·en /'krestfɔːlən/ *adj.* sad and disappointed because you have failed and you did not expect to 垂頭喪氣的；灰心失望的；沮喪的

Cret·aceous /krɪ'teɪʃəs/ *adj.* (*geology* 地) of the PERIOD between around 146 to 65 million years ago, when dinosaurs lived (until they died out); of the rocks formed during this time 白堊紀的；白堊（質）的 ▸ **the Cret·aceous** *noun* [sing.]

cre·tin /ˈkretɪn; *NAmE* ˈkriːtn/ *noun* (*informal, offensive*) a very stupid person 笨蛋；傻瓜；白痴：*Why did you do that, you cretin?* 你為什麼這樣做，你這個傻瓜？ ▸ **cret·in·ous** /ˈkretɪnəs; *NAmE* ˈkriːtnəs/ *adj.*

Creutzfeldt-Jakob disease /ˌkrɔɪtsfelt ˈjækɒb dɪziːz; *NAmE* ˈjækɔːb/ *noun* [U] (*abbr.* **CJD**) a brain disease that causes gradual loss of control of the mind and body and, finally, death. It is believed to be caused by PRIONS and is linked to BSE in cows. 克 — 雅氏病，克羅伊茨費爾特 — 雅各布病（俗稱瘋牛病，被認為由朊病毒引起並與牛海綿狀腦病有關的致命腦病）

cre·vasse /krəˈvæs/ *noun* a deep open crack, especially in ice, for example in a GLACIER （尤指冰川等的）裂縫，裂隙，冰隙

crev·ice /ˈkrevɪs/ *noun* a narrow crack in a rock or wall （岩石或牆壁的）裂縫，裂隙，裂口

crew /kruː/ *noun, verb*

■ ***noun*** **1** [C+sing./pl. v.] all the people working on a ship, plane, etc. （輪船、飛機等上面的）全體工作人員：*None of the passengers and crew were injured.* 沒有一個乘客和機組人員受傷。◇ *crew members* 全體機務人員 ➲ see also AIRCREW, CABIN CREW, FLIGHT CREW **2** [C+sing./pl. v.] all the people working on a ship, plane etc. except the officers who are in charge （輪船、飛機等上面不包括高級職員的）全體船員，全體乘務員：*the officers and crew* 負責人員和全體乘務員 **3** [C+sing./pl. v.] a group of people with special skills working together 技術人員團隊；專業團隊：*a **film/camera crew*** 電影攝製組；攝製組 ◇ *an ambulance crew* 救護車急救組 ➲ see also GROUND CREW **4** [sing.] (usually *disapproving*) a group of people 一群（或一幫、一夥）人：*The people she invited were a pretty **motley crew*** (= a strange mix of types of people). 她邀請的人相當混雜。 **5** [C+sing./pl. v.] a team of people who ROW boats in races （賽船的）划船隊員，划船隊：*a member of the Cambridge crew* 劍橋大學划船隊的隊員 **6** [U] (*NAmE*) the sport of ROWING with other people in a boat 賽艇運動：*I'm thinking of going out for crew this semester* (= joining the ROWING team). 這學期我打算參加賽艇隊。

■ ***verb*** [T, I] to be part of a crew, especially on a ship 當（尤指船上的）工作人員：**~ (sth)** *Normally the boat is crewed by five people.* 通常這條船配有五名船員。◇ **~ (for sb)** *I crewed for him on his yacht last summer.* 去年夏天我在他的遊艇上當船員。

ˈcrew cut *noun* a HAIRSTYLE for men in which the hair is cut very short 平頭（男式髮型）➲ VISUAL VOCAB page V60 ▸ **ˈcrew-cut** *adj.*：*crew-cut teenagers* 留平頭的青少年

crew·man /ˈkruːmən/ *noun* (*pl.* **-men** /-mən/) a member of a CREW, usually a man 船員，乘務員（通常為男性）

ˌcrew ˈneck *noun* a round neck on a sweater, etc. （套頭毛衣等的）圓領，水手領 ➲ VISUAL VOCAB page V63

crib /krɪb/ *noun, verb*

■ ***noun*** **1** (*NAmE*) (*BrE* **cot**) a small bed with high sides for a baby or young child （有圍欄的）幼兒牀 ➲ VISUAL VOCAB page V23 **2** a long open box that horses and cows can eat from （馬、牛的）飼料槽 SYN **manger** **3** (*BrE*) (*NAmE* **crèche**) a model of the scene of Jesus Christ's birth, placed in churches and homes at Christmas 聖誕馬槽（復現耶穌誕生的情景）**4** (*informal*) written information such as answers to questions, often used dishonestly by students in tests （考試作弊用的）夾帶：*a crib sheet* 夾帶的答案紙 **5** = CRIBBAGE **6** (*NAmE, informal*) the house, flat/apartment, etc. where sb lives 住所；公寓；居所

■ ***verb*** (**-bb-**) [I, T] **~ (sth) (from sb)** (*old-fashioned*) to dishonestly copy work from another student or from a book （學生做作業時）抄襲，剽竊

crib·bage /ˈkrɪbɪdʒ/ (also **crib**) *noun* [U] a card game in which players score points by collecting different combinations of cards. The score is kept by putting small PEGS in holes in a board. 克里巴奇牌戲（用小木釘插在有孔的木板上記分）

ˈcrib death (*NAmE*) (*BrE* **ˈcot death**) *noun* [U, C] the sudden death while sleeping of a baby that appears to be healthy 嬰兒猝死

C

crick /krɪk/ (*NAmE* also **kink**) *noun* [usually sing.] a sudden painful stiff feeling in the muscles of your neck or back （頸或背部的）痛性痙攣 ▸ **crick** *verb*：**~ sth** *I suffered a cricked neck during a game of tennis.* 我在一次網球比賽時脖子抽筋了。

cricket /ˈkrɪkɪt/ *noun* **1** [U] a game played on grass by two teams of 11 players. Players score points (called RUNS) by hitting the ball with a wooden BAT and running between two sets of vertical wooden sticks, called STUMPS. 板球（運動）：*a **cricket match/team/club/ball*** 板球比賽／運動隊／俱樂部；板球 ➲ VISUAL VOCAB page V44 **2** [C] a small brown jumping insect that makes a loud high sound by rubbing its wings together 蟋蟀；蛐蛐：*the chirping of crickets* 蟋蟀的唧唧叫聲

IDM **not ˈcricket** (*old-fashioned, BrE, informal*) unfair; not HONOURABLE 不公正；不光明正大；不光彩；見不得人

crick·et·er /ˈkrɪkɪtə(r)/ *noun* a cricket player 板球運動員

cricket·ing /ˈkrɪkɪtɪŋ/ *adj.* [only before noun] playing cricket; connected with cricket 打板球的；與板球有關的：*cricketing nations* 打板球的國家 ◇ *a cricketing jersey* 板球運動衫

cri de cœur /ˌkriː də ˈkɜː(r)/ *noun* (*pl.* **cris de cœur** /ˌkriː də ˈkɜː(r)/) (from *French*) an act of asking for sth, or protesting, in a way that shows you care deeply about sth 發自內心的要求（或抗議）；懇求；激烈抗議

cried *past tense, past part.* of CRY

crier /ˈkraɪə(r)/ *noun* = TOWN CRIER

cri·key /ˈkraɪki/ *exclamation* (*BrE, old-fashioned, informal*) used to show that sb is surprised or annoyed （驚訝或惱怒時說）哎呀，嗳喲，唷：*Crikey, is that the time?* 哎呀，都這會兒啦？

Crimbo = CHRIMBO

crime 0-w /kraɪm/ *noun*

1 0-w [U] activities that involve breaking the law 犯罪活動；不法行為：*an increase in violent crime* 暴力犯罪活動的增加 ◇ *the fight against crime* 與犯罪活動的鬥爭 ◇ *Stores spend more and more on **crime prevention** every year.* 商店每年在防止犯罪方面的花費越來越多。◇ ***petty/serious crime*** 輕微的／嚴重的犯罪 ◇ *the connection between drugs and **organized crime*** 毒品與有組織犯罪之間的聯繫 ◇ *He **turned to crime** when he dropped out of school.* 他輟學後淪為罪犯。◇ *The **crime rate** is rising.* 犯罪率正在上升。◇ ***crime fiction/novels*** (= stories about crime) 描寫犯罪活動的小說 ◇ ***crime figures/statistics*** 犯罪數字／統計數字 ◇ *She's a **crime writer*** (= she writes stories about crime). 她是罪案小說作家。 ➲ COLLOCATIONS at JUSTICE **2** 0-w [C] **~ (against sb)** an illegal act or activity that can be punished by law 罪；罪行：*to **commit a crime*** (= do sth illegal) 犯罪 ◇ *The massacre was a **crime against humanity**.* 這場大屠殺是一樁反人類的罪行。 ➲ see also WAR CRIME **3 a crime** [sing.] (*informal*) an act that you think is immoral or is a big mistake 不道德的行為；罪過：*It's a crime to waste so much money.* 揮霍這麼多錢是一種罪過。 ➲ COLLOCATIONS at next page

ˈcrime wave *noun* [sing.] a situation in which there is a sudden increase in the number of crimes that are committed 犯罪高潮

crim·inal 0-w /ˈkrɪmɪnl/ *adj., noun*

■ ***adj.*** **1** 0-w [usually before noun] (rather *formal* or *law* 律) connected with or involving crime 犯罪的；犯法的；涉及犯罪的：***criminal offences/behaviour*** 刑事犯罪；犯罪行為 ◇ ***criminal damage*** (= the crime of damaging sb's property deliberately) 刑事損害 ◇ ***criminal negligence*** (= the illegal act of sb failing to do sth that they should do, with the result that sb else is harmed) 過失犯罪 **2** 0-w [only before noun] connected to the laws that deal with crime 刑法的；刑事的：*criminal law* 刑法 ◇ *the criminal justice system* 刑事審判制度 ◇ *a criminal lawyer* 刑事訴訟律師 ◇ *to bring criminal charges against sb* 對某人提起刑事訴訟 ➲ compare CIVIL (3) **3** morally wrong 道德上錯誤的；不道德的：*This is a criminal waste of resources.* 這是一種浪費資源的可恥行為。

■ ***noun*** 0-w a person who commits a crime 罪犯：*Society does not know how to deal with **hardened criminals***

(= people who regularly commit crimes and are not sorry for what they do). 社會不知道怎樣處置慣犯。◇ (*especially NAmE*) *a* ***career criminal*** 職業罪犯 ➲ COLLOCATIONS at CRIME

crim·in·al·ity /ˌkrɪmɪˈnæləti/ *noun* [U] the fact of people being involved in crime; criminal acts 犯罪；有罪；犯罪行為

crim·in·al·ize (*BrE* also **-ise**) /ˈkrɪmɪnəlaɪz/ *verb* **1 ~ sth** to make sth illegal by passing a new law（通過新的法律）使不合法，使非法：*The use of opium was not criminalized until fairly recently.* 直到最近抽鴉片才被判定為非法。**2 ~ sb** to treat sb as a criminal 把…當罪犯對待 ▸ **crim·in·al·iza·tion, -isa·tion** /ˌkrɪmɪnəlaɪˈzeɪʃn; *NAmE* -ləˈz-/ *noun* [U]

crim·in·al·ly /ˈkrɪmɪnəli/ *adv.* according to the laws that deal with crime 刑法上；刑事上；在犯罪方面：*criminally insane* 精神不正常而犯罪的

ˌcriminal ˈrecord *noun* = RECORD (6)

crim·in·ology /ˌkrɪmɪˈnɒlədʒi; *NAmE* -ˈnɑːl-/ *noun* [U] the scientific study of crime and criminals 犯罪學 ▸ **crim·ino·logic·al** /ˌkrɪmɪnəˈlɒdʒɪkl; *NAmE* -ˈlɑːdʒ-/ *adj.* **crim·in·olo·gist** /-dʒɪst/ *noun*

crimp /krɪmp/ *verb, noun*

■ ***verb*** **1 ~ sth** to make curls in sb's hair by pressing it with a heated tool 燙髮；使（頭髮）拳曲；使（頭髮）成波形 **2 ~ sth** to press cloth or paper into small folds 把（織物或紙）壓出皺紋；使起皺 **3 ~ sth** (*NAmE, informal*) to restrict the growth or development of sth 阻止，妨礙（某事物的發展）

■ ***noun***

IDM **put a ˈcrimp in/on sth** (*NAmE, informal*) to have a bad or negative effect on sth 對…造成阻礙；對…有負面影響；損害

Crim·plene™ /ˈkrɪmpliːn/ *noun* [U] an artificial material used for making clothes, that does not get lines on it when it is folded or crushed 克林普綸（不易起皺的合成纖維布料）

crim·son /ˈkrɪmzn/ *adj.* dark red in colour 深紅色的；暗紅色的：*She went crimson* (= her face became very red because she was embarrassed). 她的臉變得通紅。▸ **crim·son** *noun* [U]

cringe /krɪndʒ/ *verb* **1** [I] to move back and/or away from sb because you are afraid 畏縮；怯退 **SYN** **cower**：*a child cringing in terror* 嚇得直退縮的小孩 **2** [I] to feel very embarrassed and uncomfortable about sth 感到尷尬不安；覺得難為情：*I cringe when I think of the poems I wrote then.* 每當我想起我那時寫的詩歌就感到很難堪。

cringe·worthy /ˈkrɪndʒwɜːði; *NAmE* -wɜːrði/ (also **ˈcringe-making**) *adj.* (both *BrE, informal*) making you feel embarrassed or uncomfortable 令人感到尷尬（或不舒服）的：*It was a cringeworthy performance from start to finish.* 從頭到尾這真是一次叫人不舒服的演出。

crin·kle /ˈkrɪŋkl/ *verb, noun*

■ ***verb*** [I, T] to become covered with or to form a lot of thin folds or lines, especially in skin, cloth or paper（尤指皮膚、布料或紙張）變皺，起皺紋：*He smiled, his* ***eyes crinkling***. 他瞇着眼睛笑了。◇ *Her face crinkled up in a smile.* 她一笑臉就皺了起來。◇ **~ sth** *The binding had faded and the pages were crinkled.* 書的封皮已經褪色，紙張也皺巴巴的。

Collocations 詞語搭配

Crime 犯罪

Committing a crime 犯罪

- **commit** a crime/a murder/a violent assault/a brutal killing/an armed robbery/fraud 犯罪／謀殺罪／暴力侵犯他人身體罪／殘殺罪／持槍搶劫罪／詐騙罪
- **be involved in** terrorism/a suspected arson attack/people smuggling/human trafficking 參與恐怖主義活動；涉嫌縱火襲擊；參與人口走私／人口販賣
- **engage/participate in** criminal activity/illegal practices/acts of mindless vandalism 參與犯罪活動／非法活動／愚昧的故意毀壞他人財產的行為
- **steal** sb's wallet/purse/(*BrE*) mobile phone/(*NAmE*) cell phone 偷某人的錢包／手機
- **rob** a bank/a person/a tourist 搶劫銀行／他人／遊客
- **break into**/(*BrE*) **burgle**/(*NAmE*) **burglarize** a house/a home/an apartment 入室盜竊
- **hijack** a plane/ship/bus 劫持飛機／輪船／公共汽車
- **smuggle** drugs/weapons/arms/immigrants 走私毒品／武器／軍火；偷運移民
- **launder** drug money (through sth)（通過…）洗毒資
- **forge** documents/certificates/passports 偽造文件／證件／護照
- **take/accept/pay sb/offer** (**sb**) a bribe 索取／接受賄賂；向（某人）行賄
- **run** a phishing/an email/an Internet scam 進行網絡釣魚／電子郵件／互聯網詐騙

Fighting crime 打擊犯罪

- **combat/fight** crime/terrorism/corruption/drug trafficking 打擊犯罪／恐怖主義／腐敗／販毒
- **prevent/stop** credit-card fraud/child abuse/software piracy 防止／阻止信用卡詐騙／虐待兒童／軟件盜版
- **deter/stop** criminals/burglars/thieves/shoplifters/vandals 威懾／阻止犯罪分子／入室盜竊者／小偷／商店扒手／故意破壞公物者
- **reduce/tackle/crack down on** knife/gun/violent/street crime 減少／處理／嚴厲打擊持刀／持槍／暴力／街頭犯罪
- **foil** a bank raid/a terrorist plot 阻截一起銀行搶劫案／一次恐怖分子的陰謀
- **help/support/protect** the victims of crime 幫助／支持／保護犯罪事件的受害者

Investigating crime 調查犯罪活動

- **report** a crime/a theft/a rape/an attack/(*especially BrE*) an incident to the police 向警方舉報不法行為／偷竊案／強姦案／襲擊事件／暴力事件
- **witness** the crime/attack/murder/incident 目擊犯罪／襲擊／謀殺／暴力事件
- **investigate** a murder/(*especially NAmE*) a homicide/a burglary/a robbery/the alleged incident 調查謀殺案件／蓄意殺人案／入室盜竊案／搶劫案／涉嫌的暴力事件
- **conduct/launch/pursue** an investigation (into …)/(*especially BrE*) a police/murder inquiry 進行／開始／繼續（對…的）調查／警方調查／謀殺案調查
- **investigate/reopen** a criminal/murder case 調查／重新審理犯罪／謀殺案件
- **examine/investigate/find fingerprints at** the crime scene/the scene of crime 仔細檢查／調查／查找犯罪現場的指紋
- **collect/gather** forensic evidence 收集法醫證據
- **uncover** new evidence/a fraud/a scam/a plot/a conspiracy/political corruption/a cache of weapons 發現新證據／詐騙／欺詐／密謀／陰謀／政治腐敗／私藏武器
- **describe/identify** a suspect/the culprit/the perpetrator/the assailant/the attacker 描述／指認嫌疑犯／罪犯／作惡者／攻擊者／襲擊者
- **question/interrogate** a suspect/witness 詢問嫌疑人／目擊證人
- **solve/crack** the case 破案

➲ more collocations at JUSTICE

■ **noun** a very thin fold or line made on paper, cloth or skin 褶痕；皺紋

crin·kly /ˈkrɪŋkli/ *adj.* **1** having a lot of thin folds or lines 多褶皺的；多皺紋的：*crinkly silver foil* 佈滿褶皺的銀箔 **2** (of hair 頭髮) having a lot of small curls or waves 多鬈髮的；多波浪的

crin·ol·ine /ˈkrɪnəlɪn/ *noun* a frame that was worn under a skirt by some women in the past in order to give the skirt a very round full shape（舊時的）裙襯，裙撐，裙架

cripes /kraɪps/ *exclamation* (*BrE, old-fashioned, informal*) used to show that sb is surprised or annoyed（表示驚訝或惱怒）天哪，啊呀

crip·ple /ˈkrɪpl/ *verb, noun*

■ **verb 1** [usually passive] **~ sb** to damage sb's body so that they are no longer able to walk or move normally 使殘廢；使跛；使成瘸子 SYN **disable**：*He was crippled by polio as a child.* 他幼年患過小兒麻痺症，結果腿就瘸了。◇ *to be crippled with arthritis* 因患關節炎而腿瘸 **2** [usually passive] **~ sb/sth** to seriously damage or harm sb/sth 嚴重毀壞（或損害）：*The pilot tried to land his crippled plane.* 飛行員試圖駕駛損壞嚴重的飛機着陸。▸ **crip·pling** *adj.*：*a crippling disease* 嚴重損害健康的疾病 ◇ *crippling debts* 導致經濟癱瘓的債務

■ **noun** (*old-fashioned* or *offensive*) a person who is unable to walk or move normally because of a disease or injury 傷殘人；殘疾人；跛子；瘸子：(*figurative*) *He's an emotional cripple* (= he cannot express his feelings). 他是個感情有缺陷的人。HELP People now use **disabled person** instead of 'cripple'. 人們現在説 disabled person，而不説 cripple。

cri·sis 🔑 /ˈkraɪsɪs/ *noun* [C, U] (*pl.* **cri·ses** /-siːz/)

1 🔑 a time of great danger, difficulty or confusion when problems must be solved or important decisions must be made 危機；危急關頭：*a* ***political/financial crisis*** 政治／金融危機 ◇ *the government's latest* ***economic crisis*** 政府最近的經濟危機 ◇ *The business is still* ***in crisis*** *but it has survived the worst of the recession.* 這家公司雖然仍處於危機之中，但已經挺過了經濟衰退最嚴重的日子。◇ *The Labour Party was facing an* ***identity crisis.*** 工黨當時正面臨着自身認同的危機。◇ *an expert in* ***crisis management*** 危機處理專家 ◇ *We provide help to families in crisis situations.* 我們對處於困境的家庭提供幫助。◇ *In times of crisis I know which friends I can turn to.* 在危難關頭我知道能投靠哪些朋友。◇ *The party was suffering a* ***crisis of confidence*** *among its supporters* (= they did not trust it any longer). 當時這個政黨在其支持者中正遭受信任危機。➲ see also MIDLIFE CRISIS **2** 🔑 a time when a problem, a bad situation or an illness is at its worst point 危難時刻；病危期：*Their marriage has reached crisis point.* 他們的婚姻已到了岌岌可危的地步。◇ *The fever has passed its crisis.* 發燒已過危險期。➲ see also CRITICAL (3)

crisp 🔑 /krɪsp/ *adj., noun, verb*

■ **adj.** (**crisp·er**, **crisp·est**) (usually *approving*) **1** 🔑 (of food 食物) (also **crispy**) pleasantly hard and dry 脆的；酥脆的：*Bake until the pastry is golden and crisp.* 把油酥糕點烤至金黃酥脆。**2** 🔑 (of fruit and vegetables 水果和蔬菜) (also **crispy**) firm and fresh 鮮脆的；脆的：*a crisp* ***apple/lettuce*** 新鮮脆生的蘋果／生菜 **3** (of paper or cloth 紙張或布料) fresh and clean; new and slightly stiff without any folds in it 潔淨的；挺括的：*a crisp new $5 bill* 一張嶄新挺括的 5 元鈔票 ◇ *a crisp white shirt* 潔淨挺括的白襯衫 **4** (of the air or the weather 空氣或天氣) pleasantly dry and cold 涼爽的；清新的；乾燥寒冷讓人舒暢的：*a crisp winter morning* 冬天一個寒冷的早晨 ◇ *The air was crisp and clear and the sky was blue.* 空氣清新，天空碧藍。**5** (of snow, leaves, etc. 雪、樹葉等) firm or dry and making a pleasant noise when crushed（壓碎時發出）脆響的：*deep, crisp snow* 踩上去咯吱作響的積雪 **6** (of sounds, images, etc. 聲音、圖像等) pleasantly clear and sharp 清脆悦耳的；清晰分明的：*The recording sounds very crisp, considering its age.* 考慮到這錄音已年代久遠，聽起來聲音還是挺清楚的。**7** (sometimes *disapproving*) (of a person's way of speaking 說話的方式) quick and confident in a way that suggests that the person is busy or is not being friendly 簡短乾脆的（表明某人忙或不友好）：*Her answer was crisp, and she gave no details.* 她的回答簡短而乾脆，沒有提供細節。▸ **crisp·ly** *adv.*：*crisply fried potatoes* 油炸脆土豆片 ◇ *'Take a seat,' she said crisply.* "坐下。"她乾脆地說。**crisp·ness** *noun* [U]：*The salad had lost its crispness.* 這色拉已經不脆了。

■ **noun 1** (also **po,tato 'crisp**) (both *BrE*) (*NAmE* **chip**, **po'tato chip**) a thin round slice of potato that is fried until hard then dried and eaten cold. Crisps are sold in bags and have many different flavours. 油炸土豆片，炸薯片（有多種風味，袋裝）➲ picture at CHIP **2** (*NAmE*) (*BrE* **crum·ble**) [U, C] a DESSERT (= a sweet dish) made from fruit that is covered with a rough mixture of flour, butter and sugar, cooked in the oven and usually served hot 水果酥，酥脆水果甜點（通常烤熟趁熱吃）：*apple crisp* 蘋果酥 IDM see BURN *v.*

■ **verb** [I, T] **~ (sth)** to become or make sth crisp（使）變脆

crisp·bread /ˈkrɪspbred/ *noun* [C, U] a thin crisp biscuit made of WHEAT or RYE, often eaten with cheese or instead of bread 薄脆麥餅乾（用小麥或黑麥製成，常與奶酪同吃，或替代麵包）

crispy /ˈkrɪspi/ *adj.* (*approving*) = CRISP：*crispy batter* 炸土豆片用的麪糊

criss-cross /ˈkrɪs krɒs; *NAmE* krɔːs/ *adj., verb*

■ **adj.** [usually before noun] with many straight lines that cross each other 十字交叉的；縱橫交錯的：*a criss-cross pattern* 十字形圖案 ▸ **criss-cross** *noun* [sing.]：*a criss-cross of streets* 縱橫交錯的街道

■ **verb** [T, I] **~ (sth)** | **~ sth (with sth)** to make a pattern on sth with many straight lines that cross each other 構成十字形（或交叉）圖案：*The city is criss-crossed with canals.* 這座城市裏運河縱橫交錯。

cri·ter·ion 🔑 AW /kraɪˈtɪəriən; *NAmE* -ˈtɪr-/ *noun* (*pl.* **cri·teria** /-riə/)

a standard or principle by which sth is judged, or with the help of which a decision is made（評判或作決定的）標準，準則，原則：*The main criterion is value for money.* 主要的標準是要划算。◇ *What criteria are used for assessing a student's ability?* 用什麼標準來評定一個學生的能力？

crit·ic /ˈkrɪtɪk/ *noun* **1** a person who expresses opinions about the good and bad qualities of books, music, etc. 批評家；評論家；評論員：*a* ***music/theatre/literary, etc. critic*** 音樂、戲劇、文學等評論家 ◇ *The critics loved the movie.* 評論家喜愛這部電影。**2** a person who expresses disapproval of sb/sth and talks about their bad qualities, especially publicly 批評者；挑剔的人：*She is one of the ruling party's most outspoken critics.* 她是最直言不諱地批評執政黨的其中一人。◇ *a critic of private health care* 對私營醫療保健服務持批評態度的人

crit·ic·al 🔑 /ˈkrɪtɪkl/ *adj.*

▸ **EXPRESSING DISAPPROVAL** 表示不贊成 **1** 🔑 expressing disapproval of sb/sth and saying what you think is bad about them 批評的；批判性的；挑剔的：*a* ***critical comment/report*** 批判性的評論／報道 ◇ *The supervisor is always very critical.* 主管總是很挑剔。◇ **~ of sb/sth** *Tom's parents were highly critical of the school.* 湯姆的父母對學校提出了強烈的批評。

▸ **IMPORTANT** 重要 **2** 🔑 extremely important because a future situation will be affected by it 極重要的；關鍵的；至關緊要的 SYN **crucial**：*a critical factor in the election campaign* 競選活動的關鍵因素 ◇ *Reducing levels of carbon dioxide in the atmosphere is* ***of critical importance.*** 減少大氣層中的二氧化碳含量極其重要。◇ *Your decision is* ***critical to*** *our future.* 你的決定對我們的將來至關重要。➲ SYNONYMS at ESSENTIAL

▸ **SERIOUS/DANGEROUS** 嚴重；危險 **3** 🔑 serious, uncertain and possibly dangerous 嚴重的；不穩定的；可能有危險的：*The first 24 hours after the operation are the most critical.* 病人手術後頭 24 小時是最危險的。◇ *a critical moment in our country's history* 我國歷史上的危急關頭 ◇ *One of the victims of the fire remains* ***in a critical condition.*** 大火的一位受害者依然病情危急。➲ see also CRISIS (2)

▸ **MAKING CAREFUL JUDGEMENTS** 判斷審慎 **4** 🔑 involving making fair, careful judgements about the good and

C

bad qualities of sb/sth 有判斷力的；判斷公正（或審慎）的：*Students are encouraged to develop critical thinking instead of accepting opinions without questioning them.* 要鼓勵學生培養判斷力，而非不懂提問，只知接收意見。▸ OF ART/MUSIC/BOOKS, ETC. 藝術、音樂、書等 **5** [only before noun] according to the judgement of critics of art, music, literature, etc. 根據（藝術、音樂、文學等）評論家的評論：*the film director's greatest critical success* 那位電影導演從評論界獲得的最大成功 ◇ *In her day she never received the **critical acclaim** (= praise from the critics) she deserved.* 她一生從未受到過評論家應當給她的讚揚。▸ **crit·ic·al·ly** /-ɪkli/ *adv.*：*She spoke critically of her father.* 她談到父親時頗有微詞。◇ *He is **critically ill** in intensive care.* 他病得很重，正處於特護之中。◇ *I looked at myself critically in the mirror.* 我對着鏡子，挑剔地打量着自己。

ˌcritical ˈmass *noun* (*physics* 物) the smallest amount of a substance that is needed for a nuclear CHAIN REACTION to take place（核鏈式反應的）臨界質量

ˌcritical ˈpath *noun* [sing.] (*technical* 術語) the order of work that should be followed to complete a project as fast and as cheaply as possible（又快又省完成項目必須遵循的）關鍵程序

ˌcritical ˈtheory *noun* [U] a way of thinking about and examining culture and literature by considering the social, historical, and IDEOLOGICAL forces that affect it and make it the way it is 批評理論，批判理論（指從社會、歷史和意識形態力量所產生的影響的角度來思考和探討文化和文學）

criti·cism 0-w /ˈkrɪtɪsɪzəm/ *noun*
1 0-w [U, C] the act of expressing disapproval of sb/sth and opinions about their faults or bad qualities; a statement showing disapproval 批評；批判；責備；指責：*The plan has attracted criticism from consumer groups.* 這項計劃引起了各消費者組織的指責。◇ *People in public life must always be **open to criticism** (= willing to accept being criticized).* 公眾人物必須隨時準備接受批評。◇ *Ben is very sensitive, he just can't **take criticism**.* 本很敏感，簡直接受不了批評。◇ *to offer sb **constructive criticism** (= that is meant to be helpful)* 給某人提出建設性的批評意見 ◇ *I didn't mean it as a criticism.* 我沒有要責備的意思。◇ ***criticisms levelled at** (= aimed at) journalists* 針對記者的批評 ◇ **~ of sb/sth** *There was **widespread criticism** of the government's handling of the disaster.* 政府對災難的處理方式遭到了普遍的批評。◇ **~ that …** *My only criticism of the house is that it is on a main road.* 我對這座房子唯一的不滿是它處於一條大路上。OPP **praise** **2** 0-w [U] the work or activity of making fair, careful judgements about the good and bad qualities of sb/sth, especially books, music, etc.（尤指對書、音樂等的）評論文章，評論：*literary criticism* 文學批評

criti·cize (*BrE* also **-ise**) 0-w /ˈkrɪtɪsaɪz/ *verb*
1 0-w [I, T] to say that you disapprove of sb/sth; to say what you do not like or think is wrong about sb/sth 批評；批判；挑剔；指責：*All you ever do is criticize!* 你就只知道批評！◇ **~ sb/sth** *The decision was criticized by environmental groups.* 這個決定受到了環保團體的批評。◇ **~ sb/sth for sth** *The government has been criticized for not taking the problem seriously.* 政府因沒有認真對待這個問題而受到指責。OPP **praise** **2** 0-w [T] **~ sth** (*BrE*) to judge the good and bad qualities of sth 評論；評價：*We were taught how to criticize poems.* 我們學習了怎樣評論詩歌。

cri·tique /krɪˈtiːk/ *noun, verb*
■ ***noun*** a piece of written criticism of a set of ideas, a work of art, etc. 評論；評論文章：*a feminist critique of Freud's theories* 從女權主義的角度對弗洛伊德理論所作的批評
■ ***verb*** **~ sth** to write or give your opinion of, or reaction to, a set of ideas, a work of art, etc. 寫評論；對…發表評論；評判：*Her job involves critiquing designs by fashion students.* 她的工作包括評判時裝專業學生的設計。

crit·ter /ˈkrɪtə(r)/ *noun* (*NAmE, informal*) a living creature 生物：*wild critters* 野生的生物

croak /krəʊk; *NAmE* kroʊk/ *verb, noun*
■ ***verb*** **1** [I] to make a rough low sound, like the sound a FROG makes 發出（像青蛙的）低沉刺耳聲；呱呱地叫 **2** [I, T] to speak or say sth with a rough low voice 用低沉而沙啞的聲音說話：*I had a sore throat and could only croak.* 我喉嚨痛，只能啞着嗓子說話。◇ **~ sth** *He managed to croak a greeting.* 他勉強用沙啞的嗓音打招呼。◇ **+ speech** *'I'm fine,' she croaked.* "我沒事。"她啞着嗓子說。**3** [I] (*slang*) to die 死；嗝氣
■ ***noun*** a rough low sound made in the throat, like the sound made by a FROG（像青蛙發出的）低沉沙啞的聲音，呱呱的叫聲

croaky /ˈkrəʊki; *NAmE* ˈkroʊ-/ *adj.* (*informal*) (of sb's voice 嗓音) deep and rough, especially because of a sore throat（尤指因嗓子疼痛而）低沉沙啞的

croc /krɒk; *NAmE* krɑːk/ *noun* (*informal*) = CROCODILE

cro·chet /ˈkrəʊʃeɪ; *NAmE* kroʊˈʃeɪ/ *noun, verb*
■ ***noun*** [U] a way of making clothes, etc. from wool or cotton using a special thick needle with a hook at the end to make a pattern of connected threads 鉤針編織 ➲ VISUAL VOCAB page V41
■ ***verb*** (**cro·chet·ing**, **cro·cheted**) [T, I] **~ (sth)** to make sth using crochet 用鉤針編織：*a crocheted shawl* 鉤針編織的披肩

crock /krɒk; *NAmE* krɑːk/ *noun* **1** **crocks** [pl.] (*old-fashioned*) cups, plates, dishes, etc. 陶器；瓦器 **2** [C] (*old use*) a large pot made of baked CLAY 瓦罐；罎子 **3** [C] (*BrE, informal*) an old person 老傢伙；老朽的人 **4** [C] (*BrE, informal*) an old car in bad condition 破舊的汽車
IDM **a ˌcrock of ˈshit** (*taboo, slang, especially NAmE*) something that is not true 屁話；胡說八道 ➲ more at GOLD *n.*

crocked /krɒkt; *NAmE* krɑːkt/ *adj.* [not before noun] (*NAmE, slang*) drunk 喝醉；醉醺醺

crock·ery /ˈkrɒkəri; *NAmE* ˈkrɑːk-/ *noun* [U] **1** (*especially BrE*) plates, cups, dishes, etc. 陶器；瓦器 **2** (*NAmE*) dishes, etc. that you use in the oven（烤箱用的）碟，盤，杯，碗

croco·dile /ˈkrɒkədaɪl; *NAmE* ˈkrɑːk-/ (also *informal* **croc**) *noun* **1** [C] a large REPTILE with a long tail, hard skin and very big JAWS. Crocodiles live in rivers and lakes in hot countries. 鱷魚 **2** [U] crocodile skin made into leather（做成皮革的）鱷魚皮：*crocodile shoes* 鱷魚皮皮鞋 **3** [C] (*BrE*) a long line of people, especially children, walking in pairs 成對縱列行進的人（尤指兒童）
IDM **ˈcrocodile tears** if sb SHEDS (= cries) **crocodile tears**, they pretend to be sad about sth, but they are not really sad at all 鱷魚的眼淚；假慈悲

ˈcrocodile clip (*especially BrE*) (also **ˈalligator clip** *especially NAmE*) *noun* an object with sharp teeth used for holding things together, that is held closed by a spring and that you squeeze to open 鱷魚嘴夾：*Use the crocodile clips to attach the cables to the battery.* 用鱷魚嘴夾把電纜接到蓄電池上。

cro·cus /ˈkrəʊkəs; *NAmE* ˈkroʊ-/ *noun* a small yellow, purple or white flower that appears in early spring 番紅花；藏紅花

croft /krɒft; *NAmE* krɔːft/ *noun* (*BrE*) a small farm or the house on it, especially in Scotland（尤指蘇格蘭的）小農場，小農場上的住宅

croft·er /ˈkrɒftə(r); *NAmE* ˈkrɔːft-/ *noun* (*BrE*) a person who rents or owns a small family farm, especially in Scotland（尤指蘇格蘭的）家庭小農場的佃戶，家庭小農場主

Crohn's disease /ˈkrəʊnz dɪziːz; *NAmE* ˈkroʊnz/ *noun* [U] a disease affecting the lower INTESTINES, in which they develop many sore areas. The disease lasts for many years and is difficult to cure. 克羅恩病，節段性腸炎（引起大腸直腸多部位長年疼痛）

crois·sant /ˈkrwæsɒ̃; *NAmE* krwɑːˈsɑ̃ː; krəˈsɑːnt/ *noun* (from *French*) a small sweet roll with a curved shape, eaten especially at breakfast 羊角麪包；新月形麪包；牛角麪包

crone /krəʊn; *NAmE* kroʊn/ *noun* (*literary*) an ugly old woman 醜陋的老太婆

crony /ˈkrəʊni; *NAmE* ˈkroʊni/ *noun* [usually pl.] (*pl.* **-ies**) (*often disapproving*) a person that sb spends a lot of time with 好友；密友：*He was playing cards with his cronies.* 他當時正與他那些狐朋狗友玩牌。

cro·ny·ism /ˈkrəʊniɪzəm; *NAmE* ˈkroʊ-/ *noun* [U] (*disapproving*) the situation in which people in power give jobs to their friends 任人唯親；任用親信

crook /krʊk/ *noun, verb, adj.*

■ **noun** **1** (*informal*) a dishonest person 騙子 SYN **criminal**：*That salesman is a real crook.* 那推銷員真是個騙子。 **2 ~ of your arm/elbow** the place where your arm bends at the elbow 臂彎；肘彎 **3** a long stick with a hook at one end, used especially in the past by SHEPHERDS for catching sheep（尤指舊時牧羊人捕羊的）曲柄杖 IDM see HOOK *n.*

■ **verb ~ sth** to bend your finger or arm 使（手指或手臂）彎曲

■ **adj.** [not usually before noun] (*AustralE, NZE, informal*) ill/sick 生病；有病；不舒服

crooked /ˈkrʊkɪd/ *adj.* **1** not in a straight line; bent or twisted 不直的；彎曲的；扭曲的：*a crooked nose/smile* 鷹鈎鼻；不自然的微笑 ◇ *a village of crooked streets* 街道彎彎曲曲的村莊 ◇ *Your glasses are on crooked.* 你的眼鏡歪了。 OPP **straight** **2** dishonest 不誠實的；欺詐的：*a crooked businessman/deal* 奸商；不正當的交易 **3 ~ (on sb)** (*AustralE, informal*) annoyed 生（某人的）氣：*It's not you I'm* **crooked on**, *it's him.* 我不是生你的氣，是生他的氣。 ▶ **crook·ed·ly** *adv.*

croon /kruːn/ *verb* [T, I] **~ (sth)** to sing sth quietly and gently 低聲哼唱：*She gently crooned a lullaby.* 她輕聲哼唱了一支搖籃曲。

croon·er /ˈkruːnə(r)/ *noun* (*old-fashioned*) a male singer who sings slow romantic songs（慢唱浪漫歌曲的）男歌手

crop 🔑 /krɒp; *NAmE* krɑːp/ *noun, verb*

■ **noun**

▸ PLANTS FOR FOOD 莊稼 **1** 🔑 [C] a plant that is grown in large quantities, especially as food 莊稼；作物：*Sugar is an important crop on the island.* 甘蔗是這個島上的一種重要作物。◇ ***crop rotation/production/yield*** 農作物輪作／生產／產量 ◇ *The crops are regularly sprayed with pesticides.* 農作物定期噴灑殺蟲劑。 ➲ COLLOCATIONS at FARMING ➲ VISUAL VOCAB pages V2, V3 ➲ see also CASH CROP **2** 🔑 [C] the amount of grain, fruit, etc. that is grown in one season（穀物、水果等一季的）收成，產量 SYN **harvest**：*a fall in this year's coffee crop* 今年咖啡產量的下降 ◇ *We are looking forward to a* ***bumper crop*** (= a very large one). 我們期盼着大豐收。

▸ GROUP OF PEOPLE 一群人 **3** [sing.] **a ~ of sth** a group of people who do sth at the same time; a number of things that happen at the same time（同時做某事的）一群人，一批人；（同時發生的）一些事情：*the current crop of trainees* 現在的這批練習生 ◇ *She is really* ***the cream of the crop*** (= the best in her group). 她的確是那批人中的精英。◇ *a* ***crop of disasters/injuries*** 一連串的災難／傷害

▸ WHIP 鞭子 **4** [C] a short WHIP used by horse riders（騎手的）短馬鞭：*a riding crop* 騎馬用的短馬鞭

▸ HAIR 頭髮 **5** [C] a very short HAIRSTYLE 短髮 **6** [sing.] **a ~ of dark, fair, etc. hair/curls** hair that is short and thick 短而密的頭髮：*He had a thick crop of black curly hair.* 他有一頭濃黑鬈曲的短髮。

▸ OF BIRD 鳥 **7** (*technical* 術語) a part of a bird's throat shaped like a bag where food is stored before it passes into the stomach 嗉囊；嗉子

■ **verb** (-pp-)

▸ HAIR 頭髮 **1** [T] **~ sth (+ adj.)** to cut sb's hair very short 剪短：*closely cropped hair* 剪得很短的頭髮 ➲ VISUAL VOCAB page V60

▸ PHOTOGRAPH 照片 **2** [T] **~ sth** (*technical* 術語) to cut off part of a photograph or picture 剪裁（照片或圖畫）

▸ OF ANIMALS 動物 **3** [T] **~ sth** to bite off and eat the tops of plants, especially grass 啃吃（青草或其他植物上面的部份）

▸ PLANTS 植物 **4** [I] (of plants 植物) to produce a crop 有收成：*The potatoes cropped well this year.* 今年馬鈴薯豐收。 **5** [T] **~ sth** to use land to grow crops 種地；種莊稼：*The river valley is intensively cropped.* 河谷裏種滿了莊稼。

PHR V **ˌcrop ˈup** to appear or happen, especially when it is not expected（尤指意外地）出現，發生 SYN **come up**：*His name just cropped up in conversation.* 交談時無意中就提到了他的名字。◇ *I'll be late—something's cropped up at home.* 我要晚一點來，家裏突然出了點事。

ˈcrop circle (also **ˈcorn circle**) *noun* a round area in a field of crops that has suddenly become flat. Some people say that crop circles were made by creatures from outer space. 麥田圈（莊稼地裏突然變平的一塊圓形地，傳說是外星生物所為）

ˈcrop dusting *noun* [U] the practice of spraying crops with chemicals such as PESTICIDES from a plane 作物噴灑（用飛機給農作物噴灑農藥等）

crop·per /ˈkrɒpə(r); *NAmE* ˈkrɑːp-/ *noun*

IDM **come a ˈcropper** (*BrE, informal*) **1** (of a person 人) to fall over 跌倒；摔倒；栽跟頭 **2** to have a failure or near disaster 失敗；慘敗：*We nearly came a cropper in the second half of the game.* 在比賽的下半場我們差一點就輸掉了。

ˈcrop top *noun* a woman's informal piece of clothing for the upper body, cut short so that the stomach can be seen（女式）露腹短上裝，露臍裝

cro·quet /ˈkrəʊkeɪ; *NAmE* kroʊˈkeɪ/ *noun* [U] a game played on grass in which players use wooden hammers (called MALLETS) to knock wooden balls through a series of HOOPS (= curved wires) 槌球（在草地上進行，以木槌擊木球穿過一連串的鐵圈）

cro·quette /krəʊˈket; *NAmE* kroʊ-/ *noun* a small amount of MASHED potato, fish, etc., shaped into a ball or tube, covered with BREADCRUMBS and fried（用土豆泥、魚餡等裹以麵包屑做成的）炸丸子，炸條塊

crore /krɔː(r)/ *number* (*plural verb* 複數動詞) (*pl.* **crore** or **crores**) (*IndE*) ten million; one hundred LAKH 一千萬

cro·sier (also **croz·ier**) /ˈkrəʊziə(r); *NAmE* ˈkroʊʒər/ *noun* a long stick, usually curved at one end, carried by a BISHOP (= a Christian priest of high rank) at religious ceremonies（主教的）牧杖，權杖

cross 🔑 /krɒs; *NAmE* krɔːs/ *noun, verb, adj.*

■ **noun**

▸ MARK ON PAPER 紙上符號 **1** 🔑 [C] a mark or an object formed by two lines crossing each other (X or +); the mark (X) is often used on paper to show sth 叉字形記號；十字形記號：*I've put a cross on the map to show where the hotel is.* 我已在地圖上打叉標出了旅館的位置。◇ *Put a tick if the answer is correct and a cross if it's wrong.* 答案正確打鈎，錯誤打叉。◇ *Sign your name on the form where I've put a cross.* 在表格上我打叉的地方簽上你的名字。◇ *Those who could not write signed with a cross.* 不會寫字的人畫十字代替簽名。 ➲ see also NOUGHTS AND CROSSES ➲ compare TICK *n.* (1)

▸ FOR PUNISHMENT 懲罰 **2** [C] a long vertical piece of wood with a shorter piece across it near the top. In the past people were hung on crosses and left to die as a punishment.（舊時用以處死人的）十字架

▸ CHRISTIAN SYMBOL 基督教標記 **3 the Cross** [sing.] the cross that Jesus Christ died on, used as a symbol of Christianity（耶穌釘死在上面的）十字架 **4** 🔑 [C] an object, a design, a piece of jewellery, etc. in the shape of a cross, used as a symbol of Christianity 十字架物品（或設計、首飾等）：*She wore a small gold cross on a chain around her neck.* 她脖子上戴了一條項鏈，上面掛着個金的小十字架。

▸ MEDAL 勳章 **5** (usually **Cross**) [C] a small decoration in the shape of a cross that is given to sb as an honour for doing sth very brave（表彰英勇行為的）十字勳章

▸ MIXTURE 混合物 **6** [C, usually sing.] **~ (between A and B)** a mixture of two different things, breeds of animal, etc. 混合物；（動物等的）雜種，雜交品種：*The play was a cross between a farce and a tragedy.* 這齣戲把鬧劇和悲劇交織為一體。◇ *A mule is a cross between a horse and a donkey.* 騾是馬和驢的雜交種。 ➲ see also HYBRID

▸ **IN SPORT 體育運動** **7** [C] (in football (SOCCER) or HOCKEY 足球或曲棍球) a kick or hit of the ball across the field rather than up or down it 橫傳 ➲ see also THE RED CROSS

IDM **have a (heavy) 'cross to bear** to have a difficult problem that makes you worried or unhappy but that you have to deal with 有本難唸的經；有苦難要忍受： *We all have our crosses to bear.* 家家有本難唸的經。

■ *verb*

▸ **GO/PUT ACROSS 穿越；使交叉** **1** [I, T] to go across; to pass or stretch from one side to the other 穿越；越過；橫過；渡過： **~ (over)** *I waved and she crossed over* (= crossed the road towards me). 我揮了揮手，她便橫穿馬路朝我走來。◇ **~ (over) (from …) (to/into …)** *We crossed from Dover to Calais.* 我們從多佛爾橫渡到加來。◇ **~ sth** *to cross a/the road* 橫穿道路 ◇ *to cross the sea/mountains* 越過大海；翻越高山 ◇ *to cross France by train* 乘火車穿越法國 ◇ *The bridge crosses the River Dee.* 這座橋橫跨迪河。◇ *A look of annoyance* ***crossed her face.*** 惱怒的神色從她臉上掠過。◇ *They crossed the finishing line together* (= in a race). 他們同時越過終點線。◇ **~ over sth** *He crossed over the road and joined me.* 他穿過馬路和我會合。 **2** [I] to pass across each other 交叉；相交： *The roads cross just outside the town.* 這些道路正好在城外交叉。◇ *The straps cross over at the back and are tied at the waist.* 帶子在背後交叉，然後繫在腰部。◇ *Our letters must have crossed in the mail* (= each was sent before the other was received). 我們的信一定是在路上交叉了。◇ *We seem to have a* ***crossed line*** (= a telephone call that interrupts another call because of a wrong connection). 我們的電話好像串線了。 **3** [T] **~ sth** to put or place sth across or over sth else 使交叉；使交疊： *to* ***cross your arms/legs*** (= place one arm or leg over the other) 交叉兩臂／雙腿 ◇ *She sat with her legs crossed.* 她蹺着二郎腿坐着。◇ *a flag with a design of two crossed keys* 有兩把鑰匙交叉圖案的旗幟

▸ **OPPOSE 反對** **4** [T] **~ sb** to oppose sb or speak against them or their plans or wishes 反對，反駁，否定（某人或計劃、意願）： *She's really nice until you cross her.* 她待人確實很好，除非你跟她作對。◇ (*literary*) *He had been* ***crossed in love*** (= the person he loved was not faithful to him). 他所愛的人背叛了他。

▸ **MIX ANIMALS/PLANTS 雜交** **5** [T] **~ A with B | ~ A and B** to make two different types of animal breed together; to mix two types of plant to form a new one 使雜交；使異種交配： *A mule is the product of a horse crossed with a donkey.* 騾是馬和驢的雜交種。◇ (*figurative*) *He behaved like an army officer crossed with a professor.* 他的舉止既像軍官又像教授。

▸ **IN SPORT 體育運動** **6** [I] (in football (SOCCER) or HOCKEY 足球或曲棍球) to kick or pass a ball sideways across the field 橫傳

▸ **DRAW LINE 畫線** **7** [T] **~ sth** to draw a line across sth 畫橫線於： *to cross your t's* (= the letters in writing) 寫 t 上面的一橫 ◇ (*BrE*) *to cross a cheque* (= to draw two lines across it so that it can only be paid through a bank account) 在支票上畫線（使支票只能經銀行賬戶兑現）

▸ **MAKE CHRISTIAN SYMBOL 做基督教的標記** **8** [T] **~ yourself** to make the sign of the cross (= the Christian symbol) on your chest （在胸口上）畫十字聖號

IDM **cross that bridge when you 'come to it** to worry about a problem when it actually happens and not before 臨機應變（不用事前操心） **cross your 'fingers** to hope that your plans will be successful (sometimes putting one finger across another as a sign of hoping for good luck) 祈求成功（有時使手指交叉為祈求好運的手勢）： *I'm crossing my fingers that my proposal will be accepted.* 但願我的建議能被採納。◇ *Keep your fingers crossed!* 祈求好運吧！ **cross my 'heart (and hope to die)** (*informal*) used to emphasize that you are telling the truth or will do what you promise 我發誓（否則不得好死）： *I saw him do it—cross my heart.* 我看見是他幹的，我可以發誓。 **cross your 'mind** (of thoughts, etc. 想法等) to come into your mind 掠過心頭；出現在腦海 **SYN** **occur to sb** ： *It never crossed my mind that she might lose* (= I was sure that she would win). 我從來沒想過她會失敗。 **,cross sb's ,palm with 'silver** to give sb money so that they will do you a favour, especially tell your FORTUNE 為得到好處而給某人錢；（尤指）付錢請人算命 **,cross sb's 'path | people's ,paths 'cross** if sb **crosses sb's path** or **their paths cross**, they meet by chance 偶然相遇；不期而遇；邂逅： *I hope I never cross her path again.* 但願我永遠不再碰見她。◇ *Our paths were to cross again many years later.* 許多年以後我們又不期而遇了。 **cross 'swords (with sb)** to fight or argue with sb （與某人）交鋒，爭論 ➲ more at DOT *v.*, WIRE *n.*

PHR V **,cross sb/sth↔'off | ,cross sb/sth 'off sth** to draw a line through a person's name or an item on a list because they/it is no longer required or involved （從名單或清單上）畫掉，刪掉： *We can cross his name off; he's not coming.* 他不來了，我們可以把他的名字畫掉了。 **,cross sth↔'out/'through** to draw a line through a word, usually because it is wrong 畫掉，刪掉（錯字） **,cross 'over (to/into sth)** to move or change from one type of culture, music, political party, etc. to another （從某種文化、音樂、政黨等）轉變，變換： *a cult movie that has crossed over to mass appeal* 由部份人推崇轉變為大眾喜愛的電影 ➲ related noun CROSSOVER

■ *adj.* (**cross·er**, **cross·est**) **~ (with sb)** (*especially BrE*) annoyed or quite angry 惱怒的；十分憤怒的；生氣的： *I was cross with him for being late.* 我因他遲到而十分生氣。◇ *Please don't* ***get cross.*** *Let me explain.* 請別發火，讓我來解釋一下。 ➲ **SYNONYMS** at ANGRY ▸ **cross·ly** *adv.* ： *'Well what did you expect?' she said crossly.* "咳，你還想要什麼？" 她氣憤地説。

cross- /krɒs; *NAmE* krɔːs/ *combining form* (in nouns, verbs, adjectives and adverbs 構成名詞、動詞、形容詞和副詞) involving movement or action from one thing to another or between two things 從一事物到另一事物的運動（或動作）；兩事物間的運動（或動作）；橫過；穿越： *cross-Channel ferries* 橫渡英吉利海峽的渡船 ◇ *cross-fertilize* 異花受粉 ◇ *crossfire* 交叉火力

cross·bar /'krɒsbɑː(r); *NAmE* 'krɔːs-/ *noun* **1** the bar joining the two vertical posts of a goal （足球球門的）橫梁 ➲ **VISUAL VOCAB** page V44 **2** the bar between the seat and the HANDLEBARS of a man's bicycle （自行車的）橫梁 ➲ **VISUAL VOCAB** page V51

'cross-bencher *noun* (*BrE*) a member of the British House of Lords who does not belong to a particular political party （英國上議院的）無黨派議員，中立議員 ▸ **'cross benches** *noun* [pl.] ： *members who sit on the cross benches* 坐在中立議員席的議員

cross·bones /'krɒsbəʊnz; *NAmE* 'krɔːsboʊnz/ *noun* [pl.] ➲ SKULL AND CROSSBONES

'cross-border *adj.* [only before noun] involving activity across a border between two countries 跨越國境的： *a cross-border raid by guerrillas* 游擊隊越過國境的襲擊

cross·bow /'krɒsbəʊ; *NAmE* 'krɔːsboʊ/ *noun* a weapon which consists of a BOW² (1) that is fixed onto a larger piece of wood, and that shoots short heavy arrows (called BOLTS) 弩；弩弓；十字弓 ➲ picture at BOLT

'cross-breed *verb, noun*

■ *verb* [T, I] **~ (sth)** to make an animal or a plant breed with a different breed; to breed with an animal or a plant of a different breed 使雜交；雜交繁育： *cross-bred sheep* 雜交羊 ▸ **,cross-'breeding** *noun* [U]

■ *noun* an animal or a plant that is a result of cross-breeding 雜交品種（動物或植物） ➲ compare HYBRID (1)

,cross-'check *verb* to make sure that information, figures etc. are correct by using a different method or system to check them （用不同的方法或系統）核查，核對；交叉檢查： **~ sth** *Cross-check your answers with a calculator.* 用計算器核對一下你的答案。◇ **~ sth against sth** *Baggage should be cross-checked against the names of individual passengers.* 必須再把行李與各位旅客的姓名核對一遍。 ▸ **'cross-check** *noun*

,cross-contam·i'n·ation *noun* [U] the process by which harmful bacteria spread from one substance to another （病菌的）交叉污染

,cross-'country *adj., adv., noun*

■ *adj.* [usually before noun], *adv.* **1** across fields or open country rather than on roads or a track 越野（的）： *cross-country running* 越野賽跑 ◇ *We rode cross-country.*

我們駕車越野前行。 **2** from one part of a country to the other, especially not using main roads or routes （尤指通過越野）橫越全國（的）： *cross-country train journeys* 穿越全國的火車旅行

▪ *noun* **1** **the cross-country** [sing.] a cross-country running or SKIING race 越野賽跑；越野滑雪比賽 **2** [U] the sport of running or SKIING across country 越野賽跑運動；越野滑雪運動 ➲ compare DOWNHILL *n.*

ˌcross-country ˈskiing (also **lang·lauf**) *noun* [U] the sport of SKIING across the countryside, rather than down mountains 越野滑雪（與高山滑雪相對） ➲ **VISUAL VOCAB** page V48

ˌcross-ˈcultural *adj.* involving or containing ideas from two or more different countries or cultures 跨文化的；涉及多種文化的

ˈcross-current *noun* **1** a current of water in a river or in the sea that flows across the main current （穿過河流或海域主流的）交叉水流 **2** [usually pl.] (*formal*) a set of beliefs or ideas that are different from others, especially from those that most people hold 岔流思想（尤指與多數人不同的信仰、觀點或看法）

ˌcross-curˈricu·lar *adj.* (*BrE*) affecting or connected with different parts of the school CURRICULUM 跨課程的；與多種課程有關的

ˌcross-ˈdressing *noun* [U] the practice of wearing clothes usually worn by a person of the opposite sex, especially for sexual pleasure （尤指為得到性快感而）穿異性服裝 **SYN** **transvestism** ▸ **ˌcross-ˈdresser** *noun*

ˌcross-eˈxamine *verb* **~ sb** to question sb carefully and in a lot of detail about answers that they have already given, especially in court（尤指在法庭上對證詞細節的）盤問，反詰： *The witness was cross-examined for over two hours.* 那位證人被盤問了兩個多小時。 ➲ **COLLOCATIONS** at JUSTICE ▸ **ˌcross-eˌxamiˈn·ation** *noun* [U, C]： *He broke down* ***under cross-examination*** (= while he was being cross-examined) *and admitted his part in the assault.* 他經不起嚴密的詰問，招認了他曾參與那次毆打。

ˌcross-ˈeyed *adj.* having one or both eyes looking towards the nose 內斜視的；對眼的；鬥眼兒的

ˌcross-ˈfertil·ize (*BrE* also **-ise**) *verb* **1** **~ sth** (*biology* 生) to FERTILIZE a plant using POLLEN from a different plant of the same SPECIES 異花授粉 **2** **~ sth** to help sth develop in a useful or positive way by mixing ideas from a different area 吸收其他領域的思想以促發展： *The study of psychology has recently been widely cross-fertilized by new discoveries in genetics.* 心理學研究最近從遺傳學的新發現中受益匪淺。 ▸ **ˌcross-ˌfertil·iˈza·tion**, **-iˈsa·tion** *noun* [U, sing.]

cross·fire /ˈkrɒsfaɪə(r); *NAmE* ˈkrɔːs-/ *noun* [U] the firing of guns from two or more directions at the same time, so that the bullets cross 交叉火力： *The doctor was killed in crossfire as he went to help the wounded.* 那位醫生去救助傷員時在交叉火力中喪生。 ◇ (*figurative*) *When two industrial giants clash, small companies can get* ***caught in the crossfire*** (= become involved and suffer as a result). 兩工業鉅頭交火時，小公司難免遭殃。

ˈcross-hatch *verb* **~ sth** (*technical* 術語) to mark or colour sth with two sets of parallel lines crossing each other 用交叉的平行線畫出（或着色）；交叉排線 ▸ **ˈcross-hatching** *noun* [U]

ˈcross head *noun* a screw with a cross shape in the top 十字頭螺釘

ˈcross-infection *noun* [U] (*medical* 醫) an occasion when sb passes an infection to sb who has a different infection 交叉感染

cross·ing /ˈkrɒsɪŋ; *NAmE* ˈkrɔːs-/ *noun* **1** a place where you can safely cross a road, a river, etc., or from one country to another（通過道路、河流等的）安全通行處；人行橫道；渡口；（從一國到另一國的）過境處： *The child was killed when a car failed to stop at the crossing.* 汽車在人行橫道線未能停車，結果把小孩撞死了。 ◇ *The next crossing point is a long way downstream.* 下一個渡口在下游方向很遠的地方。 ◇ *He was arrested by guards at the border crossing.* 他在邊境過境處被衛兵逮捕。 ➲ see also LEVEL CROSSING, PEDESTRIAN CROSSING, PELICAN CROSSING, ZEBRA CROSSING **2** a place where two lines, two roads or two tracks cross （線的）交叉點；（道路的）十字路口；（軌道的）交叉道口 **SYN** **intersection** **3** a journey across a sea or a wide river （海洋或寬闊江河的）橫渡： *a three-hour ferry crossing* 三小時的輪渡 ◇ *a rough crossing from Dover to Calais* 從多佛爾到加來波濤洶湧的橫渡 ◇ *the first Atlantic crossing* 首次橫渡大西洋 **4** an act of going from one side to another 穿越；橫越： *attempted crossings of the border* 穿越邊境未遂

cross-legged /ˌkrɒs ˈlegd; -ˈlegɪd; *NAmE* ˌkrɔːs/ *adv.* sitting on the floor with your legs pulled up in front of you and with one leg or foot over the other 盤腿 ▸ **cross-legged** *adj.*： *the cross-legged figure of the Hindu god* 盤腿打坐的印度教神像

cross·over /ˈkrɒsəʊvə(r); *NAmE* ˈkrɔːsoʊ-/ *noun* the process or result of changing from one area of activity or style of doing sth to another （活動範圍或風格的）改變，轉型，變化： *The album was an exciting jazz-pop crossover.* 這張唱片中收集了爵士樂與流行音樂兩種風格相結合的精彩作品。

cross·piece /ˈkrɒspiːs; *NAmE* ˈkrɔːs-/ *noun* (*technical* 術語) a piece of a structure or a tool that lies or is fixed across another piece 橫檔；橫杆

ˌcross-ˈplatform *adj.* (of a computer program or an electronic device 計算機程序或電子儀器) that can be used with different types of computers or programs 交叉平台的，跨平台的（能兼容不同類型的計算機或程序）

ˌcross-ˈpollin·ate *verb* **~ sth** (*biology* 生) to move POLLEN from a flower or plant onto another flower or plant so that it produces seeds 使異花傳粉；異花受粉 ▸ **ˌcross-polliˈn·ation** *noun* [U]

ˌcross-proˈmotion *noun* [C, U] (*business* 商) a set of advertisements or other activities that are designed to help a company sell two different products, or to help two companies sell their products or services together 交叉推銷（同時推銷兩種商品或兩公司相互推銷產品或服務）

ˌcross ˈpurposes *noun* [pl.] if two people are **at cross purposes**, they do not understand each other because they are talking about or aiming at different things, without realizing it （由於談論或針對不同事情而未意識到的）相互不理解，相互誤解： *I think we're talking at cross purposes; that's not what I meant at all.* 我想我們是說到兩下裏去了，我根本不是那個意思。

ˌcross-ˈquestion *verb* **~ sb** to question sb thoroughly and often in a way that seems aggressive 盤問；追問

ˌcross-reˈfer *verb* (**-rr-**) [T, I] **~ (sth) to sth** to refer to another text or part of a text, especially to give more information about sth 給…註相互參照項；將…指向參照項；交互參照： *The entry for 'polygraph' is cross-referred to the entry for 'lie detector'.* 詞條 polygraph 註有指向詞條 lie detector 的參照項。

ˌcross ˈreference *noun* **~ (to sth)** a note that tells a reader to look in another part of a book or file for further information （指向…的）參照項；交互參照

cross·roads /ˈkrɒsrəʊdz; *NAmE* ˈkrɔːsroʊdz/ *noun* (*pl.* **cross·roads**) a place where two roads meet and cross each other 十字路口： *At the next crossroads, turn right.* 在下一個十字路口向右拐。 ◇ (*figurative*) *He has reached a career crossroads* (= he must decide which way to go next in his career). 他的事業發展到了一個十字路口。 ➲ see also INTERSECTION (1), JUNCTION (1)

IDM **at a/the ˈcrossroads** at an important point in sb's life or development （人生或發展）處於關鍵時刻，在緊要關頭

ˈcross section *noun* **1** [C, U] what you see when you cut through the middle of sth so that you can see the different layers it is made of; a drawing of this view 橫截面（圖）；剖面（圖）；斷面（圖）： *a diagram representing a cross section of the human eye* 表現人眼的剖面圖 ◇ *the human eye* ***in cross section*** 人眼的剖面圖 **2** [C, usually sing.] a group of people or things that are typical of a larger group 典型的一群人（或事物）：

a representative cross section of society 一群具有代表性的社會典型人物

ˌcross-ˈselling *noun* [U] (*business* 商) the activity of selling a different extra product to a customer who is already buying a product from a company 交叉銷售（向現有顧客推銷另一產品）

C

ˈcross street *noun* (*NAmE*) a street that crosses another street 交叉的街；十字街

cross·talk /ˈkrɒstɔːk; *NAmE* ˈkrɔːs-/ *noun* [U] (*technical* 術語) a situation in which a communications system is picking up the wrong signals（通訊系統的）串話，串擾

cross·town /ˌkrɒsˈtaʊn; *NAmE* ˌkrɔːs-/ *adj.* (*NAmE*) going from one side of a town or city to the other 穿過市鎮的：*a crosstown bus* 穿越市區的公共汽車

ˈcross-trainer *noun* **1** a piece of exercise equipment that you use standing up, with parts that you push up and down with your feet and parts that you hold onto and push with your arms 多功能健身器 **2** a type of sports shoe that can be worn for more than one kind of sport 多功能運動鞋

ˈcross-training *noun* [U] the activity of training in sports other than your main sport in order to make yourself fitter and able to do your main sport better 交叉訓練（同時參加多項運動訓練提高身體素質，進而提高自己在主項上的競技水平）

cross·walk /ˈkrɒswɔːk; *NAmE* ˈkrɔːs-/ (*NAmE*) (*BrE* **peˌdestrian ˈcrossing**) *noun* a part of a road where vehicles must stop to allow people to cross 人行橫道；行人穿越道 ➲ see also ZEBRA CROSSING ➲ VISUAL VOCAB pages V2, V3

cross·wind /ˈkrɒswɪnd; *NAmE* ˈkrɔːs-/ *noun* a wind that is blowing across the direction that you are moving in 側風

cross·wise /ˈkrɒswaɪz; *NAmE* ˈkrɔːs-/ *adv.* **1** across, especially from one corner to the opposite one 橫過地；貫穿地；（尤指）對角橫穿地，斜穿地：*Cut the fabric crosswise.* 把那塊布對角剪開。 **2** in the form of a cross 成十字地；交叉地

cross·word /ˈkrɒswɜːd; *NAmE* ˈkrɔːswɜːrd/ (also **ˈcross-word puzzle**) *noun* a game in which you have to fit words across and downwards into spaces with numbers in a square diagram. You find the words by solving CLUES. 縱橫字謎；縱橫填字遊戲：*to **do a/the crossword*** 做縱橫填字遊戲 ◇ *I've finished the crossword apart from 3 across and 10 down.* 這份縱橫字謎除橫 3 豎 10 以外我都填完了。 ➲ VISUAL VOCAB page V39

crotch /krɒtʃ; *NAmE* krɑːtʃ/ (also **crutch**) *noun* **1** the part of the body where the legs join at the top, including the area around the GENITALS（人體的）胯部，兩腿分叉處 **2** the part of a pair of trousers/pants, etc. that covers the crotch 褲襠：*There's a hole in the crotch.* 褲襠上有個洞。

crot·chet /ˈkrɒtʃɪt; *NAmE* ˈkrɑːtʃ-/ (*BrE*) (*NAmE* **ˈquarter note**) *noun* (*music* 音) a note that lasts half as long as a MINIM/HALF NOTE 四分音符 ➲ picture at MUSIC

crot·chety /ˈkrɒtʃəti; *NAmE* ˈkrɑːtʃ-/ *adj.* (*informal*) bad-tempered; easily made angry 脾氣壞的；易怒的；動輒生氣的：*He was tired and crotchety.* 他累了，動不動就發火。

crotch·less /ˈkrɒtʃləs; *NAmE* ˈkrɑːtʃ-/ *adj.* (of underwear 內衣) having a hole at the CROTCH 開襠的；無襠的

crouch /kraʊtʃ/ *verb, noun*

■ ***verb*** [I] (+ **adv./prep.**) to put your body close to the ground by bending your legs under you 蹲；蹲下；蹲伏 SYN **squat**：*He **crouched down** beside her.* 他在她的旁邊蹲了下來。◇ *Doyle crouched behind a hedge.* 多伊爾蹲在籬笆後面。 ▸ **crouched** *adj.*：*She sat crouched in a corner.* 她蹲坐在一個角落裏。

PHR V **ˈcrouch over sb/sth** to bend over sb/sth so that you are very close to them or it 俯身接近：*He crouched over the papers on his desk.* 他俯身看他桌上的文件。

■ ***noun*** [sing.] a crouching position 蹲着的姿勢：*She dropped to a crouch.* 她俯身蹲了下來。

croup /kruːp/ *noun* [U] a disease of children that makes them cough a lot and have difficulty breathing 格魯布，哮吼（兒童疾病，咳得厲害，呼吸困難）

croup·ier /ˈkruːpieɪ; *NAmE* also -piər/ *noun* a person whose job is to be in charge of a gambling table and collect and pay out money, give out cards, etc.（負責收付錢、發牌等的）賭枱管理員，賭枱主持人

crou·ton /ˈkruːtɒn; *NAmE* -tɑːn/ *noun* a small piece of cold crisp fried bread served in soup or as part of a salad（放在湯或色拉裏的）油炸麵包丁

Crow /krəʊ; *NAmE* kroʊ/ *noun* (*pl.* **Crow** or **Crows**) a member of a Native American people, many of whom live in the US state of Montana 克勞人（美洲土著，很多居於美國蒙大拿州）

crow /krəʊ; *NAmE* kroʊ/ *noun, verb*

■ ***noun*** **1** a large bird, completely or mostly black, with a rough unpleasant cry 烏鴉 **2** a sound like that of a COCK/ROOSTER crowing（像雄雞的）啼叫聲，喔喔叫聲：*She gave a little crow of triumph.* 她輕輕地發出了勝利的歡呼聲。

IDM **as the ˈcrow flies** in a straight line 成直線地；筆直地：*The villages are no more than a mile apart as the crow flies.* 這些村莊直線距離相隔不超過一英里。 ➲ more at EAT, STONE *v.*

■ ***verb*** **1** [I] (of a COCK/ROOSTER 雄雞) to make repeated loud high sounds, especially early in the morning（尤指在清晨）啼叫，打鳴 **2** [I, T] (*disapproving*) to talk too proudly about sth you have achieved, especially when sb else has been unsuccessful（尤指在其他人不成功時）揚揚自得地誇口，自鳴得意 SYN **boast, gloat**：**~ (about/over sth)** *He won't stop crowing about his victory.* 他滔滔不絕地誇耀自己的勝利。◇ **+ speech** *'I've won, I've won!' she crowed.* "我贏了，我贏了！"她得意忘形地叫道。◇ **~ that ...** *He crowed that they had sold out in one day.* 他洋洋得意地炫耀他們一天內就全部售完了。 **3** [I] (*BrE*) (of a baby 嬰兒) to make happy sounds 歡叫

crow·bar /ˈkrəʊbɑː(r); *NAmE* ˈkroʊ-/ *noun* a straight iron bar, usually with a curved end, used for forcing open boxes and moving heavy objects 鐵撬棍

crowd 🔑 /kraʊd/ *noun, verb*

■ ***noun*** **1** 🔑 [C+sing./pl. v.] a large number of people gathered together in a public place, for example in the streets or at a sports game 人群；觀眾：*He pushed his way through the crowd.* 他在人群中往前擠。◇ *A small crowd had gathered outside the church.* 一小群人聚集在教堂的外面。◇ *Police had to break up the crowd.* 警方不得不驅散人群。◇ *Crowds of people poured into the street.* 人們成群結隊湧上街頭。◇ *I want to get there early to avoid the crowds.* 我想及早趕到那裏，免得擁擠。◇ *The match attracted a capacity crowd of 80 000.* 這場比賽爆滿，吸引了 8 萬名觀眾。◇ *The crowd cheered the winning hit.* 觀眾為那決勝的一擊而歡呼。◇ *crowd control* 人群控制 ◇ *crowd trouble* 群眾鬧事 ◇ *A whole crowd of us are going to the ball* (= a lot of us). 我們一大幫人要去參加那場舞會。◇ *He left the hotel surrounded by crowds of journalists.* 他在大群記者的包圍下離開了旅館。 **2** [C+sing./pl. v.] (*informal*, often *disapproving*) a particular group of people 一夥人；一幫人：*Bob introduced her to some of the usual crowd* (= people who often meet each other). 鮑勃把她介紹給常見面的幾個朋友。◇ *the bright young theatrical crowd* 這幫年輕聰明的戲劇演員 **3 the crowd** [sing.] (sometimes *disapproving*) ordinary people, not special or unusual in any way 群眾；民眾；老百姓；凡夫俗子：*We all like to think we **stand out from the crowd*** (= are different from and better than other people). 我們都喜歡認為自己勝人一籌。◇ *He prefers to be **one of the crowd**.* 他寧願做個凡夫俗子。◇ *She's quite happy to **follow the crowd**.* 她就願意隨大溜。

■ ***verb*** **1 ~ sth** to fill a place so there is little room to move 擠滿；塞滿；使…擁擠：*Thousands of people crowded the narrow streets.* 成千上萬的人把狹窄的街道擠得水泄不通。 **2 ~ sth** to fill your mind so that you can think of nothing else 湧上（心頭）；湧入（腦海）：*Memories crowded his mind.* 往事湧上他的心頭。 **3 ~ sb** (*informal*) to stand very close to sb so that they feel uncomfortable or nervous 擠，靠近，擠在一旁（以致使人不舒服或緊張）

PHR V **ˌcrowd aˈround/ˈround (sb/sth)** to gather in large numbers around sb/sth 聚集在…周圍；聚攏：*We all crowded around the stove to keep warm.* 我們都擠在爐邊取暖。◇ *Photographers were crowding around outside.* 攝影師聚集在外面。**ˌcrowd ˈin (on sb)** | **ˌcrowd ˈinto sth** (of thoughts, questions etc. 想法、問題等) to fill your mind so that you can think of nothing else 湧上（心頭）；湧入（腦海）：*Too many uncomfortable thoughts were crowding in on her.* 她心亂如麻。◇ *Memories came crowding into her mind.* 往事一齊湧上她的心頭。**ˌcrowd ˈinto/ˈonto sth** | **ˌcrowd ˈin** to move in large numbers into a small space 大批湧入（狹小的空間）：*We all crowded into her office to sing 'Happy Birthday'.* 我們全都湧進她的辦公室，唱"祝你生日快樂"。**ˌcrowd sb/sth ˈinto/ˈonto sth** | **ˌcrowd sb/sth ˈin** to put many people or things into a small space 把…裝滿（或塞滿）：*Guests were crowded into the few remaining rooms.* 客人都給塞進了剩下的幾個房間。**ˌcrowd sb/sth ˈout** to fill a place so that other people or things are kept out 把（其他人或物）排擠在外

crowd·ed 🔑 /ˈkraʊdɪd/ *adj.*
~ (with sth) **1** 🔑 having a lot of people or too many people 人（太）多的；擁擠的：*crowded streets* 擁擠的街道 ◇ *a crowded bar* 擠滿人的酒吧 ◇ *In the spring the place is crowded with skiers.* 春季這地方滿是滑雪的人。◇ *London was very crowded.* 倫敦擁擠不堪。➲ compare UNCROWDED **2** 🔑 full of sth 充滿的；擠滿的：*a room crowded with books* 堆滿書籍的房間 ◇ *We have a very crowded schedule.* 我們的日程排得滿滿的。

ˈcrowd-pleaser *noun* (*informal*) a person or performance that always pleases an audience 取悅觀眾的人（或表演）

ˈcrowd-puller *noun* (*informal*) a person or thing that always attracts a large audience 吸引大量觀眾的人（或事物）

crown 🔑 /kraʊn/ *noun, verb*

■ ***noun***

▸ **OF KING/QUEEN** 國王；女王 **1** 🔑 [C] an object in the shape of a circle, usually made of gold and PRECIOUS STONES, that a king or queen wears on his or her head on official occasions 王冠；皇冠；冕 **2 the Crown** [sing.] the government of a country, thought of as being represented by a king or queen 王國政府；王國：*land owned by the Crown* 王國的土地 ◇ *a Minister of the Crown* 王國的大臣 ◇ *Who's appearing for the Crown* (= bringing a criminal charge against sb on behalf of the state) *in this case?* 誰將在此案中代表王國政府出庭？**3 the crown** [sing.] the position or power of a king or queen 王位；王權：*She refused the crown* (= refused to become queen). 她拒絕接受王位。◇ *his claim to the French crown* 他聲稱有繼任法國王位的權利

▸ **OF FLOWERS/LEAVES** 花；樹葉 **4** [C] a circle of flowers, leaves, etc. that is worn on sb's head, sometimes as a sign of victory 花冠（戴在頭上，有時象徵勝利）

▸ **IN SPORTS COMPETITION** 體育競賽 **5** [C, usually sing.] (*informal*) the position of winning a sports competition 冠軍寶座；桂冠：*She is determined to retain her Wimbledon crown.* 她決心衛冕她的溫布爾登網球賽的冠軍寶座。

▸ **OF HEAD/HAT** 頭；帽 **6** (usually **the crown**) [sing.] the top part of the head or a hat 頭頂；帽頂 ➲ VISUAL VOCAB page V59

▸ **HIGHEST PART** 頂部 **7** (usually **the crown**) [sing.] the highest part of sth （某物的）頂部，頂端：*the crown of a hill* 山頂

▸ **ON TOOTH** 牙齒 **8** [C] an artificial cover for a damaged tooth （受損牙齒的）人造冠

▸ **SHAPE** 形狀 **9** [C] anything in the shape of a crown, especially as a decoration or a BADGE 王冠狀物（尤指飾物或徽章）

▸ **MONEY** 貨幣 **10** [C] a unit of money in several European countries 克朗（歐洲一些國家的貨幣單位）：*Czech crowns* 捷克克朗 **11** [C] an old British coin worth five SHILLINGS (= now 25p) * 5 先令的英國舊幣（等於現在的 25 便士）**IDM** see JEWEL

■ ***verb***

▸ **KING/QUEEN** 國王；女王 **1** to put a crown on the head of a new king or queen as a sign of royal power 為…加冕：**~ sb** *Queen Elizabeth was crowned in 1953.* 伊莉莎白女王加冕於 1953 年。◇ **~ sb + noun** *The prince was soon to be crowned King of England.* 王子不久就要被立為英格蘭國王了。

▸ **COVER TOP** 覆蓋頂部 **2** [usually passive] **~ sth (with sth)** to form or cover the top of sth 形成…頂部；給…加頂：*His head was crowned with a mop of brown curls.* 他長了一頭蓬亂的棕色鬈髮。

▸ **MAKE COMPLETE** 使完成 **3** [often passive] **~ sth (with sth)** to make sth complete or perfect, especially by adding an achievement, a success, etc. （尤指通過增添成就、成功等）使圓滿，使完美：*The award of the Nobel Prize has crowned a glorious career in physics.* 榮獲諾貝爾獎使其物理學研究的輝煌事業達到了頂點。◇ *Their efforts were finally crowned with success.* 他們的努力終於取得圓滿成功。

▸ **HIT ON HEAD** 擊打頭部 **4 ~ sb** (*old-fashioned, informal*) to hit sb on the head 敲（某人的）腦殼

▸ **TOOTH** 牙齒 **5 ~ sth** to put an artificial cover on a tooth （在牙齒上）鑲人造冠 **SYN** **cap**：*I've had one of my teeth crowned.* 我的一顆牙齒鑲了假齒冠。

IDM **to crown it ˈall** (*BrE, informal*) used to say that sth is the final and worst event in a series of unpleasant or annoying events （在一系列不愉快或討厭的事件中）最糟糕的是：*It was cold and raining, and, to crown it all, we had to walk home.* 天氣寒冷又下着雨，最糟的是我們得走着回家。

ˌCrown ˈColony *noun* a COLONY ruled directly by the British government 英國直轄殖民地

ˌCrown ˈCourt *noun* (in England and Wales 英格蘭和威爾士) a court which deals with criminal cases, with a judge and JURY 刑事法院（有法官和陪審團）➲ compare COUNTY COURT

crown·ing /ˈkraʊnɪŋ/ *adj.* [only before noun] making sth perfect or complete 使完美的；使圓滿的：*The cathedral is the* ***crowning glory*** *of the city.* 大教堂是這座城市至高無上的驕傲。◇ *His 'Beethoven' sculpture is seen as the crowning achievement of his career.* 人們認為他製作的貝多芬雕像是他在事業上取得的最高成就。

ˌcrown ˈjewels *noun* [pl.] the crown and other objects worn or carried by a king or queen on formal occasions 御寶（國王或女王在正式場合佩戴的飾物）

ˌCrown ˈprince *noun* (in some countries) a prince who will become king when the present king or queen dies （某些國家的）王儲，皇太子

ˌCrown prinˈcess *noun* **1** the wife of a Crown prince 王儲妃；皇太子妃 **2** (in some countries) a princess who will become queen when the present king or queen dies （某些國家的）女王儲

ˌCrown ˈprosecutor *noun* in England and Wales, a lawyer who works for the state （英格蘭和威爾士的）政府律師

ˈcrow's feet *noun* [pl.] lines in the skin around the outer corner of a person's eye （眼角的）魚尾紋

ˈcrow's nest *noun* a platform at the top of a ship's MAST (= the post that supports the sails) from which sb can see a long way and watch for land, danger, etc. 桅杆瞭望台

croz·ier = CROSIER

cru·cial 🔑 **AW** /ˈkruːʃl/ *adj.*
extremely important, because it will affect other things 至關重要的；關鍵性的 **SYN** **critical, essential**：*a* ***crucial factor/issue/decision*** 關鍵性的因素／問題／決定 ◇ *topics of crucial importance* 至關重要的課題 ◇ *The next few weeks are going to be crucial.* 今後幾個星期是關鍵。◇ **~ to/for sth** *Winning this contract is crucial to the success of the company.* 贏得這份合同對這家公司的成敗至關重要。◇ **~ that ...** *It is crucial that we get this right.* 我們把這個問題弄明白是極其重要的。◇ *Parents* ***play a crucial role*** *in preparing their child for school.* 父母對孩子做好上學的準備起着至關重要的作用。◇ *He wasn't there* ***at the crucial moment*** (= when he was needed most). 緊要關頭他卻不在那裏。➲ SYNONYMS at ESSENTIAL

C

➲ LANGUAGE BANK at EMPHASIS, VITAL ▶ **cru·cial·ly** AW /-ʃəli/ *adv.*: *crucially important* 極其重要

cru·cible /ˈkruːsɪbl/ *noun* **1** a pot in which substances are heated to high temperatures, metals are melted, etc. 坩堝；熔爐 ➲ VISUAL VOCAB page V70 **2** (*formal* or *literary*) a place or situation in which people or ideas are tested severely, often creating sth new or exciting in the process 熔爐；嚴峻的考驗；磨練

cru·ci·fix /ˈkruːsəfɪks/ *noun* a model of a cross with a figure of Jesus Christ on it, as a symbol of the Christian religion（十字架）苦像；耶穌受難像

cru·ci·fix·ion /ˌkruːsəˈfɪkʃn/ *noun* (sometimes **Cruci·fixion**) **1** [C, U] the act of killing sb by fastening them to a cross 釘死在十字架上：*the Crucifixion* (= of Jesus) 耶穌被釘在十字架上 **2** [C] a painting or other work of art representing the crucifixion of Jesus Christ 十字架苦像（耶穌受難的畫像或藝術品）

cru·ci·form /ˈkruːsɪfɔːm; *NAmE* -fɔːrm/ *adj.* (*technical* 術語) (especially of buildings 尤指建築物) in the shape of a cross 十字形的

cru·cify /ˈkruːsɪfaɪ/ *verb* (**cru·ci·fies**, **cru·ci·fy·ing**, **cru·ci·fied**, **cru·ci·fied**) **1 ~ sb** to kill sb as a punishment by fastening them to a wooden cross 把（某人）釘（或捆）在木十字架上處死 **2 ~ sb** (*informal*) to criticize or punish sb very severely 嚴厲批評；嚴懲；折磨：*The prime minister was crucified in the press for his handling of the affair.* 首相因處理此事的方式而受到新聞界的嚴厲抨擊。

crud /krʌd/ *noun* [U] (*informal*) any dirty or unpleasant substance 髒東西；污垢；渣滓

cruddy /ˈkrʌdi/ *adj.* (**crud·dier**, **crud·di·est**) (*informal, especially NAmE*) bad, dirty or of low quality 糟糕的；邋遢的；蹩腳的：*We got really cruddy service in that restaurant last time.* 我們上次在那家餐館得到的服務實在差極了。

crude /kruːd/ *adj., noun*

■ *adj.* (**cruder**, **cru·dest**) **1** simple and not very accurate but giving a general idea of sth 粗略的；簡略的；大概的：***In crude terms****, the causes of mental illness seem to be of three main kinds.* 簡略地說，導致精神病的原因看起來主要有三種。**2** (of objects or works of art 物體或藝術品) simply made, not showing much skill or attention to detail 粗糙的；粗製的：*a crude drawing of a face* 臉部的略圖 **3** (of people or the way they behave 人或行為方式) offensive or rude, especially about sex 冒犯的，粗俗的，粗魯的（尤其有關性的）SYN **vulgar**：*crude **jokes/language*** 粗俗的笑話／語言 **4** [usually before noun] (of oil and other natural substances 油和其他自然物質) in its natural state, before it has been treated with chemicals 天然的；自然的：***crude oil/metal*** 原油；未經提煉的金屬 ▶ **crude·ly** *adv.*: *a crudely drawn ship* 粗略勾畫出來的船 ◇ *To put it crudely, the poor are going without food so that the rich can drive cars.* 簡而言之，窮人無飯吃，富人才有車開。**crude·ness** *noun* [U]

■ *noun* (also ˌ**crude ˈoil**) [U] oil in its natural state, before it has been treated with chemicals 原油；石油：*50 000 barrels of crude* * 5 萬桶石油

cru·di·tés /ˈkruːdɪteɪ; *NAmE* ˌkruːdɪˈteɪ/ *noun* [pl.] (from *French*) pieces of raw vegetables that are eaten at the beginning of a meal（用餐開始食用的）生菜色拉

cru·dity /ˈkruːdəti/ *noun* [U, C] (*pl.* **-ies**) the fact of being CRUDE; an example of sth CRUDE 粗糙，簡陋，粗俗，粗魯（的事例）：*Despite the crudity of their methods and equipment, the experiment was a considerable success.* 儘管他們的方法和設備較為粗陋，那次實驗卻相當成功。◇ *the novel's structural crudities* 那部小說粗糙的結構 ◇ *The crudity of her language shocked him.* 她粗鄙的語言使他感到震驚。

cruel 0➡ /ˈkruːəl/ *adj.* (**cruel·ler**, **cruel·lest**)
1 0➡ **~** (**to sb/sth**) having a desire to cause pain and suffering 殘酷的；冷酷的；殘忍的；殘暴的：*a cruel dictator* 殘暴的獨裁者 ◇ *I can't stand people who are cruel to animals.* 我無法容忍虐待動物的人。◇ *Her eyes were cruel and hard.* 她目光冷酷逼人。◇ *Sometimes you have to **be cruel to be kind*** (= make sb suffer because it will be good for them later). 有時候為了某人好你就得對他狠。OPP **kind 2** 0➡ causing pain or suffering 引起痛苦的：*a **cruel punishment/joke*** 殘酷的懲罰；挖苦人的笑話 ◇ *Her father's death was a **cruel blow**.* 父親去世對她是一大打擊。▶ **cruel·ly** /ˈkruːəli/ *adv.*: *The dog had been cruelly treated.* 那條狗受過虐待。◇ *I was cruelly deceived.* 我被騙得慘透了。

cruelty /ˈkruːəlti/ *noun* (*pl.* **-ies**) **1** [U] **~** (**to sb/sth**) behaviour that causes pain or suffering to others, especially deliberately（尤指蓄意的）殘酷，殘忍，殘暴：*cruelty to animals* 對動物的虐待 ◇ *The deliberate cruelty of his words cut her like a knife.* 他故意說的冷言冷語對她像刀割一樣。OPP **kindness 2** [C, usually pl.] a cruel action 殘暴的行為 **3** [C, U] something that happens that seems unfair 不公；不平：*the cruelties of life* 生活中的種種不公

cruet /ˈkruːɪt/ *noun* a small container, or set of containers, for salt, pepper, oil, etc. for use on the table at meals（餐桌上的）調味瓶，一組調味瓶

cruise /kruːz/ *noun, verb*

■ *noun* a journey by sea, visiting different places, especially as a holiday/vacation 乘船遊覽；航行：*I'd love to go on a round-the-world cruise.* 我很想乘船周遊世界。◇ *a luxury cruise ship* 豪華遊輪 ➲ COLLOCATIONS at TRAVEL

■ *verb* **1** [I, T] to travel in a ship or boat visiting different places, especially as a holiday/vacation 乘船遊覽：(**+ adv./prep.**) *They cruised down the Nile.* 他們沿尼羅河而下乘船遊覽。◇ **~ sth** *We spent two weeks cruising the Bahamas.* 我們花了兩個星期乘船遊覽巴哈馬群島。**2** [I] (**+ adv./prep.**) (of a car, plane, etc. 汽車、飛機等) to travel at a steady speed 以平穩的速度行駛：*a light aircraft cruising at 4 000 feet* 一架在 4 000 英尺高度巡航的輕型飛機 ◇ *a cruising speed of 50 miles an hour* 每小時 50 英里平穩行駛的速度 **3** [I, T] (of a car, etc. or its driver 汽車等或駕駛員) to drive along slowly, especially when you are looking at or for sth（尤指查看或尋找時）慢速行駛，巡行：**+ adv./prep.** *She cruised around the block looking for a parking space.* 她繞着那個街區慢慢行駛，想找個停車的地方。◇ **~ sth** *Taxis cruised the streets, looking for fares.* 出租汽車緩慢行駛在街上招攬顧客。**4** [I] **+ adv./prep.** to win or achieve sth easily 輕而易舉贏得（或獲得）；輕取：*The home team cruised to victory.* 主隊輕鬆取勝。**5** [I, T] **~** (**sth**) (*slang*) to go around in public places looking for a sexual partner（在公共場所）尋覓性夥伴，獵豔

ˈ**cruise control** *noun* [U] a device in a vehicle that allows it to stay at the speed that the driver has chosen 巡行車速控制裝置（讓車輛以選定速度行駛）

ˌ**cruise ˈmissile** *noun* a large weapon with a WARHEAD that flies close to the ground and is guided by its own computer to an exact place 巡航導彈

cruiser /ˈkruːzə(r)/ *noun* **1** a large fast ship used in war 巡洋艦 **2** (also ˈ**cabin cruiser**) a boat with a motor and room for people to sleep, used for pleasure trips（可供住宿的）艙式遊艇 ➲ VISUAL VOCAB page V54 **3** (*NAmE*) a police car 巡邏警車

crumb /krʌm/ *noun* **1** a very small piece of food, especially of bread or cake, that has fallen off a larger piece 食物碎屑；（尤指）麪包屑，糕餅屑：*She stood up and brushed the crumbs from her sweater.* 她站起身撣掉了毛衣上的麪包屑。**2** a small piece or amount 一點；少許；少量：*a few crumbs of useful information* 點滴有用的消息 ◇ *The government's only **crumb of comfort** is that their opponents are as confused as they are.* 政府唯一聊以自慰的是反對派與他們一樣困惑不解。

crum·ble /ˈkrʌmbl/ *verb, noun*

■ *verb* **1** [I, T] to break or break sth into very small pieces（使）破碎，成碎屑：*Rice flour makes the cake less likely to crumble.* 這種糕餅用米粉做不那麼容易碎。◇ **~ sth** *Crumble the cheese over the salad.* 把乾酪弄成碎屑灑在色拉上。**2** [I] if a building or piece of land **is crumbling**, parts of it are breaking off 坍塌；損壞；崩裂：*buildings crumbling into dust* 漸漸坍塌的建築物 ◇ *crumbling stonework* 不斷破裂的石製建築 ◇ *The cliff is gradually crumbling away.* 峭壁正在逐漸崩坍。**3** [I] to begin to fail or get weaker or to come to an end（開始漸漸）衰退，衰弱；崩潰；瓦解；消亡：*a crumbling business/*

relationship 逐漸衰敗的企業；日益惡化的關係 ◇ **~ away** *All his hopes began to crumble away.* 他所有的希望開始化為泡影。◇ **~ into/to sth** *The empire finally crumbled into dust.* 這個帝國最終崩潰了。IDM see WAY *n.*

■ ***noun*** (*BrE*) (*NAmE* **crisp**) [U, C] a DESSERT (= a sweet dish) made from fruit that is covered with a rough mixture of flour, butter and sugar, cooked in the oven and usually served hot 酥皮水果甜點： *apple crumble and custard* 酥皮蘋果甜點心加蛋奶沙司

crum·bly /ˈkrʌmbli/ *adj.* that easily breaks into very small pieces 易碎的；脆的： *crumbly soil/cheese* 易碎的土壤／乾酪

crumbs /krʌmz/ *exclamation* (*old-fashioned, BrE, informal*) used to show that you are surprised（驚訝時說）哎呀，哎喲，天哪： *Oh crumbs! Is that the time?* 啊，天哪！都這會兒啦？

crummy /ˈkrʌmi/ *adj.* (*informal*) of very bad quality 劣質的；低劣的；糟糕的： *Most of his songs are pretty crummy.* 他的歌曲大多糟糕透頂。

crum·pet /ˈkrʌmpɪt/ *noun* (*BrE*) **1** [C] a small flat round cake with small holes in the top, eaten hot with butter 小圓烤餅（上層有孔，塗上黃油趁熱吃的）**2** [U] (*slang*) an offensive way of referring to people who are sexually attractive, usually women（對性感的人的蔑稱，通常指女人）

crum·ple /ˈkrʌmpl/ *verb* **1** [T, I] **~ (sth) (up) (into sth)** to crush sth into folds; to become crushed into folds 壓皺；（使）變皺，起皺： *She crumpled the letter up into a ball and threw it on the fire.* 她把那封信揉成一團扔進了火裏。◇ *This material crumples very easily.* 這種布料很容易起皺。➲ picture at SQUEEZE **2** [I] **~ (up)** if your face **crumples**, you look sad and disappointed, as if you might cry（臉部）沮喪地皺起，哭喪着 **3** [I] **~ (up)** to fall down in an uncontrolled way because you are injured, unconscious, drunk, etc.（因受傷、失去知覺、喝醉而）癱倒 SYN **collapse**： *He crumpled up in agony.* 他極度痛苦地癱倒在地。▸ **crum·pled** *adj.*： ***crumpled clothes/papers*** 皺巴巴的衣服／紙張 ◇ *A crumpled figure lay motionless in the doorway.* 門口躺着一個人，蜷縮成一團，一動不動。

ˈcrumple zone *noun* the part of a car that is designed to crumple easily if there is an accident, to protect the people in the car（汽車的）防撞緩衝區，碰撞摺皺區

crunch /krʌntʃ/ *noun, verb, adj.*

■ ***noun*** **1** [C, usually sing.] a noise like the sound of sth firm being crushed 壓碎聲；碎裂聲： *the crunch of feet on snow* 腳踩着雪發出的嘎吱嘎吱聲 ◇ *The car drew up with a crunch of gravel.* 那輛汽車在沙礫路上嘎吱一聲停了下來。 **2 the crunch** [sing.] (*informal*) an important and often unpleasant situation or piece of information 緊要關頭；困境；癥結；令人不快的重要消息： ***The crunch came*** *when she returned from America.* 她從美國回來以後，危機就出現了。◇ *He always says he'll help but* ***when it comes to the crunch*** (= when it is time for action) *he does nothing.* 他口口聲聲說一定幫忙，然而到關鍵時候卻不會行動。◇ *The crunch is that we can't afford to go abroad this year.* 癥結在於我們今年負擔不起出國的費用。 **3** [C, usually sing.] (*especially NAmE*) a situation in which there is suddenly not enough of sth, especially money（突發的）不足，短缺；（尤指）缺錢： *a* ***budget/energy/housing crunch*** 預算金額／能源／住房短缺 **4** [C] = SIT-UP

■ ***verb*** **1** [T, I] **~ (on) sth** to crush sth noisily between your teeth when you are eating 嘎吱嘎吱地嚼： *She crunched her apple noisily.* 她吃蘋果發出嘎嚓嘎嚓的聲音。 **2** [I, T] **~ (sth)** to make or cause sth to make a noise like sth hard being crushed（使）發出碎裂聲 SYN **scrunch**： *The snow crunched under our feet.* 積雪在我們腳下嘎吱作響。**3** [I] **+ adv./prep.** to move over a surface, making a loud crushing noise（在路面）行進發出響聲： *I crunched across the gravel to the front door.* 我嘎吱嘎吱走過石子路來到前門。 **4** [T] **~ sth** (*computing* 計) to deal with large amounts of data very quickly（快速大量地）處理信息；數字搗弄 ➲ see also NUMBER CRUNCHING

PHR V **ˌcrunch sth↔ˈup** to crush sth completely 徹底壓碎（或碾碎）： *He crunched up the empty pack and threw it out of the window.* 他把小空紙包壓扁後丟出了窗外。

■ ***adj.*** [only before noun] (*informal*) a **crunch** meeting, sports game, etc. is very important and may be the last chance to succeed（會議、體育競賽等）至關重要的，最後一線勝機的： *Sunday's crunch game with Leeds* 星期天與利茲隊決一雌雄的比賽

crunchy /ˈkrʌntʃi/ *adj.* (*approving*) (especially of food 尤指食物) firm and crisp and making a sharp sound when you bite or crush it 硬脆的；爽脆的；鬆脆的： *a crunchy salad* 鬆脆的色拉

cru·sade /kruːˈseɪd/ *noun, verb*

■ ***noun*** **1 ~ (for/against sth) | ~ (to do sth)** a long and determined effort to achieve sth that you believe to be right or to stop sth that you believe to be wrong（長期堅定不移的）鬥爭，運動 SYN **campaign**： *to lead a crusade against crime* 領導打擊犯罪活動的運動 ◇ *a moral crusade* 提倡道德的運動 **2** (sometimes **Crusade**) any of the wars fought in Palestine by European Christian countries against the Muslims in the Middle Ages（中世紀的）十字軍東征

■ ***verb*** [I] to make a long and determined effort to achieve sth that you believe to be right or to stop sth you believe to be wrong 長期堅定不移地奮鬥 SYN **campaign**

cru·sader /kruːˈseɪdə(r)/ *noun* a person who takes part in a crusade 十字軍戰士；（某）運動的參加者： *moral crusaders* 提倡道德運動的志士

crush 0‑w /krʌʃ/ *verb, noun*

■ ***verb*** **1** 0‑w [T] **~ sb/sth** to press or squeeze sth so hard that it is damaged or injured, or loses its shape 壓壞；壓傷；擠壓變形： *The car was completely crushed under the truck.* 小轎車被卡車壓得完全變形了。◇ *They crush the olives with a heavy wooden press.* 他們用沉重的木製壓榨機把橄欖壓碎。◇ *Several people were* ***crushed to death*** *in the accident.* 好幾個人在事故中壓死了。 **2** 0‑w [T] **~ sb/sth + adv./prep.** to push or press sb/sth into a small space 把…擠入，將…塞進（狹小的空間內）： *Over twenty prisoners were crushed into a small dark cell.* 二十多名囚犯被塞在一間黑暗狹小的牢房裏。 **3** 0‑w [T] **~ sth** to break sth into small pieces or into a powder by pressing hard 壓碎；搗碎；碾成粉末： *Add two cloves of crushed garlic.* 加入兩瓣搗碎的蒜。 ➲ picture at SQUEEZE **4** [T, I] **~ (sth)** to become or make sth full of folds or lines（使）變皺，起皺 **5** [T] **~ sb** to use violent methods to defeat people who are opposing you 鎮壓；（用暴力）制伏 SYN **put down, quash**： *The army was sent in to crush the rebellion.* 軍隊被派去平息叛亂。 **6 ~ sb** to destroy sb's confidence or happiness 破壞，毀壞（某人的信心或幸福）： *She felt completely crushed by the teacher's criticism.* 老師的批評使她覺得自己一無是處。

■ ***noun*** **1** [C, usually sing.] a crowd of people pressed close together in a small space（狹小空間中）擁擠的人群： *a big crush in the theatre bar* 劇院酒吧裏擁擠不堪的人群 ◇ *I couldn't find a way through the crush.* 人太擠，我擠不過去。 **2** [C] **~ (on sb)** a strong feeling of love, that usually does not last very long, that a young person has for sb older（通常指年輕人對年長者的短暫的）熱戀，迷戀： *a schoolgirl crush* 女學生的迷戀 ◇ *I had a huge crush on her.* 我對她愛慕至極。 **3** [U] a drink made from fruit juice 果汁飲料

ˈcrush barrier *noun* (*BrE*) a temporary metal fence used for keeping back a crowd 臨時柵欄，拒馬（用以阻擋人群）

crush·er /ˈkrʌʃə(r)/ *noun* (often in compounds 常構成複合詞) a machine or tool for crushing sth 壓碎機；壓榨機；破碎機： *a garlic crusher* 搗蒜機 ➲ VISUAL VOCAB page V26

crush·ing /ˈkrʌʃɪŋ/ *adj.* [usually before noun] used to emphasize how bad or severe sth is（強調糟糕或嚴重的程度）慘重的，毀壞性的： *a* ***crushing defeat*** *in the election* 在選舉中的慘敗 ◇ *The shipyard has been dealt another* ***crushing blow*** *with the failure to win this contract.* 由於未能贏得這份合同，造船廠又遭到了一次慘重的打擊。 ▸ **crush·ing·ly** *adv.*

crust /krʌst/ *noun* **1** [C, U] the hard outer surface of bread 麵包皮： *sandwiches with the crusts cut off* 切掉麵

包皮的三明治 **2** [C, usually sing.] a layer of PASTRY, especially on top of a PIE 糕餅（尤指餡餅）酥皮：*Bake until the crust is golden.* 把糕餅烤至外皮呈金黃色。 **3** [C, U] a hard layer or surface, especially above or around sth soft or liquid（尤指軟物或液體上面、周圍的）硬層，硬表面：*a thin crust of ice* 一層薄冰 ◇ *the earth's crust* 地殼 ➲ see also THE UPPER CRUST **IDM** see EARN

crust·acean /krʌˈsteɪʃn/ *noun* (*technical* 術語) any creature with a soft body that is divided into sections, and a hard outer shell. Most crustaceans live in water. CRABS, LOBSTERS and SHRIMPS are all crustaceans. 甲殼綱動物（如螃蟹、龍蝦和褐蝦）➲ VISUAL VOCAB page V13 ➲ compare SHELLFISH

crust·ed /ˈkrʌstɪd/ *adj.* [not usually before noun] **~ (with sth)** having a hard layer or covering of sth 有硬皮；有外殼

crusty /ˈkrʌsti/ *adj., noun*

■ *adj.* (**crust·ier**, **crusti·est**) **1** (of food 食物) having a hard outer layer 有硬皮的；有脆皮的：*fresh crusty bread* 新鮮的脆皮麪包 **2** (*informal*) (especially of older people 尤指老年人) bad-tempered; easily irritated 脾氣壞的；易發怒的：*a crusty old man* 脾氣暴躁的老人

■ *noun* (also **crustie**) (*pl.* **-ies**) (*BrE, informal*) a person who usually has no permanent home, has a dirty or untidy appearance, and rejects the way that most people live in Western society 居無定所抗拒傳統的人

crutch /krʌtʃ/ *noun* **1** one of two long sticks that you put under your arms to help you walk after you have injured your leg or foot（腿或腳受傷病人用的）腋杖：*After the accident I spent six months* ***on crutches.*** 事故後我用了六個月的腋杖。 **2** (usually *disapproving*) a person or thing that gives you help or support but often makes you depend on them too much 依靠；依賴 **3** = CROTCH

crux /krʌks/ *noun* [sing.] **the ~ (of sth)** the most important or difficult part of a problem or an issue（難題或問題的）關鍵，最難點，癥結 **SYN** **nub**：*Now we come to* ***the crux of the matter.*** 現在我們來談問題的癥結。

cry 🔑 /kraɪ/ *verb, noun*

■ *verb* (**cries**, **cry·ing**, **cried**, **cried**) **1** 🔑 [I, T] to produce tears from your eyes because you are unhappy or hurt 哭；哭泣：*It's all right. Don't cry.* 不要緊，別哭了。◇ *I just couldn't stop crying.* 我哭得停不下來。◇ **~ for sb/sth** *The baby was crying for* (= because it wanted) *its mother.* 嬰兒哭着要媽媽。◇ **~ about/over sth** *There's nothing to cry about.* 沒有什麼值得哭的。◇ **~ with sth** *He felt like crying with rage.* 他氣得想哭。◇ **+ speech** *'Waaa!' she cried.* "哇！" 她哭出聲來。◇ *I found him* ***crying his eyes out*** (= crying very much). 我看他哭得很傷心。◇ *That night she* ***cried herself to sleep.*** 那天晚上她哭着哭着就睡着了。 **2** 🔑 [I, T] to shout loudly 喊叫；呼喊；呼叫：**~ for sth** *She ran to the window and cried for help.* 她跑到窗口呼喊救命。◇ **+ speech** *'You're safe!' Tom cried in delight.* "你安全啦！" 湯姆高興地大聲説道。➲ SYNONYMS at SHOUT **3** [I] (of a bird or an animal 鳥或動物) to make a loud unpleasant noise 發出刺耳的叫聲；嗥叫；吠：*Seagulls followed the boat, crying loudly.* 海鷗追隨着那條船，高聲鳴叫着。

IDM ˌ**cry ˈfoul** (*informal*) to complain that sb else has done sth wrong or unfair 抱怨；埋怨 **cry over spilt ˈmilk** (*BrE*) (*US* **cry over spilled ˈmilk**) to waste time worrying about sth that has happened that you cannot do anything about 枉為無可挽回的事憂傷；作於事無補的擔憂：*As the saying goes—****it's no use crying over spilt milk.*** 常言道：覆水難收，後悔也於事無補。 **cry ˈwolf** to call for help when you do not need it, with the result that when you do need it people do not believe you 喊 "狼來了"；謊報險情；發假警報 **for ˌcrying out ˈloud** (*informal*) used to show you are angry or surprised（表示憤怒或驚訝）哎呀，我的天哪，真是豈有此理：*For crying out loud! Why did you have to do that?* 真是豈有此理！你為什麼非得幹那種事？➲ more at LAUGH *v.*, SHOULDER *n.*

PHR V ˌ**cry ˈoff** (*BrE, informal*) to say that you cannot do sth that you promised to do 撤回前言；取消諾言；打退堂鼓：*She said she was coming to the party, but cried off at the last moment.* 她説過她要來參加聚會，可到最後一刻又變卦了。 ˌ**cry ˈout** to make a loud sound without words because you are hurt, afraid, surprised, etc.（因傷痛、害怕、驚訝等）大叫，叫喊：*She tried to stop herself from crying out.* 她試圖控制住自己不叫出聲來。◇ *to* ***cry out in fear/alarm/pain*** 害怕／驚慌／疼痛得大叫起來 ˌ**cry ˈout/ˌcry ˈout sth** 🔑 to shout sth loudly 大聲呼喊：*She cried out for help.* 她大聲呼救。◇ *She cried out his name.* 她大聲呼喚着他的名字。◇ **+ speech** *'Help!' he cried out.* "救命啊！" 他大聲呼叫着。➲ SYNONYMS at CALL ˌ**cry ˈout for sth** (usually used in the progressive tenses 通常用於進行時) to need sth very much 迫切需要：*The company is crying out for fresh new talent.* 公司急需具有嶄新理念的人才。

■ *noun* (*pl.* **cries**) **1** 🔑 [C] a loud sound without words that expresses a strong feeling（表達強烈感情的）叫喊，叫聲：*to* ***give a cry of anguish/despair/relief/surprise/terror, etc.*** 發出痛苦、絕望、如釋重負、驚訝、恐怖等的叫聲 **2** 🔑 [C] a loud shout 大喊；大叫；呼喊：*With a cry of 'Stop thief!' he ran after the boy.* 他一邊喊 "抓賊啊！" 一邊追趕那男孩。◇ *Her answer was greeted with cries of outrage.* 她的回答引起了一片憤怒的吼叫。 **3** 🔑 [C] the sound made by a bird or an animal（鳥的）鳴叫，啼叫；（動物的）嗥叫，吠：*the cry of gulls circling overhead* 海鷗在頭頂上盤旋着發出的鳴叫 **4** 🔑 [sing.] an action or a period of crying 哭；一陣哭泣：*I felt a lot better after a good long cry.* 我痛痛快快哭了一場，好受多了。 **5** 🔑 [C] **~ (for sth)** an urgent demand or request for sth 迫切需要；懇求：*Her suicide attempt was really a* ***cry for help.*** 她企圖自殺實際上表明她迫切需要幫助。 **6** [C] (especially in compounds 尤用於構成複合詞) a word or phrase that expresses a group's beliefs and calls people to action 口號：*a battle cry* 戰鬥口號

IDM **in full ˈcry** talking or shouting loudly and in an enthusiastic way 激情吶喊；大聲疾呼：*The Leeds supporters were in full cry.* 利兹隊的球迷在激情高昂地吶喊助威。➲ more at FAR *adj.*, HUE

Vocabulary Building 詞彙擴充

Cry

To **cry** is the most general word for producing tears when you are unhappy or hurt, or when you are extremely happy. * cry 泛指因悲傷、痛苦或喜悦而流淚。

- To **sob** means to cry noisily, taking sudden, sharp breaths. * sob 意為啜泣、抽噎。
- To **wail** means to cry in a loud high voice. * wail 意為嚎啕大哭。
- To **whimper** means to cry making low, weak noises. * whimper 意為低聲啜泣、嗚咽。
- To **weep** (*literary* or *formal*) means to cry quietly for a long time. * weep（文學或正式用語）意為飲泣。

All these verbs can be used like 'say'. 以上動詞均與 say 用法相同：*'I don't want you to go,' she cried/wailed/sobbed.* "我不想你走。" 她哭／號哭／抽噎着説。

- To **be in tears** means to be crying. * be in tears 意為流淚。
- To **burst into tears** means to suddenly begin to cry. * burst into tears 意為突然哭起來。
- To **cry your eyes out** means to cry a lot or for a long time, because you are very sad. * cry one's eyes out 意為痛哭不止。

cry·baby /ˈkraɪbeɪbi/ *noun* (*pl.* **-ies**) (*informal, disapproving*) a person, especially a child, who cries too often or without good reason 愛哭的人，動不動就哭的人（尤指小孩）：*Don't be such a crybaby.* 別動不動就哭鼻子。

cry·ing /ˈkraɪɪŋ/ *adj., noun*

■ *adj.* [only before noun]

IDM **be a crying ˈshame** (*informal*) used to emphasize that you think sth is extremely bad or shocking（用於強調）極其糟糕，令人震驚：*It's a crying shame to waste all that food.* 把那些食物都浪費了，真是太不像話了。

a crying 'need (for sth) a great and urgent need for sth 迫切的需要

■ ***noun*** [U] the sound or act of crying 哭泣聲；哭泣：*the crying of terrified children* 小孩受了驚嚇的哭聲

cryo·gen·ic /ˌkraɪəˈdʒenɪk/ *adj.* (*physics* 物) involving the use of very low temperatures 低温的；致冷的：*a cryogenic storage system* 低温冷藏系統

cryo·gen·ics /ˌkraɪəˈdʒenɪks/ *noun* [U] (*physics* 物) the scientific study of the production and effects of very low temperatures 低温學 ➲ compare CRYONICS

cry·on·ics /kraɪˈɒnɪks; *NAmE* -ɑːn-/ *noun* [U] (*medical* 醫) the process of freezing a body at the moment of its death with the hope that it will be brought back to life at some future time 人體冷凍法（把人體在死亡時冷凍起來以期在將來起死回生）➲ compare CRYOGENICS

crypt /krɪpt/ *noun* a room under the floor of a church, used especially in the past as a place for burying people（尤指舊時作墓穴用的）教堂地下室

cryp·tic /ˈkrɪptɪk/ *adj.* with a meaning that is hidden or not easily understood 含義隱晦的；晦澀難懂的 **SYN** **mysterious**：*a **cryptic message/remark/smile*** 令人困惑的信息／話語／微笑 ◇ *a cryptic crossword clue* 撲朔迷離的縱橫字謎線索 ▸ **cryp·tic·al·ly** /-kli/ *adv.*：*'Yes and no,' she replied cryptically.* "又是又不是。" 她回答得很隱晦。

crypto- /ˈkrɪptəʊ; *NAmE* -toʊ/ *combining form* (in nouns 構成名詞) secret 秘密的；保密的；隱蔽的：*a crypto-communist* 地下共產黨員

crypt·og·raphy /krɪpˈtɒɡrəfi; *NAmE* -ˈtɑːɡ-/ *noun* [U] the art of writing or solving codes 密碼學；密碼術

crypto·spor·id·ium /ˌkrɪptəʊspəˈrɪdiəm; *NAmE* ˌkrɪptoʊ-/ *noun* a PARASITE found in water that causes infections inside the body 隱孢子蟲（水中寄生蟲，可引致體內受感染）

crys·tal /ˈkrɪstl/ *noun* **1** [C] a small piece of a substance with many even sides, that is formed naturally when the substance becomes solid 結晶；晶體：***ice/salt crystals*** 冰／鹽的結晶體 **2** [U, C] a clear mineral, such as QUARTZ, used in making jewellery and decorative objects 水晶（如石英，用於製作珠寶飾物）：*a pair of crystal earrings* 一對水晶耳環 **3** [U] glass of very high quality 水晶玻璃：*a **crystal chandelier/vase*** 水晶玻璃枝形吊燈／花瓶 **4** [C] (*NAmE*) a piece of glass or plastic that covers the face of a watch 石英玻璃錶護面；塑料錶護面；錶蒙子 ➲ see also LIQUID CRYSTAL DISPLAY **5** = METH

ˌcrystal 'ball *noun* a clear glass ball used by people who claim they can predict what will happen in the future by looking into it（占卜用的）水晶球：*Without a crystal ball, it's impossible to say where we'll be next year.* 沒有水晶球預卜未來，我們說不準明年處境會如何。

ˌcrystal 'clear *adj.* **1** (of glass, water, etc. 玻璃、水等) completely clear and bright 清澈透明的；晶瑩的 **2** very easy to understand; completely obvious 淺顯易懂的；顯而易見的：*I want to make my meaning crystal clear.* 我想把我的意思解釋得清清楚楚。

crys·tal·line /ˈkrɪstəlaɪn/ *adj.* **1** (*technical* 術語) made of or similar to CRYSTALS 結晶的；水晶製的；晶狀的：***crystalline structure/rocks*** 晶體結構；結晶岩 **2** (*formal*) very clear 清澈的；透明的；晶瑩的 **SYN** **transparent**：*water of crystalline purity* 清澈純淨的水

crys·tal·lize (*BrE* also **-ise**) /ˈkrɪstəlaɪz/ *verb* **1** [I, T] (of thoughts, plans, beliefs, etc. 想法、計劃、信仰等) to become clear and fixed; to make thoughts, beliefs, etc. clear and fixed 變明確；使（想法、信仰等）明確：*Our ideas began to crystallize into a definite plan.* 我們的想法開始形成了一個明確的計劃。◇ **~ sth** *The final chapter crystallizes all the main issues.* 最後一章澄清了所有的主要問題。 **2** [I, T] **~ (sth)** (*technical* 術語) to form or make sth form into CRYSTALS（使）形成晶體，結晶：*The salt crystallizes as the water evaporates.* 鹽在水分蒸發時結晶。 ▸ **crys·tal·lization, -isa·tion** /ˌkrɪstəlaɪˈzeɪʃn; *NAmE* -ləˈz-/ *noun* [U, sing.]

crys·tal·lized (*BrE* also **-ised**) /ˈkrɪstəlaɪzd/ *adj.* (especially of fruit 尤指水果) preserved in and covered with sugar 蜜餞的；用糖漬的

crystal·log·raphy /ˌkrɪstəˈlɒɡrəfi; *NAmE* -ˈlɑːɡ-/ *noun* [U] the branch of science that deals with CRYSTALS 晶體學 ▸ **crystal·log·raph·er** /ˌkrɪstəˈlɒɡrəfə(r); *NAmE* -ˈlɑːɡ-/ *noun*

crystal meth *noun* = METH

'crystal set (also **ˌcrystal 'radio**) *noun* a simple early radio which was listened to wearing HEADPHONES（早期用耳機的）晶體檢波收音機，礦石收音機

the CSA /ˌsiː es ˈeɪ/ *abbr.* the Child Support Agency (a government organization in Britain that decides how much money a parent who does not live with a child must contribute to support the child) 兒童支持局，子女撫養代理局（英國政府機構，負責向與子女分開居住的家長規定撫養費數額）

'C-section *noun* (*NAmE*) = CAESAREAN

CS gas /ˌsiː es ˈɡæs/ *noun* [U] a gas that stings the eyes, producing tears and making it difficult to breathe. CS gas is sometimes used to control crowds. 催淚性毒氣（或瓦斯）➲ see also TEAR GAS

CST /ˌsiː es ˈtiː/ *abbr.* CENTRAL STANDARD TIME

Ct (also **Ct.** especially in *NAmE*) *abbr.* (used in written addresses) COURT（用於書面地址）公寓樓，宅第：*30 Willow Ct* 威洛公寓樓 30 號

ct (also **ct.** especially in *NAmE*) *abbr.* **1** (in writing) CARAT（書寫形式）開，克拉：*an 18ct gold ring* 一枚 18 開的金戒指 **2** (in writing) CENT(S)（書寫形式）分：*50 cts* * 50 分

CTC /ˌsiː tiː ˈsiː/ *noun* (in the UK) the abbreviation for 'City Technology College' (a school in a town or city that teaches technology, science and mathematics to young people between the ages of 11 and 18) 城市技術學院（全寫為 City Technology College，在英國向 11 至 18 歲的青少年講授科技和數學的學校）

CT scan /ˌsiː ˈtiː skæn/ *noun* = CAT SCAN

cu. *abbr.* (in writing) CUBIC（書寫形式）立方的：*a volume of 2 cu. m* (= 2 cubic metres) * 2 立方米的體積

cub /kʌb/ *noun* **1** [C] a young BEAR, LION, FOX, etc.（熊、獅、狐狸等的）幼獸，崽：*a lioness guarding her cubs* 守護幼崽的母獅 **2 the Cubs** (*BrE*) (*US* **the 'Cub Scouts**) [pl.] a branch of the SCOUT ASSOCIATION for boys between the ages of eight and ten or eleven 幼童軍（八至十或十一歲的男孩組成的童子軍的一部份）：*to join the Cubs* 參加幼童軍 **3 Cub** (also **'Cub Scout**) [C] a member of the Cubs 幼童軍成員 ➲ compare BROWNIE (2), (3)

Cuban /ˈkjuːbən/ *adj., noun*

■ ***adj.*** from or connected with Cuba 古巴的

■ ***noun*** a person from Cuba 古巴人

cub·by·hole /ˈkʌbihəʊl; *NAmE* -hoʊl/ *noun* **1** a small room or a small space 小房間；斗室；狹小的空間：*My office is a cubbyhole in the basement.* 我的辦公室在地下室的一間小屋裏。 **2** (*SAfrE*) a small space or shelf facing the front seats of a car where you can keep papers, maps, etc.（汽車前排座前放紙或地圖等的）格架 ➲ compare GLOVE COMPARTMENT

cube /kjuːb/ *noun, verb*

■ ***noun*** **1** a solid or hollow figure with six equal square sides 立方體；立方形 ➲ VISUAL VOCAB page V71 **2** a piece of sth, especially food, with six sides 立方形的東西（尤指食物）：*Cut the meat into cubes.* 把肉切成丁兒。 ➲ see also ICE CUBE, STOCK CUBE, SUGAR CUBE **3** (*mathematics* 數) the number that you get when you multiply a number by itself twice 立方；三次冪：*The cube of 5 (5^3) is 125 (5×5×5).* * 5 的立方（5^3）是 125。

■ ***verb*** **1** [usually passive] **~ sth** (*mathematics* 數) to multiply a number by itself twice 求…的立方：*10 cubed is 1 000.* * 10 的立方是 1 000。 **2 ~ sth** to cut food into cubes 把（食物）切成小方塊 **SYN** **dice**

ˌcube 'root *noun* (*mathematics* 數) a number which, when multiplied by itself twice, produces a particular number 立方根：*The cube root of 64 ($\sqrt[3]{64}$) is 4.* * 64 的立方根是 4。 ➲ compare SQUARE ROOT

cubic /ˈkjuːbɪk/ *adj.* **1** (*abbr.* **cu**) [only before noun] used to show that a measurement is the volume of sth, that is the height multiplied by the length and the width 立方的：*cubic centimetres/inches/metres* 立方厘米／英寸／米 **2** measured or expressed in cubic units 用立方單位度量（或表示）的：*the cubic capacity of a car's engine* 汽車發動機汽缸的容量 **3** having the shape of a cube 立方形的：*a cubic figure* 立方形

cu·bicle /ˈkjuːbɪkl/ *noun* a small room that is made by separating off part of a larger room（大房間分隔出的）小房間，隔間：*a shower cubicle* 淋浴小單間 ◇ (*BrE*) *a changing cubicle* (= for example at a public swimming pool) 更衣室隔間 ◇ (*especially NAmE*) *an office cubicle* 辦公室的隔間

cu·bism /ˈkjuːbɪzəm/ (also **Cubism**) *noun* [U] a style and movement in early 20th century art in which objects and people are represented as GEOMETRIC shapes, often shown from many different angles at the same time（20 世紀初藝術的）立體主義，立體派 ▸ **cu·bist** (also **Cubist**) *noun*：*The exhibition includes works by the Cubists.* 這個展覽包括立體派的作品。 **cu·bist** (also **Cubist**) *adj.* [usually before noun]：*cubist paintings* 立體派的繪畫

cubit /ˈkjuːbɪt/ *noun* an ancient measurement of length, about 45 cm or the length from the elbow to the end of the fingers 腕尺（古代長度單位，約 45 厘米，或自肘至指尖的長度）

cu·boid /ˈkjuːbɔɪd/ *noun, adj.*

■ ***noun*** (*geometry* 幾何) a solid object which has six RECTANGULAR sides at RIGHT ANGLES to each other 長方體；矩形體

■ ***adj.*** shaped approximately like a CUBE 近似立方形的

ˌcub reˈporter *noun* a young newspaper REPORTER without much experience 缺少經驗的年輕記者；初出茅廬的記者

cuck·old /ˈkʌkəʊld; *NAmE* -oʊld/ *noun, verb*

■ ***noun*** (*old use, disapproving*) a man whose wife has sex with another man 妻子有外遇的人；戴綠帽子的人

■ ***verb*** (*old use*) **1 ~ sb** (of a man 男人) to make another man a cuckold by having sex with his wife 給（另一男人）戴綠帽子；與（某人）的妻子通姦 **2 ~ sb** (of a woman 女人) to make her husband a cuckold by having sex with another man 使（丈夫）戴綠帽子；使（丈夫）當王八

cuckoo /ˈkʊkuː/ *noun, adj.*

■ ***noun*** (*pl.* **-oos**) a bird with a call that sounds like its name. Cuckoos leave their eggs in the nests of other birds. 杜鵑鳥；布穀鳥 ➲ see also CLOUD CUCKOO LAND

■ ***adj.*** [not before noun] (*old-fashioned, informal*) crazy 瘋狂；狂熱

ˈcuckoo clock *noun* a clock that has a small toy bird inside that comes out every hour and marks the hours with a sound like that of a cuckoo 布穀鳥自鳴鐘（鐘內有小玩具鳥每小時出現，報時似布穀鳥叫聲）

cu·cum·ber /ˈkjuːkʌmbə(r)/ *noun* [C, U] a long vegetable with dark green skin and light green flesh, that is usually eaten raw 黃瓜 ➲ VISUAL VOCAB page V31 ➲ see also SEA CUCUMBER **IDM** see COOL *adj.*

cud /kʌd/ *noun* [U] the food that cows and similar animals bring back from the stomach into the mouth to chew again（牛等動物）反芻的食物，倒嚼的食物：*cows chewing the cud* 在咀嚼反芻食物的牛

cud·dle /ˈkʌdl/ *verb, noun*

■ ***verb*** [I, T] to hold sb/sth close in your arms to show love or affection 擁抱；摟抱 **SYN** **hug**：*A couple of teenagers were kissing and cuddling on the doorstep.* 一對年輕人在門階上親吻擁抱。◇ **~ sth (+ adj.)** *The little boy cuddled the teddy bear close.* 小男孩緊緊地摟着玩具熊。

PHR V **ˌcuddle ˈup (to/against sb/sth)** | **ˌcuddle ˈup (together)** to sit or lie very close to sb/sth 緊靠…而坐（或躺）；依偎：*She cuddled up against him.* 她依偎着他。◇ *We cuddled up together under the blanket.* 我們蓋着毯子緊貼着身子睡在一起。

■ ***noun*** [usually sing.] the action of holding sb close in your arms to show love or affection 擁抱；摟抱 **SYN** **hug**：*to give sb a cuddle* 擁抱某人

cud·dly /ˈkʌdli/ *adj.* (*informal*) (**cud·dlier**, **cud·dli·est**) **1** (*approving*) if a person is **cuddly**, they make you want to cuddle them 令人想擁抱的 **2** [only before noun] (of a child's toy 兒童玩具) soft and designed to be cuddled 柔軟而令人想摟抱的：*a cuddly rabbit* 逗人愛撫的玩具兔

cudgel /ˈkʌdʒl/ *noun, verb*

■ ***noun*** a short thick stick that is used as a weapon（用作武器的）短棒，粗短棍

IDM **take up (the) cudgels on behalf of sb/sth** (*old-fashioned*) to defend or support sb/sth strongly 堅決保衛；毅然支持

■ ***verb*** (*BrE*) (**-ll-**, *especially US* **-l-**) **~ sb** to hit sb with a cudgel 用短棒打

IDM **cudgel your ˈbrains** (*old-fashioned, BrE*) to think very hard 冥思苦想；絞盡腦汁

cue /kjuː/ *noun, verb*

■ ***noun*** **1** an action or event that is a signal for sb to do sth 暗示；提示；信號：**~ (for sth)** *Jon's arrival was a cue for more champagne.* 喬恩一來就意味着要喝更多的香檳酒了。◇ **~ (to do sth)** *I think that's my cue to explain why I'm here.* 我想這就是要我解釋一下我為什麼到這裏來。 **2** a few words or an action in a play that is a signal for another actor to do sth（戲劇的）提示，暗示，尾白：*She stood in the wings and waited for her cue to go on.* 她站在舞台側面等待着出場的提示。 **3** a long wooden stick with a leather tip, used for hitting the ball in the games of BILLIARDS, POOL and SNOOKER（枱球等的）球杆，彈子棒 ➲ VISUAL VOCAB page V40

IDM **(right) on cue** at exactly the moment you expect or that is appropriate 恰好在這時；就在這時候：*'Where is that boy?' As if on cue, Simon appeared in the doorway.* "那男孩在哪裏？" 西蒙像是接到了信號一樣剛好出現在門口。 **take your ˈcue from sb/sth** to copy what sb else does as an example of how to behave or what to do 模仿…的樣子做；學…的樣：*Investors are taking their cue from the big banks and selling dollars.* 投資者效法大銀行賣出美元。

■ ***verb*** (**cue·ing**, **cued**, **cued**) **~ sb** to give sb a signal so they know when to start doing sth 給（某人）暗示（或提示）：*Can you cue me when you want me to begin speaking?* 你要我開始講話時能給我暗示一下嗎？

ˈcue ball *noun* the ball that is hit with the cue in games such as BILLIARDS and SNOOKER（枱球等的）主球，母球 ➲ VISUAL VOCAB page V40

ˈcue card *noun* a large card held up behind a television camera so that it can be read by actors or television PRESENTERS but cannot be seen on television 提詞板，提示板（給電視演員或節目主持人看）

cuff /kʌf/ *noun, verb*

■ ***noun*** **1** [C] the end of a coat or shirt sleeve at the wrist 袖口：*a collar and cuffs of white lace* 帶白色蕾絲花邊的衣領和袖口 ➲ VISUAL VOCAB page V63 **2 cuffs** [pl.] (*informal*) = HANDCUFFS **3** (*NAmE*) (*BrE* **ˈturn-up**) [C] the bottom of the leg of a pair of trousers/pants that has been folded over on the outside（褲腳的）外翻邊，外捲邊 **4** [C] a light hit with an open hand 用掌輕拍：*to give sb a friendly cuff* 友好地輕輕拍某人一下

IDM **ˌoff the ˈcuff** (of speaking, remarks, etc. 講話、話語等) without previous thought or preparation 未經思考（或準備）；即興：*I'm just speaking off the cuff here—I haven't seen the results yet.* 我只是在這裏即興說說而已，我還沒看到結果呢。◇ *an off-the-cuff remark* 即席發言

■ ***verb*** **~ sb** to hit sb quickly and lightly with your hand, especially in a way that is not serious 用手輕快地拍（某人）：*She cuffed him lightly around his head.* 她輕輕地在他頭上拍了幾下。

cuff·link /ˈkʌflɪŋk/ *noun* [usually pl.] one of a pair of small decorative objects used for fastening shirt cuffs together（襯衫的）袖口鏈扣，袖扣：*a pair of gold cuff-links* 一對袖口金鏈扣 ➲ VISUAL VOCAB page V65

cuis·ine /kwɪˈziːn/ *noun* [U, C] (from *French*) **1** a style of cooking 烹飪；風味：*Italian cuisine* 意大利式烹飪 **2** the food served in a restaurant (usually an expensive one)（通常指昂貴的餐館中的）飯菜，菜肴：*The hotel* restaurant is noted for its excellent cuisine. 這家旅館的餐廳以美味佳肴聞名遐邇。 ➲ see also HAUTE CUISINE, NOUVELLE CUISINE

cul-de-sac /ˈkʌl də sæk/ *noun* (*pl.* **cul-de-sacs** or **culs-de-sac**) (from *French*) a street that is closed at one end 死胡同；死巷

cu·lin·ary /ˈkʌlməri; *NAmE* -neri/ *adj.* [only before noun] (*formal*) connected with cooking or food 烹飪的；食物的：*culinary skills* 烹飪技能 ◇ *Savour the culinary delights of Mexico.* 品嚐墨西哥的美味。

cull /kʌl/ *verb, noun*

■ ***verb*** **~ sth** to kill a particular number of animals of a group in order to prevent the group from getting too large 部份捕殺，宰殺（為防止動物種群量過多而殺掉其中一定數量）

PHR V **ˈcull sth from sth** to choose or collect sth from a source or several different sources 選出；挑出；採集：*an exhibition of paintings culled from regional art galleries* 從各地區畫廊中精選出來的繪畫作品展

■ ***noun*** the act of killing some animals (usually the weakest ones) of a group in order to prevent the group from getting too large （為防止動物種群量過多而通常對最弱者的）選擇性宰殺：*the annual seal cull* 每年對海豹的選擇性宰殺

cul·min·ate /ˈkʌlmɪneɪt/ *verb* [I] **~ (in/with sth)** (*formal*) to end with a particular result, or at a particular point （以某種結果）告終；（在某一點）結束：*a gun battle which culminated in the death of two police officers* 一場造成兩名警察死亡的槍戰 ◇ *Months of hard work culminated in success.* 幾個月的艱辛工作終於取得了成功。◇ *Their summer tour will culminate at a spectacular concert in London.* 在倫敦舉行的一場精彩的音樂會將為他們的夏季巡迴演出畫上句號。

cul·min·ation /ˌkʌlmɪˈneɪʃn/ *noun* [sing.] (*formal*) the highest point or end of sth, usually happening after a long time 頂點；巔峰；高潮；終點：*The reforms marked the successful culmination of a long campaign.* 這些改革標誌着一場長期運動的勝利結束。

cu·lottes /kjuːˈlɒts; *NAmE* kuːˈlɑːts/ *noun* [pl.] women's wide short trousers/pants that are made to look like a skirt 裙褲：*a pair of culottes* 一條裙褲

culp·able /ˈkʌlpəbl/ *adj.* (*formal*) responsible and deserving blame for having done sth wrong 應受責備的；難辭其咎的 ▸ **culp·abil·ity** /ˌkʌlpəˈbɪləti/ *noun* [U] **culp·ably** /ˈkʌlpəbli/ *adv.*

ˌculpable ˈhomicide *noun* [U] (*law* 律) in some countries, the crime of killing sb illegally but not deliberately （一些國家的）有罪殺人，刑事殺人 ➲ compare JUSTIFIABLE HOMICIDE

cul·prit /ˈkʌlprɪt/ *noun* **1** a person who has done sth wrong or against the law 犯錯的人；罪犯：*The police quickly identified the real culprits.* 警方很快查出了真正的罪犯。 **2** a person or thing responsible for causing a problem 肇事者；引起問題的事物：*The main culprit in the current crisis seems to be modern farming techniques.* 當前這場危機的罪魁禍首好像是現代農業技術。

cult /kʌlt/ *noun, adj.*

■ ***noun*** **1** [usually sing.] **~ (of sth)** a way of life, an attitude, an idea, etc. that has become very popular （對生活方式、態度、觀念等的）狂熱，時尚，崇拜：*the cult of physical fitness* 健身熱 ◇ *An extraordinary* ***personality cult*** *had been created around the leader.* 在這位領導人的周圍興起了一場異乎尋常的個人崇拜。 **2** a small group of people who have extreme religious beliefs and who are not part of any established religion （有極端宗教信仰的）異教團體：*Their son ran away from home and joined a cult.* 他們的兒子離家出走，加入了一個異教團體。 **3** (*formal*) a system of religious beliefs and practices 宗教信仰；宗教習俗：*the Chinese cult of ancestor worship* 中國人供奉祖先的習俗

■ ***adj.*** [only before noun] very popular with a particular group of people; treating sb/sth as a cult figure, etc. 受特定群體歡迎的；作為偶像崇拜的：*a* ***cult movie/book*** 風靡一時的電影 / 書 ◇ *The singer has become a* ***cult figure*** *in America.* 那位歌手在美國已成為人們狂熱崇拜的偶像。◇ *The cartoon has achieved* ***cult status.*** 這部動畫片達到了風靡一時的地步。◇ *The TV series has a* ***cult following*** *among young people.* 那部電視連續劇在年輕人中擁有一批狂熱的追隨者。

cul·tiv·able /ˈkʌltɪvəbl/ *adj.* (of land 土地) that can be used to grow crops 可耕作的；可耕種的

cul·ti·var /ˈkʌltɪvɑː(r)/ *noun* (*technical* 術語) a type of plant that has been deliberately developed to have particular features 栽培種；栽培品種

cul·ti·vate /ˈkʌltɪveɪt/ *verb* (*formal*) **1 ~ sth** to prepare and use land for growing plants or crops 耕；耕作：*The land around here has never been cultivated.* 這一帶的土地從未開墾過。 **2 ~ sth** to grow plants or crops 種植；栽培；培育 **SYN** **grow**：*The people cultivate mainly rice and beans.* 這裏的人們主要種植稻米和豆類。 **3 ~ sb/sth** (sometimes *disapproving*) to try to get sb's friendship or support 建立（友誼）；結交（朋友）；獲得（支持）：*He purposely tried to cultivate good relations with the press.* 他特意設法與新聞界搞好關係。◇ *It helps if you go out of your way to cultivate the local people.* 主動結交當地人大有好處。 **4 ~ sth** to develop an attitude, a way of talking or behaving, etc. 逐漸形成（某種態度、談話或舉止方式等）：*She cultivated an air of sophistication.* 她養成了一派精明練達的氣度。

cul·ti·vated /ˈkʌltɪveɪtɪd/ *adj.* **1** (of people 人) having a high level of education and showing good manners 有教養的；有修養的；舉止文雅的 **SYN** **cultured** **2** (of land 土地) used to grow crops 用於耕作的：*cultivated fields* 耕地 **3** (of plants that are also wild 野生植物) grown on a farm, etc. in order to be sold（為出售而）栽培的，培植的：*cultivated mushrooms* 培植的蘑菇 **OPP** **wild**

cul·ti·va·tion /ˌkʌltɪˈveɪʃn/ *noun* [U] **1** the preparation and use of land for growing plants or crops 耕種；種植；栽培：*fertile land that is* ***under cultivation*** (= being CULTIVATED) 肥沃的耕地 ◇ ***rice/wheat, etc. cultivation*** 水稻、小麥等的種植 ➲ see also SHIFTING CULTIVATION **2** the deliberate development of a particular relationship, quality or skill （關係的）培植；（品質或技巧的）培養：*the cultivation of a good relationship with local firms* 發展與當地公司的良好關係

cul·ti·va·tor /ˈkʌltɪveɪtə(r)/ *noun* **1** a person who CULTIVATES (= grows crops on) the land 耕種者；種植者；栽培者 **2** a machine for breaking up soil and destroying WEEDS (= plants growing where they are not wanted) 耕耘機；中耕機

cul·tural **AW** /ˈkʌltʃərəl/ *adj.* [usually before noun] **1** connected with the culture of a particular society or group, its customs, beliefs, etc. 與文化有關的；文化的：*cultural differences between the two communities* 這兩個群體之間的文化差異 ◇ *economic, social and cultural factors* 經濟、社會和文化因素 **2** connected with art, literature, music, etc. 與藝術、文學、音樂等有關的：*a cultural event* 文化活動 ◇ *Europe's cultural heritage* 歐洲的文化遺產 ◇ *The orchestra is very important for the cultural life of the city.* 管弦樂隊對這座城市的文化生活而言非常重要。 ▸ **cul·tur·al·ly** **AW** /-rəli/ *adv.*

cul·ture **AW** /ˈkʌltʃə(r)/ *noun, verb*

■ ***noun***

▸ WAY OF LIFE 生活方式 **1** [U] the customs and beliefs, art, way of life and social organization of a particular country or group 文化，文明（指國家或群體的風俗、信仰、藝術、生活方式及社會組織）：***European/Islamic/African/American, etc. culture*** 歐洲、伊斯蘭、非洲、美國等文化 ◇ *working-class culture* 工人階級的文化 **2** [C] a country, group, etc. with its own beliefs, etc. 文化（指擁有特定信仰等的國家、群體等）：*The children are taught to respect different cultures.* 孩子們受到教導要尊重不同的文化。◇ *the effect of technology on traditional cultures* 技術對各種傳統文化的影響

▸ ART/MUSIC/LITERATURE 藝術；音樂；文學 **3** [U] art, music, literature, etc., thought of as a group 文化（藝術、音樂、文學等的總稱）：*Venice is a beautiful city full of culture and history.* 威尼斯是一座具有深厚文化和歷史底蘊的美麗城市。◇ ***popular culture*** (= that is enjoyed by a lot of people) 大眾文化 ◇ *the Minister for Culture* 文化部長

▸ **BELIEFS/ATTITUDES 看法；態度 4** 🔑 [C, U] the beliefs and attitudes about sth that people in a particular group or organization share 文化（某群體或組織的一致看法和態度）: *The political cultures of the United States and Europe are very different.* 美國的政治觀和歐洲的大不相同。◇ *A culture of failure exists in some schools.* 在某些學校中存在着失敗文化。◇ *company culture* 企業文化 ◇ *We are living in a consumer culture.* 我們生活在一種消費文化之中。

▸ **GROWING/BREEDING 種植；養殖 5** [U] (*technical* 術語) the growing of plants or breeding of particular animals in order to get a particular substance or crop from them 種植；栽培；養殖；培育: *the culture of silkworms* (= for silk) 桑蠶養殖

▸ **CELLS/BACTERIA 細胞；細菌 6** [C] (*biology* 生, *medical* 醫) a group of cells or bacteria, especially one taken from a person or an animal and grown for medical or scientific study, or to produce food; the process of obtaining and growing these cells 培養細胞；培養菌；（為醫療、科研或食品生產而作細胞或細菌的）培養: *a culture of cells from the tumour* 腫瘤細胞的培養 ◇ *Yogurt is made from active cultures.* 酸奶是由活性培養菌製成的。◇ *to do/take a throat culture* 採集喉部培養細胞

■ ***verb*** **~ sth** (*biology* 生, *medical* 醫) to grow a group of cells or bacteria for medical or scientific study 培養（細胞或細菌）

cul·tured AW /ˈkʌltʃəd; *NAmE* -tʃərd/ *adj.* **1** (of people 人) well educated and able to understand and enjoy art, literature, etc. 有教養的；有修養的；文雅的 SYN **cultivated** OPP **uncultured 2** (of cells or bacteria 細胞或細菌) grown for medical or scientific study（為醫學或科學研究）培養的 **3** (of PEARLS 珍珠) grown artificially 人工養殖的

ˈ**culture shock** *noun* [C, U] a feeling of confusion and anxiety that sb may feel when they live in or visit another country 文化衝擊，文化休克（指在異國生活或訪問時的一種困惑不安的感覺）

ˈ**culture vulture** *noun* (*humorous*) a person who is very interested in serious art, music, literature, etc. 文化狂熱分子

cul·vert /ˈkʌlvət; *NAmE* -vərt/ *noun* a tunnel that carries a river or a pipe for water under a road 涵洞；（道路下面的）排水管

cum /kʌm/ *prep.* (used for linking two nouns 用於連接兩個名詞) and; as well as 和；與；及: *a bedroom-cum-study* 卧室兼作書房

cum·ber·some /ˈkʌmbəsəm; *NAmE* -bərs-/ *adj.* **1** large and heavy; difficult to carry 大而笨重的；難以攜帶的 SYN **bulky**: *cumbersome machinery* 笨重的機器 **2** slow and complicated 緩慢複雜的: *cumbersome legal procedures* 繁瑣的法律程序 **3** (of words or phrases 單詞或短語) long or complicated 冗長的；累贅的；複雜的: *The organization changed its cumbersome title to something easier to remember.* 這家機構把它那複雜累贅的名稱改得簡單好記了。

cumin /ˈkʌmɪn/ *noun* [U] the dried seeds of the cumin plant, used in cooking as a spice 蒔蘿籽；土茴香籽: *cumin seeds* 土茴香籽 ➲ VISUAL VOCAB page V32

cum laude /ˌkʊm ˈlɔːdi; ˈlaʊdeɪ/ *adv., adj.* (from *Latin*) (in the US) at the third of the three highest levels of achievement that students can reach when they finish their studies at college（美國）以優異成績（三等優異成績的第三等）: *He graduated cum laude.* 他以優等成績畢業。➲ compare MAGNA CUM LAUDE, SUMMA CUM LAUDE

cum·mer·bund /ˈkʌməbʌnd; *NAmE* -mərb-/ *noun* a wide band of silk, etc. worn around the waist, especially under a DINNER JACKET（尤指晚禮服的）寬腰帶

cu·mu·la·tive /ˈkjuːmjələtɪv; *NAmE* -leɪtɪv/ *adj.* **1** having a result that increases in strength or importance each time more of sth is added（在力量或重要性方面）聚積的，積累的，漸增的: *the* ***cumulative effect*** *of human activity on the world environment* 人類活動對世界生態環境日積月累的影響 **2** including all the amounts that have been added previously 累計的；累積的: *the monthly sales figures and the cumulative total for the past six months* 每月的銷售數字和過去六個月的累計總數 ▸ **cu·mu·la·tive·ly** *adv.*

cu·mu·lo·nim·bus /ˌkjuːmələʊˈnɪmbəs; *NAmE* -loʊ-/ *noun* [U] (*technical* 術語) a high mass of thick cloud with a flat base, often seen during THUNDERSTORMS 積雨雲（常伴有雷陣雨）

cu·mu·lus /ˈkjuːmjələs/ *noun* [U] (*technical* 術語) a type of thick white cloud 積雲

cu·nei·form /ˈkjuːnɪfɔːm; *NAmE* -fɔːrm/ *noun* [U] an ancient system of writing used in Persia and Assyria（古代波斯和亞述的）楔形文字

cun·ni·lin·gus /ˌkʌnɪˈlɪŋgəs/ *noun* [U] the act of touching a woman's sex organs with the mouth and tongue in order to give sexual pleasure 舔陰（用口和舌接觸女性生殖器）

cun·ning /ˈkʌnɪŋ/ *adj., noun*

■ ***adj.*** **1** (*disapproving*) able to get what you want in a clever way, especially by tricking or cheating sb 狡猾的；奸詐的；詭詐的 SYN **crafty, wily**: *a cunning liar* 花言巧語的騙子 ◇ *He was as cunning as a fox.* 他像狐狸一樣狡猾。 **2** clever and skilful 靈巧的；精巧的；巧妙的 SYN **ingenious**: *It was a cunning piece of detective work.* 那是一篇構思巧妙的偵探作品。▸ **cun·ning·ly** *adv.*: *The microphone was cunningly concealed in the bookcase.* 話筒被巧妙地隱藏在書櫃裏。

■ ***noun*** [U] the ability to achieve sth by tricking or cheating other people in a clever way 狡猾；詭詐；狡黠 SYN **craftiness**: *It took energy and cunning just to survive.* 既要花力氣又要有心計才能維持生存。◇ *She used low cunning* (= dishonest behaviour) *to get what she wanted.* 她用了卑鄙的欺詐手段來獲取她想得到的東西。

cunt /kʌnt/ *noun* (*taboo, slang*) **1** a woman's VAGINA and outer sexual organs 屄；女性陰部 **2** a very offensive word used to insult sb and to show anger or dislike（用於辱罵）討厭鬼，龜孫子，王八蛋: *You stupid cunt!* 你這傻屄！

cup 🔑 /kʌp/ *noun, verb*

■ ***noun* 1** 🔑 [C] a small container shaped like a bowl, usually with a handle, used for drinking tea, coffee, etc. 杯子: *a teacup* 茶杯 ◇ *a coffee cup* 咖啡杯 ◇ *a cup and saucer* 一套杯碟 ◇ *a paper cup* 紙杯 ➲ VISUAL VOCAB page V22 **2** 🔑 [C] the contents of a cup 一杯（的量）: *She drank the whole cup.* 她把那一杯全喝下去了。◇ *Would you like a cup of tea?* 你想喝杯茶嗎？ **3** 🔑 [C] a unit for measuring quantity used in cooking in the US; a metal or plastic container used to measure this quantity 杯（美國用作烹飪的計量單位）；量杯（金屬或塑料量器）: *two cups of flour and half a cup of butter* 兩杯麪粉加上半杯黃油 **4** 🔑 [C] a thing shaped like a cup 杯狀物: *an egg cup* 蛋杯 **5** 🔑 [C] a gold or silver cup on a STEM, often with two handles, that is given as a prize in a competition 獎杯；優勝杯: *She's won several cups for skating.* 她已多次榮獲滑冰比賽的獎杯。◇ *He lifted the cup for the fifth time this year* (= it was the fifth time he had won). 他今年第五次舉起了獲勝獎杯。➲ picture at MEDAL **6** 🔑 [sing.] (usually **Cup**) a sports competition in which a cup is given as a prize 優勝杯賽: *the World Cup* 世界杯賽 **7** [C] one of the two parts of a BRA that cover the breast（胸罩的）罩杯: *a C cup* 罩杯尺寸為 C 的胸罩 **8** [C, U] a drink made from wine mixed with, for example, fruit juice（由葡萄酒與果汁等調製的）混合飲料 **9** [C] (*NAmE*) (in GOLF 高爾夫球) a hollow in the ground that you must get the ball into 球洞 **10** [C] (*NAmE*) a piece of plastic that a man wears over his sex organs to protect them while he is playing a sport（體育運動時保護男子生殖器的）護杯；下身保護罩

IDM **in your ˈcups** (*old-fashioned*) having drunk too much alcohol 喝醉: *He gets very maudlin when he's in his cups.* 他酒醉就顧影自憐。 **not sb's cup of ˈtea** (*informal*) not what sb likes or is interested in 非某人所好；不合某人心意: *An evening at the opera isn't everyone's cup of tea.* 並不是所有人都喜歡晚上去聽歌劇。◇ *He's nice enough but not really my cup of tea.* 他這人挺不錯，但不是我特喜歡的那種人。➲ more at SLIP *n.*

■ ***verb*** **(-pp-) 1 ~ your hand(s) (around/over sth)** to make your hands into the shape of a bowl 使（手）窩成杯

狀：*She held the bird gently in cupped hands.* 她雙手輕輕地捧着那隻小鳥。**2 ~ sth (in your hands)** to hold sth, making your hands into a round shape 使（雙手）成圓狀托起：*He cupped her face in his hands and kissed her.* 他用雙手捧着她的臉吻她。

cup·board /ˈkʌbəd; *NAmE* -bərd/ *noun* **1** a piece of furniture with doors and shelves used for storing dishes, food, clothes, etc. 櫥櫃；食物櫃；衣櫃：*kitchen cupboards* 廚房用的櫥櫃 **2** (*BrE*) (*NAmE* **closet**) a space in a wall with a door that reaches the ground, used for storing things 壁櫥：*built-in cupboards* 壁櫥 ➲ see also AIRING CUPBOARD, BROOM CUPBOARD
IDM **the ˌcupboard is ˈbare** (*BrE*) used to say that there is no money for sth 食櫥是空的（指沒錢購買）：*They are seeking more funds but the cupboard is bare.* 他們正在尋求更多的資金，然而根本找不到。ORIGIN This expression refers to a children's nursery rhyme about Old Mother Hubbard, who had nothing in her cupboard to feed her dog. 源自一首關於老媽哈伯德的兒歌。她的食櫥裏沒有餵狗的東西。**ˈcupboard love** (*BrE*) affection that sb, especially a child, shows towards sb else in order to get sth（尤指小孩）有所企圖的親熱 ➲ more at SKELETON

cup·cake /ˈkʌpkeɪk/ (*especially NAmE*) (*BrE* also **ˈfairy cake**) *noun* a small cake, baked in a paper container shaped like a cup and often with ICING on top（常撒有糖霜的）紙杯蛋糕

ˈcup final (also **Cup Final**) *noun* (*BrE*) (especially in football (SOCCER) 尤指足球) the last match in a series of matches in a competition that gives a cup as a prize to the winners 優勝杯決賽；錦標賽決賽：*cup final tickets* 優勝杯決賽票 ◇ *the FA Cup Final* 足協杯賽決賽

cup·ful /ˈkʌpfʊl/ *noun* the amount that a cup will hold 一杯（的量）；滿杯：*3 cupfuls of water* * 3 滿杯水 ➲ see also CUP (2)

Cupid /ˈkjuːpɪd/ *noun* **1** the Roman god of love who is shown as a beautiful baby boy with wings, carrying a BOW and arrow 羅馬愛神丘比特 **2 cupid** [C] a picture or statue of a baby boy who looks like Cupid 似羅馬愛神丘比特的畫像（或雕塑）
IDM **play ˈCupid** to try to start a romantic relationship between two people 扮演丘比特角色；牽線撮合

cu·pid·ity /kjuːˈpɪdəti/ *noun* [U] (*formal*) a strong desire for more wealth, possessions, power, etc. than a person needs 貪心；貪婪 SYN **greed**

cu·pola /ˈkjuːpələ/ *noun* a round part on top of a building (like a small DOME) 圓屋頂；穹頂 ➲ VISUAL VOCAB page V14

cuppa /ˈkʌpə/ *noun* (*BrE, informal*) a cup of tea 一杯茶：*Do you fancy a cuppa?* 你想來一杯茶嗎？

cup·ping /ˈkʌpɪŋ/ *noun* [U] a way of treating pain by putting special cups on the skin and heating them so that the flow of blood to the skin increases 拔火罐；杯吸法

ˈcup tie *noun* (*BrE*) (especially in football (SOCCER) 尤指足球) a match between two teams in a competition that gives a cup as a prize to the winner 優勝杯賽比賽

cur /kɜː(r)/ *noun* (*old-fashioned, disapproving*) an aggressive dog, especially a MONGREL 惡狗；（尤指）雜種狗

cur·able /ˈkjʊərəbl; *NAmE* ˈkjʊr-/ *adj.* (of an illness 疾病) that can be cured 可醫治的；可治癒的：*Most skin cancers are curable if treated early.* 如果及早治療，多數的皮膚癌是可治好的。OPP **incurable**

cura·çao /ˌkjʊərəˈsəʊ; -ˈseɪəʊ; *NAmE* ˌkjuːrəˈsoʊ; -ˈsaʊ/ *noun* [U, C] a strong alcoholic drink made from the skin of bitter oranges 庫拉索酒（橙皮烈酒）

cur·acy /ˈkjʊərəsi; *NAmE* ˈkjʊr-/ *noun* (*pl.* **-ies**) the position of a curate; the time that sb is a curate 助理牧師的職位；助理牧師的任期

cur·ate¹ ➲ see also CURATE² /ˈkjʊərət; *NAmE* ˈkjʊrət/ *noun* (in the Anglican Church 聖公會) an assistant to a VICAR (= a priest, who is in charge of the church or churches in a particular area) 助理牧師
IDM **the/a ˌcurate's ˈegg** (*BrE*) something that has some good parts and some bad ones 好壞參半之物；瑕瑜互見之物

cur·ate² /kjʊəˈreɪt; *NAmE* kjʊˈr-/ *verb* **~ sth** to select, organize and look after the objects or works of art in a museum or art gallery, etc. 管理（博物館或畫廊等收藏品）

cura·tive /ˈkjʊərətɪv; *NAmE* ˈkjʊr-/ *adj.* (*formal*) able to cure illness 能治病的；有療效的 SYN **healing**：*the curative properties of herbs* 藥草治病的功效 ➲ compare PREVENTIVE

cur·ator /kjʊəˈreɪtə(r); *NAmE* kjʊˈr-/ *noun* a person whose job is to be in charge of the objects or works of art in a museum or art gallery, etc.（博物館或畫廊等的）館長，負責人

curb /kɜːb; *NAmE* kɜːrb/ *verb, noun*
■ *verb* **~ sth** to control or limit sth, especially sth bad 控制，抑制，限定，約束（尤指不好的事物）SYN **check**：*He needs to learn to curb his temper.* 他得學着控制自己的脾氣。◇ *A range of policies have been introduced aimed at curbing inflation.* 為了抑制通貨膨脹實施了一系列的政策。
■ *noun* **1 ~ (on sth)** something that controls and puts limits on sth 起控制（或限制）作用的事物：*curbs on government spending* 對政府開支的限制措施 **2** (*NAmE*) (*BrE* **kerb**) the edge of the raised path at the side of a road, usually made of long pieces of stone（由條石砌成的）路緣，道牙，馬路牙子：*The bus mounted the curb* (= went onto the SIDEWALK/PAVEMENT) *and hit a tree.* 那輛公交車開上路緣撞到了一棵樹上。➲ VISUAL VOCAB page V3

curb·side (*NAmE*) (*BrE* **kerb·side**) /ˈkɜːbsaɪd; *NAmE* ˈkɜːrb-/ *noun* [U] the side of the street or path near the curb/kerb 人行道靠近路緣的部份

curb·stone (*NAmE*) (*BrE* **kerb·stone**) /ˈkɜːbstəʊn; *NAmE* ˈkɜːrb-/ *noun* a block of stone or concrete in a curb/kerb 路緣石

curd /kɜːd; *NAmE* kɜːrd/ *noun* [U] (also **curds** [pl.]) a thick soft substance that is formed when milk turns sour 凝乳（牛奶變酸後形成的稠而軟的物質）

ˈcurd cheese *noun* [U, C] (*BrE*) a type of soft cheese 凝乳（軟）乾酪 ➲ compare QUARK (2)

cur·dle /ˈkɜːdl; *NAmE* ˈkɜːrdl/ *verb* **1** [I, T] **~ (sth)** when a liquid, especially milk, **curdles** or sth **curdles** it, it separates into solid and liquid parts（使）凝結，結成酸乳 **2** [I, T] **~ (sth)** if sth **curdles** your blood or makes your blood **curdle**, it makes you extremely frightened or shocked 嚇得血液凝固；使心驚膽戰 ➲ see also BLOOD-CURDLING

cure /kjʊə(r); *NAmE* kjʊr/ *verb, noun*
■ *verb* **1 ~ sb (of sth)** to make a person or an animal healthy again after an illness 治癒，治好（病人或動物）：*Will you be able to cure him, Doctor?* 醫生，你能把他治好嗎？➲ COLLOCATIONS at ILL **2 ~ sth** to make an illness go away 治好（疾病）：*TB is a serious illness, but it can be cured.* 肺結核雖然是一種嚴重的疾病，但可治癒。**3 ~ sth** to deal with a problem successfully 解決，了結（問題）：*I finally managed to cure the rattling noise in my car.* 我最終設法解決了我汽車發出的格格響聲。**4 ~ sb of sth** to stop sb from behaving in a particular way, especially a way that is bad or annoying 矯正，改正（某人的不良行為）**5 ~ sth** to treat food or TOBACCO with smoke, salt, etc. in order to preserve it（用熏、醃等方法）加工貯藏（食物或煙草）
IDM see KILL *v.*
■ *noun* **1 ~ (for sth)** a medicine or medical treatment that cures an illness 藥；藥物；療法：*the search for a cure for cancer* 對癌症治療方法的尋求 ◇ *There is no known cure but the illness can be treated.* 這種病尚沒有確切的治癒方法，但可以醫治。**2** the act of curing sb of an illness or the process of being cured 治療；療程：*Doctors cannot effect a cure if the disease has spread too far.* 假如這種疾病已擴散得厲害，醫生也無法妙手回春。◇ *The cure took six weeks.* 此療程花了六個星期。**3 ~ (for sth)** something that will solve a problem, improve a bad situation, etc.（解決問題、改善糟糕情況等的）措施，

對策：*a cure for poverty* 解決貧窮問題的措施 IDM see PREVENTION

'cure-all *noun* something that people believe can cure any problem or any disease 萬靈藥；靈丹妙藥 SYN **panacea**

C

cur·few /ˈkɜːfjuː; *NAmE* ˈkɜːrf-/ *noun* [C, U] **1** a law which says that people must not go outside after a particular time at night until the morning; the time after which nobody must go outside 宵禁令；宵禁時間：*The army imposed a dusk-to-dawn curfew.* 軍隊強制實行黃昏至黎明的宵禁。◇ *You must get home before curfew.* 你必須在實行宵禁之前回到家中。➲ COLLOCATIONS at WAR **2** (*NAmE*) a time when children must be home in the evening 兒童晚間必須在家的時間：*I have a 10 o'clock curfew.* 我得遵守晚上 10 點之前回家的規定。

curie /ˈkjʊəri; *NAmE* ˈkjʊri/ *noun* (*abbr.* **Ci**) (*physics* 物) a unit for measuring RADIOACTIVITY 居里（放射性活度單位）

curio /ˈkjʊəriəʊ; *NAmE* ˈkjʊrioʊ/ *noun* (*pl.* **-os**) a small object that is rare or unusual, often sth that people collect（常指收藏的）小件稀有物

curi·os·ity /ˌkjʊəriˈɒsəti; *NAmE* ˌkjʊriˈɑːs-/ *noun* (*pl.* **-ies**) **1** [U, sing.] **~ (about sth)** | **~ (to do sth)** a strong desire to know about sth 好奇心；求知慾：*Children show curiosity about everything.* 兒童對一切事物都顯露出好奇心。◇ *a certain curiosity to see what would happen next* 有點想知道下一步會發生什麼事的好奇心 ◇ *The letter wasn't addressed to me but I opened it* ***out of curiosity***. 那封信不是寫給我的，然而我卻出於好奇把它拆開了。◇ *His answer did not* ***satisfy my curiosity*** *at all.* 他的答覆絲毫沒有滿足我的好奇心。◇ *Sophie's* ***curiosity was aroused*** *by the mysterious phone call.* 那個神秘的電話引起了索菲的好奇心。◇ *intellectual curiosity* 求知慾 ◇ *'Why do you ask?' 'Oh, just* ***idle curiosity*** *'* (= no particular reason). "你為什麼要問？" "哦，沒什麼，好奇而已。" **2** [C] an unusual and interesting thing 罕見而有趣之物；奇物；珍品：*The museum is full of historical curiosities.* 這座博物館有許多珍奇歷史文物。

IDM **curiosity killed the 'cat** (*saying*) used to tell sb not to ask questions or try to find out about things that do not concern them 好奇心能要貓的命（讓人別提問或打聽與己無關的事情）；好管閒事；自找麻煩

curi·ous 0‑ /ˈkjʊəriəs; *NAmE* ˈkjʊr-/ *adj.*
1 0‑ **~ (about sth)** | **~ (to do sth)** having a strong desire to know about sth 求知慾強的；好奇的 SYN **inquisitive**：*They were very curious about the people who lived upstairs.* 他們對住在樓上的人感到很好奇。◇ *I was curious to find out what she had said.* 我真想弄清楚她說了些什麼。◇ *Everyone was* ***curious as to*** *why Mark was leaving.* 馬克為什麼要離去，大家都感到好奇。◇ *He is such a curious boy, always asking questions.* 他這個孩子求知慾很強，總是愛提問。 **2** 0‑ **~ (that ...)** strange and unusual 稀奇古怪；奇特；不尋常：*There was a curious mixture of people in the audience.* 觀眾中有些人混雜在一起顯得很怪。◇ *It was a curious feeling, as though we were floating on air.* 那是一種奇特的感覺，我們彷彿在空中漂浮。◇ ***It was curious that*** *she didn't tell anyone.* 她沒有告訴任何人，這很反常。▸ **curi·ous·ly** 0‑ *adv.*：*'Are you really an artist?' Sara asked curiously.* "你真是畫家嗎？" 薩拉好奇地問道。◇ *His clothes were curiously old-fashioned.* 他的衣服式樣陳舊古怪。◇ *Curiously enough, a year later exactly the same thing happened again.* 說來也怪，一模一樣的事情在一年以後又發生了。

cur·ium /ˈkjʊəriəm; *NAmE* ˈkjʊr-/ *noun* [U] (*symb.* **Cm**) a chemical element. Curium is a RADIOACTIVE metal produced artificially from PLUTONIUM. 鋦（放射性化學元素）

curl 0‑ /kɜːl; *NAmE* kɜːrl/ *verb, noun*

■ *verb* **1** 0‑ [I, T] **~ (sth)** to form or make sth form into a curl or curls 捲；（使）拳曲，變鬈曲：*His hair curls naturally.* 他的頭髮天生鬈曲。 **2** 0‑ [I, T] to form or make sth form into a curved shape（使）成拳曲狀；蜷曲：**(+ adv./prep.)** *The cat curled* ***into a ball*** *and went to sleep.* 那隻貓蜷縮成一團睡着了。◇ **~ sth (+ adv./prep.)** *She curled her legs up under her.* 她盤腿坐着。 **3** [I, T] to move while forming into a twisted or curved shape; to make sth do this（使）呈螺旋（或捲曲）狀移動；（使）旋繞；繚繞：**(+ adv./prep.)** *The smoke curled steadily upwards.* 煙裊裊上升。◇ **~ sth (+ adv./prep.)** *He turned and curled the ball around the goalkeeper.* 他轉身把球一盤，繞過了守門員。 **4** [T, I] **~ (sth)** if you **curl** your lip or your lip **curls**, you move your lip upwards and sideways to show that you think sb/sth is stupid or that you are better than they are 撇起嘴唇；撇（嘴）
IDM see TOE *n.*

PHR V **ˌcurl 'up | be ˌcurled 'up** 0‑ to lie or sit with your back curved and your arms and legs bent close to your body 蜷曲着躺（或坐）：*She curled up and closed her eyes.* 她蜷成一團，閉上了眼睛。➲ picture at CURVED **ˌcurl 'up | ˌcurl sb 'up** (*BrE, informal*) to become or make sb become very embarrassed（使）感到十分尷尬 **ˌcurl 'up | ˌcurl sth↔'up** 0‑ to form or make sth form into a tightly curled shape（使）形成緊緊的捲曲狀：*The paper started to shrivel and curl up in the heat.* 那張紙在高溫下開始起皺捲曲。

■ *noun* **1** 0‑ [C] a small bunch of hair that forms a curved or round shape（一綹）鬈髮：*Her hair was a mass of curls.* 她滿頭鬈髮。◇ *The baby had dark eyes and dark curls.* 那嬰孩長着深色的眼睛和烏黑的鬈髮。 **2** [C, U] the tendency of hair to form curls（頭髮）拳曲：*His hair had a natural curl.* 他的頭髮是自然鬈。 **3** [C] a thing that forms a curved or round shape 捲狀物；螺旋狀物：*a curl of smoke* 一縷青煙 ◇ *Decorate the cake with curls of chocolate.* 用圈狀巧克力來裝飾這個蛋糕。◇ *a contemptuous curl of the lip* (= an expression showing disapproval) 輕蔑地撇一撇嘴

curl·er /ˈkɜːlə(r); *NAmE* ˈkɜːrl-/ *noun* [usually pl.] a small plastic or metal tube which you can wrap wet hair around in order to make it curl 捲髮夾 SYN **roller**

cur·lew /ˈkɜːljuː; *NAmE* ˈkɜːrl-/ *noun* a bird with a long thin beak that curves downwards, that lives near water 鷸；杓鷸

cur·li·cue /ˈkɜːlɪkjuː; *NAmE* ˈkɜːrl-/ *noun* (*technical* 術語) a decorative curl or twist in writing or in a design（書法、圖案等的）花飾旋曲

curl·ing /ˈkɜːlɪŋ; *NAmE* ˈkɜːrlɪŋ/ *noun* [U] a game played on ice, in which players slide heavy flat stones towards a mark 冰壺，冰上溜石遊戲（將重石片滑向一目標）

'curling iron (*NAmE*) (*BrE* **tongs**, **'curling tongs**) *noun* a tool that is heated and used for curling hair 燙髮鉗；捲髮鉗

'curling tongs *noun* [pl.] (*BrE*) = CURLING IRON

curly 0‑ /ˈkɜːli; *NAmE* ˈkɜːrli/ *adj.* (**curl·ier**, **curli·est**) having a lot of curls or a curved shape 有鬈髮（或毛）的；拳曲狀的：*short curly hair* 短鬈髮 ◇ *a dog with a curly tail* 捲尾巴的狗 ➲ picture at CURVED ➲ VISUAL VOCAB page V60 OPP **straight**

ˌcurly 'endive *noun* [C, U] = CHICORY (2)

cur·mudg·eon /kɜːˈmʌdʒən; *NAmE* kɜːrˈm-/ *noun* (*old-fashioned*) a bad-tempered person, often an old one 脾氣壞的人（常指老年人）▸ **cur·mudg·eon·ly** *adj.*

cur·rant /ˈkʌrənt; *NAmE* ˈkɜːr-/ *noun* **1** a small dried GRAPE, used in cakes, etc. 小葡萄乾（用於糕餅等）：*a currant bun* 葡萄乾小圓麪包 **2** (usually in compounds 通常構成複合詞) a small black, red or white BERRY that grows in bunches on bushes 醋栗；茶藨子：*blackcurrants* 黑茶藨子 ◇ *currant bushes* 醋栗灌木叢

cur·rency AW /ˈkʌrənsi; *NAmE* ˈkɜːr-/ *noun* (*pl.* **-ies**) **1** [C, U] the system of money that a country uses 通貨；貨幣：*trading in foreign currencies* 買賣外匯 ◇ *a single European currency* 統一的歐洲貨幣 ◇ *You'll need some cash in* ***local currency*** *but you can also use your credit card.* 你將需要一些當地的貨幣現金，但也可使用信用卡。➲ see also HARD CURRENCY **2** [U] the fact that sth is used or accepted by a lot of people 通用；流行；流傳：*The term 'post-industrial' now has* ***wide currency***. "後工業化" 這個術語現已廣為使用。◇ *The qualification has* ***gained currency*** *all over the world.* 這種資格在全世界都得到了普遍認可。

cur·rent 0‑ˉ /ˈkʌrənt; *NAmE* ˈkɜːr-/ *adj., noun*

■ *adj.* **1** 0‑ˉ [only before noun] happening now; of the present time 現時發生的；當前的；現在的：*current prices* 時價 ◇ *a budget for the current year* 今年的預算 ◇ *your current employer* 你現在的雇主 ➲ note at ACTUAL **2** 0‑ˉ being used by or accepted by most people 通用的；流通的；流行的：*words that are no longer current* 已不再通用的詞

■ *noun* **1** 0‑ˉ the movement of water in the sea or a river; the movement of air in a particular direction（海洋或江河的）水流，潮流；氣流：*He swam to the shore against a* ***strong current****.* 他逆着急流游向岸邊。◇ *Birds use warm air currents to help their flight.* 鳥利用暖氣流助飛。**2** 0‑ˉ the flow of electricity through a wire, etc. 電流：*a 15 amp electrical current* * 15 安培的電流 ➲ see also AC, DC (1) **3** the fact of particular ideas, opinions or feelings being present in a group of people 思潮；潮流；趨向：*Ministers are worried by this current of anti-government feeling.* 部長們對這股反政府情緒感到擔憂。

ˈcurrent account (*BrE*) (*US* **ˈchecking account**) (*CanE*) **ˈchequing account** *noun* a type of bank account that you can take money out of at any time, and that provides you with a CHEQUEBOOK and CASH CARD 活期存款賬戶；往來賬戶 ➲ compare DEPOSIT ACCOUNT

ˌcurrent afˈfairs *noun* [pl.] events of political or social importance that are happening now 時事

cur·rent·ly 0‑ˉ /ˈkʌrəntli; *NAmE* ˈkɜːr-/ *adv.* at the present time 現時；目前；當前；時下：*The hourly charge is currently £35.* 現在每小時收費是 35 英鎊。◇ *Currently, over 500 students are enrolled on the course.* 目前有 500 多名學生註冊學習這門課程。◇ *All the options are* ***currently available****.* 所有的項目現在均可供選擇。◇ *This matter is currently being discussed.* 這個問題現正在討論之中。

cur·ricu·lar /kəˈrɪkjələ(r)/ *adj.* connected with the curriculum of a school, etc. 課程的 ➲ see also EXTRA-CURRICULAR

cur·ricu·lum /kəˈrɪkjələm/ *noun* (*pl.* **cur·ric·ula** /-lə/ or **cur·ricu·lums**) the subjects that are included in a course of study or taught in a school, college, etc.（學校等的）全部課程：*the school curriculum* 學校課程 ◇ (*BrE*) *Spanish is on the curriculum.* 西班牙語已納入課程內容。◇ (*NAmE*) *Spanish is in the curriculum.* 西班牙語已納入課程內容。➲ COLLOCATIONS at EDUCATION ➲ compare SYLLABUS

cur·ricu·lum vitae /kəˌrɪkjələm ˈviːtaɪ/ (*abbr.* **CV**) *noun* **1** (*BrE*) (*NAmE* **ré·sumé**) a written record of your education and the jobs you have done, that you send when you are applying for a job（求職用的）履歷，簡歷：*Applications with a full curriculum vitae and two references should reach the Principal by June 12th.* 申請書連同完整個人簡歷和兩份推薦信必須在 6 月 12 日以前送達校長處。**2** (also **vita**) (*US*) a record of a university/college teacher's education and where they have worked, also including a list of books and articles that they have published and courses that they have taught, used when they are applying for a job（大學教師求職用的）工作履歷

cur·ried /ˈkʌrid; *NAmE* ˈkɜːr-/ *adj.* [only before noun] cooked with hot spices 用咖喱烹調的：*curried chicken/beef/eggs, etc.* 咖喱雞、牛肉、雞蛋等

curry /ˈkʌri; *NAmE* ˈkɜːri/ *noun, verb*

■ *noun* [C, U] a S Asian dish of meat, vegetables, etc. cooked with hot spices, often served with rice 咖喱菜：*a chicken curry* 一道咖喱雞 ◇ *Would you like some more curry?* 你想再來一點咖喱燒菜嗎？

■ *verb* (**cur·ries**, **curry·ing**, **cur·ried**, **cur·ried**) **~ sth** to make curry out of meat or vegetables 以（肉或蔬菜）烹製咖喱燒菜

IDM **curry ˈfavour (with sb)** (*disapproving*) to try to get sb to like or support you by praising or helping them a lot 討好；奉承；拍馬屁

ˈcurry powder *noun* [U] a powder made from a mixture of spices, used to give a hot flavour to food, especially curry 混合辣味調料粉；（尤指）咖喱粉

curse /kɜːs; *NAmE* kɜːrs/ *noun, verb*

■ *noun* **1** (also *old-fashioned, informal* **cuss**) [C] a rude or offensive word or phrase that some people use when they are very angry 咒罵語；罵人話 SYN **oath, swear word**：*He muttered a curse at the other driver.* 他低聲咒罵另一位開車的人。**2** [C] a word or phrase that has a magic power to make sth bad happen 咒；咒語：*The family thought that they were* ***under a curse****.* 這家人認為他們受人詛咒而遭了殃。➲ compare HEX **3** [C] something that causes harm or evil 禍根；禍端；禍水：*the curse of drug addiction* 吸毒成癮的禍害 ◇ *Noise is a curse of modern city life.* 噪音是現代城市生活的一大禍根。**4 the curse** [sing.] (*old-fashioned, informal*) = MENSTRUATION

■ *verb* **1** [I] to swear 詛咒：*He hit his head as he stood up and cursed loudly.* 他站起來時撞了頭，便破口大罵。**2** [T] to say rude things to sb or think rude things about sb/sth 咒罵；詛咒；在心裏詛咒：**~ sb/sth/yourself** *She cursed her bad luck.* 她罵自己運氣不好。◇ **~ sb/sth/yourself for sth** *He cursed himself for his stupidity.* 他咒罵自己愚蠢。**3** [T] **~ sb/sth** to use a magic word or phrase against sb in order to harm them 唸咒語詛咒：*Legend has it that the whole village had been cursed by a witch.* 傳說整座村莊遭到了巫婆的詛咒。➲ compare HEX

PHR V **be ˈcursed with sth** to continuously suffer from or be affected by sth bad 不斷因…而遭殃；為…所苦；受…之害：*She seems cursed with bad luck.* 她好像運氣不好連連遭殃。

cursed *adj.* **1** /kɜːst; *NAmE* kɜːrst/ having a curse (2) on it; suffering from a curse (2) 帶有符咒的；遭受詛咒之苦的：*The necklace was cursed.* 這條項鏈上附有會給人帶來災難的符咒。◇ *The whole family seemed cursed.* 全家人彷彿都受到詛咒遭了殃。**2** /ˈkɜːsɪd; *NAmE* ˈkɜːrsɪd/ [only before noun] (*old-fashioned*) unpleasant; annoying 使人不愉快的；可恨的；討厭的

cur·sive /ˈkɜːsɪv; *NAmE* ˈkɜːrs-/ *adj.* (*technical* 術語) (of HANDWRITING 筆跡) with the letters joined together 連筆的；草書的；草寫體的

cur·sor /ˈkɜːsə(r); *NAmE* ˈkɜːrs-/ *noun* a small mark on a computer screen that can be moved and that shows the position on the screen where, for example, text will be added（計算機熒光屏上的）光標，游標 ➲ VISUAL VOCAB page V67

curs·ory /ˈkɜːsəri; *NAmE* ˈkɜːrs-/ *adj.* (often *disapproving*) done quickly and without giving enough attention to details 粗略的；倉促的 SYN **brief**, **perfunctory**：*a* ***cursory glance/examination/inspection*** 匆匆的一瞥；粗略的審查／檢查 ▸ **cur·sor·ily** /ˈkɜːsərəli; *NAmE* ˈkɜːrs-/ *adv.*

curt /kɜːt; *NAmE* kɜːrt/ *adj.* (of a person's manner or behaviour 人的舉止或行為) appearing rude because very few words are used, or because sth is done in a very quick way 簡短而失禮的；唐突無禮的 SYN **abrupt**, **brusque**：*a curt reply* 唐突無禮的答覆 ◇ *a curt nod* 草草的點頭 ◇ *His tone was curt and unfriendly.* 他說話的語調粗暴無禮。▸ **curt·ly** *adv.* **curt·ness** *noun* [U]

cur·tail /kɜːˈteɪl; *NAmE* kɜːrˈt-/ *verb* **~ sth** (*formal*) to limit sth or make it last for a shorter time 限制；縮短；減縮：*Spending on books has been severely curtailed.* 購書開支已被大大削減。◇ *The lecture was curtailed by the fire alarm going off.* 那次講座被突然鳴響的火警中斷了。▸ **cur·tail·ment** *noun* [U]：*the curtailment of civil liberties* 對公民自由的限制

cur·tain 0‑ˉ /ˈkɜːtn; *NAmE* ˈkɜːrtn/ *noun, verb*

■ *noun* **1** 0‑ˉ [C] a piece of cloth that is hung to cover a window 窗簾：*to* ***draw/pull/close the curtains*** (= to pull them across the window so they cover it) 把窗簾拉上 ◇ *to* ***draw/draw back/pull back the curtains*** (= to open them, so that the window is no longer covered) 把窗簾拉開 ◇ *It was ten in the morning but the curtains were still drawn* (= closed). 已是早上十點鐘了，可窗簾還拉着。◇ *a pair of curtains* 一對窗簾 ➲ VISUAL VOCAB page V21 ➲ see also DRAPE **2** [C] (*NAmE*) (*BrE* **ˌnet ˈcurtain**) a very thin piece of cloth that you hang at a window, which allows light to enter but stops people outside from being able to see inside 網眼簾子；紗簾 **3** 0‑ˉ [C] a piece of cloth that is hung up as a screen in a room or around a bed, for example 簾；幔；（遮隔房

C

間的）帷幔；牀帷：*a shower curtain* 淋浴簾 ➲ see also THE IRON CURTAIN **4** 🗝 [sing.] a piece of thick, heavy cloth that hangs in front of the stage in the theatre（舞台上的）幕，幕布，帷幕：*The audience was waiting for the curtain to rise* (= for the play to begin). 觀眾在等待開幕。◇ *There was tremendous applause when the curtain came down* (= the play ended). 幕落時響起了經久不息的掌聲。◇ *We left just before the* ***final curtain****.* 我們剛好在演出結束前離開。◇ (*figurative*) *The curtain has fallen on her long and distinguished career* (= her career has ended). 她那漫長而成就卓著的事業生涯已告結束。◇ (*figurative*) *It's time to face the* ***final curtain*** (= the end; death). 人生的戲該落幕了。 **5** [C, usually sing.] a thing that covers, hides or protects sth 覆蓋物；隱蔽物；防護物：*a* ***curtain of rain/smoke*** 雨 / 煙幕 ◇ *She pushed back the curtain of brown hair from her eyes.* 她把棕色的頭髮從眼前攏到腦後。

IDM **be 'curtains (for sb)** (*informal*) to be a situation without hope or that you cannot escape from 絕望的處境；無法擺脱的困境；完蛋：*When I saw he had a gun, I thought it was curtains for me.* 我一見他有槍，就想這下子我算是完了。 **bring down the 'curtain on sth | bring the 'curtain down on sth** to finish or mark the end of sth 結束；標誌着…的終結：*His sudden decision to retire brought down the curtain on a distinguished career.* 他突然決定退休結束了他成就斐然的職業生涯。

■ ***verb*** **~ sth** to provide curtains for a window or a room 給（窗戶或房間）裝上簾子

PHR V **,curtain sth↔'off** to separate an area of a room with a curtain or curtains 用簾子隔開

'curtain call *noun* the time in the theatre when the actors come to the front of the stage at the end of a play to receive the APPLAUSE of the audience（舞台演員的）謝幕

'curtain-raiser *noun* **1** **~ (to sth)** a small event that prepares for a more important one（重大事件的）前奏，序曲 **2** **~ (to sth)** a short performance before the main performance in a theatre, etc.（劇院等主要劇目演出前的）序幕，開場小戲

curtsy (also **curt·sey**) /ˈkɜːtsi; *NAmE* ˈkɜːrtsi/ *noun* (*pl.* **-ies** or **-eys**) a formal sign made by a woman in a dance or to say hello or goodbye to an important person, by bending her knees with one foot in front of the other（女子行的）屈膝禮 ▸ **curtsy** *verb* (**curt·sies, curt·sy·ing, curt·sied, curt·sied**) (also **curt·sey**) [I]：**~ (to sb)** *She curtsied to the Queen.* 她向女王行了屈膝禮。

curv·aceous /kɜːˈveɪʃəs; *NAmE* kɜːrˈv-/ *adj.* (*informal*) used in newspapers, etc. to describe a woman whose body has attractive curves（報章等描述女子）有曲線美的，體形優美的

curv·ature /ˈkɜːvətʃə(r); *NAmE* ˈkɜːrv-/ *noun* [U] (*technical* 術語) the state of being curved; the amount that sth is curved 彎曲；曲度；曲率：*the curvature of the earth* 地球的曲度 ◇ *curvature of the spine* 脊柱彎曲

curve 🗝 /kɜːv; *NAmE* kɜːrv/ *noun, verb*

■ ***noun*** **1** 🗝 a line or surface that bends gradually; a smooth bend 曲線；弧線；曲面；彎曲：*the delicate curve of her ear* 她耳朵的優美曲線 ◇ *a pattern of straight lines and curves* 直線與曲線交織的圖案 ◇ (*especially NAmE*) *a curve in the road* 道路上的拐彎處 ◇ (*especially NAmE*) *The driver lost control on a curve and the vehicle hit a tree.* 司機在拐彎處失控，撞到了一棵樹上。◇ *to plot a curve on a graph* 在圖上繪出一條曲線 ◇ (*technical* 術語) *the unemployment-income curve* (= a line on a GRAPH showing the relationship between the number of unemployed people and national income) 失業與國民收入曲線 ➲ see also LEARNING CURVE **2** (also **'curve ball**) (*NAmE*) (in BASEBALL 棒球) a ball that moves in a curve when it is thrown to the BATTER（投向擊球員的）曲線球：(*figurative*) *One of the journalists* ***threw*** *the senator* ***a curve*** (= surprised him by asking a difficult question). 一名記者向那位參議員提出了一個出乎意料的難題。

IDM **ahead of/behind the 'curve** (*especially NAmE, business* 商) in advance of or behind a particular trend 引領 / 落後於潮流：*Our expert advice will help you stay ahead of the curve.* 我們的專業建議將有助於你保持引領潮流。◇ *We've fallen behind the curve when it comes to developing new digital products.* 就開發新的數碼產品而論，我們已經落後了。

■ ***verb*** 🗝 [I, T] **~ (sth) (+ adv./prep.)** to move or make sth move in the shape of a curve; to be in the shape of a curve（使）沿曲線移動；呈曲線形：*The road curved around the bay.* 那條路沿海灣呈曲線伸展。◇ *The ball curved through the air.* 球在空中沿曲線移動。◇ *His lips curved in a smile.* 他咧嘴笑了。

curved 弧形的

bent 彎曲的

curled up 蜷成一團的

twisted 扭曲的

wavy 波狀的

curly 鬈曲的

curved 🗝 /kɜːvd; *NAmE* kɜːrvd/ *adj.* having a round shape 呈彎曲狀的；弧形的：*a curved path/roof/blade* 蜿蜒的小路；拱頂；弧形刀片

curvi·lin·ear /ˌkɜːvɪˈlɪniə(r); *NAmE* ˌkɜːrv-/ *adj.* (*formal*) consisting of a curved line or lines 曲線的；由曲線組成的

curvy /ˈkɜːvi; *NAmE* ˈkɜːrvi/ *adj.* (*informal*) having curves 有曲線的；彎曲的：*a curvy body* 富有曲線美的身段 ◇ *curvy lines* 彎彎曲曲的線條

cush·ion /ˈkʊʃn/ *noun, verb*

■ ***noun*** **1** (*NAmE* also **pil·low**) a cloth bag filled with soft material or feathers that is used, for example, to make a seat more comfortable 軟墊；坐墊；靠墊：*matching curtains and cushions* 顏色協調的窗簾與靠墊 ◇ *a floor cushion* (= a large cushion that you put on the floor to sit on) 地板坐墊 ◇ *a pile of scatter cushions* (= small cushions, often in bright colours, that you put on chairs, etc.) 一堆零星散佈的靠墊 ◇ (*figurative*) *a cushion of moss on a rock* 岩石上的一層苔蘚 ➲ VISUAL VOCAB page V21 **2** a layer of sth between two surfaces that keeps them apart（隔離兩個表面的）墊：*A hovercraft rides on a cushion of air.* 氣墊船懸浮在氣墊上行駛。 **3** [usually sing.] **~ (against sth)** something that protects you against sth unpleasant that might happen 起保護（或緩衝）作用的事物：*His savings were a comfortable cushion against financial problems.* 他的積蓄好比一個舒適的墊子，可以緩解拮据之苦。◇ *The team built up a safe cushion of two goals in the first half.* 球隊上半場射進兩球，吃了顆定心丸。 **4** (in the game of BILLIARDS, etc. 枱球等運動) the soft inside edge along each side of the table, that the balls BOUNCE off（枱球桌內側邊緣的）彈性襯裏 ➲ VISUAL VOCAB page V40

■ ***verb*** **1** **~ sth** to make the effect of a fall or hit less severe（跌倒或碰撞時）起緩衝作用，緩和衝擊：*My fall was cushioned by the deep snow.* 積雪很厚，我跌得不重。 **2** **~ sb/sth (against/from sth)** to protect sb/sth from being hurt or damaged or from the unpleasant effects of sth 緩和打擊：*The south of the country has been cushioned from the worst effects of the recession.* 國家南部保護得好，沒有受到經濟衰退造成的最惡劣影響。◇ *He broke the news of my brother's death to me, making no effort to* ***cushion the blow*** (= make the news less shocking). 他把我弟弟死亡的消息直接告訴了我，沒有試圖減輕此事對我的打擊。 **3** [usually passive] **~ sth** to make sth soft with a cushion（用墊子）使柔和，使鬆軟

cushy /ˈkʊʃi/ *adj.* (**cush·ier, cushi·est**) (*informal*, often *disapproving*) very easy and pleasant; needing little or no effort 輕鬆愉快的；安逸的；不費勁的：*a cushy job* 不費心勞神的工作

IDM **a cushy 'number** (*BrE*) an easy job; a pleasant situation that other people would like 輕鬆的工作；美差；令人羨慕的輕鬆狀態

cusp /kʌsp/ *noun* **1** (*technical* 術語) a pointed end where two curves meet (兩曲線相交的) 尖點，會切點，交點：*the cusp of a leaf* 葉尖 **2** the time when one sign of the ZODIAC ends and the next begins (黃道十二宮的) 兩宮會切的時辰：*I was born **on the cusp** between Virgo and Libra.* 我生於室女宮和天秤宮會切的時辰。◇ (*figurative*) *He was on the cusp between small acting roles and moderate fame.* 他這個配角演員現在已是小荷初露尖尖角。

cuss /kʌs/ *verb, noun*

■ ***verb*** [I, T] **~ (sb/sth)** (*old-fashioned, informal*) to swear at sb 詛咒；咒罵：*My dad used to come home drunk, shouting and cussing.* 我爹以前常常喝醉了回家，又是喊又是罵。

■ ***noun*** (*old-fashioned, informal*) **1** used with a negative adjective to describe a person (與貶義形容詞一起用於描述人) 傢伙：*He's an awkward cuss.* 他是個笨傢伙。**2** = CURSE *n.* (1)：*cuss words* 罵人話

cussed /'kʌsɪd/ *adj.* (*old-fashioned, informal*) (of people 人) not willing to be helpful 不願幫助的 **SYN** **stubborn** ▸ **cuss·ed·ly** *adv.* **cuss·ed·ness** *noun* [U]

cus·tard /'kʌstəd; *NAmE* -tərd/ *noun* **1** [U] (*especially BrE*) (*NAmE* usually ˌ**custard 'sauce**) a sweet yellow sauce made from milk, sugar, eggs and flour, usually served hot with cooked fruit, PUDDINGS, etc. 蛋奶沙司（通常與熟水果、布丁等一同食用）：*apple pie and custard* 蘋果餡餅加蛋奶沙司 **2** [C, U] a mixture of eggs, milk and sugar baked until it is firm (烤製的) 蛋奶糕，蛋撻

ˌ**custard 'pie** *noun* a flat PIE filled with sth soft and wet that looks like custard, that performers throw at each other to make people laugh (表演者互相投擲逗樂用的) 蛋奶餡餅

cus·to·dial /kʌ'stəʊdiəl; *NAmE* -'stoʊ-/ *adj.* [usually before noun] (*law* 律) **1** involving sending sb to prison 監禁的；拘留的：*The judge gave him a **custodial sentence*** (= sent him to prison). 法官判處他監禁。**2** connected with the right or duty of taking care of sb; having CUSTODY 監護權的；監管職責的；有監護權的：*The mother is usually the custodial parent after a divorce.* 離婚後母親通常擁有孩子的監護權。**OPP** **non-custodial**

cus·to·dian /kʌ'stəʊdiən; *NAmE* -'stoʊ-/ *noun* **1** a person who takes responsibility for taking care of or protecting sth 監護人；看守人；保管人：*the museum's custodians* 博物館的管理員 ◇ *a self-appointed custodian of public morals* 自封的公共道德的衛道士 **2** (*NAmE*) (*BrE* **care·taker**) (*NAmE* also, *ScotE* **jani·tor**) a person whose job is to take care of a building such as a school or a block of flats or an apartment building (建築物的) 管理員，看管人，看門人

cus·tody /'kʌstədi/ *noun* [U] **1** the legal right or duty to take care of or keep sb/sth; the act of taking care of sth/sb 監護權；保管權；監護；保管：*Who will **have custody** of the children?* 誰來負責監護這些孩子？◇ *The divorce court awarded custody to the child's mother.* 離婚法庭把監護權判給了孩子的母親。◇ *The parents were locked in a bitter battle for custody.* 雙親陷入了一場對孩子監護權的激烈爭奪之中。◇ *The bank provides **safe custody** for valuables.* 這家銀行提供對貴重物品的安全保管服務。◇ *The castle is now **in the custody of** the state.* 現在那座城堡由國家照管。➲ COLLOCATIONS at MARRIAGE **2** the state of being in prison, especially while waiting for trial (尤指在候審時的) 拘留，拘押，羈押：*After the riot, 32 people were taken into **police custody**.* 那場暴亂後，有 32 人被警方拘留。◇ (*BrE*) *He was **remanded in custody**, charged with the murder of a policeman.* 他被控謀殺一名警察，正在羈押候審。➲ see also YOUTH CUSTODY

cus·tom 0→ /'kʌstəm/ *noun, adj.*

■ ***noun*** ➲ see also CUSTOMS **1** 0→ [C, U] **~ (of doing sth)** an accepted way of behaving or of doing things in a society or a community 風俗；習俗：*an **old/ancient custom*** 舊的 / 古老的習俗 ◇ *the custom of giving presents at Christmas* 在聖誕節贈送禮品的習俗 ◇ *It's a **local custom**.* 這是當地的風俗習慣。◇ ***It is the custom** in that country for women to marry young.* 女子早婚是那個國家的風俗。**2** [sing.] (*formal* or *literary*) the way a person always behaves (個人的) 習慣，習性，慣常行為 **SYN** **habit, practice**：*It was her custom to rise early.* 早起是她的習慣。◇ *As was his custom, he knocked three times.* 一如既往，他敲了三下。**3** [U] (*BrE, formal*) (also **business** *NAmE, BrE*) the fact of a person or people buying goods or services at a shop/store or business (顧客對商店的) 惠顧，光顧：*Thank you for your custom. Please call again.* 謝謝您的惠顧，請下次再來。◇ *We've lost a lot of custom since prices went up.* 自從價格上漲以來我們失去了很多主顧。

■ ***adj.*** [only before noun] (*especially NAmE*) = CUSTOM-BUILT, CUSTOM-MADE：*a custom motorcycle* 訂製的摩托車

cus·tom·ary /'kʌstəməri; *NAmE* -meri/ *adj.* **1** if sth is **customary**, it is what people usually do in a particular place or situation 習俗的；習慣的 **SYN** **usual**：*Is it customary to tip hairdressers in this country?* 這個國家興不興給理髮師小費？**2** typical of a particular person (某人) 特有的，獨特的，典型的 **SYN** **habitual**：*She arranged everything with her customary efficiency.* 她以她特有的高效率把一切都已安排妥當。▸ **cus·tom·ar·ily** /'kʌstəmərəli; *NAmE* ˌkʌstə'merəli/ *adv.*

ˌ**custom-'built** (also **custom** especially in *NAmE*) *adj.* designed and built for a particular person (為某人) 設計建造的，訂做的

cus·tom·er 0→ /'kʌstəmə(r)/ *noun*

1 0→ a person or an organization that buys sth from a shop/store or business 顧客；主顧；客戶：*one of the shop's **best/biggest customers*** 此商店最佳 / 最大的客戶之一 ◇ *They know me—I'm a **regular customer**.* 我是老主顧，他們都認識我。◇ *the **customer service** department* 客戶服務部 ◇ *The firm has excellent customer relations.* 此公司與客戶關係極好。➲ COLLOCATIONS at SHOPPING **2** (*old-fashioned, informal*) used after an adjective to describe a particular type of person (用於形容詞之後描述某類型的人) 傢伙：*an awkward customer* 難對付的傢伙

'**customer base** *noun* [usually sing.] (*business* 商) all the people who buy or use a particular product or service (統稱某種產品或服務的) 客戶：*We need to appeal to a wider customer base.* 我們需要面向更廣泛的客戶。

'**customer-facing** *adj.* [only before noun] (*business* 商) dealing directly with customers or used by customers 面向客戶的：*customer-facing operations such as call centres* 呼叫中心之類的客戶服務 ◇ *customer-facing software applications* 面向客戶的軟件應用程序

cus·tom·ize (*BrE* also **-ise**) /'kʌstəmaɪz/ *verb* **~ sth** to make or change sth to suit the needs of the owner 訂製，訂做，改製（以滿足顧主的需要）：*You can customize the software in several ways.* 你可用幾種方法按需要編製這個軟件。▸ **cus·tom·ized** *adj.*：*a customized car* 按需要訂製的汽車

ˌ**custom-'made** (also **cus·tom** especially in *NAmE*) *adj.* designed and made for a particular person (為某人) 設計訂做的，訂製的 ➲ see also BESPOKE

cus·toms 0→ /'kʌstəmz/ *noun* [pl.]

1 0→ (usually **Customs**) (*BrE* also **Customs and Excise**) (*US* also **US Customs Service**) the government department that collects taxes on goods bought and sold and on goods brought into the country, and that checks what is brought in (政府部門) 海關：*The Customs have seized large quantities of smuggled heroin.* 海關查獲了大量走私的海洛因。◇ *a customs officer* 海關官員 **HELP** *NAmE* uses a singular verb with **customs** in this meaning. 美式英語 customs 作此義時使用單數動詞。**2** 0→ the place at a port or an airport where your bags are checked as you come into a country (港口或機場的) 海關：*to go through customs and passport control* 通過海關和交驗護照 **3** 0→ the taxes that must be paid to the government when goods are brought in from other countries 關稅；進口稅：*to pay customs on sth* 為某物繳納關稅 ◇ ***customs duty/duties*** 進口稅 ➲ SYNONYMS at TAX ➲ compare EXCISE[1]

C

ˈ**customs union** *noun* a group of states that agree to have the same taxes on imported goods 關稅同盟（締約國按統一關稅進口商品）

Synonyms 同義詞辨析

cut

slash • cut sth back • scale sth back • rationalize • downsize

These words all mean to reduce the amount or size of sth, especially of an amount of money or a business. 以上各詞均含減少、縮小之意，尤指削減經費、縮減生意。

cut to reduce sth, especially an amount of money that is demanded, spent, earned, etc. or the size of a business 指削減、縮減、裁減（尤指經費、開支、收入或生意規模）: *The President has promised to cut taxes significantly.* 總統承諾大幅度減稅。◇ *Buyers will bargain hard to cut the cost of the house they want.* 買主會竭力討價還價以壓低他們想買的房子的價格。◇ *His salary has been cut by ten per cent.* 他的薪金減少了百分之十。◇ *Could you cut your essay from 5 000 to 3 000 words?* 請把你的文章從 5 000 字刪減至 3 000 字好嗎？

slash [often passive] (*rather informal*) (often used in newspapers) to reduce sth by a large amount（常用於報章）指大幅度削減、大大降低: *The workforce has been slashed by half.* 職工人數裁減了一半。

cut sth back/cut back on sth to reduce sth, especially an amount of money or business 指削減、縮減、裁減（尤指經費或生意）: *We had to cut back production.* 我們只得減產了。

scale sth back (*especially NAmE* or *business*) to reduce sth, especially an amount of money or business 指削減、縮減、裁減（尤指經費或生意）: *The IMF has scaled back its growth forecasts for the next decade.* 國際貨幣基金組織已經調低對未來十年的增長預測。

rationalize (*BrE, business*) to make changes to a business or system, in order to make it more efficient, especially by spending less money 指對企業或制度進行合理化改革、使合理化、使有經濟效益

downsize (*business*) to make a company or organization smaller by reducing the number of jobs in it, in order to reduce costs 指公司或機構精簡人員以縮小規模，降低成本 NOTE **Downsize** is often used by people who want to avoid saying more obvious words like 'dismiss' or 'make redundant' because they sound too negative. 人們通常使用 downsize 以避免使用 dismiss 或 make redundant 等詞義直白的詞，因為這些詞聽起來過於負面。

PATTERNS

- to cut/slash/cut back on/scale back/rationalize **spending/production**
- to cut/slash/cut back on **jobs**
- to cut/slash/downsize **the workforce**
- to cut/slash/rationalize **the cost** of sth
- to cut/slash **prices/taxes/the budget**
- to cut sth/slash sth/cut sth back **drastically**

cut 0‑ᵀ /kʌt/ *verb, noun*

■ *verb* (**cut·ting, cut, cut**)

▸ **WOUND/HOLE** 傷口；破口 **1** 0‑ᵀ [T, I] to make an opening or a wound in sth, especially with a sharp tool such as a knife or scissors 切；割；割破；劃破: **~ sth** *She cut her finger on a piece of glass.* 一塊玻璃把她的手指頭劃破了。◇ **~ yourself** *He cut himself* (= his face) *shaving.* 他刮鬍子把臉刮破了。◇ **~ sth + adj.** *She had fallen and* **cut** *her head* **open**. 她摔了一跤，把頭磕破了。◇ **~ through sth** *You need a powerful saw to cut through metal.* 切割金屬需要用功率大的鋸。◇ (*figurative*) *The canoe cut through the water.* 獨木舟划破水面前行。

▸ **REMOVE WITH KNIFE** 用刀切下 **2** 0‑ᵀ [T] to remove sth or a part of sth, using a knife, etc.（用刀等從某物上）切下，割下: **~ sth (from sth)** *He cut four thick slices from the loaf.* 他從一條麪包上切下四厚片。◇ *a bunch of cut flowers* 一束剪下的花朵 ◇ **~ sb sth** *I cut them all a piece of birthday cake.* 我給他們每個人都切了一塊生日蛋糕。◇ **~ sth for sb** *I cut a piece of birthday cake for them all.* 我給他們每個人都切了一塊生日蛋糕。 **3** [T] **~ sth (in sth)** to make or form sth by removing material with a knife, etc. 切成；割成；剪成；削成；鑿成: *The climbers cut steps in the ice.* 攀登者在冰上鑿出踩腳處。◇ *Workmen* **cut a hole** *in the pipe.* 工人在管子上切了一個口。

▸ **DIVIDE** 分開 **4** 0‑ᵀ [T] to divide sth into two or more pieces with a knife, etc.（用刀等將某物）切成，割成: **~ sth** *Don't cut the string, untie the knots.* 不要剪斷繩子，把結解開。◇ **~ sth in/into sth** *He cut the loaf into thick slices.* 他把那條麪包切成了厚片。◇ *The bus was cut in two by the train.* 那輛公共汽車被火車撞成兩截。◇ *Now cut the tomatoes in half.* 把西紅柿都切成兩半。

▸ **HAIR/NAILS/GRASS, ETC.** 頭髮、指甲、草等 **5** 0‑ᵀ [T] to make sth shorter by cutting 剪短；修剪: **~ sth** *to* **cut** *your* **hair/nails** 理髮；剪指甲 ◇ *to* **cut the grass/lawn/hedge** 修剪草／草坪／樹籬 ◇ **~ sth + adj.** *He's had his* **hair cut** *really short.* 他頭髮理得真短。

▸ **RELEASE** 釋放 **6** [T] to allow sb to escape from somewhere by cutting the rope, object, etc. that is holding them（割斷繩子、某物等）讓逃跑，釋放: **~ sb (from sth)** *The injured driver had to be cut from the wreckage.* 受傷的司機不得不等到把汽車殘骸拆開才逃出來。◇ **~ sb + adj.** *Two survivors were* **cut free** *after being trapped for twenty minutes.* 兩名幸存者受困二十分鐘後才被解救出來。

▸ **CLOTHING** 服裝 **7** [T, usually passive] **~ sth + adj.** to design and make a piece of clothing in a particular way 剪裁: *The swimsuit was cut high in the leg.* 這件游泳衣的腿部開口很高。

▸ **ABLE TO CUT/BE CUT** 可切割；可被切割 **8** 0‑ᵀ [I] to be capable of cutting 可用於切割；能切割: *This knife won't cut.* 這把刀不快。 **9** [I] to be capable of being cut 可被切割: *Sandstone cuts easily.* 沙岩容易切割。

▸ **REDUCE** 減少 **10** 0‑ᵀ [T] to reduce sth by removing a part of it 削減；縮減；裁減: **~ sth** *to* **cut prices/taxes/spending/production** 削價；減稅；縮減開支；降低產量 ◇ *Buyers will bargain hard to* **cut the cost of** *the house they want.* 買主會竭力討價還價以壓低他們想買的房子的價格。◇ **~ sth by …** *His salary has been cut by ten per cent.* 他的薪金減少了百分之十。◇ **~ sth (from …) (to …)** *Could you cut your essay from 5 000 to 3 000 words?* 請把你的文章從 5 000 字刪減到 3 000 字好嗎？

▸ **REMOVE** 刪除 **11** 0‑ᵀ [T] **~ sth (from sth)** to remove sth from sth 刪剪；刪節: *This scene was cut from the final version of the movie.* 那部電影的最終版本把這場戲刪掉了。

▸ **COMPUTING** 計算機技術 **12** [I, T] **~ (sth)** to DELETE (= remove) part of a text on a computer screen in order to place it somewhere else 剪切: *You can* **cut and paste** *between different programs.* 可在不同的程序之間進行剪切和粘貼。

▸ **STOP** 停止 **13** [T] **~ sth** (*informal*) used to tell sb to stop doing sth（讓人停止做某事）: *Cut the chatter and get on with your work!* 別閒聊了，繼續幹活吧！

▸ **END** 結束 **14** [T] **~ sth** to completely end a relationship or all communication with sb 斷絕（關係）；終止（溝通）SYN **sever**: *She has cut all ties with her family.* 她已經和家人完全斷絕關係。

▸ **IN MOVIE/TV** 電影；電視 **15** [T] **~ sth** to prepare a film/movie or tape by removing parts of it or putting them in a different order 剪輯；剪接 SYN **edit** ➲ see also DIRECTOR'S CUT **16** [I] (usually used in orders 通常用於指令) to stop filming or recording 停止拍片（或錄音、錄像）: *The director shouted 'Cut!'* "停！" 導演大聲喊道。 **17** [I] **~ (from sth) to sth** (in films/movies, radio or television 電影、無線電廣播或電視) to move quickly from one scene to another 切換畫面；轉換: *The scene cuts from the bedroom to the street.* 鏡頭從卧室轉換到街道。

▸ **MISS CLASS** 曠課 **18** [T] **~ sth** (*informal, especially NAmE*) to stay away from a class that you should go to 曠（課）；缺（課）；逃學：*He's always* ***cutting class.*** 他總是曠課。

▸ **UPSET** 使不安 **19** [T] **~ sb** to hurt sb emotionally（從感情上）傷害：*His cruel remarks cut her deeply.* 他那些無情的話深深地刺痛了她的心。

▸ **IN CARD GAMES** 紙牌遊戲 **20** [I, T] **~** (**sth**) to lift and turn up a PACK/DECK of PLAYING CARDS in order to decide who is to play first, etc.（為決定誰先出牌等）切牌，抽牌：*Let's cut for dealer.* 咱們切牌決定由誰發牌吧。

▸ **GEOMETRY** 幾何學 **21** [T] **~ sth** (of a line 一條線) to cross another line（與另一條線）相交：*The line cuts the circle at two points.* 那條線與圓相交於兩點。

▸ **A TOOTH** 牙齒 **22** [T] **~ a tooth** to have a new tooth beginning to appear through the GUM 開始長（新牙）：*When did she cut her first tooth?* 她什麼時候長出了第一顆牙？

▸ **A DISC, ETC.** 激光唱片等 **23** [T] **~ a disc, etc.** to make a recording of music on a record, CD, etc. 灌製（唱片）；製作（激光唱片等）：*The Beatles cut their first disc in 1962.* 披頭士樂隊於 1962 年灌製了他們的第一張唱片。

▸ **DRUG** 毒品 **24** [T] **~ sth** (**with sth**) to mix an illegal drug such as HEROIN with another substance 把（海洛因等）與另一種物質摻和

IDM Most idioms containing **cut** are at the entries for the nouns and adjectives in the idioms, for example **cut your losses** is at **loss**. 大多數含 cut 的習語，都可在該等習語中的名詞及形容詞相關詞條找到，如 cut your losses 在詞條 loss 下。 **cut and ˈrun** (*BrE, informal*) to make a quick or sudden escape 急忙逃走；撒腿就跑 **(not) ˈcut it** (*informal*) to (not) be as good as is expected or needed（不）如預想的一般好；（不）像所需要的那麼好：*He won't cut it as a professional singer.* 他的歌藝未達到專業歌手水平。

PHR V **ˌcut aˈcross sth** **1** to affect or be true for different groups that usually remain separate 影響，符合，適用於（分離的不同群體）：*Opinion on this issue cuts across traditional political boundaries.* 人們對這個問題的看法超越了傳統的政治界限。 **2** (also **ˌcut ˈthrough sth**) to go across sth in order to make your route shorter 抄近路穿過；走近路：*I usually cut across the park on my way home.* 我回家常抄近路，打公園裏頭走。

ˌcut sth↔aˈway (from sth) to remove sth from sth by cutting 切除；割掉；砍掉；剪去：*They cut away all the dead branches from the tree.* 他們把這棵樹上的枯枝全都砍掉了。

ˌcut sth↔ˈback **1** 0-w (also **ˌcut ˈback (on sth)**) to reduce sth 減少；削減；縮減：*If we don't sell more we'll have to cut back production.* 我們若不能多銷，就必須減產。◇ *to cut back on spending* 削減開支 ➲ related noun CUTBACK **2** to make a bush, etc. smaller by cutting branches off 剪枝；修剪 **SYN** **prune**：*to cut back a rose bush* 給玫瑰叢剪枝

ˌcut sb↔ˈdown (*formal*) to kill sb 殺死（某人）：*He was cut down by an assassin's bullet.* 他被刺客的子彈擊中身亡。 **ˌcut sth↔ˈdown** 0-w to make sth fall down by cutting it at the base（自根基部份）砍倒：*to cut down a tree* 齊根砍倒一棵樹 **ˌcut sth↔ˈdown (to ...)** | **ˌcut ˈdown (on sth)** 0-w to reduce the size, amount or number of sth 削減，縮小（尺寸、數量或數目）：*We need to cut the article down to 1 000 words.* 我們得把這篇文章壓縮到 1 000 字。◇ *The doctor told him to cut down on his drinking.* 醫生勸他少喝酒。◇ *I won't have a cigarette, thanks—I'm trying to cut down* (= smoke fewer). 謝謝，我不抽了。我現在盡量少抽煙。

ˌcut ˈin **1** if a motor or an engine **cuts in**, it starts working（馬達或發動機）發動：*Emergency generators cut in.* 應急發電機啟動了。 **2** (*NAmE*) (*BrE* **ˌpush ˈin**) to go in front of other people who are waiting 加塞兒；插隊 **ˌcut ˈin (on sb/sth)** **1** to interrupt sb when they are speaking 打斷（談話）；插嘴 **SYN** **butt in**：*She kept cutting in on our conversation.* 我們談話時她老是插嘴。◇ **+ speech** *'Forget it!' she cut in.* "算了吧！" 她插嘴道。 **2** (of a vehicle or its driver 車輛或駕駛者) to move suddenly in front of another vehicle, leaving little space between the two vehicles 超車搶道 **ˌcut sb ˈin (on sth)** (*informal*) to give sb a share of the profit in a business or an activity 讓（某人）分享利潤

ˌcut sb↔ˈoff **1** [often passive] to interrupt sb who is speaking on the telephone by breaking the connection 中斷（電話通話）：*We were cut off in the middle of our conversation.* 我們電話打到一半就斷線了。 **2** to refuse to let sb receive any of your property after you die 剝奪繼承權 **SYN** **disinherit**：*He* ***cut*** *his son* ***off without a penny.*** 他完全剝奪了兒子的繼承權。 **ˌcut sb/sth↔ˈoff** **1** to interrupt sb and stop them from speaking 打斷（某人並阻止其講話）：*My explanation was cut off by loud protests.* 我的解釋被強烈的抗議聲打斷了。 **2** 0-w [often passive] to stop the supply of sth to sb 停止，中斷（供給）：*Our water supply has been cut off.* 我們斷水了。◇ *They were cut off for not paying their phone bill.* 他們未付電話費，被停機了。 **ˌcut sth↔ˈoff** **1** 0-w (also **ˌcut sth ˈoff sth**) to remove sth from sth larger by cutting 切掉；割掉；砍掉；剪掉：*He had his finger cut off in an accident at work.* 他在一次工傷中被切斷了手指。◇ (*figurative*) *The winner cut ten seconds off* (= ran the distance ten seconds faster than) *the world record.* 獲勝者比世界紀錄快了十秒。 ➲ see also CUT-OFF **2** 0-w to block or get in the way of sth 阻礙；阻擋；堵塞：*They cut off the enemy's retreat.* 他們切斷了敵人的退路。◇ *The new factory cuts off our view of the hills.* 新建的工廠擋住了我們觀山景的視線。 **ˌcut sb/sth ˈoff (from sb/sth)** 0-w [often passive] to prevent sb/sth from leaving or reaching a place or communicating with people outside a place 切斷…的去路（或來路）；使…與外界隔絕：*The army was cut off from its base.* 那支部隊與基地失去了聯絡。◇ *She feels very cut off living in the country.* 她住在鄉間感到很閉塞。◇ *He* ***cut himself off*** *from all human contact.* 他斷絕了與所有人的聯繫。

ˌcut ˈout if a motor or an engine **cuts out**, it suddenly stops working（馬達或發動機）突然熄火，停止運轉 ➲ related noun CUT-OUT **ˌcut sb↔ˈout (of sth)** to not allow sb to be involved in sth 不讓某人參與；把某人排除在…之外：*Don't cut your parents out of your lives.* 別把父母排除在你的生活之外。◇ *Furious, his mother cut him out of her will* (= refused to let him receive any of her property after she died). 他母親一怒之下，在遺囑中沒有給他任何遺產。 **ˌcut sth↔ˈout** **1** 0-w to make sth by cutting 裁剪：*She cut the dress out of some old material.* 她用一些舊布料裁剪出了那件連衣裙。◇ (*figurative*) *He's cut out a niche for himself* (= found a suitable job) *in journalism.* 他在新聞界找到了一份適合自己的工作。 ➲ related noun CUT-OUT **2** 0-w to leave sth out of a piece of writing, etc. 刪除；刪去 **SYN** **omit**：*I would cut out the bit about working as a waitress.* 我想刪掉有關做女服務員的那段工作經歷。 **3** (*informal*) used to tell sb to stop doing or saying sth annoying（讓人停止做或說惱人的事）住口，打住：*I'm sick of you two arguing—just* ***cut it out!*** 你們倆吵來吵去讓我煩死了，住口吧！ **4** to block sth, especially light 阻擋（尤指光線）：*Tall trees cut out the sunlight.* 高高的樹木遮住了陽光。 **ˌcut sth↔ˈout (of sth)** **1** 0-w to remove sth from sth larger by cutting, usually with scissors（通常用剪刀）剪下：*I cut this article out of the newspaper.* 我從報紙上剪下了這篇文章。 **2** to stop doing, using or eating sth 停止做（或使用、食用）：*I've been advised to cut sugar out of my diet.* 有人勸我飲食要忌糖。 **be ˌcut ˈout for sth** | **be ˌcut ˈout to be sth** (*informal*) to have the qualities and abilities needed for sth 具有所需素質及才能；是…的材料：*He's not cut out for teaching.* 他不適於做教學工作。◇ *He's not cut out to be a teacher.* 他不是當教師的材料。

ˌcut ˈthrough sth **1** = CUT ACROSS STH **2** (also **ˌcut sth ˈthrough sth**) to make a path or passage through sth by cutting 開闢（出路或通道）：*They used a machete to cut through the bush.* 他們用大砍刀在灌木林中劈出了一條路。◇ *The prisoners* ***cut their way through*** *the barbed wire.* 囚犯們切斷鐵絲網開出一條路逃之夭夭。

ˌcut ˈup (*NAmE, informal*) to behave in a noisy and silly way 胡鬧；吵吵嚷嚷地出洋相 **ˌcut sb↔ˈup** (*informal*) **1** to injure sb badly by cutting or hitting them（嚴重地）割傷，打傷：*He was very badly cut up in the fight.* 他在這場鬥毆中傷得很重。 **2** [usually passive] to upset sb emotionally 使傷心；使悲傷；使難受：*She was pretty cut up about them leaving.* 他們這一走使她傷心極了。

C

ˌcut sb/sth↔ˈup (*BrE*) to suddenly drive in front of another vehicle in a dangerous way（危險地）突然超車 **ˌcut sth↔ˈup** 🗝 to divide sth into small pieces with a knife, etc. 切碎；剁碎：*He cut up the meat on his plate.* 他在盤子上把肉切成小塊。

■ ***noun***

▸ **WOUND** 傷口 **1** 🗝 a wound caused by sth sharp 傷口；劃口：*cuts and bruises on the face* 臉上的傷口和挫傷 ◇ *Blood poured from the deep cut on his arm.* 鮮血從他手臂上深深的傷口中湧出。

▸ **HOLE** 開口 **2** 🗝 a hole or an opening in sth, made with sth sharp（鋒利物留下的）開口，破口：*Using sharp scissors, make a small cut in the material.* 用鋒利的剪刀在這塊布料上剪一個小口。

▸ **REDUCTION** 削減 **3** 🗝 **~ (in sth)** a reduction in amount, size, supply, etc.（數量、尺寸、供應等的）削減，減少，縮減：***price/tax/job cuts*** 減價；減稅；裁員 ◇ *They had to take a 20% cut in pay.* 他們不得不接受減薪 20%。◇ *They announced cuts in public spending.* 他們宣佈縮減公共開支。➲ see also POWER CUT, SHORT CUT

▸ **OF HAIR** 頭髮 **4** 🗝 [usually sing.] an act of cutting sb's hair; the style in which it is cut 理髮；髮型：*Your hair could do with a cut* (= it is too long). 你該理髮了。◇ *a cut and blow-dry* 理髮帶吹風 ➲ see also BUZZ CUT

▸ **OF CLOTHING** 服裝 **5** [usually sing.] the shape and style that a piece of clothing has because of the way the cloth is cut（剪裁的）款式，式樣：*the elegant cut of her dress* 她的連衣裙的典雅款式

▸ **SHARE OF MONEY** 錢的份額 **6** a share in sth, especially money（尤指錢的）份，份額：*They were rewarded with a cut of 5% from the profits.* 他們得到了佔利潤 5% 份額的酬報。

▸ **OF MOVIE/PLAY, ETC.** 電影、戲劇等 **7 ~ (in sth)** an act of removing part of a film/movie, play, piece of writing, etc. 刪剪；刪節：*The director objected to the cuts ordered by the censor.* 導演反對按審查員的指令作刪剪。◇ *She made some cuts before handing over the finished novel.* 她交定稿之前對小說作了一些刪節。

▸ **MEAT** 肉 **8** a piece of meat cut from an animal（從動物軀體上）割下的一塊肉：*a lean cut of pork* 一塊瘦豬肉 ◇ *cheap cuts of stewing lamb* 廉價的燉羊肉塊 ➲ see also COLD CUTS

IDM **a cut above sb/sth** better than sb/sth 優於；比⋯高一等；勝⋯一籌：*His latest novel is* ***a cut above the rest****.* 他最近出版的小說比其他的小說都好。**the cut and ˈthrust (of sth)** (*BrE*) the lively or aggressive way that sth is done 激烈交鋒：*the cut and thrust of political debate* 政治辯論中的唇槍舌劍

ˌcut and ˈdried *adj.* [not usually before noun] decided in a way that cannot be changed or argued about 已成定局；不容更改：*The inquiry is by no means cut and dried.* 調查之事遠未蓋棺定論。

cu·ta·ne·ous /kjuˈteɪniəs/ *adj.* (*anatomy* 解) connected with the skin 皮膚（上）的

cut·away /ˈkʌtəweɪ/ *adj., noun*

■ ***adj.*** [only before noun] (of a model or diagram 模型或圖表) with some outside parts left out, in order to show what the inside looks like 剖面的：*a cutaway picture of the inside of a nuclear reactor* 核反應堆內部的剖面圖

■ ***noun*** **1** (*especially NAmE*) **~ (to sb/sth)** (on television, in a film/movie, etc. 電視、電影等中) a picture that shows sth different from the main thing that is being shown 切出鏡頭：*There was a cutaway to Jackson's guest on the podium.* 鏡頭切換到了台上傑克遜的一位客人。**2** a model or diagram with some outside parts left out, in order to show what the inside looks like 剖面模型；剖面圖 **3** (*NAmE*) (*BrE* **ˈmorning coat**) a black or grey jacket for men, short at the front and very long at the back, worn as part of morning dress（男子日間穿的黑色或灰色）晨燕尾服，常燕尾服

cut·back /ˈkʌtbæk/ *noun* [usually pl.] **~ (in sth)** a reduction in something 削減；縮減；減少：*cutbacks in public spending* 公共開支的削減 ◇ *staff cutbacks* 裁員

ˌcut-ˈdown *adj.* [only before noun] reduced in length, size or range 縮減的；縮小的：*a cut-down version of the program* 這個程序的簡化版

cute /kjuːt/ *adj.* (**cuter**, **cutest**) **1** pretty and attractive 可愛的；漂亮迷人的：*a cute little baby* 逗人喜愛的小寶寶 ◇ (*BrE*) *an unbearably cute picture of two kittens* (= it seems SENTIMENTAL) 讓人愛得不得了的兩隻小貓的圖片 **2** (*informal, especially NAmE*) sexually attractive 有性吸引力的；性感的：*Check out those cute guys over there!* 瞧那邊那些性感的傢伙！**3** (*informal, especially NAmE*) clever, sometimes in an annoying way because a person is trying to get an advantage for himself or herself 精明的，機靈的（有時使人厭煩）：*She had a really cute idea.* 她有一個精明絕頂的主意。◇ *Don't get cute with me!* 別跟我耍滑頭！▸ **cute·ly** *adv.*：*to smile cutely* 可愛地一笑 **cute·ness** *noun* [U]

cutesy /ˈkjuːtsi/ *adj.* (*informal*) too pretty or attractive in a way that is annoying or not realistic 矯揉造作的；忸怩作態的

ˌcut ˈglass *noun* [U] glass with patterns cut in it 雕花玻璃；刻花玻璃：*a cut-glass vase* 雕花玻璃花瓶

cut·icle /ˈkjuːtɪkl/ *noun* an area of hard skin at the base of the nails on the fingers and toes（手指甲或腳趾甲根部的）表皮，薄膜 ➲ **VISUAL VOCAB** page V59

cutie /ˈkjuːti/ *noun* (*informal*) a person who is attractive or kind 俏人兒；大好人：*He's a real cutie.* 他這個人真有魅力。

cut·lass /ˈkʌtləs/ *noun* a short SWORD with a curved blade that was used as a weapon by sailors and PIRATES in the past（舊時水手和海盜用的）短劍，短彎刀

cut·lery /ˈkʌtləri/ *noun* [U] **1** (*especially BrE*) (*NAmE* usually **flat·ware**, **sil·ver·ware**) knives, forks and spoons, used for eating and serving food 餐具（刀、叉和匙）➲ **VISUAL VOCAB** page V22 **2** (*NAmE*) knives, etc. that are sharp 刀具

cut·let /ˈkʌtlət/ *noun* **1** a thick slice of meat, especially LAMB or PORK (= meat from a pig), that is cooked and served with the bone still attached 厚肉片；（尤指羊或豬）肉排 **2** (in compounds 構成複合詞) finely chopped pieces of meat, fish, vegetables, etc. that are pressed together into a flat piece, covered with BREADCRUMBS and cooked（肉、魚肉、蔬菜等剁碎後外裹麵包屑做成的）炸餅：*nut cutlets* 果仁炸餅

ˈcut-off *noun, adj.*

■ ***noun*** **1** a point or limit when you stop sth 截止點；界限：*The government announced a cut-off in overseas aid.* 政府宣佈了對外援助的限額。◇ *Is there a cut-off point between childhood and adulthood?* 童年與成年之間有分界線嗎？**2** **cut-offs** [pl.] cut-off trousers/pants 剪短的褲子：*wearing frayed cut-offs* 身着毛邊短褲

■ ***adj.*** [only before noun] (of trousers/pants 褲子) made shorter by cutting off part of the legs 褲腿剪短的：*cut-off jeans* 褲腿剪短的牛仔褲

ˈcut-out *noun* **1** a shape cut out of paper, wood, etc.（從紙、木等）剪下的圖樣：*a cardboard cut-out* 從硬紙板剪下的圖形 **2** a piece of safety equipment that stops an electric current from flowing through sth（電流的）斷流器，保險裝置：*A cut-out stops the kettle boiling dry.* 斷流裝置避免水壺燒乾。

ˌcut-ˈprice *adj.* [only before noun] (*especially BrE*) (*NAmE* usually **ˌcut-ˈrate**) **1** sold at a reduced price 減價出售的；削價的：***cut-price goods/fares*** 減價商品／票 **2** selling goods at a reduced price 出售減價商品的：*a* ***cut-price store/supermarket*** 折價商品店／超市

cut·ter /ˈkʌtə(r)/ *noun* **1** (usually in compounds 通常構成複合詞) a person or thing that cuts 切割工；剪裁工；切割工具；剪裁工具：*a pastry cutter* 油酥餅切刀 **2** **cutters** [pl.] (usually in compounds 通常構成複合詞) a tool for cutting 切割工具：*a pair of wire cutters* 一把鋼絲鉗 **3** a small fast ship 小快艇 **4** a ship's boat, used for travelling between the ship and land（行駛於大船與岸邊之間的）小艇，接應船

ˈcut-throat *adj.* [usually before noun] (of an activity 活動) in which people compete with each other in aggressive and unfair ways 競爭激烈的；殘酷無情的；不公的： *the cut-throat world of politics* 鬥得你死我活的政界

ˌcut-throat ˈrazor *noun* a RAZOR (= a tool used for shaving) with a long sharp blade 刀片長的剃鬚刀（或刮鬍刀） ➲ compare SAFETY RAZOR

cut·ting /ˈkʌtɪŋ/ *noun, adj.*

■ ***noun*** **1** (also **ˈpress cutting**) (both *BrE*) (also **clip·ping**, **ˈpress clipping** *NAmE, BrE*) an article or a story that you cut from a newspaper or magazine and keep 剪報；雜誌剪輯資料：***newspaper/press cuttings*** 剪報 **2** a piece cut off a plant that will be used to grow a new plant 插枝，插條（從植物上截取的一段供扦插的枝條） **3** (*BrE*) a narrow open passage that is dug through high ground for a road, railway/railroad or CANAL（為修道路、鐵路或運河從高地開鑿出來的）狹窄通道，路塹，河牀

■ ***adj.*** [usually before noun] **1** unkind and likely to hurt sb's feelings 尖刻的；刻薄的；挖苦人的 **SYN** biting： *a cutting remark* 尖酸刻薄的言辭 **2** (of winds 風) cold in a sharp and unpleasant way 凜冽的；刺骨的 **SYN** biting

ˈcutting board (*NAmE*) (*BrE* **ˈchopping board**) *noun* a board made of wood or plastic used for cutting meat or vegetables on 砧板；切菜板

ˌcutting ˈedge *noun* [sing.] **1 the ~** (**of sth**) the newest, most advanced stage in the development of sth（處於某事物發展的）尖端，最前沿，領先階段： *working **at the cutting edge** of computer technology* 在計算機技術的最前端工作 ➲ compare BLEEDING EDGE **2** an aspect of sth that gives it an advantage 有利方面；優勢： *We're relying on him to give the team a cutting edge.* 我們指望他給這個隊帶來優勢。

ˈcutting grass *noun* = GRASSCUTTER

ˈcutting room *noun* a room in which the different parts of a film/movie are cut and put into order（影片的）剪輯室，剪接室

cuttle·fish /ˈkʌtlfɪʃ/ *noun* (*pl.* **cuttle·fish**) a sea creature with eight arms, two TENTACLES (= long thin parts like arms) and a wide flat shell inside its body, that produces a black substance like ink when it is attacked 烏賊；墨魚；墨斗魚

cutup /ˈkʌtʌp/ *noun* (*NAmE, informal*) a person who behaves in a silly way in order to attract attention and make people laugh（引人注意和逗笑的）活寶，出盡洋相的人

CV /ˌsiː ˈviː/ (*BrE*) (*NAmE* **résumé**) *noun* the abbreviation for 'curriculum vitae' (a written record of your education and the jobs you have done, that you send when you are applying for a job) 履歷，簡歷（全寫為 curriculum vitae）： *Send a full CV with your job application.* 隨求職申請書寄上詳盡的個人履歷。 ➲ COLLOCATIONS at JOB ➲ WRITING TUTOR page WT46

cwm /kʊm/ *noun* (*geology* 地) = CORRIE

ˈC-word *noun* (*informal*, sometimes *offensive*) used to replace a word beginning with C that you do not want to say, for example the offensive swear word 'cunt', or 'cancer' * C 開頭的詞（用以替代不想說出口以 C 開頭的冒犯性髒話，如 cunt、cancer）： *An employee who uses the C-word to a colleague will be suspended.* 雇員對同事說 C 開頭的詞將被停職。◇ *I hate it when people refer to cancer as the C-word.* 我不喜歡有人把癌症說成是 C 開頭的詞。 ➲ compare F-WORD

cwt *abbr.* (*pl.* **cwt**) (in writing) HUNDREDWEIGHT（書寫形式）英擔

cwtch /kʊtʃ/ *verb* [I, T] **~** (**sb**) (*WelshE*) to be held close in sb's arms in a loving way; to hold sb in this way（被）緊緊擁抱： *Cwtch up to your mam!* 去擁抱你媽媽！ ▸ **cwtch** *noun*

-cy, -acy *suffix* (in nouns 構成名詞) **1** the state or quality of 具有…的狀態（或性質）： *infancy* 幼年 ◇ *accuracy* 精確性 **2** the status or position of 具有…的地位（或職位）： *chaplaincy* 牧靈司鐸的職位

cyan /ˈsaɪən/ *noun* [U] (*technical* 術語) a greenish-blue colour, used in printing 藍綠色，青色（用於印刷）

cy·an·ide /ˈsaɪənaɪd/ *noun* [U] a highly poisonous chemical 氰化物（劇毒化學品）

cyber- /ˈsaɪbə(r)/ *combining form* (in nouns and adjectives 構成名詞和形容詞) connected with electronic communication networks, especially the Internet 賽博，計算機的，電腦的，網絡的，網路的（尤指互聯網）： *cybernetics* 控制論 ◇ *cybercafe* 網吧

cyber·cafe /ˈsaɪbəkæfeɪ; *NAmE* ˈsaɪbər-/ *noun* a CAFE with computers on which customers can use the Internet, send emails, etc. 網吧；網咖

cyber·crime /ˈsaɪbəkraɪm; *NAmE* ˈsaɪbər-/ *noun* [U, C] crime that is committed using the Internet, for example by stealing sb's personal or bank details or infecting their computer with a virus 網絡犯罪；網路犯罪

cyber·naut /ˈsaɪbənɔːt; *NAmE* ˈsaɪbərnɔːt/ *noun* (*computing* 計) **1** a person who wears special devices in order to experience VIRTUAL REALITY 虛擬現實體驗者；虛擬實境體驗者 **2** a person who uses the Internet 網絡用戶；網民；網路使用者

cy·ber·net·ics /ˌsaɪbəˈnetɪks; *NAmE* -bərˈn-/ *noun* [U] the scientific study of communication and control, especially concerned with comparing human and animal brains with machines and electronic devices 控制論，神經機械學（對信息傳遞和控制的科學研究，尤涉及人和動物大腦與機器和電子裝置的比較） ▸ **cy·ber·net·ic** *adj.*

cyber·punk /ˈsaɪbəpʌŋk; *NAmE* -bərp-/ *noun* [U] stories set in an imaginary future world controlled by technology and computers 電腦科幻小說，電腦叛客（以受科技與電腦所控制的虛構未來世界為背景）

cyber·sex /ˈsaɪbəseks; *NAmE* ˈsaɪbər-/ *noun* [U] communication between people using the Internet which makes them sexually excited 網上性行為，網交（藉由互聯網上的溝通獲得性快感）

cyber·space /ˈsaɪbəspeɪs; *NAmE* -bərs-/ *noun* [U] the imaginary place where electronic messages, etc. exist while they are being sent between computers 網絡空間；網路空間

cyber·squat·ting /ˈsaɪbəskwɒtɪŋ; *NAmE* ˈsaɪbərskwɑːtɪŋ/ *noun* [U] the illegal activity of buying and officially recording an address on the Internet that is the name of an existing company or a well-known person, with the intention of selling it to the owner in order to make money 域名搶註，網路蟑螂的行徑（針對已成立的企業或知名人士的圖利行為） ▸ **cyber·squat·ter** *noun*

cy·borg /ˈsaɪbɔːg; *NAmE* -bɔːrg/ *noun* (in SCIENCE FICTION stories 科幻故事) a creature that is part human, part machine 電子人；半人半機器的生物

cyc·la·men /ˈsɪkləmən; *NAmE* ˈsaɪk-/ *noun* (*pl.* **cyc·la·men** or **cyc·la·mens**) a plant with pink, purple or white flowers that grow on long STEMS pointing downwards, often grown indoors 仙客來（常在室內種植，花朵下垂，呈粉紅色、紫色或白色）

cycle 🔑 **AW** /ˈsaɪkl/ *noun, verb*

■ ***noun*** **1** 🔑 a bicycle or motorcycle 自行車；摩托車： *We went for a cycle ride on Sunday.* 我們星期天騎自行車去兜風了。◇ *a **cycle route/track*** 自行車路線／車道 ➲ VISUAL VOCAB page V51 ➲ see also BIKE **2** 🔑 the fact of a series of events being repeated many times, always in the same order 循環： *the cycle of the seasons* 四季的循環 ➲ see also LIFE CYCLE **3** a complete set or series, for example of movements in a machine 整套，整個系列（如機器的運轉）： *eight cycles per second* 每秒轉動八次 ◇ *the rinse cycle* (= in a washing machine)（洗衣機的）漂洗運轉過程

■ ***verb*** 🔑 [I] (**+adv./prep.**) (*especially BrE*) to ride a bicycle; to travel by bicycle 騎自行車；騎自行車旅行： *I usually cycle home through the park.* 我通常騎自行車穿過公園回家。 ➲ compare BICYCLE, BIKE

ˈcycle lane (*BrE*) (*NAmE* **ˈbicycle lane**, *informal* **ˈbike lane**) *noun* a part of a road that only bicycles are allowed to use 自行車車道 ➲ VISUAL VOCAB page V3

ˈcycle-rickshaw *noun* a vehicle like a bicycle with three wheels, with a covered seat for passengers behind the driver, used especially in some Asian countries（一些亞洲國家的）人力三輪車

cyc·lic **AW** /ˈsaɪklɪk; ˈsɪk-/ (also **cyc·lic·al** /ˈsaɪklɪkl; ˈsɪk-/) *adj.* [usually before noun] repeated many times and always happening in the same order 循環的；週期的：*the cyclic processes of nature* 自然界的循環過程 ◇ *Economic activity often follows a cyclical pattern.* 經濟活動常常遵循週期性模式。 ▸ **cyc·lic·al·ly** *adv.*： *events that occur cyclically* 週期性出現的事情

C

cyc·ling 0‐ᴛ /ˈsaɪklɪŋ/ *noun* [U] the sport or activity of riding a bicycle 騎自行車運動（或活動）：*to go cycling* 去騎自行車 ◇ *Cycling is Europe's second most popular sport.* 騎自行車是歐洲第二種最流行的體育運動。 ◇ *cycling shorts* 自行車短運動褲 ➲ VISUAL VOCAB page V47

cyc·list /ˈsaɪklɪst/ *noun* a person who rides a bicycle 騎自行車的人 ➲ compare BICYCLIST

cyclo-cross /ˈsaɪkləʊ krɒs; *NAmE* ˈsaɪkloʊ krɔːs/ *noun* [U] the sport of racing bicycles over rough ground, which in places is too difficult to ride on so you have to carry your bicycle and run 自行車越野賽（遇到特別崎嶇的路面時需攜車跑步）

cyc·lone /ˈsaɪkləʊn; *NAmE* -kloʊn/ *noun* a violent tropical storm in which strong winds move in a circle 氣旋；旋風 ➲ compare HURRICANE, TYPHOON ▸ **cyc·lon·ic** /saɪˈklɒnɪk; *NAmE* -ˈklɑːn-/ *adj.*

Cy·clops /ˈsaɪklɒps; *NAmE* -klɑːps/ *noun* (in ancient Greek stories) a giant with only one eye in the middle of his face（古希臘神話中的）庫克羅普斯，獨眼巨人

cyclo·tron /ˈsaɪkləʊtrɒn; *NAmE* ˈsaɪkloʊtrɑːn/ *noun* (*physics* 物) a machine which makes atoms or ELECTRONS move more quickly, using electrical and MAGNETIC FIELDS 迴旋加速器

cyg·net /ˈsɪɡnət/ *noun* a young SWAN (= a large white bird with a long neck that lives on or near water) 幼天鵝

cy·lin·der /ˈsɪlɪndə(r)/ *noun* **1** a solid or hollow figure with round ends and long straight sides 圓柱；圓柱體；圓筒 ➲ VISUAL VOCAB page V71 **2** an object shaped like a cylinder, especially one used as a container（尤指用作容器的）圓筒狀物：*a gas/oxygen cylinder* 氣罐；氧氣瓶 ➲ VISUAL VOCAB page V70 **3** the hollow tube in an engine, shaped like a cylinder, inside which the PISTON moves（發動機的）氣缸：*a six-cylinder engine* 六缸發動機

IDM **working/firing on all ˈcylinders** (*informal*) using all your energy to do sth; working as well as possible 竭盡全力；盡力幹好；開足馬力

cy·lin·dric·al /səˈlɪndrɪkl/ *adj.* shaped like a cylinder 圓柱形的；圓筒狀的：*huge cylindrical gas tanks* 巨大的圓柱形貯氣罐

cym·bal /ˈsɪmbl/ *noun* a musical instrument in the form of a round metal plate. It is hit with a stick, or two cymbals are hit against each other. 鈸，鐃鈸（打擊樂器）：*a clash/crash of cymbals* 鐃鈸的敲擊聲 ➲ VISUAL VOCAB page V35

Cymru /ˈkʌmri/ *noun* the name for 'Wales' in the Welsh language（威爾士語）威爾士 ➲ see also PLAID CYMRU

cynic /ˈsɪnɪk/ *noun* **1** a person who believes that people only do things to help themselves, rather than for good or sincere reasons 認為人皆自私的人；憤世嫉俗者 **2** a person who does not believe that sth good will happen or that sth is important 悲觀者；懷疑者：*Cynics will say that there is not the slightest chance of success.* 悲觀的人會說根本不可能取得成功。 ▸ **cyni·cism** /ˈsɪnɪsɪzəm/ *noun* [U]： *In a world full of cynicism she was the one person I felt I could trust.* 在這個人人都互相猜忌的世界裏，只有她一個我認為是可以信賴的。

cyn·ic·al /ˈsɪnɪkl/ *adj.* **1** believing that people only do things to help themselves rather than for good or honest reasons 認為人皆自私的；憤世嫉俗的：*Do you have to be so cynical about everything?* 你非得懷疑一切嗎？ ◇ *a cynical view/smile* 憤世嫉俗的觀點；譏笑 **2** not believing that sth good will happen or that sth is important 悲觀的；懷疑的：*I'm a bit cynical about the benefits of the plan.* 我對這項計劃的成效有點兒懷疑。 **3** not caring that sth might hurt other people, if there is some advantage for you 只顧自己不顧他人的；見利忘義的：*a cynical disregard for the safety of others* 不顧他人安危的自私自利 ◇ *a deliberate and cynical foul* 存心惡意犯規 ▸ **cyn·ic·al·ly** /-kli/ *adv.*

cyn·o·sure /ˈsɪnəzjʊə(r); ˈsaɪn-; -ʃʊə(r); *NAmE* ˈsaɪnəʃʊr; ˈsɪn-/ *noun* [sing.] (*formal*) a person or thing that is the centre of attention 引人注目的人（或事物）；注意的中心：*Ruth was the cynosure of all eyes.* 魯思吸引了所有的目光。

cy·pher = CIPHER

cy·press /ˈsaɪprəs/ *noun* a tall straight EVERGREEN tree 柏樹

Cy·ril·lic /səˈrɪlɪk/ *adj.* the **Cyrillic** alphabet is used to write Russian, Bulgarian and some other European languages 西里爾字母的（用於俄語、保加利亞語及其他一些歐洲語言）▸ **Cy·ril·lic** *noun* [U]

cyst /sɪst/ *noun* a GROWTH containing liquid that forms in or on a person's or an animal's body and may need to be removed 囊腫；囊；包囊

cys·tic fi·bro·sis /ˌsɪstɪk faɪˈbrəʊsɪs; *NAmE* -ˈbroʊ-/ *noun* [U] a serious medical condition that some people are born with, in which GLANDS in the lungs and other organs do not work correctly. It often leads to infections and can result in early death. 囊性纖維變性；囊性纖維化

cyst·itis /sɪˈstaɪtɪs/ *noun* [U] an infection of the BLADDER, especially in women, that causes frequent, painful URINATION 膀胱炎

cy·tol·o·gy /saɪˈtɒlədʒi; *NAmE* -ˈtɑːl-/ *noun* [U] the scientific study of the structure and function of cells from living things 細胞學

cyto·megalo·virus /ˌsaɪtəʊˈmeɡələʊvaɪrəs; *NAmE* ˌsaɪtoʊˈmeɡəloʊ-/ *noun* (*medical* 醫) a virus that usually causes mild infections, but that can be serious for people with AIDS or for new babies 巨細胞病毒（對艾滋病人或新生兒有危險）

cy·to·plasm /ˈsaɪtəʊplæzəm; *NAmE* -toʊ-/ *noun* [U] (*biology* 生) all the living material in a cell, not including the NUCLEUS 細胞質；胞漿 ▸ **cy·to·plas·mic** /ˌsaɪtəʊˈplæzmɪk; *NAmE* -toʊ-/ *adj.* ➲ compare PROTOPLASM

czar, **czar·ina**, **czar·ism**, **czar·ist** = TSAR, TSARINA, TSARISM, TSARIST

D d

D /diː/ *noun, abbr., symbol*
■ ***noun*** (also **d**) [C, U] (*pl.* **Ds**, **D's**, **d's** /diːz/) **1** the fourth letter of the English alphabet 英語字母表的第 4 個字母：*'Dog' begins with (a) D/'D'.* * dog 一詞以字母 d 開頭。 **2 D** (*music* 音) the second note in the SCALE of C MAJOR * D 音（C 大調的第 2 音或音符） **3 D** the fourth highest mark/grade that a student can get for a piece of work, showing that it is not very good（學業成績）第四等，差：*He got (a) D/'D' in/for Geography.* 他的地理成績得 D 級。➲ see also D-DAY
■ ***abbr.*** (also **D.** especially in *NAmE*) (in politics in the US 美國政治) DEMOCRAT; DEMOCRATIC 民主黨人；民主黨的
■ ***symbol*** the number 500 in ROMAN NUMERALS（羅馬數字）500

d. *abbr.* **1** (in writing) died（書寫形式）去世，逝世：*Emily Clifton, d. 1865* 埃米莉•克利夫頓，卒於 1865 年 **2 d** (in the system of money used in the past in Britain) a PENNY（英國舊幣制中的）便士

-d *suffix* ➲ -ED

DA (*BrE*) (*US* **D.A.**) /ˌdiː ˈeɪ/ *abbr.* DISTRICT ATTORNEY

dab /dæb/ *verb, noun*
■ ***verb*** (**-bb-**) **1** to touch sth lightly, usually several times 輕觸，輕拍，輕拭，輕揩（幾下）：**~ sth** *She dabbed her eyes and blew her nose.* 她輕輕擦了幾下眼睛，擤了擤鼻涕。◇ **~ at sth** *He dabbed at the cut with his handkerchief.* 他用手帕輕輕按了按傷口。 **2 ~ sth + adv./prep.** to put sth on a surface with quick light movements 輕搽；輕塗；輕敷：*She dabbed a little perfume behind her ears.* 她朝耳後搽了點香水。
■ ***noun*** **1** a small amount of a liquid, cream or powder that is put on a surface in a quick gentle movement 少量，一點點（輕敷於表面的液體、乳霜或化妝用粉）：*She put a dab of perfume behind her ears.* 她朝耳後搽了點香水。 **2** an act of gently touching or pressing sth without rubbing 輕觸，輕按（但不揉擦）：*He gave the cut a quick dab with a towel.* 他麻利地用毛巾按了按傷口。 **3** a small flat fish 黃蓋鰈（小比目魚） **4** (*WelshE*) a person or thing 人；東西：*He's in hospital again.* ***Poor dab.*** 他又住醫院了，怪可憐的。

dab·ble /ˈdæbl/ *verb* **1** [I] **~ (in/with sth)** to take part in a sport, an activity, etc. but not very seriously 涉獵；涉足；淺嘗：*He dabbles in local politics.* 他開始涉足地方政壇。 **2** [T] **~ sth (in sth)** to move your hands, feet, etc. around in water 玩水；嬉水：*She dabbled her toes in the stream.* 她把腳趾浸在小河裏嬉水。

ˌdab ˈhand *noun* (*BrE, informal*) a person who is very good at doing sth or using sth 能手；高手：*He's a dab hand at cooking spaghetti.* 他是煮意大利麪的高手。◇ *She's a dab hand with a paintbrush.* 她是繪畫能手。

dacha /ˈdætʃə/ *noun* a Russian country house（俄國的）鄉間宅第，別墅

dachs·hund /ˈdæksnd; *NAmE* ˈdɑːkshʊnd/ (also *BrE informal* **ˈsausage dog**) *noun* a small dog with a long body, long ears and very short legs 獵獾狗，臘腸狗（身長、腿短、耳朵大）

dac·oit /dəˈkɔɪt/ *noun* (*IndE*) a member of a group of armed thieves 武裝匪徒；強盜

dac·tyl /ˈdæktɪl/ *noun* (*technical* 術語) a unit of sound in poetry consisting of one strong or long syllable followed by two weak or short syllables（詩歌的）揚抑抑格，長短短格

dad 🔑 /dæd/ *noun* (*informal*)
(often used as a name 常用作稱呼) father 爸爸；爹爹：*That's my dad over there.* 那是我爸爸。◇ *Do you live with your mum or your dad?* 你和媽媽還是和爸爸住在一起？◇ *Is it OK if I borrow the car, Dad?* 爸爸，借用一下汽車好嗎？

Dada /ˈdɑːdɑː/ *noun* [U] an early 20th century movement in art, literature, music and film which made fun of social and artistic conventions 達達主義（20 世紀早期興起的藝術運動，以嘲諷社會和藝術傳統為特徵） ▶ **Dada·ism** /ˈdɑːdɑːɪzəm/ *noun* [U] **Dada·ist** /ˈdɑːdɑːɪst/ *noun*

daddy /ˈdædi/ *noun* (*pl.* **-ies**) used especially by and to young children, and often as a name, to mean 'father'（尤作兒語）爸爸：*What does your daddy look like?* 你爸爸長得什麼樣？◇ *Daddy, where are you?* 爸爸，你在哪兒？◇ *Come to Daddy.* 到爸爸這兒來。

ˌdaddy-ˈlong-legs *noun* (*pl.* **daddy-long-legs**) (*informal*) **1** = CRANE FLY **2** (*NAmE*) a small creature like a spider with very long legs 長腳爺叔；盲蛛

dado /ˈdeɪdəʊ; *NAmE* -doʊ/ *noun* (*pl.* **-os**, *NAmE* **-oes**) the lower part of the wall of a room when it is a different colour or material from the top part 護壁板；牆裙

ˈdado rail *noun* a raised line around the wall of a room, that separates the dado from the upper part of the wall（牆裙頂端的）護壁條

dae·mon /ˈdiːmən/ *noun* a creature in stories from ancient Greece that is half man and half god（古希臘神話中的）半神半人的精靈

daf·fo·dil /ˈdæfədɪl/ *noun* a tall yellow spring flower shaped like a TRUMPET. It is a national symbol of Wales. 黃水仙（威爾士的民族象徵） ➲ VISUAL VOCAB page V11

daffy /ˈdæfi/ *adj.* (**daf·fier**, **daf·fi·est**) (*informal*) silly 傻的；愚蠢的

daft /dɑːft; *NAmE* dæft/ *adj.* (**daft·er**, **daft·est**) (*BrE, informal*) silly, often in a way that is amusing 笨的；傻的；愚蠢可笑的：*Don't be so daft!* 別那麼犯傻了！◇ *She's not as daft as she looks.* 她並不像看上去那麼傻。◇ *What a daft thing to say!* 這樣說真是太愚蠢了！ ▶ **daft·ness** *noun* [U]
IDM **ˌdaft as a ˈbrush** (*BrE, informal*) very silly 傻得很；愚蠢透頂

dag /dæg/ *noun* (*informal*) **1** (*AustralE, NZE*) a person who is strange or different in an amusing way 怪人；滑稽的人 **2** (*AustralE*) a person who is not fashionable 不入時的人；土包子 **3** (*AustralE, NZE*) a dirty piece of wool that hangs down from a sheep's bottom（羊屁股下面的）髒毛；羊股溝毛

dagga /ˈdæxə/ *noun* [U] (*SAfrE*) = MARIJUANA：*She was arrested for smoking dagga.* 她吸大麻被捕。

dag·ger /ˈdægə(r)/ *noun* a short pointed knife that is used as a weapon 匕首；短劍 ➲ picture at SWORD ➲ see also CLOAK-AND-DAGGER
IDM **at ˌdaggers ˈdrawn** (*BrE*) if two people are **at daggers drawn**, they are very angry with each other 劍拔弩張；勢不兩立 **look ˈdaggers at sb** to look at sb in a very angry way 對某人怒目而視

daggy /ˈdægi/ *adj.* (*AustralE, informal*) **1** not fashionable 不時髦的；過時的；土氣的：*a daggy restaurant* 土裏土氣的餐館 **2** untidy or dirty 凌亂的；骯髒的

dago /ˈdeɪgəʊ; *NAmE* -goʊ/ *noun* (*pl.* **-os** or **-oes**) (*taboo, slang*) a very offensive word for a person from Italy, Spain or Portugal 拉丁佬（對意大利人、西班牙人或葡萄牙人的蔑稱）

da·guerre·otype (also **da·guerro·type**) /dəˈgerətaɪp/ *noun* a photograph taken using an early process that used a silver plate and MERCURY gas（早期的）達蓋爾銀版照片

dah·lia /ˈdeɪliə; *NAmE* ˈdæliə/ *noun* a large brightly coloured garden flower, often shaped like a ball 大麗花屬

dai·kon /ˈdaɪkɒn; *NAmE* -kɑːn/ *noun* [U, C] = MOOLI

the Dáil /dɔɪl/ *noun* [sing.+sing./pl. v.] one of the parts of the parliament of the Republic of Ireland, whose members are elected by the people（愛爾蘭共和國的）眾議院

daily 🔑 /ˈdeɪli/ *adj., adv., noun*
■ ***adj.*** [only before noun] **1** 🔑 happening, done or produced every day 每日的；日常的：*a daily routine/visit/newspaper* 日常事務；每日一次的訪問；日報 ◇ *events affecting the* ***daily lives*** *of millions of people* 影響數百萬人日常生活的事件 ◇ *Invoices are signed* ***on a daily basis.***

D

發票按日簽發。 **2** connected with one day's work 每個工作日的；按日的：*They charge a daily rate.* 他們按日收費。

IDM **your daily 'bread** the basic things that you need to live, especially food 生計；（尤指）每日的食物

■ ***adv.*** every day 每日；每天：*The machines are inspected twice daily.* 機器每日檢查兩次。

■ ***noun*** (*pl.* **-ies**) **1** a newspaper published every day except Sunday（除星期日外每日發行的）日報：*The story was in all the dailies.* 這則新聞刊登在所有日報上。 **2** (also **,daily 'help**) (*old-fashioned, BrE*) a person employed to come to sb's house each day to clean it and do other jobs（不寄宿的）僕人

dainty /ˈdeɪnti/ *adj.* (**dain·tier**, **dain·ti·est**) **1** (of people and things 人和物) small and delicate in a way that people find attractive 嬌小的；嬌美的；精緻的；小巧的 SYN **delicate**：*dainty feet* 嬌小可愛的腳 ◇ *a dainty porcelain cup* 小巧玲瓏的瓷杯 **2** (of movements 舉止) careful, often in a way that suggests good manners 文雅的；優雅的；高雅的 SYN **delicate**：*She took a dainty little bite of the apple.* 她文雅地咬了一小口蘋果。 ▸ **dain·tily** *adv.*：*She blew her nose as daintily as possible.* 她盡量文雅地擤了擤鼻涕。 **dain·ti·ness** *noun* [U]

dai·quiri /ˈdaɪkɪri; ˈdæk-/ *noun* an alcoholic drink made from RUM mixed with fruit juice, sugar, etc. 代基里酒（由朗姆酒與果汁、糖等摻和而成）

dairy /ˈdeəri; *NAmE* ˈderi/ *noun, adj.*

■ ***noun*** (*pl.* **-ies**) **1** [C] a place on a farm where milk is kept and where butter and cheese are made 牛奶場；乳品場 **2** [C] a company that sells milk, eggs, cheese and other milk products 乳品公司；乳品店 **3** [C] (*NZE*) a small local shop（當地的）小商店，小鋪：*I went to buy a paper at the corner dairy.* 我到街角的小店去買了份報紙。 **4** [U] milk, eggs, cheese and other milk products 乳製品：*The doctor told me to eat less red meat and dairy.* 醫生告誡我要少吃紅肉和乳製品。

■ ***adj.*** [only before noun] **1** made from milk 牛奶的；奶製的；乳品的：***dairy products/produce*** 乳製品；奶類產品 **2** connected with the production of milk rather than meat 乳品業的；生產乳品的：*the dairy industry* 乳品業 ◇ ***dairy cattle/farmers*** 乳牛；乳牛場工人 ◇ ***a dairy cow/farm*** 乳牛；乳牛場

dairy·maid /ˈdeərimeɪd; *NAmE* ˈderi-/ *noun* (*old-fashioned*) a woman who works in a dairy (1) 擠奶女工；乳牛場女工

dairy·man /ˈdeərimən; *NAmE* ˈderi-/ *noun* (*pl.* **-men** /-mən/) **1** a man who works in a dairy (1) 擠奶工人；乳牛場工人 **2** a man who owns or manages a dairy (2) and sells the products 乳牛場主；乳品商

dais /ˈdeɪɪs/ *noun* a stage, especially at one end of a room, on which people stand to make speeches to an audience（尤指房間一端的）講台，高台

daisy /ˈdeɪzi/ *noun* (*pl.* **-ies**) a small wild flower with white PETALS around a yellow centre; a taller plant with similar but larger flowers 雛菊（花）；（類似雛菊，但花稍大的）菊科植物 IDM see PUSH *v.* ➲ see also MICHAELMAS DAISY ➲ VISUAL VOCAB page V11

ˈdaisy chain *noun* a string of daisies tied together to wear around the neck, etc. 雛菊花環

ˈdaisy cutter *noun* **1** (in CRICKET or BASEBALL 板球或棒球) a ball hit or thrown to roll or BOUNCE low along the ground 擦地球；地滾球；滾地球 **2** a very powerful bomb dropped from an aircraft that explodes close to the ground and causes a lot of destruction over a large area 摘菊使者（殺傷範圍大的空投炸彈）；殺傷炸彈

ˈdaisy wheel *noun* a small disc, used in some printers and TYPEWRITERS, with metal letters around the edge which print onto paper（打印機或打字機的）菊瓣字輪：*a daisy wheel printer* 菊瓣字輪打印機

daks /dæks/ *noun* [pl.] (*AustralE, NZE, informal*) trousers/pants 褲子

dal = DHAL

dala-dala /ˈdælə dælə/ *noun* (in Tanzania) a small bus used as a taxi（坦桑尼亞）出租麪包車，小巴計程車

the Dalai Lama /ˌdælaɪ ˈlɑːmə/ *noun* [sing.] the leader of Tibetan Buddhism and, in former times, the ruler of Tibet 達賴喇嘛（西藏佛教領袖，從前為西藏統治者）

dale /deɪl/ *noun* (*literary or dialect*) a valley, especially in northern England（尤指英格蘭北部的）山谷，峪：*the Yorkshire Dales* 約克郡山谷

Dalit /ˈdɑːlɪt/ *noun* (in the traditional Indian CASTE system) a member of the caste that is considered the lowest and that has the fewest advantages 達利特人，賤民（傳統印度種姓制度中地位最低、最劣勢的人）：*the Dalits' struggle for social and economic rights* 爭取社會和經濟權利的賤民鬥爭

dal·li·ance /ˈdæliəns/ *noun* [U, C] (*old-fashioned* or *humorous*) **1** the behaviour of sb who is dallying with sb/sth 嬉戲；戲弄：*It turned out to be his last dalliance with the education system.* 這一次竟成了他對教育體制最後的嘲弄。 **2** a sexual relationship that is not serious 調情；調戲

dally /ˈdæli/ *verb* (**dal·lies**, **dally·ing**, **dal·lied**, **dal·lied**) [I] (*old-fashioned*) to do sth too slowly; to take too much time making a decision 蹉跎（時光）；延誤；拖拉 PHR V **ˈdally with sb/sth** (*old-fashioned*) to treat sb/sth in a way that is not serious enough 輕率地對待；玩弄；戲弄 ➲ see also DILLY-DALLY

Dal·ma·tian /dælˈmeɪʃn/ *noun* a large dog that has short white hair with black spots 達爾馬提亞狗（帶黑色斑點的白色短毛大狗）

dam /dæm/ *noun, verb*

■ ***noun*** **1** a barrier that is built across a river in order to stop the water from flowing, used especially to make a RESERVOIR (= a lake for storing water) or to produce electricity 水壩；攔河壩 **2** (*technical* 術語) the mother of some animals, especially horses 母獸；（尤指）母馬，騾馬 ➲ compare SIRE *n.* (1) **3** = DENTAL DAM

■ ***verb*** (**-mm-**) **~ sth (up)** to build a dam across a river, especially in order to make an artificial lake for use as a water supply, etc.（在河上）築壩

dam·age /ˈdæmɪdʒ/ *noun, verb*

■ ***noun*** **1** [U] **~ (to sth)** physical harm caused to sth which makes it less attractive, useful or valuable（有形的）損壞，破壞，損失：***serious/severe/extensive/permanent/minor damage*** 重大的／嚴重的／大範圍的／永久性的／輕微的損壞 ◇ ***brain/liver etc. damage*** 腦、肝等損傷 ◇ ***fire/smoke/bomb/storm damage*** 火災損失；煙霧熏壞；炸彈毀壞；暴風雨破壞 ◇ *The earthquake caused damage to property estimated at $6 million.* 地震造成大約 600 萬元的財產損失。◇ *The storm didn't **do** much **damage**.* 暴風雨並未造成嚴重損失。◇ *Let's take a look at the damage.* 讓我們看看損失情況吧。◇ *I insist on paying for the damage.* 我堅持要賠償損失。◇ *Make sure you insure your camera against loss or damage.* 一定要給你的照相機投保，以防丟失或損壞。 **2** [U] **~ (to sb/sth)** harmful effects on sb/sth 損害；傷害：*emotional damage resulting from divorce* 離婚引起的感情傷害 ◇ *damage to a person's reputation* 對個人名譽的損害 ◇ *This could cause serious damage to the country's economy.* 這可能對國家的經濟造成嚴重破壞。◇ *I'm going—I've done enough damage here already.* 我要走了——我在這裏造成的損害已經夠大了。 **3 damages** [pl.] an amount of money that a court decides should be paid to sb by the person, company, etc. that has caused them harm or injury（法院判定的）損害賠償金：*He was ordered to pay damages totalling £30 000.* 他被責令支付總額為 3 萬英鎊的損害賠償金。◇ *They intend to sue for damages.* 他們打算起訴，要求賠償損失。◇ *Ann was awarded £6 000 (in) damages.* 安被判予 6 000 英鎊的損害賠償金。

IDM **what's the 'damage?** (*informal*) a way of asking how much sth costs 要花多少錢

■ ***verb*** **~ sth/sb** to harm or spoil sth/sb 損害；傷害；毀壞；破壞：*The fire badly damaged the town hall.* 火災使市政廳遭到嚴重破壞。◇ *Several vehicles were damaged in the crash.* 好幾輛汽車在撞車事故中損壞了。◇ *Smoking seriously damages your health.* 吸煙嚴重損害人體健康。◇ *The allegations are likely to damage his political career.* 這些指控有可能對他的政治生涯造成傷害。◇ *emotionally damaged children* 感情上受傷害的孩子 ➲ COLLOCATIONS at INJURY

Synonyms 同義詞辨析

damage

hurt • harm • impair

These words all mean to have a bad effect on sb/sth. 以上各詞均含傷害、損害之意。

damage to cause physical harm to sth, making it less attractive, useful or valuable; to have a bad effect on sb/sth's life, health, happiness or chances of success 指毀壞、破壞、傷害、損害： *The fire badly damaged the town hall.* 火災使市政廳遭到嚴重破壞。◇ *emotionally damaged children* 感情上受傷害的孩子

hurt (*rather informal*) to have a bad effect on sb/sth's life, health, happiness or chances of success 指傷害、損害： *Hard work never hurt anyone.* 努力工作絕無害處。

harm to have a bad effect on sb/sth's life, health, happiness or chances of success 指傷害、損害： *Pollution can harm marine life.* 污染會危及海洋生物。

DAMAGE, HURT OR HARM? 用 damage、hurt 還是 harm？

Hurt is slightly less formal than **damage** or **harm**, especially when it is used in negative statements. 與 damage 或 harm 相比，hurt 稍非正式，用於否定句時尤其如此： *It won't hurt him to have to wait a bit.* 等上一會兒對他無妨。◇ ~~*It won't damage/harm him to have to wait a bit.*~~ **Harm** is also often used to talk about ways in which things in the natural world such as *wildlife* and the *environment* are affected by human activity. * harm 亦常用於自然界中的事物（如野生生物和環境）受到人類活動的影響。

impair (*rather formal*) to damage sb's health, abilities or chances 指損害、削弱（健康、能力或機會）： *Even one drink can impair driving performance.* 即使一杯酒也可能影響駕駛操作。

PATTERNS

- to damage/hurt/harm/impair sb's **chances**
- to damage/hurt/harm sb's **interests/reputation**
- to damage/harm/impair sb's **health**
- to **seriously/greatly** damage/hurt/harm/impair sb/sth
- to **badly/severely** damage/hurt/impair sb/sth

ˌdamage limiˈtation (also **ˌdamage conˈtrol** especially in *NAmE*) *noun* [U] the process of trying to limit the amount of damage that is caused by sth 損害控制

dam·aging /ˈdæmɪdʒɪŋ/ *adj.* causing damage; having a bad effect on sb/sth 造成破壞的；有害的；損害的： ***damaging consequences/effects*** 破壞性的後果／影響 ◇ **~ to sb/sth** *Lead is potentially damaging to children's health.* 鉛對兒童的健康具有潛在損害。

Da·mas·cus /dəˈmæskəs/ *noun*

IDM **the road to Daˈmascus** an experience that results in a great change in a person's attitudes or beliefs 通往大馬士革之路；（觀點或信仰的）翻然轉變： *Spending a night in jail was his road to Damascus.* 在監獄裏度過的一夜徹底改變了他的人生觀。 **ORIGIN** From the story in the Bible in which St Paul hears the voice of God on the road to Damascus and becomes a Christian. 源自《聖經》故事，聖保祿在前往大馬士革的路上聽到了上帝的召喚，於是皈依基督。

dam·ask /ˈdæməsk/ *noun* [U] a type of thick cloth, usually made from silk or LINEN, with a pattern that is visible on both sides 花緞；錦緞；亞麻花緞： *a damask tablecloth* 織花桌布

dame /deɪm/ *noun* **1 Dame** (in Britain) a title given to a woman as a special honour because of the work she has done 女爵士（英國授予有貢獻的女性的榮譽稱號）： *Dame Maggie Smith* 瑪吉 • 史密斯女爵士 **2** (*old-fashioned, NAmE, informal*) a woman 女人 **3** = PANTOMIME DAME

damn /dæm/ *exclamation, adj., verb, adv., noun*

■ ***exclamation*** (also *old-fashioned* **dam·mit** /ˈdæmɪt/, **ˈdamn it**) (*informal*) a swear word that people use to show that they are annoyed, disappointed, etc.（表示厭煩、失望等）該死，他媽的，討厭： *Oh damn! I forgot he was coming.* 真該死！我把他要來這事兒給忘了。

■ ***adj.*** (also **damned**) [only before noun] (*informal*) **1** a swear word that people use to show that they are annoyed with sb/sth（表示厭煩）可惡的，討厭的，該死的： *Where's that damn book!* 那該死的書在哪兒呢！◇ *The damned thing won't start!* 這混賬東西就是發動不起來！◇ *It's none of your damn business!* 關你屁事！◇ *He's a damn nuisance!* 他真是個該死的討厭鬼！**2** a swear word that people use to emphasize what they are saying（加強語氣）十足的，完全的： *What a damn shame!* 真是太遺憾了！ **IDM** see THING

■ ***verb*** **1 ~ sb/sth** (*informal*) used when swearing at sb/sth to show that you are angry（表示憤怒）該死，混賬： *Damn you! I'm not going to let you bully me.* 你這個渾蛋！我決不讓你欺負我。◇ *Damn this machine! Why won't it work?* 這該死的機器！怎麼就是發動不起來？ **2 ~ sb** (of God 上帝) to decide that sb must suffer in hell 令（某人）下地獄 **3 ~ sb/sth** to criticize sb/sth very strongly 強烈指責；譴責；狠狠批評： *The film was damned by the critics for its mindless violence.* 這部影片因無謂的暴力受到評論家的強烈指責。

IDM **damn the consequences, expense, etc.** (*informal*) used to say that you are going to do sth even though you know it may be expensive, have bad results, etc. 置後果（或費用等）於不顧： *Let's celebrate and damn the expense!* 管它花多少錢，咱們先慶祝一番再說！ **damn sb/sth with faint ˈpraise** to praise sb/sth only a little, in order to show that you do not really like them/it 用冷漠的讚揚貶低；寓貶於褒；名褒實貶 **I'll be damned!** (*old-fashioned, informal*) used to show that you are very surprised about sth（表示驚奇）真沒想到，真叫我吃驚 **I'm damned if ...** (*informal*) used to show that you refuse to do sth or do not know sth 我決不…；我絕對不…： *I'm damned if I'll apologize!* 我決不道歉！◇ *I'm damned if I know who he is.* 我根本不認識他。 ➲ more at NEAR *adv.*

■ ***adv.*** (also **damned**) (*informal*) **1** a swear word that people use to show that they are annoyed with sb/sth（表示厭煩）該死，討厭，十足，完全： *Don't be so damn silly!* 別那麼傻了！◇ *What a damn stupid question!* 這問題問得真是愚蠢透頂！◇ *You **know damn well*** (= you know very well) *what I mean!* 我的意思你再清楚不過了！◇ *I'll damn well leave tonight* (= I am determined to). 我今晚一定得離開。 **2** a swear word that people use to emphasize what they are saying（加強語氣）非常，十分，極： *damn good* 好得不得了 ◇ *We got out pretty damned fast!* 我們一溜煙似地走了！◇ *I'm damn sure she had no idea.* 我敢肯定她不知道。

IDM **damn ˈall** (*BrE*) nothing 毫無；絲毫不；完全沒有： *I know damn all about computers.* 我對計算機一竅不通。

■ ***noun***

IDM **not care/give a ˈdamn (about sb/sth)** (*informal*) to not care at all about sb/sth（對…）毫不在乎

dam·nable /ˈdæmnəbl/ *adj.* (*old-fashioned*) bad or annoying 糟糕的；討厭的 ▸ **dam·nably** /ˈdæmnəbli/ *adv.*

dam·na·tion /dæmˈneɪʃn/ *noun* [U] the state of being in hell; the act of sending sb to hell 天譴；罰入地獄： *eternal damnation* 永罰

damned /dæmd/ *adj., adv., noun*

■ ***adj., adv.*** = DAMN

■ ***noun*** **the damned** [pl.] people who are forced to live in hell after they die 下地獄的靈魂

damned·est /ˈdæmdɪst/ *noun, adj.* (*informal*)

IDM **the damnedest ...** (*especially NAmE*) the most surprising ... 最令人驚奇；最奇妙： *It's the damnedest thing I ever saw.* 這是我見過的最奇妙的玩意。 **do/try your ˈdamnedest (to do sth)** to try as hard as you can (to do sth) 全力以赴；盡力而為；竭盡全力： *She did her* *damnedest to get it done on time.* 她竭盡全力按時把它完成了。

damn·ing /ˈdæmɪŋ/ *adj.* critical of sb/sth; suggesting that sb is guilty 譴責的；詛咒的；可以定罪的：***damning criticism/evidence*** 譴責性的批評；足以定罪的證據 ◇ *a **damning conclusion/report*** 可以定罪的結論／報告 ◇ *Her report is expected to deliver a damning indictment of education standards.* 人們預料她的報告會對教育水平予以強烈譴責。

Damo·cles /ˈdæməkliːz/ *noun* IDM see SWORD

damp 0-w /dæmp/ *adj., noun, verb*

■ ***adj.*** 0-w (**damp·er**, **damp·est**) slightly wet, often in a way that is unpleasant 潮濕的；微濕的；濕氣重的：*The cottage was cold and damp.* 這小屋又冷又濕。◇ *It feels damp in here.* 這地方使人感到潮乎乎的。◇ *damp clothes* 潮濕的衣服 ◇ *Wipe the surface with a damp cloth.* 用濕布擦表面。➲ SYNONYMS at WET ▸ **damp·ly** *adv.*: *The blouse clung damply to her skin.* 襯衫濕漉漉地貼在她身上。

IDM **a damp ˈsquib** (*BrE, informal*) an event that is disappointing because it is not as exciting or impressive as expected 啞炮；令人失望的事；令人掃興的事

■ ***noun*** [U] (*BrE*) the state of being damp; areas on a wall, etc. that are damp 潮濕；潮氣；濕氣；濕塊：*The old house smells of damp.* 這老房子散發出一股潮氣。◇ *Those marks above the window look like damp to me.* 窗子上面的那些印跡看上去像是水漬。

■ ***verb*** **~ sth** = DAMPEN：*She damped a towel and wrapped it round his leg.* 她弄濕毛巾，把它裹在他的腿上。

PHR V **ˌdamp ˈdown sth** to make an emotion or a feeling less strong 抑制，控制（情緒、感情等）**ˌdamp sth↔ˈdown** to make a fire burn more slowly or stop burning 使（火）減弱；滅火

ˈdamp course (also **ˈdamp-proof course**) *noun* (both *BrE*) a layer of material near the bottom of a wall that is used to stop damp rising from the ground（牆腳的）防潮層

damp·en /ˈdæmpən/ *verb* **1** (also *less frequent* **damp**) **~ sth** to make sth slightly wet 弄濕；使潮濕：*Perspiration dampened her face and neck.* 她的臉和脖子都汗津津的。◇ *He dampened his hair to make it lie flat.* 他把頭髮弄濕，梳得平平的。**2 ~ sth** to make sth such as a feeling or a reaction less strong 抑制，控制，減弱（感情、反應等）：*None of the setbacks could **dampen his enthusiasm** for the project.* 任何挫折都不能減弱他對這個項目的熱情。◇ *She wasn't going to let anything **dampen her spirits** today.* 她不想讓任何事情來影響她今天的興致。

damp·er /ˈdæmpə(r)/ *noun* **1** a piece of metal that can be moved to allow more or less air into a fire so that the fire burns more or less strongly（調節空氣流量，控制爐火燃燒的）風門，氣閘，擋板 **2** a device in a piano that is used to reduce the level of the sound produced（鋼琴的）制音器，減音器

IDM **put a ˈdamper on sth** (*BrE* also **put a ˈdampener on sth**) (*informal*) to make sth less enjoyable, successful, etc. 抑制；使掃興；使沮喪

damp·ness /ˈdæmpnəs/ *noun* [U] the fact or state of being damp 潮濕：*To avoid dampness, air the room regularly.* 為避免潮濕，房間要經常通風。

ˈdamp-proof course *noun* = DAMP COURSE

dam·sel /ˈdæmzl/ *noun* (*old use*) a young woman who is not married 少女；姑娘；閨女

IDM **a ˌdamsel in diˈstress** (*humorous*) a woman who needs help 落難女子；需要幫助的女子

dam·sel·fly /ˈdæmzlflaɪ/ *noun* (*pl.* **-ies**) an insect with a long thin body and two pairs of wings 豆娘

dam·son /ˈdæmzn/ *noun* a small purple fruit, like a PLUM 西洋李子（果實呈紫色，類似李子）：*a damson tree* 西洋李子樹

dan /dæn/ *noun* **1** one of the levels in KARATE or JUDO（空手道或柔道的）段 **2** a person who has reached a particular level in KARATE or JUDO 入段的空手道（或柔道）選手

dance 0-w /dɑːns; *NAmE* dæns/ *noun, verb*

■ ***noun*** **1** 0-w [C] a series of movements and steps that are usually performed to music; a particular example of these movements and steps 舞蹈；舞步：*a **dance class/routine*** 舞蹈課；一套舞蹈動作 ◇ *Find a partner and practise these new **dance steps**.* 找個舞伴來練習這些新舞步。◇ *Do you know any other Latin American dances?* 你會跳其他拉美舞蹈嗎？◇ *The next dance will be a waltz.* 接下來是華爾茲舞。**2** 0-w [U] the art of dancing, especially for entertainment 舞蹈（藝術）：*an evening of drama, music and dance* 戲劇、音樂和舞蹈晚會 ◇ ***modern/classical dance*** 現代／古典舞蹈 ◇ *a **dance company/troupe*** 舞蹈團／隊 **3** 0-w [C] an act of dancing 跳舞：*Let's have a dance.* 咱們跳個舞吧。◇ *He did a little dance of triumph.* 他興高采烈地跳了幾步舞。**4** 0-w [C] a social event at which people dance 舞會：*We hold a dance every year to raise money for charity.* 我們每年舉行一場舞會，為慈善事業募捐。**5** 0-w [C] a piece of music for dancing to 舞曲：*The band finished with a few slow dances.* 樂隊最後演奏了幾首節奏緩慢的舞曲。

IDM see LEAD[1] *v.*, SONG

■ ***verb*** **1** 0-w [I] to move your body to the sound and rhythm of music 跳舞：*Do you want to dance?* 你想跳舞嗎？◇ *He asked me to dance.* 他邀請我跳舞。◇ *They stayed up all night singing and dancing.* 他們唱啊，跳啊，一宿沒睡。◇ *They danced to the music of a string quartet.* 他們隨着弦樂四重奏樂曲跳舞。◇ *Ruth danced all evening with Richard.* 整個晚上魯思都和理查德跳舞。◇ *Ruth and Richard danced together all evening.* 魯思和理查德整晚都在一起跳舞。**2** 0-w [T] **~ sth** to do a particular type of dance 跳…舞：*to dance the tango* 跳探戈舞 ◇ *to dance a waltz* 跳華爾茲舞 **3** [I] to move in a lively way 跳躍；雀躍；輕快地移動：*The children danced around her.* 孩子們在她周圍蹦蹦跳跳。◇ *The sun shone on the sea and the waves danced and sparkled.* 太陽照在海面上，碧浪翻滾，波光粼粼。◇ *The words danced before her tired eyes.* 這些字在她疲乏的眼前晃動。

IDM **ˌdance atˈtendance on sb** (*BrE, formal*) to be with sb and do things to help and please them 討好；奉承；迎合 **ˌdance the ˈnight away** to dance for the whole evening or night 整夜（或通宵達旦）跳舞 **dance to sb's ˈtune** (*BrE*) to do whatever sb tells you to 聽從某人的指揮；唯命是從；言聽計從

ˈdance band *noun* a group of musicians who play music at dances 伴舞樂隊

ˈdance floor *noun* an area where people can dance in a hotel, restaurant, etc.（旅館、餐廳等供客人跳舞的）舞場，舞池

ˈdance hall *noun* a large public room where people pay to go and dance (more common in the past than now) 舞廳（營業性的，此義稍舊）➲ compare BALLROOM

dan·cer 0-w /ˈdɑːnsə(r); *NAmE* ˈdæn-/ *noun* a person who dances or whose job is dancing 跳舞者；舞蹈演員：*She's a fantastic dancer.* 她的舞跳得非常好。◇ *He's a dancer with the Royal Ballet.* 他是皇家芭蕾舞團的舞蹈演員。

dan·cing 0-w /ˈdɑːnsɪŋ; *NAmE* ˈdæn-/ *noun* [U] moving your body to music 跳舞；舞蹈：*dancing classes* 舞蹈課 ◇ *There was music and dancing till two in the morning.* 音樂和舞蹈一直持續到凌晨兩點。➲ see also COUNTRY DANCING at COUNTRY DANCE, LAP DANCING, POLE DANCING, TABLE DANCING

ˌD and ˈC *abbr.* DILATATION AND CURETTAGE 刮宮術

dan·delion /ˈdændɪlaɪən/ *noun* a small wild plant with a bright yellow flower that becomes a soft white ball of seeds called a **dandelion clock** 蒲公英 ➲ VISUAL VOCAB page V11

dan·di·fied /ˈdændɪfaɪd/ *adj.* (*old-fashioned, disapproving*) (of a man 男子) caring a lot about his clothes and appearance 講究衣着和外表的；好打扮的；油頭粉面的

dan·dle /ˈdændl/ *verb* **~ sb** (*old-fashioned*) to play with a baby or young child by moving them up and down on your knee 搖逗（放在膝上的孩子）

dan·druff /ˈdændrʌf/ *noun* [U] very small pieces of dead skin, seen as a white dust in a person's hair 頭皮屑

dandy /ˈdændi/ *noun, adj.*
■ **noun** (*pl.* **-ies**) (*old-fashioned*) a man who cares a lot about his clothes and appearance 講究衣着和外表的男人；好打扮的男人
■ **adj.** (*old-fashioned, especially NAmE*) very good 非常好的；極佳的

dang /dæŋ/ *adj., exclamation* (*NAmE, informal*) a mild swear word, used instead of DAMN 倒霉，該死（婉辭，與 damn 同義）: *It's just dang stupid!* 簡直太愚蠢了！

dan·ger 0→ /ˈdeɪndʒə(r)/ *noun*
1 0→ [U] **~ (of sth)** the possibility of sth happening that will injure, harm or kill sb, or damage or destroy sth 危險；風險：*Danger! Keep Out!* 危險！請勿入內！◇ *Children's lives are* ***in danger*** *every time they cross this road.* 孩子們每次過這條馬路都面臨着生命危險。◇ *Doctors said she is now* ***out of danger*** (= not likely to die). 醫生說她已脫離危險。**2** 0→ [C, U] the possibility of sth bad or unpleasant happening（壞事或不快之事發生的）可能性，危險：*There is no danger of a bush fire now.* 目前沒有山林大火之虞。◇ **~ of sth** *The building is* ***in danger of*** *collapsing.* 這棟建築有垮塌的危險。◇ *How many factory workers are* ***in danger of*** *losing their jobs?* 有多少產業工人可能失業？◇ *'Nicky won't find out, will she?' 'Oh, no, there's no danger of that.'* "尼基不會察覺吧，會嗎？" "不會，絕對不會的。" ◇ **~ that …** *There is a danger that the political disorder of the past will return.* 昔日的政治動亂可能會重演。**3** 0→ [C] **~ (to sb/sth)** a person or thing that may cause damage, or harm sb 危險的人；危險因素；危害；威脅：*Smoking is a serious danger to health.* 吸煙嚴重危害健康。◇ *Police said the man was a danger to the public.* 警方說這個男人對公眾是個危險。◇ *the hidden dangers in your home* 家裏潛在的危險因素 ➲ see also ENDANGER
IDM **be on/off the ˈdanger list** (*BrE*) to be so ill/sick that you may die; to no longer be very ill/sick 病危；病入膏肓；病勢危急（或好轉）；（病人）轉危為安

ˈdanger money (*BrE*) (*US* **ˈhazard pay**, **ˈdanger pay**) *noun* [U] extra pay for doing work that is dangerous 危險工作津貼

dan·ger·ous 0→ /ˈdeɪndʒərəs/ *adj.*
likely to injure or harm sb, or to damage or destroy sth 有危險的；引起危險的；不安全的：*a dangerous road/illness/sport* 危險的道路／疾病／運動 ◇ *dangerous levels of carbon monoxide* 達到危險程度的一氧化碳含量 ◇ *The prisoners who escaped are violent and dangerous.* 這些逃犯殘暴而危險。◇ *The situation is* ***highly dangerous***. 形勢十分危急。◇ (*BrE*) *a conviction for dangerous driving* 判危險駕駛罪 ◇ **~ for sb** *The traffic here is very dangerous for children.* 這裏的交通對孩子很危險。◇ **~ for sb to do sth** *It would be dangerous for you to stay here.* 你待在這兒不安全。▶ **dan·ger·ous·ly** *adv.*：*She was standing dangerously close to the fire.* 她站得離火太近，有危險。◇ *His father is dangerously ill* (= so ill that he might die). 他父親病情很危險。◇ *Mel enjoys living dangerously* (= doing things that involve risk or danger). 梅爾喜歡冒險活動。
IDM **dangerous ˈground** a situation or subject that is likely to make sb angry, or that involves risk 令人氣憤的場合（或話題）；危險處境：*We'd be* ***on dangerous ground*** *if we asked about race or religion.* 我們要是問到種族或宗教問題，就很可能會冒犯人。

dan·gle /ˈdæŋɡl/ *verb* **1** [I] **(+adv./prep.)** to hang or swing freely 懸垂；懸掛；懸盪；懸擺：*Gold charms dangled from her bracelet.* 她的手鐲上掛着許多金飾物。◇ *A single light bulb dangled from the ceiling.* 天花板上孤零零地懸吊着一隻燈泡。◇ *He sat on the edge with his legs dangling over the side.* 他懸垂着雙腿坐在邊緣上。**2** [T] **~ sth** to hold sth so that it hangs or swings freely 提着（某物，任其自然下垂或擺動）；來回擺動着：*She dangled her car keys nervously as she spoke.* 她說話時緊張地晃動着她那串汽車鑰匙。▶ **dan·gly** /ˈdæŋɡli/ *adj.*：*a pair of dangly earrings* 一對耳墜 ➲ VISUAL VOCAB page V65
IDM **keep/leave sb ˈdangling** (*informal*) to keep sb in an uncertain state by not telling them sth that they want to know（不對人言明而）使心裏沒底，使無把握，使拿不準：*She kept him dangling for a week before making her decision.* 她讓他忐忑不安了一個星期才作出決定。
PHR V **ˌdangle sth beˈfore/in ˈfront of sb** to offer sb sth good in order to persuade them to do sth 誘惑；吊胃口

ˌdangling parˈticiple *noun* (*grammar* 語法) a participle that relates to a noun that is not mentioned 懸垂分詞，虛懸分詞（與之相關的名詞沒有出現的分詞）
HELP 'Dangling participles' are not considered correct. In the sentence 'While walking home, my phone rang', 'walking' is a dangling participle. A correct form of the sentence would be 'While I was walking home, my phone rang'. "懸垂分詞"被認為是不正確的。在 While walking home, my phone rang 中，walking 是懸垂分詞。正確句式應是 While I was walking home, my phone rang。

Dan·ish /ˈdeɪnɪʃ/ *adj., noun*
■ **adj.** from or connected with Denmark 丹麥的
■ **noun** **1** [U] the language of Denmark 丹麥語 **2** [C] = DANISH PASTRY

ˌDanish ˈblue *noun* [U] a type of soft cheese with blue parts in it and a strong flavour 丹麥青紋軟乾酪；丹麥藍乳酪

ˌDanish ˈpastry (*especially BrE*) (also **Dan·ish** *NAmE, BrE*) *noun* a sweet cake made of light PASTRY, often containing apple, nuts, etc. and/or covered with ICING 丹麥酥皮甜餅

dank /dæŋk/ *adj.* (especially of a place 尤指地方) damp, cold and unpleasant 陰冷潮濕的；陰濕的：*a dark dank cave* 陰暗潮濕的洞穴 ▶ **dank·ness** *noun* [U]

dap·per /ˈdæpə(r)/ *adj.* (of a man 男人) small with a neat appearance and nice clothes 矮小利落的；衣冠楚楚的

dap·pled /ˈdæpld/ *adj.* marked with spots of colour, or shade 有斑點的；花斑的；斑駁的：*the cool dappled light under the trees* 樹下使人感到涼爽的斑駁的光

dapple grey (*BrE*) (*NAmE* **dapple gray**) /ˌdæpl ˈɡreɪ/ *adj.* (of a horse 馬) grey or white with darker round marks 灰（或白）色帶深色斑點的；菊花青色的 ▶ **dapple grey** *noun*

Darby and Joan /ˌdɑːbi ən ˈdʒəʊn; *NAmE* ˌdɑːrbi ən ˈdʒoʊn/ *noun* [pl.] (*BrE*) a way of referring to an old couple who are happily married 幸福的老夫妻

dare 0→ /deə(r); *NAmE* der/ *verb, noun*
■ **verb** **1** 0→ (not usually used in the progressive tenses 通常不用於進行時) to be brave enough to do sth 敢於；膽敢：*She said it as loudly as she dared.* 她壯着膽子大聲說了出來。◇ **~ (to) do sth** *He didn't dare (to) say what he thought.* 他不敢說出他的想法。◇ *They daren't ask for any more money.* 他們不敢再要錢了。◇ (*literary*) *She dared not breathe a word of it to anybody.* 她對任何人都隻字不敢提及此事。◇ *There was something,* ***dare I say it,*** *a little unusual about him.* 他這人可能有那麼一點怪。**2** [T] to persuade sb to do sth dangerous, difficult or embarrassing so that they can show that they are not afraid 激（某人做某事）；問（某人）有沒有膽量（做某事）；諒（某人）沒膽量（做某事）：**~ sb** *Go on! Take it! I dare you.* 來呀！接受吧！我諒你也不敢。◇ **~ sb to do sth** *Some of the older boys had dared him to do it.* 幾個大男孩激他，問他敢不敢幹這事。➲ note at MODAL
IDM **don't you dare!** (*informal*) used to tell sb strongly not to do sth（讓人絕不要做某事）你敢，諒你不敢：*'I'll tell her about it.' 'Don't you dare!'* "我要把這事告訴她。" "你敢！" ◇ *Don't you dare say anything to anybody.* 諒你不敢對任何人提起這事兒。**how ˈdare you, etc.** used to show that you are angry about sth that sb has done（表示氣憤）你竟然，你竟敢：*How dare you talk to me like that?* 你竟敢這樣對我說話？◇ *How dare she imply that I was lying?* 她竟敢暗示我在撒謊？**I dare say** (also **I daresay** especially in *BrE*) used when you are saying that sth is probable 我想；很可能；大概：*I dare say you know about it already.* 你大概已經知道了。
■ **noun** [usually sing.] something dangerous, difficult or embarrassing that you try to persuade sb to do, to see if they will do it 激將；挑戰：(*BrE*) *He climbed onto the*

D

roof **for a dare**. 他受到激將才爬上房頂。◇ (*NAmE*) *She learned to fly* **on a dare**. 她在激將下學會了駕駛飛機。

Grammar Point 語法說明

dare

- **Dare** (sense 1) usually forms negatives and questions like an ordinary verb and is followed by an infinitive with *to*. It is most common in the negative. * dare（第 1 義）通常與一般動詞一樣構成否定式和疑問式，後接帶 to 的動詞不定式，最常用於否定句中：*I didn't dare to ask.* 我不敢問。◇ *He won't dare to break his promise.* 他不敢食言。◇ *You told him? How did you dare?* 你告訴他了？你竟敢？◇ *I hardly dared to hope she'd remember me.* 我幾乎不敢指望她會記得我。In positive sentences a phrase like **not be afraid** is often used instead. 在肯定句中常用 not be afraid 代替：*She wasn't afraid* (= she dared) *to tell him the truth.* 她敢對他講實話。
- It can also be used like a modal verb especially in present tense negative forms in *BrE*, and is followed by an infinitive without *to*. * dare 亦可以情態動詞方式使用，尤其在英式英語中的現在時否定式，後接不帶 to 的動詞不定式：*I daren't tell her the truth.* 我不敢對她講實話。
- In spoken English, the forms of the ordinary verb are often used with an infinitive without *to*. 在英語口語中，此普通動詞的各種形式常與不帶 to 的不定式連用：*Don't you dare tell her what I said!* 諒你不敢告訴她我說的話！◇ *I didn't dare look at him.* 我不敢看他。

dare·devil /ˈdeədevl; *NAmE* ˈderd-/ *noun* a person who enjoys doing dangerous things, in a way that other people may think is stupid 魯莽大膽的人；蠻幹的人；冒失鬼：*a reckless daredevil* 輕舉妄動的冒失鬼 ▸ **dare·devil** *adj.* [only before noun]：*Don't try any daredevil stunts.* 別去做那些玩兒命的驚險動作。

dar·ing /ˈdeərɪŋ; *NAmE* ˈder-/ *adj., noun*
■ ***adj.*** brave; willing to do dangerous or unusual things; involving danger or taking risks 勇敢的；敢於冒險的：*a daring walk in space* 勇敢的太空漫步 ◇ *There are plenty of activities at the resort for the less daring.* 度假勝地有許多活動是供不太敢於冒險的人玩的。◇ *The gallery was known for putting on daring exhibitions.* 陳列館以其別具一格的展品而享有盛名。◇ *a daring strapless dress in black silk* 大膽袒露的黑綢無吊帶連衣裙 ▸ **dar·ing·ly** *adv.*
■ ***noun*** [U] courage and the willingness to take risks 大膽；勇敢；膽量：*the skill and daring of the mountain climbers* 登山者的技能和膽量

dark 🔑 /dɑːk; *NAmE* dɑːrk/ *adj., noun*
■ ***adj.*** (**dark·er**, **dark·est**)
▸ WITH LITTLE LIGHT 光線暗淡 **1** 🔑 with no or very little light, especially because it is night 黑暗的；昏暗的；陰暗的：*a dark room/street/forest* 黑暗的房間；昏暗的街道；黑黝黝的森林 ◇ *What time does it* **get dark** *in summer?* 夏天什麼時候天黑？◇ *It was dark outside and I couldn't see much.* 外面很黑，我看不清。OPP **light**
▸ COLOURS 顏色 **2** 🔑 not light; closer in shade to black than to white 深色的；暗色的：***dark blue/green/red, etc.*** 深藍色、墨綠色、深紅色等 ◇ *Darker colours are more practical and don't show stains.* 深色不顯髒，更實用。OPP **light, pale** **3** 🔑 having a colour that is close to black 近乎黑色的：*a dark suit* 深色的西服 ◇ *dark-coloured wood* 深色木材 ◇ *The dark clouds in the sky meant that a storm was coming.* 天空中的烏雲預示暴風雨即將來臨。
▸ HAIR/SKIN/EYES 頭髮；皮膚；眼睛 **4** 🔑 brown or black in colour 褐色的；黝黑的；烏黑的：*Sue has long dark hair.* 蘇留着長長的黑髮。◇ *Even if you have dark skin, you still need protection from the sun.* 即使你皮膚黝黑，仍需要防曬。 **5** 🔑 (of a person 人) having dark hair, eyes, etc. 有深色頭髮（或眼睛等）的：*a dark handsome stranger* 黑頭髮、黑眼睛的英俊陌生人 OPP **fair**
▸ MYSTERIOUS 神秘 **6** 🔑 mysterious; hidden and not known about 神秘的；隱秘的；隱藏的：*There are no dark secrets in our family.* 我們家沒有隱秘。
▸ EVIL 邪惡 **7** evil or frightening 邪惡的；陰險的；兇惡的：*There was a darker side to his nature.* 他本性中還有陰險的一面。◇ *the dark forces of the imagination* 幻想中的邪惡勢力
▸ WITHOUT HOPE 無希望 **8** unpleasant and without any hope that sth good will happen 憂鬱的；不快的；無望的：*the darkest days of Fascism* 法西斯統治下最黑暗的日子 ◇ *The film is a dark vision of the future.* 這部影片預示着黯淡無光的未來。
▸ PHONETICS 語音學 **9** (of a speech sound 語音) produced with the back part of the tongue close to the back of the mouth. In many accents of English, dark /l/ is used after a vowel, as in *ball*. 暗的 OPP **clear**
IDM **a dark ˈhorse** **1** (*BrE*) a person who does not tell other people much about their life, and who surprises other people by having interesting qualities 深藏不露的人 **2** a person taking part in a race, etc. who surprises everyone by winning 出人意料的獲勝者；黑馬 **keep sth ˈdark** (*BrE, informal*) to keep sth secret and not tell people about it 對…保密；隱瞞；隱藏
■ ***noun***
▸ NO LIGHT 無光 **1** 🔑 **the dark** [sing.] the lack of light in a place, especially because it is night 黑暗；暗處：*All the lights went out and we were left* **in the dark**. 燈全熄了，我們周圍一片黑暗。◇ *Are the children afraid of the dark?* 孩子們怕黑嗎？◇ *animals that can see in the dark* 在黑暗中能看見東西的動物
▸ COLOUR 顏色 **2** 🔑 [U] an amount of sth that is dark in colour 暗色；陰影：*patterns of light and dark* 明暗相間的圖案
IDM **after/before dark** after/before the sun goes down and it is night 天黑後／前；黃昏後／前：*Try to get home before dark.* 盡量在天黑前回家。◇ *Don't go out alone after dark.* 天黑後不要單獨外出。 **in the ˈdark (about sth)** knowing nothing about sth（對某事）全然不知：*Workers were kept in the dark about the plans to sell the company.* 工人全然不知出售公司的計劃。◇ *She arrived at the meeting as much in the dark as everyone else.* 她到會時與其他人一樣毫不知情。 **a shot/stab in the ˈdark** a guess; sth you do without knowing what the result will be 瞎猜；盲動；盲幹：*The figure he came up with was really just a shot in the dark.* 他得出的數字實際上只是瞎猜而已。➲ more at LEAP *n.*

the ˈdark ages *noun* [pl.] **1** **the Dark Ages** the period of European history between the end of the Roman Empire and the 10th century AD 黑暗時代（歐洲歷史上從羅馬帝國衰亡至公元 10 世紀的時期） **2** (often *humorous*) a period of history or a time when sth was not developed or modern 不發達的歷史時期：*Back in the dark ages of computing, in about 1980, they started a software company.* 早在計算機尚未普及的時代（約 1980 年），他們就創辦了軟件公司。

ˈdark chocolate (*BrE* also **ˈplain chocolate**) *noun* [U] dark brown chocolate with a slightly bitter taste, made without milk being added 純巧克力 ➲ compare MILK CHOCOLATE

dark·en /ˈdɑːkən; *NAmE* ˈdɑːrk-/ *verb* **1** [I, T] to become dark; to make sth dark（使）變暗，變黑：*The sky began to darken as the storm approached.* 暴風雨來臨時天空變得黑沉沉的。◇ **~ sth** *We walked quickly through the darkened streets.* 我們快步穿過黑魆魆的街道。◇ *a darkened room* 變暗了的房間 **2** [I, T] to become unhappy or angry; to make sb unhappy or angry（使）憂鬱，生氣，不快：*Her mood darkened at the news.* 聽到這消息，她的心情暗淡起來。◇ *Luke's face darkened* (= he looked angry). 盧克沉下臉來。◇ **~ sth** *It was a tragedy that darkened his later life.* 這場悲劇給他後來的歲月蒙上了陰影。
IDM **never darken my ˈdoor again** (*old-fashioned, humorous*) used to tell sb never to come to your home again 再不要跨進我的門檻；再不許踏進我的家門

ˌdark ˈglasses *noun* [pl.] glasses that have dark-coloured LENSES 墨鏡 ➲ see also SUNGLASSES

darkie /ˈdɑːki; *NAmE* ˈdɑːrki/ *noun* (*taboo, old-fashioned*) a very offensive word for a black person（蔑稱）黑人，黑鬼

dark·ling /ˈdɑːklɪŋ; *NAmE* ˈdɑːrk-/ *adj.* (*literary*) becoming dark or connected with the dark 漸暗的；昏暗的；黑暗的：*the darkling sky* 漸暗的天空

dark·ly /ˈdɑːkli; *NAmE* ˈdɑːrk-/ *adv.* **1** in a threatening or unpleasant way 威脅地；險惡地；負面地：*He hinted darkly that all was not well.* 他悲觀地暗示並非一切都順利。 **2** showing a dark colour 漆黑地；烏黑地：*Her eyes burned darkly.* 她的眼裏滿是怒火。

ˌdark ˈmatter *noun* [U] (*astronomy* 天) according to some theories, material that exists in space but does not reflect any light 暗物質（根據一些理論，指太空中不反射光的物質）

dark·ness /ˈdɑːknəs; *NAmE* ˈdɑːrk-/ *noun* [U] **1** the state of being dark, without any light 黑暗；陰暗；漆黑：*After a few minutes our eyes got used to the darkness.* 幾分鐘後我們的眼睛就適應了黑暗。◇ *The house was plunged into* ***total darkness*** *when the electricity was cut off.* 停電後，整座房子陷入一片黑暗。◇ *The sun went down and* ***darkness fell*** (= it became night). 夕陽西下，夜幕降臨。◇ *There is an extra hour of darkness on winter mornings.* 冬天的早晨天亮晚一個小時。◇ *Parking is not allowed during the* ***hours of darkness****.* 夜間禁止停放車輛。◇ *Her face was* ***in darkness****.* 她的臉處於暗處。◇ *They managed to escape* ***under cover of darkness****.* 他們設法在夜色掩護下逃跑了。 **2** the quality or state of being dark in colour 墨色；暗色；深色：*It depends on the darkness of your skin.* 這取決於你膚色的深淺。 **3** (*literary*) evil 邪惡；罪惡：*the forces of darkness* 邪惡勢力

dark·room /ˈdɑːkruːm; -rʊm; *NAmE* ˈdɑːrk-/ *noun* a room that can be made completely dark, where you can take film out of a camera and develop photographs（沖洗膠片的）暗室

ˌdark ˈstar *noun* (*astronomy* 天) an object in space similar to a star, that produces no light or very little light 暗星（太空中類似星體但不發光的物體）

dar·ling /ˈdɑːlɪŋ; *NAmE* ˈdɑːrlɪŋ/ *noun, adj.*

■ ***noun*** **1** (*informal*) a way of addressing sb that you love 親愛的；寶貝：*What's the matter, darling?* 怎麼啦，親愛的？ **2** a person who is very friendly and kind 親切友好的人：*You are a darling, Hugo.* 雨果，你真好。 **3 the ~ of sb/sth** a person who is especially liked and very popular 備受寵愛的人；寵兒：*She is the darling of the newspapers and can do no wrong.* 她是新聞界的大紅人，不可能做錯事的。

■ ***adj.*** [only before noun] (*informal*) much loved; very attractive, special, etc. 備受喜愛的；可愛的；迷人的：*My darling daughter.* 我的寶貝女兒。◇ *'Darling Henry,' the letter began.* "親愛的亨利"，信的開頭這樣寫道。

darm·stadt·ium /ˈdɑːmʃtætiəm; *NAmE* ˈdɑːrm-/ *noun* [U] (*symb.* **Ds**) a chemical element. Darmstadtium is a RADIOACTIVE element that is produced artificially. 鐽（人造放射性化學元素）

darn /dɑːn; *NAmE* dɑːrn/ *verb, noun, adj., adv.*

■ ***verb*** [T, I] **~ (sth)** to repair a hole in a piece of clothing by sewing STITCHES across the hole 織補；縫補：*to darn socks* 補襪子

IDM **ˈdarn it!** (*informal, especially NAmE*) used as a mild swear word to show that you are angry or annoyed about sth, to avoid saying 'damn' 見鬼，真氣人，真糟糕（婉辭，與 damn 同義）：*Darn it! I've lost my keys!* 真見鬼，我的鑰匙丟了！ **I'll be ˈdarned!** (*informal, especially NAmE*) used to show that you are surprised about sth（表示吃驚）真沒想到，真叫我吃驚

■ ***noun*** a place on a piece of clothing that has been repaired by darning 織補處

■ ***adj.*** (also **darned**) (*informal*) used as a mild swear word, to emphasize sth（加強語氣）該死的，討厭的：*Why don't you switch the darn thing off and listen to me!* 把那討厭的東西關掉，專心聽我講話好不好！

■ ***adv.*** (also **darned**) (*informal*) used as a mild swear word, instead of saying DAMN, to mean 'extremely' or 'very' 極其，非常（婉辭，與 damn 同義）：*You had a darn good try.* 你這一試再好不過了。◇ *It's darn cold tonight.* 今天晚上冷得要命。

darned /dɑːnd; *NAmE* dɑːrnd/ *adj., adv.* = DARN：*That's a darned good idea!* 這真是絕妙的好主意！ ▸ **darned·est** *adj.*

dart /dɑːt; *NAmE* dɑːrt/ *noun, verb*

■ ***noun*** **1** [C] a small pointed object, sometimes with feathers to help it fly, that is shot as a weapon or thrown in the game of darts 鏢；飛鏢：*a poisoned dart* 有毒的飛鏢 ➲ VISUAL VOCAB page V40 **2 darts** [U] a game in which darts are thrown at a round board marked with numbers for scoring. Darts is often played in British pubs. 擲鏢遊戲（常見於英國酒吧裏）：*a darts match* 擲鏢賽 ➲ VISUAL VOCAB page V40 **3** [sing.] a sudden quick movement 猛衝；突進；飛奔 SYN **dash**：*She* ***made a dart for*** *the door.* 她朝門口衝去。 **4** [sing.] (*literary*) a sudden feeling of a strong emotion 突發的強烈情感：*Nina felt a sudden dart of panic.* 尼娜突然感到一陣恐慌。 **5** [C] a pointed fold that is sewn in a piece of clothing to make it fit better 省縫，縫褶（為使衣服更合身而在衣料上縫去的部份）

■ ***verb*** **1** [I] **+ adv./prep.** to move suddenly and quickly in a particular direction 猛衝；突進；飛奔：*A dog darted across the road in front of me.* 一條狗突然在我面前竄過馬路。◇ *Her eyes darted around the room, looking for Greg.* 她迅速環視了一下房間，尋找格雷格。 **2** [T] to look at sb suddenly and quickly（朝某人猛然）看，瞥：**~ a glance/look (at sb)** *He darted an impatient look at Vicky.* 他不耐煩地朝維基瞥了一眼。◇ **~ sb a glance/look** *He darted Vicky an impatient look.* 他不耐煩地瞥了維基一眼。

dart·board /ˈdɑːtbɔːd; *NAmE* ˈdɑːrtbɔːrd/ *noun* a round board used in the game of darts（擲鏢遊戲的）圓靶 ➲ VISUAL VOCAB page V40

Dar·win·ism /ˈdɑːwɪnɪzəm; *NAmE* ˈdɑːr-/ *noun* [U] (*biology* 生) the theory that living things EVOLVE by NATURAL SELECTION, developed by Charles Darwin in the 19th century 達爾文主義，達爾文學說（查爾斯•達爾文於 19 世紀創立的學說，認為生物通過自然選擇而進化）▸ **Dar·win·ian** /dɑːˈwɪniən; *NAmE* dɑːr-/ *adj.*：*Darwinian ideas* 達爾文思想

dash /dæʃ/ *noun, verb*

■ ***noun***

▸ STH DONE QUICKLY 匆忙做完的事 **1** [sing.] **a ~ (for sth)** an act of going somewhere suddenly and/or quickly 猛衝；突進；急奔：*When the doors opened, there was a* ***mad dash*** *for seats.* 門一開，人們便瘋狂地朝座位奔去。◇ *a 60-mile dash to safety* 急奔 60 英里到達安全的地方◇ *He jumped off the bus and* ***made a dash for*** *the nearest bar.* 他跳下公共汽車直奔近處的酒吧。◇ *We waited for the police to leave then* ***made a dash for it*** (= left quickly in order to escape). 我們等警察離開後便迅速逃走。 **2** [sing.] an act of doing sth quickly because you do not have enough time 匆忙；匆促；倉促：*a last-minute dash to buy presents* 利用最後一點時間匆忙買禮物

▸ SMALL AMOUNT 少量 **3** [C, usually sing.] **~ (of sth)** a small amount of sth that is added to sth else 少量，少許（添加物）：*Add a dash of lemon juice.* 加少量檸檬汁。◇ *The rug adds a dash of colour to the room.* 小地毯為房間增添了點色彩。➲ compare SPLASH *n.* (4)

▸ SYMBOL 符號 **4** [C] the mark (—) used to separate parts of a sentence, often instead of a colon or in pairs instead of brackets/parentheses 破折號 ➲ compare HYPHEN

▸ RACE 賽跑 **5** [C, usually sing.] (*especially NAmE*) a race in which the people taking part run very fast over a short distance 短跑 SYN **sprint**：*the 100-meter dash* 百米賽跑

▸ WAY OF BEHAVING 行為舉止 **6** [U] (*old-fashioned, approving*) a way of behaving that combines style, enthusiasm and confidence 氣魄；活力；衝勁；銳氣

▸ PART OF CAR 汽車部件 **7** [C] (*informal*) = DASHBOARD ➲ see also PEBBLE-DASH

IDM **cut a ˈdash** (*BrE*) to look attractive in a particular set of clothes, especially in a way that makes other

D

people notice you（穿上某套衣服後）風度翩翩，引人注目：*He cut quite a dash in his uniform.* 他穿着這身制服顯得特帥。

■ *verb*

▸ GO QUICKLY 急衝 **1** [I] to go somewhere very quickly 急奔；急馳；猛衝 SYN **rush**：*I must dash* (= leave quickly), *I'm late.* 我得趕緊走，來不及了。◇ **+ adv./prep.** *She dashed off to keep an appointment.* 她急匆匆地趕去赴約。◇ *He dashed along the platform and jumped on the train.* 他沿站台猛跑，縱身跳上火車。

▸ THROW/BEAT 投擲；擊打 **2** [T, I] to throw sth or make sth fall violently onto a hard surface; to beat against a surface 猛擲；猛擊；猛撞：**~ sth + adv./prep.** *The boat was dashed repeatedly against the rocks.* 小船一次又一次撞在岩石上。◇ **+ adv./prep.** *The waves were dashing against the harbour wall.* 海浪撞擊着港灣的堤。

IDM **dash sb's 'hopes** to destroy sb's hopes by making what they were hoping for impossible 使某人的希望化為泡影（或破滅）**dash (it)! | dash it all!** (*old-fashioned, BrE*) used to show that you are annoyed about sth（表示厭煩）真見鬼，真糟糕，真混賬

PHR V **,dash sth↔'off** to write or draw sth very quickly 倉促寫出；草草畫成：*I dashed off a note to my brother.* 我急急忙忙給我弟弟寫了個字條。

dash·board /ˈdæʃbɔːd; *NAmE* -bɔːrd/ (also **fa·scia**) (also *informal* **dash** especially in *NAmE*) *noun* the part of a car in front of the driver that has instruments and controls in it（汽車上的）儀表板 ➲ VISUAL VOCAB page V52

dash·ed /dæʃt/ *adj.* [only before noun] (*BrE, old-fashioned, informal*) used as a mild swear word by some people to emphasize sth or to show they are annoyed（表示強調或不耐煩）該死的，討厭的

dash·iki /ˈdɑːʃɪki/ *noun* a loose shirt or longer piece of clothing worn by men in W Africa, often made from cloth with brightly coloured patterns 達西基（西非男子穿的花哨而寬鬆的襯衫或套衫）

dash·ing /ˈdæʃɪŋ/ *adj.* (*old-fashioned*) **1** (usually of a man 通常指男人) attractive, confident and elegant 風度翩翩的；自信的；瀟灑的：*a dashing young officer* 風度翩翩的年輕軍官 ◇ *his dashing good looks* 他英俊瀟灑的容貌 **2** (of a thing 物品) attractive and fashionable 時髦的；流行的：*his dashing red waistcoat* 他時髦的紅背心

das·tard·ly /ˈdæstədli; *NAmE* -tərd-/ *adj.* (*old-fashioned*) evil and cruel 邪惡殘忍的：*My first part was Captain O'Hagarty, a dastardly villain in a children's play.* 我演的第一個角色是奧哈格蒂船長，一部兒童劇中的惡棍。

DAT /dæt/ *abbr.* DIGITAL AUDIOTAPE

data 0➔ AW /ˈdeɪtə; *BrE* also ˈdɑːtə; *NAmE* also ˈdætə/ *noun* (used as a plural noun in technical English, when the singular is *datum* 在科技英語中用作複數名詞，其單數形式是 datum) **1** 0➔ [U, pl.] facts or information, especially when examined and used to find out things or to make decisions 數據；資料；材料：*This data was collected from 69 countries.* 這資料是從 69 個國家收集來的。◇ *the analysis/interpretation of the data* 數據分析 / 解讀 ◇ *raw data* (= that has not been analysed) 原始資料 ◇ *demographical/historical/personal data* 人口統計資料；史料；個人資料 ◇ (*technical* 術語) *These data show that most cancers are detected as a result of clinical follow-up.* 這些數據表明多數癌症是由臨牀隨訪查出的。➲ COLLOCATIONS at SCIENTIFIC **2** 0➔ [U] information that is stored by a computer（貯存在計算機中的）數據資料：*data retrieval* (= ways of storing or finding information on a computer) 數據檢索

data·bank /ˈdeɪtəbæŋk; *NAmE* also ˈdætə-/ *noun* a large amount of data on a particular subject that is stored in a computer（貯存在計算機中某一題材的）數據庫，資料庫

data·base /ˈdeɪtəbeɪs; *NAmE* also ˈdætə-/ *noun* an organized set of data that is stored in a computer and can be looked at and used in various ways（貯存在計算機中的）數據庫，資料庫

,database 'management system *noun* (*abbr.* **DBMS**) (*computing* 計) a system for organizing and managing a large amount of data 數據庫管理系統；資料庫管理系統

dat·able /ˈdeɪtəbl/ *adj.* that can be dated to a particular time 可測定日期的；可確定年代的：*pottery that is datable to the second century* 可確定產於 2 世紀的陶器

'data capture *noun* [U] the action or process of collecting data, especially using computers 數據獲取，數據搜集，資料擷取（尤指利用計算機）

'data mining *noun* [U] (*computing* 計) looking at large amounts of information that has been collected on a computer and using it to provide new information 數據採集；數據挖掘

,data 'processing *noun* [U] (*computing* 計) a series of actions that a computer performs on data to produce an output 數據處理

'data projector (also **projector**) *noun* a piece of equipment that takes data and images from a computer and shows them on a wall or large screen 數碼放映機；數碼投影儀；數位投影機 ➲ compare OVERHEAD PROJECTOR, PROJECTOR, SLIDE PROJECTOR ➲ VISUAL VOCAB page V69

,data pro'tection *noun* [U] legal restrictions that keep information stored on computers private and that control who can read it or use it 數據保護

'data set *noun* (*computing* 計) a collection of data which is treated as a single unit by a computer 數據集；資料集

'data warehouse *noun* a large amount of data which comes from different parts of a business and which is stored together 數據倉庫，數據倉貯，資料倉貯（彙集企業各部門信息的大量數據）

date 0➔ /deɪt/ *noun, verb*

■ *noun*

▸ PARTICULAR DAY 日期 **1** 0➔ [C] a particular day of the month, sometimes in a particular year, given in numbers and words 日期；日子：*'What's the date today?' 'The 10th.'* "今天幾號？" "10 號。" ◇ *Write **today's date** at the top of the page.* 在頁面頂端寫上今天的日期。◇ *We need to **fix a date** for the next meeting.* 我們得為下次會議定個日期。◇ *They haven't **set a date** for the wedding yet.* 他們尚未確定舉行婚禮的日期。◇ *I can't come on that date.* 那個日子我來不了。◇ *Please give your name, address and **date of birth**.* 請報姓名、地址和出生日期。◇ (*especially NAmE*) *name, address and **birth date*** 姓名、地址和出生日期 ◇ *There's no date on this letter.* 這封信未註明日期。➲ see also BEST-BEFORE DATE, CLOSING DATE, SELL-BY DATE

▸ PAST TIME/FUTURE 過去；將來 **2** 0➔ [sing., U] a time in the past or future that is not a particular day 年代；時期；時候：*The details can be added **at a later date**.* 細節可過些時候再補充進去。◇ *The work will be carried out **at a future date**.* 這項工作將來再做。◇ *a building of late Roman date* 羅馬時代後期的建築

▸ ARRANGEMENT TO MEET 約見 **3** 0➔ [C] (*BrE*) an arrangement to meet sb at a particular time 會晤時間；約見時間：*Call me next week and we'll try and **make a date**.* 下週打電話給我，我們爭取定個見面時間。

▸ ROMANTIC MEETING 異性約會 **4** 0➔ [C] a meeting that you have arranged with a boyfriend or girlfriend or with sb who might become a boyfriend or girlfriend 約會；幽會：*I've got a date with Lucy tomorrow night.* 明天晚上我與露西有個約會。◇ *Paul's not coming. He's got a **hot date*** (= an exciting one). 保羅不來了。他有一個朝思夜盼的幽會。➲ COLLOCATIONS at MARRIAGE ➲ see also BLIND DATE, DOUBLE DATE **5** [C] (*especially NAmE*) a boyfriend or girlfriend with whom you have arranged a date 約會對象：*My date is meeting me at seven.* 我的對象七點鐘與我見面。

▸ FRUIT 果實 **6** [C] a sweet sticky brown fruit that grows on a tree called a **date palm**, common in N Africa and W Asia（北非和西亞常見的海棗樹的）海棗

IDM **to 'date** until now 迄今為止；到目前為止；直到現在：*To date, we have received over 200 replies.* 到目前為止，我們已收到 200 多封回信。◇ *The exhibition contains some of his best work to date.* 這個展覽有他迄今為止一些最好的作品。➲ see also OUT OF DATE, UP TO DATE

■ *verb*
▸ WRITE DATE 寫日期 **1** 🔑 [T] **~ sth** to write or print the date on sth 註明日期；寫上日期： *Thank you for your letter dated 24th March.* 你 3 月 24 日來函收悉，謝謝。
▸ FIND AGE 確定年代 **2** 🔑 [T] **~ sth (at/to sth)** to say when sth old existed or was made 確定年代： *The skeleton has been dated at about 2 000 BC.* 這骨架的年代為公元前 2000 年左右。
▸ OF CLOTHES/WORDS 衣服；詞語 **3** [I] to become old-fashioned 過時；不流行： *She designs classic clothes which do not date.* 她設計的典雅式樣服裝不會過時。
▸ PERSON 人 **4** [T] **~ sb** if sth **dates** you, it shows that you are fairly old or older than the people you are with 使…顯老；顯出…的年齡大： *I was at the Woodstock festival—that dates me, doesn't it?* 我參加了伍德斯托克搖滾音樂節，那說明我老了，是不是？
▸ HAVE RELATIONSHIP 有戀愛關係 **5** [T, I] **~ (sb)** (*especially NAmE*) to have a romantic relationship with sb 與（某人）談戀愛： *She's been dating Ron for several months.* 她與羅恩談戀愛已有數月。

PHR V **ˌdate ˈback (to …)** | **ˈdate from …** 🔑 to have existed since a particular time in the past or for the length of time mentioned 追溯到；始於；自…至今： *The college dates back to medieval times.* 這所學院創辦於中世紀。◇ *The custom dates back hundreds of years.* 這一習俗可以追溯到幾百年前。◇ *a law dating from the 17th century* 自 17 世紀起沿用至今的一條法律

date·book /ˈdeɪtbʊk/ (*NAmE*) (*BrE* **diary**) *noun* a book with spaces for each day of the year in which you can write down things you have to do in the future（工作日程）記事簿 ➲ VISUAL VOCAB page V69

dated /ˈdeɪtɪd/ *adj.* old-fashioned; belonging to a time in the past 過時的；陳舊的 ➲ compare UNDATED

ˈDate Line *noun* = INTERNATIONAL DATE LINE

ˈdate rape *noun* [U] the crime of RAPING sb, committed by a person he or she has gone out with on a DATE 約會強姦（罪）

ˈdating agency (also **ˈdating service**) *noun* a business or an organization that arranges meetings between single people who want to begin a romantic relationship 婚姻介紹所： *He met his wife through a* ***computer dating agency****.* 他是通過電腦紅娘認識他妻子的。

dat·ive /ˈdeɪtɪv/ *noun* (*grammar* 語法) (in some languages 用於某些語言) the form of a noun, a pronoun or an adjective when it is the INDIRECT OBJECT of a verb or is connected with the INDIRECT OBJECT 與格（名詞、代詞或形容詞用作間接賓語時的一種形式）： *In the sentence, 'I sent her a postcard', the word 'her' is* ***in the dative****.* 在 I sent her a postcard 一句中，her 一詞處於與格。➲ compare ABLATIVE, ACCUSATIVE, GENITIVE, LOCATIVE, NOMINATIVE, VOCATIVE ▸ **dat·ive** *adj.*

datum /ˈdeɪtəm/ *noun* (*pl.* **data**) (*technical* 術語) a fact or piece of information 數據；資料 ➲ see also DATA

daub /dɔːb/ *verb, noun*
■ *verb* **~ A on, etc. B** | **~ B with A** | **+ adv./prep.** to spread a substance such as paint, mud, etc. thickly and/or carelessly onto sth（用顏料、油漆、灰泥等）塗抹，亂塗，亂畫： *The walls of the building were daubed with red paint.* 這棟建築的牆上隨意塗了一層紅色塗料。
■ *noun* **1** [U] a mixture of CLAY, etc. that was used in the past for making walls（舊時抹牆用的）粗灰泥： *walls made of* ***wattle and daub*** 用枝條和灰泥做成的牆 **2** [C] a small amount of a substance such as paint that has been spread carelessly（亂塗亂畫的）少量顏料，塗料： *a daub of lipstick* 薄薄一層唇膏 **3** [C] a badly painted picture 拙劣的畫

daugh·ter 🔑 /ˈdɔːtə(r)/ *noun*
1 🔑 a person's female child 女兒： *We have two sons and a daughter.* 我們有兩兒一女。◇ *They have three grown-up daughters.* 他們有三個成年的女兒。◇ *She's the daughter of an Oxford professor.* 她是牛津大學一位教授的女兒。➲ COLLOCATIONS at CHILD ➲ see also GOD-DAUGHTER, GRANDDAUGHTER, STEPDAUGHTER **2** (*literary*) a woman who belongs to a particular place or country, etc.（某地、某國等的）婦女： *one of the town's most famous daughters* 這座城鎮的名媛之一

ˈdaughter-in-law *noun* (*pl.* **daughters-in-law**) the wife of your son 兒媳婦 ➲ compare SON-IN-LAW

daunt /dɔːnt/ *verb* [usually passive] **~ sb** to make sb feel nervous and less confident about doing sth 使膽怯；使氣餒；使失去信心 SYN **intimidate**： *She was a brave woman but she felt daunted by the task ahead.* 她是一個勇敢的女人，但對面前的任務卻感到信心不足。▸ **daunt·ing** *adj.* SYN **intimidating**： *She has the* ***daunting task*** *of cooking for 20 people every day.* 她每天得做 20 個人的飯，這是一項可怕的任務。◇ *Starting a new job can be a* ***daunting prospect****.* 開始一項新工作有時會讓人望而卻步。 **daunt·ing·ly** *adv.*
IDM **nothing ˈdaunted** (*BrE, formal*) confident about sth difficult you have to do 無所畏懼；毫不氣餒： *Nothing daunted, the people set about rebuilding their homes.* 人們毫不氣餒，又開始重建家園。

daunt·less /ˈdɔːntləs/ *adj.* (*literary*) not easily frightened or stopped from doing sth difficult 無所畏懼的；嚇不倒的；勇敢的 SYN **resolute**

dau·phin /ˈdəʊfæ̃; -fæn; *NAmE* ˈdoʊ-/ *noun* (*old use*) the oldest son of the king of France（法國）王太子

David and Goliath /ˌdeɪvɪd ənd ɡəˈlaɪəθ/ *adj.* used to describe a situation in which a small or weak person or organization tries to defeat another much larger or stronger opponent 強弱懸殊；以弱戰強： *The match looks like being a David and Goliath contest.* 比賽看上去像是一場力量懸殊的較量。ORIGIN From the Bible story in which Goliath, a giant, is killed by the boy David with a stone. 源自《聖經》故事，巨人歌利亞被男孩大衛以石擊殺。

daw·dle /ˈdɔːdl/ *verb* [I] to take a long time to do sth or go somewhere 拖延；磨蹭；遊蕩： *Stop dawdling! We're going to be late!* 別磨蹭了，咱們快遲到了！◇ **+ adv./prep.** *They dawdled along by the river, laughing and talking.* 他們沿河邊閒逛，一路談笑風生。

dawn /dɔːn/ *noun, verb*
■ *noun* **1** [U, C] the time of day when light first appears 黎明；拂曉；破曉 SYN **daybreak, sunrise**： *They start work* ***at dawn****.* 天一亮他們就開始幹活了。◇ *It's almost dawn.* 天快亮了。◇ *We arrived in Sydney as* ***dawn broke*** (= as the first light could be seen). 黎明時分我們到達了悉尼。◇ *I woke up just before dawn.* 我正好在拂曉前醒來。◇ *summer's early dawns* 夏日早到的黎明 ◇ *He works* ***from dawn till dusk*** (= from morning till night). 他從早到晚地工作。➲ compare DUSK **2** [sing.] **~ (of sth)** the beginning or first signs of sth 開端；曙光；萌芽： *the* ***dawn of civilization/time/history*** 文明／時代／歷史的開端 ◇ *Peace marked a new dawn in the country's history.* 和平使這個國家的歷史翻開了新的一頁。IDM see BREAK *n.*, CRACK *n.*
■ *verb* **1** [I] (of a day or a period of time 一天或一個時期) to begin 開始： *The following morning dawned bright and warm.* 第二天一大早陽光和煦。◇ *A new technological age had dawned.* 新技術時代已經開始。 **2** [I] to become obvious or easy to understand 變得明朗；開始清楚： *Slowly the awful truth dawned.* 可怕的事實慢慢地清晰起來。IDM see LIGHT *n.*
PHR V **ˈdawn on sb** [no passive] if sth **dawns on you**, you begin to realize it for the first time 使開始明白；使漸漸領悟；使開始理解： **it dawns on sb that …** *Suddenly it dawned on me that they couldn't possibly have met before.* 我突然明白他們以前不可能見過面。

the ˌdawn ˈchorus *noun* [sing.] (*BrE*) the sound of birds singing very early in the morning 破曉時的鳥鳴聲

day 🔑 /deɪ/ *noun*
1 🔑 [C] a period of 24 hours 一天；一日： *I saw Tom three days ago.* 我三天前見過湯姆。◇ *'What day is it today?' 'Monday.'* "今天星期幾？" "星期一。" ◇ *We're going away* ***in a few days/in a few days' time****.* 我們過幾天就要離開了。◇ *They left* ***the day before yesterday*** (= two days ago). 他們前天就走了。◇ *We're meeting* ***the day after tomorrow*** (= in two days). 我們後天要見面。◇ *New Year's Day* 元旦 ◇ *Take the medicine three times* ***a day****.* 每日服藥三次。◇ *We can't go there today. You can go*

D

another day. 我們今天不能去那兒。你可以改天去。➲ see also FIELD DAY, OFF DAY, RED-LETTER DAY, SPORTS DAY **2** [U] the time between when it becomes light in the morning and when it becomes dark in the evening 白晝；白天：*The sun was shining **all day**.* 白天一直陽光明媚。◇ *I could sit and watch the river **all day long**.* 我可以整天坐在這裏看那條河。◇ *He works at night and sleeps **during the day**.* 他晚上幹活，白天睡覺。◇ *Nocturnal animals sleep **by day** and hunt **by night**.* 夜間活動的動物白天睡覺晚上獵食。 **3** [C, usually sing.] the hours of the day when you are awake, working, etc. 工作日；一天的活動時間：*a seven-hour **working day*** 七小時工作日 ◇ *It's been **a long day*** (= I've been very busy). 忙了一整天了。◇ *Did you have a good day?* 你這一天過得順利嗎？◇ *She didn't do a full **day's work**.* 她並沒幹一整天的工作。◇ *I took a half day off yesterday.* 昨天我休假半天。◇ (*NAmE*) *Have a nice day!* 祝你有愉快的一天！➲ see also WORKDAY **4** [C, usually pl.] a particular period of time or history 時期；時代：*in Queen Victoria's day* 在維多利亞女王時代 ◇ *the **early days** of computers* 計算機早期階段 ◇ *Most women stayed at home **in those days**.* 在那個時代大多數婦女都待在家裏。◇ (*informal*) *in the **old days*** (= in the past) 昔日 ➲ see also GLORY DAYS, HEYDAY, NOWADAYS, THE PRESENT DAY **HELP** There are many other compounds ending in **day**. You will find them at their place in the alphabet. 以 day 結尾的複合詞還有很多，可在各字母中的適當位置查到。

IDM **all in a day's 'work** part of your normal working life and not unusual 日常工作的一部份；習以為常的；不足為奇 **any day (now)** (*informal*) very soon 很快：*The letter should arrive any day now.* 信該很快就到了。**carry/win the 'day** (*formal*) to be successful against sb/sth 得勝；佔上風；取得成功：*Despite strong opposition, the ruling party carried the day.* 儘管遭到強烈反對，執政黨還是獲勝了。**day after 'day** each day repeatedly (used especially when sth is boring or annoying) 日復一日，一天又一天（尤指枯燥無味、令人厭煩）：*She hates doing the same work day after day.* 她討厭日復一日做同樣的工作。**day by 'day** all the time; a little at a time and gradually 一天天；逐日：*Day by day his condition improved.* 他的健康狀況一天天好轉。**day 'in, day 'out** every day for a long period of time 日復一日，天天（指不間斷）**a day of 'reckoning** the time when sb will have to deal with the result of sth that they have done wrong, or be punished for sth bad that they have done 遭報應的日子；受到懲罰的日子 **sb's/sth's days are 'numbered** a person or thing will not continue to live, exist or be successful for much longer （指人）死期不遠了，得意的日子屈指可數了；（指物）用不了多久了，壽命不長了：*His days as leader of the party are numbered.* 他作為黨的領袖的日子已屈指可數了。**from day 'one** (*informal*) from the beginning 從一開始；從第一天：*It's never worked from day one.* 這從一開始就行不通。**from day to 'day 1** with no thoughts or plans for the future 過一天算一天：*They live from day to day, looking after their sick daughter.* 他們過一天算一天，日復一日地照顧着生病的女兒。 **2** if a situation changes **from day to day**, it changes often 天天，一天又一天（指經常變化）：*A baby's need for food can vary from day to day.* 嬰兒對食物的需要天天都在變化。**from ˌone day to the 'next** if a situation changes **from one day to the next**, it is uncertain and not likely to stay the same each day 一天又一天（表示不知未來如何）：*I never know what to expect from one day to the next.* 一天又一天我從不知道該期待什麼。**have had your 'day** to no longer be successful, powerful, etc. 得意之時已過；風光不再；日漸衰敗：*She's had her day as a supermodel.* 她作為超級模特兒的輝煌日子已一去不復返。**have seen/known better 'days** (*humorous*) to be in poor condition 窮困潦倒；昔盛今衰；曾輝煌過：*Our car has seen better days!* 我們的汽車曾輝煌一時！**if he's, she's, etc. a 'day** (*informal*) (used when talking about sb's age) at least （談論某人年齡）至少：*He must be 70 if he's a day!* 他至少 70 歲了！**in sb's 'day 1** during the part of sb's life when they were most successful, famous, etc. （某人的）昔日盛時，鼎盛時期：*She was a great dancer in her day.* 她曾是紅極一時的舞蹈家。 **2** when sb was young 年輕時；當年：*In my day, there were plenty of jobs when you left school.* 我年輕時，畢業後就業機會很多。**in 'this day and age** now, in the modern world 當代；當今；在今天這個時代 **it's not sb's 'day** (*informal*) used when several unfortunate or unpleasant things happen on the same day 禍不單行；特別倒霉的一天：*My car broke down and then I locked myself out—it's just not my day!* 我的汽車拋錨了，我又沒帶鑰匙，真是禍不單行！**make sb's 'day** to make sb feel very happy on a particular day 使某人一天非常快活：*The phone call from Mike really made my day.* 邁克打來電話，真讓我樂了一整天。**make a day of it** (*informal*) to make a particular enjoyable activity last for a whole day instead of only part of it 痛痛快快過上一整天 **not have all 'day** to not have much time 時間不多了：*Come on! We don't have all day!* 快一點！我們的時間不多了！**of sb's 'day** during a particular period of time when sb lived 某人生活的時代：*the best player of his day* 他那個時代最優秀的運動員 ◇ *Bessie Smith was the Madonna of her day.* 貝西 • 史密斯是她那個時代的麥當娜。**of the 'day** that is served on a particular day in a restaurant （餐館）當日特別供應：*soup of the day* 當日供應的湯 **'one day** at some time in the future, or on a particular day in the past 有朝一日；（過去）某一天：*One day, I want to leave the city and move to the country.* 有朝一日，我要離開城市搬到鄉下去。◇ *One day, he walked out of the house with a small bag and never came back.* 一天，他帶了個小提包走出家門，再也沒有回來。**'one of these days** before a long time has passed 不久；日內：*One of these days you'll come back and ask me to forgive you.* 你很快就會回來請求我原諒的。**one of those 'days** (*informal*) a day when there are a lot of mistakes and a lot of things go wrong 諸事不順的日子；倒霉的日子：*It's been one of those days!* 這一天真倒霉！**'some day** at an unknown time in the future 將來有一天；總有一天：*Some day I'll be famous.* 總有一天我會成名的。**take it/things one ˌday at a 'time** (*informal*) to not think about what will happen in the future 得過且過；做一天和尚撞一天鐘；過一天算一天：*I don't know if he'll get better. We're just taking it one day at a time.* 我不知道他還能不能好，我們只有過一天算一天。**'that'll be the day** (*informal, ironic*) used when you are saying that sth is very unlikely to happen 那樣的事永遠不可能；哪有那樣的事：*Paul? Apologize? That'll be the day!* 保羅？道歉？那真是太陽從西邊出來了！**'these days** (*informal*) used to talk about the present, especially when you are comparing it with the past（尤用於拿現在和過去比較）如今，而今：*These days kids grow up so quickly.* 如今孩子們成長得真快。**'those were the days** (*informal*) used to suggest that a time in the past was happier or better than now （指過去）那才是好時光，那才是好年頭 **to the 'day** exactly 恰好；剛好；一天不差：*It's been three years to the day since we met.* 我們整整三年沒見面了。**to this 'day** even now, when a lot of time has passed 直到如今；甚至現在：*To this day, I still don't understand why he did it.* 我直到今天仍然不明白他當時為什麼那樣做。➲ more at BACK *adv.*, BORN *v.*, BREAK *n.*, CALL *v.*, CLEAR *adj.*, COLD *adj.*, DEED, DOG *n.*, EARLY *adj.*, END *n.*, END *v.*, EVIL *adj.*, FORTH, GIVE *v.*, LATE *adv.*, LIVE[1], LIVELONG, NICE, NIGHT, NINE, OLD, ORDER *n.*, OTHER *adj.*, PASS *v.*, PLAIN *adj.*, RAINY, ROME, SALAD, SAVE *v.*, TIME *n.*

'day boy *noun* (*BrE*) a boy DAY PUPIL（寄宿學校的）走讀男生

day·break /ˈdeɪbreɪk/ *noun* [U] the time of day when light first appears 黎明；拂曉；破曉；天亮 **SYN** **dawn**：*We left before daybreak.* 我們是在黎明前離開的。

'day care *noun* [U] care for small children, or for old or sick people, away from home, during the day 日託；日間護理：*Day care is provided by the company she works for.* 她工作的那家公司有日託。◇ *a day care centre* 日間託兒所

'day centre *noun* (*BrE*) a place that provides care for old or sick people during the day（老人或病人）日間護理站，日間照顧中心

day·dream /ˈdeɪdriːm/ *noun* pleasant thoughts that make you forget about the present 白日夢；幻想；空想：*She stared out of the window, lost in a daydream.*

她凝視窗外，沉浸在幻想之中。▸ **day·dream** *verb* [I] : ~ **(about sb/sth)** *I would spend hours daydreaming about a house of my own.* 我常常一連幾個小時幻想自己有一所房子。

ˈ**day girl** *noun* (*BrE*) a girl DAY PUPIL（寄宿學校的）走讀女生

Day-Glo™ /ˈdeɪ gləʊ; *NAmE* gloʊ/ *adj.* having a very bright orange, yellow, green or pink colour 日輝牌熒光色的：*Day-Glo cycling shorts* 熒光色自行車短褲

ˈ**day job** *noun* [sing.] the paid work that sb normally does 日常的有薪工作；（白天的）正職

IDM **don't give up the ˈday job** (*informal, humorous*) used to tell sb that they should continue doing what they are used to, rather than trying sth new which they are likely to fail at 別放棄白天的正職（別放棄老本行去嘗試沒有把握的新事物）：*So you want to be a writer? Well my advice is, don't give up the day job.* 這麼說你想成為一個作家了？得了，我勸你不要放棄老本行。

day·light /ˈdeɪlaɪt/ *noun* [U] the light that comes from the sun during the day 日光：*They emerged from the church into the bright daylight.* 他們走出教堂來到明亮的日光下。◇ *The street looks very different* ***in daylight.*** 大街在白天看來大不一樣。◇ *They left* ***before daylight*** (= before the sun had risen). 他們天亮前就走了。

IDM ˌ**daylight ˈrobbery** (*informal*) the fact of sb charging too much money for sth 漫天要價；敲竹槓：*You wouldn't believe some of the prices they charge; it's daylight robbery.* 他們的要價有一些你都不會相信，簡直就是在光天化日之下搶劫呀！➲ more at BROAD *adj.*

day·lights /ˈdeɪlaɪts/ *noun* [pl.]

IDM **beat/knock the (living) ˈdaylights out of sb** (*informal*) to hit sb very hard several times and hurt them very much 把某人狠揍一頓 **frighten/scare the (living) ˈdaylights out of sb** (*informal*) to frighten sb very much 嚇得某人六神無主（或魂飛魄散）

ˌ**daylight ˈsaving time** (*abbr.* **DST**) (also ˈ**daylight time**) (both *NAmE*) (*BrE* ˈ**summer time**) *noun* [U] the period during which in some countries the clocks are put forward one hour, so that it is light for an extra hour in the evening 夏令時（有些國家在夏季將時鐘撥快一小時，以節約照明能源）

day·long /ˈdeɪlɒŋ; *NAmE* -lɔːŋ/ *adj.* [only before noun] (*especially NAmE*) lasting for a whole day 全天的；整天的；終日的：*a daylong meeting* 整天的會議

ˈ**day nursery** (also **nursery**) (both *BrE*) (*NAmE* ˈ**day care center**) *noun* a place where small children are cared for while their parents are at work 日間託兒所 ➲ compare CRÈCHE (1), NURSERY SCHOOL

ˌ**day ˈoff** *noun* (*pl.* **days off**) a day on which you do not have to work 休假日；休息日：*Most weeks, Sunday is my only day off.* 我多半只有星期天才休息。◇ *Why not take a few days off?* 為什麼不休息幾天呢？

the ˌDay of ˈJudgement *noun* [sing.] = JUDGEMENT DAY

ˌ**day ˈout** *noun* (*pl.* **days out**) a trip or visit somewhere for a day 一日遊：*We had a day out in the country.* 我們在鄉下玩了一天。➲ SYNONYMS at TRIP

ˈ**day pupil** (*BrE*) (also ˈ**day student** *NAmE, BrE*) *noun* a school student who goes to a BOARDING SCHOOL but lives at home（寄宿學校的）走讀生

ˌ**day reˈlease** *noun* (*BrE*) [U] a system of allowing employees days off work for education（職工）脫產學習，脫產進修制度，進修休假制度：*time off for study on day release* 請假脫產學習的時間 ◇ *a day release course* 脫產進修課程

ˌ**day reˈturn** *noun* (*BrE*) a ticket at a reduced price for a journey to a place and back again on the same day（打了折的）當日往返車票

ˈ**day room** *noun* a room in a hospital or other institution where people can sit, relax, watch television, etc. during the day（醫院或其他機構的）日間娛樂室，日間休息室

ˈ**day school** *noun* **1** (*old-fashioned*) a private school with students who live at home and only go to school during the day 私立走讀學校；私立日校 ➲ compare BOARDING SCHOOL **2** (*BrE*) a course of education lasting one day, at which a particular topic is discussed 為期一天的專題講座：*a day school at Leeds University on women in Victorian times* 利茲大學為期一天的關於維多利亞時代婦女的專題講座

ˈ**day student** (*especially NAmE*) (*BrE* also ˈ**day pupil**) *noun* a school student who goes to a BOARDING SCHOOL but lives at home（寄宿學校的）走讀生

day·time /ˈdeɪtaɪm/ *noun* [U] the period during the day between the time when it gets light and the time when it gets dark 白天；白晝；日間：*You don't often see this bird* ***in (the) daytime.*** 這種鳥白天不常見。◇ *The park is open* ***during (the) daytime.*** 這個公園日間開放。◇ *Daytime temperatures never fell below 30°C.* 日間溫度從未低於 30 攝氏度。◇ *Please give your name and daytime phone number.* 請提供姓名和日間聯絡電話。

ˌ**day-to-ˈday** *adj.* [only before noun] **1** planning for only one day at a time 按日計劃的；逐日的；每天的：*I have organized the cleaning* ***on a day-to-day basis,*** *until our usual cleaner returns.* 我已逐日安排好清潔工作，直到我們的清潔工回來為止。**2** involving the usual events or tasks of each day 日常工作的；例行的：*She has been looking after the* ***day-to-day running*** *of the school.* 她一直在負責學校的日常管理工作。

ˈ**day trading** *noun* [U] (*finance* 財) buying and selling shares very quickly on the same day using the Internet in order to make a profit from small price changes 當日交易（用互聯網即日頻繁買賣股票，從微小差價中獲利）▸ ˈ**day trader** *noun*

ˈ**day trip** *noun* a trip or visit completed in one day 一日遊：*a day trip to France* 法國一日遊 ▸ ˈ**day tripper** *noun* (*BrE*)

day·wear /ˈdeɪweə(r); *NAmE* -wer/ *noun* [U] clothes for wearing every day, for example for working or shopping, not for special occasions 便服；日常衣服

daze /deɪz/ *noun*

IDM **in a daze** in a confused state 迷茫；茫然；恍惚：*I've been in a complete daze since hearing the news.* 自從聽到那消息，我一直茫然不知所措。

dazed /deɪzd/ *adj.* unable to think clearly, especially because of a shock or because you have been hit on the head（尤因震驚或頭部被擊）神志不清的，茫然的：*Survivors waited for the rescue boats, dazed and frightened.* 生還者不知所措，心有餘悸，等待着救援船隻。◇ *Jimmy was still dazed by the blow to his head.* 吉米由於頭部被擊，仍然神志不清。

daz·zle /ˈdæzl/ *verb, noun*

■ *verb* [often passive] **1** [T, I] ~ **(sb)** if a strong light **dazzles** you, it is so bright that you cannot see for a short time（強光等）使目眩，使眼花 **SYN** **blind**：*He was momentarily dazzled by the strong sunlight.* 強烈的陽光使他一時睜不開眼。**2** [T] ~ **sb** to impress sb a lot with your beauty, skill, etc.（美貌、技能等）使傾倒，使讚歎不已，使眼花繚亂：*He was dazzled by the warmth of her smile.* 她那溫柔的微笑使他神魂顛倒。▸ **daz·zling** *adj.* **SYN** **brilliant**：*a dazzling display of oriental dance* 令人陶醉的東方舞蹈表演 **daz·zlingly** *adv.*：*She was dazzlingly beautiful.* 她美得讓人傾倒。

■ *noun* [U, sing.] **1** the quality that bright light has that stops you from seeing clearly 耀眼眩目；眼花繚亂 **2** a thing or quality that impresses you but may prevent you from understanding or thinking clearly 令人眼花繚亂的東西（或特性）

d.b.a. /ˌdiː biː ˈeɪ/ *abbr.* (*US*) doing business as 以…公司名義營業：*Philip Smith, d.b.a. Phil's Signs* 用菲爾標誌公司名義經營的菲利普 • 史密斯

DBMS /ˌdiː biː em ˈes/ *abbr.* DATABASE MANAGEMENT SYSTEM

DC /ˌdiː ˈsiː/ *abbr.* **1** DIRECT CURRENT ➲ compare ALTERNATING CURRENT **2** District of Columbia in the US 美國哥倫比亞特區：*Washington, DC* 華盛頓（哥倫比亞特區）

DCMS /ˌdiː siː em ˈes/ *abbr.* (in Britain) Department for Culture, Media, and Sport（英國）文化、媒體和體育部

ˈD-Day *noun* [U] a date on which sth important is expected to happen 重大事情預定發生日；計劃行動開始日 **ORIGIN** From the name given to 6 June 1944, the day on which the British, US and other armies landed on the beaches of northern France in the Second World War. 源自 1944 年 6 月 6 日第二次世界大戰時，英美及其他國家的軍隊這天在法國北部海灘登陸的行動。

D

DDT /ˌdiː diː ˈtiː/ *noun* [U] a chemical used, especially in the past, for killing insects that harm crops 滴滴涕（舊時尤用作農業殺蟲劑）

de- /diː/ *prefix* (in verbs and related nouns, adjectives and adverbs 構成動詞及相關的名詞、形容詞和副詞) **1** the opposite of …的反義： *decentralization* 權力分散 **2** removing sth 除掉；去掉；取消： *to defrost the refrigerator* (= remove layers of ice from it) 給冰箱除霜

dea·con /ˈdiːkən/ *noun* **1** (in the Roman Catholic, Anglican and Orthodox Churches) a religious leader just below the rank of a priest（羅馬天主教、聖公會和東正教會的）執事，會吏 **2** (in some Nonconformist Churches) a person who is not a member of the CLERGY, but who helps a minister with church business affairs（某些不信奉英國國教的教會中協助管理教會事務的）助祭

dea·con·ess /ˌdiːkəˈnes; *NAmE* ˈdiːkənəs/ *noun* (in some Christian Churches) a woman who has duties that are similar to those of a deacon（某些基督教會中的）女執事，女會吏，女助祭

de·activ·ate /ˌdiːˈæktɪveɪt/ *verb* **~ sth** to make sth such as a device or chemical process stop working 使（儀器等）停止工作；使（化學過程）滅活化（或減活化、鈍化）： *Do you know how to deactivate the alarm?* 你知道如何讓鬧鐘不響嗎？

dead 0━ /ded/ *adj., noun, adv.*

■ ***adj.***

▸ NOT ALIVE 不活 **1** 0━ no longer alive 死的；失去生命的；枯萎的： *My mother's dead; she died in 1987.* 我母親不在了，她是 1987 年去世的。◇ *a dead person/animal* 死人；死去的動物 ◇ *dead leaves/wood/skin* 枯葉；枯木；死皮 ◇ *He was shot dead by a gunman outside his home.* 他在家門外被持槍歹徒開槍打死。◇ *Catherine's* ***dead body*** *lay peacefully on the bed.* 凱瑟琳的屍體安詳地躺在牀上。◇ *He* ***dropped dead*** (= died suddenly) *last week.* 他上星期突然就死了。◇ *The poor child looks* ***more dead than alive.*** 這孩子看上去半死不活的，真可憐。◇ (*figurative*) *In ten years he'll be* ***dead and buried*** *as a politician.* 他作為從政者十年後就不會有人記得了。

▸ IDEA/BELIEF/PLAN 想法；信念；計劃 **2** 0━ [not before noun] no longer believed in or aimed for 不再有人相信（或爭取）： *Many believe the peace plan is dead.* 許多人認為和平計劃已成泡影。◇ *Unfortunately racism is not yet dead.* 不幸的是種族歧視仍未消亡。◇ *Though the idea may be dead, it is far from being buried* (= people still talk about it, even though there is nothing new to say). 儘管這種想法可能已無人相信，但還遠沒被人遺忘。

▸ NOT USED 不用 **3** 0━ belonging to the past; no longer practised or fashionable 過時的；已廢棄的；不流行的： *Is the Western a dead art form?* 西部電影藝術形式過時了嗎？◇ *a dead language* (= one that is no longer spoken, for example Latin) 死語言（不再通用，如拉丁語）

▸ FINISHED 用完 **4** (*informal*) finished; not able to be used any more 用完了的；不能再用的： *dead matches* 擦過的火柴 ◇ *There were two dead bottles of wine on the table.* 桌子上有兩個空酒瓶。

▸ MACHINE 機器 **5** 0━ (of machines or equipment 機器或設備) not working because of a lack of power（因為缺電）不運行的，不轉動的： *a dead battery* 用完的電池 ◇ *The hard disk is dead.* 硬盤停止運行了。◇ *Suddenly the phone* ***went dead.*** 電話突然沒聲音了。

▸ PLACE 地方 **6** (*informal, disapproving*) very quiet, without activity or interest 死氣沉沉的；無活力的；無趣的： *There were no theatres, no cinemas, no coffee bars. It was dead as anything.* 那時既無劇院，又無電影院，也無咖啡館，簡直是死氣沉沉。

▸ BUSINESS 商業 **7** (*informal, disapproving*) without activity; with nobody buying or selling anything 停滯的；蕭條的： *'The market is absolutely dead this morning,' said one foreign exchange trader.* "今天早上市場蕭條極了。"一個外匯交易商說道。◇ *Winter is traditionally the dead season for the housing market.* 冬天歷來是住房市場的蕭條期。

▸ TIRED 疲勞 **8** [not usually before noun] (*informal*) extremely tired; not well 筋疲力盡；身體不好： ***half dead*** *with cold and hunger* 飢寒交迫，筋疲力盡 ◇ *She felt* ***dead on her feet*** *and didn't have the energy to question them further.* 她覺得累死了，沒有力氣繼續審問他們了。

▸ WITHOUT FEELING 無感覺 **9** [not before noun] (of a part of the body 身體部位) unable to feel because of cold, etc.（由於冷等）失去知覺，麻木 **SYN** **numb**： *My left arm had* ***gone dead.*** 我的左胳臂已經麻木了。 **10 ~ to sth** unable to feel or understand emotions 無動於衷；麻木不仁；無感覺 **SYN** **insensitive**： *He was dead to all feelings of pity.* 他毫無同情心。 **11** (especially of sb's voice, eyes or face 尤指嗓音、眼神或臉色) showing no emotion 無表情的；冷漠的；漠不關心的 **SYN** **expressionless**： *She said, 'I'm sorry, too,' in a quiet, dead voice.* 她平靜而冷漠地說："我也很抱歉。"◇ *His usually dead grey eyes were sparkling.* 他那平日冷漠的灰眼睛突然亮了起來。

▸ COMPLETE/EXACT 完全；精確 **12** [only before noun] complete or exact 完全的；精確的；全然的： *a* ***dead silence/calm*** 死寂；完全靜止 ◇ *the* ***dead centre*** *of the target* 靶子正中心 ◇ *The car gave a sudden jerk and came to a* ***dead stop.*** 汽車猛然一頓，猝然停下。◇ (*BrE*) *This horse is a* ***dead cert*** *for* (= will certainly win) *the race tomorrow.* 這匹馬明天比賽一定能贏。◇ *She crumpled to the floor* ***in a dead faint*** (= completely unconscious). 她倒在地上全然不省人事。

▸ NEVER ALIVE 無生命 **13** never having been alive 無生命的；非生物的： *dead matter* (= for example rock) 無生命物質（如岩石）◇ *a dead planet* (= one with no life on it) 無生命存在的行星

▸ IN SPORT 體育運動 **14** outside the playing area 界外的

IDM **be a dead ˈringer for sb** (*informal*) to look very like sb 酷似，極像（某人）；（和某人）一模一樣： *She's a dead ringer for a girl I used to know.* 她酷似我以前認識的一個女孩。 **(as) ˌdead as a/the ˈdodo** (*BrE, informal*) completely dead; no longer interesting or valid 完全過時；不再引人注目；失效 **(as) ˌdead as a ˈdoornail** (*informal*) completely dead 完全死了的；死僵了的 **a ˌdead ˈduck** (*informal*) a plan, an event, etc. that has failed or is certain to fail and that is therefore not worth discussing 已失敗（或注定要失敗、毫無討論價值）的計劃（或事情等） **be dead and ˈgone** (*informal*) to be dead 死了；不存在了： *You'll be sorry you said that when I'm dead and gone.* 我死後你會為你說的話感到後悔的。 **the dead hand of sth** an influence that controls or restricts sth（控制或阻礙事物發展的）影響： *We need to free business from the dead hand of bureaucracy.* 我們必須擺脫官僚主義對工作的嚴重影響。 **ˌdead in the ˈwater** a person or plan that is **dead in the water** has failed and has little hope of succeeding in the future（人或計劃）失敗，無成功希望： *His leadership campaign is dead in the water.* 他參加領導層競選無望成功。 **dead ˈmeat** (*informal*) in serious trouble 處境艱難；倒大霉： *If anyone finds out, you're dead meat.* 如果有人發現，你可要倒大霉了。 **ˌdead on arˈrival** (*abbr.* DOA) **1** (of an accident victim or other patient 事故受害者或其他病人) already dead when arriving at hospital 到達醫院時已經死亡： *She was pronounced dead on arrival.* 她在送達醫院時即被宣佈死亡。 **2** (*NAmE, informal*) very unlikely to be successful; not working when it is delivered 已不可能成功；到貨即損；到達時已無用： *The bill was dead on arrival in the Senate.* 這項法案在參議院不可能通過。◇ *The software was DOA.* 這軟件送達時已經損壞。 **ˌdead to the ˈworld** fast asleep 熟睡；沉睡；酣睡 **over ˌmy dead ˈbody** (*informal*) used to show you are strongly opposed to sth（表示強烈反對）除非我死了，我死也不： *She moves into our home over my dead body.* 除非我死了，否則她別想搬進我們家。 **sb wouldn't be seen/caught ˈdead …** (*informal*) used to say that you would not like to wear particular clothes, or to be in a particular situation（表示不願穿戴某種衣物或處於某種環境）死也不願意： *She wouldn't be seen dead in a hat.* 她最討厭戴帽子。◇ *He wouldn't be* *caught dead going to a club with his mother.* 他死也不願意跟母親一起去俱樂部。➲ more at FLOG, KNOCK *v.*

■ ***noun* the dead** **1** [pl.] people who have died 死人；死者：*The dead and wounded in that one attack amounted to 6 000.* 僅那一次進攻就死傷達 6 000 人。**2** [sing.] the state of being dead 死：*Christians believe that God raised Jesus from the dead.* 基督徒相信上帝使耶穌復活。◇ (*figurative*) *In nine years he has brought his party back from the dead almost to the brink of power.* 九年來他使黨起死回生，甚至差點成為執政黨。

IDM **in the ˌdead of ˈnight** (*BrE* also **at ˌdead of ˈnight**) in the quietest part of the night 深夜；在夜晚萬籟俱寂時：*I crept out of bed in the dead of night and sneaked downstairs.* 深夜我悄悄地從牀上爬起來，躡手躡腳地下了樓。**in the ˌdead of ˈwinter** in the coldest part of winter 在隆冬；在嚴冬

■ ***adv.*** (*informal*)

▸ **COMPLETELY 完全** **1** completely; exactly 完全地；全然地；確實地：*You're dead right!* 你完全正確！◇ (*BrE*) *a dead straight road* 筆直的道路 ◇ (*BrE*) *The train was dead on time.* 火車正點出發。◇ *He's dead against the idea.* 他堅決反對這個想法。◇ *The sight made him* ***stop dead in his tracks*** (= stop suddenly). 一看這情景，他驚呆了。◇ *She's* ***dead set on*** *getting* (= determined to get) *this new job.* 她打定主意要得到這個新工作。

▸ **VERY 非常** **2** (*BrE, informal*) very; extremely 非常；絕對；極度：*The instructions are dead easy to follow.* 這些指令很容易執行。◇ *You were dead lucky to get that job.* 你得到那份工作，真是太幸運了。◇ *I was dead scared.* 我怕得要死。

IDM **cut sb ˈdead** (*BrE*) to pretend not to have seen sb; to refuse to say hello to sb 假裝沒看見，不理睬（某人）：*She saw me, recognized me and cut me dead.* 她看見了我，也認出了我，卻不理睬我。➲ more at RIGHT *n.*

ˌdead ˈbeat (also **beat**) *adj.* [not before noun] (*informal*) very tired 筋疲力盡；疲憊不堪：*You look dead beat.* 你好像累得夠戧。

dead·beat /ˈdedbiːt/ *noun* (*informal*) **1** (*especially NAmE*) a lazy person; a person with no job and no money, who is not part of normal society 懶人；二流子；身無分文的無業者 **2** (*NAmE*) a person or company that tries to avoid paying their debts 賴賬者；賴債者；不講信用的公司 **3** (also **ˌdeadbeat ˈdad**) (*NAmE*) a father who does not live with his children and does not pay their mother any money to take care of them（不與子女同住，也不支付撫養費的）無良父親

dead·bolt /ˈdedbəʊlt; *NAmE* -boʊlt/ (*especially NAmE*) (*BrE* also **dead·lock**) *noun* a type of lock on a door that needs a key to open or close it 需用鑰匙開關的門鎖

dead·en /ˈdedn/ *verb* **~ sth** to make sth such as a sound, a feeling, etc. less strong 使（聲音、感覺等）減弱，緩和，遲鈍 **SYN** **dull**：*He was given drugs to deaden the pain.* 給了他止痛藥。▸ **dead·en·ing** *adj.* [only before noun]：*the deadening effect of alcohol on your reactions* 酒精對反應的抑制作用

ˌdead ˈend *noun* **1** a road, passage, etc. that is closed at one end 一頭封死的道路（或通道等）：*The first street we tried turned out to be a dead end.* 我們走的頭一條路，結果是條死胡同。**2** a point at which you can make no further progress in what you are doing 絕境；僵局：*We had come to a dead end in our research.* 我們的研究工作已陷入絕境。◇ *He's in a* ***dead-end job*** *in the local factory* (= one with low wages and no hope of promotion). 他在當地工廠的工作是沒有前途的。◇ *These negotiations are a* ***dead-end street*** (= they have reached a point where no further progress is possible). 談判陷入僵局。

dead·head /ˈdedhed/ *verb* **~ sth** (*BrE*) to remove dead flowers from a plant 摘掉（植物）的枯花

ˌdead ˈheat *noun* **1** (*especially BrE*) a result in a race when two of those taking part finish at exactly the same time（速度比賽中兩個參賽者）同時到達終點，成績並列 **2** (*NAmE*) a situation during a race or competition, etc. when two or more people are at the same level 勢均力敵；不分勝負；不相上下：*The two candidates are* ***in a dead heat*** *in the polls.* 兩名候選人在民意測驗中勢均力敵。

ˌdead ˈletter *noun* **1** [usually sing.] a law or an agreement that still exists but that is ignored 無人遵守的法律；形同虛設的協定；空文 **2** (*especially NAmE*) a letter that cannot be delivered to an address or to the person who sent it 死信；無法投遞（或退回）的郵件

dead·line /ˈdedlaɪn/ *noun* **~ (for sth)** a point in time by which sth must be done 最後期限；截止日期：*I prefer to* ***work to a deadline.*** 我喜歡按規定的期限完成工作。◇ *The deadline for applications is 30 April.* 交申請書的截止日期是 4 月 30 日。◇ *the January 15 deadline set by the United Nations* 聯合國規定的 1 月 15 日最後期限

dead·lock /ˈdedlɒk; *NAmE* -lɑːk/ *noun* **1** [sing., U] a complete failure to reach agreement or settle an argument 僵持；僵局；相持不下 **SYN** **stalemate**：*European agriculture ministers failed to* ***break the deadlock*** *over farm subsidies.* 歐洲各國農業部長在農業補貼問題上未能打破僵局。◇ (*BrE*) *The strike appeared to have reached deadlock.* 罷工好像已陷入僵局。◇ (*NAmE, BrE*) *The strike has reached a deadlock.* 罷工已陷入僵局。**2** (*BrE*) (also **dead·bolt** *NAmE, BrE*) [C] a type of lock on a door that needs a key to open or close it 需用鑰匙開關的門鎖 ▸ **dead·locked** *adj.* [not before noun]：*Despite months of discussion the negotiations remained deadlocked.* 儘管已討論數月，談判仍僵持不下。

ˌdead ˈloss *noun* [usually sing.] (*BrE, informal*) a person or thing that is not helpful or useful 無用的人（或物）；廢物：*He may be a very talented designer, but as a manager he's a dead loss.* 他可能是一個很有天賦的設計師，但作為經理他卻很無能。

dead·ly /ˈdedli/ *adj., adv.*

■ ***adj.*** (**dead·lier**, **dead·li·est**) **HELP** **More deadly** and **deadliest** are the usual forms. You can also use **most deadly.** 常用 more deadly 和 deadliest，亦可用 most deadly。**1** causing or likely to cause death（可能）致命的，致死的 **SYN** **lethal**：***a deadly weapon/disease*** 致命的武器 / 疾病 ◇ ***deadly poison*** 劇毒 ◇ *The cobra is one of the world's deadliest snakes.* 眼鏡蛇是世界上毒性最劇烈的蛇類之一。◇ *The terrorists have chosen to play a deadly game with the civilian population.* 恐怖分子故意要同平民百姓玩死亡遊戲。**2** [only before noun] extreme; complete 極度的；十足的；徹底的：*I'm* ***in deadly earnest.*** 我是非常認真的。◇ *We sat* ***in deadly silence.*** 我們默不作聲地坐着。◇ *They are* ***deadly enemies*** (= are full of hatred for each other). 他們是不共戴天的仇敵。**3** extremely effective, so that no defence is possible 非常有效的；無法防禦的：*His aim is deadly* (= so accurate that he can kill easily). 他彈無虛發。◇ *It was the deadly striker's 11th goal of the season.* 這是殺手前鋒本賽季的第 11 個進球。**4** (*informal*) very boring 枯燥的；令人厭煩的：*The lecture was absolutely deadly.* 這演講簡直無聊透了。

■ ***adv.*** **1** (*informal*) extremely 極其；非常：***deadly serious/dull*** 極其嚴肅認真 / 乏味 **2** = DEATHLY：***deadly pale/cold*** 死一般地蒼白；冷得要死

dead·ly night·shade /ˌdedli ˈnaɪtʃeɪd/ (also **bella·donna**) *noun* [U] a very poisonous plant with purple flowers and black BERRIES 顛茄（有毒，開紫花，結黑色漿果）

ˌdeadly ˈsin *noun* one of the seven actions for which you can go to hell, in Christian tradition 七罪宗之一，罪源，死罪（基督教指罪惡的根源）：*Greed is one of the* ***seven deadly sins.*** 貪婪是七罪宗之一。

dead·pan /ˈdedpæn/ *adj.* without any expression or emotion; often pretending to be serious when you are joking 面無表情的；不帶感情色彩的；假裝正經的：*deadpan humour* 冷面幽默

dead·weight /ˌdedˈweɪt/ *noun* [usually sing.] **1** a thing that is very heavy and difficult to lift or move（難以搬動的）重物 **2** a person or thing that makes it difficult for sth to succeed or change 重負；累贅

ˌdead ˈwood *noun* [U] people or things that have become useless or unnecessary in an organization 冗員；廢物

'dead zone *noun* **1** a place or a period of time in which nothing happens 空白地帶，空白期（沒有事情發生）：*The town is a cultural dead zone.* 這個鎮子是個文化荒原。 **2** an area which separates two places, groups of people, etc. 隔離帶：*The UN is trying to maintain a dead zone between the warring groups.* 聯合國正試圖在交戰方之間保留隔離帶。 **3** a place where a mobile/cell phone does not work because no signal can be received 盲區，靜區（無手機信號） **4** (*biology* 生) an area of water in which animals cannot live because there is not enough OXYGEN 死水區（因缺氧而使動物無法生存）

deaf /def/ *adj.* (**deaf·er**, **deaf·est**)
1 unable to hear anything or unable to hear very well 聾的：*to* ***become/go deaf*** 變聾 ◇ *She was born deaf.* 她天生耳聾。 ➲ see also STONE DEAF, TONE-DEAF **2 the deaf** *noun* [pl.] people who cannot hear 耳聾的人；聾子：*television subtitles for the deaf and hard of hearing* 為耳聾和耳背者做的電視字幕 **3** [not before noun] **~ to sth** not willing to listen or pay attention to sth 不願聽；不去注意：*He was deaf to my requests for help.* 他對我的求助充耳不聞。 ▶ **deaf·ness** *noun* [U]
IDM (as) ˌ**deaf as a 'post** (*informal*) very deaf 全聾；聾得什麼也聽不見 **fall on deaf 'ears** to be ignored or not noticed by other people 不被理睬；不被注意；被置若罔聞：*Her advice fell on deaf ears.* 她的忠告沒有受到重視。 **turn a deaf 'ear (to sb/sth)** to ignore or refuse to listen to sb/sth （對⋯）置之不理，充耳不聞：*He turned a deaf ear to the rumours.* 他對這些謠言置若罔聞。

deaf·en /'defn/ *verb* [usually passive] **1 ~ sb** to make sb unable to hear the sounds around them because there is too much noise 使震得耳朵發聾：*The noise of the siren was deafening her.* 汽笛聲震得她耳朵都快聾了。 **2 ~ sb** to make sb deaf 使聾；使聽不見

deaf·en·ing /'defnɪŋ/ *adj.* very loud 震耳欲聾的；極喧鬧的：*deafening applause* 掌聲如雷 ◇ *The noise of the machine was deafening.* 機器的轟鳴聲震耳欲聾。 ◇ *The government's response to the report has been a* ***deafening silence*** (= it was very noticeable that nothing was said or done). 政府對此報道顯然置之不理。 ▶ **deaf·en·ing·ly** *adv.*

ˌ**deaf 'mute** *noun* (sometimes *offensive*) a person who is unable to hear or speak 聾啞人

deal /diːl/ *verb, noun*
■ *verb* (**dealt**, **dealt** /delt/)
▸ CARDS 紙牌遊戲 **1** [I, T] to give cards to each player in a game of cards 發牌：*Whose turn is it to deal?* 該誰發牌了？ ◇ **~ (sth) (out) (to sb)** *Start by dealing out ten cards to each player.* 首先給每家發十張牌。 ◇ **~ sb sth** *He dealt me two aces.* 他給我發了兩張 A 牌。
▸ DRUGS 毒品 **2** [I, T] **~ (sth)** to buy and sell illegal drugs 非法買賣毒品；販毒：*You can often see people dealing openly on the streets.* 經常可以看到一些人在大街上公然買賣毒品。
IDM **deal sb/sth a 'blow | deal a 'blow to sb/sth** (*formal*) **1** to be very shocking or harmful to sb/sth 令⋯震驚；給⋯以打擊；使⋯受到傷害：*Her sudden death dealt a blow to the whole country.* 她突然逝世，舉國上下為之震驚。 **2** to hit sb/sth 給⋯一擊；打擊 ➲ more at WHEEL *v.*
PHR V **'deal in sth** **1** to buy and sell a particular product 經營，買賣（某一產品） **SYN** **trade in**：*The company deals in computer software.* 這個公司經營計算機軟件。 **2** to accept sth as a basis for your decisions, attitudes or actions 作為⋯的依據加以接受：*We don't deal in rumours or guesswork.* 我們不聽信謠言，也不胡亂猜測。 ˌ**deal sb 'in** (*informal, especially NAmE*) to include sb in an activity 將某人算在裏邊；讓某人參與：*That sounds great. Deal me in!* 這聽起來太棒了。算我一個！ ˌ**deal sth↔'out** **1** to share sth out among a group of people 分發；分配 **SYN** **distribute**：*The profits were dealt out among the investors.* 利潤分給了投資者。 **2** to say what punishment sb should have 給予（判決、處罰）：*Many judges deal out harsher sentences to men than to women.* 許多法官對男性比對女性的判決更嚴厲。 **'deal with sb** to take appropriate action in a particular situation or according to who you are talking to, managing, etc. 對付；應付；對待 **SYN** **handle**：*She is used to dealing with all kinds of people in her job.* 她已習慣於和工作中遇到的各種各樣的人打交道。 **'deal with sb/sth** to do business with a person, a company or an organization 與⋯做生意 **'deal with sth** **1** to solve a problem, perform a task, etc. 解決；處理；應付：*to deal with enquiries/issues/complaints* 處理各種詢問／問題／投訴 ◇ *Have you dealt with these letters yet?* 這些信件你處理了嗎？ ◇ *He's good at dealing with pressure.* 他善於應付壓力。 **2** to be about sth 涉及；論及；關於：*Her poems often deal with the subject of death.* 她的詩經常涉及死亡這一主題。 ➲ LANGUAGE BANK at ABOUT
■ *noun*
▸ A LOT 很多 **1** [sing.] **a good/great ~** much; a lot 大量；很多：*They spent a great deal of money.* 他們花了大量的錢。 ◇ *It took a great deal of time.* 這費了很多時間。 ◇ *I'm feeling a good deal better.* 我感覺好多了。 ◇ *We see them a great deal* (= often). 我們經常見到他們。
▸ BUSINESS AGREEMENT 商業協議 **2** [C] an agreement, especially in business, on particular conditions for buying or doing sth 協議；（尤指）交易：*to* ***make/sign/conclude/close a deal*** *(with sb)* （與某人）達成一筆交易 ◇ (*informal*) *Did you* ***cut a deal*** (= make one)? 你們交易做成了嗎？ ◇ *We* ***did a deal*** *with the management on overtime.* 我們與資方在加班問題上達成了一項協議。 ◇ *They were hoping for a better pay deal.* 他們希望達成一項提高工資的協議。 ◇ ***A deal was struck*** *after lengthy negotiations.* 經過漫長的談判終於達成了協議。 ◇ ***The deal fell through*** (= no agreement was reached). 交易沒有談成。 ◇ *I got a* ***good deal*** *on the car* (= bought it cheaply). 我這輛小汽車買得很便宜。 ◇ ***It's a deal!*** (= I agree to your terms) 就這麼辦吧！ ◇ *Listen.* ***This is the deal*** (= this is what we have agreed and are going to do). 聽着，下面是我們達成的協議。 ➲ COLLOCATIONS at BUSINESS ➲ see also PACKAGE *n.* (3)
▸ TREATMENT 待遇 **3** [C, usually sing.] the way that sb/sth is treated 待遇：*If elected, the party has promised a* ***new deal*** (= better and fairer treatment) *for teachers.* 該黨承諾如果當選將給教師更好的待遇。 ◇ *They knew they'd been given a* ***raw/rough deal*** (= been treated unfairly). 他們知道自己受到了不公正待遇。 ◇ *We tried to ensure that everyone got a* ***fair deal***. 我們曾盡力保證每個人都受到公平待遇。 ◇ *It was a* ***square deal*** *for everyone.* 這對任何人來說都是公平合理的。
▸ IN CARD GAMES 紙牌遊戲 **4** [C, usually sing.] the action of giving out cards to the players 發牌：*It's your deal.* 該你發牌了。
▸ WOOD 木材 **5** [U] (*especially BrE*) the soft pale wood of FIR or PINE trees, especially when it is cut into boards for making things 冷杉木；松木板：*a deal table* 松木桌子
IDM **what's the 'deal?** (*informal*) what is happening in the present situation? 出了什麼事；怎麼啦：*What's the deal? Do you want to go out or not?* 怎麼啦？你想不想出去？ ➲ more at BIG *adj.*, DONE *adj.*, STRIKE *v.*

'deal-breaker *noun* (*especially NAmE*) something that causes sb to reject a deal in politics or business 砸買賣的事：*The candidate's support for the war is the deal-breaker* (= people will not vote for the candidate because of it). 候選人因為支持這場戰爭而失去了選民。

deal·er /'diːlə(r)/ *noun* **1** a person whose business is buying and selling a particular product 交易商；貿易商：*an art/antique dealer* 藝術品經銷商；古董商 ◇ **~ in sth** *He's a dealer in second-hand cars.* 他經銷二手汽車。 ➲ see also WHEELER-DEALER **2** a person who sells illegal drugs 販毒者；毒品販子 **3** the person who gives out the cards in a card game （紙牌遊戲的）發牌者

deal·er·ship /'diːləʃɪp; *NAmE* -lərʃ-/ *noun* a business that buys and sells products, especially cars, for a particular company; the position of being a dealer who can buy and sell sth 專項商品（尤指汽車）經銷店；專項商品經銷：*a Ford dealership* 福特汽車經銷店

deal·ing /'diːlɪŋ/ *noun* **1 dealings** [pl.] business activities; the relations that you have with sb in business （商業）活動，往來：*Have you* ***had*** *any previous* ***dealings with*** *this company?* 你曾與這家公司有過業務往來嗎？ ◇ *I knew nothing of his business dealings.* 我對他生意上的事一概不知道。 ◇ *She has always been very polite* in her dealings with me. 她在與我交往的過程中總是彬彬有禮。**2** [U] a way of doing business with sb 經營作風；經營方式：*a reputation for **fair/honest dealing*** 經營作風正派／誠實的美名 **3** [U, C] buying and selling 買賣；交易：*drug dealing* 毒品交易 ◇ *dealings in shares* 股票交易

dealt *past tense, past part.* of DEAL

dean /diːn/ *noun* **1** (in the Anglican Church 聖公會) a priest of high rank who is in charge of the other priests in a CATHEDRAL 座堂主任牧師 **2** (also ˌ**rural ˈdean**) (*BrE*) a priest who is in charge of the priests of several churches in an area （鄉間主管若干教堂牧師的）主任牧師 **3** a person in a university who is in charge of a department of studies （大學的）學院院長，系主任 **4** (in a college or university, especially at Oxford or Cambridge) a person who is responsible for the discipline of students （大學，尤指牛津、劍橋大學的）學監 **5** (*NAmE*) = DOYEN

dean·ery /ˈdiːnəri/ *noun* (*pl.* **-ies**) **1** a group of PARISHES controlled by a dean (2) 總鐸區；（統轄若干教區的）主任牧師管轄區 **2** the office or house of a dean (1), (2) 主任牧師辦公室（或住所）

ˌ**dean's ˈlist** *noun* (in the US) a list that is published every year of the best students in a college or university （美國大學的）年度優秀學生名單

dear 🔑 /dɪə(r); *NAmE* dɪr/ *adj., exclamation, noun, adv.*

■ ***adj.*** (**dear·er**, **dear·est**) **1** 🔑 loved by or important to sb 親愛的；寶貴的；珍視的：*He's one of my dearest friends.* 他是我最親密的一位朋友。◇ **~ to sb** *Her daughter is very dear to her.* 她的女兒是她心愛的寶貝。**2** 🔑 **Dear** used at the beginning of a letter before the name or title of the person that you are writing to （用於信函抬頭的名字或頭銜前）親愛的：*Dear Sir or Madam* 親愛的先生／女士 ◇ *Dear Mrs Jones* 親愛的瓊斯太太 **3** [not usually before noun] (*BrE*) expensive; costing a lot of money 昂貴；價格高：*Everything's so dear now, isn't it?* 現在什麼東西都那麼貴，是不是？ **OPP** cheap

IDM **dear old/little ...** (*BrE*) used to describe sb in a way that shows affection （表示親昵喜愛）親愛的：*Dear old Sue! I knew she'd help.* 親愛的蘇啊！我知道她會幫忙的。◇ *Their baby's a dear little thing.* 他們的寶寶真是個小乖乖。 **hold sb/sth ˈdear** (*formal*) to care very much for sb/sth; to value sb/sth highly 非常關心；十分看重；極為珍視：*He had destroyed everything we held dear.* 他把我們珍視的一切都給毀了。➲ more at HEART, LIFE, NEAR *adj.*

■ ***exclamation*** used in expressions that show that you are surprised, upset, annoyed or worried （驚奇、不安、煩惱、擔憂等時說）啊，哎呀，糟糕，天哪：***Oh dear!*** *I think I've lost my purse!* 糟糕，我可能把錢包給丟了！◇ ***Oh dear!*** *What a shame.* 天哪，太可惜啦！◇ ***Dear me!*** *What a mess!* 哎呀，真是一團糟！◇ ***Dear oh dear!*** *What are you going to do now?* 哎呀呀，你現在怎麼辦呢？

■ ***noun*** **1** (*BrE, informal*) a kind person 仁慈的人；可愛的人：*Isn't he a dear?* 他不是很可愛嗎？◇ ***Be a dear and*** *fetch me my coat.* 勞駕把外套給我拿來。**2** used when speaking to sb you love （稱呼所愛的人）親愛的：*Would you like a drink, dear?* 喝點什麼嗎，親愛的？◇ *Come here, my dear.* 上這兒來，親愛的。**3** used when speaking to sb in a friendly way, for example by an older person to a young person or a child （對較年輕的人或孩子說話時用）親愛的，乖乖：*What's your name, dear?* 你叫什麼名字，親愛的？➲ compare DUCK *n.* (4)

■ ***adv.*** (*BrE*) at a high price 高價地；昂貴地：*to buy cheap and sell dear* 賤買貴賣 **IDM** see COST *v.*

dear·est /ˈdɪərɪst; *NAmE* ˈdɪr-/ *adj., noun*

■ ***adj.*** (*old-fashioned*) **1** used when writing to sb you love （給所愛的人寫信時用）最親愛的：*'Dearest Nina', the letter began.* "最親愛的尼娜"，信的開端這樣寫。**2** [usually before noun] that you feel deeply 深切的；由衷的：*It was her **dearest wish** to have a family.* 有一個家是她由衷的希望。

■ ***noun*** (*old-fashioned*) used when speaking to sb you love （稱呼所愛的人）親愛的：*Come (my) dearest, let's go home.* 好啦，親愛的，咱們回家吧。**IDM** see NEAR *adj.*

dearie /ˈdɪəri; *NAmE* ˈdɪri/ *noun* (*old-fashioned, BrE, informal*) used to address sb in a friendly way （表示友好的稱呼）親愛的，乖乖：*Sit down, dearie.* 坐下，親愛的。

dear·ly /ˈdɪəli; *NAmE* ˈdɪrli/ *adv.* **1** very much 非常；很：*She loves him dearly.* 她深深地愛着他。◇ *I would **dearly like/love** to know what he was thinking.* 我很想知道他在想什麼。◇ ***dearly beloved*** (= used by a minister at a Christian church service to address people) 最親愛的教友們（神職人員對參禮信眾的稱呼） **2** in a way that causes a lot of suffering or damage, or that costs a lot of money 代價極大地；高價地；昂貴地：*Success has **cost him dearly**.* 他為成功付出了高昂的代價。◇ *She **paid dearly** for her mistake.* 她因犯錯誤而付出了巨大的代價。

dearth /dɜːθ; *NAmE* dɜːrθ/ *noun* [sing.] **~ (of sth)** a lack of sth; the fact of there not being enough of sth 缺乏；不足 **SYN** **scarcity**：*There was a dearth of reliable information on the subject.* 關於這個課題還缺乏可靠資料。

death 🔑 /deθ/ *noun*

1 🔑 [C] the fact of sb dying or being killed 死；死亡：*a **sudden/violent/peaceful, etc. death*** 猝死、橫死、安詳的死等 ◇ *the anniversary of his wife's death* 他妻子的忌日 ◇ *an increase in deaths from cancer* 癌症死亡人數的增加 ◇ *He died a slow and painful death.* 他緩慢而痛苦地死去。**2** 🔑 [U] the end of life; the state of being dead 生命的終止；死亡狀態：*Two children were burnt **to death** in the fire* (= they died as a result of the fire). 兩個孩子被大火燒死。◇ *He's drinking himself **to death*** (= so that it will kill him). 他這樣喝酒非醉死不可。◇ *Police are trying to establish the **cause of death**.* 警方在設法確定死因。◇ *Do you believe in **life after death**?* 你相信來世嗎？◇ *a **death camp*** (= a place where prisoners are killed, usually in a war) 死亡集中營（常指戰爭中殺害俘虜的地方）◇ *He was **sentenced to death*** (= to be EXECUTED). 他被判處死刑。**3** 🔑 [U] **~ of sth** the permanent end or destruction of sth 永久的滅亡；毀滅；破滅：*the death of all my plans* 我所有計劃的破滅 ◇ *the death of fascism* 法西斯主義的滅亡 **4** (also **Death**) [U] (*literary*) the power that destroys life, imagined as human in form 死神：*Death is often shown in paintings as a human skeleton.* 死神在繪畫作品中常以骷髏形式出現。➲ see also SUDDEN DEATH

IDM **at death's ˈdoor** (often *humorous*) so ill/sick that you may die （因病重）生命危在旦夕；病危 **be the ˈdeath of sb** (*informal*) to worry or upset sb very much 讓某人擔心得要命；使某人深感不安：*Those kids will be the death of me.* 光為那些孩子操心就會把我累死。ˌ**do sth to ˈdeath** to do or perform sth so often that people become tired of seeing or hearing it 做煩了；看膩了；聽厭了：*That joke's been done to death.* 那個笑話都聽膩了。 **frighten/scare sb to ˈdeath** to frighten sb very much 把某人嚇得要命 **look/feel like death warmed ˈup** (*BrE*) (*NAmE* **like death warmed ˈover**) (*informal*) to look or feel very ill/sick or tired 看起來病得厲害（或疲憊不堪）；感到很不舒服（或累得要命） **put sb to death** to kill sb as a punishment 處死；處決 **SYN** **execute**：*The prisoner will be put to death at dawn.* 囚犯將在黎明時被處死。 **to death** extremely; very much 極度；非常：*to be bored to death* 膩煩得要命 ◇ *I'm **sick to death** of your endless criticism.* 你這無休止的指責真讓我煩死了。 **to the death** until sb is dead 至死；到底；永遠：*a fight to the death* 戰鬥到底 ➲ more at CATCH *v.*, CHEAT *v.*, DICE *v.*, DIE *v.*, FATE, FIGHT *v.*, FLOG, GRIM, KISS *n.*, LIFE, MATTER *n.*

death·bed /ˈdeθbed/ *noun* [usually sing.] the bed in which sb is dying or dies 臨終牀：*a **deathbed confession/conversion*** 臨終告解／皈依 ◇ *He told me the truth **on his deathbed*** (= as he lay dying). 他臨終時向我吐露了真情。◇ *She **was on her deathbed*** (= going to die very soon). 她已生命垂危。◇ (*humorous*) *You'd have to be practically on your deathbed before the doctor would come and see you!* 你非病到就要一命嗚呼的時候醫生才會來看你！

ˈ**death blow** *noun* an event that destroys or puts an end to sth 導致毀滅的事情；致命的一擊：*They thought the arrival of television would **deal a death blow** to mass*

D

cinema audiences. 他們認為電視的問世將使觀眾湧向影院的現象不復存在。

ˈdeath certificate *noun* an official document, signed by a doctor, that states the cause and time of sb's death 死亡證書

ˈdeath duty *noun* [usually pl.] (*old-fashioned, BrE*) = INHERITANCE TAX

ˈdeath knell (also **knell**) *noun* [sing.] an event that means that the end or destruction of sth will come soon 喪鐘；死亡的徵兆；預示毀滅的事件

death·less /ˈdeθləs/ *adj.* never dying or forgotten 不死的；不朽的；永恒的 SYN **immortal**：(*ironic*) *written in his usual deathless prose* (= very bad) 用他那萬世不變的筆調寫成

death·ly /ˈdeθli/ (also *less frequent* **dead·ly**) *adv.* like a dead person; suggesting death 死一般地；讓人想到死亡：*Her face was deathly pale.* 她的臉色死一般蒼白。◇ *The house was deathly still.* 房子死寂。▶ **death·ly** *adj.*：*A* ***deathly hush*** *fell over the room as he walked in.* 他進去時，房間裏變得死一般的寂靜。

ˈdeath mask *noun* a model of the face of a person who has just died, made by pressing a soft substance over their face and removing it when it becomes hard（用柔軟物質壓在死人臉上，變硬後取出製成的）死人面部模型

the ˈdeath penalty *noun* [sing.] the punishment of being killed that is used in some countries for very serious crimes 死刑；極刑：*the* ***abolition/return of the death penalty*** 廢除 / 恢復死刑 ◇ *The two men are* ***facing the death penalty.*** 這二人面臨死刑。➲ COLLOCATIONS at JUSTICE

ˈdeath rate *noun* **1** the number of deaths every year for every 1 000 people in the population of a place 死亡率（某地每年每 1 000 人的死亡人數）：*a* ***high/low death rate*** 高 / 低死亡率 **2** the number of deaths every year from a particular disease or in a particular group（某種疾病或某個群體的）死亡率：*Death rates from heart disease have risen considerably in recent years.* 近年來心臟病的死亡率大大上升了。

ˈdeath rattle *noun* [sing.] a sound sometimes heard in the throat of a dying person 臨終喉鳴

ˌdeath ˈrow *noun* [U] the cells in a prison for prisoners who are waiting to be killed as punishment for a serious crime 死囚牢房；死囚區：*prisoners* ***on death row*** 死囚區的犯人 ➲ COLLOCATIONS at JUSTICE

ˈdeath sentence *noun* the legal punishment of being killed for a serious crime 死刑：*to* ***be given/to receive the death sentence*** *for murder* 因謀殺罪被判死刑

ˈdeath's head *noun* a human SKULL (= the bone structure of the head) used as a symbol of death 骷髏頭（象徵死亡）

ˈdeath squad *noun* a group of people who are ordered by a government to kill other people, especially the government's political opponents（受命於政府謀殺政敵等的）處決小隊，暗殺小組

ˈdeath throes *noun* [pl.] **1** the final stages of sth just before it comes to an end 臨終；末日；最後階段：*The regime is now in its death throes.* 這一政權大勢已去。**2** violent pains and movements at the moment of death 臨終的劇痛；死前的掙扎

ˈdeath toll *noun* the number of people killed in an accident, a war, a disaster, etc.（事故、戰爭、災難等的）死亡人數

death·trap /ˈdeθtræp/ *noun* (*informal*) a building, vehicle, etc. that is dangerous and could cause sb's death 死亡陷阱（潛藏禍患的建築物、車輛等）：*The cars blocking the exits could turn this place into a deathtrap.* 擁塞出口的汽車會給這個地方帶來安全隱患。

ˈdeath warrant *noun* an official document stating that sb should receive the punishment of being killed for a crime that they have committed 死刑執行令：*The President* ***signed the death warrant.*** 總統簽署了死刑執行令。◇ *If you pay the ransom, you may be signing your son's death warrant.* 如果你付贖金，可能就要了你兒子的命。◇ (*figurative*) *By withdrawing the funding, the government signed the project's death warrant.* 政府撤回資金，也就是對這項工程判了死刑。

ˌdeath-watch ˈbeetle *noun* a small insect that eats into old wood, making sounds like a watch TICKING 紅毛竊蠹（專蛀舊木，發出類似錶的滴答聲的小甲蟲）

ˈdeath wish *noun* [sing.] a desire to die, often that sb is not aware of（無意識的）死亡願望

deb /deb/ *noun* (*informal*) = DEBUTANTE

de·bacle /deɪˈbɑːkl; dɪˈb-/ *noun* an event or a situation that is a complete failure and causes embarrassment 大敗；崩潰；垮台；災禍

debar /dɪˈbɑː(r)/ *verb* (**-rr-**) [usually passive] **~ sb (from sth/from doing sth)** (*formal*) to officially prevent sb from doing sth, joining sth, etc. 阻止，禁止（某人做某事、加入某團體等）：*He was debarred from holding public office.* 他被禁止擔任公職。

de·base /dɪˈbeɪs/ *verb* **~ sb/sth** to make sb/sth less valuable or respected 降低…的價值；敗壞…的名譽 SYN **devalue**：*Sport is being debased by commercial sponsorship.* 體育運動因受商業贊助而降低了聲譽。▶ **de·base·ment** *noun* [U]

de·bat·able AW /dɪˈbeɪtəbl/ *adj.* not certain because people can have different ideas and opinions about the thing being discussed 可爭辯的；有爭議的 SYN **arguable, questionable**：*a debatable point* 有爭議的觀點 ◇ ***It is highly debatable whether*** *conditions have improved for low-income families.* 低收入家庭的生活狀況是否已得到改善是一個頗有爭議的問題。

de·bate 0-w AW /dɪˈbeɪt/ *noun, verb*

■ ***noun*** [C, U] **~ (on/about/over sth)** **1** 0-w a formal discussion of an issue at a public meeting or in a parliament. In a debate two or more speakers express opposing views and then there is often a vote on the issue.（在公共集會上或議會裏就某問題進行的、常以表決結束的）辯論：*a debate on abortion* 關於墮胎的辯論 ◇ *The minister opened the debate* (= was the first to speak). 部長在辯論時率先發言。◇ *The motion* ***under debate*** (= being discussed) *was put to a vote.* 辯論中的動議已付諸表決。◇ *After a long debate, Congress approved the proposal.* 經過長時間辯論，國會通過了這項提議。➲ SYNONYMS at DISCUSSION ➲ COLLOCATIONS at POLITICS **2** 0-w an argument or discussion expressing different opinions（各自發表不同意見的）爭論，辯論，討論：*a* ***heated/wide-ranging/lively debate*** 激烈的 / 廣泛的 / 熱烈的爭論 ◇ *the current debate about tax* 目前關於稅收的討論 ◇ *There had been much debate on the issue of childcare.* 人們對兒童保育問題議論紛紛。◇ *Whether he deserves what has happened to him is* ***open to debate/a matter for debate*** (= cannot be certain or decided yet). 他是否罪有應得還有待於討論。◇ *The theatre's future is a subject of considerable debate.* 劇院的前途是一個頗有爭議的問題。

■ ***verb*** **1** 0-w [T, I] to discuss sth, especially formally, before making a decision or finding a solution（尤指正式）討論，辯論 SYN **discuss**：**~ (sth)** *Politicians will be debating the bill later this week.* 政界將在本週晚些時候討論這個議案。◇ *The question of the origin of the universe is still* ***hotly debated*** (= strongly argued about) *by scientists.* 關於宇宙起源問題，科學家仍在激烈辯論。◇ **~ whether, what, etc. ...** *The committee will debate whether to lower the age of club membership to 16.* 委員會將討論是否將參加俱樂部的年齡限制放寬到 16 歲。➲ SYNONYMS at TALK **2** [I, T] to think carefully about sth before making a decision 仔細考慮；思考；盤算：**~ (with yourself)** *She debated with herself for a while, and then picked up the phone.* 她仔細琢磨了一會兒，然後拿起了電話。◇ **~ whether, what, etc. ...** *We're debating whether or not to go skiing this winter.* 我們盤算着今年冬天是否去滑雪。◇ **~ doing sth** *For a moment he debated going after her.* 他仔細思考了片刻要不要去追求她。▶ **de·bat·ing** *noun* [U]：*a debating society at a school* 學校的辯論學會

de·bater /dɪˈbeɪtə(r)/ *noun* a person who is involved in a debate 參加討論者；爭論者

de·bauched /dɪˈbɔːtʃt/ *adj.* a **debauched** person is immoral in their sexual behaviour, drinks a lot of alcohol, takes drugs, etc. 道德敗壞的；淫蕩的；沉湎酒色的；嗜毒的 SYN **depraved, dissolute**

de·bauch·ery /dɪˈbɔːtʃəri/ *noun* [U] immoral behaviour involving sex, alcohol or drugs 道德敗壞；淫蕩；沉湎酒色（或毒品）

de·ben·ture /dɪˈbentʃə(r)/ *noun* (*BrE, finance* 財) an official document that is given by a company, showing it has borrowed money from a person and stating the interest payments that it will make to them（公司）債券

de·bili·tate /dɪˈbɪlɪteɪt/ *verb* (*formal*) **1 ~ sb/sth** to make sb's body or mind weaker 使身心衰弱；使衰竭；使虛弱：*a debilitating disease* 使人虛弱的疾病 **2 ~ sth** to make a country, an organization, etc. weaker 削弱（國家、機構等）的力量；使軟弱無力：*Prolonged strike action debilitated the industry.* 長時間的罷工削弱了這個行業的活力。

de·bil·ity /dɪˈbɪləti/ *noun* [U, C] (*pl.* **-ies**) (*formal*) physical weakness, especially as a result of illness（尤指疾病引起的）體弱，虛弱，衰弱

debit /ˈdebɪt/ *noun, verb*

■ ***noun*** **1** a written note in a bank account or other financial record of a sum of money owed or spent 借記；借方；收方：*on the debit side of an account* 賬戶的借方 ◇ (*figurative*) *On the debit side* (= a negative result will be that) *the new shopping centre will increase traffic problems.* 負面影響是新購物中心會使交通問題加劇。 **2** a sum of money taken from a bank account 借項 OPP **credit** ➲ see also DIRECT DEBIT

■ ***verb*** **~ sth** when a bank **debits** an account, it takes money from it 記入（賬戶）的借方；借記：*The money will be debited from your account each month.* 這筆錢將逐月記入你賬戶的借方。OPP **credit** ➲ COLLOCATIONS at FINANCE

ˈdebit card *noun* a plastic card that can be used to take money directly from your bank account when you pay for sth 借記卡；借方卡 ➲ compare CREDIT CARD

de·bon·air /ˌdebəˈneə(r); *NAmE* -ˈner/ *adj.* (*old-fashioned*) (usually of men 通常指男人) fashionable and confident 温文爾雅的；瀟灑的

de·brief /ˌdiːˈbriːf/ *verb* **~ sb** (**on sth**) to ask sb questions officially, in order to get information about the task that they have just completed 正式詢問，盤問（某人執行任務的情況）：*He was taken to a US airbase to be debriefed on the mission.* 他被帶到美國空軍基地彙報執行使命情況。 ➲ compare BRIEF *v.* (1) ▸ **de·brief·ing** *noun* [U, C]：*a debriefing session* 執行任務情況彙報會

deb·ris /ˈdebriː; ˈdeɪ-; *NAmE* dəˈbriː/ *noun* [U] **1** pieces of wood, metal, brick, etc. that are left after sth has been destroyed 殘骸；碎片；破片：*Emergency teams are still clearing the debris from the plane crash.* 各搶救小組仍在清理失事飛機的殘骸。 **2** (*formal*) pieces of material that are not wanted and rubbish/garbage that are left somewhere 殘渣；垃圾；廢棄物：*Clear away leaves and other garden debris from the pond.* 把池塘裏的樹葉和其他庭園垃圾清除乾淨。

debt 🗝 /det/ *noun*

1 🗝 [C] a sum of money that sb owes 借款；欠款；債務：*I need to* ***pay off*** *all my* ***debts*** *before I leave the country.* 我得在離開該國前償清所有債務。◇ *an outstanding debt of £300* 有待償還的 300 英鎊債務 ◇ *He had* ***run up*** *credit card* ***debts*** *of thousands of dollars.* 他積欠了數千元的信用卡借款。 ➲ COLLOCATIONS at FINANCE **2** 🗝 [U] the situation of owing money, especially when you cannot pay 負債情況：*He died heavily* ***in debt***. 他死時負債累累。◇ *The club is £4 million* ***in debt***. 這家俱樂部負債 400 萬英鎊。◇ *We were poor but we never* ***got into debt***. 我們窮是窮，但從不負債。◇ *It's hard to stay* ***out of debt*** *when you are a student.* 當學生很難不負債。◇ *a country's foreign debt burden* 國家的外債負擔 ➲ see also BAD DEBT **3** [C, usually sing.] the fact that you should feel grateful to sb because they have helped you or been kind to you 人情債；情義；恩情：*to* ***owe a debt of gratitude to sb*** 欠某人的情 ◇ *I would like to acknowledge my debt to my teachers.* 我想向我的老師表達我的感激之情。

IDM **be in sb's ˈdebt** (*formal*) to feel grateful to sb for their help, kindness, etc. 欠某人的人情債；受某人的恩惠；感激某人

debt·or /ˈdetə(r)/ *noun* a person, a country or an organization that owes money 債務人；借方 OPP **creditor**

debug /ˌdiːˈbʌɡ/ *verb* (**-gg-**) **~ sth** (*computing* 計) to look for and remove the faults in a computer program 排錯；調試；除錯

de·bug·ger /ˌdiːˈbʌɡə(r)/ *noun* a computer program that helps to find and correct mistakes in other programs 調試程序，排錯程序（可幫助找出並修正其他程序中的錯誤）

de·bunk /ˌdiːˈbʌŋk/ *verb* **~ sth** to show that an idea, a belief, etc. is false; to show that sth is not as good as people think it is 批判；駁斥；揭穿…的真相：*His theories have been debunked by recent research.* 最近的研究證明了他的理論不成立。

debut (also **début**) /ˈdeɪbjuː; ˈdebjuː; *NAmE* deɪˈbjuː/ *noun, verb*

■ ***noun*** the first public appearance of a performer or sports player（演員、運動員的）首次亮相；初次登台（或上場）：*He will* ***make his debut*** *for the first team this week.* 本週他將在第一支出場的隊伍中首次亮相。◇ *the band's debut album* 這個樂隊首次推出的專輯

■ ***verb*** **1** [I] (of a performer or show 演員或表演等) to make a first public appearance 首次亮相；初次登台：*The ballet will debut next month in New York.* 這齣芭蕾舞劇將於下月在紐約首演。 **2** [T] **~ sth** (*especially NAmE, business* 商) to present a new product or advertising campaign to the market 推出，首發（新產品、廣告宣傳）：*They will debut the products at the trade show.* 他們將在商品展銷會上推出新產品。

debu·tante /ˈdebjutɑːnt/ (also *informal* **deb**) *noun* a young, rich or UPPER-CLASS woman who is going to fashionable social events for the first time 首次進入上流社交場合的富家年輕女子

deca- /ˈdekə/ *combining form* (in nouns 構成名詞) ten; having ten 十；有十的：*decathlon* 十項全能運動 ➲ compare DECI-

dec·ade 🗝 AW /ˈdekeɪd; dɪˈkeɪd/ *noun*

a period of ten years, especially a continuous period, such as 1910–1919 or 2000–2009 十年，十年期（尤指一個年代）

deca·dence /ˈdekədəns/ *noun* [U] (*disapproving*) behaviour, attitudes, etc. which show a fall in standards, especially moral ones, and an interest in pleasure and enjoyment rather than more serious things 墮落；頹廢；貪圖享樂：*the decadence of modern Western society* 現代西方社會的頹廢現象

deca·dent /ˈdekədənt/ *adj.* (*disapproving*) having or showing low standards, especially moral ones, and an interest only in pleasure and enjoyment rather than serious things 墮落的；頹廢的；貪圖享樂的：*the decadent rich* 貪圖享樂的富豪 ◇ ***a decadent lifestyle/society*** 墮落的生活方式；腐朽的社會

Decaf™ (also **decaff**) (both *BrE*) (*NAmE* **decaf**) /ˈdiːkæf/ *noun* [U, C] (*informal*) decaffeinated coffee 低咖（脫咖啡因咖啡）：(*BrE*) *Regular coffee or Decaf?* 你要普通咖啡還是低咖？◇ *I'll have a decaff, please.* 請給我來一杯低咖。

de·caf·fein·ated /ˌdiːˈkæfɪneɪtɪd/ *adj.* (of coffee or tea 咖啡或茶) with most or all of the CAFFEINE removed（全）脫咖啡因的 ▸ **de·caf·fein·ated** *noun* [U, C]

decal /ˈdiːkæl/ *noun* (*NAmE*) = TRANSFER (5)

deca·litre (*US* **deca·liter**, **deka·liter**) /ˈdekəliːtə(r)/ *noun* a unit for measuring volume, equal to 10 litres 十升

deca·metre (*US* **deca·meter**, **deka·meter**) /ˈdekəmiːtə(r)/ *noun* a unit for measuring length, equal to 10 metres 十米

de·camp /dɪˈkæmp/ *verb* [I] **~** (**from …**) (**to …**) to leave a place suddenly, often secretly 逃亡；潛逃

de·cant /dɪˈkænt/ *verb* **~ sth** (**into sth**) to pour liquid, especially wine, from one container into another（把液體，尤指酒）倒入，注入

D

de·cant·er /dɪˈkæntə(r)/ *noun* a glass bottle, often decorated, that wine and other alcoholic drinks are poured into from an ordinary bottle before serving 雕花玻璃酒瓶

de·capi·tate /dɪˈkæpɪteɪt/ *verb* **~ sb/sth** to cut off sb's head 殺頭；斬首 SYN **behead**：*His decapitated body was found floating in a canal.* 人們發現他被斬首的屍體漂浮在一條水渠裏。▸ **de·capi·ta·tion** /dɪˌkæpɪˈteɪʃn/ *noun* [U, C]

deca·syl·lable /ˈdekəsɪləbl/ *noun* (*technical* 術語) a line of poetry with ten syllables 十音節詩行 ▸ **deca·syl·lab·ic** /ˌdekəsɪˈlæbɪk/ *adj.*：*a decasyllabic line* 十音節詩行

dec·ath·lete /dɪˈkæθliːt/ *noun* a person who competes in a decathlon 十項全能運動員

dec·ath·lon /dɪˈkæθlən/ *noun* a sporting event in which people compete in ten different sports 十項全能運動 ➲ compare BIATHLON, HEPTATHLON, PENTATHLON, TRIATHLON

decay 0‑ᐳ /dɪˈkeɪ/ *noun, verb*

■ ***noun*** [U] **1** 0‑ᐳ the process or result of being destroyed by natural causes or by not being cared for (= of decaying) 腐爛；腐朽：*tooth decay* 蛀牙 ◇ *The landlord had let the building* ***fall into decay***. 房東任由房子變得破爛不堪。◇ *The smell of death and decay hung over the town.* 城鎮上空瀰漫着死人和腐爛的氣味。**2** 0‑ᐳ the gradual destruction of a society, an institution, a system, etc.（社會、機構、制度等的）衰敗，衰退，衰落：***economic/moral/urban decay*** 經濟衰退；道德敗壞；城市衰落 ◇ *the decay of the old industries* 舊工業的衰敗

■ ***verb*** **1** 0‑ᐳ [I, T] **~ (sth)** to be destroyed gradually by natural processes; to destroy sth in this way（使）腐爛，腐朽 SYN **rot**：*decaying leaves/teeth/food* 爛葉；蛀齒；腐爛食物 **2** 0‑ᐳ [I] if a building or an area **decays**, its condition slowly becomes worse（建築、地方等）破敗，衰落，衰敗：*decaying inner city areas* 衰敗中的市中心區 **3** [I] to become less powerful and lose influence over people, society, etc.（力量、影響等）衰弱，衰退，衰減：*decaying standards of morality* 道德標準日趨低下

de·cease /dɪˈsiːs/ *noun* [U] (*law* 律 or *formal*) the death of a person 死亡；亡故

de·ceased /dɪˈsiːst/ *adj.* (*law* 律 or *formal*) **1** dead 死去了的；已死的；亡故的：*her deceased parents* 她已故的雙親 **2 the deceased** *noun* (*pl.* **the deceased**) a person who has died, especially recently 死者；已故者

de·ceit /dɪˈsiːt/ *noun* [U, C] dishonest behaviour that is intended to make sb believe sth that is not true; an example of this behaviour 欺騙，欺詐（行為）；詭計 SYN **deception**：*He was accused of lies and deceit.* 他被指控撒謊和欺詐。◇ *Everyone was involved in this web of deceit.* 所有人都牽涉到這起詐騙勾當之中了。◇ *Their marriage was an illusion and a deceit.* 他們的婚姻是虛假的，不真實的。

de·ceit·ful /dɪˈsiːtfl/ *adj.* (*formal*) behaving in a dishonest way by telling lies and making people believe things that are not true 不誠實的；騙人的 SYN **dishonest** ▸ **de·ceit·ful·ly** /-fəli/ *adv.* **de·ceit·ful·ness** *noun* [U]

de·ceive /dɪˈsiːv/ *verb* **1** [T] to make sb believe sth that is not true 欺騙；矇騙；誑騙：**~ sb** *Her husband had been deceiving her for years.* 她丈夫多年來一直在欺騙她。◇ **~ sb into doing sth** *She deceived him into handing over all his savings.* 她把他所有的積蓄都騙了出來。➲ SYNONYMS at CHEAT **2** [T] **~ yourself** (**that** ...) to refuse to admit to yourself that sth unpleasant is true 欺騙（自己）：*You're deceiving yourself if you think he'll change his mind.* 如果你認為他會改變主意，那你是在欺騙自己。**3** [T, I] **~ (sb)** to make sb have a wrong idea about sb/sth 使人誤信；誤導 SYN **mislead**：*Unless my eyes deceive me, that's his wife.* 如果我沒有看錯的話，那是他的妻子。➲ see also DECEPTIVE ▸ **de·ceiver** *noun*
IDM see FLATTER

> **WORD FAMILY**
> deceive *verb*
> deceit *noun*
> deceitful *adj.*
> deception *noun*
> deceptive *adj.*

de·cel·er·ate /ˌdiːˈseləreɪt/ *verb* (*formal*) **1** [I, T] **~ (sth)** to reduce the speed at which a vehicle is travelling（使）減速行駛；降低運行速度 **2** [I, T] **~ (sth)** to become or make sth become slower（使）減緩，變慢 SYN **slow down**：*Economic growth decelerated sharply in June.* 六月份經濟增長大幅度減緩。OPP **accelerate** ▸ **de·cel·er·ation** /ˌdiːseləˈreɪʃn/ *noun* [U]

De·cem·ber 0‑ᐳ /dɪˈsembə(r)/ *noun* [U, C] (*abbr.* **Dec.**) the 12th and last month of the year 十二月 HELP To see how **December** is used, look at the examples at **April**. * December 的用法見詞條 April 下的示例。

de·cency /ˈdiːsnsi/ *noun* **1** [U] honest, polite behaviour that follows accepted moral standards and shows respect for others 正派；得體；彬彬有禮：*Her behaviour showed a total lack of* ***common decency***. 她的舉止顯示她連起碼的禮節都不懂。◇ *Have you no* ***sense of decency***? 你禮貌都不懂嗎？◇ *He might* ***have had the decency to*** *apologize.* 他其實應該道個歉的。**2 the decencies** [pl.] (*formal*) standards of behaviour in society that people think are acceptable 禮儀；行為準則：*the basic decencies of civilized society* 文明社會的基本行為準則

de·cent /ˈdiːsnt/ *adj.* **1** of a good enough standard or quality 像樣的；相當不錯的；尚好的：(*informal*) *a decent meal/job/place to live* 相當不錯的飯菜／工作／住所 ◇ *I need a decent night's sleep.* 我需要好好地睡上一夜。**2** (of people or behaviour 人或行為舉止) honest and fair; treating people with respect 正派的；公平的；合乎禮節的：*ordinary, decent, hard-working people* 勤勞、正派的普通人 ◇ *Everyone said he was a decent sort of guy.* 人人都說他是個品行端正的小伙子。**3** acceptable to people in a particular situation 得體的；合宜的；適當的：*a decent burial* 體面的葬禮 ◇ *That dress isn't decent.* 那件連衣裙不夠雅觀。◇ *She ought to have waited for a decent interval before getting married again.* 她再次嫁人也應該適當等上一段時間。**4** (*informal*) wearing enough clothes to allow sb to see you 穿好了衣服的；適宜於見人的：*I can't go to the door—I'm not decent.* 我不能去開門，我還沒穿好衣服。➲ compare INDECENT (1) ▸ **de·cent·ly** *adv.*
IDM **to do the decent ˈthing** to do what people or society expect, especially in a difficult situation（尤指在困境中）做人心所向的事，做體面事：*He did the decent thing and resigned.* 他做得很體面，辭職了。

de·cen·tral·ize (*BrE* also **-ise**) /ˌdiːˈsentrəlaɪz/ *verb* [T, I] **~ (sth)** to give some of the power of a central government, organization, etc. to smaller parts or organizations around the country 分散，下放（權力）；將…的權力下放：*decentralized authority/administration* 下放了的權力／行政權 OPP **centralize** ▸ **de·cen·tral·iza·tion, -isa·tion** /ˌdiːˌsentrəlaɪˈzeɪʃn; *NAmE* -ləˈz-/ *noun* [U, sing.]

de·cep·tion /dɪˈsepʃn/ *noun* **1** [U] the act of deliberately making sb believe sth that is not true (= of DECEIVING them) 欺騙；矇騙；誆騙 SYN **deceit**：*a drama full of lies and deception* 充滿謊言和欺騙的一齣戲 ◇ *He was accused of obtaining property by deception.* 他被指控騙取錢財。**2** [C] a trick intended to make sb believe sth that is not true 詭計；騙術；騙局 SYN **deceit**：*The whole episode had been a cruel deception.* 整個經歷都是殘酷的騙局。

de·cep·tive /dɪˈseptɪv/ *adj.* likely to make you believe sth that is not true 欺騙性的；誤導的；騙人的 SYN **misleading**：*a deceptive advertisement* 虛假廣告 ◇ *Appearances can often be deceptive* (= things are not always what they seem to be). 外表常常靠不住。◇ *the deceptive simplicity of her writing style* (= it seems simple but is not really) 她那看似簡單實則不然的寫作風格 ▸ **de·cep·tive·ly** *adv.*：*a deceptively simple idea* 貌似簡單的想法

deci- /ˈdesɪ-/ *combining form* (in nouns; often used in units of measurement 構成名詞，常用於計量單位) one tenth 十分之一：*decilitre* 分升 ➲ compare DECA-

deci·bel /ˈdesɪbel/ *noun* a unit for measuring how loud a sound is 分貝（聲音強度的單位）

de·cide 0→ /dɪˈsaɪd/ *verb*

WORD FAMILY
decide *verb*
decision *noun* (≠ indecision)
decisive *adj.* (≠ indecisive)
undecided *adj.*

1 0→ [I, T] to think carefully about the different possibilities that are available and choose one of them 對…作出抉擇；決定；選定：*It's up to you to decide.* 這事由你來決定吧。◇ **~ between A and B** *It was difficult to decide between the two candidates.* 很難在這兩個候選人之間決定取捨。◇ **~ against sth** *They decided against taking legal action.* 他們決定不提起訴訟。◇ **~ what, whether, etc. …** *I can't decide what to wear.* 我拿不定主意穿什麼。◇ **~ (that) …** *She decided (that) she wanted to live in France.* 她決定要住在法國。◇ **~ to do sth** *We've decided not to go away after all.* 我們到底還是決定不離開。◇ **~ sth** *We might be hiring more people but nothing has been decided yet.* 我們或許會再多雇些人，不過現在什麼都還沒定下來。◇ **it is decided (that) …** *It was decided (that) the school should purchase new software.* 已經決定學校要購買新軟件。➲ SYNONYMS at CHOOSE **2** [T, I] (*law* 律) to make an official or legal judgement 裁決；判決：**~ sth** *The case will be decided by a jury.* 這案件將由陪審團裁決。◇ **~ for/in favour of sb | ~ in sb's favour** *The Appeal Court decided in their favour.* 上訴法院作出了有利於他們的裁定。◇ **~ against sb** *It is always possible that the judge may decide against you.* 法官判你敗訴總是有可能的。**3** [T, I] to affect the result of sth 影響（或決定）…的結果：**~ (sth)** *A mixture of skill and good luck decided the outcome of the game.* 技術和運氣結合在一起決定了比賽的結果。◇ **~ if, whether, etc. …** *A number of factors decide whether a movie will be successful or not.* 一部電影成功與否是由許多因素決定的。**4** [T] to be the reason why sb does sth 成為（某人）做某事的原因：*For most customers, price is* ***the deciding factor***. 對大多數顧客來説，價格是決定性因素。◇ **~ sb (to do sth)** *They offered me free accommodation for a year, and that decided me.* 他們願意免費為我提供一年的住宿，這就使我下定了決心。

PHR V **deˈcide on/upon sth** 0→ to choose sth from a number of possibilities 決定；選定：*We're still trying to decide on a venue.* 我們仍然在設法選定一個會場。

de·cided /dɪˈsaɪdɪd/ *adj.* **1** [only before noun] obvious and definite 明顯的；明白無誤的；確實無疑的：*His height was a decided advantage in the job.* 幹這項工作，他的身高是明顯優勢。**2** (*especially BrE*) having very strong opinions 堅定的；堅決的；果斷的：*She was a very decided young woman, eager to do some good in the world.* 她是一個非常堅定的年輕女子，渴望在世上做點有益的事。◇ *The child is very decided about what she wants and doesn't want.* 這孩子對她想要和不想要的東西非常有主見。➲ compare UNDECIDED

de·cided·ly /dɪˈsaɪdɪdli/ *adv.* **1** (used with an adjective or adverb 與形容詞或副詞連用) definitely and in an obvious way 確實；肯定；顯然：*Amy was looking decidedly worried.* 埃米看上去顯然是憂心忡忡。**2** (*BrE*) in a way that shows that you are sure and determined about sth 果斷地；堅決地；堅定地：*'I won't go,' she said decidedly.* "我不去。" 她果斷地説。

de·cider /dɪˈsaɪdə(r)/ *noun* [usually sing.] the game, race, etc. that will decide who the winner is in a competition 決勝局；決賽

de·cidu·ous /dɪˈsɪdʒuəs; -dju-/ *adj.* (of a tree, bush etc. 樹、灌木等) that loses its leaves every year 落葉的 ➲ compare EVERGREEN ➲ VISUAL VOCAB page V10

decile /ˈdesaɪl; *NAmE* also ˈdesl/ *noun* (*statistics* 統計) one of ten equal groups into which a collection of things or people can be divided according to the DISTRIBUTION of a particular VARIABLE 十分位數：*families in the top decile of income* (= the 10% of families with the highest income) 收入排在前十分位的家庭

deci·litre (*especially US* **deci·liter**) /ˈdesiliːtə(r)/ *noun* a unit for measuring liquids. There are 10 decilitres in a litre. 分升；十分之一升

deci·mal /ˈdesɪml/ *adj.*, *noun*

▪ ***adj.*** based on or counted in tens or tenths 十進位的；小數的：*the decimal system* 十進制

▪ ***noun*** (also **ˌdecimal ˈfraction**) a FRACTION (= a number less than one) that is shown as a dot or point followed by the number of tenths, HUNDREDTHS, etc. 小數：*The decimal 0.61 stands for 61 hundredths.* 小數 0.61 代表 61%。➲ compare VULGAR FRACTION

deci·mal·ize (*BrE* also **-ise**) /ˈdesɪməlaɪz/ *verb* **1 ~ sth** to change a system of coins or weights and measurements to a decimal system 把（幣制或度量衡）改為十進制 **2 ~ sth** to express an amount using the decimal system instead of the system it is already expressed in 把（數量）化為小數：*The question asks you to decimalize the fraction ⅞.* 這道題要求你將分數 ⅞ 化為小數。▸ **deci·mal·iza·tion, -isa·tion** /ˌdesɪməlaɪˈzeɪʃn; *NAmE* -ləˈz-/ *noun* [U]

ˌdecimal ˈplace *noun* the position of a number after a decimal point 小數位：*The figure is* ***accurate to*** *two* ***decimal places***. 這個數精確到小數點後兩位。

ˌdecimal ˈpoint *noun* a dot or point used to separate the whole number from the tenths, HUNDREDTHS, etc. of a decimal, for example in 0.61 小數點

deci·mate /ˈdesɪmeɪt/ *verb* **1** [usually passive] **~ sth** to kill large numbers of animals, plants or people in a particular area 大量毀滅，大批殺死（某地區的動物、植物或人）：*The rabbit population was decimated by the disease.* 這種疾病使大批兔子死亡。**2 ~ sth** (*informal*) to severely damage sth or make sth weaker 嚴重破壞；大大削弱：*Cheap imports decimated the British cycle industry.* 廉價進口產品嚴重削弱了英國的自行車工業。▸ **deci·ma·tion** /ˌdesɪˈmeɪʃn/ *noun* [U]

deci·metre (*especially US* **deci·meter**) /ˈdesɪmiːtə(r)/ *noun* a unit for measuring length. There are 10 decimetres in a metre. 分米；十分之一米

de·cipher /dɪˈsaɪfə(r)/ *verb* **~ sth** to succeed in finding the meaning of sth that is difficult to read or understand 破譯，辨認（難認、難解的東西）：*to decipher a code* 破譯密碼 ◇ *Can anyone decipher his handwriting?* 有誰能辨認他的字跡？➲ see also INDECIPHERABLE

de·ci·sion 0→ /dɪˈsɪʒn/ *noun*

1 0→ [C] **~ (on/about sth) | ~ (to do sth)** a choice or judgement that you make after thinking and talking about what is the best thing to do （作出的）決定，抉擇：*to* ***make a decision*** (= to decide) 作出決定 ◇ (*BrE*) *to* ***take a decision*** (= to decide) 作出決定 ◇ *We need a decision on this by next week.* 我們得在下週前就這一問題作出決定。◇ *Who* ***took the decision*** *to go ahead with the project?* 是誰決定開始這項工程的？◇ *He is really bad at* ***making decisions***. 他的確不善於決策。◇ *We finally* ***reached a decision*** (= decided after some difficulty). 我們終於作出了抉擇。◇ *We must* ***come to a decision*** *about what to do next by tomorrow.* 我們必須最晚明天就下一步做什麼作出決定。◇ *a big* (= an important) *decision* 一項重大的抉擇 ◇ *The final decision is yours.* 最終的決定權屬於你。◇ *It's a difficult decision for any doctor.* 這對任何醫生來説都是一個困難的決定。◇ *The editor's decision is final.* 編輯定了就不再改了。◇ *Mary is the decision-maker in the house.* 家裏的事瑪麗説了算。**2** (also **de·cisive·ness**) [U] the ability to decide sth clearly and quickly 決斷（力）；果斷：*This is not a job for someone who lacks decision.* 不果斷的人不適宜做這工作。OPP **indecision** **3** [U] the process of deciding sth 作決定；決策：*The moment of decision had arrived.* 決策的時刻已經到了。

deˈcision-making *noun* [U] the process of deciding about sth important, especially in a group of people or in an organization 決策 ▸ **deˈcision-maker** *noun*

de·cisive /dɪˈsaɪsɪv/ *adj.* **1** very important for the final result of a particular situation 決定性的；關鍵的：***a decisive factor/victory/battle*** 決定性的因素／勝利／戰役 ◇ *She has* ***played a decisive role*** *in the peace negotiations.* 她在和談中起了關鍵作用。◇ ***a decisive step*** (= an important action that will change a situation) *towards a cleaner environment* 朝着更清潔的環境邁出的關鍵一步 ➲ SYNONYMS at ESSENTIAL **2** able to decide sth quickly and with confidence 堅決的；果斷的；決斷的：*decisive management* 果斷的管理層 ◇ *The government must take* *decisive action on gun control.* 政府必須在槍支管制方面採取果斷措施。OPP **indecisive** ▸ **de·cisive·ly** *adv.*

de·cisive·ness /dɪˈsaɪsɪvnəs/ *noun* [U] = DECISION (2)

deck /dek/ *noun, verb*

■ **noun** **1** the top outside floor of a ship or boat 甲板；艙面：*I was the only person* ***on deck*** *at that time of night.* 夜裏當時只有我一個人在甲板上。◇ *As the storm began, everyone disappeared* ***below deck(s)***. 暴風雨來臨時，所有的人都躲到甲板下面去了。**2** one of the floors of a ship or a bus（船或公共汽車的）一層，層面：*the* ***upper/lower/main deck*** *of a ship* 船的上層／下層／主甲板 ◇ *We sat on the top deck of the bus.* 我們坐在公共汽車的上層。◇ *My cabin is on deck C.* 我的艙位在 C 層甲板。➲ see also DOUBLE-DECKER (1), FLIGHT DECK, SINGLE-DECKER **3** (also ˌ**deck of ˈcards**) (both *especially NAmE*) a complete set of 52 PLAYING CARDS 一副（52 張紙牌）➲ **VISUAL VOCAB** page V37 **4** a wooden floor that is built outside the back of a house where you can sit and relax（屋後供憩息的）木製平台 ➲ **VISUAL VOCAB** page V19 **5** a part of a SOUND SYSTEM that records and/or plays sounds on a disc or tape（唱機的）轉盤裝置；（音響系統的）走帶機構，錄音座：*a* ***cassette/tape deck*** 盒式錄音帶／磁帶轉動機械裝置 **IDM** see CLEAR *v.*, HAND *n.*, HIT *v.*

■ **verb** **1** [often passive] **~ sb/sth (out) (in/with sth)** to decorate sb/sth with sth 裝飾；佈置；打扮：*The room was decked out in flowers and balloons.* 房間裏裝點着鮮花和氣球。**2 ~ sb** (*informal*) to hit sb very hard so that they fall to the ground 用力擊倒；打倒在地；揍趴下

deck·chair /ˈdektʃeə(r); *NAmE* -tʃer/ *noun* a folding chair with a seat made from a long strip of material on a wooden or metal frame, used for example on a beach（沙灘等用的）帆布摺疊椅 ➲ **VISUAL VOCAB** page V19

deck·hand /ˈdekhænd/ *noun* a worker on a ship who does work that is not skilled 艙面水手；普通水手

deck·ing /ˈdekɪŋ/ *noun* [U] wood used to build a floor (called a DECK) in the garden/yard next to or near a house（房屋外的）平台木板

ˈ**deck shoe** *noun* a flat shoe made of strong cloth or soft leather, with a soft SOLE which does not slip 平底帆布鞋，平底軟皮鞋（鞋底防滑）

de·claim /dɪˈkleɪm/ *verb* [T, I] **~ (against) sth | ~ that … | + speech** (*formal*) to say sth loudly; to speak loudly and with force about sth you feel strongly about, especially in public（尤指在公眾前）慷慨激昂地宣講，慷慨陳辭：*She declaimed the famous opening speech of the play.* 她慷慨激昂地朗誦了這齣戲中著名的開場白。◇ *He declaimed against the evils of alcohol.* 他慷慨陳辭，猛烈抨擊酗酒的罪惡。

dec·lam·ation /ˌdekləˈmeɪʃn/ *noun* (*formal*) **1** [U] the act of speaking or of expressing sth to an audience in a formal way 朗誦；雄辯 **2** [C] a speech or piece of writing that strongly expresses feelings and opinions 慷慨激昂的演說（辭）

de·clama·tory /dɪˈklæmətəri; *NAmE* -tɔːri/ *adj.* (*formal*) expressing feelings or opinions in a strong way in a speech or a piece of writing 慷慨陳辭的；雄辯演說的

dec·lar·ation /ˌdekləˈreɪʃn/ *noun* **1** [C, U] an official or formal statement, especially about the plans of a government or an organization; the act of making such a statement 公告；宣告；宣言：*to* ***issue/sign a declaration*** 發佈／簽署公告 ◇ *the declaration of war* 宣戰 ◇ *the Declaration of Independence* (= of the United States)（美國）獨立宣言 **2** [C] a written or spoken statement, especially about what people feel or believe 聲明（書）；宣佈；表白；宣稱：*a* ***declaration of love/faith/guilt*** 表白愛情；表達信念；宣判有罪 ➲ **SYNONYMS** at STATEMENT **3** [C] an official written statement giving information 申報（單）：*a declaration of income* 收益申報表 ◇ *customs declarations* (= giving details of goods that have been brought into a country) 報關單（帶入境內物品的詳細清單）

the Decla̩ration of Indeˈpendence *noun* [sing.] the document which stated that the thirteen British COLONIES in America were independent of Britain. It was adopted on July 4, 1776.《獨立宣言》（1776 年 7 月 4 日正式通過，宣佈在北美的十三個英國殖民地脫離英國獨立）

de·clara·tive /dɪˈklærətɪv/ *adj.* (*grammar* 語法) (of a sentence 句子) in the form of a simple statement 陳述的

Synonyms 同義詞辨析

declare

state • indicate • announce

These words all mean to say sth, usually firmly and clearly and often in public. 以上各詞均含表明、宣稱、宣佈之意。

declare (*rather formal*) to say sth officially or publicly; to state sth firmly and clearly 指公佈、宣佈、表明、宣稱：*to declare war* 宣戰 ◇ *The painting was declared to be a forgery.* 這幅畫被判定為贋品。

state (*rather formal*) to formally write or say sth, especially in a careful and clear way 指陳述、說明、聲明：*He has already stated his intention to run for election.* 他已聲明打算參加競選。

indicate (*rather formal*) to state sth, sometimes in a way that is slightly indirect 指表明、暗示：*During our meeting, he indicated his willingness to cooperate.* 在我們會晤期間，他提及了合作的意願。

announce to tell people officially about a decision or plans; to give information about sth in a public place, especially through a loudspeaker; to say sth in a loud and/or serious way 指宣佈、宣告、（通過廣播）通知：*They haven't formally announced their engagement yet.* 他們還沒有正式宣佈訂婚。◇ *Has our flight been announced yet?* 廣播通知了我們的航班沒有？

DECLARE OR ANNOUNCE? 用 declare 還是 announce？

Declare is used more often for giving judgements; **announce** is used more often for giving facts.

* declare 較常用於表明意見、看法；announce 較常用於說明事實：~~*The painting was announced to be a forgery.*~~ ◇ ~~*They haven't formally declared their engagement yet.*~~

PATTERNS

- to declare/state/indicate/announce **that …**
- to declare/state sb/sth **to be** sth
- to declare/state/indicate/announce **your intention** to do sth
- to declare/state/announce sth **formally/publicly/officially**
- to declare/state/announce sth **firmly/confidently**

de·clare 0ᵯ /dɪˈkleə(r); *NAmE* dɪˈkler/ *verb*

1 0ᵯ [T] to say sth officially or publicly 公佈；宣佈；宣告：**~ sth** *The government has declared a state of emergency.* 政府已宣佈進入緊急狀態。◇ *Germany* ***declared war on*** *France on 1 August 1914.* 德國在 1914 年 8 月 1 日向法國宣戰。◇ *The government has* ***declared war on*** (= officially stated its intention to stop) *illiteracy.* 政府已宣佈要掃除文盲。◇ **~ that …** *The court declared that strike action was illegal.* 法庭宣判罷工為非法。◇ **~ sth + noun** *The area has been declared a national park.* 這地區已公佈為國家公園。◇ **~ sth to be sth** *The painting was declared to be a forgery.* 這幅畫被判定為贋品。◇ **~ sth + adj.** *The contract was declared void.* 這份合同被宣佈無效。◇ *I declare this bridge open.* 我宣佈這座大橋正式啟用。**2** 0ᵯ [T] to state sth firmly and clearly 表明；宣稱；斷言：**+ speech** *'I'll do it!' Tom declared.* "讓我來！"湯姆果斷地說。◇ **~ that …** *He declared that he was in love with her.* 他聲稱他已愛上她。◇ **~ sth** *Few people dared to declare their opposition to the regime.* 很少有人敢宣稱他們反對這個政權。◇ **~ yourself + adj./noun** *She declared herself extremely hurt by his lack of support.* 她說自己非常傷心，因為他沒有得到支持。**3** 0ᵯ [T] **~ sth** to tell the tax authorities how much money you have earned 申報（收益）：*All income must be declared.* 所有收益必須申報。**4** 🗝 [T] **~ sth** to tell customs officers (= at the border of a country) that you are carrying goods on which you should pay tax 申報（應納稅品）：*Do you have anything to declare?* 你有什麼要申報的嗎？**5** [I] (in CRICKET 板球) to decide to end your INNINGS (= the period during which your team is BATTING) before all your players have BATTED（在擊球員還未全部出局時）宣佈結束賽局，宣佈停止擊球

PHR V **deˌclare aˈgainst sb/sth** (*BrE, formal*) to say publicly that you do not support sb/sth 聲明反對；表示不贊成 **deˈclare for sb/sth** (*BrE, formal*) to say publicly that you support sb/sth 聲明支持；表示贊成

de·clared /dɪˈkleəd; *NAmE* -ˈklerd/ *adj.* [only before noun] stated in an open way so that people know about it 公開宣佈（或聲明、表態）的 **SYN** **professed**：*the government's declared intention to reduce crime* 政府公開宣佈的減少犯罪的計劃

de·clas·sify /ˌdiːˈklæsɪfaɪ/ *verb* (**de·clas·si·fies, de·clas·si·fy·ing, de·clas·si·fied, de·clas·si·fied**) **~ sth** to state officially that secret government information is no longer secret 將（政府機密文件）解密：*declassified* ***information/documents*** 已解密的情報／文件 **OPP** **classify** ▸ **de·clas·si·fi·ca·tion** /ˌdiːˌklæsɪfɪˈkeɪʃn/ *noun* [U]

de·clen·sion /dɪˈklenʃn/ *noun* (*grammar* 語法) **1** [C] a set of nouns, adjectives or pronouns that change in the same way to show CASE, number and GENDER（名詞、形容詞或代詞顯示性、數、格的）變格 **2** [U] the way in which some sets of nouns, adjectives and pronouns change their form or endings to show CASE, number or GENDER（名詞、形容詞和代詞顯示性、數、格的）詞形變化

de·cline 🗝 **AW** /dɪˈklaɪn/ *noun, verb*

▪ ***noun*** 🗝 [C, usually sing., U] **~ (in sth)** | **~ (of sth)** a continuous decrease in the number, value, quality, etc. of sth（數量、價值、質量等的）減少，下降，衰落，衰退：*a* ***rapid/sharp/gradual decline*** 迅速／急劇／逐漸下降 ◇ ***urban/economic decline*** 城市衰落；經濟衰退 ◇ *The company reported a small decline in its profits.* 公司報告其利潤略有減少。◇ *An increase in cars has resulted in the decline of public transport.* 汽車的增加導致了公共交通的減少。◇ *The town* ***fell into*** *(****a****)* ***decline*** (= started to be less busy, important, etc.) *after the mine closed.* 這個鎮在礦井關閉後開始衰落。◇ *Industry in Britain has been* ***in decline*** *since the 1970s.* 英國工業自 20 世紀 70 年代以來一直在走下坡路。

▪ ***verb*** **1** 🗝 [I] (rather *formal*) to become smaller, fewer, weaker, etc. 減少；下降；衰弱；衰退：*Support for the party continues to decline.* 對該黨的支持繼續下降。◇ *The number of tourists to the resort declined by 10% last year.* 去年到這個勝地旅遊的人數減少了 10%。◇ *Her health was declining rapidly.* 她的健康狀況迅速惡化。**2** [I, T] (*formal*) to refuse politely to accept or to do sth 謝絕；婉言拒絕 **SYN** **refuse**：*I offered to give them a lift but they declined.* 我主動提議開車送他們，但他們婉言謝絕了。◇ **~ sth** *to* ***decline an offer/invitation*** 謝絕對方的主動幫助／邀請 ◇ **~ to do sth** *Their spokesman declined to comment on the allegations.* 他們的發言人拒絕對這些指控加以評論。**3** [I, T] **~ (sth)** (*grammar* 語法) if a noun, an adjective or a pronoun **declines**, it has different forms according to whether it is the subject or the object of a verb, whether it is in the singular or plural, etc. When you **decline** a noun, etc., you list these forms.（根據名詞、形容詞或代詞在句中的作用）變格，使發生詞形變化 ➲ compare CONJUGATE

IDM **sb's declining ˈyears** (*literary*) the last years of sb's life 暮年；晚年

de·clut·ter (also **de-clut·ter**) /diːˈklʌtə(r)/ *verb* [I, T] to remove things that you do not use so that you have more space and can easily find things when you need them 清除，清理（無用雜物）：*Moving is a good opportunity to declutter.* 搬家是清理無用雜物的好時機。◇ **~ sth** *a 7-step plan to help you declutter your home* 幫你把家清掃一淨的 7 步驟計劃

de·code /ˌdiːˈkəʊd; *NAmE* -ˈkoʊd/ *verb* **1 ~ sth** to find the meaning of sth, especially sth that has been written in code 解（碼）；破譯（尤指密碼）**SYN** **decipher** **2 ~ sth** to receive an electronic signal and change it into pictures that can be shown on a television screen 譯解（電子信號）：*decoding equipment* 電子信號譯解設備 **3 ~ sth** (*linguistics* 語言) to understand the meaning of sth in a foreign language 譯解，理解（外文）➲ compare ENCODE

de·coder /ˌdiːˈkəʊdə(r); *NAmE* -ˈkoʊ-/ *noun* a device that changes an electronic signal into a form that people can understand, such as sound and pictures（電子信號）解碼器，譯碼機：*a* ***satellite/video decoder*** 衞星／視頻解碼器

dé·col·le·tage /ˌdeɪkɒlˈtɑːʒ; *NAmE* -kɑːləˈt-/ (also **dé·col·leté** /deɪˈkɒlteɪ; *NAmE* ˌdeɪkɑːlˈteɪ/) *noun* (from *French*) the top edge of a woman's dress, etc. that is designed to be very low in order to show her shoulders and the top part of her breasts（女裝的）低胸露肩領 ▸ **dé·col·leté** *adj.*

de·col·on·iza·tion (*BrE* also **-isa·tion**) /diːˌkɒlənaɪˈzeɪʃn; *NAmE* -ˌkɑːlənəˈz-/ *noun* [U] the process of a COLONY or COLONIES becoming independent 非殖民（地）化；殖民地獨立

de·com·mis·sion /ˌdiːkəˈmɪʃn/ *verb* **~ sth** to officially stop using weapons, a nuclear power station, etc. 正式停止使用（武器、核電站等）

de·com·pose /ˌdiːkəmˈpəʊz; *NAmE* -ˈpoʊz/ *verb* **1** [I, T] to be destroyed gradually by natural chemical processes 腐爛 **SYN** **decay, rot**：*a decomposing corpse* 正在腐爛的屍體 ◇ *As the waste materials decompose, they produce methane gas.* 廢物腐爛時會產生沼氣。◇ **~ sth** *a decomposed body* 已經腐爛了的屍體 **2** [T, I] **~ (sth) (into sth)** (*technical* 術語) to divide sth into smaller parts; to divide into smaller parts（使）分解 ▸ **de·com·pos·ition** /ˌdiːkɒmpəˈzɪʃn; *NAmE* -kɑːm-/ *noun* [U]：*the decomposition of organic waste* 有機垃圾的分解

de·com·press /ˌdiːkəmˈpres/ *verb* **1** [I, T] **~ (sth)** to have the air pressure in sth reduced to a normal level or to reduce it to its normal level（使）減壓；（給）卸壓 **2** [T] **~ sth** (*computing* 計) to return files, etc. to their original size after they have been COMPRESSED 解壓縮（將壓縮文件等恢復到原大小）**OPP** **compress**

de·com·pres·sion /ˌdiːkəmˈpreʃn/ *noun* [U] **1** a reduction in air pressure; the act of reducing the pressure of the air 減壓；卸壓：*a* ***decompression chamber*** (= a piece of equipment that DIVERS sit in so that they can return slowly to normal air pressure after being deep in the sea) 減壓艙（潛水員深海作業後坐在其中恢復到正常氣壓）◇ ***decompression sickness*** (= severe pain and difficulty in breathing experienced by DIVERS who come back to the surface of deep water too quickly) 減壓病（潛水員從深水迅速回到水面後感到的劇痛和呼吸困難）➲ see also BENDS at BEND *n.* (2) **2** (*technical* 術語) the act or process of allowing sth that has been compressed (= made smaller) to fill the space that it originally took up 解壓縮（將壓縮的東西恢復到原位）

de·com·pres·sor /ˌdiːkəmˈpresə(r)/ *noun* (*BrE*) **1** (*technical* 術語) a device for reducing pressure in a vehicle's engine（機動車發動機的）減壓裝置，減壓器 **2** (*computing* 計) a computer program which returns files, etc. to their original size after they have been COMPRESSED 解壓縮程序

de·con·gest·ant /ˌdiːkənˈdʒestənt/ *noun* a medicine that helps sb with a cold to breathe more easily 減充血藥：*a nasal decongestant* 鼻塞通藥

de·con·se·crate /ˌdiːˈkɒnsɪkreɪt; *NAmE* -ˈkɑːn-/ *verb* **~ sth** (*religion* 宗) to stop using sth, especially a building, for a religious purpose 停止把（建築物等）用於宗教目的；把…改作俗用：*a deconsecrated church* 改作俗用的教堂 ▸ **de·con·se·cra·tion** *noun* [U]

de·con·struct /ˌdiːkənˈstrʌkt/ *verb* **~ sth** (*technical* 術語) (in literature and philosophy 文學和哲學) to analyse a text in order to show that there is no fixed meaning within the text but that the meaning is created each time in the act of reading 解構分析（文本沒有固定意義，而在每次的閱讀中才構建出意義）

D

D

Collocations 詞語搭配

Decorating and home improvement 裝飾和改善房屋

Houses 房屋

- **refurbish/renovate/**(*BrE*) **do up** a building/a house 整修／翻新／修繕樓房／房屋
- **convert** a building/house/room into homes/offices/(*especially NAmE*) apartments/(*BrE*) flats 把樓房／房子／房間改建成住房／辦公室／公寓
- **extend/enlarge** a house/building/room/kitchen 擴建／擴大房屋／樓房／房間／廚房
- **build** (*BrE*) an extension (to the back/rear of a house)/(*NAmE*) an addition (on/to sth)/(*BrE*) a conservatory（在房子後面）擴建；（在某處）增建；建造暖房
- **knock down/demolish** a house/home/building/wall 推倒／拆除房子／住房／樓房／牆壁
- **knock out/through** the wall separating two rooms 將兩個房間的隔牆打通

Decoration 裝飾

- **furnish/paint/**(*especially BrE*) **decorate** a home/house/apartment/flat/room 佈置／油漆／裝飾住房／房子／公寓套房／單元房／房間
- **be decorated** in bright colours/(*especially US*) colors/in a traditional style/with flowers/with paintings 用明亮的色彩／傳統風格／花朵／繪畫裝飾
- **paint/plaster** the walls/ceiling 給牆壁／天花板上塗料／抹灰
- **hang/put up/strip off/remove** the wallpaper 貼／除牆紙
- **install/replace/remove** the bathroom fixtures/(*BrE*) fittings 安裝／更換／拆除浴室的固定裝置／附加設備
- **build/put up** shelves 搭架子
- **lay** wooden flooring/timber decking/floor tiles/a carpet/a patio 鋪設木地板／平台木板／地磚／地毯／露台
- **put up/hang/take down** a picture/painting/poster/curtain 掛上／取下圖畫／繪畫／海報／簾子

DIY/home improvement 自己動手；房屋改造

- **do** (*BrE*) DIY/carpentry/the plumbing/the wiring 自己動手做；做木匠活；鋪設管道；鋪設電路
- **make** home improvements 改造房屋
- **add/install** central heating/underfloor heating/insulation 添加／安裝中央供暖系統／地暖系統／隔熱材料
- **fit/install** double-glazing/a smoke alarm 安裝雙層玻璃／煙霧報警器
- **insulate** your house/your home/the walls/the pipes/the tanks/(*especially BrE*) the loft 在房子／住房／牆壁／管道／熱水箱／閣樓裏加隔熱裝置
- **fix/repair** a roof/a leak/a pipe/the plumbing/a leaking (*especially BrE*) tap/(*NAmE usually*) faucet 維修房頂／裂縫／管子／管道系統／漏水的水龍頭
- **block/clog (up)/unblock/unclog** a pipe/sink 堵住／疏通管道／洗滌池
- **make/drill/fill** a hole 開／鑽／填一個洞
- **hammer (in)/pull out/remove** a nail 錘進／拔出釘子
- **tighten/untighten/loosen/remove** a screw 擰緊／擰鬆／擰開螺絲釘
- **saw/cut/treat/stain/varnish/paint** wood 鋸／切割／加工木料；給木料上色／上清漆／上油漆

de·con·struc·tion /ˌdiːkənˈstrʌkʃn/ *noun* [U] (*technical* 術語) (in literature and philosophy 文學和哲學) a theory that states that it is impossible for a text to have one fixed meaning, and emphasizes the role of the reader in the production of meaning 解構理論（文本不可能只有一個固定意義，強調讀者在意義構建過程中的作用）➲ compare STRUCTURALISM ▸ **de·con·struc·tion·ist** *noun, adj.*：*a deconstructionist critic/approach* 解構分析評論家／方法

de·con·tam·in·ate /ˌdiːkənˈtæmɪneɪt/ *verb* **~ sth** to remove harmful substances from a place or thing 清除有害物質；排除…的污染：*the process of decontaminating areas exposed to radioactivity* 清除受輻射污染地區有害物質的過程 ▸ **de·con·tam·in·ation** /ˌdiːkənˌtæmɪˈneɪʃn/ *noun* [U]

de·con·trol /ˌdiːkənˈtrəʊl; *NAmE* -ˈtroʊl/ *verb* (**-ll-**) **~ sth** (*formal, especially NAmE*) if a government **decontrols** sth, it removes legal controls from it 解除對…的控制；撤銷對…的管制 SYN **deregulate** ▸ **de·con·trol** *noun* [U]

decor /ˈdeɪkɔː(r); *NAmE* deɪˈkɔːr/ *noun* [U, C, usually sing.] the style in which the inside of a building is decorated（建築內部的）裝飾佈局，裝飾風格：*interior decor* 室內裝飾風格 ◇ *the restaurant's elegant new decor* 餐館內部別致的新裝潢

dec·or·ate 0-w /ˈdekəreɪt/ *verb* **1** 0-w [T] **~ sth (with sth)** to make sth look more attractive by putting things on it 裝飾；裝潢：*They decorated the room with flowers and balloons.* 他們用花和氣球裝飾了房間。◇ *The cake was decorated to look like a car.* 這蛋糕裝飾得像一輛汽車。**2** 0-w [I, T] (*especially BrE*) to put paint, WALLPAPER, etc. on the walls and ceilings of a room or house 粉刷；油漆；糊牆紙：*I hate decorating.* 我討厭粉刷牆壁。◇ *He has his own painting and decorating business.* 他經營自己的油漆和粉刷牆壁生意。◇ **~ sth** *We need to decorate the sitting room.* 我們需要將客廳粉刷一下。◇ *The sitting room needs decorating.* 客廳需要粉刷。**3** 0-w [T] **~ sth** to be placed on sth in order to make it look more attractive 點綴；裝點 SYN **adorn**：*Photographs of actors decorated the walls of the restaurant.* 演員的照片裝點着餐館的牆壁。**4** [T, usually passive] **~ sb (for sth)** to give sb a MEDAL as a sign of respect for sth they have done 授給（某人）勳章（或獎章）

dec·or·ation 0-w /ˌdekəˈreɪʃn/ *noun* **1** 0-w [C, usually pl.] a thing that makes sth look more attractive on special occasions 裝飾品：*Christmas decorations* 聖誕節裝飾品 ◇ *a table decoration* 餐桌裝飾物 **2** 0-w [U, C] a pattern, etc. that is added to sth and that stops it from being plain 裝飾圖案：*the elaborate decoration on the carved wooden door* 木雕門上精美的裝飾圖案 **3** 0-w [U] the style in which sth is decorated 裝飾風格：*a Chinese theme in the interior decoration* 室內裝飾的中國情調 **4** [U] (*BrE*) the act or process of decorating sth such as the inside of a house by painting it, etc.（房屋內部等的）裝飾，裝潢 **5** [C] a MEDAL that is given to sb as an honour 勳章；獎章

dec·ora·tive 0-w /ˈdekərətɪv; *NAmE* ˈdekəreɪtɪv/ *adj.* (of an object or a building 物體或建築) decorated in a way that makes it attractive; intended to look attractive or pretty 裝飾性的；作裝飾用的：*The mirror is functional yet decorative.* 這鏡子能照人，但也有裝飾作用。◇ *purely decorative arches* 純屬裝飾性的拱門

ˌdecorative ˈarts *noun* [pl.] artistic activities which produce objects which are useful and beautiful at the same time（實用美觀兼備的）裝飾藝術

dec·or·ator /ˈdekəreɪtə(r)/ *noun* a person whose job is painting and decorating houses（房屋的）油漆匠，裱糊匠

dec·or·ous /ˈdekərəs/ *adj.* (*formal*) polite and appropriate in a particular social situation; not shocking 禮貌得體的；端莊穩重的 SYN **proper**：*a decorous kiss* 禮貌得體的一吻 ▸ **dec·or·ous·ly** *adv.*

de·corum /dɪˈkɔːrəm/ *noun* [U] (*formal*) polite behaviour that is appropriate in a social situation 禮貌得體；端莊穩重 SYN **propriety**

dé·coup·age /ˌdeɪkuːˈpɑːʒ/ *noun* [U] (*art* 美術) the art of decorating furniture or other objects by cutting out pictures or designs on paper and sticking them onto the surface 剪紙裝飾藝術

de·couple /diːˈkʌpl/ *verb* **~ sth (from sth)** (*formal*) to end the connection or relationship between two things (使兩事物)分離，隔斷

decoy /ˈdiːkɔɪ/ *noun* [C] **1** an animal or a bird, or a model of one, that attracts other animals or birds, especially so that they can be shot by people who are hunting them (誘捕鳥獸的)動物，假獸，假鳥 **2** a thing or a person that is used to trick sb into doing what you want them to do, going where you want them to go, etc. 誘餌；誘惑物；用作誘餌的人 ▸ **decoy** /dɪˈkɔɪ/ *verb* **~ sth**

de·crease *verb, noun*

■ *verb* /dɪˈkriːs/ [I, T] (rather *formal*) to become or make sth become smaller in size, number, etc. (使大小、數量等)減少，減小，降低：**~ (from sth) (to sth)** *The number of new students decreased from 210 to 160 this year.* 今年新生人數從 210 減少到 160。◇ *a decreasing population* 逐漸減少的人口 ◇ **~ by sth** *The price of wheat has decreased by 5%.* 小麥價格降低了 5%。◇ **~ in sth** *This species of bird is decreasing in numbers every year.* 這種鳥的數量在逐年減少。◇ **~ sth** *People should decrease the amount of fat they eat.* 人們應減少脂肪的攝入量。**OPP increase**

■ *noun* /ˈdiːkriːs/ [C, U] the process of reducing sth or the amount that sth is reduced by 減少；降低；減少量 **SYN reduction**：**~ (in sth)** *There has been some decrease in military spending this year.* 今年的軍費開支有所減少。◇ **~ (of sth)** *a decrease of nearly 6% in the number of visitors to the museum* 參觀博物館人數下降將近 6% **OPP increase**

de·cree /dɪˈkriː/ *noun, verb*

■ *noun* **1** [C, U] an official order from a ruler or a government that becomes the law 法令；政令：*to* ***issue/sign a decree*** 頒佈 / 簽署法令 ◇ *a leader who rules* ***by decree*** (= not in a DEMOCRATIC way) 專制統治者 **2** [C] a decision that is made in court (法院的)裁定，判決

■ *verb* (**de·cree·ing**, **de·creed**, **de·creed**) [T, I] to decide, judge or order sth officially 裁定；判決；頒佈：**~ (sth)** *The government decreed a state of emergency.* 政府下令進入緊急狀態。◇ **~ what, how, etc. …** *We cannot decree what the committee should do.* 我們不能命令委員會做什麼。◇ **it is decreed that …** *It was decreed that the following day would be a holiday.* 法令宣佈第二天為休假日。

de,cree 'absolute *noun* [sing.] (*BrE*, *law* 律) an order from a court that finally ends a marriage, making the two people divorced (法院對離婚訴訟的)絕對判決，最終判決：*The period between the decree nisi and the decree absolute was six weeks.* 離婚判決令和最終判決之間的期限當時為六個星期。

decree nisi /dɪˌkriː ˈnaɪsaɪ/ *noun* [sing.] (*BrE*, *law* 律) an order from a court that a marriage will end after a fixed amount of time unless there is a good reason why it should not (法院對離婚訴訟的)非絕對判決，初期判決

de·crepit /dɪˈkrepɪt/ *adj.* (of a thing or person 物或人) very old and not in good condition or health 衰老的；老朽的；破舊的

de·crepi·tude /dɪˈkrepɪtjuːd; *NAmE* -tuːd/ *noun* [U] (*formal*) the state of being old and in poor condition or health 衰老；老朽；破舊

de·crim·in·al·ize (*BrE* also **-ise**) /diːˈkrɪmɪnəlaɪz/ *verb* **~ sth** to change the law so that sth is no longer illegal (改變法律以)使合法化：*There are moves to decriminalize some soft drugs.* 已採取步驟使某些軟毒品合法化。**OPP criminalize** ▸ **de·crim·in·al·iza·tion**, **-isa·tion** /diːˌkrɪmɪnəlaɪˈzeɪʃn; *NAmE* -ləˈz-/ *noun* [U]

decry /dɪˈkraɪ/ *verb* (**de·cries**, **de·cry·ing**, **de·cried**, **de·cried**) **~ sb/sth (as sth)** (*formal*) to strongly criticize sb/sth, especially publicly (公開)譴責；(強烈)批評 **SYN condemn**：*The measures were decried as useless.* 這些措施受到指責，說是不起作用。

de·crypt /diːˈkrɪpt/ *verb* **~ sth** (*computing* 計) to change information that is in code into ordinary language so that it can be understood by anyone 脫密；給…解密 **OPP encrypt** ▸ **de·cryp·tion** /diːˈkrɪpʃn/ *noun* [U] **OPP encryption**

dedi·cate /ˈdedɪkeɪt/ *verb* **1** to give a lot of your time and effort to a particular activity or purpose because you think it is important 把…奉獻給 **SYN devote**：**~ yourself/sth to sth** *She dedicates herself to her work.* 她獻身於自己的工作。◇ **~ yourself/sth to doing sth** *He dedicated his life to helping the poor.* 他畢生致力於幫助窮人。 **2 ~ sth to sb** to say at the beginning of a book, a piece of music or a performance that you are doing it for sb, as a way of thanking them or showing respect (在書、音樂或演出的前部)題獻辭：*This book is dedicated to my parents.* 謹以此書獻給我的父母。 **3** to hold an official ceremony to say that a building or an object has a special purpose or is special to the memory of a particular person 為…舉行奉獻典禮；為(建築物等)舉行落成典禮：**~ sth** *The chapel was dedicated in 1880.* 這座小教堂於 1880 年舉行獻堂典禮。◇ **~ sth to sb/sth** *A memorial stone was dedicated to those who were killed in the war.* 為陣亡將士紀念碑舉行了落成典禮。

dedi·cated /ˈdedɪkeɪtɪd/ *adj.* **1** working hard at sth because it is very important to you 獻身的；專心致志的；一心一意的 **SYN committed**：*a dedicated teacher* 富有獻身精神的教師◇ **~ to sth** *She is dedicated to her job.* 她對工作專心致志。 **2** [only before noun] designed to do only one particular type of work; used for one particular purpose only 專用的；專門用途的：*Software is exported through a dedicated satellite link.* 軟件通過專用衛星線路出口。

dedi·ca·tion /ˌdedɪˈkeɪʃn/ *noun* **1** [U] **~ (to sth)** (*approving*) the hard work and effort that sb puts into an activity or purpose because they think it is important 獻身；奉獻 **SYN commitment**：*hard work and dedication* 勤奮和奉獻 **2** [C] a ceremony that is held to show that a building or an object has a special purpose or is special to the memory of a particular person (建築物等的)落成典禮 **3** [C] the words that are used at the beginning of a book, a piece of music, a performance, etc. to offer it to sb as a sign of thanks or respect (書、音樂或演出前部的)獻辭

de·duce **AW** /dɪˈdjuːs; *NAmE* dɪˈduːs/ *verb* (*formal*) to form an opinion about sth based on the information or evidence that is available 推論；推斷；演繹 **SYN infer**：**~ sth (from sth)** *We can deduce a lot from what people choose to buy.* 從人們選購的東西可以作出多方面的推斷。◇ **~ (from sth) that, what, how, etc. …** *Can we deduce from your silence that you do not approve?* 你保持沉默，我們是否可以據此而推斷出你不贊成？ ➲ see also DEDUCTION ▸ **de·du·cible** /dɪˈdjuːsəbl; *NAmE* -ˈduːs-/ *adj.*

de·duct /dɪˈdʌkt/ *verb* [often passive] to take away money, points, etc. from a total amount (從總量中)扣除，減去 **SYN subtract**：**~ sth** *Ten points will be deducted for a wrong answer.* 答錯一題扣十分。◇ **~ sth from sth** *The cost of your uniform will be deducted from your wages.* 制服費將從你的工資中扣除。

de·duct·ible /dɪˈdʌktəbl/ *adj., noun*

■ *adj.* that can be taken away from an amount of money you earn, from tax, etc. 可扣除的；可減免的：*These costs are deductible from profits.* 這些費用可從利潤中扣除。◇ *tax-deductible expenses* (= that you do not have to pay tax on) 可減免稅款的開支

■ *noun* (*NAmE*) (*BrE* **ex·cess**) the part of an insurance claim that a person has to pay while the insurance company pays the rest 免賠額；自負額：*a policy with a very high deductible* 免賠額極高的保單

de·duc·tion **AW** /dɪˈdʌkʃn/ *noun* **1** [U, C] the process of using information you have in order to understand a particular situation or to find the answer to a problem 演繹；推論；推理：*He arrived at the solution by a simple process of deduction.* 他通過一番簡單的推理得出了解決問題的方法。◇ *If my deductions are correct, I can tell you who the killer was.* 如果我的推論正確的話，我可

以告訴你誰是兇手。➲ compare INDUCTION (3) ➲ see also DEDUCE **2** [U, C] the process of taking an amount of sth, especially money, away from a total; the amount that is taken away 扣除（額）；減去（數）: *deductions from your pay for tax, etc.* 從工資中扣除稅金等的數額 ◇ *tax deductions* 稅金扣除額

D

de·duct·ive /dɪˈdʌktɪv/ *adj.* [usually before noun] using knowledge about things that are generally true in order to think about and understand particular situations or problems 演繹的；推論的；推理的: ***deductive logic/reasoning*** 演繹邏輯 / 推理 ➲ compare INDUCTIVE (1)

deed /diːd/ *noun* **1** (*formal, literary*) a thing that sb does that is usually very good or very bad 行為；行動 **SYN** **act**: *a **brave/charitable/evil/good deed*** 勇敢的行為；善舉；惡行；善行 ◇ *a tale of heroic deeds* 英雄事跡的故事 **2** (often plural in (*BrE*) 在英式英語中常用複數) a legal document that you sign, especially one that proves that you own a house or a building（尤指房產）契約，證書: *the deeds of the house* 房契 ➲ **COLLOCATIONS** at HOUSE ➲ see also TITLE DEED
IDM **your good deed for the ˈday** a helpful, kind thing that you do（所做的）好事，善事

ˌdeed of ˈcovenant *noun* (*BrE*) an agreement to pay a regular amount of money to sb/sth, especially a charity, that means that they also receive the tax that would have to be paid on this money 付款契據（承諾定期捐款的契約，受款人可兼獲為此款所應繳的稅額）: *Signing a deed of covenant makes £1 worth £1.33.* 簽署一張付款契據就使 1 英鎊價值變為 1.33 英鎊。

ˈdeed poll *noun* [U, sing.] (*BrE*) a legal document signed by only one person, especially in order to change their name 單務契約，單邊契據（由一方簽立，尤為更改姓名）: *Smith changed his name **by deed poll** to Jervis-Smith.* 史密斯通過單邊契據將自己的名字更改為傑維斯－史密斯。

dee·jay /ˈdiːdʒeɪ/ *noun, verb*
■ ***noun*** (*informal*) = DISC JOCKEY
■ ***verb*** [I] to perform as a DISC JOCKEY, especially in a club 當音樂唱片節目主持人；當唱片騎師

deem /diːm/ *verb* **~ sth + noun/adj.** | **~ sth to be sth** | **~ (that)** ... (*formal*) (not usually used in the progressive tenses 通常不用於進行時) to have a particular opinion about sth 認為；視為；相信 **SYN** **consider**: *The evening was deemed a great success.* 大家認為這次晚會非常成功。◇ *She **deemed it** prudent not to say anything.* 她認為什麼都不說是明智的。◇ *They would take any action **deemed necessary**.* 他們會採取認為必要的任何行動。

deep 🔑 /diːp/ *adj., adv., noun*

WORD FAMILY
deep *adj., adv.*
deeply *adv.*
deepen *verb*
depth *noun*

■ ***adj.*** (**deep·er**, **deep·est**)
▸ **TOP TO BOTTOM** 由頂向底 **1** 🔑 having a large distance from the top or surface to the bottom 深的；厚的: *a deep hole/well/river* 很深的洞 / 井 / 河 ◇ *deep water/snow* 深水；厚雪 **OPP** **shallow**
▸ **FRONT TO BACK** 由前向後 **2** 🔑 having a large distance from the front edge to the furthest point inside 縱深的；寬的: *a deep cut/wound* 很深的劃口 / 傷口 ◇ *a deep space* 深邃的空間 **OPP** **shallow**
▸ **MEASUREMENT** 量度 **3** 🔑 used to describe or ask about the depth of sth 有…深的: *The water is only a few inches deep.* 這水只有幾英寸深。◇ *How deep is the wound?* 傷口有多深？
▸ **-DEEP** 有…深 **4** (in adjectives 構成形容詞) as far up or down as the point mentioned 遠至…的；有…深的: *The water was only waist-deep so I walked ashore.* 水只有齊腰深，所以我涉水上了岸。**5** (in adjectives 構成形容詞) in the number of rows mentioned, one behind the other 成…排的；有…層的: *They were standing three-deep at the bar.* 他們在吧枱前站成三排。
▸ **BREATH/SIGH** 呼吸；歎息 **6** 🔑 [usually before noun] taking in or giving out a lot of air 深（呼吸）的: *She took a deep breath.* 她深深地吸了一口氣。◇ *He gave a deep sigh.* 他深深地歎了一口氣。
▸ **SOUNDS** 聲音 **7** 🔑 low 深沉的；低沉的: *I heard his deep warm voice filling the room.* 我聽到他低沉暖人的話語在整個房間裏迴盪。◇ *a **deep roar/groan*** 低沉的轟鳴聲 / 呻吟聲
▸ **COLOURS** 顏色 **8** 🔑 strong and dark 深的: *a rich deep red* 鮮豔的深紅色 **OPP** **pale**
▸ **SLEEP** 睡眠 **9** 🔑 a person in a **deep** sleep is difficult to wake 酣睡的；沉睡的: *to be in a **deep sleep/trance/coma*** 酣睡；昏睡；昏迷 **OPP** **light**
▸ **SERIOUS** 嚴重 **10** 🔑 extreme or serious 極度的；嚴重的: *He's **in deep trouble**.* 他陷入極度困境之中。◇ *a deep economic recession* 嚴重的經濟衰退 ◇ *The affair had exposed deep divisions within the party.* 這件事暴露出黨內的嚴重分歧。◇ *a place of great power and of deep significance* 具有重大影響力和深遠意義的地方
▸ **EMOTIONS** 情感 **11** 🔑 strongly felt 強烈的；深切的；衷心的 **SYN** **sincere**: *deep respect* 深深的敬意 ◇ *a deep sense of loss* 強烈的失落感
▸ **KNOWLEDGE** 知識 **12** 🔑 showing great knowledge or understanding 淵博的；深刻的: *a deep understanding* 深刻的理解
▸ **DIFFICULT TO UNDERSTAND** 難以理解 **13** 🔑 difficult to understand 深奧的；難懂的；難解的 **SYN** **profound**: *This discussion's getting too deep for me.* 這討論越來越深奧，使我難以理解。◇ *He pondered, as if over some deep philosophical point.* 他沉思着，彷彿在思索某個深奧的哲學問題。
▸ **INVOLVED** 深陷 **14 ~ in sth** fully involved in an activity or a state 專心；全神貫注；深陷: *to be **deep in thought/conversation*** 陷入深思；專心談話 ◇ *He is often so deep in his books that he forgets to eat.* 他常常專心於讀書以致忘了吃飯。◇ *The firm ended up **deep in debt**.* 這家公司最後債台高築。
▸ **PERSON** 人 **15** if a person is **deep**, they hide their real feelings and opinions 深沉的；摸不透的；城府深的: *She's always been a deep one, trusting no one.* 她這個人一直城府很深，對誰也不相信。
▸ **IN SPORT** 體育運動 **16** to or from a position far down or across the field 靠近對方端線的；靠近外場線的: *a deep ball from Beckham* 貝克漢姆踢到靠近對方端線的球 ➲ see also DEPTH
IDM **go off the ˈdeep end** (*informal*) to suddenly become very angry or emotional（突然）火冒三丈，大發脾氣，非常激動 **in deep ˈwater(s)** (*informal*) in trouble or difficulty 在困境中；在危難中 **jump/be thrown in at the ˈdeep end** (*informal*) to start or be made to start a new and difficult activity that you are not prepared for（使）陷入未曾料到的艱難處境，一籌莫展: *Junior hospital doctors are thrown in at the deep end in their first jobs.* 醫院的初級醫生開始工作時會遇上未曾料到的困難。➲ more at DEVIL, SHIT *n.*
■ ***adv.*** 🔑 (**deep·er**, **deep·est**) **~ (below, into, under, etc.)** a long way below the surface of sth or a long way inside or into sth 深深地；在深處；至深處: *Dig deeper!* 再挖深點！◇ *The miners were trapped deep underground.* 礦工被困在地下深處。◇ *whales that feed deep beneath the waves* 在大海深處進食的鯨魚 ◇ *He gazed deep into her eyes.* 他深深凝視着她的眼睛。◇ *They sat and talked **deep into the night*** (= until very late). 他們坐着談話，一直談到深夜。◇ *deep in the forest* 在森林深處 ◇ *He stood with his hands deep in his pockets.* 他雙手深插在衣袋裏站着。
IDM **deep ˈdown 1** if you know sth **deep down**, you know your true feelings about sth, although you may not admit them to yourself 在內心深處；在心底: *Deep down I still loved him.* 我在內心深處仍然愛着他。**2** if sth is true **deep down**, it is really like that, although it may not be obvious to people 本質上；實際上；事實上: *He seems confident but deep down he's quite insecure.* 他好像很有信心，實際上卻沒什麼把握。**go/run ˈdeep** (of emotions, beliefs, etc. 情感、信仰等) to be felt in a strong way, especially for a long time 強烈；深厚；深入內心: *Dignity and pride run deep in this community.* 尊嚴和驕傲已深深扎根於這個群體之中。➲ more at DIG *v.*, STILL *adj.*
■ ***noun*** [sing.] **the deep** (*literary*) the sea 海；海洋

ˌdeep-ˈdyed *adj.* (*NAmE*) having a particular characteristic or opinion very strongly 特性明顯的；立場鮮明的；十足的: *a deep-dyed socialist* 不折不扣的社會主義者

Which Word? 詞語辨析

deep / deeply

- The adverbs **deep** and **deeply** can both mean 'a long way down or into something'. **Deep** can only mean this and is more common than **deeply** in this sense. It is usually followed by a word like *into* or *below*. 副詞 deep 和 deeply 均含由上到下或從外到裏距離大的意思。deep 只含此義，而且用於此義時較 deeply 通用，其後通常接 into 或 below： *We decided to go deeper into the jungle.* 我們決定繼續深入叢林。
- **Deeply** usually means 'very much'. * deeply 常指非常之意： *deeply in love* 深愛 ◇ *deeply shocked* 大為震驚 You can use **deep down** (but not **deeply**) to talk about a person's real nature. 表示人的本性、心地可用 deep down（但不能用 deeply）： *She can seem stern, but deep down she's a very kind person.* 她看上去可能嚴厲，其實心地非常善良。◇ ~~*She can seem stern, but deeply she's a very kind person.*~~

deep·en /ˈdiːpən/ *verb* **1** [I, T] **~ (sth) (into sth)** if an emotion or a feeling **deepens**, or if sth **deepens** it, it becomes stronger（使情感、感覺等）加強，變強烈： *Their friendship soon deepened into love.* 他們的友誼很快發展成為愛情。 **2** [I, T] **~ (sth)** to become worse; to make sth worse（使）變糟，惡化，嚴重： *Warships were sent in as the crisis deepened.* 危機加重時艦艇便奉命來到現場。◇ *a deepening economic recession* 越來越嚴重的經濟衰退 **3** [I, T] to become deeper; to make sth deeper（使）變深；加深： *The water deepened gradually.* 水漸漸變深了。◇ *His frown deepened.* 他的眉頭皺得更緊了。◇ **~ sth** *There were plans to deepen a stretch of the river.* 曾經有過加深一段河道的計劃。 **4** [T] **~ sth** to improve your knowledge or understanding of sth 增長（知識）；加深（理解）： *an opportunity for students to deepen their understanding of different cultures* 學生加深理解不同文化的機會 **5** [I, T] **~ (sth)** if colour or light **deepens** or if sth **deepens** it, it becomes darker（使色澤、光線等）變濃；（使）變昏暗： *deepening shadows* 越來越暗的陰影 **6** [I, T] **~ (sth) (to sth)** if a sound or voice **deepens** or if you **deepen** it, it becomes lower or you make it lower（使聲音）變低沉： *His voice deepened to a growl.* 他的聲音變成了低沉的怒吼。 **7** [I] if your breathing **deepens**, you breathe more deeply than usual 深（呼吸）；喘（大氣）

ˌdeep ˈfreeze (*BrE*) (*US* **Deep·freeze™**, **ˌdeep ˈfreezer**) *noun* = FREEZER

ˌdeep-ˈfrozen *adj.* preserved at an extremely low temperature 低温冷藏的

ˌdeep-ˈfry *verb* [usually passive] **~ sth** to cook food in oil that covers it completely 油炸： *deep-fried chicken pieces* 油炸雞塊

deep·ly 🗝 /ˈdiːpli/ *adv.*
1 🗝 very; very much 很；非常；極其： *She is deeply religious.* 她非常虔誠。◇ *They were deeply disturbed by the accident.* 這個事故使他們深感不安。◇ *Opinion is* ***deeply divided*** *on this issue.* 對這個問題的意見分歧很大。◇ ***deeply rooted*** *customs/ideas* 根深蒂固的習俗／思想 ◇ ***deeply held*** *beliefs/convictions/views* (= that sb feels very strongly) 堅定不移的信仰／信念／觀點 **2** 🗝 used with some verbs to show that sth is done in a very complete way（與某些動詞連用）深刻地，強烈地，深沉地： *to* ***breathe/sigh/exhale deeply*** (= using all of the air in your lungs) 深呼吸；深深地歎息；長長地呼氣 ◇ ***sleep deeply*** (= in a way that makes it difficult for you to wake up) 酣睡 ◇ *to* ***think deeply*** (= about all the aspects of sth) 沉思 **3** 🗝 to a depth that is quite a long way from the surface of sth 至深處： *to drill deeply into the wood*（鑽頭）往木頭深處鑽 ➲ note at DEEP

ˌdeep-ˈrooted, **ˌdeep-ˈseated** *adj.* [usually before noun] (of feelings and beliefs 感情和信仰) very fixed and strong; difficult to change or to destroy 根深蒂固的；強烈的；堅定的： *a deep-rooted desire* 強烈的願望 ◇ *The country's political divisions are deep-seated.* 這個國家的政治分歧根深蒂固。

ˈdeep-sea (also *less frequent* **ˈdeep-water**) *adj.* [only before noun] of or in the deeper parts of the sea 深海的： *a deep-sea diver* 深海潛水員 ◇ ***deep-sea fishing/diving*** 深海捕魚／潛水

ˌdeep-ˈset *adj.* (*formal*) eyes that are **deep-set** seem to be quite far back in a person's face（眼睛）深陷的

ˌdeep-ˈsix *verb* [usually passive] **~ sth** (*NAmE, informal*) to decide not to do or use sth that you had planned to do or use 放棄；拋棄；丟棄： *Plans to build a new mall were deep-sixed after protests from local residents.* 修建新室內購物中心的計劃由於當地居民反對而擱置。

the ˌDeep ˈSouth *noun* [sing.] the southern states of the US, especially Georgia, Alabama, Mississippi, Louisiana and South Carolina 美國南部諸州（尤指佐治亞、亞拉巴馬、密西西比、路易斯安那和南卡羅來納州）

ˈdeep structure (also **ˈD-structure**) *noun* (*grammar* 語法) the basic relationships between the different parts of a sentence, which show how we think when we are using language 深層結構 ➲ compare SURFACE STRUCTURE

ˌdeep vein thromˈbosis *noun* [U, C] (*abbr.* **DVT**) (*medical* 醫) a serious condition caused by a blood CLOT (= a thick mass of blood) forming in a VEIN 深靜脈血栓： *Passengers on long-haul flights are being warned about the risks of deep vein thrombosis.* 長途航班上的乘客須注意可能出現深靜脈血栓。

deer /dɪə(r); *NAmE* dɪr/ *noun* (*pl.* **deer**) an animal with long legs, that eats grass, leaves, etc. and can run fast. Most male deer have ANTLERS (= horns shaped like branches). There are many types of deer. 鹿： *a herd of deer* 一群鹿 ◇ *a deer park* 鹿苑 ➲ see also FALLOW DEER, RED DEER, REINDEER, ROE DEER, DOE, FAWN *n.* (1), STAG

deer·stalk·er /ˈdɪəstɔːkə(r); *NAmE* ˈdɪrs-/ *noun* a cap with two PEAKS, one in front and one behind, and two pieces of cloth which are usually tied together on top but can be folded down to cover the ears 獵鹿帽（前後各有一帽舌，兩塊護耳可繫於帽頂）

def /def/ *adj.* (*slang*) excellent 極好的；很棒的： *a def band* 出色的樂隊

de·face /dɪˈfeɪs/ *verb* **~ sth** to damage the appearance of sth especially by drawing or writing on it 損傷…的外貌（尤指亂塗、亂寫） ▸ **de·face·ment** *noun* [U]

de facto /ˌdeɪ ˈfæktəʊ; *NAmE* -toʊ/ *adj.* [usually before noun] (from *Latin, formal*) existing as a fact although it may not be legally accepted as existing 實際上存在的（不一定合法）： *The general took de facto control of the country.* 這位將軍實際上控制了整個國家。 ▸ **de facto** *adv.*： *He continued to rule the country de facto.* 實際上，他繼續統治着這個國家。 ➲ compare DE JURE

defae·cate, **defae·ca·tion** (*BrE*) = DEFECATE, DEFECATION

def·am·ation /ˌdefəˈmeɪʃn/ *noun* [U, C] (*formal*) the act of damaging sb's reputation by saying or writing bad or false things about them 破壞名譽；誹謗；中傷： *The company sued for defamation.* 這家公司因受到誹謗而提起訴訟。

de·fama·tory /dɪˈfæmətri; *NAmE* -tɔːri/ *adj.* (*formal*) (of speech or writing 說話或文章) intended to harm sb by saying or writing bad or false things about them 誣衊的；誹謗的；中傷的

de·fame /dɪˈfeɪm/ *verb* **~ sb/sth** (*formal*) to harm sb by saying or writing bad or false things about them 誣衊；誹謗；中傷

de·fault /dɪˈfɔːlt; ˈdiːfɔːlt/ *noun, verb*
■ ***noun*** **1** [U, C] failure to do sth that must be done by law, especially paying a debt 違約（尤指未償付債務）： *The company is in default on the loan.* 這家公司拖欠借款。◇ *Mortgage defaults have risen in the last year.* 按揭借款違約在近一年裏呈上升趨勢。 **2** [U, C, usually sing.] (*computing* 計) what happens or appears if you do not make any other choice or change 默認；系統設定值；預置值： *The default option is to save your work every five minutes.* 默認設置為每五分鐘存盤一次。◇ *On this*

D

screen, 256 colours is the default. 這個顯示屏的系統設定值是 256 色。

IDM **by de'fault** 1 a game or competition can be won **by default** if there are no other people, teams, etc. taking part（比賽）因其他參賽者不到場，由於對手缺席（而勝出） 2 if sth happens **by default**, it happens because you have not made any other decision or choices which would make things happen in a different way 由於沒有特別作出決定（或選擇） **in de'fault of sth** (*formal*) because of a lack of sth 由於缺乏…；因為沒有…：*They accepted what he had said **in default of** any evidence to disprove it.* 由於缺乏相反的證據，他們相信了他的話。

■ *verb* **1** [I] **~ (on sth)** to fail to do sth that you legally have to do, especially by not paying a debt 違約，不履行義務（尤指不償還債務）：*to default on a loan/debt* 拖欠借款 / 債務 ◇ *defaulting borrowers/tenants* 不償還債務的借款人；拖欠租金的承租人 **2** [I] **~ (to sth)** (*computing* 計) to happen when you do not make any other choice or change 默認；預設；預置 ▸ **de·fault·er** *noun*：*mortgage defaulters* 按揭借款違約者

de·feat 0-w /dɪ'fiːt/ *verb*, *noun*

■ *verb* **1** 0-w **~ sb/sth** to win against sb in a war, competition, sports game, etc. 擊敗；戰勝 SYN **beat**：*He defeated the champion in three sets.* 他三盤擊敗了冠軍。◇ *a defeated army* 敗軍 **2** 0-w **~ sth** to stop sth from being successful 使失敗；阻撓；挫敗：*The motion was defeated by 19 votes.* 這項動議以 19 票反對被否決。◇ *Staying late at the office to discuss shorter working hours rather **defeats the object of the exercise!*** 遲遲待在辦公室討論縮短工作時間恰恰是在阻撓這一目標的實現！ **3 ~ sb** (*formal*) if sth **defeats** you, you cannot understand it 困惑；難住：*The instruction manual completely defeated me.* 這操作指南把我完全弄糊塗。

■ *noun* **1** 0-w [U, C] failure to win or to be successful 失敗；戰敗；挫敗：*The party faces defeat in the election.* 這個黨面臨選舉失敗。◇ *a **narrow/heavy defeat*** 惜敗；慘敗 ◇ *The world champion has only had two defeats in 20 fights.* 這個世界冠軍在 20 場賽事中只敗過兩場。◇ *They finally had to **admit defeat*** (= stop trying to be successful). 他們最後只得認輸。 **2** 0-w [C, usually sing.] the act of winning a victory over sb/sth 擊敗；戰勝：*the defeat of fascism* 戰勝法西斯主義

de·feat·ist /dɪ'fiːtɪst/ *adj.* expecting not to succeed, and showing it in a particular situation 失敗主義（者）的：*a **defeatist attitude/view*** 失敗主義的態度 / 觀點 ▸ **de·feat·ist** *noun*：*He is a pessimist and a defeatist.* 他是悲觀主義者，也是失敗主義者。 **de·feat·ism** *noun* [U]

defe·cate (*BrE* also **defae·cate**) /'defəkeɪt; 'diː-/ *verb* [I] (*formal*) to get rid of solid waste from your body through your BOWELS 排便 ▸ **defe·ca·tion** (*BrE* also **defae·ca·tion**) /ˌdefə'keɪʃn; ˌdiː-/ *noun* [U]

de·fect *noun*, *verb*

■ *noun* /'diːfekt; dɪ'fekt/ a fault in sth or in the way it has been made which means that it is not perfect 缺點；缺陷；毛病：*a speech defect* 言語缺陷 ◇ *a defect in the glass* 玻璃杯的缺陷

■ *verb* /dɪ'fekt/ [I] **~ (from sth) (to sth)** to leave a political party, country, etc. to join another that is considered to be an enemy 背叛；叛變；投敵 ▸ **de·fec·tion** /dɪ'fekʃn/ *noun* [U, C]：**~ (from sth) (to sth)** *There have been several defections from the ruling party.* 執政黨已有好幾位黨員倒戈。 **de·fect·or** *noun*

de·fect·ive /dɪ'fektɪv/ *adj.* having a fault or faults; not perfect or complete 有缺點的；有缺陷的；有毛病的 SYN **faulty**：*defective goods* 有缺陷的商品 ◇ *Her hearing was found to be slightly defective.* 經檢查，她的聽力有點缺陷。 ▸ **de·fect·ive·ly** *adv.* **de·fect·ive·ness** *noun* [U]

de·fence 0-w (*especially US* **de·fense**) /dɪ'fens/ *noun*

▸ **PROTECTION AGAINST ATTACK** 防禦 **1** 0-w [U] the act of protecting sb/sth from attack, criticism, etc. 防禦；保護；保衛：*soldiers who died **in defence of** their country* 為保衛祖國而獻身的戰士 ◇ *When her brother was criticized she **leapt to his defence**.* 她的哥哥受到批評時，她馬上跳出來衛護。◇ *What points can be raised in defence of this argument?* 有什麼論點能提出來為這個說法辯護呢？◇ *I have to say **in her defence** that she knew nothing about it beforehand.* 我得為她說句話，她事先並不知道此事。 ➲ see also SELF-DEFENCE **2** 0-w [C, U] **~ (against sth)** something that provides protection against attack from enemies, the weather, illness, etc. 防禦物；防務；防禦能力：*The town walls were built as a defence against enemy attacks.* 城牆是為防禦敵人襲擊而修建的。◇ *The harbour's sea defences are in poor condition.* 港口的海防工事狀況很差。◇ *The body has natural **defence mechanisms** to protect it from disease.* 人體具有先天性防禦機制以抵抗疾病。◇ *Humour is a more effective defence than violence.* 幽默是比暴力更有效的防禦武器。 **3** 0-w [U] the organization of the people and systems that are used by a government to protect a country from attack 國防機構；國防體系：(*BrE*) *the Ministry of Defence* 國防部 ◇ (*NAmE*) *the Department of Defense* 國防部 ◇ *Further cuts in defence spending are being considered.* 目前正在考慮進一步削減國防開支。

▸ **SUPPORT** 支持 **4** [C] something that is said or written in order to support sth 辯解；辯白：*a defence of Marxism* 為馬克思主義辯解

▸ **LAW** 法律 **5** [C] what is said in court to prove that a person did not commit a crime; the act of presenting this argument in court 辯護；辯詞；答辯：*Her defence was that she was somewhere completely different at the time of the crime.* 她的辯詞是案發時她根本就不在現場。◇ *He wanted to conduct his own defence.* 他想自己為自己辯護。 **6 the defence** [sing.+sing./pl. v.] the lawyer or lawyers whose job is to prove in court that a person did not commit a crime 被告方；辯方 ➲ compare PROSECUTION (2)

▸ **IN SPORT** 體育運動 **7** [sing., U] the players who must prevent the other team from scoring; the position of these players on the sports field 防守隊員；防守；後衛：*Welford cut through the defence to score the winning goal.* 韋爾福特突破防守射進了制勝的一球。◇ (*BrE*) *She plays **in defence**.* 她打防守。◇ (*NAmE*) *He plays **on defense**.* 他打防守。 ➲ compare ATTACK *n.* (8), OFFENSE (2) **8** [C] a contest, game, etc. in which the previous winner or winners compete in order to try to win again 衛冕賽：*Barcelona's defence of the Champions League title* 歐洲冠軍聯賽巴塞羅納隊的冠軍衛冕賽

de·fence·less (*especially US* **de·fense·less**) /dɪ'fensləs/ *adj.* weak; not able to protect yourself; having no protection 軟弱的；不能自衛的；無防禦的：*defenceless children* 沒有自衛能力的兒童 ◇ *The village is defenceless against attack.* 這個村莊毫無防禦能力。 ▸ **de·fence·less·ness** (*especially US* **de·fense·less·ness**) *noun* [U]

de·fend 0-w /dɪ'fend/ *verb*

▸ **PROTECT AGAINST ATTACK** 防禦 **1** 0-w [T, I] to protect sb/sth from attack 防禦；保護；保衛：**~ sb/yourself/sth** *Troops have been sent to defend the borders.* 已派出部隊去守衛邊疆。◇ **~ sb/yourself/sth from/against sb/sth** *All our officers are trained to defend themselves against knife attacks.* 我們所有的警察都接受過自衛訓練，能夠對付持刀襲擊。◇ **~ against sb/sth** *It is impossible to defend against an all-out attack.* 防禦全面進攻是不可能的。

▸ **SUPPORT** 支持 **2** 0-w [T] to say or write sth in support of sb/sth that has been criticized 辯解；辯白：**~ sth** *How can you defend such behaviour?* 你怎能為這種行為辯解呢？◇ **~ sb/yourself/sth from/against sb/sth** *Politicians are skilled at defending themselves against their critics.* 從政者都善於為自己辯解，反駁別人的批評。

▸ **IN SPORT** 體育運動 **3** [I, T] **~ (sth)** (in sports 體育運動) to protect your own goal to stop your opponents from scoring 防守 OPP **attack**

▸ **IN COMPETITIONS** 競賽 **4** [T] **~ sth** to take part in a competition that you won the last time and try to win it again 參加比賽（或選舉）保住（頭銜、席位等）：*He is **defending champion**.* 他在參加衛冕賽。◇ *She will be **defending her title** at next month's championships.* 她將在下月的錦標賽上爭取蟬聯冠軍。◇ (*politics* 政) *He intends to defend his seat in the next election.* 他想在下屆選舉中尋求連任。

▸ **LAW** 法律 **5** [T, I] **~ (sb/yourself)** to act as a lawyer for sb who has been charged with a crime 進行辯護；當辯護律師：*He has employed one of the UK's top lawyers* to defend him. 他請了英國一位頂尖律師為他辯護。 ➲ compare PROSECUTE (2)

de·fend·ant /dɪˈfendənt/ *noun* the person in a trial who is accused of committing a crime, or who is being sued by another person 被告人；被告 ➲ COLLOCATIONS at JUSTICE ➲ compare ACCUSED, PLAINTIFF

de·fend·er /dɪˈfendə(r)/ *noun* **1** a player who must stop the other team from scoring in games such as football (SOCCER), HOCKEY, etc. 防守隊員；後衛 **2** a person who defends and believes in protecting sth 守衛者；保護人；防禦者： *a passionate defender of human rights* 狂熱的人權衛士

de·fense (*especially US*) = DEFENCE

de·fens·ible /dɪˈfensəbl/ *adj.* **1** able to be supported by reasons or arguments that show that it is right or should be allowed 可辯解的；合乎情理的；有正當理由的： *Is abortion morally defensible?* 墮胎從道德上講合乎情理嗎？ OPP **indefensible 2** (of a place 地方) able to be defended from an attack 可防禦的；可守護的

de·fen·sive /dɪˈfensɪv/ *adj.*, *noun*

■ *adj.* **1** protecting sb/sth against attack 防禦的；保護的；保衛的： *a defensive measure* 防禦措施 ◇ *Troops took up a defensive position around the town.* 部隊在全城採取了守勢。 ➲ compare OFFENSIVE *adj.* (3) **2** behaving in a way that shows that you feel that people are criticizing you 戒備的；懷有戒心的；自衛的： *Don't ask him about his plans—he just gets defensive.* 別問他有什麼計劃，他老存有戒心。 **3** (*sport* 體) connected with trying to prevent the other team or player from scoring points or goals 防守的： *defensive play* 防守型打法 ➲ compare OFFENSIVE *adj.* (4) ▶ **de·fen·sive·ly** *adv.* **de·fen·sive·ness** *noun* [U]

■ *noun*

IDM **on/onto the deˈfensive** acting in a way that shows that you expect to be attacked or criticized; having to defend yourself 處於防禦姿態；處於戒備狀態；採取守勢： *Their questions about the money put her on the defensive.* 他們問到錢的問題時，她就警覺起來。◇ *Warnings of an enemy attack forced the troops onto the defensive.* 敵軍顯示出進攻的跡象，部隊不得不進入戒備狀態。

deˌfensive ˈmedicine *noun* [U] (*especially NAmE*) medical treatment that involves more tests, operations, etc. than a person really needs because a doctor is worried that a claim or complaint may be made against them in court if they make a mistake in the treatment they give 防禦性治療，自衛性治療（醫生擔心因誤診被起訴而讓病人做過多的化驗、手術等）

defer /dɪˈfɜː(r)/ *verb* (**-rr-**) **~ (doing) sth** (*formal*) to delay sth until a later time 推遲；延緩；展期 SYN **put off**： *The department deferred the decision for six months.* 這個部門推遲了六個月才作決定。◇ *She had applied for deferred admission to college.* 她已申請延期入學。 ▶ **de·fer·ment**, **de·fer·ral** /dɪˈfɜːrəl/ *noun* [U, C]

PHR V **deˈfer to sb/sth** (*formal*) to agree to accept what sb has decided or what they think about sb/sth because you respect him or her 遵從；聽從；順從： *We will defer to whatever the committee decides.* 我們遵從委員會的任何決定。

def·er·ence /ˈdefərəns/ *noun* [U] behaviour that shows that you respect sb/sth 尊重；遵從；聽從： *The women wore veils* ***in deference to*** *the customs of the country.* 這些婦女戴着面紗是遵從這個國家的習俗。◇ *The flags were lowered* ***out of deference to*** *the bereaved family.* 降旗是出於對死者家屬的尊重。 ▶ **def·er·en·tial** /ˌdefəˈrenʃl/ *adj.* **def·er·en·tial·ly** /-ʃəli/ *adv.*

de·fi·ance /dɪˈfaɪəns/ *noun* [U] open refusal to obey sb/sth 違抗；反抗；拒絕服從： *a look/an act/a gesture of defiance* 反抗的神色／行動／表示 ◇ *Nuclear testing was resumed* ***in defiance of*** *an international ban.* 儘管國際上明令禁止，核試驗又在進行了。

deˈfiance campaign *noun* (in South Africa in the past, especially in the period after 1952) a series of activities in which black people refused to obey laws that were not fair 抗法運動（尤指 1952 年之後，南非黑人拒絕遵守不公平的法律規定）

de·fi·ant /dɪˈfaɪənt/ *adj.* openly refusing to obey sb/sth, sometimes in an aggressive way 公然違抗的；反抗的；挑釁的： *a defiant teenager* 一個反叛的少年 ◇ *The terrorists sent a defiant message to the government.* 恐怖分子向政府發出了挑戰書。 ▶ **de·fi·ant·ly** *adv.*

de·fib·ril·la·tion /ˌdiːfɪbrɪˈleɪʃn/ *noun* [U] (*medical* 醫) the use of a controlled electric shock from a defibrillator to return the heart to its natural rhythm 心臟除顫（用電擊）

de·fib·ril·la·tor /diːˈfɪbrɪleɪtə(r)/ *noun* (*medical* 醫) a piece of equipment used to control the movements of the heart muscles by giving the heart a controlled electric shock 去纖顫器（通過電擊心臟控制心肌運動）

de·fi·ciency /dɪˈfɪʃnsi/ *noun* (*pl.* **-ies**) (*formal*) **1** [U, C] **~ (in/of sth)** the state of not having, or not having enough of, sth that is essential 缺乏；缺少；不足 SYN **shortage**： *Vitamin deficiency in the diet can cause illness.* 飲食中缺乏維生素可能導致疾病。◇ *a deficiency of Vitamin B* 缺乏維生素 B **2** [C] **~ (in/of sth)** a fault or a weakness in sth/sb that makes it or them less successful 缺點；缺陷： *deficiencies in the computer system* 計算機系統的種種缺陷

de·fi·cient /dɪˈfɪʃnt/ *adj.* (*formal*) **1 ~ (in sth)** not having enough of sth, especially sth that is essential 缺乏的；缺少的；不足的： *a diet that is deficient in vitamin A* 缺乏維生素 A 的飲食 **2** not good enough 有缺點的；有缺陷的： *Deaf people are sometimes treated as being mentally deficient.* 耳聾的人有時被看作智力不健全。

def·icit /ˈdefɪsɪt/ *noun* **1** (*economics* 經) the amount by which money spent or owed is greater than money earned in a particular period of time 赤字；逆差；虧損： *a* ***budget/trade deficit*** 預算赤字；貿易逆差 ◇ *The trade balance has been* ***in deficit*** *for the past five years.* 過去五年來貿易狀況一直是逆差。 ➲ COLLOCATIONS at INTERNATIONAL ➲ compare SURPLUS *n.* (2) **2** (*formal*) the amount by which sth, especially an amount of money, is too small or smaller than sth else 不足額；缺款額；缺少： *There's a deficit of $3 million in the total needed to complete the project.* 完成這項工程所需資金中有 300 萬元的虧空。◇ *The team has to come back from a 2–0 deficit in the first half.* 這支隊得扳回上半場 0:2 的落後局面。

de·fied *past tense, past part.* of DEFY

de·file¹ /dɪˈfaɪl/ *verb* **~ sth** (*formal* or *literary*) to make sth dirty or no longer pure, especially sth that people consider important or holy 弄髒；玷污；糟蹋；褻瀆： *Many victims of burglary feel their homes have been defiled.* 許多家門被撬的人都感到自己的家被玷污了。◇ *The altar had been defiled by vandals.* 聖壇受到破壞公物者的肆意踐踏。 ▶ **de·file·ment** *noun* [U, C]

de·file² /dɪˈfaɪl; ˈdiːfaɪl/ *noun* (*formal*) a narrow way through mountains 山中狹徑

de·fine 0-w AW /dɪˈfaɪn/ *verb*

1 0-w to say or explain what the meaning of a word or phrase is 解釋（詞語的含義）；給…下定義： **~ sth** *The term 'mental illness' is difficult to define.* "精神病"這個詞很難下定義。◇ **~ sth as sth** *Life imprisonment is defined as 60 years under state law.* 按照州法律終身監禁定義為 60 年。 **2** 0-w to describe or show sth accurately 闡明；明確；界定： **~ sth** *We need to define the task ahead very clearly.* 我們需要明確今後的任務。◇ *The difficulty of a problem was* ***defined in terms of*** *how long it took to complete.* 問題的難易度是以解決這個問題所花時間的長短而定的。◇ **~ what, how, etc. …** *It is difficult to define what makes him so popular.* 很難解釋清楚什麼原因使他如此走紅。 **3 ~ sth** to show clearly a line, shape or edge 畫出…的線條；描出…的外形；確定…的界線；界定： *The mountain was* ***sharply defined*** *against the sky.* 那座山在天空的襯托下顯得輪廓分明。 ▶ **de·fin·able** AW *adj.* ➲ LANGUAGE BANK at next page

deˌfined ˈbenefit *noun* a fixed amount of money that will be paid by a PENSION PLAN, especially when this amount is based on your salary at the end of your working life and the number of years you worked（養老金計劃的）固定福利金，月退俸

D

Language Bank 用語庫

define

Defining terms 為術語下定義

- **It is important to clarify what is meant by** climate change. 說清楚"氣候變化"的含義很重要。
- Climate change **can/may be defined as** 'the long-term fluctuations in temperature, precipitation, wind and other aspects of the earth's climate'. 氣候變化可以被定義為"地球氣候在溫度、降雨量、風力及其他方面的長期波動"。
- **A generally accepted definition of** global warming **is** the gradual increase in the overall temperature of the earth's atmosphere due to the greenhouse effect. 對於全球變暖，普遍接受的一種定義是：由於受到溫室效應的影響，地球大氣層總體溫度逐漸上升。
- The greenhouse effect **is defined** by the author **as** the process by which heat from the sun is trapped in the earth's atmosphere, causing the temperature of the earth to rise. 作者將溫室效應定義為：地球大氣層鎖住來自太陽的熱量，導致地球溫度上升的過程。
- The author **uses the term** climate change **to refer to** any significant change in measures of climate lasting for an extended period. 作者使用"氣候變化"這個術語來指代任何持續較長時間的氣候的顯著變化。
- **The term** 'carbon footprint' **refers to** the amount of carbon dioxide released into the atmosphere as a result of the activities of an individual or organization. "碳足跡"這個術語指的是由於個人和組織的活動排放到大氣層中的二氧化碳的量。
- Scientists suggest that increased carbon dioxide in the atmosphere will result in an increase in global temperatures, and **the term** 'global warming' **is used** to describe this phenomenon. 科學家認為大氣層中二氧化碳的增加會導致全球氣溫上升，"全球變暖"這個術語就是用來描述這種現象的。

➲ Language Bank at FIRST

de͵fined contri'bution *noun* fixed payments that are made to a PENSION PLAN, where the amount that will be paid out can change（養老金計劃的）固定供款

de·fin·ing /dɪ'faɪnɪŋ/ *adj.* = RESTRICTIVE (2)

de'fining vocabulary *noun* a set of carefully chosen words used to write the explanations in some dictionaries（詞典的）釋義詞彙

def·in·ite 🔑 AW /'defɪnət/ *adj., noun*

■ *adj.* **1** 🔑 **~ (that …)** sure or certain; unlikely to change 肯定的；確定的；不會改變的：*Can you give me a definite answer by tomorrow?* 你最晚明天能給我一個確定的答覆嗎？◇ *Is it definite that he's leaving?* 他肯定要離開嗎？◇ *I've heard rumours, but nothing definite.* 我聽到一些流言，但都不確定。◇ *a definite offer of a job* 明確給予一份工作 ◇ *I'm not sure—I can find out* **for definite** *if you like.* 我沒把握，如果你想要，我可以去核實。◇ *That's definite then, is it?* 那麼，那是確切的了，是嗎？◇ *They have very definite ideas on how to bring up children.* 關於如何培養孩子，他們有非常明確的想法。➲ SYNONYMS at CERTAIN **2** 🔑 easily or clearly seen or understood; obvious 清楚的；明顯的 SYN **clear**：*The look on her face was a definite sign that something was wrong.* 一看她的神色就知道出事了。◇ *There was a definite feeling that things were getting worse.* 人們明顯感到事情越來越糟。**3** [not before noun] **~ (about sth)** | **~ (that …)** (of a person 人) sure that sth is true or that sth is going to happen and stating it to other people 肯定；有把握：*I'm definite about this.* 我對這事毫無疑問。

■ *noun* [sing.] (*informal*) sth that you are certain about or that you know will happen; sb who is sure to do sth 肯定的事（或人）：*'We're moving our office to Glasgow.' 'That's a definite, is it?'* "我們的辦事處要搬到格拉斯哥去。""這事兒定了，是嗎？"◇ *'Is Sarah coming to the party?' 'Yes, she's a definite.'* "薩拉要來參加聚會嗎？""是的，她肯定來。"

͵definite 'article *noun* (*grammar* 語法) the word *the* in English, or a similar word in another language 定冠詞（如英語中的 the）➲ compare INDEFINITE ARTICLE

def·in·ite·ly 🔑 AW /'defɪnətli/ *adv.*

1 🔑 (*informal*) a way of emphasizing that sth is true and that there is no doubt about it 肯定；沒問題；當然；確實：*I definitely remember sending the letter.* 我記得這封信肯定發出去了。◇ *'Was it what you expected?' 'Yes, definitely.'* "那是你所期待的嗎？""當然是。"◇ *'Do you plan to have children?' 'Definitely not!'* "你們打算要孩子嗎？""絕對沒這個打算！"◇ *Some old people want help; others most definitely do not.* 有些老人想要得到幫助，有些卻根本不需要。**2** 🔑 in a way that is certain or that shows that you are certain 確切地；明確地；清楚地：*The date of the move has not been definitely decided yet* (= it may change). 搬遷日期還未完全確定下來。◇ *Please say definitely whether you will be coming or not.* 請說清楚，你來還是不來。

def·in·ition 🔑 AW /͵defɪ'nɪʃn/ *noun*

1 🔑 [C, U] an explanation of the meaning of a word or phrase, especially in a dictionary; the act of stating the meanings of words and phrases（尤指詞典裏的詞或短語的）釋義，解釋：*clear simple definitions* 簡單明瞭的釋義 ◇ *Neighbours* **by definition** *live close by* (= this is what being a neighbour means). 按照釋義，"鄰居"就是住在鄰近地方的人。➲ LANGUAGE BANK at DEFINE **2** 🔑 [C] what an idea, etc. means 定義：*What's your definition of happiness?* 你對幸福的定義是什麼？**3** [U] the quality of being clear and easy to see 清晰度：*The definition of the digital TV pictures is excellent.* 數字電視圖像的清晰度很高。

de·fini·tive AW /dɪ'fɪnətɪv/ *adj.* **1** final; not able to be changed 最後的；決定性的；不可更改的：*a* ***definitive agreement/answer/statement*** 最後的協議／答覆／聲明 ◇ *The* ***definitive version*** *of the text is ready to be published.* 正式的文本很快就要發表了。**2** [usually before noun] considered to be the best of its kind and almost impossible to improve 最佳的；最完整可靠的：*the definitive biography of Einstein* 最完整可靠的愛因斯坦傳記 ▸ **de·fini·tive·ly** *adv.*

de·flate *verb* **1** /dɪ'fleɪt; ͵diː-/ [T, I] **~ (sth)** to let air or gas out of a tyre, BALLOON, etc.; to become smaller because of air or gas coming out 放掉（輪胎、氣球等的）氣；（使）癟下來 **2** /dɪ'fleɪt/ [T, often passive] **~ sb/sth** to make sb feel less confident; to make sb/sth feel or seem less important 使泄氣；挫敗…的銳氣：*All the criticism had left her feeling totally deflated.* 所有這些批評使她徹底失去了信心。**3** /͵diː'fleɪt/ [T] **~ sth** (*economics* 經) to reduce the amount of money being used in a country so that prices fall or stay steady 緊縮（通貨）➲ compare INFLATE (3), REFLATE

de·fla·tion /͵diː'fleɪʃn/ *noun* [U] **1** (*economics* 經) a reduction in the amount of money in a country's economy so that prices fall or remain the same 通貨緊縮 ➲ COLLOCATIONS at ECONOMY **2** the action of air being removed from sth 放氣；抽氣；泄氣 OPP **inflation** ▸ **de·fla·tion·ary** /͵diː'fleɪʃənri; *NAmE* -neri/ *adj.*：*deflationary policies* 通貨緊縮政策

de·flect /dɪ'flekt/ *verb* **1** [I, T] to change direction or make sth change direction, especially after hitting sth（尤指擊中某物後）偏斜，轉向，使偏斜，使轉向：*The ball deflected off Reid's body into the goal.* 球打在里德身上反彈進球門。◇ **~ sth** *He raised his arm to try to deflect the blow.* 他舉起手臂試圖擋開這一擊。**2** [T] **~ sth** to succeed in preventing sth from being directed towards you 轉移；引開 SYN **divert**：*All attempts to* ***deflect attention*** *from his private life have failed.* 本想轉移人們對他私生活的注意，但一切努力都失敗了。◇ *She sought to* ***deflect criticism*** *by blaming her family.* 她責怪她的家人，企圖轉移對她的批評。**3** [T] **~ sb (from sth)** to prevent sb from doing sth that they are determined to do 阻止（某人做已決定做的事）：*The government will not be deflected from its commitments.* 政府決不會因任何阻礙而放棄承諾。

de·flec·tion /dɪˈflekʃn/ *noun* [U, C, usually sing.] a sudden change in the direction that sth is moving in, usually after it has hit sth; the act of causing sth to change direction（常指擊中某物後）突然轉向，偏斜，偏離：*the angle of deflection* 偏斜度 ◇ *the deflection of the missile away from its target* 導彈偏離目標 ◇ *The goal was scored with a deflection off the goalkeeper.* 這個入球是球打在守門員身上反彈入網的。

de·flower /ˌdiːˈflaʊə(r)/ *verb* **~ sb** (*old-fashioned, literary*) to have sex with a woman who has not had sex before 姦污（處女）；奪去（女子）的貞操

defog /ˌdiːˈfɒg; *NAmE* -ˈfɔːg; -ˈfɑːg/ *verb* (**-gg-**) [T, I] **~ (sth)** (*NAmE*) (*BrE* **de·mist**) to remove the CONDENSATION from a car's windows so that you can see clearly 除去（汽車玻璃上的）霧水

de·fo·liant /ˌdiːˈfəʊliənt; *NAmE* -ˈfoʊ-/ *noun* [C, U] a chemical that removes the leaves from plants, sometimes used as a weapon in war 落葉劑（有時用作軍事武器）

de·foli·ate /ˌdiːˈfəʊlieɪt; *NAmE* -ˈfoʊ-/ *verb* **~ sth** (*technical* 術語) to destroy the leaves of trees or plants, especially with chemicals （尤指用化學物質）除去…的葉 ▸ **de·foli·ation** /ˌdiːˌfəʊliˈeɪʃn; *NAmE* -ˌfoʊ-/ *noun* [U]

de·for·est /ˌdiːˈfɒrɪst; *NAmE* -ˈfɔːr-; -ˈfɑːr-/ (also **dis·af·for·est**) *verb* [usually passive] **~ sth** to cut down and destroy all the trees in a place 砍掉…樹林；毀掉…森林：*Two thirds of the region has been deforested in the past decade.* 在過去十年裏這個地區的森林有三分之二被毀掉。

de·for·est·ation /ˌdiːˌfɒrɪˈsteɪʃn; *NAmE* -ˌfɔːr-; -ˌfɑːr-/ *noun* [U] the act of cutting down or burning the trees in an area 毀林；濫伐森林；燒林 ➲ **COLLOCATIONS** at ENVIRONMENT ➲ **VISUAL VOCAB** page V6 ➲ compare AFFORESTATION, REFORESTATION

de·form /dɪˈfɔːm; *NAmE* -ˈfɔːrm/ *verb* **~ sth** to change or spoil the usual or natural shape of sth 改變…的外形；損毀…的形狀；使成畸形：*The disease had deformed his spine.* 疾病導致他脊柱變形。

de·form·ation /ˌdiːfɔːˈmeɪʃn; *NAmE* -fɔːrˈm-/ *noun* **1** [U] the process or result of changing and spoiling the normal shape of sth 損形；變形；畸形 **2** [C] a change in the normal shape of sth as a result of injury or illness 破相；變醜；殘廢：*a deformation of the spine* 脊柱的畸變

de·formed /dɪˈfɔːmd; *NAmE* -ˈfɔːrmd/ *adj.* (of a person or a part of the body 人或身體部位) having a shape that is not normal because it has grown wrongly 畸形的；變形的：*She was born with deformed hands.* 她的雙手天生畸形。

de·form·ity /dɪˈfɔːməti; *NAmE* -ˈfɔːrm-/ *noun* (*pl.* **-ies**) [C, U] a condition in which a part of the body is not the normal shape because of injury, illness or because it has grown wrongly（身體部位的）畸形 **SYN** **malformation**：*Drugs taken during pregnancy may cause physical deformity in babies.* 妊娠期服用的藥物可能引起嬰兒身體畸形。

DEFRA /ˈdefrə/ *abbr.* (in Britain) Department for Environment, Food and Rural Affairs （英國）環境食物農業事務部

de·frag·ment /ˌdiːfrægˈment/ (also *informal* **de·frag** /ˌdiːˈfræg/) *verb* **~ sth** (*computing* 計) to organize the files on a computer so that information relating to each file is stored in the same area, so the computer works faster 整理（計算機磁盤）碎片

de·fraud /dɪˈfrɔːd/ *verb* [I, T] to get money illegally from a person or an organization by tricking them 騙取，詐取（…的錢財）：*All three men were charged with conspiracy to defraud.* 三人均被控密謀詐騙。◇ **~ sb (of sth)** *They were accused of defrauding the company of $14 000.* 他們被控詐騙該公司 14 000 元。

de·fray /dɪˈfreɪ/ *verb* **~ costs/expenses** (*formal*) to give sb back the money that they have spent on sth 支付，付給（已開支的款項）

de·frock /ˌdiːˈfrɒk; *NAmE* -ˈfrɑːk/ *verb* [usually passive] **~ sb** to officially remove a priest from his or her job, because he or she has done sth wrong 免去（行為不端的牧師）之聖職：*a defrocked priest* 被免職的祭司

de·frost /ˌdiːˈfrɒst; *NAmE* -ˈfrɔːst/ *verb* **1** [I, T] to become or make sth warmer, especially food, so that it is no longer frozen 解凍，使解凍（尤指食物）：*It will take about four hours to defrost.* 解凍要花四小時左右。◇ **~ sth** *Make sure you defrost the chicken completely before cooking.* 一定要讓凍雞化透後再烹調。 **2** [T, I] **~ (sth)** when you **defrost** a fridge/refrigerator or FREEZER, or when it **defrosts**, you remove the ice from it 給（冰箱或冷凍櫃）除霜；除霜 ➲ compare DE-ICE, MELT (1), THAW *v.* (3), UNFREEZE (1) **3** [T] **~ sth** (*NAmE*) to remove ice from the surface of a car's windows 除去（汽車玻璃上的）冰霜 ▸ **de·frost·er** *noun*

deft /deft/ *adj.* **1** (of a person's movements 人的動作) skilful and quick 熟練的；靈巧的；機敏的：***deft hands/fingers/footwork*** 靈活的手／手指／步法 ◇ *He finished off the painting with a few deft strokes of the brush.* 他用畫筆熟練地勾上幾筆，這幅畫就完成了。 **2** skilful 熟練的；有技巧的：*her deft command of the language* 她對這種語言的充分掌握 ▸ **deft·ly** *adv.*：*I threw her a towel which she deftly caught.* 我扔給她一塊毛巾，她敏捷地接住了。◇ *They deftly avoided answering my questions.* 他們機智地避開了我的問題。 **deft·ness** *noun* [U]

de·funct /dɪˈfʌŋkt/ *adj.* (*formal*) no longer existing, operating or being used 已滅絕的；不再起作用的；不再使用的

de·fuse /ˌdiːˈfjuːz/ *verb* **1 ~ sth** to stop a possibly dangerous or difficult situation from developing, especially by making people less angry or nervous 緩和；平息：*Local police are trying to defuse racial tension in the community.* 當地的警察竭力緩和這個社區種族間的緊張局面。 **2 ~ sth** to remove the FUSE from a bomb so that it cannot explode 拆除（炸彈的）引信

defy /dɪˈfaɪ/ *verb* (**de·fies**, **defy·ing**, **de·fied**, **de·fied**)

> **WORD FAMILY**
> **defy** *verb*
> **defiance** *noun*
> **defiant** *adj.*

1 ~ sb/sth to refuse to obey or show respect for sb in authority, a law, a rule, etc. 違抗；反抗；蔑視：*I wouldn't have dared to defy my teachers.* 我可不敢不聽老師的話。◇ *Hundreds of people today defied the ban on political gatherings.* 今天有數百人違抗禁止政治集會的規定。 **2 ~ belief, explanation, description, etc.** to be impossible or almost impossible to believe, explain, describe, etc. 不可能，無法（相信、解釋、描繪等）：*a political move that defies explanation* 無法解釋的政治舉動 ◇ *The beauty of the scene defies description.* 景色之美簡直難以描繪。 **3 ~ sth** to successfully resist sth to a very unusual degree 經受住；頂住；抗住：*The baby boy **defied all the odds** and survived* (= stayed alive when it seemed certain that he would die). 這名男嬰九死一生活了下來。

IDM **I defy you/anyone to do sth** used to say that sb should try to do sth, as a way of emphasizing that you think it is impossible to do it 激，挑動（某人盡力做你認為不可能的事）：*I defy anyone not to cry at the end of the film.* 我倒要看看有誰在電影結尾時不哭。

deg. *abbr.* DEGREE(S)：*26 deg. C* * 26 攝氏度

de·gen·er·ate *verb, adj., noun*

■ ***verb*** /dɪˈdʒenəreɪt/ [I] to become worse, for example by becoming lower in quality or weaker 惡化；蛻變；衰退 **SYN** **deteriorate**：*Her health degenerated quickly.* 她的健康狀況迅速惡化。◇ **~ into sth** *The march degenerated into a riot.* 示威遊行變成了暴動。

■ ***adj.*** /dɪˈdʒenərət/ **1** having moral standards that have fallen to a level that is very low and unacceptable to most people 墮落的；頹廢的：*a degenerate popular culture* 頹廢的大眾文化 **2** (*technical* 術語) having returned to a simple structure; lacking sth that is usually present 退化的；簡併的 ▸ **de·gen·er·acy** /dɪˈdʒenərəsi/ *noun* [U]

■ ***noun*** /dɪˈdʒenerət/ a person whose behaviour shows moral standards that have fallen to a very low level 墮落的人

D

de·gen·er·ation /dɪˌdʒenəˈreɪʃn/ *noun* [U] the process of becoming worse or less acceptable in quality or condition 蛻化；衰退；墮落：*social/moral degeneration* 社會倒退；道德淪喪 ◇ *Intensive farming in the area has caused severe degeneration of the land.* 這個地區的集約化農業使得土壤嚴重貧瘠化。

de·gen·era·tive /dɪˈdʒenərətɪv/ *adj.* (*technical* 術語) (of an illness 疾病) getting or likely to get worse as time passes（隨着時間的推移）變性的，退化的：*degenerative diseases such as arthritis* 諸如關節炎之類的變性病

de·grad·able /dɪˈɡreɪdəbl/ *adj.* (*especially NAmE, technical* 術語) that can be changed to a simpler form 可降級的；可降低的；可降解的 ➲ see also BIODEGRADABLE

deg·rad·ation /ˌdeɡrəˈdeɪʃn/ *noun* [U] **1** a situation in which sb has lost all SELF-RESPECT and the respect of other people 墮落；落泊，潦倒（的境況）：*the degradation of being sent to prison* 被關進監獄的落泊境況 **2** (*technical* 術語) the process of sth being damaged or made worse 毀壞，惡化（過程）：*environmental degradation* 環境惡化

de·grade /dɪˈɡreɪd/ *verb* **1** [T] **~ sb** to show or treat sb in a way that makes them seem not worth any respect or not worth taking seriously 降低…身分；侮辱…的人格；使受屈辱：*This poster is offensive and degrades women.* 這張海報冒失無禮，有辱女性尊嚴。 **2** [I, T] **~ (sth)** (*technical* 術語) to change or make sth change to a simpler chemical form（使）退化，降解；分解 **3** [T] **~ sth** (*technical* 術語) to make sth become worse, especially in quality 降低，削弱（尤指質量）

de·grad·ing /dɪˈɡreɪdɪŋ/ *adj.* treating sb as if they have no value, so that they lose their SELF-RESPECT and the respect of other people 有辱人格的；降低身分的；貶低的：*the inhuman and degrading treatment of prisoners* 犯人所受的不人道和侮辱性待遇

de·grease /ˌdiːˈɡriːs/ *verb* **~ sth** to remove GREASE or oil from sth 除去油脂（或油污）

de·gree 🔑 /dɪˈɡriː/ *noun*
1 🔑 [C] a unit for measuring angles 度，度數（角的量度單位）：*an angle of ninety degrees (90°)* * 90 度角 **2** 🔑 [C] (*abbr.* **deg.**) a unit for measuring temperature 度，度數（溫度單位）：*Water freezes at 32 degrees Fahrenheit (32°F) or zero/nought degrees Celsius (0°C).* 水在 32 華氏度或零攝氏度結冰。 **3** 🔑 [C, U] the amount or level of sth 程度：*Her job demands a high degree of skill.* 她的工作要求有高超的技能。◇ *I agree with you **to a certain degree**.* 我在某種程度上同意你的觀點。◇ *To what degree can parents be held responsible for a child's behaviour?* 父母應在多大程度上對孩子的行為負責呢？◇ *Most pop music is influenced, to a greater or lesser degree, by the blues.* 多數流行音樂都不同程度地受到布魯斯音樂的影響。 **4** 🔑 [C] the qualification obtained by students who successfully complete a university or college course（大學）學位：*My brother has a master's degree from Harvard.* 我哥哥有哈佛大學的碩士學位。◇ *She has a degree in Biochemistry from Queen's University.* 她有女王大學的生物化學學位。◇ *a four-year degree course* 四年的學位課程 ➲ COLLOCATIONS at EDUCATION **5** [C] (*BrE*) a university or college course, normally lasting three years or more（大學通常三年或以上的）學位課程：*I'm hoping to do a chemistry degree.* 我希望攻讀化學學位課程。 **6** [C] a level in a scale of how serious sth is 嚴重程度（或級別）：*murder in the first degree* (= of the most serious kind) 第一等級謀殺（最嚴重）◇ *first-degree murder* 第一等級謀殺 ◇ *third-degree* (= very serious) *burns* 三度燒傷（非常嚴重）
IDM **by de'grees** slowly and gradually 逐漸地；漸漸地：*By degrees their friendship grew into love.* 他們的友誼逐漸發展成為愛情。➲ more at NTH

de·hu·man·ize (*BrE* also **-ise**) /ˌdiːˈhjuːmənaɪz/ *verb* **~ sb** to make sb lose their human qualities such as kindness, pity, etc. 使喪失人性；使無人性：*the dehumanizing effects of poverty and squalor* 貧窮和骯髒的環境造成喪失人性的結果 ▶ **de·hu·man·iza·tion, -isa·tion** /ˌdiːˌhjuːmənaɪˈzeɪʃn; *NAmE* -nəˈz-/ *noun* [U]

de·hu·midi·fier /ˌdiːhjuːˈmɪdɪfaɪə(r)/ *noun* an electrical machine for removing water from the air 抽濕機；除濕機；乾燥機 ➲ see also HUMIDIFIER

de·hy·drate /diːˈhaɪdreɪt; ˌdiːhaɪˈdreɪt/ *verb* **1** [T, usually passive] **~ sth** to remove the water from sth, especially food, in order to preserve it 使（食物）脱水 **2** [I, T] to lose too much water from your body; to make a person's body lose too much water（身體）失水，脱水；使（身體）脱水：*Runners can dehydrate very quickly in this heat.* 天這樣熱，賽跑運動員很快會脱水。◇ **~ sb** *the dehydrating effects of alcohol* 酒精引起的脱水 ▶ **de·hy·dra·tion** /ˌdiːhaɪˈdreɪʃn/ *noun* [U]：*to suffer from dehydration* 受脱水之苦 **de·hy·drated** /ˌdiːhaɪˈdreɪtɪd/ *adj.*：*Drink lots of water to avoid becoming dehydrated.* 要大量飲水，以免脱水。

de-ice /ˌdiː ˈaɪs/ *verb* **~ sth** to remove the ice from sth 除去…上的冰 ➲ compare DEFROST (2), MELT (1), THAW *v.* (3), UNFREEZE (1)

de-icer /ˌdiː ˈaɪsə(r)/ *noun* [C, U] a substance that is put on a surface to remove ice or to stop it from forming 除冰劑；防固劑

deic·tic /ˈdaɪktɪk; ˈdeɪktɪk/ *adj.* (*linguistics* 語言) relating to a word or expression whose meaning depends on who says it, where they are, who they are talking to, etc., for example 'you', 'me', 'here', 'next week'（指詞或表達方式）指示的（如 you、me、here、next week 等）

deify /ˈdeɪɪfaɪ; ˈdiːɪfaɪ/ *verb* (**dei·fies, dei·fy·ing, dei·fied, dei·fied**) **~ sb** (*formal*) to treat or worship sb as a god 把（某人）奉若神明；把（某人）尊為神；崇拜 ▶ **dei·fi·ca·tion** /ˌdeɪɪfɪˈkeɪʃn; ˌdiːɪfɪˈkeɪʃn/ *noun* [U]：*the deification of medieval kings* 對中世紀國王的神化

deign /deɪn/ *verb* **~ to do sth** (*disapproving*) to do sth in a way that shows you think you are too important to do it 屈尊，俯就，降低身分（做某事） **SYN** **condescend**：*She just grunted, not deigning to look up from the page.* 她只咕噥了一聲，繼續看書，不屑抬起頭來看一眼。

deism /ˈdeɪɪzəm; ˈdiːɪz-/ *noun* [U] belief in God, especially a God that created the universe but does not take part in it 自然神論，理神論（認為上帝創造世界後讓其自然運行） ▶ **deist** /ˈdeɪɪst; ˈdiːɪst/ *noun* **de·is·tic** /deɪˈɪstɪk; diːˈɪ-/ *adj.*

deity /ˈdeɪəti; ˈdiːəti/ *noun* (*pl.* **-ies**) **1** [C] a god or GODDESS 神；女神：*Greek/Roman/Hindu deities* 希臘/羅馬/印度教諸神 **2 the Deity** [sing.] (*formal*) God 上帝；天主

deixis /ˈdeɪksɪs; ˈdaɪksɪs/ *noun* [U] (*linguistics* 語言) the function or use of DEICTIC words or expressions (= ones whose meaning depends on where, when or by whom they are used) 指示功能；指示詞的使用

déjà vu /ˌdeɪʒɑː ˈvuː/ *noun* [U] (from *French*) the feeling that you have previously experienced sth which is happening to you now 似曾經歷過的感覺：*I had a strong sense of déjà vu as I entered the room.* 進這房間時我有一種似曾來過的強烈感覺。

de·ject·ed /dɪˈdʒektɪd/ *adj.* unhappy and disappointed 沮喪的；情緒低落的；垂頭喪氣的 **SYN** **despondent**：*She looked so dejected when she lost the game.* 她輸掉比賽時情緒顯得非常低落。 ▶ **de·ject·ed·ly** *adv.*

de·jec·tion /dɪˈdʒekʃn/ *noun* [U] a feeling of unhappiness and disappointment 沮喪；情緒低落；垂頭喪氣

de jure /ˌdeɪ ˈdʒʊəri; *NAmE* ˈdʒʊri/ *adj., adv.* (from *Latin, law* 律) according to the law 根據法律；在法律上：*He held power de jure and de facto* (= both according to the law and in reality). 他無論在法律上還是實際上都大權在握。➲ compare DE FACTO

deka·liter /ˈdekəliːtə(r)/ *noun* (*US*) = DECALITRE

deka·meter /ˈdekəmiːtə(r)/ *noun* (*US*) = DECAMETRE

dekko /ˈdekəʊ; *NAmE* -koʊ/ *noun*
IDM **have a dekko (at sth)** (*old-fashioned, BrE, slang*) to look (at sth) 看，望（某物）；（對…）看一眼 **ORIGIN** From the Hindi word for 'look!', used by the British army in India in the past. 源自印地語表示"看！"的詞，過去由駐印度英軍使用。

delay 🔑 /dɪˈleɪ/ *noun, verb*

■ ***noun*** **1** 🔑 [C] a period of time when sb/sth has to wait because of a problem that makes sth slow or late 延遲（或耽擱、拖延）的時間：*Commuters will face long delays on the roads today.* 路遠乘車上下班的人今天要在路上耽誤很多時間了。◇ *We apologize for the delay in answering your letter.* 來信收悉，遲覆為歉。◇ *a delay of two hours/a two-hour delay* 兩小時的延誤 ➲ COLLOCATIONS at TRAVEL **2** 🔑 [C, U] a situation in which sth does not happen when it should; the act of delaying 延期；耽擱；延誤：*There's no time for delay.* 沒有時間了，不能拖延了。◇ *Report it to the police **without delay*** (= immediately). 趕快將此事報告警方。

■ ***verb*** **1** 🔑 [I, T] to not do sth until a later time or to make sth happen at a later time 延遲；延期；推遲 SYN **defer**：*Don't delay—call us today!* 別拖延——今天就給我們打電話！◇ **~ sth** *The judge will delay his verdict until he receives medical reports on the offender.* 法官將推遲判決，直到收到有關違法者的醫療報告。◇ *She's suffering a **delayed reaction*** (= a reaction that did not happen immediately) *to the shock.* 她正在承受着衝擊所帶來的滯後反應。◇ **~ doing sth** *He delayed telling her the news, waiting for the right moment.* 他沒有馬上把消息告訴她，等有了適當的時機再説。**2** 🔑 [T] **~ sb** to make sb late or force them to do sth more slowly 使遲到；使耽擱；使拖延 SYN **hold up**：*Thousands of commuters were delayed for over an hour.* 數千名乘車上下班的人被耽擱了一個多小時。◇ *The government is accused of using **delaying tactics*** (= deliberately doing sth to delay a process, decision, etc.). 政府被指責故意採取拖延戰術。

de·lect·able /dɪˈlektəbl/ *adj.* **1** (of food and drink 食物或飲料) extremely pleasant to taste, smell or look at 美味可口的；香甜的；宜人的 SYN **delicious**：*the delectable smell of freshly baked bread* 新烤麪包的香味 **2** (*humorous*) (of a person 人) very attractive 嫵媚動人的；有迷惑力的；有吸引力的：*his delectable body* 他健美的身體

de·lect·ation /ˌdiːlekˈteɪʃn/ *noun* [U] (*formal* or *humorous*) enjoyment or entertainment 享受；愉快；娛樂 SYN **delight**

dele·gate *noun, verb*

■ ***noun*** /ˈdelɪɡət/ a person who is chosen or elected to represent the views of a group of people and vote and make decisions for them 代表；會議代表：*The conference was attended by delegates from 56 countries.* 此次會議有來自 56 個國家的代表出席。

■ ***verb*** /ˈdelɪɡeɪt/ **1** [I, T] to give part of your work, power or authority to sb in a lower position than you 授（權）；把（工作、權力等）委託（給下級）：*Some managers find it difficult to delegate.* 有些經理認為難以做到知人善任。◇ **~ (sth) (to sb)** *The job had to be delegated to an assistant.* 這工作得交給助手負責。**2** [T] **~ sb to do sth** [usually passive] to choose sb to do sth 選派（某人做某事）：*I've been delegated to organize the Christmas party.* 我被選派來組織聖誕聚會。

dele·ga·tion /ˌdelɪˈɡeɪʃn/ *noun* **1** [C+sing./pl. v.] a group of people who represent the views of an organization, a country, etc. 代表團：*the Dutch delegation to the United Nations* 出席聯合國會議的荷蘭代表團 ◇ *a delegation of teachers* 教師代表團 ➲ COLLOCATIONS at INTERNATIONAL **2** [U] the process of giving sb work or responsibilities that would usually be yours 委託；委派：*delegation of authority/decision-making* 授予權力／決策權

de·lete /dɪˈliːt/ *verb* **~ sth (from sth)** to remove sth that has been written or printed, or that has been stored on a computer 刪去；刪除：*Your name has been deleted from the list.* 你的名字已從名單上刪掉。◇ *This command deletes files from the directory.* 這一指令把文檔從目錄中刪除。◇ (*BrE*) *Mr/Mrs/Ms* (***delete as appropriate***) 先生／太太／女士（酌情刪除）➲ COLLOCATIONS at EMAIL ▸ **de·le·tion** /dɪˈliːʃn/ *noun* [U, C]：*He made several deletions to the manuscript.* 他在原稿上刪去了好幾處。

dele·teri·ous /ˌdeləˈtɪəriəs; *NAmE* -ˈtɪr-/ *adj.* (*formal*) harmful and damaging 有害的；造成傷害的；損害的

deli /ˈdeli/ *noun* = DELICATESSEN

de·lib·er·ate 🔑 *adj., verb*

■ ***adj.*** /dɪˈlɪbərət/ **1** 🔑 done on purpose rather than by accident 故意的；蓄意的；存心的 SYN **intentional, planned**：*a deliberate act of vandalism* 故意毀壞公物的行為 ◇ *The speech was a deliberate attempt to embarrass the government.* 這一發言蓄意使政府難堪。OPP **unintentional** **2** (of a movement or an action 動作或行為) done slowly and carefully 不慌不忙的；小心翼翼的；從容不迫的：*She spoke in a slow and deliberate way.* 她説話慢條斯理不慌不忙。

■ ***verb*** /dɪˈlɪbəreɪt/ [I, T] (*formal*) to think very carefully about sth, usually before making a decision 仔細考慮；深思熟慮；反複思考：*The jury deliberated for five days before finding him guilty.* 陪審團認真討論了五天才認定他有罪。◇ **~ (on) whether, what, etc. …** *They deliberated (on) whether to continue with the talks.* 他們仔細考慮了是否繼續談判的問題。

de·lib·er·ate·ly 🔑 /dɪˈlɪbərətli/ *adv.* **1** 🔑 done in a way that was planned, not by chance 故意；蓄意；存心 SYN **intentionally, on purpose**：*She's been deliberately ignoring him all day.* 她故意整天都不理他。**2** slowly and carefully 不慌不忙地；小心翼翼地；從容不迫地：*He packed up his possessions slowly and deliberately.* 他慢慢地、小心翼翼地收拾好自己的物品。

de·lib·er·ation /dɪˌlɪbəˈreɪʃn/ *noun* (*formal*) **1** [U, C, usually pl.] the process of carefully considering or discussing sth 細想；考慮；商議；審議：*After ten hours of deliberation, the jury returned a verdict of 'not guilty'.* 經過十小時的商議，陪審團宣告了"無罪"的裁決。◇ *The deliberations of the committee are completely confidential.* 委員會的審議過程是絕對保密的。**2** [U] the quality of being slow and careful in what you say or do（説話或辦事）緩慢，從容，審慎：*She signed her name with great deliberation.* 她非常審慎地簽上了自己的名字。

deli·cacy /ˈdelɪkəsi/ *noun* (*pl.* **-ies**) **1** [U] the quality of being, or appearing to be, easy to damage or break 柔軟（性）；脆弱；嬌嫩：*the delicacy of the fabric* 織物的柔軟性 **2** [U] the quality of being done carefully and gently 仔細；溫柔：*the delicacy of his touch* 他那溫柔的撫摸 **3** [U] very careful behaviour in a difficult situation so that nobody is offended 周到；體貼 SYN **tact**：*She handled the situation with great sensitivity and delicacy.* 她慎重而周到地處理了這個情況。**4** [U] the fact that a situation is difficult and sb may be easily offended 棘手；微妙：*I need to talk to you about a matter of some delicacy.* 我需要與你談個有點棘手的問題。**5** [C] a type of food considered to be very special in a particular place 精美的食物；佳肴 SYN **speciality**：*local delicacies* 當地的美味佳肴

deli·cate 🔑 /ˈdelɪkət/ *adj.*

1 🔑 easily damaged or broken 易損的；易碎的；脆弱的 SYN **fragile**：*delicate china teacups* 易碎的瓷茶杯 ◇ *The eye is one of the most delicate organs of the body.* 眼睛是人體最嬌貴的器官之一。◇ *the delicate ecological balance of the rainforest* 熱帶雨林極易被破壞的生態平衡 ◇ *Babies have very delicate skin.* 嬰兒的皮膚非常嬌嫩。◇ *a cool wash cycle for delicate fabrics* 精細織物冷洗程序 **2** 🔑 (of a person 人) not strong and easily becoming ill/sick 虛弱的；纖弱的：*a **delicate child/constitution*** 纖弱的孩子／體質 **3** 🔑 small and having a beautiful shape or appearance 纖細的；微小的；精美的；小巧玲瓏的：*his delicate hands* 他纖細的手 **4** 🔑 made or formed in a very careful and detailed way 精緻的；精細的；精密的：*the delicate mechanisms of a clock* 鐘的精密機件 **5** 🔑 showing or needing skilful, careful or sensitive treatment 熟練的；需要技巧的；需要小心處理的；微妙的：*I admired your delicate handling of the situation.* 我佩服你應付這種局面的嫻熟技巧。◇ *a delicate problem* 微妙的問題 ◇ *The delicate surgical operation took five hours.* 這精細的外科手術花了五個小時。**6** 🔑 (of colours, flavours and smells 顏色、味道、氣味) light and pleasant; not strong 柔和的；清淡可口的；清香的 SYN **subtle**：*a **delicate fragrance/flavour*** 清新的芳香；鮮美的味道 ◇ *a river scene painted in delicate watercolours* 用柔和的水彩畫的河景 ▸ **deli·cate·ly** *adv.*：*He*

D

stepped delicately over the broken glass. 他小心翼翼地跨過碎玻璃。◇ *delicately balanced flavours* 精心調配的味道

deli·ca·tes·sen /ˌdelɪkəˈtesn/ (also **deli**) *noun* a shop/store or part of one that sells cooked meats and cheeses, and special or unusual foods that come from other countries（出售熟肉、乾酪和進口風味食品的）熟食店，熟食櫃枱

D

de·li·cious /dɪˈlɪʃəs/ *adj.* **1** having a very pleasant taste or smell 美味的；可口的；芬芳的：*Who cooked this? It's delicious.* 誰做的？味道好極了。**2** (*literary*) extremely pleasant or enjoyable 令人愉快的；令人開心的；宜人的：*the delicious coolness of the breeze* 微風送爽 ▸ **de·li·cious·ly** *adv.*：*deliciously creamy soup* 可口的奶油湯

de·light /dɪˈlaɪt/ *noun, verb*

■ *noun* **1** [U] a feeling of great pleasure 高興；愉快；快樂 SYN **joy**：*a feeling of* ***sheer/pure delight*** 十分高興的心情 ◇ *The children squealed* ***with delight*** *when they saw the puppy.* 孩子們看到小狗時高興得大聲尖叫。◇ *She won the game easily,* ***to the delight of*** *all her fans.* 這場比賽她贏得很輕鬆，令所有的崇拜者大為高興。◇ *He* ***takes*** *(****great****)* ***delight in*** (= enjoys) *proving others wrong.* 他以證實別人出錯為（一大）快事。➲ SYNONYMS at PLEASURE **2** [C] something that gives you great pleasure 令人高興的事；樂事；樂趣 SYN **joy**：*This guitar is a delight to play.* 這吉他彈起來很愜意。◇ *the delights of living in the country* 生活在鄉村的樂趣

■ *verb* ~ **sb** to give sb a lot of pleasure and enjoyment 使高興；使愉快；使快樂：*This news will delight his fans all over the world.* 這消息將使全世界崇拜他的人都感到高興。

PHR V **deˈlight in sth/doing sth** [no passive] to enjoy doing sth very much, especially sth that makes other people feel embarrassed, uncomfortable, etc. 以…為樂（尤指做使別人感到尷尬、不舒服的事）

de·light·ed /dɪˈlaɪtɪd/ *adj.* very pleased 高興的；愉快的；快樂的：*a delighted smile* 愉快的微笑 ◇ **~ to do sth** *I'd be absolutely delighted to come.* 我非常樂意前來。◇ **~ that …** *I was delighted that you could stay.* 你能留下來我很高興。◇ **~ by/at sth** *She was delighted by/at the news of the wedding.* 聽到婚禮的消息她很高興。◇ **~ with sth** *I was delighted with my presents.* 我對我收到的禮物很滿意。➲ SYNONYMS at GLAD ▸ **de·light·ed·ly** *adv.*

de·light·ful /dɪˈlaɪtfl/ *adj.* very pleasant 使人快樂的；令人愉快的；宜人的 SYN **charming**：*a delightful book/restaurant/town* 令人愉快的書；舒適的餐館；宜人的城鎮 ◇ *a delightful child* 討人喜歡的孩子 ➲ SYNONYMS at WONDERFUL ▸ **de·light·ful·ly** /dɪˈlaɪtfəli/ *adv.*

de·limit /diˈlɪmɪt/ *verb* ~ **sth** (*formal*) to decide what the limits of sth are 定…的界限；限定；界定

de·lin·eate /dɪˈlɪnieɪt/ *verb* ~ **sth** (*formal*) to describe, draw or explain sth in detail（詳細地）描述，描畫，解釋：*Our objectives need to be precisely delineated.* 我們的目標需詳細解釋清楚。◇ *The ship's route is clearly delineated on the map.* 這條船的航線清楚地標在地圖上。▸ **de·lin·ea·tion** /dɪˌlɪniˈeɪʃn/ *noun* [U, C]

de·lin·quency /dɪˈlɪŋkwənsi/ *noun* [U, C] (*pl.* **-ies**) bad or criminal behaviour, usually of young people（常指青年人的）犯罪，違法行為：*an increase in juvenile delinquency* 青少年犯罪的增加

de·lin·quent /dɪˈlɪŋkwənt/ *adj.* **1** (especially of young people or their behaviour 尤指青年人或其行為) showing a tendency to commit crimes 有違法傾向的：*delinquent teenagers* 不良青少年 **2** (*NAmE, finance* 財) having failed to pay money that is owed 拖欠債務的；欠債未還的：*a delinquent borrower* 欠債未還的借款人 **3** (*NAmE, finance* 財) (of a sum of money 款項) not having been paid in time 到期未付的：*a delinquent loan* 逾期未還的貸款 ▸ **de·lin·quent** *noun* ➲ see also JUVENILE DELINQUENT

deli·quesce /ˌdelɪˈkwes/ *verb* (*formal*) **1** [I] to become liquid as a result of decaying（因腐爛而）融解 **2** [I] (*chemistry* 化) to become liquid as a result of absorbing water from the air 潮解 ▸ **deli·ques·cence** /ˌdelɪˈkwesns/ *noun* [U]

de·li·ri·ous /dɪˈlɪriəs; *BrE* also -ˈlɪəriəs/ *adj.* **1** in an excited state and not able to think or speak clearly, usually because of fever 極度亢奮的，精神錯亂的，語無倫次的（常由發燒引起）：*He became delirious and couldn't recognize people.* 他已精神錯亂，誰都不認得了。**2** extremely excited and happy 極度興奮的；特別愉快的：*The crowds were delirious with joy.* 人群欣喜若狂。▸ **de·li·ri·ous·ly** *adv.*

de·lir·ium /dɪˈlɪriəm; *BrE* also -ˈlɪəriəm/ *noun* [U] a mental state where sb becomes delirious, usually because of illness 譫妄，神志失常，說胡話（常由疾病引起）：*fits of delirium* 一陣陣胡言亂語

delirium tremens /dɪˌlɪriəm ˈtriːmenz; *BrE* also -ˌlɪəriəm/ *noun* [U] (*medical* 醫) = DTs

de·liver /dɪˈlɪvə(r)/ *verb*

▸ TAKE GOODS/LETTERS 送貨 / 信 **1** [T, I] to take goods, letters, etc. to the person or people they have been sent to; to take sb somewhere 遞送；傳送；交付；運載：**~ sth** *Do you have your milk delivered?* 你的牛奶是讓別人送嗎？◇ **~ (sth) to sb/sth** *Leaflets have been delivered to every household.* 傳單已發送到每家每戶。◇ **~ (to sb/sth)** *We promise to deliver within 48 hours.* 我們承諾在 48 小時內送到。

▸ GIVE SPEECH 發表演說 **2** [T] **~ sth** to give a speech, talk, etc. or other official statement 發表；宣佈；發佈：*She is due to deliver a lecture on genetic engineering.* 根據安排她要作一個關於遺傳工程的演講。◇ *He delivered his lines confidently.* 他信心十足地說了他的台詞。◇ *The jury finally delivered its verdict.* 陪審團終於宣佈了裁決。

▸ KEEP PROMISE 履行諾言 **3** [I, T] to do what you promised to do or what you are expected to do; to produce or provide what people expect you to 履行諾言；不負所望；兌現：*He has promised to finish the job by June and I am sure he will deliver.* 他答應在六月底完成這項工作，我相信他會履行諾言。◇ **~ on sth** *She always delivers on her promises.* 她總是信守諾言。◇ **~ sth** *If you can't deliver improved sales figures, you're fired.* 如果你不能按照要求提高銷售額，就會被解雇。◇ *The team delivered a stunning victory last night.* 昨晚這個隊不負眾望，大獲全勝。

▸ GIVE TO SB'S CONTROL 交某人控制 **4** [T] **~ sb/sth (up/over) (to sb)** (*formal*) to give sb/sth to sb else so that they are under this person's control 交出；交付；移交：*They delivered their prisoner over to the invading army.* 他們把俘虜交給了侵略軍。

▸ BABY 嬰兒 **5** [T] **~ a baby** to help a woman to give birth to a baby 助產；接生：*The baby was delivered by Caesarean section.* 這個嬰兒是剖腹產下的。**6** [T] **be delivered of a baby** (*formal*) to give birth to a baby 分娩；生孩子：*She was delivered of a healthy boy.* 她生下一個健康的男孩兒。

▸ THROW 投擲 **7** [T] **~ sth** to throw or aim sth 投擲；把…瞄準；用…對準：*He* ***delivered the blow*** (= hit sb hard) *with all his force.* 他打這一下使出了全身的力氣。

▸ RESCUE 解救 **8** [T] **~ sb (from sth)** (*old use*) to rescue sb from sth bad 解救；拯救；使擺脫 SYN **save** IDM see GOODS, SIGN *v.*

de·liver·able /dɪˈlɪvərəbl/ *noun* [usually pl.] a product that a company promises to have ready for a customer 應交付的產品：*computer software deliverables* 應交付的計算機軟件

de·liv·er·ance /dɪˈlɪvərəns/ *noun* [U] **~ (from sth)** (*formal*) the state of being rescued from danger, evil or pain 解救；拯救；解脫

de·liv·ery /dɪˈlɪvəri/ *noun* (*pl.* **-ies**)

1 [U, C] the act of taking goods, letters, etc. to the people they have been sent to 傳送；遞送；交付：*a delivery van* 廂式送貨車 ◇ *Please pay for goods* ***on delivery*** (= when you receive them). 請貨到付款。◇ *Allow 28 days* ***for delivery.*** 請留出 28 天送貨時間。◇ *Is there a* ***postal/mail delivery*** *on Saturdays?* 星期六送郵件嗎？◇ (*formal*) *When can you* ***take delivery of*** (= be available to receive) *the car?* 你何時能提取那輛汽車？◇ (*figurative*) *the delivery of public services* 提供公共事業服務 **2** [C, U] the process of giving birth to a baby 分娩：*an* ***easy/difficult delivery*** 順 / 難產 ◇ *a* ***delivery room/ward*** (= in a hospital, etc.) 產房；產科病房 **3** [sing.] the way in which sb speaks, sings a song, etc. in public

演講方式；表演風格：*The beautiful poetry was ruined by her poor delivery.* 這優美的詩被她拙劣的朗誦給糟蹋了。**4** [C] a ball that is thrown, especially in CRICKET or BASEBALL 投球（尤指板球或棒球）：*a fast delivery* 一個快投球 **IDM** see CASH *n.*

dell /del/ *noun* (*literary*) a small valley with trees growing in or around it（裏面或周圍有樹的）小山谷

de·louse /ˌdiːˈlaʊs/ *verb* **~ sb/sth** to remove LICE (= small insects) from sb's hair or from an animal's coat 除去（頭髮或動物皮毛上的）虱子

Del·phic /ˈdelfɪk/ *adj.* **1** relating to the ancient Greek ORACLE at Delphi (= the place where people went to ask the gods for advice or information about the future) 德爾斐神諭的 **2** (often **delphic**) (*formal*) with a meaning that is deliberately hidden or difficult to understand 隱晦的；難以理解的：*a delphic utterance* 令人費解的話

del·phin·ium /delˈfɪniəm/ *noun* a tall garden plant with blue or white flowers growing up its STEM 翠雀；飛燕草屬（高株園藝植物，開藍花或白花）

DELTA /ˈdeltə/ *noun* [U] the abbreviation for 'Diploma in English Language Teaching to Adults' (a British qualification from the University of Cambridge for experienced teachers of English as a foreign language) 成人英語教學文憑（全寫為 Diploma in English Language Teaching to Adults，英國劍橋大學為有經驗的、教授英語作為外語的教師頒發的資格證書）

delta /ˈdeltə/ *noun* **1** the fourth letter of the Greek alphabet (Δ, δ) 希臘字母表的第 4 個字母 **2** an area of land, shaped like a triangle, where a river has split into several smaller rivers before entering the sea 三角洲：*the Nile Delta* 尼羅河三角洲

del·toids /ˈdeltɔɪdz/ (also *informal* **delts** /delts/) *noun* [pl.] (*anatomy* 解) the thick triangle-shaped muscles that cover the shoulder joints 三角肌（覆蓋於肩關節）

de·lude /dɪˈluːd/ *verb* to make sb believe sth that is not true 欺騙；哄騙 **SYN** **deceive**：**~ sb** *You poor deluded creature.* 你這上了當的可憐蟲。◇ **~ yourself** *He's deluding himself if he thinks it's going to be easy.* 他要是以為那事很容易，那就是自己欺騙自己。◇ **~ sb/yourself into doing sth** *Don't be deluded into thinking that we are out of danger yet.* 不要誤以為我們已脫離危險。◇ **~ yourself that ...** *She had been deluding herself that he loved her.* 她一直欺騙自己說他愛着她。➲ see also DELUSION

del·uge /ˈdeljuːdʒ/ *noun, verb*

■ ***noun*** [usually sing.] **1** a sudden very heavy fall of rain 暴雨；大雨；洪水 **SYN** **flood** **2** a large number of things that happen or arrive at the same time 湧現的事物；蜂擁而至的事物：*a **deluge of calls/complaints/letters*** 接連不斷的電話；沒完沒了的投訴；紛至沓來的信件

■ ***verb*** **1 ~ sb/sth (with sth)** [usually passive] to send or give sb/sth a large number of things at the same time 使湧來；使充滿 **SYN** **flood, inundate**：*We have been deluged with applications for the job.* 申請這個工作的求職信使我們應接不暇。**2** [often passive] **~ sth** (*formal*) to flood a place with water 泛濫；淹沒：*The campsite was deluged by a flash flood.* 露營地被突發的洪水淹沒。

de·lu·sion /dɪˈluːʒn/ *noun* **1** [C] a false belief or opinion about yourself or your situation 錯覺；謬見；妄想：*the delusions of the mentally ill* 精神病患者的妄想 ◇ *Don't go getting **delusions of grandeur*** (= a belief that you are more important than you actually are). 不要變得妄自尊大。**2** [U] the act of believing or making yourself believe sth that is not true 欺騙；哄騙

de·lu·sive /dɪˈluːsɪv/ (also **de·lu·sory** /dɪˈluːsəri; -zəri/) *adj.* (*formal*) not real or true 不真實的；虛假的 **SYN** **deceptive**

de luxe (also **de·luxe**) /ˌdə ˈlʌks; ˈlʊks/ *adj.* [usually before noun] of a higher quality and more expensive than usual 高級的；豪華的 **SYN** **luxury**：*a de luxe hotel* 豪華旅館

delve /delv/ *verb* [I] **+ adv./prep.** to search for sth inside a bag, container, etc.（在手提包、容器等中）翻找 **SYN** **dig**：*She delved in her handbag for a pen.* 她在手提包裏翻找鋼筆。

PHR V **ˌdelve ˈinto sth** to try hard to find out more information about sth 探索；探究；查考：*She had started to delve into her father's distant past.* 她開始探究她父親久已逝去的歲月。

Dem. *abbr.* (in politics in the US 美國政治) DEMOCRAT; DEMOCRATIC 民主黨人；民主黨的

dema·gogue /ˈdeməɡɒɡ; *NAmE* -ɡɑːɡ/ *noun* (*disapproving*) a political leader who tries to win support by using arguments based on emotion rather than reason 蠱惑民心的政客 ▸ **dema·gog·ic** /ˌdeməˈɡɒɡɪk; *NAmE* -ˈɡɑːɡ-/ *adj.* **dema·gogy** /ˈdeməɡɒɡi; *NAmE* -ɡɑːɡi/ *noun* [U]

D

Synonyms 同義詞辨析

demand

require • expect • insist • ask

These words all mean to say that sb should do or have sth. 以上各詞均含要求之意。

demand to ask for sth very firmly; to say very firmly that sb should have or do sth 指強烈要求、堅決要求：*She demanded an immediate explanation.* 她強烈要求立即作出解釋。

require [often passive] (*rather formal*) to make sb do or have sth, especially because it is necessary according to a law or set of rules or standards 指要求做（某事）、達到（某水平）、（尤指根據法規）規定：*All candidates will be required to take a short test.* 所有候選人都要做一個小測驗。

expect to demand that sb should do, have or be sth, especially because it is their duty or responsibility 指要求、認為應得、指望，尤因義務或責任：*I expect to be paid promptly for the work.* 我要求即時付工錢。

insist to demand that sth happens or that sb agrees to do sth 指堅決要求、堅持：*I didn't want to go but he insisted.* 我並不想去，但他硬要我去。◇ *We insist on the highest standards at all times.* 我們始終堅持最高標準。

ask to expect or demand sth 指期望、要求：*You're asking too much of him.* 你對他要求過分了。

DEMAND, EXPECT OR ASK? 用 demand、expect 還是 ask？

Ask is not as strong as **demand** or **expect**, both of which can be more like a command. * ask 不如 demand 和 expect 語氣強烈，demand 和 expect 更像命令。

PATTERNS

- to demand/require/expect/ask sth **of/from** sb
- to demand/require/expect/insist/ask **that ...**
- to require/expect/ask sb **to do sth**
- to demand/require/expect/ask **a lot/too much/a great deal**
- to **be too much to** expect/ask

de·mand 🔑 /dɪˈmɑːnd; *NAmE* dɪˈmænd/ *noun, verb*

■ ***noun*** **1** 🔑 [C] **~ (for sth/that ...)** a very firm request for sth; sth that sb needs（堅決的）要求；所需之物：*a demand for higher pay* 增加工資的要求 ◇ *demands that the law on gun ownership should be changed* 要求修改槍械持有法的呼聲 ◇ *firms attempting to **meet/satisfy** their customers' **demands*** (= to give them what they are asking for) 盡力滿足客戶要求的商行 **2** 🔑 **demands** [pl.] **~ (of sth)** | **~ (on sb)** things that sb/sth makes you do, especially things that are difficult, make you tired, worried, etc.（尤指困難、使人勞累、令人擔憂等的）要求：*the demands of children/work* 孩子煩人的事；工作中累人的事 ◇ *Flying **makes** enormous **demands** on pilots.* 駕駛飛機對飛行員要求很高。**3** 🔑 [U, C] **~ (for sth/sb)** the desire or need of customers for goods or services which they want to buy or use（顧客的）需求，需要：*to meet the demand for a product* 滿足對某產品的需求 ◇ *There's an increased demand for organic produce these days.*

目前對有機農產品有更大的需求。◇ *Demand is exceeding supply.* 供不應求。➲ COLLOCATIONS at ECONOMY

IDM **by popular de'mand** because a lot of people have asked for sth 由於許多人的要求；由於普遍要求：*By popular demand, the play will run for another week.* 應廣大觀眾要求，這齣戲將加演一週。**in de'mand** 🔑 wanted by a lot of people 需求大：*Good secretaries are always in demand.* 優秀的秘書總是很搶手。**on de'mand** done or happening whenever sb asks 一經要求：*Feed the baby on demand.* 寶寶需要時再餵食。◇ *on-demand printing of books* 書籍承索即印 ➲ see also SUPPLY AND DEMAND

D

■ *verb* **1** 🔑 to ask for sth very firmly 強烈要求：**~ sth** *She demanded an immediate explanation.* 她強烈要求立即作出解釋。◇ **~ that ...** *The UN has demanded that all troops be withdrawn.* 聯合國已要求撤出所有部隊。◇ (*BrE* also) *They are demanding that all troops should be withdrawn.* 他們強烈要求所有部隊撤離。◇ **~ to do sth** *I demand to see the manager.* 我堅決要求見經理。◇ **+ speech** *'Who the hell are you?' he demanded angrily.* "你到底是誰？"他氣勢洶洶地查問道。➲ SYNONYMS at ASK **2** 🔑 **~ sth** to need sth in order to be done successfully 需要：*This sport demands both speed and strength.* 這項運動既需要速度也需要體力。

de·mand·ing /dɪˈmɑːndɪŋ; *NAmE* -ˈmæn-/ *adj.* **1** (of a piece of work 工作) needing a lot of skill, patience, effort, etc. 要求高的；需要高技能（或耐性等）的；費力的：*The work is physically demanding.* 這工作需要有很好的體力。➲ SYNONYMS at DIFFICULT **2** (of a person 人) expecting a lot of work or attention from others; not easily satisfied 要求極嚴的；苛求的；難滿足的：*a demanding boss/child* 苛刻的老闆；難滿足的孩子 OPP **undemanding**

de·mar·cate /ˈdiːmɑːkeɪt; *NAmE* -mɑːrk-/ *verb* **~ sth** (*formal*) to mark or establish the limits of sth 標出…的界線；給…劃界：*Plots of land have been demarcated by barbed wire.* 一塊塊土地都用帶刺的鐵絲網圈了起來。

de·mar·ca·tion /ˌdiːmɑːˈkeɪʃn; *NAmE* -mɑːrˈk-/ *noun* [U, C] a border or line that separates two things, such as types of work, groups of people or areas of land（工種、人群、土地等的）劃分，區分，界線：*It was hard to draw clear lines of demarcation between work and leisure.* 在工作和閒暇之間很難劃出明確的界限。◇ *social demarcations* 社會階層的劃分

de·mean /dɪˈmiːn/ *verb* **1 ~ yourself** to do sth that makes people have less respect for you 降低身分；失去尊重：*I wouldn't demean myself by asking for charity.* 我決不低三下四地乞求施捨。**2 ~ sb/sth** to make people have less respect for sb/sth 貶低；貶損；使失尊嚴 SYN **degrade**：*Such images demean women.* 這些形象有損婦女尊嚴。

de·mean·ing /dɪˈmiːnɪŋ/ *adj.* putting sb in a position that does not give them the respect that they should have 降低身分的；失去尊嚴的 SYN **humiliating**：*He found it demeaning to work for his former employee.* 他覺得為自己以前的雇員工作有失體面。

de·mean·our (*especially US* **de·meanor**) /dɪˈmiːnə(r)/ *noun* [U] (*formal*) the way that sb looks or behaves 外表；風度；行為；舉止：*He maintained a professional demeanour throughout.* 他始終保持着專業人才的風度。

de·men·ted /dɪˈmentɪd/ *adj.* **1** (*especially BrE*) behaving in a crazy way because you are extremely upset or worried 極度焦躁不安的；憂慮失常的；發狂的：*I've been nearly demented with worry about you.* 我一直為你擔心，都快發瘋了。**2** (*old-fashioned* or *medical* 醫) having a mental illness 痴呆的；發狂的 ▸ **de·men·ted·ly** *adv.*

de·men·tia /dɪˈmenʃə/ *noun* [U] (*medical* 醫) a serious mental DISORDER caused by brain disease or injury, that affects the ability to think, remember and behave normally 痴呆；精神錯亂 ➲ see also SENILE DEMENTIA

dem·er·ara sugar /ˌdeməreərə ˈʃʊɡə(r); *NAmE* -rerə/ *noun* [U] (*BrE*) a type of rough brown sugar 德梅拉拉蔗糖

de·merge /ˌdiːˈmɜːdʒ; *NAmE* -ˈmɜːrdʒ/ *verb* [T, I] **~ (sth)** (*BrE, business* 商) to separate a company into smaller companies, usually into the companies that had previously been joined together; to be split in this way 將（合併公司）分拆；（公司）分拆

de·mer·ger /ˌdiːˈmɜːdʒə(r); *NAmE* -ˈmɜːrdʒ-/ *noun* [C, U] (*BrE, business* 商) the act of separating a company from a larger company, especially when they had previously been joined together（尤指合併公司的）分拆

de·merit /diːˈmerɪt/ *noun* (*formal*) **1** [usually pl.] a fault in sth or a disadvantage of sth 過失；缺點；短處：*the merits and demerits of the scheme* 這個方案的優缺點 **2** (*NAmE*) a mark on sb's school record showing that they have done sth wrong（學校給學生記的）過失分：*You'll get three demerits if you're caught smoking on school grounds.* 在校內抽煙一經發現將被記過失分三分。

de·mesne /dəˈmeɪn/ *noun* **1** (in the past) land attached to a MANOR (= large house) that was kept by the owners for their own use（舊時）領主自留地產 **2** (*old use*) a region or large area of land 地區；地域

demi- /ˈdemi/ *prefix* (in nouns 構成名詞) half; partly 半；部份：*demigod* 半神半人

demi·god /ˈdemiɡɒd; *NAmE* -ɡɑːd/ *noun* **1** a minor god, or a BEING that is partly a god and partly human 次神；半神半人 **2** a ruler or other person who is treated like a god 尊為神明的統治者；被神化的人物

demi·john /ˈdemidʒɒn; *NAmE* -dʒɑːn/ *noun* a very large bottle with a narrow opening at the top, for holding and transporting water, wine, etc. 小口大肚瓶；細頸大瓶

de·mili·tar·ize (*BrE* also **-ise**) /ˌdiːˈmɪlɪtəraɪz/ *verb* [usually passive] **~ sth** to remove military forces from an area 從…撤軍；使非軍事化：***a demilitarized zone*** 非軍事區 OPP **militarize** ▸ **de·mili·tar·iza·tion**, **-isa·tion** /ˌdiːˌmɪlɪtəraɪˈzeɪʃn; *NAmE* -rəˈz-/ *noun* [U]

demi-monde /ˌdemi ˈmɒnd; *NAmE* ˈmɑːnd/ *noun* [sing.] (from *French*) people whose behaviour or beliefs prevent them from being fully accepted as part of the main group in society 不完全獲得社會接受的人；行為（或信仰）不受社會尊重的人

de·mise /dɪˈmaɪz/ *noun* [sing.] **1** the end or failure of an institution, an idea, a company, etc. 終止；失敗；倒閉 **2** (*formal* or *humorous*) death 死亡；逝世；一命嗚呼：*his **imminent/sudden/sad demise*** 他死到臨頭；他的猝死；他悲慘的死亡

de·mist /ˌdiːˈmɪst/ (*BrE*) (*NAmE* **de·fog**) *verb* **~ sth** to remove the CONDENSATION from a car's windows so that you can see clearly 除去（汽車玻璃上的）霧水

de·mist·er /ˌdiːˈmɪstə(r)/ *noun* a device, spray, etc. that removes CONDENSATION, especially from the windows of a car（尤指汽車擋風玻璃的）除霧器

demi·urge /ˈdemiɜːdʒ; *NAmE* -ɜːrdʒ/ *noun* (*literary*) **1** a BEING that is responsible for creating the world 巨匠造物主（創世者）**2** a BEING that controls the part of the world which is not spiritual 巨匠造物主（物質世界的控制者）

demo /ˈdeməʊ; *NAmE* -moʊ/ *noun, verb*

■ *noun* (*pl.* **-os**) (*informal*) **1** (*especially BrE*) = DEMONSTRATION (1)：*They all went on the demo.* 他們都參加了示威遊行。**2** = DEMONSTRATION (2)：*I'll **give you a demo**.* 我來給你作個示範。**3** a record or tape with an example of sb's music on it 試樣唱片；錄音樣帶：*a demo tape* 一盤錄音樣帶

■ *verb* **~ sth** to use sth, especially a piece of software, to show sb or to see for yourself how it works 試用（尤指軟件）；演示；示範：*He demoed the new program he had just created.* 他演示了他剛編寫的新程序。◇ *Can I demo the software before I buy it?* 在購買此軟件之前，我能先試用一下嗎？

demo- *prefix* (in nouns, adjectives and adverbs 構成名詞、形容詞和副詞) connected with people or population 與人（或人口）有關的：*democracy* 民主 ◇ *democratic* 民主的

demob /ˌdiːˈmɒb; *NAmE* -ˈmɑːb/ *verb* (**-bb-**) [usually passive] **~ sb** (*BrE, informal*) = DEMOBILIZE：*He was demobbed in 1946.* 他於 1946 年復員。▸ **demob** *noun* [U] (*BrE*)

de·mo·bil·ize (*BrE* also **-ise**) /dɪˈməʊbəlaɪz; *NAmE* -ˈmoʊ-/ (also *BrE informal* **demob**) *verb* **~ sb** to release sb from military service, especially at the end of a war

（尤指戰後）使退伍，使復員 ➲ compare MOBILIZE (3) ▸ **de·mo·bil·iza·tion, -isa·tion** /dɪˌməʊbəlaɪˈzeɪʃn; *NAmE* -ˌmoʊbələˈz-/ *noun* [U]

dem·oc·racy /dɪˈmɒkrəsi; *NAmE* -ˈmɑːk-/ *noun* (*pl.* **-ies**) **1** [U] a system of government in which all the people of a country can vote to elect their representatives 民主；民主政體；民主制度：*parliamentary democracy* 議會民主 ◇ *the principles of democracy* 民主原則 **2** [C] a country which has this system of government 民主國家：*Western democracies* 西方民主國家 ◇ *I thought we were supposed to be living in a democracy.* 我還以為我們應該是生活在一個民主國家裏。 **3** [U] fair and equal treatment of everyone in an organization, etc., and their right to take part in making decisions 民主精神；民主權利；民主：*the fight for justice and democracy* 為正義和民主的鬥爭

demo·crat /ˈdeməkræt/ *noun* **1** a person who believes in or supports democracy 民主主義者 **2 Democrat** (*abbr.* **D**, **Dem.**) a member or supporter of the Democratic Party of the US（美國）民主黨黨員，民主黨人，民主黨支持者 ➲ compare REPUBLICAN *n.* (2)

demo·crat·ic /ˌdeməˈkrætɪk/ *adj.* **1** (of a country, state, system, etc. 國家、政府、制度等) controlled by representatives who are elected by the people of a country; connected with this system 民主的；民主政體的；民主制度的：*a democratic country* 民主國家 ◇ *a democratic system* 民主制度 ◇ *democratic government* 民主政府 **2** based on the principle that all members have an equal right to be involved in running an organization, etc. 民主權利的：*democratic participation* 民主參與 ◇ *a democratic decision* 民主決策 **3** based on the principle that all members of society are equal rather than divided by money or social class 有民主精神的；平等的：*a democratic society* 民主社會 ◇ *democratic reforms* 民主改革 **4 Democratic** (*abbr.* **Dem.**, **D**) connected with the Democratic Party in the US（美國）民主黨的：*the Democratic senator from Oregon*（美國）俄勒岡州的民主黨參議員 ▸ **demo·crat·ic·al·ly** /-kli/ *adv.*：*a democratically elected government* 民主選舉的政府 ◇ *democratically controlled* 民主監管的 ◇ *The decision was taken democratically.* 這是通過民主討論作出的決策。

the Demo'cratic Party *noun* [sing.] one of the two main political parties in the US, usually considered to be in favour of social reform 民主黨（美國兩大主要政黨之一，通常被視為社會改革的支持者）➲ compare THE REPUBLICAN PARTY

dem·oc·ra·tize (*BrE* also **-ise**) /dɪˈmɒkrətaɪz; *NAmE* -ˈmɑːk-/ *verb* **~ sth** (*formal*) to make a country or an institution more democratic 使民主化 ▸ **dem·oc·ra·tiza·tion, -isa·tion** /dɪˌmɒkrətaɪˈzeɪʃn; *NAmE* -ˌmɑːkrətəˈz-/ *noun* [U]

demo·graph·ic /ˌdeməˈɡræfɪk/ *noun, adj.*

▪ *noun* **1 demographics** [pl.] (*statistics* 統計) data relating to the population and different groups within it 人口統計數據：*the demographics of radio listeners* 電台聽眾統計數據 **2** [sing.] (*business* 商) a group of customers who are of a similar age, the same sex, etc. 同類客戶群體：*The products are designed to appeal to a young demographic.* 這些產品是為吸引年輕一代客戶而設計的。◇ *the 18–30 demographic* * 18 至 30 歲的客戶群

▪ *adj.* relating to the population and different groups within it 人口的；人口學的：***demographic changes/trends/factors*** 人口結構變化／發展趨勢／統計要素 ▸ **demo·graph·ic·al·ly** *adv.*

demo·graph·ics /ˌdeməˈɡræfɪks/ *noun* [pl.] (*statistics* 統計) data relating to the population and different groups within it 人口統計數據：*the demographics of radio listeners* 電台聽眾統計數據

dem·og·raphy /dɪˈmɒɡrəfi; *NAmE* -ˈmɑːɡ-/ *noun* [U] the changing number of births, deaths, diseases, etc. in a community over a period of time; the scientific study of these changes 人口統計；人口統計學；人口學：*the social demography of Africa* 非洲社會人口統計 ▸ **dem·og·raph·er** /dɪˈmɒɡrəfə(r); *NAmE* -ˈmɑːɡ-/ *noun*

de·mol·ish /dɪˈmɒlɪʃ; *NAmE* -ˈmɑːl-/ *verb* **1 ~ sth** to pull or knock down a building 拆毀，拆除（建築物）：*The factory is due to be demolished next year.* 這個工廠定於明年拆除。 **2 ~ sth** to destroy sth accidentally（意外）毀壞，破壞：*The car had skidded across the road and demolished part of the wall.* 汽車打滑衝過馬路，把部份牆撞塌了。 **3 ~ sth** to show that an idea or theory is completely wrong 推翻，駁倒（觀點或理論）：*A recent book has demolished this theory.* 最近出版的一本書推翻了這種理論。 **4 ~ sb/sth** to defeat sb easily and completely 輕易戰勝；徹底打敗：*They demolished New Zealand 44–6 in the final.* 他們在決賽中以 44:6 大敗新西蘭隊。 **5 ~ sth** (*BrE, informal*) to eat sth very quickly 狼吞虎嚥地吃；貪婪地吃：*The children demolished their burgers and chips.* 孩子們狼吞虎嚥地吃了漢堡包和炸土豆條。 ▸ **demo·li·tion** /ˌdeməˈlɪʃn/ *noun* [U, C]：*The whole row of houses is scheduled for demolition.* 整排房子均預定拆除。◇ *His speech did a very effective* ***demolition job*** *on the government's proposals.* 他的發言非常成功地駁倒了政府的提案。

ˌdemolition 'derby (*NAmE*) *noun* [C] a type of race in which the competing cars are allowed to hit each other 破壞性賽車（參賽車輛可以相互碰撞）

demon /ˈdiːmən/ *noun* **1** an evil spirit 惡魔；魔鬼：*demons torturing the sinners in Hell* 地獄裏折磨罪人的魔鬼 **2** (*informal*) a person who does sth very well or with a lot of energy 技藝出眾的人；精力充沛的人：*He skis like a demon.* 他滑雪技藝超群。 **3** something that causes a person to worry and makes them unhappy（使人擔憂和不快的）邪惡事物：*the demons of jealousy* 惡魔一樣的嫉妒心

IDM **the demon 'drink** (*BrE, humorous*) alcoholic drink 含酒精飲料

de·mon·ic /diˈmɒnɪk; *NAmE* -ˈmɑːn-/ *adj.* connected with, or like, a demon 惡魔的；魔鬼似的；惡魔般的：*demonic forces* 邪惡勢力 ◇ *a demonic appearance* 魔鬼般的外表

de·mon·ize (*BrE* also **-ise**) /ˈdiːmənaɪz/ *verb* **~ sb/sth** to describe sb/sth in a way that is intended to make other people think of them or it as evil or dangerous 把…描繪成魔鬼（或危險人物等）；將…妖魔化：*He was demonized by the right-wing press.* 他被右翼報章描寫成了魔鬼。 ▸ **de·mon·iza·tion, -isa·tion** /ˌdiːmənaɪˈzeɪʃn/ *noun* [U]

dem·on·strable AW /dɪˈmɒnstrəbl; *NAmE* -ˈmɑːn-; *BrE* also ˈdemənstrəbl/ *adj.* (*formal*) that can be shown or proved 明顯的；可表明的；可論證的；可證明的：*a demonstrable need* 明顯的需要 ▸ **dem·on·strably** AW /-bli/ *adv.*：*demonstrably unfair* 顯然不公平

dem·on·strate 🔑 AW /ˈdemənstreɪt/ *verb* **1** 🔑 [T] to show sth clearly by giving proof or evidence 證明；證實；論證；說明：**~ that …** *These results demonstrate convincingly that our campaign is working.* 這些結果有力地證明，我們的運動正在發揮作用。◇ **~ sth (to sb)** *Let me demonstrate to you some of the difficulties we are facing.* 我來向你說明一下我們面臨的一些困難。◇ **~ how, what, etc. …** *His sudden departure had demonstrated how unreliable he was.* 他突然離去，這說明他是多麼不可靠。◇ **~ sb/sth to be sth** *The theories were demonstrated to be false.* 這些理論已被證明是錯誤的。◇ **it is demonstrated that …** *It has been demonstrated that this drug is effective.* 這藥已證實是有效的。➲ LANGUAGE BANK at EVIDENCE **2** [T] **~ sth** to show by your actions that you have a particular quality, feeling or opinion 表達；表露；表現；顯露 SYN **display**：*You need to demonstrate more self-control.* 你得表現出更強的自制力。◇ *We want to demonstrate our commitment to human rights.* 我們想表明我們為人權而獻身。 **3** 🔑 [T] to show and explain how sth works or how to do sth 示範；演示：**~ sth (to sb)** *Her job involves demonstrating new educational software.* 她的工作包括演示新的教學軟件。◇ **~ (to sb) how, what, etc. …** *Let me demonstrate to you how it works.* 讓我來為你演示一下它是怎麼運行的。 **4** 🔑 [I] to take part in a public meeting or march, usually as a protest or to show support for sth 遊行示威 SYN **protest**：**~ (against sth)** *students demonstrating against the war* 參加反戰示威遊行的學生 ◇ **~ (in favour/support of sth)** *They are demonstrating in favour of free*

D

higher education. 他們參加示威遊行，要求實行免費高等教育。

de·mon·stra·tion AW /ˌdemənˈstreɪʃn/ *noun* **1** (also *informal* **demo** especially in *BrE*) [C] ~ (**against sb/sth**) a public meeting or march at which people show that they are protesting against or supporting sb/sth 遊行示威： *to* ***take part in/go on a demonstration*** 參加 / 進行示威遊行 ◇ *to* ***hold/stage a demonstration*** 舉行示威遊行 ◇ ***mass demonstrations*** *in support of the exiled leader* 支持流亡領導人的群眾集會 ◇ *anti-government demonstrations* 反政府示威遊行 ◇ *a* ***peaceful/violent demonstration*** 和平 / 暴力示威 ➲ compare MARCH *n.* (1) **2** (also *informal* **demo**) [C, U] an act of showing or explaining how sth works or is done 示範；示範表演；演示： *We were given a brief demonstration of the computer's functions.* 我們看了這種計算機各種功能的簡短演示。◇ *a practical demonstration* 實際操作示範 ◇ *We provide demonstration of videoconferencing over the Internet.* 我們通過互聯網演示視頻會議。 **3** [C, U] an act of giving proof or evidence for sth 證明；證實；論證；說明： *a demonstration of the connection between the two sets of figures* 論證這兩組數字間的聯繫 ◇ *a demonstration of how something that seems simple can turn out to be very complicated* 說明看似簡單的東西實際上可能非常複雜 **4** [C] an act of showing a feeling or an opinion 表達；表露；表現；顯露： *a public demonstration of affection* 公開表露愛慕之情 ◇ *a demonstration of support for the reforms* 表示對改革的支持

de·mon·stra·tive AW /dɪˈmɒnstrətɪv; *NAmE* -ˈmɑːn-/ *adj.*, *noun*

■ ***adj.*** **1** showing feelings openly, especially feelings of affection 公開表露感情（尤指愛慕之情）的；感情外露的： *Some people are more demonstrative than others.* 有些人更容易流露感情。◇ *a demonstrative greeting* 熱情的問候 **2** (*grammar* 語法) used to identify the person or thing that is being referred to 指示的： *'This' and 'that' are demonstrative pronouns.* * this 和 that 是指示代詞。 ▸ **de·mon·stra·tive·ly** AW *adv.*

■ ***noun*** (*grammar* 語法) a demonstrative pronoun or determiner 指示代詞；限定詞；指示代名詞

dem·on·stra·tor AW /ˈdemənstreɪtə(r)/ *noun* **1** a person who takes part in a public meeting or march in order to protest against sb/sth or to show support for sb/sth （集會或遊行的）示威者 **2** a person whose job is to show or explain how sth works or is done 示範者；演示者

de·mor·al·ize (*BrE* also **-ise**) /dɪˈmɒrəlaɪz; *NAmE* -ˈmɔːr-/ *verb* [usually passive] ~ **sb** to make sb lose confidence or hope 使泄氣；使意志消沉；使士氣低落 SYN **dishearten**： *Constant criticism is enough to demoralize anybody.* 頻繁的批評足以使任何人意志消沉。 ▸ **de·mor·al·ized**, **-ised** *adj.*： *The workers here seem very demoralized.* 這裏的工人顯得十分沮喪。 **de·mor·al·iz·ing**, **-is·ing** *adj.*： *the demoralizing effects of unemployment* 失業造成的使人沮喪的後果 **de·mor·al·iza·tion**, **-isa·tion** /dɪˌmɒrəlaɪˈzeɪʃn; *NAmE* -ˌmɔːrələˈz-/ *noun* [U]

de·mote /ˌdiːˈməʊt; *NAmE* -ˈmoʊt/ *verb* [often passive] ~ **sb** (**from sth**) (**to sth**) to move sb to a lower position or rank, often as a punishment 使降級，使降職，使降低地位（常作為懲罰） OPP **promote** ▸ **de·mo·tion** /ˌdiːˈməʊʃn; *NAmE* -ˈmoʊ-/ *noun* [C, U]

dem·ot·ic /dɪˈmɒtɪk; *NAmE* -ˈmɑːt-/ *adj.* (*formal*) used by or typical of ordinary people 民眾的；通俗的；大眾化的

de·mo·tiv·ate /ˌdiːˈməʊtɪveɪt; *NAmE* -ˈmoʊ-/ *verb* ~ **sb** to make sb feel that it is not worth making an effort 使失去動力；使變得消極： *Failure can demotivate students.* 失敗會挫傷學生的積極性。 ▸ **de·mo·tiv·at·ing** *adj.* **de·mo·tiv·ated** *adj.* **de·mo·tiv·ation** /ˌdiːməʊtɪˈveɪʃn; *NAmE* -moʊ-/ *noun* [U]

demur /dɪˈmɜː(r)/ *verb*, *noun*

■ ***verb*** (**-rr-**) [I] (+ **speech**) (*formal*) to say that you do not agree with sth or that you refuse to do sth 表示反對；提出異議；拒絕： *At first she demurred, but then finally agreed.* 她一開始表示反對，但最終還是同意了。

■ ***noun***

IDM **without de'mur** (*formal*) without objecting or hesitating 毫無異議；毫不猶豫： *They accepted without demur.* 他們接受了，沒有提出異議。

de·mure /dɪˈmjʊə(r); *NAmE* dɪˈmjʊr/ *adj.* **1** (of a woman or a girl 女子) behaving in a way that does not attract attention to herself or her body; quiet and serious 嫻靜的；端莊的 SYN **modest**： *a demure young lady* 嫻靜的年輕女士 **2** suggesting that a woman or girl is demure 顯得（女子）莊重的 SYN **modest**： *a demure smile* 矜持的微笑 ◇ *a demure navy blouse with a white collar* 嚴肅莊重的白領海軍軍服上衣 ▸ **de·mure·ly** *adv.*

de·mys·tify /ˌdiːˈmɪstɪfaɪ/ *verb* (**de·mys·ti·fies**, **de·mys·ti·fy·ing**, **de·mys·ti·fied**, **de·mys·ti·fied**) ~ **sth** to make sth easier to understand and less complicated by explaining it in a clear and simple way 使明白易懂；深入淺出地解釋 ▸ **de·mys·ti·fi·ca·tion** /ˌdiːˌmɪstɪfɪˈkeɪʃn/ *noun* [U]

den /den/ *noun* **1** the hidden home of some types of wild animal 獸穴；獸窩： *a* ***bear's/lion's den*** 熊的 / 獅子的洞穴 **2** (*disapproving*) a place where people meet in secret, especially for some illegal or immoral activity 窩點，窩子（尤指非法或邪惡活動秘密聚會處）： *a den of thieves* 賊窩 ◇ *a* ***drinking/gambling den*** 酗酒窩點；賭窟 ◇ *He thought of New York as* ***a den of iniquity***. 他把紐約視為罪惡的淵藪。 **3** (*NAmE*) a room in a house where people go to relax, watch television, etc. 休息室 **4** (*old-fashioned*, *BrE*, *informal*) a room in a house where a person can work or study without being disturbed 書齋；書房： *He would often retire to his den.* 他往往是回自己的書房去。 **5** a secret place, often made roughly with walls and a roof, where children play （兒童的）隱蔽玩耍處： *They made themselves a den in the woods.* 他們在樹林裏為自己搭了個窩，在裏面玩。 IDM see BEARD *v.*, LION

de·nation·al·ize (*BrE* also **-ise**) /ˌdiːˈnæʃnəlaɪz/ *verb* ~ **sth** to sell a company or an industry so that it is no longer owned by the government 使私有化；使非國有化 SYN **privatize** OPP **nationalize** ▸ **de·nation·al·iza·tion**, **-isa·tion** /ˌdiːˌnæʃnəlaɪˈzeɪʃn; *NAmE* -ləˈz-/ *noun* [U]

den·drite /ˈdendraɪt/ (also **den·dron** /ˈdendrɒn; *NAmE* -drɑːn/) *noun* (*biology* 生) a short branch at the end of a nerve cell, which receives signals from other cells 樹突（位於神經元末端的細分支，接收其他神經元傳來的衝動） ➲ compare AXON ▸ **den·drit·ic** /ˌdenˈdrɪtɪk/ *adj.*： *dendritic cells* 樹突細胞

dengue /ˈdeŋgi/ (also **ˈdengue fever**, **ˈbreakbone fever**) *noun* [U] a disease caused by a virus carried by MOSQUITOES, that is found in tropical areas and causes fever and severe pain in the joints 登革熱（由蚊子傳播的熱帶疾病，症狀為發燒和關節劇痛）

deni·able AW /dɪˈnaɪəbl/ *adj.* that can be denied 可否認的；可拒絕的 OPP **undeniable**

de·nial AW /dɪˈnaɪəl/ *noun* **1** [C] ~ (**of sth/that ...**) a statement that says sth is not true or does not exist 否認；否定： *the prisoner's repeated denials of the charges against him* 囚犯再三否認對他的指控 ◇ *The terrorists issued a denial of responsibility for the attack.* 恐怖分子發表聲明，否認對這次襲擊負責。◇ *an official denial that there would be an election before the end of the year* 對年底前將進行選舉的正式否認 **2** [C, U] (a) ~ **of sth** a refusal to allow sb to have sth they have a right to expect 拒絕給予，剝奪（應有的權利）： *the denial of basic human rights* 剝奪基本人權 **3** [U] (*psychology* 心) a refusal to accept that sth unpleasant or painful is true 拒絕接受，拒不承認（令人不快、痛苦的事）： *The patient is still in denial.* 病人仍然拒不接受事實。

den·ier /ˈdeniə(r)/ *noun* (*especially BrE*) a unit for measuring how fine threads of NYLON, silk, etc. are 旦（測量尼龍線、絲線等的纖度單位）： *15 denier stockings* * 15 旦的長襪

deni·grate /ˈdenɪgreɪt/ *verb* ~ **sb/sth** (*formal*) to criticize sb/sth unfairly; to say sb/sth does not have any value or is not important 詆譭；誹謗；貶低 SYN **belittle**： *I didn't intend to denigrate her achievements.* 我不是想貶低她的成績。 ▸ **deni·gra·tion** /ˌdenɪˈgreɪʃn/ *noun* [U]

denim /ˈdenɪm/ *noun* **1** [U] a type of strong cotton cloth that is usually blue and is used for making clothes, especially jeans 藍粗棉布；勞動布；牛仔布：*a denim jacket* 牛仔布夾克衫 ➲ VISUAL VOCAB page V61 **ORIGIN** From the French *serge de Nîmes*, meaning 'serge (= a type of cloth) from the town of Nîmes'. 源自法語 serge de Nîmes，意為尼姆城產的嗶嘰。 **2 denims** [pl.] (*old-fashioned*) trousers/pants made of denim 牛仔褲 **SYN jeans**

deni·zen /ˈdenɪzn/ *noun* (*formal* or *humorous*) a person, an animal or a plant that lives, grows or is often found in a particular place （某地區的）居民，常客，動物，植物 **SYN inhabitant**：*polar bears, denizens of the frozen north* 北極熊，在冰天雪地的北方生活的動物 ◇ *the denizens of the local pub* 當地酒吧的常客

de·nom·in·ate /dɪˈnɒmɪneɪt; *NAmE* -ˈnɑːm-/ *verb* **1 ~ sth (in sth)** to express an amount of money using a particular unit 以（某種貨幣）為單位：*The loan was denominated in US dollars.* 這筆貸款是以美元計算的。 **2 ~ sb (as) sth** (*formal*) to give sth a particular name or description 將…命名為；稱…為：*These payments are denominated as 'fees' rather than 'salary'.* 付出的這幾筆款子稱為"費用"而不是"工資"。

de·nom·in·ation /dɪˌnɒmɪˈneɪʃn; *NAmE* -ˌnɑːm-/ *noun* (*formal*) **1** a branch of the Christian Church （基督教）教派，宗派：*Christians of all denominations attended the conference.* 基督教所有教派的人都出席了這次會議。 **2** a unit of value, especially of money （尤指錢的）面額，面值：*coins and banknotes of various denominations* 各種面額的硬幣和紙幣

de·nom·in·ation·al /dɪˌnɒmɪˈneɪʃənl; *NAmE* -ˌnɑːm-/ *adj.* belonging to a particular branch of the Christian Church （基督教）教派的，宗派的

de·nom·in·ator /dɪˈnɒmɪneɪtə(r); *NAmE* -ˈnɑːm-/ *noun* (*mathematics* 數) the number below the line in a FRACTION showing how many parts the whole is divided into, for example 4 in ¾ 分母 ➲ compare NUMERATOR, COMMON DENOMINATOR (1)

de·nota·tion **AW** /ˌdiːnəʊˈteɪʃn; *NAmE* -noʊ-/ *noun* (*technical* 術語) the act of naming sth with a word; the actual object or idea to which the word refers 指稱；指稱之物；指稱意義；外延 ➲ compare CONNOTATION ▸ **de·nota·tion·al** /ˌdiːnəʊˈteɪʃnl; *NAmE* -noʊ-/ *adj.*

de·note **AW** /dɪˈnəʊt; *NAmE* dɪˈnoʊt/ *verb* (*formal*) **1 ~ sth | ~ that …** to be a sign of sth 標誌；預示；象徵 **SYN indicate**：*A very high temperature often denotes a serious illness.* 高燒常常表示病得很重。 **2 ~ sth | ~ what, when, etc. …** to mean sth 表示；意指 **SYN represent**：*In this example 'X' denotes the time taken and 'Y' denotes the distance covered.* 在這個例子中，X 表示所用的時間，Y 表示所行的距離。 ◇ *The red triangle denotes danger.* 紅色三角形表示危險。 ◇ *Here 'family' denotes mother, father and children.* 此處的 family 指母親、父親和孩子。 ➲ compare CONNOTE

de·noue·ment (also **dé·noue·ment**) /ˌdeɪˈnuːmɒ̃; *NAmE* ˌdeɪnuːˈmɑ̃ː/ *noun* (from *French*) the end of a play, book, etc., in which everything is explained or settled; the end result of a situation （戲劇、書籍等的）結局，收場；（事情的）結果

de·nounce /dɪˈnaʊns/ *verb* **1** to strongly criticize sb/sth that you think is wrong, illegal, etc. 譴責；指責；斥責：**~ sb/sth** *She publicly denounced the government's handling of the crisis.* 她公開譴責政府處理這場危機的方式。 ◇ **~ sb/sth as sth** *The project was denounced as a scandalous waste of public money.* 這項工程被斥責為揮霍公款，令人憤慨。 **2** to tell the police, the authorities, etc. about sb's illegal political activities 告發（某人從事非法政治活動）：**~ sb as sth** *They were denounced as spies.* 他們被揭發是間諜。 ◇ **~ sb (to sb)** *Many people denounced their neighbours to the secret police.* 許多人向秘密警察告發自己的鄰居。 ➲ see also DENUNCIATION

dense /dens/ *adj.* (**dens·er, dens·est**) **1** containing a lot of people, things, plants, etc. with little space between them 密集的；稠密的：*a* ***dense crowd/forest*** 密集的人群；密林 ◇ *areas of dense population* 人口密集地區 **2** difficult to see through 濃密的；濃重的 **SYN thick**：***dense fog/smoke/fumes*** 濃霧／煙；濃烈的氣體 **3** (*informal*) stupid 愚笨的；遲鈍的；笨拙的：*How can you be so dense?* 你怎麼會這麼笨？ **4** difficult to understand because it contains a lot of information （信息量大得）難理解的，難懂的：*a dense piece of writing* 難懂的文章 **5** (*technical* 術語) heavy in relation to its size 密度大的；密實的：*Less dense substances move upwards to form a crust.* 密度小的物質向上浮動並形成一硬層。 ▸ **dense·ly** *adv.*：*a* ***densely populated*** *area* 人口密集地區 ◇ ***densely covered/packed*** 蓋得／包得嚴實的

dens·ity /ˈdensəti/ *noun* (*pl.* **-ies**) **1** [U] the quality of being dense; the degree to which sth is dense 密集；稠密；密度；濃度：*population density* 人口密度 ◇ *low density forest* 低密度森林 **2** [C, U] (*physics* 物) the thickness of a solid, liquid or gas measured by its mass per unit of volume 密度（固體、液體或氣體單位體積的質量）：*the density of a gas* 一種氣體的密度 **3** [U] (*computing* 計) the amount of space available on a disk for recording data 密度（磁盤存貯數據的可用空間）：*a* ***high/double density*** *floppy* 高密度／雙密度軟盤

dent /dent/ *verb, noun*

■ *verb* **1 ~ sth** to make a hollow place in a hard surface, usually by hitting it 使凹陷；使產生凹痕：*The back of the car was badly dented in the collision.* 汽車尾部被撞後嚴重凹陷。 **2 ~ sth** to damage sb's confidence, reputation, etc. 損害，傷害，挫傷（信心、名譽等）：*It seemed that nothing could dent his confidence.* 似乎任何事情都不會使他的信心受挫。

■ *noun* a hollow place in a hard surface, usually caused by sth hitting it 凹痕；凹坑；凹部：*a large dent in the car door* 車門上一大塊凹陷

IDM **make, etc. a ˈdent in sth** to reduce the amount of sth, especially money 減少，削減（尤指資金）：*The lawyer's fees will make a dent in our finances.* 律師費將耗去我們一部份資金。

dent·al /ˈdentl/ *adj.* [only before noun] **1** connected with teeth 牙齒的；牙科的：***dental disease/care/treatment/health*** 牙齒疾病／護理／治療／健康 ◇ *a dental appointment* 牙科預約 ◇ *dental records* 牙科病歷 ◇ (*BrE*) *a dental surgery* (= where a dentist sees patients) 牙科診所 **2** (*phonetics* 語音) (of a consonant 輔音) produced with the tongue against the upper front teeth, for example /θ/ and /ð/ in *thin* and *this* 齒音的

ˈdental dam (also **dam**) *noun* **1** a small rubber sheet used by dentists to keep a tooth separate from the other teeth 橡皮障（牙醫用的牙齒阻隔膜） **2** a small rubber sheet used to protect the mouth during sex （性交時用的）口腔保護膜；口交保險膜

ˈdental floss (also **floss**) *noun* [U] a type of thread that is used for cleaning between the teeth 潔牙線；牙線

ˈdental hygienist *noun* (*especially NAmE*) = HYGIENIST

ˈdental surgeon *noun* (*formal*) = DENTIST (1)

den·tine /ˈdentiːn/ (*NAmE* also **den·tin** /ˈdentɪn/) *noun* [U] (*biology* 生) the hard substance that forms the main part of a tooth under the ENAMEL 牙質；牙本質；齒質

den·tist 0→ /ˈdentɪst/ *noun*
1 0→ (also *formal* **ˈdental surgeon**) a person whose job is to take care of people's teeth 牙科醫生 **2 dentist's** a place where a dentist sees patients 牙科診所：*an appointment at the dentist's* 牙科診所的門診預約

den·tis·try /ˈdentɪstri/ *noun* [U] **1** the medical study of the teeth and mouth 牙科學 **2** the work of a dentist 牙科醫術；牙醫的工作：*preventive dentistry* 預防牙科

den·ti·tion /denˈtɪʃn/ *noun* [U, C] (*technical* 術語) the arrangement or condition of a person's or animal's teeth 齒系（人或動物的牙列或牙齒狀況）

den·tures /ˈdentʃəz; *NAmE* -tʃərz/ *noun* [pl.] artificial teeth on a thin piece of plastic (= a PLATE), worn by sb who no longer has all their own teeth 托牙；假牙 ▸ **den·ture** *adj.*：*denture adhesive* 托牙黏膠 ➲ compare FALSE TEETH, PLATE *n.* (14)

de·nude /dɪˈnjuːd; *NAmE* dɪˈnuːd/ *verb* [usually passive] **~ sth (of sth)** (*formal*) to remove the covering, features,

D

etc. from sth, so that it is exposed 剝光；使裸露；使光秃：*hillsides denuded of trees* 光禿禿沒有樹的山坡

de·nun·ci·ation /dɪˌnʌnsiˈeɪʃn/ *noun* [C, U] **~ (of sb/sth)** (*formal*) an act of criticizing sb/sth strongly in public 公開譴責；斥責；指責：*an angry denunciation of the government's policies* 憤怒譴責政府的政策 ◇ *All parties joined in bitter denunciation of the terrorists.* 所有黨派同仇敵愾地痛斥恐怖分子。➲ see also DENOUNCE

D

Denver boot /ˈdenvə buːt; *NAmE* -vər/ (also **boot**) (both *US*) (*BrE* **clamp**, **ˈwheel clamp**) *noun* a device that is attached to the wheel of a car that has been parked illegally, so that it cannot be driven away 車輪夾鎖（用於鎖住違章停放的車輛）

deny 🔑 AW /dɪˈnaɪ/ *verb* (**de·nies**, **deny·ing**, **de·nied**, **de·nied**)

> **WORD FAMILY**
> **deny** *verb*
> **denial** *noun*
> **undeniable** *adj.*
> **undeniably** *adv.*

1 🔑 to say that sth is not true 否認；否定：**~ sth** *to deny a claim/a charge/an accusation* 否認某種說法 / 指控 / 指責 ◇ *The spokesman refused either to confirm or deny the reports.* 發言人對那些報道不置可否。◇ **~ (that)** … *She denied (that) there had been any cover-up.* 她否認有任何隱瞞。◇ ***There's no denying** (the fact) **that** quicker action could have saved them.* 無可否認，如果行動快一點，本來是救得了他們的。◇ **it is denied that** … ***It can't be denied that** we need to devote more resources to this problem.* 無可否認，我們需要投入更多的資源來解決這個問題。◇ **~ doing sth** *He denies attempting to murder his wife.* 他否認企圖謀殺妻子。 **2** 🔑 **~ sth** to refuse to admit or accept sth 拒絕承認；拒絕接受：*She denied all knowledge of the incident.* 她矢口否認知曉此事的任何情況。◇ *The department denies responsibility for what occurred.* 這個部門拒絕為所發生的事承擔責任。 **3** (*formal*) to refuse to allow sb to have sth that they want or ask for 拒絕；拒絕給予：**~ sb sth** *They were denied access to the information.* 他們試圖取得這個情報被拒。◇ **~ sth to sb** *Access to the information was denied to them.* 他們無法得到這個情報。 **4 ~ yourself** (**sth**) (*formal*) to refuse to let yourself have sth that you would like to have, especially for moral or religious reasons（尤因道德或宗教原因）節制，克制，戒絕

de·odor·ant /diˈəʊdərənt; *NAmE* diˈoʊ-/ *noun* [C, U] a substance that people put on their bodies to prevent or hide unpleasant smells 除臭劑，解臭劑（用於消除體臭）：*(a) roll-on deodorant* 滾搽式除臭劑 ➲ see also ANTIPERSPIRANT

dep. *abbr.* (in writing) DEPART(S); DEPARTURE （書寫形式）離開，出發 ➲ compare ARR. (1)

de·part /dɪˈpɑːt; *NAmE* dɪˈpɑːrt/ *verb* (rather *formal*) **1** [I, T] to leave a place, especially to start a trip 離開；離去；起程；出發 OPP **arrive**：**~ (for …) (from …)** *Flights for Rome depart from Terminal 3.* 飛往羅馬的班機從 3 號航空站出發。◇ *She waited until the last of the guests had departed.* 她一直等到最後一個客人離開。◇ **~ sth** (*NAmE*) *The train departed Amritsar at 6.15 p.m.* 火車在下午 6 點 15 分離開了阿姆利則。 **2** [I, T] (*NAmE*) to leave your job 離職：*the departing president* 行將卸任的總裁 ◇ **~ sth** *He departed his job December 16.* 他於 12 月 16 日離職。➲ see also DEPARTURE

IDM **depart this ˈlife** to die. People say 'depart this life' to avoid saying 'die'. 離開人世，去世，亡故（委婉說法，與 die 同義）

PHR V **deˈpart from sth** to behave in a way that is different from usual 違反，背離（常規）：*Departing from her usual routine, she took the bus to work.* 她一反常態乘公共汽車上班了。

de·part·ed /dɪˈpɑːtɪd; *NAmE* -ˈpɑːrt-/ *adj.* [only before noun] (*formal*) **1** dead. People say 'departed' to avoid saying 'dead'. 去世的，已故的（委婉說法，與 dead 同義）：*your dear departed brother* 你摯愛的亡兄 **2 the departed** *noun* (*pl.* **the de·part·ed**) the person who has died 去世者；亡故者

de·part·ment 🔑 /dɪˈpɑːtmənt; *NAmE* -ˈpɑːrt-/ *noun* (*abbr.* **Dept**) a section of a large organization such as a government, business, university, etc. 部；司；局；處；系；（醫院的）科；部門：*the Department of Trade and Industry* 工業貿易署 ◇ *the Treasury Department* 財政部 ◇ ***a government/university, etc. department*** 政府部門、大學學系等 ◇ *the **marketing/sales, etc. department*** 營銷、銷售等部門 ◇ *the children's department* (= in a large store) 兒童用品部 ◇ *the English department* 英語系 ➲ see also POLICE DEPARTMENT, THE STATE DEPARTMENT

IDM **be sb's department** (*informal*) to be sth that sb is responsible for or knows a lot about 某人的職責範圍（或知識範圍）：*Don't ask me about it—that's her department.* 這事別問我，那是她的職責範圍。

de·part·ment·al /ˌdiːpɑːtˈmentl; *NAmE* -pɑːrt-/ *adj.* [only before noun] connected with a department rather than with the whole organization 部門的；分部的：*a departmental manager* 部門經理

deˈpartment store *noun* a large shop/store that is divided into several parts, each part selling a different type of goods 百貨公司；大百貨商店

de·par·ture 🔑 /dɪˈpɑːtʃə(r); *NAmE* -ˈpɑːrt-/ *noun* **1** 🔑 [C, U] **~ (from …)** the act of leaving a place; an example of this 離開；起程；出發：*His sudden departure threw the office into chaos.* 他的突然離去使整個辦公室陷入一片混亂。◇ *Flights should be confirmed 48 hours before departure.* 航班應在起飛前 48 小時予以確認。◇ *They had received no news of him since his departure from the island.* 自從他離開這座島後，他們再沒聽過他的消息。OPP **arrival** **2** 🔑 [C] a plane, train, etc. leaving a place at a particular time（在特定時間）離開的飛機（或火車等）：*arrivals and departures* 到站和離站航班 ◇ *All departures are from Manchester.* 所有離站班次都從曼徹斯特出發。◇ *the **departure lounge/time/gate*** 候機（或車）室；離站時間；登機（或上車）口 ◇ *the **departures board*** 離站時刻牌 OPP **arrival** **3** [C] **~ (from sth)** an action that is different from what is usual or expected 背離；違反；逾越：*It was a radical departure from tradition.* 這從根本上違背了傳統。◇ *Their latest single represents **a new departure** for the band.* 他們最新推出的單曲唱片體現了這支樂隊的新嘗試。

IDM see POINT *n.*

de·pend 🔑 /dɪˈpend/ *verb*

IDM **deˈpending on** 🔑 according to 視乎；決定於：*Starting salary varies from £26 000 to £30 500, depending on experience.* 起薪為 26 000 至 30 500 英鎊不等，依個人經驗而定。◇ *He either resigned or was sacked, depending on who you talk to.* 他或是辭職了，或是被辭退了，這要看你跟誰講了。 **that deˈpends | it (all) deˈpends** 🔑 used to say that you are not certain about sth because other things have to be considered 那得看情況：*'Is he coming?' 'That depends. He may not have the time.'* "他來嗎？" "那要看情況。他不一定有時間。" ◇ *I don't know if we can help—it all depends.* 我不知道我們能不能幫上忙，一切都得看情況而定。◇ *I might not go. It depends how tired I am.* 我不一定去。這要看我累不累。◇ *'Your job sounds fun.' 'It depends what you mean by 'fun'.'* "你的工作聽起來很有樂趣。" "這就要看你說的'樂趣'是什麼意思了。" ◇ *I shouldn't be too late. But it depends if the traffic's bad.* 我應該不會太遲。不過這取決於交通是否擁擠了。

PHR V **deˈpend on/upon sb/sth** **1** 🔑 to rely on sb/sth and be able to trust them 依靠；信賴：*He was the sort of person you could depend on.* 他這個人你是可以信賴的。◇ **~ sb/sth to do sth** *He knew he could depend upon her to deal with the situation.* 他知道可以依靠她來應付這種局面。➲ SYNONYMS at TRUST **2** 🔑 to be sure or expect that sth will happen 確信；相信；指望 SYN **count on**：***Depend upon it*** (= you can be sure) *we won't give up.* 請相信，我們決不會放棄。◇ **~ sb/sth doing sth** *Can we depend on you coming in on Sunday?* 我們能指望你星期天來參加嗎？◇ (*formal*) *You can depend on his coming in on Sunday.* 你放心，他星期天一定來參加。◇ **~ sb/sth to do sth** (*ironic*) *You can depend on her to be* (= she always is) *late.* 她保準遲到。 **deˈpend on/upon sb/sth (for sth)** 🔑 (not usually used in the progressive tenses 通常不用於進行時) to need money, help, etc.

from sb/sth else for a particular purpose 需要，依靠（提供資金、幫助等）: *The community depends on the shipping industry for its survival.* 這個社區靠航運業維持生活。◇ *I don't want to depend too much on my parents.* 我不想過度依靠父母。**de'pend on/upon sth** (not used in the progressive tenses 不用於進行時) to be affected or decided by sth 受…的影響；由…決定；取決於: *Does the quality of teaching depend on class size?* 教學質量取決於每個班的人數嗎？◇ *It would depend on the circumstances.* 這要視情況而定。◇ **~ how, what, etc. …** *Whether we need more food depends on how many people turn up.* 我們是否需要更多的食物，這要視到場人數而定。

Grammar Point 語法說明

depend on

- In informal English, it is quite common to say **depend** rather than **depend on** before words like *what, how* or *whether.* 在非正式英語中，在 what、how 或 whether 等詞前常用 depend 而非 depend on: *It depends what you mean by 'hostile'.* 那得看你所説的 hostile 的含義。In formal written English, **depend** should always be followed by *on* or *upon.* 在正式的書面英語中，depend 後總是跟 on 或 upon: *It depends on how you define the term 'hostile'.* 那得看你怎麼定義 hostile 這個詞。*Upon* is more formal and less frequent than *on.* * upon 較正式，不如 on 常用。

de·pend·able /dɪˈpendəbl/ *adj.* that can be relied on to do what you want or need 可信賴的；可靠的 SYN **reliable** ▸ **de·pend·abil·ity** /dɪˌpendəˈbɪləti/ *noun* [U]

de·pend·ant /dɪˈpendənt/ (*BrE, CanE*) (also **de·pend·ent** *NAmE, BrE*) *noun* a person, especially a child, who depends on another person for a home, food, money, etc. 受扶養者（尤指孩子）；靠他人生活者；受扶養的家屬

de·pend·ence /dɪˈpendəns/ *noun* [U] **1 ~ (on/upon sb/sth)** the state of needing the help and support of sb/sth in order to survive or be successful（生存或成功必需的）依靠，依賴，依存: *his dependence on his parents* 他對父母的依賴 ◇ *Our relationship was based on mutual dependence.* 我們的關係建立在相互依存的基礎上。◇ *the dependence of Europe on imported foods* 歐洲對進口食物的依賴 ◇ *financial/economic dependence* 財政／經濟依賴 OPP **independence 2** (also **de·pend·ency**) the state of being ADDICTED to sth (= unable to stop taking or using it) 癮: ***drug/alcohol dependence*** 毒癮；酒癮 **3 ~ of A and B** (*technical* 術語) the fact of one thing being affected by another 相關（性）；相依（性）: *the close dependence of soil and landforms* 土壤和地貌的密切相關

de·pend·ency /dɪˈpendənsi/ *noun* (*pl.* **-ies**) **1** [U] **~ (on/upon sb/sth)** the state of relying on sb/sth for sth, especially when this is not normal or necessary（尤指不正常或不必要的）依靠，依賴: *financial dependency* 財政上的依賴 ◇ *Their aim is to reduce people's dependency on the welfare state.* 他們旨在減少人們對福利制度的依賴。◇ *the **dependency culture*** (= a way of life in which people depend too much on money from the government) 依賴文化（過分依賴政府資助）➲ compare CODEPENDENCY **2** [C] a country, an area, etc. that is controlled by another country 附屬國；附屬地 **3** = DEPENDENCE (2)

de·pend·ent /dɪˈpendənt/ *adj., noun*

■ ***adj.*** **1** needing sb/sth in order to survive or be successful 依靠的；依賴的: *a woman with several dependent children* 一個女人帶着幾個未自立的孩子 ◇ **~ on/upon sb/sth** *You can't be dependent on your parents all your life.* 你不可能一輩子靠父母生活。◇ **~ on/upon sb/sth for sth** *The festival is heavily dependent on sponsorship for its success.* 這次節日慶祝活動成功與否，在很大程度上就看贊助了。**2 ~ on/upon sth** ADDICTED to sth (= unable to stop taking or using it) 有癮的: *to be dependent on drugs* 有毒癮 **3 ~ on/upon sth** (*formal*) affected or decided by sth 受…的影響；取決於: *A child's development is dependent on many factors.* 孩子的成長受多種因素影響。◇ *The price is dependent on how many extras you choose.* 價格取決於你挑選額外收費項目的多少。

■ ***noun*** (*especially NAmE*) = DEPENDANT

de,pendent 'clause *noun* (*grammar* 語法) = SUBORDINATE CLAUSE

de,pendent 'variable *noun* (*mathematics* 數) a VARIABLE whose value depends on another variable 因變量；因變數

de·per·son·al·ize (*BrE* also **-ise**) /diːˈpɜːsənəlaɪz; *NAmE* -ˈpɜːrs-/ *verb* **~ sth** [often passive] to make sth less personal so that it does not seem as if humans with feelings and personality are involved 使非個性化；使不摻雜個人感情

de·pict /dɪˈpɪkt/ *verb* (rather *formal*) **1** to show an image of sb/sth in a picture 描繪；描畫: **~ sb/sth (as sb/sth)** *a painting depicting the Virgin and Child* 一幅描繪童貞瑪利亞和聖子耶穌的畫 ◇ **~ sb/sth doing sth** *The artist had depicted her lying on a bed.* 畫家畫了她躺在牀上。**2** to describe sth in words, or give an impression of sth in words or with a picture 描寫；描述；刻畫: **~ sb/sth** *The novel depicts French society in the 1930s.* 這部小説描述了 20 世紀 30 年代的法國社會。◇ **~ sb/sth as sb/sth** *The advertisements depict smoking as glamorous and attractive.* 這些廣告把吸煙描繪得充滿刺激和富有吸引力。▸ **de·pic·tion** /dɪˈpɪkʃn/ *noun* [U, C]: *They object to the movie's depiction of gay people.* 他們反對這部影片對同性戀者的刻畫。

de·pila·tor /ˈdepɪleɪtə(r); *NAmE* dɪˈpɪlətɔːr/ *noun* a device which removes hair from your body by pulling it out 拔毛器；脱毛器

de·pila·tory /dɪˈpɪlətri; *NAmE* -tɔːri/ *noun* (*pl.* **-ies**) a substance used for removing body hair 脱毛劑 ▸ **de·pila·tory** *adj.* [only before noun]: *depilatory creams* 脱毛乳膏

de·plane /diːˈpleɪn/ *verb* [I] (*NAmE*) to get off a plane 下飛機 SYN **disembark**

de·plete /dɪˈpliːt/ *verb* [usually passive] **~ sth** (*formal*) to reduce sth by a large amount so that there is not enough left 大量減少；耗盡；使枯竭: *Food supplies were severely depleted.* 食物供應已嚴重不足。▸ **de·ple·tion** /dɪˈpliːʃn/ *noun* [U]: *ozone depletion* 臭氧耗損 ◇ *the depletion of fish stocks* 魚量消耗殆盡

de·plor·able /dɪˈplɔːrəbl/ *adj.* (*formal*) very bad and unacceptable, often in a way that shocks people 糟透的；令人震驚的；令人憤慨的 SYN **appalling**: *a deplorable incident* 令人憤慨的事件 ◇ *They were living in the most deplorable conditions.* 他們生活在最糟糕的環境裏。◇ *The acting was deplorable.* 那演技糟透了。▸ **de·plor·ably** /-əbli/ *adv.*: *They behaved deplorably.* 他們的表現糟透了。◇ ***deplorably high/low/bad*** 高／低／糟得令人吃驚

de·plore /dɪˈplɔː(r)/ *verb* **~ sth** (*formal*) to strongly disapprove of sth and criticize it, especially publicly 公開譴責；強烈反對: *Like everyone else, I deplore and condemn this killing.* 我同所有人一樣強烈譴責這樁兇殺案。

de·ploy /dɪˈplɔɪ/ *verb* **1 ~ sb/sth** (*technical* 術語) to move soldiers or weapons into a position where they are ready for military action 部署，調度（軍隊或武器）: *2 000 troops were deployed in the area.* 那個地區部署了 2 000 人的部隊。◇ *At least 5 000 missiles were deployed along the border.* 沿邊境至少部署了 5 000 枚導彈。**2 ~ sth** (*formal*) to use sth effectively 有效地利用；調動: *to **deploy arguments/resources*** 利用論據／資源 ▸ **de·ploy·ment** *noun* [U, C]

de·popu·late /ˌdiːˈpɒpjuleɪt; *NAmE* -ˈpɑːp-/ *verb* [usually passive] **~ sth** to reduce the number of people living in a place 使人口減少: *Whole stretches of land were laid waste and depopulated.* 一片片土地荒蕪，人口減少。▸ **de·popu·la·tion** /ˌdiːˌpɒpjuˈleɪʃn; *NAmE* -ˌpɑːp-/ *noun* [U]

de·port /dɪˈpɔːt; *NAmE* dɪˈpɔːrt/ *verb* **~ sb** to force sb to leave a country, usually because they have broken the law or because they have no legal right to be there 把（違法者或無合法居留權的人）驅逐出境；遞解出境

D

D

▸ **de·port·ation** /ˌdiːpɔːˈteɪʃn; *NAmE* -pɔːrˈt-/ *noun* [C, U]：*Several of the asylum seekers now face deportation.* 尋求避難的人中有幾個正面臨遞解出境。◇ *a deportation order* 驅逐出境令

de·port·ee /ˌdiːpɔːˈtiː; *NAmE* -pɔːr-/ *noun* a person who has been DEPORTED or is going to be deported 被驅逐出境者；被判處驅逐出境者

de·port·ment /dɪˈpɔːtmənt; *NAmE* -ˈpɔːrt-/ *noun* [U] (*formal*) **1** (*BrE*) the way in which a person stands and moves 風度；儀態：*lessons for young ladies in deportment and etiquette* 年輕女士的禮儀課 **2** (*old-fashioned, especially NAmE*) the way in which a person behaves 行為；舉止

de·pose /dɪˈpəʊz; *NAmE* dɪˈpoʊz/ *verb* **~ sb** to remove sb, especially a ruler, from power 罷免；廢黜：*The president was deposed in a military coup.* 總統在軍事政變中被廢黜。

de·posit 🔑 /dɪˈpɒzɪt; *NAmE* -ˈpɑːz-/ *noun, verb*

■ ***noun***

▸ MONEY 錢 **1** 🔑 [usually sing.] **a ~ (on sth)** a sum of money that is given as the first part of a larger payment 訂金；訂錢 SYN **down payment**：*They normally ask you to pay $100 (as a) deposit.* 他們通常要求付 100 元（作為）訂金。◇ (*BrE*) *We've put down a 5% deposit on the house.* 我們已支付了房款的 5% 作為訂金。 ➲ SYNONYMS at PAYMENT ➲ COLLOCATIONS at HOUSE **2** 🔑 [usually sing.] a sum of money that is paid by sb when they rent sth and that is returned to them if they do not lose or damage the thing they are renting 押金：*to pay a deposit* 付押金 **3** a sum of money that is paid into a bank account 存款：*Deposits can be made at any branch.* 在任何一家分行都可以存錢。OPP **withdrawal** ➲ COLLOCATIONS at FINANCE **4** (in the British political system) the amount of money that a candidate in an election to Parliament has to pay, and that is returned if he/she gets enough votes 競選保證金（英國議員候選人預付，獲得足夠的票數則退還）：*All the other candidates **lost their deposits**.* 所有其餘候選人都失掉了競選保證金。

▸ SUBSTANCE 物質 **5** a layer of a substance that has formed naturally underground（地下自然形成的）沉積物，沉積層：***mineral/gold/coal deposits*** 礦牀；金礦；煤藏 **6** a layer of a substance that has been left somewhere, especially by a river, flood, etc., or is found at the bottom of a liquid（尤指河流、洪水、液體等的）沉積物，淤積物：*The rain left a deposit of mud on the windows.* 雨水在窗上留下一層泥。◇ *fatty deposits in the arteries of the heart* 心動脈中的脂肪沉積

■ ***verb***

▸ PUT DOWN 放下 **1 ~ sb/sth + adv./prep.** to put or lay sb/sth down in a particular place 放下；放置：*She deposited a pile of books on my desk.* 她把一摞書放在我的書桌上。◇ (*informal*) *I was whisked off in a taxi and deposited outside the hotel.* 一輛出租車匆匆把我送到旅館外面，讓我下了車。

▸ LEAVE SUBSTANCE 留存物質 **2 ~ sth** (especially of a river or a liquid 尤指河流或液體) to leave a layer of sth on the surface of sth, especially gradually and over a period of time 使沉積；使沉澱；使淤積：*Sand was deposited which hardened into sandstone.* 沙經沉積固結形成沙岩。

▸ MONEY 錢 **3** 🔑 **~ sth** to put money into a bank account（錢）存入銀行；存儲：*Millions were deposited in Swiss bank accounts.* 巨額款項存入了瑞士的銀行賬戶。**4** 🔑 **~ sth** to pay a sum of money as the first part of a larger payment; to pay a sum of money that you will get back if you return in good condition sth that you have rented 付訂金；付保證金；付押金

▸ PUT IN SAFE PLACE 存放 **5 ~ sth (in sth)** | **~ sth (with sb/sth)** to put sth valuable or important in a place where it will be safe 寄放，寄存（貴重物品）：*Guests may deposit their valuables in the hotel safe.* 旅客可將貴重物品寄存在旅館的保險櫃裏。

deˈposit account *noun* (*BrE*) a type of account at a bank or BUILDING SOCIETY that pays interest on money that is left in it 定期存款賬戶 ➲ compare CURRENT ACCOUNT

de·pos·ition /ˌdepəˈzɪʃn/ *noun* **1** [U, C] (*technical* 術語) the natural process of leaving a layer of a substance on rocks or soil; a substance left in this way 沉積（物）；沉澱（物）；淤積（物）：***marine/river deposition*** 海洋 / 河流沉積物 **2** [U, C] the act of removing sb, especially a ruler, from power 罷免；廢黜：*the deposition of the King* 廢黜國王 **3** [C] (*law* 律) a formal statement, taken from sb and used in court 證詞；口供書

de·pos·it·or /dɪˈpɒzɪtə(r); *NAmE* -ˈpɑːz-/ *noun* a person who puts money in a bank account 儲戶；存戶

de·posi·tory /dɪˈpɒzɪtri; *NAmE* dɪˈpɑːzətɔːri/ *noun* (*pl.* **-ies**) a place where things can be stored 貯藏室；存放處；倉庫

depot /ˈdepəʊ; *NAmE* ˈdiːpoʊ/ *noun* **1** a place where large amounts of food, goods or equipment are stored（大量物品的）貯藏處，倉庫：*an arms depot* 軍械庫 **2** (*BrE*) a place where buses or other vehicles are kept and repaired 車庫；修車廠 **3** (*NAmE*) a small station where trains or buses stop 火車小站；公共汽車小站

de·prave /dɪˈpreɪv/ *verb* **~ sb** (*formal*) to make sb morally bad 使墮落；使腐化；敗壞 SYN **corrupt**：*In my view this book would deprave young children.* 我認為這本書會腐蝕兒童。

de·praved /dɪˈpreɪvd/ *adj.* (*formal*) morally bad 道德敗壞的；墮落的；腐化的 SYN **wicked, evil**：*This is the work of a depraved mind.* 這是思想墮落者所為。

de·prav·ity /dɪˈprævəti/ *noun* [U] (*formal*) the state of being morally bad 墮落；腐化 SYN **wickedness**：*a life of depravity* 腐化的生活

dep·re·cate /ˈdeprəkeɪt/ *verb* **~ sth** (*formal*) to feel and express strong disapproval of sth 對…表示極不贊成；強烈反對 ▸ **dep·re·cat·ing** (also *less frequent* **dep·re·ca·tory** /ˌdeprəˈkeɪtəri; *NAmE* ˈdeprɪkətɔːri/) *adj.*：*a deprecating comment* 表示反對的評論 **dep·re·cat·ing·ly** *adv.*

de·pre·ci·ate /dɪˈpriːʃieɪt/ *verb* **1** [I] to become less valuable over a period of time 貶值；跌價：*New cars start to depreciate as soon as they are on the road.* 新車一上路就開始貶值。◇ *Shares continued to depreciate on the stock markets today.* 今日股市股價繼續下跌。OPP **appreciate 2** [T] **~ sth** (*business* 商) to reduce the value, as stated in the company's accounts, of a particular ASSET over a particular period of time 折舊：*The bank depreciates PCs over a period of five years.* 這家銀行把個人計算機分五年折舊。 **3** [T] **~ sth** (*formal*) to make sth seem unimportant or of no value 貶低；輕視：*I had no intention of depreciating your contribution.* 我並不想貶低你的貢獻。▸ **de·pre·ci·ation** /dɪˌpriːʃiˈeɪʃn/ *noun* [U]：*currency depreciation* 通貨貶值 ◇ *the depreciation of fixed assets* 固定資產折舊

dep·re·da·tion /ˌdeprəˈdeɪʃn/ *noun* [usually pl.] (*formal*) acts that cause damage to people's property, lives, etc. 掠奪；劫掠

de·press 🔑 AW /dɪˈpres/ *verb*

1 🔑 to make sb sad and without enthusiasm or hope 使抑鬱；使沮喪；使消沉；使失去信心：**~ sb** *Wet weather always depresses me.* 陰雨天總使我心情抑鬱。◇ **it depresses sb to do sth** *It depresses me to see so many young girls smoking.* 看到這麼多女孩抽煙令我感到很沮喪。 **2 ~ sth** to make trade, business, etc. less active 使蕭條；使不景氣：*The recession has depressed the housing market.* 經濟衰退導致住房市場不景氣。 **3 ~ sth** to make the value of prices or wages lower 降低（價格）；減少（工資）：*to **depress wages/prices*** 減少工資；降低價格 **4 ~ sth** (*formal*) to press or push sth down, especially part of a machine 按，壓，推下（尤指機器部件）：*to depress the clutch pedal* (= when driving)（開車時）踩離合器踏板

de·pres·sant /dɪˈpresnt/ *noun* (*medical* 醫) a drug which slows the rate of the body's functions 抑制藥

de·pressed 🔑 AW /dɪˈprest/ *adj.*

1 🔑 very sad and without hope 抑鬱的；沮喪的；意志消沉的：*She felt very depressed about the future.* 她感到前途無望。 **2** 🔑 suffering from the medical condition of DEPRESSION 患抑鬱症的 **3** (of a place or an industry

地方或行業) without enough economic activity or jobs for people 不景氣的；蕭條的；經濟困難的： *an attempt to bring jobs to depressed areas* 給經濟蕭條地區創造就業機會的努力 **4** having a lower amount or level than usual 低於一般水準的；降低了的；削弱了的： *depressed prices* 降低了的價格

de·press·ing AW /dɪˈpresɪŋ/ *adj.* making you feel very sad and without enthusiasm 令人抑鬱的；令人沮喪的；令人消沉的： *a **depressing sight/thought/experience*** 令人沮喪的景象／想法／經歷 ◇ *Looking for a job these days can be very depressing.* 如今求職有時會令人非常沮喪。 ▸ **de·press·ing·ly** *adv.*： *a depressingly familiar experience* 令人感到膩煩的經歷

de·pres·sion AW /dɪˈpreʃn/ *noun* **1** [U] a medical condition in which a person feels very sad and anxious and often has physical SYMPTOMS such as being unable to sleep, etc. 抑鬱症；精神憂鬱： *clinical depression* 臨牀抑鬱症 ◇ *She suffered from severe depression after losing her job.* 她失業後患了嚴重的抑鬱症。 ➲ see also POST-NATAL DEPRESSION, POST-PARTUM DEPRESSION **2** [U, C] the state of feeling very sad and without hope 抑鬱；沮喪；消沉： *There was a feeling of gloom and depression in the office when the news of the job cuts was announced.* 裁員消息宣佈時辦公室裏一片憂鬱和沮喪的氣氛。 **3** [C, U] a period when there is little economic activity and many people are poor or without jobs 蕭條期；經濟衰退；不景氣： *The country was in the grip of (an) economic depression.* 當時國家處於經濟蕭條期。◇ *the great Depression of the 1930s* * 20 世紀 30 年代的經濟大蕭條 **4** [C] (*formal*) a part of a surface that is lower than the parts around it 窪地；凹地；坑 SYN **hollow**： *Rainwater collects in shallow depressions on the ground.* 雨水積在地上的淺坑裏。 **5** [C] (*technical* 術語) a weather condition in which the pressure of the air becomes lower, often causing rain 低氣壓；氣壓降低 ➲ compare ANTICYCLONE

de·pres·sive /dɪˈpresɪv/ *adj., noun*
■ ***adj.*** connected with the medical condition of depression 患抑鬱症的；抑鬱的： *depressive illness* 抑鬱症
■ ***noun*** a person who is suffering from the medical condition of depression 抑鬱症患者 ➲ see also MANIC-DEPRESSIVE

de·pres·sor /dɪˈpresə(r)/ *noun* = TONGUE DEPRESSOR

de·priv·ation /ˌdeprɪˈveɪʃn/ *noun* [U] the fact of not having sth that you need, like enough food, money or a home; the process that causes this 貧困；喪失；剝奪： *neglected children suffering from social deprivation* 遭社會遺棄無人照管的孩子 ◇ *sleep deprivation* 睡眠剝奪 ◇ *the deprivation of war* (= the suffering caused by not having enough of some things) 戰時的物品匱乏

de·prive /dɪˈpraɪv/ *verb*
PHR V **deˈprive sb/sth of sth** to prevent sb from having or doing sth, especially sth important 剝奪；使喪失；使不能享有： *They were imprisoned and deprived of their basic rights.* 他們遭到監禁並被剝奪了基本權利。◇ *Why should you **deprive yourself** of such simple pleasures?* 你為什麼連這種簡單的娛樂也不讓自己享受一下呢？

de·prived /dɪˈpraɪvd/ *adj.* without enough food, education, and all the things that are necessary for people to live a happy and comfortable life 貧窮的；貧困的；窮苦的： *a **deprived childhood/background/area*** 貧窮的童年／出身／地區 ◇ ***economically/emotionally/socially deprived*** 經濟困難的；感情失落的；社會遺棄的 ➲ SYNONYMS at POOR

Dept (also **Dept.** especially in *NAmE*) *abbr.* (in writing) department（書寫形式）部，部門，系

depth /depθ/ *noun*
▸ MEASUREMENT 量度 **1** [C, U] the distance from the top or surface to the bottom of sth 向下的距離；深（度）；縱深： *What's the depth of the water here?* 這兒的水有多深？◇ *Water was found **at a depth of** 30 metres.* 在 30 米深處找到了水。◇ *They dug down **to a depth of** two metres.* 他們挖到兩米深。◇ *Many dolphins can dive to depths of 200 metres.* 許多海豚可潛到 200 米深。◇ *The oil well extended several hundreds of feet **in depth**.* 油井向下延伸了數百英尺。◇ *the depth of a cut/wound/crack* 劃口／傷口／裂口深度 **2** [C, U] the distance from the front to the back of sth 向裏的距離；深（度）；寬（度）： *The depth of the shelves is 30 centimetres.* 書架的深度為 30 厘米。
▸ OF FEELINGS 感覺 **3** [U] the strength and power of feelings 深厚；誠摯；強烈： *the depth of her love* 她那愛情之深
▸ OF KNOWLEDGE 知識 **4** [U] (*approving*) the quality of knowing or understanding a lot of details about sth; the ability to provide and explain these details 淵博；深刻；洞察力： *a writer of great wisdom and depth* 有卓越智慧和洞察力的作家 ◇ *a job that doesn't require any great **depth of knowledge*** 不需要多麼高深知識的工作 ◇ *His ideas lack depth.* 他的想法缺乏深度。
▸ DEEPEST PART 最深處 **5** [C, usually pl.] the deepest, most extreme or serious part of sth 最深處；深淵；極限： *the **depths of the ocean*** 海洋深處 ◇ *to live **in the depths of the country*** (= a long way from a town) 住在偏遠地區 ◇ *in the **depths of winter*** (= when it is coldest) 在隆冬季節 ◇ *She was **in the depths of despair**.* 她處於絕望的深淵。◇ *He gazed into the depths of her eyes.* 他深深凝視着她的眼睛。◇ *Her paintings reveal **hidden depths*** (= unknown and interesting things about her character). 她的畫揭示出她隱藏的性格特徵。
▸ OF COLOUR 顏色 **6** [U] the strength of a colour 濃度；強度： *Strong light will affect the depth of colour of your carpets and curtains.* 強烈的陽光會使你的地毯和窗簾褪色。
▸ PICTURE/PHOTOGRAPH 畫；照片 **7** [U] (*technical* 術語) the quality in a work of art or a photograph which makes it appear not to be flat 立體感 ➲ see also DEEP
IDM **ˌin ˈdepth** in a detailed and thorough way 全面；深入；詳細： *I haven't looked at the report in depth yet.* 我還沒有細看這份報告。◇ *an in-depth study* 深入研究 **be out of your ˈdepth** **1** (*BrE*) to be in water that is too deep to stand in with your head above water 在水深沒頂（或夠不着底）的地方 **2** to be unable to understand sth because it is too difficult; to be in a situation that you cannot control 非某人所能理解；為某人力所不及： *He felt totally out of his depth in his new job.* 他感到自己根本不能勝任這新工作。 ➲ more at PLUMB *v.*

ˈdepth charge *noun* a bomb that is set to explode underwater, used to destroy SUBMARINES（用以摧毀潛艇的）深水炸彈

ˌdepth of ˈfield (also **ˌdepth of ˈfocus**) *noun* (*technical* 術語) the distance between the nearest and the furthest objects that a camera can produce a clear image of at the same time 景深（照相機能同時清晰拍攝的最近和最遠物體之間的距離）

depu·ta·tion /ˌdepjuˈteɪʃn/ *noun* [C+sing./pl. v.] a small group of people who are asked or allowed to act or speak for others 代表團

de·pute /dɪˈpjuːt/ *verb* **~ sb to do sth** [often passive] (*formal*) to give sb else the authority to represent you or do sth for you 授（權）；把（權）委託給 SYN **delegate**： *He was deputed to put our views to the committee.* 他獲授權向委員會表達我們的觀點。

depu·tize (*BrE* also **-ise**) /ˈdepjutaɪz/ *verb* [I] **~ (for sb)** to do sth that sb in a higher position than you would usually do 擔任代表；充當代理人： *Ms Green has asked me to deputize for her at the meeting.* 格林女士請我代表她出席會議。

dep·uty /ˈdepjuti/ *noun* (*pl.* **-ies**) **1** a person who is the next most important person below a business manager, a head of a school, a political leader, etc. and who does the person's job when he or she is away 副手；副職；代理： *I'm acting as deputy till the manager returns.* 我在經理回來之前代行他的職務。◇ *the deputy head of a school* 副校長 **2** the name for a member of parliament in some countries（某些國家的）議員 **3** (in the US) a police officer who helps the SHERIFF of an area（美國協助地方治安官辦案的）警官

de·racin·ate /ˌdiːˈræsmeɪt/ *verb* **~ sb** (*formal*) to force sb to leave the place or situation in which they feel comfortable 迫使（某人）離開熟悉的環境；使離開根據地 ▸ **de·racin·ated** /ˌdiːˈræsmeɪtɪd/ *adj.*

de·rail /dɪˈreɪl/ *verb* [I, T] (of a train 火車) to leave the track; to make a train do this（使）脫軌，出軌：*The train derailed and plunged into the river.* 火車脫軌栽進了河裏。◇ **~ sth** (*figurative*) *This latest incident could derail the peace process.* 最近這個事件可能會攪亂和平進程。▸ **de·rail·ment** *noun* [C, U]

D

de·rail·leur /dɪˈreɪljə(r)/ *noun* (*technical* 術語) a type of gear on a bicycle that works by lifting the chain from one gear wheel to another larger or smaller one 撥鏈器，變速器（自行車換擋裝置）

de·ranged /dɪˈreɪndʒd/ *adj.* unable to behave and think normally, especially because of mental illness 精神錯亂的；精神失常的；瘋狂的：*mentally deranged* 精神錯亂◇ *a deranged attacker* 瘋狂的攻擊者 ▸ **de·range·ment** *noun* [U]：*He seemed to be on the verge of total derangement.* 他似乎已瀕臨精神崩潰的邊緣。

derby /ˈdɑːbi; *NAmE* ˈdɜːrbi/ *noun* (*pl.* **-ies**) **1** (*NAmE*) = BOWLER (2) **2** (*BrE*) a sports competition between teams from the same area or town 德比，同城大戰（同地區兩隊間的比賽）：*a **local derby** between the two North London sides* 兩支北倫敦隊之間的一場本地德比 ◇ *a derby match* 地區體育比賽 **3** a race or sports competition 速度比賽；體育競賽：*a motorcycle derby* 摩托車大賽 ➲ see also DEMOLITION DERBY **4 Derby** used in the name of several horse races which happen every year 德比馬賽（特指幾個一年一度的馬賽）：*the Epsom Derby* 埃普瑟姆馬賽◇ *the Kentucky Derby* 肯塔基馬賽

de·regu·late AW /ˌdiːˈregjuleɪt/ *verb* [often passive] **~ sth** to free a trade, a business activity, etc. from rules and controls 撤銷對（貿易、商業活動等）的管制；解除控制 SYN **decontrol**：*deregulated financial markets* 放寬了管制的金融市場 ▸ **de·regu·la·tion** AW /ˌdiːˌreguˈleɪʃn/ *noun* [U] **de·regu·la·tory** /ˌdiːˈregjələtəri; *NAmE* -tɔːri/ *adj.* [only before noun]：*deregulatory reforms* 撤銷管制的改革

dere·lict /ˈderəlɪkt/ *adj.*, *noun*
■ ***adj.*** (especially of land or buildings 尤指土地或建築物) not used or cared for and in bad condition 荒廢的；被棄置的；破舊的：***derelict land/buildings/sites*** 荒廢的土地；被廢棄的建築物；破舊的遺址
■ ***noun*** (*formal*) a person without a home, a job or property 無家可歸者；乞丐；社會棄兒 SYN **vagrant**：*derelicts living on the streets* 流落街頭的乞丐

dere·lic·tion /ˌderəˈlɪkʃn/ *noun* (*formal*) **1** [U] the state of being derelict 荒廢；棄置；破舊不堪：***industrial/urban dereliction*** 工業／城市廢墟◇ *a house in a state of dereliction* 破舊不堪的房屋 **2** [U, sing.] **~ of duty** (*formal* or *law* 律) the fact of deliberately not doing what you ought to do, especially when it is part of your job 玩忽職守；瀆職：*The police officers were found guilty of serious **dereliction of duty**.* 這些警察被判犯有嚴重瀆職罪。

de·ride /dɪˈraɪd/ *verb* [often passive] **~ sb/sth (as sth)** | **+ speech** (*formal*) to treat sb/sth as ridiculous and not worth considering seriously 嘲笑；愚弄；揶揄 SYN **mock**：*His views were derided as old-fashioned.* 他的觀點被當作舊思想受到嘲弄。

de ri·gueur /ˌdə rɪˈgɜː(r)/ *adj.* [not before noun] (from *French*) considered necessary if you wish to be accepted socially 合乎禮節；按照習俗；按照時尚：*Evening dress is de rigueur at the casino.* 按照習俗在賭場要穿晚禮服。

de·ri·sion /dɪˈrɪʒn/ *noun* [U] a strong feeling that sb/sth is ridiculous and not worth considering seriously, shown by laughing in an unkind way or by making unkind remarks 嘲笑；取笑；奚落 SYN **scorn**：*Her speech was greeted with howls of derision.* 她的演講受到陣陣嘲笑。◇ *He became an object of universal derision.* 他成了眾人嘲弄的對象。

de·ri·sive /dɪˈraɪsɪv/ (also *less frequent* **de·ri·sory**) *adj.* unkind and showing that you think sb/sth is ridiculous 嘲笑的；嘲弄的；取笑的：*She gave a short, derisive laugh.* 她譏諷地笑了笑。▸ **de·ri·sive·ly** *adv.*

de·ri·sory /dɪˈraɪsəri/ *adj.* (*formal*) **1** too small or of too little value to be considered seriously 少得可笑的；少得可憐的；不屑一顧的 SYN **laughable**：*They offered us a derisory £10 a week.* 他們每週給我們 10 英鎊，少得可憐。**2** = DERISIVE

der·iv·ation AW /ˌderɪˈveɪʃn/ *noun* [U, C] the origin or development of sth, especially a word（尤指詞語的）起源，由來，派生：*a word of Greek derivation* 由希臘語派生的詞

de·riva·tive AW /dɪˈrɪvətɪv/ *noun*, *adj.*
■ ***noun*** a word or thing that has been developed or produced from another word or thing 派生詞；衍生字；派生物；衍生物：*'Happiness' is a derivative of 'happy'.* * happiness 是 happy 的派生詞。◇ *Crack is a highly potent and addictive derivative of cocaine.* 強效純可卡因是一種藥效極強、容易使人上癮的可卡因製劑。
■ ***adj.*** (usually *disapproving*) copied from sth else; not having new or original ideas 模仿他人的；缺乏獨創性的：*a **derivative design/style*** 沿襲前人的設計／樣式

de·rive 0-w AW /dɪˈraɪv/ *verb*
PHR V **de'rive from sth** | **be de'rived from sth** 0-w to come or develop from sth 從…衍生出；起源於；來自：*The word 'politics' is derived from a Greek word meaning 'city'.* * politics 一詞源自希臘語，意思是 city。**de'rive sth from sth 1** (*formal*) to get sth from sth（從…中）得到，獲得：*He derived great pleasure from painting.* 他從繪畫中得到極大的樂趣。**2** (*technical* 術語) to obtain a substance from sth（從…中）提取：*The new drug is derived from fish oil.* 這種新藥是從魚油中提煉出來的。

derma·titis /ˌdɜːməˈtaɪtɪs; *NAmE* ˌdɜːrm-/ *noun* [U] (*medical* 醫) a skin condition in which the skin becomes red, swollen and sore 皮炎

derma·tolo·gist /ˌdɜːməˈtɒlədʒɪst; *NAmE* ˌdɜːrməˈtɑːl-/ *noun* a doctor who studies and treats skin diseases 皮膚病醫生；皮膚病專家

derma·tol·ogy /ˌdɜːməˈtɒlədʒi; *NAmE* ˌdɜːrməˈtɑːl-/ *noun* [U] the scientific study of skin diseases 皮膚病學 ▸ **derma·to·logi·cal** /ˌdɜːmətəˈlɒdʒɪkl; *NAmE* ˌdɜːrmətəˈlɑːdʒ-/ *adj.*

der·mis /ˈdɜːmɪs; *NAmE* ˈdɜːr-/ *noun* [U] (*biology* 生) the skin 真皮

dero·gate /ˈderəgeɪt/ *verb* **~ sth** (*formal*) to state that sth or sb is without worth 貶低；貶損
PHR V **'derogate from sth** to ignore a responsibility or duty 迴避責任

dero·ga·tion /ˌderəˈgeɪʃn/ *noun* [U, C] (*formal*) **1** an occasion when a rule or law is allowed to be ignored（對法規等的）背離 **2** words or actions which show that sb or sth is considered to have no worth 含有貶義的言辭（或行為）

de·roga·tory /dɪˈrɒgətri; *NAmE* dɪˈrɑːgətɔːri/ *adj.* (*formal*) showing a critical attitude towards sb 貶低的；貶義的 SYN **insulting**：***derogatory remarks/comments*** 貶斥的言辭／評論

der·rick /ˈderɪk/ *noun* **1** a tall machine used for moving or lifting heavy weights, especially on a ship; a type of CRANE 轉臂起重機；（尤指船上的）吊杆式起重機 **2** a tall structure over an OIL WELL for holding the DRILL (= the machine that makes the hole in the ground for getting the oil out)（油井的）井架，鑽塔

derring-do /ˌderɪŋ ˈduː/ *noun* [U] (*old-fashioned, humorous*) brave actions, like those in adventure stories 大膽冒險行為；英勇行為

der·vish /ˈdɜːvɪʃ; *NAmE* ˈdɜːrvɪʃ/ *noun* a member of a Muslim religious group whose members make a promise to stay poor and live without comforts or pleasures. They perform a fast lively dance as part of their worship. 托鉢僧，苦行僧（屬伊斯蘭教，狂舞為其禮拜儀式的一部份）：*He threw himself around the stage like a whirling dervish.* 他在台上轉圈，如同跳旋轉舞蹈的托鉢僧一樣。

de·sal·in·ation /ˌdiːˌsælɪˈneɪʃn/ *noun* [U] the process of removing salt from sea water（海水的）脫鹽：*a desalination plant* 脫鹽工廠

de·scale /ˌdiːˈskeɪl/ *verb* **~ sth** (*BrE*) to remove the SCALE (= the hard white material left on pipes, etc. by water when it is heated) from sth 除去（熱水管道等的）水垢

des·cant /ˈdeskænt/ *noun* (*music* 音) a tune that is sung or played at the same time as, and usually higher than, the main tune 高於主音的旋律

ˌdescant reˈcorder (*BrE*) (*NAmE* **soˌprano reˈcorder**) *noun* (*music* 音) the most common size of RECORDER (= a musical instrument in the shape of a pipe that you blow into), with a high range of notes 高音豎笛

des·cend /dɪˈsend/ *verb* **1** [I, T] (*formal*) to come or go down from a higher to a lower level 下來；下去；下降：*The plane began to descend.* 飛機開始降落。◇ *The results, ranked* ***in descending order*** (= from the highest to the lowest) *are as follows …* 結果按遞減順序排列如下… ◇ **~ sth** *She descended the stairs slowly.* 她緩慢地走下樓梯。**OPP** **ascend** **2** [I] (*formal*) (of a hill, etc. 山等) to slope downwards 下斜；下傾：*At this point the path descends steeply.* 小路從這裏陡然而下。**OPP** **ascend** **3** [I] (*literary*) (of night, DARKNESS, a mood, etc. 夜晚、黑暗、情緒等) to arrive and begin to affect sb/sth 降臨；來臨 **SYN** **fall**：*Night descends quickly in the tropics.* 熱帶地區黑夜來得快。◇ **~ on/upon sb/sth** *Calm descended on the crowd.* 人群平靜下來。

PHR V **be desˈcended from sb** to be related to sb who lived a long time ago 是某人的後裔：*He claims to be descended from a Spanish prince.* 他聲稱是一位西班牙王子的後裔。 **desˈcend into sth** [no passive] (*formal*) to gradually get into a bad state 逐漸陷入：*The country was descending into chaos.* 這個國家陷入一片混亂。 **desˈcend on/upon sb/sth** to visit sb/sth in large numbers, sometimes unexpectedly 突然大批來訪：*Hundreds of football fans descended on the city.* 數百名足球迷蜂擁入城。 **desˈcend to sth** [no passive] to do sth that makes people stop respecting you 降低身分去做；竟做出；墮落到…地步：*They descended to the level of personal insults.* 他們竟卑鄙到進行人身侮辱的地步。

des·cend·ant /dɪˈsendənt/ *noun* **1** a person's **descendants** are their children, their children's children, and all the people who live after them who are related to them 後裔；後代；子孫：*He was an O'Conor and a* ***direct descendant*** *of the last High King of Ireland.* 他屬於奧康納家族，是愛爾蘭最後一位君王的嫡系後裔。◇ *Many of them are descendants of the original settlers.* 他們中許多人都是早期移民的後裔。**2** something that has developed from sth similar in the past（由過去類似物發展來的）派生物

des·cent /dɪˈsent/ *noun* (*formal*) **1** [C, usually sing.] an action of coming or going down 下降；下傾：*The plane began its descent to Heathrow.* 飛機開始向希思羅機場降落。◇ (*figurative*) *the country's swift descent into anarchy* 國家迅速陷入無政府狀態 **OPP** **ascent** **2** [C] a slope going downwards 斜坡；坡道：*There is a gradual descent to the sea.* 有一片斜坡緩緩伸延到海邊。**OPP** **ascent** **3** [U] a person's family origins 血統；祖籍；祖先；出身 **SYN** **ancestry**：*to be of Scottish descent* 祖籍是蘇格蘭 ◇ **~ from sb** *He traces his line of descent from the Stuart kings.* 他的家族可追溯到斯圖亞特王朝。

de·scribe 0-π /dɪˈskraɪb/ *verb*
1 0-π to say what sb/sth is like 描述；形容；把…稱為：**~ sb/sth (to/for sb)** *Can you describe him to me?* 你能向我描述一下他的樣子嗎？◇ **~ sb/sth as sth** *The man was described as tall and dark, and aged about 20.* 據描述這男人高個子，深色皮膚，年齡在 20 歲左右。◇ *Jim was described by his colleagues as 'unusual'.* 吉姆被同事們稱為"不尋常"的人。◇ **~ how, what, etc. …** *Describe how you did it.* 談談你是怎樣做這事的。◇ **~ (sb/sth) doing sth** *Several people described seeing strange lights in the sky.* 好幾個人都說看到天上出現了奇異光芒。 **2 ~ sth** (*formal or technical* 術語) to make a movement which has a particular shape; to form a particular shape 沿…形狀移動；畫出…圖形；形成…形狀：*The shark described a circle around the shoal of fish.* 這條鯊魚圍繞着魚群游動。▶ **de·scrib·able** *adj.*

de·scrip·tion 0-π /dɪˈskrɪpʃn/ *noun*
1 0-π [C, U] **~ (of sb/sth)** a piece of writing or speech that says what sb/sth is like; the act of writing or saying in words what sb/sth is like 描寫（文字）；形容；說明：*to give a* ***detailed/full description*** *of the procedure* 對程序作詳細的／詳盡的說明 ◇ *a* ***brief/general description*** *of the software* 軟件的簡要／概括性說明 ◇ *Police have issued a description of the gunman.* 警方發佈通告，描述了持槍歹徒的特徵。◇ *'Scared stiff' is an apt description of how I felt at that moment.* "嚇得呆若木雞"是我當時感受的貼切描述。◇ *a personal pain that goes* ***beyond description*** (= is too great to express in words) 難以言表的個人痛苦 ◇ *the novelist's powers of description* 小說家的敘述才能 **2** [C] **of some, all, every, etc. ~** of some, etc. type 類型：*boats of every description / all descriptions* 各種類型的船 ◇ *Their money came from trade of some description.* 他們的錢是做某種生意賺來的。◇ *medals, coins and things of that description* 紀念章、硬幣以及諸如此類的東西

IDM **answer/fit a description (of sb/sth)** to be like a particular person or thing 與描述的…相像：*A child answering the description of the missing boy was found safe and well in London yesterday.* 昨天在倫敦發現了一個與失蹤男孩情況相符的孩子，安然無恙。➲ more at BEGGAR *v.*

de·scrip·tive /dɪˈskrɪptɪv/ *adj.* **1** saying what sb/sth is like; describing sth 描寫的；敘述的；說明的：*the descriptive passages in the novel* 小說中的描寫性段落 ◇ *The term I used was meant to be purely descriptive* (= not judging). 我所用的措辭是純敘述性的（並非作出判斷）。 **2** (*linguistics* 語言) saying how language is actually used, without giving rules for how it should be used 描寫性的（描述語言的實際應用而非使用規則）**OPP** **prescriptive**

de·scrip·tor /dɪˈskrɪptə(r)/ *noun* (*linguistics* 語言) a word or expression used to describe or identify sth 敘詞

des·cry /dɪˈskraɪ/ *verb* (**des·cries**, **des·cry·ing**, **des·cried**, **des·cried**) **~ sb/sth** (*literary*) to suddenly see sb/sth 突然看到；突然發現

dese·crate /ˈdesɪkreɪt/ *verb* **~ sth** to damage a holy thing or place or treat it without respect 褻瀆（聖物或聖地）：*desecrated graves* 被褻瀆的墳墓 ▶ **dese·cra·tion** /ˌdesɪˈkreɪʃn/ *noun* [U]：*the desecration of a cemetery* 褻瀆墓地 ◇ (*figurative*) *the desecration of the countryside by new roads* 新公路糟蹋了鄉村

de·seg·re·gate /ˌdiːˈsegrɪgeɪt/ *verb* **~ sth** to end the policy of SEGREGATION in a place in which people of different races are kept separate in public places, etc. 廢除…的種族隔離 ▶ **de·seg·re·ga·tion** /ˌdiːˌsegrɪˈgeɪʃn/ *noun* [U]

de·select /ˌdiːsɪˈlekt/ *verb* **1 ~ sb** if the local branch of a political party in Britain **deselects** the existing Member of Parliament, it does not choose him or her as a candidate at the next election（英國）取消（某人）的候選人資格，否決（某人）為下屆候選人 **2 ~ sth** (*computing* 計) to remove sth from the list of possible choices on a computer menu（從計算機選單上）撤銷選定 ▶ **de·selec·tion** *noun* [U]

de·sen·si·tize (*BrE* also **-ise**) /ˌdiːˈsensətaɪz/ *verb* [usually passive] **1 ~ sb/sth (to sth)** to make sb/sth less aware of sth, especially a problem or sth bad, by making them become used to it 使（對不好的事）不再敏感：*People are increasingly becoming desensitized to violence on television.* 大眾對電視上的暴力鏡頭越來越麻木了。 **2 ~ sb/sth** (*technical* 術語) to treat sb/sth so that they will stop being sensitive to physical or chemical changes, or to a particular substance 使脫敏；降低敏感作用 ▶ **de·sen·si·tiza·tion**, **-isa·tion** /ˌdiːˌsensətaɪˈzeɪʃn; *NAmE* -təˈz-/ *noun* [U]

des·ert 0-π *noun, verb*
■ ***noun*** 0-π /ˈdezət; *NAmE* ˈdezərt/ ➲ see also DESERTS [C, U] a large area of land that has very little water and very few plants growing on it. Many deserts are covered by sand. 沙漠；荒漠；荒原：*the Sahara Desert* 撒哈拉大沙漠 ◇ *Somalia is mostly desert.* 索馬里大部份地區都是荒漠。◇ *burning desert sands* 沙漠裏灼熱的沙 ◇ (*figurative*) *a cultural desert* (= a place without any culture) 文化沙漠

■ *verb* /dɪˈzɜːt; *NAmE* dɪˈzɜːrt/ **1** [T] **~ sb** to leave sb without help or support 拋棄，離棄，遺棄（某人） **SYN abandon**：*She was deserted by her husband.* 她被丈夫遺棄了。 **2** [T, often passive] **~ sth** to go away from a place and leave it empty 捨棄，離棄（某地方） **SYN abandon**：*The villages had been deserted.* 這些村莊已經荒無人煙了。◇ *The owl seems to have deserted its nest.* 這隻貓頭鷹似乎不要這個窩了。 **3** [I, T] **~ (sth)** to leave the armed forces without permission 擅離（部隊）；逃走；開小差：*Large numbers of soldiers deserted as defeat became inevitable.* 戰敗已成定局，許多士兵開小差跑了。 **4** [T] **~ sth (for sth)** to stop using, buying or supporting sth 廢棄；放棄；撇下不管：*Why did you desert teaching for politics?* 你為什麼棄教從政呢？ **5** [T] **~ sb** if a particular quality **deserts** you, it is not there when you need it 背離；使失望：*Her courage seemed to desert her for a moment.* 她一時間似乎失去了勇氣。 ▸ **de·ser·tion** /dɪˈzɜːʃn; *NAmE* -ˈzɜːr-/ *noun* [U, C]：*She felt betrayed by her husband's desertion.* 她感到丈夫遺棄她辜負了她的心。◇ *The army was badly affected by desertions.* 開小差使部隊大受影響。 **IDM** see SINK *v.*

ˈdesert boot *noun* a SUEDE boot that just covers the ankle 沙漠靴（齊踝深的幼山羊皮皮靴）

des·ert·ed /dɪˈzɜːtɪd; *NAmE* -ˈzɜːrt-/ *adj.* **1** (of a place 地方) with no people in it 無人居住的；空寂無人的：*deserted streets* 空無一人的街道 **2** left by a person or people who do not intend to return 被拋棄的；被遺棄的；被捨棄的 **SYN abandoned**：*a deserted village* 被捨棄的村莊◇ *deserted wives* 遭遺棄的妻子

de·sert·er /dɪˈzɜːtə(r); *NAmE* -ˈzɜːrt-/ *noun* a person who leaves the army, navy, etc. without permission (= DESERTS) 逃兵；開小差的人

desert·ifi·ca·tion /dɪˌzɜːtɪfɪˈkeɪʃn; *NAmE* -ˌzɜːrt-/ *noun* [U] (*technical* 術語) the process of becoming or making sth a desert 沙漠化

ˌdesert ˈisland *noun* a tropical island where no people live 荒無人煙的熱帶島

des·erts /dɪˈzɜːts; *NAmE* dɪˈzɜːrts/ *noun* [pl.]
IDM **sb's (just) deserts** what sb deserves, especially when it is sth bad 應得的懲罰；報應：*The family of the victim said that the killer had* ***got his just deserts*** *when he was jailed for life.* 受害者家屬說殺人犯被判終身監禁是得到了他應有的懲罰。

de·serve /dɪˈzɜːv; *NAmE* dɪˈzɜːrv/ *verb* (not used in the progressive tenses 不用於進行時) if sb/sth **deserves** sth, it is right that they should have it, because of the way they have behaved or because of what they are 值得；應得；應受：**~ sth** *You deserve a rest after all that hard work.* 辛苦勞累那麼久，你該休息一下了。◇ *The report deserves careful consideration.* 這報告應該給予認真考慮。◇ *One player in particular deserves a mention.* 有一名運動員特別值得表揚。◇ *What have I done to deserve this?* 我做了什麼事而要得到這樣待遇呢？◇ **~ to do sth** *They didn't deserve to win.* 他們不該贏。◇ *He deserves to be locked up for ever for what he did.* 他做了這樣的事，應該終身監禁。◇ **~ doing sth** *Several other points deserve mentioning.* 其他幾點值得一提。
IDM **sb deˌserves a ˈmedal** (*informal*) used to say that you admire sb because they have done sth difficult or unpleasant（用以誇獎某人完成了艱巨任務）應給某人授勳 **ˌget what you deˈserve | deˌserve all/everything you ˈget** (*informal*) used to say that you think sb has earned the bad things that happen to them 罪有應得 ➲ more at TURN *n.*

de·served·ly /dɪˈzɜːvɪdli; *NAmE* -ˈzɜːrv-/ *adv.* in the way that is deserved; correctly 應得地；恰如其分地；理所當然地：*The restaurant is deservedly popular.* 這餐館為大眾喜愛是理所當然的。◇ *He has just been chosen for the top job, and* ***deservedly so.*** 他剛被選中擔任這一要職，這是理所當然的。

de·serv·ing /dɪˈzɜːvɪŋ; *NAmE* -ˈzɜːrv-/ *adj.* **~ (of sth)** (*formal*) that deserves help, praise, a reward, etc. 值得的；應得的：*to give money to a deserving cause* 把錢捐給值得贊助的事業◇ *This family is one of the most deserving cases.* 這是最應當得到幫助的一戶人家。◇ *an issue deserving of attention* 值得注意的問題 **OPP undeserving**

dés·ha·billé /ˌdezæbiːˈjeɪ/ (also **dis·ha·bille** /ˌdɪsəˈbiːl; -ˈbiː/) *noun* [U] (*formal* or *humorous*) the state of wearing no clothes or very few clothes 赤身裸體；一絲不掛；衣不蔽體：*in a state of déshabillé* 一絲不掛

des·ic·cated /ˈdesɪkeɪtɪd/ *adj.* **1** (of food 食物) dried in order to preserve it 脫水的；乾燥法保存的：*desiccated coconut* 椰子乾 **2** (*technical* 術語) completely dry 乾涸的；枯竭的：*treeless and desiccated soil* 無樹的荒蕪乾旱土壤

des·ic·ca·tion /ˌdesɪˈkeɪʃn/ *noun* [U] (*technical* 術語) the process of becoming completely dry 乾涸；枯竭

de·sid·er·atum /dɪˌzɪdəˈrɑːtəm; -ˈreɪtəm/ *noun* (*pl.* **desid·erata** /-ɑːtə; -eɪtə/) (from *Latin, formal*) a thing that is wanted or needed 想望的東西；需要的東西

de·sign **AW** /dɪˈzaɪn/ *noun, verb*
■ *noun*
▸ **ARRANGEMENT** 佈置 **1** [U, C] the general arrangement of the different parts of sth that is made, such as a building, book, machine, etc. 設計；佈局；安排：*The basic design of the car is very similar to that of earlier models.* 這種汽車的基本設計與早期的型號非常相似。◇ *special new design features* 特別的新型設計風格◇ *The magazine will appear in a new design from next month.* 從下月起這本雜誌將以新的設計問世。
▸ **DRAWING/PLAN/MODEL** 圖樣；方案；模型 **2** [U] the art or process of deciding how sth will look, work, etc. by drawing plans, making models, etc. 設計藝術；構思：*a course in art and design* 美術及設計課程◇ *a design studio* 設計室◇ *computer-aided design* 計算機輔助設計◇ *the design and development of new products* 新產品的設計和開發 ➲ see also INTERIOR DESIGN **3** [C] **~ (for sth)** a drawing or plan from which sth may be made 設計圖樣；設計方案：*designs for aircraft* 飛機的設計圖樣◇ *new and original designs* 別具一格的新型設計方案
▸ **PATTERN** 圖案 **4** [C] an arrangement of lines and shapes as a decoration 裝飾圖案；花紋 **SYN pattern**：***floral/abstract/geometric designs*** 花卉／抽象／幾何圖案◇ *The tiles come in a huge range of colours and designs.* 瓷磚有各種各樣的顏色和圖案。
▸ **INTENTION** 意圖 **5** [U, C] a plan or an intention 打算；意圖；目的：*It happened—whether* ***by accident or design***—*that the two of them were left alone after all the others had gone.* 不知道是偶然還是有意安排，其他人走後，竟然只剩下他們兩個人。◇ *It is all part of his* ***grand design.*** 這都是他那宏圖大略的一部份。
IDM **have designs on sb** (*formal* or *humorous*) to want to start a sexual relationship with sb 企圖佔有某人；存心與某人發生性關係；對…存心不良 **have designs on sth** (*formal*) to be planning to get sth for yourself, often in a way that other people do not approve of 企圖將某物據為己有；圖謀得到某物；打…的鬼主意：*Rumours spread that the Duke had designs on the crown* (= wanted to make himself king). 謠傳公爵覬覦王位。
■ *verb*
▸ **DRAW PLANS** 設計 **1** to decide how sth will look, work, etc., especially by drawing plans or making models 設計；製圖；構思：**~ sth** *to design a car/a dress/an office* 設計汽車／連衣裙／辦公室◇ *a badly designed kitchen* 設計很糟糕的廚房◇ **~ sth for sb/sth** *They asked me to design a poster for the campaign.* 他們請我為這次運動設計一張海報。◇ **~ sb sth** *Could you design us a poster?* 你能為我們設計一張海報嗎？
▸ **PLAN STH** 計劃 **2** **~ sth** to think of and plan a system, a way of doing sth, etc. 計劃；籌劃；制訂：*We need to design a new syllabus for the third year.* 我們需要為三年級學生制訂一個新的課程大綱。
▸ **FOR SPECIAL PURPOSE** 特定目的 **3** [usually passive] to make, plan or intend sth for a particular purpose or use 製造；設計；意欲：**~ sth (for sth)** *The method is specifically designed for use in small groups.* 這方法是專為小組活動設計的。◇ **~ sth (as sth)** *This course is primarily designed as an introduction to the subject.* 這門課程開設的主要目的是教授這門學科的概論。◇ **~ sth to do sth** *The programme is designed to help people who have been out*

of work for a long time. 這項計劃的目的是為長期失業者提供幫助。

des·ig·nate *verb, adj.*

■ ***verb*** /ˈdezɪɡneɪt/ [often passive] (*formal*) **1** to say officially that sb/sth has a particular character or name; to describe sb/sth in a particular way 命名；指定；認定：**~ sb/sth (as) sth** *This area has been designated (as) a National Park.* 本區已定為國家公園。◇ **~ sb/sth (as being/having sth)** *Several pupils were designated as having moderate or severe learning difficulties.* 幾名學生被認定有中等或嚴重學習困難。◇ *a designated nature reserve* 指定的自然保護區 ◇ *designated seats for the elderly* 老人專座 **2** to choose or name sb for a particular job or position 選定，指派，委任（某人任某職）：**~ sb/sth** *The director is allowed to designate his/her successor.* 主任獲准選定自己的繼任人。◇ **~ sb (as) sth** *Who has she designated (as) her deputy?* 她委任了誰為她的副手？◇ **~ sb to do sth** *the man designated to succeed the president* 被指派接替主席職務的男人 **3 ~ sth (by sth)** to show sth using a particular mark or sign 標明；標示；指明：*The different types are designated by the letters A, B and C.* 不同的類型分別用字母 A、B 和 C 標明。

■ ***adj.*** /ˈdezɪɡneɪt; -nət/ [after noun] (*formal*) chosen to do a job but not yet having officially started it（已受委派）尚未上任；（已當選）尚未就職：*an interview with the director designate* 與未到任主任的面談

ˌdesignated ˈdriver *noun* (*informal*) the person who agrees to drive and not drink alcohol when people go to a party, a bar, etc. 指定駕車人（同意去聚會、酒吧等不飲酒而為他人開車）

ˌdesignated ˈhitter *noun* (in BASEBALL 棒球) a player who is named at the start of the game as the person who will hit the ball in place of the PITCHER 指定擊球員（比賽開始即指定為擊球手而非投球手）

des·ig·na·tion /ˌdezɪɡˈneɪʃn/ *noun* (*formal*) **1** [U] **~ (as sth)** the action of choosing a person or thing for a particular purpose, or of giving them or it a particular status 選定；指定；委任：*The district is under consideration for designation as a conservation area.* 正在考慮將這個地區指定為保護區。**2** [C] a name, title or description 名稱；稱號；稱呼：*Her official designation is Financial Controller.* 她的正式職銜是財務總監。

de·sign·er **AW** /dɪˈzaɪnə(r)/ *noun, adj.*

■ ***noun*** a person whose job is to decide how things such as clothes, furniture, tools, etc. will look or work by making drawings, plans or patterns 設計者；構思者：*a **fashion/jewellery, etc. designer*** 時裝、珠寶等設計師 ◇ *an industrial designer* 工業設計師

■ ***adj.*** [only before noun] made by a famous designer; expensive and having a famous brand name 由著名設計師設計的；標有設計師姓名的；名牌的：*designer jeans* 名牌牛仔褲 ◇ *designer labels* 設計師品牌 ◇ *designer water* 名牌飲用水 ◇ *He had a trendy haircut, an earring and **designer stubble*** (= a short beard, grown for two or three days and thought to look fashionable). 他理了個時髦的髮型，戴着一隻耳環，還留着形似設計師的鬍子茬。➲ COLLOCATIONS at FASHION

deˌsigner ˈbaby *noun* (used especially in newspapers 尤用於報紙) a baby that is born from an EMBRYO which was selected from a number of embryos produced using IVF, for example because the parents want a baby that can provide cells to treat a brother's or sister's medical condition 訂製嬰兒，設計嬰兒（借助體外受精技術選取胚胎而生出的嬰兒，以提供細胞治療兄弟姐妹的病）

deˌsigner ˈdrug *noun* a drug produced artificially, usually one that is illegal 人造毒品

de·sir·able /dɪˈzaɪərəbl/ *adj.* **1** (*formal*) that you would like to have or do; worth having or doing 想望的；可取的；值得擁有的；值得做的：*She chatted for a few minutes about the qualities she considered **desirable in** a secretary.* 她用了幾分鐘談了談她認為一個秘書應有的品質。◇ *Such measures are desirable, if not essential.* 這些措施即使不是必要，也是可取的。◇ *The house has many desirable features.* 這棟房子有許多吸引人的特點。◇ *highly desirable* 非常可取 ◇ **~ that** (*BrE*) *It is **desirable that** interest rates should be reduced.* 利率下調是可取的。◇ (*NAmE*) *It is **desirable that** interest rates be reduced.* 利率下調是可取的。◇ **~ (for sb) (to do sth)** *It is no longer **desirable for** adult children to live with their parents.* 孩子長大成人後便不再想與父母住在一起了。**OPP** **undesirable** **2** (of a person 人) causing other people to feel sexual desire 引起性慾的；性感的 ▸ **de·sir·abil·ity** /dɪˌzaɪərəˈbɪləti/ *noun* [U]：(*formal*) *No one questions the desirability of cheaper fares.* 沒有人質疑票價下調是件好事。

D

de·sire 🗝 /dɪˈzaɪə(r)/ *noun, verb*

■ ***noun*** **1** 🗝 [C, U] a strong wish to have or do sth 願望；慾望；渴望：*enough money to satisfy all your desires* 足夠的錢來滿足你所有的慾望 ◇ **~ for sth** *a strong desire for power* 強烈的權力慾 ◇ **~ to do sth** *She felt an overwhelming desire to return home.* 她感到想回家的願望難以遏制。◇ (*formal*) *I have no desire* (= I do not want) *to discuss the matter further.* 我不想再談此事。◇ (*formal*) *He has expressed a desire to see you.* 他表示想見見你。**2** [U, C] **~ (for sb)** a strong wish to have sex with sb 情慾；肉慾；性慾：*She felt a surge of love and desire for him.* 她對他驟生愛意，慾火攻心。**3** [C, usually sing.] a person or thing that is wished for 想望的人；渴望的事物：*When she agreed to marry him he felt he had achieved **his heart's desire**.* 當她答應嫁給他時，他感到終於得到了自己的心上人。

■ ***verb*** (not used in the progressive tenses 不用於進行時) **1** 🗝 (*formal*) to want sth; to wish for sth 渴望；期望；想望：**~ sth** *We all desire health and happiness.* 我們都渴望健康和幸福。◇ *The house had everything you could desire.* 這房子你要什麼有什麼。◇ *The medicine did not achieve **the desired effect**.* 這種藥未達到預期效果。◇ **~ (sb/sth) to do sth** *Fewer people desire to live in the north of the country.* 想住在這個國家北方的人減少了。**2 ~ sb** to be sexually attracted to sb 被（某人）吸引；對（某人）產生性慾：*He still desired her.* 他依然戀着她。

IDM **leave a lot, much, something, etc. to be deˈsired** to be bad or unacceptable 還有許多（或一些等）需要改進的地方

de·sir·ous /dɪˈzaɪərəs/ *adj.* [not before noun] **~ (of sth / of doing sth)** | **~ (to do sth)** (*formal*) having a wish for sth; wanting sth 渴望；想望；希望：*At that point Franco was desirous of prolonging the war.* 那時，佛朗哥希望戰爭能延續下去。

de·sist /dɪˈzɪst; dɪˈsɪst/ *verb* [I] **~ (from sth/from doing sth)** (*formal*) to stop doing sth 停止；結束：*They agreed to desist from the bombing campaign.* 他們同意停止大規模轟炸。

desk 🗝 /desk/ *noun*

1 🗝 a piece of furniture like a table, usually with drawers in it, that you sit at to read, write, work, etc. 書桌；寫字枱；辦公桌：*He used to be a pilot but now he has **a desk job**.* 他曾是飛行員，但現在做辦公室工作。➲ VISUAL VOCAB page V69 **2** 🗝 a place where you can get information or be served at an airport, a hotel, etc.（機場、旅館等的）問訊枱，服務枱，工作枱：*the check-in desk*（機場）驗票領取登機卡處 ◇ *the reception desk* 服務枱 ➲ see also CASH DESK, FRONT DESK **3** an office at a newspaper, television company, etc. that deals with a particular subject（報社、電視台等的）辦公處，部，室，組：*the sports desk* 體育部 ➲ see also CITY DESK, NEWS DESK

ˈdesk clerk *noun* (*NAmE*) = CLERK (4)

de·skill /diːˈskɪl/ *verb* **~ sth** (*technical* 術語) to reduce the amount of skill that is needed to do a particular job 減低（某工作）的技術要求 ▸ **de·skill·ing** *noun* [U]

desk·top /ˈdesktɒp; *NAmE* -tɑːp/ *noun* **1** the top of a desk 桌面 **2** a screen on a computer which shows the ICONS of the programs that can be used 桌面（顯示使用程序圖標的計算機屏幕）➲ VISUAL VOCAB page V68 **3** = DESKTOP COMPUTER

ˌdesktop comˈputer (also **desk·top**) *noun* a computer with a keyboard, screen and main processing unit, that fits on a desk 枱式計算機；枱式電腦；桌上型電腦 ➲ compare LAPTOP, NOTEBOOK (3)

D

desktop 'publishing *noun* [U] (*abbr.* **DTP**) the use of a small computer and a printer to produce a small book, a magazine or other printed material 桌面出版，桌上排版（用小型電腦和打印機從事出版業務）

deso·late *adj., verb*
■ **adj.** /'desələt/ **1** (of a place 地方) empty and without people, making you feel sad or frightened 無人居住的；荒無人煙的；荒涼的：*a bleak and desolate landscape* 一片荒涼的景色 **2** very lonely and unhappy 孤獨淒涼的；不幸的；憂傷的 **SYN** **forlorn**
■ **verb** /'desəleɪt/ [usually passive] **~ sb** (*literary*) to make sb feel sad and without hope 使感到悲慘；使感到淒涼；使悲傷絕望：*She had been desolated by the death of her friend.* 朋友的去世使她感到十分悲傷。

deso·la·tion /ˌdesə'leɪʃn/ *noun* [U] (*formal*) **1** the feeling of being very lonely and unhappy 孤寂；悲哀；憂傷 **2** the state of a place that is ruined or destroyed and offers no joy or hope to people 廢墟；荒蕪；荒涼：*a scene of utter desolation* 滿目瘡痍的景象

des·pair /dɪ'speə(r); *NAmE* dɪ'sper/ *noun, verb*
■ **noun** [U] the feeling of having lost all hope 絕望：*She uttered a cry of despair.* 她發出了絕望的叫聲。◇ *A deep sense of despair overwhelmed him.* 深深的絕望使他痛苦不堪。◇ *He gave up the struggle* ***in despair***. 他絕望地放棄了鬥爭。◇ *One harsh word would send her into* ***the depths of despair***. 一句嚴厲的話就會使她陷入極度的絕望之中。◇ *Eventually,* ***driven to despair***, *he threw himself under a train.* 他被迫得走投無路，最後卧軌自殺。➲ see also DESPERATE
IDM **be the despair of sb** to make sb worried or unhappy, because they cannot help 令某人擔心（或絕望）：*My handwriting was the despair of my teachers.* 我的字寫得很差，使老師們感到十分失望。➲ more at COUNSEL *n.*
■ **verb** [I] to stop having any hope that a situation will change or improve 絕望；失去希望；喪失信心：*Don't despair! We'll think of a way out of this.* 別灰心！我們會找到出路的。◇ **~ of sth/sb** *I despair of him; he can't keep a job for more than six months.* 我對他都絕望了，他做任何工作都不超過半年。◇ **~ of doing sth** *They'd almost despaired of ever having children.* 他們對生孩子幾乎不抱任何希望了。

des·pair·ing /dɪ'speərɪŋ; *NAmE* -'sper-/ *adj.* showing or feeling the loss of all hope 表示絕望的；感到絕望的；沒有希望的：*a* ***despairing cry/look/sigh*** 絕望的呼聲／神情／歎息 ◇ *With every day that passed he became ever more despairing.* 隨着日子一天天過去，他越來越絕望。
▸ **des·pair·ing·ly** *adv.*：*She looked despairingly at the mess.* 她一看這亂糟糟的樣子，心就涼了。

des·patch (*BrE*) = DISPATCH

des·per·ado /ˌdespə'rɑːdəʊ; *NAmE* -doʊ/ *noun* (*pl.* **-oes** or **-os**) (*old-fashioned*) a man who does dangerous and criminal things without caring about himself or other people 暴徒；歹徒；亡命之徒

des·per·ate 🔑 /'despərət/ *adj.*
1 🔑 feeling or showing that you have little hope and are ready to do anything without worrying about danger to yourself or others（因絕望而）不惜冒險的，不顧一切的，拚命的：*The prisoners grew increasingly desperate.* 犯人因絕望而越來越膽大妄為。◇ *Stores are getting desperate after two years of poor sales.* 兩年來銷路不暢，商店不惜冒起險來。◇ *Somewhere out there was a desperate man, cold, hungry, hunted.* 那外面有個男人又冷又餓，還有人抓他，走投無路了。◇ *I heard sounds of a desperate struggle in the next room.* 我聽到隔壁房間裏有拚命掙扎的聲音。 **2** 🔑 [usually before noun] (of an action 行為) giving little hope of success; tried when everything else has failed 絕望的；孤注一擲的；鋌而走險的：*a* ***desperate bid*** *for freedom* 孤注一擲爭取自由的努力 ◇ *She clung to the edge* ***in a desperate attempt*** *to save herself.* 為了活命，她拚命抓住邊緣。◇ *His increasing financial difficulties forced him to take* ***desperate measures***. 不斷增加的經濟困難迫使他採取了鋌而走險的辦法。◇ *Doctors were fighting a* ***desperate battle*** *to save the little girl's life.* 醫生們不惜一切地奮力搶救小女孩的生命。 **3** 🔑 [not usually before noun] needing or wanting sth very much 非常需要；極想；渴望：**~ (for sth)** *He was so desperate for a job he would have done anything.* 他當時太想找份工作了，什麼事都願意幹。◇ (*informal*) *I'm desperate for a cigarette.* 我很想抽支煙。◇ **~ (to do sth)** *I was absolutely desperate to see her.* 我極想見到她。 **4** 🔑 (of a situation 情況) extremely serious or dangerous 極嚴重的；極危險的；很危急的：*The children are* ***in desperate need*** *of love and attention.* 這些孩子非常需要愛心和關懷。◇ *They face a desperate shortage of clean water.* 他們面臨乾淨用水的嚴重短缺。▸ **des·per·ate·ly** 🔑 *adv.*：***desperately ill/unhappy/lonely*** 病得厲害；極為不快；極其孤獨 ◇ *He took a deep breath, desperately trying to keep calm.* 他深深地吸了口氣，竭盡全力保持鎮定。◇ *They desperately wanted a child.* 他們非常想要一個孩子。◇ *She looked desperately around for a weapon.* 她在四下裏找，急於弄到一件武器。

des·per·ation /ˌdespə'reɪʃn/ *noun* [U] the state of being desperate 絕望；拚命；鋌而走險：***In desperation***, *she called Louise and asked for her help.* 在走投無路的情況下，她給路易絲打了個電話請她幫忙。◇ *There was a note of desperation in his voice.* 聽他的語氣他急得要命。◇ *an act of sheer desperation* 完全絕望的行為

de·spic·able /dɪ'spɪkəbl; *rarely* 'despɪkəbl/ *adj.* (*formal*) very unpleasant or evil 令人厭惡的；可鄙的；卑鄙的：*a* ***despicable act/crime*** 卑鄙的行為／罪行 ◇ *I hate you! You're despicable.* 我恨你！你真卑鄙。

de·spise /dɪ'spaɪz/ *verb* **~ sb/sth** (not used in the progressive tenses 不用於進行時) to dislike and have no respect for sb/sth 鄙視；蔑視；看不起：*She despised gossip in any form.* 她對任何形式的流言蜚語都嗤之以鼻。◇ *He despised himself for being so cowardly.* 他為自己如此怯懦而自慚形穢。➲ SYNONYMS at HATE

de·spite 🔑 **AW** /dɪ'spaɪt/ *prep.*
1 🔑 used to show that sth happened or is true although sth else might have happened to prevent it 即使；儘管 **SYN** **in spite of**：*Her voice was shaking despite all her efforts to control it.* 儘管她竭盡全力控制自己，聲音仍然在顫抖。◇ *Despite applying for hundreds of jobs, he is still out of work.* 儘管他申請了數百個工作，但仍然在失業中。◇ *She was good at physics* ***despite the fact that*** *she found it boring.* 儘管她認為物理枯燥無味，她卻學得很好。➲ LANGUAGE BANK at HOWEVER **2** **despite yourself** used to show that sb did not intend to do the thing mentioned 儘管（自己）不願意 **SYN** **in spite of**：*He had to laugh despite himself.* 他不想笑，但還是忍不住笑了出來。

de·spoil /dɪ'spɔɪl/ *verb* **~ sth (of sth)** (*literary*) to steal sth valuable from a place; to make a place less attractive by damaging or destroying it 搶劫；掠奪；蹂躪；破壞 **SYN** **plunder**

des·pond /dɪ'spɒnd; *NAmE* -'spɑːnd/ *noun* [U] ➲ SLOUGH OF DESPOND

des·pond·ent /dɪ'spɒndənt; *NAmE* -'spɑːn-/ *adj.* **~ (about sth)** | (*especially NAmE*) **~ (over sth)** sad, without much hope 苦惱的；沮喪的；泄氣的；失望的 **SYN** **dejected**：*She was becoming increasingly despondent about the way things were going.* 她對情況的發展越來越失望。
▸ **des·pond·ency** /dɪ'spɒndənsi; *NAmE* -'spɑːn-/ *noun* [U]：*a mood of despondency* 沮喪的心情 ◇ *Life's not all gloom and despondency.* 生活並不都是悲觀和失望。
des·pond·ent·ly *adv.*

des·pot /'despɒt; *NAmE* 'despɑːt/ *noun* a ruler with great power, especially one who uses it in a cruel way 專制統治者；專制君主；暴君：*an enlightened despot* (= one who tries to use his/her power in a good way) 開明的專制君主 ▸ **des·pot·ic** /dɪ'spɒtɪk; *NAmE* -'spɑːt-/ *adj.*：***despotic power/rule*** 至高無上的權力；專制統治

des·pot·ism /'despətɪzəm/ *noun* [U] the rule of a despot 專制統治；獨裁制；暴政

des res /ˌdez 'rez/ *noun* [usually sing.] (*BrE, humorous*) an attractive house, especially a large one (from the words 'desirable residence') 理想的房子（desirable residence 的縮略形式）

des·sert /dɪ'zɜːt; *NAmE* dɪ'zɜːrt/ *noun* [U, C] sweet food eaten at the end of a meal（飯後）甜點，甜食：*What's for dessert?* 餐後甜點吃什麼？◇ *a rich chocolate dessert*

膩人的巧克力甜點 ◊ *a dessert wine* 餐末甜酒 ◊ (*BrE*) *the dessert trolley* (= a table on wheels from which you choose your dessert in a restaurant)（餐廳內）送甜點的手推車 ➲ COLLOCATIONS at RESTAURANT ➲ compare AFTERS, PUDDING (1), SWEET *n.* (2)

des·sert·spoon /dɪ'zɜːtspuːn; *NAmE* -'zɜːrt-/ *noun* **1** a spoon of medium size 中型匙；點心匙 ➲ VISUAL VOCAB page V22 **2** (also **des·sert·spoon·ful** /-fʊl/) the amount a dessertspoon can hold 一點心匙（的量）

de·sta·bil·ize (*BrE* also **-ise**) /ˌdiː'steɪbəlaɪz/ *verb* ~ **sth** to make a system, country, government, etc. become less firmly established or successful 使（制度、國家、政府等）動搖；使不安定；使不穩定：*Terrorist attacks were threatening to destabilize the government.* 恐怖襲擊威脅着政府的穩定。◊ *The news had a destabilizing effect on the stock market.* 這消息引起了股市的動盪。➲ compare STABILIZE ▸ **de·sta·bil·iza·tion, -isa·tion** /ˌdiːˌsteɪbəlaɪ'zeɪʃn; *NAmE* -lə'z-/ *noun* [U]

des·tin·ation /ˌdestɪ'neɪʃn/ *noun, adj.*

■ ***noun*** a place to which sb/sth is going or being sent 目的地；終點：*popular **holiday destinations** like the Bahamas* 像巴哈馬那樣深受大眾喜愛的度假勝地 ◊ *to **arrive at/reach your destination*** 到達目的地 ◊ *Our luggage was checked all the way through to our **final destination**.* 我們的行李一直被託運到最終目的地。

■ ***adj.*** ~ **hotel/store/restaurant, etc.** a hotel, store, etc. that people will make a special trip to visit 預訂的旅館、要去的商店等

des·tined /'destɪnd/ *adj.* (*formal*) **1** having a future which has been decided or planned at an earlier time, especially by FATE 預定；注定；（尤指）命中注定：~ **for sth** *He was destined for a military career, like his father before him.* 他命中注定要步父親的後塵，過戎馬生涯。◊ ~ **to do sth** *We seem destined never to meet.* 我們似乎是命中注定無緣相見。**2** ~ **for** ... on the way to or intended for a place 開往；運往；前往 SYN **bound for**：*goods destined for Poland* 運往波蘭的貨物

des·tiny /'destəni/ *noun* (*pl.* **-ies**) **1** [C] what happens to sb or what will happen to them in the future, especially things that they cannot change or avoid 命運；天命；天數：*the destinies of nations* 國家的命運 ◊ *He wants to be in control of his own destiny.* 他想要掌握自己的命運。**2** [U] the power believed to control events 主宰事物的力量；命運之神 SYN **fate**：*I believe there's some force guiding us—call it God, destiny or fate.* 我總認為有某種力量在指引着我們，稱之為上帝也罷，天意也罷，還是命運也罷。➲ SYNONYMS at LUCK

des·ti·tute /'destɪtjuːt; *NAmE* -tuːt/ *adj.* **1** without money, food and the other things necessary for life 貧困的；貧窮的；赤貧的：*When he died, his family was left completely destitute.* 他死時家裏一貧如洗。**2 the destitute** *noun* [pl.] people who are destitute 窮人；貧民 **3** ~ **of sth** (*formal*) lacking sth 缺乏；沒有；毫無：*They seem destitute of ordinary human feelings.* 他們似乎一點人情味都沒有。▸ **des·ti·tu·tion** /ˌdestɪ'tjuːʃn; *NAmE* -'tuːʃn/ *noun* [U]：*homelessness and destitution* 無家可歸且一無所有

de·stock /ˌdiː'stɒk; *NAmE* -'stɑːk/ *verb* [I, T] ~ (**sth**) (*BrE, business* 商) to reduce the amount of goods in a shop/store, the amount of materials kept available for making sth in a factory, etc. 減少存貨；減少庫存

de-stress /ˌdiː 'stres/ *verb* [I, T] ~ (**sb/yourself**) to relax after working hard or experiencing stress; to reduce the amount of stress that you experience 放鬆；舒緩壓力；減少壓力：*De-stress yourself with a relaxing bath.* 舒舒服服洗個澡放鬆一下。

de·stroy 🔑 /dɪ'strɔɪ/ *verb*

> **WORD FAMILY**
> destroy *verb*
> destroyer *noun*
> destruction *noun*
> destructive *adj.*
> indestructible *adj.*

1 🔑 ~ **sth/sb** to damage sth so badly that it no longer exists, works, etc. 摧毀；毀滅；破壞：*The building was completely destroyed by fire.* 這棟建築物被大火徹底焚燬了。◊ *They've destroyed all the evidence.* 他們銷毀了一切證據。◊ *Heat gradually destroys vitamin C.* 加熱會逐漸破壞維生素 C。◊ *You have destroyed my hopes of happiness.* 你毀掉了我得到幸福的希望。◊ *Failure was slowly destroying him* (= making him less and less confident and happy). 失敗漸漸地把他毀了。**2** ~ **sth** to kill an animal deliberately, usually because it is sick or not wanted（因動物有病或不再需要而）殺死，消滅，人道毀滅：*The injured horse had to be destroyed.* 這匹馬受了傷，只好送它回老家了。➲ see also SOUL-DESTROYING

des·troy·er /dɪ'strɔɪə(r)/ *noun* **1** a small fast ship used in war, for example to protect larger ships 驅逐艦 **2** a person or thing that destroys 破壞者；毀滅者：*Sugar is the destroyer of healthy teeth.* 糖會危害健全的牙齒。

de·struc·tion 🔑 /dɪ'strʌkʃn/ *noun* [U] the act of destroying sth; the process of being destroyed 摧毀；毀滅；破壞：*the destruction of the rainforests* 對熱帶雨林的破壞 ◊ *weapons of mass destruction* 大規模殺傷性武器 ◊ *a tidal wave bringing **death and destruction** in its wake* 海嘯以及隨之而來的死亡與破壞 ◊ *The central argument is that capitalism **sows the seeds of its own destruction*** (= creates the forces that destroy it). 主要論點是資本主義播下了自我毀滅的種子。

de·struc·tive /dɪ'strʌktɪv/ *adj.* causing destruction or damage 引起破壞（或毀滅）的；破壞（或毀滅）性的：*the destructive power of modern weapons* 現代武器的毀滅性力量 ◊ *the destructive effects of anxiety* 焦慮的破壞性影響 ➲ compare CONSTRUCTIVE ▸ **de·struc·tive·ly** *adv.* **de·struc·tive·ness** *noun* [U]

des·ul·tory /'desəltri; *NAmE* -tɔːri/ *adj.* (*formal*) going from one thing to another, without a definite plan and without enthusiasm 漫無目的的；無條理的；隨意的：*I wandered about in a desultory fashion.* 我漫無目的地四處遊蕩。◊ *a desultory conversation* 漫無邊際的談話 ▸ **des·ul·tor·ily** *adv.*

Det *abbr.* (*BrE*) (in writing) DETECTIVE（書寫形式）偵探：*Det Insp* (= Inspector) *Cox* 考克斯探長

de·tach /dɪ'tætʃ/ *verb* **1** [T, I] to remove sth from sth larger; to become separated from sth 拆卸；（使）分開，脱離：~ **sth** *Detach the coupon and return it as soon as possible* 將表格撕下後儘快寄回。◊ ~ **sth from sth** *One of the panels had become detached from the main structure.* 一塊鑲板已從主體結構上脱落。◊ ~ (**from sth**) *The skis should detach from the boot if you fall.* 要是你跌倒了，滑雪板就該脱離靴子。➲ compare ATTACH (1) **2** [T] ~ **yourself** (**from sb/sth**) (*formal*) to leave or separate yourself from sb/sth 掙脱；擺脱；離開：*She detached herself from his embrace.* 她掙脱了他的擁抱。◊ (*figurative*) *I tried to detach myself from the reality of these terrible events.* 我盡力使自己從這些可怕事件的現實中擺脱出來。**3** [T] ~ **sb/sth** (*technical* 術語) to send a group of soldiers, etc. away from the main group, especially to do special duties 派遣；分遣；分派

de·tach·able /dɪ'tætʃəbl/ *adj.* that can be taken off 可拆卸的；可分開的 SYN **removable**：*a coat with a detachable hood* 帶有活風帽的外套

de·tached /dɪ'tætʃt/ *adj.* **1** (of a house 房子) not joined to another house on either side 單獨的；獨立的；不連接的 ➲ VISUAL VOCAB page V17 ➲ compare SEMI-DETACHED **2** showing a lack of feeling 不帶感情的；超然的；冷漠的 SYN **indifferent**：*She wanted him to stop being so cool, so detached, so cynical.* 她希望他不再那麼冷酷無情，那麼無動於衷，那麼憤世嫉俗。**3** (*approving*) not influenced by other people or by your own feelings 客觀的；公正的；無偏見的 SYN **impartial**：*a detached observer* 客觀的觀察者

de·tach·ment /dɪ'tætʃmənt/ *noun* **1** [U] the state of not being involved in sth in an emotional or personal way 超然；超脱；冷漠：*He answered with an air of detachment.* 他回答時帶着冷漠的神態。◊ *She felt a sense of detachment from what was going on.* 她對眼前發生的事感到很超然。OPP **involvement** **2** [U] (*approving*) the state of not being influenced by other people or by your own feelings 公正；客觀；獨立：*In judging these issues a degree of critical detachment is required.* 在裁決這些爭議時須要有一定程度的公正判斷力。**3** [C] a group of soldiers, ships, etc. sent away from a larger group, especially to do special duties 分遣隊；支隊；特遣小分隊：*a detachment of artillery* 炮兵支隊 **4** [U] the act of detaching sth; the process of being detached from sth 拆卸；分離；分遣：*to suffer detachment of the retina* 出現視網膜脱落

de·tail /ˈdiːteɪl; *US* also dɪˈteɪl/ *noun, verb*

D

■ **noun**

▸ **FACTS/INFORMATION** 事實；信息 **1** [C] a small individual fact or item; a less important fact or item 細微之處；枝節；瑣事：*an expedition planned down to the last detail* 計劃詳盡的探險 ◇ *He stood still, absorbing every detail of the street.* 他一動不動地站着，不放過街上的每一細微之處。◇ *Tell me the main points now; leave* ***the details*** *till later.* 現在把要點告訴我，細節留到以後再説。 **2** [U] the small facts or features of sth, when you consider them all together 詳情；全部細節：*This issue will be discussed* ***in*** *more* ***detail*** *in the next chapter.* 這個問題將在下一章詳細論述。◇ *The research has been carried out with scrupulous* ***attention to detail***. 研究工作一絲不苟地完成了。◇ *He had* ***an eye for detail*** (= noticed and remembered small details). 他很善於發現並記住細節。◇ *The fine detail of the plan has yet to be worked out.* 這個方案的具體細節尚未制訂出來。 **3** **details** [pl.] information about sth 具體情況；（關於某事物的）資料，消息：*Please supply the following details: name, age and sex.* 請提供下列資料：姓名、年齡及性別。◇ *Further details and booking forms are available on request.* 備有詳細資料和訂購單以供索取。◇ *They didn't give any details about the game.* 他們沒有提供這場比賽的具體情況。◇ *'We had a terrible time—' 'Oh, spare me the details* (= don't tell me any more).' "我們倒霉透了——" "唉呀，別給我細說了。"

▸ **SMALL PARTS** 細部 **4** [C, U] a small part of a picture or painting; the smaller or less important parts of a picture, pattern, etc. when you consider them all together（照片、繪畫等的）細部，局部，次要部份：*This is a detail from the 1844 Turner painting.* 這是透納 1844 年畫作的一小部份。◇ *a huge picture with a lot of detail in it* 一幅有很多細微之處的巨型畫

▸ **SOLDIERS** 士兵 **5** [C] a group of soldiers given special duties 特遣隊；小分隊；支隊

IDM **go into 'detail(s)** to explain sth fully 詳細敍述；逐一說明：*I can't go into details now; it would take too long.* 我現在不能細說，太費工夫。

■ **verb**

▸ **GIVE FACTS/INFORMATION** 詳述 **1 ~ sth** to give a list of facts or all the available information about sth 詳細列舉；詳細說明；詳述：*The brochure details all the hotels in the area and their facilities.* 這本小冊子詳細介紹了當地所有旅館及其設施。

▸ **ORDER SOLDIER** 派遣士兵 **2** [often passive] **~ sb (to do sth)** to give an official order to sb, especially a soldier, to do a particular task 派遣；選派；分遣：*Several of the men were detailed to form a search party.* 幾名士兵被派組成一個搜索隊。

▸ **CLEAN CAR** 清洗汽車 **3 ~ sth** (*NAmE*) to clean a car extremely thoroughly 徹底清洗（汽車）：*He got work for a while detailing cars.* 他找到一個清洗汽車的臨時工作。

de·tailed /ˈdiːteɪld; *NAmE* also dɪˈteɪld/ *adj.* giving many details and a lot of information; paying great attention to details 詳細的；細緻的；精細的：*a* ***detailed description/analysis/study*** 詳細的描述／分析／研究 ◇ *He gave me* ***detailed instructions*** *on how to get there.* 他詳細地告訴我如何到達那裏。

de·tail·ing /ˈdiːteɪlɪŋ; *NAmE* also dɪˈteɪlɪŋ/ *noun* [U] small details put on a building, piece of clothing, etc., especially for decoration（建築、服裝等的）裝飾細部

de·tain /dɪˈteɪn/ *verb* **1 ~ sb** to keep sb in an official place, such as a police station, a prison or a hospital, and prevent them from leaving 拘留；扣押：*One man has been detained for questioning.* 一個男人被拘留審問。 **2 ~ sb** (*formal*) to delay sb or prevent them from going somewhere 耽擱；留住；阻留：*I'm sorry—he'll be late; he's been detained at a meeting.* 對不起——他要晚點到，他因會議耽擱了。➲ see also DETENTION

de·tain·ee /ˌdiːteɪˈniː/ *noun* a person who is kept in prison, usually because of his or her political opinions（通常因政治主張）被拘留者，被扣押者

de·tect **AW** /dɪˈtekt/ *verb* **~ sth** to discover or notice sth, especially sth that is not easy to see, hear, etc. 發現；查明；偵察出：*The tests are designed to detect the disease early.* 這些檢查旨在早期查出疾病。◇ *an instrument that can detect small amounts of radiation* 能檢測微量輻射的儀器 ◇ *Do I detect a note of criticism?* 這裏面是不是好像帶有批評的意味？➲ SYNONYMS at NOTICE ▸ **de·tect·able** **AW** *adj.*: *The noise is barely detectable by the human ear.* 這種聲音人的耳朵幾乎是察覺不到的。 **OPP** **undetectable**

de·tec·tion **AW** /dɪˈtekʃn/ *noun* [U] the process of detecting sth; the fact of being detected 偵查；探測；察覺；發現：*crime prevention and detection* 犯罪的預防和偵查 ◇ *Last year the detection rate for car theft was just 13%.* 去年汽車盜竊案的偵破率僅為 13%。◇ *Many problems, however, escape detection.* 然而許多問題卻未被察覺。◇ *Early detection of cancers is vitally important.* 癌症的早期查出是極為重要的。

de·tect·ive **AW** /dɪˈtektɪv/ *noun* (*abbr.* **Det**) **1** a person, especially a police officer, whose job is to examine crimes and catch criminals 偵探；警探：*Detective Inspector (Roger) Brown*（羅傑）布朗探長 ◇ *detectives from the anti-terrorist squad* 反恐怖主義小組的偵探 ◇ *a* ***detective story/novel*** 偵探故事／小說 ➲ see also STORE DETECTIVE **2** a person employed by sb to find out information about sb/sth 私人偵探 ➲ see also PRIVATE DETECTIVE

de·tect·or **AW** /dɪˈtektə(r)/ *noun* a piece of equipment for discovering the presence of sth, such as metal, smoke, EXPLOSIVES or changes in pressure or temperature 探測器；偵察器；檢測器：*a smoke detector* 煙霧檢測器

dé·tente (also **de·tente** especially in *NAmE*) /ˌdeɪˈtɑːnt/ *noun* [U] (from *French, formal*) an improvement in the relationship between two or more countries which have been unfriendly towards each other in the past（國際緊張關係的）緩和，改善

de·ten·tion /dɪˈtenʃn/ *noun* **1** [U] the state of being kept in a place, especially a prison, and prevented from leaving 拘留；扣押；監禁：*a sentence of 12 months' detention in a young offender institution* 在青少年教養院拘禁 12 個月的判決 ◇ *police powers of arrest and detention* 警方的逮捕和拘留權 ◇ *allegations of torture and detention without trial* 拷打和未經審判便進行關押的指控 ◇ *a detention camp* 拘留營 **2** [U, C] the punishment of being kept at school for a time after other students have gone home 放學後留校，留堂（處罰學生）：*They can't give me (a) detention for this.* 他們不能因為這事罰我課後留下來。➲ see also DETAIN

de'tention centre (*BrE*) (*NAmE* **de'tention center**) *noun* **1** a place where young people who have committed offences are kept in detention 少年管教所；少年觀護所 **2** a place where people are kept in detention, especially people who have entered a country illegally（尤指非法入境者的）收容所，拘留營

deter /dɪˈtɜː(r)/ *verb* (**-rr-**) [T, I] **~ (sb) (from sth/from doing sth)** to make sb decide not to do sth or continue doing sth, especially by making them understand the difficulties and unpleasant results of their actions 制止；阻止；威懾；使不敢：*I told him I wasn't interested, but he wasn't deterred.* 我已告訴他我不感興趣，可他卻不罷休。◇ *The high price of the service could deter people from seeking advice.* 這麼高的服務費可能使咨詢者望而卻步。➲ see also DETERRENT

de·ter·gent /dɪˈtɜːdʒənt; *NAmE* -ˈtɜːrdʒ-/ *noun* [U, C] a liquid or powder that helps remove dirt, for example from clothes or dishes 洗滌劑；去垢劑；洗衣粉

de·teri·or·ate /dɪˈtɪəriəreɪt; *NAmE* -ˈtɪr-/ *verb* [I] to become worse 變壞；惡化；退化：*Her health deteriorated rapidly, and she died shortly afterwards.* 她的健康狀況急劇惡化，不久便去世了。◇ *deteriorating weather conditions* 不斷惡化的天氣狀況 ◇ **~ into sth** *The discussion quickly deteriorated into an angry argument.* 這場討論迅速演變成憤怒的爭吵。▸ **de·teri·or·ation**

/dɪˌtɪəriəˈreɪʃn; *NAmE* -ˌtɪr-/ *noun* [U, C] : *a serious deterioration in relations between the two countries* 兩國關係的嚴重惡化

de·ter·min·able /dɪˈtɜːmɪnəbl; *NAmE* -ˈtɜːrm-/ *adj.* (*formal*) that can be found out or calculated 可確定的；可查明的；可計算出的：*During the third month of pregnancy the sex of the child becomes determinable.* 孩子的性別在妊娠期第三個月便可查明。

de·ter·min·ant /dɪˈtɜːmɪnənt; *NAmE* -ˈtɜːrm-/ *noun* (*formal*) a thing that decides whether or how sth happens 決定因素；決定條件

de·ter·min·ate /dɪˈtɜːmɪnət; *NAmE* -ˈtɜːrm-/ *adj.* (*formal*) fixed and definite 固定的；限定的；確定的：*a sentence with a determinate meaning* 具有確定意義的句子 OPP **indeterminate**

de·ter·min·ation /dɪˌtɜːmɪˈneɪʃn; *NAmE* -ˌtɜːrm-/ *noun*
1 [U] the quality that makes you continue trying to do sth even when this is difficult 決心；果斷；堅定：***fierce/grim/dogged determination*** 強烈的／不屈不撓的／頑強的決心 ◇ *He fought the illness with courage and determination.* 他勇敢頑強地與疾病作鬥爭。◇ *They had survived by sheer determination.* 他們全憑堅強的決心幸存下來。◇ **~ to do sth** *I admire her determination to get it right.* 我讚賞她非把事情弄清楚的決心。 **2** [U] (*formal*) the process of deciding sth officially （正式）決定，確定，規定：*factors influencing the determination of future policy* 影響未來決策的各種因素 **3** [U, C] (*technical* 術語) the act of finding out or calculating sth 查明；測定；計算：*Both methods rely on the accurate determination of the pressure of the gas.* 兩種方法都依賴於對氣體壓力的準確測定。

de·ter·mine /dɪˈtɜːmɪn; *NAmE* -ˈtɜːrm-/ *verb* (*formal*)
1 [T] to discover the facts about sth; to calculate sth exactly 查明；測定；準確算出 SYN **establish** : **~ sth** *An inquiry was set up to determine the cause of the accident.* 已展開調查以確定事故原因。◇ **~ what, whether, etc.** … *We set out to determine exactly what happened that night.* 我們着手查明那天晚上發生的事情。◇ **it is determined that** … *It was determined that she had died of natural causes.* 已確認她是自然死亡。 **2** [T] **~ sth** | **~ what, whether, etc.** … to make sth happen in a particular way or be of a particular type 決定；形成；支配；影響：*Age and experience will be* ***determining factors*** *in our choice of candidate.* 年齡和經驗是我們選擇候選人的決定因素。◇ *Upbringing plays an important part in determining a person's character.* 後天培養對於一個人性格的形成起着重要作用。 **3** [T] to officially decide and/or arrange sth 確定；裁決；安排：**~ sth** *A date for the meeting has yet to be determined.* 會議日期尚待確定。◇ **~ (that)** … *The court determined (that) the defendant should pay the legal costs.* 法庭裁決由被告支付訴訟費用。 **4** [T, I] **~ to do sth** | **~ (that)** … | **~ on sth** to decide definitely to do sth 決定，決心（做某事）：*They determined to start early.* 他們決定早點出發。

de·ter·mined /dɪˈtɜːmɪnd; *NAmE* -ˈtɜːrm-/ *adj.*
1 [not before noun] **~ (to do sth)** if you are **determined** to do sth, you have made a firm decision to do it and you will not let anyone prevent you 決心；決定；決意：*I'm determined to succeed.* 我決心要獲得成功。 **2** showing a person's determination to do sth 堅定的；堅決的；果斷的：*a determined effort to stop smoking* 堅決戒煙的努力 ◇ *The proposal had been dropped in the face of determined opposition.* 這項建議因遭到堅決反對而撤銷。 IDM see BOUND *adj.* ▸ **de·ter·mined·ly** *adv.*

de·ter·miner /dɪˈtɜːmɪnə(r); *NAmE* -ˈtɜːrm-/ *noun* (*grammar* 語法) (abbreviation *det.* in this dictionary 本詞典縮略為 det.) a word such as *the*, *some*, *my*, etc. that comes before a noun to show how the noun is being used 限定詞（置於名詞前起限定作用，如 the、some、my 等）

de·ter·min·ism /dɪˈtɜːmɪnɪzəm; *NAmE* -ˈtɜːrm-/ *noun* [U] (*philosophy* 哲) the belief that people are not free to choose what they are like or how they behave, because these things are decided by their surroundings and other things over which they have no control 決定論（排除自由意志，認為個性或行為均由環境和自己不能控制的因素所決定） ▸ **de·ter·min·is·tic** /dɪˌtɜːmɪˈnɪstɪk; *NAmE* -ˌtɜːrm-/ *adj.*

de·ter·rent /dɪˈterənt; *NAmE* -ˈtɜːr-/ *noun* **~ (to sb/sth)** a thing that makes sb less likely to do sth (= that deters them) 威懾因素；遏制力：*Hopefully his punishment will act as a deterrent to others.* 對他的懲罰但願能起到殺一儆百的作用。◇ *the country's* ***nuclear deterrents*** (= nuclear weapons that are intended to stop an enemy from attacking) 這個國家核武器的威懾力 ▸ **de·ter·rence** /dɪˈterəns; *NAmE* -ˈtɜːr-/ *noun* [U] (*formal*) **de·ter·rent** *adj.* : *a deterrent effect* 遏制作用

D

de·test /dɪˈtest/ *verb* (not used in the progressive tenses 不用於進行時) **~ sb/sth** | **~ doing sth** to hate sb/sth very much 厭惡；憎恨；討厭 SYN **loathe** : *They detested each other on sight.* 他們互相看着就不順眼。 ⊃ SYNONYMS at HATE ▸ **de·test·ation** /ˌdiːteˈsteɪʃn/ *noun* [U]

de·test·able /dɪˈtestəbl/ *adj.* that deserves to be hated 可憎的；可恨的；令人討厭的：*All terrorist crime is detestable, whoever the victims.* 無論受害者是誰，一切恐怖主義罪行都是可憎的。

de·throne /ˌdiːˈθrəʊn; *NAmE* -ˈθroʊn/ *verb* **~ sb** to remove a king or queen from power; to remove sb from a position of authority or power 廢黜（國王或女王）；撵下台；免（某人）的職；罷（某人）的官

det·on·ate /ˈdetəneɪt/ *verb* [I, T] **~ (sth)** to explode, or to make a bomb or other device explode （使）爆炸；引爆；起爆：*Two other bombs failed to detonate.* 另外兩枚炸彈未引爆。 ⊃ SYNONYMS at EXPLODE

det·on·ation /ˌdetəˈneɪʃn/ *noun* [C, U] an explosion; the action of making sth explode 爆炸；起爆；引爆

det·on·ator /ˈdetəneɪtə(r)/ *noun* a device for making sth, especially a bomb, explode 引爆裝置；雷管；起爆管

de·tour /ˈdiːtʊə(r); *NAmE* -tʊr/ *noun, verb*
■ ***noun*** **1** a longer route that you take in order to avoid a problem or to visit a place 繞行的路；迂迴路；兜圈子：*We had to make a detour around the flooded fields.* 我們只得繞道避開被洪水淹沒的田野。◇ *It's well worth making a detour to see the village.* 繞道去參觀一下這村子很是值得。 **2** (*NAmE*) (*BrE* **di·ver·sion**) a road or route that is used when the usual one is closed 臨時繞行路；臨時支路
■ ***verb*** [I, T] (*NAmE*) **~ (sb/sth) (to …)** to take a longer route in order to avoid a problem or to visit a place; to make sb/sth take a longer route （使）繞道，繞行：*The President detoured to Chicago for a special meeting.* 總統繞道到芝加哥參加一個特別會議。

detox /ˈdiːtɒks; *NAmE* -tɑːks/ *noun* [U] (*informal*) **1** the process of removing harmful substances from your body by only eating and drinking particular things 排毒（通過控制飲食種類將有害物質排出體外） **2** = DETOXIFICATION : *a detox clinic* 戒癮（診）所 ◇ *He's gone into detox.* 他進了戒毒所。

de·toxi·fi·ca·tion /diːˌtɒksɪfɪˈkeɪʃn; *NAmE* -ˌtɑːks-/ (also *informal* **detox**) *noun* [U] treatment given to people to help them stop drinking alcohol or taking drugs 戒酒；戒毒：*a detoxification unit* 戒毒所

de·tox·ify /ˌdiːˈtɒksɪfaɪ; *NAmE* -ˈtɑːks-/ *verb* (**de·toxi·fies**, **de·toxi·fy·ing**, **de·toxi·fied**, **de·toxi·fied**) **1 ~ sth** to remove harmful substances or poisons from sth 排毒；解毒；去毒；除去…的毒素 **2 ~ sb** to treat sb in order to help them stop drinking too much alcohol or taking drugs 戒酒；戒毒

de·tract /dɪˈtrækt/ *verb*
PHR V **de'tract from sth** | **de'tract sth from sth** (not used in the progressive tenses 不用於進行時) to make sth seem less good or enjoyable 減損；毀損；貶低 SYN **take away from** : *He was determined not to let anything detract from his enjoyment of the trip.* 他下決心這次旅行不讓任何事情影響他的興致。

de·tract·or /dɪˈtræktə(r)/ *noun* [usually pl.] (especially *formal*) a person who tries to make sb/sth seem less good or valuable by criticizing it 詆譭者；貶低者；惡意批評者

de·train /ˌdiːˈtreɪn/ *verb* [I, T] ~ **(sb)** (*formal*) to leave a train or make sb leave a train（使）下火車

det·ri·ment /ˈdetrɪmənt/ *noun* [U, C, usually sing.] (*formal*) the act of causing harm or damage; sth that causes harm or damage 傷害；損害；造成傷害（或損害）的事物

D

IDM **to the detriment of sb/sth | to sb/sth's detriment** resulting in harm or damage to sb/sth（結果）不利於，有害於，有損於：*He was engrossed in his job to the detriment of his health.* 他全身心地投入工作結果損害了他的健康。 **without detriment (to sb/sth)** not resulting in harm or damage to sb/sth（結果）無害於，無損於

det·ri·ment·al /ˌdetrɪˈmentl/ *adj.* ~ **(to sb/sth)** (*formal*) harmful 有害的；不利的 SYN **damaging**：*the sun's **detrimental effect** on skin* 日光對皮膚的有害影響 ◇ *The policy will be detrimental to the peace process.* 這項政策將不利於和平進程。 ▸ **det·ri·men·tal·ly** /-təli/ *adv.*

de·tritus /dɪˈtraɪtəs/ *noun* [U] **1** (*technical* 術語) natural waste material that is left after sth has been used or broken up 風化物；殘渣；腐殖質：*organic detritus from fish and plants* 魚和植物的有機殘渣 **2** (*formal*) any kind of rubbish/garbage that is left after an event or when sth has been used 瓦礫；碎石；垃圾；廢物 SYN **debris**：*the detritus of everyday life* 日常生活垃圾

de trop /ˌdə ˈtrəʊ; *NAmE* ˈtroʊ/ *adj.* [not before noun] (from *French*, *formal*) not wanted, especially in a social situation with other people（尤指在社交場合）不受歡迎，不需要，多餘

deuce /djuːs; *NAmE* duːs/ *noun* **1** [U, C] (in TENNIS 網球) the situation when both players have 40 as a score, after which one player must win two points one after the other in order to win the game 局末平分 **2** [C] (*NAmE*) a PLAYING CARD with two PIPS on it 二點的紙牌：*the deuce of clubs* 梅花二 **3 the deuce** [sing.] (*old-fashioned, informal*) used in questions to show that you are annoyed（用於問句中表示煩惱、厭惡）到底，究竟：*What the deuce is he doing?* 他到底在幹什麼？

deuced /djuːst; *NAmE* also duːst/ *adj.* [only before noun] (*old use*) used for emphasizing feelings, especially anger, disappointment or surprise（強調生氣、失望、驚訝等感情）非常的，極其的：*The man's a deuced fool!* 那個男人真是個傻瓜！ ▸ **deuced** *adv.*：*It's deuced awkward.* 那事真令人難堪。

deur·me·kaar /ˌdjɜːməˈkɑː(r); *NAmE* ˌdjɜːrm-/ *adj.* (*SAfrE, informal*) in a confused state 混亂的；迷惑的

deus ex machina /ˌdeɪʊs eks ˈmækɪnə/ *noun* [sing.] (*literary*) an unexpected power or event that saves a situation that seems without hope, especially in a play or novel（尤指劇本或小說中）扭轉乾坤之力量

deu·ter·ium /djuːˈtɪəriəm; *NAmE* -ˈtɪr-; duːˈt-/ *noun* [U] (*symb.* D) (*chemistry* 化) an ISOTOPE (= a different form) of HYDROGEN with twice the mass of the usual isotope 氘，重氫（氫的同位素）

Deutsch·mark /ˈdɔɪtʃmɑːk; *NAmE* -mɑːrk/ (also **mark**) *noun* (*abbr.* **DM**) the former unit of money in Germany (replaced in 2002 by the euro) 德國馬克（德國貨幣單位，於 2002 年為歐元所取代）

de·value /ˌdiːˈvæljuː/ *verb* **1** [I, T] ~ **(sth)** (**against sth**) (*finance* 財) to reduce the value of the money of one country when it is exchanged for the money of another country 使（貨幣）貶值 OPP **revalue** **2** [T] ~ **sth** to give a lower value to sth, making it seem less important than it really is 降低…的價值；貶低：*Work in the home is often ignored and devalued.* 家務勞動常常被忽視和貶低。 ▸ **de·valu·ation** /ˌdiːˌvæljuˈeɪʃn/ *noun* [C, U]：*There has been a further small devaluation against the dollar.* 兑美元的比值繼續小幅下跌。

Deva·nag·ari /ˌdeɪvəˈnɑːɡəri; ˌdev-/ *noun* [U] the alphabet used to write Sanskrit, Hindi and some other Indian languages 天城體文字，伽里字母（用於梵語、印地語等印度語）

dev·as·tate /ˈdevəsteɪt/ *verb* **1** ~ **sth** to completely destroy a place or an area 徹底破壞；摧毀；毀滅：*The bomb devastated much of the old part of the city.* 這顆炸彈炸毀了舊城的一大片地方。 **2** [often passive] ~ **sb** to make sb feel very shocked and sad 使震驚；使極為憂傷；使極為悲痛

dev·as·tated /ˈdevəsteɪtɪd/ *adj.* extremely upset and shocked（極度）不安的，混亂的，震驚的：*His family is absolutely devastated.* 他的一家感到極為震驚。

dev·as·tat·ing /ˈdevəsteɪtɪŋ/ *adj.* **1** causing a lot of damage and destruction 破壞性極大的；毀滅性的 SYN **disastrous**：*a **devastating explosion/fire/cyclone*** 毀滅性的爆炸 / 火災 / 旋風 ◇ *Oil spills are having a **devastating effect** on coral reefs in the ocean.* 石油泄漏對海洋裏的珊瑚礁有着毀滅性影響。 ◇ *He received devastating injuries in the accident.* 他在這次事故中受到致命傷害。 ◇ *It will be a **devastating blow** to the local community if the factory closes.* 如果這家工廠倒閉，將給當地居民以毀滅性的打擊。 **2** extremely shocking to a person 令人震驚的；駭人的：*the devastating news that her father was dead* 她父親去世的驚人消息 **3** impressive and powerful 給人印象深刻的；令人欽佩的；強有力的：*his devastating performance in the 100 metres* 他在 100 米賽跑中的驚人表現 ◇ *Her smile was devastating.* 她的笑容令人傾倒。 ◇ *a devastating attack on the President's economic record* 針對總統的經濟政績發動的猛烈抨擊 ▸ **dev·as·tat·ing·ly** *adv.*：*a devastatingly handsome man* 富有魅力的美男子

dev·as·ta·tion /ˌdevəˈsteɪʃn/ *noun* [U] great destruction or damage, especially over a wide area（尤指大面積的）毀滅，破壞，蹂躪：*The bomb caused widespread devastation.* 炸彈造成大面積破壞。

de·velop 0‒ /dɪˈveləp/ *verb*

▸ **GROW BIGGER/STRONGER** 發展；壯大 **1** 0‒ [I, T] to gradually grow or become bigger, more advanced, stronger, etc.; to make sth do this（使）成長，發展，壯大：*The child is developing normally.* 這孩子發育正常。 ◇ ~ **(from sth) (into sth)** *The place has rapidly developed from a small fishing community into a thriving tourist resort.* 這地方由原來的小漁村迅速發展成一個繁榮的旅遊勝地。 ◇ ~ **sth (from sth) (into sth)** *She developed the company from nothing.* 她白手起家創辦了這家公司。

▸ **NEW IDEA/PRODUCT** 新思想 / 產品 **2** 0‒ [T] ~ **sth** to think of or produce a new idea, product, etc. and make it successful 開發；研製：*The company develops and markets new software.* 這家公司開發並銷售新軟件。 ➲ SYNONYMS at MAKE

▸ **DISEASE/PROBLEM** 疾病；問題 **3** 0‒ [I, T] ~ **(sth)** to begin to have sth such as a disease or a problem; to start to affect sb/sth 患（病）；出現（問題）；（疾病）開始侵襲；（問題）開始影響：*Her son developed asthma when he was two.* 她的兒子兩歲時患了哮喘。 ◇ *The car developed engine trouble and we had to stop.* 汽車發動機出了故障，我們只好停下來。

▸ **HAPPEN/CHANGE** 發生；變化 **4** 0‒ [I] to start to happen or change, especially in a bad way（尤指開始向壞的方面）發展，變化：*A crisis was rapidly developing in the Gulf.* 海灣危機迅速加劇。 ◇ *We need more time to see how things develop before we take action.* 我們採取行動之前需要有更多時間觀察情況的發展。

▸ **BECOME BETTER** 變得更好 **5** 0‒ [T, I] ~ **(sth)** to start to have a skill, ability, quality, etc. that becomes better and stronger; to become better and stronger 加強；增強；發揮：*He's developed a real flair for management.* 他在管理方面已經變得很有一套。 ◇ *Their relationship has developed over a number of years.* 多年來他們的情誼日益深厚。

▸ **BUILD HOUSES** 建房 **6** 0‒ [T] ~ **sth** to build new houses, factories, etc. on an area of land, especially land that was not being used effectively before 修建；開發：*The site is being developed by a French company.* 這塊地正由一家法國公司開發利用。

▸ **IDEA/STORY** 想法；敍述 **7** [T] ~ **sth** to make an idea, a story, etc. clearer by explaining it further 詳盡闡述；闡明 SYN **elaborate on**：*She develops the theme more fully in her later books.* 她在後來寫的書中更詳盡地闡明了這個主題。

▸ **PHOTOGRAPHS** 照片 **8** [T] ~ **sth** to treat film which has

been used to take photographs with chemicals so that the pictures can be seen 使（膠捲）顯影；顯像；沖洗（膠片）：*I had the film developed yesterday.* 我昨天把膠捲拿去沖印了。

de·veloped /dɪˈveləpt/ *adj.* **1** (of a country, society, etc. 國家、社會等) having many industries and a complicated economic system 發達的；高度發展的：*financial aid to less developed countries* 對欠發達國家的經濟援助 ◇ *The average citizen in the* ***developed world*** *uses over 155kg of paper per year.* 發達國家中普通公民每年的用紙量超過 155 公斤。➲ compare UNDERDEVELOPED **2** in an advanced state 先進的；成熟的：*children with highly developed problem-solving skills* 具有非常熟練解決問題能力的孩子 ➲ see also WELL DEVELOPED

de·vel·op·er /dɪˈveləpə(r)/ *noun* **1** [C] a person or company that buys land or buildings in order to build new houses, shops/stores, etc., or to improve the old ones, and makes a profit from doing this（房地產）開發商，開發公司：*property developers* 房地產開發商 **2** [C] a person or a company that designs and creates new products（新產品的）開發者，研製者：*a software developer* 軟件開發人員 **3** [U] a chemical substance that is used for developing photographs from a film 顯影劑；顯色劑

de·vel·op·ing /dɪˈveləpɪŋ/ *adj.* [only before noun] (of a country, society, etc. 國家、社會等) poor, and trying to make its industry and economic system more advanced 發展中的：***developing countries/nations/economies*** 發展中國家 / 經濟體 ➲ compare UNDERDEVELOPED

de·vel·op·ment 🔑 /dɪˈveləpmənt/ *noun*

▸ GROWTH 發展 **1** 🔑 [U] the gradual growth of sth so that it becomes more advanced, stronger, etc. 發展；發育；成長；壯大：*a baby's development in the womb* 胎兒在子宮內的發育 ◇ *the development of basic skills such as literacy and numeracy* 諸如識字與識數等基本技能的發展 ◇ *career development* 職業的發展

▸ NEW PRODUCT 新產品 **2** 🔑 [U, C] the process of producing or creating sth new or more advanced; a new or advanced product 開發；研製；研製成果：*the development of vaccines against tropical diseases* 熱帶疾病疫苗的研製 ◇ *developments in aviation technology* 航空技術的開發成果 ◇ *This piece of equipment is an exciting new development.* 這台設備是一項振奮人心的最新研究成果。➲ see also RESEARCH AND DEVELOPMENT

▸ NEW EVENT 新事態 **3** 🔑 [C] a new event or stage that is likely to affect what happens in a continuing situation（新的）發展事態，進展情況，發展階段：*the latest developments in the war* 戰爭的最新進展情況 ◇ *Are there further developments in the investigation?* 調查有新的進展嗎？

▸ NEW BUILDINGS 新建築 **4** 🔑 [C] a piece of land with new buildings on it 新建住宅區；新開發區：*a* ***commercial/business/housing development*** 商業開發區；新建住宅區 ➲ see also RIBBON DEVELOPMENT **5** 🔑 [U] the process of using an area of land, especially to make a profit by building on it, etc.（尤指房地產的）開發：*He bought the land for development.* 他買了這塊地準備開發。

de·vel·op·men·tal /dɪˌveləpˈmentl/ *adj.* **1** in a state of developing or being developed 發育中的；進化中的；開發中的：*The product is still at a developmental stage.* 這種產品仍處於研製階段。**2** connected with the development of sb/sth 發展的；成長的；進化的：*developmental psychology* 發展心理學 ▸ **de·vel·op·men·tal·ly** *adv.*

deˈvelopment area *noun* (*BrE*) an area where new industries are encouraged in order to create jobs 開發區

de·vi·ant /ˈdiːviənt/ *adj.* different from what most people consider to be normal and acceptable 不正常的；異常的；偏離常軌的：***deviant behaviour/sexuality*** 偏常行為 / 性行為 ▸ **de·vi·ant** *noun*：*sexual deviants* 性偏離者 **de·vi·ance** /-viəns/, **de·vi·ancy** /ˈdiːviənsi/ *noun* [U]：*a study of social deviance and crime* 對社會偏常行為和犯罪行為的研究

de·vi·ate AW /ˈdiːvieɪt/ *verb* [I] ~ (**from sth**) to be different from sth; to do sth in a different way from what is usual or expected 背離；偏離；違背：*The bus had to deviate from its usual route because of a road closure.* 因為道路封閉，公共汽車只得繞道而行。◇ *He never deviated from his original plan.* 他從未偏離自己最初的計劃。

de·vi·ation AW /ˌdiːviˈeɪʃn/ *noun* **1** [U, C] ~ (**from sth**) the act of moving away from what is normal or acceptable; a difference from what is expected or acceptable 背離；偏離；違背：*deviation from the previously accepted norms* 違背事先接受的準則 ◇ *sexual deviation* 性慾倒錯 ◇ *a deviation from the plan* 違背計劃 **2** [C] ~ (**from sth**) (*technical* 術語) the amount by which a single measurement is different from the average 偏差：*a compass deviation of 5°* (= from true north) 羅盤偏差 5 度（相對正北而言）➲ see also STANDARD DEVIATION

de·vice 🔑 AW /dɪˈvaɪs/ *noun*
1 🔑 an object or a piece of equipment that has been designed to do a particular job 裝置；儀器；器具；設備：*a water-saving device* 節水裝置 ◇ *electrical labour-saving devices around the home* 節省勞力的各種家用電器 **2** a bomb or weapon that will explode 炸彈；爆炸性武器；爆炸裝置：*A powerful device exploded outside the station.* 一枚威力巨大的炸彈在車站外爆炸了。◇ *the world's first atomic device* 世界第一枚原子彈 **3** a method of doing sth that produces a particular result or effect 手段；策略；方法；技巧：*Sending advertising by email is very successful as a marketing device.* 作為一種營銷手段，用電子郵件發送廣告是非常成功的。**4** a plan or trick that is used to get sth that sb wants 花招；計謀；詭計：*The report was a device used to hide rather than reveal problems.* 這份報告不是揭露問題而是為掩蓋問題而耍的花招。

IDM **leave sb to their own deˈvices** to leave sb alone to do as they wish, and not tell them what to do 聽任某人自行其是；對某人不加干涉

devil /ˈdevl/ *noun* **1 the Devil** (in the Christian, Jewish and Muslim religions 基督教、猶太教和伊斯蘭教) the most powerful evil BEING 魔王；魔鬼；撒旦 SYN **Satan** **2** an evil spirit 魔鬼；惡魔：*They believed she was possessed by devils.* 他們認為她是魔鬼附身。**3** (*informal*) a person who behaves badly, especially a child 淘氣鬼；冒失鬼；調皮鬼：*a naughty little devil* 小淘氣鬼 **4** (*informal*) used to talk about sb and to emphasize an opinion that you have of them（強調對某人的看法）人，傢伙：*I miss the old devil, now that he's gone.* 老傢伙這一走，我還真想他。◇ *She's off to Greece for a month—lucky devil!* 她休假去希臘一個月，真夠幸運的！

IDM **be a ˈdevil** (*BrE*) people say **Be a devil!** to encourage sb to do sth that they are not sure about doing（用以鼓勵）別怕，勇敢點：*Go on, be a devil, buy both of them.* 來，怕什麼，兩個都買了吧。**better the ˌdevil you ˈknow (than the ˌdevil you ˈdon't)** (*saying*) used to say that it is easier and wiser to stay in a bad situation that you know and can deal with rather than change to a new situation which may be much worse 熟悉的魔鬼比不熟悉的魔鬼好；不要嫌熟悉的環境不好，換個不熟悉的環境可能更糟 **between the ˌdevil and the ˌdeep blue ˈsea** in a difficult situation where there are two equally unpleasant or unacceptable choices 進退維谷；左右為難 **the ˈdevil** (*old-fashioned*) very difficult or unpleasant 非常困難；令人非常不快：*These berries are the devil to pick because they're so small.* 這些漿果太小了，很難摘。**the ˌdevil looks after his ˈown** (*saying*) bad people often seem to have good luck 壞人多好運；壞蛋自有鬼照顧；惡人自有惡人幫 **the devil makes work for idle ˈhands** (*saying*) people who do not have enough to do often start to do wrong 人閒生是非：*She blamed the crimes on the local jobless teenagers. 'The devil makes work for idle hands,' she would say.* 她認為那些違法活動是當地的無業青少年所為，總是說："人一閒，惹麻煩"。**a ˈdevil of a job/time** (*old-fashioned*) a very difficult or unpleasant job or time 費力（或令人討厭）的事；難熬（或令人不快）的日子：*I've had a devil of a job finding you.* 我費了九牛二虎之力才找到你。**go to the ˈdevil!** (*old-fashioned, informal*) used, in an unfriendly way, to tell sb to go away 滾開；見鬼去；去你的 **like the ˈdevil** (*old-fashioned, informal*) very hard, fast, etc. 拚命；賣力；飛快：*We ran like the*

D

devil. 我們跑得飛快。**speak/talk of the 'devil** (*informal*) people say **speak/talk of the devil** when sb they have been talking about appears unexpectedly 說到某人，某人就到：*Well, speak of the devil—here's Alice now!* 嗬，說曹操，曹操就到——瞧，艾麗斯這就來啦！**what, where, who, why, etc. the 'devil ...** (*old-fashioned*) used in questions to show that you are annoyed or surprised（用於問句表示煩惱或吃驚）究竟…，到底…：*What the devil do you think you're doing?* 你到底以為自己在幹什麼？➲ more at PAY *v.*, SELL *v.*

D

devil·ish /'devəlɪʃ/ *adj.* **1** cruel or evil 殘忍邪惡的；惡毒的：*a devilish conspiracy* 惡毒的陰謀活動 **2** morally bad, but in a way that people find attractive 魔鬼似的，惡魔似的（但具吸引力）：*He was handsome, with a devilish charm.* 他英俊漂亮，具有魔鬼般的迷惑力。

devil·ish·ly /'devəlɪʃli/ *adv.* (*old-fashioned*) extremely; very 極其；非常：*a devilishly hot day* 酷熱的一天

dev·illed (*BrE*) (*US* **dev·iled**) /'devld/ *adj.* cooked in a thick liquid containing hot spices 用辣味濃湯燉的

,devil-may-'care *adj.* [usually before noun] cheerful and not worrying about the future 樂天的；無憂無慮的；無所顧忌的

dev·il·ment /'devlmənt/ (also **dev·il·ry** /'devlri/) *noun* (*formal*) wild behaviour that causes trouble 搗亂；惡作劇 SYN **mischief**

,devil's 'advocate *noun* a person who expresses an opinion that they do not really hold in order to encourage a discussion about a subject 故意唱反調的人；故意持不同意見的人：*Often the interviewer will need to* ***play devil's advocate*** *in order to get a discussion going.* 採訪者常常需要故意唱唱反調以使訪談繼續下去。

de·vi·ous /'diːviəs/ *adj.* **1** behaving in a dishonest or indirect way, or tricking people, in order to get sth 不誠實的；不直率的；欺詐的 SYN **deceitful, underhand**：*a devious politician* 不誠實的政治家 ◇ *He got rich by devious means.* 他不擇手段大發橫財。**2 ~ route/path** a route or path that is not straight but has many changes in direction; not direct 迂迴的（路線）；曲折的（道路）：*a devious route from the airport* 出機場的曲折路線 ▸ **de·vi·ous·ly** *adv.* **de·vi·ous·ness** *noun* [U]

de·vise /dɪ'vaɪz/ *verb* **~ sth** to invent sth new or a new way of doing sth 發明；設計；想出 SYN **think up**：*A new system has been devised to control traffic in the city.* 控制城市交通的新系統已經設計出來。

de·voice /,diː'vɔɪs/ *verb* **~ sth** (*phonetics* 語音) to make a speech sound, usually a consonant, VOICELESS 使（輔音等）清化

de·void /dɪ'vɔɪd/ *adj.* **~ of sth** completely lacking in sth 完全沒有；缺乏：*The letter was devoid of warmth and feeling.* 這封信既無熱情又無感情。

de·vo·lu·tion /,diːvə'luːʃn; *NAmE* ,dev-/ *noun* [U] the act of giving power from a central authority or government to an authority or a government in a local region（中央政府向地方政府的）權力下放，權力轉移，分權

de·volve /dɪ'vɒlv; *NAmE* -'vɑːlv/ *verb*

PHR V **de'volve on/upon sb/sth** (*formal*) **1** if property, money, etc. **devolves on/upon** you, you receive it after sb else dies（財產、金錢等遺產）轉給，傳給，移交 **2** if a duty, responsibility, etc. **devolves on/upon** you, it is given to you by sb at a higher level of authority（職責、責任等）交由…接替，委託…承擔 **de'volve sth to/on/upon sb** to give a duty, responsibility, power, etc. to sb who has less authority than you（將職責、責任、權力等）移交，轉交，委任：*The central government devolved most tax-raising powers to the regional authorities.* 中央政府將大部份徵稅權移交給了地方當局。

de·volved /dɪ'vɒlvd; *NAmE* -'vɑːlvd/ *adj.* if power or authority is **devolved**, it has been passed to sb who has less power（職權）已移交的，下放的，委任的：*devolved responsibility* 已移交的責任 ◇ *a system of devolved government* 治理權力下放制

de·vote 0┳ AW /dɪ'vəʊt; *NAmE* dɪ'voʊt/ *verb*

PHR V **de'vote yourself to sb/sth** 0┳ to give most of your time, energy, attention, etc. to sb/sth 獻身；致力；專心：*She devoted herself to her career.* 她全力傾注於自己的事業。**de'vote sth to sth** 0┳ to give an amount of time, attention, etc. to sth 把…用於：*I could only devote two hours a day to the work.* 我一天只能在這個工作上花兩個小時。

de·voted 0┳ /dɪ'vəʊtɪd; *NAmE* -'voʊt-/ *adj.* **~ (to sb/sth)** having great love for sb/sth and being loyal to them 摯愛的；忠誠的；全心全意的：*They are devoted to their children.* 他們深愛着自己的孩子。◇ *a devoted son/friend/fan* 孝子；忠誠的朋友；狂熱的崇拜者 ➲ SYNONYMS at LOVE ▸ **de·voted·ly** *adv.*

de·votee /,devə'tiː/ *noun* **1 ~ (of sb/sth)** a person who admires and is very enthusiastic about sb/sth（狂熱的）崇拜者，愛好者：*a devotee of science fiction* 科幻小說的狂熱愛好者 **2 ~ (of sb/sth)** a very religious person who belongs to a particular group 虔誠的宗教信徒：*devotees of Krishna*（印度教）黑天的虔誠信徒

de·vo·tion AW /dɪ'vəʊʃn; *NAmE* -'voʊ-/ *noun* **1** [U, sing.] **~ (to sb/sth)** great love, care and support for sb/sth 摯愛；關愛；關照：*His devotion to his wife and family is touching.* 他對妻子和家人的關愛感人至深。**2** [U, sing.] **~ (to sb/sth)** the action of spending a lot of time or energy on sth 奉獻；忠誠；專心；熱心 SYN **dedication**：*her* ***devotion to duty*** 她對職責的忠誠 ◇ *Her devotion to the job left her with very little free time.* 她全身心投入工作，幾乎沒有閒暇。**3 devotions** [pl.] prayers and other religious practices 宗教敬拜

de·vo·tion·al /dɪ'vəʊʃənl; *NAmE* -'voʊ-/ *adj.* (of music, etc. 音樂等) connected with or used in religious services 用於祈禱的；宗教儀式的

de·vour /dɪ'vaʊə(r)/ *verb* **1 ~ sth** to eat all of sth quickly, especially because you are very hungry（尤指因飢餓而）狼吞虎嚥地吃光 SYN **gobble up 2** to read or look at sth with great interest and enthusiasm 津津有味地看；如飢似渴地讀：*She devoured everything she could lay her hands on: books, magazines and newspapers.* 無論是書、雜誌，還是報紙，只要能弄到手，她都看得津津有味。**3 ~ sb/th** (*formal*) to destroy sb/sth 吞沒；吞噬；毀滅 SYN **engulf**：*Flames devoured the house.* 大火吞噬了這棟房子。

IDM **be devoured by sth** to be filled with a strong emotion that seems to control you 心中充滿（強烈的情感）：*She was devoured by envy and hatred.* 她心中充滿嫉妒和憎恨。

de·vout /dɪ'vaʊt/ *adj.* (of a person 人) believing strongly in a particular religion and obeying its laws and practices 篤信宗教的；虔誠的：*a devout Christian/Muslim* 虔誠的基督徒／穆斯林 ▸ **de·vout·ly** *adv.*：*a devoutly Catholic region* 篤信天主教的地區 ◇ *She devoutly (= very strongly) hoped he was telling the truth.* 她誠摯地希望他講的是實情。

dew /djuː; *NAmE* duː/ *noun* [U] the very small drops of water that form on the ground, etc. during the night 露；露水：*The grass was wet with early morning dew.* 清晨的露水使得青草濕漉漉的。

dew·berry /'djuːbəri; *NAmE* 'duːberi; 'djuː-/ *noun* (*pl.* **-ies**) a small soft black or blue-black fruit like a BLACKBERRY, or the bush that it grows on 露莓（漿果）；露莓（灌木）

dew·drop /'djuːdrɒp; *NAmE* 'duːdrɑːp/ *noun* a small drop of dew or other liquid 露珠；水珠

Dewey decimal classification /,djuːi 'desɪml klæsɪfɪ'keɪʃn; *NAmE* also ,duːi/ (also **'Dewey system**) *noun* [sing.] an international system for arranging books in a library 杜威十進分類法（圖書館藏書分類法）

'dew point *noun* [sing.] (*technical* 術語) the temperature at which air can hold no more water. Below this temperature the water comes out of the air in the form of drops. 露點（空氣中水氣含量達到飽和的氣温，低於此温度時水氣從空氣中析出凝成水珠）

dewy /'djuːi; *NAmE* duːi/ *adj.* wet with DEW 露水打濕的；帶露水的

ˌdewy-ˈeyed *adj.* (*disapproving*) showing emotion about sth, perhaps with a few tears in the eyes 動感情的；感傷的；淚汪汪的 **SYN** **sentimental**

dex·ter·ity /dekˈsterəti/ *noun* [U] skill in using your hands or your mind（手）靈巧，熟練；（思維）敏捷，靈活：*You need manual dexterity to be good at video games.* 玩好電子遊戲手要靈巧。◇ ***mental/verbal dexterity*** 智能；說話技巧

dex·ter·ous (also **dex·trous**) /ˈdekstrəs/ *adj.* (*formal*) skilful with your hands; skilfully done 靈巧的；熟練的；敏捷的 ▸ **dex·ter·ous·ly** (also **dex·trous·ly**) *adv.*

dex·trose /ˈdekstrəʊz; -əʊs; *NAmE* -oʊz; -oʊs/ *noun* [U] (*chemistry* 化) a form of GLUCOSE (= a type of natural sugar) 葡萄糖，右旋糖（一種天然糖）

DFID /ˌdiː ef aɪ ˈdiː/ *abbr.* (in Britain) Department for International Development（英國）國際發展部

dhal (also **dal**) /dɑːl/ *noun* [U] a S Asian dish made from LENTILS or other PULSES (= seeds from certain plants) 印度扁豆（菜肴）

dhania /ˈdɑːniə/ *noun* [U] (*EAfrE, IndE, SAfrE*) the leaves or seeds of the CORIANDER plant, used to flavour food 香菜葉，香菜籽（用作調味料）

dhan·sak /ˈdʌnsɑːk; ˈdænsæk/ *noun* an Indian meat or vegetable dish cooked with LENTILS and CORIANDER 兵豆香菜燉肉，炒兵豆香菜（印度菜肴）

dharma /ˈdɑːmə; *NAmE* ˈdɑːr-/ *noun* [U] (in Indian religion 印度宗教) truth or law that affects the whole universe 法，達摩（影響整個宇宙的真理或規則）

dharna /ˈdɜːnə; -nɑː; *NAmE* ˈdɜːrn-/ *noun* (*IndE*) **1** an act of lying flat on the floor with your face down as an act of worship in a TEMPLE 達爾那（在寺廟中伏地朝拜）**2** a form of protest in which a group of people refuse to leave a factory, public place, etc. 靜坐抗議

dhoti /ˈdəʊti; *NAmE* ˈdoʊti/ *noun* a long piece of cloth worn by Hindu men. It is sometimes tied round the waist, with the lower part passed between the legs and put into the cloth at the back, so that the knees are usually covered.（印度男子的）腰布

dhow /daʊ/ *noun* an Arab ship with one large sail in the shape of a triangle 阿拉伯三角帆船

dhurrie (also **durrie**) /ˈdʌri/ *noun* a heavy cotton RUG (= small carpet) from S Asia 達里（南亞產小塊厚棉地毯）

DI /ˌdiː ˈaɪ/ *abbr.* Detective Inspector (a British police officer of middle rank) 探長（英國中級警官）：*DI Ross* 羅斯探長

di- /daɪ/ *combining form* (*chemistry* 化) (in nouns that are names of chemical COMPOUNDS 構成化合物名詞) containing two atoms or groups of the type mentioned 含有兩個原子的；含有兩組…物質的：*carbon dioxide* 二氧化碳

dia·betes /ˌdaɪəˈbiːtiːz/ *noun* [U] a medical condition which makes the patient produce a lot of URINE and feel very thirsty. There are several types of diabetes. 糖尿病；多尿症

dia·bet·ic /ˌdaɪəˈbetɪk/ *adj., noun*
▪ ***adj.*** **1** having or connected with diabetes 糖尿病的；患糖尿病的：*She's diabetic.* 她患有糖尿病。◇ *a diabetic patient* 糖尿病患者 ◇ *diabetic complications* 糖尿病併發症 **2** suitable for or used by sb who has diabetes 適合糖尿病患者的；專供糖尿病患者吃的：*a diabetic diet* 適合糖尿病患者的飲食
▪ ***noun*** a person who suffers from DIABETES 糖尿病患者

dia·bol·ical /ˌdaɪəˈbɒlɪkl; *NAmE* -ˈbɑːl-/ *adj.* **1** (*informal, especially BrE*) extremely bad or annoying 糟糕透頂的；煩人的；討厭的 **SYN** **terrible**：*The traffic was diabolical.* 交通狀況糟糕透了。**2** (also *less frequent* **dia·bol·ic** /ˌdaɪəˈbɒlɪk; *NAmE* -ˈbɑːl-/) morally bad and evil; like a DEVIL 道德敗壞的；邪惡的；惡魔似的 ▸ **dia·bol·ic·al·ly** /-kli/ *adv.*

dia·chron·ic /ˌdaɪəˈkrɒnɪk; *NAmE* -ˈkrɑːn-/ *adj.* (*technical* 術語) relating to the way sth, especially a language, has developed over time（尤指語言研究）歷時的 ➲ compare SYNCHRONIC

dia·crit·ic /ˌdaɪəˈkrɪtɪk/ *noun* (*linguistics* 語言) a mark such as an accent, placed over, under or through a letter in some languages, to show that the letter should be pronounced in a different way from the same letter without a mark 附加符號（置於字母上方、下方或穿過字母，表示發音不同，如重音符號）▸ **dia·crit·ic·al** /-ˈkrɪtɪkl/ *adj.*：*diacritical marks* 變音符

D

dia·dem /ˈdaɪədem/ *noun* a crown, worn especially as a sign of royal power 王冠；冕

di·aer·esis (*BrE*) (*US* **di·er·esis**) /daɪˈerəsɪs/ (*pl.* **di·aer·eses**, **di·er·eses** /-siːz/) *noun* (*technical* 術語) the mark placed over a vowel to show that it is pronounced separately, as in *naïve* 分音符（標在元音上面，表示單獨發音，如 naïve）

diag·nose /ˈdaɪəgnəʊz; ˌdaɪəgˈnəʊz; *NAmE* -ˈnoʊs/ *verb* [T, I] to say exactly what an illness or the cause of a problem is 診斷（疾病）；判斷（問題的原因）：**~ (sth)** *The test is used to diagnose a variety of diseases.* 此項化驗可用於診斷多種疾病。◇ **~ sth as sth** *The illness was diagnosed as cancer.* 此病診斷為癌症。◇ **~ sb with sth** *He has recently been diagnosed with angina.* 他最近被診斷出患有心絞痛。◇ **~ sb (as) sth** *He was diagnosed (as) a diabetic when he was 64.* 他 64 歲時被診斷患有糖尿病。◇ **~ sb + adj./noun** *He was diagnosed (a) diabetic.* 他被診斷患有糖尿病。➲ COLLOCATIONS at ILL

diag·no·sis /ˌdaɪəgˈnəʊsɪs; *NAmE* -ˈnoʊ-/ *noun* [C, U] (*pl.* **diag·noses** /-siːz/) **~ (of sth)** the act of discovering or identifying the exact cause of an illness or a problem 診斷；（問題原因的）判斷：*diagnosis of lung cancer* 肺癌的診斷 ◇ *They are waiting for the doctor's diagnosis.* 他們正在等待醫生的診斷結果。◇ *An accurate* ***diagnosis was made*** *after a series of tests.* 準確的診斷是在一系列的化驗後作出的。

diag·nos·tic /ˌdaɪəgˈnɒstɪk; *NAmE* -ˈnɑːs-/ *adj., noun*
▪ ***adj.*** [usually before noun] (*technical* 術語) connected with identifying sth, especially an illness 診斷的；判斷的：*to carry out* ***diagnostic assessments/tests*** 進行診斷性評估／化驗 ◇ *specific conditions which are diagnostic of AIDS* 診斷為艾滋病的具體症狀
▪ ***noun*** (*computing* 計) **1** (also **ˌdiagˈnostic program**) [C] a program used for identifying a computer fault 診斷程序，診斷程式（診斷計算機的錯誤）**2** [C] a message on a computer screen giving information about a fault 診斷提示（計算機錯誤的顯示）**3** **diagnostics** [U] the practice or methods of diagnosis 診斷；診斷法

di·ag·onal /daɪˈægənl/ *adj., noun*
▪ ***adj.*** (of a straight line 直線) at an angle; joining two opposite sides of sth at an angle 斜線的；對角線的：*diagonal stripes* 斜紋 ▸ **di·ag·onal·ly** /-nəli/ *adv.*：*Walk diagonally across the field to the far corner and then turn left.* 斜着穿過這塊地到遠處的拐角處，然後朝左轉。
▪ ***noun*** a straight line that joins two opposite sides of sth at an angle; a straight line that is at an angle 對角線；斜線

dia·gram 0→ /ˈdaɪəgræm/ *noun*
a simple drawing using lines to explain where sth is, how sth works, etc. 簡圖；圖解；圖表；示意圖：*a diagram of the wiring system* 線路系統圖 ◇ *The results are shown in diagram 2.* 結果顯示在表 2 上。▸ **dia·gram·mat·ic** /ˌdaɪəgrəˈmætɪk/ *adj.* **dia·gram·mat·ic·al·ly** /-kli/ *adv.*

dial /ˈdaɪəl/ *noun, verb*
▪ ***noun*** **1** the face of a clock or watch, or a similar control on a machine, piece of equipment or vehicle that shows a measurement of time, amount, speed, temperature, etc. 錶盤；刻度盤；標度盤；儀表盤：*an alarm clock with a luminous dial* 夜光鬧鐘 ◇ *Check the tyre pressure on the dial.* 檢查一下儀表盤顯示的車胎壓力。➲ see also SUNDIAL **2** the round control on a radio, cooker/stove, etc. that you turn in order to adjust sth, for example to choose a particular station or to choose a particular temperature（收音機、爐、灶等的）調節盤，控制盤 **3** the round part on some older telephones, with holes for the fingers, that you move around to call a

particular number（舊式電話機的）撥號盤

■ *verb* (-ll-, *NAmE* -l-) [T, I] **~** (sth) to use a telephone by pushing buttons or turning the dial to call a number 撥（電話號碼）：*He dialled the number and waited.* 他撥號後便等着通話。◇ *Dial 0033 for France.* 打電話到法國撥 0033。➲ COLLOCATIONS at PHONE

dia·lect /ˈdaɪəlekt/ *noun* [C, U] the form of a language that is spoken in one area with grammar, words and pronunciation that may be different from other forms of the same language 地方話；土話；方言：*the Yorkshire dialect* 約克郡方言 ➲ compare ACCENT *n.* (1), IDIOLECT ▸ **dia·lect·al** /ˌdaɪəˈlektl/ *adj.*

dia·lect·ic /ˌdaɪəˈlektɪk/ *noun* [sing.] (also *less frequent* **dia·lect·ics** [U]) **1** (*philosophy* 哲) a method of discovering the truth of ideas by discussion and logical argument and by considering ideas that are opposed to each other 辯證法 **2** (*formal*) the way in which two aspects of a situation affect each other 對立（一個情況的兩個方面彼此影響）▸ **dia·lect·ic·al** /-kl/ *adj.*

dia,lectical ma'terialism *noun* [U] (*philosophy* 哲) the Marxist theory that all change results from opposing social forces, which come into conflict because of material needs 辯證唯物主義（馬克思主義理論，認為所有變化都由相對立的社會力量引起，而對立源於物質需求產生的衝突）

dial·ler (*BrE*) (*NAmE* **dial·er**) /ˈdaɪələ(r)/ *noun* a computer program or piece of equipment which calls telephone numbers automatically 自動撥號程序；自動撥號器

'dialling code (also **code**) *noun* (*BrE*) the numbers that are used for a particular town, area or country, in front of an individual telephone number（電話的）區號：*international dialling codes* 國際區號 ➲ compare AREA CODE

'dialling tone (*BrE*) (*NAmE* **'dial tone**) *noun* the sound that you hear when you pick up a telephone that means you can make a call（電話的）撥號音

'dialog box (*BrE* also **'dialogue box**) *noun* a box that appears on a computer screen asking the user to choose what they want to do next（計算機屏幕上的）對話窗，對話框 ➲ VISUAL VOCAB page V67

dia·logue (*NAmE* also **dia·log**) /ˈdaɪəlɒɡ; *NAmE* -lɑːɡ; -lɔːɡ/ *noun* [C, U] **1** conversations in a book, play, or film/movie（書、戲劇或電影中的）對話，對白：*The novel has long descriptions and not much dialogue.* 這部小說描述多對話少。◇ *dialogues for language learners* 供語言學習者學習的對話 ➲ SYNONYMS at DISCUSSION **2** a formal discussion between two groups or countries, especially when they are trying to solve a problem, end a disagreement, etc.（尤指集體或國家間為解決問題、結束爭端等進行的）對話：*The President told waiting reporters there had been a constructive dialogue.* 總統告訴等候的記者，剛才進行了一次富有建設性的對話。➲ compare MONOLOGUE

'dial-up *adj.* [only before noun] using a telephone line and a MODEM to connect your computer to the Internet 撥號上網的

di·aly·sis /ˌdaɪˈæləsɪs/ *noun* [U] (*technical* 術語) a process for separating substances from a liquid, especially for taking waste substances out of the blood of people with damaged KIDNEYS 滲析，透析（尤指將廢物從腎病病人的血液中分離出來）：***kidney/renal dialysis*** 腎透析 ◇ *a dialysis machine* 透析機

dia·manté /ˌdiːəˈmɒnteɪ; *NAmE* ˌdiːəmɑːnˈteɪ/ *adj.* decorated with glass that is cut to look like diamonds 鑲嵌鑽石狀玻璃飾品的；珠光的：*diamanté earrings* 珠光耳環

dia·man·tine /ˌdaɪəˈmæntiːn/ *adj.* (*technical* 術語) **1** made from, or looking like, diamonds（像）鑽石的 **2** very hard or strong 堅硬的；堅固的

diam·eter /daɪˈæmɪtə(r)/ *noun* **1** a straight line going from one side of a circle or any other round object to the other side, passing through the centre 直徑；對徑：*the diameter of a tree trunk* 樹幹的直徑 ◇ *The dome is 42.3 metres **in diameter**.* 這個穹頂直徑為 42.3 米。➲ VISUAL VOCAB page V71 ➲ compare RADIUS (1) **2** (*technical* 術語) a measurement of the power of an instrument to MAGNIFY sth 放大率；放大倍數：*a lens magnifying 300 diameters* (= making sth look 300 times larger than it really is) 放大 300 倍的透鏡

dia·met·ric·al /ˌdaɪəˈmetrɪkl/ *adj.* [usually before noun] **1** used to emphasize that people or things are completely different 截然相反的；完全不同的：*He's the **diametrical opposite** of his brother.* 他和他的弟弟截然不同。**2** relating to the DIAMETER of sth 直徑的

dia·met·ric·al·ly /ˌdaɪəˈmetrɪkli/ *adv.* **~ opposed/opposite** completely different 完全（不同）；截然（相反）：*We hold diametrically opposed views.* 我們的觀點大相逕庭。

dia·mond 🔑 /ˈdaɪəmənd/ *noun*
1 🔑 [U, C] a clear PRECIOUS STONE of pure CARBON, the hardest substance known. Diamonds are used in jewellery and also in industry, especially for cutting glass. 金剛石；鑽石：*a ring with a diamond in it* 鑽石戒指 ◇ *a **diamond ring/necklace*** 鑽石戒指 / 項鏈 ◇ *She was wearing her diamonds* (= jewellery with diamonds in it). 她戴着鑽石首飾。◇ *The lights shone like diamonds.* 燈光像鑽石一樣閃閃發亮。➲ see also ROUGH DIAMOND **2** 🔑 [C] a shape with four straight sides of equal length and with angles that are not RIGHT ANGLES 菱形 **3 diamonds** [pl., U] one of the four SUITS (= sets) in a PACK/DECK of cards. The cards are marked with red diamond shapes.（紙牌的）方塊：*the ten of diamonds* 方塊十 ➲ VISUAL VOCAB page V37 **4** [C] a card of this SUIT（一張）方塊牌：*You must play a diamond if you have one.* 如果你有方塊就必須出。**5** [C] (in BASEBALL 棒球) the space inside the lines that connect the four BASES; also used to mean the whole BASEBALL field 內場；棒球場

,dia·mond in the 'rough (*NAmE*) *noun* a person who has many good qualities even though they do not seem to be very polite, educated, etc. 外粗內秀的人

,dia·mond 'ju·bi·lee *noun* [usually sing.] the 60th anniversary of an important event, especially of sb becoming king/queen; a celebration of this event 鑽石大慶，60 週年慶典（尤指國王或女王登基 60 週年紀念日）➲ compare GOLDEN JUBILEE, SILVER JUBILEE

,dia·mond 'wed·ding (*BrE*) (*NAmE* **,dia·mond an·ni·'ver·sary**) (also **,dia·mond 'wed·ding an·ni·ver·sary** *NAmE, BrE*) *noun* the 60th anniversary of a wedding 鑽石婚（結婚 60 週年紀念）➲ compare GOLDEN WEDDING, RUBY WEDDING, SILVER WEDDING

dia·mor·phine /ˌdaɪəˈmɔːfiːn; *NAmE* -ˈmɔːrf-/ *noun* [U] a powerful drug that is made from OPIUM and used to reduce pain 二乙酰嗎啡，海洛因（用以鎮痛）

di·aper /ˈdaɪəpə(r); *NAmE* ˈdaɪpər/ (*NAmE*) *noun* a piece of soft cloth or other thick material that is folded around a baby's bottom and between its legs to absorb and hold its body waste 尿布：*a diaper rash* 尿布疹

di·aph·an·ous /daɪˈæfənəs/ *adj.* (*formal*) (of cloth 布料) so light and fine that you can almost see through it 輕柔細密的；半透明的

dia·phragm /ˈdaɪəfræm/ *noun* **1** (*anatomy* 解) the layer of muscle between the lungs and the stomach, used especially to control breathing 膈；膈膜；橫膈膜 **2** (*BrE* also **cap**) a rubber or plastic device that a woman places inside her VAGINA before having sex to prevent SPERM from entering the WOMB and making her pregnant 子宮帽（避孕用具）**3** any thin piece of material used to separate the parts of a machine, etc.（機器等的）隔膜，隔板 **4** (*technical* 術語) a thin disc used to turn electronic signals into sound and sound into electronic signals in telephones, LOUDSPEAKERS, etc.（電話機、揚聲器等的）膜片，膜件，振動膜

diar·ist /ˈdaɪərɪst/ *noun* a person who writes a diary, especially one that is later published 日記作者；日誌記載者：*Samuel Pepys, the famous 17th century diarist* 塞繆爾•佩皮斯，17 世紀著名的日記作者

diar·rhoea (*BrE*) (*NAmE* **diar·rhea**) /ˌdaɪəˈrɪə; *NAmE* -ˈriːə/ (also *informal* **the runs**) *noun* [U] an illness in which waste matter is emptied from the BOWELS much more frequently than normal, and in liquid form 腹瀉：

Symptoms include diarrhoea and vomiting. 症狀有腹瀉和嘔吐。

diary /ˈdaɪəri/ *noun* (*pl.* **-ies**)
1 (*BrE*) (*NAmE* **date·book**) a book with spaces for each day of the year in which you can write down things you have to do in the future（工作日程）記事簿：*a desk diary* 枱式記事簿 ◇ *I'll make a note of our next meeting in my diary.* 我將把下次會議的事記在我的記事簿上。➲ VISUAL VOCAB page V69 **2** a book in which you can write down the experiences you have each day, your private thoughts, etc. 日記；日記簿：*Do you **keep a diary**?* (= write one regularly)? 你有寫日記嗎？➲ see also JOURNAL (3), VIDEO DIARY ➲ note at AGENDA

dias·pora /daɪˈæspərə/ *noun* [sing.] (*formal*) **1 the dias·pora** the movement of the Jewish people away from their own country to live and work in other countries（猶太人的）大流散 **2** the movement of people from any nation or group away from their own country（任何民族或群體的）大移居

di·atom·ic /ˌdaɪəˈtɒmɪk; *NAmE* -ˈtɑːmɪk/ *adj.* (*chemistry* 化) consisting of two atoms 雙原子的

dia·ton·ic /ˌdaɪəˈtɒnɪk; *NAmE* -ˈtɑːn-/ *adj.* (*music* 音) using only the notes of the appropriate MAJOR or MINOR SCALE 用自然音階的 ➲ compare CHROMATIC

dia·tribe /ˈdaɪətraɪb/ *noun* ~ (**against sb/sth**) (*formal*) a long and angry speech or piece of writing attacking and criticizing sb/sth（無休止的）指責；（長篇）抨擊，譴責：*He launched a bitter diatribe against the younger generation.* 他對年輕一代發起了猛烈的抨擊。

di·aze·pam /daɪˈæzəpæm/ *noun* [U] (*medical* 醫) a drug that is used to make people feel less anxious and more relaxed 苯甲二氮䓬；安定

dibs /dɪbz/
IDM **dibs on …** (*NAmE*) (*BrE* **bags (I) …**) (*informal*) used to claim sth as yours before sb else can claim it …是我的；我要求…

dice /daɪs/ *noun, verb*
▪ **noun** (*pl.* **dice**) **1** (also **die** especially in *NAmE*) [C] a small CUBE of wood, plastic, etc., with a different number of spots on each of its sides, used in games of chance 骰子；色子：*a pair of dice* 一對骰子 ◇ *to **roll/throw/shake the dice*** 滾／擲／搖骰子 **2** [U] a game played with dice 擲骰遊戲；擲骰賭博：*We played dice all night.* 我們擲了一夜的骰子。➲ VISUAL VOCAB page V38
IDM **no ˈdice** (*informal, especially NAmE*) used to show that you refuse to do sth, or that sth cannot be done（表示拒絕做或某事做不成）不行，不成，沒門兒：*'Did you get that job?' 'No dice.'* "你得到那份工作了嗎？" "沒門兒啊。" ➲ more at LOAD *v.*
▪ **verb** ~ **sth** to cut meat, vegetables, etc. into small square pieces 將（肉、菜等）切成小方塊；將…切成丁：*diced carrots* 胡蘿蔔丁 ➲ VISUAL VOCAB page V28
IDM **dice with death** (*informal*) to risk your life by doing sth that you know is dangerous 冒生命危險；玩命

dicey /ˈdaɪsi/ *adj.* (*informal*) uncertain and dangerous 沒把握的；不可靠的；危險的 SYN **risky**

di·chot·omy /daɪˈkɒtəmi; *NAmE* -ˈkɑːt-/ *noun* [usually sing.] (*pl.* **-ies**) ~ (**between A and B**) (*formal*) the separation that exists between two groups or things that are completely opposite to and different from each other 一分為二；二分法

dick /dɪk/ *noun* (*taboo, slang*) **1** a man's PENIS 雞巴；屌 **2** = DICKHEAD ➲ see also CLEVER DICK

dick·ens /ˈdɪkɪnz/ *noun* **the dickens** (*old-fashioned, informal*) **1** used in questions instead of 'devil' to show that you are annoyed or surprised（用於問句代替 devil，表示煩惱或吃驚）究竟，到底：*Where the dickens did he go?* 他究竟上哪兒去了？**2** (*NAmE*) used when you are saying how attractive, etc. sb is（某人）…極了，太…了，多麼…啊：*cute as the dickens* 可愛極了

Dick·ens·ian /dɪˈkenziən/ *adj.* connected with or typical of the novels of Charles Dickens, which often describe social problems and bad social conditions 狄更斯文體的；具有狄更斯小說特點的；類似狄更斯筆下描述的：*a Dickensian slum* 類似狄更斯筆下的貧民窟

dicker /ˈdɪkə(r)/ *verb* [I] ~ (**with sb**) (**over sth**) (*especially NAmE*) to argue about or discuss sth with sb, especially in order to agree on a price 討價還價；議價；講價 SYN **bargain**

dick·head /ˈdɪkhed/ (also **dick**) *noun* (*taboo, slang*) a very rude way of referring to sb, especially a man, that you think is stupid 笨蛋，蠢貨，蠢傢伙（尤用於辱罵男性）SYN **idiot**

D

dicky /ˈdɪki/ *adj., noun*
▪ **adj.** (*old-fashioned, BrE, informal*) not healthy; not working correctly 虛弱的；有病的；工作不正常的：*a dicky heart* 虛弱的心臟
▪ **noun** (also **dickey**) (*pl.* **dickies** or **dickeys**) (*IndE*) the BOOT/TRUNK of a car（汽車後部的）行李廂

ˈdicky bird *noun* (*BrE*) (used by or when speaking to young children 兒語) a bird 鳥兒；小鳥兒
IDM **not say, hear, etc. a dicky bird** (*BrE, informal*) to say, hear, etc. nothing 什麼也沒說（或沒聽見等）：*He won't say a dicky bird, but we think he knows who did it.* 他什麼都不肯說，但是我們認為他知道是誰幹的。ORIGIN This idiom is from rhyming slang, in which 'dicky bird' stands for 'word'. 源自同韻俚語，其中 dicky bird（小鳥兒）代表 word。

di·coty·ledon /ˌdaɪkɒtɪˈliːdən; *NAmE* -kɑːt-/ (also **dicot** /ˈdaɪkɒt; *NAmE* -kɑːt/) *noun* (*biology* 生) a plant whose seeds form EMBRYOS that produce two leaves 雙子葉植物 ➲ compare MONOCOTYLEDON

Dicta·phone™ /ˈdɪktəfəʊn; *NAmE* -foʊn/ *noun* a small machine used to record people speaking, so that their words can be played back later and written down 口述錄音機

dic·tate *verb, noun*
▪ **verb** /dɪkˈteɪt; *NAmE* ˈdɪkteɪt/ **1** [T, I] ~ (**sth**) (**to sb**) to say words for sb else to write down 口述：*He dictated a letter to his secretary.* 他向秘書口授信稿。**2** [T] to tell sb what to do, especially in an annoying way（尤指以令人厭煩的方式）指使，強行規定：~ **sth** (**to sb**) *They are in no position to **dictate terms*** (= tell other people what to do). 他們沒有資格發號施令。◇ ~ **how, what, etc. …/that …** *What right do they have to dictate how we live our lives?* 他們有什麼權利強行規定我們該怎樣生活？**3** [T, I] to control or influence how sth happens 支配；擺佈；決定 SYN **determine**：~ (**sth**) *When we take our vacations is very much dictated by Greg's work schedule.* 我們什麼時候休假在很大程度上取決於格雷格的工作時間安排。◇ ~ **where, what, etc. …** *It's generally your job that dictates where you live now.* 一般說來，你住在什麼地方是由你的工作決定的。◇ ~ **that …** *The social conventions of the day dictated that she should remain at home with her parents.* 那時的社會習俗規定她必須留在家裏，與她父母在一起。
PHR V **dicˈtate to sb** [often passive] to give orders to sb, often in a rude or aggressive way 任意指使某人；向某人發號施令：*She refused to be dictated to by anyone.* 她不願受任何人擺佈。
▪ **noun** /ˈdɪkteɪt/ [usually pl.] (*formal*) an order or a rule that you must obey 命令；規定：*to follow the dictates of fashion* 趕時髦

dic·ta·tion /dɪkˈteɪʃn/ *noun* **1** [U] the act of speaking or reading so that sb can write down the words 口述 **2** [C, U] a test in which students write down what is being read to them, especially in language lessons 聽寫

dic·ta·tor /dɪkˈteɪtə(r); *NAmE* ˈdɪkteɪtər/ *noun* (*disapproving*) **1** a ruler who has complete power over a country, especially one who has gained it using military force 獨裁者 **2** a person who behaves as if they have complete power over other people, and tells them what to do 發號施令者；專橫的人

dic·ta·tor·ial /ˌdɪktəˈtɔːriəl/ *adj.* (*disapproving*) **1** connected with or controlled by a dictator 獨裁的；專政的：*a dictatorial ruler* 獨裁統治者 ◇ *a dictatorial regime* 獨裁政權 **2** using power in an unreasonable way by telling people what to do and not listening to their views or wishes 發號施令的；專橫的；盛氣凌人的：

dictatorial behaviour 專橫的行為 ▸ **dic·ta·tori·al·ly** /-əli/ *adv.*

dic·ta·tor·ship /ˌdɪk'teɪtəʃɪp; *NAmE* -tərʃ-/ *noun* **1** [C, U] government by a dictator 獨裁；專政 ➲ COLLOCATIONS at POLITICS **2** [C] a country that is ruled by a dictator 獨裁國家

D

dic·tion /'dɪkʃn/ *noun* [U] **1** the way that sb pronounces words 吐字；發音方式：*clear diction* 清晰的吐字 **2** (*technical* 術語) the choice and use of words in literature 措辭；用語；用詞

dic·tion·ary 🔑 /'dɪkʃənri; *NAmE* -neri/ *noun* (*pl.* **-ies**) **1** 🔑 a book that gives a list of the words of a language in alphabetical order and explains what they mean, or gives a word for them in a foreign language 詞典；字典；辭書：*a Spanish-English dictionary* 西班牙語－英語詞典 **2** a book that explains the words that are used in a particular subject 專業術語大全；專業詞典：*a dictionary of mathematics* 數學詞典 **3** a list of words in electronic form, for example stored in a computer's SPELLCHECKER 電子詞典

dic·tum /'dɪktəm/ *noun* (*pl.* **dicta** /-tə/ or **dic·tums**) (*formal*) a statement that expresses sth that people believe is always true or should be followed 名言；格言

did /dɪd/ ➲ DO[1]

di·dac·tic /daɪ'dæktɪk/ *adj.* (*formal*) **1** designed to teach people sth, especially a moral lesson 道德說教的；教誨的；教導的：*didactic art* 道德說教藝術 **2** (usually *disapproving*) telling people things rather than letting them find out for themselves 說教似的；好教訓人的 ▸ **di·dac·tic·al·ly** /-kli/ *adv.*

did·dle /'dɪdl/ *verb* **~ sb (out of sth)** (*BrE, informal*) to get money or some advantage from sb by cheating them 欺騙；哄騙；騙取 SYN **cheat**

diddly /'dɪdli/ (also **ˌdiddly-'squat**) *noun* (*NAmE, informal*) (used in negative sentences 用於否定句) not anything; nothing 一點也不；毫不；根本不：*She doesn't know diddly about it.* 她根本不知道這事兒。

did·dums /'dɪdəmz/ *exclamation, noun* (*BrE, informal*)
■ ***exclamation*** used for showing sympathy, especially in a way which is not sincere（表示同情，尤指不真心地）好啦，乖
■ ***noun*** used when addressing sb to show sympathy, especially when you are not being sincere（用作稱呼以示同情，尤指不真心地）小可憐，小乖乖：*Is Diddums OK?* 小可憐沒事了吧？

diddy /'dɪdi/ *adj.* (*BrE, informal*) very small 很小的；袖珍的：*a diddy little camera* 袖珍照相機

didg·eri·doo /ˌdɪdʒəri'du:/ *noun* (*pl.* **-oos**) an Australian musical instrument consisting of a long wooden tube which you blow through to produce a variety of deep sounds 狄潔里都號角（澳大利亞土著用的低沉音木管樂器）

didi /'di:di:/ *noun* (*IndE*) **1** an older sister 姐姐：*Didi taught me how to read.* 姐姐教我讀書。 **2** used after the name of an older female cousin of the same generation（用於堂、表姐名字後）姐 **3** used when speaking to an older female who is not related to you, as a title showing respect（尊稱比自己年齡大的女子）姐：*Didi, could you help me with this bag?* 大姐，幫我抬一下這個袋子好嗎？

didn't /'dɪdnt/ *short form* did not

die 🔑 /daɪ/ *verb, noun*
■ ***verb*** (**dies, dying, died, died**) **1** 🔑 [I, T] to stop living 死；死亡；凋謝：*Her husband died suddenly last week.* 她的丈夫上週猝死。◇ *That plant's died.* 那植物已經枯萎。◇ **~ of/from sth** *to die of/from cancer* 死於癌症 ◇ **~ for sth** *He died for his beliefs.* 他為自己的信仰獻身。◇ *I'll never forget it* **to my dying day** (= until I die). 我將終生不忘。◇ (*informal*) ***I nearly died*** *when I saw him there* (= it was very embarrassing). 看到他在那裏我簡直無地自容。◇ **~ sth** *to die a violent/painful/natural, etc. death* 橫死、痛苦地死去、盡其天年等 ◇ **+ adj.** *She died young.* 她年紀輕輕就死了。◇ *At least they died happy.* 至少他們死時很幸福。◇ **+ noun** *He died a poor man.* 他在貧困中死去。 **2** 🔑 [I] to stop existing; to disappear 消失；消亡；滅亡：*The old customs are dying.* 舊的習俗正在消亡。◇ *His secret died with him* (= he never told anyone). 他的秘密隨同他一起進了墳墓。◇ *The words died on my lips* (= I stopped speaking). 我話到嘴邊又縮回去了。 **3** [I] (of a machine 機器) to stop working 停止運轉：*The engine spluttered and died.* 發動機劈劈啪啪響了一陣後便熄火了。◇ *My car just* ***died on me.*** 我的汽車開着開着就壞了。

IDM **be 'dying for sth/to do sth** 🔑 (*informal*) to want sth or want to do sth very much 渴望；極想：*I'm dying for a glass of water.* 我真想喝杯水。◇ *I'm dying to know what happened.* 我很想知道發生了什麼事兒。 **die a/the 'death** (*BrE, informal*) to fail completely 徹底失敗；完全消失：*The play got terrible reviews and quickly died a death.* 這齣戲被批得一無是處，很快就收場了。 **die in your 'bed** to die because you are old or ill/sick 壽終正寢 **die 'laughing** to find sth extremely funny 可笑極了；笑死人：*I nearly died laughing when she said that.* 她說那話時，我差點給笑死。 **old ˌhabits, ˌtraditions, etc. die 'hard** used to say that things change very slowly（舊習慣、傳統等）難以改變，根深蒂固 **to 'die for** (*informal*) if you think sth is **to die for**, you really want it, and would do anything to get it 就是去死也要；不管怎麼樣都要：*She was wearing a dress to die for.* 她穿了一條漂亮得要命的連衣裙。 ➲ more at CROSS *v.*, FLY *n.*, SAY *v.*

PHR V **ˌdie a'way** 🔑 to become gradually weaker or fainter and finally disappear 逐漸減弱；逐漸模糊；逐漸消失：*The sound of their laughter died away.* 他們的笑聲漸漸消失了。 **ˌdie 'back** if a plant **dies back**, it loses its leaves but remains alive（植物）葉凋而不死 **ˌdie 'down** to become gradually less strong, loud, noticeable, etc. 逐漸變弱；逐漸平息；逐漸暗淡：*The flames finally died down.* 火焰越來越小，最後熄滅了。◇ *When the applause had died down, she began her speech.* 掌聲平息後她便開始演講了。 **ˌdie 'off** to die one after the other until there are none left 相繼死去；先後死去 **ˌdie 'out** 🔑 to stop existing 滅絕；消失：*This species has nearly died out because its habitat is being destroyed.* 因棲息地正受到破壞，這一物種已瀕於滅絕。

■ ***noun*** **1** a block of metal with a special shape, or with a pattern cut into it, that is used for shaping other pieces of metal such as coins, or for making patterns on paper or leather 模具；衝模；壓模 **2** (*especially NAmE*) = DICE (1)

IDM **the die is cast** (*saying*) used to say that an event has happened or a decision has been made that cannot be changed 事已成定局；木已成舟

'die-cast *adj.* (of a metal object 金屬物品) made by pouring liquid metal into a MOULD and allowing it to cool 壓鑄成形的

die·hard /'daɪhɑ:d; *NAmE* -hɑ:rd/ *adj.* strongly opposing change and new ideas 頑固的；因循守舊的；死硬的：*diehard supporters of the exiled king* 頑固支持流亡國王的人 ▸ **die·hard** *noun*：*A few diehards are trying to stop the reforms.* 有些頑固分子試圖阻止改革。

diesel /'di:zl/ *noun* **1** (also **'diesel fuel**, **'diesel oil**) [U] a type of heavy oil used as a fuel instead of petrol/gas 柴油：*a* ***diesel engine*** (= one that burns diesel) 柴油發動機 ◇ ***diesel cars/locomotives/trains*** 柴油汽車／機車／火車 ➲ compare PETROL **2** [C] a vehicle that uses diesel fuel 柴油車；內燃機車：*Our new car is a diesel.* 我們的新車是柴油車。

diet 🔑 /'daɪət/ *noun, verb*
■ ***noun*** **1** 🔑 [C, U] the food that you eat and drink regularly 日常飲食；日常食物：*to have a* ***healthy, balanced diet*** 有健康和均衡的飲食 ◇ *the Japanese diet of rice, vegetables and fish* 米飯、蔬菜和魚這些日本人常吃的食物 ◇ *to receive advice on diet* 接受飲食建議 **2** 🔑 [C] a limited variety or amount of food that you eat for medical reasons or because you want to lose weight; a time when you only eat this limited variety or amount 規定飲食（為健康或減肥等目的）；規定飲食的時期：*a* ***low-fat, salt-free diet*** 低脂肪無鹽的飲食 ◇ ***diet drinks*** (= with fewer CALORIES than normal) 低熱量飲料 ◇ *I decided to* ***go on a diet*** (= to lose weight) *before my*

holiday. 我決定在休假前節食。 **3** [sing.] **a ~ of sth** (*disapproving*) a large amount of a restricted range of activities 大量單調的活動；大量單一的東西： *Children today are brought up on a diet of television cartoons and soap operas.* 如今的孩子是看電視上的動畫片和肥皂劇長大的。 ▶ **diet·ary** /ˈdaɪətəri; *NAmE* -teri/ *adj.* [usually before noun]： ***dietary advice/changes/habits*** 飲食建議／變化／習慣 ◇ *dietary fibre* 飲食纖維素

■ ***verb*** [I] to eat less food or only food of a particular type in order to lose weight 節食；進行規定飲食 SYN **be on a diet**： *She's always dieting but she never seems to lose any weight.* 她總是在節食，但體重好像並未減少。

diet·er /ˈdaɪətə(r)/ *noun* a person who is trying to lose weight on a diet 節食者；限制飲食的人

diet·et·ics /ˌdaɪəˈtetɪks/ *noun* [U] the scientific study of diet and healthy eating 飲食學 ▶ **diet·et·ic** *adj.*： *dietetic advice* 飲食建議

diet·itian (also **diet·ician**) /ˌdaɪəˈtɪʃn/ *noun* a person whose job is to advise people on what kind of food they should eat to keep healthy 營養學家

dif·fer /ˈdɪfə(r)/ *verb* **1** [I] to be different from sb/sth 相異；有區別；不同於：*They hold differing views.* 他們持有不同的觀點。◇ **A ~s from B** *French differs from English in this respect.* 在這方面法語不同於英語。◇ **A and B ~** (**from each other**) *French and English differ in this respect.* 在這方面法語和英語不同。◇ **~ between A and B** *Ideas on childcare may differ considerably between the parents.* 在撫育兒童方面父母的觀點可能迥然不同。 ➲ LANGUAGE BANK at CONTRAST **2** [I] to disagree with sb 意見相左；持不同看法；不同意： **~ (with sb) (about/on/over sth)** *I have to differ with you on that.* 在那一點上我不能同意你的看法。◇ **~ (as to sth)** *Medical opinion differs as to how to treat the disease.* 關於如何治療這種疾病醫學界有不同的看法。 IDM see AGREE, BEG

dif·fer·ence 0⁻ /ˈdɪfrəns/ *noun*

1 0⁻ [C, U] **~ (between A and B)** | **~ (in sth)** the way in which two people or things are not like each other; the way in which sb/sth has changed 差別；差異；不同（之處）；變化（之處）：*There are no significant differences between the education systems of the two countries.* 這兩國的教育制度沒有大的差別。◇ *He was studying the complex similarities and differences between humans and animals.* 他在研究人和動物之間錯綜複雜的相似與不同之處。◇ *There's no difference in the results.* 各種結果沒有差別。◇ *I can never **tell the difference*** (= distinguish) *between the twins.* 我從來都分不清這對雙胞胎。◇ *She noticed a **marked difference** in the children on her second visit.* 她第二次來訪時注意到孩子們發生了明顯的變化。◇ *There's **a world of difference** between liking someone and loving them.* 喜歡一個人和愛一個人有天壤之別。◇ ***What a difference!** You look great with your hair like that.* 真是判若兩人！你梳這種髮型顯得太好看了。 OPP **similarity** ➲ LANGUAGE BANK at CONTRAST

2 0⁻ [sing., U] **~ (in sth)** (**between A and B**) the amount that sth is greater or smaller than sth else 差；差額：*There's not much difference in price between the two computers.* 這兩種計算機價格上沒有多大的差別。◇

Collocations 詞語搭配

Diet and exercise 節食和鍛煉

Weight 體重

- **put on/gain/lose** weight/a few kilos/a few pounds 增加／減少體重／幾公斤／幾磅
- **watch/control/struggle with** your weight 關注／控制體重；努力減肥
- **be/become** seriously overweight/underweight 已經／變得嚴重超重／體重不足
- **be/become** clinically/morbidly obese 已經是／變成臨牀／病態肥胖
- **achieve/facilitate/promote/stimulate** weight loss 達到減輕體重的目的；促進減肥
- **slim down to** 70 kilos/(*BrE*) 11 stone/(*especially NAmE*) 160 pounds 減肥到 70 公斤／11 英石／160 磅
- **combat/prevent/tackle/treat** obesity 遏制／防止／解決／治療肥胖
- **develop/have/suffer from/struggle with/recover from** anorexia/bulimia/an eating disorder 患上／對抗／治癒厭食症／貪食症／飲食失調症
- **be on/go on/follow** a crash/strict diet 採用快速減肥食譜；嚴格節食
- **have/suffer from** a negative/poor body image 有不好的身體形象
- **have/develop** a positive/healthy body image 具有／促成好的／健康的身體形象

Healthy eating 健康的飲食

- **eat** a balanced diet/healthily/sensibly 吃得均衡／健康／合理
- **get/provide/receive** adequate/proper nutrition 獲得／提供／得到充足的／合適的營養
- **contain/get/provide** essential nutrients/vitamins/minerals 含有／得到／提供必需的營養素／維生素／礦物質
- **be high/low in** calories/fat/fibre/(*especially US*) fiber/protein/vitamin D/Omega-3 fatty acids 熱量／脂肪／纖維素／蛋白質／維生素 D／歐米加 3 脂肪酸含量高／低
- **contain (no)/use/be full of/be free from** additives/chemical preservatives/artificial sweeteners（不）含／使用／含有大量／不含添加劑／化學防腐劑／人工甜味劑
- **avoid/cut down on/cut out** alcohol/caffeine/fatty foods 避免攝取／減少／戒酒／咖啡因／高脂食物
- **stop/give up**/(*especially NAmE*) **quit** smoking 戒煙

Exercise 鍛煉

- (*BrE*) **take** regular exercise 經常鍛煉
- **do** moderate/strenuous/vigorous exercise 做適度／劇烈運動
- **play** football/hockey/tennis 玩足球／曲棍球／網球
- **go** cycling/jogging/running 騎自行車；慢跑；跑步
- **go to/visit**/(*especially NAmE*) **hit/work out at** the gym 去健身房鍛煉
- **strengthen/tone/train** your stomach muscles 增強／鍛煉腹肌
- **contract/relax/stretch/use/work** your lower-body muscles 收縮／放鬆／伸展／使用／鍛煉下肢的肌肉
- **build (up)/gain** muscle 增強肌肉
- **improve/increase** your stamina/energy levels/physical fitness 增強耐力／體能／體質
- **burn/consume/expend** calories 消耗熱量

Staying healthy 保持健康

- **be/get/keep/stay** healthy/in shape/(*especially BrE*) fit 身體健康；變得／保持健康
- **lower** your cholesterol/blood pressure 降低膽固醇／血壓
- **boost/stimulate/strengthen** your immune system 增強免疫力
- **prevent/reduce the risk of** heart disease/high blood pressure/diabetes/osteoporosis 預防／減少患心臟病／高血壓／糖尿病／骨質疏鬆的風險
- **reduce/relieve/manage/combat** stress 緩解／控制壓力
- **enhance/promote** relaxation/physical and mental well-being 有助於身體放鬆／身心健康

D

There's an age difference of six years between the boys (= one is six years older than the other). 這兩個男孩的年齡相差六歲。◇ *I'll lend you £500 and you'll have to find the difference* (= the rest of the money that you need). 我借給你 500 英鎊，其餘的你自己解決。◇ *We measured the difference in temperature.* 我們測量了溫度的變化。 **3** [C] a disagreement between people 意見分歧；不和： *We **have our differences**, but she's still my sister.* 我們之間雖然不和，但她仍舊是我的妹妹。◇ *Why don't you **settle your differences** and be friends again?* 你們為什麼不消除隔閡，言歸於好呢？◇ *There was **a difference of opinion** over who had won.* 在誰獲勝的問題上發生了爭執。

IDM **make a, no, some, etc. difference (to/in sb/sth)** 🔑 to have an effect/no effect on sb/sth 有（或沒有、有些等）作用，關係，影響： *The rain didn't make much difference to the game.* 這場雨對比賽沒多大影響。◇ *Your age shouldn't make any difference to whether you get the job or not.* 你能否得到這工作應該與你的年齡無關。◇ *Changing schools made a **big difference** to my life.* 轉學對我的一生有着重大影響。◇ *What difference will it make if he knows or not?* 他知不知道有什麼關係嗎？◇ *I don't think it makes **a lot of difference** what colour it is* (= it is not important). 我認為顏色無關緊要。◇ *'Shall we go on Friday or Saturday?' 'It makes no difference (to me).'* "我們星期五還是星期六去？" "（我）無所謂。" **make all the 'difference (to sb/sth)** to have an important effect on sb/sth; to make sb feel better 關係重大；大不相同；使更好受： *A few kind words at the right time make all the difference.* 在適當的時候說幾句體貼話效果迥然不同。 **same 'difference** (*informal*) used to say that you think the differences between two things are not important 差不多一樣： *'That's not a xylophone, it's a glockenspiel.' 'Same difference.'* "那不是木琴而是鐘琴。" "反正都差不多。" **with a 'difference** (*informal*) (after nouns 用於名詞後) used to show that sth is interesting or unusual 引人注目；與眾不同： *The traditional backpack with a difference—it's waterproof.* 這個跟傳統背包不同，它能防水。➲ more at BURY, SINK *v.*, SPLIT *v.*, WORLD

British/American 英式/美式英語

different from / to / than

- **Different from** is the most common structure in both *BrE* and *NAmE*. **Different to** is also used in *BrE*. * different from 在英式英語和美式英語中均為最通用的結構。different to 亦用於英式英語： *Paul's very different from/to his brother.* 保羅與他的哥哥大不一樣。◇ *This visit is very different from/to last time.* 這次訪問與上一次的大不相同。
- In *NAmE* people also say **different than**. 美式英語亦有 different than 的說法： *Your trains are different than ours.* 你們的火車與我們的不一樣。◇ *You look different than before.* 你看上去與從前不一樣了。
- Before a clause you can also use **different from** (and **different than** in *NAmE*). 從句前亦可用 different from（美式英語用 different than）： *She looked different from what I'd expected.* ◇ *She looked different than (what) I'd expected.* 她看上去與我想像的不一樣。

dif·fer·ent 🔑 /ˈdɪfrənt/ *adj.*
1 🔑 **~ (from/to/than sb/sth)** not the same as sb/sth; not like sb/sth else 不同的；有區別的；有差異的： *American English is significantly different from British English.* 美式英語與英式英語有很大差異。◇ (*BrE*) *It's very different to what I'm used to.* 這與我所習慣的大不相同。◇ (*NAmE*) *He saw he was no different than anybody else.* 他認為他與其他人沒什麼兩樣。◇ *It's different now than it was a year ago.* 現在同一年前不一樣了。◇ *People often give very different accounts of the same event.* 人們常常對同一件事有非常不同的敘述。◇ *My son's terribly untidy; my daughter's **no different**.* 我兒子邋遢極了，女兒也不比他強。**OPP** **similar** **2** 🔑 [only before noun] separate and individual 分別的；各別的；各種的： *She offered us five different kinds of cake.* 她給我們提供了五種不同的蛋糕。◇ *The programme was about customs in different parts of the country.* 這個節目介紹全國各地的風俗習慣。◇ *They are sold in many different colours.* 這些有多種顏色供選購。◇ *I looked it up in three different dictionaries.* 我分別在三本詞典裏查找過。 **3** [not usually before noun] (*informal*) unusual; not like other people or things 不平常；與眾不同；別致： *'Did you enjoy the play?' 'Well, it was certainly different!'* "你喜歡這齣戲嗎？" "哦，的確不同凡響！" ▸ **dif·fer·ent·ly** 🔑 *adv.*: *Boys and girls may behave differently.* 男孩兒和女孩兒的表現可能不同。◇ *The male bird has a differently shaped head.* 雄鳥的頭形有點特別。

IDM **a different kettle of fish** (*informal*) a completely different situation or person from the one previously mentioned 另一碼事；截然不同的人 ➲ more at COMPLEXION, KNOW *v.*, MARCH *v.*, MATTER *n.*, PULL *v.*, SING *v.*, TELL

dif·fer·en·tial /ˌdɪfəˈrenʃl/ *noun, adj.*
■ *noun* **1** **~ (between A and B)** a difference in the amount, value or size of sth, especially the difference in rates of pay for people doing different work in the same industry or profession 差別；差額；差價；（尤指同行業不同工種的）工資級差： ***wage/pay/income differentials*** 工資/收入差異 **2** (also **ˌdifferential ˈgear**) a gear that makes it possible for a vehicle's back wheels to turn at different speeds when going around corners（汽車）差動齒輪，分速器，差速器行星齒輪
■ *adj.* [only before noun] (*formal*) showing or depending on a difference; not equal 差別的；以差別而定的；有區別的： *the differential treatment of prisoners based on sex and social class* 按性別和社會階層區別對待犯人 ◇ *differential rates of pay* 工資級差

ˌdifferential ˈcalculus *noun* [U] (*mathematics* 數) a type of mathematics that deals with quantities that change in time. It is used to calculate a quantity at a particular moment. 微分學 ➲ compare INTEGRAL CALCULUS

diffeˌrential eˈquation *noun* (*mathematics* 數) an EQUATION that involves FUNCTIONS (= quantities that can vary) and their rates of change 微分方程

dif·fer·en·ti·ate **AW** /ˌdɪfəˈrenʃieɪt/ *verb* **1** [I, T] to recognize or show that two things are not the same 區分；區別；辨別 **SYN** **distinguish**: **~ (between) A and B** *It's difficult to differentiate between the two varieties.* 這兩個品種很難辨別。◇ **~ A (from B)** *I can't differentiate one variety from another.* 我無法將這幾個品種區別開來。 **2** [T] **~ sth (from sth)** to be the particular thing that shows that things or people are not the same 表明…間的差別；構成…間差別的特徵 **SYN** **distinguish**: *The male's yellow beak differentiates it from the female.* 雄鳥黃色的喙是與雌鳥相區別的主要特徵。 **3** [I] **~ between A and B** to treat people or things in a different way, especially in an unfair way （尤指不公正地）差別對待，區別對待 **SYN** **discriminate** ▸ **dif·fer·en·ti·ation** **AW** /ˌdɪfəˌrenʃiˈeɪʃn/ *noun* [U]

dif·fi·cult 🔑 /ˈdɪfɪkəlt/ *adj.*
1 🔑 **~ (for sb) (to do sth)** not easy; needing effort or skill to do or to understand 困難的；費力的；難做的；難解的： *a difficult problem/task/exam* 難題；艱巨的任務；很難的考試 ◇ ***It's difficult** for them to get here much before seven.* 他們很難在七點以前早早地來到這裏。◇ *It's really difficult to read your writing.* 你的筆跡真是難以辨認。◇ *Your writing is really difficult to read.* 你的筆跡真是難以辨認。◇ *She **finds it** very **difficult** to get up early.* 她覺得很難早起。 **2** 🔑 full of problems; causing a lot of trouble 問題很多的；充滿艱難困苦的；麻煩的： *to be in a **difficult position/situation*** 處於困境 ◇ *My boss is **making life** very **difficult** for me.* 我的老闆總是給我找麻煩。◇ *13 is a difficult age.* * 13 歲是個容易出問題的年齡。 **3** 🔑 (of people 人) not easy to please; not helpful 難以討好的；難以取悅的；不願幫助的 **SYN** **awkward**: *a difficult child/customer/boss* 難哄的孩子；難對付的顧客；難討好的老闆 ◇ *Don't pay any attention to her—she's just being difficult.* 別理她，她不過是在故意刁難。

IDM see JOB, LIFE

Synonyms 同義詞辨析

difficult

hard • challenging • demanding • taxing

These words all describe sth that is not easy and requires a lot of effort or skill to do. 以上各詞均形容事情困難、費力、難做。

difficult not easy; needing effort or skill to do or understand 指困難的、費力的、難做的、難懂的：*The exam questions were quite difficult.* 考題相當難。◇ *It is difficult for young people to find jobs around here.* 年輕人要在這裏附近找到工作很難。

hard not easy; needing effort or skill to do or understand 指困難的、費力的、難做的、難懂的：*I always found languages quite hard at school.* 在學校讀書時我總覺得語言很難學。◇ *It was one of the hardest things I ever did.* 這是我做過的最難的事情之一。

DIFFICULT OR HARD? 用 difficult 還是 hard？

Hard is slightly less formal than **difficult**. It is used particularly in the structure *hard to believe/say/find/take, etc.*, although **difficult** can also be used in any of these examples. * hard 較 difficult 稍非正式，主要用於 hard to believe/say/find/take 等結構中，不過 difficult 亦可用於上述結構。

challenging (*approving*) difficult in an interesting way that tests your ability 指困難而有意思的、有挑戰性的、考驗能力的

demanding difficult to do or deal with and needing a lot of effort, skill or patience 指要求高的、費力的、需要高技能或耐性的：*It is a technically demanding piece of music to play.* 演奏這一段音樂需要有很高的技藝。

taxing (often used in negative statements) difficult to do and needing a lot of mental or physical effort（常用於否定句）指繁重的、費力的、傷腦筋的：*This shouldn't be too taxing for you.* 這對你來說不至於太費勁。

PATTERNS

- difficult/hard/challenging/demanding/taxing **for** sb
- difficult/hard **to do sth**
- **physically** difficult/hard/challenging/demanding/taxing
- **technically** difficult/challenging/demanding
- **mentally/intellectually** challenging/demanding/taxing

dif·fi·culty 0-w /ˈdɪfɪkəlti/ *noun* (*pl.* **-ies**)
1 0-w [C, usually pl., U] a problem; a thing or situation that causes problems 困難；難題；難事；困境：*the difficulties of English syntax* 英語句法的難點 ◇ *children with severe learning difficulties* 學習上有嚴重困難的孩子 ◇ *We've* ***run into difficulties/difficulty*** *with the new project.* 我們在這項新工程中遇到了難題。◇ *He* ***got into difficulties*** *while swimming and had to be rescued.* 他游泳時遇險，只好靠人營救。◇ *The bank is* ***in difficulty/difficulties****.* 這家銀行處境困難。◇ *It was a time fraught with difficulties and frustration.* 這是一個充滿困難和挫折的時期。 **2** 0-w [U] the state or quality of being hard to do or to understand; the effort that sth involves 艱難；困難；費勁；辛苦：*I had considerable difficulty (in) persuading her to leave.* 我費了好大的勁說服她離開。◇ *I had no difficulty (in) making myself understood.* 我毫不費力地表達了自己的意思。◇ *The changes were made with surprisingly little difficulty.* 這些變化幾乎沒有遇到阻力，簡直不可思議。◇ *He spoke slowly and with great difficulty.* 他話說得很慢，而且很吃力。◇ *We found the house* ***without difficulty****.* 我們輕而易舉就找到了這棟房子。◇ *They discussed the difficulty of studying abroad.* 他們討論了到國外學習的困難。 **HELP** You cannot say 'have difficulty to do sth'. 不能說 have difficulty to do sth：~~*I had difficulty to persuade her to leave.*~~ **3** 0-w [U] how hard sth is 困難程度；難度：*varying levels of difficulty* 不同的難度 ◇ *questions of increasing difficulty* 難度不斷增加的問題

dif·fi·dent /ˈdɪfɪdənt/ *adj.* **~ (about sth)** not having much confidence in yourself; not wanting to talk about yourself 缺乏自信的；膽怯的；羞怯的 **SYN** **shy**：*a* ***diffident manner/smile*** 畏首畏尾的態度；羞怯的一笑 ◇ *He was modest and diffident about his own success.* 他很謙虛，不願談及自己的成功。 ▸ **dif·fi·dence** /-dəns/ *noun* [U]：*She overcame her natural diffidence and spoke with great frankness.* 她克服了膽怯的毛病，非常坦率地說出了自己的想法。 **dif·fi·dent·ly** *adv.*

dif·fract /dɪˈfrækt/ *verb* **~ sth** (*physics* 物) to break up a stream of light into a series of dark and light bands or into the different colours of the SPECTRUM（使光束）衍射 ▸ **dif·frac·tion** /dɪˈfrækʃn/ *noun* [U]

dif·fuse *adj., verb*
■ *adj.* /dɪˈfjuːs/ **1** spread over a wide area 彌漫的；擴散的；漫射的：*diffuse light* 漫射光 ◇ *a diffuse community* 居住分散的社群 **2** not clear or easy to understand; using a lot of words 不清楚的；難解的；冗長的；囉嗦的：*a diffuse style of writing* 冗贅的文體 ▸ **dif·fuse·ly** *adv.* **dif·fuse·ness** *noun* [U]
■ *verb* /dɪˈfjuːz/ **1** [T, I] **~ (sth)** (*formal*) to spread sth or become spread widely in all directions 傳播；普及；使分散；散佈：*The problem is how to diffuse power without creating anarchy.* 問題在於如何將權力分散而不造成無政府狀態。◇ *Technologies diffuse rapidly.* 技術普及非常快。 **2** [I, T] **~ (sth)** (*technical* 術語) if a gas or liquid **diffuses** or **is diffused** in a substance, it becomes slowly mixed with that substance（使氣體或液體）擴散，彌漫，滲透 **3** [T] **~ sth** (*formal*) to make light shine less brightly by spreading it in many directions（使光）模糊，漫射，漫散：*The moon was fuller than the night before, but the light was diffused by cloud.* 月亮比頭一天晚上更圓，但因雲層遮掩而月光朦朧。 ▸ **dif·fu·sion** /dɪˈfjuːʒn/ *noun* [U]

dif·fu·ser /dɪˈfjuːzə(r)/ *noun* **1** a device used in photography to avoid dark shadows or areas which are too bright（攝影用的）漫射體，柔光鏡 **2** a part that is attached to a HAIRDRYER to spread the hot air around the head and dry the hair more gently（吹風機的）擴散器

dig 0-w /dɪɡ/ *verb, noun*
■ *verb* (**dig·ging, dug, dug** /dʌɡ/) **1** 0-w [I, T] to make a hole in the ground or to move soil from one place to another using your hands, a tool or a machine 掘（地）；鑿（洞）；挖（土）：**~ (for sth)** *to dig for coal/gold/Roman remains* 挖煤；採掘黃金；掘地探尋古羅馬遺跡 ◇ *They dug deeper and deeper but still found nothing.* 他們越挖越深卻仍一無所獲。◇ *I think I'll* ***do some digging*** *in the garden.* 我想我該給花園鬆鬆土了。◇ **~ sth** *to* ***dig a ditch/grave/hole/tunnel*** 挖溝；挖墳；挖洞；挖隧道 ◇ (*BrE*) *I've been digging the garden.* 我一直在花園鬆土。 **2** [T] **~ sth** to remove sth from the ground with a tool 掘得；（採）掘出：*I'll dig some potatoes for lunch.* 我要挖點土豆作午餐。 **3** [I] **(+ adv./prep.)** to search in sth in order to find an object in sth 尋找，搜尋（物品）：*I dug around in my bag for a pen.* 我在包裏到處翻找筆。 **4** [T] **~ sth** (*old-fashioned, slang*) to approve of or like sth very much 贊成；看中；喜歡

IDM **dig ˈdeep (into sth)** **1** to search thoroughly for information 探究；搜集；細查：*You'll need to dig deep into the records to find the figures you want.* 你必須仔細查閱檔案才能找到你需要的數字。 **2** to try hard to provide the money, equipment, etc. that is needed 盡力提供（所需金錢、設備等）：*We're asking you to dig deep for the earthquake victims.* 我們請求你們盡力為地震災民提供財物。 **dig your ˈheels/ˈtoes in** to refuse to do sth or to change your mind about sth 拒不讓步；固執己見：*They dug in their heels and would not lower the price.* 他們說什麼也不肯降價。 **dig (deep) in/into your pocket(s), savings, etc.** to spend a lot of your own money on sth 慷慨解囊；花費；掏腰包 **dig sb in the ˈribs** to push your finger or your elbow into sb's side, especially to attract their attention（尤指為引起注意用手指或胳膊肘）捅某人一下 **dig yourself into a ˈhole**

D

to get yourself into a bad situation that will be very difficult to get out of 使自己陷入困境；使自己處境尷尬 **dig your own 'grave | dig a 'grave for yourself** to do sth that will have very harmful results for you 自掘墳墓；自取滅亡；自己害自己

PHR V **,dig 'in** (*informal*) **1** used to tell sb to start to eat 開始吃吧： *Help yourselves, everybody! Dig in!* 請大家隨意，開始吃吧！ **2** to wait, or deal with a difficult situation, with great patience 耐心等待；忍耐；忍受： *There is nothing we can do except dig in and wait.* 我們除了耐心等待別無他法。 **,dig sth↔'in 1** to mix soil with another substance by digging the two substances together（把…）摻進土中，混入土壤： *The manure should be well dug in.* 肥料應均勻地混入土壤。 **2** to push sth into sth else（把…）戳進，插入： *He dug his fork into the steak.* 他把餐叉叉進牛排。 **,dig yourself 'in** (of soldiers 士兵) to protect yourself against an attack by making a safe place in the ground 掘壕防守；挖掩體藏身 **,dig 'into sth 1** (*informal*) to start to eat food with enthusiasm 開始津津有味地吃；開始貪婪地吃： *She dug into her bowl of pasta.* 她津津有味地吃着碗裏的麪條。 **2** to push or rub against your body in a painful or uncomfortable way 擠痛，磨痛，碰痛（身體部位）： *His fingers dug painfully into my arm.* 他的手指把我的手臂給抓痛了。 **3** to find out information by searching or asking questions 探究；探尋；探詢： *Will you dig a little into his past and see what you find?* 你稍微探究一下他的過去看看能發現什麼，好嗎？ **,dig sth 'into sth 1** to mix soil with another substance by digging the two substances together（把…）摻進土中，混入土壤 **2** to push or press sth into sth else（把…）戳進，插入，壓入： *She dug her hands deeper into her pockets.* 她把兩手深深地插進衣服口袋裏。 **,dig sb/sth↔'out (of sth) 1** to remove sb/sth from somewhere by digging the ground around them or it 挖掘出： *More than a dozen people were dug out of the avalanche alive.* 十多個埋在雪崩下的人被挖了出來，仍然活着。 **2** to find sth that has been hidden or forgotten for a long time 找出，發掘，發現（藏着的或被遺忘的東西）： *I went to the attic and dug out Grandad's medals.* 我到閣樓裏發現了祖父的勳章。 **,dig sth↔'over** to prepare ground by digging the soil to remove stones, etc. 翻（地）；翻挖；刨（地） **,dig sth↔'up 1** to break the ground into small pieces before planting seeds, building sth, etc.（在播種或建築前）掘地，平整土地： *They are digging up the football field to lay a new surface.* 他們正在把足球場挖開鋪一層新地面。 **2** to remove sth from the ground by digging 掘起；挖掘出： *An old Roman vase was dug up here last month.* 上個月在此地出土了一個古羅馬花瓶。 **3** to discover information about sb/sth 發現；搜集；查明 SYN **unearth**： *Tabloid newspapers love to dig up scandal.* 通俗小報都熱衷於刨醜聞。

■ ***noun*** ➲ see also DIGS **1** a small push with your finger or elbow（用手指或肘部）輕碰，輕戳，輕推： *She gave him **a dig in the ribs**.* 她輕輕地戳了一下他的肋部。 **2 ~ (at sb/sth)** a remark that is intended to annoy or upset sb 挖苦；嘲諷： *He kept making sly little digs at me.* 他總是拐彎抹角地挖苦我。◇ *to **have a dig at sb/sth*** 嘲諷某人／某事 **3** an occasion when an organized group of people dig in the ground to discover old buildings or objects, in order to find out more about their history 考古發掘 SYN **excavation**： *to go on a dig* 進行考古發掘 ◇ *an archaeological dig* 一次考古發掘

the dig·er·ati /ˌdɪdʒəˈrɑːti/ *noun* [pl.] (*humorous*) people who are very good at using computers or who use computers a lot 電腦高手；電腦專家 ➲ compare LITERATI

di·gest *verb, noun*

■ ***verb*** /daɪˈdʒest; dɪ-/ **1** [T, I] **~ (sth)** when you **digest** food, or it **digests**, it is changed into substances that your body can use 消化： *Humans cannot digest plants such as grass.* 人不能消化草類植物。◇ *You should allow a little time after a meal for the food to digest.* 飯後你應該留點時間讓食物消化。 **2** [T] **~ sth** to think about sth so that you fully understand it 領會；領悟；理解： *He paused, waiting for her to digest the information.* 他停了一會兒，等她慢慢領會這一信息。

■ ***noun*** /ˈdaɪdʒest/ a short report containing the most important facts of a longer report or piece of writing; a collection of short reports 摘要；概要；文摘；彙編： *a monthly news digest* 每月新聞摘要

di·gest·ible /daɪˈdʒestəbl; dɪ-/ *adj.* easy to digest; pleasant to eat or easy to understand 易消化的；口感好的；易理解的；可領會的 OPP **indigestible**

di·ges·tion /daɪˈdʒestʃən; dɪ-/ *noun* **1** [U] the process of digesting food 消化 ➲ compare INDIGESTION **2** [C, usually sing.] the ability to digest food 消化能力： *to have a **good/poor digestion*** 消化能力強／弱

di·gest·ive /daɪˈdʒestɪv; dɪ-/ *adj.* [only before noun] connected with the digestion of food 消化的；和消化有關的： *the **digestive system/tract*** 消化系統／道 ◇ *digestive problems* 消化問題

di'gestive biscuit (also **digestive**) *noun* (*BrE*) a round sweet biscuit made from WHOLEMEAL flour, sometimes covered with chocolate 消化餅乾；粗麪餅乾： *a packet of chocolate digestives* 一包巧克力粗麪餅乾

di'gestive system *noun* the series of organs inside the body that digest food 消化系統

dig·ger /ˈdɪɡə(r)/ *noun* **1** a large machine that is used for digging up the ground 挖掘機 **2** a person or an animal that digs 挖掘者；有挖掘習性的動物 ➲ see also GOLD-DIGGER **3** (*AustralE, NZE, old-fashioned, informal*) a man 男人；傢伙；老兄

digit /ˈdɪdʒɪt/ *noun* **1** any of the numbers from 0 to 9（從 0 到 9 的任何一個）數字，數位： *The number 57306 contains five digits.* 數字 57 306 是個五位數。◇ *a four-digit number* 四位數 **2** (*anatomy* 解) a finger, thumb or toe 手指；拇指；腳趾

digit·al /ˈdɪdʒɪtl/ *adj., noun*

■ ***adj.*** **1** using a system of receiving and sending information as a series of the numbers one and zero, showing that an electronic signal is there or is not there 數字信息系統的；數碼的；數字式的；數位的： *a digital camera* 數碼照相機 ◇ *digital terrestrial and digital satellite broadcasting* 數字陸上廣播和數字衛星廣播 **2** (of clocks, watches, etc. 鐘錶等) showing information by using figures, rather than with HANDS that point to numbers 數字顯示的： *a **digital clock/watch*** 數字鐘／錶 ➲ picture at CLOCK ➲ compare ANALOGUE *adj.* (2) ▸ **digit·al·ly** /-təli/ *adv.*： *digitally remastered tapes* 以數字方式重新灌製的錄音帶

■ ***noun*** [U] digital television 數字電視；數位電視： *How long have you had digital?* 你們有數字電視多長時間了？ ◇ *With digital you can choose the camera angle you want.* 有了數字電視你就可以選擇你想要的攝像角度。

digi·talis /ˌdɪdʒɪˈteɪlɪs; *NAmE* also -ˈtælɪs/ *noun* [U] (*medical* 醫) a drug made from the FOXGLOVE plant, that helps the heart muscle to work 洋地黃（一種強心劑）；強心苷

digit·al·ize (*BrE* also **-ise**) /ˈdɪdʒɪtəlaɪz/ *verb* **~ sth** = DIGITIZE

,digital re'cording *noun* [C, U] a recording in which sounds or pictures are represented by a series of numbers showing that an electronic signal is there or is not there; the process of making a recording in this way 數字錄製品；數字錄製；數位錄製品；數位錄製

,digital 'signature *noun* (*computing* 計) a way of secretly adding sb's name to an electronic message or document to prove the identity of the person who is sending it and show that the data has not been changed at all 數字簽名；數位簽名

,digital 'television *noun* **1** [U] the system of broadcasting television using digital signals 數字電視（系統）；數位電視（系統） **2** [C] a television set that can receive digital signals 數字電視機；數位電視機

digit·ize (*BrE* also **-ise**) /ˈdɪdʒɪtaɪz/ (also **digit·al·ize**) *verb* **~ sth** to change data into a DIGITAL form that can be easily read and processed by a computer（使數據）數字化，數位化： *a digitized map* 一張數字化地圖

di·glos·sia /daɪˈɡlɒsiə; *NAmE* -ˈɡlɔːs-; -ˈɡlɑːs-/ *noun* [U] (*linguistics* 語言) a situation in which two languages or two forms of a language are used under different conditions in a community 雙語現象，雙變體現象（兩

種語言或一種語言的兩種變體並存於一個語言集體中）▸ **di·glos·sic** *adj.*

dig·ni·fied /ˈdɪɡnɪfaɪd/ *adj.* calm and serious and deserving respect 莊重的；莊嚴的；有尊嚴的：*a dignified person/manner/voice* 有尊嚴的人；莊重的舉止；莊嚴的聲音 ◇ *Throughout his trial he maintained a dignified silence.* 在整個審訊過程中，他始終沉默以保持尊嚴。**OPP** **undignified**

dig·nify /ˈdɪɡnɪfaɪ/ *verb* (**dig·ni·fies**, **dig·ni·fy·ing**, **dig·ni·fied**) (*formal*) **1 ~ sb/sth** to make sb/sth seem impressive 使有尊嚴；使崇高；使顯貴；使增輝：*The mayor was there to dignify the celebrations.* 市長的光臨為慶祝活動增輝。**2 ~ sth** to make sth appear important when it is not really 使顯得堂皇；抬高…的身價；美化：*I'm not going to dignify his comments by reacting to them.* 我才不會理睬他的評論以抬高其身價呢。

dig·ni·tary /ˈdɪɡnɪtəri; *NAmE* -teri/ *noun* (*pl.* **-ies**) a person who has an important official position 顯貴；要人；達官貴人 **SYN** **VIP**

dig·nity /ˈdɪɡnəti/ *noun* [U] **1** a calm and serious manner that deserves respect 莊重；莊嚴；尊嚴：*She accepted the criticism with quiet dignity.* 她大度地接受了批評。**2** the fact of being given honour and respect by people 尊貴；高貴；高尚：*the dignity of work* 工作的光榮 ◇ *The terminally ill should be allowed to die with dignity.* 應該允許垂危病人死得有尊嚴。**3** a sense of your own importance and value 自豪；自尊；自重：*It's difficult to preserve your dignity when you have no job and no home.* 一個無家無業的人難以保持自己的尊嚴。

IDM **beˌneath your ˈdignity** below what you see as your own importance or worth 有失尊嚴；有失身分；有失體面 **ˌstand on your ˈdignity** (*formal*) to demand to be treated with the respect that you think that you deserve 要求受到應有的禮遇；保持尊嚴

di·graph /ˈdaɪɡrɑːf; *NAmE* -ɡræf/ *noun* a combination of two letters representing one sound, for example 'ph' and 'sh' in English 雙字母（兩個相連字母表達單個音素）

di·gress /daɪˈɡres/ *verb* [I] (*formal*) to start to talk about sth that is not connected with the main point of what you are saying 離題；偏離主題 ▸ **di·gres·sion** /daɪˈɡreʃn/ *noun* [C, U]：*After several digressions, he finally got to the point.* 說了幾句題外話後，他終於言歸正傳。

digs /dɪɡz/ *noun* [pl.] (*old-fashioned*, *informal*) a room or rooms that you rent to live in 租住的住所；住處 **SYN** **lodgings**

dike *noun* = DYKE

dik·tat /ˈdɪktæt; *NAmE* dɪkˈtæt/ *noun* [C, U] (*disapproving*) an order given by a government, for example, that people must obey 強制執行的命令；勒令：*an EU diktat from Brussels* 來自布魯塞爾歐盟的命令 ◇ *government by diktat* 用專制手段統治

di·lapi·dated /dɪˈlæpɪdeɪtɪd/ *adj.* (of furniture and buildings 傢具和建築物) old and in very bad condition 破舊的；破爛的；年久失修的 **SYN** **ramshackle** ▸ **di·lapi·da·tion** /dɪˌlæpɪˈdeɪʃn/ *noun* [U]：*in a state of dilapidation* 處於破舊狀態

dila·ta·tion /ˌdaɪləˈteɪʃn; ˌdɪlə-; *BrE* also ˌdaɪleɪ-/ *noun* [U] (*medical* 醫) the process of becoming wider (= of becoming dilated), or the action of making sth become wider 膨脹；擴大；擴張

dilaˌtation and curetˈtage (also **D and C**) *noun* (*medical* 醫) an operation in which the CERVIX is opened and material is removed from the UTERUS, for example after a MISCARRIAGE 刮宮術

di·late /daɪˈleɪt/ *verb* [I, T] to become or to make sth larger, wider or more open 擴大；（使）膨脹，擴張：*Her eyes dilated with fear.* 她嚇得瞪大了眼睛。◇ **~ sth** *dilated pupils/nostrils* 擴大了的瞳孔；張大了的鼻孔 ◇ *Red wine can help to dilate blood vessels.* 紅葡萄酒有助於擴張血管。**OPP** **contract** ▸ **dila·tion** /daɪˈleɪʃn/ *noun* [U, C]

dila·tory /ˈdɪlətəri; *NAmE* -tɔːri/ *adj.* **~ (in doing sth)** (*formal*) not acting quickly enough; causing delay 拖拉的；拖延的；延誤的：*The government has been dilatory in dealing with the problem of unemployment.* 政府遲遲未解決失業問題。

dildo /ˈdɪldəʊ; *NAmE* -doʊ/ *noun* (*pl.* **dildos** or **dildoes**) an object shaped like a PENIS that is used for sexual pleasure 人造陰莖；假陽具；女子性快樂器

di·lemma /dɪˈlemə; daɪ-/ *noun* a situation which makes problems, often one in which you have to make a very difficult choice between things of equal importance （進退兩難的）窘境，困境 **SYN** **predicament**：*to face a dilemma* 面臨左右為難的困境 ◇ *to be in a dilemma* 處於進退兩難的境地 **IDM** see HORN *n.*

D

dil·et·tante /ˌdɪləˈtænti/ *noun* (*pl.* **dil·et·tanti** /-tiː/ or **dil·et·tan·tes**) (*disapproving*) a person who does or studies sth but is not serious about it and does not have much knowledge 淺薄的涉獵者；淺嘗輒止者；半吊子；半瓶醋 ▸ **di·let·tante** *adj.*：*a dilettante artist* 粗通藝術的人

dili·gence /ˈdɪlɪdʒəns/ *noun* [U] (*formal*) careful and thorough work or effort 勤勉；勤奮；用功：*She shows great diligence in her schoolwork.* 她上學非常用功。

dili·gent /ˈdɪlɪdʒənt/ *adj.* (*formal*) showing care and effort in your work or duties 孜孜不倦的；勤勉的；刻苦的：*a **diligent student/worker*** 勤奮的學生／工人 ▸ **dili·gent·ly** *adv.*

dill /dɪl/ *noun* [U] a plant with yellow flowers whose leaves and seeds have a strong taste and are used in cooking as a HERB. Dill is often added to vegetables kept in VINEGAR. 蒔蘿，土茴香（味衝，用作佐料）：*dill pickles* 加了土茴香的泡菜 ➲ VISUAL VOCAB page V32

dilly-dally /ˈdɪli dæli/ *verb* (**dilly-dallies**, **dilly-dallying**, **dilly-dallied**, **dilly-dallied**) [I] (*old-fashioned*, *informal*) to take too long to do sth, go somewhere or make a decision 磨蹭；猶豫 **SYN** **dawdle**

di·lute /daɪˈluːt; *BrE* also -ˈljuːt/ *verb*, *adj.*

▪ ***verb*** **1 ~ sth (with sth)** to make a liquid weaker by adding water or another liquid to it 稀釋；沖淡 **SYN** **water down**：*The paint can be diluted with water to make a lighter shade.* 這顏料可用水稀釋以使色度淡一些。**2 ~ sth** to make sth weaker or less effective 削弱；降低；使降低效果 **SYN** **water down**：*Large classes dilute the quality of education that children receive.* 大班上課會降低孩子所受教育的質量。▸ **di·lu·tion** /daɪˈluːʃn; *BrE* also -ˈljuːʃn/ *noun* [U]：*the dilution of sewage* 污水的稀釋處理 ◇ *This is a serious dilution of their election promises.* 這是對他們競選時許下的諾言大打折扣。

▪ ***adj.*** (also **di·luted**) (of a liquid 液體) made weaker by adding water or another substance 稀釋了的；沖淡了的：*a **dilute acid/solution*** 稀釋酸液／溶液

dim /dɪm/ *adj.*, *verb*

▪ ***adj.*** (**dim·mer**, **dim·mest**)

▸ LIGHT 光線 **1** not bright 暗淡的；昏暗的；微弱的：*the dim glow of the fire in the grate* 壁爐裏微弱的火光 ◇ *This light is too dim to read by.* 這光線太暗，看不了書。

▸ PLACE 地方 **2** where you cannot see well because there is not much light 不明亮的；光線暗淡的；昏暗的：*a dim room/street* 昏暗的房間／街道

▸ SHAPE 形狀 **3** that you cannot see well because there is not much light 不分明的；不清楚的；朦朧的；隱約的：*the dim outline of a house in the moonlight* 月光下影影綽綽的房子的輪廓 ◇ *I could see a dim shape in the doorway.* 我模模糊糊看見門口有個人影。

▸ EYES 眼睛 **4** not able to see well 看不清的；視力差的；模糊的：*His eyesight is getting dim.* 他的視力越來越差。

▸ MEMORIES 記憶 **5** that you cannot remember or imagine clearly 不清晰的；模糊的 **SYN** **vague**：*dim memories* 模糊的記憶 ◇ *She had a dim recollection of the visit.* 她依稀記得那次訪問。◇ (*humorous*) *in the **dim and distant** past* 在遙遠的過去

▸ PERSON 人 **6** (*informal, especially BrE*) not intelligent 遲鈍的；愚笨的；愚蠢的：*He's very dim.* 他很遲鈍。

▸ SITUATION 境況 **7** not giving any reason to have hope; not good 不明朗的；不樂觀的：*Her future career prospects look dim.* 她的事業前景看來很暗淡。

▸ **dim·ness** *noun* [U]：*It took a while for his eyes to adjust to the dimness.* 過了好一陣他的眼睛才適應了這昏暗的地方。➲ see also DIMLY

D

IDM **take a dim view of sb/sth** to disapprove of sb/sth; to not have a good opinion of sb/sth 對…持不贊成（或懷疑）態度；對…沒有好感： *She took a dim view of my suggestion.* 她對我的建議持否定態度。

■ *verb* (-mm-)

▸ LIGHT 光線 **1** [I, T] **~ (sth)** if a light **dims** or if you **dim** it, it becomes or you make it less bright （使）變暗淡，變微弱，變昏暗： *The lights in the theatre dimmed as the curtain rose.* 幕布升起，劇場內的燈光暗了下來。

▸ FEELING/QUALITY 感覺；品質 **2** [I, T] **~ (sth)** if a feeling or quality **dims**, or if sth **dims** it, it becomes less strong （使）減弱，變淡漠，失去光澤： *Her passion for dancing never dimmed over the years.* 這些年來她對跳舞的熱情一直不減。

dime /daɪm/ *noun* a coin of the US and Canada worth ten cents （美國，加拿大的）十分硬幣，十分錢

IDM **a ˌdime a ˈdozen** (*NAmE*) (*BrE* **ˌtwo/ˌten a ˈpenny**) very common and therefore not valuable 普通得不值錢；（因常見而）價值低

ˈdime novel *noun* (*NAmE, old-fashioned*) a cheap popular novel, usually an exciting adventure or romantic story 一角錢小說，廉價通俗小說（常為刺激歷險或愛情小說）

di·men·sion AW /daɪˈmenʃn; dɪ-/ *noun* **1** a measurement in space, for example the height, width or length of sth 維（構成空間的因素）： *We measured the dimensions of the kitchen.* 我們測量了廚房的面積。◇ *computer design tools that work in three dimensions* 計算機三維設計工具 ➲ see also THE FOURTH DIMENSION (1) **2** [usually pl.] the size and extent of a situation 大小；規模；程度；範圍： *a problem of considerable dimensions* 一個涉及面相當廣的問題 **3** an aspect, or way of looking at or thinking about sth 方面；側面： *Her job added a new dimension to her life.* 她的工作為她的生活增添了新的內容。◇ *the social dimension of unemployment* 失業的社會性層面

-dimensional AW /daɪˈmenʃənl; dɪ-/ *combining form* (in adjectives 構成形容詞) having the number of dimensions mentioned …維的： *a multidimensional model* 多維模型 ➲ see also MULTIDIMENSIONAL, THREE-DIMENSIONAL, TWO-DIMENSIONAL

ˈdime store *noun* (*old-fashioned, NAmE*) = FIVE-AND-DIME

di·min·ish AW /dɪˈmɪnɪʃ/ *verb* **1** [I, T] **~ (sth)** to become or to make sth become smaller, weaker, etc. 減少；（使）減弱，縮減；降低 SYN **decrease**： *The world's resources are rapidly diminishing.* 世界資源正在迅速減少。◇ *His influence has diminished with time.* 隨着時間的推移，他的影響已不如從前了。◇ *Our efforts were producing* ***diminishing returns*** (= we achieved less although we spent more time or money). 我們不斷付出努力，但收效卻越來越小。 **2** [T] **~ sb/sth** to make sb/sth seem less important than they really are 貶低；貶損；輕視 SYN **belittle**： *I don't wish to diminish the importance of their contribution.* 我並不想貶低他們所作貢獻的重要性。

diˌminished responsiˈbility *noun* [U] (*BrE, law* 律) a state in which a person who is accused of a crime is not considered to be responsible for their actions, because they are mentally ill （因精神失常）減輕的罪責： *He was found not guilty of murder on the grounds of diminished responsibility.* 他未被判謀殺罪是基於精神失常而減輕了刑事責任。

di·minu·endo /dɪˌmɪnjuˈendəʊ; *NAmE* -doʊ/ *noun* (*pl.* **-os**) [C, U] (*music* 音) a gradual decrease in how loudly a piece of music is played or sung 漸弱 OPP **crescendo**

dim·in·ution AW /ˌdɪmɪˈnjuːʃn; *NAmE* -ˈnuːʃn/ *noun* **~ (of/in sth)** (*formal*) **1** [U] the act of reducing sth or of being reduced 減少；縮減；降低： *the diminution of political power* 政權的削弱 **2** [C, usually sing.] a reduction; an amount reduced 縮小；減少；縮小量；減少量： *a diminution in population growth* 人口增長幅度的縮小

di·minu·tive /dɪˈmɪnjətɪv/ *adj., noun*

■ *adj.* (*formal*) very small 極小的；特小的；微小的： *She was a diminutive figure beside her husband.* 她同丈夫比起來就像個小人。

■ *noun* **1** a word or an ending of a word that shows that sb/sth is small, for example *piglet* (= a young pig), *kitchenette* (= a small kitchen) 指小詞，指小詞綴（如 piglet 小豬，kitchenette 小廚房） **2** a short informal form of a word, especially a name （單詞，尤指名字的）非正式縮略形式： *'Nick' is a common diminutive of 'Nicholas'.* * Nick 是 Nicholas 的常用簡稱。

dimly /ˈdɪmli/ *adv.* not very brightly or clearly 暗淡地；昏暗地；模糊地： *a dimly lit room* 燈光昏暗的房間 ◇ *I was* ***dimly aware*** (= only just aware) *of the sound of a car in the distance.* 我隱隱約約聽到遠處有汽車的聲音。◇ *I did remember, but only dimly.* 我的確記得，只是記不太清楚了。

ˈdim·mer switch (also **dim·mer**) *noun* **1** a switch that allows you to make an electric light brighter or less bright 調光器；調光開關；亮度調節開關 **2** (*NAmE*) (*BrE* **ˈdip switch**) a switch that allows you to make the front lights on a car point downwards （汽車的）前燈垂光開關

dimple /ˈdɪmpl/ *verb, noun*

■ *verb* [I] to make a hollow place appear on each of your cheeks, especially by smiling 使現酒窩；使現笑靨

■ *noun* **1** a small hollow place in the skin, especially in the cheek or chin 酒窩；笑靨： *She had a dimple which appeared when she smiled.* 她一笑就現出酒窩。 **2** any small hollow place in a surface 淺凹；小凹；小坑： *a pane of glass with a dimple pattern* 帶淺凹形圖案的窗玻璃 ▸ **dimpled** /ˈdɪmpld/ *adj.*： *a dimpled chin* 有酒窩的臉

dim sum /ˌdɪm ˈsʌm/ (also **dim sim** /ˌdɪm ˈsɪm/) *noun* [U] (from *Chinese*) a Chinese dish or meal consisting of small pieces of food wrapped in sheets of DOUGH 點心（中式食品）

ˌdim-ˈwitted *adj.* (*informal*) stupid 愚笨的；傻的： *a dim-witted child* 傻孩子 ▸ **dim·wit** *noun*

din /dɪn/ *noun* [sing.] a loud, unpleasant noise that lasts for a long time 喧囂聲；嘈雜聲；吵鬧聲 SYN **racket**： *The children were making an awful din.* 孩子們吵得厲害。

dinar /ˈdiːnɑː(r)/ *noun* a unit of money in Serbia and various countries in the Middle East and N Africa 第納爾（塞爾維亞以及中東和北非多國的貨幣單位）

din-dins /ˈdɪndɪnz/ (*BrE*) (*NAmE* **din-din** /ˈdɪndɪn/) *noun* [U] (*humorous*) (used when talking to a baby or a pet 對嬰孩或寵物的用語) food 食物；好吃的

dine /daɪn/ *verb* [I] (*formal*) to eat dinner 進餐；用飯： *We dined with my parents at a restaurant in town.* 我們同我父母在鎮裏一家餐館吃飯。 ➲ COLLOCATIONS at RESTAURANT

PHR V **ˈdine on sth** (*formal*) to have a particular type of food for dinner 正餐吃…；以…作正餐 **ˌdine ˈout** to eat dinner in a restaurant or sb else's home 下館子；外出進餐 **ˌdine ˈout on sth** (*informal*) to tell other people about sth that has happened to you, in order to make them interested in you 吹噓自己的經歷以引起他人對你的興趣（或重視） IDM see WINE *v.*

diner /ˈdaɪnə(r)/ *noun* **1** a person eating a meal, especially in a restaurant （尤指餐館的）就餐者： *a restaurant capable of seating 100 diners* 可容納 100 人就餐的餐館 **2** (*especially NAmE*) a small, usually cheap, restaurant （常指較便宜的）小餐館，小飯店： *a road-side diner* 路邊小餐館

din·ero /dɪˈneərəʊ; *NAmE* dɪˈneroʊ/ *noun* [U] (*informal, especially NAmE*, from *Spanish*) money 錢

din·ette /daɪˈnet/ *noun* (*especially NAmE*) a small room or part of a room for eating meals 小飯廳；小餐室

ding /dɪŋ/ *noun, verb*

■ *noun* **1** (*NAmE*) a blow, especially one that causes slight damage to a car, etc. （尤指造成汽車上的凹痕、劃痕等的）一擊： *I got a ding in my rear fender.* 我汽車後面的擋泥板撞癟了一處。 **2** used to represent the sound made by a bell 叮噹；丁零： *The lift came to a halt with a loud 'ding'.* 電梯"叮"一聲停下了。

■ *verb* **1** [I] to make a sound like a bell 叮噹（或丁零）作響： *The computer just dings when I press a key.* 我一按鍵，電腦就發出叮的一聲。 **2** [T] **~ sth** (*NAmE*) to cause slight damage to a car, etc. 使（汽車等）輕微受損：*I dinged my passenger door.* 我把乘客門撞壞了一點。**3** [T] **~ sb** (*NAmE*) to hit sb 打：(*figurative*) *My department got dinged by the budget cuts.* 因預算縮減，我的部門受到一定的影響。

ding·bat /ˈdɪŋbæt/ *noun* (*NAmE, slang*) a stupid person 笨蛋；蠢貨；傻瓜

ding-dong /ˈdɪŋ dɒŋ; *NAmE* dɔːŋ/ *noun* **1** [U] used to represent the sound made by a bell（鐘、鈴聲）叮噹：*I rang the doorbell. Ding-dong! No answer.* 我按了按門鈴。叮噹！可沒有人應門。**2** (*BrE, informal*) an argument or fight 辯論；爭吵：*They were having a real ding-dong on the doorstep.* 他們在門前大吵起來。

dinghy /ˈdɪŋi; ˈdɪŋɡi/ *noun* (*pl.* **-ies**) **1** a small open boat that you sail or ROW 小艇；敞篷小船；小舢板：*a sailing dinghy* 小帆船 ➲ **VISUAL VOCAB** page V54 ➲ compare YACHT **2** = RUBBER DINGHY

dingo /ˈdɪŋɡəʊ; *NAmE* -ɡoʊ/ *noun* (*pl.* **-oes**) a wild Australian dog 澳洲野犬

dingy /ˈdɪndʒi/ *adj.* (**din·gier**, **din·gi·est**) dark and dirty 又黑又髒的；昏暗的；骯髒的：*a dingy room/hotel* 又黑又髒的房間 / 旅館 ◇ *dingy curtains/clothes* 髒得發黑的窗簾 / 衣服 ▸ **din·gi·ness** *noun* [U]

ˈ**dining car** (*BrE* also ˈ**restaurant car**) *noun* a coach/car on a train in which meals are served（火車的）餐車

ˈ**dining room** *noun* a room that is used mainly for eating meals in 餐室；餐廳；飯廳 ➲ **VISUAL VOCAB** page V22

ˈ**dining table** *noun* a table for having meals on 餐桌 ➲ compare DINNER TABLE ➲ **VISUAL VOCAB** page V22

dink /dɪŋk/ *noun* (also ˈ**drop shot**) (in TENNIS 網球) a soft hit that makes the ball land on the ground without BOUNCING much 吊球 ▸ **dink** *verb* **~ sth**

din·kum /ˈdɪŋkəm/ *adj.* (*AustralE, NZE, informal*) (of an article or a person 物品或人) real or genuine 真實的；真正的：*If you're dinkum, I'll help you.* 如果你的身分真實無假，我就幫你。➲ see also FAIR DINKUM

dinky /ˈdɪŋki/ *adj.* (*informal*) **1** (*BrE, approving*) small and neat in an attractive way 小巧的；小而精緻的：*What a dinky little hat!* 多麼漂亮的小帽子啊！**2** (*NAmE, disapproving*) too small 微不足道的；不起眼的；無足輕重的：*I grew up in a dinky little town that didn't even have a movie theater.* 我生長在一個無名小鎮，那裏連個電影院都沒有。

din·ner 🔑 /ˈdɪnə(r)/ *noun*
1 🔑 [U, C] the main meal of the day, eaten either in the middle of the day or in the evening（中午或晚上吃的）正餐，主餐：*It's time for dinner.* 該吃飯了。◇ *When do you* **have dinner**? 你什麼時間吃主餐？◇ *What time do you serve dinner?* 你們什麼時候供應主餐？◇ *Let's invite them to dinner tomorrow.* 我們明天請他們吃飯吧。◇ *What shall we have* **for dinner** *tonight?* 我們今晚吃什麼好呢？◇ *It's your turn to cook dinner.* 該你做飯了。◇ *She didn't eat much dinner.* 她沒吃多少飯。◇ *I never eat a big dinner.* 我向來飯量不大。◇ *Christmas dinner* 聖誕大餐 ◇ *a three-course dinner* 三道菜的正餐 ◇ *I'd like to take you out* **to dinner** *tonight.* 今天晚上我想帶你出去吃飯。◇ (*BrE*) **school dinners** (= meals provided at school in the middle of the day) 學校午餐 ➲ **COLLOCATIONS** at RESTAURANT ➲ note at MEAL **2** 🔑 [C] a large formal social gathering at which dinner is eaten 宴會：*The club's annual dinner will be held on 3 June.* 俱樂部一年一度的宴會將於 6 月 3 日舉行。➲ see also DINNER PARTY
IDM ˌ**done like a** ˈ**dinner** (*AustralE, NZE, informal*) completely defeated 徹底被打敗；一敗塗地 ➲ more at DOG *n.*

ˈ**dinner dance** *noun* a social event in the evening that includes a formal meal and dancing 餐後有舞會的正式宴會

ˈ**dinner jacket** (*BrE*) (also **tux·edo** *NAmE, BrE*) *noun* a black or white jacket worn with a BOW TIE at formal occasions in the evening（男式，配蝶形領結的）晚禮服，無尾禮服 ➲ compare TAILS at TAIL *n.* (6)

ˈ**dinner lady** (*BrE*) (*US* ˈ**lunch lady**) *noun* a woman whose job is to serve meals to children in schools（學校裏照顧孩子吃飯的）女服務員

ˈ**dinner party** *noun* a social event at which a small group of people eat dinner at sb's house（在家裏舉行的）宴會；家宴

ˈ**dinner service** *noun* a set of matching plates, dishes, etc. for serving a meal 成套餐具

ˈ**dinner suit** (*BrE*) (also **tux·edo** *NAmE, BrE*) *noun* a DINNER JACKET and trousers/pants, worn with a BOW TIE at formal occasions in the evening（男式，配蝶形領結的）成套無尾晚禮服

ˈ**dinner table** *noun* (often **the dinner table**) [usually sing.] the table at which people are eating dinner; an occasion when people are eating together 餐桌；同一桌進餐：*conversation at the dinner table* 席間交談 ➲ compare DINING TABLE

ˈ**dinner theater** *noun* (*NAmE*) a restaurant where you see a play after your meal 餐館劇院（餐後有戲劇表演）

ˈ**dinner time** *noun* the time at which dinner is normally eaten 正餐時間

din·ner·ware /ˈdɪnəweə(r); *NAmE* ˈdɪnərwer/ *noun* [U] (*NAmE*) plates, dishes, etc. used for serving a meal 餐具

dino·saur /ˈdaɪnəsɔː(r)/ *noun* **1** an animal that lived millions of years ago but is now EXTINCT (= it no longer exists). There were many types of dinosaur, some of which were very large. 恐龍 **2** (*disapproving*) a person or thing that is old-fashioned and cannot change in the changing conditions of modern life 守舊落伍的人；過時落後的東西

dint /dɪnt/ *noun*
IDM **by dint of sth/of doing sth** (*formal*) by means of sth 借助；憑藉；由於：*He succeeded by dint of hard work.* 他靠艱苦的努力獲得了成功。

dio·cese /ˈdaɪəsɪs/ *noun* (*pl.* **dio·ceses** /ˈdaɪəsiːz/) (in the Christian Church 基督教會) a district for which a BISHOP is responsible 教區；主教轄區 ▸ **dio·cesan** /daɪˈɒsɪsn; *NAmE* -ˈɑːs-/ *adj.*

diode /ˈdaɪəʊd; *NAmE* -oʊd/ *noun* (*technical* 術語) an electronic device in which the electric current passes in one direction only, for example a SILICON CHIP（電子）二極管

Dio·nys·iac /ˌdaɪəˈnɪziæk/ (also **Dio·nys·ian** /ˌdaɪəˈnɪziən/) *adj.* (*formal*) **1** relating to the ancient Greek god Dionysus（古希臘酒神）狄俄尼索斯的；酒與狂歡之神的 **2** relating to the physical senses and the emotions, especially when they are expressed without control 感情慾望的（尤指放縱的）➲ compare APOLLONIAN

di·optre (*especially US* **di·opter**) /daɪˈɒptə(r); *NAmE* -ˈɑːp-/ *noun* (*physics* 物) a unit for measuring the power of a LENS to REFRACT light (= make it change direction) 屈光度（透鏡放大率的單位）

di·op·trics /daɪˈɒptrɪks; *NAmE* -ˈɑːp-/ *noun* [U] (*physics* 物) the scientific study of REFRACTION (= the way light changes direction when it goes through glass, etc.) 折射光學 ▸ **di·op·tric** /daɪˈɒptrɪk; *NAmE* -ˈɑːp-/ *adj.*

dio·rama /ˌdaɪəˈrɑːmə; *NAmE* also -ˈræmə/ *noun* a model representing a scene with figures, especially in a museum 透景畫（博物館廣泛使用）

di·ox·ide /daɪˈɒksaɪd; *NAmE* -ˈɑːks-/ *noun* [U, C] (*chemistry* 化) a substance formed by combining two atoms of OXYGEN and one atom of another chemical element 二氧化物 ➲ see also CARBON DIOXIDE

di·oxin /daɪˈɒksɪn; *NAmE* -ˈɑːks-/ *noun* a chemical used in industry and farming. Most dioxins are poisonous. 二噁英；二氧（雜）芑；戴奧辛

dip /dɪp/ *verb, noun*
■ *verb* (**-pp-**) **1** [T] to put sth quickly into a liquid and take it out again 蘸；浸：**~ sth (into sth)** *He dipped the brush into the paint.* 他拿畫筆蘸了蘸顏料。◇ **~ sth (in)** *Dip your hand in to see how hot the water is.* 把手伸進去看看水有多熱。◇ *The fruit had been dipped in chocolate.* 這水果蘸過巧克力醬。**2** [I, T] to go downwards or to a lower level; to make sth do this（使）下降，下沉 **SYN** **fall**：(+ **adv./prep.**) *The sun dipped below the*

horizon. 太陽落到地平線下了。◇ *Sales for this quarter have dipped from 38.7 million to 33 million.* 本季度銷售額從 3 870 萬下降到 3 300 萬。◇ *The road dipped suddenly as we approached the town.* 我們向鎮裏駛近時道路陡然下斜。◇ **~ sth (+ adv./prep.)** *The plane dipped its wings.* 機翼向下傾斜。 **3** [T] **~ sth** (*BrE*) if you **dip** your HEADLIGHTS when driving a car at night, you make the light from them point down so that other drivers do not have the light in their eyes 把（汽車前燈的）遠光調為近光 **4** [T] **~ sth** when farmers **dip** animals, especially sheep, they put them in a bath of a liquid containing chemicals in order to kill insects, etc. 給（牲畜，尤指綿羊）洗藥浴

IDM **dip into your 'pocket** (*informal*) to spend some of your own money on sth 花錢；掏腰包 **dip a 'toe in/into sth | dip a 'toe in/into the water** (*informal*) to start doing sth very carefully to see if it will be successful or not 涉足試試；試做

PHR V **,dip 'into sth** **1** to put your hand into a container to take sth out 把手伸進（…裏取東西）：*She dipped into her purse and took out some coins.* 她從錢包裏掏出一些硬幣。 **2** to read or watch only parts of sth 瀏覽；略為過目；涉獵：*I have only had time to dip into the report.* 這份報告我來不及細看，只是草草瀏覽了一遍。 **3** to take an amount from money that you have saved 提取（款項）；動用（存款）：*We took out a loan for the car because we didn't want to dip into our savings.* 因為不想動用存款，我們申請了一筆貸款買汽車。

■ ***noun*** **1** [C] (*informal*) a quick swim 游一游；泡一泡：*Let's **go for a dip** before breakfast.* 我們早飯前去游一會兒泳吧。 **2** [C] a decrease in the amount or success of sth, usually for only a short period（通常指暫時的）減少，下降，衰退 **SYN** **fall**：*a sharp **dip in** profits* 利潤急劇下降 **3** [C] a place where a surface suddenly drops to a lower level and then rises again 凹陷處；低窪處：*a dip in the road* 路上的凹陷處 ◇ *Puddles had formed in the dips.* 低窪處形成了一個個水坑。 **4** [C, U] a thick mixture into which pieces of food are dipped before being eaten 調味醬（用食物來蘸着吃） **5** [U, C] a liquid containing a chemical into which sheep and other animals can be dipped in order to kill insects on them 藥浴液，清洗液（用於綿羊或其他牲畜洗浴以殺死身上的蟲子） **6** [sing.] **~ into sth** a quick look at sth 瀏覽；草草翻閱：*A brief dip into history serves to confirm this view.* 隨便翻閱一下歷史就足以證實這種觀點。 **7** [C, usually sing.] a quick movement of sth down and up（降而復升的）一動：*He gave a dip of his head.* 他點了點頭。 ➲ see also LUCKY DIP

diph·theria /dɪfˈθɪəriə; *NAmE* -ˈθɪriə; dɪp-/ *noun* [U] a serious infectious disease of the throat that causes difficulty in breathing 白喉

diph·thong /ˈdɪfθɒŋ; ˈdɪp-; *NAmE* -θɑːŋ; -θɔːŋ/ *noun* (*phonetics* 語音) a combination of two vowel sounds or vowel letters, for example the sounds /aɪ/ in *pipe* /paɪp/ or the letters *ou* in *doubt* 二合元音；複合元音；雙元音；雙元音字母組合；雙母音 ▸ **diph·thong·al** /dɪfˈθɒŋɡl; dɪp-; *NAmE* -ˈθɑːŋɡl; -ˈθɔːŋɡl/ *adj.*

dip·lod·ocus /dɪˈplɒdəkəs; ˌdɪpləˈdəʊkəs; *NAmE* -ˈplɑːd-; -ˈdoʊk-/ *noun* a very large DINOSAUR with a long thin neck and tail 梁龍（頸部和尾巴細長的大恐龍）

dip·loid /ˈdɪplɔɪd/ *adj.* (*biology* 生) (of a cell 細胞) containing two complete sets of CHROMOSOMES, one from each parent 二倍體的（含有兩套染色體）➲ compare HAPLOID

dip·loma /dɪˈpləʊmə; *NAmE* -ˈploʊ-/ *noun* **1** (*BrE*) a course of study at a college or university 文憑課程：*a two-year diploma course* 二年制的文憑課程 ◇ *She is taking a diploma in management studies.* 她在攻讀管理學文憑課程。 **2** a document showing that you have completed a course of study or part of your education 畢業文憑：*a High School diploma* 高中畢業文憑

dip·lo·macy /dɪˈpləʊməsi; *NAmE* -ˈploʊ-/ *noun* [U] **1** the activity of managing relations between different countries; the skill in doing this 外交；外交技巧；外交手腕：*international diplomacy* 國際外交 ◇ *Diplomacy is better than war.* 採取外交手段勝於訴諸戰爭。➲ COLLOCATIONS at INTERNATIONAL **2** skill in dealing with people in difficult situations without upsetting or offending them（處理人際關係的）手腕，手段，策略 **SYN** **tact** ➲ see also SHUTTLE DIPLOMACY

dip·lo·mat /ˈdɪpləmæt/ *noun* **1** (also *old-fashioned* **dip·lo·ma·tist**) a person whose job is to represent his or her country in a foreign country, for example, in an EMBASSY 外交官 **2** a person who is skilled at dealing with other people 善於交際的人；通權達變的人；圓通的人；有手腕的人

dip·lo·mat·ic /ˌdɪpləˈmætɪk/ *adj.* **1** connected with managing relations between countries (= DIPLOMACY) 外交的；從事外交的：*a diplomatic crisis* 外交危機 ◇ *Attempts are being made to settle the dispute by diplomatic means.* 正在努力通過外交途徑解決爭端。◇ *to **break off/establish/restore diplomatic relations** with a country* 與某國斷絕／建立／恢復外交關係 **2** having or showing skill in dealing with people in difficult situations 有手腕的；靈活變通的；策略的；圓通的 **SYN** **tactful**：*a diplomatic answer* 圓通的回答 ▸ **dip·lo·mat·ic·al·ly** /-kli/ *adv.*：*The country remained diplomatically isolated.* 這個國家在外交上仍然受到孤立。◇ *'Why don't we take a break for coffee?' she suggested diplomatically.* "我們何不停下來喝杯咖啡呢？"她婉轉地提議道。

,diplo,matic 'bag (*BrE*) (*US* **,diplo,matic 'pouch**) *noun* a container that is used for sending official letters and documents between a government and its representatives in another country and that cannot be opened by customs officers 外交郵袋，外交信袋（海關官員不能拆封）

,diplo'matic corps *noun* (usually **the diplomatic corps**) [C+sing./pl. v.] (*pl.* **diplomatic corps**) all the DIPLOMATS who work in a particular city or country 外交使團

,diplo,matic im'munity *noun* [U] special rights given to diplomats working in a foreign country which mean they cannot be arrested, taxed, etc. in that country 外交豁免權；外交特權

the Diplo'matic Service (*especially BrE*) (*NAmE* usually **the 'Foreign Service**) *noun* [sing.] the government department concerned with representing a country in foreign countries 外交部門

dip·lo·ma·tist /dɪˈpləʊmətɪst; *NAmE* -ˈploʊ-/ *noun* (*old-fashioned*) = DIPLOMAT

di·pole /ˈdaɪpəʊl; *NAmE* -poʊl/ *noun* (*physics* 物) a pair of separated POLES, one positive and one negative 偶極子

dip·per /ˈdɪpə(r)/ *noun* a bird that lives near rivers 河烏 ➲ see also BIG DIPPER

dippy /ˈdɪpi/ *adj.* (*informal*) stupid; crazy 笨的；傻的；腦子有問題的

dipso·maniac /ˌdɪpsəˈmeɪniæk/ *noun* a person who has a strong desire for alcoholic drink that they cannot control 嗜酒狂；間發性酒狂 **SYN** **alcoholic**

dip·stick /ˈdɪpstɪk/ *noun* **1** a long straight piece of metal used for measuring the amount of liquid in a container, especially the amount of oil in an engine 浸量尺；（尤指發動機的）油尺 **2** (*informal*) a stupid person 笨蛋；傻瓜

'dip switch (*BrE*) (*NAmE* **'dim·mer switch**) *noun* a switch that allows you to make the front lights on a car point downwards（汽車的）前燈垂光開關

dip·tych /ˈdɪptɪk/ *noun* (*technical* 術語) a painting, especially a religious one, with two wooden panels that can be closed like a book（尤指宗教的）對摺畫，雙聯畫

dire /ˈdaɪə(r)/ *adj.* (**direr**, **dir·est**) **1** [usually before noun] (*formal*) very serious 極其嚴重的；危急的：*living in dire poverty* 生活赤貧 ◇ ***dire warnings/threats*** 嚴重的警告／威脅 ◇ *Such action may have **dire consequences**.* 這種行為可能產生嚴重後果。◇ *We're **in dire need of** your help.* 我們急需你的幫助。◇ *The firm is **in dire straits*** (= in a very difficult situation) *and may go bankrupt.* 這家公司已陷入極度困境之中，可能會破產。 **2** (*BrE, informal*) very bad 極糟的；極差的：*The acting was dire.* 這表演糟透了。

dir·ect 🔑 /dəˈrekt; dɪ-; daɪ-/ *adj., verb, adv.*

■ ***adj.***

‣ **NOBODY/NOTHING IN BETWEEN** 直接 **1** 🔑 [usually before noun] happening or done without involving other people, actions, etc. in between 直接的；親自的；親身的： *They are in direct contact with the hijackers.* 他們與劫機者直接聯繫。◇ *His death was a direct result of your action.* 他的死是你的行為直接造成的後果。◇ *We are looking for somebody with direct experience of this type of work.* 我們在尋找對這種工作有過親身體驗的人。◇ *This information has* **a direct bearing on** (= it is closely connected with) *the case.* 這一信息與此論據有直接關係。 **OPP** **indirect**

‣ **JOURNEY/ROUTE** 旅程；路線 **2** 🔑 going in the straightest line between two places without stopping or changing direction 筆直的；逕直的；最近的： *the most* ***direct route/course*** 最直接的路線／航線◇ *a* ***direct flight*** (= a flight that does not stop) 直飛航班◇ *There's a* ***direct train*** *to Leeds* (= it may stop at other stations but you do not have to change trains). 有一班直達利茲的火車。◇ *a* ***direct hit*** (= a hit that is accurate and does not touch sth else first) 直接命中 **OPP** **indirect**

‣ **HEAT/LIGHT** 熱；光 **3** 🔑 [only before noun] with nothing between sth and the source of the heat or light 直射的： *Protect your child from direct sunlight by using a sunscreen.* 給孩子搽點防曬霜以防日光直接照射。

‣ **SAYING WHAT YOU MEAN** 直爽 **4** 🔑 saying exactly what you mean in a way that nobody can pretend not to understand 直爽的；直率的；坦率的： *a* ***direct answer/question*** 直截了當的回答；坦率的問題◇ *You'll have to get used to his direct manner.* 你可得慢慢習慣他這種直率的態度。 **OPP** **indirect** ➲ SYNONYMS at HONEST

‣ **EXACT** 恰好 **5** [only before noun] exact 正好的；恰好的： *That's the* ***direct opposite*** *of what you told me yesterday.* 那與你昨天告訴我的截然相反。◇ *a* ***direct quote*** (= one using a person's exact words) 直接引語

‣ **RELATIONSHIP** 關係 **6** [only before noun] related through parents and children rather than brothers, sisters, aunts, etc. 直系的；嫡系的： *a direct descendant of the country's first president* 國家第一任總統的嫡系後裔 **OPP** **indirect**

■ ***verb***

‣ **AIM** 目標 **1** 🔑 [T] to aim sth in a particular direction or at a particular person 把…對準（某方向或某人）： **~ sth at sth/sb** *The machine directs a powerful beam at the affected part of the body.* 這種機器將很強的射線對準身體感染部位。◇ *Was that remark directed at me?* 那話是衝着我來的嗎？◇ **~ sth to/towards sth/sb** *There are three main issues that we need to direct our attention to.* 我們需要注意的主要有三個問題。◇ **~ sth against sth/sb** *Most of his anger was directed against himself.* 他主要是生自己的氣。

‣ **CONTROL** 控制 **2** 🔑 [T] **~ sb/sth** to control or be in charge of sb/sth 管理；監督；指導： *A new manager has been appointed to direct the project.* 已任命一位新經理來管理這項工程。◇ *He was asked to take command and* ***direct operations.*** 他奉命統率並指揮作戰行動。

‣ **MOVIE/PLAY/MUSIC** 電影；戲劇；音樂 **3** 🔑 [I, T] to be in charge of actors in a play, or a film/movie, or musicians in an ORCHESTRA, etc. 導演（戲劇或電影）；指揮（管弦樂隊）： *She prefers to act rather than direct.* 她寧願當演員，不願當導演。◇ **~ sb/sth** *The movie was directed by Steven Spielberg.* 這部電影是由史蒂文・斯皮爾伯格導演的。◇ *She now directs a large choir.* 她目前擔任一個大合唱團的指揮。 ➲ COLLOCATIONS at CINEMA

‣ **SHOW THE WAY** 指路 **4** 🔑 [T] **~ sb (to ...)** to tell or show sb how to get to somewhere or where to go 給（某人）指路；為（某人）領路： *Could you direct me to the station?* 請問到車站怎麼走？◇ *A police officer was directing the traffic.* 一名警察在指揮交通。 ➲ SYNONYMS at TAKE

‣ **GIVE ORDER** 下達命令 **5** [T] *(formal)* to give an official order 指示；命令 **SYN** **order**： **~ sb to do sth** *The police officers had been directed to search the building.* 警察奉命搜查這棟大樓。◇ **~ that ...** *The judge directed that the mother be given custody of the children.* 法官判決孩子由母親監護。◇ (*BrE* also) *The judge directed that the mother should be given custody of the children.* 法官判決孩子由母親監護。 ➲ SYNONYMS at ORDER

‣ **LETTER/COMMENT** 信函；意見 **6** [T] **~ sth to ...** *(formal)* to send a letter, etc. to a particular place or to a particular person 把（信件等）寄至；交予： *Direct any complaints to the Customer Services department.* 將投訴寄至用戶服務部。

■ ***adv.***

‣ **JOURNEY/ROUTE** 旅程；路線 **1** without stopping or changing direction 直接；逕直： *We flew direct to Hong Kong.* 我們直飛香港。◇ *The 10.40 goes direct to Leeds.* * 10:40 這班火車直達利茲。

‣ **NOBODY IN BETWEEN** 親自 **2** without involving other people 親自；直接： *I prefer to deal with him direct.* 我更願意直接跟他打交道。

di,rect 'access *noun* [U] (*computing* 計) the ability to get data immediately from any part of a computer file 直接存取；隨機訪問

di,rect 'action *noun* [U, C] the use of strikes, protests, etc. instead of discussion in order to get what you want 直接行動（用罷工、抗議等方式達到目的）

di,rect 'current *noun* [C, U] (*abbr.* DC) an electric current that flows in one direction only 直流電 ➲ compare ALTERNATING CURRENT

di,rect 'debit *noun* [U, C] (*BrE*) an instruction to your bank to allow sb else to take an amount of money from your account on a particular date, especially to pay bills 直接借記；直接扣賬： *We pay all our bills* ***by direct debit.*** 我們以直接借記方式支付所有賬單。 ➲ compare STANDING ORDER

di,rect de'posit *noun* [U] (*NAmE*) the system of paying sb's wages straight into their bank account 直接將工資轉入銀行賬戶

dir·ec·tion 🔑 /dəˈrekʃn; dɪ-; daɪ-/ *noun*

‣ **WHERE TO** 去向 **1** 🔑 [C, U] the general position a person or thing moves or points towards 方向；方位： *Tom went off* ***in the direction of*** *home.* 湯姆朝家的方向去了。◇ *She glanced* ***in his direction.*** 她朝他那個方向瞥了一眼。◇ *The aircraft was flying in a northerly direction.* 飛機正向北飛去。◇ *The road was blocked in both directions.* 這條路往返方向都堵死了。◇ *They hit a truck coming in* ***the opposite direction.*** 他們撞上一輛迎面開來的卡車。◇ *Has the wind* ***changed direction?*** 風向變了嗎？◇ *When the police arrived, the crowd scattered* ***in all directions.*** 警察趕到後，人群便向四面八方散開了。◇ *I lost all* ***sense of direction*** (= I didn't know which way to go). 我完全迷失了方向。

‣ **DEVELOPMENT** 發展 **2** 🔑 [C, U] the general way in which a person or thing develops 趨勢；動向： *The exhibition provides evidence of several new directions in her work.* 這個展覽表明她的創作有幾個新動向。◇ *I am very unhappy with the direction the club is taking.* 我對俱樂部的發展趨勢很不滿意。◇ *It's only a small improvement, but at least it's* ***a step in the right direction.*** 雖然這只是小小的改進，但至少是朝正確方向邁出的一步。

‣ **WHERE FROM** 來自 **3** [C] the general position a person or thing comes or develops from 方面： *Support came from an unexpected direction.* 一個出人意料的來源提供了幫助。◇ *Let us approach the subject from a different direction.* 咱們從一個不同的角度來探討這個題目吧。

‣ **PURPOSE** 目的 **4** 🔑 [U] a purpose; an aim 目的；目標： *We are looking for somebody with a clear* ***sense of direction.*** 我們想找一個有明確目標的人。◇ *Once again her life felt lacking in direction.* 她的人生似乎又沒了方向。

‣ **INSTRUCTIONS** 說明 **5** 🔑 [C, usually pl.] instructions about how to do sth, where to go, etc. 用法說明；操作指南；旅行指南： *Let's stop and ask for directions.* 咱們停下來問問路吧。◇ *Simple directions for assembling the model are printed on the box.* 模型裝配的簡要說明印在盒子上。

‣ **CONTROL** 控制 **6** 🔑 [U] the art of managing or guiding sb/sth 管理；指導： *All work was produced by the students* ***under the direction of*** *John Williams.* 所有作品都是在約翰・威廉斯的指導下由學生創作完成的。

‣ **FILM/MOVIE** 電影 **7** [U] the instructions given by sb directing a film/movie （電影導演的）指點，指示： *There is some clever direction and the film is very well* *shot.* 由於導演指導有方，影片拍得非常成功。**IDM** see PULL *v.*

dir·ec·tion·al /dəˈrekʃənl; dɪ-; daɪ-/ *adj.* (*technical* 術語) **1** producing or receiving signals, sound, etc. better in one particular direction（發出或接收信號、聲音等）定向的，指向的：*a* ***directional microphone/aerial*** 定向傳聲器／天線 **2** connected with the direction in which sth is moving 方向的：*directional stability* 方向穩定性

dir·ec·tion·less /dəˈrekʃənləs; dɪ-; daɪ-/ *adj.* (*formal*) without a direction or purpose 無方向的；無目標的

dir·ect·ive /dəˈrektɪv; dɪ-; daɪ-/ *noun, adj.*

■ ***noun*** an official instruction 指示；命令：*The EU has issued a new set of directives on pollution.* 歐盟發佈了一系列關於污染的新指令。

■ ***adj.*** (*formal*) giving instructions 指示的；指導的：*They are seeking a central, directive role in national energy policy.* 他們正尋求在國家能源政策方面起中心指導作用。

dir·ect·ly O‑w /dəˈrektli; dɪ-; daɪ-/ *adv., conj.*

■ ***adv.*** **1** O‑w in a direct line or manner 直接地；逕直地；坦率地：*He drove her directly to her hotel.* 他駕車直接把她送到了她下榻的旅館。◇ *She looked directly at us.* 她正視着我們。◇ *He's directly responsible to the boss.* 他直接對老闆負責。◇ *We have not been directly affected by the cuts.* 我們並未直接受到裁減的影響。**OPP** **indirectly** **2** O‑w exactly in a particular position 正；正好地；恰好：***directly opposite/below/ahead*** 正對面；正下方；前方◇ *They remain directly opposed to these new plans.* 他們仍舊截然反對這些新方案。**3** immediately 立即；立刻：*She left directly after the show.* 演出一結束，她馬上就走了。**4** (*old-fashioned, BrE*) soon 過一會兒；很快 **SYN** **shortly**：*Tell them I'll be there directly.* 告訴他們我一會兒就到。

■ ***conj.*** (*BrE*) as soon as 一…就…：*I went home directly I had finished work.* 我一幹完活就回家了。

di,rect ˈmail *noun* [U] advertisements that are sent to people through the post/mail 直接郵寄的廣告

di,rect ˈmarketing *noun* [U] the business of selling products or services directly to customers who order by mail or by telephone instead of going to a shop/store 直接營銷（通過郵寄或電話直接向顧客銷售產品或推銷服務）

the diˈrect method *noun* [sing.] a way of teaching a foreign language using only that language and not treating the study of grammar as the most important thing（外語）直接教學法（只以目標語為教學語言，不以學習語法為最重要）

dir·ect·ness /dəˈrektnəs; dɪ-; daɪ-/ *noun* [U] the quality of being simple and clear, so that it is impossible not to understand 直接；直截了當；坦率：*'What's that?' she asked with her usual directness.* "那是什麼？"她以慣用的坦率語氣問道。

di,rect ˈobject *noun* (*grammar* 語法) a noun, noun phrase or pronoun that refers to a person or thing that is directly affected by the action of a verb 直接賓語；直接受詞：*In 'I met him in town', the word 'him' is the direct object.* 在 I met him in town 中，him 是直接賓語。➲ compare INDIRECT OBJECT

dir·ect·or O‑w /dəˈrektə(r); dɪ-; daɪ-/ *noun* **1** O‑w one of a group of senior managers who run a company 董事；理事；經理：*the* ***managing director*** 總經理◇ *an* ***executive/non-executive director*** 執行／非執行董事◇ *He's on* ***the board of directors****.* 他是董事會成員。**2** O‑w a person who is in charge of a particular activity or department in a company, a college, etc.（某一活動的）負責人；（公司部門的）主任，經理；（學院的）院長：*the musical director* 音樂總監◇ *a regional director* 地區主管◇ *the director of education* 教育局長 **3** O‑w a person in charge of a film/movie or play who tells the actors and staff what to do（電影或戲劇的）導演 ➲ compare PRODUCER (2)

dir·ect·or·ate /dəˈrektərət; dɪ-; daɪ-/ *noun* **1** a section of a government department in charge of one particular activity（政府）部門：*the environmental directorate* 環境部門 **2** the group of directors who run a company 董事會；理事會 **SYN** **board of directors**

di,rector ˈgeneral *noun* (*especially BrE*) the head of a large organization, especially a public organization 署長；局長；（尤指公共機構的）總管：*the director general of the BBC* 英國廣播公司總裁

dir·ect·or·ial /ˌdaɪrekˈtɔːriəl/ *adj.* [only before noun] connected with the position or work of a director, especially of a director of films/movies 主管的；（尤指）導演的；指揮的：*The film marks her directorial debut.* 這部電影是她作為導演初露頭角的標誌。

Di,rector of ,Public Proseˈcutions *noun* (*abbr.* **DPP**) (in England and Wales) a public official whose job is to decide whether people who are suspected of a crime should be brought to trial（英格蘭和威爾士的）檢察官

diˈrector's chair *noun* a folding wooden chair with crossed legs, a seat and back made of cloth, and sides on which you can rest your arms 導演椅，輕便摺疊椅（木製扶手椅，以帆布作座面、椅背）➲ VISUAL VOCAB page V21

diˈrector's cut *noun* a version of a film/movie, usually released some time after the original is first shown, that is exactly how the director wanted it to be（電影的）導演剪輯版

dir·ect·or·ship /dəˈrektəʃɪp; dɪ-; daɪ-; *NAmE* -tərʃ-/ *noun* the position of a company director; the period during which this is held 董事的職位；董事的任期

dir·ec·tory /dəˈrektəri; dɪ-; daɪ-/ *noun* (*pl.* **-ies**) **1** a book containing lists of information, usually in alphabetical order, for example people's telephone numbers or the names and addresses of businesses in a particular area 名錄；電話號碼簿；公司名錄：*a* ***telephone/trade directory*** 電話號碼簿；商行名錄◇ *a directory of European Trade Associations* 歐洲同業公會名錄 **2** a file containing a group of other files or programs in a computer（計算機文件或程序的）目錄

di,rectory enˈquiries (*BrE*) (*NAmE* **di,rectory asˈsistance** or *informal* **in·for·ma·tion**) *noun* [U+sing./pl. v.] a telephone service that you can use to find out a person's telephone number 電話號碼查詢台

di,rect ˈrule *noun* [U] government of a region by a central government, when that region has had its own government in the past 直轄

di,rect ˈspeech *noun* [U] (*grammar* 語法) a speaker's actual words; the use of these in writing 說話者原話；直接引語；直接敍述法：*Only direct speech should go inside inverted commas.* 只有直接引語應放在引號內。➲ compare INDIRECT SPEECH, REPORTED SPEECH

di,rect ˈtax *noun* (*technical* 術語) a tax which is collected directly from the person who pays it, for example income tax 直接稅（如所得稅）➲ compare INDIRECT TAX ▶ **di,rect taxˈation** *noun* [U]

dirge /dɜːdʒ; *NAmE* dɜːrdʒ/ *noun* **1** a song sung in the past at a funeral or for a dead person 哀歌；輓歌 **2** (*informal, disapproving*) any song or piece of music that is too slow and sad 悽慘的歌曲（或樂曲）

diri·gible /ˈdɪrɪdʒəbl/ *adj., noun*

■ ***adj.*** (*formal*) able to be guided or steered 可駕駛的；可操縱的：*a dirigible balloon* 可操控的熱氣球

■ ***noun*** an AIRSHIP 飛艇

dirk /dɜːk; *NAmE* dɜːrk/ *noun* a long heavy pointed knife that was used as a weapon in Scotland in the past（舊時蘇格蘭人用的）長匕首

dirndl /ˈdɜːndl; *NAmE* ˈdɜːrndl/ *noun* (from *German*) a very full wide skirt, pulled in tightly at the waist; a dress with a skirt like this and a closely fitting top 阿爾卑斯村姑裙（束腰寬襬）；阿爾卑斯村姑式連衣裙（有緊胸褡和束腰寬襬裙）

dirt O‑w /dɜːt; *NAmE* dɜːrt/ *noun* [U] **1** O‑w any substance that makes sth dirty, for example dust, soil or mud 污物；塵土；爛泥：*His clothes were covered in dirt.* 他的衣服沾滿了污垢。◇ *First remove any grease or dirt from the surface.* 先把表面的油污或塵土去掉。**2** O‑w (*especially NAmE*) loose earth or soil 鬆土；泥土；散土：*He picked up a handful of dirt and threw it at* them. 他抓起一把土朝他們扔過去。◇ *Pack the dirt firmly round the plants.* 將植物周圍的土培實。◇ *They lived in a shack with a dirt floor.* 他們住在土地板的棚屋裏。 ➲ SYNONYMS at SOIL **3** (*informal*) unpleasant or harmful information about sb that could be used to damage their reputation, career, etc. 醜聞；流言蜚語：*Do you have any dirt on the new guy?* 你知道新來的那個人的醜聞嗎？ **4** (*informal*) = EXCREMENT：*dog dirt* 狗屎 **IDM** see DISH *v.*, TREAT *v.*

'dirt bike *noun* a motorcycle designed for rough ground, especially for competitions（尤指用於比賽的）越野摩托車 ➲ VISUAL VOCAB page V51

ˌdirt 'cheap *adj., adv.* (*informal*) very cheap 非常便宜（的）：*It was dirt cheap.* 這太便宜了。◇ *I got it dirt cheap.* 我買得非常便宜。

'dirt farmer *noun* (*NAmE*) a farmer who has poor land and does not make much money, and who does not pay anyone else to work on the farm 自耕農

ˌdirt 'poor *adj.* (*NAmE, informal*) extremely poor 極貧困的；極貧窮的

'dirt road (*NAmE* also **'dirt track**) *noun* a rough road in the country that is made from hard earth 土路

'dirt track *noun* **1** (*NAmE*) = DIRT ROAD **2** a track made of CINDERS, soil, etc. used for motorcycle racing 煤渣跑道（供摩托車比賽用）：*a dirt-track race* 煤渣跑道賽車

dirty 🔑 /'dɜːti; *NAmE* 'dɜːrti/ *adj., verb, adv.*

■ *adj.* (**dirt·ier**, **dirti·est**)

▸ **NOT CLEAN** 不潔 **1** 🔑 not clean 骯髒的；齷齪的；污穢的：*dirty hands/clothes* 髒手／衣服 ◇ *a dirty mark* 污跡 ◇ *Try not to get too dirty!* 別把身上弄得太髒！◇ *I always get given the dirty jobs* (= jobs that make you become dirty). 讓我幹的總是些髒活。

▸ **OFFENSIVE** 冒犯 **2** 🔑 [usually before noun] connected with sex in an offensive way 下流的；色情的；黃色的；猥褻的：*a* ***dirty joke/book*** 下流的笑話；黃色的書 ◇ *He's got a* ***dirty mind*** (= he often thinks about sex). 他滿腦子下流事兒。

▸ **UNPLEASANT/DISHONEST** 令人不快；不誠實 **3** [usually before noun] (*informal*) unpleasant or dishonest 令人厭惡的；卑鄙的；不誠實的：*a dirty lie* 卑鄙的謊言 ◇ *She's a dirty player.* 她是個沒有體育道德的運動員。◇ *He's a great man for doing the dirty jobs* (= jobs which are unpleasant because they involve being dishonest or mean to people). 他這個人最會幹傷天害理的事。

▸ **COLOURS** 顏色 **4** [only before noun] dull 不鮮明的；暗淡的：*a dirty brown carpet* 暗褐色的地毯

▸ **DRUGS** 毒品 **5** (*NAmE, slang*) using illegal drugs 吸毒的

IDM **be a dirty 'word** to be a subject or an idea that people think is bad or immoral 犯忌的字眼；犯忌的話題；忌諱的想法；淫穢字眼：*Profit is not a dirty word around here.* 在這裏，贏利不是一個犯忌的字眼。 **(do sb's) 'dirty work** (to do) the unpleasant or dishonest jobs that sb else does not want to do（幹）沒人願幹的事，卑鄙的勾當 **do the 'dirty on sb** (*BrE, informal*) to cheat sb who trusts you; to treat sb badly or unfairly 欺騙，出賣，虧待（某人）：*I'd never do the dirty on my friends.* 我決不出賣朋友。 **ˌdown and 'dirty** (*NAmE, informal*) **1** behaving in an unfair or aggressive way, especially because you want to win 不正當競爭的；不擇手段的：*The candidate again got down and dirty with his rival.* 這名候選人又開始用下作的手段對付他的競爭對手。 **2** rude and shocking 粗暴無禮的；惡劣的：*The singer got down and dirty at the club last night and made headlines again.* 這個歌手昨晚在俱樂部的無恥行為使他又上了報紙的頭版頭條。 **give sb a dirty 'look** to look at sb in a way that shows you are annoyed with them 厭惡地瞪某人一眼；給某人一個白眼 ➲ more at HAND *n.*, WASH *v.*

■ *verb* (**dirt·ies**, **dirty·ing**, **dirt·ied**, **dirt·ied**) **~ sth** to make sth dirty 弄髒；使變髒

■ *adv.*

IDM **dirty great/big** (*BrE, informal*) used to emphasize how large sth is 非常大的；很大的：*When I turned round he was pointing a dirty great gun at me.* 我轉過身來，他以一支老大的槍對準我。 **play 'dirty** (*informal*) to behave or play a game in an unfair way 幹卑鄙勾當；（比賽）犯規 ➲ more at TALK *v.*

Synonyms 同義詞辨析

dirty

dusty • filthy • muddy • soiled • grubby • stained

These words all describe sb/sth that is not clean. 以上各詞均形容人或事物不乾淨、骯髒。

dirty not clean; covered with dust, soil, mud, oil, etc. 指骯髒的、齷齪的、污穢的：*If your hands are dirty, go and wash them.* 要是你的手髒了，就去洗一洗。

dusty full of dust; covered with dust 指佈滿灰塵的、灰塵覆蓋的：*There were shelves full of dusty books.* 有些書架上全是佈滿灰塵的書。

filthy very dirty and unpleasant 指骯髒的、污穢的：*It's absolutely filthy in here.* 這裏面髒得不得了。

muddy full of or covered in mud 指沾滿泥的、泥濘的：*Don't you come in here with those muddy boots on!* 你不要穿着那雙沾滿泥漿的靴子進來！

soiled (*rather formal*) dirty, especially with waste from the body 指骯髒的、齷齪的，尤指有人體排泄物的：*soiled nappies/diapers* 髒尿布

grubby (*rather informal*) rather dirty, usually because it has not been washed 通常指因未經洗滌而骯髒的、邋遢的、污穢的：*He hoped she wouldn't notice his grubby shirt cuffs.* 他希望她不會注意到他骯髒的襯衫袖口。

stained (often in compounds) covered with stains; marked with a stain (= a dirty mark that is difficult to remove)（常構成複合詞）指污漬斑斑的、沾有污漬的：*a pair of paint-stained jeans* 一條沾滿油漆的牛仔褲

PATTERNS

- dirty/dusty/filthy/muddy/soiled/grubby/stained **clothes**
- dirty/dusty/filthy/grubby **hands**
- a dirty/dusty/filthy **room**
- **to get** dirty/dusty/filthy/muddy/stained

'dirty bomb *noun* a bomb which contains RADIOACTIVE material "髒彈"；放射性炸彈

ˌdirty old 'man *noun* (*informal*) an older man whose interest in sex or in sexually attractive young people is considered to be offensive or not natural for sb of his age 老色鬼

ˌdirty 'trick *noun* **1** [usually pl.] dishonest, secret and often illegal activity by a political group or other organization that is intended to harm the reputation or success of an opponent 卑鄙伎倆；造謠中傷：*a dirty tricks campaign* 骯髒卑鄙的競選運動 **2** an unpleasant and dishonest act 卑鄙的勾當；奸詐：*What a dirty trick to play!* 玩的手段太卑鄙了！

ˌdirty week'end *noun* (*BrE, humorous*) a weekend spent away with a sexual partner, often in secret 與性伴侶廝混的週末

dis (also **diss**) /dɪs/ *verb* (**-ss-**) **~ sb** (*informal, especially NAmE*) to show a lack of respect for sb, especially by saying insulting things to them 看不起，作踐（尤指用侮辱性言辭）

dis- /dɪs/ *prefix* (in adjectives, adverbs, nouns and verbs 構成形容詞、副詞、名詞和動詞) not; the opposite of 不；非；相反；相對：*dishonest* 不誠實 ◇ *disagreeably* 不合意地 ◇ *disadvantage* 不利條件 ◇ *disappear* 消失

dis·abil·ity /ˌdɪsə'bɪləti/ *noun* (*pl.* **-ies**) **1** [C] a physical or mental condition that means you cannot use a part of your body completely or easily, or that you cannot learn easily（某種）缺陷，障礙：***a physical/mental disability*** 生理缺陷；心理障礙 ◇ *people with severe learning disabilities* 具有嚴重學習障礙的人 **2** [U] the state of not being able to use a part of your body completely or easily; the state of not being able to learn easily

（指狀態、身心、學習等方面的）缺陷，障礙：*He qualifies for help on the grounds of disability.* 他因身有殘疾有資格得到幫助。➲ note at DISABLED

dis·able /dɪsˈeɪbl/ *verb* **1** **~ sb** to injure or affect sb permanently so that, for example, they cannot walk or cannot use a part of their body 使喪失能力；使傷殘：*He was disabled in a car accident.* 他在車禍中殘廢了。◊ *a disabling condition* 導致殘障的疾病 **2** **~ sth** to make sth unable to work so that it cannot be used 使無效；使不能運轉：*The burglars gained entry to the building after disabling the alarm.* 竊賊破壞警報器後便得以進入大樓。

D

dis·abled 🔑 /dɪsˈeɪbld/ *adj.* **1** 🔑 unable to use a part of your body completely or easily because of a physical condition, illness, injury, etc.; unable to learn easily 喪失能力的；有殘疾的；無能力的：***physically/mentally disabled*** 有生理殘疾的；有智力缺陷的 ◊ *severely disabled* 嚴重傷殘 ◊ *He was born disabled.* 他天生殘疾。◊ *facilities for disabled people* 殘疾人使用的設施 **2** **the disabled** *noun* [pl.] people who are disabled 殘疾人；傷殘者：*caring for the sick, elderly and disabled* 關心老弱病殘

Which Word? 詞語辨析

disabled / handicapped

- **Disabled** is the most generally accepted term to refer to people with a permanent illness or injury that makes it difficult for them to use part of their body completely or easily. **Handicapped** is slightly old-fashioned and many people now think it is offensive. People also now prefer to use the word **disability** rather than **handicap**. The expression **disabled people** is often preferred to **the disabled** because it sounds more personal. * disabled 是最廣為接受的用語，指殘疾人或傷殘人。handicapped 稍為過時，現在許多人認為該詞意含冒犯。現在人們喜歡用 disability 而非 handicap。disabled people 比 the disabled 更為人所接受，原因是聽起來較個人化。
- **Disabled** and **disability** can be used with other words to talk about a mental condition. * disabled 和 disability 可與其他詞連用表示智力狀況：*mentally disabled* 有智力缺陷的 ◊ *learning disabilities* 學習障礙
- If somebody's ability to hear, speak or see has been damaged but not destroyed completely, they have **impaired hearing/speech/sight** (or **vision**). They can be described as **visually/hearing impaired** or **partially sighted**. 聽力、說話能力或視力受到損害但未完全喪失，用 impaired hearing/speech/sight（或 vision）表示，或形容某人為 visually/hearing impaired（視力／聽力受損的）或 partially sighted（視力有缺陷的）：*The museum has special facilities for blind and partially sighted visitors.* 博物館有專門設備供失明和視力有缺陷的參觀者使用。

dis·able·ment /dɪsˈeɪblmənt/ *noun* [U] (*formal*) the state of being disabled or the process of becoming disabled 殘廢；傷殘；失去能力：*The insurance policy covers sudden death or disablement.* 保險單上包括突然死亡或傷殘。

dis·abuse /ˌdɪsəˈbjuːz/ *verb* **~ sb (of sth)** (*formal*) to tell sb that what they think is true is, in fact, not true 去掉（某人）的錯誤想法；使省悟

dis·ad·van·tage 🔑 /ˌdɪsədˈvɑːntɪdʒ; *NAmE* -ˈvæn-/ *noun* [C, U] something that causes problems and tends to stop sb/sth from succeeding or making progress 不利因素；障礙；不便之處：*a* ***serious/severe/considerable disadvantage*** 嚴重的／重大的不利條件 ◊ **~ (of sth)** *One major* ***disadvantage*** *of the area is the lack of public transport.* 這個地區的一大不便之處就是缺少公共交通工具。◊ **~ (to sth)** *There are disadvantages to the plan.* 這個計劃有諸多不利因素。◊ *What's the* ***main disadvantage****?* 主要的不利條件是什麼？◊ *I was* ***at a disadvantage*** *compared to the younger members of the team.* 與隊裏較年輕的隊員相比，我處於不利地位。◊ *The fact that he didn't speak a foreign language* ***put him at a*** *distinct* ***disadvantage****.* 他不會說外語使他處於明顯的不利地位。◊ *I hope my lack of experience won't* ***be to my disadvantage****.* 但願我的經驗不足不會使我吃虧。◊ *The advantages of the scheme far* ***outweighed the disadvantages****.* 這個計劃的優點遠遠超過了缺點。◊ *Many children in the class suffered severe social and economic disadvantage.* 班上許多孩子都來自社會地位低下並且經濟困難的家庭。**OPP** advantage ▶ **dis·ad·van·tage** *verb* **~ sb/sth**

dis·ad·van·taged /ˌdɪsədˈvɑːntɪdʒd; *NAmE* -ˈvæn-/ *adj.* **1** not having the things, such as education, or enough money, that people need in order to succeed in life 弱勢的；社會地位低下的 **SYN** deprived：***disadvantaged groups/children*** 生活條件差的群體／孩子 ◊ *a severely disadvantaged area* 極貧困地區 **OPP** advantaged ➲ SYNONYMS at POOR **2** **the disadvantaged** *noun* [pl.] people who are disadvantaged 下層社會

dis·ad·van·ta·geous /ˌdɪsædvænˈteɪdʒəs/ *adj.* **~ (to/for sb)** (*formal*) causing sb to be in a worse situation compared to other people 不利的；不便的：*The deal will not be disadvantageous to your company.* 這項交易不會對你公司不利。**OPP** advantageous

dis·af·fect·ed /ˌdɪsəˈfektɪd/ *adj.* no longer satisfied with your situation, organization, belief, etc. and therefore not loyal to it 不滿的：*Some disaffected members left to form a new party.* 部份不滿的成員已脫黨另立新黨。▶ **dis·af·fec·tion** /ˌdɪsəˈfekʃn/ *noun* [U]：*There are signs of growing disaffection amongst voters.* 選民中出現日漸不滿的跡象。

dis·af·fili·ate /ˌdɪsəˈfɪlieɪt/ *verb* [I, T] **~ (sth) (from sth)** to end the link between a group, a company or an organization and a larger one（使）脫離，退出：*The local club has disaffiliated from the National Athletic Association.* 當地俱樂部已退出全國體育聯合會。▶ **dis·af·fili·ation** /ˌdɪsəfɪliˈeɪʃn/ *noun* [U]

dis·agree 🔑 /ˌdɪsəˈɡriː/ *verb* **1** 🔑 [I] if two people **disagree** or one person **disagrees** with another about sth, they have a different opinion about it 不同意；持不同意見；有分歧：*Even friends disagree sometimes.* 即便是朋友有時也有分歧。◊ *No, I disagree. I don't think it would be the right thing to do.* 不，我不贊成。我認為這樣做不合適。◊ **~ (with sb) (about/on/over sth)** *He disagreed with his parents on most things.* 他在多數事情上都與父母意見不一。◊ *Some people disagree with this argument.* 有些人不同意這一論點。◊ **~ that …** *Few would disagree that students learn best when they are interested in the topic.* 學生對自己感興趣的題目學得最好，這一點幾乎所有人都不會有異議。**2** 🔑 [I] if statements or reports **disagree**, they give different information 不符；不一致 **OPP** agree

PHR V **disaˈgree with sb** if sth, especially food, **disagrees** with you, it has a bad effect on you and makes you feel ill/sick（尤指食物）對（某人）不適宜，使不舒服 **disaˈgree with sth/with doing sth** 🔑 to believe that sth is bad or wrong; to disapprove of sth 不贊成；反對：*I disagree with violent protests.* 我不贊成暴力抗議。

dis·agree·able /ˌdɪsəˈɡriːəbl/ *adj.* (*formal*) **1** not nice or enjoyable 不合意的；令人不快的；討厭的 **SYN** unpleasant：*a disagreeable smell/experience/job* 難聞的氣味；令人不快的經歷；不合意的工作 **2** (of a person 人) rude and unfriendly 不友善的；難相處的 **SYN** unpleasant：*a disagreeable bad-tempered man* 一個脾氣不好難以相處的男人 **OPP** agreeable ▶ **dis·agree·ably** /-əbli/ *adv.*

dis·agree·ment 🔑 /ˌdɪsəˈɡriːmənt/ *noun* **1** 🔑 [U, C] a situation where people have different opinions about sth and often argue 意見不一；分歧；爭論：**~ (about/on/over/as to sth)** *Disagreement arose about exactly how to plan the show.* 在如何擬訂具體演出計劃的問題上出現了分歧。◊ *disagreement on the method to be used* 在要採用的方法上的爭論 ◊ *There is considerable disagreement over the safety of the treatment.* 這種療法

是否安全爭論很大。◇ ~ (**between A and B**) *It was a source of disagreement between the two states.* 這就是兩國紛爭的一個根源。◇ ~ (**among …**) *There is disagreement among archaeologists as to the age of the sculpture.* 考古學家在這尊雕塑的年代問題上意見不一。◇ ~ (**with sb**) *They have had several disagreements with their neighbours.* 他們與鄰居發生過好幾次爭吵。OPP **agreement** **2** [U, C] ~ **between A and B** a difference between two things that should be the same 不符；不一致：*The comparison shows considerable disagreement between theory and practice.* 這一對比表明理論和實踐之間有相當大的差距。

dis·allow /ˌdɪsəˈlaʊ/ *verb* ~ **sth** [often passive] (*formal*) to officially refuse to accept sth because it is not valid 不准許；不接受；駁回：*to **disallow a claim/an appeal*** 不接受要求；駁回上訴 ◇ *The second goal was disallowed.* 第二個進球被判無效。⇨ compare ALLOW (6)

dis·am·bigu·ate /ˌdɪsæmˈbɪɡjueɪt/ *verb* ~ **sth** (*technical* 術語) to show clearly the difference between two or more words, phrases, etc. which are similar in meaning 消除歧義

dis·ap·pear 🔑 /ˌdɪsəˈpɪə(r); *NAmE* -ˈpɪr/ *verb* **1** 🔑 [I] (+ **adv./prep.**) to become impossible to see 消失；不見 SYN **vanish**：*The plane disappeared behind a cloud.* 飛機消失在雲層裏。◇ *Lisa watched until the train **disappeared from view**.* 莉薩一直看着火車從視線中消失。 **2** 🔑 [I] to stop existing 不復存在；滅絕；消亡 SYN **vanish**：*Her nervousness quickly disappeared once she was on stage.* 她一走上台緊張情緒便迅速消失了。◇ *The problem won't just disappear.* 這個問題不會就這樣不了了之的。◇ *Our countryside is disappearing at an alarming rate.* 我們的農村地區正在以驚人的速度消亡。 **3** 🔑 [I] to be lost or impossible to find 失踪；丢失 SYN **vanish**：*I can never find a pen in this house. They disappear as soon as I buy them.* 我在家裏從來找不到一支筆。每次我一買來就不翼而飛。◇ ~ **from sth** *The child disappeared from his home some time after four.* 這孩子四點多的時候就離家不見了。▶ **dis·ap·pear·ance** /-ˈpɪərəns; *NAmE* -ˈpɪr-/ *noun* [U, C]：*the disappearance of many species of plants and animals from our planet* 許多動植物物種從我們這顆行星上的消失 ◇ *Police are investigating the disappearance of a young woman.* 警方正在調查一位年輕女子的失踪案。IDM see ACT *n.*, FACE *n.*

dis·ap·point 🔑 /ˌdɪsəˈpɔɪnt/ *verb* **1** 🔑 [T, I] ~ (**sb**) | (**it disappoints sb that …**) to make sb feel sad because sth that they hope for or expect to happen does not happen or is not as good as they hoped 使失望：*Her decision to cancel the concert is bound to disappoint her fans.* 她決定取消這場音樂會，肯定會使她的歌迷失望。◇ *I hate to disappoint you, but I'm just not interested.* 我不想使你掃興，但我確實不感興趣。◇ *The movie had disappointed her* (= it wasn't as good as she had expected). 這部電影使她失望。◇ *His latest novel does not disappoint.* 他最近發表的這部小說沒有使人失望。 **2** [T] ~ **sth** to prevent sth that sb hopes for from becoming a reality 使破滅；使落空：*The new government had soon disappointed the hopes of many of its supporters.* 新政府不久便使許多支持者的希望破滅了。

dis·ap·point·ed 🔑 /ˌdɪsəˈpɔɪntɪd/ *adj.* upset because sth you hoped for has not happened or been as good, successful, etc. as you expected 失望的；沮喪的；失意的：~ (**at/by sth**) *They were **bitterly disappointed** at the result of the game.* 他們對比賽結果極為失望。◇ *I was disappointed by the quality of the wine.* 這酒的質量令我失望。◇ ~ (**in/with sb/sth**) *I'm disappointed in you—I really thought I could trust you!* 你真讓我失望，我原以為可以相信你的！◇ *I was very disappointed with myself.* 我對自己感到非常失望。◇ ~ (**to see, hear, etc.**) *He was disappointed to see she wasn't at the party.* 看到她沒來參加晚會，他感到很失望。◇ ~ (**that …**) *I'm disappointed (that) it was sold out.* 全都賣完了，我感到很失望。◇ ~ (**not**) **to be …** *She was disappointed not to be chosen.* 她沒有被選中感到很沮喪。

dis·ap·point·ing 🔑 /ˌdɪsəˈpɔɪntɪŋ/ *adj.* not as good, successful, etc. as you had hoped; making you feel disappointed 令人失望的；令人沮喪的；令人掃興的：*a disappointing result/performance* 令人失望的結果／演出 ◇ *The outcome of the court case was disappointing for the family involved.* 訴訟案的結果使得涉及本案的這家人非常失望。▶ **dis·ap·point·ing·ly** *adv.*：*The room was disappointingly small.* 房間小得令人失望。

dis·ap·point·ment 🔑 /ˌdɪsəˈpɔɪntmənt/ *noun* **1** 🔑 [U] sadness because sth has not happened or been as good, successful, etc. as you expected or hoped 失望；沮喪；掃興：*Book early for the show to avoid disappointment.* 欲看演出，從速訂票，以免向隅。◇ ***To our great disappointment**, it rained every day of the trip.* 這次旅行天天下雨，讓我們大失所望。◇ *He found it difficult to hide his disappointment when she didn't arrive.* 她沒有來，他感到很難掩飾自己內心的沮喪。 **2** 🔑 [C] a person or thing that is disappointing 使人失望的人（或事物）；令人掃興的人（或事物）：*a **bitter/major disappointment*** 令人極度失望／大失所望的事 ◇ *That new restaurant was a big disappointment.* 那家新餐館使人大失所望。◇ ~ **to sb** *I always felt I was a disappointment to my father.* 我總覺得我使父親失望了。

dis·ap·pro·ba·tion /ˌdɪsˌæprəˈbeɪʃn/ *noun* [U] (*formal*) disapproval of sb/sth that you think is morally wrong （對不道德的人或事）反對，不認可

dis·ap·proval 🔑 /ˌdɪsəˈpruːvl/ *noun* [U] ~ (**of sb/sth**) a feeling that you do not like an idea, an action or sb's behaviour because you think it is bad, not suitable or going to have a bad effect on sb else 不贊成；反對：*disapproval of his methods* 不贊同他的方法 ◇ *to show/express disapproval* 表明／表示反對 ◇ *He shook his head **in disapproval**.* 他搖了搖頭，表示反對。◇ *She looked at my clothes **with disapproval**.* 她不滿意地看着我的衣服。OPP **approval**

dis·ap·prove 🔑 /ˌdɪsəˈpruːv/ *verb* [I, T] to think that sb/sth is not good or suitable; to not approve of sb/sth 不贊成；不同意；反對：*She wants to be an actress, but her parents disapprove.* 她想當演員，可是她父母不同意。◇ ~ **of sb/sth** *He **strongly disapproved** of the changes that had been made.* 他強烈反對已進行的變革。◇ ~ **sth** (*NAmE*) *A solid majority disapproves the way the president is handling the controversy.* 大多數人都反對總統處理爭論的方式。OPP **approve**

dis·ap·prov·ing 🔑 /ˌdɪsəˈpruːvɪŋ/ *adj.* showing that you do not approve of sb/sth 不贊成的；表示反對的；不以為然的：*a **disapproving glance/tone/look*** 不以為然的一瞥／語氣／樣子 OPP **approving** ▶ **dis·ap·prov·ing·ly** *adv.*：*He looked disapprovingly at the row of empty wine bottles.* 他不以為然地看了看那排空酒瓶。

dis·arm /dɪsˈɑːm; *NAmE* -ˈɑːrm/ *verb* **1** [T] ~ **sb** to take a weapon or weapons away from sb 繳（某人）的械；解除（某人）的武裝：*Most of the rebels were captured and disarmed.* 大部份叛亂分子被俘獲並解除了武裝。 **2** [I] (of a country or a group of people 國家或集體) to reduce the size of an army or to give up some or all weapons, especially nuclear weapons 裁軍，解除武裝，裁減軍備（尤指核武器） **3** [T] ~ **sb** to make sb feel less angry or critical 消釋（某人）的怒氣（或批評）：*He disarmed her immediately by apologizing profusely.* 他一再向她道歉，馬上便消釋了她的怒氣。⇨ compare ARM

dis·arma·ment /dɪsˈɑːməmənt; *NAmE* -ˈɑːrm-/ *noun* [U] the fact of a country reducing the size of its armed forces or the number of weapons, especially nuclear weapons, that it has 裁軍，裁減軍備（尤指核武器）：*nuclear disarmament* 核裁軍 ◇ *disarmament talks* 裁軍談判 ⇨ compare ARMAMENT

dis·arm·ing /dɪsˈɑːmɪŋ; *NAmE* -ˈɑːrm-/ *adj.* making people feel less angry or suspicious than they were before 使人消氣的；解人疑慮的：*a disarming smile* 使人消氣的微笑 ▶ **dis·arm·ing·ly** *adv.*：*disarmingly frank* 坦率得使人放心

dis·ar·range /ˌdɪsəˈreɪndʒ/ *verb* [usually passive] ~ **sth** (*formal*) to make sth untidy 使紊亂；弄亂

dis·array /ˌdɪsəˈreɪ/ *noun* [U] a state of confusion and lack of organization in a situation or a place 混亂；紊亂：*The peace talks broke up **in disarray**.* 和談在混亂

D

中破裂了。◇ *Our plans were* **thrown into disarray** *by her arrival.* 我們的計劃因她的到來而陷入一片混亂。

dis·as·sem·ble /ˌdɪsəˈsembl/ *verb* **1** [T] **~ sth** to take apart a machine or structure so that it is in separate pieces 拆卸；拆開：*We had to completely disassemble the engine to find the problem.* 我們只好把發動機全部拆開以尋找故障原因。OPP **assemble** **2** [T] **~ sth** (*computing* 計) to translate sth from computer code into a language that can be read by humans 反彙編（將計算機編碼譯成普通語言）**3** [I] (*formal*) (of a group of people 人群) to move apart and go away in different directions 散開；分散：*The concert ended and the crowd disassembled.* 音樂會結束，人群便散去了。

dis·as·sem·bler /ˌdɪsəˈsemblə(r)/ *noun* (*computing* 計) a program used to disassemble computer code 反彙編程序；反組譯器

dis·as·so·ci·ate /ˌdɪsəˈsəʊʃieɪt; -ˈsəʊs-; *NAmE* -ˈsoʊ-/ *verb* = DISSOCIATE (1)

dis·as·ter 0→ /dɪˈzɑːstə(r); *NAmE* -ˈzæs-/ *noun* **1** 0→ [C] an unexpected event, such as a very bad accident, a flood or a fire, that kills a lot of people or causes a lot of damage 災難；災禍；災害 SYN **catastrophe**：*an* **air disaster** 空難 ◇ *environmental disasters* 環境災難 ◇ *Thousands died in the disaster.* 數千人在這場災禍中喪生。◇ *a* **natural disaster** (= one that is caused by nature) 自然災害 **2** 0→ [C, U] a very bad situation that causes problems 不幸；禍患：*Losing your job doesn't have to be such a disaster.* 丟了工作不一定就是大難臨頭。◇ **Disaster struck** *when the wheel came off.* 車輪脫落，災難就來了。◇ *financial disaster* 嚴重的財政危機 ◇ *Letting her organize the party is a* **recipe for disaster** (= something that is likely to go badly wrong). 讓她來組織這次聚會非壞事不可。**3** 0→ [C, U] (*informal*) a complete failure 徹底失敗的人（或事）：*As a teacher, he's a disaster.* 他當老師壓根兒就不稱職。◇ *The play's first night was a total disaster.* 這齣戲頭一晚就徹底演砸了。IDM see WAIT *v.*

diˈsaster area *noun* **1** a place where a disaster has happened and which needs special help 災區 **2** (*informal*) a place or situation that has a lot of problems, is a failure, or is badly organized 問題成堆的地方；災難性局面

dis·as·trous /dɪˈzɑːstrəs; *NAmE* -ˈzæs-/ *adj.* very bad, harmful or unsuccessful 極糟糕的；災難性的；完全失敗的 SYN **catastrophic**, **devastating**：*a disastrous harvest/fire/result* 嚴重歉收／火災；災難性的結果 ◇ *Lowering interest rates could have disastrous consequences for the economy.* 降低利率可能給經濟帶來災難性後果。▸ **dis·as·trous·ly** *adv.*：*How could everything go so disastrously wrong?* 怎麼會事事都出這麼大的錯呢？

dis·avow /ˌdɪsəˈvaʊ/ *verb* **~ sth** (*formal*) to state publicly that you have no knowledge of sth or that you are not responsible for sth/sb 不承認；否認；拒絕對…承擔責任：*They disavowed claims of a split in the party.* 他們否認了黨內出現分裂的說法。▸ **dis·avowal** /-ˈvaʊəl/ *noun* [C, U]

dis·band /dɪsˈbænd/ *verb* [T, I] **~ (sb/sth)** to stop sb/sth from operating as a group; to separate or no longer operate as a group 解散；解體；散夥：*They set about disbanding the terrorist groups.* 他們開始解散恐怖主義組織。◇ *The committee formally disbanded in August.* 委員會於八月份正式解散。▸ **dis·band·ment** *noun* [U]

dis·bar /dɪsˈbɑː(r)/ *verb* (-rr-) [usually passive] **~ sb (from sth/from doing sth)** to stop a lawyer from working in the legal profession, especially because he or she has done sth illegal 取消（某人）的律師資格

dis·be·lief /ˌdɪsbɪˈliːf/ *noun* [U] the feeling of not being able to believe sth 不信；懷疑：*He stared at me* **in disbelief**. 他滿腹疑惑地盯着我。◇ *To enjoy the movie you have to* **suspend your disbelief** (= pretend to believe sth, even if it seems very unlikely). 要欣賞這部電影就得暫且相信那些甚至不可能發生的事。➲ compare BELIEF (3), UNBELIEF

dis·be·lieve /ˌdɪsbɪˈliːv/ *verb* [T, I] (not used in the progressive tenses 不用於進行時) **~ (sth)** (*formal*) to not believe that sth is true or that sb is telling the truth 不信；懷疑：*Why should I disbelieve her story?* 我為什麼要懷疑她的說法呢？▸ **dis·be·liev·ing** *adj.*：*a disbelieving look/smile/laugh* 懷疑的表情／微笑／笑聲 **dis·be·liev·ing·ly** *adv.*

PHR V **disbeˈlieve in sth** to not believe that sth exists 懷疑，不信（某物存在）

dis·burse /dɪsˈbɜːs; *NAmE* -ˈbɜːrs/ *verb* **~ sth** (*formal*) to pay money to sb from a large amount that has been collected for a purpose（從資金中）支付，支出 ▸ **dis·burse·ment** *noun* [U, C]：*the disbursement of funds* 撥款 ◇ *aid disbursements* 援助款項的支出額

disc 0→ (also **disk** especially in *NAmE*) /dɪsk/ *noun* **1** 0→ a thin flat round object 圓盤；圓片：*He wears an identity disc around his neck.* 他脖子上掛着圓形身分牌。**2** 0→ = CD：*This recording is available online or* **on disc**. 這錄音可在線獲取，也可購買激光唱片。**3** 0→ (*BrE*) a disk for a computer（計算機）磁盤，磁碟 **4** (*old-fashioned*) = RECORD (2) **5** a structure made of CARTILAGE between the bones of the back 椎間盤：*He's been off work with a* **slipped disc** (= one that has moved from its correct position, causing pain). 他因椎間盤突出一直未上班。

dis·card *verb, noun*

■ **verb** /dɪsˈkɑːd; *NAmE* -ˈkɑːrd/ **1** [T] (*formal*) to get rid of sth that you no longer want or need 丟棄；拋棄：**~ sb/sth** *The room was littered with discarded newspapers.* 房間裏到處是亂扔的報紙。◇ *He had discarded his jacket because of the heat.* 因天氣炎熱他脫掉了夾克。◇ (*figurative*) *She could now discard all thought of promotion.* 她現在可以打消晉升的念頭了。◇ **~ sb/sth as sth** *10% of the data was discarded as unreliable* * 10% 的數據因不可靠而被廢棄。**2** [T, I] **~ (sth)** (in card games 紙牌遊戲) to get rid of a card that you do not want 墊（牌）；打出（無用的牌）

■ **noun** /ˈdɪskɑːd; *NAmE* -kɑːrd/ a person or thing that is not wanted or thrown away, especially a card in a card game 被拋棄的人（或物）；（尤指紙牌遊戲中）墊出的牌

ˈdisc brake *noun* [usually pl.] a BRAKE that works by two surfaces pressing onto a disc in the centre of a wheel 盤型制動

dis·cern /dɪˈsɜːn; *NAmE* -ˈsɜːrn/ *verb* (not used in the progressive tenses 不用於進行時) (*formal*) **1** to know, recognize or understand sth, especially sth that is not obvious 覺察出；識別；瞭解 SYN **detect**：**~ sth** *It is possible to discern a number of different techniques in her work.* 從她的作品中可以瞭解到許多不同的創作手法。◇ *He discerned a certain coldness in their welcome.* 他覺察到他們的接待有點冷淡。◇ **~ how, whether, etc.** … *It is often difficult to discern how widespread public support is.* 瞭解公眾支持的廣泛程度常常是困難的。◇ **~ that** … *I quickly discerned that something was wrong.* 我很快覺察到出了問題。**2** **~ sth** to see or hear sth, but not very clearly（依稀）看出，分辨出，聽出 SYN **make out**：*We could just discern the house in the distance.* 我們只能勉強分辨出遠處的房子。▸ **dis·cern·ible** *adj.* (*formal*) SYN **perceptible**：*There is often no discernible difference between rival brands.* 相互競爭的品牌之間往往看不出明顯的區別。◇ *His face was barely discernible in the gloom.* 在黑暗中很難看得清他的臉。

dis·cern·ing /dɪˈsɜːnɪŋ; *NAmE* -ˈsɜːrn-/ *adj.* (*approving*) able to show good judgement about the quality of sb/sth 有識別力的；有眼力的；有洞察力的

dis·cern·ment /dɪˈsɜːnmənt; *NAmE* -ˈsɜːrn-/ *noun* [U] (*formal, approving*) the ability to show good judgement about the quality of sb/sth 識別能力；洞察力 SYN **discrimination**：*He shows great discernment in his choice of friends.* 他選擇朋友很有眼光。

dis·charge *verb, noun*

■ **verb** /dɪsˈtʃɑːdʒ; *NAmE* -ˈtʃɑːrdʒ/ (*formal*)

▸ FROM HOSPITAL/JOB 醫院；工作 **1** [T, usually passive] **~ sb (from sth)** to give sb official permission to leave a place or job; to make sb leave a job 准許（某人）離開；解雇：*Patients were being discharged from the hospital too early.* 病人都過早獲准出院。◇ *She had discharged herself* against medical advice. 她不聽醫囑擅自出院了。◇ *He was discharged from the army following his injury.* 他受傷後就退伍了。◇ *She was discharged from the police force for bad conduct.* 她因行為不檢被革除出警察隊伍。

▸ FROM PRISON/COURT 監獄；法庭 **2** [T, often passive] **~ sb** to allow sb to leave prison or court 釋放：*He was **conditionally discharged** after admitting the theft.* 他承認偷盜行為後被有條件地釋放了。

▸ GAS/LIQUID 氣體；液體 **3** [I, T] when a gas or a liquid **discharges** or **is discharged**, or sb **discharges** it, it flows somewhere 排出；放出；流出：**~ (into sth)** *The river is diverted through the power station before discharging into the sea.* 這條河改道經水電站後流入大海。◇ **~ sth (into sth)** *The factory was fined for discharging chemicals into the river.* 這家工廠因往河裏排放化學物質而被罰款。

▸ FORCE/POWER 力量；電力 **4** [T, I] **~ (sth)** (*technical* 術語) to release force or power 發（力）；放（電）：*Lightning is caused by clouds discharging electricity.* 閃電是由雲層放電產生的。

▸ DUTY 職責 **5** [T] **~ sth** to do everything that is necessary to perform and complete a particular duty 盡（職）；完成；履行：*to **discharge your duties/responsibilities/obligations*** 履行職責／責任／義務 ◇ *to **discharge a debt*** (= to pay it) 清償債務

▸ GUN 槍 **6** [T] **~ sth** to fire a gun, etc. 射出；開火

■ ***noun*** /ˈdɪstʃɑːdʒ; *NAmE* -tʃɑːrdʒ/ (*formal*)

▸ OF LIQUID/GAS 液體；氣體 **1** [U, C] the action of releasing a substance such as a liquid or gas; a substance that comes out from inside somewhere 排出（物）；放出（物）；流出（物）：*a ban on the discharge of toxic waste* 禁止有毒廢物的排放 ◇ *thunder and lightning caused by electrical discharges* 由放電產生的雷電 ◇ ***nasal/vaginal discharge*** (= from the nose/VAGINA) 鼻涕；陰道分泌物

▸ FROM HOSPITAL/JOB 醫院；工作 **2** [U, C] **~ (from sth)** the act of officially allowing sb, or of telling sb, to leave somewhere, especially sb in a hospital or the army 獲准離開；免職；出院；退伍

▸ OF DUTY 職責 **3** [U] the act of performing a task or a duty or of paying money that is owed 履行；執行；（債務的）清償：*the **discharge of debts/obligations*** 債務的清償；義務的履行

dis·ciple /dɪˈsaɪpl/ *noun* **1** a person who believes in and follows the teachings of a religious or political leader 信徒；門徒；追隨者 SYN **follower**：*a disciple of the economist John Maynard Keynes* 經濟學家約翰 • 梅納德 • 凱恩斯的信徒 **2** (according to the Bible) one of the people who followed Jesus Christ and his teachings when he was living on earth, especially one of the twelve APOSTLES（《聖經》中耶穌的）門徒，十二宗徒之一

dis·cip·lin·ar·ian /ˌdɪsəplɪˈneəriən; *NAmE* -ˈner-/ *noun* a person who believes in using rules and punishments for controlling people 嚴格紀律信奉者；嚴格執行紀律者：*She's a very strict disciplinarian.* 她執行紀律非常嚴格。

dis·cip·lin·ary /ˈdɪsəplɪnəri; ˌdɪsəˈplɪnəri; *NAmE* ˈdɪsəpləneri/ *adj.* connected with the punishment of people who break rules 有關紀律的；執行紀律的；懲戒性的：*a disciplinary hearing* (= to decide if sb has done sth wrong) 紀律審訊 ◇ *The company will be taking **disciplinary action** against him.* 公司將對他進行紀律處分。

dis·cip·line 🔑 /ˈdɪsəplɪn/ *noun, verb*

■ ***noun*** **1** 🔑 [U] the practice of training people to obey rules and orders and punishing them if they do not; the controlled behaviour or situation that results from this training 訓練；訓導；紀律；風紀：*The school has a reputation for high standards of discipline.* 這所學校因紀律嚴格而名聞遐邇。◇ *Strict discipline is imposed on army recruits.* 新兵受嚴格的紀律約束。◇ *She keeps good discipline in class.* 她嚴格執行課堂紀律。 **2** [C] a method of training your mind or body or of controlling your behaviour; an area of activity where this is necessary 訓練方法；行為準則；符合準則的行為：*Yoga is a good discipline for learning to relax.* 瑜伽是一種學習放鬆的有效方法。 **3** [U] the ability to control your behaviour or the way you live, work, etc. 自制力；遵守紀律：*He'll never get anywhere working for himself—he's got no discipline.* 他為自己工作是不會有什麼成就的，他毫無自制力。 ➲ see also SELF-DISCIPLINE **4** [C] (*formal*) an area of knowledge; a subject that people study or are taught, especially in a university 知識領域；（尤指大學的）學科，科目

■ ***verb*** **1 ~ sb (for sth)** to punish sb for sth they have done 懲罰；處罰：*The officers were disciplined for using racist language.* 這些軍官因使用種族歧視性語言而受到懲罰。 **2 ~ sb** to train sb, especially a child, to obey particular rules and control the way they behave 訓練；訓導；管教：*a guide to the best ways of disciplining your child* 管教子女最佳方法指南 **3** to control the way you behave and make yourself do things that you believe you should do 自我控制；嚴格要求（自己）：**~ yourself** *Dieting is a matter of disciplining yourself.* 節食是自我控制的問題。◇ **~ yourself to do sth** *He disciplined himself to exercise at least three times a week.* 他規定自己每週至少鍛煉三次。 ▸ **dis·cip·lined** *adj.*：*a disciplined army/team* 紀律嚴明的軍隊／團隊 ◇ *a disciplined approach to work* 嚴格的工作態度

ˈdisc jockey *noun* (*abbr.* **DJ**) (also *informal* **dee·jay**) a person whose job is to introduce and play recorded popular music, on radio or television or at a club（電台、電視台、俱樂部）唱片節目主持人

dis·claim /dɪsˈkleɪm/ *verb* (*formal*) **1 ~ sth** to state publicly that you have no knowledge of sth, or that you are not responsible for sth 否認；拒絕承認 SYN **deny**：*She disclaimed any knowledge of her husband's whereabouts.* 她否認知道丈夫的下落。◇ *The rebels disclaimed all responsibility for the explosion.* 叛亂分子否認對這次爆炸事件負有任何責任。 **2 ~ sth** to give up your right to sth, such as property or a title 放棄（財產、頭銜等的）權利 SYN **renounce**

dis·claim·er /dɪsˈkleɪmə(r)/ *noun* **1** (*formal*) a statement in which sb says that they are not connected with or responsible for sth, or that they do not have any knowledge of it 免責聲明 **2** (*law* 律) a statement in which a person says officially that they do not claim the right to do sth 棄權聲明（書）

dis·close /dɪsˈkləʊz; *NAmE* -ˈkloʊz/ *verb* (*formal*) **1** to give sb information about sth, especially sth that was previously secret 揭露；透露；泄露 SYN **reveal**：**~ sth (to sb)** *The spokesman refused to disclose details of the takeover to the press.* 發言人拒絕向新聞界透露公司收購的詳細情況。◇ **~ that …** *The report discloses that human error was to blame for the accident.* 報告披露這次事故是人為失誤造成的。◇ **it is disclosed that …** *It was disclosed that two women were being interviewed by the police.* 據透露，警方當時正和兩名婦女面談。◇ **~ what, whether, etc. …** *I cannot disclose what we discussed.* 我不能泄露我們討論的內容。 **2 ~ sth** to allow sth that was hidden to be seen 使顯露；使暴露 SYN **reveal**：*The door swung open, disclosing a long dark passage.* 門開了，露出一條昏暗的長通道。

dis·clo·sure /dɪsˈkləʊʒə(r); *NAmE* -ˈkloʊ-/ *noun* (*formal*) **1** [U] the act of making sth known or public that was previously secret or private 揭露；透露；公開 SYN **revelation**：*the newspaper's disclosure of defence secrets* 報紙對防務內幕的披露 **2** [C] information or a fact that is made known or public that was previously secret or private 透露的秘聞；公開的事情；暴露的事實 SYN **revelation**：*startling disclosures about his private life* 對他的私生活聳人聽聞的披露

disco /ˈdɪskəʊ; *NAmE* ˈdɪskoʊ/ (*pl.* **-os**) *noun* **1** (also *old-fashioned* **disco·theque**) a club or party where people dance to recorded pop music 迪斯科舞廳（或舞會）：***disco music/dancing*** 迪斯科樂曲／舞 ◇ *the youth club disco* 青年俱樂部迪斯科舞廳 **2** the lights and sound equipment for such an event 迪斯科舞會的燈光及音響設備

disc·og·raphy /dɪsˈkɒɡrəfi; *NAmE* -ˈkɑːɡ-/ *noun* (*pl.* **disc·og·raph·ies**) **1** [C] all of the music that has been performed, written or collected by a particular person; a list of this music（某人的）音樂演唱集（或作品集、

作品收藏集），唱片分類目錄 **2** [U] the study of musical recordings or collections 音樂錄音（或作品集）研究

dis·col·or·ation (*BrE* also **dis·col·our·ation**) /dɪsˌkʌləˈreɪʃn/ *noun* **1** [U] the process of becoming discoloured 變色；褪色：*discoloration caused by the sun* 因日照引起的褪色 **2** [C] a place where sth has become discoloured 變色處；褪色處

D

dis·col·our (*especially US* **dis·color**) /dɪsˈkʌlə(r)/ *verb* [I, T] to change colour, or to make the colour of sth change, in a way that makes it look less attractive（使）變色，褪色：*Plastic tends to discolour with age.* 塑料久而久之便會褪色。◇ **~ sth** *The pipes were beginning to rust, discolouring the water.* 管子開始生銹，水都變顏色了。

dis·comfit /dɪsˈkʌmfɪt/ *verb* [often passive] **~ sb** (*literary*) to make sb feel confused or embarrassed 使困惑；使窘迫；使尷尬 ▸ **dis·com·fit·ure** /dɪsˈkʌmfɪtʃə(r)/ *noun* [U]：*He was clearly taking delight in her discomfiture.* 他顯然以她的窘迫為樂。

dis·com·fort /dɪsˈkʌmfət; *NAmE* -fərt/ *noun, verb*

■ ***noun*** (*formal*) **1** [U] a feeling of slight pain or of being physically uncomfortable 輕微的病痛；不舒服；不適：*You will experience some minor discomfort during the treatment.* 治療中你會稍感不適。◇ *abdominal discomfort* 腹部不適 **2** [U] a feeling of worry or embarrassment 不安；不自在；尷尬 SYN **unease**：*John's presence caused her considerable discomfort.* 約翰在場使她頗感尷尬。**3** [C] something that makes you feel uncomfortable or causes you a slight feeling of pain 使人不舒服的事物；苦事；痛苦

■ ***verb*** [often passive] **~ sb** (*formal*) to make sb feel anxious or embarrassed 使不舒服；使不安；使尷尬

dis·com·pose /ˌdɪskəmˈpəʊz; *NAmE* -ˈpoʊz/ *verb* **~ sb** (*formal*) to disturb sb and make them feel anxious 擾亂；使不安；使心煩意亂 SYN **disconcert, disturb** ▸ **dis·com·pos·ure** /ˌdɪskəmˈpəʊʒə(r); *NAmE* -ˈpoʊ-/ *noun* [U]

dis·con·cert /ˌdɪskənˈsɜːt; *NAmE* -ˈsɜːrt/ *verb* **~ sb** to make sb feel anxious, confused or embarrassed 使不安；使困惑；使尷尬 SYN **disturb**：*His answer rather disconcerted her.* 他的回答使她頗感難堪。▸ **dis·con·cert·ed** *adj.*：*I was disconcerted to find that everyone else already knew it.* 我發現別人都已知道此事，感到甚是尷尬。**dis·con·cert·ing** *adj.*：*She had the disconcerting habit of saying exactly what she thought.* 她怎麼想的就怎麼說，這種習慣令人非常難堪。**dis·con·cert·ing·ly** *adv.*

dis·con·nect /ˌdɪskəˈnekt/ *verb* **1** [T] **~ sth (from sth)** to remove a piece of equipment from a supply of gas, water or electricity 切斷（煤氣、水或電的供應）：*First, disconnect the boiler from the water mains.* 先將鍋爐與供水總管斷開。**2** [T] **~ sb/sth** [usually passive] to officially stop the supply of telephone lines, water, electricity or gas to a building 切斷（電話服務）；停止供應（水、電或煤氣）：*You may be disconnected if you do not pay the bill.* 若不付賬單就可能停止供應。**3** [T] **~ sth (from sth)** to separate sth from sth 使分離；使脫離：*The ski had become disconnected from the boot.* 滑雪板與靴子脫離了。**4** [T] **~ sb** [usually passive] to break the contact between two people who are talking on the telephone 使（電話線路）中斷：*We were suddenly disconnected.* 我們的電話突然斷線了。**5** [T, I, often passive] to end a connection to the Internet（與互聯網）斷開：**~ sb (from sth)** *I keep getting disconnected when I'm online.* 我連網時不斷掉線。◇ **~ (from sth)** *My computer crashes every time I disconnect from the Internet.* 我每次下網，計算機都會突然死機。OPP **connect** ▸ **dis·con·nec·tion** *noun* [U, C]

dis·con·nect·ed /ˌdɪskəˈnektɪd/ *adj.* **1** not related to or connected with the things or people around 分離的；斷開的；無關聯的：***disconnected images/thoughts/ideas*** 互不相關的形象／思想／意見 ◇ *I felt disconnected from the world around me.* 我感到已與周圍世界隔絕。**2** (of speech or writing 講話或寫作) with the parts not connected in a logical order 不連貫的；無條理的 SYN **disjointed, incoherent**

dis·con·so·late /dɪsˈkɒnsələt; *NAmE* -ˈkɑːn-/ *adj.* (*formal*) very unhappy and disappointed 憂鬱的；沮喪的；鬱鬱寡歡的 SYN **dejected** ▸ **dis·con·so·late·ly** *adv.*

dis·con·tent /ˌdɪskənˈtent/ (also **dis·con·tent·ment** /ˌdɪskənˈtentmənt/) *noun* [U, C] **~ (at/over/with sth)** a feeling of being unhappy because you are not satisfied with a particular situation; sth that makes you have this feeling 不滿；感到不滿的事情 SYN **dissatisfaction**：*There is widespread discontent among the staff at the proposed changes to pay and conditions.* 員工對改變工資和環境的建議普遍不滿。➲ compare CONTENTMENT

dis·con·tent·ed /ˌdɪskənˈtentɪd/ *adj.* **~ (with sth)** unhappy because you are not satisfied with your situation 不滿的；不滿足的 SYN **dissatisfied** OPP **contented** ▸ **dis·con·tent·ed·ly** *adv.*

dis·con·tinue /ˌdɪskənˈtɪnjuː/ *verb* (*formal*) **1 ~ (doing) sth** to stop doing, using or providing sth, especially sth that you have been doing, using or providing regularly 停止；終止；中斷：*It was decided to discontinue the treatment after three months.* 三個月後決定終止治療。**2** [usually passive] **~ sth** to stop making a product 停止，終止（生產）：*a sale of discontinued china* 已停止生產的瓷器的出售

dis·con·tinu·ity /dɪsˌkɒntɪˈnjuːəti; *NAmE* -ˌkɑːntəˈnuː-/ *noun* (*pl.* **-ies**) (*formal*) **1** [U] the state of not being continuous 不連貫；不連續：*discontinuity in the children's education* 兒童教育缺乏連貫性 **2** [C] a break or change in a continuous process 中斷；間斷；停頓：*Changes in government led to discontinuities in policy.* 政府的更迭導致政策無以為繼。OPP **continuity**

dis·con·tinu·ous /ˌdɪskənˈtɪnjuəs/ *adj.* (*formal*) not continuous; stopping and starting again 不連續的；間斷的；斷續的 SYN **intermittent**

dis·cord /ˈdɪskɔːd; *NAmE* -kɔːrd/ *noun* **1** [U] (*formal*) disagreement; arguing 不一致；不和；紛爭：***marital/family discord*** 夫妻／家庭不和 ◇ *A note of discord surfaced during the proceedings.* 事件進程中出現了意見分歧。OPP **concord** ➲ compare HARMONY (1) **2** [C, U] (*music* 音) a combination of musical notes that do not sound pleasant together 不協和和弦 ➲ compare HARMONY (2)

dis·cord·ant /dɪsˈkɔːdənt; *NAmE* -ˈkɔːrd-/ *adj.* **1** [usually before noun] (*formal*) not in agreement; combining with other things in a way that is strange or unpleasant 不一致的；不協調的；不和的：*discordant views* 相互衝突的觀點 **2** (of sounds 聲音) not sounding pleasant together 不和諧的 OPP **harmonious**

disco·theque /ˈdɪskətek/ *noun* (*old-fashioned*) = DISCO (1)

dis·count 🔑 *noun, verb*

■ ***noun*** 🔑 /ˈdɪskaʊnt/ [C, U] an amount of money that is taken off the usual cost of sth 折扣 SYN **reduction**：*to **get/give/offer a discount*** 得到／給予／提供折扣 ◇ ***discount rates/prices*** 貼現率；折扣價 ◇ **~ (on/off sth)** *They're offering a 10% discount on all sofas this month.* 本月他們給沙發售價統統打九折。◇ *They were selling everything **at a discount*** (= at reduced prices). 他們銷售的所有商品都打折。◇ *a **discount shop*** (= one that regularly sells goods at reduced prices) 打折商店 ◇ *Do you give any discount?* 你們打折嗎？➲ COLLOCATIONS at SHOPPING

■ ***verb*** /dɪsˈkaʊnt; *NAmE* also ˈdɪskaʊnt/ **1** (*formal*) to think or say that sth is not important or not true 認為…不重要；對…不全信；低估 SYN **dismiss**：**~ sth** *We cannot **discount the possibility** of further strikes.* 我們不能低估再次發生罷工的可能性。◇ **~ sth as sth** *The news reports were being discounted as propaganda.* 人們認為這些新聞報道不過是為了宣傳，不可全信。**2 ~ sth** to take an amount of money off the usual cost of sth; to sell sth at a discount 打折扣；打折出售 SYN **reduce**：*discounted prices/fares* 打折價／票價

dis·counter /ˈdɪskaʊntə(r)/ (also ˈ**discount store**) *noun* a shop/store that sells things very cheaply, often in large quantities or from a limited range of goods 折扣商店；廉價商店

ˈ**discount rate** *noun* (*finance* 財) **1** the minimum rate of interest that banks in the US and some other countries must pay when they borrow money from other banks（美國及其他一些國家的）銀行同業拆息 **2** the amount that the price of a BILL OF EXCHANGE is reduced by when it is bought before it reaches its full value（匯票）貼現率 **3** the rate at which an investment increases in value each year（投資）折現率

dis·cour·age /dɪsˈkʌrɪdʒ; *NAmE* -ˈkɜːr-/ *verb* **1** to try to prevent sth or to prevent sb from doing sth, especially by making it difficult to do or by showing that you do not approve of it 阻攔；阻止；勸阻：**~ (doing) sth** *a campaign to discourage smoking among teenagers* 勸阻青少年吸煙的運動 ◇ **~ sb** *I leave a light on when I'm out to discourage burglars.* 我出門時開着燈以防夜盜闖入。◇ **~ sb from doing sth** *His parents tried to discourage him from being an actor.* 他的父母試圖阻止他去當演員。 **2** to make sb feel less confident or enthusiastic about doing sth 使灰心；使泄氣；使喪失信心 SYN **dishearten**：**~ sb** *Don't be discouraged by the first failure—try again!* 這才是第一次失敗，別灰心喪氣，再試一次吧！◇ **~ sb from doing sth** *The weather discouraged people from attending.* 這天氣使得人們不願到場出席。 OPP **encourage** ▸ **dis·cour·aged** *adj.* [not usually before noun] SYN **disheartened**：*Learners can feel very discouraged if an exercise is too difficult.* 如果練習太難，學習者就可能感到沒信心。 **dis·cour·aging** *adj.*：*a* **discouraging experience/response/result** 令人泄氣的經歷／回答／結果 **dis·cour·aging·ly** *adv.*

dis·cour·age·ment /dɪsˈkʌrɪdʒmənt; *NAmE* -ˈkɜːr-/ *noun* **1** [U] a feeling that you no longer have the confidence or enthusiasm to do sth 泄氣；灰心：*an atmosphere of discouragement and despair* 灰心絕望的氣氛 **2** [U] the action of trying to stop sth 阻止；阻攔；勸阻：*the government's discouragement of political protest* 政府對政治抗議的阻攔 **3** [C] a thing that discourages sb from doing sth 使人泄氣的事物；挫折：*Despite all these discouragements, she refused to give up.* 儘管遇到這麼多挫折，她仍不氣餒。

dis·course *noun, verb*

■ *noun* /ˈdɪskɔːs; *NAmE* -kɔːrs/ **1** [C, U] (*formal*) a long and serious treatment or discussion of a subject in speech or writing 論文；演講：*a discourse on issues of gender and sexuality* 關於性別和性行為的論文 ◇ *He was hoping for some lively political discourse at the meeting.* 他希望在會上聽到些生動的政治演講。 **2** [U] (*linguistics* 語言) the use of language in speech and writing in order to produce meaning; language that is studied, usually in order to see how the different parts of a text are connected 話語；語篇：***spoken/written discourse*** 口頭／書面語段 ◇ *discourse analysis* 語篇分析

■ *verb* /dɪsˈkɔːs; *NAmE* -ˈkɔːrs/

PHR V **disˈcourse on/upon sth** (*formal*) to talk or give a long speech about sth that you know a lot about 講述；論述

ˈdiscourse marker *noun* (*grammar* 語法) a word or phrase that organizes spoken language into different parts, for example 'Well …' or 'On the other hand …' 話語標記

dis·cour·teous /dɪsˈkɜːtiəs; *NAmE* -ˈkɜːrt-/ *adj.* (*formal*) having bad manners and not showing respect for other people 不禮貌的；失禮的；粗魯的 SYN **impolite** OPP **courteous** ⇨ SYNONYMS at RUDE

dis·cour·tesy /dɪsˈkɜːtəsi; *NAmE* -ˈkɜːrt-/ *noun* [U, C] (*pl.* **-ies**) (*formal*) behaviour or an action that is not polite 失禮的行為；粗魯的舉動

dis·cover 🔑 /dɪˈskʌvə(r)/ *verb*

1 🔑 **~ sth** to be the first person to become aware that a particular place or thing exists（第一個）發現：*Cook is credited with discovering Hawaii.* 人們把發現夏威夷的功勞歸於庫克。◇ *Scientists around the world are working to discover a cure for AIDS.* 全世界的科學家都在努力尋找治療艾滋病的方法。 **2** 🔑 to find sb/sth that was hidden or that you did not expect to find（出乎意料地）發現，找到，發覺：**~ sb/sth** *Police discovered a large stash of drugs while searching the house.* 警方搜查這棟房子時發現裏面藏着一大批毒品。◇ *We discovered this beach while we were sailing around the island.* 我們在圍繞這個海島航行時發現了這個海灘。◇ **~ sb/sth doing sth** *He was discovered hiding in a shed.* 他被發現原來藏在棚屋裏。◇ **~ sb/sth + adj.** *She was discovered dead at her home in Leeds.* 她被發現死在利茲的家裏。 **3** 🔑 to find out about sth; to find some information about sth 瞭解到；認識到；查明：**~ sth** *I've just discovered hang-gliding!* 我剛知道有懸掛式滑翔運動！◇ **~ (that)** … *It was a shock to discover (that) he couldn't read.* 得知他不識字真令人震驚。◇ **~ why, how, etc.** … *We never did discover why she gave up her job.* 我們一直弄不清楚她為什麼辭職。◇ **it is discovered that** … *It was later discovered that the diaries were a fraud.* 後來查明這些日記完全是偽造的。◇ **sb/sth is discovered to be/have** … *He was later discovered to be seriously ill.* 後來才瞭解到他患了重病。 **4** [often passive] **~ sb** to be the first person to realize that sb is very good at singing, acting, etc. and help them to become successful and famous 發現，發掘（人才）：*The singer was discovered while still at school.* 這個歌唱家在上學的時候就受到賞識了。 ▸ **dis·cov·er·er** *noun*：*the discoverer of penicillin* 第一個發現青黴素的人

dis·cov·ery 🔑 /dɪˈskʌvəri/ *noun* (*pl.* **-ies**)

1 🔑 [C, U] an act or the process of finding sb/sth, or learning about sth that was not known about before 發現；發覺：**~ (of sth)** *the discovery of antibiotics in the 20th century* * 20 世紀抗生素的發現 ◇ *The discovery of a child's body in the river has shocked the community.* 在河裏發現一個孩子的屍體使社區大為震驚。◇ *the discovery of new talent in the art world* 藝術界新秀的發現 ◇ *Researchers in this field have* **made** *some important new* **discoveries**. 這個領域的研究人員有了一些重大的新發現。◇ *He saw life as a voyage of discovery.* 他把生命看作是一次探索未知世界的航行。◇ **~ (that …)** *She was shocked by the discovery that he had been unfaithful.* 她發覺他不忠時感到非常震驚。 **2** 🔑 [C] a thing, fact or person that is found or learned about for the first time 被發現的事物（或真相、人）：*The drug is not a new discovery—it's been known about for years.* 這種藥並不是什麼新發現，多年前便為人所知。

dis·credit /dɪsˈkredɪt/ *verb, noun*

■ *verb* **1 ~ sb/sth** to make people stop respecting sb/sth 敗壞…的名聲；使喪失信譽；使丟臉：*The photos were deliberately taken to discredit the President.* 這些蓄意拍攝的照片旨在敗壞總統的名聲。◇ *a discredited* ***government/policy*** 名譽掃地的政府；失去信譽的政策 **2 ~ sth** to make people stop believing that sth is true; to make sth appear unlikely to be true 使不相信；使懷疑；使不可置信：*These theories are now largely discredited among linguists.* 這些理論現已大多受到語言學家的質疑。

■ *noun* [U] (*formal*) damage to sb's reputation; loss of respect 名譽喪失；信譽喪失；丟臉：*Violent football fans* **bring discredit on** *the teams they support.* 狂暴的足球迷敗壞了他們所支持球隊的聲譽。◇ *Britain,* **to its discredit**, *did not speak out against these atrocities.* 英國沒有公開反對這些殘暴行為，使其名譽掃地。⇨ compare CREDIT *n.* (7)

dis·cred·it·able /dɪsˈkredɪtəbl/ *adj.* (*formal*) bad and unacceptable; causing people to lose respect 不光彩的；有損信譽的；丟臉的

dis·creet /dɪˈskriːt/ *adj.* careful in what you say or do, in order to keep sth secret or to avoid causing embarrassment or difficulty for sb（言行）謹慎的，慎重的，考慮周到的 SYN **tactful**：*He was always very discreet about his love affairs.* 他對談戀愛一向十分慎重。◇ *You ought to make a few discreet enquiries before you sign anything.* 你應該審慎地詢問清楚再簽字。 ▸ **dis·creet·ly** *adv.*：*She coughed discreetly to announce her presence.* 她審慎地咳了一聲以讓人注意自己在場。

> **WORD FAMILY**
> **discreet** *adj.* (≠ indiscreet)
> **discretion** *noun*
> (≠ indiscretion)

dis·crep·ancy /dɪsˈkrepənsi/ *noun* (*pl.* **-ies**) [C, U] a difference between two or more things that should be the same 差異；不符合；不一致：**~ (in sth)** *wide discrepancies in prices quoted for the work* 這項工作的報價出入很大 ◇ **~ (between A and B)** *What are the reasons for the discrepancy between girls' and boys' performance in school?* 女生和男生在學校表現不同的原因何在呢？

D

D

dis·crete AW /dɪˈskriːt/ *adj.* (*formal* or *technical* 術語) independent of other things of the same type 分離的；互不相連的；各別的 SYN **separate**：*The organisms can be divided into discrete categories.* 有機體可分為許多互不相聯的種類。▸ **dis·crete·ly** AW *adv.* **dis·crete·ness** *noun* [U]

dis·cre·tion AW /dɪˈskreʃn/ *noun* [U] **1** the freedom or power to decide what should be done in a particular situation 自行決定的自由；自行決定權：*I'll leave it up to you to* **use your discretion**. 我把這件事留給你自己斟酌決定。◇ *How much to tell terminally ill patients is* **left to the discretion of** *the doctor.* 讓晚期病人知道多少病情由醫生自行決定。**2** care in what you say or do, in order to keep sth secret or to avoid causing embarrassment to or difficulty for sb; the quality of being DISCREET 謹慎；慎重；審慎：*This is confidential, but I know that I can rely on your discretion.* 這是機密，不過我知道你靠得住。➲ compare INDISCRETION
IDM **at sb's diˈscretion** according to what sb decides or wishes to do 由某人斟酌決定；按照某人的意願：*Bail is granted at the discretion of the court.* 由法庭決定准予保釋。◇ *There is no service charge and tipping is at your discretion.* 不收服務費，給不給小費由你自行決定。 **diˌscretion is the ˌbetter part of ˈvalour** (*saying*) you should avoid danger and not take unnecessary risks 謹慎即大勇；慎重為勇敢之本

dis·cre·tion·ary AW /dɪˈskreʃənəri; *NAmE* -neri/ *adj.* [usually before noun] (*formal*) decided according to the judgement of a person in authority about what is necessary in each particular situation; not decided by rules 自行決定的；酌情行事的；便宜行事的：*You may be eligible for a discretionary grant for your university course.* 讀大學課程可能會有資格獲得學校自行決定是否發放的助學金。

dis·crim·in·ate AW /dɪˈskrɪmɪneɪt/ *verb* **1** [I, T] to recognize that there is a difference between people or things; to show a difference between people or things 區別；辨別；區分 SYN **differentiate, distinguish**：**~ (between A and B)** *The computer program was unable to discriminate between letters and numbers.* 這計算機程序不能辨別字母與數字。◇ **~ sth** *When do babies learn to discriminate voices?* 嬰兒什麼時候學會辨別嗓音呢？◇ **~ A from B** *A number of features discriminate this species from others.* 有些特徵使這一物種與其他物種區別開來。**2** [I] to treat one person or group worse/better than another in an unfair way 區別對待；歧視；偏袒：**~ (against sb)** | **~ (in favour of sb)** *practices that discriminate against women and in favour of men* 重男輕女的做法 ◇ **~ (on the grounds of sth)** *It is illegal to discriminate on grounds of race, sex or religion.* 因種族、性別或宗教信仰而有所歧視是非法的。

dis·crim·in·at·ing /dɪˈskrɪmɪneɪtɪŋ/ *adj.* (*approving*) able to judge the good quality of sth 有識別力的；有辨別力的；有鑒賞力的 SYN **discerning**：*a* **discriminating audience/customer** 有鑒賞力的觀眾／顧客

dis·crim·in·ation AW /dɪˌskrɪmɪˈneɪʃn/ *noun* **1** [U] the practice of treating sb or a particular group in society less fairly than others 區別對待；歧視；偏袒：***age/racial/sex/sexual discrimination*** (= because of sb's age, race or sex) 年齡／種族／性別歧視 ◇ **~ against sb** *discrimination against the elderly* 歧視老人 ◇ **~ in favour of sb** *discrimination in favour of the young* 厚待年輕人 ◇ **~ on the grounds of sth** *discrimination on the grounds of race, gender, or sexual orientation* 按照種族、性別或性取向給予區別對待 ➲ COLLOCATIONS at RACE ➲ see also POSITIVE DISCRIMINATION **2** [U] (*approving*) the ability to judge what is good, true, etc. 識別力；辨別力；鑒賞力 SYN **discernment**：*He showed great discrimination in his choice of friends.* 他在擇友方面頗具慧眼。**3** (*formal*) [U, C] the ability to recognize a difference between one thing and another; a difference that is recognized 區別；識別；辨別：*to learn discrimination between right and wrong* 學會分辨是非 ◇ *fine discriminations* 細微區別

dis·crim·in·atory /dɪˈskrɪmɪnətəri; *NAmE* dɪˈskrɪmɪnətɔːri/ *adj.* unfair; treating sb or one group of people worse than others 區別對待的；不公正的；歧視的：***discriminatory practices/rules/measures*** 不公正的做法／規定／措施 ◇ ***sexually/racially discriminatory*** *laws* 性別／種族歧視性法律

dis·cur·sive /dɪsˈkɜːsɪv; *NAmE* -ˈkɜːrs-/ *adj.* (*formal*) (of a style of writing or speaking 書面或口頭表達方式) moving from one point to another without any strict structure 東拉西扯的；離題的；不着邊際的：*the discursive style of the novel* 這部小說的散漫風格

Synonyms 同義詞辨析

discussion

conversation • dialogue • talk • debate • consultation • chat • gossip

These are all words for an occasion when people talk about sth. 以上各詞均表示交談、談論。

discussion a detailed conversation about sth that is considered to be important 指重要事情的討論、談論、商討：*Discussions are still taking place between the two leaders.* 兩位領導人仍在進行討論。

conversation a talk, usually a private or informal one, involving two people or a small group; the activity of talking in this way 通常指私下的或非正式的交談、談話：*a telephone conversation* 電話交談

dialogue conversations in a book, play or film 指書、戲劇或電影中的對話、對白：*The novel has long descriptions and not much dialogue.* 這部小說描述多對話少。A **dialogue** is also a formal discussion between two groups, especially when they are trying to solve a problem or end a dispute. * dialogue 亦指兩個團體間為解決問題或結束爭端進行的正式對話、討論、交換意見：*The President told waiting reporters there had been a constructive dialogue.* 總統告訴等候的記者，剛才進行了一次富有建設性的對話。

talk a conversation or discussion, often one about a problem or sth important for the people involved 常指就某個問題或對有關人員重要的事情進行的交談、談話、討論、商討：*I had a long talk with my boss about my career prospects.* 我和老闆就我的事業前景進行了一次長談。

debate a formal discussion of an issue at a public meeting or in a parliament. In a debate two or more speakers express opposing views and then there is often a vote on the issue. 指公共集會上或議會裏就某問題進行的、常以表決結束的辯論：*a debate on prison reform* 關於監獄制度改革的辯論

consultation a formal discussion between groups of people before a decision is made about sth 指團體間在決策前進行的咨詢、商討、磋商：*There have been extensive consultations between the two countries.* 兩國之間進行了廣泛磋商。

chat a friendly informal conversation; informal talking 指友好的非正式交談、聊天 NOTE The countable use of **chat** is especially British English. * chat 作可數名詞尤用於英式英語：*I just called in for a chat about the kids.* 我只是打電話來隨便聊聊孩子的事情。

gossip a conversation about other people and their private lives 指關於他人及其私生活的閒談、閒聊、說長道短：*We had a good gossip about the boss.* 我們講了好一會兒老闆的閒話。

PATTERNS

- a discussion/conversation/dialogue/talk/debate/consultation/chat/gossip **about** sth
- a discussion/conversation/dialogue/debate/consultation **on** sth
- **in (close)** discussion/conversation/dialogue/debate/consultation **with** sb
- to **have** a discussion/conversation/dialogue/talk/debate/consultation/chat/gossip **with** sb
- to **hold** a discussion/conversation/debate/consultation

dis·cus /ˈdɪskəs/ *noun* **1** [C] a heavy flat round object thrown in a sporting event 鐵餅（體育運動用品） **2 the discus** [sing.] the event or sport of throwing a discus as far as possible 擲鐵餅；擲鐵餅比賽 ➲ VISUAL VOCAB page V46

dis·cuss 🔑 /dɪˈskʌs/ *verb* **1** 🔑 to talk about sth with sb, especially in order to decide sth 討論；談論；商量： **~ sth with sb** *Have you discussed the problem with anyone?* 你與誰商量過這個問題嗎？ ◇ **~ sth** *I'm not prepared to discuss this on the phone.* 我不想在電話裏談論此事。◇ **~ when, what, etc. …** *We need to discuss when we should go.* 我們需要商量一下什麼時候動身。◇ **~ (sb/sth) doing sth** *We briefly discussed buying a second car.* 我們草草商量過再買一輛汽車的事兒。**HELP** You cannot say 'discuss about sth'：~~*I discussed about my problem with my parents.*~~ Look also at **discussion**. 不能說 discuss about sth。不作 I discussed about my problem with my parents. 另見 discussion。➲ SYNONYMS at TALK **2** 🔑 **~ sth** | **~ what, how, etc. …** to write or talk about sth in detail, showing the different ideas and opinions about it 詳述；論述： *This topic will be discussed at greater length in the next chapter.* 這個題目將在下一章裏詳細論述。➲ LANGUAGE BANK at ABOUT ➲ SYNONYMS at EXAMINE

dis·cus·sion 🔑 /dɪˈskʌʃn/ *noun* [U, C] **1** 🔑 the process of discussing sb/sth; a conversation about sb/sth 討論；商討： *a* ***topic/subject for discussion*** 討論的題目／主題 ◇ *After considerable discussion, they decided to accept our offer.* 他們經過反複討論後決定接受我們的報價。◇ *The plans have been* ***under discussion*** (= being talked about) *for a year now.* 這些計劃至今已討論一年了。◇ *Discussions are still taking place between the two leaders.* 兩位領導人仍在進行討論。◇ **~ (with sb) (about/on sb/sth)** *We* ***had a discussion*** *with them about the differences between Britain and the US.* 我們和他們討論了英美兩國的不同之處。 **2** 🔑 **~ (of sth)** a speech or a piece of writing that discusses many different aspects of a subject 詳述；論述： *Her article is a discussion of the methods used in research.* 她這篇文章論述的是研究中使用的方法。

dis·dain /dɪsˈdeɪn/ *noun, verb*

■ *noun* [U, sing.] the feeling that sb/sth is not good enough to deserve your respect or attention 鄙視；蔑視；鄙棄 **SYN** **contempt**： *to treat sb* ***with disdain*** 鄙視某人 ◇ **~ for sb/sth** *a disdain for the law* 對法律的藐視

■ *verb* (*formal*) **1 ~ sb/sth** to think that sb/sth is not good enough to deserve your respect 鄙視；蔑視；鄙棄： *She disdained his offer of help.* 他提出要幫助，遭到她的鄙棄。 **2 ~ to do sth** to refuse to do sth because you think that you are too important to do it 不屑（做某事）： *He disdained to turn to his son for advice.* 他不屑向自己的兒子請教。

dis·dain·ful /dɪsˈdeɪnfl/ *adj.* **~ (of sb/sth)** showing disdain 輕視的；鄙視的；倨傲的 **SYN** **contemptuous, dismissive**： *She's always been disdainful of people who haven't been to college.* 她總是瞧不起那些未唸過大學的人。▸ **dis·dain·ful·ly** /-fəli/ *adv.*

dis·ease 🔑 /dɪˈziːz/ *noun* [U, C] **1** 🔑 an illness affecting humans, animals or plants, often caused by infection 病；疾病： ***heart/liver/kidney, etc. disease*** 心臟病、肝病、腎病等 ◇ *health measures to prevent the* ***spread of disease*** 預防疾病傳播的保健措施 ◇ *an* ***infectious/contagious disease*** (= one that can be passed to sb very easily) 傳染病；接觸性傳染病 ◇ *It is not known what causes the disease.* 這種病的起因不明。◇ *protection against sexually transmitted diseases* 性傳播疾病的預防 ◇ *He suffers from a rare blood disease.* 他患有一種罕見的血液病。 ➲ COLLOCATIONS at ILL **2** [C] (*formal*) something that is very wrong with people's attitudes, way of life or with society 弊端；惡疾；痼疾： *Greed is a disease of modern society.* 貪婪是現代社會的惡疾。

dis·eased /dɪˈziːzd/ *adj.* suffering from a disease 有病的；患病的；不健康的： *diseased tissue* 有病的組織 ◇ *the diseased social system* 病態的社會制度

dis·em·bark /ˌdɪsɪmˈbɑːk; *NAmE* -ˈbɑːrk/ *verb* [I] **~ (from sth)** (*formal*) to leave a vehicle, especially a ship or an aircraft, at the end of a journey 下（車、船、飛機等） **OPP** **embark** ▸ **dis·em·bark·ation** /ˌdɪsˌembɑːˈkeɪʃn; *NAmE* -bɑːrˈk-/ *noun* [U]

dis·em·bod·ied /ˌdɪsɪmˈbɒdid; *NAmE* -ˈbɑːdid/ *adj.* [usually before noun] **1** (of sounds 聲音) coming from a person or place that cannot be seen or identified 從看不到的人（或地方）發出的： *a disembodied voice* 不見其人的說話聲 **2** separated from the body 脱離肉體的： *disembodied spirits* 遊魂

Synonyms 同義詞辨析

disease

illness • disorder • infection • condition • ailment • bug

These are all words for a medical problem. 以上各詞均表示健康問題。

disease a medical problem affecting humans, animals or plants, often caused by infection 常指人、動植物感染的病、疾病： *He suffers from a rare blood disease.* 他患有一種罕見的血液病。

illness a medical problem, or a period of suffering from one 指病、疾病、患病期： *She died after a long illness.* 她久病不癒而亡。

DISEASE OR ILLNESS? 用 disease 還是 illness？

Disease is used to talk about more severe physical medical problems, especially those that affect the organs. **Illness** is used to talk about both more severe and more minor medical problems, and those that affect mental health. * disease 指較嚴重的身體疾病，尤其是影響身體器官的疾病。illness 指重病或小病均可，也可指精神上的疾病： ~~*heart/kidney/liver illness*~~ ◇ ~~*mental disease*~~ **Disease** is not used about a period of illness. * disease 不指患病期： ~~*she died after a long disease*~~

disorder (*rather formal*) an illness that causes a part of the body to stop functioning correctly 指失調、紊亂、不適、疾病： *a rare disorder of the liver* 一種罕見的肝病 **NOTE** A **disorder** is generally not infectious. **Disorder** is used most frequently with words relating to mental problems, for example *psychiatric, personality, mental* and *eating*. When it is used to talk about physical problems, it is most often used with *blood, bowel* and *kidney*, and these are commonly *serious, severe* or *rare*. * disorder 一般不傳染，多與有關精神問題的詞連用，如 psychiatric/personality/mental/eating disorder（精神錯亂；人格障礙；精神紊亂；進食障礙）。談到身體方面的問題常與下列詞連用，如 blood/bowel/kidney disorder（血液病；腸道失調；腎臟疾病），這些疾病一般用 serious、severe 或 rare 等詞修飾。

infection an illness that is caused by bacteria or a virus and that affects one part of the body 指由細菌或病毒引起的身體某部位的感染或傳染疾病： *a throat infection* 喉部感染

condition a medical problem that you have for a long time because it is not possible to cure it 指因不可治癒而長期患有的疾病： *a heart condition* 心臟病

ailment (*rather formal*) an illness that is not very serious 指輕病、小恙： *childhood ailments* 兒童期小病

bug (*informal*) an infectious illness that is usually fairly mild 指輕微的傳染病、小病： *a nasty flu bug* 嚴重的流感

PATTERNS

- to **have/suffer from** a(n) disease/illness/disorder/infection/condition/ailment/bug
- to **catch/contract/get/pick up** a(n) disease/illness/infection/bug

D

dis·em·bowel /ˌdɪsɪmˈbaʊəl/ *verb* (**-ll-**, *especially US* **-l-**) **~ sb/sth** to take the stomach, BOWELS and other organs out of a person or animal 取出…的內臟；開…的膛

dis·en·chant·ed /ˌdɪsɪnˈtʃɑːntɪd; *NAmE* -ˈtʃænt-/ *adj.* **~ (with sb/sth)** no longer feeling enthusiasm for sb/sth; not believing sth is good or worth doing 不再着迷的；不再抱幻想的 SYN **disillusioned**：*He was becoming disenchanted with his job as a lawyer.* 他對自己的律師工作漸漸地不抱幻想了。▸ **dis·en·chant·ment** *noun* [U]：*a growing* ***sense/feeling of disenchantment*** *with his job* 對他的工作越來越感到失望

dis·en·fran·chise /ˌdɪsɪnˈfræntʃaɪz/ *verb* **~ sb** to take away sb's rights, especially their right to vote 剝奪（某人）的權利（尤指選舉權）OPP **enfranchise**

dis·en·gage /ˌdɪsɪnˈɡeɪdʒ/ *verb* **1** [T, I] (*formal*) to free sb/sth from the person or thing that is holding them or it; to become free （使）脫離，鬆開；解脫：**~ yourself (from sb/sth)** *She gently disengaged herself from her sleeping son.* 她輕輕地放下懷中熟睡的兒子。◇ (*figurative*) *They wished to disengage themselves from these policies.* 他們希望能擺脫這些政策的束縛。◇ **~ (sth/sb) (from sth/sb)** *to disengage the clutch* (= when driving a car)（開車時）鬆開離合器◇ *We saw the booster rockets disengage and fall into the sea.* 我們看到火箭助推器脫落後墜入大海。 **2** [I, T] **~ (sth)** (*technical* 術語) if an army **disengages** or sb **disengages** it, it stops fighting and moves away （使）停止交戰，脫離接觸 ➲ compare ENGAGE ▸ **dis·en·gage·ment** *noun* [U]

dis·en·tan·gle /ˌdɪsɪnˈtæŋɡl/ *verb* **1 ~ sth (from sth)** to separate different arguments, ideas, etc. that have become confused 理順，分清，清理出（混亂的論據、想法等）：*It's not easy to disentangle the truth from the official statistics.* 從官方統計資料中理出真實情況並不容易。 **2 ~ sth/sb (from sth)** to free sb/sth from sth that has become wrapped or twisted around it or them 使解脫；使脫出；使擺脫：*He tried to disentangle his fingers from her hair.* 他竭力將手指從她纏繞的頭髮中掙脫出來。◇ (*figurative*) *She has just disentangled herself from a painful relationship.* 她剛剛擺脫一段痛苦的感情。 **3 ~ sth** to get rid of the twists and knots in sth 解開…的結；理順：*He was sitting on the deck disentangling a coil of rope.* 他坐在甲板上解開一捆繩索。➲ compare ENTANGLE

dis·equi·lib·rium /ˌdɪsˌiːkwɪˈlɪbriəm; ˌdɪsˌek-/ *noun* [U] (*formal* or *technical* 術語) a loss or lack of balance in a situation 不平衡；失調

dis·es·tab·lish AW /ˌdɪsɪˈstæblɪʃ/ *verb* **~ sth** (*formal*) to end the official status of a national Church 廢除（國教）的法定地位：*a campaign to disestablish the Church of England* 廢除英國國教運動 ▸ **dis·es·tab·lish·ment** AW *noun* [U]

dis·favour (*especially US* **dis·favor**) /dɪsˈfeɪvə(r)/ *noun* [U] (*formal*) the feeling that you do not like or approve of sb/sth 不喜歡；不贊成

dis·fig·ure /dɪsˈfɪɡə(r); *NAmE* -ɡjər/ *verb* **~ sb/sth** to spoil the appearance of a person, thing or place 損毀…的外形；使變醜；毀容：*Her face was disfigured by a long red scar.* 她臉上一條紅色的長疤使她破相了。▸ **dis·fig·ure·ment** *noun* [U, C]：*He suffered permanent disfigurement in the fire.* 那場火災永久毀了他的面容。

dis·gorge /dɪsˈɡɔːdʒ; *NAmE* -ˈɡɔːrdʒ/ *verb* (*formal*) **1 ~ sth** to pour sth out in large quantities 大量湧出；傾泄出：*The pipe disgorges sewage into the sea.* 這管道將污水排入大海。 **2 ~ sb/sth** if a vehicle or building **disgorges** people, they come out of it in large numbers （從交通工具、建築物裏）湧出：*The bus disgorged a crowd of noisy children.* 公共汽車上湧下來一群嘰嘰喳喳的孩子。

dis·grace /dɪsˈɡreɪs/ *noun, verb*

■ ***noun*** **1** [U] the loss of other people's respect and approval because of the bad way sb has behaved 丟臉；恥辱；不光彩 SYN **shame**：*Her behaviour has* ***brought disgrace on*** *her family.* 她的行為使家人蒙羞。◇ *The swimmer was sent home from the Olympics* ***in disgrace***. 這位游泳運動員很不光彩地從奧運會上被遣送回國。◇ *There is no disgrace in being poor.* 貧窮不是恥辱。◇ *Sam was* ***in disgrace*** *with his parents.* 薩姆已失寵於他的父母。 **2** [sing.] **a ~ (to sb/sth)** a person or thing that is so bad that people connected with them or it feel or should feel ashamed 令人感到羞恥的人（或事）：*Your homework is an absolute disgrace.* 你做的作業太丟人了。◇ *That sort of behaviour is* ***a disgrace to*** *the legal profession.* 那種行為是法律界的恥辱。◇ *The state of our roads is a national disgrace.* 我們的道路狀況是國家的恥辱。◇ ***It's a disgrace that*** (= it is very wrong that) *they are paid so little.* 他們的報酬如此微薄，太不像話了。

■ ***verb*** **1** to behave badly in a way that makes you or other people feel ashamed 使丟臉；使蒙受恥辱：**~ yourself** *I disgraced myself by drinking far too much.* 我喝酒過多出了洋相。◇ **~ sb/sth** *He had disgraced the family name.* 他玷污了家族的名聲。 **2 be disgraced** to lose the respect of people, usually so that you lose a position of power 使名譽掃地；使失勢；使失去地位：*He was publicly disgraced and sent into exile.* 他被當眾貶謫，放逐異鄉。◇ *a disgraced politician/leader* 失勢的從政者 / 領導人

dis·grace·ful /dɪsˈɡreɪsfl/ *adj.* very bad or unacceptable; that people should feel ashamed about 不光彩的；可恥的；丟臉的：*His behaviour was absolutely disgraceful!* 他的行為真可恥！◇ *It's disgraceful that none of the family tried to help her.* 家裏竟無人肯幫助她，太不像話了。◇ *a disgraceful waste of money* 可恥的金錢浪費 ▸ **dis·grace·ful·ly** /-fəli/ *adv.*

dis·grun·tled /dɪsˈɡrʌntld/ *adj.* annoyed or disappointed because sth has happened to upset you 不滿的；不高興的：*disgruntled employees* 不滿的雇員◇ **~ at sb/sth** *I left feeling disgruntled at the way I'd been treated.* 我受到如此對待因而憤然離去。

dis·guise /dɪsˈɡaɪz/ *verb, noun*

■ ***verb*** **1** to change your appearance so that people cannot recognize you 假扮；裝扮；偽裝：**~ sb** *The hijackers were heavily disguised.* 劫持者偽裝得嚴嚴實實。◇ **~ sb as sb/sth** *They got in disguised as security guards.* 他們裝扮成保安人員混了進去。◇ **~ yourself (as sb/sth)** *She disguised herself as a boy.* 她女扮男裝。 **2 ~ sth** to hide sth or change it, so that it cannot be recognized 掩蔽；掩飾 SYN **conceal**：*She made no attempt to disguise her surprise.* 她沒有掩飾自己驚奇的心情。◇ *It was a* ***thinly disguised*** *attack on the President.* 明眼人一下就能看出這是在攻擊總統。◇ *She couldn't* ***disguise the fact that*** *she felt uncomfortable.* 她無法掩飾她那不安的心情。➲ SYNONYMS at HIDE

■ ***noun*** **1** [C, U] a thing that you wear or use to change your appearance so that people do not recognize you 偽裝物；化裝用具：*She wore glasses and a wig as a disguise.* 她用眼鏡和假髮偽裝起來。◇ *The star travelled* ***in disguise*** (= wearing a disguise). 這位明星化了裝去旅行。◇ (*figurative*) *A vote for the Liberal Democrats is just a Labour vote* ***in disguise***. 投自由民主黨的票不過是改頭換面投工黨的票。 **2** [U] the art of changing your appearance so that people do not recognize you 假扮；裝扮；偽裝：*He is a master of disguise.* 他是偽裝能手。IDM see BLESSING

dis·gust 0ₙ /dɪsˈɡʌst/ *noun, verb*

■ ***noun*** 0ₙ [U] a strong feeling of dislike or disapproval for sb/sth that you feel is unacceptable, or for sth that looks, smells, etc. unpleasant 厭惡；憎惡；反感：**~ (at/with sth)** *She expressed her disgust at the programme by writing a letter of complaint.* 她寫了封投訴信，表示對這個節目的反感。◇ **~ (for sb)** *I can only feel disgust for these criminals.* 對這些罪犯我只感到憎惡。◇ *The idea fills me* ***with disgust***. 這個想法實在令我惡心。◇ *He walked away* ***in disgust***. 他感到厭惡，就走開了。◇ ***Much to my disgust***, *they refused to help.* 他們不肯幫忙，令我極其憤慨。◇ *She wrinkled her nose* ***in disgust*** *at the smell.* 她聞到那氣味，惡心地皺起了鼻子。

■ ***verb*** 0ₙ **~ sb** if sth **disgusts** you, it makes you feel shocked and almost ill/sick because it is so unpleasant 使作嘔；使厭惡；使反感：*The level of violence in the film really disgusted me.* 影片中的暴力程度實在讓我反感。

dis·gust·ed 0ₙ /dɪsˈɡʌstɪd/ *adj.* feeling or showing disgust 厭惡的；憎惡的；反感的：**~ (at/by sb/sth)** *I was disgusted at/by the sight.* 我一看就

恶心。◇ ~ (**with sb/sth/yourself**) *I was disgusted with myself for eating so much.* 我吃得太多，自己也覺得無地自容。◇ ~ (**to see, hear, etc. ...**) *He was disgusted to see such awful living conditions.* 看到如此糟糕的生活環境他覺得很氣憤。▸ **dis·gust·ed·ly** *adv.*：*'This champagne is warm!', he said disgustedly.* "這香檳酒是温的！"他氣憤地說。

dis·gust·ing 0‑ᴍ /dɪsˈɡʌstɪŋ/ *adj.* **1** 0‑ᴍ extremely unpleasant 極糟的；令人不快的 SYN **revolting**：*The kitchen was in a disgusting state when she left.* 她離開時廚房裏一片狼藉。◇ *What a disgusting smell!* 這氣味真難聞！**2** 0‑ᴍ unacceptable and shocking 令人厭惡的；令人氣憤的 SYN **despicable, outrageous**：*I think it's disgusting that they're closing the local hospital.* 他們要關閉這家地方醫院，我認為這太讓人氣憤了。◇ *His language is disgusting* (= he uses a lot of offensive words). 他的言語不堪入耳。

Synonyms 同義詞辨析

disgusting

foul • revolting • repulsive • offensive • gross

These words all describe sth, especially a smell, taste or habit, that is extremely unpleasant and often makes you feel slightly ill. 以上各詞尤指氣味、味道或習慣令人很不舒服而且常令人惡心。

disgusting extremely unpleasant and making you feel slightly ill 指令人不快的、使人厭惡的、令人惡心的、使人作嘔的：*What a disgusting smell!* 這氣味真難聞！

foul dirty, and tasting or smelling bad 指骯髒惡臭的、難聞的、惡心的：*She could smell his foul breath.* 她聞得到他的口臭。

revolting extremely unpleasant and making you feel slightly ill 指令人不快的、使人厭惡的、令人惡心的、使人作嘔的：*The stew looked revolting.* 這燜菜看上去令人作嘔。

DISGUSTING OR REVOLTING? 用 disgusting 還是 revolting？

Both of these words are used to describe things that smell and taste unpleasant, unpleasant personal habits and people who have them. There is no real difference in meaning, but **disgusting** is more frequent, especially in spoken English. 以上兩詞均指氣味、味道、個人習慣和有這些習慣的人令人惡心、使人厭惡，在含義上沒有實質的區別，只是 disgusting 更常用，尤其是在英語口語中。

repulsive (*rather formal*) extremely unpleasant in a way that offends you or makes you feel slightly ill 指使人厭惡的、令人反感的、十分討厭的 NOTE **Repulsive** usually describes people, their behaviour or habits, which you may find offensive for physical or moral reasons. * repulsive 通常指人或其行為習慣刺激感官或有違道德而令人厭惡。

offensive (*formal*) (especially of smells) extremely unpleasant 尤指氣味令人不適的、令人惡心的、使人厭惡的

gross (*informal*) (of a smell, taste or personal habit) extremely unpleasant 指氣味、味道或個人習慣令人很不舒服的、令人惡心的、使人厭惡的

PATTERNS

- disgusting/repulsive/offensive **to sb**
- to **find sb/sth** disgusting/revolting/repulsive/offensive
- to **smell/taste** disgusting/foul/gross
- a(n) disgusting/foul/revolting/offensive/gross **smell**
- a disgusting/revolting/gross **habit**
- disgusting/offensive/gross **behaviour**
- a disgusting/revolting/repulsive **man/woman/person**

dis·gust·ing·ly /dɪsˈɡʌstɪŋli/ *adv.* **1** (sometimes *humorous*) extremely (in a way that other people feel jealous of) 極其，極端，非常（以致使人忌妒）：*He looked disgustingly healthy when he got back from the Bahamas.* 他從巴哈馬群島回來時看上去健康得令人眼紅。**2** in a disgusting way 令人作嘔地；令人厭惡地；討厭地：*disgustingly dirty* 髒得令人作嘔

dish 0‑ᴍ /dɪʃ/ *noun, verb*

■ *noun* **1** 0‑ᴍ [C] a flat shallow container for cooking food in or serving it from 碟；盤：*a glass dish* 玻璃盤 ◇ *an ovenproof dish* 耐熱盤 ◇ *a baking/serving dish* 烤盤；上食物的盤子 ◇ *They helped themselves from a large dish of pasta.* 他們從一大盤意大利麪中取一些吃。➲ VISUAL VOCAB page V22 **2** 0‑ᴍ **the dishes** [pl.] the plates, bowls, cups, etc. that have been used for a meal and need to be washed（待清洗的）餐具：*I'll **do the dishes*** (= wash them). 我來洗碗。**3** 0‑ᴍ [C] food prepared in a particular way as part of a meal 一道菜；菜肴：*a vegetarian/fish dish* 一道素菜；一盤魚 ◇ *This makes an excellent hot **main dish**.* 這就是一道絕好的熱主菜。◇ *I can recommend the chef's **dish of the day**.* 我可推薦今天的主廚特餐。➲ see also SIDE DISH **4** [C] any object that is shaped like a dish or bowl 盤狀物；碟狀物：*a soap dish* 肥皂碟 ➲ VISUAL VOCAB page V24 ➲ see also SATELLITE DISH **5** [C] (*informal*) a sexually attractive person 性感的人；對異性有迷惑力的人：*What a dish!* 真性感！

■ *verb*

IDM ˌ**dish the ˈdirt (on sb)** (*informal*) to tell people unkind or unpleasant things about sb, especially about their private life 說（某人）的閒話；揭（某人）的短 ˌ**dish it ˈout** (*disapproving*) to criticize other people 數落；指責；批評：*He enjoys dishing it out, but he really can't take it* (= cannot accept criticism from other people). 他喜歡指責別人，而自己卻一點批評都接受不了。

PHR V ˌ**dish sth↔ˈout 1** (*informal*) to give sth, often to a lot of people or in large amounts 大量提供；分發：*Students dished out leaflets to passers-by.* 學生向過路人散發傳單。◇ *She's always dishing out advice, even when you don't want it.* 即使你不想聽，她仍然沒完沒了地建議這建議那。**2** to serve food onto plates for a meal 把（食物）分到盤裏（以便用餐）：*Can you dish out the potatoes, please?* 你給大家分一下土豆好嗎？ˌ**dish ˈup | ˌdish sth↔ˈup** to serve food onto plates for a meal 把（食物）盛到盤裏（以便用餐）ˌ**dish ˈup sth** to offer sth to sb, especially sth that is not very good 提供，供給（尤指不太好的東西）

dis·ha·bille /ˌdɪsəˈbiːl; -ˈbiː/ *adj.* = DÉSHABILLÉ

dis·har·mony /dɪsˈhɑːməni; *NAmE* -ˈhɑːrm-/ *noun* [U] (*formal*) a lack of agreement about important things, which causes bad feelings between people or groups of people 不協調；不和諧；不一致：***marital/racial/social disharmony*** 夫妻不和；種族分歧；社會不協調 OPP **harmony**

dish·cloth /ˈdɪʃklɒθ; *NAmE* -klɔːθ/ (*NAmE* usually **dish·rag**) *noun* a cloth for washing dishes 洗碟布；洗碗布 ➲ VISUAL VOCAB page V25

dis·heart·en /dɪsˈhɑːtn; *NAmE* -ˈhɑːrtn/ *verb* ~ **sb** to make sb lose hope or confidence 使沮喪；使失去信心；使灰心 SYN **discourage**：*Don't let this defeat dishearten you.* 不要因這次失敗而氣餒。▸ **dis·heart·ened** *adj.*：*a disheartened team* 喪失信心的團隊 **dis·heart·en·ing** /-ˈhɑːtnɪŋ; *NAmE* -ˈhɑːrt-/ *adj.*：*a disheartening experience* 令人沮喪的經歷

dish·ev·elled /dɪˈʃevld/ (*especially BrE*) (*NAmE* usually **dish·ev·eled**) *adj.* (of hair, clothes or sb's general appearance 頭髮、衣着或外表) very untidy 凌亂的；不整潔的；衣冠不整的 SYN **unkempt**：*He looked tired and dishevelled.* 他衣冠不整，顯得很疲倦。

dis·hon·est 0‑ᴍ /dɪsˈɒnɪst; *NAmE* -ˈɑːn-/ *adj.* not honest; intending to trick people 不誠實的；騙人的；欺騙性的：*Beware of dishonest traders in the tourist areas.* 在旅遊區一定要謹防奸商。◇ *I don't like him, and it would be dishonest of me to pretend otherwise.* 我不喜歡他，如果假裝喜歡，那就是我不誠實了。OPP **honest** ▸ **dis·hon·est·ly** 0‑ᴍ *adv.* **dis·hon·esty** *noun* [U]

D

D

dis·hon·our (*especially US* **dis·honor**) /dɪsˈɒnə(r); *NAmE* -ˈɑːn-/ *noun, verb*

■ ***noun*** [U] (*formal*) a loss of honour or respect because you have done sth immoral or unacceptable 不名譽；恥辱；丟臉

■ ***verb*** (*formal*) **1 ~ sb/sth** to make sb/sth lose the respect of other people 使喪失名譽；使蒙受恥辱；使丟臉：*You have dishonoured the name of the school.* 你敗壞了學校的名聲。 **2 ~ sth** to refuse to keep an agreement or promise 違背，違反（協議或諾言）：*He had dishonoured nearly all of his election pledges.* 他幾乎違背了所有的競選諾言。 OPP **honour**

dis·hon·our·able (*especially US* **dis·hon·or·able**) /dɪsˈɒnərəbl; *NAmE* -ˈɑːn-/ *adj.* not deserving respect; immoral or unacceptable 不名譽的；不光彩的；可恥的：*It would have been dishonourable of her not to keep her promise.* 她要是不履行諾言就不光彩了。◇ *He was given a* ***dishonourable discharge*** (= an order to leave the army for unacceptable behaviour). 他被開除了軍籍。 OPP **honourable** ▸ **dis·hon·our·ably** /-nərəbli/ *adv.*

dish·pan /ˈdɪʃpæn/ *noun* (*NAmE*) a bowl for washing plates, etc. in 洗碟盆；洗碗盆

dish·rag /ˈdɪʃræɡ/ *noun* (*NAmE*) = DISHCLOTH

dish·towel /ˈdɪʃtaʊəl/ (*NAmE*) (*BrE* **ˈtea towel**, **ˈtea cloth**) *noun* a small towel used for drying cups, plates, knives, etc. after they have been washed（擦拭已洗餐具的）擦碗布，抹布 ➲ VISUAL VOCAB page V25

dish·wash·er /ˈdɪʃwɒʃə(r); *NAmE* -wɔːʃ-; -wɑːʃ-/ *noun* **1** a machine for washing plates, cups, etc. 洗碗碟機：*to* ***load/stack the dishwasher*** 將碗碟放在/碼在洗碟機裏 ➲ VISUAL VOCAB page V25 **2** a person whose job is to wash plates, etc., for example in a restaurant 洗碟工；洗碗工

dish·water /ˈdɪʃwɔːtə(r)/ *noun* [U] water that sb has used to wash dirty plates, etc. 洗過碗碟的水；泔水 IDM ▸ see DULL *adj.*

dishy /ˈdɪʃi/ *adj.* (**dish·ier**, **dishi·est**) (*old-fashioned, informal, especially BrE*) (of a person 人) physically attractive 性感的；有魅力的

dis·il·lu·sion /ˌdɪsɪˈluːʒn/ *verb* **~ sb** to destroy sb's belief in or good opinion of sb/sth 使醒悟；使不再抱幻想；使幻想破滅：*I hate to disillusion you, but not everyone is as honest as you.* 我實在不願把實情告訴你，但並非人人都像你那樣誠實。 ▸ **dis·il·lu·sion** *noun* [U] = DISILLUSIONMENT

dis·il·lu·sioned /ˌdɪsɪˈluːʒnd/ *adj.* **~ (by/with sb/sth)** disappointed because the person you admired or the idea you believed to be good and true now seems without value 大失所望的；不再抱幻想的；幻想破滅的 SYN **disenchanted**：*I soon became disillusioned with the job.* 我不久便對這個工作不再抱幻想了。

dis·il·lu·sion·ment /ˌdɪsɪˈluːʒnmənt/ (also **dis·il·lu·sion**) *noun* [U, sing.] **~ (with sth)** the state of being disillusioned 醒悟；不再抱幻想；幻想破滅 SYN **disenchantment**：*There is widespread disillusionment with the present government.* 人們對現政府普遍感到失望。

dis·in·cen·tive /ˌdɪsɪnˈsentɪv/ *noun* [C] a thing that makes sb less willing to do sth 起抑制作用的事物；遏制因素 OPP **incentive**

dis·in·clin·ation /ˌdɪsˌɪnklɪˈneɪʃn/ *noun* [sing., U] (*formal*) a lack of willingness to do sth; a lack of enthusiasm for sth 不情願；不樂意；無意：*There was a general disinclination to return to the office after lunch.* 午飯後人們一般都不樂意回辦公室辦公。

dis·in·clined /ˌdɪsɪnˈklaɪnd/ *adj.* [not before noun] **~ (to do sth)** (*formal*) not willing 不情願；不樂意；無意於 SYN **reluctant**：*He was strongly disinclined to believe anything that she said.* 她說什麼他都堅決不肯相信。

dis·in·fect /ˌdɪsɪnˈfekt/ *verb* **1 ~ sth** to clean sth using a substance that kills bacteria 給…消毒：*to disinfect a surface/room/wound* 給表面/房間/傷口消毒 **2 ~ sth** to run a computer program to get rid of a computer virus 消（計算機）病毒；掃除（電腦）病毒 ▸ **dis·in·fec·tion** *noun* [U]

dis·in·fect·ant /ˌdɪsɪnˈfektənt/ *noun* [U, C] a substance that disinfects 消毒劑；殺菌劑：*a strong smell of disinfectant* 嗆人的消毒劑氣味

dis·in·for·ma·tion /ˌdɪsˌɪnfəˈmeɪʃn; *NAmE* -fərˈm-/ *noun* [U] false information that is given deliberately, especially by government organizations（尤指政府機構故意發佈的）虛假信息，假消息

dis·in·genu·ous /ˌdɪsɪnˈdʒenjuəs/ *adj.* [not usually before noun] (*formal*) not sincere, especially when you pretend to know less about sth than you really do 不真誠；不誠實；假裝不知道：*It would be disingenuous of me to claim I had never seen it.* 要說我從未看到過，那就是言不由衷了。 ➲ compare INGENUOUS ▸ **dis·in·genu·ous·ly** *adv.*

dis·in·herit /ˌdɪsɪnˈherɪt/ *verb* **~ sb** to prevent sb, especially your son or daughter, from receiving your money or property after your death 剝奪（某人）的繼承權 ➲ compare INHERIT (1)

dis·in·hibit /ˌdɪsɪnˈhɪbɪt/ *verb* **~ sb** (*formal*) to help sb to stop feeling shy so that they can relax and show their feelings 使不再拘謹；使不再拘束 ▸ **dis·in·hib·ition** /ˌdɪsɪnhɪˈbɪʃn/ *noun* [U]

dis·in·te·grate /dɪsˈɪntɪɡreɪt/ *verb* **1** [I] to break into small parts or pieces and be destroyed 碎裂；解體；分裂：*The plane disintegrated as it fell into the sea.* 飛機墜入大海時解體了。 **2** [I] to become much less strong or united and be gradually destroyed 衰微；瓦解；崩潰 SYN **fall apart**：*The authority of the central government was rapidly disintegrating.* 中央政府的權力在迅速瓦解。 ▸ **dis·in·te·gra·tion** /dɪsˌɪntɪˈɡreɪʃn/ *noun* [U]：*the gradual disintegration of traditional values* 傳統價值觀念的逐漸淡薄

dis·in·ter /ˌdɪsɪnˈtɜː(r)/ *verb* (**-rr-**) (*formal*) **1 ~ sth** to dig up sth, especially a dead body, from the ground 從地下掘出（尤指屍體） OPP **inter 2 ~ sth (from sth)** to find sth that has been hidden or lost for a long time 發現（埋藏或丟失很久的東西）；使顯現

dis·in·ter·est /dɪsˈɪntrəst; -trest/ *noun* [U] **1 ~ (in sth)** lack of interest 無興趣；不關心；冷漠：*His total disinterest in money puzzled his family.* 他對金錢毫無興趣使他的家人感到迷惑不解。 **2** the fact of not being involved in sth 客觀；公正

dis·in·ter·est·ed /dɪsˈɪntrəstɪd; -trestɪd/ *adj.* **1** not influenced by personal feelings, or by the chance of getting some advantage for yourself 客觀的；無私的；公正的 SYN **impartial, objective, unbiased**：*a* ***disinterested onlooker/spectator*** 不偏不倚的旁觀者/觀眾 ◇ *Her advice appeared to be disinterested.* 她的建議似乎是客觀公正的。 **2** (*informal*) not interested 無興趣的；不關心的；冷漠的 ➲ note at INTERESTED ▸ **dis·in·ter·est·ed·ly** *adv.*

dis·in·vest /ˌdɪsɪnˈvest/ *verb* [I] **~ (from sth)** (*business* 商) to stop investing money in a company, industry or country; to reduce the amount of money invested 撤資；減少（對…的）投資

dis·in·vest·ment /ˌdɪsɪnˈvestmənt/ *noun* [U] (*finance* 財) the process of reducing the amount of money that you have invested in a particular company, industry, etc. 減少投資；抽回投資

dis·joint·ed /dɪsˈdʒɔɪntɪd/ *adj.* not communicated or described in a clear or logical way; not connected 不連貫的；支離破碎的；雜亂無章的 SYN **disconnected, incoherent**

dis·junc·tion /dɪsˈdʒʌŋkʃn/ (also *less frequent* **dis·junc·ture** /dɪsˈdʒʌŋktʃə(r)/) *noun* **~ (between A and B)** (*formal*) a difference between two things that you would expect to be in agreement with each other 分離；分裂

disk 0**m** /dɪsk/ *noun*
1 0**m** (*especially NAmE*) = DISC：*Red blood cells are roughly the shape of a disk.* 紅細胞大致呈圓盤狀。 **2** 0**m** (also **magˌnetic ˈdisk**) (*computing* 計) a device for storing information on a computer, with a MAGNETIC surface that records information received in electronic form 磁盤；磁碟 ➲ see also FLOPPY DISK, HARD DISK

ˈdisk drive *noun* a device that passes data between a disk and the memory of a computer or from one disk or computer to another 驅動器 ➲ VISUAL VOCAB page V66

disk·ette /dɪsˈket/ *noun* = FLOPPY DISK

dis·like 🔑 /dɪsˈlaɪk/ *verb, noun*

■ *verb* 🔑 (rather *formal*) to not like sb/sth 不喜愛；厭惡：**~ sb/sth** *Why do you dislike him so much?* 你為什麼那麼討厭他呢？◇ *He* ***disliked it*** *when she behaved badly in front of his mother.* 他討厭她在他母親面前舉止失當。◇ **~ doing sth** *I dislike being away from my family.* 我不喜歡同家人分開。◇ ***Much as she disliked*** *going to funerals* (= although she did not like it at all), *she knew she had to be there.* 儘管她很不喜歡參加葬禮，但她知道她必須去。◇ **~ sb/sth doing sth** *He disliked her staying away from home.* 他不願意讓她住在外面。➲ SYNONYMS at HATE OPP **like**

■ *noun* **1** 🔑 [U, sing.] **~ (of/for sb/sth)** a feeling of not liking sb/sth 不喜愛；厭惡；反感：*He did not try to hide his dislike of his boss.* 他沒有掩飾自己對上司的反感。◇ *She* ***took an instant dislike to*** *the house and the neighbourhood.* 她一下子就對那棟房子以及鄰近地區產生了反感。 **2** 🔑 [C, usually pl.] a thing that you do not like 不喜歡的事物；討厭的事物：*I've told you all my* ***likes and dislikes.*** 我喜歡什麼，不喜歡什麼，都對你說了。

dis·locate /ˈdɪsləkeɪt; *NAmE* -loʊk-; dɪsˈloʊ-/ *verb* **1 ~ sth** to put a bone out of its normal position in a joint 使（骨頭）脫位；使脫臼：*He dislocated his shoulder in the accident.* 他在事故中肩膀脫臼了。◇ *a dislocated finger* 脫臼的手指 ➲ COLLOCATIONS at INJURY **2 ~ sth** to stop a system, plan etc. from working or continuing in the normal way 擾亂（制度、計劃等）；使混亂；使運轉不正常 SYN **disrupt** ▸ **dis·loca·tion** /ˌdɪsləˈkeɪʃn; *NAmE* -loʊ-/ *noun* [C, U]：*a dislocation of the shoulder* 肩膀脫臼 ◇ *These policies could cause severe economic and social dislocation.* 這些政策可能引起嚴重的經濟和社會混亂。

dis·lodge /dɪsˈlɒdʒ; *NAmE* -ˈlɑːdʒ/ *verb* (*formal*) **1 ~ sth (from sth)** to force or knock sth out of its position（把某物）強行去除，取出，移動：*The wind dislodged one or two tiles from the roof.* 大風從屋頂上颳下了一兩片瓦來。 **2 ~ sb (from sth)** to force sb to leave a place, position or job（把某人）逐出，趕出，驅逐出：*The rebels have so far failed to dislodge the President.* 叛亂分子至今未能把總統趕下台。

dis·loyal /dɪsˈlɔɪəl/ *adj.* **~ (to sb/sth)** not loyal or faithful to your friends, family, country, etc.（對國家、家庭等）不忠實的，不忠誠的；（對朋友等）不守信義的：*He was accused of being disloyal to the government.* 他被指控對政府不忠。▸ **dis·loy·alty** /-ˈlɔɪəlti/ *noun* [U]

dis·mal /ˈdɪzməl/ *adj.* **1** causing or showing sadness 憂鬱的；淒涼的；慘淡的；陰沉的 SYN **gloomy, miserable**：*dismal conditions/surroundings/weather* 悲慘的狀況；淒涼的環境；陰沉的天氣 **2** (*informal*) not skilful or successful; of very low quality 不熟練的；差勁的；不怎麼樣的：*The singer gave a dismal performance of some old songs.* 那歌手唱了幾首老歌，唱得也不怎麼樣。◇ *Their recent attempt to increase sales has been a* ***dismal failure.*** 他們最近努力提高銷售量，全是白費勁。▸ **dis·mal·ly** /-məli/ *adv.*：*I tried not to laugh but failed dismally* (= was completely unsuccessful). 我想盡量忍着不笑，但根本忍不住。

dis·man·tle /dɪsˈmæntl/ *verb* **1 ~ sth** to take apart a machine or structure so that it is in separate pieces 拆開，拆卸（機器或結構）：*I had to dismantle the engine in order to repair it.* 我得把發動機拆開來修理。◇ *The steel mill was dismantled piece by piece.* 鋼廠已經一塊塊拆散了。 **2 ~ sth** to end an organization or system gradually in an organized way（逐漸）廢除，取消：*The government was in the process of dismantling the state-owned industries.* 政府正在着手逐步廢除國有企業。▸ **dis·mant·ling** *noun* [U]

dis·may /dɪsˈmeɪ/ *noun, verb*

■ *noun* [U] a worried, sad feeling after you have received an unpleasant surprise 詫異；驚愕；灰心；喪氣：*She could not hide her dismay at the result.* 她無法掩飾自己對這一結果的惶恐不安。◇ *He looked at her* ***in dismay.*** 他詫異地看着她。◇ ***To her dismay,*** *her name was not on the list.* 使她難過的是，名單上沒有她的名字。◇ *The news has been greeted* ***with dismay*** *by local business leaders.* 當地商界領袖聽到這消息都感到很喪氣。

■ *verb* **~ sb** to make sb feel shocked and disappointed 使詫異；使驚愕；使失望：*Their reaction dismayed him.* 他們的反應使他感到驚愕。▸ **dis·mayed** *adj.*：**~ (at/by sth)** *He was dismayed at the change in his old friend.* 他對老朋友變化之大感到震驚。◇ *The suggestion was greeted by a dismayed silence.* 大家對這個建議感到驚愕，誰都不吭聲。◇ **~ (to find, hear, see, etc. …)** *They were dismayed to find that the ferry had already left.* 他們發現渡船已經離開，感到很失望。

dis·mem·ber /dɪsˈmembə(r)/ *verb* **1 ~ sth** to cut or tear the dead body of a person or an animal into pieces 分割…的軀體；肢解 **2 ~ sth** (*formal*) to divide a country, an organization, etc. into smaller parts 分割；瓜分 ▸ **dis·mem·ber·ment** *noun* [U]

dis·miss 🔑 /dɪsˈmɪs/ *verb*

1 🔑 to decide that sb/sth is not important and not worth thinking or talking about 不予考慮；摒棄；對…不屑一提 SYN **wave aside**：**~ sb/sth** *I think we can safely dismiss their objections.* 我認為我們對他們的異議完全可以不予理會。◇ **~ sb/sth as sth** *Vegetarians are no longer dismissed as cranks.* 素食主義者不再被當作怪人。◇ *He dismissed the opinion polls as worthless.* 他認為民意測驗毫無用處而不予考慮。◇ *The suggestion should not be* ***dismissed out of hand*** (= without thinking about it). 這建議不應當直接就被摒棄。 **2** 🔑 to put thoughts or feelings out of your mind 去除，消除，摒除（思想、感情等）：**~ sth** *Dismissing her fears, she climbed higher.* 她排除了恐懼，爬得更高了。◇ **~ sb/sth from sth** *He dismissed her from his mind.* 他揮去了對她的思念。 **3** 🔑 **~ sb (from sth)** to officially remove sb from their job 解雇；免職；開除 SYN **fire, sack**：*She claims she was unfairly dismissed from her post.* 她聲稱自己被無理免職。 **4 ~ sb** to send sb away or allow them to leave 讓（某人）離開；把（某人）打發走；解散：*At 12 o'clock the class was dismissed.* * 12 點下課了。 **5 ~ sth** (*law* 律) to say that a trial or legal case should not continue, usually because there is not enough evidence 駁回；不受理：*The case was dismissed.* 此案已被駁回。 **6 ~ sb** (in CRICKET 板球) to end the INNINGS of a player or team 使（球員或球隊）退場；使出局

dis·missal /dɪsˈmɪsl/ *noun* **1** [U, C] the act of dismissing sb from their job; an example of this 解雇；開除；撤職：*He still hopes to win his claim against* ***unfair dismissal.*** 他聲稱遭無理解雇，仍然希望贏得申訴。◇ *The dismissals followed the resignation of the chairman.* 董事長辭職後緊接着就是解雇人員。 **2** [U] the failure to consider sth as important 不予考慮；不予理會；摒棄：*Her casual dismissal of the threats seemed irresponsible.* 她對這些威脅毫不在乎而不予理會，似乎很不負責任。 **3** [U, C] (*law* 律) the act of not allowing a trial or legal case to continue, usually because there is not enough evidence 駁回（訴訟）；不予受理：*the dismissal of the appeal* 駁回上訴 **4** [U, C] the act of sending sb away or allowing them to leave 解散；打發走 **5** [U, C] (in CRICKET 板球) the end of the INNINGS of a player or team（球員或球隊的）退場，出局

dis·mis·sive /dɪsˈmɪsɪv/ *adj.* **~ (of sb/sth)** showing that you do not believe a person or thing to be important or worth considering 輕蔑的；鄙視的 SYN **disdainful**：*a* ***dismissive gesture/tone*** 輕蔑的手勢／語調 ▸ **dis·mis·sive·ly** *adv.*：*to shrug/wave dismissively* 輕蔑地聳聳肩／揮揮手

dis·mount /dɪsˈmaʊnt/ *verb* [I] **~ (from sth)** (*formal*) to get off a horse, bicycle or motorcycle 下（馬、自行車、摩托車）OPP **mount**

dis·obedi·ence /ˌdɪsəˈbiːdiəns/ *noun* [U] failure or refusal to obey 不服從；不順從；違抗 ➲ see also CIVIL DISOBEDIENCE OPP **obedience**

dis·obedi·ent /ˌdɪsəˈbiːdiənt/ *adj.* failing or refusing to obey 不服從的；不順從的；違抗的：*a disobedient child* 不聽話的孩子 OPP **obedient**

D

dis·obey /ˌdɪsəˈbeɪ/ *verb* [T, I] **~ (sb/sth)** to refuse to do what a person, law, order, etc. tells you to do; to refuse to obey 不服從；不順從；違抗：*He was punished for disobeying orders.* 他因違抗命令而受到懲罰。OPP **obey**

dis·obli·ging /ˌdɪsəˈblaɪdʒɪŋ/ *adj.* deliberately not helpful 不肯幫忙的；不合作的：*a disobliging manner* 不合作的態度

D

dis·order /dɪsˈɔːdə(r); *NAmE* -ˈɔːrd-/ *noun* **1** [U] *(formal)* an untidy state; a lack of order or organization 雜亂；混亂；淩亂：*His financial affairs were* ***in*** *complete* ***disorder***. 他的錢財完全是一筆糊塗賬。◇ *The room was in a state of disorder.* 房間淩亂不堪。OPP **order 2** [U] *(formal)* violent behaviour of large groups of people 騷亂；動亂：*an outbreak of rioting and* ***public disorder*** 暴亂和公眾騷亂的爆發 ➲ compare ORDER (3) **3** [C, U] *(medical* 醫*)* an illness that causes a part of the body to stop functioning correctly 失調；紊亂；不適；疾病：***a blood/bowel, etc. disorder*** 血液病、鬧肚子等 ◇ ***eating disorders*** 進食障礙 ◇ *He was suffering from some form of psychiatric disorder.* 他患有某種類型的精神錯亂。➲ SYNONYMS at DISEASE

dis·ordered /dɪsˈɔːdəd; *NAmE* -ˈɔːrdərd/ *adj.* **1** showing a lack of order or control 雜亂的；混亂的；淩亂的：*disordered hair* 亂七八糟的頭髮 ◇ *a disordered state* 混亂狀態 OPP **ordered 2** *(technical* 術語*)* suffering from a mental or physical disorder （身心）失調的，紊亂的，錯亂的：*emotionally disordered children* 有情緒障礙的孩子

dis·or·der·ly /dɪsˈɔːdəli; *NAmE* -ˈɔːrdərli/ *adj.* [usually before noun] *(formal)* **1** (of people or behaviour 人或行為) showing lack of control; publicly violent or noisy 難駕馭的；目無法紀的；騷亂的：*disorderly conduct* 目無法紀的行為 ◇ *They were arrested for being* ***drunk and disorderly***. 他們因醉酒滋事而被捕。**2** untidy 雜亂的；混亂的；淩亂的：*newspapers in a disorderly pile by the door* 門邊亂七八糟的一堆報紙 OPP **orderly**

disˌorderly ˈhouse *noun* *(law* 律*)* *(old use)* a BROTHEL (= place where people pay to have sex) 妓院

dis·or·gan·ized (*BrE* also **-ised**) /dɪsˈɔːɡənaɪzd; *NAmE* -ˈɔːrɡ-/ (also *less frequent* **un·or·gan·ized**, **-ised**) *adj.* badly planned; not able to plan or organize well 計劃不周的；缺乏組織的；雜亂無章的：*It was a hectic disorganized weekend.* 這個週末忙亂得一塌糊塗。◇ *She's so disorganized.* 她太缺乏條理了。➲ compare ORGANIZED (2), (3) ▶ **dis·or·gan·iza·tion**, **-isa·tion** /dɪsˌɔːɡənaɪˈzeɪʃn; *NAmE* -ˌɔːrɡənəˈz-/ *noun* [U]

dis·orien·tate /dɪsˈɔːriənteɪt/ (*BrE*) (also **dis·orient** /dɪsˈɔːrient/ *NAmE, BrE*) *verb* **1 ~ sb** to make sb unable to recognize where they are or where they should go 使迷失方向：*The darkness had disorientated him.* 黑暗使他迷失了方向。**2 ~ sb** to make sb feel confused 使迷惘；使不知所措；使無所適從：*Ex-soldiers can be disorientated by the transition to civilian life.* 退伍軍人轉去過平民生活可能會感到茫然。➲ compare ORIENT ▶ **dis·orien·tated** (also **dis·orient·ed**) *adj.*：*She felt shocked and totally disorientated.* 她感到震驚而茫然不知所措。**dis·orien·ta·tion** /dɪsˌɔːriənˈteɪʃn/ *noun* [U]

dis·own /dɪsˈəʊn; *NAmE* -ˈoʊn/ *verb* **~ sb/sth** to decide that you no longer want to be connected with or responsible for sb/sth 與…斷絕關係；否認對…的責任：*Her family disowned her for marrying a foreigner.* 她的家人因她嫁給了外國人而與她斷絕關係。

dis·par·age /dɪˈspærɪdʒ/ *verb* **~ sb/sth** *(formal)* to suggest that sb/sth is not important or valuable 貶低；輕視 SYN **belittle**：*I don't mean to disparage your achievements.* 我並不想貶低你的成就。▶ **dis·par·age·ment** *noun* [U] **dis·para·ging** *adj.*：*disparaging remarks* 貶損的言辭 **dis·para·ging·ly** *adv.*：*He spoke disparagingly of his colleagues.* 他言辭之中很是看不起同事。

dis·par·ate /ˈdɪspərət/ *adj.* *(formal)* **1** made up of parts or people that are very different from each other 由不同的人（或事物）組成的：*a disparate group of individuals* 三教九流的一幫人 **2** (of two or more things 兩種或以上的事物) so different from each other that they cannot be compared or cannot work together 迥然不同的；無法比較的

dis·par·ity /dɪˈspærəti/ *noun* [U, C] (*pl.* **-ies**) *(formal)* a difference, especially one connected with unfair treatment （尤指因不公正對待引起的）不同，不等，差異，懸殊：*the wide disparity between rich and poor* 貧富懸殊

dis·pas·sion·ate /dɪsˈpæʃənət/ *adj.* *(approving)* not influenced by emotion 不動感情的；冷靜的；不帶偏見的 SYN **impartial**：*taking a calm, dispassionate view of the situation* 以冷靜、客觀公正的觀點看待形勢 ◇ *a dispassionate observer* 冷靜的旁觀者 ▶ **dis·pas·sion·ate·ly** *adv.*

dis·patch (*BrE* also **des·patch**) /dɪˈspætʃ/ *verb, noun*

■ *verb* **1 ~ sb/sth (to …)** *(formal)* to send sb/sth somewhere, especially for a special purpose 派遣；調遣；派出：*Troops have been dispatched to the area.* 部隊已派往那個地區。◇ *A courier was dispatched to collect the documents.* 已派人去取文件。**2 ~ sth (to sb/sth)** *(formal)* to send a letter, package or message somewhere 發出，發送（郵件、包裹、信息）：*Goods are dispatched within 24 hours of your order reaching us.* 訂單到達我方 24 小時內發貨。**3 ~ sb/sth** *(formal)* to deal or finish with sb/sth quickly and completely 迅速處理；迅速辦妥；迅速完成：*He dispatched the younger player in straight sets.* 他連續幾盤迅速擊敗了那位比他年輕的選手。**4 ~ sb/sth** *(old-fashioned)* to kill a person or an animal 殺死；處決

■ *noun* **1** [U] *(formal)* the act of sending sb/sth somewhere 派遣；調遣；發送：*More food supplies are ready for immediate dispatch.* 更多的食品供應已備妥即刻發運。**2** [C] a message or report sent quickly from one military officer to another or between government officials （軍事人員或政府官員之間的）急件，快信 **3** [C] a report sent to a newspaper by a journalist who is working in a foreign country （駐外國記者發給報刊的）新聞報道，電訊：*dispatches from the war zone* 從戰區發來的報道

IDM **with diˈspatch** *(formal)* quickly and efficiently 迅速而有效

diˈspatch box (also **deˈspatch box**) (both *BrE*) *noun* **1** [C] a container for carrying official documents 公文箱 **2 the Dispatch Box** [sing.] a box on a table in the centre of the House of Commons in the British parliament, which ministers stand next to when they speak 英國下議院中央置於大臣站立發言處旁邊的箱子

dis·patch·er /dɪˈspætʃə(r)/ *noun* **1** *(NAmE)* a person whose job is to see that trains, buses, planes, etc. leave on time （火車、公交車、飛機等的）調度員 **2** a person whose job is to send emergency vehicles to where they are needed （應急車輛的）調度員

diˈspatch rider (also **deˈspatch rider**) *noun* (both *BrE*) a person whose job is to carry messages or packages by motorcycle （騎摩托車的）通信員，信使

dis·pel /dɪˈspel/ *verb* (**-ll-**) **~ sth** to make sth, especially a feeling or belief, go away or disappear 驅散，消除（尤指感覺或信仰）：*His speech dispelled any fears about his health.* 他的發言消除了人們對他身體健康的擔心。

dis·pens·able /dɪˈspensəbl/ *adj.* [not usually before noun] not necessary; that can be got rid of 不必要；可有可無；不重要：*They looked on music and art lessons as dispensable.* 他們認為音樂課和美術課是可有可無的。OPP **essential, indispensable**

dis·pens·ary /dɪˈspensəri/ *noun* (*pl.* **-ies**) **1** a place in a hospital, shop/store, etc. where medicines are prepared for patients （醫院、商店等的）藥房，配藥處 **2** *(old-fashioned)* a place where patients are treated, especially one run by a charity （尤指慈善機構的）醫務室，診所

dis·pen·sa·tion /ˌdɪspenˈseɪʃn/ *noun* **1** [C, U] special permission, especially from a religious leader, to do sth that is not usually allowed or legal （尤指宗教領袖給予的）豁免，寬免：*She needed a special dispensation to remarry.* 她需要得到義務寬免才能再婚。◇ *The sport's ruling body gave him dispensation to compete in national competitions.* 體育運動管理機構特許他參加全國性的體育比賽。**2** [U] *(formal)* the act or process of providing sth, especially by sb in authority 分配；施與；實施：*the dispensation of justice* 執法 **3** [C] *(technical* 術語*)* a political or religious system that operates in a country at a particular time （某一國家某一時期的政治、宗教）制度

dis·pense /dɪˈspens/ *verb* **1 ~ sth (to sb)** (*formal*) to give out sth to people 分配；分發：*The machine dispenses a range of drinks and snacks.* 這台機器發售各種飲料和小吃。 **2 ~ sth (to sb)** (*formal*) to provide sth, especially a service, for people 施與，提供（尤指服務）：*The organization dispenses free health care to the poor.* 這個機構為窮人提供免費醫療。◇ *to* ***dispense justice/advice*** 執法；給予忠告 **3 ~ sth** to prepare medicine and give it to people, as a job 配（藥）；發（藥）：*to dispense a prescription* 按處方配藥◇ (*BrE*) *to dispense medicine* 發藥◇ (*BrE*) *a dispensing chemist* 藥劑師

PHR V **diˈspense with sb/sth** to stop using sb/sth because you no longer need them or it 摒棄；不再需要；不再用 **SYN do away with**：*Debit cards dispense with the need for cash altogether.* 有借記卡就完全不需要用現金了。◇ *I think we can* ***dispense with the formalities*** (= speak openly and naturally to each other). 我想我們就免去客套吧。

dis·pens·er /dɪˈspensə(r)/ *noun* a machine or container holding money, drinks, paper towels, etc. that you can obtain quickly, for example by pulling a handle or pressing buttons 自動取款機；自動售貨機；自動取物器：*a soap dispenser* 皂液瓶 ➲ **VISUAL VOCAB** pages V24, V69 ➲ see also CASH DISPENSER

disˈpensing chemist *noun* (*BrE*) = CHEMIST (1)

dis·pers·al /dɪˈspɜːsl; *NAmE* dɪˈspɜːrsl/ *noun* [U, C] (*formal*) the process of sending sb/sth in different directions; the process of spreading sth over a wide area 分散；疏散；散佈：*police trained in crowd dispersal* 在疏散人群方面受過訓練的警察◇ *the dispersal of seeds* 種子的傳播

dis·perse /dɪˈspɜːs; *NAmE* dɪˈspɜːrs/ *verb* **1** [I, T] to move apart and go away in different directions; to make sb/sth do this（使）分散，散開，疏散，驅散：*The fog began to disperse.* 霧開始散了。◇ *The* ***crowd dispersed*** *quickly.* 人群很快便散開了。◇ **~ sb/sth** *Police dispersed the protesters with tear gas.* 警察用催淚彈驅散了抗議者。 **2** [T, I] **~ (sth)** to spread or to make sth spread over a wide area 散佈；散發；傳播 **SYN scatter**：*The seeds are dispersed by the wind.* 這些種子由風傳播。

dis·per·sion /dɪˈspɜːʃn; *NAmE* dɪˈspɜːrʒn/ *noun* [U] (*technical* 術語) the process by which people or things are spread over a wide area 分散；散開；散佈

dis·pirited /dɪˈspɪrɪtɪd/ *adj.* having no hope or enthusiasm 氣餒的；垂頭喪氣的；心灰意懶的：*She looked tired and dispirited.* 她顯得疲倦而且神情沮喪。➲ compare SPIRITED

dis·pir·it·ing /dɪˈspɪrɪtɪŋ/ *adj.* making sb lose their hope or enthusiasm 令人沮喪的；使人氣餒的：*a* ***dispiriting experience/failure*** 令人沮喪的經歷／失敗

dis·place **AW** /dɪsˈpleɪs/ *verb* [often passive] (*formal*) **1 ~ sb/sth** to take the place of sb/sth 取代；替代；置換 **SYN replace**：*Gradually factory workers have been displaced by machines.* 工廠的工人已逐漸被機器取代。◇ (*technical* 術語) *The ship displaces 58 000 tonnes* (= as a way of measuring its size). 這艘輪船的排水量為 58 000 噸。 **2 ~ sb** to force people to move away from their home to another place 迫使（某人）離開家園：*Around 10 000 people have been displaced by the fighting.* 大約 1 萬人因戰爭而背井離鄉。 **3 ~ sth** to move sth from its usual position 移動；挪開；轉移：*Check for roof tiles that have been displaced by the wind.* 檢查一下屋頂上是否有瓦被風颳得挪位。 **4 ~ sb** (*especially NAmE*) to remove sb from a job or position 撤職；免職；使失業：*displaced workers* 辭退的工人

diˌsplaced ˈperson *noun* (*pl.* **diˌsplaced ˈpersons**) (*technical* 術語) a REFUGEE 難民；流亡者

dis·place·ment **AW** /dɪsˈpleɪsmənt/ *noun* [U] **1** (*formal*) the act of displacing sb/sth; the process of being displaced 取代；替代；移位；免職：*the largest displacement of civilian population since World War Two* 自第二次世界大戰以來最大規模的平民遷移 **2** [C] (*physics* 物) the amount of a liquid moved out of place by sth floating or put in it, especially a ship floating in water 排水量：*a ship with a displacement of 10 000 tonnes* 排水量為 1 萬噸的船

disˈplacement activity *noun* **1** [U] things that you do in order to avoid doing what you are supposed to be doing 逃避職責的活動 **2** (*biology* 生, *psychology* 心) [U, C] behaviour in animals or humans that seems to have no connection with the situation in which it is performed, resulting from two conflicting urges 替換活動，移位活動（人或動物由於對立的驅力而表現出不相宜的行為）

dis·play **0-w** **AW** /dɪˈspleɪ/ *verb, noun*

■ ***verb*** **1** **0-w** [T] **~ sth (to sb)** to put sth in a place where people can see it easily; to show sth to people 陳列；展出；展示 **SYN exhibit**：*The exhibition gives local artists an opportunity to display their work.* 這次展覽為當地藝術家提供了展示自己作品的機會。◇ *She displayed her bruises for all to see.* 她將自己身上青一塊紫一塊的傷痕露出來給大家看。 **2** **0-w** [T] **~ sth** to show signs of sth, especially a quality or feeling 顯示，顯露，表現（尤指特性或情感）：*I have rarely seen her display any sign of emotion.* 我難得見到她將喜怒形於色。◇ *These statistics display a definite trend.* 這些統計數據表現出一種明顯的趨勢。 **3** **0-w** [T] **~ sth** (of a computer, etc. 計算機等) to show information 顯示：*The screen will display the username in the top right-hand corner.* 屏幕將在右上角顯示用戶名稱。◇ *This column displays the title of the mail message.* 這一欄顯示郵件標題。 **4** [I] (*technical* 術語) (of male birds and animals 雄性的鳥獸) to show a special pattern of behaviour that is intended to attract a female bird or animal（為求偶）作炫耀行為

■ ***noun*** **1** **0-w** an arrangement of things in a public place to inform or entertain people or advertise sth for sale 陳列；展覽：*a beautiful floral display outside the Town Hall* 市政廳外陳設的美麗的花◇ *a window display* 櫥窗陳列◇ *a display cabinet* 陳列櫃 **2** **0-w** an act of performing a skill or of showing sth happening, in order to entertain 展示；表演：*a firework display* 煙火表演◇ *a breathtaking display of aerobatics* 驚險的特技飛行表演 **3** an occasion when you show a particular quality, feeling or ability by the way that you behave（特性、情感或能力的）顯示，表現，表露：*a display of affection/strength/wealth* 愛的流露；實力的顯示；財富的炫耀 **4** the words, pictures, etc. shown on a computer screen（計算機屏幕上的）顯示，顯像：*a high resolution colour display* 高分辨率彩色顯示 ➲ see also LIQUID CRYSTAL DISPLAY, VDU

IDM **on diˈsplay** **0-w** put in a place where people can look at it 陳列；展出 **SYN on show**：*Designs for the new sports hall are on display in the library.* 新體育館的設計圖展示在圖書館裏。◇ *to put sth on* ***temporary/permanent display*** 臨時／長期展出某物

disˈplay bin (*BrE* also **ˈdump bin**) *noun* a box in a shop/store for displaying goods, especially goods whose prices have been reduced（商店）陳列櫃；（尤指）減價貨品櫃

dis·please /dɪsˈpliːz/ *verb* **~ sb** (*formal*) to make sb feel upset, annoyed or not satisfied 使惱怒；使生氣；使不悅 **OPP please** ▸ **dis·pleased** *adj.*：**~ (with sb/sth)** *Are you displeased with my work?* 你對我的工作不滿意嗎？◇ **~ (at sth)** *She was not displeased at the effect she was having on the young man.* 她並沒有為自己對那個年輕人產生的影響而感到不快。 **dis·pleas·ing** *adj.*：**~ (to sb/sth)** *His remarks were clearly not displeasing to her.* 他的話顯然並沒使她不快。

dis·pleas·ure /dɪsˈpleʒə(r)/ *noun* [U] **~ (at/with sb/sth)** (*formal*) the feeling of being upset and annoyed 煩惱；生氣；不悅 **SYN annoyance**：*She made no attempt to hide her displeasure at the prospect.* 她沒有掩飾自己對前景並不樂觀。➲ compare PLEASURE

dis·port /dɪˈspɔːt; *NAmE* dɪˈspɔːrt/ *verb* **~ yourself** (*old-fashioned* or *humorous*) to enjoy yourself by doing sth active 作樂；自娛自樂

dis·pos·able **AW** /dɪˈspəʊzəbl; *NAmE* -ˈspoʊ-/ *adj.* [usually before noun] **1** made to be thrown away after use 用後即丟棄的；一次性的：*disposable gloves/razors* 一次性手套／剃刀◇ (*BrE*) *disposable nappies* 一次性尿布◇ (*NAmE*) *disposable diapers* 一次性尿布 **2** (*finance* 財) available for use 可動用的；可自由支配的：***disposable assets/capital/resources*** 可支配資產／資本／資源◇ *a person's* *disposable income* (= money they are free to spend after paying taxes, etc.) 個人可支配（稅後）收入

dis·pos·ables /dɪ'spəʊzəblz; *NAmE* -'spoʊ-/ *noun* [pl.] items such as NAPPIES/DIAPERS and CONTACT LENSES that are designed to be thrown away after use 用後即丟棄的物品，一次性物品（如尿布、隱形眼鏡片）

dis·posal AW /dɪ'spəʊzl; *NAmE* -'spoʊ-/ *noun* **1** [U] the act of getting rid of sth 去掉；清除；處理：*a bomb disposal squad* 炸彈清除小組 ◇ *sewage disposal systems* 污水處理系統 ◇ *the disposal of nuclear waste* 核廢料的處理 **2** [C] (*business* 商) the sale of part of a business, property, etc.（企業、財產等的）變賣，讓與 **3** [C] (*NAmE*) = WASTE-DISPOSAL UNIT

IDM **at your/sb's disposal** available for use as you prefer/sb prefers 任某人處理；供某人任意使用；由某人自行支配：*He will have a car at his disposal for the whole month.* 他將有一輛汽車歸他使用一個月。◇ *Well, I'm at your disposal* (= I am ready to help you in any way I can). 好吧，我聽候你的吩咐。

dis·pose AW /dɪ'spəʊz; *NAmE* dɪ'spoʊz/ *verb* (*formal*) **1 ~ sth/sb + adv./prep.** to arrange things or people in a particular way or position 排列；佈置；安排 **2 ~ sb to/toward(s) sth | ~ sb to do sth** to make sb behave in a particular way 使傾向於；使有意於；使易於：*a drug that disposes the patient towards sleep* 使病人想睡覺的藥

PHR V **di'spose of sb/sth** **1** to get rid of sb/sth that you do not want or cannot keep 去掉；清除；銷毀：*the difficulties of disposing of nuclear waste* 處理核廢料的困難 ◇ *to dispose of stolen property* 銷贓 **2** to deal with a problem, question or threat successfully 應付；解決；處理：*That seems to have disposed of most of their arguments.* 這樣就似乎把他們的大部份論點都駁倒了。**3** to defeat or kill sb 擊敗；殺死：*It took her a mere 20 minutes to dispose of her opponent.* 她僅用了 20 分鐘就擊敗了對手。

dis·posed AW /dɪ'spəʊzd; *NAmE* dɪ'spoʊzd/ *adj.* [not before noun] (*formal*) **1 ~ (to do sth)** willing or prepared to do sth 傾向於；有意於；樂意：*I'm not disposed to argue.* 我無意爭論。◇ *You're most welcome to join us if you feel so disposed.* 你若有意參加，我們非常歡迎。**2** (following an adverb 用於副詞後) **~ to/towards sb/sth** having a good/bad opinion of a person or thing 對…有好感（或惡感）：*She seems favourably disposed to the move.* 她似乎對這一行動持贊同態度。➲ see also ILL-DISPOSED, WELL DISPOSED

dis·pos·ition /ˌdɪspə'zɪʃn/ *noun* **1** [C, usually sing.] (*formal*) the natural qualities of a person's character 性格；性情 SYN **temperament**：*to have a cheerful disposition* 性情開朗 ◇ *people of a nervous disposition* 神經質的人 **2** [C, usually sing.] **~ to/towards sth | ~ to do sth** (*formal*) a tendency to behave in a particular way 傾向；意向：*to have/show a disposition towards violence* 有／表現出暴力傾向 **3** [C, usually sing.] (*formal*) the way sth is placed or arranged 排列；佈置；安排 SYN **arrangement** **4** [C, U] (*law* 律) a formal act of giving property or money to sb（財產、金錢的）處置，讓與

dis·pos·sess /ˌdɪspə'zes/ *verb* [usually passive] **~ sb (of sth)** (*formal*) to take sb's property, land or house away from them 剝奪，奪去（某人的財產、土地、房屋）▶ **dis·pos·ses·sion** /ˌdɪspə'zeʃn/ *noun* [U]

the dis·pos·sessed /ˌdɪspə'zest/ *noun* [pl.] people who have had property taken away from them 被剝奪財產者

dis·pro·por·tion AW /ˌdɪsprə'pɔːʃn; *NAmE* -'pɔːrʃn/ *noun* [U, C] (*formal*) the state of two things not being at an equally high or low level; an example of this 不相稱；不均衡；不成比例；不相稱（或不均衡、不成比例）的東西：**~ (between A and B)** *the disproportion between the extra responsibilities and the small salary increase* 額外的責任與小幅增加的薪金之間的不相稱 ◇ **~ (of A to B)** *a profession with a high disproportion of male to female employees* 男女雇員比例嚴重失調的職業

dis·pro·por·tion·ate AW /ˌdɪsprə'pɔːʃənət; *NAmE* -'pɔːrʃ-/ *adj.* **~ (to sth)** too large or too small when compared with sth else 不成比例的；不相稱的；太大（或太小）的：*The area contains a disproportionate number of young middle-class families.* 此地年輕的中產階級家庭特別多。➲ compare PROPORTIONATE ▶ **dis·pro·por·tion·ately** AW *adv.*：*The lower-paid spend a disproportionately large amount of their earnings on food.* 低工資者將收入花在食物上的比例很大。

dis·prove /ˌdɪs'pruːv/ *verb* **~ sth** to show that sth is wrong or false 證明…是錯誤（或虛假）的：*The theory has now been disproved.* 這一理論現已證明是錯誤的。OPP **prove**

dis·put·able /dɪ'spjuːtəbl/ *adj.* (*formal*) that can or should be questioned or argued about 可質疑的；有爭辯餘地的；可商榷的 ➲ compare INDISPUTABLE

dis·pu·ta·tion /ˌdɪspju'teɪʃn/ *noun* [C, U] (*formal*) a discussion about sth that people cannot agree on 爭論；辯論；討論

dis·pute *noun*, *verb*

■ *noun* /dɪ'spjuːt; 'dɪspjuːt/ [C, U] an argument or a disagreement between two people, groups or countries; discussion about a subject where there is disagreement 爭論；辯論；爭端；糾紛：**~ (between A and B)** *a dispute between the two countries about the border* 兩國間的邊界爭端 ◇ **~ (over/about sth)** *the latest dispute over fishing rights* 最近關於捕魚權的爭端 ◇ ***industrial/pay disputes*** 勞資／工資糾紛 ◇ *The union is **in dispute with** management over working hours.* 工會與資方在工時問題上發生糾紛。◇ *The cause of the accident was still **in dispute*** (= being argued about). 事故的原因仍在爭議之中。◇ *The matter was settled **beyond dispute** by the court judgment* (= it could no longer be argued about). 此問題已由法庭判決，不容爭辯。◇ *His theories are **open to dispute*** (= can be disagreed with). 他的理論值得商榷。

■ *verb* /dɪ'spjuːt/ **1** [T] to question whether sth is true and valid 對…提出質詢；對…表示異議（或懷疑）：**~ sth** *These figures have been disputed.* 有人對這些數字提出了質疑。◇ *to **dispute a decision/claim*** 對某項決定／權利要求提出異議 ◇ *The family wanted to dispute the will.* 家屬想對遺囑提出質疑。◇ **~ that …** *No one is disputing that there is a problem.* 沒有人否認現在有問題。◇ **~ whether, how, etc. … | it is disputed whether, how, etc. …** *It is disputed whether the law applies in this case.* 有人對這項法律是否適用於這個案例提出質疑。**2** [T, I] **~ (sth)** to argue or disagree strongly with sb about sth, especially about who owns sth 爭論；辯論；爭執：*disputed territory* 有爭議的領土 ◇ *The issue remains **hotly disputed**.* 這個問題至今仍在激烈地辯論中。**3** [T] **~ sth** to fight to get control of sth or to win sth 爭奪；競爭：*On the last lap three runners were disputing the lead.* 在最後一圈，三名賽跑者在爭奪領先地位。

dis·qual·ify /dɪs'kwɒlɪfaɪ; *NAmE* -'kwɑːl-/ *verb* (**dis·quali·fies**, **dis·quali·fy·ing**, **dis·quali·fied**, **dis·quali·fied**) to prevent sb from doing sth because they have broken a rule or are not suitable 使不合格；使不適合；取消（某人）的資格 SYN **bar**：**~ sb (from sth)** *He was disqualified from the competition for using drugs.* 他因使用違禁藥被取消比賽資格。◇ **~ sb (from doing sth)** (*BrE*) *You could be disqualified from driving for up to three years.* 你可能會被取消駕駛資格達三年之久。◇ **~ sb (for sth)** *A heart condition disqualified him for military service.* 心臟病使他不符合服兵役的條件。▶ **dis·quali·fi·ca·tion** /dɪsˌkwɒlɪfɪ'keɪʃn; *NAmE* -ˌkwɑːl-/ *noun* [C, U]：*Any form of cheating means automatic disqualification.* 任何形式的作弊都意味着自動取消資格。

dis·quiet /dɪs'kwaɪət/ *noun* [U] **~ (about/over sth)** (*formal*) feelings of worry and unhappiness about sth 不安；憂慮；煩惱 SYN **unease**：*There is considerable public disquiet about the safety of the new trains.* 公眾對新型列車的安全深感憂慮。

dis·quiet·ing /dɪs'kwaɪətɪŋ/ *adj.* (*formal*) causing worry and unhappiness 令人不安的；使人憂慮的

dis·quisi·tion /ˌdɪskwɪ'zɪʃn/ *noun* (*formal*) a long complicated speech or written report on a particular subject 專題演講；專題論文；專題報告

dis·re·gard /ˌdɪsrɪ'gɑːd; *NAmE* -'gɑːrd/ *verb*, *noun*

■ *verb* **~ sth** (*formal*) to not consider sth; to treat sth as unimportant 不理會；不顧；漠視 SYN **ignore**：*The* *board completely disregarded my recommendations.* 董事會完全無視我的建議。◇ *Safety rules were disregarded.* 安全規定被忽視了。

■ ***noun*** [U] **~ (for/of sb/sth)** (*formal*) the act of treating sb/sth as unimportant and not caring about them/it 漠視；忽視：*She shows a total disregard for other people's feelings.* 她絲毫不顧及別人的感受。

dis·re·pair /ˌdɪsrɪˈpeə(r); *NAmE* -ˈper/ *noun* [U] a building, road, etc. that is in a state of **disrepair** has not been taken care of and is broken or in bad condition 失修；破敗；破損：*The station quickly* ***fell into disrepair*** *after it was closed.* 車站關閉後很快便破敗不堪。

dis·rep·ut·able /dɪsˈrepjətəbl/ *adj.* that people consider to be dishonest and bad 名聲不好的；不名譽的；不光彩的：*She spent the evening with her disreputable brother Stefan.* 她同聲名狼藉的弟弟斯蒂芬一起度過了這個傍晚。◇ *a disreputable area of the city* 城裏破舊骯髒的地方 **OPP** **respectable** ➲ compare REPUTABLE

dis·re·pute /ˌdɪsrɪˈpjuːt/ *noun* [U] (*formal*) the fact that sb/sth loses the respect of other people 喪失名譽；壞名聲：*The players' behaviour on the field is likely to* ***bring*** *the game* ***into disrepute****.* 球員在賽場上的表現很可能使這場比賽臭名遠揚。

dis·res·pect /ˌdɪsrɪˈspekt/ *noun, verb*

■ ***noun*** [U, C] **~ (for/to sb/sth)** a lack of respect for sb/sth 不尊敬；無禮；輕蔑：*disrespect for the law/the dead* 藐視法律；對死者的不敬 ◇ ***No disrespect intended*** *sir. It was just a joke.* 先生，絕無不敬之意。這不過是個玩笑而已。▸ **dis·res·pect·ful** /-fl/ *adj.* **~ (to sb/sth)** **dis·res·pect·ful·ly** /-fəli/ *adv.*

■ ***verb*** **~ sb/sth** (*informal*) to speak about or treat sb/sth without respect 不尊敬；對…無禮：*They were accused of disrespecting the country's flag.* 他們被控褻瀆國旗。
HELP Some people consider that it is not correct to use **disrespect** as a verb, and that you should use the noun instead, especially in formal and written English. 有人認為 disrespect 用作動詞不恰當，應作名詞使用，尤其在正式和書面英語中：*They were accused of treating the country's flag with disrespect.*

dis·robe /dɪsˈrəʊb; *NAmE* -ˈroʊb/ *verb* [I, T] **~ (sb)** (*formal* or *humorous*) to take off your or sb else's clothes; to take off clothes worn for an official ceremony 脫去（某人）的衣服；脫衣服；脫去制服（或禮服）：*She went behind the screen to disrobe.* 她到屏風後面去換裝。

dis·rupt /dɪsˈrʌpt/ *verb* **~ sth** to make it difficult for sth to continue in the normal way 擾亂；使中斷；打亂：*Demonstrators succeeded in disrupting the meeting.* 示威者成功地擾亂了會議。◇ *Bus services will be disrupted tomorrow because of the bridge closure.* 明日公共汽車服務將因大橋停止通行而受影響。▸ **dis·rup·tion** /dɪsˈrʌpʃn/ *noun* [U, C]：*We aim to help you move house with minimum disruption to yourself.* 我們的宗旨是幫您搬家的時候，盡量減少給您帶來的不便。◇ *disruptions to rail services* 對鐵路交通的干擾 ◇ *The strike caused serious disruptions.* 罷工造成了嚴重的混亂。

dis·rup·tive /dɪsˈrʌptɪv/ *adj.* causing problems, noise, etc. so that sth cannot continue normally 引起混亂的；擾亂性的；破壞性的：*She had a disruptive influence on the rest of the class.* 她攪擾了班上其他的學生。

diss = DIS

dis·sat·is·fac·tion /ˌdɪsˌsætɪsˈfækʃn/ *noun* [U] **~ (with/at sb/sth)** a feeling that you are not pleased and satisfied 不快；不悅；不滿意：*Many people have expressed their dissatisfaction with the arrangement.* 許多人表示對這一安排不滿。**OPP** **satisfaction**

dis·sat·is·fied /dɪsˈsætɪsfaɪd; dɪˈsæt-/ *adj.* not happy or satisfied with sb/sth（對…）不滿的，不高興的，不滿意的：*dissatisfied customers* 不滿的顧客 ◇ **~ with sb/sth** *If you are dissatisfied with our service, please write to the manager.* 對於服務如有不滿，請函告經理。**OPP** **satisfied** ➲ compare UNSATISFIED

dis·sect /dɪˈsekt; daɪ-/ *verb* **1** **~ sth** to cut up a dead person, animal or plant in order to study it 解剖（人或動植物）**2** **~ sth** to study sth closely and/or discuss it in great detail 仔細研究；詳細評論；剖析：*Her latest novel was dissected by the critics.* 評論家對她最近出版的一部小說作了詳細剖析。**3** **~ sth** to divide sth into smaller pieces, areas, etc. 把…分成小塊：*The city is dissected by a network of old canals.* 古老的運河網將這座城市分割開來。▸ **dis·sec·tion** /dɪˈsekʃn; daɪ-/ *noun* [U, C]：*anatomical dissection* 解剖分析 ◇ *Your enjoyment of a novel can suffer from too much analysis and dissection.* 對一部小說過多的剖析可能會影響你閱讀的樂趣。

dis·sem·ble /dɪˈsembl/ *verb* [I, T] **~ (sth)** (*formal*) to hide your real feelings or intentions, often by pretending to have different ones 掩蓋，掩飾（真實感情或意圖）：*She was a very honest person who was incapable of dissembling.* 她是一個非常誠實的人，不會偽裝。

dis·sem·in·ate /dɪˈsemɪneɪt/ *verb* **~ sth** (*formal*) to spread information, knowledge, etc. so that it reaches many people 散佈，傳播（信息、知識等）：*Their findings have been* ***widely disseminated****.* 他們的研究成果已經廣為傳播。▸ **dis·sem·in·ation** /dɪˌsemɪˈneɪʃn/ *noun* [U]

dis·sen·sion /dɪˈsenʃn/ *noun* [U] (*formal*) disagreement between people or within a group 意見分歧；（派性）紛爭；不和：*dissension within the government* 政府內部的意見分歧

dis·sent /dɪˈsent/ *noun, verb*

■ ***noun*** (*formal*) **1** [U] the fact of having or expressing opinions that are different from those that are officially accepted（與官方的）不同意見，異議：***political/religious dissent*** 政治觀點／宗教信仰上的分歧 **2** [C] (*NAmE*) a judge's statement giving reasons why he or she disagrees with a decision made by the other judges in a court case（訴訟案中某法官對其他法官判決的）異議，不同意見

■ ***verb*** [I] **~ (from sth)** (*formal*) to have or express opinions that are different from those that are officially accepted（對官方意見）不同意，持異議：*Only two ministers dissented from the official view.* 只有兩位部長與官方持不同的觀點。▸ **dis·sent·ing** *adj.*：***dissenting groups/voices/views/opinion*** 持不同意見的團體；反對的呼聲；不同的觀點；異議

dis·sent·er /dɪˈsentə(r)/ *noun* a person who does not agree with opinions that are officially or generally accepted（對官方或普遍認可的意見）持異議者，持不同意見者

dis·ser·ta·tion /ˌdɪsəˈteɪʃn; *NAmE* -sərˈt-/ *noun* **~ (on sth)** a long piece of writing on a particular subject, especially one written for a university degree 專題論文；（尤指）學位論文 ➲ **WRITING TUTOR** page WT16

dis·ser·vice /dɪsˈsɜːvɪs; dɪˈsɜː-; *NAmE* -ˈsɜːrv-/ *noun* [sing.]
IDM **do sb a disˈservice** to do sth that harms sb and the opinion that other people have of them 損害；傷害；危害；中傷

dis·si·dent /ˈdɪsɪdənt/ *noun* a person who strongly disagrees with and criticizes their government, especially in a country where this kind of action is dangerous 持不同政見者 ▸ **dis·si·dence** /ˈdɪsɪdəns/ *noun* [U] **dis·si·dent** *adj.*

dis·simi·lar **AW** /dɪˈsɪmɪlə(r)/ *adj.* **~ (from/to sb/sth)** (*formal*) not the same 不一樣的；不同的；不相似的：*These wines are* ***not dissimilar*** (= are similar). 這些葡萄酒都差不多。**OPP** **similar** ▸ **dis·simi·lar·ity** /ˌdɪsɪmɪˈlærəti/ *noun* [C, U]

dis·simu·late /dɪˈsɪmjuleɪt/ *verb* [T, I] **~ (sth)** (*formal*) to hide your real feelings or intentions, often by pretending to have different ones 掩蓋，掩飾（真實感情或意圖）**SYN** **dissemble** ▸ **dis·simu·la·tion** /dɪˌsɪmjuˈleɪʃn/ *noun* [U]

dis·si·pate /ˈdɪsɪpeɪt/ *verb* (*formal*) **1** [I, T] to gradually become or make sth become weaker until it disappears（使）消散，消失；驅散：*Eventually, his anger dissipated.* 他的憤怒終於平息了。◇ **~ sth** *Her laughter soon dissipated the tension in the air.* 她的笑聲很快消除了緊張氣氛。**2** [T] **~ sth** to waste sth, such as time or money, especially by not planning the best way of using it 揮霍，浪費，消磨（時間、金錢等）**SYN** **squander**

dis·si·pated /ˈdɪsɪpeɪtɪd/ *adj.* (*disapproving*) enjoying activities that are harmful such as drinking too much alcohol 放蕩的；花天酒地的

D

D

dis·si·pa·tion /ˌdɪsɪˈpeɪʃn/ *noun* [U] (*formal*) **1** the process of disappearing or of making sth disappear 消散；驅散：*the dissipation of energy in the form of heat* 以熱量形式耗散的能量 **2** the act of wasting money or spending money until there is none left 揮霍；浪費：*concerns about the dissipation of the country's wealth* 對揮霍國家財富的憂慮 **3** (*disapproving*) behaviour which is enjoyable but has a harmful effect on you 放蕩；縱情逸慾

dis·so·ci·ate /dɪˈsəʊʃieɪt; -ˈsəʊs-; *NAmE* -ˈsoʊ-/ *verb* **1** (also **dis·as·so·ci·ate**) **~ yourself/sb from sb/sth** to say or do sth to show that you are not connected with or do not support sb/sth; to make it clear that sth is not connected with a particular plan, action, etc. 否認同…有關係；聲明不支持；表明無關：*He tried to dissociate himself from the party's more extreme views.* 他極力表明自己並不贊成該黨較為偏激的觀點。◇ *They were determined to dissociate the UN from any agreement to impose sanctions.* 他們決心阻止聯合國同意實施制裁。**2 ~ sb/sth (from sth)** (*formal*) to think of two people or things as separate and not connected with each other 把…分開（或看作是無關聯的）：*She tried to dissociate the two events in her mind.* 她試圖從思想上將這兩件事分開。**OPP** **associate** ▸ **dis·so·ci·ation** /dɪˌsəʊʃiˈeɪʃn; -ˌsəʊs-; *NAmE* -ˌsoʊ-/ *noun* [U]

dis·sol·ute /ˈdɪsəluːt/ *adj.* (*formal, disapproving*) enjoying immoral activities and not caring about behaving in a morally acceptable way 放縱的；放蕩的；道德淪喪的

dis·so·lution /ˌdɪsəˈluːʃn/ *noun* [U] **~ (of sth)** (*formal*) **1** the act of officially ending a marriage, a business agreement or a parliament（婚姻關係的）解除；（商業協議的）終止；（議會的）解散 **2** the process in which sth gradually disappears 消失；消亡：*the dissolution of barriers of class and race* 階級和種族隔閡的消除 **3** the act of breaking up an organization, etc. 解體；瓦解；分裂

dis·solve 🔑 /dɪˈzɒlv; *NAmE* -ˈzɑːlv/ *verb* **1** 🔑 [I] **~ (in sth)** (of a solid 固體) to mix with a liquid and become part of it 溶解：*Salt dissolves in water.* 鹽溶解於水。◇ *Heat gently until the sugar dissolves.* 慢慢加熱直到糖溶解為止。**2** 🔑 [T] **~ sth (in sth)** to make a solid become part of a liquid 使（固體）溶解：*Dissolve the tablet in water.* 把藥片溶於水中。**3** [T] **~ sth** to officially end a marriage, business agreement or parliament 解除（婚姻關係）；終止（商業協議）；解散（議會）：*Their marriage was dissolved in 1999.* 他們於 1999 年解除了婚姻關係。◇ *The election was announced and parliament was dissolved.* 宣佈選舉後，議會解散了。**4** [I, T] to disappear; to make sth disappear 消除；（使）消失，消散：*When the ambulance had gone, the crowd dissolved.* 救護車離開後人群便散開了。◇ **~ sth** *His calm response dissolved her anger.* 他平靜的回答化解了她的怒氣。**5** [I] **~ into laughter, tears, etc.** to suddenly start laughing, crying, etc. 禁不住（笑起來或哭起來等）：*When the teacher looked up, the children dissolved into giggles.* 教師抬頭看時，孩子們不禁格格笑起來。◇ *Every time she heard his name, she dissolved into tears.* 每當聽到他的名字時，她都禁不住淚流滿面。**6** [T, I] to remove or destroy sth, especially by a chemical process; to be destroyed in this way（尤以化學手段）除去，毀掉；（被）破壞：**~ sth (away)** *a new detergent that dissolves stains* 新型去污洗滌劑 ◇ **~ (away)** *All the original calcium had dissolved away.* 所有原始鈣都被破壞了。

dis·son·ance /ˈdɪsənəns/ *noun* **1** [C, U] (*music* 音) a combination of musical notes that do not sound pleasant together 不協和（音）；不諧和（音）**OPP** **consonance 2** [U] (*formal*) lack of agreement 不和諧；不協調；不一致 ▸ **dis·son·ant** /ˈdɪsənənt/ *adj.*：*dissonant voices/notes* 刺耳的聲音；不協和音

dis·suade /dɪˈsweɪd/ *verb* **~ sb (from sth/from doing sth)** to persuade sb not to do sth 勸（某人）勿做（某事）；勸阻：*I tried to dissuade him from giving up his job.* 我勸過他不要放棄自己的工作。◇ *They were going to set off in the fog, but were dissuaded.* 他們原打算在霧中出發，但被勸阻了。

dis·taff /ˈdɪstɑːf; *NAmE* ˈdɪstæf/ *noun* a stick that was used in the past for holding wool when it was spun by hand（舊時手工紡紗用的）紡紗杆，繞線杆
IDM **on the distaff side** (*old-fashioned*) on the woman's side of the family 母系的

dis·tal /ˈdɪstl/ *adj.* (*anatomy* 解) located away from the centre of the body or at the far end of sth 遠端的；末梢的：*the distal end of the tibia* 脛骨遠端

dis·tance 🔑 /ˈdɪstəns/ *noun, verb*
■ ***noun*** **1** 🔑 [C, U] the amount of space between two places or things 距離；間距：*a* ***short/long distance*** 短／長距離 ◇ *the distance of the earth from the sun* 太陽到地球的距離 ◇ ***a distance of*** *200 kilometres* ＊ 200 公里的距離 ◇ *What's the distance between New York City and Boston/from New York City to Boston?* 紐約市離波士頓有多遠？◇ *In the US, distance is measured in miles.* 在美國，測量距離以英里作單位。◇ *The beach is* ***within walking distance*** *of my house* (= you can walk there easily). 海灘離我家很近，走幾步路就到了。◇ *Paul has to drive very long distances as part of his job.* 開長途車是保羅工作的一部份。◇ *Our parents live some* ***distance away*** (= quite far away). 我們的父母住的地方相當遠。➲ see also LONG-DISTANCE, MIDDLE-DISTANCE, OUTDISTANCE **2** 🔑 [U] being far away in space or in time（空間的）遙遠；（時間的）久遠，間隔：*Distance is no problem on the Internet.* 在互聯網上距離已不成為問題。**3** 🔑 [sing.] a point that is a particular amount of space away from sth else 遠方；遠處：*You'll never get the ball in from that distance.* 你絕不可能從那麼遠的地方把球投進去。**4** [C, usually sing., U] a difference or lack of a connection between two things（兩事物之間的）差異，無關：*The distance between fashion and art remains as great as ever.* 時尚與藝術之間的差別之大依然如故。◇ *The government is keen to* ***put some distance between*** *itself and these events* (= show that there is no connection between them). 政府急於表示本身與這些事件無關。◇ (*BrE*) *Eddie is,* ***by some distance*** (= by a great amount), *the funniest character in the show.* 埃迪顯然是這個節目中最有趣的人物。**5** [U, C] a situation in which there is a lack of friendly feelings or of a close relationship between two people or groups of people 冷淡；疏遠：*The coldness and distance in her voice took me by surprise.* 她話語中透出的冷淡和疏遠使我感到意外。
IDM **at/from a 'distance** from a place or time that is not near; from far away 離一段距離；從遠處；遙遠地；久遠地：*She had loved him at a distance for years.* 她曾經暗暗愛了他好多年。**go the (full) 'distance** to continue playing in a competition or sports contest until the end（比賽）打完全場，賽足全局：*Nobody thought he would last 15 rounds, but he went the full distance.* 誰都以為他堅持不到 15 個回合，可是他卻打完了全場。**in/into the 'distance** 🔑 far away but still able to be seen or heard 在遠處；在遠方：*We saw lights in the distance.* 我們看到了遠處的點點燈光。◇ *Alice stood staring into the distance.* 艾麗斯站着凝視遠方。**keep sb at a 'distance** to refuse to be friendly with sb; to not let sb be friendly towards you 對…冷淡；同…疏遠；與…保持一定距離 **keep your 'distance (from sb/sth) 1** to make sure you are not too near sb/sth（與…）保持距離 **2** to avoid getting too friendly or involved with a person, group, etc. 疏遠；避免（與…）親近；避免介入：*She was warned to keep her distance from Charles if she didn't want to get hurt.* 有人告誡她說，如果不想受到傷害，就與查爾斯離得遠一點。➲ more at SHOUTING, SPIT *v.*, STRIKE *v.*
■ ***verb*** **~ yourself/sb/sth (from sb/sth)** to become, or to make sb/sth become, less involved or connected with sb/sth 拉開距離；與…疏遠：*When he retired, he tried to distance himself from politics.* 退休後，他便盡量使自己置身於政治之外。◇ *It's not always easy for nurses to distance themselves emotionally.* 對護士來說，使自己不動感情總是不容易。

'distance learning *noun* [U] a system of education in which people study at home with the help of special Internet sites and television and radio programmes, and send or email work to their teachers 遠程學習

dis·tant /ˈdɪstənt/ *adj.* **1** far away in space or time 遙遠的；遠處的；久遠的：*the distant sound of music* 遠處的

音樂聲 ◇ *distant stars/planets* 遙遠的恒星／行星 ◇ *The time we spent together is now a distant memory.* 我們一起度過的時光現已成為久遠的記憶。◇ *(formal) The airport was about 20 kilometres distant.* 機場在大約 20 公里遠的地方。◇ *a star 30 000 light years distant from the Earth* 離地球 3 萬光年遠的恒星 ◇ *(figurative) Peace was just a distant hope* (= not very likely). 和平只是遙不可及的希望而已。 **2** ~ **(from sth)** not like sth else 不相似的；不同的 **SYN** **remote**：*Their life seemed utterly distant from his own.* 他們的生活與他自己的生活似乎完全不同。 **3** [only before noun] (of a person 人) related to you but not closely 遠親的；遠房的：*a* ***distant cousin/aunt/relative*** 遠房堂兄弟／姑母／親戚 **4** not friendly; not wanting a close relationship with sb 不友好的；冷淡的；疏遠的：*Pat sounded very cold and distant on the phone.* 從電話裏聽起來帕特非常冷淡和疏遠。 **5** not paying attention to sth but thinking about sth completely different 心不在焉的；恍惚的；出神的：*There was a distant look in her eyes; her mind was obviously on something else.* 她眼神恍惚，顯然心裏在想着別的什麼事兒。 ▶ **dis·tant·ly** *adv.*：*Somewhere, distantly, he could hear the sound of the sea.* 他能聽到在遠處某個地方的海浪聲。◇ *We're distantly related.* 我們是遠親。◇ *Holly smiled distantly.* 霍利恍惚地笑了笑。

IDM **the (ˌdim and) ˌdistant ˈpast** a long time ago 很久以前；遙遠的過去：*stories from the distant past* 很久以前的故事 **in the not too ˌdistant ˈfuture** not a long time in the future but fairly soon 在不久的將來

dis·taste /dɪsˈteɪst/ *noun* [U, sing.] a feeling that sb/sth is unpleasant or offensive 不喜歡；反感；厭惡：*He looked around the filthy room in distaste.* 他厭惡地環顧着這骯髒的房間。◇ **~ for sb/sth** *a distaste for politics of any sort* 對任何形式的政治的反感

dis·taste·ful /dɪsˈteɪstfl/ *adj.* *(formal)* unpleasant or offensive 使人不愉快的；令人反感的；討厭的

dis·tem·per /dɪˈstempə(r)/ *noun* [U] **1** an infectious disease of animals, especially cats and dogs, that causes fever and coughing 瘟熱（動物，尤指貓、狗的傳染病） **2** *(BrE)* a type of paint that is mixed with water and used on walls 刷牆水粉；水漿塗料

dis·tend /dɪˈstend/ *verb* [I, T] ~ **(sth)** *(formal* or *medical* 醫) to swell or make sth swell because of pressure from inside（使）膨脹，腫脹：*starving children with huge distended bellies* 鼓着浮腫肚子的捱餓兒童 ▶ **dis·ten·sion** /dɪˈstenʃn/ *noun* [U]：*distension of the stomach* 胃脹

dis·til *(NAmE* also **dis·till**) /dɪˈstɪl/ *verb* (**-ll-**) **1** ~ **sth (from sth)** to make a liquid pure by heating it until it becomes a gas, then cooling it and collecting the drops of liquid that form 蒸餾；用蒸餾法提取：*to distil fresh water from sea water* 用蒸餾法從海水中提取淡水 ◇ *distilled water* 蒸餾水 **2** ~ **sth** to make sth such as a strong alcoholic drink in this way 用蒸餾法製造（酒等）：*The factory distils and bottles whisky.* 這家工廠用蒸餾法釀造瓶裝威士忌酒。 **3** ~ **sth (from/into sth)** *(formal)* to get the essential meaning or ideas from thoughts, information, experiences, etc. 吸取…的精華；提煉；濃縮：*The notes I made on my travels were distilled into a book.* 我的旅行筆記精選彙編成了一本書。 ▶ **dis·til·la·tion** /ˌdɪstɪˈleɪʃn/ *noun* [C, U]：*the distillation process* 蒸餾過程

dis·til·late /ˈdɪstɪleɪt/ *noun* [U, C] *(technical* 術語) a substance which is formed by distilling a liquid 餾出物；餾出液；餾分

dis·til·ler /dɪˈstɪlə(r)/ *noun* a person or company that produces SPIRITS (= strong alcoholic drinks) such as WHISKY by distilling them（採用蒸餾法的）釀酒者，釀酒公司

dis·til·lery /dɪˈstɪləri/ *noun* (*pl.* **-ies**) a factory where strong alcoholic drink is made by the process of distilling（採用蒸餾法的）釀酒廠

dis·tinct **AW** /dɪˈstɪŋkt/ *adj.* **1** easily or clearly heard, seen, felt, etc. 清晰的；清楚的；明白的；明顯的：*There was a distinct smell of gas.* 有一股明顯的煤氣味。◇ *His voice was quiet but every word was distinct.* 他說話聲音不大，但字字清晰。 **2** clearly different or of a different kind 截然不同的；有區別的；不同種類的：*The results of the survey fell into two distinct groups.* 調查結果分為截然不同的兩組。◇ **~ from sth** *Jamaican reggae music is quite distinct from North American jazz or blues.* 牙買加的雷蓋音樂完全不同於北美的爵士樂或布魯斯音樂。◇ *rural areas,* ***as distinct from*** *major cities* 完全不同於大城市的農村地區 **3** [only before noun] used to emphasize that you think an idea or situation definitely exists and is important 確定無疑的；確實的；確切的 **SYN** **definite**：*Being tall gave Tony a distinct advantage.* 托尼個子高是個明顯的優勢。◇ *I had the distinct impression I was being watched.* 我確實感到有人在監視我。◇ *A strike is now a distinct possibility.* 目前罷工確有可能發生。 ▶ **dis·tinct·ly** **AW** *adv.*：*I distinctly heard someone calling me.* 我清楚地聽到有人在叫我。◇ *a distinctly Australian accent* 明顯的澳大利亞口音 ◇ *He could remember everything very distinctly.* 他什麼事都能記得清清楚楚。 **dis·tinct·ness** *noun* [U]

dis·tinc·tion **AW** /dɪˈstɪŋkʃn/ *noun* **1** [C] ~ **(between A and B)** a clear difference or contrast especially between people or things that are similar or related 差別；區別；對比：*distinctions between traditional and modern societies* 傳統社會和現代社會的差別 ◇ *Philosophers did not use to* ***make a distinction*** *between arts and science.* 哲學家過去習慣不把藝術和科學區別開來。◇ *We need to* ***draw a distinction*** *between the two events.* 我們得把兩起事件區別開來。 **2** [U] the quality of being excellent or important 優秀；傑出；卓越：*a writer of distinction* 優秀作家 **3** [sing.] the quality of being sth that is special 特質；特點；不同凡響：*She* ***had the distinction of*** *being the first woman to fly the Atlantic.* 她不同凡響，是第一個飛越大西洋的女子。 **4** [U] ~ **(between A and B)** the separation of people or things into different groups 區分；分清；辨別：*The new law* ***makes no distinction*** *between adults and children* (= treats them equally). 這項新法規對成人和孩子同樣適用。◇ *All groups are entitled to this money* ***without distinction.*** 所有團體一律有權得到這筆款項。 **5** [C, U] a special mark/grade or award that is given to sb, especially a student, for excellent work（尤指給學生的）優等評分，榮譽，獎賞：*Naomi got a distinction in maths.* 內奧米的數學得了優等。◇ *He graduated* ***with distinction.*** 他以優異成績畢業。

dis·tinct·ive **AW** /dɪˈstɪŋktɪv/ *adj.* having a quality or characteristic that makes sth different and easily noticed 獨特的；特別的；有特色的 **SYN** **characteristic**：*clothes with a distinctive style* 式樣獨特的衣服 ◇ *The male bird has distinctive white markings on its head.* 雄鳥的頭上有明顯的白色斑紋。 ▶ **dis·tinct·ive·ly** **AW** *adv.*：*a distinctively nutty flavour* 特別的堅果味道

dis·tin·guish 0→ /dɪˈstɪŋɡwɪʃ/ *verb*
1 0→ [I, T] to recognize the difference between two people or things 區分；辨別；分清 **SYN** **differentiate**：**~ between A and B** *At what age are children able to distinguish between right and wrong?* 兒童到什麼年齡才能明辨是非？◇ **~ A from B** *It was hard to distinguish one twin from the other.* 很難分辨出一對孿生兒誰是誰。◇ **~ A and B** *Sometimes reality and fantasy are hard to distinguish.* 有時候現實和幻想很難區分。 **2** 0→ [T] (not used in the progressive tenses 不用於進行時) **~ A (from B)** to be a characteristic that makes two people, animals or things different 成為…的特徵；使具有…的特色；使有別於：*What was it that distinguished her from her classmates?* 是什麼使得她有別於班上其他同學呢？◇ *The male bird is distinguished from the female by its red beak.* 雄鳥喙紅色，有別於雌鳥。◇ *Does your cat have any distinguishing marks?* 你的貓有什麼特殊斑紋嗎？ **3** [T] (not used in the progressive tenses 不用於進行時) **~ sth** to be able to see or hear sth 看清；認出；聽出 **SYN** **differentiate, make out**：*I could not distinguish her words, but she sounded agitated.* 我聽不清她說的話，但聽得出她很激動。 **4** [T] **~ yourself (as sth)** to do sth so well that people notice and admire you 使出眾；使著名；使受人青睞：*She has already distinguished herself as an athlete.* 作為運動員她已享有盛名。 ▶ **dis·tin·guish·able** /dɪˈstɪŋɡwɪʃəbl/ *adj.*：**~ (from sb/sth)** *The male bird is easily distinguishable from the female.* 這種鳥很容易辨認雌雄。◇ *The coast was barely distinguishable in the mist.* 在霧中很難看清海岸。

D

D

dis·tin·guished /dɪˈstɪŋɡwɪʃt/ *adj.* **1** very successful and admired by other people 卓越的；傑出的；著名的：*a distinguished career in medicine* 在醫學領域的輝煌生涯 **2** having an appearance that makes sb look important or that makes people admire or respect them 顯得重要的；高貴的；有尊嚴的：*I think grey hair makes you look very distinguished.* 我認為灰白的頭髮使你看上去很有尊嚴。

dis·tort AW /dɪˈstɔːt; *NAmE* dɪˈstɔːrt/ *verb* **1 ~ sth** to change the shape, appearance or sound of sth so that it is strange or not clear 使變形；扭曲；使失真：*a fairground mirror that distorts your shape* 露天遊樂場的哈哈鏡 ◇ *The loudspeaker seemed to distort his voice.* 他的聲音從喇叭裏傳出來好像失真了。**2 ~ sth** to twist or change facts, ideas, etc. so that they are no longer correct or true 歪曲；曲解：*Newspapers are often guilty of distorting the truth.* 報章常犯歪曲事實的錯誤。◇ *The article gave a distorted picture of his childhood.* 這篇文章對他的童年作了歪曲的描述。▸ **dis·tort·ion** AW /dɪˈstɔːʃn; *NAmE* dɪˈstɔːrʃn/ *noun* [C, U]：*modern alloys that are resistant to wear and distortion* 耐磨、防變形的新型合金 ◇ *a distortion of the facts* 對事實的歪曲

dis·tract /dɪˈstrækt/ *verb* **~ sb/sth (from sth)** to take sb's attention away from what they are trying to do 轉移（注意力）；分散（思想）；使分心 SYN **divert**：*You're distracting me from my work.* 你使我不能專心工作。◇ *Don't talk to her—she's very easily distracted.* 不要同她講話——她的注意力很容易分散。◇ *It was another attempt to* ***distract attention*** *from the truth.* 這又是企圖分散人們對事實真相的注意力。▸ **dis·tract·ing** *adj.*：*distracting thoughts* 令人分心的想法 ◇ *a distracting noise* 使人心煩意亂的嘈雜聲

dis·tract·ed /dɪˈstræktɪd/ *adj.* **~ (by sb/sth)** unable to pay attention to sb/sth because you are worried or thinking about sth else 注意力分散的；思想不集中的 ▸ **dis·tract·ed·ly** *adv.*

dis·trac·tion /dɪˈstrækʃn/ *noun* **1** [C, U] a thing that takes your attention away from what you are doing or thinking about 分散注意力的事；使人分心的事：*I find it hard to work at home because there are too many distractions.* 我發覺在家裏工作很難，因為使人分心的事太多。◇ *cinema audiences looking for distraction* 尋求解悶的電影觀眾 **2** [C] an activity that amuses or entertains you 娛樂；消遣

IDM **to diˈstraction** so that you become upset, excited or angry, and not able to think clearly 到心煩意亂（或激動、氣憤）的地步：*The children are* ***driving me to distraction*** *today.* 今天孩子們鬧得我心煩意亂。

dis·trac·tor /dɪˈstræktə(r)/ *noun* **1** a person or thing that takes your attention away from what you should be doing 使分心的人（或物）**2** one of the wrong answers in a MULTIPLE-CHOICE test（多項選擇題中的）干擾項

dis·traught /dɪˈstrɔːt/ *adj.* extremely upset and anxious so that you cannot think clearly 心煩意亂的；心急如焚的；發狂的

dis·tress /dɪˈstres/ *noun, verb*

■ ***noun*** [U] **1** a feeling of great worry or unhappiness; great suffering 憂慮；悲傷；痛苦：*The newspaper article caused the actor considerable distress.* 報上的文章給這位演員帶來極大的痛苦。◇ *She was obviously* ***in distress*** *after the attack.* 她受到攻擊後顯然很痛苦。◇ *deep emotional distress* 感情上的深深痛苦 **2** suffering and problems caused by not having enough money, food, etc. 貧困；窘迫；困苦 SYN **hardship**：*economic/financial distress* 經濟拮据；財政困難 **3** a situation in which a ship, plane, etc. is in danger or difficulty and needs help（船、飛機等）遇難，遇險：***a distress signal*** (= a message asking for help) 求救信號 ◇ *It is a rule of the sea to help another boat* ***in distress.*** 救助別的遇難船是海上的規則。IDM see DAMSEL

■ ***verb*** to make sb feel very worried or unhappy 使憂慮；使悲傷；使苦惱：**~ sb** *It was clear that the letter had deeply distressed her.* 這封信顯然使她極為悲傷。◇ **~ yourself** *Don't distress yourself* (= don't worry). 你別犯愁了。

dis·tressed /dɪˈstrest/ *adj.* **1** upset and anxious 煩惱的；憂慮的；苦惱的：*He was too distressed and confused to answer their questions.* 他非常苦惱而困惑，無法回答他們的問題。**2** suffering pain; in a poor physical condition 痛苦的；身體虛弱的：*When the baby was born, it was blue and distressed.* 這嬰兒出生時全身發青，非常虛弱。**3** (of a piece of clothing or furniture 衣服或傢具) made to look older and more worn than it really is 刻意磨損以顯古風的：*a distressed leather jacket* 仿古皮夾克 **4** (*formal* or *business* 商) having problems caused by lack of money 貧困的；窘迫的；受經濟困擾的：*They buy up financially distressed companies.* 他們收購陷入財務危機的公司。◇ *The charity helps kids in distressed situations.* 這個慈善機構幫助處於困境的兒童。

dis·tress·ing /dɪˈstresɪŋ/ *adj.* making you feel extremely upset, especially because of sb's suffering 使人痛苦的；令人苦惱的 ▸ **dis·tress·ing·ly** *adv.*

dis·trib·ute 🔑 AW /dɪˈstrɪbjuːt; ˈdɪstrɪbjuːt/ *verb* **1** 🔑 to give things to a large number of people; to share sth between a number of people 分發；分配：**~ sth** *The newspaper is distributed free.* 本報免費派發。◇ **~ sth to sb/sth** *The organization distributed food to the earthquake victims.* 這個機構向地震災民分發了食品。◇ **~ sth among sb/sth** *The money was distributed among schools in the area.* 這筆款項是在本地區的學校中分配的。**2** 🔑 **~ sth** to send goods to shops/stores and businesses so that they can be sold 分銷：*Who distributes our products in the UK?* 誰在英國經銷我們的產品？**3** 🔑 [often passive] **~ sth** to spread sth, or different parts of sth, over an area 使散開；使分佈；分散：*Make sure that your weight is evenly distributed.* 要確保你的重量分佈均勻。

dis·tri·bu·tion 🔑 AW /ˌdɪstrɪˈbjuːʃn/ *noun* **1** 🔑 [U, C] the way that sth is shared or exists over a particular area or among a particular group of people 分配；分佈：*the unfair distribution of wealth* 財富分配不公 ◇ *The map shows the distribution of this species across the world.* 地圖上標明了這一物種在全世界的分佈情況。◇ *They studied the geographical distribution of the disease.* 他們研究了這種疾病的地域分佈情況。**2** 🔑 [U] the act of giving or delivering sth to a number of people 分發；分送：*the distribution of food and medicines to the flood victims* 向遭受洪災的難民分發食品和藥物 ◇ *He was arrested on drug distribution charges.* 他被指犯分銷毒品罪而遭逮捕。**3** 🔑 [U] (*business* 商) the system of transporting and delivering goods（商品）運銷，經銷，分銷：*distribution costs* 經銷成本 ◇ *worldwide distribution systems* 全球經銷系統 ◇ *marketing, sales and distribution* 營銷、銷售和經銷 ▸ **dis·tri·bu·tion·al** AW /-ʃənl/ *adj.*

distriˈbution board *noun* (*BrE, physics* 物) a board that contains the connections for several electrical CIRCUITS 配電板；配電盤

dis·tribu·tive AW /dɪˈstrɪbjətɪv/ *adj.* [usually before noun] (*business* 商) connected with distribution of goods 經銷的；分銷的

dis·tribu·tor AW /dɪˈstrɪbjətə(r)/ *noun* **1** a person or company that supplies goods to shops/stores, etc. 經銷商；分銷商：*Japan's largest software distributor* 日本最大的軟件分銷公司 **2** a device in an engine that sends electric current to the SPARK PLUGS（發動機的）配電器，配電盤

dis·trict 🔑 /ˈdɪstrɪkt/ *noun* **1** 🔑 an area of a country or town, especially one that has particular features 地區；區域：*the City of London's financial district* 倫敦市的金融區 **2** 🔑 one of the areas which a country, town or state is divided into for purposes of organization, with official BOUNDARIES (= borders) 區；管區；行政區：*a* ***tax/postal district*** 稅務區；郵政區 ◇ *a school district* 學區 ◇ *congressional districts* 議會選區 ◇ *district councils* 區議會

ˌdistrict aˈttorney *noun* (*abbr.* DA) (in the US) a lawyer who is responsible for bringing criminal charges against sb in a particular area or state（美國）地方檢察官

ˌdistrict ˈcourt *noun* (in the US) a court that deals with cases in a particular area （美國）區域法院

ˌdistrict ˈnurse *noun* (in Britain) a nurse who visits patients in their homes （英國上門護理的）區域護士

dis·trust /dɪsˈtrʌst/ *noun, verb*

■ ***noun*** [U, sing.] a feeling of not being able to trust sb/sth 不信任；懷疑：*They looked at each other with distrust.* 他們心懷戒備地相互看着對方。◇ **~ of sb/sth** *He has a deep distrust of all modern technology.* 他對所有現代技術都深表懷疑。▸ **dis·trust·ful** /-fl/ *adj.*：*distrustful of authority* 不相信權威

■ ***verb*** **~ sb/sth** to feel that you cannot trust or believe sb/sth 不信任；懷疑：*She distrusted his motives for wanting to see her again.* 她懷疑他想再見她一面是別有用心。➲ compare MISTRUST

Which Word? 詞語辨析

distrust / mistrust

- There is very little difference between these two words, but **distrust** is more common and perhaps slightly stronger. If you are sure that someone is acting dishonestly or cannot be relied on, you are more likely to say that you **distrust** them. If you are expressing doubts and suspicions, on the other hand, you would probably use **mistrust**. 這兩個詞意義差別很小，但 distrust 更通用，或許語氣稍強。確信某人不誠實或不可信較常用 distrust，而表示猜疑、疑慮、不信任則大概要用 mistrust。

dis·turb 0┳ /dɪˈstɜːb; *NAmE* -ˈstɜːrb/ *verb*

1 0┳ **~ sb/sth** to interrupt sb when they are trying to work, sleep, etc. 打擾；干擾；妨礙：*I'm sorry to disturb you, but can I talk to you for a moment?* 對不起，打擾你一下，我能跟你談一會兒嗎？◇ *If you get up early, try not to disturb everyone else.* 如果你起得早，盡量不要打擾別人。◇ ***Do not disturb*** (= a sign placed on the outside of the door of a hotel room, office, etc.) 請勿打擾（旅館房間、辦公室等門上的提示牌）◇ *She awoke early after a disturbed night.* 她折騰了一夜，很早就醒了。**2** 0┳ **~ sth** to move sth or change its position 攪亂；弄亂；搞亂：*Don't disturb the papers on my desk.* 別把我寫字枱上的文件弄亂了。**3** 0┳ to make sb worry 使焦慮；使不安；使煩惱：**~ sb** *The letter shocked and disturbed me.* 這封信使我感到震驚和不安。◇ **it disturbs sb to do sth** *It disturbed her to realize that she was alone.* 她意識到自己孤單一人，心裏感到很不安。

dis·turb·ance /dɪˈstɜːbəns; *NAmE* -ˈstɜːrb-/ *noun* **1** [U, C, usually sing.] actions that make you stop what you are doing, or that upset the normal state that sth is in; the act of disturbing sb/sth or the fact of being disturbed （受）打擾，干擾，妨礙：*The building work is creating constant noise, dust and disturbance.* 建築施工不斷製造噪音、灰塵和干擾。◇ *a disturbance in the usual pattern of events* 對平常事情發展狀況的干擾◇ *the disturbance of the local wildlife by tourists* 遊客對當地野生動物的滋擾 **2** [C] a situation in which people behave violently in a public place 騷亂；騷動；動亂：*serious disturbances in the streets* 街上的嚴重騷亂◇ *He was charged with causing a disturbance after the game.* 他被指控在比賽結束後製造騷亂。**3** [U, C] a state in which sb's mind or a function of the body is upset and not working normally 障礙；失調；紊亂：*emotional disturbance* 情緒失常

dis·turbed /dɪˈstɜːbd; *NAmE* -ˈstɜːrbd/ *adj.* **1** mentally ill, especially because of very unhappy or shocking experiences 有精神病的；心理不正常的；精神紊亂的：*a special school for emotionally disturbed children* 為精神異常兒童開辦的特殊學校 ➲ **SYNONYMS** at MENTALLY **2** unhappy and full of bad or shocking experiences 不幸的；多災多難的；坎坷的：*The killer had a disturbed family background.* 那名殺手出身於一個坎坷不幸的家庭。**3** very anxious and unhappy about sth 心神不安的；心煩意亂的；煩惱的：*I was deeply disturbed and depressed by the news.* 這消息使我深感不安和沮喪。➲ compare UNDISTURBED

dis·turb·ing 0┳ /dɪˈstɜːbɪŋ; *NAmE* -ˈstɜːrb-/ *adj.* making you feel anxious and upset or shocked 引起煩惱的；令人不安的；引起恐慌的：*a disturbing piece of news* 一則令人不安的消息 ▸ **dis·turb·ing·ly** *adv.*

dis·unite /ˌdɪsjuˈnaɪt/ *verb* [usually passive] **~ sb/sth** (*formal*) to make a group of people unable to agree with each other or work together 使不統一；使不和；使紛爭：*a disunited political party* 四分五裂的政黨

dis·unity /dɪsˈjuːnəti/ *noun* [U] (*formal*) a lack of agreement between people 不統一；不團結；不和：*disunity within the Conservative party* 保守黨內部的不統一 **OPP** **unity**

dis·use /dɪsˈjuːs/ *noun* [U] a situation in which sth is no longer being used 不用；廢棄：*The factory* ***fell into disuse*** *twenty years ago.* 這家工廠二十年前就廢棄了。

dis·used /ˌdɪsˈjuːzd/ *adj.* [usually before noun] no longer used 不再使用的；廢棄的：*a disused station* 廢棄的車站 ➲ compare UNUSED[1]

ditch /dɪtʃ/ *noun, verb*

■ ***noun*** a long channel dug at the side of a field or road, to hold or take away water 溝；渠 ➲ **VISUAL VOCAB** pages V2, V3

■ ***verb*** **1** [T] **~ sth/sb** (*informal*) to get rid of sth/sb because you no longer want or need it/them 擺脫；拋棄；丟棄：*The new road building programme has been ditched.* 新的道路建設計劃已廢棄。◇ *He ditched his girlfriend.* 他把女朋友給甩了。**2** [T, I] **~ (sth)** if a pilot **ditches** an aircraft, or if it **ditches**, it lands in the sea in an emergency 使（飛機）在海上緊急降落；（在海上）迫降 **3** [T] **~ school** (*NAmE, informal*) to stay away from school without permission 逃學；曠課

ditch·water /ˈdɪtʃwɔːtə(r)/ *noun* [U] **IDM** see DULL *adj.*

dither /ˈdɪðə(r)/ *verb, noun*

■ ***verb*** [I] to hesitate about what to do because you are unable to decide 猶豫不決；躊躇：*Stop dithering and get on with it.* 別再猶豫了，繼續幹吧。◇ **~ over sth** *She was dithering over what to wear.* 她拿不定主意穿什麼好。

■ ***noun*** [sing.] (*informal*) **1** a state of not being able to decide what you should do 猶豫不決；躊躇：*I'm* ***in a dither*** *about who to invite.* 我拿不定主意邀請誰。**2** a state of excitement or worry 緊張；焦慮；慌亂：*Don't get yourself* ***in a dither*** *over everything.* 不要什麼事都緊張兮兮。

di·tran·si·tive /daɪˈtrænsətɪv; -ˈtrænz-/ *adj.* (*grammar* 語法) (of verbs 動詞) used with two objects. In the sentence 'I gave her the book', for example, the verb 'give' is ditransitive and 'her' and 'the books' are both objects. 雙及物的；（後接）雙賓語的

ditsy = DITZY

ditto /ˈdɪtəʊ; *NAmE* -toʊ/ *noun, adv.*

■ ***noun*** (*abbr.* **do.**) (*symb.* **"**) used, especially in a list, underneath a particular word or phrase, to show that it is repeated and to avoid having to write it again （尤用於表格中）同上，同前

■ ***adv.*** (*informal*) used instead of a particular word or phrase, to avoid repeating it （代替某一詞語以免重複）同樣，也一樣：*The waiters were rude and unhelpful, the manager ditto.* 這些服務員態度生硬，服務不周，經理也一樣。

ditty /ˈdɪti/ *noun* (*pl.* **-ies**) (often *humorous*) a short simple song 小曲；小調

ditzy (also **ditsy**) /ˈdɪtsi/ *adj.* (*informal, especially NAmE*) (usually of a woman 通常指女性) silly; not able to be trusted to remember things or to think in an organized way 傻的；愚蠢的；忘性大的；糊塗的

di·ur·et·ic /ˌdaɪjuˈretɪk/ *noun* (*medical* 醫) a substance that causes an increase in the flow of URINE 利尿藥 ▸ **di·ur·et·ic** *adj.*：***diuretic drugs/effects*** 利尿藥／效果

di·ur·nal /daɪˈɜːnl; *NAmE* -ˈɜːrnl/ *adj.* **1** (*biology* 生) (of animals 動物) active during the day 日間活動的；晝行性的 **OPP** **nocturnal** **2** (*astronomy* 天) taking one day 週日的：*the diurnal rotation of the earth* 地球的週日自轉

Div. *abbr.* (in writing) DIVISION（書寫形式）部門，級，師：*League Div. 1* (= in football/SOCCER) 甲級聯賽（足球）

diva /'di:və/ *noun* a famous woman singer, especially an OPERA singer 著名女歌唱家（尤指歌劇女主角）

Di·vali = DIWALI

D

divan /dɪ'væn; *NAmE* 'daɪvæn/ *noun* **1** (also **di,van 'bed**) (both *BrE*) a bed with a thick base and a MATTRESS 厚墊睡榻 ➲ **VISUAL VOCAB** page V23 **2** a long low soft seat without a back or arms（無靠背和扶手的）矮長沙發

dive /daɪv/ *verb, noun*

■ *verb* (**dived, dived**, *NAmE* also **dove** /doʊv; *NAmE* doʊv/, **dived**)

▸ **JUMP INTO WATER** 跳水 **1** [I] **~ (from/off sth) (into sth)** | **~ (in)** to jump into water with your head and arms going in first 跳水（頭和雙臂先入水）：*We dived into the river to cool off.* 我們一頭跳進河裏，涼快一下。

▸ **UNDERWATER** 水下 **2** (usually **go diving**) [I] to swim underwater wearing breathing equipment, collecting or looking at things（戴呼吸裝備）潛水：*to dive for pearls* 潛水採珠 ◇ *The main purpose of his holiday to Greece was to go diving.* 他到希臘度假的主要目的就是去潛水。➲ see also DIVING **3** [I] to go to a deeper level underwater 下潛；潛到更深的水下：*The whale dived as the harpoon struck it.* 鯨被魚叉射中後下潛。

▸ **OF BIRDS/AIRCRAFT** 鳥；飛機 **4** [I] to go steeply down through the air 俯衝：*The seagulls soared then dived.* 海鷗翱翔着，然後俯衝下來。➲ see also NOSEDIVE

▸ **OF PRICES** 價格 **5** [I] to fall suddenly 突然下降；暴跌 **SYN** **plunge**：*The share price dived from 49p to an all-time low of 40p.* 股價從 49 便士暴跌到 40 便士的歷史最低位。

▸ **MOVE/JUMP/FALL** 移動；跳躍；跌下 **6** [I] (*informal*) to move or jump quickly in a particular direction, especially to avoid sth, to try to catch a ball, etc. 撲，衝，奔（以避開某物、接球等）：**~ for sth** *We heard an explosion and* **dived for cover** (= got into a place where we would be protected). 我們聽到一聲爆炸便伏身找掩護。◇ *The goalie dived for the ball, but missed it.* 守門員一個魚躍向球撲去，可是沒有撲到。◇ **+ adv./prep.** *It started to rain so we dived into the nearest cafe.* 天下起雨來，我們立即鑽進一家最近的咖啡館。**7** [I] (in football (SOCCER), HOCKEY, etc. 足球、曲棍球等) to fall deliberately when sb TACKLES you, so that the REFEREE awards a FOUL（對方阻截時）假摔

PHR V **'dive into sth** (*informal*) to put your hand quickly into sth such as a bag or pocket 迅速將手伸入（包或口袋裏）：*She dived into her bag and took out a couple of coins.* 她立即將手伸進包裏拿出幾枚硬幣。

■ *noun*

▸ **JUMP INTO WATER** 跳水 **1** a jump into deep water with your head first and your arms in front of you（頭和雙臂先入水的）跳水：*a spectacular high dive* (= from high above the water) 精彩的高台跳水

▸ **UNDERWATER** 水下 **2** an act of going underwater and swimming there with special equipment（戴呼吸裝備的）潛水：*a dive to a depth of 18 metres* 潛到 18 米水深處

▸ **OF BIRDS/AIRCRAFT** 鳥；飛機 **3** an act of suddenly flying downwards 撲；衝；俯衝

▸ **BAR/CLUB** 酒吧；夜總會 **4** (*informal*) a bar, music club, etc. that is cheap, and perhaps dark or dirty 下等酒吧；低級夜總會

▸ **FALL** 跌倒 **5** (*BrE*) (in football (SOCCER), HOCKEY, etc. 足球、曲棍球等) a deliberate fall that a player makes when sb TACKLES them, so that the REFEREE awards a FOUL（遇到阻截時的）假摔，故意跌倒

IDM **make a 'dive (for sth)** to suddenly move or jump forward to do sth or reach sb/sth 迅速移動；猛然一跳；撲躍：*The goalkeeper made a dive for the ball.* 守門員一個魚躍向球撲去。 **take a 'dive** (*informal*) to suddenly get worse 突然下降；暴跌：*Profits really took a dive last year.* 去年利潤確實跌得很厲害。

'dive-bomb *verb* **~ sb/sth** (of an aircraft, a bird, etc. 飛機、鳥等) to dive steeply through the air and attack sb/sth 俯衝轟炸；俯衝攻擊

diver /'daɪvə(r)/ *noun* **1** a person who works underwater, usually with special equipment（通常有專用裝備的）潛水員：*a deep-sea diver* 深海潛水員 ➲ compare FROGMAN **2** a person who jumps into the water with their head first and their arms in front of them 跳水者；跳水運動員

di·verge /daɪ'vɜ:dʒ; *NAmE* -'vɜ:rdʒ/ *verb* (*formal*) **1** [I] to separate and go in different directions 分叉；岔開：*The parallel lines appear to diverge.* 這些平行線像是岔開了。◇ *We went through school and college together, but then our paths diverged.* 我們從小學到大學一直在一起，但後來就分道揚鑣了。◇ **~ from sth** *The coastal road diverges from the freeway just north of Santa Monica.* 沿海公路與這條高速公路就在聖莫尼卡以北處岔開。◇ *Many species have diverged from a single ancestor.* 許多物種都是同宗演變而來的。 **2** [I] **~ (from sth)** (*formal*) (of opinions, views, etc. 意見、觀點等) to be different 分歧；相異：*Opinions diverge greatly on this issue.* 在這個問題上意見分歧很大。 **3** [I] **~ from sth** to be or become different from what is expected, planned, etc. 偏離；背離；違背：*to diverge from the norm* 與常態不符 ◇ *He diverged from established procedure.* 他違背了既定程序。 **OPP** **converge** ▸ **di·ver·gence** /daɪ'vɜ:dʒəns; *NAmE* -'vɜ:rdʒ-/ *noun* [C, U] *a wide divergence of opinion* 嚴重的意見分歧 **di·ver·gent** /-dʒənt/ *adj.* **divergent paths/opinions** 岔路；歧見

divers /'daɪvəz; *NAmE* -vərz/ *adj.* [only before noun] (*old use*) of many different kinds 各種各樣的；不同種類的；形形色色的

di·verse **AW** /daɪ'vɜ:s; *NAmE* -'vɜ:rs/ *adj.* very different from each other and of various kinds 不同的；相異的；多種多樣的；形形色色的：*people from diverse cultures* 不同文化背景的人 ◇ *My interests are very diverse.* 我的興趣非常廣泛。

di·ver·sify **AW** /daɪ'vɜ:sɪfaɪ; *NAmE* -'vɜ:rs-/ *verb* (**di·ver·si·fies, di·ver·si·fy·ing, di·ver·si·fied, di·ver·si·fied**) **1** [I, T] **~ (sth) (into sth)** (especially of a business or company 尤指企業或公司) to develop a wider range of products, interests, skills, etc. in order to be more successful or reduce risk 增加…的品種；從事多種經營；擴大業務範圍 **SYN** **branch out**：*Farmers are being encouraged to diversify into new crops.* 目前正鼓勵農民兼種新的農作物。 **2** [I, T] to change or to make sth change so that there is greater variety（使）多樣化，變化，不同：*Patterns of family life are diversifying.* 家庭生活模式正在變得多樣化。◇ **~ sth** *The culture has been diversified with the arrival of immigrants.* 隨着外來移民的到來，這裏的文化變得多元化了。 ▸ **di·ver·si·fi·ca·tion** **AW** /daɪ,vɜ:sɪfɪ'keɪʃn; *NAmE* -,vɜ:rs-/ *noun* [U]

di·ver·sion /daɪ'vɜ:ʃn; *NAmE* -'vɜ:rʒn/ *noun* **1** [C, U] the act of changing the direction that sb/sth is following, or what sth is used for 轉向；轉移；偏離：*a river diversion project* 河流改道工程 ◇ *We made a short diversion to go and look at the castle.* 我們繞了一小段路去參觀城堡。◇ *the diversion of funds from the public to the private sector of industry* 資金從公有企業向私有企業的轉移 **2** [C] something that takes your attention away from sb/sth while sth else is happening 轉移視線（或注意力）的事物：*For the government, the war was a welcome diversion from the country's economic problems.* 政府歡迎這場戰爭，因為它轉移了人們對國家經濟問題的注意力。◇ *A smoke bomb* **created a diversion** *while the robbery took place.* 劫案發生時，一枚煙霧彈轉移了人們的視線。 **3** [C] (*BrE*) (*NAmE* **de·tour**) a road or route that is used when the usual one is closed 臨時繞行路；臨時支路：*Diversions will be signposted.* 臨時支路都將設置路標。 **4** [C] (*formal*) an activity that is done for pleasure, especially because it takes your attention away from sth else 消遣；娛樂 **SYN** **distraction**：*The party will make a pleasant diversion.* 這個聚會將是一個很不錯的消遣活動。◇ *The city is full of diversions.* 城市裏各種娛樂活動比比皆是。

di·ver·sion·ary /daɪ'vɜ:ʃənəri; *NAmE* -'vɜ:rʒəneri/ *adj.* intended to take sb's attention away from sth 轉移注意力的

di·ver·sity AW /daɪˈvɜːsəti; NAmE -ˈvɜːrs-/ noun **1** [U, C, usually sing.] a range of many people or things that are very different from each other 差異（性）；不同（點） SYN **variety**：*the biological diversity of the rainforests* 熱帶雨林的生物多樣性 ◇ *a great/wide/rich diversity of opinion* 意見紛紜 **2** [U] the quality or fact of including a range of many people or things 多樣性；多樣化：*There is a need for greater diversity and choice in education.* 教育方面需要更加多元化和更大的選擇性。➲ COLLOCATIONS at RACE

di·vert /daɪˈvɜːt; NAmE -ˈvɜːrt/ verb **~ sb/sth (from sth) (to sth) 1** to make sb/sth change direction 使轉向；使繞道；轉移：*Northbound traffic will have to be diverted onto minor roads.* 北行車輛將不得不繞次要道路行駛。**2 ~ sth** to use money, materials, etc. for a different purpose from their original purpose 改變（資金、材料等）的用途 **3 ~ sth** to take sb's thoughts or attention away from sth 轉移（某人）的注意力；使分心 SYN **distract**：*The war diverted people's attention away from the economic situation.* 戰爭把民眾的注意力從經濟狀況上移開了。**4 ~ sb** (*formal*) to entertain people 娛樂；供消遣：*Children are easily diverted.* 孩子們很容易被逗樂。

di·vert·ing /daɪˈvɜːtɪŋ; NAmE -ˈvɜːrt-/ adj. (*formal*) entertaining and amusing 娛樂的；消遣性的；有趣的

di·vest /daɪˈvest/ verb (*formal*) **1 ~ sb/yourself of sth** to remove clothes 使（某人）脫去（衣服）：*He divested himself of his jacket.* 他脫去了短上衣。**2 ~ yourself of sth** to get rid of sth 處理掉；丟棄：*The company is divesting itself of some of its assets.* 公司正在處理掉它的部份財產。**3 ~ sb/sth of sth** to take sth away from sb/sth 使解除；使擺脫：*After her illness she was divested of much of her responsibility.* 她生病後便給解除了許多責任。

di·vest·ment /daɪˈvestmənt/ noun [U, C] (*finance* 財) the act of selling the shares you have bought in a company or of taking money away from where you have invested it 轉讓股份；撤銷投資

di·vide 0‑w /dɪˈvaɪd/ verb, noun

> **WORD FAMILY**
> divide *verb, noun*
> division *noun*
> divisive *adj.*

■ **verb**

▸ SEPARATE 分開 **1** 0‑w [I, T] to separate or make sth separate into parts （使）分開，分散，分割，分成… SYN **split up**：**~ (up) (into sth)** *The cells began to divide rapidly.* 細胞開始迅速分裂。◇ **~ sth (up) (into sth)** *A sentence can be divided up into meaningful segments.* 一個句子可以劃分成有意義的各個部份。**2** 0‑w [T] to separate sth into parts and give a share to each of a number of different people, etc. 分配；分享；分擔 SYN **share (out)**：**~ sth (up/out)** *Jack divided up the rest of the cash.* 傑克把餘下的現金分了。◇ **~ sth (up/out) between/among sb** *We divided the work between us.* 我們共同分擔這項工作。**3** 0‑w [T] **~ sth (between A and B)** to use different parts of your time, energy, etc. for different activities, etc. 把（時間、精力等）分別用於：*He divides his energies between politics and business.* 他把精力一部份用在政治上，一部份用在業務上。**4** 0‑w [T] **~ A from B** (*formal*) to separate two people or things 使分離；使分開：*Can it ever be right to divide a mother from her child?* 讓母子分離難道還有對的時候？**5** [T] **~ sth (off)** | **~ A from B** to be the real or imaginary line or barrier that separates two people or things 是…的分界線；分隔；把…隔開 SYN **separate (off)**：*A fence divides off the western side of the grounds.* 籬笆把庭院的西面隔開。**6** 0‑w [I] (of a road 道路) to separate into two parts that lead in different directions 分岔：*Where the path divides, keep right.* 來到岔口就靠右。

▸ CAUSE DISAGREEMENT 引起分歧 **7** 0‑w [T] **~ sb/sth** to make two or more people disagree 使產生分歧；使意見不一 SYN **split**：*The issue has divided the government.* 這個問題在政府中引起了意見分歧。

▸ MATHEMATICS 數學 **8** 0‑w [T, I] **~ (sth) by sth** to find out how many times one number is contained in another 除以：*30 divided by 6 is 5 (30 ÷ 6 = 5).* * 30 除以 6 等於 5。**9** [I, T] **~ (sth) into sth** to be able to be multiplied to give another number 除：*5 divides into 30 6 times.* * 5 除 30 等於 6。

IDM **di,vide and 'rule** to keep control over people by making them disagree with and fight each other, therefore not giving them the chance to unite and oppose you together 分而治之：*a policy of divide and rule* 分而治之的政策 ➲ more at MIDDLE *n.*

■ **noun** [usually sing.]

▸ DIFFERENCE 不同 **1** a difference between two groups of people that separates them from each other 不同；差異；分歧：*the North/South divide* 南北分歧 ◇ **~ between A and B** *the divide between Catholics and Protestants in Northern Ireland* 北愛爾蘭的天主教徒和新教徒之間的分歧

▸ BETWEEN RIVERS 河流之間 **2** (*especially NAmE*) a line of high land that separates two systems of rivers 分水嶺；分水線 SYN **watershed** IDM see BRIDGE *v.*

div·ided /dɪˈvaɪdɪd/ adj. (of a group or an organization 團體或組織) split by disagreements or different opinions 分裂的；有分歧的：*The government is divided on this issue.* 政府在這個問題上意見不統一。◇ *a deeply divided society* 四分五裂的社會 ◇ *The regime is profoundly **divided against itself**.* 這一政體內部徹底分裂了。

di,vided 'highway (*NAmE*) (*BrE* **,dual 'carriageway**) noun a road with a strip of land in the middle that divides the lines of traffic moving in opposite directions （中央有分隔帶的）雙幅車行道，雙向車道

divi·dend /ˈdɪvɪdend/ noun **1** an amount of the profits that a company pays to people who own shares in the company 紅利；股息；股利：*dividend payments of 50 cents a share* 每股 50 分的股息支付 **2** (*BrE*) a money prize that is given to winners in the FOOTBALL POOLS （足球彩票的）彩金 IDM see PAY *v.*

div·ider /dɪˈvaɪdə(r)/ noun **1** [C] a thing that divides sth 分隔物；分開物：*a room divider* (= a screen or door that divides a room into two parts) 房間分隔板（屏風或門）**2 dividers** [pl.] an instrument made of two long thin metal parts joined together at the top, used for measuring lines and angles 分線規；兩腳規：*a pair of dividers* 一副分線規

di'viding line noun [usually sing.] **1** something that marks the separation between two things or ideas （兩種事物或思想的）分界線，界限：*There is no clear dividing line between what is good and what is bad.* 是非之間沒有明確的界限。**2** a place that separates two areas （分隔兩個地區的）地界，分界線：*The river was chosen as a dividing line between the two districts.* 兩個地區以這條河流為界。

div·in·ation /ˌdɪvɪˈneɪʃn/ noun [U] the act of finding out and saying what will happen in the future 占卜；預測；預言

di·vine /dɪˈvaɪn/ adj., verb

■ **adj. 1** [usually before noun] coming from or connected with God or a god 天賜的；上帝的；神的：***divine law/love/will*** 天道；上帝的慈愛；天意 ◇ ***divine intervention*** (= help from God to change a situation) 上帝之祐 **2** (*old-fashioned*) wonderful; beautiful 絕妙的；非凡的；極美的 ▸ **di·vine·ly** *adv.*

■ **verb 1** [T] **~ what, whether, etc. …** | **~ sth** (*formal*) to find out sth by guessing 猜到；領悟：*She could divine what he was thinking just by looking at him.* 她一看就知道他在想什麼。**2** [T, I] **~ (sth)** to search for underground water using a stick in the shape of a Y, called a **divining rod** （用丫形杖）探測（地下水）

di,vine 'right noun [U, sing.] **1** (in the past) the belief that the right of a king or queen to rule comes directly from God rather than from the agreement of the people （舊時的）君權神授說 **2** a right that sb thinks they have to do sth, without needing to ask anyone else （自認為）應有的權利，天賦的權利：*No player has a divine right to be in this team.* 沒有哪名選手天生就有權待在這個隊裏。

div·ing /ˈdaɪvɪŋ/ noun [U] **1** the sport or activity of diving into water with your head and arms first 跳水；跳水運動：*a diving competition* 跳水比賽 **2** the activity of swimming underwater using special breathing equipment（戴呼吸裝備的）潛水：*I'd love to* **go diving** *in the Aegean.* 我很想到愛琴海去潛水。◇ *a diving suit* 潛水服 ➲ see also SKIN-DIVING

'diving bell *noun* a container that has a supply of air and that is open at the bottom, in which a person can be carried down to the deep ocean 潛水鐘（內貯空氣、底部有開口，潛入深海用）

D

'diving board *noun* a board at the side of or above a swimming pool from which people can jump or DIVE into the water 跳水板（游泳池設施）

div·in·ity /dɪˈvɪnəti/ *noun* (*pl.* **-ies**) **1** [U] the quality of being a god or like God 神性：*the divinity of Christ* 基督的神性 **2** [C] a god or GODDESS 神；女神：*Roman/ Greek/Egyptian divinities* 羅馬／希臘／埃及神祇 **3** [U] the study of the nature of God and religious belief 神學 SYN **theology**：*a doctor of Divinity* 神學博士

div·is·ible /dɪˈvɪzəbl/ *adj.* [not before noun] **~ (by sth)** that can be divided, usually with nothing remaining 可除；可除盡：*8 is divisible by 2 and 4, but not by 3.* * 8 可被 2 和 4 除盡，但不能被 3 除盡。OPP **indivisible**

div·ision 0→ /dɪˈvɪʒn/ *noun*

▸ INTO SEPARATE PARTS 分成若干部份 **1** 0→ [U, sing.] the process or result of dividing into separate parts; the process or result of dividing sth or sharing it out 分開；分隔；分配；（分出來的）部份：*cell division* 細胞分裂 ◇ **~ of sth** *a fair division of time and resources* 時間和資源的合理分配 ◇ **~ of sth between A and B** *the division of labour between the sexes* 男女分工 ◇ **~ (of sth) into sth** *the division of the population into age groups* 把人口分成不同的年齡組

▸ MATHEMATICS 數學 **2** 0→ [U] the process of dividing one number by another 除（法）：*the division sign* (÷) 除號 ➲ compare MULTIPLICATION ➲ see also LONG DIVISION

▸ DISAGREEMENT/DIFFERENCE 不一致；差異 **3** 0→ [C, U] a disagreement or difference in opinion, way of life, etc., especially between members of a society or an organization 分歧；不和；差異：**~ (in/within sth)** *There are* **deep divisions** *in the party over the war.* 黨內對於這場戰爭存在着嚴重的分歧。◇ *the work of healing the divisions within society* 彌合社會內部分歧的工作 ◇ **~ (between A and B)** *divisions between rich and poor* 貧富差異 ◇ ***social/ class divisions*** 社會分化；階級對立

▸ PART OF ORGANIZATION 部門 **4** [C+sing./pl. v.] (*abbr.* **Div.**) a large and important unit or section of an organization（機構的）部門：*the company's sales division* 公司銷售部

▸ IN SPORT 體育運動 **5** [C+sing./pl. v.] (*abbr.* **Div.**) (in Britain) one of the group of teams that a sport competition is divided into, especially in football (SOCCER)（英國體育運動，尤指足球比賽的）級：*the* ***first division/division one*** 甲級 ◇ *a first-division team* 甲級隊

▸ PART OF ARMY 軍隊編制 **6** [C+sing./pl. v.] (*abbr.* **Div.**) a unit of an army, consisting of several BRIGADES or REGIMENTS 師：*the Guards Armoured Division* 禁衛裝甲師

▸ BORDER 邊界 **7** [C] a line that divides sth 分界線：*A hedge forms the division between their land and ours.* 他們的土地與我們的土地之間以一道樹籬隔開。

▸ IN PARLIAMENT 議會 **8** [C] (*technical* 術語) the separation of members of the British parliament into groups to vote for or against sth（英國議會的）分組表決：*The Bill was read without a division.* 議案未經分組表決就宣讀通過了。

div·ision·al /dɪˈvɪʒənl/ *adj.* [only before noun] belonging to or connected with a DIVISION (= a section of the army or department of an organization) 部門的；師的：*the* ***divisional commander/headquarters*** 師長／部

di'vision bell *noun* a bell which is rung in the British parliament when it is time for a DIVISION (8)（英國議會的）分組表決鐘

di'vision lobby *noun* one of the two halls in the British parliament to which members go when there is a DIVISION (8)（英國議會的）分組表決廳

div·isive /dɪˈvaɪsɪv/ *adj.* (*disapproving*) causing people to be split into groups that disagree with or oppose each other 造成不和的；引起分歧的；製造分裂的：*He believes that unemployment is socially divisive.* 他認為失業會引起社會分化。➲ see also DIVIDE *v.* (7) ▸ **div·isive·ly** *adv.* **div·isive·ness** *noun* [U]

div·isor /dɪˈvaɪzə(r)/ *noun* (*mathematics* 數) a number by which another number is divided 除數；除子 ➲ compare REMAINDER (2)

di·vorce 0→ /dɪˈvɔːs; *NAmE* dɪˈvɔːrs/ *noun, verb*

■ ***noun*** **1** 0→ [U, C] the legal ending of a marriage 離婚：*The marriage* **ended in divorce** *in 1996.* 這樁婚姻在 1996 年以離婚告終。◇ *an increase in the* **divorce rate** (= the number of divorces in a year) 離婚率的增長 ◇ *They have agreed to* **get a divorce**. 他們已同意離婚。◇ ***Divorce proceedings*** (= the legal process of divorce) *started today.* 今日已提起離婚訴訟。➲ COLLOCATIONS at MARRIAGE ➲ compare SEPARATION (3) **2** [C, usually sing.] (*formal*) **~ (between A and B)** a separation; the ending of a relationship between two things 分離；脫離：*the divorce between religion and science* 宗教與科學的分裂

■ ***verb*** **1** 0→ [T, I] **~ (sb)** to end your marriage to sb legally 與（某人）離婚；判（某人）離婚：*They're* **getting divorced**. 他們要離婚了。◇ *She's divorcing her husband.* 她與丈夫在鬧離婚。◇ *I'd heard they're divorcing.* 我聽說他們要離婚了。**2** [T, often passive] **~ sb/sth from sth** (*formal*) to separate a person, an idea, a subject, etc. from sth; to keep two things separate 使分離；使脫離：*They believed that art should be divorced from politics.* 他們認為藝術應該與政治分開。◇ *When he was depressed, he felt utterly divorced from reality.* 他沮喪時便感到完全脫離了現實。

di·vorcé /dɪˌvɔːˈseɪ; *NAmE* dɪˌvɔːrˈseɪ/ *noun* (*NAmE*) a man whose marriage has been legally ended 離婚的男子

di·vorced 0→ /dɪˈvɔːst; *NAmE* -ˈvɔːrst/ *adj.*

1 0→ no longer married 離婚的；離異的：*Many divorced men remarry and have second families.* 許多離婚的男子再婚組成了新的家庭。◇ *My parents are divorced.* 我的父母離婚了。◇ *Are they going to* **get divorced**? 他們打算離婚嗎？➲ COLLOCATIONS at MARRIAGE **2 ~ from sth** (*formal*) appearing not to be affected by sth; separate from sth 表現得不受影響的；脫離…的：*He seems completely divorced from reality.* 他似乎完全脫離了現實。

di·vor·cee /dɪˌvɔːˈsiː; *NAmE* dɪˌvɔːrˈseɪ/ *noun* (*BrE*) a person whose marriage has been legally ended, especially a woman 離婚的人（尤指女子）

di·vorcée /dɪˌvɔːˈseɪ; *NAmE* dɪˌvɔːrˈseɪ/ *noun* (*NAmE*) a woman whose marriage has been legally ended 離婚女子；離異女子

divot /ˈdɪvət/ *noun* a piece of grass and earth that is dug out by accident, for example by a CLUB when sb is playing GOLF（打高爾夫球等時不小心削起的）一塊草皮和泥土

di·vulge /daɪˈvʌldʒ/ *verb* **~ sth (to sb)** | **~ what, whether, etc. ...** (*formal*) to give sb information that is supposed to be secret 泄露，透露（秘密）SYN **reveal**：*Police refused to divulge the identity of the suspect.* 警方拒絕透露嫌疑犯的身分。

divvy /ˈdɪvi/ *verb* (**div·vies, divvy·ing, div·vied, div·vied**)

PHR V **ˌdivvy sth↔ˈup** (*informal*) to divide sth, especially money into two or more parts 分，分攤，分享（尤指金錢）

Di·wali (also **Di·vali**) /diːˈwɑːli/ *noun* [U] a Hindu festival that is held in the autumn/fall, celebrated by lighting CANDLES and CLAY lamps, and with FIREWORKS 排燈節（印度教秋季節日）

Dix·ie /ˈdɪksi/ *noun* [U] an informal name for the south-eastern states of the US 迪克西（美國東南部各州的非正式統稱）

Dixie·land /ˈdɪksilænd/ *noun* [U] a type of traditional JAZZ 迪克西蘭爵士樂 ➲ see also TRAD

DIY /ˌdiː aɪ ˈwaɪ/ *noun* [U] (*BrE*) the abbreviation for 'do-it-yourself' (the activity of making, repairing or decorating things in the home yourself, instead of paying sb to do it) 自己動手（全寫為 do-it-yourself，相對於雇人做）：*a DIY store* * DIY 商店 ➲ COLLOCATIONS at DECORATE ➲ VISUAL VOCAB page V20

di·zy·got·ic twin /ˌdaɪzaɪˌɡɒtɪk ˈtwɪn; *NAmE* -ɡɑːtɪk/ (also **di·zyg·ous twin** /daɪˌzaɪɡəs ˈtwɪn/) *adj.* (*technical* 術語) = FRATERNAL TWIN ➲ compare MONOZYGOTIC TWIN

dizzy /ˈdɪzi/ *adj.* (**diz·ziest**, **diz·zi·est**) **1** feeling as if everything is spinning around you and that you are not able to balance 頭暈目眩的；眩暈的 **SYN** **giddy**：*Climbing so high made me* ***feel dizzy***. 爬那麼高使我感到頭暈目眩。◇ *I suffer from* ***dizzy spells*** (= short periods when I am dizzy). 我患有陣發性頭暈。 **2** making you feel dizzy; making you feel that a situation is changing very fast 使人眩暈的；使人頭昏眼花的；使人感到變化太快的 **SYN** **giddy**：*the dizzy descent from the summit* 從山頂陡然而下令人目眩的山坡◇ *the dizzy pace of life in Hong Kong* 香港令人目眩的生活節奏 **3** (*informal, especially NAmE*) silly or stupid 愚蠢的；笨的 **SYN** **giddy**：*a dizzy blonde* 金髮傻妞 ▸ **diz·zily** *adv.* **diz·zi·ness** *noun* [U]

IDM **the dizzy ˈheights (of sth)** (*informal*) an important or impressive position 重要的職位；顯赫的地位：*She dreamed of reaching the dizzy heights of stardom.* 她夢想達到超級巨星的地位。

dizzy·ing /ˈdɪziɪŋ/ *adj.* making you feel dizzy 使人眩暈的；使人頭昏眼花的：*The car drove past at a dizzying speed.* 汽車風馳電掣地駛過。

DJ /ˈdiː dʒeɪ/ *noun, verb*

■ ***noun*** **1** the abbreviation for DISC JOCKEY（電台、電視台、俱樂部）唱片節目主持人（全寫為 disc jockey） **2** (*BrE*) the abbreviation for DINNER JACKET（男式）晚禮服，無尾禮服（全寫為 dinner jacket）

■ ***verb*** (**DJ's**, **DJ'ing**, **DJ'd**, **DJ'd**) [I] to perform as a DISC JOCKEY, especially in a club 做音樂節目主持人（尤指在俱樂部）

djinn /dʒɪn/ *noun* (in Arabian stories) a spirit with magic powers（阿拉伯神話）神怪，神靈，精靈 **SYN** **genie**

DLitt (*NAmE* **D.Litt**) /ˌdiː ˈlɪt/ *noun* the abbreviation for 'Doctor of Letters' (a university degree at the highest level, awarded for a long record of academic research, or as an HONORARY degree to recognize sb's contribution to society) 文學博士（全寫為 Doctor of Letters，大學最高學位或榮譽學位）

DMA /ˌdiː em ˈeɪ/ *noun* [U] the abbreviation for 'direct memory access' (a system that allows a device attached to a computer to take data from the computer's memory without using the CENTRAL PROCESSING UNIT) 直接存貯器存取，直接內存存取（全寫為 direct memory access，無須使用中央處理器）

DMs /ˌdiː ˈemz/ *noun* (*informal*) = DR MARTENS

DNA /ˌdiː en ˈeɪ/ *noun* [U] (*chemistry* 化) deoxyribonucleic acid (the chemical in the cells of animals and plants that carries GENETIC information and is a type of NUCLEIC ACID) 脫氧核糖核酸（動植物的細胞中帶有基因信息的化學物質）：*a DNA test* * DNA 測試

ˌDNA ˈfingerprinting *noun* [U] = GENETIC FINGERPRINTING

do¹ 🔑 /də; du; *strong form* duː/ *verb, auxiliary verb, noun* ➲ IRREGULAR VERBS at page R5 ➲ see also DO²

■ ***verb***

▸ **ACTION** 行為 **1** 🔑 [T] **~ sth** used to refer to actions that you do not mention by name or do not know about 做，幹，辦（某事）：*What are you doing this evening?* 你今晚打算做什麼？◇ *We will do what we can to help.* 我們會盡力幫助。◇ *Are you doing anything tomorrow evening?* 你明晚有事嗎？◇ *The company ought to do something about the poor service.* 公司應該對劣等服務採取點措施。◇ *What have you done to your hair?* 你的頭髮是怎麼搞的？◇ *There's* ***nothing to do*** (= no means of passing the time in an enjoyable way) *in this place.* 這地方沒什麼好玩的。◇ *There's* ***nothing we can do*** *about it* (= we can't change the situation). 這種事情我們毫無辦法。◇ ***What can I do for you*** (= how can I help)? 我能為您做點什麼？

▸ **BEHAVE** 表現 **2** [I] to act or behave in the way mentioned（以某種方式）做，行動，表現：**~ as …** *Do as you're told!* 叫你怎麼做你就怎麼做！◇ *They are free to do as they please.* 他們想怎麼做就怎麼做。◇ **+ adv./prep.** *You* ***would do well to*** (= I advise you to) *consider all the options before buying.* 你購買之前最好對各種選擇都考慮一下。

▸ **SUCCEED/PROGRESS** 順利進行；進展 **3** 🔑 [I] **+ adv./prep.** used to ask or talk about the success or progress of sb/sth（問詢或談論時用）進展，進行：*How is the business doing?* 生意好嗎？◇ *She* ***did well*** *out of* (= made a big profit from) *the deal.* 她從這筆交易中賺了不少錢。◇ *He's* ***doing very well*** *at school* (= his work is good). 他在學校裏學習很不錯。◇ *Both mother and baby are* ***doing well*** (= after the birth of the baby). 母子平安。◇ (*informal*) ***How are you doing*** (= how are you)? 你好嗎？

▸ **TASK/ACTIVITY** 任務；活動 **4** 🔑 [T] **~ sth** to work at or perform an activity or a task 從事（工作）；進行（活動）；執行（任務）：*I'm doing some research on the subject.* 我正就這一課題進行研究。◇ *I have a number of things to do today.* 我今天有些事情要做。◇ *I do aerobics once a week.* 我每週做一次健美操。◇ *Let's do* (= meet for) *lunch.* 咱們一起吃頓午飯吧。◇ (*informal*) *Sorry. I don't do funny* (= I can't be funny). 對不起。我可不是開玩笑。 **5** [T] **~ sth** used with nouns to talk about tasks such as cleaning, washing, arranging, etc.（與名詞連用，表示打掃、清洗、整理等）：*to do* (= wash) *the dishes* 洗碗碟◇ *to do* (= arrange) *the flowers* 插花◇ *I like the way you've done your hair.* 我喜歡你梳的髮式。 **6** [T] to perform the activity or task mentioned **~ the ironing, cooking, shopping, etc.** 做，從事（熨燙、烹調、購物、演戲、寫作等）：*I like listening to the radio when I'm doing the ironing.* 我喜歡邊熨衣服邊聽收音機。◇ **~ some, a little, etc. acting, writing, etc.** *She did a lot of acting when she was at college.* 她在大學時演過很多戲。

▸ **JOB** 職業 **7** 🔑 [T] **~ sth** (usually used in questions 通常用於疑問句) to work at sth as a job 從事（職業）：***What do you do*** (= what is your job)? 你幹什麼工作？◇ *What does she want to do when she leaves school?* 她畢業後想幹什麼？◇ *What did she* ***do for a living***? 她過去幹哪一行為生？◇ *What's Tom doing these days?* 湯姆最近在幹什麼？

▸ **STUDY** 學習 **8** [T] **~ sth** to learn or study sth 學習；攻讀：*I'm doing physics, biology and chemistry.* 我在學物理、生物和化學。◇ *Have you done any* (= studied anything by) *Keats?* 你讀過濟慈的作品嗎？

▸ **SOLVE** 解決 **9** [T] **~ sth** to find the answer to sth; to solve sth 解答；解決：*I can't do this sum.* 我不會做這道算術題。◇ *Are you good at doing crosswords?* 你擅長填縱橫字謎嗎？

▸ **MAKE** 製作 **10** 🔑 [T] to produce or make sth 做出；製作：**~ sth** ***to do a drawing/painting/sketch*** 畫畫；繪畫；畫素描◇ *Does this pub do* (= provide) *lunches?* 這家酒館供應午餐嗎？◇ *Who's doing* (= organizing and preparing) *the food for the wedding reception?* 誰在承辦婚宴的酒席？◇ **~ sth for sb** *I'll do a copy for you.* 我將為你複印一份。◇ **~ sb sth** *I'll do you a copy.* 我將複印一份給你。 ➲ SYNONYMS at MAKE

▸ **PERFORM** 演出 **11** [T] **~ sth** to perform or produce a play, an OPERA, etc. 演出，編排（戲劇、歌劇等）：*The local dramatic society is doing 'Hamlet' next month.* 地方戲劇社準備下月演出《哈姆雷特》。

▸ **COPY SB** 仿效 **12** [T] **~ sb/sth** to copy sb's behaviour or the way sb speaks, sings, etc., especially in order to make people laugh 仿效，模仿，扮演（尤以令人發笑）：*He does a great Elvis Presley.* 他把埃爾維斯•普雷斯利模仿得維妙維肖。◇ *Can you do a Welsh accent?* 你能模仿威爾士口音嗎？

▸ **FINISH** 完成 **13** [I, T] to finish sth 完成；做完：**have/be done** *Sit there and wait till I've done.* 坐在那兒等到我做完。◇ **have/be done doing sth** *I've done talking—let's get started.* 我的話說完了，咱們開始吧。◇ **get sth done** *Did you get your article done in time?* 你的論文按時完成了嗎？

▸ **TRAVEL** 旅行 **14** [T] **~ sth** to travel a particular distance 走過，旅行過（一段路程）：*How many miles did you do during your tour?* 你走了多少英里的旅程？◇ *My car does 40 miles to the gallon* (= uses one gallon of petrol/gas to travel 40 miles). 我的汽車每耗一加侖汽油可行駛 40 英里。 **15** [T] **~ sth** to complete a journey/trip 走完，完成（旅程）：*We did the round trip in two hours.* 我們兩小時打了個來回。

▸ **SPEED 速度 16** [T] **~ sth** to travel at or reach a particular speed 以…速度行進；達到…速度：*The car was doing 90 miles an hour.* 汽車以每小時 90 英里的速度行駛。

▸ **VISIT 參觀 17** [T] **~ sth** (*informal*) to visit a place as a tourist 參觀；遊覽；在…觀光：*We did Tokyo in three days.* 我們在東京遊覽了三天。

▸ **SPEND TIME 度過 18** 🔑 [T] **~ sth** to spend a period of time doing sth 度過（一段時間）：*She did a year at college, but then dropped out.* 她在大學讀了一年書，但後來就輟學了。◇ *He did six years* (= in prison) *for armed robbery.* 他因持械搶劫罪服了六年刑。

▸ **DEAL WITH 處理 19** [T] **~ sb/sth** to deal with or attend to sb/sth 處理；照料：*The hairdresser said she could do me* (= cut my hair) *at three.* 理髮師說她三點鐘可以給我理髮。

▸ **BE SUITABLE/ENOUGH 適合；足夠 20** [I, T] to be suitable or be enough for sb/sth 適合；足夠：*'Can you lend me some money?' 'Sure— **will $20 do?**'* "你能借給我一點錢嗎？" "當然可以，20 元夠嗎？" ◇ **~ for sb/sth** *These shoes **won't do** for the party.* 這雙鞋聚會時穿不合適。◇ **~ as sth** *The box will **do fine as** a table.* 這個箱子用作桌子還蠻不錯。◇ **~ sb (+ adv./prep.)** (*especially BrE*) *This room **will do me** nicely, thank you* (= it has everything I need). 這房間對我很合適，謝謝你。

▸ **COOK 烹調 21** [T] **~ sth** to cook sth 烹製；煮；燒；煎：*How would you like your steak done?* 你的牛排要幾成熟？

▸ **CHEAT 欺騙 22** [T, usually passive] **~ sb** (*BrE, informal*) to cheat sb 欺騙：*This isn't a genuine antique—you've been done.* 這不是真正的古董——你上當了。

▸ **PUNISH 懲罰 23** [T] **~ sb (for sth)** (*BrE, informal*) to punish sb 懲罰；處罰：*They did him for tax evasion.* 他們因他逃稅而處罰了他。◇ *She **got done** for speeding.* 她因超速行駛而受到處罰。

▸ **STEAL 偷竊 24** [T] **~ sth** (*informal*) to steal from a place（從某地方）盜竊；搶劫（某地方）：*The gang did a warehouse and a supermarket.* 那幫匪徒搶劫了一個倉庫和一家超級市場。

▸ **TAKE DRUGS 吸毒 25** [T] **~ sth** (*informal*) to take an illegal drug 吸（毒）：*He doesn't smoke, drink or **do drugs**.* 他不抽煙，不喝酒，也不吸毒。

▸ **HAVE SEX 性交 26** [T] **~ it** (*slang*) to have sex 性交

IDM Most idioms containing **do** are at the entries for the nouns and adjectives in the idioms, for example **do a bunk** is at **bunk**. 大多數含 do 的習語，都可在該等習語中的名詞及形容詞相關詞條找到，如 do a bunk 在詞條 bunk 下。 **be/have to do with sb/sth** 🔑 to be about or connected with sb/sth 關於；與…有關係（或有聯繫）：*'What do you want to see me about?' 'It's to do with that letter you sent me.'* "你想見我有什麼事？" "是關於你寫給我的那封信。" **have (got) something, nothing, a lot, etc. to do with sb/sth** used to talk about how much sb/sth is connected with sb/sth 與…有些（毫無、有很大等）關係：*Her job has something to do with computers.* 她的工作與計算機有些關係。◇ *'How much do you earn?' 'What's it got to do with you?'* "你掙多少錢？" "這跟你有什麼關係？" ◇ *Hard work has a lot to do with* (= is an important reason for) *her success.* 努力工作是她成功的重要原因。◇ *We don't have very much to do with our neighbours* (= we do not speak to them very often). 我們與鄰居沒什麼來往。◇ *I'd have nothing to do with him, if I were you.* 如果我是你，我就不會跟他有任何瓜葛。 **it won't 'do** (*especially BrE*) used to say that a situation is not acceptable and should be changed or improved（表示情況不令人滿意、需要改變或改進）那不行，這不合適：*This is the third time you've been late this week; it simply won't do.* 這是你本週第三次遲到了，這可不行啊。 **not 'do anything/a lot/much for sb** (*informal*) used to say that sth does not make sb look attractive 並不使某人漂亮一些 / 很多：*That hairstyle doesn't do anything for her.* 那種髮型並不使她更漂亮。 **ˌnothing 'doing** (*informal*) used to refuse a request（拒絕請求）不行，辦不到：*'Can you lend me ten dollars?' 'Nothing doing!'* "你能借給我十塊錢嗎？" "不行！" **no you 'don't** (*informal*) used to show that you intend to stop sb from doing sth that they were going to do 不，你辦不到；不，我不許你這樣做；你敢：*Sharon went to get into the taxi. 'Oh no you don't,' said Steve.* 沙倫走過去要上出租車。"喔，不，你不許走。" 史蒂夫說道。 **that 'does it** (*informal*) used to show that you will not accept sth any longer（表示不願再接受）行了，得了，夠了：*That does it, I'm off. I'm not having you swear at me like that.* 夠了，我就要不客氣了。我不能容忍你那樣跟我罵罵咧咧的。 **that's 'done it** (*informal*) used to say that an accident, a mistake, etc. has spoiled or ruined sth 這下可糟了；這下可完了：*That's done it. You've completely broken it this time.* 這下可完了。你這回是把它徹底弄壞了。 **that will 'do** used to order sb to stop doing or saying sth（下令制止行動或說話）行啦，夠啦：*That'll do, children—you're getting far too noisy.* 行啦，孩子們，你們簡直吵死人了。 **what do you do for sth?** used to ask how sb manages to obtain the thing mentioned 你是怎麼設法獲得…的：*What do you do for entertainment out here?* 你在這裏有什麼消遣？ **what is sb/sth doing ...?** used to ask why sb/sth is in the place mentioned 為什麼在…地方：*What are these shoes doing on my desk?* 這些鞋怎麼在我的書桌上呢？

PHR V **ˌdo aˈway with sb/yourself** (*informal*) to kill sb/yourself 殺死，幹掉（某人）；自殺 **ˌdo aˈway with sth** (*informal*) to stop doing or having sth; to make sth end 廢除；取消；結束 **SYN** **abolish**：*He thinks it's time we did away with the monarchy.* 他認為我們該廢除君主制了。 **ˌdo sb/sth 'down** (*BrE, informal*) to criticize sb/sth unfairly 詆譭；說…的壞話 **'do for sb/sth** [usually passive] (*informal*) to ruin, destroy or kill sb/sth 毀滅；破壞；殺死：*Without that contract, we're done for.* 要是沒有那份合同，我們就完蛋了。 **ˌdo sb/yourself 'in** (*informal*) **1** to kill sb/yourself 殺死，幹掉（某人）；自殺 **2** [usually passive] to make sb very tired 使筋疲力盡；使疲乏至極：*Come and sit down—you look done in.* 過來坐坐吧，你看樣子累壞了。 **ˌdo sth↔'in** (*informal*) to injure a part of the body 傷害（身體某部位）：*He did his back in lifting heavy furniture.* 他抬重傢具時扭傷了腰背。 **ˌdo sb 'out of sth** (*informal*) to unfairly prevent sb from having what they ought to have（用不正當手段）阻止某人擁有，剝奪：*She was done out of her promotion.* 她受人算計而未獲得提升。 **ˌdo sb 'over** (*informal, especially BrE*) to attack and beat sb severely 猛擊；痛打；毒打；狠揍：*He was done over by a gang of thugs.* 他被一群暴徒毒打了一頓。 **ˌdo sth↔'over** **1** to clean or decorate sth again 重新清理；重新裝飾：*The paintwork will need doing over soon.* 需要儘快重新油漆一遍。 **2** (*NAmE*) to do sth again 重做；重複；再做一遍：*She insisted that everything be done over.* 她堅持全部返工。 **3** (*BrE, informal*) to enter a building by force and steal things 入室盜竊：*He got home to find that his flat had been done over.* 他回到家後發現公寓裏被盜了。 **ˌdo 'up** to be fastened 固定住；扣上；綁緊：*The skirt does up at the back.* 這條裙子在後面繫扣。 **ˌdo sth↔'up** **1** 🔑 to fasten a coat, skirt, etc. 扣上（外套、裙子等）：*He never bothers to do his jacket up.* 他向來都懶得扣外衣。 **OPP** **undo 2** to make sth into a package 包起來；紮起來 **SYN** **wrap**：*She was carrying a package done up in brown paper.* 她提着一個牛皮紙包。 **3** (*BrE*) to repair and decorate a house, etc. 修繕，整修，裝飾（房屋等）：*He makes money by buying old houses and doing them up.* 他靠買舊房整修翻新賺錢。 **ˌdo yourself 'up** (*informal*) to make yourself more attractive by putting on MAKE-UP, attractive clothes, etc. 梳妝，打扮（自己） **'do sth with sb/sth** 🔑 used in negative sentences and questions with *what* 用於否定句和與 what 連用的疑問句：*I don't know what to do with* (= how to use) *all the food that's left over.* 我不知道怎樣處理所有這些剩飯剩菜。◇ *What have you done with* (= where have you put) *my umbrella?* 你把我的傘弄到哪裏去了？◇ *What have you been doing with yourselves* (= how have you been passing the time)? 你這一向是怎麼過的？ ➲ see also CAN'T BE DOING WITH at CAN[1], COULD DO WITH at COULD **ˌdo withˈout (sb/sth)** 🔑 to manage without sb/sth 沒有…也行；沒有…而設法應付：*She can't do **without** a secretary.* 她不能沒有秘書。◇ *If they can't get it to us in time, we'll just have to do without.* 如果他們不能及時給我們拿來，我們就只好將就了。◇ **~ doing sth** (*ironic*) *I **could have done without** being* (= I wish I had not been) *woken up at three in the morning.* 其實用不着在凌晨三點鐘就把我叫醒。

■ ***auxiliary verb*** (**does** /dʌz/, **did** /dɪd/, **done** /dʌn/) **1** used before a full verb to form negative sentences and questions（用於實義動詞前構成否定句和疑問句）：*I don't like fish.* 我不喜歡魚。◇ *They didn't go to Paris.* 他們沒去巴黎。◇ *Don't forget to write.* 別忘了寫信。◇ *Does she speak French?* 她會說法語嗎？ **2** used to make QUESTION TAGS (= short questions at the end of statements)（構成附加疑問句）：*You live in New York, don't you?* 你住在紐約，不是嗎？◇ *She doesn't work here, does she?* 她不在這裏工作，對吧？ **3** used to avoid repeating a full verb（代替實義動詞以避免重複）：*He plays better than he did a year ago.* 他的球比一年前打得好了。◇ *She works harder than he does.* 她工作比他努力。◇ *'Who won?' 'I did.'* "誰贏了？" "我贏了。" ◇ *'I love peaches.' '**So do I.**'* "我愛吃桃子。" "我也愛吃。" ◇ *'I don't want to go back.' '**Neither do I.**'* "我不想回去。" "我也不想。" **4** used when no other auxiliary verb is present, to emphasize what you are saying（句中無其他助動詞時，用以加強語氣）：*He does look tired.* 他的確顯得很疲倦。◇ *She did at least write to say thank you.* 她至少還寫了信道謝。◇ (*BrE*) *Do shut up!* 把嘴給我閉上！ **5** used to change the order of the subject and verb when an adverb is moved to the front（副詞移置句首時，用以改變主語和動詞的語序）：*Not only does she speak Spanish, she's also good with computers.* 她不僅會說西班牙語，還精通計算機。

■ ***noun*** /duː/ (*pl.* **dos** or **do's** /duːz/) (*BrE, informal*) a party; a social event 社交聚會；社交活動：*Are you having a big do for your birthday?* 你打算舉行大型生日宴會嗎？

IDM **dos and don'ts** (also **do's and don'ts**) (*informal*) rules that you should follow 規則；注意事項：*Here are some dos and don'ts for exercise during pregnancy.* 這是妊娠期間鍛煉的一些注意事項。➲ more at FAIR *adj.*

Vocabulary Building 詞彙擴充

Household jobs: do or make? 家務活：用 do 還是 make？

- To talk about jobs in the home you can use such phrases as **wash the dishes**, **clean the kitchen floor**, **set the table**, etc. In conversation the verb **do** is often used instead. 做家務活可用下列短語表示：wash the dishes（洗餐具）、clean the kitchen floor（擦洗廚房地板）、set the table（擺餐具）等，在口語中常用動詞 do 取代：*Let me do the dishes.* 我來洗碗吧。◇ *Michael said he would do the kitchen floor.* 邁克爾說他來擦洗廚房地板。◇ *It's your turn to do the table.* 輪到你擺餐具了。 **Do** is often used with nouns ending *-ing*. * do 常與以 -ing 結尾的名詞連用：*to do the shopping/cleaning/ironing/vacuuming* 買東西；打掃衞生；熨衣服；用吸塵器吸塵
- The verb **make** is used especially in the phrase **make the beds** and when you are talking about preparing or cooking food. 動詞 make 尤用於短語 make the beds 中及談論烹調時：*He makes a great lasagne.* 他做的寬麪條真好吃。◇ *I'll make breakfast while you're having a shower.* 你淋浴時我就做早餐。 You can also say **get**, **get ready** and, especially in *NAmE*, **fix** for preparing meals. 做飯亦可用 get、get ready 和 fix（尤用於美式英語）等詞：*Can you get dinner while I put the kids to bed?* 我弄孩子上牀睡覺時你做飯行嗎？◇ *Sit down — I'll fix supper for you.* 坐下吧，我給你做晚飯。

do² /dəʊ; *NAmE* doʊ/ *noun* = DOH ➲ see also DO¹

do. *abbr.* DITTO 同上；同前

DOA /ˌdiː əʊ ˈeɪ; *NAmE* -oʊ-/ *abbr.* = DEAD ON ARRIVAL at DEAD *adj.*

do·able /ˈduːəbl/ *adj.* (*informal*) **1** [not usually before noun] able to be done 可做；可行：*It's not doable by Friday.* 這事星期五之前做不了。➲ compare FEASIBLE **2** (*BrE*) sexually attractive 性感的

D.O.B. *abbr.* date of birth 出生日期

dob /dɒb; *NAmE* dɑːb/ *verb* (**-bb-**) (*BrE, informal*)

PHR V ˌ**dob sb ˈin (to sb) for sth/for doing sth** to tell sb about sth that another person has done wrong 向（某人）告發另一人：*Sue dobbed me in to the teacher.* 蘇向老師告了我一狀。

Dobermann (pinscher) (also **Doberman (pinscher)** especially in *NAmE*) /ˌdəʊbəmən ˈpɪnʃə(r)/; *NAmE* ˌdoʊbərmən/ *noun* a large dog with short dark hair, often used for guarding buildings 多伯曼氏短尾狗

doc /dɒk; *NAmE* dɑːk/ *noun* (*informal, especially NAmE*) a way of addressing or talking about a doctor（稱呼或談論時用語）醫生，大夫

do·cent /ˈdəʊsnt; *NAmE* ˈdoʊ-/ *noun* (*NAmE*) **1** a teacher at some universities who is not a regular member of the department（某些大學的）非正式教授，臨時教師 **2** a person whose job is to show tourists around a museum, etc. and talk to them about it（博物館等場所的）講解員，嚮導

do·cile /ˈdəʊsaɪl; *NAmE* ˈdɑːsl/ *adj.* quiet and easy to control 馴服的；易駕馭的；易控制的：*a docile child/horse* 聽話的孩子；溫馴的馬 ▸ **do·cile·ly** /-saɪlli; *NAmE* -səli/ *adv.* **do·cil·ity** /dəʊˈsɪləti; *NAmE* dɑːˈs-/ *noun* [U]

dock /dɒk; *NAmE* dɑːk/ *noun, verb*

■ ***noun*** **1** [C] a part of a port where ships are repaired, or where goods are put onto or taken off them 船塢；船埠；碼頭：*dock workers* 碼頭工人 ◇ *The ship was **in dock**.* 船泊在船塢。➲ see also DRY DOCK **2 docks** [pl.] a group of docks in a port and the buildings around them that are used for repairing ships, storing goods, etc. 港區 **3** [C] (*NAmE*) = JETTY **4** [C] (*NAmE*) a raised platform for loading vehicles or trains（供運貨汽車或鐵路貨車裝卸貨物的）月台 **5** [C] the part of a court where the person who has been accused of a crime stands or sits during a trial（法庭的）被告席：*He's been **in the dock** (= on trial for a crime) several times already.* 他已受審多次。➲ COLLOCATIONS at JUSTICE **6** [U] a wild plant of northern Europe with large thick leaves that can be rubbed on skin that has been stung by NETTLES to make it less painful 酸模（北歐闊葉野草，可用來揉擦被蕁麻刺傷的皮膚以止痛）：*dock leaves* 酸模葉

■ ***verb*** **1** [I, T] **~ (sth)** if a ship **docks** or you **dock** a ship, it sails into a HARBOUR and stays there（使船）進港，停靠碼頭，進入船塢：*The ferry is expected to dock at 6.* 渡船預計在 6 點停靠碼頭。 **2** [I, T] **~ (sth)** if two SPACECRAFT **dock**, or **are docked**, they are joined together in space（使太空船在外層空間）對接：*Next year, a technology module will be docked on the space station.* 明年將有一個技術艙與航天站對接。 **3** [T] to take away part of sb's wages, etc. 扣除（部份工資等）：**~ sth** *If you're late, your wages will be docked.* 如果你遲到了，就要扣你的工資。◇ **~ sth from/off sth** *They've docked 15% off my pay for this week.* 本週他們扣掉了我 15% 的工資。 **4** [T] **~ sth** (*computing* 計) to connect a computer to a DOCKING STATION 入塢（將電腦連接到擴展塢） OPP **undock** **5** [T] **~ sth** to cut an animal's tail short 剪短（動物的尾巴）

dock·er /ˈdɒkə(r); *NAmE* ˈdɑːk-/ *noun* a person whose job is moving goods on and off ships 碼頭工人

Dock·ers™ /ˈdɒkəz; *NAmE* ˈdɑːkərz/ *noun* [pl.] a US make of trousers/pants made of cotton（美國）道克斯全棉長褲

docket /ˈdɒkɪt; *NAmE* ˈdɑːk-/ *noun* **1** (*business* 商) a document or label that shows what is in a package, which goods have been delivered, which jobs have been done, etc.（載明包裹、發貨、完工等情況的）單據，標籤 **2** (*NAmE*) (also **ˈdocket sheet**) a list of cases to be dealt with in a particular court 備審案件目錄表；法院積案清單 **3** (*NAmE*) a list of items to be discussed at a meeting 議程

ˈdocking station *noun* (*computing* 計) a device to which a LAPTOP computer can be connected so that it can be used like a DESKTOP computer（手提電腦的）電腦塢，擴展塢

dock·land /ˈdɒklænd; *NAmE* ˈdɑːk-/ *noun* [U] (also **dock·lands** [pl.]) (*BrE*) the district near DOCKS (= the place where ships are loaded and unloaded in a port) 港區陸

域；碼頭區：*plans to further redevelop Bristol's docklands* 進一步開發布里斯托爾港區陸域的方案

dock·side /ˈdɒksaɪd; *NAmE* ˈdɑːk-/ *noun* [sing.] the area around the DOCKS (= the place where ships are loaded and unloaded) in a port 碼頭邊；碼頭鄰區；塢邊

dock·yard /ˈdɒkjɑːd; *NAmE* ˈdɑːkjɑːrd/ *noun* an area with DOCKS (= the place where ships are loaded and unloaded in a port) and equipment for building and repairing ships 造船廠；修船廠

D

ˌDoc ˈMartens *noun* (*informal*) = DR MARTENS

doc·tor /ˈdɒktə(r); *NAmE* ˈdɑːk-/ *noun, verb*

■ *noun* (*abbr.* **Dr**) **1** a person who has been trained in medical science, whose job is to treat people who are ill/sick or injured 醫生；大夫：*You'd better **see a doctor** about that cough.* 你最好找醫生治治你的咳嗽。◇ *Doctor Staples* (= as a title/form of address) 斯特普爾斯醫生 **2** **doctor's** a place where a doctor sees patients 診所：*an appointment at the doctor's* 診所的預約門診 **3** a person who has received the highest university degree 博士：*a Doctor of Philosophy/Law* 哲學/法學博士 ◇ *Doctor Franks* (= as a title/form of address) 弗蘭克斯博士 **4** (*especially NAmE*) used as a title or form of address for a dentist（用作頭銜或稱呼）牙醫

IDM **just what the doctor ˈordered** (*humorous*) exactly what sb wants or needs 正是所需之物

■ *verb* **1 ~ sth** to change sth in order to trick sb 篡改；偽造 SYN **falsify**：*He was accused of doctoring the figures.* 他被指控篡改數字。**2 ~ sth** to add sth harmful to food or drink 將有害物摻入（食物或飲料）中：*The wine had been doctored.* 這葡萄酒裏摻入了有害物質。**3 ~ sth** (*informal*) to remove part of the sex organs of an animal 閹割（動物）SYN **neuter**

doc·tor·al /ˈdɒktərəl; *NAmE* ˈdɑːk-/ *adj.* [only before noun] connected with a doctorate 博士的；博士學位的：(*BrE*) *a doctoral thesis* 博士學位論文 ◇ (*NAmE*) *a doctoral dissertation* 博士學位論文

doc·tor·ate /ˈdɒktərət; *NAmE* ˈdɑːk-/ *noun* the highest university degree 博士學位：*She's studying for her doctorate.* 她正在攻讀博士學位。

doc·trin·aire /ˌdɒktrɪˈneə(r); *NAmE* ˌdɑːktrəˈner/ *adj.* (*disapproving*) strictly following a theory in all circumstances, even if there are practical problems or disagreement 空談理論的；脫離實際的；教條主義的：*a doctrinaire communist* 一名着重教條的共產主義者 ◇ ***doctrinaire attitudes/beliefs/policies*** 教條主義的態度/信條/政策

doc·tri·nal /dɒkˈtraɪnl; *NAmE* ˈdɑːktrənl/ *adj.* (*formal*) relating to a doctrine or doctrines 教義的；學說的；主義的：*the doctrinal position of the English church* 英國國教教義的地位 ◇ (*disapproving*) *a rigidly doctrinal approach* 硬搬教條的方法 ▸ **doc·tri·nal·ly** *adv.*

doc·trine /ˈdɒktrɪn; *NAmE* ˈdɑːk-/ *noun* **1** [C, U] a belief or set of beliefs held and taught by a Church, a political party, etc. 教義；主義；學說；信條：*the doctrine of parliamentary sovereignty* 議會主權學說 ◇ *Christian doctrine* 基督教教義 **2** **Doctrine** [C] (*US*) a statement of government policy（政府政策的）正式聲明：*the Monroe Doctrine* 門羅主義

docu·drama /ˈdɒkjudrɑːmə; *NAmE* ˈdɑːk-/ *noun* a film/movie, usually made for television, in which real events are shown in the form of a story 紀實電影；紀實電視劇；文獻影片（或電視片）

docu·ment AW *noun, verb*

■ *noun* /ˈdɒkjumənt; *NAmE* ˈdɑːk-/ **1** an official paper or book that gives information about sth, or that can be used as evidence or proof of sth 文件；公文；文獻；證件：*legal documents* 法律文件 ◇ *travel documents* 旅行證件 ◇ *Copies of the relevant documents must be filed at court.* 有關文件副本必須送交法院備案。◇ *One of the documents leaked to the press was a memorandum written by the head of the security police.* 泄露給報界的文件中有一份是秘密警察局長寫的備忘錄。**2** a computer file that contains text that has a name that identifies it（計算機）文檔，文件：*Save the document before closing.* 在關閉文檔前存盤。➲ VISUAL VOCAB page V68

■ *verb* /ˈdɒkjument; *NAmE* ˈdɑːk-/ **1 ~ sth** to record the details of sth 記錄，記載（詳情）：*Causes of the disease have been well documented.* 這種疾病的起因已有完備的記載。**2 ~ sth** to prove or support sth with documents 用文件證明（或證實）：*documented evidence* 有文件證明的證據

docu·men·tary /ˌdɒkjuˈmentri; *NAmE* ˌdɑːk-/ *noun, adj.*

■ *noun* (*pl.* **-ies**) a film or a radio or television programme giving facts about sth 紀錄片；紀實廣播（或電視）節目：*a television documentary about/on the future of nuclear power* 關於核能前景的紀實電視片 ➲ COLLOCATIONS at TELEVISION

■ *adj.* [only before noun] **1** consisting of documents 文件的；文獻的；由文件（或文獻）組成的：***documentary evidence/sources/material*** 書面證據；文件來源；文獻資料 **2** giving a record of or report on the facts about sth, especially by using pictures, recordings, etc. of people involved 紀錄的；紀實的：*a documentary film about the war* 關於那場戰爭的紀錄片

docu·men·ta·tion AW /ˌdɒkjumenˈteɪʃn; *NAmE* ˌdɑːk-/ *noun* [U] **1** the documents that are required for sth, or that give evidence or proof of sth 必備資料；證明文件：*I couldn't enter the country because I didn't have all the necessary documentation.* 我不能入境是因為我證明文件不齊備。**2** the act of recording sth in a document; the state of being recorded in a document 文件記載；文獻記錄；歸檔：*the documentation of an agreement* 協議的歸檔

ˈdocument case *noun* a soft flat case without a handle, usually made from leather, plastic, etc., and used for holding and carrying documents 公文包；文件套

docu·soap /ˈdɒkjusəʊp; *NAmE* ˈdɑːkjusoʊp/ *noun* (*BrE*) a television programme about the lives of real people, presented as entertainment 紀實肥皂劇；紀實電視娛樂節目 ➲ see also SOAP OPERA

DOD /ˌdiː əʊ ˈdiː; *NAmE* oʊ/ *abbr.* Department of Defense (the government department in the US that is responsible for defence)（美國）國防部

dod·der·ing /ˈdɒdərɪŋ; *NAmE* ˈdɑːd-/ (*BrE* also **dod·dery** /ˈdɒdəri; *NAmE* ˈdɑːd-/) *adj.* weak, slow and not able to walk in a steady way, especially because you are old（尤指因年邁）衰弱而步履蹣跚的

dod·dle /ˈdɒdl; *NAmE* ˈdɑːdl/ *noun* [sing.] (*BrE, informal*) a task or an activity that is very easy 輕而易舉的事 SYN **cinch**：*The first year of the course was an absolute doddle.* 第一年的課程簡直太容易了。◇ *The machine is a doddle to set up and use.* 這機器的安裝和使用都很簡單。

do·deca·he·dron /ˌdəʊdekəˈhiːdrən; -ˈhed-; *NAmE* ˌdoʊ-/ *noun* (*geometry* 幾何) a solid figure with twelve flat sides 十二面體

do·deca·phon·ic /ˌdəʊdekəˈfɒnɪk; *NAmE* ˌdoʊdekəˈfɑːnɪk/ *adj.* (*music* 音) = TWELVE-NOTE

dodge /dɒdʒ; *NAmE* dɑːdʒ/ *verb, noun*

■ *verb* **1** [T, I] to move quickly and suddenly to one side in order to avoid sb/sth 閃開；躲開；避開：**~ sth** *He ran across the road, dodging the traffic.* 他躲開來往的車輛跑過馬路。◇ **(+ adv./prep.)** *The girl dodged behind a tree to hide from the other children.* 這女孩閃身躲到樹後不讓其他孩子看見。**2** [T] (rather *informal*) to avoid doing sth, especially in a dishonest way（尤指不誠實地）逃避：**~ sth** *He dodged his military service.* 他弄虛作假逃避了服兵役。◇ **~ doing sth** *She tried to dodge paying her taxes.* 她想方設法逃稅。

■ *noun* (*informal*) a clever and dishonest trick, played in order to avoid sth 推脫的計策；逃避的詭計；騙人的伎倆：*a tax dodge* 逃稅花招 ◇ *When it comes to getting off work, he knows all the dodges.* 說到請假歇班，他什麼花招都想得出。

dodge·ball /ˈdɒdʒbɔːl; *NAmE* ˈdɑːdʒ-/ *noun* [U] (*NAmE*) a game in which teams of players form circles and try to hit other teams with a large ball 躲球遊戲，躲避球（參加者圍成一個圈，以一大球投擲圈中人）

dodgem /ˈdɒdʒəm; *NAmE* ˈdɑːdʒəm/ *noun* (*BrE*) **1 the dodgems** [pl.] a ride at a FUNFAIR in which people drive small electric cars around a track, trying to chase and hit the other cars 開碰碰車：*The kids wanted to go on the dodgems.* 孩子們想去玩碰碰車。**2** (also **ˈdodgem car**) (also **ˈbumper car** *NAmE, BrE*) one of the small electric cars that you drive in the dodgems 碰碰車

dodger /ˈdɒdʒə(r); *NAmE* ˈdɑːdʒ-/ *noun* (*informal*) a person who dishonestly avoids doing sth 逃避者；迴避者；躲避者：*tax dodgers* 逃稅者 ◇ *a crackdown on fare dodgers on trains* 對火車逃票者的嚴厲打擊 ➲ see also DRAFT DODGER

dodgy /ˈdɒdʒi; *NAmE* ˈdɑːdʒi/ *adj.* (*BrE, informal*) (**dodgi·er, dodgi·est**) **1** seeming or likely to be dishonest 狡猾的；狡詐的；可疑的 SYN **suspicious**：*He made a lot of money, using some very dodgy methods.* 他採用一些極其狡詐的手段賺了許多錢。◇ *I don't want to get involved in anything dodgy.* 我不想牽連進任何欺騙勾當。 **2** not working well; not in good condition 有毛病的；運轉不良的；狀況不佳的：*I can't play—I've got a dodgy knee.* 我不能玩了，我的膝蓋出了毛病。◇ *The marriage had been distinctly dodgy for a long time.* 這樁婚姻長期以來明顯有問題。 **3** involving risk, danger or difficulty 冒險的；危險的；困難的：*If you get into any dodgy situations, call me.* 如果你遇上什麼難事，給我打電話。

dodo /ˈdəʊdəʊ; *NAmE* ˈdoʊdoʊ/ *noun* (*pl.* **-os**) **1** a large bird that could not fly and that is now EXTINCT (= no longer exists) 渡渡鳥（不能飛行，現已滅絕） **2** (*NAmE*) a stupid person 笨人；蠢人 IDM see DEAD *adj.*

DOE /ˌdiː əʊ ˈiː; *NAmE* oʊ/ *abbr.* Department of Energy (the US government department that plans and controls the development of the country's sources of energy)（美國）能源部

doe /dəʊ; *NAmE* doʊ/ *noun* a female DEER, RABBIT or HARE 雌鹿；雌兔 ➲ compare BUCK (2), HIND, STAG

doer /ˈduːə(r)/ *noun* (*approving*) a person who does things rather than thinking or talking about them 實幹的人；身體力行者；實行者：*We need fewer organizers and more doers.* 我們需要的是少些組織者，多些實幹者。

does /dʌz/ ➲ DO[1]

doesn't /ˈdʌznt/ *short form* does not

doff /dɒf; *NAmE* dɑːf; dɔːf/ *verb, adj.*

■ *verb* **~ sth** (*old-fashioned*) to take off your hat, especially to show respect for sb/sth 脱（帽）致意

■ *adj.* (*SAfrE, informal*) stupid 笨的；愚昧無知的

dog 0‑ /dɒg; *NAmE* dɔːg/ *noun, verb*

■ *noun* **1** 0‑ [C] an animal with four legs and a tail, often kept as a pet or trained for work, for example hunting or guarding buildings. There are many types of dog, some of which are wild. 狗；犬：*I took the dog for a walk.* 我遛狗去了。◇ *I could hear a dog barking.* 我聽到犬吠聲。◇ *dog food* 狗食 ◇ *guard dogs* 看家狗 ◇ *a dog and her puppies* 母狗和它的狗崽兒 ➲ see also GUIDE DOG, GUN DOG, HEARING DOG, LAPDOG (1), PRAIRIE DOG, SHEEPDOG, SNIFFER DOG, TRACKER DOG **2** [C] a male dog, FOX or WOLF 公狗；公狐；公狼 ➲ compare BITCH (1) **3 the dogs** [pl.] (*BrE, informal*) GREYHOUND racing 賽狗；靈猩賽 **4** [C] (*informal, especially NAmE*) a thing of low quality; a failure 蹩腳貨；失敗：*Her last movie was an absolute dog.* 她的最後一部影片徹底砸鍋了。 **5** [C] (*informal*) an offensive way of describing a woman who is not considered attractive 醜女人 **6** [C] (*informal, disapproving*) used, especially after an adjective, to describe a man who has done sth bad（尤用於形容詞後）傢伙，小人，無賴：*You dirty dog!* 你這個下流坯！ ➲ see also HOT DOG (2), SHAGGY-DOG STORY, TOP DOG, WATCHDOG

IDM **a ˌdog and ˈpony show** (*NAmE, informal, disapproving*) an event that is planned only in order to impress people so that they will support or buy sth（為公關或促銷而舉行的）造勢活動 **(a case of) ˌdog eat ˈdog** a situation in business, politics, etc. where there is a lot of competition and people are willing to harm each other in order to succeed 殘酷無情的競爭；損人利己的角逐；相互殘殺：*I'm afraid in this line of work it's a case of dog eat dog.* 恐怕在這種行業中競爭是殘酷無情的。◇ *We're operating in a dog-eat-dog world.* 我們是在一個殘酷競爭的世界裏經營。 **a ˌdog in the ˈmanger** a person who stops other people from enjoying what he or she cannot use or does not want 佔馬槽的狗 **a dog's ˈbreakfast/ˈdinner** (*BrE, informal*) a thing that has been done badly 亂七八糟；一團糟 SYN **mess**：*He's made a real dog's breakfast of these accounts.* 他把這些賬目搞得簡直一塌糊塗。 **a ˈdog's life** an unhappy life, full of problems or unfair treatment 悲慘的生活；牛馬不如的生活 **every dog has his/its ˈday** (*saying*) everyone has good luck or success at some point in their life 人人皆有得意日 **give a dog a bad ˈname** (*saying*) when a person already has a bad reputation, it is difficult to change it because others will continue to blame or suspect him/her 惡名難洗；名聲一毀，萬難挽回 **go to the ˈdogs** (*NAmE* also **go to hell in a ˈhandbasket**) (*informal*) to get into a very bad state 敗落；大不如前：*This firm's gone to the dogs since the new management took over.* 這家公司自新的管理人員接手以來日漸衰敗。 **not have a ˈdog's chance** to have no chance at all 毫無機會；絕無可能：*He hasn't a dog's chance of passing the exam.* 他根本不可能通過這次考試。 **why keep a ˌdog and bark yourˈself?** (*informal, saying*) if sb can do a task for you, there is no point in doing it yourself 既然有人代勞，何必自己操勞 ➲ more at HAIR, RAIN *v.*, SICK *adj.*, SLEEP *v.*, TAIL *n.*, TEACH

■ *verb* (**-gg-**) **1 ~ sb/sth** (of a problem or bad luck 問題或不幸) to cause you trouble for a long time 困擾；折磨；糾纏：*He had been dogged by bad health all his life.* 他一生多病，備受折磨。 **2 ~ sb/sth** to follow sb closely 跟踪；尾隨：*She had the impression that someone was dogging her steps.* 她感覺到有人在尾隨她。

ˈdog biscuit *noun* a small hard biscuit fed to dogs 餵狗的小塊硬餅乾；狗食餅乾

dog·box /ˈdɒgbɒks; *NAmE* ˈdɔːgbɑːks/ *noun*

IDM **be in the ˈdogbox** (*SAfrE*) = BE IN THE DOGHOUSE at DOGHOUSE

dog·catch·er /ˈdɒgkætʃə(r); *NAmE* ˈdɔːg-/ (*NAmE*, becoming *old-fashioned*) (*NAmE formal* **ˌanimal conˈtrol officer**, *BrE* **ˈdog warden**) *noun* a person whose job is to catch dogs and cats that are walking freely in the streets and do not seem to have a home 捕狗員（負責捕捉街上的流浪貓狗）

ˈdog collar *noun* **1** a COLLAR for a dog 狗項圈 **2** (*informal*) a stiff white COLLAR fastened at the back and worn by some Christian priests（聖職人員穿的）白色硬領；牧師領

ˈdog days *noun* [pl.] the hottest period of the year 三伏天；酷暑期

ˈdog-eared *adj.* (of a book 書) used so much that the corners of many of the pages are turned down 捲角的；翻舊了的

ˌdog-ˈend *noun* (*BrE, informal*) the end of a cigarette that has been smoked 煙頭；香煙屁股

dog·fight /ˈdɒgfaɪt; *NAmE* ˈdɔːg-/ *noun* **1** a fight between aircraft in which they fly around close to each other（戰鬥機的）近距離空戰 **2** a struggle between two people or groups in order to win sth 爭鬥；格鬥；混戰 **3 dog fight** a fight between dogs, especially one that is arranged illegally, for entertainment 狗打架；（尤指非法的）鬥狗 ▸ **dog·fight·ing** *noun* [U]

dog·fish /ˈdɒgfɪʃ; *NAmE* ˈdɔːg-/ *noun* (*pl.* **dog·fish**) a small SHARK (= an aggressive sea fish with very sharp teeth) 狗鯊（小型鯊魚，極富攻擊性）

dog·ged /ˈdɒgɪd; *NAmE* ˈdɔːg-/ *adj.* [usually before noun] (*approving*) showing determination; not giving up easily 頑強的；堅持不懈的 SYN **tenacious**：***dogged determination/persistence*** 頑強的決心／毅力 ◇ *their dogged defence of the city* 他們對城市的嚴防死守 ▸ **dog·ged·ly** *adv.* SYN **tenaciously** **dog·ged·ness** *noun* [U] SYN **tenacity**

dog·gerel /ˈdɒgərəl; *NAmE* ˈdɔːg-; ˈdɑːg-/ *noun* [U] poetry that is badly written or ridiculous, sometimes because the writer has not intended it to be serious 蹩腳詩；打油詩；歪詩

doggo /ˈdɒɡəʊ; NAmE ˈdɔːɡoʊ/ *adv.* **lie ~** (*old-fashioned, informal*) to lie still and quiet, so that other people will not notice you 隱蔽地；隱伏着

dog·gone /ˈdɒɡɒn; NAmE ˈdɔːɡɔːn/ *adj.* [only before noun], *adv., exclamation* (*NAmE, informal*) used to show that you are annoyed or surprised（表示惱怒或驚訝）該死的，討厭的，他媽的：*Where's the doggone key?* 這該死的鑰匙上哪兒去了？◇ *Don't drive so doggone fast.* 別他媽開這麼快呀。◇ *Well, doggone it!* 唉，真該死！

doggy /ˈdɒɡi; NAmE ˈdɔːɡi/ *noun, adj.*
▪ *noun* (also **dog·gie**) (*pl.* **-ies**) (*informal*) a child's word for a dog（兒語）小狗，汪汪，狗狗
▪ *adj.* [only before noun] of or like a dog 狗的；像狗一樣的：*a doggy smell* 一股狗騷味

ˈdoggy bag (also **ˈdoggie bag**) *noun* (*informal*) a bag for taking home any food that is left after a meal in a restaurant 剩菜袋（餐館裝剩菜回家用的袋子）

ˈdoggy-paddle *noun* = DOG-PADDLE

ˈdog handler *noun* a police officer who works with a trained dog 警犬訓練員

dog·house /ˈdɒɡhaʊs; NAmE ˈdɔːɡ-/ (*NAmE*) (*BrE* **ken·nel**) *noun* a small shelter for a dog to sleep in 狗窩；犬舍
IDM **be in the doghouse** (*informal, NAmE, BrE*) if you are **in the doghouse**, sb is annoyed with you because of sth that you have done 受冷落；失體面；丟臉

dogie /ˈdəʊɡi; NAmE ˈdoʊɡi/ *noun* (*NAmE*) a young cow that has lost its mother 孤犢

ˈdog-leg *noun* a sharp bend, especially in a road or on a GOLF COURSE（道路的）急轉彎；（高爾夫球場的）彎曲球道，拐形擊球區

dogma /ˈdɒɡmə; NAmE ˈdɔːɡmə/ *noun* [U, C] (often *disapproving*) a belief or set of beliefs held by a group or organization, which others are expected to accept without argument 教義；教理；信條；教條：***political/religious/party dogma*** 政治／宗教／政黨信條 ◇ *one of the central dogmas of the Church* 這個教會的核心教義之一

dog·mat·ic /dɒɡˈmætɪk; NAmE dɔːɡ-/ *adj.* (*disapproving*) being certain that your beliefs are right and that others should accept them, without paying attention to evidence or other opinions 自以為是的；教條的；武斷的：*a **dogmatic approach*** 武斷的方法 ◇ *There is a danger of becoming too dogmatic about teaching methods.* 在教學方法上存在着過分教條主義的危險。▸ **dog·mat·ic·al·ly** /-kli/ *adv.*

dog·ma·tism /ˈdɒɡmətɪzəm; NAmE ˈdɔːɡ-/ *noun* [U] (*disapproving*) behaviour and attitudes that are dogmatic 教條主義；獨斷論；武斷

ˌdo-ˈgooder *noun* (*informal, disapproving*) a person who tries to help other people but who does it in a way that is annoying 幫倒忙的人；幫忙不得法的人

ˈdog-paddle (also **ˈdoggy-paddle**) *noun* [U] a simple swimming stroke, with short quick movements like those of a dog in the water 狗爬式（游泳）

dogs·body /ˈdɒɡzbɒdi; NAmE ˈdɔːɡzbɑːdi/ *noun* (*pl.* **-ies**) (*BrE, informal*) a person who does all the boring jobs that nobody else wants to do, and who is treated as being less important than other people 勤雜工；幹雜活的人

dog·sled /ˈdɒɡsled; NAmE ˈdɔːɡ-/ *noun* (*NAmE*) a SLEDGE (= a vehicle that slides over snow) pulled by dogs, used especially in Canada and Alaska（尤用於加拿大和阿拉斯加的）狗拉雪橇

ˈdog tag *noun* (*NAmE, slang*) a small piece of metal that US soldiers wear round their necks with their name and number on it（美國士兵掛在頸部的）身分識別牌

ˌdog-ˈtired *adj.* [not usually before noun] (*informal*) very tired 極度疲乏；累極了 **SYN** **exhausted**

ˈdog warden (*BrE*) (*NAmE* becoming *old-fashioned* **dog·catch·er**, *formal* **animal control officer**) *noun* a person whose job is to catch dogs and cats that are walking freely in the streets and do not seem to have a home 捕狗員（負責捕捉街上的流浪貓狗）

dog·wood /ˈdɒɡwʊd; NAmE ˈdɔːɡ-/ *noun* [U, C] a bush or small tree with red or pink BERRIES and red STEMS, that grows in northern regions; the hard wood of this tree 梾木；梾木的木材

DoH *abbr.* (in Britain) Department of Health（英國）衛生部

d'oh /dəʊ; NAmE doʊ/ *exclamation* (*informal*) used when you have just said or done sth that you know is stupid 唉，哦（用以表示自己言行失當）：*D'oh! That was the biggest mistake ever.* 唉！那是我犯過的最大錯誤。
ORIGIN Used by Homer Simpson in *The Simpsons* television series. 源自電視系列片《辛普森一家》中霍默・辛普森的用語。

doh (also **do**) /dəʊ; NAmE doʊ/ *noun* (*music* 音) the 1st and 8th note of a MAJOR SCALE 大調音階的第 1 音和第 8 音

DOI /ˌdiː əʊ ˈaɪ; NAmE oʊ/ *abbr.* **1** (*computing* 計) digital object identifier (a series of numbers and letters that identifies a particular text or document published in electronic form on the Internet) 數字對象識別碼，數位對象識別碼（用以識別在互聯網上發表的電子文本或文檔的數字和字母序列）**2** Department of the Interior (the US government department responsible for protecting the country's environment)（美國）內務部（負責國內環保事務）

doily /ˈdɔɪli/ *noun* (*pl.* **-ies**) **1** a small circle of paper or cloth with a pattern of very small holes in it, that you put on a plate under a cake or SANDWICHES（糕點盤上的）網眼紙墊圈，網眼布墊圈 **2** (*NAmE*) a small decorative MAT that you put on top of a piece of furniture（置於傢具上的）裝飾小墊

doing /ˈduːɪŋ/ *noun* [C, usually pl., U] a thing done or caused by sb 所做的事；發生的事；所作所為：*I've been hearing a lot about your doings recently.* 我最近不斷聽到很多關於你的所作所為。◇ *I promise you this was none of my doing* (= I didn't do it). 我向你保證這不是我幹的。
IDM **take some ˈdoing | take a lot of ˈdoing** to be hard work; to be difficult 費勁；有困難：*Getting it finished by tomorrow will take some doing.* 要在明天完成有點難度。

ˌdo-it-yourˈself *noun* [U] (*especially BrE*) = DIY：*The materials you need are available from any good do-it-yourself store.* 所需材料可以從任何好的 DIY 商店買到。

dojo /ˈdəʊdʒəʊ; NAmE ˈdoʊdʒoʊ/ *noun* (*pl.* **-os**) (from *Japanese*) a hall or school where JUDO or other similar MARTIAL ARTS (= fighting sports) are practised 柔道館；柔道學校；武術學校

Dolby™ /ˈdɒlbi; ˈdəʊlbi; NAmE ˈdɔːlbi; ˈdoʊlbi/ *noun* [U] a system for reducing background noise in sound recordings 杜比降噪系統

dol·drums /ˈdɒldrəmz; NAmE ˈdoʊl-/ *noun* [pl.] (usually **the doldrums**) **1** the state of feeling sad or depressed 憂鬱；鬱悶；消沉；沒精打采：*He's been **in the doldrums** ever since she left him.* 自從她離開他以來，他一直很消沉。**2** a lack of activity or improvement 無生氣；停滯；蕭條：*The bond market normally revives after the summer doldrums.* 債券市場通常在夏天蕭條期後開始復蘇。◇ *Despite these measures, the economy remains **in the doldrums**.* 儘管採取了這些措施，經濟仍然停滯不前。**ORIGIN** From the place in the ocean near the equator where there are sudden periods of calm. A sailing ship caught in this area can be stuck there because of a lack of wind. 源自近赤道海洋上的無風帶，帆船到此可能因無風而無法航行。

dole /dəʊl; NAmE doʊl/ *noun, verb*
▪ *noun* [sing.] (usually **the dole**) (*BrE, informal*) money paid by the state to unemployed people 失業救濟金：*He's been **on the dole*** (= without a job) *for a year.* 他領失業救濟金已一年了。◇ *The government is changing the rules for claiming dole.* 政府正在修改申領失業救濟金的規定。◇ *lengthening dole queues* 排隊領取失業救濟金人數的不斷增多 ◇ *We could all be **in the dole queue** on Monday* (= have lost our jobs). 我們都可能在星期一站在領取失業救濟金的隊伍裏。⇨ COLLOCATIONS at UNEMPLOYMENT

■ *verb*

PHR V **ˌdole sth↔ˈout (to sb)** (*informal*) to give out an amount of food, money, etc. to a number of people in a group 發放，發給（食物、錢等）；施捨

dole·ful /ˈdəʊlfl; *NAmE* ˈdoʊlfl/ *adj.* very sad 憂鬱的；悲傷的 **SYN** **mournful**： *a **doleful expression/face/song*** 憂鬱的表情；愁苦的臉；令人悲傷的歌 ◇ *a doleful looking man* 哭喪着臉的男人 ▸ **dole·ful·ly** /-fəli/ *adv.*

doll /dɒl; *NAmE* dɑːl/ *noun, verb*

■ *noun* **1** a child's toy in the shape of a person, especially a baby or a child 玩偶；玩具娃娃： *a rag doll* (= one made out of cloth) 布娃娃 **2** (*old-fashioned, informal, especially NAmE*) a word used to describe a pretty or attractive woman, now often considered offensive 俊妞，甜姐兒，美人兒（現多認為意含冒犯）： *She's quite a doll.* 她真是個美人兒。

■ *verb*

PHR V **ˌdoll sb/yourself ˈup** (*informal*) to make sb/yourself look attractive for a party, etc., with fashionable clothes （把…）打扮得花枝招展，裝扮得漂漂亮亮： *Are you **getting dolled up** for the party?* 你要把自己打扮起來去參加聚會嗎？

dol·lar 🔑 /ˈdɒlə(r); *NAmE* ˈdɑːl-/ *noun*

1 🔑 [C] (*symb.* **$**) the unit of money in the US, Canada, Australia and several other countries 元（美國、加拿大、澳大利亞等國的貨幣單位）： *You will be paid in American dollars.* 你的報酬將以美元支付。➲ compare BUCK (1) ➲ see also TOP DOLLAR **2** 🔑 [C] a BANKNOTE or coin worth one dollar 一元（紙幣或硬幣）： *Do you have a dollar?* 你有一元錢嗎？◇ *a dollar bill* 一元鈔票 **3** **the dollar** [sing.] (*finance* 財) the value of the US dollar compared with the value of the money of other countries 美元（幣值）： *The dollar closed two cents down.* 美元收跌兩美分。**IDM** see BET *v.*, MILLION

dol·lar·ize (*BrE* also **-ise**) /ˈdɒləraɪz; *NAmE* ˈdɑːl-/ *verb* [T, I] **~ (sth)** (of a country 國家) to start using the US dollar as its own CURRENCY （使）美元化 ▸ **dol·lar·iza·tion, -isa·tion** /ˌdɒləraɪˈzeɪʃn; *NAmE* ˌdɑːl-/ *noun* [U]

doll·house /ˈdɒlhaʊs; *NAmE* ˈdɑːl-/ (*NAmE*) (*BrE* **ˈdoll's house**) *noun* a toy house with small furniture and sometimes DOLLS in it for children to play with （兒童放玩偶的）玩具小屋，娃娃屋 ➲ VISUAL VOCAB page V37

dol·lop /ˈdɒləp; *NAmE* ˈdɑːləp/ *noun* (*informal*) **1** a lump of soft food, often dropped from a spoon 一團，一塊（從勺中掉落的軟食）： *a dollop of whipped cream* 一團攪打的奶油 **2** an amount of sth 少量；些許；一點兒： *A dollop of romance now and then is good for everybody.* 時而來點兒浪漫對每個人都是好事。

ˈdoll's house (*BrE*) (*NAmE* **doll·house**) *noun* a toy house with small furniture and sometimes DOLLS in it for children to play with （兒童放玩偶的）玩具小屋，娃娃屋 ➲ VISUAL VOCAB page V37

dolly /ˈdɒli; *NAmE* ˈdɑːli; ˈdɔːli/ *noun* (*pl.* **-ies**) **1** a child's word for a DOLL （兒語）娃娃，洋娃娃 **2** (*especially NAmE*) a low platform on wheels for moving heavy objects （搬運重物的）台車，滑動台架

ˈdolly bird *noun* (*old-fashioned, BrE, informal*) a way of referring to a young woman who is considered attractive but not very intelligent 傻美妞

dol·men /ˈdɒlmen; *NAmE* ˈdoʊl-/ *noun* a pair or group of vertical stones with a large flat stone on top, built in ancient times to mark a place where sb was buried 石室冢墓（在一組豎石頂端置大石板）

dol·or·ous /ˈdɒlərəs; *NAmE* ˈdoʊl-/ *adj.* [usually before noun] (*literary*) feeling or showing great sadness 悲痛的；悲哀的

dol·phin /ˈdɒlfɪn; *NAmE* ˈdɑːl-/ *noun* a sea animal (a MAMMAL) that looks like a large fish with a pointed mouth. Dolphins are very intelligent and often friendly towards humans. There are several types of dolphin. 海豚： *a school of dolphins* 一群海豚 ➲ compare PORPOISE

dol·phin·arium /ˌdɒlfɪˈneəriəm; *NAmE* ˌdɑːlfɪˈneriəm/ *noun* (*pl.* **dol·phin·ariums** or **dol·phin·aria** /-riə/) a building with a pool where people can go to see dolphins, especially ones who have been trained to do tricks 海豚（表演）館

dolt /dəʊlt; *NAmE* doʊlt/ *noun* (*disapproving*) a stupid person 笨蛋；傻瓜 **SYN** **idiot** ▸ **dol·tish** *adj.*

-dom *suffix* (in nouns 構成名詞) **1** the condition or state of（表示狀況或狀態）： *freedom* 自由 ◇ *martyrdom* 殉難 **2** the rank of; an area ruled by（表示職位、地位、領域）： *kingdom* 王國 **3** the group of（表示群體、集體）： *officialdom* 官員

do·main **AW** /dəˈmeɪn; dəʊ-; *NAmE* doʊ-/ *noun* **1** an area of knowledge or activity; especially one that sb is responsible for （知識、活動的）領域，範圍，範疇： *The care of older people is being placed firmly within the domain of the family.* 照顧老人正被確認為是家庭範圍的事。◇ *Physics used to be very much a male domain.* 物理學曾在很大程度上是男性佔據的領域。➲ see also PUBLIC DOMAIN **2** lands owned or ruled by a particular person, government, etc., especially in the past （尤指舊時個人、國家等所擁有或統治的）領土，領地，勢力範圍： *The Spice Islands were within the Spanish domains.* 香料群島曾是西班牙的領地。**3** (*computing* 計) a set of websites on the Internet which end with the same group of letters, for example '.com', '.org' 域；定義域 **4** (*mathematics* 數) the range of possible values of a particular VARIABLE 區域；定義域

doˈmain name *noun* (*computing* 計) a name which identifies a website or group of websites on the Internet 域名

dome /dəʊm; *NAmE* doʊm/ *noun* **1** a round roof with a CIRCULAR base 穹頂；圓屋頂： *the dome of St Paul's Cathedral* 聖保羅大教堂的穹頂 ➲ VISUAL VOCAB pages V2, V14 **2** a thing or a building shaped like a dome 圓頂狀物；穹狀建築物： *his bald dome of a head* 他圓溜溜的禿頂 **3** (*NAmE*) (in names 用於名稱) a sports STADIUM whose roof is shaped like a dome 圓頂體育場： *the Houston Astrodome* 休斯敦阿斯托洛圓頂運動場

domed /dəʊmd; *NAmE* doʊmd/ *adj.* [usually before noun] having or shaped like a dome 有圓頂的；圓頂狀的；半球形的： *a **domed forehead/ceiling*** 隆起的前額；圓頂篷

do·mes·tic 🔑 **AW** /dəˈmestɪk/ *adj., noun*

■ *adj.* **1** 🔑 [usually before noun] of or inside a particular country; not foreign or international 本國的；國內的： ***domestic affairs/politics*** 國內事務／政治 ◇ ***domestic flights*** (= to and from places within a country) 國內航班 ◇ *Output consists of both exports and sales on the domestic market.* 產量包括出口和國內市場銷售兩部份。**OPP** **foreign** **2** 🔑 [only before noun] used in the home; connected with the home or family 家用的；家庭的；家務的： *domestic appliances* 家用器具 ◇ *domestic chores* 家務瑣事 ◇ *the growing problem of **domestic violence*** (= violence between members of the same family) 日趨嚴重的家庭暴力問題 ◇ ***domestic service*** (= the work of a servant in a large house) （傭人的）家務服務 **3** liking home life; enjoying or good at cooking, cleaning the house, etc. 喜愛家庭生活的；享受家庭樂趣的；樂於操持家務的： *I'm not a very domestic sort of person.* 我不是那種很喜歡待在家裏的人。**4** 🔑 (of animals 動物) kept on farms or as pets; not wild 馴養的；作寵物飼養的；非野生的 ▸ **do·mes·tic·al·ly** **AW** /-kli/ *adv.*： *domestically produced goods* 本國產品

■ *noun* **1** (also **ˌdomestic ˈhelp**, **ˌdomestic ˈworker**) a servant who works in sb's house, doing the cleaning and other jobs 家傭；傭人 **2** (*BrE, informal*) a fight between two members of the same family 家庭糾紛；家庭矛盾： *The police were called to sort out a domestic.* 已叫警察來解決家庭糾紛。

do·mes·ti·cate **AW** /dəˈmestɪkeɪt/ *verb* **1 ~ sth** to make a wild animal used to living with or working for humans 馴養，馴化（動物） **2 ~ sth** to grow plants or crops for human use 栽培，培育（植物或農作物） **SYN** **cultivate** **3 ~ sb** (often *humorous*) to make sb good at cooking, caring for a house, etc.; to make sb enjoy home life 使精於家務；使喜家居： *Some men are very hard to domesticate.* 有些男人很難做好家務活。▸ **do·mes·ti·cated** **AW** *adj.*： *domesticated animals* 馴養的動物 ◇ *They've become a lot more domesticated since they got married.* 他們婚後

戀家多了。 **do·mes·ti·ca·tion** /dəˌmestɪˈkeɪʃn/ *noun* [U]：*the domestication of cattle* 牛的馴養

do·mes·ti·city /ˌdəʊmeˈstɪsəti; ˌdɒm-; NAmE ˌdoʊ-; ˌdɑːm-/ *noun* [U] home or family life 家庭生活：*an atmosphere of happy domesticity* 幸福的家庭生活氣氛

doˌmestic ˈscience *noun* (*old-fashioned, BrE*) = HOME ECONOMICS

D

ˈdome tent *noun* a tent which forms the shape of a dome 圓頂帳篷 ➲ compare FRAME TENT, RIDGE TENT

domi·cile /ˈdɒmɪsaɪl; NAmE ˈdɑːm-; ˈdoʊm-/ *noun* (*formal* or *law* 律) the place where sb lives, especially when it is stated for official or legal purposes（尤指正式或法律意義的）住處，住所，定居地

domi·ciled /ˈdɒmɪsaɪld; NAmE ˈdɑːm-; ˈdoʊm-/ *adj.* [not before noun] (*formal* or *law* 律) living in a particular place 定居；在固定住所生活：*to be domiciled in the United Kingdom* 在英國定居

domi·cil·iary /ˌdɒmɪˈsɪliəri; NAmE ˌdɑːməˈsɪlieri; ˌdoʊ-/ *adj.* [only before noun] (*formal*) in sb's home 在住所的；在家中的：*a* ***domiciliary visit*** (= for example, by a doctor) 家訪 ◇ ***domiciliary care/services/treatment*** 家訪護理 / 服務；出診

dom·in·ant AW /ˈdɒmɪnənt; NAmE ˈdɑːm-/ *adj.* **1** more important, powerful or noticeable than other things 首要的；佔支配地位的；佔優勢的；顯著的：*The firm has achieved a dominant position in the world market.* 這家公司在國際市場上佔有舉足輕重的地位。◇ *The dominant feature of the room was the large fireplace.* 這間屋子要數那個大壁爐最顯眼了。 **2** (*biology* 生) a **dominant** GENE causes a person to have a particular physical characteristic, for example brown eyes, even if only one of their parents has passed on this GENE（基因）顯性的，優勢的 ➲ compare RECESSIVE ▶ **dom·in·ance** AW /ˈdɒmɪnəns; NAmE ˈdɑː-/ *noun* [U]：*to achieve/assert dominance over sb* 取得對某人的支配地位 ◇ *political/economic dominance* 政治 / 經濟上的優勢

dom·in·ate 🔑 AW /ˈdɒmɪneɪt; NAmE ˈdɑːm-/ *verb* **1** 🔑 [T, I] **~ (sb/sth)** to control or have a lot of influence over sb/sth, especially in an unpleasant way 支配；控制；左右；影響：*As a child he was dominated by his father.* 他小時候由父親主宰一切。◇ *He tended to dominate the conversation.* 他不時左右着交談的內容。◇ *She always says a lot in meetings, but she doesn't dominate.* 她在會上總是滔滔不絕，但她左右不了局面。 **2** 🔑 [T] **~ sth** to be the most important or noticeable feature of sth 在…中具有最重要（或明顯）的特色：*The train crash dominated the news.* 火車相撞事故成了最重要的新聞。 **3** [T] **~ sth** to be the largest, highest or most obvious thing in a place 在…中最顯眼的位置；俯視；高聳於：*The cathedral dominates the city.* 大教堂俯視全城。 **4** [T, I] **~ (sth)** (*sport* 體) to play much better than your opponent in a game（在比賽中）佔有優勢，佔據主動，控制戰局：*Arsenal dominated the first half of the match.* 阿森納隊在上半場比賽中佔據上風。▶ **dom·in·ation** AW /ˌdɒmɪˈneɪʃn; NAmE ˌdɑː-/ *noun* [U]：*political domination* 政治上的支配 ◇ *companies fighting for domination of the software market* 爭取控制軟件市場的公司

dom·in·atrix /ˌdɒmɪˈneɪtrɪks; NAmE ˌdɑːm-/ *noun* (*pl.* **dom·in·atri·ces** /ˌdɒmɪˈneɪtrɪsiːz; NAmE ˌdɑːm-/, **dom·in·atrixes**) a woman who controls a man during sex, often using violence to give sexual pleasure 虐戀女主人（性生活中常以性虐待等制伏男子）

dom·in·eer·ing /ˌdɒmɪˈnɪərɪŋ; NAmE ˌdɑːməˈnɪr-/ *adj.* (*disapproving*) trying to control other people without considering their opinions or feelings 專斷的：*a cold and domineering father* 冷漠而專制的父親 ◇ *a domineering manner* 專斷的態度

Do·min·ic·an /dəˈmɪnɪkən/ *noun* a member of a Christian group of MONKS or NUNS following the rules of St Dominic 道明會士 ▶ **Do·min·ic·an** *adj.*

do·min·ion /dəˈmɪniən/ *noun* **1** [U] **~ (over sb/sth)** (*literary*) authority to rule; control 統治（權）；管轄；支配：*Man has dominion over the natural world.* 人類擁有對自然界的統治權。◇ *Soon the whole country was under his sole dominion.* 不久，他便獨攬了整個國家的大權。 **2** [C] (*formal*) an area controlled by one ruler 領土；版圖：*the vast dominions of the Roman Empire* 羅馬帝國的遼闊疆域 **3** (often **Dominion**) [C] (in the past 舊時) any of the countries of the British Commonwealth that had their own government 英聯邦自治領 ➲ compare COLONY, PROTECTORATE (1)

dom·ino /ˈdɒmɪnəʊ; NAmE ˈdɑːmənoʊ/ *noun* (*pl.* **-oes**) **1** [C] a small flat block, often made of wood, marked on one side with two groups of dots representing numbers, used for playing games 多米諾骨牌 ➲ VISUAL VOCAB page V38 **2 dominoes** [U] a game played with a set of dominoes, in which players take turns to put them onto a table 多米諾骨牌遊戲

ˈdomino effect *noun* [usually sing.] a situation in which one event causes a series of similar events to happen one after the other 多米諾（骨牌）效應；連鎖反應

dom·pas /ˈdɒmpʌs; NAmE ˈdɔːm-/ *noun* (*SAfrE, informal, disapproving*) (in South Africa in the past) the official document that black people had to carry with them to prove their identity and where they could live or work（舊時南非黑人的）身分證，居住證

don /dɒn; NAmE dɑːn/ *noun, verb*

■ ***noun*** **1** (*BrE*) a teacher at a university, especially Oxford or Cambridge（尤指牛津大學和劍橋大學的）大學教師 ➲ see also DONNISH **2** (*informal*) the leader of a group of criminals involved with the Mafia 黑手黨頭目

■ ***verb*** (**-nn-**) **~ sth** (*formal*) to put clothes, etc. on 披上；穿上；戴上：*He donned his jacket and went out.* 他穿上短上衣出去了。

do·nate /dəʊˈneɪt; NAmE ˈdoʊneɪt/ *verb* **1 ~ sth (to sb/sth)** to give money, food, clothes, etc. to sb/sth, especially a charity（尤指向慈善機構）捐贈，贈送：*He donated thousands of pounds to charity.* 他向慈善事業捐款數千英鎊。 **2 ~ sth (to sb/sth)** to allow doctors to remove blood or a body organ in order to help sb who needs it 獻（血）；捐（血）；捐獻（器官）：*All donated blood is tested for HIV and other infections.* 對所有捐獻的血都要進行艾滋病病毒和其他傳染病病毒檢驗。

do·na·tion /dəʊˈneɪʃn; NAmE doʊ-/ *noun* [C, U] something that is given to a person or an organization such as a charity, in order to help them; the act of giving sth in this way 捐贈物；捐贈；贈送：**~ (to sb/sth)** *to make* ***a donation*** *to charity* 向慈善事業捐贈 ◇ ***a generous/large/small donation*** 慷慨 / 大量 / 少量捐助 ◇ **~ (of …)** *a donation of £200/a £200 donation* * 200 英鎊的捐款 ◇ *The work of the charity is funded by voluntary donations.* 這家慈善機構工作所需資金是人們自願捐贈的。◇ ***organ donation*** (= allowing doctors to use an organ from your body after your death in order to save a sick person's life) 器官捐獻

done /dʌn/ *adj., exclamation* ➲ see also DO[1] *v., auxiliary verb*

■ ***adj.*** [not before noun] **1** finished; completed 完畢；了結；結束：*When you're done, perhaps I can say something.* 等你說完，也許我可以說點什麼。◇ **~ with** *I'll be glad when this job is* ***over and done with.*** 這個工作徹底完成後我就高興了。 **2** (of food 食物) cooked enough 煮熟；熟了：*The meat isn't quite done yet.* 這肉還不太熟。 **3** (*BrE*) socially acceptable, especially among people who have a strict set of social rules 合乎禮儀；合乎規矩；得體：*At school, it simply wasn't done to show that you cared for anything except cricket.* 在學校裏，除了板球外，你對什麼都不感興趣，這顯然不對。

IDM **be ˈdone for** (*informal*) to be in a very bad situation; to be certain to fail 處境艱難；注定完蛋；肯定不行：*Unless we start making some sales, we're done for.* 如果我們還賣不出去，那我們就完了。◇ *When he pointed the gun at me, I thought I was done for* (= about to die). 他把槍對準我時，我還以為我死定了。 **be/get ˈdone for sth/for doing sth** (*BrE, informal*) to be caught and punished for doing sth illegal but not too serious 因輕微違法行為受罰：*I got done for speeding on my way back.* 我在返回的路上因超速行駛而受罰。 **be done ˈin** (*informal*) to be extremely tired 累得夠受；精疲力竭 SYN **be exhausted** **be the ˌdone ˈthing** (*BrE*) to be socially acceptable behaviour 是合乎禮儀的行為；是得

體的行為 **be/have 'done with sb/sth** to have finished dealing with sb, or doing or using sth 與（某人）斷絕關係；做完（某事）；用完（某物）：*If you've done with that magazine, can I have a look at it?* 如果你已看完那本雜誌，給我看看行嗎？ **a ˌdone 'deal** an agreement or a plan that has been finally completed or agreed 達成的協議；決定了的計劃：*The merger is by no means a done deal yet.* 合併之事遠未成定局。 **done and 'dusted** (*BrE, informal*) completely finished 完全結束；徹底完成：*That's my article for the magazine done and dusted.* 這就是我為該雜誌寫的文章，已經脫稿。 **have 'done with it** (*BrE*) to do sth unpleasant as quickly as possible, so that it is finished 趕快了結，儘快做完（令人不愉快的事）：*Why not tell her you're quitting and have done with it?* 為什麼不告訴她你打算辭職，儘快把這件事了結呢？ ➲ more at EASY *adv.*, HARD *adv.*, SOON

■ ***exclamation*** used to show that you accept an offer（接受提議）行，好：*'I'll give you £800 for it.' 'Done!'* "我出 800 英鎊買它。" "成交！"

doner kebab /ˌdɒnə kɪ'bæb; *NAmE* ˌdoʊnər/ *noun* (*BrE*) thin slices of cooked meat, usually served with PITTA bread 烤羊肉片，沙威瑪（常切片夾入麵包中食用） ➲ see also KEBAB

donga /'dɒŋgə; *NAmE* 'dɑːŋgə; 'dɔːŋgə/ *noun* (*SAfrE*) a deep channel in the ground that is formed by the action of water（水流沖出的）深溝；陡岸乾溝：*The car slid into a donga at the side of the road.* 汽車滑進了路旁邊的深溝。

don·gle /'dɒŋgl; *NAmE* 'dɑːŋgl; 'dɔːŋgl/ *noun* (*computing* 計) **1** a cable that is used to attach a computer to a telephone system or to another computer 電話（或網絡）連線 **2** a device or code that is needed in order to use protected software（軟件的）保護鎖，加密狗

Don Juan /ˌdɒn 'dʒuːən; ˌdɒn 'hwɑːn; *NAmE* ˌdɑːn/ *noun* (*informal*) a man who has sex with a lot of women 唐璜；風流浪蕩子；濫交的男子 **ORIGIN** From the name of a character from Spanish legend who was skilled at persuading women to have sex with him. 源自西班牙傳說中人物的姓名，此人擅長勾引女人和其發生關係。

don·key /'dɒŋki; *NAmE* 'dɔːŋ-; 'dɑːŋ-/ *noun* an animal of the horse family, with short legs and long ears. People ride donkeys or use them to carry heavy loads. 驢

IDM **'donkey's years** (*BrE, informal*) a very long time 很長時間：*We've known each other for donkey's years.* 我們已認識多年。 ➲ more at TALK *v.*

'donkey jacket *noun* (*BrE*) a thick short coat, usually dark blue, worn especially by people working outside（尤指野外作業工人穿的深藍色）短厚外衣

'donkey work *noun* [U] (*informal*) the hard boring part of a job or task 單調的苦差事

don·nish /'dɒnɪʃ; *NAmE* 'dɑːn-/ *adj.* (*BrE*) (usually of a man 通常指男人) serious and concerned with academic rather than practical matters 學究式的：*He has a somewhat donnish air about him.* 他身上有點學究氣。

donor /'dəʊnə(r); *NAmE* 'doʊ-/ *noun* **1** a person or an organization that makes a gift of money, clothes, food, etc. to a charity, etc. 捐贈者；捐贈機構：*international aid donors* (= countries which give money, etc. to help other countries) 國際援助國 ◇ *She is one of the charity's main donors.* 她是這一慈善機構的主要捐贈者之一。 **2** a person who gives blood or a part of his or her body to be used by doctors in medical treatment 獻血者；器官捐獻者：*a blood donor* 獻血者 ◇ *The heart transplant will take place as soon as a suitable donor can be found.* 一找到合適的捐獻者即可進行心臟移植手術。◇ *donor organs* 捐獻的器官 ◇ *a donor card* (= a card that you carry giving permission for doctors to use parts of your body after your death) 器官捐獻卡（持有者同意死後將器官捐獻）

don't /dəʊnt; *NAmE* doʊnt/ *short form* do not

ˌdon't-'know *noun* a person who does not have a strong opinion about a question which they are asked in an OPINION POLL（回答問卷）沒有明確意見的人：*A quarter of all the people surveyed were don't-knows.* 參加問卷調查的所有人中有四分之一沒有表示明確意見。

donut *noun* (*especially NAmE*) = DOUGHNUT

doo·dah /'duːdɑː/ (*BrE*) (*NAmE* **doo·dad** /'duːdæd/) *noun* (*informal*) a small object whose name you have forgotten or do not know（忘掉名稱或叫不出名目的）小裝置，小玩意兒

doo·dle /'duːdl/ *verb* [I] to draw lines, shapes, etc., especially when you are bored or thinking about sth else（尤指厭煩或心不在焉時）亂塗，胡寫亂畫：*I often doodle when I'm on the phone.* 我講電話時常常信手亂畫。 ▸ **doo·dle** *noun*

doo·fus /'duːfəs/ *noun* (*NAmE, informal*) a stupid person 蠢人；笨蛋

doo·hickey /'duːhɪki/ *noun* (*NAmE, informal*) a small object whose name you have forgotten or do not know, especially part of a machine 那玩意兒（尤指忘掉名稱或叫不出名目的機器部件）

doo·lal·ly /duː'læli/ *adj.* [not before noun] (*BrE, informal*) crazy 發瘋；瘋了：*The poor chap's gone doolally.* 這可憐的小伙子瘋了。

doom /duːm/ *noun, verb*

■ ***noun*** [U] death or destruction; any terrible event that you cannot avoid 死亡；毀滅；厄運；劫數：***to meet your doom*** 死亡 ◇ *She had* ***a sense of impending doom*** (= felt that sth very bad was going to happen). 她預感到厄運已經逼近。

IDM **ˌdoom and 'gloom** | **ˌgloom and 'doom** a general feeling of having lost all hope, and of PESSIMISM (= expecting things to go badly) 悲觀失望；無望；前景暗淡：*Despite the obvious setbacks, it is not all doom and gloom for the England team.* 儘管明顯多次受挫，但對英格蘭隊來說絕非勝利無望。 **ˌprophet of 'doom** | **'doom merchant** a person who predicts that things will go very badly 末日預言者：*The prophets of doom who said television would kill off the book were wrong.* 認為電視會扼殺書籍的悲觀預言家完全錯了。

■ ***verb*** [usually passive] **~ sb/sth (to sth)** | **~ sb/sth to do sth** to make sb/sth certain to fail, suffer, die, etc. 使…注定失敗（或遭殃、死亡等）：*The plan was* ***doomed to failure***. 這個計劃注定要失敗。◇ *The marriage was* ***doomed from the start***. 這樁婚姻從一開始就注定要破裂。

'doom-laden *adj.* [usually before noun] predicting or leading to death or destruction 預示滅亡的；導致毀滅的：*doom-laden economic forecasts* 經濟注定要崩潰的預報

doom·sayer /'duːmseɪə(r)/ (*especially NAmE*) (*BrE* also **doom·ster** /'duːmstə(r)/) *noun* a person who says that sth very bad is going to happen 凶事預示者；預言災難者

dooms·day /'duːmzdeɪ/ *noun* [sing.] the last day of the world when Christians believe that everyone will be judged by God 最後審判日，世界末日（基督教認為在這一天世人都將接受上帝的審判）

IDM **till 'doomsday** (*informal*) a very long time; for ever 直到世界末日；很長時間；永遠：*This job's going to take me till doomsday.* 這項工作要花去我一生一世的心血。

doomy /'duːmi/ *adj.* (**doom·ier**, **doomi·est**) suggesting disaster and unhappiness 顯示災難（或厄運）的；令人沮喪的：*doomy predictions* 不祥的預測 ◇ *Their new album is their doomiest.* 他們的新專輯是他們最失敗的作品。

Doona™ /'duːnə/ *noun* (*AustralE*) a large cloth bag that is filled with feathers or other soft material and that you have on top of you in bed to keep yourself warm 多納（羽絨）被 **SYN** **duvet**

door 🔑 /dɔː(r)/ *noun*

1 🔑 [C] a piece of wood, glass, etc. that is opened and closed so that people can get in and out of a room, building, car, etc.; a similar thing in a cupboard/closet 門：*a* ***knock on the door*** 敲門 ◇ *to* ***open/shut/close/slam/lock/bolt*** *the door* 開門；關門；砰地關上門；鎖門；拴門 ◇ *to* ***answer the door*** (= to go and open it because sb has knocked on it or rung the bell) 應門（聽到敲門或門鈴響後去開門）◇ *the* ***front/back door*** (= at the entrance at the front/back of a building) 前 / 後門 ◇ *the bedroom door* 卧室門 ◇ *the door frame* 門框 ◇

a four-door saloon car 四門轎車 ◇ *the fridge door* 冰箱門 ◇ *Shut the door!* 把門關上！◇ *Close the door behind you, please.* 請隨手關門。◇ *The door closed behind him.* 他一出門，門就關上了。➲ VISUAL VOCAB pages V25, V52 ➲ see also BACK-DOOR, FIRE DOOR, FRENCH DOOR, OPEN DOOR, REVOLVING DOOR (1), SLIDING DOOR, STABLE DOOR, STAGE DOOR, SWING DOOR, TRAPDOOR **2** [C] the space when a door is open 出入口；門口：*Marc appeared through a door at the far end of the room.* 馬克從房間另一端的門口出現。◇ (*informal*) *She's just arrived—she's just* ***come in the door***. 她剛到，剛踏進門。◇ (*informal*) *He walked* ***out the door***. 他出門去了。**3** [C] the area close to the entrance of a building 門邊；門旁：*There's somebody* ***at the door*** (= at the front door of a house). 門口有人。◇ *'Can I help you?' asked the man at the door.* "我能為您效勞嗎？"門邊的男子問道。➲ see also DOORWAY **4** [C] a house, room, etc. that is a particular number of houses, rooms, etc. away from another 棟；住戶；人家：*the family that lives three doors up from us* 住在與我們相隔三戶的那戶人家 ◇ *Our other branch is just a few doors down the road.* 我們的另一家分店沿路過幾個門面就到。➲ see also NEXT DOOR **5** [U] (*BrE*) the amount of money made by selling tickets for an event 票房收入 SYN **gate**：*50% of the door will go to the Red Cross.* * 50% 的票房收入將捐給紅十字會。

IDM **be on the door** to work at the entrance to a theatre, club, etc., for example collecting tickets from people as they enter 把門（在戲院、夜總會等門口做檢票等工作） **close/shut the 'door on sth** to make it unlikely that sth will happen 使不可能；拒…於門外；把…的門堵死：*She was careful not to close the door on the possibility of further talks.* 她十分注意不讓進一步談判的大門關上。**(from) ,door to 'door** from building to building 從一棟房子到另一棟房子；從一處到另一處；挨家挨戶：*The journey takes about an hour door to door.* 全程大約要花一個小時。◇ *a door-to-door salesman* 走家串戶的推銷員 **(open) the door to sth** (to provide) the means of getting or reaching sth; (to create) the opportunity for sth（為…提供）達到目的的手段；（為…創造）機會：*The agreement will open the door to increased international trade.* 此協議將會提供增長國際貿易的機會。◇ *Our courses are the door to success in English.* 我們的課程是通向掌握英語的成功之路。**lay sth at sb's 'door** (*formal*) to say that sb is responsible for sth that has gone wrong 把…歸咎於某人；認為某人應對…負責 **leave the door 'open (for sth)** to make sure that there is still the possibility of doing sth 不把門堵死；保留可能性 **out of 'doors** not inside a building 在戶外；露天：*You should spend more time out of doors in the fresh air.* 你應多花點時間在戶外透透新鮮空氣。**shut/slam the door in sb's face 1** to shut a door hard when sb is trying to come in 將某人拒之門外；讓某人吃閉門羹 **2** to refuse to talk to sb or meet them, in a rude way 拒絕同某人談話；拒絕見某人 **to sb's door** directly to sb's house 直接到某人的家：*We promise to deliver to your door within 48 hours of you ordering.* 我們承諾在接到訂單後 48 小時內送貨上門。➲ more at BACK *adj.*, BARN, BEAT *v.*, CLOSE[1] *v.*, CLOSED, DARKEN, DEATH, FOOT *n.*, OPEN *v.*, SHOW *v.*, STABLE DOOR, WOLF *n.*

door·bell /'dɔːbel; *NAmE* 'dɔːrbel/ *noun* a bell with a button outside a house that you push to let the people inside know that you are there 門鈴：*to ring the doorbell* 按門鈴

,do-or-'die *adj.* having or needing great determination 一往無前的；破釜沉舟的：*a do-or-die attitude* 孤注一擲的態度

'door furniture *noun* [U] (*BrE, technical* 術語) the handles, KNOCKERS, etc. on a door 門配件

door·keeper /'dɔːkiːpə(r); *NAmE* 'dɔːrk-/ *noun* a person who guards the entrance to a large building, especially to check on people going in 看門人；守門人

door·knob /'dɔːnɒb; *NAmE* 'dɔːrnɑːb/ *noun* a type of round handle for a door, that you turn in order to open the door 球形門拉手

'door knocker *noun* = KNOCKER (1)

door·man /'dɔːmən; *NAmE* 'dɔːrmən/ *noun* (*pl.* **-men** /-mən/) a man, often in uniform, whose job is to stand at the entrance to a large building such as a hotel or a theatre, and open the door for visitors, find them taxis, etc.（旅館、劇院等門口身着制服的）門廳侍者 ➲ compare PORTER (3)

door·mat /'dɔːmæt; *NAmE* 'dɔːrmæt/ *noun* **1** a small piece of strong material near a door that people can clean their shoes on 門口地墊；門口擦鞋墊 **2** (*informal*) a person who allows other people to treat them badly but usually does not complain 逆來順受的可憐蟲；受氣包

door·nail /'dɔːneɪl; *NAmE* 'dɔːrn-/ *noun* IDM see DEAD *adj.*

door·step /'dɔːstep; *NAmE* 'dɔːrs-/ *noun, verb*

■ *noun* **1** a step outside a door of a building, or the area that is very close to the door 門階：*The police turned up on their doorstep at 3 o'clock this morning.* 今天凌晨 3 點，警察出現在他們的住所門前。➲ VISUAL VOCAB page V17 **2** (*BrE, informal*) a thick piece of bread, usually one that is made into a SANDWICH（常用以做三明治的）厚麪包片

IDM **on the/your 'doorstep** very close to where a person lives 在某人的住所旁：*The nightlife is great with bars and clubs right on the doorstep.* 有這些酒吧和夜總會在家門口，夜生活真是棒極了。

■ *verb* (**-pp-**) [T, I] **~ (sb)** (*BrE*) when a journalist **doorsteps** sb, he or she goes to the person's house to try to speak to them, even if they do not want to say anything（記者）登門採訪，蹲守

door·stop /'dɔːstɒp; *NAmE* 'dɔːrstɑːp/ *noun* a thing that is used to stop a door from closing or to prevent it from hitting and damaging a wall when it is opened（防止門關閉的）制門器；（防止門開時撞牆的）門碰頭

door·way /'dɔːweɪ; *NAmE* 'dɔːrweɪ/ *noun* an opening into a building or a room, where the door is 出入口；門口；門道：*She stood* ***in the doorway*** *for a moment before going in.* 她在門口站了一會兒才進去。◇ *homeless people sleeping in shop doorways* 露宿商店門口無家可歸的人

doo·zy (also **doo·zie**) /'duːzi/ *noun* (*pl.* **-ies**) (*NAmE, informal*) something that is very special or unusual 異乎尋常的東西；獨特的事物

dop /dɒp; *NAmE* dɑːp/ *noun, verb* (*SAfrE, informal*)

■ *noun* an alcoholic drink 酒：*Let's* ***have a dop***. 咱們喝杯酒吧。

■ *verb* (**-pp-**) **1** [I, T] **~ (sth)** to drink alcohol, especially in large amounts（尤指大量地）喝酒；狂飲：*They lay around dopping all day.* 他們一整天無所事事都在狂飲。**2** [T] **~ sth** (*slang*) to not pass a test or an exam; to not be successful in completing a period of study at a school, university, etc. 考試不及格；學期（或學年）成績不合格：*I dopped my first year at varsity.* 我在大學的第一年學習很糟糕。

dopa·mine /'dəʊpəmiːn; *NAmE* 'doʊ-/ *noun* [U] a chemical produced by nerve cells which has an effect on other cells 多巴胺（神經細胞產生的一種作用於其他細胞的化學物質）

dope /dəʊp; *NAmE* doʊp/ *noun, verb*

■ *noun* **1** [U] (*informal*) a drug that is taken illegally for pleasure, especially CANNABIS or, in the US, HEROIN 麻醉劑，毒品（尤指大麻，在美國尤指海洛因）**2** [U] a drug that is taken by a person or given to an animal to affect their performance in a race or sport 興奮劑：*The athlete failed a* ***dope test*** (= a medical test showed that he had taken such drugs). 這個運動員未能通過藥檢。**3** [C] (*informal*) a stupid person 笨蛋；呆子；蠢貨 SYN **idiot 4** [U] **the ~ (on sb/sth)** (*informal*) information on sb/sth, especially details that are not generally known 內幕消息；情報：*Give me the dope on the new boss.* 把新上司的底細告訴我吧。

■ *verb* **1 ~ sb/sth** to give a drug to a person or an animal in order to affect their performance in a race or sport 給…用興奮劑 **2 ~ sb/sth** to give sb a drug, often in their food or drink, in order to make them unconscious; to put a drug in food, etc. 給…服麻醉劑；在（食物、飲料）中摻麻醉劑：*Thieves doped a guard dog and stole*

$10 000 worth of goods. 盜賊將看門狗麻醉後偷走了價值1萬元的東西。◇ *The wine was doped.* 這酒摻有麻醉藥。
3 [usually passive] **~ sb (up)** (*informal*) if sb is **doped** or **doped up**, they cannot think clearly or act normally because they are under the influence of drugs 給…用麻醉藥；使昏昏沉沉；使藥力發作

dopey /ˈdəʊpi; *NAmE* ˈdoʊpi/ *adj.* (*informal*) (**dopi·er**, **dopi·est**) **1** rather stupid 愚笨的；遲鈍的；呆頭呆腦的：*a dopey grin* 齜牙咧嘴的傻笑 **2** not fully awake or thinking clearly, sometimes because you have taken a drug 被麻醉的；迷迷糊糊的；昏昏沉沉的：*I felt dopey and drowsy after the operation.* 手術後我感到迷迷糊糊，昏昏欲睡。

dop·pel·gän·ger /ˈdɒplɡæŋə(r); -ɡeŋ-; *NAmE* ˈdɑːpl-/ *noun* (from *German*) a person's **doppelgänger** is another person who looks exactly like them 相貌一樣的人

the Dop·pler effect /ˈdɒplər ɪfekt; *NAmE* ˈdɑːp-/ *noun* [sing.] (*physics* 物) the way that sound waves, light waves, etc. change according to the direction that the source is moving in with relation to the person who is observing 多普勒效應（即聲波、光波等按聲源、光源等相對於觀察者的傳播方向的變化而變化）

ˈ**Doppler shift** *noun* (*physics* 物) the change in sound, colour, etc. caused by the Doppler effect 多普勒頻移（多普勒效應引起的聲、色等的變化）

Dorian Gray /ˌdɔːriən ˈɡreɪ/ *noun* [usually sing.] a person who continues to look young and beautiful, even though they are growing older or behaving in an immoral way（不受年齡增長或行為不端影響）永遠年輕貌美的人：*He's a real Dorian Gray, apparently untouched by the ageing process.* 他像是不受衰老過程的影響，青春永駐。**ORIGIN** From the story by Oscar Wilde, *The Picture of Dorian Gray*, in which Dorian Gray is a beautiful young man who behaves in an immoral way. He secretly keeps a painting of himself, which gradually changes, making him look older and more evil in it. Dorian himself continues to look young and beautiful. 源自奧斯卡·王爾德的小說《道林·格雷的肖像》，主人公道林·格雷年輕俊美但品行不端。在他秘密收藏的一幅畫像中，他的形象逐漸變得更加衰老與醜惡，而他本人卻一直年輕俊美如昔。

Doric /ˈdɒrɪk; *NAmE* ˈdɔːrɪk; ˈdɑːrɪk/ *adj.* [usually before noun] (*architecture* 建) used to describe the oldest style of ARCHITECTURE in ancient Greece that has thick plain columns and no decoration at the top 多立克式的（古典希臘建築風格，柱身和柱頭形式簡樸）：*a Doric column/temple* 多立克式圓柱／廟宇

dork /dɔːk; *NAmE* dɔːrk/ *noun* (*informal*) a stupid or boring person that other people laugh at（受人嘲笑的）呆子，無聊乏味之人 ▶ **dorky** *adj.*

dorm /dɔːm; *NAmE* dɔːrm/ *noun* (*informal*) = DORMITORY

dor·mant /ˈdɔːmənt; *NAmE* ˈdɔːrm-/ *adj.* not active or growing now but able to become active or to grow in the future 休眠的；蟄伏的；暫停活動的 **SYN** **inactive**：*a dormant volcano* 休眠火山 ◇ *During the winter the seeds **lie dormant** in the soil.* 冬天，種子在土壤中休眠。**OPP** **active** ▶ **dor·mancy** /ˈdɔːmənsi; *NAmE* ˈdɔːrm-/ *noun* [U]

ˌ**dormer** ˈ**window** (also **dormer**) *noun* a vertical window in a room that is built into a sloping roof 老虎窗；（建在斜屋頂上的豎式）屋頂窗，天窗 ➲ VISUAL VOCAB page V17

dor·mi·tory /ˈdɔːmətri; *NAmE* ˈdɔːrmətɔːri/ *noun* (*pl.* **-ies**) (also *informal* **dorm**) **1** a room for several people to sleep in, especially in a school or other institution 宿舍；學生宿舍 **2** (*NAmE*) (*BrE* ˌ**hall of** ˈ**residence**, **hall**) a building for university or college students to live in（大學）學生宿舍

ˈ**dormitory town** (*BrE*) (*NAmE* ˈ**bedroom community**, ˈ**bedroom suburb**) *noun* a town that people live in and from where they travel to work in a bigger town or city 郊外住宅區

dor·mouse /ˈdɔːmaʊs; *NAmE* ˈdɔːrm-/ *noun* (*pl.* **dor·mice** /-maɪs/) a small animal like a mouse, with a tail covered in fur 睡鼠

dorp /dɔːp; *NAmE* dɔːrp/ *noun* (*SAfrE*, *informal*) a small town or village in the country 小鎮；村莊

dor·sal /ˈdɔːsl; *NAmE* ˈdɔːrsl/ *adj.* [only before noun] (*technical* 術語) on or connected with the back of a fish or an animal（魚或動物）背部的，背上的，背側的：*a shark's dorsal fin* 鯊魚的背鰭 ➲ VISUAL VOCAB page V12

dory /ˈdɔːri/ *noun* (*pl.* **-ies**) a narrow fish that has a deep body and that can open its mouth very wide 海魴

DOS /dɒs; *NAmE* dɔːs/ *abbr.* (*computing* 計) disk operating system 磁盤操作系統；DOS 系統

dosa /ˈdəʊsə; *NAmE* ˈdoʊ-/ *noun* a southern Indian PANCAKE made with rice flour 多莎餅（印度南部的一種米粉薄餅）

dos·age /ˈdəʊsɪdʒ; *NAmE* ˈdoʊ-/ *noun* [usually sing.] an amount of sth, usually a medicine or a drug, that is taken regularly over a particular period of time（通常指藥的）劑量：*a **high/low dosage*** 大／小劑量 ◇ *to **increase/reduce the dosage*** 增加／減少劑量 ◇ *Do not exceed the **recommended dosage**.* 切勿超過規定劑量。

dos and don'ts ➲ DO[1] *n.*

dose /dəʊs; *NAmE* doʊs/ *noun*, *verb*

■ *noun* **1** an amount of a medicine or a drug that is taken once, or regularly over a period of time（藥的）一劑，一服：*a **high/low/lethal dose*** 大／小／致死劑量 ◇ *Repeat the dose after 12 hours if necessary.* 如果需要，12 小時後再服一劑。**2** (*informal*) an amount of sth 一份；一次；一點：*A dose of flu kept me off work.* 一場感冒使得我上不了班。◇ *Workers at the nuclear plant were exposed to high doses of radiation.* 核電站的工作人員受到大量輻射。◇ *I can cope with her **in small doses*** (= for short amounts of time). 我只能跟她應付片刻。
IDM **like a dose of** ˈ**salts** (*old-fashioned*, *BrE*, *informal*) very fast and easily 迅速輕易地；一下子 ➲ more at MEDICINE

■ *verb* **~ sb/yourself (up) (with sth)** to give sb/yourself a medicine or drug 給（某人）服藥：*She dosed herself up with vitamin pills.* 她給自己服了一些維生素片。◇ *He was heavily dosed with painkillers.* 他服用了大量止痛藥。

dosh /dɒʃ; *NAmE* dɑːʃ/ *noun* [U] (*BrE*, *slang*) money 錢

doss /dɒs; *NAmE* dɑːs/ *verb*, *noun*

■ *verb* (*BrE*, *slang*) **1** [I] **~ (down)** to sleep somewhere, especially somewhere uncomfortable or without a real bed（尤指在不舒適或簡陋的地方）睡覺，過夜：*You can doss down on my floor.* 你可以在我的地板上睡。**2** [I] **~ (about/around)** to spend your time not doing very much 混時間：*We were just dossing about in lessons today.* 今天我們只是在課堂上混時間。

■ *noun* (*BrE*) something that does not need much effort 輕鬆的事；不費力的事

doss·er /ˈdɒsə(r); *NAmE* ˈdɑːs-/ *noun* (*BrE*) **1** a person who has no permanent home and who lives and sleeps on the streets or in cheap HOSTELS 流浪者；露宿街頭者；住廉價旅館者 **2** (*informal*) a person who is very lazy 懶人

doss·house /ˈdɒshaʊs; *NAmE* ˈdɑːs-/ (*BrE*) (*NAmE* **flop·house**) *noun* (*informal*) a cheap place to stay for people who have no home（供流浪者投宿的）廉價客店

dos·sier /ˈdɒsieɪ; *NAmE* ˈdɔːs-; ˈdɑːs-/ *noun* (*formal*) a collection of documents that contain information about a person, an event or a subject 材料彙編；卷宗；檔案 **SYN** **file**：*to **assemble/compile a dossier*** 彙總／彙編材料 ◇ **~ on sb/sth** *We have a dossier on him.* 我們有他的檔案。

dot 🔑 /dɒt; *NAmE* dɑːt/ *noun*, *verb*

■ *noun* **1** 🔑 a small round mark, especially one that is printed 點；小點；小圓點：*There are dots above the letters i and j.* 字母 i 和 j 上面都有一點。◇ *Text and graphics are printed at 300 dots per inch.* 文字和插圖按每英寸 300 點的解析度打印。◇ *The helicopters appeared as two black dots on the horizon.* 直升機像兩個小黑點出現在地平線上。➲ SYNONYMS at PATCH **2** 🔑 (*computing* 計) a symbol like a full stop/period used to separate parts of a DOMAIN NAME, a URL or an email address

D

點（用以分隔域名、統一資源地址、電子郵件地址的組成部份）

IDM **on the 'dot** (*informal*) exactly on time or at the exact time mentioned 準時；在指定時刻：*The taxi showed up on the dot.* 出租車準時到了。◇ *Breakfast is served at 8 on the dot.* * 8 點整開早飯。➲ more at YEAR

■ **verb** (-tt-) **1 ~ sth** to put a dot above or next to a letter or word 打點於；在（字母上方、字母或單詞旁邊）加點：*Why do you never dot your i's?* 你為什麼從不在字母 i 上加點呢？ **2** [usually passive] **~ sth** to spread things or people over an area; to be spread over an area 星羅棋佈於；遍佈：*The countryside was* **dotted with** *small villages.* 鄉間有星羅棋佈的小村莊。◇ *Small villages dot the countryside.* 小村莊星羅棋佈於鄉間。◇ *There are lots of Italian restaurants* **dotted around** *London.* 倫敦到處都有意大利餐館。 **3** to put very small amounts of sth in a number of places on a surface 使佈滿；點綴：**~ A on/over B** *Dot the cream all over your face.* 將乳霜均勻地搽在臉上。◇ **~ B with A** *Dot your face with the cream.* 將乳霜搽在臉上。

IDM **dot your ˌi's and cross your 't's** to pay attention to the small details when you are finishing a task（完成任務時）一絲不苟，注重細節

dot·age /ˈdəʊtɪdʒ; *NAmE* ˈdoʊ-/ *noun*

IDM **be in your dotage** to be old and not always able to think clearly 年老昏聵；年老糊塗

dot-com (also **dot·com**) /ˌdɒt ˈkɒm; *NAmE* ˌdɑːt ˈkɑːm/ *noun* a company that sells goods and services on the Internet, especially one whose address ends '.com'（尤指網址末尾為 .com 的）網絡公司，網路公司：*The weaker dot-coms have collapsed.* 實力較弱的網絡公司倒閉了。◇ *a dot-com millionaire* 一位網絡公司富翁

dote /dəʊt; *NAmE* doʊt/ *verb*

PHR V **'dote on/upon sb** to feel and show great love for sb, ignoring their faults 溺愛；寵愛；過分喜愛：*He dotes on his children.* 他溺愛他的孩子。➲ **SYNONYMS** at LOVE

dot·ing /ˈdəʊtɪŋ; *NAmE* ˈdoʊtɪŋ/ *adj.* [only before noun] showing a lot of love for sb, often ignoring their faults 溺愛的；寵愛的

ˌdot 'matrix printer *noun* a machine that prints letters, numbers, etc. formed from very small dots 點陣打印機；點陣印表機

dot·ted /ˈdɒtɪd; *NAmE* ˈdɑːt-/ *adj.* **1** covered in dots 有斑點的；星羅棋佈的 **2** [only before noun] (*music* 音) (of a musical note 音符) followed by a dot to show that it is one and a half times the length of the same note without the dot 加附點的

ˌdot·ted 'line *noun* a line made of dots 點線；虛線：*Country boundaries are shown on this map as dotted lines.* 這張地圖上國界以虛線標出。◇ *Fold along the dotted line.* 沿虛線摺疊。◇ *Write your name on the dotted line.* 把名字填在虛線上。**IDM** see SIGN *v.*

dotty /ˈdɒti; *NAmE* ˈdɑːti/ *adj.* (**dot·tier**, **dot·ti·est**) (*old-fashioned, BrE, informal*) **1** slightly crazy or silly 瘋瘋癲癲的；半痴的；低能的 **SYN** **eccentric** **2 ~ about sb/sth** having romantic feelings for sb; being enthusiastic about sth 迷戀；充滿熱情；着迷

double 🔑 /ˈdʌbl/ *adj., det., adv., noun, verb*

■ **adj.** [usually before noun]

▸ TWICE AS MUCH/MANY 兩倍 **1** 🔑 twice as much or as many as usual 兩倍的；加倍的：*a double helping* 一客雙份的食物 ◇ *two double whiskies* 兩杯雙份的威士忌酒

▸ WITH TWO PARTS 成雙 **2** 🔑 having or made of two things or parts that are equal or similar 雙的；成雙的；成對的：*double doors* 雙扇門 ◇ *a double-page advertisement* 雙頁廣告 ◇ *'Otter' is spelt with a double t.* * otter 一詞的拼寫中有兩個 t。◇ *My extension is two four double 0 (2400).* 我的分機號碼是 2400。

▸ FOR TWO PEOPLE 雙人 **3** 🔑 made for two people or things 供兩者用的；雙人的：*a* **double bed/room** 雙人牀／房間 ➲ **VISUAL VOCAB** page V23 ➲ compare SINGLE *adj.* (4)

▸ COMBINING TWO THINGS 雙重 **4** 🔑 combining two things or qualities 雙重的：*a* **double meaning/purpose/aim** 雙重意義／目的／目標 ◇ *It has the double advantage of being both easy and cheap.* 它具有既方便又便宜的雙重優點。

■ **det.** 🔑

▸ TWICE AS MUCH/MANY 兩倍 twice as much or as many as 兩倍的；雙倍的：*His income is double hers.* 他的收入是她的兩倍。◇ *He earns double what she does.* 他掙的錢是她的兩倍。◇ *We need double the amount we already have.* 我們需要現有數量的兩倍。

■ **adv.** 🔑

▸ IN TWO PARTS 成雙 in twos or in two parts 雙雙地；成對地：*I thought I was* **seeing double** (= seeing two of sth). 我以為我是看到重影了。◇ *Fold the blanket double.* 把毯子對摺起來。◇ *I had to* **bend double** *to get under the table.* 我必須弓着身子才能鑽到桌子底下。

■ **noun**

▸ TWICE AS MUCH/MANY 兩倍 **1** 🔑 [U] twice the number or amount 兩倍；兩倍數；兩倍量：*He gets paid double for doing the same job I do.* 他與我做同樣的工作，但報酬卻比我多一倍。

▸ ALCOHOLIC DRINK 酒精飲料 **2** [C] a glass of strong alcoholic drink containing twice the usual amount 一杯雙份的烈酒：*Two Scotches, please—and make those doubles, will you?* 請來兩杯蘇格蘭威士忌，兩杯都要雙份的，好嗎？

▸ PERSON/THING 人；物 **3** [C] a person or thing that looks exactly like another 酷似的人；極相似的對應物：*She's the double of her mother.* 她和她母親長得一模一樣。 **4** [C] an actor who replaces another actor in a film/movie to do dangerous or other special things（電影中的）替身演員 ➲ see also BODY DOUBLE

▸ BEDROOM 臥室 **5** [C] = DOUBLE ROOM：*Is that a single or a double you want?* 你要的是單人房間還是雙人房間？➲ compare SINGLE *n.* (3)

▸ IN SPORT 體育運動 **6 doubles** [U+sing./pl. v.] a game, especially of TENNIS, in which one pair plays another 雙打（尤指網球）：*mixed doubles* (= in which each pair consists of a man and a woman) 混合雙打 ➲ compare SINGLES at SINGLE *n.* (6) **7 the double** [sing.] the fact of winning two important competitions or beating the same player or team twice, in the same season or year（在同一賽季或年份）雙料冠軍，兩次獲勝，兩次打敗同一對手

IDM **at the 'double** (*BrE*) (*NAmE* **on the 'double**) (*informal*) quickly; hurrying 迅速地；儘快地；趕緊 **ˌdouble or 'quits** (*BrE*) (*NAmE* **ˌdouble or 'nothing**) (in gambling 賭博) a risk in which you could win twice the amount you pay, or you could lose all your money 要麼贏雙倍，要麼輸得精光

■ **verb**

▸ BECOME TWICE AS MUCH/MANY 加倍 **1** 🔑 [I, T] to become, or make sth become, twice as much or as many（使）加倍；是…的兩倍：*Membership almost doubled in two years.* 兩年內會員數目幾乎翻了一番。◇ **~ sth** *Double all the quantities in the recipe to make enough for eight people.* 把菜譜上的量都增加一倍以夠八人用餐。

▸ FOLD 摺疊 **2** [T] **~ sth (over)** to bend or fold sth so that there are two layers 把…對摺；摺疊：*She doubled the blanket and put it under his head.* 她把毯子摺疊起來給他做枕頭。

▸ IN BASEBALL 棒球 **3** [I] to hit the ball far enough for you to get to second BASE 以二壘打使上二壘；擊出二壘安打：*He doubled to left field.* 他將球擊向左外場而跑上了二壘。

PHR V **'double as sth | ˌdouble 'up as sth** to have another use or function as well as the main one 兼任；兼作：*The kitchen doubles as a dining room.* 這廚房兼做飯廳。 **ˌdouble 'back** to turn back and go in the direction you have come from 循原路折回 **ˌdouble 'up (on sth/with sb)** (*informal*) to form a pair in order to do sth or to share sth 合用；同享：*We'll have to double up on books; there aren't enough to go around.* 因為書不夠人手一冊，我們只好合用了。◇ *They only have one room left: you'll have to double up with Peter.* 他們只剩下一個房間，你只好與彼得合住了。 **ˌdouble 'up/'over | ˌdouble sb 'up/'over** to bend or to make your body bend over quickly, for example because you are in pain

（使）彎腰，弓身：*Jo doubled up with laughter.* 喬笑彎了腰。◇ *I was doubled over with pain.* 我痛得直不起身子。

Synonyms 同義詞辨析

double / dual

These adjectives are frequently used with the following nouns. 這兩個形容詞常與下列名詞連用：

double ~	dual ~
bed	purpose
doors	function
figures	role
standards	approach
thickness	citizenship

- **Dual** describes something that has two parts, uses or aspects. * dual 描述有兩個部份、兩種用途或兩個方面的事物。
- **Double** can be used with a similar meaning, but when it is used to describe something that has two parts, the two parts are usually the same or very similar. * double 具有相似的意思，但所描述事物的兩個部份通常是相同或相似的。
- **Double**, but not **dual**, can describe something that is made for two people or things, or is twice as big as usual. 指供給兩人或兩事物的東西或較平常大一倍的東西用 double，不用 dual。

ˈdouble act *noun* two people who work together, usually to entertain an audience 雙人戲；雙簧

ˌdouble-ˈaction *adj.* [usually before noun] **1** working in two ways 雙效的；雙功能的：*double-action tablets* 雙效藥片 **2** (of a gun 槍) needing two separate actions for preparing to fire and firing 雙動式的（準備射擊和射擊需分別進行的）

ˌdouble ˈagent *noun* a person who is a SPY for a particular country, and also for another country which is an enemy of the first one 雙重間諜

ˌdouble ˈbar *noun* (*music* 音) a pair of vertical lines at the end of a piece of music 複縱線（劃分段落或結束樂曲時用）

ˌdouble-ˈbarrelled (*especially US* **ˌdouble-ˈbarreled**) *adj.* [usually before noun] **1** (of a gun 槍) having two BARRELS (= places where the bullets come out) 雙管的 **2** (*BrE*) (of a family name 姓) having two parts, sometimes joined by a hyphen, for example 'Day-Lewis' 由兩部份組成的 **3** (of a plan, etc. 計劃等) having two parts, and therefore likely to be effective 雙重目的的；雙作用的

ˌdouble ˈbass (also **bass**) *noun* the largest musical instrument in the VIOLIN family, that plays very low notes 低音提琴；低音大提琴 ➲ VISUAL VOCAB page V34

ˌdouble ˈbill (*NAmE* also **ˌdouble ˈfeature**) *noun* two films/movies, television programmes, etc. that are shown one after the other 連場，雙場（兩場電影、兩個電視節目等連續播放）

ˌdouble ˈbind *noun* [usually sing.] a situation in which it is difficult to choose what to do because whatever you choose will have negative results 兩難境地

ˌdouble-ˈblind *adj.* [only before noun] (of a test 測試) conducted so that neither the organizer nor any other people involved know any information which might influence the results 雙盲的（策動者和參與者都不知道可能影響結果的信息）：*A randomized double-blind study was carried out to test the drug's effectiveness.* 進行了隨機雙盲研究以測試藥效。

ˌdouble ˈbluff *noun* a way of trying to trick sb by telling them the truth while hoping that they think you are lying 虛實並用的詐騙（以實相告而期望對方以為有詐）

ˌdouble-ˈbook *verb* [often passive] **~ sth** to promise the same room, seat, table, etc. to two different people at

the same time 重複預訂（將同一房間、座位、餐桌等同時預訂給不同的人）➲ compare OVERBOOK ▸ **ˌdouble-ˈbooking** *noun* [C, U]

ˌdouble-ˈbreasted *adj.* a **double-breasted** jacket or coat has two front parts so that one part covers the other when the buttons are done up, and two rows of buttons can be seen（上衣、外套）雙排鈕扣的 ➲ compare SINGLE-BREASTED

ˌdouble-ˈcheck *verb* [T, I] **~ (sth)** | **~ (that)** ... to check sth for a second time or with great care 復核；復查；仔細審核：*I'll double-check the figures.* 我將對這些數字進行復核。▸ **ˌdouble-ˈcheck** *noun*

ˌdouble ˈchin *noun* a fold of fat under a person's chin, that looks like another chin 雙下巴

ˌdouble-ˈclick *verb* [I, T] **~ (on) sth** (*computing* 計) to choose a particular function or item on a computer screen, etc. by pressing one of the buttons on a mouse twice quickly 雙擊（鼠標鍵）

ˌdouble ˈcream *noun* [U] (*BrE*) thick cream which contains a lot of fat and can be mixed so that it is no longer liquid 濃奶油 ➲ compare SINGLE CREAM

ˌdouble-ˈcross *verb* **~ sb** to cheat or trick sb who trusts you (usually in connection with sth illegal or dishonest) 欺騙；叛賣；出賣：*He double-crossed the rest of the gang and disappeared with all the money.* 他騙了其他同夥攜款潛逃了。▸ **ˌdouble-ˈcross** *noun* [usually sing.]

ˌdouble ˈdate *noun* an occasion when two couples go out together on a DATE 雙約會，四人約會（兩對情侶一同赴約）▸ **ˌdouble-ˈdate** *verb* [I]

ˌdouble-ˈdealer *noun* (*informal*) a dishonest person who cheats other people 兩面派；暗箭傷人者 ▸ **ˌdouble-ˈdealing** *noun* [U]

ˌdouble-ˈdecker *noun* **1** a bus with two floors, one on top of the other 雙層公共汽車 ➲ VISUAL VOCAB page V57 ➲ compare SINGLE-DECKER **2** (*NAmE*) a SANDWICH made from three pieces of bread with two layers of food between them 雙層三明治

ˌdouble-ˈdensity *adj.* (*computing* 計) (of a computer disk 計算機磁盤) able to hold twice the amount of data as other older disks of the same size 倍密度的；雙倍容量的

ˌdouble ˈdigits *noun* [pl.] (*NAmE*) = DOUBLE FIGURES ▸ **ˌdouble-ˈdigit** *adj.* (*NAmE*) = DOUBLE-FIGURE

ˌdouble ˈDutch *noun* [U] (*BrE*, *informal*) speech or writing that is impossible to understand, and that seems to be nonsense 晦澀的言語（或文字）；莫名其妙的話

ˌdouble-ˈedged *adj.* **1** (of a knife, etc. 刀等) having two cutting edges 雙刃的 **2** (of a remark, comment, etc. 言語、評論等) having two possible meanings 意義雙關的；可有兩種解釋的；模稜兩可的 SYN **ambiguous** **3** having two different parts or uses, often parts that contrast with each other 有雙重效果的，有雙重作用的（常指形成鮮明對比的兩部份）：*the double-edged quality of life in a small town—security and boredom* 小城鎮生活的雙重性——安全但乏味

IDM **be a double-edged ˈsword/ˈweapon** to be sth that has both advantages and disadvantages 既有優點也有缺點；是一把雙刃劍

double en·ten·dre /ˌduːbl ɒ̃ˈtɒ̃drə; *NAmE* ɑːˈtɑ̃ːdrə/ *noun* (from *French*) a word or phrase that can be understood in two different ways, one of which usually refers to sex（通常帶有猥褻含意的）雙關語

ˌdouble-entry ˈbookkeeping *noun* [U] (*business* 商) a system of keeping financial records in which each piece of business is recorded as a CREDIT in one account and a DEBIT in another 複式記賬法，複式簿記（將每個賬項分別登入貸記和借記）

ˌdouble ˈfault *noun* (in TENNIS 網球) the loss of a point caused by a player not SERVING correctly twice 雙發失誤（因兩次發球失誤輸掉的一分）▸ **ˌdouble-ˈfault** *verb* [I]

ˌdouble ˈfeature *noun* (*NAmE*) = DOUBLE BILL

D

D

ˌ**double ˈfigures** (*especially BrE*) (*NAmE* usually ˌ**double ˈdigits**) *noun* [pl.] used to describe a number that is not less than 10 and not more than 99 兩位數： *Inflation is in **double figures**.* 通貨膨脹率達兩位數。 ▸ ˌ**double-ˈfigure** (*especially BrE*) (*NAmE* usually ˌ**double-ˈdigit**) *adj.* [only before noun]： *a double-figure pay rise* 兩位數的工資漲幅

ˌ**double ˈglazing** *noun* [U] (*especially BrE*) windows that have two layers of glass with a space between them, designed to make the room warmer and to reduce noise 雙層玻璃窗 ➲ COLLOCATIONS at DECORATE ▸ ˌ**double-ˈglaze** *verb* **~ sth** ˌ**double-ˈglazed** *adj.*： *double-glazed windows* 雙層玻璃窗

ˌ**double-ˈheader** *noun* (*NAmE*) (in BASEBALL 棒球) two games that are played on the same day, traditionally on a Sunday, and usually by the same two teams 一日連賽兩場（傳統上在星期日，通常為相同的兩個隊）

ˌ**double ˈhelix** *noun* (*biology* 生) the structure of DNA, consisting of two connected long thin pieces that form a SPIRAL shape 雙螺旋（脫氧核糖核酸的結構）

ˌ**double ˈjeopardy** *noun* [U] (in US law 美國法律) the fact of taking sb to court twice for the same crime, or punishing sb twice for the same reason. This is not allowed under the Fifth AMENDMENT of the US CONSTITUTION.（對同一罪行的）重複起訴，（因同一原因的）兩次懲罰（這種情況為美國憲法第五修正案所禁止）

ˌ**double-ˈjointed** *adj.* having joints in your fingers, arms, etc. that allow you to bend them both backwards and forwards 有雙關節的；關節能前後彎曲的

ˌ**double ˈlife** *noun* a life of a person who leads two different lives which are kept separate from each other, usually because one of them involves secret, often illegal or immoral, activities 雙重人格的生活（常指其中一重人格涉及非法或不道德行為）： *to **live/lead a double life*** 過着雙重人格的生活

ˌ**double ˈnegative** *noun* (*grammar* 語法) a negative statement containing two negative words. 'I didn't say nothing' is a double negative because it contains two negative words, 'n't' and 'nothing'. This use is not considered correct in standard English. 雙重否定（I didn't say nothing 是雙重否定句，包含 n't 和 nothing 兩個否定詞，此用法在標準英語中被視為不正確）

ˌ**double-ˈpark** *verb* [T, I, usually passive] **~ (sth)** to park a car or other vehicle beside one that is already parked in a street 並排停放（將車停在已停放於路邊的車輛旁）： *A car stood double-parked almost in the middle of the road.* 一輛車並排停在路邊另一輛車旁，幾乎佔據了路的中央。 ◇ *I'll have to rush—I'm double-parked.* 我得趕緊點，我這是並排停車。

ˌ**double ˈplay** *noun* (*NAmE*) (in BASEBALL 棒球) a situation in which two players are put out (= made to finish their attempt at scoring a RUN) 雙殺

ˌ**double ˈquick** *adv.* (*BrE, informal*) very quickly 飛快；快極了 ▸ ˌ**double-ˈquick** *adj.* [only before noun]： *The TV was repaired in **double-quick time**.* 這電視機一會兒就修好了。

ˌ**double ˈrhyme** *noun* [U] (in poetry 詩歌) a pair of words which have two parts ending with the same sounds, for example 'reading' and 'speeding' 雙重韻律詞對，雙韻詞對（有兩處末尾發音相同的兩個詞，如 reading 和 speeding）

ˌ**double ˈroom** (also **double**) *noun* a bedroom for two people 雙人房間

double·speak /ˈdʌblspiːk/ (also ˈ**double·talk**) *noun* [U] language that is intended to make people believe sth which is not true, or that can be understood in two different ways 欺人之談；模稜兩可的用詞；含糊其辭的說法

ˌ**double ˈstandard** *noun* a rule or moral principle that is unfair because it is used in one situation, but not in another, or because it treats one group of people in a way that is different from the treatment of another 雙重標準；雙重道德標準

doub·let /ˈdʌblət/ *noun* a short, tightly fitting jacket worn by men from the 14th to the 17th century（14–17 世紀男子穿的）緊身短上衣： *dressed in **doublet and hose*** 穿着緊身衣褲

ˌ**double ˈtake** *noun* if you **do a double take**, you wait for a moment before you react to sth that has happened, because it is very surprising 愣了一會兒才恍然大悟的反應

double·talk /ˈdʌbltɔːk/ *noun* [U] = DOUBLESPEAK

double·think /ˈdʌblθɪŋk/ *noun* [U] the act of holding two opposite opinions or beliefs at the same time; the ability to do this 雙重思想，雙重思考（同時保持兩種矛盾的看法或信仰）；雙重思考能力

ˌ**double ˈtime** *noun* [U] twice sb's normal pay, that they earn for working at times which are not normal working hours（付給加班者的）雙倍工資

ˌ**double ˈvision** *noun* [U] if you have **double vision**, you can see two things where there is actually only one 複視（將一個物體看成兩個影像）

doub·loon /dʌˈbluːn/ *noun* (in the past) a Spanish gold coin 達布隆（西班牙舊時的金幣）

doubly /ˈdʌbli/ *adv.* (used before adjectives 置於形容詞前) **1** more than usual 更加；越發；倍加： ***doubly difficult/hard/important*** 越發困難／努力／重要 ◇ *I made doubly sure I locked all the doors when I went out.* 我一再查看所有的門都鎖好後才出門。 **2** in two ways; for two reasons 在兩方面；由於雙重原因： *I was doubly attracted to the house—by its size and its location.* 我喜歡這房子有兩方面的原因 —— 大小合適而且地點好。

doubt 0-w /daʊt/ *noun, verb*

■ ***noun*** 0-w [U, C] a feeling of being uncertain about sth or not believing sth 疑惑；疑問；不確定；不相信： *a feeling of doubt and uncertainty* 遲疑不定的感受 ◇ **~ (about sth)** ***There is some doubt** about the best way to do it.* 這件事怎麼做才是最佳辦法有點吃不準。 ◇ *The article **raised doubts** about how effective the new drug really was.* 這篇文章對這種新藥的實效有多大提出了疑問。 ◇ **~ (that ...)** ***There is no doubt** at all that we did the right thing.* 毫無疑問我們做得對。 ◇ **~ (as to sth)** *If you are **in any doubt as to whether** you should be doing these exercises, consult your doctor.* 如果你拿不準是否應進行這些運動，咨詢一下醫生好了。 ◇ *New evidence has **cast doubt on** the guilt of the man jailed for the crime.* 新的證據使人們對這個犯罪入獄的男子是否有罪產生了懷疑。 ◇ *She knew **without a shadow of a doubt** that he was lying to her.* 她十分清楚他在對她撒謊。 ◇ *Whether he will continue to be successful in future is **open to doubt**.* 他今後能否繼續獲得成功值得懷疑。 ➲ LANGUAGE BANK at IMPERSONAL

IDM **beyond (any) ˈdoubt** in a way that shows that sth is completely certain 無疑；確實： *The research showed beyond doubt that smoking contributes to heart disease.* 這項研究確實表明吸煙會導致心臟病。 ◇ (*law* 律) *The prosecution was able to establish **beyond reasonable doubt** that the woman had been lying.* 控方能夠確切無疑地證實這個女人一直在撒謊。 **be in ˈdoubt** 0-w to be uncertain 不肯定；不確定；拿不準： *The success of the system is not in doubt.* 這種制度的成功確定無疑。 **have your ˈdoubts (about sth)** to have reasons why you are not certain about whether sth is good or whether sth good will happen（有理由）不相信；對（某事）持懷疑態度： *I've had my doubts about his work since he joined the firm.* 自從他加入事務所以來，我對他的工作一直有懷疑。 ◇ *It may be all right. Personally, I have my doubts.* 這或許行，但我個人持懷疑態度。 **if in ˈdoubt** used to give advice to sb who cannot decide what to do 如果沒把握；如果拿不準： *If in doubt, wear black.* 拿不定主意就穿黑色衣服。 ˌ**no ˈdoubt** **1** 0-w used when you are saying that sth is probable 無疑；很可能： *No doubt she'll call us when she gets there.* 她到達那裏時必定會給我們打電話。 **2** 0-w used when you are saying that sth is certainly true 無疑；確實地： *He's made some great movies. There's **no doubt about it**.* 他拍了一些非常出色的影片，這一點是毫無疑問的。 **without/beyond ˈdoubt** 0-w used when you are giving your opinion and emphasizing the point that you are making 毫無疑問；的確： *This meeting has been, without doubt, one of the most useful* *we have had so far.* 這無疑是我們迄今為止最有用的一次會議。➲ more at BENEFIT *n.*

■ *verb* **1** to feel uncertain about sth; to feel that sth is not true, will probably not happen, etc. 懷疑；無把握；不能肯定；認為…未必可能：**~ sth** *There seems no reason to doubt her story.* 似乎沒有理由懷疑她所說的話。◇ *'Do you think England will win?'—' **I doubt it**.'* "你認為英格蘭隊會取勝嗎？" "不一定。" ◇ **~ (that)** … *I never doubted (that) she would come.* 我從未懷疑過她會來。◇ **~ whether, if, etc.** … *I **doubt whether/if** the new one will be any better.* 我不敢肯定這個新的是否會好些。**2 ~ sb/sth** to not trust sb/sth; to not believe sb 懷疑；不相信；不信任：*I had no reason to doubt him.* 我沒有理由不相信他。▸ **doubt·er** *noun*

doubt·ful /ˈdaʊtfl/ *adj.* **1** (of a person 人) not sure; uncertain and feeling doubt 拿不定主意；不確定；懷疑 SYN **dubious**：**~ (about sth)** *Rose was doubtful about the whole idea.* 羅斯對整個設想持懷疑態度。◇ **~ (about doing sth)** *He was doubtful about accepting extra work.* 他拿不定主意是否接受額外工作。**2** unlikely; not probable 未必；難說；不大可能：**~ (if …)** *It's doubtful if this painting is a Picasso.* 這未必就是畢加索的畫。◇ **~ (that …)** *With her injuries it's doubtful that she'll ever walk again.* 她多處受傷，今後能否行走還很難說。◇ **~ (whether …)** *It's doubtful whether the car will last another year.* 這輛汽車未必還能用上一年。◇ **~ (for sth)** *He is injured and is doubtful for the game tomorrow* (= unlikely to play). 他受了傷，明天未必能參賽。**3** [not usually before noun] (of a thing 事情) uncertain and likely to get worse 不明朗；懸而未定；可能變糟：*At the beginning of the war things were looking very doubtful.* 戰爭剛開始時，形勢看上去很不明朗。**4** [only before noun] of low value; probably not genuine or of a quality that you can rely on 低劣的；未必是真的；靠不住的 SYN **dubious**：*This wine is of doubtful quality.* 這酒的質量有問題。▸ **doubt·ful·ly** /-fəli/ *adv.*

doubt·ing Thomas /ˌdaʊtɪŋ ˈtɒməs; *NAmE* ˈtɑːm-/ *noun* [sing.] (*old-fashioned*) a person who is unlikely to believe sth until they see proof of it 懷疑一切的人；多疑的人；有證據才相信的人 ORIGIN From St Thomas in the Bible, who did not believe that Jesus Christ had risen from the dead until he saw and touched his wounds. 源自《聖經》中的多馬，他直到看見和觸摸到耶穌基督的傷口才相信耶穌已從死裏復活。

doubt·less /ˈdaʊtləs/ *adv.* (also *less frequent* **doubt·less·ly**) almost certainly 大概；幾乎肯定地 SYN **without doubt**：*He would doubtless disapprove of what Kelly was doing.* 他大概不會贊同凱利做的事。

douche /duːʃ/ *noun* a method of washing inside a woman's VAGINA using a stream of water（婦女陰道）沖洗法，灌洗法 ▸ **douche** *verb* [I, T] **~ (sth)**

dough /dəʊ; *NAmE* doʊ/ *noun* **1** [U, sing.] a mixture of flour, water, etc. that is made into bread and PASTRY（用於製麵包和糕點的）生麪糰：*Knead the dough on a floured surface.* 在撒了麪粉的案板上揉麪糰。**2** [U] (*old-fashioned, slang*) money 錢

dough·nut (also **donut** especially in *NAmE*) /ˈdəʊnʌt; *NAmE* ˈdoʊ-/ *noun* a small cake made of fried dough, usually in the shape of a ring, or round and filled with jam/jelly, fruit, cream, etc. 炸麪圈，甜甜圈（常含果醬、水果、奶油等）

doughty /ˈdaʊti/ *adj.* (*old-fashioned*) brave and strong 勇敢強悍的

doula /ˈduːlə/ *noun* (*NAmE*) a woman whose role is to provide emotional support to a woman who is giving birth 產婦陪護（給產婦以心理支持）➲ compare MIDWIFE

dour /ˈdaʊə(r); *BrE* also dʊə(r); *NAmE* also dʊr/ *adj.* **1** (of a person 人) giving the impression of being unfriendly and severe 冷酷的；嚴厲的 **2** (of a thing, a place, or a situation 事物、地方或情況) not pleasant; with no features that make it lively or interesting 令人不快的；無生氣的：*The city, drab and dour by day, is transformed at night.* 這座城市白天死氣沉沉、單調乏味，晚上就完全變了樣。◇ *The game proved to be a dour struggle, with both men determined to win.* 這次比賽結果成為一場惡戰，因為兩個人都志在必得。▸ **dour·ly** *adv.*

douse (also **dowse**) /daʊs/ *verb* **1 ~ sth (with sth)** to stop a fire from burning by pouring water over it; to put out a light 澆滅（火）；熄（燈）**2 ~ sb/sth (in/with sth)** to pour a lot of liquid over sb/sth; to SOAK sb/sth in liquid 往…上潑水；把…浸在液體裏：*The car was doused in petrol and set alight.* 這輛汽車被澆上汽油點燃了。

dove[1] /dʌv/ *noun* **1** a bird of the PIGEON family. The white dove is often used as a symbol of peace. 鴿子（白鴿常作為和平的象徵）：*A dove cooed softly.* 一隻鴿子輕柔地咕咕叫。◇ *He wore a dove-grey suit.* 他穿了一套鴿灰色西裝。➲ see also TURTLE DOVE **2** a person, especially a politician, who prefers peace and discussion to war 鴿派人物，温和派人物（尤指願意和平與談判而不願戰爭的從政者）OPP **hawk**

dove[2] /dəʊv; *NAmE* doʊv/ (*NAmE*) *past tense of* DIVE

dove·cote /ˈdʌvkɒt; ˈdʌvkəʊt; *NAmE* -kɑːt; -koʊt/ (also **dove·cot** /ˈdʌvkɒt; *NAmE* -kɑːt/) *noun* a small building for DOVES or PIGEONS to live in 鴿房；鴿舍；鴿棚

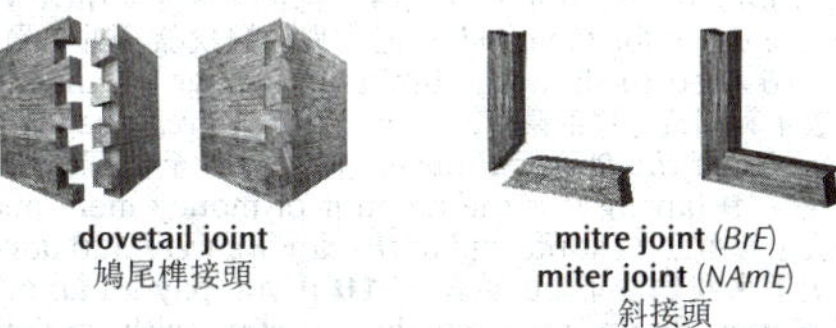

dovetail joint 鳩尾榫接頭

mitre joint (*BrE*) miter joint (*NAmE*) 斜接頭

dove·tail /ˈdʌvteɪl/ *verb, noun*

■ *verb* [I, T] (*formal*) **~ (sth) (with/into sth)** if two things **dovetail** or if one thing **dovetails** with another, they fit together well 吻合；與…吻合：*My plans dovetailed nicely with hers.* 我的計劃與她的計劃正好吻合。

■ *noun* (also **ˌdovetail ˈjoint**) a joint for fixing two pieces of wood together 鳩尾榫接頭

dov·ish /ˈdʌvɪʃ/ *adj.* preferring to use peaceful discussion rather than military action in order to solve a political problem 温和派的；鴿派的 OPP **hawkish**

dow·ager /ˈdaʊədʒə(r)/ *noun* **1** a woman of high social rank who has a title from her dead husband（具有亡夫頭銜的）孀居貴婦：*the dowager Duchess of Norfolk* 諾福克公爵遺孀 **2** (*informal*) an impressive, usually rich, old woman 氣度不凡的老年貴婦人

dowdy /ˈdaʊdi/ *adj.* (**dow·dier**, **dow·di·est**) **1** (of a woman 女人) not attractive or fashionable 缺乏魅力的；不時髦的；過時的 **2** (of a thing 物件) dull or boring and not attractive 單調的；不雅致的；不美觀的 SYN **drab**：*a dowdy dress* 單調的連衣裙

dow·el /ˈdaʊəl/ (also **ˈdowel rod**) *noun* a small piece of wood, plastic, etc. in the shape of a CYLINDER, used to fix larger pieces of wood, plastic, etc. together 暗榫

dowel·ling (*BrE*) (*US* **dowel·ing**) /ˈdaʊəlɪŋ/ *noun* [U] short pieces of wooden, metal or plastic ROD that are used for holding parts of sth together 榫釘

the Dow Jones Index /ˌdaʊ ˈdʒəʊnz ɪndeks; *NAmE* ˈdʒoʊnz/ (also **ˌDow ˈJones average, the ˈDow**) *noun* [sing.] a list of the share prices of 30 US industrial companies that can be used to compare the prices to previous levels 道瓊斯（工業平均）指數

down /daʊn/ *adv., prep., verb, adj., noun*

■ *adv.* HELP For the special uses of **down** in phrasal verbs, look at the entries for the verbs. For example **climb down** is in the phrasal verb section at **climb**. * down 在短語動詞中的特殊用法見有關動詞詞條。如 climb down 在詞條 climb 的短語動詞部份。**1** to or at a lower place or position 向下；朝下；在下面：*She jumped down off the chair.* 她跳下椅子。◇ *He looked down at her.* 他低頭看着她。◇ *We watched as the sun went down.* 我們看着夕陽西沉。◇ *She bent down to pick up her glove.* 她俯身撿起了手套。◇ *Mary's not down yet* (= she is still upstairs). 瑪麗還沒下樓呢。◇ *The baby* *can't keep any food down* (= in her body). 這嬰兒吃什麼吐什麼。 **2** ⊶ from a standing or vertical position to a sitting or horizontal one（坐、倒、躺）下： *Please sit down.* 請坐。◇ *He had to go and lie down for a while.* 他不得不去躺一會兒。 **3** ⊶ at a lower level or rate 在較低水平；下降；下跌： *Prices have gone down recently.* 最近物價下降了。◇ *We're already two goals down* (= the other team has two goals more). 我們已落後對方兩球。 ➲ LANGUAGE BANK at FALL **4** ⊶ used to show that the amount or strength of sth is lower, or that there is less activity（數量、力量、活動等）減少，減弱，降低： *Turn the music down!* 把音樂聲關小點！◇ *The class settled down and she began the lesson.* 課堂安靜下來她便開始上課了。 **5** (in a CROSSWORD 縱橫填字遊戲) reading from top to bottom, not from side to side 由上至下： *I can't do 3 down.* 我填不出第 3 個豎行。 **6** ⊶ to or in the south of a country 向南方；在南方： *They flew down to Texas.* 他們乘飛機南下去得克薩斯州了。◇ *Houses are more expensive down south.* 南邊的房屋價格要貴些。 **7** ⊶ on paper; on a list（寫）在紙上；（列）在表格上： *Did you get that down?* 你寫下來了嗎？◇ *I always write everything down.* 我不管什麼事情都記下來。◇ *Have you got me down for the trip?* 你把我列入這次旅行的名單了嗎？ **8** used to show the limits in a range or an order（表示範圍或順序的限度）下至，直至： *Everyone will be there, from the Principal down.* 從校長下至每個人都將到場。 **9** having lost the amount of money mentioned 失去（錢數）： *At the end of the day we were £20 down.* 一天下來我們少了 20 英鎊。 **10** if you pay an amount of money **down**, you pay that to start with, and the rest later（錢）先付，預付 **11** (*informal*) used to say how far you have got in a list of things you have to do 已完成數量（或進度）： *Well, I've seen six apartments so far. That's six down and four to go!* 好啦，到目前為止我已看了六套公寓房。看完六套還有四套要去看呢！ **12** (*informal*) to or at a local place such as a shop/store, pub, etc. 到，去，在（當地的商店、酒館等地方）： *I'm just going down to the post office.* 我正要到郵局去。◇ *I saw him down at the shops.* 我剛才看到他在那邊的商店裏。 **HELP** In informal British English, **to** and **at** are often left out after **down** in this sense. 在非正式的英式英語中，down 作此義時後面的 to 和 at 經常省略： *He's gone down the shops.*

IDM **be down to sb** (*informal*) to be the responsibility of sb 是某人的責任；由某人負責： *It's down to you to check the door.* 檢查門是否關好是你的事。 **be down to sb/sth** to be caused by a particular person or thing 由…引起（或造成）： *She claimed her problems were down to the media.* 她聲稱她的問題是媒體造成的。 **be down to sth** to have only a little money left 只剩下（一點兒錢）： *I'm down to my last dollar.* 我只剩下最後一塊錢了。 **be/go down with sth** to have or catch an illness 患…病；得…病 **down through sth** (*formal*) during a long period of time 在（相當長的一段）時間內： *Down through the years this town has seen many changes.* 多年來這座城鎮發生了許多變化。 **down to the last, smallest, final, etc. sth** including every small part or detail of sth 非常詳盡地：*She organized everything down to the last detail.* 她每件事情都安排得滴水不漏。 **down 'under** (*informal*) to or in Australia and/or New Zealand 到，向，在（澳大利亞和／或新西蘭） **down with sb/sth** used to say that you are opposed to sth, or to a person 打倒： *The crowds chanted 'Down with NATO!'* 人群有節奏地反複高喊"打倒北約！" ➲ more at MAN *n.*

■ ***prep.*** **1** ⊶ from a high or higher point on sth to a lower one（從高處）向下，往下： *The stone rolled down the hill.* 石頭滾下山坡。◇ *Tears ran down her face.* 淚水順着她的臉龐流下來。◇ *Her hair hung down her back to her waist.* 她的長髮披在背上直垂腰際。 **2** ⊶ along; towards the direction in which you are facing 沿着；順着；朝着： *He lives just down the street.* 他就住在街那頭。◇ *Go down the road till you reach the traffic lights.* 沿着這條路一直走到紅綠燈處。◇ *There's a bridge a mile down the river from here.* 從這裏沿河而下一英里處有座橋。 **3** all through a period of time 貫穿…時間；遍及…時期： *an exhibition of costumes down the ages* (= from all periods of history) 歷代服裝展覽

■ ***verb*** (*informal*) **1** ~ **sth** to finish a drink or eat sth quickly（一下子）喝下，吃下，嚥下： *We downed our coffees and left.* 我們一口氣喝完咖啡就離開了。 **2** ~ **sb/sth** to force sb/sth down to the ground 使倒下；擊倒： *to down a plane* 擊落一架飛機

IDM **,down 'tools** (*BrE*) (of workers 工人) to stop work; to go on strike 撂下工作；罷工

■ ***adj.*** [not before noun] **1** (*informal*) sad or depressed 悲哀；沮喪；情緒低落： *I feel a bit down today.* 我今天有點悶悶不樂。 **2** (of a computer or computer system 計算機或計算機系統) not working 停機；停止運行： *The system was down all morning.* 這系統整個上午都停機。 ➲ see also DOWNTIME (1) **IDM** see HIT *v.*, KICK *v.*, LUCK *n.*, MOUTH *n.*

■ ***noun*** ➲ see also DOWNS **1** [U] the very fine soft feathers of a bird（鳥的）絨羽，絨毛： *duck down* 鴨絨 **2** [U] fine soft hair 絨毛；軟毛；汗毛 ➲ see also DOWNY **3** [C] (in AMERICAN FOOTBALL 美式足球) one of a series of four chances to carry the ball forward ten yards that a team is allowed. These series continue until the team loses the ball or fails to go forward ten yards in four downs. 進攻分段，10 碼進攻（球隊可向前推進 10 碼持球進攻的四次機會。球隊在連續四次進攻中失球或未能推進 10 碼即不能繼續）

IDM **have a 'down on sb/sth** (*BrE, informal*) to have a bad opinion of a person or thing 對…評價不好；瞧不起；厭惡 ➲ more at UP *n.*

,down and 'out *adj.* (of a person 人) **1** without money, a home or a job, and living on the streets 窮困潦倒；一無所有： *a novel about being down and out in London* 一部以倫敦的流浪生活為題材的小說 **2** certain to be defeated 必輸無疑的；必定失敗的

'down-and-out *noun* a person without money, a home or a job, who lives on the streets 窮困潦倒的人；無家可歸的人

,down at 'heel *adj.* looking less attractive and fashionable than before, usually because of a lack of money 潦倒的；寒酸的： *The town has become very down at heel.* 這座城鎮已變得破敗不堪。◇ *a down-at-heel hotel* 寒酸的旅館

down·beat /'daʊnbi:t/ *adj.* (*informal*) **1** dull or depressing; not having much hope for the future 沉悶的；令人沮喪的；悲觀的： *The overall mood of the meeting was downbeat.* 整個會場的氣氛是沉悶的。 **OPP** **upbeat** **2** not showing strong feelings or enthusiasm 不強烈的；消沉的；無熱情的

down·cast /'daʊnkɑ:st; *NAmE* -kæst/ *adj.* **1** (of eyes 眼睛) looking down 向下的；低垂的： *Eyes downcast, she continued eating.* 她低垂雙眼，繼續吃。 **2** (of a person or an expression 人或表情) sad or depressed 悲哀的；沮喪的；垂頭喪氣的 **SYN** **dejected**： *A group of downcast men stood waiting for food.* 一群人垂頭喪氣地站在那兒等着吃飯。

down·draught (*BrE*) (*NAmE* **down·draft**) /'daʊndrɑ:ft; *NAmE* -dræft/ *noun* a downward movement of air, for example down a CHIMNEY 下曳氣流；（煙囪等的）倒灌風

down·er /'daʊnə(r)/ *noun* (*informal*) **1** [usually pl.] a drug, especially a BARBITURATE, that relaxes you or makes you want to sleep 鎮靜藥，抑制藥（尤指巴比土酸鹽） ➲ compare UPPER *n.* (2) **2** an experience that makes you feel sad or depressed 令人悲哀（或沮喪）的經歷： *Not getting the promotion was a real downer.* 未得到提升真讓人很沮喪。◇ *He's really **on a downer*** (= very depressed). 他確實很鬱悶。

down·fall /'daʊnfɔ:l/ *noun* [sing.] the loss of a person's money, power, social position, etc.; the thing that causes this 衰落；衰敗；垮台；衰落（或衰敗、垮台）的原因： *The sex scandal finally led to his downfall.* 這樁緋聞最終使他身敗名裂。◇ *Greed was her downfall.* 貪得無厭就是她墮落的緣由。

down·grade /,daʊn'greɪd/ *verb* **1** ~ **sb/sth** (**from sth**) (**to sth**) to move sb/sth down to a lower rank or level 使降職；使降級： *She's been downgraded from principal to vice-principal.* 她已從校長降職為副校長。 **2** ~ **sth/sb** to make sth/sb seem less important or valuable than it/they really are 貶低；降低；低估 ➲ compare

UPGRADE ▸ **down·grad·ing** *noun* [U, C] ： *a downgrading of diplomatic relations* 外交關係降格

down·heart·ed /ˌdaʊnˈhɑːtɪd; *NAmE* -ˈhɑːrtɪd/ *adj.* [not before noun] feeling depressed or sad 情緒低落；垂頭喪氣；悲哀： *We're disappointed by these results but we're not downhearted.* 我們對這些結果感到失望，但是並未喪失信心。

down·hill *adv., adj., noun*

■ ***adv.*** /ˌdaʊnˈhɪl/ towards the bottom of a hill; in a direction that goes down 向山下；向下： *to* ***run/walk/cycle downhill*** 跑 / 走 / 騎車下山 OPP **uphill**

IDM **ˌgo downˈhill** to get worse in quality, health, etc. （質量、健康等）每況愈下，走下坡路，惡化 SYN **deteriorate**： *Their marriage went downhill after the first child was born.* 自第一個孩子出生後他們的婚姻便開始走下坡路了。

■ ***adj.*** /ˌdaʊnˈhɪl/ going or sloping towards the bottom of a hill 下山的；下坡的；下斜的： *a downhill path* 下山的路 OPP **uphill**

IDM **be (all) downhill | be ˌdownhill all the ˈway** (*informal*) **1** to be easy compared to what came before（與前面的相比較）容易： *It's all downhill from here. We'll soon be finished.* 從這以後就容易了。我們很快就會結束。 **2** to become worse or less successful 每況愈下；走下坡路；不斷惡化： *It's been all downhill for his career since then, with four defeats in five games.* 從那時起他的戰績便江河日下，五場比賽輸掉了四場。◇ *I started work as a journalist and it was downhill all the way for my health.* 我開始當記者後，身體每況愈下。

■ ***noun*** /ˈdaʊnhɪl/ [U] the type of SKIING in which you go directly down a mountain; a race in which people SKI down a mountain （滑雪）速降，速降比賽 ➲ VISUAL VOCAB page V48 ➲ compare CROSS-COUNTRY

ˌdown-ˈhome *adj.* (*NAmE*) used to describe a person or thing that reminds you of a simple way of life, typical of the country, not the town 淳樸的；鄉村的；有鄉土味的

Down·ing Street /ˈdaʊnɪŋ striːt/ *noun* [sing.] (not used with *the* 不與 the 連用) a way of referring to the British prime minister and government, taken from the name of the street where the prime minister lives 唐寧街，英國首相，英國政府（英國首相官邸所在街道的名稱）： *Downing Street issued a statement late last night.* 昨天深夜唐寧街發表了一項聲明。

down·light·er /ˈdaʊnlaɪtə(r)/ (also **down·light** /ˈdaʊnlaɪt/) *noun* a light on a wall which shines downwards（安裝於牆壁上的）下照燈具 ➲ compare UPLIGHTER

down·link /ˈdaʊnlɪŋk/ *noun* a communications link by which information is received from space or from an aircraft 下行鏈路，下鏈（從太空或飛行器接收信號的通訊方式）▸ **down·link** *verb*： **~ sth** *Any organization can downlink the program without charge.* 任何機構都可以免費下載這一程序。

down·load *verb, noun*

■ ***verb*** /ˌdaʊnˈləʊd; *NAmE* -ˈloʊd/ **~ sth** (*computing* 計) to move data to a smaller computer system from a larger one 下載；下裝 OPP **upload** ➲ COLLOCATIONS at EMAIL ➲ compare LOAD *v.* (5)

■ ***noun*** /ˈdaʊnləʊd; *NAmE* -loʊd/ (*computing* 計) data which is downloaded from another computer system 已下載的數據資料 ▸ **down·load·able** /ˌdaʊnˈləʊdəbl; *NAmE* -ˈloʊd-/ *adj.*

down·low /ˈdaʊnləʊ; *NAmE* -loʊ/ *noun, adj.*

■ ***noun*** **the downlow** [sing.] (*informal*) **~ on (sb/sth)** the true facts about sb/sth, especially those considered most important to know（有關…的）實情，重要事實 SYN **low-down**： *the website that gives you the downlow on the best movies* 為您提供最優秀電影情報的網站

IDM **on the ˈdownlow** secretly; not wanting other people to discover what you are doing 秘密地；暗中

■ ***adj.*** [only before noun] (*slang*) used to refer to a man who appears to be HETEROSEXUAL, but secretly has sex with men 隱秘同性戀男子的

down·mark·et /ˌdaʊnˈmɑːkɪt; *NAmE* -ˈmɑːrkɪt/ (*BrE*) (*NAmE* **down·scale**) *adj.* (*disapproving*) cheap and of poor quality 價廉質次的；下品的；低檔的： *The company wants to break away from its downmarket image.* 這家公司想擺脱它面向低消費階層的形象。 OPP **upmarket** ▸ **down·mark·et** *adv.*： *To get more viewers the TV station was forced to* ***go downmarket.*** 為了爭取更多觀眾，電視台不得不迎合低收入階層。

down·most /ˈdaʊnməʊst; *NAmE* -moʊst/ *adj.* (*especially BrE*) nearest to the ground or lower level 最下面的；最低的 ▸ **down·most** *adv.*

ˌdown ˈpayment *noun* a sum of money that is given as the first part of a larger payment（分期付款的）首期付款；預付金；訂金： *We are saving for a down payment on a house.* 我們正攢錢支付買房的首付金。 ➲ COLLOCATIONS at HOUSE

down·pipe /ˈdaʊnpaɪp/ (*BrE*) (*US* **ˈfall-pipe**) *noun* a pipe for carrying water from a roof down to the ground or to a DRAIN 落水管；雨水管

down·play /ˌdaʊnˈpleɪ/ *verb* **~ sth** to make people think that sth is less important than it really is 對…輕描淡寫；使輕視；貶低 SYN **play down**： *The coach is downplaying the team's poor performance.* 教練對這個隊的拙劣表現不以為然。

down·pour /ˈdaʊnpɔː(r)/ *noun* [usually sing.] a heavy fall of rain that often starts suddenly 傾盆大雨；暴雨；驟雨

down·right /ˈdaʊnraɪt/ *adj.* [only before noun] used as a way of emphasizing sth negative or unpleasant（強調反面的或令人不快的事物）徹頭徹尾的，十足的，完全的： *There was suspicion and even downright hatred between them.* 他們之間相互懷疑甚至極度仇恨。▸ **downright** *adv.*： *She couldn't think of anything to say that wasn't downright rude.* 她除了破口大罵之外再也說不出什麼。◇ *It's not just stupid—it's downright dangerous.* 這豈止是愚蠢，簡直是危險。

down·river /ˌdaʊnˈrɪvə(r)/ *adv.* = DOWNSTREAM

downs /daʊnz/ *noun* **the downs** [pl.] an area of open land with low hills, especially in southern England（尤指英格蘭南部的）開闊的丘陵地

down·scale /ˌdaʊnˈskeɪl/ (*NAmE*) (*BrE* **down·mark·et**) *adj.* (*disapproving*) cheap and of poor quality 價廉質次的；下品的；低檔的 OPP **upscale** ▸ **down·scale** *adv.*

down·shift /ˈdaʊnʃɪft/ *verb* **1** [I] (*NAmE*) to change to a lower gear in a vehicle（車輛）調到低速擋，換低擋 **2** [I] to change to a job or style of life where you may earn less but which puts less pressure on you and involves less stress 減慢節奏（為減輕壓力而更換工作或生活方式） ➲ COLLOCATIONS at TOWN ▸ **down·shift** *noun* [C, U] **down·shift·er** *noun*

down·side /ˈdaʊnsaɪd/ *noun* [sing.] the disadvantages or less positive aspects of sth 缺點；不利方面 OPP **upside**

down·size /ˈdaʊnsaɪz/ *verb* [I, T] **~ (sth)** (*business* 商) to reduce the number of people who work in a company, business, etc. in order to reduce costs（公司、企業等）裁員，精減 ➲ SYNONYMS at CUT ▸ **down·siz·ing** *noun* [U]

down·spout /ˈdaʊnspaʊt/ *noun* (*NAmE*) = DRAINPIPE (1)

ˈDown's syndrome (*NAmE* usually **ˈDown syndrome**) *noun* [U] a medical condition, caused by a fault with one CHROMOSOME, in which a person is born with particular physical characteristics and a mental ability that is below average 唐氏綜合症

down·stage /ˈdaʊnsteɪdʒ/ *adv.* towards the front of the stage in a theatre 向舞台前部 OPP **upstage** ▸ **downstage** *adj.*

down·stairs 🔑 /ˌdaʊnˈsteəz; *NAmE* -ˈsterz/ *adv., noun*

■ ***adv.*** 🔑 down the stairs; on or to a floor or a house or building lower than the one you are on, especially the one at ground level 順樓梯而下；在樓下；往樓下： *She rushed downstairs and burst into the kitchen.* 她衝下樓闖進廚房。◇ *Wait downstairs in the hall.* 在樓下大廳裏等着。 OPP **upstairs** ▸ **down·stairs** 🔑 *adj.* [only before noun]： *a downstairs bathroom* 樓下的盥洗室

■ ***noun*** 🔑 [sing.] the lower floor of a house or building, especially the one at ground level 樓下（尤指地面的一

D

層）: *We're painting the downstairs.* 我們在粉刷底層。 **OPP** **upstairs**

down·stream /ˌdaʊnˈstriːm/ *adv., adj.*
■ (also *less frequent* **down·river**) **adv. ~ (of/from sth)** in the direction in which a river flows 順流而下；在下游方向：*to **drift/float downstream*** 順水漂流／漂浮而下 ◇ *downstream of/from the bridge* 橋的下游方向 **OPP** **upstream**
■ **adj. 1** (also *less frequent* **down·river**) in a position along a river which is nearer the sea 在下游的：*downstream areas* 下游地區 **OPP** **upstream 2** happening as a consequence of sth that has happened earlier 引發的；導致的：*downstream effects* 隨之產生的後果

D

down·swing /ˈdaʊnswɪŋ/ *noun* [usually sing.] **1 ~ (in sth)** a situation in which sth gets worse or decreases over a period of time 惡化趨勢；向下走勢；下降：*the current downswing in the airline industry* 航空業目前的滑坡狀況 ◇ *He is on a career downswing.* 他在事業上正走下坡路。 **OPP** **upswing 2** (in GOLF 高爾夫球) the downward movement of a CLUB when a player is about to hit the ball 下揮杆

ˈDown syndrome *noun* [U] (*NAmE*) = DOWN'S SYNDROME

down·tick /ˈdaʊntɪk/ *noun* [C, usually sing.] (*NAmE, economics* 經) a small decrease in the level or value of sth, especially in the price of shares（尤指股價的）微跌，微落：*The shares were bought **on a downtick**.* 這些股票是在小幅下跌時買進的。 **OPP** **uptick**

down·time /ˈdaʊntaɪm/ *noun* [U] **1** the time during which a machine, especially a computer, is not working（尤指計算機的）停機時間，停止運行時間 ➲ compare UPTIME **2** (*especially NAmE*) the time when sb stops working and is able to relax 停工；休息：*Everyone needs a little downtime.* 大家都需要休息一下。

ˌdown to ˈearth *adj.* (*approving*) sensible and practical, in a way that is helpful and friendly 務實的；切合實際的

down·town /ˌdaʊnˈtaʊn/ *adv.* (*especially NAmE*) in or towards the centre of a city, especially its main business area 在市中心，往市中心（尤指商業中心區）：*to go/work downtown* 到商業中心區去；在商業中心區工作 ➲ COLLOCATIONS at TOWN ➲ compare MIDTOWN, TOWN CENTRE, UPTOWN ▸ **ˈdown·town** *adj.*：*a downtown store* 鬧市區的商店 **ˈdown·town** *noun* [U]：*a hotel in the heart of downtown* 市區中心的旅館

down·trend /ˈdaʊntrend/ *noun* [sing.] a situation in which business activity or performance decreases or becomes worse over a period of time（經濟活動或運作情況的）下降趨勢 **OPP** **uptrend**

down·trod·den /ˈdaʊntrɒdn; *NAmE* -trɑːdn/ *adj.* **downtrodden** people are treated so badly by the people with authority and power that they no longer have the energy or ability to fight back 受欺壓的；被蹂躪的；被踐踏的

down·turn /ˈdaʊntɜːn; *NAmE* -tɜːrn/ *noun* [usually sing.] **~ (in sth)** a fall in the amount of business that is done; a time when the economy becomes weaker（商業經濟的）衰退，下降，衰退期：*a **downturn in sales/trade/business*** 銷量／貿易／生意下跌 ◇ *the economic downturn of 2008/2009* * 2008／2009 年的經濟衰退 **OPP** **upturn**

down·ward 🔑 /ˈdaʊnwəd; *NAmE* -wərd/ *adj.* [usually before noun] moving or pointing towards a lower level 下降的；向下的：*the downward slope of a hill* 向下的山坡 ◇ *the downward trend in inflation* 通貨膨脹的下降趨勢 ◇ *She was trapped in a **downward spiral** of personal unhappiness.* 她陷入了個人不幸的漩渦難以自拔。 **OPP** **upward** ▸ **down·ward·ly** *adv.*

down·wards 🔑 /ˈdaʊnwədz; *NAmE* -wərdz/ (also **down·ward** especially in *NAmE*) *adv.* towards the ground or towards a lower level 向下：*She was lying **face downwards** on the grass.* 她俯臥在草地上。◇ *The garden sloped gently downwards to the river.* 花園向河邊呈緩坡傾斜。◇ *It was a policy welcomed by world leaders from the US president downwards.* 這一政策受到了美國總統乃至全世界領導人的歡迎。 **OPP** **upwards** ➲ LANGUAGE BANK at FALL

down·wind /ˌdaʊnˈwɪnd/ *adv.* in the direction in which the wind is blowing 順風地；在下風處：*sailing downwind* 順風航行 ◇ **~ of sth** *Warnings were issued to people living downwind of the fire to stay indoors.* 已經向住在火勢下風處的人們發出不要出門的警告。 **OPP** **upwind** ▸ **down·wind** *adj.*

downy /ˈdaʊni/ *adj.* covered in sth very soft, especially hair or feathers 絨毛覆蓋的；長着絨毛的；毛茸茸的 ➲ see also DOWN *n.* (1)

dowry /ˈdaʊri/ *noun* (*pl.* **-ies**) **1** money and/or property that, in some societies, a wife or her family must pay to her husband when they get married（新娘家給新郎的）嫁妝，陪嫁 **2** money and/or property that, in some societies, a husband must pay to his wife's family when they get married（新郎給新娘家的）彩禮，財禮

dowse /daʊz/ *verb* **1** [I] to look for underground water or minerals by using a special stick or long piece of metal that moves when it comes near water, etc. 用探測杆探尋（地下水或礦藏） **2** = DOUSE ▸ **dow·ser** *noun*

ˈdowsing rod *noun* a stick used when dowsing for water or minerals underground（探測地下水或礦藏的）探測杆

doxy /ˈdɒksi; *NAmE* ˈdɑːksi/ *noun* (*pl.* **-ies**) (*old use*) **1** a woman who is sb's lover 情婦 **2** a PROSTITUTE 妓女

doyen /ˈdɔɪən/ (*NAmE* usually **dean**) *noun* the most respected or most experienced member of a group or profession（某團體或職業中的）老前輩，資格最老者，元老：*Richard Dawkins, the doyen of evolutionary biologists* 理查德•道金斯——進化生物學家的泰斗

doy·enne /dɔɪˈen/ *noun* the most respected or most experienced woman member of a group or profession 地位最高的女子；資格最老的女子：*Martha Graham, the doyenne of American modern dance* 瑪莎•格雷厄姆——美國現代舞之母

doz. *abbr.* (in writing) DOZEN（書寫形式）（一）打，十二個：*2 doz. eggs* 兩打雞蛋

doze /dəʊz; *NAmE* doʊz/ *verb, noun*
■ **verb** [I] to sleep lightly for a short time 打瞌睡；打盹兒；小睡 ➲ SYNONYMS at SLEEP
PHR V **ˌdoze ˈoff** to go to sleep, especially during the day（尤指在日間）打瞌睡，打盹兒：*She dozed off in front of the fire.* 她在爐火前打起盹兒來。
■ **noun** [sing.] a short period of sleep, usually during the day（通常在日間的）瞌睡，小睡：*I had a doze on the train.* 我在火車上打了個盹兒。

dozen 🔑 /ˈdʌzn/ *noun, det.* (*pl.* **dozen**)
1 🔑 [C] (*abbr.* **doz.**) a group of twelve of the same thing（一）打；十二個：*Give me a dozen, please.* 請給我來一打。◇ *two dozen eggs* 兩打雞蛋 ◇ *three dozen red roses* 三打紅玫瑰 ➲ see also BAKER'S DOZEN **2** 🔑 [C] a group of approximately twelve people or things 十來個；十幾個；十多個：*several dozen/a few dozen people* 數十／幾十個人 ◇ *The company employs no more than **a couple of dozen** people.* 這家公司頂多雇用了幾十個人。◇ *Only about **half a dozen** people turned up.* 只有六七個人到了。◇ *There was only space for a **half-dozen** tables.* 只有擺六張桌子的地方。 **3** 🔑 **dozens** [pl.] (*informal*) a lot of people or things 許多；很多：*They arrived **in dozens*** (= in large numbers). 他們大批到達了。◇ **~ of sth** *I've been there dozens of times.* 我到過那裏很多次了。
IDM see DIME, NINETEEN, SIX

dozy /ˈdəʊzi; *NAmE* ˈdoʊzi/ *adj.* (*informal*) **1** not looking or feeling awake 想睡的；昏昏欲睡的；睏倦的 **2** (*BrE*) stupid; not intelligent 愚笨的；不聰明的

DPhil /ˌdiː ˈfɪl/ *noun* (*BrE*) the abbreviation for 'Doctor of Philosophy' 哲學博士（全寫為 Doctor of Philosophy）：*to **be/have/do a DPhil*** 是哲學博士；有／攻讀哲學博士學位 ◇ *James Mendelssohn DPhil* 哲學博士詹姆斯•門德爾松

dpi /ˌdiː piː ˈaɪ/ *abbr.* (*computing* 計) dots per inch (a measure of how clear the images produced by a printer, SCANNER, etc. are) 每英寸點數，點每英寸（打印機、掃描儀等的清晰度參數）

D

DPP /ˌdiː piː ˈpiː/ *abbr.* (in England and Wales) DIRECTOR OF PUBLIC PROSECUTIONS（英格蘭和威爾士的）檢察官

Dr (*BrE*) (also **Dr.** *NAmE, BrE*) *abbr.* **1** (in writing) Doctor（書寫形式）醫生，博士：*Dr (Jane) Walker*（簡）沃克博士 **2** (in street names) DRIVE（用於街道名）路，大道

drab /dræb/ *adj.* (**drab·ber**, **drab·best**) without interest or colour; dull and boring 單調乏味的；無光彩的；無生氣的：*a cold drab little office* 冷冰冰的小辦公室 ◇ *drab women, dressed in browns and greys* 身着棕灰二色衣服毫無光彩的女人 ▸ **drab·ness** *noun* [U]

drabs /dræbz/ *noun* IDM see DRIBS

drachma /ˈdrækmə/ *noun* (*pl.* **drachmas** or **drachmae** /ˈdrækmiː/) the former unit of money in Greece (replaced in 2002 by the euro) 德拉克馬（希臘貨幣單位，於 2002 年為歐元所取代）

dra·co·nian /drəˈkəʊniən; *NAmE* -ˈkoʊ-/ *adj.* (*formal*) (of a law, punishment, etc. 法律、懲罰等) extremely cruel and severe 德拉古式的；嚴酷的；殘忍的 ORIGIN From **Draco**, a legislator in ancient Athens who gave severe punishments for crimes, especially the punishment of being killed. 源自古雅典立法者德拉古，他嚴懲犯罪，尤其是施以死刑。

Drac·ula /ˈdrækjələ/ *noun* a character in many horror films who is a VAMPIRE. Vampires appear at night and suck the blood of their victims. 吸血鬼德古拉（恐怖電影角色）ORIGIN From the novel *Dracula* by Bram Stoker. 源自布拉姆 • 斯托克的小説《吸血鬼德古拉》(Dracula)。

draft ⁰ᵛ AW /drɑːft; *NAmE* dræft/ *noun, adj., verb*

■ *noun* **1** ⁰ᵛ [C] a rough written version of sth that is not yet in its final form 草稿；草案；草圖：*I've made a **rough draft** of the letter.* 我已經寫好這封信的草稿。◇ *This is only the first draft of my speech.* 這只是我演講的初稿。◇ *the **final draft*** (= the final version) 定稿 ◇ *The legislation is still in **draft form**.* 這條法規還只是項草案。◇ *a **draft constitution/treaty/agreement*** 憲法／條約／協議草案 **2** [C] (*finance* 財) a written order to a bank to pay money to sb 匯票：*Payment must be made **by bank draft** drawn on a UK bank.* 付款必須用英國銀行承兑的匯票。 **3 the draft** [sing.] (*especially US*) = CONSCRIPTION **4** [sing.] (*NAmE*) a system in which professional teams in some sports choose players each year from among college students 運動員選拔制（某些職業運動隊每年在大學生中選拔新隊員）**5** [C] (*NAmE*) = DRAUGHT *n.* (1)：*Can you shut the door? There's a draft in here.* 你關上門好嗎？這裏有穿堂風。

■ *adj.* (*NAmE*) = DRAUGHT

■ *verb* (also **draught** especially in *BrE*) **1** ⁰ᵛ **~ sth** to write the first rough version of sth such as a letter, speech or book 起草；草擬：*to **draft** a constitution/contract/bill* 起草憲法／合同／法案 ◇ *I'll draft a letter for you.* 我來為你草擬一封信。 **2 ~ sb + adv./prep.** to choose people and send them somewhere for a special task 選派；抽調：*Extra police are being drafted in to control the crowds.* 現正在另外抽調警察去控制人群。 **3** [usually passive] **~ sb** (*NAmE*) = CONSCRIPT：*They were drafted into the army.* 他們應徵入伍。

ˈdraft dodger *noun* (*NAmE, disapproving*) a person who illegally tries to avoid doing military service 逃避兵役者 ➲ compare CONSCIENTIOUS OBJECTOR

draft·ee /ˌdrɑːfˈtiː; *NAmE* ˌdræfˈtiː/ *noun* (*US*) = CONSCRIPT

draft·er /ˈdrɑːftə(r); *NAmE* ˈdræftər/ *noun* **1** a person who prepares a rough version of a plan, document, etc.（計劃、文件等的）起草人，擬稿者 **2** (*NAmE*) = DRAFTSMAN (2)

drafts·man /ˈdrɑːftsmən; *NAmE* ˈdræftsmən/, **drafts·woman** /ˈdrɑːftswʊmən; *NAmE* ˈdræftswʊmən/ *noun* (*pl.* **-men** /-mən/, **-women** /-wɪmɪn/) **1** (*NAmE*) = DRAUGHTSMAN, DRAUGHTSWOMAN **2** (*NAmE* also **drafter**) a person who writes official or legal documents（正式或法律文件的）起草人：*the draftsmen of the constitution* 憲法起草人

drafts·man·ship (*NAmE*) = DRAUGHTSMANSHIP

drafts·per·son /ˈdrɑːftspɜːsn; *NAmE* ˈdræftspɜːrsn/ *noun* (*NAmE*) = DRAUGHTSPERSON

drafty /ˈdræfti/ (*NAmE*) = DRAUGHTY

drag ⁰ᵛ /dræɡ/ *verb, noun*

■ *verb* (-gg-)

▸ PULL 拉 **1** ⁰ᵛ [T] (+ **adv.prep.**) to pull sb/sth along with effort and difficulty（使勁而吃力地）拖，拉，拽，扯：*I dragged the chair over to the window.* 我把椅子拖到了窗口那邊。◇ *They dragged her from her bed.* 他們把她從牀上拽了起來。➲ SYNONYMS at PULL

▸ MOVE SLOWLY 緩慢移動 **2** [T, I] to move yourself slowly and with effort 緩慢而費力地移動（或行進）：**~ yourself + adv./prep.** *I managed to drag myself out of bed.* 我總算硬撐着從牀上爬了起來。◇ **+ adv./prep.** *She always drags behind when we walk anywhere.* 我們每走到什麼地方她都慢慢騰騰吃力地跟在後面。

▸ PERSUADE SB TO GO 勸人走 **3** [T] **~ sb/yourself + adv./prep.** to persuade sb to come or go somewhere they do not really want to come or go to 生拉硬拽；勸人勉強來（或去）：*I'm sorry to drag you all this way in the heat.* 對不起，這麼熱的天硬拉着你跑了那麼遠。◇ *The party was so good I couldn't drag myself away.* 這聚會太好玩了，我捨不得離開。

▸ OF TIME 時間 **4** [I] (of time or an event 時間或活動) to pass very slowly 過得很慢；拖沓地進行：*Time dragged terribly.* 時間過得真慢。◇ *The meeting really dragged.* 這會議開得真拖拉。➲ see also DRAG ON

▸ TOUCH GROUND 觸到地上 **5** [I, T] to move, or make sth move, partly touching the ground（使）在地上拖着移動：*This dress is too long—it drags on the ground when I walk.* 這條連衣裙太長了，我走路時會拖在地上。◇ **~ sth** *He was dragging his coat in the mud.* 他的外套拖在泥裏。

▸ SEARCH RIVER 在河中搜索 **6** [T] **~ sth (for sb/sth)** to search the bottom of a river, lake, etc. with nets or hooks 用網（或鈎）搜索（河或湖底）：*They dragged the canal for the murder weapon.* 他們用拖網沿運河打撈兇器。

▸ COMPUTING 計算機技術 **7** [T] **~ sth + adv./prep.** to move some text, an ICON, etc. across the screen of a computer using the mouse（用鼠標）拖動

IDM **drag your ˈfeet/ˈheels** to be deliberately slow in doing sth or in making a decision 故意拖拉；故意延遲（作出決定）➲ more at BOOTSTRAP

PHR V **ˌdrag ˈby** (of time 時間) to pass very slowly 過得很慢；拖沓地進行：*The last few weeks of the summer really dragged by.* 夏天最後的幾個星期過得真是慢啊。 **ˌdrag sb↔ˈdown** to make sb feel weak or unhappy 使虛弱（或不愉快）**ˌdrag sb/sth↔ˈdown (to sth)** to bring sb/sth to a lower social or economic level, a lower standard of behaviour, etc. 使社會地位（或經濟地位、行為標準等）下降：*If he fails, he'll drag us all down with him.* 要是他失敗了，他會使我們大家連同他一起毀掉的。 **ˌdrag sth/sb ˈinto sth | ˌdrag sth/sb↔ˈin** **1** to start to talk about sth/sb that has nothing to do with what is being discussed 把毫不相干的事（或人）插入談論；毫無必要地扯到：*Do you have to drag politics into everything?* 你什麼事都非要把政治扯進去嗎？ **2** to try to get sb who is not connected with a situation involved in it 硬讓毫無關係的人捲入；硬把…拉進去：*Don't drag the children into our argument.* 不要硬讓孩子也捲入我們的爭論。 **ˌdrag ˈon** (*disapproving*) to go on for too long 拖得太久；持續太久：*The dispute has dragged on for months.* 這場爭論沒完沒了地持續了數月。 **ˌdrag sth↔ˈout** to make sth last longer than necessary 不必要地拖延；使持續過久 SYN **prolong**：*Let's not drag out this discussion—we need to reach a decision.* 別讓這場討論拖得太久，我們得作出決定。 **ˌdrag sth ˈout of sb** to make sb say sth they do not want to say 強迫某人説出；套某人的話：*We dragged a confession out of him.* 我們硬逼着他招了供。 **ˌdrag sth↔ˈup** to mention an unpleasant story, fact, etc. that people do not want to remember or talk about 提起（不願回憶或談論的事）：*Why do you have to keep dragging up my divorce?* 你為什麼非要老提我離婚的事呢？

■ *noun*

▸ BORING PERSON/THING 令人厭煩的人／事 **1** [sing.] (*informal*) a boring person or thing; sth that is annoying

令人厭煩的人；乏味無聊的事：*He's such a drag.* 他真惹人討厭。◇ *Walking's a drag—let's drive there.* 步行太累了，咱們開車去吧。◇ *Having to work late every day is a drag.* 每天都得晚下班可真討厭。

▸ SB/STH STOPPING PROGRESS 阻礙前進的人／事物 **2** [sing.] **a ~ on sb/sth** (*informal*) a person or thing that makes progress difficult 累贅；拖累；絆腳石：*He came to be seen as a drag on his own party's prospects.* 他逐漸被看成是阻礙自己的黨走向未來的絆腳石。

▸ ON CIGARETTE 香煙 **3** [C] (*informal*) an act of breathing in smoke from a cigarette, etc. 抽一口；吸一口 SYN **draw**：*She took a long drag on her cigarette.* 她長長地抽了一大口煙。

▸ WOMEN'S CLOTHES 女裝 **4** [U] (*informal*) clothes that are usually worn by the opposite sex (usually women's clothes worn by men) 異性服裝（通常指男子穿的女裝）：*He performed in drag.* 他身着女裝演出。◇ *a drag queen* (= a man who dresses in women's clothes, usually in order to entertain people) 男扮女裝者（通常以娛樂他人為目的）

▸ PHYSICS 物理 **5** [U] the force of the air that acts against the movement of an aircraft or other vehicle（作用於飛機或其他交通工具的）空氣阻力 ➲ compare LIFT *n.* (5) ➲ see also MAIN DRAG

,drag-and-'drop *adj.* (*computing* 計) relating to the moving of ICONS, etc. on a screen using the mouse（鼠標的）拖放功能

dra·gée /'drɑːʒeɪ; *NAmE* drɑː'ʒeɪ/ *noun* **1** a sweet with a hard covering 糖衣夾心糖 **2** a very small silver or gold-coloured ball, used for decorating cakes（裝飾蛋糕的）小銀珠

drag·net /'drægnet/ *noun* **1** a net which is pulled through water to catch fish, or along the ground to catch animals（捕魚的）拖網；捕獵網 **2** a thorough search, especially for a criminal 徹底搜查；（尤指對罪犯的）拉網式搜捕

dragon /'drægən/ *noun* **1** (in stories) a large aggressive animal with wings and a long tail, that can breathe out fire（傳說中的）龍 **2** (*disapproving, especially BrE*) a woman who behaves in an aggressive and frightening way 悍婦；母夜叉

'dragon boat *noun* a long narrow boat of traditional Chinese design that is used for racing and that is moved through the water by a lot of people using PADDLES. It is decorated to look like a dragon. 龍舟；龍船

dragon·fly /'drægənflaɪ/ *noun* (*pl.* **-ies**) an insect with a long thin body, often brightly coloured, and two pairs of large transparent wings. Dragonflies are often seen over water. 蜻蜓 ➲ VISUAL VOCAB page V13

drag·oon /drə'guːn/ *noun, verb*

■ *noun* a soldier in the past who rode a horse and carried a gun（舊時的攜槍）騎兵

■ *verb*

PHR V **dra'goon sb into sth/into doing sth** (*formal*) to force or persuade sb to do sth that they do not want to do 迫使就範；勉強人做（不願做的事）SYN **coerce**

'drag race *noun* a race between specially adapted cars over a short distance 短程高速汽車賽 ▸ **'drag racing** *noun* [U]

drag·ster /'drægstə(r)/ *noun* a car that is used in a drag race 參加短程高速賽的賽車

drain /dreɪn/ *verb, noun*

■ *verb* **1** [T, I] **~ (sth)** to make sth empty or dry by removing all the liquid from it; to become empty or dry in this way 排空；（使）流光；放乾：*Drain and rinse the pasta.* 把通心粉瀝過一過水。◇ *The marshes have been drained.* 沼澤地裏的水已排乾。◇ *You will need to drain the central heating system before you replace the radiator.* 你得先把中央供暖系統的水排淨再更換散熱器。◇ *The swimming pool drains very slowly.* 游泳池裏的水排得很慢。◇ *Leave the dishes to drain.* 把碟子控乾。➲ COLLOCATIONS at COOKING **2** [T, I] to make liquid flow away from sth; to flow away（使）流走，流出：**~ sth (from/out of sth)** *We had to drain the oil out of the engine.* 我們必須把發動機裏的機油全部放掉。◇ **~ sth away/off** *Drain off the excess fat from the meat.* 把肉裏面多餘的油瀝掉。◇ **~ away/off** *She pulled out the plug and the water drained away.* 她拔掉塞子，讓水流走了。◇ (*figurative*) *My anger slowly drained away.* 我的怒火慢慢平息下來。◇ **~ into sth** *The river drains into a lake.* 這條河流入湖中。◇ **~ from/out of sth** *All the colour drained from his face when I told him the news* 我把這消息告訴他時他臉色變得煞白。◇ **~ of sth** *His face drained of colour.* 他的臉上血色全無。 **3** [T] **~ sth** to empty a cup or glass by drinking everything in it 喝光；喝乾：*In one gulp, he drained the glass.* 他一口喝乾了杯中的水。◇ *She quickly drained the last of her drink.* 她一下子就把最後一點兒酒喝掉了。 **4** [T] to make sb/sth weaker, poorer, etc. by using up their/its strength, money, etc. 使（精力、金錢等）耗盡：**~ sb/sth** *My mother's hospital expenses were slowly draining my income.* 我母親的住院開銷把我的收入漸漸耗光了。◇ *an exhausting and draining experience* 令人精疲力竭的一段經歷◇ **~ sb/sth of sth** *I felt drained of energy.* 我感到筋疲力盡。

■ *noun* **1** [C] a pipe that carries away dirty water or other liquid waste 下水道；排水管：*We had to call in a plumber to unblock the drain.* 我們只得叫個管子工來疏通下水道。◇ *The drains* (= the system of pipes) *date from the beginning of the century.* 下水道排水系統是本世紀初修的。 **2** [C] (*BrE*) (*US* **grate**, **'sewer grate**) a frame of metal bars over the opening to a drain in the ground 下水道孔蓋 **3** (*US*) (*BrE* **plug·hole**) [C] a hole in a bath/BATHTUB, SINK, etc. where the water flows away and into which a plug fits（浴缸、水池等的）排水孔，滲水孔，漏眼 ➲ VISUAL VOCAB page V24 **4** [sing.] **a ~ on sb/sth** a thing that uses a lot of the time, money, etc. that could be used for sth else 消耗；耗竭；耗費：*Military spending is a huge drain on the country's resources.* 軍費開支是對國家資源的巨大耗費。➲ see also BRAIN DRAIN

IDM **(go) down the 'drain** (*BrE* also **(go) down the 'plughole**) (*informal*) (to be) wasted; (to get) very much worse（被）浪費掉；（變得）非常糟糕：*It's just money down the drain, you know.* 你要知道，這是白白丟錢。◇ *Safety standards have gone down the drain.* 安全標準根本不管用了。➲ more at LAUGH *v.*

drain·age /'dreɪnɪdʒ/ *noun* [U] **1** the process by which water or liquid waste is drained from an area 排水；放水：*a **drainage system/channel/ditch*** 排水系統／渠／溝◇ *The area has good natural drainage.* 這個地區有良好的天然排水系統。 **2** a system of drains 排水系統

drained /dreɪnd/ *adj.* [not usually before noun] very tired and without energy 精疲力竭；無精打采：*She suddenly felt totally drained.* 她突然感到精疲力竭。◇ *The experience left her **emotionally drained**.* 這次經歷使得她在感情上心灰意懶。

'draining board (*BrE*) (*NAmE* **'drain·board**) *noun* the area next to a kitchen SINK where cups, plates, etc. are put for the water to run off, after they have been washed（廚房洗滌池邊控乾洗過的杯、碟等的）滴水板 ➲ VISUAL VOCAB page V25

drain·pipe /'dreɪnpaɪp/ *noun* **1** (*NAmE* also **down·spout**) a pipe that carries RAINWATER from the roof of a building to a DRAIN（把雨水從屋頂輸送到下水道的）雨水管，排水管 ➲ VISUAL VOCAB page V17 ➲ picture at PIPE **2** a pipe that carries dirty water or other liquid waste away from a building（排放建築物內污水的）排水管，泄水管

drake /dreɪk/ *noun* a male DUCK 公鴨 ➲ see also DUCKS AND DRAKES

dram /dræm/ *noun* (*especially ScotE*) a small amount of an alcoholic drink, especially WHISKY 少量的酒（尤指威士忌）

drama 🔑 AW /'drɑːmə/ *noun*

1 🔑 [C] a play for the theatre, television or radio 戲；劇：*a **costume/historical, etc. drama*** 古裝、歷史等劇 **2** 🔑 [U] plays considered as a form of literature 戲劇文學；戲劇藝術；戲劇：***classical/Elizabethan/modern, etc. drama*** 古典戲劇、伊麗莎白時代的戲劇、現代戲劇等 ◇ *a drama critic* 戲劇評論家◇ *drama school* 戲劇學校◇ *a drama student* 學習戲劇藝術的學生◇ *I studied English* *and Drama at college.* 我在大學學的是英語和戲劇。 **3** [C] an exciting event 戲劇性事件；戲劇性情節：*A powerful human drama was unfolding before our eyes.* 一個極富人情味的戲劇性事件在我們的眼前上演了。 **4** [U] the fact of being exciting 激動；興奮；刺激：*You couldn't help being thrilled by the drama of the situation.* 這充滿激情的場面令人不禁激動不已。

IDM **make a drama out of sth** to make a small problem or event seem more important or serious than it really is 小題大做；大驚小怪

'drama queen *noun* (*informal, disapproving*) a person who behaves as if a small problem or event is more important or serious than it really is 大驚小怪的人；小題大做的人

dra·mat·ic AW /drəˈmætɪk/ *adj.*
1 (of a change, an event, etc. 變化、事件等) sudden, very great and often surprising 突然的；巨大的；令人吃驚的：*a **dramatic increase/fall/change/improvement*** 暴漲；暴跌；巨變；巨大的改進 ◇ ***dramatic results/developments/news*** 出人意料的結果；突飛猛進的發展；令人吃驚的消息 ◇ *The announcement had a **dramatic effect** on house prices.* 這項公告對房屋價格產生了巨大的影響。 **2** exciting and impressive 激動人心的；引人注目的；給人印象深刻的：*a dramatic victory* 激動人心的勝利 ◇ *They watched dramatic pictures of the police raid on TV.* 他們在電視上看到了警察突擊搜捕的激動人心的畫面。 ➲ SYNONYMS at EXCITING **3** [usually before noun] connected with the theatre or plays 戲劇的；有關戲劇的；戲劇藝術的：*a local dramatic society* 地方戲劇協會 **4** exaggerated in order to create a special effect and attract people's attention 戲劇性的；戲劇般的；誇張做作的：*He flung out his arms in a **dramatic gesture**.* 他誇張地張開雙臂。◇ *Don't be so dramatic!* 別那麼誇張做作！ ▶ **dra·mat·ic·al·ly** AW /-kli/ *adv.*：*Prices have fallen dramatically.* 價格突然暴跌。◇ *Events could have developed in a dramatically different way.* 事情本來可以發展成另一種局面。◇ *'At last!' she cried dramatically.* "終於成功了！" 她激動地叫起來。

dra,matic 'irony *noun* [U] a situation in a play when a character's words carry an extra meaning to the audience because they know more than the character, especially about what is going to happen 戲劇性諷示（指觀眾比劇中人更能領會其台詞的言外之意）

dra·mat·ics /drəˈmætɪks/ *noun* [pl.] behaviour that does not seem sincere because it is exaggerated or too emotional 誇張的行為；做作的感情表露 ➲ see also AMATEUR DRAMATICS

drama·tis per·sonae /ˌdræmətɪs pɜːˈsəʊnaɪ; *NAmE* pɜːrˈsoʊ-/ *noun* [pl.] (from *Latin, formal*) all the characters in a play in the theatre 全體劇中人物；（統稱）一齣戲的演員

drama·tist AW /ˈdræmətɪst/ *noun* a person who writes plays for the theatre, television or radio 劇作家；編劇 SYN **playwright**：*a TV dramatist* 電視劇編劇

drama·tize (*BrE* also **-ise**) AW /ˈdræmətaɪz/ *verb*
1 [T] **~ sth** to present a book, an event, etc. as a play or a film/movie 將…改編成劇本；搬上（舞台或銀幕）
2 [T, I] **~ (sth)** to make sth seem more exciting or important than it really is 使戲劇化；戲劇性地表現；誇張：*Don't worry too much about what she said—she tends to dramatize things.* 別太在意她說的話——她往往言過其實。 ▶ **drama·tiza·tion, -isa·tion** AW /ˌdræmətaɪˈzeɪʃn; -təˈz-/ *noun* [U, C]：*a television dramatization of the trial* 根據那次審判改編成的電視劇

drama·turgy /ˈdræmətɜːdʒi; *NAmE* -tɜːrdʒi/ *noun* [U] (*formal*) the study or activity of writing dramatic texts 編劇研究；編劇

dram·edy /ˈdrɑːmədi; *NAmE* ˈdræm-/ *noun* (*pl.* **-ies**) (*NAmE*) a television programme that is intended to be both humorous and serious 電視情景喜劇（融合幽默與嚴肅成分）

drank *past tense* of DRINK

drape /dreɪp/ *verb, noun*
■ *verb* **1 ~ sth around/over/across, etc. sth** to hang clothes, materials, etc. loosely on sb/sth 將（衣服、織物等）懸掛，披：*She had a shawl draped around her shoulders.* 她肩上披着一條圍巾。◇ *He draped his coat over the back of the chair.* 他把外衣搭在座椅背上。◇ *She draped a cover over the old sofa.* 她把套子罩在舊沙發上。
2 ~ sb/sth in/with sth to cover or decorate sb/sth with material 遮蓋；蓋住；裝飾：*walls draped in ivy* 長滿常春藤的牆 **3 ~ sth around/round/over, etc. sth** to allow part of your body to rest on sth in a relaxed way 使（身體部位）放鬆地搭在…上：*His arm was draped casually around her shoulders.* 他隨意地將手臂搭在她的雙肩上。
■ *noun* (*especially NAmE*) (*NAmE* also **dra·pery**) [usually pl.] a long thick curtain（厚長的）簾子，帷簾，帷幕：*blue velvet drapes* 藍色絲絨帷簾

draper /ˈdreɪpə(r)/ *noun* (*old-fashioned, BrE*) **1** a person who owns or manages a shop that sells cloth, curtains, etc. 布商；布料零售商；紡織品商 **2 draper's** (*pl.* **drapers**) a shop/store that sells cloth, curtains, etc. 布店；紡織品店

dra·pery /ˈdreɪpəri/ *noun* (*pl.* **-ies**) **1** [U] (also **dra·per·ies** [pl.]) cloth or clothing hanging in loose folds 垂褶布（或織物）：*a cradle swathed in draperies and blue ribbon* 紮着打褶裝飾織物和藍色緞帶的搖籃 **2** [C, usually pl.] (*NAmE*) = DRAPE **3** [U] (*old-fashioned*) cloth and materials for sewing sold by a draper（布商出售的）織物，布料 ➲ compare DRY GOODS (2)

dras·tic /ˈdræstɪk; *BrE* also ˈdrɑːs-/ *adj.* extreme in a way that has a sudden, serious or violent effect on sth 極端的；急劇的；嚴厲的；猛烈的：***drastic measures/changes*** 嚴厲的措施；劇烈的變化 ◇ *The government is threatening to **take drastic action**.* 政府警告說要採取斷然措施。◇ *a drastic shortage of food* 食物的極度短缺 ◇ *Talk to me before you do anything drastic.* 你採取任何重大行動之前要跟我談談。 ▶ **dras·tic·al·ly** /-kli/ *adv.*：*Output has been drastically reduced.* 產量已急劇下降。◇ *Things have started to go drastically wrong.* 情況變得完全失控。

drat /dræt/ *exclamation* (*old-fashioned, informal*) used to show that you are annoyed（表示厭煩）見鬼，討厭，該死，倒霉：*Drat! I forgot my key.* 真見鬼！我忘帶鑰匙了。 ▶ **drat·ted** *adj.* [only before noun]：(*old-fashioned, BrE, informal*) *This dratted pen won't work.* 這該死的筆寫不出字來。

draught /drɑːft/ (*BrE*) (*NAmE* **draft**) *noun, adj., verb*
■ *noun* **1** [C] a flow of cool air in a room or other confined space 穿堂風；通風氣流；通風：*There's a draught in here.* 這兒有一股冷風。◇ *A cold draught of air blew in from the open window.* 一股寒氣從敞開的窗戶吹了進來。◇ *I was sitting **in a draught**.* 我坐在風口上。
2 [C] (*formal*) one continuous action of swallowing liquid; the amount swallowed 一飲（的量）：*He took a deep draught of his beer.* 他喝了一大口啤酒。 **3** [C] (*old use* or *literary*) medicine in a liquid form 藥水；飲劑：*a sleeping draught* (= one that makes you sleep) 一服安眠飲劑 **4 draughts** (*BrE*) (*NAmE* **check·ers**) [U] a game for two players using 24 round pieces on a board marked with black and white squares 國際跳棋；西洋跳棋 **5** [C] (*BrE*) (*NAmE* **check·er**) one of the round pieces used in a game of draughts（國際跳棋的）棋子；（西洋跳棋的）棋子
IDM **on 'draught** (*BrE*) (of beer 啤酒) taken from a large container (= a BARREL) 從桶中吸取的；散裝的：*This beer is not available on draught* (= it is available only in bottles or cans). 這種啤酒不賣散裝。
■ *adj.* **1** [usually before noun] served from a large container (= a BARREL) rather than in a bottle 零售的；散裝的：*draught beer* 散裝啤酒 **2** [only before noun] used for pulling heavy loads 拖曳重載用的：*a draught horse* 役馬
■ *verb* (*especially BrE*) = DRAFT

draught·board /ˈdrɑːftbɔːd; *NAmE* ˈdræftbɔːrd/ (*BrE*) (*NAmE* **'check·er·board**) *noun* a board with black and white squares, used for playing DRAUGHTS/CHECKERS 國際跳棋棋盤；西洋跳棋棋盤

'draught excluder (*BrE*) (*NAmE* **'weather strip**) *noun* [C, U] a piece of material that helps to prevent cold air coming through a door, window, etc. （門窗等的）擋風簾

draughts·man /ˈdrɑːftsmən/ (*BrE*) (*NAmE* **drafts·man**) *noun* (*pl.* **-men** /-mən/) **1** a person whose job is to draw detailed plans of machinery, buildings, etc. 製圖員 **2** a person who draws 繪畫者：*He's a poor draughtsman.* 他不擅長繪畫。➲ see also DRAUGHTSWOMAN, DRAUGHTSPERSON

D

draughts·man·ship (*BrE*) (*NAmE* **drafts·man·ship**) /ˈdrɑːftsmənʃɪp; *NAmE* ˈdræfts-/ *noun* [U] the ability to draw well 畫圖才能；繪畫天賦：*You have to admire her superb draughtsmanship.* 你不得不佩服她那一流的繪畫水平。

draughts·person /ˈdrɑːftspɜːsn/ (*BrE*) (*NAmE* **drafts·person**) *noun* a draughtsman or a draughtswoman 製圖員；繪畫者

draughts·woman /ˈdrɑːftswʊmən/ (*BrE*) (*NAmE* **drafts·woman** /ˈdræfts-/) *noun* (*pl.* **-women** /-wɪmɪn/) **1** a woman whose job is to draw detailed plans of machinery, buildings, etc. 女製圖員 ➲ note at GENDER **2** a woman who draws 女繪畫者 ➲ see also DRAUGHTSMAN

draughty /ˈdrɑːfti/ (*BrE*) (*NAmE* **drafty**) *adj.* (**draught·ier**, **draughti·est**) (of a room, etc. 房間等) uncomfortable because cold air is blowing through 有過堂風的；有冷風吹過的：*a draughty room/corridor* 有過堂風的房間／走廊

Dra·vid·ian /drəˈvɪdiən/ *adj.* connected with a group of languages spoken in southern India and in Sri Lanka, or with the people who speak these languages （印度南部和斯里蘭卡）達羅毗荼諸語的，達羅毗荼人的

draw 🔑 /drɔː/ *verb*, *noun*

■ **verb** (**drew** /druː/, **drawn** /drɔːn/)

▸ MAKE PICTURES 繪畫 **1** 🔑 [I, T] to make pictures, or a picture of sth, with a pencil, pen or CHALK (but not paint) （用鉛筆、鋼筆或粉筆）畫，描繪，描畫：*You draw beautifully.* 你的畫畫得真好。◇ **~ sth** *to* **draw a picture/diagram/graph** 畫畫／示意圖／曲線圖 ◇ *She drew a house.* 她畫了一棟房屋。◇ *He drew a circle in the sand with a stick.* 他用枝條在沙地上畫了一個圓。◇ (*figurative*) *The report drew a grim picture of inefficiency and corruption.* 這份報告描繪了一幅辦事效率低下和貪污腐化的可怕景象。➲ COLLOCATIONS at ART

▸ PULL 拖；拉 **2** 🔑 [T] **~ sth/sb + adv./prep.** to move sth/sb by pulling it or them gently 拖（動）；拉（動）；牽引：*He drew the cork out of the bottle.* 他把瓶塞拔了出來。◇ *I drew my chair up closer to the fire.* 我把椅子向火旁拉近了點。◇ *She drew me onto the balcony.* 她把我拉到陽台上。◇ *I tried to* **draw him aside** (= for example where I could talk to him privately). 我設法把他拉到了一邊。◇ (*figurative*) *My eyes were drawn to the man in the corner.* 角落裏的那個男人引起了我的注意。➲ SYNONYMS at PULL **3** [T] **~ sth** (of horses, etc. 馬匹等) to pull a vehicle such as a CARRIAGE 拉，拖（車）：*The Queen's coach was drawn by six horses.* 女王的御駕是由六匹馬拉的。◇ *a horse-drawn carriage* 馬車

▸ CURTAINS 窗簾 **4** [T] **~ sth** to open or close curtains, etc. 拉（窗簾、簾子）：*The blinds were drawn.* 窗簾拉上了。◇ *It was getting dark so I switched on the light and drew the curtains.* 天快黑了，我便打開燈，拉上了窗簾。◇ *She drew back the curtains and let the sunlight in.* 她拉開窗簾讓陽光照進來。

▸ MOVE 移動 **5** [I] **+ adv./prep.** to move in the direction mentioned （向某個方向）移動，行進：*The train drew into the station.* 火車徐徐駛入車站。◇ *The train drew in.* 火車進站了。◇ *The figures in the distance seemed to be drawing closer.* 遠處的人影好像越來越近。◇ *Their car* **drew alongside** *ours.* 他們的汽車與我們的並排行駛。◇ (*figurative*) *Her retirement is drawing near.* 她快退休了。◇ (*figurative*) *The meeting was* **drawing to a close**. 會議快結束了。

▸ WEAPON 武器 **6** [T, I] **~** (**sth**) (**on sb**) to take out a weapon, such as a gun or a SWORD, in order to attack sb 拔出；抽出；掏出：*She drew a revolver on me.* 她拔出左輪手槍對準我。◇ *He came towards them with his sword drawn.* 他手持出鞘的劍向他們走來。

▸ ATTRACT 吸引 **7** [T] to attract or interest sb 吸引；招引；使感興趣：**~ sb** *The movie is drawing large audiences.* 這部影片吸引了大批觀眾。◇ *The course draws students from all over the country.* 這課程吸引了來自全國各地的學生。◇ **~ sb to sth** *Her screams drew passers-by to the scene.* 她的驚叫聲把過路人吸引到了現場。

▸ GET REACTION 引起反應 **8** [T] to produce a reaction or response 產生，引起，激起（反應或回應）：**~ sth** *The plan has drawn a lot of criticism.* 這個計劃引來眾多批評。◇ **~ sth from sb** *The announcement drew loud applause from the audience.* 公告博得觀眾的熱烈掌聲。

▸ MAKE SB TALK 使人說話 **9** [T] **~ sb** (**about/on sth**) [often passive] to make sb say more about sth 使說出；使吐露：*Spielberg refused to be drawn on his next movie.* 斯皮爾伯格拒絕透露他下一部影片的任何消息。

▸ CONCLUSION 結論 **10** [T] **~ sth** (**from sth**) to have a particular idea after you have studied sth or thought about it 獲取；得出；推斷出：*What conclusions did you draw from the report?* 你從這個報告中得出了什麼結論？◇ *We can draw some lessons for the future from this accident.* 我們可以從這起事故中為今後吸取教訓。

▸ COMPARISON 比較 **11** [T] **~ sth** to express a comparison or a contrast 進行，作（比較或對比）：*to* **draw an analogy/a comparison/a parallel/a distinction** *between two events* 對兩件事進行類比／比較；找出兩件事之間的相似之處／區別

▸ CHOOSE 選擇 **12** [I, T] to decide sth by picking cards, tickets or numbers by chance 抽（籤、牌）；抓（鬮）：*We drew for partners.* 我們抓鬮決定夥伴。◇ **~ sth** *They had to* **draw lots** *to decide who would go.* 他們只得抽籤決定誰去。◇ *He drew the winning ticket.* 他抽到中彩券了。◇ *Names were drawn from a hat for the last few places.* 從帽子裏抽籤來決定最後幾個名額。◇ *Italy has been drawn against Spain in the first round.* 第一輪比賽的抽籤結果是意大利隊對西班牙隊。◇ **~ sb/sth to do sth** *Italy has been drawn to play Spain.* 抽籤結果是意大利隊對西班牙隊。

▸ GAME 比賽 **13** [I, T] to finish a game without either team winning 以平局結束；不分勝負：*England and France drew.* 英格蘭隊和法國隊打平。◇ *England and France drew 3–3.* 英格蘭隊與法國隊打成三平。◇ **~ with/against sb** *England drew with/against France.* 英格蘭隊與法國隊打成平局。◇ **~ sth** *England drew their game against France.* 英格蘭隊與法國隊的比賽未分勝負。

▸ MONEY 錢 **14** [T] to take money or payments from a bank account or post office 提取；領取；支取 SYN **withdraw**：**~ sth out** (**of sth**) *I drew out £200.* 我取了 200 英鎊。◇ *Can I draw $80 out of my account?* 我可以從我的賬戶上提取 80 元錢嗎？◇ **~ sth** (**from sth**) *She went to the post office to draw her pension.* 她到郵局去領取她的養老金。◇ **~ sth on sth** *The cheque was drawn on his personal account.* 這張支票從他的個人賬戶中支付。

▸ LIQUID/GAS 液體；氣體 **15** [T] **~ sth** (**+adv./prep.**) to take or pull liquid or gas from somewhere 抽出；吸出：*to draw water from a well* 從井中抽水 ◇ *The device draws gas along the pipe.* 這裝置將氣體順着管子抽出來。

▸ SMOKE/AIR 煙；空氣 **16** [I, T] to breathe in smoke or air 抽（煙）；吸（氣）：**~ at/on sth** *He drew thoughtfully on his pipe.* 他若有所思地抽着煙斗。◇ **~ sth in** *She breathed deeply, drawing in the fresh mountain air.* 她深深地呼吸着山上的新鮮空氣。

IDM **draw a ˈblank** to get no response or result 無回音；無結果；無收穫：*So far, the police investigation has drawn a blank.* 到目前為止警方的調查毫無結果。 **draw ˈblood** to make sb BLEED 使流血 **draw ˈbreath** (*BrE*) (*US* **draw a ˈbreath**) **1** to stop doing sth and rest 停下來歇口氣：*She talks all the time and hardly stops to draw breath.* 她一直滔滔不絕，幾乎沒停下來喘口氣。 **2** (*literary*) to live; to be alive 生存；活着：*He was as kind a man as ever drew breath.* 他是世上少有的大善人。 **draw sb's ˈfire** to make sb direct their anger, criticism, etc. at you, so that others do not have to face it （為掩護他人）吸引…的火力，轉移視線 **draw a ˈline under sth** (*BrE*) to say that sth is finished and not worth discussing any more 到…為止；就…打住 **draw the ˈline** (**at sth/at doing sth**) to refuse to do sth; to set a limit 拒絕做；給…定界限：*I don't mind helping, but I draw the line at doing everything myself.* 我幫忙倒無所

謂，但可不能什麼事都讓我做。◇ *We would have liked to invite all our relatives, but you have to draw the line somewhere.* 我們本倒是願意邀請所有親戚的，但你總得有個限度呀。 **draw the 'line (between sth and sth)** to distinguish between two closely related ideas 劃界線；區分（兩個密切相關的思想）： *Where do you draw the line between genius and madness?* 天才和瘋狂之間如何劃界呢？ **,draw the short 'straw** (*BrE*) (*NAmE* **get the ,short end of the 'stick**) to be the person in a group who is chosen or forced to perform an unpleasant duty or task 抽到倒霉籤；被派做苦差事： *I drew the short straw and had to clean the toilets.* 我抽到了下下籤，只得打掃廁所了。 **,draw 'straws (for sth)** to decide on sb to do or have sth, by choosing pieces of paper, etc. 抽籤（決定某事）： *We drew straws for who went first.* 我們抽籤決定誰先去。 ➲ more at BATTLE *n.*, BEAD *n.*, DAGGER, HEIGHT, HORN *n.*, LOT *n.*, SIDE *n.*

PHR V **,draw 'back** to move away from sb/sth 移開；後退： *He came close but she drew back.* 他一步步靠近，而她卻一步步向後退。 **,draw 'back (from sth/from doing sth)** to choose not to take action, especially because you feel nervous 退縮；撤銷；撤回： *We drew back from taking our neighbours to court.* 我們撤回了對鄰居的起訴。 **,draw sth↔'down** | **,draw 'down** (*especially NAmE*) to reduce a supply of sth that has been created over a period of time; to be reduced 減少；下降： *There are many life events that can unexpectedly draw down savings.* 生活中許多意想不到的事情都可能會花費存款。◇ *If we don't cut costs our reserves will draw down.* 如果我們不削減開支，儲備金就會減少。 ➲ related noun DRAWDOWN **,draw sth↔'down (from sth)** | **,draw 'down on sth** (*especially NAmE*) (*BrE* usually **draw**) (*finance* 財) to take money from a fund that a bank, etc. has made available 提取，動用（資金）： *The company has already drawn down €600 million of its €725 million credit line.* 公司已從 7.25 億歐元的授信額度中動用了 6 億歐元。◇ *They can draw down on the loan at any time.* 他們可以隨時提取這筆貸款。 ➲ related noun DRAWDOWN **'draw sth from sb/sth** to take or obtain sth from a particular source （從…中）得到，獲得： *to **draw support/comfort/strength** from your family* 從家人那裏得到支持／安慰／力量◇ *She drew her inspiration from her childhood experiences.* 她從兒時的經歷中獲得靈感。 **,draw 'in** to become dark earlier in the evening as winter gets nearer （天黑）漸早；（白晝）漸短： *The nights/days are drawing in.* 天黑得越來越早了。 **'draw sb into sth/into doing sth** | **,draw sb↔'in** to involve sb or make sb take part in sth, although they may not want to take part at first 使捲入；使參與： *youngsters drawn into a life of crime* 身不由己捲入犯罪活動的年輕人◇ *The book starts slowly, but it gradually draws you in.* 這本書開始時情節展開得很慢，但漸漸地就把你給完全吸引住了。 **,draw sth↔'off** to remove some liquid from a larger supply 抽出；排掉： *The doctor drew off some fluid to relieve the pressure.* 醫生排掉了一些液體以緩解壓力。 **,draw 'on** if a time or a season **draws on**, it passes （時光）漸漸過去，荏苒： *Night was drawing on.* 夜漸深了。 **'draw on/upon sth** to use a supply of sth that is available to you 憑藉；利用；動用： *I'll have to draw on my savings.* 我只得動用我的存款了。◇ *The novelist draws heavily on her personal experiences.* 這位小說家運用很多她的親身經歷為素材。 **,draw 'out** to become lighter in the evening as summer gets nearer （天黑）漸晚；（白晝）漸長： *The days/evenings are drawing out.* 白晝越來越長了。 **,draw sb↔'out** to encourage sb to talk or express themselves freely 使暢所欲言 **,draw sth↔'out** to make sth last longer than usual or necessary 拖延；拉長： *She drew the interview out to over an hour.* 她拖拖沓沓採訪了一個多小時。 ➲ see also LONG-DRAWN-OUT **,draw 'up** if a vehicle **draws up**, it arrives and stops （車輛）到達某處停下，停止： *The cab drew up outside the house.* 出租車在房子外面停了下來。 **,draw sth↔'up** to make or write sth that needs careful thought or planning 擬訂；制訂；起草： *to draw up a contract/list* 擬訂合同／名單

■ ***noun***

▸ **CHOOSING** 選擇 **1** (*US* also **draw·ing**) [usually sing.] **~ (for sth)** the act of choosing sth, for example the winner of a prize or the teams who play each other in a competition, usually by taking pieces of paper, etc. out of a container without being able to see what is written on them 抽彩；抽獎；抽籤： *the draw for the second round of the Champions League* 歐洲冠軍聯賽第二輪抽籤◇ *The draw for the raffle takes place on Saturday.* 星期六進行抽彩。

▸ **SPORTS/GAMES** 體育運動；比賽 **2** (*especially BrE*) a game in which both teams or players finish with the same number of points 平局；和局；不分勝負： *The match ended in a two-all draw.* 比賽以二平結束。◇ *He managed to hold Smith to a draw* (= to stop him from winning when he seemed likely to do so). 他總算與史密斯打了個平局。 ➲ compare TIE *n.* (5) **3** (*NAmE* usually **draw·ing**) a competition in which the winners are chosen in a draw 由抽籤決定贏家的競賽： *a prize draw* 抽獎 ➲ compare LOTTERY (1) **4** (*BrE*) a sports match for which the teams or players are chosen in a draw 由抽籤決定對手的比賽： *Liverpool have an away draw against Manchester United.* 利物浦隊抽的籤是在客場與曼徹斯特聯隊進行比賽。 **5** [usually sing.] a set of matches for which the teams or players are chosen in a draw 由抽籤決定對手的系列比賽： *There are only two seeded players left in the top half of the draw.* 在抽籤系列比賽的上半區就只剩下兩名種子選手了。

▸ **ATTRACTION** 吸引力 **6** a person, a thing or an event that attracts a lot of people 有吸引力的人（或事物） **SYN** **attraction** ： *She is currently one of the biggest draws on the Irish music scene.* 她是目前愛爾蘭音樂界最受歡迎的人物之一。

▸ **SMOKE** 煙 **7** an act of breathing in the smoke from a cigarette 吸煙 **SYN** **drag**

IDM **be quick/fast on the 'draw** **1** (*informal*) to be quick to understand or react in a new situation 領悟敏捷；反應迅速： *You can't fool him—he's always quick on the draw.* 你騙不了他，他腦筋一向很快。 **2** to be quick at pulling out a gun in order to shoot it 拔槍迅速 ➲ more at LUCK *n.*

draw·back /ˈdrɔːbæk/ *noun* **~ (of/to sth)** | **~ (of/to doing sth)** a disadvantage or problem that makes sth a less attractive idea 缺點；不利條件 **SYN** **disadvantage, snag** ： *The main drawback to it is the cost.* 它的主要缺點是成本高。◇ *This is the one major drawback of the new system.* 這是新系統的一大弊端。

draw·bridge /ˈdrɔːbrɪdʒ/ *noun* a bridge that can be pulled up, for example to stop people from entering a castle or to allow ships to pass under it 開合橋；活動吊橋

draw·down /ˈdrɔːdaʊn/ *noun* [C, U] **~ (on sth)** **1** the act of reducing a supply of sth that has been created over a period of time; the amount used 消耗；消耗量；洩降： *The cold winter has led to a larger-than-expected drawdown on oil stocks.* 寒冬使石油儲備消耗量高出預料。 **2** (*finance* 財) the act of using money that is available to you; the amount used 動用資金；動用資金額： *a drawdown of cash from the company's reserves* 從公司儲備金中支取的一筆錢

drawer 🔑 *noun*

1 🔑 /drɔː(r)/ a part of a piece of furniture such as a desk, used for keeping things in. It is shaped like a box and has a handle on the front for pulling it out. 抽屜： *in the **top/middle/bottom drawer** of the desk* 寫字枱的上層／中層／下層抽屜 ➲ **VISUAL VOCAB** pages V22, V23, V26 ➲ see also CHEST OF DRAWERS, TOP DRAWER **2** /ˈdrɔːə(r)/ (*formal*) a person who writes a cheque 開票人；出票人

drawers /drɔːz; *NAmE* drɔːrz/ *noun* [pl.] (*old-fashioned*) KNICKERS or UNDERPANTS, especially ones that cover the upper parts of the legs （長）內褲

draw·ing 🔑 /ˈdrɔːɪŋ/ *noun* **1** 🔑 [C] a picture made using a pencil or pen rather than paint 圖畫；素描畫： *a **pencil/charcoal drawing*** 鉛筆畫；炭筆畫◇ *a drawing of a yacht* 遊艇的素描畫◇ *He **did/made a drawing** of the old farmhouse.* 他畫了一幅古老農舍的素描。 ➲ **SYNONYMS** at PICTURE ➲ **COLLOCATIONS** at ART **2** 🔑 [U] the art or skill of making pictures, plans, etc. using a

D

pen or pencil 繪畫（藝術）；製圖（技巧）：*I'm not very good at drawing.* 我不擅長繪畫。◇ *technical drawing* 工藝製圖 **3** (*NAmE*) = DRAW *n.* (1), (3)

ˈdrawing board *noun* a large flat board used for holding a piece of paper while a drawing or plan is being made 繪畫板；圖畫板；製圖板

IDM **(go) back to the ˈdrawing board** to start thinking about a new way of doing sth after a previous plan or idea has failed （失敗後）另起爐灶，從頭開始 **on the ˈdrawing board** being prepared or considered 在籌劃階段；在設計中：*It's just one of several projects on the drawing board.* 這只是正在籌劃的幾個項目中的一個。

ˈdrawing pin (*BrE*) (*NAmE* **thumb·tack**, **tack**) *noun* a short pin with a large round flat head, used especially for fastening paper to a board or wall 圖釘 ➲ VISUAL VOCAB page V69

ˈdrawing power (*NAmE*) (*BrE* **ˈpulling power**) *noun* [U] the ability of sb/sth to attract people 吸引力；誘惑力

ˈdrawing room *noun* (*formal* or *old-fashioned*) a room in a large house in which people relax and guests are entertained 起居室；客廳 ➲ compare LIVING ROOM

drawl /drɔːl/ *verb* [T, I] **+ speech** | **~ (sth)** to speak or say sth slowly with vowel sounds that are longer than usual （拉長調子）慢吞吞地說話：*'Hi there!' she drawled lazily.* "喂，你好！" 她拖着長腔懶洋洋地說。◇ *He had a smooth drawling voice.* 他說起話來油嘴滑舌，帶着拖腔。▸ **drawl** *noun* [sing.]：*She spoke in a slow southern drawl.* 她帶着南方的拖腔慢條斯理地講話。

drawn /drɔːn/ *adj.* (of a person or their face 人或人臉) looking pale and thin because the person is ill/sick, tired or worried （因身體不適、疲倦或憂慮）憔悴的，蒼白的 ➲ see also DRAW *v.*

ˌdrawn-ˈout *adj.* = LONG-DRAWN-OUT

draw·string /ˈdrɔːstrɪŋ/ *noun* a piece of string sewn inside the material at the top of a bag, pair of trousers/pants, etc. that can be pulled tighter in order to make the opening smaller（穿在袋口、褲腰等上的）拉繩，拉帶，束帶：*They fasten with a drawstring.* 它們是用拉繩繫緊的。➲ VISUAL VOCAB page V63

dray /dreɪ/ *noun* a low flat vehicle pulled by horses and used in the past for carrying heavy loads, especially BARRELS of beer 平板馬車（舊時運重載如桶裝啤酒）

dread /dred/ *verb, noun*

▪ *verb* to be very afraid of sth; to fear that sth bad is going to happen 非常害怕；極為擔心：**~ sth** *This was the moment he had been dreading.* 這是他一直最擔心的時刻。◇ **~ doing sth** *I dread being sick.* 我特別害怕生病。◇ **~ sb doing sth** *She dreads her husband finding out.* 她生怕丈夫察覺出來。◇ **~ to do sth** *I dread to think what would happen if there really was a fire here.* 我不敢想像假如這兒真的發生火災會是什麼情景。◇ **~ that …** *I both hoped and dreaded that he would come.* 我既希望又害怕他來。

▪ *noun* [U, C, usually sing.] a feeling of great fear about sth that might or will happen in the future; a thing that causes this feeling 恐懼；令人懼怕的事物：*The prospect of growing old* ***fills me with dread.*** 想到人會一天天老下去便使我充滿恐懼。◇ *She has an irrational dread of hospitals.* 她莫名其妙地害怕醫院。◇ *The committee members* ***live in dread of*** (= are always worried about) *anything that may cause a scandal.* 委員會成員整天提心吊膽，生怕有什麼事會引起流言蜚語。◇ *My greatest dread is that my parents will find out.* 我最擔心的就是父母會察覺出來。

dread·ed /ˈdredɪd/ (also *formal* **dread**) *adj.* [only before noun] causing fear 令人害怕的；可怕的：*The dreaded moment had finally arrived.* 可怕的時刻終於來到了。◇ (*humorous*) *Did I hear the dreaded word 'homework'?* 我是不是聽到"家庭作業"這可怕的字眼了？

dread·ful /ˈdredfl/ *adj.* (*especially BrE*) **1** very bad or unpleasant 糟糕透頂的；討厭的；令人不快的：*What dreadful weather!* 多麼討厭的天氣！◇ *What a dreadful thing to say!* 話說得太難聽了！◇ *It's dreadful the way they treat their staff.* 他們對待雇員的方式糟糕透了。◇ *How dreadful!* 多討厭啊！◇ *Jane* ***looked dreadful*** (= looked ill or tired). 簡看上去臉色很不好。➲ SYNONYMS at TERRIBLE **2** [only before noun] used to emphasize how bad sth is （強調糟糕的程度）極其的，極壞的 SYN **terrible**：*She's making a dreadful mess of things.* 她把事情搞得一塌糊塗。◇ *I'm afraid there's been a dreadful mistake.* 恐怕是出了大錯。**3** [usually before noun] causing fear or suffering 可怕的；令人畏懼的；使人痛苦的 SYN **terrible**：*a dreadful accident* 可怕的事故 ◇ *They suffered dreadful injuries.* 他們嚴重受傷。

dread·ful·ly /ˈdredfəli/ *adv.* (*especially BrE*) **1** extremely; very much 極其；極端；非常：*I'm dreadfully sorry.* 我感到非常抱歉。◇ *I miss you dreadfully.* 我非常想念您。**2** very badly 糟糕地；厲害地；嚴重地：*They suffered dreadfully during the war.* 他們在戰爭中遭受了巨大的痛苦。

dread·locks /ˈdredlɒks; *NAmE* -lɑːks/ (also *informal* **dreads** /dredz/) *noun* [pl.] hair that is twisted into long thick pieces that hang down from the head, worn especially by RASTAFARIANS （尤指拉斯塔法里教派成員蓄的）"駭人"長髮綹 ➲ VISUAL VOCAB page V60

dread·nought /ˈdrednɔːt/ *noun* a type of ship used in war in the early 20th century （20 世紀初期的）無畏艦

dream 0→ /driːm/ *noun, verb*

▪ *noun* **1** 0→ [C] a series of images, events and feelings that happen in your mind while you are asleep 夢；睡夢：*I had a vivid dream about my old school.* 我做了一個非常逼真的夢，夢見了我的母校。◇ *I thought someone came into the bedroom, but it was just a dream.* 我還以為有人進了卧室，原來只是一場夢。◇ *'Goodnight. Sweet dreams.'* "晚安。祝你做個好夢。" ➲ compare NIGHTMARE ➲ see also WET DREAM **2** 0→ [C] a wish to have or be sth, especially one that seems difficult to achieve 夢想；理想；願望：*Her lifelong dream was to be a famous writer.* 她的畢生願望就是成為名作家。◇ *He wanted to be rich but it was an impossible dream.* 他想發財，然而這是不可能實現的夢想。◇ *If I win, it will be a* ***dream come true.*** 如果我贏了，那就是夢想成真。◇ *She tried to turn her dream of running her own business into reality.* 她努力實現自己做生意的夢想。◇ ***a dream car/house/job, etc.*** 夢寐以求的汽車、房子、工作等 ◇ *I've finally found the man* ***of my dreams.*** 我終於找到了理想中的男人。◇ *a chance to* ***fulfil a*** *childhood* ***dream*** 實現童年夢想的機會 ◇ *It was the end of all my hopes and dreams.* 我的希望和夢想全都破滅了。➲ see also PIPE DREAM **3** 0→ [sing.] a state of mind or a situation in which things do not seem real or part of normal life 夢幻狀態；恍惚；出神：*She walked around* ***in a dream*** *all day.* 她整天都在夢遊似的到處轉悠。➲ see also DAYDREAM **4** [sing.] (*informal*) a beautiful or wonderful person or thing 夢一般美妙的人（或事物）；極美好的人（或事物）：*That meal was an absolute dream.* 那頓飯真是太棒了。

IDM **go/work like a ˈdream** **1** to work very well 性能極佳；十分有效：*My new car goes like a dream.* 我的新汽車性能好極了。**2** to happen without problems, in the way that you had planned 毫無困難；非常順利；完美 **in your ˈdreams** (*informal*) used to tell sb that sth they are hoping for is not likely to happen 你妄想；你在做夢：*'I'll be a manager before I'm 30.' 'In your dreams.'* "我要在 30 歲前當經理。" "你做夢。" **like a bad ˈdream** (of a situation 處境) so unpleasant that you cannot believe it is true 噩夢般令人難以置信：*In broad daylight the events of the night before seemed like a bad dream.* 在大白天裏，前一天夜裏發生的事情就像噩夢般令人難以置信。➲ more at WILD *adj.*

▪ *verb* (**dreamt**, **dreamt** /dremt/) or (**dreamed**, **dreamed**) **1** 0→ [I, T] to experience a series of images, events and feelings in your mind while you are asleep 做夢：*Did I talk in my sleep? I must have been dreaming.* 我說夢話了嗎？我肯定是在做夢。◇ **~ of/about sb/sth** *I dreamt about you last night.* 我昨晚夢見你了。◇ **~ sth** *Did it really happen or did I just dream it?* 這是真的嗎？還是我在做夢？◇ **~ (that) …** *I dreamt (that) I got the job.* 我夢見自己得到了那份工作。**2** 0→ [I, T] to imagine and think about sth that you would like to happen 想像；夢想：**~ of/about sth** *She dreams of running her own business.* 她夢想自己開業做生意。◇ *It was the kind of* trip most of us only dream about. 對我們大多數人來說，這樣的旅行只是夢想。◇ **~ of/about doing sth** (*informal*) *I* ***wouldn't dream of*** *going without you* (= I would never go without you). 你不去，我絕對不會去。◇ **~ sth** *Who'd have dreamt it? They're getting married.* 誰會料到？他們要結婚了。◇ **~ (that)** … *I never dreamt (that) I'd actually get the job.* 我做夢也沒想到會真的得到這份工作。

PHR V **,dream sth a'way** to waste time just thinking about things you would like to do without actually doing anything 夢幻似的度過；在遐想中虛度 **,dream 'on** (*informal*) you say **dream on** to tell sb that an idea is not practical or likely to happen 痴心妄想 **,dream sth↔'up** (*informal*) to have an idea, especially a very unusual or silly one 憑空想出，虛構出（尤指荒誕不經的事） SYN **think up**： *Trust you to dream up a crazy idea like this!* 你這個人就是會想出這種荒唐的主意來！

dream·boat /'dri:mbəʊt; *NAmE* -boʊt/ *noun* (*old-fashioned, informal*) a man who is very attractive 富有魅力的男子；迷人的男子

dreamcatcher 捕夢網

dream·catch·er /'dri:mkætʃə(r)/ *noun* a ring containing a decorated net, originally made by Native Americans, and thought to give its owner good dreams 捕夢網（最初由美洲土著製作的一種帶裝飾網兜的圓環，據信能給主人帶來好夢）

dream·er /'dri:mə(r)/ *noun* **1** (*sometimes disapproving*) a person who has ideas or plans that are not practical or realistic 夢想家；空想家；不切實際的人 **2** (*usually disapproving*) a person who does not pay attention to what is happening around them, but thinks about other things instead 做白日夢的人；出神的人；神不守舍的人 **3** a person who dreams 做夢的人： *Dreamers do not always remember their dreams.* 做夢的人並不總能記住自己的夢。

dream·land /'dri:mlænd/ *noun* [U] (*especially BrE, disapproving*) a pleasant but not very realistic situation that only exists in your mind 夢境；幻想世界；理想世界： *You must be living in dreamland if you think he'll change his mind.* 如果你認為他會改變主意那你一定是在做夢。

dream·less /'dri:mləs/ *adj.* (of sleep 睡眠) without dreams; deep and peaceful 無夢的；酣暢安寧的

dream·like /'dri:mlaɪk/ *adj.* as if existing or happening in a dream 似在夢中的；如夢的；夢幻（般）的

'dream team *noun* the best possible combination of people for a particular competition or activity 夢之隊；最佳陣容；最佳組合

'dream ticket *noun* [sing.] (used especially in newspapers about candidates for an election) a combination of people who, together, are considered to be the best（尤用於報章，指大選的候選人）夢幻組合，最佳組合，最佳陣容

Dream·time /'dri:mtaɪm/ *noun* [U] = ALCHERINGA

dream·world /'dri:mwɜ:ld; *NAmE* -wɜ:rld/ *noun* a world that is not like the real world; a person's idea of reality that is not realistic 幻想世界；理想世界；不現實的想法： *If he thinks it's easy to get a job, he's* ***living in a dreamworld***. 如果他認為找工作很容易，那他就是在做白日夢。

dreamy /'dri:mi/ *adj.* (**dream·ier, dreami·est**) **1** looking as though you are thinking about other things and not paying attention to what is happening around you 做白日夢的；心不在焉的： *She had a dreamy look in her eyes.* 她眼裏帶着心不在焉的神色。 **2** (of a person or an idea 人或想法) having a lot of imagination, but not very realistic 愛幻想的（不切實際）： *Paul was dreamy and not very practical.* 保羅喜歡幻想，不太講究實際。 **3** as if you are in a dream or asleep 似在夢中的；模糊的；朦朧的；恍惚的： *He moved in the dreamy way of a man in a state of shock.* 他像受到驚嚇似的恍恍惚惚。 **4** (*informal*) pleasant and gentle; that makes you feel relaxed 怡然的；恬靜的；輕鬆的： *a slow, dreamy melody* 緩慢柔和的旋律 **5** (*informal*) beautiful; wonderful 漂亮的；美妙的；極好的： *What's he like? I bet he's really dreamy.* 他長得如何？我敢說他一定很俊。 ▸ **dream·ily** /-ɪli/ *adv.* **dreami·ness** *noun* [U]

dreary /'drɪəri; *NAmE* 'drɪri/ *adj.* (**drear·ier, dreari·est**) that makes you feel sad; dull and not interesting 令人沮喪的；沉悶的；枯燥無味的 SYN **dull**： *a dreary winter's day* 陰沉的冬日 ◇ *a* ***dreary film*** 枯燥無味的影片 ◇ *a long and dreary journey on the train* 火車上漫長而乏味的旅程 ▸ **drear·ily** /'drɪərəli; *NAmE* 'drɪr-/ *adv.* **dreari·ness** *noun* [U]

dreck /drek/ *noun* [U] (*slang, especially NAmE*) something that you think is of very bad quality 極低劣的東西；蹩腳貨： *The movie is utter dreck.* 那電影完全是一堆垃圾。

dredge /dredʒ/ *verb* **1** [T, I] **~ (sth) (for sth)** to remove mud, stones, etc. from the bottom of a river, CANAL, etc. using a boat or special machine, to make it deeper or to search for sth 疏濬；清淤；挖掘： *They're dredging the harbour so that larger ships can use it.* 他們正在疏濬港灣以便大船駛入。◇ *They dredge the bay for gravel.* 他們在挖掘海灣沙礫。 **2** [T] **~ sth (up) (from sth)** to bring sth up from the bottom of a river, etc. using a boat or special machine 打撈；採撈；撈取： *waste dredged (up) from the seabed* 從海底打撈出的廢物 **3** [T] **~ sth in/with sth** to cover food lightly with sugar, flour, etc.（用糖、麵粉等）撒，塗： *Dredge the top of the cake with icing sugar.* 把糖霜撒在蛋糕面上。

PHR V **,dredge sth↔'up 1** (*usually disapproving*) to mention sth that has been forgotten, especially sth unpleasant or embarrassing 重提，翻出（已遺忘的令人不快的往事）： *The papers keep trying to dredge up details of his past love life.* 這些報紙老是翻出他以往愛情生活的瑣事。 **2** to manage to remember sth, especially sth that happened a long time ago 追憶；回憶： *Now she was dredging up memories from the depths of her mind.* 這時，她回憶起內心深處的往事。

dredger /'dredʒə(r)/ *noun* a boat or machine that is used to clear mud, etc. from the bottom of a river, or to make the river wider 挖泥船；疏濬船

dregs /dregz/ *noun* [pl.] **1** the last drops of a liquid, mixed with little pieces of solid material that are left in the bottom of a container 殘渣；沉澱物： *coffee dregs* 咖啡渣 **2** the worst and most useless parts of sth 渣滓；糟粕： *the dregs of society* 社會渣滓 **3** (*literary*) the last parts of sth 殘餘： *the last dregs of daylight* 最後的餘暉

dreich /dri:x/ *adj.* (*ScotE*) dull and depressing 沉悶陰鬱的： *dreich weather on the Scottish coast* 蘇格蘭沿海地區陰鬱的天氣

drench /drentʃ/ *verb* [often passive] to make sb/sth completely wet 使濕透 SYN **soak**： **~ sb/sth** *We were caught in the storm and got drenched to the skin.* 我們遇上了暴雨，淋得渾身透濕。◇ **~ sb/sth in/with sth** *His face was drenched with sweat.* 他滿頭大汗。◇ (*figurative*) *She drenched herself in perfume.* 她渾身灑滿香水。
➲ SYNONYMS at WET

dress 🗝 /dres/ *noun, verb*

■ ***noun***

▸ CLOTHES 衣服 **1** 🗝 [C] a piece of women's clothing that is made in one piece and covers the body down to the legs, sometimes reaching to below the knees, or to the ankles 連衣裙： *a long white dress* 白色的長連衣裙 ◇ *a*

D

wedding dress 婚紗 ➲ VISUAL VOCAB page V61 ➲ see also COCKTAIL DRESS, EVENING DRESS (2), SUNDRESS **2** [U] clothes for either men or women 衣服：*to wear **casual/formal dress*** 穿便服／禮服 ◇ *He has no **dress sense*** (= no idea of how to dress well). 他毫無服裝品味。 ➲ SYNONYMS at CLOTHES ➲ see also EVENING DRESS (1), FANCY DRESS, HEADDRESS, MORNING DRESS

D

■ *verb*

▸ CLOTHES 衣服 **1** [I, T] to put clothes on yourself/sb 穿衣服；給（某人）穿衣服：**~ (in sth)** *I dressed quickly.* 我很快穿好了衣服。◇ **~ sb (in sth)** *She dressed the children in their best clothes.* 她給孩子們穿上了最漂亮的衣服。◇ *Get up and **get dressed**!* 起牀穿衣服了！ OPP **undress** ➲ COLLOCATIONS at FASHION **2** [I, T] to wear a particular type or style of clothes 穿…的服裝：*to **dress well/badly/fashionably/comfortably*** 穿得好／不好／時髦／舒適 ◇ **~ for/in/as sth** *You should dress for cold weather today.* 你今天應該穿防寒的衣服。◇ *She always dressed entirely in black.* 她一向全身黑色裝束。◇ **~ sb (for/in/as sth)** *He was dressed as a woman* (= he was wearing women's clothes). 他打扮得像個女人。 ➲ COLLOCATIONS at FASHION **3** [I] to put on formal clothes 穿正式服裝：*Do they expect us to dress for dinner?* 他們要求我們穿正式服裝赴宴嗎？ **4** [T] **~ sb** to provide clothes for sb 為…提供服裝：*He dresses many of Hollywood's most famous young stars.* 他為好萊塢許多最著名的年輕明星提供服裝。

▸ WOUND 傷口 **5** [T] **~ sth** to clean, treat and cover a wound 清洗，包紮，敷裹（傷口）：*The nurse will dress that cut for you.* 護士將為你包紮那個傷口。

▸ FOOD 食物 **6** [T] **~ sth** to prepare food for cooking or eating（烹調前）準備，處理；（食用前）給…加調味醬：*to **dress a salad*** (= put oil or VINEGAR, etc. on it) 給色拉加調味醬（放油、醋等）◇ *to **dress a chicken*** (= take out the parts you cannot eat) 給雞去毛開膛

▸ DECORATE 裝飾 **7** [T] **~ sth** (*formal*) to decorate or arrange sth 裝飾；佈置：*to dress a shop window* (= arrange a display of clothes or goods in it) 佈置櫥窗

▸ STONE/WOOD/LEATHER 石頭；木材；皮革 **8** [T] **~ sth** to prepare a material such as stone, wood, leather, etc. for use 加工；處理；修整 IDM see MUTTON, PART *n.*

PHR V ˌ**dress ˈdown** to wear clothes that are more informal than those you usually wear, for example in an office（與平時比較）穿着隨便 ˌ**dress sb ˈdown** to criticize or be angry with sb because they have done sth wrong 訓斥；責罵 ➲ related noun DRESSING-DOWN ˌ**dress ˈup** to wear clothes that are more formal than those you usually wear 穿上盛裝；穿上正裝 ˌ**dress ˈup** | ˌ**dress sb ˈup** to put on special clothes, especially to pretend to be sb/sth different 裝扮；喬裝打扮：*Kids love dressing up.* 孩子們都喜歡裝扮成別人玩兒。◇ *The boys were all dressed up as pirates.* 這些男孩子都裝扮成了海盜。◇ (*BrE*) *dressing-up clothes* 孩子裝扮成別人玩的服裝 ◇ (*NAmE*) *dress-up clothes* 孩子裝扮成別人玩的服裝 ˌ**dress sth ˈup** to present sth in a way that makes it seem better or different 裝飾；修飾；掩飾：*However much you try to dress it up, office work is not glamorous.* 無論你怎樣誇飾，辦公室工作都不令人嚮往。

dress·age /ˈdresɑːʒ/ *noun* [U] a set of controlled movements that a rider trains a horse to perform; a competition in which these movements are performed 花式騎術動作；花式騎術比賽

ˌ**dress ˈcircle** (*especially BrE*) (*NAmE* usually ˌ**first ˈbalcony**) *noun* the first level of seats above the ground floor in a theatre（劇院）樓廳前座，二樓正座

ˈ**dress code** *noun* rules about what clothes people should wear at work（工作時的）着裝規定：*The company has a strict dress code—all male employees are expected to wear suits.* 公司有嚴格的着裝規定：所有男職員都要穿西服。

dressed /drest/ *adj.* [not before noun]

1 wearing clothes and not naked or wearing clothes for sleeping 穿着衣服：*Hurry up and **get dressed**.* 快點穿上衣服。◇ *fully dressed* 穿戴整齊的 ◇ *I can't go to the door—I'm not dressed yet.* 我沒法去開門，我還沒穿好衣服呢。 **2** wearing clothes of a particular type 穿着…服裝：*smartly dressed* 衣着講究 ◇ **~ in ...** *The bride was dressed in white.* 新娘身穿白色禮服。◇ *He was casually dressed in jeans and a T-shirt.* 他穿着很隨便的牛仔褲和T恤衫。

IDM **dressed to ˈkill** (*informal*) wearing the kind of clothes that will make people notice and admire you 打扮得引人注目；穿着特別顯眼 **dressed (up) to the ˈnines** (*informal*) wearing very elegant or formal clothes 衣飾華麗；穿着講究 ➲ more at MUTTON

dress·er /ˈdresə(r)/ *noun* **1** (also ˌ**Welsh ˈdresser**) (*BrE*) a large piece of wooden furniture with shelves in the top part and cupboards below, used for displaying and storing cups, plates, etc. 食具櫥；碗櫥 **2** (*NAmE*) = CHEST OF DRAWERS **3** (used with an adjective 與形容詞連用) a person who dresses in the way mentioned 穿着…的人；衣着…者：*a snappy dresser* 穿着漂亮的人 **4** (in a theatre 劇院) a person whose job is to take care of an actor's clothes for a play and help him/her to get dressed 服裝員；服裝師

dress·ing /ˈdresɪŋ/ *noun* **1** (also ˈ**salad dressing**) [C, U] a thin sauce used to add flavour to salads, usually made from oil, VINEGAR, salt, pepper, etc.（拌製色拉用的）調料 ➲ see also FRENCH DRESSING **2** [U] (*NAmE*) = STUFFING (1) **3** [C] a piece of soft material placed over a wound in order to protect it（保護傷口的）敷料 **4** [U] the act of putting on clothes 穿衣；穿戴；打扮：*Many of our patients need help with dressing.* 我們的許多病人需要有人幫助穿衣。 ➲ see also CROSS-DRESSING, POWER DRESSING, WINDOW DRESSING

ˌ**dressing-ˈdown** *noun* [sing.] (*old-fashioned, informal*) an occasion when sb speaks angrily to a person because they have done sth wrong 訓斥；責罵

ˈ**dressing gown** (*BrE*) (*NAmE* **bath·robe**, **robe**) *noun* a long loose piece of clothing, usually with a belt, worn indoors over night clothes, for example when you first get out of bed 晨衣，晨袍（起牀後套於睡衣外在室內穿的寬鬆長罩衫，通常有束帶） ➲ VISUAL VOCAB page V63

ˈ**dressing room** *noun* **1** a room for changing your clothes in, especially one for actors or, in British English, for sports players（演員的）化妝間；（在英式英語中指運動員的）更衣室 **2** a small room next to a bedroom in some large houses, in which clothes are kept and people get dressed 梳妝室 **3** (*NAmE*) = FITTING ROOM

ˈ**dressing table** (*NAmE* also **van·ity**, ˈ**vanity table**) *noun* a piece of bedroom furniture like a table with drawers and a mirror on top 梳妝枱 ➲ VISUAL VOCAB page V23

dress·maker /ˈdresmeɪkə(r)/ *noun* a person who makes women's clothes, especially as a job（女裝）裁縫 ▸ **dress·mak·ing** *noun* [U]

ˌ**dress reˈhearsal** *noun* the final practice of a play in the theatre, using the clothes and lights that will be used for the real performance 彩排：(*figurative*) *The earlier protests had just been dress rehearsals for full-scale revolution.* 早期的抗議僅僅是大革命開始前的預演。

ˈ**dress shirt** *noun* **1** a white shirt worn on formal occasions with a BOW TIE and suit（白色、打蝶形領結的）西服襯衫，禮服襯衫 **2** (*NAmE*) a smart shirt with long sleeves, which can be worn with a tie（可打領帶的）長袖正裝襯衫

ˈ**dress uniform** *noun* [U] a uniform that army, navy, etc. officers wear for formal occasions and ceremonies 軍禮服

dressy /ˈdresi/ *adj.* (**dress·ier**, **dressi·est**) **1** (of clothes 衣服) elegant and formal 漂亮雅致的；講究的；正式的 **2** (of people 人) liking to wear elegant or fashionable clothes 衣着講究的；穿着時髦的

drew *past tense* of DRAW

drey /dreɪ/ *noun* the home of a SQUIRREL 松鼠窩

drib·ble /ˈdrɪbl/ *verb, noun*

■ *verb* **1** [I, T] **~ (sth)** to let SALIVA or another liquid come out of your mouth and run down your chin 流口水；垂涎 SYN **drool** **2** [I] **+ adv./prep.** to fall in small drops or in a thin stream 一點一滴地落下；細流：*Melted wax* *dribbled down the side of the candle.* 熔化了的蠟一滴滴從蠟燭邊上流下。 **3** [T] **~ sth (into/over/onto sth)** to pour sth slowly, in drops or a thin stream 使滴出；使成細流 SYN **drizzle, trickle**：*Dribble a little olive oil over the salad.* 在色拉上面滴點橄欖油。 **4** [T, I] **~ (sth) (+ adv./prep.)** (in football (SOCCER) and some other sports 足球及其他某些體育運動) to move the ball along with several short kicks, hits or BOUNCES 運球；帶球；盤球：*She dribbled the ball the length of the field.* 她帶球從後場跑到前場。◇ *He dribbled past two defenders and scored a magnificent goal.* 他帶球越過兩個防守隊員，射入非常精彩的一球。

■ ***noun*** **1** [C] a very small amount of liquid, in a thin stream 小滴；細流：*a dribble of blood* 一滴血 ◇ *Add just a dribble of oil.* 只加一點點油。 **2** [U] (*especially BrE*) SALIVA (= liquid) from a person's mouth 口水：*There was dribble all down the baby's front.* 這嬰兒胸前淌滿了口水。 **3** [C] the act of dribbling the ball in a sport 運球；帶球；盤球

dribs /drɪbz/ *noun* [pl.]

IDM **in ˌdribs and ˈdrabs** (*informal*) in small amounts or numbers over a period of time 少量；一點一滴；零零星星：*She paid me in dribs and drabs, not all at once.* 她一點一點地付給我錢，而不是一次付清。

dried *past tense, past part. of* DRY

ˌdried ˈfruit *noun* [U, C] fruit (for example, CURRANTS or RAISINS) that has been dried to be used in cooking or eaten on its own 乾果，果乾兒（如葡萄乾）

drier = DRYER ➲ see also DRY *adj.*

dri·est ➲ DRY *adj.*

drift /drɪft/ *noun, verb*

■ ***noun***

▸ **SLOW MOVEMENT** 緩緩流動 **1** [sing., U] a slow steady movement from one place to another; a gradual change or development from one situation to another, especially to sth bad 流動；趨勢；逐漸變化（尤指向壞的方面）：*a population drift away from rural areas* 農村地區的人口外流 ◇ *attempts to halt the drift towards war* 制止逐步走上戰爭道路的努力

▸ **OF SHIP** 船舶 **2** [U] the movement of a ship or plane away from its direction because of currents or wind（船隻或飛機的）偏航，航差

▸ **OF SEA/AIR** 海水；空氣 **3** [U, C] the movement of the sea or air 水流；氣流；流動 SYN **current**：*the general direction of drift on the east coast* 東海岸海水的總體流向 ◇ *He knew the hidden drifts in that part of the river.* 他對那段河道中的暗流非常清楚。

▸ **OF SNOW** 雪 **4** [C] a large pile of sth, especially snow, made by the wind 吹聚物；雪堆：*The road was blocked by deep drifts of snow.* 道路被風吹來的厚厚積雪阻塞。 ➲ see also SNOWDRIFT

▸ **OF FLOWERS** 花 **5** [C] a large mass of sth, especially flowers 大叢的花；叢生的植物：*Plant daffodils in informal drifts.* 隨便種幾叢黃水仙。

▸ **MEANING** 意義 **6** [sing.] the general meaning of what sb says or writes 大意；主旨；要點 SYN **gist**：*Do you* ***catch my drift****?* 你大概明白我的意思嗎？◇ *My German isn't very good, but I* ***got the drift*** *of what she said.* 我的德語不太好，但我大致明白她說的意思。 ➲ see also CONTINENTAL DRIFT

■ ***verb***

▸ **MOVE SLOWLY** 緩緩流動 **1** [I] (+ **adv./prep.**) to move along smoothly and slowly in water or air 漂流；漂移；飄：*Clouds drifted across the sky.* 朵朵浮雲在空中飄過。◇ *The empty boat drifted out to sea.* 空船向海上漂去。 **2** [I] **+ adv./prep.** to move or go somewhere slowly 緩緩移動；緩慢行走：*The crowd drifted away from the scene of the accident.* 人群漸漸從事故現場散去。◇ *Her gaze drifted around the room.* 她的目光緩緩掃視了一下室內。

▸ **WITHOUT PURPOSE** 漫無目的 **3** [I] (**+ adv./prep.**) to happen or change, or to do sth without a particular plan or purpose 無意間發生；無目的地轉變；順其自然地做：*I didn't intend to be a teacher—I just drifted into it.* 我並沒打算過當老師，只是順其自然就當了。◇ *He hasn't decided what to do yet—he's just drifting.* 他還沒決定做什麼，只是順其自然。◇ *The conversation drifted onto politics.* 談話不知不覺就轉到政治方面來了。

▸ **INTO STATE/SITUATION** 狀態；情況 **4** [I] **~ in/into sth** to go from one situation or state to another without realizing it 無意間進入；不知不覺陷入：*Finally she drifted into sleep.* 最後她不知不覺地睡着了。◇ *The injured man tried to speak but soon drifted into unconsciousness.* 受傷的男人想說點什麼，但一會兒就不省人事了。

▸ **OF SNOW/SAND** 雪；沙 **5** [I] to be blown into large piles by the wind 吹積；堆積：*drifting sand* 堆積的沙 ◇ *Some roads are closed because of drifting.* 有些道路因積雪而封閉。

▸ **FLOAT** 漂浮 **6** [T] **+ adv./prep.** to make sth float somewhere 使漂流；使漂浮：*The logs are drifted downstream to the mill.* 原木順流而下漂到木材加工廠。

PHR V **ˌdrift aˈpart** to become less friendly or close to sb 逐漸疏遠：*As children we were very close, but as we grew up we just drifted apart.* 孩提時我們親密無間，但長大後我們就逐漸疏遠了。 **ˌdrift ˈoff (to sleep)** to fall asleep 入睡；睡着：*I didn't hear the storm. I must have drifted off by then.* 我沒有聽見暴風雨，那時一定是睡着了。

drift·er /ˈdrɪftə(r)/ *noun* (*disapproving*) a person who moves from one job or place to another with no real purpose 漂泊者；盲流

ˈdrift net *noun* a very large net used by fishing boats. The net has weights at the bottom and FLOATS at the top and is allowed to hang in the sea. 流網；漂網

drift·wood /ˈdrɪftwʊd/ *noun* [U] wood that the sea carries up onto land, or that floats on the water 浮木，漂流木（海水沖上岸或在水中漂流的木頭）

drill /drɪl/ *noun, verb*

■ ***noun*** **1** [C] a tool or machine with a pointed end for making holes 鑽；鑽頭；鑽牀；鑽機：*an electric drill* 電鑽 ◇ *a pneumatic drill* 風鑽 ◇ *a hand drill* 手鑽 ◇ *a dentist's drill* 牙鑽 ◇ *a drill bit* (= the pointed part at the end of the drill) 鑽頭 ➲ **VISUAL VOCAB** page V20 **2** [C, U] a way of learning sth by means of repeated exercises 練習；訓練 **3** [C, U] a practice of what to do in an emergency, for example if there is a fire（應對緊急情況的）演習：*a fire drill* 消防演習 **4** [U] military training in marching, the use of weapons, etc. 軍事訓練；操練：*rifle drill* 步槍操練 **5 the drill** [sing.] (*old-fashioned, BrE*) the correct or usual way to do sth 正確的步驟；常規；程序 SYN **procedure**：*What's the drill for claiming expenses?* 報銷費用的手續是什麼？ **6** [U] a type of strong cotton cloth 粗斜紋布 **7** [C] a machine for planting seeds in rows 條播機

■ ***verb*** **1** [T, I] to make a hole in sth, using a drill 鑽（孔）；打（眼）：**~ sth** *Drill a series of holes in the frame.* 在構架上鑽一串孔。◇ **~ (for sth)** *They're* ***drilling for oil*** *off the Irish coast.* 他們在愛爾蘭沿海鑽井採油。◇ **~ (through sth)** *He drilled through the wall by mistake.* 他誤將牆壁鑽穿了。 **2** [T] to teach sb to do sth by making them repeat it a lot of times 培訓；訓練：**~ sb to do sth** *The children were drilled to leave the classroom quickly when the fire bell rang.* 孩子們接受了如何在火警鐘拉響時迅速離開教室的訓練。◇ **~ sb** *a well-drilled team* 訓練有素的隊伍 ◇ **~ sb in sth** *Recruits are drilled in basic techniques over the five-day course.* 新兵接受為期五天的基本技能訓練。 **3** [T] **~ sb** to train soldiers to perform military actions 進行軍事訓練；操練

PHR V **ˌdrill ˈdown** (*computing* 計 or *business* 商) to go to deeper levels of an organized set of data in order to find more detail, especially on a computer or a website 自頂向下搜索；向下鑽取：*Navigation is good and there's a display to show how far you've drilled down.* 導航很好，可以顯示你正在看哪一級信息。 **ˈdrill sth into sb** to make sb remember or learn sth by repeating it often 反複訓練某人；向某人反複灌輸：*It was drilled into us at an early age never to drop litter.* 我們從小就被叮囑絕不能亂扔垃圾。

drily (also **dryly**) /ˈdraɪli/ *adv.* ➲ see also DRY **1** if sb speaks **drily**, they are being humorous, but not in an obvious way 幽默而不形於色地：*'That's a lovely purple suit you're wearing,' she said drily.* "你穿的這件紫色套裝真夠可愛。"她不動聲色地諷刺說。 **2** in a way that

D

shows no emotion 冷冰冰地；冷淡地；不動感情地：*He smiled drily and leaned back in his chair.* 他冷冷地笑了笑，隨即靠在椅背上。**3** in a way that shows that there is no liquid present 乾燥地：*She coughed drily.* 她乾咳着。◇ *He swallowed drily and nodded.* 他乾嚥了一下，然後點了點頭。

D

drink 🔑 /drɪŋk/ *noun, verb*

■ ***noun*** **1** 🔑 [C, U] a liquid for drinking; an amount of a liquid that you drink 飲料；一杯，一份，一口（飲料）：*Can I* ***have a drink****?* 給我來一杯飲料好嗎？◇ *soft drinks* (= cold drinks without alcohol) 軟飲料（不含酒精）◇ *a drink of water* 一杯水 ◇ *food and drink* 食物和飲料 ◇ *She took a drink from the glass and then put it down.* 她喝了一口飲料，然後放下杯子。**2** 🔑 [C, U] alcohol or an alcoholic drink; sth that you drink on a social occasion 酒；酒精飲料：*They went* ***for a drink****.* 他們去了喝酒。◇ *The drinks are on me* (= I'll pay for them). 酒錢由我付。◇ *I need* ***a stiff drink*** (= a very strong drink). 我要一杯烈酒。◇ (*BrE*) *He's got* ***a drink problem****.* 他有貪杯的毛病。◇ (*NAmE*) *He has a* ***drinking problem****.* 他有貪杯的毛病。◇ (*humorous*) *The children are enough to* ***drive me to drink****.* 這些孩子足以逼得我酗起酒來。◇ (*BrE*) *They came home* ***the worse for drink*** (= drunk). 他們喝得酩酊大醉地回到家裏。◇ *She* ***took to drink*** (= often drank too much alcohol) *after her marriage broke up.* 婚姻破裂後，她染上了酗酒的惡習。**3 drinks** [pl.] (*BrE*) a social occasion where you have alcoholic drinks 酒宴；酒會：*Would you like to come for drinks on Sunday?* 星期天來參加酒宴好嗎？◇ *a drinks party* 酒會 **IDM** see DEMON, MEAT

■ ***verb*** (**drank** /dræŋk/, **drunk** /drʌŋk/) **1** 🔑 [T, I] **~ (sth)** to take liquid into your mouth and swallow it 喝；飲：*What would you like to drink?* 你想喝點什麼？◇ *In hot weather, drink plenty of water.* 天熱時要多喝水。◇ *I don't drink coffee.* 我不喝咖啡。◇ *He was drinking straight from the bottle.* 他直接對着酒瓶喝酒。**2** 🔑 [I, T] to drink alcohol, especially when it is done regularly 喝酒；（尤指）酗酒：*He doesn't drink.* 他不喝酒。◇ *Don't* ***drink and drive*** (= drive a car after drinking alcohol). 切勿酒後駕車。◇ *She's been drinking heavily since she lost her job.* 她失業後便常常酗酒。◇ **~ sth** *I drank far too much last night.* 我昨天晚上喝得酩酊大醉。◇ **~ yourself + adj.** *He had drunk himself unconscious on vodka.* 他喝伏特加酒喝得不省人事。➲ see also DRUNK *adj.* (1)

IDM **drink sb's 'health** (*BrE*) to wish sb good health as you lift your glass, and then drink from it 為某人的健康乾杯 **drink like a 'fish** to drink a lot of alcohol regularly（習慣性）飲酒過度，酗酒，豪飲 **ˌdrink sb under the 'table** (*informal*) to drink more alcohol than sb else without becoming as drunk as they are（拚酒量）喝倒某人；喝到使某人醉倒 ➲ more at EAT, HORSE *n.*

PHR V **ˌdrink sth↔'in** to look at or listen to sth with great interest and enjoyment 盡情地欣賞；如飢似渴地傾聽；陶醉於：*We just stood there drinking in the scenery.* 我們就站在那兒盡情欣賞景色。**'drink to sb/sth** to wish sb good luck, health or success as you lift your glass and then drink from it 為…乾杯（或祝酒）**SYN** **toast**：*All raise your glasses and drink to Katie and Tom!* 大家舉起杯為凱蒂和湯姆祝福吧！**ˌdrink 'up | ˌdrink (sth)↔'up** to drink all of sth （把…）喝完：*Drink up and let's go.* 喝完了咱們走吧。◇ *Come on, drink up your juice.* 快，把果汁喝完。

drink·able /'drɪŋkəbl/ *adj.* **1** clean and safe to drink 可飲用的 **2** pleasant to drink 好喝的：*a very drinkable wine* 很好喝的葡萄酒

ˌdrink-'driver (*BrE*) (also **ˌdrunk 'driver** *NAmE, BrE*) *noun* a person who drives a vehicle after drinking too much alcohol 酒後駕車者

ˌdrink-'driving (also **ˌdrunken 'driving**) (both *BrE*) (also **'drunk driving** *NAmE, BrE*) *noun* [U] driving a vehicle after drinking too much alcohol 酒後駕車

drink·er /'drɪŋkə(r)/ *noun* **1** a person who drinks alcohol regularly, especially sb who drinks too much 飲酒者；（尤指）酗酒者，酒徒：*a* ***heavy/moderate drinker*** 酒鬼；有節制的飲酒者 **2** (after a noun 置於名詞後) a person who regularly drinks the particular drink mentioned 常飲…酒者；常喝…飲料者：*a coffee drinker* 常喝咖啡的人

drink·ing /'drɪŋkɪŋ/ *noun* [U] the act of drinking alcohol 喝酒；飲酒：*Drinking is not advised during pregnancy.* 建議妊娠期不要飲酒。◇ *There are tough penalties for drinking and driving.* 酒後駕車刑罰很重。

'drinking box *noun* (*CanE*) a small cardboard box of juice, etc. that has a drinking straw with it that can be pushed through a small hole in the top （帶吸管的）盒裝飲料

'drinking chocolate *noun* [U] (*BrE*) a sweet chocolate powder or a hot drink made from this powder mixed with hot milk and/or water 甜巧克力粉；巧克力熱飲 ➲ compare COCOA

'drinking fountain (*especially BrE*) (*NAmE* usually **'water fountain**) *noun* a device that supplies water for drinking in public places （設於公共場所的）噴泉式飲水器

'drinking straw *noun* = STRAW (3)

ˌdrinking-'up time *noun* [U] (*BrE*) in Britain, the time between when a pub stops serving drinks and when it closes, when people are allowed to finish drinks that they bought earlier （在英國酒吧停止售酒但在打烊前允給顧客的）飲完殘酒時間

'drinking water *noun* [U] water that is safe for drinking 飲用水

drip /drɪp/ *verb, noun*

■ ***verb*** (**-pp-**) **1** [I] (**+ adv./prep.**) (of liquid 液體) to fall in small drops 滴下：*She was hot and sweat dripped into her eyes.* 她很熱，汗水滴入雙眼。◇ *Water was dripping down the walls.* 水從牆上滴落下來。**2** [I, T] to produce drops of liquid 滴出；滴水：*The tap was dripping.* 龍頭在滴水。◇ **+ adv./prep.** *Her hair dripped down her back.* 她頭髮上的水順着後背滴落下來。◇ **~ sth (+adv./prep.)** *Be careful, you're dripping paint everywhere!* 小心點，你把顏料滴得到處都是！**3** [I, T] to contain or hold a lot of sth 含有；充滿；充溢：**~ with sth** *The trees were dripping with fruit.* 樹上掛滿了果子。◇ **~ sth** *His voice dripped sarcasm.* 他的話語中充滿了譏諷。

■ ***noun*** **1** [sing.] the sound or action of small drops of liquid falling continuously 滴落；滴水聲；滴答聲：*The silence was broken only by the steady drip, drip of water from the roof.* 只有屋頂上滴答滴答持續不斷的滴水聲打破了寂靜。**2** [C] a small drop of liquid that falls from sth 水滴；滴液：*We put a bucket under the hole in the roof to catch the drips.* 我們在屋頂漏洞下放了一個水桶接水滴。**3** (*NAmE* also **IV**) [C] (*medical* 醫) a piece of equipment that passes liquid food, medicine or blood very slowly through a tube into a patient's VEIN（靜脈）滴注器，點滴瓶：*She's been put* ***on a drip****.* 她一直在輸液。**4** [C] (*informal, becoming old-fashioned*) a boring or stupid person with a weak personality 怯懦討厭的人；愚蠢膽怯的人 **SYN** **wimp**：*Don't be such a drip—come and join in the fun!* 別犯傻了，過來一起玩吧！

ˌdrip-'dry *adj.* made of a type of cloth that will dry quickly without CREASES when you hang it up wet （衣服）快速滴乾的，滴乾免熨的

'drip-feed *verb* (**drip-fed, drip-fed**) **~ sb/sth** to give sb sth in separate small amounts 餵飼；分做小量點滴給予 ▸ **'drip feed** *noun* [U, C]：*the steady drip feed of leaked documents in the papers* 泄露的文件一點點接連在報紙上出現

drip·ping /'drɪpɪŋ/ *adj., noun*

■ ***adj.*** **~ (with sth)** very wet 濕淋淋的：*Her face was dripping with sweat.* 她臉上汗水淋淋。◇ *His clothes were still* ***dripping wet****.* 他的衣服還是濕淋淋的。◇ (*figurative*) *His wife came in, dripping with diamonds.* 他的妻子渾身珠光寶氣地走了進來。

■ ***noun*** [U] fat that comes out of meat when it is cooked, often kept for frying other food in （烤肉時滴下的）油

drip·py /'drɪpi/ *adj.* (**drip·pier, drip·pi·est**) (*informal*) **1** boring, stupid and weak or SENTIMENTAL 愚懦脆弱的；婆婆媽媽的：*her drippy boyfriend* 她那婆婆媽媽的男朋友 **2** in a liquid state, and likely to fall in drops 濕漉漉的；滴水的：*drippy paint* 濕淋淋的油漆 ◇ *a drippy* *nose* (= with drops of liquid falling from it) 淌鼻涕的鼻子 ▸ **drip·pily** *adv.* **drip·pi·ness** *noun* [U]

drive 0→ /draɪv/ *verb, noun*

■ *verb* (drove /drəʊv; *NAmE* droʊv/, **driven** /ˈdrɪvn/)

▸ VEHICLE 交通工具 **1** 0→ [I, T] to operate a vehicle so that it goes in a particular direction 駕駛；開車： *Can you drive?* 你會開車嗎？◇ *Don't drive so fast!* 別開得那麼快！◇ *I drove to work this morning.* 我今天早上開車去上班。◇ *Shall we drive* (= go there by car) *or go by train?* 我們開車去還是乘火車去？◇ **~ sth** *He drives a taxi* (= that is his job). 他是開出租車的。➲ COLLOCATIONS at DRIVING **2** 0→ [T] **~ sb** (**+ adv./prep.**) to take sb somewhere in a car, taxi, etc. 駕車送（人）： *Could you drive me home?* 你可以開車送我回家嗎？➲ SYNONYMS at TAKE **3** 0→ [T] **~ sth** to own or use a particular type of vehicle 擁有（或駕駛）…汽車：*What car do you drive?* 你開什麼車？

▸ MACHINE 機器 **4** 0→ [T, usually passive] **~ sth** to provide the power that makes a machine work 驅動；推動： *a steam-driven locomotive* 蒸汽機車

▸ MAKE SB DO STH 使人做某事 **5** 0→ [T] **~ sb** (**+ adv./prep.**) to force sb to act in a particular way 迫使；驅使： *The urge to survive drove them on.* 求生的慾望驅使他們繼續下去。◇ *You're driving yourself too hard.* 你把自己弄得太累了。 **6** 0→ [T] to make sb very angry, crazy, etc. or to make them do sth extreme 迫使（某人生氣、發瘋或做出極端事情）： **~ sb + adj.** *to* **drive** *sb* **crazy/mad/insane** 把某人逼得發瘋／發狂／失去理智◇ **~ sb to do sth** *Hunger drove her to steal.* 飢餓迫使她去偷竊。◇ **~ sb to sth** *Those kids are driving me to despair.* 那些孩子讓我都快絕望了。◇ (*humorous*) *It's enough to* **drive you to drink** (= to make you start drinking too much alcohol). 這種事足以逼得人拚命喝酒。

▸ MAKE SB/STH MOVE 使移動 **7** [T] **~ sb/sth + adv./prep.** to force sb/sth to move in a particular direction 驅趕；趕走；驅逐： *to drive sheep into a field* 把羊群趕到田野裏◇ *The enemy was driven back.* 敵人被擊退了。

▸ CAUSE STH TO MAKE PROGRESS 推動 **8** [T] **~ sth** to influence sth or cause it to make progress 激勵；促進；推進： *This is the main factor driving investment in the area.* 這是推動在這個地區投資的主要因素。

▸ HIT/PUSH 擊；推 **9** [T] **~ sth + adv./prep.** to force sth to go in a particular direction or into a particular position by pushing it, hitting it, etc. 擊；打；敲；推： *to drive a nail into a piece of wood* 把釘子釘進一塊木頭

▸ MAKE A HOLE 打洞 **10** [T] **~ sth + adv./prep.** to make an opening in or through sth by using force 鑿；挖掘： *They drove a tunnel through the solid rock.* 他們鑿出一條穿過堅固岩石的隧道。

Collocations 詞語搭配

Driving 駕駛

Having a car 擁有一輛汽車

- **have/own/**(*BrE*) **run** a car 有一輛汽車
- **ride** a motorcycle/motorbike 騎摩托車
- **drive/prefer/use** an automatic/a manual/(*NAmE, informal*) a stick shift 開／喜歡／用自動擋／手動擋汽車
- **have/get** your car **serviced/fixed/repaired** 給汽車做一次保養／維修一下／修理一下
- **buy/sell** a used car/(*especially BrE*) a second-hand car 買／賣二手車
- **take/pass/fail** a (*BrE*) driving test/(*both NAmE*) driver's test/road test 參加／通過／未通過駕照考試／道路試驗
- **get/obtain/have/lose/carry** a/your (*BrE*) driving licence/(*NAmE*) driver's license 得到／擁有／丟失／攜帶駕照

Driving 駕駛

- **put on/fasten/**(*NAmE*) **buckle/wear/undo** your seat belt/safety belt 繫上／解開安全帶
- **put/turn/leave** the key in the ignition 把鑰匙插進點火開關；轉動鑰匙點火；把鑰匙留在點火開關
- **start** the car/engine 發動汽車／引擎
- (*BrE*) **change/**(*NAmE*) **shift/put sth into gear** 換擋；掛上擋
- **press/put your foot on** the brake pedal/clutch/accelerator 踩剎車／離合器／油門
- **release** the clutch/(*especially BrE*) the handbrake/(*both NAmE*) the emergency brake/the parking brake 鬆開離合器／手閘
- **drive/park/reverse** the car 駕車；停車；倒車
- (*BrE*) **indicate** left/right 示意左轉／右轉
- (*especially NAmE*) **signal** that you are turning left/right 示意左轉／右轉
- **take/miss** (*BrE*) the turning/(*especially NAmE*) the turn 拐彎；錯過拐彎處
- **apply/hit/slam on** the brake(s) 踩剎車；猛踩剎車
- **beep/honk/**(*especially BrE*) **toot/**(*BrE*) **sound** your horn 按喇叭

Problems and accidents 問題及事故

- a car **skids/crashes** (**into sth**)/**collides** (**with sth**) 車打滑／撞上（某物）/（與某物）相撞
- **swerve to avoid** an oncoming car/a pedestrian 猛地轉彎以避開迎面來的車／行人
- **crash/lose control of** the car 撞車；車失控
- **have/be in/be killed in/survive** a car crash/a car accident/(*NAmE*) a car wreck/a hit-and-run 出車禍／肇事逃逸事故；在車禍／肇事逃逸事故中喪生；幸免於車禍／肇事逃逸事故
- **be run over/knocked down by** a car/bus/truck 被汽車／公交車／大卡車軋過／撞倒
- **dent/hit** (*BrE*) the bonnet/(*NAmE*) the hood 撞凹／撞上引擎蓋
- **break/crack/shatter** (*BrE*) the windscreen/(*NAmE*) the windshield 打碎擋風玻璃
- **blow/**(*especially BrE*) **burst/puncture** (*BrE*) a tyre/(*NAmE*) a tire 爆胎；扎破輪胎
- **get/have** (*BrE*) a flat tyre/a flat tire/a puncture 胎癟了；輪胎被扎破了
- **inflate/change/fit/replace/check** a tyre/tire 給輪胎充氣；更換／安裝／更換／檢查輪胎

Traffic and driving regulations 交通法規

- **be caught in/get stuck in/sit in** a traffic jam 遇上堵車
- **cause** congestion/tailbacks/traffic jams/gridlock 引起交通堵塞
- **experience/face** lengthy delays 經歷／面臨長時間的延誤
- **beat/avoid** the traffic/the rush hour 避開交通高峰時段
- **break/observe/**(*NAmE*) **drive** the speed limit 超速行駛；遵守速度限制；限速行駛
- **be caught on** (*BrE*) a speed camera 被測速攝像機逮住
- **stop sb for/pull sb over for/**(*BrE, informal*) **be done for** speeding 因超速被要求停車／停靠路邊／被逮住
- (*both informal*) **run/**(*BrE*) **jump** a red light/the lights 闖紅燈
- **be arrested for/charged with** (*BrE*) drink-driving/(*both US*) driving under the influence (DUI)/driving while intoxicated (DWI) 因酒後／醉酒駕車被逮捕／起訴
- **be banned/**(*BrE*) **disqualified** from driving 被禁止駕車；被取消駕駛資格

D

▸ IN SPORT 體育運動 **11** [T, I] **~ (sth) (+ adv./prep.)** to hit a ball with force, sending it forward 猛抽，猛擊（球）: *to drive the ball into the rough* (= in GOLF) 將球擊入長草區（高爾夫球） ▸ WIND/WATER 風；水 **12** [T] **~ sth (+ adv./prep.)** to carry sth along 吹；捲；颳；沖: *Huge waves drove the yacht onto the rocks.* 巨浪將快艇沖到岩石上。 **13** [I] **(+ adv./prep.)** to fall or move rapidly and with great force 猛落；急速驅進: *The waves drove against the shore.* 波浪沖擊着岸邊。

IDM **drive a coach and 'horses through sth** to spoil sth, for example a plan 毀掉，糟蹋，破壞（計劃等） **drive sth 'home (to sb)** to make sb understand or accept sth by saying it often, loudly, angrily, etc. 把…講透徹；闡明；使充分理解: *You will really need to drive your point home.* 你的確需要把你的觀點闡釋清楚。 **what sb is 'driving at** (*informal*) the thing sb is trying to say 某人的用意；某人話中的意思: *I wish I knew what they were driving at.* 我要是知道他們的用意就好了。 ➲ more at GROUND *n.*, HARD *adj.*, SNOW *n.*

PHR V **,drive a'way | ,drive sb/sth a'way** 🔑 to leave in a vehicle; to take sb away in a vehicle 驅車離開；駕車送走: *We heard him drive away.* 我們聽到他驅車離去了。◇ *Someone drove the car away in the night.* 有人夜裏把車開走了。 **,drive sb a'way** 🔑 to make sb not want to stay or not want to go somewhere 使離去；使不願久留；使不想去（某地）: *Her constant nagging drove him away.* 她不斷的嘮叨把他給趕跑了。◇ *Terrorist threats are driving away tourists.* 恐怖分子的威脅嚇跑了觀光客。 **,drive 'off** **1** 🔑 (of a driver, car, etc. 駕駛者、汽車等) to leave 驅車離去；駛去: *The robbers drove off in a stolen vehicle.* 劫匪駕駛着一輛偷來的汽車逃跑了。 **2** (in GOLF 高爾夫球) to hit the ball to begin a game 開（球） **,drive sb/sth↔'off** to force sb/sth to go back or away 擊退；趕走: *The defenders drove off each attack.* 防守隊員擊退了每一次進攻。 **,drive 'on** to continue driving 驅車繼續行駛: *Don't stop—drive on!* 不要停，繼續往前開！ **,drive sb/sth↔'out (of sth)** to make sb/sth disappear or stop doing sth 驅散；消除；使停止: *New fashions drive out old ones.* 新款式服裝使舊的款式不再流行。 **,drive sth↔'up/'down** to make sth such as prices rise or fall quickly 抬高（或壓低）；使上升（或下跌）

■ ***noun***

▸ IN/OF VEHICLE 交通工具 **1** 🔑 [C] a journey in a car or other vehicle 驅車旅行；駕車路程: *Let's **go for a drive**.* 咱們開車去兜兜風吧。◇ *It's a three-hour drive to London.* 到倫敦要三小時的駕車路程。 **2** [C, U] the equipment in a vehicle that takes power from the engine to the wheels 傳動（或驅動）裝置: *the drive shaft* 驅動軸 ◇ *a car with four-wheel drive* 四輪驅動汽車 ◇ *a **left-/right-hand drive** car* (= a car where the driver and the controls are on the left/right) 左／右座駕駛的汽車 ▸ OUTSIDE HOUSE 住宅外面 **3** (also **drive·way**) [C] a wide hard path or a private road that leads from the street to a house（從街道通向住宅的寬闊或私人的）車道: *There were two cars parked **in/on** the drive.* 車道上停了兩輛汽車。 ➲ VISUAL VOCAB page V17 ▸ EFFORT 努力 **4** [C] an organized effort by a group of people to achieve sth（團體為達到某目的而進行的）有組織的努力，運動: *a **recruitment/export/economy drive*** 徵兵／出口／經濟運動 ◇ **~ for sth** *a drive for greater efficiency* 為提高效率而進行的運動 ◇ **~ to do sth** *the government's drive to reduce energy consumption* 政府為減少能源消耗而發起的運動 ➲ SYNONYMS at CAMPAIGN ▸ DESIRE/ENERGY 慾望；精力 **5** [C, U] a strong desire or need in people（人的）強烈慾望，本能需求: *a strong sexual drive* 強烈的性慾 **6** [U] (*approving*) a strong desire to do things and achieve sth; great energy 衝勁；幹勁；精力: *He'll do very well—he has tremendous drive.* 他會幹得很出色的，他幹勁十足。 ▸ IN SPORT 體育運動 **7** [C] a long hard hit or kick 猛擊；猛踢: *She has a strong forehand drive* (= in TENNIS). 她正手擊球強而有力。◇ *He scored with a brilliant 25-yard drive.* 他在 25 碼外一腳勁射入球得分。 ▸ COMPUTING 計算機技術 **8** [C] the part of a computer that reads and stores information on disks or tapes 驅動器: *a 750GB hard drive* * 750 吉字節的硬盤 ◇ *a CD drive* 光盤驅動器 ➲ VISUAL VOCAB page V66 ➲ see also DISK DRIVE ▸ GAMES 遊戲 **9** [C] (*BrE*) a social occasion when a lot of people compete in a game such as WHIST or BINGO（惠斯特或賓戈紙牌遊戲）比賽；玩紙牌的聚會 ▸ ANIMALS/ENEMY 動物；敵人 **10** [C] an act of chasing animals or the enemy and making them go into a smaller area, especially in order to kill or capture them 驅趕；趕攏；（尤指）圍攻，圍殲 ▸ ROAD 路 **11 Drive** (*abbr.* **Dr**) used in the names of roads（用於路名）路，大道: *21 Island Heights Drive* 艾蘭海茨路 21 號

'drive bay *noun* (*computing* 計) a space inside a computer for a DISK DRIVE（磁盤）驅動器槽

'drive-by *adj.* (*NAmE*) [only before noun] a **drive-by** shooting, etc. is done from a moving car（槍擊等）飛車而過發射的: *a drive-by killing* 從行駛汽車上開槍殺人 ▸ **'drive-by** *noun*

'drive-in *noun* a place where you can watch films/movies, eat, etc. without leaving your car "免下車"電影院（或餐館等）: *We stopped at a drive-in for a hamburger.* 我們在一家"免下車"餐館停下來吃漢堡包。◇ *drive-in movies* "免下車"露天電影院

drivel /ˈdrɪvl/ *noun, verb*

■ ***noun*** [U] (*informal, disapproving*) silly nonsense 蠢話；傻話；廢話: *How can you watch that drivel on TV?* 你怎麼能看電視上那種胡説八道的東西？

■ ***verb*** (**-ll-**, *US* **-l-**) [I] **~ (on) (about sth)** (usually used in the progressive tenses 通常用於進行時) to keep talking about silly or unimportant things 老是説傻話；喋喋不休地説無聊話

driven /ˈdrɪvn/ *adj.* **1** (of a person 人) determined to succeed, and working very hard to do so 奮發努力的；發憤圖強的 **2 -driven** (in compounds 構成複合詞) influenced or caused by a particular thing 受…影響的；由…造成的: *a market-driven economy* 市場導向的經濟 ◇ *a character-driven movie* 以人物為主的電影 ➲ see also DRIVE, DROVE, DRIVEN *v.*

driver 🔑 /ˈdraɪvə(r)/ *noun*

1 🔑 a person who drives a vehicle 駕駛員；司機；駕車者: *a **bus/train/ambulance/taxi driver*** 公共汽車／火車／救護車／出租車司機 ◇ *She climbed into the driver's seat.* 她爬上了駕駛座。◇ (*BrE*) *a **learner driver*** (= one who has not yet passed a driving test) 學開車的人 ◇ (*NAmE*) *a **student driver*** 實習駕駛的人 ◇ *The car comes equipped with a driver's airbag.* 這輛汽車裝有駕駛員安全氣囊。 ➲ see also BACK-SEAT DRIVER **2** (in GOLF 高爾夫球) a CLUB with a wooden head 球杆 **3** (*computing* 計) software that controls the sending of data between a computer and a piece of equipment that is attached to it, such as a printer 驅動程序 **4** one of the main things that influence sth or cause it to make progress 驅動因素: *Housing is a key driver of the economy.* 住房是個促使經濟增長的主要因素。 IDM see SEAT *n.*

'driver's license (*NAmE*) (*BrE* **'driving licence**) *noun* an official document that shows that you are qualified to drive 駕駛執照；駕照

'driver's test *noun* (*NAmE*) = DRIVING TEST

drive·shaft /ˈdraɪvʃɑːft; *NAmE* -ʃæft/ *noun* a long thin part of a machine that turns round and round and sends power from the engine to another part of the machine（機器的）主動軸，驅動軸

'drive-through (also **'drive-thru**) *noun* (*NAmE*) a restaurant, bank, etc. where you can be served without having to get out of your car 不必下車即可得到服務的餐館（或銀行等）

'drive time *noun* [U] a time during the day when many people are driving their cars, for example to or from work（如上下班交通高峰的）開車時間 ▸ **'drive-time** *adj.*: *a drive-time radio show* 駕車時間廣播節目

drive·way /ˈdraɪvweɪ/ *noun* = DRIVE (3): *There was a car parked **in/on** the driveway.* 有一輛汽車停在車道上。

driv·ing 🔑 /ˈdraɪvɪŋ/ *noun, adj.*

■ ***noun*** 🔑 [U] the way that sb drives a vehicle; the act of driving 行車的方式；駕駛；行車: *dangerous driving* 危險駕駛 ◇ *driving lessons* 駕駛課程 IDM see SEAT *n.*

▪ *adj.* [only before noun] **1** strong and powerful; having a strong influence in making sth happen 強有力的；起推動作用的；推動的：*Who was* ***the driving force*** (= the person with the strongest influence) *in the band?* 誰是樂隊的主力？ **2** (of rain, snow, etc. 雨、雪等) falling very fast and at an angle 猛烈的；傾瀉而下的

ˈdriving licence (*BrE*) (*NAmE* **ˈdriver's license**) *noun* an official document that shows that you are qualified to drive 駕駛執照；駕照

ˈdriving range *noun* a place where people can practise hitting GOLF balls 高爾夫球練習場

ˈdriving school *noun* a business that gives people lessons in how to drive a car, etc. 駕駛學校

ˈdriving test (*NAmE* also **ˈdriver's test**, **ˈroad test**) *noun* a test that must be passed before you are qualified to drive a car, etc. 駕照考試

ˌdriving under the ˈinfluence *noun* [U] (*abbr.* **DUI**) (*US*) (in some states in the US 美國某些州) the crime of driving a vehicle after drinking too much alcohol. It is a less serious crime than 'driving while intoxicated'. 酒後開車罪（較酒醉開車罪輕）

ˌdriving while inˈtoxicated *noun* [U] (*abbr.* **DWI**) (*US*) the crime of driving a vehicle after drinking too much alcohol 酒醉開車罪

driz·zle /ˈdrɪzl/ *verb, noun*

▪ *verb* **1** [I] when **it is drizzling**, it is raining lightly 下毛毛雨；下濛濛細雨 **2** [T] **~ sth (over sth)** to pour a small amount of liquid over the surface of sth （毛毛雨似的）灑落 SYN **dribble**

▪ *noun* [U, sing.] light fine rain 毛毛細雨 ▸ **driz·zly** /ˈdrɪzli/ *adj.*：*a dull, drizzly morning* 陰雨濛濛的早上

DRM /ˌdiː ɑːr ˈem/ *abbr.* (*computing* 計) digital rights management (actions and devices that are used by the owners of software or information to prevent people from copying it from the Internet) 數字版權管理；數位著作權管理（指軟件或信息擁有者為防止互聯網盜版行為所採用的措施或裝置）

Dr Mar·tens™ /ˌdɒktə ˈmɑːtɪnz; *NAmE* ˌdɑːktər ˈmɑːrtnz/ (also *informal* **Doc Martens**, **DMs**) *noun* [pl.] a type of comfortable heavy boot or shoe with LACES 馬丁斯醫生靴（舒適的繫帶厚靴或鞋子）

drogue /drəʊg; *NAmE* droʊg/ *noun* a small PARACHUTE, used to pull a larger one from its bag 引導傘，拖曳傘（將大降落傘從袋子中拉出的小型降落傘）

droit de seigneur /ˌdrwʌ də senˈjɜː(r)/ *noun* [U] (from *French*) the right of a lord to have sex with a woman of lower social rank on her wedding night, said to exist in the Middle Ages （據傳中世紀領主對其封臣新娘的）初夜權

droll /drəʊl; *NAmE* droʊl/ *adj.* (*old-fashioned* or *ironic*) amusing, but not in a way that you expect 離奇可笑的；滑稽古怪的

drom·ed·ary /ˈdrɒmədəri; *NAmE* ˈdrɑːmədəri/ *noun* (*pl.* **-ies**) an animal of the CAMEL family, with only one HUMP, that lives in desert countries 單峰駝

drone /drəʊn; *NAmE* droʊn/ *noun, verb*

▪ *noun* **1** [usually sing.] a continuous low noise 嗡嗡聲：*the distant drone of traffic* 遠處車輛往來發出的嗡嗡聲 **2** [usually sing.] a continuous low sound made by some musical instruments, for example the BAGPIPES, over which other notes are played or sung; the part of the instrument that makes this noise 伴音（如風笛等發出的持續音）；伴音管（或弦等） **3** a male BEE that does not work 雄蜂 ➲ compare QUEEN BEE (1), WORKER (4) **4** a person who is lazy and gives nothing to society while others work （不勞動，依賴他人為生的）寄生蟲 **5** an aircraft without a pilot, controlled from the ground 無人駕駛飛機

▪ *verb* [I] to make a continuous low noise 嗡嗡叫；嗡嗡響：*A plane was droning in the distance.* 飛機在遠處嗡嗡地響。◇ *a droning voice* 嗡嗡的響聲

PHR V **ˌdrone ˈon (about sth)** to talk for a long time in a boring way 嘮嘮叨叨地說

drongo /ˈdrɒŋgəʊ; *NAmE* ˈdrɑːŋgoʊ/ *noun* (*pl.* **-os** or **-oes**) **1** a shiny black bird with a long tail 捲尾（毛色光亮的長尾黑鳥） **2** (*AustralE, NZE, slang*) a stupid person 傻瓜；笨蛋

drool /druːl/ *verb* **1** [I] to let SALIVA (= liquid) come out of your mouth 垂涎；淌口水 SYN **dribble**：*The dog was* ***drooling at the mouth.*** 狗嘴裏淌着口水。 **2** [I] **~ (over sb/sth)** (*disapproving*) to show in a silly or exaggerated way that you want or admire sb/sth very much （對…）垂涎欲滴，過分痴迷：*teenagers drooling over photos of movie stars* 對電影明星照片如痴如醉的青少年

droop /druːp/ *verb* **1** [I] to bend, hang or move downwards, especially because of being weak or tired（尤指因衰弱或疲勞）低垂，垂落，垂下：*She was so tired, her eyelids were beginning to droop.* 她太疲倦了，眼瞼開始往下垂。 **2** [I] to become sad or depressed 沮喪；消沉；垂頭喪氣：*Our spirits drooped when we heard the news.* 聽到這消息，我們情緒低落下來。 ▸ **droop** *noun* [sing.]：*the slight droop of her mouth* 她的嘴微微下垂 **droopy** *adj.*：*a droopy moustache* 耷拉着的小鬍子

drop 0-w /drɒp; *NAmE* drɑːp/ *verb, noun*

▪ *verb* (**-pp-**)

▸ FALL 落下 **1** 0-w [I, T] to fall or allow sth to fall by accident （意外地）落下，掉下，使落下：*The climber slipped and dropped to his death.* 攀登者一失足掉下去摔死了。◇ **~ sth** *Be careful not to drop that plate.* 小心別把那盤子摔了。 **2** 0-w [I, T] to fall or make sth fall deliberately （故意）降下，使降落，使落下：**+ adv./prep.** *He staggered in and dropped into a chair.* 他蹣跚着走進來，一屁股坐在椅子上。◇ **~ sth (+ adv./prep.)** *Medical supplies are being dropped into the stricken area.* 正在向災區空投醫藥用品。◇ (*BrE*) *He dropped his trousers* (= undid them and let them fall). 他鬆開腰帶，褲子掉下去。◇ (*NAmE*) *He dropped his pants.* 他鬆開腰帶，褲子掉下去。 **3** [I] (*informal*) to fall down or be no longer able to stand because you are extremely tired 累倒；累垮：*I feel* ***ready to drop.*** 我感到快累垮了。◇ *She expects everyone to work till they drop.* 她巴不得人人都幹到累垮為止。

▸ BECOME WEAKER/LESS 變弱；減少 **4** 0-w [I, T] to become or make sth weaker, lower or less （使）變弱，降低，減少 SYN **fall**：*The temperature has dropped considerably.* 溫度已大大降低。◇ *At last the wind dropped.* 風勢終於減弱了。◇ *His* ***voice dropped*** *to a whisper.* 他的聲音已放低到輕聲細語了。◇ *The Dutch team have dropped to fifth place.* 荷蘭隊已降至第五名。◇ *The price of shares dropped by 14p.* 股價下跌了 14 便士。◇ *Shares* ***dropped in price*** *by 14p.* 股價下跌了 14 便士。◇ **~ sth** *She* ***dropped her voice*** *dramatically.* 她突然壓低了聲音。◇ *You must drop your speed in built-up areas.* 在樓房密集區必須放慢車速。 ➲ LANGUAGE BANK at FALL

▸ EYES 眼睛 **5** [I, T] **your eyes/gaze ~** | **~ your eyes/gaze** (*formal*) to look down 垂下（眼睛）；垂視：*Her eyes dropped to her lap.* 她雙目低垂，看着自己的腿。

▸ SLOPE DOWNWARDS 向下傾斜 **6** [I] **~ (away) (from sth)** to slope steeply downwards 急劇傾斜而下：*In front of them the valley dropped sharply away from the road.* 他們前面的山谷從路旁急劇傾斜而下。

▸ DELIVER/SEND 運送；發送 **7** [T] to stop so that sb can get out of a car, etc.; to deliver sth on the way to somewhere else 中途卸客；中途卸貨：**~ sb/sth** *Can you drop me near the bank?* 你可以讓我在銀行附近下車嗎？◇ **~ sb/sth off** *You left your jacket, but I can drop it off on my way to work tomorrow.* 你忘了拿你的短上衣，不過我可以在明天上班的路上順便捎給你。 **8** [T] **~ sb a line/note** to send a short letter to sb 寄，送，寫（信）：*Drop me a line when you get there.* 你到那兒後給我寫封信。

▸ LEAVE OUT 略去 **9** [T] **~ sb/sth (from sth)** to leave sb/sth out by accident or deliberately 遺漏；省略；不予考慮：*She's been dropped from the team because of injury.* 她因受傷而未被列入隊員名單。◇ *He spoke with a cockney accent and* ***dropped his aitches*** (= did not pronounce the letter 'h' at the start of words). 他講話帶着倫敦東區的口音，把詞首的 h 音給吞掉了。

▸ FRIENDS 朋友 **10** [T] **~ sb** to stop seeing sb socially 不再與（某人）往來；同（某人）斷絕聯繫：*She's dropped most of her old friends.* 她已與多數老朋友停止了來往。

D

▸ STOP 停止 **11** [T] **~ sth** to stop doing or discussing sth; to not continue with sth 停止；終止；放棄：*I dropped German* (= stopped studying it) *when I was 14.* 我 14 歲後就沒再學德語。◇ *Drop everything and come at once!* 放下所有事情趕快來吧！◇ *Look, can we just drop it* (= stop talking about it)? 喂，這事兒能不能就談到這兒？◇ *I think we'd better drop the subject.* 我認為我們最好不要談這個話題。◇ *Let's drop the formalities—please call me Mike.* 咱們不必拘禮，叫我邁克好了。◇ *The police decided to drop the charges against her.* 警方決定撤回對她的指控。

▸ HINT 暗示 **12** [T] **~ a hint** to say or do sth in order to show sb, in an indirect way, what you are thinking 暗示；透露

▸ IN KNITTING 編織 **13** [T] **~ a stitch** to let a STITCH go off the needle 漏，脫，掉（針）

IDM **drop the 'ball** (*NAmE, informal*) to make a mistake and spoil sth that you are responsible for 犯錯；處理失當 **drop a 'brick/'clanger** (*BrE, informal*) to say sth that offends or embarrasses sb, although you did not intend to 失言傷人；出言不慎 **drop 'dead** **1** (*informal*) to die suddenly and unexpectedly 暴斃；突然死去；猝死 **2** (*informal*) used to tell sb, rudely, to stop annoying you, INTERFERING, etc. 別煩人；別打擾；別搗亂 ➲ see also DROP-DEAD **drop sb 'in it** (*BrE, informal*) to put sb in an embarrassing situation, especially by telling a secret that you should not have told（尤指因泄露秘密）使尷尬，使狼狽不堪 **drop 'names** to mention famous people you know or have met in order to impress others 提及自己認識或見過的名人以抬高身價 ➲ related noun NAME-DROPPING **,drop your 'bundle** (*AustralE, NZE, informal*) to suddenly not be able to think clearly; to act in a stupid way because you have lost control over yourself 突然發蒙；失態 **let sb/sth 'drop** **1** to do or say nothing more about sb/sth 不再提起；放棄：*I suggest we let the matter drop.* 我建議咱們別再提及此事。**2** to mention sb/sth in a conversation, by accident or as if by accident（好像是）無意中說出：*He let it drop that the Prime Minister was a close friend of his.* 他有意無意地提起首相是他的密友。➲ more at BOTTOM *n.*, FLY *n.*, HEAR, JAW *n.*, LAP *n.*, PENNY

PHR V **,drop a'way** to become weaker or less 減弱；減少：*She could feel the tension drop away.* 她感到緊張氣氛緩和了下來。**,drop 'back/be'hind | ,drop be'hind sb** to move or fall into position behind sb else 後退；落後；落在⋯後面：*We cannot afford to drop behind our competitors.* 我們可擔當不起落後於競爭對手的後果。**,drop 'by/'in/'round | ,drop 'in on sb | ,drop 'into sth** to pay an informal visit to a person or a place 順便訪問；順便進入：*Drop by sometime.* 有空兒來坐坐。◇ *I thought I'd drop in on you while I was passing.* 我曾想路過時順便來看看你。◇ *Sorry we're late—we dropped into the pub on the way.* 對不起，我們遲到了。我們半路上順便到酒館坐了坐。**,drop 'off** (*BrE, informal*) **1** to fall into a light sleep 打盹兒；小睡 SYN **fall asleep**：*I dropped off and missed the end of the film.* 我打了個盹兒，錯過了影片的結尾。**2** to become fewer or less 減少；下降：*Traffic in the town has dropped off since the bypass opened.* 自從這條旁道通車後，城裏來往的車輛就減少了。**,drop 'out (of sth)** **1** 🗝 to no longer take part in or be part of sth 不再參加；退出；脫離：*He has dropped out of active politics.* 他已不再積極參政了。◇ *a word that has dropped out of the language* 該語言中已廢棄的一個詞 **2** 🗝 to leave school, college, etc. without finishing your studies 退學；輟學：*She started a degree but dropped out after only a year.* 她在攻讀學位僅一年後就退學了。➲ related noun DROPOUT (1) **3** to reject the ideas and ways of behaving that are accepted by the rest of society 拒絕傳統社會 ➲ related noun DROPOUT (2)

■ *noun*

▸ OF LIQUID 液體 **1** 🗝 [C] a very small amount of liquid that forms a round shape 滴；水珠：*drops of rain* 雨滴 ◇ *a drop of blood* 一滴血 ➲ see also RAINDROP, TEARDROP **2** 🗝 [C, usually sing.] a small quantity of a liquid 少量；微量；一點點：*Could I have a drop more milk in my coffee, please?* 請給我在咖啡裏多加點牛奶好嗎？◇ *I haven't touched a drop* (= drunk any alcohol) *all evening.* 整個晚上我滴酒未沾。

▸ FALL 下降 **3** 🗝 [C, usually sing.] **~ (in sth)** a fall or reduction in the amount, level or number of sth 下降；下跌；減少：*a drop in prices/temperature, etc.* 價格、溫度等下降 ◇ *a dramatic/sharp drop in profits* 利潤大幅度/急劇下降 ◇ *a five per cent drop* 下跌百分之五 ➲ LANGUAGE BANK at FALL

▸ DISTANCE 距離 **4** [sing.] a distance down from a high point to a lower point 下落的距離；落差：*There was a sheer drop of fifty metres to the rocks below.* 距下面的岩石有五十米的垂直距離。◇ *a twenty-foot drop* 二十英尺的落差

▸ MEDICINE 藥 **5 drops** [pl.] a liquid medicine that you put one drop at a time into your eyes, ears or nose 滴劑：*eye drops* 眼藥水

▸ DELIVERING 運送 **6** [C] the act of delivering sb/sth in a vehicle or by plane; the act of dropping sth 運送；空投：*Aid agencies are organizing food drops to civilians in the war zone.* 援助機構正組織向戰區平民運送食品。◇ *a parachute drop* 降落傘空投

▸ SWEET/CANDY 糖果 **7** [C] a small round sweet/candy of the type mentioned 球狀糖果：*fruit drops* 水果糖 ◇ *cough drops* (= sweets/candy to help a cough) 止咳糖

IDM **at the ,drop of a 'hat** immediately; without hesitating 立即；毫不遲疑：*The company can't expect me to move my home and family at the drop of a hat.* 公司不可能指望我立即搬家。**a ,drop in the 'ocean** (*BrE*) (*NAmE* **a ,drop in the 'bucket**) an amount of sth that is too small or unimportant to make any real difference to a situation 滄海一粟；九牛一毛

'drop cloth (*NAmE*) (*BrE* **'dust sheet**) *noun* a large sheet that is used to protect floors, furniture, etc. from dust or paint（地板、傢具等的）防塵罩，苫布

,drop-'dead *adv.* (*informal*) used before an adjective to emphasize that sb/sth is attractive in a very noticeable way（用於形容詞前，強調非常引人注目）以令人絕倒方式，極其，非常：*a drop-dead gorgeous Hollywood star* 令人瞠目的好萊塢豔星

,drop-down 'menu *noun* (*computing* 計) a menu that appears on a computer screen when you choose it, and that stays there until you choose one of the functions on it 下拉式選單 ➲ VISUAL VOCAB page V67

'drop goal *noun* (in RUGBY 橄欖球) a goal scored by dropping the ball onto the ground and kicking it over the CROSSBAR as it BOUNCES 越過球門橫木得分；碰球入門

,drop 'handlebars *noun* [pl.] low curved handles on a bicycle 自行車車把

'drop-in *adj.* [only before noun] able to be visited without arranging a fixed time first 可隨時造訪的；無須預約的：*a drop-in centre* 開放式中心

'drop kick *noun* (in RUGBY 橄欖球) a kick made by dropping the ball onto the ground and kicking it as it BOUNCES 踢落地球 ▸ **'drop-kick** *verb* **~ sth**

drop·let /ˈdrɒplət; *NAmE* ˈdrɑːp-/ *noun* a small drop of a liquid 小滴

drop·out /ˈdrɒpaʊt; *NAmE* ˈdrɑːp-/ *noun* **1** a person who leaves school or college before they have finished their studies 輟學者；退學者：*college dropouts* 大學肄業生 ◇ *a university with a high dropout rate* 退學率高的大學 **2** a person who rejects the ideas and ways of behaving that are accepted by the rest of society 拒絕傳統社會的人

drop·per /ˈdrɒpə(r); *NAmE* ˈdrɑːp-/ *noun* a short glass tube with a hollow rubber end used for measuring medicine or other liquids in drops 滴管 ➲ VISUAL VOCAB page V70

drop·pings /ˈdrɒpɪŋz; *NAmE* ˈdrɑːp-/ *noun* the solid waste matter of birds and animals (usually small animals)（鳥、小動物的）糞

'drop shot *noun* = DINK

dropsy /ˈdrɒpsi; *NAmE* ˈdrɑːpsi/ *noun* [U] (*old-fashioned*) = OEDEMA

'drop zone *noun* the area in which sb/sth should land after being dropped from an aircraft 空投區；空降區

dros·oph·ila /drɒˈsɒfɪlə; *NAmE* drəˈsɑːfɪlə/ (*pl.* **dros·oph·ila**) *noun* a small fly that feeds on fruit and is often used in scientific research 果蠅（常用於實驗）

dross /drɒs; *NAmE* drɔːs; drɑːs/ *noun* [U] **1** (*especially BrE*) something of very low quality; the least valuable part of sth 劣質品；糟粕：*mass-produced dross* 成批生產的劣質品 **2** (*technical* 術語) a waste substance, especially that separated from a metal when it is melted 廢料；（尤指金屬熔化的）浮渣

drought /draʊt/ *noun* [U, C] a long period of time when there is little or no rain 久旱；旱災：*two years of severe drought* 兩年的嚴重旱災 ◇ *one of the worst droughts on record* 有記載以來最嚴重的旱災之一

drove /drəʊv; *NAmE* droʊv/ *noun* [usually pl.] a large number of people or animals, often moving or doing sth as a group（移動的）人群，畜群：*droves of tourists* 成群的遊客 ◇ *People were leaving the countryside **in droves** to look for work in the cities.* 一批一批的人離開農村到城裏找工作。➲ see also DRIVE *v.* (7), (9)

drover /ˈdrəʊvə(r); *NAmE* ˈdroʊv-/ *noun* a person who moves groups of cows or sheep from one place to another, especially to market 趕牛羊牲畜者；趕畜群上市者

drown /draʊn/ *verb* **1** [I, T] to die because you have been underwater too long and you cannot breathe; to kill sb in this way（使）淹死，溺死：*Two children drowned after falling into the river.* 兩個孩子掉進河裏淹死了。◇ *He had attempted to rescue the drowning man.* 他曾試圖去救那個溺水的男人。◇ **~ sb/sth/yourself** *She tried to drown herself.* 她試圖投水自殺。◇ *He was drowned at sea.* 他淹死在海裏。◇ *They had drowned the unwanted kittens.* 他們把沒人要的小貓淹死了。**2** [T] **~ sth (in sth)** to make sth very wet; to completely cover sth in water or another liquid 浸透；淹沒；浸泡 SYN **drench**：*The fruit was drowned in cream.* 水果在奶油裏泡過。**3** [T] **~ sb/sth (out)** (of a sound 聲音) to be louder than other sounds so that you cannot hear them 壓過；蓋沒；淹沒：*She turned up the radio to drown out the noise from next door.* 她開大了收音機的音量以壓過隔壁房間的吵鬧聲。▸ **drown·ing** *noun* [U, C]：*death by drowning* 溺水身亡 ◇ *Alcohol plays a part in an estimated 30% of drownings.* 估計有 30% 的溺水是酒精的作用所致。

IDM **drown your ˈfears/ˈloneliness/ˈsorrows, etc.** (especially *humorous*) to get drunk in order to forget your problems 借酒壯膽／解寂寞／澆愁等

drowse /draʊz/ *verb* [I] to be in a light sleep or almost asleep 打瞌睡；打盹；假寐

drowsy /ˈdraʊzi/ *adj.* (**drows·ier**, **drowsi·est**) **1** tired and almost asleep 睏倦的；昏昏欲睡的 SYN **sleepy**：*The tablets may make you feel drowsy.* 這些藥片可能會使你昏昏欲睡。**2** making you feel relaxed and tired 使人鬆弛的；令人疲乏的；使人睏倦的：*a drowsy afternoon in the sunshine* 陽光照耀下使人睏倦的下午 ▸ **drows·ily** /-ɪli/ *adv.* **drow·si·ness** *noun* [U]：*The drugs tend to cause drowsiness.* 這些藥常常使人昏昏欲睡。

drub·bing /ˈdrʌbɪŋ/ *noun* (*informal*) (in a sport 體育運動) a situation where one team easily beats another 輕取；輕易戰勝：*We **gave them a drubbing** in the match on Saturday.* 我們在星期六的比賽中輕而易舉地打敗了他們。

drudge /drʌdʒ/ *noun* a person who has to do long hard boring jobs 苦工；做繁重無聊工作的人

drudg·ery /ˈdrʌdʒəri/ *noun* [U] hard boring work 單調乏味的苦差事；繁重無聊的工作

drug 🔑 /drʌg/ *noun, verb*

■ *noun* **1** 🔑 an illegal substance that some people smoke, INJECT, etc. for the physical and mental effects it has 毒品：*He does not smoke or **take drugs**.* 他既不抽煙也不吸毒。◇ *teenagers experimenting with drugs* 試用毒品的青少年 ◇ *I found out Steve was **on drugs*** (= regularly used drugs). 我發現史蒂夫已吸毒成癮。◇ *drug and alcohol abuse* 吸毒和酗酒 ◇ *a **hard*** (= very harmful) ***drug** such as heroin* 海洛因之類的硬毒品（毒性很大）◇ *a **soft drug*** (= one that is not considered very harmful) 軟毒品（毒性不太大）◇ *Drugs have been seized with a street value of two million dollars.* 黑市價值二百萬元的毒品已被查獲。◇ *She was a **drug addict*** (= could not stop using drugs). 她是個吸毒成癮的人。◇ *He was charged with **pushing drugs*** (= selling them). 他被控販毒。◇ (*informal*) *I don't **do drugs*** (= use them). 我不吸毒。◇ *drug rehabilitation* 吸毒者的康復訓練 **2** 🔑 a substance used as a medicine or used in a medicine 藥；藥物：*prescribed drugs* 處方藥 ◇ *The doctor put me on a course of pain-killing drugs.* 醫生讓我服一個療程的止痛藥。◇ *drug companies* 藥品公司 ◇ *The drug has some bad side effects.* 這種藥有些嚴重的副作用。➲ COLLOCATIONS at ILL ➲ see also DESIGNER DRUG

■ *verb* (**-gg-**) **1 ~ sb/sth** to give a person or an animal a drug, especially to make them unconscious, or to affect their performance in a race or competition 使服麻醉藥；用藥麻醉；使服興奮劑：*He was drugged and bundled into the back of the car.* 他被麻醉後塞入汽車後座。◇ *It's illegal to drug horses before a race.* 比賽前給馬服用興奮劑是違法的。**2 ~ sth** to add a drug to sb's food or drink to make them unconscious or SLEEPY（在食物或飲料中）投放麻醉藥，下麻醉藥：*Her drink must have been drugged.* 她的飲料中肯定被摻了麻醉藥。

IDM **be drugged up to the ˈeyeballs** to have taken or been given a lot of drugs 已服用大量毒品

ˈdrug dealer *noun* a person who sells illegal drugs 毒品販

drug·gie (*BrE* also **drug·gy**) /ˈdrʌgi/ *noun* (*pl.* **-ies**) (*informal*) a person who takes illegal drugs regularly 吸毒者；有毒癮的人

drug·ging /ˈdrʌgɪŋ/ *noun* [U] the act of taking a drug, especially an illegal one 服藥；（尤指）吸毒：*They were feeling the effects of drinking and drugging all night.* 他們酗酒吸毒，整夜恍惚迷離。

drug·gist /ˈdrʌgɪst/ *noun* (*NAmE*) **1** (also **chem·ist**, **disˈpensing chemist** both *BrE*) a person whose job is to prepare and sell medicines, and who works in a shop 藥劑師；藥商 **2** = PHARMACIST (1)

drug·gy /ˈdrʌgi/ *adj., noun*

■ *adj.* (**drug·gier**, **drug·gi·est**) (*informal*) using or involving illegal drugs 吸毒的；毒品的

■ *noun* (*BrE*) = DRUGGIE

ˈdrug peddler *noun* = PEDDLER (1)

drug·store 🔑 /ˈdrʌgstɔː(r)/ *noun* (*NAmE*) a shop/store that sells medicines and also other types of goods, for example COSMETICS（兼售化妝品等的）藥房 ➲ compare PHARMACY (1) ➲ see also CHEMIST (2)

Druid /ˈdruːɪd/ *noun* a priest of an ancient Celtic religion 德魯伊特（古代凱爾特人的祭司）

drum 🔑 /drʌm/ *noun, verb*

■ *noun* **1** 🔑 a musical instrument made of a hollow round frame with plastic or skin stretched tightly across one or both ends. You play it by hitting it with sticks or with your hands. 鼓：*a bass drum* 大鼓 ◇ *Tony Cox on drums* 鼓手托尼•考克斯 ◇ *to play the drums* 擊鼓 ◇ *a regular drum beat* 節奏均勻的擊鼓聲 ➲ VISUAL VOCAB page V35 **2** a large container for oil or chemicals, shaped like a CYLINDER（裝油或化學劑的）大桶：*a 50 gallon drum* 容積為 50 加侖的桶 ◇ *an oil drum* 油桶 **3** a thing shaped like a drum, especially part of a machine 鼓狀物；（尤指機器上的）鼓輪，滾筒：*The mixture flows to a revolving drum where the water is filtered out.* 混合劑流過旋轉着的滾筒時水分便從中濾出。

IDM **beat/bang the ˈdrum (for sb/sth)** (*especially BrE*) to speak with enthusiasm in support of sb/sth（為…）竭力鼓吹，搖旗吶喊 ➲ more at MARCH *v.*

■ *verb* (**-mm-**) **1** [I] to play a drum 打鼓；擊鼓 **2** [T, I] **~ (sth) on sth** to make a sound by hitting a surface again and again 連續敲擊…使發出咚咚聲；不停地擊打：*Impatiently, he **drummed his fingers** on the table.* 他不耐煩地用手指嗒嗒地敲擊桌子。

IDM **ˈdrum sth into sb's head** = DRUM STH INTO SB

PHR V **ˈdrum sth into sb** to make sb remember sth by repeating it a lot of times 向某人反複灌輸；對某人反複講述：*We had it drummed into us that we should never talk to strangers.* 我們曾被反複叮囑千萬不要與陌生人講話。**ˌdrum sb ˈout (of sth)** [usually passive] to force sb to leave an organization as a punishment for doing sth wrong 開除；轟走；驅逐 ,**drum sth↔'up** to try hard to get support or business 竭力爭取（支持）；兜攬（生意）：*He had flown to the north of the country to drum up support for the campaign.* 他已乘飛機到國家的北方去努力爭取對這一運動的支持。

D

,drum and 'bass (also **,drum 'n' 'bass**) *noun* [U] a type of electronic dance music developed in Britain in the early 1990s, which has a fast drum beat and a strong slower BASS beat 鼓與貝司，鼓打貝司（20 世紀 90 年代初在英國出現的電子音樂舞曲，以快速的鼓節奏和強勁緩慢的貝司節奏為特點）

drum·beat /ˈdrʌmbiːt/ *noun* the sound that a beat on a drum makes 擊鼓聲

'drum kit *noun* a set of drums 成套鼓樂器 ➲ VISUAL VOCAB page V35

drum·lin /ˈdrʌmlɪn/ *noun* (*geology* 地) a very small hill formed by the movement of a GLACIER (= a large moving mass of ice)（冰川形成的）鼓丘

'drum machine *noun* an electronic musical instrument that produces the sound of drums 電子鼓

,drum 'major *noun* the leader of a marching band of musicians, especially in the army（尤指軍樂隊的）行進樂隊指揮

,drum majo'rette (*especially BrE*) (*NAmE* usually **ma·jor·ette**) *noun* a girl in special brightly coloured clothes who walks in front of a marching band, spinning, throwing and catching a long stick (called a BATON)（行進樂隊中身着豔麗服裝、舞動指揮棒的）女領隊

drum·mer /ˈdrʌmə(r)/ *noun* a person who plays a drum or drums 鼓手 IDM see MARCH *v.*

drum·ming /ˈdrʌmɪŋ/ *noun* [U, sing.] **1** the act of playing a drum; the sound of a drum being played 擊鼓；鼓聲 **2** a continuous sound or feeling like the beats of a drum 擊鼓似的咚咚聲；似擊鼓一樣連續不停的感覺：*the steady drumming of the rain on the tin roof* 雨點打在鐵皮屋頂上發出的有節奏的嗒嗒聲

,drum 'n' 'bass *noun* = DRUM AND BASS

drum·stick /ˈdrʌmstɪk/ *noun* **1** a stick used for playing a drum 鼓槌 ➲ VISUAL VOCAB page V35 **2** the lower part of the leg of a chicken or other bird that is cooked and eaten as food 熟雞（或家禽）腿下段；下段雞（或家禽）腿肉：***a chicken/turkey drumstick*** 雞 / 火雞腿下段

drunk 🔑 /drʌŋk/ *adj.*, *noun* ➲ see also DRINK *v.*

■ *adj.* **1** 🔑 [not usually before noun] having drunk so much alcohol that it is impossible to think or speak clearly（酒）醉：*She was too drunk to remember anything about the party.* 她喝得酩酊大醉，聚會上的事什麼都記不得了。◇ *His only way of dealing with his problems was to go out and* ***get drunk***. 他解決煩心事的唯一辦法就是出去喝個爛醉。◇ *They got drunk on vodka.* 他們喝伏特加酒醉倒了。◇ *Police arrested him for being* ***drunk and disorderly*** (= violent or noisy in a public place because of being drunk). 他因醉酒妨害治安被警方逮捕。OPP **sober** **2 ~ with sth** (*formal*) in a great state of excitement because of a particular emotion or situation 陶醉；沉醉；飄飄然；忘乎所以：*drunk with success* 因成功而飄飄然

IDM **(as) drunk as a 'lord** (*BrE*) (*NAmE* **(as) drunk as a 'skunk**) (*informal*) very drunk 爛醉如泥 ➲ more at BLIND *adv.*, ROARING

■ *noun* a person who is drunk or who often gets drunk 醉漢；酒鬼；酗酒者

drunk·ard /ˈdrʌŋkəd; *NAmE* -ərd/ *noun* (*old-fashioned*) a person who gets drunk very often 酒鬼；醉鬼 SYN **alcoholic**

,drunk 'driver (*especially NAmE*) (*BrE* also **,drink-'driver**) *noun* a person who drives a vehicle after drinking too much alcohol 醉酒駕車者

'drunk driving (*especially NAmE*) (*BrE* also **,drink-'driving**, **,drunken 'driving**) *noun* [U] driving a vehicle after drinking too much alcohol 醉酒駕車

drunk·en /ˈdrʌŋkən/ *adj.* [only before noun] **1** drunk or often getting drunk 醉的；常醉的；酗酒的：*a drunken driver* 喝醉的司機 ◇ *She was often beaten by her drunken husband.* 她常常遭到酗酒丈夫的毒打。 **2** showing the effects of too much alcohol; involving people who are drunk 酒醉引起的；醉漢的：*He came home to find her in a drunken stupor.* 他回到家裏發現她處於酒後恍惚狀態。◇ *a drunken brawl* 酒後鬧事 ▸ **drunk·en·ly** *adv.*：*He staggered drunkenly to his feet.* 他醉醺醺地蹣跚着站起來。 **drunk·en·ness** *noun* [U]

,drunken 'driving *noun* [U] (*BrE*) = DRINK-DRIVING

'drunk tank *noun* (*informal, humorous, especially NAmE*) a place where people are put by the police because they are drunk 醉漢監禁室：*He spent the night in the drunk tank.* 他在酒鬼監禁室過夜了。

dry 🔑 /draɪ/ *adj.*, *verb*

■ *adj.* (**drier**, **dri·est**)

▸ NOT WET 乾 **1** 🔑 not wet, damp or sticky; without water or MOISTURE 乾的；乾燥的：*Is my shirt dry yet?* 我的襯衣乾了嗎？◇ *Store onions in a cool dry place.* 把洋蔥存放在涼爽乾燥的地方。◇ *I'm afraid this cake has turned out very dry.* 恐怕這個蛋糕烤得太乾。◇ *Her mouth felt* ***as dry as a bone*** (= completely dry). 她感到口乾舌燥。◇ *When the paint is completely dry, apply another coat.* 油漆乾透後再塗上一層。◇ *It was high summer and the rivers were dry* (= had no water in them). 正值盛夏，河流都乾涸了。OPP **wet** ➲ see also BONE DRY

▸ LITTLE RAIN 雨少 **2** 🔑 with very little rain 雨少的；乾旱的；乾燥的：*weeks of hot* ***dry weather*** 連續幾週炎熱乾燥的天氣 ◇ *the* ***dry season*** 旱季 ◇ *I hope it* ***stays dry*** *for our picnic.* 希望別下雨，我們好去野餐。◇ *Rattlesnakes occur in the warmer, drier parts of North America.* 響尾蛇出現在北美溫暖乾燥的地區。OPP **wet**

▸ SKIN/HAIR 皮膚；頭髮 **3** without the natural oils that makes it soft and healthy 乾性的；無水分的：*a shampoo for dry hair* 適合乾性髮質的洗髮劑

▸ COUGH 咳嗽 **4** that does not produce any PHLEGM (= the thick liquid that forms in the nose and throat) 乾咳的：*a dry hacking cough* 猛烈的乾咳

▸ BREAD 麪包 **5** eaten on its own without any butter, jam, etc. 無黃油（或果醬等）的：*Breakfast consisted of dry bread and a cup of tea.* 早餐有不塗黃油的麪包和一杯茶。

▸ WINE 葡萄酒 **6** not sweet 無甜味的；乾的：*a crisp dry white wine* 爽口的乾白葡萄酒 ◇ *a dry sherry* 乾雪利酒 OPP **sweet**

▸ HUMOUR 幽默 **7** (*approving*) very clever and expressed in a quiet way that is not obvious; often using IRONY 機敏的；不形於色的；不露聲色的：*He was a man of few words with a delightful dry sense of humour.* 他話不多，卻富有不形於色的幽默感，讓人很欣賞。

▸ WITHOUT EMOTION 無感情 **8** not showing emotion 不動感情的；冷冰冰的：*a dry voice* 冷冰冰的聲音

▸ BORING 乏味 **9** not interesting 乾巴巴的；枯燥乏味的：*Government reports tend to make dry reading.* 政府報告讀起來往往枯燥無味。

▸ WITHOUT ALCOHOL 無酒 **10** without alcohol; where it is illegal to buy, sell or drink alcohol 無酒的；禁酒的；戒酒的：*We had a dry wedding* (= no alcoholic drinks were served). 我們舉行了一個無酒的婚禮。◇ *a dry county/state* 禁酒的郡 / 州

▸ THIRSTY 口渴 **11** (*informal, especially BrE*) thirsty; that makes you thirsty 口渴的；令人口渴的：*I'm a bit dry.* 我有點渴。◇ *This is dry work.* 這是使人覺得口渴的工作。 ▸ **dryly** *adv.* = DRILY **dry·ness** *noun* [U]

IDM **milk/suck sb/sth 'dry** to get from sb/sth all the money, help, information, etc. they have, usually giving nothing in return 榨乾…的錢財；耗盡…的精力；掏盡…的信息 **not a dry eye in the 'house** (*humorous*) used to say that everyone was very emotional about sth 全場無人不流淚；全場無不為之動容：*There wasn't a dry eye in the house when they announced their engagement.* 他們宣佈訂婚時大夥眼睛全濕了。 **run 'dry** to stop supplying water; to be all used so that none is left 乾涸；枯竭；耗盡：*The wells in most villages in the region have run dry.* 這個地區多數村莊的水井都已乾涸。◇ *Vaccine supplies started to run dry as the flu outbreak reached epidemic proportions.* 由於流感爆發已大肆流行，

疫苗供應開始消耗殆盡。➲ more at BLEED, HIGH *adj.*, HOME *adv.*, POWDER *n.*, SQUEEZE *v.*

■ *verb* (dries, dry·ing, dried, dried) [I, T] to become dry; to make sth dry （使）變乾；（把…）弄乾：*Be careful. The paint hasn't dried yet.* 小心點，油漆還沒有乾。◇ *You wash the dishes and I'll dry.* 你洗盤子，我來擦乾。◇ **~ sth** *Use this towel to dry your hands.* 用這條毛巾擦乾你的手。◇ *dry your hair* 弄乾頭髮 ◇ *to* ***dry your eyes/tears*** (= stop crying) 擦乾眼睛／眼淚

PHR V **ˌdry ˈoff** | **ˌdry sb/sth↔ˈoff** to become dry or make sth dry （使）變乾；弄乾：*We went swimming and then lay in the sun to dry off.* 我們去了游泳，然後就躺在太陽下曬乾。◇ *We dried our boots off by the fire.* 我們把靴子放在火旁烘乾。 **ˌdry ˈout** | **ˌdry sb↔ˈout** (*informal*) to stop drinking alcohol after you have continuously been drinking too much; to cure sb of drinking too much alcohol （使）戒酒癮：*He went to an expensive clinic to dry out.* 他到一家費用昂貴的診所戒酒癮。 **ˌdry ˈout** | **ˌdry sth↔ˈout** to become or to allow sth to become dry, in a way that is not wanted （使）變乾，乾透：*Water the plant regularly, never letting the soil dry out.* 經常給植物澆水，別讓土壤乾透了。◇ *Hot sun and cold winds can soon dry out your skin.* 火辣辣的太陽和寒風可使你的皮膚很快變乾燥。 **ˌdry ˈup 1** (of rivers, lakes, etc. 河流、湖泊等) to become completely dry 乾涸：*During the drought the river dried up.* 旱災期間，河流都乾涸了。 **2** if a supply of sth **dries up**, there is gradually less of it until there is none left 枯竭；耗盡：*As she got older, offers of modelling work began to dry up.* 隨着她年齡漸長，邀請她做模特兒的工作已越來越少。 **3** to suddenly stop talking because you do not know what to say next （因不知該說什麼而）突然住口，突然說不出話來 **ˌdry ˈup** | **ˌdry sth↔ˈup** (*BrE*) to dry dishes with a towel after you have washed them 擦乾（剛洗的盤子）：*I'll wash and you can dry up.* 我洗盤子，你可以擦乾。

dryad /ˈdraɪæd/ *noun* (in stories) a female spirit who lives in a tree （傳說中的）林中女仙，樹精

ˌdry ˈcell *noun* the type of cell in a **dry battery** which contains chemicals only in solid form 乾電池

ˌdry-ˈclean (also **clean**) *verb* **~ sth** to clean clothes using chemicals instead of water 乾洗：*This garment must be dry-cleaned only.* 這件衣服只可乾洗。➲ SYNONYMS at CLEAN ▸ **ˌdry-ˈcleaning** *noun* [U]

ˌdry-ˈcleaner's *noun* = CLEANER (3)

ˌdry ˈdock *noun* [C, U] an area in a port from which the water can be removed, used for building or repairing ships 乾船塢

dryer (also **drier**) /ˈdraɪə(r)/ *noun* (especially in compounds 尤用於構成複合詞) a machine for drying sth 烘乾機；脫水機；乾燥機：*a hairdryer* 吹風機 ➲ see also SPIN DRYER, TUMBLE DRYER

ˌdry-ˈeyed *adj.* [not before noun] not crying 不哭；無淚；哭不出：*She remained dry-eyed throughout the trial.* 整個審訊過程中她沒掉一滴眼淚。

ˈdry goods *noun* [pl.] **1** (*BrE*) types of food that are solid and dry, such as tea, coffee and flour 乾貨 **2** (*old-fashioned, NAmE*) cloth and things that are made out of cloth, such as clothes and sheets 紡織品（如衣服、被單等）：*a dry goods store* 紡織品商店 ➲ compare DRAPERY (3)

ˌdry ˈice *noun* [U] solid CARBON DIOXIDE used for keeping food, etc. cold or for producing special effects in the theatre 乾冰；固態二氧化碳

ˌdry ˈland *noun* [U] land, rather than sea 陸地（有別於海洋）**SYN** **terra firma**：*It was a great relief to be back* ***on dry land*** *after such a rough crossing.* 渡過洶湧澎湃的大海回到陸地後使人感到如釋重負。

dryly = DRILY

ˌdry ˈmilk (*US*) (*BrE* **ˈmilk powder**, **ˌpowdered ˈmilk**) *noun* [U] dried milk in the form of a powder 奶粉

ˌdry-ˈroasted *adj.* cooked in an oven without adding oil or fat 乾烤的，乾焙的（不加油脂）：*dry-roasted peanuts* 乾烤花生

ˌdry ˈrot *noun* [U] **1** wood that has decayed and turned to powder （木材）乾腐病，乾朽 **2** any FUNGUS that causes this decay 乾腐菌

ˌdry ˈrun *noun* [usually sing.] a complete practice of a performance or way of doing sth, before the real one 排練；演習 **SYN** **dummy run**

ˈdry slope (also **ˈdry-ski slope**) *noun* a steep slope with a special surface for practising SKIING （練習用）人造滑雪斜坡

dry·stone wall /ˌdraɪstəʊn ˈwɔːl; *NAmE* -stoʊn/ *noun* (*BrE*) (*NAmE* **ˈdry wall**) a stone wall built without MORTAR (= a substance used in building to hold bricks or stones together) between the stones 乾砌石牆

dry·suit /ˈdraɪsuːt; *BrE* also -sjuːt/ *noun* a piece of clothing that fits the whole body closely and keeps water out, worn by people swimming underwater or sailing 潛水衣 ➲ compare WETSUIT

ˈdry wall *noun* [U] (*NAmE*) **1** = PLASTERBOARD **2** (*BrE* **dry·stone wall**) a stone wall built without MORTAR (= a substance used in building to hold bricks or stones together) between the stones 乾砌石牆

DSL /ˌdiː es ˈel/ *abbr.* (*computing* 計) digital subscriber line (a way of sending electronic data at high speed along ordinary telephone lines, used for supplying the Internet to homes, businesses, etc.) 數字用戶線；數位用戶迴路

DST /ˌdiː es ˈtiː/ *abbr.* DAYLIGHT SAVING TIME

DT /ˌdiː ˈtiː/ *noun* [U] (*BrE*) the abbreviation for design and technology (a school subject in which students learn about the role of technology in modern life and also design and make things for themselves) 設計與技術（全寫為 design and technology，學校科目，講授技術在現代生活中的作用以及實用設計技巧）

DTI /ˌdiː tiː ˈaɪ/ *abbr.* (in Britain) Department of Trade and Industry （英國）貿易工業部

DTP /ˌdiː tiː ˈpiː/ *abbr.* DESKTOP PUBLISHING

DTs (*BrE*) (*US* **D.T.'s**) /ˌdiː ˈtiːz/ *noun* [pl.] the abbreviation for 'delirium tremens' (a physical condition in which people who drink too much alcohol feel their body shaking and imagine that they are seeing things that are not really there) 震顫性譫妄（全寫為 delirium tremens，喝酒太多導致身體震顫和出現幻覺）

dual /ˈdjuːəl; *NAmE* ˈduːəl/ *adj.* [only before noun] having two parts or aspects 兩部份的；雙重的；雙的：*his dual role as composer and conductor* 他兼任作曲家和指揮的雙重角色 ◇ *She has* ***dual nationality*** (= is a citizen of two different countries). 她具有雙重國籍。◇ *The piece of furniture serves a dual purpose as a cupboard and as a table.* 這件傢具有兩個用途，既作食櫥也作飯桌。➲ SYNONYMS at DOUBLE ➲ see also DUAL-PURPOSE

ˌdual ˈcarriageway (*BrE*) (*NAmE* **diˌvided ˈhighway**) *noun* a road with a strip of land in the middle that divides the lines of traffic moving in opposite directions （中央有分隔帶的）雙幅車行道，雙向車道

ˌdual conˈtrols *noun* [pl.] two sets of instruments for controlling a vehicle or aircraft, so that a teacher, for example, can take control from the driver（車輛或飛機的）複式控制裝置，複式操縱裝置 ▸ **ˌdual conˈtrol** *adj.*：*a dual-control vehicle* 有複式操縱裝置的汽車

dual·ism /ˈdjuːəlɪzəm; *NAmE* ˈduː-/ *noun* [U] **1** (*philosophy* 哲) the theory that there are two opposite principles in everything, for example good and evil 二元論 **2** (*formal*) the state of having two parts 雙重性；二元性 ▸ **dual·ist**, **dual·ist·ic** *adj.* **dual·ist** *noun*

dual·ity /djuːˈæləti; *NAmE* duː-/ *noun* [U, C] (*pl.* **-ies**) (*formal*) the state of having two parts or aspects 雙重性；二元性

ˌdual-ˈpurpose *adj.* that can be used for two different purposes 雙重目的的；兩用的：*a dual-purpose vehicle* (= for carrying passengers or goods) 兩用汽車（載客或載貨）

D

dub /dʌb/ verb, noun

■ **verb** (-bb-) **1 ~ sb + noun** to give sb/sth a particular name, often in a humorous or critical way 把…戲稱為；給…起綽號：*The Belgian actor Jean-Claude Van Damme has been dubbed 'Muscles from Brussels'.* 比利時演員讓・克勞德・范・達默一直被戲稱為"布魯塞爾肌肉"。**2 ~ sth (into sth)** to replace the original speech in a film/movie or television programme with words in another language 為（影片或電視節目）配音；譯製：*an American movie dubbed into Italian* 用意大利語配音的美國影片 ➲ compare SUBTITLE **3 ~ sth** (*especially BrE*) to make a piece of music by mixing sounds from different recordings 混聲錄製，混錄（音樂）

■ **noun** [U] a type of West Indian music or poetry with a strong beat（西印度群島的）強節奏音樂，強節拍詩歌

du·bi·ety /dju:ˈbaɪəti; *NAmE* ˌdu:-/ noun [U] (*formal*) the fact of being uncertain 猶豫；懷疑；疑惑

du·bi·ous /ˈdju:biəs; *NAmE* ˈdu:-/ adj. **1** [not usually before noun] **~ (about sth)/(about doing sth)** (of a person 人) not certain and slightly suspicious about sth; not knowing whether sth is good or bad 懷疑；無把握；拿不準 SYN **doubtful**：*I was rather dubious about the whole idea.* 我對這整個想法很懷疑。**2** (*disapproving*) probably not honest 可疑的；不可信的；靠不住的；不誠實的 SYN **suspicious**：*They indulged in some highly dubious business practices to obtain their current position in the market.* 他們採取了一些極為可疑的商業手段以取得目前在市場上的地位。**3** that you cannot be sure about; that is probably not good 不確定的；不一定好的：*They consider the plan to be of dubious benefit to most families.* 他們認為這項計劃對大多數家庭不一定有好處。◇ (*ironic*) *She had the dubious honour of being the last woman to be hanged in England* (= it was not an honour at all). 她成為英國最後一個受絞刑的女子，這或許也算得上是榮幸之至吧。▶ **du·bi·ous·ly** adv.

ˌDublin Bay ˈprawn noun = LANGOUSTINE

dub·nium /ˈdʌbniəm; *NAmE* ˈdu:b-/ noun [U] (*symb.* **Db**) a RADIOACTIVE chemical element. Dubnium is produced when atoms COLLIDE (= crash into each other). 鉗（放射性化學元素）

ducal /ˈdju:kl; *NAmE* ˈdu:kl/ adj. [only before noun] of or belonging to a DUKE 公爵的；公爵領地的

ducat /ˈdʌkət/ noun (in the past) a gold coin used in many European countries 達克特（舊時在多個歐洲國家通用的金幣）

duch·ess /ˈdʌtʃəs/ noun **1** the wife of a DUKE 公爵夫人：*the Duchess of York* 約克公爵夫人 **2** a woman who has the rank of a DUKE 女公爵

duchy /ˈdʌtʃi/ noun (*pl.* -ies) (also **duke·dom**) an area of land that is owned and controlled by a DUKE or DUCHESS 公爵領地

duck /dʌk/ noun, verb

■ **noun 1** (*pl.* **ducks** or **duck**) [C] a common bird that lives on or near water and has short legs, WEBBED feet (= feet with thin pieces of skin between the toes) and a wide beak. There are many types of duck, some of which are kept for their meat or eggs. 鴨：*wild ducks* 野鴨 ◇ *duck eggs* 鴨蛋 ➲ VISUAL VOCAB page V12 **2** [C] a female duck 母鴨 ➲ compare DRAKE **3** [U] meat from a duck 鴨肉：*roast duck with orange sauce* 烤鴨蘸橘子醬 **4** (also **duckie**, **ducks**, **ducky**) [C, usually sing.] (*BrE, informal*) a friendly way of addressing sb（表示友好的稱呼）乖乖，寶貝兒：*Anything else, duck?* 還有別的事嗎，寶貝兒？➲ compare DEAR, LOVE **5 a duck** [sing.] (in CRICKET 板球) a BATSMAN's score of zero 零分：*He was out for a duck.* 他因得了零分而出局。➲ see also LAME DUCK, SITTING DUCK

IDM **get/have (all) your ˌducks in a ˈrow** (*especially NAmE*) to have made all the preparations needed to do sth; to be well organized 為某事做充分準備；把事情安排得井井有條 **(take to sth) like a ˌduck to ˈwater** (to become used to sth) very easily, without any problems or fears 像鴨子入水般容易，輕而易舉，毫不困難，毫無畏懼（習慣於某事）：*She has taken to teaching like a duck to water.* 她教起書來駕輕就熟。➲ more at DEAD adj., WATER n.

■ **verb 1** [I, T] to move your head or body downwards to avoid being hit or seen 低下頭，彎下身（以免被打中或看見）：*He had to duck as he came through the door.* 他穿過門口時得彎下身來。◇ **~ (down) (behind/under sth)** *We ducked down behind the wall so they wouldn't see us.* 我們弓身躲在牆後不讓他們看見。◇ *He just managed to* **duck out of sight**. 他總算躲開了別人的視線。◇ **~ sth** *She ducked her head and got into the car.* 她低着頭進了汽車。**2** [T] **~ sth** to avoid sth by moving your head or body out of the way 躲閃；躲避 SYN **dodge**：*He ducked the first few blows then started to fight back.* 他躲開最先幾拳後便開始反擊。**3** [I] **+ adv./prep.** to move somewhere quickly, especially in order to avoid being seen 迅速行進，飛快行走（以免被看見）：*She ducked into the adjoining room as we came in.* 我們進來時她轉身躲進了隔壁房間。**4** [I, T] (rather *informal*) to avoid a difficult or unpleasant duty or responsibility 逃避，迴避，推脱，推諉（職責或責任）：**~ out of sth** *It's his turn to cook dinner, but I bet he'll try to duck out of it.* 輪到他做飯了，但我敢打賭他會想方設法逃避的。◇ **~ sth** *The government is ducking the issue.* 政府是在迴避這個問題。**5** (*NAmE* also **dunk**) [T] **~ sb** to push sb underwater and hold them there for a short time 把…按入水中：*The kids were ducking each other in the pool.* 孩子們在池塘裏相互把對方按入水中。

ˌduck-billed ˈplatypus noun = PLATYPUS

duck·boards /ˈdʌkbɔ:dz; *NAmE* -bɔ:rdz/ noun [pl.] long narrow wooden boards used to make a path over wet ground（用窄長木板做鋪在濕地上的）鋪道板，墊路板

duck·ling /ˈdʌklɪŋ/ noun [C, U] a young duck; the meat of a young duck 小鴨；幼鴨；小鴨肉 ➲ see also UGLY DUCKLING

ˌducks and ˈdrakes noun [U] (*BrE*) a game in which you make flat stones BOUNCE across the surface of water 打水漂（遊戲）

ˌduck ˈsoup noun [U] (*NAmE, informal*) a problem that is easy to deal with, or an opponent who is easy to defeat 容易處理的問題；容易打敗的對手

duck·weed /ˈdʌkwi:d/ noun [U] a very small plant that grows on the surface of still water 浮萍

ducky /ˈdʌki/ noun, adj.

■ **noun** (*BrE, informal*) = DUCK n. (4)

■ **adj.** (**duck·ier, ducki·est**) (*NAmE, old-fashioned* or *humorous*) very pleasant 順心如願的；令人十分愉快的：*Everything is just ducky.* 一切順順當當的。

duct /dʌkt/ noun **1** a pipe or tube carrying liquid, gas, electric or telephone wires, etc.（傳送液體、氣體、電線、電話線等的）管道，管子：*a heating/ventilation duct* 加熱導管；通風道 **2** a tube in the body or in plants through which liquid passes（人體或植物體內輸送液體的）管，導管：*the bile duct* 膽管

duc·tile /ˈdʌktaɪl/ adj. (*technical* 術語) (of a metal 金屬) that can be made into a thin wire 可拉成細絲的；可延展的；有延性的

duct·ing /ˈdʌktɪŋ/ noun [U] **1** a system of ducts 管道（或導管）系統 **2** material in the form of a duct or ducts 管狀材料：*a short piece of ducting* 一小截管狀材料

ˈduct tape noun [U] (*NAmE*) very strong cloth tape that is sticky on one side, often used for repairing things or covering holes in pipes 強力膠布（常用於維修或粘貼管道漏洞）

dud /dʌd/ noun, adj.

■ **noun 1** [C] (*informal*) a thing that is useless, especially because it does not work correctly 不中用的東西；廢物：*Two of the fireworks in the box were duds.* 盒子裏的煙火有兩個是沒爆開的廢品。**2 duds** [pl.] (*slang*) clothes 衣裳

■ **adj.** [only before noun] useless; that does not work correctly 無用的；不中用的；出故障的：*a dud battery* 廢電池 ◇ *a dud cheque* (= written by sb who has not enough money in their bank account) 空頭支票

dude /du:d; *BrE* also dju:d/ noun (*slang, especially NAmE*) a man 男人：*He's a real cool dude.* 他真是個帥哥。◇ *Hey, dude, what's up?* 喂，哥們兒，怎麼啦？

ˈdude ranch *noun* an American RANCH (= a large farm) where people can go on holiday/vacation and do the sort of activities that COWBOYS do （美國的）度假牧場，度假農場 **ORIGIN** From an old meaning of the word *dude*, a man from the city who wears fashionable clothes. 源自 dude 一詞的舊義，指衣着時髦的城市男人。

dudgeon /ˈdʌdʒən/ *noun* **IDM** see HIGH *adj.*

due /djuː; *NAmE* duː/ *adj., noun, adv.*

■ ***adj.***

▸ CAUSED BY 由於 **1** [not before noun] **~ to sth/sb** caused by sb/sth; because of sb/sth 由於；因為：*The team's success was largely due to her efforts.* 這個隊的成功主要是她努力的結果。◇ *Most of the problems were due to human error.* 多數問題都是人為錯誤造成的。◇ *The project had to be abandoned due to a lack of government funding.* 這項工程由於缺乏政府的資助而不得不放棄。➲ LANGUAGE BANK at BECAUSE **HELP** Some people think that it is more correct to use **owing to** to mean 'because of' after a verb or at the beginning of a clause, as **due** is an adjective. 有人認為在動詞之後或從句之首用 owing to 表示"因為"更合適，因為 due 是形容詞。

▸ EXPECTED 預期 **2** [not before noun] arranged or expected 預定；預期；預計：*When's the baby due?* 寶寶什麼時候出世？◇ *The next train is due in five minutes.* 下一班火車預定在五分鐘後抵達。◇ (*especially NAmE*) *My essay's due next Friday* (= it has to be given to the teacher by then). 我的論文下週五必須交。◇ **~ to do sth** *Rose is due to start school in January.* 羅斯一月份就要開始上學了。◇ **~ for sth** *The band's first album is due for release later this month.* 這個樂隊的第一張唱片預定在本月下旬發行。

▸ OWED 欠款 **3** [not usually before noun] when a sum of money is **due**, it must be paid immediately 到期：*Payment is due on 1 October.* 付款期限為 10 月 1 日。**4** [not before noun] **~** (**to sb**) owed to sb as a debt, because it is their right or because they have done sth to deserve it 應支付；應給予；應歸於：*Have they been paid the money that is due to them?* 他們應得的錢付給他們了嗎？◇ *Our thanks are due to the whole team.* 我們要向全隊致謝。**5** [not before noun] owed sth; deserving sth 應有；應得到：**~ sth** *I'm still due 15 days' leave.* 我還應有 15 天的休假。◇ **~ for sth** *She's due for promotion soon.* 她很快該晉升了。

▸ SUITABLE/RIGHT 適當；合適 **6** [only before noun] (*formal*) that is suitable or right in the circumstances 適當的；恰當的；合適的：*After due consideration, we have decided to appoint Mr Davis to the job.* 經過充分考慮之後，我們決定委任戴維斯先生負責這項工作。◇ *to make due allowance for sth* 適當考慮某事 ◇ (*BrE*) *He was charged with driving without **due care and attention**.* 他被控魯莽駕駛。➲ compare UNDUE

IDM **in ˌdue ˈcourse** at the right time and not before 在適當的時候；到一定的時候：*Your request will be dealt with in due course.* 你的要求將在適當的時候予以處理。➲ more at RESPECT *n.*

■ ***noun*** **1 your/sb's ~** [U] a thing that should be given to sb by right 應有的權利；應得到的東西：*He received a large reward, which was no more than his due* (= than what he deserved). 他得到重賞，這也是他應該得到的。◇ *She's a slow worker, but **to give her her due*** (= to be fair to her), *she does try very hard.* 她做事很慢，但說句公道話，她確實很盡力。**2 dues** [pl.] charges, for example to be a member of a club 應繳款（如俱樂部會費）：*to pay your dues* 交你的會費

■ ***adv.*** **~ north/south/east/west** exactly; in a straight line 正向；正對着：*to sail due east* 向正東航行 ◇ *The village lies five miles due north of York.* 這個村莊位於約克正北五英里處。

ˌdue ˈdate *noun* [usually sing.] the date on or by which sth, especially a sum of money, is owed or expected （尤指欠款的）到期日，滿期日

duel /ˈdjuːəl; *NAmE* ˈduːəl/ *noun* **1** a formal fight with weapons between two people, used in the past to settle a disagreement, especially over a matter of honour （舊時為解決紛爭的）決鬥：*to **fight/win a duel*** 進行/贏得決鬥 ◇ *to **challenge sb to a duel*** 向某人挑戰要求決鬥 **2** a competition or struggle between two people or groups （雙方的）競爭，鬥爭：*a verbal duel* 舌戰

▸ **duel** *verb* (-ll-, *US* -l-) [I]：*The two men duelled to the death.* 兩個男人雙雙在決鬥中喪命。

du·el·ling (*US* **du·el·ing**) /ˈdjuːəlɪŋ; *NAmE* ˈduːəlɪŋ/ *noun* [U] the practice of fighting duels 決鬥

ˌdue ˈprocess of law (also **ˌdue ˈprocess**) *noun* [U] (*law* 律) (in the US) the right of a citizen to be treated fairly, especially the right to a fair trial 正當法律程序（美國公民得到公正待遇的權利，尤指公正審判）

duet /djuˈet; *NAmE* duˈet/ (also *less frequent* **duo**) *noun* a piece of music for two players or singers 二重奏（曲）；二重唱（曲）：*a piano duet* 鋼琴二重奏曲 ➲ compare SOLO *n.* (1), TRIO (2), (3)

duff /dʌf/ *adj., noun, verb*

■ ***adj.*** (*BrE, informal*) useless; that does not work as it should 無用的；失靈的；出故障的：*He sold me a duff radio.* 他賣給我一台不響的收音機。

■ ***noun*** (*NAmE, informal*) a person's bottom 屁股；臀部

IDM **up the ˈduff** (*BrE, slang*) pregnant 懷孕：*He got her up the duff.* 他使她懷孕了。

■ ***verb***

PHR V **ˌduff sb↔ˈup** (*BrE, informal*) to hit or kick sb severely 痛擊；猛踢；毒打 **SYN** **beat up**

duf·fel bag (also **duf·fle bag**) /ˈdʌfl bæg/ *noun* **1** (*BrE*) a bag made out of cloth, shaped like a tube and closed by a string around the top. It is usually carried over the shoulder. 筒狀帆布包（或旅行包）**2** (*NAmE*) (*BrE* **hold-all**) a large bag made of strong cloth or soft leather, used when you are travelling for carrying clothes, etc. （用帆布或軟皮製造的）大旅行袋 ➲ VISUAL VOCAB page V64

duf·fel coat (also **duf·fle coat**) /ˈdʌfl kəʊt; *NAmE* koʊt/ *noun* a heavy coat made of wool, that usually has a HOOD and is fastened with TOGGLES 粗呢外衣（常連帽及用棒形套扣）

duf·fer /ˈdʌfə(r)/ *noun* (*BrE, informal*) a person who is stupid or unable to do anything well 笨蛋；傻瓜；不中用的人

dug *past tense, past part.* of DIG

du·gong /ˈduːgɒŋ; ˈdjuː-; *NAmE* ˈduːgɑːŋ; -gɔːŋ/ *noun* a large sea animal with thick greyish skin, which lives mainly in the Indian Ocean and eats plants 儒艮，海牛（主要生活於印度洋的大型銀灰色厚皮海洋動物）

dug·out /ˈdʌgaʊt/ *noun* **1** a rough shelter made by digging a hole in the ground and covering it, used by soldiers 防空洞；地下掩體 **2** a shelter by the side of a football (SOCCER) or BASEBALL field where a team's manager, etc. can sit and watch the game 球員席（足球或棒球場邊供球隊教練、候補隊員等就座觀賽）**3** (also **ˌdugout caˈnoe**) a CANOE (= a type of light narrow boat) made by cutting out the inside of a tree TRUNK 獨木舟

DUI /ˌdiː juː ˈaɪ/ *abbr.* (*NAmE*) = DRIVING UNDER THE INFLUENCE

du jour /duː ˈʒʊə(r); *NAmE* duː ˈʒʊr/ *adj.* [after noun] (*informal, humorous*) very popular or important now 流行的；熱門的；當下重要的；時下最夯的：*This age group is the target group du jour.* 這個年齡組是眼下受關注的目標組。◇ *Facebook is the Internet phenomenon du jour.* 臉書（Facebook）網站是當前互聯網上很時髦的現象。**ORIGIN** From French, meaning 'of the day'. 源自法語，意思是"當今的"。

duke /djuːk; *NAmE* duːk/ *noun* **1** a NOBLEMAN of the highest rank 公爵：*the Duke of Edinburgh* 愛丁堡公爵 **2** (in some parts of Europe, especially in the past) a male ruler of a small independent state （尤指舊時歐洲部份地區小公國的）君主 ➲ see also ARCHDUKE, DUCHESS, DUCHY, GRAND DUKE (1)

duke·dom /ˈdjuːkdəm; *NAmE* ˈduːk-/ *noun* **1** the rank or position of a duke 公爵的爵位；公爵的地位 **2** = DUCHY

dulce /ˈdʌlseɪ/ *noun* [C, U] (*US*) a sweet food or drink, especially a sweet or jam 甜食；甜飲料

dul·cet /ˈdʌlsɪt/ *adj.* [only before noun] (*humorous* or *ironic*) sounding sweet and pleasant 甜美的；悦耳動聽的；

美妙的：*I thought I recognized your* ***dulcet tones*** (= the sound of your voice). 我還以為是你那甜美的嗓音呢。

dul·ci·mer /ˈdʌlsɪmə(r)/ *noun* **1** a musical instrument that you play by hitting the metal strings with two HAMMERS 大揚琴；洋琴 **2** a musical instrument with strings, popular in American traditional music, that you lay on your knee and play with your fingers 杜西莫琴（美國傳統撥弦樂器）

D

dull /dʌl/ *adj., verb*

■ ***adj.*** (**dull·er**, **dull·est**)

▸ BORING 乏味 **1** not interesting or exciting 枯燥無味的；無聊的；令人生厭的 SYN **dreary**：*Life in a small town could be deadly dull.* 小城鎮的生活可能會非常沒意思。◇ *The first half of the game was pretty dull.* 上半場比賽打得十分沉悶。◇ *There's* ***never a dull moment*** *when John's around.* 只要約翰在就不會有沉悶的時候。 ➲ SYNONYMS at BORING

▸ LIGHT/COLOURS 光；色彩 **2** not bright or shiny 不明亮的；不鮮明的；無光澤的：*a dull grey colour* 暗灰色 ◇ *dull, lifeless hair* 無光澤、無彈性的頭髮 ◇ *Her eyes were dull.* 她目光呆滯。

▸ WEATHER 天氣 **3** not bright, with a lot of clouds 陰沉的；昏暗的；多雲的 SYN **overcast**：*It was a dull, grey day.* 那是一個陰沉昏暗的日子。

▸ SOUNDS 聲音 **4** not clear or loud 不清晰的；隱約的；低沉的：*The gates shut behind him with a dull thud.* 他走出後，大門砰的一聲悶響關上了。

▸ PAIN 疼痛 **5** not very severe, but continuous 隱隱約約的：*a* ***dull ache/pain*** 隱隱的疼痛

▸ PERSON 人 **6** slow in understanding 遲鈍的；愚笨的 SYN **stupid**：*a dull pupil* 腦子遲鈍的小學生

▸ TRADE 貿易 **7** (*especially NAmE*) not busy; slow 蕭條的；不景氣的；呆滯的：*Don't sell into a dull market.* 不要到蕭條的市場去推銷。

▸ **dull·ness** *noun* [U] **dully** /ˈdʌlli/ *adv.*：*'I suppose so,' she said dully.* "我看是這樣。" 她木然說道。◇ *His leg ached dully.* 他的腿隱隱作痛。

IDM (**as**) **dull as ˈditchwater** (*BrE*) (*US* (**as**) **dull as ˈdish-water**) extremely boring 索然無味；無聊透頂 ➲ more at WORK *n.*

■ ***verb***

▸ PAIN 疼痛 **1** [T, I] **~ (sth)** (of pain or an emotion 疼痛或感情) to become or be made weaker or less severe 減輕；（使）變麻木：*The tablets they gave him dulled the pain for a while.* 他們給他的藥片暫時緩解了疼痛。

▸ PERSON 人 **2** [T] **~ sb** to make a person slower or less lively 使遲鈍；使不活潑：*He felt dulled and stupid with sleep.* 他睡得迷迷糊糊，昏頭昏腦。

▸ COLOURS/SOUNDS 色彩；聲音 **3** [I, T] to become or to make sth less bright, clean or sharp（使）變得無光澤，變模糊，變低沉：*His eyes dulled and he slumped to the ground.* 他眼前一黑重重地倒在地上。◇ **~ sth** *The endless rain seemed to dull all sound.* 連綿不斷的陰雨似乎使所有的聲音都變得沉悶起來。

dull·ard /ˈdʌlɑːd; *NAmE* -lɑːrd/ *noun* (*old-fashioned*) a stupid person with no imagination（毫無想像力的）笨蛋，蠢人

dulls·ville /ˈdʌlzvɪl/ *noun* [U] (*NAmE, informal*) a place or situation which is extremely boring 沉悶乏味的地方（或狀況）

ˌdull-ˈwitted *adj.* (*old-fashioned*) not understanding quickly or easily 悟性低的；理解力差的 SYN **stupid**

duly /ˈdjuːli; *NAmE* ˈduːli/ *adv.* **1** (*formal*) in the correct or expected manner 適當地；恰當地：*The document was duly signed by the inspector.* 這份文件已由檢查員簽妥。 **2** at the expected and correct time 按時地；準時地；適時地：*They duly arrived at 9.30 in spite of torrential rain.* 儘管下着傾盆大雨，他們仍在 9:30 準時到達了。➲ compare UNDULY

dumb /dʌm/ *adj., verb*

■ ***adj.*** (**dumb·er**, **dumb·est**) **1** (*old-fashioned*, sometimes *offensive*) unable to speak 啞的；不能說話的：*She was born* ***deaf and dumb***. 她天生又聾又啞。 HELP **Dumb** used in this meaning is old-fashioned and can be offensive. It is better to use **speech-impaired** instead. * dumb 用於此義是過時用法，可能意含冒犯，最好以 speech-impaired 代之。 **2** temporarily not speaking or refusing to speak 一時說不出話的；不肯開口的：*We were all* ***struck dumb*** *with amazement.* 我們都驚訝得說不出話來。◇ *We sat there in dumb silence.* 我們坐在那裏，默然無語。 **3** (*informal, especially NAmE*) stupid 愚蠢的；傻的；笨的：*That was a pretty dumb thing to do.* 做那樣的事太愚蠢了。◇ *If the police question you,* ***act dumb*** (= pretend you do not know anything). 如果警察盤問，你就一問三不知。◇ *In her early movies she played* ***a dumb blonde***. 在她早期的電影中，她扮演傻乎乎的金髮女郎。 ▸ **dumb·ly** *adv.*：*'Are you all right?' Laura nodded dumbly.* "你身體好嗎？" 勞拉默默地點了點頭。 **dumb·ness** *noun* [U]

■ ***verb***

PHR V **ˌdumb ˈdown | ˌdumb sth↔ˈdown** (*disapproving*) to make sth less accurate or EDUCATIONAL, and of worse quality, by trying to make it easier for people to understand（為使公眾更易理解而）降低…的標準，減少…的專業性教育內容 ▸ **ˌdumbing ˈdown** *noun* [U]

ˌdumb ˈanimal *noun* [usually pl.] (*BrE*) an animal, especially when seen as deserving pity（尤指可憐巴巴的）啞巴牲口

ˈdumb-ass *adj.* [only before noun] (*NAmE, taboo, slang*) stupid 愚蠢的；笨頭笨腦的

ˈdumb-bell *noun* **1** a short bar with a weight at each end, used for making the arm and shoulder muscles stronger 啞鈴 ➲ VISUAL VOCAB page V42 **2** (*NAmE, informal*) a stupid person 笨蛋；蠢貨；傻瓜

dumb·found /dʌmˈfaʊnd/ *verb* **~ sb** to surprise or shock sb so much that they are unable to speak 使驚呆：*His reply dumbfounded me.* 他的回答使我啞然。

dumb·found·ed /dʌmˈfaʊndɪd/ (also *less frequent* **dumb·struck** /ˈdʌmstrʌk/) *adj.* unable to speak because of surprise 驚呆了的：*The news left her dumbfounded.* 這消息把她驚呆了。

dumbo /ˈdʌmbəʊ; *NAmE* -boʊ/ *noun* (*pl.* **-oes**) (*informal*) a stupid person 笨蛋；蠢貨；呆子

ˌdumb ˈwaiter *noun* a small lift/elevator for carrying food and plates from one floor to another in a restaurant（餐廳樓層間運送食物和餐具的）升降架

dum·dum /ˈdʌmdʌm/ (also **ˌdumdum ˈbullet**) *noun* a bullet that spreads out and breaks into many pieces when it hits sb 達姆彈（擊入目標體內後爆開） ORIGIN It is named after the factory at Dumdum near Calcutta in India, where such bullets were originally made. They are now illegal. 源自於印度加爾各答附近一家工廠的廠名，這種子彈起初在此生產。現在達姆彈屬於非法。

dummy /ˈdʌmi/ *noun, adj., verb*

■ ***noun*** (*pl.* **-ies**) **1** [C] a model of a person, used especially when making clothes or for showing them in a shop window（尤指縫製或陳列服裝用的）人體模型：*a tailor's dummy* 裁縫店的模型人 ➲ see also MANNEQUIN (1) **2** [C] a thing that seems to be real but is only a copy of the real thing 仿製品；仿造物 **3** [C] (*NAmE, informal*) a stupid person 笨蛋；蠢貨：*Don't just stand there, you dummy.* 別在那兒乾站着，你這個蠢貨。 **4** [C] (in some sports 某些體育運動) an occasion when you pretend to make a particular move and then do not do so 假動作 **5** [C] (*BrE*) (*NAmE* **paci·fier**) a specially shaped rubber or plastic object for a baby to suck 橡皮奶嘴；橡皮奶頭 **6** [U] (in card games, especially BRIDGE 紙牌遊戲，尤指橋牌) the cards which are placed facing upwards on the table and which can be seen by all the players 明手牌

■ ***adj.*** [only before noun] made to look real, although it is actually a copy which does not work 假的 SYN **replica**：*a dummy bomb* 空包彈

■ ***verb*** [T, I] (in football (SOCCER) 足球) to pretend to make a particular move in order to confuse your opponent 做假動作：**~ sth** *She dummied a shot that brought the goalie to her knees.* 她一個假射門使守門員雙膝跪到地上。◇ **+ adv./prep.** *He dummied past five defenders, then shot at the near post.* 他以假動作晃過五個防守隊員，接着把球射向近門柱。

ˌdummy ˈrun *noun* (*BrE*) a practice attack, performance, etc. before the real one 演習；試演 SYN **dry run**

dump 0-- /dʌmp/ *verb, noun*

■ *verb*

▸ **GET RID OF** 丟棄 **1** 0-- **~ sth** to get rid of sth you do not want, especially in a place which is not suitable（尤指在不合適的地方）丟棄，扔掉，傾倒：*Too much toxic waste is being dumped at sea.* 太多的有毒廢料在向大海裏傾倒。◇ *The dead body was just dumped by the roadside.* 這具死屍就扔在路邊。**2 ~ sb/sth (on sb)** (*informal*) to get rid of sb/sth or leave them for sb else to deal with 丟下；拋棄；推卸：*He's got no right to keep dumping his problems on me.* 他沒有權利總是把他的問題推到我身上。**3 ~ sth** (*business* 商) to get rid of goods by selling them at a very low price, often in another country（常向國外）傾銷，拋售

▸ **PUT DOWN** 放下 **4 ~ sth** to put sth down in a careless or untidy way 隨便堆放；亂放：*Just dump your stuff over there—we'll sort it out later.* 就把你的東西堆在那兒吧——我們以後再整理。

▸ **END RELATIONSHIP** 斷絕關係 **5 ~ sb** (*informal*) to end a romantic relationship with sb 與（某人）結束戀愛關係：*Did you hear he's dumped his girlfriend?* 他已把女朋友給甩了，你聽說了嗎？

▸ **COMPUTING** 計算機技術 **6 ~ sth** to copy information and move it somewhere to store it（內存信息）轉貯，轉存

IDM see LAP *n.*

PHR V **'dump on sb** (*informal, especially NAmE*) to criticize sb severely or treat them badly 非難；虧待

■ *noun* ➲ see also DUMPS

▸ **FOR WASTE** 垃圾 **1** 0-- a place where waste or rubbish/garbage is taken and left 垃圾場；廢物堆：(*BrE*) *a* ***rubbish dump*** 垃圾場 ◇ (*NAmE*) *a* ***garbage dump*** 垃圾場 ◇ *the municipal dump* 市政垃圾場 ◇ *a toxic/nuclear* ***waste dump*** 有毒／核廢料堆 **2** (also **'mine dump**) (*SAfrE*) a hill that is formed when waste sand from the production of gold is piled in one place over a period of time 廢渣堆；尾礦堆

▸ **DIRTY PLACE** 髒地方 **3** (*informal, disapproving*) a dirty or unpleasant place 髒地方；邋遢場所；令人討厭的地方：*How can you live in this dump?* 你怎麼會住在這種骯髒地方？

▸ **FOR WEAPONS** 武器 **4** a temporary store for military supplies 軍需品臨時存放處：*an ammunition dump* 彈藥臨時堆積處

▸ **COMPUTING** 計算機技術 **5** an act of copying data stored in a computer; a copy or list of the contents of this data 轉貯；轉存；轉貯數據 ➲ see also SCREEN DUMP

▸ **WASTE FROM BODY** 糞便 **6** [C] (*slang*) an act of passing waste matter from the body through the BOWELS 拉屎：*to have a dump* 拉屎

'dump bin (*BrE*) (also **dis'play bin** *US, BrE*) *noun* a box in a shop/store for displaying goods, especially goods whose prices have been reduced（商店）陳列櫃；（尤指）減價貨品櫃

dump·er /'dʌmpə(r)/ *noun* (*especially NAmE*) a person who throws away dangerous or harmful things, especially in the wrong place 亂扔危險（或有害）物品者

'dumper truck (*BrE*) (*NAmE* **'dump truck**) *noun* a vehicle for carrying earth, stones, etc. in a container which can be lifted up for the load to fall out 自卸貨車；翻斗車 ➲ **VISUAL VOCAB** page V58

dump·ing /'dʌmpɪŋ/ *noun* [U] the act or practice of dumping sth, especially dangerous substances（尤指危險物質的）傾倒，傾卸：*a ban on the dumping of radioactive waste at sea* 禁止向海裏傾倒放射性廢物

'dumping ground *noun* [usually sing.] a place where sth that is not wanted is dumped 垃圾傾倒場

dump·ling /'dʌmplɪŋ/ *noun* **1** a small ball of DOUGH (= a mixture of flour, fat and water) that is cooked and served with meat dishes 小麪糰；湯糰；餃子：*chicken with herb dumplings* 芳草雞肉餃子 **2** a small ball of PASTRY, often with fruit in it, eaten as a DESSERT 小麪糰；水果湯糰；水果布丁：*apple dumplings* 蘋果布丁

dumps /dʌmps/ *noun* [pl.]

IDM **down in the 'dumps** (*informal*) feeling unhappy 悶悶不樂；沮喪 **SYN** **depressed**

Dump·ster™ /'dʌmpstə(r)/ (*NAmE*) (*BrE* **skip**) *noun* a large open container for putting old bricks, rubbish/garbage, etc. in. The Dumpster is then loaded on a lorry/truck and taken away. 大垃圾桶（裝工地廢料、垃圾等，由卡車拖走）

'dump truck (*NAmE*) (*BrE* **'dumper truck**) *noun* a vehicle for carrying earth, stones, etc. in a container which can be lifted up for the load to fall out 自卸貨車；翻斗車 ➲ **VISUAL VOCAB** page V58

dumpy /'dʌmpi/ *adj.* (especially of a person 尤指人) short and fat 矮胖的

dun /dʌn/ *adj.* greyish-brown in colour 棕灰色的；灰褐色的；暗褐色的 ▸ **dun** *noun* [U]

dunce /dʌns/ *noun* (*old-fashioned*) a person, especially a child at school, who is stupid or slow to learn 愚笨的人；（尤指）遲鈍的學生

,dunce's 'cap (*BrE*) (*NAmE* **'dunce cap**) *noun* a pointed hat that was sometimes given in the past to a child in a class at school who was slow to learn（舊時有時給學習遲緩學生戴的）笨蛋圓錐帽

Dun·dee cake /dʌn'di: keɪk/ *noun* [C, U] a fruit cake, usually decorated with ALMONDS (= a type of nut) 鄧迪水果杏仁蛋糕

dun·der·head /'dʌndəhed; *NAmE* 'dʌndər-/ *noun* (*informal*) a silly or stupid person 傻瓜；笨蛋

dune /dju:n; *NAmE* du:n/ (also **'sand dune**) *noun* a small hill of sand formed by the wind, near the sea or in a desert（風吹積成的）沙丘 ➲ **VISUAL VOCAB** pages V4, V5

'dune buggy *noun* = BEACH BUGGY

dung /dʌŋ/ *noun* [U] solid waste from animals, especially from large ones（尤指大型動物的）糞 **SYN** **manure**：*cow dung* 牛糞

dun·garees /,dʌŋgə'ri:z/ *noun* [pl.] **1** (*BrE*) (*NAmE* **overalls**, **'bib overalls**) a piece of clothing that consists of trousers/pants with an extra piece of cloth covering the chest, held up by strips of cloth over the shoulders 工裝褲；背帶工作服：*a pair of dungarees* 一條工裝褲 ◇ *His dungarees were covered in grease.* 他的工裝褲上沾滿了油污。➲ picture at OVERALL **2** (*NAmE*) heavy cotton trousers/pants for working in 粗布工作褲；勞動布工裝褲

dun·geon /'dʌndʒən/ *noun* a dark underground room used as a prison, especially in a castle（尤指城堡中的）地牢，土牢

dung·heap /'dʌŋhi:p/ (also **dung·hill** /'dʌŋhɪl/) *noun* a large pile of dung, especially on a farm（尤指農莊上的）糞堆

dunk /dʌŋk/ *verb* **1** [T] **~ sth (in/into sth)** to put food quickly into liquid before eating it（吃前將食物放入液體中）浸一浸，泡一泡：*She sat reading a magazine, dunking cookies in her coffee.* 她坐着一邊看雜誌一邊將曲奇餅在咖啡裏蘸一下再吃。**2** [T] **~ sb/sth** (*especially NAmE*) to push sb underwater for a short time, as a joke; to put sth into water（開玩笑地將某人按入水中）浸一下；浸，泡（某物）：*The camera survived being dunked in the river.* 這照相機在河裏泡了一下還沒壞。**3** [I, T] **~ (sth)** (in BASKETBALL 籃球) to jump very high and put the ball through the BASKET with great force from above 把（球）扣入籃內；扣籃；灌籃

dunno /də'nəʊ; *NAmE* də'noʊ/ (*non-standard*) a way of writing the informal spoken form of 'I don't know' 我不知道（I don't know 的非正式寫法）

dunny /'dʌni/ *noun* (*pl.* **-ies**) (*AustralE, NZE, informal*) a toilet 廁所；茅廁

dunt /dʌnt/ *verb* **~ sth** (**+ adv./prep.**) (*ScotE*) to hit or knock sb or sth 擊打；敲擊 ▸ **dunt** *noun*

duo /'dju:əʊ; *NAmE* 'du:oʊ/ *noun* (*pl.* **-os**) **1** two people who perform together or are often seen or thought of together 一對表演者；搭檔：*the comedy duo Laurel and Hardy* 勞雷爾和哈迪這對喜劇搭檔 ➲ compare TRIO (1) **2** = DUET

duo·de·num /,dju:ə'di:nəm; *NAmE* ,du:ə-/ *noun* (*pl.* **duo·de·nums** or **duo·dena** /-'di:nə/) (*anatomy* 解) the first part of the small INTESTINE, next to the stomach 十二指腸 ➲ VISUAL VOCAB page V59 ➲ compare ILEUM, JEJUNUM ▸ **duo·denal** /ˌdjuːəˈdiːnl; NAmE ˌduːə-/ adj.: *a duodenal ulcer* 十二指腸潰瘍

du·op·oly /djuːˈɒpəli; NAmE duːˈɑː-/ noun (pl. -ies) (business 商) **1** a right to trade in a particular product or service, held by only two companies or organizations（商品或服務的）兩強壟斷 **2** a group of two companies or organizations who hold a duopoly 兩強壟斷集團 ➲ compare MONOPOLY (1)

the DUP /ˌdiː juː ˈpiː/ abbr. the Democratic Unionist Party (a political party in Northern Ireland that wants it to remain a part of the United Kingdom) 民主統一黨（主張北愛爾蘭歸屬聯合王國的北愛爾蘭政黨）

du·patta /dʊˈpʌtə/ noun a long piece of material worn around the head and neck by women in S Asia, usually with a SALWAR or GHAGRA（南亞女子戴的）圍巾，頭巾

dupe /djuːp; NAmE duːp/ verb, noun

▪ *verb* to trick or cheat sb 詐騙；哄騙；欺騙：**~ sb** *They soon realized they had been duped.* 他們很快便意識到自己上當了。◇ **~ sb into doing sth** *He was duped into giving them his credit card.* 他上當受騙把信用卡交給了他們。

▪ *noun* (formal) a person who is tricked or cheated 上當受騙者

du·plex /ˈdjuːpleks; NAmE ˈduː-/ noun (especially NAmE) **1** a building divided into two separate homes 連棟式的兩棟住宅；聯式房屋 ➲ VISUAL VOCAB page V16 **2** a flat/apartment with rooms on two floors 佔兩層樓的公寓套房；複式住宅；躍層公寓

du·pli·cate verb, adj., noun

▪ *verb* /ˈdjuːplɪkeɪt; NAmE ˈduː-/ **1** [often passive] **~ sth** to make an exact copy of sth 複製；複印；複寫：*a duplicated form* 複製的表格 **2 ~ sth** to do sth again, especially when it is unnecessary（尤指不必要時）重複，再做一次：*There's no point in duplicating work already done.* 重複別人已經做過的工作毫無意義。▸ **du·pli·ca·tion** /ˌdjuːplɪˈkeɪʃn; NAmE ˌduː-/ noun [U, C]

▪ *adj.* /ˈdjuːplɪkət; NAmE ˈduː-/ [only before noun] exactly like sth else; made as a copy of sth else 完全一樣的；複製的；副本的：*a duplicate invoice* 發票副本

▪ *noun* /ˈdjuːplɪkət; NAmE ˈduː-/ one of two or more things that are the same in every detail 完全一樣的東西；複製品；副本 SYN **copy**：*Is this a duplicate or the original?* 這是副本還是正本？

IDM **in duplicate** (of documents, etc. 文件等) as two copies that are exactly the same in every detail 一式兩份的：*to prepare a contract in duplicate* 準備一式兩份的合同 ➲ compare TRIPLICATE

du·pli·city /djuːˈplɪsəti; NAmE duː-/ noun [U] (formal) dishonest behaviour that is intended to make sb believe sth which is not true 欺騙，奸詐（行為）SYN **deceit** ▸ **du·pli·ci·tous** /djuːˈplɪsɪtəs; NAmE duː-/ adj.

dur·able /ˈdjʊərəbl; NAmE ˈdʊr-/ adj. likely to last for a long time without breaking or getting weaker 耐用的；持久的：*durable plastics* 耐用塑料 ◇ *negotiations for a durable peace* 為持久和平而進行的談判 ▸ **dur·abil·ity** /ˌdjʊərəˈbɪləti; NAmE ˌdʊr-/ noun [U]：*the durability of gold* 金子的耐久性 ➲ see also CONSUMER DURABLES

ˌdurable ˈgoods (NAmE) (BrE **conˌsumer ˈdurables**) noun [pl.] (business 商) goods which are expected to last for a long time after they have been bought, such as cars, televisions, etc. 耐用消費品（如汽車、電視機等）

dur·ation AW /djuˈreɪʃn; NAmE du-/ noun [U] (formal) the length of time that sth lasts or continues 持續時間；期間：*The school was used as a hospital for the duration of the war.* 戰爭期間這所學校用作醫院。◇ *a contract of three years' duration* 三年期的合同

IDM **for the duration** (informal) until the end of a particular situation 直到…結束；在整個…期間

dura·tive /ˈdjʊərətɪv; NAmE ˈdʊr-/ adj. (grammar 語法) (of a verb tense, a word, etc. 動詞時態、詞語等) describing an action that continues for some time 持續（性）的；延續的

dur·ess /djuˈres; NAmE du-/ noun [U] (formal) threats or force that are used to make sb do sth 脅迫；強迫：*He signed the confession* **under duress**. 他被迫無奈在供狀上簽了字。

Durex™ /ˈdjʊəreks; NAmE ˈdʊr-/ noun (pl. **Durex**) (BrE) a CONDOM 杜蕾斯避孕套

dur·ian /ˈdʊəriən; NAmE ˈdʊr-/ noun a large tropical fruit with a strong unpleasant smell but a sweet flavour 榴蓮 ➲ VISUAL VOCAB page V30

dur·ing 🔑 /ˈdjʊərɪŋ; NAmE ˈdʊr-/ prep. **1** 🔑 all through a period of time 在…期間：*during the 1990s* 在 20 世紀 90 年代 ◇ *There are extra flights to Colorado during the winter.* 冬季有飛往科羅拉多的增開航班。◇ *Please remain seated during the performance.* 演出期間請不要站起來。**2** 🔑 at some point in a period of time 在…期間的某個時候：*He was taken to the hospital during the night.* 他在夜間被送到醫院。◇ *I only saw her once during my stay in Rome.* 我在羅馬逗留期間只見過她一次。HELP **During** is used to say when something happens; **for** answers the question 'how long?'. * during 表示某事發生的時間，for 則回答 how long 的問題：*I stayed in London for a week.* ◇ ~~*I stayed in London during a week.*~~

durrie noun = DHURRIE

durum /ˈdjʊərəm; NAmE ˈdʊrəm/ (also **ˌdurum ˈwheat**) noun [U] a type of hard WHEAT, used to make PASTA 硬質小麥（用於製作意大利麪食）

dusk /dʌsk/ noun [U] the time of day when the light has almost gone, but it is not yet dark 黃昏；傍晚 SYN **twilight**：*The street lights go on* **at dusk**. 街燈在黃昏時分亮起來。➲ compare DAWN (1)

dusky /ˈdʌski/ adj. (literary) not very bright; dark or soft in colour 昏暗的；暗淡的；（顏色）暗的，柔和的：*the dusky light inside the cave* 洞中昏暗的光線 ◇ *dusky pink* 暗粉紅色

dust 🔑 /dʌst/ noun, verb

▪ *noun* **1** 🔑 [U] a fine powder that consists of very small pieces of sand, earth, etc. 沙土；塵土：*A cloud of dust rose as the truck drove off.* 卡車開過時揚起一片灰塵。◇ *The workers wear masks to avoid inhaling the dust.* 工人們戴着面罩避免吸入塵土。➲ see also COSMIC DUST ➲ SYNONYMS at SOIL **2** 🔑 the fine powder of dirt that forms in buildings, on furniture, floors, etc.（建築物內、傢具或地板等上的）灰塵，塵埃：*The books were all covered with dust.* 書上積滿了灰塵。◇ *There wasn't a* **speck of dust** *anywhere in the room.* 屋子裏處處一塵不染。◇ *That guitar's been sitting* **gathering dust** (= not being used) *for years now.* 那把吉他現已塵封多年。**3** a fine powder that consists of very small pieces of a particular substance 粉塵；粉末：**coal/gold dust** 煤 / 金粉 ➲ see also DUSTY

IDM **leave sb in the ˈdust** (NAmE) to leave sb far behind 把某人遠遠拋在後面；使望塵莫及 **let the dust settle** | **wait for the dust to settle** to wait for a situation to become clear or certain 待形勢明朗；待情況清楚 ➲ more at BITE v.

▪ *verb* **1** 🔑 [I, T] to clean furniture, a room, etc. by removing dust from surfaces with a cloth 擦去…的灰塵；擦灰：*I broke the vase while I was dusting.* 我擦灰塵時將花瓶打碎了。◇ **~ sth** *Could you dust the sitting room?* 你把起居室擦一擦好嗎？**2** [T] **~ sth (+ adv./prep.)** to remove dirt from sb/sth/yourself with your hands or a brush 撣去；擦去；刷去：*She dusted some ash from her sleeve.* 她撣去袖子上的灰末。**3** [T] **~ sth (with sth)** to cover sth with fine powder 把（粉末）撒於；撒（粉）：*Dust the cake with sugar.* 把糖撒在蛋糕上。IDM see DONE adj.

PHR V **ˌdust sb/sth↔ˈdown** (especially BrE) to remove dust, dirt, etc. from sb/sth 除去…的灰塵：*Mel stood up and dusted herself down.* 梅爾站起來拍掉了身上的塵土。**ˌdust sb/sth↔ˈoff** to remove dust, dirt, etc. from sb/sth 除去…的灰塵：(figurative) *For the concert, he dusted off some of his old hits.* 為了這次音樂會，他重溫了他的一些曾紅極一時的老歌。

dust·ball /ˈdʌstbɔːl/ (also **ˈdust bunny**) noun (NAmE) a mass of dust and small pieces of thread, hair, material, etc.（由灰塵和細小線段、毛髮、布料等形成的）塵球，塵埃團

dust·bin /ˈdʌstbɪn/ (*BrE*) (*NAmE* **ˈgarbage can**, **ˈtrash can**) *noun* a large container with a lid, used for putting rubbish/garbage in, usually kept outside the house（常置於房外的）垃圾桶，垃圾箱 ➲ note at RUBBISH

ˈdust bowl *noun* an area of land that has been turned into desert by lack of rain or too much farming 乾旱塵暴區；風沙侵蝕區

dust·cart /ˈdʌstkɑːt; *NAmE* -kɑːrt/ (*BrE*) (*NAmE* **ˈgarbage truck**) *noun* a vehicle for collecting rubbish/garbage from outside houses, etc. 垃圾車

ˈdust cover *noun* **1** = DUST JACKET **2** a hard or soft plastic cover on a piece of equipment, etc. that protects it when it is not being used 防塵罩；防塵套

ˈdust devil *noun* a small column of dust over land, caused by the wind 塵捲風

dust·er /ˈdʌstə(r)/ *noun* **1** a cloth for removing dust from furniture 抹布；擦布；撣子 ➲ VISUAL VOCAB page V20 **2** (*old-fashioned, NAmE*) a piece of clothing that you wear over your other clothes when you are cleaning the house, etc.（打掃清潔時穿的）防塵罩衫 **3** (*NAmE*) a long coat that was worn by COWBOYS（牛仔穿的）防塵長外衣

ˈdust jacket (also **ˈdust cover**) *noun* a paper cover on a book that protects it but that can be removed（書的）護封，包封

dust·man /ˈdʌstmən/ *noun* (*pl.* **-men** /-mən/) (also *informal* **bin·man**, *formal* **ˈrefuse collector**) (all *BrE*) (*NAmE* **ˈgarbage man**) a person whose job is to remove waste from outside houses, etc. 垃圾工 ➲ note at RUBBISH

ˈdust mite (also **ˈhouse dust mite**) *noun* a very small creature that lives in houses and can cause ALLERGIES 塵蟎（可引起過敏）

dust·pan /ˈdʌstpæn/ *noun* a small flat container with a handle into which dust is brushed from the floor 畚箕 ➲ VISUAL VOCAB page V20

ˈdust sheet (*BrE*) (*NAmE* **ˈdrop cloth**) *noun* a large sheet that is used to protect floors, furniture, etc. from dust or paint（地板、傢具等的）防塵罩，苫布

ˈdust storm *noun* a storm that carries clouds of dust in the wind over a wide area 塵暴

ˈdust-up *noun* (*BrE, informal*) an argument or fight 吵架；爭吵；打架

dusty /ˈdʌsti/ *adj.* (**dust·ier**, **dusti·est**) **1** full of dust; covered with dust 佈滿灰塵的；灰塵覆蓋的：*a dusty road* 塵土飛揚的路 ◊ *piles of dusty books* 一摞一摞佈滿灰塵的書 ➲ SYNONYMS at DIRTY **2** (of a colour 顏色) not bright; dull 土灰色的；灰暗的；無光澤的：*dusty pink* 土灰粉紅色

Dutch /dʌtʃ/ *adj.* of or connected with the Netherlands, its people or its language 荷蘭的；荷蘭人的；荷蘭語的
IDM **go Dutch (with sb)** to share the cost of sth with sb（同某人）各付各的賬，平攤費用

ˌDutch ˈauction *noun* a sale in which the price of an item is reduced until sb offers to buy it 荷蘭式拍賣（把價格逐步降低到有人願買為止）

ˌDutch ˈbarn *noun* (*BrE*) a farm building without walls that has a roof supported on poles, and is used for storing HAY (= dried grass), etc.（無牆的）乾草棚

ˌDutch ˈcourage *noun* [U] (*BrE, informal*) the false courage or confidence that a person gets from drinking alcohol 酒後之勇

ˌDutch ˈdoor (*NAmE*) (*BrE* **ˌstable ˈdoor**) *noun* a door which is divided into two parts so that the top part can be left open while the bottom part is kept shut 馬廐式兩截門（上下兩部份可分別開關）

ˌDutch ˈelm disease *noun* [U] a disease that kills ELM trees 榆樹荷蘭病

duti·ful /ˈdjuːtɪfl; *NAmE* ˈduː-/ *adj.* doing everything that you are expected to do; willing to obey and to show respect 盡職的；順從的；恭敬的 SYN **obedient**：*a* ***dutiful daughter/son/wife*** 孝順的女兒／兒子；賢惠的妻子 ▸ **duti·ful·ly** /-fəli/ *adv.*

duty 🔑 /ˈdjuːti; *NAmE* ˈduːti/ *noun* (*pl.* **-ies**)
1 🔑 [C, U] something that you feel you have to do because it is your moral or legal responsibility 責任；義務；本分：*It is my duty to report it to the police.* 把這事報告給警方是我的責任。◊ *Local councillors* ***have a duty to*** *serve the community.* 地方議員有義務為社區服務。◊ *I don't want you to visit me simply out of* ***a sense of duty****.* 我希望你不只是出於責任感才來看我。◊ *your duties as a parent* 你作為父母的責任 ◊ *to* ***do your duty*** *for your country* 為祖國盡己任 **2** 🔑 [U] the work that is your job 上班；值班：***Report for duty*** *at 8 a.m.* 早上 8 點鐘報到上班。➲ see also NIGHT DUTY **3** 🔑 **duties** [pl.] tasks that are part of your job 職責；任務：*I spend a lot of my time on administrative duties.* 我在行政管理事務上花了大量時間。◊ *Your duties will include setting up a new computer system.* 你的職責將包括建立一個新的計算機系統。➲ see also HEAVY-DUTY ➲ SYNONYMS at TASK **4** 🔑 [C, U] a tax that you pay on things that you buy, especially those that you bring into a country 税；（尤指進口貨品）關税：***customs/excise/import duties*** 關税；消費税；進口税 ◊ **~ on sth** *duty on wine and beer* 葡萄酒和啤酒税 ➲ SYNONYMS at TAX ➲ see also DEATH DUTY, STAMP DUTY
IDM **on/off duty** 🔑 (of nurses, police officers, etc. 護士、警官等) working/not working at a particular time 值（或下）班；值（或不值）勤：*Who's on duty today?* 今天誰值班？◊ *What time do you go off duty?* 你什麼時候下班？ ➲ see also OFF-DUTY ➲ more at BOUNDEN, LINE *n.*

ˌduty-ˈbound *adj.* [not before noun] (*formal*) having to do sth because it is your duty 責無旁貸；義不容辭：*I felt duty-bound to help him.* 我覺得幫助他責無旁貸。

ˌduty-ˈfree *adj.* (of goods 商品) that you can bring into a country without paying tax on them 免關税的：*duty-free cigarettes* 免税香煙 ▸ **ˌduty-ˈfree** *adv.* **ˌduty-ˈfree** *noun* (*BrE, informal*)：*We bought a load of duty-frees* (= duty-free goods) *at the airport.* 我們在機場買了許多免税商品。

ˌduty-ˈfree shop (also **ˌduty-ˈfree**) *noun* a shop/store in an airport or on a ship, etc. that sells goods such as cigarettes, alcohol, PERFUME, etc. without tax on them（機場內、船上等的）免税商店

ˈduty officer *noun* the officer, for example in the police, army, etc., who is on duty at a particular time in a particular place（警察、軍隊等的）值勤官，值班員

duvet /ˈduːveɪ; *NAmE* also duːˈveɪ/ (also **ˌcontinental ˈquilt**, **quilt**) *noun* (all *BrE*) a large cloth bag that is filled with feathers or other soft material and that you have on top of you in bed to keep yourself warm 羽絨被：*a* ***duvet cover*** (= a cover that you can wash, that you put over a duvet) 羽絨被套 ➲ VISUAL VOCAB page V23

ˈduvet day *noun* (*BrE, informal*) a day when you stay at home instead of going to work because you feel tired and want to rest but are not ill 羽絨被擁臥日；偷懶假日；偷閒日 ➲ compare PERSONAL DAY

DVD 🔑 /ˌdiː viː ˈdiː/ *noun* a disk on which large amounts of information, especially photographs and video, can be stored, for use on a computer or **DVD player** (the abbreviation for 'digital videodisc' or 'digital versatile disc') 數字影碟，數碼（多功能）光碟（全寫為 digital videodisc 或 digital versatile disc）：*a DVD-ROM drive* 只讀型 DVD 存貯驅動器 ◊ *Is it available* ***on DVD*** *yet?* 這個現在有 DVD 版了嗎？ ➲ COLLOCATIONS at CINEMA ➲ VISUAL VOCAB page V66

DVD-A /ˌdiː viː diː ˈeɪ/ *noun* a type of DVD that stores sound of very high quality (the abbreviation for 'digital versatile disc audio') 音頻 DVD，音訊光碟（全寫為 digital versatile disc audio）

ˌDVˈD burn·er (also **ˌDVˈD writer**) *noun* a piece of equipment used for recording from a computer onto a DVD * DVD 刻錄機；光碟燒錄機

DVD-R /ˌdiː viː diː ˈɑː(r)/ *noun* a type of DVD that you can use only once to record data (the abbreviation for

D

'digital versatile disc recordable') 一次寫入式 DVD，可寫入光碟（全寫為 digital versatile disc recordable）

DVD-ROM /ˌdiː viː diː ˈrɒm; NAmE ˈrɑːm/ *noun* a type of DVD that allows you to store data but not to record it (the abbreviation for 'digital versatile disc read-only memory') 只讀型 DVD，唯讀光碟（全寫為 digital versatile disc read-only memory）

D

DVD-RW /ˌdiː viː diː ɑː ˈdʌbljuː; NAmE ɑːr/ *noun* a type of DVD that you can use many times to record data (the abbreviation for 'digital versatile disc rewritable') 可擦寫 DVD，可重寫光碟（全寫為 digital versatile disc rewritable）

DVR /ˌdiː viː ˈɑː(r)/ *noun* a device that records video onto a hard disk or other memory device, using digital technology (the abbreviation for 'digital video recorder') 數字視頻錄像機，數位視訊錄影機（全寫為 digital video recorder）SYN PVR

DVT /ˌdiː viː ˈtiː/ *abbr.* DEEP VEIN THROMBOSIS

dwaal /dwɑːl/ *noun* (*SAfrE*) a confused or very relaxed state of mind 迷惑；惘然：*I was in a complete dwaal.* 我一片茫然。

dwarf /dwɔːf; NAmE dwɔːrf/ *noun, adj., verb*

■ ***noun*** (*pl.* **dwarfs** or **dwarves** /dwɔːvz; NAmE dwɔːrvz/) **1** (in stories) a creature like a small man, who has magic powers and who is usually described as living and working under the ground, especially working with metal（神話中會魔法的）小矮人 **2** (*sometimes offensive*) an extremely small person, who will never grow to a normal size because of a physical problem; a person suffering from DWARFISM 矮子；侏儒 HELP There is no other word that is generally considered more acceptable. 普遍認為沒有比這更易於接受的用詞。

■ ***adj.*** [only before noun] (of a plant or an animal 植物或動物) much smaller than the normal size 矮小的：*dwarf conifers* 矮小的針葉樹

■ ***verb*** **~ sth** to make sth seem small or unimportant compared with sth else 使顯得矮小；使相形見絀：*The old houses were dwarfed by the huge new tower blocks.* 這些舊房子在新建的高樓大廈的映襯下顯得十分矮小。

dwarf·ism /ˈdwɔːfɪzəm; NAmE ˈdwɔːrf-/ *noun* the medical condition of being a dwarf. People who suffer from this condition are very short and often have short arms and legs. 侏儒症

ˌdwarf ˈplanet *noun* a round object in space that goes around the sun but is not as large as a planet and does not clear other objects from its path 矮行星（以軌道繞着太陽的天體，未能清除在軌跡上的其他天體）：*the dwarf planets Pluto, Ceres, Eris, Makemake and Haumea* 冥王星、穀神星、鬩神星、鳥神星和妊神星等五顆矮行星 ➲ compare PLUTOID

dweeb /dwiːb/ *noun* (*slang, especially NAmE*) a person, especially a boy or a man, who does not have good social skills and is not fashionable（尤指男孩或男人）不合群的人，不合時尚的人，怪人

dwell /dwel/ *verb* (**dwelt**, **dwelt**) or (**dwelled**, **dwelled**) [I] **+ adv./prep.** (*formal* or *literary*) to live somewhere 居住；棲身：*For ten years she dwelled among the nomads of North America.* 她在北美遊牧民中生活了十年。

PHR V **ˈdwell on/upon sth** **1** to think or talk a lot about sth, especially sth it would be better to forget 老是想着，嘮叨（尤指最好應忘記的事）：*So you made a mistake, but there's no need to dwell on it.* 你是錯了，不過不必老是想着這事兒。 **2** to look at sth for a long time 細看；凝視

dwell·er /ˈdwelə(r)/ *noun* (especially in compounds 尤用於構成複合詞) a person or an animal that lives in the particular place that is mentioned 居民；居住者；棲身者：*apartment dwellers* 公寓房客

dwell·ing /ˈdwelɪŋ/ *noun* (*formal*) a house, flat/apartment, etc. where a person lives 住宅；住所；公寓：*The development will consist of 66 dwellings and a number of offices.* 新建樓區將由 66 棟住房和一些辦公用房組成。

ˈdwelling house *noun* (*BrE, law* 律) a house that people live in, not one that is used as an office, etc. 住宅

ˈdwelling place *noun* (*old-fashioned*) the place where sb lives 住處

DWI /ˌdiː dʌbljuː ˈaɪ/ *abbr.* (*US*) DRIVING WHILE INTOXICATED

dwin·dle /ˈdwɪndl/ *verb* [I] to become gradually less or smaller（逐漸）減少，變小，縮小：*dwindling audiences* 越來越少的觀眾 ◇ **~ (away) (to sth)** *Support for the party has dwindled away to nothing.* 支持這個黨派的人漸漸化為烏有。◇ **~ (from sth) (to sth)** *Membership of the club has dwindled from 70 to 20.* 俱樂部會員人數已從 70 減少到 20。

DWP /ˌdiː dʌbljuː ˈpiː/ *abbr.* (in Britain) Department for Work and Pensions（英國）就業和退休保障部

dyad /ˈdaɪæd/ *noun* **1** (*technical* 術語) something that consists of two parts 二分體；二聯體：*the mother-child dyad* 母子二分體 **2** (*mathematics* 數) an OPERATOR which is the combination of two VECTORS 並矢；並向量 ▸ **dyad·ic** /daɪˈædɪk/ *adj.*

dye /daɪ/ *verb, noun*

■ ***verb*** (**dyes**, **dye·ing**, **dyed**, **dyed**) to change the colour of sth, especially by using a special liquid or substance 給…染色；染：**~ sth** *to dye fabric* 染織物 ◇ **~ sth + adj.** *She dyed her hair blonde.* 她把頭髮染成了金黃色。➲ see also TIE-DYE

■ ***noun*** [C, U] a substance that is used to change the colour of things such as cloth or hair 染料；染液：*black dye* 黑色染料 ◇ *hair dye* 染髮液 ◇ ***natural/chemical/vegetable dyes*** 天然 / 化學 / 植物染料

ˌdyed in the ˈwool *adj.* [usually before noun] (*usually disapproving*) having strong beliefs or opinions that are never going to change（信仰、觀念等）根深蒂固的：*dyed-in-the-wool traditionalists* 徹頭徹尾的傳統主義者 ORIGIN From the idea that wool which was dyed in its raw state gave a more even and lasting colour. 源自染羊毛的方法，即給未加工的羊毛染色，使顏色更均勻、持久。

dying 🔑 /ˈdaɪɪŋ/ *adj.*

1 🔑 [only before noun] connected with or happening at the time of sb's death 臨終的；臨死的；垂死的：*I will remember it **to my dying day**.* 我至死都不會忘記此事。◇ *her **dying wishes/words*** 她的臨終遺願 / 遺言 **2** **the dying** *noun* [pl.] people who are dying 垂死者；臨終者：*doctors who care for the dying* 照看臨終病人的醫生 IDM see BREATH ➲ see also DIE *v.*

dyke (also **dike**) /daɪk/ *noun* **1** a long thick wall that is built to stop water flooding onto a low area of land, especially from the sea 堰；堤；壩 **2** (*especially BrE*) a channel that carries water away from the land 渠；溝；壕溝 SYN **ditch** **3** (*taboo, slang*) a word for a LESBIAN, that is usually offensive 女同性戀者（常意含冒犯）

dy·nam·ic AW /daɪˈnæmɪk/ *noun, adj.*

■ ***noun*** **1** **dynamics** [pl.] the way in which people or things behave and react to each other in a particular situation（人或事物）相互作用的方式，動態：*the dynamics of political change* 政治變化動態 ◇ ***group dynamics*** (= the way in which members of a group react to each other) 成員的互動 **2** **dynamics** [U] the science of the forces involved in movement 力學；動力學：*fluid dynamics* 流體力學 ➲ compare STATIC *n.* (3) **3** [sing.] (*formal*) a force that produces change, action or effects 動力 **4** **dynamics** [pl.] (*music* 音) changes in volume in music 力度；力度變化

■ ***adj.*** **1** (*approving*) (of a person 人) having a lot of energy and a strong personality 充滿活力的；精力充沛的；個性強的：*a dynamic leader* 一位活力充沛的領導者 **2** (of a process 過程) always changing and making progress 動態的；發展變化的 OPP **static** **3** (*physics* 物) (of a force or power 力或動力) producing movement 力的；動力的 OPP **static** **4** (*linguistics* 語言) (of verbs 動詞) describing an action rather than a state. **Dynamic** verbs (for example *eat*, *grow*, *knock*, *die*) can be used in the progressive tenses. 動態的 ➲ compare STATIVE (2) ▸ **dy·nam·ic·al·ly** AW /-kli/ *adv.*

dyna·mism /ˈdaɪnəmɪzəm/ *noun* [U] energy and enthusiasm to make new things happen or to make things succeed 精力；活力；勁頭

dyna·mite /ˈdaɪnəmaɪt/ *noun, verb*

■ ***noun*** [U] **1** a powerful EXPLOSIVE 黃色炸藥；甘油炸藥；達納炸藥：*a stick of dynamite* 一根達納炸藥 **2** a thing that is likely to cause a violent reaction or a lot of trouble 具有爆炸性的事物；（可能）引起轟動的事物；具有隱患的事物：*The abortion issue is political dynamite.* 墮胎問題在政治上是個爆炸性的議題。**3** (*informal, approving*) an extremely impressive or exciting person or thing 轟動一時的人（或事物）：*Their new album is dynamite.* 他們的新唱片引起轟動。

■ ***verb*** **~ sth** to destroy or damage sth using dynamite 炸毀；爆破

dy·namo /ˈdaɪnəməʊ; *NAmE* -moʊ/ *noun* (*pl.* **-os**) **1** a device for turning MECHANICAL energy (= energy from movement) into electricity; a GENERATOR 發電機 **2** (*informal*) a person with a lot of energy 精力充沛的人：*the team's midfield dynamo* 這個隊的中場主力隊員 ◇ *She's a* ***human dynamo****.* 她是個精力充沛的人。

dyn·asty /ˈdɪnəsti; *NAmE* ˈdaɪ-/ *noun* (*pl.* **-ies**) **1** a series of rulers of a country who all belong to the same family 王朝；朝代：*the Nehru-Gandhi dynasty* 尼赫魯—甘地王朝 **2** a period of years during which members of a particular family rule a country 朝；代 ▸ **dyn·as·tic** /dɪˈnæstɪk; *NAmE* daɪ-/ *adj.* [usually before noun]：*dynastic history* 王朝統治史

dys·en·tery /ˈdɪsəntri; *NAmE* -teri/ *noun* [U] an infection of the BOWELS that causes severe DIARRHOEA with loss of blood 痢疾

dys·func·tion /dɪsˈfʌŋkʃn/ *noun* [U, C] **1** (*medical* 醫) the fact of a part of the body not working normally（身體）功能障礙：*He's suffering from sexual dysfunction caused by depression.* 他因抑鬱而患上性功能障礙。**2** the situation when the relationships within a society, family, etc. are not working normally（社會、家庭等內部的）關係失衡：*a tale of loneliness and family dysfunction* 一個關於孤獨與家庭關係失衡的故事

dys·func·tion·al /dɪsˈfʌŋkʃənl/ *adj.* (*technical* 術語) not working normally or properly 機能失調的；功能障礙的：*children from dysfunctional families* 有缺陷家庭的子女

dys·lexia /dɪsˈleksiə/ *noun* [U] a slight DISORDER of the brain that causes difficulty in reading and spelling, for example, but does not affect intelligence 誦讀困難 ▸ **dys·lex·ic** /dɪsˈleksɪk/ *adj.*：*He's dyslexic.* 他患誦讀困難症。**dys·lex·ic** *noun*：*writing courses for dyslexics* 為誦讀困難患者開設的寫字班

dys·mor·phia /dɪsˈmɔːfiə; *NAmE* -ˈmɔːrf-/ *noun* [U] (*medical* 醫) a condition in which a part of the body grows larger than normal 畸形，變形（身體部位的過度增長症）▸ **dys·morph·ic** /dɪsˈmɔːfɪk; *NAmE* -ˈmɔːrf-/ *adj.*

dys·pep·sia /dɪsˈpepsiə; *NAmE* dɪsˈpepʃə/ *noun* [U] (*medical* 醫) pain caused by difficulty in DIGESTING food 消化不良 SYN **indigestion**

dys·pep·tic /dɪsˈpeptɪk/ *adj.* **1** (*medical* 醫) connected with or suffering from dyspepsia 消化不良的；患消化不良的 **2** (*formal*) bad-tempered 脾氣壞的；暴躁的

dys·phoria /dɪsˈfɔːriə/ *noun* [U] (*medical* 醫) a state of worry or general unhappiness 病理性心境惡劣 ➲ compare EUPHORIA ▸ **dys·phor·ic** /dɪsˈfɒrɪk; *NAmE* -ˈfɔːr-/ *adj.*

dys·prax·ia /dɪsˈpræksiə/ *noun* [U] a condition of the brain which causes children to have difficulties, for example with physical movement, with writing neatly, and with organizing themselves（兒童）運用障礙

dys·pro·sium /dɪsˈprəʊziəm; *NAmE* -ˈproʊ-/ *noun* [U] (*symb.* **Dy**) a chemical element. Dysprosium is a soft silver-white metal used in nuclear research. 鏑（用於核研究）

dys·to·pia /dɪsˈtəʊpiə; *NAmE* -ˈtoʊ-/ *noun* an imaginary place or state in which everything is extremely bad or unpleasant 反烏托邦，反面假想國，敵托幫（極度惡劣的假想處境或狀況）➲ compare UTOPIA ▸ **dys·to·pian** /dɪsˈtəʊpiən; *NAmE* -ˈtoʊ-/ (also **dys·top·ic** /dɪsˈtɒpɪk; *NAmE* -ˈtɑːp-/) *adj.*

dys·trophy ➲ MUSCULAR DYSTROPHY

Ee

E /iː/ *noun, abbr.*

■ ***noun*** (also **e**) [C, U] (*pl.* **Es, E's, e's** /iːz/) **1** the fifth letter in the English alphabet 英語字母表的第 5 個字母： *'Egg' begins with (an) E/'E'.* * egg 一詞以字母 e 開頭。 **2 E** (*music* 音) the third note in the SCALE of C MAJOR * E 音（C 大調的第 3 音或音符） **3 E** the fifth highest mark/grade that a student can get for a piece of work, showing that it is very bad（學業成績）第五等，劣： *He got an* **E** ***in/for*** *French.* 他的法語成績得 E 級。 ➲ see also E-NUMBER

■ ***abbr.*** **1** East; Eastern 東方（的）；東部（的）： *E Asia* 東亞 **2** (*slang*) the drug ECSTASY 搖頭丸；迷幻藥： *She had taken an E.* 她吃了一顆搖頭丸。

e- /iː/ *combining form* (in nouns and verbs 構成名詞和動詞) connected with the use of electronic communication, especially the Internet, for sending information, doing business, etc. 電子的；電子通信的： *e-commerce* 電子商務 ◇ *e-business* 電子商務 ➲ see also E-FIT, EMAIL

each 0-π /iːtʃ/ *det., pron.*
used to refer to every one of two or more people or things, when you are thinking about them separately（兩個或以上的人或物中）各自，各個，每個： *Each answer is worth 20 points.* 每題為 20 分。◇ *Each of the answers is worth 20 points.* 每題為 20 分。◇ *The answers are worth 20 points each.* 這些答題每題為 20 分。◇ *'Red or blue?' 'I'll take one of each, please.'* "紅的還是藍的？" "請一樣給我一個。" ◇ *We each have our own car.* 我們各人都有自己的汽車。◇ *There aren't enough books for everyone to have one each.* 沒有足夠的書給每人發一本。◇ *They lost $40 each.* 他們每人損失了 40 元。◇ *Each day that passed he grew more and more desperate.* 一天天過去，他變得越來越絕望。

Grammar Point 語法説明

each / every

■ **Each** is used in front of a singular noun and is followed by a singular verb. * each 用於單數名詞前，後接單數動詞： *Each student has been given his or her own email address.* 每個學生都得到自己的電子郵件地址。 The use of *his* or *her* sometimes sounds slightly formal and it is becoming more common to use the plural pronoun *their.* 有時候 his 或 her 聽起來有點正式，故日漸普遍使用複數代詞 their： *Each student has been given their own email address.* 每個學生都得到自己的電子郵件地址。

■ When **each** is used after a plural subject, it has a plural verb. * each 用於複數主語後，謂語動詞用複數： *They each have their own email address.* 他們每個人都有自己的電子郵件地址。

■ **Every** is always followed by a singular verb. * every 後總是接單數動詞： *Every student in the class is capable of passing the exam.* 班上每個同學都有能力通過這次考試。

■ **Each of**, **each one of** and **every one of** are followed by a plural noun or pronoun, but the verb is usually singular. * each of、each one of 與 every one of 後接複數名詞或代詞，但謂語動詞通常用單數： *Each (one) of the houses was slightly different.* 每座房子都稍有不同。◇ *I bought a dozen eggs and every one of them was bad.* 我買了一打雞蛋，個個都是壞的。 A plural verb is more informal. 用複數動詞則較非正式。

each 'other 0-π *pron.*
used as the object of a verb or preposition to show that each member of a group does sth to or for the other members（用作動詞或介詞的賓語）互相，彼此： *Don and Susie really loved each other* (= he loved her and she loved him). 唐和蘇茜確實相親相愛。◇ *They looked at each other and laughed.* 他們彼此看了看便笑了起來。◇ *We can wear each other's clothes.* 我們可以相互換着衣服穿。

ˌeach 'way *adv., adj.* (*BrE*) if you bet money **each way** on a race, you win if your horse, etc. comes first, second or third in the race 下注於首三名之一，一注三贏（指賽馬等下的賭注為前三名之一）： *She put £5 each way on the favourite.* 她用 5 英鎊，在熱門馬上投注獨贏及位置。◇ *an each-way bet* 獨贏及位置的賭注

eager /ˈiːɡə(r)/ *adj.* very interested and excited by sth that is going to happen or about sth that you want to do 熱切的；渴望的；渴求的 SYN **keen**： *eager crowds outside the stadium* 體育場外急不可耐的人群◇ **~ for sth** *She is eager for* (= wants very much to get) *her parents' approval.* 她渴望得到父母的讚許。◇ **~ to do sth** *Everyone in the class seemed eager to learn.* 班上每個人似乎都熱愛學習。◇ *They're* ***eager to please*** (= wanting to be helpful). 他們竭力討好。 ▸ **eager·ly** *adv.*： *the band's eagerly awaited new CD* 人們熱切等待着的樂隊的新唱片 **eager·ness** *noun* [U, sing.]： *I couldn't hide my eagerness to get back home.* 我無法掩飾想回家的渴望。

ˌeager 'beaver *noun* (*informal*) an enthusiastic person who works very hard 幹活特別賣力的人；對工作極有熱忱的人

eagle /ˈiːɡl/ *noun* **1** a large BIRD OF PREY (= a bird that kills other creatures for food) with a sharp curved beak and very good sight 雕： *eagles soaring overhead* 在上空翱翔的雕 ➲ see also BALD EAGLE, GOLDEN EAGLE **2** (in GOLF 高爾夫球) a score of two strokes less than the standard score for a hole (= two under PAR) 鷹擊（比標準杆少打兩杆） ➲ compare BIRDIE (2), BOGEY (4)

ˌeagle 'eye *noun* [usually sing.] if sb has an **eagle eye**, they watch things carefully and are good at noticing things 敏鋭的眼光；鋭利的目光： *Nothing escaped our teacher's eagle eye.* 任何事情都逃不過我們老師那鋭利的目光。 ▸ **ˌeagle-'eyed** *adj.* SYN **hawk-eyed**： *An eagle-eyed tourist found the suspicious package.* 一位眼尖的遊客發現了可疑的包裹。

eag·let /ˈiːɡlət/ *noun* a young eagle 雛雕；小雕

EAL /ˌiː eɪ ˈel/ *abbr.* (in the UK and Ireland) English as an additional language (refers to the teaching of English in schools to children whose first language is not English)（英國和愛爾蘭）作為附加語言的英語（教學對象為第一語言非英語的中小學生） ➲ compare EFL, ESL, ESOL

EAP /ˌiː eɪ ˈpiː/ *abbr.* ENGLISH FOR ACADEMIC PURPOSES

ear 0-π /ɪə(r); *NAmE* ɪr/ *noun*
1 0-π [C] either of the organs on the sides of the head that you hear with 耳；耳朵： *an ear infection* 耳朵感染 ◇ *the* ***inner/outer ear*** 內 / 外耳◇ *She whispered something in his ear.* 她對他耳語了幾句。◇ *He put his hands over his ears.* 他用雙手捂住耳朵。◇ *She's had her ears pierced.* 她扎了耳朵眼兒。◇ *The elephant flapped its ears.* 大象拍打着雙耳。◇ *He was always there with a sympathetic ear* (= a willingness to listen to people). 他總是願意傾聽別人的心聲。 ➲ VISUAL VOCAB page V59 ➲ see also CAULIFLOWER EAR, GLUE EAR, MIDDLE EAR **2 -eared** (in adjectives 構成形容詞) having the type of ears mentioned 有…耳朵的；耳朵…的： *a long-eared owl* 長耳貓頭鷹 **3** [sing.] an ability to recognize and copy sounds well 靈敏的聽力；辨音力： *You need a good ear to master the piano.* 彈好鋼琴需要有敏鋭的辨音能力。 **4** [C] the top part of a grain plant, such as WHEAT, that contains the seeds（穀類植物的）穗： *ears of corn* 玉米穗 ➲ VISUAL VOCAB page V32

IDM **be all 'ears** (*informal*) to be waiting with interest to hear what sb has to say 全神貫注地聽；聚精會神地聽： *'Do you know what he said?' 'Go on—I'm all ears.'* "你知道他說什麼了嗎？" "講吧 —— 我洗耳恭聽。" **be out on your 'ear** (*informal*) to be forced to leave (a job, etc.) 被迫離開（工作崗位等）；被攆出去 **be up to your ears in sth** to have a lot of sth to deal with 深陷於；埋頭於；忙於： *We're up to our ears in work.* 我們工作忙得不可開交。 **sth comes to/reaches sb's 'ears** somebody hears about sth, especially when other people already know about it 傳到…的耳朵裏： *News of his affair* *eventually reached her ears.* 他的緋聞終於傳到她耳朵裏。**sb's 'ears are burning** a person thinks that other people are talking about them, especially in an unkind way（感到有人議論自己，尤指説閒話而）耳朵發熱：*'I bumped into your ex-wife last night.' 'I thought I could feel my ears burning!'* "我昨天晚上偶然遇到你的前妻。" "怪不得我好像覺得耳朵發熱呢！" **sb's 'ears are flapping** (*BrE, informal*) a person is trying to listen to sb else's conversation 某人正豎着耳朵聽 **go in 'one ear and out the 'other** (*informal*) (of information, etc. 消息等) to be forgotten quickly 一隻耳朵進另一隻耳朵出；被當作耳邊風：*Everything I tell them just goes in one ear and out the other.* 我無論對他們説什麼都只被當作耳邊風。**have sth coming out of your 'ears** (*informal*) to have a lot of sth, especially more than you need 有的是某物（形容大量擁有，甚至超過所需）**have sb's ear | have the ear of sb** to be able to give sb advice, influence them, etc. because they trust you 在某人那裏説得上話；使某人聽得進去：*He had the ear of the monarch.* 他在君主那裏説得上話。**keep/have your ear to the 'ground** to make sure that you always find out about the most recent developments in a particular situation 注意看動向；掌握最新發展情況 **play (sth) by 'ear** to play music by remembering how it sounds rather than by reading it 憑記憶演奏；不看樂譜彈奏 **play it by 'ear** (*informal*) to decide how to deal with a situation as it develops rather than by having a plan to follow 見機行事；隨機應變；根據情況需要行動：*I don't know what they'll want when they arrive—we'll have to play it by ear.* 我不知道他們到達時想要什麼，我們只有見機行事了。**shut/close your 'ears to sth** to refuse to listen to sth（對…）充耳不聞，置之不理：*She decided to shut her ears to all the rumours.* 她拿定主意對所有的謠言置之不理。**smile/grin/beam from ear to 'ear** to be smiling, etc. a lot because you are very pleased about sth 眉開眼笑；笑得合不攏嘴 **with half an 'ear** without giving your full attention to what is being said, etc. 心不在焉地聽 ➲ more at BELIEVE, BEND *v.*, BOX *n.*, BOX *v.*, COCK *v.*, DEAF, EASY *adj.*, FEEL *v.*, FLEA, LEND, MUSIC, OPEN *adj.*, PIG *n.*, PRICK *v.*, RING² *v.*, SILK, THICK *adj.*, WALL *n.*, WET *adj.*, WORD *n.*

ear·ache /ˈɪəreɪk; *NAmE* ˈɪr-/ *noun* [U, C] pain inside the ear 耳痛：*to have (an) earache* 患耳痛

ear·bash·ing /ˈɪəbæʃɪŋ; *NAmE* ˈɪr-/ *noun* [sing.] (*BrE, informal*) an occasion where sb criticizes a person in an angry way 對某人的憤怒指責

ear·bud /ˈɪəbʌd; *NAmE* ˈɪr-/ *noun* [usually pl.] a very small HEADPHONE that is worn inside the ear 耳塞 ➲ **VISUAL VOCAB** page V66

'ear drops *noun* [pl.] liquid medicine that can be put into the ears 滴耳藥水；滴耳劑

ear·drum /ˈɪədrʌm; *NAmE* ˈɪr-/ *noun* the piece of thin tightly stretched skin inside the ear which is moved by sound waves, making you able to hear 耳膜；鼓膜：*a perforated eardrum* 鼓膜穿孔

ear·ful /ˈɪəfʊl; *NAmE* ˈɪrfʊl/ *noun* [sing.] (*informal*) if sb gives you an **earful**, they tell you for a long time how angry they are about sth 長時間的投訴（或牢騷）

ear·hole /ˈɪəhəʊl; *NAmE* ˈɪrhoʊl/ *noun* (*informal*) the outer opening of the ear 耳孔

earl /ɜːl; *NAmE* ɜːrl/ *noun* a NOBLEMAN of high rank 伯爵：*the Earl of Essex* 埃塞克斯伯爵 ➲ see also COUNTESS

,Earl 'Grey *noun* [U] a type of tea flavoured with BERGAMOT 伯爵茶（用香檸檬調味）

earli·est /ˈɜːliɪst; *NAmE* ˈɜːrl-/ *noun* [sing.] **the earliest** the time before which sth cannot happen 最早；最早時間：*The earliest we can finish is next Friday.* 我們最早能在下星期五完成。◇ *We can't finish before next Friday **at the earliest**.* 我們最早也要到下星期五才能完成。

'ear lobe (also **lobe**) *noun* the soft part at the bottom of the ear 耳垂 ➲ **VISUAL VOCAB** page V59

early 0‑ₙ /ˈɜːli; *NAmE* ˈɜːrli/ *adj., adv.*

■ *adj.* (**earl·ier**, **earli·est**) **1** 0‑ₙ near the beginning of a period of time, an event etc. 早期的；初期的；早先的：*the early morning* 清晨 ◇ *my earliest memories* 我最早的記憶 ◇ *The project is still in the early stages.* 這個項目仍處於初期階段。◇ *the early 1990s* * 20 世紀 90 年代初 ◇ *in **the early days of** space exploration* (= when it was just beginning) 在太空探索初期 ◇ *The earliest possible date I can make it is the third.* 我最早也要到三號才有時間。◇ *He's in his early twenties.* 他二十出頭。◇ *Mozart's early works* (= those written at the beginning of his career) 莫扎特的早期作品 ◇ *Early booking is essential, as space is limited.* 座位有限，務必早日預訂。**2** 0‑ₙ arriving, or done before the usual, expected or planned time 早到的；提前的；提早的：*You're early! I wasn't expecting you till seven.* 你來得真早！我還以為你七點鐘才能到呢。◇ *The bus was ten minutes early.* 公共汽車早到了十分鐘。◇ *an early breakfast* 一早吃的早餐 ◇ *Let's **make an early start** tomorrow.* 咱們明天一早就出發吧。◇ *She's an **early riser*** (= she gets up early in the morning). 她是個習慣於早起的人。◇ *He learnt to play the piano at an **early age**.* 他早年就學會了彈鋼琴。◇ *early potatoes* (= that are ready to eat at the beginning of the season) 早造的土豆 **OPP** late ▸ **earli·ness** *noun* [U]

IDM **an 'early bird** (*humorous*) a person who gets up, arrives, etc. very early 早起者；早到者；趕早者；捷足先登者 **at your earliest con'venience** (*business* 商) as soon as possible 儘早；儘快：*Please telephone at your earliest convenience.* 請儘早打電話。**the ,early bird catches the 'worm** (*saying*) the person who takes the opportunity to do sth before other people will have an advantage over them 捷足先登；捷足先得 **it's early 'days (yet)** (*BrE*) used to say that it is too soon to be sure how a situation will develop 為時尚早；言之過早 ➲ more at BRIGHT *adj.*, HOUR, NIGHT

■ *adv.* (**earl·ier**, **earli·est**) **1** 0‑ₙ near the beginning of a period of time, an event, a piece of work, etc. 在早期；在初期；在開始階段：***early in the week/year/season/morning*** 一週開始時；年初；季度初；一大早 ◇ *The best rooms go to those who book earliest.* 最早預訂者可得最好的房間。◇ *We arrived early the next day.* 我們第二天很早就到達了。◇ *He started writing music as early as 1989.* 他早在 1989 年就開始作曲了。**OPP** late **2** 0‑ₙ before the usual, expected or planned time 提早；提前：*The bus came five minutes early.* 公共汽車早到了五分鐘。◇ *I woke up early this morning.* 我今天早上醒得早。◇ *The baby arrived earlier than expected.* 嬰兒早產了。**OPP** late **3** 0‑ₙ **earlier** before the present time or the time mentioned 先前；早些時候；…之前：*As I mentioned earlier …* 正如我先前所提到的… ◇ *a week earlier* 一週前 ◇ *She had seen him earlier in the day.* 她在那天早些時候已見過他。**OPP** later

IDM **early 'on** 0‑ₙ at an early stage of a situation, relationship, period of time, etc. 在初期；在開始階段；早先：*I knew quite early on that I wanted to marry her.* 我老早就知道我想娶她。

,early 'closing *noun* [U] (*BrE*) the practice of closing shops on a particular afternoon every week (now no longer very common) 提早打烊，提前停止營業（指商店每週的某個下午不開門，現已不常見）

,early 'warning *noun* [U, sing.] a thing that tells you in advance that sth serious or dangerous is going to happen 預先警報：*an early warning of heart disease* 心臟病的早期症狀 ◇ *an early warning system* (= of enemy attack) 預警系統

ear·mark /ˈɪəmɑːk; *NAmE* ˈɪrmɑːrk/ *verb, noun*

■ *verb* [usually passive] to decide that sth will be used for a particular purpose, or to state that sth will happen to sb/sth in the future 指定…的用途；預先安排，確定（未來發生的事情）：**~ sb/sth (for sb/sth)** *The money had been earmarked for spending on new school buildings.* 這筆款項已指定用於新校舍建設。◇ *The factory has been earmarked for closure.* 這家工廠已被指定關閉。◇ **~ sb/sth (as sb/sth)** *She was earmarked early as a possible champion.* 人們早就認定她有可能奪冠。

■ *noun* [usually pl.] (*NAmE*) a feature or quality that is typical of sb/sth 標記；特徵：*The incident has all the earmarks of a terrorist attack.* 這一事件具有恐怖襲擊的所有特徵。

ear·muffs /ˈɪəmʌfs; *NAmE* ˈɪrmʌfs/ *noun* [pl.] a pair of coverings for the ears connected by a band across the

E

top of the head, and worn to protect the ears, especially from cold（尤指禦寒用的）耳罩，耳套，護耳：*a pair of earmuffs* 一副耳套

earn /ɜːn; NAmE ɜːrn/ *verb* **1** [T, I] to get money for work that you do 掙得；賺得；掙錢：**~ (sth)** *He earns about $40 000 a year.* 他一年大約掙 4 萬元。◇ *She **earned a living** as a part-time secretary.* 她靠做兼職秘書為生。◇ *She must **earn a fortune*** (= earn a lot of money). 她準是掙了一大筆錢。◇ *All the children are earning now.* 所有子女都在掙錢了。◇ **~ sb sth** *His victory in the tournament earned him $50 000.* 他在這次錦標賽中獲勝，掙得了 5 萬元。➲ COLLOCATIONS at FINANCE **2** [T] **~ sth** to get money as profit or interest on money you lend, have in a bank, etc. 生（利）；獲（利）：*Your money would earn more in a high-interest account.* 你的錢放在高利息賬戶裏可獲利更多。**3** [T] to get sth that you deserve, usually because of sth good you have done or because of the good qualities you have 應得；博得；贏得：**~ sth** *He earned a reputation as an expert on tax law.* 他贏得了稅法專家的美名。◇ *As a teacher, she had earned the respect of her students.* 作為教師，她贏得了學生的尊敬。◇ *I need a rest. I think I've earned it, don't you?* 我需要休息一下。我覺得應該讓我歇一歇，你說是不是？◇ *She's having a well-earned rest this week.* 她本週休假，這完全是應當的。◇ **~ sb sth** *His outstanding ability earned him a place on the team.* 他非凡的能耐為他在隊中贏得了一席之地。

IDM ˌ**earn a/your ˈcrust** (*BrE, informal*) to earn enough money to live on 掙錢餬口；謀生 ˌ**earn your ˈkeep 1** to do useful or helpful things in return for being allowed to live or stay somewhere 掙口飯吃；為有棲身之處而工作 **2** to be worth the amount of time or money that is being spent 值得所花的時間（或金錢）：*He felt he no longer deserved such a high salary. He just wasn't earning his keep.* 他認為他不應再得到那麼高的薪金了。他根本不配拿那麼多錢。➲ more at SPUR *n.*

ˌ**earned ˈrun** *noun* (in BASEBALL 棒球) a RUN scored without the help of errors by the opposing team 投手責任失分

earn·er /ˈɜːnə(r); NAmE ˈɜːrn-/ *noun* **1** a person who earns money for a job that they do 掙錢者；掙工資者：***high/low earners*** 高薪 / 低薪的人 ➲ see also WAGE EARNER **2** an activity or a business that makes a profit 贏利活動；賺錢的生意：*Tourism is the country's biggest foreign currency earner.* 旅遊業是這個國家賺取外匯最多的行業。◇ (*BrE, informal*) *Her new business has turned out to be a **nice little earner**.* 她新開的商店結果還真賺不少錢呢。

earn·est /ˈɜːnɪst; NAmE ˈɜːrn-/ *adj.* very serious and sincere 非常認真的；誠實的；真誠的：*an earnest young man* 非常認真的年輕人 ◇ *Despite her earnest efforts, she could not find a job.* 儘管她已盡心竭力，但是仍然找不到工作。▸ **earn·est·ly** *adv.* **earn·est·ness** *noun* [U]

IDM **in ˈearnest 1** more seriously and with more force or effort than before（更加）嚴肅地，認真地，堅定地：*The work on the house will **begin in earnest** on Monday.* 這棟房子的修建工作將在星期一正式開始。**2** very serious and sincere about what you are saying and about your intentions; in a way that shows that you are serious 鄭重其事；當真：*You may laugh but I'm in **deadly earnest**.* 你可以笑，不過我可是正經八百的。◇ *I could tell she spoke in earnest.* 我看得出她是鄭重其事地說的。

earn·ings /ˈɜːnɪŋz; NAmE ˈɜːrn-/ *noun* [pl.] **1** the money that you earn for the work that you do 薪水；工資；收入：*a rise in average earnings* 平均收入的增加 ◇ *compensation for loss of earnings caused by the accident* 由於事故造成收入損失的賠償 ➲ SYNONYMS at INCOME **2** the profit that a company makes 利潤；收益；盈利：*earnings per share* 每股收益 ◇ *export earnings* 出口利潤 ➲ COLLOCATIONS at BUSINESS

ˌ**earnings-reˈlated** *adj.* (*BrE*) (of payments, etc. 付款等) connected to and changing according to the amount of money that you earn 與收入掛鉤的；按收益計算的：*an earnings-related pension scheme* 與收入掛鉤的退休金計劃

ear·phones /ˈɪəfəʊnz; NAmE ˈɪrfoʊnz/ *noun* [pl.] = HEADPHONES

ear·piece /ˈɪəpiːs; NAmE ˈɪrpiːs/ *noun* the part of a telephone or piece of electrical equipment that you hold next to or put into your ear so that you can listen（電話）聽筒；耳機；耳塞

ˈ**ear-piercing** *adj., noun*
■ ***adj.*** [only before noun] very high, loud and unpleasant 刺耳的；尖厲的：*an ear-piercing scream* 一聲刺耳的尖叫
■ ***noun*** [U] the practice of making small holes in sb's ears so jewellery can be put in them 穿耳洞；扎耳朵眼兒

ear·plug /ˈɪəplʌɡ; NAmE ˈɪrp-/ *noun* [usually pl.] a piece of soft material that you put into your ear to keep out noise or water 耳塞（用以擋噪音、防水）

ear·ring /ˈɪərɪŋ; NAmE ˈɪrɪŋ/ *noun* a piece of jewellery that you fasten in or on your ear 耳環；耳飾：*a pair of earrings* 一對耳環 ➲ VISUAL VOCAB page V65

ear·set /ˈɪəset; NAmE ˈɪrset/ *noun* a piece of equipment that fits into your ear and has a MICROPHONE attached to it. It is connected to a telephone and allows you to use the telephone without using your hands.（電話）耳機，免提裝置

ear·shot /ˈɪəʃɒt; NAmE ˈɪrʃɑːt/ *noun*

IDM **out of ˈearshot (of sb/sth)** too far away to hear sb/sth or to be heard 在聽力範圍之外：*We waited until Ted was safely out of earshot before discussing it.* 我們一直等到特德保準聽不見時才討論這事。**within ˈearshot (of sb/sth)** near enough to hear sb/sth or to be heard 在聽力範圍之內：*As she came within earshot of the group, she heard her name mentioned.* 她剛走近到能聽見這群人說話聲時便聽到有人提她的名字。

ˈ**ear-splitting** *adj.* extremely loud 極響的；震耳欲聾的

earth /ɜːθ; NAmE ɜːrθ/ *noun, verb*
■ ***noun*** **1** (also **Earth**, **the Earth**) [U, sing.] the world; the planet that we live on 世界；地球：***the planet Earth*** 地球這顆行星 ◇ *the history of **life on earth*** 地球上的生命史 ◇ *the earth's ozone layer* 地球的臭氧層 ◇ *The earth revolves around the sun.* 地球繞着太陽轉。◇ *I must be the happiest person **on earth**!* 我一定是世界上最幸福的人！**2** [U, sing.] land; the hard surface of the world that is not the sea or the sky; the ground 陸地；地面；大地：*After a week at sea, it was good to feel the earth beneath our feet again.* 出海一週後，重新踏上陸地感到很愉快。◇ *You could feel the earth shake as the truck came closer.* 卡車開近時會感覺到地面在震動。➲ SYNONYMS at FLOOR **3** [U] the substance that plants grow in 土；泥；泥土：*a **clod/lump/mound of earth*** 一塊土；一團泥；一堆土 ➲ SYNONYMS at SOIL **4** [C] the hole where an animal, especially a FOX, lives 獸穴；（尤指狐狸棲息的）洞穴 **5** (*BrE*) (*NAmE* **ground**) [C, usually sing.] a wire that connects an electric CIRCUIT with the ground and makes it safe（接）地線

IDM **charge, cost, pay, etc. the ˈearth** (*BrE, informal*) to charge, etc. a lot of money 收（或花、付等）很多錢 **come back/down to ˈearth (with a ˈbang/ˈbump)** | **bring sb (back) down to ˈearth (with a ˈbang/ˈbump)** (*informal*) to return, or to make sb return, to a normal way of thinking or behaving after a time when they have been very excited, not very practical, etc.（使）從幻想中清醒過來，回到現實中來 ➲ see also DOWN TO EARTH **go to ˈearth/ˈground** (*BrE*) to hide, especially to escape from sb who is chasing you 躲藏起來（以免被捉住）**how, why, where, who, etc. on ˈearth** (*informal*) used to emphasize the question you are asking when you are surprised or angry or cannot think of an obvious answer（加強疑問句的語氣）到底，究竟：*What on earth are you doing?* 你究竟在幹什麼？◇ *How on earth can she afford that?* 她怎麼可能負擔得起呢？**be, feel, look, taste, etc. like nothing on ˈearth** (*informal*) to be, feel, look, taste, etc. very bad 感到（或顯得、嚐起來等）非常糟糕，非常難受 **on ˈearth** used after negative nouns or pronouns to emphasize what you are saying（用於否定名詞或代詞之後表示強調）在世界上，在人世間：*Nothing on earth would persuade me to go with him.* 無論什麼都不能說服我跟他一塊兒走。**run sb/sth to ˈearth/ˈground** (*BrE*) to find sb/sth after looking hard for a long time（長期搜尋後）終於找到

➲ more at END *n.*, FACE *n.*, MOVE *v.*, PROMISE *v.*, SALT *n.*, WIPE *v.*

■ *verb* (*BrE*) (*NAmE* **ground**) [usually passive] **~ sth** to make electrical equipment safe by connecting it to the ground with a wire 把（電線）接地

earth·bound /ˈɜːθbaʊnd; *NAmE* ˈɜːrθ-/ *adj.* **1** unable to leave the surface of the earth （只在）地球上的，陸地的，地面上的： *birds and their earthbound predators* 鳥和地面上捕食它們的動物 **2** (*literary*) not spiritual or having much imagination 世俗的；物質世界的

earth·en /ˈɜːθn; *NAmE* ˈɜːrθn/ *adj.* [only before noun] **1** (of floors or walls 地面或牆) made of earth 泥土做的；土製的 **2** (of objects 物體) made of baked CLAY 陶製的： *earthen pots* 陶罐

earth·en·ware /ˈɜːθnweə(r); *NAmE* ˈɜːrθnwer/ *adj.* made of very hard baked CLAY 陶製的： *an earthenware bowl* 陶碗 ▸ **earth·en·ware** *noun* [U]

earth·ling /ˈɜːθlɪŋ; *NAmE* ˈɜːrθ-/ *noun* (in SCIENCE FICTION stories) a word used by creatures from other planets to refer to a person living on the earth （科幻小說中外星人用語）地球人

earth·ly /ˈɜːθli; *NAmE* ˈɜːrθ-/ *adj.* [usually before noun] **1** (*literary*) connected with life on earth and not with any spiritual life 人間的；塵世的；世俗的： *the sorrows of this earthly life* 今生今世的不幸 **2** (often used in questions and negatives for emphasis 常用於疑問句或否定句以加強語氣) possible 可能的： *There's* ***no earthly reason*** *why you shouldn't go.* 你完全沒有理由不去。◇ *What earthly difference is my opinion going to make?* 我的意見會有什麼作用呢？◇ *He didn't have an earthly chance of getting the job.* 他根本就不可能得到這份工作。

ˈ**earth mother** *noun* **1** (also **Earth Mother**) a GODDESS who represents the earth as the source of life; a GODDESS of FERTILITY （象徵生命之源的）大地母親；（主生殖繁衍的）女神 **2** (*informal*) a woman who seems very suited to being a mother 天生的母親

ˈ**earth mover** *noun* a vehicle or machine that digs up large quantities of soil 推土機；挖土車

earth·quake /ˈɜːθkweɪk; *NAmE* ˈɜːrθ-/ (also *informal* **quake**) *noun* a sudden, violent shaking of the earth's surface 地震

ˈ**earth science** *noun* [C, U] a science concerned with studying the earth or part of it. Geography and GEOLOGY are both earth sciences. 地球科學，地學（包括地理學和地質學）➲ compare LIFE SCIENCES, NATURAL SCIENCE

ˈ**earth-shatter·ing** *adj.* having a very great effect and of great importance 震撼世界的；影響深遠的；極其重大的： *an earth-shattering discovery* 驚天動地的發現

earth·work /ˈɜːθwɜːk; *NAmE* ˈɜːrθwɜːrk/ *noun* [usually pl.] a large bank of earth that was built long ago in the past and used as a defence 土壘（舊時防禦用的工事）

earth·worm /ˈɜːθwɜːm; *NAmE* ˈɜːrθwɜːrm/ *noun* a common long thin WORM that lives in soil 蚯蚓

earthy /ˈɜːθi; *NAmE* ˈɜːrθi/ *adj.* (**earth·ier**, **earthi·est**) **1** concerned with the body, sex, etc. in an open and direct way that some people find rude or embarrassing 粗俗的；庸俗的；不文雅的： *an earthy sense of humour* 粗俗的幽默感 **2** of or like earth or soil 泥土的；泥土似的；有泥土氣息的： *earthy colours* 泥土的顏色 ▸ **earthi·ness** *noun* [U]

ˈ**ear trumpet** *noun* a device shaped like a TRUMPET, used in the past by people who could not hear well （舊時的）號角狀助聽器

ear·wax /ˈɪəwæks; *NAmE* ˈɪrwæks/ *noun* [U] the yellow substance produced inside the ear to protect it 耵聹；耳垢

ear·wig /ˈɪəwɪɡ; *NAmE* ˈɪrwɪɡ/ *noun* a small brown insect with a long body and two curved pointed parts called PINCERS that stick out at the back end of its body 蠼螋；地蜈蚣；土蚣

ease 🔑 /iːz/ *noun, verb*

■ *noun* [U] **1** 🔑 lack of difficulty 容易；輕易；不費勁： *He passed the exam* ***with ease.*** 他輕而易舉地通過了考試。◇ *The ease with which she learns languages is astonishing.* 她學習語言之輕鬆令人驚訝。◇ *This computer is popular for its good design and* ***ease of use.*** 這種計算機因設計巧妙、簡單易用而廣受歡迎。◇ *All important points are numbered* ***for ease of*** *reference* (= so that you can find them easily). 全部重點均編了號碼以便查閱。 **2** the state of feeling relaxed or comfortable without worries, problems or pain 舒適；安逸；自在；無憂無慮： *In his retirement, he lived a life of ease.* 他退休後過着悠閒舒適的生活。

IDM **(stand) at ˈease** used as a command to soldiers to tell them to stand with their feet apart and their hands behind their backs（對士兵的命令用語）稍息 ➲ compare ATTENTION *n.* (5) **at (your) ˈease** relaxed and confident and not nervous or embarrassed 舒適；自由自在；無拘無束： *I never feel completely at ease with him.* 我跟他在一起總感到不是很自在。 **put sb at (their) ˈease** to make sb feel relaxed and confident, not nervous or embarrassed 使舒適；使自在；使不受拘束 ➲ more at ILL *adj.*, MIND *n.*

■ *verb* **1** 🔑 [I, T] to become or to make sth less unpleasant, painful, severe, etc.（使）寬慰；減輕；緩解 **SYN** **alleviate**： *The pain immediately eased.* 疼痛立刻減輕了。◇ **~ sth** *This should help ease the pain.* 這該有助於減輕痛楚。◇ *The plan should ease traffic congestion in the town.* 這項計劃對城裏的交通擁擠狀況應該有所緩解。◇ *It would* ***ease my mind*** (= make me less worried) *to know that she was settled.* 知道她已安頓下來會使我放心些。 **2** [I, T] to move, or to move sb/sth, slowly and carefully （使）小心緩緩地移動： **+ adv./prep.** *He eased slowly forwards.* 他緩緩向前移動。◇ **~ sb/sth + adv./prep.** *She eased herself into a chair.* 她輕手輕腳地坐到椅子上。◇ *He eased off* (= took off) *his shoes.* 他慢慢地脫下鞋子。 **3** [T] **~ sth** to make sth easier 使…容易些： *Ramps have been built to ease access for the disabled.* 為方便殘疾人的出入修建了坡道。 **4** [T, I] **~ (sth)** to make sth or to become less tight and more relaxed （使）緩和，放鬆 **SYN** **relax**： *Ease your grip on the wheel a little.* 握方向盤的手放鬆一點。 **5** [I, T] **~ (sth)** to become or make sth lower in price or value 降低；（使）貶值 **SYN** **reduce**： *Share prices eased back from yesterday's levels.* 股價從昨天的水平上回落了。

PHR V **ˈease into sth** | **ˈease yourself/sb into sth** to become or help sb to become familiar with sth new, especially a new job 熟悉，使熟悉（新事物，尤指新工作） **ˌease ˈoff** | **ˌease ˈoff sth** to become or make sth become less strong, unpleasant, etc. 減輕；放鬆： *We waited until the traffic had eased off.* 我們一直等到交通緩解。◇ *Ease off the training a few days before the race.* 比賽前幾天要減輕訓練強度。 **ˌease sb↔ˈout (of sth)** to force sb to leave a job or position of authority, especially by making it difficult or unpleasant for them over a period of time（尤指故意為難）迫使某人離開（工作崗位等） **ˌease ˈup** **1** to reduce the speed at which you are travelling 放慢速度 **2** to become less strong, unpleasant, etc. 減輕；緩和；放鬆

ease·ful /ˈiːzfl/ *adj.* (*literary*) that provides comfort or peace 舒適的；安閒的

easel /ˈiːzl/ *noun* a wooden frame to hold a picture while it is being painted 畫架 ➲ VISUAL VOCAB page V41

ease·ment /ˈiːzmənt/ *noun* [U] **1** (*law* 律) the right to cross or use sb's land for a particular purpose 地役權（穿越或徵用某人土地的權利） **2** (*literary*) a state or feeling of peace or happiness 安逸；安樂

eas·ily 🔑 /ˈiːzəli/ *adv.*

1 🔑 without problems or difficulty 容易地；輕易地；不費力地： *I can easily finish it tonight.* 我今晚能毫不費力地把它完成。◇ *The museum is easily accessible by car.* 開車可以方便地到達博物館。 **2** very probably; very likely 很可能；多半： *Are you sure you locked the gate? You could easily have forgotten.* 你肯定鎖上大門了嗎？你很可能是忘了。◇ *The situation might* ***all too easily*** *have become a disaster.* 這形勢本來是極有可能成為一場大災難的。 **3 ~ the best, nicest, etc.** without doubt; definitely 無疑；肯定： *It's easily the best play I've seen this year.* 這無疑是我今年看過的最好的一齣戲。 **4** quickly; more quickly than is usual 一會兒；不多久：*I get bored easily.* 我易生厭倦。◇ *He's easily distracted.* 他注意力很容易分散。

east 🔑 /iːst/ *noun, adj., adv.*

■ ***noun*** [U, sing.] (*abbr.* **E**) **1** 🔑 (usually **the east**) the direction that you look towards to see the sun rise; one of the four main points of the COMPASS 東；東方：*Which way is east?* 哪邊是東？◇ *A gale was blowing from the east.* 大風從東面吹來。◇ *a town **to the east of*** (= further east than) *Chicago* 芝加哥以東的一個城鎮 ➲ picture at COMPASS ➲ compare NORTH, SOUTH, WEST **2** 🔑 (also **East**) the eastern part of a country, region or city 東部；東邊：*I was born in the East, but now live in San Francisco.* 我出生在東部，但現住在舊金山。**3** 🔑 **the East** the countries of Asia, especially China, Japan and India 亞洲國家，東方國家（尤指中國、日本和印度）**4** **the East** (in the past) the Communist countries of Central and Eastern Europe （舊時）中歐和東歐共產主義國家：*East-West relations* 東西方關係

■ ***adj.*** [only before noun] **1** 🔑 (also **East**) (*abbr.* **E**) in or towards the east 東方的；向東的；東部的：*East Africa* 東非 ◇ *They live on the east coast.* 他們住在東海岸。**2** 🔑 an **east wind** blows from the east 東風的；東方吹來的 ➲ compare EASTERLY

■ ***adv.*** 🔑 towards the east 向東；朝東：*The house faces east.* 房子朝東。

east·bound /ˈiːstbaʊnd/ *adj.* travelling or leading towards the east 東行的；向東的：*eastbound traffic* 東行交通 ◇ *the eastbound carriageway of the motorway* 高速公路的東行車道

ˌEast Coast ˈFever *noun* [U] a disease that cows in Africa can get by being bitten by a TICK (= a small insect), and which can kill them 東海岸熱（病）（非洲牛被蜱叮咬引起的疾病，可導致死亡）

the ˌEast ˈEnd *noun* an area of East London traditionally connected with working people 倫敦東區（傳統上為工人居住區）▶ **ˌEast ˈEnder** *noun*：*He's a real East Ender.* 他是一個地道的倫敦東區人。

Easter /ˈiːstə(r)/ *noun* **1** [U, C] (also **ˌEaster ˈDay**, **ˌEaster ˈSunday**) (in the Christian religion) a Sunday in March or April when Christians remember the death of Christ and his return to life 復活節（紀念耶穌復活，在三月或四月的一個星期日）**2** (also **East·er·time**) the period that includes Easter Day and the days close to it 復活節期間：*the Easter holidays/vacation* 復活節假期

ˈEaster egg *noun* **1** an egg made of chocolate that is given as a present and eaten at Easter 復活節巧克力蛋 **2** an egg with a shell that is painted and decorated at Easter 復活節彩蛋（復活節時彩繪或裝飾的雞蛋）

east·er·ly /ˈiːstəli; *NAmE* -ərli/ *adj., noun*

■ ***adj.*** [only before noun] **1** in or towards the east 東方的；向東的；東部的：*travelling in an easterly direction* 向東行走 **2** [usually before noun] (of winds 風) blowing from the east 從東方吹來的：*a cold easterly wind* 寒冷的東風 ➲ compare EAST

■ ***noun*** (*pl.* **-ies**) a wind that blows from the east 東風

east·ern 🔑 /ˈiːstən; *NAmE* -ərn/ *adj.*

1 🔑 (also **Eastern**) (*abbr.* **E**) [only before noun] located in the east or facing east 東方的；向東的；東部的：*eastern Spain* 西班牙東部 ◇ *Eastern Europe* 東歐 ◇ *the eastern slopes of the mountain* 東山坡 **2** 🔑 (usually **Eastern**) connected with the part of the world that is to the east of Europe （歐洲以東的）亞洲國家的，東方國家的：*Eastern cookery* 東方烹飪

ˌEastern ˈDaylight Time *noun* [U] (*abbr.* **EDT**) the time used in the summer in the eastern US and Canada, which is four hours earlier than GMT 東部日光節約時間，東部夏令時間（美國和加拿大東部的夏季時間，比格林尼治平時早四個小時）

east·ern·er /ˈiːstənə(r); *NAmE* ˈiːstərnər/ *noun* a person who comes from or lives in the eastern part of a country, especially the US 東方人；（尤指）美國東部人

east·ern·most /ˈiːstənməʊst; *NAmE* -ərnmoʊst/ *adj.* furthest east 最東的；最東端的；最東部的：*the easternmost city in Europe* 歐洲最東邊的城市

the ˌEastern ˌOrthodox ˈChurch *noun* = THE ORTHODOX CHURCH

ˌEastern ˈStandard Time *noun* [U] (*abbr.* **EST**) (also **Eastern time**) the time used in the winter in the eastern US and Canada, which is five hours earlier than GMT 東部標準時間，東部冬令時間（美國和加拿大東部的冬季時間，比格林尼治平時早五個小時）

ˈEastern time *noun* [U] the standard time in the eastern US and parts of Canada 東部時間（美國東部和加拿大部份地區的標準時間）

East·er·time /ˈiːstətaɪm; *NAmE* ˈiːstərt-/ *noun* [U, C] = EASTER (2)

ˌEast ˈIndian *noun* a person whose family originally came from the Indian SUBCONTINENT 印度次大陸人 ▶ **ˌEast ˈIndian** *adj.*

ˌeast-north-ˈeast *noun* [sing.] (*abbr.* **ENE**) the direction at an equal distance between east and north-east 東東北；東北東 ▶ **ˌeast-north-ˈeast** *adv.*

ˌeast-south-ˈeast *noun* [sing.] (*abbr.* **ESE**) the direction at an equal distance between east and south-east 東東南；東南東 ▶ **ˌeast-south-ˈeast** *adv.*

east·wards /ˈiːstwədz; *NAmE* -wərdz/ (also **east·ward**) *adv.* towards the east 向東；朝東：*to **go/look/turn eastwards*** 向東走／看／轉 ▶ **east·ward** *adj.*：*in an eastward direction* 向東

easy 🔑 /ˈiːzi/ *adj., adv.*

■ ***adj.*** (**eas·ier**, **easi·est**) **1** 🔑 not difficult; done or obtained without a lot of effort or problems 容易的；輕易的；不費力的：*an easy exam/job* 容易的考試／工作 ◇ *He didn't **make it easy** for me to leave.* 他並沒有輕易讓我離開。◇ *Their house isn't the easiest place to get to.* 他們的房子可不容易到。◇ *vegetables that are easy to grow* 容易種植的蔬菜 ◇ *Several schools are **within easy reach*** (= not far away). 幾所學校都在附近不遠處。◇ *It can't be easy for her, on her own with the children.* 她一個人帶着這些孩子絕非易事。◇ *It's easy for you to tell me to keep calm, but you're not in my position.* 你叫我保持冷靜當然容易，那是你沒到我這份上。OPP **hard** **2** 🔑 comfortable, relaxed and not worried 舒適的；安逸的；安心的：*I'll agree to anything for **an easy life**.* 只要有安逸舒適的生活我什麼都同意。◇ *I don't feel easy about letting the kids go out alone.* 讓孩子們單獨出去我不放心。OPP **uneasy** **3** [only before noun] open to attack; not able to defend yourself 易受攻擊的；無自衞能力的；容易吃虧的：*She's an easy target for their criticisms.* 她很容易成為他們抨擊的目標。◇ *The baby fish are easy prey for birds.* 這些小魚很容易為鳥類捕獲。**4** [only before noun] pleasant and friendly 隨和的；平易近人的 SYN **easy-going**：*He had a very easy manner.* 他很容易相與。OPP **awkward** **5** [not usually before noun] (*informal, disapproving*) (of women 女人) willing to have sex with many different people 水性楊花；輕浮；放蕩 ➲ see also EASILY ▶ **easi·ness** *noun* [U]

IDM **as ˌeasy as ˈanything/as ˈpie/as ABˈC/as falling off a ˈlog** (*informal*) very easy or very easily 十分容易；極容易；輕而易舉 **ˌeasy ˈmoney** money that you get without having to work very hard for it 來得容易的錢 **ˌeasy on the ˈear/ˈeye** (*informal*) pleasant to listen to or look at 好聽／好看的；悅耳／悅目的 **have an easy ˈtime (of it)** (*BrE*) to have no difficulties or problems 日子好過；過得舒適；毫無困難 **I'm ˈeasy** (*BrE, informal*) used to say that you do not have a strong opinion when sb has offered you a choice 我隨便；我好辦；我無所謂：*'Do you want to watch this or the news?' 'Oh, I'm easy. It's up to you.'* "你想看這個節目還是看新聞？" "噢，我隨便。你決定吧。" **of easy ˈvirtue** (*old-fashioned*) (of a woman 女人) willing to have sex with anyone 水性楊花；輕浮；放蕩 **on ˈeasy street** enjoying a comfortable way of life with plenty of money 環境舒適；生活優裕；安定富足 **take the easy way ˈout** to end a difficult situation by choosing the simplest solution even if it is not the best one 以最簡單的方法解決難題；快刀斬亂麻 ➲ more at FREE *adj.*, OPTION *n.*, REACH *n.*, RIDE *n.*, TOUCH *n.*

▪ *adv.* (**eas·ier**, **easi·est**) used to tell sb to be careful when doing sth 小心；慢些；輕點：*Easy with that chair—one of its legs is loose.* 小心搬動那椅子，有一條腿鬆了。
IDM **breathe/rest 'easy** to relax and stop worrying 安下心；鬆口氣：*You can rest easy—I'm not going to tell anyone.* 你儘管放心，我不會告訴任何人的。**be ˌeasier ˌsaid than 'done** (*saying*) to be much more difficult to do than to talk about 說時容易做時難；談何容易：*'Why don't you get yourself a job?' 'That's easier said than done.'* "你怎麼不給自己找個工作呢？" "那談何容易呀。" **ˌeasy 'come, ˌeasy 'go** (*saying*) used to mean that sb does not care very much about money or possessions especially if they spend it or lose sth 來得容易去得快；易得則易失 **ˌeasy 'does it** (*informal*) used to tell sb to do sth, or move sth, slowly and carefully 小心些；別急；悠着點 **go 'easy on sb** (*informal*) used to tell sb to treat a person in a gentle way and not to be too angry or severe 對某人溫和（或寬容）些：*Go easy on her—she's having a really hard time at the moment.* 對她寬容些吧，她目前的處境真是很艱難。**go 'easy on/with sth** (*informal*) used to tell sb not to use too much of sth 省着點；少用些；別浪費：*Go easy on the sugar.* 糖要省着點用。**not come 'easy (to sb)** to be difficult for sb to do（對某人來說）並非易事：*Talking about my problems doesn't come easy to me.* 要講關於自己的問題，對我來說並不容易。**ˌstand 'easy** used as a command to soldiers who are already standing AT EASE to tell them that they can stand in an even more relaxed way（對士兵的命令用語）原地休息 **ˌtake it 'easy** (*informal*) used to tell sb not to be worried or angry 別急；沉住氣；從容點：*Take it easy! Don't panic.* 沉住氣！不要驚慌。**ˌtake it/things 'easy** to relax and avoid working too hard or doing too much 放鬆；休息；別過分勞累：*The doctor told me to take it easy for a few weeks.* 醫生叫我休息幾週。

'easy-care *adj.* (of clothes or cloth 衣服或布料) not needing to be ironed after washing 免熨燙的

ˌeasy 'chair *noun* a large comfortable chair 安樂椅：*to sit in an easy chair* 坐在安樂椅上

ˌeasy-'going *adj.* relaxed and happy to accept things without worrying or getting angry 悠閒的；隨和的；不慌不忙的

ˌeasy 'listening *noun* [U] music that is pleasant and relaxing but that some people think is not very interesting（不用費神欣賞的）悅耳樂曲

easy-peasy /ˌiːzi ˈpiːzi/ *adj.* (*BrE, informal*) (used especially by children 尤為兒語) very easy 簡單得很；容易極了

eat 🔑 /iːt/ *verb* (**ate** /et; eɪt; *NAmE* eɪt/, **eaten** /ˈiːtn/)
1 🔑 [I, T] to put food in your mouth, chew it and swallow it 吃：*I was too nervous to eat.* 我緊張得飯都吃不下。◇ *She doesn't eat sensibly* (= doesn't eat food that is good for her). 她飲食不合理。◇ **~ sth** *I don't eat meat.* 我不吃肉。◇ *Would you like something to eat?* 你想吃點什麼嗎？◇ *I couldn't eat another thing* (= I have had enough food). 我再也吃不下了。➲ COLLOCATIONS at DIET
2 🔑 [I] to have a meal 吃飯；用餐：*Where shall we eat tonight?* 我們今晚在哪兒吃飯？◇ *We ate at a pizzeria in town.* 我們在城裏一家比薩餅店用餐。
IDM **ˌeat sb a'live** (*informal*) **1** to criticize or punish sb severely because you are extremely angry with them（對某人極為氣憤而）尖銳批評，嚴厲懲罰，橫加指責 **2** to defeat sb completely in an argument, a competition, etc.（辯論、比賽等中）大敗某人，完全戰勝某人：*The defence lawyers are going to eat you alive tomorrow.* 辯護律師明天一定會徹底打敗你們。**3** [usually passive] (of insects, etc. 昆蟲等) to bite sb many times（多次）叮，蜇：*I was being eaten alive by mosquitoes.* 蚊子要把我活活吃了。**ˌeat, drink and be 'merry** (*saying*) said to encourage sb to enjoy life now, while they can, and not to think of the future 行樂要及時 **eat your 'heart out!** (*informal*) used to compare two things and say that one of them is better（比較兩事物）比…還好：*Look at him dance! Eat your heart out, Fred Astaire* (= he dances even better than Fred Astaire). 看看他跳的舞！比弗雷德•阿斯泰爾跳得還好。**eat your 'heart out (for sb/sth)** (*especially BrE*) to feel very unhappy, especially because you want sb/sth you cannot have（尤因不能擁有所渴求的人或事物而）極度不快 **eat humble 'pie** (*BrE*) (*NAmE* **eat 'crow**) to say and show that you are sorry for a mistake that you made 認錯；道歉；賠罪 **ORIGIN** From a pun on the old word **umbles**, meaning 'offal', which was considered to be food for poor people. 源自古詞umbles 的雙關諧音，意為 "內臟"，被認為是窮人的食物。**eat like a 'horse** (*informal*) to eat a lot 吃得很多：*She may be thin, but she eats like a horse.* 她或許是瘦了點，但吃得卻很多。**eat out of your/sb's 'hand** to trust sb and be willing to do what they say 甘願聽命於某人；順從某人：*She'll have them eating out of her hand in no time.* 她很快就會讓他們俯首帖耳的。**eat sb out of ˌhouse and 'home** (*informal*, often *humorous*) to eat a lot of sb else's food 把某人吃窮 **eat your 'words** to admit that what you said was wrong 收回前言；承認說錯 **I could eat a 'horse** (*informal*) used to say that you are very hungry 我餓極了 **I'll eat my 'hat** (*informal*) used to say that you think sth is very unlikely to happen（認為某事不太可能發生）我才不信，那才怪，絕不可能：*If she's here on time, I'll eat my hat!* 她要是準時到這兒那才怪咧！**what's eating him, etc.?** (*informal*) used to ask what sb is annoyed or worried about（某人）為何苦惱（或擔憂）➲ more at CAKE *n.*, DOG *n.*
PHR V **ˌeat sth↔a'way** to reduce or destroy sth gradually 侵蝕；腐蝕；逐漸破壞 **SYN** **erode**：*The coastline is being eaten away year by year.* 海岸線年復一年地被侵蝕着。**ˌeat a'way at sth/sb** **1** to reduce or destroy sth gradually 侵蝕；腐蝕；逐漸破壞：*Woodworm had eaten away at the door frame.* 木蛀蟲將門框一點點蛀壞了。◇ *His constant criticism ate away at her self-confidence.* 他不斷的批評使她逐漸喪失了自信心。**2** to worry sb over a period of time（一段時間內）使某人苦惱，使某人擔心 **'eat into sth** **1** to use up a part of sth, especially sb's money or time 消耗，花掉，耗費（尤指金錢或時間）：*Those repair bills have really eaten into my savings.* 那些修理賬單已經耗掉我相當一部份積蓄。**2** to destroy or damage the surface of sth 腐蝕，損壞（物體表面）：*Rust had eaten into the metal.* 這金屬已經銹壞。**ˌeat 'out** 🔑 to have a meal in a restaurant, etc. rather than at home 上館子吃飯；在外用餐：*Do you feel like eating out tonight?* 你今晚想下館子嗎？**ˌeat 'up | ˌeat sth↔'up** 🔑 to eat all of sth 吃完；吃光：*Eat up! We've got to go out soon.* 都吃光！我們得馬上出去。◇ *Come on. Eat up your potatoes.* 快點兒。把土豆都吃掉。**ˌeat sb 'up** [usually passive] to fill sb with a particular emotion so that they cannot think of anything else（情感）使沉迷，使焦慮，使糾纏：*She was eaten up by regrets.* 她後悔不已。**ˌeat sth↔'up** to use sth in large quantities（大量地）耗費，花費，損耗：*Legal costs had eaten up all the savings she had.* 訴訟費耗掉了她所有的積蓄。

eat·able /ˈiːtəbl/ *adj.* good enough to be eaten 可吃的；可食用的 ➲ see also EDIBLE

eater /ˈiːtə(r)/ *noun* (usually after an adjective or a noun 通常用於形容詞或名詞後) a person or an animal that eats a particular thing or in a particular way（以某種方式）吃…的人，吃…的動物：*We're not great meat eaters.* 我們肉吃得不多。◇ *He's a big eater* (= he eats a lot). 他飯量很大。

eat·ery /ˈiːtəri/ (*pl.* **-ies**) *noun* (*informal, especially NAmE*) a restaurant or other place that serves food 餐館；飲食店

'eat-in *adj.* [only before noun] (of a kitchen 廚房) big enough for eating in as well as cooking in 可供用餐的

eat·ing /ˈiːtɪŋ/ *noun* [U] the act of eating sth 吃；飲食：*healthy eating* 有益健康的飲食 **IDM** see PROOF *n.*

'eating apple *noun* (*BrE*) any type of apple that can be eaten raw 可生吃的蘋果 ➲ compare COOKING APPLE

'eating disorder *noun* an emotional DISORDER that causes eating habits that are not normal, for example ANOREXIA 飲食功能失調症

eats /iːts/ *noun* [pl.] (*informal*) food, especially at a party（尤指聚會上的）小吃

eau de cologne /ˌəʊ də kəˈləʊn; *NAmE* ˌoʊ də kəˈloʊn/ *noun* [U] = COLOGNE

eau de toilette /ˌəʊ də twɑːˈlet; *NAmE* ˌoʊ/ *noun* [C, U] PERFUME that contains a lot of water and does not smell very strong 淡香水

eaves /iːvz/ *noun* [pl.] the lower edges of a roof that stick out over the walls 屋簷：*birds nesting under the eaves* 在屋簷下築巢的鳥 ➲ VISUAL VOCAB page V17

eaves·drop /ˈiːvzdrɒp; *NAmE* -drɑːp/ *verb* (-pp-) [I] **~ (on sb/sth)** to listen secretly to what other people are saying 偷聽，竊聽（其他人談話）：*We caught him eavesdropping outside the window.* 我們撞見他正在窗外偷聽。▸ **eaves·drop·per** *noun*

eaves·trough /ˈiːvztrɒf; *NAmE* -trɔːf; -trɑːf/ *noun* (*CanE*) = GUTTER (1)

eBay™ /ˈiːbeɪ/ *noun* [U] a website on the Internet where people can AUCTION goods (= sell them to the person who offers the most money for them) 易趣（網站）（經營拍賣）：*He buys rare baseball cards on eBay.* 他從易趣網上購買珍稀的棒球卡。▸ **eBay** *verb* **~ sth**

ebb /eb/ *noun, verb*

■ ***noun*** **the ebb** [usually sing.] the period of time when the sea flows away from the land 落潮；退潮：*the ebb tide* 退潮

IDM **the ˌebb and ˈflow (of sth/sb)** the repeated, often regular, movement from one state to another; the repeated change in level, numbers or amount 漲落；盛衰；起伏；消長：*the ebb and flow of the seasons* 四時更迭 ◇ *She sat in silence enjoying the ebb and flow of conversation.* 她默默地坐在那兒，饒有興致地聽着時高時低的談話聲。➲ more at LOW *adj.*

■ ***verb*** **1** [I] (*formal*) (of the TIDE in the sea 海潮) to move away from the land 退；落 SYN **go out** OPP **flow** **2** [I] **~ (away)** to become gradually weaker or less 衰弱；衰退；減退 SYN **decrease**：*The pain was ebbing.* 疼痛逐漸減輕了。◇ *As night fell, our enthusiasm began to ebb away.* 我們的熱情隨着夜晚的降臨而漸漸低落下來。

Ebola fever /iːˈbəʊlə fiːvə(r); əˈbəʊlə; *NAmE* -ˈboʊ-; fiːvər/ *noun* [U] a very serious disease, caused by a virus, which causes internal parts of the body to lose blood and usually ends in death 埃博拉熱病（致命出血熱，由病毒引起）

Eb·on·ics /eˈbɒnɪks; *NAmE* -ˈbɑːn-/ *noun* [U] a type of English spoken by many African Americans that has been considered by some people to be a separate language 烏語，美國黑人英語（有些人認為是一種語言而非方言）

ebony /ˈebəni/ *noun, adj.*

■ ***noun*** [U] the hard black wood of various tropical trees 烏木；黑檀：*an ebony carving* 一件烏木雕刻

■ ***adj.*** black in colour 烏黑的：*ebony skin* 黝黑的皮膚

ˈe-book *noun* a book that is displayed on a computer screen or on an electronic device that is held in the hand, instead of being printed on paper 電子書

ebul·li·ent /ɪˈbʌliənt; -ˈbʊl-/ *adj.* (*formal*) full of confidence, energy and good humour 充滿自信的；精力充沛的；熱情洋溢的：*The Prime Minister was in ebullient mood.* 首相興致勃勃。▸ **ebul·li·ence** /-əns/ *noun* [U] **ebul·li·ent·ly** *adv.*

ˈe-cash *noun* [U] a system for sending and receiving payments using the Internet 電子現金（互聯網付費和收費系統）

ec·cen·tric /ɪkˈsentrɪk/ *adj.* considered by other people to be strange or unusual 古怪的；異乎尋常的：*eccentric behaviour/clothes* 古怪的行為；奇裝異服 ◇ *an eccentric aunt* 怪僻的大嬸 ▸ **ec·cen·tric** *noun*：*Most people considered him a harmless eccentric.* 多數人都認為他是一個無傷大雅的怪人。 **ec·cen·tric·al·ly** /-kli/ *adv.*

ec·cen·tri·city /ˌeksenˈtrɪsəti/ (*pl.* -ies) *noun* **1** [U] behaviour that people think is strange or unusual; the quality of being unusual and different from other people 古怪行為；反常：*As a teacher, she had a reputation for eccentricity.* 她身為教師，以行為古怪而出名。◇ *Arthur was noted for the eccentricity of his clothes.* 阿瑟以穿奇裝異服而著稱。**2** [C, usually pl.] an unusual act or habit 怪行；怪癖：*We all have our little eccentricities.* 我們都有些小怪癖。

Ec·cles cake /ˈeklz keɪk/ *noun* a small flat cake made from PASTRY with RAISINS inside 埃克爾斯葡萄乾小餅

ec·cle·si·as·tic /ɪˌkliːziˈæstɪk/ *noun* (*formal*) a priest or minister in the Christian Church（基督教）教士，聖職人員

ec·cle·si·as·tic·al /ɪˌkliːziˈæstɪkl/ *adj.* [usually before noun] connected with the Christian Church 基督教會的；與基督教會有關的

ECG /ˌiː siː ˈdʒiː/ (*NAmE* also **EKG**) *noun* the abbreviation for 'electrocardiogram' (a medical test that measures and records electrical activity of the heart) 心電圖，心動電流圖（全寫為 electrocardiogram）

ech·elon /ˈeʃəlɒn; *NAmE* -lɑːn/ *noun* **1** [usually pl.] a rank or position of authority in an organization or a society 職權的等級；階層：*the **lower/upper/top/higher echelons** of the Civil Service* 公務員的低層／上層／最高層／高層 **2** an arrangement of soldiers, planes, etc. in which each one is behind and to the side of the one in front（士兵、飛機等的）梯形編隊，梯隊

ech·idna /ɪˈkɪdnə/ (also **ˌspiny ˈanteater**) *noun* an Australasian animal which has a long nose, sharp CLAWS on its feet, and sharp SPINES on its body, and which eats insects 針鼴，針食蟻獸（澳大拉西亞長吻食蟻獸）

ech·in·acea /ˌekɪˈneɪsiə; -ʃə/ *noun* [U, C] a plant similar to a DAISY, that is thought to help the body heal itself and fight infection 松果菊屬植物，紫錐菊（類似雛菊，據信有助於身體自癒及抗感染）

echo /ˈekəʊ; *NAmE* ˈekoʊ/ *noun, verb*

■ ***noun*** (*pl.* -oes) **1** the reflecting of sound off a wall or inside a confined space so that a noise appears to be repeated; a sound that is reflected back in this way 回響；回聲；回音：*There was an echo on the phone and I couldn't hear clearly.* 電話裏有回音，我聽不清楚。◇ *The hills sent back a faint echo.* 座座山丘傳來微弱的回聲。◇ *the echo of footsteps running down the corridor* 沿走廊跑的腳步回聲 **2** the fact of an idea, event, etc. being like another and reminding you of it; sth that reminds you of sth else 映現；暗示；啟示；反響：*Yesterday's crash has grim echoes of previous disasters.* 昨天的撞車事故使人想起之前那些令人痛心的災難。**3** an opinion or attitude that agrees with or repeats one already expressed or thought 共鳴；附和；重複：*His words were an echo of what she had heard many times before.* 他的話跟她以往多次聽到過的話重複。◇ *The speech **found an echo** in the hearts of many of the audience* (= they agreed with it). 這次演講在許多聽眾的心中引起共鳴。

■ ***verb*** (echoes, echo·ing, echoed, echoed) **1** [I] if a sound **echoes**, it is reflected off a wall, the side of a mountain, etc. so that you can hear it again 回響；迴盪 SYN **reverberate**：*Her footsteps echoed in the empty room.* 她的腳步聲在空蕩蕩的屋子裏回響着。◇ *The gunshot echoed through the forest.* 槍炮聲在林中迴盪。**2** [I, T] to send back and repeat a sound; to be full of a sound 發出回聲；產生回響；充滿回聲 SYN **reverberate**：*The whole house echoed.* 整個房子充滿回聲。◇ **~ to/with sth** *The street echoed with the cries of children.* 街上迴盪着孩子的哭聲。◇ **~ sth (back)** *The valley echoed back his voice.* 山谷裏迴盪着他的聲音。**3** [T] **~ sth** to repeat an idea or opinion because you agree with it 重複，附和（想法或看法）：*This is a view echoed by many on the right of the party.* 這是黨內許多右翼分子都重複過的觀點。**4** [T] **+ speech** | **~ sth** to repeat what sb else has just said, especially because you find it surprising（尤因感到意外而）重複…話，模仿：*'He's gone!' Viv echoed.* "他去了！"維夫重複道。

echo·loca·tion /ˌekəʊləʊˈkeɪʃn; *NAmE* ˌekoʊloʊ-/ *noun* [U] the use of reflected sound waves for finding things, especially by creatures such as DOLPHINS and BATS（尤指海豚、蝙蝠等動物的）回聲定位

echt /ext/ *adj.* (from *German*) genuine and typical 真正的；典型的；十足的 ▸ **echt** *adv.*：*echt Viennese cream cakes* 真正的維也納奶油蛋糕

eclair /ɪˈkleə(r); *NAmE* ɪˈkler/ *noun* a long thin cake for one person, made of light PASTRY, filled with cream and usually with chocolate on top（巧克力）長形泡夫；奶油鬆餅；奶油酥餅

eclamp·sia /ɪˈklæmpsiə/ *noun* [U] a condition in which a pregnant woman has high blood pressure and CONVULSIONS, which can be dangerous to the woman and the baby 子癇（懷孕引起高血壓和驚厥，對產婦母子造成威脅）➲ compare PRE-ECLAMPSIA

eclec·tic /ɪˈklektɪk/ *adj.* (*formal*) not following one style or set of ideas but choosing from or using a wide variety 不拘一格的；兼收並蓄的：*She has very eclectic tastes in literature.* 她在文學方面的興趣非常廣泛。▸ **eclec·tic·al·ly** /-tɪkli/ *adv.* **eclec·ti·cism** /ɪˈklektɪsɪzəm/ *noun* [U]

eclipse /ɪˈklɪps/ *noun, verb*

■ **noun 1** [C] an occasion when the moon passes between the earth and the sun so that you cannot see all or part of the sun for a time; an occasion when the earth passes between the moon and the sun so that you cannot see all or part of the moon for a time 日蝕；月蝕：*an* ***eclipse of the sun/moon*** 日蝕；月蝕 ◇ *a* ***total/partial eclipse*** 全蝕；偏蝕 **2** [sing., U] a loss of importance, power, etc. especially because sb/sth else has become more important, powerful, etc.（重要性、權勢等的）喪失，黯然失色，暗淡：*The election result marked the eclipse of the right wing.* 選舉結果標誌着右翼的失勢。◇ *Her work was* ***in eclipse*** *for most of the 20th century.* 她的作品在 20 世紀大部份時間裏都湮沒無聞。

■ **verb 1** [often passive] **~ sth** (of the moon, the earth, etc. 月球、地球等) to cause an eclipse 遮住…的光 **2 ~ sb/sth** to make sb/sth seem dull or unimportant by comparison 使失色；使相形見絀；使喪失重要性 SYN **outshine, overshadow**：*Though a talented player, he was completely eclipsed by his brother.* 他雖是個天才運動員，但與他的哥哥相比就黯然失色了。

eco- /ˈiːkəʊ; *NAmE* ˈiːkoʊ/ *combining form* (in nouns, adjectives and adverbs 構成名詞、形容詞和副詞) connected with the environment 環境的；生態的：*eco-friendly* 環保的 ◇ *eco-warriors* (= people who protest about damage to the environment) 生態保護鬥士 ◇ *ecoterrorism* (= the use of force or violent action in order to protest about damage to the environment) 過激環保行為（用暴力行動來抗議對環境的破壞）

eco·cide /ˈiːkəʊsaɪd; *NAmE* ˈiːkoʊ-/ *noun* [U] the destruction of the natural environment, especially when this is deliberate（尤指蓄意的）生態破壞，環境破壞

ˌeco-ˈfriend·ly *adj.* not harmful to the environment 對環境無害的；環保的：*eco-friendly products* 環保型產品

E. coli /ˌiː ˈkəʊlaɪ; *NAmE* -ˈkoʊ-/ *noun* [U] a type of bacteria that lives inside humans and some animals, some forms of which can cause FOOD POISONING 大腸桿菌

eco·logic·al /ˌiːkəˈlɒdʒɪkl; *NAmE* -ˈlɑːdʒ-/ *adj.* **1** connected with the relation of plants and living creatures to each other and to their environment 生態的；生態學的：*We risk upsetting the ecological balance of the area.* 我們有可能破壞這個地區的生態平衡。◇ *an ecological disaster* (= one that alters the whole balance of ecology in an area) 生態災難 **2** interested in and concerned about the ecology of a place 關注生態環境的；主張生態保護的：*the ecological movement* 生態保護運動 ▸ **eco·logic·al·ly** /-kli/ *adv.*：*The system is both practical and* ***ecologically sound.*** 這個系統不但切合實際，從生態學觀點來看也是合理的。

ecoˌlogical ˈfootprint *noun* a measure of the amount of the earth's resources used by a person or a population that lives in a particular way 生態足跡（測定個人或群體生活所消耗地球資源的指標）：*the ecological footprint of the average Canadian* 普通加拿大人的生態足跡

ecolo·gist /iˈkɒlədʒɪst; *NAmE* iˈkɑːl-/ *noun* **1** a scientist who studies ecology 生態學家 **2** a person who is interested in ecology and believes the environment should be protected 生態保護論者

ecol·ogy /iˈkɒlədʒi; *NAmE* iˈkɑːl-/ *noun* [U] the relation of plants and living creatures to each other and to their environment; the study of this 生態；生態學：***plant/animal/human ecology*** 植物／動物／人類生態學 ◇ *the ecology movement* 生態保護運動 ◇ *Oil pollution could damage the* ***fragile ecology*** *of the coral reefs.* 石油污染可能破壞珊瑚礁脆弱的生態環境。

Synonyms 同義詞辨析

economic

financial • commercial • monetary • budgetary

These words all describe activities or situations that are connected with the use of money, especially by a business or country. 以上各詞尤用於企業或國家的經濟活動或狀況。

economic connected with the trade, industry and development of wealth of a country, an area or a society 指國家、地區或社會經濟的、經濟上的、經濟學的：*This book deals with the social, economic and political issues of the period.* 這本書論及了那個時期的社會、經濟和政治問題。

financial connected with money and finance 指財政的、財務的、金融的：*She had got into financial difficulties.* 她陷入了財務困境。◇ *Tokyo is a major financial centre.* 東京是主要的金融中心。

commercial connected with the buying and selling of goods and services 指貿易的、商業的

monetary (*formal* or *finance*) connected with money, especially all the money in a country 指貨幣的、錢的，尤指一國的金融：*closer European monetary union* 更為緊密的歐洲貨幣聯盟

budgetary (*finance*) connected with a budget (= the money available or a plan of how it will be spent) 指財政預算的

PATTERNS

- economic/financial/commercial/monetary/budgetary **affairs/decisions**
- the economic/financial/commercial/budgetary **climate**
- the economic/financial/commercial **side** of sth
- a(n) economic/financial/commercial **centre**

eco·nom·ic 0-m AW /ˌiːkəˈnɒmɪk; ˌekə-; *NAmE* -ˈnɑːm-/ *adj.* **1** 0-m [only before noun] connected with the trade, industry and development of wealth of a country, an area or a society 經濟的；經濟上的；經濟學的：*social, economic and political issues* 社會、經濟和政治問題 ◇ ***economic growth/cooperation/development/reform*** 經濟增長／合作／發展／改革 ◇ *the government's economic policy* 政府的經濟政策 ◇ *economic history* 經濟史 ◇ *the current economic climate* 目前的經濟形勢 **2** 0-m (of a process, a business or an activity 工序、業務或活動) producing enough profit to continue 有利可圖的；可賺錢的；合算的 SYN **profitable** OPP **uneconomic** ➲ SYNONYMS at SUCCESSFUL

Which Word? 詞語辨析

economic / economical

- **Economic** means 'connected with the economy of a country or an area, or with the money that a society or an individual has'. * economic 意為與國家、地區、社會或個人經濟有關的：*the government's economic policy* 政府的經濟政策 ◇ *the economic aspects of having children* 養孩子在經濟上的考慮

➲ see also ECONOMY (1)

- **Economical** means 'spending money or using something in a careful way that avoids waste'. * economical 意為經濟實惠的、節儉的、節約的：*It is usually economical to buy washing powder in large quantities.* 大量購買洗衣粉通常要省錢些。

➲ see also ECONOMY (3)

E

eco·nom·ic·al **AW** /ˌiːkəˈnɒmɪkl; ˌekə-; *NAmE* -ˈnɑːm-/ *adj.* **1** providing good service or value in relation to the amount of time or money spent 經濟的；實惠的： *an economical car to run* (= one that does not use too much petrol/gas) 節油型汽車 ◇ *It would be more economical to buy the bigger size.* 買尺寸大點的更實惠。 **OPP** **uneconomical** **2** using no more of sth than is necessary 節儉的；節約的；簡潔的： *an economical use of space* 節約利用空間 ◇ *an economical prose style* (= one that uses no unnecessary words) 簡煉的散文文體 **OPP** **uneconomical** **3** not spending more money than necessary 精打細算的；省錢的 **SYN** **frugal**： *He was economical in all areas of his life.* 他在生活的各個方面都精打細算。

IDM **economical with the ˈtruth** a way of saying that sb has left out some important facts, when you do not want to say that they are lying 沒把實話全講出來（婉指某人隱瞞了一些重要事實）

eco·nom·ic·al·ly **AW** /ˌiːkəˈnɒmɪkli; ˌekə-; *NAmE* -ˈnɑːm-/ *adv.* **1** in a way connected with the trade, industry and development of wealth of a country, an area or a society 在經濟上；在經濟學上： *The factory is no longer economically viable.* 這家工廠已沒有經濟效益了。◇ *Economically, the centre of Spain has lost its dominant role.* 西班牙中部在經濟上已失去了其主導地位。◇ *the **economically active/inactive** population* (= those who are employed/unemployed) 就業／失業人口 **2** in a way that provides good service or value in relation to the amount of time or money spent 經濟地；實惠地： *I'll do the job as economically as possible.* 我一定盡可能高效率地工作。 **3** in a way that uses no more of sth than is necessary 節儉地；節約地；節省地；簡潔地： *The design is intended to use space as economically as possible.* 這個設計方案是為了盡可能節省空間。◇ *She writes elegantly and economically.* 她寫作典雅而簡煉。

ˌeconomic ˈmigrant *noun* a person who moves from their own country to a new country in order to find work or have a better standard of living 經濟移民（以找工作或尋求更高生活水平為目的）： *They claimed they were political refugees and not economic migrants.* 他們宣稱自己是政治難民，不是經濟移民。

eco·nom·ics **AW** /ˌiːkəˈnɒmɪks; ˌekə-; *NAmE* -ˈnɑːm-/ *noun* **1** [U] the study of how a society organizes its money, trade and industry 經濟學： *He studied politics and economics at Yale.* 他曾在耶魯大學學習政治學和經濟學。◇ *Keynesian/Marxist economics* 凱恩斯主義／馬克思主義經濟學 ➲ see also HOME ECONOMICS **2** [pl., U] the way in which money influences, or is organized within an area of business or society 經濟情況；經濟因素；經濟意義： *The economics of the project are very encouraging.* 這項工程的經濟情況非常令人鼓舞。

econo·mist **AW** /ɪˈkɒnəmɪst; *NAmE* ɪˈkɑːn-/ *noun* a person who studies or writes about economics 經濟學家；經濟專家

econo·mize (*BrE* also **-ise**) /ɪˈkɒnəmaɪz; *NAmE* ɪˈkɑːn-/ *verb* [I] **~ (on sth)** to use less money, time, etc. than you normally use 節省；節約；節儉： *Old people often try to economize on heating, thus endangering their health.* 老年人常常想方設法節約用暖氣，結果損害了他們的健康。 ➲ SYNONYMS at SAVE

econ·omy 🔑 **AW** /ɪˈkɒnəmi; *NAmE* ɪˈkɑːn-/ *noun* (*pl.* -ies)
1 🔑 (often **the economy**) [C] the relationship between production, trade and the supply of money in a particular country or region 經濟；經濟情況；經濟結構： *The economy is in recession.* 經濟處於衰退之中。◇ *the world economy* 世界經濟 ◇ *a market economy* (= one

Collocations 詞語搭配

The economy 經濟

Managing the economy 管理經濟

- **handle/run/manage** the economy 管理經濟
- **boost** investment/spending/employment/growth 加快投資／支出／就業；加快增長速度
- **stimulate** demand/the economy/industry 刺激需求／經濟／工業
- **cut/reduce** investment/spending/borrowing 削減投資／支出／借貸
- **reduce/curb/control/keep down** inflation 減少／遏制通貨膨脹
- **create/fuel** growth/demand/a boom/a bubble 創造／刺激增長／需求／經濟繁榮／經濟泡沫
- **encourage/foster/promote/stimulate/stifle** innovation/competition 鼓勵／促進／刺激／抑制創新／競爭
- **encourage/work with/compete with** the private sector 鼓勵私營部門；與私營部門合作／競爭
- **increase/boost/promote** US/agricultural exports 增加／促進美國／農業出口
- **ban/restrict/block** cheap/foreign imports 禁止／限制／阻止廉價／進口產品
- the economy **grows/expands/shrinks/contracts/slows (down)/recovers/improves/is booming** 經濟增長／擴張／收縮／萎縮／減緩／復蘇／改善／繁榮
- **enjoy** an economic/housing/property boom 享受經濟／住房／房地產的繁榮期

Economic problems 經濟問題

- **push up/drive up** prices/costs/inflation 抬高價格／成本；加快通貨膨脹
- **damage/hurt/destroy** industry/the economy 破壞工業／經濟
- **cause/lead to/go into/avoid/escape** recession 引起／導致／進入／避開經濟衰退
- **experience/suffer** a recession/downturn 經歷／遭受經濟衰退
- **fight/combat** inflation/deflation/unemployment 抵抗通貨膨脹／通貨緊縮／失業
- **cause/create** inflation/poverty/unemployment 導致／造成通貨膨脹／貧窮／失業
- **create/burst** a housing/stock market bubble 造成／引爆住房／股票市場泡沫
- **cause/trigger** a stock market crash/the collapse of the banking system 引起股市崩盤／銀行系統崩潰
- **face/be plunged into** a financial/an economic crisis 面臨／陷入財政／經濟危機
- **be caught in/experience** cycles of boom and bust 陷入／經歷週期性繁榮與蕭條

Public finance 公共財政

- **cut/reduce/slash/increase/double** the defence/(*especially US*) defense/education/aid budget 削減／大幅削減／增加／加倍國防／教育／援助預算
- **increase/boost/slash/cut** public spending 增加／大幅削減／削減公共支出
- **increase/put up/raise/cut/lower/reduce** taxes 提高／降低稅收
- **raise/cut/lower/reduce** interest rates 提高／降低利率
- **ease/loosen/tighten** monetary policy 放寬／收緊貨幣政策
- **balance** the (state/federal) budget 平衡（州／聯邦）預算
- **achieve/maintain** a balanced budget 達到／保持預算平衡
- **run** a ($4 trillion) budget deficit/surplus 有（4 萬億元的）預算赤字／盈餘

➲ more collocations at POLITICS, VOTE

in which the price is fixed according to both cost and demand) 市場經濟 **2** [C] a country, when you are thinking about its economic system（就經濟體制而言）國家；經濟制度：*Ireland was one of the fastest-growing economies in Western Europe in the 1990s.* 在 20 世紀 90 年代愛爾蘭是西歐經濟發展最快的國家之一。 **3** [C, U] the use of the time, money, etc. that is available in a way that avoids waste 節約；節省；節儉：*We need to make substantial economies.* 我們需要厲行節約。◇ *It's a **false economy** to buy cheap clothes* (= it seems cheaper but it is not really since they do not last very long). 買便宜衣服實際上划不來。◇ *She writes with a great economy of words* (= using only the necessary words). 她寫作文字非常簡煉。◇ (*BrE*) *We're on an **economy drive** at home* (= trying to avoid waste and spend as little money as possible). 我們正在家裏實行勤儉節約。◇ *Buy the large **economy pack*** (= the one that gives you better value for money). 買大包的實惠裝吧。◇ *to fly **economy** (**class**)* (= by the cheapest class of air travel) 乘坐經濟艙 ◇ *an economy fare* (= the cheapest) 經濟艙票價

e'conomy class syndrome *noun* [U] (*BrE*) the fact of a person suffering from DEEP VEIN THROMBOSIS after they have travelled on a plane. This condition is thought to be more common among people who travel in the cheapest seats because they do not have space to move their legs much. 經濟艙綜合症，經濟艙症候群（在飛機上空間狹窄的經濟艙中久坐不動而導致深靜脈血栓形成）

eco·sys·tem /'i:kəʊsɪstəm; *NAmE* 'i:koʊ-/ *noun* all the plants and living creatures in a particular area considered in relation to their physical environment 生態系統 ➲ COLLOCATIONS at ENVIRONMENT

eco·ter·ror·ism /'i:kəʊterərɪzəm; *NAmE* 'i:koʊ-/ *noun* [U] **1** violent activities which are done in order to draw attention to issues relating to the environment 過激環保行為（為引起對環境問題的關注而實施暴力行動） **2** deliberate damage to the environment, done in order to draw attention to a political issue 生態恐怖主義（為引起對某政治問題的關注而蓄意破壞環境） ▸ **eco·ter·ror·ist** *noun*

eco·tour·ism /'i:kəʊtʊərɪzəm; -tɔ:r-; *NAmE* 'i:koʊtʊr-/ *noun* [U] organized holidays/vacations that are designed so that the tourists damage the environment as little as possible, especially when some of the money they pay is used to protect the local environment and animals 生態旅遊 ▸ **eco·tour·ist** /'i:kəʊtʊərɪst; -tɔ:r-; *NAmE* 'i:koʊtʊr-/ *noun*

eco·type /'i:kəʊtaɪp; *NAmE* 'i:koʊ-/ *noun* (*biology* 生) the type or race of a plant or animal that has adapted to live in particular local conditions 生態型（已適應特定局部條件的植物或動物種類）

ecru /'eɪkru:; 'ekru:/ *noun* a light brown or cream colour 淡褐色；米色

ec·stasy /'ekstəsi/ *noun* (*pl.* **-ies**) **1** [U, C] a feeling or state of very great happiness 狂喜；陶醉；入迷 SYN **bliss** **2** **Ecstasy** [U] (*abbr.* **E**) an illegal drug, taken especially by young people at parties, clubs, etc. 搖頭丸；迷幻藥

ec·stat·ic /ɪk'stætɪk/ *adj.* very happy, excited and enthusiastic; feeling or showing great enthusiasm 狂喜的；熱情極高的 SYN **delighted**：*Sally was ecstatic about her new job.* 薩莉對她的新工作高興得發狂。◇ ***ecstatic applause/praise/reviews*** 狂熱的鼓掌／讚美／評論 ➲ SYNONYMS at EXCITED ▸ **ec·stat·ic·al·ly** /-kli/ *adv.*

-ec·tomy *combining form* (in nouns 構成名詞) a medical operation in which part of the body is removed 切除術；截除：*appendectomy* (= removal of the APPENDIX) 闌尾切除術

ec·top·ic /ek'tɒpɪk; *NAmE* -'tɑ:p-/ *adj.* (*medical* 醫) in an **ectopic** PREGNANCY, the baby starts to develop outside the mother's WOMB（妊娠）異位的，子宮外的

ecto·plasm /'ektəʊplæzəm; *NAmE* 'ektoʊ-/ *noun* [U] **1** (*biology* 生) (*old-fashioned*) the outer layer of the jelly-like substance inside cells 外質（細胞的外胚層質） ➲ compare ENDOPLASM **2** a substance which is said to come from the body of sb who is communicating with the spirit of a dead person, allowing the spirit to have a form 外質（據信為神鬼附體者身上滲出的物質，可能形成死者的外形）

ecu·men·ic·al /ˌi:kju:'menɪkl; ˌekju:-/ *adj.* involving or uniting members of different branches of the Christian Church 基督宗教合一的；大公的

ecu·men·ism /ɪ'kju:mənɪzəm/ *noun* [U] the principle or aim of uniting different branches of the Christian Church（基督宗教）合一運動精神，大公主義

ec·zema /'eksɪmə; *NAmE* ɪg'zi:mə/ *noun* [U] a skin condition in which areas of skin become red, rough and ITCHY 濕疹

-ed, -d *suffix* **1** (in adjectives 構成形容詞) having; having the characteristics of 有…的；有…特徵的；以…為特徵的：*talented* 天才的 ◇ *bearded* 長鬍鬚的 ◇ *diseased* 患病的 **2** (makes the past tense and past participle of regular verbs 構成規則動詞的過去時和過去分詞)：*hated* 恨 ◇ *walked* 走路 ◇ *loved* 愛

ed. (also **Ed.**) *abbr.* EDITED (BY), EDITION, EDITOR：*'Eighteenth Century Women Poets', Ed. Lonsdale* 朗斯代爾主編的《十八世紀女詩人》◇ *7th ed.* 第七版

Edam /'i:dæm/ *noun* [U, C] a type of round yellow Dutch cheese that is covered with red WAX 埃丹乾酪（荷蘭球形乾酪，色黃，外塗紅蠟）

eddy /'edi/ *noun, verb*

■ ***noun*** (*pl.* **-ies**) a movement of air, dust or water in a circle（空氣、灰塵或水的）漩渦，渦流

■ ***verb*** (**ed·dies**, **eddy·ing**, **ed·died**, **ed·died**) [I] (of air, dust, water, etc. 空氣、灰塵、水等) to move around in a circle 起漩渦；旋轉 SYN **swirl**：*The waves swirled and eddied around the rocks.* 波浪翻滾着在岩石周圍打旋。

edema (*NAmE*) (*BrE* **oe·dema**) /ɪ'di:mə/ *noun* [U] (*medical* 醫) a condition in which liquid collects in the spaces inside the body and makes it swell 水腫

Eden /'i:dn/ (also **the ˌGarden of 'Eden**) *noun* [sing.] (in the Bible《聖經》) the beautiful garden where Adam and Eve, the first humans, lived before they did sth God had told them not to and were sent away, often seen as a place of happiness and INNOCENCE 伊甸園（人類始祖背叛上帝前居住的樂園）

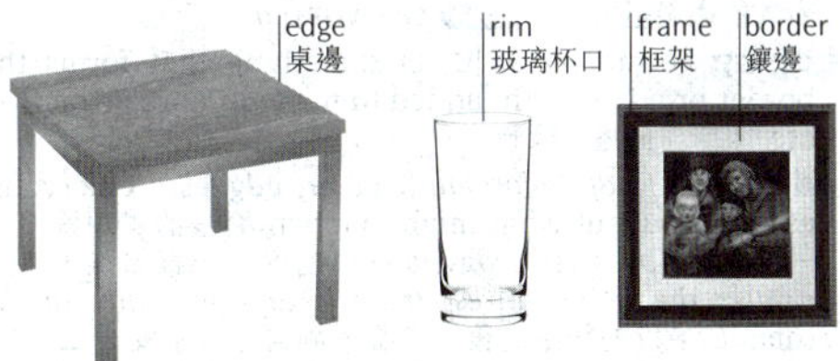

edge /edʒ/ *noun, verb*

■ ***noun*** **1** [C] the outside limit of an object, a surface or an area; the part furthest from the centre 邊；邊緣；邊線；邊沿：*He stood **on the edge of** the cliff.* 他站在懸崖邊上。◇ *a big house **on/at the edge of town*** 城邊的一棟大房子 ◇ *Don't put that glass so near the edge of the table.* 別把那隻玻璃杯放在離桌邊太近的地方。◇ *I sat down at the water's edge.* 我在水邊坐了下來。◇ *Stand the coin on its edge.* 讓硬幣豎起來。➲ see also LEADING EDGE **2** [C] the sharp part of a blade, knife or SWORD that is used for cutting 刀口；刀刃；利刃：*Be careful—it has a sharp edge.* 小心點，這刀刃很鋒利。➲ VISUAL VOCAB page V26 ➲ see also KNIFE-EDGE **3** (usually **the edge**) [sing.] the point at which sth, especially sth bad, may begin to happen（尤指災難的）邊緣 SYN **brink**, **verge**：*They had brought the country to the edge of disaster.* 他們使國家瀕臨災難。➲ see also CUTTING EDGE **4** [sing.] a slight advantage over sb/sth（微弱的）優勢：*The company needs to improve its **competitive edge**.* 公司需要提高它的競爭力。◇ **~ on/over sb/sth** *They have the edge on us.* 他們略勝我們一籌。 **5** [sing.] a strong, often exciting, quality 銳利；敏銳；尖銳：*Her show now has a hard political edge to it.* 她現在的表演具有強烈的政治性。 **6** [sing.] a sharp tone of voice, often showing anger 尖刻的聲調；憤怒的語氣：*He did his best to remain calm, but there was a distinct edge to his voice.* 儘管他竭力保持鎮靜，話音裏仍明顯帶有怒氣。 **7 -edged** (in adjectives 構成形容詞) having the type of edge or edges mentioned 有…邊的；有…棱的；有…鋒的：*a lace-edged handkerchief* 有網眼花邊的手絹 ➲ see also GILT-EDGED

IDM **be on 'edge** to be nervous, excited or bad-tempered 緊張不安；激動；煩躁 ➲ SYNONYMS at NERVOUS **on the edge of your 'seat** very excited and giving your full attention to sth 異常興奮；極為激動；有濃厚興趣：*The game had the crowd on the edge of their seats.* 這場比賽使觀眾興奮不已。 **take the 'edge off sth** to make sth less strong, less bad, etc. 減弱；使變鈍；挫傷…的銳氣：*The sandwich took the edge off my appetite.* 這份三明治使我食慾大減。 ➲ more at FRAY *v.*, RAZOR, ROUGH *adj.*, TEETER, TOOTH

■ *verb* **1** [I, T] to move or to move sth slowly and carefully in a particular direction（使）徐徐移動，漸漸移動：**+ adv./prep.** *She edged a little closer to me.* 她慢慢地向我靠近了一些。◇ *I edged nervously past the dog.* 我緊張不安地從狗旁邊慢慢走過去。◇ **~ sth + adv./prep.** *Emily edged her chair forward.* 埃米莉把椅子慢慢地向前挪動。 **2** [T, usually passive] **~ sth (with/in sth)** to put sth around the edge of sth 給…加邊：*The handkerchief is edged with lace.* 這條手絹鑲着網眼花邊。 **3** [I] **+ adv./prep.** to increase or decrease slightly 略為增加（或減少）：*Prices edged up 2% in the year to December.* 到十二月為止的年度價格上漲了 2%。

PHR V **,edge sb/sth↔'out (of sth)** to move sb from their position or job gradually, especially when they are not fully aware of what is happening 逐漸將…排擠出：*She was edged out of the company by the new director.* 新上任的經理一步步把她排擠出了公司。

,edge 'city *noun* (*NAmE*) a large area of buildings on the edge of a city, usually near a main road 邊緣城，衛星城（通常位於主幹公路旁）

edge·ways /ˈedʒweɪz/ (*BrE*) (*NAmE* **edge·wise** /-waɪz/) *adv.* with the edge upwards or forwards; on one side 邊向上（或向前）；側着；斜着：*You'll only get the desk through the door if you turn it edgeways.* 你要把書桌側着才能搬過這道門。 **IDM** see WORD *n.*

edging /ˈedʒɪŋ/ *noun* [U, C] something that forms the border or edge of sth, added to make it more attractive, etc. 邊緣；飾邊；緣飾

edgy /ˈedʒi/ *adj.* (*informal*) (**edgi·er**, **edgi·est**) **1** nervous, especially about what might happen 緊張的；煩躁不安的：*She's been very edgy lately.* 她近來一直煩躁不安。◇ *After the recent unrest there is an edgy calm in the capital.* 最近的騷亂之後，首都平靜得令人不安。 **2** (of a film/movie, book, piece of music, etc. 電影、書籍、樂曲等) having a sharp exciting quality 緊張的；激動人心的：*a clever, edgy film* 一部情節巧妙、扣人心弦的電影 ▸ **edgi·ly** *adv.*：*'I'm not sure I can make it tomorrow,' he said edgily.* "我不敢肯定明天能完成。" 他緊張不安地說。 **edgi·ness** *noun* [U, sing.]

EDI /ˌiː diː ˈaɪ/ *noun* [U] (*computing* 計) the abbreviation for 'electronic data interchange' (a system that is used in business for sending information between different companies' computer systems) 電子數據交換系統（全寫為 electronic data interchange，公司間局域網傳送系統）

ed·ible /ˈedəbl/ *adj.* fit or suitable to be eaten; not poisonous 適宜食用的；（無毒而）可以吃的：*The food at the hotel was barely edible.* 這家旅館的食物簡直不能入口。◇ *edible fungi/snails/flowers* 可食用的真菌類植物／蝸牛／花

edict /ˈiːdɪkt/ *noun* [U, C] (*formal*) an official order or statement given by sb in authority 法令；命令；敕令 **SYN** **decree**

edi·fi·ca·tion /ˌedɪfɪˈkeɪʃn/ *noun* [U] (*formal* or *humorous*) the improvement of sb's mind or character 教化；啟迪；陶冶：*The books were intended for the edification of the masses.* 這些書旨在教化民眾。

edi·fice /ˈedɪfɪs/ *noun* (*formal*) a large impressive building 大廈；宏偉建築：*an imposing edifice* 一座宏偉的建築 ◇ (*figurative*) *Their new manifesto hardly threatens to bring the **whole edifice of** capitalism crashing down.* 他們要使整個資本主義大廈崩塌的新宣言幾乎完全起不了威脅作用。◇ (*figurative*) *an edifice of lies* 謊話連篇

edify /ˈedɪfaɪ/ *verb* (**edi·fies**, **edify·ing**, **edi·fied**, **edi·fied**) [I, T] **~ sb** (*formal*) to improve people's minds or characters by teaching them about sth 教化；啟迪；教誨

edify·ing /ˈedɪfaɪɪŋ/ *adj.* (*formal* or *humorous*) likely to improve your mind or your character 啟迪的；有啟發意義的；起教化作用的

edit **AW** /ˈedɪt/ *verb* **1** [T, I] **~ (sth)** to prepare a piece of writing, a book, etc. to be published by correcting the mistakes, making improvements to it, etc. 編輯，編纂，校訂（文章、書籍等）：*I know that this draft text will need to be edited.* 我知道這篇草稿需要校訂。◇ *This is the edited version of my speech* (= some parts have been taken out). 這是我的演講稿選編本。 **2** [T] **~ sth** to prepare a book to be published by collecting together and arranging pieces of writing by one or more authors 編選；編纂；編集：*He's editing a book of essays by Isaiah Berlin.* 他正在編輯一本以賽亞 • 伯林的散文集。 **3** [T, I] **~ (sth)** (*computing* 計) to make changes to text or data on screen（屏幕）編輯：*You can download the file and edit it on your computer.* 你可以把文件下載，在計算機上編輯。 **4** [T] **~ sth** when sb **edits** a film/movie, television programme, etc. they take what has been filmed or recorded and decide which parts to include and in which order 剪輯，剪接（影片、電視節目等）：*They're showing the **edited highlights** of last month's game.* 他們正在放映上月比賽的精彩片段剪輯。 ➲ COLLOCATIONS at CINEMA **5** [T] **~ sth** to be responsible for planning and publishing a newspaper, magazine, etc. (= to be the EDITOR) 主編（報紙、雜誌等）：*She used to edit a women's magazine.* 她曾主編過一本女性雜誌。 ▸ **edit** *noun*：*I had time to do a quick edit of my essay before handing it in.* 我呈交論文之前有點時間，很快地校訂了一遍。

PHR V **,edit sth↔'out (of sth)** to remove words, phrases or scenes from a book, programme, etc. before it is published or shown（從書、節目中）刪除，刪掉，刪節 **SYN** **cut out**：*They edited out references to her father in the interview.* 他們刪掉了採訪中提到她父親的部份。

edit·able /ˈedɪtəbl/ *adj.* (*computing* 計) (of text or software 文本或軟件) that can be EDITED by the user（用戶）可編輯的：*an editable document* 可編輯文檔

edi·tion 🔑 **AW** /ɪˈdɪʃn/ *noun*

1 🔑 the form in which a book is published 版本（出版形式）：*a **paperback/hardback edition*** 平裝／精裝本 ◇ *She collects **first editions** of Victorian novels.* 她收集維多利亞時代的初版小說。◇ *the electronic edition of 'The Guardian'*《衛報》的電子版 **2** 🔑 a particular newspaper or magazine, or radio or television programme, especially one in a regular series（報紙、雜誌的）一份；（廣播、電視節目的）一期，一輯：*Tonight's edition of 'Panorama' looks at unemployment.* 今晚這輯《全景》探討的是失業問題。 **3** 🔑 (*abbr.* **ed.**) the total number of copies of a book, newspaper or magazine, etc. published at one time（書、報紙、雜誌等的）一版印刷總數，版次：*The dictionary is now in its eighth edition.* 本詞典現在是第八版。◇ *The article appeared in the evening edition of 'The Mercury'.* 這篇文章刊登在《信使報》的晚間版上。 ➲ see also LIMITED EDITION ➲ compare IMPRESSION (7)

edi·tor 🔑 **AW** /ˈedɪtə(r)/ *noun*

1 🔑 a person who is in charge of a newspaper, magazine, etc., or part of one, and who decides what should be included（報紙、雜誌等的）主編，編輯：*the editor of the Washington Post*《華盛頓郵報》的主編 ◇ *the **sports/financial/fashion, etc. editor*** 體育、財經、時尚等編輯 **2** 🔑 a person who prepares a book to be published, for example by checking and correcting the text, making improvements, etc.（書籍的）編輯，校訂者，審校者 ➲ see also COPY EDITOR, SUBEDITOR **3** a person who prepares a film/movie, radio or television programme for being shown or broadcast by deciding what to include, and what order it should be in（影片、電台或電視節目的）剪輯員，剪接師 **4** a person who works as a journalist for radio or television reporting on a particular area of news（電台或電視的）記者，編輯：*our economics editor* 本台經濟新聞的記者 **5** a person who chooses texts written by one or by several writers and prepares them to be published in a book（書籍的）編者：*She's the editor of a new collection of ghost stories.* 她編了一部新版鬼故事集。**6** (*computing* 計) a program that allows you to change stored text or data 編輯程序 ▸ **edit·or·ship** *noun* [U]：*the editorship of 'The Times'*《泰晤士報》的編輯工作

edi·tor·ial AW /ˌedɪˈtɔːriəl/ *adj., noun*

■ *adj.* [usually before noun] connected with the task of preparing sth such as a newspaper, a book or a television or radio programme, to be published or broadcast 編輯的；編者的；主編的：*the magazine's editorial staff* 雜誌的全體編輯人員 ◇ *an editorial decision* 編輯的決定

■ *noun* (*BrE* also **lead·er**, ˌ**leading** ˈ**article**) an important article in a newspaper, that expresses the editor's opinion about an item of news or an issue; in the US also a comment on radio or television that expresses the opinion of the STATION or network（報章的）社論；（美國電台或電視台的）評論

edi·tor·ial·ize (*BrE* also **-ise**) /ˌedɪˈtɔːriəlaɪz/ *verb* **1** [I] to express your opinions rather than just reporting the news or giving the facts（在報道中）加入意見：*He accused the BBC of editorializing in its handling of the story.* 他指責英國廣播公司在報道這則新聞時摻雜了主觀評論。**2** [I] (*NAmE*) to express an opinion in an editorial 發表社論：*Yesterday the Washington Post editorialized on this subject.* 昨天《華盛頓郵報》就這一課題發表了社論。

ˈ**edit suite** *noun* a room containing electronic equipment for EDITING material recorded on video 錄像編輯室；影像製作室

EDT /ˌiː diː ˈtiː/ *abbr.* EASTERN DAYLIGHT TIME

edu·cate 🔑 /ˈedʒukeɪt/ *verb*

1 🔑 [often passive] **~ sb** to teach sb over a period of time at a school, university, etc.（在學校）教育：*She was educated in the US.* 她是在美國受教育的。◇ *He was educated at his local comprehensive school and then at Oxford.* 他先在地方綜合學校上學，然後在牛津大學接受教育。**2** 🔑 to teach sb about sth or how to do sth 教導；教養；訓練：**~ sb (in/on sth)** *Children need to be educated on the dangers of drug-taking.* 有必要教導兒童吸毒的危害。◇ **~ sb to do sth** *The campaign is intended to educate the public to respect the environment.* 這一運動旨在教育公眾愛護環境。

edu·cated 🔑 /ˈedʒukeɪtɪd/ *adj.*

1 🔑 **-educated** having had the kind of education mentioned; having been to the school, college or university mentioned 受過…教育（或訓練）的；上過…學校的：*privately educated children* 受過私立教育的孩子 ◇ *a British-educated lawyer* 受英國教育的律師 ◇ *He's a Princeton-educated Texan.* 他是受過普林斯頓大學教育的得克薩斯人。**2** 🔑 having had a high standard of education; showing a high standard of education 受過良好教育（或訓練）的；有教養的：*an educated and articulate person* 有教養而且善於表達的人 ◇ *the educated elite* 受過良好教育的英才 ◇ *He spoke in an educated voice.* 他說話很斯文。

IDM **an** ˌ**educated** ˈ**guess** a guess that is based on some degree of knowledge, and is therefore likely to be correct 基於一定知識的猜測

edu·ca·tion 🔑 /ˌedʒuˈkeɪʃn/ *noun*

1 🔑 [U, sing.] a process of teaching, training and learning, especially in schools or colleges, to improve knowledge and develop skills（尤指學校）教育：*primary/elementary education* 初等／基礎教育 ◇ *secondary education* 中等教育 ◇ *further/higher/post-secondary education* 繼續／高等／中學後教育 ◇ *students in full-time education* 接受全日制教育的學生 ◇ *adult education classes* 成人教育班 ◇ *a college/university education* 大學教育 ◇ *the state education system* 國家教育體制 ◇ *a man of little education* 沒受過多少教育的人 ◇ *She completed her formal education in 1995.* 她在 1995 年完成正規學業。**2** 🔑 [U, sing.] a particular kind of teaching or training 教育；培養；訓練：*health education* 健康教育 **3** 🔑 (also **Education**) [U] the institutions or people involved in teaching and training 教育機構；教育界人士：*the Education Department* 教育部 ◇ *the Department of Health, Education and Welfare* 衛生、教育和福利部 ◇ *There should be closer links between education and industry.* 教育界與產業界之間應該有更緊密的聯繫。**4** 🔑 (usually **Education**) [U] the subject of study that deals with how to teach 教育學：*a College of Education* 教育學院 ◇ *a Bachelor of Education degree* 教育學學士 ◇ *She's an education major.* 她主修教育學。**5** [sing.] (often *humorous*) an interesting experience that teaches you sth 有教益的經歷：*The rock concert was quite an education for my parents!* 這場搖滾樂音樂會真讓我父母大受教益！ ➲ COLLOCATIONS at next page

edu·ca·tion·al /ˌedʒuˈkeɪʃənl/ *adj.* connected with education; providing education 教育的；有關教育的；有教育意義的：*children with special educational needs* 需要特殊教育的孩子 ◇ *an educational psychologist* 教育心理學家 ◇ *an educational visit* 教育訪問 ◇ ***educational games/toys*** (= that teach you sth as well as amusing you) 寓教於樂的遊戲／玩具 ◇ *Watching television can be very educational.* 看電視可以使人受到很多教益。▸ **edu·ca·tion·al·ly** /-ʃənəli/ *adv.*：*Children living in inner-city areas may be educationally disadvantaged.* 居住在市中心貧民區的孩子在教育方面可能條件較差。◇ (*old-fashioned*) *educationally subnormal* 學習能力低下

edu·ca·tion·al·ist /ˌedʒuˈkeɪʃənəlɪst/ (also **edu·ca·tion·ist** /ˌedʒuˈkeɪʃənɪst/) *noun* a specialist in theories and methods of teaching 教育家；教育學家

edu·ca·tive /ˈedjukətɪv/ *adj.* (*formal*) that teaches sth 教育的；有教育作用的：*the educative role of the community* 社區的教育作用

edu·ca·tor /ˈedʒukeɪtə(r)/ *noun* (*formal*) **1** a person whose job is to teach or educate people 教育工作者；教師：*adult educators* (= who teach adults) 成人教育教師 **2** (*especially NAmE*) a person who is an expert in the theories and methods of education 教育學家；教育家 ➲ see also EDUCATIONALIST

edu·tain·ment /ˌedjuˈteɪnmənt/ *noun* [U] products such as books, television programmes and especially computer software that both educate and entertain 寓教於樂型產品（指教育兼娛樂的書籍、電視節目，尤其是電腦軟件等）

Ed·ward·ian /edˈwɔːdiən; *NAmE* -ˈwɔːrd-/ *adj.* from the time of the British king Edward VII (1901–1910) 英王愛德華七世時代的（1901–1910）：*an Edwardian terraced house* 一座愛德華七世時代的排房 ▸ **Ed·ward·ian** *noun*

-ee *suffix* (in nouns 構成名詞) **1** a person affected by an action 受動者；受益者：*employee* 雇員 ➲ compare -ER (1), -OR **2** a person described as or concerned with 稱為…的人；與…有關的人：*absentee* 缺席者 ◇ *refugee* 難民

EEG /ˌiː iː ˈdʒiː/ *noun* the abbreviation for 'electroencephalogram' (a medical test that measures and records electrical activity in the brain) 腦電圖（全寫為 electroencephalogram）

eejit /ˈiːdʒɪt/ *noun* (*informal, IrishE, ScotE, disapproving*) a way of saying IDIOT which represents the way it is pronounced by some people 白痴，傻瓜（代表一些人對 idiot 的讀音方式）

eek /iːk/ *exclamation* used to express fear or surprise（表示害怕或驚訝）呀，咦：*Eek! It moved!* 咦！它動了！

eel /iːl/ *noun* [C, U] a long thin sea or FRESHWATER fish that looks like a snake. There are several types of eel, some of which are used for food. 鰻；鰻鱺：*jellied eels* 鰻魚凍

e'en /iːn/ *adv.* (*literary*) = EVEN

e'er /eə(r); *NAmE* er/ *adv.* (*literary*) = EVER

-eer *suffix* **1** (in nouns 構成名詞) a person concerned with 與…有關的人：*auctioneer* 拍賣商 ◇ *mountaineer* 登山運動員 **2** (in verbs 構成動詞) (often *disapproving*) to be concerned with 與…有關：*profiteer* 牟取暴利 ◇ *commandeer* 強佔

E

eerie /ˈɪəri; *NAmE* ˈɪri/ *adj.* strange, mysterious and frightening 怪異的；神秘的；恐怖的 SYN **uncanny**: *an eerie yellow light* 神秘兮兮的黃燈 ◇ *I found the silence underwater really eerie.* 我發覺水下的寂靜很恐怖。▶ **eer·ily** /ˈɪərəli; *NAmE* ˈɪr-/ *adv.* **eeri·ness** *noun* [U]

eff /ef/ *verb*

IDM **eff and ˈblind** (*BrE, informal*) to use swear words 咒罵；詛咒：*There was a lot of effing and blinding going on.* 咒罵聲沒完沒了。

PHR V **ˌeff ˈoff** (*taboo, BrE*) a rude way of telling sb to go away, used instead of 'fuck off' 滾蛋，滾開（代替 fuck off）➲ see also EFFING

ef·face /ɪˈfeɪs/ *verb* **~ sth** (*formal*) to make sth disappear; to remove sth 消除；抹去；擦掉 ➲ see also SELF-EFFACING

ef·fect 0-w /ɪˈfekt/ *noun, verb*

■ *noun* **1** 0-w [C, U] **~ (on sb/sth)** a change that sb/sth causes in sb/sth else; a result 效應；影響；結果：*the effect of heat on metal* 熱對金屬產生的效應 ◇ ***dramatic/long-term effects*** 巨大的影響；長期效應 ◇ *to learn to distinguish between* ***cause and effect*** 學會分清因果 ◇ *the beneficial effects of exercise* 鍛煉的好處 ◇ *Modern farming methods can have an* ***adverse effect*** *on the environment.* 現代農業耕作方法可能對環境造成負面影響。◇ *Her criticisms* ***had the effect of*** *discouraging him completely.* 她批評的結果是使他完全喪失了信心。◇ *Despite her ordeal, she seems to have suffered no* ***ill effects***. 她儘管備受磨難，但好像並未受到不利影響。◇ *I can certainly* ***feel the effects of*** *too many late nights.* 我當然能感覺到熬夜太多產生的影響。◇ *'I'm feeling really depressed.' 'The winter here has that effect sometimes.'* "我真感到抑鬱。" "這兒的冬天有時候就會產生這種影響。" ◇ *I tried to persuade him, but with little or no effect.* 我試圖說服他，但卻無濟於事。➲ LANGUAGE BANK at CONSEQUENTLY ➲ note at AFFECT ➲ see also GREENHOUSE EFFECT, KNOCK-ON, SIDE EFFECT **2** 0-w [C, U] a particular look, sound or impression that sb, such as an artist or a writer, wants to create（藝術家或作家等所要創造的特定）外觀，聲響，印象，效果：*The overall effect of the painting is overwhelming.* 這幅畫的總體效果氣勢磅礴。◇ *The stage lighting gives the effect of a moonlit scene.* 這種舞台燈光能產生月下景色的效果。◇ *Add a scarf for a casual effect.* 再圍上一條圍巾以顯得隨便些。◇ *He only behaves like that* ***for effect*** (= in order to impress people). 他那樣表現不過是為了譁眾取寵。➲ see also SOUND EFFECT, SPECIAL EFFECTS **3 effects** [pl.] (*formal*) your personal possessions（個人）財產，所有物，財物 SYN **belongings**: *The insurance policy covers all baggage and personal effects.* 這份保險單為全部行李和個人財產提供保險。

IDM **bring/put sth into efˈfect** 0-w to cause sth to come into use 使生效；實行；實施：*The recommendations will soon be put into effect.* 這些建議即將付諸實施。

Collocations 詞語搭配

Education 教育

Learning 學習

- **acquire/get/lack** (an) education/training/(*BrE*) (some) qualifications 獲得／缺少教育／培訓／資格
- **receive/provide sb with** training/tuition 得到／給某人提供培訓／指導
- **develop/design/plan** a curriculum/(*especially BrE*) course/(*NAmE*) program/syllabus 制訂課程方案／教學大綱
- **give/go to/attend** a class/lesson/lecture/seminar 講課；上課；舉辦／參加／出席研討會
- **hold/run/conduct** a class/seminar/workshop 辦班；舉辦研討會／講習班
- **sign up for/take** a course/classes/lessons 報名參加／修讀課程

School 學校

- **go to/start** preschool/kindergarten/nursery school 上學前班／幼兒園／託兒所
- **be in the first, second, etc.** (*NAmE*) grade/(*especially BrE*) year (at school) 在讀一／二…年級
- **study/take/drop** history/chemistry/German, etc. 修讀／放棄修歷史課／化學課／德語課…
- (*BrE*) **leave/finish/drop out of**/(*NAmE*) **quit** school 離校；完成學業；輟學；退學
- (*NAmE*) **graduate** high school/college 高中／大學畢業

Problems at school 在學校遇到的問題

- **be the victim/target of** bullying 成為被欺負的受害者／對象
- (*BrE*) **play truant from**/(*both BrE, informal*) **bunk off/skive off** school (= not go to school when you should) 逃學
- (*both especially NAmE*) **skip/cut** class/school 逃課；逃學
- (*BrE*) **cheat** in/(*NAmE*) cheat on an exam/a test 考試作弊
- **get/be given** a detention (for doing sth)（因做了某事）被罰放學後留校
- **be expelled from/be suspended from** school 被學校開除／暫時停學

Work and exams 功課和考試

- **do** your homework/(*BrE*) revision/a project on sth 做家庭作業；複習功課；對…進行專題研究
- **work on/write/do/submit** an essay/a dissertation/a thesis/an assignment/(*NAmE*) a paper 寫／提交文章／學位論文／畢業論文／作業／論文
- **finish/complete** your dissertation/thesis/studies/coursework 完成學位論文／畢業論文／學業／課程作業
- **hand in**/(*NAmE*) **turn in** your homework/essay/assignment/paper 提交家庭作業／文章／作業／論文
- **study/prepare**/(*BrE*) **revise**/(*NAmE*) **review**/(*NAmE, informal*) **cram** for a test/an exam 為應考而學習／準備／複習／臨時死記硬背
- **take**/(*both BrE*) **do/sit** a test/an exam 參加考試
- (*especially BrE*) **mark**/(*especially NAmE*) **grade** homework/a test 給作業／考試打分
- (*BrE*) **do well in**/(*NAmE*) **do well on**/(*informal, especially NAmE*) **ace** a test/an exam 在考試中取得好成績
- **pass/fail**/(*informal, especially NAmE*) **flunk** a test/an exam/a class/a course/a subject 測驗／考試／課程／學科及格／不及格

University 大學

- **apply to/get into/go to/start** college/(*BrE*) university 申請／上／開始上大學
- **leave/graduate from** law school/college/(*BrE*) university (with a degree in computer science) 離開／畢業於法學院；離開大學；大學畢業（取得計算機科學的學位）
- **study for/take**/(*BrE*) **do/complete** a law degree/a degree in physics 攻讀／讀完法學學位／物理學位課程
- (*both NAmE*) **major/minor** in biology/philosophy 主修／副修生物學／哲學
- **earn/receive/be awarded/get/have/hold** a master's degree/a bachelor's degree/a PhD in economics 獲得／被授予／拿到／擁有經濟學碩士學位／學士學位／博士學位

come into ef'fect 🔑 to come into use; to begin to apply 生效；開始實施： *New controls come into effect next month.* 下月開始實施新的管制措施。 **in ef'fect** **1** used when you are stating what the facts of a situation are 實際上；事實上： *In effect, the two systems are identical.* 實際上，這兩種系統完全一樣。◇ *His wife had, in effect, run the government for the past six months.* 過去的六個月實際上是他的妻子在執政。 **2** (of a law or rule 法律或規則) in use 在實施中；有效： *These laws are in effect in twenty states.* 這些法律在二十個州有效。 **take ef'fect** **1** to start to produce the results that are intended 開始起作用；見效： *The aspirins soon take effect.* 阿司匹林藥片見效快。**2** to come into use; to begin to apply 生效；開始實施：*The new law takes effect from tomorrow.* 新法令明日起生效。 **to the effect that …** | **to this/that ef'fect** used to show that you are giving the general meaning of what sb has said or written rather than the exact words 大意是；意思是；有這個（或那個）意思： *He left a note to the effect that he would not be coming back.* 他留下一張字條，大意是他不回來了。◇ *She told me to get out—or* ***words to that effect.*** 她叫我滾開，或說了類似的話。 **to good, great, dramatic, etc. ef'fect** producing a good, successful, dramatic, etc. result or impression 富有成效；效果良好 **to no ef'fect** not producing the result you intend or hope for 毫無效果；毫無成效；不起作用： *We warned them, but to no effect.* 我們曾告誡過他們，但沒起任何作用。 **with immediate effect** | **with effect from …** (*formal*) starting now; starting from … 立即生效；從…起開始生效： *The government has cut interest rates with effect from the beginning of next month.* 政府已削減利率，從下月初起開始生效。

■ ***verb*** **~ sth** (*formal*) to make sth happen 使發生；實現；引起： *to* ***effect a cure/change/recovery*** 產生療效；引起變化；實現復蘇 ➲ note at AFFECT

ef·fect·ive 🔑 /ɪˈfektɪv/ *adj.* **1** 🔑 producing the result that is wanted or intended; producing a successful result 產生預期結果的；有效的： *Long prison sentences can be a very effective deterrent for offenders.* 判處長期監禁可對違法者起到強有力的威懾作用。◇ *Aspirin is a simple but highly effective treatment.* 阿司匹林藥片治療方法簡便，效果卻非常顯著。◇ *drugs that are effective against cancer* 治療癌症的有效藥物◇ *I admire the effective use of colour in her paintings.* 我很欣賞她繪畫作品中的色彩效果。 **OPP** **ineffective** ➲ see also COST-EFFECTIVE **2** [only before noun] in reality, although not officially intended 實際的；事實上的： *the effective, if not the actual, leader of the party* 雖未居其位卻實際上是黨的領導人◇ *He has now taken effective control of the country.* 他目前已實際上控制了這個國家。 **3** (*formal*) (of laws and rules 法律和規則) coming into use 生效的；起作用的： *The new speed limit on this road becomes effective from 1 June.* 這條路的新限速規定自6月1日起生效。 ▸ **ef·fect·ive·ness** (also *less frequent* **ef·fect·iv·ity** /ˌɪfekˈtɪvɪti/) *noun* [U]： *to check the effectiveness of the security system* 檢查安全系統的有效性

ef·fect·ive·ly 🔑 /ɪˈfektɪvli/ *adv.* **1** 🔑 in a way that produces the intended result or a successful result 有效地：*The company must reduce costs to compete effectively.* 公司要有效地參與競爭必須降低成本。◇ *You dealt with the situation very effectively.* 你這次應付這種局面很有一套。 **OPP** **ineffectively** **2** used when you are saying what the facts of a situation are 實際上；事實上： *He was very polite but effectively he was telling me that I had no chance of getting the job.* 他彬彬有禮，但實際上卻是在告訴我，我不可能得到這份工作。

ef·fect·or /ɪˈfektə(r)/ *noun* (*biology* 生) an organ or a cell in the body that is made to react by sth outside the body 效應器（對外界刺激做出反應的身體器官或細胞）

ef·fec·tual /ɪˈfektʃuəl/ *adj.* (*formal*) (of things, not people 指物，不指人) producing the result that was intended 有效的；奏效的 **SYN** **effective**：*an effectual remedy* 有效的療法 ➲ compare INEFFECTUAL ▸ **ef·fec·tual·ly** *adv.*

ef·fec·tu·ate /ɪˈfektʃueɪt/ *verb* **~ sth** (*formal*) to make sth happen 使發生；實現 **SYN** **cause**

ef·fem·in·ate /ɪˈfemɪnət/ *adj.* (*disapproving*) (of a man or a boy 男人或男孩) looking, behaving or sounding like a woman or a girl 女人氣的 ▸ **ef·fem·in·acy** /ɪˈfemɪnəsi/ *noun* [U]

ef·fer·ves·cent /ˌefəˈvesnt; *NAmE* ˌefərˈv-/ *adj.* **1** (*approving*) (of people and their behaviour 人或其行為) excited, enthusiastic and full of energy 興高采烈的；熱情洋溢的；充滿活力的 **SYN** **bubbly** **2** (of a liquid 液體) having or producing small bubbles of gas 冒泡的；起沫的 **SYN** **fizzy** ▸ **ef·fer·ves·cence** /ˌefəˈvesns; *NAmE* ˌefərˈv-/ *noun* [U]

ef·fete /ɪˈfiːt/ *adj.* (*disapproving*) **1** weak; without the power that it once had 衰弱的；衰敗的；喪失權力的 **2** (of a man 男人) without strength; looking or behaving like a woman 軟弱的；女人氣的

ef·fi·ca·cious /ˌefɪˈkeɪʃəs/ *adj.* (*formal*) (of things, not of people 指物，不指人) producing the result that was wanted or intended 有效的；奏效的；靈驗的 **SYN** **effective**： *They hope the new drug will prove especially efficacious in the relief of pain.* 他們希望這種新藥能在緩解疼痛方面產生特效。

ef·fi·cacy /ˈefɪkəsi/ *noun* [U] (*formal*) the ability of sth, especially a drug or a medical treatment, to produce the results that are wanted（尤指藥物或治療方法的）功效，效驗，效力 **SYN** **effectiveness**

ef·fi·ciency /ɪˈfɪʃnsi/ *noun* **1** [U] the quality of doing sth well with no waste of time or money 效率；效能；功效： *improvements in efficiency at the factory* 工廠效率的提高◇ *I was impressed by the efficiency with which she handled the crisis.* 她應變效率之高給我留下了深刻的印象。 **2** **efficiencies** [pl.] ways of wasting less time and money or of saving time or money 提高功效的方法： *We are looking at our business to see where savings and efficiencies can be made.* 我們正在研究我們的經營情況，看是否有可以節約和提高功效的地方。**3** [U] (*technical* 術語) the relationship between the amount of energy that goes into a machine or an engine, and the amount that it produces（能源的）效率，功率 **4** [C] = EFFICIENCY APARTMENT

ef'ficiency apartment (also **ef'ficiency unit**, **ef·fi·ciency**) *noun* (*NAmE*) a small flat/apartment with one main room for living, cooking and sleeping in and a separate bathroom 公寓式小套房，開放式套房（起居室、廚房和寢區在同一個房間裏，有獨立盥洗室）

ef·fi·cient 🔑 /ɪˈfɪʃnt/ *adj.* doing sth well and thoroughly with no waste of time, money, or energy 效率高的；有功效的： *an efficient secretary* 效率高的秘書◇ *efficient heating equipment* 效能好的供暖設備◇ *the efficient use of energy* 能源的有效利用◇ *As we get older, our bodies become less efficient at burning up calories.* 隨着一天天衰老，我們的身體消耗熱量的功能逐漸減弱。◇ *fuel-efficient cars* (= that do not use much fuel) 節能汽車 **OPP** **inefficient** ▸ **ef·fi·cient·ly** 🔑 *adv.*： *a very efficiently organized event* 組織效率極高的活動

ef·figy /ˈefɪdʒi/ *noun* (*pl.* **-ies**) **1** a statue of a famous person, a SAINT or a god（名人、聖人或神的）雕像，塑像： *stone effigies in the church* 教堂裏的石雕像 **2** a model of a person that makes them look ugly（醜化人的）模擬像，畫像： *The demonstrators burned a crude effigy of the president.* 示威者焚燬了總統的醜化像。

eff·ing (also **f-ing**) /ˈefɪŋ/ *adj.* [only before noun] (*taboo, slang*) a swear word that many people find offensive that is used to emphasize a comment or an angry statement; used instead of saying 'fucking' 該死的，他媽的（避而不說 fucking）

ef·flor·es·cence /ˌefləˈresns/ *noun* [U, C] **1** (*formal*) the most developed stage of sth 全盛期；最輝煌期 **2** (*chemistry* 化) the powder which appears on the surface of bricks, rocks, etc. when water EVAPORATES（磚、岩石等表面的）風化物，粉化物

ef·flu·ent /ˈefluənt/ *noun* [U, C] (*formal*) liquid waste, especially chemicals produced by factories, or SEWAGE 廢水，污水（尤指工廠排出的化學廢料）

E

ef·fort 🔑 /ˈefət; *NAmE* ˈefərt/ *noun*
1 🔑 [U, C] the physical or mental energy that you need to do sth; sth that takes a lot of energy 氣力；努力；費力的事：*You should **put** more **effort into** your work.* 你應該更加努力地工作。◇ *A lot of effort has gone into making this event a success.* 為使這次活動成功費了很大的勁。◇ *It's a long climb to the top, but well worth the effort.* 爬到頂上路程很長，雖然費力卻很值得。◇ *Getting up this morning was quite an effort* (= it was difficult). 今天早上起牀相當費力。◇ (*BrE*) ***With (an) effort*** (= with difficulty) *she managed to stop herself laughing.* 她好不容易才忍住了笑。**2** 🔑 [C] an attempt to do sth especially when it is difficult to do 艱難的嘗試；試圖；盡力：*a **determined/real/special effort*** 堅決的／真正的／特別的努力 ◇ *to **make an effort*** 作出努力 ◇ *I didn't really feel like going out, but I am glad I **made the effort**.* 我當時並不很想出去，不過我很慶幸還是出去了。◇ **~ (to do sth)** *The company has laid off 150 workers **in an effort to** save money.* 公司為節省資金遣散了 150 名工人。◇ *The local clubs are **making every effort** to interest more young people.* 地方俱樂部正在盡一切努力來吸引更多的年輕人。◇ *We need to make a **concerted effort** to finish on time.* 我們需要通力合作才能按時完成。◇ *I spent hours cleaning the house, but there isn't much to show **for all my efforts**.* 我花了幾個小時來打掃房子，但費了這麼大力氣卻看不到多少效果。◇ *With an **effort of will** he resisted the temptation.* 他憑自己的意志頂住了這一誘惑。◇ *The project was a **joint/group** effort.* 這項工程是共同／集體努力的結果。**3** [C] (usually after a noun 通常置於名詞後) a particular activity that a group of people organize in order to achieve sth 有組織的活動：*the Russian space effort* 俄羅斯航天計劃 ◇ *the United Nations' peacekeeping effort* 聯合國的維和行動 **4** [C] the result of an attempt to do sth 努力的結果；成就：*I'm afraid this essay is a poor effort.* 很抱歉，這篇文章寫得不好。
IDM see BEND *v.*

ef·fort·less /ˈefətləs; *NAmE* ˈefərt-/ *adj.* needing little or no effort, so that it seems easy 不需費力的；容易的：*She dances with effortless grace.* 她跳舞動作優美，輕鬆自如。◇ *He made playing the guitar look effortless.* 他彈起吉他來顯得輕鬆自如。▶ **ef·fort·less·ly** *adv.* **ef·fort·less·ness** *noun* [U]

ef·front·ery /ɪˈfrʌntəri/ *noun* [U] (*formal*) behaviour that is confident and very rude, without any feeling of shame 厚顏無恥的行為；傲慢魯莽的舉止 **SYN** **nerve**

ef·ful·gent /ɪˈfʌldʒənt/ *adj.* (*literary*) shining brightly 燦爛的；光輝的 ▶ **ef·ful·gence** /ɪˈfʌldʒəns/ *noun* [U]

ef·fu·sion /ɪˈfjuːʒn/ *noun* [C, U] **1** (*technical* 術語) something, especially a liquid, that flows out of sb/sth; the act of flowing out 流出（物）；溢出（物）**2** (*formal*) the expression of feelings in an exaggerated way; feelings that are expressed in this way （感情）過分流露，迸發，傾瀉；過分流露的感情

ef·fu·sive /ɪˈfjuːsɪv/ *adj.* showing much or too much emotion 感情過分流露的；太動感情的；奔放的：*an effusive welcome* 非常熱烈的歡迎 ◇ *He was effusive in his praise.* 他極盡溢美之詞。▶ **ef·fu·sive·ly** *adv.*

E-fit™ /ˈiːfɪt/ *noun* (*BrE*) a picture of a person who is wanted by the police, made using a computer program that puts together and makes changes to pictures of different features of faces, based on information that is given by sb who has seen the person（根據目擊者的描述用計算機拼合成的）通緝犯畫像 ➲ compare IDENTIKIT, PHOTOFIT

EFL /ˌiː ef ˈel/ *abbr.* (*BrE*) English as a foreign language (refers to the teaching of English to people for whom it is not the first language) 非母語的英語教學；作為外語的英語教學 ➲ compare EAL, EAP, ESL, ESOL

ˈe-friend *noun* = E-PAL

EFTA /ˈeftə/ *abbr.* European Free Trade Association (an economic association of some European countries) 歐洲自由貿易聯盟

e.g. 🔑 /ˌiː ˈdʒiː/ *abbr.* for example (from Latin 'exempli gratia') 例如（源自拉丁文 exempli gratia）：*popular pets, e.g. cats and dogs* 人們喜愛的寵物，如貓和狗

Language Bank 用語庫

e.g.

Giving examples 舉例

- The website has a variety of interactive exercises (**e.g.** matching games, crosswords and quizzes). 這個網站有各種各樣的互動練習（比如：配對遊戲、縱橫填字遊戲和智力測試）。
- The website has a variety of interactive exercises, **including** matching games, crosswords and quizzes. 這個網站有各種各樣的互動練習，包括配對遊戲、縱橫填字遊戲和智力測試。
- Web 2.0 technologies, **such as** wikis, blogs and social networking sites, have changed the way that people use the Internet. * Web 2.0 技術，比如維基、博客及社交網站，改變了人們使用互聯網的方式。
- Many websites now allow users to contribute information. **A good example of this is** the 'wiki', a type of website that anyone can edit. 現在許多網站都允許用戶撰寫信息。維基就是一個很好的例子，它是一種任何人都可以編輯的網站。
- Wikis vary in how open they are. **For example**, some wikis allow anybody to edit content, while others only allow registered users to do this. 各維基網的開放程度不同。比如，有些維基網允許任何人編輯內容，另一些則只允許註冊用戶進行內容編輯。
- Wikis vary in how open they are. Some wikis, **for example / for instance**, allow anybody to edit content, while others only allow registered users to do this. 各維基網的開放程度不同。比如，有些維基網允許任何人編輯內容，另一些則只允許註冊用戶進行內容編輯。
- More and more people read their news on the Internet. **To take one example,** over 14 million people now read the online version of 'The Oxford Herald'. 越來越多的人在網上閱讀新聞。舉個例子來說，現在有超過 1 400 萬人閱讀《牛津先驅報》的網絡版本。
- Online newspapers are now more popular than paper ones. 'The Oxford Herald' **is a case in point** . Its print circulation has fallen in recent years, while its website attracts millions of users every month. 現在，網絡報紙比紙質報紙更受歡迎。《牛津先驅報》就是一個很好的例子。近年來，其印刷版發行量趨於減少，但其網站每個月卻吸引上千萬的用戶。

➲ note at EXAMPLE
➲ Language Banks at ADDITION, ARGUE, EVIDENCE, ILLUSTRATE

egali·tar·ian /iˌɡælɪˈteəriən; *NAmE* -ˈter-/ *adj.* based on, or holding, the belief that everyone is equal and should have the same rights and opportunities 主張人人平等的；平等主義的 ▶ **egali·tar·ian** *noun*：*He described himself as 'an egalitarian'.* 他自稱為"平等主義者"。**egali·tar·ian·ism** /-ɪzəm/ *noun* [U]

egg 🔑 /eɡ/ *noun, verb*
■ ***noun*** **1** 🔑 [C] a small OVAL object with a thin hard shell produced by a female bird and containing a young bird; a similar object produced by a female fish, insect, etc.（鳥類的）蛋；（魚、昆蟲等的）卵：*The female sits on the eggs until they hatch.* 雌鳥伏在蛋上直到孵化。◇ *The fish lay thousands of eggs at one time.* 這種魚一次產卵數千個。◇ *crocodile eggs* 鱷魚蛋 ➲ **COLLOCATIONS** at LIFE ➲ **VISUAL VOCAB** pages V12, V13 **2** 🔑 [C, U] a bird's egg, especially one from a chicken, that is eaten as food（用作食物的）禽蛋；（尤指）雞蛋：*a **boiled egg*** 煮蛋 ◇ *bacon and eggs* 熏肉加煎蛋 ◇ ***fried/poached/scrambled eggs*** 煎蛋；荷包蛋；炒蛋 ◇ *Bind the mixture together with a little beaten egg.* 用少許打過的蛋將混合料攪拌在一起。◇ *You've got some egg on your shirt.* 你的襯衣上沾了些蛋。◇ ***egg yolks/whites*** 蛋黃；蛋白 ◇ *egg noodles*

雞蛋麪 ◇ *ducks'/quails' eggs* 鴨蛋；鵪鶉蛋 ◇ *a chocolate egg* (= made from chocolate in the shape of an egg) 巧克力蛋 ➲ see also EASTER EGG, SCOTCH EGG **3** [C] (in women and female animals 婦女和雌性動物) a cell that combines with a SPERM to create a baby or young animal 卵子；卵細胞 SYN **ovum**：*The male sperm fertilizes the female egg.* 雄性的精子使雌性的卵子受精。◇ *an egg donor* 卵子捐贈者 ➲ see also NEST EGG

IDM **a ˈgood egg** (*old-fashioned, informal*) a person who you can rely on to behave well 好人；正人君子 **have ˈegg on/all over your face** (*informal*) to be made to look stupid 顯得愚蠢；出醜；丟臉：*They were left with egg on their faces when only ten people showed up.* 只有十人到場，他們感到很丟面子。 **put all your eggs in one ˈbasket** to rely on one particular course of action for success rather than giving yourself several different possibilities 寄希望於一件事情上；孤注一擲 ➲ more at CHICKEN *n.*, CURATE[1], KILL *v.*, OMELETTE, SURE *adv.*, TEACH

■ *verb*

PHR V **ˌegg sb↔ˈon** (*informal*) to encourage sb to do sth, especially sth that they should not do 鼓動；慫恿；煽動：*He hit the other boy again and again as his friends egged him on.* 他在朋友的煽動下一次又一次地打了另一個男孩。

ˌegg-and-ˈspoon race *noun* (*BrE*) a race, usually run by children, in which those taking part have to hold an egg balanced in a spoon 湯匙盛蛋賽跑（通常為兒童比賽，賽跑者須手持盛雞蛋的湯匙）

ˈegg cup *noun* a small cup for holding a boiled egg（盛放煮蛋的）蛋杯 ➲ VISUAL VOCAB page V22

egg·head /ˈeghed/ *noun* (*informal, disapproving* or *humorous*) a person who is very intelligent and is only interested in studying 學究

egg·nog /ˈegnɒg; *NAmE* -nɑːg; -nɔːg/ (*BrE* also **ˈegg flip**) *noun* [U, C] an alcoholic drink made by mixing beer, wine, etc. with eggs and milk 蛋奶酒（用啤酒、葡萄酒等和蛋、牛奶攪拌而成）

egg·plant /ˈegplɑːnt; *NAmE* -plænt/ (*NAmE*) (*BrE* **au·ber·gine**) *noun* [C, U] a vegetable with shiny dark purple skin and soft white flesh 茄子 ➲ VISUAL VOCAB page V31

ˌegg ˈroll *noun* (*NAmE*) a type of SPRING ROLL in which the PASTRY is made with eggs 炸蛋捲；蛋皮春捲

egg·shell /ˈegʃel/ *noun* **1** [C, U] the hard thin outside of an egg 蛋殼 **2** [U] (*BrE*) a type of paint that is smooth but not shiny when it dries 蛋殼漆（乾後平滑無光）

ˈegg timer *noun* a device that you use to measure the time needed to boil an egg 煮蛋計時器

ego /ˈiːgəʊ; ˈegəʊ; *NAmE* ˈiːgoʊ/ *noun* (*pl.* **-os**) **1** your sense of your own value and importance 自我價值感：*He has the biggest ego of anyone I've ever met.* 他是我所見的最自負的人。◇ *Winning the prize really* ***boosted her ego.*** 獲得這個獎項大大增強了她的自尊心。 **2** (*psychology* 心) the part of the mind that is responsible for your sense of who you are (= your identity) 自我 ➲ compare SUPEREGO ➲ see also ALTER EGO ➲ compare ID

ego·cen·tric /ˌegəʊˈsentrɪk; ˌiːg-; *NAmE* ˌiːgoʊ-/ *adj.* thinking only about yourself and not about what other people need or want 以自我為中心的；自私自利的 SYN **selfish**

ego·ism /ˈegəʊɪzəm; ˈiːg-; *NAmE* -goʊ-/ (also **egot·ism** /ˈegətɪzəm; ˈiːg-/) *noun* [U] (*disapproving*) the fact of thinking that you are better or more important than anyone else 利己主義；自高自大；自負；自我主義 ▸ **ego·is·tic** /ˌegəʊˈɪstɪk; ˌiːg-; *NAmE* -goʊ-/ (also **egot·is·tic·al** /ˌegəˈtɪstɪkl; ˌiːgə-/, **egot·is·tic** /ˌegəˈtɪstɪk; ˌiːgə-/) *adj.* **egot·is·tic·al·ly** /-kli/ *adv.*

ego·ist /ˈegəʊɪst; ˈiːg-; *NAmE* ˈiːgoʊ-/ (also **egot·ist** /ˈegətɪst; ˈiːgə-/) *noun* (*disapproving*) a person who thinks that he or she is better than other people and who thinks and talks too much about himself or herself 利己主義者；自高自大者；自我主義者

ego·mania /ˌegəʊˈmeɪniə; ˌiːgəʊ-; *NAmE* ˌiːgoʊ-/ *noun* [U] a mental condition in which sb is interested in themselves or concerned about themselves in a way that is not normal 極端利己；病態自我中心主義 ▸ **ego·maniac** /ˌegəʊˈmeɪniæk; ˌiːgəʊ-; *NAmE* ˌiːgoʊ-/ *noun* **ego·ma·ni·acal** /ˌegəʊməˈnaɪəkl; ˌiːgəʊ-; *NAmE* ˌiːgoʊ-/ *adj.*

ˈego-surfing *noun* [U] (often *humorous*) the activity of searching the Internet to find places where your own name has been mentioned 自我衝浪，自我搜尋（在互聯網上搜索提及自己名字的網頁）

ˈego trip *noun* (usually *disapproving*) an activity that sb does because it makes them feel good and important 自我表現；自我滿足的行為

egre·gious /ɪˈgriːdʒiəs/ *adj.* (*formal*) extremely bad 極糟的；極壞的

e·gress /ˈiːgres/ *noun* [U] (*formal*) the act of leaving a place 離開；外出 ➲ compare ACCESS *n.* (1), INGRESS

egret /ˈiːgrət/ *noun* a bird of the HERON family, with long legs and long white tail feathers 白鷺

Egypt·ology /ˌiːdʒɪpˈtɒlədʒi; *NAmE* -ˈtɑːl-/ *noun* [U] the study of the language, history and culture of ancient Egypt 埃及學（研究古埃及的語言、歷史和文化） ▸ **Egyp·tolo·gist** /ˌiːdʒɪpˈtɒlədʒɪst; *NAmE* -ˈtɑːl-/ *noun*

eh /eɪ/ *exclamation* (*BrE*) (*NAmE* usually **huh**) **1** the sound that people make when they want sb to repeat sth（請對方再說一遍）嗯，什麼：*'I'm not hungry.' 'Eh?' 'I said I'm not hungry.'* "我不餓。" "嗯？" "我說我不餓。" **2** the sound that people make when they want sb to agree or reply（徵求對方同意或答覆）是嗎，好嗎，嗯：*So what do you think, eh?* 那你是怎麼想的，嗯？ **3** the sound people make when they are surprised（表示驚奇）啊：*Another new dress, eh!* 呵，又是一件新連衣裙！

Eid (also **Id**) /iːd/ *noun* one of the two main Muslim festivals, either **Eid ul-Fitr** /ˌiːd ʊl ˈfɪtrə/ at the end of Ramadan, or **Eid ul-Adha** /ˌiːd ʊl ˈɑːdə/ which celebrates the end of the PILGRIMAGE to Mecca and Abraham's SACRIFICE of a sheep 開齋節，宰牲節（伊斯蘭教的兩個主要節日之一，開齋節在齋月的最後一天，宰牲節以亞伯拉罕的羊作祭品慶祝麥加朝聖結束）

ei·der·down /ˈaɪdədaʊn; *NAmE* -dərd-/ *noun* (*BrE*) a thick, warm cover for a bed, filled with feathers or other soft material, and usually placed on top of a sheet and BLANKETS 羽絨被；（用輕軟物作芯子的）軟被

eider duck /ˈaɪdə dʌk; *NAmE* ˈaɪdər/ *noun* a large DUCK with soft feathers, that lives in northern countries 絨鴨，棉鳧（生活在北方國家）

eight /eɪt/

1 *number* 8 八 HELP There are examples of how to use numbers at the entry for **five**. 數詞用法示例見 five 條。 **2** *noun* a team of eight people who ROW a long narrow boat in races; the boat they row 八人划船隊；由八人划的船 ➲ see also FIGURE OF EIGHT

eight·een /ˌeɪˈtiːn/ *number*

18 十八 ▸ **eight·eenth** /ˌeɪˈtiːnθ/ *ordinal number, noun* HELP There are examples of how to use ordinal numbers at the entry for **fifth**. 序數詞用法示例見 fifth 條。

eighth /eɪtθ/ *ordinal number, noun*

■ ***ordinal number*** 8th 第八 HELP There are examples of how to use ordinal numbers at the entry for **fifth**. 序數詞用法示例見 fifth 條。

■ ***noun*** each of eight equal parts of sth 八分之一

ˈeighth note (*NAmE*) (*BrE* **qua·ver**) *noun* (*music* 音) a note that lasts half as long as a CROTCHET/QUARTER NOTE 八分音符 ➲ picture at MUSIC

eighty /ˈeɪti/

1 *number* 80 八十 **2** *noun* **the eight·ies** [pl.] numbers, years or temperatures from 80 to 89 八十幾；八十年代 ▸ **eight·ieth** /ˈeɪtiəθ/ *ordinal number, noun* HELP There are examples of how to use ordinal numbers at the entry for **fifth**. 序數詞用法示例見 fifth 條。

IDM **in your eighties** between the ages of 80 and 89 * 80 多歲

eina /ˈemɑː/ *exclamation* (*SAfrE*) used to express sudden pain（突然疼痛時發出的聲音）哎唷，啊：*Eina! That was sore!* 哎唷！好痛！

ein·stein·ium /amˈstaɪniəm/ *noun* [U] (*symb.* **Es**) a chemical element. Einsteinium is a RADIOACTIVE element produced artificially from PLUTONIUM and other elements. 鑀（放射性化學元素）

ei·stedd·fod /aɪˈsteðvɒd; *NAmE* -vɑːd/ *noun* (*WelshE*) a type of festival, held in Wales, in which there are singing, music and poetry competitions 艾斯特福德節（威爾士的一種節日，有歌唱、音樂和詩作比賽）

E

ei·ther /ˈaɪðə(r); ˈiːðə(r)/ *det., pron., adv.*

■ ***det., pron.* 1** one or the other of two; it does not matter which（兩者中的）任何一個：*You can park on either side of the street.* 這條街兩邊都可停車。◇ *You can keep one of the photos. Either of them—whichever you like.* 你可以保留一張照片。兩張裏任選一張，你喜歡的。◇ *There are two types of qualification—either is acceptable.* 有兩種資格證明，任何一種都可以接受。➲ note at NEITHER **2** each of two（兩者中的）每個，各方：*The offices on either side were empty.* 兩邊的辦公室都是空的。◇ *There's a door at either end of the corridor.* 走廊兩端各有一道門。

■ ***adv.* 1** used after negative phrases to state that a feeling or situation is similar to one already mentioned（用於否定詞組後）也：*Pete can't go and I can't either.* 皮特不能去，我也不能。◇ (*NAmE, informal*) *'I don't like it.' 'Me either.'* (= Neither do I.) "我不喜歡這個。" "我也不喜歡。" **2** used to add extra information to a statement（補充時說）而且：*I know a good Italian restaurant. It's not far from here, either.* 我知道一家很好的意大利餐館，而且離這兒不遠。 **3 either ... or ...** used to show a choice of two things（對兩事物的選擇）要麼…要麼，不是…就是，或者…或者：*Well, I think she's either Czech or Slovak.* 嗯，我看她不是捷克人就是斯洛伐克人。◇ *I'm going to buy either a camera or a DVD player with the money.* 我打算用這筆錢買一架照相機或者 DVD 機。◇ *Either he could not come or he did not want to.* 他要麼是不能來要麼就是不想來。➲ note at NEITHER ➲ compare OR (1)

ejacu·late /iˈdʒækjuleɪt/ *verb* **1** [I, T] **~ (sth)** when a man or a male animal **ejaculates**, SEMEN comes out through the PENIS 射精 **2 + speech** (*old-fashioned*) to say or shout sth suddenly 突然說出；喊出；喊叫 SYN **exclaim**

ejacu·la·tion /iˌdʒækjuˈleɪʃn/ *noun* **1** [C, U] the act of ejaculating; the moment when SPERM comes out of a man's PENIS 射精：*premature ejaculation* 早泄 **2** [C] (*formal*) a sudden shout or sound that you make when you are angry or surprised（憤怒或吃驚時）突然喊出，叫喊 SYN **exclamation**

eject /iˈdʒekt/ *verb* **1** [T] **~ sb (from sth)** (*formal*) to force sb to leave a place 驅逐；逐出；趕出 SYN **throw out**：*Police ejected a number of violent protesters from the hall.* 警察將一些暴力抗議者趕出了會議廳。 **2** [T] **~ sth (from sth)** to push sth out suddenly and with a lot of force 噴出；噴射；排出：*Used cartridges are ejected from the gun after firing.* 空彈殼在射擊後從槍裏彈出。 **3** [I] (of a pilot) to escape from an aircraft that is going to crash, sometimes using an EJECTOR SEAT（飛行員在飛機墜毀前從彈射座椅）彈出 **4** [T, I] **~ (sth)** when you **eject** a tape, disk, etc., or when it **ejects**, it comes out of the machine after you have pressed a button（按鍵後磁帶、磁盤等）彈出；使彈出 ▸ **ejec·tion** /iˈdʒekʃn/ *noun* [U, C]

eject·or seat /iˈdʒektə siːt; *NAmE* -tər/ (*US* also **ejection seat**) *noun* a seat that allows a pilot to be thrown out of an aircraft in an emergency（飛行員在緊急情況下從飛機中彈出用的）彈射座椅

eke /iːk/ *verb*

PHR V **ˌeke sth↔ˈout 1** to make a small supply of sth such as food or money last longer by using only small amounts of it（靠節省用量）使…的供應持久；節約使用：*She managed to eke out her student loan till the end of the year.* 她想方設法節約用錢使學生貸款維持到了年底。 **2 ~ a living, etc.** to manage to live with very little money 竭力維持生計；勉強度日

EKG /ˌiː keɪ ˈdʒiː/ *abbr.* (*NAmE*) = ECG

elab·or·ate *adj., verb*

■ ***adj.*** /ɪˈlæbərət/ [usually before noun] very complicated and detailed; carefully prepared and organized 複雜的；詳盡的；精心製作的：*elaborate designs* 精心的設計 ◇ *She had prepared a very elaborate meal.* 她做了一頓精美的飯菜。◇ *an elaborate computer system* 精密的計算機系統 ▸ **elab·or·ate·ly** *adv.*：*an elaborately decorated room* 精心裝飾的房間 **elab·or·ate·ness** *noun* [U]

■ ***verb*** /ɪˈlæbəreɪt/ **1** [I, T] to explain or describe sth in a more detailed way 詳盡闡述；詳細描述：**~ (on/upon sth)** *He said he was resigning but did not elaborate on his reasons.* 他說他準備辭職但未詳細說明原因。◇ **~ sth** *She went on to elaborate her argument.* 她進而詳盡闡述了她的論點。 **2** [T] **~ sth** to develop a plan, an idea, etc. and make it complicated or detailed 詳細制訂；精心製作：*In his plays he takes simple traditional tales and elaborates them.* 他在劇本裏採用了一些簡單的傳統故事並加以發揮。 ▸ **elab·or·ation** /ɪˌlæbəˈreɪʃn/ *noun* [U, C]：*The importance of the plan needs no further elaboration.* 這個計劃的重要性無須贅述。

elan /eɪˈlɒ̃; eɪˈlæn; *NAmE* eɪˈlɑ̃ː/ *noun* [U] (from *French, literary*) great enthusiasm and energy, style and confidence 活力和風格

eland /ˈiːlənd/ *noun* (*pl.* **eland** or **elands**) a large African ANTELOPE with curled horns 大角斑羚（非洲大羚羊）

elapse /ɪˈlæps/ *verb* [I] (not usually used in the progressive tenses 通常不用於進行時) (*formal*) if a period of time **elapses**, it passes（時間）消逝，流逝 SYN **go by**：*Many years elapsed before they met again.* 過了許多年他們才再次相見。

eˌlapsed ˈtime *noun* [U] (*technical* 術語) used to describe the time that passes between the start and end of a project or a computer operation, in contrast to the actual time needed to do a particular task which is part of the project（一項工程的）實耗時間；（計算機一次操作的）運行時間

elas·tic /ɪˈlæstɪk/ *noun, adj.*

■ ***noun*** [U] material made with rubber, that can stretch and then return to its original size 橡皮圈（或帶）；鬆緊帶：*This skirt needs some new elastic in the waist.* 這條裙子需要換一根鬆緊腰帶。

■ ***adj.* 1** made with elastic 橡皮圈（或帶）的：*an elastic headband* 鬆緊頭帶 **2** able to stretch and return to its original size and shape 有彈性的；有彈力的：*elastic materials* 彈性材料 **3** that can change or be changed 靈活的；可改變的；可伸縮的：*Our plans are fairly elastic.* 我們的計劃有相當大的靈活性。

elas·ti·cated /ɪˈlæstɪkeɪtɪd/ (*BrE*) (*NAmE* **elas·ti·cized** /ɪˈlæstɪsaɪzd/) *adj.* (of clothing, or part of a piece of clothing 衣服或衣服某部份) made using elastic material that can stretch 彈性物質織成的；織入橡皮筋的；有鬆緊帶的：*a skirt with an elasticated waist* 有鬆緊腰帶的裙子

eˌlastic ˈband *noun* (*BrE*) = RUBBER BAND ➲ VISUAL VOCAB page V69

elas·ti·city /ˌiːlæˈstɪsəti; ˌelæ-; ɪˌlæ-/ *noun* [U] the quality that sth has of being able to stretch and return to its original size and shape (= of being elastic) 彈性；彈力

elas·tin /ɪˈlæstɪn/ *noun* [U] (*biology* 生) a natural substance that stretches easily, found in the skin, the heart and other body TISSUES 彈性蛋白（存在於皮膚、心臟等身體組織）

elasto·mer /ɪˈlæstəmə(r)/ *noun* (*chemistry* 化) a natural or artificial chemical that behaves like rubber 彈性體；高彈體

elated /iˈleɪtɪd/ *adj.* **~ (at/by sth)** very happy and excited because of sth good that has happened, or will happen 興高采烈的；歡欣鼓舞的；喜氣洋洋的：*They were elated at the result.* 他們對這一結果感到歡欣鼓舞。◇ *I was elated by the prospect of the new job ahead.* 我為眼前新工作的前景所鼓舞。➲ SYNONYMS at EXCITED

ela·tion /iˈleɪʃn/ *noun* [U] a feeling of great happiness and excitement 興高采烈；歡欣鼓舞；喜氣洋洋

elbow 0-π /ˈelbəʊ; *NAmE* -boʊ/ *noun*, *verb*

■ ***noun*** **1** 0-π the joint between the upper and lower parts of the arm where it bends in the middle 肘；肘部：*She jabbed him with her elbow.* 她用胳膊肘捅他。◇ *He's fractured his elbow.* 他肘部骨折。➲ VISUAL VOCAB page V59 **2** 0-π the part of a piece of clothing that covers the elbow（衣服的）肘部：*The jacket was worn at the elbows.* 這件夾克衫的肘部磨破了。**3** a part of a pipe, CHIMNEY, etc. where it bends at a sharp angle（管子、煙囪等的）彎處，彎頭

IDM **get the ˈelbow** (*BrE, informal*) to be told by sb that they no longer want to have a relationship with you; to be told to go away 被排斥；被甩；被攆走 **give sb the ˈelbow** (*BrE, informal*) to tell sb that you no longer want to have a relationship with them; to tell sb to go away 排斥；甩掉；攆走 ➲ more at KNOW *v.*, POWER *n.*, RUB *v.*

■ ***verb*** **~ sb/sth (+adv./prep.)** to push sb with your elbow, usually in order to get past them 用肘推；用肘擠：*She elbowed me out of the way to get to the front of the line.* 她用肘部把我推開朝隊伍前面擠。◇ *He elbowed his way through the crowd.* 他從人群中擠了過去。

ˈelbow grease *noun* [U] (*informal*) the effort used in physical work, especially in cleaning or polishing sth 苦幹；（尤指費勁的）清潔，擦拭

ˈelbow room *noun* [U] (*informal*) enough space to move or walk in 足夠的活動空間；足以走進的地方

elder /ˈeldə(r)/ *adj.*, *noun*

■ ***adj.*** **1** [only before noun] (of people, especially two members of the same family 指人，尤指同一家庭裏兩個成員) older 年紀較長的：*my elder brother* 我的哥哥 ◇ *his elder sister* 他的姐姐 **2 the elder** used without a noun immediately after it to show who is the older of two people（後面不緊跟名詞，指兩者中的）較年長者：*the elder of their two sons* 他們的兩個兒子中年紀較大的那個 **3 the elder** (*formal*) used before or after sb's name to show that they are the older of two people who have the same name（用於人名前或後，指同名的兩個人中）年齡較大的一個：*the elder Pitt* 老皮特 ◇ *Pitt the elder* 老皮特 ➲ note at OLD ➲ compare THE YOUNGER at YOUNG *adj.* (6)

■ ***noun*** **1 elders** [pl.] people of greater age, experience and authority 長者；長輩；元老：*Children have no respect for their elders nowadays.* 現今的孩子對長輩一點兒也不尊敬。◇ *the village elders* (= the old and respected people of the village) 村裏德高望重的長輩 **2 my, etc. elder** [sing.] (*formal*) a person older than me, etc. 比…年長的人：*He is her elder by several years.* 他比她年長幾歲。**3** [C] an official in some Christian churches（某些基督教會中的）長老 **4** [C] a small tree with white flowers with a sweet smell (**elderflowers**) and bunches of small black BERRIES (**elderberries**) 接骨木

IDM **your ˌelders and ˈbetters** people who are older and wiser than you and whom you should respect 前輩；長者

ˈelder abuse *noun* [U] the crime of harming or stealing from an old person, committed by sb who is trusted to care for or help them 虐待老人；虐老

elder·berry /ˈeldəberi; *NAmE* ˈeldərb-/ *noun* (*pl.* **-ies**) a small black BERRY that grows in bunches on an elder tree 接骨木果

elder·care /ˈeldəkeə(r); *NAmE* ˈeldərker/ *noun* [U] (*especially NAmE*) help for old people, especially services such as special homes and medical care 老年照料；老年保健；老年照護：*nursing homes and other eldercare facilities* 養老院等老年護理設施

elder·flower /ˈeldəflaʊə(r); *NAmE* ˈeldərf-/ *noun* the flower of the elder tree, used to make wines and other drinks 接骨木花（用於製作果酒等飲料）

eld·er·ly 0-π /ˈeldəli; *NAmE* -ərli/ *adj.*

1 0-π (of people 人) used as a polite word for 'old' 年紀較大的，上了年紀的（婉辭，與 old 同義）：*an elderly couple* 一對老年夫婦 ◇ *elderly relatives* 年老的親戚 ➲ SYNONYMS at OLD **2 the elderly** *noun* [pl.] people who are old 老人；上了年紀的人

ˌelder ˈstatesman *noun* **1** an old and respected politician or former politician whose advice is still valued because of his or her long experience 政界元老 **2** any experienced and respected person whose advice or work is valued 資深前輩；德高望重的老前輩：*an elder statesman of golf* 高爾夫球的元老

eld·est /ˈeldɪst/ *adj.* **1** (of people, especially of three or more members of the same family 指人，尤指同一家庭裏三個或以上成員) oldest 年齡最大的：*Tom is my eldest son.* 湯姆是我的長子。**2 the eldest** used without a noun immediately after it to show who is the oldest of three or more people（後面不緊跟名詞，指三個或以上的人中）年齡最大的人：*the eldest of their three children* 他們的三個子女中最大的那個 ➲ note at OLD

eld·ritch /ˈeldrɪtʃ/ *adj.* [usually before noun] (*literary*) strange and frightening 怪異可怕的；駭人的：*an eldritch screech* 駭人的怪叫聲

elect 0-π /ɪˈlekt/ *verb*, *adj.*

■ ***verb*** **1** 0-π to choose sb to do a particular job by voting for them 選舉；推選：**~ sb/sth** *an* ***elected assembly/leader/representative*** 選出的議會／領導人／代表 ◇ *the newly elected government* 新選的政府 ◇ **~ sb to sth** *She became the first black woman to be elected to the Senate.* 她成為第一個被選進參議院的黑人婦女。◇ **~ sb (as) sth** | **~ sb + noun** *He was elected (as) MP for Oxford East.* 他被選為牛津東區的議員。➲ COLLOCATIONS at VOTE **2 ~ to do sth** (*formal*) to choose to do sth 選擇，決定（做某事）：*Increasing numbers of people elect to work from home nowadays.* 現在越來越多的人選擇在家工作。

■ ***adj.*** **1** used after nouns to show that sb has been chosen for a job, but is not yet doing that job（用於名詞後）當選而尚未就職的，候任的：*the president elect* 候任總統 **2 the elect** *noun* [pl.] (*religion* 宗) people who have been chosen to be saved from punishment after death 上帝的選民

elec·tion 0-π /ɪˈlekʃn/ *noun*

1 0-π [U, C] the process of choosing a person or a group of people for a position, especially a political position, by voting 選舉，推選（尤指從政）：***election campaigns/results*** 競選運動；選舉結果 ◇ *to* ***win/lose an election*** 在選舉中獲勝／失敗 ◇ *to* ***fight an election*** 參加競選 ◇ *to* ***vote in an election*** 參加投票選舉 ◇ *In America, presidential* ***elections are held*** *every four years.* 美國每四年舉行一次總統選舉。◇ *The prime minister is about to* ***call*** (= announce) ***an election.*** 首相即將宣佈舉行大選。◇ (*especially BrE*) *How many candidates are* ***standing for election****?* 有多少候選人參加競選？◇ (*especially NAmE*) *to* ***run for election*** 參加競選 ➲ COLLOCATIONS at VOTE **2** 0-π [U] the fact of having been chosen by election 當選：**~ (as sth)** *We welcome his election as president.* 我們歡迎他當選總統。◇ **~ (to sth)** *a year after her election to the committee* 她獲選入該委員會之後一年 ➲ see also BY-ELECTION, GENERAL ELECTION ➲ SYNONYMS at next page

elec·tion·eer·ing /ɪˌlekʃəˈnɪərɪŋ; *NAmE* -ˈnɪr-/ *noun* [U] the activity of making speeches and visiting people to try to persuade them to vote for a particular politician or political party in an election 競選活動；拉選票

elect·ive /ɪˈlektɪv/ *adj.*, *noun*

■ ***adj.*** [usually before noun] (*formal*) **1** using or chosen by election 選舉的；由選舉產生的；選任的：*an elective democracy* 民主選舉的國家 ◇ *an elective assembly* 選舉產生大會 ◇ *an elective member* 選任的成員 ◇ *He had never held elective office* (= a position which is filled by election). 他從未擔任過經選舉獲得的職務。**2** having the power to elect 有選舉權的：*an elective body* 有選舉權的機構 **3** (of medical treatment 醫療) that you choose to have; that is not urgent 可選擇的；非急需的 SYN **optional**：*elective surgery* 非急需施行的手術 **4** (of a course or subject 課程或科目) that a student can choose 可選擇的；選修的 SYN **optional**

■ ***noun*** (*especially NAmE*) a course or subject at a college or school which a student can choose to do 選修課程；選修科目

elect·or /ɪˈlektə(r)/ *noun* a person who has the right to vote in an election 有選舉權的人；選民

E

Synonyms 同義詞辨析

election

vote • poll • referendum • ballot

These are all words for an event in which people choose a representative or decide sth by voting. 以上各詞均表示選舉或投票表決。

election an occasion on which people officially choose a political representative or government by voting 指選舉、推選，尤指政治選舉：*Who did you vote for in the last election?* 上次選舉中你把票投給了誰？

vote an occasion on which a group of people vote for sb/sth 指投票、選舉、表決：*They took a vote on who should go first.* 他們以投票方式決定誰先走。

poll (*journalism*) the process of voting in an election（新聞）指選舉投票、計票：*They suffered a defeat **at the polls**.* 他們在投票選舉中慘遭失敗。

referendum an occasion on which all the adults in a country can vote on a particular issue 指全民投票、全民公決

ballot the system of voting by marking an election paper, especially in secret; an occasion on which a vote is held 尤指無記名投票選舉、投票表決：*The leader will be chosen by secret ballot.* 領導人將通過無記名投票選舉產生。NOTE **Ballot** is usually used about a vote within an organization rather than an occasion on which the public vote. * ballot 通常用於機構內部的選舉，而非公開的投票選舉。

PATTERNS

- a **national/local** election/vote/poll/referendum/ballot
- to **have/hold/conduct** a(n) election/vote/poll/referendum/ballot

elect·or·al /ɪ'lektərəl/ *adj.* [only before noun] connected with elections 有關選舉的：***electoral systems/reforms*** 選舉制度／改革 ▸ **elect·or·al·ly** /-rəli/ *adv.*：*an electorally effective campaign* 富有成效的競選運動

e,lectoral 'college *noun* **1 the Electoral College** (in the US) a group of people who come together to elect the President and Vice-President, based on the votes of people in each state 總統選舉團（在美國由各州總統選舉人推選組成，集中在一起選舉總統和副總統）**2** (*BrE*) a group of people who are chosen to represent the members of a political party, etc. in the election of a leader 領袖選舉團（經推選組成，代表政黨黨員選舉領導人）

e,lectoral 'register (also **e,lectoral 'roll**) *noun* (in Britain) the official list of people who have the right to vote in a particular area（英國）選民登記冊

elect·or·ate /ɪ'lektərət/ *noun* [C+sing./pl. v.] **1** the people in a country or an area who have the right to vote, thought of as a group（一國或一地區的）全體選民：*Only 60% of the electorate voted in the last election.* 上次選舉只有 60% 的選民參加了投票。➲ COLLOCATIONS at VOTE **2** (*AustralE, NZE*) = CONSTITUENCY (1)

elec·tric 0┳ /ɪ'lektrɪk/ *adj., noun*

■ ***adj.*** **1** 0┳ [usually before noun] connected with electricity; using, produced by or producing electricity 電的；用電的；電動的；發電的：*an electric motor* 電動機 ◇ *an **electric light/guitar, etc.*** 電燈、電吉他等 ◇ *an **electric current/charge*** 電流／荷 ◇ *an electric generator* 發電機 ◇ *an **electric plug/socket/switch*** (= that carries electricity) 電源插頭／插座／開關 ➲ see also ELECTRIC SHOCK, ELECTRICAL STORM **2** full of excitement; making people excited 充滿刺激的；令人激動的 SYN **electrifying**：*The atmosphere was electric.* 氣氛很熱烈。

■ ***noun*** [U] (*informal*) used to refer to the supply of electricity to a building 供電：*The electric will be off tomorrow.* 明天停電。◇ *I've paid the electric* (= the bill for the supply of electricity). 我已經付電費了。

Synonyms 同義詞辨析

electric / electrical

These adjectives are frequently used with the following nouns. 這兩個形容詞常與下列名詞連用：

electric ~	electrical ~
light	equipment
guitar	wiring
drill	signal
chair	engineer
shock	shock

■ **Electric** is usually used to describe something that uses or produces electricity. You use **electrical** with more general nouns such as *equipment* and *wiring* and things that are concerned with electricity. * electric 通常指使用或產生電力的。electrical 與更籠統的名詞如 equipment（電氣設備）和 wiring（供電線路），以及與電有關的事物搭配：*an electrical fault* 電故障 However, the distinction is not always so clear now. 不過現在兩者的區別並不總是如此明顯：*an electric/electrical company* 電力公司 ◇ *an electric/electrical current* 電流 ◇ *an electric/electrical shock* 觸電

elec·tric·al 0┳ /ɪ'lektrɪkl/ *adj.* connected with electricity; using or producing electricity 電的；用電的；發電的：*an electrical fault in the engine* 發動機的電力故障 ◇ ***electrical equipment/appliances*** 電氣設備；電器 ◇ ***electrical power/energy*** 電力；電能 ▸ **elec·tric·al·ly** /-kli/ *adv.*：*a car with electrically operated windows* 帶電動窗的汽車 ◇ *electrically charged particles* 帶電粒子

e,lectrical engi'neering *noun* [U] the design and building of machines and systems that use or produce electricity; the study of this subject 電機工程；電機工程學 ▸ **e,lectrical engi'neer** *noun*

e,lectrical 'storm (*BrE* also **e,lectric 'storm**) *noun* a violent storm in which electricity is produced in the atmosphere 電暴；雷暴

e,lectric 'blanket *noun* a BLANKET for a bed that is heated by electricity passing through the wires inside it (usually used under the bottom sheet of the bed) 電熱毯

e,lectric 'blue *noun* [U] a bright or METALLIC blue colour 鋼青色；鐵藍色

e,lectric 'chair (usually **the electric chair**) (also *informal* **the chair**) *noun* [sing.] (especially in the US) a chair in which criminals are killed by passing a powerful electric current through their bodies; the method of EXECUTION which uses this chair（尤指美國處決犯人的）電椅，電刑：*He was sent to the electric chair.* 他被送上電椅處決。◇ *They face death by the electric chair.* 他們面臨着被電刑處死。

e,lectric 'fence *noun* a wire fence through which an electric current can be passed 電籬笆；電鐵絲網

elec·tri·cian /ɪˌlek'trɪʃn/ *noun* a person whose job is to connect, repair, etc. electrical equipment 電工；電器技師

elec·tri·city 0┳ /ɪˌlek'trɪsəti/ *noun* **1** 0┳ [U] a form of energy from charged ELEMENTARY PARTICLES, usually supplied as electric current through cables, wires, etc. for lighting, heating, driving machines, etc. 電；電能：*a waste of electricity* 浪費電 ◇ *The electricity is off* (= there is no electric power supply). 停電了。**2** [U, sing.] a feeling of great emotion, excitement, etc. 強烈的感情；激動；興奮

e,lectric 'razor *noun* = SHAVER

elec·trics /ɪ'lektrɪks/ *noun* [pl.] (*BrE, informal*) the system of electrical wires in a house, car or machine（房屋、

汽車或機器的）電力系統，電路：*There's a problem with the electrics.* 電路有問題。

e,lectric 'shock (also **shock**) *noun* a sudden painful feeling that you get when electricity passes through your body 電休克；觸電；電擊

elec·tri·fi·ca·tion /ɪˌlektrɪfɪˈkeɪʃn/ *noun* [U] the process of changing sth so that it works by electricity 電氣化

elec·trify /ɪˈlektrɪfaɪ/ *verb* (**elec·tri·fies**, **elec·tri·fy·ing**, **elec·tri·fied**, **elec·tri·fied**) **1** [usually passive] **~ sth** to make sth work by using electricity; to pass an electrical current through sth 使電氣化；使通電；使帶電：*The railway line was electrified in the 1950s.* 這條鐵路線在 20 世紀 50 年代就以電力推動。◇ *He had all the fences around his home electrified.* 他把房子周圍的鐵絲網都通了電。 **2 ~ sb** to make sb feel very excited and enthusiastic about sth 使激動；使興奮：*Her performance electrified the audience.* 她的表演使觀眾興奮不已。

elec·tri·fy·ing /ɪˈlektrɪfaɪɪŋ/ *adj.* very exciting 令人激動的；使人興奮的：*The dancers gave an electrifying performance.* 舞蹈演員們的表演激動人心。

elec·tro- /ɪˈlektrəʊ; *NAmE* -troʊ/ *combining form* (in nouns, adjectives, verbs and adverbs 構成名詞、形容詞、動詞和副詞) connected with electricity 電的：*electromagnetism* 電磁

elec·tro·car·dio·gram /ɪˌlektrəʊˈkɑːdiəʊɡræm; *NAmE* ɪˌlektroʊˈkɑːrdioʊ-/ *noun* = ECG

elec·tro·con·vul·sive therapy /ɪˌlektrəʊkənˈvʌlsɪv θerəpi; *NAmE* -troʊ-/ (also **e'lec·tro·shock ther·apy**) *noun* [U] a medical treatment of mental illness that passes electricity through the patient's brain 電休克治療；電抽搐治療；電痙攣治療

elec·tro·cute /ɪˈlektrəkjuːt/ *verb* [usually passive] **~ sb** to injure or kill sb by passing electricity through their body 使觸電受傷（或死亡）；用電刑處死：*The boy was electrocuted when he wandered onto a railway track.* 那名男孩閒逛時踩到鐵軌上觸電死亡。◇ *He was electrocuted in Virginia in 2006* (= punished by being killed in the electric chair). 他於 2006 年在弗吉尼亞州被電刑處死。 ▸ **elec·tro·cu·tion** /ɪˌlektrəˈkjuːʃn/ *noun* [U]：*Six people were drowned; five died from electrocution.* 六人淹死，五人觸電身亡。◇ *He was sentenced to death by electrocution.* 他被判電刑處死。

elec·trode /ɪˈlektrəʊd; *NAmE* -troʊd/ *noun* either of two points (or TERMINALS) by which an electric current enters or leaves a battery or other electrical device 電極 ➲ see also ANODE, CATHODE

elec·tro·dynam·ics /ɪˌlektrəʊdaɪˈnæmɪks; *NAmE* -troʊ-/ *noun* [U] (*physics* 物) the study of the way that electric currents and MAGNETIC FIELDS affect each other 電動力學

elec·tro·enceph·alo·gram /ɪˌlektrəʊɪnˈsefələɡræm; -ˈkefələ-; *NAmE* -troʊɪnˈsef-/ *noun* = EEG

elec·troly·sis /ɪˌlekˈtrɒləsɪs; *NAmE* -ˈtrɑːl-/ *noun* [U] **1** the destruction of the roots of hairs by means of an electric current, as a beauty treatment 電解（除毛）術（美容方法） **2** (*chemistry* 化) the separation of a liquid (or electrolyte) into its chemical parts by passing an electric current through it 電解

elec·tro·lyte /ɪˈlektrəlaɪt/ *noun* (*chemistry* 化) a liquid that an electric current can pass through, especially in an electric cell or battery 電解液；電解質 ▸ **elec·tro·ly·tic** /ɪˌlektrəˈlɪtɪk/ *adj.*

elec·tro·mag·net /ɪˈlektrəʊmæɡnət; *NAmE* -troʊ-/ *noun* (*physics* 物) a piece of metal which becomes MAGNETIC when electricity is passed through it 電磁體

elec·tro·mag·net·ic /ɪˌlektrəʊmæɡˈnetɪk; *NAmE* -troʊ-/ *adj.* (*physics* 物) having both electrical and MAGNETIC characteristics (or PROPERTIES) 電磁的：*an electromagnetic wave/field* 電磁波 / 場

elec·tro·mag·net·ism /ɪˌlektrəʊˈmæɡnətɪzəm; *NAmE* -troʊ-/ *noun* [U] (*physics* 物) the production of a MAGNETIC FIELD by means of an electric current, or of an electric current by means of a MAGNETIC FIELD 電磁

elec·tron /ɪˈlektrɒn; *NAmE* -trɑːn/ *noun* (*physics* 物) a very small piece of matter (= a substance) with a negative electric charge, found in all atoms 電子 ➲ see also NEUTRON, PROTON

elec·tron·ic 🔑 /ɪˌlekˈtrɒnɪk; *NAmE* -ˈtrɑːnɪk/ *adj.* [usually before noun]
1 🔑 (of a device 裝置) having or using many small parts, such as MICROCHIPS, that control and direct a small electric current 電子的；電子器件的：*an electronic calculator* 電子計算器 ◇ *electronic music* 電子音樂 ◇ *This dictionary is available in electronic form.* 本詞典有電子版本。 **2** 🔑 concerned with electronic equipment 電子設備的；電子器件的：*an electronic engineer* 電子工程師

elec·tron·ic·al·ly /ɪˌlekˈtrɒnɪkli; *NAmE* -ˈtrɑːn-/ *adv.* in an electronic way, or using a device that works in an electronic way 用電子方法；用電子裝置：*to process data electronically* (= using a computer) 進行電子數據處理

ˌelectronic ˈmail *noun* [U] (*formal*) = EMAIL *n.* (1)

ˌelectronic ˈorganizer *noun* a very small computer which can be carried around, used for storing information such as addresses and important dates 電子記事簿

ˌelectronic ˈpublishing *noun* [U] the business of publishing books in a form that can be read on a computer, for example as CD-ROMs 電子出版

elec·tron·ics /ɪˌlekˈtrɒnɪks; *NAmE* -ˈtrɑːn-/ *noun* **1** [U] the branch of science and technology that studies electric currents in electronic equipment 電子學 **2** [U] the use of electronic technology, especially in developing new equipment 電子技術的應用：*the electronics industry* 電子工業 **3 electronics** [pl.] the electronic CIRCUITS and COMPONENTS (= parts) used in electronic equipment 電子電路；電子器件：*a fault in the electronics* 電子電路故障

elecˌtronic ˈtagging *noun* [U] the system of attaching an electronic device to a person so that the police, etc. know where the person is 電子標識跟踪系統（附於人體，以便警方等知道其行踪）

eˌlectron ˈmicroscope *noun* a very powerful MICROSCOPE that uses ELECTRONS instead of light 電子顯微鏡

elec·tro·plate /ɪˈlektrəpleɪt/ *verb* [usually passive] **~ sth** to cover sth with a thin layer of metal using ELECTROLYSIS 電鍍

elec·tro·shock ther·apy /ɪˈlektrəʊʃɒk θerəpi; *NAmE* -troʊʃɑːk/ *noun* = ELECTROCONVULSIVE THERAPY

elec·tro·stat·ic /ɪˌlektrəʊˈstætɪk; *NAmE* -troʊ-/ *adj.* (*physics* 物) used to talk about electric charges that are not moving, rather than electric currents 靜電的

ele·gant 🔑 /ˈelɪɡənt/ *adj.*
1 🔑 (of people or their behaviour 人或其舉止) attractive and showing a good sense of style 優美的；文雅的 **SYN** **stylish**：*She was tall and elegant.* 她身材修長，優雅大方。 **2** 🔑 (of clothes, places and things 衣服、地方和物品) attractive and designed well 漂亮雅致的；陳設講究的；精美的 **SYN** **stylish**：*an elegant dress* 高雅的連衣裙 ◇ *an elegant room/restaurant* 雅致的房間 / 餐廳 **3** (of a plan or an idea 計劃或想法) clever but simple 簡煉的；簡潔的；簡明的：*an elegant solution to the problem* 解決這個問題的簡要方法 ▸ **ele·gance** /ˈelɪɡəns/ *noun* [U]：*She dresses with casual elegance.* 她的穿着隨意而不失雅致。◇ *His writing combines elegance and wit.* 他的文章典雅而風趣。 **ele·gant·ly** *adv.*：*elegantly dressed* 穿着考究 ◇ *elegantly furnished* 佈置精美

ele·giac /ˌelɪˈdʒaɪək/ *adj.* (*formal* or *literary*) expressing sadness, especially about the past or people who have died 輓歌的；哀悼的；傷感的

elegy /ˈelədʒi/ *noun* (*pl.* **-ies**) a poem or song that expresses sadness, especially for sb who has died 輓詩；輓歌；哀歌

elem·ent 🔑 **AW** /ˈelɪmənt/ *noun*
▸ **PART/AMOUNT** 部份；數量 **1** 🔑 [C] **~ (in/of sth)** a necessary or typical part of sth 要素；基本部份；典型部份：*Cost was a* **key element** *in our decision.* 成本是我們決策時考慮的一個重要因素。◇ *The story has all the*

E

elements of a soap opera. 這個故事有肥皂劇的所有要素。◇ Customer relations is an important element of the job. 與客戶的關係是這個工作的重要部份。 **2** [C, usually sing.] **~ of surprise, risk, truth, etc.** a small amount of a quality or feeling 少量；有點；有些： *We need to preserve the element of surprise.* 我們得保留一些使人感到意外的東西。◇ *There appears to be an element of truth in his story.* 他的話似乎有點事實根據。
▸ GROUP OF PEOPLE 集團 **3** [C, usually pl.] a group of people who form a part of a larger group or society（大團體或社會中的）一組，一群，一夥： ***moderate/radical** elements within the party* 黨內的溫和派 / 激進派 ◇ *unruly elements in the school* 學校裏難管教的人
▸ CHEMISTRY 化學 **4** [C] a simple chemical substance that consists of atoms of only one type and cannot be split by chemical means into a simpler substance. Gold, OXYGEN and CARBON are all elements. 元素（如金、氧、碳）➲ compare COMPOUND *n.* (2)
▸ EARTH/AIR/FIRE/WATER 土；空氣；火；水 **5** [C] one of the four substances: earth, air, fire and water, which people used to believe everything else was made of 要素（舊時認為土、空氣、火和水是構成一切物質的四大要素）
▸ WEATHER 天氣 **6 the elements** [pl.] the weather, especially bad weather（尤指惡劣的）天氣： *Are we going to brave the elements and go for a walk?* 我們要冒着風雨去散步嗎？◇ *to be exposed to the elements* 經受風吹雨打
▸ BASIC PRINCIPLES 基本原理 **7 elements** [pl.] the basic principles of a subject that you have to learn first（學科的）基本原理，基礎，綱要 SYN **basics**： *He taught me the elements of map-reading.* 他教我看地圖的基本方法。
▸ ENVIRONMENT 環境 **8** [C, usually sing.] a natural or suitable environment, especially for an animal（尤指動物的）自然環境，適宜的環境： *Water is a fish's natural element.* 水是魚的天然生活環境。
▸ ELECTRICAL PART 電器元件 **9** [C] the part of a piece of electrical equipment that gives out heat 電熱元件；電熱絲： *The kettle needs a new element.* 這個電壺需要一根新電熱絲。
IDM **in your 'element** doing what you are good at and enjoy 如魚得水；得心應手： *She's really in her element at parties.* 她在社交聚會上真是如魚得水。 **out of your 'element** in a situation that you are not used to and that makes you feel uncomfortable 處於不適宜的環境；不得其所

elem·en·tal /ˌelɪˈmentl/ *adj.* [usually before noun] (*formal*) **1** wild and powerful; like the forces of nature 狂暴的；猛烈的；似自然力的： *the elemental fury of the storm* 暴風雨的肆虐 **2** basic and important 基本的；主要的；重要的： *an elemental truth* 基本事實

elem·en·tary /ˌelɪˈmentri/ *adj.* **1** in or connected with the first stages of a course of study 初級的；基礎的： *an elementary English course* 基礎英語課程 ◇ *a book for elementary students* 初學者課本 ◇ *at an elementary level* 處於初級水平 ➲ compare PRIMARY *adj.* (3), SECONDARY (3) **2** of the most basic kind 基本的： *the elementary laws of economics* 基本經濟法則 ◇ *an elementary mistake* 基本錯誤 **3** very simple and easy 簡單的；容易的： *elementary questions* 簡單的問題

ˌelementary 'particle *noun* (*physics* 物) any of the different types of very small pieces of matter (= a substance) smaller than an atom 基本粒子

ˌele'mentary school (also *informal* **'grade school**) *noun* (in the US) a school for children between the ages of about 6 and 12（美國）小學

ele·phant /ˈelɪfənt/ *noun* a very large animal with thick grey skin, large ears, two curved outer teeth called TUSKS and a long nose called a TRUNK. There are two types of elephant, the African and the Asian. 象： *herds of elephants/elephant herds* 象群 ◇ *a baby elephant* 幼象 ➲ see also WHITE ELEPHANT
IDM **the ˌelephant in the 'room** a problem or question that everyone knows about but does not mention because it is easier not to discuss it 明擺着的難題；眾所周知卻避而不談的事： *The elephant in the room was the money that had to be paid in bribes.* 難題明擺着，就是要付賄款。

ele·phant·ia·sis /ˌelɪfənˈtaɪəsɪs/ *noun* [U] (*medical* 醫) a condition in which part of the body swells and becomes very large because the LYMPHATIC system is blocked 象皮病（因淋巴系統阻塞而引起的身體腫脹）

ele·phant·ine /ˌelɪˈfæntaɪn; *NAmE* -tiːn/ *adj.* (*formal* or *humorous*) very large and CLUMSY; like an elephant 龐大的；笨重的；似象一樣的

ele·vate /ˈelɪveɪt/ *verb* **1** (*formal*) to give sb/sth a higher position or rank, often more important than they deserve 提拔，晉升，提升（到不應有的位置）SYN **raise, promote**： **~ sb/sth (to sth)** *He elevated many of his friends to powerful positions within the government.* 他將許多朋友都提拔到政府部門的要職上。◇ **~ sth (into sth)** *It was an attempt to elevate football to a subject worthy of serious study.* 這是試圖將足球拔高成一門學科來進行嚴肅的研究。 **2 ~ sth** (*technical* 術語 or *formal*) to lift sth up or put sth in a higher position 舉起；抬起： *It is important that the injured leg should be elevated.* 將受傷的腿抬高是很重要的。 **3 ~ sth** (*technical* 術語) to make the level of sth increase 提高；使升高： *Smoking often elevates blood pressure.* 抽煙常常使血壓升高。 **4 ~ sth** (*formal*) to improve a person's mood, so that they feel happy 使情緒高昂；使精神振奮；使興高采烈： *The song never failed to elevate his spirits.* 這首歌總使他精神振奮。

ele·vated /ˈelɪveɪtɪd/ *adj.* [usually before noun] **1** high in rank 高貴的；職位高的： *an elevated status* 高貴的身分 **2** (*formal*) having a high moral or INTELLECTUAL level 高尚的；睿智的： *elevated language/sentiments/thoughts* 高尚的語言 / 情操 / 思想 **3** higher than the area around; above the level of the ground 高的；升高的；高出地面的： *The house is in an elevated position, overlooking the town.* 這棟房子地勢較高，可以俯瞰全鎮。◇ *an **elevated highway/railway/road*** (= one that runs on a bridge above the ground or street) 高架公路 / 鐵路 / 道路 **4** (*technical* 術語) higher than normal 偏高的： *elevated blood pressure* 血壓偏高

ele·vat·ing /ˈelɪveɪtɪŋ/ *adj.* making people think about serious and interesting subjects 發人深思的；有啟發的；有趣的： *Reading this essay was an elevating experience.* 閱讀這篇短文很有啟發。

ele·va·tion /ˌelɪˈveɪʃn/ *noun* **1** [U] (*formal*) the process of sb getting a higher or more important rank 提拔；晉級；提升： *his elevation to the presidency* 他提升到主席的職位 **2** [C, usually sing.] (*technical* 術語) the height of a place, especially its height above sea level（某地方的）高度；（尤指）海拔： *The city is at an elevation of 2 000 metres.* 這座城市海拔 2 000 米。 **3** [C] (*formal*) a piece of ground that is higher than the area around 高地；高處 **4** [C] (*architecture* 建) one side of a building, or a drawing of this by an ARCHITECT（建築物的）立面圖，立視圖： *the **front/rear/side elevation** of a house* 房子的正面 / 後面 / 側面立視圖 ➲ compare PLAN *n.* (4) **5** [U, sing.] (*technical* 術語) an increase in the level or amount of sth（水平或數量的）提高，升高，增加： *elevation of blood sugar levels* 血糖升高

ele·va·tor /ˈelɪveɪtə(r)/ *noun* **1** (*NAmE*) (*BrE* **lift**) a machine that carries people or goods up and down to different levels in a building or a mine 電梯；升降機： *It's on the fifth floor, so we'd better take the elevator.* 那是在六樓上，我們最好乘電梯。 **2** a place for storing large quantities of grain 穀倉；糧倉 **3** a part in the tail of an aircraft that is moved to make it go up and down（飛行器的）升降舵 ➲ VISUAL VOCAB page V53

eleven /ɪˈlevn/ **1** *number* 11 十一 **2** *noun* a team of eleven players for football (SOCCER), CRICKET or HOCKEY（足球、板球或曲棍球）十一人隊： *She was chosen for the first eleven.* 她被選派首發上場。 ▸ **elev·enth** /ɪˈlevnθ/ *ordinal number, noun* HELP There are examples of how to use ordinal numbers at the entry for **fifth**. 序數詞用法示例見 fifth 條。
IDM **at the eˌleventh 'hour** at the last possible moment; just in time 在最後時刻；剛好來得及

e͵leven-ˈplus *noun* (usually **the eleven-plus**) [sing.] an exam that all children used to take in Britain at the age of eleven to decide which type of SECONDARY SCHOOL they should go to. It is still taken in a few areas. 十一歲兒童入學考試（英國舊時舉行的升中學甄別考試，現仍在少數地區實行）

elev·enses /ɪˈlevnzɪz/ *noun* [U] (*old-fashioned, BrE, informal*) a very small meal, for example biscuits with tea or coffee, that people sometimes have at about eleven o'clock in the morning（上午十一時左右吃的）午前茶點

ELF /elf/ *abbr.* (*linguistics* 語言) English as a lingua franca 作為共同語言的英語；通用英語

elf /elf/ *noun* (*pl.* **elves** /elvz/) (in stories) a creature like a small person with pointed ears, who has magic powers（故事中的）精靈，小妖精

elfin /ˈelfɪn/ *adj.* (of a person or their features 人或容貌) small and delicate 小巧玲瓏的：*an elfin face* 小巧清秀的臉龐

elicit /iˈlɪsɪt/ *verb* **~ sth (from sb)** (*formal*) to get information or a reaction from sb, often with difficulty 引出；探出；誘出：*I could elicit no response from him.* 我從他那裏套不出任何反應。◇ *Her tears elicited great sympathy from her audience.* 她的眼淚博得觀眾的無限同情。▸ **elicit·ation** /i͵lɪsɪˈteɪʃn/ *noun* [U]

elide /iˈlaɪd/ *verb* **~ sth** (*phonetics* 語音) to leave out the sound of part of a word when you are pronouncing it 省略（詞的部份）發音：*The 't' in 'often' may be elided.* * often 中的 t 可以不發音。➲ see also ELISION

eli·gible /ˈelɪdʒəbl/ *adj.* **1** a person who is **eligible** for sth or to do sth, is able to have or do it because they have the right qualifications, are the right age, etc. 有資格的；合格的；具備條件的：**~ (for sth)** *Only those over 70 are eligible for the special payment.* 只有 70 歲以上的人才有資格領取這項專款。◇ **~ (to do sth)** *When are you eligible to vote in your country?* 在你們國家幾歲才有資格投票選舉呢？ **OPP** **ineligible** **2** an **eligible** young man or woman is thought to be a good choice as a husband/wife, usually because they are rich or attractive（指認為可做夫妻的男女）合意的，合適的，中意的 ▸ **eli·gi·bil·ity** /͵elɪdʒəˈbɪləti/ *noun* [U]

elim·in·ate **AW** /ɪˈlɪmɪneɪt/ *verb* **1** to remove or get rid of sth/sb 排除；清除；消除：**~ sth/sb** *Credit cards eliminate the need to carry a lot of cash.* 有了信用卡就用不着攜帶很多現金。◇ **~ sth/sb from sth** *The police have eliminated two suspects from their investigation.* 警方通過調查已經排除了兩名嫌疑犯。◇ *This diet claims to eliminate toxins from the body.* 這種飲食據稱具有排除體內毒素的作用。**2 ~ sb (from sth)** [usually passive] to defeat a person or a team so that they no longer take part in a competition, etc.（比賽中）淘汰 **SYN** **knock out**：*All the English teams were eliminated in the early stages of the competition.* 所有英國隊伍在比賽初期就被淘汰了。**3 ~ sb** (*formal*) to kill sb, especially an enemy or opponent 消滅，殺死（尤指敵人或對手）：*Most of the regime's left-wing opponents were eliminated.* 這個政權的左翼反對派多數已被除掉。▸ **elim·in·ation** **AW** /ɪ͵lɪmɪˈneɪʃn/ *noun* [U, C]：*the **elimination of disease/poverty/crime*** 消除疾病 / 貧困 / 犯罪 ◇ *There were three eliminations in the first round of the competition.* 比賽第一輪淘汰了三個隊。◇ *the elimination of toxins from the body* 排除體內毒素

e͵limiˈnation reaction *noun* (*chemistry* 化) a chemical reaction which involves the separation of a substance from other substances 消除反應（一種物質從其他物質分離的化學反應）

eli·sion /ɪˈlɪʒn/ *noun* [U, C] (*phonetics* 語音) the act of leaving out the sound of part of a word when you are pronouncing it, as in *we'll, don't* and *let's* 省音，省略部份讀音（如 we'll、don't 和 let's）➲ see also ELIDE

elite /eɪˈliːt; ɪˈliːt/ *noun* [C+sing./pl. v.] a group of people in a society, etc. who are powerful and have a lot of influence, because they are rich, intelligent, etc. 上層集團；（統稱）掌權人物，社會精英：*a member of the **ruling/intellectual elite*** 上層統治集團的成員；知識界的精英 ◇ *Public opinion is influenced by the small elite who control the media.* 輿論為少數控制着新聞媒介的上層人士所左右。◇ *In these countries, only the elite can afford an education for their children.* 在這些國家裏，只有上層人士才供得起子女上學。▸ **elite** *adj.* [only before noun]：*an elite group of senior officials* 一批出類拔萃的高級官員 ◇ *an elite military academy* 精英官事學院

elit·ism /eɪˈliːtɪzəm; ɪ-/ *noun* [U] (often *disapproving*) **1** a way of organizing a system, society, etc. so that only a few people (= an elite) have power or influence 精英統治；精英主義：*Many people believe that private education encourages elitism.* 許多人認為私立教育助長精英主義。**2** the feeling of being better than other people that being part of an elite encourages 高人一等的優越感 ▸ **elit·ist** *adj.*：*an elitist model of society* 精英統治的社會模式 ◇ *She accused him of being elitist.* 她指責他自以為高人一等。 **elit·ist** *noun*

elixir /ɪˈlɪksə(r); *BrE* also -sɪə(r)/ *noun* (*literary*) a magic liquid that is believed to cure illnesses or to make people live for ever 聖水；靈丹妙藥；長生不老藥：*the **elixir of life/youth*** 長生不老 / 永葆青春藥

Eliza·bethan /ɪ͵lɪzəˈbiːθn/ *adj.* connected with the time when Queen Elizabeth I was queen of England (1558–1603) 伊麗莎白女王一世時代的 ▸ **Eliza·bethan** *noun*：*Shakespeare was an Elizabethan.* 莎士比亞是伊麗莎白女王一世時代的人。

elk (*BrE*) **moose** (*NAmE*) 駝鹿

wapiti (*NAmE also* **elk**) 美洲赤鹿

elk /elk/ *noun* (*pl.* **elk** or **elks**) **1** (*BrE*) a large DEER that lives in the north of Europe, Asia and N America. In N America it is called a MOOSE. 駝鹿，麋鹿（生活於北歐、亞洲和北美洲，北美洲稱 moose） **2** (*NAmE*) = WAPITI **3** **Elk** a member of the Benevolent and Protective Order of Elks, a US social organization that gives money to charity（美國）厄爾克思慈善互助會會員（捐款給慈善機構）

ell /el/ *noun* a unit used in the past for measuring cloth, equal to about 45 inches or 115 centimetres 埃爾（舊時量布的長度單位，相當於大約 45 英寸或 115 厘米）

el·lipse /ɪˈlɪps/ *noun* (*technical* 術語) a regular OVAL shape, like a circle that has been squeezed on two sides 橢圓 ➲ VISUAL VOCAB page V71

el·lip·sis /ɪˈlɪpsɪs/ *noun* (*pl.* **el·lip·ses** /-siːz/) [C, U] **1** (*grammar* 語法) the act of leaving out a word or words from a sentence deliberately, when the meaning can be understood without them（詞在句子中的）省略 **2** three dots (...) used to show that a word or words have been left out 省略號

el·lip·tic·al /ɪˈlɪptɪkl/ *adj.* **1** (*grammar* 語法) with a word or words left out of a sentence deliberately 省略的；隱晦的：*an elliptical remark* (= one that suggests more than is actually said) 隱晦的話 **2** (also *less frequent* **el·lip·tic** /ɪˈlɪptɪk/) (*geometry* 幾何) connected with or in the form of an ELLIPSE 橢圓的；橢圓形的 ▸ **el·lip·tic·al·ly**

/-kli/ *adv.* : *to speak/write elliptically* 說得 / 寫得晦澀難懂

Ellis Island /ˌelɪs ˈaɪlənd/ *noun* a small island near New York City that from 1892 to 1943 was the official place of entry for people coming to live in the US from other countries 埃利斯島（美國紐約市附近的小島，1892 至 1943 年間是美國的移民檢查站）

elm /elm/ *noun* **1** [C, U] (also **'elm tree**) a tall tree with broad leaves 榆樹 : *a line of stately elms* 一排雄偉壯觀的榆樹 ◇ *The hedgerows were planted with elm.* 這一排排樹籬是用榆樹植成的。 **2** [U] the hard wood of the elm tree 榆木

E

El Niño /ˌel ˈniːnjəʊ; NAmE -joʊ/ *noun* [U] a set of changes in the weather system near the coast of northern Peru and Ecuador that happens every few years, causing the surface of the Pacific Ocean there to become warmer and having severe effects on the weather in many parts of the world 厄爾尼諾現象，聖嬰現象（南美洲西海岸每隔數年一次海溫升高的現象，導致太平洋水溫上升，嚴重影響全球多處氣候） ⮌ compare LA NIÑA

elo·cu·tion /ˌeləˈkjuːʃn/ *noun* [U] the ability to speak clearly and correctly, especially in public and pronouncing the words in a way that is considered to be socially acceptable 演講技巧；演說術

elong·ate /ˈiːlɒŋɡeɪt; NAmE ɪˈlɔːŋ-; ɪˈlɑːŋ-/ *verb* [I, T] **~ (sth)** to become longer; to make sth longer（使）變長，伸長；拉長 **SYN** **lengthen** ▸ **elonga·tion** /ˌiːlɒŋˈɡeɪʃn; NAmE ˌiːlɔːŋ-; ˌiːlɑːŋ-/ *noun* [U] : *the elongation of vowel sounds* 元音拖長

elong·ated /ˈiːlɒŋɡeɪtɪd; NAmE ɪˈlɔːŋ-; ɪˈlɑːŋ-/ *adj.* long and thin, often in a way that is not normal 細長的；拉得又細又長的 : *Modigliani's women have strangely elongated faces.* 莫迪里阿尼畫中的婦女都長着奇長無比的臉。

elope /ɪˈləʊp; NAmE ɪˈloʊp/ *verb* [I] **~ (with sb)** to run away with sb in order to marry them secretly 私奔 ▸ **elope·ment** /ɪˈləʊpmənt; NAmE ɪˈloʊp-/ *noun* [C, U]

elo·quent /ˈeləkwənt/ *adj.* **1** able to use language and express your opinions well, especially when you are speaking in public 雄辯的；有口才的；流利的 : *an **eloquent speech/speaker*** 雄辯的演講 / 演講人 **2** (of a look or movement 表情或動作) able to express a feeling 傳神的 : *His eyes were eloquent.* 他的眼睛很傳神。 ▸ **elo·quence** /ˈeləkwəns/ *noun* [U] : *a speech of passionate eloquence* 熱情洋溢的演講 ◇ *the eloquence of his smile* 他意味深長的微笑 **elo·quent·ly** *adv.* : *She spoke eloquently on the subject.* 她講起這個題目來滔滔不絕。 ◇ *His face expressed his grief more eloquently than any words.* 他那張臉比任何言語都更清楚地表達了他的憂傷。

else 🔑 /els/ *adv.*
(used in questions or after *nothing, nobody, something, anything*, etc. 用於疑問句或 nothing、nobody、something、anything 等之後) **1** 🔑 in addition to sth already mentioned 其他的；別的 : *What else did he say?* 他還說了些什麼？ ◇ *I don't want anything else, thanks.* 我不要別的東西了，謝謝。 ◇ *I'm taking a few clothes and some books, not much else.* 我帶了幾件衣服和一些書，別的就不多了。 **2** 🔑 different 另外的；不同的 : *Ask somebody else to help you.* 另請個人來幫幫你吧。 ◇ *Haven't you got anything else to wear?* 你沒有其他穿的了嗎？ ◇ *Why didn't you come? Everybody else was there.* 你為什麼沒來呢？其他所有的人都來了。 ◇ *Yes I did give it to her. What else could I do?* 是的，我的確給她了。我還能怎麼辦呢？

IDM **or else 1** 🔑 if not 要不然；否則 **SYN** **otherwise** : *Hurry up or else you'll be late.* 快點，否則你就要遲到了。 ◇ *They can't be coming or else they'd have called.* 他們不會來，不然他們就打電話了。 **2** 🔑 used to introduce the second of two possibilities（表示另一種可能）或者，也許 : *He either forgot or else decided not to come.* 他或許忘了，或許決定不來。 **3** (*informal*) used to threaten or warn sb（威脅或警告）否則的話，要不然的話 : *Just shut up, or else!* 住口，不然的話，哼！

else·where 🔑 /ˌelsˈweə(r); NAmE -ˈwer/ *adv.*
in, at or to another place 在（或去、到）別處 : *The answer to the problem must be sought elsewhere.* 這個問題的答案必須在別處尋找。 ◇ *Our favourite restaurant was closed, so we had to go elsewhere.* 我們最喜歡的餐館已關門了，所以我們只好到別處去。 ◇ *Elsewhere, the weather today has been fairly sunny.* 今天其他地方的天氣都比較晴朗。 ◇ *Prices are higher here than elsewhere.* 這裏的價格比其他地方高。

ELT /ˌiː el ˈtiː/ *abbr.* (*BrE*) English Language Teaching (the teaching of English to people for whom it is not the first language)（對英語為非第一語言者的）英語教學

elu·ci·date /iˈluːsɪdeɪt/ *verb* [T, I] (*formal*) to make sth clearer by explaining it more fully 闡明；解釋；說明 **SYN** **explain** : **~ (sth)** *He elucidated a point of grammar.* 他解釋了一個語法要點。 ◇ *Let me elucidate.* 讓我來說明一下吧。 ◇ **~ what, how, etc. …** *I will try to elucidate what I think the problems are.* 我將盡力闡明我認為問題的所在。 ▸ **elu·ci·da·tion** /iˌluːsɪˈdeɪʃn/ *noun* [U, C] : *Their objectives and methods require further elucidation.* 他們的目標和方法都需要進一步闡明。

elude /iˈluːd/ *verb* **1 ~ sb/sth** to manage to avoid or escape from sb/sth, especially in a clever way（尤指機敏地）避開，逃避，躲避 : *The two men managed to elude the police for six weeks.* 這兩個男人想方設法逃避警方追捕達六個星期。 **2 ~ sb** if sth **eludes** you, you are not able to achieve it, or not able to remember or understand it 使達不到；使不記得；使不理解 : *He was extremely tired but sleep eluded him.* 他累極了，卻睡不着。 ◇ *They're a popular band but chart success has eluded them so far.* 他們是一支很受歡迎的樂隊，但到目前為止還未能在流行唱片榜上取得佳績。 ◇ *Finally he remembered the tiny detail that had eluded him the night before.* 他終於想起了前一天晚上想不起來的細節。

elu·sive /iˈluːsɪv/ *adj.* difficult to find, define, or achieve 難找的；難以解釋的；難以達到的 : *Eric, as elusive as ever, was nowhere to be found.* 埃里克神出鬼沒，哪兒也找不着。 ◇ *the elusive concept of 'literature'* "文學"這一難以解釋的概念 ◇ *A solution to the problem of toxic waste is **proving elusive**.* 有毒廢料這個問題日見難以解決。 ▸ **elu·sive·ly** *adv.* **elu·sive·ness** *noun* [U]

elver /ˈelvə(r)/ *noun* a young EEL 幼鰻

elves *pl.* of ELF

Elys·ian /ɪˈlɪziən; NAmE ɪˈliːʒən/ *adj.* (*literary*) relating to heaven or to a place of perfect happiness 埃律西昂的；樂園的

IDM **the ˌElysian ˈFields** (in ancient Greek stories 古希臘傳說) a wonderful place where some people were taken by the gods after death 埃律西昂田野，埃律西昂（獲得不朽生命者所去的樂園）

em- ⮌ EN-

'em /əm/ *pron.* (*informal*) = THEM : *Don't let 'em get away.* 別讓他們跑掉。

ema·ci·ated /ɪˈmeɪʃieɪtɪd; ɪˈmeɪs-/ *adj.* thin and weak, usually because of illness or lack of food（常指因疾病或缺少食物而）消瘦的，憔悴的，虛弱的 ▸ **ema·ci·ation** /ɪˌmeɪsiˈeɪʃn/ *noun* [U] : *She was very thin, almost to the point of emaciation.* 她很瘦，幾乎到了憔悴的地步。

email 🔑 (also **e-mail**) /ˈiːmeɪl/ *noun, verb*
■ *noun* **1** 🔑 (also *formal* **ˌelectronic ˈmail**) [U] a way of sending messages and data to other people by means of computers connected together in a network 電子郵件（通信方式）: *to send a message by email* 以電郵發送一條信息 **2** 🔑 [C, U] a message sent by email 電子郵件 ⮌ WRITING TUTOR page WT40
■ *verb* 🔑 [T, I] to send a message to sb by email（給…）發電子郵件；用電郵發送 : **~ (sb)** *Patrick emailed me yesterday.* 帕特里克昨天給我發電郵了。 ◇ **~ sth (to sb)** *I'll email the documents to her.* 我將用電郵把這些文件發送給她。 ◇ **~ sb sth** *I'll email her the documents.* 我將用電郵把這些文件發送給她。

em·an·ate /ˈeməneɪt/ *verb* **~ sth** (*formal*) to produce or show sth 產生；表現；顯示 : *He emanates power and confidence.* 他表現出力量和信心。 ▸ **em·an·ation** /ˌeməˈneɪʃn/ *noun* [C, U]

PHR V **ˈemanate from sth** to come from sth or somewhere 發源於；從…發出 **SYN** **issue from**：*The sound of loud music emanated from the building.* 喧鬧的音樂聲是從那棟樓房裏傳出來的。◇ *The proposal originally emanated from the UN.* 這個建議最初是由聯合國提出的。

eman·ci·pate /ɪˈmænsɪpeɪt/ *verb* [often passive] **~ sb (from sth)** (*formal*) to free sb, especially from legal, political or social restrictions 解放；使不受（法律、政治或社會的）束縛 **SYN** **set free**：*Slaves were not emancipated until 1863 in the United States.* 美國奴隸直到 1863 年才獲得自由。▶ **eman·ci·pated** *adj.*：*Are women now fully emancipated* (= with the same rights and opportunities as men)? 現在女性已經徹底解放了嗎？◇ *an emancipated young woman* (= one with modern ideas about women's place in society) 一位思想解放的年輕女士 **eman·ci·pa·tion** /ɪˌmænsɪˈpeɪʃn/ *noun* [U]：*the emancipation of slaves* 奴隸的解放

emas·cu·late /iˈmæskjuleɪt/ *verb* [often passive] (*formal*) **1 ~ sb/sth** to make sb/sth less powerful or less effective 削弱；使無力；使失去效力 **2 ~ sb** to make a man feel that he has lost his male role or qualities 使（男人）柔弱；使無男子氣 ▶ **emas·cu·la·tion** /iˌmæskjuˈleɪʃn/ *noun* [U]

em·balm /ɪmˈbɑːm/ *verb* **~ sth** to prevent a dead body from decaying by treating it with special substances to preserve it 對（屍體）進行防腐處理 ▶ **em·balm·er** /ɪmˈbɑːmə(r)/ *noun*

em·bank·ment /ɪmˈbæŋkmənt/ *noun* **1** a wall of stone or earth made to keep water back or to carry a road or railway/railroad over low ground 堤；堤岸；堤圍；（公路或鐵路）路堤 **2** a slope made of earth or stone that rises up from either side of a road or railway/railroad（公路或鐵路兩側的）護坡

em·bargo /ɪmˈbɑːɡəʊ; *NAmE* ɪmˈbɑːrɡoʊ/ *noun, verb*

■ ***noun*** (*pl.* -oes) an official order that bans trade with another country 禁止貿易令；禁運 **SYN** **boycott**：*an **arms embargo*** 武器禁運 ◇ **~ (on sth)** *an embargo on arms sales to certain countries* 禁止向某些國家出售武器的法令 ◇ *a **trade embargo** against certain countries* 對某些國家的貿易禁運 ◇ *to **impose/enforce/lift an embargo*** 實行／實施／取消貿易禁令 ➲ COLLOCATIONS at INTERNATIONAL

■ ***verb*** (em·bar·goes, em·bargo·ing, em·bar·goed, em·bar·goed) **~ sth** to place an embargo on sth 禁止…的貿易；禁運 **SYN** **boycott**：*There have been calls to embargo all arms shipments to the region.* 曾有人呼籲禁止所有武器運往這個地區。

em·bark /ɪmˈbɑːk; *NAmE* ɪmˈbɑːrk/ *verb* [I, T] (*formal*) to get onto a ship; to put sth onto a ship 上船；裝船：*We stood on the pier and watched as they embarked.* 我們站在突碼頭上目送他們登船。◇ **~ sb/sth** *They embarked the troops by night.* 他們讓部隊在夜晚之前上了船。**OPP** **disembark** ▶ **em·bark·ation** /ˌembɑːˈkeɪʃn/ *noun* [U, C]：*Embarkation will be at 14:20 hours.* 上船時間是 14:20。

PHR V **emˈbark on/upon sth** (*formal*) to start to do sth new or difficult 從事，着手，開始（新的或艱難的事情）：*She is about to embark on a diplomatic career.* 她即將開始外交生涯。

em·bar·rass 0-ᴡ /ɪmˈbærəs/ *verb*

1 0-ᴡ to make sb feel shy, awkward or ashamed, especially in a social situation（尤指在社交場合）使窘迫，使尷尬：**~ sb** *Her questions about my private life embarrassed me.* 她詢問我的私生活使我感到很尷尬。◇ *I didn't want to embarrass him by kissing him in front of his friends.* 我並不想當着他的朋友吻他而使他感到難堪。◇ **it embarrasses sb to do sth** *It embarrassed her to meet strange men in the corridor at night.* 夜裏在走廊上遇見陌生男人使她感到很不好意思。**2** 0-ᴡ **~ sb** to cause problems or difficulties for sb 使困惑；使為難；使陷入困境：*The*

Collocations 詞語搭配

Email and the Internet 電子郵件和互聯網

Email 電子郵件

- **receive/get/open** an email 收到／打開電郵
- **write/send/answer/forward/delete** an email 寫／發送／回覆／轉發／刪除電郵
- **check/read/access** your email 查收／閱讀／讀取電郵
- **block/filter (out)** junk/spam/unsolicited email 阻止／過濾垃圾／非索求的電郵
- **exchange** email addresses 交換電郵地址
- **open/check** your inbox 打開／查看收件箱
- junk mail **fills/floods/clogs** your inbox 垃圾電郵塞滿了收件箱
- **have/set up** an email account 擁有／創建電郵賬號
- **open/send/contain** an attachment 打開／發送／包含附件
- **sign up for/receive** email alerts 註冊使用／收到電郵提醒

Connecting to the Internet 連接到互聯網

- **use/access/log onto** the Internet/the Web 使用／登錄互聯網
- **go** online/on the Internet 上網
- **have** a high-speed/dial-up/broadband/wireless (Internet) connection 有高速／撥號／寬帶／無線網絡連接
- **access/connect to/locate** the server 登錄／連接到／定位服務器
- **use/open/close/launch** a/your web browser 使用／打開／關閉／開啟網頁瀏覽器
- **browse/surf/search/scour** the Internet/the Web 上網瀏覽／搜索
- **send/contain/spread/detect** a(n) (computer/email) virus 發送／含有／傳播／發現（電腦／郵件）病毒
- **update** your anti-virus software 升級殺毒軟件
- **install/use/configure** a firewall 安裝／使用／設置防火牆
- **accept/enable/block/delete** cookies 接受／啟用／阻止／刪除網絡餅乾

Using the Internet 使用互聯網

- **visit/check** a website/an Internet site/sb's blog 訪問／查看網站／互聯網站點／某人的博客
- **create/design/launch** a website/social networking site 創建／設計／啟用一個網站／社交網站
- **start/write/post/read** a blog 創建／寫／發佈／讀博客
- **update** your blog/a website 更新博客／網站內容
- **be in/meet sb in/go into/enter** an Internet chat room 在／偶遇某人在／進入網絡聊天室
- **download/upload** music/software/a song/a podcast/a file/a copy of sth 下載／上傳音樂／軟件／一首歌／一個播客／一個文件／一個…的備份
- **share** information/data/files 共享信息／數據／文件
- **post** a comment/message on a website/an online message board/a web forum/an internet chat room 在網站上／網絡留言板上／網絡論壇上／網絡聊天室裏發佈評論／信息
- **stream** video/audio/music/content over the Internet 在互聯網上流播視頻／音頻／音樂／內容
- **join/participate in/visit/provide** a(n) (web-based/web/online/Internet/discussion) forum 加入／訪問／提供網絡論壇
- **generate/increase/monitor** Internet traffic 產生／增加／監管網絡信息流量

speech was deliberately designed to embarrass the prime minister. 這個發言是故意為難首相。

em·bar·rassed /ɪmˈbærəst/ *adj.* **1** (of a person or their behaviour 人或行為) shy, awkward or ashamed, especially in a social situation（尤指在社交場合）窘迫的，尷尬的，害羞的：*I've never felt so embarrassed in my life!* 我一生中從未感到如此難堪過！◇ *Her remark was followed by an embarrassed silence.* 她的話講完後，接下來便是難堪的沉默。◇ **~ about sth** *She's embarrassed about her height.* 她因自己個子高而困窘。◇ **~ at sth** *He felt embarrassed at being the centre of attention.* 他因自己成為眾人注目的中心而感到很尷尬。◇ **~ to do sth** *Some women are too embarrassed to consult their doctor about the problem.* 有些婦女太害羞，不願就這個問題向醫生咨詢。➲ note at ASHAMED **2 financially ~** (*informal*) not having any money; in a difficult financial situation 拮据的；經濟困難的

em·bar·rass·ing /ɪmˈbærəsɪŋ/ *adj.* **1** making you feel shy, awkward or ashamed 使人害羞的（或難堪的、慚愧的）：*an* ***embarrassing mistake/question/situation*** 令人難堪的錯誤／問題／處境 ◇ *It can be embarrassing for children to tell complete strangers about such incidents.* 讓孩子們向素不相識的人講述這樣的事情可能是難為了他們。◇ *It was so embarrassing having to sing in public.* 非得在眾人面前唱歌太令人難為情了。**2** causing sb to look stupid, dishonest, etc. 使顯得愚蠢的（或不誠實等的）：*The report is likely to prove highly embarrassing to the government.* 這份報告可能會讓政府非常尷尬。▸ **em·bar·rass·ing·ly** *adv.*：*The play was embarrassingly bad.* 這齣戲很糟，令人難堪。

em·bar·rass·ment /ɪmˈbærəsmənt/ *noun* **1** [U] shy, awkward or guilty feelings; a feeling of being embarrassed 害羞；窘迫；愧疚；難堪：*I nearly died of embarrassment when he said that.* 他說那話差點兒把我給難堪死了。◇ *I'm glad you offered—it saved me the embarrassment of having to ask.* 你願意幫忙我很高興，省得我厚着臉皮來問你。◇ *Much* ***to her embarrassment*** *she realized that everybody had been listening to her singing.* 她意識到大家一直在聽她唱歌，感到很不好意思。**2** [C] **~ (to/for sb)** a situation which causes problems for sb 使人為難的處境；困境：*Her resignation will be a severe embarrassment to the party.* 她的辭職將使黨處於極度的困境。**3** [C] **~ (to sb)** a person who causes problems for another person or other people and makes them feel embarrassed 令人為難（或難堪、尷尬）的人

IDM **an embarrassment of ˈriches** so many good things that it is difficult to choose just one 好東西多得難以選擇

em·bassy /ˈembəsi/ *noun* (*pl.* **-ies**) **1** a group of officials led by an AMBASSADOR who represent their government in a foreign country 大使館；（統稱）使館官員：*embassy officials* 大使館官員 ◇ *to inform the embassy of the situation* 向大使館報告形勢 **2** the building in which an embassy works 大使館（指館舍）：*a demonstration outside the Russian Embassy* 在俄羅斯大使館外的示威遊行 ➲ compare CONSULATE, HIGH COMMISSION

em·bat·tled /ɪmˈbætld/ *adj.* **1** surrounded by problems and difficulties 被困擾的；處境艱難的；危機四伏的：*the embattled party leader* 處境艱難的黨的領導人 **2** (of an army, a city, etc. 軍隊、城市等) involved in war; surrounded by the enemy 捲入戰爭的；被敵人包圍的

embed (also **imbed**) /ɪmˈbed/ *verb* (**-dd-**) [usually passive] **1 ~ sth (in sth)** to fix sth firmly into a substance or solid object 把…牢牢地嵌入（或插入、埋入）：*an operation to remove glass that was embedded in his leg* 取出扎入他腿部玻璃的手術 ◇ *The bullet embedded itself in the wall.* 子彈射進了牆裏。◇ (*figurative*) *These attitudes are deeply embedded in our society* (= felt very strongly and difficult to change). 這些看法在我們這個社會中根深蒂固。**2 ~ sb** to send a journalist, photographer, etc. to an area where there is fighting, so that he or she can travel with the army and report what is happening 派遣（戰地記者、攝影記者等）：*embedded reporters in the war zone* 戰區特派記者 **3 ~ sth** (*linguistics* 語言) to place a sentence inside another sentence. In the sentence 'I'm aware that she knows', *she knows* is an embedded sentence. 嵌入（在 I'm aware that she knows 句中，she knows 為內嵌句）

em·bel·lish /ɪmˈbelɪʃ/ *verb* (*formal*) **1 ~ sth** to make sth more beautiful by adding decorations to it 美化；裝飾；佈置 SYN **decorate** **2 ~ sth** to make a story more interesting by adding details that are not always true 對…加以渲染（或發揮）；潤飾；對…添枝加葉 SYN **embroider** ▸ **em·bel·lish·ment** *noun* [U, C]：*Good pasta needs very little embellishment.* 好的意大利麪食用不着過多裝飾。◇ *a 16th century church with 18th century embellishments* 具有 18 世紀裝飾藝術的 16 世紀教堂

ember /ˈembə(r)/ *noun* [usually pl.] a piece of wood or coal that is not burning but is still red and hot after a fire has died 餘火未盡的木塊（或煤塊）

em·bez·zle /ɪmˈbezl/ *verb* [T, I] **~ (sth)** to steal money that you are responsible for or that belongs to your employer 盜用，挪用，貪污，侵吞（款項）：*He was found guilty of embezzling $150 000 of public funds.* 他被判犯有盜用 15 萬元公款罪。▸ **em·bezzle·ment** *noun* [U]：*She was found guilty of embezzlement.* 她被判犯有貪污罪。**em·bez·zler** /ɪmˈbezlə(r)/ *noun*

em·bit·ter /ɪmˈbɪtə(r)/ *verb* **~ sb** to make sb feel angry or disappointed about sth over a long period of time 使怨憤；使沮喪；使苦惱 ▸ **em·bit·tered** *adj.*：*a sick and embittered old man* 身患疾病、牢騷滿腹的老人 ◇ *an embittered laugh* 苦笑

em·bla·zon /ɪmˈbleɪzn/ (also **blazon**) *verb* [usually passive] to decorate sth with a design, a symbol or words so that people will notice it easily（用圖案、符號或文字醒目地）裝飾：**~ A with B** *baseball caps emblazoned with the team's logo* 飾有球隊標識的棒球帽 ◇ **~ B on, across, etc. A** *The team's logo was emblazoned on the baseball caps.* 球隊標識醒目地印在棒球帽上。

em·blem /ˈembləm/ *noun* **~ (of sth) 1** a design or picture that represents a country or an organization（代表國家或組織的）徽章，標記，圖案：*America's national emblem, the bald eagle* 美國的國徽 —— 白頭鷲 ◇ *the club emblem* 俱樂部的徽章 **2** something that represents a perfect example or a principle 象徵；標誌：*The dove is an emblem of peace.* 鴿子是和平的象徵。

em·blem·at·ic /ˌembləˈmætɪk/ *adj.* **~ (of sth)** (*formal*) **1** that represents or is a symbol of sth 標誌的；象徵（性）的 SYN **representative** **2** that is considered typical of a situation, an area of work, etc. 特有的；典型的；有代表性的 SYN **typical**：*The violence is emblematic of what is happening in our inner cities.* 這種暴力行為正標示了我們市中心貧民區的狀況。

em·bodi·ment /ɪmˈbɒdimənt; *NAmE* -ˈbɑːd-/ *noun* [usually sing.] **~ of sth** (*formal*) a person or thing that represents or is a typical example of an idea or a quality（體現一種思想或品質的）典型，化身 SYN **epitome**：*He is the embodiment of the young successful businessman.* 他是成功青年企業家的典型。

em·body /ɪmˈbɒdi; *NAmE* ɪmˈbɑːdi/ *verb* (**em·bodies**, **em·body·ing**, **em·bodied**, **em·bodied**) **1** to express or represent an idea or a quality 具體表現，體現，代表（思想或品質）SYN **represent**：**~ sth** *a politician who embodied the hopes of black youth* 代表黑人青年希望的政治家 ◇ **be embodied in sth** *the principles embodied in the Declaration of Human Rights* 體現在《人權宣言》中的原則 **2 ~ sth** (*formal*) to include or contain sth 包括；包含；收錄：*This model embodies many new features.* 這種型號具有許多新特點。

em·bold·en /ɪmˈbəʊldən; *NAmE* -ˈboʊl-/ *verb* **1** [usually passive] (*formal*) to make sb feel braver or more confident 使增加勇氣；使更有膽量；使更有信心：**~ sb** *Emboldened by the wine, he went over to introduce himself to her.* 他借酒壯膽，走上前去向她作自我介紹。◇ **~ sb to do sth** *With such a majority, the administration was emboldened to introduce radical new policies.* 政府有了這大多數人的支持，才敢推行激進的新政策。**2 ~ sth** (*technical* 術語) to make a piece of text appear in BOLD print 將（文本）變成粗體

em·bol·ism /ˈembəlɪzəm/ *noun* (*medical* 醫) a condition in which a BLOOD CLOT or air bubble blocks an ARTERY in the body 栓塞（動脈被栓子堵塞）

em·bolus /ˈembələs/ *noun* (*pl.* **em·boli** /-laɪ; -liː/) (*medical* 醫) a BLOOD CLOT, air bubble, or small object that causes an embolism 栓子

em·boss /ɪmˈbɒs; *NAmE* ɪmˈbɔːs; ɪmˈbɑːs/ *verb* [usually passive] to put a raised design or piece of writing on paper, leather, etc. 壓印浮凸字體（或圖案）；凹凸印：**~ A with B** *stationery embossed with the hotel's name* 凸印旅館名稱的信箋和信封 ◇ **~ B on A** *The hotel's name was embossed on the stationery.* 旅館的名字凸印在信箋和信封上。▶ **em·bossed** *adj.*：*embossed stationery* 有凸起圖案的文具

em·bouch·ure /ˌɒmbʊˈʃʊə(r); *NAmE* ˌɑːmbʊˈʃʊr/ *noun* (*music* 音) **1** the shape of the mouth when playing a WIND INSTRUMENT 嘴唇法（吹奏管樂器時的口形）**2** the MOUTHPIECE of a FLUTE（長笛的）吹孔

em·brace /ɪmˈbreɪs/ *verb* **1** [I, T] (*formal*) to put your arms around sb as a sign of love or friendship 抱；擁抱 **SYN** **hug**：*They embraced and promised to keep in touch.* 他們互相擁抱，許諾將保持聯繫。◇ **~ sb** *She embraced her son warmly.* 她熱情地擁抱着兒子。**2 ~ sth** (*formal*) to accept an idea, a proposal, a set of beliefs, etc., especially when it is done with enthusiasm 欣然接受，樂意採納（思想、建議等）；信奉（宗教、信仰等）：*to embrace democracy/feminism/Islam* 信奉民主／女權主義／伊斯蘭教 **3 ~ sth** (*formal*) to include sth 包括；包含：*The talks embraced a wide range of issues.* 這些談話涉及的問題非常廣泛。▶ **em·brace** *noun* [C, U]：*He held her in a warm embrace.* 他熱烈地擁抱着她。◇ *There were tears and embraces as they said goodbye.* 他們分別時又是流淚，又是擁抱。◇ *the country's eager embrace of modern technology* 這個國家對現代技術的熱切尋求

em·bras·ure /ɪmˈbreɪʒə(r)/ *noun* (*architecture* 建) an opening in a wall for a door or window, wider on the inside than on the outside 斜面門（或窗）洞（兩側向內漸寬）

em·bro·ca·tion /ˌembrəˈkeɪʃn/ *noun* [U] a liquid for rubbing on sore muscles to make them less painful, for example after too much exercise 擦劑（用於緩解因運動量過大而造成的肌肉疼痛）

em·broi·der /ɪmˈbrɔɪdə(r)/ *verb* **1** [T, I] to decorate cloth with a pattern of STITCHES usually using coloured thread 在…上刺繡：**~ A on B** *She embroidered flowers on the cushion covers.* 她在這些靠墊套上繡了花。◇ **~ B with A** *She embroidered the cushion cover with flowers.* 她在靠墊套上繡了花。◇ **~ (sth)** *an embroidered blouse* 繡花女襯衫 ◇ *She sat in the window, embroidering.* 她坐在窗前繡花。**2** [T] **~ sth** to make a story more interesting by adding details that are not always true 加以渲染（或潤飾）；對…添枝加葉 **SYN** **embellish**

em·broi·dery /ɪmˈbrɔɪdəri/ *noun* **1** [U, C] patterns that are sewn onto cloth using threads of various colours; cloth that is decorated in this way 繡花；刺繡圖案；刺繡品：*a beautiful piece of embroidery* 一件美麗的刺繡品 ◇ *Indian embroideries* 印度刺繡品 **2** [U] the skill or activity of decorating cloth in this way 刺繡技法；刺繡 ⊃ VISUAL VOCAB page V41

em·broil /ɪmˈbrɔɪl/ *verb* [often passive] **~ sb/yourself (in sth)** (*formal*) to involve sb/yourself in an argument or a difficult situation 使捲入（糾紛）；使陷入（困境）；使糾纏於：*He became embroiled in a dispute with his neighbours.* 他與鄰居們發生了爭執。◇ *I was reluctant to embroil myself in his problems.* 我不願意捲入到他的問題中去。

em·bryo /ˈembriəʊ; *NAmE* -brioʊ/ *noun* (*pl.* **-os**) a young animal or plant in the very early stages of development before birth, or before coming out of its egg or seed, especially a human egg in the first eight weeks after FERTILIZATION 胚；胚胎；（尤指受孕後八週內的）人類胚胎：*human embryos* 人的胚胎 ◇ (*figurative*) *the embryo of an idea* 一種想法的雛形 ◇ *an embryo politician* (= one who is not yet very experienced) 尚未成熟的政治家

IDM **in embryo** existing but not yet fully developed 在胚胎階段；在萌芽時期；尚未成熟：*The idea already existed in embryo in his earlier novels.* 這個想法在他早期的小說中已初見端倪。

em·bry·ology /ˌembriˈɒlədʒi; *NAmE* -ˈɑːl-/ *noun* [U] the scientific study of the development of embryos 胚胎學 ▶ **em·bryo·logic·al** /ˌembriəˈlɒdʒɪkl; *NAmE* -ˈlɑːdʒ-/ *adj.* **em·bry·olo·gist** /ˌembriˈɒlədʒɪst; *NAmE* -ˈɑːl-/ *noun*

em·bry·on·ic /ˌembriˈɒnɪk; *NAmE* -ˈɑːnɪk/ *adj.* [usually before noun] **1** (*formal*) in an early stage of development 胚胎期的；萌芽期的；未成熟的：*The plan, as yet, only exists in embryonic form.* 這個計劃迄今為止還只是在醞釀之中。**2** (*technical* 術語) of an embryo 胚的；胚胎的：*embryonic cells* 胚胎細胞

emcee /emˈsiː/ *noun* (*NAmE*, *informal*) **1** a person who introduces guests or entertainers at a formal occasion 司儀；（演出的）主持人 **SYN** **master of ceremonies** **2** an MC (3) at a club or party（夜總會或聚會的）說唱樂歌詞朗讀者 ▶ **emcee** *verb* [I, T] **~ (sth)**

emend /iˈmend/ *verb* **~ sth** (*formal*) to remove the mistakes in a piece of writing, especially before it is printed 校訂，校改，修改（文稿）**SYN** **correct**

emend·ation /ˌiːmenˈdeɪʃn/ *noun* [C, U] (*formal*) a letter or word that has been changed or corrected in a text; the act of making changes to a text 校訂的內容；修改的意見；校訂；修改

em·er·ald /ˈemərəld/ *noun* **1** [C, U] a bright green PRECIOUS STONE 祖母綠；綠寶石；翡翠：*an emerald ring* 綠寶石戒指 **2** (also ˌ**emerald** ˈ**green**) [U] a bright green colour 翡翠綠；綠寶石色 ▶ **em·er·ald** (also ˌ**emerald** ˈ**green**) *adj.*

the ˌ**Emerald** ˈ**Isle** *noun* [sing.] (*literary*) a name for Ireland 綠寶石島（愛爾蘭的別稱）

emerge 🔑 **AW** /iˈmɜːdʒ; *NAmE* iˈmɜːrdʒ/ *verb* **1** 🔑 [I] to come out of a dark, confined or hidden place（從隱蔽處或暗處）出現，浮現，露出：**~ (from sth)** *The swimmer emerged from the lake.* 游泳者從湖水中浮出來。◇ *She finally emerged from her room at noon.* 中午，她終於從房間裏出來了。◇ **~ (into sth)** *We emerged into bright sunlight.* 我們來到明媚的陽光下。**2** 🔑 [I, T] (of facts, ideas, etc. 事實、意見等) to become known 暴露；露出真相；被知曉 **SYN** **transpire**：*No new evidence emerged during the investigation.* 調查過程中未發現新證據。◇ **it emerges that …** *It emerged that the company was going to be sold.* 事已清楚，這家公司準備出售。**3** 🔑 [I] to start to exist; to appear or become known 露頭；顯現；顯露：*After the elections opposition groups began to emerge.* 經過選舉，反對派開始露頭。◇ *the emerging markets of South Asia* 正在興起的南亞市場 ◇ **~ as sth** *He emerged as a key figure in the campaign.* 他已初露頭角，成為這次運動的主要人物。**4** [I] **~ (from sth)** to survive a difficult situation or experience（從困境或苦難經歷中）幸存下來，擺脫出來：*She emerged from the scandal with her reputation intact.* 她在醜聞中安然無恙，名聲絲毫未受影響。▶ **emer·gence** **AW** /-dʒəns/ *noun* [U]：*the island's emergence from the sea 3 000 years ago* * 3 000 年前這個島從大海中露出 ◇ *the emergence of new technologies* 新技術的出現

emer·gency 🔑 /iˈmɜːdʒənsi; *NAmE* iˈmɜːrdʒ-/ *noun* (*pl.* **-ies**) [C, U] a sudden serious and dangerous event or situation which needs immediate action to deal with it 突發事件；緊急情況：*The government has declared a* ***state of emergency*** *following the earthquake.* 地震發生後政府已宣佈進入緊急狀態。◇ *This door should only be used* ***in an emergency***. 這道門只能在緊急情況下使用。◇ *the emergency exit* (= to be used in an emergency) 緊急出口 ◇ *The government had to take emergency action.* 政府只得採取緊急措施。◇ *The pilot made an emergency landing in a field.* 飛行員在一片農田裏緊急着陸。◇ *I always have some extra cash with me* ***for emergencies***. 我總是隨身多帶點現金以備急需。◇ *The government has been granted* ***emergency powers*** (= to deal with an emergency). 政府已被授予應急權力。

eˈmergency brake *noun* (*NAmE*) **1** = HANDBRAKE ➲ **VISUAL VOCAB** page V52 **2** a BRAKE on a train that can be pulled in an emergency（火車的）緊急剎車

eˈmergency room (*NAmE*) (*abbr.* **ER**) (*BrE* **ˌaccident and eˈmergency**) *noun* the part of a hospital where people who need urgent treatment are taken（醫院）急診室

eˈmergency services *noun* [pl.] (*BrE*) the public organizations that deal with emergencies: the police, fire, ambulance and COASTGUARD services 應急服務機構（治安、消防、救護和海岸警衛）➲ compare FIRST RESPONDER

emer·gent AW /iˈmɜːdʒənt; *NAmE* iˈmɜːrdʒ-/ *adj.* [usually before noun] new and still developing 新興的；處於發展初期的：***emergent nations/states*** 新興民族 / 國家

emeri·tus /iˈmerɪtəs/ *adj.* (often **Emeritus**) used with a title to show that a person, usually a university teacher, keeps the title as an honour, although he or she has stopped working（常指大學教師）退休後保留頭銜的，榮譽退休的：*the Emeritus Professor of Biology* 榮譽退休的生物學教授 HELP In *NAmE* the form **Emerita** /iˈmerɪtə/ is used for women. 在美式英語中 Emerita 用於女性：*Professor Emerita Mary Judd*

emery /ˈeməri/ *noun* [U] a hard mineral used especially in powder form for polishing things and making them smooth 金剛砂，剛玉粉（其粉末尤用作磨料）

ˈemery board *noun* a small strip of wood or cardboard covered in emery, used for shaping your nails 指甲砂銼 ➲ **VISUAL VOCAB** page V24

emet·ic /iˈmetɪk/ *noun* (*medical* 醫) a substance that makes you VOMIT (= bring up food from the stomach) 催吐藥；催吐劑 ▸ **emet·ic** *adj.*

emi·grant /ˈemɪɡrənt/ *noun* a person who leaves their country to live in another 移居外國的人；移民：*emigrant workers* 移居國外的工人 ◇ *emigrants to Canada* 移居加拿大的人 ➲ compare IMMIGRANT

emi·grate /ˈemɪɡreɪt/ *verb* [I] **~ (from …) (to …)** to leave your own country to go and live permanently in another country 移居國外；移民 ➲ compare IMMIGRATE ▸ **emi·gra·tion** /ˌemɪˈɡreɪʃn/ *noun* [U, C]：*the mass emigration of Jews from Eastern Europe* 猶太人從東歐往其他地區的大批移居 ➲ compare IMMIGRATION (1)

émi·gré /ˈemɪɡreɪ/ *noun* (from *French*) a person who has left their own country, usually for political reasons（通常因政治原因移居外國的）流亡者，逃亡者 SYN **exile**

emi·nence /ˈemɪnəns/ *noun* **1** [U] (*formal*) the quality of being famous and respected, especially in a profession（尤指在某專業中）卓越，著名，顯赫：*a man of political eminence* 政壇上出類拔萃的人 **2** [C] **His/Your Eminence** a title used in speaking to or about a CARDINAL (= a priest of the highest rank in the Roman Catholic Church)（天主教中對樞機主教的尊稱）最可敬的樞機：*Their Eminences will see you now.* 最可敬的樞機現在要見你。 **3** [C] (*old-fashioned* or *formal*) an area of high ground 高地；山丘

emi·nent /ˈemɪnənt/ *adj.* [usually before noun] **1** (of people 人) famous and respected, especially in a particular profession（尤指在某專業中）卓越的，著名的，顯赫的：*an eminent architect* 著名的建築師 **2** (of good qualities 良好品質) unusual; excellent 非凡的；傑出的：*a man of eminent good sense* 極其明智的人

ˌeminent doˈmain *noun* [U] (*NAmE, law* 律) the right to force sb to sell land or a building if it is needed by the government（政府對私有財產的）徵用權，支配權；土地徵收權

emi·nent·ly /ˈemɪnəntli/ *adv.* (*formal*) (used to emphasize a positive quality 強調良好品質) very; extremely 非常；特別；極其：*She seems eminently suitable for the job.* 她看來非常適合這個工作。

emir (also **amir**) /eˈmɪə(r); ˈeɪmɪə(r); *NAmE* eˈmɪr; eɪˈmɪr/ *noun* the title given to some Muslim rulers 埃米爾（對某些穆斯林統治者的尊稱）：*the Emir of Kuwait* 科威特的埃米爾

emir·ate /ˈemɪərət; ˈemɪrət; *NAmE* ˈemərət/ *noun* **1** the position of an emir 埃米爾的職位 **2** an area of land that is ruled over by an emir 埃米爾的管轄地；酋長國：*the United Arab Emirates* 阿拉伯聯合酋長國 **3** the period of time that an emir rules 埃米爾統治期

emis·sary /ˈemɪsəri; *NAmE* -seri/ *noun* (*pl.* **-ies**) (*formal*) a person who is sent to deliver an official message, especially from one country to another, or to perform a special task 特使；密使 SYN **envoy**

emis·sion /iˈmɪʃn/ *noun* **1** [U] (*formal*) the production or sending out of light, heat, gas, etc.（光、熱、氣等的）發出，射出，排放：*the emission of carbon dioxide into the atmosphere* 向大氣排放二氧化碳 ◇ *emission controls* 排放管制 **2** [C] gas, etc. that is sent out into the air 排放物；散發物；排泄物：*The government has pledged to clean up industrial emissions.* 政府已保證要清除工業排放物。 ➲ **COLLOCATIONS** at ENVIRONMENT

eˈmissions trading *noun* = CARBON TRADING

emit /iˈmɪt/ *verb* (**-tt-**) **~ sth** (*formal*) to send out sth such as light, heat, sound, gas, etc. 發出，射出，散發（光、熱、聲音、氣等）：*The metal container began to emit a clicking sound.* 金屬容器開始發出咔嗒咔嗒的聲音。 ◇ *Sulphur gases were emitted by the volcano.* 硫磺氣體由火山噴發出來。

Em·men·tal (also **Em·men·thal**) /ˈeməntɑːl/ *noun* [U] a type of Swiss cheese, with holes in it 埃曼塔爾乾酪（多孔瑞士乾酪）

Emmy /ˈemi/ *noun* (*pl.* **-ies**) one of the awards given every year in the US for achievement in the making of television programmes 艾美獎（美國每年頒發的電視節目及演出獎項之一）

emo /ˈiːməʊ; *NAmE* ˈiːmoʊ/ *noun* (*pl.* **emos**) **1** [U] a style of rock music that developed from PUNK, but has more complicated musical arrangements and deals with more emotional subjects 情感核搖滾樂，情感核（基於朋客搖滾樂，音樂編排更複雜，主題更富於情感） **2** [C] a person who likes emo music and often follows emo fashion, wearing tight jeans and having long black hair. Emos are typically supposed to be emotional and sensitive and full of ANGST. 情感核樂迷（常追隨時尚，穿緊身牛仔褲，蓄黑色長髮，以衝動、敏感、憂慮為特徵）

emol·li·ent /iˈmɒliənt; *NAmE* iˈmɑːl-/ *adj., noun*

■ ***adj.*** (*formal*) **1** making a person or situation calmer in the hope of keeping relations peaceful 使平靜的；使緩和的 SYN **soothing**：*an emollient reply* 令人寬慰的回答 **2** (*technical* 術語) used for making your skin soft or less painful 潤膚的；護膚的 SYN **soothing**：*an emollient cream* 潤膚霜

■ ***noun*** [C, U] (*technical* 術語) a liquid or cream that is used to make the skin soft 潤膚劑；潤膚霜

emolu·ment /ɪˈmɒljumənt; *NAmE* ɪˈmɑːl-/ *noun* [usually pl.] (*formal*) money paid to sb for work they have done, especially to sb who earns a lot of money（尤指付給高收入者的）酬金，薪水，工資

emote /ɪˈməʊt; *NAmE* ɪˈmoʊt/ *verb* [I] to show emotion in a very obvious way 強烈地表現（或表露）感情

emoti·con /ɪˈməʊtɪkɒn; *NAmE* ɪˈmoʊtɪkɑːn/ *noun* (*computing* 計) a short set of keyboard symbols that represents the expression on sb's face, used in email, etc. to show the feelings of the person sending the message. For example :-) represents a smiling face (when you look at it sideways). 情感符號，表情符號（如 :-) 表示笑臉）

emo·tion 0-w /ɪˈməʊʃn; *NAmE* ɪˈmoʊʃn/ *noun* [C, U] a strong feeling such as love, fear or anger; the part of a person's character that consists of feelings 強烈的感情；激情；情感；情緒：*He lost control of his emotions.* 他對自己的情緒失去了控制。 ◇ *They expressed mixed emotions at the news.* 他們對這個消息表現出複雜的感情。 ◇ ***Emotions are running high*** (= people are feeling very excited, angry, etc.). 群情激動起來。 ◇ *The decision was based on emotion rather than rational thought.* 這個決定不是基於理性的思考而是基於感情作出的。 ◇ *She* *showed no emotion at the verdict.* 她對這一裁定無動於衷。◇ *Mary was overcome with emotion.* 瑪麗激動得不能自持。

emo·tion·al 🗝 /ɪˈməʊʃənl; *NAmE* ɪˈmoʊ-/ *adj.* **1** 🗝 [usually before noun] connected with people's feelings (= with the emotions) 感情的；情感的；情緒的：*emotional problems/needs* 情感問題 / 需求 ◇ *emotional stress* 情緒緊張 ◇ *a child's emotional and intellectual development* 兒童的情感和智力發展 ◇ *Mothers are often the ones who provide **emotional support** for the family.* 母親通常是家庭的情感支柱。**2** 🗝 causing people to feel strong emotions 激起感情的；有感染力的；激動人心的 **SYN** **emotive**：*emotional language* 有感染力的語言 ◇ *abortion and other **emotional issues*** 墮胎和其他使人情緒激動的問題 **3** 🗝 (sometimes *disapproving*) showing strong emotions, sometimes in a way that other people think is unnecessary 情緒激動的；感情衝動的：*an **emotional outburst/response/reaction*** 感情爆發；情緒激動的回答 / 反應 ◇ *They made an emotional appeal for help.* 他們情緒激動地懇求救助。◇ *He tends to **get emotional** on these occasions.* 他在這些場合往往容易感情衝動。▶ **emo·tion·al·ly** 🗝 /-ʃənəli/ *adv.*：*emotionally disturbed children* 情緒異常的孩子 ◇ *I try not to become emotionally involved.* 我盡量在感情上不受到影響。◇ *They have suffered physically and emotionally.* 他們遭受了肉體上和感情上的折磨。◇ *an emotionally charged atmosphere* 群情激昂的氣氛

eˌmotional inˈtelligence *noun* [U] the ability to understand your emotions and those of other people and to behave appropriately in different situations 情緒智力（指理解情感、在不同場合下舉止得體的能力）

emo·tion·less /ɪˈməʊʃənləs; *NAmE* ɪˈmoʊ-/ *adj.* not showing any emotion 沒有感情的；冷漠的：*an emotionless voice* 冷漠的聲音

emo·tive /iˈməʊtɪv; *NAmE* iˈmoʊ-/ *adj.* causing people to feel strong emotions 激起感情的；有感染力的；激動人心的 **SYN** **emotional**：***emotive language/words*** 有感染力的語言 / 話語 ◇ *Capital punishment is a highly **emotive issue**.* 死刑是極易引起激烈爭論的問題。

em·panel = IMPANEL

em·pa·thize (*BrE* also **-ise**) /ˈempəθaɪz/ *verb* [I] **~ (with sb/sth)** to understand another person's feelings and experiences, especially because you have been in a similar situation 有同感；產生共鳴；表同情

em·pathy /ˈempəθi/ *noun* [U] the ability to understand another person's feelings, experience, etc. 同感；共鳴；同情：**~ (with sb/sth)** *the writer's imaginative empathy with his subject* 作者把想像中的感情投入到筆下的人物 ◇ **~ (for sb/sth)** *empathy for other people's situations* 對他人所處境況的同情 ◇ **~ (between A and B)** *The empathy between the two women was obvious.* 顯然這兩個女人心靈相通。

em·peror /ˈempərə(r)/ *noun* the ruler of an empire 皇帝：*the Roman emperors* 古羅馬皇帝 ◇ *the Emperor Napoleon* 拿破侖皇帝 ➲ see also EMPRESS

IDM **the ˌemperor has no ˈclothes** used to describe a situation in which everybody suddenly realizes that they were mistaken in believing that sb/sth was very good, important, etc. 原來皇帝沒有穿衣服；恍然大悟；如夢初醒：*Soon investors will realize that the emperor has no clothes and there will be a big sell-off in stocks.* 投資者很快會瞭解事實真相，股票將被大肆拋售。**ORIGIN** From the story of *The Emperor's New Clothes* by Hans Christian Andersen, in which the emperor is tricked into thinking he is wearing beautiful new clothes and everyone pretends to admire them, until a little boy points out that he is naked. 這句話源自漢斯 • 克里斯蒂安 • 安徒生的童話《皇帝的新裝》。在這個童話中，皇帝被欺騙，以為自己穿上了美麗的新衣，所有人都假裝讚賞其衣服光彩耀人，直至一個小男孩說出他赤身裸體的真相時才恍然大悟。

em·phasis 🗝 **AW** /ˈemfəsɪs/ *noun* (*pl.* **em·phases** /-siːz/) [U, C] **1** 🗝 special importance that is given to sth 強調；重視；重要性 **SYN** **stress**：**~ (on/upon sth)** *The emphasis is very much on learning the spoken language.* 重點主要放在學習口語上。◇ *to **put/lay/place emphasis** on sth* 強調 / 重視某事 ◇ *We provide all types of information, **with an emphasis on** legal advice.* 我們提供各種信息服務，尤其是法律咨詢。◇ *There has been **a shift of emphasis** from manufacturing to service industries.* 重點已經從製造業向服務行業轉移。◇ *The course has a vocational emphasis.* 這門課程着重職業培訓。◇ *The examples we will look at have quite different emphases.* 我們將要觀察的例子所強調的重點很不相同。**2** 🗝 the extra force given to a word or phrase when spoken, especially in order to show that it is important; a way of writing a word (for example drawing a line underneath it) to show that it is important（對某個詞或短語的）強調，加重語氣，重讀 **SYN** **stress**：*'I can assure you,' she added with emphasis, 'the figures are correct.'* "我可以向你保證，" 她加重語氣補充道，"這些數字是正確的。"

E

Language Bank 用語庫

emphasis

Highlighting an important point 強調重點

- This case **emphasizes/highlights** the importance of honest communication between managers and employees. 這個事例凸顯出經理與員工之間坦誠交流的重要性。
- Effective communication skills are **essential/crucial/vital**. 有效的交流技巧是至關重要的。
- **It should be noted that** this study considers only verbal communication. Non-verbal communication is not dealt with here. 應該注意的是本研究只考查了言語交流，在此沒有涉及非言語交流。
- **It is important to remember that/An important point to remember is that** non-verbal communication plays a key role in getting your message across. 非言語交流在傳遞信息過程中起到至關重要的作用，記住這一點非常重要。
- Communication is not only about the words you use but also your body language and, **especially/above all**, the effectiveness with which you listen. 交流不僅涉及使用的詞語，同時也涉及身體語言，尤其與能否有效聽取對方的話有關。
- I would like to **draw attention to** the role of listening in effective communication. 我想讓大家注意到傾聽在有效交流中扮演的角色。
- Choose your words carefully: **in particular**, avoid confusing and ambiguous language. 注意用詞，特別是避免使用令人費解和有歧義的語言。
- Finally, and perhaps **most importantly**, you must learn to listen as well as to speak. 最後，也許是最重要的，你不僅要學會說還要學會聽。

➲ note at ESSENTIAL

➲ Language Bank at VITAL

em·pha·size 🗝 (*BrE* also **-ise**) **AW** /ˈemfəsaɪz/ *verb* **1** 🗝 to give special importance to sth 強調；重視；着重 **SYN** **stress**：**~ sth** *His speech emphasized the importance of attracting industry to the town.* 他的發言強調了吸引工業到城鎮的重要性。◇ **~ that …** *She emphasized that their plan would mean sacrifices and hard work.* 她強調說他們的計劃意味着犧牲和辛勤工作。◇ **~ how, what, etc. …** *He emphasized how little was known about the disease.* 他着重指出對這種疾病所知甚少。◇ **it must/should be emphasized that …** *It should be emphasized that this is only one possible explanation.* 應該強調的是，這只是一種可能的解釋。◇ **+ speech** *'This must be our top priority,' he emphasized.* "這必須成為我們的當務之急。" 他強調說。➲ LANGUAGE BANK at EMPHASIS **2** 🗝 **~ sth** to make sth more noticeable 使突出；使明顯：*She swept her hair back from her face to emphasize her high cheekbones.* 她把頭髮朝臉後攏時，高高的顴骨顯得更為突出。**3** 🗝 **~ sth** to give extra force to a word or phrase when you are speaking, especially to show that it is important 重讀，強調（詞或短語）；加強…的語氣 ➲ SYNONYMS at STRESS

em·phat·ic AW /ɪmˈfætɪk/ *adj.* **1** an **emphatic** statement, answer, etc. is given with force to show that it is important 強調的；有力的：*an **emphatic denial/rejection*** 斷然的否認／拒絕 **2** (of a person 人) making it very clear what you mean by speaking with force 明確表示的；加強語氣的：*He was emphatic that he could not work with her.* 他強調他不能與她共事。 **3** an **emphatic** victory, win, or defeat is one in which one team or player wins by a large amount（勝負）明顯的，突出的，顯著的 ▸ **em·phat·ic·al·ly** AW /-kli/ *adv.*：*'Certainly not,' he replied emphatically.* "當然不。"他斷然回答道。◇ *She is emphatically opposed to the proposals.* 她堅決反對這些建議。◇ *He has always emphatically denied the allegations.* 他一直斷然否認這些指控。◇ *The proposal was emphatically defeated.* 這個建議已被斷然否決。

em·phy·se·ma /ˌemfɪˈsiːmə/ *noun* [U] (*medical* 醫) a condition that affects the lungs, making it difficult to breathe 肺氣腫

em·pire 0━ /ˈempaɪə(r)/ *noun* **1** 0━ a group of countries or states that are controlled by one ruler or government 帝國：*the Roman empire* 羅馬帝國 **2** 0━ a group of commercial organizations controlled by one person or company 大企業；企業集團：*a business empire* 大型企業集團

ˈempire-ˌbuilding *noun* [U] (usually *disapproving*) the process of obtaining extra land, authority, etc. in order to increase your own power or position（為增加自己的權力或地位）擴展疆土（或加強權力等）；營造帝國

ˈEmpire line *noun* a style of women's dress with the WAISTLINE positioned just below the breasts and a low-cut neck（連衣裙的）高腰線

em·pir·ic·al AW /ɪmˈpɪrɪkl/ *adj.* [usually before noun] (*formal*) based on experiments or experience rather than ideas or theories 以實驗（或經驗）為依據的；經驗主義的：***empirical evidence/knowledge/research*** 實踐經驗的證明；從實際經驗中獲得的知識；以實驗為基礎的研究 ◇ *an **empirical study*** 經驗式研究 OPP **theoretical** ▸ **em·pir·ic·al·ly** AW /-kli/ *adv.*：*Such claims need to be tested empirically.* 這類斷言需要實踐來檢驗。

em·piri·cism AW /ɪmˈpɪrɪsɪzəm/ *noun* [U] (*philosophy* 哲) the use of experiments or experience as the basis for your ideas; the belief in these methods 實證論；經驗主義；經驗論 ▸ **em·piri·cist** /-sɪst/ *adj.*：*an empiricist theory* 經驗主義理論 **em·piri·cist** *noun*：*the English empiricist, John Locke* 英國經驗主義者約翰·洛克

em·place·ment /ɪmˈpleɪsmənt/ *noun* (*technical* 術語) a position that has been specially prepared so that a large gun can be fired from it 炮台；炮位

em·ploy 0━ /ɪmˈplɔɪ/ *verb, noun*

■ *verb* **1** 0━ to give sb a job to do for payment 雇用：**~ sb** *How many people does the company employ?* 這家公司雇用了多少人？◇ **~ sb as sth** *For the past three years he has been employed as a firefighter.* 三年來他一直受雇當消防員。◇ **~ sb to do sth** *A number of people have been employed to deal with the backlog of work.* 已雇來一些人處理積壓的工作。➲ COLLOCATIONS at JOB ➲ see also SELF-EMPLOYED, UNEMPLOYED **2** 0━ **~ sth** (*formal*) to use sth such as a skill, method, etc. for a particular purpose 應用；運用；使用：*He criticized the repressive methods employed by the country's government.* 他指責了這個國家政府採取的鎮壓手段。◇ *The police had to employ force to enter the building.* 警察不得不強行進入大樓。

IDM **be employed in doing sth** if a person or their time is **employed in doing sth**, the person spends time doing that thing 從事於，忙於（做某事）：*She was employed in making a list of all the jobs to be done.* 她忙着把要做的所有工作列一個清單。

■ *noun* [U]

IDM **in sb's emˈploy | in the emˈploy of sb** (*formal*) working for sb; employed by sb 替某人工作；為某人所雇用

em·ploy·able /ɪmˈplɔɪəbl/ *adj.* having the skills and qualifications that will make sb want to employ you 具備受雇條件的；適宜雇用的

em·ploy·ee 0━ /ɪmˈplɔɪiː/ *noun* a person who is paid to work for sb 受雇者；雇工；雇員：*The firm has over 500 employees.* 這家公司有 500 多名雇員。◇ *government employees* 政府雇員 ◇ ***employee rights/relations*** 雇員權利／關係

em·ploy·er 0━ /ɪmˈplɔɪə(r)/ *noun* a person or company that pays people to work for them 雇用者；雇主；老闆：*They're very good employers* (= they treat the people that work for them well). 他們是非常好的雇主。◇ *one of the largest employers in the area* 這個地區最大的雇主之一

em·ploy·ment 0━ /ɪmˈplɔɪmənt/ *noun* **1** 0━ [U, C] work, especially when it is done to earn money; the state of being employed 工作；職業；受雇：*to be in **paid employment*** 有拿工資的工作 ◇ ***full-time/part-time employment*** 全職／兼職工作 ◇ ***conditions/terms of employment*** 雇傭條件／條款 ◇ *Graduates are finding it more and more difficult to find employment.* 畢業生感到找工作越來越難。◇ *pensions from previous employments* 以前工作的退休金 ➲ SYNONYMS at WORK ➲ COLLOCATIONS at JOB, UNEMPLOYMENT **2** 0━ [U] the situation in which people have work 就業：*The government is aiming at **full employment**.* 政府在力求達到全面就業。◇ *Changes in farming methods have badly affected employment in the area.* 耕作方法的改變嚴重影響了這個地區的就業。OPP **unemployment** **3** [U] the act of employing sb 雇用：*The law prevented the employment of children under ten in the cotton mills.* 法律禁止棉紡廠雇用十歲以下的童工。 **4** [U] **~ (of sth)** (*formal*) the use of sth 使用；利用：*the employment of artillery in the capture of the town* 在攻城時使用大炮

emˈployment agency *noun* a business that helps people to find work and employers to find workers 職業介紹所

emˌployment triˈbunal (also **inˌdustrial triˈbunal**) *noun* (*BrE*) a type of court that can decide on disagreements between employees and employers 勞資裁判庭；勞資仲裁庭：*She took her case to an employment tribunal.* 她向勞資裁判庭提起訴訟。

em·por·ium /emˈpɔːriəm/ *noun* (*pl.* **em·por·iums** or **em·poria** /-riə/) **1** (*old-fashioned*) a large shop/store 大百貨商店；大型商場 **2** a shop/store that sells a particular type of goods 專門店：*an arts and crafts emporium* 工藝品商店

em·power /ɪmˈpaʊə(r)/ *verb* [often passive] **1 ~ sb (to do sth)** (*formal*) to give sb the power or authority to do sth 授權；給（某人）…的權力 SYN **authorize**：*The courts were empowered to impose the death sentence for certain crimes.* 法院有權因某些罪行判處罪犯死刑。 **2 ~ sb (to do sth)** to give sb more control over their own life or the situation they are in 增加（某人的）自主權；使控制局勢：*The movement actively empowered women and gave them confidence in themselves.* 這場運動使女性更能主動掌握自己的命運，對自己充滿信心。▸ **em·power·ment** *noun* [U]：*the empowerment of the individual* 讓個人掌握自己的命運

emp·ress /ˈemprəs/ *noun* **1** a woman who is the ruler of an empire 女皇：*the Empress of Egypt* 埃及女皇 **2** the wife of an EMPEROR 皇后

emp·ties /ˈemptiz/ *noun* [pl.] empty bottles or glasses 空瓶；空玻璃杯

emp·ti·ness /ˈemptinəs/ *noun* [U, sing.] **1** a feeling of being sad because nothing seems to have any value 空虛：*There was an aching emptiness in her heart.* 她的內心有一種隱隱作痛的空虛感。 **2** the fact that there is nothing or nobody in a place 空無；空曠：*The silence and emptiness of the house did not scare her.* 房子的空寂並未使她感到害怕。 **3** (*formal*) a place that is empty 空地：*He stared out at the vast emptiness that was the sea.* 他放眼向遼闊無際的海洋望去。

empty 0━ /ˈempti/ *adj., verb*

■ *adj.* (**emp·tier**, **emp·ti·est**) **1** 0━ with no people or things inside 空的：*an empty box/glass* 空盒／杯 ◇ *empty hands*

(= not holding anything) 空手 ◇ *an empty plate* (= with no food on it) 空盤子 ◇ *The theatre was* ***half empty***. 劇場空了一半。◇ *an empty house/room/bus* 空着的房子 / 房間 / 公共汽車 ◇ *Is this an empty chair* (= a chair that nobody else is using)? 這張椅子沒人坐嗎？◇ *The house had been* ***standing empty*** (= without people living in it) *for some time.* 這房子已經有一段時間沒人住了。◇ *It's not good to drink alcohol* ***on an empty stomach*** (= without having eaten something). 空腹飲酒不好。◇ **~ of sth** (*formal*) *The room was empty of furniture.* 房間裏什麼傢具都沒有。 **2** [usually before noun] (of sth that sb says or does 言語或行動) with no meaning; not meaning what is said 空洞的；說話不算數的；無誠意的 **SYN** **hollow**：*empty words* 空話 ◇ *an empty promise* 兌現不了的承諾 ◇ *an empty gesture aimed at pleasing the crowds* 旨在取悅觀眾的裝腔作勢 **3** (of a person, or a person's life 人或其生活) unhappy because life does not seem to have a purpose, usually after sth sad has happened 空虛的；無意義的；無目的的：*Three months after his death, she still felt empty.* 他死後三個月她仍然感到心裏很空虛。◇ *My life seems empty without you.* 沒有你，我的生活似乎就沒有了意義。 **4 ~ of sth** without a quality that you would expect to be there 沒有；缺乏；無：*words that were empty of meaning* 無意義的話 ▸ **emp·ti·ly** *adv.*：*She stood staring emptily into space.* 她站着茫然地凝視遠方。

■ *verb* (**emp·ties**, **empty·ing**, **emp·tied**, **emp·tied**) **1** [T] to remove everything that is in a container, etc. 倒空；騰空；掏空：**~ sth** *He emptied the ashtrays, washed the glasses and went to bed.* 他倒掉煙灰缸裏的灰，洗完杯子就上牀睡覺了。◇ *He emptied his glass and asked for a refill.* 他乾了一杯，又要求再斟滿一杯。◇ **~ sth out** *I emptied out my pockets but could not find my keys.* 我把口袋裏的東西都掏了出來，仍然找不到我的鑰匙。◇ **~ sth out of sth** *She emptied the water out of the vase.* 她把水從花瓶裏倒了出來。◇ **~ sth of sth** *The room had been emptied of all furniture.* 房間裏所有的傢具都搬走了。◇ (*figurative*) *She emptied her mind of all thoughts of home.* 她打消了想家的所有念頭。 **2** [I] to become empty 變空：*The streets soon emptied when the rain started.* 雨下起來時街上很快便空無一人。◇ **~ out** *The tank empties out in five minutes.* 箱裏的液體五分鐘就流乾了。 **3** [T] **~ sth** (**out**) to take out the contents of sth and put them somewhere else 把…移出，把…騰出（置於別處）：*She emptied the contents of her bag onto the table.* 她把包裏的東西全倒在了桌子上。◇ *Many factories emptied their waste into the river.* 許多工廠都將廢料倒進了這條河裏。 **4** [T] **~ sth** to make sure that everyone leaves a room, building, etc.（把…）撤出，撤離；撤空 **SYN** **evacuate**：*Police had instructions to empty the building because of a bomb threat.* 由於炸彈的威脅，警方奉命將人撤離這棟大樓。 **5** [I] to flow or move out from one place to another 流入；湧進：**~ into/onto sth** *The Rhine empties into the North Sea.* 萊茵河流入北海。◇ **~ out into/onto sth** *Fans emptied out onto the streets after the concert.* 音樂會結束後，樂迷湧到大街上。

ˌempty-ˈhanded *adj.* [not usually before noun] without getting what you wanted; without taking sth to sb 一無所獲；空手：*The robbers fled empty-handed.* 搶劫犯一無所獲地逃走了。◇ *She visited every Sunday and never arrived empty-handed.* 她每個星期天都來拜訪，沒有哪一次不帶禮物。

ˌempty-ˈheaded *adj.* (*disapproving*) unable to think or behave in an intelligent way 沒頭腦的；傻的；無知的

the ˌempty ˈnest *noun* [sing.] the situation that parents are in when their children have grown up and left home 空巢（子女長大離家後家長獨守家中）

ˌempty ˈnester *noun* [usually pl.] a parent whose children have grown up and left home 空巢家長

EMS /ˌiː em ˈes/ *noun* **1** [U] the abbreviation for 'enhanced message service' (a system for sending pictures, music and long written messages from one mobile/cell phone to another) 增強型信息服務（全寫為 enhanced message service，手機傳送圖片、音樂和長條信息的系統） **2** [C] a message sent by EMS 增強型信息；音畫信息；增強型簡訊

EMU /ˌiː em ˈjuː/ *abbr.* Economic and Monetary Union (of the European Union)（歐盟）經濟和貨幣聯盟

emu /ˈiːmjuː/ *noun* a large Australian bird that can run fast but cannot fly 鴯鶓（澳洲大型鳥，善跑但不會飛）

emu·late /ˈemjuleɪt/ *verb* **1 ~ sb/sth** (*formal*) to try to do sth as well as sb else because you admire them 努力趕上；同…看齊：*She hopes to emulate her sister's sporting achievements.* 她希望在運動成績方面趕上她姐姐。 **2 ~ sth** (*computing* 計) (of a computer program, etc. 計算機程序等) to work in the same way as another computer, etc. and perform the same tasks 仿真；模仿 ▸ **emu·la·tion** /ˌemjuˈleɪʃn/ *noun* [U, C]

emu·la·tor /ˈemjuleɪtə(r)/ *noun* (*computing* 計) a device or piece of software that makes it possible to use programs, etc. on one type of computer even though they have been designed for a different type 仿真器；仿真程序

emul·si·fier /ɪˈmʌlsɪfaɪə(r)/ *noun* (*chemistry* 化) a substance that is added to food to make the different substances in them combine to form a smooth mixture（食品）乳化劑

emul·sify /ɪˈmʌlsɪfaɪ/ *verb* (**emul·si·fies**, **emul·si·fy·ing**, **emul·si·fied**, **emul·si·fied**) [I, T] **~** (**sth**) (*technical* 術語) if two liquids of different thicknesses **emulsify** or **are emulsified**, they combine to form a smooth mixture（使）乳化

emul·sion /ɪˈmʌlʃn/ *noun* [C, U] **1** any mixture of liquids that do not normally mix together, such as oil and water 乳狀液；乳濁液；乳劑 **2** (also **eˈmulsion paint**) (*BrE*) a type of paint used on walls and ceilings that dries without leaving a shiny surface 乳膠漆（乾後無光澤） **3** (*technical* 術語) a substance on the surface of PHOTOGRAPHIC film that makes it sensitive to light 感光乳劑

en- /ɪn/ (also **em-** /ɪm/ before *b*, *m* or *p*) *prefix* (in verbs 構成動詞) **1** to put into the thing or condition mentioned 置於…之中；使處於…狀態；賦予：*encase* 置於箱中 ◇ *endanger* 使遭危險 ◇ *empower* 授權 **2** to cause to be 使；使成為：*enlarge* 擴大 ◇ *embolden* 使更有膽量

-en *suffix* **1** (in verbs 構成動詞) to make or become 使；使成為；變得：*blacken* 使變黑 ◇ *sadden* 使悲傷 **2** (in adjectives 構成形容詞) made of; looking like 由…製成（或構成）的；像…一樣的：*wooden* 木製的 ◇ *golden* 金的

en·able **AW** /ɪˈneɪbl/ *verb*
1 ~ sb to do sth to make it possible for sb to do sth 使能夠；使有機會 **SYN** **allow**：*The software enables you to create your own DVDs.* 這個軟件可用來自製 DVD。◇ *a new programme to enable older people to study at college* 使老年人有機會在大學學習的新方案 **2** to make it possible for sth to happen or exist by creating the necessary conditions 使成為可能；使可行；使實現 **SYN** **allow**：**~ sth to do sth** *Insulin enables the body to use and store sugar.* 胰島素使人體能夠利用和貯存糖分。◇ **~ sth** *a new train line to enable easier access to the stadium* 到體育場更為便捷的新列車線路 ➲ LANGUAGE BANK at PROCESS

-enabled /ɪˈneɪbld/ *adj.* (in compound adjectives 構成複合形容詞) (*computing* 計) that can be used with a particular system or technology, especially the Internet 能與某一系統（或技術）使用的：*web-enabled phones* 具有上網功能的電話

eˈnabling act *noun* a law which allows a person or an organization to do sth, especially to make rules 授權法

enact /ɪˈnækt/ *verb* **1** [often passive] **~ sth** | **it is enacted that …** (*law* 律) to pass a law 通過（法律）：*legislation enacted by parliament* 由議會通過的法律 **2** [often passive] **~ sth** (*formal*) to perform a play or act a part in a play 扮演；擔任…角色；演出：*scenes from history enacted by local residents* 由當地居民參加演出的歷史場面 **3 be enacted** (*formal*) to take place 發生；進行；舉行 **SYN** **be played out**：*They seemed unaware of the drama being enacted a few feet away from them.* 他們對於正在咫尺之外上演的戲劇性事件似乎渾然不知。

E

en·act·ment /ɪˈnæktmənt/ *noun* [U, C] (*law* 律) the process of a law becoming official; a law which has been made official（法律、法案、法令的）制訂，通過，頒佈；法律；法規

en·amel /ɪˈnæml/ *noun* **1** [U, C] a substance that is melted onto metal, pots, etc. and forms a hard shiny surface to protect or decorate them; an object made from enamel 搪瓷；琺瑯；搪瓷製品：*a chipped enamel bowl* 脫落搪瓷的碗 ◇ *a handle inlaid with enamel* 有琺瑯鑲飾的把手 ◇ *an exhibition of enamels and jewellery* 搪瓷藝術品和珠寶首飾展覽 **2** [U] the hard white outer layer of a tooth（牙齒的）琺瑯質，釉質 **3** (also **eˌnamel ˈpaint**) [U, C] a type of paint that dries to leave a hard shiny surface 瓷漆；瓷釉

en·am·elled (*especially US* **en·am·eled**) /ɪˈnæmld/ *adj.* [usually before noun] covered or decorated with enamel 上了瓷漆（或瓷釉）的；用搪瓷（或琺瑯）裝飾的

en·am·oured (*especially US* **en·amored**) /ɪˈnæməd; *NAmE* -ərd/ *adj.* **1** (*formal*) (often in negative sentences 常用於否定句) liking sth a lot 愛好；喜歡：**~ of sth** *He was less than enamoured of the music.* 他不大愛好這種音樂。◇ **~ with sth** (*humorous*) *I'm not exactly enamoured with the idea of spending a whole day with them.* 我不是很喜歡一整天都跟他們待在一起的想法。 **2 ~ of/with sb** (*literary*) in love with sb 迷戀，傾心於（某人）

en bloc /ˌɒ̃ ˈblɒk; *NAmE* ˌɑ̃ː ˈblɑːk/ *adv.* (from *French*) as a group rather than separately 整體；全部；一起；統統：*There are reports of teachers resigning en bloc.* 有一些關於教師集體辭職的報道。

enc. = ENCL.

en·camp /ɪnˈkæmp/ *verb* [I, T] (*formal*) if a group of people **encamp** or **are encamped** somewhere, they set up a camp or have set up a camp there（使）紮營，露營

en·camp·ment /ɪnˈkæmpmənt/ *noun* a group of tents, HUTS, etc. where people live together, usually for only a short period of time（常指臨時居住的）營房，營地：*a military encampment* 軍營

en·cap·su·late /ɪnˈkæpsjuleɪt/ *verb* **~ sth (in sth)** (*formal*) to express the most important parts of sth in a few words, a small space or a single object 簡述；概括；壓縮 **SYN** **sum up**：*The poem encapsulates many of the central themes of her writing.* 這首詩概括了她許多著作的核心主題。▸ **en·cap·su·la·tion** *noun* [U, C]

en·case /ɪnˈkeɪs/ *verb* [often passive] **~ sth (in sth)** (*formal*) to surround or cover sth completely, especially to protect it 把…裝箱（或圍住、包起）：*The reactor is encased in concrete and steel.* 核反應堆由鋼筋混凝土圍住。

en·cash /ɪnˈkæʃ/ *verb* **~ sth** (*BrE, formal*) to exchange a cheque, etc. for money 把（支票等）兌現；把…變為現錢 **SYN** **cash** ▸ **en·cash·ment** *noun* [U, C]

-ence ➲ -ANCE

en·ceph·al·itis /enˌsefəˈlaɪtəs; -ˌkefə-/ *noun* [U] (*medical* 醫) a condition in which the brain becomes swollen, caused by an infection or ALLERGIC reaction 腦炎

en·ceph·al·op·athy /enˌsefəˈlɒpəθi; -ˌkefə-; *NAmE* -ˈlɑːp-/ *noun* [U] (*medical* 醫) a disease in which the functioning of the brain is affected by infection, BLOOD POISONING, etc. 腦病 ➲ see also BSE

en·chant /ɪnˈtʃɑːnt; *NAmE* -ˈtʃænt/ *verb* **1 ~ sb** (*formal*) to attract sb strongly and make them feel very interested, excited, etc. 使着迷；使陶醉 **SYN** **delight** **2 ~ sb/sth** to place sb/sth under a magic SPELL (= magic words that have special powers) 使着魔；對…用魔法（或唸咒語） **SYN** **bewitch**

en·chant·ed /ɪnˈtʃɑːntɪd; *NAmE* -ˈtʃæntɪd/ *adj.* **1** placed under a SPELL (= magic words that have special powers) 中魔法的；着了魔的；施過魔法的：*an* ***enchanted forest/kingdom*** 被施了魔法的森林／王國 **2** (*formal*) filled with great pleasure 狂喜的；極樂的 **SYN** **delighted**：*He was enchanted to see her again after so long.* 與她久別重逢，他欣喜不已。

en·chant·er /ɪnˈtʃɑːntə(r); *NAmE* -ˈtʃæn-/ *noun* (in stories) a man who has magic powers that he uses to control people（故事中）施魔法的人，巫師

en·chant·ing /ɪnˈtʃɑːntɪŋ; *NAmE* -ˈtʃæntɪŋ/ *adj.* attractive and pleasing 迷人的；令人陶醉的；使人喜悅的 **SYN** **delightful**：*an enchanting view* 迷人的景色 ▸ **en·chant·ing·ly** *adv.*

en·chant·ment /ɪnˈtʃɑːntmənt; *NAmE* -ˈtʃænt-/ *noun* **1** [U] (*formal*) a feeling of great pleasure 狂喜；陶醉 **2** [U] the state of being under a magic SPELL 着迷；着魔：*It was a place of deep mystery and enchantment.* 這是一個極其神秘和迷人的地方。 **3** [C] (*literary*) = SPELL *n.* (3)：*They had been turned to stone by an enchantment.* 他們被魔法變成了石頭。

en·chant·ress /ɪnˈtʃɑːntrəs; *NAmE* -ˈtʃæn-/ *noun* **1** (in stories) a woman who has magic powers that she uses to control people（故事中）施魔法的女人，巫婆 **2** (*literary*) a woman that men find very attractive and interesting 迷人的女子

en·chil·ada /ˌentʃɪˈlɑːdə/ *noun* (from *Spanish*) a Mexican dish consisting of a TORTILLA filled with meat and covered with a spicy sauce（墨西哥）辣肉餡玉米捲

IDM **the whole enchilˈada** (*informal*) the whole thing; everything 整個；全部；所有 ➲ more at BIG *adj.*

en·cir·cle /ɪnˈsɜːkl; *NAmE* ɪnˈsɜːrkl/ *verb* **~ sb/sth** (*formal*) to surround sb/sth completely in a circle 環繞；圍繞；包圍：*Jack's arms encircled her waist.* 傑克的雙臂摟着她的腰。◇ *The island is encircled by a coral reef.* 這個島周圍都是珊瑚礁。▸ **en·circle·ment** *noun* [U]

encl. (also **enc.**) *abbr.* (*business* 商) enclosed (used on business letters to show that another document is being sent in the same envelope) 隨函附上的，附上的（用於商業信函）

en·clave /ˈenkleɪv/ *noun* an area of a country or city where the people have a different religion, culture or NATIONALITY from those who live in the country or city that surrounds it 飛地（某國或某市境內隸屬外國或外市，具有不同宗教、文化或民族的領土）

en·close /ɪnˈkləʊz; *NAmE* ɪnˈkloʊz/ *verb* **1** [usually passive] **~ sth (in/with sth)** to build a wall, fence, etc. around sth（用牆、籬笆等）把…圍起來：*The yard had been enclosed with iron railings.* 院子用鐵柵欄圍了起來。◇ *The land was enclosed in the seventeenth century* (= in Britain, when public land was made private property). 這塊地在 17 世紀被圈為私有。◇ (*figurative*) *All translated words should be enclosed in brackets.* 所有譯文都應用括號括起來。 **2 ~ sth** (especially of a wall, fence, etc. 尤指牆、籬笆等) to surround sth 圍住：*Low hedges enclosed the flower beds.* 矮樹籬把花壇圍了起來。◇ (*figurative*) *She felt his arms enclose her.* 她感到他雙臂摟住了她。 **3 ~ sth (with sth)** to put sth in the same envelope, package, etc. as sth else 附入；隨函（或包裹等）附上：*Please return the completed form, enclosing a recent photograph.* 請將填好的表格寄回，並附上近照一張。

en·closed /ɪnˈkləʊzd; *NAmE* ɪnˈkloʊzd/ *adj.* **1** with walls, etc. all around（用牆等）圍住的，封閉的：*Do not use this substance in an enclosed space.* 切勿在不透氣的地方使用此物質。 **2** (*abbr.* **encl.**) sent with a letter, etc. 隨函附上的；附上的：*Please complete the enclosed application form.* 請填好隨函所附的申請表。◇ *Please* ***find enclosed*** *a cheque for £100.* 隨函附上 100 英鎊支票一張。 **3** (of religious communities 宗教團體) having little contact with the outside world 與外界隔絕的

en·clos·ure /ɪnˈkləʊʒə(r); *NAmE* -ˈkloʊ-/ *noun* **1** [C] a piece of land that is surrounded by a fence or wall and is used for a particular purpose 圈佔地；圈用地；圍場：*a wildlife enclosure* 野生動物圍場 **2** [U, C] the act of placing a fence or wall around a piece of land 圈地：*the enclosure of common land in the seventeenth century* * 17 世紀對公用地的圈佔 **3** [C] something that is placed in an envelope with a letter（信中）附件

en·code /ɪnˈkəʊd; *NAmE* ɪnˈkoʊd/ *verb* **1 ~ sth** to change ordinary language into letters, symbols, etc. in order to send secret messages 把…譯成電碼（或密碼） **2 ~ sth** (*computing* 計) to change information into a form that can be processed by a computer 把…編碼 **3 ~ sth** (*linguistics* 語言) to express the meaning of sth in a foreign language 把…譯成外語 ➲ compare DECODE

en·co·mium /en'kəʊmiəm; *NAmE* -'koʊm-/ *noun* (*pl.* **en·co·miums** or **en·co·mia** /en'kəʊmiə; *NAmE* -'koʊm-/) (*formal*) a speech or piece of writing that praises sb or sth highly 高度讚揚的話（或文章）；頌辭

en·com·pass /ɪn'kʌmpəs/ *verb* (*formal*) **1 ~ sth** to include a large number or range of things 包含，包括，涉及（大量事物）：*The job encompasses a wide range of responsibilities.* 這項工作涉及的職責範圍很廣。◇ *The group encompasses all ages.* 這個小組各種年齡的人都有。**2 ~ sth** to surround or cover sth completely 包圍；圍繞；圍住：*The fog soon encompassed the whole valley.* 大霧很快籠罩了整個山谷。

en·core /'ɒŋkɔː(r); *NAmE* 'ɑːŋ-/ *noun, exclamation*

■ ***noun*** an extra short performance given at the end of a concert or other performance; a request for this made by an audience calling out （音樂會或其他演出結束時）加演的節目；（觀眾要求的）再演一個；安可：*She played a Chopin waltz as an encore.* 她應聽眾的要求又加演了一首肖邦的圓舞曲。◇ *The group got three encores.* 樂團三次得到觀眾"再來一個"的請求。

■ ***exclamation*** an audience calls out **encore!** at the end of a concert to ask the performer to play or sing another piece of music （在音樂會結束時觀眾喊的）再來一個，再唱一首，再奏一曲

en·coun·ter 🔑 AW /ɪn'kaʊntə(r)/ *verb, noun*

■ ***verb*** **1** 🔑 **~ sth** to experience sth, especially sth unpleasant or difficult, while you are trying to do sth else 遭遇，遇到（尤指令人不快或困難的事） SYN **meet with, run into**：*We encountered a number of difficulties in the first week.* 我們在第一週遇到了一些困難。◇ *I had never encountered such resistance before.* 我以前從未遇到過這麼大的阻力。 **2** 🔑 **~ sb/sth** (*formal*) to meet sb, or discover or experience sth, especially sb/sth new, unusual or unexpected 偶然碰到；意外地遇見；與…邂逅 SYN **come across**：*She was the most remarkable woman he had ever encountered.* 她是他所見到過的最出色的女性。

■ ***noun*** **1** 🔑 a meeting, especially one that is sudden, unexpected or violent （尤指突然、意外或暴力的）相遇，邂逅，遭遇，衝突：**~ (with sb/sth)** *Three of them were killed in the subsequent encounter with the police.* 他們中有三個人後來在與警察的衝突中被殺死。◇ **~ (between A and B)** *The story describes the extraordinary encounter between a man and a dolphin.* 這個故事描述了一個男人與一隻海豚之間的奇遇。◇ *a chance encounter* 偶然相遇 ◇ *I've had a number of* ***close encounters*** (= situations that could have been dangerous) *with bad drivers.* 我好幾次都險些與技術不佳的司機相撞。◇ *It was his first sexual encounter* (= first experience of sex). 那是他的第一次性經歷。 **2** a sports match against a particular player or team （體育）比賽，交鋒：*She has beaten her opponent in all of their previous encounters.* 她在以前的所有交鋒中都擊敗了這個對手。 **3** (*IndE*) an incident in which police shoot dead a suspected criminal 警察擊斃嫌疑犯事件

en'counter group *noun* a group of people who meet regularly in order to help each other with emotional and PSYCHOLOGICAL problems 交心心理治療團體，會心團體（成員定期聚集）

en·cour·age 🔑 /ɪn'kʌrɪdʒ; *NAmE* -'kɜːr-/ *verb*
1 🔑 to give sb support, courage or hope 支持；鼓勵；激勵：**~ sb in sth** *My parents have always encouraged me in my choice of career.* 在我選擇職業時父母總是鼓勵我。◇ **~ sb** *We were greatly encouraged by the positive response of the public.* 公眾所持的肯定態度給了我們極大的鼓舞。 **2** 🔑 **~ sb to do sth** | **~ doing sth** to persuade sb to do sth by making it easier for them and making them believe it is a good thing to do 鼓動；勸告；慫恿：*Banks actively encourage people to borrow money.* 銀行積極鼓動人們貸款。 **3** 🔑 to make sth more likely to happen or develop 促進；助長；刺激：**~ sth (in sb/sth)** *They claim that some computer games encourage violent behaviour in young children.* 他們聲稱有些電腦遊戲助長兒童的暴力行為。◇ **~ sb to do sth** *Music and lighting are used to encourage shoppers to buy more.* 音樂和燈光用於刺激購物者買更多的東西。◇ **~ doing sth** *Technology encourages multitasking.* 技術進步促進多工處理。 OPP **discourage** ▸ **en·cour·aging** *adj.* [not usually before noun]：*This month's unemployment figures are not very encouraging.* 這個月的失業統計數字不太樂觀。◇ *You could try being a little more encouraging!* 你可以試着多給人一些鼓勵嘛！ **en·cour·aging·ly** *adv.*：*to smile encouragingly* 表示鼓勵地微微一笑 ◇ *The attendance was encouragingly high.* 出席人數之多令人振奮。

en·cour·age·ment 🔑 /ɪn'kʌrɪdʒmənt; *NAmE* -'kɜːr-/ *noun* [U, C, usually sing.]
the act of encouraging sb to do sth; something that encourages sb 鼓舞；鼓勵；起激勵作用的事物：*a few words of encouragement* 幾句鼓勵的話 ◇ *He needs all the support and encouragement he can get.* 他需要所能得到的一切支持和鼓勵。◇ *With a little encouragement from his parents he should do well.* 只要父母給點鼓勵，他應該會幹得很好。◇ **~ (to sb) (to do sth)** *She was given every encouragement to try something new.* 她得到充分的鼓勵去嘗試新事物。◇ *Her words were a great encouragement to them.* 她的話對他們是極大的鼓舞。 OPP **discouragement**

en·croach /ɪn'krəʊtʃ; *NAmE* ɪn'kroʊtʃ/ *verb* (*formal*) **1** [I] **~ (on/upon sth)** (*disapproving*) to begin to affect or use up too much of sb's time, rights, personal life, etc. 侵佔（某人的時間）；侵犯（某人的權利）；擾亂（某人的生活）：*I won't encroach on your time any longer.* 我再也不會佔用你的時間了。◇ *He never allows work to encroach upon his family life.* 他從不讓工作擾亂他的家庭生活。 **2** [I] **~ (on/upon sth)** to slowly begin to cover more and more of an area 侵蝕，蠶食（地區）：*The growing town soon encroached on the surrounding countryside.* 這個不斷擴大的城鎮不久便將周圍的農村變成了市區。◇ *the encroaching tide* (= that is coming in) 不斷湧向陸地的潮水 ▸ **en·croach·ment** *noun* [U, C]：**~ (on/upon sth)** *the regime's many encroachments on human rights* 這個政權種種侵犯人權的行為

en·crust·ation /ˌenkrʌ'steɪʃn/ *noun* = INCRUSTATION

en·crust·ed /ɪn'krʌstɪd/ *adj.* **~ (with/in sth)** covered with a thin hard layer of sth; forming a thin hard layer on sth 硬殼覆蓋的；形成硬外層的：*a crown encrusted with diamonds* 鑲滿鑽石的王冠 ◇ *encrusted blood* 已凝結的血

en·crypt /ɪn'krɪpt/ *verb* **~ sth** (*computing* 計) to put information into a special code, especially in order to prevent people from looking at it without authority 把…加密（或編碼） OPP **decrypt** ▸ **en·cryp·tion** /ɪn'krɪpʃn/ *noun* [U] OPP **decryption**

en·cum·ber /ɪn'kʌmbə(r)/ *verb* [usually passive] (*formal*) **1 ~ sb/sth (with sth)** to make it difficult for sb to do sth or for sth to happen 妨礙；阻礙；拖累：*The police operation was encumbered by crowds of reporters.* 警方的行動被成群的記者所妨礙。 **2 ~ sb/sth (with sth)** to be large and/or heavy and make it difficult for sb to move 大（或重）得難以移動；使負擔沉重：*The frogmen were encumbered by their diving equipment.* 沉重的潛水裝備使蛙人步履維艱。

en·cum·brance /ɪn'kʌmbrəns/ *noun* (*formal*) a person or thing that prevents sb from moving easily or from doing what they want 妨礙者；累贅；障礙物 SYN **burden**：*I felt I was being an encumbrance to them.* 我感到自己成了他們的累贅。

-ency ➲ -ANCY

en·cyc·lic·al /ɪn'sɪklɪkl/ *noun* an official letter written by the Pope and sent to all Roman Catholic BISHOPS 教宗通諭

en·cyc·lo·pe·dia (*BrE* also **-pae·dia**) /ɪnˌsaɪklə'piːdiə/ *noun* a book or set of books giving information about all areas of knowledge or about different areas of one particular subject, usually arranged in alphabetical order; a similar collection of information on a website or CD-ROM （紙質、網絡或光盤版）百科全書；（某一學科的）專科全書：*an* ***online encyclopedia*** 一部網絡百科全書

en·cyclo·pe·dic (*BrE* also **-paedic**) /ɪnˌsaɪkləˈpiːdɪk/ *adj.* **1** connected with encyclopedias or the type of information found in them 百科全書的；百科知識的：*encyclopedic information* 百科知識 ◇ *an encyclopedic dictionary* 百科詞典 **2** having a lot of information about a wide variety of subjects; containing complete information about a particular subject 包含各種學科的；知識淵博的；博學的：*She has an encyclopedic knowledge of natural history.* 她具有廣博的自然史知識。

end 🗝 /end/ *noun, verb*

■ ***noun***

▸ **FINAL PART** 最後部份 **1** 🗝 the final part of a period of time, an event, an activity or a story（時間、事件、活動或故事的）終止，終結，結局，結尾：*at the end of the week* 在週末 ◇ *We didn't leave until the* ***very end***. 我們直到最後才離開。◇ *the end of the book* 書的末尾 ◇ *We had to hear about the whole journey* ***from beginning to end***. 我們只好從頭到尾把整個旅行情況聽完。◇ *It's the end of an era.* 這是一個時代的終結。

▸ **FURTHEST PART** 末端 **2** 🗝 the part of an object or a place that is the furthest away from its centre 末端；盡頭；末梢：*Turn right at the end of the road.* 在路的盡頭向右轉。◇ *I joined the end of the queue.* 我站在了這隊伍的最後。◇ *Go to the end of the line!* 到這條隊的最後去！◇ *You've got something on the end of your nose.* 你的鼻尖上有點東西。◇ *Tie the ends of the string together.* 把繩子兩端繫在一起。◇ *That's his wife sitting at* ***the far end*** *of the table.* 坐在桌子遠端的那位就是他妻子。◇ *These two products are from opposite ends of the price range.* 這兩種產品一種是價格最高的，一種是價格最低的。◇ *We've travelled from one end of Mexico to the other.* 我們從墨西哥的一端旅行到了另一端。◇ *They live in the end house.* 他們住在最後的那座房子。➲ see also BIG END, DEAD END, EAST END, SPLIT END, TAIL END

▸ **FINISH** 結束 **3** 🗝 a situation in which sth does not exist any more 結束；破滅：*the end of all his dreams* 他所有夢想的破滅 ◇ *The meeting* ***came to an end*** (= finished). 會議結束了。◇ *The war was finally* ***at an end***. 戰爭終於結束了。◇ *The coup* ***brought*** *his corrupt regime* ***to an end***. 政變結束了他的腐敗統治。◇ *There's no* ***end in sight*** *to the present crisis.* 目前的危機無望結束。◇ *They have* ***called for an end to*** *violence.* 他們呼籲停止暴力。◇ *That was by no means the end of the matter.* 事情決不可能到此為止。

▸ **AIM** 目的 **4** an aim or a purpose 目的；目標：*They are prepared to use violence in pursuit of their ends.* 他們準備使用暴力來達到目的。◇ *She is exploiting the current situation for her own ends.* 她在利用目前的形勢來達到自己的目的。◇ ***With this end in view*** (= in order to achieve this) *they employed 50 new staff.* 為了達到這個目標他們雇用了 50 名新職員。◇ *We are willing to make any concessions necessary* ***to this end*** (= in order to achieve this). 為達到此目的我們願作出任何必要的讓步。
➲ SYNONYMS at TARGET

▸ **PART OF ACTIVITY** 部份活動 **5** [usually sing.] a part of an activity with which sb is concerned, especially in business（尤指經營活動的）部份，方面：*We need somebody to handle the marketing end of the business.* 我們需要有人來處理業務的推廣。◇ *Are there any problems at your end?* 你那邊有什麼問題嗎？◇ *I have kept my end of the bargain.* 我已履行了我方的協議條件。

▸ **OF TELEPHONE LINE/JOURNEY** 電話線；旅程 **6** [usually sing.] either of two places connected by a telephone call, journey, etc. 端點；終點：*I answered the phone but there was no one* ***at the other end***. 我接了電話，但線路的另一端沒有人。◇ *Jean is going to meet me at* ***the other end***. 瓊打算在那邊終點站接我。

▸ **OF SPORTS FIELD** 運動場 **7** one of the two halves of a sports field 半邊球場：*The teams changed ends at half-time.* 上半場結束時雙方交換了場地。

▸ **PIECE LEFT** 剩餘物 **8** (*BrE*) a small piece that is left after sth has been used 剩餘物；殘餘；殘片：*a cigarette end* 煙蒂 ➲ see also FAG END, LOOSE END, ODDS AND ENDS

▸ **DEATH** 死亡 **9** [usually sing.] a person's death. People say 'end' to avoid saying 'death'. 辭世，過世（婉辭，與 death 同義）：*She came to* ***an untimely end*** (= died young). 她英年早逝。◇ *I was with him at the end* (= when he died). 他臨終時我在他身邊。◇ (*literary*) *He* ***met his end*** (= died) *at the Battle of Waterloo.* 他在滑鐵盧戰役中陣亡。

IDM **at the ˌend of the ˈday** (*BrE, informal*) used to introduce the most important fact after everything has been considered（考慮到所有情況後引出最重要的事實）最終，到頭來：*At the end of the day, he'll still have to make his own decision.* 最終，他還得自己拿主意。 **a bad/sticky ˈend** (*BrE*) something unpleasant that happens to sb, for example punishment or a violent death, usually because of their own actions 不愉快的結局；可悲的下場：*He'll* ***come to a sticky end*** *one of these days if he carries on like that.* 如果他繼續那樣下去，總有一天會落得個可悲的下場。 **be at the end of sth** to have almost nothing left of sth 所剩無幾；到…的盡頭（或極限）：*I'm at the end of my patience.* 我已忍無可忍。◇ *They are at the end of their food supply.* 他們的食物儲備已消耗殆盡。 **be at the ˌend of your ˈtether** (*BrE*) (*NAmE* **be at the ˌend of your ˈrope**) to feel that you cannot deal with a difficult situation any more because you are too tired, worried, etc. 筋疲力盡；智窮力竭；山窮水盡 **be the ˈend** (*BrE, informal*) when you say that people or situations are **the end**, you mean that you are annoyed with them 令人討厭；惹人煩惱；讓人無法容忍 **an ˌend in itˈself** a thing that is itself important and not just a part of sth more important 本身重要的事 **the end justifies the ˈmeans** (*saying*) bad or unfair methods of doing sth are acceptable if the result of that action is good or positive 只要目的正當，可以不擇手段 **(reach) the end of the ˈline/ˈroad** (to reach) the point at which sth can no longer continue in the same way（達到）盡頭，極限；窮途末路：*A defeat in the second round marked the end of the line for last year's champion.* 第二局的失利表明去年的冠軍得主已衛冕無望。 **end of ˈstory** (*informal*) (*NAmE* also **end of ...**) used when you are stating that there is nothing more that can be said or done about sth 情況就是這樣；就這麼辦 **ˌend to ˈend** in a line, with the ends touching 首尾相接連成一行：*They arranged the tables end to end.* 他們將桌子連接起來排成一行。 **get/have your ˈend away** (*BrE, slang*) to have sex 性交 **go to the ˌends of the ˈearth** to do everything possible, even if it is difficult, in order to get or achieve sth 走遍天涯海角；歷盡千辛萬苦：*I'd go to the ends of the earth to see her again.* 哪怕走遍天涯海角我也要再見她一面。 **in the ˈend 1** 🗝 after a long period of time or series of events 最後；終於：*He tried various jobs and in the end became an accountant.* 他嘗試過各種各樣的工作，最後當上了會計。 **2** 🗝 after everything has been considered 到頭來；最終：*You can try your best to impress the interviewers but in the end it's often just a question of luck.* 你可以盡最大的努力給主持面試的人留下深刻的印象，不過最終常常要視乎運氣。 **keep your ˈend up** (*BrE, informal*) to continue to be cheerful in a difficult situation（在困境中）不泄氣，保持樂觀 **make (both) ends ˈmeet** to earn just enough money to be able to buy the things you need 使收支相抵；勉強維持生計：*Many families struggle to make ends meet.* 許多家庭只能勉強維持生計。 **no ˈend** (*informal*) very much 極其；非常：*It upset me no end to hear they'd split up.* 聽說他們要離婚，我感到非常不安。 **no ˈend of sth** (*informal*) a lot of sth 無數；大量；許多：*We had no end of trouble getting them to agree.* 我們費了九牛二虎之力才使他們同意。 **not the end of the ˈworld** (*informal*) not the worst thing that could happen to sb 天不會塌下來；不是滅頂之災：*Failing one exam is not the end of the world.* 一次考試不及格並非世界末日。 **on ˈend 1** in a vertical position 豎着；直立着：*It'll fit if you stand it on end.* 如果把它豎着就放得進去了。 **2** for the stated length of time, without stopping 連續地；不斷地：*He would disappear for* ***weeks on end***. 他常常是連續幾週不見人影。 **put an ˈend to yourself | put an ˈend to it all** to kill yourself 自殺；一了百了 ➲ more at BEGINNING, BITTER *adj.*, BURN *v.*, DEEP *adj.*, HAIR, HEAR, LIGHT *n.*, LOOSE END, MEANS, RECEIVE, ROUGH *adj.*, SHARP *adj.*, SHORT *adj.*, THIN *adj.*, WIT, WRONG *adj.*

■ ***verb*** 🗝 [I, T] to finish; to make sth finish 結束；終止：*The road ends here.* 這條路到此為止。◇ *How does the* *story end?* 這個故事結局如何？◇ *The speaker ended by suggesting some topics for discussion.* 演講者最後給出了幾個討論話題。◇ **~ with sth** *Her note ended with the words: 'See you soon.'* 她的便條以“再見”結束。◇ **~ sth** *They decided to end their relationship.* 他們決定斷絕關係。◇ **~ sth with sth** *They ended the play with a song.* 他們以一首歌曲結束了這齣戲。◇ **+ speech** *'And that was that,' she ended.* “就這樣了。”她最後說。

IDM **a/the sth to end all sths** used to emphasize how large, important, exciting, etc. you think sth is 最大（或最重要、最激動人心等）的…： *The movie has a car chase to end all car chases.* 這部影片的汽車追逐場面非常刺激。 **ˌend your ˈdays/ˈlife (in sth)** to spend the last part of your life in a particular state or place（在某種狀態下或某處）度過餘生，安度晚年： *He ended his days in poverty.* 他在貧窮中度過餘生。 **ˌend in ˈtears** (*BrE, informal*) if you say that sth will **end in tears**, you are warning sb that what they are doing will have an unhappy or unpleasant result（告誡時說）以痛苦而告終，結局悲慘 **ˈend it all | ˌend your ˈlife** to kill yourself 自殺；一了百了

PHR V **ˈend in sth** [no passive] **1** to have sth as an ending 以…結尾；末端是： *The word I'm thinking of ends in '-ous'.* 我想到的這個詞以 ous 結尾。 **2** to have sth as a result 以…為結果；以…告終： *Their long struggle ended in failure.* 他們的長期努力以失敗告終。◇ *The debate ended in uproar.* 那場辯論最後以大吵大鬧收場。 **ˌend ˈup** to find yourself in a place or situation that you did not intend or expect to be in 最終成為；最後處於：**~ doing sth** *I ended up doing all the work myself.* 結果所有的活兒都是我一個人幹了。◇ **+ adv./prep.** *If you go on like this you'll end up in prison.* 如果你繼續這樣，早晚得進監獄。◇ **+ adj.** *If he carries on driving like that, he'll end up dead.* 如果他繼續那樣開車，總有一天會把命都丟掉。

en·dan·ger /ɪnˈdeɪndʒə(r)/ *verb* **~ sb/sth** to put sb/sth in a situation in which they could be harmed or damaged 使遭危險；危及；危害： *The health of our children is being endangered by exhaust fumes.* 我們孩子的健康正受到排放出的廢氣損害。◇ *That one mistake seriously endangered the future of the company.* 僅那一個失誤就嚴重地危及了公司的未來。◇ *The sea turtle is an* ***endangered species*** (= it may soon no longer exist). 海龜是瀕危物種。

en·dear /ɪnˈdɪə(r); *NAmE* -ˈdɪr/ *verb*

PHR V **enˈdear sb/yourself to sb** to make sb/yourself popular 使受歡迎（或喜愛、愛慕）： *Their policies on taxation didn't endear them to voters.* 他們的稅收政策並沒使他們受到選民的歡迎。◇ *She was a talented teacher who endeared herself to all who worked with her.* 她是一位深受同事喜愛的有才華的教師。

en·dear·ing /ɪnˈdɪərɪŋ; *NAmE* -ˈdɪr-/ *adj.* causing people to feel affection 令人愛慕的；惹人喜愛的；討人喜歡的 **SYN** **lovable**： *an endearing habit* 討人喜歡的習慣 ▸ **en·dear·ing·ly** *adv.*

en·dear·ment /ɪnˈdɪəmənt; *NAmE* -ˈdɪrm-/ *noun* [C, U] a word or an expression that is used to show affection 表示愛慕的話語；親熱的表示： *They were whispering endearments to each other.* 他們彼此低聲傾吐着愛慕之情。◇ *'Darling' is a term of endearment.* “親愛的”是一種昵稱。

en·deav·our (*especially US* **en·deavor**) /ɪnˈdevə(r)/ *noun, verb*

■ ***noun*** [U, C] (*formal*) an attempt to do sth, especially sth new or difficult（尤指新的或艱苦的）努力，嘗試： *Please make every endeavour to arrive on time.* 請盡全力按時到達。◇ *advances in the field of scientific endeavour* 在科學探索領域的進步 ◇ *The manager is expected to use his or her best endeavours to promote the artist's career.* 經理人應以最大的努力來推動一位演藝人的事業發展。

■ ***verb*** **~ to do sth** (*formal*) to try very hard to do sth 努力；盡力；竭力 **SYN** **strive**： *I will endeavour to do my best for my country.* 我將竭盡全力報效祖國。

en·dem·ic /enˈdemɪk/ *adj.* regularly found in a particular place or among a particular group of people and difficult to get rid of 地方性的；（某地或某集體中）特有的，流行的，難擺脫的： **~ (in …)** *Malaria is endemic in many hot countries.* 瘧疾是許多氣候炎熱國家的流行病。◇ *Corruption is endemic in the system.* 腐敗在這種制度下普遍存在。◇ **~ (among …)** *an attitude endemic among senior members of the profession* 此行業中的資深者普遍持有的看法 ◇ **~ (to …)** *species endemic to* (= only found in) *Madagascar* 馬達加斯加特有的物種 ◇ *the endemic problem of racism* 普遍存在的種族主義問題 ➲ compare PANDEMIC

end·game /ˈendgeɪm/ *noun* **1** the final stage of a game of CHESS（棋賽的）尾盤，殘局 **2** the final stage of a political process（政治進程的）最後階段

end·ing 0-w /ˈendɪŋ/ *noun*

1 0-w the last part of a story, film/movie, etc.（故事、電影等的）結尾，結局： *His stories usually have a* ***happy ending***. 他的故事通常有一個美滿的結局。 **OPP** **opening** **2** 0-w the act of finishing sth; the last part of sth 結束；終結；最後部份： *the anniversary of the ending of the Pacific War* 太平洋戰爭結束的週年紀念日 ◇ *It was the perfect ending to the perfect day.* 那是美好一天的圓滿結束。 **3** 0-w the last part of a word, that is added to a main part 詞尾；字尾： *verb endings* 動詞詞尾 ◇ *a* ***masculine/feminine ending*** 陽性／陰性詞尾

en·dive /ˈendaɪv; -dɪv/ *noun* [C, U] **1** (*BrE*) (*NAmE* **chic·ory**, **ˌcurly ˈendive**, **fri·sée** [U]) a plant with green curly leaves that are eaten raw as a vegetable（捲葉）歐洲菊苣 **2** (*NAmE*) (*BrE* **chic·ory**) a small pale green plant with bitter leaves that are eaten raw or cooked as a vegetable. The root can be dried and used with or instead of coffee. 菊苣（根乾燥後可與咖啡同飲或作其代用品）

end·less /ˈendləs/ *adj.* **1** very large in size or amount and seeming to have no end 無止境的；無垠的；無窮無盡的；不計其數的 **SYN** **limitless**： *endless patience* 無限的耐心 ◇ *endless opportunities for making money* 無數掙錢的機會 ◇ *The possibilities are endless.* 存在着無限的可能性。◇ *an endless list of things to do* 列不完的要做的事 ◇ *We don't have an endless supply of money, you know.* 你要知道，我們沒有取之不盡的資金供給。 **2** continuing for a long time and seeming to have no end 永久的；不斷的；無休止的： *an endless round of parties and visits* 沒完沒了一個又一個的社交聚會和訪問 ◇ *The journey seemed endless.* 旅程似乎沒有盡頭。◇ *I've had enough of their endless arguing.* 我聽夠了他們無休止的爭吵。 **3** (*technical* 術語) (of a LOOP, etc. 環狀物) having the ends joined together so it forms one piece 兩端連接的；環狀的： *an endless loop of tape* 環狀帶 ▸ **end·less·ly** *adv.*： *She talks endlessly about her problems.* 她喋喋不休地談論着自己的問題。◇ *an endlessly repeated pattern* 不斷重複的模式

end·note /ˈendnəʊt; *NAmE* -noʊt/ *noun* a note printed at the end of a book or section of a book（書末或章節末的）尾註 ➲ **WRITING TUTOR** page WT18

endo·crine /ˈendəʊkrɪn; -kraɪn; *NAmE* ˈendəkrɪn/ *adj.* (*biology* 生) connected with GLANDS that put HORMONES and other products directly into the blood 內分泌腺的；內分泌的： *the endocrine system* 內分泌系統 ➲ compare EXOCRINE

endo·crin·ology /ˌendəʊkrɪˈnɒlədʒi; *NAmE* ˌendoʊkrəˈnɑːl-/ *noun* [U] (*medical* 醫) the part of medicine concerning the endocrine system and HORMONES 內分泌學 ▸ **endo·crin·olo·gist** /-dʒɪst/ *noun*

en·dog·amy /enˈdɒgəmi; *NAmE* -ˈdɑːg-/ *noun* [U] (*technical* 術語) the custom of marrying only people from your local community 族內婚，內婚制（只在一個群體內部通婚的風俗） ➲ compare EXOGAMY

en·dogen·ous /enˈdɒdʒənəs; *NAmE* -ˈdɑːdʒ-/ *adj.* (*medical* 醫) (of a disease or SYMPTOM 疾病或症狀) having no obvious cause 內源性的；內生的 ➲ compare EXOGENOUS

endo·plasm /ˈendəʊplæzəm; *NAmE* ˈendoʊ-/ *noun* [U] (*biology* 生) (*old-fashioned*) the more liquid inner layer of the jelly-like substance inside cells（細胞）內質 ➲ compare ECTOPLASM (1)

en·dor·phin /enˈdɔːfɪn; *NAmE* -ˈdɔːrf-/ *noun* (*biology* 生) a HORMONE produced in the brain that reduces the

E

feeling of pain 內啡肽，腦內啡（內分泌激素，有鎮痛作用）

en·dorse /ɪnˈdɔːs; NAmE ɪnˈdɔːrs/ *verb* **1 ~ sth** to say publicly that you support a person, statement or course of action（公開）贊同，支持，認可：*I wholeheartedly endorse his remarks.* 我真誠地贊同他的話。◇ *Members of all parties endorsed a ban on land mines.* 各黨派成員都贊同禁用地雷。**2 ~ sth** to say in an advertisement that you use and like a particular product so that other people will want to buy it（在廣告中）宣傳，代言（某一產品）**3 ~ sth** to write your name on the back of a cheque so that it can be paid into a bank account（在支票背面）簽名，背書 **4** [usually passive] **~ sth** (BrE) to write details of a driving offence on sb's DRIVING LICENCE（在駕駛執照上）記錄違章事項：*You risk having your licence endorsed.* 你這樣做駕照可能被記錄違章。

en·dorse·ment /ɪnˈdɔːsmənt; NAmE -ˈdɔːrs-/ *noun* [C, U] **1** a public statement or action showing that you support sb/sth（公開的）贊同，支持，認可：*The election victory is a clear endorsement of their policies.* 競選成功顯然是對他們政策的支持。◇ *a letter of endorsement* 認可證書 **2** a statement made in an advertisement, usually by sb famous or important, saying that they use and like a particular product（通常由名人或要人在廣告中為某一產品的）宣傳，代言 **3** (BrE) details of a driving offence written on sb's DRIVING LICENCE（駕駛執照上的）違章記錄

en·do·scope /ˈendəskəʊp; NAmE -skoʊp/ *noun* an instrument used in medical operations which consists of a very small camera on a long thin tube which can be put into a person's body so that the parts inside can be seen 內鏡；內窺鏡；內腔鏡

en·dos·co·py /enˈdɒskəpi; NAmE -ˈdɑːsk-/ *noun* [C, U] (pl. -ies) (medical 醫) a medical operation in which an endoscope is put into a person's body so that the parts inside can be seen 內鏡檢查；內窺鏡檢查

endo·skel·eton /ˈendəʊskelɪtn; NAmE ˈendoʊ-/ *noun* (anatomy 解) the bones inside the body of an animal that give it shape and support 內骨骼（動物體內的支撐骨架）➲ compare EXOSKELETON

endo·sperm /ˈendəʊspɜːm; NAmE ˈendoʊspɜːrm/ *noun* [U] (biology 生) the part of the plant seed that provides food for the EMBRYO 胚乳

endo·ther·mic /ˌendəʊˈθɜːmɪk; NAmE ˌendoʊˈθɜːrmɪk/ *adj.* (chemistry 化) (of a chemical reaction 化學反應) needing heat in order to take place 吸熱的 ➲ compare EXOTHERMIC

endow /ɪnˈdaʊ/ *verb* **~ sth** to give a large sum of money to a school, a college or another institution to provide it with an income（向學校等機構）捐錢，捐贈，資助

PHR V **be enˈdowed with sth** (formal) to naturally have a particular feature, quality, etc. 天生賦有，生來具有（某種特性、品質等）：*She was endowed with intelligence and wit.* 她天資聰穎。➲ see also WELL ENDOWED **enˈdow sb/sth with sth** (formal) **1** to believe or imagine that sb/sth has a particular quality 認為…具有某種品質：*She had endowed Marcus with the qualities she wanted him to possess.* 她認為馬庫斯具有她所期望的品質。**2** to give sth to sb/sth 給予；賦予：*to endow sb with a responsibility* 賦予某人以責任

en·dow·ment /ɪnˈdaʊmənt/ *noun* (formal) **1** [C, U] money that is given to a school, a college or another institution to provide it with an income; the act of giving this money 捐款；捐贈；資助 **2** [C, usually pl.] a quality or an ability that you are born with 天賦；天資；才能

enˈdowment mortgage *noun* (BrE) a type of MORTGAGE (= money borrowed to buy property) in which money is regularly paid into an endowment policy. At the end of a particular period of time this money is then used to pay back the money that was borrowed. 定期人壽保險按揭；兩全人壽保險按揭 ➲ compare REPAYMENT MORTGAGE

enˈdowment policy *noun* (BrE) a type of life insurance in which a person regularly pays money to an insurance company, and receives a sum of money from them at the end of a particular period of time 定期人壽保險，兩全人壽保險（保險期內死亡或期滿生存均可得到保險金）

end·paper /ˈendpeɪpə(r)/ *noun* (technical 術語) a blank or decorated page stuck inside the front or back cover of a book 扉頁；襯頁

ˈend product *noun* something that is produced by a particular activity or process 製成品

ˌend reˈsult *noun* [usually sing.] the final result of a particular activity or process 最終結果

ˈend run *noun* (in AMERICAN FOOTBALL 美式足球) an attempt by the person carrying the ball to run around the end of the line of defending players 端線迂迴進攻

en·dur·ance /ɪnˈdjʊərəns; NAmE -ˈdʊr-/ *noun* [U] the ability to continue doing sth painful or difficult for a long period of time without complaining 忍耐力；耐久力：*He showed remarkable endurance throughout his illness.* 他在整個生病期間表現出非凡的忍耐力。◇ *They were humiliated* ***beyond endurance***. 他們被羞辱到忍無可忍的地步。◇ *This event tests both physical and mental endurance.* 該比賽項目既是對體力也是對心理承受力的考驗。◇ *powers of endurance* 耐力 ◇ *The party turned out to be more of an* ***endurance test*** *than a pleasure.* 這次聚會結果成了一次耐力測試，而不是一件樂事。

en·dure /ɪnˈdjʊə(r); NAmE -ˈdʊr/ *verb* (formal) **1** [T] to experience and deal with sth that is painful or unpleasant, especially without complaining 忍耐；忍受 SYN **bear**：**~ sth** *They had to endure a long wait before the case came to trial.* 在此案審理前他們只得忍受長時間的等待。◇ *She could not endure the thought of parting.* 一想到分別她就無法忍受。◇ *The pain was almost too great to endure.* 痛苦得幾乎難以忍受。◇ (formal) *a love that endures all things and never fails* 可經受一切考驗的永不凋謝的愛情 ◇ **~ doing sth** *He can't endure being defeated.* 他無法忍受失敗。◇ **~ to do sth** *He can't endure to be defeated.* 他無法忍受失敗。**2** [I] to continue to exist for a long time 持續；持久 SYN **last**：*a success that will endure* 將會持續的成功 ▸ **en·dur·able** /ɪnˈdjʊərəbl; NAmE -ˈdʊr-/ *adj.*：*I felt that life was no longer endurable.* 我感到生活再也無法忍受。OPP **unendurable**

en·dur·ing /ɪnˈdjʊərɪŋ; NAmE -ˈdʊr-/ *adj.* lasting for a long time 持久的；耐久的：*enduring memories* 永存的記憶 ◇ *What is the reason for the game's enduring appeal?* 這種遊戲為什麼具有經久不衰的吸引力呢？▸ **en·dur·ing·ly** *adv.*：*an enduringly popular style* 一直流行的式樣

ˌend-ˈuser *noun* a person who actually uses a product rather than one who makes or sells it, especially a person who uses a product connected with computers（尤指計算機產品的）最終用戶，直接用戶，終端用戶

end·ways /ˈendweɪz/ (also **end·wise** /-waɪz/) *adv.* **1** (also **ˌendways/ˌendwise ˈon**) (of an object 物體) with one end facing up, forwards, or towards the person who is looking at it 末端朝上（或向前）地；豎着：*We turned the table endways to get it through the doors.* 我們把桌子腳朝上豎着以便挪進門。◇ *The first picture was taken from the side of the building, and the second one endways on.* 第一張照片照的是樓房側面，第二張照的是樓房正面。**2** with the end of one thing touching the end of another 首尾相連地；兩端相接地：*The stones are laid down endways to make a path.* 石頭一塊接一塊地鋪成小路。

ˈend zone *noun* the area at the end of an AMERICAN FOOTBALL field into which the ball must be carried or passed in order to score points（美式足球的）端區，球門區

enema /ˈenəmə/ *noun* a liquid that is put into a person's RECTUM (= the opening through which solid waste leaves the body) in order to clean out the BOWELS, especially before a medical operation; the act of cleaning out the bowels in this way 灌腸劑；（尤指手術前的）灌腸

enemy 0‑w /ˈenəmi/ *noun* (*pl.* **-ies**)
1 0‑w [C] a person who hates sb or who acts or speaks against sb/sth 敵人；仇人；反對者：*He has a lot of enemies in the company.* 他在公司裏有很多對頭。◇ *After just one day, she had already* ***made an enemy of*** *her manager.* 剛過一天她就已經與經理為敵了。◇ *It is rare to find a prominent politician with few* ***political enemies.*** 沒有什麼政敵的傑出從政者是罕見的。◇ *The state has a duty to protect its citizens against external enemies.* 國家有義務保護本國公民不受外敵侵犯。◇ *Birds are the* ***natural enemies*** *of many insect pests* (= they kill them). 鳥類是許多害蟲的天敵。➲ see also ENMITY **2** 0‑w **the enemy** [sing.+sing./pl. v.] a country that you are fighting a war against; the soldiers, etc. of this country 敵國；敵軍；敵兵：*The enemy was/were forced to retreat.* 敵軍被迫撤退了。◇ ***enemy forces/aircraft/territory*** 敵軍；敵機；敵佔區 ◇ *behind* ***enemy lines*** (= the area controlled by the enemy) 在敵後 ➲ COLLOCATIONS at WAR **3** 0‑w [C] **~ (of sth)** (*formal*) anything that harms sth or prevents it from being successful 危害物；大敵：*Poverty and ignorance are the enemies of progress.* 貧窮和愚昧阻礙進步。**IDM** see WORST *adj.*

en·er·get·ic **AW** /ˌenəˈdʒetɪk; *NAmE* ˌenərˈdʒ-/ *adj.* having or needing a lot of energy and enthusiasm 精力充沛的；充滿活力的；需要能量的；積極的：*He knew I was energetic and dynamic and would get things done.* 他知道我精力充沛、生氣勃勃，會把事情辦成的。◇ *an energetic supporter* 熱情支持者 ◇ *The heart responds well to energetic exercise.* 心臟對劇烈運動反應良好。◇ *For the more energetic* (= people who prefer physical activities), *we offer windsurfing and diving.* 我們為喜歡劇烈運動的人準備了帆板和潛水運動。◇ *I think I'd prefer something a little less energetic.* 我想我更喜歡不太劇烈的活動。▸ **en·er·get·ic·al·ly** **AW** /-kli/ *adv.*

en·er·gize (*BrE* also **-ise**) /ˈenədʒaɪz; *NAmE* ˈenərdʒ-/ *verb* **1 ~ sb** to make sb enthusiastic about sth 使充滿熱情 **2 ~ sb** to give sb more energy, strength, etc. 給（某人）增添能量（或精力、活力、幹勁）：*a refreshing and energizing fruit drink* 提神並增加能量的果汁飲料 **3 ~ sth** (*technical* 術語) to supply power or energy to a machine, an atom, etc. 提供電力（或能量）；使通電

en·ergy 0‑w **AW** /ˈenədʒi; *NAmE* -ərdʒi/ *noun*
1 0‑w [U] the ability to put effort and enthusiasm into an activity, work, etc. 精力；活力；幹勁：*It's a waste of time and energy.* 那是浪費時間和精力。◇ *She's always* ***full of energy.*** 她總是充滿活力。◇ ***nervous energy*** (= energy produced by feeling nervous) 精神緊張而產生的精力 **2 energies** [pl.] the physical and mental effort that you use to do sth 精力；力量：*She put all her energies into her work.* 她把全部精力都投入到工作中去了。◇ ***creative/destructive energies*** 創造／毀滅力 **3** 0‑w [U] a source of power, such as fuel, used for driving machines, providing heat, etc. 能源：***solar/nuclear energy*** 太陽能；核能 ◇ *It is important to conserve energy.* 節省能源十分重要。◇ *an energy crisis* (= for example when fuel is not freely available) 能源危機 ➲ COLLOCATIONS at ENVIRONMENT **4** [U] (*physics* 物) the ability of matter or RADIATION to work because of its mass, movement, electric charge, etc. 能；能量：***kinetic/potential, etc. energy*** 動能、勢能等

ener·vate /ˈenəveɪt; *NAmE* ˈenərv-/ *verb* **~ sb** (*formal*) to make sb feel weak and tired 使感到衰弱（或虛弱、無力）：*an enervating disease/climate* 使人衰弱的疾病；使人感到乏力的氣候 ▸ **en·er·va·tion** /ˌenəˈveɪʃn; *NAmE* ˌenərˈv-/ *noun* [U]

en·fant ter·rible /ˌɒ̃fɒ̃ teˈriːbl; *NAmE* ˌɑːfɑː/ *noun* (*pl.* **en·fants ter·ribles** /ˌɒ̃fɒ̃ teˈriːbl; *NAmE* ˌɑːfɑː/) (from *French*) a person who is young and successful and whose behaviour and ideas may be unusual and may shock or embarrass other people 少年得志不可一世的人

en·fee·ble /ɪnˈfiːbl/ *verb* **~ sb/sth** (*formal*) to make sb/sth weak 使衰弱；使虛弱；使無力 ▸ **en·fee·bled** *adj.*

en·fold /ɪnˈfəʊld; *NAmE* ɪnˈfoʊld/ *verb* (*literary*) **1 ~ sb/sth (in sth)** to hold sb in your arms in a way that shows affection 擁抱；摟抱 **SYN** **embrace**：*She lay quietly, enfolded in his arms.* 她靜靜地躺在他懷裏。**2 ~ sb/sth (in sth)** to surround or cover sb/sth completely 包趕；圍住；裹住：*Darkness spread and enfolded him.* 黑暗瀰漫開來，將他籠罩。

en·force **AW** /ɪnˈfɔːs; *NAmE* ɪnˈfɔːrs/ *verb* **1 ~ sth (on/against sb/sth)** to make sure that people obey a particular law or rule 強制執行，強行實施（法律或規定）：*It's the job of the police to enforce the law.* 警察的工作就是執法。◇ *The legislation will be difficult to enforce.* 這一法規將難以實施。◇ *United Nations troops enforced a ceasefire in the area.* 聯合國軍隊在該地區強制執行停火命令。**2 ~ sth (on sb)** to make sth happen or force sb to do sth 強迫；迫使：*You can't enforce cooperation between the players.* 隊員間的配合並非強迫命令而成。▸ **en·force·able** /-əbl/ *adj.*：*A gambling debt is not legally enforceable.* 賭債不能通過法律手段強制償還。**en·force·ment** **AW** *noun* [U]：*strict enforcement of regulations* 規章的嚴格執行 ◇ ***law enforcement*** *officers* 執法官員

en·forced **AW** /ɪnˈfɔːst; *NAmE* ɪnˈfɔːrst/ *adj.* that sb is forced to do or experience without being able to control it 強迫的；強制性的：*a period of enforced absence* 不得不離開的一段時間

en·for·cer /ɪnˈfɔːsə(r); *NAmE* -fɔːrs-/ *noun* a person whose responsibility is to make sure that other people perform the actions they are supposed to, especially in a government 實施者；強制執行者

en·fran·chise /ɪnˈfræntʃaɪz/ *verb* [usually passive] **~ sb** (*formal*) to give sb the right to vote in an election 給（某人）選舉權 **OPP** **disenfranchise** ▸ **en·fran·chise·ment** /ɪnˈfræntʃɪzmənt/ *noun* [U]

eng. *abbr.* (*BrE*) (in writing) engineer; engineering（書寫形式）工程師，工程，工程學

en·gage 0‑w /ɪnˈgeɪdʒ/ *verb*
1 0‑w [T] **~ sth** (*formal*) to succeed in attracting and keeping sb's attention and interest 吸引住（注意力、興趣）：*It is a movie that engages both the mind and the eye.* 這是一部令人賞心悅目的影片。**2** 0‑w [T] **~ sb (as sth) | ~ sth | ~ sb to do sth** (*formal*) to employ sb to do a particular job 雇用；聘用：*He is currently engaged as a consultant.* 他現在受雇為顧問。**3** [I] **~ (with sth/sb)** to become involved with and try to understand sth/sb 與…建立密切關係；盡力理解：*She has the ability to engage with young minds.* 她能夠與年輕人心意相通。**4** [T, I] **~ (sb)** (*formal*) to begin fighting with sb 與（某人）交戰；與（某人）開戰：*to engage the enemy* 與敵人交戰 **5** [I, T] when a part of a machine **engages**, or when you **engage** it, it fits together with another part of the machine and the machine begins to work（使）銜接，齧合：*The cogwheels are not engaging.* 齒輪未齧合在一起。◇ **~ with sth** *One cogwheel engages with the next.* 齒輪一個個齧合在一起。◇ **~ sth** *Engage the clutch before selecting a gear.* 先踩離合器再掛擋。**OPP** **disengage**
PHR V **en'gage in sth | en'gage sb in sth** (*formal*) to take part in sth; to make sb take part in sth（使）從事，參加：*Even in prison, he continued to engage in criminal activities.* 他甚至在監獄裏還繼續從事犯罪活動。◇ *She tried desperately to* ***engage him in conversation.*** 她用盡辦法要他跟她談話。

en·gaged 0‑w /ɪnˈgeɪdʒd/ *adj.*
1 0‑w (*formal*) busy doing sth 忙於；從事於：**~ (in sth)** *They are engaged in talks with the Irish government.* 他們正忙着與愛爾蘭政府談判。◇ *They were engaged in conversation.* 他們正談得來勁。◇ **~ (on sth)** *He is now engaged on his second novel.* 他正埋頭寫他的第二部小說。◇ *I can't come to dinner on Tuesday—I'm* ***otherwise engaged*** (= I have already arranged to do something else). 我星期二不能來參加宴會，我有別的安排。**2** 0‑w having agreed to marry sb 已訂婚：*When did you* ***get engaged****?* 你們什麼時候訂的婚？◇ *an engaged couple* 已訂婚的一對 ◇ **~ to sb** *She's engaged to Peter.* 她與彼得訂了婚。◇ *They are engaged to be married* (= to each other). 他們已經訂婚。➲ COLLOCATIONS at MARRIAGE **3** 0‑w (*BrE*) (*NAmE* **busy**) (of a telephone line 電話線) being used 被佔用的；使用中的：*I couldn't get through—the line's engaged.* 我打不通電話，線路忙。◇ *I phoned earlier but you were engaged* (= using your phone). 我早先打過電

話，但你那邊佔線。◇ *the* **engaged** *tone/signal* 忙音；佔線信號 ➲ COLLOCATIONS at PHONE **4** (*BrE*) (of a public toilet/bathroom 公共衞生間) being used 佔用着；使用中 **OPP** **vacant**

en·gage·ment /ɪnˈɡeɪdʒmənt/ *noun*
▸ **BEFORE MARRIAGE 婚前** **1** [C] an agreement to marry sb; the period during which two people are engaged 訂婚；訂婚期間：*Their engagement was announced in the local paper.* 他們訂婚的消息已在當地報紙上公佈。◇ **~ (to sb)** *She has* **broken off her engagement** *to Charles.* 她已解除同查爾斯的婚約。◇ *an engagement party* 訂婚宴會◇ *a long/short engagement* 長／短婚約期
▸ **ARRANGEMENT TO DO STH 約定** **2** [C] an arrangement to do sth at a particular time, especially sth official or sth connected with your job（尤指正式的或與工作有關的）約定，約會，預約：*an* **engagement book/diary** 預約簿／日誌◇ *He has a number of social engagements next week.* 他下週有幾次社交約會。◇ *It was her first* **official engagement**. 那是她第一次正式約會。◇ *I had to refuse because of a* **prior engagement**. 我因為已經有預約只好拒絕了。
▸ **FIGHTING 戰鬥** **3** [C, U] (*technical* 術語) fighting between two armies, etc. 戰鬥；交戰：*The general tried to avoid an engagement with the enemy.* 將軍竭力避免與敵軍交火。
▸ **BEING INVOLVED 聯繫** **4** [U] **~ (with sb/sth)** (*formal*) being involved with sb/sth in an attempt to understand them/it（與…的）密切關係；（對…的）瞭解：*Her views are based on years of engagement with the problems of the inner city.* 她的觀點是以多年對內城區問題的瞭解為基礎的。
▸ **EMPLOYMENT 雇用** **5** [U, C] (*BrE*) an arrangement to employ sb; the process of employing sb 雇用；聘用：*The terms of engagement are to be agreed in writing.* 聘用條款應有書面協議。

enˈgagement ring *noun* a ring that a man gives to a woman when they agree to get married 訂婚戒指

en·gaging /ɪnˈɡeɪdʒɪŋ/ *adj.* interesting or pleasant in a way that attracts your attention 有趣的；令人愉快的；迷人的：*an engaging smile* 迷人的微笑 ▸ **en·ga·ging·ly** *adv.*

en·gen·der /ɪnˈdʒendə(r)/ *verb* **~ sth** (*formal*) to make a feeling or situation exist 產生，引起（某種感覺或情況）：*The issue engendered controversy.* 這個問題引起了爭論。

en·gine /ˈendʒɪn/ *noun*
1 the part of a vehicle that produces power to make the vehicle move 發動機；引擎：*a* **diesel/petrol engine** 柴油／汽油發動機◇ *My car had to have a new engine.* 我的汽車得換一個新發動機。◇ *engine trouble* 發動機故障◇ *I* **switched/turned the engine off**. 我關掉了發動機。➲ VISUAL VOCAB page V51 ➲ see also INTERNAL-COMBUSTION ENGINE, JET ENGINE, TRACTION ENGINE **2** (also **loco·mo·tive**) a vehicle that pulls a train 火車頭；機車 ➲ VISUAL VOCAB page V58 **3** **-engined** (in adjectives 構成形容詞) having the type or number of engines mentioned 有…型發動機的；有…個引擎的：*a twin-engined speedboat* 雙引擎快艇 ➲ see also FIRE ENGINE, SEARCH ENGINE

ˈengine driver (*BrE*, becoming *old-fashioned*) (*NAmE* **en·gin·eer**) *noun* a person whose job is driving a railway/railroad engine 火車司機；機車司機

en·gin·eer /ˌendʒɪˈnɪə(r); *NAmE* -ˈnɪr/ *noun, verb*
■ ***noun*** **1** a person whose job involves designing and building engines, machines, roads, bridges, etc. 工程師；設計師 ➲ see also CHEMICAL ENGINEER at CHEMICAL ENGINEERING, CIVIL ENGINEER at CIVIL ENGINEERING, ELECTRICAL ENGINEER at ELECTRICAL ENGINEERING, LIGHTING ENGINEER, MECHANICAL ENGINEER at MECHANICAL ENGINEERING, SOFTWARE ENGINEER, SOUND ENGINEER **2** a person who is trained to repair machines and electrical equipment 機修工；技師；技工：*They're sending an engineer to fix the phone.* 他們會派一名技師來安裝電話。**3** a person whose job is to control and repair engines, especially on a ship or an aircraft（船上的）輪機手；（飛機上的）機械師：*a flight engineer* 空勤機械師◇ *the chief engineer on a cruise liner* 遊輪的輪機長 **4** (*NAmE*) (*BrE* **ˈengine driver**) a person whose job is driving a railway/railroad engine 火車司機；機車司機 **5** a soldier trained to design and build military structures 工兵
■ ***verb*** **1 ~ sth** (often *disapproving*) to arrange for sth to happen or take place, especially when this is done secretly in order to give yourself an advantage 密謀策劃 **SYN** **contrive**：*She engineered a further meeting with him.* 她精心安排又和他見了一面。**2** [usually passive] **~ sth** to design and build sth 設計製造：*The car is beautifully engineered and a pleasure to drive.* 這輛汽車設計完美，工藝精良，開起來過癮。**3 ~ sth** to change the GENETIC structure of sth 改變…的基因（或遺傳）結構 **SYN** **genetically modify**：*genetically engineered crops* 轉基因農作物

en·gin·eer·ing /ˌendʒɪˈnɪərɪŋ; *NAmE* -ˈnɪr-/ *noun* [U]
1 the activity of applying scientific knowledge to the design, building and control of machines, roads, bridges, electrical equipment, etc. 工程：*The bridge is a triumph of modern engineering.* 這座橋是現代工程的一大成就。➲ compare REVERSE ENGINEERING **2** (also **ˌengineering ˈscience**) the study of engineering as a subject 工程學：*a degree in engineering* 工程學學位 ➲ see also CHEMICAL ENGINEERING, CIVIL ENGINEERING, ELECTRICAL ENGINEERING, GENETIC ENGINEERING, MECHANICAL ENGINEERING, SOCIAL ENGINEERING

ˈengine room *noun* **1** the part of a ship where the engines are（船舶）機艙 **2** the part of an organization where most of the important activity takes place or important decisions are made（機構的）決策部門

Eng·lish /ˈɪŋɡlɪʃ/ *noun, adj.*
■ ***noun*** **1** [U, C] the language, originally of England, now spoken in many other countries and used as a language of international communication throughout the world 英語；英文：*She speaks good English.* 她英語說得很好。◇ *I need to improve my English.* 我需要提高我的英語水平。◇ *world Englishes* 世界各地的英語 **2** [U] English language or literature as a subject of study（作為一門學科的）英語語言文學；英語學科：*a degree in English* 英語學位◇ *English is my best subject.* 英語是我學得最好的一門科目。**3** **the English** [pl.] the people of England (sometimes wrongly used to mean the British, including the Scots, the Welsh and the Northern Irish) 英格蘭人（有時誤用以指包括蘇格蘭、威爾士和北愛爾蘭人在內的英國人）**IDM** see PLAIN *adj.*
■ ***adj.*** connected with England, its people or its language 英格蘭的；英格蘭人的；英語的：*the English countryside* 英格蘭鄉村◇ *an English man/woman* 英格蘭男人／女人◇ *typically English attitudes* 典型的英國式作風◇ *an English dictionary* 英語詞典 ➲ note at BRITISH

ˌEnglish ˈbreakfast *noun* [C, U] a large breakfast, usually consisting of CEREAL (= food made from grain), cooked BACON and eggs, TOAST and tea or coffee 英式早餐（通常包括麥片類、熏豬肉片、雞蛋、烤麵包片以及茶或咖啡）➲ compare CONTINENTAL BREAKFAST

ˌEnglish for ˌAcademic ˈPurposes (*abbr.* **EAP**) *noun* [U] the teaching of English for people who are using English for study, but whose first language is not English 學術英語教學（對象為母語非英語者）

ˌEnglish ˈhorn *noun* (*especially NAmE*) = COR ANGLAIS

Eng·lish·man /ˈɪŋɡlɪʃmən/ *noun* (*pl.* **-men** /-mən/) a man from England 英格蘭（男）人；英國（男）人
IDM **an ˌEnglishman's ˌhome is his ˈcastle** (*BrE*) (*US* **a ˌman's ˌhome is his ˈcastle**) (*saying*) a person's home is a place where they can be private and safe and do as they like 英國人的家就是他的城堡

ˌEnglish ˈmuffin (*NAmE*) (*BrE* **muf·fin**) *noun* a type of round flat bread roll, usually TOASTED and eaten hot with butter 英格蘭鬆餅，英式鬆餅（通常烤熱加黃油吃）

ˌEnglish ˈrose *noun* an attractive girl with fair skin and an appearance that is thought to be typical of English people 英國玫瑰少女（皮膚白皙、有典型英國人長相的美麗少女）

Eng·lish·woman /ˈɪŋɡlɪʃwʊmən/ *noun* (*pl.* **-women** /-wɪmɪn/) a woman from England 英格蘭女人

en·gorge /ɪnˈɡɔːdʒ; *NAmE* ɪnˈɡɔːrdʒ/ *verb* **~ sth** (*technical* 術語) to cause sth to become filled with blood or another liquid and to swell 使充血；使漲滿液體

en·grave /ɪnˈɡreɪv/ *verb* [often passive] to cut words or designs on wood, stone, metal, etc. 在…上雕刻（字或圖案）：**~ A (with B)** *The silver cup was engraved with his name.* 銀杯上刻有他的名字。◇ **~ B on A** *His name was engraved on the silver cup.* 他的名字刻在了銀杯上。

IDM **be enˌgraved ˌon/in your ˈheart, ˈmemory, ˈmind, etc.** to be sth that you will never forget because it affected you so strongly 牢記，銘記，深深印入（心中、記憶中、頭腦中等）

en·graver /ɪnˈɡreɪvə(r)/ *noun* a person whose job is to cut words or designs on wood, stone, metal, etc. 雕刻師；雕刻工；鐫版工

en·grav·ing /ɪnˈɡreɪvɪŋ/ *noun* **1** [C] a picture made by cutting a design on a piece of metal and then printing the design on paper 版畫；雕版印刷品 **2** [U] the art or process of cutting designs on wood, stone, metal, etc. 雕刻（術）；鐫版術 ➲ COLLOCATIONS at ART

en·gross /ɪnˈɡrəʊs; *NAmE* ɪnˈɡroʊs/ *verb* **~ sb** if sth **engrosses** you, it is so interesting that you give it all your attention and time 使全神貫注；佔去（某人的）全部注意力和時間 ▸ **en·gross·ing** /ɪnˈɡrəʊsɪŋ; *NAmE* -ˈɡroʊs-/ *adj.*：*an engrossing problem* 引人關注的問題

en·grossed /ɪnˈɡrəʊst; *NAmE* ɪnˈɡroʊst/ *adj.* **~ (in/with sth)** so interested or involved in sth that you give it all your attention 全神貫注的；聚精會神的；專心致志的：*She was engrossed in conversation.* 她聚精會神地談話。

en·gulf /ɪnˈɡʌlf/ *verb* (*formal*) **1 ~ sb/sth** to surround or to cover sb/sth completely 包圍；吞沒；淹沒：*He was engulfed by a crowd of reporters.* 他被一群記者團團圍住。◇ *The vehicle was* ***engulfed in flames.*** 汽車被大火吞沒。 **2 ~ sb/sth** to affect sb/sth very strongly 嚴重影響：*Fear engulfed her.* 她陷入深深的恐懼之中。

en·hance **AW** /ɪnˈhɑːns; *NAmE* -ˈhæns/ *verb* **~ sth** to increase or further improve the good quality, value or status of sb/sth 提高；增強；增進：*This is an opportunity to enhance the reputation of the company.* 這是提高公司聲譽的機會。◇ *the skilled use of make-up to enhance your best features* 熟練地利用化妝以突出最嫵媚的容貌 ▸ **en·hanced** **AW** *adj.*：*enhanced efficiency* 提高了的效率 **en·hance·ment** **AW** *noun* [U, C]：*equipment for the enhancement of sound quality* 音質提升設備 ◇ *software enhancements* 軟件增強設備

en·hancer /ɪnˈhɑːnsə(r); *NAmE* -ˈhæns-/ *noun* (*technical* 術語) a substance or device that is designed to improve sth 增強子（劑）；增強器；放大器：*flavour enhancers* 增味劑

en·igma /ɪˈnɪɡmə/ *noun* a person, thing or situation that is mysterious and difficult to understand 神秘的人；費解的事物；令人困惑的處境 **SYN** **mystery, puzzle**

en·ig·mat·ic /ˌenɪɡˈmætɪk/ *adj.* mysterious and difficult to understand 神秘的；費解的；令人困惑的：*an enigmatic smile* 神秘的笑 ▸ **en·ig·mat·ic·al·ly** /-kli/ *adv.*：*'I might,' he said enigmatically.* "我也許會的。"他神秘地說道。

en·jambe·ment (also **en·jamb·ment**) /ɪnˈdʒæmbmənt/ *noun* [U, C] (from *French*, *technical* 術語) the fact of a sentence continuing beyond the end of a line of poetry（詩句的）跨行 ➲ compare CAESURA

en·join /ɪnˈdʒɔɪn/ *verb* **1** [often passive] **~ sb to do sth** | **~ sth** (*formal*) to order or strongly advise sb to do sth; to say that a particular action or quality is necessary 命令；責令；囑咐 **2 ~ sb from doing sth** (*law* 律) to legally prevent sb from doing sth, for example with an INJUNCTION 禁止

enjoy 🔑 /ɪnˈdʒɔɪ/ *verb*
1 🔑 [T] to get pleasure from sth 享受…的樂趣；欣賞；喜愛：**~ sth** *We thoroughly enjoyed our time in New York.* 我們在紐約的時間過得十分快活。◇ *Thanks for a great evening. I really* ***enjoyed it.*** 非常感謝你，我今晚玩得很開心。◇ **~ doing sth** *I enjoy playing tennis and squash.* 我喜歡打網球和壁球。 **2** 🔑 [T] **~ yourself** to be happy and get pleasure from what you are doing 過得快活；玩得痛快；得到樂趣：*They all enjoyed themselves at the party.* 他們在聚會上都玩得非常痛快。 **3** [T] **~ sth** (*formal*) to have sth good that is an advantage to you 享有；享受：*People in this country enjoy a high standard of living.* 這個國家的人民享有很高的生活水平。◇ *He's always enjoyed good health.* 他一直都很健康。 **4** [I] **enjoy!** (*informal*) used to say that you hope sb gets pleasure from sth that you are giving them or recommending to them（祝願時說）玩痛快些，過愉快些，好好欣賞：*Here's that book I promised you. Enjoy!* 這就是我答應給你的那本書。好好欣賞吧！

Grammar Point 語法說明

enjoy

Note the following patterns. 注意下列句型：

- *I enjoyed myself at the party.* 我在聚會上玩得很開心。◇ ~~*I enjoyed at the party.*~~
- *Thanks. I really enjoyed it.* 謝謝，我真的很開心。◇ ~~*Thanks. I really enjoyed.*~~
- *I enjoy playing basketball.* 我喜歡打籃球。◇ ~~*I enjoy to play basketball.*~~
- *I enjoy reading very much.* 我非常喜歡閱讀。◇ ~~*I enjoy very much reading.*~~
- *I hope you enjoy your trip.* 祝你旅途愉快。◇ ~~*I hope you enjoy with your trip.*~~

en·joy·able 🔑 /ɪnˈdʒɔɪəbl/ *adj.*
giving pleasure 有樂趣的；使人快樂的；令人愉快的：*an enjoyable weekend/experience* 令人愉快的週末／經歷 ◇ ***highly/really/thoroughly/very enjoyable*** 令人非常愉快 ▸ **en·joy·ably** /-əbli/ *adv.*：*The evening passed enjoyably.* 這個晚上過得很愉快。

en·joy·ment 🔑 /ɪnˈdʒɔɪmənt/ *noun*
1 🔑 [U] the pleasure that you get from sth 愉快；快樂；樂趣：*He spoiled my enjoyment of the game by talking all through it.* 他一直在講話，破壞了我看比賽的興致。◇ *The rules are there to ensure everyone's safety and enjoyment.* 這些規定是為了保證每個人的安全和快樂。◇ *Children seem to have lost their enjoyment in reading.* 孩子們似乎已失去閱讀的興趣。◇ *I get a lot of enjoyment from my grandchildren.* 我從孫子孫女們那兒得到很多樂趣。 ➲ SYNONYMS at FUN **2** [C] something that gives you pleasure 樂事；令人愉快的事：*Children like to share interests and enjoyments with their parents.* 孩子們喜歡同父母一起分享各種興趣和樂事。 **3** [U] **~ of sth** (*formal*) the fact of having and using sth 享有；享受：*the enjoyment of equal rights* 平等權利的享有

en·large /ɪnˈlɑːdʒ; *NAmE* -ˈlɑːrdʒ/ *verb* **1** [T, I] **~ (sth)** to make sth bigger; to become bigger 擴大；擴充；擴展；增大：*There are plans to enlarge the recreation area.* 已經有了擴大娛樂場地的計劃。◇ *Reading will enlarge your vocabulary.* 閱讀能擴大詞彙量。 **2** [T, usually passive] **~ sth** to make a bigger copy of a photograph or document 放大（照片或文件）：*We're going to have this picture enlarged.* 我們準備將這張照片放大。 ▸ **en·larged** *adj.*：*an enlarged heart* 肥大的心臟

PHR V **enˈlarge on/upon sth** (*formal*) to say or write more about sth that has been mentioned 詳述；細說 **SYN** **elaborate**

en·large·ment /ɪnˈlɑːdʒmənt; *NAmE* -ˈlɑːrdʒ-/ *noun* **1** [U, sing.] **~ (of sth)** the process or result of sth becoming or being made larger 擴大；擴充；擴展；增大：*the enlargement of the company's overseas business activities* 公司海外業務的擴展 ◇ *There was widespread support for* ***EU enlargement*** (= the fact of more countries joining). 歐盟擴大得到了廣泛的支持。 **2** [C] something that has been made larger, especially a photograph 擴大物，放大物（尤指照片）：*If you like the picture I can send you an enlargement of it.* 如果你喜歡這照片，我可以給你寄一張放大的。**OPP** **reduction**

E

E

en·lar·ger /ɪnˈlɑːdʒə(r); *NAmE* -ˈlɑːrdʒ-/ *noun* a piece of equipment for making photographs larger or smaller（照片）放大機

en·light·en /ɪnˈlaɪtn/ *verb* **~ sb** (*formal*) to give sb information so that they understand sth better 啟發；開導；闡明：*She didn't enlighten him about her background.* 她未向他講明自己的出身背景。▸ **en·light·en·ing** *adj.*: *It was a very enlightening interview.* 那次面談讓人很受啟發。

en·light·ened /ɪnˈlaɪtnd/ *adj.* [usually before noun] (*approving*) having or showing an understanding of people's needs, a situation, etc. that is not based on old-fashioned attitudes and PREJUDICE 開明的；有見識的；擺脫偏見的：***enlightened opinions/attitudes/ideas*** 開明的見解 / 態度 / 想法

en·light·en·ment /ɪnˈlaɪtnmənt/ *noun* **1** [U] knowledge about and understanding of sth; the process of understanding sth or making sb understand it 啟迪；啟發；開導；開明：*The newspapers provided little enlightenment about the cause of the accident.* 報章對事故原因並未解釋清楚。◇ *spiritual enlightenment* 心靈啟迪 ➲ COLLOCATIONS at RELIGION **2 the Enlightenment** [sing.] the period in the 18th century when many writers and scientists began to argue that science and reason were more important than religion and tradition（18 世紀歐洲的）啟蒙運動

en·list /ɪnˈlɪst/ *verb* **1** [T] to persuade sb to help you or to join you in doing sth 爭取，謀取（幫助、支持或參與）：**~ sth/sb (in sth)** *They hoped to **enlist the help of** the public in solving the crime.* 他們希望尋求公眾協助破案。◇ **~ sb (as sth)** *We were enlisted as helpers.* 我們應邀協助。◇ **~ sb to do sth** *We were enlisted to help.* 我們應邀協助。**2** [I, T] to join or to make sb join the armed forces（使）入伍；徵募；從軍 SYN **call up, conscript, draft**：*They both enlisted in 1915.* 他倆都是 1915 年入伍的。◇ **~ as sth** *to enlist as a soldier* 入伍當兵 ◇ **~ sb (in/into/for/as sth)** *He was enlisted into the US Navy.* 他應徵加入了美國海軍。▸ **en·list·ment** *noun* [U]: *the enlistment of expert help* 尋求專家的幫助 ◇ *his enlistment in the Royal Air Force* 他應徵加入皇家空軍

en·list·ed /ɪnˈlɪstɪd/ *adj.* (*especially US*) (of a member of the army, etc. 部隊等的一員) having a rank that is below that of an officer 士兵的：*enlisted men and women* 男兵和女兵 ◇ *enlisted personnel* 應徵入伍人員

en·liven /ɪnˈlaɪvn/ *verb* **~ sth** (*formal*) to make sth more interesting or more fun 使更有生氣（或活力）

en masse /ˌɒ̃ ˈmæs; *NAmE* ˌɑ̃ː/ *adv.* (from *French*) all together, and usually in large numbers 一起；全體

en·mesh /ɪnˈmeʃ/ *verb* [usually passive] **~ sb/sth (in sth)** (*formal*) to involve sb/sth in a bad situation that it is not easy to escape from 使陷入，使捲入（困境）

en·mity /ˈenməti/ *noun* [U, C] (*pl.* **-ies**) feelings of hatred towards sb 敵意；敵對；仇恨：*personal enmities and political conflicts* 個人仇恨和政治衝突 ◇ *Her action earned her the enmity of two or three colleagues.* 她的行動激起了兩三個同事對她的怨恨。◇ **~ between A and B** *the traditional problem of the enmity between Protestants and Catholics* 新教徒和天主教徒之間歷來仇視的問題 ➲ see also ENEMY (1)

en·noble /ɪˈnəʊbl; *NAmE* ɪˈnoʊbl/ *verb* (*formal*) **1** [usually passive] **~ sb** to make sb a member of the NOBILITY 封（某人）為貴族 **2 ~ sb/sth** to give sb/sth a better moral character 使更崇高；使更高尚；使更尊貴：*In a strange way she seemed ennobled by her grief.* 奇怪的是，憂傷使她顯得更加高貴。▸ **en·noble·ment** *noun* [U]

ennui /ɒnˈwiː; *NAmE* ɑːn-/ *noun* [U] (from *French, literary*) feelings of being bored and not satisfied because nothing interesting is happening 無聊；厭倦；倦怠

en·ol·ogy (*US*) (*BrE* **oen·ology**) /iːˈnɒlədʒi; *NAmE* -ˈnɑːl-/ *noun* [U] (*technical* 術語) the study of wine 葡萄釀酒學；葡萄酒釀造學

eno·phile (*US*) (*BrE* **oeno·phile**) /ˈiːnəfaɪl/ *noun* (*formal*) a person who knows a lot about wine 葡萄酒行家

enor·mity AW /ɪˈnɔːməti; *NAmE* ɪˈnɔːrm-/ *noun* (*pl.* **-ies**) **1** [U] **the ~ of sth** (of a problem, etc. 問題等) the very great size, effect, etc. of sth; the fact of sth being very serious 巨大；深遠影響；嚴重性：*the enormity of the task* 任務的艱巨性 ◇ *People are still coming to terms with the enormity of the disaster.* 人們仍在忍受這一災難帶來的嚴重惡果。◇ *The full enormity of the crime has not yet been revealed.* 這一罪行的嚴重性還沒有充分揭示出來。**2** [C, usually pl.] (*formal*) a very serious crime 滔天罪行；罪大惡極：*the enormities of the Hitler regime* 希特勒政權的滔天罪行

enor·mous 0-w AW /ɪˈnɔːməs; *NAmE* ɪˈnɔːrməs/ *adj.* extremely large 巨大的；龐大的；極大的 SYN **huge, immense**：*an enormous house/dog* 巨大的房子；大狗 ◇ *an **enormous amount** of time* 大量的時間 ◇ *enormous interest* 濃厚的興趣 ◇ *The problems facing the President are enormous.* 總統面臨的問題是巨大的。

enor·mous·ly AW /ɪˈnɔːməsli; *NAmE* ɪˈnɔːrm-/ *adv.* very; very much 非常；極其：***enormously rich/powerful/grateful*** 非常富有 / 強大 / 感激 ◇ *The price of wine varies enormously depending on where it comes from.* 不同產地的葡萄酒價格差別很大。◇ *She was looking forward to the meeting enormously.* 她急切期待着這次聚會。

enough 0-w /ɪˈnʌf/ *det., pron., adv.*

■ ***det.*** 0-w used before plural or uncountable nouns to mean 'as many or as much as sb needs or wants'（用於複數或不可數名詞前）足夠的，充足的，充分的 SYN **sufficient**：*Have you made enough copies?* 你複印的份數夠嗎？◇ *Is there enough room for me?* 有足夠的地方給我嗎？◇ *I didn't have enough clothes to last a week.* 我的衣服不夠一週穿的。◇ *Don't ask me to do it. I've got enough problems as it is.* 別讓我做這件事。我目前的問題已夠多了。◇ (*old-fashioned*) *There was food enough for all.* 所有人都有足夠的食物。HELP Although **enough** after a noun now sounds old-fashioned, **time enough** is still fairly common. 儘管 enough 置於名詞後似乎有點過時，但 time enough 仍然相當常用：*There'll be time enough to relax when you've finished your work.*

■ ***pron.*** 0-w as many or as much as sb needs or wants 足夠；充分；充足：*Six bottles should be enough.* 六瓶應該夠了。◇ *Have you had enough (= to eat)?* 你吃飽了嗎？◇ *If enough of you are interested, we'll organize a trip to the theatre.* 如果你們中有足夠多的人感興趣，我們就組織去看一場戲。◇ *There was **nowhere near enough** for everybody.* 沒有離每個人都近的地方。◇ *We've nearly run out of paper. Do you think there's enough for today?* 我們的紙差不多已用完了。你看今天夠用嗎？

IDM **e'nough already** (*informal, especially NAmE*) used to say that sth is annoying or boring and that you want it to stop 行了；早已夠了 **eˌnough is e'nough** (*saying*) used when you think that sth should not continue any longer（認為不應再繼續）夠了，行了，適可而止 **eˌnough 'said** used to say that you understand a situation and there is no need to say any more 無須再講；不必多說：*'He's a politician, remember.' 'Enough said.'* "記住，他是一個政客。" "不用多說了。" **have had e'nough (of sth/sb)** used when sth/sb is annoying you and you no longer want to do, have or see it or them 對…已厭煩透了；再也忍受不住；受夠了：*I've had enough of driving the kids around.* 我已厭煩駕車帶孩子們到處去。

■ ***adv.*** (used after verbs, adjectives and adverbs 用於動詞、形容詞和副詞後) **1** 0-w to the necessary degree 足夠地；充分地；充足地：*I hadn't trained enough for the game.* 對這次比賽我訓練得不夠。◇ *This house isn't big enough for us.* 這房子對我們來說不夠大。◇ *She's old enough to decide for herself.* 她已到自己做決定的年齡了。◇ *We didn't leave early enough.* 我們離開得不夠早。◇ *Tell them it's just **not good enough**.* 告訴他們這確實不夠好。**2** 0-w to an acceptable degree, but not to a very great degree 相當；尚：*He seemed pleasant enough to me.* 他對我似乎已相當和氣了。**3** 0-w to a degree that you do not wish to get any greater 十分；很：*I hope my job's safe. Life is hard enough as it is.* 希望我的工作安穩。生活照現在這樣已經夠苦了。

IDM **ˌcuriously, ˌfunnily, ˌoddly, ˌstrangely, etc. e'nough** used to show that sth is surprising（表示驚

奇）奇怪的是，說來也奇怪： *Funnily enough, I said the same thing myself only yesterday.* 奇怪的是，就在昨天我自己也說過同樣的話。 ⮑ more at FAIR *adj.*, FAR *adv.*, LIKE *adv.*, MAN *n.*, NEAR *adv.*, RIGHT *adj.*, SURE *adv.*

en pas·sant /ˌɒ̃ 'pæsɒ̃; *NAmE* ˌɑːn pɑː'sɑːn/ *adv.* (from *French*) while talking about sth else and without giving much information 順便；附帶地： *He mentioned en passant that he was going away.* 他順便提到他要離開。

en·quire (*especially BrE*) (also **inquire** *NAmE, BrE*) /ɪn'kwaɪə(r)/ *verb* [I, T] (rather *formal*) to ask sb for some information 詢問；打聽： **~ (about sb/sth)** *I called the station to enquire about train times.* 我打電話到車站詢問火車時刻。 ◇ **~ (as to sb/sth)** *She enquired as to your whereabouts.* 她打聽你的下落。 ◇ **~ why, where, etc. …** *Might I enquire why you have not mentioned this until now?* 請問你為什麼直到現在才提及此事呢？ ◇ **~ sth** *He enquired her name.* 他打聽她的姓名。 ◇ **+ speech** *'What is your name?' he enquired.* "您叫什麼名字？"他詢問道。 ⮑ SYNONYMS at ASK **HELP** In British English people sometimes distinguish between **enquire** and **inquire**, using **enquire** for the general meaning of 'ask for information' and **inquire** for the more particular meaning of 'officially investigate'. 在英式英語中，人們有時會區分 enquire 和 inquire 的用法，用 enquire 表示一般意義上的詢問、打聽，用 inquire 表示特別意義上的探究、查詢、調查： *I called to enquire about train times.* 我打電話詢問火車時刻表。 ◇ *A committee will inquire into the allegations.* 一個委員會將調查這些指控。 However, you can use either spelling in either meaning. In American English **inquire** is usually used in both meanings. 不過兩種拼寫用於兩個意思均可。在美式英語中，通常兩種意思均用 inquire。

PHR V **en'quire after sb** (*formal*) to ask for information about sb, especially about their health or about what they are doing 向某人問好（或問候） **en'quire into sth** to find out more information about sth 調查；查究；查問 **SYN** **investigate**： *A committee was appointed to enquire into the allegations.* 一個委員會已受命調查這些指控。 **en'quire sth of sb** (*formal*) to ask sb sth 向某人打聽（或詢問、瞭解）： **(+ speech)** *'Will you be staying for lunch?' she enquired of Charles.* "留下吃午飯好嗎？"她向查爾斯問道。

en·quir·er (*especially BrE*) (also **in·quirer** *NAmE, BrE*) /ɪn'kwaɪərə(r)/ *noun* (*formal*) a person who asks for information 詢問者；調查者

en·quir·ing (also **in·quir·ing** especially in *NAmE*) /ɪn'kwaɪərɪŋ/ *adj.* [usually before noun] **1** showing an interest in learning new things 愛探索的；好奇的；好問的： *a child with an enquiring mind* 有好奇心的孩子 **2** asking for information 探詢的；探究的： *an enquiring look* 探詢的神色 ▸ **en·quir·ing·ly** (also **in·quir·ing·ly** especially in *NAmE*) *adv.*

en·quiry 🗝 (*especially BrE*) (also **in·quiry** *NAmE, BrE*) /ɪn'kwaɪəri; *NAmE* usually 'ɪnkwəri/ *noun* (*pl.* **-ies**) **1** 🗝 [C] an official process to find out the cause of sth or to find out information about sth 調查；查究；查問： *a* ***murder enquiry*** 謀殺案調查 ◇ **~ into sth** *a* ***public enquiry*** *into the environmental effects of the proposed new road* 擬建新路對環境影響的公開調查 ◇ *to* ***hold/order an enquiry*** *into the affair* 對此事進行調查；責令調查此事 ⮑ COLLOCATIONS at CRIME **2** 🗝 [C] a request for information about sb/sth; a question about sb/sth 詢問；打聽： *a telephone enquiry* 電話查詢 ◇ **~ (from sb) (about sb/sth)** *We received over 300 enquiries about the job.* 我們收到 300 多個關於這項工作的查詢。 ◇ *enquiries from prospective students* 未來學生的詢問 ◇ *I'll have to* ***make a few enquiries*** (= try to find out about it) *and get back to you.* 我得打聽打聽再給你答覆。 ◇ (*BrE*) *Two men have been* ***helping police with their enquiries*** (= are being questioned about a crime, but have not been charged with it). 兩名男子一直在協助警方調查。 **3** [U] the act of asking questions or collecting information about sb/sth 查詢；探究；探索： *scientific enquiry* 科學探索 ◇ *The police are following several* ***lines of enquiry***. 警方正沿着幾條線索進行調查。 ◇ *a committee of enquiry* 調查委員會 **4** **enquiries** [pl.] (*BrE*) a place where you can get information 問訊處： *Ask at enquiries to see if your bag has been handed in.* 到問訊處看看是否有人交來了你的包。 ⮑ see also DIRECTORY ENQUIRIES **HELP** In British English people sometimes distinguish between **enquiry** and **inquiry**, using **enquiry** for the general meaning of 'a request for information' and **inquiry** for the more particular meaning of 'official investigation'. 在英式英語中，人們有時會區分 enquiry 和 inquiry 的用法，用 enquiry 表示一般意義上的詢問、打聽，用 inquiry 表示特別意義上的探究、查詢、調查： *enquiries from prospective students* 未來學生的詢問 ◇ *a murder inquiry* 謀殺案調查 However, you can use either spelling in either meaning. In American English **inquiry** is usually used in both meanings. 不過兩種拼寫用於兩個意思均可。在美式英語中，通常兩種意思均用 inquiry。

E

en·rage /ɪn'reɪdʒ/ *verb* [usually passive] **~ sb** to make sb very angry 使異常憤怒；激怒；觸怒 **SYN** **infuriate**

en·rap·ture /ɪn'ræptʃə(r)/ *verb* [usually passive] **~ sb** (*formal*) to give sb great pleasure or joy 使欣喜若狂；使興高采烈 **SYN** **enchant**

en·rap·tured /ɪn'ræptʃəd; *NAmE* -ərd/ *adj.* (*formal*) filled with great pleasure or joy 狂喜的；欣喜萬分的；陶然的 **SYN** **enchanted**

en·rich /ɪn'rɪtʃ/ *verb* **1** to improve the quality of sth, often by adding sth to it 充實；使豐富；使飽含（某物）： **~ sth** *The study of science has enriched all our lives.* 科學研究豐富了我們的整個生活。 ◇ **~ sth with sth** *Most breakfast cereals are enriched with vitamins.* 多數穀類早餐食物都加添了維生素。 **2 ~ sb/sth** to make sb/sth rich or richer 使富有；使富裕： *a nation enriched by oil revenues* 靠石油收入富裕起來的國家 ◇ *He used his position to enrich himself.* 他利用職位之便斂財。 ▸ **en·rich·ment** *noun* [U]

enrol /ɪn'rəʊl; *NAmE* ɪn'roʊl/ (*especially US* **en·roll**) *verb* (**-ll-**) [I, T] to arrange for yourself or for sb else to officially join a course, school, etc. （使）加入；註冊；登記： *You need to enrol before the end of August.* 你必須在八月底前註冊。 ◇ (*BrE*) *to enrol on a course* 註冊學習一門課程 ◇ (*NAmE*) *to enroll in a course* 註冊學習一門課程 ◇ **~ sb** *The centre will soon be ready to enrol candidates for the new programme.* 中心將很快為新課程的招生做好準備。

en·rol·lee /ɪnˌrəʊ'liː; *NAmE* ɪnˌroʊ-/ *noun* (*NAmE*) a person who has officially joined a course, an organization, etc. 入學者；被錄用者；入會者

en·rol·ment (*especially US* **en·roll·ment**) /ɪn'rəʊlmənt; *NAmE* -'roʊl-/ *noun* [U, C] the act of officially joining a course, school, etc.; the number of people who do this 入學，註冊，登記（人數）： *Enrolment is the first week of September.* 九月份的第一週註冊。 ◇ *School enrolments are currently falling.* 目前學校的註冊人數在減少。

en route /ˌɒ̃ 'ruːt; ˌɒn; *NAmE* ˌɑː; ˌɑːn/ *adv.* (from *French*) on the way; while travelling from/to a particular place 在途中；在路上： *We stopped for a picnic en route.* 我們在途中停下來野餐。 ◇ **~ (from …) (to …)** *The bus broke down en route from Boston to New York.* 公共汽車在從波士頓到紐約的途中拋錨了。 ◇ (*BrE*) **~ (for …)** *a plane en route for Heathrow* 在飛往希思羅機場途中的飛機

en·sconce /ɪn'skɒns; *NAmE* -'skɑːns/ *verb* **be ensconced (+adv./prep.)** | **~ yourself (+adv./prep.)** (*formal*) if you **are ensconced** or **ensconce yourself** somewhere, you are made or make yourself comfortable and safe in that place or position 安置；使安頓；使安坐

en·sem·ble /ɒn'sɒmbl; *NAmE* ɑːn'sɑːmbl/ *noun* **1** [C+sing./pl. v.] a small group of musicians, dancers or actors who perform together 樂團，劇團，舞劇團（全體成員）： *a* ***brass/wind/string, etc. ensemble*** 銅管樂器、管樂器、弦樂器等合奏組 ◇ *The ensemble is/are based in Lyons.* 這個樂團總部設在里昂。 **2** [C, usually sing.] (*formal*) a number of things considered as a group 全體；整體 **3** [C, usually sing.] a set of clothes that are worn together 全套服裝

en·shrine /ɪn'ʃraɪn/ *verb* [usually passive] **~ sth (in sth)** (*formal*) to make a law, right, etc. respected or official, especially by stating it in an important written document 把（法律、權利等）奉為神聖；把…莊嚴地載入：

These rights are enshrined in the country's constitution. 這些權利已莊嚴地載入國家憲法。

en·shroud /ɪn'ʃraʊd/ *verb* **~ sth** (*literary*) to cover or surround sth completely so that it cannot be seen or understood 掩蓋；遮蔽；籠罩

en·sign /'ensən/ *noun* **1** a flag flown on a ship to show which country it belongs to （表明國籍的）艦旗，商船旗：*the White Ensign* (= the flag of the British Navy) 英國海軍旗 **2** an officer of low rank in the US navy （美國）海軍少尉：*Ensign Marshall* 馬歇爾海軍少尉

E

en·slave /ɪn'sleɪv/ *verb* [usually passive] **1 ~ sb** to make sb a SLAVE 使成為奴隸；奴役 **2 ~ sb/sth (to sth)** (*formal*) to make sb/sth completely depend on sth so that they cannot manage without it 使受控制；征服；制伏 ▸ **en·slave·ment** *noun* [U]

en·snare /ɪn'sneə(r); *NAmE* ɪn'sner/ *verb* **~ sb/sth** (*formal*) to make sb/sth unable to escape from a difficult situation or from a person who wants to control them 使入陷阱（或圈套、困境）**SYN** **trap**：*young homeless people who become ensnared in a life of crime* 陷入犯罪活動的無家可歸的年輕人

ensue /ɪn'sjuː; *NAmE* -'suː/ *verb* [I] (*formal*) to happen after or as a result of another event 接着發生；因而產生 **SYN** **follow**：*An argument ensued.* 緊接着的是一場爭論。▸ **en·su·ing** *adj.*：*He had become separated from his parents in the ensuing panic.* 在隨後的慌亂中他便與父母分散了。

en suite /ˌɒ̃ 'swiːt; *NAmE* ˌɑ̃ː/ *adj.*, *adv.* (*BrE*, from *French*) (of a bathroom 浴室) joined onto a bedroom and for use only by people in that bedroom 與卧室配套的：*Each bedroom in the hotel has a bathroom en suite/an en suite bathroom.* 旅館裏每間卧室都帶浴室。◇ *an en suite bedroom* (= a bedroom with an en suite bathroom) 帶浴室的卧室 ◇ *en suite facilities* 與卧室配套的設備 ➲ VISUAL VOCAB page V23

en·sure 🔑 **AW** (also **in·sure** especially in *NAmE*) /ɪn'ʃʊə(r); -'ʃɔː(r); *NAmE* ɪn'ʃʊr/ *verb* to make sure that sth happens or is definite 保證；擔保；確保：**~ sth** *The book ensured his success.* 這本書使他篤定會成功。◇ **~ sb sth** *Victory ensured them a place in the final.* 勝利確保了他們晉級決賽。◇ **~ (that)** ... *Please ensure (that) all lights are switched off.* 請確保將所有燈都關掉。

ENT /ˌiː en 'tiː/ *abbr.* ear, nose and throat (as a department in a hospital) （醫院的）耳鼻喉科

-ent ➲ -ANT

en·tail /ɪn'teɪl/ *verb* to involve sth that cannot be avoided 牽涉；須要；使必要 **SYN** **involve**：**~ sth** *The job entails a lot of hard work.* 這工作需要十分艱苦的努力。◇ **be entailed in sth** *The girls learn exactly what is entailed in caring for a newborn baby.* 姑娘們學的是怎樣照看新生兒。◇ **~ (sb) doing sth** *It will entail driving a long distance every day.* 這意味着每天都要長途開車。

en·tan·gle /ɪn'tæŋgl/ *verb* [usually passive] **1 ~ sb/sth (in/with sth)** to make sb/sth become caught or twisted in sth 使糾纏；纏住；套住：*The bird had* **become entangled** *in the wire netting.* 那隻小鳥被鐵絲網纏住了。 **2** to involve sb in a difficult or complicated situation 使捲入；使陷入：**~ sb in sth** *He* **became entangled** *in a series of conflicts with the management.* 他捲入了與管理層的一系列衝突之中。◇ **~ sb with sb** *She didn't want to* **get entangled** (= emotionally involved) *with him.* 她不想與他有瓜葛。

en·tangle·ment /ɪn'tæŋglmənt/ *noun* **1** [C] a difficult or complicated relationship with another person or country 瓜葛；牽連 **2** [U] the act of becoming entangled in sth; the state of being entangled 糾纏；纏住：*Many dolphins die each year from entanglement in fishing nets.* 每年都有許多海豚被捕魚網纏繞致死。 **3 en·tangle·ments** [pl.] (*technical* 術語) barriers made of BARBED WIRE, used to stop an enemy from getting close 鐵絲網（用以阻止敵人靠近）

en·tente /ɒn'tɒnt; *NAmE* ɑːn'tɑːnt/ *noun* [U, sing.] (from *French*) a friendly relationship between two countries （國家間的）友好關係：*the Franco-Russian entente* 法俄友好關係

en·tente cor·di·ale /ˌɒntɒnt ˌkɔːdi'ɑːl; *NAmE* ˌɑːntɑːnt ˌkɔːrd-/ *noun* [U, sing.] (from *French*) a friendly relationship between two countries, especially between Britain and France （尤指英法兩國間的）友好關係

enter 🔑 /'entə(r)/ *verb*

▸ **COME/GO IN** 進來；進去 **1** 🔑 [I, T] (not usually used in the passive 通常不用於被動語態) (*formal*) to come or go into sth 進來；進去；進入：*Knock before you enter.* 進來前先敲門。◇ **~ sth** *Someone entered the room behind me.* 有人跟着我進了房間。◇ *Where did the bullet enter the body?* 子彈從哪個部位穿入身體的？◇ (*figurative*) *A note of defiance entered her voice.* 她的聲音裏帶有蔑視的口氣。◇ (*figurative*) *It never* **entered my head** (= I never thought) *that she would tell him about me.* 我從未想到過她會把我的事告訴他。

▸ **JOIN INSTITUTION/START WORK** 加入機構；開始從事 **2** 🔑 [T, no passive] **~ sth** (*formal*) to become a member of an institution; to start working in an organization or a profession 成為…的一員；加入；開始從事：*to* **enter** *a school/college/university* 考入學校／學院／大學 ◇ *to* **enter politics** 開始從政 ◇ *to* **enter Parliament** (= become an MP) 成為英國議會議員 ◇ *to* **enter the Church** (= become a priest) 成為神職人員

▸ **BEGIN ACTIVITY** 開始活動 **3** [T] **~ sth** to begin or become involved in an activity, a situation, etc. 開始參加；開始進入；着手進行：*to* **enter** *a relationship/conflict/war* 建立關係；發生衝突；參戰 ◇ *Several new firms have now entered the market.* 有幾家新公司已打入市場。◇ *The investigation has entered a new phase.* 調查已進入新階段。◇ *The strike is entering its fourth week.* 罷工正進入第四週。

▸ **EXAM/COMPETITION** 考試；比賽 **4** 🔑 [T, I] to put your name on the list for an exam, a race, a competition, etc.; to do this for sb 報名參加，為…報名參加（考試、比賽等）：**~ sth** *1 000 children entered the competition.* * 1 000 名孩子報名參加了比賽。◇ **~ sb/sth in sth** *Irish trainers have entered several horses in the race.* 愛爾蘭馴馬師讓好幾匹馬參加了比賽。◇ **~ sb/sth for sth** *How many students have been entered for the exam?* 讓多少學生參加了考試？◇ **~ (for sth)** *Only four British players have entered for the championship.* 只有四名英國運動員報名參加錦標賽。

▸ **WRITE INFORMATION** 記錄信息 **5** [T] to put names, numbers, details, etc. in a list, book or computer 登記，錄入，輸入（姓名、號碼、詳細資料等）：**~ sth (in sth)** *Enter your name and occupation in the boxes* (= on a form). 將姓名和職業填入（表格的）方框裏。◇ **~ sth (into sth)** *to enter data into a computer* 將數據輸入計算機 ◇ **~ sth (on sth)** *to enter figures on a spreadsheet* 將數字輸入電腦表格

▸ **SAY OFFICIALLY** 正式說 **6** [T] **~ sth** (*formal*) to say sth officially so that it can be recorded （正式）提出：*to* **enter a plea** *of not guilty* (= at the beginning of a court case) （在訴訟案件開始時）提出無罪的抗辯 ◇ *to enter an offer* 報價 ➲ see also ENTRANCE[1], ENTRY **IDM** see FORCE *n.*, NAME *n.*

PHR V **'enter into sth** (*formal*) **1** to begin to discuss or deal with sth 開始討論；着手處理：*Let's not enter into details at this stage.* 咱們現階段不要討論細節問題。 **2** to take an active part in sth 積極參加；投入：*They* **entered into the spirit** *of the occasion* (= began to enjoy and feel part of it). 他們開始感受到了節慶的氣氛。 **3** [no passive] to form part of sth or have an influence on sth 成為…的一部份；影響：*This possibility never entered into our calculations.* 我們從未估計到這種可能性。◇ *Your personal feelings shouldn't enter into this at all.* 這根本就不應該摻雜進你個人的感情。 **'enter into sth (with sb)** to begin sth or become involved in sth 開始；進入；參與：*to enter into an agreement* 訂立協議 ◇ *to enter into negotiations* 開始談判 **'enter on/upon sth** (*formal*) to start to do sth or become involved in it 開始；着手；參與：*to enter on a new career* 開始新的職業生涯

en·ter·ic /en'terɪk/ *adj.* (*medical* 醫) connected with the INTESTINES 腸的

en·ter·itis /ˌentə'raɪtəs/ *noun* [U] (*medical* 醫) a painful infection in the INTESTINES that usually causes DIARRHOEA 小腸炎 ➲ see also GASTROENTERITIS

en·ter·prise /'entəpraɪz; *NAmE* -tərp-/ *noun* **1** [C] a company or business 公司；企業單位；事業單位：*an enterprise with a turnover of $26 billion* 營業額 260 億元的公司 ◇ ***state-owned/public enterprises*** 國有企業；公共事業單位 ◇ *small and medium-sized enterprises* 中小型企業 **2** [C] a large project, especially one that is difficult（尤指艱巨而重大的）規劃，事業 **SYN** **venture**：*his latest business enterprise* 他最新的企業規劃 ◇ *a **joint enterprise*** 共同事業 **3** [U] the development of businesses by the people of a country rather than by the government 企業發展；企業經營；企業活動：*grants to encourage enterprise in the region* 鼓勵這個地區企業發展的撥款 ◇ *an enterprise culture* (= in which people are encouraged to develop small businesses) 經商文化（鼓勵發展小型企業）➲ see also FREE ENTERPRISE, PRIVATE ENTERPRISE **4** [U] (*approving*) the ability to think of new projects and make them successful 事業心；進取心；創業精神 **SYN** **initiative**：*a job in which enterprise is rewarded* 事業進取精神有所回報的工作

en·ter·pris·ing /'entəpraɪzɪŋ; *NAmE* -tərp-/ *adj.* (*approving*) having or showing the ability to think of new projects or new ways of doing things and make them successful 有事業心的；有進取心的；有創業精神的

en·ter·tain 0- /ˌentə'teɪn; *NAmE* -tər't-/ *verb* **1** 0- [I, T] to invite people to eat or drink with you as your guests, especially in your home （尤指在自己家中）招待，款待：*The job involves a lot of entertaining.* 這項工作需要經常設宴招待客人。◇ **~ sb** *Barbecues are a favourite way of entertaining friends.* 烤肉野餐是最受人喜愛的待客方式。 **2** 0- [T, I] **~ (sb) (with sth)** to interest and amuse sb in order to please them 使有興趣；使快樂；娛樂：*He entertained us for hours with his stories and jokes.* 他講故事說笑話，逗我們樂了好幾個小時。◇ *The aim of the series is both to entertain and inform.* 這套系列節目是為了寓教於樂。 **3** [T] (not used in the progressive tenses 不用於進行時) **~ sth** (*formal*) to consider or allow yourself to think about an idea, a hope, a feeling, etc. 心存，懷有（想法、希望、感覺等）：*He had **entertained hopes** of a reconciliation.* 他曾對和解抱有希望。◇ *to **entertain a doubt/suspicion*** 持懷疑態度

en·ter·tain·er 0- /ˌentə'teɪnə(r); *NAmE* -tər't-/ *noun* a person whose job is amusing or interesting people, for example, by singing, telling jokes or dancing（歌唱、說笑話、舞蹈等的）演員，表演者，藝人

en·ter·tain·ing 0- /ˌentə'teɪnɪŋ; *NAmE* -tər't-/ *adj.* interesting and amusing 有趣的；娛樂的；使人愉快的：*an entertaining speech/evening* 妙趣橫生的演講；令人開心的晚會 ◇ *I found the talk both informative and entertaining.* 我認為這次演講知識與趣味並重。◇ *She was always so funny and entertaining.* 她總是那麼風趣，令人愉快。➲ SYNONYMS at FUNNY ▸ **en·ter·tain·ing·ly** *adv.*

en·ter·tain·ment 0- /ˌentə'teɪnmənt; *NAmE* -tər't-/ *noun* **1** 0- [U, C] films/movies, music, etc. used to entertain people; an example of this 娛樂片；文娛節目；表演會；娛樂活動：*radio, television and other forms of entertainment* 廣播、電視和其他形式的娛樂活動 ◇ *There will be **live entertainment** at the party.* 聯歡會上將有現場表演節目。◇ *It was typical **family entertainment**.* 這是典型的家庭娛樂活動。◇ *The entertainment was provided by a folk band.* 這個文娛節目由民歌樂隊演出。◇ *Local entertainments are listed in the newspaper.* 本地的娛樂活動刊登在報上。◇ *The show was good **entertainment value**.* 這場演出有很大的娛樂價值。 **2** [U] the act of entertaining sb 招待；款待；娛樂：*a budget for the entertainment of clients* 用於招待客戶的專項開支

en·thral (*BrE*) (*NAmE* **en·thrall**) /ɪn'θrɔːl/ *verb* (**-ll-**) [T, I, usually passive] **~ (sb)** if sth **enthrals** you, it is so interesting, beautiful, etc. that you give it all your attention 迷住；吸引住 **SYN** **entrance**：*The child watched, enthralled by the bright moving images.* 這孩子看着那明亮的移動的影像，被迷住了。▸ **en·thral·ling** *adj.*：*an enthralling performance* 迷人的表演

en·throne /ɪn'θrəʊn; *NAmE* ɪn'θroʊn/ *verb* [usually passive] **~ sb** when a king, queen or important member of a Church is **enthroned**, they sit on a THRONE (= a special chair) in a ceremony to mark the beginning of their rule 使登基；使即位 ▸ **en·throne·ment** *noun* [U, C]

E

Synonyms 同義詞辨析

entertainment

fun • recreation • relaxation • play • pleasure • amusement

These are all words for things or activities used to entertain people when they are not working. 以上各詞均指休閒、娛樂或相關活動。

entertainment films, television, music, etc. used to entertain people 指娛樂片、文娛節目、表演會等：*There are three bars, with live entertainment seven nights a week.* 有三家酒吧一個星期七個晚上都有現場表演節目。

fun (*rather informal*) behaviour or activities that are not serious but come from a sense of enjoyment 指嬉戲、逗樂、玩笑：*It wasn't serious—it was all done **in fun**.* 那不是認真的，全是鬧着玩的。◇ *We didn't mean to hurt him. It was just **a bit of fun**.* 我們並非有意要傷害他，只不過是開個玩笑罷了。◇ *The lottery provides **harmless fun** for millions.* 彩票抽獎為數百萬人提供無傷大雅的娛樂。

recreation (*rather formal*) things people do for enjoyment when they are not working 指娛樂、消遣：*His only form of recreation is playing football.* 他唯一的娛樂就是踢足球。

relaxation (*rather formal*) things people do to rest and enjoy themselves when they are not working; the ability to relax 指休閒活動、消遣：*I go hill-walking for relaxation.* 我要是想活動活動，就到山上走走。

RECREATION OR RELAXATION? 用 recreation 還是 relaxation？

Both these words can be used for a wide range of activities, physical and mental, but **relaxation** is sometimes used for gentler activities than **recreation**. 以上兩詞均可指各種體力和精神活動，但 relaxation 有時指較 recreation 輕鬆的活動：*I play the flute in a wind band for recreation.* 我在管樂隊吹長笛消遣。◇ *I listen to music for relaxation.* 我聽音樂放鬆心情。

play things that people, especially children, do for enjoyment rather than as work 尤指孩子遊戲、玩耍、娛樂：*the happy sounds of children **at play*** 兒童嬉戲的歡鬧聲

pleasure the activity of enjoying yourself, especially in contrast to working 指玩樂、休閒，尤與工作相對：*Are you in Paris **for business or pleasure**?* 你來巴黎公幹還是遊玩？

amusement the fact of being entertained by sth 指娛樂、消遣、遊戲：*What do you do for amusement round here?* 你在這兒以什麼消遣？

PATTERNS

- to do sth **for** entertainment/fun/recreation/relaxation/pleasure/amusement
- to **provide** entertainment/fun/recreation/relaxation/amusement

E

en·thuse /ɪn'θjuːz; *NAmE* -'θuːz/ *verb* **1** [I, T] to talk in an enthusiastic and excited way about sth 充滿熱情地說；熱烈地講：**~ (about/over sth/sb)** *The article enthused about the benefits that the new system would bring.* 本文熱情讚揚了新制度將帶來的好處。◇ **+ speech** *'It's a wonderful idea', he enthused.* "這真是個絕妙的主意。"他讚歎地說。◇ **~ that …** *The organizers enthused that it was their most successful event yet.* 組織者讚歎地說這是他們迄今為止最成功的活動。**2** [usually passive] **~ sb (with sth)** to make sb feel very interested and excited 使熱衷；使熱心；使激動：*Everyone present was enthused by the idea.* 在場的每一個人都為這種想法感到激動。

en·thu·si·asm 0-π /ɪn'θjuːziæzəm; *NAmE* -'θuː-/ *noun* **1** 0-π [U] a strong feeling of excitement and interest in sth and a desire to become involved in it 熱情；熱心；熱忱：**~ (for sth)** *I can't say I share your enthusiasm for the idea.* 我可不像你那樣，對這個想法那樣熱心。◇ *He had a real enthusiasm for the work.* 他的確熱衷於這項工作。◇ **~ (for doing sth)** *She never lost her enthusiasm for teaching.* 她從未失去過教書的熱忱。◇ *The news was greeted with a lack of enthusiasm by those at the meeting.* 與會者對這消息未表現出多少興趣。◇ *'I don't mind,' she said, without much enthusiasm.* "我不在乎。"她不冷不熱地說。◇ *full of enthusiasm* 充滿熱情 **2** [C] (*formal*) something that you are very interested in and spend a lot of time doing 熱衷的事物；激發熱情的事物

en·thu·si·ast /ɪn'θjuːziæst; *NAmE* -'θuː-/ *noun* **1 ~ (for/of sth)** a person who is very interested in sth and spends a lot of time doing it 熱衷於…的人；熱心者；愛好者：*a football enthusiast* 足球愛好者 ◇ *an enthusiast of jazz* 爵士樂愛好者 **2 ~ (for/of sth)** a person who approves of sth and shows enthusiasm for it 熱烈支持者；熱情贊成者：*enthusiasts for a united Europe* 熱烈贊成建立統一歐洲的人

en·thu·si·as·tic 0-π /ɪnˌθjuːzi'æstɪk; *NAmE* -ˌθuː-/ *adj.* feeling or showing a lot of excitement and interest about sb/sth 熱情的；熱心的；熱烈的；滿腔熱忱的：*an enthusiastic supporter* 熱心的支持者 ◇ *an enthusiastic welcome* 熱烈歡迎 ◇ **~ about sb/sth** *You don't sound very enthusiastic about the idea.* 你好像對這個想法不太感興趣。◇ **~ about doing sth** *She was even less enthusiastic about going to Spain.* 她對去西班牙更是不感興趣。▸ **en·thu·si·as·tic·al·ly** 0-π /-kli/ *adv.*

en·tice /ɪn'taɪs/ *verb* to persuade sb/sth to go somewhere or to do sth, usually by offering them sth 誘使；引誘 SYN **persuade**：**~ sb/sth (+ adv./prep.)** *The bargain prices are expected to entice customers away from other stores.* 低廉的價格意在把顧客從其他商店吸引過來。◇ *The animal refused to be enticed from its hole.* 那隻動物怎麼引誘也不肯出洞。◇ **~ sb into doing sth** *He was not enticed into parting with his cash.* 他沒有因為誘惑而掏錢。◇ **~ sb to do sth** *Try and entice the child to eat by offering small portions of their favourite food.* 給少許孩子愛吃的食物，設法誘使他們吃飯。▸ **en·tice·ment** *noun* [C, U]：*The party is offering low taxation as its main enticement.* 這個黨正提出低稅收，以此作為其主要的誘人舉措。

en·ticing /ɪn'taɪsɪŋ/ *adj.* something that is **enticing** is so attractive and interesting that you want to have it or know more about it 有誘惑力的；誘人的；有吸引力的：*The offer was too enticing to refuse.* 這提議太有誘惑力，使人難以拒絕。▸ **en·ticing·ly** *adv.*

en·tire 0-π /ɪn'taɪə(r)/ *adj.* [only before noun] (used when you are emphasizing that the whole of sth is involved 用以強調涉及全部) including everything, everyone or every part 全部的；整個的；完全的 SYN **whole**：*The entire village was destroyed.* 整個村莊都給毀了。◇ *I wasted an entire day on it.* 我為此浪費了整整一天。◇ *I have never in my entire life heard such nonsense!* 我一生中從未聽到過這樣的廢話！◇ *The disease threatens to wipe out the entire population.* 這種疾病有可能毀滅整個族群。

en·tire·ly 0-π /ɪn'taɪəli; *NAmE* ɪn'taɪərli/ *adv.* in every way possible; completely 全部地；完整地；完全地：*I entirely agree with you.* 我完全同意你的看法。◇ *I'm not entirely happy about the proposal.* 我對這個建議並不十分滿意。◇ *That's an entirely different matter.* 那完全是另一碼事。◇ *The audience was almost entirely female.* 觀眾幾乎全是女性。

en·tir·ety /ɪn'taɪərəti/ *noun* [sing.] (*formal*) **the ~ of sth** the whole of sth 全部；全體；整體

IDM **in its/their en'tirety** as a whole, rather than in parts 作為整體；整個地；全面地：*The poem is too long to quote in its entirety.* 這首詩太長，不能全部引用。

en·title 0-π /ɪn'taɪtl/ *verb*
1 0-π [often passive] to give sb the right to have or to do sth 使享有權利；使符合資格：**~ sb to sth** *You will be entitled to your pension when you reach 65.* 你到 65 歲就有資格領取養老金。◇ *Everyone's entitled to their own opinion.* 人人都有權發表自己的意見。◇ **~ sb to do sth** *This ticket does not entitle you to travel first class.* 你拿這張票不能坐頭等艙。**2** 0-π [usually passive] **~ sth + noun** to give a title to a book, play, etc. 給…命名（或題名）：*He read a poem entitled 'Salt'.* 他朗誦一首題為《鹽》的詩。

en·title·ment /ɪn'taɪtlmənt/ *noun* (*formal*) **1** [U] **~ (to sth)** the official right to have or do sth （擁有某物或做某事的）權利，資格：*This may affect your entitlement to compensation.* 這可能影響你索賠的權利。**2** [C] something that you have an official right to; the amount that you have the right to receive 有權得到的東西；應得的數額：*Your contributions will affect your pension entitlements.* 你繳納的養老金分攤額將會影響你領取養老金的數額。**3** [C] (*NAmE*) a government system that provides financial support to a particular group of people（以特定群體為對象的）政府津貼制：*a reform of entitlements* 政府津貼制度的改革 ◇ *Medicaid, Medicare and other entitlement programs* 醫療援助制度、老年保健醫療制度以及其他政府津貼計劃

en·tity AW /'entəti/ *noun* (*pl.* **-ies**) (*formal*) something that exists separately from other things and has its own identity 獨立存在物；實體：*The unit has become part of a larger department and no longer exists as a* ***separate entity***. 這個單位已附屬於一個大的部門，不再作為一個實體獨立存在。◇ *These countries can no longer be viewed as a* ***single entity***. 這些國家不能再被看成是一個單獨的實體。

en·tomb /ɪn'tuːm/ *verb* [usually passive] (*formal*) **1 ~ sb/sth (in sth)** to bury or completely cover sb/sth so that they cannot get out, be seen, etc. 掩埋；埋葬 **2 ~ sb/sth (in sth)** to put a dead body in a TOMB 把（屍體）葬入墳墓

en·to·mol·ogy /ˌentə'mɒlədʒi; *NAmE* -'mɑːl-/ *noun* [U] the scientific study of insects 昆蟲學 ▸ **en·to·mo·logic·al** /ˌentəmə'lɒdʒɪkl; *NAmE* -'lɑːdʒ-/ *adj.* **en·to·molo·gist** /ˌentə'mɒlədʒɪst; *NAmE* -'mɑːl-/ *noun*

en·tou·rage /'ɒnturɑːʒ; *NAmE* 'ɑːn-/ *noun* [C+sing./pl. v.] a group of people who travel with an important person （統稱）隨行人員，隨從

en·tr'acte /'ɒntrækt; 'ɒ̃t-; *NAmE* 'ɑːntrækt; ɑːn'trækt/ *noun* (from *French*) **1** (*formal*) the time between the different parts of a play, show, etc.（戲劇、演出等的）幕間休息 SYN **interval 2** a short performance between the different parts of a play, show, etc. 幕間插演的節目；幕間表演

en·trails /'entreɪlz/ *noun* [pl.] the organs inside the body of a person or an animal, especially their INTESTINES 內臟；（尤指）腸 SYN **innards, insides**

en·trance[1] 0-π /'entrəns/ *noun*
➲ see also ENTRANCE[2]
▸ **DOOR/GATE** 門 **1** 0-π [C] **~ (to sth)** a door, gate, passage, etc. used for entering a room, building or place 大門（口）；入口（處）；通道：*the entrance to the museum/the museum entrance* 博物館入口處 ◇ *A lighthouse marks the entrance to the harbour.* 燈塔是進入海港的標誌。◇ *the* ***front/back/side entrance*** *of the house* 房子的前門／後門／側門 ◇ *an* ***entrance hall/lobby*** 門廳 ◇ *I'll meet you at the* ***main entrance***. 我在正門和你碰面。➲ compare EXIT *n.* (1)

▸ **GOING IN** 進入 **2** [C, usually sing.] the act of entering a room, building or place, especially in a way that attracts the attention of other people 進入；出場；登場： *His sudden entrance took everyone by surprise.* 他的突然出場使所有人都感到意外。◇ *A fanfare signalled the entrance of the king.* 響亮的喇叭聲是國王駕到的信號。◇ *She **made her entrance** after all the other guests had arrived.* 她在其他所有客人都到達後才入場。◇ *The hero **makes his entrance*** (= walks onto the stage) *in Scene 2.* 男主角在第 2 場出場。 **3** [U] **~ (to sth)** the right or opportunity to enter a building or place 進入權；進入機會： *They were refused entrance to the exhibition.* 他們被拒於展覽會門外。◇ *The police were unable to **gain entrance** to the house.* 警方未能得到進入這棟房子的許可。◇ (*BrE*) *an **entrance fee*** (= money paid to go into a museum, etc.) 入場費

▸ **BECOMING INVOLVED** 捲入 **4** [C] **~ (into sth)** the act of becoming involved in sth 捲入；參與： *The company made a dramatic entrance into the export market.* 這家公司戲劇性地打入了出口市場。

▸ **TO CLUB/INSTITUTION** 俱樂部；機構 **5** [U] permission to become a member of a club, society, university, etc.（俱樂部、社團、大學等的）准許加入，進入許可： *a university entrance exam* 大學入學考試 ◇ *entrance requirements* 入學要求 ◇ **~ (to sth)** *Entrance to the golf club is by sponsorship only.* 只有通過贊助才能加入這個高爾夫球俱樂部。 ➲ compare ENTRY

en·trance² /ɪnˈtrɑːns; *NAmE* -ˈtræns/ *verb* [usually passive] **~ sb** (*formal*) to make sb feel great pleasure and admiration so that they give sb/sth all their attention 使狂喜；使入迷 SYN **enthral** : *He listened to her, entranced.* 他聽她講話聽得出了神。 ➲ see also ENTRANCE¹ ▸ **en·tran·cing** *adj.* : *entrancing music* 令人陶醉的音樂

ˈentrance hall *noun* (*especially BrE*) a large room inside the entrance of a large or public building 門廳

en·trant /ˈentrənt/ *noun* **1 ~ (to sth)** a person who has recently joined a profession, university, etc. 新職員；新生；新會員；新成員： *new women entrants to the police force* 新加入警察部隊的女警察 ◇ *university entrants* 大學新生 **2 ~ (to sth)** a person or an animal that enters a race or a competition; a person that enters an exam 參賽者（或動物）；考生

en·trap /ɪnˈtræp/ *verb* (-pp-) [often passive] (*formal*) **1 ~ sb/sth** to put or catch sb/sth in a place or situation from which they cannot escape 使入陷阱（或圈套、困境等） SYN **trap** **2 ~ sb (into doing sth)** to trick sb, and encourage them to do sth, especially to commit a crime, so that they can be arrested for it 誘捕；誘騙；欺騙

en·trap·ment /ɪnˈtræpmənt/ *noun* [U] (*law* 律) the illegal act of tricking sb into committing a crime so that they can be arrested for it（非法）誘捕，誘人犯罪

en·treat /ɪnˈtriːt/ *verb* (*formal*) to ask sb to do sth in a serious and often emotional way 懇求；乞求 SYN **beg, implore** : **~ sb** *Please help me, I entreat you.* 請幫幫我吧，求你了。◇ **~ sb to do sth** *She entreated him not to go.* 她懇求他不要走。◇ **~ (sb) + speech** *'Please don't go,' she entreated (him).* "不要離開我。" 她懇求（他）說。

en·treaty /ɪnˈtriːti/ *noun* (*pl.* **-ies**) [C, U] (*formal*) a serious and often emotional request 懇求；乞求

en·trée /ˈɒntreɪ; *NAmE* ˈɑːn-/ *noun* (from *French*) **1** [C] (in a restaurant or at a formal meal) the main dish of the meal or a dish served before the main course（餐廳裏或正式宴會上的）主菜，主菜前的小菜 **2** [U, C] **~ (into/to sth)** (*formal*) the right or ability to enter a social group or institution 入場權；進入許可；進入資格

en·trench (also **in·trench**) /ɪnˈtrentʃ/ *verb* [usually passive] **~ sth** (sometimes *disapproving*) to establish sth very firmly so that it is very difficult to change 使處於牢固地位；牢固確立： *Sexism is **deeply entrenched** in our society.* 性別歧視在我們這個社會根深蒂固。◇ ***entrenched attitudes/interests/opposition*** 頑固的態度；固有的利益；頑固的反對

en·trench·ment /ɪnˈtrentʃmənt/ *noun* **1** [U] the fact of sth being firmly established 牢固確立；根深蒂固 **2** [C, usually pl.] a system of TRENCHES (= long narrow holes dug in the ground by soldiers to provide defence) 塹壕；戰壕

entre·pôt /ˈɒntrəpəʊ; *NAmE* ˈɑːntrəpoʊ/ *noun* (from *French*) a port or other place where goods are brought for import and export 轉口港；轉運口岸

entre·pre·neur /ˌɒntrəprəˈnɜː(r); *NAmE* ˌɑːn-/ *noun* a person who makes money by starting or running businesses, especially when this involves taking financial risks 創業者，企業家（尤指涉及財務風險的） ▸ **en·tre·pre·neur·ial** /-ˈnɜːriəl/ *adj.* : *entrepreneurial skills* 辦企業的能力 **entre·pre·neur·ship** *noun* [U]

en·tropy /ˈentrəpi/ *noun* [U] **1** (*technical* 術語) a way of measuring the lack of order that exists in a system 無序狀態測量法 **2** (*physics* 物) (*symb.* **S**) a measurement of the energy that is present in a system or process but is not available to do work 熵（系統或過程中不能用來做功的能量的度量） **3** a complete lack of order 無序狀態： *In the business world, entropy rules.* 在商業世界中，無序狀態主宰一切。 ▸ **en·trop·ic** /enˈtrɒpɪk; -ˈtrəʊp-; *NAmE* -ˈtrɑːp-/ *adj.* **en·trop·ical·ly** /-kli/ *adv.*

en·trust /ɪnˈtrʌst/ *verb* (*formal*) to make sb responsible for doing sth or taking care of sb 委託；交託；託付： **~ A (to B)** *He entrusted the task to his nephew.* 他把這任務託付給了他的姪兒。◇ **~ B with A** *He entrusted his nephew with the task.* 他把這任務託付給了他的姪兒。

entry 🔑 /ˈentri/ *noun* (*pl.* **-ies**)

▸ **GOING IN** 進入 **1** 🔑 [C, U] an act of going into or getting into a place 進入（指行動）： *She **made her entry** to the sound of thunderous applause.* 她在雷鳴般的掌聲中走了進來。◇ *The children were surprised by the sudden entry of their teacher.* 老師突然進來使孩子們感到意外。◇ **~ (into sth)** *How did the thieves **gain entry** into the building?* 竊賊是怎樣進入大樓的？ **2** 🔑 [U] the right or opportunity to enter a place 進入（指權利、機會）： ***No Entry*** (= for example, on a sign) 禁止入內 ◇ **~ (to/into sth)** *Entry to the museum is free.* 這座博物館免費參觀。◇ *to **be granted/refused entry** into the country* 准予 / 禁止入境

▸ **JOINING GROUP** 加入集體 **3** 🔑 [U] **~ (into sth)** the right or opportunity to take part in sth or become a member of a group 參與，加入（指權利、機會）： *countries seeking entry into the European Union* 尋求加入歐盟的國家 ◇ *the entry of women into the workforce* 婦女加入勞動大軍

▸ **IN COMPETITION** 比賽 **4** 🔑 [C] something that you do, write or make to take part in a competition, for example answering a set of questions 參賽作品；競賽答題： *There have been some impressive entries in the wildlife photography section* (= impressive photographs). 野生動物攝影部份已有一些上佳參賽作品。◇ *The closing date for entries is 31 March.* 遞交參賽作品的截止日期是 3 月 31 日。◇ *The sender of the first correct entry drawn will win a weekend for two in Venice.* 第一個寄出正確的競賽答題者將獲得兩人在威尼斯度週末的機會。 **5** [U] the act of taking part in a competition, race, etc. 參賽： *Entry is open to anyone over the age of 18.* * 18 歲以上的人均可參賽。◇ *an entry form* 參賽表格 **6** [sing.] the total number of people who are taking part in a competition, race, etc. 參賽人數： *There's a record entry for this year's marathon.* 參加本年度馬拉松比賽的人數創下最高紀錄。

▸ **WRITTEN INFORMATION** 書面資料 **7** 🔑 [C] an item, for example a piece of information, that is written or printed in a dictionary, an account book, a diary, etc. 項目；條目；詞條；賬目；記錄： *an encyclopedia entry* 百科全書的一個條目 ◇ **~ (in sth)** *There is no entry in his diary for that day.* 他的日記裏沒有那天的記錄。 **8** [U] the act of recording information in a computer, book, etc. 登記；登錄；錄入： *More keyboarding staff are required for data entry.* 需要更多的鍵盤錄入人員來負責輸入資料。

▸ **DOOR/GATE** 門 **9** (also **entry·way** /ˈentriweɪ/) (both *NAmE*) [C] a door, gate or passage where you enter a building; an entrance hall 大門；入口處；通道；門廳： *You can leave your umbrella in the entry.* 你可以把傘放在入口處。

ˈentry-level *adj.* [usually before noun] **1** (of a product 產品) basic and suitable for new users who may later move on to a more advanced product 適合初級用戶的；入門級的：*an entry-level computer* 供初學者使用的計算機 **2** (of a job 工作) at the lowest level in a company（公司中）最初級的

Entry·phone™ /ˈentrifəʊn; *NAmE* -foʊn/ *noun* (*BrE*) a type of telephone on the wall next to the entrance to a building enabling a person inside the building to speak to a person outside before opening the door 應門對講機

E

en·twine /ɪnˈtwaɪn/ *verb* [usually passive] **1** ~ **sth** (**with/in/around sth**) to twist or wind sth around sth else 盤繞；纏繞：*They strolled through the park, with arms entwined.* 他們挽着胳膊漫步穿過公園。**2 be entwined (with sth)** to be very closely involved or connected with sth 與…密切相關（或緊密相聯）：*Her destiny was entwined with his.* 她與他的命運緊密相聯。

ˈE-number *noun* (*BrE*) a number beginning with the letter E that is printed on packs and containers to show what artificial flavours and colours have been added to food and drink; an artificial flavour, colour, etc. added to food and drink * E 數（於包裝上註明食品或飲料中添加劑的含量）；食品添加劑：*This sauce is full of E-numbers.* 這種調味汁盡是人造香料和色素。

enu·mer·ate /ɪˈnjuːməreɪt; *NAmE* ɪˈnuː-/ *verb* ~ **sth** (*formal*) to name things on a list one by one 列舉；枚舉 ▸ **enu·mer·ation** /ɪˌnjuːməˈreɪʃn; *NAmE* ɪˌnuː-/ *noun* [U, C]

enun·ci·ate /ɪˈnʌnsieɪt/ *verb* **1** [T, I] ~ (**sth**) | + **speech** to say or pronounce words clearly 清楚地唸（字）；清晰地發（音）：*She enunciated each word slowly and carefully.* 她每個字都唸得又慢又仔細。**2** [T] ~ **sth** (*formal*) to express an idea clearly and exactly 清楚地表明；闡明：*He enunciated his vision of the future.* 他闡明了自己對未來的看法。▸ **enun·ci·ation** /ɪˌnʌnsiˈeɪʃn/ *noun* [U]

en·ur·esis /ˌenjʊəˈriːsɪs; *NAmE* ˌenjʊˈriː-/ *noun* [U] (*medical* 醫) URINATION (= letting waste liquid flow from the body) that is not under sb's control, especially in the case of a child who is asleep 遺尿（症）；（尤指兒童）尿牀

en·velop /ɪnˈveləp/ *verb* ~ **sb/sth** (**in sth**) (*formal*) to wrap sb/sth up or cover them or it completely 包住；裹住；蓋住：*She was enveloped in a huge white towel.* 她裹在一條白色大毛巾裏。◇ *Clouds enveloped the mountain tops.* 雲霧籠罩着山頂。▸ **en·velop·ment** *noun* [U]

en·vel·ope 🔑 /ˈenvələʊp; ˈɒn-; *NAmE* ˈenvəloʊp; ˈɑːn-/ *noun*
1 🔑 a flat paper container used for sending letters in 信封 ➲ VISUAL VOCAB page V69：*writing paper and envelopes* 信紙和信封 ◇ *an* ***airmail/padded/prepaid envelope*** 航空 / 有墊料夾層的 / 預付郵資信封 ➲ see also PAY ENVELOPE, SAE, SASE **2** a flat container made of plastic for keeping papers in 塑料封套；塑料封皮；塑膠封套 IDM see PUSH *v.*

en·vi·able /ˈenviəbl/ *adj.* something that is **enviable** is the sort of thing that is good and that other people want to have too 令人羨慕的；引起忌妒的：*He is in the* ***enviable position*** *of having two job offers to choose from.* 他有兩份工作可選，真讓人羨慕。OPP **unenviable** ▸ **en·vi·ably** /-bli/ *adv.*：*an enviably mild climate* 暖和得讓人羨慕的氣候

en·vi·ous /ˈenviəs/ *adj.* ~ (**of sb/sth**) wanting to be in the same situation as sb else; wanting sth that sb else has 羨慕的；忌妒的：*Everyone is so envious of her.* 人人都那麼羨慕她。◇ *They were envious of his success.* 他們忌妒他的成功。◇ *He saw the envious look in the other boy's eyes.* 他看到了另一個男孩眼裏那羨慕的目光。▸ **en·vi·ous·ly** *adv.*：*They look enviously at the success of their European counterparts.* 他們看着歐洲同行的成功，羨慕不已。➲ see also ENVY

en·vir·on·ment 🔑 AW /ɪnˈvaɪrənmənt/ *noun*
1 🔑 [C, U] the conditions that affect the behaviour and development of sb/sth; the physical conditions that sb/sth exists in（影響個體行為或事物發展的）環境；客觀環境：*a pleasant* ***working/learning environment*** 令人愉快的工作 / 學習環境 ◇ *An unhappy* ***home environment*** *can affect a child's behaviour.* 不幸的家庭環境可能對孩子的行為造成影響。◇ *They have created an environment in which productivity should flourish.* 他們創造了一種可以大大提高生產力的環境。◇ *the political environment* 政治環境 ◇ *tests carried out in a controlled environment* 在受控環境下進行的試驗 **2** 🔑 **the environment** [sing.] the natural world in which people, animals and plants live 自然環境；生態環境：*the Department of the Environment* 環境事務部 ◇ *measures to protect the environment* 保護環境的措施 ◇ *pollution of the environment* 環境污染 ◇ *damage to the environment* 對環境的破壞 **3** [C] (*computing* 計) the complete structure within which a user, computer or program operates（運行）環境；工作平台；軟件包：*a desktop development environment* 桌面開發環境

Synonyms 同義詞辨析

environment

setting • surroundings • background

These are all words for the type of place in which sb/sth exists or is situated. 以上各詞均指人或事物生存或所處的環境。

environment the conditions in a place that affect the behaviour and development of sb/sth 指影響人或事物的行為或發展的環境：*An unhappy* ***home environment*** *can affect children's behaviour.* 不幸的家庭環境可能對孩子的行為造成影響。◇ *a pleasant* ***working environment*** 令人愉快的工作環境

setting a place or situation of a particular type, in which sth happens or exists 指事物所處的環境或發生的背景：*The island provided an idyllic setting for the concert.* 這島為音樂會提供了優美的田園佈景。

surroundings everything that is around or near sb/sth 指周圍的環境：*The huts blend in perfectly with their surroundings.* 這些棚屋與周圍的環境渾然一體，非常和諧。

background the things or area behind or around the main objects or people that are in a place or picture 指對主要人物、事物起襯托作用的事物、背景：*The mountains in the background were capped with snow.* 遠處的山巒白雪覆蓋。

PATTERNS

- **in** (a/an) environment/setting/surroundings
- (a/an) **new/unfamiliar** environment/setting/surroundings
- sb/sth's **immediate** environment/surroundings
- (a) **dramatic** setting/background

en·vir·on·men·tal 🔑 AW /ɪnˌvaɪrənˈmentl/ *adj.* [usually before noun]
1 🔑 connected with the natural conditions in which people, animals and plants live; connected with the environment 自然環境的；生態環境的；有關環境的：*the environmental impact of pollution* 污染對環境的影響 ◇ ***environmental issues/problems*** 環境問題 ◇ *an* ***environmental group/movement*** (= that aims to improve or protect the natural environment) 環境保護組織 / 運動 ◇ *environmental damage* 環境破壞 **2** 🔑 connected with the conditions that affect the behaviour and development of sb/sth（有關影響個體或事物行為或發展）環境的：*environmental influences* 環境影響 ◇ *an environmental health officer* 環境衞生檢查官員 ▸ **en·vir·on·men·tal·ly** AW /-təli/ *adv.*：*an environmentally sensitive area* (= one that is easily damaged or that contains rare animals, plants, etc.) 生態環境脆弱的地區 ◇ *environmentally damaging* 對環境有害的

en·vir·on·men·tal·ist AW /ɪnˌvaɪrənˈmentəlɪst/ *noun* a person who is concerned about the natural environment and wants to improve and protect it 環境保護論者 ▸ **en·vir·on·ment·al·ism** *noun* [U]

en,vironmentally 'friendly (also **en,vironment-'friendly**) *adj.* (of products 產品) not harming the environment 環保的；不損害環境的：*environmentally friendly packaging* 環保包裝

en·vir·ons /ɪn'vaɪrənz/ *noun* [pl.] (*formal*) the area surrounding a place 周圍地區：*Berlin and its environs* 柏林及其周圍地區 ◇ *people living in the immediate environs of a nuclear plant* 居住在核電站附近地區的人

en·vis·age /ɪn'vɪzɪdʒ/ (*especially BrE*) (*NAmE* usually **en·vis·ion**) *verb* to imagine what will happen in the future 想像；設想；展望：**~ sth** *What level of profit do you envisage?* 你預計會有什麼樣的利潤水平？◇ **~ (sb) doing sth** *I can't envisage her coping with this job.* 我無法設想她如何應付這個工作。◇ **it is envisaged that …** *It is envisaged that the talks will take place in the spring.* 談判預期在春季舉行。◇ **~ that …** *I envisage that the work will be completed next year.* 我預計這項工作將在明年完成。◇ **~ how, where, etc. …** *It is difficult to envisage how people will react.* 很難設想人們將有什麼反應。➲ SYNONYMS at IMAGINE

en·vi·sion /ɪn'vɪʒn/ *verb* **1 ~ sth** (*formal*) to imagine what a situation will be like in the future, especially a situation you intend to work towards 展望；想像：*They envision an equal society, free of poverty and disease.* 他們嚮往一個沒有貧窮和疾病的平等社會。➲ SYNONYMS at IMAGINE **2** (*especially NAmE*) = ENVISAGE：*They didn't envision any problems with the new building.* 他們沒想到這棟新樓會有什麼問題。

envoy /'envɔɪ/ *noun* a person who represents a government or an organization and is sent as a representative to talk to other governments and organizations 使者；使節；（談判等的）代表 SYN **emissary**

envy /'envi/ *noun, verb*

▪ ***noun*** [U] the feeling of wanting to be in the same situation as sb else; the feeling of wanting sth that sb else has 羨慕；忌妒 SYN **jealousy**：**~ (of sb)** *He couldn't conceal his envy of me.* 他掩飾不住對我的忌妒。◇ **~ (at/of sth)** *She felt a pang of envy at the thought of his success.* 她想到他的成功便感到一陣忌妒的痛苦。◇ *They looked **with envy** at her latest purchase.* 他們羨慕地看着她最近買到的東西。◇ *Her colleagues were **green with envy*** (= they had very strong feelings of envy). 她的同事都非常眼紅。

IDM **be the envy of sb/sth** to be a person or thing that other people admire and that causes feelings of envy 成為羨慕（或忌妒）的對象；成為羨慕（或忌妒）的東西：*British television is the envy of the world.* 英國電視節目令世人羨慕。➲ see also ENVIABLE, ENVIOUS

▪ ***verb*** (**en·vies**, **envy·ing**, **en·vied**, **en·vied**) **1** to wish you had the same qualities, possessions, opportunities, etc. as sb else 羨慕；忌妒：**~ sb** *He envied her—she seemed*

Collocations 詞語搭配

The environment 環境

Environmental damage 環境破壞

- **cause/contribute to** climate change/global warming 引起氣候變化／全球變暖
- **produce** pollution/CO_2/greenhouse (gas) emissions 產生污染／二氧化碳／溫室氣體排放
- **damage/destroy** the environment/a marine ecosystem/the ozone layer/coral reefs 破壞環境／海洋生態系統／臭氧層／珊瑚礁
- **degrade** ecosystems/habitats/the environment 使生態系統／棲息地／環境退化
- **harm** the environment/wildlife/marine life 危害環境／野生動物／海洋生物
- **threaten** natural habitats/coastal ecosystems/a species with extinction 構成對自然棲息地／沿海生態系統／物種滅絕的威脅
- **deplete** natural resources/the ozone layer 大量損耗自然資源／臭氧層
- **pollute** rivers and lakes/waterways/the air/the atmosphere/the environment/oceans 污染河流湖泊／航道／空氣／大氣層／環境／海洋
- **contaminate** groundwater/the soil/food/crops 污染地下水／土壤／食物／莊稼
- **log** forests/rainforests/trees 採伐森林／熱帶雨林／樹木

Protecting the environment 保護環境

- **address/combat/tackle** the threat/effects/impact of climate change 設法解決／防止／應對氣候變化帶來的威脅／影響／衝擊
- **fight/take action on/reduce/stop** global warming 對抗／採取行動應對／減緩／阻止全球變暖
- **limit/curb/control** air/water/atmospheric/environmental pollution 控制空氣／水／大氣／環境污染
- **cut/reduce** pollution/greenhouse gas emissions 減少污染／溫室氣體排放
- **offset** carbon/CO_2 emissions 抵消碳／二氧化碳的排放
- **reduce** (the size of) your carbon footprint 減少碳足跡（量）
- **achieve/promote** sustainable development 實現／促進可持續發展
- **preserve/conserve** biodiversity/natural resources 保持生物多樣性；保護自然資源
- **protect** endangered species/a coastal ecosystem 保護瀕危物種／沿海生態系統
- **prevent/stop** soil erosion/overfishing/massive deforestation/damage to ecosystems 防止／阻止水土流失／過度捕撈／大面積森林砍伐／對生態系統的破壞
- **raise** awareness of environmental issues 增強環境意識
- **save** the planet/the rainforests/an endangered species 拯救地球／熱帶雨林／瀕危物種

Energy and resources 能源和資源

- **conserve/save/consume/waste** energy 保護／節約／消耗／浪費能源
- **manage/exploit/be rich in** natural resources 管理／開發／有豐富的自然資源
- **dump/dispose of** hazardous/toxic/nuclear waste 傾倒／處理有害／有毒／核廢料
- **dispose of/throw away** litter/(*especially BrE*) rubbish/(*especially NAmE*) garbage/(*NAmE*) trash/sewage 處理／扔掉垃圾／廢物／污水
- **use/be made from** recycled/recyclable/biodegradable material 使用回收／可回收／可生物降解材料；由回收／可回收／可生物降解材料製成
- **recycle** bottles/packaging/paper/plastic/waste 回收瓶子／包裝材料／紙／塑料／廢品
- **promote/encourage** recycling/sustainable development/the use of renewable energy 促進／鼓勵回收利用／可持續發展／使用可再生能源
- **develop/invest in/promote** renewable energy 研發／投資／推動可再生能源
- **reduce** your dependence/reliance on fossil fuels 減少對化石燃料的依賴
- **get/obtain/generate/produce** electricity from wind, solar and wave power/renewable sources 利用風、太陽能、潮汐／可再生能源發電
- **build/develop** a (50-megawatt/offshore) wind farm 修建一座（50 兆瓦／海上）風力發電站
- **install/be fitted with/be powered by** solar panels 安裝太陽能板；由太陽能板提供動力

to have everything she could possibly want. 他羨慕她，她似乎要什麼有什麼。◇ **~ sth** *She has always envied my success.* 她一直忌妒我的成功。◇ **~ sb sth** *I envied him his good looks.* 我羨慕他的英俊。◇ **~ sb doing sth** *I envy you having such a close family.* 我羨慕你有這麼一個關係緊密的家庭。 **2** to be glad that you do not have to do what sb else has to do 慶幸（不必做別人非做不可的事）： **not ~ sb** *It's a difficult situation you're in. I don't envy you.* 你的處境很困難，我不會羨慕你。◇ **not ~ sb sth** *I don't envy her that job.* 我不羨慕她有那份工作。

E

en·zyme /ˈenzaɪm/ *noun* (*biology* 生) a substance, produced by all living things, which helps a chemical change happen or happen more quickly, without being changed itself 酶

eo·lian (*NAmE*) (*BrE* **ae·olian**) /iːˈəʊliən; *NAmE* iːˈoʊ-/ *adj.* (*technical* 術語) connected with or caused by the action of the wind 風的；風成的

eon (*especially NAmE*) (*BrE* usually **aeon**) /ˈiːən/ *noun* **1** (*formal*) an extremely long period of time; thousands of years 極漫長的時間；千萬年 **2** (*geology* 地) a major division of time, divided into ERAS 宙（地質學上的年代分期，下分代）： *eons of geological history* 數以億萬年計的地質史

ˈe-pal (also **ˈe-friend**) *noun* a person that you make friends with by sending emails, often sb you have never met 網友（通過電子郵件交流）

ep·aul·ette (*especially BrE*) (*NAmE* usually **ep·aulet**) /ˈepəlet/ *noun* a decoration on the shoulder of a coat, jacket, etc., especially when part of a military uniform（尤指軍服上的）肩章，肩飾

épée /eˈpeɪ; ˈepeɪ/ *noun* **1** [C] a SWORD used in the sport of FENCING 重劍，銳劍（擊劍運動用） **2** [U] (*NAmE*) the sport of FENCING with an épée 重劍，銳劍（運動項目）

ephem·era /ɪˈfemərə/ *noun* [pl.] things that are important or used for only a short period of time 只在短期內有用的事物： *a collection of postcards, tickets and other ephemera* 明信片、票證和其他短時效物品的收藏系列

ephem·eral /ɪˈfemərəl/ *adj.* (*formal*) lasting or used for only a short period of time 短暫的；瞬息的 **SYN** **short-lived**

epic /ˈepɪk/ *noun, adj.*

■ ***noun*** **1** [C, U] a long poem about the actions of great men and women or about a nation's history; this style of poetry 敘事詩；史詩： *one of the great Hindu epics* 偉大的印度教史詩之一 ◇ *the creative genius of Greek epic* 富有創造力的希臘史詩天才 ➲ compare LYRIC *n.* (1) **2** [C] a long film/movie or book that contains a lot of action, usually about a historical subject 史詩般的電影（或書） **3** [C] (sometimes *humorous*) a long and difficult job or activity that you think people should admire 壯舉；驚人之舉： *Their four-hour match on Centre Court was an epic.* 他們在中心球場歷時四個小時的比賽是一個壯舉。

■ ***adj.*** [usually before noun] **1** having the features of an epic 具有史詩性質的；史詩般的： *an epic poem* 史詩般的詩 ➲ compare LYRIC *adj.* (1) **2** taking place over a long period of time and involving a lot of difficulties 漫長而艱難的；艱苦卓絕的： *an* ***epic journey/struggle*** 漫長而艱難的旅程；艱苦卓絕的鬥爭 **3** very great and impressive 宏大的；壯麗的；給人深刻印象的： *a tragedy of* ***epic proportions*** 巨大的不幸

epi·cene /ˈepɪsiːn/ *adj.* **1** (*formal*) having characteristics of both the male and female sex or of neither sex in particular 兼具男女兩性特徵的；缺乏性特徵的： *epicene beauty* 兼具陽剛和陰柔之美 **2** (*grammar* 語法) (of a word 詞) having one form to represent male and female 通性的： *You can write* ***'s/he'*** *as an* ***epicene*** *pronoun when you are not referring to men or women in particular.* 不特指男性或女性時可以寫成 s / he 表示通性代詞。

epi·centre (*especially US* **epi·cen·ter**) /ˈepɪsentə(r)/ *noun* **1** the point on the earth's surface where the effects of an EARTHQUAKE are felt most strongly 震中；震央 **2** (*formal*) the central point of sth 中心；焦點；集中點

epi·cure /ˈepɪkjʊə(r); *NAmE* -kjʊr/ *noun* (*formal*) a person who enjoys food and drink of high quality and knows a lot about it 講究飲食的人；美食家

epi·cur·ean /ˌepɪkjʊəˈriːən; *NAmE* ˌepɪkjʊˈr-/ *adj.* (*formal*) devoted to pleasure and enjoying yourself 享樂的；吃喝玩樂的 ▸ **epi·cur·ean·ism** /ˌepɪkjʊəˈriːənɪzəm; *NAmE* ˌepɪkjʊˈriːən-/ *noun* [U]

epi·dem·ic /ˌepɪˈdemɪk/ *noun* **1** a large number of cases of a particular disease happening at the same time in a particular community 流行病： *the outbreak of a flu epidemic* 流感的爆發 ◇ *an epidemic of measles* 麻疹的流行 **2** a sudden rapid increase in how often sth bad happens（壞事迅速的）泛濫，蔓延： *an epidemic of crime in the inner cities* 內城區犯罪活動盛行 ▸ **epi·dem·ic** *adj.*： *Car theft is now reaching* ***epidemic proportions****.* 汽車偷盜現已近泛濫成災。➲ compare PANDEMIC

epi·demi·ology /ˌepɪˌdiːmiˈɒlədʒi; *NAmE* -ˈɑːl-/ *noun* [U] the scientific study of the spread and control of diseases 流行病學 ▸ **epi·demi·ologic·al** /ˌepɪˌdiːmiəˈlɒdʒɪkl; *NAmE* -ˈlɑːdʒ-/ *adj.* **epi·demi·olo·gist** /ˌepɪˌdiːmiˈɒlədʒɪst; *NAmE* -ˈɑːl-/ *noun*

epi·der·mis /ˌepɪˈdɜːmɪs; *NAmE* -ˈdɜːrm-/ *noun* [sing., U] (*anatomy* 解) the outer layer of the skin 表皮

epi·dural /ˌepɪˈdjʊərəl; *NAmE* usually -ˈdʊr-/ *noun* (*medical* 醫) an ANAESTHETIC that is put into the lower part of the back so that no pain is felt below the waist 硬膜外麻醉： *Some mothers choose to have an epidural when giving birth.* 有些母親分娩時選擇硬膜外麻醉。

epi·glot·tis /ˌepɪˈɡlɒtɪs; *NAmE* -ˈɡlɑːtɪs/ *noun* (*anatomy* 解) a thin piece of TISSUE behind the tongue that prevents food or drink from entering the lungs 會厭

epi·gram /ˈepɪɡræm/ *noun* a short poem or phrase that expresses an idea in a clever or amusing way 詼諧短詩；警句；雋語 ▸ **epi·gram·mat·ic** /ˌepɪɡrəˈmætɪk/ *adj.*

epi·graph /ˈepɪɡrɑːf; *NAmE* -ɡræf/ *noun* a line of writing, short phrase, etc. on a building or statue, or as an introduction to part of a book（建築物或雕塑的）刻文，銘文；（書籍卷首或章節前的）引言，題辭

epi·lepsy /ˈepɪlepsi/ *noun* [U] a DISORDER of the nervous system that causes a person to become unconscious suddenly, often with violent movements of the body 癲癇；羊癲風；羊角風 ▸ **epi·lep·tic** /ˌepɪˈleptɪk/ *adj.*： *an epileptic fit* 癲癇發作 **epi·lep·tic** *noun*： *Is she an epileptic?* 她是癲癇病患者嗎？

epi·logue /ˈepɪlɒɡ; *NAmE* -lɔːɡ; -lɑːɡ/ *noun* a speech, etc. at the end of a play, book, or film/movie that comments on or acts as a conclusion to what has happened（劇本、書籍、電影的）收場白，尾聲，後記，跋 ➲ compare PROLOGUE

Epiph·any /ɪˈpɪfəni/ *noun* a Christian festival, held on the 6 January, in memory of the time when the MAGI came to see the baby Jesus at Bethlehem 顯現節，主顯節（1 月 6 日紀念賢士朝拜耶穌）

epis·cop·acy /ɪˈpɪskəpəsi/ *noun* [U] government of a church by BISHOPS 主教制（以主教為主體管理教會）

epis·cop·al /ɪˈpɪskəpl/ *adj.* **1** connected with a BISHOP or BISHOPS 主教的： *episcopal power* 主教管轄權 **2** (usually **Episcopal**) (also **Epis·co·pa·lian**) (of a Christian Church 基督教) that is governed by BISHOPS 主教制的： *the Episcopal Church* (= the Anglican Church in Scotland and the US)（蘇格蘭和美國的）聖公會

Epis·co·pa·lian /ɪˌpɪskəˈpeɪliən/ *noun* a member of the Episcopal Church（蘇格蘭和美國的）聖公會教徒

epis·co·pate /ɪˈpɪskəpət/ *noun* [usually sing.] (*religion* 宗) **1 the episcopate** the BISHOPS of a particular church or area 主教團（統稱某教會或地區的主教） **2** the job of BISHOP or the period of time during which sb is bishop 主教職位；主教任期

episi·ot·omy /ɪˌpiːsiˈɒtəmi; *NAmE* -ˈɑːtəmi/ *noun* (*pl.* **-ies**) (*medical* 醫) a cut that is sometimes made at the opening of a woman's VAGINA to make the birth of a baby easier or safer 會陰切開術

epi·sode /ˈepɪsəʊd; *NAmE* -soʊd/ *noun* **1** an event, a situation, or a period of time in sb's life, a novel, etc. that is important or interesting in some way（人生的）

一段經歷；（小說的）片段，插曲 SYN **incident**：*I'd like to try and forget the whole episode.* 我倒想盡量把那段經歷全部忘掉。◇ *One of the funniest episodes in the book occurs in Chapter 6.* 書中最有趣的片段之一在第 6 章。**2** one part of a story that is broadcast on television or radio in several parts（電視連續劇或廣播劇的）一集

epi·sod·ic /ˌepɪˈsɒdɪk; *NAmE* -ˈsɑːd-/ *adj.* (*formal*) **1** happening occasionally and not at regular intervals 偶爾發生的；不定期的 **2** (of a story, etc. 故事等) containing or consisting of many separate and different events 由鬆散片段組成的；有許多片段的：*My memories of childhood are hazy and episodic.* 我兒時的回憶是一些朦朦朧朧的鬆散片段。

epi·stem·ic /ˌepɪˈstiːmɪk; -ˈstem-/ *adj.* (*formal*) relating to knowledge 知識的；認識的

epis·te·mol·ogy /ɪˌpɪstəˈmɒlədʒi; *NAmE* -ˈmɑːl-/ *noun* [U] the part of philosophy that deals with knowledge 認識論

epis·tle /ɪˈpɪsl/ *noun* **1 Epistle** any of the letters in the New Testament of the Bible, written by the first people who followed Christ 使徒書信，宗徒書信（《〈聖經〉新約》書卷）：*the Epistles of St Paul* 聖保羅書信 **2** (*formal* or *humorous*) a long, serious letter on an important subject（文體鄭重、內容重要、篇幅較長的）書信

epis·tol·ary /ɪˈpɪstələri; *NAmE* -leri/ *adj.* (*formal*) written or expressed in the form of letters 書信的；用書信表達的；書信體的：*an epistolary novel* 書信體小說

epi·taph /ˈepɪtɑːf; *NAmE* -tæf/ *noun* **1** words that are written or said about a dead person, especially words on a GRAVESTONE 悼文；祭文；（尤指）墓誌銘，碑文 **2 ~ (to sb/sth)** something which is left to remind people of a particular person, a period of time or an event 遺物；遺存；遺跡：*These slums are an epitaph to the housing policy of the 1960s.* 這些貧民窟是 20 世紀 60 年代住房政策的遺跡。

epi·thet /ˈepɪθet/ *noun* **1** an adjective or phrase that is used to describe sb/sth's character or most important quality, especially in order to give praise or criticism（尤用於褒貶人或事物特徵或性質的）表述形容詞，修飾語：*The film is long and dramatic but does not quite earn the epithet 'epic'.* 這部影片篇幅長，戲劇性強，不過還不能譽為"史詩"。**2** (*especially NAmE*) an offensive word or phrase that is used about a person or group of people 別稱；綽號；諢名：*Racial epithets were scrawled on the walls.* 牆上塗寫着一些帶有種族歧視的稱謂。

epit·ome /ɪˈpɪtəmi/ *noun* [sing.] **the ~ of sth** (*formal*) a perfect example of sth 典型；典範 SYN **embodiment**：*He is the epitome of a modern young man.* 他是現代青年男子的典範。◇ *clothes that are the epitome of good taste* 典型的高品味服裝

epit·om·ize (*BrE* also **-ise**) /ɪˈpɪtəmaɪz/ *verb* **~ sth** to be a perfect example of sth 成為…的典範（或典型）：*The fighting qualities of the team are epitomized by the captain.* 這個隊的戰鬥精神從隊長身上體現出來。◇ *These movies seem to epitomize the 1950s.* 這些影片似乎就是 20 世紀 50 年代的縮影。

epoch /ˈiːpɒk; *NAmE* ˈepək/ *noun* (*formal* or *literary*) **1** a period of time in history, especially one during which important events or changes happen 時代；紀元；時期 SYN **era**：*The death of the emperor marked the end of an epoch in the country's history.* 皇帝駕崩標誌着該國歷史上一個時代的結束。**2** (*geology* 地) a length of time which is a division of a PERIOD 世（地質年代，紀下分世）：*geological epochs* 地質世

ˈepoch-making *adj.* (*formal*) having a very important effect on people's lives and on history 劃時代的；開創新紀元的；意義重大的

epo·nym /ˈepənɪm/ *noun* (*technical* 術語) a person or thing, or the name of a person or thing, from which a place, an invention, a discovery, etc. gets its name 名祖（姓名或名稱被用以命名地方、發明、發現等的人或物）

epony·mous /ɪˈpɒnɪməs; *NAmE* ɪˈpɑːn-/ *adj.* [only before noun] the **eponymous** character of a book, play, film/movie, etc. is the one mentioned in the title（與標題）同名的 SYN **titular**：*Don Quixote, eponymous hero of the great novel by Cervantes* 堂吉訶德——塞萬提斯巨著中與書同名的主人公

epoxy /ɪˈpɒksi; *NAmE* ɪˈpɑːksi/ *noun* [U, C] (*pl.* **-ies**) (also **eˌpoxy ˈresin**) a type of strong glue 環氧樹脂

ep·si·lon /ˈepsɪlɒn; epˈsaɪlɒn; *NAmE* ˈepsɪlɑːn/ *noun* the fifth letter of the Greek alphabet (Ε, ϵ) 希臘字母表的第 5 個字母

Epsom salts /ˌepsəm ˈsɔːlts/ *noun* [pl.] a white powder that can be mixed with water and used as a medicine or LAXATIVE 瀉鹽

equ·able /ˈekwəbl/ *adj.* (*formal*) **1** calm and not easily upset or annoyed 寧靜的；平和的；不易惱怒的：*an equable temperament* 平和的性情 **2** (of weather 天氣) keeping a steady temperature with no sudden changes 穩定的；變化小的；溫差小的 ▸ **equ·ably** /ˈekwəbli/ *adv.*

equal 🔑 /ˈiːkwəl/ *adj.*, *noun*, *verb*

■ ***adj.*** **1** 🔑 the same in size, quantity, value, etc. as sth else（大小、數量、價值等）相同的，同樣的；相等的：*There is an equal number of boys and girls in the class.* 這個班男女生人數相等。◇ *two pieces of wood equal in length/of equal length* 兩塊長度相同的木頭 ◇ **~ to sb/sth** *One unit of alcohol is equal to half a pint of beer.* 一單位酒精等於半品脫啤酒。HELP You can use **exactly**, **precisely**, **approximately**, etc. with **equal** in this meaning. * equal 作此義可與 exactly、precisely、approximately 等詞連用。**2** 🔑 having the same rights or being treated the same as other people, without differences such as race, religion or sex being considered 平等的；同等的：***equal rights/pay*** 平等的權利；同酬 ◇ *The company has an **equal opportunities** policy* (= gives the same chances of employment to everyone). 這家公司的政策是人人機會均等。◇ *the desire for a more equal society* (= in which everyone has the same rights and chances) 對更平等的社會的嚮往 HELP You can use **more** with **equal** in this meaning. * equal 作此義可與 more 連用。**3 ~ to sth** (*formal*) having the necessary strength, courage and ability to deal with sth successfully（力氣、勇氣、能力）相當的；能勝任的；能應付的：*I hope that he proves equal to the challenge.* 我希望他最後能應付這一挑戰。➲ see also EQUALLY

IDM **on ˌequal ˈterms (with sb)** having the same advantages and disadvantages as sb else（與某人）處於平等的地位：*Can our industry compete on equal terms with its overseas rivals?* 我們的工業能與海外對手以平等的地位競爭嗎？➲ more at THING

■ ***noun*** 🔑 a person or thing of the same quality or with the same status, rights, etc. as another 同等的人；相等物：*She treats the people who work for her as her equals.* 她以平等的身分對待為她工作的人。◇ *Our cars are the equal of those produced anywhere in the world.* 我們的汽車可與世界上任何地方生產的汽車媲美。

IDM **be without ˈequal | have no ˈequal** (*formal*) to be better than anything else or anyone else of the same type 無與倫比；無敵；無比：*He is a player without equal.* 他是個無與倫比的運動員。**ˌsome (people, members, etc.) are more equal than ˈothers** (*saying*) although the members of a society, group, etc. appear to be equal, some, in fact, get better treatment than others 有些（人、成員等）比其他的更平等 ORIGIN This phrase is used by one of the pigs in the book 'Animal Farm' by George Orwell: 'All animals are equal but some animals are more equal than others.' 本短語來自喬治 • 奧威爾所著的《動物莊園》中一頭豬所說的話："所有的動物都平等，但有些動物比其他的動物更平等。" ➲ more at FIRST *n.*

■ ***verb*** (-ll-, *US* -l-) **1** 🔑 *linking verb* + **noun** to be the same in size, quantity, value, etc. as sth else（大小、數量、價值等）與…相等，等於：*2x plus y equals 7* (2x+y=7). * 2x 加 y 等於 7。◇ *A metre equals 39.38 inches.* * 1 米等於 39.38 英寸。**2** 🔑 **~ sth** to be as good as sth else or do sth to the same standard as sb else 比得上；敵得過：*This achievement is unlikely ever to be equalled.* 這一成就可能任何時候都沒有能與之匹敵的。◇ *Her hatred of religion is equalled only by her loathing for politicians.* 只有對政客的厭惡才能與她對宗教的憎恨同日而語。◇

E

With his last jump he equalled the world record. 他的最後一跳平了世界紀錄。 **3 ~ sth** to lead to or result in sth 導致；結果為： *Cooperation equals success.* 合作意味着成功。

equal·ity /iˈkwɒləti; *NAmE* iˈkwɑː-/ *noun* [U] the fact of being equal in rights, status, advantages, etc. 平等；均等；相等： ***racial/social/sexual equality*** 種族 / 社會 / 男女平等 ◇ *equality of opportunity* 機會均等 ◇ *the principle of equality before the law* (= the law treats everyone the same) 法律面前人人平等的原則 ◇ *Don't you believe in equality between men and women?* 難道你不相信男女平等嗎？ OPP **inequality** ➲ COLLOCATIONS at RACE

E

equal·ize (*BrE* also **-ise**) /ˈiːkwəlaɪz/ *verb* **1** [T] **~ sth** to make things equal in size, quantity, value, etc. in the whole of a place or group 使平等；使均等；使相等： *a policy to equalize the distribution of resources throughout the country* 使資源在全國分佈均衡的政策 **2** [I] (*BrE*) (especially in football (SOCCER) 尤指足球) to score a goal that makes the score of both teams equal 打成平局；扳平比分： *Rooney equalized early in the second half.* 魯尼在下半場比賽開始後不久將比分扳平。 ▸ **equal·iza·tion, -isa·tion** /ˌiːkwəlaɪˈzeɪʃn; *NAmE* -ləˈz-/ *noun* [U]

equal·izer (*BrE* also **-iser**) /ˈiːkwəlaɪzər/ *noun* [usually sing.] (*BrE*) (especially in football (SOCCER) 尤指足球) a goal that makes the score of both teams equal 扳平比分的得分： *Rooney scored the equalizer.* 魯尼進了一球，扳平了比分。

equal·ly 🔑 /ˈiːkwəli/ *adv.*
1 🔑 to the same degree; in the same or in a similar way 平等地；同樣地： *Diet and exercise are equally important.* 飲食和鍛煉同樣重要。◇ *This job could be done **equally well** by a computer.* 這個工作用計算機同樣可以做得很好。◇ *We try to treat every member of staff equally.* 我們盡可能平等對待每一位工作人員。 **2** 🔑 in equal parts, amounts, etc. 平均地；相等地；均等地： *The money was divided equally among her four children.* 這筆錢在她的四個孩子中平分了。◇ *They share the housework equally.* 他們平均分擔家務。 **3** used to introduce another phrase or idea that adds to and is as important as what you have just said（引出同樣重要的內容）同樣，此外，也： *I'm trying to do what is best, but equally I've got to consider the cost.* 我在想盡力做得最好，但同時我也得考慮費用。

ˈequals sign (also **ˈequal sign**) *noun* the symbol (=), used in mathematics 等號

equa·nim·ity /ˌekwəˈnɪməti/ *noun* [U] (*formal*) a calm state of mind which means that you do not become angry or upset, especially in difficult situations（尤指處於困境時的）鎮靜，沉着，冷靜： *She accepted the prospect of her operation **with equanimity**.* 她心情平靜地接受了動手術的可能性。

equate AW /iˈkweɪt/ *verb* **~ sth (with sth)** to think that sth is the same as sth else or is as important 同等看待；使等同： *Some parents equate education with exam success.* 有些父母認為教育就是考試成績優秀。◇ *I don't see how you can equate the two things.* 我不明白你怎麼能把這兩件事等同起來。

PHR V **eˈquate to sth** to be equal to sth else 相當於；等於： *A $5 000 raise equates to 25%.* 加薪 5 000 元相當於增加了 25%。

equa·tion AW /iˈkweɪʒn/ *noun* **1** [C] (*mathematics* 數) a statement showing that two amounts or values are equal, for example 2x + y = 54 方程；方程式；等式 **2** [U, sing.] the act of making sth equal or considering sth as equal (= of equating them) 相等；等同看待： *The equation of wealth with happiness can be dangerous.* 把財富與幸福等同起來可能是危險的。 **3** [C, usually sing.] a problem or situation in which several things must be considered and dealt with（多種因素的）平衡，綜合體： *When children **enter the equation**, further tensions may arise within a marriage.* 有了孩子以後，緊張的情況可能增加，影響婚姻中的平衡關係。

equa·tor /iˈkweɪtə(r)/ (usually **the equator**) *noun* [sing.] an imaginary line around the earth at an equal distance from the North and South Poles 赤道

equa·tor·ial /ˌekwəˈtɔːriəl/ *adj.* near the equator or typical of a country that is near the equator 赤道的；赤道附近的；赤道地區特有的： *equatorial rainforests* 赤道地區的雨林 ◇ *an equatorial climate* 赤道氣候

equerry /ɪˈkweri; ˈekwəri/ *noun* (*pl.* **-ies**) a male officer who acts as an assistant to a member of a royal family 王室侍從官

eques·trian /ɪˈkwestriən/ *adj.* [usually before noun] connected with riding horses, especially as a sport 騎術的： *equestrian events at the Olympic Games* 奧林匹克運動會的騎術比賽項目 ➲ VISUAL VOCAB page V46

eques·tri·an·ism /ɪˈkwestriənɪzəm/ *noun* [U] **1** the skill or sport of riding horses（騎）馬術 **2** an Olympic sport consisting of SHOWJUMPING, DRESSAGE and THREE-DAY EVENTING 馬術（運動項目）

equi- /ˈiːkwɪ-; ˈek-/ *combining form* (in nouns, adjectives and adverbs 構成名詞、形容詞和副詞) equal; equally 相等的；相等地： *equidistant* 等距 ◇ *equilibrium* 平衡

equi·dis·tant /ˌiːkwɪˈdɪstənt; ˌek-/ *adj.* [not before noun] **~ (from sth)** (*formal*) equally far from two or more places 等距離；等距： *All points on a circle are equidistant from the centre.* 圓周上各點離圓心的距離相等。

equi·lat·eral tri·angle /ˌiːkwɪˌlætərəl ˈtraɪæŋɡl/ *noun* (*geometry* 幾何) a triangle whose three sides are all the same length 等邊三角形 ➲ VISUAL VOCAB page V71

equi·lib·rium /ˌiːkwɪˈlɪbriəm; ˌek-/ *noun* [U, sing.]
1 a state of balance, especially between opposing forces or influences 平衡；均衡；均勢： *The point at which the solid and the liquid are **in equilibrium** is called the freezing point.* 固體和液體的平衡點叫做冰點。◇ *Any disturbance to the body's state of equilibrium can produce stress.* 對身體平衡狀態的任何干擾都可能產生壓力。◇ *We have achieved an equilibrium in the economy.* 我們已在經濟上達到平衡。 **2** a calm state of mind and a balance of emotions（心情、情緒）平靜，安寧；心理平衡： *He sat down to try and recover his equilibrium.* 他坐了下來，努力恢復平靜。

equine /ˈekwaɪn; ˈiːk-; *NAmE* ˈiːk-/ *adj.* (*formal*) connected with horses; like a horse 馬的；馬科的；似馬的

equi·noc·tial /ˌiːkwɪˈnɒkʃl; ˌek-; *NAmE* -ˈnɑːk-/ *adj.* connected with an equinox 二分點的；晝夜平分時的；春分（或秋分）的

equi·nox /ˈiːkwɪnɒks; ˈek-; *NAmE* -nɑːks/ *noun* one of the two times in the year (around 20 March and 22 September) when the sun is above the EQUATOR and day and night are of equal length 二分時刻；晝夜平分時；春分；秋分： *the **spring/autumn equinox*** 春分；秋分

equip AW /ɪˈkwɪp/ *verb* (**-pp-**) **1** to provide yourself/sb/sth with the things that are needed for a particular purpose or activity 配備；裝備 SYN **kit out** ： **~ sth** *to be **fully/poorly equipped*** 裝備齊全 / 簡陋 ◇ *She got a bank loan to rent and equip a small workshop.* 她向銀行貸款，為成立一個小工作室租地方和買設備。◇ **~ yourself/sb/sth (with sth) (for sth)** *He equipped himself with a street plan.* 他隨身帶着一張街道平面圖。◇ *The centre is **well equipped** for canoeing and mountaineering.* 本中心有齊全的划船和登山設備。 **2 ~ sb (for sth) | ~ sb (to do sth)** to prepare sb for an activity or task, especially by teaching them what they need to know 使有所準備；使有能力： *The course is designed to equip students for a career in nursing.* 此課程旨在使學生能夠勝任護理工作。

equip·ment 🔑 AW /ɪˈkwɪpmənt/ *noun* [U]
1 🔑 the things that are needed for a particular purpose or activity 設備；器材： *a useful **piece of equipment** for the kitchen* 一件有用的廚房設備 ◇ *office equipment* 辦公室設備 ◇ *new equipment for the sports club* 體育俱樂部的新器材 ➲ VISUAL VOCAB page V70 **2** the process of providing a place or person with necessary things 配備；裝備： *The equipment of the photographic studio was expensive.* 這個攝影室的裝備花費巨大。

Synonyms 同義詞辨析

equipment

material • gear • kit • apparatus

These are all words for the things that you need for a particular purpose or activity. 以上各詞均指特定目的或活動所需的材料、設備、器材。

equipment the things that are needed for a particular purpose or activity 指特定目的或活動所需的設備、器材： *camping equipment* 野營裝備 ◇ *a piece of equipment* 一件設備

material things that are needed for a particular activity 指特定活動所需的材料： *household cleaning materials* 家用清潔劑 ◇ *teaching material* 教材

EQUIPMENT OR MATERIAL? 用 equipment 還是 material？

Equipment is usually solid things, especially large ones. **Materials** may be liquids, powders or books, CDs, etc. containing information, as well as small solid items. * equipment 通常指固體材料，尤其是大型設備器材；material 除指小型固體材料外，還可指液體、粉狀物、書籍、信息光盤等。

gear the equipment or clothes needed for a particular activity 指某種活動所需的設備、用具、衣服： *Skiing gear can be expensive.* 滑雪用具有時會很昂貴。

kit a set of tools or equipment that you use for a particular purpose 指用於特定目的的成套工具、成套設備： *a first-aid kit* 一套急救用品 ◇ *a tool kit* 一套工具

apparatus the tools or other pieces of equipment that are needed for a particular activity or task 指特定活動或任務所需的儀器、器械、裝置： *breathing apparatus for firefighters* 消防員用的呼吸器 ◇ *laboratory apparatus* 實驗室儀器 NOTE **Apparatus** is used especially for scientific, medical or technical purposes. * apparatus 尤用於科學、醫學或技術等方面。

PATTERNS

- **electrical/electronic** equipment/gear/apparatus
- **sports** equipment/gear/kit
- **camping** equipment/gear
- a **piece of** equipment/apparatus

equi·poise /ˈiːkwɪpɔɪz; ˈek-/ *noun* [U] (*formal*) a state of balance 平衡；均勢

equit·able /ˈekwɪtəbl/ *adj.* (*formal*) fair and reasonable; treating everyone in an equal way 公平合理的；公正的 SYN **fair** OPP **inequitable** ▸ **equit·ably** /-bli/ *adv.*

Equity /ˈekwəti/ *noun* [U] the TRADE/LABOR UNION for actors in the UK, the US and some other countries （英、美等國的）演員工會

equity /ˈekwəti/ *noun* **1** [U] (*finance* 財) the value of a company's shares; the value of a property after all charges and debts have been paid （公司的）股本；資產淨值 ➲ see also NEGATIVE EQUITY **2 equities** [pl.] (*finance* 財) shares in a company which do not pay a fixed amount of interest （公司的）普通股 **3** [U] (*formal*) a situation in which everyone is treated equally 公平；公正 SYN **fairness** OPP **inequity** **4** [U] (*law* 律) (*especially BrE*) a system of natural justice allowing a fair judgement in a situation which is not covered by the existing laws 衡平法

equiva·lent 🔑 AW /ɪˈkwɪvələnt/ *adj., noun*

■ *adj.* 🔑 equal in value, amount, meaning, importance, etc. （價值、數量、意義、重要性等）相等的，相同的： *250 grams or an equivalent amount in ounces* * 250 克或與之等量的盎司 ◇ **~ to sth** *Eight kilometres is roughly equivalent to five miles.* 八公里約等於五英里。 ▸ **equiva·lence** AW /-ləns/ *noun* [U]： (*formal*) *There is no straightforward equivalence between economic progress and social well-being.* 經濟進步與社會福利之間絕非輕易等同。

■ *noun* 🔑 a thing, amount, word, etc. that is equivalent to sth else 相等的東西；等量；對應詞： *Send €20 or the equivalent in your own currency.* 寄 20 歐元或等值的貴國貨幣。 ◇ **~ of/to sth** *Creutzfeldt-Jakob disease, the human equivalent of BSE* 克羅伊茨費爾特 — 雅各布病，相當於瘋牛病的人類疾病 ◇ *Breathing such polluted air is the equivalent of* (= has the same effect as) *smoking ten cigarettes a day.* 呼吸污染這麼嚴重的空氣等於每天抽十支煙。 ◇ *The German 'Gymnasium' is the closest equivalent to the grammar school in England.* 德語 Gymnasium 基本上相當於英格蘭的文法學校。

E

equivo·cal /ɪˈkwɪvəkl/ *adj.* (*formal*) **1** (of words or statements 言語或陳述) not having one clear or definite meaning or intention; able to be understood in more than one way 模棱兩可的；意義雙關的；含糊其詞的 SYN **ambiguous**： *She gave an equivocal answer, typical of a politician.* 她的回答模棱兩可，是典型的政客做法。 **2** (of actions or behaviour 行動或行為) difficult to understand or explain clearly or easily 難以理解的；難以解釋清楚的： *The experiments produced equivocal results.* 這些實驗產生的結果難以理解。 ➲ see also UNEQUIVOCAL

equivo·cate /ɪˈkwɪvəkeɪt/ *verb* [I, T] (+ **speech**) (*formal*) to talk about sth in a way that is deliberately not clear in order to avoid or hide the truth （故意）含糊其詞，支吾，搪塞

equivo·ca·tion /ɪˌkwɪvəˈkeɪʃn/ *noun* [C, U] (*formal*) a way of behaving or speaking that is not clear or definite and is intended to avoid or hide the truth 含糊其詞；支吾；搪塞

ER /ˌiː ˈɑː(r)/ *abbr.* EMERGENCY ROOM

er /ɜː(r)/ (also **erm**) *exclamation* (*BrE*) the sound that people make when they are deciding what to say next （思索接着說什麼時發出的聲音）哦，嗯： *'Will you do it?' 'Er, yes, I suppose so.'* "你會幹這事兒嗎？" "哦，會的，我想我會。"

-er *suffix* **1** (in nouns 構成名詞) a person or thing that …的人（或物）： *lover* 情人 ◇ *computer* 計算機 ➲ compare -EE (1), -OR **2** (in nouns 構成名詞) a person or thing that has the thing or quality mentioned 具有…的人（或物）： *three-wheeler* 三輪車 ◇ *foreigner* 外國人 **3** (in nouns 構成名詞) a person concerned with 與…有關的人： *astronomer* 天文學家 ◇ *philosopher* 哲學家 **4** (in nouns 構成名詞) a person belonging to 屬於…的人： *New Yorker* 紐約人 **5** (makes comparative adjectives and adverbs 構成形容詞和副詞的比較級)： *wider* 較寬 ◇ *bigger* 較大 ◇ *happier* 更幸福 ◇ *sooner* 更早 ➲ compare -EST

era /ˈɪərə; *NAmE* ˈɪrə; ˈerə/ *noun* **1** a period of time, usually in history, that is different from other periods because of particular characteristics or events 時代；年代；紀元： *the Victorian/modern/post-war era* 維多利亞女王 / 當今 / 戰後時代 ◇ *When she left the firm, it was the* **end of an era** (= things were different after that). 她離開公司後，一個時代結束了（後來的情況就大不一樣了）。 **2** (*geology* 地) a length of time which is a division of an AEON 代（地質年代，宙下分代）

eradi·cate /ɪˈrædɪkeɪt/ *verb* to destroy or get rid of sth completely, especially sth bad 根除；消滅；杜絕 SYN **wipe out**： **~ sth** *Diphtheria has been virtually eradicated in the United States.* 在美國白喉幾乎已經絕跡。 ◇ **~ sth from sth** *We are determined to eradicate racism from our sport.* 我們決心要杜絕體育競技活動中的種族歧視現象。 ▸ **eradi·ca·tion** /ɪˌrædɪˈkeɪʃn/ *noun* [U]

erase /ɪˈreɪz; *NAmE* ɪˈreɪs/ *verb* **1** to remove sth completely 清除；消除；消滅： **~ sth** *She tried to erase* **the memory** *of that evening.* 她試圖忘卻那天晚上的事。 ◇ **~ sth from sth** *All doubts were suddenly* **erased from his mind**. 他心中所有的疑慮突然一掃而空了。 ◇ *You cannot erase injustice from the world.* 任何人都不可能讓不公平的現象從世界上消失。 **2 ~ sth** to make a mark or sth you have written disappear, for example by rubbing it, especially in order to correct it 擦掉，抹掉（筆跡等）： *He had erased the wrong word.* 他擦去了寫錯的

字。◇ *All the phone numbers had been erased.* 所有的電話號碼都被抹掉了。**3 ~ sth** to remove a recording from a tape or information from a computer's memory 抹去，清洗（磁帶上的錄音或存貯器中的信息）：*Parts of the recording have been erased.* 部份錄音已被抹掉。

eraser /ɪˈreɪzə(r); *NAmE* ɪˈreɪsər/ (*NAmE* or *formal*) (*BrE* also **rub·ber**) *noun* a small piece of rubber or a similar substance, used for removing pencil marks from paper; a piece of soft material used for removing CHALK marks from a BLACKBOARD 橡皮擦；黑板擦 ➲ VISUAL VOCAB page V69

E

eras·ure /ɪˈreɪʒə(r)/ *noun* [U] (*formal*) the act of removing or destroying sth 擦掉；抹掉；消除；消滅；刪除：*the accidental erasure of important computer files* 計算機上重要文件的意外刪除

er·bium /ˈɜːbiəm; *NAmE* ˈɜːrb-/ *noun* [U] (*symb.* **Er**) a chemical element. Erbium is a soft silver-white metal. 鉺

ere /eə(r); *NAmE* er/ *conj.*, *prep.* (*old use* or *literary*) before 在…之前：*Ere long* (= soon) *they returned.* 他們不久就回來了。

erect /ɪˈrekt/ *adj.*, *verb*

■ *adj.* **1** (*formal*) in a vertical position 垂直的；豎直的；直立的 SYN **straight**：*Stand with your arms by your side and your head erect.* 手放兩邊，昂首站立。**2** (of the PENIS or NIPPLES 陰莖或乳頭) larger than usual, stiff and standing up because of sexual excitement（因性興奮）勃起的，堅挺的

■ *verb* (*formal*) **1 ~ sth** to build sth 建立；建造：*The church was erected in 1582.* 此教堂建於 1582 年。➲ SYNONYMS at BUILD **2 ~ sth** to put sth in position and make it stand vertical 豎立；搭起 SYN **put sth up**：*Police had to erect barriers to keep crowds back.* 警察得設立路障來阻截人群。◇ *to erect a tent* 搭帳篷 ➲ SYNONYMS at BUILD **3 ~ sth** to create or establish sth 創立；設立：*to erect trade barriers* 設置貿易壁壘

erect·ile /ɪˈrektaɪl; *NAmE* also ɪˈrektl/ *adj.* (*biology* 生) (of a part of the body 身體部位) able to become stiff and stand up 能勃起的：*erectile tissue* 勃起組織

erec·tion /ɪˈrekʃn/ *noun* **1** [C] if a man has an **erection**, his PENIS is hard and stands up because he is sexually excited（陰莖）勃起：*to **get/have an erection*** 勃起 **2** [U] (*formal*) the act of building sth or putting it in a vertical position 建造；豎立：*the erection of scaffolding around the building* 建築物周圍鷹架的搭建 **3** [C] (*formal*) a structure or building, especially a large one（尤指大型）結構，建築物

erg /ɜːg; *NAmE* ɜːrg/ *noun* a unit of work or energy 爾格（功或能量單位）

erga·tive /ˈɜːgətɪv; *NAmE* ˈɜːrg-/ *adj.* (*grammar* 語法) (of verbs 動詞) able to be used in both a TRANSITIVE and an INTRANSITIVE way with the same meaning, where the object of the transitive verb is the same as the subject of the intransitive verb 作格的（可在不改變詞義的情況下同時用作及物和不及物的動詞，作及物動詞時的賓語與作不及物動詞時的主語一致）：*The verb 'grow' is ergative because you can say 'She grew flowers in her garden' or 'Flowers grew in her garden'.* * grow 為作格動詞，因為既可以說 She grew flowers in her garden，也可以說 Flowers grew in her garden。➲ compare CAUSATIVE (2), INCHOATIVE ▸ **er·ga·tive·ly** *adv.*

ergo /ˈɜːgəʊ; *NAmE* ˈɜːrgoʊ/ *adv.* (from *Latin*, *formal* or *humorous*) therefore 因此；所以

er·go·nom·ic /ˌɜːgəˈnɒmɪk; *NAmE* ˌɜːrgəˈnɑːm-/ *adj.* designed to improve people's working conditions and to help them work more efficiently 工效學的；人類工程學的：*ergonomic design* 提高工效的設計 ▸ **er·go·nom·ic·al·ly** *adv.*：*The layout is hard to fault ergonomically.* 這一設計從工效學方面看幾乎無懈可擊。

er·go·nom·ics /ˌɜːgəˈnɒmɪks; *NAmE* ˌɜːrgəˈnɑːm-/ *noun* [U] the study of working conditions, especially the design of equipment and furniture, in order to help people work more efficiently 工效學，人類工程學（研究如何改善工作條件，提高工作效率）

erm /ɜːm/ *exclamation* (*BrE*) = ER：*'Shall we go?' 'Erm, yes, let's.'* "咱們走吧？" "喔，好的，咱們走。"

er·mine /ˈɜːmɪn; *NAmE* ˈɜːrmɪn/ *noun* [U] the white winter fur of the STOAT, used especially to decorate the formal clothes of judges, kings, etc. 白色鼬皮（尤用於法官、國王等的服飾）

erode AW /ɪˈrəʊd; *NAmE* ɪˈroʊd/ *verb* [often passive] **1** [T, I] to gradually destroy the surface of sth through the action of wind, rain, etc.; to be gradually destroyed in this way 侵蝕；腐蝕；風化 SYN **wear away**：**~ sth (away)** *The cliff face has been steadily eroded by the sea.* 峭壁表面逐漸被海水侵蝕。◇ **~ (away)** *The rocks have eroded away over time.* 這些岩石隨着時間的推移逐漸風化了。**2** [T, I] **~ (sth)** to gradually destroy sth or make it weaker over a period of time; to be destroyed or made weaker in this way 逐漸毀壞；削弱；損害：*Her confidence has been slowly eroded by repeated failures.* 她的自信心因屢屢失敗慢慢消磨掉了。◇ *Mortgage payments have been eroded* (= decreased in value) *by inflation.* 償還的按揭貸款因通貨膨脹而降值。▸ **ero·sion** AW /ɪˈrəʊʒn; *NAmE* ɪˈroʊʒn/ *noun* [U]：*the erosion of the coastline by the sea* 海水對海岸線的侵蝕 ◇ *soil erosion* 水土流失 ◇ *the erosion of her confidence* 對她信心的削弱

er·ogen·ous zone /ɪˈrɒdʒənəs zəʊn; *NAmE* ɪˈrɑːdʒənəs zoʊn/ *noun* an area of the body that gives sexual pleasure when it is touched 性慾發生區；性敏感區；性感帶

Eros /ˈɪərɒs; *NAmE* ˈɪrɑːs; ˈerɑːs/ *noun* [U] (*formal*) sexual love or desire 性愛；性慾

erot·ic /ɪˈrɒtɪk; *NAmE* ɪˈrɑːtɪk/ *adj.* showing or involving sexual desire and pleasure; intended to make sb feel sexual desire 性慾的；性愛的；色情的：*erotic art* 色情藝術 ◇ *an erotic fantasy* 性幻想 ▸ **erot·ic·al·ly** /-kli/ *adv.*

erot·ica /ɪˈrɒtɪkə; *NAmE* ɪˈrɑːt-/ *noun* [U] books, pictures, etc. that are intended to make sb feel sexual desire 色情書畫；色情作品

eroti·cism /ɪˈrɒtɪsɪzəm; *NAmE* ɪˈrɑːt-/ *noun* [U] the fact of expressing or describing sexual feelings and desire, especially in art, literature, etc.（尤指藝術、文學作品等中的）色情描寫

err /ɜː(r); *NAmE* er/ *verb* [I] (*old-fashioned*, *formal*) to make a mistake 犯錯誤；做錯事；出差錯：*To err is human …* 犯錯人皆難免…

IDM **err on the side of sth** to show too much of a good quality 過於；失之：*I thought it was better **to err on the side of caution*** (= to be too careful rather than take a risk). 我認為寧可過於謹慎也不要冒風險。

er·rand /ˈerənd/ *noun* a job that you do for sb that involves going somewhere to take a message, to buy sth, deliver goods, etc. 差使；差事：*He often **runs errands** for his grandmother.* 他經常給他的祖母跑腿兒。◇ *Her boss sent her **on an errand** into town.* 老闆派她進城辦事去了。➲ see also FOOL'S ERRAND

er·rant /ˈerənt/ *adj.* [only before noun] (*formal* or *humorous*) **1** doing sth that is wrong; not behaving in an acceptable way 犯錯誤的；行為不當的；出格的 **2** (of a husband or wife 丈夫或妻子) not sexually faithful 對配偶不忠的

er·rat·ic /ɪˈrætɪk/ *adj.*, *noun*

■ *adj.* (often *disapproving*) not happening at regular times; not following any plan or regular pattern; that you cannot rely on 不規則的；不確定的；不穩定的；不可靠的 SYN **unpredictable**：*The electricity supply here is quite erratic.* 這裏的電力供應相當不穩定。◇ *She had learnt to live with his sudden changes of mood and erratic behaviour.* 她已經學會適應他那變幻莫測的情緒和難以捉摸的行為。◇ *Mary is a gifted but erratic player* (= she does not always play well). 瑪麗是一名有天賦的運動員，但發揮不太穩定。▸ **er·rat·ic·al·ly** /-kli/ *adv.*：*He was obviously upset and was driving erratically.* 他顯然心煩意亂，開起車來搖晃不定。

■ *noun* (also **er,ratic ˈblock**, **er,ratic ˈboulder**) (*geology* 地) a large rock that is different from the rock around and was left behind when a large mass of ice melted 漂礫；漂石

er·ratum /eˈrɑːtəm/ *noun* [usually pl.] (*pl.* **er·rata** /-tə/) (*technical* 術語) a mistake in a book (shown in a list at the back or front) 書刊中的文字錯誤（複數 errata 為勘誤表，列於書前或書後）

er·ro·ne·ous AW /ɪˈrəʊniəs; *NAmE* ɪˈroʊ-/ *adj.* (*formal*) not correct; based on wrong information 錯誤的：***erroneous conclusions/assumptions*** 錯誤的結論／假設 ▸ **er·ro·ne·ous·ly** AW *adv.*

error 0‑ AW /ˈerə(r)/ *noun* [C, U] a mistake, especially one that causes problems or affects the result of sth 錯誤；差錯；謬誤：*No payments were made last week because of a computer error.* 由於計算機出錯，上週未付任何款項。◇ **~ in sth** *There are too many errors in your work.* 你的工作失誤太多。◇ **~ in doing sth** *I think you have made an error in calculating the total.* 我想你在計算總數時出了差錯。◇ *A simple* ***error of judgement*** *meant that there was not enough food to go around.* 一個簡單的判斷錯誤就意味着食物不夠每人一份。◇ *a* ***grave error*** (= a very serious mistake) 嚴重錯誤 ◇ *a* ***glaring error*** (= a mistake that is very obvious) 明顯的錯誤 ◇ *The delay was due to* ***human error*** (= a mistake made by a person rather than by a machine). 延誤是人為錯誤造成的。◇ *The computer system was switched off* ***in error*** (= by mistake). 計算機系統被不慎關閉。◇ *There is no* ***room for error*** *in this job.* 這項工作決不允許出差錯。➲ **SYNONYMS** at MISTAKE ➲ see also MARGIN OF ERROR

IDM **see, realize, etc. the ˌerror of your ˈways** (*formal* or *humorous*) to realize or admit that you have done sth wrong and decide to change your behaviour 知過即改；承認自己的做法不對並決心改正 ➲ more at TRIAL *n.*

ˈerror message *noun* (*computing* 計) a message that appears on a computer screen which tells you that you have done sth wrong or that the program cannot do what you want it to do 錯誤信息（在計算機屏幕上出現，表示有錯誤）

er·satz /ˈeəzæts; *NAmE* ˈersɑːts/ *adj.* artificial and not as good as the real thing or product 人造的，代用的，合成的（因而質量不如真品）：*ersatz coffee* 咖啡替代品

Erse /ɜːs; *NAmE* ɜːrs/ *noun* [U] (*old-fashioned*) the Scottish or Irish Gaelic language 蘇格蘭（或愛爾蘭）蓋爾語；埃爾斯語 ➲ compare GAELIC, IRISH *n.* (1)

erst·while /ˈɜːstwaɪl; *NAmE* ˈɜːrst-/ *adj.* [only before noun] (*formal*) former; that until recently was the type of person or thing described but is not any more 以前的；先前的；過去的；往昔的：*an erstwhile opponent* 以前的對手 ◇ *His erstwhile friends turned against him.* 他先前的朋友轉而與他作對。

eru·dite /ˈerudaɪt/ *adj.* (*formal*) having or showing great knowledge that is gained from academic study 博學的；有學問的 SYN **learned**

eru·di·tion /ˌeruˈdɪʃn/ *noun* [U] (*formal*) great academic knowledge 博學；學問

erupt /ɪˈrʌpt/ *verb* **1** [I, T] when a VOLCANO **erupts** or burning rocks, smoke, etc. **erupt** or **are erupted**, the burning rocks, etc. are thrown out from the volcano（火山）爆發；（岩漿、煙等）噴出：*The volcano could erupt at any time.* 這座火山隨時可能爆發。◇ **~ from sth** *Ash began to erupt from the crater.* 火山灰開始從火山口噴出。◇ **~ sth** *An immense volume of rocks and molten lava was erupted.* 大量岩石和熔岩噴發出來。➲ **SYNONYMS** at EXPLODE **2** [I] to start happening, suddenly and violently 突然發生；爆發 SYN **break out**：*Violence erupted outside the embassy gates.* 大使館門外突然發生了暴亂。◇ **~ into sth** *The unrest erupted into revolution.* 動亂爆發為革命。 **3** [I, T] to suddenly express your feelings very strongly, especially by shouting loudly 突然發出（尤指叫喊）：*When Davis scored for the third time the crowd erupted.* 戴維斯第三次得分，觀眾歡聲雷動。◇ **~ in/into sth** *My father just erupted into fury.* 我父親勃然大怒。◇ **+ speech** *'How dare you?' she erupted.* "你竟敢這樣？" 她突然大聲叫道。 **4** [I] (of spots, etc. 斑點等) to suddenly appear on your skin 突然（在皮膚上）出現：*A rash had erupted all over his chest.* 他的胸部突然出滿疹子。▸ **erup·tion** /ɪˈrʌpʃn/ *noun* [C, U]：*a major volcanic eruption* 火山大爆發 ◇ *an eruption of violent protest* 暴力抗議的爆發 ◇ *skin rashes and eruptions* 皮疹和疹子

erup·tive /ɪˈrʌptɪv/ *adj.* relating to or produced by the ERUPTION of a VOLCANO 火山爆發的；火山噴發的

-ery, -ry *suffix* (in nouns 構成名詞) **1** the group or class of …群體（或類）的事物：*greenery* 綠色植物 ◇ *gadgetry* 小巧裝置 **2** the state or character of …狀態（或性質）：*bravery* 勇氣 ◇ *rivalry* 競爭 **3** the art or practice of …的藝術（或技術）：*cookery* 烹飪 ◇ *archery* 射箭 **4** a place where sth is made, grows, lives, etc. 做（或生長、住）的地方：*bakery* 麵包店 ◇ *orangery* 柑橘園

eryth·ro·cyte /ɪˈrɪθrəsaɪt/ *noun* (*biology* 生) = RED BLOOD CELL

es·cal·ate /ˈeskəleɪt/ *verb* [I, T] to become or make sth greater, worse, more serious, etc.（使）逐步擴大，不斷惡化，加劇：**~ (into sth)** *The fighting escalated into a full-scale war.* 這場交戰逐步擴大為全面戰爭。◇ ***the escalating costs*** *of health care* 逐漸增加的保健費用 ◇ **~ sth (into sth)** *We do not want to escalate the war.* 我們不想讓戰爭升級。 ▸ **es·cal·ation** /ˌeskəˈleɪʃn/ *noun* [C, U]：*an escalation in food prices* 食品價格的不斷上漲 ◇ *further escalation of the conflict* 衝突的進一步加劇

es·cal·ator /ˈeskəleɪtə(r)/ *noun* moving stairs that carry people between different floors of a large building 自動扶梯；電扶梯；滾梯

es·cal·ope /ˈeskəlɒp; eˈskæləp; *NAmE* ɪˈskɑːləp; ɪˈskæ-/ *noun* a thin slice of meat with no bones in it, often covered with BREADCRUMBS and fried 薄肉片（常裹以麵包屑油炸）：*escalopes of veal* 小牛肉片

es·cap·ade /ˌeskəˈpeɪd; ˈeskəpeɪd/ *noun* an exciting adventure (often one that people think is dangerous or stupid)（常指危險或愚蠢的）冒險行為，惡作劇：*Isabel's latest romantic escapade* 伊莎貝爾最近的戀愛鬧劇

es·cape 0‑ /ɪˈskeɪp/ *verb, noun*

■ ***verb*** **1** 0‑ [I] to get away from a place where you have been kept as a prisoner or not allowed to leave（從監禁或管制中）逃跑，逃走，逃出：*Two prisoners have escaped.* 兩名犯人逃走了。◇ **~ from sb/sth** *He escaped from prison this morning.* 他今天早上從監獄裏逃跑了。 **2** 0‑ [I, T] to get away from an unpleasant or dangerous situation（從不愉快或危險處境中）逃脫，擺脫，逃避：**~ (from sth)** *She managed to escape from the burning car.* 她終於從燃燒的汽車裏逃了出來。◇ **~ (into sth)** (*figurative*) *As a child he would often escape into a dream world of his own.* 小時候他常常躲進自己的夢幻世界中。◇ **~ sth** *They were glad to have* ***escaped the clutches*** *of winter for another year.* 他們很高興又一年躲過了寒冬的魔爪。 **3** 0‑ [T, no passive] to avoid sth unpleasant or dangerous 避開，避免（不愉快或危險的事物）：**~ sth** *She was lucky to escape punishment.* 她逃脫懲罰真是幸運。◇ *The pilot* ***escaped death*** *by seconds.* 這名飛行員幸能在生死瞬間逃出生天。◇ ***There was no escaping*** *the fact that he was overweight.* 他身體超重這一事實是無法迴避的。◇ **~ doing sth** *He* ***narrowly escaped*** *being killed.* 他險些喪命。 **4** 0‑ [I] to suffer no harm or less harm than you would expect（沒有受傷或只受了一點傷害而）逃脫，幸免於難：**~ (with sth)** *I was lucky to escape with minor injuries.* 我只受了一點輕傷逃出來真是萬幸。◇ **+ adj.** *Both drivers* ***escaped unhurt.*** 兩個駕駛員都幸免於難，安然無恙。 **5** [T, no passive] **~ sb/sth** to be forgotten or not noticed 被忘掉；被忽視；未被注意：*Her name escapes me* (= I can't remember it). 我記不起她的名字了。◇ *It might have* ***escaped your notice,*** *but I'm very busy at the moment.* 也許你沒注意到，可我此刻忙得不可開交。 **6** [I] (of gases, liquids, etc. 氣體、液體等) to get out of a container, especially through a hole or crack 漏出；泄漏；滲出：*Put a lid on to prevent heat escaping.* 蓋上蓋子，以免熱氣跑了。◇ *toxic waste escaping into the sea* 流入大海的有毒廢料 **7** [T, I] **~ (sth)** (of a sound 聲音) to come out from your mouth without you intending it to（不自覺地）由…發出：*A groan escaped her lips.* 她不由得發出一聲呻吟。

■ ***noun*** **1** 0‑ [C, U] **~ (from sth)** the act or a method of escaping from a place or an unpleasant or dangerous situation 逃跑；逃脫；逃避：*an escape from a prisoner* *of war camp* 從戰俘營中逃出 ◇ *I had a* ***narrow escape*** (= I was lucky to have escaped). 我是死裏逃生。◇ *There was no hope of escape from her disastrous marriage.* 她無望從不幸的婚姻中解脱出來。◇ *He took an elaborate* ***escape route*** *from South Africa to Britain.* 他周密安排了一條路線從南非逃往英國。◇ *As soon as he turned his back, she would* ***make her escape****.* 他一轉身，她就逃跑。➲ see also FIRE ESCAPE **2** [sing., U] a way of forgetting sth unpleasant or difficult for a short time 逃避現實；解脱；消遣：*For her, travel was an escape from the boredom of her everyday life.* 對她來説，旅行就是逃離乏味的日常生活。**3** [C] the fact of a liquid, gas, etc. coming out of a pipe or container by accident; the amount that comes out 漏出，溢出，滲出（量）：*an escape of gas* 漏氣 **4** [U] (also **e'scape key** [C]) (*computing* 計) a button on a computer keyboard that you press to stop a particular operation or leave a program * Esc 鍵；退出鍵：*Press escape to get back to the menu.* 按 Esc 鍵，退回到選單。

IDM **make ˌgood your eˈscape** (*formal*) to manage to escape completely 成功地逃脱 ➲ more at BARN

esˈcape clause *noun* a part of a contract which states the conditions under which the contract may be broken（合約的）免責條款，例外條約

es·caped /ɪˈskeɪpt/ *adj.* [only before noun] having escaped from a place 逃跑了的：*an escaped prisoner/lion* 逃犯；脱逃的獅子

es·capee /ɪˌskeɪˈpiː/ *noun* (*formal*) a person or an animal that has escaped from somewhere, especially sb who has escaped from prison 逃亡者；脱逃的動物；（尤指）逃犯

es·cap·ism /ɪˈskeɪpɪzəm/ *noun* [U] an activity, a form of entertainment, etc. that helps you avoid or forget unpleasant or boring things 逃避現實；解脱方法：*the pure escapism of adventure movies* 驚險電影的純娛樂性 ◇ *For John, books are a* ***form of escapism****.* 對約翰來説，看書是一種消遣形式。▸ **es·cap·ist** /-pɪst/ *adj.*

es·cap·olo·gist /ˌeskəˈpɒlədʒɪst; *NAmE* -ˈpɑːl-/ *noun* a performer who escapes from ropes, chains, boxes, etc. 擅長表演從捆紮的繩索（或箱子等）中脱身的魔術演員；脱逃術表演者

es·carp·ment /ɪˈskɑːpmənt; *NAmE* ɪˈskɑːrp-/ *noun* a steep slope that separates an area of high ground from an area of lower ground 陡坡；懸崖；峭壁

ES cell /ˌiː ˈes sel/ *noun* (*biology* 生) the abbreviation for 'embryonic stem cell' (a STEM CELL taken from an EMBRYO soon after it is formed) 胚胎幹細胞（全寫為 embryonic stem cell，從形成之初的胚胎上提取的幹細胞）

eschat·ology /ˌeskəˈtɒlədʒi; *NAmE* -ˈtɑːl-/ *noun* [U] (*religion* 宗) the part of THEOLOGY concerned with death and judgement 末世論（神學中關於死亡和審判的論述）▸ **eschat·ologic·al** /eˌskætəˈlɒdʒɪkl; *NAmE* -ˈlɑːdʒ-/ *adj.*

es·chew /ɪsˈtʃuː/ *verb* **~ sth** (*formal*) to deliberately avoid or keep away from sth（有意地）避開，迴避，避免

es·cort *noun, verb*

■ ***noun*** /ˈeskɔːt; *NAmE* ˈeskɔːrt/ **1** [C, U] a person or group of people or vehicles that travels with sb/sth in order to protect or guard them 護送者；護衛隊；護衛艦（或車隊、飛機）：*Armed escorts are provided for visiting heads of state.* 來訪的國家元首由武裝衛隊護送。◇ *Prisoners are taken to court* ***under police escort****.* 囚犯由警察押送帶上法庭。**2** [C] (*formal* or *old-fashioned*) a person, especially a man, who takes sb to a particular social event 陪同某人參加社交活動的人（尤指男人）**3** [C] a person, especially a woman, who is paid to go out socially with sb 受雇陪同某人外出社交的人（尤指女人）：*an escort service/agency* 社交陪伴服務社

■ ***verb*** /ɪˈskɔːt; *NAmE* ɪˈskɔːrt/ **~ sb** (**+ adv./prep.**) to go with sb to protect or guard them or to show them the way 護衛；護送：*The President arrived, escorted by twelve soldiers.* 總統在十二名衛兵的護送下到達。➲ SYNONYMS at TAKE

es·cudo /eˈskuːdəʊ; *NAmE* -doʊ/ *noun* (*pl.* **-os**) the unit of money in Cape Verde, and formerly in Portugal (replaced in Portugal in 2002 by the euro) 埃斯庫多（佛得角貨幣單位，以及葡萄牙原貨幣單位，在葡萄牙於 2002 年已為歐元所取代）

es·cut·cheon /ɪˈskʌtʃən/ *noun* **1** a flat piece of metal around a KEYHOLE, door handle, or light switch 孔罩；鎖眼蓋；門把手蓋板；電燈開關板 **2** a SHIELD that has a COAT OF ARMS on it 盾形飾牌

-ese *suffix* **1** (in adjectives and nouns 構成形容詞和名詞) of a country or city; a person who lives in a country or city; the language spoken there …國（或城市）的；…國（或城市）的人；…國（或城市）的語言：*Chinese* 中國的 ◇ *Viennese* 維也納的 **2** (in nouns 構成名詞) (often *disapproving*) the style or language of …文體（或用語）：*journalese* 新聞文體 ◇ *officialese* 官場用語

esker /ˈeskə(r)/ *noun* (*geology* 地) a long narrow area of small stones and earth that has been left by a large mass of ice that has melted 蛇丘（由冰川融化後留下的沙礫和土形成的狹長脊）

Es·kimo /ˈeskɪməʊ; *NAmE* -moʊ/ *noun* (*pl.* **Es·kimo** or **Es·kimos**) (sometimes *offensive*) a member of a race of people from northern Canada, and parts of Alaska, Greenland and Siberia. Some of these people prefer to use the name Inuit. 愛斯基摩人（有些喜歡 Inuit（因努伊特人）這個名稱）➲ compare INUIT

Esky™ /ˈeski/ *noun* (*pl.* **-ies**) (*AustralE*) a bag or box which keeps food or drinks cold and which can be used for a PICNIC 埃斯基冷藏袋（或盒）（可用於野餐）

ESL /ˌiː es ˈel/ *abbr.* (in the US and Canada) English as a second language (refers to the teaching of English as a foreign language to people who are living in a country in which English is either the first or second language)（美國和加拿大）作為第二語言的英語（指對生活在英語為第一或第二語言的國家的人的英語教學）➲ compare EAL, EFL, ESOL

ESOL /ˈiːsɒl; *NAmE* -sɑːl/ *abbr.* (in the UK and Ireland) English for speakers of other languages (refers to the teaching of English as a foreign language to people who are living in a country in which English is either the first or second language)（英國和愛爾蘭）操其他語言者的英語（指對生活在英語為第一或第二語言的國家的人的英語教學）➲ compare EAL, EFL, ESL

esopha·gus (*NAmE*) (*BrE* **oe·sopha·gus**) /iˈsɒfəgəs; *NAmE* iˈsɑː-/ *noun* (*pl.* **-pha·guses** or **-ph·agi** /-gaɪ/) (*anatomy* 解) the tube through which food passes from the mouth to the stomach 食道；食管 **SYN** **gullet** ➲ VISUAL VOCAB page V59

eso·ter·ic /ˌesəˈterɪk; ˌiːsə-/ *adj.* (*formal*) likely to be understood or enjoyed by only a few people with a special knowledge or interest 只有內行才懂的；難領略的

ESP /ˌiː es ˈpiː/ *abbr.* **1** English for specific/special purposes (the teaching of English for scientific, technical, etc. purposes to people whose first language is not English)（科技等方面的）專業英語，專門用途英語（教學對象第一語言並非英語）**2** extrasensory perception (the ability to know things without using the senses of sight, hearing, etc., for example to know what people are thinking or what will happen in the future) 超感知覺

esp. *abbr.* (in writing) especially（書寫形式）尤其，特別

es·pa·drille /ˈespədrɪl/ *noun* a light shoe made of strong cloth with a SOLE made of rope 帆布便鞋（鞋底用繩子編織而成）

es·pal·ier /ɪˈspæliə(r)/ *noun* **1** a tree or SHRUB that is grown flat along a wooden or wire frame on a wall 棚樹；牆樹；樹籬 **2** the frame that such a tree grows along 籬架；攀架

es·pe·cial /ɪˈspeʃl/ *adj.* [only before noun] (*BrE, formal*) greater or better than usual; special in some way or for a particular group 格外的；特別的；特殊的：*a matter of especial importance* 特別重要的事情 ◇ *The lecture will be of especial interest to history students.* 學歷史的學生會對這個講座特別有興趣。➲ compare SPECIAL *adj.* (5)

es·pe·cial·ly /ɪˈspeʃəli/ *adv.* (*abbr.* **esp.**)
1 more with one person, thing, etc. than with others, or more in particular circumstances than in others 尤其；特別；格外 SYN **particularly**：*The car is quite small, especially if you have children.* 這輛汽車很小，如果有孩子就尤其顯得小。◇ *Teenagers are very fashion conscious, especially girls.* 青少年，尤其是女孩，很注重時尚。◇ *I love Rome, especially in the spring.* 我喜愛羅馬，尤其是春天的羅馬。 ➲ LANGUAGE BANK at EMPHASIS **2** for a particular purpose, person, etc. 專門；特地：*I made it especially for you.* 這是我特地為你做的。**3** very much; to a particular degree 十分；非常：*I wasn't feeling especially happy that day.* 那天我並不十分高興。◇ *'Do you like his novels?' 'Not especially.'* "你喜歡他的小説嗎？" "不十分喜歡。"

Which Word? 詞語辨析

especially / specially

- **Especially** usually means 'particularly'. * especially 通常表示尤其、特別：*She loves all sports, especially swimming.* 她喜愛各種運動，尤其是游泳。 It is not placed first in a sentence. 該詞不用於句首：*I especially like sweet things.* 我特別喜歡吃甜食。 ~~*Especially I like sweet things.*~~
- **Specially** usually means 'for a particular purpose' and is often followed by a past participle, such as *designed*, *developed* or *made*. * specially 通常表示特意地、專門地，其後常接 designed、developed 或 made 等過去分詞：*a course specially designed to meet your needs* 為滿足你們的需要專門開設的課程 ◇ *She has her clothes specially made in Paris.* 她的衣服是特意在巴黎訂做的。
- In *BrE*, **especially** and **specially** are often used in the same way and it can be hard to hear the difference when people speak. **Specially** is less formal. 在英式英語中，especially 和 specially 常具有相同的用法，說話時很難聽出其區別。specially 較非正式：*I bought this especially/specially for you.* 這是我特意為你買的。◇ *It is especially/specially important to remember this.* 記住這一點尤為重要。
- The adjective for both **especially** and **specially** is usually **special**. * especially 和 specially 的形容詞通常為 special。

Es·per·anto /ˌespəˈræntəʊ; *NAmE* -toʊ/ *noun* [U] an artificial language invented in 1887 as a means of international communication, based on the main European languages but with easy grammar and pronunciation 世界語（1887 年公佈的一種人造國際語言，源自歐洲諸語言）

es·pi·on·age /ˈespiənɑːʒ/ *noun* [U] the activity of secretly getting important political or military information about another country or of finding out another company's secrets by using SPIES 間諜活動；諜報活動；刺探活動 SYN **spying**：*Some of the commercial activities were a cover for espionage.* 有些商業活動是為間諜活動提供掩護。◇ *She may call it research; I call it industrial espionage.* 她可以稱之為研究，可我稱它為產業情報刺探。 ➲ see also COUNTER-ESPIONAGE

es·plan·ade /ˌespləˈneɪd/ *noun* a level area of open ground in a town for people to walk along, often by the sea or a river（常指城鎮中海濱、河畔供人散步的）廣場，空地

es·pouse /ɪˈspaʊz/ *verb* **~ sth** (*formal*) to give your support to a belief, policy, etc. 支持，擁護，贊成（信仰、政策等）：*They espoused the notion of equal opportunity for all in education.* 他們贊同在教育方面人人機會均等的觀念。 ▸ **es·pousal** /ɪˈspaʊzl/ *noun* [U, sing.]：**~ of sth** *his recent espousal of populism* 他最近對民粹主義的支持

es·presso /eˈspresəʊ; *NAmE* -soʊ/ *noun* (*pl.* **-os**) **1** [U] strong black coffee made by forcing steam or boiling water through GROUND coffee 蒸餾咖啡（讓蒸汽或開水通過磨碎的咖啡豆製成的濃咖啡）**2** [C] a cup of espresso 一杯蒸餾咖啡

es·prit de corps /eˌspriː də ˈkɔː(r)/ *noun* [U] (from *French*) feelings of pride, care and support for each other, etc. that are shared by the members of a group 集體榮譽感；團隊精神

espy /eˈspaɪ/ *verb* (**espies**, **espy·ing**, **espied**, **espied**) **~ sb/sth** (*literary*) to see sb/sth suddenly 突然看見 SYN **catch sight of**, **spy**

Esq. *abbr.* **1** (*old-fashioned, especially BrE*) Esquire (a polite title written after a man's name, especially on an official letter addressed to him. If Esq. is used, Mr. is not then used) 先生（寫信時用於男子名後的尊稱。如果用了 Esq.，便不再用 Mr.）：*Edward Smith, Esq.* 愛德華•史密斯先生 **2** (*NAmE*) used as a title after the name of a male or female lawyer（對男、女律師的稱謂）…律師

-esque *suffix* (in adjectives 構成形容詞) in the style of … 風格（或樣式）的：*statuesque* 雕像般的 ◇ *Kafkaesque* 卡夫卡風格的

-ess *suffix* (in nouns 構成名詞) female 女…；雌…；母…：*lioness* 母獅子 ◇ *actress* 女演員 ➲ note at GENDER

essay *noun, verb*
■ ***noun*** /ˈeseɪ/ **1** **~ (on sth)** a short piece of writing by a student as part of a course of study（作為課程作業，學生寫的）文章，短文：*an essay on the causes of the First World War* 關於第一次世界大戰起因的文章 ➲ WRITING TUTOR pages WT10-WT19 **2** **~ (on sth)** a short piece of writing on a particular subject, written in order to be published（用來刊登的）論說文，小品文 **3** **~ (in sth)** (*formal*) an attempt to do sth 企圖；嘗試：*His first essay in politics was a complete disaster.* 他初次涉足政壇便碰得頭破血流。
■ ***verb*** /eˈseɪ/ **~ sth** (*literary*) to try to do sth 企圖；試圖

es·say·ist /ˈeseɪɪst/ *noun* a person who writes essays to be published 論說文（或小品文）作者

es·sence /ˈesns/ *noun* **1** [U] **~ (of sth)** the most important quality or feature of sth, that makes it what it is 本質；實質；精髓：*His paintings capture the essence of France.* 他的畫描繪出法國的神韻。◇ ***In essence*** (= when you consider the most important points), *your situation isn't so different from mine.* 從本質上講，你我的情況並非相差很遠。 **2** [U, C] a liquid taken from a plant, etc. that contains its smell and taste in a very strong form 香精；精油：*essence of rosewood* 黃檀木香精 ◇ (*BrE*) ***coffee/vanilla/almond essence*** 咖啡／香草／杏仁香精 ➲ see also EXTRACT *n.* (2)
IDM **of the ˈessence** necessary and very important 必不可少；非常重要：*In this situation **time is of the essence*** (= we must do things as quickly as possible). 在這種情況下，時間是至關重要的。

es·sen·tial /ɪˈsenʃl/ *adj., noun*
■ ***adj.*** **1** completely necessary; extremely important in a particular situation or for a particular activity 完全必要的；必不可少的；極其重要的 SYN **vital**：***an essential part/ingredient/component** of sth* 某事物必不可少的一部份／成分／組成部份 ◇ *essential services such as gas, water and electricity* 諸如燃氣、水、電等基本公用事業 ◇ *The museum is closed while essential repairs are being carried out.* 博物館正在進行大修，在此期間暫停開放。◇ *Even in small companies, computers are an essential tool.* 即使在小公司裏，計算機也是必不可少的工具。◇ **~ to sth** *Money is not essential to happiness.* 金錢對於幸福並非必不可少。◇ **~ for sth** *Experience is essential for this job.* 對於這個工作，經驗是非常重要的。◇ **it is essential to do sth** *It is essential to keep the two groups separate.* 將這兩組分開是完全必要的。◇ **it is essential that …** *It is essential that you have some experience.* 你須要有些經驗。 ➲ compare INESSENTIAL, NON-ESSENTIAL OPP **dispensable** ➲ LANGUAGE BANK at EMPHASIS, VITAL **2** [only before noun] connected with the most important aspect or basic nature of sb/sth 本質的；基本的；根本的 SYN **fundamental**：*The essential difference between Sara and me is in our attitude to money.* 我與

薩拉的根本區別在於我們對金錢的態度。◇ *The essential character of the town has been destroyed by the new road.* 這個城鎮的主要特色被這條新公路毀了。

■ ***noun*** [usually pl.] **1** something that is needed in a particular situation or in order to do a particular thing 必不可少的東西；必需品：*I only had time to pack the **bare essentials*** (= the most necessary things). 我只來得及裝上最基本的用品。◇ *The studio had all the essentials like heating and running water.* 工作室裏具備所有的基本設施，如暖氣裝置和自來水。**2** an important basic fact or piece of knowledge about a subject 要點；要素；實質：*the essentials of English grammar* 英語語法基礎

E

es·sen·tial·ly /ɪˈsenʃəli/ *adv.* when you think about the true, important or basic nature of sb/sth 本質上；根本上；基本上 SYN **basically, fundamentally**：*There are three **essentially different** ways of tackling the problem.* 解決這個問題有三種本質上完全不同的方法。◇ *The pattern is **essentially the same** in all cases.* 這種模式在所有情況下基本相同。◇ *Essentially, what we are suggesting is that the firm needs to change.* 說到底，我們的建議是公司必須思變。◇ *He was, essentially, a teacher, not a manager.* 他本質上來說是個教師而不是經理。◇ *The article was essentially concerned with her relationship with her parents* (= it dealt with other things, but this was the most important). 本文主要是關於她與父母的關係。

es,sential 'oil *noun* an oil taken from a plant, used because of its strong smell for making PERFUME and in AROMATHERAPY 精油；香精

Essex girl /ˈesɪks ɡɜːl/ *noun* (*BrE, humorous, disapproving*) a name used especially in jokes to refer to a type of young woman who is not intelligent, dresses badly, talks in a loud and ugly way, and is very willing to have sex 埃塞克斯女郎（尤用於笑話，指愚笨、邋遢、講話沒修養、隨便與人發生關係的女子）

EST /ˌiː es ˈtiː/ *abbr.* EASTERN STANDARD TIME

-est *suffix* (makes superlative adjectives and adverbs 構成形容詞和副詞的最高級)：*widest* 最寬◇ *biggest* 最大◇ *happiest* 最幸福◇ *soonest* 最早 ➲ compare -ER (5)

es·tab·lish AW /ɪˈstæblɪʃ/ *verb* **1** **~ sth** to start or create an organization, a system, etc. that is meant to last for a long time 建立；創立；設立 SYN **set up**：*The committee was established in 1912.* 這個委員會創立於 1912 年。◇ *The new treaty establishes a free trade zone.* 新條約設立了自由貿易區。**2** **~ sth** to start having a relationship, especially a formal one, with another person, group or country 建立（尤指正式關係）：*The school has established a successful relationship with the local community.* 這所學校與當地社區建立了良好的關係。**3** **~ sb/sth/yourself (in sth) (as sth)** to hold a position for long enough or succeed in sth well enough to make people accept and respect you 確立；使立足；使穩固：*By then she was established as a star.* 那時她作為明星的地位已經確立。◇ *He has just set up his own business but it will take him a while to **get established**.* 他剛建立起自己的公司，但要站穩腳跟還得花上一段時間。**4** **~ sth** to make people accept a belief, claim, custom etc. 使…獲得接受；使…得到認可：*It was this campaign that established the paper's reputation.* 正是這場運動確立了這家報紙的聲譽。◇ *Traditions get established over time.* 傳統是隨着時間的推移而得到認可的。**5** to discover or prove the facts of a situation 查實；確定；證實 SYN **ascertain**：**~ sth** *Police are still trying to establish the cause of the accident.* 警方仍在努力確定事故的原因。◇ **~ that ...** *They have established that his injuries were caused by a fall.* 他們已經證實他是摔傷的。◇ **~ where, what, etc. ...** *We need to establish where she was at the time of the shooting.* 我們需要查實槍擊發生時她在何處。◇ **it is established that ...** *It has since been established that the horse was drugged.* 此後便證實那匹馬被注射了麻醉藥。

es·tab·lished AW /ɪˈstæblɪʃt/ *adj.* [only before noun] **1** respected or given official status because it has existed or been used for a long time 已確立的；已獲確認的；確定的：*They are an established company with a good reputation.* 他們是一家地位穩固、信譽良好的公司。

Synonyms 同義詞辨析

essential

vital • crucial • critical • decisive • indispensable

These words all describe sb/sth that is extremely important and completely necessary because a particular situation or activity depends on them. 以上各詞均表示極其重要、完全必要、必不可少。

essential extremely important and completely necessary, because without it sth cannot exist, be made or be successful 指極其重要的、完全必要的、必不可少的：*Experience is essential for this job.* 對於這個工作，經驗是非常重要的。

vital essential 指極其重要的、完全必要的、必不可少的：*The police play a vital role in our society.* 警察在我們的社會中起着極其重要的作用。

ESSENTIAL OR VITAL? 用 essential 還是 vital？

These words have the same meaning but there can be a slight difference in tone. **Essential** is used to state a fact or opinion with authority. **Vital** is often used when there is some anxiety felt about sth, or a need to persuade sb that a fact or opinion is true, right or important. **Vital** is less often used in negative statements. 以上兩詞意義相同，但語氣稍有區別。essential 用以說明事實或表明權威意見，vital 常用於對某事感到急迫或需要使人信服某一事實或意見確實、正確或重要等情況。vital 較少用於否定句：*It was vital to show that he was not afraid.* 最重要的是要表現出他毫無畏懼。◇ ~~*Money is not vital to happiness.*~~

crucial extremely important because a particular situation or activity depends on it 指至關重要的、關鍵的：*It is crucial that we get this right.* 我們把這個問題弄明白是極其重要的。

critical extremely important because a particular situation or activity depends on it 指至關重要的、關鍵的：*Your decision is critical to our future.* 你的決定對我們的將來至關重要。

CRUCIAL OR CRITICAL? 用 crucial 還是 critical？

These words have the same meaning but there can be a slight difference in context. **Critical** is often used in technical matters of business or science; **crucial** is often used to talk about matters that may cause anxiety or other emotions. 以上兩詞意義相同，但使用場合稍有區別。critical 常用於商業或科學的技術問題，crucial 常用於可能引起焦慮或其他情感方面的問題。

decisive of the greatest importance in affecting the final result of a particular situation 指決定性的、關鍵的：*She has played a decisive role in the peace negotiations.* 她在和談中起了關鍵作用。

indispensable essential; too important to be without 指必需的、不可或缺的：*Cars have become an indispensable part of our lives.* 汽車已成了我們生活中必不可少的一部份。

PATTERNS

- essential/vital/crucial/critical/decisive/indispensable **for** sth
- essential/vital/crucial/critical/indispensable **to** sth
- essential/vital/crucial/critical **that** ...
- essential/vital/crucial/critical **to do sth**
- a(n) essential/vital/crucial/critical/decisive/indispensable **part/factor**
- **of** vital/crucial/critical/decisive **importance**
- **absolutely** essential/vital/crucial/critical/decisive/indispensable

◇ *This unit is now an established part of the course.* 這個單元現在為本課程既定的一部份。 ➲ see also WELL ESTABLISHED **2** (of a person 人) well known and respected in a job, etc. that they have been doing for a long time 著名的；成名的；公認的： *an established actor* 著名演員 **3** (of a Church or a religion 教會或宗教) made official for a country 成為國教的

es·tab·lish·ment AW /ɪˈstæblɪʃmənt/ *noun* **1** [C] (*formal*) an organization, a large institution or a hotel 機構；大型機關；企業；旅館： *an educational establishment* 教育機構 ◇ *a research establishment* 研究機構 ◇ *The hotel is a comfortable and well-run establishment.* 這家旅館既舒適，經營又良好。 **2** (usually **the Establishment**) [sing.+sing./pl. v.] (often *disapproving*) the people in a society or a profession who have influence and power and who usually do not support change （通常反對變革的）當權派，權勢集團；（統稱）權威人士： *the **medical/military/political, etc. establishment*** 醫學界、軍界、政界等當權派 ◇ *young people rebelling against the Establishment* 反對當權者的年輕人 **3** [U] the act of starting or creating sth that is meant to last for a long time 建立；創立；確立： *The speaker announced the establishment of a new college.* 發言人宣佈了新學院的成立。 ◇ *the establishment of diplomatic relations between the countries* 國家間外交關係的建立

es·tate 0- AW /ɪˈsteɪt/ *noun*
1 0- [C] a large area of land, usually in the country, that is owned by one person or family（通常指農村的）大片私有土地，莊園 **2** 0- [C] (*BrE*) an area of land with a lot of houses or factories of the same type on it 住宅區；工業區；工廠區： *She lives in a tower block on an estate in London.* 她住在倫敦某住宅區的一棟高樓裏。 ➲ see also COUNCIL ESTATE, HOUSING ESTATE, INDUSTRIAL ESTATE, TRADING ESTATE **3** (*law* 律) [C, U] all the money and property that a person owns, especially everything that is left when they die 個人財產；（尤指）遺產： *Her estate was left to her daughter.* 她的遺產全部留給了女兒。 **4** [C] (*BrE*) = ESTATE CAR

e'state agent (*BrE*) (*NAmE* **Real·tor™**, **'real estate agent**) *noun* a person whose job is to sell houses and land for people 房地產經紀人 ➲ **COLLOCATIONS** at HOUSE

e'state car (also **estate**) (both *BrE*) (*NAmE* **'station wagon**) *noun* a car with a lot of space behind the back seats and a door at the back for loading large items 旅行轎車；客貨兩用小汽車 ➲ **VISUAL VOCAB** page V52

e'state sale *noun* (*NAmE*) a sale of the possessions of a person who has died or is moving to another house 遺物出售；（搬遷戶的）舊物變賣

e'state tax *noun* [U] (*NAmE*) = INHERITANCE TAX

es·teem /ɪˈstiːm/ *noun, verb*
■ ***noun*** [U] (*formal*) great respect and admiration; a good opinion of sb 尊重；敬重；好評： *She is **held in high esteem** by her colleagues.* 她深受同事們的敬重。 ◇ *Please accept this small gift as a token of our esteem.* 小小禮物，聊表敬意，請笑納。 ➲ see also SELF-ESTEEM
■ ***verb*** (*formal*) (not used in the progressive tenses 不用於進行時) **1** [usually passive] **~ sb/sth** to respect and admire sb/sth very much 尊重；敬重： *a **highly esteemed** scientist* 深受敬重的科學家 **2 ~ sb/sth + noun** (*old-fashioned, formal*) to think of sb/sth in a particular way 把…看作；認為： *She was esteemed the perfect novelist.* 她被認為是完美的小說家。

ester /ˈestə(r)/ *noun* (*chemistry* 化) a sweet-smelling substance that is formed from an ORGANIC acid and an alcohol 酯（由有機酸和乙醇形成的芳香物質）

es·thete, **es·thet·ic** (*NAmE*) = AESTHETE, AESTHETIC

es·tim·able /ˈestɪməbl/ *adj.* (*old-fashioned* or *formal*) deserving respect and admiration 值得尊重的；值得敬佩的

es·ti·mate 0- AW *noun, verb*
■ ***noun*** /ˈestɪmət/ **1** 0- a judgement that you make without having the exact details or figures about the size, amount, cost, etc. of sth（對大小、數量、成本等的）估計；估價： *I can give you a **rough estimate** of the amount of wood you will need.* 我可以粗略估計一下你所需要的木材量。 ◇ *a **ballpark estimate*** (= an approximate estimate) 大致相近的估計 ◇ *official government estimates of traffic growth over the next decade* 政府對今後十年交通增長的正式估計 ◇ *At least 5 000 people were killed, and that's a **conservative estimate*** (= the real figure will be higher). 至少 5 000 人喪生，這還是個保守的估計。 **2** 0- a statement of how much a piece of work will probably cost 估計的成本；估價
■ ***verb*** 0- /ˈestɪmeɪt/ [often passive] to form an idea of the cost, size, value etc. of sth, but without calculating it exactly 估計；估價；估算： **~ sth (at sth)** *The satellite will cost an estimated £400 million.* 這顆衛星估計要耗資 4 億英鎊。 ◇ *Police estimate the crowd at 30 000.* 警方估計聚集的人有 3 萬。 ◇ **~ sth to do sth** *The deal is estimated to be worth around $1.5 million.* 這筆交易估計價值 150 萬元左右。 ◇ **~ (that)** … *We estimated (that) it would cost about €5 000.* 我們估計要花費大約 5 000 歐元。 ◇ **it is estimated (that)** … *It is estimated (that) the project will last four years.* 據估計，這項工程將需時四年。 ◇ **~ how many, large, etc.** … *It is hard to estimate how many children suffer from dyslexia.* 很難估計有多少孩子患有誦讀困難症。

es·ti·ma·tion AW /ˌestɪˈmeɪʃn/ *noun* (*formal*) **1** [sing.] a judgement or opinion about the value or quality of sb/sth 判斷；評價；看法： *Who is the best candidate **in your estimation**?* 你認為誰是最合適的人選？ ◇ *Since he left his wife he's certainly **gone down in my estimation*** (= I have less respect for him). 他離棄妻子後我對他的看法便不如以前了。 ◇ *She **went up in my estimation*** (= I have more respect for her) *when I discovered how much charity work she does.* 我發現她做了這麼多慈善工作，我就比以前尊敬她了。 **2** [C] a judgement about the levels or quantity of sth（對水平、數量的）估計： *Estimations of our total world sales are around 50 million.* 我們在全世界的總銷售量估計在 5 000 萬左右。

es·tranged /ɪˈstreɪndʒd/ *adj.* (*formal*) **1** [usually before noun] no longer living with your husband or wife（夫妻）分居的： *his estranged wife Emma* 他分居的妻子埃瑪 **2 ~ (from sb)** no longer friendly, loyal or in contact with sb（與某人）疏遠的，分手的： *He became estranged from his family after the argument.* 那場爭吵後他便與家人疏遠了。 **3 ~ (from sth)** no longer involved in or connected with sth, especially sth that used to be important to you（尤指與過去某重要事物）脫離的，決裂的： *She felt estranged from her former existence.* 她感到自己已脫離了過去的生活方式。

es·trange·ment /ɪˈstreɪndʒmənt/ *noun* [U, C] (*formal*) the state of being estranged; a period of being estranged 疏遠（的一段時間）；分居（期）： **~ (from sb/sth)** *a period of estrangement from his wife* 他與妻子分居期間 ◇ **~ (between A and B)** *The misunderstanding had caused a seven-year estrangement between them.* 這場誤會使得他們七年互不往來。

es·tro·gen (*NAmE*) (*BrE* **oes·tro·gen**) /ˈiːstrədʒən; *NAmE* ˈes-/ *noun* [U] a HORMONE produced in women's OVARIES that causes them to develop the physical and sexual features that are characteristic of females and that causes them to prepare their body to have babies 雌激素 ➲ compare PROGESTERONE, TESTOSTERONE

es·trus (*NAmE*) (*BrE* **oes·trus**) /ˈiːstrəs; *NAmE* ˈestrəs/ *noun* [U] (*technical* 術語) a period of time in which a female animal is ready to have sex（雌性動物的）動情期

es·tu·ary /ˈestʃuəri; *NAmE* -eri/ (*pl.* **-ies**) *noun* the wide part of a river where it flows into the sea（江河入海的）河口，河口灣： *the Thames estuary* 泰晤士河河口 ➲ **VISUAL VOCAB** pages V4, V5

ˌEstuary 'English *noun* [U] a way of speaking which has features of standard English and of the type of English that is typical of London, used by many people in the south-east of England 港灣英語（兼具標準英語和英格蘭東南部人使用的倫敦英語的特點）

ETA /ˌiː tiː ˈeɪ/ *abbr.* estimated time of arrival (the time at which an aircraft, a ship, etc. is expected to arrive)（航班等的）預計到達時間 ➲ compare ETD

E

eta /ˈiːtə/ *noun* the 7th letter of the Greek alphabet (Η, η) 希臘字母表的第 7 個字母

ˈe-tailing *noun* [U] the business of selling goods to the public over the Internet 網上零售；網路零售： *E-tailing in the US broke all records last year.* 去年美國的網上零售業打破了所有紀錄。 ▸ **ˈe-tailer** *noun*： *America's leading e-tailers* 美國主要的網上零售商

et al. /ˌet ˈæl/ *abbr.* (used especially after names) and other people or things (from Latin 'et alii/alia') 等人，等物，等等（源自拉丁文 et alii/alia）： *research by West et al., 1996* 韋斯特等人 1996 年所做的研究

etc. 0-π /ˌet ˈsetərə; ˌɪt/ *abbr.* used after a list to show that there are other things that you could have mentioned (the abbreviation for 'et cetera') 以及諸如此類；以及其他；等等： *Remember to take some paper, a pen, etc.* 記住帶些紙、筆等東西。◇ *We talked about the contract, pay, etc.* 我們討論了合同、工資等問題。

et cet·era /ˌet ˈsetərə; ˌɪt/ = ETC.

etch /etʃ/ *verb* **1** [T, I] to cut lines into a piece of glass, metal, etc. in order to make words or a picture 蝕刻，鑿出（玻璃、金屬等上的文字或圖畫）： **~ (A) (in/into/on B)** *a glass tankard with his initials etched on it* 刻有他姓名首字母的玻璃大酒杯 ◇ **~ B (with A)** *a glass tankard etched with his initials* 刻有他姓名首字母的玻璃大酒杯 **2** [T, usually passive] (*literary*) if a feeling is **etched** on sb's face, or sb's face is **etched** with a feeling, that feeling can be seen very clearly（臉上）流露出： **~ A in/into/on B** *Tiredness was etched on his face.* 從他的臉上可以看出他疲憊不堪。◇ **~ B with A** *His face was etched with tiredness.* 從他的臉上可以看出他疲憊不堪。 **3** [T, usually passive] **~ sth (+ adv./prep.)** to make a strong clear mark or pattern on sth 銘刻；畫出…的輪廓： *a mountain etched* (= having a clear outline) *against the sky* 在天空映襯下輪廓清晰的山

IDM **be etched on your ˈheart/ˈmemory/ˈmind** if sth is **etched** on your memory, you remember it because it has made a strong impression on you 銘記在心；永誌不忘；牢記心頭

etch·ing /ˈetʃɪŋ/ *noun* [C, U] a picture that is printed from an etched piece of metal; the art of making these pictures 蝕刻畫；蝕刻術；蝕刻法

ETD /ˌiː tiː ˈdiː/ *abbr.* estimated time of departure (the time at which an aircraft, ship, etc. is expected to leave)（航班等的）預計離開時間 ➲ compare ETA

eter·nal /ɪˈtɜːnl; *NAmE* ɪˈtɜːrnl/ *adj.* **1** without an end; existing or continuing forever 不朽的；永久的；永恆的： *the promise of eternal life in heaven* 在天國永生的許諾 ◇ *She's an eternal optimist* (= she always expects that the best will happen). 她是個永遠的樂觀主義者。◇ *eternal truths* (= ideas that are always true and never change) 永恆的真理 **2** [only before noun] (*disapproving*) happening often and seeming never to stop 無休止的；永不停止的；沒完沒了的 **SYN** **constant**： *I'm tired of your eternal arguments.* 我煩透了你們那沒完沒了的爭論。 ▸ **eter·nal·ly** /ɪˈtɜːnəli; *NAmE* -ˈtɜːrn-/ *adv.*： *I'll be eternally grateful to you for this.* 我將為此永遠感激你。◇ *women trying to look eternally young* 試圖永葆青春的女人 **IDM** see HOPE *n.*

eˌternal ˈtriangle *noun* a situation where two people are in love with or having a sexual relationship with the same person 三角戀愛

eˌternal ˈverity *noun* [usually pl.] (*formal*) an essential basic moral principle 基本道德原則

eter·nity /ɪˈtɜːnəti; *NAmE* ɪˈtɜːrn-/ *noun* **1** [U] (*formal*) time without end, especially life continuing without end after death 永恆；永生；不朽： *There will be rich and poor for all eternity.* 貧富將永遠存在。◇ *They believed that their souls would be condemned to burn in hell for eternity.* 他們相信他們的靈魂會受到懲罰，在地獄裏永受煎熬。 **2** **an eternity** [sing.] (*informal*) a period of time that seems to be very long or to never end（似乎）無窮無盡的一段時間： *After what **seemed like an eternity** the nurse returned with the results of the test.* 過了漫長的一段時間後護士才拿着檢驗結果回來。

eth /eð/ *noun* (*phonetics* 語音) the letter ð that was used in Old English to represent the sounds /θ/ and /ð/ and later written as *th*. This letter is now used as a PHONETIC symbol for the sound /ð/, as in *this*. */ð/ 音符號（古英語中用以表示 /θ/ 和 /ð/ 音的字母，後寫作 th）。

eth·ane /ˈiːθeɪn/ *noun* [U] (*symb.* C_2H_6) (*chemistry* 化) a gas that has no colour or smell and that can burn. Ethane is found in natural gas and mineral oil. 乙烷（無色無味的可燃氣體）

etha·nol /ˈeθənɒl; *NAmE* -nɔːl; -nɑːl/ (also **ˌethyl ˈalcohol**) *noun* [U] (*chemistry* 化) the type of alcohol in alcoholic drinks, also used as a fuel or SOLVENT 乙醇

eth·ene /ˈeθiːn/ *noun* [U] = ETHYLENE

ether /ˈiːθə(r)/ *noun* [U] **1** a clear liquid made from alcohol, used in industry as a SOLVENT and, in the past, in medicine to make people unconscious before an operation 醚；乙醚 **2** **the ether** (*old use* or *literary*) the upper part of the sky 蒼穹；蒼天；太空： *Her words disappeared into the ether.* 她的話消失在九霄雲外。 **3** **the ether** the air, when it is thought of as the place in which radio or electronic communication takes place 以太（指無線電和電子通訊可傳播的空間）

ether·eal /iˈθɪəriəl; *NAmE* iˈθɪr-/ *adj.* (*formal*) extremely delicate and light; seeming to belong to another, more spiritual, world 優雅的；輕飄的；縹緲的；超凡的： *ethereal music* 優雅的音樂 ◇ *her ethereal beauty* 她飄逸的美

Ether·net /ˈiːθənet; *NAmE* ˈiːθərnet/ *noun* [sing.] (*computing* 計) a system for connecting a number of computer systems to form a network 以太網

ethic **AW** /ˈeθɪk/ *noun* **1** **ethics** [pl.] moral principles that control or influence a person's behaviour 道德準則；倫理標準： ***professional/business/medical ethics*** 職業／商業道德；醫德 ◇ *to draw up a **code of ethics*** 擬定一份道德規範 ◇ *He began to question the ethics of his position.* 他開始對他的立場是否符合道德準則提出質疑。 **2** [sing.] a system of moral principles or rules of behaviour 道德體系；行為準則： *a strongly defined work ethic* 明確規定的工作守則 ◇ *the Protestant ethic* 新教倫理 **3** **ethics** [U] the branch of philosophy that deals with moral principles 倫理學；道德學

eth·ic·al **AW** /ˈeθɪkl/ *adj.* **1** connected with beliefs and principles about what is right and wrong（有關）道德的；倫理的： ***ethical issues/standards/questions*** 有關道德的問題；道德標準／問題 ◇ *the **ethical problems** of human embryo research* 人類胚胎研究的倫理問題 **2** morally correct or acceptable 合乎道德的： *Is it ethical to promote cigarettes through advertising?* 通過廣告推銷香煙合乎道德嗎？◇ ***ethical investment*** (= investing money in businesses that are considered morally acceptable) 合乎道德的投資 ▸ **eth·ic·al·ly** **AW** /-kli/ *adv.*： *The committee judged that he had not behaved ethically.* 委員會裁定他的行為違背了道德標準。

eth·nic **AW** /ˈeθnɪk/ *adj.*, *noun*

■ *adj.* **1** connected with or belonging to a nation, race or people that shares a cultural tradition 民族的；種族的： ***ethnic groups/communities*** 族群；種族社區 ◇ ***ethnic strife/tensions/violence*** (= between people from different races or peoples) 種族衝突／緊張形勢／暴力 ◇ *ethnic Albanians living in Germany* 生活在德國的阿爾巴尼亞族人 **2** typical of a country or culture that is very different from modern Western culture and therefore interesting for people in Western countries 具有民族特色的；異國風味的： ***ethnic clothes/jewellery/cooking*** 具有民族特色的服裝／珠寶首飾／烹調 ▸ **eth·nic·al·ly** /-kli/ *adv.*： *an ethnically divided region* 種族分裂地區

■ *noun* (*especially NAmE*) a person from an ETHNIC MINORITY 少數民族的人

ˌethnic ˈcleansing *noun* [U] (used especially in news reports) the policy of forcing the people of a particular race or religion to leave an area or a country 種族清洗 ➲ COLLOCATIONS at WAR

eth·ni·city **AW** /eθˈnɪsəti/ *noun* [U] (*technical* 術語) the fact of belonging to a particular race 種族淵源；種族

特點：*Many factors are important, for example class, gender, age and ethnicity.* 許多因素都很重要，如階級、性別、年齡和種族。

ˌethnic miˈnority *noun* a group of people from a particular culture or of a particular race living in a country where the main group is of a different culture or race 少數民族

ethno·cen·tric /ˌeθnəʊˈsentrɪk; *NAmE* ˌeθnoʊ-/ *adj.* based on the ideas and beliefs of one particular culture and using these to judge other cultures 種族（或民族）中心主義的；種族（或民族）優越感的：*a white, ethnocentric school curriculum* 以白種人為中心的學校課程 ▸ **ethno·cen·trism** *noun* [U]

eth·nog·raph·er /eθˈnɒɡrəfə(r); *NAmE* -ˈnɑːɡ-/ *noun* a person who studies different races and cultures 人種誌（或人種論）研究者

eth·nog·raphy /eθˈnɒɡrəfi; *NAmE* -ˈnɑːɡ-/ *noun* [U] the scientific description of different races and cultures 人種誌；人種論 ▸ **ethno·graph·ic** /ˌeθnəˈɡræfɪk/ *adj.*：*ethnographic research* 人種誌研究

eth·no·logy /eθˈnɒlədʒi; *NAmE* -ˈnɑːl-/ *noun* [U] the scientific study and comparison of human races 人種學；民族學 ▸ **ethno·logic·al** /ˌeθnəˈlɒdʒɪkl; *NAmE* -ˈlɑːdʒ-/ *adj.* **eth·nolo·gist** /eθˈnɒlədʒɪst; *NAmE* -ˈnɑːl-/ *noun*

ethos /ˈiːθɒs; *NAmE* ˈiːθɑːs/ *noun* [sing.] (*formal*) the moral ideas and attitudes that belong to a particular group or society（某團體或社會的）道德思想，道德觀：*an ethos of public service* 公益服務的道德意識

ethyl /ˈeθɪl; ˈiːθaɪl/ *adj.* [only before noun] (*chemistry* 化) containing the group of atoms C_2H_5, formed from ETHANE 含乙基的：*ethyl acetate* 乙酸乙酯

ˌethyl ˈalcohol *noun* [U] (*chemistry* 化) = ETHANOL

ethyl·ene /ˈeθɪliːn/ (also **eth·ene**) *noun* [U] (*symb.* C_2H_4) (*chemistry* 化) a gas which is present in coal, CRUDE OIL, and NATURAL GAS 乙烯

eth·yne /ˈiːθaɪn; *NAmE* ˈeθ-/ *noun* [U] (*symb.* C_2H_2) the chemical name for ACETYLENE 乙炔

ˈe-ticket (*US* **ˈE-ticket™**) *noun* a ticket, for example a plane ticket, that you buy over the Internet and receive by email. Your purchase details are stored on computer so you do not need a paper ticket. 電子票

eti·ol·ated /ˈiːtiəleɪtɪd/ *adj.* **1** (*biology* 生) if a plant is **etiolated** it is pale because it does not receive enough light（植物因吸收光線不足而）黃化的 **2** (*formal*) lacking force and energy 無力的；虛弱的

eti·ology (*NAmE*) (*BrE* **aeti·ology**) /ˌiːtiˈɒlədʒi; *NAmE* -ˈɑːl-/ *noun* [U] (*medical* 醫) the scientific study of the causes of disease 病原學；病因學

eti·quette /ˈetɪket; -kət/ *noun* [U] the formal rules of correct or polite behaviour in society or among members of a particular profession（社會或行業中的）禮節，禮儀，規矩：*advice on etiquette* 在禮節方面的忠告 ◇ ***medical/legal/professional etiquette*** 醫學界的／法律界的／行業規矩 ➲ see also NETIQUETTE

Eton·ian /iːˈtəʊniən; *NAmE* -ˈtoʊ-/ *noun* a person who is or was a student at the English private school Eton College（英國）伊頓公學學生，伊頓公學校友

-ette *suffix* (in nouns 構成名詞) **1** small 小：*kitchenette* 小廚房 **2** female 女性：*usherette* 女引座員

étude /ˈeɪtjuːd; *NAmE* also -tuːd/ (from *French*, *especially NAmE*) (*BrE* also **study**) *noun* (*music* 音) a piece of music designed to give a player practice in technical skills 練習曲

ety·mol·ogy /ˌetɪˈmɒlədʒi; *NAmE* -ˈmɑːl-/ *noun* (*pl.* **-ies**) **1** [U] the study of the origin and history of words and their meanings 詞源學 **2** [C] the origin and history of a particular word 詞源 ▸ **etymo·logic·al** /ˌetɪməˈlɒdʒɪkl; *NAmE* -ˈlɑːdʒ-/ *adj.*：*an etymological dictionary* 詞源詞典

EU /ˌiː ˈjuː/ *abbr.* EUROPEAN UNION

eu·ca·lyp·tus /ˌjuːkəˈlɪptəs/ *noun* [C, U] (*pl.* **eu·ca·lyp·tuses** or **eu·ca·lyp·ti** /-taɪ/) (also **eucaˈlyptus tree**, **ˈgum tree**) a tall straight tree with leaves that produce an oil with a strong smell, that is used in medicine. There are several types of eucalyptus and they grow especially in Australasia. 桉樹，尤加利樹（尤產於澳大拉西亞）➲ **VISUAL VOCAB** page V12

Eu·char·ist /ˈjuːkərɪst/ *noun* [sing.] a ceremony in the Christian Church during which people eat bread and drink wine in memory of the last meal that Christ had with his DISCIPLES; the bread and wine taken at this ceremony（基督教）聖祭禮，聖餐，聖體聖血 ➲ see also COMMUNION (1), MASS (1)

Eu·clid·ean geom·etry /juːˌklɪdiən dʒiˈɒmətri; *NAmE* -ˈɑːm-/ *noun* [U] the system of GEOMETRY based on the work of Euclid 歐幾里德幾何

eu·gen·ics /juːˈdʒenɪks/ *noun* [U] the study of methods to improve the mental and physical characteristics of the human race by choosing who may become parents 優生學；人種改良學 ▸ **eu·gen·ic** *adj.* **eu·gen·ist** /juːˈdʒiːnɪst/ (also **eu·geni·cist** /juːˈdʒenɪsɪst/) *noun*

eu·lo·gize (*BrE* also **-ise**) /ˈjuːlədʒaɪz/ *verb* **~ sb/sth** (**as sth**) (*formal*) to praise sb/sth very highly 稱讚；頌揚；讚頌：*He was eulogized as a hero.* 他被讚譽為英雄。▸ **eu·lo·gis·tic** /ˌjuːləˈdʒɪstɪk/ *adj.*

eu·logy /ˈjuːlədʒi/ *noun* [C, U] (*pl.* **-ies**) **1 ~** (**of/to sb/sth**) a speech or piece of writing praising sb/sth very much 頌辭；頌文：*a eulogy to marriage* 婚禮頌辭 **2 ~** (**for/to sb**) (*especially NAmE*) a speech given at a funeral praising the person who has died（頌揚死者的）悼辭，悼文

eu·nuch /ˈjuːnək/ *noun* **1** a man who has been CASTRATED, especially one who guarded women in some Asian countries in the past 閹人；太監 **2** (*formal*) a person without power or influence 無權力（或影響）的人：*a political eunuch* 政治"閹人"

eu·phem·ism /ˈjuːfəmɪzəm/ *noun* **~** (**for sth**) an indirect word or phrase that people often use to refer to sth embarrassing or unpleasant, sometimes to make it seem more acceptable than it really is 委婉語；委婉說法：*'Pass away' is a euphemism for 'die'.* "去世"是"死"的委婉語。◇ *'User fees' is just a politician's euphemism for taxes.* "用戶費"不過是政治家對"稅款"的委婉說法。▸ **eu·phem·is·tic** /ˌjuːfəˈmɪstɪk/ *adj.*：*euphemistic language* 委婉的語言 **eu·phem·is·tic·al·ly** /ˌjuːfəˈmɪstɪkli/ *adv.*：*The prison camps were euphemistically called 'retraining centres'.* 戰俘營被委婉地稱作"再訓練中心"。

eu·pho·ni·ous /juːˈfəʊniəs; *NAmE* -ˈfoʊ-/ *adj.* (*formal*) (of a sound, word, etc. 聲音、詞等) pleasant to listen to 悅耳的；動聽的；和諧的 ▸ **eu·pho·ny** /ˈjuːfəni/ *noun* [U]

eu·pho·nium /juːˈfəʊniəm; *NAmE* -ˈfoʊ-/ *noun* a large BRASS musical instrument like a TUBA 尤風寧號

eu·phoria /juːˈfɔːriə/ *noun* [U] an extremely strong feeling of happiness and excitement that usually lasts only a short time（通常指持續時間較短的）極度愉快的心情，極度興奮的情緒 ▸ **eu·phor·ic** /juːˈfɒrɪk; *NAmE* -ˈfɔːr-/ *adj.*：*My euphoric mood could not last.* 我興奮的心情持久不了。➲ **SYNONYMS** at EXCITED

Eur·asian /juˈreɪʒn; -ˈreɪʃn/ *adj.*, *noun*

■ ***adj.*** **1** of or connected with both Europe and Asia 歐亞的：*the Centre for Russian and Eurasian Studies* 俄羅斯和歐亞研究中心 **2** having one Asian parent and one parent who is white or from Europe 歐亞混血兒的

■ ***noun*** a person with one Asian parent and one parent who is white or from Europe 歐亞混血兒：*Singapore Eurasians* 新加坡的歐亞混血兒

eur·eka /juˈriːkə/ *exclamation* used to show pleasure at having found sth, especially the answer to a problem（因找到某物，尤指問題的答案而高興）我發現了，我找到了

euˈreka moment *noun* the moment when you suddenly understand sth important, have a great idea, or find the answer to a problem 頓悟時刻；突發靈感的一刻

eu·rhyth·mics (*BrE*) (*NAmE* **eu·ryth·mics**) /juˈrɪðmɪks/ *noun* [U] a form of exercise which combines physical movement with music and speech 韻律（體）操

Euro /ˈjʊərəʊ; *NAmE* ˈjʊroʊ/ *adj.* (*informal*) (used especially in newspapers) connected with Europe, especially the European Union 歐洲的；歐盟的：*Euro rules* 歐盟條例

euro /ˈjʊərəʊ; *NAmE* ˈjʊroʊ/ *noun* (*symb.* €) (*pl.* **euros** or **euro**) the unit of money of some countries of the European Union 歐元（歐盟中某些國家的貨幣單位）：*The price is given in dollars or euros.* 價格用美元或歐元標出。◇ *I paid five euros for it.* 買這我花了五歐元。◇ *10 million euro* * 1 000 萬歐元 ◇ *a 30-million-euro deal* * 3 000 萬歐元的交易 ◇ *the value of* ***the euro*** *against the dollar* 歐元對美元的比值

E

Euro- /ˈjʊərəʊ; *NAmE* ˈjʊroʊ/ *combining form* (in nouns and adjectives 構成名詞和形容詞) connected with Europe or the European Union 歐洲的；歐盟的：*a Euro-MP* 歐洲議會議員 ◇ *Euro-elections* 歐盟選舉

Euro·crat /ˈjʊərəkræt; *NAmE* ˈjʊr-/ *noun* (sometimes *disapproving*) an official of the European Union, especially a senior one 歐盟官員（尤指高級官員）

Euro·land /ˈjʊərəʊlænd; *NAmE* ˈjʊroʊ-/ *noun* [U] = EUROZONE

Eur·ope /ˈjʊərəp; *NAmE* ˈjʊrəp/ *noun* [U] **1** the continent next to Asia in the east, the Atlantic Ocean in the west, and the Mediterranean Sea in the south 歐洲：***western/eastern/central Europe*** 西歐；東歐；中歐 **2** the European Union 歐盟：*countries wanting to join Europe* 想加入歐盟的國家 ◇ *He's very pro-Europe.* 他非常支持歐盟。 **3** (*BrE*) all of Europe except for Britain（除英國以外的）全歐洲：*British holidaymakers in Europe* 在歐洲度假的英國人

Euro·pean /ˌjʊərəˈpiːən; *NAmE* jʊr-/ *adj.*, *noun*

■ ***adj.*** **1** of or connected with Europe 歐洲的；全歐的：*European languages* 歐洲的語言 **2** of or connected with the European Union 歐盟的：*European law* 歐盟的法律 ◇ *our European partners* 我們的歐盟夥伴

■ ***noun*** **1** a person from Europe, or whose ANCESTORS came from Europe 歐洲人；祖籍歐洲的人；歐洲人的後裔 **2** (*BrE*) a person who supports the principles and aims of the European Union 歐盟支持者；歐盟擁護者：*a good European* 歐盟的堅定擁護者

the ˌEuropean Comˈmission *noun* [sing.] the group of people who are responsible for the work of the European Union and for suggesting new laws 歐盟委員會，歐盟執委會（負責歐盟工作和新法規的提出）

Euro·pean·ize (*BrE* also **-ise**) /ˌjʊərəˈpiːənaɪz; *NAmE* jʊr-/ *verb* **1 ~ sb/sth** to make sb/sth feel or seem European 歐化；使具有歐洲風味：*a Europeanized American* 一名歐化的美國人 **2 ~ sth** to put sth under the control of the European Union 使受歐盟管轄 ▸ **Euro·pean·iza·tion, -isa·tion** /ˌjʊərəpiːənaɪˈzeɪʃn; *NAmE* jʊr-/ *noun* [U]

the ˌEuropean ˈParliament *noun* [sing.] the group of people who are elected in the countries of the European Union to make and change its laws 歐洲議會（由歐盟各國選舉產生，負責法律的制訂和修改）

ˌEuropean ˈplan *noun* [sing.] (*NAmE*) a system of charging for a hotel room only, without meals 歐式旅館收費制（只收客房費，不含餐飲）➲ compare BED AND BREAKFAST (1), FULL BOARD, HALF BOARD

the ˌEuropean ˈUnion *noun* [sing.] (*abbr.* **EU**) an economic and political organization, based in Brussels, that many European countries belong to 歐洲聯盟，歐盟（總部設在布魯塞爾）

euro·pium /jʊəˈrəʊpiəm; *NAmE* jʊˈroʊ-/ *noun* [U] (*symb.* **Eu**) a chemical element. Europium is a silver-white metal used in colour television screens. 銪（用於彩電屏幕）

ˌEuro-ˈsceptic *noun* a person, especially a British politician, who is opposed to closer links with the European Union 反對與歐盟有密切聯繫的人（尤指英國政界人士）▸ **ˌEuro-ˈsceptic** *adj.*

Euro·vision /ˈjʊərəvɪʒn; *NAmE* ˈjʊr-/ *noun* [sing.] an organization of European television companies that share news and programmes 歐洲電視網（由歐洲各電視公司組成，可共享新聞和電視節目）：*the Eurovision Song Contest* 歐洲電視網歌曲大賽

the Euro·zone /ˈjʊərəʊzəʊn; *NAmE* ˈjʊroʊzoʊn/ *noun* [sing.] (also **Euro·land**) the countries in the European Union that use the euro as a unit of money 歐元區

Eus·ta·chian tube /juːˈsteɪʃn tjuːb/ *noun* (*anatomy* 解) a narrow tube that joins the throat to the middle ear 咽鼓管；耳咽管

eu·tha·nasia /ˌjuːθəˈneɪziə; *NAmE* -ˈneɪʒə/ *noun* [U] the practice (illegal in most countries) of killing without pain a person who is suffering from a disease that cannot be cured 安樂死 SYN **mercy killing**：*They argued in favour of legalizing* ***voluntary euthanasia*** (= people being able to ask for euthanasia themselves). 他們據理力爭讓自願安樂死合法化。

eu·than·ize (*BrE* also **-ise**) /ˈjuːθənaɪz/ *verb* **~ sb/sth** (*especially NAmE*) to kill a sick or injured animal or person by giving them drugs so that they die without pain 使（人或動物）安樂死 SYN **put sth down, put sth to sleep**

eu·troph·ic /juːˈtrɒfɪk; *NAmE* -ˈtroʊf-/ *adj.* (*technical* 術語) (of a lake, river, etc. 湖、河等) containing too many food substances that encourage plants to grow, which then kill animal life by using too much OXYGEN from the water 富營養的

eu·trophi·ca·tion /juːtrəfɪˈkeɪʃn/ *noun* [U] (*technical* 術語) the process of too many plants growing on the surface of a river, lake, etc., often because chemicals that are used to help crops grow have been carried there by rain （常因雨水帶來的化肥造成水體的）富營養化

evacu·ate /ɪˈvækjueɪt/ *verb* **1** [T] to move people from a place of danger to a safer place （把人從危險的地方）疏散，轉移，撤離：**~ sth** *Police evacuated nearby buildings.* 警方已將附近大樓的居民疏散。◇ **~ sb (from …) (to …)** *Children were evacuated from London to escape the bombing.* 為躲避轟炸，孩子們都撤離了倫敦。 **2** [T, I] **~ (sth)** to move out of a place because of danger, and leave the place empty （從危險的地方）撤出，搬出，撤空：*Employees were urged to evacuate their offices immediately.* 已敦促各雇員立即從辦公室撤出。◇ *Locals were told to evacuate.* 當地居民已收到撤離的通知。 **3** [T] **~ sth** (*formal*) to empty your BOWELS 排空（胃腸）；排泄（糞便）▸ **evacu·ation** /ɪˌvækjuˈeɪʃn/ *noun* [U, C]：*the emergency evacuation of thousands of people after the earthquake* 地震後數千人的緊急疏散

evac·uee /ɪˌvækjuˈiː/ *noun* a person who is sent away from a place because it is dangerous, especially during a war 被疏散者；撤離者

evade /ɪˈveɪd/ *verb* **1 ~ (doing) sth** to escape from sb/sth or avoid meeting sb 逃脫；躲開；躲避：*For two weeks they evaded the press.* 他們有兩週一直避而不見記者。◇ *He managed to* ***evade capture.*** 他設法逃脫了抓捕。 **2 ~ (doing) sth** to find a way of not doing sth, especially sth that legally or morally you should do 逃避，規避（尤指法律或道德責任）：*to evade payment of taxes* 逃稅 ◇ *She is trying to* ***evade all responsibility*** *for her behaviour.* 她在試圖逃避應為自己的行為承擔的所有責任。 **3** to avoid dealing with or talking about sth 迴避，避開（處理或談論某事）：**~ sth** *Come on, don't you think you're* ***evading the issue?*** 得了吧，你不認為你是在迴避這個問題嗎？◇ **~ doing sth** *to evade answering a question* 避而不答某一問題 **4 ~ sb** (*formal*) to not come or happen to sb 想不出；不發生 SYN **elude**：*The answer evaded him* (= he could not think of it). 他答不上來。➲ see also EVASION, EVASIVE

evalu·ate AW /ɪˈvæljueɪt/ *verb* to form an opinion of the amount, value or quality of sth after thinking about it carefully 估計；評價；評估 SYN **assess**：**~ sth** *Our research attempts to evaluate the effectiveness of the different drugs.* 我們的研究試圖對不同藥物的療效進行評估。◇ **~ how, whether, etc. …** *We need to evaluate how well the policy is working.* 我們需要對這一政策產生的效果作出評價。▸ **evalu·ation** AW /ɪˌvæljuˈeɪʃn/ *noun* [C, U]：*an evaluation of the health care system* 對保健制度的評價 **evalu·ative** AW /ɪˈvæljuətɪv/ *adj.*

evan·es·cent /ˌiːvəˈnesnt; *NAmE* usually ˌev-/ *adj.* (*literary*) disappearing quickly from sight or memory 瞬息即逝的；迅速遺忘的 ▶ **evan·es·cence** *noun* [U]

evan·gel·ic·al /ˌiːvænˈdʒelɪkl/ *adj.*, *noun*

■ ***adj.*** **1** of or belonging to a Christian group that emphasizes the authority of the Bible and the importance of people being saved through faith 基督教福音派的：*They're evangelical Christians.* 他們是福音派基督徒。 **2** wanting very much to persuade people to accept your views and opinions 熱衷於傳播自己觀點的：*He delivered his speech with evangelical fervour.* 他發表演說時熱烈鼓吹自己的思想。 ▶ **evan·gel·ic·al·ism** *noun* [U]

■ ***noun*** a member of the evangelical branch of the Christian Church 基督教福音派教徒

evan·gel·ist /ɪˈvændʒəlɪst/ *noun* **1** a person who tries to persuade people to become Christians, especially by travelling around the country holding religious meetings or speaking on radio or television（基督教）佈道者 ➲ see also TELEVANGELIST **2** **Evangelist** one of the four writers (Matthew, Mark, Luke, John) of the books called the GOSPELS in the Bible 福音作者，聖史（寫作《聖經》中四部福音的人）▶ **evan·gel·ism** *noun* [U] **evan·gel·ist·ic** /ɪˌvændʒəˈlɪstɪk/ *adj.*：*an evangelistic meeting* 佈道會

evan·gel·ize (*BrE* also **-ise**) /ɪˈvændʒəlaɪz/ *verb* **~ sb** to try to persuade people to become Christians 傳播福音；使皈依基督教

evap·or·ate /ɪˈvæpəreɪt/ *verb* **1** [I, T] if a liquid **evaporates** or if sth **evaporates** it, it changes into a gas, especially steam（使）蒸發，揮發：*Heat until all the water has evaporated.* 加熱直至水全部蒸發。◇ **~ sth** *The sun is constantly evaporating the earth's moisture.* 太陽使地球上的濕氣不斷蒸發。 **2** [I] to disappear, especially by gradually becoming less and less（逐漸）消失，消散，衰減：*Her confidence had now completely evaporated.* 她的信心已消失殆盡。 ▶ **evap·or·ation** /ɪˌvæpəˈreɪʃn/ *noun* [U]

eˌvaporated ˈmilk *noun* [U] thick sweet milk sold in cans, often served with fruit instead of cream（罐裝）甜煉乳

eˈvaporating dish *noun* (*technical* 術語) a dish in which scientists heat a liquid, so that it leaves a solid when it has disappeared 蒸發皿 ➲ **VISUAL VOCAB** page V70

eva·sion /ɪˈveɪʒn/ *noun* [C, U] **1** the act of avoiding sb or of avoiding sth that you are supposed to do 躲避；規避；逃避；迴避：*His behaviour was an evasion of his responsibilities as a father.* 他的行為是逃避為父之責。 ◇ *She's been charged with* ***tax evasion***. 她被控逃稅。 **2** a statement that sb makes that avoids dealing with sth or talking about sth honestly and directly 遁詞；藉口；託辭：*His speech was full of evasions and half-truths.* 他的發言盡是些遁詞和真假參半的說法。 ➲ see also EVADE

eva·sive /ɪˈveɪsɪv/ *adj.* not willing to give clear answers to a question 迴避提問的；推託的；推諉的 **SYN** **cagey**：***evasive answers/comments/replies*** 含糊其詞的回答 / 意見 / 答覆 ◇ *Tessa was evasive about why she had not been at home that night.* 特薩對她那天晚上不在家的原因避而不談。 ▶ **eva·sive·ly** *adv.*：*'I'm not sure,' she replied evasively.* "我不敢確定。" 她躲躲閃閃地答道。 **eva·sive·ness** *noun* [U]

IDM **take evasive action** to act in order to avoid danger or an unpleasant situation 採取迴避行動（以避免危險或不愉快的處境）

eve /iːv/ *noun* **1** the day or evening before an event, especially a religious festival or holiday（尤指宗教節假日的）前夜，前夕：*Christmas Eve* (= 24 December) 聖誕前夕（12 月 24 日）◇ *a New Year's Eve party* (= on 31 December) 除夕晚會 ◇ ***on the eve of*** *the election* 在選舉前夕 **2** (*old use* or *literary*) evening 傍晚；黃昏

even 🔑 /ˈiːvn/ *adv.*, *adj.*, *verb*

■ ***adv.*** **1** 🔑 used to emphasize sth unexpected or surprising（強調出乎意料）甚至，連，即使：*He never even opened the letter* (= so he certainly didn't read it). 他根本沒打開過那封信。◇ *It was cold there even in summer* (= so it must have been very cold in winter). 那兒即使夏天也很冷。◇ *Even a child can understand it* (= so adults certainly can). 這就連小孩子也能理解。 ◇ *She didn't even call to say she wasn't coming.* 她甚至沒打電話來說一聲她不來了。 **2** 🔑 used when you are comparing things, to make the comparison stronger（用以加強比較）甚至更，愈加，還：*You know even less about it than I do.* 你對此事的瞭解甚至還不如我。◇ *She's even more intelligent than her sister.* 她甚至比她姐姐還聰明。 **3** used to introduce a more exact description of sb/sth（引出更精確的說法）甚至可以說，其實，實際上：*It's an unattractive building, ugly even.* 這棟建築毫不美觀，甚至可以說難看。 ➲ note at ALTHOUGH

IDM **even as** (*formal*) just at the same time as sb does sth or as sth else happens 正當；恰好在…時候：*Even as he shouted the warning the car skidded.* 他正在高喊注意時，汽車就打滑了。 **even if/though** 🔑 despite the fact or belief that; no matter whether 即使；縱然；雖然：*I'll get there, even if I have to walk.* 我就是走也要走到那兒去。◇ *I like her, even though she can be annoying at times.* 儘管她有時可能很煩人，我還是喜歡她。 ➲ note at ALTHOUGH **ˌeven ˈnow/ˈthen** **1** 🔑 despite what has/had happened 甚至到現在（或那時）；即便是這樣（或那樣）；儘管如此（或那樣）：*I've shown him the photographs but even now he won't believe me.* 我把照片給他看了，即便是這樣他仍然不相信我。◇ *Even then she would not admit her mistake.* 甚至到那時她還是不肯認錯。 **2** (*formal*) at this or that exact moment 恰好在這時（或那時）：*The troops are even now preparing to march into the city.* 部隊此刻正在準備向城裏開進。 **ˌeven ˈso** 🔑 despite that 儘管如此；即使那樣：*There are a lot of spelling mistakes; even so, it's quite a good essay.* 儘管有許多拼寫錯誤，它仍不失為一篇佳作。 ➲ more at LESS *adv.*

■ ***adj.***

▸ **SMOOTH/LEVEL** 平滑；平 **1** 🔑 smooth, level and flat 平滑的；平的；平坦的：*You need an even surface to work on.* 你需要有個平面在上面工作。 **OPP** **uneven**

▸ **NOT CHANGING** 不變 **2** 🔑 not changing very much in amount, speed, etc.（數量、速度等）變化不大的，均勻的，平穩的：*an even temperature all year* 常年溫度變化不大 ◇ *Children do not learn at an even pace.* 孩子學東西時快時慢。 **OPP** **uneven**

▸ **EQUAL** 相等 **3** 🔑 (of an amount of sth 數量) equal or the same for each person, team, place, etc. 相等的；均等的：*Our scores are now even.* 我們的比分現在相等。◇ *the even distribution of food* 食物的平均分配 **OPP** **uneven** **4** 🔑 (of two people or teams 兩人或兩隊) equally balanced or of an equal standard 均衡的；不相上下的；同一水平的：*an even contest* 勢均力敵的競賽 ◇ *The two players were pretty even.* 這兩個運動員不分上下。 **OPP** **uneven**

▸ **NUMBERS** 數目 **5** 🔑 that can be divided exactly by two 雙數的；偶數的：*4, 6, 8, 10 are all* ***even numbers***. *4、6、8、10 都是偶數。 **OPP** **odd**

▸ **SAME SIZE** 大小相同 **6** equally spaced and the same size 勻稱的；均勻的；同樣大小的：*even features/teeth* 勻稱的面容；整齊的牙齒 **OPP** **uneven**

▸ **CALM** 平靜 **7** calm; not changing or becoming upset 鎮靜的；穩重的；平和的，溫和的：*She has a very even temperament.* 她的性情非常平和。◇ *He spoke in a steady, even voice.* 當時他說話的聲音平穩而鎮靜。 ▶ **even·ness** /ˈiːvənnəs/ *noun* [U]

IDM **be ˈeven** (*informal*) to no longer owe sb money or a favour 了賬；扯平；兩清；兩抵 **be/get ˈeven (with sb)** (*informal*) to cause sb the same amount of trouble or harm as they have caused you（向某人）報復；（跟某人）算賬，扯平：*I'll get even with you for this, just you wait.* 這事我會找你算賬的，等着瞧吧。 **break ˈeven** to complete a piece of business, etc. without either losing money or making a profit 收支平衡；不賠不賺：*The company just about broke even last year.* 這家公司去年接近收支平衡。 **have an even ˈchance (of doing sth)** to be equally likely to do or not do sth（做某事）有一半的機會；正反各半的可能性：*She has more than an even chance of winning tomorrow.* 她明天多半會贏。 **on an even ˈkeel** living, working or happening in a calm way, with no sudden changes, especially after a

E

difficult time（生活、工作等經歷困難後）平穩下來，順順當當 ➲ more at HONOUR *n.*

■ *verb*

IDM ˌ**even the ˈscore** to harm or punish sb who has harmed or cheated you in the past 結清宿怨；攞平

PHR V ˌ**even ˈout** to become level or steady, usually after varying a lot（在多變之後）變平坦，穩定下來：*House prices keep rising and falling but they should eventually even out.* 房價一直時漲時落，但最終應該會趨於穩定。 ˌ**even sth↔ˈout** to spread things equally over a period of time or among a number of people 平均分配；平均分攤：*He tried to even out the distribution of work among his employees.* 他盡量把工作平均分配給雇員。 ˌ**even sth↔ˈup** to make a situation or a competition more equal 使拉平；使相等；使平衡

E

ˌ**even-ˈhanded** *adj.* completely fair, especially when dealing with different groups of people 不偏不倚的；公正的；公平的

even·ing 🔑 /ˈiːvnɪŋ/ *noun*

1 🔑 [C, U] the part of the day between the afternoon and the time you go to bed 晚上；傍晚：*I'll see you tomorrow evening.* 我明天晚上來看你。◇ *Come over on Thursday evening.* 星期四晚上過來。◇ *What do you usually do* ***in the evening****?* 你晚上通常幹什麼？◇ *She's going to her sister's* ***for the evening****.* 她打算晚上到姐姐家去。◇ *the long winter evenings* 冬季漫長的夜晚 ◇ *the evening performance* 晚上的演出 ➲ see also GOOD EVENING **2** [C] an event of a particular type happening in the evening 晚會；晚間活動：*a musical evening at school* (= when music is performed) 學校的音樂晚會 ▸ **even·ings** *adv.*：(*especially NAmE*) *He works evenings.* 他晚上工作。 IDM see OTHER

ˈ**evening class** *noun* a course of study for adults in the evening 夜校課程：*an evening class in car maintenance* 夜校的汽車維修課程 ◇ *to* ***go to/attend evening classes*** 上夜校

ˈ**evening dress** *noun* **1** [U] elegant clothes worn for formal occasions in the evening 晚禮服：*Everyone was in evening dress.* 人人都身着晚禮服。 **2** [C] a woman's long formal dress 女裝晚禮服

ˌ**evening ˈprimrose** *noun* [C, U] a plant with yellow flowers that open in the evening, sometimes used as a medicine 月見草（晚間開黃花，有時作藥用）

the ˌ**evening ˈstar** *noun* [sing.] the planet Venus, when it is seen in the western sky after the sun has set 昏星（即太陽落山後出現於西方天空的金星）

even·ly /ˈiːvnli/ *adv.* **1** in a smooth, regular or equal way 平滑地；有規律地；均勻地；相等地：*Make sure the paint covers the surface evenly.* 要確保油漆均勻地塗在表面上。◇ *She was fast asleep, breathing evenly.* 她睡熟了，呼吸很平穩。◇ ***evenly spaced*** *at four cm apart* 以四厘米的間隔均勻分佈 **2** with equal amounts for each person or in each place 平均地；均等地：***evenly distributed/divided*** 平均分配／分開 ◇ *Incidence of the disease is fairly* ***evenly spread*** *across Europe.* 這種疾病的發生率在歐洲各地相當平均。◇ *The two teams are very* ***evenly matched*** (= are equally likely to win). 這兩個隊勢均力敵。 **3** calmly; without showing any emotion 平靜地；鎮靜地；平和地：*'I warned you not to phone me,' he said evenly.* "我告誡過你不要給我打電話。" 他平靜地說。

ˌ**even ˈmoney** *noun* (*BrE* also **evens** [pl.]) (in betting 賭博) ODDS that give an equal chance of winning or losing and that mean a person has the chance of winning the same amount of money that he or she has bet 同額賭注；均等的輸贏機會

even·song /ˈiːvnsɒŋ; *NAmE* -sɔːŋ; -sɑːŋ/ *noun* [U] the service of evening prayer in the Anglican Church（聖公會的）晚禱 ➲ compare MATINS, VESPERS

event 🔑 /ɪˈvent/ *noun*

1 🔑 a thing that happens, especially sth important 發生的事情；（尤指）重要事情，大事：*The election was the main event of 2008.* 那次選舉是 2008 年的重大事件。◇ *In the light of later events the decision was proved right.* 從後來發生的事看，這一決定證明是正確的。◇ *The decisions we take now may influence* ***the course of events*** (= the way things happen) *in the future.* 我們現在作出的決定可能會對未來事情的發展產生影響。◇ *Everyone was frightened by the strange* ***sequence of events****.* 人人都因接二連三發生的怪事感到驚恐。◇ ***In the normal course of events*** (= if things had happened as expected) *she would have gone with him.* 要是事情發展順利的話，她已同他一塊兒走了。 **2** 🔑 a planned public or social occasion 公開活動；社交場合：*a fund-raising event* 籌款活動 ◇ *the social event of the year* 本年度最重要的社交活動 **3** one of the races or competitions in a sports programme（體育運動的）比賽項目：*The 800 metres is the fourth event of the afternoon.* * 800 米賽是下午的第四項比賽。 ➲ see also FIELD EVENT, TRACK EVENT

IDM **after the eˈvent** (*BrE*) after sth has happened 事情發生後；事後：*Anyone can be wise after the event.* 事後聰明誰都會。 **in ˈany event | at ˈall events** used to emphasize or show that sth is true or will happen in spite of other circumstances 不管怎樣；無論如何 SYN **in any case**：*I think she'll agree to do it but in any event, all she can say is 'no'.* 我想她會同意做的，但無論怎樣，她只能說 "不"。 **in the eˈvent** when the situation actually happened 結果；到頭來：*I got very nervous about the exam, but in the event, I needn't have worried; it was really easy.* 我對考試提心吊膽，但其實我本不必擔心，這次考試的確很容易。 **in the event of sth | in the event that sth happens** 🔑 if sth happens 如果…發生；萬一；倘若：*In the event of an accident, call this number.* 萬一發生事故就撥這個號碼。◇ *Sheila will inherit everything in the event of his death.* 他一旦故去，所有財產都由希拉繼承。 **in ˈthat event** if that happens 如果是那樣的話；如果那種事情發生：*In that event, we will have to reconsider our offer.* 如果是那樣的話，我們就得重新考慮我們的建議。 ➲ more at HAPPY, WISE *adj.*

ˌ**even-ˈtempered** *adj.* not easily made angry or upset 性情平和的

event·ful /ɪˈventfl/ *adj.* full of things that happen, especially exciting, important or dangerous things 充滿大事的；多事故的；多變故的：*an eventful day/life/journey* 不平凡的一天；多姿多彩的一生／旅程

even·tide /ˈiːvntaɪd/ *noun* [U] (*old use* or *literary*) evening 黃昏；薄暮

event·ing /ɪˈventɪŋ/ (also ˌ**three-day eˈventing**) *noun* [U] the sport of taking part in competitions riding horses. These are often held over three days and include riding across country, jumping and DRESSAGE. 馬術比賽，馬術三日賽（包括越野賽、超越障礙賽和花式騎術）

even·tual AW /ɪˈventʃuəl/ *adj.* [only before noun] happening at the end of a period of time or of a process 最後的；最終的；結果的：*the eventual winner of the tournament* 錦標賽的最終勝利者 ◇ *It is impossible to predict what the eventual outcome will be.* 無法預測最終結果會怎麼樣。◇ *The village school may face eventual closure.* 這所鄉村學校可能面臨最後被關閉。

even·tu·al·ity AW /ɪˌventʃuˈæləti/ *noun* (*pl.* **-ies**) (*formal*) something that may possibly happen, especially sth unpleasant（尤指令人不快的）可能發生的事情，可能出現的結果：*We were prepared for* ***every eventuality****.* 我們已做好準備應付任何可能出現的情況。◇ *The money had been saved* ***for just such an eventuality****.* 錢積攢下來就是為應付這樣的意外。

even·tu·al·ly 🔑 AW /ɪˈventʃuəli/ *adv.* at the end of a period of time or a series of events 最後；終於：*Our flight eventually left five hours late.* 我們的班機最終晚了五個小時起飛。◇ *I'll get round to mending it eventually.* 我最後會抽出時間來修理它的。◇ *She hopes to get a job on the local newspaper and eventually work for 'The Times'.* 她希望先在當地報社找一份工作，而最後可以到《泰晤士報》工作。 HELP Use **finally** for the last in a list of things. 列舉事物中的最後一項用 finally。

even·tu·ate /ɪˈventʃueɪt/ *verb* [I] (*formal*) to happen as a result of sth 導致；最終造成

ever 0→ /ˈevə(r)/ *adv.*
1 0→ used in negative sentences and questions, or sentences with *if* to mean 'at any time'（用於否定句和疑問句，或與 if 連用的句子）在任何時候，從來：*Nothing ever happens here.* 這兒從未發生過任何事。◇ *Don't you ever get tired?* 難道你從來不累嗎？◇ *If you're ever in Miami, come and see us.* 你要是什麼時候到了邁阿密，就來看看我們吧。◇ *'Have you ever thought of changing your job?' 'No, never/No I haven't.'* "你想過換一下工作嗎？" "沒有，從未想過。" ◇ *'Have you ever been to Rome?' 'Yes, I have, actually. Not long ago.'* "你去過羅馬嗎？" "是的，我確實去過，就在不久前。" ◇ *She* **hardly ever** (= almost never) *goes out.* 她幾乎從不出門。◇ *We see them very seldom,* **if ever**. 我們難得見到他們。◇ (*informal*) *I'll* **never ever** *do that again!* 我再也不會幹那種事了！ **2** 0→ used for emphasis when you are comparing things（進行比較時用以加強語氣）以往任何時候，曾經：*It was raining harder than ever.* 當時下着前所未有的大雨。◇ *It's my* **best ever** *score.* 這是我得到過的最好分數。 **3** (*rather formal*) all the time or every time; always 不斷地；總是；始終：*Paul, ever the optimist, agreed to try again.* 保羅這個永遠的樂觀主義者答應再試一次。◇ *She married the prince and they* **lived happily ever after**. 她與王子成了婚，從此過着幸福的生活。◇ *He said he would love her* **for ever** (**and ever**). 他説會永遠愛她。◇ *Their debts grew ever larger* (= kept increasing). 他們的債務不斷增加。◇ *the ever-growing problem* 日趨嚴重的問題 ◇ *an ever-present danger* 始終存在的危險 **4** used after *when, why*, etc. to show that you are surprised or shocked（用於 when、why 等之後表示驚訝）究竟，到底：*Why ever did you agree?* 你究竟為什麼要同意？

IDM **all sb ever does is …** used to emphasize that sb does the same thing very often, usually in an annoying way 某人只會／就知道做某事：*All he ever does is grumble about things.* 他只會抱怨。 **did you 'ever (…)!** (*old-fashioned, informal*) used to show that you are surprised or shocked（表示驚訝）你曾…過嗎：*Did you ever hear anything like it?* 你聽到過這種事嗎？ **ever since (…)** 0→ continuously since the time mentioned 自從；自…以後；從…起：*He's had a car ever since he was 18.* 他從 18 歲起就有汽車了。◇ *I was bitten by a dog once and I've been afraid of them ever since.* 我曾被狗咬過，自那以後就一直害怕狗。 **'ever so/'ever such a** (*informal, especially BrE*) very; really 非常；很；確實；的確：*He looks ever so smart.* 他樣子很帥。◇ *She's ever such a nice woman.* 她是個非常好的女人。◇ *It's ever so easy.* 這非常容易。 **if ˌever there 'was (one)** (*informal*) used to emphasize that sth is certainly true（用以加強語氣）確實，無可置疑，真正地：*That was a disaster if ever there was one!* 那確實是場災難！ **was/is/does, etc. sb 'ever!** (*informal, especially NAmE*) used to emphasize sth you are talking about 確實如此；千真萬確；一點兒不差：*'You must have been upset by that.' 'Was I ever!'* "你一定曾為那事而心煩了。" "可不是嘛！" **yours 'ever/ever 'yours** sometimes used at the end of an informal letter, before you write your name（有時用於非正式書信末尾署名前）你的永遠的朋友

ever·green /ˈevəɡriːn; *NAmE* ˈevərɡ-/ *noun* a tree or bush that has green leaves all through the year 常青樹；常綠樹 ➲ VISUAL VOCAB page V10 ➲ compare CONIFER, DECIDUOUS ▸ **ever·green** *adj.*：*evergreen shrubs* 常青灌木 ◇ (*figurative*) *a new production of Rossini's evergreen* (= always popular) *opera* 經久不衰的羅西尼歌劇的重新製作

ever·last·ing /ˌevəˈlɑːstɪŋ; *NAmE* ˌevərˈlæstɪŋ/ *adj.*
1 continuing for ever; never changing 永久的；永恆的；經久不變的 SYN **eternal**：*everlasting life/love* 永生；永恆的愛 ◇ *an everlasting memory of her smile* 她的微笑留下的永久回憶 ◇ **To his everlasting credit**, *he never told anyone what I'd done.* 值得永遠稱讚的是他從未把我做的事告訴過任何人。 **2** (*disapproving*) continuing too long; repeated too often 冗長的；持續過長的；重複太多的 SYN **constant, interminable, never-ending**：*I'm tired of your everlasting complaints.* 我討厭你沒完沒了的抱怨。 ▸ **ever·last·ing·ly** *adv.*

ever·more /ˌevəˈmɔː(r); *NAmE* ˌevərˈm-/ (also **for ever'more**) *adv.* (*literary*) always 始終；永遠

every 0→ /ˈevri/ *det.*
1 0→ used with singular nouns to refer to all the members of a group of things or people（與單數名詞連用，指整體中的）每一個，每個：*She knows every student in the school.* 她認識學校裏的每一個學生。◇ *I could hear every word they said.* 他們説的每句話我都能聽見。◇ *We enjoyed every minute of our stay.* 我們逗留期間每一分鐘都過得很愉快。◇ *Every day seemed the same to him.* 對他來説似乎天天都一樣。◇ **Every single** *time he calls, I'm out.* 他每次打電話來我都不在家。◇ *I read* **every last** *article in the newspaper* (= all of them). 報紙上的每一篇文章我都讀。◇ *They were watching her every movement.* 他們注視着她的每一個動作。◇ *Every one of their CDs has been a hit.* 他們的每一張激光唱片都曾經非常流行。➲ note at EACH **2** 0→ all possible 所有可能的；完全可能的：*We wish you every success.* 我們祝你萬事如意。◇ *He had every reason to be angry.* 他完全有理由感到憤怒。 **3** 0→ used to say how often sth happens or is done（表示發生的頻率）每，每逢，每隔：*The buses go every 10 minutes.* 公共汽車每隔 10 分鐘發一班車。◇ *We had to stop every few miles.* 我們每走幾英里就得停一停。◇ *One in every three marriages ends in divorce.* 三分之一的婚姻都以離婚告終。◇ *He has every third day off* (= he works for two days then has one day off then works for two days and so on). 他每隔兩天休息一天。◇ *We see each other* **every now and again**. 我們偶爾相見。◇ **Every now and then** *he regretted his decision.* 他有時為自己的決定後悔。

IDM **every other** 0→ each ALTERNATE one (= the first, third, fifth, etc. one, but not the second, fourth, sixth, etc.) 每隔一個：*They visit us every other week.* 他們隔週來看我們一次。

every·body 0→ /ˈevribɒdi; *NAmE* -bɑːdi; -bʌdi/ *pron.* = EVERYONE：*Everybody knows Tom.* 人人都認識湯姆。◇ *Have you asked everybody?* 你每個人都問了嗎？◇ *Didn't you like it?* **Everybody else** *did.* 你不喜歡嗎？其他所有人都喜歡。

every·day /ˈevrideɪ/ *adj.* [only before noun] used or happening every day or regularly; ordinary 每天的；每日發生的；日常的：*everyday objects* 日常物品 ◇ *The Internet has become part of* **everyday life**. 互聯網已成為日常生活的一部份。◇ *a small dictionary for everyday use* 常用小詞典

Every·man /ˈevrimæn/ *noun* [sing.] an ordinary or typical person 普通人；常人：*a story of Everyman* 尋常百姓的故事

every·one 0→ /ˈevriwʌn/ (also **every·body**) *pron.* every person; all people 每人；人人；所有人：*Everyone cheered and clapped.* 人人都鼓掌歡呼。◇ *Everyone has a chance to win.* 每個人都有機會贏。◇ *Everyone brought their partner to the party.* 所有人都攜伴參加聚會。◇ (*formal*) *Everyone brought his or her partner to the party.* 每個人都攜伴參加聚會。◇ *The police questioned everyone in the room.* 警方盤問了房間裏的每一個人。◇ *The teacher commented on everyone's work.* 老師對每個人的作業都給了評語。◇ **Everyone else** *was there.* 其他所有人都在那兒。

every·place /ˈevripleɪs/ *adv.* (*NAmE*) = EVERYWHERE

every·thing 0→ /ˈevriθɪŋ/ *pron.* (with a singular verb 與單數動詞連用)
1 0→ all things 每件事；所有事物；一切：*Everything had gone.* 一切都過去了。◇ *When we confronted him, he denied everything.* 我們與他當面對質時，他什麼都不承認。◇ *Take this bag, and leave* **everything else** *to me.* 把這個包拿走，其他所有東西都給我留下。◇ *She seemed to* **have everything**—*looks, money, intelligence.* 她似乎什麼都有了——美貌、金錢和智慧。 **2** 0→ the situation now; life generally 形勢；情況；生活：*Everything in the capital is now quiet.* 目前首都的形勢很平靜。◇ *'How's everything with you?' 'Fine, thanks.'* "你一切都好嗎？" "很好，謝謝。" **3** 0→ the most important thing 最重要的東西；最要緊的事情：*Money isn't everything.* 金錢不是最重要的。◇ *My family* **means everything** *to me.* 對我來説家庭意味着一切。

E

IDM **and everything** (*informal*) and so on; and other similar things 以及其他；等等：*Have you got his name and address and everything?* 你知道他的名字、地址及其他情况吗？◇ *She told me about the baby and everything.* 她向我讲了小宝宝和其他的情况。

every·where 0‑π /ˈevriweə(r); *NAmE* -wer/ (*NAmE* also **every·place**) *adv., pron., conj.* in, to or at every place; all places 處處；到處；各個地方；所有地方：*I've looked everywhere.* 我各處都看過了。◇ *He follows me everywhere.* 我無論去哪兒他都跟着我。◇ *We'll have to eat here—**everywhere else** is full.* 我們只好在這兒吃飯了，其他地方都客滿。◇ *Everywhere we went was full of tourists.* 我們所到之處遊客人頭攢動。

E

evict /ɪˈvɪkt/ *verb* **~ sb (from sth)** to force sb to leave a house or land, especially when you have the legal right to do so（尤指依法從房屋或土地上）驅逐，趕出，逐出：*A number of tenants have been evicted for not paying the rent.* 一些房客因不付房租被趕了出來。▸ **evic·tion** /ɪˈvɪkʃn/ *noun* [U, C]：*to face eviction from your home* 面臨着被趕出家門

Language Bank 用語庫

evidence

Giving proof 提供證據

- **There is clear evidence that** TV advertising influences what children buy. 有明確的證據表明電視廣告影響兒童的購買行為。
- **It is clear** from numerous studies **that** TV advertising influences what children buy. 眾多研究清楚地表明電視廣告影響兒童的購買行為。
- Recent research **demonstrates** that TV advertising influences children's spending habits. 最近的研究表明電視廣告影響兒童的消費習慣。
- Many parents think that TV advertising influences their children. This view **is supported by** the findings of a recent study, which **show** a clear link between television advertisements and children's spending habits. 許多家長認為電視廣告對他們的孩子會產生影響。這一觀點得到近期的研究結果的支持，即電視廣告和兒童消費習慣之間有明顯的關聯。
- The findings also **reveal** that most children are unaware of the persuasive purpose of advertising. 這些研究結果還顯示大多數兒童沒有意識到廣告的說服意圖。
- **There is little evidence that** children understand the persuasive intent of advertising. 幾乎沒有證據表明兒童能夠理解廣告的說服意圖。
- The results **contradict** claims that advertising is unrelated to children's spending habits. 這些研究結果否定了廣告與兒童消費習慣無關的說法。
- Manufacturers argue that it is difficult to **prove** that advertising alone influences what children buy. 生產廠商爭辯說，很難證明單憑廣告就能影響兒童的購買行為。

➲ Language Banks at ARGUE, E.G., ILLUSTRATE

evi·dence 0‑π AW /ˈevɪdəns/ *noun, verb*

■ *noun* **1** 0‑π [U, C] the facts, signs or objects that make you believe that sth is true 根據；證明；證據：**~ (of sth)** *There is convincing evidence of a link between exposure to sun and skin cancer.* 有可靠證據表明日光曝曬與皮膚癌之間有聯繫。◇ *The room bore evidence of a struggle.* 房間裏有搏鬥過的痕跡。◇ **~ (for sth)** *We found further scientific evidence for this theory.* 我們找到了進一步證實這種理論的科學根據。◇ **~ (that ...)** *There is **not a shred of evidence** that the meeting actually took place.* 沒有絲毫證據表明這個會議確已舉行。◇ **~ (to suggest, show, etc.)** *Have you any evidence to support this allegation?* 你有證據支持這種說法嗎？◇ ***On the evidence of*** *their recent matches, it is unlikely the Spanish team will win the cup.* 從西班牙隊最近的比賽情況看，他們不太可能奪冠。**2** 0‑π [U] the information that is used in court to try to prove sth（法庭上的）證據，證詞，人證，物證：*I was asked to **give evidence*** (= to say what I knew, describe what I had seen, etc.) *at the trial.* 我被要求審訊時出庭作證。◇ *He was released when the judge ruled there was no evidence against him.* 法官裁決沒有證明他有罪的證據，他獲得釋放了。➲ COLLOCATIONS at JUSTICE ➲ see also CIRCUMSTANTIAL (1)

IDM **(be) in ˈevidence** present and clearly seen 顯眼；顯而易見：*The police were much in evidence at today's demonstration.* 在今天的示威集會上警察隨處可見。**turn King's/Queen's ˈevidence** (*BrE*) (*US* **turn state's ˈevidence**) to give information against other criminals in order to get a less severe punishment 提供同犯的罪證，揭發其他案犯（以減輕所受懲罰）➲ compare PLEA-BARGAINING ➲ more at BALANCE *n.*

■ *verb* [usually passive] **~ sth** (*formal*) to prove or show sth; to be evidence of sth 證明；表明；作為…的證據 SYN **testify to**：*The legal profession is still a largely male world, **as evidenced by** the small number of women judges.* 法律界在很大程度上仍然是男人的世界，這一點從女法官的人數屈指可數即可得到證實。

evi·dent AW /ˈevɪdənt/ *adj.* clear; easily seen 清楚的；顯而易見的；顯然的 SYN **obvious**：*The orchestra played with evident enjoyment.* 管弦樂隊演奏得興致勃勃。◇ **~ (to sb) (that ...)** *It has now become evident to us that a mistake has been made.* 我們現已清楚知道出了差錯。◇ **~ in/from sth** *The growing interest in history is clearly evident in the number of people visiting museums and country houses.* 從參觀博物館和鄉村住宅的人數明顯看出人們對歷史越來越感興趣。➲ SYNONYMS at CLEAR ➲ see also SELF-EVIDENT

evi·den·tial AW /ˌevɪˈdenʃl/ *adj.* [usually before noun] (*formal*) providing or connected with evidence 提供證據的；作證的：*The necessary evidential basis for her claim is lacking.* 她的訴求缺乏必要的基本憑據。

evi·dent·ly AW /ˈevɪdəntli/ *adv.* **1** clearly; that can be seen or understood easily 明顯地；顯然地 SYN **obviously**：*She walked slowly down the road, evidently in pain.* 她沿路慢慢地走着，顯然很痛苦。◇ *'I'm afraid I couldn't finish the work last night.' 'Evidently not.'* "對不起，昨天晚上我沒能完成工作。" "顯然完不成。" **2** according to what people say 據說 SYN **apparently**：*Evidently, she had nothing to do with the whole affair.* 據說，她與整件事情毫無關係。

evil 0‑π /ˈiːvl; ˈiːvɪl/ *adj., noun*

■ *adj.* **1** 0‑π (of people 人) enjoying harming others; morally bad and cruel 惡毒的；邪惡的：*an evil man* 惡棍 ◇ *an evil grin* 獰笑 **2** 0‑π having a harmful effect on people; morally bad 有害的；道德敗壞的：*evil deeds* 惡行 ◇ *the evil effects of racism* 種族主義的惡劣影響 **3** 0‑π connected with the DEVIL and with what is bad in the world 惡魔的；罪惡的：*evil spirits* 邪靈 **4** extremely unpleasant 討厭的；令人作嘔的；使人不舒服的：*an evil smell* 難聞的氣味

IDM **the evil ˈhour/ˈday/ˈmoment** (often *humorous*) the time when you have to do sth difficult or unpleasant 倒霉的時候（或日子、時刻）➲ more at BREW *n.*, GENIUS *n.*

■ *noun* (*formal*) **1** 0‑π [U] a force that causes bad things to happen; morally bad behaviour 邪惡；罪惡；惡行：*the eternal struggle between good and evil* 善與惡永不休止的鬥爭 ◇ *the forces of evil* 邪惡勢力 ◇ *You cannot pretend there's no evil in the world.* 你不能睜着眼睛瞎說世界上沒有罪惡。OPP **good** **2** 0‑π [C, usually pl.] a bad or harmful thing; the bad effect of sth 害處；壞處；弊端：*the evils of drugs/alcohol* 毒品／酒的害處 ◇ *social evils* 社會弊端
IDM see LESSER, NECESSARY

ˈevil-doer *noun* (*formal*) a person who does very bad things 作惡的人；壞人

the ˌevil ˈeye *noun* [sing.] the magic power to harm sb by looking at them 惡毒的眼光，惡目（傳說能傷人）

evil·ly /ˈiːvəli/ *adv.* in a morally bad or very unpleasant way 邪惡地；陰險地：*to grin evilly* 獰笑 ◇ *to look evilly at sb* 邪惡地看着某人

evince /ɪ'vɪns/ *verb* **~ sth** (*formal*) to show clearly that you have a feeling or quality 表明，表現，顯示（感情或品質）：*He evinced a strong desire to be reconciled with his family.* 他表現出與家人和好的強烈願望。

evis·cer·ate /ɪ'vɪsəreɪt/ *verb* **~ sth** (*formal*) to remove the inner organs of a body 切除內臟；切除…的內部器官 SYN **disembowel**

evoca·tive /ɪ'vɒkətɪv; *NAmE* ɪ'vɑːk-/ *adj.* making you think of or remember a strong image or feeling, in a pleasant way 引起記憶的；喚起感情的：***evocative smells/sounds/music*** 引起回憶的氣味／聲音／音樂◇ **~ of sth** *Her new book is wonderfully evocative of village life.* 她的新書喚起人們對鄉村生活的美好感情。

evoke /ɪ'vəʊk; *NAmE* ɪ'voʊk/ *verb* **~ sth** (*formal*) to bring a feeling, a memory or an image into your mind 引起，喚起（感情、記憶或形象）：*The music **evoked memories** of her youth.* 這樂曲勾起了她對青年時代的回憶。◇ *His case is unlikely to evoke public sympathy.* 他的情況不大可能引起公眾的同情。▶ **evo·ca·tion** /ˌiːvəʊ'keɪʃn; *NAmE* ˌiːvoʊ-/ *noun* [C, U]：*a brilliant evocation of childhood in the 1940s* 喚起對 20 世紀 40 年代童年生活的美好回憶

evo·lu·tion AW /ˌiːvə'luːʃn; ˌev-/ *noun* [U] **1** (*biology* 生) the gradual development of plants, animals, etc. over many years as they adapt to changes in their environment 進化：*the evolution of the human species* 人類的進化◇ *Darwin's theory of evolution* 達爾文的進化論 **2** the gradual development of sth 演變；發展；漸進：*In politics Britain has preferred evolution to revolution* (= gradual development to sudden violent change). 英國在政治上寧願漸進而不願革命。

evo·lu·tion·ary AW /ˌiːvə'luːʃənri; ˌev-; *NAmE* -neri/ *adj.* connected with evolution; connected with gradual development and change 進化的；演變的；逐漸發展的：*evolutionary theory* 進化論◇ *evolutionary change* 逐漸演變 ▶ **evo·lu·tion·ar·ily** *adv.*

evo·lu·tion·ist AW /ˌiːvə'luːʃnɪst; ˌev-/ *noun, adj.*
■ ***noun*** a person who believes in the theories of EVOLUTION and NATURAL SELECTION 進化論者
■ ***adj.*** relating to the theories of EVOLUTION and NATURAL SELECTION 進化論的 ▶ **evo·lu·tion·ism** /ˌiːvə'luːʃnɪzəm; ˌev-/ *noun*

evolve AW /i'vɒlv; *NAmE* i'vɑːlv/ *verb* **1** [I, T] to develop gradually, especially from a simple to a more complicated form; to develop sth in this way（使）逐漸形成，逐步發展，逐漸演變：**~ (from sth) (into sth)** *The idea evolved from a drawing I discovered in the attic.* 這種想法是從我在閣樓裏發現的一幅畫得到啟發的。◇ *The company has evolved into a major chemical manufacturer.* 這家公司已逐步發展成一家大型的化工廠。◇ **~ sth (from sth)** *Each school must evolve its own way of working.* 每所學校必須發展出自己的辦學方式。 **2** [I, T] (*biology* 生) (of plants, animals, etc. 動植物等) to develop over time, often many generations, into forms that are better adapted to survive changes in their environment 進化；演化：**~ (from sth)** *The three species evolved from a single ancestor.* 這三種生物從同一祖先進化而來。◇ **~ sth** *The dolphin has evolved a highly developed jaw.* 海豚已經進化形成高度發達的下頜。

ewe /juː/ *noun* a female sheep 母羊；雌羊；牝羊 ➲ compare RAM *n.* (1)

ewer /'juːə(r)/ *noun* a large JUG used in the past for carrying water（舊時提水用的）大口水壺，大口水罐

ex /eks/ *noun, prep.*
■ ***noun*** (*pl.* **exes**) (*informal*) a person's former wife, husband or partner 前妻；前夫；以前的性伴侶：*The children are spending the weekend with my ex and his new wife.* 孩子們與我的前夫及其新夫人在一起度週末。
■ ***prep.*** (*BrE*) not including sth 不包括；除…之外：*The price is £1 500 ex VAT.* 價格為 1 500 英鎊，不包括增值稅。

ex- 0┳ /eks/ *prefix* (in nouns 構成名詞) former 前任：*ex-wife* 前妻◇ *ex-president* 前總裁

ex·acer·bate /ɪg'zæsəbeɪt; *NAmE* ɪg'zæsərb-/ *verb* **~ sth** (*formal*) to make sth worse, especially a disease or problem 使惡化；使加劇；使加重 SYN **aggravate**：*The symptoms may be exacerbated by certain drugs.* 這些症狀可能會因為某些藥物而加重。▶ **ex·acer·ba·tion** *noun* [U, C]

exact 0┳ /ɪg'zækt/ *adj., verb*
■ ***adj.*** **1** 0┳ correct in every detail 精確的；準確的 SYN **precise**：*She gave an exact description of the attacker.* 她對襲擊者的特徵作了精確的描述。◇ ***an exact copy/replica*** *of the painting* 那幅畫的精確複製品◇ *We need to know the exact time the incident occurred.* 我們需要瞭解事情發生的確切時間。◇ *What were his exact words?* 他的原話是什麼？◇ *She's in her mid-thirties—thirty-six **to be exact**.* 她三十五歲左右，確切地說是三十六歲。◇ *The colours were an exact match.* 顏色極為協調。◇ *He started to phone me at the exact moment I started to phone him* (= at the same time). 他開始給我打電話時，我也正好開始給他打電話。◇ *Her second husband was **the exact opposite** of her first* (= completely different). 她的第二任丈夫與第一任截然不同。 **2** 0┳ (of people 人) very accurate and careful about details 嚴謹的；嚴格的；一絲不苟的 SYN **meticulous, precise** **3** (of a science 科學) using accurate measurements and following set rules 精密的；嚴密的 SYN **precise**：*Assessing insurance risk can never be an exact science.* 估定承保的風險永遠不會成為一門精確的科學。▶ **exact·ness** *noun* [U]
■ ***verb*** (*formal*) **1 ~ sth (from sb)** to demand and get sth from sb 要求；索取：*She was determined to exact a promise from him.* 她決意要他作出許諾。 **2** to make sth bad happen to sb 迫使；強迫；強求：**~ sth** *He exacted* (= took) *a terrible revenge for their treatment of him.* 他因受他們的虐待而痛加報復。◇ **~ sth from sb** *Stress can exact a high price from workers* (= can affect them badly). 壓力可能迫使工人付出昂貴的代價。▶ **exac·tion** /ɪg'zækʃn/ *noun* [C, U] (*formal*)

exact·ing /ɪg'zæktɪŋ/ *adj.* needing or demanding a lot of effort and care about details 需要付出很大努力的；要求小心仔細的；要求嚴格的 SYN **demanding**：*exacting work* 艱巨的工作◇ *products designed to meet the exacting standards of today's marketplace* 為符合當今市場嚴格的標準而設計的產品◇ *He was an exacting man to work for.* 他對手下的人要求極為嚴格。

exac·ti·tude /ɪg'zæktɪtjuːd; *NAmE* -tuːd/ *noun* [U] (*formal*) the quality of being very accurate and exact 精確性；準確性；嚴密性

exact·ly 0┳ /ɪg'zæktli/ *adv.*
1 0┳ used to emphasize that sth is correct in every way or in every detail 精確地；準確地；確切地 SYN **precisely**：*I know exactly how she felt.* 我完全清楚她的感受。◇ *Do exactly as I tell you.* 按我說的照辦。◇ *It happened almost exactly a year ago.* 這事情發生差不多正好一年了。◇ *It's exactly nine o'clock.* 現在是九點整。◇ *You haven't changed at all—you still look **exactly the same**.* 你一點沒變，看上去依然是老樣子。◇ *His words had **exactly the opposite** effect.* 他的話產生了截然相反的效果。◇ *Your answer is exactly right.* 你的回答完全正確。◇ *It was a warm day, if not exactly hot.* 這一天即使算不上熱，也是一個暖和的日子。 **2** 0┳ (*informal*) used to ask for more information about sth（要求得到更多信息）究竟，到底：*Where exactly did you stay in France?* 你究竟待在法國什麼地方？◇ (*disapproving*) *Exactly what are you trying to tell me?* 你到底想對我說什麼？ **3** 0┳ used as a reply, agreeing with what sb has just said, or emphasizing that it is correct（答語，表示贊同或強調正確）一點不錯，正是如此，完全正確：*'You mean somebody in this room must be the murderer?' 'Exactly.'* "你的意思是這屋子裏肯定有人是兇手？" "正是。"

IDM **not exactly** (*informal*) **1** 0┳ used when you are saying the opposite of what you really mean（說反話時用）根本不，決不，一點也不：*He wasn't exactly pleased to see us—in fact he refused to open the door.* 他根本不願見我們，事實上他連門都不開。◇ *It's not exactly beautiful, is it?* (= it's ugly) 這一點也不美，是嗎？ **2** 0┳ used when you are correcting sth that sb has said（糾正對方剛說過的話）不完全：*'So he told you you'd got the job?' 'Not exactly, but he said they were impressed with me.'* "如此看來，他對你說你得到這份工

作了？”“不完全是這樣，不過他說我給他們留下了深刻的印象。”

ex·ag·ger·ate /ɪɡˈzædʒəreɪt/ *verb* [I, T] to make sth seem larger, better, worse or more important than it really is 誇張；誇大；言過其實：*The hotel was really filthy and I'm not exaggerating.* 我不是誇張，這旅店真的很髒。◇ **~ sth** *He tends to exaggerate the difficulties.* 他往往誇大困難。◇ *I'm sure he exaggerates his Irish accent* (= tries to sound more Irish than he really is). 我肯定他故意把愛爾蘭口音說得很重。◇ *Demand for the product has been greatly exaggerated.* 對這項產品的需求給過分誇大了。

ex·ag·ger·ated /ɪɡˈzædʒəreɪtɪd/ *adj.* **1** made to seem larger, better, worse or more important than it really is or needs to be 誇張的；誇大的；言過其實的：*to make* ***greatly/grossly/wildly exaggerated*** *claims* 提出極為過分的索償 ◇ *She has an exaggerated sense of her own importance.* 她自視過高。**2** (of an action 行為) done in a way that makes people notice it 故作姿態的；矯揉造作的：*He looked at me with exaggerated surprise.* 他故作吃驚地看着我。▸ **ex·ag·ger·ated·ly** *adv.*

ex·ag·ger·ation /ɪɡˌzædʒəˈreɪʃn/ *noun* [C, usually sing., U] a statement or description that makes sth seem larger, better, worse or more important than it really is; the act of making a statement like this 誇張；誇大；言過其實：*a* ***slight/gross/wild exaggeration*** 有點／明顯的／胡亂的誇張 ◇ *It would be an exaggeration to say I knew her well—I only met her twice.* 說我非常瞭解她不免言過其實，我只見過她兩次。◇ *It's no exaggeration to say that most students have never read a complete Shakespeare play.* 說大多數同學從未讀過一部完整的莎士比亞戲劇一點也不誇張。◇ *He told his story simply and without exaggeration.* 他簡單扼要、毫不誇張地講述了自己的故事。

exalt /ɪɡˈzɔːlt/ *verb* (*formal*) **1 ~ sb** (**to sth**) to make sb rise to a higher rank or position, sometimes to one that they do not deserve 提拔，提升（有時指不該得到的職位）**2 ~ sb/sth** to praise sb/sth very much 表揚；褒揚；高度讚揚

exalt·ation /ˌeɡzɔːlˈteɪʃn/ *noun* [U] (*formal*) **1** a feeling of very great joy or happiness 興奮；興高采烈 **2** an act of raising sth/sb to a high position or rank 提高；晉升；提拔：*the exaltation of emotion above logical reasoning* 把情感提高到邏輯推理之上

exalt·ed /ɪɡˈzɔːltɪd/ *adj.* **1** (*formal or humorous*) of high rank, position or great importance 地位高的；高貴的；顯赫的：*She was the only woman to rise to such an exalted position.* 她是唯一晉升到如此顯赫地位的女人。◇ *You're moving in very exalted circles!* 你這是出入於顯貴要人的圈子呀！**2** (*formal*) full of great joy and happiness 興奮的；興高采烈的：*I felt exalted and newly alive.* 我感到興高采烈，充滿新的活力。

More About 補充說明

exams

- **Exam** is the usual word for a written, spoken or practical test at school or college, especially an important one that you need to do in order to get a qualification. **Examination** is a very formal word. A **test** is something that students might be given in addition to, or sometimes instead of, regular exams, to see how much they have learned. A very short informal test is called a **quiz** in *NAmE*. **Quiz** in both *NAmE* and *BrE* also means a contest in which people try to answer questions. * exam 為常用詞，指學校的筆試、口試或實習考試，尤指為取得學歷必須參加的重要考試。examination 是很正式的詞。test 是指除正規考試外，對學生所學知識的測驗，有時也取代正規考試。在美式英語中非正規的小測驗稱為 quiz；在美式英語和英式英語中 quiz 亦指問答競賽：*a trivia quiz* 難題問答競賽 ◇ *a quiz show* 問答競賽節目

exam /ɪɡˈzæm/ (also *formal* **exam·in·ation**) *noun* **1** a formal written, spoken or practical test, especially at school or college, to see how much you know about a subject, or what you can do（筆頭、口頭或實習）考試：*to* ***take an exam*** 參加考試 ◇ *to* ***pass/fail an exam*** 考試合格／不合格 ◇ *an* ***exam paper*** 試卷 ◇ *I got my* ***exam results*** *today.* 我今天得到了考試成績。◇ *A lot of students suffer from* ***exam nerves***. 許多學生考試怯陣。◇ (*BrE*) *I hate* ***doing exams***. 我不喜歡參加考試。◇ (*BrE, formal*) *to* ***sit an exam*** 參加考試 ◇ (*BrE*) *to* ***mark an exam*** 閱卷評分 ◇ (*NAmE*) *to* ***grade an exam*** 閱卷評分 ◇ (*BrE*) *She did well* ***in her exams***. 她考試考得好。◇ (*NAmE*) *She did well* ***on her exams***. 她考試考得好。➲ COLLOCATIONS at EDUCATION **2** (*NAmE*) a medical test of a particular part of the body（對身體特定部位進行的）檢查；體檢：*an eye exam* 眼睛檢查

exam·in·ation /ɪɡˌzæmɪˈneɪʃn/ *noun* **1** [C] (*formal*) = EXAM：*to sit an examination in mathematics* 參加數學考試 ◇ *successful candidates in GCSE examinations* 通過普通中等教育證書考試的考生 ◇ *Applicants are selected for jobs on the results of a competitive examination.* 競聘者按遴選考試結果擇優錄用。**HELP** Use: ***take/do/sit an examination*** not ~~*write an examination*~~. 可以說 take/do/sit an examination，不作 write an examination。**2** [U, C] the act of looking at or considering sth very carefully 審查；調查；考查；考察：*Careful examination of the ruins revealed an even earlier temple.* 仔細考察這片廢墟後發現了一座更為古老的廟宇。◇ ***On closer examination*** *it was found that the signature was not genuine.* 經過進一步認真檢查發現簽名是偽造的。◇ *Your proposals are still* ***under examination***. 你的提議仍在審查之中。◇ *The issue needs* ***further examination***. 這個問題需要進一步考查。◇ *The chapter concludes with a brief examination of some of the factors causing family break-up.* 本章結束時簡要考查了引起家庭破裂的某些因素。**3** [C] a close look at sth/sb, especially to see if there is anything wrong or to find the cause of a problem（仔細的）檢查，檢驗：*a medical examination* 體格檢查 ◇ *a post-mortem examination* 驗屍 ➲ see also CROSS-EXAMINATION at CROSS-EXAMINE

exam·ine /ɪɡˈzæmɪn/ *verb* **1** to consider or study an idea, a subject, etc. very carefully 審查；調查；考查；考察：**~ sth** *These ideas will be examined in more detail in Chapter 10.* 這些觀點將在第 10 章作更為詳細的探討。◇ **~ how, what, etc.** … *It is necessary to examine how the proposals can be carried out.* 有必要調查一下怎樣才能實施這些方案。➲ LANGUAGE BANK at ABOUT **2** to look at sb/sth closely, to see if there is anything wrong or to find the cause of a problem（仔細地）檢查，檢驗：**~ sb/sth** *The doctor examined her but could find nothing wrong.* 醫生給她做了檢查，但沒發現什麼問題。◇ **~ sth/sb for sth** *The goods were examined for damage on arrival.* 貨物到達時檢查是否有破損。➲ SYNONYMS at CHECK **3 ~ sb** (**in/on sth**) (*formal*) to give sb a test to see how much they know about a subject or what they can do 考，測驗（某人）：*The students will be examined in all subjects at the end of term.* 期末時學生須要參加所有學科的考試。◇ *You are only being examined on this semester's work.* 現在只考你在本學期學的課程。**4 ~ sb** (*law* 律) to ask sb questions formally, especially in court（尤指在法庭上）審問，查問 ➲ see also CROSS-EXAMINE **IDM** see NEED *v.*

exam·inee /ɪɡˌzæmɪˈniː/ *noun* a person who is being tested to see how much they know about a subject or what they can do; a person who is taking an exam 應試人；參加考試者

exam·in·er /ɪɡˈzæmɪnə(r)/ *noun* **1** a person who writes the questions for, or marks/grades, a test of knowledge or ability 主考人；考官：*The papers are sent to* ***external examiners*** (= ones not connected with the students' school or college). 試卷送到校外主考人那裏。**2** (*especially NAmE*) a person who has the official duty to check that things are being done correctly and according to the rules of an organization; a person who officially examines sth 審查人；檢查人 ➲ see also MEDICAL EXAMINER

Synonyms 同義詞辨析

examine

analyse • review • study • discuss

These words all mean to think about, study or describe sb/sth carefully, especially in order to understand them, form an opinion of them or make a decision about them. 以上各詞均含思量、審查、調查、研究之意。

examine to think about, study or describe an idea, subject or piece of work very carefully 指審查、調查、考查、考察：*These ideas will be examined in more detail in Chapter 10.* 這些觀點將在第 10 章作更為詳細的探討。

analyse/analyze to examine the nature or structure of sth, especially by separating it into its parts, in order to understand or explain it 指分析：*The job involves gathering and analysing data.* 這項工作需要搜集和分析資料。◇ *He tried to analyse his feelings.* 他試圖分析自己的感情。

review to examine sth again, especially so that you can decide if it is necessary to make changes 指複查、檢討，以做必要的修改：*The government will review the situation later in the year.* 政府將在今年晚些時候重新檢討形勢。

study to examine sb/sth in order to understand them or it 指研究、調查：*We will study the report carefully before making a decision.* 我們將認真研究這份報告，然後再作決定。

EXAMINE OR STUDY? 用 examine 還是 study？

You **examine** sth in order to understand it or to help other people understand it, for example by describing it in a book; you **study** sth in order to understand it yourself. 為理解或幫助別人理解某事，如在書中探討，用 examine；為使自己理解某事，用 study。

discuss to write or talk about sth in detail, showing the different ideas and opinions about it 指詳述、論述：*This topic will be discussed at greater length in the next chapter.* 這個主題將在下一章裏詳細論述。

PATTERNS

- to examine/analyse/review/study/discuss **what/how/whether …**
- to examine/analyse/review/study/discuss the **situation/vidence**
- to examine/analyse/review/study/discuss sth **carefully/critically/systematically/briefly**

ex·ample 0-w /ɪɡ'zɑːmpl; *NAmE* -'zæmpl/ *noun* **1** 0-w **~ (of sth)** something such as an object, a fact or a situation that shows, explains or supports what you say 實例；例證；例子：*Can you give me an example of what you mean?* 你能給我舉個實例來解釋你的意思嗎？◇ *This dictionary has many examples of how words are used.* 這部詞典有許多關於詞語用法的示例。◇ *Just to give you an example of his generosity—he gave me his old car and wouldn't take any money for it.* 且給你舉個例子來說明他的慷慨吧 —— 他把他的舊汽車給了我，而且分文不取。◇ *It is important to cite examples to support your argument.* 引用實例來證明你的論點是重要的。➲ LANGUAGE BANK at E.G. **2** 0-w **~ (of sth)** a thing that is typical of or represents a particular group or set 典型；範例；樣品：*This is a good example of the artist's early work.* 這是這位藝術家早期作品的範例。◇ *It is a* ***perfect example*** *of a medieval castle.* 這是最典型的中世紀城堡。◇ *Japan is often quoted as the* ***prime example*** *of a modern industrial nation.* 人們經常舉例把日本作為現代工業國家的典範。◇ *It is a* ***classic example*** *of how not to design a new city centre.* 這對於如何設計新市中心是個絕佳的反面教材。 **3** 0-w a person or their behaviour that is thought to be a good model for others to copy 榜樣；楷模；模範：**~ (to sb)** *Her courage is an example to us all.* 她的勇氣是我們大家的榜樣。◇ *He* ***sets an example*** *to the other students.* 他為其他同學樹立了榜樣。◇ **~ (of sth)** *She is a* ***shining example*** *of what people with disabilities can achieve.* 她為殘疾人有所作為樹立了光輝的榜樣。◇ *He is a captain who leads* ***by example***. 他是個以身作則的隊長。 **4** a person's behaviour, either good or bad, that other people copy 樣板；榜樣：*It would be a mistake to* ***follow his example***. 仿效他的做法是錯誤的。

IDM **for example** 0-w (*abbr.* e.g.) used to emphasize sth that explains or supports what you are saying; used to give an example of what you are saying 例如；譬如：*There is a similar word in many languages, for example in French and Italian.* 在許多語言，譬如法語和意大利語中都有相似的詞。◇ *The report is incomplete; it does not include sales in France, for example.* 這份報告不完整，例如在法國的銷售情況就沒包括進去。◇ *It is possible to combine Computer Science with other subjects, for example Physics.* 將計算機科學與其他學科，如物理學，結合起來是可能的。➲ LANGUAGE BANK at E.G. **make an example of sb** to punish sb as a warning to others not to do the same thing 懲罰某人以儆戒他人；用某人來殺一儆百

Synonyms 同義詞辨析

example

case • instance • specimen • illustration

These are all words for a thing or situation that is typical of a particular group or set, and is sometimes used to support an argument. 以上各詞均指事例、實例、例證。

example something such as an object, a fact or a situation that shows, explains or supports what you say; a thing that is typical of or represents a particular group or set 指實例、例證、典型、範例、樣品：*Can you give me an example of what you mean?* 你能給我舉個實例來解釋你的意思嗎？

case a particular situation or a situation of a particular type; a situation that relates to a particular person or thing 指具體情況、事例、實例、特定情況：*In some cases people have had to wait several weeks for an appointment.* 在某些情況下，人們必須等上好幾週才能得到約見。

instance (*rather formal*) a particular situation or a situation of a particular type 指例子、事例、實例：*The report highlights a number of instances of injustice.* 這篇報道重點列舉了一些不公正的實例。

specimen an example of sth, especially an animal or plant 尤指動植物的樣品、實例：*The aquarium has some interesting specimens of unusual tropical fish.* 水族館裏有一些罕見的熱帶魚，很有趣。

illustration (*rather formal*) a story, an event or an example that clearly shows the truth about sth 指說明事實的故事、實例、示例：*The statistics are a clear illustration of the point I am trying to make.* 這些統計數字清楚地闡明了我要陳述的要點。

EXAMPLE OR ILLUSTRATION? 用 example 還是 illustration？

An **illustration** is often used to show that sth is true. An **example** is used to help to explain sth. * illustration 常用以表示事物的真實性，example 用以解釋說明。

PATTERNS

- a(n) example/case/instance/specimen/illustration **of sth**
- **in** a particular case/instance
- **for** example/instance

ex·as·per·ate /ɪɡ'zæspəreɪt; *BrE* also -'zɑːsp-/ *verb* **~ sb** to annoy or irritate sb very much 使煩惱；使惱怒；激怒 **SYN** **infuriate** ▶ **ex·as·per·ation** /ɪɡˌzæspə'reɪʃn; *BrE* also -ˌzɑːsp-/ *noun* [U]：*He shook his head in exasperation.* 他惱怒地搖了搖頭。◇ *a groan/look/sigh of exasperation* 惱怒的哼聲／樣子／歎息聲

E

ex·as·per·ated /ɪɡˈzæspəreɪtɪd; *BrE* also -ˈzɑːsp-/ *adj.* extremely annoyed, especially if you cannot do anything to improve the situation 惱怒的；煩惱的；憤怒的 SYN **infuriated**：*'Why won't you answer me?' he asked in an exasperated voice.* "你為什麼不願意回答我？"他憤怒地問道。◇ *She was becoming exasperated with all the questions they were asking.* 她開始對他們問的所有問題感到惱火。▸ **ex·as·per·ated·ly** *adv.*

ex·as·per·at·ing /ɪɡˈzæspəreɪtɪŋ; *BrE* also -ˈzɑːsp-/ *adj.* extremely annoying 使人惱怒的；惹人生氣的 SYN **infuriating**

E

ex·cav·ate /ˈekskəveɪt/ *verb* **1** to dig in the ground to look for old buildings or objects that have been buried for a long time; to find sth by digging in this way 發掘，挖出（古建築或古物）：**~ sth** *The site has been excavated by archaeologists.* 這個遺址已被考古學家發掘出來。◇ **~ sth from sth** *pottery and weapons excavated from the burial site* 從墓地挖掘出的陶器和兵器 **2 ~ sth** (*formal*) to make a hole, etc. in the ground by digging 挖掘，開鑿，挖空（洞、隧道等）：*The body was discovered when builders excavated the area.* 建築工人挖地時發現了這具屍體。

ex·cav·ation /ˌekskəˈveɪʃn/ *noun* **1** [C, U] the activity of digging in the ground to look for old buildings or objects that have been buried for a long time（對古建築或古物的）發掘，挖掘 **2** [C, usually pl.] a place where people are digging to look for old buildings or objects 發掘現場：*The excavations are open to the public.* 發掘現場對公眾開放。 **3** [U] the act of digging, especially with a machine 挖掘；開鑿；挖土

ex·cav·ator /ˈekskəveɪtə(r)/ *noun* **1** a large machine that is used for digging and moving earth 挖掘機；挖土機 ➲ VISUAL VOCAB page V58 **2** a person who digs in the ground to look for old buildings and objects 發掘者

ex·ceed AW /ɪkˈsiːd/ *verb* (*formal*) **1 ~ sth** to be greater than a particular number or amount 超過（數目或數量）：*The price will not exceed £100.* 價格不會超過 100 英鎊。◇ *His achievements have* **exceeded expectations.** 他的成就出乎預料。 **2 ~ sth** to do more than the law or an order, etc. allows you to do 超越（法律、命令等）的限制：*She was exceeding the speed limit* (= driving faster than is allowed). 當時她超速駕駛。◇ *The officers had exceeded their authority.* 這些官員超越了他們的權限。➲ see also EXCESS

ex·ceed·ing·ly /ɪkˈsiːdɪŋli/ *adv.* (*formal, becoming old-fashioned*) extremely; very; very much 極其；非常；很 SYN **exceptionally**

excel /ɪkˈsel/ *verb* (-ll-) **1** [I] to be very good at doing sth 擅長；善於；突出：**~ (in/at sth)** *She has always excelled in foreign languages.* 她的外語從來都是出類拔萃。◇ *As a child he excelled at music and art.* 他小時候擅長音樂和美術。◇ **~ (at doing sth)** *The team excels at turning defence into attack.* 這個隊善於打防守反擊。 **2** [T] **~ yourself** (*BrE*) to do extremely well and even better than you usually do 勝過平時：*Rick's cooking was always good but this time he really excelled himself.* 里克的烹飪技術一直不錯，但這次簡直是好上加好。

ex·cel·lence /ˈeksələns/ *noun* [U] the quality of being extremely good 優秀；傑出；卓越：*a reputation for academic excellence* 因學術上的傑出成就而獲得的聲譽 ◇ **~ in sth** *The hospital is recognized as* **a centre of excellence** *in research and teaching.* 這所醫院已被確認為成就卓著的教學和研究中心。➲ see also PAR EXCELLENCE

Ex·cel·lency /ˈeksələnsi/ *noun* **His/Her/Your Excellency** (*pl.* -ies) a title used when talking to or about sb who has a very important official position, especially an AMBASSADOR（對身居要職的人，尤其是大使的尊稱）閣下：*Good evening, your Excellency.* 晚上好，閣下。◇ *their Excellencies the French and Spanish Ambassadors* 法國和西班牙大使閣下

ex·cel·lent 0-w /ˈeksələnt/ *adj.* **1** 0-w extremely good 優秀的；傑出的；極好的：*an excellent meal* 一頓美味佳肴 ◇ *excellent service* 優質服務 ◇ *At $300 the bike is* **excellent value.** 這輛自行車 300 塊錢太合算了。◇ *She speaks excellent French.* 她法語說得好極了。◇ (*informal*) *It was absolutely excellent.* 這簡直太好了。 **2** 0-w used to show that you are very pleased about sth or that you approve of sth（用以表示愉快或贊同）好極了，妙極了：*You can all come? Excellent!* 你們都能來？太好了！▸ **ex·cel·lent·ly** *adv.*

Synonyms 同義詞辨析

excellent

outstanding • perfect • superb

These words all describe sth that is extremely good. 以上各詞均形容某事物極好。

excellent extremely good 指優秀的、傑出的、極好的 NOTE **Excellent** is used especially about standards of service or of sth that sb has worked to produce. * excellent 尤用於修飾服務或產品的質量標準：*The rooms are excellent value at $20 a night.* 這些房間一晚 20 元太合算了。◇ *He speaks excellent English.* 他英語說得棒極了。NOTE **Excellent** is also used to show that you are very pleased about sth or that you approve of sth. * excellent 亦用以表示愉快或贊同：*You can all come? Excellent!* 你們都能來？太好了！

outstanding extremely good 指優秀的、傑出的、出色的 NOTE **Outstanding** is used especially about how well sb does sth or how good sb is at sth. * outstanding 尤指在做某事上或某方面傑出：*an outstanding achievement* 傑出的成績

perfect extremely good 指極好的、很好的 NOTE **Perfect** is used especially about conditions or how suitable sth is for a purpose. * perfect 尤指條件狀況極好或很合適：*Conditions were perfect for walking.* 這些環境最適合散步。◇ *She came up with the perfect excuse.* 她想出了極好的藉口。

superb (*informal*) extremely good or impressive 指極佳的、卓越的、出色的：*The facilities at the hotel are superb.* 旅館的設施棒極了。

PATTERNS

- a(n) excellent/outstanding/perfect/superb **job/performance**
- a(n) excellent/outstanding/superb **achievement**
- **really/absolutely/quite** excellent/outstanding/perfect/superb

ex·cept 0-w /ɪkˈsept/ *prep., conj., verb*

▪ ***prep.*** 0-w (also **exˈcept for**) used before you mention the only thing or person about which a statement is not true（用於所言不包括的人或事物前）除…之外 SYN **apart from**：*We work every day except Sunday.* 我們除星期天外每天都工作。◇ *They all came except Matt.* 除馬特外他們都來了。◇ *I had nothing on except for my socks.* 我除了短襪什麼都還沒穿。➲ note at BESIDES

▪ ***conj.*** 0-w **~ (that)** ... used before you mention sth that makes a statement not completely true 除了；只是 SYN **apart from the fact that**：*I didn't tell him anything except that I needed the money.* 我什麼都沒告訴他，只是說我需要錢。◇ *Our dresses were the same except mine was red.* 我們的連衣裙是一樣的，只是我的那件是紅色。

▪ ***verb*** [usually passive] (*formal*) to not include sb/sth 不包括；不計；把…除外：**~ sb/sth** *The sanctions ban the sale of any products excepting medical supplies and food.* 國際制裁禁止銷售醫藥用品和食物以外的任何產品。◇ *Tours are arranged all year round (January excepted).* 全年都提供觀光旅遊（一月份除外）。◇ **~ sb/sth from sth** *Children under five are excepted from the survey.* 五歲以下的兒童不在調查之列。IDM see PRESENT *adj.*

ex·cep·tion 0-w /ɪkˈsepʃn/ *noun*

1 0-w a person or thing that is not included in a general statement 一般情況以外的人（或事物）；例外：*Most of the buildings in the town are modern, but the church is an exception.* 城裏大多是現代建築，不過教堂是個例外。◇ *With very few exceptions, private schools get the best exam results.* 私立學校的考試成績是最好的，很少有例外情況。◇ *Nobody had much money at the time and I was* *no exception.* 那時候誰都沒有很多錢，我也不例外。 ➲ LANGUAGE BANK at EXCEPT **2** a thing that does not follow a rule 規則的例外；例外的事物： *Good writing is unfortunately **the exception rather than the rule*** (= it is unusual). 可惜優秀的文字作品真是可遇不可求。◇ *There are always a lot of exceptions to grammar rules.* 語法規則總是有很多例外。

IDM **the exception that proves the 'rule** (*saying*) people say that sth is **the exception that proves the rule** when they are stating sth that seems to be different from the normal situation, but they mean that the normal situation remains true in general 反證規律的例外；足以證明普遍性的例外： *Most electronics companies have not done well this year, but ours is the exception that proves the rule.* 今年多數電子公司都不景氣，而我們公司卻是普遍中的例外。**make an ex'ception** to allow sb not to follow the usual rule on one occasion 允許有例外；讓…成為例外： *Children are not usually allowed in, but I'm prepared to make an exception in this case.* 兒童一般不允許入內，不過這次我可以破例。 **take ex'ception to sth** to object strongly to sth; to be angry about sth （強烈地）反對；生…的氣： *I take great exception to the fact that you told my wife before you told me.* 你還沒告訴我就先對我妻子講了，為此我非常生氣。◇ *No one could possibly take exception to his comments.* 任何人都不可能對他的意見提出異議。 **with the ex'ception of** except; not including 除…之外；不包括…在內： *All his novels are set in Italy with the exception of his last.* 他的小說除最後一部外全是以意大利為背景。 ➲ LANGUAGE BANK at EXCEPT **without ex'ception** used to emphasize that the statement you are making is always true and everyone or everything is included 一律；無一例外： *All students without exception must take the English examination.* 所有學生都必須參加英語考試，無一例外。

Language Bank 用語庫

except

Making an exception 說明例外的情況

- She wrote all of the songs on the album **except for** the final track. 除最後一首歌外，這張專輯中所有歌曲都是她寫的。
- **Apart from/aside from** the final track, all of the songs on the album were written by her. 除最後一首歌外，這張專輯中所有歌曲都是她寫的。
- The songwriting—**with a few minor exceptions**—is of a very high quality. 除了幾首歌美中不足以外，歌曲創作質量非常高。
- With only **one or two exceptions**, the songwriting is of a very high quality. 歌曲創作質量非常高，僅有一兩首歌例外。
- The majority of the compositions are less than three minutes long, **with the notable exception of** the title track. 大多數曲目的長度都不超過三分鐘，只有與專輯同名的曲目是明顯的例外。
- **With the exception of** the title track, this album is a huge disappointment. 這張專輯令人大失所望，只有與專輯同名的曲目還過得去。
- Here is a list of all the band's CDs, **excluding** unofficial 'bootleg' recordings. 這是這個樂隊所有 CD 的清單，不包括未經批准非法錄製的作品。

ex·cep·tion·al /ɪk'sepʃənl/ *adj.* **1** unusually good 傑出的；優秀的；卓越的 SYN **outstanding**： *At the age of five he showed exceptional talent as a musician.* 他五歲時就表現出非凡的音樂才能。◇ *The quality of the recording is **quite exceptional**.* 錄音質量相當不錯。 **2** very unusual 異常的；特別的；罕見的： *This deadline will be extended only **in exceptional circumstances**.* 只有在特殊情況下才會延長最後期限。 OPP **unexceptional**

ex·cep·tion·al·ly /ɪk'sepʃənəli/ *adv.* **1** used before an adjective or adverb to emphasize how strong or unusual the quality is （用於形容詞和副詞之前表示強調）罕見，特別，非常： *The weather, even for January, was exceptionally cold.* 這種天氣即使在一月份也算得上非常寒冷。◇ *I thought Bill played exceptionally well.* 我認為比爾的球打得特別好。 **2** only in unusual circumstances 只有在特殊情況下；例外地： *Exceptionally, students may be accepted without formal qualifications.* 在特殊情況下，也可能接受無正式文憑的學生。

ex·cerpt /'eksɜːpt; *NAmE* -sɜːrpt/ *noun* **~ (from sth)** a short piece of writing, music, film, etc. taken from a longer whole 摘錄；節選；（音樂、電影的）片段 ▸ **ex·cerpt** *verb* ： **~ sth (from sth)** *The document was excerpted from an unidentified FBI file.* 此文件摘自來源不明的聯邦調查局檔案。

ex·cess *noun, adj.*

■ ***noun*** /ɪk'ses/ **1** [sing., U] more than is necessary, reasonable or acceptable 超過；過度；過分： *You can throw away any excess.* 凡多餘的你都可以扔掉。◇ **~ of sth** *Are you suffering from an excess of stress in your life?* 你生活中的壓力太大嗎？◇ *In an excess of enthusiasm I agreed to work late.* 我一時熱情過度答應了工作到很晚。◇ *He started drinking **to excess** after losing his job.* 他失業後便開始酗酒了。◇ *The increase will not be **in excess of*** (= more than) *two per cent.* 增加幅度不會超過百分之二。 **2** [C, U] an amount by which sth is larger than sth else 過多的量；超過的量： *We cover costs up to £600 and then you pay the excess.* 我們最多支付 600 英鎊的費用，超過的部份由你支付。 **3** [C, usually sing.] (*BrE*) (*NAmE* **de·duct·ible**) the part of an insurance claim that a person has to pay while the insurance company pays the rest 免賠額；自負額： *There is an excess of £100 on each claim under this policy.* 本保險單每次索賠均有 100 英鎊的免賠額。 **4 excesses** [pl.] extreme behaviour that is unacceptable, illegal or immoral 放肆行為；越軌行為： *We need a free press to curb government excesses.* 我們需要新聞自由來約束政府的越軌行為。

■ ***adj.*** /'ekses/ [only before noun] in addition to an amount that is necessary, usual or legal 超額的；額外的；附加的；過度的： *Excess food is stored as fat.* 多餘的食物作為脂肪貯存起來。◇ *Driving with excess alcohol in the blood is a serious offence.* 血液裏酒精含量過高時駕車是嚴重的違法行為。

excess 'baggage *noun* [U] bags, cases, etc. taken on to a plane that weigh more than the amount each passenger is allowed to carry without paying extra （需另收運費的）超重行李

ex·ces·sive /ɪk'sesɪv/ *adj.* greater than what seems reasonable or appropriate 過分的；過度的： *They complained about the excessive noise coming from the upstairs flat.* 他們抱怨樓上發出的噪音太大。◇ *The amounts she borrowed were not excessive.* 她借的數量沒有超額。◇ *Excessive drinking can lead to stomach disorders.* 酗酒可能引起胃病。 ▸ **ex·ces·sive·ly** *adv.* ： *excessively high prices* 過高的價格

ex·change /ɪks'tʃeɪndʒ/ *noun, verb*

■ ***noun***

▸ GIVING AND RECEIVING 交換 **1** [C, U] an act of giving sth to sb or doing sth for sb and receiving sth in return 交換；互換；交流；掉換： *The exchange of prisoners took place this morning.* 今天早上交換了俘虜。◇ *We need to promote an open exchange of ideas and information.* 我們需要促進思想和信息的公開交流。◇ *an **exchange of glances/insults*** 互換眼色；相互侮辱◇ *an **exchange of fire*** (= between enemy soldiers) 交火◇ *I buy you lunch and you fix my computer. Is that a **fair exchange**?* 我請你吃午飯，你給我修計算機，這算是公平交易吧？◇ *Would you like my old TV **in exchange for** this camera?* 用我的舊電視機換這架照相機，你願意嗎？◇ *I'll type your report if you'll babysit **in exchange**.* 如果你願意代我照看孩子，我就把這個報告給你打出來。 ➲ see also PART EXCHANGE

▸ CONVERSATION/ARGUMENT 交談；爭論 **2** [C] a conversation or an argument 交談；對話；爭論： *There was only time for a brief exchange.* 只有簡短的交談時間。◇ *The Prime Minister was involved in a **heated exchange** with opposition MPs.* 首相參與了和反對黨議員的激烈爭論。

E

▸ **OF MONEY** 金錢 **3** 🔑 [U] the process of changing an amount of one CURRENCY (= the money used in one country) for an equal value of another 兌換；匯兌：*currency exchange facilities* 貨幣兌換服務 ◇ *Where can I find the best* ***exchange rate/rate of exchange****?* 在什麼地方才能獲得最好的兌換價？ ➲ see also FOREIGN EXCHANGE

▸ **BETWEEN TWO COUNTRIES** 兩國之間 **4** 🔑 [C] an arrangement when two people or groups from different countries visit each other's homes or do each other's jobs for a short time（不同國家人或團體之間的）交流，互訪：*Our school does an exchange with a school in France.* 我們學校與法國的一所學校進行交流。◇ *Nick went on the French exchange.* 尼克到法國去作互訪了。◇ *trade and cultural exchanges with China* 與中國的貿易和文化交流

▸ **BUILDING** 建築物 **5** (often **Exchange**) [C] (in compounds 構成複合詞) a building where business people met in the past to buy and sell a particular type of goods 交易所：*the old Corn Exchange* 古老的穀物交易所 ➲ see also STOCK EXCHANGE

▸ **TELEPHONE** 電話 **6** [C] = TELEPHONE EXCHANGE

■ *verb*

▸ **GIVE AND RECEIVE** 交換 **1** 🔑 to give sth to sb and at the same time receive the same type of thing from them 交換；交流；掉換：**~ sth** *to* ***exchange ideas/news/information*** 交流思想；互通消息；交流信息 ◇ *Juliet and David* ***exchanged glances*** (= they looked at each other). 朱麗葉和戴維相互看了看對方。◇ *Everyone in the group exchanged email addresses.* 所有的組員都相互交換了電子郵件地址。◇ **~ sth with sb** *I shook hands and exchanged a few words with the manager.* 我和經理握了握手，交談了幾句。◇ *The two men* ***exchanged blows*** (= hit each other). 兩個男人相互毆打起來。

▸ **MONEY/GOODS** 金錢；商品 **2** 🔑 to give or return sth that you have and get sth different or better instead 兌換；交易；更換 **SYN** **change**：**~ sth** *If it doesn't fit, take it back and the store will exchange it.* 如果不合適就把它拿回來，商店將給你更換。◇ **~ A for B** *You can exchange your currency for dollars in the hotel.* 你可在旅館把你的錢兌換成美元。

▸ **CONTRACTS** 契約 **3 ~ contracts** (*especially BrE*) to sign a contract with the person that you are buying sth from, especially a house or land 交換（尤指房屋或土地買賣的契約）**IDM** see WORD *n.*

ex·change·able /ɪks'tʃeɪndʒəbl/ *adj.* that can be exchanged 可交換的；可交易的；可兌換的；可更換的：*These tokens are exchangeable for DVDs only.* 這些贈券只能換 DVD 盤。

ex·chequer /ɪks'tʃekə(r)/ *noun* [sing.] **1** (often **the Exchequer**) (in Britain) the government department that controls public money（英國）財政部 **SYN** **treasury** ➲ see also CHANCELLOR OF THE EXCHEQUER **2** the public or national supply of money 公共財源；國庫；金庫：*This resulted in a considerable loss to the exchequer.* 這使國庫遭受了重大損失。

ex·cise¹ /'eksaɪz/ *noun* [U] a government tax on some goods made, sold or used within a country 國內貨物稅；消費稅：*new excise duties on low-alcohol drinks* 低酒精飲料新的消費稅 ◇ *a sharp increase in vehicle excise* 機動車消費稅的劇增 ◇ *an excise officer* (= an official whose job is to collect excise) 國內消費稅務官 ➲ compare CUSTOMS (3)

ex·cise² /ɪk'saɪz/ *verb* **~ sth** (**from sth**) (*formal*) to remove sth completely 切除；刪除：*Certain passages were excised from the book.* 書中某些段落已刪去。

ex·ci·sion /ɪk'sɪʒn/ *noun* [U, C] (*formal* or *technical* 術語) the act of removing sth completely from sth; the thing removed 切除；刪除；切除物

ex·cit·able /ɪk'saɪtəbl/ *adj.* (of people or animals 人或動物) likely to become easily excited 易激動的；易興奮的：*a class of excitable ten-year-olds* 一群易興奮的十歲兒童 ▸ **ex·cit·abil·ity** /ɪkˌsaɪtə'bɪləti/ *noun* [U]

ex·cite 🔑 /ɪk'saɪt/ *verb*

1 🔑 **~ sb** to make sb feel very pleased, interested or enthusiastic, especially about sth that is going to happen 使激動；使興奮：*The prospect of a year in India greatly excited her.* 有望在印度待上一年使她激動萬分。**2** to make sb nervous or upset and unable to relax 刺激；使緊張不安：**~ sb** *Try not to excite your baby too much before bedtime.* 睡覺前盡量別使寶寶太興奮。◇ **~ yourself** *Don't excite yourself* (= keep calm). 別激動。**3** to make sb feel a particular emotion or react in a particular way 激發；引發；引起 **SYN** **arouse**：**~ sth** *to* ***excite attention/criticism/curiosity*** 引起注意 / 批評 / 好奇心 ◇ *The news has certainly* ***excited comment*** (= made people talk about it). 這消息已經使人們議論紛紛了。◇ **~ sth in sb** *The European Parliament is not an institution which excites interest in voters.* 歐洲議會是個激不起選民興趣的機構。**4 ~ sb** to make sb feel sexual desire 激發（性慾）**SYN** **arouse** **5 ~ sth** (*formal*) to make a part of the body or part of a physical system more active 使（身體部位或身體系統某部位）活動；刺激…的活動 **SYN** **stimulate**

ex·cited 🔑 /ɪk'saɪtɪd/ *adj.*

1 🔑 feeling or showing happiness and enthusiasm 激動的；興奮的：**~ (about sth)** *The children were excited about opening their presents.* 孩子們對打開禮物感到興奮不已。◇ **~ (at sth)** *I'm really excited at the prospect of working abroad.* 我對有希望到國外工作着實很激動。◇ **~ (by sth)** *Don't get too excited by the sight of your name in print.* 不要一看到你的名字出現在出版物中就過分激動。◇ **~ (to do sth)** *He was very excited to be asked to play for Wales.* 入選威爾士隊使他非常興奮。◇ *The new restaurant is* ***nothing to get excited about*** (= not particularly good). 這家新餐館沒什麼值得特別激動的地方。◇ *An excited crowd of people gathered around her.* 一群激動的人聚集在她周圍。**2** nervous or upset and unable to relax 受刺激的；緊張不安的：*Some horses become excited when they're in traffic.* 有些馬在車流中會受驚。**3** feeling sexual desire 性興奮的 **SYN** **aroused** ▸ **ex·cited·ly** *adv.*：*She waved excitedly as the car approached.* 汽車開近時她激動地揮着手。

Synonyms 同義詞辨析

excited

ecstatic • elated • euphoric • rapturous • exhilarated

These words all describe feeling or showing happiness and enthusiasm. 以上各詞均指激動、興奮。

excited feeling or showing happiness and enthusiasm 指激動的、興奮的：*The kids were excited about the holiday.* 孩子們對假期興奮不已。

ecstatic very happy, excited and enthusiastic; showing this enthusiasm 指狂喜的、熱情極高的：*Sally was ecstatic about her new job.* 薩莉對她的新工作高興得發狂。

elated happy and excited because of sth good that has happened or will happen 指興高采烈的、歡欣鼓舞的、喜氣洋洋的：*I was elated with the thrill of success.* 我為成功的喜悅所鼓舞。

euphoric very happy and excited, but usually only for a short time 指極度愉快的、興奮的，通常持續時間較短：*My euphoric mood could not last.* 我興奮的心情持久不了。

rapturous expressing extreme pleasure or enthusiasm 指興高采烈的、狂喜的、熱烈的：*He was greeted with rapturous applause.* 他受到熱烈的鼓掌歡迎。

exhilarated happy and excited, especially after physical activity 尤指身體活動後感到高興的、興奮的、激動的：*She felt exhilarated with the speed.* 這種速度令她興奮不已。

PATTERNS

- to **feel** excited/elated/euphoric/exhilarated
- to be excited/ecstatic/elated/euphoric **at** sth
- to be excited/ecstatic/elated **about** sth
- to be excited/elated/exhilarated **by** sth
- to be ecstatic/elated/exhilarated **with** sth

ex·cite·ment 🔑 /ɪk'saɪtmənt/ *noun*
1 🔑 [U] the state of feeling excited 激動；興奮；刺激：*The news caused great excitement among her friends.* 這消息使她的朋友們興奮不已。◇ *to feel a **surge/thrill/shiver of excitement*** 感到一陣激動 ◇ *He was flushed **with excitement** at the thought.* 他想到這就激動得滿臉通紅。◇ *The dog leapt and wagged its tail **in excitement**.* 狗興奮得搖着尾巴跳來跳去。◇ ***In her excitement** she dropped her glass.* 她一激動把杯子摔了。 **2** [C] (*formal*) something that you find exciting 令人激動（或興奮）的事：*The new job was not without its excitements.* 這個新工作並非枯燥無味。

ex·cit·ing 🔑 /ɪk'saɪtɪŋ/ *adj.* causing great interest or excitement 令人激動的；使人興奮的：*one of the most exciting developments in biology in recent years* 近年來生物學上最令人振奮的發展之一 ◇ *They waited and waited for something exciting to happen.* 他們等啊等啊，等待着激動人心的事情發生。◇ *an **exciting prospect/possibility*** 令人激動的前景／可能性 ◇ *an **exciting story/discovery*** 激動人心的故事／發現 ▸ **ex·cit·ing·ly** *adv.*

Synonyms 同義詞辨析

exciting

dramatic • heady • thrilling • exhilarating

These words all describe an event, experience or feeling that causes excitement. 以上各詞均指事情、經歷或感受令人激動、興奮。

exciting causing great interest or excitement 指令人激動的、使人興奮的：*This is one of the most exciting developments in biology in recent years.* 這是近年來生物學上最令人振奮的發展之一。

dramatic (of events or scenes) exciting and impressive（指事情或情景）激動人心的，引人注目的，給人印象深刻的：*They watched dramatic pictures of the police raid on TV.* 他們在電視上看到了警察突擊搜捕的激動人心的畫面。

heady having a strong effect on your senses; making you feel excited and hopeful 指強烈作用於感官的、使興奮的、使抱有希望的：*the heady days of youth* 令人陶醉的年輕時代

thrilling exciting and enjoyable 指驚險的、緊張的、扣人心弦的、令人興奮不已的：*Don't miss next week's thrilling episode!* 別錯過下週扣人心弦的那一集！

exhilarating very exciting and enjoyable 指使人興奮的、令人激動的、令人高興的：*My first parachute jump was an exhilarating experience.* 我第一次跳傘的經歷很令人激動。

EXCITING, THRILLING OR EXHILARATING? 用 exciting、thrilling 還是 exhilarating？

Exhilarating is the strongest of these words and **exciting** the least strong. **Exciting** is the most general and can be used to talk about any activity, experience, feeling or event that excites you. **Thrilling** is used especially for contests and stories where the ending is uncertain. **Exhilarating** is used especially for physical activities that involve speed and/or danger. 在這組詞中 exhilarating 語氣最強，exciting 語氣最弱。exciting 最通用，可用於任何令人激動的活動、經歷、感受或事情；thrilling 尤用於結局難測的比賽和故事；exhilarating 尤用於涉及高速度和／或危險的體育活動。

PATTERNS

- a(n) exciting/dramatic/heady/thrilling/exhilarating **experience/moment**
- a(n) exciting/dramatic/heady **atmosphere**
- a(n) exciting/dramatic/thrilling **finish/finale/victory/win**

ex·claim /ɪk'skleɪm/ *verb* [I, T] to say sth suddenly and loudly, especially because of strong emotion or pain（尤因強烈的情感或痛苦而）驚叫，呼喊：*She opened her eyes and exclaimed in delight at the scene.* 看到這情景，她瞪着眼睛，高興得大叫起來。◇ **+ speech** *'It isn't fair!', he exclaimed angrily.* "這不公平！"他氣憤地喊道。◇ **~ that ...** *She exclaimed that it was useless.* 她大叫說這是無效的。 ➲ SYNONYMS at CALL

ex·clam·ation /ˌekskləˈmeɪʃn/ *noun* a short sound, word or phrase spoken suddenly to express an emotion. *Oh!*, *Look out!* and *Ow!* are exclamations. 感歎；感歎語；感歎詞：*He gave an exclamation of surprise.* 他發出一聲驚歎。

excla'mation mark (*especially BrE*) (*NAmE* usually **excla'mation point**) *noun* the mark (!) that is written after an exclamation 感歎號

ex·clama·tory /ɪk'sklæmətri; ek-; *NAmE* -tɔːri/ *adj.* (*formal*) (of language 語言) expressing surprise or strong feelings 表示感歎的；驚歎的

ex·clude 🔑 **AW** /ɪk'skluːd/ *verb* **1** 🔑 **~ sth (from sth)** to deliberately not include sth in what you are doing or considering 不包括；不放在考慮之列：*The cost of borrowing has been excluded from the inflation figures.* 通脹數字未包括借貸費用。◇ *Try excluding fat from your diet.* 平時用餐時試一試不吃含脂肪的食物。◇ *Buses run every hour, Sundays excluded.* 公共汽車每小時一班，星期天除外。 **OPP** **include** **2** 🔑 **~ sb/sth (from sth)** to prevent sb/sth from entering a place or taking part in sth 防止…進入；阻止…參加；把…排斥在外：*Women are still excluded from some London clubs.* 倫敦有些俱樂部仍然拒絕婦女參加。◇ (*BrE*) *Concern is growing over the number of children excluded from school* (= not allowed to attend because of bad behaviour). 對遭學校開除的兒童人數之眾，人們越來越表關注。◇ *She felt excluded by the other girls* (= they did not let her join in what they were doing). 她感到自己受到其他女孩子的排斥。 **3 ~ sth** to decide that sth is not possible 排除（…的可能性）；認為…不可能：*We should not **exclude the possibility** of negotiation.* 我們不應該排除談判的可能性。◇ *The police have excluded theft as a motive for the murder.* 警方已排除這起謀殺案中有偷竊的動機。 **OPP** **include**

ex·clud·ing 🔑 **AW** /ɪk'skluːdɪŋ/ *prep.* not including 不包括；除…外：*Lunch costs £10 per person, excluding drinks.* 午餐每人 10 英鎊，酒水除外。 ➲ LANGUAGE BANK at EXCEPT

ex·clu·sion **AW** /ɪk'skluːʒn/ *noun* **1** [U] **~ (of sb/sth) (from sth)** the act of preventing sb/sth from entering a place or taking part in sth 排斥；排除在外：*He was disappointed with his exclusion from the England squad.* 他對自己沒給選進英格蘭隊感到失望。◇ *Exclusion of air creates a vacuum in the bottle.* 瓶子裏的空氣排除後就產生真空。◇ *Memories of the past filled her mind **to the exclusion of** all else.* 她滿腦子全是對過去的回憶，其他事情都不想了。 **2** [C] a person or thing that is not included in sth 不包括在內的人（或事物）；被排除在外的人（或事物）：*Check the list of exclusions in the insurance policy.* 檢查一下保險單上不包括的項目。 **3** [U] **~ (of sth)** the act of deciding that sth is not possible 排除；認為不可能：*the exclusion of robbery as a motive* 排除搶劫動機 **4** [U, C] (*BrE*) a situation in which a child is banned from attending school because of bad behaviour 開除學籍：*the exclusion of disruptive students from school* 把搗蛋的學生開除出學校 ◇ *Two exclusions from one school in the same week is unusual.* 一所學校在一週內就有兩起開除學生的事是少有的。 **OPP** **inclusion**

ex·clu·sion·ary **AW** /ɪk'skluːʒənri/ *adj.* (*formal*) designed to prevent a particular person or group of people from taking part in sth or doing sth 排斥（性）的；排除在外的

ex'clusion order *noun* (*BrE*) an official order not to go to a particular place（進入某場所的）禁令：*The judge placed an exclusion order on him, banning him from city centre shops.* 法官給他下了禁令，禁止他進入市中心的店鋪。

E

ex'clusion zone *noun* an area where people are not allowed to enter because it is dangerous or is used for secret activities 禁區

ex·clu·sive AW /ɪk'skluːsɪv/ *adj.*, *noun*

■ **adj.** **1** only to be used by one particular person or group; only given to one particular person or group (個人或集體)專用的，專有的，獨有的，獨佔的：*The hotel has exclusive access to the beach.* 這家旅館有通向海灘的專用通道。◇ *exclusive rights to televise the World Cup* 世界杯賽的獨家電視播放權 ◇ *His mother has told 'The Times' about his death in an exclusive interview* (= not given to any other newspaper). 他的母親在接受《泰晤士報》的獨家採訪時談到他的死亡。 **2** (of a group, society, etc. 團體、社團等) not very willing to allow new people to become members, especially if they are from a lower social class 排外的；不願接收新成員的：*He belongs to an exclusive club.* 他參加的是一個不輕易吸收新會員的俱樂部。 **3** of a high quality and expensive and therefore not often bought or used by most people 高檔的；豪華的；高級的：*an exclusive hotel* 高級旅館 ◇ *exclusive designer clothes* 高檔名牌服裝 **4** not able to exist or be a true statement at the same time as sth else 排斥的；排他的：*The two options are not **mutually exclusive*** (= you can have them both). 這兩種選擇並不相互排斥。 **5 ~ of sb/sth** not including sb/sth 不包括；不算；除…外：*The price is for accommodation only, exclusive of meals.* 此價只包括住宿，飯費除外。 OPP **inclusive** ▸ **ex·clu·sive·ly** AW *adv.*：*a charity that relies almost exclusively on voluntary contributions* 幾乎全靠自願捐贈的慈善機構 **ex·clu·sive·ness** *noun* [U]

■ **noun** an item of news or a story about famous people that is published in only one newspaper or magazine 獨家新聞；獨家專文；獨家報道

ex·clu·siv·ity /ˌekskluː'sɪvəti/ (also **ex·clu·sive·ness** /ɪk'skluːsɪvnəs/) *noun* [U] the quality of being exclusive 排他性；專有權；獨特性：*The resort still preserves a feeling of exclusivity.* 這個度假勝地仍然保持着特有的情調。◇ *a designer whose clothes have not lost their exclusiveness* 設計的服裝不失獨特風格的設計師

ex·com·mu·ni·cate /ˌekskə'mjuːnɪkeɪt/ *verb* **~ sb** (**for sth**) to punish sb by officially stating that they can no longer be a member of a Christian Church, especially the Roman Catholic Church 絕罰(開除教籍)(尤指天主教) ▸ **ex·com·mu·ni·ca·tion** /ˌekskəˌmjuːnɪ'keɪʃn/ *noun* [U, C]

ex·cori·ate /ˌeks'kɔːrieɪt/ *verb* **1 ~ sth** (*medical* 醫) to irritate a person's skin so that it starts to come off 擦破，擦傷，剝落(皮膚) **2 ~ sb/sth** (*formal*) to criticize sb/sth severely 嚴厲指責；痛斥 ▸ **ex·cori·ation** *noun* [U, C]

ex·cre·ment /'ekskrɪmənt/ *noun* [U] (*formal*) solid waste matter that is passed from the body through the BOWELS 糞便；排泄物 SYN **faeces**：*the pollution of drinking water by untreated human excrement* 未經處理的人體排泄物對飲用水的污染 ▸ **ex·cre·men·tal** *adj.*

ex·cres·cence /ɪk'skresns/ *noun* (*formal*) an ugly lump that has grown on a part of an animal's body or on a plant 贅生物；贅疣；瘤：(*figurative*) *The new office block is an excrescence* (= it is very ugly). 這座新辦公樓很是煞風景。

ex·creta /ɪk'skriːtə/ *noun* [U] (*formal*) solid and liquid waste matter passed from the body (身體的)排泄物：*human excreta* 人體排泄物

ex·crete /ɪk'skriːt/ *verb* [I] (*technical* 術語) to pass solid or liquid waste matter from the body 排泄 ▸ **ex·cre·tion** /ɪk'skriːʃn/ *noun* [U, C]

ex·cre·tory /ɪks'kriːtəri; *NAmE* 'ekskrətɔːri/ *adj.* (*biology* 生) connected with getting rid of waste matter from the body 排泄的；有排泄功能的：*the excretory organs* 排泄器官

ex·cru·ci·at·ing /ɪk'skruːʃieɪtɪŋ/ *adj.* extremely painful or bad 極痛苦的；極壞的；糟糕透頂的：*The pain in my back was excruciating.* 我的背疼痛難忍。◇ *She groaned at the memory, suffering all over again the excruciating embarrassment of those moments.* 她在回憶中呻吟，又一次飽嚐那時所經歷的極度困窘。 ➲ SYNONYMS at PAINFUL ▸ **ex·cru·ci·at·ing·ly** *adv.*：*excruciatingly uncomfortable* 極不舒服 ◇ ***excruciatingly painful/boring/embarrassing*** 極其痛苦／乏味／難堪

ex·cul·pate /'ekskʌlpeɪt/ *verb* **~ sb** (*formal*) to prove or state officially that sb is not guilty of sth 證明(或宣佈)無罪；為(某人)開脫 ▸ **ex·cul·pa·tion** *noun* [U]

ex·cur·sion /ɪk'skɜːʃn; *NAmE* ɪk'skɜːrʒn/ *noun* **1** a short journey made for pleasure, especially one that has been organized for a group of people (尤指集體)遠足，短途旅行：*They've gone **on an excursion** to York.* 他們到約克旅遊去了。 ➲ SYNONYMS at TRIP **2 ~ into sth** (*formal*) a short period of trying a new or different activity (短期的)涉足，涉獵：*After a brief excursion into drama, he concentrated on his main interest, which was poetry.* 他短暫涉獵過戲劇之後便把全部精力投入到他的主要興趣——詩歌中去了。

ex·cus·able /ɪk'skjuːzəbl/ *adj.* [not usually before noun] that can be excused 可原諒；可諒解 SYN **forgivable**：*Doing it once was just about excusable—doing it twice was certainly not.* 這種事幹一次還可以原諒，幹兩次就絕對不能了。 OPP **inexcusable**

ex·cuse 0-w *noun*, *verb*

■ **noun** /ɪk'skjuːs/ **1** 0-w a reason, either true or invented, that you give to explain or defend your behaviour 藉口；理由；辯解：*Late again! What's your excuse this time?* 又遲到了！你這次有什麼藉口？◇ **~ (for sth)** *There's **no excuse for** such behaviour.* 這種行為說不過去。◇ **~ (for doing sth)** *His excuse for forgetting her birthday was that he had lost his diary.* 他辯解說因為日記本丟了才忘了她的生日。◇ *You don't have to **make excuses** for her* (= try to think of reasons for her behaviour). 你不必為她辯解了。◇ *It's late. I'm afraid I'll have to **make my excuses*** (= say I'm sorry, give my reasons and leave). 時間不早了。很抱歉，我得告辭了。 ➲ SYNONYMS at REASON **2** 0-w a good reason that you give for doing sth that you want to do for other reasons (正當的)理由，藉口：**~ (for sth/for doing sth)** *It's just an excuse for a party.* 這只是藉故一起聚會。◇ **~ (to do sth)** *It gave me an excuse to take the car.* 這使我有理由開車去。 **3** a very bad example of sth 拙劣樣品；蹩腳貨：*Why get involved with that pathetic excuse for a human being?* 為什麼要與那個討厭的傢伙混在一起？ **4** (*NAmE*) a note written by a parent or doctor to explain why a student cannot go to school or sb cannot go to work 假條(家長或醫生寫明請假或給假理由)

■ **verb** /ɪk'skjuːz/ **1** 0-w to forgive sb for sth that they have done, for example not being polite or making a small mistake 原諒；寬恕：**~ sth** *Please excuse the mess.* 這裏凌亂不堪，請見諒。◇ **~ sb** *You must excuse my father—he's not always that rude.* 你一定要原諒我父親，他並不總是那樣粗暴無禮。◇ **~ sb for sth/for doing sth** *I hope you'll excuse me for being so late.* 我來得這麼晚，希望你能原諒。◇ (*BrE*) *You **might be excused for** thinking that Ben is in charge* (= he is not, but it is an easy mistake to make). 你誤以為是本在負責，這是情有可原的。◇ **~ sb doing sth** (*formal*) *Excuse my interrupting you.* 對不起，打擾你一下。 **2** 0-w **~ sth | ~ sb/yourself** (**for sth/for doing sth**) to make your or sb else's behaviour seem less offensive by finding reasons for it 為…辯解(或找理由) SYN **justify**：*Nothing can excuse such rudeness.* 如此粗暴無禮不能原諒。 **3 ~ sb/yourself** (**from sth**) to allow sb to leave; to say in a polite way that you are leaving 准許…離開；請求准予離開；(離開前)請求原諒：*Now if you'll excuse me, I'm a very busy man.* 如果可以，我先行一步了。我很忙。◇ *She excused herself and left the meeting early.* 她說了聲"請原諒"就提前離開了會場。 **4** [usually passive] **~ sb** (**from sth/from doing sth**) | **~ sb sth** to allow sb to not do sth that they should normally do 同意免除；同意免做：*She was excused from giving evidence because of her age.* 因年齡關係她獲准不予作證。

IDM **ex'cuse me** **1** 0-w used to politely get sb's attention, especially sb you do not know (引起尤其是陌生人的注意)勞駕，請原諒：*Excuse me, is this the way to the station?* 勞駕，這是去車站的路嗎？ **2** 0-w used to politely ask sb to move so that you can get past them (客氣地請人讓路)對不起，勞駕，借光：*Excuse me, could you* *let me through?* 對不起，能讓我過去嗎？ **3** ⊶ used to say that you are sorry for interrupting sb or behaving in a slightly rude way（因打擾別人或失禮表示歉意）對不起，請原諒： *Guy sneezed loudly. 'Excuse me,' he said.* 蓋伊大聲打了個噴嚏，然後說了聲"對不起"。 **4** ⊶ used to disagree politely with sb（婉轉地表示不贊成）對不起，請原諒，很抱歉： *Excuse me, but I don't think that's true.* 很抱歉，我認為這不是真的。 **5** ⊶ used to politely tell sb that you are going to leave or talk to sb else（婉轉地要求離開或要與另外的人講話）對不起，請原諒，抱歉： *'Excuse me for a moment,' she said and left the room.* 她說了聲"很抱歉，失陪一會兒"就離開了房間。 **6** ⊶ (*especially NAmE*) used to say sorry for pushing sb or doing sth wrong（因擠着別人或做錯了事表示歉意）對不起，請原諒，很抱歉： *Oh, excuse me. I didn't see you there.* 啊呀，對不起，我沒看到你在那裏。 **7** ⊶ **excuse me?** (*NAmE*) used when you did not hear what sb said and you want them to repeat it（沒聽清楚，請對方再說一遍）對不起，請再說一遍 ➲ more at FRENCH *n.*

ˌex-diˈrectory *adj.* (*BrE*) (of a person or telephone number 人或電話號碼) not listed in the public telephone book, at the request of the owner of the telephone. The telephone company will not give ex-directory numbers to people who ask for them. 未列入電話號碼簿的（經用戶要求電話公司不向詢問人提供其電話號碼）： *an ex-directory number* 未列入電話簿的電話號碼 ◇ *She's ex-directory.* 她的名字未列入電話號碼簿。 ➲ see also UNLISTED (2)

exeat /ˈeksiæt/ *noun* (*BrE*) permission from an institution such as a BOARDING SCHOOL to be away from it for a period of time（寄宿學校等機構的）短期外出許可，短假許可

exec /ɪɡˈzek/ *noun* (*informal*) an executive in a business（公司的）經理，管理人員

exe·crable /ˈeksɪkrəbl/ *adj.* (*formal*) very bad 糟糕的；拙劣的；極壞的 SYN **terrible**

exe·cut·able /ɪɡˈzekjətəbl/ *adj.* (*computing* 計) (of a file or program 文件或程序) that can be run by a computer 可執行的

exe·cute /ˈeksɪkjuːt/ *verb* **1** [usually passive] **~ sb** (**for sth**) to kill sb, especially as a legal punishment（尤指依法）處決，處死： *He was executed for treason.* 他因叛國罪被處死。◇ *The prisoners were executed by firing squad.* 這些犯人已由行刑隊槍決。 **2 ~ sth** (*formal*) to do a piece of work, perform a duty, put a plan into action, etc. 實行；執行；實施： *They drew up and executed a plan to reduce fuel consumption.* 他們制訂並實施了一項降低燃料消耗的計劃。◇ *The crime was very cleverly executed.* 這一犯罪活動實施得非常巧妙。◇ *Check that the computer has executed your commands.* 檢查一下計算機是否已執行指令。 **3 ~ sth** (*formal*) to successfully perform a skilful action or movement 成功地完成（技巧或動作）： *The pilot executed a perfect landing.* 飛行員完成了一個非常嫻熟的着陸動作。 **4 ~ sth** (*formal*) to make or produce a work of art 製作，做成（藝術品）： *Picasso also executed several landscapes at Horta de San Juan.* 畢加索還在奧爾塔 — 德聖胡安畫了幾幅風景畫。 **5 ~ sth** (*law* 律) to follow the instructions in a legal document; to make a document legally valid 執行（法令）；使（法律文件）生效

exe·cu·tion /ˌeksɪˈkjuːʃn/ *noun* **1** [U, C] the act of killing sb, especially as a legal punishment 處決： *He faced execution by hanging for murder.* 他因謀殺罪要以絞刑處死。◇ *Over 200 executions were carried out last year.* 去年執行了 200 多起死刑。 **2** [U] (*formal*) the act of doing a piece of work, performing a duty, or putting a plan into action 實行；執行；實施： *He had failed in the execution of his duty.* 他未能履行職責。◇ *The idea was good, but the execution was poor.* 這個主意倒不錯，可實施情況不理想。 **3** [U] (*formal*) skill in performing or making sth, such as a piece of music or work of art 表演；（樂曲的）演奏；（藝術品的）製作： *Her execution of the piano piece was perfect.* 她把那段鋼琴曲演奏得非常完美。 **4** [U] (*law* 律) the act of following the instructions in a legal document, especially those in sb's WILL（尤指遺囑的）執行 IDM see STAY *n.*

exe·cu·tion·er /ˌeksɪˈkjuːʃənə(r)/ *noun* a public official whose job is to execute criminals 行刑者；死刑執行者

ex·ecu·tive ⊶ /ɪɡˈzekjətɪv/ *noun, adj.*

■ ***noun*** **1** ⊶ [C] a person who has an important job as a manager of a company or an organization（公司或機構的）經理，主管領導，管理人員： ***advertising/business/sales, etc. executives*** 廣告、業務、銷售等主管 ◇ *a **chief/senior/top executive** in a computer firm* 一家計算機公司的總裁／資深主管／高層主管 **2** [C+sing./pl. v.] a group of people who run a company or an organization（統稱公司或機構的）行政領導，領導層： *The union's executive has/have yet to reach a decision.* 工會領導層還有待作出決策。 **3 the executive** [sing.+sing./pl. v.] the part of a government responsible for putting laws into effect（政府的）行政部門 ➲ compare JUDICIARY, LEGISLATURE

■ ***adj.*** [only before noun] **1** ⊶ connected with managing a business or an organization, and with making plans and decisions 經營管理的；經理的；決策的： *She has an executive position in a finance company.* 她在一家金融公司擔任主管。◇ ***executive decisions/duties/jobs/positions*** 經營管理的決策／職責／工作／職位 ◇ *the executive dining room* 管理人員食堂 **2** having the power to put important laws and decisions into effect 有執行權的；實施的；行政的： *executive authority* 行政當局 ◇ *an **executive board/body/committee/officer*** 執行董事會；行政機構；執行委員會；行政長官 ◇ *Executive power is held by the president.* 執行權由董事長掌握。 **3** ⊶ expensive; for the use of sb who is considered important 高級的；供重要人物使用的： *an **executive car/home*** 高級汽車／住宅 ◇ *an **executive suite*** (= in a hotel)（旅館的）貴賓套房 ◇ *an **executive lounge*** (= at an airport)（機場的）貴賓休息室

the eˈxecutive branch *noun* [sing.] (in the US) the part of the government that is controlled by the President（美國總統掌管的）政府行政部門

eˌxecutive ˈprivilege *noun* [U] (in the US) the right of the President and the executive part of the government to keep official documents secret 行政特權，總統特權（美國總統和政府行政部門對官方文件保密的特權）

ex·ecu·tor /ɪɡˈzekjətə(r)/ *noun* (*technical* 術語) a person, bank, etc. that is chosen by sb who is making their WILL to follow the instructions in it 遺囑執行人（或銀行等）

exe·gesis /ˌeksɪˈdʒiːsɪs/ *noun* [U, C] (*pl.* **exe·geses** /-siːz/) (*formal*) the detailed explanation of a piece of writing, especially religious writing（尤指宗教著作的）詮釋；解經；釋經

ex·em·plar /ɪɡˈzemplɑː(r)/ *noun* (*formal*) a person or thing that is a good or typical example of sth 模範；榜樣；典型；範例 SYN **model**

ex·em·plary /ɪɡˈzempləri/ *adj.* **1** providing a good example for people to copy 典範的；可作榜樣的；可作楷模的： *Her behaviour was exemplary.* 她的行為堪作楷模。◇ *a man of exemplary character* 一個具有模範品德的人 **2** [usually before noun] (*law* 律 or *formal*) (of punishment 懲罰) severe; used especially as a warning to others 嚴厲的；儆戒性的；懲戒性的

ex·em·plify /ɪɡˈzemplɪfaɪ/ *verb* (**ex·em·pli·fies**, **ex·em·pli·fy·ing**, **ex·em·pli·fied**, **ex·em·pli·fied**) [often passive] (*formal*) **1 ~ sth** to be a typical example of sth 是…的典型（或典範、榜樣）： *Her early work is exemplified in her book, 'A Study of Children's Minds'.* 她的《兒童思維研究》一書是她早期的代表作。◇ *His food exemplifies Italian cooking at its best.* 他的菜肴體現了意大利烹飪的精髓。 **2 ~ sth** to give an example in order to make sth clearer 舉例說明；例證；例示 SYN **illustrate**： *She exemplified each of the points she was making with an amusing anecdote.* 她的每一個論點都用一個佚聞趣事來說明。 ▸ **ex·em·pli·fi·ca·tion** /ɪɡˌzemplɪfɪˈkeɪʃn/ *noun* [U, C]

ex·empt /ɪɡˈzempt/ *adj., verb*

■ ***adj.*** [not before noun] **~** (**from sth**) if sb/sth is **exempt** from sth, they are not affected by it, do not have to do it, pay it, etc. 免除（責任、付款等）；獲豁免： *The*

E

interest on the money is exempt from tax. 這筆錢的利息免稅。◇ Some students are exempt from certain exams. 有些學生可免除某些考試。▶ **-exempt** (in compounds, forming adjectives 構成複合形容詞): tax-exempt donations to charity 給慈善機構的免稅捐款

■ *verb* ~ **sb/sth (from sth/from doing sth)** (formal) to give or get sb's official permission not to do sth or not to pay sth they would normally have to do or pay 免除；豁免：*His bad eyesight exempted him from military service.* 他因視力不好而免服兵役。◇ *In 1983, charities were exempted from paying the tax.* * 1983 年慈善團體均免付稅款。

ex·emp·tion /ɪɡˈzempʃn/ *noun* **1** [U, C] ~ **(from sth)** official permission not to do sth or pay sth that you would normally have to pay 免除；豁免：*She was given exemption from the final examination.* 她已獲准期末免試。**2** [C] a part of your income that you do not have to pay tax on （部份收入的）免稅：*a tax exemption on money donated to charity* 給慈善機構的捐款免稅

ex·er·cise 0-π /ˈeksəsaɪz; *NAmE* -sərs-/ *noun, verb*

■ *noun*

▸ **ACTIVITY/MOVEMENTS** 活動；運動 **1** 0-π [U] physical or mental activity that you do to stay healthy or become stronger （身體或思想的）活動，鍛煉，運動：*Swimming is good exercise.* 游泳是有益的運動。◇ *I don't get **much exercise** sitting in the office all day.* 我整天坐在辦公室很少運動。◇ *The mind needs exercise as well as the body.* 大腦同身體一樣需要鍛煉。◇ ***vigorous/gentle exercise*** 劇烈的／平和的運動 ◇ (BrE) *to take exercise* 鍛煉 ➲ COLLOCATIONS at DIET **2** 0-π [C] a set of movements or activities that you do to stay healthy or develop a skill （保持健康或培養技能的）一套動作，訓練活動，練習：***breathing/relaxation/stretching exercises*** 呼吸／放鬆／伸展運動 ◇ *exercises for the piano* 鋼琴練習 ◇ *Repeat the exercise ten times on each leg.* 每條腿重複做十次這種動作。

▸ **QUESTIONS** 問題 **3** 0-π [C] a set of questions in a book that tests your knowledge or practises a skill 習題；練習：*grammar exercises* 語法練習 ◇ *Do exercise one for homework.* 家庭作業做習題一。

▸ **USE OF POWER/RIGHT/QUALITY** 權力／權利的行使；品質的運用 **4** [U] ~ **of sth** the use of power, a skill, a quality or a right to make sth happen 行使；運用；使用：*the exercise of power by the government* 政府權力的行使 ◇ *the exercise of discretion* 自行決定權的行使

▸ **FOR PARTICULAR RESULT** 為某結果 **5** [C] an activity that is designed to achieve a particular result （為達到特定結果的）活動：*a communications exercise* 通信演習 ◇ *In the end it proved a pointless exercise.* 這最終證明是一項毫無意義的活動。◇ ~ **in sth** *an exercise in public relations* 公關活動 ◇ *Staying calm was an exercise in self-control.* 保持鎮定是一種自我控制活動。

▸ **FOR SOLDIERS** 士兵 **6** [C, usually pl.] a set of activities for training soldiers （士兵的）操練，演習，演練：*military exercises* 軍事演習

▸ **CEREMONIES** 儀式 **7** **exercises** [pl.] (NAmE) ceremonies 典禮；儀式：*college graduation exercises* 大學畢業典禮

■ *verb*

▸ **USE POWER/RIGHT/QUALITY** 行使權力／權利；運用品質 **1** 0-π [T] ~ **sth** (formal) to use your power, rights or personal qualities in order to achieve sth 行使；使用；運用：*When she appeared in court she exercised her right to remain silent.* 她出庭時行使了自己保持沉默的權利。◇ *He was a man who exercised considerable influence over people.* 他是個對別人有相當影響的人。

▸ **DO PHYSICAL ACTIVITY** 體力鍛煉 **2** 0-π [I, T] to do sports or other physical activities in order to stay healthy or become stronger; to make an animal do this 鍛煉；訓練；操練：*an hour's class of exercising to music* 音樂伴奏下的一小時健身操課 ◇ *How often do you exercise?* 你多長時間鍛煉一次？◇ ~ **sth** *Horses need to be exercised regularly.* 馬需要有規律的訓練。**3** [T] ~ **sth** to give a part of the body the movement and activity it needs to keep strong and healthy 鍛煉（身體某部位）：*These movements will exercise your arms and shoulders.* 這些動作將鍛煉你的手臂和肩膀。

▸ **BE ANXIOUS** 焦慮 **4** [usually passive] ~ **sb/sth (about sth)** (formal) if sb is **exercised** about sth, they are very anxious about it 使焦慮；使不安；使煩惱

ˈ**exercise ball** (also ˈ**Swiss ball™**) *noun* a large ball that you can sit on when doing exercises to make your muscles work in a different way 健身球

ˈ**exercise bike** *noun* a bicycle that does not move forward but is used for getting exercise indoors （室內使用的）健身腳踏車 ➲ VISUAL VOCAB page V42

ˈ**exercise book** *noun* **1** (BrE) (NAmE **note·book**) a small book for students to write their work in 練習本 ➲ VISUAL VOCAB page V70 **2** (NAmE) (BrE **work·book**) a book with exercises in it, often with spaces for students to write answers in, to help them practise what they have learnt 練習冊；作業本

exert /ɪɡˈzɜːt; *NAmE* ɪɡˈzɜːrt/ *verb* **1** ~ **sth** to use power or influence to affect sb/sth 運用；行使；施加：*He exerted all his authority to make them accept the plan.* 他利用他的所有權力讓他們接受這個計劃。◇ *The moon exerts a force on the earth that causes the tides.* 月球對地球的吸引力引起潮汐。**2** ~ **yourself** to make a big physical or mental effort 努力；竭力：*In order to be successful he would have to exert himself.* 他必須努力才能成功。

ex·er·tion /ɪɡˈzɜːʃn; *NAmE* -ˈzɜːrʃ-/ *noun* **1** [U] (also **exertions** [pl.]) physical or mental effort; the act of making an effort 努力；盡力；費力：*She was hot and breathless from the exertion of cycling uphill.* 她騎車上山累得全身發熱，喘不過氣來。◇ *He needed to relax after the exertions of a busy day at work.* 他忙碌工作了一天後需要休息。**2** [sing.] the use of power to make sth happen 行使；運用；施加：*the **exertion of force/strength/authority*** 使用武力；使勁；行使權力

exe·unt /ˈeksiʌnt/ *verb* [I] (from Latin) used in a play as a written instruction that tells two or more actors to leave the stage （劇本中的說明，兩個或以上演員）退場，下場 ➲ compare EXIT *v.* (3)

ex·foli·ate /eksˈfəʊlieɪt; *NAmE* -ˈfoʊ-/ *verb* [I, T] ~ **(sth)** to remove dead cells from the surface of skin in order to make it smoother 使表皮剝脫 ▶ **ex·foli·ation** *noun* [U]

ex gra·tia /ˌeks ˈɡreɪʃə/ *adj.* (from Latin) given or done as a gift or favour, not because there is a legal duty to do it 作為禮物的；作為恩惠的：*ex gratia payments* 通融付款 ▶ **ex gra·tia** *adv.*：*The sum was paid ex gratia.* 這是所付的一筆特惠款。

ex·hale /eksˈheɪl/ *verb* [I, T] (formal) to breathe out the air or smoke, etc. in your lungs 呼出，吐出（肺中的空氣、煙等）；呼氣：*He sat back and exhaled deeply.* 他仰坐着深深地呼氣。◇ ~ **sth** *She exhaled the smoke through her nose.* 她從鼻子裏噴出煙霧。OPP **inhale** ▶ **ex·hal·ation** /ˌekshəˈleɪʃn/ *noun* [U, C]

ex·haust /ɪɡˈzɔːst/ *noun, verb*

■ *noun* **1** [U] waste gases that come out of a vehicle, an engine or a machine （車輛、發動機或機器排出的）廢氣：*car **exhaust fumes/emissions*** 汽車排出的廢氣；汽車排放物 ➲ VISUAL VOCAB page V6 **2** (also **exˈhaust pipe**) (also **tail·pipe** especially in NAmE) [C] a pipe through which exhaust gases come out 排氣管：*My car needs a new exhaust.* 我的汽車需要一個新排氣管。➲ VISUAL VOCAB page V52

■ *verb* **1** to make sb feel very tired 使筋疲力盡；使疲憊不堪 SYN **wear out**：~ **sb** *Even a short walk exhausted her.* 即使走一段短路，她也疲憊不堪了。◇ ~ **yourself** *There's no need to exhaust yourself clearing up—we'll do it.* 你不必筋疲力盡地收拾，我們會做的。**2** ~ **sth** to use all of sth so that there is none left 用完；花光；耗盡：*Within three days they had exhausted their supply of food.* 他們在三天之內就把所有糧食吃光了。◇ *Don't give up until you have exhausted all the possibilities.* 只要還有可能就別放棄。**3** ~ **sth** to talk about or study a subject until there is nothing else to say about it 詳盡討論（或研究）：*I think we've exhausted that particular topic.* 我認為我們已把那個題目討論透徹了。

ex·haust·ed /ɪɡˈzɔːstɪd/ *adj.* **1** very tired 筋疲力盡的；疲憊不堪的：*I'm exhausted!* 我累死了！◇ *to feel **completely/utterly exhausted*** 感到筋疲力盡 ◇ *The exhausted climbers were rescued by helicopter.* 筋疲力盡的登山者由直升機營救出來。**2** completely used or finished 用完的；耗盡的；枯竭的：*You cannot grow crops on exhausted land.* 貧瘠的土地上種不了莊稼。

ex·haust·ing /ɪɡˈzɔːstɪŋ/ *adj.* making you feel very tired 使人疲憊不堪的；令人筋疲力盡的：*an exhausting day at work* 工作得筋疲力盡的一天 ◇ *I find her exhausting—she never stops talking.* 我發現她真讓人疲累 —— 她總是不停地說話。

ex·haus·tion /ɪɡˈzɔːstʃən/ *noun* [U] **1** the state of being very tired 筋疲力盡；疲憊不堪：*suffering from* ***physical/mental/nervous exhaustion*** 身體／精神／神經衰弱 ◇ *Her face was grey with exhaustion.* 她疲憊得臉色發白。 **2** (*formal*) the act of using sth until it is completely finished 耗盡；用盡；枯竭：*the exhaustion of natural resources* 自然資源的枯竭

ex·haust·ive /ɪɡˈzɔːstɪv/ *adj.* including everything possible; very thorough or complete 詳盡的；徹底的；全面的：***exhaustive research/tests*** 徹底的研究／測試 ◇ *This list is not intended to be exhaustive.* 這份清單不求詳盡無遺。 ▸ **ex·haust·ive·ly** *adv.*：*Every product is exhaustively tested before being sold.* 每件產品銷售前都經過全面檢驗。

exˈhaust pipe *noun* = EXHAUST *n.* (2)

ex·hibit 🔑 **AW** /ɪɡˈzɪbɪt/ *verb, noun*

■ *verb* **1** 🔑 [T, I] to show sth in a public place for people to enjoy or to give them information 展覽；展出：**~ sth (at/in …)** *They will be exhibiting their new designs at the trade fairs.* 他們將在商品交易會上展出他們新的設計。◇ **~ (at/in …)** *He exhibits regularly in local art galleries.* 他經常在當地的畫廊舉辦畫展。 **2** [T] **~ sth** (*formal*) to show clearly that you have or feel a particular feeling, quality or ability 表現，顯示，顯出（感情、品質或能力） **SYN** **display**：*The patient exhibited signs of fatigue and memory loss.* 病人表現出疲勞和記憶力喪失的跡象。

■ *noun* **1** 🔑 an object or a work of art put in a public place, for example a museum, so that people can see it （一件）展覽品，陳列品 **2** a thing that is used in court to prove that sb is guilty or not guilty （在法庭上出示的）物證，證據：*The first exhibit was a knife which the prosecution claimed was the murder weapon.* 當庭出示的第一件物證就是原告稱為殺人兇器的一把刀。 **3** 🔑 (*NAmE*) = EXHIBITION (1)：*The new exhibit will tour a dozen US cities next year.* 這批新展品明年將在美國十二個城市巡迴展出。

ex·hib·ition 🔑 **AW** /ˌeksɪˈbɪʃn/ *noun*

1 🔑 (*especially BrE*) (*NAmE* usually **ex·hibit**) [C] a collection of things, for example works of art, that are shown to the public （一批）展覽品：*Have you seen the Picasso exhibition?* 你看過畢加索的畫展嗎？◇ *an exhibition of old photographs* 老照片展 ➲ COLLOCATIONS at ART **2** [U] **~ of sth** the act of showing sth, for example works of art, to the public 展覽；展出：*She refused to allow the exhibition of her husband's work.* 她拒不允許展出她丈夫的作品。 **3** [sing.] **an ~ of sth** (*formal*) the act of showing a skill, a feeling, or a kind of behaviour （技能、感情或行為的）表現，顯示，表演：*We were treated to an exhibition of the footballer's speed and skill.* 足球運動員表現出的速度和技術，真讓我們大飽眼福。◇ *an appalling exhibition of bad manners* 極其惡劣無禮的行為 **4** [C] (*BrE*) an amount of money that is given as a prize to a student 獎學金

IDM **make an exhiˈbition of yourself** (*disapproving*) to behave in a bad or stupid way in public 出洋相；當眾出醜

ex·hib·ition·ism /ˌeksɪˈbɪʃənɪzəm/ *noun* [U] **1** (*disapproving*) behaviour that is intended to make people notice or admire you 表現癖；表現狂；出風頭 **2** (*psychology* 心) the mental condition that makes sb want to show their sexual organs in public 裸露癖；露陰癖；露陰狂

ex·hib·ition·ist /ˌeksɪˈbɪʃənɪst/ *noun* (usually *disapproving*) a person who likes to make other people notice him or her 好出風頭者；好表現者：*Children are natural exhibitionists.* 兒童天生好表現自己。

ex·hib·it·or /ɪɡˈzɪbɪtə(r)/ *noun* a person or a company that shows their work or products to the public 參展者；參展商

ex·hil·ar·ate /ɪɡˈzɪləreɪt/ *verb* **~ sb** to make sb feel very happy and excited 使高興；使興奮；使激動：*Speed had always exhilarated him.* 速度總讓他感到興奮。 ▸ **ex·hil·ar·ated** *adj.*：*I felt exhilarated after a morning of skiing.* 我滑了一上午的雪興奮不已。 ➲ SYNONYMS at EXCITED **ex·hil·ar·ation** /ɪɡˌzɪləˈreɪʃn/ *noun* [U]：*the exhilaration of performing on stage* 在舞台上演出的激動心情

ex·hil·ar·at·ing /ɪɡˈzɪləreɪtɪŋ/ *adj.* very exciting and enjoyable 使人興奮的；令人激動的；令人高興的：*My first parachute jump was an exhilarating experience.* 我第一次跳傘的經歷很令人激動。 ➲ SYNONYMS at EXCITING

E

ex·hort /ɪɡˈzɔːt; *NAmE* ɪɡˈzɔːrt/ *verb* (*formal*) to try hard to persuade sb to do sth 規勸；敦促；告誡 **SYN** **urge**：**~ sb to do sth** *The party leader exhorted his members to start preparing for government.* 該黨領袖敦促黨員着手準備籌建政府的工作。◇ **~ sb to sth** *They had been exhorted to action.* 已經告誡他們採取行動。◇ **~ (sb) + speech** *'Come on!' he exhorted (them).* "快點！" 他敦促（他們）道。 ▸ **ex·hort·ation** /ˌeɡzɔːˈteɪʃn; *NAmE* -zɔːrˈt-/ *noun* [C, U]

ex·hume /eksˈhjuːm; ɪɡˈzjuːm; *NAmE* ɪɡˈzuːm/ *verb* [usually passive] **~ sth** (*formal*) to remove a dead body from the ground especially in order to examine how the person died （為檢查死因）掘出（屍首） **SYN** **dig up** ▸ **ex·hum·ation** /ˌekshjuːˈmeɪʃn/ *noun* [U]

exi·gency /ˈeksɪdʒənsi; ɪɡˈzɪdʒ-/ *noun* [C, usually pl., U] (*pl.* **-ies**) (*formal*) an urgent need or demand that you must deal with 急切需要；迫切要求 **SYN** **demand**

ex·igu·ous /eɡˈzɪɡjuəs/ *adj.* (*formal*) very small in size or amount; hardly enough 微小的；稀少的；不夠的

exile /ˈeksaɪl; ˈeɡzaɪl/ *noun, verb*

■ *noun* **1** [U, sing.] the state of being sent to live in another country that is not your own, especially for political reasons or as a punishment 流放；流亡；放逐：*to be/live* ***in exile*** 在流放中；過流放生活 ◇ *to be forced/sent* ***into exile*** 被迫／被流放 ◇ *to go* ***into exile*** 流亡 ◇ *a place of exile* 流放地 ◇ *He returned after 40 years of exile.* 他流放 40 年後歸來。 **2** [C] a person who chooses, or is forced to live away from his or her own country 流亡國外者；被流放者；離鄉背井者：*political exiles* 政治流亡者 ◇ *a* ***tax exile*** (= a rich person who moves to another country where taxes are lower) 遷居低稅國家的富人

■ *verb* [usually passive] **~ sb (from …)** to force sb to leave their country, especially for political reasons or as a punishment; to send sb into exile 流放；放逐：*the party's exiled leaders* 該黨的流亡領袖

exist 🔑 /ɪɡˈzɪst/ *verb*

1 🔑 [I] (not used in the progressive tenses 不用於進行時) to be real; to be present in a place or situation 存在；實際上有：*Does life exist on other planets?* 其他行星上有生命嗎？◇ *The problem only exists in your head, Jane.* 這個問題不過是你的想像，簡。◇ *Few of these monkeys still exist in the wild.* 這些野生的猴子已為數不多了。◇ *On his retirement the post will* ***cease to exist***. 他退休後這個職位就不會存在。◇ *The charity exists to support victims of crime.* 設立這個慈善機構是為了援助罪案受害者。 **2** [I] **~ (on sth)** to live, especially in a difficult situation or with very little money（尤指在困境或貧困中）生活，生存：*We existed on a diet of rice.* 我們靠吃大米過活。◇ *They can't exist on the money he's earning.* 他們靠他掙的那點錢無法維持生活。

ex·ist·ence 🔑 /ɪɡˈzɪstəns/ *noun*

1 🔑 [U] the state or fact of being real or living or of being present 存在；實有：*I was unaware of his existence until today.* 直到今天我才知道有他這麼個人。◇ *This is the oldest Hebrew manuscript* ***in existence***. 這是現存最古老的希伯來語手稿。◇ *Pakistan* ***came into existence*** *as an independent country in 1947.* 巴基斯坦在 1947 年成為了獨立國家。◇ *a crisis that threatens the industry's continued existence* 對這一行業的繼續生存構成威脅的危機 **2** 🔑 [C] a way of living especially when this is difficult or boring （尤指艱難或無聊的）生活，生活方式：*The family endured a miserable existence in a cramped* *apartment.* 這家人在狹小的公寓裏艱難度日。◇ *We led a poor but happy enough existence as children.* 我們兒時的生活雖然貧窮卻過得很愉快。◇ *They eke out a precarious existence* (= they have hardly enough money to live on). 他們勉強維持着朝不保夕的生活。◇ *The peasants depend on a good harvest for their **very existence*** (= in order to continue to live). 農民靠豐收才能活命。

ex·ist·ent /ɪɡˈzɪstənt/ *adj., noun*
■ **adj.** (*formal*) existing; real 存在的；實有的：*creatures existent in nature* 自然界中現存的生物 OPP **non-existent**
■ **noun** (*philosophy* 哲) a thing that is real and exists 存在（或實有）的事物：*The self is the only knowable existent.* 自我是唯一可知的存在物。

ex·ist·en·tial /ˌeɡzɪˈstenʃəl/ *adj.* [only before noun] **1** (*formal*) connected with human existence 關於人類存在的；與人類存在有關的 **2** (*philosophy* 哲) connected with the theory of existentialism（關於）存在主義的

ex·ist·en·tial·ism /ˌeɡzɪˈstenʃəlɪzəm/ *noun* [U] (*philosophy* 哲) the theory that humans are free and responsible for their own actions in a world without meaning 存在主義 ▸ **ex·ist·en·tial·ist** /-ʃəlɪst/ *noun*：*Sartre was an existentialist.* 薩特是個存在主義者。**ex·ist·en·tial·ist** *adj.*：*existentialist theory* 存在主義理論

ex·ist·ing /ɪɡˈzɪstɪŋ/ *adj.* [only before noun] found or used now 現存的；現行的：*New laws will soon replace existing legislation.* 新法律即將取代現行法規。

exit 🔑 /ˈeksɪt; ˈeɡzɪt/ *noun, verb*
■ **noun 1** 🔑 a way out of a public building or vehicle 出口；通道；太平門：*Where's the exit?* 出口在哪兒？◇ *There is a **fire exit** on each floor of the building.* 這棟建築每層樓都有個消防通道。◇ *The **emergency exit** is at the back of the bus.* 緊急出口在公共汽車的尾部。➲ compare ENTRANCE[1] (1) **2** 🔑 an act of leaving, especially of an actor from the stage 退出；離去；（尤指演員）退場：*The heroine **made her exit** to great applause.* 女主角在熱烈的掌聲中退場。◇ *He made a quick exit to avoid meeting her.* 他迅速離去以避免見到她。◇ *an **exit visa*** (= a stamp in a passport giving sb permission to leave a particular country) 出境簽證 **3** 🔑 a place where vehicles can leave a road to join another road（車輛可以從一道路駛出進入另一道路的）出口，出路：*Leave the roundabout at the second exit.* 在第二個出口處駛離環島。◇ *Take the exit for Brno.* 從通往布爾諾的出口駛出。
■ **verb 1** [I, T] (*formal*) to go out; to leave a building, stage, vehicle, etc. 出去；離去；退場：(+ **adv./prep.**) *The bullet entered her back and exited through her chest.* 子彈從她背部穿胸而過。◇ *We exited via a fire door.* 我們從防火安全門走了出去。◇ **~ sth** *As the actors exited the stage the lights went on.* 演員們退場時燈光便亮了起來。**2** [I, T] to finish using a computer program 退出（計算機程序）：**~ (from sth)** *To exit from this page, press the return key.* 退出本頁面按返回鍵。◇ **~ sth** *I exited the database and switched off the computer.* 我退出數據庫後關掉了計算機。**3** [I] **exit ...** used in the instructions printed in a play to say that an actor must leave the stage（劇本裏的指示）退場，退下 ➲ compare EXEUNT

ˈexit exam (also *formal* **exit examination**) *noun* (*especially NAmE*) an exam that you take at the end of the last year in school or at the end of a period of training 畢業考試；結業考試：*a high school exit exam* 中學畢業考試

ˈexit poll *noun* in an **exit poll** immediately after an election, people are asked how they voted, in order to predict the result of the election 出口民調；投票後民調

ex libris /ˌeks ˈlɪbrɪs; ˈliːb-/ *adv.* written in the front of a book before the name of the person the book belongs to（寫於書前頁的藏書者姓名前）…的藏書，…的藏本：*ex libris David Harries* 戴維 • 哈里斯藏書

exo·crine /ˈeksəʊkraɪn; -krɪn; *NAmE* ˈeksəkrɪn; -kriːn/ *adj.* (*biology* 生) connected with GLANDS that do not put substances directly into the blood but export their product through tubes for use outside the body 外分泌腺的；外分泌的：*exocrine glands* 外分泌腺 ➲ compare ENDOCRINE

exo·dus /ˈeksədəs/ *noun* [sing.] **~ (from ...) (to ...)** (*formal or humorous*) a situation in which many people leave a place at the same time（大批人同時）離開，外出，出去：*the **mass exodus** from Paris to the country in the summer* 夏日大批人從巴黎外出到鄉村

ex of·fi·cio /ˌeks əˈfɪʃiəʊ; *NAmE* -ʃioʊ/ *adj.* (from Latin, *formal*) included or allowed because of your job, position or rank 出於工作（或職位、職權）的；（由於工作、職位或職權而成為的）當然的：*an ex officio member of the committee* 委員會的當然委員 ▸ **ex of·fi·cio** *adv.*

ex·og·amy /ekˈsɒɡəmi; *NAmE* -ˈsɑːɡ-/ *noun* [U] (*technical* 術語) marriage outside your family or CASTE (= division of society) 族外婚；外婚制 ➲ compare ENDOGAMY ▸ **ex·og·am·ous** /ekˈsɒɡəməs; *NAmE* -ˈsɑːɡ-/ *adj.*

ex·ogen·ous /ekˈsɒdʒənəs; ɪk-; *NAmE* ekˈsɑːdʒ-/ *adj.* (*medical* 醫) (of a disease or SYMPTOM 疾病或症狀) having a cause that is outside the body 外源性的 ➲ compare ENDOGENOUS

ex·on·er·ate /ɪɡˈzɒnəreɪt; *NAmE* -ˈzɑːn-/ *verb* **~ sb (from sth)** (*formal*) to officially state that sb is not responsible for sth that they have been blamed for 宣佈（某人）無罪；免除責任：*The police report exonerated Lewis from all charges of corruption.* 警方的報告免除了對劉易斯貪污的所有指控。▸ **ex·on·er·ation** /ɪɡˌzɒnəˈreɪʃn; *NAmE* -ˌzɑːnə-/ *noun* [U]

ex·or·bi·tant /ɪɡˈzɔːbɪtənt; *NAmE* -ˈzɔːrb-/ *adj.* (*formal*) (of a price 價格) much too high 過高的；高得離譜的：***exorbitant costs/fares/fees/prices/rents*** 過高的花費／交通費／收費／價格／租金 ▸ **ex·or·bi·tant·ly** *adv.*：*Prices are exorbitantly high in this shop.* 這家商店的價格高得離譜。

ex·or·cism /ˈeksɔːsɪzəm; *NAmE* -sɔːrs-/ *noun* [U, C] **1** the act of getting rid of an evil spirit from a place or a person's body by prayers or magic; a ceremony where this is done（用祈禱或法術）驅魔，驅邪，驅邪的儀式 **2** (*formal*) the act of making yourself forget a bad experience or memory（不愉快的經歷或記憶的）消除，忘掉

ex·or·cist /ˈeksɔːsɪst; *NAmE* -sɔːrs-/ *noun* a person who makes evil spirits leave a place or a person's body by prayers or magic（用祈禱或法術）驅邪的法師，驅魔者

ex·or·cize (*BrE* also **-ise**) /ˈeksɔːsaɪz; *NAmE* -sɔːrs-/ *verb* **1 ~ sth (from sb/sth)** to make an evil spirit leave a place or sb's body by special prayers or magic（用祈禱或法術）祛除（邪惡），驅魔 **2 ~ sth (from sth)** (*formal*) to remove sth that is bad or painful from your mind 消除，除去（不好的或痛苦的想法）：*She had managed to exorcize these unhappy memories from her mind.* 她終於把這些不愉快的記憶從頭腦中抹掉了。

exo·skel·eton /ˈeksəʊskelɪtn; *NAmE* ˈeksoʊ-/ *noun* (*biology* 生) a hard outer covering that protects the bodies of certain animals, such as insects（昆蟲等動物的）外骨骼 ➲ compare ENDOSKELETON

exo·ther·mic /ˌeksəʊˈθɜːmɪk; *NAmE* ˌeksoʊˈθɜːrmɪk/ *adj.* (*chemistry* 化) (of a chemical reaction 化學反應) producing heat 放熱的 ➲ compare ENDOTHERMIC

exot·ic /ɪɡˈzɒtɪk; *NAmE* ɪɡˈzɑːtɪk/ *adj.* from or in another country, especially a tropical one; seeming exciting and unusual because it is connected with foreign countries 來自異國（尤指熱帶國家）的；奇異的；異國情調的；異國風味的：*brightly-coloured **exotic flowers/plants/birds*** 色彩鮮豔的異國花卉／植物／鳥兒◇ *She travels to all kinds of exotic locations all over the world.* 她走遍了全世界所有具有奇異風情的地方。▸ **exot·ic·al·ly** /-kli/ *adv.*：*rainbows of exotically coloured blooms* 奇異的七彩花彩虹

exot·ica /ɪɡˈzɒtɪkə; *NAmE* ɪɡˈzɑːt-/ *noun* [U] unusual and exciting things, especially from other countries（尤指來自異國的）奇異事物，異族事物

eˌxotic ˈdancer *noun* an entertainer who dances with very few clothes on, or who removes clothes while dancing 脱衣舞女；豔舞女郎

exoti·cism /ɪɡˈzɒtɪsɪzəm; *NAmE* ɪɡˈzɑːt-/ *noun* [U] (*formal*) the quality of being exciting and unusual that sth has because it is connected with foreign countries 異國情調；外國風情

ex·pand 0-w AW /ɪkˈspænd/ *verb* **1** 0-w [I, T] to become greater in size, number or importance; to make sth greater in size, number or importance 擴大，增加，增強（尺碼、數量或重要性）：*Metals expand when they are heated.* 金屬受熱會膨脹。◇ *Student numbers are expanding rapidly.* 學生人數在迅速增加。◇ *A child's vocabulary expands through reading.* 孩子的詞彙量通過閱讀得到擴大。◇ *The waist expands to fit all sizes.* 腰部可鬆可緊，適合任何尺碼。◇ **~ sth** *In breathing the chest muscles expand the ribcage and allow air to be sucked into the lungs.* 呼吸時胸部肌肉使胸廓擴大讓空氣吸入肺部。◇ *The new system expanded the role of family doctors.* 新體制擴大了家庭醫生的作用。◇ *There are no plans to expand the local airport.* 目前沒有擴建地方機場的計劃。OPP **contract 2** 0-w [I, T] if a business **expands** or **is expanded**, new branches are opened, it makes more money, etc. 擴展，發展（業務）：*an expanding economy* (= with more businesses starting and growing) 不斷發展的經濟 ◇ **~ sth** *We've expanded the business by opening two more stores.* 我們增開了兩家商店以擴展業務。**3** [I] to talk more; to add details to what you are saying 細談；詳述；詳細闡明：*I repeated the question and waited for her to expand.* 我把問題重複了一遍，等着她詳細回答。

PHR V **exˈpand on/upon sth** to say more about sth and add some details 詳述；充分敍述；詳細闡明：*Could you expand on that point, please?* 請你把那一點詳細說明一下好嗎？

ex·pand·able /ɪkˈspændəbl/ *adj.* (*technical* 術語) that can be expanded 可擴張的；可擴充的；可膨脹的：*an expandable briefcase* 可伸縮公文包 ◇ **~ to sth** *The system has 1GB RAM, expandable to 4GB.* 這個系統的內存為 1 千兆字節，可擴充到 4 千兆字節。

ex·panse /ɪkˈspæns/ *noun* **~ (of sth)** a wide and open area of sth, especially land or water 一大片，廣闊，寬廣，浩瀚（尤指陸地或海洋）：*a* ***wide/vast expanse*** *of blue sky* 廣闊 / 無垠的藍天 ◇ *flat expanses of open farmland* 平坦而遼闊的農田

ex·pan·sion AW /ɪkˈspænʃn/ *noun* [U, C] an act of increasing or making sth increase in size, amount or importance 擴張；擴展；擴大；膨脹：*a period of rapid economic expansion* 經濟迅猛發展期 ◇ *Despite the recession the company is confident of further expansion.* 儘管經濟衰退，公司對進一步擴展仍充滿信心。◇ *The book is an expansion of a series of lectures given last year.* 本書是去年舉行的系列講座的擴充。

ex·pan·sion·ary /ɪkˈspænʃənri/ *adj.* (*formal*) encouraging economic expansion 刺激經濟擴張的：*This budget will have a net expansionary effect on the economy.* 本預算對經濟的發展最終會有促進作用。

exˈpansion card (also **ˈadd-in**) *noun* (*computing* 計) a CIRCUIT BOARD that can be put into a computer to give it more memory or make it able to do more things 擴展卡

ex·pan·sion·ism AW /ɪkˈspænʃənɪzəm/ *noun* [U] (sometimes *disapproving*) the belief in and process of increasing the size and importance of sth, especially in a country or a business 擴張主義；擴張政策：*the economic expansionism of America* 美國的經濟擴張主義 ◇ ***military/territorial expansionism*** 軍事 / 領土擴張主義 ▸ **ex·pan·sion·ist** /-ʃənɪst/ *adj.*：*expansionist policies* 擴張主義政策 **ex·pan·sion·ist** *noun*：*He was a ruthless expansionist.* 他是個殘酷的擴張主義者。

ex·pan·sive AW /ɪkˈspænsɪv/ *adj.* **1** covering a large amount of space 廣闊的；遼闊的；浩瀚的：*She opened her arms wide in an expansive gesture of welcome.* 她豪爽地張開雙臂以示歡迎。◇ *landscape with expansive skies* 以遼闊藍天為背景的風景 **2** covering a large subject area, rather than trying to be exact and use few words 廣泛的；全面的：*We need to look at a more expansive definition of the term.* 我們需要考慮這個用語所包含的更廣泛意義。◇ *The piece is written in his usual expansive style.* 這篇文章是以他慣常的洋洋灑灑的風格寫成的。**3** friendly and willing to talk a lot 友善健談的；開朗的：*She was clearly relaxed and in an expansive mood.* 她顯然悠閒自在，心情豁達開朗。**4** (especially of a period of time 尤指一段時間) encouraging economic EXPANSION 刺激經濟擴展的：*In the expansive 1990s bright graduates could advance rapidly.* 在經濟發展快速的 20 世紀 90 年代，有才華的大學畢業生可以發展很快。▸ **ex·pan·sive·ly** *adv.*：*He waved his arms expansively.* 他豪爽地揮舞着雙臂。**ex·pan·sive·ness** *noun* [U]

ex·pati·ate /ɪkˈspeɪʃieɪt/ *verb*

PHR V **exˈpatiate on/upon sth** (*formal*) to write or speak in detail about a subject 詳述；細說；闡述

ex·patri·ate /ˌeksˈpætriət; *NAmE* -ˈpeɪt-/ (also *informal* **expat** /ˌeksˈpæt/) *noun* a person living in a country that is not their own 居住在國外的人；僑民：*American expatriates in Paris* 居住在巴黎的美國人 ▸ **ex·patri·ate** *adj.* [only before noun]：*expatriate Britons in Spain* 居住在西班牙的英國人 ◇ *expatriate workers* 在國外工作的人

Language Bank 用語庫

expect

Discussing predictions 談論預測

- The number of people using mobile phones to purchase goods and services is **expected/likely** to more than double by the end of 2015. 到 2015 年底，使用手機購買商品和服務的人數預計 / 可能會是現在的兩倍多。
- Experts have **predicted/forecast** that the number of people using their mobile phones to pay for goods and services should exceed 190 million in 2015. 專家已經預言，到 2015 年使用手機支付商品和服務費用的人數將超過 1.9 億。
- This figure **is set to** reach 200 million by 2016. 到 2016 年這個數字可能會達到 2 億。
- **By** 2015, 800 million mobile phone users worldwide **will** be participating in social networks via their phone. 到 2015 年，全球將有 8 億手機用戶通過手機參與社交網絡。
- Sales of mobile phones in 2009 were lower **than expected**. * 2009 年的手機銷量低於預期。
- The company's announcement of 1.26 billion handsets sold for the year is **in line with predictions**. 公司宣佈本年度手機銷量為 12.6 億部，符合預期。

➲ Language Banks at FALL, ILLUSTRATE, INCREASE, PROPORTION

ex·pect 0-w /ɪkˈspekt/ *verb* **1** 0-w [T] to think or believe that sth will happen or that sb will do sth 預料；預期；預計：**~ sth** *We are expecting a rise in food prices this month.* 我們預計這個月的食物價格會上漲。◇ **~ sth from sb/sth** *Don't expect sympathy from me!* 休想得到我的同情！◇ **~ sth of sb/sth** *That's not the sort of behaviour I expect of you!* 我不敢相信你竟有那樣的行為！◇ **~ to do sth** *You can't expect to learn a foreign language in a few months.* 不要指望在幾個月內就能學會一門外語。◇ *I looked back,* ***half expecting*** *to see someone following me.* 我回過頭去，預計可能看到有人跟蹤我。◇ **~ sb/sth to do sth** *House prices are expected to rise sharply.* 預計房價會急劇上漲。◇ *Do you really expect me to believe you?* 你真以為我會相信你嗎？◇ **~ (that) …** *Many people were expecting (that) the peace talks would break down.* 許多人預料和平談判會破裂。◇ **it is expected that …** *It is expected that the report will suggest some major reforms.* 預計這個報告會提出一些重大的改革。**2** 0-w [T] (often used in the progressive tenses 常用於進行時) to be waiting for sb/sth to arrive, as this has been arranged 等待；期待；盼望：**~ sb/sth** *to expect a visit/call/letter from sb* 等待某人的來訪 / 電話 / 來信 ◇ *Are you expecting visitors?* 你在等客人嗎？◇ *We were expecting him yesterday.* 我們昨天一直在等他。

◇ **~ sb to do sth** *We were expecting him to arrive yesterday.* 我們一直盼望着他昨天到達。 **3** 🔑 to demand that sb will do sth because it is their duty or responsibility 要求；期望；指望： **~ sth (from sb)** *Her parents expected high standards from her.* 她的父母對她的期望很高。◇ *He's still getting over his illness, so don't expect too much from him.* 他仍處於康復期，所以不要對他期望過高。◇ **~ sth (of sb)** *Are you clear what is expected of you?* 你清楚大家對你的期望嗎？◇ **~ sb to do sth** *They expected all their children to be high achievers.* 他們期望自己所有的孩子都大有作為。◇ **~ to do sth** *I expect to be paid promptly for thework.* 我希望立即給付工錢。➲ SYNONYMS at DEMAND **4** 🔑 [I, T] (*informal, especially BrE*) (not used in the progressive tenses 不用於進行時) used when you think sth is probably true 猜想；認為；料想： *'Will you be late?' '**I expect so.**'* "你會遲到嗎？" "我想會的。" ◇ *'Are you going out tonight?' '**I don't expect so.**'* "你今晚要出去嗎？" "我想不會吧。" ◇ **~ (that ...)** *'Who's eaten all the cake?' 'Tom, I expect/I expect it was Tom.'* "誰把蛋糕都吃光了？" "我想是湯姆吧。" HELP 'That' is nearly always left out. * that 幾乎總是被省略。➲ compare UNEXPECTED

IDM **be expecting a baby/child** 🔑 (*informal*) to be pregnant 懷孕；懷胎： *Ann's expecting a baby in June.* 安六月份要生孩子。 **be (only) to be ex'pected** to be likely to happen; to be quite normal 可能發生；可以預料；相當正常： *A little tiredness after taking these drugs is to be expected.* 服用這些藥後有點倦意是正常的。 **what (else) do you ex'pect?** (*informal*) used to tell sb not to be surprised by sth 那有什麼大驚小怪的；那還用得着驚奇嗎；那還用說嗎： *She swore at you? What do you expect when you treat her like that?* 她用粗話罵你了？你那樣待她那還用說嗎？

ex·pect·ancy /ɪk'spektənsi/ *noun* [U] the state of expecting or hoping that sth, especially sth good or exciting, will happen 預料；預期；期待；盼望： *There was **an air of expectancy** among the waiting crowd.* 等待的人群有一種期盼的心情。➲ see also LIFE EXPECTANCY

ex·pect·ant /ɪk'spektənt/ *adj.* **1** hoping for sth, especially sth good and exciting 期待的；預期的；期望的： *children with expectant faces waiting for the fireworks to begin* 帶着期盼的神情等待煙火表演的孩子們 ◇ *A sudden roar came from the expectant crowd.* 期待的人群中突然發出一聲咆哮。 **2 ~ mother/father/parent** used to describe sb who is going to have a baby soon or become a father 未來的（母親、父親、父母） ▸ **ex·pect·ant·ly** *adv.*： *She looked at him expectantly.* 她滿懷期望地看着他。◇ *waiting expectantly* 滿懷期望地等待

ex·pect·ation 🔑 /ˌekspek'teɪʃn/ *noun*
1 🔑 [U, C] a belief that sth will happen because it is likely 預料；預期；期待： **~ (of sth)** *We are confident in our expectation of a full recovery.* 我們滿懷信心地期待着完全康復。◇ **~ (that ...)** *There was a general expectation that he would win.* 普遍認為他會獲勝。◇ *The expectation is that property prices will rise.* 預計地產價格會上漲。◇ *I applied for the post more in hope than expectation.* 我申請這個職位是希望多於期待。◇ ***Contrary to expectations**, interest rates did not rise.* 出乎意料的是利率並未上升。◇ ***Against all expectations**, she was enjoying herself.* 完全沒想到她過得非常快活。 **2** 🔑 [C, usually pl., U] a hope that sth good will happen 希望；盼望： *She went to college with great expectations.* 她滿懷希望地進入大學。◇ *There was an air of expectation and great curiosity.* 有着一種期待和神秘的氣氛。◇ *The results exceeded our expectations.* 結果比我們希望的還好。◇ *The numbers attending fell short of expectations.* 出席的人數比預期的要少。◇ *The event did not **live up to expectations**.* 這項活動有負眾望。 **3** 🔑 [C, usually pl.] a strong belief about the way sth should happen or how sb should behave 期望；指望： *Some parents have unrealistic expectations of their children.* 有些父母對孩子的指望不切實際。◇ *Unfortunately the new software has failed to **meet expectations**.* 遺憾的是新軟件並不理想。

ˌexpectation of 'life *noun* [U] = LIFE EXPECTANCY

ex·pect·ed 🔑 /ɪk'spektɪd/ *adj.* that you think will happen 預料的；預期的： *Double the expected number of people came to the meeting.* 出席會議的人數比預期的多一倍。◇ *this year's expected earnings* 今年的預計收入 ➲ compare UNEXPECTED

ex·pec·tor·ant /ɪk'spektərənt/ *noun* (*medical* 醫) a cough medicine that helps you to get rid of thick liquid (= PHLEGM) from the lungs 祛痰藥

ex·pec·tor·ate /ɪk'spektəreɪt/ *verb* [I] (*formal*) to cough and make PHLEGM come up from your lungs into your mouth so you can SPIT it out 咳出（痰） ▸ **ex·pec·tor·ation** /ɪkˌspektə'reɪʃn/ *noun* [U]

ex·pe·di·ent /ɪk'spiːdiənt/ *noun, adj.*
■ ***noun*** an action that is useful or necessary for a particular purpose, but not always fair or right 權宜之計；應急辦法： *The disease was controlled **by the simple expedient of** not allowing anyone to leave the city.* 採取了禁止所有人出城的簡單應急辦法使疾病得到了控制。
■ ***adj.*** [not usually before noun] (of an action 行動) useful or necessary for a particular purpose, but not always fair or right 得當；可取；合宜；權宜之計： *The government has clearly decided that a cut in interest rates would be politically expedient.* 政府顯然認為削減利率是政治上的權宜之計。 OPP **inexpedient** ▸ **ex·pe·di·ency** /-ənsi/ *noun* [U]： *He acted out of expediency, not principle.* 他的行為是出於權宜之計而非原則。 **ex·pe·di·ent·ly** *adv.*

ex·ped·ite /'ekspədaɪt/ *verb* **~ sth** (*formal*) to make a process happen more quickly 加快；加速 SYN **speed up**： *We have developed rapid order processing to expedite deliveries to customers.* 我們已開發了快速處理訂單的方法以便迅速將貨物交給顧客。

ex·ped·ition /ˌekspə'dɪʃn/ *noun* **1** an organized journey with a particular purpose, especially to find out about a place that is not well known 遠征；探險；考察： *to **plan/lead/go on an expedition** to the North Pole* 計劃 / 帶隊 / 去北極探險 **2** the people who go on an expedition 遠征隊；探險隊；考察隊： *Three members of the Everest expedition were killed.* 三名珠穆朗瑪峰探險隊員遇難。 **3** (sometimes *humorous*) a short trip that you make when you want or need sth （短途的）旅行，出行： *a shopping expedition* 外出購物 ➲ SYNONYMS at TRIP

ex·ped·ition·ary force /ˌekspə'dɪʃənri fɔːs; *NAmE* -neri fɔːrs/ *noun* a group of soldiers who are sent to another country to fight in a war（派往國外參戰的）遠征軍

ex·ped·itious /ˌekspə'dɪʃəs/ *adj.* (*formal*) that works well without wasting time, money, etc. 迅速而有效的；迅速完成的 SYN **efficient** ▸ **ex·ped·itious·ly** *adv.*

expel /ɪk'spel/ *verb* (**-ll-**) **1 ~ sb (from sth)** to officially make sb leave a school or an organization 把…開除（或除名）： *She was expelled from school at 15.* 她 15 歲時被學校開除了。◇ *Olympic athletes expelled for drug-taking* 因服禁藥被取消比賽資格的奧運會運動員 ➲ COLLOCATIONS at EDUCATION **2 ~ sb (from sth)** to force sb to leave a country 驅逐出境： *Foreign journalists are being expelled.* 外國記者被驅逐出境。 **3 ~ sth (from sth)** (*technical* 術語) to force air or water out of a part of the body or from a container 排出；噴出： *to expel air from the lungs* 用力呼出肺裏的氣 ➲ see also EXPULSION

ex·pend /ɪk'spend/ *verb* **~ sth (in/on sb)** | **~ sth (in/on/doing sth)** (*formal*) to use or spend a lot of time, money, energy, etc. 花費；消費；耗費： *She expended all her efforts on the care of home and children.* 她把所有精力都花在照顧家庭和孩子上。

ex·pend·able /ɪk'spendəbl/ *adj.* (*formal*) if you consider people or things to be **expendable**, you think that you can get rid of them when they are no longer needed, or think it is acceptable if they are killed or destroyed 可犧牲的；可消耗的；可毀滅的 SYN **dispensable**

ex·pend·iture /ɪk'spendɪtʃə(r)/ *noun* [U, C] **1** the act of spending or using money; an amount of money spent 花費；消費；費用；開支： *a reduction in **public/government/military expenditure*** 公共 / 政府 / 軍費開支的削減 ◇ *plans to increase expenditure on health* 增加醫療保健開支的計劃 ◇ *The budget provided for a total expenditure of £27 billion.* 預算案規定支出總額為 270 億英鎊。➲ SYNONYMS at COST **2** the use of energy, time, materials, etc.（精力、時間、材料等的）耗費，消耗：*the expenditure of emotion* 感情耗費 ◇ *This study represents a major expenditure of time and effort.* 這項研究意味着要耗費大量的時間和精力。 ➲ compare INCOME

Synonyms 同義詞辨析

expensive

costly • overpriced • pricey

These words all describe sth that costs a lot of money. 以上各詞均用於花錢多的事物。

expensive costing a lot of money; charging high prices 指昂貴的、花錢多的、價格高的：*I can't afford it—it's just too expensive for me.* 我買不起，對我來說這太貴了。◇ *an expensive restaurant* 高檔餐館

costly (*rather formal*) costing a lot of money, especially more than you want to pay 指昂貴的、花錢多的、價錢比願意付的為高：*You want to avoid costly legal proceedings if you can.* 如果能夠的話你希望避免昂貴的法律訴訟。

overpriced too expensive; costing more than it is worth 指價格太高的、過於昂貴的：*ridiculously overpriced designer clothes* 貴得離譜的名牌衣服

pricey (*informal*) expensive 指昂貴的、價格高的：*Houses in the village are now too pricey for local people to afford.* 如今該村莊的房價太高，當地人根本買不起。

dear [not usually before noun] (*BrE*) expensive 指昂貴、價格高：*Everything's so dear now, isn't it?* 現在什麼東西都那麼貴，是不是？ **NOTE** This word is starting to become rather old-fashioned. 這詞已開始有些過時了。

PATTERNS

- expensive/costly/overpriced/pricey **for** sb/sth
- expensive/costly **to do sth**
- **very/too/fairly/quite/pretty** expensive/costly/pricey

ex·pense 🔑 /ɪk'spens/ *noun*
1 🔑 [U] the money that you spend on sth 費用；價錢：*The garden was transformed **at great expense**.* 花園改建花了一大筆費用。◇ ***No expense was spared*** (= they spent as much money as was needed) *to make the party a success.* 為使聚會成功多大費用都在所不惜。◇ *He's arranged everything, **no expense spared**.* 他不惜代價把一切安排得井井有條。◇ *She always travels first-class regardless of expense.* 無論費用多高她總是乘頭等艙。◇ *The results are well worth the expense.* 有這些結果花的錢很值。 ➲ SYNONYMS at PRICE **2** 🔑 [C, usually sing.] something that makes you spend money 花錢的東西；開銷：*Running a car is a big expense.* 養一輛車開銷很大。 **3** 🔑 **expenses** [pl.] money spent in doing a particular job, or for a particular purpose 開支；花費；費用：***living/household/medical/legal, etc. expenses*** 生活費用；家庭開支；醫療、律師等費用 ◇ *Can I give you something towards expenses?* 在開支方面我能為你做點什麼嗎？◇ *financial help to meet the expenses of an emergency* 供緊急情況下開支的經濟援助 ◇ *The payments he gets barely cover his expenses.* 他幾乎是入不敷出。 ➲ SYNONYMS at COST **4** 🔑 **expenses** [pl.] money that you spend while you are working and which your employer will pay back to you later（向雇主報銷的）費用，開支，花銷，業務費用：*You can claim back your **travelling/travel** expenses.* 你可以報銷差旅費。◇ (*BrE*) *to take a client out for a meal **on expenses*** 用業務費請客戶外出就餐 ◇ *an **all-expenses-paid** trip* 費用全數報銷的公差 ➲ SYNONYMS at COST
IDM **at sb's expense** **1** paid for by sb 由某人付錢；由某人負擔費用：*We were taken out for a meal at the company's expense.* 公司出錢請我們外出就餐。 **2** if you make a joke **at sb's expense**, you laugh at them and make them feel silly 在某人受損的情況下；以某人為代價；跟某人開玩笑 **at the expense of sb/sth** with loss or damage to sb/sth 在犧牲（或損害）…的情況下：*He built up the business at the expense of his health.* 他以自己的健康為代價逐步建立起這個企業。 **go to the expense of sth/of doing sth** | **go to a lot of, etc. expense** to spend money on sth 把錢用在…上；花錢於：*They went to all the expense of redecorating the house and then they moved.* 他們不惜一切代價重新裝飾這房子，可後來又搬走了。 **put sb to the expense of sth/of doing sth** | **put sb to a lot of, etc. expense** to make sb spend money on sth 使某人花錢（於…）；使某人負擔費用：*Their visit put us to a lot of expense.* 他們的來訪使我們破費不小。 ➲ more at OBJECT *n.*

E

ex'pense account *noun* an arrangement by which money spent by sb while they are at work is later paid back to them by their employer; a record of money spent in this way 報銷賬目；費用賬戶

ex·pen·sive 🔑 /ɪk'spensɪv/ *adj.* costing a lot of money 昂貴的；花錢多的；價格高的：*an expensive car/restaurant/holiday* 昂貴的汽車；高檔的餐館；花費大的假日 ◇ *Art books are expensive to produce.* 美術書籍製作成本高。◇ *I can't afford it, it's too expensive.* 我買不起，太貴了。◇ *Making the wrong decision could **prove expensive**.* 錯誤的決策可能會付出昂貴的代價。◇ *That dress was an **expensive mistake**.* 那件連衣裙看走眼買貴了。 **OPP** **inexpensive** ▸ **ex·pen·sive·ly** *adv.*：*expensively dressed/furnished* 穿着／陳設華貴 ◇ *There are other restaurants where you can eat less expensively.* 還有其他一些餐館價錢稍微便宜些。

ex·peri·ence 🔑 /ɪk'spɪəriəns; *NAmE* -'spɪr-/ *noun, verb*
■ ***noun*** **1** 🔑 [U] the knowledge and skill that you have gained through doing sth for a period of time; the process of gaining this（由實踐得來的）經驗；實踐：*to have over ten years' teaching experience* 有十多年教學經驗 ◇ *Do you have any **previous experience** of this type of work?* 你以前幹過這種工作嗎？◇ *a doctor with **experience in** dealing with patients suffering from stress* 在治療受到壓力的病人方面很有經驗的醫生 ◇ *My lack of **practical experience** was a disadvantage.* 我缺少實際經驗是個不利條件。◇ *She didn't get paid much but it was all **good experience**.* 她得到的報酬雖然不高，但有極好的體驗。◇ *He gained valuable experience whilst working on the project.* 從事這項工程使他獲得了寶貴的經驗。◇ *We all **learn by experience**.* 我們都從經驗中學習。 ➲ see also WORK EXPERIENCE **2** 🔑 [U] the things that have happened to you that influence the way you think and behave 經歷；閱歷：*Experience has taught me that life can be very unfair.* 經歷使我懂得人生有時是很不公平的。◇ *It is important to try and **learn from experience**.* 努力從經驗中學習是重要的。◇ ***In my experience**, very few people really understand the problem.* 據我的經驗看，真正理解這個問題的人很少。◇ *She knew **from past experience** that Ann would not give up easily.* 她憑以往的經驗知道安是不會輕易放棄的。◇ *The book is based on **personal experience**.* 本書是以個人經歷為基礎的。◇ ***direct/first-hand experience** of poverty* 對貧窮的直接／親身感受 **3** 🔑 [C] an event or activity that affects you in some way（一次）經歷，體驗：*an enjoyable/exciting/unusual/unforgettable, etc. experience* 愉快、激動人心、異乎尋常、難以忘記等的經歷 ◇ **~ (of sth)** *It was her first experience of living alone.* 那是她第一次體驗單獨生活。◇ *Living in Africa was very different from home and **quite an experience*** (= unusual for us). 生活在非洲完全不同於在家裏，那真是一次不同尋常的經歷。◇ *I had a bad experience with fireworks once.* 我放煙火有過一次不愉快的遭遇。◇ *He seems to have had some sort of religious experience.* 他似乎有某種宗教體驗。 **4** **the ... experience** [sing.] events or knowledge shared by all the members of a particular group in society, that influences the way they think and behave 傳統：*musical forms like jazz that emerged out of the Black American experience* 諸如爵士樂這類起源於美國黑人傳統的音樂形式
IDM **put sth down to ex'perience** (also **chalk sth up to ex'perience**) used to say that sb should think of a failure as being sth that they can learn from 從…中吸取教訓：*We lost a lot of money, but we just put it down to experience.* 我們損失了很多錢，只當是吃一塹長一智了。

E

■ *verb* **1** ⊶ **~ sth** to have a particular situation affect you or happen to you 經歷；經受；遭受：*The country experienced a foreign currency shortage for several months.* 這個國家經歷了幾個月的外匯短缺。◇ *Everyone experiences these problems at some time in their lives.* 每個人在人生的某個階段都會經歷這些問題。**2** ⊶ **~ sth** to have and be aware of a particular emotion or physical feeling 感受；體會；體驗：*to experience pain/pleasure/unhappiness* 感受痛苦／愉快／不幸 ◇ *I experienced a moment of panic as I boarded the plane.* 我上飛機時曾一度感到恐慌。

ex·peri·enced ⊶ /ɪkˈspɪəriənst; *NAmE* -ˈspɪr-/ *adj.* **1** ⊶ having knowledge or skill in a particular job or activity 有經驗的；熟練的：*an experienced teacher* 經驗豐富的教師 ◇ **~ in sth/in doing sth** *He's very experienced in looking after animals.* 他養動物很有經驗。**2** ⊶ having knowledge as a result of doing sth for a long time, or having had a lot of different experiences 有閱歷的；有見識的；老練的：*She's very young and not very experienced.* 她很年輕，還不太老練。◇ *an experienced traveller* (= sb who has travelled a lot) 閱歷豐富的旅行者 OPP **inexperienced**

ex·peri·en·tial /ɪkˌspɪəriˈenʃl; *NAmE* -ˌspɪr-/ *adj.* (*formal* or *technical* 術語) based on or involving experience 經驗得來的；來自經驗的；經驗的：*experiential knowledge* 由經驗得來的知識 ◇ *experiential learning methods* 由經驗得來的學習方法

ex·peri·ment ⊶ /ɪkˈsperɪmənt/ *noun, verb*

■ *noun* [C, U] **1** ⊶ a scientific test that is done in order to study what happens and to gain new knowledge 實驗；試驗：*to* **do/perform/conduct an experiment** 做／進行實驗 ◇ *proved* **by experiment** 經過實驗證明 ◇ *laboratory experiments* 實驗室實驗 ◇ *Many people do not like the idea of experiments on animals.* 許多人不贊成在動物身上做試驗。➲ COLLOCATIONS at SCIENTIFIC **2** ⊶ a new activity, idea or method that you try out to see what happens or what effect it has 嘗試；實踐：*I've never cooked this before so it's an experiment.* 我以前從未做過這種菜，所以這是一個嘗試。◇ **~ in sth** *the country's brief experiment in democracy* 這個國家對民主的短暫嘗試

■ *verb* **1** ⊶ [I] **~ (on sb/sth)** | **~ (with sth)** to do a scientific experiment or experiments 做試驗；進行實驗：*Some people feel that experimenting on animals is wrong.* 有人覺得利用動物做實驗是錯誤的。**2** ⊶ [I] **~ (on sb/sth)** | **~ (with sth)** to try or test new ideas, methods, etc. to find out what effect they have 嘗試；試用：*I experimented until I got the recipe just right.* 我不斷地嘗試，直至找到正合適的烹飪法為止。◇ *He wanted to experiment more with different textures in his paintings.* 他想在自己的繪畫中更多地嘗試不同的紋理結構。▶ **ex·peri·ment·er** *noun*

ex·peri·men·tal /ɪkˌsperɪˈmentl/ *adj.* **1** based on new ideas, forms or methods that are used to find out what effect they have 以實驗（或試驗）為基礎的；實驗性的；試驗性的：*experimental teaching methods* 試驗性教學方法 ◇ ***experimental theatre/art/music*** 實驗戲劇／藝術／音樂 ◇ *The equipment is still at the experimental stage.* 這種設備仍處於試驗階段。**2** connected with scientific experiments 科學實驗的；科學試驗的：***experimental conditions/data/evidence*** 實驗環境／數據／證據 ▶ **ex·peri·men·tal·ly** /-təli/ *adv.*：*This theory can be confirmed experimentally.* 這種理論可通過實驗得到證實。◇ *The new drug is being used experimentally on some patients.* 這種新藥正由某些病人試用。◇ *He moved his shoulder experimentally to see if it still hurt.* 他試着動了動肩看看還疼不疼。

ex·peri·men·ta·tion /ɪkˌsperɪmenˈteɪʃn/ *noun* [U] (*formal*) the activity or process of experimenting 實驗；試驗：*experimentation with new teaching methods* 用新的教學方法實驗 ◇ *Many people object to experimentation on embryos.* 許多人反對用胚胎做實驗。

ex·pert ⊶ AW /ˈekspɜːt; *NAmE* -pɜːrt/ *noun, adj.*

■ *noun* ⊶ a person with special knowledge, skill or training in sth 專家；行家；能手：*a computer/medical expert* 計算機／醫學專家 ◇ **~ (at/in/on sth)** *an expert in child psychology* 兒童心理學家 ◇ *an expert on modern literature* 現代文學研究專家 ◇ **~ (at/in/on doing sth)** *He's an expert at getting his own way.* 他在如何達到自己的目的方面很在行。◇ *Don't ask me—I'm no expert!* 不要問我，我不是行家！

■ *adj.* ⊶ done with, having or involving great knowledge or skill 熟練的；內行的；專家的；經驗（或知識）豐富的：*to* **seek expert advice/an expert opinion** 徵求專家意見 ◇ *an expert driver* 技術高超的駕駛員 ◇ *We need some expert help.* 我們需要一些內行的幫助。◇ **~ (at/in sth)** *They are all expert in this field.* 他們都是這個領域的行家。◇ **~ (at/in doing sth)** *She's expert at making cheap but stylish clothes.* 她擅長做便宜但雅致的服裝。➲ compare INEXPERT ▶ **ex·pert·ly** AW *adv.*：*The roads were icy but she stopped the car expertly.* 道路結了冰，可她卻非常熟練地把車停了下來。◇ *The music was expertly performed.* 樂曲演奏得非常嫻熟。

ex·pert·ise AW /ˌekspɜːˈtiːz; *NAmE* -pɜːrˈt-/ *noun* [U] expert knowledge or skill in a particular subject, activity or job 專門知識；專門技能；專長：***professional/scientific/technical, etc.*** *expertise* 專業、科學、技術等知識 ◇ *We have the expertise to help you run your business.* 我們有幫助你經營自己業務的專門知識。◇ **~ in sth/in doing sth** *They have considerable expertise in dealing with oil spills.* 他們在解決溢油問題方面非常在行。

ˌexpert ˈsystem *noun* (*computing* 計) a computer system that can provide information and expert advice on a particular subject. The program asks users a series of questions about their problem and gives them advice based on its store of knowledge.（計算機）專家系統

ex·pi·ate /ˈekspieɪt/ *verb* **~ sth** (*formal*) to accept punishment for sth that you have done wrong in order to show that you are sorry 為（所犯罪過）接受懲罰；贖（罪）：*He had a chance to confess and expiate his guilt.* 他有認錯和贖罪的機會。▶ **ex·pi·ation** /ˌekspiˈeɪʃn/ *noun* [U, sing.]

ex·pir·ation /ˌekspəˈreɪʃn/ *noun* [U] (*NAmE, formal*) = EXPIRY

expiˈration date *noun* (*NAmE*) (*BrE* **exˈpiry date**) the date after which an official document, agreement, etc. is no longer valid, or after which sth should not be used or eaten（文件、協議等的）到期日，截止日期；（物品、食品等的）有效期：*Check the expiration date on your passport.* 檢查一下你護照上的有效期。◇ *The expiration date on this yogurt was November 20.* 這酸奶的食用期限到 11 月 20 日。

ex·pire /ɪkˈspaɪə(r)/ *verb* **1** [I] (of a document, an agreement, etc. 文件、協議等) to be no longer valid because the period of time for which it could be used has ended（因到期而）失效，終止；到期 SYN **run out**：*When does your driving licence expire?* 你的駕照什麼時候到期？**2** [I] (of a period of time, especially one during which sb holds a position of authority 一段時間，尤指職權的任期) to end 屆滿：*His term of office expires at the end of June.* 他的任期六月底屆滿。**3** [I] (*literary*) to die 逝世；去世；故去 ➲ see also UNEXPIRED ▶ **ex·pired** *adj.*：*an expired passport* 過期的護照

ex·piry /ɪkˈspaɪəri/ (*especially BrE*) (*NAmE* usually *formal* **ex·pir·ation**) *noun* [U] an ending of the period of time when an official document can be used, or when an agreement is valid（文件、協議等的）滿期，屆期，到期：*the expiry of a fixed-term contract* 定期合同的滿期 ◇ *The licence can be renewed on expiry.* 執照期滿時可延期。

exˈpiry date (*BrE*) (*NAmE* **expiˈration date**) *noun* the date after which an official document, agreement, etc. is no longer valid, or after which sth should not be used or eaten（文件、協議等的）到期日，截止日期；（物品、食品等的）有效期：*Check the expiry date of your credit cards.* 查看一下你的信用卡的有效期。

ex·plain ⊶ /ɪkˈspleɪn/ *verb* **1** ⊶ [T, I] to tell sb about sth in a way that makes it easy to understand 解釋；說明；闡明：**~ (sth) (to sb)** *First, I'll explain the rules*

WORD FAMILY
explain *verb*
explanation *noun*
explanatory *adj.*
explicable *adj.*
(≠ inexplicable)

of the game. 首先我要說明一下遊戲規則。◇ *It was difficult to explain the problem to beginners.* 對初學者解釋這個問題很難。◇ *'Let me explain!' he added helpfully.* "讓我來說明一下！" 他熱心地補充道。◇ **~ that …** *I explained that an ambulance would be coming soon.* 我解釋說救護車很快就到。◇ **~ who, how, etc. …** *He explained who each person in the photo was.* 他一一介紹了照片裏的人。◇ **~ to sb who, how, etc. …** *She explained to them what to do in an emergency.* 她向他們說明了緊急情況下應採取的行動。◇ **+ speech** *'It works like this,' she explained.* "它是這樣運作的。" 她解釋道。◇ **it is explained that …** *It was explained that attendance was compulsory.* 所給的解釋是必須到場。 **2** 🔑 [I, T] to give a reason, or be a reason, for sth 說明（…的）原因；解釋（…的）理由： *She tried to explain but he wouldn't listen.* 她試圖辯解，可他根本不聽。◇ **~ that …** *Alex explained that his car had broken down.* 亞歷克斯解釋說他的汽車出了毛病。◇ **~ why, how, etc. …** *Well, that doesn't explain why you didn't phone.* 嗳，那不是你不打電話的理由。◇ **~ sth (to sb)** *scientific findings that help explain the origins of the universe* 有助於解釋宇宙起源的科學發現 ◇ *The government now has to explain its decision to the public.* 政府現在必須向公眾解釋決策的理由。◇ (*informal*) *Oh well then, that* ***explains it*** (= I understand now why sth happened). 噢，原來是這麼回事。 **HELP** You cannot say 'explain me, him, her, etc.' 不能說 explain me/him/her 等： *Can you explain the situation to me?* ◇ ~~*Can you explain me the situation?*~~ ◇ *I'll explain to you why I like it.* ◇ ~~*I'll explain you why I like it.*~~

IDM **ex'plain yourself** **1** 🔑 to give sb reasons for your behaviour, especially when they are angry or upset because of it 為自己的行為作說明（或解釋）： *I really don't see why I should have to explain myself to you.* 我真不明白我為什麼非要向你解釋我的行為不可。 **2** 🔑 to say what you mean in a clear way 把自己的意思解釋清楚： *Could you explain yourself a little more—I didn't understand.* 請把你的意思說得更清楚一點，我還是不明白。

PHR V **ex,plain sth↔a'way** to give reasons why sth is not your fault or why sth is not important 為…作辯解

ex·plan·ation 🔑 /ˌekspləˈneɪʃn/ *noun* **1** 🔑 [C, U] a statement, fact, or situation that tells you why sth happened; a reason given for sth 解釋；說明；闡述；理由： *The most likely explanation is that his plane was delayed.* 最可能的解釋是他的飛機晚點了。◇ *to* ***offer/provide an explanation*** 給予解釋 ◇ **~ (for sth)** *I can't think of any possible explanation for his absence.* 我想不出他缺席的任何理由。◇ **~ (for doing sth)** *She didn't* ***give an*** *adequate* ***explanation*** *for being late.* 她沒有給出充分的理由說明遲到的原因。◇ **~ (of sth)** *The book opens with an explanation of why some drugs are banned.* 本書在開篇闡述了禁用某些藥物的原因。◇ **~ (as to why …)** *an explanation as to why he had left early* 關於他提早離開的原因說明 ◇ *She left the room abruptly* ***without explanation.*** 她未作解釋就突然離開了房間。◇ *'I had to see you,' he said, by way of explanation.* "我當時必須來找你。" 他解釋道。 ➲ SYNONYMS at REASON **2** 🔑 [C] a statement or piece of writing that tells you how sth works or makes sth easier to understand 解釋性說法；說明性文字： *For a full explanation of how the machine works, turn to page 5.* 關於機器運作原理的詳細說明，請翻閱第 5 頁。

ex·plana·tory /ɪkˈsplænətri; *NAmE* -tɔːri/ *adj.* [usually before noun] giving the reasons for sth; intended to describe how sth works or to make sth easier to understand 解釋的；說明的；闡述的： *There are explanatory notes at the back of the book.* 書後有註解。 ➲ see also SELF-EXPLANATORY

ex·ple·tive /ɪkˈspliːtɪv; *NAmE* ˈeksplətɪv/ *noun* (*formal*) a word, especially a rude word, that you use when you are angry, or in pain（憤怒或痛苦時用的）穢語，咒罵語，感歎語 **SYN** **swear word**

ex·plic·able /ɪkˈsplɪkəbl; ˈeksplɪkəbl/ *adj.* [not usually before noun] (*formal*) that can be explained or understood 可解釋；可說明；可理解： *His behaviour is only explicable in terms of* (= because of) *his recent illness.* 他的行為只能用他最近患病來解釋。 **OPP** **inexplicable**

ex·pli·cate /ˈeksplɪkeɪt/ *verb* **~ sth** (*formal*) to explain an idea or a work of literature in a lot of detail 詳細解釋，詳細分析（想法或文學作品） ▸ **ex·pli·ca·tion** /ˌekspləˈkeɪʃn/ *noun* [C, U]

ex·pli·cit **AW** /ɪkˈsplɪsɪt/ *adj.* **1** (of a statement or piece of writing 陳述或文章) clear and easy to understand 清楚明白的；易於理解的： *He gave me very explicit directions on how to get there.* 他清楚地向我說明了去那兒的路線。 **2** (of a person 人) saying sth clearly, exactly and openly（說話）清晰的，明確的；直言的；坦率的 **SYN** **frank**： *She was quite explicit about why she had left.* 她對自己離開的原因直言不諱。 **3** said, done or shown in an open or direct way, so that you have no doubt about what is happening 直截了當的；不隱晦的；不含糊的： *The reasons for the decision should be made explicit.* 應該直截了當給出決定的理由。◇ *She made some very explicit references to my personal life.* 她毫不隱諱地談到了我的私生活。◇ *a sexually explicit film* 一部有露骨性愛場面的影片 ➲ compare IMPLICIT ▸ **ex·pli·cit·ly** **AW** *adv.*： *The report states explicitly that the system was to blame.* 報告明確指出問題出在制度上。 ➲ compare IMPLICITLY **ex·pli·cit·ness** *noun* [U]： *He didn't like the degree of sexual explicitness in the film.* 他不喜歡那部電影裏性愛露骨的程度。

ex·plode 🔑 /ɪkˈspləʊd; *NAmE* ɪkˈsploʊd/ *verb*

> **WORD FAMILY**
> **explode** *verb*
> **explosion** *noun*
> **explosive** *adj., noun*
> **unexploded** *adj.*

▸ **BURST VIOLENTLY** 爆炸 **1** 🔑 [I, T] to burst or make sth burst loudly and violently, causing damage 爆炸；爆破；爆裂 **SYN** **blow up**： *Bombs were exploding all around the city.* 城裏到處都響起炸彈的爆炸聲。◇ **~ sth** *There was a huge bang as if someone had exploded a rocket outside.* 突然一聲巨響，彷彿有人在外面引爆了火箭似的。◇ *Bomb disposal experts exploded the device under controlled conditions.* 炸彈銷毀專家在受控條件下引爆了這個裝置。 ➲ compare IMPLODE (1)

▸ **GET ANGRY/DANGEROUS** 變得憤怒／危急 **2** [I, T] (of a person or situation 人或形勢) to suddenly become very angry or dangerous 勃然（大怒）；大發（雷霆）；突然發生（危險）： **~ (with sth)** *Suddenly Charles exploded with rage.* 查爾斯勃然大怒。◇ **~ (into sth)** *The protest exploded into a riot.* 抗議爆發成一場暴亂。◇ **+ speech** *'Of course there's something wrong!' Jem exploded.* "當然是出了毛病！" 傑姆大發雷霆道。

▸ **EXPRESS EMOTION** 表達感情 **3** [I] **~ (into/with sth)** to suddenly express an emotion 突然爆發，迸發（感情）： *We all exploded into wild laughter.* 我們都一下子大笑起來。

▸ **MOVE SUDDENLY** 突然行動 **4** [I] **~ (into sth)** to suddenly and quickly do sth; to move suddenly with a lot of force 突然做起…來；突然活躍起來： *After ten minutes the game exploded into life.* 比賽在十分鐘後突然激烈起來。

▸ **MAKE LOUD NOISE** 發出巨響 **5** [I] to make a sudden very loud noise 突然發出巨響： *Thunder exploded overhead.* 雷聲在頭頂上炸開。

▸ **INCREASE QUICKLY** 激增 **6** [I] to increase suddenly and very quickly in number 突增；激增： *the exploding world population* 迅猛增長的世界人口

▸ **SHOW STH IS NOT TRUE** 推翻 **7** [T] **~ sth** to show that sth is not true, especially sth that people believe 推翻；駁倒；破除： *At last, a women's magazine to explode the myth that thin equals beautiful.* 終於有一家女性雜誌起來推翻瘦就是美的迷思。 ➲ SYNONYMS at next page

ex·ploded /ɪkˈspləʊdɪd; *NAmE* -ˈsploʊ-/ *adj.* (*technical* 術語) (of a drawing or diagram 圖樣或圖表) showing the parts of sth separately but also showing how they are connected to each other 分解的 ➲ compare UNEXPLODED

ex·ploit **AW** *verb, noun*

■ *verb* /ɪkˈsplɔɪt/ **1** **~ sth** (*disapproving*) to treat a person or situation as an opportunity to gain an advantage for yourself 利用（…為自己謀利）： *He exploited his father's name to get himself a job.* 他利用他父親的名聲為

自己找到一份工作。◇ *She realized that her youth and inexperience were being exploited.* 她意識到自己的年輕和缺乏經驗正受人利用。 **2 ~ sb** (*disapproving*) to treat sb unfairly by making them work and not giving them much in return 剝削；榨取： *What is being done to stop employers from exploiting young people?* 目前有什麼措施制止雇主剝削年輕人呢？ **3 ~ sth** to use sth well in order to gain as much from it as possible 運用；利用；發揮： *She fully exploits the humour of her role in the play.* 她在劇中把她那個角色的幽默發揮得淋漓盡致。 **4** to develop or use sth for business or industry 開發；開採；開拓： **~ sth** *No minerals have yet been exploited in Antarctica.* 南極洲的礦藏還未開採。◇ **~ sth for sth** *countries exploiting the rainforests for hardwood* 為獲取硬木而開發熱帶雨林的國家 ▸ **ex·ploit·er** *noun* [C]

■ ***noun*** /ˈeksplɔɪt/ [usually pl.] a brave, exciting or interesting act 英勇（或激動人心、引人注目）的行為： *the daring exploits of Roman heroes* 古羅馬英雄的英勇壯舉

ex·ploit·ation **AW** /ˌeksplɔɪˈteɪʃn/ *noun* [U] **1** (*disapproving*) a situation in which sb treats sb else in an unfair way, especially in order to make money from their work 剝削；榨取： *the exploitation of children* 對兒童的剝削 **2** the use of land, oil, minerals, etc. 開發；開採；開拓： *commercial exploitation of the mineral resources in Antarctica* 南極洲礦物資源的商業開採 **3** (*disapproving*) the fact of using a situation in order to get an advantage for yourself（出於私利的）利用： *exploitation of the situation for his own purposes* 利用這種局勢達到他自己的目的

Synonyms 同義詞辨析

explode

blow up • go off • burst • erupt • detonate

These are all words that can be used when sth bursts apart violently, causing damage or injury. 以上各詞均可表示爆炸、爆破、爆裂。

explode to burst loudly and violently, causing damage; to make sth burst in this way 指爆炸、爆破、爆裂、引爆： *The jet smashed into a hillside and exploded.* 噴氣式飛機撞上山坡爆炸了。◇ *The bomb was exploded under controlled conditions.* 炸彈在受控條件下被引爆了。

blow (sth) up to be destroyed by an explosion; to destroy sth by an explosion 指爆炸、（被）炸毀： *A police officer was killed when his car blew up.* 一名警員在其汽車爆炸時遇難。

go off (of a bomb) to explode; (of a gun) to be fired 指（炸彈）爆炸、（槍）開火： *The bomb went off in a crowded street.* 炸彈在擠滿人的大街上爆炸了。 **NOTE** When used about guns, the choice of **go off** (instead of 'be fired') can suggest that the gun was fired by accident. 用 go off（而非 be fired）可指槍支走火。

burst to break open or apart, especially because of pressure from inside; to make sth break in this way 指（使）爆裂、脹開： *That balloon's going to burst.* 那氣球馬上要爆了。

erupt (of a volcano) to throw out burning rocks and smoke; (of burning rocks and smoke) to be thrown out of a volcano 指（火山）爆發、（岩漿、煙）噴出

detonate (*rather formal*) (of a bomb) to explode; to make a bomb explode 指（炸彈）爆炸、使（炸彈）爆炸、引爆、起爆： *Two other bombs failed to detonate.* 另外兩枚炸彈沒有爆炸。

PATTERNS

- a **bomb** explodes/blows up/goes off/bursts/detonates
- a **car/plane/vehicle** explodes/blows up
- a **firework/rocket** explodes/goes off

ex·ploit·ative /ɪkˈsplɔɪtətɪv/ (*NAmE* also **ex·ploit·ive** /ɪkˈsplɔɪtɪv/) *adj.* treating sb unfairly in order to gain an advantage or to make money 剝削的；榨取的

ex·plor·ation /ˌekspləˈreɪʃn/ *noun* [C, U] **1** the act of travelling through a place in order to find out about it or look for sth in it 勘探；勘查；探索： *the exploration of space* 對宇宙空間的探索 ◇ *oil exploration* (= searching for oil in the ground) 石油勘探 **2** an examination of sth in order to find out about it 探究；研究；探測： *the book's explorations of the human mind* 本書對人類思維的研究

ex·plora·tory /ɪkˈsplɒrətri; *NAmE* ɪkˈsplɔːrətɔːri/ *adj.* done with the intention of examining sth in order to find out more about it 探索的；探究的；探測的；勘探的： *exploratory surgery* 探索性手術 ◇ *exploratory drilling for oil* 鑽井勘探石油

ex·plore **0-w** /ɪkˈsplɔː(r)/ *verb*
1 **0-w** [T, I] to travel to or around an area or a country in order to learn about it 勘探；探索；考察： **~ sth (for sth)** *The city is best explored on foot.* 最好是徒步探索這個城市。◇ *They explored the land to the south of the Murray River.* 他們勘查了墨累河以南的地區。◇ **~ (for sth)** *As soon as we arrived on the island we were eager to explore.* 我們一來到島上就急不可耐地考察起來。◇ *companies exploring for* (= searching for) *oil* 石油勘探公司 **2** **0-w** [T] **~ sth** to examine sth completely or carefully in order to find out more about it 探究；調查研究；探索；探討 **SYN** **analyse**： *These ideas will be explored in more detail in Chapter 7.* 這些想法將在第 7 章裏作更詳細的探討。 ➲ LANGUAGE BANK at ABOUT **3** [T] **~ sth** to feel sth with your hands or another part of the body（用手或另一身體部位）觸摸，探查： *She explored the sand with her toes.* 她用腳趾觸探沙子。 ➲ see also UNEXPLORED

ex·plorer /ɪkˈsplɔːrə(r)/ *noun* a person who travels to unknown places in order to find out more about them 探險者；勘探者；考察者

Exˈplorer Scout (*US*) (*BrE* **ˈVenture Scout**) *noun* a member of the senior branch of the SCOUT ASSOCIATION for young people between the ages of 15 or 16 and 20 深資童軍，奮進童子軍（15 或 16 歲至 20 歲）

ex·plo·sion **0-w** /ɪkˈspləʊʒn; *NAmE* -ˈsploʊ-/ *noun*
1 **0-w** [C, U] the sudden violent bursting and loud noise of sth such as a bomb exploding; the act of deliberately causing sth to explode 爆炸，爆破，爆裂（聲）： *a* ***bomb/nuclear/gas explosion*** 炸彈／核／氣體爆炸 ◇ *There were two loud explosions and then the building burst into flames.* 兩聲巨響之後建築物便燃燒起來。◇ *Bomb Squad officers carried out a* ***controlled explosion*** *of the device.* 炸彈處理小組人員在受控條件下引爆了這一裝置。◇ *300 people were injured in the explosion.* 有 300 人在爆炸中受傷。 **2** **0-w** [C] a large, sudden or rapid increase in the amount or number of sth 突增；猛增；激增： *a population explosion* 人口激增 ◇ *an explosion of interest in learning Japanese* 學習日語的興趣陡然上升 **3** [C] (*formal*) a sudden, violent expression of emotion, especially anger（感情，尤指憤怒的）突然爆發，迸發 **SYN** **outburst**

ex·plo·sive /ɪkˈspləʊsɪv; -zɪv; *NAmE* -ˈsploʊ-/ *adj.*, *noun*

■ ***adj.*** **1** easily able or likely to explode 易爆炸的；可能引起爆炸的： *an* ***explosive device*** (= a bomb) 爆炸裝置（炸彈）◇ *an explosive mixture of chemicals* 易爆化學混合物 **2** likely to cause violence or strong feelings of anger or hatred 易爆發的；可能引起衝動的；爆炸性的： *a potentially explosive situation* 可能引起爆炸性反應的形勢 **3** often having sudden violent or angry feelings 暴躁的： *an explosive temper* 暴躁的脾氣 **4** increasing suddenly and rapidly 突增的；猛增的；激增的： *the explosive growth of the export market* 出口市場的急劇擴大 **5** (of a sound 聲音) sudden and loud 爆發的 ▸ **ex·plo·sive·ly** *adv.*

■ ***noun*** [C, U] a substance that is able or likely to cause an explosion 炸藥；爆炸物： *plastic explosives* 塑性炸藥 ◇ *The bomb was packed with several pounds of* ***high explosive.*** 這枚炸彈裝有幾磅烈性炸藥。

ex·po·nent /ɪk'spəʊnənt; *NAmE* -'spoʊ-/ *noun* **1** a person who supports an idea, theory, etc. and persuades others that it is good（觀點、理論等的）擁護者，鼓吹者，倡導者 SYN **proponent**：*She was* ***a leading exponent*** *of free trade during her political career* 她從政期間是自由貿易的主要倡導者。 **2** a person who is able to perform a particular activity with skill（某種活動的）能手，大師：*the most famous exponent of the art of mime* 最著名的啞劇表演藝術大師 **3** (*mathematics* 數) a raised figure or symbol that shows how many times a quantity must be multiplied by itself, for example the figure 4 in a^4 指數；冪

ex·po·nen·tial /ˌekspə'nenʃl/ *adj.* **1** (*mathematics* 數) of or shown by an exponent 指數的；冪的；由指數表示的：*2^4 is an exponential expression.* * 2^4 是個指數式。◇ *an* ***exponential curve/function*** 指數曲線 / 函數 **2** (*formal*) (of a rate of increase 增長率) becoming faster and faster 越來越快的：***exponential growth/increase*** 越來越快的增長 ▸ **ex·po·nen·ti·al·ly** /-ʃəli/ *adv.*：*to increase exponentially* 呈指數增長

ex·port O→ AW *verb, noun*

■ ***verb*** /ɪk'spɔːt; *NAmE* ɪk'spɔːrt/ **1** O→ [T, I] **~ (sth) (to sb)** to sell and send goods to another country 出口；輸出：*The islands export sugar and fruit.* 這些島出口糖和水果。◇ *90% of the engines are exported to Europe.* * 90% 的發動機都出口到歐洲。 **2** [T] **~ sth (+ adv./prep.)** to introduce an idea or activity to another country or area 傳播，輸出（思想或活動）：*American pop music has been exported around the world.* 美國流行音樂已傳播到世界各地。 **3** [T] **~ sth** (*computing* 計) to send data to another program, changing its form so that the other program can read it 輸出；移出；調出 OPP **import**

■ ***noun*** /'ekspɔːt; *NAmE* 'ekspɔːrt/ **1** O→ [U] the selling and transporting of goods to another country 出口；輸出：*a ban on the export of live cattle* 禁止活牛出口◇ *Then the fruit is packaged* ***for export***. 然後水果便包裝出口。◇ *export earnings* 出口收益◇ *an export licence* 出口許可證 **2** O→ [C, usually pl.] a product that is sold to another country 出口產品；輸出品：*the country's major exports* 該國的主要出口產品◇ *a fall in the value of exports* 出口產品值的下跌 OPP **import** ➲ COLLOCATIONS at ECONOMY

ex·port·ation /ˌekspɔː'teɪʃn; *NAmE* ˌekspɔːr't-/ *noun* [U] the process of sending goods to another country for sale 出口；輸出 OPP **importation**

ex·port·er AW /ek'spɔːtə(r); *NAmE* ek'spɔːrt-/ *noun* a person, company or country that sells goods to another country 出口商；出口公司；出口國：*the world's* ***largest/major/leading exporter*** *of cars* 世界上最大的 / 重要的 / 主要的汽車輸出國◇ *The country is now a* ***net exporter*** *of fuel* (= it exports more than it imports). 目前這個國家是燃料淨輸出國。 OPP **importer**

ex·pose O→ AW /ɪk'spəʊz; *NAmE* ɪk'spoʊz/ *verb*

▸ SHOW STH HIDDEN 使顯露 **1** O→ to show sth that is usually hidden 暴露；顯露；露出 SYN **reveal**：**~ sth** *He smiled suddenly, exposing a set of amazingly white teeth.* 他突然一笑，露出一口雪白的牙齒。◇ *Miles of sand are exposed at low tide.* 在退潮時數英里的沙灘就會顯現出來。◇ *My job as a journalist is to expose the truth.* 我作為記者的職責就是揭露真相。◇ **~ sth to sb** *He did not want to expose his fears and insecurity to anyone.* 他不想向任何人顯露他的恐懼與不安。

▸ SHOW TRUTH 揭露事實 **2** O→ **~ sb/sth (as sth)** to tell the true facts about a person or a situation, and show them/it to be immoral, illegal, etc. 揭露；揭穿：*She was exposed as a liar and a fraud.* 她說謊和欺騙的面目被揭穿了。◇ *He threatened to expose the racism that existed within the police force.* 他揚言要把警隊內部存在的種族歧視公之於眾。

▸ TO STH HARMFUL 有害事物 **3** O→ **~ sb/sth/yourself (to sth)** to put sb/sth in a place or situation where they are not protected from sth harmful or unpleasant 使面臨，使遭受（危險或不快）：*to expose yourself to ridicule* 讓自己受到嘲笑◇ *Do not expose babies to strong sunlight.* 不要讓嬰孩受到強烈的陽光照射。

▸ GIVE EXPERIENCE 給予經驗 **4 ~ sb to sth** to let sb find out about sth by giving them experience of it or showing them what it is like 使接觸；使體驗：*We want to expose the kids to as much art and culture as possible.* 我們想讓孩子們盡量受到藝術和文化薰陶。

▸ FILM IN CAMERA 照相機膠片 **5 ~ sth** to allow light onto the film inside a camera when taking a photograph 曝光

▸ YOURSELF 自己 **6 ~ yourself** a man who **exposes** himself, shows his sexual organs in public in a way that is offensive to other people 當眾露陰 ➲ see also EXPOSURE

ex·posé /ek'spəʊzeɪ; *NAmE* ˌekspoʊ'zeɪ/ *noun* an account of the facts of a situation, especially when these are shocking or have deliberately been kept secret（尤指對令人震驚或故意保密的事實的）陳述，闡述，揭露

ex·posed AW /ɪk'spəʊzd; *NAmE* ɪk'spoʊzd/ *adj.* **1** (of a place 地方) not protected from the weather by trees, buildings or high ground 無遮蔽的；不遮擋風雨的 **2** (of a person 人) not protected from attack or criticism 易受攻擊（或批評）的；無保護的：*She was left feeling exposed and vulnerable.* 她感到自己孤立無助，非常脆弱。 **3** (*finance* 財) likely to experience financial losses 風險高的；很可能遭受經濟損失的

ex·pos·ition /ˌekspə'zɪʃn/ *noun* (*formal*) **1** [C, U] a full explanation of a theory, plan, etc.（理論、計劃等的）解釋，說明，闡述：*a clear and detailed exposition of their legal position* 對他們的法律地位清楚而詳盡的說明 **2** [C] an event at which people, businesses, etc. show and sell their goods; a TRADE FAIR（產品的）展銷；商品交易會；產品博覽會

ex·posi·tory /ɪk'spɒzətri; *NAmE* ɪk'spɑːzətɔːri/ *adj.* (*formal*) intended to explain or describe sth 闡述的；解釋的；說明性的：*The film suffers from too much expository dialogue.* 這部影片的敗筆在於論說性對話過多。

ex·pos·tu·late /ɪk'spɒstʃuleɪt; *NAmE* ɪk'spɑːs-/ *verb* [I] (+ **speech**) (*formal*) to argue, disagree or protest about sth 爭論；爭執；抗議 ▸ **ex·pos·tu·la·tion** /ɪkˌspɒstʃu'leɪʃn; *NAmE* ɪkˌspɑːs-/ *noun* [U, C]

ex·pos·ure AW /ɪk'spəʊʒə(r); *NAmE* -'spoʊ-/ *noun*

▸ TO STH HARMFUL 有害事物 **1** [U] **~ (to sth)** the state of being in a place or situation where there is no protection from sth harmful or unpleasant 面臨，遭受（危險或不快）：*prolonged exposure to harmful radiation* 長時間接觸有害輻射◇ (*finance* 財) *the company's exposure on the foreign exchange markets* (= to the risk of making financial losses) 公司面對外匯市場的風險

▸ SHOWING TRUTH 揭露事實 **2** [U] the state of having the true facts about sb/sth told after they have been hidden because they are bad, immoral or illegal 揭露：*exposure as a liar and a fraud* 說謊者和騙子的面目被揭露◇ *the exposure of illegal currency deals* 對非法交易貨幣的揭露

▸ ON TV/IN NEWSPAPERS, ETC. 電視、報章等 **3** [U] the fact of being discussed or mentioned on television, in newspapers, etc.（在電視、報紙等上的）亮相，被報道 SYN **publicity**：*Her new movie has had a lot of exposure in the media.* 她的新電影媒體有很多報道。

▸ MEDICAL CONDITION 身體狀況 **4** [U] a medical condition caused by being out in very cold weather for too long without protection 挨凍；受寒：*Two climbers were brought in suffering from exposure.* 兩名登山者因凍僵被帶了進來。

▸ FILM IN CAMERA 照相機膠片 **5** [C] a length of film in a camera that is used to take a photograph（照一張照片的）軟片，底片，膠片：*There are three exposures left on this roll of film.* 這捲膠捲還有三張沒拍。 **6** [C] the length of time for which light is allowed to reach the film when taking a photograph 曝光時間：*I used a long exposure for this one.* 我這張照片用了長一點的曝光時間。

▸ SHOWING STH HIDDEN 使暴露 **7** [U] the act of showing sth that is usually hidden 暴露；顯露 ➲ see also INDECENT EXPOSURE

ex·pound /ɪk'spaʊnd/ *verb* [T, I] (*formal*) to explain sth by talking about it in detail 詳解；詳述；闡述：**~ sth (to sb)** *He expounded his views on the subject to me at great length.* 他詳細地向我闡述了他在這個問題上的觀點。◇ **~ on sth** *We listened as she expounded on the government's new policies.* 我們聽她詳細講解了政府的新政策。

ex·press 0ꟷ /ɪk'spres/ *verb, adj., adv., noun*

■ *verb* **1** 0ꟷ to show or make known a feeling, an opinion, etc. by words, looks or actions 表示；表達；表露：**~ sth** *Teachers have expressed concern about the changes.* 教師們對這些變化表示憂慮。◇ *His views have been expressed in numerous speeches.* 他已在無數次發言中表達了自己的觀點。◇ *to* ***express fears/doubts/reservations*** 表示擔心 / 懷疑 / 保留意見 ◇ *to* ***express interest/regret/surprise*** 表示關注 / 遺憾 / 驚訝 ◇ **~ how, what, etc. …** ***Words cannot express*** *how pleased I am.* 言語無法表達我的愉快心情。➲ see also UNEXPRESSED **2** 0ꟷ to speak, write or communicate in some other way what you think or feel 表達（自己的思想感情）：**~ yourself** *Teenagers often have difficulty expressing themselves.* 十來歲的孩子在表達思想方面常常有困難。◇ **~ yourself + adv./prep.** *Perhaps I have not expressed myself very well.* 我大概未把自己的意思表達清楚。◇ *She expresses herself most fully in her paintings.* 她把自己的感情在畫作中表現得淋漓盡致。◇ (*formal*) **~ yourself + adj.** *They expressed themselves delighted.* 他們表示他們很高興。 **3 ~ itself** (**+ adv./prep.**) (*formal*) (of a feeling 感覺) to become obvious in a particular way 顯而易見；不言自明：*Their pleasure expressed itself in a burst of applause.* 他們的喜悅從一陣熱烈的掌聲中表現出來。 **4** (*mathematics* 數) to represent sth in a particular way, for example by symbols（用符號等）表示，代表：**~ sth as sth** *The figures are expressed as percentages.* 這些數字用百分數表示。◇ **~ sth in sth** *Educational expenditure is often expressed in terms of the amount spent per student.* 教育經費通常以用於每個學生的開支表示。 **5 ~ sth** (**from sth**) to remove air or liquid from sth by pressing it 壓榨，擠壓出（空氣或液體）：*Coconut milk is expressed from grated coconuts.* 椰子汁是從擦碎的椰肉裹榨出來的。 **6 ~ sth** (**to sb/sth**) (*NAmE*) to send sth by express post 快遞郵寄（或發送）：*As soon as I receive payment I will express the book to you.* 我一收到款就把書用快遞給你寄去。

■ *adj.* [only before noun] **1** 0ꟷ travelling very fast; operating very quickly 特快的；快速的；快遞的：*an* ***express bus/coach/train*** 特快公共汽車 / 長途汽車 / 列車 ◇ *express delivery services* 快遞服務 **2** 0ꟷ (of a letter, package, etc. 信件、包裹等) sent by express service 用快遞寄送的：*express mail* 特快郵件 **3** 0ꟷ (*NAmE*) (of a company that delivers packages 郵遞公司) providing an express service 提供快遞服務的：*an air express company* 航空快遞公司 **4** (*formal*) (of a wish or an aim 願望或目的) clearly and openly stated 明確的；明白表示的 SYN **definite**：*It was his* ***express wish*** *that you should have his gold watch after he died.* 他明確表示死後把金錶留給你。◇ *I came here with the* ***express purpose*** *of speaking with the manager.* 我特意來這裏與經理面談。

■ *adv.* using a special fast service 使用快速服務：*I'd like to send this express, please.* 勞駕，我要寄快遞。

■ *noun* **1** (also **ex'press train**) [C] a fast train that does not stop at many places 特快列車：*the 8.27 express to Edinburgh* * 8:27 開往愛丁堡的特快列車 ◇ *the Trans-Siberian Express* 橫穿西伯利亞的特快列車 **2** (also ˌ**special de'livery**) [U] (*BrE*) a service for sending or transporting things quickly 快件服務；快遞服務；快運服務

ex·pres·sion 0ꟷ /ɪk'spreʃn/ *noun*

▸ SHOWING FEELINGS/IDEAS 表達感情 / 思想 **1** 0ꟷ [U, C] things that people say, write or do in order to show their feelings, opinions and ideas 表示；表達；表露：*an expression of support* 表示支持 ◇ *Expressions of sympathy flooded in from all over the country.* 同情之意潮水般地從全國各地湧來。◇ ***Freedom of expression*** (= freedom to say what you think) *is a basic human right.* 言論自由是基本的人權。◇ (*formal*) *The poet's anger* ***finds expression in*** (= is shown in) *the last verse of the poem.* 詩人的憤怒在詩的最後一節表達出來。◇ *Only in his dreams does he* ***give expression to*** *his fears.* 只有在夢裏他的恐懼才能得以表露。

▸ ON FACE 臉上 **2** 0ꟷ [C] a look on a person's face that shows their thoughts or feelings 表情；神色 SYN **look**：*There was a worried expression on her face.* 她臉上流露出擔心的神色。◇ *an* ***expression of amazement/disbelief/horror*** 驚訝 / 不相信 / 恐怖的神色 ◇ *His expression changed from surprise to one of amusement.* 他的神情由驚變喜。◇ *The expression in her eyes told me something was wrong.* 她的眼神告訴我出事了。◇ *facial expressions* 面部表情

▸ WORDS 詞語 **3** 0ꟷ [C] a word or phrase 詞語；措辭；表達方式：*an old-fashioned expression* 陳舊的表達方式 ◇ (*informal*) *He's a pain in the butt,* ***if you'll pardon the expression.*** 請原諒我這麼說，他是一個討厭透頂的傢伙。➲ SYNONYMS at WORD

▸ IN MUSIC/ACTING 音樂；表演 **4** [U] a strong show of feeling when you are playing music, speaking, acting, etc.（演奏樂曲、説話、表演等時流露的）感情，表情：*Try to put a little more expression into it!* 盡量注入更多的感情！

▸ MATHEMATICS 數學 **5** [C] a group of signs that represent an idea or a quantity 式；表達式

ex·pres·sion·ism /ɪk'spreʃənɪzəm/ (also **Expression·ism**) *noun* [U] a style and movement in early 20th century art, theatre, cinema and music that tries to express people's feelings and emotions rather than showing events or objects in a realistic way 表現主義 ▸ **ex·pres·sion·ist** /-ʃənɪst/ (also **Expressionist**) *noun, adj.*

ex·pres·sion·less /ɪk'spreʃənləs/ *adj.* not showing feelings, thoughts, etc. 無表情的；呆板的：*an* ***expressionless face/tone/voice*** 呆板的面孔 / 聲調 / 聲音 ➲ compare EXPRESSIVE (1)

ex·pres·sive /ɪk'spresɪv/ *adj.* **1** showing or able to show your thoughts and feelings 富於表情的；有表現力的；意味深長的：*She has wonderfully expressive eyes.* 她有一雙會説話的眼睛。◇ *the expressive power of his music* 他的音樂的表現力 ➲ compare EXPRESSIONLESS **2** [not before noun] **~ of sth** (*formal*) showing sth; existing as an expression of sth 表現；表達；表示：*Every word and gesture is expressive of the artist's sincerity.* 這位藝術家的真誠從一言一行中表現出來。▸ **ex·pres·sive·ly** *adv.* **ex·pres·sive·ness** *noun* [U]

ex'press lane *noun* (*NAmE*) **1** part of a road on which certain vehicles can travel faster because there is less traffic 快車道 **2** a place in a shop/store where customers can pay without having to wait for a long time（購物場所收銀結賬的）快速通道：*Customers with ten items or less can use the express lane.* 購買十件商品以內的顧客可使用快速購物通道。➲ compare CHECKOUT (1), TILL *n.* (2)

ex·press·ly /ɪk'spresli/ *adv.* (*formal*) **1** clearly; definitely 清楚地；明確地；確切地：*She was expressly forbidden to touch my papers.* 已經明確禁止她動我的文件。 **2** for a special and deliberate purpose 特意；專程 SYN **especially**：*The rule was introduced expressly for this purpose.* 這項規則是為此特意提出的。

ex·press·way /ɪk'spresweɪ/ *noun* (in the US) a wide road that allows traffic to travel fast through a city or other area where many people live（美國）高速公路

ex·pro·pri·ate /eks'prəʊprieɪt; *NAmE* -'proʊ-/ *verb* **1 ~ sth** (*formal* or *law* 律) (of a government or an authority 政府或權力機構) to officially take away private property from its owner for public use 徵用，沒收（私有財產） **2 ~ sth** (*formal*) to take sb's property and use it without permission 侵佔（他人財產）▸ **ex·pro·pri·ation** /ˌeksˌprəʊpri'eɪʃn; *NAmE* -ˌproʊ-/ *noun* [U]

ex·pul·sion /ɪk'spʌlʃn/ *noun* **1** [U, C] **~** (**from …**) the act of forcing sb to leave a place; the act of EXPELLING sb 驅逐；逐出：*These events led to the expulsion of senior diplomats from the country.* 這些事件導致一些高級外交官被驅逐出境。 **2** [U, C] **~** (**from …**) the act of sending sb away from a school or an organization, so that they can no longer belong to it; the act of EXPELLING sb 開除；除名：*The headteacher threatened the three girls with expulsion.* 校長以開除來威脅這三名女學生。◇ *The club faces expulsion from the football league.* 這家俱樂部面臨被足協開除。 **3** [U] **~** (**from …**) (*formal*) the act of sending or driving a substance out of your body or a container 排出

ex·punge /ɪk'spʌndʒ/ *verb* **~ sth (from sth)** (*formal*) to remove or get rid of sth, such as a name, piece of information or a memory, from a book or list, or from your mind 抹去；除去；刪去 **SYN** **erase**：*Details of his criminal activities were expunged from the file.* 他犯罪活動的詳細情況已從檔案中刪去。◇ *What happened just before the accident was expunged from his memory.* 事故前一刻發生的事他都記不得了。

ex·pur·gate /'ekspəgeɪt; *NAmE* -pərg-/ *verb* **~ sth** [usually passive] (*formal*) to remove or leave out parts of a piece of writing or a conversation when printing or reporting it, because you think those parts could offend people 刪除…中的不當之處；略去…中的不雅之處

ex·quis·ite /ɪk'skwɪzɪt; 'ekskwɪzɪt/ *adj.* **1** extremely beautiful or carefully made 精美的；精緻的：*exquisite craftsmanship* 精美的工藝 **2** (*formal*) (of a feeling 感覺) strongly felt 劇烈的；強烈的 **SYN** **acute**：***exquisite pain/pleasure*** 劇烈的疼痛；極大的快樂 **3** (*formal*) delicate and sensitive 微妙的；雅致的；敏銳的；敏感的：*The room was decorated in exquisite taste.* 這個房間的裝飾情趣高雅。◇ *an exquisite sense of timing* 時間安排上恰到好處的感覺 ▸ **ex·quis·ite·ly** *adv.*

ˌex-'service *adj.* (*BrE*) having previously been a member of the army, navy, etc. 退役的；退伍的：*ex-service personnel* 退伍人員

ˌex-'service·man, **ˌex-'service·woman** *noun* (*pl.* **-men** /-mən/, **-women** /-wɪmɪn/) (*BrE*) a person who used to be in the army, navy, etc. 退役軍人；復員軍人

ext. *abbr.* (used as part of a telephone number) EXTENSION（用於電話號碼）電話分機線，分機號碼：*Ext. 4299* 分機號碼 4299

ex·tant /ek'stænt; 'ekstənt/ *adj.* (*formal*) (of sth very old 古老的東西) still in existence 尚存的；現存的：*extant remains of the ancient wall* 尚存的古城牆遺跡

ex·tem·pore /ek'stempəri/ *adj.* (*formal*) spoken or done without any previous thought or preparation 即席的；即興的；無準備的 **SYN** **impromptu** ▸ **ex·tem·pore** *adv.*

ex·tem·por·ize (*BrE* also **-ise**) /ɪk'stempəraɪz/ *verb* [I] (*formal*) to speak or perform without preparing or practising 即席發言；即興表演 **SYN** **improvise** ▸ **ex·tem·por·iza·tion**, **-isa·tion** /ɪkˌstempəraɪ'zeɪʃn; *NAmE* -rə'z-/ *noun* [U]

ex·tend 🔑 /ɪk'stend/ *verb*

▸ **MAKE LONGER/LARGER/WIDER** 延長；擴大；擴展 **1** 🔑 [T] **~ sth** to make sth longer or larger 使伸長；擴大；擴展：*to extend a fence/road/house* 擴建護欄／公路／房子 ◇ *There are plans to extend the no-smoking area.* 現已有擴大無煙區的計劃。 **2** 🔑 [T] **~ sth** to make sth last longer 延長；使延期：*to **extend a deadline/visa*** 延長最後期限／簽證 ◇ *The show has been extended for another six weeks.* 展覽會又延長了六週。◇ *Careful maintenance can **extend the life** of your car.* 精心保養可延長汽車壽命。 **3** 🔑 [T] **~ sth** to make a business, an idea, an influence, etc. cover more areas or operate in more places 擴大…的範圍（或影響）：*The company plans to extend its operations into Europe.* 公司打算將業務擴展到歐洲。◇ *The school is extending the range of subjects taught.* 學校正在拓寬授課學科的範圍。

▸ **INCLUDE** 包括 **4** [I] **+ adv./prep.** to relate to or include sb/sth 適用於；包括：*The offer does not extend to employees' partners.* 這項優惠不包括雇員的伴侶。◇ *His willingness to help did not extend beyond making a few phone calls.* 他的樂意幫助只不過限於打幾個電話罷了。

▸ **COVER AREA/TIME/DISTANCE** 涉及範圍／時間／距離 **5** [I] **+ adv./prep.** to cover a particular area, distance or length of time 涉及（範圍）；延伸（距離）；延續（時間）：*Our land extends as far as the river.* 我們的土地一直延伸到河邊。◇ *His writing career extended over a period of 40 years.* 他的寫作生涯超過了 40 年。 **6** [I] **+ adv./prep.** to make sth reach sth or stretch 使達到；使延伸：*to extend a rope between two posts* 在兩根柱子間拉根繩子

▸ **PART OF BODY** 身體部位 **7** [T] **~ sth** to stretch part of your body, especially an arm or a leg, away from yourself 伸展，舒展，展開（尤指手臂或腿）：*He extended his hand to* (= offered to shake hands with) *the new employee.* 他伸出手來與新雇員握手。◇ (*figurative*) *to **extend the hand of friendship** to* (= try to have good relations with) *another country* 向另一個國家伸出友誼之手

▸ **OFFER/GIVE** 提供；給予 **8** [T] (*formal*) to offer or give sth to sb 提供；給予：**~ sth to sb** *I'm sure you will join me in extending a very warm welcome to our visitors.* 我肯定你們會同我一起向來訪者表示熱烈的歡迎。◇ *to extend hospitality to overseas students* 殷勤款待外國留學生 ◇ *The bank refused to extend credit to them* (= to lend them money). 銀行拒絕向他們提供信貸。◇ **~ sb sth** *to extend sb an invitation* 向某人發出邀請

▸ **USE EFFORT/ABILITY** 努力；盡力 **9** [T, often passive] **~ sb/sth/yourself** to make sb/sth use all their effort, abilities, supplies, etc. 使竭盡全力：*Jim didn't really have to extend himself in the exam.* 吉姆大可不必為這次考試那麼拚命。◇ *Hospitals were already fully extended because of the epidemic.* 這場流行病已使各醫院疲於奔命。➲ see also EXTENSION, EXTENSIVE

ex·tend·able (also **ex·tend·ible**) /ɪk'stendəbl/ *adj.* that can be made longer, or made valid for a longer time 可延長的；可延伸的；可延期的：*an extendable ladder* 伸縮梯 ◇ *The visa is for 14 days, extendable to one month.* 此簽證有效期為 14 天，可延期到一個月。

ex·tend·ed /ɪk'stendɪd/ *adj.* [only before noun] long or longer than usual or expected 延長了的；擴展了的：*an extended lunch hour* 延長了的午餐時間

exˌtended 'family *noun* a family group with a close relationship among the members that includes not only parents and children but also uncles, aunts, grandparents, etc. 大家庭（幾代同堂的家庭）➲ compare NUCLEAR FAMILY

ex·ten·sion 🔑 /ɪk'stenʃn/ *noun*

▸ **INCREASING INFLUENCE** 擴大影響 **1** 🔑 [U, C] **~ (of sth)** the act of increasing the area of activity, group of people, etc. that is affected by sth 擴大；延伸：*the extension of new technology into developing countries* 新技術向發展中國家的傳播 ◇ *a gradual extension of the powers of central government* 中央政府權力的逐漸擴大 ◇ *The bank plans various extensions to its credit facilities.* 銀行計劃從各個方面擴展信貸服務。

▸ **OF BUILDING** 建築 **2** 🔑 [C] **~ (to sth)** (*BrE*) (*NAmE* **addition**) a new room or rooms that are added to a house 增加的房間 ➲ COLLOCATIONS at DECORATE **3** 🔑 [C] a new part that is added to a building 擴建部份；增建部份：*a planned two-storey extension to the hospital* 計劃在醫院增建一棟兩層的樓

▸ **EXTRA TIME** 增加的時間 **4** 🔑 [C] **~ (of sth)** an extra period of time allowed for sth 延期；延長期；放寬的期限：*He's been granted an extension of the contract for another year.* 他的合同獲得延期一年。◇ *a visa extension* 延長簽證 ◇ (*BrE*) *The pub had an extension* (= was allowed to stay open longer) *on Christmas Eve.* 這家酒吧已獲准在聖誕前夕延長營業時間。

▸ **TELEPHONE** 電話 **5** 🔑 [C] (*abbr.* **ext.**) an extra telephone line connected to a central telephone in a house or to a SWITCHBOARD in a large building. In a large building, each extension usually has its own number. 電話分機線；分機號碼：*We have an extension in the bedroom.* 我們的臥室裏有一個分機。◇ *What's your extension number?* 你的分機號碼是多少？◇ *Can I have extension 4332 please?* 請接 4332 號分機。

▸ **MAKING STH LONGER/LARGER** 延伸；擴大 **6** [U, C] the act of making sth longer or larger; the thing that is made longer and larger 延長；擴大；延長（或擴大）的事物：*The extension of the subway will take several months.* 擴建地鐵需用幾個月時間。◇ *extensions to the original railway track* 原有鐵路線的若干延伸路線 ◇ ***hair extensions*** (= pieces of artificial hair that are added to your hair to make it longer) 接長的假髮

▸ **COLLEGE/UNIVERSITY** 學院；大學 **7** [C] a part of a college or university that offers courses to students who are not studying FULL-TIME; a programme of study for these students（為非全日制學生開設的）進修部，進修課：*La Salle Extension University* 拉薩爾大學進修部 ◇ *extension courses* 大學進修課程

E

▸ COMPUTING 計算機技術 **8** the set of three letters that are placed after a dot at the end of the name of a file and that show what type of file it is 擴展名；副檔名
▸ ELECTRICAL 電的 **9** [C] (*BrE*) = EXTENSION LEAD

IDM **by exˈtension** (*formal*) taking the argument or situation one stage further 引申；再則：*The blame lies with the teachers and, by extension, with the Education Service.* 應受指責的是教師，再則就是教育機構。

exˈtension agent *noun* (in the US) a person who works for a state university in a country area, and whose job is to give advice to farmers, do research into farming, etc.（美國鄉村州立大學的）農業技術推廣研究員

E

exˈtension lead (also **extension**) (both *BrE*) (*NAmE* **exˈtension cord**) *noun* an extra length of electric wire, used when the wire on an electrical device is not long enough 接長線路，延長線（電器上的電線加長部份）

ex·ten·sive 0̶ /ɪkˈstensɪv/ *adj.*
1 0̶ covering a large area; great in amount 廣闊的；廣大的；大量的：*The house has extensive grounds.* 這棟房子有寬敞的庭院。◇ *The fire caused extensive damage.* 火災造成了巨大的損失。◇ *She suffered extensive injuries in the accident.* 她在事故中受了重傷。◇ *Extensive repair work is being carried out.* 大規模的修繕工作正在進行。◇ *an extensive range of wines* 各種各樣的葡萄酒
2 0̶ including or dealing with a wide range of information 廣泛的；廣博的 SYN **far-reaching**：*Extensive research has been done into this disease.* 對這種疾病已進行了廣泛研究。◇ *His knowledge of music is extensive.* 他音樂知識很廣博。▸ **ex·ten·sive·ly** *adv.*：*a spice used extensively in Eastern cooking* 東方烹飪大量使用的香料 ◇ *She has travelled extensively.* 她遊歷甚廣。

ex·ten·sor /ɪkˈstensə(r); *NAmE* -sɔːr; *BrE* also ekˈs-/ (also **exˈtensor muscle**) *noun* (*anatomy* 解) a muscle that allows you to make part of your body straight or stretched out 伸肌 ➲ compare FLEXOR

ex·tent 0̶ /ɪkˈstent/ *noun* [sing., U]
1 0̶ how large, important, serious, etc. sth is 程度；限度：*It is difficult to assess the* ***full extent*** *of the damage.* 損失情況難以全面估計。◇ *She was exaggerating the* ***true extent*** *of the problem.* 她誇大了問題的嚴重性。◇ *I was amazed at the extent of his knowledge.* 他知識之淵博令我驚奇。 **2** the physical size of an area 大小；面積；範圍：*You can't see the* ***full extent*** *of the beach from here.* 從這兒不能看到海灘全貌。

IDM **to … extent** 0̶ used to show how far sth is true or how great an effect it has 到…程度；在…程度上：*To a* ***certain extent****, we are all responsible for this tragic situation.* 我們都在一定程度上對這悲慘的局面負有責任。◇ *He had changed* ***to such an extent*** (= so much) *that I no longer recognized him.* 他變得我簡直認不出了。◇ ***To some extent*** *what she argues is true.* 她的論證在某種程度上是符合事實的。◇ *The pollution of the forest has seriously affected plant life and,* ***to a lesser extent****, wildlife.* 森林污染嚴重影響了植物的生存，其次也對野生動物造成了影響。◇ ***To what extent*** *is this true of all schools?* 這在多大程度上符合所有學校的實際情況？◇ *The book discusses* ***the extent to which*** (= how much) *family life has changed over the past 50 years.* 本書論述了近 50 年來家庭生活的變化程度。➲ LANGUAGE BANK at GENERALLY

ex·tenu·at·ing /ɪkˈstenjueɪtɪŋ/ *adj.* [only before noun] (*formal*) showing reasons why a wrong or illegal act, or a bad situation, should be judged less seriously or excused 情有可原的；可減輕的：*There were* ***extenuating circumstances*** *and the defendant did not receive a prison sentence.* 因為有可減輕罪行的情節，所以被告未被判刑。

ex·ter·ior /ɪkˈstɪəriə(r); *NAmE* -ˈstɪr-/ *noun, adj.*
■ ***noun*** **1** [C] the outside of sth, especially a building（尤指建築物的）外部，外觀，表面，外貌：*The exterior of the house needs painting.* 房子外牆需要油漆。OPP **interior**
2 [sing.] the way that sb appears or behaves, especially when this is very different from their real feelings or character（人的）外貌，外表：*Beneath his confident exterior, he was desperately nervous.* 他表面上自信，內心極度緊張。
■ ***adj.*** [usually before noun] on the outside of sth; done or happening outdoors 外面的；外部的；外表的；戶外的：***exterior walls/surfaces*** 外牆；外層表面 ◇ *The filming of the exterior scenes was done on the moors.* 外景是在高沼地拍攝的。OPP **interior**

ex·ter·min·ate /ɪkˈstɜːmɪneɪt; *NAmE* -ˈstɜːrm-/ *verb* **~ sb/sth** to kill all the members of a group of people or animals 滅絕；根除；消滅；毀滅 SYN **wipe out** ▸ **ex·ter·min·ation** /ɪkˌstɜːmɪˈneɪʃn; *NAmE* -ˌstɜːrm-/ *noun* [U]

ex·tern /ˈekstɜːn; *NAmE* -tɜːrn/ *noun* (*US*) a person who works in an institution but does not live there, especially a doctor or other worker in a hospital（尤指）非住院醫生，非住院的醫院員工

ex·ter·nal AW /ɪkˈstɜːnl; *NAmE* ɪkˈstɜːrnl/ *adj.* **1** connected with or located on the outside of sth/sb 外部的；外面的：*the external walls of the building* 建築物的外牆 ◇ *The lotion is* ***for external use*** *only* (= only for the skin and must not be swallowed). 此護膚液僅限外用。
2 happening or coming from outside a place, an organization, your particular situation, etc. 外界的；外來的；在外的：*A combination of internal and external factors caused the company to close down.* 內外因結合導致了公司的倒閉。◇ *external pressures on the economy* 外部因素對經濟的壓力 ◇ *Many external influences can affect your state of mind.* 許多外在因素都可能影響人的心情。 **3** coming from or arranged by sb from outside a school, a university or an organization 來自（學校或機構）以外的；外來的：(*BrE*) ***external examiners/assessors*** 校外主考人／評定人 ◇ *An external auditor will verify the accounts.* 外部審計員將核實這些賬目。
4 connected with foreign countries 與外國有關的；對外的：*The government is committed to reducing the country's external debt.* 政府決心減少國家的外債。◇ *the Minister of State for External Affairs* 外交大臣 OPP **internal** ▸ **ex·ter·nal·ly** AW /ɪkˈstɜːnəli; *NAmE* -ˈstɜːrn-/ *adv.*：*The building has been restored externally and internally.* 這棟建築內外均已修復。◇ *The university has many externally funded research projects.* 這所大學有許多外界資助的研究項目。

exˌternal ˈear *noun* (*anatomy* 解) the parts of the ear outside the EARDRUM 外耳

ex·ter·nal·ity AW /ˌekstɜːˈnæləti; *NAmE* -stɜːrˈn-/ *noun* **1** [C] (*economics* 經) a consequence of an industrial or commercial activity which affects other people or things without this being reflected in market prices 外部性，界外效應（工商業活動所產生的影響，但不通過市場價格反映）：*Pollution is a negative externality that imposes a cost—reduced happiness—on the victims.* 污染是一種負面外部效應，使部份人的幸福被犧牲而成為受害者。 **2** [U] (*philosophy* 哲) the fact of existing outside the person or thing that is aware of it 外在性；客觀性：*man's externality to an indifferent natural world* 相對於冷漠自然界的人類外在性

ex·ter·nal·ize (*BrE* also **-ise**) AW /ɪkˈstɜːnəlaɪz; *NAmE* -ˈstɜːrn-/ *verb* **~ sth** (*formal*) to show what you are thinking and feeling by what you say or do（以言行）表達；使（思想、感情）表露出來 ➲ compare INTERNALIZE ▸ **ex·ter·nal·iza·tion**, **-isa·tion** AW /ɪkˌstɜːnəlaɪˈzeɪʃn; *NAmE* -ˌstɜːrn-/ *noun* [U]

ex·ter·nals /ɪkˈstɜːnlz; *NAmE* -ˈstɜːrn-/ *noun* [pl.] (*formal*) the outer appearance of sth 外表；外觀；外貌

ex·tinct /ɪkˈstɪŋkt/ *adj.* **1** (of a type of plant, animal, etc. 某種植物、動物等) no longer in existence 不再存在的；已滅絕的；絕種的：*an extinct species* 已滅絕的物種 ◇ *to become extinct* 絕種 **2** (of a type of person, job or way of life 某種類型的人、工作或生活方式) no longer in existence in society 絕跡的；消亡了的；廢除了的：*Servants are now almost extinct in modern society.* 在現代社會裏奴僕已近乎不復存在。 **3** (of a VOLCANO 火山) no longer active 不再活躍的；死的 OPP **active**

ex·tinc·tion /ɪkˈstɪŋkʃn/ *noun* [U, C] a situation in which a plant, an animal, a way of life, etc. stops existing（植物、動物、生活方式等的）滅絕，絕種，消亡：*a tribe* ***threatened with extinction/in danger of extinction*** 面臨消亡威脅／有消亡危險的部落 ◇ *The mountain gorilla* *is on the verge of extinction.* 居住在山區的大猩猩已瀕臨滅絕。◇ *We know of several mass extinctions in the earth's history.* 我們知道地球歷史上出現過幾次大規模的滅絕。

ex·tin·guish /ɪkˈstɪŋɡwɪʃ/ *verb* (*formal*) **1 ~ sth** to make a fire stop burning or a light stop shining 熄滅；撲滅 **SYN put out**: *Firefighters tried to extinguish the flames.* 消防隊員奮力救火。◇ *All lights had been extinguished.* 所有燈光都熄滅了。 **2 ~ sth** to destroy sth 毀滅；消滅；使破滅: *News of the bombing extinguished all hope of peace.* 轟炸的消息使和平的希望全部破滅。

ex·tin·guish·er *noun* = FIRE EXTINGUISHER

ex·tirp·ate /ˈekstəpeɪt; *NAmE* -tərp-/ *verb* **~ sth** (*formal*) to destroy or get rid of sth that is bad or not wanted 消滅，根除，除掉（壞的或不需要的事物） ▸ **ex·tir·pa·tion** /ˌekstəˈpeɪʃn; *NAmE* -tərˈp-/ *noun* [U]

extol /ɪkˈstəʊl; *NAmE* ɪkˈstoʊl/ *verb* (-ll-) (*formal*) to praise sb/sth very much 讚揚；頌揚；稱讚: **~ sb/sth** *Doctors often **extol the virtues** of eating less fat.* 醫生常常宣揚少吃脂肪的好處。◇ **~ sb/sth as sth** *She was extolled as a genius.* 她被譽為天才。

ex·tort /ɪkˈstɔːt; *NAmE* ɪkˈstɔːrt/ *verb* **~ sth (from sb)** to make sb give you sth by threatening them 敲詐；勒索；強奪: *The gang extorted money from over 30 local businesses.* 這幫歹徒向當地 30 多家企業勒索過錢財。 ▸ **ex·tor·tion** /ɪkˈstɔːʃn; *NAmE* ɪkˈstɔːrʃn/ *noun* [U, C]: *He was arrested and charged with extortion.* 他因敲詐勒索罪被拘捕和控告。

ex·tor·tion·ate /ɪkˈstɔːʃənət; *NAmE* -ˈstɔːrʃ-/ *adj.* (*rather informal, disapproving*) (of prices, etc. 價格等) much too high 過於昂貴的；過高的 **SYN excessive, outrageous**: *They are offering loans at extortionate rates of interest.* 他們在放高利貸。 ▸ **ex·tor·tion·ate·ly** *adv.*: *extortionately priced* 價格過於昂貴的

extra 🔑 /ˈekstrə/ *adj., noun, adv.*

■ ***adj.*** 🔑 more than is usual, expected, or than exists already 額外的；分外的；外加的；附加的 **SYN additional**: *Breakfast is provided at no extra charge.* 供應早餐，不另收費。◇ *The conference is going to be a lot of extra work.* 這次會議將有很多額外工作。◇ *an extra pint of milk* 外加的一品脫牛奶 ◇ *The government has promised an extra £1 billion for health care.* 政府承諾為醫療保健再撥款 10 億英鎊。◇ *Take extra care on the roads this evening.* 今晚在路上要格外小心。 ➲ see also EXTRA TIME

■ ***noun*** **1** 🔑 a thing that is added to sth that is not usual, standard or necessary and that costs more 額外的事物；另外收費的事物: *The monthly fee is fixed and there are no **hidden extras*** (= unexpected costs). 月費是固定的，沒有未言明的額外開支。◇ (*BrE*) *Metallic paint is **an optional extra*** (= a thing you can choose to have or not, but must pay more for if you have it). 噴金屬漆是自由選擇的，要額外收費。 **2** a person who is employed to play a very small part in a film/movie, usually as a member of a crowd（電影裏的）臨時演員，群眾演員

■ ***adv.*** **1** 🔑 in addition; more than is usual, expected or exists already 額外；另外；外加: *to **charge/pay/cost extra*** 另外收費；另付；額外花費 ◇ *I need to earn a bit extra this month.* 我這個月需要掙點外快。◇ *The rate for a room is £30, but breakfast is extra.* 一個房間收費 30 英鎊，但早餐另付。 **2** 🔑 (with an adjective or adverb 與形容詞或副詞連用) more than usually 特別；格外；分外: *You need to be extra careful not to make any mistakes.* 你要格外小心，別犯錯誤。◇ *an extra large T-shirt* 一件特大號的 T 恤衫 ◇ *She tried extra hard.* 她特別努力。

extra- /ˈekstrə/ *prefix* (in adjectives 構成形容詞) **1** outside; beyond 在…之外；超出；越出: *extramarital sex* 婚外性行為 ◇ *extraterrestrial beings* 外星人 **2** (*informal*) very; more than usual 非常；格外；十分: *extra-thin* 特別瘦 ◇ *extra-special* 十分特別

ex·tract **AW** *noun, verb*

■ ***noun*** /ˈekstrækt/ **1** [C] **~ (from sth)** a short passage from a book, piece of music, etc. that gives you an idea of what the whole thing is like 摘錄；選錄；選曲；節錄: *The following extract is taken from her new novel.* 下面一段摘自她的新小說。 **2** [U, C] a substance that has been obtained from sth else using a particular process 提取物；濃縮物；精；汁: *yeast extract* 酵母萃 ◇ *face cream containing natural plant extracts* 含有天然植物提取物的面霜 ◇ (*NAmE*) *vanilla extract* 香草精 ➲ see also ESSENCE (2)

■ ***verb*** /ɪkˈstrækt/ **1 ~ sth (from sb/sth)** to remove or obtain a substance from sth, for example by using an industrial or a chemical process 提取；提煉: *a machine that extracts excess moisture from the air* 抽濕機 ◇ *to extract essential oils from plants* 從植物中提取香精油 **2 ~ sth (from sb/sth)** to obtain information, money, etc., often by taking it from sb who is unwilling to give it 索取，設法得到（不願提供的信息、錢財等）: *Journalists managed to extract all kinds of information about her private life.* 記者們終於得到了有關她私生活的各種情況。 **3 ~ sth (from sb/sth)** to choose information, etc. from a book, a computer, etc. to be used for a particular purpose 選取；摘錄；選錄: *This article is extracted from his new book.* 本文選自他的新書。 **4 ~ sth (from sb/sth)** (*formal* or *technical* 術語) to take or pull sth out, especially when this needs force or effort（用力）取出，拔出: *The dentist may decide that the wisdom teeth need to be extracted.* 牙醫可能會認為智牙需要拔掉。◇ *He rifled through his briefcase and extracted a file.* 他在公文包內搜索一番，取出一份文件。 **5 ~ sth (from sb/sth)** (*formal*) to get a particular feeling or quality from a situation 獲得，得到（某種感覺或品質） **SYN derive**: *They are unlikely to extract much benefit from the trip.* 他們不大可能從這次旅行中獲得很多益處。

ex·trac·tion **AW** /ɪkˈstrækʃn/ *noun* **1** [U, C] the act or process of removing or obtaining sth from sth else 提取；提煉；拔出；開採: ***oil/mineral/coal, etc. extraction*** 石油、礦物、煤等的開採 ◇ *the extraction of salt from the sea* 從海水中提取鹽 **2** [U] **of ... extraction** (*formal*) having a particular family origin（有…）血統；族裔: *an American of Hungarian extraction* 匈牙利血統的美國人 **3** [C] (*technical* 術語) the removal of a tooth 拔牙

ex·tract·ive /ɪkˈstræktɪv; ek-/ *adj.* (*technical* 術語) relating to the process of removing or obtaining sth, especially minerals 提取的；提煉的；（尤指礦物）冶煉的: *extractive industries* 冶金工業

ex·tract·or /ɪkˈstræktə(r)/ *noun* **1** (also **exˈtractor fan**) a device that removes hot air, unpleasant smells, etc. from a room 排氣扇；抽油煙機 **2** a device or machine that removes sth from sth else 提取器；抽出器: *a juice extractor* 榨汁機

ˌextra-curˈricu·lar *adj.* [usually before noun] not part of the usual course of work or studies at a school or college 課外的；課程以外的: *She's involved in many **extra-curricular activities**.* 她參加了許多課外活動。

extra·dite /ˈekstrədaɪt/ *verb* **~ sb (to ...) (from ...)** to officially send back sb who has been accused or found guilty of a crime to the country where the crime was committed 引渡（嫌犯或罪犯）: *The British government attempted to extradite the suspects from Belgium.* 英國政府試圖從比利時引渡犯罪嫌疑人。 ▸ **extra·di·tion** /ˌekstrəˈdɪʃn/ *noun* [U, C]: *the extradition of terrorist suspects* 對恐怖分子嫌疑犯的引渡 ◇ *an extradition treaty* 引渡條約 ◇ *to start extradition proceedings* 啟動引渡程序

extra·judi·cial /ˌekstrədʒuˈdɪʃl/ *adj.* happening outside the normal power of the law 未按法律程序的；法庭以外的

extra·mar·it·al /ˌekstrəˈmærɪtl/ *adj.* happening outside marriage 婚外的: *an extramarital affair* 婚外情

extra·mural /ˌekstrəˈmjʊərəl; *NAmE* -ˈmjʊrəl/ *adj.* [usually before noun] **1** (*BrE*) arranged by a university, college, etc. for people who only study PART-TIME 校外的（高等院校為非本科生而設的）: ***extramural education/studies/departments*** 校外教育／學習／課程部 ➲ see also EXTENSION (7) **2** (*formal*) happening or existing outside or separate from a place, an organization, etc.（地方、機構等）之外的，外部的，以外的: *The hospital provides extramural care to patients who do not need to be admitted.* 這家醫院對無須住院的病人提供院外護理。

E

E

ex·tra·ne·ous /ɪkˈstremiəs/ *adj.* (*formal*) not directly connected with the particular situation you are in or the subject you are dealing with 沒有直接聯繫的；無關的 SYN **irrelevant**：*We do not want any extraneous information on the page.* 我們不希望這一頁上有任何無關的信息。◇ **~ to sth** *We shall ignore factors extraneous to the problem.* 我們應該撇開與此問題無直接聯繫的因素。

extra·or·din·aire /ɪkˌstrɔːdɪˈneə(r); *NAmE* ɪkˌstrɔːrdɪˈner/ *adj.* (from *French, approving*, often *humorous*) used after nouns to say that sb is a good example of a particular kind of person（用於名詞後）卓越的，傑出的，非凡的：*Houdini, escape artist extraordinaire* 烏丹尼 —— 擅長表演脫身術的傑出魔術師

extra·or·din·ary 0‑w /ɪkˈstrɔːdnri; *NAmE* ɪkˈstrɔːrdəneri/ *adj.*
1 0‑w unexpected, surprising or strange 意想不到的；令人驚奇的；奇怪的 SYN **incredible**：*It's extraordinary that he managed to sleep through the party.* 真想不到他竟然從聚會開始一直睡到結束。◇ *What an extraordinary thing to say!* 真是咄咄怪事！ **2** 0‑w not normal or ordinary; greater or better than usual 不平常的；不一般的；非凡的；卓越的：*an extraordinary achievement* 卓越的成就 ◇ *She was a truly extraordinary woman.* 她是位非常傑出的女性。◇ *They went to extraordinary lengths to explain their behaviour.* 他們竭力為自己的行為辯解。
➲ compare ORDINARY **3** [only before noun] (*formal*) (of a meeting, etc. 會議等) arranged for a special purpose and happening in addition to what normally or regularly happens 特別的；臨時的：*An extraordinary meeting was held to discuss the problem.* 舉行了特別會議討論這個問題。 **4** (following nouns 緊接名詞之後) (*technical* 術語) (of an official 官員) employed for a special purpose in addition to the usual staff 特派的；特命的：*an envoy extraordinary* 特使 ▸ **extra·or·din·ar·ily** /ɪkˈstrɔːdnrəli; *NAmE* ɪkˌstrɔːrdəˈnerəli/ *adv.*：*He behaves extraordinarily for someone in his position.* 對他那種地位的人來說，他的行為很特別。◇ *extraordinarily difficult* 特別困難 ◇ *She did extraordinarily well.* 她幹得特別好。

exˌtraordinary renˈdition *noun* = RENDITION (2)

ex·trapo·late /ɪkˈstræpəleɪt/ *verb* [I, T] (*formal*) to estimate sth or form an opinion about sth, using the facts that you have now and that are valid for one situation and supposing that they will be valid for the new one 推斷；推知；外推：**~ (from/to sth)** *The figures were obtained by extrapolating from past trends.* 這些數字是從過去的趨勢推斷出來的。◇ **~ sth (from/to sth)** *We have extrapolated these results from research done in other countries.* 我們從其他國家所做的研究中推斷出這些結果。
▸ **ex·trapo·la·tion** /ɪkˌstræpəˈleɪʃn/ *noun* [U, C]：*Their age can be determined by extrapolation from their growth rate.* 它們的年齡可從其生長速度來推定。

extra·sens·ory perception /ˌekstrəˌsensəri pəˈsepʃn; *NAmE* pərˈs-/ *noun* [U] = ESP (2)

extra·solar /ˌekstrəˈsəʊlə(r); *NAmE* -ˈsoʊlər/ *adj.* [usually before noun] (*technical* 術語) (of a planet, etc. 行星等) located outside our SOLAR SYSTEM 在太陽系之外的

extra·ter·res·trial /ˌekstrətəˈrestriəl/ *noun, adj.*
■ ***noun*** (in stories) a creature that comes from another planet; a creature that may exist on another planet（故事中的）天外來客，外星人，外星生物
■ ***adj.*** connected with life existing outside the planet Earth 地球外的；外星球的；宇宙的：***extraterrestrial beings/life*** 外星人 / 生命

extra·ter·ri·tor·ial /ˌekstrəterəˈtɔːriəl/ *adj.* (of a law 法律) valid outside the country where the law was made 治外法權的；域外的

ˌextra ˈtime (*BrE*) (*NAmE* **over·time**) *noun* [U] (*sport* 體) a set period of time that is added to the end of a sports game, etc., if there is no winner at the end of the normal period（體育比賽等的）加時，加時賽：*They won by a single goal after extra time.* 他們在加時賽中僅踢進一球即獲勝。

ex·trava·gance /ɪkˈstrævəgəns/ *noun* **1** [U] the act or habit of spending more money than you can afford or than is necessary 奢侈；揮霍；鋪張浪費 **2** [C] something that you buy although it costs a lot of money, perhaps more than you can afford or than is necessary 奢侈品：*Going to the theatre is our only extravagance.* 去劇院看戲是我們唯一的奢侈享受。 **3** [C, U] something that is impressive or noticeable because it is unusual or extreme 富麗堂皇；豪華；奢華：*the extravagance of Strauss's music* 施特勞斯音樂作品的富麗堂皇

ex·trava·gant /ɪkˈstrævəgənt/ *adj.* **1** spending a lot more money or using a lot more of sth than you can afford or than is necessary 奢侈的；揮霍的；鋪張浪費的：*I felt very extravagant spending £100 on a dress.* 我覺得花 100 英鎊買一條連衣裙太奢侈了。◇ *She's got very extravagant tastes.* 她有很奢侈的嗜好。◇ *Residents were warned not to be* ***extravagant with*** *water, in view of the low rainfall this year.* 鑒於今年降雨量少，居民被告誡不得浪費用水。 **2** costing a lot more money than you can afford or is necessary 過於昂貴的：*an extravagant present* 昂貴的禮物 **3** (of ideas, speech or behaviour 想法或言行) very extreme or impressive but not reasonable or practical 無節制的；過分的；放肆的；不切實際的 SYN **exaggerated**：*the* ***extravagant claims/promises*** *of politicians* 政客的誇大其詞 / 不切實際的承諾 ▸ **ex·trava·gant·ly** *adv.*：*extravagantly expensive* 極為昂貴 ◇ *extravagantly high hopes* 奢望

ex·trava·ganza /ɪkˌstrævəˈgænzə/ *noun* a large, expensive and impressive entertainment 鋪張華麗的娛樂表演

ex·tra·vert = EXTROVERT

ˌextra ˈvirgin *adj.* used to describe good quality oil obtained the first time that OLIVES are pressed（橄欖油）優質初榨的：*extra virgin olive oil* 優質初榨橄欖油

ex·treme 0‑w /ɪkˈstriːm/ *adj., noun*
■ ***adj.*** **1** 0‑w [usually before noun] very great in degree 極度的；極大的：*We are working under extreme pressure at the moment.* 目前我們正在極大的壓力下工作。◇ *people living in extreme poverty* 生活在極度貧困中的人 ◇ *The heat in the desert was extreme.* 沙漠中極其炎熱。 **2** 0‑w not ordinary or usual; serious or severe 異乎尋常的；嚴重的；嚴厲的：*Children will be removed from their parents only* ***in extreme circumstances****.* 只有在極端情況下才會讓孩子離開父母。◇ *Don't go doing anything extreme like leaving the country.* 千萬不要做出諸如離開國家之類的極端行為。◇ *It was the most* ***extreme example*** *of cruelty to animals I had ever seen.* 這是我見過的最嚴重的虐待動物的事例。◇ *extreme weather conditions* 極端惡劣的天氣狀況 **3** 0‑w (of people, political organizations, opinions, etc. 人、政治組織、意見等) far from what most people consider to be normal, reasonable or acceptable 極端的；偏激的；過分的：***extreme left-wing/right-wing*** *views* 極左 / 極右觀點 OPP **moderate 4** [only before noun] as far as possible from the centre, the beginning or in the direction mentioned 遠離中心的；末端的；盡頭的：*Kerry is in the extreme west of Ireland.* 凱里位於愛爾蘭的最西端。◇ *She sat on the extreme edge of her seat.* 她坐在座位最邊上。
■ ***noun*** **1** a feeling, situation, way of behaving, etc. that is as different as possible from another or is opposite to it 極端不同的感情（或境況、行為方式等）；完全相反的事物：*extremes of love and hate* 愛和恨兩種截然不同的感情 ◇ *He used to be very shy, but now he's gone to the* ***opposite extreme*** (= changed from one extreme kind of behaviour to another). 他以前很靦腆，現在卻走向了另一個極端。 **2** the greatest or highest degree of sth 極端；極度；極限：*extremes of cold, wind or rain* 嚴寒、狂風、暴雨

IDM **go, etc. to exˈtremes | take sth to exˈtremes** to act or be forced to act in a way that is far from normal or reasonable 走極端；被迫採取極端行為：*It's embarrassing the extremes he'll go to in order to impress his boss.* 他為了給上司留下深刻印象，不惜走極端，真令人難堪。◇ *Taken to extremes, this kind of behaviour can be dangerous.* 這種行為如果走向極端則可能是非常危險的。
in the exˈtreme (*formal*) to a great degree 極度；極端；非常：*The journey would be dangerous in the extreme.* 這段旅程將會是極其危險的。

exˈtreme fighting *noun* [U] = ULTIMATE FIGHTING

ex·treme·ly 🔑 /ɪk'striːmli/ *adv.* (usually with adjectives and adverbs 通常與形容詞和副詞連用) to a very high degree 極其；極端；非常：*extremely important/useful/complicated* 極為重要／有用／複雜◇ *She found it extremely difficult to get a job.* 她發覺找工作極其困難。

ex,treme 'sports *noun* [pl.] sports that are extremely exciting to do and often dangerous, for example SKYDIVING and BUNGEE JUMPING 極限運動 ➲ VISUAL VOCAB pages V49, V50

ex,treme 'unction *noun* [U] (*religion* 宗) (*old use*) in the Catholic Church, the ceremony of BLESSING sick or dying people 傅油聖事（天主教為病人或臨終者做的聖事）：*He was given extreme unction.* 他接受了終傅聖事。

ex·tre·mis ➲ IN EXTREMIS

ex·trem·ism /ɪk'striːmɪzəm/ *noun* [U] political, religious, etc. ideas or actions that are extreme and not normal, reasonable or acceptable to most people 極端主義；過激論：*political extremism* 政治上的極端主義

ex·trem·ist /ɪk'striːmɪst/ *noun* (usually *disapproving*) a person whose opinions, especially about religion or politics, are extreme, and who may do things that are violent, illegal, etc. for what they believe 極端主義者；極端分子；過激分子：***left-wing/right-wing/political/religious extremists*** 左翼／右翼／政治／宗教極端主義者 ▸ **ex·trem·ist** *adj.* [usually before noun]：***extremist attacks/groups/policies*** 過激分子的攻擊；極端分子組織；極端主義政策

ex·trem·ity /ɪk'streməti/ *noun* (*pl.* **-ies**) **1** [C] the furthest point, end or limit of sth 末端；端點；盡頭：*The lake is situated at the eastern extremity of the mountain range.* 湖位於山脈最東端。 **2** [C, U] the degree to which a situation, a feeling, an action, etc. is extreme, difficult or unusual 極端；極度；極限：*the extremities/extremity of pain* 極度疼痛 **3 extremities** [pl.] (*formal*) the parts of your body that are furthest from the centre, especially your hands and feet （人體的）四肢，手足

ex·tri·cate /'ekstrɪkeɪt/ *verb* (*formal*) **1 ~ sb/sth/yourself (from sth)** to escape or enable sb to escape from a difficult situation （使）擺脫，脫離，脫出：*He had managed to extricate himself from most of his official duties.* 他終於擺脫了大部份公務。 **2 ~ sb/sth/yourself (from sth)** to free sb/sth or yourself from a place where they/it or you are trapped 解救；救出；掙脫：*They managed to extricate the pilot from the tangled control panel.* 他們設法把困在控制盤裏的飛行員救了出來。

ex·trin·sic /eks'trɪnsɪk; -zɪk/ *adj.* (*formal*) not belonging naturally to sb/sth; coming from or existing outside sb/sth rather than within them 非固有的；非本質的；外在的；外來的：*extrinsic factors* 外在因素 ➲ compare INTRINSIC

ex·tro·vert (also *less frequent* **ex·tra·vert**) /'ekstrəvɜːt; *NAmE* -vɜːrt/ *noun* a lively and confident person who enjoys being with other people 性格外向者；活潑自信的人 OPP **introvert** ▸ **ex·tro·vert·ed** (*BrE* also **ex·tro·vert**) *adj.*

ex·trude /ɪk'struːd/ *verb* **1** [T, I] **~ (sth) (from sth)** (*formal*) to force or push sth out of sth; to be forced or pushed in this way （被）擠壓出，排出，噴出：*Lava is extruded from the volcano.* 熔岩從火山中噴出。 **2** [T] **~ sth** (*technical* 術語) to shape metal or plastic by forcing it through a hole （把金屬或塑料）擠壓成，壓製 ▸ **ex·tru·sion** /ɪk'struːʒn/ *noun* [U]

ex·tru·sive /ɪk'struːsɪv/ *adj.* (*geology* 地) (of rock 岩石) that has been pushed out of the earth by a VOLCANO （火山）噴出的

ex·uber·ant /ɪɡ'zjuːbərənt; *NAmE* -'zuː-/ *adj.* **1** full of energy, excitement and happiness 精力充沛的；熱情洋溢的；興高采烈的：*She gave an exuberant performance.* 她的表演熱情洋溢。◇ *an* ***exuberant personality/imagination*** 充滿活力的個性；豐富的想像力◇ *a picture painted in exuberant reds and yellows* 用鮮豔的紅黃兩色畫的畫 **2** (of plants, etc. 植物等) strong and healthy; growing quickly and well 繁茂的；茂盛的；茁壯的 ▸ **ex·uber·ance** /-rəns/ *noun* [U]：*We can excuse his behaviour as youthful exuberance.* 年輕人精力旺盛，所以他的行為我們可以原諒。 **ex·uber·ant·ly** *adv.*

exude /ɪɡ'zjuːd; *NAmE* -'zuːd/ *verb* **1** [T, I] **~ (sth) | ~ (from sb)** if you **exude** a particular feeling or quality, or it **exudes** from you, people can easily see that you have it 流露，顯露（感覺或品質）；（感覺或品質）顯現：*She exuded confidence.* 她顯得信心十足。 **2** [T, I] if sth **exudes** a liquid or smell, or a liquid or smell **exudes** from somewhere, the liquid, etc. comes out slowly 流出，滲出（液體）；散發出（氣味）；（從某處）滲出，散發出來：**~ sth** *The plant exudes a sticky fluid.* 這種植物分泌出一種黏液。◇ **~ (from sth)** *An awful smell exuded from the creature's body.* 這生物身上發出難聞的氣味。

exult /ɪɡ'zʌlt/ *verb* [I, T] (*formal*) to feel and show that you are very excited and happy because of sth that has happened 歡欣鼓舞；興高采烈；喜形於色：**~ (at/in sth)** *He leaned back, exulting at the success of his plan.* 他向後一靠，為自己計劃的成功而得意揚揚。◇ **+ speech** *'We won!' she exulted.* "我們贏了！"她欣喜若狂道。

ex·ult·ant /ɪɡ'zʌltənt/ *adj.* **~ (at sth)** (*formal*) feeling or showing great pride or happiness especially because of sth exciting that has happened 歡欣鼓舞的；興高采烈的；得意揚揚的 SYN **triumphant** ▸ **ex·ult·ant·ly** *adv.*

ex·ult·ation /ˌeɡzʌl'teɪʃn/ *noun* [U] (*formal*) great pride or happiness, especially because of sth exciting that has happened 得意；歡悅；興高采烈

-ey ➲ -Y (1)

eye 🔑 /aɪ/ *noun, verb*

■ ***noun***

▸ PART OF BODY 身體部位 **1** 🔑 [C] either of the two organs on the face that you see with 眼睛：*The suspect has dark hair and green eyes.* 嫌疑犯有着一頭黑髮和一雙綠眼睛。◇ *to* ***close/open*** *your* ***eyes*** 閉上／睜開眼睛◇ *to* ***drop/lower*** *your* ***eyes*** (= to look down) 眼睛朝下看◇ *There were tears in his eyes.* 他眼裏噙着淚水。◇ *I have something in my eye.* 我的眼睛裏有點什麼東西。◇ *to make/avoid* ***eye contact*** *with sb* (= to look/avoid looking at them at the same time as they look at you) 與／避免與某人目光接觸◇ ***All eyes were on*** *him* (= everyone was looking at him) *as he walked on to the stage.* 他走上台時所有的目光都注視着他。 ➲ COLLOCATIONS at PHYSICAL ➲ VISUAL VOCAB page V59 ➲ see also BLACK EYE, COMPOUND EYE, LAZY EYE, SHUT-EYE **2 -eyed** (in adjectives 構成形容詞) having the type or number of eyes mentioned 有…眼睛的；有…隻眼的：*a blue-eyed blonde* 藍眼睛的金髮女郎◇ *a one-eyed monster* 獨眼怪物

▸ ABILITY TO SEE 視力 **3** 🔑 [sing.] the ability to see 視力；眼力：*A surgeon needs a good eye and a steady hand.* 做外科醫生眼要準，手要穩。 ➲ see also EAGLE EYE

▸ WAY OF SEEING 眼光 **4** [C, usually sing.] a particular way of seeing sth 眼光；視角：*He looked at the design* ***with the eye of*** *an engineer.* 他以工程師的眼光看這個設計。◇ *She viewed the findings with a critical eye.* 她以批判的眼光看待這些研究結果。◇ ***To my eye,*** *the windows seem out of proportion.* 在我看來，這些窗子似乎不成比例。

▸ OF NEEDLE 針 **5** [C] the hole in the end of a needle that you put the thread through 針鼻兒；針眼

▸ ON CLOTHES 衣服 **6** [C] a small thin piece of metal curved round, that a small hook fits into, used for fastening clothes 風紀扣扣眼；金屬環眼：*It fastens with* ***a hook and eye.*** 它是用風紀扣扣上的。 ➲ VISUAL VOCAB page V63

▸ OF STORM 風暴 **7** [sing.] **the ~ of a/the storm, tornado, hurricane, etc.** a calm area at the centre of a storm, etc. 風眼（風暴等的中心平靜區）

▸ ON POTATO 馬鈴薯 **8** [C] a dark mark on a potato from which another plant will grow 芽眼 ➲ see also BULLSEYE, CATSEYE, THE EVIL EYE, FISHEYE LENS, RED-EYE

IDM **be all 'eyes** to be watching sb/sth carefully and with a lot of interest 極注意地看；留神地看；全神貫注地看；目不轉睛 **before/in front of sb's (very) eyes** in sb's presence; in front of sb 當着某人的面；就在某人的眼皮底下：*He had seen his life's work destroyed before his very eyes.* 他曾看到他畢生的勞動成果就在自己的眼前

E

毀於一旦。 **be up to your eyes in sth** to have a lot of sth to deal with 忙於；埋頭於；深陷於： *We're up to our eyes in work.* 我們工作忙得不可開交。 **cast/run an eye/your eyes over sth** to look at or examine sth quickly 用眼光瞥（或掃）；匆匆查看；粗略地看一看： *Could you just run your eyes over this report?* 你就粗略地看一下這報告可以嗎？ **clap/lay/set eyes on sb/sth** (*informal*) (usually used in negative sentences 通常用於否定句) to see sb/sth 看見；注意到： *I haven't clapped eyes on them for weeks.* 我幾週沒見到他們了。◇ *I hope I never set eyes on this place again!* 我希望永遠不再見到這個地方！ **an ˌeye for an ˈeye (and a ˌtooth for a ˈtooth)** (*saying*) used to say that you should punish sb by doing to them what they have done to you or to sb else 以眼還眼；以牙還牙 **sb's eyes are bigger than their ˈstomach** used to say that sb has been GREEDY by taking more food than they can eat（表示貪吃）眼大肚皮小，眼饞肚飽 **for sb's eyes ˈonly** to be seen only by a particular person 只供某人讀（或看）： *I'll lend you the letters but they're for your eyes only.* 我會把這些信借給你，但只准你一個人看。 **get your ˈeye in** (*BrE*) (in ball games 球類運動) to practise so that you are able to judge more clearly how fast and where the ball is going 能進行準確判斷（球的速度和方向） **have an eye for sth** to be able to judge if things look attractive, valuable, etc. 對…有鑒賞力（或識別力、眼力）： *I've never had much of an eye for fashion.* 我對時裝從來沒多少鑒賞力。◇ *She has an eye for a bargain.* 她善識便宜貨。 **have eyes in the back of your ˈhead** to be aware of everything that is happening around you, even things that seem difficult or impossible to see 腦後長眼；眼光敏銳；什麼都能覺察到 **have (got) eyes like a ˈhawk** to be able to notice or see everything 洞察一切；眼尖： *She's bound to notice that chipped glass. The woman has eyes like a hawk!* 她一定會注意到那隻破損的玻璃杯。這個女人的眼睛可尖呢！ **have one eye/half an eye on sth** to look at or watch sth while doing sth else, especially in a secret way so that other people do not notice 做另一件事的同時（悄悄）注意： *During his talk, most of the delegates had one eye on the clock.* 他講話時大部份代表邊聽邊悄悄看鐘。 **have your ˈeye on sb 1** 🔑 to be watching sb carefully, especially to check that they do not do anything wrong 密切注視；盯住；監視 **2** to be thinking about asking sb out, offering sb a job, etc. because you think they are attractive, good at their job, etc. 看中；看上： *He's got his eye on the new girl in your class.* 他看中了你們班上新來的那個女孩。 **have your ˈeye on sth** to be thinking about buying sth 想得到；想買到 **in the eyes of the ˈlaw, ˈworld, etc.** according to the law, most people in the world, etc. 從（法律、世人等）的觀點看；就…而言 **in ˈsb's eyes** (*BrE* also **to ˈsb's eyes**) in sb's opinion or according to the way that they see the situation 按某人的意見；在某人眼裏；依某人看： *She can do no wrong in her father's eyes.* 在她父親看來，她不可能做壞事。 **keep an eye on sb/sth** 🔑 to take care of sb/sth and make sure that they are not harmed, damaged, etc. 照看；留神；留意： *We've asked the neighbours to keep an eye on the house for us while we are away.* 我們已請鄰居在我們外出時幫我們照看一下房子。 **keep an eye open/out (for sb/sth)** to look for sb/sth while you are doing other things 密切注意；提防；警覺： *Police have asked residents to keep an eye out for anything suspicious.* 警方呼籲居民密切注意一切可疑的情況。 **keep your eye on the ˈball** to continue to give your attention to what is most important 眼睛盯着大事；密切注意關鍵問題 **keep your ˈeyes peeled/skinned (for sb/sth)** to look carefully for sb/sth 留心；注意；仔細查找： *We kept our eyes peeled for any signs of life.* 我們注意尋找任何生命的跡象。 **look sb in the ˈeye(s)/ˈface** (usually used in negative sentences and questions 通常用於否定句和疑問句) to look straight at sb without feeling embarrassed or ashamed（坦然或問心無愧地）直視某人，正視某人： *Can you look me in the eye and tell me you're not lying?* 你能問心無愧地看着我說你沒撒謊嗎？◇ *I'll never be able to look her in the face again!* 我再也不能坦然地面對她了！ **make ˈeyes at sb | give sb the ˈeye** to look at sb in a way that shows that you find them sexually attractive 向某人送秋波；向某人拋媚眼： *He's definitely giving you the eye!* 他肯定是在向你眉目傳情！ **ˌmy ˈeye!** (*BrE, old-fashioned, informal*) used to show that you do not believe sb/sth（表示不相信）： *'It's an antique.' 'An antique, my eye!'* "這是件文物。" "是文物才怪！" **not see eye to ˈeye with sb (on sth)** to not share the same views as sb about sth 與某人看法不一致（或意見不盡相同）；與…不敢苟同 **not (be able to) take your ˈeyes off sb/sth** to find sb/sth so interesting, attractive, etc. that you watch them all the time 目不轉睛地盯着；始終注視着 **one in the eye (for sb/sth)** (*informal*) a result, action, etc. that represents a defeat or disappointment for sb/sth 失敗；挫折；失望： *The appointment of a woman was one in the eye for male domination.* 任命女性擔任這個職位是對男權統治的嚴重打擊。 **only have eyes for/have eyes only for sb** to be in love with only one particular person 只鍾情於某人；只愛某人： *He's only ever had eyes for his wife.* 他始終只愛自己的妻子。 **see, look at, etc. sth through sb's eyes** to think about or see sth the way that another person sees it 從別人的角度看： *Try looking at it through her eyes for a change.* 試試設身處地站在她的角度想想這事吧。 **shut/close your eyes to sth** 🔑 to pretend that you have not noticed sth so that you do not have to deal with it（對…）視而不見，熟視無睹，置若罔聞 **take your eye off the ˈball** to stop giving your attention to what is most important 不再關注重要問題 **under the (watchful) eye of sb** being watched carefully by sb 在某人的密切注視下；在某人的監視下： *The children played under the watchful eye of their father.* 孩子們在父親悉心看護下玩耍。 **what the eye doesn't ˈsee (the heart doesn't ˈgrieve over)** (*saying*) if a person does not know about sth that they would normally disapprove of, then it cannot hurt them 眼不見（心不煩）；眼不見為淨： *What does it matter if I use his flat while he's away? What the eye doesn't see ...!* 我趁他外出時用他的公寓有什麼關係呢？反正他又看不見！ **with an eye for/on/to the main chance** (*BrE*, usually *disapproving*) with the hope of using a particular situation in order to gain some advantage for yourself 瞅機會撈一把 **with an eye to sth/to doing sth** with the intention of doing sth 着眼於；目的在於；試圖： *He bought the warehouse with an eye to converting it into a hotel.* 他買這個倉庫是為了將它改建成一家旅館。 **with your eyes ˈopen** fully aware of the possible problems or results of a particular course of action 明知後果如何；明知有問題；心中有數： *I went into this with my eyes open so I guess I only have myself to blame.* 我是明明知道做這事的後果的，所以我想只能責怪我自己。 **with your eyes ˈshut/ˈclosed** having enough experience to be able to do sth easily 輕車熟路；毫不費力： *I've made this trip so often, I could do it with my eyes shut.* 我經常走這條路，閉着眼睛都能找到。 ➲ more at APPLE, BAT *v.*, BEAUTY, BELIEVE, BIRD *n.*, BLIND *adj.*, BLINK *n.*, CATCH *v.*, CLOSE² *adj.*, COCK *v.*, CORNER *n.*, DRY *adj.*, EASY *adj.*, FAR *adv.*, FEAST *v.*, HIT *v.*, MEET *v.*, MIND *n.*, NAKED, OPEN *adj.*, OPEN *v.*, PLEASE *v.*, PUBLIC *adj.*, PULL *v.*, ROVING, SIGHT *n.*, TWINKLING, WEATHER *n.*

■ ***verb*** (**eye·ing** or **eying**, **eyed**, **eyed**) **~ sb/sth (+ adv./prep.)** to look at sb/sth carefully, especially because you want sth or you are suspicious of sth 注視；審視；細看： *to eye sb suspiciously* 懷疑地注視着某人 ◇ *He couldn't help eyeing the cakes hungrily.* 他飢不可耐地盯着蛋糕。◇ *They eyed us with alarm.* 他們警覺地注視着我們。

PHR V **ˌeye sb↔ˈup** (*informal*) to look at sb in a way that shows you have a special interest in them, especially a sexual interest 色迷迷地打量着某人

eye·ball /ˈaɪbɔːl/ *noun, verb*

■ ***noun*** the whole of the eye, including the part inside the head that cannot be seen 眼球；眼珠 ➲ VISUAL VOCAB page V59

IDM **ˌeyeball to ˈeyeball (with sb)** very close to sb and looking at them, especially during an angry conversation, meeting, etc.（與某人）面對面，怒目相視，對峙： *The protesters and police stood eyeball to eyeball.* 抗議者與警察劍拔弩張。◇ *an eyeball-to-eyeball confrontation* 面對面的對抗 **be up to your eyeballs in sth** to have a lot of sth to deal with 忙於；埋頭於；深陷於：*They're up to their eyeballs in work.* 他們的工作忙得不可開交。➲ more at DRUG *v.*

■ ***verb* ~ sb/sth** (*informal*) to look at sb/sth in a way that is very direct and not always polite or friendly 瞪着；逼視；盯住

eye·bath /ˈaɪbɑːθ; *NAmE* -bæθ/ *noun* a small container that you put a liquid in to wash your eye with 洗眼杯

eye·brow /ˈaɪbraʊ/ (also **brow**) *noun* [usually pl.] the line of hair above the eye 眉；眉毛 ➲ COLLOCATIONS at PHYSICAL ➲ VISUAL VOCAB page V59

IDM **be up to your eyebrows in sth** to have a lot of sth to deal with 忙於；埋頭於；深陷於：*He's in it* (= trouble) *up to his eyebrows.* 他深陷於困境之中。➲ more at RAISE *v.*

ˈ**eyebrow pencil** *noun* a type of make-up in the form of a pencil, used for emphasizing or improving the shape of the EYEBROWS 眉筆

ˈ**eye candy** *noun* [U] (*informal*) a person or thing that is attractive but not intelligent or useful 有魅力但不聰明的人；中看不中用的東西

ˈ**eye-catching** *adj.* (of a thing 事物) immediately noticeable because it is particularly interesting, bright or attractive 惹人注意的；引人注目的：*an eye-catching advertisement* 醒目的廣告

eye·ful /ˈaɪfʊl/ *noun* **1** an amount of sth such as liquid or dust that has been thrown, or blown into your eye 滿眼 **2** (*informal*) a person or thing that is beautiful or interesting to look at 悅目的人（或物）；美人；好看的東西

IDM **have/get an eyeful (of sth)** (*BrE, informal*) to look carefully at sth that is interesting or unusual 一飽眼福；好好看一看

eye·glass /ˈaɪɡlɑːs; *NAmE* -ɡlæs/ *noun* **1** a LENS for one eye used to help you see more clearly with that eye 鏡片；單片眼鏡 **2 eyeglasses** (*NAmE*) = GLASSES at GLASS *n.* (6)

eye·lash /ˈaɪlæʃ/ (also **lash**) *noun* [usually pl.] one of the hairs growing on the edge of the EYELIDS 睫；睫毛：*false eyelashes* 假睫毛 ◇ *She just* ***flutters her eyelashes*** *and the men come running!* 她只要眨一下眼睫毛，男人們便忙不迭地跑過來！➲ COLLOCATIONS at PHYSICAL ➲ VISUAL VOCAB page V59 IDM see BAT *v.*

eye·let /ˈaɪlət/ *noun* a hole with a metal ring around it in a piece of cloth or leather, normally used for passing a rope or string through（供穿繩、線用的）圓孔眼

ˈ**eye level** *noun* [U] the height of a person's eyes 視線的水平高度：*Computer screens should be at eye level.* 計算機屏幕應該與眼睛齊平。◇ *an eye-level grill* 與眼睛齊平的鐵柵欄

eye·lid /ˈaɪlɪd/ (also **lid**) *noun* either of the pieces of skin above and below the eye that cover it when you BLINK or close the eye 眼瞼；眼皮 ➲ VISUAL VOCAB page V59 IDM see BAT *v.*

eye·line /ˈaɪlaɪn/ *noun* the direction that sb is looking in 視線

eye·liner /ˈaɪlaɪnə(r)/ (also **liner**) *noun* [U] a type of make-up, usually black, that is put around the edge of the eyes to make them more noticeable and attractive（化妝的）眼線 ➲ VISUAL VOCAB page V60

ˈ**eye-opener** *noun* [usually sing.] an event, experience, etc. that is surprising and shows you sth that you did not already know 使人大開眼界的事情（或經歷等）：*Travelling around India was a real eye-opener for me.* 周遊印度真讓我開了眼界。

eye·patch /ˈaɪpætʃ/ *noun* a piece of material worn over one eye, usually because the eye is damaged 眼罩（通常因眼睛受傷而戴）

eye·piece /ˈaɪpiːs/ *noun* the piece of glass (= a LENS) at the end of a TELESCOPE or MICROSCOPE that you look through（望遠鏡或顯微鏡的）目鏡 ➲ picture at BINOCULARS ➲ VISUAL VOCAB page V70

eye·shadow /ˈaɪʃædəʊ; *NAmE* -doʊ/ *noun* [C, U] a type of coloured make-up that is put on the skin above the eyes (= the EYELIDS) to make them look more attractive 眼影 ➲ VISUAL VOCAB page V60

eye·sight /ˈaɪsaɪt/ *noun* [U] the ability to see 視力；目力：*to have* ***good/bad/poor eyesight*** 視力好／不好／差 ◇ *an eyesight test* 視力測試

eye·sore /ˈaɪsɔː(r)/ *noun* a building, an object, etc. that is unpleasant to look at 礙眼的建築；醜陋的東西；令人厭惡的東西：*That old factory is a real eyesore!* 那老工廠實在礙眼！

ˈ**eye strain** *noun* [U] a condition of the eyes caused, for example, by a long period of reading or looking at a computer screen 眼疲勞

ˈ**eye teeth** *noun* [pl.]

IDM **give your eye teeth for sth/to do sth** (*BrE, informal*) used when you are saying that you want sth very much 迫切想要；巴不得有：*I'd give my eye teeth to own a car like that.* 我巴不得有一輛那樣的汽車。

eye·wall /ˈaɪwɔːl/ *noun* (*technical* 術語) a thick ring of cloud around the EYE (= calm area at the centre) of a HURRICANE（颶風）眼壁

eye·wash /ˈaɪwɒʃ; *NAmE* -wɔːʃ; -wɑːʃ/ *noun* [U] (*old-fashioned, informal*) words, promises, etc. that are not true or sincere 空話；假話；口惠

ˈ**eye-watering** *adj.* (*informal, especially BrE*) so high or extreme that it is difficult or painful to think about it（高得）難以想像的；令人心痛的；催人落淚的：*eye-watering fare increases* 超乎想像的交通票價飆升 ▸ **eye-wateringly** *adv.*：*eye-wateringly high interest rates* 難以承受的高利率

eye·wear /ˈaɪweə(r); *NAmE* -wer/ *noun* [U] (*formal*) things worn on the eyes such as glasses or CONTACT LENSES（隱形）眼鏡

eye·wit·ness /ˈaɪwɪtnəs/ *noun* a person who has seen a crime, accident, etc. and can describe it afterwards 目擊者；見證人：*an eyewitness account of the suffering of the refugees* 目擊者對難民苦難遭遇的敍述 ➲ SYNONYMS at WITNESS ➲ see also WITNESS *n.* (1)

eyrie (*especially BrE*) (*NAmE* usually **aerie**) /ˈɪəri; ˈeəri; ˈaɪəri; *NAmE* ˈɪri; ˈeri/ *noun* **1** a nest that is built high up among rocks by a BIRD OF PREY (= a bird that kills other creatures for food) such as an EAGLE（在岩石高處築的）猛禽巢，鷹巢 **2** a room or building in a high place, especially one that is difficult to reach and from which sb can see what is happening below（尤指難以接近的）高處的房屋

ˈ**e-zine** *noun* a magazine published in electronic form on the Internet 電子雜誌

Ff

F /ef/ *noun, abbr.*

■ ***noun*** (also **f**) [C, U] (*pl.* **Fs, F's, f's** /efs/) **1** the 6th letter of the English alphabet 英語字母表的第 6 個字母：*'Fox' begins with (an) F/'F'.* * fox 一詞以字母 f 開頭。**2 F** (*music* 音) the fourth note in the SCALE of C MAJOR * F 音（C 大調的第 4 音或音符）**3** the 6th highest mark/grade that a student can get for a piece of work, showing that it is very bad and the student has failed（學業成績）第六等，不及格：*He got (an) F/'F' in/for Chemistry.* 他的化學成績不及格。➲ see also F-WORD

■ ***abbr.*** **1** FAHRENHEIT 華氏度：*Water freezes at 32°F.* 水在 32 華氏度結冰。**2** (*BrE*) (in academic titles 學術頭銜) FELLOW of 會員：*FRCM* (= Fellow of the Royal College of Music) 皇家音樂學院研究員 **3** FARAD 法拉（電容單位）

Synonyms 同義詞辨析

fabric

cloth • material • textile

These are all words for woven or knitted cotton, silk, wool, etc., used for making things such as clothes and curtains, and for covering furniture. 以下詞彙均指織物、布料。

fabric woven or knitted cotton, silk, wool, etc., used for making things such as clothes and curtains, and for covering furniture 指織物、布料：*cotton fabric* 棉織物 ◇ *furnishing fabrics* 室內裝飾織物 **NOTE** **Fabric** is often fairly strong material, and is often used when talking about covering furniture or making curtains. * fabric 常指較結實的材料，常用於指蓋傢具、做窗簾的織物。

cloth fabric made by weaving or knitting cotton, wool, silk, etc. 指織物、布料：*His bandages had been made from strips of cloth.* 他的繃帶是用布條做的。**NOTE** **Cloth** is often fairly light material, especially in a form that has not been printed, treated, or prepared for use in any way. **Cloth** is frequently used in talking about buying and selling woven material. * cloth 常指較輕的材料，尤指尚未印花、處理或加工的織物。cloth 常指買賣的織物、布料。

material fabric used for making clothes, curtains, etc. 指布料：*'What material is this dress made of?' 'Cotton.'*"這件裙子是用什麼料子做的？""棉布。" **NOTE** **Material** is a more general word than **fabric** or **cloth** as it has the related meaning of 'a substance that things can be made from'. It is not used when it might not be clear which type of material is meant. * material 較 fabric 或 cloth 含義更廣，因為該詞含材料、原料等相關意義。不清楚布料類型就不用該詞：~~*furnishing material*~~ ◇ ~~*the material industry*~~ ◇ ~~*a material manufacturer*~~

textile any type of fabric made by weaving or knitting 指紡織品：*He owns a factory producing a range of textiles.* 他擁有一家工廠，生產一系列紡織品。◇ *the textile industry* 紡織工業 **NOTE** **Textile** is used mostly when talking about the business of making woven materials. The industry of making textiles is called **textiles**. * textile 多用於指織物生產業，生產紡織品的產業叫 textiles：*He got a job in textiles.* 他在紡織行業找到一份工作。

PATTERNS

- **woven/cotton/woollen** fabric/cloth/material/textiles
- **synthetic** fabric/material/textiles
- **printed** fabric/cloth/textiles
- **furnishing/curtain/dress** fabric/material

f (*BrE*) (also **f.** *NAmE, BrE*) *abbr.* **1** female 女的；女性的 **2** (*grammar* 語法) feminine 陰性的；女性的 **3** (*music* 音) loudly (from Italian 'forte')（演奏或歌唱）強，強有力（源自意大利語 forte）

F-1 visa /ˌef wʌn ˈviːzə/ *noun* a document that allows sb from another country to enter the US as a student（美國）外國學生簽證

FA /ˌef ˈeɪ/ *noun* [sing.] **the FA** the abbreviation for 'Football Association' (the organization that controls the sport of football (SOCCER) in England and Wales)（英格蘭和威爾士的）足球協會（全寫為 Football Association）

fa = FAH

fab /fæb/ *adj.* (*BrE, informal*) extremely good 極好的

fable /ˈfeɪbl/ *noun* **1** [C, U] a traditional short story that teaches a moral lesson, especially one with animals as characters; these stories considered as a group 寓言；寓言故事：*Aesop's Fables* 伊索寓言 ◇ *a land rich in fable* 寓言之鄉 **2** [U, C] a statement, or an account of sth, that is not true 謊言；不實之詞；無稽之談

fabled /ˈfeɪbld/ *adj.* (*literary* or *humorous*) famous and often talked about, but rarely seen 傳說中的 **SYN** **legendary**：*a fabled monster* 傳說中的怪物 ◇ *For the first week he never actually saw the fabled Jack.* 第一週他實際上沒見到傳聞已久的傑克。

fab·ric /ˈfæbrɪk/ *noun* **1** [U, C] material made by WEAVING wool, cotton, silk, etc., used for making clothes, curtains, etc. and for covering furniture 織物；布料：*cotton fabric* 棉織物 ◇ *furnishing fabrics* 室內裝飾織品 **2** [sing.] **the ~ (of sth)** (*formal*) the basic structure of a society, an organization, etc. that enables it to function successfully（社會、機構等的）結構：*a trend which threatens the very **fabric of society*** 威脅社會基本結構的趨勢 ➲ SYNONYMS at STRUCTURE **3** [sing.] **the ~ (of sth)** the basic structure of a building, such as the walls, floor and roof（建築物的）結構（如牆、地面、屋頂）

fab·ri·cate /ˈfæbrɪkeɪt/ *verb* [often passive] **1 ~ sth** to invent false information in order to trick people 編造；捏造 **SYN** **make up**：*The evidence was totally fabricated.* 這個證據純屬偽造。**2 ~ sth** (*technical* 術語) to make or produce goods, equipment, etc. from various different materials 製造；裝配；組裝 **SYN** **manufacture** ▸ **fab·ri·ca·tion** /ˌfæbrɪˈkeɪʃn/ *noun* [C, U] (*formal*)：*Her story was a complete fabrication from start to finish.* 她的敘述從頭至尾都是編造出來的。

fabu·list /ˈfæbjəlɪst/ *noun* (*formal*) a person who invents or tells stories 寓言作家；講故事的人

fabu·lous /ˈfæbjələs/ *adj.* **1** (*informal*) extremely good 極好的；絕妙的：*a fabulous performance* 精彩的表演 ◇ *Jana is a fabulous cook.* 詹娜的廚藝堪稱一絕。➲ SYNONYMS at GREAT **2** (*formal*) very great 很大的；巨大的：***fabulous wealth/riches/beauty*** 大量財產；非常美麗 **3** [only before noun] (*literary*) appearing in FABLES 寓言中的；神話似的：*fabulous beasts* 傳說中的野獸

fabu·lous·ly /ˈfæbjələsli/ *adv.* (*formal*) extremely 極其；非常：***fabulously wealthy/rich*** 極為富有

fa·cade /fəˈsɑːd/ *noun* **1** the front of a building（建築物的）正面，立面 **2** [usually sing.] the way that sb/sth appears to be, which is different from the way sb/sth really is（虛假的）表面，外表：*She managed to maintain a facade of indifference.* 她設法繼續裝作漠不關心的樣子。◇ *Squalor and poverty lay behind the city's glittering facade.* 表面的繁華掩蓋了這座城市的骯髒和貧窮。

face 🔑 /feɪs/ *noun, verb*

■ ***noun***

▸ **FRONT OF HEAD** 頭的正面 **1** 🔑 the front part of the head between the FOREHEAD and the chin 臉；面孔：*a pretty/round/freckled face* 漂亮的／圓的／有雀斑的面孔 ◇ *He buried his face in his hands.* 他雙手掩面。◇ *You should have seen the look **on her face** when I told her!* 我告訴她的時候你真該看到她的臉色！◇ *The expression on his face never changed.* 他的面部表情總是一成不變。➲ VISUAL VOCAB page V59

▸ **EXPRESSION** 表情 **2** 🔑 an expression that is shown on sb's face 面部表情：*a **sad/happy/smiling face*** 悲哀／幸福的面容；笑臉 ◇ *Her **face lit up*** (= showed happiness) *when she spoke of the past.* 她講到往事時就面露喜色。

◇ *His* ***face fell*** (= showed disappointment, sadness, etc.) *when he read the headlines.* 他讀大標題時臉沉了下來。◇ *Sue's* ***face was a picture*** (= she looked very surprised, angry, etc.) *as she listened to her husband's speech.* 蘇聽她丈夫講話時，臉上露出又驚又氣的表情。

▸ **-FACED** 面容… **3** (in adjectives 構成形容詞) having the type of face or expression mentioned 有…面容的；有…表情的： *pale-faced* 面色蒼白 ◇ *grim-faced* 表情嚴肅

▸ **PERSON** 人 **4** (in compounds 構成複合詞) used to refer to a person of the type mentioned （某類型的）人： *She looked around for a* ***familiar face.*** 她環顧四周想找個熟人。◇ *a well-known face on our television screens* 電視屏幕上的一位名人 ◇ *It's nice to see some* ***new faces*** *here this evening.* 今晚在這兒見到一些新面孔真是太好了。◇ *I'm fed up of seeing the* ***same old faces*** *every time we go out!* 每個社交場合都只見到那些舊面孔，我都膩了。

▸ **SIDE/SURFACE** 面；表面 **5** a side or surface of sth （某物的）面，表面： *the north face of the mountain* 山的北坡 ◇ *The birds build their nests in the rock face.* 這些鳥在岩壁上築巢。◇ *How many faces does a cube have?* 立方體有幾個面？ ➲ see also COALFACE

▸ **FRONT OF CLOCK** 鐘面 **6** the front part of a clock or watch 鐘面；錶盤 ➲ picture at CLOCK

▸ **CHARACTER/ASPECT** 特徵；方面 **7 ~ of sth** the particular character of sth （事物的某種）特徵： *the changing face of Britain* 大不列顛變化中的特徵 **8 ~ of sth** a particular aspect of sth 方面： *the unacceptable face of capitalism* 資本主義不可接受的方面 ➲ see also IN-YOUR-FACE, TYPEFACE, VOLTE-FACE

IDM **disappear/vanish off the face of the 'earth** to disappear completely 完全消失；消逝得無影無踪： *Keep looking—they can't just have vanished off the face of the earth.* 繼續找，他們不可能就從此消失得無影無踪的。 **sb's face doesn't fit** used to say that sb will not get a particular job or position because they do not have the appearance, personality, etc. that the employer wants, even when this should not be important 長相不合格；性格不合適： *It doesn't matter how well qualified you are, if your face doesn't fit, you don't stand a chance.* 資歷多好也沒用，如果人家看你不對眼，你就不會有機會。 **sb's face is like 'thunder | sb has a face like 'thunder** somebody looks very angry 某人怒氣沖沖；某人滿面怒容 **ˌface to 'face (with sb)** close to and looking at sb （與某人）面對面： *The two have never met face to face before.* 兩個人過去從未見過面。 **ˌface to 'face with sth** in a situation where you have to accept that sth is true and deal with it 面對某種處境： *She was at an early age brought face to face with the horrors of war.* 她年幼時就面臨戰爭的恐怖。 **ˌface 'up/'down 1** (of a person 人) with your face and stomach facing upwards/downwards 面朝上／朝下： *She lay face down on the bed.* 她俯卧在牀上。 **2** with the front part or surface facing upwards/downwards 正面朝上／朝下；表面衝上／衝下： *Place the card face up on the pile.* 把紙牌正面朝上放在這一疊的上面。 **have the 'face to do sth** (*BrE, informal*) to do sth that other people think is rude or shows a lack of respect without feeling embarrassed or ashamed 居然有臉幹某事；恬不知恥做某事 **in sb's 'face** (*NAmE, informal*) annoying sb by criticizing them or telling them what to do all the time 批評某人，支使某人（使人惱火） **in the face of 'sth 1** despite problems, difficulties, etc. 即使面對（問題、困難等）： *She showed great courage in the face of danger.* 面對危險她表現出了巨大的勇氣。 **2** as a result of sth 由於；因為： *He was unable to deny the charges in the face of new evidence.* 面對新的證據，他無法否認被控告的罪。 **lose 'face** to be less respected or look stupid because of sth you have done 丟臉；失面子 SYN **be humiliated** **on the 'face of it** (*informal*) used to say that sth seems to be good, true, etc. but that this opinion may need to be changed when you know more about it 表面上看： *On the face of it, it seems like a great deal.* 表面上看來好像很多。 **pull/make 'faces/a 'face (at sb)** to produce an expression on your face to show that you do not like sb/sth or in order to make sb laugh （對某人）耷拉着臉，板着臉，做鬼臉： *What are you pulling a face at now?* 你幹嗎板着臉？ **put your 'face on** (*informal*) to put on MAKE-UP 化妝 **set your face against sb/sth** (*especially BrE*) to be determined to oppose sb/sth 堅決反對某人／事物： *Her father had set his face against the marriage.* 她的父親堅決反對這門親事。 **to sb's 'face** if you say sth **to sb's face**, you say it to them directly rather than to other people 當着某人的面 ➲ compare BEHIND SB'S BACK at BACK **'what's his/her face** (*informal*) used to refer to a person whose name you cannot remember （指記不起姓名的人）叫…的人： *Are you still working for what's her face?* 你還在為那個叫什麼的女人幹活？ ➲ more at BLOW *v.*, BLUE *adj.*, BRAVE *adj.*, DOOR, EGG *n.*, EYE *n.*, FEED *v.*, FLAT *adv.*, FLY *v.*, LAUGH *v.*, LONG *adj.*, NOSE *n.*, PLAIN *adj.*, PRETTY *adj.*, SAVE *v.*, SHOW *v.*, SHUT *v.*, SLAP *n.*, STARE *v.*, STRAIGHT *adj.*, WIPE *v.*, WRITE

Vocabulary Building 詞彙擴充

Expressions on your face 面部表情

- To **beam** is to have a big happy smile on your face. * beam 指笑逐顏開。
- To **frown** is to make a serious, angry or worried expression by bringing your eyebrows closer together so that lines appear on your forehead. * frown 指皺眉、蹙額。
- To **glare** or **glower** is to look in an angry, aggressive way. * glare 和 glower 指怒目而視、咄咄逼人地瞪眼。
- To **grimace** is to make an ugly expression with your face to show pain, disgust, etc. * grimace 指因痛苦、厭惡等而面目扭曲。
- To **scowl** is to look at someone in an angry or annoyed way. * scowl 指怒視。
- To **smirk** is to smile in a silly or unpleasant way that shows that you are pleased with yourself, know something that other people do not know, etc. * smirk 指傻笑、得意地笑，以示自鳴得意、知他人所不知等。
- To **sneer** is to show that you have no respect for someone by turning your upper lip upwards. * sneer 指翹起上唇嗤笑、譏笑，以示輕蔑。

These words can also be used as nouns. 以上各詞亦可作名詞： *She looked up with a puzzled frown.* 她抬起頭來，困惑地皺着眉頭。◇ *He gave me an icy glare.* 他冷冰冰地怒視着我。◇ *a grimace of pain* 痛得扭曲的臉

■ *verb*

▸ **BE OPPOSITE** 面對 **1** [T, I] to be opposite sb/sth; to have your face or front pointing towards sb/sth or in a particular direction 面對；面向；正對： **~ sb/sth** *She turned and faced him.* 她轉過身來面對着他。◇ *Most of the rooms face the sea.* 多數房間朝海。◇ **+ adv./prep.** *The terrace faces south.* 露台朝南。◇ *a north-facing wall* 面北的牆 ◇ *Stand with your feet apart and your hands facing upwards.* 兩腳叉開站着，雙手向上。◇ *Which direction are you facing?* 你面朝哪個方向？

▸ **SB/STH DIFFICULT** 難對付的人／事物 **2** [T] if you **face** a particular situation, or it **faces** you, you have to deal with it 面臨，必須對付（某情況）： **~ sth** *the problems faced by one-parent families* 單親家庭面對的問題 ◇ *The company is facing a financial crisis.* 公司正面臨財政危機。◇ **be faced with sth** *She's faced with a difficult decision.* 她眼前有一項難作的決定。 **3** [T] **~ sth** to accept that a difficult situation exists, although you would prefer not to 承認，正視（現實）： *It's not always easy to face the truth.* 承認事實並不總是一件容易的事。◇ *She had to* ***face the fact that*** *her life had changed forever.* 她得正視她的生活已永遠改變了這一事實。◇ ***Face facts****—she isn't coming back.* 面對現實吧，她不會回來了。◇ ***Let's face it****, we're not going to win.* 我們得承認，我們贏不了啦。 **4** [T] if you **can't face** sth unpleasant, you feel unable or unwilling to deal with it （感到不能）對付；（不願）處理： **~ sth** *I just can't face work today.* 我今天就是沒法工作。◇ **~ doing sth** *I can't face seeing them.* 我真不願意見到他們。 **5** [T] **~ sb** to talk to or deal with sb, even though this is difficult or

unpleasant（明知不好辦而）交談，應付：*How can I face Tom? He'll be so disappointed.* 我怎樣才能和湯姆談呢？他會很失望的。
▸ COVER SURFACE 覆蓋表面 **6** [T, usually passive] **~ sth with sth** to cover a surface with another material（以另一物）覆蓋表面：*a brick building faced with stone* 石料貼面的磚建築物
IDM **face the 'music** (*informal*) to accept and deal with criticism or punishment for sth you have done 接受批評（或懲罰）：*The others all ran off, leaving me to face the music.* 其他人都跑掉了，留下我來捱罰。
PHR V **,face sb↔'down** to oppose or beat sb by dealing with them directly and confidently（威風凜凜地）把某人壓制下去 **,face 'off** (*especially NAmE*) **1** to start a game such as ICE HOCKEY（冰球等）開球：*Both teams are ready to face off.* 兩隊都準備好了開球。**2** to get ready to argue, fight or compete with sb 準備好辯論（或戰鬥、比賽）：*The candidates are preparing to face off on TV tonight.* 今夜候選人準備在電視上進行辯論。➲ related noun FACE-OFF **,face 'up to sth** 🗝 to accept and deal with sth that is difficult or unpleasant 敢於面對，勇於正視（困難或不快之事）：*She had to face up to the fact that she would never walk again.* 她必須敢於面對現實：她再也不能走路了。

Face·book™ /'feɪsbʊk/ *noun* a SOCIAL NETWORKING website 臉譜網站；臉書網站；社交網站；臉書

'face card (*especially NAmE*) (*BrE* also **'court card**) *noun* a PLAYING CARD with a picture of a king, queen or JACK on it 人頭牌，花牌（紙牌的 K、Q 或 J）➲ VISUAL VOCAB page V37

face·cloth /'feɪsklɒθ; *NAmE* -klɔːθ/ *noun* (*BrE*) = FLANNEL (2)

'face cream *noun* [U, C] a thick cream that you put on your face to clean the skin or keep it soft 面霜；雪花膏

face·less /'feɪsləs/ *adj.* [usually before noun] (*disapproving*) having no noticeable characteristics or identity 無個性的；缺乏特徵的；身分不明的：*faceless bureaucrats* 千人一面的官僚主義者 ◇ *faceless high-rise apartment blocks* 千篇一律的高層公寓大樓

face·lift /'feɪslɪft/ *noun* [usually sing.] **1** a medical operation in which the skin on a person's face is made tighter in order to make them look younger 去皺整容手術；面部拉皮手術：*to have a facelift* 接受去皺整容手術 **2** changes made to a building or place to make it look more attractive（建築物、地方的）翻新，整修：*The town has recently been given a facelift.* 該鎮最近進行了整修。

'face-off *noun* **1** (*informal, especially NAmE*) an argument or a fight 辯論；搏鬥：*a face-off between the presidential candidates* 總統候選人之間的辯論 **2** the way of starting play in a game of ICE HOCKEY（冰球賽的）開球

'face pack *noun* (*BrE*) a substance that you put on your face and take off after a short period of time, used to clean your skin 面膜（潔淨面部皮膚用）

'face powder *noun* powder that you put on your face to make it look less shiny 撲面粉；敷面粉

'face-saving *adj.* [only before noun] intended to protect sb's reputation and to avoid embarrassment 保全面子的：*a face-saving compromise* 體面的妥協

facet /'fæsɪt/ *noun* **1 ~ (of sth)** a particular part or aspect of sth（事物的）部份，方面：*Now let's look at another facet of the problem.* 現在咱們看問題的另一面。**2** one of the flat sides of a JEWEL（寶石的）小平面，琢面

'face time *noun* [U] (*NAmE, informal*) time that you spend talking face-to-face (= in person) to people you work with, rather than speaking on the phone or sending emails（與同事等的）面對面（交流）時間

fa·cetious /fə'siːʃəs/ *adj.* trying to appear amusing and intelligent at a time when other people do not think it is appropriate, and when it would be better to be serious 亂引人發笑的；不問場合要聰明的 **SYN** **flippant**：*a **facetious comment/remark*** 不當的滑稽評論；不問場合要聰明的議論 ◇ *Stop being facetious; this is serious.* 別亂開玩笑，這是個嚴肅的事。▸ **fa·cetious·ly** *adv.* **fa·cetious·ness** *noun* [U]

,face-to-'face *adj.* involving people who are close together and looking at each other 面對面的：*a face-to-face conversation* 面談 ◇ *I deal with customers on the phone and rarely meet them face-to-face.* 我用電話和客戶打交道，很少和他們見面。▸ **face-to-face** *adv.*：*He opened the door and **came face-to-face with** a burglar.* 他打開門和竊賊打了個照面。◇ (*figurative*) *She was brought face-to-face with the horrors of war.* 她直面了戰爭的恐怖。

,face 'value *noun* [U, sing.] the value of a stamp, coin, ticket, etc. that is shown on the front of it（郵票、錢幣、票等的）票面價值，面值
IDM **take sth at face 'value** to believe that sth is what it appears to be, without questioning it 相信表面：*Taken at face value, the figures look very encouraging.* 若只看表面，數字很令人鼓舞。◇ *You shouldn't take anything she says at face value.* 她的話你絕對不能只相信表面。

fa·cia = FASCIA (1), (3), (4)

fa·cial /'feɪʃl/ *adj., noun*
■ ***adj.*** [usually before noun] connected with a person's face; on a person's face 面部的：*a facial expression* 面部表情 ◇ *facial hair* 面部毫毛 ▸ **fa·cial·ly** /'feɪʃəli/ *adv.*：*Facially the two men were very different.* 這兩個男人的臉型迥異。
■ ***noun*** a beauty treatment in which a person's face is cleaned using creams, steam, etc. in order to improve the quality of the skin 面部護理；美容

fa·cile /'fæsaɪl; *NAmE* 'fæsl/ *adj.* (*disapproving*) **1** produced without effort or careful thought 輕率作出的；不動腦筋的 **SYN** **glib**：*a **facile remark/generalization*** 信口開河；隨意概括 **2** [only before noun] (*formal*) obtained too easily and having little value 輕易可得的；得來容易的：*a facile victory* 唾手可得的勝利

fa·cili·tate **AW** /fə'sɪlɪteɪt/ *verb* **~ sth** (*formal*) to make an action or a process possible or easier 促進；促使；使便利：*The new trade agreement should facilitate more rapid economic growth.* 新貿易協定應當會加快經濟發展。◇ *Structured teaching facilitates learning.* 有條理的教導有利於學習。▸ **fa·cili·ta·tion** **AW** /fə,sɪlɪ'teɪʃn/ *noun* [U, sing.]

fa·cili·ta·tor **AW** /fə'sɪlɪteɪtə(r)/ *noun* **1** a person who helps sb do sth more easily by discussing problems, giving advice, etc. rather than telling them what to do 誘導者：*The teacher acts as a facilitator of learning.* 教師是學習的誘導者。**2** (*formal*) a thing that helps a process take place 促進（或推動）…的事物

fa·cil·ity 🗝 **AW** /fə'sɪləti/ *noun*
1 🗝 **facilities** [pl.] buildings, services, equipment, etc. that are provided for a particular purpose 設施；設備：***sports/leisure facilities*** 體育／消閒設施 ◇ *conference facilities* 會議設施 ◇ ***shopping/banking/cooking facilities*** 商店／銀行設施；炊事設備 ◇ *The hotel has special facilities for welcoming disabled people.* 這家旅館有專供殘疾人使用的設施。◇ *All rooms have **private facilities*** (= a private bathroom). 每一個房間都有專用的浴室。**2** [C] a special feature of a machine, service, etc. that makes it possible to do sth extra（機器等的）特別裝置；（服務等的）特色：*a bank account with an overdraft facility* 提供透支服務的銀行賬戶 ◇ *a facility for checking spelling* 檢查拼寫的設備 **3** [C] a place, usually including buildings, used for a particular purpose or activity（供特定用途的）場所：*the world's largest nuclear waste facility* 世界最大的核廢料處理場所 ◇ *a new health care facility* 新保健中心 **4** [sing., U] **~ (for sth)** a natural ability to learn or do sth easily（學習、做事的）天資，才能，天賦：*She has a facility for languages.* 她有語言天賦。

fa·cing /'feɪsɪŋ/ *noun* **1** [C, U] a layer of brick, stone, etc. that covers the surface of a wall to make it look more attractive（建築物的）飾面，面層 **2** [C, U] a layer of stiff material sewn around the inside of the neck, ARMHOLES, etc. of a piece of clothing to make them stronger 領口襯裏，袖口貼邊，鑲邊（使衣服耐穿）**3** **facings** [pl.] the COLLAR, CUFFS, etc. of a piece of clothing that are made in a different colour or material（不同質地或顏色的）領子（或袖口等）

fac·sim·ile /fæk'sɪməli/ *noun* **1** [C] an exact copy of sth 摹本；傳真本；複製本：*a facsimile edition* 摹本版 ◇ *a manuscript reproduced* ***in facsimile*** 精確複製的手稿 **2** [C, U] (*formal*) = FAX *n.*：*a facsimile machine* 傳真機

fact 🔑 /fækt/ *noun*
1 🔑 [sing.] **~ (that ...)** used to refer to a particular situation that exists 現實；實際情況：*I could no longer ignore the fact that he was deeply unhappy.* 我再不能對他深感不快這個事實不聞不問了。◇ ***Despite the fact that*** *she was wearing a seat belt, she was thrown sharply forward.* 儘管她繫了安全帶，還是被猛然拋前。◇ ***Due to the fact that*** *they did not read English, the prisoners were unaware of what they were signing.* 這些囚犯由於看不懂英語，不知道自己在簽什麼。◇ *She was happy* ***apart from the fact that*** *she could not return home.* 除了不能回家之外，她很快活。◇ *Voluntary work was particularly important* ***in view of the fact that*** *women were often forced to give up paid work on marriage.* 鑒於婦女一結婚就常常被迫放棄有報酬工作的事實，義務工作尤其重要。◇ *How do you account for the fact that unemployment is still rising?* 你如何解釋失業人數仍在增加這個現實？◇ ***The fact remains*** *that we are still two teachers short.* 實際情況是我們還缺少兩名教師。◇ *The mere fact of being poor makes such children criminals in the eyes of the police.* 只因為貧窮就使得這群兒童成為警方眼中的罪犯。➲ LANGUAGE BANK at HOWEVER **2** 🔑 [C] a thing that is known to be true, especially when it can be proved（可證實的）事實，真相：*Isn't it a fact that the firm is losing money?* 公司正在虧本，這難道不是事實嗎？◇ (*informal*) *I haven't spoken to anyone in English for days* ***and that's a fact.*** 我有好多天沒和任何人說英語了，事實就是這樣。◇ *I* ***know for a fact*** (= I am certain) *that she's involved in something illegal.* 我肯定她捲入了非法活動。◇ *The judge instructed both lawyers to* ***stick to the facts*** *of the case.* 法官責令雙方律師要緊扣案情。◇ *First, some basic facts about healthy eating!* 首先，說說健康飲食的幾點基本事實！◇ *The report is based on* ***hard facts*** (= information that can be proved to be true). 這個報告是以鐵的事實為根據的。◇ *If you're going to make accusations, you'd better* ***get your facts right*** (= make sure your information is correct). 你要是打算控告最好把證據弄確鑿。◇ *It's about time you learnt to* ***face (the) facts*** (= accepted the truth about the situation). 現在該是你學會正視現實的時候了。**3** 🔑 [U] things that are true rather than things that have been invented 真實的事物；真實情況：*The story is based on fact.* 這個故事是根據真人真事寫的。◇ *It's important to distinguish fact from fiction.* 區別真實和虛構是重要的。

IDM **,after the 'fact** after sth has happened or been done, when it is too late to prevent it or change it 事後：*On some vital decisions employees were only informed after the fact.* 有一些重大決策雇員只在事後才獲悉。 **the fact (of the matter) is (that) ...** used to emphasize a statement, especially one that is the opposite of what has just been mentioned（用以強調，尤其與剛提到的相反）事實上是，實際情況是：*A new car would be wonderful but the fact of the matter is that we can't afford one.* 有新車好是好，不過實際情況是我們買不起。 **a ,fact of 'life** a situation that cannot be changed, especially one that is unpleasant 生活的（不快）現實 **,facts and 'figures** accurate and detailed information 準確的信息；精確的資料；確實的情報：*I've asked to see all the facts and figures before I make a decision.* 我已要求在看到所有的確切信息後再作決定。 **the ,facts of 'life** the details about sex and about how babies are born, especially as told to children（尤指對兒童講的）性知識 **the facts speak for them'selves** it is not necessary to give any further explanation about sth because the information that is available already proves that it is true 事實足以說明一切 **in (actual) fact** **1** 🔑 used to give extra details about sth that has just been mentioned（補充細節）確切地說：*I used to live in France; in fact, not far from where you're going.* 我曾在法國住過；確切地說，離你要去的地方不遠。**2** 🔑 used to emphasize a statement, especially one that is the opposite of what has just been mentioned（用以強調，尤其與剛提到的相反）事實上，實際上：*I thought the work would be difficult. In actual fact, it's very easy.* 我原以為這工作會很難，事實上卻很容易。➲ LANGUAGE BANK at HOWEVER

Is that a 'fact? (*informal*) used to reply to a statement that you find interesting or surprising, or that you do not believe（回答認為有趣、驚奇或不相信的說法）是真的嗎：*'She says I'm one of the best students she's ever taught.' 'Is that a fact?'* "她說我是她教過的最好的學生之一。" "真的是這樣嗎？" ➲ more at MATTER *n.*, POINT *n.*

'fact-finding *adj.* [only before noun] done in order to find out information about a country, an organization, a situation, etc. 實情調查的：*a* ***fact-finding mission/visit*** 實情調查團；查訪

fac·tion /'fækʃn/ *noun* **1** [C] a small group of people within a larger one whose members have some different aims and beliefs to those of the larger group（大團體中的）派系，派別，小集團：*rival factions within the administration* 政府中的對立派別 ➲ COLLOCATIONS at POLITICS **2** [U] opposition, disagreement, etc. that exists between small groups of people within an organization or political party 派系鬥爭；內訌：*a party divided by faction and intrigue* 因派系和陰謀詭計搞得四分五裂的政黨 **3** [U] films/movies, books, etc. that combine fact with FICTION (= imaginary events) 紀實與虛構相結合的電影（或書等）

fac·tion·al /'fækʃənl/ *adj.* [only before noun] connected with the factions of an organization or political party 派系的；派別的：*factional conflict* 派系衝突 ▸ **fac·tion·al·ism** *noun* [U]

fac·ti·tious /fæk'tɪʃəs/ *adj.* (*formal*) not genuine but created deliberately and made to appear to be true 人為的；虛假的

fac·toid /'fæktɔɪd/ *noun* **1** something that is widely accepted as a fact, although it is probably not true 仿真陳述（很可能不真實但給信以為真）**2** a small piece of interesting information, especially about sth that is not very important 有趣消息（尤指有關不太重要事情的）：*Here's a pop factoid for you.* 告訴你一個廣為流傳的趣聞。

fac·tor 🔑 **AW** /'fæktə(r)/ *noun, verb*
■ ***noun*** **1** 🔑 [C] one of several things that cause or influence sth 因素；要素：*economic factors* 經濟因素 ◇ *The closure of the mine was the* ***single most important*** *factor in the town's decline.* 礦山的關閉是這個鎮衰落的最重要的因素。◇ *the* ***key/crucial/deciding factor*** 關鍵的／至關重要的／決定性的因素 ➲ LANGUAGE BANK at CAUSE **2** [C] (*mathematics* 數) a number that divides into another number exactly 因子；因數：*1, 2, 3, 4, 6 and 12 are the factors of 12.* * 1、2、3、4、6 和 12 是 12 的因子。**3** [C] the amount by which sth increases or decreases（增或減的）數量，倍數：*The real wage of the average worker has increased by a factor of over ten in the last 70 years.* 近 70 年來工人的實際工資平均增長超過了十倍。**4** [C] a particular level on a scale of measurement 係數：*a suntan lotion with a protection factor of 10* 防護係數為 10 的防曬油 ◇ *The wind-chill factor will make it seem colder.* 風寒係數使人覺得比實際溫度更冷一些。**5** [U] (*medical* 醫) a substance in the blood that helps the CLOTTING process. There are several types of this substance 凝血因子：*Haemophiliacs have no factor 8 in their blood.* 血友病患者的血液中缺乏凝血因子 VIII。
IDM see FEEL-GOOD
■ ***verb***
PHR V **,factor sth↔'in | factor sth↔into sth** (*technical* 術語) to include a particular fact or situation when you are thinking about or planning sth 把…因素包括進去：*Remember to factor in staffing costs when you are planning the project.* 規劃該項目時，記住要把雇人費用這個因素考慮進去。

fac·tor VIII (also **factor 8**, **factor eight**) /,fæktər 'eɪt/ *noun* [U] (*biology* 生) a substance in the blood that helps it to CLOT (= become thick) 因子 VIII；凝血因子 VIII

fac·tor·ial /fæk'tɔːriəl/ *noun* (*mathematics* 數) the result when you multiply a whole number by all the numbers below it 階乘：*5! (= factorial 5) is 120 (= 5 × 4 × 3 × 2 × 1).* * 5!（5 的階乘）為 120（即 5 × 4 × 3 × 2 × 1）。

F

fac·tor·ize (*BrE* also **-ise**) /ˈfæktəraɪz/ *verb* **~ sth** (*mathematics* 數) to express a number in terms of its FACTORS *n.* (2) 因數分解；因式分解；將…分解成因子

fac·tory /ˈfæktri; -təri/ *noun* (*pl.* **-ies**) a building or group of buildings where goods are made 工廠；製造廠：*a car factory* 汽車製造廠 ◇ *factory workers* 工廠工人

Synonyms 同義詞辨析

factory

plant • mill • works • yard • workshop • foundry

These are all words for buildings or places where things are made or where industrial processes take place. 以上各詞均指工廠、車間、工場、製造廠。

factory a building or group of buildings where goods are made 指工廠、製造廠：*a chocolate/cigarette/clothing factory* 巧克力廠；香煙廠；製衣廠

plant a factory or place where power is produced or an industrial process takes place 指發電廠、工廠：*a nuclear power plant* 核電廠 ◇ *a manufacturing plant* 製造廠

mill a factory that produces a particular type of material 指（生產特定材料的）工廠、製造廠：*a cotton/paper/textile/woollen mill* 棉紡廠；造紙廠；紡織廠；毛紡廠

works (often in compounds) a place where things are made or an industrial process takes place（常構成複合詞）指工廠、製造廠：*a brickworks* 磚廠 ◇ *a steelworks* 煉鋼廠 ◇ *Raw materials were carried to the works by barge.* 原材料由駁船運到工廠。

yard (usually in compounds) an area of land used for building sth（通常構成複合詞）指建造某物的區域、場地：*a shipyard* 船塢

workshop a room or building in which things are made or repaired using tools or machinery 指車間、工場、作坊：*a car repair workshop* 汽車修理廠

foundry a factory where metal or glass is melted and made into different shapes or objects 指鑄造廠、玻璃廠：*an iron foundry* 鑄鐵廠

PATTERNS

- a **car/chemical/munitions** factory/plant
- an **engineering** plant/works
- to **manage/run** a factory/plant/mill/works/yard/workshop/foundry
- to **work in/at** a factory/plant/mill/yard/workshop/foundry
- factory/mill/foundry **owners/managers/workers**

ˈfactory farm *noun* (*BrE*) a type of farm in which animals are kept inside in small spaces and are fed special food so that a large amount of meat, milk, etc. is produced as quickly and cheaply as possible 工廠化農場 ➲ compare BATTERY FARM ▶ **ˈfactory farming** *noun* [U]

ˌfactory ˈfloor *noun* (often **the factory floor**) [sing.] the part of a factory where the goods are actually produced 廠房；車間：*Jobs are at risk, not just* ***on the factory floor*** (= among the workers, rather than the managers) *but throughout the business.* 職位不保，不僅對車間工人如此，而且危及整個行業。

ˈfactory ship *noun* a large ship used for catching fish, that has equipment for cleaning and freezing the fish on board 捕魚加工船（有加工冰凍設備）

ˈfactory shop (*BrE*) (also **ˈfactory store**, **ˈfactory outlet** *NAmE, BrE*) *noun* a shop/store in which goods are sold directly by the company that produces them at a cheaper price than normal 廠家直銷店；工廠直營店

fac·to·tum /fækˈtəʊtəm; *NAmE* -ˈtoʊ-/ *noun* (*formal* or *humorous*) a person employed to do a wide variety of jobs for sb 勤雜工；事務總管

ˈfact sheet *noun* a piece of paper or an electronic document giving information about a subject, especially (in Britain) one discussed on a radio or television programme（尤指英國廣播或電視節目中有關討論題目的）資料頁，資料電子文件

fac·tual /ˈfæktʃuəl/ *adj.* based on or containing facts 根據事實的；事實的；真實的：*a factual account of events* 事件的如實報道 ◇ *factual information* 事實信息 ◇ *The essay contains a number of factual errors.* 文章中有一些與事實不符的錯誤。▶ **fact·ual·ly** /-tʃuəli/ *adv.*: *factually correct* 與事實相符

fac·ulty /ˈfæklti/ *noun* (*pl.* **-ies**) **1** [C, usually pl.] any of the physical or mental abilities that a person is born with 官能；天賦：*the faculty of sight* 視覺 ◇ *She retained her mental faculties* (= the ability to think and understand) *until the day she died.* 她直到臨終那天一直保持着思維和理解能力。◇ *to be* ***in full possession of your faculties*** (= be able to speak, hear, see, understand, etc.) 擁有一切官能（能夠說、聽、看見、理解等）**2** [sing.] **~ of/for (doing) sth** (*formal*) a particular ability for doing sth 才能；能力：*the faculty of understanding complex issues* 理解複雜問題的能力 ◇ *He had a faculty for seeing his own mistakes.* 他具有看到自己錯誤的能力。**3** [C] a department or group of related departments in a college or university（高等院校的）系，院：*the Faculty of Law* 法學院 ◇ *the Arts Faculty* 文學院 **4** [C+sing./pl. v.] all the teachers in a faculty of a college or university（高等院校中院、系的）全體教師：*the Law School faculty* 法學院全體教師 ◇ *a faculty meeting* 全體教師會議 ◇ *faculty members* 全系教師 **5** [C, U] (often **the faculty**) (*NAmE*) all the teachers of a particular university or college（某高等院校的）全體教師：*faculty members* 全系教師

fad /fæd/ *noun* something that people are interested in for only a short period of time 一時的風尚；短暫的狂熱 SYN **craze**：*the* ***latest/current fad*** 最新／當前的時尚 ◇ *a fad for physical fitness* 一陣健身狂熱 ◇ *Rap music proved to be more than just a* ***passing fad****.* 事實證明，說唱音樂並不是曇花一現。

faddy /ˈfædi/ *adj.* (*BrE, informal, disapproving*) liking some things and not others, especially food, in a way that other people think is unreasonable 口味不尋常的；（尤指）挑食的，偏食的：*a faddy eater* 過分挑食的人 ▶ **fad·di·ness** *noun* [U]

fade /feɪd/ *verb* **1** [I, T] to become or to make sth become paler or less bright（使）變淡，變暗：*The curtains had faded in the sun.* 窗簾已經給曬褪了色。◇ **~ from sth** *All colour had faded from the sky.* 天上的顏色都褪去了。◇ **~ sth** *The sun had faded the curtains.* 太陽把窗簾曬褪了色。◇ *He was wearing faded blue jeans.* 他穿着褪色的藍牛仔褲。**2** [I] to disappear gradually 逐漸消逝；逐漸消失：*Her smile faded.* 她的笑容逐漸消失。◇ **~ away** *Hopes of reaching an agreement seem to be fading away.* 達成協議的希望看來已逐漸渺茫。◇ *The laughter faded away.* 笑聲逐漸消逝。◇ **~ to/into sth** *His voice faded to a whisper* (= gradually became quieter). 他的聲音越來越小，變成了耳語。◇ *All other issues* ***fade into insignificance*** *compared with the struggle for survival.* 與掙扎求存相比，所有其他問題都顯得不重要了。**3** [I] if a sports player, team, actor, etc. **fades**, they stop playing or performing as well as they did before（運動員、運動隊、演員等）走下坡路，衰退，衰落：*Black faded on the final bend.* 布萊克在最後一個彎道處速度慢了下來。
IDM see WOODWORK
PHR V **ˌfade aˈway** (of a person 人) to become very weak or ill/sick and die 衰弱；病重死亡：*In the last weeks of her life she simply faded away.* 她在生命的最後幾個星期已是草枯燈油盡了。**ˌfade ˈin/ˈout** to become clearer or louder/less clear or quieter（畫面）淡入／淡出，漸顯／漸隱；（聲音）漸強／漸弱：*George saw the monitor black out and then a few words faded in.* 喬治看見屏幕變暗，接着出現了幾個字。**ˌfade sth ˈin/ˈout** to make a picture or a sound clearer or louder/less clear or quieter 使（畫面）淡入／淡出；使漸顯／漸隱；使（聲音）漸強／漸弱：*Fade out the music at the end of the scene.* 在這個場景的末尾把音樂減弱。

'fade-out *noun* [U, C] (in cinema, broadcasting, etc. 電影、廣播等) the process of making a sound or an image gradually disappear; an occasion when this happens（畫面）淡出，漸隱；（聲音）漸弱

fader /ˈfeɪdə(r)/ *noun* (*technical* 術語) a piece of equipment used to make sounds or images gradually appear or disappear 音量控制器；光量控制器

fae·ces (*BrE*) (*NAmE* **feces**) /ˈfiːsiːz/ *noun* [pl.] (*formal*) solid waste material that leaves the body through the ANUS 糞便 **SYN** **excrement** ▸ **fae·cal** (*BrE*) (*NAmE* **fecal**) /ˈfiːkl/ *adj.* [only before noun]

faff /fæf/ *verb, noun* (*BrE, informal*)

■ *verb*

PHR V **,faff a'bout/a'round** to spend time doing things in a way that is not well organized and that does not achieve much 磨蹭：*Stop faffing about and get on with it!* 別磨磨蹭蹭的，快些幹！

■ *noun* [U, sing.] a lot of activity that is not well organized and that may cause problems or be annoying 忙亂：*There was the usual faff of finding somewhere to park the car.* 找地方停車照例又是一番忙亂。

fag /fæg/ *noun* **1** [C] (*BrE, informal*) = CIGARETTE **2** (also **fag·got**) [C] (*NAmE, taboo, slang*) an offensive word for a male HOMOSEXUAL（蔑稱）男同性戀者 **3** [sing.] (*BrE, informal*) something that is boring and tiring to do 苦工；苦差事：*It's too much of a fag to go out.* 外出活動真叫人吃不消。 **4** [C] (*BrE*) (especially in the past) a boy at a PUBLIC SCHOOL who has to do jobs for an older boy（尤指舊時）公學中受高年級男生使喚的低年級男生

,fag 'end *noun* (*BrE, informal*) **1** [C] the last part of a cigarette that is left after it has been smoked 煙蒂；香煙頭 **2** [sing.] **the ~ of sth** the last part of sth, especially when it is less important or interesting（尤指不重要或索然無味的）結尾，末尾：*I only caught the fag end of their conversation.* 我僅聽到他們談話的結尾。

fagged /fægd/ (also **,fagged 'out**) *adj.* [not before noun] (*BrE, informal*) very tired 筋疲力盡；累得要死 **SYN** **exhausted**

IDM **I can't be 'fagged (to do sth)** used to say that you are too tired or bored to do sth（讓我做某事）我可吃不消

fag·got /ˈfægət/ *noun* **1** (*BrE*) a ball of finely chopped meat mixed with bread, baked or fried and eaten hot 烤肉丸；炸肉丸 **2** (*NAmE*) = FAG (2) **3** a bunch of sticks tied together, used for burning on a fire 柴把；柴捆

'fag hag *noun* (*slang, offensive*) a woman who likes to spend time with HOMOSEXUAL men 喜歡與男同性戀者交往的女性

fah (also **fa**) /fɑː/ *noun* (*music* 音) the fourth note of a MAJOR, SCALE 大調音階的第 4 音

'fah-fee *noun* [U] (*SAfrE*) an illegal game in which you risk money on a particular number being chosen 推筒子，押寶（一種對所選點數押錢賭博的遊戲）

Fahr·en·heit /ˈfærənhaɪt/ *adj.* (*abbr.* **F**) of or using a scale of temperature in which water freezes at 32° and boils at 212° 華氏溫度計的，華氏的（冰點為 32 度，沸點為 212 度）：*fifty degrees Fahrenheit* 五十華氏度 ▸ **Fahr·en·heit** *noun* [U]：*to give the temperature in Fahrenheit* 以華氏表示溫度

fail 0→ /feɪl/ *verb, noun*

■ *verb*

▸ **NOT SUCCEED** 不成功 **1** 0→ [I, T] to not be successful in achieving sth 失敗；未能（做到）：*Many diets fail because they are boring.* 許多規定飲食因單調乏味都不奏效。◇ *a failing school* 一所失敗的學校 ◇ **~ in sth** *I failed in my attempt to persuade her.* 我未能説服她。◇ **~ to do sth** *She failed to get into art college.* 她未能進入藝術學院。◇ *The song* ***can't fail*** *to be a hit* (= definitely will be a hit). 這首歌不可能不流行起來。

▸ **NOT DO STH** 未做某事 **2** 0→ [I] to not do sth 未做；未履行（某事）：**~ to do sth** *He failed to keep the appointment.* 他未履約。◇ *She never fails to email every week.* 每週她必定發電子郵件。◇ ***I fail to see*** (= I don't understand) *why you won't even give it a try.* 我不懂為什麼你連試一試都不願意。◇ **~ in sth** *He felt he would be failing in his duty if he did not report it.* 他認為如果不報告就是他失職。

▸ **TEST/EXAM** 測驗；考試 **3** 0→ [T, I] to not pass a test or an exam; to decide that sb/sth has not passed a test or an exam 不及格；評定不及格：**~ (sth)** *He failed his driving test.* 他駕駛執照考試不及格。◇ *She was disqualified after failing a drugs test.* 她藥檢未通過，被取消了資格。◇ *What will you do if you fail?* 如果你考試失敗打算幹什麼？◇ **~ sb** *The examiners failed over half the candidates.* 主考人員評定，半數以上考生不及格。 **OPP** **pass**

▸ **OF MACHINES/PARTS OF BODY** 機器；身體部位 **4** [I] to stop working 出故障；失靈：*The brakes on my bike failed half way down the hill.* 我的自行車下山途中車閘失靈了。

▸ **OF HEALTH/SIGHT** 健康；視力 **5** [I] (especially in the progressive tenses 尤用於進行時) to become weak 衰退：*Her eyesight is failing.* 她的視力日漸衰退。◇ *His last months in office were marred by failing health.* 由於健康惡化，他最後幾個月的工作大受影響。

▸ **DISAPPOINT SB** 使失望 **6** [T] **~ sb** to disappoint sb; to be unable to help when needed 使失望；有負於；無能為力：*When he lost his job, he felt he had failed his family.* 他失去工作以後，感到辜負了家庭。◇ *She tried to be brave, but her courage failed her.* 她想勇敢，但卻鼓不起勇氣。◇ (*figurative*) ***Words fail me*** (= I cannot express how I feel). 我無法表達自己的感受。

▸ **NOT BE ENOUGH** 不足 **7** [I] to not be enough when needed or expected 不足；缺乏：*The crops failed again last summer.* 上個夏季莊稼又歉收了。◇ *The rains had failed and the rivers were dry.* 雨量不足，河流乾涸。

▸ **OF COMPANY/BUSINESS** 公司；企業 **8** [I] to be unable to continue 倒閉；破產：*Several banks failed during the recession.* 經濟衰退期間有幾家銀行倒閉了。

IDM **if all else 'fails** used to suggest sth that sb can do if nothing else they have tried is successful 實在不行的話（還可以…）：*If all else fails, you can always sell your motorbike.* 如果所有別的辦法都不行，你總還可以賣掉摩托車。

■ *noun* the result of an exam in which a person is not successful（考試）不及格：*I got three passes and one fail.* 我考試三門及格，一門不及格。 **OPP** **pass**

IDM **without 'fail** **1** when you tell sb to do sth **without fail**, you are telling them that they must do it 務必；一定：*I want you here by two o'clock without fail.* 我要你兩點鐘務必來到這裏。 **2** always 總是；必定：*He emails every week without fail.* 他每週必定發電子郵件。

failed /feɪld/ *adj.* [only before noun] not successful 失敗的；不成功的：*a failed writer* 不成功的作家 ◇ *a failed coup* 流產政變

,failed 'state *noun* a country in which the government is so weak that it has lost control of the structures of the state and other groups have more power 失敗國家（政府軟弱無能，而其他團體擁有更多權力）

fail·ing /ˈfeɪlɪŋ/ *noun, prep.*

■ *noun* [usually pl.] a weakness or fault in sb/sth 弱點；缺點：*She is aware of her own failings.* 她瞭解自己的弱點。◇ *The inquiry acknowledges failings in the judicial system.* 這次調查承認司法制度有缺陷。

■ *prep.* used to introduce a suggestion that could be considered if the one just mentioned is not possible 如果不能；如果沒有：*Ask a friend to recommend a doctor or,* ***failing that****, ask for a list in your local library.* 請朋友推薦一位醫生，如果辦不到就向當地圖書館要一份名單。

'fail-safe *adj.* [usually before noun] (of machinery or equipment 機器或設備) designed to stop working if anything goes wrong 有自動保險裝置的；具有自動防止故障性能的：*a* ***fail-safe device/mechanism/system*** 故障保護裝置／機械裝置／系統

fail·ure 0→ /ˈfeɪljə(r)/ *noun*

▸ **NOT SUCCESSFUL** 不成功 **1** 0→ [U] lack of success in doing or achieving sth 失敗：*The success or failure of the plan depends on you.* 這項計劃的成敗取決於你。◇ *The attempt was* ***doomed to failure****.* 這項嘗試注定失敗。◇ *All my efforts* ***ended in failure****.* 我的一切努力最後都無濟於事。◇ *the problems of economic failure and increasing unemployment* 經濟失敗和失業人數增加的問題 ◇ *She is still coming to terms with the failure of her marriage.*

F

她還在努力適應婚姻失敗的事實。**OPP success** **2** [C] a person or thing that is not successful 失敗的人（或事物）：*The whole thing was a complete failure.* 整個事情徹底失敗了。◇ *He was a failure as a teacher.* 他當教師並不成功。**OPP success**

▸ **NOT DOING STH** 未做某事 **3** [U, C] **~ to do sth** an act of not doing sth, especially sth that you are expected to do 未做，未履行（應做之事）：*the failure of the United Nations to maintain food supplies* 聯合國未能維持糧食供應 ◇ *Failure to comply with the regulations will result in prosecution.* 不遵守規章制度將被起訴。

▸ **OF MACHINE/PART OF BODY** 機器；身體部位 **4** [U, C] the state of not working correctly or as expected; an occasion when this happens 故障；失靈：*patients suffering from* ***heart/kidney, etc. failure*** 心臟、腎等衰竭的病人 ◇ *A power failure plunged everything into darkness.* 停電使一切陷入黑暗。◇ *The cause of the crash was given as engine failure.* 撞車事故的原因被認定是發動機故障。

▸ **OF BUSINESS** 企業 **5** [C, U] **business ~** a situation in which a business has to close because it is not successful 倒閉

▸ **OF CROP/HARVEST** 莊稼；收成 **6** [U, C] **crop/harvest ~** a situation in which crops do not grow correctly and do not produce food 歉收

fain /feɪn/ *adv.* (*old use*) willingly or with pleasure 欣然；樂意地：*I would fain do as you ask.* 聽候你的吩咐。

faint /feɪnt/ *adj., verb, noun*

■ ***adj.*** (**faint·er**, **faint·est**) **1** that cannot be clearly seen, heard or smelt （光、聲、味）微弱的，不清楚的：*a* ***faint glow/glimmer/light*** 微弱的光亮／閃光／光 ◇ *a faint smell of perfume* 淡淡的香水味 ◇ *We could hear their voices growing fainter as they walked down the road.* 他們沿路走遠時我們聽見他們的說話聲逐漸模糊。◇ *His breathing became faint.* 他的呼吸變得微弱了。**2** very small; possible but unlikely 微小的；可能性不大的 **SYN slight**：*There is still a faint hope that she may be cured.* 她的病還有一點點希望可以治癒。◇ *They don't have the faintest chance of winning.* 他們毫無獲勝的可能。**3** not enthusiastic 不熱情的；不積極的：*a faint show of resistance* 軟弱無力裝模作樣的抵抗 ◇ *a faint smile* 淡淡一笑 **4** [not before noun] feeling weak and tired and likely to become unconscious 昏眩；快要昏厥：*She suddenly felt faint.* 她突然感到快要昏倒。◇ *The walkers were faint from hunger.* 那些走路的人餓得頭昏眼花。▸ **faint·ly** *adv.*：*She smiled faintly.* 她淡淡地笑了一下。◇ *He looked faintly embarrassed.* 他顯得有點難堪。

IDM **not have the 'faintest (idea)** (*informal*) to not know anything at all about sth 完全不知道：*I didn't have the faintest idea what you meant.* 我一點也不明白你的意思。➲ more at DAMN *v.*

■ ***verb*** [I] to become unconscious when not enough blood is going to your brain, usually because of the heat, a shock, etc. 昏厥 **SYN pass out**：*to faint from hunger* 餓昏過去 ◇ *Suddenly the woman in front of me fainted.* 我面前的女人突然昏倒了。◇ (*informal*) *I almost fainted* (= I was very surprised) *when she told me.* 她告訴我時我吃驚得差點昏過去。

■ ***noun*** [sing.] the state of becoming unconscious 昏厥：*He fell to the ground in a dead faint.* 他跌倒在地，昏死過去。

ˌfaint-'hearted *adj., noun*

■ ***adj.*** lacking confidence and not brave; afraid of failing 膽怯的；怯懦的 **SYN cowardly**

■ ***noun***

IDM **ˌnot for the ˌfaint-'hearted** not suitable for people who lack confidence or who get frightened easily 不適合缺乏信心的人；不適合膽怯之人：*The climb is* ***not for the faint-hearted*** (= is only for people who are brave). 攀岩絕不是膽小的人做的事。

faint·ness /'feɪntnəs/ *noun* [U] the state of feeling weak and tired and likely to become unconscious 眩暈；昏厥

fair /feə(r); *NAmE* fer/ *adj., adv., noun*

■ ***adj.*** (**fair·er**, **fair·est**)

▸ **ACCEPTABLE/APPROPRIATE** 可接受；恰當 **1** acceptable and appropriate in a particular situation 合理的；恰當的；適當的：*a fair deal/wage/price/question* 公平交易；合理的工資；公道的價格；恰當的問題 ◇ *The punishment was very fair.* 這個處罰很公正。◇ **~ to sb** (**to do sth**) *Was it really fair to him to ask him to do all the work?* 要他做所有的工作對他真的公平嗎？◇ **~ on sb** (**to do sth**) *It's not fair on the students to keep changing the timetable.* 不斷改動時間表，這樣對待學生不恰當。◇ **~ to do sth** ***It's only fair*** *to add that they were not told about the problem until the last minute.* 要補充說明以下情況才合理，即他們是最後一刻才獲知這個問題。◇ *I think* ***it is fair to say that*** *they are pleased with this latest offer.* 我認為恰當地說，他們對最新的這一次提議很滿意。◇ **~ that …** *It seems only fair that they should give us something in return.* 似乎他們應該給我們點什麼作為回報才像話。◇ ***To be fair****, she behaved better than we expected.* 說句公道話，她表現得比我們預期的要好。◇ (*especially BrE*) *'You should really have asked me first.' 'Right, okay,* ***fair comment****.'* "你本來應該先問我。" "對，是的，是這樣。" **OPP unfair**

▸ **TREATING PEOPLE EQUALLY** 一視同仁 **2** treating everyone equally and according to the rules or law （按法律、規定）平等待人的，秉公辦事的，公正的：*She has always been scrupulously fair.* 她總是一絲不苟地秉公辦事。◇ *demands for a fairer distribution of wealth* 更加公平分配財富的要求 ◇ **~ (to sb)** *We have to be fair to both players.* 我們必須公正對待雙方運動員。◇ *to receive a fair trial* 得到公正審判 ◇ *free and fair elections* 自由公正的選舉 ◇ ***It's not fair!*** *He always gets more than me.* 這不公平！他得到的總比我多。◇ *The new tax is fairer than the old system.* 新稅制比舊稅制公正。**OPP unfair**

▸ **QUITE LARGE** 相當大 **3** [only before noun] quite large in number, size or amount （數量、大小）相當大的：*A fair number of people came along.* 有相當多的人來了。◇ *a fair-sized town* 一座不小的市鎮 ◇ *We've still got* ***a fair bit*** (= quite a lot) *to do.* 我們還有相當多的事要做。

▸ **QUITE GOOD** 相當好 **4** (*especially BrE*) quite good 相當好的；不錯的：*There's* ***a fair chance*** *that we might win this time.* 這次我們可能勝算很大。◇ *It's a fair bet that they won't turn up.* 我敢打賭，他們不會出席。◇ *I have a fair idea of what happened.* 我相當瞭解發生的事。◇ *His knowledge of French is only fair.* 他的法語知識還算可以。

▸ **HAIR/SKIN** 頭髮；皮膚 **5** pale in colour 淺色的；白皙的：*a fair complexion* 白皙的膚色 ◇ *She has long fair hair.* 她有一頭淺色長髮。◇ *All her children are fair* (= they all have fair hair). 她的孩子們都長着淺色的頭髮。**OPP dark**

▸ **WEATHER** 天氣 **6** bright and not raining 晴朗的 **SYN fine**：*a fair and breezy day* 風和日麗的日子 **7** (*literary*) (of winds 風) not too strong and blowing in the right direction 順風的：*They set sail with the first fair wind.* 順風一起他們就揚帆出航了。

▸ **BEAUTIFUL** 美麗 **8** (*literary* or *old use*) beautiful 美麗的：*a fair maiden* 美麗的少女

IDM **ˌall's ˌfair in ˌlove and 'war** (*saying*) in some situations any type of behaviour is acceptable to get what you want 在情場和戰場上可以不擇手段 **be 'fair!** (*informal*) used to tell sb to be reasonable in their judgement of sb/sth 要講道理：*Be fair! She didn't know you were coming.* 要講道理！她不知道你要來。**by fair means or 'foul** using dishonest methods if honest ones do not work 不擇手段 **a fair crack of the 'whip** (*BrE, informal*) a reasonable opportunity to show that you can do sth （做某事的）合理機會：*I felt we weren't given a fair crack of the whip.* 我覺得我們沒有得到合理的機會。**fair e'nough** (*informal, especially BrE*) used to say that an idea or suggestion seems reasonable （指想法、建議）有道理，說得對，行：*'We'll meet at 8.' 'Fair enough.'* "我們在 8 點鐘見面。" "行。" ◇ *If you don't want to come, fair enough, but let Bill know.* 你要是不想來，可以，不過要讓比爾知道。**fair's 'fair** (*informal*) (*BrE* also **fair 'dos/'do's**) used, especially as an exclamation, to say that you think that an action, decision, etc. is acceptable and appropriate because it means that everyone will be treated fairly （尤用作感歎詞，表示認為行動、決定等可以接受）彼此都要公平，應該公正才是：*Fair's fair—you can't expect them to cancel everything just because you can't make it.* 彼此都要公平，不可能就因為你不能出席就指望他們取消一切。**(give sb)**

a fair 'hearing (to allow sb) the opportunity to give their opinion of sth before deciding if they have done sth wrong, often in court （給某人）申辯機會；（讓某人接受）公平審訊：*I'll see that you get a fair hearing.* 我務必使你有說明觀點的機會。 **(give sb/get) a fair 'shake** (*NAmE, informal*) (to give sb/get) fair treatment that gives you the same chance as sb else （給某人/得到）公平待遇 **(more than) your fair share of sth** (more than) an amount of sth that is considered to be reasonable or acceptable （超過）合理的數量，恰當的數量：*He has more than his fair share of problems.* 他的問題過多。◇ *I've had my fair share of success in the past.* 過去我已經取得了應有的成功。 **fair to 'middling** (*old-fashioned*) not particularly good or bad 一般水平；不過不失 **it's a fair 'cop** (*BrE, informal, humorous*) used by sb who is caught doing sth wrong, to say that they admit that they are wrong （當場被抓獲時說）這是罪有應得，抓得有理

■ ***adv.*** according to the rules; in a way that is considered to be acceptable and appropriate 按照規則；公正地；公平合理地：*Come on, you two, fight fair!* 得了，你們倆，要按規則比賽！◇ *They'll respect you as long as you* ***play fair*** (= behave honestly). 只要為人正直，別人就會尊敬你。

IDM **fair and 'square | fairly and 'squarely** **1** honestly and according to the rules 誠實；光明正大：*We won the election fair and square.* 我們光明正大地競選獲勝。 **2** (*BrE*) in a direct way that is easy to understand 直截了當：*I told him fair and square to pack his bags.* 我直截了當讓他收拾好行李走人。 **3** (*BrE*) exactly in the place you were aiming for 不偏不斜：*I hit the target fair and square.* 我不偏不斜正中靶子。 **set fair (to do sth/for sth)** (*BrE*) having the necessary qualities or conditions to succeed 有成功的素質；具備成功的條件：*She seems set fair to win the championship.* 她似乎具備奪冠的條件。◇ *Conditions were set fair for stable economic development.* 形勢適合經濟穩定發展。 ➲ more at SAY *v.*

■ ***noun***

▸ **ENTERTAINMENT** 娛樂 **1** (*BrE* also **fun·fair**) (*NAmE* also **car·ni·val**) a type of entertainment in a field or park at which people can ride on large machines and play games to win prizes 露天遊樂場：*Let's take the kids to the fair.* 咱們帶孩子們到遊樂場吧。◇ *all the fun of the fair* 露天遊樂園的一切樂趣 **2** (*NAmE*) a type of entertainment in a field or park at which farm animals and products are shown and take part in competitions （評比農畜產品的）集市：*the* ***county/state fair*** 縣/州農畜產品集市 **3** (*BrE*) = FETE

▸ **BUSINESS** 商業 **4** an event at which people, businesses, etc. show and sell their goods 商品交易會；展銷會：*a world trade fair* 世界交易會 ◇ *a craft/a book/an antique fair* 工藝品展銷會；書市；古玩交易會

▸ **ANIMAL MARKET** 牲畜市場 **5** (*BrE*) (in the past) a market at which animals were sold （舊時）牲畜市場：*a horse fair* 馬市

▸ **JOBS** 工作 **6 job/careers ~** an event at which people who are looking for jobs can get information about companies who might employ them 職業介紹會；就業展覽會

ˌfair 'copy *noun* (*BrE*) a neat version of a piece of writing 謄清本；清稿

ˌfair 'dinkum *adj., adv.* (*AustralE, NZE, informal*) **1** used to emphasize that sth is genuine or true, or to ask whether it is （強調或詢問真實性）：*It's a fair dinkum Aussie wedding.* 那是地道的澳大利亞婚禮。◇ *'Burt's just told me he's packing up in a month.' 'Fair dinkum?'* "伯特剛才跟我說，再過一個月他就收拾行李走人。" "真的嗎？" **2** used to emphasize that behaviour is acceptable （強調行為可接受）：*They were asking a lot for the car, but fair dinkum considering how new it is.* 他們這輛車的要價很高，但考慮到車子很新，還是可以接受的。

the ˌfairer 'sex *noun* = THE FAIR SEX

ˌfair 'game *noun* [U] if a person or thing is said to be **fair game**, it is considered acceptable to play jokes on them, criticize them, etc. 可開玩笑（或嘲弄、作弄）的對象：*The younger teachers were considered fair game by most of the kids.* 多數小孩認為年輕教師是可作弄的對象。

fair·ground /ˈfeəɡraʊnd; *NAmE* ˈferɡ-/ *noun* **1** an outdoor area where a FAIR with entertainments is held 露天遊樂場 **2** [usually pl.] (*NAmE*) a place where a FAIR showing farm animals, farm products, etc. is held 農畜產品集市場地：*the Ohio State Fairgrounds* 俄亥俄州農畜產品集市場地 **3** [usually pl.] (*NAmE*) a place where companies and businesses hold a FAIR to show their products 商品交易會場址；展銷會場地：*the Milan trade fairgrounds* 米蘭交易會場址

ˌfair-'haired *adj.* with light or blonde hair 淺色頭髮的；金髮的

fair·ly 🔑 /ˈfeəli; *NAmE* ˈferli/ *adv.*

1 🔑 (before adjectives and adverbs 用於形容詞和副詞前) to some extent but not very 一定地；相當地：*a fairly easy book* 一本相當淺易的書 ◇ *a fairly typical reaction* 相當典型的反應 ◇ *I know him fairly well, but I wouldn't say we were really close friends.* 我相當瞭解他，但並不是說我們是真正的密友。◇ *I go jogging fairly regularly.* 我算是很常去慢跑鍛煉。◇ *We'll have to leave fairly soon* (= before very long). 我們不久得離開。◇ *I'm fairly certain I can do the job.* 我有相當把握能幹這項工作。◇ *The report was fairly incomprehensible.* 這份報告相當難懂。◇ *I think you'll find it fairly difficult* (= you do not want to say that it is very difficult). 我認為你會覺得它相當難。 ➲ note at QUITE **2** 🔑 in a fair and reasonable way; honestly 公平合理地；公正地：*He has always treated me very fairly.* 他待我一直很公正。◇ *Her attitude could fairly be described as hostile.* 公平而論，她的態度可以說是懷有敵意。 **3** (*old-fashioned*) used to emphasize sth that you are saying （用以強調）簡直，竟然：*The time fairly raced by.* 時間過得真快。

IDM **fairly and squarely** = FAIR AND SQUARE

ˌfair-'minded *adj.* (of people 人) looking at and judging things in a fair and open way 公正的；不偏不倚的

fair·ness /ˈfeənəs; *NAmE* ˈfernəs/ *noun* [U] **1** the quality of treating people equally or in a way that is reasonable 公正性；公平合理性：*the fairness of the judicial system* 司法制度的公正性 **2** (of skin or hair 皮膚或頭髮) a pale colour 白皙；淺色：*A tan emphasized the fairness of her hair.* 曬黑的皮膚更加襯托出了她的頭髮顏色有多淺。

IDM **in (all) fairness (to sb)** used to introduce a statement that defends sb who has just been criticized, or that explains another statement that may seem unreasonable 要公正對待，不能怪（某人）：*In all fairness to him, he did try to stop her leaving.* 不能怪他，他確實曾設法阻止她離開。

ˌfair 'play *noun* [U] the fact of playing a game or acting honestly, fairly and according to the rules 按規則比賽；公平辦事：*a player admired for his* ***sense of fair play*** 因公正比賽而受人尊敬的運動員 ◇ *The task of the organization is to* ***ensure fair play*** *when food is distributed to the refugees.* 該組織的任務就是把糧食分給難民時要保證公平合理。

IDM **fair 'play to sb** (*BrE, informal*) used to express approval when sb has done sth that you think is right or reasonable （表示讚許）做得對，公道，公平合理

the ˌfair 'sex (also **the ˌfairer 'sex**) *noun* [sing.+sing./pl. v.] (*old-fashioned*) women 女性；婦女

ˌfair-'trade *adj.* involving trade which supports producers in developing countries by paying fair prices and making sure that workers have good working conditions and fair pay 公平貿易的（尤指支持發展中國家在價格、工人工資等方面實行公平政策）

fair·way /ˈfeəweɪ; *NAmE* ˈferweɪ/ *noun* (in GOLF 高爾夫球) the long strip of short grass that you must hit the ball along before you get to the GREEN and the hole 球道 ➲ VISUAL VOCAB page V40 ➲ compare THE ROUGH at ROUGH *n.* (1)

'fair-weather *adj.* [only before noun] (*disapproving*) (of people 人) behaving in a particular way or doing a particular activity only when it is pleasant for them 同甘不共苦的；只在順境中的：***a fair-weather friend*** (= sb who stops being a friend when you are in trouble) 不能共患難的朋友

fairy /ˈfeəri; *NAmE* ˈferi/ *noun* (*pl.* **-ies**) **1** (in stories) a creature like a small person, who has magic powers（故事中的）小仙人，仙子，小精靈：*a good/wicked fairy* 善良的仙子；邪惡的精靈 ➲ see also TOOTH FAIRY **2** (*slang, disapproving*) an offensive word for a HOMOSEXUAL man 兔子（男同性戀者）

ˈ**fairy cake** (*BrE*) (also **cup·cake** *NAmE, BrE*) *noun* a small cake, baked in a paper container shaped like a cup and often with ICING on top（常撒有糖霜的）紙杯蛋糕

ˌ**fairy ˈgodmother** *noun* a person who rescues you when you most need help 恩人；救星

F

fairy·land /ˈfeərilænd; *NAmE* ˈferi-/ *noun* **1** [U] the home of FAIRIES 仙國；仙界 **2** [sing.] a beautiful, special or unusual place 仙境；奇境：*The toyshop is a fairyland for young children.* 玩具店是孩子們的仙境。

ˈ**fairy lights** *noun* [pl.] (*BrE*) small coloured electric lights used for decoration, especially on a tree at Christmas（尤指掛在聖誕樹上的）彩色小燈

ˈ**fairy tale** (also ˈ**fairy story**) *noun* **1** a story about magic or FAIRIES, usually for children 童話（故事） **2** a story that sb tells that is not true; a lie 不實之詞；謊言：*Now tell me the truth: I don't want any more of your fairy stories.* 現在跟我說實話：我不想再聽你胡編亂謅了。

ˈ**fairy-tale** *adj.* typical of sth in a fairy tale 童話的；童話式的：*a fairy-tale castle on an island* 島上的一座神奇城堡 ◇ *a fairy-tale wedding in the cathedral* 在大教堂舉行的童話般的婚禮

fait ac·com·pli /ˌfeɪt əˈkɒmpliː; *NAmE* əˈkɑːm-/ *noun* [usually sing.] (*pl.* **faits ac·com·plis** /ˌfeɪz əˈkɒmpliː; *NAmE* əˈkɑːm-/) (from *French*) something that has already happened or been done and that you cannot change 既成事實

faith 0━ /feɪθ/ *noun*

1 0━ [U] **~ (in sb/sth)** trust in sb's ability or knowledge; trust that sb/sth will do what has been promised 信任；相信；信心：*I have great faith in you—I know you'll do well.* 我對你有信心，我知道你會幹好的。◇ *We've* **lost faith in** *the government's promises.* 我們不再相信政府的承諾。◇ *Her friend's kindness has* **restored her faith in** *human nature.* 朋友的善意使她恢復了對人性的信心。◇ *He has* **blind faith** (= unreasonable trust) *in doctors' ability to find a cure.* 他盲目相信醫生有妙手回春的能力。 **2** 0━ [U, sing.] strong religious belief 宗教信仰；信德：*to lose your faith* 失去信德 ◇ *Faith is stronger than reason.* 信德比理智更有力。➲ COLLOCATIONS at RELIGION **3** 0━ [C] a particular religion（某一）宗教：*the Christian faith* 基督教 ◇ *The children are learning to understand people of different faiths.* 孩子們在學會理解不同宗教信仰的人。 **4** [U] **good ~** the intention to do sth right 誠意；善意：*They handed over the weapons as a gesture of good faith.* 他們交出武器以示誠意。

IDM **break/keep faith with sb** to break/keep a promise that you have made to sb; to stop/continue being loyal to sb 對某人不守信用／守信用；不忠誠／忠誠於某人 **in bad ˈfaith** knowing that what you are doing is wrong 存心不良；背信棄義地 **in good ˈfaith** believing that what you are doing is right; believing that sth is correct 真誠；誠心誠意：*We printed the report in good faith but have now learnt that it was incorrect.* 我們好意印發了這份報告，但現在才知道它並不正確。➲ more at PIN *v.*

faith·ful 0━ /ˈfeɪθfl/ *adj.*

1 0━ staying with or supporting a particular person, organization or belief 忠實的；忠誠的 **SYN** **loyal**：*a* **faithful** *servant/friend/dog* 忠實的僕人／朋友／狗 ◇ *She was rewarded for her 40 years' faithful service with the company.* 她為公司忠誠服務了 40 年，因而獲得獎賞。◇ *I have been a faithful reader of your newspaper for many years.* 我是貴報多年來的忠實讀者。◇ **~ to sb/sth** *He* **remained faithful** *to the ideals of the party.* 他對黨的理想堅貞不移。 **2** **the faithful** *noun* [pl.] people who believe in a religion; the loyal supporters of a political party（宗教的）忠實信徒；（政黨的）忠誠支持者：*The president will keep the support of the* **party faithful**. 總統將繼續獲得忠誠黨員的擁護。 **3** 0━ (of a wife, husband or partner 夫妻或性伴侶) **~ (to sb)** not having a sexual relationship with anyone else 忠誠的；忠貞的 **OPP** **unfaithful** **4** true and accurate; not changing anything 如實的；絲毫不變的：*a* **faithful** *copy/account/description* 精確的副本；如實的敘述／描述 ◇ **~ to sth** *His translation manages to be faithful to the spirit of the original.* 他的譯文做到了忠於原文的精神。 **5** [only before noun] able to be trusted; that you can rely on 可信任的；可信賴的：*my faithful old car* 我那忠實的老爺車 ▸ **faith·ful·ness** *noun* [U]：*faithfulness to tradition* 對傳統的恪守 ◇ *She had doubts about his faithfulness.* 她懷疑他的忠誠。

faith·ful·ly 0━ /ˈfeɪθfəli/ *adv.*

1 0━ accurately; carefully 準確地；如實地；仔細地：*to follow instructions faithfully* 嚴格遵循指示 ◇ *The events were faithfully recorded in her diary.* 這些事件在她的日記中如實地記錄了下來。 **2** 0━ in a loyal way; in a way that you can rely on 忠實地；忠誠地：*He had supported the local team faithfully for 30 years.* 他忠實地支持當地球隊 30 年。◇ *She promised faithfully not to tell anyone my secret.* 她保證恪守諾言，不把我的秘密告訴任何人。

IDM **Yours faithfully** 0━ (*BrE*) used at the end of a formal letter before you sign your name, when you have addressed sb as 'Dear Sir/Dear Madam, etc.' and not by their name（正式信末署名前的套語）➲ WRITING TUTOR page WT37

ˈ**faith healing** *noun* [U] a method of treating a sick person through the power of belief and prayer 信仰醫治（通過信心、祈禱治療病人）▸ ˈ**faith healer** *noun*

faith·less /ˈfeɪθləs/ *adj.* (*formal*) not loyal; that you cannot rely on or trust 不忠誠的；不可信任的；不可信賴的：*a faithless friend* 不忠實的朋友

ˈ**faith school** *noun* (*BrE*) a school especially for children of a particular religion 信眾學校（為某種宗教的信仰者特設）：*He called for new faith schools to be created.* 他呼籲設立新的信眾學校。➲ compare PAROCHIAL SCHOOL

fa·jitas /fəˈhiːtəs/ *noun* [pl.] (from *Spanish*) a Mexican dish of strips of meat and/or vegetables wrapped in a soft TORTILLA and often served with sour cream（墨西哥）肉絲蔬菜玉米捲餅（常佐以酸奶油）

fake /feɪk/ *adj., noun, verb*

■ ***adj.*** **1** (*disapproving*) not genuine; appearing to be sth it is not 假的 **SYN** **counterfeit**：*fake designer clothing* 冒牌的名設計師服裝 ◇ *a fake American accent* 偽裝的美國口音 **2** made to look like sth else 冒充的；偽造的 **SYN** **imitation**：*a jacket in fake fur* 人造毛皮短上衣 ◇ *Don't go out in the sun—get a fake tan from a bottle.* 別頂着太陽出去了，擦點棕褐色油裝作太陽曬的就行了。➲ SYNONYMS at ARTIFICIAL

■ ***noun*** **1** an object such as a work of art, a coin or a piece of jewellery that is not genuine but has been made to look as if it is 假貨；贋品：*All the paintings proved to be fakes.* 所有這些畫結果證實都是贋品。 **2** a person who pretends to be what they are not in order to cheat people 冒充者

■ ***verb*** **1** [T] **~ sth** to make sth false appear to be genuine, especially in order to cheat sb 偽造；冒充：*She faked her mother's signature on the document.* 她冒充母親的筆跡在文件上簽字。◇ *He arranged the accident in order to fake his own death.* 他策劃了這次事故以便造成自己死亡的假象。 **2** [T, I] **~ (sth)** to pretend to have a particular feeling, illness, etc. 假裝，佯裝，裝出（某種感情、有病等）：*She's not really sick—she's just* **faking it**. 她並不是真的病了，不過是假裝的。◇ *He faked a yawn.* 他裝着打了一個哈欠。▸ **faker** *noun*

fakie /ˈfeɪki/ *noun* (*informal*) a movement backwards on a SKATEBOARD or SNOWBOARD（用滑板或滑雪板的）倒滑，倒溜

fakir (also **faquir**) /ˈfeɪkɪə(r); *NAmE* fəˈkɪr/ *noun* a Muslim (or sometimes a Hindu) who lives without possessions and survives by receiving food and money from other people（伊斯蘭教或印度教）托缽僧

fala·fel (also **fela·fel**) /fəˈlæfl/ *noun* [U, C] (*pl.* **fala·fel** or **fala·fels**) a Middle Eastern dish consisting of small balls formed from crushed CHICKPEAS, usually eaten with flat bread; one of these balls 炸豆丸子（中東食品，用鷹嘴豆泥製成，常與麵包一起吃）

fal·con /ˈfɔːlkən; *NAmE* ˈfælkən/ *noun* a BIRD OF PREY (= a bird that kills other creatures for food) with long pointed wings 隼

fal·con·er /ˈfɔːlkənə(r); *NAmE* ˈfælkənər/ *noun* a person who keeps and trains falcons, often for hunting （為狩獵活動）養隼者；訓練隼者

fal·con·ry /ˈfɔːlkənri; *NAmE* ˈfæl-/ *noun* [U] the art or sport of breeding falcons and training them to hunt other birds or animals 鷹獵

fall 0ᵂ /fɔːl/ *verb, noun*

■ *verb* (**fell** /fel/, **fall·en** /ˈfɔːlən/)

▸ **DROP DOWN** 落下 **1** 0ᵂ [I] to drop down from a higher level to a lower level 落下；下落；掉落；跌落：*September had come and the leaves were starting to fall.* 已到九月了，樹葉開始凋落。◇ *They were injured by falling rocks.* 他們被落石砸傷了。◇ **+ adv./prep.** *Several of the books had fallen onto the floor.* 這些書有幾本掉到了地上。◇ *One of the kids fell into the river.* 小孩中有一個掉進了河裏。◇ *The handle had fallen off the drawer.* 抽屜的拉手掉了。◇ *He fell 20 metres onto the rocks below.* 他掉到下面 20 米處的岩石上。◇ *The rain was falling steadily.* 雨不停地下着。

▸ **STOP STANDING** 倒下 **2** 0ᵂ [I] to suddenly stop standing 突然倒下；跌倒；倒塌：*She slipped on the ice and fell.* 她在冰上滑了一跤。◇ **+ adv./prep.** *I **fell over** and cut my knee.* 我摔倒了，劃破了膝蓋。◇ *The house looked as if it was about to fall down.* 房子看起來好像就要倒塌似的。➲ see also FALLEN

▸ **OF HAIR/MATERIAL** 毛髮；材料 **3** 0ᵂ [I] **+ adv./prep.** to hang down 下垂；低垂：*Her hair fell over her shoulders in a mass of curls.* 她的鬈髮披肩。

▸ **SLOPE DOWNWARDS** 向下傾斜 **4** 0ᵂ [I] **~ (away/off)** to slope downwards 向下傾斜：*The land falls away sharply towards the river.* 地勢向河邊陡然傾斜。

▸ **DECREASE** 減少 **5** 0ᵂ [I] to decrease in amount, number or strength （數量）減少，下降；（強度）減小：*Their profits have fallen by 30 per cent.* 他們的利潤減少了 30%。◇ *Prices continued to fall on the stock market today.* 今天股票市場價格繼續下跌。◇ *The temperature fell sharply in the night.* 夜間溫度陡降。◇ *falling birth rates* 下降的出生率 ◇ *Her voice fell to a whisper.* 她的聲音變小，成了耳語。◇ **+ noun** *Share prices fell 30p.* 股價下跌了 30 便士。OPP rise

▸ **BE DEFEATED** 被打敗 **6** [I] to be defeated or captured 被打敗；淪陷；失守：*The coup failed but the government fell shortly afterwards.* 政變雖然流產，但是不久以後政府便垮台了。◇ **~ to sb** *Troy finally fell to the Greeks.* 特洛伊城最終被希臘人攻陷。

▸ **DIE IN BATTLE** 陣亡 **7** [I] (*literary*) to die in battle; to be shot 陣亡；被擊斃：*a memorial to those who fell in the two world wars* 兩次世界大戰陣亡將士紀念碑

▸ **BECOME** 變成 **8** 0ᵂ [I] to pass into a particular state; to begin to be sth 進入（某狀態）；開始變成（某事物）：**+ adj.** *He had fallen asleep on the sofa.* 他在沙發上睡着了。◇ *The book fell open at a page of illustrations.* 書翻開在有插圖的那一頁。◇ *The room had fallen silent.* 整個房間都變得靜悄悄的。◇ *She fell ill soon after and did not recover.* 不久後她就病倒了，而且未能痊癒。◇ **~ into sth** *I had fallen into conversation with a man on the train.* 在火車上我和一個男人攀談起來。◇ *The house had fallen into disrepair.* 這棟房子已年久失修。◇ **+ noun** *She knew she must not fall prey to his charm.* 她清楚自己絕不可以被他迷住。

▸ **HAPPEN/OCCUR** 發生 **9** [I] (*literary*) to come quickly and suddenly 突然來到；突然出現 SYN **descend**：*A sudden silence fell.* 突然一片鴉雀無聲。◇ *Darkness falls quickly in the tropics.* 在熱帶地區夜幕降臨迅速。◇ **~ on sb/sth** *An expectant hush fell on the guests.* 客人們即時安靜了下來，期待着將要發生的事。**10** [I] **+ adv./prep.** to happen or take place 發生：*My birthday falls on a Monday this year.* 今年我的生日適逢星期一。**11** [I] **+ adv./prep.** to move in a particular direction or come in a particular position（向某方向）移動；落（在某位置上）：*My eye fell on (= I suddenly saw) a curious object.* 我突然見到了一樣奇怪的東西。◇ *Which syllable does the stress fall on?* 重音在哪個音節？◇ *A shadow fell across her face.* 一片陰影掠過她的臉龐。

▸ **BELONG TO GROUP** 屬於群體 **12** [I] **+ adv./prep.** to belong to a particular class, group or area of responsibility 屬於（某類、群體、責任範圍）：*Out of over 400 staff there are just 7 that fall into this category.* * 400 多個職員中只有 7 人屬於這一類。◇ *This case falls outside my jurisdiction.* 這個案件不屬於我的管轄範圍。◇ *This falls under the heading of scientific research.* 這一項屬於科研類目。

IDM Idioms containing **fall** are at the entries for the nouns and adjectives in the idioms, for example **fall by the wayside** is at **wayside**. 含 fall 的習語，都可在該等習語中的名詞及形容詞相關詞條找到，如 fall by the wayside 在詞條 wayside 下。

PHR V ˌ**fall aˈbout** (*BrE, informal*) to laugh a lot 捧腹大笑；笑得前仰後合：**~ doing sth** *We all fell about laughing.* 我們都笑得前仰後合。

ˌ**fall aˈpart** **1** to be in very bad condition so that parts are breaking off 破碎；破裂：*My car is falling apart.* 我的汽車要散架了。**2** to have so many problems that it is no longer possible to exist or function 破裂；崩潰：*Their marriage finally fell apart.* 他們的婚姻終於破裂了。◇ *The deal fell apart when we failed to agree on a price.* 我們在價格上未能達成一致意見，生意吹了。

ˌ**fall aˈway** to become gradually fewer or smaller; to disappear （逐漸）減少；減小；消失；消散：*His supporters fell away as his popularity declined.* 隨着他的名望下降，他的支持者漸漸離他而去。◇ *The market for their products fell away to almost nothing.* 他們產品的市場幾乎萎縮到零。◇ *All our doubts fell away.* 我們的一切疑慮都煙消雲散。◇ *The houses fell away as we left the city.* 隨着我們離城市越來越遠，房屋也逐漸在視線中消失了。

ˌ**fall ˈback** **1** to move or turn back 後退；撤退；退卻 SYN **retreat**：*The enemy fell back as our troops advanced.* 我軍部隊挺進，敵軍向後撤退。**2** to decrease in value or amount （價值）降低；（數量）減少 ˌ**fall ˈback on sb/sth** [no passive] to go to sb for support; to have sth to use when you are in difficulty 求助於；借助於；轉而依靠：*I have a little money in the bank to fall back on.* 我在銀行還有一點錢，需要時可以動用。◇ *She fell back on her usual excuse of having no time.* 她以慣用的藉口推說沒有時間。➲ related noun FALLBACK

ˌ**fall beˈhind (sb/sth)** to fail to keep level with sb/sth 落後；落在…後面：*She soon fell behind the leaders.* 她很快就落在領頭者的後面。ˌ**fall beˈhind with sth** (also ˌ**fall beˈhind on sth** especially in *NAmE*) to not pay or do sth at the right time 拖欠（付款）；沒有及時做：*They had fallen behind on their mortgage repayments.* 他們拖欠了按揭還款。◇ *He's fallen behind with his school work again.* 他又沒有按時做學校作業了。

ˌ**fall ˈdown** to be shown to be not true or not good enough 不實；不能令人滿意；不夠好：*And that's where the theory falls down.* 這就是該理論的不足之處。➲ see also FALL *v.* (2)

ˈ**fall for sb** [no passive] (*informal*) to be strongly attracted to sb; to fall in love with sb 愛上；傾心於：*They fell for each other instantly.* 他倆一見鍾情。ˈ**fall for sth** [no passive] (*informal*) to be tricked into believing sth that is not true 信以為真：*I'm surprised you fell for that trick.* 我感到驚奇，你竟中了那個詭計。

ˌ**fall ˈin** if soldiers **fall in**, they form lines 集合；列隊：*The sergeant ordered his men to fall in.* 中士命令士兵集合。ˌ**fall ˈin with sb/sth** [no passive] (*BrE*) to agree to sth 同意；贊成：*She fell in with my idea at once.* 她立刻同意了我的主意。

ˈ**fall into sth** to be able to be divided into sth 可以分為；能夠分成：*My talk falls naturally into three parts.* 我的講話可以自然分成三個部份。

ˌ**fall ˈoff** to decrease in quantity or quality 數量減少；質量下降：*Attendance at my lectures has fallen off considerably.* 聽我講課的學生大大減少了。OPP rise

ˈ**fall on/upon sb/sth** [no passive] (*especially BrE*) **1** to attack or take hold of sb/sth with a lot of energy and enthusiasm 襲擊；向…進攻；撲向；抓住：*They fell on him with sticks.* 他們用棍棒襲擊他。◇ *The children fell*

F

on the food and ate it greedily. 孩子們撲向食物，狼吞虎嚥地吃起來。 **2** to be the responsibility of sb（責任）落在…身上；由…負擔：*The full cost of the wedding fell on us.* 整個婚禮費用由我們負擔了。

ˌfall ˈout 1 to become loose and drop 掉落；脫落：*His hair is falling out.* 他的頭髮在脫落。 **2** if soldiers **fall out**, they leave their lines and move away 原地解散；離開隊列 **ˌfall ˈout (with sb)** (*BrE*) to have an argument with sb so that you are no longer friendly with them（與某人）吵翻，鬧翻

ˌfall ˈover (*informal*) (of a computer or program 計算機或程序) to stop working suddenly（突然）發生故障，不運轉，死機：*My spreadsheet keeps falling over.* 我的電子表格程序不斷出故障。 **ˌfall ˈover sb/sth** [no passive] to hit your foot against sth when you are walking and fall, or almost fall 被…絆倒；幾乎被…絆倒 **SYN trip over**：*I rushed for the door and fell over the cat in the hallway.* 我衝向門口，在過道被貓絆了一跤。 ➲ see also FALL *v.* (2) **ˌfall ˈover yourself to do sth** (*informal*) to try very hard or want very much to do sth 特別賣力；迫不及待；煞費苦心；不遺餘力：*He was falling over himself to be nice to me.* 他盡力對我友好。

ˌfall ˈthrough to not be completed, or not happen 落空；失敗；成為泡影：*Our plans fell through because of lack of money.* 我們的計劃由於缺錢而落空了。

ˈfall to sb to become the duty or responsibility of sb（職責、責任）落在…身上；應由…做：*With his partner away, all the work now fell to him.* 他的搭檔走了以後，工作現在全落在他的身上。 ◇ **it falls to sb to do sth** *It fell to me to inform her of her son's death.* 把她兒子死訊通知她的差事落在了我的頭上。 **ˈfall to sth** (*literary*) to begin to do sth 開始做；幹起來：**~ doing sth** *She fell to brooding about what had happened to her.* 她開始憤憤地思忖着自己的遭遇。

■ ***noun***

▸ **ACT OF FALLING** 落下 **1** 🗝 [C] an act of falling 落下；下落；跌落；掉落：*I had a bad fall and broke my arm.* 我重重地跌了一跤，摔斷了手臂。 ◇ *She was killed in a fall from a horse.* 她從馬背上掉下來摔死了。

▸ **OF SNOW/ROCKS** 雪；岩石 **2** 🗝 [C] **~ (of sth)** an amount of snow, rocks, etc. that falls or has fallen（雪、岩石等的）降落：*a heavy fall of snow* 一場大雪 ◇ *a rock fall* 岩崩

▸ **WAY STH FALLS/HAPPENS** 下落；發生 **3** [sing.] **~ of sth** the way in which sth falls or happens 下落；發生：*the fall of the dice* 骰子的擲出 ◇ *the dark fall of her hair* (= the way her hair hangs down) 她那垂瀉的黑髮

▸ **OF WATER** 水 **4 falls** [pl.] (especially in names 尤用於名稱) a large amount of water falling down from a height 瀑布 **SYN waterfall**：*The falls upstream are full of salmon.* 瀑布的上游一帶盛產鮭魚。 ◇ *Niagara Falls* 尼亞加拉瀑布

▸ **AUTUMN** 秋 **5** 🗝 [C] (*NAmE*) = AUTUMN：*in the fall of 2009* 在 2009 年的秋天 ◇ *last fall* 去年秋天 ◇ *fall weather* 秋季天氣

▸ **DECREASE** 減少 **6** 🗝 [C] **~ (in sth)** a decrease in size, number, rate or level（大小）減小；（數量）減少；（比率、水平）降低：*a steep fall in profits* 利潤的驟降 ◇ *a big fall in unemployment* 失業人數的大大減少 **OPP rise**

▸ **DEFEAT** 失敗 **7** 🗝 [sing.] **~ (of sth)** a loss of political, economic, etc. power or success; the loss or defeat of a city, country, etc. in war（政權的）垮台；（經濟的）崩潰；（城市、國家的）淪陷，滅亡：*the fall of the Roman Empire* 羅馬帝國的滅亡 ◇ *the* ***rise and fall*** *of British industry* 英國工業的興衰 ◇ *the fall of Berlin* 柏林的淪陷

▸ **LOSS OF RESPECT** 喪失尊敬 **8** [sing.] a situation in which a person, an organization, etc. loses the respect of other people because they have done sth wrong（威信的）驟降：*the TV preacher's spectacular* ***fall from grace*** 電視佈道者威信的遽降

▸ **IN BIBLE** 《聖經》 **9 the Fall** [sing.] the occasion when Adam and Eve did not obey God and had to leave the Garden of Eden 人類墮落（指亞當和夏娃違背上帝意旨而被迫離開伊甸園）

IDM **break sb's ˈfall** to stop sb from falling onto sth hard 緩和某人的跌勢；防止某人跌得很重：*Luckily, a bush broke his fall.* 幸虧有灌木接着，他摔得不重。 **take the ˈfall (for sb/sth)** (*informal, especially NAmE*) to accept responsibility or punishment for sth that you did not do, or did not do alone 替…承擔責任；成為…的替罪羊：*He took the fall for his boss and resigned.* 他成了老闆的替罪羊，辭職了。 ➲ more at PRIDE *n.*, RIDE *v.*

Language Bank 用語庫

fall

Describing a decrease 描述下降

- Car crime in Oxford **fell significantly** last year. 去年牛津的汽車犯罪顯著下降。
- Car crime **fell** by about a quarter over a 12-month period. * 12 個月內汽車犯罪下降了約四分之一。
- The number of stolen vehicles **dropped** from 1 013 to 780, **a fall of** 26 per cent. 被盜汽車數量從 1 013 輛減少到 780 輛，下降了 26%。
- According to this data, 780 vehicles were stolen, 26% **down** on the previous year. 根據這份數據，780 輛車被盜，比去年下降了 26%。
- There was an 11% **drop** in reported thefts from motor vehicles, from 1 871 to 1 737. 機動車財物盜竊案件數量下降了 11%，從 1 871 下降到 1 737。
- These figures show that, as far as car crime is concerned, **the main trend is downwards**. 這些數據表明，就汽車犯罪而言，大趨勢是下降的。

➲ Language Banks at EXPECT, ILLUSTRATE, INCREASE, PROPORTION

fal·la·cious /fəˈleɪʃəs/ *adj.* (*formal*) wrong; based on a false idea 謬誤的：*a fallacious argument* 謬誤的論據

fal·lacy /ˈfæləsi/ *noun* (*pl.* **-ies**) **1** [C] a false idea that many people believe is true 謬見；謬論；謬誤：***It is a fallacy*** *to say that the camera never lies.* 說照相機絕不騙人，這是謬見。 **2** [U, C] a false way of thinking about sth 思維方式謬誤；謬誤推理：*He detected the fallacy of her argument.* 他發覺她論據中的推理謬誤。 ➲ see also PATHETIC FALLACY

fall·back /ˈfɔːlbæk/ *noun* a plan or course of action that is ready to be used in an emergency if other things fail 應變計劃；退路：*What's our fallback if they don't come up with the money?* 要是他們拿不出錢，我們如何應變？ ◇ *We need a* ***fallback position*** *if they won't do the job.* 如果他們不幹這個工作，我們就需要一個應變的方案。

fall·en /ˈfɔːlən/ *adj.* [only before noun] **1** lying on the ground, after falling 倒下的；落下的；落在地上的：*a fallen tree* 倒下的樹 **2** (*formal*) (of a soldier 士兵) killed in a war 陣亡的 ➲ see also FALL *v.*

ˌfallen ˈwoman *noun* (*old-fashioned*) a way of describing a woman in the past who had a sexual relationship with sb who was not her husband 墮落的婦女（舊時指有姦情的）

ˈfall guy *noun* (*especially NAmE*) a person who is blamed or punished for sth wrong that another person has done 代人受過者；替罪羊 **SYN scapegoat**

fall·ible /ˈfæləbl/ *adj.* able to make mistakes or be wrong 會犯錯誤的：*Memory is selective and fallible.* 記憶有選擇性而且會出錯。 ◇ *All human beings are fallible.* 人人都難免犯錯誤。 **OPP infallible** ▸ **fal·li·bil·ity** /ˌfæləˈbɪləti/ *noun* [U]：*human fallibility* 人易犯的錯誤

ˈfalling-off *noun* [sing.] (*BrE*) = FALL-OFF

ˌfalling-ˈout *noun* (*informal*) [sing.] a situation where people are no longer friends, caused by a disagreement or an argument 失和；鬧翻：*Dave and I* ***had a falling-out.*** 戴夫和我鬧翻了。

ˌfalling ˈstar *noun* = SHOOTING STAR

ˈfall-off (*BrE* also *less frequent* **ˈfalling-off**) *noun* [sing.] **~ (in sth)** a reduction in the number, amount or quality of sth（數量的）減少；（質量的）降低：*a recent fall-off in sales* 近來銷售量的減少

Fal·lo·pian tube (also **fal·lo·pian tube**) /fəˌləʊpiən ˈtjuːb; *NAmE* fəˈloʊpiən tuːb/ *noun* (*anatomy* 解) one of the two tubes in the body of a woman or female animal along which eggs pass from the OVARIES to the UTERUS 輸卵管

fall·out /ˈfɔːlaʊt/ *noun* [U] **1** dangerous RADIOACTIVE dust that is in the air after a nuclear explosion（核爆炸後的）放射性墜塵 **2** the bad results of a situation or an action 後果；餘波

fal·low /ˈfæləʊ; NAmE -loʊ/ *adj.* **1** (of farm land 農田) not used for growing crops, especially so that the quality of the land will improve 休耕的；休閒的：*Farmers are now paid to let their land **lie fallow**.* 農民讓土地休耕現在得到了回報。 **2** (of a period of time 一段時期) when nothing is created or produced; not successful 休閒的；休眠的；不成功的：*Contemporary dance is coming onto the arts scene again after a long fallow period.* 當代舞蹈經過一段長時期銷聲匿跡以後現在又回到了藝術舞台。

ˈfallow deer *noun* a small European DEER with white spots on its back 黇鹿（有白色斑點）

ˈfall-pipe (*US*) (*BrE* **down·pipe**) *noun* a pipe for carrying water from a roof down to the ground or to a DRAIN（從房頂到地面排水的）落水管，雨水管

false 🗝 /fɔːls/ *adj.*

▸ NOT TRUE 不真實 **1** 🗝 wrong; not correct or true 錯誤的；不正確的；不真實的：*A whale is a fish. True or false?* 鯨魚是魚，對還是錯？◇ *Predictions of an early improvement in the housing market proved false.* 認為房屋市場很快就好轉的預測結果證明是錯誤的。◇ *She gave false information to the insurance company.* 她向保險公司提供了不真實的資料。◇ *He used a false name to get the job.* 他用假名得到了這份工作。

▸ NOT NATURAL 非天生 **2** 🗝 not natural 非天生的；人造的；假的 SYN **artificial**：*false teeth/eyelashes* 假牙／睫毛 ◇ *a false beard* 假鬍子 ➲ SYNONYMS at ARTIFICIAL

▸ NOT GENUINE 偽造 **3** 🗝 not genuine, but made to look real to cheat people 假的；偽造的：*a false passport* 假護照

▸ NOT SINCERE 不真誠 **4** (of people's behaviour 人的行為) not real or sincere 表裏不一的；不真誠的：*false modesty* 假謙虛 ◇ *She flashed him a false smile of congratulation.* 她向他虛情假意地微微一笑表示祝賀。

▸ WRONG/MISTAKEN 錯誤 **5** 🗝 [usually before noun] wrong or mistaken, because it is based on sth that is not true or correct 錯誤的：*a **false argument/assumption/belief*** 錯誤的論據／假設／信念 ◇ *to give a **false impression** of wealth* 給人以富有的假象 ◇ *to lull sb into a **false sense of security*** (= make sb feel safe when they are really in danger) 哄某人產生虛假的安全感 ◇ *They didn't want to raise any **false hopes**, but they believed her husband had escaped capture.* 他們並不想讓人心存奢望，但是他們相信她的丈夫已逃脱追捕。◇ *Buying a cheap computer is a **false economy*** (= will not actually save you money). 買廉價計算機看似省錢，但其實並不划算。

▸ NOT FAITHFUL 不忠實 **6** (*literary*) (of people 人) not faithful 不忠實的；不忠誠的：*a false lover* 不忠誠的情人 ▸ **false·ly** *adv.*：*to be falsely accused of sth* 被誣告某事 ◇ *She smiled falsely at his joke.* 她聽了他的笑話假裝笑了。

IDM **by/under/on false preˈtences** by pretending to be sth that you are not, in order to gain some advantage for yourself 靠欺詐手段；以虛假的藉口：*She was accused of obtaining money under false pretences.* 她被控詐騙錢財。➲ more at RING² *v.*

ˌfalse aˈlarm *noun* a warning about a danger that does not happen; a belief that sth bad is going to happen, when it is not 假警報；虛驚：*The fire service was called out but it was a false alarm.* 消防人員接到報警後出動，但這是假報火警。

ˌfalse beˈginner *noun* a person who has a basic knowledge of a language, but has started to study it again from the beginning 二次初學者（對某一語言雖已有基本知識但又從頭學習）

ˌfalse ˈdawn *noun* [usually sing.] (*formal*) a situation in which you think that sth good is going to happen but it does not 假曙光；虛幻的希望：*a false dawn for the economy* 經濟復蘇的假象

ˌfalse ˈfriend *noun* **1** a person who seems to be your friend, but who is not loyal and cannot be trusted 不忠實的朋友 **2** a word in a foreign language that looks similar to a word in your own language, but has a different meaning（與某外國語的）同形異義詞：*The English word 'sensible' and the French word 'sensible' are false friends.* 英語的 sensible 一詞和法語的 sensible 一詞同形異義。

false·hood /ˈfɔːlshʊd/ *noun* (*formal*) **1** [U] the state of not being true; the act of telling a lie 虛假；說謊：*to test the truth or falsehood of her claims* 檢驗她陳述的真偽 **2** [C] a statement that is not true 不實之詞；謊言 SYN **lie**

ˌfalse imˈprisonment *noun* [U] (*law* 律) the crime of illegally keeping sb as a prisoner somewhere 私禁；非法拘禁；非法拘留

ˌfalse ˈmemory *noun* (*psychology* 心) a memory of sth that did not actually happen（對事實上並未發生的事情的）偽記憶

ˌfalse ˈmove *noun* [usually sing.] an action that is not allowed or not recommended and that may cause a bad result（可能引起不良後果的）不允行為，不明智行動：***One false move** and the bomb might blow up.* 一步弄錯，炸彈就可能會爆炸。

ˌfalse ˈrib *noun* = FLOATING RIB

ˌfalse ˈstart *noun* **1** an attempt to begin sth that is not successful 不成功的開端；起步失誤：*After a number of false starts, she finally found a job she liked.* 她起初失敗了幾次，之後終於找到了喜歡的工作。 **2** (*sport* 體) a situation when sb taking part in a race starts before the official signal has been given 起跑犯規；搶跑

ˌfalse ˈteeth *noun* [pl.] a set of artificial teeth used by sb who has lost their natural teeth（整副的）假牙 ➲ compare DENTURES

fal·setto /fɔːlˈsetəʊ; NAmE -toʊ/ *noun* (*pl.* **-os**) an unusually high voice, especially the voice that men use to sing very high notes（尤指男高音的）假聲

fal·sies /ˈfɔːlsiz/ *noun* [pl.] (*informal*) pieces of material used inside a BRA to make a woman's breasts seem larger 胸罩襯墊；襯墊義乳

fals·ify /ˈfɔːlsɪfaɪ/ *verb* (**fal·si·fies**, **fal·si·fy·ing**, **fal·si·fied**, **fal·si·fied**) **~ sth** (*formal*) to change a written record or information so that it is no longer true 篡改，偽造（文字記錄、信息）▸ **fal·si·fi·ca·tion** /ˌfɔːlsɪfɪˈkeɪʃn/ *noun* [U, C]：*the deliberate falsification of the company's records* 對公司記錄的蓄意篡改

fal·sity /ˈfɔːlsəti/ *noun* [U] the state of not being true or genuine 虛假；不真實；錯誤 OPP **truth**

Fal·staff·i·an /fɔːlˈstɑːfiən; NAmE -ˈstæf-/ *adj.* (*literary*) fat, cheerful and eating and drinking a lot 法爾斯塔夫式的（源於莎士比亞筆下人物，外形肥胖且喜狂歡闊飲）：*My uncle was a Falstaffian figure.* 我的叔叔是個法爾斯塔夫式的人物。ORIGIN From Sir John Falstaff, a character in several plays by William Shakespeare. 源自莎士比亞筆下幾部戲劇中的人物法爾斯塔夫（Sir John Falstaff）。

fal·ter /ˈfɔːltə(r)/ *verb* **1** [I] to become weaker or less effective 衰弱；衰退；衰落 SYN **waver**：*The economy shows no signs of faltering.* 經濟沒有衰退的跡象。◇ *Her courage never faltered.* 她從未氣餒過。 **2** [I, T] (+ **speech**) to speak in a way that shows that you are not confident（嗓音）顫抖；結巴地說；支吾其詞：*His voice faltered as he began his speech.* 他開始演講時說話結結巴巴。 **3** [I] to walk or behave in a way that shows that you are not confident 蹣跚；搖晃；猶豫；畏縮：*She walked up to the platform without faltering.* 她健步走上了講台。◇ *He never faltered in his commitment to the party.* 他對黨始終忠貞不渝。▸ **fal·ter·ing** /ˈfɔːltərɪŋ/ *adj.*：*the faltering peace talks* 一波三折的和平談判 ◇ *the baby's first faltering steps* 嬰兒學步時搖搖晃晃的腳步

fame 🗝 /feɪm/ *noun* [U]

the state of being known and talked about by many people 名聲；聲譽；名氣：*to **achieve/win** instant **fame*** 立即獲得／迅即贏得名聲 ◇ *to **rise/shoot to fame** overnight* 一夜之間成名 ◇ *Andrew Lloyd Webber of 'Evita' fame* (= famous for 'Evita') 以《埃維塔》成名的安德魯・勞埃德・韋伯 ◇ *The town's only **claim to fame** is that there* *was once a riot there.* 這個鎮唯一出名之處就是那裏有過一次暴亂。◇ *She went to Hollywood in search of* ***fame and fortune.*** 她為追逐名利去了好萊塢。➲ see also FAMOUS

famed /feɪmd/ *adj.* **~ (for sth)** very well known 著名的 **SYN renowned**： *Las Vegas, famed for its casinos* 以賭場著名的拉斯韋加斯 ◇ *a famed poet and musician* 一位大名鼎鼎的詩人和音樂家 ➲ see also FAMOUS

fa·mil·ial /fəˈmɪliəl/ *adj.* [only before noun] (*formal*) **1** related to or typical of a family 家庭的；家族的 **2** (*medical* 醫) (of diseases, conditions, etc. 疾病、情況等) affecting several members of a family 家庭遺傳的；家族共有的： *familial left-handedness* 家族遺傳的左撇子

F

fa·mil·iar 🔑 /fəˈmɪliə(r)/ *adj.*
1 🔑 well known to you; often seen or heard and therefore easy to recognize 熟悉的；常見到的；常聽說的： *to* ***look/sound/taste familiar*** 看／聽／嚐起來熟悉 ◇ *He's a familiar figure in the neighbourhood.* 他在這個地區是大家熟悉的人物。◇ *Something about her voice was vaguely familiar.* 她的聲音有點耳熟。◇ **~ to sb** *The smell is very familiar to everyone who lives near a bakery.* 住在麵包店附近的人都很熟悉這種氣味。◇ *Violent attacks are becoming* ***all too familiar*** (= sadly familiar). 暴力攻擊變成了司空見慣的現象。**OPP unfamiliar** **2** 🔑 **~ with sth** knowing sth very well 通曉；熟悉： *an area with which I had been familiar since childhood* 我自幼就瞭若指掌的一個地區 ◇ *Are you familiar with the computer software they use?* 你熟悉他們使用的計算機軟件嗎？ **OPP unfamiliar** **3 ~ (with sb)** (of a person's behaviour 人的行為) very informal, sometimes in a way that is unpleasant 隨便的： *You seem to be on very familiar terms with your tutor.* 你似乎和你的導師之間很隨便。◇ *After a few drinks her boss started getting too familiar for her liking.* 老闆幾杯酒下肚以後就開始令她覺得過分親昵。

fa·mil·iar·ity /fəˌmɪliˈærəti/ *noun* [U] **1 ~ (with sth)** | **~ (to sb)** the state of knowing sb/sth well; the state of recognizing sb/sth 熟悉；通曉；認識： *His familiarity with the language helped him enjoy his stay.* 他通曉這種語言，所以逗留期間過得很愜意。◇ *When she saw the house, she had a feeling of familiarity.* 她見到這座房子就有一種熟悉的感覺。**2** a friendly informal manner 友好隨便；親近： *She addressed me with an easy familiarity that made me feel at home.* 她和我談話親切隨和，使我不感到拘束。

IDM **familiarity breeds conˈtempt** (*saying*) knowing sb/sth very well may cause you to lose admiration and respect for them/it 過分親密就會有所侮慢

fa·mil·iar·ize (*BrE* also **-ise**) /fəˈmɪliəraɪz/ *verb* **~ yourself/sb (with sth)** to learn about sth or teach sb about sth, so that you/they start to understand it（使）熟悉，瞭解，通曉 **SYN acquaint**： *You'll need time to familiarize yourself with our procedures.* 你需要時間熟悉我們的程序。▸ **fa·mil·iar·iza·tion, -isa·tion** /fəˌmɪliəraɪˈzeɪʃn; *NAmE* -rəˈz-/ *noun* [U]

fa·mil·iar·ly /fəˈmɪliəli; *NAmE* -ərli/ *adv.* **1** in a friendly and informal manner, sometimes in a way that is too informal to be pleasant 友好隨便地；親昵地： *John Hunt, familiarly known to his friends as Jack* 約翰 • 亨特，朋友昵稱他為傑克 ◇ *He touched her cheek familiarly.* 他親昵地碰了碰她的面頰。**2** in the way that is well known to people 人們熟悉地： *The elephant's nose or, more familiarly, trunk, is the most versatile organ in the animal kingdom.* 象的鼻子，俗稱為 trunk，是動物界中功能最多的器官。

fam·ily 🔑 /ˈfæməli/ *noun, adj.*
■ **noun** (*pl.* **-ies**) **1** 🔑 [C+sing./pl. v.] a group consisting of one or two parents and their children 家，家庭（包括父母子女）： *the other members of my family* 我家的其他成員 ◇ *Almost every family in the country owns a television.* 這個國家幾乎家家都有一台電視機。◇ *All my family enjoy skiing.* 我們全家都喜歡滑雪。◇ ***one-parent/single-parent families*** 單親家庭 ◇ *a family of four* 四口之家 ◇ *families with young children* 有小孩的家庭 ➲ see also BLENDED FAMILY, NUCLEAR FAMILY **2** 🔑 [C+sing./pl. v., U] a group consisting of one or two parents, their children and close relations（大）家庭（包括父母子女及近親）；親屬： *All our family came to Grandad's eightieth birthday party.* 我們所有親屬都來參加了祖父的八十壽宴。◇ *The support of* ***family and friends*** *is vital.* 親友的支持極為重要。◇ *We've only told the* ***immediate family*** (= the closest relations). 我們只告訴了直系親屬。◇ *the* ***Royal Family*** (= the children and close relations of the king or queen) 王室 ◇ *I always think of you as* ***one of the family.*** 我一直把你當成自家人。◇ (*informal*) *She's family* (= she is a relation). 她是我們家的人。➲ see also EXTENDED FAMILY **3** 🔑 [C+sing./pl. v.] all the people who are related to each other, including those who are now dead 家族： *Some families have farmed in this area for hundreds of years.* 有些家族在這個地區務農有幾百年了。◇ *This painting has* ***been in our family*** *for generations.* 這幅畫是我們家的傳家寶。**4** 🔑 [C+sing./pl. v., U] a couple's or a person's children, especially young children 子女；（尤指）年幼子女： *They have a large family.* 他們的子女成群。◇ *I addressed it to Mr and Mrs Jones and family.* 我以此致瓊斯伉儷及子女。◇ *Do they plan to* ***start a family*** (= have children)? 他們打算生孩子嗎？◇ *to* ***bring up/raise a family*** 撫育／撫養孩子 ➲ COLLOCATIONS at CHILD **5** 🔑 [C] a group of related animals and plants; a group of related things, especially languages（動植物）科；（尤指語言）語族： *Lions belong to the cat family.* 獅屬於貓科。◇ *the Germanic family of languages* 日耳曼語族

IDM **(be/get) in the ˈfamily way** (*old-fashioned, informal*) (to be/become) pregnant 懷孕；有喜 **run in the ˈfamily** to be a common feature in a particular family 為一家人所共有；世代相傳： *Heart disease runs in the family.* 這家人都有心臟病。

■ **adj.** [only before noun] **1** 🔑 connected with the family or a particular family 家庭的： *family life* 家庭生活 ◇ *your family background* 你的家庭背景 **2** 🔑 owned by a family 一家所有的： *a family business* 家庭企業 **3** 🔑 suitable for all members of a family, both adults and children 適合全家人的： *a family show* 家庭節目

the ˈFamily Division *noun* [sing.] in the UK, the part of the High Court which deals with cases that affect families, for example when people get divorced or adopt a child（英國高等法院的）家事法庭

ˌfamily ˈdoctor *noun* (*informal, especially BrE*) = GENERAL PRACTITIONER

ˈfamily man *noun* a man who has a wife or partner and children; a man who enjoys being at home with his wife or partner and children 有妻室兒女的人；戀家的男人；喜歡在家享受天倫之樂的男人： *I see he's become a family man.* 我發覺他已有妻室兒女。◇ *a devoted family man* 忠於家庭的男人

ˈfamily name *noun* the part of your name that shows which family you belong to 姓 ➲ compare SURNAME

ˌfamily ˈplanning *noun* [U] the process of controlling the number of children you have by using CONTRACEPTION 計劃生育；家庭計劃

ˌfamily ˈpractitioner *noun* (*especially BrE*) = GENERAL PRACTITIONER

ˈfamily room *noun* **1** (*NAmE*) a room in a house where the family can relax, watch television, etc. 家庭娛樂室 **2** a room in a hotel for three or four people to sleep in, especially parents and children（旅館的）家庭間 **3** (in Britain) a room in a pub where children are allowed to sit（英國小酒吧裏的）兒童休息室

ˌfamily ˈtree *noun* a diagram that shows the relationship between members of a family over a long period of time 家譜；家譜圖： *How far back can you trace your family tree?* 你的家譜可以追溯到多少代？

fam·ine /ˈfæmɪn/ *noun* [C, U] a lack of food during a long period of time in a region 饑荒： *a severe famine* 嚴重饑荒 ◇ *disasters such as floods and famine* 水災和饑荒這一類災難 ◇ *the threat of* ***widespread famine*** *in the area* 區內大範圍的饑荒威脅 ◇ *to raise money for* ***famine relief*** 為賑濟饑荒籌款

fam·ished /ˈfæmɪʃt/ *adj.* [not usually before noun] (*informal, becoming old-fashioned*) very hungry 很餓 **SYN starving**： *When's lunch? I'm famished!* 什麼時候吃午飯？我餓得要死了！

fam·ous 0-■ /ˈfeɪməs/ *adj.* known about by many people 著名的；出名的：*a famous artist/hotel* 著名的藝術家 / 旅館 ◇ *the most famous lake in Italy* 意大利最著名的湖 ◇ *One day, I'll be* **rich and famous**. 總有一天我會名利雙收。◇ **~ for sth** *He became internationally famous for his novels.* 他以小說享譽國際。◇ **~ as sth** *She was more famous as a writer than as a singer.* 她作為作家比作為歌手名聲要大。➲ see also FAME, INFAMOUS, NOTORIOUS, WORLD-FAMOUS

IDM **ˌfamous ˌlast ˈwords** (*saying*) people sometimes say **Famous last words!** when they think sb is being too confident about sth that is going to happen 吹牛，胡扯（表示某人盲目樂觀）：*'Everything's under control.' 'Famous last words!'* "一切都在掌握之中。" "淨吹牛！" **ORIGIN** This phrase refers to a collection of quotations of the dying words of famous people. 這個短語原指名人臨終遺言語錄選編。

fam·ous·ly /ˈfeɪməsli/ *adv.* in a way that is famous 著名地；出名地：*Some newspapers, most famously the New York Times, refuse to print the word Ms.* 有些報紙，其中最著名的是《紐約時報》，拒不刊用 Ms 這個詞。

IDM **get on/along ˈfamously** (*informal, becoming old-fashioned*) to have a very good relationship 和睦相處；相處極好

fans 扇

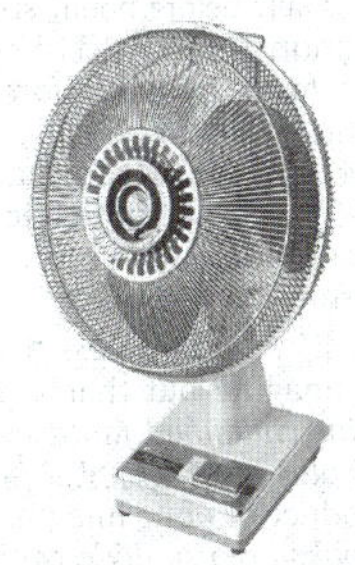

fan 0-■ /fæn/ *noun, verb*

■ *noun* **1** 0-■ a person who admires sb/sth or enjoys watching or listening to sb/sth very much 迷；狂熱愛好者；狂熱仰慕者：*movie fans* 電影迷 ◇ *crowds of football fans* 一群群足球迷 ◇ *a big fan of Madonna* 麥當娜的狂熱仰慕者 ◇ ***fan mail*** (= letters from fans to the person they admire) 狂熱仰慕者的來信 **2** 0-■ a machine with blades that go round to create a current of air 風扇：*to switch on the electric fan* 開電扇 ◇ *a fan heater* 風扇式加熱器 ➲ see also EXTRACTOR (1) **3** a thing that you hold in your hand and wave to create a current of cool air 扇子 **IDM** see SHIT *n.*

■ *verb* (-nn-) **1 ~ sb/sth/yourself** to make air blow onto sb/sth by waving a fan, your hand, etc. 扇（風）：*He fanned himself with a newspaper to cool down.* 他用一張報紙給自己扇涼。 **2 ~ sth** to make a fire burn more strongly by blowing on it 扇，吹（使火更旺）：*Fanned by a westerly wind, the fire spread rapidly through the city.* 火借助西風迅速蔓延全城。 **3 ~ sth** (*literary*) to make a feeling, an attitude, etc. stronger 煽起；激起 **SYN** **fuel**：*His reluctance to answer her questions simply fanned her curiosity.* 他不爽快地回答她的問題，這就激起了她的好奇心。

IDM **fan the ˈflames (of sth)** to make a feeling such as anger, hatred, etc. worse 煽風點火；煽動（情緒）：*His writings fanned the flames of racism.* 他的寫作煽起了種族主義情緒。

PHR V **ˌfan ˈout | ˌfan sth↔ˈout** to spread out or spread sth out over an area（使）展開，散開，成扇形散開：*The police fanned out to surround the house.* 警察散開包圍了這座房子。◇ *The bird fanned out its tail feathers.* 這隻鳥把尾羽展成扇形。

fan·at·ic /fəˈnætɪk/ *noun* **1** (*informal*) a person who is extremely enthusiastic about sth 入迷者 **SYN** **enthusiast**：*a* ***fitness/crossword, etc. fanatic*** 熱衷於健美、縱橫填字遊戲等的人 **2** (*disapproving*) a person who holds extreme or dangerous opinions 極端分子；狂熱信徒 **SYN** **extremist**：*religious fanatics* 狂熱的宗教信徒 ▸ **fan·at·ic·al** /-kl/ *adj.*：*a fanatical supporter* 狂熱的支持者 ◇ *fanatical anti-royalists* 狂熱的反君主制度者 ◇ *a fanatical interest in football* 對足球入迷 ◇ *She's fanatical about healthy eating.* 她對健康飲食着了迷。**fan·at·ic·al·ly** /-kli/ *adv.*：*fanatically fit* 健美狂熱的

fan·ati·cism /fəˈnætɪsɪzəm/ *noun* [U] (*disapproving*) extreme beliefs or behaviour, especially in connection with religion or politics（尤指宗教、政治上的）狂熱，入迷 **SYN** **extremism**

ˈfan belt *noun* a belt that operates the machinery that cools a car engine（帶動冷卻汽車引擎散熱器的）風扇皮帶

fan·boy /ˈfænbɔɪ/ *noun* (*informal*) a person, especially a boy or young man, who is extremely interested in sth such as a particular type of music or software 迷（尤指痴迷某種音樂、軟件等的男孩或年輕男子）：*a Nintendo fanboy* 任天堂電玩迷 ◇ *Linux fanboys* * Linux 操作系統迷

fan·ci·able /ˈfænsiəbl/ *adj.* (*BrE, informal*) sexually attractive 性感的

fan·cier /ˈfænsiə(r)/ *noun* (usually in compounds 通常構成複合詞) (*especially BrE*) a person who has a special interest in sth, especially sb who keeps or breeds birds, animals or plants 愛好者；（尤指）飼養迷，園藝迷：*a pigeon fancier* 喜歡養鴿子的人

fan·ci·ful /ˈfænsɪfl/ *adj.* **1** (*disapproving*) based on imagination and not facts or reason 空想的；想像的 **2** (of things 物件) decorated in an unusual style that shows imagination 裝飾獨出心裁的；式樣奇特的；花哨的：*a fanciful gold border* 別出心裁的金色鑲邊 ▸ **fan·ci·ful·ly** /-fəli/ *adv.*

ˈfan club *noun* an organization that a person's fans belong to and that sends them information, etc. about that person …迷俱樂部；影迷（或歌迷、球迷等）會

fancy 0-■ /ˈfænsi/ *verb, noun, adj.*

■ *verb* (**fan·cies**, **fancy·ing**, **fan·cied**, **fan·cied**) **1** 0-■ [T] (*BrE, informal*) to want sth or want to do sth 想要；想做 **SYN** **feel like**：**~ sth** *Fancy a drink?* 想喝一杯嗎？◇ *She didn't fancy* (= did not like) *the idea of going home in the dark.* 她不喜歡在黑夜裏回家。◇ **~ doing sth** *Do you fancy going out this evening?* 今晚你想不想外出？ **2** 0-■ [T] **~ sb** (*BrE, informal*) to be sexually attracted to sb 對…有性幻想；傾慕：*I think she fancies me.* 我覺得她對我動心了。 **3** [T] **~ yourself** (*BrE, informal, disapproving*) to think that you are very popular, attractive or intelligent 自負；自命不凡：*He started to chat to me and I could tell that he really fancied himself.* 他和我聊起天來，我看得出他確實自以為了不起。 **4** [T] (*BrE*) to like the idea of being sth or to believe, often wrongly, that you are sth 自認為是；自命為：**~ yourself (as) sth** *She fancies herself (as) a serious actress.* 她自以為是嚴肅的演員。◇ **~ yourself + adv./prep.** **5** [I, T] **Fancy!** (*BrE, informal, becoming old-fashioned*) used to show that you are surprised or shocked by sth（表示驚奇或震驚）真想不到，竟然：*Fancy! She's never been in a plane before.* 真想不到！她竟然從未坐過飛機。◇ **~ doing sth** *Fancy meeting you here!* 竟然在這兒遇到你！◇ **~ sth** *'She remembered my name after all those years.' '****Fancy that!****'* "過了那麼多年她還記得我的名字。" "真是不可思議！" **6** [T] (*BrE*) **~ sb/sth** to think that sb/sth will win or be successful at sth, especially in a race 認為…會成功；（尤指速度競賽）認為…要贏：*Which horse do you fancy in the next race?* 下一輪賽馬你認為哪匹馬會贏？◇ *He's hoping to get the job but I don't* ***fancy his chances.***

F

他希望得到那份工作，不過我認為他的機會不大。**7** [T] **~ (that)** … (*literary*) to believe or imagine sth 認為；想像：*She fancied (that) she could hear footsteps.* 她覺得好像聽到了腳步聲。

■ ***noun*** (*pl.* **-ies**) **1** [C, U] something that you imagine; your imagination 想像的事物；想像（力） SYN **fantasy**：*night-time fancies that disappear in the morning* 在早上逝去的夜間幻覺 ◇ *a child's wild **flights of fancy*** 孩子的異想天開 **2** [sing.] a feeling that you would like to have or to do sth 想要；愛好 SYN **whim**：*She said she wanted a dog but it was only a passing fancy.* 她說想要一條狗，但這不過是一時心血來潮。**3** [C, usually pl.] (*BrE*) a small decorated cake 花色小蛋糕

F

IDM **as/whenever, etc. the fancy 'takes you** as/whenever, etc. you feel like doing sth 當（或無論何時等）想做某事時：*We bought a camper van so we could go away whenever the fancy took us.* 我們買了一輛野營車，所以我們啥時想去野營就可以去。**catch/take sb's 'fancy** to attract or please sb 吸引某人；中某人的意：*She looked through the hotel advertisements until one of them caught her fancy.* 她仔細查看旅館廣告，終於有一家中了她的意。**take a 'fancy to sb/sth** (*especially BrE*) to start liking sb/sth, often without an obvious reason 喜歡上，愛上（常指沒有明顯原因）➲ more at TICKLE *v.*

■ ***adj.*** (**fan·cier**, **fan·ci·est**) **1** unusually complicated, often in an unnecessary way; intended to impress other people 異常複雜的；太花哨的：*a kitchen full of fancy gadgets* 有各式各樣小裝置的廚房 ◇ *They added a lot of fancy footwork to the dance.* 他們給這個舞蹈增加了許多複雜的舞步。◇ *He's always using fancy legal words.* 他總是使用異常複雜的法律詞語。OPP **simple** **2** [only before noun] (especially of small things 尤指小物件) with a lot of decorations or bright colours 精緻的；有精美裝飾的；絢麗的；花哨的：*fancy goods* (= things sold as gifts or for decoration) 飾物禮品 ➲ compare PLAIN (3) **3** (sometimes *disapproving*) expensive or connected with an expensive way of life 昂貴的；奢華的：*fancy restaurants with fancy prices* 價格昂貴的豪華餐廳 ◇ *Don't come back with any fancy ideas.* 別用任何大手大腳花錢的想法回敬我了。**4** (*NAmE*) (of food 食物) of high quality 優質的；高檔的

ˌfancy 'dress *noun* [U] (*BrE*) clothes that you wear, especially at parties, to make you appear to be a different character 化裝服；化裝舞會服：*guests **in fancy dress*** 身着化裝服的客人們 ◇ *a fancy-dress party* 化裝晚會 ➲ see also COSTUME (2), MASQUERADE (2)

ˌfancy-'free *adj.* free to do what you like because you are not emotionally involved with anyone 無拘束的；逍遙自在的：*I was still **footloose and fancy-free*** (= free to enjoy myself) *in those days.* 當時我仍然毫無牽掛、逍遙自在呢。

'fancy man, 'fancy woman *noun* (*old-fashioned, informal, disapproving*) the man/woman with whom a person is having a romantic relationship, especially when one or both of them is married to sb else （尤指一方或雙方已婚的）情夫，情婦

fan·dango /fænˈdæŋɡəʊ; *NAmE* -ɡoʊ/ *noun* (*pl.* **fan·dan·goes** or **fan·dangos**) [C] a lively Spanish dance; a piece of music for this dance 凡丹戈舞（節奏歡快的西班牙舞蹈）；凡丹戈舞曲

fan·fare /ˈfænfeə(r); *NAmE* -fer/ *noun* **1** [C] a short loud piece of music that is played to celebrate sb/sth important arriving 號角花彩，號角齊鳴（歡迎儀式等上奏的響亮短曲）**2** [U, C] a large amount of activity and discussion on television, in newspapers, etc. to celebrate sb/sth（為慶祝而在媒體上的）喧耀：*The product was launched amid much fanfare worldwide.* 這個產品在世界各地隆重推出。

'fan fiction *noun* [U] a type of literature, usually written on the Internet, by people who admire a particular novel, film/movie, etc., with characters taken from these stories 同人小說（由某小說、電影等的愛好者創作，人物取自原作，常為網絡文學）

fang /fæŋ/ *noun* [usually pl.] either of two long sharp teeth at the front of the mouths of some animals, such as a snake or dog 尖牙；犬齒；（蛇的）毒牙 ➲ VISUAL VOCAB page V13

'F angles *noun* [pl.] = CORRESPONDING ANGLES

fan·light /ˈfænlaɪt/ (*NAmE* also **tran·som**) *noun* a small window above a door or another window 氣窗（門或窗上方的小窗）

Fanny /ˈfæni/ *noun* IDM see SWEET *adj.*

fanny /ˈfæni/ *noun* (*pl.* **-ies**) **1** (*BrE, taboo, slang*) the female sex organs 女性生殖器；陰部 **2** (*slang, especially NAmE*) a person's bottom 屁股

'fanny pack (*NAmE*) (*BrE* **bum·bag**) *noun* (*informal*) a small bag attached to a belt and worn around the waist, to keep money, etc. in（圍在腰間，放錢物的）腰包 ➲ VISUAL VOCAB page V64

fan·ta·sia /fænˈteɪziə/ *noun* a piece of music in a free form, often based on well-known tunes 幻想曲

fan·ta·size (*BrE* also **-ise**) /ˈfæntəsaɪz/ *verb* [I, T] **~ (about sth)** | **~ (that …)** to imagine that you are doing sth that you would like to do, or that sth that you would like to happen is happening, even though this is very unlikely 想像；幻想；做白日夢：*He sometimes fantasized about winning the gold medal.* 他有時幻想贏得金牌的情景。▸ **fan·ta·sist** /ˈfæntəsɪst/ *noun*

fan·tas·tic /fænˈtæstɪk/ *adj.* **1** (*informal*) extremely good; excellent 極好的；了不起的 SYN **great, brilliant**：*a fantastic beach in Australia* 澳大利亞一個旖旎的海灘 ◇ *a fantastic achievement* 了不起的成就 ◇ *The weather was absolutely fantastic.* 天氣十分宜人。◇ *You've got the job? Fantastic!* 你得到那工作了？太好了！➲ SYNONYMS at GREAT **2** (*informal*) very large; larger than you expected 很大的；大得難以置信的 SYN **enormous, amazing**：*The response to our appeal was fantastic.* 我們的呼籲引起十分強烈的反應。◇ *The car costs a fantastic amount of money.* 這輛車的價錢貴得嚇人。**3** (also *less frequent* **fan·tas·tic·al**) [usually before noun] strange and showing a lot of imagination 怪誕的；荒誕不經的；富於想像的 SYN **weird**：*fantastic dreams of forests and jungles* 關於森林和熱帶叢林的怪夢 **4** impossible to put into practice 不切實際的；無法實現的：*a **fantastic** scheme/project* 不切實際的計劃／方案 ▸ **fan·tas·tic·al·ly** /fænˈtæstɪkli/ *adv.*：*fantastically successful* 極其成功 ◇ *a fantastically shaped piece of stone* 一塊奇形怪狀的石頭

fan·tasy /ˈfæntəsi/ *noun* (*pl.* **-ies**) **1** [C] a pleasant situation that you imagine but that is unlikely to happen 幻想；想像：*his childhood fantasies about becoming a famous football player* 他兒時想成為著名足球運動員的幻想 **2** [C] a product of your imagination 想像產物；幻想作品：*Her books are usually escapist fantasies.* 她的書通常是逃避現實的幻想作品。**3** [U] the act of imagining things; a person's imagination 幻想；想像：*a work of fantasy* 幻想作品 ◇ *Stop living in a **fantasy world**.* 別再生活在幻想世界中了。

ˌfantasy 'football *noun* [U] a competition in which you choose players to make your own imaginary team, and score points according to the performance of the real players 夢幻足球（虛幻比賽方式，組成想像中的球隊，根據球員的實際比賽表現計算得分）

fan·zine /ˈfænziːn/ *noun* a magazine that is written and read by fans of a musician, sports team, etc.（音樂、體育等方面的）愛好者雜誌

fao *abbr.* (*BrE*) used in writing to mean 'for the attention of' (written on a document or letter to say who should deal with it)（書面語）請…注意；（文件或書信用語）由…處理，由…辦理 ➲ see also ATTN

FAQ /ˌef eɪ ˈkjuː/ *abbr.* used in writing to mean 'frequently asked questions' 常問問題（全寫為 frequently asked questions，書寫形式）

fa·quir = FAKIR

far /fɑː(r)/ *adv., adj.*

■ ***adv.*** (**far·ther**, **far·thest** or **fur·ther**, **fur·thest**)

▸ **DISTANCE** 距離 **1** a long distance away 遠：*We didn't go far.* 我們沒有走遠。◇ *Have you come far?* 你是遠道來的嗎？◇ *It's not far to the beach.* 到海灘不遠。◇ *There's not far to go now.* 現在離得不遠了。◇ **~ (from, away, below, etc.)** *The restaurant is not far from here.* 餐廳離這兒不遠。◇ *countries as far apart as Japan and Brazil*

像日本和巴西這樣相隔遙遠的國家◇ *He looked down at the traffic far below.* 他俯視下方遠處的行駛的車輛。◇ *Far away in the distance, a train whistled.* 遠處有一輛火車鳴笛。◇ *The farther north they went, the colder it became.* 他們愈往北去，天氣就變得愈冷。◇ *a concert of music from* ***near and far*** 來自四面八方的音樂的演奏會 **HELP** In positive sentences it is more usual to use **a long way**. 肯定句較常用 a long way：*We went a long way.* ◇ ~~*We went far.*~~ ◇ *The restaurant is a long way from here.* **2** used when you are asking or talking about the distance between two places or the distance that has been travelled or is to be travelled（問到或談及距離時說）有多遠，遠（至）：*How far is it to your house from here?* 從這兒到你家有多遠？◇ *How much further is it?* 還有多遠？◇ *We'll go by train* ***as far as*** *London, and then take a bus.* 我們坐火車到倫敦，然後轉乘公共汽車。◇ *We didn't go* ***as far as*** *the others.* 我們不如其他人走得遠。◇ *I'm not sure I can walk* ***so far***. 我沒有把握能步行這麼遠。

▸ **TIME** 時間 **3** a long time from the present; for a large part of a particular period of time 久；遠：**~ back** *The band made their first record as far back as 1990.* 這個樂隊早在 1990 年就錄製了他們的第一張唱片。◇ **~ ahead** *Let's try to plan further ahead.* 咱們盡量計劃得更長遠些。◇ **~ into sth** *We worked far into the night.* 我們工作到深夜。

▸ **DEGREE** 程度 **4** very much; to a great degree 非常；很大程度上；遠遠；大大：*That's a far better idea.* 那個主意好得多。◇ *There are* ***far more*** *opportunities for young people than there used to be.* 現在年輕人的機會比過去多得多。◇ *It had been a success* ***far beyond*** *their expectations.* 成功之大遠遠超過他們的預期。◇ *He's fallen far behind in his work.* 他的工作大大落後了。◇ *She always gives us* ***far too much*** *homework.* 她總是讓我們做多得不得了的家庭作業。 **5** used when you are asking or talking about the degree to which sth is true or possible（問到或談及程度時說）有多大，直（至）：*How far can we trust him?* 我們能夠信任他到什麼程度？◇ *His parents supported him* ***as far as*** *they could.* 他的父母全力支持他。◇ *Plan your route in advance, using main roads* ***as far as possible***. 預先安排好你的路線，盡量走大路。

▸ **PROGRESS** 進展 **6** used to talk about how much progress has been made in doing or achieving sth 進展程度：*How far have you got with that report?* 你那個報告寫得怎麼樣了？◇ *I read* ***as far as*** *the third chapter.* 我讀到了第三章。⊃ note at FARTHER

IDM **as far as the eye can/could 'see** to the HORIZON (= where the sky meets the land or sea) 極目所盡：*The bleak moorland stretched on all sides as far as the eye could see.* 荒涼的曠野向四面伸展開去，一望無際。 **as far as I 'know | as far as I can re'member, 'see, 'tell, etc.** used to say that you think you know, remember, understand, etc. sth but you cannot be completely sure, especially because you do not know all the facts 就我所知；盡我所記得的；依我看：*As far as we knew, there was no cause for concern.* 就我們所知，沒有什麼需要擔心的。◇ *As far as I can see, you've done nothing wrong.* 依我看，你沒有做錯任何事。◇ *She lived in Chicago, as far as I can remember.* 據我所記得的，她過去住在芝加哥。 **as/so far as 'I am concerned** used to give your personal opinion on sth 就我而言：*As far as I am concerned, you can do what you like.* 就我而言，你想幹什麼就可以幹什麼。 **as/so far as sb/sth is concerned | as/so far as sb/sth goes** used to give facts or an opinion about a particular aspect of sth 就…而言 **as/so far as it 'goes** to a limited degree, usually less than is sufficient 在一定程度上（通常指不足）：*It's a good plan as far as it goes, but there are a lot of things they haven't thought of.* 這計劃還算不錯，不過還有很多事情没有考慮到。 **by 'far** (used with comparative or superlative adjectives or adverbs 與形容詞、副詞的比較級或最高級連用) by a great amount 大大地；…得多：*The last of these reasons is by far the most important.* 這些理由中最後一條比其他的重要得多。◇ *Amy is the smartest by far.* 埃米顯然最聰明。 **carry/take sth too 'far** to continue doing sth beyond reasonable limits 做得過分 **far and a'way** (followed by comparative or superlative adjectives 後接形容詞比較級或最高級) by a very great amount 遠為；大大地：*She's far and away the best player.* 她是當之無愧的最佳選手。 **far and 'wide** over a large area 到處；各處；廣泛地：*They searched far and wide for the missing child.* 他們四處搜尋失踪的小孩。 **far be it from me to do sth (but ...)** (*informal*) used when you are just about to disagree with sb or to criticize them and you would like them to think that you do not really want to do this（要表示不同意和批評但又希望對方感到自己並非真正想要這樣做）：*Far be it from me to interfere in your affairs but I would like to give you just one piece of advice.* 我絕不想干涉你的事，我只不過想給你一個忠告。 **far from sth/from doing sth** almost the opposite of sth or of what is expected 幾乎相反；遠非：*It is far from clear* (= it is not clear) *what he intends to do.* 他打算怎樣做一點都不清楚。◇ *Computers, far from destroying jobs, can create employment.* 計算機遠非破壞就業，而是能創造就業。 **far 'from it** (*informal*) used to say that the opposite of what sb says is true 完全相反；絕非；遠非如此：*'You're not angry then?' 'Far from it. I've never laughed so much in my life.'* "那麼你不生氣？" "非但沒有生氣，我一生中還沒有這樣笑過呢。" **go 'far** (of people 人) to be very successful in the future 有遠大前程：*She is very talented and should go far.* 她天賦很高，會很有出息。 **go far enough** (used in questions and negative sentences 用於疑問句和否定句) to achieve all that is wanted 達到目的：*The new legislation is welcome but does not go far enough.* 新法規受到歡迎，但力度還不夠大。◇ *Do these measures go far enough?* 這些措施能不能解決問題？◇ (*disapproving*) *Stop it now. The joke has gone far enough* (= it has continued too long). 行啦，這玩笑開得太久了。 **go so/as far as to ...** to be willing to go to extreme or surprising limits in dealing with sth 竟然；甚至：*I wouldn't go as far as to say that he's a liar* (= but I think he may be slightly dishonest). 我倒不想說他是個騙子（不過我認為他可能有點不老實）。 **go too 'far | go 'this/'that far** to behave in an extreme way that is not acceptable 走得太遠；做得過分：*He's always been quite crude, but this time he's gone too far.* 他一向很粗魯，但這次太過分了。◇ *I never thought she'd go this far.* 我絕沒有想到她會做得這麼過分。 **in so/as 'far as** to the degree that 到…程度；在…範圍：*That's the truth, in so far as I know it.* 就我所知，那是真實情況。 **not far 'off/'out/'wrong** (*informal*) almost correct 幾乎正確：*Your guess wasn't far out at all.* 你猜得幾乎一點不錯。 **not go 'far 1** (of money 錢) to not be enough to buy a lot of things 不夠買，買不了（許多東西）：*Five pounds doesn't go very far these days.* 這年頭五英鎊買不了多少東西。 **2** (of a supply of sth 某物的供應) to not be enough for what is needed 不充足；不夠用：*Four bottles of wine won't go far among twenty people.* 四瓶酒不夠二十人喝。 **'so far | 'thus far** until now; up to this point 到目前為止；迄今為止；到這點為止：*What do you think of the show so far?* 到目前為止你覺得這場演出怎麼樣？◇ *Detectives are so far at a loss to explain the reason for his death.* 至今偵探仍茫然無法解釋他的死因。 **,so 'far** (*informal*) only to a limited degree 僅到一定程度；只在有限範圍內：*I trust him only so far.* 我只相信他到這個程度。 **,so far, so 'good** (*saying*) used to say that things have been successful until now and you hope that they will continue to be successful, but you know that the task, etc. is not finished yet 到目前為止，一切還算順利 ⊃ more at AFIELD, FEW *adj.*, NEAR *adv.*

■ ***adj.*** (**far·ther**, **far·thest** or **fur·ther**, **fur·thest**) [only before noun]

▸ **DISTANT** 距離大 **1** at a greater distance away from you 較遠的：*I saw her on the* ***far side*** *of the road.* 我看見她在馬路那頭。◇ *at the* ***far end*** *of the room* 在房間的另一頭◇ *They made for an empty table in the* ***far corner***. 他們走向遠處那個角落的空桌子。 **2** at the furthest point in a particular direction（某方向的）最遠的，遠端的：*the* ***far north*** *of Scotland* 蘇格蘭的最北邊◇ *Who is that on the* ***far left*** *of the photograph?* 相片上最左邊的那個人是誰？◇ *She is on the* ***far right*** *of the party* (= holds extreme RIGHT-WING political views). 她是黨內的極右分子。 **3** (*old-fashioned* or *literary*) a long distance away 遠的；遠方的；遙遠的：*a far country* 遠方的國家

IDM **a far cry from sth** a very different experience from sth 和…相去甚遠；與…大相逕庭 SYN **remote**

Farad /ˈfærəd/ *noun* (*abbr.* F) (*physics* 物) a unit for measuring CAPACITANCE 法拉（電容單位）

far·away /ˈfɑːrəweɪ/ *adj.* [only before noun] **1** a long distance away 遠的；遠方的；遙遠的 SYN **distant**：*a war in a faraway country* 在一個遠方國家發生的戰爭 **2 a ~ look/expression** an expression on your face that shows that your thoughts are far away from your present surroundings 心不在焉的；恍惚的；出神的 SYN **distant**

F

farce /fɑːs; *NAmE* fɑːrs/ *noun* **1** [C, U] a funny play for the theatre based on ridiculous and unlikely situations and events; this type of writing or performance 滑稽戲（劇本）；鬧劇（劇本）；笑劇（劇本）：*a bedroom farce* (= a funny play about sex) 牀上笑劇 **2** [C] a situation or an event that is so unfair or badly organized that it becomes ridiculous 荒唐的事情；鬧劇：*The trial was a complete farce.* 這次審判完全是一場鬧劇。

far·ci·cal /ˈfɑːsɪkl; *NAmE* ˈfɑːrs-/ *adj.* ridiculous and not worth taking seriously 荒唐的；荒謬的；可笑的：*It was a farcical trial.* 那是一次荒唐的審判。◇ *a situation verging on the farcical* 近乎荒唐的場面

fare /feə(r); *NAmE* fer/ *noun, verb*

■ *noun* **1** [C, U] the money that you pay to travel by bus, plane, taxi, etc. 車費；船費；飛機票價：***bus/taxi fares*** 公共汽車費；出租汽車費 ◇ ***train/rail fares*** 火車票價 ◇ *Children travel (at) half fare.* 兒童交通費減半。◇ *When do they start paying full fare?* 他們什麼時候開始買全票？➲ see also AIRFARE ➲ note at RATE **2** [C] a passenger in a taxi 出租車乘客；計程車乘客：*The taxi driver picked up a fare at the station.* 計程車司機在車站接了一名乘客。**3** [U] (*old-fashioned* or *formal*) food that is offered as a meal 飯菜：*The restaurant provides good traditional fare.* 這家餐廳提供傳統風味佳餚。

■ *verb* [I] **~ well, badly, better, etc.** to be successful/unsuccessful in a particular situation 成功（或不成功、更好等）SYN **get on**：*The party fared very badly in the last election.* 該黨上次競選情況很糟。

the ˌFar ˈEast *noun* China, Japan and other countries of E and SE Asia 遠東（中國、日本等東亞及東南亞諸國）➲ compare THE MIDDLE EAST ▶ **ˌFar ˈEastern** *adj.*

fare·well /ˌfeəˈwel; *NAmE* ˌferˈwel/ *noun, exclamation, verb*

■ *noun* [C, U] the act of saying goodbye to sb 告別；辭行：*She said her farewells and left.* 她告別後就離開了。◇ *a **farewell party/drink**, etc.* 歡送會、惜別酒會等

■ *exclamation* (*old use* or *formal*) goodbye 再見；再會

■ *verb* **~ sb** (*AustralE*) to arrange a ceremony or party for sb because they are leaving 為…舉行送別儀式（或宴會）：*The troops were farewelled at a ceremony in Darwin.* 為軍隊舉辦的送別儀式在達爾文舉行。

ˌfar-ˈfetched *adj.* very difficult to believe 難以置信的；牽強的：*The whole story sounds very far-fetched.* 整個敍述聽起來很難以置信。

ˌfar-ˈflung *adj.* [usually before noun] (*literary*) **1** a long distance away 遙遠的：*expeditions to the far-flung corners of the world* 去世界偏遠地方的探險 **2** spread over a wide area 分佈廣的；廣泛的：*a newsletter that helps to keep all our far-flung graduates in touch* 使我們分佈在各地的畢業生保持聯繫的通訊

ˌfar ˈgone *adj.* [not before noun] (*informal*) very ill/sick, crazy or drunk 病重；精神失常；爛醉：*She was too far gone to understand anything we said to her.* 她已神志不清，聽不懂我們向她說的任何話。

farm 0-n /fɑːm; *NAmE* fɑːrm/ *noun, verb*

■ *noun* **1** 0-n an area of land, and the buildings on it, used for growing crops and/or keeping animals 農場：*a 200-hectare farm* 一個 200 公頃的農場 ◇ ***a farm worker/labourer*** 農場工人 ◇ ***farm buildings/machinery*** 農場建築物；農業機械 ◇ *to live/work **on a farm*** 在農場居住／工作 ➲ COLLOCATIONS at FARMING ➲ VISUAL VOCAB pages V2, V3 **2** 0-n the main house on a farm, where the farmer lives 農舍 **3** (especially in compounds 尤用於構成複合詞) a place where particular fish or animals are bred 養殖場；飼養場：*a trout/mink/pig farm* 鱒魚養殖場；水貂飼養場；養豬場 ➲ see also BATTERY FARM, COLLECTIVE FARM, DAIRY FARM at DAIRY *adj.* (2), FACTORY FARM, FUNNY FARM, HEALTH FARM, TRUCK FARM, WIND FARM

■ *verb* [I, T] to use land for growing crops and/or keeping animals 務農；種田；從事畜牧業：*The family has farmed in Kent for over two hundred years.* 這個家族在肯特務農兩百多年了。◇ **~ sth** *They farm dairy cattle.* 他們飼養奶牛。◇ *He farmed 200 acres of prime arable land.* 他耕種了 200 英畝良田。◇ *organically farmed produce* 有機種植農產品 IDM see BUY *v.*

PHR V **ˌfarm sb↔ˈout (to sb)** (*BrE, disapproving*) to arrange for sb to be cared for by other people 託（別人）照看某人 **ˌfarm sb/sth↔ˈout to sb** to send out work for other people to do 把工作包給（某人）：*The company farms out a lot of work to freelancers.* 這家公司把大量工作包給了個體人員。

ˈfarm belt *noun* (*US*) an area where there are a lot of farms 農場密集地區

farm·er 0-n /ˈfɑːmə(r); *NAmE* ˈfɑːrm-/ *noun* a person who owns or manages a farm 農場主；農人

ˈfarmers' market *noun* a place where farmers sell food directly to the public 農貿市場；農產品市場

farm·hand /ˈfɑːmhænd; *NAmE* ˈfɑːrm-/ (*NAmE* also **ˈfield hand**) *noun* a person who works for a farmer 農場工人

farm·house /ˈfɑːmhaʊs; *NAmE* ˈfɑːrm-/ *noun* the main house on a farm, where the farmer lives 農場住宅，農舍（農場主的主要住房）➲ VISUAL VOCAB pages V2, V3

farm·ing 0-n /ˈfɑːmɪŋ; *NAmE* ˈfɑːrmɪŋ/ *noun* [U] the business of managing or working on a farm 務農；農場經營：*to take up farming* 從事農業 ◇ ***sheep/fish, etc. farming*** 牧羊、養魚等 ◇ *organic farming* 有機耕作 ◇ *modern farming methods* 現代耕作方法 ◇ *a farming community* 農業社區

farm·land /ˈfɑːmlænd; *NAmE* ˈfɑːrm-/ *noun* [U, pl.] land that is used for farming 農田；耕地：*250 acres of farmland* * 250 英畝耕地 ◇ *the prosperous farmlands of Picardy* 皮卡第的富饒農田

farm·stead /ˈfɑːmsted; *NAmE* ˈfɑːrm-/ *noun* (*NAmE* or *formal*) a FARMHOUSE and the buildings near it 農舍及附近建築物

farm·yard /ˈfɑːmjɑːd; *NAmE* ˈfɑːrmjɑːrd/ *noun* an area that is surrounded by farm buildings 農家庭院 ➲ VISUAL VOCAB pages V2, V3

ˌfar-off *adj.* [only before noun] **1** a long distance away 遙遠的 SYN **distant, faraway, remote**：*a far-off land* 一個遙遠的國度 **2** a long time ago 很久以前的；久遠的 SYN **distant**：*memories of those far-off days* 久遠往昔的回憶

far·rago /fəˈrɑːɡəʊ; *NAmE* -ɡoʊ/ *noun* [usually sing.] (*pl.* **-oes** or **-os**) (*formal, disapproving*) a confused mixture of different things 大雜燴；混雜物 SYN **hotchpotch**

ˌfar-ˈreaching *adj.* likely to have a lot of influence or many effects 影響深遠的；廣泛的：***far-reaching consequences/implications*** 影響深遠的後果；意味深長 ◇ ***far-reaching changes/reforms*** 意義深遠的變革／改革

far·rier /ˈfæriə(r)/ *noun* a person whose job is making and fitting HORSESHOES for horses' feet 蹄鐵工

far·row /ˈfærəʊ; *NAmE* -roʊ/ *noun, verb*

■ *noun* **1** a group of baby pigs that are born together to the same mother（同時生出的）一窩子豬 SYN **litter** **2** an act of giving birth to pigs 產子豬

■ *verb* [I] (of a female pig 母豬) to give birth 產子豬

Farsi /ˈfɑːsiː; *NAmE* ˈfɑːrsiː/ *noun* [U] = PERSIAN (2)

ˌfar-ˈsighted *adj.* **1** having or showing an understanding of the effects in the future of actions that you take now, and being able to plan for them 有遠見的；深謀遠慮的：*the most far-sighted of politicians* 最有遠見的政治家 ◇ *a far-sighted decision* 有遠見的決定 **2** (*especially NAmE*) = LONG-SIGHTED ▶ **ˌfar-ˈsighted·ness** *noun* [U]

fart /fɑːt; *NAmE* fɑːrt/ *verb, noun*

■ ***verb*** [I] (*taboo, slang*) to let air from the BOWELS come out through the ANUS, especially when it happens loudly 放屁；（尤指）放響屁 **HELP** A more polite way of expressing this is 'to break wind'. 較為禮貌的說法是 to break wind。

PHR V ˌ**fart aˈround** (*BrE* also ˌ**fart aˈbout**) (*taboo, slang*) to waste time by behaving in a silly way 閒蕩；浪蕩

■ ***noun*** (*taboo, slang*) **1** an act of letting air from the BOWELS come out through the ANUS, especially when it happens loudly 放屁；（尤指）放響屁 **2** an unpleasant, boring or stupid person 討厭的人；令人厭煩的人；蠢人

Collocations 詞語搭配

Farming 農場經營

Growing food and raising animals 種植糧食和飼養動物

- **plant** trees/seeds/crops/vines/barley 植樹；播種；種莊稼；種植葡萄樹；種大麥
- **grow/produce** corn/wheat/rice/fruit 種植 / 生產玉米 / 小麥 / 大米 / 水果
- **plough/**(*NAmE*) **plow** land/a field 耕地；犁田
- **sow/harvest** seeds/crops/fields 播種 / 收穫穀粒 / 農作物 / 莊稼
- **spread** manure/fertilizer on sth 給…施撒糞肥 / 肥料
- **cultivate/irrigate/water/contaminate** crops/plants/fields/land 耕作 / 灌溉 / 澆灌 / 污染莊稼 / 植物 / 田地 / 土地
- **damage/destroy/lose** your crop 損害 / 毀壞 / 損失農作物
- **ripen/pick** fruit/berries/grapes 催熟 / 採摘水果 / 漿果 / 葡萄
- **press/dry/ferment** grapes 壓榨 / 晾乾 / 發酵葡萄
- **grind/thresh** grain/corn/wheat 磨 / 打穀物 / 玉米 / 小麥
- **raise/rear/keep** chickens/poultry/cattle/pigs 飼養雞 / 家禽 / 牛 / 豬
- **raise/breed/feed/graze** livestock/cattle/sheep 飼養 / 餵養 / 放養家畜 / 牛 / 羊
- **kill/slaughter** livestock 屠宰家畜
- **preserve/smoke/cure/salt** meat 防腐保存 / 熏 / 加工貯藏 / 用鹽醃製肉

Modern farming 現代農場經營

- **run** a fish farm/an organic dairy 經營養魚場 / 有機乳品場
- **engage in/be involved in** intensive (pig/fish) farming 從事集約型（生豬 / 漁業）養殖
- **use/apply** (chemical/organic) fertilizer/insecticides/pesticides 使用（化學 / 有機）肥料 / 殺蟲劑
- **begin/do/conduct** field trials of GM (= genetically modified) crops 開始 / 進行轉基因作物的田間試驗
- **grow/develop** GM crops/seeds/plants/foods 種植 / 研發轉基因作物 / 種子 / 植物 / 糧食
- **fund/invest in** genetic engineering/research 資助 / 投資基因工程 / 研究
- **improve/increase** crop yields 提高 / 增加糧食產量
- **face/suffer from/alleviate** food shortages 面臨 / 遭受 / 緩解食物短缺
- **label** food that contains GMOs (= genetically modified organisms) 給含有轉基因生物的食品貼標籤
- **eliminate/reduce** farm subsidies 取消 / 減少農業補貼
- **oppose/be against** factory farming/GM food 反對工廠化養殖 / 轉基因食品
- **promote/encourage/support** organic/sustainable farming 促進 / 鼓勵 / 支持有機 / 可持續農耕

far·ther 0‑w /ˈfɑːðə(r); *NAmE* ˈfɑːrð-/ *adv., adj.*

■ ***adv.*** 0‑w (comparative of *far* * far 的比較級) at or to a greater distance in space or time （時間或空間上）更遠，較遠： *farther north/south* 再往北 / 南 ◇ ***farther along*** *the road* 沿路繼續往前 ◇ *I can't go* ***any farther***. 我再也走不動了。◇ *As a family we grew* ***farther and farther*** *apart.* 我們一家人越來越疏遠了。◇ *We watched their ship moving gradually* ***farther away***. 我們望着他們的船漸漸遠去。◇ *How much farther is it?* 還有多遠？◇ *They hadn't got any farther with the work* (= they had made no progress). 他們的工作毫無進展。 **IDM** see AFIELD

■ ***adj.*** 0‑w (comparative of *far* * far 的比較級) at a greater distance in space, direction or time （空間、方向或時間上）更遠的，較遠的： *the farther shore of the lake* 湖的彼岸

Which Word? 詞語辨析

farther / further / farthest / furthest

- These are the comparative and superlative forms of **far**. 以上為 far 的比較級和最高級形式。
- To talk about distance, use either **farther, farthest** or **further, furthest**. In *BrE*, **further, furthest** are the most common forms and in *NAmE*, **further** and **farthest**. 表示距離既可用 farther、farthest，也可用 further、furthest。英式英語最常用 further、furthest，美式英語最常用 further、farthest： *I have to travel further/farther to work now.* 現在我得走更遠的路去上班。
- To talk about the degree or extent of something, **further/furthest** are usually preferred. 表示事物的程度或幅度通常宜用 further/furthest： *Let's consider this point further.* 讓我們更深入地考慮這一點。
- **Further**, but not **farther**, can also mean 'more' or 'additional'. * further 亦可表示更加或進一步，farther 則無此意： *Are there any further questions?* 還有什麼問題嗎？ This sounds very formal in *NAmE*. 這在美式英語中是很正式的用法。

far·thest 0‑w /ˈfɑːðɪst; *NAmE* ˈfɑːrð-/ (also **fur·thest**) *adv., adj.*

■ ***adv.*** 0‑w (superlative of *far* * far 的最高級) at or to the greatest distance in space or time （空間或時間上）最遠，最久： *the house* ***farthest away*** *from the road* 離這條路最遠的那棟房子 ◇ *a competition to see who could throw (the) farthest* 擲遠比賽

■ ***adj.*** 0‑w (superlative of *far* * far 的最高級) at the greatest distance in space, direction or time （空間、方向或時間上）最遠的，最久的： *the farthest point of the journey* 旅程的最遠端 ◇ *the part of the garden farthest from the house* 花園離房子最遠的那部份

far·thing /ˈfɑːðɪŋ; *NAmE* ˈfɑːrðɪŋ/ *noun* in the past, a British coin worth one quarter of an old penny 法尋（英國舊硬幣，值 ¼ 舊便士）

far·thin·gale /ˈfɑːðɪŋɡeɪl; *NAmE* ˈfɑːr-/ *noun* in the past, a thick piece of material or set of large rings worn under a woman's skirt to give it a wide round shape （舊時用以撐開女裙的）裙撐，裙環

fa·scia /ˈfeɪʃə/ *noun* (*BrE*) **1** (also **facia**) = DASHBOARD **2** (also ˈ**fascia board**) a board on the roof of a house, at the end of the RAFTERS 封簷板；挑口板 **3** (also **facia**) a board above the entrance of a shop/store, with the name of the shop on it （商店入口上方的）招牌 **4** (also **facia**) the hard cover on a mobile phone/cell phone 手機蓋

fas·cin·ate /ˈfæsmeɪt/ *verb* [T, I] **~ (sb)** to attract or interest sb very much 深深吸引；迷住： *China has always fascinated me.* 中國一直令我心馳神往。◇ *It was a question that had fascinated him since he was a boy.* 這是他自幼就着迷的問題。◇ *The private lives of movie* *stars never fail to fascinate.* 電影明星的私生活總讓人津津樂道。

fas·cin·ated /ˈfæsɪneɪtɪd/ *adj.* very interested 入迷的；極感興趣的：*The children watched, fascinated, as the picture began to appear.* 電影開始以後孩子們入迷地觀看着。◇ **~ by sth** *I've always been fascinated by his ideas.* 我總是對他的想法極感興趣。◇ **~ to see, learn, etc.** *They were fascinated to see that it was similar to one they had at home.* 他們發現這個和他們家中的那個相似，極感興趣。

fas·cin·at·ing /ˈfæsɪneɪtɪŋ/ *adj.* extremely interesting and attractive 極有吸引力的；迷人的：*a fascinating story/subject* 迷人的故事；趣味無窮的話題 ◇ *The results of the survey made fascinating reading.* 調查結果令人讀起來饒有興味。◇ *It's* ***fascinating to see*** *how different people approach the problem.* 看到不同的人怎樣處理這個問題真是有趣極了。◇ *I fail to see what women find so fascinating about him.* 我就看不出他哪一點使女人神魂顛倒。➲ SYNONYMS at INTERESTING ▸ **fas·cin·at·ing·ly** *adv.*

fas·cin·ation /ˌfæsɪˈneɪʃn/ *noun* **1** [C, usually sing.] a very strong attraction, that makes sth very interesting 魅力；極大的吸引力：*Water* ***holds a fascination for*** *most children.* 水對多數孩子都有極大的吸引力。◇ *The fascination of the game lies in trying to guess what your opponent is thinking.* 這個遊戲的魅力就在於要努力去猜對手在想什麼。 **2** [U, sing.] the state of being very attracted to and interested in sb/sth 入迷；着迷：*The girls listened* ***in fascination*** *as the story unfolded.* 故事情節逐漸展開，小女孩都入迷地聽着。◇ **~ for/with sb/sth** *the public's enduring fascination with the Royal Family* 公眾對王室的經久不衰的興趣

fas·cism (also **Fascism**) /ˈfæʃɪzəm/ *noun* [U] an extreme RIGHT-WING political system or attitude which is in favour of strong central government and which does not allow any opposition 法西斯主義

fas·cist (also **Fascist**) /ˈfæʃɪst/ *noun* **1** a person who supports fascism 法西斯主義者 **2** a way of referring to sb that you disapprove of because they have RIGHT-WING attitudes 極右分子 ▸ **fas·cist** *adj.*：*a fascist state* 法西斯國家 ◇ *fascist sympathies* 極右分子的支持

fash·ion 0┳ /ˈfæʃn/ *noun, verb*

■ ***noun*** **1** 0┳ [U, C] a popular style of clothes, hair, etc. at a particular time or place; the state of being popular（衣服、髮式等的）流行款式，時興式樣：*dressed in the latest fashion* 穿着入時 ◇ *the new season's fashions* 新季度的流行款式 ◇ *Long skirts have* ***come into fashion*** *again.* 長裙又時興起來了。◇ *Jeans are still* ***in fashion.*** 牛仔褲仍然流行。◇ *Some styles never* ***go out of fashion.*** 有些款式永遠不會過時。 **2** 0┳ [C] a popular way of behaving, doing an activity, etc.（行為、活動等的）時尚，時興：*The fashion at the time was for teaching mainly the written language.* 那時教學時興的主要是書面語。◇ *Fashions in art and literature come and go.* 文藝的潮流總是曇花一現。 **3** 0┳ [U] the business of making or selling clothes in new and different styles 時裝業：***a fashion designer/magazine/show*** 時裝設計師／雜誌／表演 ◇ *the world of fashion* 時裝界 ◇ *the fashion industry* 時裝業

IDM ▸ **after a ˈfashion** to some extent, but not very well 還過得去；還算可以：*I can play the piano, after a fashion.* 我會彈鋼琴，不過馬馬虎虎。 **after the fashion of sb/sth** (*formal*) in the style of sb/sth 模仿…的式樣；像…的風格：*The new library is very much after the fashion of Nash.* 這座新圖書館很像納什的風格。 **in (a) ... ˈfashion** (*formal*) in a particular way 以…方式：*How could they behave in such a fashion?* 他們的態度怎麼會這樣呢？◇ *She was proved right, in dramatic fashion, when the whole department resigned.* 整個部門的人都辭

Collocations 詞語搭配

Clothes and fashion 服裝與時尚

Clothes 衣服

- **be wearing** a new outfit/bright colours/fancy dress/fur/uniform 穿着一身新衣裳／鮮豔的服裝／化裝舞會服／毛皮衣服／制服
- **be** (**dressed**) **in** black/red/jeans and a T-shirt/your best suit/leather/silk/rags (= very old torn clothes) 穿着黑色衣服／紅色衣服／牛仔褲和 T 恤／最好的西服／皮衣／絲綢衣服／破衣爛衫
- **be dressed for** work/school/dinner/a special occasion 穿好衣服準備上班／上學／赴晚宴／出席特殊場合
- **be dressed as** a man/woman/clown/pirate 打扮成男人／女人／小丑／海盜
- **wear/dress in** casual/designer/second-hand clothes 穿休閒服／名牌服裝／二手衣服
- **wear** jewellery/(*especially US*) jewelry/accessories/a watch/glasses/contact lenses/perfume 佩戴珠寶首飾／飾品／手錶／眼鏡／隱形眼鏡；噴香水
- **have** a cowboy hat/red dress/blue suit **on** 戴着牛仔帽；穿着紅色連衣裙／藍色西服
- **put on/take off** your clothes/coat/shoes/helmet 穿上／脫下衣服／外套／鞋子；戴上／取下頭盔
- **pull on/pull off** your coat/gloves/socks 穿上／脫下外套；戴上／脫下手套；穿上／脫下襪子
- **change into/get changed into** a pair of jeans/your pyjamas/(*especially US*) your pajamas 換上牛仔褲／睡衣

Appearance 外貌

- **change/enhance/improve** your appearance 改變／提升／改善形象
- **create/get/have/give sth** a new/contemporary/retro look 塑造／獲得／擁有／給某物以新的／現代的／復古的外貌
- **brush/comb/shampoo/wash/blow-dry** your hair 梳／用洗髮劑洗／洗／吹頭髮
- **have/get** a haircut/your hair cut/a new hairstyle 理髮；換一個新髮型
- **have/get** a piercing/your nose pierced 穿孔；穿鼻孔
- **have/get** a tattoo/a tattoo done (on your arm)/a tattoo removed 有紋身；在（胳膊上）刺花紋；去除紋身
- **have/get** a makeover/cosmetic surgery 做整容手術
- **use/wear/apply/put on** make-up/cosmetics 使用化妝品；化妝

Fashion 時尚

- **follow/keep up with** (the) fashion/the latest fashions 追求時尚；趕時髦
- **spend/waste money on** designer clothes 把錢花在／浪費在名牌服裝上
- **be** fashionably/stylishly/well **dressed** 衣着時尚／新潮／考究
- **have** good/great/terrible/awful **taste** in clothes 着裝很有品味／品味很差
- **update/revamp** your wardrobe 更新服裝
- **be in/come into/go out of** fashion 流行；開始流行；不再流行
- **be** (**back/very much**) in vogue（又開始／非常）流行
- **create** a style/trend/vogue for sth 為…創造了一種風格／趨勢／潮流
- **organize/put on** a fashion show 策劃／舉辦時裝秀
- **show/unveil** a designer's spring/summer collection 展示／首次推出一位設計師的春／夏裝系列
- **sashay/strut** down the catwalk/(*NAmE also*) runway 走 T 型台
- **be on/do** a photo/fashion shoot 做專業攝影／時裝攝影

了職，這惹人注目的事證明她是對的。 **like it's going out of 'fashion** (*informal*) used to emphasize that sb is doing sth or using sth a lot 做得很多；大量使用；大肆花費： *She's been spending money like it's going out of fashion.* 她花錢一直大手大腳。 ➲ see also PARROT-FASHION

■ *verb* to make or shape sth, especially with your hands（尤指用手工）製作，使成形，塑造： **~ A (from/out of B)** *She fashioned a pot from the clay.* 她用黏土製成一個罐。 ◇ **~ B (into A)** *She fashioned the clay into a pot.* 她用黏土製成一個罐。

fash·ion·able 🗝 /ˈfæʃnəbl/ *adj.* **1** 🗝 following a style that is popular at a particular time 流行的；時興的；時髦的： *fashionable clothes/furniture/ideas* 時髦的服裝/傢具/思想 ◇ *It's becoming fashionable to have long hair again.* 現在又開始流行蓄長髮了。 ◇ *Such thinking is fashionable among right-wing politicians.* 在政界右翼人士中這種想法很流行。 **2** 🗝 used or visited by people following a current fashion, especially by rich people 時髦人物使用的；（尤指）有錢人常光顧的： *a fashionable address/resort/restaurant* 時髦人物常去的地點/勝地/餐館 ◇ *She lives in a very fashionable part of London.* 她住在倫敦一個高級住宅區。 **OPP unfashionable** ➲ compare OLD-FASHIONED ▸ **fash·ion·ably** /-əbli/ *adv.* ： *fashionably dressed* 穿着時髦 ◇ *His wife was blonde and fashionably thin.* 他的妻子一頭金髮，苗條入時。

'fashion-conscious *adj.* aware of the latest fashions and wanting to follow them 趕時髦的；講究時髦的： *fashion-conscious teenagers* 趕時髦的青少年

'fashion designer *noun* a person who designs fashionable clothes 時裝設計師

Synonyms 同義詞辨析

fast / quick / rapid

These adjectives are frequently used with the following nouns. 這些形容詞常與下列名詞連用：

fast ~	quick ~	rapid ~
car	glance	change
train	look	growth
bowler	reply	increase
pace	decision	decline
lane	way	progress

- **Fast** is used especially to describe a person or thing that moves or is able to move at great speed. * fast 尤用以描述高速運動的人或事物。
- **Quick** is more often used to describe something that is done in a short time or without delay. * quick 較常用以描述迅速或立即完成的事。
- **Rapid**, **swift** and **speedy** are more formal words. * rapid、swift 和 speedy 較正式。
- **Rapid** is most commonly used to describe the speed at which something changes. It is not used to describe the speed at which something moves or is done. * rapid 最常用於描述事物變化的速度，而非運動或完成的速度： ~~*a rapid train*~~ ◇ ~~*We had a rapid coffee.*~~
- **Swift** usually describes something that happens or is done quickly and immediately. * swift 通常用以描述事物發生或完成的速度快而及時： *a swift decision* 迅即作出的決定 ◇ *The government took swift action.* 政府立即採取了行動。
- **Speedy** has a similar meaning. * speedy 具有相似的意義： *a speedy recovery* 迅速康復 It is used less often to talk about the speed at which something moves. 該詞較少指事物運動速度快： ~~*a speedy car*~~
- For the use of **fast** and **quick** as adverbs, see the usage note at QUICK. 關於 fast 和 quick 作副詞的用法，見 quick 詞條的用法說明。

'fashion-forward *adj.* more modern than the current fashion 超時尚的；超時髦的；超前於流行款式的： *We tend to be traditional rather than fashion-forward in our designs.* 我們的設計傾向於傳統而非超前於流行款式。

fash·ion·ista /ˌfæʃnˈiːstə/ *noun* (used especially in newspapers 尤用於報章) a fashion DESIGNER, or a person who is always dressed in a fashionable way 時裝設計師；穿着入時的人

'fashion show *noun* an occasion where people can see new designs of clothes being worn by fashion models 時裝表演

'fashion statement *noun* something that you wear or own that is new or unusual and is meant to draw attention to you 時尚宣言（為引人注目而穿戴或擁有的奇裝異服）： *This shirt is great for anyone who wants to **make a fashion statement**.* 要求着裝別樹一幟的人穿這件襯衫最合適。

'fashion victim *noun* a person who always wears the newest fashions even if they do not suit him or her 時尚受害者（盲目趕時髦的人）

fast 🗝 /fɑːst; *NAmE* fæst/ *adj.*, *adv.*, *verb*, *noun*

■ *adj.* (**fast·er**, **fast·est**)

▸ **QUICK** 快速 **1** 🗝 moving or able to move quickly 快的；迅速的；敏捷的： *a fast car/horse* 速度快的汽車/馬 ◇ *the world's fastest runner* 世界最快的賽跑運動員 **2** 🗝 happening in a short time or without delay 迅速發生的；立即發生的： *the fastest rate of increase for years* 多年來最高的增長率 ◇ *a fast response time* 迅速的反應時間 **3** 🗝 able to do sth quickly 動作迅速的；頭腦靈活的： *a fast learner* 領悟快的學習者

▸ **SURFACE** 物體表面 **4** producing or allowing quick movement 可供快速運動的： *a **fast road/pitch*** 快車道；平整的球場 ➲ see also FAST LANE

▸ **WATCH/CLOCK** 鐘錶 **5** [not before noun] showing a time later than the true time 走得快： *I'm early—my watch must be fast.* 我早了，我的錶肯定快了。 ◇ *That clock's ten minutes fast.* 那座鐘快十分鐘。

▸ **PHOTOGRAPHIC FILM** 照相膠片 **6** (*technical* 術語) very sensitive to light, and therefore useful when taking photographs in poor light or of sth that is moving very quickly 感光快的

▸ **FIRMLY FIXED** 牢牢固定 **7** (of a boat, etc. 船等) firmly fixed and safe 繫牢的；穩固的： *He **made** the boat **fast**.* 他把船繫牢了。

▸ **COLOURS IN CLOTHES** 衣服顏色 **8** not likely to change or to come out when washed 不褪色的 **HELP** There is no noun related to **fast**. Use **speed** in connection with vehicles, actions, etc.; **quickness** is used about thinking. * fast 沒有派生的名詞。關於交通工具、行動等的速度用 speed；關於思維則用 quickness。

IDM **fast and 'furious** (of films/movies, shows, etc. 電影、演出等) full of rapid action and sudden changes 情節節奏快且變化多端： *In his latest movie, the action is fast and furious.* 在他的最新電影中，情節起伏跌宕。 **a fast 'talker** a person who can talk very quickly and easily, but who cannot always be trusted 快嘴快舌但不可信賴的人 **a fast 'worker** (*informal*) a person who knows how to get what they want quickly, especially when beginning a sexual relationship with sb 善於迅速達到目的的人；（尤指戀愛方面）善於一下子獲得青睞的人 ➲ more at BUCK *n.*, DRAW *n.*, HARD *adj.*, PULL *v.*

■ *adv.* (**fast·er**, **fast·est**)

▸ **QUICKLY** 快速 **1** 🗝 quickly 快；快速；迅速： *Don't drive so fast!* 別把車開得這麼快！ ◇ *How fast were you going?* 當時你們走得有多快？ ◇ *I can't go any faster.* 我不能走得更快了。 ◇ *The water was rising fast.* 水迅猛上漲。 ◇ *Her heart beat faster.* 她的心跳加快。 ◇ (*formal*) *Night was fast approaching.* 黑夜迅速降臨。 ◇ *a fast-flowing stream* 湍急的溪流 ➲ note at QUICK **2** 🗝 in a short time; without delay 不久；立即： *Children grow up so fast these days.* 如今孩子們長得真快。 ◇ *Britain is **fast becoming** a nation of fatties.* 英國不久就要變成一個胖子國了。 ◇ *The police said that they had reacted as fast as they could.* 警方說他們已儘快作出了反應。

F

▸ **FIRMLY** 牢固 **3** ⊶ firmly; completely 牢固地；完全地：*Within a few minutes she was **fast asleep** (= sleeping deeply).* 幾分鐘後她就沉睡了。◇ *The boat was **stuck fast** (= unable to move) in the mud.* 船深陷在淤泥裏動彈不得。**HELP** There is no noun related to **fast**. Use **speed** in connection with vehicles, actions, etc.; **quickness** is used about thinking. * fast 沒有派生的名詞。關於交通工具、行動等的速度用 speed；關於思維則用 quickness。

IDM **as fast as your ˌlegs can ˈcarry you** as quickly as you can 儘快 **hold ˈfast to sth** (*formal*) to continue to believe in an idea, etc. despite difficulties 堅持（某種思想等）**play fast and ˈloose (with sb/sth)** (*old-fashioned*) to treat sb/sth in a way that shows that you feel no responsibility or respect for them 反覆無常；若即若離；玩弄 **stand ˈfast/ˈfirm** to refuse to move back; to refuse to change your opinions 堅定不移；不讓步；不改變主張 ➲ more at THICK *adv.*

■ ***verb*** [I] to eat little or no food for a period of time, especially for religious or health reasons 節食；禁食；齋戒：*Muslims fast during Ramadan.* 伊斯蘭教徒在齋月期間齋戒。

■ ***noun*** a period during which you do not eat food, especially for religious or health reasons 禁食期；齋戒期：*to go on a fast* 開始禁食 ◇ *to break (= end) your fast* 開齋

fast·ball /ˈfɑːstbɔːl; *NAmE* ˈfæst-/ *noun* (in BASEBALL 棒球) a ball that is thrown at the PITCHER's fastest speed（投手投出的）快速球

ˌfast ˈbowler (also **ˌpace ˈbowler**, **pace·man**) *noun* (in CRICKET 板球) a person who BOWLS very fast 快速球投手

ˌfast ˈbreeder (also **ˌfast ˌbreeder reˈactor**) *noun* a REACTOR in a nuclear power station in which the reaction that produces energy is not made slower 快中子增殖反應堆；快滋生反應器

fas·ten ⊶ /ˈfɑːsn; *NAmE* ˈfæsn/ *verb*
1 ⊶ [T, I] to close or join together the two parts of sth; to become closed or joined together（使兩部份）繫牢，紮牢，結牢，扣緊 **SYN** **do up**：**~ sth** *Fasten your seatbelts, please.* 請繫好安全帶。◇ **~ sth up** *He fastened up his coat and hurried out.* 他扣好大衣就匆匆出去了。◇ **~ (up)** *The dress fastens at the back.* 這件連衣裙是在後背繫扣的。**OPP** **unfasten** **2** ⊶ [T, I] **~ (sth)** to close sth firmly so that it will not open; to be closed in this way（使）關緊，蓋好：*Fasten the gates securely so that they do not blow open.* 把大門閂好以免被風吹開。◇ *The window wouldn't fasten.* 這扇窗子關不嚴。**OPP** **unfasten** **3** ⊶ [T] **~ sth + adv./prep.** to fix or place sth in a particular position, so that it will not move 使牢固；使固定：*He fastened back the shutters.* 他把活動護窗拉開繫緊。**4** ⊶ [T] **~ A to B** | **~ A and B (together)** to attach or tie one thing to another thing（使兩物）繫牢，紮牢，結牢，扣牢：*He fastened the papers together with a paper clip.* 他用迴形針別好了文件。**5** [T, I] if you **fasten** your arms around sb, your teeth into sth, etc., or if your arms, teeth, etc. **fasten** around, into, etc. sb/sth, you hold the person/thing firmly with your arms, etc. 握住；抓牢；咬住：**~ sth + adv./prep.** *The dog fastened its teeth in his leg.* 狗死死咬着他的腿。◇ **+ adv./prep.** *His hand fastened on her arm.* 他用手牢牢抓住她的胳膊。**6** [T, I] **~ (sth) (on sb/sth)** if you **fasten** your eyes on sb/sth or your eyes **fasten** on sb/sth, you look at them for a long time 盯住：*He fastened his gaze on her face.* 他盯着她的臉。

PHR V **ˈfasten on(to) sb/sth** to choose or follow sb/sth in a determined way 抓住；對…鍥而不捨；堅決跟隨；糾纏 **SYN** **latch on to sb/sth**

fas·ten·er /ˈfɑːsnə(r); *NAmE* ˈfæs-/ (also **fas·ten·ing**) *noun* a device, such as a button or a zip/zipper, used to close a piece of clothing; a device used to close a window, suitcase, etc. tightly 鈕扣；拉鏈；扣件 ➲ VISUAL VOCAB page V63

fas·ten·ing /ˈfɑːsnɪŋ; *NAmE* ˈfæs-/ *noun* **1** = FASTENER **2** the place where sth, especially a piece of clothing, fastens; the way sth fastens（尤指衣服的）扣處，扣法：*The trousers have a fly fastening.* 這條褲子是前開口的。

ˌfast ˈfood *noun* [U] hot food, such as HAMBURGERS and chips/fries, that is served very quickly and can be taken away to be eaten in the street 快餐；速食：*fast-food restaurants* 快餐店 ➲ compare SLOW FOOD

ˌfast-ˈforward *verb* **1** [T, I] **~ (sth)** to wind a tape or video forward without playing it 使（錄音帶或錄像帶）快進 **2** [I] **~ to sth** | **+ adv./prep.** to move quickly forwards in time, especially to a later point in a story（尤指故事情節）迅速進入：*The action then fast-forwards to Ettore as a young man.* 情節很快發展到埃多勒的青年時代。▸ **ˌfast ˈforward** *noun* [U]：*Press fast forward to advance the tape.* 按下快進鍵向前轉帶子。◇ *the fast-forward button* 快進按鈕

fas·tidi·ous /fæˈstɪdiəs/ *adj.* **1** being careful that every detail of sth is correct 一絲不苟的；嚴謹的 **SYN** **meticulous**：*Everything was planned in fastidious detail.* 樣樣都一絲不苟地計劃好了。◇ *He was fastidious in his preparation for the big day.* 他認真仔細地準備着這個盛大的日子。**2** (sometimes *disapproving*) not liking things to be dirty or untidy 講究整潔的；有潔癖的：*She wasn't very fastidious about personal hygiene.* 她不過分講究個人衛生。▸ **fas·tidi·ous·ly** *adv.* **fas·tidi·ous·ness** *noun* [U]

ˈfast lane *noun* [sing.] the part of a major road such as a MOTORWAY or INTERSTATE where vehicles drive fastest（高速公路或州際公路上的）快車道

IDM **in the ˈfast lane** where things are most exciting and where a lot is happening 在生活的快車道上；享受豐富多彩的生活：*He had a good job, plenty of money and he was enjoying **life in the fast lane**.* 他有份好工作，錢又多，盡情享受着豐富多彩的生活。

fast·ness /ˈfɑːstnəs; *NAmE* ˈfæs-/ *noun* (*literary*) a place that is thought to be safe because it is difficult to get to or easy to defend 要塞；堡壘 **SYN** **stronghold**

ˈfast track *noun* [sing.] a quick way to achieve sth, for example a high position in a job 快速晉升之道；迅速成功之路 ▸ **ˈfast-track** *adj.*：*the fast-track route to promotion* 快速晉升之道 ◇ *fast-track graduates* 快速獲得學位者

ˈfast-track *verb* **~ sb/sth** to make sb's progress in achieving sth, for example a high position in a job, quicker than usual 加速…的進程

fat ⊶ /fæt/ *adj.*, *noun*

> **WORD FAMILY**
> fat *adj.*
> fatty *adj.*
> fatten *verb*
> fattening *adj.*

■ ***adj.*** (**fat·ter**, **fat·test**) **1** ⊶ (of a person's or an animal's body 人或動物的身體) having too much flesh on it and weighing too much 肥的；肥胖的：*a big fat man/woman* 大胖男人／女人 ◇ *You'll **get fat** if you eat so much chocolate.* 你如果吃這麼多巧克力是會發胖的。◇ *He grew fatter and fatter.* 他愈來愈胖了。◇ *fat flabby legs* 肥胖鬆弛的雙腿 **OPP** **thin** **2** ⊶ thick or wide 厚的；寬大的：*a fat volume on American history* 厚厚的一冊美國史 **3** [only before noun] (*informal*) large in quantity; worth a lot of money 大量的；值錢的：*a **fat sum/profit*** 一大筆款子；豐厚的利潤 ◇ *He gave me a nice fat cheque.* 他給了我一張大額支票。▸ **fat·ness** *noun* [U]：*Fatness tends to run in families.* 肥胖往往有遺傳性。

IDM **(a) fat ˈchance (of sth/doing sth)** (*informal*) used for saying that you do not believe sth is likely to happen 不大可能發生：*'They might let us in without tickets.' 'Fat chance of that!'* "他們也許會讓我們免票入場。" "別痴心妄想了！" **a fat lot of good, use, etc.** (*informal*) not at all good or useful 差極了；毫無用處：*Paul can't drive so he was a fat lot of use when I broke my arm.* 保羅不會開車，所以我手臂骨折時他一點忙也沒幫上。**it's not ˌover until the fat lady ˈsings** (*saying*) used for saying that a situation may still change, for example that a contest, election, etc. is not finished yet, and sb still has a chance to win it 最後才能見輸贏；不到最後，結果難料

■ ***noun*** **1** ⊶ [U] a white or yellow substance in the bodies of animals and humans, stored under the skin 脂肪；肥肉：*excess body fat* 多餘的體內脂肪 ◇ *This ham has too much fat on it.* 這塊火腿肥肉太多。➲ COLLOCATIONS at DIET **2** ⊶ [C, U] a solid or liquid substance from animals or plants, treated so that it becomes pure for use in cooking（烹調用的）動植物油：*Cook the meat in shallow fat.* 用少許油煎肉。 **3** [C, U] animal and vegetable fats, when you are thinking of them as part of what a person eats（人體攝入的動植物）脂肪：*You should cut down on fats and carbohydrates.* 你應該減少攝入脂肪和碳水化合物。◇ *foods which are* ***low in fat*** 低脂肪食物 ◇ *reduced-fat margarines* 低脂人造黃油 IDM see CHEW *v.*, LIVE[1]

Vocabulary Building 詞彙擴充

Saying that somebody is fat 形容人肥胖

- **Fat** is the most common and direct word, but it is not polite to say to someone that they are fat. * fat 最通用，意思最直接，但當面說某人 fat 不禮貌：*Does this dress make me look fat?* 我穿這連衣裙顯胖嗎？◇ ~~*You're looking fat now.*~~
- **Overweight** is a more neutral word. * overweight 是比較中性的詞：*I'm a bit overweight.* 我有點超重。It can also mean too fat, especially so that you are not fit. 這詞亦含過胖之意，尤指身體不健康。
- **Large** or **heavy** is less offensive than **fat**. 與 fat 相比，large 或 heavy 含冒犯意較少：*She's a rather large woman.* 她是個大塊頭。 **Big** describes someone who is tall as well as fat. * big 指人又高又胖：*Her sister is a big girl, isn't she?* 她姐姐塊頭挺大的，是嗎？
- **Plump** means slightly fat in an attractive way, often used to describe women. * plump 常用於形容女性豐滿。
- **Chubby** is used mainly to describe babies and children who are fat in a pleasant, healthy-looking way. * chubby 主要用以形容嬰兒和孩子健康可愛、胖乎乎的樣子：*the baby's chubby cheeks* 嬰兒胖乎乎的臉蛋
- **Tubby** (*informal*) is used in a friendly way to describe people who are short and round, especially around the stomach. * tubby（非正式）用於善意地描述矮胖的人，尤指肚子圓滾滾的。
- **Stocky** is a neutral word and means fairly short, broad and strong. * stocky 是中性詞，意為矮壯。
- **Stout** is often used to describe older people who have a round and heavy appearance. * stout 常用以描述圓胖壯實的較年長者：*a short stout man with a bald head* 一個矮壯禿頂男人
- **Flabby** describes flesh that is fat and loose. * flabby 指肌肉肥胖鬆弛，有冒犯意：*exercises to firm up flabby thighs* 使大腿鬆弛肌肉結實的鍛煉
- **Obese** is used by doctors to describe people who are so fat that they are unhealthy. It is also used in a general way to mean 'really fat'. * obese 是醫學用語，指患肥胖症，亦可泛指十分肥胖。

Note that although people talk a lot about their own size or weight, it is generally not considered polite to refer to a person's large size or their weight when you talk to them. 注意：雖然人們常談論自己的身材和體重，但一般認為當面說人肥胖是不禮貌的。

➲ note at THIN

fatal /ˈfeɪtl/ *adj.* **1** causing or ending in death 致命的：*a* ***fatal accident/blow/illness*** 致命的事故／一擊／疾病 ◇ *a* ***potentially fatal*** *form of cancer* 潛在致死型癌症 ◇ *If she gets ill again it could* ***prove fatal.*** 如果她再患病，就會有性命之憂。➲ compare MORTAL (2) **2** causing disaster or failure 災難性的；毀滅性的；導致失敗的：*a* ***fatal error/mistake*** 災難性的錯誤 ◇ *Any delay would be fatal.* 任何延誤都可能導致失敗。◇ *There was a* ***fatal flaw*** *in the plan.* 計劃中有一個致命的缺陷。◇ *It'd be fatal to try and stop them now.* 現在要試圖制止他們就會導致災難性後果。▸ **fa·tal·ly** /-təli/ *adv.*：*fatally injured/wounded* 受致命傷 ◇ *The plan was* ***fatally flawed*** *from the start.* 這個計劃一開始就有致命的缺陷。

fa·tal·ism /ˈfeɪtəlɪzəm/ *noun* [U] the belief that events are decided by FATE and that you cannot control them; the fact of accepting that you cannot prevent sth from happening 宿命論 ▸ **fa·tal·ist** *noun*：*I'm a fatalist.* 我是宿命論者。

fa·tal·is·tic /ˌfeɪtəˈlɪstɪk/ *adj.* showing a belief in FATE and feeling that you cannot control events or stop them from happening 宿命論的；聽天由命的 ▸ **fa·tal·is·tic·al·ly** /ˌfeɪtəˈlɪstɪkəli/ *adv.*

fa·tal·ity /fəˈtæləti/ *noun* (*pl.* **-ies**) **1** [C] a death that is caused in an accident or a war, or by violence or disease（事故、戰爭、疾病等中的）死亡：*Several people were injured, but there were no fatalities.* 有幾個人受傷，但沒有人死亡。 **2** [U] the fact that a particular disease will result in death（疾病的）致命性：*to reduce the fatality of certain types of cancer* 降低某些癌症的致命性 ◇ *Different forms of cancer have different fatality rates.* 不同類型的癌症死亡率也不同。 **3** [U] the belief or feeling that we have no control over what happens to us 宿命；聽天由命；天數：*A sense of fatality gripped her.* 一種命中注定的意識控制着她。

ˈfat camp *noun* [U, C] an organized holiday/vacation for fat children during which they are helped to lose weight 兒童減肥假期訓練營

ˈfat cat *noun* (*informal, disapproving*) a person who earns, or who has, a lot of money (especially when compared to people who do not earn so much) 大亨；闊老

fate /feɪt/ *noun* **1** [C] the things, especially bad things, that will happen or have happened to sb/sth 命中注定的事（尤指壞事）；命運的安排：***The fate of*** *the three men is unknown.* 這三個人命運未卜。◇ *She sat outside, waiting to find out her fate.* 她坐在外面，等待命運對她作出的安排。◇ *The court will* ***decide our fate/fates.*** 法庭將決定我們的命運。◇ *Each of the managers* ***suffered the same fate.*** 每一個經理命運都是如此。◇ *The government had* ***abandoned*** *the refugees* ***to their fate.*** 政府拋棄了難民，讓他們聽天由命。◇ *From that moment* ***our fate was sealed*** (= our future was decided). 從那時起我們的命運就已經注定了。 **2** [U] the power that is believed to control everything that happens and that cannot be stopped or changed 命運；天數；定數；天意：*Fate was kind to me that day.* 那天我很幸運。◇ *By a strange* ***twist of fate****, Andy and I were on the same plane.* 由於命運的奇特安排，我和安迪乘坐了同一架飛機。➲ SYNONYMS at LUCK

IDM **a fate worse than ˈdeath** (often *humorous*) a terrible thing that could happen（可能發生的）極可怕的事 ➲ more at TEMPT

fated /ˈfeɪtɪd/ *adj.* **1 ~ (to do sth)** unable to escape a particular fate; certain to happen because everything is controlled by fate 命中注定的；命運決定的 SYN **destined**：*We were fated never to meet again.* 我們注定了永遠不能再相見。◇ *He believes that everything in life is fated.* 他相信生命中的一切都是注定的。 **2** = ILL-FATED

fate·ful /ˈfeɪtfl/ *adj.* [usually before noun] having an important, often very bad, effect on future events 對未來有重大（負面）影響的：*She looked back now to* ***that fateful day*** *in December.* 她現在回顧十二月裏那決定性的一天。

ˌfat-ˈfree *adj.* not containing any fat 不含脂肪的：*fat-free yogurt* 脫脂酸奶

father 0-w /ˈfɑːðə(r)/ *noun, verb*

■ *noun* **1** 0-w a male parent of a child or an animal; a person who is acting as the father to a child 父親；爸爸：*Ben's a wonderful father.* 本是個極好的父親。◇ *You've been* ***like a father*** *to me.* 你對我一直像父親一樣。◇ *Our new boss is a* ***father of three*** (= he has three children). 我們的新老闆是三個孩子的父親。◇ *He was a wonderful father to both his natural and adopted children.* 他對親生的和領養的子女都很好。◇ (*old-fashioned*) *Father, I cannot lie to you.* 爸爸，我不能對你說謊。➲ see also GODFATHER, GRANDFATHER, STEPFATHER **2 fathers** [pl.] (*literary*) a person's ANCESTORS (= people who are related to you who lived in the past) 祖先：*the land of our fathers* 我們祖先的土地 ➲ see also FOREFATHER **3 ~ (of sth)** the first man to introduce a new

F

way of thinking about sth or of doing sth 創始人；奠基者；先驅；鼻祖：*Henry Moore is considered to be the father of modern British sculpture.* 亨利・穆爾被認為是現代英國雕塑之父。➲ see also FOUNDING FATHER **4 Father** used by Christians to refer to God 天父；上帝：*Father, forgive us.* 天父，寬恕我們吧。◇ *God the Father* 天父 **5 Father** (*abbr.* **Fr**) the title of a priest, especially in the Roman Catholic Church and the Orthodox Church（尤指天主教和東正教的）神父：*Father Dominic* 道明神父 ➲ see also HOLY FATHER

IDM from ˌfather to ˈson from one generation of a family to the next 從父到子；世代相傳 **like ˌfather, like ˈson** (*saying*) used to say that a son's character or behaviour is similar to that of his father 有其父必有其子 ➲ more at OLD, WISH *n.*

F

■ ***verb* 1 ~ sb** to become the father of a child by making a woman pregnant 成為父親；做父親：*He claims to have fathered over 20 children.* 他聲稱有 20 多個親生子女。**2 ~ sth** to create new ideas or a new way of doing sth 創立（新思想）；創造，發明（新方法）

ˌFather ˈChristmas *noun* (*BrE*) = SANTA CLAUS

ˈfather figure *noun* an older man that sb respects because he will advise and help them like a father 父親般的人；受尊敬的人；長者

father·hood /ˈfɑːðəhʊd; *NAmE* -ðərhʊd/ *noun* [U] the state of being a father 父親的地位（或身分）

ˈfather-in-law *noun* (*pl.* **fathers-in-law**) the father of your husband or wife 岳父；公公；丈夫（或妻子）的父親 ➲ compare MOTHER-IN-LAW

father·land /ˈfɑːðəlænd; *NAmE* -ðərlænd/ *noun* [usually sing.] (*old-fashioned*) (used especially about Germany) the country where a person, or their family, was born, especially when they feel very loyal towards it 祖國（尤用以指德國）

father·less /ˈfɑːðələs; *NAmE* -ðərləs/ *adj.* [usually before noun] without a father, either because he has died or because he does not live with his children 沒有父親的：***fatherless children/families*** 沒有父親的孩子/家庭

father·ly /ˈfɑːðəli; *NAmE* -ðərli/ *adj.* typical of a good father 父親的；慈父般的：*fatherly advice* 慈父般的忠告 ◇ *He keeps a fatherly eye on his players.* 他像父親一樣照管着他的球員。

ˈFather's Day *noun* a day when fathers receive cards and gifts from their children, usually the third Sunday in June 父親節（通常為六月的第三個星期日）

ˌFather ˈTime *noun* an imaginary figure who represents time and looks like an old man carrying a SCYTHE and an HOURGLASS 時間老人（手拿鐮刀和沙漏、象徵時間的虛構人物）

fathom /ˈfæðəm/ *verb, noun*

■ ***verb*** to understand or find an explanation for sth 理解；徹底瞭解；弄清真相：**~ sb/sth (out)** *It is hard to fathom the pain felt at the death of a child.* 喪子之痛是難以體會的。◇ **~ (out) what, where, etc. …** *He couldn't fathom out what the man could possibly mean.* 他弄不清這個男人的意思。

■ ***noun*** a unit for measuring the depth of water, equal to 6 feet or 1.8 metres 英尋（測量水深單位，合 6 英尺或 1.8 米）：*The ship sank in 20 fathoms.* 船沉在水下 20 英尋處。◇ (*figurative*) *She kept her feelings hidden fathoms deep.* 她把感情深深地隱藏在心中。

fa·tigue /fəˈtiːɡ/ *noun* **1** [U] a feeling of being extremely tired, usually because of hard work or exercise 疲勞；勞累 **SYN exhaustion, tiredness**：*physical and mental fatigue* 身體和精神的疲勞 ◇ *Driver fatigue was to blame for the accident.* 這個事故是駕駛員疲勞所致。◇ *I was dropping with fatigue and could not keep my eyes open.* 我快要累倒了，眼睛也睜不開了。**2** [U] (usually after another noun 通常置於另一名詞後) a feeling of not wanting to do a particular activity any longer because you have done too much of it 厭倦：*battle fatigue* 戰鬥疲勞 **3** [U] weakness in metal or wood caused by repeated bending or stretching（金屬或木材的）疲勞：*The wing of the plane showed signs of **metal fatigue**.* 機翼顯示出金屬疲勞的跡象。**4 fatigues** [pl.] loose clothes worn by soldiers（士兵穿的）工作服 **5 fatigues** [pl.] (*especially NAmE*) duties, such as cleaning and cooking, that soldiers have to do, especially as a punishment 士兵雜役（尤指作為懲罰，如做打掃、幫廚）

fa·tigued /fəˈtiːɡd/ *adj.* [not usually before noun] (*formal*) very tired, both physically and mentally 身心交瘁；精疲力竭 **SYN exhausted**

fa·tiguing /fəˈtiːɡɪŋ/ *adj.* (*formal*) very tiring, both physically and mentally 令人身心交瘁的；勞心勞力的 **SYN exhausting**

fatso /ˈfætsəʊ; *NAmE* -soʊ/ *noun* (*pl.* **-oes**) = FATTY

fat·ten /ˈfætn/ *verb* [T, I] **~ (sb/sth) (up)** to make sb/sth fatter, especially an animal before killing it for food; to become fatter（使）長胖，長肥；（尤指動物宰殺前）育肥：*The piglets are taken from the sow to be fattened for market.* 這些小豬從母豬身邊帶走，好育肥上市。◇ *She's very thin after her illness—but we'll soon fatten her up.* 她病後瘦得很，不過我們會使她迅速胖起來的。

fat·ten·ing /ˈfætnɪŋ/ *adj.* (of food 食物) likely to make you fat 要使人發胖的：*fattening cakes* 吃了會發胖的蛋糕

fat·tism /ˈfætɪzəm/ *noun* [U] unfair treatment of people because of their large body size 胖人歧視 ▶ **fat·tist** *adj.*

fatty /ˈfæti/ *adj., noun*

■ ***adj.*** (**fat·tier, fat·ti·est**) containing a lot of fat; consisting of fat 富含脂肪的；肥胖的；脂肪的：*fatty foods* 高脂食物 ◇ *fatty tissue* 脂肪組織

■ ***noun*** (*pl.* **-ies**) (also **fatso**) (*informal, disapproving*) a fat person 胖子：*Britain is fast becoming a nation of fatties.* 英國很快就會變成胖子國。

ˌfatty ˈacid *noun* (*chemistry* 化) an acid that is found in fats and oils 脂肪酸

fatu·ous /ˈfætʃuəs/ *adj.* (*formal*) stupid 愚蠢的；愚昧的：*a fatuous comment/grin* 愚蠢的話語；齜牙咧嘴的傻笑 ▶ **fatu·ous·ly** *adv.*

fatwa /ˈfætwɑː/ *noun* a decision or order made under Islamic law 法特瓦（伊斯蘭律法的裁決或教令）

fau·cet 🔑 /ˈfɔːsɪt/ (*NAmE*) (*BrE* **tap**) *noun* a device that controls the flow of water from a pipe 龍頭；旋塞：*the **hot/cold faucet*** 熱水/冷水龍頭 ◇ ***to turn a faucet on/off*** 開/關龍頭 ➲ picture at PLUG ➲ VISUAL VOCAB pages V24, V25

fault 🔑 /fɔːlt/ *noun, verb*

■ ***noun***

▸ **RESPONSIBILITY** 責任 **1** 🔑 [U] the responsibility for sth wrong that has happened or been done 責任；過錯；過失：*Why should I say sorry when it's not **my fault**?* 不是我的錯為什麼要我道歉？◇ *It's nobody's fault.* 誰都沒有錯。◇ **~ (that …)** *It was **his fault** that we were late.* 我們遲到責任在他。◇ **~ (for doing sth)** *It's **your own fault** for being careless.* 你粗心大意是你自己的過失。◇ *Many people live in poverty **through no fault of their own**.* 很多人生活貧困並非他們自己有什麼過錯。◇ *I think the owners are **at fault*** (= responsible) *for not warning us.* 我認為業主沒有提醒我們是有責任的。

▸ **IN SB'S CHARACTER** 人品 **2** 🔑 [C] a bad or weak aspect of sb's character 弱點；缺點 **SYN shortcoming**：*He's proud of his children and blind to their faults.* 他為孩子們感到自豪，對他們的缺點視而不見。◇ *I love her **for all her faults*** (= in spite of them). 儘管她有這麼多缺點，我還是愛她。

▸ **STH WRONG** 錯事 **3** 🔑 [C] something that is wrong or not perfect; something that is wrong with a machine or system that stops it from working correctly 缺陷；毛病；故障 **SYN defect**：*The book's virtues far outweigh its faults.* 這本書優點遠遠大於缺點。◇ *The system, **for all its faults**, is the best available at the moment.* 這個系統雖然缺點不少，卻是現有最好的一個。◇ *a major fault in the design* 設計中的一個重大失誤 ◇ *a structural fault* 結構缺陷 ◇ *an electrical fault* 電路故障

▸ **IN TENNIS** 網球 **4** [C] a mistake made when SERVING 發球失誤：*He has served a number of **double faults** in this set.* 他在這盤發球出現了一些雙誤。

▸ **GEOLOGY** 地質 **5** [C] a place where there is a break that is longer than usual in the layers of rock in the earth's

CRUST（地殼岩層的）斷層：*the San Andreas fault* 聖安德烈亞斯斷層 ◇ *a fault line* 斷層線

IDM **to a 'fault** used to say that sb has a lot, or even too much, of a particular good quality（良好品質）過分，過度：*She is generous to a fault.* 她過分慷慨。➲ more at FIND *v.*

■ ***verb*** **~ sb/sth** (often used in negative sentences with *can* and *could* 常與 can 和 could 連用於否定句) to find a mistake or a weakness in sb/sth 發現錯誤；找出缺點 **SYN** **criticize**：*Her colleagues could not fault her dedication to the job.* 她的同事認為她的敬業精神是無可挑剔的。◇ *He had always been polite—she couldn't fault him on that.* 他總是彬彬有禮，在這方面她對他無可指摘。

'fault-finding *noun* [U] the act of looking for faults in sb/sth 找岔子；挑剔

fault·less /'fɔːltləs/ *adj.* having no mistakes 沒有錯誤的；無缺點的；完美無缺的 **SYN** **perfect**：*faultless English* 完美的英語 ▸ **fault·less·ly** *adv.*

faulty /'fɔːlti/ *adj.* **1** not perfect; not working or made correctly 不完美的；有錯誤的；有缺陷的 **SYN** **defective**：*Ask for a refund if the goods are faulty.* 商品如有缺陷，可要求退款。◇ *faulty workmanship* 不完美的做工 ◇ *an accident caused by a faulty signal* 錯誤信號造成的事故 **2** (of a way of thinking 思想方法) wrong or containing mistakes, often resulting in bad decisions 錯誤的；有錯誤的：*faulty reasoning* 錯誤推理

faun /fɔːn/ *noun* (in ancient Roman stories) a god of the woods, with a man's face and body and a GOAT'S legs and horns 農牧神（見於古羅馬故事，呈人面人身羊腿羊角）

fauna /'fɔːnə/ *noun* [U, C] all the animals living in an area or in a particular period of history（某地區或某時期的）動物群：*the local **flora and fauna*** (= plants and animals) 當地動植物群 ◇ (*technical* 術語) *land and marine faunas* 陸地和海洋動物區系

Faust·ian /'faʊstiən/ *adj.* (*formal*) **~ bargain/pact/agreement** an agreement in which sb agrees to do sth bad or dishonest, in return for money, success or power 浮士德式的（交易或協議）（為獲得財富、成功或權力而不擇手段）**ORIGIN** From **Faust**, who, according to the German legend, sold his soul to the Devil in return for many years of power and pleasure. 源自德國傳說中的人物浮士德（Faust），他將靈魂出賣給了魔鬼，以換取多年的權力和享樂。

faute de mieux /ˌfəʊt də 'mjɜː; *NAmE* ˌfoʊt/ *adv.* (from *French*) because there is nothing else that is better 因無更好的：*We were obliged, faute de mieux, to drink the local beverage.* 因為沒有更好的飲料，我們只好將就着喝當地的。

Fauve /fəʊv; *NAmE* foʊv/ *noun* a member of a group of French painters who were important in Fauvism（法國）野獸派核心畫家

Fauv·ism /'fəʊvɪzəm; *NAmE* 'foʊv-/ *noun* [U] (*art* 美術) a style of painting that uses bright colours and in which objects and people are represented in a non-realistic way. It was popular in Paris for a short period from 1905. 野獸主義（一種繪畫風格，以鮮明色彩和非現實主義方式表現物體和人物，從 1905 年起在巴黎流行一時）

faux /fəʊ; *NAmE* foʊ/ *adj.* artificial, but intended to look or seem real 人造的；仿製的：*The chairs were covered in faux animal skin.* 椅子外層是人造獸皮。◇ *His accent was so faux.* 他的口音聽上去很假。

faux pas /ˌfəʊ 'pɑː; *NAmE* ˌfoʊ/ *noun* (*pl.* **faux pas** /ˌfəʊ 'pɑːz; *NAmE* ˌfoʊ/) (from *French*) an action or a remark that causes embarrassment because it is not socially correct 有失檢點；失態；失禮；失言

fava bean /'fɑːvə biːn/ (*NAmE*) (*BrE* ˌ**broad 'bean**) *noun* a type of round, pale green BEAN. Several fava beans grow together inside a fat POD. 蠶豆

fave /feɪv/ *noun* (*informal*) a favourite person or thing 特別喜愛的人（或事物）：*That song is one of my faves.* 這是我特別喜愛的歌曲之一。▸ **fave** *adj.*：*her fave TV show* 她特別喜愛的電視節目

fa·vela /fæ'velə/ *noun* (from *Portuguese*) a poor area in or near a Brazilian city, with many small houses that are close together and in bad condition（巴西城市或邊緣的）棚戶區，貧民窟 ➲ compare SHANTY TOWN

fa·vour 0➔ (*especially US* **favor**) /'feɪvə(r)/ *noun, verb*

■ ***noun***

▸ **HELP** 幫助 **1** 0➔ [C] a thing that you do to help sb 幫助；好事；恩惠：*Could you **do me a favour** and pick up Sam from school today?* 今天你能幫我個忙去學校接薩姆嗎？◇ *Can I **ask a favour**?* 請幫個忙行嗎？◇ *I would never ask for any favours from her.* 我再也不會請她幫任何忙了。◇ *I'm going **as a favour** to Ann, not because I want to.* 我去是給安一個面子，而不是我想去。◇ *I'll ask Steve to take it. He **owes me a favour**.* 我要請史蒂夫接受，他欠我一個人情。◇ *Thanks for helping me out. I'll **return the favour*** (= help you because you have helped me) *some time.* 多謝你幫了我個大忙。總有一天我會報答你的。◇ ***Do yourself a favour*** (= help yourself) *and wear a helmet on the bike.* 要照顧自己，騎車戴上頭盔。

▸ **APPROVAL** 贊同 **2** 0➔ [U] approval or support for sb/sth 贊同；支持：*The suggestion to close the road has **found favour with*** (= been supported by) *local people.* 關閉這條路的建議已得到當地人的支持。◇ *The programme has **lost favour** with viewers recently.* 近來這個節目已不受觀眾歡迎。◇ *an athlete who **fell from favour** after a drugs scandal* 在毒品醜聞以後不再受人喜愛的運動員 ◇ (*formal*) *The government **looks with favour upon*** (= approves of) *the report's recommendations.* 政府贊同報告所提出的建議。◇ *She's not **in favour with*** (= supported or liked by) *the media just now.* 目前她沒有媒體的捧場。◇ *It seems Tim is **back in favour** with the boss* (= the boss likes him again). 看來蒂姆又贏得了老闆的好感。

▸ **BETTER TREATMENT** 優惠 **3** [U] treatment that is generous to one person or group in a way that seems unfair to others 特別照顧；偏袒；偏愛 **SYN** **bias**：*As an examiner, she showed no favour to any candidate.* 作為主考人她沒有偏袒任何應試者。

▸ **PARTY GIFT** 聚會小禮物 **4 favors** [pl.] (*NAmE*) = PARTY FAVORS

▸ **SEX** 性 **5 favours** [pl.] (*old-fashioned*) agreement to have sex with sb 同意性交：*demands for sexual favours* 對性交的要求

IDM **do sb no 'favours** to do sth that is not helpful to sb or that gives a bad impression of them 無助於某人；給某人留下壞印象：*You're not doing yourself any favours, working for nothing.* 你幹活不取報酬，對自己沒有任何好處。◇ *The orchestra did Beethoven no favours.* 這個交響樂團沒有把貝多芬的樂曲演奏好。 **do me a 'favour!** (*informal*) used in reply to a question that you think is silly（回答認為是愚蠢的問題）得了吧：*'Do you think they'll win?' 'Do me a favour! They haven't got a single decent player.'* "你認為他們會贏嗎？" "得了吧！他們連一個像樣的運動員都沒有。" **in favour (of sb/sth)** **1** 0➔ if you are **in favour** of sb/sth, you support and agree with them/it 贊同；支持：*He argued in favour of a strike.* 他據理力爭主張罷工。◇ *There were 247 votes in favour* (*of the motion*) *and 152 against.* 有 247 票贊成（動議），152 票反對。◇ *I'm **all in favour of*** (= completely support) *equal pay for equal work.* 我完全支持同工同酬。◇ *Most of the 'don't knows' in the opinion polls **came down in favour of*** (= eventually chose to support) *the Democrats.* 在民意測驗中多數未作決定的選民最終決定支持民主黨人。 **2** in exchange for another thing (because the other thing is better or you want it more) 為獲得（更好或更需要的事物）：*He abandoned teaching in favour of a career as a musician.* 他棄教從事音樂。 **in sb's favour** **1** if sth is **in sb's favour**, it gives them an advantage or helps them 有利於某人；有助於某人：*The exchange rate is in our favour at the moment.* 目前匯率對我們有利。◇ *She was willing to bend the rules in Mary's favour.* 她願意放寬規定以有利於瑪麗。 **2** a decision or judgement that is **in sb's favour** benefits that person or says that they were right（決定）對某人有利；（判決）判某人正確 ➲ more at CURRY *v.*, FEAR *n.*, STACKED

■ ***verb***

▸ **PREFER** 較喜歡 **1 ~ sth | ~ (sb) doing sth** to prefer one system, plan, way of doing sth, etc. to another 較喜歡；

F

選擇：*Many countries favour a presidential system of government.* 很多國家選擇總統制政府。
▸ **TREAT BETTER** 優惠 **2 ~ sb** to treat sb better than you treat other people, especially in an unfair way 優惠；特別照顧；偏袒：*The treaty seems to favour the US.* 這項條約似乎偏向美國。
▸ **HELP** 幫助 **3 ~ sth** to provide suitable conditions for a particular person, group, etc. 有助於；有利於：*The warm climate favours many types of tropical plants.* 温暖的氣候對多種熱帶植物生長有利。
▸ **LOOK LIKE PARENT** 外貌像父母 **4 ~ sb** (*old-fashioned* or *NAmE*) to look like one of your parents or older relations 外貌像，長得像（父母或長輩）：*She definitely favours her father.* 她酷似她父親。

F

fa·vour·able (*especially US* **fa·vor·able**) /ˈfeɪvərəbl/ *adj.* **1** making people have a good opinion of sb/sth 給人好印象的：*She* ***made a favourable impression*** *on his parents.* 她給他的父母留下了好印象。◇ *The biography shows him in a favourable light.* 傳記刻畫出了他的正面形象。 **2** positive and showing your good opinion of sb/sth 肯定的；贊同的；支持的：*favourable comments* 好評 **3 ~ (to/for sb/sth)** good for sth and making it likely to be successful or have an advantage 有利的；有助於…的 SYN **advantageous**：*The terms of the agreement are favourable to both sides.* 協議條款對雙方都有利。◇ *favourable economic conditions* 有利的經濟環境 **4** fairly good and not too expensive 好而不貴的；優惠的：*They offered me a loan on very* ***favourable terms.*** 他們提出以十分優惠的條件貸款給我。OPP **unfavourable** ▸ **fa·vour·abil·ity** (*especially US* **fa·vor·abil·ity**) /ˌfeɪvərəˈbɪləti/ *noun* [U] **fa·vour·ably** (*especially US* **fa·vor·ably**) /-əbli/ *adv.*：*He speaks very favourably of your work.* 他對你的工作十分讚賞。◇ *These figures compare favourably with last year's.* 這些數字比去年的好多了。◇ *I was very favourably impressed with her work.* 她的工作給我留下了很好的印象。

fa·voured (*especially US* **favored**) /ˈfeɪvəd; *NAmE* -vərd/ *adj.* **1** treated in a special way or receiving special help or advantages in a way that may seem unfair 受到寵愛的；得到偏愛的；獲得優惠的：*a member of the President's favoured circle of advisers* 總統寵愛的顧問班子中的一員 **2** preferred by most people 大眾喜愛的：*the favoured candidate* 公眾喜愛的候選人 **3** (*formal*) particularly pleasant and worth having 稱心如意的；中意的：*Their house is in a very favoured position near the park.* 他們的房子在公園附近一個很愜意的地段。

fa·vour·ite 🔑 (*especially US* **fa·vor·ite**) /ˈfeɪvərɪt/ *adj.*, *noun*
■ ***adj.*** 🔑 liked more than others of the same kind 特別受喜愛的：*It's one of my favourite movies.* 這是我特別喜歡的電影之一。◇ *Who is your favourite writer?* 誰是你特別喜歡的作家？◇ *January is my least favourite month.* 一月是我最不喜歡的月份。➲ SYNONYMS at CHOICE
IDM **sb's favourite 'son 1** a performer, politician, sports player, etc., who is popular where they were born 故鄉的驕子（可指演員、政治家、運動員等） **2** (in the US) a candidate for president who is supported by his or her own state in the first part of a campaign（美國大選第一階段）本州支持的總統候選人
■ ***noun* 1** 🔑 a person or thing that you like more than the others of the same type 特別喜愛的人（或事物）：*These biscuits are great favourites with the children.* 孩子們特別喜歡這種餅乾。◇ *This song is a* ***particular favourite*** *of mine.* 我尤其喜愛這首歌曲。◇ *The band played all my* ***old favourites.*** 樂隊演奏了所有我最喜歡的老曲子。◇ *Which one's your favourite?* 你最喜歡哪一個？◇ *The programme has become a* ***firm favourite*** *with young people.* 這個節目已着實贏得了年輕人的喜愛。 **2** 🔑 a person who is liked better by sb and receives better treatment than others 受寵的人；得到偏愛的人：*She loved all her grandchildren but Ann was her favourite.* 她愛所有的孫兒孫女，但最寵安。 **3** the horse, runner, team, etc. that is expected to win（比賽中）被認為最有希望的獲勝者：*The favourite came third.* 那個可望奪魁者得了第三名。◇ **~ (for sth)** *Her horse is the* ***hot favourite*** *for the race.* 她的馬在這次賽馬中奪魁的呼聲最高。◇ **~ (to do sth)** *AC Milan, the* ***hot favourites*** *to win the Champions League* * AC 米蘭隊，歐洲冠軍聯賽的奪標大熱門 **4** the person who is expected by most people to get a particular job or position（取得職位等的）最有希望者：**~ (for sth)** *She's the favourite for the job.* 她最有希望得到這份工作。◇ **~ (to do sth)** *She's the favourite to succeed him as leader.* 她最有希望接替他成為領導人。

fa·vour·it·ism (*especially US* **fa·vor·it·ism**) /ˈfeɪvərɪtɪzəm/ *noun* [U] (*disapproving*) the act of unfairly treating one person better than others because you like them better 偏愛；偏袒：*The students accused the teacher of favouritism.* 學生指責老師有偏心。

fawn /fɔːn/ *adj.*, *noun*, *verb*
■ ***adj.*** light yellowish-brown in colour 淺黃褐色的：*a fawn coat* 淺黃褐色外套
■ ***noun* 1** [C] a DEER less than one year old（不足一歲的）幼鹿 **2** [U] a light yellowish-brown colour 淺黃褐色
■ ***verb*** [I] **~ (on/over sb)** (*disapproving*) to try to please sb by praising them or paying them too much attention 恭維；討好；巴結

fax /fæks/ *noun*, *verb*
■ ***noun*** (also *formal* **fac·sim·ile**) **1** (also **'fax machine**) [C] a machine that sends and receives documents in an electronic form along telephone wires and then prints them 傳真機：*Do you have a fax?* 你有傳真機嗎？ **2** [U] a system for sending documents using a fax machine 傳真（系統）：*Can you send it to me* ***by fax?*** 你能用傳真把它發給我嗎？◇ *What is your fax number?* 你的傳真號碼是多少？ **3** [C] a letter or message sent by fax 傳真信件；傳真電文；明電：*Did you get my fax?* 你收到我的傳真信件沒有？◇ *You can send faxes by email from your computer.* 你可以通過計算機用電子郵件發送傳真信件。➲ COLLOCATIONS at PHONE
■ ***verb*** to send sb a document, message, etc. by fax 傳真（文檔、信件等）：**~ sb sth** *Could you fax me the latest version?* 你可不可以把最新版本傳真給我？◇ **~ sth to sb** *Could you fax it to me?* 你能把它傳真給我嗎？◇ **~ sth** *I faxed the list of hotels through to them.* 我把旅館名單傳真給了他們。

faze /feɪz/ *verb* **~ sb** [often passive] (*informal*) to make you feel confused or shocked, so that you do not know what to do 使慌亂；使驚慌失措；使困窘 SYN **disconcert**：*She wasn't fazed by his comments.* 她並沒有因他的話而驚慌失措。◇ *He looked as if nothing could faze him.* 他顯得鎮靜自若，遇事不驚。

FBI /ˌef biː ˈaɪ/ *abbr.* Federal Bureau of Investigation (the police department in the US that is controlled by the national government and that is responsible for dealing with crimes that affect more than one state)（美國）聯邦調查局

FC /ˌef ˈsiː/ *abbr.* (*BrE*) football club 足球俱樂部：*Liverpool FC* 利物浦足球俱樂部

FCE /ˌef siː ˈiː/ *noun* [U] the abbreviation for 'First Certificate in English' (a British test that measures a person's ability to speak and write English as a foreign language at an UPPER-INTERMEDIATE level) 第一英語證書考試，中高級英語認證考試（全寫為 First Certificate in English，英語作為外語的中高級口語和寫作的英國考試）：*When are you* ***taking FCE?*** 你何時參加第一英語證書考試？

FCO /ˌef siː ˈəʊ; *NAmE* ˈoʊ/ *abbr.* FOREIGN AND COMMONWEALTH OFFICE 外交和聯邦事務部

FDA /ˌef diː ˈeɪ/ *abbr.* Food and Drug Administration (the US government department that is responsible for making sure that food and drugs are safe to be sold)（美國）食品及藥物管理局

FE /ˌef ˈiː/ *abbr.* (in Britain) FURTHER EDUCATION（英國）繼續教育，進修教育

fealty /ˈfiːəlti/ *noun* [U] (*old use*) a promise to be loyal to sb, especially a king or queen（尤指對君主的）效忠宣誓

fear 🔑 /fɪə(r); *NAmE* fɪr/ *noun*, *verb*
■ ***noun*** 🔑 [U, C] the bad feeling that you have when you are in danger, when sth bad might happen, or when a particular thing frightens you 害怕；懼怕；擔憂：*Her eyes showed no fear.* 她的眼神無絲毫畏懼。◇ *The child was shaking* ***with fear.*** 小孩嚇得發抖。◇ **~ (of sb/sth)** (**a**) ***fear of the dark/spiders/flying, etc.*** 害怕黑暗、蜘蛛、

坐飛機等 ◇ *We lived **in constant fear of** losing our jobs.* 我們一直生活在擔心失去工作的陰影裏。◇ **~ (for sb/sth)** *her fears for her son's safety* 她對兒子安全的擔憂 ◇ *Alan spoke of his **fears for the future**.* 艾倫談到了他對未來的擔憂。◇ **~ (that ...)** *the fear that he had cancer* 他對患癌症的恐懼 ◇ *The doctor's report confirmed our worst fears.* 醫生的報告證實了我們最大的擔憂。

IDM **for fear of sth/of doing sth | for fear (that) ...** to avoid the danger of sth happening 唯恐，以免（發生危險）：*We spoke quietly for fear of waking the guards.* 我們悄悄說話，以免驚醒警衛。◇ *I had to run away for fear (that) he might one day kill me.* 我只好逃走，生怕他有一天把我殺了。 **in ˌfear of your ˈlife** feeling frightened that you might be killed 害怕會喪生；為生命安全擔憂 **ˌno ˈfear** (*BrE, informal*) used to say that you definitely do not want to do sth（表示決不願做某事）絕不，當然不：*'Are you coming climbing?' 'No fear!'* "你來爬山嗎？" "當然不！" **put the fear of ˈGod into sb** to make sb very frightened, especially in order to make them do sth 恐嚇；（尤指）威脅某人服從 **without fear or ˈfavour** (*formal*) in a fair way 公正地；不偏不倚 ➲ more at FOOL *n.*, STRIKE *v.*

■ *verb* **1** [T] to be frightened of sb/sth or frightened of doing sth 害怕；畏懼；懼怕：**~ sb/sth** *All his employees fear him.* 他的雇員都怕他。◇ *to fear death/persecution/the unknown* 怕死；害怕遭迫害／未知的事物 ◇ *Don't worry, you have **nothing to fear from** us.* 別擔心，你一點也不必害怕我們。◇ **~ to do sth** (*formal*) *She feared to tell him the truth.* 她不敢把真相告訴他。◇ **~ doing sth** (*formal*) *She feared going out at night.* 她不敢晚上出去。 **2** [T, I] to feel that sth bad might have happened or might happen in the future 擔心；擔憂：**~ sth** *She has been missing for three days now and police are beginning to **fear the worst*** (= think that she is dead). 現在她已經失踪三天了，警方擔心發生了最壞的情況（認為她已死亡）。◇ **~ sb/sth + adj.** *Hundreds of people are feared dead.* 好幾百人恐遭不測。◇ **be feared to be/have sth** *Women and children are feared to be among the victims.* 大家擔心受害者中有婦女兒童。◇ **it is feared (that) ...** *It is feared (that) he may have been kidnapped.* 人們擔心他可能被綁架了。◇ **~ (that) ...** *She feared (that) he might be dead.* 她擔心他可能死了。◇ ***Never fear/Fear not*** (= Don't worry), *I shall return.* 別擔心，我會回來的。 **3 I fear** [I] (*formal*) used to tell sb that you think that sth bad has happened or is true（引出不好的事情）恐怕：*They are unlikely to get here on time, I fear.* 恐怕他們不大可能準時到達這裏。◇ *'He must be dead then?' '**I fear so.**'* "那麼他肯定死了？" "恐怕是這樣。" ◇ *'She's not coming back?' '**I fear not.**'* "她不打算回來了？" "我想是的。"

PHR V **ˈfear for sb/sth** to be worried about sb/sth 為…擔心（或擔憂）：*We fear for his safety.* 我們擔心他的安全。◇ *He feared for his mother, left alone on the farm.* 他為獨自一人留在農場的母親擔憂。

fear·ful /ˈfɪəfl; *NAmE* ˈfɪrfl/ *adj.* **1** (*formal*) nervous and afraid 擔心；擔憂；憂慮：**~ (for sb)** *Parents are ever fearful for their children.* 父母總是為子女擔憂。◇ **~ (of sth/of doing sth)** *fearful of an attack* 擔心遭到襲擊 ◇ **~ (that ...)** *She was fearful that she would fail.* 她生怕失敗。 **2** [only before noun] (*formal*) terrible and frightening 可怕的；嚇人的；恐懼的 **3** (*old-fashioned, informal*) extremely bad 極壞的；極糟的：*We made a fearful mess of the room.* 我們把房間弄得一團糟。 ▸ **fear·ful·ly** /-fəli/ *adv.*：*We watched fearfully.* 我們憂心忡忡地觀察着。◇ *fearfully* (= extremely) *expensive* 貴得嚇人 **fear·ful·ness** *noun* [U]

fear·less /ˈfɪələs; *NAmE* ˈfɪrləs/ *adj.* (*approving*) not afraid, in a way that people admire 不怕的；無畏的；大膽的：*a fearless mountaineer* 無畏的登山運動員 ▸ **fear·less·ly** *adv.* **fear·less·ness** *noun* [U]

fear·some /ˈfɪəsəm; *NAmE* ˈfɪrsəm/ *adj.* (*formal*) making people feel very frightened 很可怕的；十分嚇人的

feas·ible /ˈfiːzəbl/ *adj.* that is possible and likely to be achieved 可行的；行得通的 **SYN** **practicable**：*a feasible plan/suggestion/idea* 可行的計劃／建議／想法 ◇ *It's just not feasible to manage the business on a part-time basis.* 兼職管理業務是搞不好的。 **OPP** **unfeasible** ▸ **feasi·bil·ity** /ˌfiːzəˈbɪləti/ *noun* [U]：*a **feasibility study** on the proposed new airport* 關於建議中新機場的可行性研究 ◇ *I doubt the feasibility of the plan.* 我懷疑這個計劃的可行性。

feast /fiːst/ *noun, verb*

■ *noun* **1** a large or special meal, especially for a lot of people and to celebrate sth 盛宴；宴會：*a wedding feast* 婚筵 **2** a day or period of time when there is a religious festival（宗教的）節日，節期：*the feast of Christmas* 聖誕佳節 ◇ *a feast day* 一個宗教節日 **3** [usually sing.] a thing or an event that brings great pleasure 使人歡快的事物（或活動）：*a feast of colours* 五彩繽紛 ◇ *The evening was a real feast for music lovers.* 這個晚會真是讓音樂愛好者大飽耳福。

■ *verb* [I] **~ (on sth)** to eat a large amount of food, with great enjoyment 盡情享用（美味佳肴）

IDM **feast your ˈeyes (on sb/sth)** to look at sb/sth and get great pleasure 盡情欣賞；大飽眼福；賞心悅目

ˌFeast of ˈTabernacles *noun* [U] = SUCCOTH

ˌFeast of ˈWeeks *noun* [U] = SHAVUOTH

feat /fiːt/ *noun* (*approving*) an action or a piece of work that needs skill, strength or courage 技藝；武藝；功績；英勇事跡：*The tunnel is a brilliant feat of engineering.* 這條隧道是工程方面的光輝業績。◇ *to **perform/attempt/achieve** astonishing **feats*** 表演驚人的技藝；爭取／取得驚人的功績 ◇ *That was **no mean feat*** (= it was difficult to do). 那是偉大的成就。

Synonyms 同義詞辨析

fear

terror • panic • alarm • fright

These are all words for the bad feeling you have when you are afraid. 以上各詞均表示害怕時的恐慌情緒。

fear the bad feeling that you have when you are in danger, when sth bad might happen, or when a particular thing frightens you 指害怕、懼怕、擔憂：*(a) fear of flying* 害怕坐飛機 ◇ *She showed no fear.* 她毫無懼色。

terror a feeling of extreme fear 指驚恐、恐懼、驚駭：*Her eyes were wild with terror.* 她的眼睛裏充滿了恐懼。

panic a sudden feeling of great fear that cannot be controlled and prevents you from thinking clearly 指驚恐、恐慌：*I had a sudden moment of panic.* 我突然一陣驚慌。

alarm fear or worry that sb feels when sth dangerous or unpleasant might happen 指驚恐、驚慌、恐慌：*The doctor said there was **no cause for alarm**.* 醫生說不必驚慌。

fright a feeling of fear, usually sudden 通常指突如其來的驚嚇、恐怖：*She cried out in fright.* 她嚇得大聲叫喊。

FEAR OR FRIGHT? 用 fear 還是 fright？

Fright is a reaction to sth that has just happened or is happening now. Use **fear**, but not **fright**, to talk about things that always frighten you and things that may happen in the future. * fright 指對剛剛發生或正在發生的事情的反應。對一直使人害怕的事物和對未來可能發生的事情感到擔憂應該用 fear，而不能用 fright：~~*I have a fright of spiders.*~~ ◇ ~~*his fright of what might happen*~~

PATTERNS

- a fear/terror **of** sth
- **in** fear/terror/panic/alarm/fright
- fear/terror/panic/alarm **that** ...
- to be **filled with** fear/terror/panic/alarm
- **a feeling of** fear/terror/panic/alarm

F

fea·ther 0→ /ˈfeðə(r)/ *noun, verb*

■ **noun** 0→ one of the many soft light parts covering a bird's body 羽毛；翎毛：*a peacock feather* 孔雀羽毛 ◊ *a feather pillow* (= one containing feathers) 羽絨枕頭 ➲ VISUAL VOCAB page V12

IDM **a ˈfeather in your cap** an action that you can be proud of 可引以自豪的行為 ORIGIN This idiom comes from the Native American custom of giving a feather to sb who had been very brave in battle. 此習語源自美國土著的風俗，把一根羽毛獎賞給在戰鬥中表現英勇的人。 ➲ more at BIRD, KNOCK *v.*, RUFFLE *v.*, SMOOTH *v.*

■ **verb**

F

IDM **feather your (own) ˈnest** to make yourself richer, especially by spending money on yourself that should be spent on sth else 中飽私囊 ➲ more at TAR *v.*

ˌfeather-ˈbed *verb* (-dd-) **~ sb/sth** (*BrE*) to make things easy for sb, especially by giving them money or good conditions of work（尤指提供金錢或良好條件）使安逸，使輕鬆，嬌養，溺愛

ˌfeather ˈboa (also **boa**) *noun* a long thin piece of clothing like a SCARF, made of feathers and worn over the shoulders by women, especially in the past（舊時女用）羽毛圍巾

ˈfeather-brained *adj.* (*informal, disapproving*) very silly 渾頭渾腦的

ˌfeather ˈduster *noun* a stick with feathers on the end of it that is used for cleaning 羽毛撣子 ➲ VISUAL VOCAB page V20

fea·thered /ˈfeðəd; *NAmE* -ðərd/ *adj.* covered with feathers or having feathers 覆蓋着羽毛的；有羽毛的

fea·ther·weight /ˈfeðəweɪt; *NAmE* ˈfeðərw-/ *noun* a BOXER weighing between 53.5 and 57 kilograms, heavier than a BANTAMWEIGHT 次輕量級拳擊手，羽量級拳擊手（體重 53.5 至 57 公斤）

fea·thery /ˈfeðəri/ *adj.* light and soft; like feathers 輕軟的；羽毛似的

fea·ture 0→ AW /ˈfiːtʃə(r)/ *noun, verb*

■ **noun** [C] **1** 0→ something important, interesting or typical of a place or thing 特色；特徵；特點：*An interesting feature of the city is the old market.* 這座城市的一個有趣特徵就是古老的市場。◊ *Teamwork is a* ***key feature*** *of the training programme.* 團隊合作是這項訓練計劃的重要特點。◊ *Which features do you look for when choosing a car?* 你挑選轎車時要着重哪些特點？◊ *The software has no particular* ***distinguishing features****.* 這個軟件沒有明顯的特點。◊ *geographical features* 地勢 ➲ see also WATER FEATURE **2** 0→ [usually pl.] a part of sb's face such as their nose, mouth and eyes 面容的一部份（如鼻、口、眼）：*his strong handsome features* 他輪廓分明的英俊面孔 ◊ *Her eyes are her most* ***striking feature****.* 她容貌中最引人注目的是她的雙眼。**3** 0→ **~ (on sb/sth)** (in newspapers, on television, etc.) a special article or programme about sb/sth（報章、電視等的）特寫，專題節目：*a special feature on education* 關於教育的專題文章 **4** (*old-fashioned*) the main film/movie in a cinema programme（電影的）正片，故事片

■ **verb** **1** 0→ [T] to include a particular person or thing as a special feature 以…為特色；是…的特徵：**~ sb/sth as sb/sth** *The film features Cary Grant as a professor.* 這部電影由卡里 • 格蘭特飾演一位教授。◊ **~ sb/sth** *The latest model features alloy wheels and an electronic alarm.* 最新款式的特色是合金車輪和電子報警器。◊ *Many of the hotels featured in the brochure offer special deals for weekend breaks.* 小冊子列舉的多家旅館都有週末假日特別優待。**2** 0→ [I] **~ (in sth)** to have an important part in sth 起重要作用；佔重要地位：*Olive oil and garlic feature prominently in his recipes.* 橄欖油和大蒜在他的食譜中是重要的材料。

ˈfeature film *noun* a main film/movie with a story, rather than a DOCUMENTARY, etc. 故事片

ˈfeature-length *adj.* [usually before noun] of the same length as a typical film/movie（影片）達到正片應有長度的

fea·ture·less /ˈfiːtʃələs; *NAmE* -tʃərl-/ *adj.* without any qualities or noticeable characteristics 沒有特色的；平淡無奇的：*The countryside is flat and featureless.* 這鄉村一馬平川，平淡無奇。

fe·brile /ˈfiːbraɪl; *NAmE* also ˈfeb-/ *adj.* **1** (*formal*) nervous, excited and very active 狂熱的：*a product of her febrile imagination* 她狂想的產物 **2** (*medical* 醫) (of an illness 疾病) caused by fever 發熱引起的；熱性的；發熱的

Feb·ru·ary 0→ /ˈfebruəri; *NAmE* -ueri/ *noun* [U, C] (*abbr.* **Feb.**) the 2nd month of the year, between January and March 二月 HELP To see how **February** is used, look at the examples at **April**. * February 的用法見詞條 April 下的示例。

feces (*NAmE*) (*BrE* **fae·ces**) /ˈfiːsiːz/ *noun* [pl.] (*formal*) solid waste material that leaves the body through the ANUS 糞便 SYN **excrement** ▸ **fecal** (*NAmE*) (*BrE* **fae·cal**) /ˈfiːkl/ *adj.* [only before noun]

feck·less /ˈfekləs/ *adj.* having a weak character; not behaving in a responsible way 品格差的；不負責任的：*Her husband was a charming, but lazy and feckless man.* 她的丈夫討人喜歡，但卻是個懶惰沒有出息的人。▸ **feck·less·ness** *noun* [U]

fe·cund /ˈfiːkənd; ˈfek-/ *adj.* (*formal*) **1** able to produce a lot of children, crops, etc. 生殖力旺盛的；多產的 SYN **fertile** **2** producing new and useful things, especially ideas 有發明創造力的；（尤指）能提出新穎想法的 ▸ **fe·cund·ity** /fɪˈkʌndəti/ *noun* [U]

Fed /fed/ *noun* (*US, informal*) **1** [C] an officer of the FBI or another federal organization（美國）聯邦調查局官員，聯邦政府官員 **2** **the Fed** [sing.] = THE FEDERAL RESERVE

fed *past tense, past part.* of FEED

fed·eral 0→ AW /ˈfedərəl/ *adj.*

1 0→ having a system of government in which the individual states of a country have control over their own affairs, but are controlled by a central government for national decisions, etc. 聯邦制的：*a federal republic* 聯邦共和國 **2** 0→ (within a federal system, for example the US and Canada) connected with national government rather than the local government of an individual state（在美國、加拿大等聯邦制下）聯邦政府的：*a federal law* 聯邦法 ◊ *state and federal income taxes* 州政府和聯邦政府徵收的所得稅 ▸ **fed·er·al·ly** *adv.*：*federally funded health care* 由聯邦政府撥款的保健

the ˌFederal ˌBureau of Investiˈgation *noun* [sing.] = FBI

fed·er·al·ist /ˈfedərəlɪst/ *noun* a supporter of a federal system of government 聯邦主義者 ▸ **fed·er·al·ism** /ˈfedərəlɪzəm/ *noun* [U]：*European federalism* 歐洲聯邦主義 **fed·er·al·ist** *adj.*：*a federalist future in Europe* 歐洲聯邦主義的未來

the ˌFederal Reˈserve System (also **the Federal Reserve**) *noun* (*abbr.* **the FRS**) (also *informal* **the Fed**) [sing.] the organization that controls the supply of money in the US（美國）聯邦儲備體制，聯邦準備制度

fed·er·ate /ˈfedəreɪt/ *verb* [I] (*technical* 術語) (of states, organizations, etc. 州、組織、機構等) to unite under a central government or organization while keeping some local control 結成聯邦；組成同盟

fed·er·ation AW /ˌfedəˈreɪʃn/ *noun* **1** [C] a country consisting of a group of individual states that have control over their own affairs but are controlled by a central government for national decisions, etc. 聯邦：*the Russian Federation* 俄羅斯聯邦 **2** [C] a group of clubs, TRADE/LABOR UNIONS, etc. that have joined together to form an organization（俱樂部、工會等的）聯合會：*the International Tennis Federation* 國際網球聯合會 **3** [U] the act of forming a federation 聯邦；同盟；聯盟：*Many MPs are against federation in Europe.* 許多議會議員反對歐洲結成聯邦。

fe·dora /fɪˈdɔːrə/ *noun* a low soft hat with a curled BRIM 淺頂捲簷軟呢帽

ˌfed ˈup *adj.* [not before noun] (*informal*) bored or unhappy, especially with a situation that has continued for too long 厭煩；厭倦；不愉快：*You look fed up.*

What's the matter? 你滿臉不高興的樣子。怎麼啦？◇ **~ with sb/sth** *People are fed up with all these traffic jams.* 人們厭煩這麼多的交通堵塞。◇ *In the end, I just* ***got fed up with*** *his constant complaining.* 他不停地發牢騷，終於使我厭煩。◇ *I wish he'd get a job. I'm* ***fed up with it*** (= with the situation). 但願他能找到工作。這樣下去我都煩死了。◇ **~ with doing sth** *I'm fed up with waiting for her.* 我等她等煩了。**HELP** Some people say 'fed up of sth' in informal British English, but this is not considered correct in standard English. 非正式英式英語中，有人說 fed up of sth，但在規範英語中，此用法被視為不正確。

fee **AW** /fiː/ *noun*
1 an amount of money that you pay for professional advice or services 專業服務費；咨詢費；報酬：*legal fees* 律師費 ◇ *Does the bank* ***charge a fee*** *for setting up the account?* 在這家銀行開立賬戶要收費嗎？◇ *fee-paying schools* (= that you have to pay to go to) 收費學校 ➲ SYNONYMS at RATE **2** an amount of money that you pay to join an organization, or to do sth （加入組織或做某事付的）費：*membership fees* 會費 ◇ *There is no* ***entrance fee*** *to the gallery.* 這個美術陳列館不收門票。

fee·ble /ˈfiːbl/ *adj.* (**fee·bler** /ˈfiːblə(r)/, **feeb·lest** /ˈfiːblɪst/)
1 very weak 虛弱的；衰弱的：*a feeble old man* 衰弱的老人 ◇ *The heartbeat was feeble and irregular.* 心搏無力，心律不齊。**2** not effective; not showing determination or energy 無效的；缺乏決心的；無力的：*a feeble argument/excuse/joke* 無力的證據；站不住腳的藉口；乾巴巴的笑話 ◇ *a feeble attempt to explain* 無力的試圖解釋 ◇ *Don't be so feeble! Tell her you don't want to go.* 別那麼軟弱了！告訴她你不想去。▸ **feeble·ness** *noun* [U] **feebly** /ˈfiːbli/ *adv.*

ˌfeeble-ˈminded *adj.* **1** (*old use, offensive*) having less than usual intelligence 弱智的；低能的；愚笨的 **2** weak and unable to make decisions 意志薄弱的；優柔寡斷的；無決斷的

feed /fiːd/ *verb, noun*

■ **verb** (**fed**, **fed** /fed/)

▸ **GIVE/EAT FOOD** 提供／吃食物 **1** [T] to give food to a person or an animal 給（人或動物）食物；餵養；飼養：**~ sb/sth/yourself** *Have you fed the cat yet?* 你餵了貓沒有？◇ *The baby can't feed itself yet* (= can't put food into its own mouth). 這個嬰兒還不能自己吃東西。◇ **~ sb/sth (on) sth** *The cattle are fed (on) barley.* 牛要餵大麥。◇ **~ sth to sb/sth** *The barley is fed to the cattle.* 牛餵的是大麥。**2** [I] (of a baby or an animal 嬰兒或動物) to eat food 進食：*Slugs and snails feed at night.* 蛞蝓和蝸牛夜間進食。➲ see also FEED ON/OFF STH **3** [T] **~ sb** to provide food for a family or group of people 養，養活（全家、一群人）：*They have a large family to feed.* 他們要養活一大家人。◇ *There's enough here to feed an army.* 這兒的東西足以養活一支軍隊。

▸ **PLANT** 植物 **4** [T] **~ sth** to give a plant a special substance to make it grow 施（肥等）：*Feed the plants once a week.* 每星期要給這些花草施一次肥。

▸ **GIVE ADVICE/INFORMATION** 提供意見／信息 **5** [T] to give advice, information, etc. to sb/sth 提供（意見或信息等）；灌輸：**~ sb sth** *We are constantly fed gossip and speculation by the media.* 媒體不斷給我們灌輸流言蜚語和猜測臆斷。◇ **~ sth to sb** *Gossip and speculation are constantly fed to us by the media.* 媒體不斷把流言蜚語和猜測臆斷灌輸給我們。

▸ **SUPPLY** 供給 **6** [T] to supply sth to sb/sth 供給；供應：**~ A (with B)** *The electricity line is fed with power through an underground cable.* 這條電線的電源是通過地下電纜傳輸的。◇ **~ B into A** *Power is fed into the electricity line through an underground cable.* 電力通過地下電纜傳輸到這條電線。

▸ **PUT INTO MACHINE** 放進機器中 **7** [T] to put or push sth into or through a machine 把…放進機器；將…塞進機器：**~ A (with B)** *He fed the meter with coins.* 他把硬幣投入停車計時收費器。◇ **~ B into A** *He fed coins into the meter.* 他把硬幣投入停車計時收費器。◇ **~ sth into/through sth** *The fabric is fed through the machine.* 布料放進了機器。

▸ **SATISFY NEED** 滿足需要 **8** [T] **~ sth** to satisfy a need, desire, etc. and keep it strong 滿足（需要、願望、慾望等）：*For drug addicts, the need to feed the addiction takes priority over everything else.* 對於吸毒者來說滿足毒癮勝過一切。

IDM **ˌfeed your ˈface** (*informal*, usually *disapproving*) to eat a lot of food or too much food 大吃一頓；吃得過飽 ➲ more at BITE *v.*

PHR V **ˌfeed ˈback (into/to sth)** to have an influence on the development of sth by reacting to it in some way 反過來影響（事物的發展）：*What the audience tells me feeds back into my work.* 觀眾給我提的意見反過來對我的作品起到了促進作用。**ˌfeed (sth)↔ˈback (to sb)** to give information or opinions about sth, especially so that it can be improved 反饋，反應（信息或意見）：*Test results will be fed back to the schools.* 測驗的成績將反饋給各學校。**ˈfeed into sth** to have an influence on the development of sth 對…的發展產生影響：*The report's findings will feed into company policy.* 公司的政策將會考慮到報告的調研結果。**ˈfeed on/off sth** **1** (of an animal 動物) to eat sth 以…為食：*Butterflies feed on the flowers of garden plants.* 蝴蝶以園林中草木的花為食。**2** (often *disapproving*) to become stronger because of sth else 因…而壯大；從…中得到滋養：*Racism feeds on fear.* 恐懼心理會助長種族主義。**ˌfeed ˈthrough (to sb/sth)** to reach sb/sth after going through a process or system 最終得以提供給：*It will take time for the higher rates to feed through to investors.* 需要時日投資者才能最終得到較高的回報率。**ˌfeed sb↔ˈup** (*BrE*) to give a lot of food to sb to make them fatter or stronger （用大量食物）養肥，養壯

■ **noun**

▸ **MEAL FOR BABY/ANIMAL** 嬰兒／動物的食物 **1** [C] a meal of milk for a young baby; a meal for an animal （嬰兒的）一次餵奶，一餐；（動物的）一次餵給的飼料：*her morning feed* 她早上的一次餵奶

▸ **FOR ANIMALS/PLANTS** 動植物 **2** [U, C] food for animals or plants 動物的飼料；植物的肥料：*winter feed for the horses* 馬的冬季飼料

▸ **FOR MACHINE** 機器 **3** [U] material supplied to a machine （機器的）進料 **4** [C] a pipe, device, etc. which supplies a machine with sth （機器的）進料裝置，進料器：*the cold feed to the water cylinder* 水缸的冷進水管 ◇ *The printer has an automatic paper feed.* 這台打印機有自動進紙裝置。

▸ **LARGE MEAL** 豐盛膳食 **5** [C] (*informal*) a large meal 豐盛的一餐：*They needed a bath and a good feed.* 他們需要洗個澡，飽餐一頓。

▸ **TELEVISION PROGRAMMES** 電視節目 **6** [U] (*NAmE*) television programmes that are sent from a central station to other stations in a network; the system of sending out these programmes （電視中心台）網絡供給節目（系統）：*network feed* 網絡供給節目系統

feed·back /ˈfiːdbæk/ *noun* [U] **1** advice, criticism or information about how good or useful sth or sb's work is 反饋的意見（或信息）：*I'd appreciate some feedback on my work.* 如果有人對我的工作提出意見我將感激不盡。◇ *The teacher will* ***give you feedback*** *on the test.* 老師會對你的測驗提供反饋信息。◇ *We need both positive and negative feedback from our customers.* 我們需要顧客正反兩方面的反饋意見。**2** the unpleasant noise produced by electrical equipment such as an AMPLIFIER when some of the power returns to the system （電器的）反饋噪音

feed·bag /ˈfiːdbæg/ (*NAmE*) (*BrE* **nose·bag**) *noun* a bag containing food for a horse, that you hang from its head （掛在馬頭上的）飼料袋

feed·er /ˈfiːdə(r)/ *noun, adj.*

■ **noun** **1** (used with an adjective or a noun 與形容詞或名詞連用) an animal or plant that eats a particular thing or eats in a particular way （動植物）進某種食物者，以…方式進食者：*plankton feeders* 以浮游生物為食者 **2** a part of a machine that supplies sth to another part of the machine （機器的）進料器，供給裝置 **3** a container filled with food for birds or animals 鳥食罐；飼料槽

■ **adj.** [only before noun] **1** (of roads, rivers, etc. 道路、河流等) leading to a bigger road, etc. 匯入主幹道（或河等）的：*a* ***feeder road*** *to the motorway/freeway* 匯入高

F

速公路的支路 **2** supplying goods, services, etc. to a large organization（向大機構）供應商品的，提供服務的 **3** (*NAmE*) (of animals on a farm 飼養場中的動物) kept to be killed and used for meat 育肥備宰的；供肉食的

'feeder school *noun* (*BrE*) a school from which most of the children go to a particular SECONDARY SCHOOL or college in the same area 直屬學校（學生畢業後大多進入本地區特定中學或高校）

feed·ing /ˈfiːdɪŋ/ *noun* [U] the act of giving food to a person, an animal or a plant 餵食；飼養；施肥：*breast/bottle feeding* 母乳 / 奶瓶餵養

'feeding bottle *noun* (*BrE*) a plastic bottle with a rubber top which a baby or young animal can suck milk through 奶瓶

F

'feeding frenzy *noun* **1** an occasion when a group of SHARKS or other fish attack sth（鯊魚等魚群的）瘋狂捕食 **2** a situation in which a lot of people compete with each other in an excited way because they want to get sth（對某物的）集體狂熱追求，瘋狂競爭

the Feeding of the Five 'Thousand *noun* [sing.] a situation in which a lot of people need to be given food 眾人求食的場面：*I made breakfast for all my son's friends—it was like the Feeding of the Five Thousand.* 我為兒子的所有朋友做了早餐，就像供應食物給五千人一樣。**ORIGIN** From the Bible story in which Jesus is said to have fed 5 000 people with five loaves of bread and two fish. 源自《聖經》中耶穌用五個餅和兩條魚讓 5 000 人吃飽的故事。

feed·stuff /ˈfiːdstʌf/ *noun* [U] (also **feedstuffs** [pl.]) food for farm animals, especially food that has been processed（尤指經加工的）飼料 **SYN** **feed** ➲ compare FOODSTUFF

feel 🔑 /fiːl/ *verb, noun*

■ *verb* (**felt**, **felt** /felt/)

▸ **WELL/SICK/HAPPY/SAD, ETC.** 健康、不適、愉快、悲傷等 **1** 🔑 *linking verb* to experience a particular feeling or emotion 覺得；感到；體會到：**+ adj.** *The heat made him feel faint.* 炎熱使他覺得快要暈倒了。◇ *She sounded more confident than she felt.* 她的語氣聽起來比她本人的感覺要有信心。◇ *I was feeling guilty.* 我感到歉疚。◇ *You'll feel better after a good night's sleep.* 你晚上睡個好覺就會覺得舒服些。◇ *She felt betrayed.* 她感到被出賣了。◇ *I feel sorry for him.* 我為他感到可惜。◇ **+ adv./prep.** *How are you feeling today?* 你今天覺得怎麼樣？◇ *I know exactly how you feel* (= I feel sympathy for you). 我完全理解你的心情。◇ *Luckily I was feeling in a good mood.* 幸好我當時情緒好。◇ **~ sth** *He seemed to feel no remorse at all.* 他當時似乎一點也不感到懊悔。◇ **+ noun** *Standing there on stage I felt a complete idiot.* 我站在舞台上覺得簡直是一個大傻瓜。◇ **~ like sth** *I felt like a complete idiot.* 我感到完全像個傻瓜。

▸ **BE/BECOME AWARE** 發覺；意識到 **2** 🔑 [T] (not usually used in the progressive tenses 通常不用於進行時) to notice or be aware of sth because it is touching you or having a physical effect on you（通過觸覺）注意到，意識到，感覺到 **SYN** **sense**：**~ sth** *I could feel the warm sun on my back.* 我背上感受到了陽光的溫暖。◇ *She could not feel her legs.* 她的雙腿失去了知覺。◇ *He felt a hand on his shoulder.* 他感到有隻手在他肩上。◇ **~ sb/sth/yourself doing sth** *He felt a hand touching his shoulder.* 他感到有隻手在觸摸他的肩膀。◇ *She could feel herself blushing.* 她可以感到臉都紅了。◇ **~ sb/sth/yourself do sth** *I felt something crawl up my arm.* 我覺得有個東西順着手臂往上爬。◇ *We felt the ground give way under our feet.* 我們感覺到腳下的土地下陷了。 **3** 🔑 [T] (not usually used in the progressive tenses 通常不用於進行時) **~ sth** to become aware of sth even though you cannot see it, hear it, etc. 感到，感覺到（抽象事物）**SYN** **sense**：*Can you feel the tension in this room?* 你能感覺到這房間裏的緊張氣氛嗎？

▸ **GIVE IMPRESSION** 留下印象 **4** 🔑 *linking verb* (not used in the progressive tenses 不用於進行時) to give you a particular feeling or impression 給…感覺；有印象；感受到：**+ adj.** *It felt strange to be back in my old school.* 我回到母校有一種生疏的感覺。◇ *My mouth felt completely dry.* 我感到口乾舌燥。◇ **~ like sth** *The interview only took ten minutes, but it felt like hours.* 面試只用了十分鐘，但覺得像幾個小時似的。◇ *It feels like rain* (= seems likely to rain). 好像快要下雨了。◇ **~ as if/though** ... *Her head felt as if it would burst.* 她覺得頭要爆裂了。◇ *It felt as though he had run a marathon.* 他感到好像跑了一個馬拉松似的。◇ *How does it feel to be alone all day?* 整天獨自一個人的感受如何？**HELP** In spoken English people often use **like** instead of **as if** or **as though** in this meaning, especially in *NAmE*. 英語口語中，尤其是美式英語，常用 like 代替 as if 或 as though 表示此義：*He felt like he'd run a marathon.* This is not considered correct in written *BrE*. 書面英式英語中，此用法被視為不正確。

▸ **TOUCH** 觸摸 **5** 🔑 *linking verb* (not used in the progressive tenses 不用於進行時) to have a particular physical quality which you become aware of by touching 摸起來；手感：**+ adj.** *The water feels warm.* 這水摸着很暖。◇ *Its skin feels really smooth.* 它的皮摸起來真光滑。◇ **~ like sth** *This wallet feels like leather.* 這個錢包摸上去像是皮的。 **6** 🔑 [T] to deliberately move your fingers over sth in order to find out what it is like 觸；摸：**~ sth** *Can you feel the bump on my head?* 你能摸到我頭上那個腫塊嗎？◇ *Try to tell what this is just by feeling it.* 憑手摸摸說出這是什麼東西？◇ **~ how, what, etc. ...** *Feel how rough this is.* 摸摸這有多粗糙。

▸ **THINK/BELIEVE** 認為；相信 **7** 🔑 [T, I] (not usually used in the progressive tenses 通常不用於進行時) to think or believe that sth is the case; to have a particular opinion or attitude 以為；認為；相信：**~ (that)** ... *We all felt (that) we were unlucky to lose.* 我們都認為我們輸了是運氣不好。◇ *I felt (that) I had to apologize.* 我以為我得道歉。◇ **~ it to be sth** *She felt it to be her duty to tell the police.* 她認為她有責任報警。◇ **~ it + noun** *She felt it her duty to tell the police.* 她認為報警是她的義務。◇ **~ it + adj.** *I felt it advisable to do nothing.* 我覺得最好不要作出行動。◇ **(+ adv./prep.)** *This is something I feel strongly about.* 這事令我感觸頗深。◇ *This decision is, I feel, a huge mistake.* 我認為這個決定是個天大的錯誤。➲ SYNONYMS at THINK

▸ **BE STRONGLY AFFECTED** 強烈影響 **8** 🔑 [T] **~ sth** to experience the effects or results of sth, often strongly 受（強烈）影響；（深深）體驗到：*He feels the cold a lot.* 他很怕冷。◇ *Cathy was really feeling the heat.* 凱茜真的感到很熱。◇ *She felt her mother's death very deeply.* 她深感喪母之痛。◇ *The effects of the recession are being felt everywhere.* 經濟衰退的影響無所不在。◇ *We all felt the force of her arguments.* 我們都體會到了她的論據的分量。

▸ **SEARCH WITH HANDS** 用手摸索 **9** 🔑 [I] **~ (in sth/about/around, etc.) (for sth)** to search for sth with your hands, feet, etc.（用手、足等）摸索，尋找，探索：*He felt in his pockets for some money.* 他在口袋裏摸着想找一些錢。◇ *I had to feel about in the dark for the light switch.* 我得在黑暗中摸索尋找電燈開關。

IDM **,feel your 'age** to realize that you are getting old, especially compared with people you are with who are younger than you（尤指與較年輕者比）感到自己上年紀了，意識到自己老了 **feel your 'ears burning** to think or imagine that other people are talking about you 覺得耳朵在發燒（認為或猜測別人在說自己） **feel 'free (to do sth)** (*informal*) used to tell sb that they are allowed to do sth（表示允許）可以隨便做某事：*Feel free to ask questions if you don't understand.* 你要是不懂，可以隨便提問。◇ *'Can I use your phone?' 'Feel free.'* "我能用你的電話嗎？""隨便用吧。" **feel 'good** 🔑 to feel happy, confident, etc. 感到愉快（或有信心等）：*It makes me feel good to know my work is appreciated.* 我知道我的工作得到賞識後感到很高興。 **feel (it) in your 'bones (that ...)** to be certain about sth even though you do not have any direct proof and cannot explain why you are certain 心中感到；本能預感到；直覺確信：*I know I'm going to fail this exam—I can feel it in my bones.* 我知道這次考試我過不了關，我有這種直覺。 **feel like sth/like doing sth** 🔑 (*informal*) to want to have or do sth 想要某物；想做某事：*I feel like a drink.* 我想喝一杯。◇ *We all felt like celebrating.* 我們都想慶祝一番。◇ *We'll go for a walk if you feel like it.* 要是你願意，我們去散散步。 **feel the 'pinch** (*informal*) to not have enough money 手頭拮据；經濟困難：*Lots of* people who have lost their jobs are starting to feel the pinch.* 大量失業者開始感到日子不好過了。 **feel 'sick** (*especially BrE*) to feel as though you will VOMIT soon 覺得要嘔吐；想吐：*Mum! I feel sick.* 媽媽！我覺得惡心。 **feel ˌsick to your 'stomach** (*NAmE*) to feel as though you will VOMIT soon 覺得要嘔吐；想吐 **feel your 'way** **1** to move along carefully, for example when it is dark, by touching walls, objects, etc.（如在黑暗中）摸索着走動 **2** to be careful about how you do things, usually because you are in a situation that you are not familiar with（在新環境中）謹慎行事：*She was new in the job, still feeling her way.* 她對這項工作不熟悉，還在摸索着幹。 **not feel your'self** to not feel healthy and well 覺得身體不好；感到身體不舒服 ➲ more at DEATH, FLATTER, HARD *adv.*, HONOUR *n.*, HONOUR *v.*, JELLY, MARK *n.*, MILLION, PRESENCE, SMALL *adj.*

PHR V **'feel for sb** to have sympathy for sb 同情，憐憫（某人）：*I really felt for her when her husband died.* 她的丈夫去世，我確實同情她。◇ *I do feel for you, honestly.* 說真的，我確實同情你。 **ˌfeel sb↔'up** (*informal*) to touch sb sexually, especially when they do not want you to 猥褻 **SYN** **grope** **ˌfeel 'up to sth** to have the strength and energy to do or deal with sth 覺得有精力（做某事）；感到有能力（處理某事）：*Do we have to go to the party? I really don't feel up to it.* 我們是不是一定得去參加這次聚會？我實在沒有精力應付了。◇ **~ doing sth** *After the accident she didn't feel up to driving.* 她在事故以後，開車已力不從心。

■ ***noun*** [sing.]

▸ **TOUCH** 觸摸 **1** **the feel** the feeling you get when you touch sth or are touched 觸覺；手感：*You can tell it's silk by the feel.* 你一摸就知道這是絲綢。◇ *She loved the feel of the sun on her skin.* 她喜歡太陽照在皮膚上的感覺。 **2** an act of feeling or touching 觸摸；摸：*I had a feel of the material.* 我摸了一下這種織物。

▸ **IMPRESSION** 印象 **3** the impression that is created by a place, situation, etc.; atmosphere（場所、情況等給人的）印象，感受；氣氛：*It's a big city but it has the feel of a small town.* 這是座大城市，卻給人一個小城鎮的印象。◇ *The room has a comfortable feel to it.* 這個房間令人感到舒適。

IDM **get the feel of sth/of doing sth** to become familiar with sth or with doing sth 開始熟悉，開始熟悉做（某事）：*I haven't got the feel of the brakes in this car yet.* 我還沒有掌握這輛車的剎車性能。 **have a feel for sth** to have an understanding of sth or be naturally good at doing it 善於理解某事物；有…的天才：*She has a real feel for languages.* 她有語言天才。

feel·er /'fiːlə(r)/ *noun* [usually pl.] either of the two long thin parts on the heads of some insects and of some animals that live in shells that they use to feel and touch things with（某些昆蟲和貝殼動物的）觸角，觸鬚 **SYN** **antenna**

IDM **put out 'feelers** (*informal*) to try to find out what people think about a particular course of action before you do it 試探

'feel-good *adj.* making you feel happy and pleased about life 使人愉悅的：*a feel-good movie* 令人愉悅的電影

IDM **the 'feel-good factor** (*BrE*) (used especially in newspapers, etc.) the feeling of confidence in the future that is shared by many people（尤用於報章等）前景美好的氛圍

feel·ing 🔑 /'fiːlɪŋ/ *noun*

▸ **STH THAT YOU FEEL** 感覺 **1** 🔑 [C] **~ (of sth)** something that you feel through the mind or through the senses（內心和感官的）感覺，感觸：*a feeling of hunger/excitement/sadness, etc.* 飢餓、興奮、悲傷等的感覺 ◇ *guilty feelings* 內疚感 ◇ *I've got a tight feeling in my stomach.* 我覺得胃部脹痛。◇ (*informal*) *'I really resent the way he treated me.' '**I know the feeling** (= I know how you feel).'* "我實在氣憤他如此待我。""我理解你的感受。" ◇ *'I'm going to miss you.' '**The feeling's mutual** (= I feel exactly the same).'* "我會想念你的。""我也是。"

▸ **IDEA/BELIEF** 想法；信念 **2** 🔑 [sing.] the idea or belief that a particular thing is true or a particular situation is likely to happen 想法；看法；信念 **SYN** **impression**：**~ (of sth)** *He suddenly had the feeling of being followed.* 他突然覺得被跟踪了。◇ **~ (that …)** *I got the feeling that he didn't like me much.* 我的感覺是他並不很喜歡我。◇ *I had a nasty feeling that we were lost.* 我有個不祥的預感：我們迷路了。

▸ **ATTITUDE/OPINION** 態度；意見 **3** 🔑 [U, C] an attitude or opinion about sth 態度；意見：*The general feeling of the meeting was against the decision.* 會議上普遍的意見是反對這個決定。◇ **~ (about/on sth)** *I don't have any strong feelings about it one way or the other.* 我對此既不特別喜歡，也不特別討厭。◇ *She **had mixed feelings** about giving up her job.* 她對辭去工作感到又喜又憂。◇ *My own feeling is that we should buy the cheaper one.* 我個人的意見是我們應該買較便宜的那個。◇ *Public feeling is being ignored by the government.* 公眾的意見遭到了政府忽視。

▸ **EMOTIONS** 情感 **4** 🔑 **feelings** [pl.] a person's emotions rather than their thoughts or ideas 情感；感情：*He hates talking about his feelings.* 他討厭談他的感情。◇ *I didn't mean to **hurt your feelings** (= offend you).* 我不是故意傷害你的感情。 **5** 🔑 [U, C] strong emotion 激動；激情；強烈情緒：*She spoke **with feeling** about the plight of the homeless.* 她激動地講述了無家可歸者的困境。◇ ***Feelings are running high** (= people are very angry or excited).* 群情激奮。

▸ **UNDERSTANDING** 理解 **6** 🔑 [U] the ability to understand sb/sth or to do sth in a sensitive way 理解力；領悟力；敏感：*He played the piano with great feeling.* 他演奏鋼琴十分投入。◇ **~ for sb/sth** *She has a wonderful feeling for colour.* 她的色感特強。

▸ **SYMPATHY/LOVE** 同情；愛 **7** [U, pl.] **~ (for sb/sth)** sympathy or love for sb/sth 同情；愛：*You have no feeling for the sufferings of others.* 你對他人的痛苦毫無同情心。◇ *I still **have feelings** for her (= feel attracted to her in a romantic way).* 我仍然愛她。

▸ **PHYSICAL** 身體 **8** 🔑 [U] the ability to feel physically 身體感覺；知覺：*I've lost all feeling in my legs.* 我的雙腿已完全失去知覺。

▸ **ATMOSPHERE** 氣氛 **9** [sing.] the atmosphere of a place, situation, etc.（場所、情況等給人的）氣氛：*They have managed to recreate the feeling of the original theatre.* 他們設法再現了老戲院原來的氣氛。

IDM **bad/ill 'feeling** (also **bad/ill 'feelings** especially in *NAmE*) anger between people, especially after an argument or disagreement 惡感；交惡；不滿；反感：*There was a lot of bad feeling between the two groups of students.* 這兩群學生互懷敵意。 ➲ more at HARD *adj.*, SINK *v.*, SPARE *v.*

feel·ing·ly /'fiːlɪŋli/ *adv.* with strong emotion 激情地；激動地 **SYN** **emotionally**：*He spoke feelingly about his dead father.* 他談起他死去的父親時激動不已。

feet *pl.* of FOOT

feign /feɪn/ *verb* **~ sth** | **~ to do sth** (*formal*) to pretend that you have a particular feeling or that you are ill/sick, tired, etc. 假裝，裝作，佯裝（有某種感覺或生病、疲倦等）：*He survived the massacre by feigning death.* 他裝死才在大屠殺中死裏逃生。◇ *'Who cares?' said Alex, feigning indifference.* "有誰在乎？"亞歷克斯佯作漠不關心地說。

feint /feɪnt/ *noun, verb*

■ ***noun*** (especially in sport) a movement that is intended to make your opponent think you are going to do one thing when you are really going to do sth else（尤指體育運動中的）假動作，佯攻，虛晃

■ ***verb*** [I] (especially in sport 尤用於體育運動) to confuse your opponent by making them think you are going to do one thing when you are really going to do sth else 做假動作；佯攻；虛晃

feisty /'faɪsti/ *adj.* (**feist·ier**, **feisti·est**) (*informal, approving*) (of people 人) strong, determined and not afraid of arguing with people 堅決而據理力爭的

fela·fel = FALAFEL

feld·spar /'feldspɑː(r)/ *noun* [U, C] a type of white or red rock 長石

fe·lici·tous /fə'lɪsɪtəs/ *adj.* (*formal* or *literary*) (especially of words 尤指言辭) chosen well; very suitable; giving a good result 貼切的；恰當的；妥帖的 **SYN** **apt, happy**：

F

a felicitous turn of phrase 貼切的措辭 ▸ **fe·lici·tous·ly** *adv.*

fe·li·city /fəˈlɪsəti/ *noun* (*pl.* **-ies**) (*formal* or *literary*) **1** [U] great happiness 幸福；十分快樂 **2** [U] the quality of being well chosen or suitable 貼切；恰當；得體 **3 feli·cities** [pl.] well-chosen or successful features, especially in a speech or piece of writing（尤指講話或文章中的）精彩之處，言辭巧妙，措辭恰當

fe·line /ˈfiːlaɪn/ *adj., noun*

▪ ***adj.*** like a cat; connected with an animal of the cat family 貓似的；貓科動物的：*She walks with feline grace.* 她步履如貓般輕盈。

▪ ***noun*** (*formal*) a cat; an animal of the cat family 貓；貓科動物

F

fell /fel/ *noun, verb, adj.* ➲ see also FALL

▪ ***noun*** a hill or an area of hills in northern England（英格蘭北部的）小山，丘陵地區

▪ ***verb* 1 ~ sth** to cut down a tree 砍伐（樹木）**2 ~ sb** (*literary*) to make sb fall to the ground 擊倒，打倒（某人）：*He felled his opponent with a single blow.* 他一拳擊倒了對手。

▪ ***adj.*** (*literary*) very evil or violent 邪惡的；殘暴的

IDM **at/in one fell swoop** all at the same time; in a single action, especially a sudden or violent one 一下子；一舉

fella (also **fell·er**) /ˈfelə(r)/ *noun* (*informal*) **1** an informal way of referring to a man 夥伴；夥計；小伙子；哥們兒 **2** an informal way of referring to sb's boyfriend 男朋友：*Have you met her new fella?* 你見到她的新男朋友沒有？

fel·late /fəˈleɪt; *NAmE* also ˈfeleɪt/ *verb* **~ sb** (*formal*) to perform FELLATIO on a man 吮吸（…的）陰莖；（為…）口交

fel·la·tio /fəˈleɪʃiəʊ; *NAmE* -ʃioʊ/ *noun* [U] (*formal*) the practice of touching a man's PENIS with the tongue and lips to give sexual pleasure 吮吸陰莖；口交

fel·low 🔑 /ˈfeləʊ; *NAmE* ˈfeloʊ/ *noun, adj.*

▪ ***noun* 1** 🔑 (*informal*, becoming *old-fashioned*) a way of referring to a man or boy 男人；男孩；小伙子；傢伙；哥兒們：*He's a nice old fellow.* 他這位老兄人不錯。➲ see also FELLA **2** [usually pl.] a person that you work with or that is like you; a thing that is similar to the one mentioned 同事；同輩；同類；配對物：*She has a very good reputation among her fellows.* 她在同事中的口碑甚佳。◇ *Many caged birds live longer than their fellows in the wild.* 許多籠中鳥比野外同類鳥的壽命長。**3** (*BrE*) a senior member of some colleges or universities（某些學院或大學的）董事：*a fellow of New College, Oxford* 牛津大學新學院董事 **4** a member of an academic or professional organization（學術或專業團體的）會員：*a fellow of the Royal College of Surgeons* 皇家外科醫生學會會員 **5** (*especially NAmE*) a GRADUATE student who holds a FELLOWSHIP（接受獎學金的）研究生：*a graduate fellow* 接受獎學金的研究生 ◇ *a teaching fellow* 兼任教學的研究生

▪ ***adj.*** 🔑 [only before noun] used to describe sb who is the same as you in some way, or in the same situation 同類的；同事的；同伴的；同情況的：***fellow members/citizens/workers*** 同一組織的成員；同胞；同事 ◇ *my* ***fellow passengers*** *on the train* 和我同火車的旅伴

ˌfellow ˈfeeling *noun* [U, C] a feeling of sympathy for sb because you have shared similar experiences 遭遇相同而同情；同病相憐；同感

fel·low·ship /ˈfeləʊʃɪp; *NAmE* -loʊ-/ *noun* **1** [U] (*formal*) a feeling of friendship between people who do things together or share an interest 夥伴關係；友誼；交情 **2** [C] an organized group of people who share an interest, aim or belief（具有共同利益、目的或信仰的）團體，協會，聯誼會 **3** [C] (*especially BrE*) the position of being a senior member of a college or university（學院或大學的）董事職位 **4** [C] an award of money to a GRADUATE student to allow them to continue their studies or to do research 研究生獎學金 **5** [C, U] the state of being a member of an academic or professional organization（學術或專業團體的）會員資格：*to be elected to fellowship of the British Academy* 當選為英國人文社會科學院的院士

ˌfellow-ˈtrav·el·ler *noun* **1** a person who is travelling to the same place as another person 旅伴 **2** a person who agrees with the aims of a political party, especially the Communist party, but is not a member of it 同路人（政黨的支持者，尤指贊同共產黨的黨外人）

felon /ˈfelən/ *noun* (*especially NAmE*, *law* 律) a person who has committed a felony 重罪犯

fe·loni·ous /fəˈləʊniəs; *NAmE* -ˈloʊ-/ *adj.* (*formal*) relating to or involved in crime 罪行的；犯罪的

fel·ony /ˈfeləni/ *noun* [C, U] (*pl.* **-ies**) (*US* or *old-fashioned*, *law* 律) the act of committing a serious crime such as murder or RAPE; a crime of this type 重罪；重刑罪：*a charge of felony* 對犯重罪的指控 ➲ compare MISDEMEANOUR (2)

felt /felt/ *noun* [U] a type of soft thick cloth made from wool or hair that has been pressed tightly together 毛氈：*a felt hat* 氈帽 ➲ see also FEEL, FELT, FELT *v.*

ˌfelt-tip ˈpen (also **ˈfelt tip**, **ˌfelt-tipped ˈpen**) *noun* a pen that has a point made of felt 氈頭筆

fe·male 🔑 /ˈfiːmeɪl/ *adj., noun*

▪ ***adj.* 1** 🔑 being a woman or a girl 女的；女性的：*a female student/employee/artist* 女學生／雇員／藝術家 ◇ *Two of the candidates must be female.* 候選人中必須有兩名是女性。**2** 🔑 of the sex that can lay eggs or give birth to babies 雌的；母的：*a female cat* 母貓 **3** 🔑 of women; typical of women; affecting women 女性的；婦女的；女性特有的：*female characteristics* 女性特徵 ◇ *the female role* 婦女的角色 ➲ compare FEMININE (1) **4** (*biology* 生) (of plants and flowers 植物和花) that can produce fruit 能結果實的；雌性的；有雌蕊的 **5** (*technical* 術語) (of electrical equipment 電氣設備) having a hole that another part fits into 陰的；內孔的；凹的：*a female plug* 內孔插頭 **OPP** **male**

▪ ***noun* 1** 🔑 an animal that can lay eggs or give birth to babies; a plant that can produce fruit 雌性動物；雌性植物；雌株 **2** 🔑 (*formal*) a woman or a girl 女子：*More females than males are employed in the factory.* 這家工廠雇用的女性比男性多。**OPP** **male**

femi·nine /ˈfemənɪn/ *adj., noun*

▪ ***adj.* 1** having the qualities or appearance considered to be typical of women; connected with women（指氣質或外貌）女性特有的，女性的，婦女的：*That dress makes you look very feminine.* 那件衣服你穿起來很有麗人風韻。◇ *He had delicate, almost feminine, features.* 他面目清秀，五官很像女性。◇ *the traditional feminine role* 傳統的女性角色 ➲ compare FEMALE *adj.* (3), MASCULINE *adj.* (1) **2** (*grammar* 語法) belonging to a class of words that refer to female people or animals and often have a special form 陰性的：*Some people prefer not to use the feminine form 'actress' and use the word 'actor' for both sexes.* 有些人不喜歡使用 actress 這一陰性形式，而用 actor 一詞代表兩個性別。**3** (*grammar* 語法) (in some languages 用於某些語言) belonging to a class of nouns, pronouns or adjectives that have feminine GENDER not MASCULINE or NEUTER（指名詞、代詞或形容詞陰性的）：*The French word for 'table' is feminine.* 法語的 table 一詞是陰性。

▪ ***noun*** (*grammar* 語法) **1 the feminine** [sing.] the feminine GENDER (= form of nouns, adjectives and pronouns) 陰性（指名詞、形容詞和代詞的形式）**2** [C] a feminine word or word form 陰性詞（形式）➲ compare MASCULINE, NEUTER *adj.*

femi·nin·ity /ˌfeməˈnɪnəti/ *noun* [U] the fact of being a woman; the qualities that are considered to be typical of women 女子氣質；女氣；陰柔

femi·nism /ˈfemənɪzəm/ *noun* [U] the belief and aim that women should have the same rights and opportunities as men; the struggle to achieve this aim 女權主義；女權運動

femi·nist /ˈfemənɪst/ *noun* a person who supports the belief that women should have the same rights and opportunities as men 女權主義者；女權運動者 ▸ **femi·nist** *adj.* [usually before noun]：*feminist demands/ideas/*

theories 男女平等的要求 / 思想 / 理論 ◇ *the feminist movement* 女權運動

femi·nize (*BrE* also **-ise**) /ˈfemənaɪz/ *verb* **1 ~ sb** to make sb more like a woman 使女性化；使更像女人 **2 ~ sth** to make sth involve more women 增加女性成員：*Offices became increasingly feminized during the 1960s.* * 20 世紀 60 年代期間辦公室的女職員越來越多。

femme /fem/ *adj.* (sometimes *offensive*) (of a HOMOSEXUAL person) having qualities typical of a woman（同性戀者）女人氣的，脂粉氣的，婆 ➲ compare BUTCH (1)

femme fa·tale /ˌfæm fəˈtɑːl; *NAmE* ˌfem fəˈtæl/ *noun* (*pl.* **femmes fa·tales** /ˌfæm fəˈtɑːl; -z; *NAmE* ˌfem fəˈtæl/) (from *French*) a very beautiful woman that men find sexually attractive but who brings them trouble or unhappiness 禍水紅顏

femto- /ˈfemtəʊ; *NAmE* -toʊ/ *combining form* (*technical* 術語) (in units of measurement 用於計量單位) 10^{-15} 飛（母托）；毫微微；千萬億分之一：*a femtosecond* 毫微微秒

femur /ˈfiːmə(r)/ *noun* (*pl.* **fe·murs** or **fem·ora** /ˈfemərə/) (*anatomy* 解) the THIGH BONE 股骨 ➲ VISUAL VOCAB page V59 ▸ **fem·oral** /ˈfemərəl/ *adj.* [only before noun]

fen /fen/ *noun* an area of low flat wet land, especially in the east of England（尤指英格蘭東部）低位沼澤，沼澤

fence 🔑 /fens/ *noun*, *verb*

■ ***noun*** **1** 🔑 a structure made of wood or wire supported with posts that is put between two areas of land as a BOUNDARY, or around a garden/yard, field, etc. to keep animals in, or to keep people and animals out 柵欄；籬笆；圍欄 ➲ VISUAL VOCAB pages V3, V19 **2** a structure that horses must jump over in a race or a competition（障礙賽馬中的）障礙物 **3** (*informal*) a criminal who buys and sells stolen goods 買賣贓物者；銷贓犯 **IDM** see GRASS *n.*, MEND *v.*, SIDE *n.*, SIT

■ ***verb*** **1** [T] **~ sth** to surround or divide an area with a fence（用柵欄、籬笆或圍欄）圍住，隔開：*His property is fenced with barbed wire.* 他的房地產四周圍有帶刺的鐵絲網。 ➲ see also UNFENCED **2** [I] to take part in the sport of FENCING 參加擊劍運動 **3** [I] **~ (with sb)** to speak to sb in a clever way in order to gain an advantage in the conversation 搪塞；支吾；迴避

PHR V **ˌfence sb/sth↔ˈin** [often passive] **1** to surround sb/sth with a fence（用柵欄、籬笆或圍欄）圍住，關住 **2** to restrict sb's freedom 限制自由 **SYN** **hem sb in**：*She felt fenced in by domestic routine.* 她感到被日常家務束縛住了。 **ˌfence sth↔ˈoff** [often passive] to divide one area from another with a fence（用柵欄、籬笆、圍欄）隔開

ˈfence-mending *noun* [U] an attempt to improve relations between two people or groups and to try to find a solution to a disagreement between them 友好關係的修復；修好

fen·cer /ˈfensə(r)/ *noun* a person who takes part in the sport of FENCING 擊劍運動員

fen·cing /ˈfensɪŋ/ *noun* [U] **1** the sport of fighting with long thin SWORDS 擊劍運動 ➲ VISUAL VOCAB page V47 **2** fences; wood, wire, or other material used for making fences 柵欄；籬笆；圍欄；築柵欄用的材料：*The factory is surrounded by electric fencing.* 工廠有電網圍着。

fend /fend/ *verb*

PHR V **ˌfend for yourˈself** to take care of yourself without help from anyone else 照料自己；自謀生計：*His parents agreed to pay the rent for his apartment but otherwise left him to fend for himself.* 他的父母同意替他付房租，其他的則讓他自己解決。 **ˌfend sth/sb↔ˈoff** **1** to defend or protect yourself from sth/sb that is attacking you 抵擋，擋開，避開（攻擊） **SYN** **fight off, ward off**：*The police officer fended off the blows with his riot shield.* 那名警察用防暴盾牌抵擋攻擊。 **2** to protect yourself from difficult questions, criticisms, etc., especially by avoiding them 避開，迴避（難題、批評等） **SYN** **ward off**：*She managed to fend off questions about new tax increases.* 她設法避開了關於新增賦稅的問題。

fend·er /ˈfendə(r)/ *noun* **1** (*NAmE*) (*BrE* **wing**) a part of a car that is above a wheel（汽車的）擋泥板；翼子板 ➲ VISUAL VOCAB page V52 **2** (*NAmE*) (*BrE* **mud·guard**) a curved cover over a wheel of a bicycle（自行車的）擋泥板 **3** a frame around a FIREPLACE to prevent burning coal or wood from falling out 壁爐的柵欄 **4** a soft solid object such as an old tyre or a piece of rope that is hung over the side of a boat so the boat is not damaged if it touches another boat, a wall, etc. 護舷墊（懸掛在船舷的輪胎、繩子等，起防碰損作用）

ˈfender bender *noun* (*NAmE*, *informal*) a car accident in which there is not a lot of damage 不嚴重的撞車事故；輕微車禍

feng shui /ˌfeŋ ˈʃuːi; ˌfʌŋ ˈʃweɪ/ *noun* [U] (from *Chinese*) a Chinese system for deciding the right position for a building and for placing objects inside a building in order to make people feel comfortable and happy 風水

Fen·ian /ˈfiːniən/ *noun* **1** a member of an organization formed in the 1850s in the US and Ireland in order to end British rule in Ireland 芬尼運動成員（19 世紀 50 年代在美國和愛爾蘭成立組織，致力爭取愛爾蘭脱離英國統治） **2** (*informal*, *taboo*) (especially in Northern Ireland 尤用於北愛爾蘭) an offensive word for a Catholic 芬尼亞人（對天主教徒的蔑稱）

fen·land /ˈfenlænd; -lənd/ *noun* [U, C] an area of low flat wet land in the east of England（英格蘭東部的）沼澤地帶

fen·nel /ˈfenl/ *noun* [U] a vegetable that has a thick round STEM with a strong taste. The seeds and leaves are also used in cooking. 茴香（莖作蔬菜，籽和葉亦用於烹調） ➲ VISUAL VOCAB page V31

fenu·greek /ˈfenjʊɡriːk/ *noun* [U] a plant with hard yellow-brown seeds that are used in S Asian cooking as a spice 葫蘆巴（種子用於南亞食物調味）

feral /ˈferəl/ *adj.* (of animals 動物) living wild, especially after escaping from life as a pet or on a farm 野生的（尤指餵養後逃脱的）：*feral cats* 野貓

fe·ring·hee /fəˈrɪŋɡi/ *noun* a word used in some Asian countries for any person with a white skin, especially a European or an American（一些亞洲國家用詞，尤指歐洲或美洲的）白人

fer·mata /fɜːˈmɑːtə; *NAmE* fɜːrˈm-/ *noun* (*music* 音) (*especially NAmE*) = PAUSE

fer·ment *verb*, *noun*

■ ***verb*** /fəˈment; *NAmE* fərˈm-/ [I, T] to experience a chemical change because of the action of YEAST or bacteria, often changing sugar to alcohol; to make sth change in this way （使）發酵：*Fruit juices ferment if they are kept for too long.* 果汁存放過久就會發酵。 ◇ (*figurative*) *A blend of emotions fermented inside her.* 她百感交集，激動不已。 ◇ **~ sth** *Red wine is fermented at a higher temperature than white.* 紅葡萄酒發酵的溫度比白葡萄酒高。 ▸ **fer·men·ta·tion** /ˌfɜːmenˈteɪʃn; *NAmE* ˌfɜːrm-/ *noun* [U]

■ ***noun*** /ˈfɜːment; *NAmE* ˈfɜːrm-/ [U, sing.] (*formal*) a state of political or social excitement and confusion（政治或社會上的）動亂，騷動，紛擾：*The country is in ferment.* 這個國家動盪不安。

fer·mium /ˈfɜːmiəm; *NAmE* ˈfɜːrm-/ *noun* [U] (*symb.* **Fm**) a chemical element. Fermium is a very rare RADIOACTIVE metal. 鐨（罕有的放射性化學元素）

fern /fɜːn; *NAmE* fɜːrn/ *noun* [C, U] a plant with large delicate leaves and no flowers that grows in wet areas or is grown in a pot. There are many types of fern. 蕨；蕨類植物 ➲ VISUAL VOCAB page V11 ▸ **ferny** *adj.*

fer·ocious /fəˈrəʊʃəs; *NAmE* -ˈroʊ-/ *adj.* very aggressive or violent; very strong 兇猛的；殘暴的；猛烈的 **SYN** **savage**：*a ferocious beast/attack/storm* 猛獸；猛烈的進攻；狂風暴雨 ◇ *a man driven by ferocious determination* 為強烈的決心所驅使的人 ◇ *ferocious opposition to the plan* 對這個計劃激烈的反對 ▸ **fer·ocious·ly** *adv.*

fer·ocity /fəˈrɒsəti; *NAmE* fəˈrɑːs-/ *noun* [U] violence; aggressive behaviour 殘暴；兇猛；兇惡：*The police were shocked by the ferocity of the attack.* 警方對那起攻擊的兇殘感到震驚。

fer·ret /ˈferɪt/ *noun, verb*

■ ***noun*** a small aggressive animal with a long thin body, kept for chasing RABBITS from their holes, killing RATS, etc. 雪貂（身體細長，飼養用於驅兔滅鼠）

■ ***verb*** **1** [I] **~ (about/around) (for sth)** (*informal*) to search for sth that is lost or hidden among a lot of things 搜索，四處搜尋，翻找（丟失或藏匿的東西）：*She opened the drawer and ferreted around for her keys.* 她打開抽屜，翻找她的鑰匙。 **2** [I] to hunt RABBITS, RATS, etc. using ferrets 用雪貂獵兔（或捕鼠等）

PHR V **ˌferret sb/sth↔ˈout** (*informal*) to discover information or to find sb/sth by searching thoroughly, asking a lot of questions, etc. 搜索出；搜尋出；查獲

F

Fer·ris wheel /ˈferɪs wiːl/ (*especially NAmE*) (*BrE* also **ˌbig ˈwheel**) *noun* a large wheel which stands in a vertical position at an AMUSEMENT PARK, with seats hanging at its edge for people to ride in（遊樂場的）摩天輪，大轉輪

fer·rite /ˈferaɪt/ *noun* [U] **1** a chemical containing iron, used in electrical devices such as AERIALS/ANTENNAS 鐵氧體（用於製作天線等電氣設備） **2** a form of pure iron that is found in steel which contains low amounts of CARBON（存在於鋼中的）鐵素體，純粒鐵

ferro·mag·net·ic /ˌferəʊmæɡˈnetɪk; *NAmE* ˌferoʊ-/ *adj.* (*physics* 物) having the kind of MAGNETISM which iron has 鐵磁的

fer·rous /ˈferəs/ *adj.* [only before noun] (*technical* 術語) containing iron; connected with iron 含鐵的；鐵的

fer·rule /ˈferuːl; *NAmE* ˈferəl/ *noun* a piece of metal or rubber that covers the end of an umbrella or a stick to protect it（棍杖、傘頂端的）金屬包箍，橡皮包頭

ferry /ˈferi/ *noun, verb*

■ ***noun*** (*pl.* **-ies**) a boat or ship that carries people, vehicles and goods across a river or across a narrow part of the sea 渡船；擺渡：*the cross-channel ferry service* 橫渡海峽輪渡服務 ◇ *We caught the ferry at Ostend.* 我們在奧斯坦德趕上了渡船。◇ *the Dover-Calais ferry crossing* 多佛爾 — 加來輪渡 ◇ *the Staten Island ferry* 往返斯塔滕島的渡船 ➲ COLLOCATIONS at TRAVEL ➲ VISUAL VOCAB page V54

■ ***verb*** (**fer·ries, ferry·ing, fer·ried, fer·ried**) [T, I] **~ (sb/sth) (+ adv./prep.)** to carry people or goods in a boat or other vehicle from one place to another, often for a short distance and as a regular service 渡運；擺渡：*He offered to ferry us across the river in his boat.* 他提出坐他的船載我們渡河。◇ *The children need to be ferried to and from school.* 孩子們上學放學需要擺渡。

ˈferry boat *noun* a boat that is used as a ferry 渡船

ferry·man /ˈferimən/ *noun* (*pl.* **-men** /-mən/) a person in charge of a ferry across a river 渡船船工；渡船主

fer·tile /ˈfɜːtaɪl; *NAmE* ˈfɜːrtl/ *adj.* **1** (of land or soil 土地或土壤) that plants grow well in 肥沃的；富饒的：*a fertile region* 富饒的地區 **OPP** **infertile** **2** (of people, animals or plants 人或動植物) that can produce babies, young animals, fruit or new plants 能生育的；可繁殖的；能結果的：*The treatment has been tested on healthy fertile women under the age of 35.* 這個療法已對 35 歲以下能生育的健康婦女進行了試驗。**OPP** **infertile** ➲ compare STERILE (1) **3** [usually before noun] that produces good results; that encourages activity 能產生好結果的；促進的：*a fertile partnership* 有成效的合夥關係 ◇ *The region at the time was* ***fertile ground*** *for revolutionary movements* (= there were the necessary conditions for them to develop easily). 當時該地區是革命運動的沃土。**4** [usually before noun] (of a person's mind or imagination 人的思想或想像力) that produces a lot of new ideas 點子多的；想像力豐富的：*the product of a* ***fertile imagination*** 想像力豐富的產物

fer·til·ity /fəˈtɪləti; *NAmE* fərˈt-/ *noun* [U] the state of being fertile 富饒；豐產；能生育性；可繁殖性；想像力豐富：*the fertility of the soil/land* 土壤的肥沃；土地的豐饒 ◇ *a god of fertility* 豐收之神 ◇ *fertility treatment* (= medical help given to a person to help them have a baby) 不孕症治療 **OPP** **infertility**

fer·til·ize (*BrE* also **-ise**) /ˈfɜːtəlaɪz; *NAmE* ˈfɜːrt-/ *verb* **1 ~ sth** to put POLLEN into a plant so that a seed develops; to join SPERM with an egg so that a baby or young animal develops 使受粉；使受精；使受胎；使受孕：*Flowers are often fertilized by bees as they gather nectar.* 花常在蜜蜂採蜜時受粉。◇ *a fertilized egg* 受精卵 **2 ~ sth** to add a substance to soil to make plants grow more successfully 施肥於 ▶ **fer·til·iza·tion, -isa·tion** /ˌfɜːtəlaɪˈzeɪʃn; *NAmE* ˌfɜːrtələˈz-/ *noun* [U]：*Immediately after fertilization, the cells of the egg divide.* 卵受精後細胞立即開始分裂。◇ *the fertilization of soil with artificial chemicals* 給土壤施化肥

fer·til·izer (*BrE* also **-iser**) /ˈfɜːtəlaɪzə(r); *NAmE* ˈfɜːrt-/ *noun* [C, U] a substance added to soil to make plants grow more successfully 肥料：***artificial/chemical fertilizers*** 人工／化學肥料 ➲ COLLOCATIONS at FARMING

fer·vent /ˈfɜːvənt; *NAmE* ˈfɜːrv-/ *adj.* [usually before noun] having or showing very strong and sincere feelings about sth 熱情的；熱誠的；熱烈的 **SYN** **ardent**：*a* ***fervent admirer/believer/supporter*** 熱誠的仰慕者；虔誠的信徒；熱情的支持者 ◇ *a* ***fervent belief/hope/desire*** 虔誠的信仰；熱望；強烈的願望 ▶ **fer·vent·ly** *adv.*

fer·vid /ˈfɜːvɪd; *NAmE* ˈfɜːrvɪd/ *adj.* (*formal*) feeling sth too strongly; showing feelings that are too strong 情感異常強烈的；激昂的；充滿激情的 ▶ **fer·vid·ly** *adv.*

fer·vour (*especially US* **fer·vor**) /ˈfɜːvə(r); *NAmE* ˈfɜːrv-/ *noun* [U] very strong feelings about sth 熱情；熱誠；熱烈 **SYN** **enthusiasm**：*She kissed him with unusual fervour.* 她特別熱烈地吻着他。◇ *religious/patriotic fervour* 宗教狂熱；愛國熱忱

fess /fes/ *verb*

PHR V **ˌfess ˈup** (*NAmE, informal*) to admit that you have done sth wrong 供認；坦白 **SYN** **own up**

-fest /fest/ *combining form* (in nouns 構成名詞) a festival or large meeting involving a particular activity or with a particular atmosphere 節日；聯歡；大型聚會：*a jazzfest* 爵士音樂節 ◇ *a talkfest* (= a session involving long discussions) 漫談會 ◇ (usually *disapproving*) *a lovefest* (= an event in which people show too much affection for each other that may not be genuine) 愛筵

fes·ter /ˈfestə(r)/ *verb* **1** [I] (of a wound or cut 傷口或破口) to become badly infected 化膿；潰爛：***festering sores/wounds*** 膿瘡；化膿傷口 **2** [I] (of bad feelings or thoughts 不快的情感或思想) to become much worse because you do not deal with them successfully 更加苦惱；愈益惡化

fes·ti·val 🔑 /ˈfestɪvl/ *noun*

1 🔑 a series of performances of music, plays, films/movies, etc., usually organized in the same place once a year; a series of public events connected with a particular activity or idea（音樂、戲劇、電影等的）會演，節：*the Edinburgh festival* 愛丁堡藝術節 ◇ *the Cannes film festival* 戛納電影節 ◇ *a beer festival* 啤酒節 ◇ *a rock festival* (= where bands perform, often outdoors and over a period of several days) 搖滾樂會演 **2** 🔑 a day or period of the year when people stop working to celebrate a special event, often a religious one 節日；節期；喜慶日 ➲ see also HARVEST FESTIVAL

fes·tive /ˈfestɪv/ *adj.* **1** typical of a special event or celebration 節日的；喜慶的；歡樂的：*a festive occasion* 喜慶場合 ◇ *The whole town is in* ***festive mood.*** 全城喜氣洋洋。 **2** (*BrE*) connected with the period when people celebrate Christmas 聖誕節的：*the* ***festive season/period*** 聖誕節／期間 ◇ *festive decorations* 聖誕節裝飾

fes·tiv·ity /feˈstɪvəti/ *noun* **1** **festivities** [pl.] the activities that are organized to celebrate a special event 慶祝活動 **2** [U] the happiness and enjoyment that exist when people celebrate sth 歡慶；歡樂：*The wedding was an occasion of great festivity.* 這個婚禮是喜慶盛事。◇ *an air of festivity* 歡慶的氣氛

fes·toon /feˈstuːn/ *verb, noun*

■ ***verb*** [usually passive] **~ sb/sth (with sth)** to decorate sb/sth with flowers, coloured paper, etc., often as part of a celebration 給…飾以花彩；結綵於；張燈結綵

■ ***noun*** a chain of lights, coloured paper, flowers, etc., used to decorate sth 彩燈；花彩

Fest·schrift /ˈfestʃrɪft/ *noun* (from *German*) a collection of articles published in honour of a SCHOLAR（紀念某學者的）紀念文集

feta cheese /ˌfetə ˈtʃiːz/ (also **feta**) *noun* [U] a type of Greek cheese made from sheep's milk（希臘的）羊奶乾酪

fetal (*especially NAmE*) (*BrE* usually **foe·tal**) /ˈfiːtl/ *adj.* [only before noun] connected with a fetus; typical of a fetus 胎兒的；胎的：*fetal abnormalities* 胎兒異常 ◇ *She lay curled up in a* **fetal position**. 她像胎兒一樣蜷曲地躺著。

ˌfetal ˈalcohol syndrome *noun* [U] (*medical* 醫) a condition in which a child's mental and physical development are damaged because the mother drank too much alcohol while she was pregnant 胎兒酒精綜合症

fetch 0-w /fetʃ/ *verb*

1 0-w (*especially BrE*) to go to where sb/sth is and bring them/it back（去）拿來；（去）請來：**~ sb/sth** *to fetch help / a doctor* 去請人幫助；去請醫生 ◇ *The inhabitants have to walk a mile to fetch water.* 居民得走一英里路去取水。◇ *She's gone to fetch the kids from school.* 她去學校接孩子了。◇ **~ sb sth** *Could you fetch me my bag?* 你能幫我去取我的包嗎？ **2 ~ sth** to be sold for a particular price 售得，賣得（某價）SYN **sell for**：*The painting is expected to fetch $10 000 at auction.* 這幅畫預計拍賣可得 10 000 元。

IDM **fetch and ˈcarry (for sb)** to do a lot of little jobs for sb as if you were their servant（為某人）打雜，當聽差，跑腿

PHR V **ˌfetch ˈup** (*informal, especially BrE*) to arrive somewhere without planning to 偶然來到；意外到達：*And then, a few years later, he somehow fetched up in Rome.* 後來，過了幾年，他不知怎麼到了羅馬。

fetch·ing /ˈfetʃɪŋ/ *adj.* (*informal*) (especially of a person or their clothes 尤指人或穿的衣服) attractive 吸引人的；迷人的；動人的 ▸ **fetch·ing·ly** *adv.*

fete (also **fête**) /feɪt/ *noun, verb*

■ *noun* **1** (also **fair**) (both *BrE*) (*NAmE* **car·ni·val**) an outdoor entertainment at which people can play games to win prizes, buy food and drink, etc., usually arranged to make money for a special purpose 露天遊樂會；義賣遊樂會：*the* **school/village/church fete** 學校／村莊／教堂義賣會 **2** (*NAmE*) a special occasion held to celebrate sth 慶祝活動；園遊會：*a charity fete* 慈善慶典

■ *verb* [usually passive] **~ sb** (*formal*) to welcome, praise or entertain sb publicly 盛情款待；公開讚揚

fetid /ˈfetɪd/ (*BrE less frequent* **foe·tid**) *adj.* [usually before noun] (*formal*) smelling very unpleasant 惡臭的 SYN **stinking**

fet·ish /ˈfetɪʃ/ *noun* **1** (usually *disapproving*) the fact that a person spends too much time doing or thinking about a particular thing 迷戀；癖：*She has a fetish about cleanliness.* 她有潔癖。◇ *He makes a fetish of his work.* 他迷上了他的工作。**2** the fact of getting sexual pleasure from a particular object（從某物獲得性快感的）戀物：*to have a leather fetish* 有戀皮革的癖 **3** an object that some people worship because they believe that it has magic powers 奉若神明之物；物神 ▸ **fet·ish·ism** *noun* [U]：*a magazine specializing in rubber fetishism* 專登橡膠戀物的雜誌 ◇ *the importance of animal fetishism in the history of Egypt* 埃及史上崇拜動物的重要性 **fet·ish·ist** *noun*：*a leather fetishist* 有戀皮革癖者 **fet·ish·is·tic** /ˌfetɪˈʃɪstɪk/ *adj.*

fet·ish·ize (*BrE* also **-ise**) /ˈfetɪʃaɪz/ *verb* **1 ~ sth** to spend too much time thinking about or doing sth 沉迷於思考（或做）… **2 ~ sth** to get sexual pleasure from thinking about or looking at a particular thing 對…有戀物癖

fet·lock /ˈfetlɒk; *NAmE* -lɑːk/ *noun* the part at the back of a horse's leg, just above its HOOF, where long hair grows 球節（馬蹄上面有叢毛的部份）

fet·ter /ˈfetə(r)/ *verb, noun*

■ *verb* [usually passive] **1 ~ sb** (*literary*) to restrict sb's freedom to do what they want 束縛；限制，抑制（某人的自由） **2 ~ sb** to put chains around a prisoner's feet 給（囚犯）上腳鐐 SYN **shackle**

■ *noun* **1** [usually pl.] (*literary*) something that stops sb from doing what they want 束縛；桎梏；羈絆：*They were at last freed from the fetters of ignorance.* 他們終於從愚昧無知的束縛中解脫出來。 **2 fetters** [pl.] chains that are put around a prisoner's feet 腳鐐 SYN **chains, shackles**

fet·tle /ˈfetl/ *noun*

IDM **in fine/good ˈfettle** (*old-fashioned, informal*) healthy; in good condition 健康；身心俱佳；狀況良好

fetus (*especially NAmE*) (*BrE* usually **foe·tus**) /ˈfiːtəs/ *noun* a young human or animal before it is born, especially a human more than eight weeks after FERTILIZATION 胎兒；胎

feud /fjuːd/ *noun, verb*

■ *noun* an angry and bitter argument between two people or groups of people that continues over a long period of time 長期不和；爭吵不休；世仇；夙怨：**~ (between A and B)** *a long-running feud between the two artists* 兩個藝術家之間的夙怨 ◇ **~ (with sb)** *a feud with the neighbours* 與鄰不睦 ◇ *a family feud* (= within a family or between two families) 家族世仇 ◇ **~ (over sb/sth)** *a feud over money* 為錢爭吵不休

■ *verb* [I] **~ (with sb)** to have an angry and bitter argument with sb over a long period of time 長期爭鬥；爭吵不休；世代結仇 ▸ **feud·ing** *noun* [U]：*stories of bitter feuding between rival drug dealers* 勢不兩立的毒販之間瘋狂爭鬥的故事

feu·dal /ˈfjuːdl/ *adj.* [usually before noun] connected with or similar to feudalism 封建（制度）的：*the feudal system* 封建制度

feu·dal·ism /ˈfjuːdəlɪzəm/ *noun* [U] the social system that existed during the Middle Ages in Europe in which people were given land and protection by a NOBLEMAN, and had to work and fight for him in return 封建制度；封建主義 ▸ **feu·dal·ist·ic** /ˌfjuːdəˈlɪstɪk/ *adj.*

fever 0-w /ˈfiːvə(r)/ *noun*

1 0-w [C, U] a medical condition in which a person has a temperature that is higher than normal 發燒；發熱：*He has a high fever.* 他發高燒。◇ *Aspirin should help reduce the fever.* 阿司匹林能夠退燒。➲ COLLOCATIONS at ILL ➲ compare TEMPERATURE (2) **2** 0-w [C, U] (*old-fashioned*) (used mainly in compounds 主要用於構成複合詞) a particular type of disease in which sb has a high temperature 熱（病）：*She caught a fever on her travels in Africa, and died.* 她在非洲旅行時患熱病而死。➲ see also GLANDULAR FEVER, HAY FEVER, RHEUMATIC FEVER, SCARLET FEVER, YELLOW FEVER **3** [sing.] **~ (of sth)** a state of nervous excitement 激動不安；興奮緊張：*He waited for her arrival in a fever of impatience.* 他焦急不安地等待她的到來。 **4** [U] (especially in compounds 尤用於構成複合詞) great interest or excitement about sth 狂熱：*election fever* 選舉熱

ˈfever blister *noun* (*NAmE*) = COLD SORE

fe·vered /ˈfiːvəd; *NAmE* -vərd/ *adj.* [only before noun] **1** showing great excitement or worry 非常激動的；焦慮不安的：**fevered excitement/speculation** 興奮異常；焦急不安的猜測 ◇ *a* **fevered imagination/mind** (= that imagines strange things) 馳騁的想像力；奇想聯翩 **2** suffering from a fever 發燒的；發熱的：*She mopped his* **fevered brow**. 她擦了他那發燒的前額。

fever·few /ˈfiːvəfjuː; *NAmE* ˈfiːvər-/ *noun* [U] a plant of the DAISY family, sometimes used as a medicine 小白菊（可作藥用）

fe·ver·ish /ˈfiːvərɪʃ/ *adj.* **1** [usually before noun] showing strong feelings of excitement or worry, often with a lot of activity or quick movements 激動的；焦慮不安的：*The whole place was a scene of* **feverish activity**. 整個地方都是一片緊張匆忙的景象。◇ *a state of feverish excitement* 異常激動的狀態 ◇ *feverish with longing* 十分渴望 **2** suffering from a fever; caused by a fever 發燒的；發燒引起的：*She was aching and feverish.* 她疼痛發燒。◇ *a feverish cold/dream* 伴有發燒的感冒；發燒引起的夢 ▸ **fe·ver·ish·ly** *adv.*：*The team worked feverishly to the November deadline.* 這個隊搶在十一月最後期限前拚命工作。◇ *Her mind raced feverishly.* 她思潮起伏。

F

'fever pitch *noun* [U, C] a very high level of excitement or activity 高度興奮；極為激動；狂熱：*Speculation about his future had* ***reached fever pitch****.* 關於他的前途的猜測達到了狂想的地步。◇ *Excitement has been* ***at fever pitch*** *for days.* 狂熱的興奮持續了好些日子。

few 🔑 /fjuː/ *det., adj., pron.*

■ ***det., adj.*** (**fewer**, **few·est**) **1** 🔑 used with plural nouns and a plural verb to mean 'not many'（與複數名詞和複數動詞連用）不多，很少：*Few people understand the difference.* 很少有人瞭解這個差別。◇ *There seem to be fewer tourists around this year.* 今年來訪的旅遊者似乎少了。◇ *Very few students learn Latin now.* 現在學拉丁語的學生少得很。 **2** 🔑 (usually **a few**) used with plural nouns and a plural verb to mean 'a small number', 'some'（與複數名詞和複數動詞連用）有些，幾個：*We've had a few replies.* 我們已得到了一些答覆。◇ *I need a few things from the store.* 我需要從商店買些東西。◇ ***Quite a few*** *people are going to arrive early.* 相當多的人打算早到。◇ *I try to visit my parents* ***every few weeks****.* 我盡量每隔幾個星期看望一次父母。

IDM **,few and ,far be'tween** not frequent; not happening often 稀少；稀疏；不常發生

■ ***pron.*** **1** 🔑 not many people, things or places 很少人（或事物、地方）：*Very few of his books are worth reading.* 他的書值得讀的太少了。◇ *You can pass with* ***as few as*** *25 points.* 只需要 25 分就可以及格。◇ (*formal*) *Few will argue with this conclusion.* 很少有人會不同意這個結論。 **2** 🔑 **a few** a small number of people, things or places; some 有些（人、事物、地方）；一些：*I recognized a few of the other people.* 我認出了一些其他的人。◇ *I've seen most of his movies. Only a few are as good as his first one.* 他的電影多數我都看過。只有少數幾部能與他的第一部媲美。◇ *Could you give me a few more details?* 你能再給我提供一些詳情嗎？ **3** 🔑 **fewer** not as many as 不和…一般多；少於：*Fewer than 20 students passed all the exams.* 不到 20 個學生考試全部及格。◇ *There are* ***no fewer than*** *100 different species in the area.* 這個地區有不少於 100 個的不同物種。 **HELP** Look at the note at **less**. 參看 less 詞條下的註釋。 **4** **the few** used with a plural verb to mean 'a small group of people'（與複數動詞連用）少數人：*Real power belongs to the few.* 真正的權力掌握在少數人手中。◇ *She was one of* ***the chosen few*** (= the small group with special rights). 她屬於少數享有特權的人。

IDM **quite a 'few** 🔑 (*BrE* also **a good 'few**) a fairly large number 相當多；不少：*I've been there quite a few times.* 我去過那裏好多次了。 **have 'had a few** (*informal*) to have had enough alcohol to make you drunk 喝醉了；已醉

fey /feɪ/ *adj.* (*literary*, sometimes *disapproving*) (usually of a person 通常指人) sensitive and rather mysterious or strange; not acting in a very practical way 古怪易衝動的；有點故弄玄虛的；不講求實際的

fez /fez/ *noun* (*pl.* **fezzes**) a round red hat with a flat top and a TASSEL but no BRIM, worn by men in some Muslim countries（一些穆斯林國家男人戴的平頂有纓無邊）紅圓帽

ff *abbr.* (*music* 音) very loudly (from Italian 'fortissimo')（演奏或歌唱）很強（源自意大利語 fortissimo）

ff. *abbr.* written after the number of a page or line to mean 'and the following pages or lines' 及以後各頁（或各行）：*See pp. 96 ff.* 見 96 頁及以後各頁。

fi·ancé /fiˈɒnseɪ; -ˈɑːns-; *NAmE* ˌfiːɑːnˈseɪ/ *noun* the man that a woman is engaged to 未婚夫：*Linda and her fiancé were there.* 琳達和她的未婚夫在那裏。➲ COLLOCATIONS at MARRIAGE

fi·an·cée /fiˈɒnseɪ; *NAmE* ˌfiːɑːnˈseɪ/ *noun* the woman that a man is engaged to 未婚妻：*Paul and his fiancée were there.* 保羅和他的未婚妻在那裏。➲ COLLOCATIONS at MARRIAGE

Fianna Fáil /ˌfiænə ˈfɔɪl/ *noun* [sing.+sing./pl. v.] one of the two main political parties in the Republic of Ireland, on the political left 替天行道士兵黨（愛爾蘭共和國兩大政黨之一，左傾黨派，有時稱作共和黨）➲ compare FINE GAEL

fi·asco /fiˈæskəʊ; *NAmE* fiˈæskoʊ/ *noun* (*pl.* **-os**, *NAmE* also **-oes**) (*informal*) something that does not succeed, often in a way that causes embarrassment 慘敗；可恥的失敗；尷尬的結局 **SYN** **disaster**：*What a fiasco!* 真是使人下不了台！

fiat /ˈfiːæt; ˈfaɪæt/ *noun* [C, U] (*formal*) an official order given by sb in authority（當權者的）法令，命令，諭 **SYN** **decree**

fib /fɪb/ *noun, verb*

■ ***noun*** (*informal*) a statement that is not true; a lie about sth that is not important 謊言；（無關緊要的）小謊，瞎話：*Stop* ***telling fibs****.* 別再撒謊了。

■ ***verb*** (**-bb-**) [I] (*informal*) to tell a lie, usually about sth that is not important 撒謊；說瞎話：*Come on, don't fib! Where were you really last night?* 得了吧，不要撒謊了！昨夜你到底在哪兒？ ▸ **fib·ber** *noun*：*You fibber!* 你騙人！

Fi·bo·nacci ser·ies /ˌfɪbəˈnɑːtʃi sɪəriːz; *NAmE* sɪriːz/ *noun* (*mathematics* 數) a series of numbers in which each number is equal to the two numbers before it added together. Starting from 1, the series is 1, 1, 2, 3, 5, 8, 13, etc. 斐波那契數列（其中每數等於前面兩數之和）

fibre (*especially US* **fiber**) /ˈfaɪbə(r)/ *noun* **1** [U] the part of food that helps to keep a person healthy by keeping the BOWELS working and moving other food quickly through the body（食物中的）纖維素 **SYN** **roughage**：***dietary fibre*** 飲食纖維素 ◇ *Dried fruits are especially* ***high in fibre****.* 乾水果的纖維素含量尤其高。◇ *a* ***high-/low-fibre diet*** 纖維素含量高／低的飲食 **2** [C, U] a material such as cloth or rope that is made from a mass of natural or artificial threads（織物或繩等的）纖維：*nylon and other* ***man-made fibres*** 尼龍和其他人造纖維 **3** [C] one of the many thin threads that form body TISSUE, such as muscle, and natural materials, such as wood and cotton（人或動物身體組織及天然物質的）纖維：***cotton/wood/nerve/muscle fibres*** 棉／木／神經／肌肉纖維 ◇ (*literary*) *She loved him with every fibre of her being.* 她一心一意地愛他。➲ see also MORAL FIBRE, OPTICAL FIBRE

fibre·board (*especially US* **fiber·board**) /ˈfaɪbəbɔːd; *NAmE* ˈfaɪbərbɔːrd/ *noun* [U] a building material made of wood or other plant fibres pressed together to form boards 纖維板

fibre·glass (*especially US* **fiber-**) /ˈfaɪbəɡlɑːs; *NAmE* ˈfaɪbərɡlæs/ (*BrE* also **ˌglass 'fibre**) (*US* also **ˌglass 'fiber**) *noun* [U] a strong light material made from glass fibres and plastic, used for making boats, etc. 玻璃纖維

ˌfibre 'optics (*especially US* **ˌfiber 'optics**) *noun* [U] the use of thin fibres of glass, etc. for sending information in the form of light signals 光導纖維；光纖 ▸ **ˌfibre-'optic** (*especially US* **ˌfiber-'optic**) *adj.*：*fibre-optic cables* 光纜

fi·brin /ˈfaɪbrɪn; ˈfɪb-/ *noun* [U] (*biology* 生) a PROTEIN that stops blood from flowing or being lost from a wound 纖維蛋白，血纖蛋白（有凝血作用）

fi·brino·gen /faɪˈbrɪnədʒən; fɪˈb-/ *noun* [U] (*biology* 生) a PROTEIN in the blood from which fibrin is produced 凝血因子 I；血纖蛋白原；纖維蛋白原

fibro /ˈfaɪbrəʊ; *NAmE* -oʊ/ *noun* (*pl.* **-os**) (*AustralE*) **1** [U] a mixture of sand, CEMENT, and plant FIBRES, used as a building material 石棉水泥（以沙子、水泥及植物纖維混合而成的建築材料） **2** [C] a house that is built mainly of such material 石棉水泥房

fi·broid /ˈfaɪbrɔɪd/ *noun* (*medical* 醫) a mass of cells that form a lump, usually found in the wall of a woman's UTERUS（通常長在子宮壁上的）纖維瘤

fi·broma /faɪˈbrəʊmə; *NAmE* -ˈbroʊ-/ *noun* (*medical* 醫) a harmless lump that grows inside the body（體內生長的）纖維瘤

fi·brous /ˈfaɪbrəs/ *adj.* [usually before noun] (*technical* 術語) made of many fibres; looking like fibres 纖維構成的；纖維狀的：*fibrous tissue* 纖維組織

fib·ula /ˈfɪbjələ/ *noun* (*pl.* **fibu·lae** /ˈfɪbjəliː/ or **fibu·las**) (*anatomy* 解) the outer bone of the two bones in the lower part of the leg between the knee and the ankle 腓骨 ➲ VISUAL VOCAB page V59 ➲ see also TIBIA

fickle /ˈfɪkl/ *adj.* (*disapproving*) **1** changing often and suddenly 易變的；無常的：*The weather here is notoriously fickle.* 這裏的天氣出了名的變化無常。◇ *the fickle world of fashion* 千變萬化的時裝界 **2** (of a person 人) often changing their mind in an unreasonable way so that you cannot rely on them 反覆無常的：*a fickle friend* 靠不住的朋友 ▸ **fickle·ness** *noun* [U]：*the fickleness of the English climate* 英國氣候的變幻不定

fic·tion /ˈfɪkʃn/ *noun* **1** [U] a type of literature that describes imaginary people and events, not real ones 小說：*a work of popular fiction* 通俗小說作品 ◇ *historical/romantic fiction* 歷史／言情小說 OPP **non-fiction** ➲ COLLOCATIONS at LITERATURE ➲ see also SCIENCE FICTION **2** [C, U] a thing that is invented or imagined and is not true 虛構的事；假想之物：*For years he managed to keep up the fiction that he was not married.* 多年來他設法一直給人一種未婚的假象。IDM see TRUTH

fic·tion·al /ˈfɪkʃənl/ *adj.* not real or true; existing only in stories; connected with fiction 虛構的；小說（中）的：*fictional characters* 虛構的人物 ◇ *a fictional account of life on a desert island* 對荒島生活的虛構描述 ◇ *fictional techniques* 小說技巧 OPP **real-life**

fic·tion·al·ize (*BrE* also **-ise**) /ˈfɪkʃənəlaɪz/ *verb* [usually passive] **~ sth** to write a book or make a film/movie about a true story, but changing some of the details, characters, etc. 把（真人真事）改編成小說（或電影）：*a fictionalized account of his childhood* 關於他童年的小說式描述

fic·ti·tious /fɪkˈtɪʃəs/ *adj.* invented by sb rather than true 虛構的；虛假的：*All the places and characters in my novel are fictitious* (= they do not exist in real life). 我小說中的人物地點純屬虛構。

fid·dle /ˈfɪdl/ *verb, noun*

■ ***verb*** **1** [I] **~ (with sth)** to keep touching or moving sth with your hands, especially because you are bored or nervous（尤指厭煩或緊張地）不斷摸弄，不停擺弄：*He was fiddling with his keys while he talked to me.* 和我談話時他不停地擺弄鑰匙。**2** [T] **~ sth** (*informal*) to change the details or figures of sth in order to try to get money dishonestly, or gain an advantage 篡改；偽造；對…做手腳：*to fiddle the accounts* 篡改賬目 ◇ *She **fiddled the books*** (= changed a company's financial records) *while working as an accountant.* 她當會計時對賬簿做了手腳。**3** [I] (*informal*) to play music on the VIOLIN 拉小提琴

PHR V **ˌfiddle aˈbout/aˈround** to spend your time doing things that are not important 虛度光陰；瞎混 **ˌfiddle aˈbout/aˈround with sth** | **ˈfiddle with sth** **1** to keep touching sth or making small changes to sth because you are not satisfied with it 不斷擺弄；不停對…作小修小改：*I've been fiddling about with this design for ages.* 我不斷地修改這個設計已經好長時間了。**2** to touch or move the parts of sth in order to try to change it or repair it 撥弄，擺弄（為改變或修理某物）：*Who's been fiddling with the TV again?* 誰又在擺弄電視機了？

■ ***noun*** (*informal*) **1** [C] = VIOLIN **2** [C] (*BrE*) something that is done dishonestly to get money 欺詐；騙錢行為；騙局 SYN **fraud**：***an insurance/tax, etc. fiddle*** 保險、納稅等騙局 **3** [sing.] (*BrE*) an act of moving sth or adjusting sth in order to make it work 修理；調整；擺弄 **4** [sing.] (*BrE*) something that is difficult to do 難事

IDM **be on the ˈfiddle** (*BrE*) to be doing sth dishonest to get money 搞騙錢勾當 **play second ˈfiddle (to sb/sth)** to be treated as less important than sb/sth; to have a less important position than sb/sth else 當第二把手；居次要地位；當副手 ➲ more at FIT *adj.*

fid·dler /ˈfɪdlə(r)/ *noun* a person who plays the VIOLIN, especially to play FOLK MUSIC 小提琴手（尤指演奏民間音樂者）

fiddle·sticks /ˈfɪdlstɪks/ *exclamation* (*old-fashioned, informal*) used to say that you disagree with sb（表示不同意）胡扯，廢話

fid·dling /ˈfɪdlɪŋ/ *adj.* [usually before noun] (*informal*) small, unimportant and often annoying 瑣碎的；繁瑣的

fid·dly /ˈfɪdli/ *adj.* (*BrE, informal*) (**fid·dlier, fid·dli·est**) difficult to do or use because small objects are involved 微小難弄的；需要手巧的；精巧難使用的：*Changing a fuse is one of those fiddly jobs I hate.* 換保險絲是我不願幹的麻煩事之一。

fi·del·ity /fɪˈdeləti/ *noun* [U] **1 ~ (to sth)** (*formal*) the quality of being loyal to sb/sth 忠誠；忠實；忠貞：*fidelity to your principles* 對原則的忠誠不移 **2 ~ (to sb)** the quality of being faithful to your husband, wife or partner by not having a sexual relationship with anyone else（對丈夫、妻子或性伴侶的）忠貞，忠實，忠誠：***marital/sexual fidelity*** 婚姻／性的忠貞 OPP **infidelity** **3 ~ (of sth) (to sth)** (*formal*) the quality of being accurate 準確性；精確性：*the fidelity of the translation to the original text* 對原文翻譯的準確性 ➲ see also HIGH FIDELITY

fidget /ˈfɪdʒɪt/ *verb, noun*

■ ***verb*** [I] **~ (with sth)** to keep moving your body, your hands or your feet because you are nervous, bored, excited, etc. 坐立不安；煩躁：*Sit still and stop fidgeting!* 坐好，不要動來晃去的！

■ ***noun*** a person who is always fidgeting 坐立不安的人

fidgety /ˈfɪdʒɪti/ *adj.* (*informal*) (of a person 人) unable to remain still or quiet, usually because of being bored or nervous 坐立不安的 SYN **restless**

fidu·ciary /fɪˈdjuːʃəri; *NAmE* also fɪˈduːʃieri/ *adj., noun* (*law* 律)

■ ***adj.*** involving trust, especially in a situation where a person or company controls money or property belonging to others 信託的；信用的；（尤指）受委託的，受信託的：*the company's fiduciary duty to its shareholders* 公司對股東負有的受託責任

■ ***noun*** (*pl.* **-ies**) a person or company that is in a position of trust, especially when it involves controlling money or property belonging to others（尤指財產）受信託人（或公司）

fief /fiːf/ (also **fief·dom** /ˈfiːfdəm/) *noun* **1** (*law* 律) (*old use*) an area of land, especially a rented area for which the payment is work, not money 土地；（尤指）采邑，封地 **2** an area or a situation in which sb has control or influence 領域；勢力範圍：*She considers the office as her own private fiefdom.* 她把辦公室視為她的私人領地。

field 🔑 /fiːld/ *noun, verb*

■ ***noun***

▸ **AREA OF LAND** 田地 **1** 🔑 [C] an area of land in the country used for growing crops or keeping animals in, usually surrounded by a fence, etc. 田；地；牧場：*People were working in the fields.* 人們在田間勞動。◇ *a ploughed field* 已耕地 ◇ *a field of wheat* 麥田 ◇ *We camped in a field near the village.* 我們在靠近村莊的地裏露營。➲ COLLOCATIONS at FARMING ➲ VISUAL VOCAB pages V2, V3 **2** [C] (usually in compounds 通常構成複合詞) an area of land used for the purpose mentioned（作某種用途的）場地：*a landing field* 降落場 ◇ *a medal for bravery in the field* (*of battle*) 作戰英勇獎章 ➲ see also AIRFIELD, BATTLEFIELD, MINEFIELD **3** 🔑 [C] (usually in compounds 通常構成複合詞) a large area of land covered with the thing mentioned; an area from which the thing mentioned is obtained（覆蓋…的或有…的）大片地方：*ice fields* 冰原 ◇ *gas fields*（天然）氣田 ➲ see also COALFIELD, GOLDFIELD, OILFIELD, SNOWFIELD

▸ **SUBJECT/ACTIVITY** 學科；活動 **4** 🔑 [C] a particular subject or activity that sb works in or is interested in 專業；學科；界；領域 SYN **area**：*famous **in the field of** music* 音樂界著名的 ◇ *All of them are experts in their chosen field.* 他們在各自選定的專業中都是專家。◇ *This discovery has opened up a whole new field of research.* 這個發現開闢了一個嶄新的研究領域。

▸ **PRACTICAL WORK** 實地工作 **5** [C] (usually used as an adjective 通常用作形容詞) the fact of people doing practical work or study, rather than working in a library or laboratory 實地；野外：*a **field study/investigation*** 實地研究／調查 ◇ ***field research/methods*** 野外研究；實習方法 ◇ *essential reading for those working **in the field*** 實地工作者必備讀物 ➲ see also FIELD TRIP, FIELDWORK

F

▸ IN SPORT 體育運動 **6** (BrE also **pitch**) [C] (usually in compounds 通常構成複合詞) an area of land used for playing a sport on 運動場： *a* ***baseball/rugby/football, etc. field*** 棒球、橄欖球、足球等場地 ◇ *a sports field* 運動場 ◇ *Today they* ***take the field*** (= go on to the field to play a game) *against county champions Essex.* 今天他們登場與郡冠軍隊埃塞克斯隊比賽。 ➲ see also PLAYING FIELD **7** (in CRICKET and BASEBALL 板球和棒球) [sing.+sing./pl. v.] the team that is trying to catch the ball rather than hit it 守隊 **8** [sing.+sing./pl. v.] all the people or animals competing in a particular sports event（比賽項目的）全體參賽者： *The field includes three world-record holders.* 參賽運動員中有三位世界紀錄的保持者。

▸ IN BUSINESS 商業 **9** [sing.+sing./pl. v.] all the people or products competing in a particular area of business 行業： *They* ***lead the field*** *in home entertainment systems.* 他們在家庭娛樂設備行業中居領先地位。

▸ PHYSICS 物理學 **10** [C] (usually in compounds 通常構成複合詞) an area within which the force mentioned has an effect 場： *the earth's gravitational field* 地球引力場 ◇ *an electro-magnetic field* 電磁場

▸ COMPUTING 計算機技術 **11** [C] part of a record that is a separate item of data 字段；信息組；欄： *You will need to create separate fields for first name, surname and address.* 名字、姓氏和地址要各自編成單獨的輸入欄。

IDM **leave the field 'clear for sb | leave sb in possession of the 'field** to enable sb to be successful in a particular area of activity because other people or groups have given up competing with them 為…的勝利鋪平道路；為…的成功掃清障礙 **play the 'field** (*informal*) to have sexual relationships with a lot of different people 性濫交；亂搞男女關係

■ *verb*

▸ CANDIDATE/TEAM 候選人；隊 **1** [T] **~ sb/sth** to provide a candidate, speaker, team, etc. to represent you in an election, a competition, etc. 使參加競選；使參加比賽： *Each of the main parties fielded more than 300 candidates.* 每個主要政黨都選派出 300 多名候選人。◇ *England fielded a young side in the World Cup.* 英格蘭派出了一支年輕的隊伍參加世界杯賽。

▸ IN CRICKET/BASEBALL 板球；棒球 **2** [I] to be the person or the team that catches the ball and throws it back after sb has hit it 擔任守隊（隊員）；任守方： *He won the toss and chose to field first.* 他在擲硬幣時猜中了，選擇先作守方。 **3** [T] **~ sth** to catch the ball and throw it back 接，擲還（球）： *He fielded the ball expertly.* 他熟練地把球接住了。

▸ QUESTIONS 問題 **4** [T] **~ sth** to receive and deal with questions or comments 處理，應付（問題或意見）： *The BBC had to field more than 300 phone calls after last night's programme.* 英國廣播公司在昨夜的節目播出以後，不得不答覆了 300 多次電話。

'field day (*NAmE*) (*BrE* **'sports day**) *noun* a special day at school when there are no classes and children compete in sports events（學校的）運動會

IDM **have a 'field day** (*NAmE, BrE*) to be given the opportunity to do sth that you enjoy, especially sth that other people do not approve of 有展現本領的機會，有機會大幹一番（尤指他人不贊同的事）： *The tabloid press had a field day with the latest government scandal.* 這家小報利用最近的政府醜聞大做文章。

field·er /'fiːldə(r)/ *noun* (*BrE* also **fields·man**) (in CRICKET and BASEBALL 板球和棒球) a member of the team that is trying to catch the ball rather than hit it 守場員；外場手；外野手

'field event *noun* [usually pl.] a sport done by ATHLETES that is not a race, for example jumping or throwing the JAVELIN 田賽項目（如跳高或標槍） ➲ VISUAL VOCAB page V46 ➲ compare TRACK EVENT

'field glasses *noun* [pl.] = BINOCULARS

'field goal *noun* **1** (in AMERICAN FOOTBALL or RUGBY 美式足球或橄欖球) a goal scored by kicking the ball over the bar of the goal 點球；球越過球門橫木得分的球 **2** (in BASKETBALL 籃球) a goal scored by throwing the ball through the net during normal play 投球中籃

'field hand *noun* (*NAmE*) = FARMHAND

'field hockey (*NAmE*) (*BrE* **hockey**) *noun* [U] a game played on a field by two teams of 11 players, with curved sticks and a small hard ball. Teams try to hit the ball into the other team's goal. 曲棍球 ➲ VISUAL VOCAB page V44

'field hospital *noun* a temporary hospital near a BATTLEFIELD 野戰醫院

'field house *noun* (*NAmE*) **1** a building at a sports field where people can change their clothes, have a shower, etc.（運動場的）更衣室，淋浴間 **2** a building where sports events are held, with seats for people to watch（比賽用）室內運動場，體育館

field·ing /'fiːldɪŋ/ *noun* [U] (in CRICKET and BASEBALL 板球和棒球) the activity of catching and returning the ball 接住並擲還球；守備

,field 'marshal *noun* (*abbr.* **FM**) an officer of the highest rank in the British army（英國）陸軍元帥： *Field Marshal Montgomery* 蒙哥馬利陸軍元帥

'field officer *noun* **1** a person in a company or other organization whose job involves practical work in a particular area or region（公司等的）派駐地區工作人員，地區工作人員 **2** an officer of high rank in the army (= a MAJOR, LIEUTENANT COLONEL or COLONEL) 陸軍校官

,field of 'fire *noun* (*pl.* **fields of fire**) the area that you can hit when shooting from a particular position 射界

,field of 'vision (also **,field of 'view** or *technical* 術語 **,visual 'field**) *noun* (*pl.* **fields of vision/view**, **visual fields**) the total amount of space that you can see from a particular point without moving your head 視野

fields·man /'fiːldzmən/ *noun* (*pl.* **-men** /-mən/) (*BrE*) = FIELDER

'field sports *noun* [pl.] (*BrE*) outdoor sports such as hunting, fishing and shooting 野外運動（如打獵、釣魚、射擊）

'field-test *verb* **~ sth** to test sth, such as a piece of equipment, in the place where it will be used 對（設備等）做現場試驗 ▸ **'field test** *noun*： *Laboratory and field tests have been conducted.* 已進行實驗室試驗和現場試驗。

'field trip *noun* a journey made by a group of people, often students, to study sth in its natural environment（常指學生）野外考察，實地考察，戶外教學： *We went on a geology field trip.* 我們去進行地質野外考察。

field·work /'fiːldwɜːk; *NAmE* -wɜːrk/ *noun* [U] research or study that is done in the real world rather than in a library or laboratory 實地研究；野外考察 ▸ **field·worker** *noun*

fiend /fiːnd/ *noun* **1** a very cruel or unpleasant person 惡魔般的人；殘忍的人；令人憎惡的人 **2** (*informal*) (used after another noun 用於另一名詞後) a person who is very interested in the thing mentioned …迷；…狂；愛好者 SYN **fanatic**： *a crossword fiend* 縱橫填字遊戲愛好者 **3** an evil spirit 魔鬼；惡魔

fiend·ish /'fiːndɪʃ/ *adj.* [usually before noun] **1** cruel and unpleasant 惡魔般的；殘忍的；令人憎惡的： *a fiendish act* 殘忍的行為 ◇ *shrieks of fiendish laughter* 惡魔般的尖笑聲 **2** (*informal*) extremely clever and complicated, often in an unpleasant way（常令人不快地）巧妙複雜的： *a puzzle of fiendish complexity* 深奧複雜的謎 ◇ *a fiendish plan* 巧妙複雜的計劃 **3** (*informal*) extremely difficult 極其困難的： *a fiendish problem* 大難題

fiend·ish·ly /'fiːndɪʃli/ *adv.* (*informal*) very; extremely 很；極其： ***fiendishly clever/complicated*** 極其巧妙 / 複雜

fierce /fɪəs; *NAmE* fɪrs/ *adj.* (**fier·cer**, **fier·cest**) **1** (especially of people or animals 尤指人或動物) angry and aggressive in a way that is frightening 兇猛的；兇狠的；兇殘的： *a fierce dog* 惡狗 ◇ *Two fierce eyes glared at them.* 一雙兇狠的眼睛對着他們怒目而視。◇ *He suddenly looked fierce.* 他突然面露兇相。◇ *She spoke in a fierce whisper.* 她惡狠狠地低聲說話。 **2** (especially of actions or emotions 尤指動作或情感) showing strong feelings or a lot of activity, often in a way that is violent 狂熱的；強烈的；猛烈的： *fierce loyalty* 極度的忠誠 ◇ *the scene of* *fierce fighting* 激烈戰鬥的場面 ◇ *He launched a fierce attack on the Democrats.* 他對民主黨人發動了猛烈的攻擊。◇ *Competition from abroad became fiercer in the 1990s.* 在 20 世紀 90 年代來自國外的競爭加劇。 **3** (of weather conditions or temperatures 天氣或溫度) very strong in a way that could cause damage 狂暴的；惡劣的：*fierce wind* 狂風 ◇ *the fierce heat of the flames* 火焰的熾熱高溫 ▸ **fierce·ly** *adv.*: *'Let go of me,' she said fiercely.* "放開我。" 她極為氣憤地說道。◇ *fiercely competitive* 競爭激烈的 ◇ *The aircraft was burning fiercely.* 飛機猛烈地燃燒着。 **fierce·ness** *noun* [U]

IDM **something 'fierce** (*NAmE, informal*) very much; more than usual 十分；特別：*I sure do miss you something fierce!* 我真的非常想念你！

fiery /'faɪəri/ *adj.* [usually before noun] (**fier·ier**, **fieri·est**) **1** looking like fire; consisting of fire 火一般的；火的：*fiery red hair* 火紅的頭髮 ◇ *The sun was now sinking, a fiery ball of light in the west.* 西邊的太陽像一個發光的火球正在下沉。 **2** quickly or easily becoming angry 暴躁的；易怒的：*She has a **fiery temper**.* 她脾氣暴躁。◇ *a fiery young man* 動輒發怒的年輕人 **3** showing strong emotions, especially anger 充滿激情的；（尤指）怒氣沖沖的 **SYN** **passionate**：*a fiery look* 怒容滿面 **4** (of food or drink 食物或飲料) causing a part of your body to feel as if it is burning 辣的：*a fiery Mexican dish* 味辣的墨西哥菜肴

fi·esta /fi'estə/ *noun* (from *Spanish*) a public event when people celebrate and are entertained with music and dancing, usually connected with a religious festival in countries where the people speak Spanish （通常指說西班牙語國家的）宗教節日，節日

FIFA /'fi:fə/ *abbr.* (from *French*) Fédération Internationale de Football Association (the international organization that controls the sport of football (SOCCER)) 國際足球聯合會；國際足球總會；國際足球協會

fife /faɪf/ *noun* a musical instrument like a small FLUTE that plays high notes and is used with drums in military music 小橫笛（用於軍樂中與鼓合奏）

fif·teen 0→ /,fɪf'ti:n/ **1** 0→ *number* 15 十五 **2** *noun* a team of RUGBY UNION players 聯合會橄欖球隊：*He's in the first fifteen.* 他是聯合會橄欖球球隊隊員。 ▸ **fif·teenth** 0→ /,fɪf'ti:nθ/ *ordinal number, noun* **HELP** There are examples of how to use ordinal numbers at the entry for **fifth**. 序數詞用法示例見 fifth 條。

fifth 0→ /fɪfθ/ *ordinal number, noun*

■ ***ordinal number*** 0→ 5th 第五：*Today is the fifth (of May).* 今天是（五月）五號。◇ *the fifth century BC* 公元前五世紀 ◇ *It's her fifth birthday.* 這是她五歲生日。◇ *My office is on the fifth floor.* 我的辦公室在六樓。◇ *It's the fifth time that I've been to America.* 這是我第五次去美國了。◇ *Her mother had just given birth to another child, her fifth.* 她的母親剛又生了孩子，她的第五個孩子。◇ *the world's fifth-largest oil exporter* 世界第五大石油輸出國 ◇ *He finished fifth in the race.* 他賽跑得了第五名。◇ *Edward V* (= Edward the Fifth) 愛德華五世

■ ***noun*** 0→ each of five equal parts of sth 五分之一：*She cut the cake into fifths.* 她把蛋糕切成五塊。◇ *He gave her a fifth of the total amount.* 他給了她總數的五分之一。

IDM **take/plead the 'fifth** (*US*) to make use of the right to refuse to answer questions in court about a crime, because you may give information which will make it seem that you are guilty （在法庭上）拒絕回答，避而不答 **ORIGIN** From the **Fifth Amendment** of the US Constitution, which guarantees this right. 源自《美國憲法》第五條修正案，該條保障這種權利。

,fifth 'column *noun* a group of people working secretly to help the enemy of the country or organization they are in 第五縱隊（為所在國家或組織的敵人秘密工作的一群人） ▸ **,fifth 'columnist** *noun*

,fifth gene'ration *adj.* (*computing* 計) relating to a type of computer that is starting to be developed which uses ARTIFICIAL INTELLIGENCE 第五代的；人工智能機的

fifth·ly /'fɪfθli/ *adv.* used to introduce the fifth of a list of points you want to make in a speech or piece of writing （用於列舉）第五：*Fifthly, we need to consider the effect on the local population.* 第五，我們必須考慮對當地居民的影響。

fifty 0→ /'fɪfti/ **1** 0→ *number* 50 五十 **2** *noun* **the fifties** [pl.] numbers, years or temperatures from 50 to 59 五十幾；五十年代：*She was born in the fifties.* 她是五十年代出生的。 ▸ **fif·ti·eth** 0→ /'fɪftiəθ/ *ordinal number, noun* **HELP** There are examples of how to use ordinal numbers at the entry for **fifth**. 序數詞用法示例見 fifth 條。

IDM **in your 'fifties** between the ages of 50 and 59 * 50 多歲：*He retired in his fifties.* 他在五十多歲時退休了。

,fifty-'fifty *adj., adv.* (*informal*) divided equally between two people, groups or possibilities 對半（的）；各半（的）；平分（的）；二一添作五：*Costs are to be shared on **a fifty-fifty basis** between the government and local businesses.* 費用由政府和當地企業均攤。◇ *She has **a fifty-fifty chance** of winning* (= an equal chance of winning or losing). 她獲勝的可能性是百分之五十。◇ *Let's split this fifty-fifty.* 咱們把這平分了吧。

,fifty 'pence (also **,fifty pence 'piece**, **50p** /,fɪfti 'pi:/) *noun* a British coin worth 50 pence （英國硬幣）50 便士：*Put a fifty pence in the machine.* 把一枚五十便士硬幣投進機器。◇ *Have you got a 50p?* 你有沒有 50 便士的硬幣？

fig /fɪg/ *noun* a soft sweet fruit that is full of small seeds and often eaten dried 無花果：*a fig tree* 無花果樹 ➲ VISUAL VOCAB page V30

IDM **not care/give a 'fig (for sb/sth)** (*old-fashioned, BrE, informal*) not to care at all about sth; to think that sth is not important 對…絲毫不在乎；完全不把…放在心上；認為…毫無價值

fig. *abbr.* **1** (in writing) FIGURE （書寫形式）圖，表：*See fig. 3.* 見圖表 3。 **2** (in writing) FIGURATIVE(LY) （書寫形式）比喻的，譬如說

fight 0→ /faɪt/ *verb, noun*

■ ***verb*** (**fought**, **fought** /fɔ:t/)

▸ IN WAR/BATTLE 戰爭；戰鬥 **1** 0→ [I, T] to take part in a war or battle against an enemy 打仗；戰鬥；作戰：*soldiers trained to fight* 受過作戰訓練的士兵 ◇ *He fought in Vietnam.* 他在越南打過仗。◇ **~ against sb** *My grandfather fought against the Fascists in Spain.* 我的祖父曾經在西班牙與法西斯分子作戰。◇ **~ sb/sth** *to fight **a war/battle*** 打仗；作戰 ◇ *They gathered soldiers to fight the invading army.* 他們召集士兵對抗入侵的軍隊。 ➲ COLLOCATIONS at WAR

▸ STRUGGLE/HIT 搏鬥；打擊 **2** 0→ [I, T] **~ (sb)** to struggle physically with sb 搏鬥；打鬥；打架：*My little brothers are always fighting.* 我的小弟弟們總在打架。◇ *She'll **fight like a tiger** to protect her children.* 她為了保護孩子，可以兇得像隻老虎。

▸ IN CONTEST 競賽 **3** 0→ [T, I] to take part in a contest against sb 參加（競賽）；競爭：**~ sb/sth (for sth)** *to **fight an election/a campaign*** 參加競選／爭取權益的運動 ◇ **~ for sth** *She's fighting for a place in the national team.* 她正努力爭取加入國家隊。

▸ OPPOSE 反對 **4** 0→ [T, I] **~ (sth)** to try hard to stop, deal with or oppose sth bad 極力反對；與…作鬥爭：*to **fight racism/corruption/poverty, etc.*** 與種族主義、腐敗、貧困等作鬥爭 ◇ *Workers are fighting the decision to close the factory.* 工人在極力反對關閉工廠的決定。◇ *The fire crews had problems fighting the blaze.* 消防隊員撲滅那場大火困難重重。◇ *We will fight for as long as it takes.* 我們要一直鬥爭到底。

▸ TRY TO GET/DO STH 爭取 **5** [I, T] to try very hard to get sth or to achieve sth 努力爭取；為…而鬥爭：**~ (for sth)** *He's still fighting for compensation after the accident.* 他還在力爭事故後的賠償。◇ **~ your way ...** *She gradually fought her way to the top of the company.* 她努力奮鬥，逐漸登上公司的高位。◇ **~ to do sth** *Doctors fought for more than six hours to save his life.* 醫生搶救了六個多小時來拯救他的生命。 ➲ SYNONYMS at CAMPAIGN

▸ ARGUE 爭辯 **6** [I] **~ (with sb) (about/over sth)** to have an argument with sb about sth 爭辯：*It's a trivial matter and not worth fighting about.* 這是一樁小事，不值得為之爭辯。

▸ **IN BOXING** 拳擊 **7** [I, T] **~ (sb)** to take part in a BOXING match 參加（拳擊比賽）：*Doctors fear he may never fight again.* 醫生認為他可能再也不能重返拳壇了。
▸ **LAW** 法律 **8** [T, I] to try to get what you want in court（為…）和某人打官司：**~ (sb) for sth** *He fought his wife for custody of the children.* 他和妻子打官司爭取孩子的監護權。◇ **~ sth** *I'm determined to fight the case.* 我決意要打這場官司。▸ **fight·ing** ⊶ *noun* [U]：*Fighting broke out in three districts of the city last night.* 昨夜這座城市有三個區發生了戰鬥。◇ *outbreaks of street fighting* 巷戰的爆發

IDM **fight your/sb's corner** (*BrE*) to defend your/sb's position against other people 維護地位、立場等 **fight ˌfire with ˈfire** to use similar methods in a fight or an argument to those your opponent is using 以眼還眼，以牙還牙 **ˌfight for (your) ˈlife** to make a great effort to stay alive, especially when you are badly injured or seriously ill（尤指嚴重傷病時）與死亡作鬥爭 **a ˌfighting ˈchance** a small chance of being successful if a great effort is made 要努力奮鬥才有的一線成功機會 **fighting ˈfit** extremely fit or healthy 十分健壯；彪悍 **fighting ˈspirit** a feeling that you are ready to fight very hard for sth or to try sth difficult 鬥志；戰鬥精神 **fighting ˈtalk** comments or remarks that show that you are ready to fight very hard for sth 戰鬥性的言論：*What we want from the management is fighting talk.* 我們要求資方的是發表戰鬥宣言。 **fight a ˌlosing ˈbattle** to try to do sth that you will probably never succeed in doing 打一場無望取勝的仗；雖必敗無疑猶作奮鬥 **fight ˈshy of sth/of doing sth** to be unwilling to accept sth or do sth, and to try to avoid it 不願接受（或做）某事；迴避；躲避：*Successive governments have fought shy of such measures.* 一屆接一屆政府均不願採取這些措施。 **fight to the ˈdeath/ˈfinish** to fight until one of the two people or groups is dead, or until one person or group defeats the other 打到有一方倒下；一決雌雄 **fight ˌtooth and ˈnail** to fight in a very determined way for what you want 堅決鬥爭；全力以赴地鬥爭：*The residents are fighting tooth and nail to stop the new development.* 居民為制止新的建房開發計劃正在全力以赴進行鬥爭。 **fight your own battles** to be able to win an argument or get what you want without anyone's help 獨力戰勝；獨自奮鬥成功：*I wouldn't get involved—he's old enough to fight his own battles.* 我不想參與，他已經長大，能獨自應付了。➲ more at LIVE[1]

PHR V **ˌfight ˈback (against sb/sth)** to resist strongly or attack sb who has attacked you 奮力抵抗；還擊：*Don't let them bully you. Fight back!* 別讓他們欺侮你。要還擊！◇ *It is time to fight back against street crime.* 現在是打擊街頭犯罪行為的時候了。 **ˌfight sth↔ˈback/ˈdown** to try hard not to do or show sth, especially not to show your feelings 忍住，抑制住（尤指情感）：*I was fighting back the tears.* 我強忍住眼淚。◇ *He fought down his disgust.* 他強忍住心裏的厭惡。 **ˌfight sb/sth↔ˈoff** to resist sb/sth by fighting against them/it 抵抗；擊退：*The jeweller was stabbed as he tried to fight the robbers off.* 珠寶商在試圖抵抗強盜時被刺傷了。 **ˌfight ˈout sth | ˌfight it ˈout** to fight or argue until an argument has been settled 以鬥爭方式解決；辯論出結果：*The conflict is still being fought out.* 仍在通過戰鬥解決這次衝突。◇ *They hadn't reached any agreement so we left them to fight it out.* 他們未有達成協議，所以我們讓他們爭出個結果。

■ *noun*
▸ **STRUGGLE** 搏鬥 **1** ⊶ [C] a struggle against sb/sth using physical force 搏鬥；打鬥；打架：**~ (with sb/sth)** *He got into a fight with a man in the bar.* 他在酒吧裏和一個男人鬥毆。◇ *a street/gang fight* 街頭／幫派打鬥◇ **~ (between A and B)** *A fight broke out between rival groups of fans.* 比賽雙方球迷打了起來。◇ *a world title fight* (= fighting as a sport, especially BOXING) 一場世界冠軍爭奪戰（尤指拳擊）
▸ **TRYING TO GET/DO STH** 爭取 **2** ⊶ [sing.] the work of trying to destroy, prevent or achieve sth 鬥爭：**~ (against sth)** *the fight against crime* 打擊罪行◇ **~ (for sth)** *a fight for survival* 為生存而奮鬥◇ **~ (to do sth)** *Workers won their fight to stop compulsory redundancies.* 工人在阻止強制性裁員的鬥爭中取得了勝利。
▸ **COMPETITION** 競賽 **3** [sing.] a competition or an act of competing, especially in a sport（尤指體育運動）比賽，競賽：*The team* **put up a good fight** (= they played well) *but were finally beaten.* 這個隊打得不錯，但最後還是輸了。◇ *She now* **has a fight on her hands** (= will have to play very well) *to make it through to the next round.* 現在她得表現突出才能進入下一輪比賽。
➲ SYNONYMS at CAMPAIGN
▸ **ARGUMENT** 爭論 **4** ⊶ [C] **~ (with sb) (over/about sth)** (*especially NAmE*) an argument about sth 爭論；爭吵：*Did you have a fight with him?* 你和他爭辯了？◇ *We had a fight over money.* 我們為錢吵了一架。
▸ **BATTLE/WAR** 戰鬥；戰爭 **5** [C] a battle, especially for a particular place or position 戰鬥（尤指為奪取某一地方或位置）：*In the fight for Lemburg, the Austrians were defeated.* 在爭奪倫貝格的戰鬥中，奧地利人戰敗了。
▸ **DESIRE TO FIGHT** 鬥志 **6** [U] the desire or ability to keep fighting for sth 鬥志；戰鬥力：*In spite of many defeats, they still had plenty of fight left in them.* 他們儘管多次失敗，但仍然鬥志昂揚。

IDM **a fight to the ˈfinish** a sports competition, election, etc. between sides that are so equal in ability that they continue fighting very hard until the end（體育比賽、選舉等的）直到最後才能決出勝負的鬥爭 ➲ more at PICK *v.*, SPOIL *v.*

Synonyms 同義詞辨析

fight

clash • brawl • struggle • scuffle

These are all words for a situation in which people try to defeat each other using physical force. 以上各詞均指搏鬥、打鬥、打架。

fight a situation in which two or more people try to defeat each other using physical force 指搏鬥、打鬥、打架：*He got into a fight with a man in the bar.* 他在酒吧裏和一個男人鬥毆。

clash (*journalism*) a short fight between two groups of people（新聞）指兩群人之間短暫的打鬥、打架、衝突：*Clashes broke out between police and demonstrators.* 警方與示威者發生了衝突。

brawl a noisy and violent fight involving a group of people, usually in a public place 通常指一群人在公共場合喧鬧、鬥毆、鬧事：*a drunken brawl in a bar* 在酒吧裏酒後鬧事

struggle a fight between two people or groups of people, especially when one of them is trying to escape, or to get sth from the other 指搏鬥、扭打，尤指搶奪、掙扎脱身：*There were no signs of a struggle at the murder scene.* 在謀殺現場沒有打鬥痕跡。

scuffle a short and not very violent fight or struggle 指短暫而不太激烈的扭打、衝突：*He was involved in a scuffle with a photographer.* 他和一名攝影記者發生了肢體衝撞。

PATTERNS

- a fight/clash/brawl/struggle/scuffle **over** sth
- **in** a fight/brawl/struggle/scuffle
- a **violent** fight/clash/struggle
- to **be in/get into/be involved in** a fight/clash/brawl/scuffle
- a fight/clash/brawl/scuffle **breaks out**

fight·back /ˈfaɪtbæk/ *noun* [usually sing.] (*BrE*) an effort by a person, group or team to get back to a strong position that they have lost 回擊；反攻

fight·er /ˈfaɪtə(r)/ *noun* **1** (also **ˈfighter plane**) a fast military plane designed to attack other aircraft 戰鬥機；殲擊機：*a* **jet fighter** 噴氣式戰鬥機◇ *a* **fighter pilot** 戰鬥機駕駛員◇ *fighter bases* 戰鬥機基地 ➲ VISUAL VOCAB page V53 **2** a person who fights 戰士；戰鬥者；拳擊手 ➲ see also FIREFIGHTER, FREEDOM FIGHTER, PRIZE-FIGHTER at PRIZEFIGHT **3** (*approving*) a person who does not give up hope or admit that they are defeated 鬥士；奮鬥者

ˈ**fighter-bomber** *noun* a military plane that can fight other planes in the air and also drop bombs 戰鬥轟炸機

ˈ**fig leaf** *noun* **1** a leaf of a FIG tree, traditionally used for covering the sex organs of naked bodies in paintings and on statues 無花果樹葉（傳統上用作裸體畫像或雕像的遮陰物） **2** a thing that is used to hide an embarrassing fact or situation 遮羞布

fig·ment /ˈfɪɡmənt/ *noun*

IDM **a figment of sb's imagiˈnation** something that sb has imagined and that does not really exist 憑空想像的事物；臆造的東西；虛構的事

fig·ura·tive /ˈfɪɡərətɪv; *NAmE* also ˈfɪɡjə-/ *adj.* [usually before noun] **1** (of language, words, phrases, etc. 語言、詞語等) used in a way that is different from the usual meaning, in order to create a particular mental picture. For example, 'He exploded with rage' shows a figurative use of the verb 'explode'. 比喻的 ➲ compare LITERAL (1), METAPHORICAL **2** (of paintings, art, etc. 繪畫、藝術等) showing people, animals and objects as they really look 形象的：*a figurative artist* 形象藝術家 ➲ compare ABSTRACT (3) ▸ **fig·ura·tive·ly** *adv.*：*She is, figuratively speaking, holding a gun to his head.* 打個比方說，她正拿槍對着他的腦袋。

fig·ure 🔑 /ˈfɪɡə(r); *NAmE* ˈfɪɡjər/ *noun, verb*

▪ ***noun***

▸ **NUMBERS** 數 **1** 🔑 [C, usually pl.] a number representing a particular amount, especially one given in official information（代表數量，尤指官方資料中的）數字：*the latest* ***trade/sales/unemployment, etc. figures*** 最新的貿易、銷售、失業等數字 ◇ *By 2009, this figure had risen to 14 million.* 到 2009 年為止，這個數字已經增長到 1 400 萬。◇ *Experts put the real figure at closer to 75%.* 專家們估計真實的數字較接近於 75%。 **2** 🔑 [C] a symbol rather than a word representing one of the numbers between 0 and 9 數字符號；字碼；位數：*Write the figure '7' on the board.* 把數碼 7 寫在黑板上。◇ *a six-figure salary* (= over 100 000 pounds or dollars) 六位數的薪水（即超過 10 萬英鎊或元）◇ *His salary is now in six figures.* 他的薪水現在是六位數。➲ see also DOUBLE FIGURES, SINGLE FIGURES **3** 🔑 **fig·ures** [pl.] (*informal*) the area of mathematics that deals with adding, multiplying, etc. numbers 算術 **SYN** **arithmetic**：*Are you any good at figures?* 你的算術好嗎？◇ *I'm afraid I don't* ***have a head for figures*** (= I am not good at adding, etc.). 恐怕我沒有算術頭腦。

▸ **PERSON** 人 **4** 🔑 [C] a person of the type mentioned 人物；人士：*a* ***leading figure*** *in the music industry* 音樂界一位主要人物 ◇ *a political figure* 政治人物 ◇ *a figure of authority* 當權者 ➲ see also FATHER FIGURE, MOTHER FIGURE **5** 🔑 [C] the shape of a person seen from a distance or not clearly（遠處人的）輪廓；（隱約可見的）人影：*a tall figure in black* 一個黑衣高個子人影

▸ **SHAPE OF BODY** 體形 **6** 🔑 [C] the shape of the human body, especially a woman's body that is attractive 身材；體形；（尤指）身段：*She's always had a good figure.* 她身材一向很好。◇ *I'm watching my figure* (= trying not to get fat). 我一直注意保持身材。➲ COLLOCATIONS at PHYSICAL

▸ **IN PAINTING/STORY** 繪畫；故事 **7** [C] a person or an animal in a drawing, painting, etc., or in a story（繪畫或故事中的）人，動物：*The central figure in the painting is the artist's daughter.* 畫中間那個人是畫家的女兒。

▸ **STATUE** 造像 **8** [C] a statue of a person or an animal（人、動物的）雕像，塑像：*a bronze figure of a horse* 一座馬的銅像

▸ **PICTURE/DIAGRAM** 圖表 **9** [C] (*abbr.* **fig.**) a picture, diagram, etc. in a book, that is referred to by a number（書中的）圖，表：*The results are illustrated in figure 3 opposite.* 結果已在對頁圖表 3 中顯示。

▸ **GEOMETRY** 幾何 **10** [C] a particular shape formed by lines or surfaces 圖形：*a five-sided figure* 五邊形 ◇ *a solid figure* 立體圖形

▸ **MOVEMENT ON ICE** 冰上動作 **11** [C] a pattern or series of movements performed on ice（冰上表演動作的）花樣

IDM **be/become a figure of ˈfun** to be/become sb that other people laugh at 是嘲笑的對象；成為笑柄 **cut a ... ˈfigure** (of a person 人) to have a particular appearance 顯出…的樣子；顯得：*He cut a striking figure in his white dinner jacket.* 他穿着白色晚禮服顯得十分出眾。 **put a figure on sth** to say the exact price or number of sth 定價；說出…的準確數字 ➲ more at FACT

▪ ***verb***

▸ **BE IMPORTANT** 重要 **1** 🔑 [I] to be part of a process, situation, etc. especially an important part 是重要部份；是…的部份 **SYN** **feature**：*My feelings about the matter didn't seem to figure at all.* 我對這個問題的意見似乎根本無足輕重。◇ **~ (as sth) (in/on/among sth)** *Do I still figure in your plans?* 在你的計劃中還包括我嗎？◇ *The question of the peace settlement is likely to* ***figure prominently*** *in the talks.* 和平解決的問題很可能是這次談判的突出重點。◇ *It did not figure high on her list of priorities.* 這沒有列入她最優先考慮辦理的事項。

▸ **THINK/DECIDE** 認為；認定 **2** [T] (*informal*) to think or decide that sth will happen or is true 認為，認定（某事將發生或屬實）：**~ (that) ...** *I figured (that) if I took the night train, I could be in Scotland by morning.* 我認為，如果我坐夜班火車，早上就可以到達蘇格蘭。◇ *We figured the sensible thing to do was to wait.* 我們判定，明智的做法是等待。◇ **~ sth** *That's what I figured.* 這就是我的看法。◇ **~ why, whether, etc. ...** *He tried to figure why she had come.* 他想弄清楚她怎麼來了。

▸ **CALCULATE** 計算 **3** [T] **~ sth (at sth)** (*NAmE*) to calculate an amount or the cost of sth 計算（數量或成本）：*We figured the attendance at 150 000.* 我們估計有 15 萬人參加。

IDM **go ˈfigure** (*NAmE, informal*) used to say that you do not understand the reason for sth, or that you do not want to give an explanation for sth because you think it is obvious 搞不懂；明擺着不用解釋：*People are more aware of the risks of smoking nowadays, but more young women are smoking than ever. Go figure!* 現在人們更加瞭解吸煙的危害，但吸煙的年輕女性倒比以往多了。真讓人搞不懂！ **it/that figures** used to say that sth was expected or seems logical（表示應該或似乎合乎邏輯）有道理，合乎情理：*'John called in sick.' 'That figures, he wasn't feeling well yesterday.'* "約翰打電話來說他病了。" "這合乎情理，他昨天就感到不舒服。" ◇ (*disapproving*) *'She was late again.' 'Yes, that figures.'* "她又遲到了。" "是呀，她總是這樣。"

PHR V ˈ**figure on sth** | ˈ**figure on (sb/sth) doing sth** to plan sth or to do sth; to expect sth (to happen) 計劃；打算；預料到 **SYN** **plan on**：*I hadn't figured on getting home so late.* 我沒有估計到這麼晚才回到家。 ˌ**figure sb/sth↔ˈout** **1** 🔑 to think about sb/sth until you understand them/it 弄懂；弄清楚；弄明白 **SYN** **work out**：*We couldn't figure her out.* 我們摸不透她。◇ **~ how, what, etc. ...** *I can't figure out how to do this.* 我弄不懂怎樣做這件事。 **2** 🔑 to calculate an amount or the cost of sth 計算（數量或成本） **SYN** **work out**：**~ how, what, etc. ...** *Have you figured out how much the trip will cost?* 旅行要花多少費用你算出來沒有？

fig·ured /ˈfɪɡəd; *NAmE* ˈfɪɡjərd/ *adj.* [only before noun] (*technical* 術語) decorated with a small pattern 飾以圖案的：*figured pottery* 繪有圖案的陶器

fig·ure·head /ˈfɪɡəhed; *NAmE* -ɡjərh-/ *noun* **1** a person who is in a high position in a country or an organization but who has no real power or authority 有名無實的領導人；傀儡 **2** a large wooden statue, usually representing a woman, that used to be fixed to the front end of a ship（過去的）艏飾像

ˈ**figure-hugging** *adj.* [usually before noun] (of a piece of clothing 衣服) tight in an attractive way that shows the shape of a woman's body 緊身的；包身的；烘托線條的

ˌ**figure of ˈeight** (*BrE*) (*NAmE* ˌ**figure ˈeight**) *noun* (*pl.* **figures of eight, figure eights**) a pattern or movement that looks like the shape of the number 8（圖案、運動的）8 字形

ˌ**figure of ˈspeech** *noun* (*pl.* **figures of speech**) a word or phrase used in a different way from its usual meaning in order to create a particular mental picture or effect 修辭格；修辭手段

'figure-skating *noun* [U] a type of ICE SKATING in which you cut patterns in the ice and do jumps and spins 花樣滑冰；花式溜冰 ➲ compare SPEED SKATING

fig·ur·ine /'fɪgəriːn; *NAmE* ˌfɪgjə'riːn/ *noun* a small statue of a person or an animal used as a decorative object（人、動物的）小雕像，小塑像

fila·ment /'fɪləmənt/ *noun* **1** a thin wire in a LIGHT BULB that produces light when electricity is passed through it（電燈泡的）燈絲；絲極 **2** (*technical* 術語) a long thin piece of sth that looks like a thread 細絲；絲狀物：*glass/metal filaments* 玻璃 / 金屬絲

F

fil·bert /'fɪlbət; *NAmE* -bərt/ *noun* (*especially NAmE*) = HAZELNUT

filch /fɪltʃ/ *verb* **~ sth** (*informal*) to steal sth, especially sth small or not very valuable 偷（尤指小的或不貴重的物品）SYN **pinch**

file 0→ AW /faɪl/ *noun, verb*

■ *noun* **1** 0→ a box or folded piece of card for keeping loose papers together and in order 文件夾；卷宗：*a box file* 文件箱 ◇ *A stack of files awaited me on my desk.* 我桌上有一堆文件正待我去處理。➲ VISUAL VOCAB page V69 **2** 0→ a collection of information stored together in a computer, under a particular name（計算機的）文件，檔案：*to* ***access/copy/create/delete/download/save a file*** 存取 / 複製 / 建立 / 刪除 / 下載 / 保存文件 ◇ *Every file on the same disk must have a different name.* 同一磁盤上的每一個文件都必須有不同的文件名。➲ see also PDF **3** 0→ a file and the information it contains, for example about a particular person or subject 檔案：*secret police files* 警方秘密檔案 ◇ *Your application will be kept* ***on file*** (= in a file, to be used later). 你的申請書將存檔。◇ **~ on sb** *to* ***have/open/keep a confidential file*** *on sb* 有 / 設立 / 保存某人的機密檔案 ◇ *Police have reopened the file* (= have started collecting information again) *on the missing girl.* 警方對失蹤的女孩已重新建檔調查。 **4** a metal tool with a rough surface for cutting or shaping hard substances or for making them smooth 銼；銼刀 ➲ VISUAL VOCAB page V20 ➲ see also NAIL FILE **5** a line of people or things, one behind the other 排成一行的人（或物）：*They set off* ***in file*** *behind the teacher.* 他們跟在教師後面魚貫出發。

IDM **(in) single 'file** (also *old-fashioned* **(in) Indian file**) (in) one line, one behind the other 一路縱隊；單行：*They made their way in single file along the cliff path.* 他們一個接着一個沿懸崖小徑前進。

■ *verb* **1** [T] to put and keep documents, etc. in a particular place and in a particular order so that you can find them easily; to put a document into a file 把（文件等）歸檔：**~ sth (+ adv./prep.)** *The forms should be filed alphabetically.* 這些表格應該按字母順序歸檔。◇ *Please file it in my 'Research' file.* 請把它歸入我的研究類檔案。◇ **~ sth away** *I filed the letters away in a drawer.* 我把信件存放到抽屜裏了。 **2** [I, T] (*law* 律) to present sth so that it can be officially recorded and dealt with 提起（訴訟）；提出（申請）；送交（備案）：**~ for sth** *to file for divorce* 提交離婚申請書 ◇ **~ sth** *to* ***file a claim/complaint/petition/lawsuit*** 提出索賠 / 申訴；呈交訴狀；提起訴訟 ◇ **~ to do sth** *He filed to divorce his wife.* 他提交了與妻子離婚的申請。 **3** [T] **~ sth** (of a journalist 記者) to send a report or a story to your employer 發送（報道給報社） **4** [I] **+ adv./prep.** to walk in a line of people, one after the other, in a particular direction 排成一行行走：*The doors of the museum opened and the visitors began to file in.* 博物館開門了，參觀者魚貫而入。 **5** [T] **~ sth (away/down, etc.)** to cut or shape sth or make sth smooth using a file 銼平；銼去；銼薄；銼光滑：*to file your nails* 把指甲銼光滑

'file cabinet (*NAmE*) (*BrE* **'filing cabinet**) *noun* a piece of office furniture with deep drawers for storing files 文件櫃；檔案櫃 ➲ VISUAL VOCAB page V69

'file clerk (*NAmE*) (*BrE* **'filing clerk**) *noun* a person whose job is to FILE letters, etc. and do general office tasks 檔案管理員；資料員

file·name /'faɪlneɪm/ *noun* (*computing* 計) a name given to a computer file in order to identify it 文件名；檔案名

'file sharing *noun* [U] the practice of sharing computer files with other people over the Internet or another computer network 文件共享：*Illegal music file-sharing sites have spread through the Net.* 非法的音樂文件共享網站已遍佈互聯網。

filet *noun* (*NAmE*) = FILLET

fil·ial /'fɪliəl/ *adj.* [usually before noun] (*formal*) connected with the way children behave towards their parents 子女（對父母）的：***filial affection/duty*** 子女的親情 / 孝道

fili·bus·ter /'fɪlɪbʌstə(r)/ *noun* (*especially NAmE*) a long speech made in a parliament in order to delay a vote（議會中為拖延表決的）冗長演說 ▶ **fili·bus·ter** *verb* [I]

fili·gree /'fɪlɪgriː/ *noun* [U] delicate decoration made from gold or silver wire 金銀絲飾品

fil·ing /'faɪlɪŋ/ *noun* **1** [U] the act of putting documents, letters, etc. into a file 存檔；歸檔 **2** [C] (*especially NAmE*) something that is placed in an official record 存檔檔案；歸檔記錄：*a bankruptcy filing* 破產檔案 **3 filings** [pl.] very small pieces of metal, made when a larger piece of metal is filed 銼屑：*iron filings* 鐵銼屑

'filing cabinet (*BrE*) (*NAmE* **'file cabinet**) *noun* a piece of office furniture with deep drawers for storing files 文件櫃；檔案櫃 ➲ VISUAL VOCAB page V69

'filing clerk (*BrE*) (*NAmE* **'file clerk**) *noun* a person whose job is to FILE letters, etc. and do general office tasks 檔案管理員

Fi·li·pino /ˌfɪlɪ'piːnəʊ; *NAmE* -noʊ/ *noun, adj.*

■ *noun* (*pl.* **-os**) **1** [C] a person from the Philippines 菲律賓人 **2** [U] the language of the Philippines 菲律賓語

■ *adj.* connected with the Philippines, its people or their language 菲律賓的；菲律賓人的；菲律賓語的

fill 0→ /fɪl/ *verb, noun*

■ *verb*

▸ MAKE FULL 使充滿 **1** 0→ [T, I] to make sth full of sth; to become full of sth（使）充滿，裝滿，注滿，填滿：**~ sth** *Please fill this glass for me.* 請把這個杯子給我倒滿。◇ *to fill a vacuum/void* 填補真空 / 空間 ◇ *The school is* ***filled to capacity****.* 這所學校已經滿員。◇ *Smoke filled the room.* 房間裏煙霧彌漫。◇ *The wind filled the sails.* 風吹帆張。◇ *A Disney film can always fill cinemas* (= attract a lot of people to see it). 迪斯尼電影總是讓電影院座滿。◇ **~ sth with sth** *to fill a hole with earth/a bucket with water* 用泥土把洞填起來；把水桶裝滿水 ◇ **~ sth + adj.** *Fill a pan half full of water.* 給平底鍋裝半鍋水。◇ **~ (with sth)** *The room was filling quickly.* 房間很快就擠滿了人。◇ *Her eyes suddenly filled with tears.* 她的眼裏突然噙滿了淚水。◇ *The sails filled with wind.* 帆脹滿了風。

▸ BLOCK HOLE 堵洞 **2** 0→ [T] **~ sth (with sth)** to block a hole with a substance 堵塞，填補（洞、孔）：*The crack in the wall had been filled with plaster.* 牆上的洞已用灰泥堵上了。◇ *I need to have two teeth filled* (= to have FILLINGS put in them). 我有兩顆牙要補。◇ (*figurative*) *The product has* ***filled a gap*** *in the market.* 這個產品填補了市場的空白。

▸ WITH FEELING 感情 **3** 0→ [T] **~ sb (with sth)** to make sb have a strong feeling 使充滿（感情）：*We were all filled with admiration for his achievements.* 我們都十分佩服他的成就。

▸ WITH SMELL/SOUND/LIGHT 氣味；聲；光 **4** 0→ [T] **~ sth (with sth)** if a smell, sound or light **fills** a place, it is very strong, loud or bright and easy to notice 使遍及；瀰漫；佈滿；照滿

▸ -FILLED 充滿… **5** (in adjectives 構成形容詞) full of the thing mentioned 充滿…的：*a smoke-filled room* 煙霧瀰漫的房間 ◇ *a fun-filled day* 充滿歡樂的一天

▸ A NEED 需要 **6** [T] **~ sth** to stop people from continuing to want or need sth 滿足：*More nurseries will be built to fill the need for high-quality child care.* 將建立更多的託兒所以滿足高質量兒童保育的需要。

▸ JOB 工作 **7** [T] **~ sth** to do a job, have a role or position, etc. 擔任；充任：*He fills the post satisfactorily* (= performs his duties well). 他很盡職。◇ *The team needs someone to fill the role of manager very soon.* 該隊迫切需要一個人來擔任經理。 **8** [T] **~ sth** to appoint sb to a job 派人擔任：*The vacancy has already been filled.* 該空缺已有人接任。

▸ TIME 時間 **9** [T] **~ sth (up)** to use up a particular period of time doing sth 耗去；打發；消磨：*How do you fill your day now that you've retired?* 現在你已退休了，怎樣打發你的日子？

▸ WITH FOOD 食物 **10** [T] **~ sb/yourself (up) (with sth)** (*informal*) to make sb/yourself feel unable to eat any more （使）吃飽：*The kids filled themselves with snacks.* 孩子們吃點心吃飽了。

▸ AN ORDER 訂單 **11** [T] **~ sth** if sb **fills** an order or a PRESCRIPTION, they give the customer what they have asked for （按訂單）供應；交付（訂貨）；（按藥方）配藥 ➲ see also UNFILLED

IDM **fill sb's shoes/boots** to do sb's job in an acceptable way when they are not there 妥善代職 ➲ more at BILL *n.*

PHR V **ˌfill ˈin (for sb)** to do sb's job for a short time while they are not there 暫時代替；臨時補缺 **ˌfill sth↔ˈin 1** (*BrE*) to complete a form, etc. by writing information on it 填寫（表格等）：*to fill in an application form* 填寫申請表 ◇ *To order, fill in the coupon on p 54.* 訂貨填寫 54 頁上的訂貨單。 **2** to fill sth completely 填滿；塞滿：*The hole has been filled in.* 洞已填平。 **3** to spend time doing sth while waiting for sth more important 消磨，打發（時間）：*He filled in the rest of the day watching television.* 他看電視打發了那天餘下的時光。 **4** to complete a drawing, etc. by covering the space inside the outline with colour 給（圖畫等）最後着色 **ˌfill sb ˈin (on sth)** to tell sb about sth that has happened 向…提供（情況） **ˌfill ˈout** to become larger, rounder or fatter 膨脹；擴張；長胖；長肥 **ˌfill sth↔ˈout** = FILL STH IN (1) **ˌfill ˈup (with sth) | ˌfill sth↔ˈup (with sth)** to become completely full; to make sth completely full 充滿；（使）填滿；裝滿：*The ditches had filled up with mud.* 溝渠中塞滿了淤泥。◇ *to fill up the tank with oil* 把油罐裝滿油

■ ***noun*** [sing.] **1 your ~ (of sth/sb)** as much of sth/sb as you are willing to accept 填滿…的量；足夠…的量：*I've had my fill of entertaining for one week.* 我已足足享受了一週的娛樂活動。 **2 your ~ (of food/drink)** as much as you can eat/drink 吃飽的量；喝足的量

fill·er /ˈfɪlə(r)/ *noun* **1** [U, C] a substance used to fill holes or cracks, especially in walls before painting them 填充物，填料（尤用於漆牆前填孔或縫） **2** [C] (*informal*) something that is not important but is used to complete sth else because nothing better is available 充數的東西；填補空白之物：*The song was originally a filler on their first album.* 這首歌在他們第一張專輯中本來是用來湊時間的。 ➲ see also STOCKING FILLER

ˈfiller cap *noun* a lid for covering the end of the pipe through which petrol/gas is put into a vehicle （汽車）加油口蓋，管蓋

fil·let /ˈfɪlɪt; *NAmE* fɪˈleɪ/ *noun, verb*

■ ***noun*** (*NAmE* also **filet**) [C, U] a piece of meat or fish that has no bones in it 無骨肉片；去骨魚片：*plaice fillets* 鰈魚片 ◇ *a fillet of cod* 一片鱈魚片 ◇ *fillet steak* 無骨牛排

■ ***verb*** **~ sth** to remove the bones from a piece of fish or meat; to cut fish or meat into fillets 剔去（魚、肉的）骨頭；把（魚、肉）切成片

fill·ing /ˈfɪlɪŋ/ *noun, adj.*

■ ***noun*** **1** [C] a small amount of metal or other material used to fill a hole in a tooth （補牙的）填料：*I had to have two fillings at the dentist's today.* 我今天不得不在牙科診所補了兩顆牙。 **2** [C, U] food put inside a SANDWICH, cake, PIE, etc. （糕點等的）餡：*a sponge cake with cream and jam filling* 奶油果醬作餡的海綿蛋糕 ◇ *a wide range of sandwich fillings* 各種各樣的三明治餡 **3** [C, U] soft material used to fill CUSHIONS, PILLOWS, etc. （枕頭、靠墊等的）填充物，填料

■ ***adj.*** (of food 食物) making your stomach feel full 能填飽肚子的：*This cake is very filling.* 這種餅很能填飽肚子。

ˈfilling station *noun* = GAS STATION, PETROL STATION

fil·lip /ˈfɪlɪp/ *noun* [sing.] **a ~ (to/for sth)** (*formal*) a thing or person that causes sth to improve suddenly 起推動作用的人（或事物） SYN **boost**：*A drop in interest rates gave a welcome fillip to the housing market.* 降低利率給房屋市場帶來利好刺激。

ˈfill-up *noun* an occasion when a car is completely filled up with petrol/gas （汽車）加滿油

filly /ˈfɪli/ *noun* (*pl.* **-ies**) a young female horse 小牝馬 ➲ compare COLT (1), MARE

film 0‑w /fɪlm/ *noun, verb*

■ ***noun***

▸ MOVING PICTURES 電影 **1** 0‑w [C] (*especially BrE*) (*NAmE* usually **movie**) a series of moving pictures recorded with sound that tells a story, shown on television or at the cinema/movie theater 電影；影片：*Let's go to the cinema— **there's a good film on** this week.* 咱們去看電影吧，本週在上映一部好片子。◇ *Let's stay in and **watch a film**.* 咱們待在家裏看電影吧。◇ *a **horror/documentary/feature film*** 恐怖片；紀錄片；故事片 ◇ *a **silent film*** (= one recorded without sound) 無聲電影 ◇ *an international **film festival*** 國際電影節 ◇ *a **film crew/critic/director/producer*** 電影攝製組／評論家／導演／製作人 ◇ *the **film version** of the novel* 由同名小說改編的電影版本 ◇ *to **make/shoot a film*** 製作／拍攝電影 ➲ COLLOCATIONS at CINEMA **2** 0‑w [U] (*especially BrE*) (*NAmE* usually **the movies** [pl.]) (*BrE* also **the cin·ema**) the art or business of making films/movies 電影製作藝術；電影業：*to study film and photography* 學習電影製作和攝影 ◇ *the film industry* 電影業 ➲ compare CINEMA (3) **3** 0‑w [U] moving pictures of real events, shown for example on television 新聞片 SYN **footage**：*television news film of the riots* 這場暴亂的電視新聞片 ◇ *The accident was captured/caught **on film**.* 事故已給拍攝下來。

▸ IN CAMERAS 攝影機；攝像機 **4** 0‑w [U, C] thin plastic that is sensitive to light, used for taking photographs and making films/movies; a roll of this plastic, used in cameras 膠片；膠捲；底片：*a **roll of film*** 一捲膠捲 ◇ *a 35mm film* * 35 毫米膠片 ◇ *She put a new film in her camera.* 她在相機裏裝上新膠捲。◇ *to **have a film developed*** 讓人沖洗膠捲

▸ THIN LAYER 薄層 **5** [C, usually sing.] **~ (of sth)** a thin layer of sth, usually on the surface of sth else 薄薄的一層；薄膜 SYN **coat, coating, layer**：*Everything was covered in a film of dust.* 所有的東西都蒙上了一層灰塵。 ➲ see also CLING FILM

■ ***verb*** 0‑w [I, T] to make a film/movie of a story or a real event 拍攝電影：*They are filming in Moscow right now.* 目前他們正在莫斯科拍電影。◇ **~ sth** *The show was filmed on location in New York.* 這次演出是在紐約取景錄製的。◇ **~ sb/sth doing sth** *Two young boys were filmed stealing CDs on the security video.* 兩個少年偷唱片時被保安錄像機拍攝了下來。 ▸ **film·ing** *noun* [U]：*Filming was delayed because of bad weather.* 由於天氣惡劣，拍攝受阻了。

ˈfilm-goer (*especially BrE*) (*NAmE* usually **movie·goer**) (*BrE* also **ˈcinema-goer**) *noun* a person who goes to the cinema/movies, especially when they do it regularly （經常）上電影院的人；愛看電影者

film·ic /ˈfɪlmɪk/ *adj.* [only before noun] (*formal*) connected with films/movies 電影的；與電影有關的

ˈfilm-maker *noun* a person who makes films/movies 電影製作人 ▸ **ˈfilm-making** *noun* [U]

film noir /ˌfɪlm ˈnwɑː(r)/ *noun* (from *French*) **1** [U] a style of making films/movies in which there are strong feelings of fear or evil; films/movies made in this style 黑色電影（充滿恐懼、邪惡色彩） **2** [C] (*pl.* **films noirs** /ˌfɪlm ˈnwɑː(r)/) a film made in this style 黑色影片

film·og·raphy /ˌfɪlˈmɒɡrəfi; *NAmE* -ˈmɑːɡ-/ *noun* (*pl.* **-ies**) a list of films/movies made by a particular actor or director, or a list of films/movies that deal with a particular subject （演員、導演或某主題的）電影作品年表，影片目錄

ˈfilm star (*especially BrE*) (*NAmE* usually **ˈmovie star**) *noun* a male or female actor who is famous for being in films/movies 電影明星

F

film·strip /ˈfɪlmstrɪp/ *noun* a series of images on a film, through which light is shone to show them on a screen 幻燈片

filmy /ˈfɪlmi/ *adj.* [usually before noun] thin and almost transparent 薄而幾乎透明的 SYN **sheer**：*a filmy cotton blouse* 薄如蟬翼的女棉襯衫

Filo·fax™ /ˈfaɪləʊfæks; *NAmE* -loʊ-/ *noun* a small book with pages that can be added or removed easily, used for writing notes, addresses, etc. in 菲洛法克斯活頁記事本 ➲ see also PERSONAL ORGANIZER

filo pastry /ˈfiːləʊ ˌpeɪstri; *NAmE* ˈfiːloʊ/ (also **filo**) *noun* [U] a type of thin PASTRY, used in layers 油酥千層餅

F

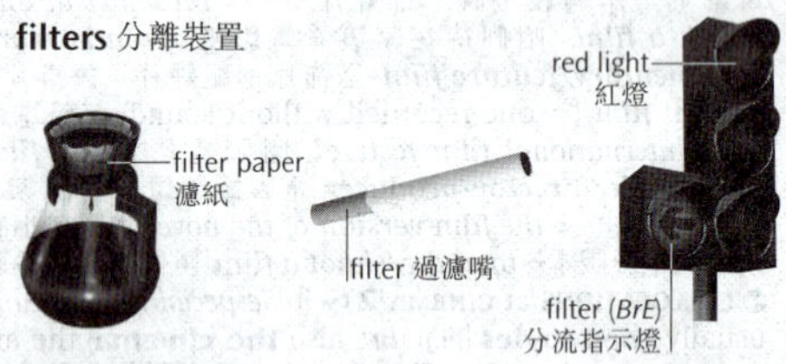

fil·ter /ˈfɪltə(r)/ *noun, verb*

■ *noun* **1** a device containing paper, sand, chemicals, etc. that a liquid or gas is passed through in order to remove any materials that are not wanted 濾器；過濾器：*an air/oil filter* 空氣過濾器；濾油器 ◇ *a coffee/water filter* 咖啡過濾器；濾水器 ◇ *filter paper for the coffee machine* 咖啡機濾紙 ◇ *He smokes cigarettes without filters.* 他吸沒有過濾嘴的香煙。➲ VISUAL VOCAB pages V25, V70 **2** a device that allows only particular types of light or sound to pass through it 濾光器；濾聲器；濾波器 **3** (*computing* 計) a program that stops certain types of electronic information, email, etc. being sent to a computer 篩選（過濾）程序 **4** (*BrE*) a light on a set of TRAFFIC LIGHTS showing that traffic can turn left or right while traffic that wants to go straight ahead must wait（交通紅燈指示不得直行的同時，表示可左轉或右轉的）分流指示燈

■ *verb* **1** [T] **~ sth** to pass liquid, light, etc. through a special device, especially to remove sth that is not wanted 過濾：*All drinking water must be filtered.* 所有飲用水必須經過過濾。◇ *Use a sun block that filters UVA effectively.* 使用能有效濾掉長波紫外線的防曬霜。◇ (*figurative*) *My secretary is very good at filtering my calls* (= making sure that calls that I do not want do not get through). 我的秘書很會替我過濾電話。➲ see also FILTRATION **2** [T] **~ sth** to use a special program to check the content of emails or websites before they are sent to your computer（用程序）篩選，過濾 **3** [I] **+ adv./prep.** (of people 人) to move slowly in a particular direction 緩行：*The doors opened and people started filtering through.* 門開了，人們開始徐徐通過。**4** [I] **+ adv./prep.** (of information, news, etc. 信息、新聞等) to slowly become known 慢慢傳開；走漏：*More details about the crash are filtering through.* 關於這場空難的具體情況慢慢披露了。**5** [I] **+ adv./prep.** (of light or sound 光或聲) to come into a place slowly or in small amounts 滲入；透過：*Sunlight filtered in through the curtains.* 陽光從窗簾透了進來。**6** [I] (*BrE*) (of traffic at traffic lights 交通指示燈處的交通) to turn left at traffic lights while other vehicles wanting to go straight ahead or turn right must wait 僅可左轉行駛

PHR V **ˌfilter sth↔ˈout** **1** to remove sth that you do not want from a liquid, light, etc. by using a special device or substance 過濾掉：*to filter out dust particles/light/impurities* 過濾掉塵粒；濾光；用過濾法除雜質 **2** to remove sb/sth that you do not want from a large number of people or things using a special system, device, etc.（用專門的系統、裝置等）過濾掉，篩除，淘汰掉：*The test is used to filter out candidates who may be unsuitable.* 這個測驗是用來淘汰不適合的求職者。◇ *The software filters out Internet sites whose content is not suitable for children.* 這個軟件可篩除含兒童不宜內容的互聯網網站。

ˈfilter tip *noun* a filter at the end of a cigarette that removes some of the harmful substances from the smoke; a cigarette that has this filter（香煙的）過濾嘴

filth /fɪlθ/ *noun* [U] **1** any very dirty and unpleasant substance 污物；污穢：*The floor was covered in grease and filth.* 地板上滿是油垢和污物。**2** words, magazines, etc. that are connected with sex and that are considered very rude and offensive 下流言辭；淫穢書刊：*How can you read such filth?* 你怎麼能看這種淫穢讀物？**3 the filth** [U] (*BrE, slang*) an offensive word for the police（罵人話）警察；雷子

filthy /ˈfɪlθi/ *adj., adv.*

■ *adj.* (**filth·ier, filthi·est**) **1** very dirty and unpleasant 骯髒的；污穢的：*filthy rags/streets* 骯髒的破布／街道 ◇ *It's filthy in here!* 這裏面髒得很！➲ SYNONYMS at DIRTY **2** very rude and offensive and usually connected with sex 下流的；淫穢的；猥褻的：*filthy language/words* 下流的語言／言辭 ◇ *He's got a **filthy mind*** (= is always thinking about sex). 他滿腦子淫亂思想。**3** (*informal*) showing anger 氣憤的：*He was in a **filthy mood**.* 他氣憤不已。◇ *She has a **filthy temper**.* 她脾氣暴躁。◇ *Ann gave him a **filthy look**.* 安氣憤地瞧了他一眼。**4** (*BrE, informal*) (of the weather 天氣) cold and wet 寒冷潮濕的；惡劣的；糟糕的：*Isn't it a filthy day?* 今天可不是又冷又濕嗎？▶ **filth·ily** *adv.* **filthi·ness** *noun* [U]

■ *adv.* (*informal*) **1 ~ dirty** extremely dirty 極其骯髒的 **2 ~ rich** so rich that you think the person is too rich and you find it offensive 富得流油的

fil·trate /ˈfɪltreɪt/ *noun* (*chemistry* 化) a liquid that has passed through a FILTER 濾液

fil·tra·tion /fɪlˈtreɪʃn/ *noun* [U] (*chemistry* 化) the process of FILTERING a liquid or gas 過濾；濾清；濾除

fin /fɪn/ *noun* **1** a thin flat part that sticks out from the body of a fish, used for swimming and keeping balance（魚的）鰭 ➲ VISUAL VOCAB page V12 **2** a thin flat part that sticks out from the body of a vehicle, an aircraft, etc., used for improving its balance and movement 鰭狀物，翼（車輛、航空器等用以保持平衡等的突出窄扁部份）：*tail fins* 垂直尾翼 ➲ VISUAL VOCAB page V53

fin·agle /fɪˈneɪɡl/ *verb* [T, I] **~ (sth)** (*informal, especially NAmE*) to behave dishonestly or to obtain sth dishonestly 欺詐；騙取：*He finagled some tickets for tonight's big game.* 他騙到了幾張今晚大賽的門票。

final 🔑 AW /ˈfaɪnl/ *adj., noun*

■ *adj.* **1** 🔑 [only before noun] being or happening at the end of a series of events, actions, statements, etc. 最終的；最後的：*his final act as party leader* 他作為黨的領袖所採取的最後行動 ◇ *The referee blew the final whistle.* 裁判吹響了終場的哨聲。◇ *The project is in its final stages.* 這個項目到了最後階段。◇ *I'd like to return to the final point you made.* 我想再談談你所說的最後一點。➲ LANGUAGE BANK at PROCESS **2** 🔑 [only before noun] being the result of a particular process（指結果）最終的，最後的：*the final product* 成品 ◇ *No one could have predicted the final outcome.* 誰也沒有預想到最終結果會是這樣。**3** 🔑 that cannot be argued with or changed 決定性的；不可改變的；最終的：*The judge's **decision is final**.* 法官的判決是最終判決。◇ *Who has the **final say** around here?* 這裏誰有最後決定權？◇ *I'll give you $500 for it, and that's my **final offer**!* 我出價 500 元，不再加價！◇ *I'm not coming, **and that's final**!* (= I will not change my mind) 我不來，就這麼定了！IDM see ANALYSIS, STRAW, WORD *n.*

■ *noun* **1** 🔑 [C] the last of a series of games or competitions in which the winner is decided 決賽：*She reached the final of the 100m hurdles.* 她取得了 100 米跨欄的決賽權。◇ *the 2010 World Cup Finals* (= the last few games in the competition) * 2010 年世界盃決賽階段 ◇ *The winner of each contest goes through to the **grand final**.* 每場比賽的勝者進入最後的決賽。➲ see also QUARTER-FINAL, SEMI-FINAL **2 finals** [pl.] (*BrE*) the last exams taken by university students at the end of their final year 大學畢業考試：*to **sit/take your finals*** 參加

大學畢業考試 **3** [C] (*NAmE*) an exam taken by school, university or college students at the end of a SEMESTER or QUARTER, usually in a topic that they will not study again 期終結業考試；期終考試

,final 'clause *noun* (*grammar* 語法) a clause that expresses purpose or intention, for example one that follows 'in order that' or 'so that' 目的從句，目的子句（如 in order that、so that 等引導的從句）

fi·nale /fɪ'nɑːli; *NAmE* fɪ'næli/ *noun* **1** the last part of a show or a piece of music （演出的）終場，結局；（音樂的）終曲，末樂章：*the rousing finale of Beethoven's Ninth Symphony* 貝多芬第九交響曲激動人心的末樂章◇*The festival ended with a* ***grand finale*** *in Hyde Park.* 節日的壓軸活動是在海德公園舉行的盛大演出。 **2 ~ (to sth)** (after an adjective 置於形容詞後) an ending to sth of the type mentioned 結尾：*a fitting finale to the day's events* 當天活動的圓滿結束

fi·nal·ist /'faɪnəlɪst/ *noun* a person who takes part in the final of a game or competition 參加決賽者：*an Olympic finalist* 奧運會決賽運動員

fi·nal·ity AW /faɪ'næləti/ *noun* [U] the quality of being final and impossible to change 終結；定局；不可改變性：*the finality of death* 死亡的不可改變性◇*There was a note of finality in his voice.* 他的話有斬釘截鐵的意味。

fi·nal·ize (*BrE* also **-ise**) AW /'faɪnəlaɪz/ *verb* **~ sth** to complete the last part of a plan, trip, project, etc. 把（計劃、旅行、項目等）最後定下來；定案：*to* ***finalize*** *your* ***plans/arrangements*** 把計劃／安排最後確定下來◇*They met to finalize the terms of the treaty.* 他們會晤確定條約的條款。 ▶ **fi·nal·iza·tion, -isa·tion** *noun* [U]

fi·nal·ly 🔑 AW /'faɪnəli/ *adv.*
1 🔑 after a long time, especially when there has been some difficulty or delay 終於；最終 SYN **eventually**：*The performance finally started half an hour late.* 延遲了半小時以後演出終於開始了。◇*I finally managed to get her attention.* 我終於設法引起了她的注意。◇*When they finally arrived it was well past midnight.* 他們最後到達時已是第二天的淩晨。 **2** 🔑 used to introduce the last in a list of things （用於列舉）最後 SYN **lastly**：*And finally, I would like to thank you all for coming here today.* 最後，我感謝大家今天的光臨。 ➲ LANGUAGE BANK at FIRST, PROCESS **3** 🔑 in a way that ends all discussion about sth 徹底地；決定性地：*The matter was not finally settled until later.* 這事後來才得到徹底解決。

fi·nance 🔑 AW /'faɪnæns; faɪ'næns; fə'næns/ *noun, verb*
▪ *noun* **1** 🔑 (*especially BrE*) (*NAmE* usually **fi·nan·cing**) [U] **~ (for sth)** money used to run a business, an activity or a project 資金：*Finance for education comes from taxpayers.* 教育經費來自納稅人。 **2** 🔑 [U] the activity of managing

F

Collocations 詞語搭配

Finance 財務

Income 收入

- **earn** money/cash/(*informal*) a fortune 掙錢；掙一大筆錢
- **make** money/a fortune/(*informal*) a killing on the stock market 在股市上賺錢／賺一大筆錢／發大財
- **acquire/inherit/amass** wealth/a fortune 獲得／繼承／積累財富／一大筆錢
- **build up** funds/savings 積累資金／存款
- **get/receive/leave** (sb) an inheritance/a legacy 得到／（給某人）留下遺產
- **live on** a low wage/a fixed income/a pension 靠低微的工資／固定收入／養老金過活
- **get/receive/draw/collect** a pension 領取養老金
- **depend/be dependent on** (*BrE*) benefits/(*NAmE*) welfare/social security 靠福利金／社會保障金過活

Expenditure 開支；支出

- **spend** money/your savings/(*informal*) a fortune on … 把錢／存款／一大筆錢花在…上
- **invest/put** your savings in … 投資／把儲蓄金用於…
- **throw away/waste/**(*informal*) **shell out** money on … 把錢浪費／花費巨資在…上
- **lose** your money/inheritance/pension 失去錢財／遺產／養老金
- **use up/**(*informal*) **wipe out** all your savings 把儲蓄用光
- **pay (in)** cash 用現金支付
- **use/pay by** a credit/debit card 用信用卡／借記卡支付
- **pay by/make out a/write sb a/accept a** (*BrE*) cheque/(*US*) check 用支票支付；開支票；給某人開支票；接受支票
- **change/exchange** money/currency/(*BrE*) traveller's cheques/(*US*) traveler's checks 兑換錢／貨幣／旅行支票
- **give/pay/leave (sb)** a deposit 預付（某人）訂金

Banks 銀行

- **have/hold/open/close/freeze** a bank account/an account 持有／開立／註銷／凍結銀行賬戶
- **credit/debit/pay sth into/take money out of** your account 記入賬戶的貸方／借方；把錢存入賬戶／從賬戶中取出
- **deposit** money/funds in your account 往賬戶裏存錢／存入資金
- **withdraw** money/cash/£30 from an ATM, etc. 從自動提款機等取錢／現金／30 英鎊
- (*formal*) **make** a deposit/withdrawal 存款；取款
- **find/go to/use** (*especially NAmE*) an ATM/(*BrE*) a cash machine/dispenser 找到／去／使用自動提款機
- **be in** credit/**in** debit/**in** the black/**in** the red/overdrawn 賬面有錢／虧空；有盈餘；透支

Personal finance 個人理財

- **manage/handle/plan/run/**(*especially BrE*) **sort out** your finances 管理／處理／計劃／經營管理／整頓財務問題
- **plan/manage/work out/stick to a** budget 計劃／管理／制訂／嚴格執行預算
- **offer/extend** credit (to sb) （給某人）提供貸款
- **arrange/take out** a loan/an overdraft 商定／獲得貸款／透支額
- **pay back/repay** money/a loan/a debt 償還錢／貸款／債務
- **pay for sth in** (*especially BrE*) instalments/(*NAmE usually*) installments 以分期付款購買某物

Financial difficulties 財務困難

- **get into** debt/financial difficulties 陷入債務／財務困難
- **be short of/**(*informal*) **be strapped for** cash 缺錢
- **run out of/owe** money 錢用光了；欠錢
- **face/get/**(*informal*) **be landed with** a bill for £ … 面對／收到一張…英鎊的賬單
- **can't afford** the cost of … /payments/rent 承擔不起…的費用／款項／房租
- **fall behind with/**(*especially NAmE*) **fall behind on** the mortgage/repayments/rent 拖欠按揭貸款／分期償還款項／房租
- **incur/run up/accumulate** debts 帶來／積欠／累積債務
- **tackle/reduce/settle** your debts 處理／減少／付清債務

money, especially by a government or commercial organization 財政；金融；財務： *the Minister of Finance* 財政部長 ◇ *the* ***finance director/department*** 財務主任；財務科 ◇ *a diploma in banking and finance* 銀行學與金融學文憑 ◇ *the world of* ***high finance*** (= finance involving large companies or countries) 高級金融界（關乎大公司或國家的金融） **3** **finances** [pl.] the money available to a person, an organization or a country; the way this money is managed （個人、組織、國家的）財力，財源，財務管理： ***government/public/personal finances*** 政府／公共／個人財力 ◇ *It's about time you sorted out your finances.* 現在是你整頓財務狀況的時候了。◇ *Moving house put a severe strain on our finances.* 搬家使我們的經濟十分緊張。

F

■ *verb* **~ sth** to provide money for a project 提供資金 SYN **fund**： *The building project will be financed by the government.* 這個建築項目將由政府出資。◇ *He took a job to finance his stay in Germany.* 他找了一份工作以賺錢支付在德國逗留的費用。

'finance company (*BrE* also **'finance house**) *noun* a company that lends money to people or businesses （向個人或公司貸款的）信貸公司，金融公司

fi·nan·cial AW /faɪ'nænʃl; fə'næ-/ *adj.* [usually before noun]
1 connected with money and finance 財政的；財務的；金融的： *financial services* 金融服務 ◇ *to give financial advice* 提供財務咨詢 ◇ *to be in* ***financial difficulties*** 處於財務困難之中 ◇ *an independent* ***financial adviser*** 獨立財務顧問 ◇ *Tokyo and New York are major* ***financial centres.*** 東京和紐約是主要的金融中心。 ➲ SYNONYMS at ECONOMIC **2** (*AustralE, NZE, informal*) having money 有錢的 ▸ **fi·nan·cial·ly** AW /-ʃəli/ *adv.*： *She is still* ***financially dependent*** *on her parents.* 她在經濟上仍然依靠父母。◇ *Financially, I'm much better off than before.* 我的經濟狀況比過去好多了。◇ *Such projects are not* ***financially viable*** *without government funding.* 沒有政府專款，這樣的項目在資金上是不可行的。

fi,nancial 'aid *noun* [U] (*NAmE*) money that is given or lent to students at a university or college who cannot pay the full cost of their education （高等院校的）助學金，助學貸款： *to apply for financial aid* 申請助學金

the Fi,nancial Times 'index *noun* = FTSE INDEX

fi,nancial 'year (*BrE*) (*BrE* also **'tax year**) (*NAmE* **,fiscal 'year**) *noun* [usually sing.] a period of twelve months over which the accounts and taxes of a company or a person are calculated 財政年度；會計年度： *the current financial year* 本財政年度

fi·nan·cier AW /faɪ'nænsiə(r); fə-; *NAmE* ,fɪnən'sɪr/ *noun* a person who lends large amounts of money to businesses 金融家；理財家

fi·nan·cing /'faɪnænsɪŋ; faɪ'nænsɪŋ; fə'nænsɪŋ/ *noun* [U] (*NAmE*) = FINANCE： *The project will only go ahead if they can raise the necessary financing.* 只有籌集到必要的資金，這個項目才能得以進行。

finch /fɪntʃ/ *noun* (often in compounds 常構成複合詞) a small bird with a short beak. There are several types of finch. 雀科小鳥 ➲ VISUAL VOCAB page V12 ➲ see also BULLFINCH, CHAFFINCH, GOLDFINCH

find /faɪnd/ *verb, noun*
■ *verb* (**found, found** /faʊnd/)
▸ BY CHANCE 偶然 **1** [T] to discover sb/sth unexpectedly or by chance （意外或偶然地）發現，碰到： **~ sb/sth** *Look what I've found!* 看我發現了什麼！◇ *We've found a great new restaurant near the office.* 我們在辦公處附近發現了一家挺好的新餐館。◇ **~ sb/sth + adj.** *A whale was found washed up on the shore.* 一頭鯨被發現沖到了岸上。
▸ BY SEARCHING 通過搜尋 **2** [T] to get back sth/sb that was lost after searching for it/them 找到；找回： **~ sth for sb** *Can you find my bag for me?* 你能幫我找找我的包嗎？◇ **~ sb sth** *Can you find me my bag?* 你能幫我找找我的包嗎？◇ **~ sb/sth** *I wanted to talk to him but he was* ***nowhere to be found.*** 我想和他談談，但哪兒也找不到他。◇ **~ sb/sth + adj.** *The child was found safe and well.* 小孩找到了，安然無恙。
▸ BY STUDYING/THINKING 通過研究／思考 **3** [T] to discover sth/sb by searching, studying or thinking carefully （經尋找、研究或思考）發現，查明，找出，求得： **~ sth/sb** *scientists trying to find a cure for cancer* 努力尋找癌症療法的科學家 ◇ *I managed to find a solution to the problem.* 我設法找出了解決問題的辦法。◇ *I'm having trouble finding anything new to say on this subject.* 在這個課題上要提出什麼新看法，我有困難。◇ *Have they found anyone to replace her yet?* 他們找到了代替她的人沒有？◇ **~ sth for sb** *Can you find a hotel for me?* 你能給我找一家旅館嗎？◇ **~ sb sth** *Can you find me a hotel?* 你能給我找一家旅館嗎？
▸ BY EXPERIENCE/TESTING 通過體驗／試驗 **4** [T] to discover that sth is true after you have tried it, tested it or experienced it 發現（某事屬實）： **~ (that)** ... *I find (that) it pays to be honest.* 我發現老實人不吃虧。◇ *The report found that 30% of the firms studied had failed within a year.* 據報告稱，調查過的公司有 30% 一年內倒閉了。◇ **~ sb/sth + adj./noun** *We found the beds very comfortable.* 我們發現這些牀非常舒適。◇ **~ sb/sth to be/do sth** *They found him to be charming.* 他們覺得他很招人喜歡。◇ *Her blood was found to contain poison.* 她的血液中發現有毒素。◇ **it is found that** ... ***It was found that*** *her blood contained poison.* 她的血液中發現有毒素。
▸ HAVE OPINION/FEELING 有意見／看法 **5** [T] to have a particular feeling or opinion about sth 認為；感到： **~ sth + adj.** *You may find your illness hard to accept.* 你可能覺得難以接受自己患病。◇ *You may* ***find it hard*** *to accept your illness.* 你可能覺得難以相信自己患病。◇ *I find it amazing that they're still together.* 他們還在一起，這使我大吃一驚。◇ **~ sth + noun** *She* ***finds it a strain*** *to meet new people.* 她和生人見面總感到局促不安。 ➲ SYNONYMS at REGARD
▸ HAVE/MAKE AVAILABLE 現有；使現有 **6** [T] **~ sth** to have sth available so that you can use it 現有（可用）： *I keep meaning to write, but never seem to find (the) time.* 我一直打算寫信，但總找不到時間。◇ *How are we going to find £5 000 for a car?* 我們哪裏有 5 000 英鎊買車呢？
▸ IN UNEXPECTED SITUATIONS 處於意外狀況 **7** [T] to discover sb/sth/yourself doing sth or in a particular situation, especially when this is unexpected 發現，發覺（處於某狀態、在做某事）： **~ sb/sth/yourself + adv./prep.** *She woke up and found herself in a hospital bed.* 她醒來發覺自己躺在醫院的牀上。◇ **~ sb/sth/yourself + adj.** *We came home and found him asleep on the sofa.* 我們回到家發現他在沙發上睡着了。◇ **~ sb/sth/yourself doing sth** *I suddenly found myself running down the street.* 我不知不覺突然在街上跑了起來。◇ **~ (that)** ... *I was disappointed to find that they had left already.* 我發現他們已經離開了，覺得很失望。
▸ REACH 達到；到達 **8** [T] **~ sth** (of things 事物) to arrive at sth naturally; to reach sth 自然到達；達到： *Water will always find its own level.* 水總會自行流平。◇ *Most of the money finds its way to the people who need it.* 多數的錢都會輾轉傳到需要的人的手中。◇ *The criticism found its mark* (= had the effect intended). 批評擊中了要害。
▸ EXIST/GROW 存在；生長 **9** [T] **~ sth + adv./prep.** used to say that sth exists, grows, etc. somewhere （在某處）存在，生長： *These flowers are found only in Africa.* 這些花僅見於非洲。◇ *You'll find this style of architecture all over the town.* 全城到處可見這種風格的建築。
▸ IN COURT 法庭 **10** [T, I] (*formal*) to make a particular decision in a court case 裁決；判決： **~ sb + adj.** *The jury found him guilty.* 陪審團裁決他有罪。◇ *How do you find the accused?* 你如何裁定被告？◇ **~ in sb's favour** *The court found in her favour.* 法庭判決對她有利。
IDM **all 'found** (*old-fashioned, BrE*) with free food and accommodation in addition to your wages （工資外）加免費食宿 **find fault (with sb/sth)** to look for and discover mistakes in sb/sth; to complain about sb/sth 找碴兒；挑錯；抱怨；挑剔 **find your 'feet** to become able to act independently and with confidence 已能獨立而有信心地工作；已適應新環境： *I only recently joined the firm so I'm still finding my feet.* 我最近才加入這家公司，所以還在適應過程中。 **find it in your heart/yourself to do sth** (*literary*) to be able or willing to do sth 能做某事；願意幹某事： *Can you find it in your heart to forgive her?* 你能夠做到寬恕她嗎？◇ *He couldn't find it in himself to trust anyone again.* 他再也不願意相

信任何人了。**find your 'voice/'tongue** to be able to speak or express your opinion 能說出自己的看法；能表達自己的意見 **find your way (to ...)** to discover the right route (to a place) 找到正確的路（去某處）：*I hope you can find your way home.* 希望你能找到回家的路。**find your/its 'way (to/into ...)** to come to a place or a situation by chance or without intending to 偶然來到；無意中處於：*He eventually found his way into acting.* 他弄到最後竟幹起了演藝這一行。**take sb as you 'find them** to accept sb as they are without expecting them to behave in a special way or have special qualities 接受某人的現狀；承認某人的情況（別無指望）➲ more at BEARING, MATCH *n.*, NOWHERE

PHR V **'find for/against sb** [no passive] (*law* 律) to make a decision in favour of/against sb in a court case 作出對…有利（或不利）的裁決；判…勝訴（或敗訴）：*The jury found for the defendant.* 陪審團作出了對被告有利的裁決。**,find 'out (about sth/sb)** | **,find 'out sth (about sth/sb)** 🔑 to get some information about sth/sb by asking, reading, etc. 查明，弄清（情況）：*She'd been seeing the boy for a while, but didn't want her parents to find out.* 她和這個男孩約會已有一段時間了，但不想讓父母知道。◇ *I haven't found anything out about him yet.* 我還沒有發現有關他的什麼情況。◇ **~ what, when, etc.** ... *Can you find out what time the meeting starts?* 你能查清楚會議什麼時候開始嗎？◇ **~ that** ... *We found out later that we had been at the same school.* 後來我們才弄清楚我們是校友。**,find sb 'out** to discover that sb has done sth wrong 查出（壞人）；識破：*He had been cheating the taxman but it was years before he was found out.* 他過去一直在欺騙稅務部門，只是多年以後才被查出來。

■ ***noun*** a thing or person that has been found, especially one that is interesting, valuable or useful 發現物，被發現的人（尤指有趣、有價值或有用者）：*an important archaeological find* 考古的重大發現 ◇ *Our new babysitter is **a real find**.* 我們新來的臨時保母是難得的好保母。

find·er /'faɪndə(r)/ *noun* a person who finds sth 發現者；尋得者 ➲ see also VIEWFINDER

IDM **,finders 'keepers** (*saying*) (often used by children 兒童常用語) anyone who finds sth has a right to keep it 誰找到是誰的；誰撿到的歸誰

fin de siècle /,fæ̃ də 'sjekl/ *adj.* (from *French*) typical of the end of the 19th century, especially of its art, literature and attitudes（尤指文學、藝術、看法）十九世紀末的

find·ing /'faɪndɪŋ/ *noun* **1** [usually pl.] information that is discovered as the result of research into sth 調查發現；調研結果：*The findings of the commission will be published today.* 委員會的調查結果將於今天公佈。➲ COLLOCATIONS at SCIENTIFIC **2** (*law* 律) a decision made by the judge or JURY in a court case 判決；裁決

fine 🔑 /faɪn/ *adj., adv., noun, verb*

■ ***adj.*** (**finer, fin·est**)

▸ VERY GOOD 很好 **1** 🔑 [usually before noun] of high quality; good 高質量的；美好的：*a very fine performance* 十分精彩的演出 ◇ *fine clothes/wines/workmanship* 漂亮的衣服；美酒；精湛的工藝 ◇ *a particularly fine example of Saxon architecture* 撒克遜式建築的優秀範例 ◇ *Jim has made a fine job of the garden.* 吉姆把花園拾掇得漂漂亮亮。◇ *people who enjoy the **finer things** in life* (= for example art, good food, etc.) 享受生活中美好事物的人 ◇ *He tried to appeal to their **finer feelings*** (= feelings of duty, love, etc.). 他試圖打動他們更美好的情感（即責任感、愛等）。◇ *It was his **finest hour*** (= most successful period) *as manager of the England team.* 那是他作為英格蘭隊經理的鼎盛時期。

▸ VERY WELL 很不錯 **2** 🔑 (of a person 人) in good health 健康的；身體很好的：*'How are you?' 'Fine, thanks.'* "你好嗎？""很好，謝謝。" ◇ *I was **feeling fine** when I got up this morning.* 今天早上我起牀時感覺很好。➲ SYNONYMS at WELL

▸ ACCEPTABLE/GOOD ENOUGH 可接受；夠好 **3** 🔑 (also used as an exclamation 亦作感歎詞) used to tell sb that an action, a suggestion or a decision is acceptable（指行為、建議、決定）可接受：*'I'll leave this here, OK?' 'Fine.'* "我把這個留在這兒，可以嗎？""可以。" ◇ *'Bob wants to know if he can come too.' **'That's fine by me.'*** "鮑勃想知道他是否也能來。""我認為沒問題。" **4** 🔑 used to say you are satisfied with sth（表示滿意）很好，不錯，滿意：*Don't worry. Your speech was fine.* 別擔心。你的講話挺好的。◇ *You go on without me. **I'll be fine**.* 沒有我你繼續吧，我沒事的。◇ *'Can I get you another drink?' 'No, thanks. **I'm fine**.'* "我可以再給你取一杯嗎？""不，謝謝。我夠了。" ◇ (*ironic*) *This is a **fine*** (= terrible) ***mess** we're in!* 我們的處境好狼狽啊！◇ (*ironic*) ***You're a fine one to talk!*** (= you are not in a position to criticize, give advice, etc.) 哪有你說話的份！

▸ ATTRACTIVE 有吸引力 **5** 🔑 [usually before noun] pleasing to look at 好看的；漂亮的：*a fine view* 美景 ◇ *a fine-looking woman* 漂亮女人 ◇ *a fine figure of a man* 身材俊美的男人

▸ DELICATE 精緻 **6** 🔑 [usually before noun] attractive and delicate 精巧的；精美的：*fine bone china* 精緻的骨灰瓷 ◇ *She has inherited her mother's fine features* (= a small nose, mouth, etc.). 她遺傳了她母親的清秀面容。

▸ WEATHER 天氣 **7** 🔑 (*especially BrE*) bright and not raining 晴朗的：*a fine day/evening* 晴朗的一天／晚上 ◇ *I hope it **stays fine** for the picnic.* 我希望野餐那天還是晴天。

▸ VERY THIN 纖細 **8** 🔑 very thin or narrow 纖細的；很細的：*fine blond hair* 纖細的金髮 ◇ *a fine thread* 細線 ◇ *a brush with a fine tip* 筆頭尖細的畫筆

▸ DETAIL/DISTINCTIONS 細節；差別 **9** [usually before noun] difficult to see or describe 難以看出的；很難描述的 **SYN** **subtle**：*You really need a magnifying glass to appreciate all the fine detail.* 確實需要放大鏡才能欣賞到一切細微之處。◇ *There's no need to make such **fine distinctions**.* 沒有必要區分出如此細微的差別。◇ *There's **a fine line** between love and hate* (= it is easy for one to become the other). 愛恨只有一線之隔。

▸ WITH SMALL GRAINS 小顆粒 **10** made of very small grains 小顆粒製成的；顆粒細微的：*fine sand* 細沙 ◇ *Use a finer piece of sandpaper to finish.* 用細砂紙最後磨光。**OPP** **coarse**

▸ PERSON 人 **11** [only before noun] that you have a lot of respect for 值得尊敬的；傑出的：*He was a fine man.* 他是個優秀的人。

▸ WORDS/SPEECHES 詞語；話語 **12** sounding important and impressive but unlikely to have any effect 漂亮的；虛飾的；辭藻華麗的：*His speech was full of fine words which meant nothing.* 他的演講華而不實。

▸ METALS 金屬 **13** (*technical* 術語) containing only a particular metal and no other substances that reduce the quality 純的；無雜質的：*fine gold* 純金

IDM **get sth down to a fine 'art** (*informal*) to learn to do sth well and efficiently 把…學到家；學得非常在行：*I spend so much time travelling that I've got packing down to a fine art.* 我常常旅行，這就把打點行李學到家了。**not to put too fine a 'point on it** used to emphasize sth that is expressed clearly and directly, especially a criticism 直截了當地說，不客氣地說（尤指批評）：*Not to put too fine a point on it, I think you are lying.* 不客氣地說，我認為你在撒謊。➲ more at CHANCE *n.*, FETTLE, LINE *n.*

■ ***adv.*** (*informal*) in a way that is acceptable or good enough 可接受；夠好；蠻不錯：*Keep going like that—you're **doing fine**.* 就這樣做下去，你做得蠻不錯嘛。◇ *Things were **going fine** until you showed up.* 你一露面就把事情搞糟了。◇ *That arrangement **suits me fine**.* 那種安排對我很合適。◇ (*BrE*) *An omelette will **do me fine*** (= will be enough for me). 一份攤雞蛋我就夠了。

IDM **cut it/things 'fine** (*informal*) to leave yourself just enough time to do sth 把時間扣得很緊；時間上不留餘地：*If we don't leave till after lunch we'll be cutting it very fine.* 我們要是午飯以後才走，時間就緊得很了。

■ ***noun*** 🔑 a sum of money that must be paid as punishment for breaking a law or rule 罰金；罰款：*a parking fine* 違規停車罰款 ◇ *Offenders will be liable to a **heavy fine*** (= one that costs a lot of money). 違者須付巨額罰金。◇ *She has already paid over $2 000 in fines.* 她已經付了 2 000 多元罰金。➲ SYNONYMS at RATE ➲ COLLOCATIONS at JUSTICE

■ ***verb*** 🔑 [often passive] to make sb pay money as an official punishment 對…處以罰款：**~ sb (for sth/for doing sth)** *She was fined for speeding.* 她因超速而被罰款。◇ **~ sb sth (for sth/for doing sth)** *The company* *was fined £20 000 for breaching safety regulations.* 這家公司因違反安全條例而被罰款 2 萬英鎊。

fine ˈart *noun* [U] (also **fine ˈarts** [pl.]) forms of art, especially painting, drawing and SCULPTURE, that are created to be beautiful rather than useful 藝術（尤指繪畫和雕塑）

Fine Gael /ˌfiːnə ˈɡeɪl/ *noun* [sing.+sing./pl. v.] the more conservative of the two main political parties in the Republic of Ireland 統一黨（愛爾蘭共和國兩大政黨之一，保守黨派）➲ compare FIANNA FÁIL

fine·ly 🔑 /ˈfaɪnli/ *adv.* **1** 🔑 into very small grains or pieces 成顆粒；細微地；細小地：*finely chopped herbs* 剁得很細的草藥 **2** 🔑 in a beautiful or impressive way 華麗地；優雅地：*a finely furnished room* 陳設雅致的房間 **3** 🔑 in a very delicate or exact way 精緻地；精巧地；精確地：*a finely tuned engine* 精確調整的發動機 ◇ *The match was finely balanced throughout.* 比賽自始至終不分上下。

fine·ness /ˈfaɪnnəs/ *noun* [U] **1** the quality of being made of thin threads or lines very close together 纖細；精細度；細度：*fineness of detail* 詳情的細微 **2** (*technical* 術語) the quality of sth 純度；成色：*the fineness of the gold* 黃金的成色

the ˌfine ˈprint (*NAmE*) (*BrE* **the ˌsmall ˈprint**) *noun* [U] the important details of an agreement or a legal document that are usually printed in small type and are therefore easy to miss（協議或法律文件中易於被忽略但重要的）小號字附加條款

fin·ery /ˈfaɪnəri/ *noun* [U] (*formal*) brightly coloured and elegant clothes and jewellery, especially those that are worn for a special occasion 高雅華麗的衣服；精美高貴的飾物

fi·nesse /fɪˈnes/ *noun, verb*

■ **noun** [U] great skill in dealing with people or situations, especially in a delicate way 手腕；策略；手段

■ **verb** (*especially NAmE*) **1 ~ sth** to deal with sth in a way that is clever but slightly dishonest 用策略對付某事：*to finesse a deal* 略施小計達成一樁交易 **2 ~ sth** to do sth with a lot of skill or style 巧妙地做；派頭十足地做

ˌfine-tooth ˈcomb (also **ˌfine-toothed ˈcomb**) *noun* a COMB in which the pointed parts are thin and very close together 細齒梳子

IDM **go over/through sth with a fine-tooth/fine-toothed comb** to examine or search sth very carefully 十分認真地檢查；非常仔細地搜查

ˌfine-ˈtune *verb* **~ sth** to make very small changes to sth so that it is as good as it can possibly be 對…微調 ▸ **ˌfine-ˈtuning** *noun* [U]：*The system is set up but it needs some fine-tuning.* 該系統已裝配好，但需要一些細小調整。

f-ing /ˈefɪŋ/ *adj.* [only before noun] (*taboo, slang*) = EFFING

fin·ger 🔑 /ˈfɪŋɡə(r)/ *noun, verb*

■ **noun** **1** 🔑 one of the four long thin parts that stick out from the hand (or five, if the thumb is included) 手指：*She* ***ran her fingers*** *through her hair.* 她用手指梳理頭髮。◇ *Hold the material between finger and thumb.* 用拇指和另一指拿住這個材料。◇ *He was about to speak but she raised a finger to her lips.* 他正要說話，但她舉手捂唇示意。➲ **COLLOCATIONS** at PHYSICAL ➲ see also BUTTERFINGERS, FOREFINGER, GREEN FINGERS, INDEX FINGER, LITTLE FINGER, MIDDLE FINGER, RING FINGER **2 -fingered** (in adjectives 構成形容詞) having the type of fingers mentioned; having or using the number of fingers mentioned 有…手指的；有（或用）…手指的：*long-fingered* 長手指的 ◇ *nimble-fingered* 手指靈敏的 ◇ *a four-fingered chord* 四指彈奏的和弦 ➲ see also LIGHT-FINGERED **3** the part of a glove that covers the finger（手套的）指部 **4 ~ (of sth)** a long narrow piece of bread, cake, land, etc. 狹長物（如麵包、糕餅、土地等）：*a finger of toast* 長條吐司 ◇ *chocolate fingers* 巧克力條 ➲ see also FISH FINGER

IDM **the ˌfinger of susˈpicion** if **the finger of suspicion** points or is pointed at sb, they are suspected of having committed a crime, being responsible for sth, etc. 嫌疑所指 **get, pull, etc. your ˈfinger out** (*BrE, informal*) used to tell sb to start doing some work or making an effort 幹起來；加把勁：*You're going to have to pull your finger out if you want to pass this exam.* 如果你想通過這次考試就得多加把勁。 **give sb the ˈfinger** (*NAmE, informal*) to raise your middle finger in the air with the back part of your hand facing sb, done to be rude to sb or to show them that you are angry 向某人豎起中指（手背向外以表示侮辱） **have a finger in every ˈpie** (*informal*) to be involved in a lot of different activities and have influence over them, especially when other people think that this is annoying 多管閒事；到處干預 **have, etc. your ˈfingers in the till** (*BrE, informal*) to be stealing money from the place where you work 偷自己工作單位的錢；內盜；監守自盜 **have/keep your finger on the ˈpulse (of sth)** to always be aware of the most recent developments in a particular situation 保持瞭解…的最新情況；掌握…的脈搏 **lay a ˈfinger on sb** (usually used in negative sentences 通常用於否定句) to touch sb with the intention of hurting them physically 觸碰，動…的一根毫毛（意欲傷害某人）：*I never laid a finger on her.* 我從來沒有碰過她。 **not put your finger on sth** to not be able to identify what is wrong or different about a particular situation 看不出（問題所在）；說不出（差別）：*There was something odd about him but I couldn't put my finger on it.* 他有些古怪，但我說不出到底是什麼。 **put/stick two ˈfingers up at sb** (*BrE, informal*) to form the shape of a V with the two fingers nearest your thumb and raise your hand in the air with the back part of it facing sb, done to be rude to them or to show them that you are angry（手背向某人做出 V 形手勢表示侮辱）➲ see also V-SIGN **work your fingers to the ˈbone** to work very hard 拚命幹活 ➲ more at BURN *v.*, COUNT *v.*, CROSS *v.*, LIFT *v.*, POINT *v.*, SLIP *v.*, SNAP *v.*, STICKY *adj.*, THUMB *n.*

■ **verb** **1 ~ sth** to touch or feel sth with your fingers 用手指觸摸：*Gary sat fingering his beard, saying nothing.* 加里坐着用手捋着鬍子，一言不發。 **2 ~ sb (for sth)** | **~ sb (as sth)** (*informal, especially NAmE*) to accuse sb of doing sth illegal and tell the police about it 告發；告密：*Who fingered him for the burglaries?* 誰告發他入室盜竊？

fin·ger·board /ˈfɪŋɡəbɔːd; *NAmE* ˈfɪŋɡərbɔːrd/ *noun* a flat strip on the neck of a musical instrument such as a GUITAR or VIOLIN, against which the strings are pressed to play different notes（吉他或小提琴等的）指板

ˈfinger bowl *noun* a small bowl of water for washing your fingers during a meal（用餐時用的）洗指碗

ˈfinger food *noun* [U, C] pieces of food that you can easily eat with your fingers 便於用手指取食的食物

fin·ger·ing /ˈfɪŋɡərɪŋ/ *noun* [U, C] the positions in which you put your fingers when playing a musical instrument（演奏樂器的）指法

fin·ger·mark /ˈfɪŋɡəmɑːk; *NAmE* ˈfɪŋɡərmɑːrk/ *noun* [usually pl.] (*especially BrE*) a mark made by a finger, for example on a clean surface 指痕；指跡

fin·ger·nail /ˈfɪŋɡəneɪl; *NAmE* -ɡərn-/ *noun* the thin hard layer that covers the outer tip of each finger 手指甲 ➲ **VISUAL VOCAB** page V59

fin·ger·print /ˈfɪŋɡəprɪnt; *NAmE* -ɡərp-/ *noun* a mark made by the pattern of lines on the tip of a person's finger, often used by the police to identify criminals 指紋；指印 ➲ **SYNONYMS** at MARK ➲ see also GENETIC FINGERPRINT ▸ **fin·ger·print** *verb* **~ sb**

fin·ger·print·ing /ˈfɪŋɡəprɪntɪŋ; *NAmE* -ɡərp-/ *noun* [U] the practice of recording sb's fingerprints, often used by the police to identify criminals 取（罪犯等的）指紋印；蓋手印 ➲ see also DNA FINGERPRINTING, GENETIC FINGERPRINTING

fin·ger·tip /ˈfɪŋɡətɪp; *NAmE* -ɡərt-/ *noun* [usually pl.] the end of the finger that is furthest from the hand 指尖

IDM **have sth at your ˈfingertips** to have the information, knowledge, etc. that is needed in a particular situation and be able to find it easily and use it quickly 掌握（信息等）；熟悉，精通（知識等）；對…瞭如指掌；有…隨時可供使用 **to your ˈfingertips** (*BrE*) in every way 完全；十足： *She's a perfectionist to her fingertips.* 她是個道道地地的完美主義者。

fin·ial /ˈfɪniəl/ *noun* **1** (*architecture* 建) a decorative part at the top of a roof, wall, etc.（屋頂、牆頭等的）尖頂飾 **2** a decorative part that fits on the end of a curtain pole（簾杆的）裝飾頭 ➲ VISUAL VOCAB page V21

fin·icky /ˈfɪnɪki/ *adj.* **1** (*disapproving*) too worried about what you eat, wear, etc.; disliking many things（對衣食等）過分講究的，過分挑剔的 SYN **fussy**： *a finicky eater* 過分挑食者 **2** needing great care and attention to detail 需認真仔細對待的；需要注意細節的 SYN **fiddly**： *It's a very finicky job.* 這是個很細緻的工作。

fin·ish 🔑 /ˈfɪnɪʃ/ *verb, noun*

■ *verb* **1** 🔑 [T, I] to stop doing sth or making sth because it is complete 完成；做好： **~ (sth)** *Haven't you finished your homework yet?* 難道你還沒有完成家庭作業嗎？◇ *She finished law school last year.* 她去年畢業於法學院。◇ *I thought you'd never finish!* 我還以為你會完成不了呢！◇ *a beautifully finished piece of furniture* 一件做工精美的傢具 ◇ *He* ***put the finishing touches*** *to his painting* (= did the things that made it complete). 他在畫上作了最後幾處潤色。◇ **~ doing sth** *Be quiet! He hasn't finished speaking.* 安靜！他還沒有講完。◇ **+ speech** *'And that was all,' she finished.* "情況就這些。" 她結束時說。 **2** 🔑 [I, T] to come to an end; to bring sth to an end（使）結束：*The play finished at 10.30.* 比賽於 10:30 結束。◇ **~ with sth** *The symphony finishes with a flourish.* 交響樂在響亮的樂曲聲中結束。◇ **~ sth** *A cup of coffee finished the meal perfectly.* 飯後一杯咖啡，美餐圓滿結束。 **3** 🔑 [T] **~ sth (off/up)** to eat, drink or use what remains of sth 吃完，喝光，用盡（所剩之物）： *He finished off his drink with one large gulp.* 他一大口喝完了飲料。◇ *We might as well finish up the cake.* 我們倒不如把蛋糕吃完。 **4** 🔑 [I] to be in a particular state or position at the end of a race or a competition（賽跑、競賽）得…名；獲…成績： **+ adj.** *She was delighted to finish second.* 她為競賽得了第二名而高興。◇ *The dollar finished the day slightly down.* 當日結束時美元匯率略有下跌。◇ **+ adv./prep.** *He finished 12 seconds outside the world record.* 他的賽跑成績比世界紀錄慢 12 秒。 **5** [T] **~ sb (off)** (*informal*) to make sb so tired or impatient that they cannot do any more 使筋疲力盡；使失去耐心： *Climbing that hill really finished me off.* 登那座山真把我累得筋疲力盡。◇ *A lecture from my parents now would just finish me.* 現在父母教訓我簡直會使我受不了。

PHR V ˌ**finish sb/sth↔ˈoff** (*informal*) to destroy sb/sth, especially sb/sth that is badly injured or damaged 殺死，徹底摧毀（已嚴重受傷或受損的人或事物）： *The hunter moved in to finish the animal off.* 獵人逼到近前了結了那隻動物。 ˌ**finish sth↔ˈoff** 🔑 to do the last part of sth; to make sth end by doing one last thing 完成；作最後加工： *I need about an hour to finish off this report.* 我需要一小時左右完成這篇報告。◇ *They finished off the show with one of their most famous songs.* 他們用自己的一首最著名的歌曲作演出的壓台戲。 ˌ**finish ˈup ...** (*BrE*) to be in a particular state or at a particular place after a series of events 結果成為；以…終結；最終來到： **+ adj.** *If you're not careful, you could finish up seriously ill.* 你要是不小心，可能到頭來會得場大病。 ˈ**finish with sb** **1** (*BrE*) to end a relationship with sb 與（某人）斷絕關係： *She finished with her boyfriend last week.* 上星期她和男友分手了。 **2** to stop dealing with a person 停止和（某人）打交道： *He'll regret he ever said it once I've finished with him.* 我不再和他打交道，他就會後悔他說過那句話。 ˈ**finish with sth** **1** to no longer need to use sth 不再需用（某物）： *When you've finished with the book, can I see it?* 這本書你看完以後我能看嗎？ **2** (*BrE, informal*) to stop doing sth 不再做（某事）： *I've finished with gambling.* 我已戒賭了。 **finish (up) with sth** to have sth at the end 最後得到；以…結束： *We had a five-course lunch and finished up with coffee and mints.* 我們這頓午餐吃了五道菜，最後是咖啡和薄荷糖。◇ *To finish with, we'll listen to a few songs.* 最後我們將聽幾首歌。

■ *noun* **1** 🔑 [C, usually sing.] the last part or the end of sth 最後部份；結尾；結局： *a dramatic finish to the race* 賽跑的戲劇性結局 ◇ *It was* ***a close finish***, *as they had predicted.* 正如他們所預料的，比賽結果難分上下。◇ *They won in the end but it was a* ***tight finish***. 他們終於贏了，但比分十分接近。◇ *The story was a lie* ***from start to finish***. 這樣的講述自始至終都是騙人的。◇ *I want to see the job through* ***to the finish***. 我要看這項工作做完為止。 ➲ see also PHOTO FINISH **2** 🔑 [C, U] the last covering of paint, polish, etc. that is put onto the surface of sth; the condition of the surface 末道漆；拋光；（漆完拋光後的）成品表面： *a* ***gloss/matt finish*** 光澤／無光表面 ◇ *furniture available in a range of finishes* 有各種光澤處理的傢具 **3** [C, U] the final details that are added to sth to make it complete 最後精細加工： *The bows will give a feminine finish to the curtains.* 窗簾最後配上蝴蝶結顯出女性的柔美。 IDM see FIGHT *v.*

fin·ished 🔑 /ˈfɪnɪʃt/ *adj.*

1 🔑 [not before noun] no longer doing sth or dealing with sb/sth 完成；不再與…打交道： *I won't be finished for another hour.* 我還得一小時以後才能完成。◇ **~ with sb/sth** *I'm not finished with you yet.* 你我之間的交道還沒有完。 **2** 🔑 [not before noun] no longer powerful, effective or able to continue 垮台；失敗；完蛋： *If the newspapers find out, he's finished in politics.* 如果報界發現這些問題，他的政治生涯就完了。◇ *Their marriage was finished.* 他們的婚姻破裂了。 **3** 🔑 [usually before noun] fully completed, especially in a particular way 完成了的： *the* ***finished product/article*** 成品；脫稿的文章 ◇ *a beautifully finished suit* 做工精美的一套西服

fin·ish·er /ˈfɪnɪʃə(r)/ *noun* a person or an animal that finishes a race, etc.（賽跑等的）到達終點者

ˈ**fin·ish·ing line** (*BrE*) (*NAmE* ˈ**finish line**) *noun* the line across a sports track, etc. that marks the end of a race（體育比賽跑道的）終點線： *The two horses crossed the finishing line together.* 兩匹馬同時越過終點線。

ˈ**fin·ish·ing school** *noun* a private school where young women from rich families are taught how to behave in fashionable society 精修學校（為富家女子學習上流社會行為所辦的私立學校）

fi·nite AW /ˈfaɪnaɪt/ *adj.* **1** having a definite limit or fixed size 有限的；有限制的： *a finite number of possibilities* 為數有限的可能 ◇ *The world's resources are finite.* 世界的資源是有限的。 OPP **infinite** **2** (*grammar* 語法) a **finite** verb form or clause shows a particular tense, PERSON and NUMBER 限定的： *'Am', 'is', 'are', 'was' and 'were' are the finite forms of 'be'; 'being', and 'been' are the non-finite forms.* * am、is、are、was 和 were 是 be 的限定形式，being 和 been 是非限定形式。 OPP **non-finite**

fink /fɪŋk/ *noun* (*informal, especially NAmE*) an unpleasant person 討厭鬼；卑鄙小人

fiord = FJORD

fir /fɜː(r)/ (also ˈ**fir tree**) *noun* an EVERGREEN forest tree with leaves like needles 樅；冷杉 ➲ VISUAL VOCAB page V10

ˈ**fir cone** (*BrE*) (also **cone** *NAmE, BrE*) *noun* the hard fruit of the fir tree 冷杉球果 ➲ VISUAL VOCAB page V10

fire 🔑 /ˈfaɪə(r)/ *noun, verb*

■ *noun*

▸ STH BURNING 燃燒的東西 **1** 🔑 [U] the flames, light and heat, and often smoke, that are produced when sth burns 火： *Most animals are afraid of fire.* 大多數動物怕火。 **2** 🔑 [U, C] flames that are out of control and destroy buildings, trees, etc. 失火；火災： *The car was now* ***on fire***. 小轎車在燃燒。◇ *The warehouse has been badly damaged by fire.* 倉庫因失火損壞嚴重。◇ *Several youths had* ***set fire to*** *the police car* (= had made it start burning). 幾個年輕人縱火焚燒警車。◇ *A candle had* ***set*** *the curtains* ***on fire***. 蠟燭把窗簾燃起來了。◇ *These thatched roofs frequently* ***catch fire*** (= start to burn). 這些茅草屋頂屢屢着火。◇ ***forest fires*** 森林大火 ◇ *Five people died in a house fire last night.* 有五人死於昨夜的住宅火災。◇ *A small fire had started in the kitchen.* 廚房失火了，燃起了一股小小的火苗。◇ ***Fires*** *were* ***breaking out*** *everywhere.* 到處都在發生火災。◇ *It took two hours to* ***put out the fire*** (= stop it burning). 用了兩小時才把火撲滅。

▸ **FOR HEATING/COOKING** 取暖；烹飪 **3** [C] a pile of burning fuel, such as wood or coal, used for cooking food or heating a room 爐火；灶火： *to **make/build a fire*** 生火 ◇ *a **log/coal fire*** 柴／煤火 ◇ *Sam had **lit a fire** to welcome us home.* 薩姆點燃爐火歡迎我們回家。◇ *Come and get warm by the fire.* 到爐火邊來取暖。◇ *We sat in front of a **roaring fire**.* 我們坐在熊熊的爐火面前。➲ see also BONFIRE, CAMPFIRE **4** [C] (*especially BrE*) a piece of equipment for heating a room 取暖器；暖氣裝置： *a **gas/electric fire*** 煤氣／電取暖器 ◇ *Shall I put the fire on?* 我打開暖氣好嗎？➲ see also HEATER

▸ **FROM GUNS** 槍支 **5** [U] shots from guns 射擊；火力： *a burst of machine-gun fire* 一陣機槍射擊 ◇ *to **return fire*** (= to fire back at sb who is shooting at you) 用槍炮還擊 ◇ *The gunmen **opened fire on*** (= started shooting at) *the police.* 持槍歹徒向警察開火。◇ *Their vehicle **came under fire*** (= was being shot at). 他們的車遭到射擊。◇ *He ordered his men to **hold their fire*** (= not to shoot). 他命令士兵停止射擊。◇ *A young girl was **in the line of fire*** (= between the person shooting and what he/she was shooting at). 有一個女孩處於射程之內。

▸ **ANGER/ENTHUSIASM** 憤怒；熱情 **6** [U] very strong emotion, especially anger or enthusiasm 激情；憤怒；熱情： *Her eyes were full of fire.* 她的雙眼充滿激情的火花。

IDM **be/come under 'fire** to be criticized severely for sth you have done 受到嚴厲批評；遭到猛烈批判： *The health minister has come under fire from all sides.* 衛生部長受到來自各方的責難。 **hang/hold 'fire** to delay or be delayed in taking action （使行動）延遲；（使）遲緩： *The project had hung fire for several years for lack of funds.* 這個項目因缺少資金耽擱了好幾年。 **on 'fire** giving you a painful burning feeling 火辣辣；火燒火燎的： *He couldn't breathe. His chest was on fire.* 他無法呼吸。他的胸部火辣辣地疼痛。 **play with 'fire** to act in a way that is not sensible and take dangerous risks 玩火；冒險 ➲ more at BALL *n.*, BAPTISM, DRAW *v.*, FIGHT *v.*, FRYING PAN, HOUSE *n.*, IRON *n.*, SMOKE *n.*, WORLD

■ ***verb***

▸ **SHOOT** 射擊 **1** [I, T] to shoot bullets from a gun 射擊；開火；開槍： *The officer ordered his men to fire.* 軍官下令士兵射擊。◇ **~ on sb/sth** *Soldiers fired on the crowd.* 軍人朝人群開槍。◇ **~ sth** *They ran away as soon as the first shot was fired.* 第一槍剛響他們就跑了。◇ **~ (sth) (into sth)** *He fired the gun into the air.* 他朝天鳴槍。◇ **~ (sth) (at sb/sth)** *Missiles were fired at the enemy.* 向敵人發射了導彈。➲ COLLOCATIONS at WAR **2** [I, T] (of a gun 槍) to shoot bullets out 射出（子彈）： *We heard the sound of guns firing.* 我們聽見槍炮射擊聲。◇ **~ sth** *A starter's pistol fires only blanks.* 初學者的手槍發射的只是空彈。 **3** [T] **~ sth** to shoot an arrow 射（箭）： *She fired an arrow at the target.* 她瞄準靶子射箭。

▸ **FROM JOB** 工作 **4** [T] **~ sb** to force sb to leave their job 解雇；開除 **SYN** **sack**： *We had to fire him for dishonesty.* 他不誠實，我們不得不開除他。◇ *She got fired from her first job.* 她第一次工作就被解雇。◇ *He was responsible for **hiring and firing** staff.* 他負責招聘和解雇職員。➲ COLLOCATIONS at UNEMPLOYMENT

▸ **MAKE SB ENTHUSIASTIC** 使充滿激情 **5** [T] **~ sb (with sth)** to make sb feel very excited about sth or interested in sth 激勵；激起熱情；使充滿熱情： *The talk had fired her with enthusiasm for the project.* 這次談話激起了她對這個項目的熱情。◇ *His imagination had been fired by the film.* 這部電影激發了他的想像力。

▸ **OF ENGINE** 發動機 **6** [I] when an engine **fires**, an electrical SPARK is produced that makes the fuel burn and the engine start to work 點火；發動

▸ **-FIRED** 燃…的 **7** (in adjectives 構成形容詞) using the fuel mentioned in order to operate 以…為燃料的： *gas-fired central heating* 煤氣集中供暖

▸ **CLAY OBJECTS** 陶器 **8** [T] **~ sth** to heat a CLAY object to make it hard and strong 燒製（陶器、磚等）： *to fire pottery* 燒製陶器 ◇ *to fire bricks in a kiln* 在窰內燒磚

IDM **fire 'questions, 'insults, etc. at sb** to ask sb a lot of questions one after another or make a lot of comments very quickly 對某人發出連珠炮似的問題（或辱罵等）： *The room was full of journalists, all firing questions at them.* 滿屋的記者向他們接二連三地提問題。➲ more at CYLINDER

PHR V **,fire a'way** (*informal*) used to tell sb to begin to speak or ask a question （讓人）開始說，開始問： *'I've got a few questions.' 'OK then, fire away.'* "我有幾個問題。" "好，那就問吧。" **,fire sth↔'off** **1** to shoot a bullet from a gun 開槍；射擊： *They fired off a volley of shots.* 他們舉槍齊射。 **2** to write or say sth to sb very quickly, often when you are angry （常指憤怒地）連珠炮似地說，奮筆疾書： *He fired off a letter of complaint.* 他奮筆寫了一封投訴信。◇ *She spent an hour firing off emails to all concerned.* 她花了一個小時氣沖沖地向有關各方發電郵。 **,fire sb↔'up** to make sb excited or interested in sth 激起熱情；使充滿激情： *She's all fired up about her new job.* 她對新工作充滿熱情。 **,fire sth↔'up** (*informal*) to start a machine, piece of equipment, computer program, etc. 發動（機器）；啟動（設備、程序等）： *We need to fire up one of the generators.* 我們需要開動一台發電機。◇ *Let me fire up another window* (= on the computer screen). 讓我再打開一個窗口。

'fire alarm *noun* a bell or other device that gives people warning of a fire in a building 火警鐘；火警報警器： *Who set off the fire alarm?* 誰拉響了火警報警器？

fire·arm /'faɪərɑːm; *NAmE* -ɑːrm/ *noun* (*formal*) a gun that can be carried （便攜式的）槍： *The police were issued with firearms.* 警察都配發了小型槍支。

fire·ball /'faɪəbɔːl; *NAmE* 'faɪərb-/ *noun* a bright ball of fire, especially one at the centre of an explosion （尤指在爆炸中心的）火球

fire·bomb /'faɪəbɒm; *NAmE* 'faɪərbɑːm/ *noun* a bomb that makes a fire start burning after it explodes 燃燒彈 ▸ **fire·bomb** *verb* **~ sth**

fire·brand /'faɪəbrænd; *NAmE* 'faɪərb-/ *noun* a person who is always encouraging other people to take strong political action, often causing trouble 挑動政治爭端者；煽動動亂者

fire·break /'faɪəbreɪk; *NAmE* 'faɪərb-/ *noun* a thing that stops a fire from spreading, for example a special door or a strip of land in a forest that has been cleared of trees 火障（如防火安全門、防火帶、防火線）➲ see also FIRE LINE

fire·brick /'faɪəbrɪk; *NAmE* 'faɪər-/ *noun* [U, C] (*technical* 術語) brick which is not destroyed by very strong heat; an individual block of this 耐火磚

'fire brigade (also **'fire service**) (both *BrE*) (*NAmE* **'fire department**) *noun* [C+sing./pl. v.] an organization of people who are trained and employed to put out fires and to rescue people from fires; the people who belong to this organization 消防隊；消防署： *to call out the fire brigade* 叫消防隊來 ◇ *The fire brigade were there in minutes.* 幾分鐘後消防隊就到了現場。

fire·bug /'faɪəbʌɡ; *NAmE* 'faɪər-/ *noun* (*informal*) a person who deliberately starts fires 放火者；縱火狂

fire·crack·er /'faɪəkrækə(r); *NAmE* 'faɪərk-/ *noun* a small FIREWORK that explodes with a loud noise 鞭炮；爆竹

'fire de·part·ment (*NAmE*) (*BrE* **'fire brigade**, **'fire service**) *noun* [usually sing.] an organization of people who are trained and employed to put out fires and to rescue people from fires; the people who belong to this organization 消防隊；消防隊員

'fire door *noun* a heavy door that is used to prevent a fire from spreading in a building （建築物內的）防火安全門

'fire drill (*BrE* also **'fire practice**) *noun* [C, U] a practice of what people must do in order to escape safely from a fire in a building 消防演習

'fire-eater *noun* an entertainer who pretends to eat fire 吞火表演者

'fire engine (*NAmE* also **'fire truck**) *noun* a special vehicle that carries equipment for fighting large fires 消防車；救火車

'fire es·cape *noun* metal stairs or a LADDER on the outside of a building, which people can use to escape from a fire 太平梯（在建築物外部，用以逃離火場）➲ VISUAL VOCAB page V16

'fire extinguisher (also **ex·tin·guish·er**) *noun* a metal container with water or chemicals inside for putting out small fires 滅火器

fire·fight /ˈfaɪəfaɪt; *NAmE* ˈfaɪərf-/ *noun* (*technical* 術語) a battle where guns are used, involving soldiers or the police 交火；火戰；炮戰

fire·fight·er /ˈfaɪəfaɪtə(r); *NAmE* ˈfaɪərf-/ *noun* a person whose job is to put out fires 消防隊員 ➲ see also FIREMAN ▸ **fire·fight·ing** *noun* [U]：*firefighting equipment/vehicles* 消防設備／車輛

fire·fly /ˈfaɪəflaɪ; *NAmE* ˈfaɪərf-/ *noun* (*pl.* **-ies**) (*NAmE* also **'lightning bug**) a flying insect with a tail that shines in the dark 螢火蟲

fire·guard /ˈfaɪəɡɑːd; *NAmE* ˈfaɪərɡɑːrd/ (*NAmE* also **'fire screen**) *noun* a metal frame that is put in front of a fire in a room to prevent people from burning themselves（室內取暖爐的）爐欄，爐擋

'fire hose *noun* a long tube that is used for directing water onto fires 消防水龍帶；消防水管

fire·house /ˈfaɪəhaʊs; *NAmE* ˈfaɪərh-/ *noun* (*US*) a FIRE STATION in a small town（小城鎮的）消防站

'fire hydrant (also **hy·drant**) *noun* a pipe in the street through which water can be sent using a PUMP in order to put out fires or to clean the streets 消防栓；消防龍頭

fire·light /ˈfaɪəlaɪt; *NAmE* ˈfaɪərl-/ *noun* [U] the light that comes from a fire in a room（室內的）爐火光

fire·light·er /ˈfaɪəlaɪtə(r); *NAmE* ˈfaɪərl-/ (*BrE*) (*NAmE* **'fire·start·er**) *noun* [C, U] a block of material that burns easily and is used to help start a coal or wood fire（生爐子的）引火物，火種

'fire line *noun* (*NAmE*) a strip of land that has been cleared in order to stop a fire from spreading 防火帶；防火線 ➲ see also FIREBREAK

fire·man /ˈfaɪəmən; *NAmE* ˈfaɪərmən/ *noun* (*pl.* **-men** /-mən/) a person, usually a man, whose job is to put out fires 消防隊員 ➲ see also FIREFIGHTER ➲ note at GENDER

fire·place /ˈfaɪəpleɪs; *NAmE* ˈfaɪərp-/ *noun* an open space for a fire in the wall of a room 壁爐 ➲ VISUAL VOCAB page V21

fire·power /ˈfaɪəpaʊə(r); *NAmE* ˈfaɪərp-/ *noun* [U] the number and size of guns that an army, a ship, etc. has available（軍隊、艦船等的）火力：(*figurative*) *The company has enormous financial firepower.* 這家公司財力雄厚。

'fire prac·tice *noun* [C, U] (*BrE*) = FIRE DRILL

fire·proof /ˈfaɪəpruːf; *NAmE* ˈfaɪərp-/ *adj.* able to resist great heat without burning or being badly damaged 防火的；耐火的：*a fireproof door* 防火門 ◇ *a fireproof dish* (= that can be heated in an oven) 耐火盤

'fire-raiser *noun* (*BrE*) a person who starts a fire deliberately 縱火者；放火者 SYN **arsonist** ▸ **'fire-raising** *noun* [U]

fire-retard·ant /ˈfaɪə rɪˌtɑːdənt; *NAmE* ˈfaɪər rɪˌtɑːrd-/ (also **'flame-retardant**) *adj.* [usually before noun] that makes a fire burn more slowly 阻燃的

'fire sale *noun* **1** a sale at low prices of things that a company or person owns, usually in order to pay debts（抵債）大甩賣：*The company was forced to have a fire sale of its assets.* 公司被迫低價拋售其資產償還債務。**2** a sale of goods at low prices because they have been damaged by a fire or because they cannot be stored after a fire 火災後大甩賣

'fire screen *noun* **1** (*NAmE*) = FIREGUARD **2** a screen, often decorative, that is put in front of an open fire in a room to protect people from the heat or from SPARKS, or to hide it when it is not lit 擋火隔板

'fire ser·vice *noun* [usually sing.] (*BrE*) = FIRE BRIGADE

fire·side /ˈfaɪəsaɪd; *NAmE* ˈfaɪərs-/ *noun* [usually sing.] the part of a room beside the fire 爐邊：*sitting by the fireside* 坐在爐邊

'fire starter (*NAmE*) (*BrE* **fire·light·er**) *noun* a block of material that burns easily and is used to help start a coal or wood fire（生爐子的）引火物

fire·start·er /ˈfaɪəstɑːtə(r); *NAmE* ˈfaɪərstɑːrtər/ *noun* (*NAmE*) **1** a device that allows you to start a fire, usually by hitting a piece of FLINT (= a hard grey stone) against a piece of steel 打火石點火器具 **2** (*BrE* **fire·light·er**) a block of material that burns easily and is used to help start a coal or wood fire（生爐子的）引火物 **3** a person who commits the crime of deliberately setting fire to sth 縱火罪犯；蓄意縱火者 SYN **arsonist**

'fire station *noun* a building for a FIRE BRIGADE or FIRE DEPARTMENT and its equipment 消防站

fire·storm /ˈfaɪəstɔːm; *NAmE* ˈfaɪərstɔːrm/ *noun* a very large fire, usually started by bombs, that is not under control and is made worse by the winds that it causes（尤指爆炸引起的）風暴性大火

'fire trap *noun* a building that would be very dangerous if a fire started there, especially because it would be difficult for people to escape 發生火災時難以逃生的建築物

'fire truck *noun* (*NAmE*) = FIRE ENGINE

fire·wall /ˈfaɪəwɔːl; *NAmE* ˈfaɪərw-/ *noun* (*computing* 計) a part of a computer system that prevents people from getting at information without permission, but still allows them to receive information that is sent to them 防火牆（防止竊取計算機信息的系統）➲ COLLOCATIONS at EMAIL

fire·water /ˈfaɪəwɔːtə(r); *NAmE* ˈfaɪər-/ *noun* [U] (*informal*) strong alcoholic drink 烈酒；燒酒

fire·wood /ˈfaɪəwʊd; *NAmE* ˈfaɪərwʊd/ *noun* [U] wood that has been cut into pieces to be used for burning in fires 木柴

fire·work /ˈfaɪəwɜːk; *NAmE* ˈfaɪərwɜːrk/ *noun* **1** [C] a small device containing powder that burns or explodes and produces bright coloured lights and loud noises, used especially at celebrations 煙火；煙花：(*BrE*) *to let off a few fireworks* 放幾個煙火 ◇ (*NAmE*) *to set off a few fireworks* 放幾個煙火 ◇ *a firework(s) display* 放煙火 **2 fireworks** [pl.] a display of fireworks 煙火表演；煙花表演；放煙火：*When do the fireworks start?* 什麼時候開始放煙火？ **3 fireworks** [pl.] (*informal*) strong or angry words; exciting actions 激烈的言辭；憤怒的話語；令人激動的行動：*There'll be fireworks when he finds out!* 他要是發覺了就會大發雷霆！

fir·ing /ˈfaɪərɪŋ/ *noun* **1** [U] the action of firing guns 射擊；發射；開火；開槍；開炮：*There was continuous firing throughout the night.* 整夜槍炮不息。**2** [U, C] (*especially NAmE*) the action of forcing sb to leave their job 解雇：*teachers protesting against the firing of a colleague* 因一位同事被開除而抗議的教師們 ◇ *She's responsible for the hirings and firings.* 她負責雇用和解雇。

'firing line *noun*

IDM **be in the 'firing line** (*BrE*) (*NAmE* **be on the 'firing line**) **1** to be in a position where you can be shot at 處於射程以內 **2** to be in a position where people can criticize or blame you 處於易受批評（或責備）的地位：*The employment secretary found himself in the firing line over recent job cuts.* 勞工部長因近期的職位削減而備受責難。

'firing squad *noun* [C+sing./pl. v., U] a group of soldiers who are ordered to shoot and kill sb who is found guilty of a crime 行刑隊（對判死刑的犯人執行槍決）：*He was executed by (a) firing squad.* 他被行刑隊執行槍決。

fir·kin /ˈfɜːkɪn; *NAmE* ˈfɜːrkɪn/ *noun* (*old use*) **1** a small BARREL (= a round container with flat ends), used mainly for liquids, butter or fish（盛液體、黃油、魚等的）小桶 **2** a unit for measuring volume, equal to about 41 litres 桶（容量單位，相當於 41 公升）

firm 0‑π /fɜːm; *NAmE* fɜːrm/ *noun, adj., adv., verb*

■ ***noun*** 0‑π a business or company 商行；商號；公司：*an engineering firm* 工程公司 ◇ *a firm of accountants* 會計事務所 ➲ COLLOCATIONS at BUSINESS

■ ***adj.*** (**firm·er**, **firm·est**) **1** 0‑π fairly hard; not easy to press into a different shape 堅固的；堅硬的；結實的：*a firm bed/mattress* 結實的牀／牀墊 ◇ *These peaches are still*

F

firm. 這些桃子還很硬。◇ *Bake the cakes until they are firm to the touch.* 把糕餅烤到摸來有硬感為止。 **2** 🔑 not likely to change 堅定的；確定的；堅決的： *a* ***firm believer*** *in socialism* 堅定信仰社會主義的人 ◇ *a* ***firm agreement/date/decision/offer/promise*** 鞏固的協議；確定的日期；不能更改的決定；實盤；堅決的保證 ◇ ***firm beliefs/conclusions/convictions/principles*** 堅定不移的信仰；定論；堅定的信念 / 原則 ◇ *She is a* ***firm favourite with*** *the children.* 孩子們着實喜歡她。◇ *We have no* ***firm evidence*** *to support the case.* 我們沒有確鑿的證據支持這個論點。◇ *They remained* ***firm friends.*** 他們依然友情甚篤。 **3** 🔑 strongly fixed in place 牢固的；穩固的 **SYN** **secure**： *Stand the fish tank on a firm base.* 把魚缸放在牢固的基座上。◇ *No building can stand without firm foundations, and neither can a marriage.* 沒有穩固的基礎，建築就不牢靠，婚姻也是如此。 **4** 🔑 (of sb's voice or hand movements 聲音或手勢) strong and steady 強有力的；堅決的： *'No,' she repeated, her voice firmer this time.* "不。"她重複說，這次語氣較前堅決。◇ *With a* ***firm grip*** *on my hand, he pulled me away.* 他緊握我的手把我拉開。◇ *Her handshake was cool and firm.* 她握手鎮定而有力。 **5** (of sb's behaviour, position or understanding of sth 行為、處境或理解) strong and in control 牢牢控制的；嚴格的；掌握的： *to exercise* ***firm control/discipline/leadership*** 實施嚴格的控制 / 紀律 / 領導 ◇ *Parents must* ***be firm with*** *their children.* 父母必須對子女嚴格。◇ *The company now has a* ***firm footing*** *in the marketplace.* 現在這家公司在市場上已站穩了腳跟。◇ *This book will give your students a* ***firm grasp of*** *English grammar.* 這本書將使學生牢固地掌握英語語法。◇ *We need to keep a* ***firm grip*** *on the situation.* 我們需要牢牢地掌握局面。 **6** [usually before noun] **~ (against sth)** (of a country's money, etc. 貨幣等) not lower than another 堅挺的： *The euro remained firm against the dollar, but fell against the yen.* 歐元對美元依然堅挺，但對日元的匯率則下跌。 ➲ see also FIRMLY ▶ **firm·ness** *noun* [U]

IDM **be on firm 'ground** to be in a strong position in an argument, etc. because you know the facts（在辯論等中）立場堅定，對事實確信無疑： *Everyone agreed with me, so I knew I was on firm ground.* 每個人都同意我的意見，所以我知道自己立場穩固了。 **a firm 'hand** strong control or discipline 牢固控制；嚴格紀律；鐵腕： *Those children need a firm hand to make them behave.* 那些孩子得嚴加管教。 **take a firm 'line/'stand (on/against sth)** to make your beliefs known and to try to make others follow them（對…）採取堅定的立場（或態度）： *We need to take a firm line on tobacco advertising.* 我們需要對煙草廣告採取強硬的態度。◇ *They took a firm stand against drugs in the school.* 他們堅決反對校園吸毒現象。

■ ***adv.***

IDM **hold 'firm (to sth)** (*formal*) to believe sth strongly and not change your mind 堅信；堅持： *She held firm to her principles.* 她堅持自己的原則。 **stand 'fast/'firm** to refuse to move back; to refuse to change your opinions 堅定不移；不讓步；堅持自己的觀點

■ ***verb*** **1** [T] **~ sth** to make sth become stronger or harder 使強壯；使堅固；使堅實： *Firm the soil around the plant.* 把植物周圍的土弄緊實。◇ *This product claims to firm your body in six weeks.* 這個產品據稱能在六週內使身體強壯。 **2** [I] **~ (to/at ...)** (*finance* 財) (of shares, prices, etc. 股票、物價等) to become steady or rise steadily 堅挺；穩步上漲： *Rank's shares firmed 3p to 696p.* 蘭克公司的股票漲了 3 便士，升至 696 便士。

PHR V **,firm 'up** to become harder or more solid 變堅固；變堅實： *Put the mixture somewhere cool to firm up.* 把混合物放在一個地方冷卻變硬。 **,firm 'up sth** **1** to make arrangements more final and fixed 最後落實；敲定： *The company has not yet firmed up its plans for expansion.* 公司的擴大計劃尚未最後落實。◇ *The precise details still have to be firmed up.* 準確的細節仍需最後敲定。 **2** to make sth harder or more solid 使堅固；使堅硬；使堅實： *A few weeks of aerobics will firm up that flabby stomach.* 幾個星期的有氧健身運動將使鬆弛的腹部結實。

F

firma·ment /ˈfɜːməmənt; *NAmE* ˈfɜːrm-/ *noun* **the firmament** [sing.] (*old use* or *literary*) the sky 天空；蒼穹： (*figurative*) *a rising star in the literary firmament* 文壇上一顆冉冉升起的新星

firm·ly 🔑 /ˈfɜːmli; *NAmE* ˈfɜːrm-/ *adv.* in a strong or definite way 堅定地；堅固地： *'I can manage,' she said firmly.* "我應付得了。"她堅定地說。◇ *It is now firmly established as one of the leading brands in the country.* 現在它已穩穩地確立為國內主要品牌之一。◇ *Keep your eyes firmly fixed on the road ahead.* 密切注視路的前方。

firm·ware /ˈfɜːmweə(r); *NAmE* ˈfɜːrmwer/ *noun* [U] (*computing* 計) a type of computer software that is stored in such a way that it cannot be changed or lost 固件；固化軟件；韌體

first 🔑 /fɜːst; *NAmE* fɜːrst/ *det., ordinal number, adv., noun*

■ ***det., ordinal number*** **1** 🔑 happening or coming before all other similar things or people; 1st 第一： *his first wife* 他的第一個妻子 ◇ *It was the first time they had ever met.* 這是他們初次見面。◇ *I didn't take the first bus.* 我沒有乘坐首班公共汽車。◇ *students in their first year at college* 大學一年級學生 ◇ *your first impressions* 你的初步印象 ◇ *She resolved to do it at the first (= earliest) opportunity.* 她決定一有機會就去做。◇ *King Edward I (= pronounced 'King Edward the First')* 英王愛德華一世 ◇ *the first of May/May 1st* * 5 月 1 日 ◇ *His second book is better than his first.* 他的第二部書比第一部好。 **2** 🔑 the most important or best 最重要的；首要的；最優秀的： *Your first duty is to your family.* 你首要的是對家庭盡責。◇ *She won first prize in the competition.* 她在競賽中獲得一等獎。◇ *an issue of the first importance* 最重要的問題

IDM Most idioms containing **first** are at the entries for the nouns and adjectives in the idioms, for example **on first acquaintance** is at **acquaintance**. 大多數含有 first 的習語位於該習語中名詞和形容詞所在的詞條，如 first acquaintance 位於 acquaintance 詞條。 **there's a first time for everything** (*saying, humorous*) the fact that sth has not happened before does not mean that it will never happen 沒有發生的事情並不意味着永遠不會發生；什麼事情都有第一次

■ ***adv.*** **1** 🔑 before anyone or anything else; at the beginning 首先；第一；最初： *'Do you want a drink?' 'I'll finish my work first.'* "你想喝杯飲料嗎？""我要先完成工作。"◇ *First I had to decide what to wear.* 首先我得決定穿什麼。◇ *Who* ***came first*** *in the race (= who won)?* 賽跑誰第一？◇ *It plunged nose first into the river.* 它一頭跳入水中。 **2** 🔑 for the first time 第一次；首次： *When did you first meet him?* 你和他初次見面是何時？ **3** 🔑 used to introduce the first of a list of points you want to make in a speech or piece of writing（列舉時用）第一，首先 **SYN** **firstly**： *This method has two advantages: first it is cheaper and second it is quicker.* 這個方法有兩個優點：一是更便宜，二是較快。 ➲ LANGUAGE BANK at PROCESS **4** used to emphasize that you are determined not to do sth（強調不願意）寧可，寧願： *She swore that she wouldn't apologize—she'd die first!* 她發誓決不道歉，寧死也不！

IDM **at 'first** at or in the beginning 起初；起先： *I didn't like the job much at first.* 起初我並不很喜歡這個工作。◇ *At first I thought he was shy, but then I discovered he was just not interested in other people.* 起先我以為他靦腆，後來才發現他對別人沒興趣。◇ (*saying*) *If at first you don't succeed, try, try again.* 一次不成功就反複嘗試。 ➲ note at FIRSTLY **come 'first** to be considered more important than anything else 首要；第一；首先要考慮的： *In any decision she makes, her family always comes first.* 她作任何決定都是家庭第一。 **,first and 'foremost** more than anything else 首要的是；首先： *He does a little teaching, but first and foremost he's a writer.* 他幹一點教學，但首要的是寫作。 **,first and 'last** in every way that is important; completely 從各方面看；完全地： *She regarded herself, first and last, as a musician.* 她認為她自己是一個不折不扣的音樂家。 **,first 'come, ,first 'served** (*saying*) people will be dealt with, seen, etc. strictly in the order in which they arrive 先來先接待；先到先供應；按先來後到對待： *Tickets are available on a first come, first served basis.* 票先來先買，售完為止。

ˌ**first of ˈall 1** before doing anything else; at the beginning 第一；首先：*First of all, let me ask you something.* 首先，讓我問你一件事。➲ LANGUAGE BANK at PROCESS **2** as the most important thing 最重要；首先：*The content of any article needs, first of all, to be relevant to the reader.* 任何文章的內容都首先要與讀者有關。➲ note at FIRSTLY ˌ**first ˈoff** (*informal, especially BrE*) before anything else 首先：*First off, let's see how much it'll cost.* 首先咱們看看這要花多少錢。ˌ**first ˈup** (*BrE, informal*) to start with; before anything else 第一；首先 ˌ**put sb/sth ˈfirst** to consider sb/sth to be more important than anyone/anything else 認為…最重要；把…放在第一位：*She always puts her children first.* 她總是把子女放在第一位。➲ more at FOOT *n.*, HEAD *n.*, SAFETY

■ *noun* **1** **the first** [C] (*pl.* **the first**) the first person or thing mentioned; the first person or thing to do a particular thing 第一個人（或事物）：*I was the first in my family to go to college.* 我是我們家第一個大學生。◇ *Sheila and Jim were the first to arrive.* 希拉和吉姆最先到的。◇ *I'd be* ***the first to admit*** (= I will most willingly admit) *I might be wrong.* 我非常願意承認我可能錯了。◇ ***The first I heard about*** *the wedding* (= the first time I became aware of it) *was when I saw it in the local paper.* 我最初知道他們結婚的消息是從當地報紙上看到的。**2** [C, usually sing.] an achievement, event, etc., never done or experienced before 空前的成就；前所未有的事情：*We went on a cruise, a first for both of us.* 我倆都是平生第一次去海上旅遊。**3** (also ˌ**first ˈgear**) [U] the lowest gear on a car, bicycle, etc. that you use when you are moving slowly（汽車、自行車等的）頭擋，最低擋：*He stuck the car* ***in first*** *and revved.* 他掛上了頭擋，開動了汽車。**4** [C] **~ (in sth)** the highest level of university degree at British universities（英國大學學位）最高成績，優等成績：*She* ***got a first*** *in maths at Exeter.* 她在埃克塞特大學畢業，獲數學一級優等學位。➲ compare SECOND[1] *n.* (7), THIRD *n.* (2)

IDM ˌ**first among ˈequals** the person or thing with the highest status in a group 第一把手；首要的事物 **from the (very) ˈfirst** from the beginning 從一開始：*They were attracted to each other from the first.* 他倆一見傾心。**from ˌfirst to ˈlast** from beginning to end; during the whole time 從頭至尾；自始至終：*It's a fine performance that commands attention from first to last.* 這是個精彩的演出，自始至終都扣人心弦。

Language Bank 用語庫

first

Ordering your points 梳理要點

- This study has **the following** aims: **first**, to investigate how international students in the UK use humour; **second**, to examine how jokes can help to establish social relationships; and, **third**, to explore the role that humour plays in helping overseas students adjust to life in the UK. 本研究有以下幾個目的：第一，調查在英國的留學生如何運用幽默；第二，考察笑話如何幫助建立社交關係；第三，探究幽默對留學生適應英國生活所起的作用。
- **Let us begin by** identifying some of the popular joke genres in the UK. 首先我們來辨別一下流行於英國的一些笑話類型。
- **Next, let us turn to/Next, let us consider** the question of gender differences in the use of humour. 接下來，我們來探討一下運用幽默的性別差異問題。
- **Finally/Lastly**, let us briefly examine the role of humour in defining a nation's culture. 最後，我們來簡略地探討一下幽默在界定民族文化中所起的作用。

➲ notes at FIRSTLY, LASTLY

➲ Language Banks at CONCLUSION, PROCESS

ˌ**first ˈaid** *noun* [U] simple medical treatment that is given to sb before a doctor comes or before the person can be taken to a hospital 急救：*to give first aid* 進行急救 ◇ *a first-aid course* 急救課程

ˌ**first ˈaider** *noun* (*BrE*) a person who is trained to give first aid 急救員

the ˌFirst Aˈmendment *noun* [sing.] the statement in the US Constitution that protects freedom of speech and religion and the right to meet in peaceful groups（美國憲法）第一修正案（保護言論與信仰自由以及和平結社權）

ˌ**first ˈbalcony** *noun* (*NAmE*) = DRESS CIRCLE

ˌ**first ˈbase** *noun* (in BASEBALL 棒球) the first of the BASES that players must touch 一壘：*He didn't make it past first base.* 他未能跑過一壘。

IDM **not get to first ˈbase (with sth/sb)** (*informal, especially NAmE*) to fail to make a successful start in a project, relationship, etc.; to fail to get through the first stage（工程、關係等）未能順利開始，未能跨出第一步

first·born /ˈfɜːstbɔːn; *NAmE* ˈfɜːrstbɔːrn/ *noun* (*old-fashioned*) a person's first child 頭胎；長子；長女 ▸ **first·born** *adj.* [only before noun]：*their firstborn son* 他們的長子

ˌ**first ˈclass** *noun, adv.*

■ *noun* [U] **1** the best and most expensive seats or accommodation on a train, plane or ship 頭等座位（或車廂、艙）：*There is more room in first class.* 頭等艙更寬敞。**2** (in Britain) the class of mail that is delivered most quickly 第一類郵件（在英國投遞最快的郵件）：*First class costs more.* 第一類郵件郵資較高。**3** (in the US) the class of mail that is used for letters 第一類郵件（在美國用於投遞信件和明信片）**4** the highest standard of degree given by a British university 一級優等學位（英國大學學位等級）

■ *adv.* **1** using the best and most expensive seats or accommodation in a train, plane or ship 乘坐頭等座位（或車廂、艙）：*to travel first class* 乘頭等艙旅行 **2** (in Britain) by the quickest form of mail（英國）按最快投遞郵件：*I sent the package first class on Monday.* 我於星期一以最快投遞郵件寄出包裹。**3** (in the US) by the class of mail that is used for letters（美國）按第一類郵件

ˌ**first-ˈclass** *adj.* **1** [usually before noun] in the best group; of the highest standard 第一流的；一級的；一等的；最優的 **SYN** **excellent**：*a first-class novel* 最佳小說 ◇ *a first-class writer* 一流作家 ◇ *The car was in first-class condition.* 當時車子處於最佳狀態。◇ *I know a place where the food is first-class.* 我知道有一個品嚐一流美食的地方。**2** [only before noun] connected with the best and most expensive way of travelling on a train, plane or ship（座位、車廂、艙位）頭等的：*first-class rail travel* 乘頭等車廂旅行 ◇ *a first-class cabin/seat/ticket* 頭等艙／座位／票 **3** [only before noun] (in Britain) connected with letters, packages, etc. that are delivered most quickly, or that cost more to send 第一類的（英國郵件等級，投遞最快）：***first-class mail/post/postage/stamps*** 第一類郵件／郵資／郵票 **4** [only before noun] used to describe a university degree of the highest class from a British university 一級優等的（英國大學學位）：*She was awarded a first-class degree in English.* 她獲得一級優等英語學位。

ˈ**first cost** *noun* [C, U] (*economics* 經) = PRIME COST

ˌ**first ˈcousin** *noun* = COUSIN (1)

ˈ**first degree** *noun* (*especially BrE*) an academic qualification given by a university or college, for example a BA or BSc, that is given to sb who does not already have a degree in that subject（大學的）初級學位，學士學位：*What was your first degree in?* 你的學士學位是哪一科？◇ *to study geography at first-degree level* 攻讀地理學學士學位

ˌ**first-deˈgree** *adj.* [only before noun] **1** (*especially NAmE*) **~ murder, assault, robbery, etc.** murder, etc. of the most serious kind 第一等級（謀殺、人身侵犯或搶劫等罪）**2 ~ burns** burns of the least serious of three kinds, affecting only the surface of the skin 一度（燒傷）➲ compare SECOND-DEGREE, THIRD-DEGREE

ˌfirst ˈdown *noun* (in AMERICAN FOOTBALL 美式足球) **1** the first of a series of four DOWNS (= chances to move the ball forward ten yards)（四次十碼進攻中的）第一次進攻，首攻 **2** the chance to start a new series of four DOWNS because your team has succeeded in going forward ten yards（成功推進十碼之後的）新一輪四次十碼進攻權

ˌfirst eˈdition *noun* one of the copies of a book that was produced the first time the book was printed（書籍的）第一版，初版

ˌfirst-ˈever *adj.* [only before noun] never having happened or been experienced before 首次的：*his first-ever visit to London* 他對倫敦的初次訪問 ◇ *the first-ever woman vice-president* 第一位女副總統

the ˌfirst ˈfamily *noun* [sing.] the family of the President of the United States 第一家庭（美國總統的家庭）

ˌfirst ˈfinger *noun* = INDEX FINGER

ˌfirst ˈfloor (usually **the first floor**) *noun* [sing.] **1** (*BrE*) the level of a building above the ground level 地面以上的一層：*Menswear is on the first floor.* 男裝在第二層。 **2** (*NAmE*) (*BrE* **ˌground ˈfloor**) the floor of a building that is at the same level as the ground outside 底層，底樓，一樓（建築物與外面地面相平的一層）▶ **ˌfirst-ˈfloor** *adj.* [only before noun]：*a first-floor flat/apartment* 二樓的一套公寓房／（公寓）套房 ➲ note at FLOOR

ˌfirst-ˈfoot *verb* **~ sb** to be the first person to enter sb's house in the New Year. First-footing is a Scottish custom.（蘇格蘭風俗）作為新年第一位訪客 ▶ **ˌfirst-ˈfooter** *noun*

ˈfirst fruit *noun* [usually pl.] the first result of sb's work or effort（工作、努力的）初步成果，最初收穫

ˌfirst geneˈration *noun* [sing.] **1** people who have left their country to go and live in a new country; the children of these people（移民的）第一代；第一代移民的子女 **2** the first type of a machine to be developed（研製的機器的）第一代：*the first generation of personal computers* 第一代個人電腦 ▶ **ˌfirst-geneˈration** *adj.*：*first-generation Caribbeans in the UK* 在英國的第一代加勒比海移民

ˌfirst-ˈhand *adj.* [only before noun] obtained or experienced yourself 第一手的；直接的：*to have first-hand experience of poverty* 親身體驗過貧窮 ➲ compare SECOND-HAND ▶ **ˌfirst-ˈhand** *adv.*：*to experience poverty first-hand* 親身體驗貧窮

ˌFirst ˈLady *noun* [usually sing.] **1 the First Lady** (in the US) the wife of the President 第一夫人（美國的總統夫人）**2** (*NAmE*) the wife of the leader of a state 元首夫人 **3** (usually **first lady**) the woman who is thought to be the best in a particular profession, sport, etc. 女傑：*the first lady of country music* 鄉村音樂最佳女歌手

ˌfirst ˈlanguage *noun* the language that you learn to speak first as a child; the language that you speak best 母語；第一語言：*His first language is Welsh.* 他的母語是威爾士語。➲ compare SECOND LANGUAGE

ˌfirst lieuˈtenant *noun* **1** an officer in the navy with responsibility for managing a ship, etc. 艦務官 **2** an officer in the US army and AIR FORCE just below the rank of a captain（美國陸軍和空軍的）中尉 **3** (*informal*) a person who is the next most important to sb 第二把手

ˌfirst ˈlight *noun* [U] the time when light first appears in the morning 黎明；破曉；曙光 SYN **dawn, daybreak**：*We left at first light.* 我們黎明時離去。

first·ly /ˈfɜːstli; *NAmE* ˈfɜːrst-/ *adv.* used to introduce the first of a list of points you want to make in a speech or piece of writing（用於列舉）第一，首先：*There are two reasons for this decision: firstly …* 做此決定理由有二：第一… ➲ LANGUAGE BANK at FIRST

ˌfirst ˈmate (also **ˌfirst ˈofficer**) *noun* the officer on a commercial ship just below the rank of captain or MASTER（商船的）大副

ˌfirst ˈminister (also **First Minister**) *noun* the leader of the ruling political party in some regions or countries, for example in Scotland 首席部長（一些地區或國家中執政黨的領袖）

Which Word? 詞語辨析

firstly / first of all / at first

- **Firstly** and **first** (**of all**) are used to introduce a series of facts, reasons, opinions, etc. * firstly 和 first (of all) 均用以引出一系列事實、理由、意見等：*The brochure is divided into two sections, dealing firstly with basic courses and secondly with advanced ones.* 小冊子分為兩部份：第一部份涉及基礎課程，第二部份涉及高階課程。 **Firstly** is more common in *BrE* than in *NAmE*. * firstly 在英式英語中比在美式英語中更通用。
- **At first** is used to talk about the situation at the beginning of a period of time, especially when you are comparing it with a different situation at a later period. * at first 用以講述最初階段的情況，尤指與後來的不同情況相比較：*Maggie had seen him nearly every day at first. Now she saw him much less.* 起初瑪吉幾乎每天都見到他，現在見到他的次數少得多了。

ˈfirst name (also **ˈgiven name** especially in *NAmE*) *noun* a name that was given to you when you were born, that comes before your family name 名字：*His first name is Tom and his surname is Green.* 他叫湯姆，姓格林。◇ *Please give all your first names.* 請給出姓以外的全名。◇ (*BrE*) *to be* ***on first-name terms*** *with sb* (= to call them by their first name as a sign of a friendly informal relationship) 與某人以名字相稱 ◇ (*NAmE*) *to be* ***on a first-name basis*** 關係密切直呼其名

ˌFirst ˈNations *noun* [pl.] (*CanE*) the Aboriginal peoples of Canada, not including the Inuit or Metis 原部落居民（不包括因努伊特人或混血的加拿大土著居民）

ˌfirst ˈnight *noun* **1** the first public performance of a play, film/movie, etc.（戲劇、電影等的）首場，首次上演 **2** (*NAmE*) a public celebration of NEW YEAR'S EVE 除夕的公眾慶祝活動

ˌfirst ofˈfender *noun* a person who has been found guilty of a crime for the first time 初犯

ˌfirst ˈofficer *noun* = FIRST MATE

ˌfirst-ˌpast-the-ˈpost *adj.* [only before noun] (of a system of elections 選舉體制) in which only the person who gets the most votes is elected 得票最多者當選的 ➲ compare PROPORTIONAL REPRESENTATION

the ˌfirst ˈperson *noun* [sing.] **1** (*grammar* 語法) a set of pronouns and verb forms used by a speaker to refer to himself or herself, or to a group including himself or herself 第一人稱：*'I am' is the first person singular of the present tense of the verb 'to be'.* * I am 是動詞 to be 現在時的第一人稱單數。◇ *'I', 'me', 'we' and 'us' are first-person pronouns.* * I、me、we 和 us 是第一人稱代詞。 **2** a way of writing a novel, etc. as if one of the characters is telling the story using the word *I* 以第一人稱敍述的文體：*a novel written* ***in the first person*** 以第一人稱寫作的小說 ➲ compare THE SECOND PERSON, THE THIRD PERSON

ˌfirst ˈprinciples *noun* [pl.] the basic ideas on which a theory, system or method is based 基本原理；基本原則：*I think we should go back to first principles.* 我認為我們應該回到基本原則上。

ˌfirst-ˈrate *adj.* of the highest quality 第一流的；質量最優的；優等的 SYN **excellent**：*a first-rate swimmer* 優秀游泳運動員 ◇ *The food here is absolutely first-rate.* 這裏的食物絕對是第一流的。

ˌfirst reˈfusal *noun* [U] (*BrE*) the right to decide whether to accept or refuse sth before it is offered to others 優先取捨權：*Will you give me first refusal on the car, if you decide to sell it?* 如果你決定出售這輛車，給我優先購買權好嗎？

first responder /ˌfɜːst rɪˈspɒndə(r); *NAmE* ˌfɜːrst rɪˈspɑːndər/ *noun* (*especially NAmE*) a person such as a member of the police or fire department in a position to arrive first at an emergency, who has been trained to give basic medical treatment 第一反應人員（指接受過

培訓在緊急情況下首先到達現場施行基本救治的人，如警察或消防隊員）➲ compare EMERGENCY SERVICES

ˈfirst school *noun* (in Britain) a school for children between the ages of 5 and 8 or 9（英國）第一學校（學生為 5 至 8、9 歲的兒童）

ˌfirst ˈstrike *noun* an attack on an enemy made before they attack you 先發制人；首先發起攻擊

ˈfirst-time *adj.* [only before noun] doing or experiencing sth for the first time 首次的；第一次的：*houses for first-time buyers* 供應給首次購房者的房屋 ◇ *a computer program designed for first-time users* 為初次用戶設計的計算機程序

ˌfirst-ˈtimer *noun* a person who does sth for the first time 初次…者：*conference first-timers* 初次與會人員

ˌFirst ˈWorld *noun* [sing.] the rich industrial countries of the world 第一世界（指富有的工業國）➲ compare THE THIRD WORLD

the ˌFirst World ˈWar (also **ˌWorld War ˈI**) *noun* [sing.] the war that was fought mainly in Europe between 1914 and 1918 第一次世界大戰（1914 至 1918 年間，主戰場在歐洲）

firth /fɜːθ; *NAmE* fɜːrθ/ *noun* (especially in Scottish place names) a narrow strip of the sea that runs a long way into the land, or a part of a river where it flows into the sea（尤用於蘇格蘭地名）狹長海灣，河流入海口：*the Moray Firth* 馬里灣 ◇ *the Firth of Clyde* 克萊德灣

fis·cal /ˈfɪskl/ *adj.* connected with government or public money, especially taxes 財政的；國庫的；國家歲入的：***fiscal policies/reforms*** 財政政策／改革 ▸ **fis·cal·ly** *adv.* ➲ see also PROCURATOR FISCAL

ˌfiscal ˈyear (*NAmE*) (*BrE* **fiˌnancial ˈyear**, **ˈtax year**) *noun* [usually sing.] a period of twelve months over which the accounts and taxes of a company or a person are calculated 財政年度；會計年度

fish 🔑 /fɪʃ/ *noun, verb*

▪ **noun** (*pl.* **fish** or **fishes**) HELP **Fish** is the usual plural form. The older form, **fishes**, can be used to refer to different kinds of fish. * fish 是通常的複數形式，較古老的形式 fishes 可用於表示不同種類的魚。 **1** 🔑 [C] a creature that lives in water, breathes through GILLS, and uses FINS and a tail for swimming 魚：*They caught several fish.* 他們捉到了幾條魚。◇ ***tropical/marine/freshwater fish*** 熱帶／海／淡水魚 ◇ ***shoals*** (= groups) ***of fish*** 魚群 ◇ *a **fish tank/pond*** 魚缸／池 ◇ *There are about 30 000 species of fish in the world.* 世界上約有 3 萬種魚。◇ *The list of endangered species includes nearly 600 fishes.* 瀕臨滅絕物種的名單中列有將近 600 種魚。◇ *Fish stocks in the Baltic are in decline.* 波羅的海的魚類資源逐漸減少。➲ COLLOCATIONS at LIFE ➲ VISUAL VOCAB page V12 ➲ see also COARSE FISH, FLATFISH, SEA FISH, SHELLFISH, WET FISH **2** 🔑 [U] the flesh of fish eaten as food 魚肉：***frozen/smoked/fresh fish*** 凍／熏／鮮魚 ◇ *fish pie* 魚肉餡餅

IDM **a ˌfish out of ˈwater** a person who feels uncomfortable or awkward because he or she is in surroundings that are not familiar 離水之魚；在陌生環境不得其所的人 **have bigger/other fish to ˈfry** to have more important or more interesting things to do 還有更重要的事情要做；另有他圖 **neither ˌfish nor ˈfowl** neither one thing nor another 非驢非馬；不倫不類 **an odd/a queer ˈfish** (*old-fashioned, BrE*) a person who is slightly strange or crazy 古怪的人；有些荒唐的人 **there are plenty more fish in the ˈsea** there are many other people or things that are as good as the one sb has failed to get 海裏的魚有的是；還有很多一樣好的（人或事物）➲ more at BIG *adj.*, COLD *adj.*, DIFFERENT, DRINK *v.*, SHOOT *v.*

▪ **verb 1** 🔑 [I] to try to catch fish with a hook, nets, etc. 釣魚；捕魚：*The trawler was fishing off the coast of Iceland.* 拖網漁船在冰島沿海捕魚。◇ **~ for sth** *You can fish for trout in this stream.* 你可以在這條小溪釣鱒魚。**2** 🔑 [I] **go fishing** to spend time fishing for pleasure 釣魚；捕魚：*Let's go fishing this weekend.* 咱們這個週末去釣魚吧。**3** [T] **~ sth** (**for sth**) to try to catch fish in the area of water mentioned 在…捕魚（或釣魚）：*They fished the loch for salmon.* 他們在狹長海灣裏釣鮭魚。**4** [I] **+ adv./prep.** to search for sth, using your hands 摸找：*She fished around in her bag for her keys.* 她在包裏摸找鑰匙。

PHR V **ˈfish for sth** to try to get sth, or to find out sth, although you are pretending not to 旁敲側擊地打聽；轉彎抹角地謀取：*to fish for compliments/information* 轉彎抹角地謀取恭維／打聽情況 **ˌfish sth/sb↔ˈout (of sth)** to take or pull sth/sb out of a place（從…中）取出，拿出，拖出：*She fished a piece of paper out of the pile on her desk.* 她從桌上一大堆紙中抽出了一張。◇ *They fished a dead body out of the river.* 他們從河裏撈起了一具屍體。

ˌfish and ˈchips *noun* [U] a dish of fish that has been fried in BATTER served with CHIPS/FRIES, and usually bought in the place where it has been cooked and eaten at home, etc., especially in Britain 炸魚加土豆條；炸魚薯條：*Three portions of fish and chips, please.* 請來三份炸魚薯條。◇ *a fish and chip shop* 炸魚薯條店

fish·bowl /ˈfɪʃbəʊl; *NAmE* -boʊl/ *noun* = GOLDFISH BOWL

fish·cake /ˈfɪʃkeɪk/ *noun* (*especially BrE*) pieces of fish mixed with MASHED potato made into a flat round shape, covered with BREADCRUMBS and fried 魚餅（魚肉拌土豆泥煎成）

fish·er /ˈfɪʃə(r)/ *noun* (*especially NAmE*) = FISHERMAN

fish·er·man /ˈfɪʃəmən; *NAmE* ˈfɪʃərmən/ *noun* (*pl.* **-men** /-mən/) a person who catches fish, either as a job or as a sport 漁民；釣魚的人 ➲ compare ANGLER

fisher·woman /ˈfɪʃəwʊmən; *NAmE* ˈfɪʃər-/ *noun* (*pl.* **-women** /-wɪmɪn/) a woman who catches fish, either as a job or as a sport 女漁民；漁婦；女釣魚愛好者 ➲ compare ANGLER ➲ note at GENDER

fish·ery /ˈfɪʃəri/ *noun* (*pl.* **-ies**) **1** a part of the sea or a river where fish are caught in large quantities 漁場：*a herring fishery* 鯡魚漁場 ◇ ***coastal/freshwater fisheries*** 沿海／淡水漁場 **2** = FISH FARM：*a trout fishery* 鱒魚養殖場

fish-eye lens /ˌfɪʃaɪ ˈlenz/ *noun* a camera LENS with a wide angle that gives the view a curved shape 魚眼鏡頭；超廣角鏡頭

ˈfish farm (also **fish·ery**) *noun* a place where fish are bred as a business 養魚場

ˌfish ˈfinger (*BrE*) (*NAmE* **ˌfish ˈstick**) *noun* a long narrow piece of fish covered with BREADCRUMBS or BATTER, usually frozen and sold in packs 魚條（塗有麪包屑或麪糊的魚肉條，通常冷凍後小包裝出售）

ˈfish hook *noun* a sharp metal hook for catching fish, that has a point which curves backwards to make it difficult to pull out 魚鈎；釣鈎 ➲ picture at HOOK

fish·ing 🔑 /ˈfɪʃɪŋ/ *noun* [U] the sport or business of catching fish 釣魚；捕魚業（或活動）：*They often **go fishing**.* 他們常去釣魚。◇ *deep-sea fishing* 深海捕魚 ◇ *a fishing boat* 小漁船 ◇ *fishing grounds* 漁場 ◇ *We enjoyed a day's fishing by the river.* 我們在河邊享受了一天垂釣之樂。

ˈfishing line *noun* [C, U] a long thread with a sharp hook attached, that is used for catching fish（帶釣鈎的）釣線，釣絲

ˈfishing rod (also **rod**) (*NAmE* also **ˈfishing pole**) *noun* a long wooden or plastic stick with a fishing line and hook attached, that is used for catching fish 釣竿

ˈfishing tackle *noun* [U] equipment used for catching fish 漁具

ˈfish knife *noun* a knife with a broad blade and without a sharp edge, used for eating fish（吃魚用的）餐刀 ➲ VISUAL VOCAB page V22

fish·mon·ger /ˈfɪʃmʌŋɡə(r)/ *noun* (*especially BrE*) **1** a person whose job is to sell fish in a shop 魚販；魚商 **2 fish·mon·ger's** (*pl.* **fish·mon·gers**) a shop that sells fish 魚店

fish·net /ˈfɪʃnet/ *noun* [U] a type of cloth made of threads that produce a pattern of small holes like a net 網眼織物：*fishnet stockings* 網眼長襪

ˈ**fish slice** (*BrE*) (also **spat·ula** *NAmE, BrE*) *noun* a kitchen UTENSIL that has a broad flat blade with narrow holes in it, attached to a long handle, used for turning and lifting food when cooking 煎魚鍋鏟（鏟面有細長孔）➲ VISUAL VOCAB page V26

ˌ**fish ˈstick** (*NAmE*) (*BrE* ˌ**fish ˈfinger**) *noun* a long narrow piece of fish covered with BREADCRUMBS or BATTER, usually frozen and sold in packs 魚條（塗有麪包屑或麪糊的魚肉條，通常冷凍後小包裝出售）

fish·tail /ˈfɪʃteɪl/ *verb* [I] if a vehicle **fishtails**, the back end slides from side to side（車輛）擺尾行駛

fish·wife /ˈfɪʃwaɪf/ *noun* (*pl.* **-wives** /-waɪvz/) (*disapproving*) a woman with a loud voice and bad manners 罵街的潑婦；粗野的女人

fishy /ˈfɪʃi/ *adj.* (**fish·ier, fishi·est**) **1** (*informal*) that makes you suspicious because it seems dishonest 可疑的；值得懷疑的 SYN **suspicious**：*There's something fishy going on here.* 這兒有點不大對頭。 **2** smelling or tasting like a fish（像）魚味的；有魚腥味的：*What's that fishy smell?* 那是什麼腥味？

fis·sile /ˈfɪsaɪl; *NAmE* ˈfɪsl/ *adj.* (*physics* 物) capable of nuclear FISSION 可裂變的：*fissile material* 可裂變物質

fis·sion /ˈfɪʃn/ *noun* [U] **1** (also ˌ**nuclear ˈfission**) (*physics* 物) the act or process of splitting the NUCLEUS (= central part) of an atom, when a large amount of energy is released （核）裂變，分裂 ➲ compare FUSION (2) **2** (*biology* 生) the division of cells into new cells as a method of reproducing cells 細胞分裂；裂殖 **3** (*chemistry* 化) the breaking of a chemical BOND between two atoms （鍵）斷裂；裂變

fis·sure /ˈfɪʃə(r)/ *noun* (*technical* 術語) a long deep crack in sth, especially in rock or in the earth （岩石、土地等中深長的）裂縫，裂隙 ▸ **fis·sured** *adj.*

fist /fɪst/ *noun* a hand when it is tightly closed with the fingers bent into the PALM 拳；拳頭：*He punched me with his fist.* 他用拳頭猛擊我。◇ *She* ***clenched her fists*** *to stop herself trembling.* 她緊握雙拳，克制顫抖。◇ *He got into a* ***fist fight*** *in the bar.* 他在酒吧與人揮拳鬥毆。➲ see also HAM-FISTED, TIGHT-FISTED

IDM **make a better, good, poor, etc. fist of sth** (*BrE, old-fashioned, informal*) to make a good, bad, etc. attempt to do sth 試圖把（或未能把）某事做得很成功 ➲ more at IRON *adj.*, MONEY

fist·ful /ˈfɪstfʊl/ *noun* a number or an amount of sth that can be held in a fist 一把（的量）：*a fistful of coins* 一把硬幣

fisti·cuffs /ˈfɪstɪkʌfs/ *noun* [pl.] (*old-fashioned* or *humorous*) a fight in which people hit each other with their FISTS 拳鬥；互毆

fis·tula /ˈfɪstjʊlə; *NAmE* ˈfɪstʃələ/ *noun* (*medical* 醫) an opening between two organs of the body, or between an organ and the skin, that would not normally exist, caused by injury, disease, etc. 瘻；瘻管

fit 🔑 /fɪt/ *verb, adj., noun*

■ *verb* (**fit·ting, fit·ted, fit·ted**) (*NAmE* usually **fit·ting, fit, fit** except in the passive 用於被動語態者除外)

▸ **RIGHT SIZE/TYPE** 恰當的大小／類型 **1** 🔑 [I, T] (not used in the progressive tenses 不用於進行時) to be the right shape and size for sb/sth（形狀和尺寸）適合，合身：*I tried the dress on but it didn't fit.* 我試穿了那連衣裙，但不合身。◇ *That jacket fits well.* 那件短上衣很合身。◇ *a close-fitting dress* 緊身連衣裙 ◇ **~ sb/sth** *I can't find clothes to fit me.* 我找不到合身的衣服。◇ *The key doesn't fit the lock.* 這把鑰匙打不開這把鎖。 **2** 🔑 [I] to be of the right size, type or number to go somewhere （大小、式樣、數量適合）可容納，裝進：*I'd like to have a desk in the room but it won't fit.* 我想在房間放一張桌子，但是擱不下。◇ **+ adv./prep.** *All the kids will fit in the back of the car.* 所有的孩子都可以坐到車的後排。 **3** [T, often passive] **~ sb** (**for sth**) to put clothes on sb and make them the right size and shape 試穿（衣服）：*I'm going to be fitted for my wedding dress today.* 今天我要去試穿結婚禮服。

▸ **PUT STH SOMEWHERE** 安置 **4** 🔑 [T] to put or fix sth somewhere 安置，安裝（在某處）：**~ sth + adv./prep.** *They fitted a smoke alarm to the ceiling.* 他們把煙霧報警器安裝在天花板上。◇ **~ sth with sth** *The rooms were all fitted with smoke alarms.* 所有的房間都安裝了煙霧報警器。 **5** 🔑 [I, T] to put or join sth in the right place 合上；蓋上；組合；組裝：**~ + adv./prep.** *The glass fits on top of the jug to form a lid.* 這個玻璃杯放在大罐口上恰好當個蓋子。◇ *How do these two parts* ***fit together***? 這兩部份如何拼在一起呢？◇ **~ sth + adv./prep.** *We fitted together the pieces of the puzzle.* 我們把拼圖玩具的各部份拼合在了一起。

▸ **AGREE/MATCH** 一致；相稱 **6** 🔑 [I, T] (not used in the progressive tenses 不用於進行時) to agree with, match or be suitable for sth; to make sth do this （使）與…一致，和…相稱，符合：*Something doesn't quite fit here.* 這裏有點不大協調。◇ **~ into sth** *His pictures don't fit into any category.* 他的畫哪一類也算不上。◇ **~ sth** *The facts certainly fit your theory.* 這些事實和你的說法絲毫不差。◇ *The punishment ought to fit the crime.* 罰需當罪。◇ **~ sth to sth** *We should fit the punishment to the crime.* 我們應該根據罪行量刑。

▸ **MAKE SUITABLE** 使適合 **7** [T] (*especially BrE*) to make sb/sth suitable for a particular job 使適合，使勝任（某工作）：**~ sb/sth for sth** *His experience fitted him perfectly for the job.* 他的經驗使他完全勝任這項工作。◇ **~ sb/sth to do sth** *His experience fitted him to do the job.* 他的經驗使他適合幹這個工作。➲ see also FITTED (4)

IDM **fit** (**sb**) **like a ˈglove** to be the perfect size or shape for sb（大小、形狀）完全合適，恰好合身 ➲ more at BILL *n.*, CAP *n.*, DESCRIPTION, FACE *n.*

PHR V ˌ**fit sb/sth↔ˈin** | ˌ**fit sb/sth ˈin/ˈinto sth** **1** 🔑 to find time to see sb or to do sth 找到時間（見某人、做某事）：*I'll try and fit you in after lunch.* 我盡量午飯後抽時間見你。◇ *I had to fit ten appointments into one morning.* 我得在一個上午安排十個約見。 **2** 🔑 to find or have enough space for sb/sth in a place 找到足夠的地方；有足夠空間：*We can't fit in any more chairs.* 我們沒有地方再擺更多的椅子了。 ˌ**fit ˈin** (**with sb/sth**) 🔑 to live, work, etc. in an easy and natural way with sb/sth （與…）合得來；適應：*He's never done this type of work before; I'm not sure how he'll fit in with the other people.* 他過去從未幹過這種工作，很難說他是否會與其他人配合得好。◇ *Where do I fit in?* 哪裏有適合我的地方？◇ *Do these plans fit in with your arrangements?* 這些計劃和你的安排有衝突嗎？ ˌ**fit sb/sth↔ˈout/ˈup** (**with sth**) to supply sb/sth with all the equipment, clothes, food, etc. they need 向…提供所需的東西（如裝備、設備、衣服、糧食等）SYN **equip**：*to fit out a ship before a long voyage* 給要遠航的輪船提供必需品 ◇ *The room has been fitted out with a stove and a sink.* 這個房間安裝有爐子和洗滌槽。 ˌ**fit sb↔ˈup** (**for sth**) (*BrE, informal*) to make it look as if sb is guilty of a crime they have not committed 誣陷某人（犯某事）SYN **frame**：*I didn't do it—I've been fitted up!* 這事不是我幹的，我遭到誣陷了！

■ *adj.* (**fit·ter, fit·test**)

▸ **HEALTHY** 健康 **1** 🔑 healthy and strong, especially because you do regular physical exercise 健壯的；健康的：*Top athletes have to be very fit.* 頂級運動員體格必須十分健壯。◇ **~** (**to do sth**) (*BrE*) *He won't be fit to play in the match on Saturday.* 他身體不適，不能在星期六出場比賽。◇ *She tries to* ***keep fit*** *by jogging every day.* 她每天慢跑以保持健康。◇ **~** (**for sth**) (*BrE*) *He's had a bad cold and isn't fit enough for work yet.* 他得了重感冒，還不能上班。◇ *I feel really* ***fighting fit*** (= very healthy and full of energy). 我覺得十分健康，精力充沛。◇ *The government aims to make British industry leaner and fitter* (= employing fewer people and with lower costs). 政府旨在使英國的工業更加簡而精。OPP **unfit** ➲ SYNONYMS at WELL ➲ see also KEEP-FIT

▸ **SUITABLE** 合適 **2** 🔑 suitable; of the right quality; with the right qualities or skills （質量、素質或技能）適合的，恰當的，合格的：**~ for sb/sth** *The food was not fit for human consumption.* 這食物不適合人吃。◇ *It was a meal* ***fit for a king*** (= of very good quality). 這飯菜夠得上御膳。◇ *The children seem to think I'm only fit for cooking and washing!* 孩子們似乎以為我只配做飯洗衣！◇ **~ to do sth** *Your car isn't fit to be on the road!* 你的車

子還不適合上馬路！◇ *He's so angry he's **in no fit state** to see anyone.* 他氣成這個樣子，不適合見人。◇ (*formal*) *This is not a fit place for you to live.* 這個地方不適合你居住。**OPP unfit**

▸ READY 準備好 **3 ~ to do sth** (*BrE, informal*) ready or likely to do sth extreme 可能（或準備）做某事至極端程度：*They worked until they were **fit to drop*** (= so tired that they were likely to fall down). 他們一直工作到快要累趴下了。◇ *I've eaten so much I'm **fit to burst**.* 我吃得太多，肚子快要撐破了。◇ *She was laughing **fit to burst*** (= very much). 她笑得肚子都要破了。

▸ ATTRACTIVE 誘人 **4** (*BrE, informal*) sexually attractive 性感迷人的

IDM **(as) ˌfit as a ˈfiddle** (*informal*) in very good physical condition 非常健康 **see/think ˈfit (to do sth)** (*formal*) to consider it right or acceptable to do sth; to decide or choose to do sth 認為（做某事）恰當（或適合）；決定，願意（做某事）：*You must do as you think fit* (= but I don't agree with your decision). 你認為怎麼合適就怎麼幹（但我不同意你的決定）。◇ *The newspaper did not see fit to publish my letter* (= and I criticize it for that). 那份報紙認為我的信件不宜發表（而我批評這種看法）。➲ more at SURVIVAL

■ ***noun***

▸ ILLNESS 疾病 **1** [C] a sudden attack of an illness, such as EPILEPSY, in which sb becomes unconscious and their body may make violent movements（癲癇等的）突發，發作；昏厥；痙攣 **SYN convulsion**：*to have an epileptic fit* 癲癇發作 ◇ *Her fits are now controlled by drugs.* 她的病現已用藥物控制，沒有發作。

▸ OF COUGHING/LAUGHTER 咳嗽；笑 **2** [C] a sudden short period of coughing or of laughing, that you cannot control 一陣（忍不住的咳嗽、笑）**SYN bout**：*a fit of coughing* 一陣咳嗽 ◇ *He had us all **in fits** (**of laughter**) with his jokes.* 他的笑話使我們都笑得前仰後合。

▸ OF STRONG FEELING 強烈感情 **3** [C] a short period of very strong feeling（強烈感情）發作，衝動：*to act in a fit **of anger/rage/temper/pique*** 一陣憤怒 / 狂怒 / 怒火 / 惱怒之下採取行動 ➲ see also HISSY FIT

▸ OF CLOTHING 衣服 **4** [C, U] (often with an adjective 常與形容詞連用) the way that sth, especially a piece of clothing, fits（尤指衣服）適合，合身：*a **good/bad/close/perfect fit*** 很 / 不合身；貼身；完全合身

▸ MATCH 匹配 **5** [C] **~ (between A and B)** the way that two things match each other or are suitable for each other 匹配；相配：*We need to work out the best fit between the staff required and the staff available.* 我們得算出所需人員與現有人員之間的最佳配比。

IDM **by/in ˌfits and ˈstarts** frequently starting and stopping again; not continuously 間歇地；一陣一陣地：*Because of other commitments I can only write my book in fits and starts.* 由於還承擔着其他任務，我只能斷斷續續地寫書。 **have/throw a ˈfit** (*informal*) to be very shocked, upset or angry 大為震驚；非常心煩意亂；大發脾氣：*Your mother would have a fit if she knew you'd been drinking!* 要是你母親知道你一直喝酒，會很生氣的！

fit·ful /ˈfɪtfl/ *adj.* happening only for short periods; not continuous or regular 斷斷續續的；一陣陣的；間歇的：*a fitful night's sleep* 夜間時睡時醒 ▸ **fit·ful·ly** /ˈfɪtfəli/ *adv.*：*to sleep fitfully* 睡睡醒醒

fit·ment /ˈfɪtmənt/ *noun* [usually pl.] (*BrE, technical* 術語) a piece of furniture or equipment, especially one that is made for and fixed in a particular place（尤指為固定位置訂做的）傢具，設備

fit·ness /ˈfɪtnəs/ *noun* [U] **1** the state of being physically healthy and strong 健壯；健康：*a magazine on health and fitness* 衞生與健康雜誌 ◇ *a **fitness instructor/class/test*** 健美教練 / 班；健康合格檢查 ◇ *a high level of physical fitness* 高水平體質 ➲ COLLOCATIONS at DIET **2** the state of being suitable or good enough for sth 適合（某事物或做某事）：**~ for sth** *He convinced us of his fitness for the task.* 他使我們相信他適合做這項工作。◇ **~ to do sth** *There were doubts about her fitness to hold office.* 她是否稱職還有疑慮。

ˈfitness centre (*BrE*) (*NAmE* **ˈfitness center**) *noun* a place where people go to do physical exercise in order to stay or become healthy and fit 健身中心

fit·ted /ˈfɪtɪd/ *adj.* **1** [only before noun] (*especially BrE*) (of furniture 傢具) built to be fixed into a particular space（按放置的地方）訂做的 **SYN built-in**：***fitted wardrobes/cupboards*** 訂做的衣櫥 / 櫥櫃 ➲ VISUAL VOCAB page V23 **2** [only before noun] (*especially BrE*) (of a room 房間) with matching cupboards and other furniture built for the space and fixed in place 有訂做配套傢具的：*a **fitted kitchen/bedroom*** 有訂做配套設備的廚房；有訂做配套傢具的卧室 **3** [only before noun] (of clothes 衣服) made to follow the shape of the body 訂做的；合身的：*a fitted jacket* 合身的短上衣 **OPP loose** **4 ~ for/to sth** | **~ to do sth** (*especially BrE*) suitable; with the right qualities and skills 合適的；恰當的；勝任的：*She was well fitted to the role of tragic heroine.* 她很適合演悲劇女主角。 **5 ~ with sth** having sth as equipment 有…設備的：*Insurance costs will be reduced for houses fitted with window locks.* 窗戶有鎖的房子保險費用降低。

ˌfitted ˈcarpet *noun* (*BrE*) a carpet that is cut and fixed to cover the floor of a room completely（鋪滿房間地板的）訂做的地毯 ➲ VISUAL VOCAB page V23 ➲ see also WALL-TO-WALL CARPET at WALL-TO-WALL (1)

fit·ter /ˈfɪtə(r)/ *noun* **1** a person whose job is to put together or repair equipment 裝配工；修理工；鉗工：*a gas fitter* 煤氣設備裝修工 **2** a person whose job is to cut and fit clothes or carpets, etc. 試衣裁縫；試樣裁縫；地毯安裝工

fit·ting /ˈfɪtɪŋ/ *adj.*, *noun*

■ ***adj.*** **1** (*formal*) suitable or right for the occasion 適合（某場合）的；恰當的 **SYN appropriate**：*The award was a **fitting tribute** to her years of devoted work.* 這個獎項是對她多年全心全意工作的恰如其分的褒獎。◇ *A fitting end to the meal would be a glass of port.* 餐後一杯波爾圖葡萄酒是挺合適的。◇ ***It is fitting that** the new centre for European studies should be in a university that teaches every European language.* 新的歐洲研究中心應設在教授各種歐洲語言的大學裏才合適。 **2 -fitting** (in adjectives 構成形容詞) having a particular FIT 合身的；合…適的：*a tight-fitting dress* 貼身的連衣裙

■ ***noun*** **1** [usually pl.] a small part on a piece of equipment or furniture（設備或傢具的）小配件，附件：*light fittings* 燈具配件 ◇ *a pine cupboard with brass fittings* 黃銅鑲配的松木櫥櫃 **2** [usually pl.] (*BrE*) items in a house such as a cooker, lights or shelves that are usually fixed but that you can take with you when you move to a new house 可拆除裝置（如櫥、灶、燈、擱架）➲ compare FIXTURE (2) **3** an occasion when you try on a piece of clothing that is being made for you to see if it fits 試衣

ˈfitting room (*NAmE* also **ˈdressing room**) *noun* a room or CUBICLE in a shop/store where you can put on clothes to see how they look（商店的）試衣室，試衣間

five 0‑ /faɪv/ *number*

5 五：*There are only five cookies left.* 只剩下五塊曲奇了。◇ *five of Sweden's top financial experts* 五個一流的瑞典金融專家 ◇ *Ten people were invited but only five turned up.* 邀請了十人，只有五人出席。◇ *Do you have change for five dollars?* 你有五元零錢嗎？◇ *a five-month contract* 一項為期五個月的合同 ◇ *Look at page five.* 見第五頁。◇ *Five and four is nine.* 五加四等於九。◇ *Three fives are fifteen.* 三個五等於十五。◇ *I can't read your writing—is this meant to be a five?* 我看不懂你的筆跡 —— 這個是不是五字？◇ *The bulbs are planted in threes or fives* (= groups of three or five). 這些鱗莖植物是三五株在一起種植的。◇ *We moved to America when I was five* (= five years old). 我五歲時我們移居到美國。◇ *Shall we meet at five* (= at five o'clock)*, then?* 那麼我們五點鐘見面好嗎？➲ see also HIGH FIVE

IDM **ˌgive sb ˈfive** (*informal*) to hit the inside of sb's hand with your hand as a way of saying hello or to celebrate a victory 與某人擊掌問候（或慶祝勝利）：*Give me five!* 咱們擊掌相慶吧！➲ more at NINE

ˌfive-and-ˈdime (also **ˈdime store**) *noun* (*old-fashioned, NAmE*) a shop/store that sells a range of cheap goods 廉價品店

F

ˌfive-a-ˈside *noun* [U] (*BrE*) a game of football (SOCCER) played indoors with five players on each team（室內）五人足球

five·fold /ˈfaɪvfəʊld; *NAmE* -foʊld/ *adj., adv.* ➲ -FOLD

ˌfive o'clock ˈshadow *noun* [sing.] (*informal*) the dark colour that appears on a man's chin and face when the hair has grown a little during the day （早上刮臉後下午又長出的）鬍鬚茬兒

ˌfive ˈpence (also ˌ**five pence ˈpiece**, **5p**) *noun* a British coin worth five pence （英國）五便士硬幣：*Have you got a five pence?* 你有一枚五便士硬幣嗎？

fiver /ˈfaɪvə(r)/ *noun* (*informal*) **1** (*BrE*) £5 or a five-pound note * 5 英鎊；五英鎊鈔票：*Can you lend me a fiver?* 你能借我五英鎊嗎？ **2** (*NAmE, old-fashioned*) $5 or a five-dollar bill * 5 美元；五美元鈔票

fives /faɪvz/ *noun* [U] a game played especially in British PUBLIC SCHOOLS in which players hit a ball with their hand or a BAT against the walls of a COURT 英式牆手球（用手或球拍對牆擊球，流行於英國公學）

ˈfive-star *adj.* [usually before noun] **1** having five stars in a system that measures quality. Five stars usually represents the highest quality 五星級的（表示最優質）：*a five-star hotel* 五星級旅館 **2** (*NAmE*) having the highest military rank, and wearing a uniform which has five stars on it （軍階）五星級的：*a five-star general* 五星上將

fix 0→ /fɪks/ *verb, noun*

■ *verb*

▸ **ATTACH** 附；繫 **1** 0→ ~ **sth (+ adv./prep.)** (*especially BrE*) to put sth firmly in a place so that it will not move 使固定；安裝：*to fix a shelf to the wall* 把擱架固定在牆上 ◇ *to fix a post in the ground* 把柱子固定在地上 ◇ (*figurative*) *He noted every detail so as to fix the scene in his mind.* 他留意着每一個細節以便牢記這一幕。

▸ **ARRANGE** 安排 **2** 0→ ~ **sth** to decide on a date, a time, an amount, etc. for sth 決定，確定（日期、時間、數量等） SYN **set**：*Has the date of the next meeting been fixed?* 下次會議的日期確定了沒有？◇ *They fixed the rent at £100 a week.* 他們把租金定為每週 100 英鎊。◇ *Their prices are fixed until the end of the year* (= will not change before then). 他們的價格一直到年底固定不變。 **3** to arrange or organize sth 安排；組織：~ **sth (for sb)** *I'll fix a meeting.* 我要安排一次會議。◇ ~ **sth up (for sb)** *You have to fix visits up in advance with the museum.* 你得預先和博物館聯繫安排好參觀事宜。◇ ~ **sth with sth** (*informal*) *Don't worry, I'll* **fix it with** *Sarah.* 別着急，我會和薩拉商量安排好的。◇ ~ **(up) (for sb) to do sth** *I've fixed up (for us) to go to the theatre next week.* 我已安排好（我們）下星期去看戲。

▸ **POSITION/TIME** 位置；時間 **4** ~ **sth** to discover or say the exact position, time, etc. of sth 找到，確定，說出（確切位置、時間等）：*We can fix the ship's exact position at the time the fire broke out.* 我們可以確定發生火災時那艘船的確切位置。

▸ **REPAIR** 修理 **5** 0→ ~ **sth** to repair or correct sth 修理；校準；校正：*The car won't start—can you fix it?* 這輛車發動不起來了，你能修理一下嗎？◇ *I've fixed the problem.* 我已解決了這個問題。

▸ **FOOD/DRINK** 食物；飲料 **6** (*especially NAmE*) to provide or prepare sth, especially food 提供，準備（尤指食物）：~ **sb sth** *Can I fix you a drink?* 我給你弄杯飲料好嗎？◇ ~ **sth for sb** *Can I fix a drink for you?* 我給你弄杯飲料好嗎？◇ ~ **sth** *I'll fix supper.* 我來準備晚餐。

▸ **HAIR/FACE** 頭髮；面孔 **7** ~ **sth** (*especially NAmE*) to make sth such as your hair or face neat and attractive 梳洗；整理；收拾：*I'll fix my hair and then I'll be ready.* 我梳梳頭就準備好了。

▸ **RESULT** 結果 **8** [often passive] ~ **sth** (*informal*) to arrange the result of sth in a way that is not honest or fair 操縱；作弊：*I'm sure the race was fixed.* 我肯定這場比賽有人操縱。

▸ **PUNISH** 懲罰 **9** ~ **sb** (*informal*) to punish sb who has harmed you and stop them doing you any more harm 懲罰；收拾：*Don't worry—I'll fix him.* 別擔憂，我會收拾他的。

▸ **IN PHOTOGRAPHY** 攝影 **10** ~ **sth** (*technical* 術語) to treat film for cameras, etc. with a chemical so that the colours do not change or become less bright 定（影）；定（色）

▸ **ANIMAL** 動物 **11** ~ **sth** (*NAmE, informal*) to make an animal unable to have young by means of an operation 閹割（家畜） ➲ see also NEUTER (1)

IDM **fix sb with a ˈlook, ˈstare, ˈgaze, etc.** to look directly at sb for a long time 定睛凝視（某人）：*He fixed her with an angry stare.* 他生氣地盯着她。➲ more at AIN'T

PHR V **ˈfix on sb/sth** to choose sb/sth 選定；決定：*They've fixed on Paris for their honeymoon.* 他們已選定在巴黎度蜜月。 **ˈfix sth on sb/sth** [often passive] if your eyes or your mind are **fixed on** sth, you are looking at or thinking about sth with great attention 集中（目光、注意力、思想等）於 ˌ**fix sth**↔ˈ**up** to repair, decorate or make sth ready 修理；裝飾；準備好：*They fixed up the house before they moved in.* 他們把房子裝修了以後才遷入。 ˌ**fix sb ˈup (with sb)** (*informal*) to arrange for sb to have a meeting with sb who might become a boyfriend or girlfriend 給…介紹（男友、女友） ˌ**fix sb ˈup (with sth)** (*informal*) to arrange for sb to have sth; to provide sb with sth 向某人提供；給某人準備；安頓：*I'll fix you up with a place to stay.* 我會給你安排住處的。

■ *noun*

▸ **SOLUTION** 解決 **1** [C] (*informal*) a solution to a problem, especially an easy or temporary one （尤指簡單、暫時的）解決方法：*There is no* **quick fix** *for the steel industry.* 鋼鐵工業的問題沒有即時解決的辦法。

▸ **DRUG** 毒品 **2** [sing.] (*informal*) an amount of sth that you need and want frequently, especially an illegal drug such as HEROIN（致癮的東西，尤指毒品的）一次用量：*to get yourself a fix* 給自己注射一劑毒品 ◇ *I need a fix of coffee before I can face the day.* 我總需要喝足咖啡才有精神應付一天的工作。

▸ **DIFFICULT SITUATION** 困境；窘境 **3** [sing.] a difficult situation 困境；窘境 SYN **mess**：*We've got ourselves* **in a fix** *about this.* 在這個問題上我們已陷入了困境。

▸ **ON POSITION** 位置 **4** [sing.] the act of finding the position of a ship or an aircraft （船或飛機的）方位確定，定位：*They managed to* **get a fix** *on the yacht's position.* 他們設法確定了快艇的方位。

▸ **UNDERSTANDING** 理解 **5** [sing.] (*informal*) an act of understanding sth 理解；瞭解：*He tried to* **get a fix** *on the young man's motives, but he just couldn't understand him.* 他努力瞭解這個年輕人的動機，但就是弄不清楚。

▸ **DISHONEST RESULT** 不正當結果 **6** [sing.] (*informal*) a thing that is dishonestly arranged; a trick 受操縱的事；勾當；搞鬼：*Her promotion was a fix, I'm sure!* 我肯定她的提升有內幕！

fix·ated /fɪkˈseɪtɪd/ *adj.* [not before noun] ~ **(on sb/sth)** always thinking and talking about sb/sth in a way that is not normal （對…）異常依戀，固戀

fix·ation /fɪkˈseɪʃn/ *noun* **1** [C] a very strong interest in sb/sth, that is not normal or natural （對…的）異常依戀，固戀；癖：*a mother fixation* 戀母情結 ◇ ~ **with/on sb/sth** *He's got this fixation with cleanliness.* 他有潔癖。 **2** [U] (*technical* 術語) the process of a gas becoming solid 固定（指氣態變成固態的過程）：*nitrogen fixation* 氮的固定

fixa·tive /ˈfɪksətɪv/ *noun* [C, U] **1** a substance that is used to prevent colours or smells from changing or becoming weaker, for example in photography, art or the making of PERFUME 定影劑；定色劑；防（香味）揮發劑 **2** a substance that is used to stick things together or keep things in position 固定劑

fixed 0→ /fɪkst/ *adj.*

1 0→ staying the same; not changing or able to be changed 固定的；不變的；不能變的：*fixed prices* 固定價格 ◇ *a fixed rate of interest* 固定利率 ◇ *people living on* **fixed incomes** 靠固定收入生活的人們 ◇ *The money has been invested for a* **fixed period**. 這筆款項已作定期投資。➲ see also ABODE **2** 0→ (often *disapproving*) (of ideas and wishes 思想和期望) held very firmly; not easily changed 不易改變的；執著的：*My parents had* **fixed ideas** *about what I should become.* 父母對我應該成為什麼樣的人有定見。 **3** [only before noun] (of expressions on sb's face 面部表情) not changing and not sincere 呆板的；不變的： *He greeted all his guests with a fixed smile on his face.* 他對所有的客人都以一貫笑容相迎。

IDM **how are you, etc. 'fixed (for sth)?** (*informal*) used to ask how much of sth a person has, or to ask about arrangements 你有多少…；你…的安排如何： *How are you fixed for cash?* 你有多少現金？◇ *How are we fixed for Saturday* (= have we arranged to do anything)? 星期六我們有什麼安排？

fixed 'assets *noun* [pl.] (*business* 商) land, buildings and equipment that are owned and used by a company 固定資產

fixed 'costs *noun* [pl.] (*business* 商) the costs that a business must pay that do not change even if the amount of work produced changes 固定成本

fix·ed·ly /ˈfɪksɪdli/ *adv.* continuously, without looking away, but often with no real interest 凝視地；目不轉睛地： *to* **stare/gaze fixedly** *at sb/sth* 凝視／目不轉睛地盯着某人／某物

,fixed-'term *adj.* [only before noun] a **fixed-term** contract, etc. is one that only lasts for the agreed period of time 定期的

,fixed-'wing *adj.* [only before noun] used to describe aircraft with wings that remain in the same position, rather than HELICOPTERS, etc. 固定機翼的

fixer /ˈfɪksə(r)/ *noun* **1** (*informal*) a person who arranges things for other people, sometimes dishonestly（有時用不正當的手段）代人安排者，代人疏通者： *a great political fixer* 一位傑出的政治調停人 **2** a chemical substance used in photography to prevent a photograph from changing and becoming too dark 定影劑；定色劑

,fixer-'upper *noun* (*NAmE, informal*) a house or flat/apartment that is cheap because it needs a lot of repair work when you buy it 待修廉價房

fix·ings /ˈfɪksɪŋz/ *noun* [pl.] (*NAmE*) = TRIMMING (1)： *a hamburger with all the fixings* 有各種配料的漢堡包

fix·ity /ˈfɪksəti/ *noun* [U] (*formal*) the quality of being firm and not changing 固定性；穩定性

fix·ture /ˈfɪkstʃə(r)/ *noun* **1** (*BrE*) a sports event that has been arranged to take place on a particular date and at a particular place（定期定點舉行的）體育活動，體育節： *an annual fixture* 一年一度的體育節 ◇ *Saturday's fixture against Liverpool* 定於星期六與利物浦隊的比賽 ◇ *the season's fixture list* 這個季度的體育活動項目表 **2** a thing such as a bath/BATHTUB or a toilet that is fixed in a house and that you do not take with you when you move house 固定設施（如房屋內安裝的浴缸或抽水馬桶）：(*BrE*) *The price of the house includes* **fixtures and fittings**. 房屋價格包括固定裝置和附加設備。◇ (*figurative*) *He has stayed with us so long he seems to have become* **a permanent fixture**. 他在我們這裏待了很久，好像成了我們的固定成員。➲ COLLOCATIONS at DECORATE ➲ compare FITTING *n.* (2)

fizz /fɪz/ *verb, noun*

■ ***verb*** [I] when a liquid **fizzes**, it produces a lot of bubbles and makes a long sound like an 's' 起泡發嘶嘶聲： *Champagne was fizzing in the glass.* 杯裏的香檳酒嘶嘶地冒泡。◇ (*figurative*) *Share prices are fizzing.* 股價活力十足。◇ **~ with sth** (*figurative*) *He started to fizz with enthusiasm.* 他開始熱情奔放起來。

■ ***noun*** **1** [U, sing.] the small bubbles of gas in a liquid（液體中的）氣泡： (*figurative*) *There is plenty of fizz and sparkle in the show.* 演出精彩，妙趣橫生。◇ (*figurative*) *The fizz has gone out of the market.* 市場已杳無生氣。**2** [U, sing.] the sound that is made by bubbles of gas in a liquid, or a sound similar to this（液體中的）氣泡嘶嘶聲，嘶嘶聲，劈啪聲： *the fizz of a firework* 煙火的劈啪聲 **3** [U] (*BrE, informal*) a drink that has a lot of bubbles of gas, especially CHAMPAGNE 起泡飲料（尤指香檳）

fizz·er /ˈfɪzə(r)/ *noun* (*AustralE, NZE, informal*) a failure 失敗： *The party was a fizzer.* 聚會搞砸了。

fiz·zle /ˈfɪzl/ *verb* [I] when sth, especially sth that is burning, **fizzles**, it makes a sound like a long 's'（火等）發出嘶嘶聲 **SYN** **hiss**

PHR V **,fizzle 'out** (*informal*) to gradually become less successful and end in a disappointing way（順利開始）結果失敗，終成泡影；虎頭蛇尾

fizzy /ˈfɪzi/ *adj.* (*BrE*) (**fizz·ier**, **fizzi·est**) (of a drink 飲料) having bubbles of gas in it 起泡的 **SYN** **sparkling**： *fizzy drinks* 起泡飲料 **OPP** **still**

fjord (also **fiord**) /ˈfjɔːd; *NAmE* ˈfjɔːrd/ *noun* a long narrow strip of sea between high CLIFFS, especially in Norway（尤指挪威兩岸峭壁間的）峽灣

flab /flæb/ *noun* [U] (*informal, disapproving*) soft, loose flesh on a person's body（人體）鬆弛的肌肉

flab·ber·gast·ed /ˈflæbəgɑːstɪd; *NAmE* ˈflæbərgæstɪd/ *adj.* [not usually before noun] (*informal*) extremely surprised and/or shocked 大吃一驚；目瞪口呆 **SYN** **astonished**

flabby /ˈflæbi/ *adj.* (*informal, disapproving*) (**flab·bier**, **flab·bi est**) **1** having soft, loose flesh; fat（肌肉）鬆弛的；肥胖的： *flabby thighs* 肥胖的大腿 **2** weak; with no strength or force 軟弱的；無力的： *a flabby grip* 無力的一握 ◇ *a flabby argument* 無力的論據

flac·cid /ˈflæsɪd; ˈflæk-/ *adj.* (*formal*) soft and weak; not firm and hard 軟弱的；鬆弛的；不結實的： *flaccid breasts* 鬆弛的乳房

flack /flæk/ *noun* **1** [U] = FLAK **2** [C] (*NAmE, informal*) = PRESS AGENT

flag 0→ /flæg/ *noun, verb*

■ ***noun*** **1** 0→ a piece of cloth with a special coloured design on it that may be the symbol of a particular country or organization, or may have a particular meaning. A flag can be attached to a pole or held in the hand 旗： *the Italian flag* 意大利國旗 ◇ *the flag of Italy* 意大利國旗 ◇ *The hotel* **flies the** *European Union* **flag**. 這家旅館懸掛着歐盟的旗幟。◇ *The American* **flag was flying**. 美國國旗飄揚。◇ *All the* **flags were at half mast** (= in honour of a famous person who has died). 到處都下半旗致哀。◇ *The black and white flag went down, and the race began.* 黑白旗落下，賽跑開始了。➲ VISUAL VOCAB pages V2, V3 ➲ see also BLUE FLAG **2** used to refer to a particular country or organization and its beliefs and values 旗幟（指某國家或組織及其信仰和價值觀）： *to swear allegiance to the flag* 面對旗幟作效忠宣誓 ◇ *He was working under the flag of the United Nations.* 他在聯合國工作。**3** 0→ a piece of cloth that is attached to a pole and used as a signal or MARKER in various sports（體育運動的）信號旗，標誌旗 **4** a flower that is a type of IRIS and that grows near water 菖蒲；鳶尾；香蒲： *yellow flags* 黃菖蒲 **5** = FLAGSTONE

IDM **fly/show/wave the 'flag** to show your support for your country, an organization or an idea to encourage or persuade others to do the same 表示並號召擁護自己的國家（或某組織、某思想） **keep the 'flag flying** to represent your country or organization 代表自己的國家（或組織）： *Our exporters keep the flag flying at international trade exhibitions.* 我們的出口商在國際貿易展覽會上代表我們的國家參展。➲ more at RED *adj.*

■ ***verb*** (**-gg-**) **1** [T] **~ sth** to put a special mark next to information that you think is important 標示（重要處）： *I've flagged the paragraphs that we need to look at in more detail.* 我已用記號標出我們需要更仔細研究的段落。**2** [I] to become tired, weaker or less enthusiastic 疲乏；變弱；熱情衰減： *It had been a long day and the children were beginning to flag.* 這一天真漫長，孩子們都累得打起蔫來。◇ *Her confidence had never flagged.* 她的信心從未減弱。◇ ***flagging support/enthusiasm*** 日益減少的支持；漸漸低落的熱情

PHR V **,flag sb/sth↔'down** to signal to the driver of a vehicle to stop by waving at them 揮旗（或揮手）示意停車 **,flag sth↔'up** (*BrE*) to draw attention to sth 引起對…的注意： *The report flagged up the dangers of underage drinking.* 這篇報道引起大眾對未成年人飲酒危害的關注。

'flag day *noun* **1** (*BrE*) a day when money is collected in public places for a charity, and people who give money receive a small paper STICKER 募捐售旗日 **2** **Flag Day** 14 June, the anniversary of the day in 1777 when the

Stars and Stripes became the national flag of the United States 美國國旗紀念日（6 月 14 日）

fla·gel·late /ˈflædʒəleɪt/ *verb* **~ sb/yourself** (*formal*) to WHIP yourself or sb else, especially as a religious punishment or as a way of experiencing sexual pleasure 鞭笞（自己或他人，尤作為一種宗教懲罰或為獲得性快感）▸ **fla·gel·la·tion** /ˌflædʒəˈleɪʃn/ *noun* [U]

ˌflag ˈfootball *noun* [U] (*NAmE*) a type of AMERICAN FOOTBALL played without the usual form of TACKLING. A TACKLE is made instead by pulling a piece of cloth from an opponent's WAISTBAND.（美式）奪旗橄欖球（擒抱方式不同於一般的美式足球，而是從對方的腰帶上拽出一塊織物）➲ compare TOUCH FOOTBALL

F

flagged /flæɡd/ *adj.* covered with large flat stones (called FLAGSTONES) 鋪石板的：*a flagged floor* 石板地面

ˌflag of conˈvenience *noun* a flag of a foreign country that is used by a ship from another country for legal or financial reasons 方便旗（指船由於法律或經濟上的原因掛外國國旗）

flagon /ˈflæɡən/ *noun* a large bottle or similar container, often with a handle, in which wine, etc. is sold or served 大肚短頸瓶；大酒壺

flag·pole /ˈflæɡpəʊl; *NAmE* -poʊl/ (also **flag·staff**) *noun* a tall pole on which a flag is hung 旗杆 ➲ VISUAL VOCAB pages V2, V3

fla·grant /ˈfleɪɡrənt/ *adj.* (of an action 行動) shocking because it is done in a very obvious way and shows no respect for people, laws, etc. 駭人聽聞的；公然的；罪惡昭彰的 SYN **blatant**：*a flagrant abuse of human rights* 粗暴的踐踏人權 ◇ *He showed a flagrant disregard for anyone else's feelings.* 他公然蔑視任何人的感情。▸ **fla·grant·ly** *adv.*

fla·grante ➲ IN FLAGRANTE

flag·ship /ˈflæɡʃɪp/ *noun* **1** the main ship in a FLEET of ships in the navy 旗艦 **2** [usually sing.] the most important product, service, building, etc. that an organization owns or produces（某組織機構的）最重要產品，最佳服務項目，主建築物，王牌：*The company is opening a new flagship store in London.* 這家公司將在倫敦新開一家旗艦店。

flag·staff /ˈflæɡstɑːf; *NAmE* -stæf/ *noun* = FLAGPOLE

flag·stone /ˈflæɡstəʊn; *NAmE* -stoʊn/ (also **flag**) *noun* a large flat square piece of stone that is used for floors, paths, etc. 石板（方形，用於鋪地面、小徑等）

ˈflag-waving *noun* [U] the expression of strong national feelings, especially in a way that people disapprove of 強烈民族情緒；（尤指）沙文主義的表現

flail /fleɪl/ *verb, noun*

■ *verb* **1** [I, T] **~ (sth) (about/around)** to move around without control; to move your arms and legs around without control 亂動；胡亂擺動：*The boys flailed around on the floor.* 男孩子們在地板上任意地動來動去。◇ *He was running along, his arms flailing wildly.* 他向前跑，拚命擺動雙臂。**2** [T] **~ sb/sth** to hit sb/sth very hard, especially with a stick（尤指用棍棒）猛擊，猛打

■ *noun* a tool that has a long handle with a stick swinging from it, used especially in the past to separate grains of WHEAT from their dry outer covering, by beating the WHEAT 連枷（舊時長柄脫粒農具）

flair /fleə(r); *NAmE* fler/ *noun* **1** [sing., U] **~ for sth** a natural ability to do sth well 天資；天賦；天分 SYN **talent**：*He **has a flair for** languages.* 他有學語言的天分。**2** [U] a quality showing the ability to do things in an interesting way that shows imagination 才華；資質：*artistic flair* 藝術魅力 ◇ *She dresses with real flair.* 她衣着甚有品味。

flak (also **flack**) /flæk/ *noun* [U] **1** guns on the ground that are shooting at enemy aircraft; bullets from these guns 高射炮；高射炮火 **2** (*informal*) severe criticism 嚴厲批評；抨擊：*He's **taken a lot of flak** for his left-wing views.* 他的左傾觀點受到了廣泛指責。◇ *She **came in for a lot of flak** from the press.* 她遭到報界猛烈抨擊。

flake /fleɪk/ *noun, verb*

■ *noun* **1** a small, very thin layer or piece of sth, especially one that has broken off from sth larger 小薄片；（尤指）碎片：***flakes of snow/paint*** 雪花；剝落的片片油漆 ◇ *dried onion flakes* 乾洋蔥皮片 ➲ see also CORNFLAKES, SNOWFLAKE, SOAP FLAKES **2** (*NAmE, informal*) a person who is strange or unusual or who forgets things easily 古怪的人；奇特的人；健忘的人

■ *verb* **1** [I] **~ (off)** to fall off in small thin pieces（成小薄片）脫落，剝落：*You could see bare wood where the paint had flaked off.* 油漆剝落處可以看見光禿禿的木頭。◇ *His skin was dry and flaking.* 他的皮膚乾燥，脫皮屑。**2** [T, I] **~ (sth)** to break sth, especially fish or other food into small thin pieces; to fall into small thin pieces 把（魚、食物等）切成薄片：*Flake the tuna and add to the sauce.* 把金槍魚切成片，加上調味汁。◇ *flaked almonds* 杏仁片

PHR V **ˌflake ˈout 1** (*informal*) to lie down or fall asleep because you are extremely tired（疲倦得）倒下，睡着：*When I got home he'd already flaked out on the bed.* 我到家時他已累倒在牀上。**2** (*NAmE, informal*) to begin to behave in a strange way 行為古怪起來

ˈflak jacket *noun* a heavy jacket without sleeves that has metal inside it to make it stronger, and is worn by soldiers and police officers to protect them from bullets 防彈背心

flaky /ˈfleɪki/ *adj.* **1** tending to break into small, thin pieces 易碎成小薄片的；易剝落的：*flaky pastry* 酥餅 ◇ *dry flaky skin* 乾燥易脫皮屑的皮膚 **2** (*informal*) (of a person 人) behaving in a strange or unusual way; tending to forget things 行為古怪的；好忘事的 **3** (*especially BrE, informal, computing* 計) that does not work well or often stops working 運行不正常的；經常出問題的：*I found the software a bit flaky.* 我發現這個軟件有點問題。▸ **flaki·ness** *noun* [U]

flambé /ˈflɒmbeɪ; *NAmE* flɑːmˈbeɪ/ *adj.* [after noun] (from *French*) (of food 食物) covered with alcohol, especially BRANDY and allowed to burn for a short time 火燒（澆上白蘭地等酒後點燃上桌）▸ **flambé** *verb* **~ sth** ➲ VISUAL VOCAB page V27

flam·boy·ant /flæmˈbɔɪənt/ *adj.* **1** (of people or their behaviour 人或行為) different, confident and exciting in a way that attracts attention 炫耀的；賣弄的：***a flamboyant gesture/style/personality*** 炫耀的手勢／作風／個性 **2** brightly coloured and noticeable 豔麗的；絢麗奪目的：***flamboyant clothes/designs*** 豔麗的衣服；華麗的設計 ▸ **flam·boy·ance** /-ˈbɔɪəns/ *noun* [U] **flam·boy·ant·ly** *adv.*

flame 0‑π /fleɪm/ *noun, verb*

■ *noun* **1** 0‑π [C, U] a hot bright stream of burning gas that comes from sth that is on fire 火焰；火舌：*the tiny yellow flame of a match* 火柴小小的黃色火焰 ◇ *The flames were growing higher and higher.* 熊熊火焰越來越高。◇ *The building was **in flames*** (= was burning). 大樓失火了。◇ *The plane **burst into flame(s)*** (= suddenly began burning strongly). 飛機突然猛烈燃燒起來。◇ *Everything **went up in flames*** (= was destroyed by fire). 一切都毀於大火。➲ VISUAL VOCAB page V70 **2** [U] a bright red or orange colour 鮮紅色；橘紅色；橙黃色：*a flame-red car* 橘紅色的汽車 **3** [C] (*literary*) a very strong feeling 強烈的感情；激情：*a flame of passion* 激情的烈火 ➲ see also OLD FLAME **4** [C] (*informal*) an angry or insulting message sent to sb by email or on the Internet 火藥味電郵（或互聯網信息）IDM see FAN *v.*

■ *verb* **1** [I] (+ **adj.**) (*literary*) to burn with a bright flame 燃燒：*The logs flamed on the hearth.* 木柴在壁爐牀裏燃燒。◇ (*figurative*) *Hope flamed in her.* 她燃起了希望之火。**2** [I, T] (+ **adj.**) | **~ (sth)** (*literary*) (of a person's face 人臉) to become red as a result of a strong emotion; to make sth become red（因強烈情緒而）變紅，使變紅：*Her cheeks flamed with rage.* 她憤怒得兩頰通紅。**3** [T] **~ sb** (*informal*) to send sb an angry or insulting message by email or on the Internet 發送火藥味電郵（或互聯網信息）

fla·menco /fləˈmeŋkəʊ; *NAmE* -koʊ/ *noun* (*pl.* **-os**) **1** [U, C] a fast exciting Spanish dance that is usually danced to music played on a GUITAR 弗拉門科舞（一種西班牙舞，節奏快而強烈，吉他伴奏）：*flamenco dancing* 跳弗拉門

科舞 ◇ *to dance the flamenco* 跳弗拉門科舞 **2** [U] the GUITAR music that is played for this dance 弗拉門科舞吉他樂曲

flame·proof /ˈfleɪmpruːf/ *adj.* made of or covered with a special material that will not burn easily 耐火的；防火的

flame-retard·ant /ˈfleɪm rɪˌtɑːdənt; *NAmE* -ˌtɑːrd-/ *adj.* = FIRE-RETARDANT

ˈflame-thrower *noun* a weapon like a gun that shoots out burning liquid or flames and is often used for clearing plants from land 噴火器；火焰噴射器

flam·ing /ˈfleɪmɪŋ/ *adj.* [only before noun] **1** full of anger 滿腔怒火的；激動的：*a **flaming argument/temper*** 激烈的爭論；暴躁的脾氣 **2** burning and covered in flames 燃燒的；冒火焰的：*Flaming fragments were still falling from the sky.* 燃燒着的碎片還在不斷地從天而降。 **3** (*BrE, informal*) used to emphasize that you are annoyed（強調惱怒）可惡的，討厭的：*You flaming idiot!* 你這個討厭的笨蛋！ **4** bright red or orange in colour 鮮紅色的；橙黃色的；橘紅色的：*flaming (red) hair* 火焰般的（紅）頭髮 ◇ *a flaming sunset* 嫣紅的晚霞

fla·mingo /fləˈmɪŋgəʊ; *NAmE* -goʊ/ *noun* (*pl.* **-oes** or **-os**) a large pink bird with long thin legs and a long neck, that lives near water in warm countries 紅鸛，火烈鳥，紅鶴（熱帶大涉禽，羽色粉紅，腿細長，長頸）

flam·mable /ˈflæməbl/ (also **in·flam·mable** especially in *BrE*) *adj.* that can burn easily 易燃的；可燃的：***highly flammable** liquids* 高度易燃的液體 **OPP** **non-flammable**

flan /flæn/ *noun* [C, U] **1** (*especially BrE*) an open PIE made of PASTRY or cake filled with eggs and cheese, fruit, etc.（蛋糊）果餡餅：*a mushroom/strawberry flan* 蘑菇餡餅；草莓餡餅 ◇ *Have some more flan.* 再吃一點果餡餅。 ➲ compare QUICHE, TART *n.* (1) **2** (*NAmE*) (*BrE* **crème caramel**) a cold DESSERT (= a sweet dish) made from milk, eggs and sugar 焦糖蛋奶（冷甜食）

flange /flændʒ/ *noun* an edge that sticks out from an object and makes it stronger or (as in a wheel of a train) keeps it in the correct position 凸緣；法蘭；（火車的）輪緣

flank /flæŋk/ *noun, verb*

■ ***noun*** **1** the side of sth such as a building or mountain（建築物、山等的）側面 **2** the left or right side of an army during a battle, or a sports team during a game（軍隊或運動隊的）翼側，側面，側翼 **3** the side of an animal between the RIBS and the hip（動物的）脅腹

■ ***verb*** **1 be flanked by sb/sth** to have sb/sth on one or both sides 側面（或兩側）有：*She left the courtroom flanked by armed guards.* 她在武裝警衛護送下離開法庭。 **2 ~ sth** to be placed on one or both sides of sth 位於…的側翼；在…側面：*They drove through the cotton fields that flanked Highway 17.* 他們駕車穿過了 17 號公路側面的棉田。

flank·er /ˈflæŋkə(r)/ *noun* an attacking player in RUGBY or AMERICAN FOOTBALL（橄欖球或美式足球）邊鋒

flan·nel /ˈflænl/ *noun* **1** [U] a type of soft light cloth, containing cotton or wool, used for making clothes 法蘭絨：*a flannel shirt* 法蘭絨襯衣 ◇ *a grey flannel suit* 一套灰法蘭絨西服 **2** (also **face·cloth**) (both *BrE*) (*NAmE* **wash·cloth**) [C] a small piece of cloth used for washing yourself（洗擦身體用的）毛巾：*a face flannel* 洗臉毛巾 ➲ VISUAL VOCAB page V24 **3 flannels** [pl.] trousers/pants made of flannel 法蘭絨男褲 **4** [U] (*BrE, informal*) words that do not have much meaning and that avoid telling sb what they want to know 兜圈子的話語；應付性言語

flan·nel·ette /ˌflænəˈlet/ *noun* [U] a type of soft cotton cloth, used especially for making sheets and NIGHT-CLOTHES 絨布，棉法蘭絨（尤用於製作牀單和睡衣）

flap /flæp/ *noun, verb*

■ ***noun***

▸ **FLAT PIECE OF PAPER, ETC.** 平整的紙等 **1** [C] a flat piece of paper, cloth, metal, etc. that is attached to sth along one side and that hangs down or covers an opening（附於某物的）片狀下垂物，封蓋，口蓋，袋蓋：*the flap of an envelope* 信封的封蓋 ◇ *I zipped the tent flaps shut.* 我拉上了帳篷門簾的拉鏈。 ➲ see also CAT FLAP ➲ VISUAL VOCAB page V69

▸ **MOVEMENT** 動作 **2** [C, usually sing.] a quick often noisy movement of sth up and down or from side to side（上下或左右）拍打，振（翅），拍擊：*With a flap of its wings, the bird was gone.* 鳥撲打着翅膀飛走了。◇ *the flap of the sails* 風帆的鼓脹

▸ **WORRY/EXCITEMENT** 憂慮；激動 **3** [sing.] (*informal, especially BrE*) a state of worry, confusion and excitement 憂慮；困惑；激動：*She **gets in a flap** over the slightest thing.* 極小的事也能令她不安。

▸ **PUBLIC DISAGREEMENT** 公眾不同意 **4** [sing.] (*NAmE*) public disagreement, anger or criticism caused by sth a public figure has said or done 公眾不同意；群眾憤怒；大眾批評：*the flap about the President's business affairs* 公眾對總統公務的批評

▸ **PART OF AIRCRAFT** 飛行器部份 **5** [C] (*technical* 術語) a part of the wing of an aircraft, on the rear of the wing, that can be moved up or down to control upward or downward movement（飛機的）襟翼 ➲ VISUAL VOCAB page V53

▸ **PHONETICS** 語音學 **6** [C] = TAP (6)

■ ***verb*** (**-pp-**)

▸ **MOVE QUICKLY** 快速動作 **1** [T, I] **~ (sth)** if a bird **flaps** its wings, or if its wings **flap**, they move quickly up and down 振（翅）**SYN** **beat** *The bird flapped its wings and flew away.* 鳥振翅飛去。◇ *The gulls flew off, wings flapping.* 海鷗撲打着雙翅飛走了。 **2** [I, T] to move or to make sth move up and down or from side to side, often making a noise（上下或左右）拍打，拍擊，擺動：**(+ adv./prep.)** *The sails flapped in the breeze.* 風帆在微風中擺動。◇ *Two large birds flapped (= flew) slowly across the water.* 兩隻大鳥振翅緩緩飛過水面。◇ **~ sth** *She walked up and down, flapping her arms to keep warm.* 她來回走動，揮動着雙臂使身體暖和起來。◇ *A gust of wind flapped the tents.* 一陣風吹動了帳篷。

▸ **BE WORRIED/EXCITED** 憂慮；激動 **3** [I] (*BrE, informal*) to behave in an anxious or excited way 憂慮；激動：*There's no need to flap—I've got everything under control.* 不必擔心，一切都已在我控制之中。

▸ **PHONETICS** 語音學 **4** [T] **~ sth** = TAP (7) **IDM** see EAR

flap·jack /ˈflæpdʒæk/ *noun* **1** [U, C] (*BrE*) a thick soft biscuit made from OATS, butter, sugar and SYRUP 燕麥甜餅 **2** [C] (*NAmE*) a thick PANCAKE 煎餅；烤餅

flap·per /ˈflæpə(r)/ *noun* a fashionable young woman in the 1920s who was interested in modern ideas and was determined to enjoy herself（20 世紀 20 年代不受傳統拘束的）新潮女郎

flare /fleə(r); *NAmE* fler/ *verb, noun*

■ ***verb*** **1** [I] to burn brightly, but usually for only a short time or not steadily（短暫）燒旺；（搖曳着）燃燒；（火光）閃耀：*The match flared and went out.* 火柴閃亮了一下就熄了。◇ *The fire flared into life.* 火旺了起來。◇ (*figurative*) *Colour flared in her cheeks.* 她兩頰泛起了紅暈。 **2** [I] **~ (up)** (especially of anger and violence 尤指憤怒和暴力) to suddenly start or become much stronger 突發；加劇 **SYN** **erupt** *Violence flared when the police moved in.* 警察逼近時爆發了暴力行為。◇ ***Tempers flared** towards the end of the meeting.* 會議快結束時群情激憤。 ➲ related noun FLARE-UP (1) **3** [T, I] (**+ speech**) to say sth in an angry and aggressive way 發怒地說；粗暴地說：*'You should have told me!' she flared at him.* "你應該告訴我的！" 她氣沖沖地對他說。 **4** [I] (of clothes 衣服) to become wider towards the bottom 底部展開；呈喇叭形：*The sleeves are tight to the elbow, then flare out.* 袖子在肘部收緊，接着逐漸展開。 **5** [T, I] **~ (sth)** if a person or an animal **flares** their NOSTRILS (= the openings at the end of the nose), or if their nostrils **flare**, they become wider, especially as a sign of anger（尤指因氣憤）使鼻孔張開，（鼻翼）張開，搧動：*The horse backed away, its nostrils flaring with fear.* 馬向後驚退，嚇得鼻翼搧動。

PHR V **ˌflare ˈup** **1** (of flames, a fire, etc. 火焰、火等) to suddenly start burning more brightly 突然旺起來 ➲ related noun FLARE-UP (3) **2** (of a person 人) to suddenly become angry 突然發怒 ➲ related noun

FLARE-UP (1) **3** (of an illness, injury, etc. 疾病、損傷等) to suddenly start again or become worse 復發；突然加劇 ➲ related noun FLARE-UP (2)

■ ***noun*** **1** [usually sing.] a bright but unsteady light or flame that does not last long （短暫的）旺火；（搖曳的）光；（閃耀的）火光：*The flare of the match lit up his face.* 火柴的光照亮了他的臉。 **2** a device that produces a bright flame, used especially as a signal; a flame produced in this way 閃光裝置；閃光信號燈；照明彈：*The ship sent up distress flares to attract the attention of the coastguard.* 這艘船點起了遇險信號以引起海岸警衛隊的注意。 **3** a shape that becomes gradually wider 逐漸展開；喇叭形：*a skirt with a slight flare* 下襬略張的裙子 **4 flares** (*BrE* also ˌ**flared 'trousers**) [pl.] (*informal*) trousers/pants that become very wide at the bottom of the legs 喇叭褲：*a pair of flares* 一條喇叭褲

flared /fleəd; *NAmE* flerd/ *adj.* (of clothes 衣服) wider at the bottom edge than at the top 底部展開的；喇叭形的

'flare-up *noun* [usually sing.] **1** a sudden expression of angry or violent feeling （怒氣、激烈情緒等）爆發 **SYN outburst**：*a flare-up of tension between the two sides* 雙方劍拔弩張 **2** (of an illness 疾病) a sudden painful attack, especially after a period without any problems or pain 突發；（尤指）復發 **3** the fact of a fire suddenly starting to burn again more strongly than before 驟燃；突然發出火焰：*a flare-up of the bushfires* 林區大火的猛燃

flash 0-π /flæʃ/ *verb, noun, adj.*

■ ***verb***

▸ **SHINE BRIGHTLY** 照耀 **1** 0-π [I, T] to shine very brightly for a short time; to make sth shine in this way （使）閃耀，閃光：*Lightning flashed in the distance.* 遠處電光閃閃。◇ *the flashing blue lights of a police car* 警車閃爍的藍燈 ◇ **+ adv./prep.** *A neon sign flashed on and off above the door.* 門上方霓虹燈忽明忽暗地閃爍着。◇ **~ sth** *The guide flashed a light into the cave.* 導遊用手電筒照射洞穴。

▸ **GIVE SIGNAL** 發出信號 **2** 0-π [T, I] to use a light to give sb a signal 用光發出信號：**~ sth (at sb)** *Red lights flashed a warning at them.* 紅燈閃亮向他們發出警告。◇ **~ sb (sth)** *Red lights flashed them a warning.* 紅燈閃亮向他們發出警告。◇ **~ at sb** *Why is that driver flashing at us?* 那個司機為什麼向我們閃燈？

▸ **SHOW QUICKLY** 快速顯示 **3** [T] **~ sth at sb** to show sth to sb quickly （快速地）出示，顯示：*He flashed his pass at the security officer.* 他向保安員亮了一下通行證。

▸ **MOVE QUICKLY** 快速移動 **4** [I] **+ adv./prep.** to move or pass very quickly 飛速運動；掠過：*The countryside flashed past the train windows.* 鄉村景色從火車窗外飛掠而過。◇ *A look of terror flashed across his face.* 他臉上掠過驚恐的神色。

▸ **OF THOUGHTS/MEMORIES** 思想；記憶 **5** [I] **+ adv./prep.** to come into your mind suddenly 突然想到；猛然想起：*A terrible thought flashed through my mind.* 一個可怕的想法閃過我的腦海。

▸ **ON SCREEN** 屏幕 **6** [I, T] to appear on a television screen, computer screen, etc. for a short time; to make sth do this （使）閃現，映出，顯示：*A message was flashing on his pager.* 他的尋呼機上閃現出一則信息。◇ **~ (sth) (up)** *His name was flashed up on the screen.* 屏幕上顯示出了他的名字。

▸ **SEND NEWS** 發送消息 **7** [T] **~ sth + adv./prep.** to send information quickly by radio, computer, etc. （通過無線電、計算機等）快速發送（信息）：*News of their triumph was flashed around the world.* 他們勝利的消息迅速傳遍了全世界。

▸ **SHOW EMOTION** 顯露情感 **8** [I] **(+ adv./prep.)** (*literary*) to show a strong emotion suddenly and quickly 突然顯露（強烈情感）：*Her eyes flashed with anger.* 她眼中閃出怒火。

▸ **OF A MAN** 男子 **9** [I] (*informal*) if a man **flashes**, he shows his sexual organs in public 當眾暴露性器官

IDM **flash sb a 'smile, 'look, etc.** to smile, look, etc. at sb suddenly and quickly 向…微微一笑（或瞥一眼）

PHR V ˌ**flash sth a'round** (*disapproving*) to show sth to other people in order to impress them 炫耀（某物）：*He's always flashing his money around.* 他總是在炫耀他的金錢。 ˌ**flash 'back (to sth)** **1** if your mind **flashes back** to sth, you remember sth that happened in the past 回憶；回想；回顧：*Her thoughts flashed back to their wedding day.* 她回憶起他們婚禮那一天的情景。 ➲ related noun FLASHBACK (2) **2** if a film/movie **flashes back** to sth, it shows things that happened at an earlier time, for example at an earlier part of sb's life （電影）閃回，倒敘 ➲ related noun FLASHBACK (1) **3** to reply very quickly and/or angrily 迅即答覆；憤怒回答 ˌ**flash 'by/'past** (of time 時間) to go very quickly 飛逝：*The morning has just flashed by.* 這個上午轉眼就過去了。 **'flash on sth** (*US, informal*) to suddenly remember or think of sth 突然回想起；猛地想到：*I flashed on an argument I had with my sister when we were kids.* 我突然回想起小時候和姐姐的一次爭吵。 **'flash on sb** [no passive] if sth **flashes on you**, you suddenly realize it 突然意識到；猛然領悟：**it flashes on sb that …** *It flashed on me that he was the man I'd seen in the hotel.* 我頓時認出他就是我在旅館裏看到的那個人。

■ ***noun***

▸ **LIGHT** 光 **1** 0-π [C] a sudden bright light that shines for a moment and then disappears 閃光；閃耀：*a* ***flash of lightning*** 一道閃電 ◇ *Flashes of light were followed by an explosion.* 陣陣閃光後就是一聲爆炸的巨響。◇ *There was* ***a blinding flash*** *and the whole building shuddered.* 一道眩目的閃光過後，整棟大樓顫抖起來。

▸ **SIGNAL** 信號 **2** 0-π [C] the act of shining a light on sth, especially as a signal （尤指信號燈）閃亮

▸ **IN PHOTOGRAPHY** 攝影 **3** 0-π [C, U] a piece of equipment that produces a bright light for a very short time, used for taking photographs indoors, when it is dark, etc.; the use of this when taking a photograph 閃光燈：*a camera with a built-in flash* 有內置閃光燈的照相機 ◇ *I'll need flash for this shot.* 拍這個鏡頭我需要閃光燈。◇ *flash photography* 閃光攝影術 ➲ VISUAL VOCAB page V41

▸ **OF BRIGHT COLOUR** 鮮明顏色 **4** 0-π [C] **~ of sth** the sudden appearance for a short time of sth bright（明亮的東西）閃現：*a flash of white teeth* 閃露潔白的牙齒 ◇ *On the horizon, she saw a flash of silver—the sea!* 她看見天邊閃現一片銀色——大海！

▸ **SUDDEN IDEA/EMOTION** 突然想法；突發情感 **5** [C] **~ of sth** a particular feeling or idea that suddenly comes into your mind or shows in your face （想法的）突現；（情感的）突發：*a* ***flash of anger/inspiration, etc.*** 怒上心頭、靈感閃現等

▸ **NEWS** 新聞 **6** [C] = NEWSFLASH

▸ **ON UNIFORM** 制服 **7** [C] (*BrE*) a band or small piece of cloth worn on a military uniform to show a person's rank （佩戴在軍服上的）徽章，肩章，臂章

▸ **ON BOOK/PACK** 書；小包 **8** [C] a band of colour or writing across a book, pack, etc. 彩條；文字條

▸ **COMPUTING** 計算機技術 **9 Flash™** [U] a program which creates moving images for websites * Flash 網站動畫程序

IDM **a ˌflash in the 'pan** a sudden success that lasts only a short time and is not likely to be repeated 曇花一現 **in/like a 'flash** very quickly and suddenly 轉瞬間；立即 ➲ more at QUICK *adj.*

■ ***adj.*** (*BrE, informal, disapproving*) attracting attention by being large or expensive, or by having expensive clothes, etc. 龐大的；昂貴的；穿着奢華的：*a flash car* 外表華麗的轎車 ◇ *He's very flash, isn't he?* 他穿着十分奢華，不是嗎？

flash·back /'flæʃbæk/ *noun* **1** [C, U] a part of a film/movie, play, etc. that shows a scene that happened earlier in time than the main story （電影或戲劇的）閃回，倒敘，倒敘片段：*The events that led up to the murder were shown in a series of flashbacks.* 通過一系列倒敘展現出了導致謀殺的各個情節。◇ *The reader is told the story* ***in flashback***. 故事是以倒敘手法向讀者講述的。 **2** [C] a sudden, very clear, strong memory of sth that happened in the past that is so real you feel that you are living through the experience again （往事的）閃回

flash·bulb /'flæʃbʌlb/ *noun* a small electric BULB that can be attached to a camera to take photographs indoors or when it is dark （照相機的）閃光燈泡

'flash card *noun* a card with a word or picture on it, that teachers use during lessons 教學卡片；識字卡；字卡

'flash drive (also **US'B drive**, **'pen drive**) (*NAmE* also **'thumb drive**) *noun* (*computing* 計) a small memory device that can be used to store data from a computer and to move it from one computer to another 閃存盤；閃盤；U 盤；隨身碟 SYN **memory stick** ➲ VISUAL VOCAB page V66

flash·er /ˈflæʃə(r)/ *noun* **1** (*informal*) a man who shows his sexual organs in public, especially in order to shock or frighten women （男子）暴露狂 **2** a device that turns a light on and off quickly 閃光裝置 **3** (*NAmE*) a light on a vehicle that you can turn on and off quickly as a signal （車用）閃光燈：*four-way flashers* (= four lights that flash together to warn other drivers of possible danger) 四向閃光燈

'flash flood *noun* a sudden flood of water caused by heavy rain （暴雨引起的）暴洪

flash·gun /ˈflæʃɡʌn/ *noun* a piece of equipment that holds and operates a bright light that is used to take photographs indoors or when it is dark （攝影用的）閃光槍

flash·ing /ˈflæʃɪŋ/ *noun* [U] (also **flashings** [pl.]) a strip of metal put on a roof where it joins a wall to prevent water getting through （房頂與牆交接處的）防雨板，蓋片

flash·light /ˈflæʃlaɪt/ (*especially NAmE*) (*BrE* also **torch**) *noun* a small electric lamp that uses batteries and that you can hold in your hand 手電筒

'flash memory *noun* [U] (*computing* 計) computer memory that does not lose data when the power supply is lost 閃速存貯，閃速存貯器，快閃記憶體（斷電時不丟失數據）

flash·mob /ˈflæʃmɒb; *NAmE* -mɑːb/ *noun* a large group of people who arrange (by mobile/cell phone or email) to gather together in a public place at exactly the same time, spend a short time doing sth there and then quickly all leave at the same time 快閃族，快閃黨（通過手機或電郵相約同一時間在公共場所速聚速散的一大群人）▸ **flash·mob·ber** *noun* **flash·mob·bing** *noun* [U]

flash·point /ˈflæʃpɔɪnt/ *noun* [C, U] a situation or place in which violence or anger starts and cannot be controlled（暴力或憤怒的）一觸即發，危機即將爆發的地點：*Tension in the city is rapidly reaching flashpoint.* 這座城市處於緊張狀態，大有一觸即發之勢。◇ *potential flashpoints in the south of the country* 該國南部潛在的暴力爆發點

flashy /ˈflæʃi/ *adj.* (**flash·ier**, **flashi·est**) (*informal*, usually *disapproving*) **1** (of things 物品) attracting attention by being bright, expensive, large, etc. 俗豔的；（因昂貴、巨大等）顯眼的：*a flashy hotel* 奢華的旅館 ◇ *I just want a good reliable car, nothing flashy.* 我只要一輛性能可靠的轎車，不要華而不實的那種。 **2** (of people 人) attracting attention by wearing expensive clothes, etc. 穿着奢華的 **3** intended to impress by looking very skilful 炫耀技藝的：*He specializes in flashy technique, without much depth.* 他就會些沒有深度的花招。▸ **flash·ily** *adv.*：*flashily dressed* 穿着豔俗的

flask /flɑːsk; *NAmE* flæsk/ *noun* **1** a bottle with a narrow top, used in scientific work for mixing or storing chemicals 燒瓶 ➲ VISUAL VOCAB page V70 **2** (*BrE*) = VACUUM FLASK：*a **flask of tea/coffee*** 一保溫瓶的茶／咖啡 ➲ compare THERMOS **3** (*especially NAmE*) (*BrE* also **'hip flask**) a small flat bottle made of metal or glass and often covered with leather, used for carrying alcohol 小扁酒瓶（用金屬或玻璃製成，常帶皮套，隨身攜帶）

flat 🔑 /flæt/ *adj., noun, adv., verb*

■ *adj.* (**flat·ter**, **flat·test**)

▸ LEVEL 平 **1** 🔑 having a level surface, not curved or sloping 水平的；平坦的：*low buildings with flat roofs* 平頂矮建築物 ◇ *People used to think the earth was flat.* 人們曾經認為地球是平的。◇ *Exercise is the only way to get a flat stomach after having a baby.* 產後只有通過鍛煉才能使腹部收平。◇ *The sails hung limply in the flat calm* (= conditions at sea when there is no wind and the water is completely level). 風平浪靜，風帆無力地垂掛着。**2** 🔑 (of land 土地) without any slopes or hills 平坦的：*The road stretched ahead across the flat landscape.* 公路向前延伸，經過一片平坦的地。 **3** 🔑 (of surfaces 表面) smooth and even; without lumps or holes 平滑的：*I need a flat surface to write on.* 我需要一個平面在上面寫字。◇ *We found a large flat rock to sit on.* 我們找了一塊可以坐的大而平滑的石頭。

▸ NOT HIGH 不高 **4** 🔑 broad but not very high 扁平的：*Chapattis are a kind of flat Indian bread.* * chapatti 是一種印度薄餅。◇ *flat shoes* (= with no heels or very low ones) 平跟鞋；平底鞋

▸ DULL 枯燥 **5** dull; lacking interest or enthusiasm 枯燥的；無趣的；缺乏熱情的：*He felt very flat after his friends had gone home.* 他的朋友們回家後，他感到興味索然。

▸ VOICE 嗓音 **6** not showing much emotion; not changing much in tone 平淡的；單調的：*Her voice was flat and expressionless.* 她的聲音平淡而呆板。

▸ COLOURS/PICTURES 顏色；圖畫 **7** very smooth, with no contrast between light and dark, and giving no impression of depth 色彩單調的；無反差的；無景深的：*Acrylic paints can be used to create large, flat blocks of colour.* 丙烯顏料可用來創作單一色調的大幅圖塊。

▸ BUSINESS 商業 **8** not very successful because very little is being sold 不景氣的；蕭條的；生意清淡的：*The housing market has been flat for months.* 房屋市場已有好幾個月處於低迷狀態。

▸ REFUSAL/DENIAL 拒絕；否認 **9** [only before noun] not allowing discussion or argument; definite 斷然的；絕對的：*Her request was met with a flat refusal.* 她的請求被斷然拒絕。◇ *He gave a flat 'No!' to one reporter's question.* 他對一名記者提問直截了當地答覆"不！"

▸ IN MUSIC 音樂 **10** used after the name of a note to mean a note a SEMITONE/HALF TONE lower 降音的；降半音的：*That note should be B flat, not B.* 那個音應該是降 B 音，而不是 B 音。➲ picture at MUSIC OPP **sharp** ➲ compare NATURAL *adj.* (9) **11** below the correct PITCH (= how high or low a note sounds) 低於標準音高的；偏低的：*The high notes were slightly flat.* 這些高音略為偏低。OPP **sharp**

▸ DRINK 飲料 **12** no longer having bubbles in it; not fresh 走了氣的；不新鮮的：*The soda was warm and had gone flat.* 這汽水是溫的，已走了氣。

▸ BATTERY 電池 **13** (*BrE*) unable to supply any more electricity 電用完了的

▸ TYRE 輪胎 **14** not containing enough air, usually because of a hole 癟了的；撒了氣的

▸ FEET 足 **15** with no natural raised curves underneath 扁平的；足弓平坦的 ➲ see also FLAT-FOOTED (1) ▸ **flat·ness** *noun* [U]

IDM **and ˌthat's 'flat!** (*BrE, informal*) that is my final decision and I will not change my mind 這就是最後決定：*You can't go and that's flat!* 你不能去，就這樣！ **as ˌflat as a 'pancake** completely flat 完全平的 ➲ more at BACK *n.*, SPIN *n.*

■ *noun*

▸ ROOMS 房間 **1** 🔑 [C] (*BrE*) a set of rooms for living in, including a kitchen, usually on one floor of a building 一套房間；公寓；單元房：*Do you live in a flat or a house?* 你住的是一層公寓還是一座房子？◇ *They're renting a **furnished flat** on the third floor.* 他們租了四樓的一層帶傢具的公寓。◇ *a ground-floor flat* 一樓的一套單元房 ◇ *a new **block of flats*** 一棟新建的公寓樓 ◇ *Many large old houses have been converted into flats.* 許多大的老房子已改建成單元房。◇ *Children from the flats* (= the block of flats) *across the street were playing outside.* 街對面公寓樓裏的兒童正在戶外玩耍。➲ COLLOCATIONS at HOUSE ➲ VISUAL VOCAB page V16 ➲ compare APARTMENT (1)

▸ LEVEL PART 平面部份 **2** [sing.] **the ~ of sth** the flat level part of sth （某物的）平面部份：*He beat on the door with the flat of his hand.* 他用手掌打門。◇ *the flat of a sword* 劍面

▸ LAND 土地 **3** [C, usually pl.] an area of low flat land, especially near water （尤指水邊的）平地；低窪地：*salt flats* 鹽灘 ➲ see also MUDFLAT

▸ HORSE RACING 賽馬 **4 the flat, the Flat** [sing.] (*BrE*) the season for racing horses on flat ground with no jumps 無障礙平地賽馬季節

▸ IN MUSIC 音樂 **5** [C] a note played a SEMITONE/HALF TONE lower than the note that is named. The written symbol is (♭). 降半音；降音；降號：*There are no sharps or flats in the key of C major.* * C 大調中沒有升半音和降半音。OPP **sharp** ➲ compare NATURAL *n.* (2)

▸ TYRE 輪胎 **6** [C] (*especially NAmE*) a tyre that has lost air, usually because of a hole 癟了的輪胎；撒了氣的輪胎：*We got a flat on the way home.* 我們在回家的路上有一個輪胎漏氣癟了。◇ *We had to stop to fix a flat.* 我們得停車修一下撒了氣的輪胎。

F

▸ IN THEATRE 劇院 **7** [C] (*technical* 術語) a vertical section of SCENERY used on a theatre stage 平面佈景；佈景屏

▸ SHOES 鞋 **8 flats** (also **flat·ties**) [pl.] (*informal*) shoes with a very low heel 平跟鞋；平底鞋：*a pair of flats* 一雙平跟鞋 ➲ VISUAL VOCAB page V64

IDM **on the 'flat** (*BrE*) on level ground, without hills or jumps (= for example in horse racing) 在平地上

■ *adv.* (*comparative* **flat·ter**, no *superlative*)

▸ LEVEL 水平地 **1** spread out in a level, straight position, especially against another surface（尤指貼着另一表面）平直地，平躺地：*Lie flat and breathe deeply.* 平躺做深呼吸。◇ *They pressed themselves flat against the tunnel wall as the train approached.* 火車接近時他們身體緊貼着隧道壁。

▸ REFUSING/DENYING 拒絕；否認 **2** (*BrE*) (*NAmE* ˌ**flat 'out**) (*informal*) in a definite and direct way 斷然；直截了當地：*She told me flat she would not speak to me again.* 她直截了當地跟我說她再不會理我了。◇ *I made them a reasonable offer but they turned it down flat.* 我向他們提出一個合理建議，但是他們斷然拒絕了。

▸ IN MUSIC 音樂 **3** lower than the correct PITCH (= how high or low a note sounds) 低於標準音高：*He sings flat all the time.* 他總是唱低了音。OPP **sharp**

IDM **fall 'flat** if a joke, a story, or an event **falls flat**, it completely fails to amuse people or to have the effect that was intended（笑話、故事、事件等）完全失敗，根本未達到預期效果 **fall flat on your 'face 1** to fall so that you are lying on your front 趴倒在地 **2** to fail completely, usually causing embarrassment（顏面丟盡地）徹底失敗：*His next television venture fell flat on its face.* 他的下一個電視項目丟人現眼，徹底失敗了。**flat 'broke** (*BrE* also **stony 'broke**) (*informal*) completely BROKE (= without money) 窮得一個子兒也沒有；一貧如洗；窮得叮噹響 **flat 'out** (*informal*) **1** as fast or as hard as possible 全速；全力以赴：*Workers are working flat out to meet the rise in demand for new cars.* 為滿足對新轎車需求的增加，工人正全力以赴地工作。**2** (*especially NAmE*) in a definite and direct way; completely 直截了當；斷然：*I told him flat out 'No'.* 我斬釘截鐵地告訴他"不"。◇ *It's a 30-year mortgage we just flat out can't handle.* 這是一宗我們根本無法處理的 30 年按揭貸款業務。➲ see also FLAT-OUT **in … 'flat** (*informal*) used with an expression of time to say that sth happened or was done very quickly, in no more than the time stated（與表達時間的詞語連用，表示發生或做得很快）才…，只用了…，整：*They changed the wheel in three minutes flat* (= in only three minutes). 他們僅用三分鐘就換好了輪胎。

■ *verb* (**-tt-**) [I] (*AustralE, NZE*) to live in or share a flat/apartment 住公寓；夥住公寓：*My sister Zoe flats in Auckland.* 我妹妹佐伊住在奧克蘭的一棟公寓裏。

flat·bed /ˈflætbed/ *noun* **1** (*computing* 計) = FLATBED SCANNER **2** (also ˌ**flatbed 'truck**, ˌ**flatbed 'trailer**) (*especially NAmE*) an open truck or TRAILER without high sides, used for carrying large objects 平板車；平板拖車

ˌ**flatbed 'scanner** (also **flat'bed**) *noun* (*computing* 計) a SCANNER (= device for copying pictures and documents so that they can be stored on a computer) on which the picture or document can be laid flat for copying 平板掃描儀；平台式掃描器 ➲ VISUAL VOCAB pages V66, V69

ˌ**flat 'cap** *noun* (*BrE*) = CLOTH CAP

flat·car /ˈflætkɑː(r)/ *noun* (*NAmE*) a coach/car on a train without a roof or sides, used for carrying goods（鐵路）平板貨車，敞車

ˌ**flat-'chested** *adj.* (of a woman 婦女) having small breasts 平胸的；乳房小的

flat·fish /ˈflætfɪʃ/ *noun* (*pl.* **flat·fish**) any sea fish with a flat body, for example a PLAICE 比目魚（扁平海魚，如鰈）

ˌ**flat-'footed** *adj.* **1** without naturally raised curves (= ARCHES) under the feet 平足的；扁平足的 **2** (*especially NAmE*) not prepared for what is going to happen 無準備的：*They were **caught flat-footed** by the attack.* 他們冷不防遭到了攻擊。

flat·head /ˈflæthed/ *adj.* **1** (of a SCREWDRIVER 螺絲刀) with a straight end rather than a cross-shaped end 平頭的；一字頭的 ➲ compare PHILLIPS

flat·let /ˈflætlət/ *noun* (*BrE*) a very small flat/apartment 公寓小套間；小套房

flat·line /ˈflætlaɪn/ *verb* (*informal*) **1** [I] to die 死；斷氣 **2** [I] to be at a low level and fail to improve or increase 處於低潮；沒有起色

flat·ly /ˈflætli/ *adv.* **1** in a way that is very definite and will not be changed 斷然；斬釘截鐵地 SYN **absolutely**：*to **flatly** deny/reject/oppose sth* 斷然否認 / 拒絕 / 反對某事 ◇ *I **flatly refused** to spend any more time helping him.* 我斷然拒絕再花時間幫助他。**2** in a dull way with very little interest or emotion 枯燥地；無趣地；缺乏熱情地：*'Oh, it's you,' she said flatly.* "哦，是你。"她冷冷地說。

flat·mate /ˈflætmeɪt/ (*BrE*) (*NAmE* **'room·mate**) *noun* a person who shares a flat/apartment with one or more others 合住公寓套間者；同公寓房客

ˌ**flat-'out** *adj.* [only before noun] (*especially NAmE*) definite and direct; complete 直截了當的；完全的：*His story was full of contradictions and flat-out lies.* 他的話充滿矛盾和不折不扣的謊言。▸ ˌ**flat-'out** *adv.*：*She just flat-out hated me.* 她就是恨透了我。➲ see also FLAT OUT (2) at FLAT *adv.*

'**flat-pack** *noun* (*BrE*) a piece of furniture that is sold in pieces in a flat box and that you have to build yourself 扁平盒裝組件傢具（買主自己拼裝）

ˌ**flat-'panel** *adj.* = FLAT-SCREEN

'**flat racing** *noun* [U] the sport of horse racing over flat ground with no jumps 無障礙平地賽馬 ➲ compare STEEPLECHASE (1)

ˌ**flat 'rate** *noun* a price that is the same for everyone and in all situations 統一價格；統一收費率：*Interest is charged at a flat rate of 11%.* 利息按標準比率 11% 收取。

ˌ**flat-'screen** (also ˌ**flat-'panel**) *adj.* [only before noun] **~ television/TV/computer/monitor, etc.** a type of television or computer monitor that is very thin when compared with the traditional type（電視或電腦顯示器）平面的，平板的，超薄的 ➲ VISUAL VOCAB pages V21, V66

ˌ**flat 'spin** *noun* (*technical* 術語) a movement of an aircraft in which it goes gradually downwards while flying around in almost horizontal circles（飛機的）水平螺旋下降，平面旋轉下降

IDM **in a flat 'spin** very confused, worried or excited 慌亂；驚慌失措；緊張激動

flat·ten /ˈflætn/ *verb* **1** [I, T] to become or make sth become flat or flatter （使）變平；把…弄平：*The cookies will flatten slightly while cooking.* 曲奇烤時會略微變平。◇ **~ sth** *These exercises will help to flatten your stomach.* 這些身體鍛煉有助你腹部變平。◇ *He flattened his hair down with gel.* 他用髮膠把頭髮弄平。**2** [T] **~ sth** to destroy or knock down a building, tree, etc. 摧毀，推倒，弄倒（建築物、樹木等）：*Most of the factory was flattened by the explosion.* 工廠的大部份被爆炸夷為平地。**3** [T] **~ sb** (*informal*) to defeat sb easily in a competition, an argument, etc. 輕易擊敗對手 SYN **smash, thrash**：*Our team was flattened this evening!* 今晚我們隊被打得落花流水！ **4** [T] **~ sb** (*informal*) to hit sb very hard so that they fall down 擊倒；打倒：*He flattened the intruder with a single punch.* 他一拳就把闖入者打倒

在地。◇ *I'll flatten you if you do that again!* 你要再那樣我就把你揍趴下！

PHR V **ˌflatten sth/yourself aˈgainst/ˈon sb/sth** to press sth/your body against sb/sth 使平貼；把…緊貼着：*She flattened her nose against the window and looked in.* 她把鼻子緊貼着窗戶朝裏瞧。◇ *Greg flattened himself against the wall to let me pass.* 格雷格身體緊靠着牆讓我通過。 **ˌflatten ˈout 1** to gradually become completely flat 逐漸變平：*The hills first rose steeply then flattened out towards the sea.* 山巒起初拔地而起，然後逐漸平坦，伸向大海。 **2** to stop growing or going up 停止生長；不再長高；停止上升：*Export growth has started to flatten out.* 出口增長已逐漸緩了下來。 **ˌflatten sth↔ˈout** to make sth completely flat 使變平

flat·ter /ˈflætə(r)/ *verb* **1** [T] **~ sb** to say nice things about sb, often in a way that is not sincere, because you want them to do sth for you or you want to please them 奉承；討好；向…諂媚：*Are you trying to flatter me?* 你是想討好我？ **2** [T] **~ yourself (that …)** to choose to believe sth good about yourself and your abilities, especially when other people do not share this opinion 自命不凡：*'How will you manage without me?' 'Don't flatter yourself.'* "沒有我看你怎麼辦！" "別自以為了不起。" **3** [T] **~ sb** to make sb seem more attractive or better than they really are 使顯得更漂亮（或更好）：*That colour doesn't flatter many people.* 那種顏色很多人都不適宜。◇ *The scoreline flattered England* (= they did not deserve to get such a high score). 英格蘭隊在積分榜上的位置大大超過了其實力。 ▸ **flat·ter·er** /ˈflætərə(r)/ *noun*

IDM **be/feel ˈflattered** to be pleased because sb has made you feel important or special 被奉承得高興；感到榮幸：*He was flattered by her attention.* 她的關注使他感到格外高興。◇ *I felt flattered at being asked to give a lecture.* 承蒙邀請來演講，我深感榮幸。 **ˌflatter to deˈceive** (*BrE*) if sth **flatters to deceive**, it appears to be better, more successful, etc. than it really is 顯得比實際好；看似比實際成功

flat·ter·ing /ˈflætərɪŋ/ *adj.* **1** making sb look more attractive 使人顯得更漂亮的：*a flattering dress* 穿上去使人更漂亮的連衣裙 **2** saying nice things about sb/sth 奉承的；阿諛的；討好的：*flattering remarks* 奉承話 **3** making sb feel pleased and special 奉承的；使人感到榮幸的：*I found it flattering that he still recognized me after all these years.* 過了這麼多年他還認得我，使我覺得榮幸。

flat·tery /ˈflætəri/ *noun* [U] praise that is not sincere, especially in order to obtain sth from sb 奉承；阿諛；討好；恭維：*You're too intelligent to fall for his flattery.* 你很聰明，不會受他的阿諛奉承所惑。

IDM **flattery will get you ˈeverywhere/ˈnowhere** (*informal, humorous*) praise that is not sincere will/will not get you what you want 阿諛奉承將會使你如願以償（或無濟於事）

flat·ties /ˈflætiz/ *noun* [pl.] = FLAT *n.* (8)

ˈflat-top *noun* a HAIRSTYLE in which the hair is cut short and flat across the top 平頂頭，平頭（髮型） ➲ VISUAL VOCAB page V60

flatu·lence /ˈflætjʊləns; *NAmE* -tʃə-/ *noun* [U] an uncomfortable feeling caused by having too much gas in the stomach 腸胃氣脹

flatu·lent /ˈflætjʊlənt; *NAmE* -tʃə-/ *adj.* **1** (*disapproving*) sounding important and impressive in a way that exaggerates the truth or facts 浮誇的；浮華的 **2** suffering from too much gas in the stomach 患腸胃氣脹的

flat·ware /ˈflætweə(r); *NAmE* -wer/ *noun* [U] (*NAmE*) **1** = SILVERWARE (2) **2** flat dishes such as plates and SAUCERS 扁平餐具（如盤子、茶碟等）

flat·worm /ˈflætwɜːm; *NAmE* -wɜːrm/ *noun* a very simple WORM with a flat body 扁形動物；扁蟲

flaunt /flɔːnt/ *verb* (*disapproving*) **1** [T] **~ sth** to show sth you are proud of to other people, in order to impress them 炫耀；誇示；誇耀；賣弄：*He did not believe in flaunting his wealth.* 他不相信擺闊有什麼好處。◇ *She openly flaunted her affair with the senator.* 她公開誇耀與參議員的戀情。 **2** [T] **~ yourself** to behave in a confident and sexual way to attract attention （性感地）招搖過市

IDM **if you've ˌgot it, ˈflaunt it** (*humorous, saying*) used to tell sb that they should not be afraid of allowing other people to see their qualities and abilities 有什麼能耐施出來瞧瞧

flaut·ist /ˈflɔːtɪst; *NAmE* ˈflaʊtɪst/ (*BrE*) (*NAmE* **flut·ist**) *noun* a person who plays the FLUTE 長笛手

fla·von·oid /ˈfleɪvənɔɪd/ *noun* (*chemistry* 化) a type of substance that is found in some plants such as tomatoes, which is thought to protect against some types of cancer and heart disease 類黃酮（存在於西紅柿等植物中，據信對某些癌症和心臟病有防治作用）

fla·vour 🔑 (*especially US* **fla·vor**) /ˈfleɪvə(r)/ *noun, verb*

▪ *noun* **1** 🔑 [U] how food or drink tastes （食物或飲料的）味道 **SYN** **taste**：*The tomatoes **give** extra **flavour** to the sauce.* 番茄使調味汁別有風味。◇ *It is stronger **in flavour** than other Dutch cheeses.* 這比其他荷蘭乾酪的味道要濃。 **2** 🔑 [C] a particular type of taste（某種）味道：*This yogurt comes in ten different flavours.* 這種酸乳酪有十種不同的味道。◇ *a wine with a delicate fruit flavour* 有淡淡的水果味的葡萄酒 **3** (*NAmE*) = FLAVOURING **4** 🔑 [sing.] a particular quality or atmosphere 特點；特色；氣氛 **SYN** **ambience**：*the distinctive flavour of South Florida* 南佛羅里達的獨特風情 ◇ *Foreign visitors help to **give a** truly international **flavour** to the occasion.* 外國客人使這個場合顯出一種真正國際性的氣氛。 **5** [sing.] **a/the ~ of sth** an idea of what sth is like 像…的想法：*I have tried to convey something of the flavour of the argument.* 我試圖表達某種類似論據的東西。 **6** (*computing* 計) a particular type of sth, especially computer software 衍生系統

IDM **flavour of the ˈmonth** (*especially BrE*) a person or thing that is very popular at a particular time 風靡一時的人（或事物）

▪ *verb* 🔑 **~ sth (with sth)** to add sth to food or drink to give it more flavour or a particular flavour 給（食物或飲料）調味；加味於

fla·voured (*especially US* **fla·vored**) /ˈfleɪvəd; *NAmE* -vərd/ *adj.* **1 -flavoured** having the type of flavour mentioned 有…味道的：*lemon-flavoured sweets/candy* 檸檬味糖果 **2** having had flavour added to it 添加了味道的：*flavoured yogurt* 有添加味道的酸奶

fla·vour·ing (*especially US* **fla·vor·ing**) /ˈfleɪvərɪŋ/ (*NAmE* also **fla·vor**) *noun* [U, C] a substance added to food or drink to give it a particular flavour 調味品；調味香料：*orange/vanilla flavouring* 橙/香草調味香料 ◇ *This food contains no artificial flavourings.* 這種食品不含人工調味品。

fla·vour·less (*especially US* **fla·vor·less**) /ˈfleɪvələs; *NAmE* -ərləs/ *adj.* having no flavour 無味的；沒有味道的：*The meat was tough and flavourless.* 這肉咬不動，又沒有滋味。

fla·vour·some /ˈfleɪvəsəm; *NAmE* -vərs-/ (*especially US* **fla·vor·ful** /ˈfleɪvəfʊl; *NAmE* -vərf-/) *adj.* having a lot of flavour 多味的；味道豐富的；很有滋味的

flaw /flɔː/ *noun* **1** a mistake in sth that means that it is not correct or does not work correctly 錯誤；缺點 **SYN** **defect, fault**：*The argument is full of fundamental flaws.* 這段論述充滿根本性的錯誤。◇ **~ in sth** *The report reveals **fatal flaws** in security at the airport.* 報告揭示了機場安全的致命缺陷。 **2 ~ (in sth)** a crack or fault in sth that makes it less attractive or valuable 裂痕；裂隙；瑕疵 **3 ~ (in sb/sth)** a weakness in sb's character （性格上的）弱點，缺點：*There is always a flaw in the character of a tragic hero.* 悲劇主角總有性格上的缺點。

flawed /flɔːd/ *adj.* having a flaw; damaged or spoiled 有錯誤的；有缺點的；有瑕疵的：***seriously/fundamentally/fatally flawed*** 有嚴重/根本/致命缺點 ◇ *a flawed argument* 有錯誤的論點 ◇ *the book's flawed heroine* 書中有弱點的女主角

flaw·less /ˈflɔːləs/ *adj.* without FLAWS and therefore perfect 完美的；無瑕的 **SYN** **perfect**：*a flawless complexion/performance* 無瑕疵的面容；完美的表演◇

F

Her English is almost flawless. 她的英語幾乎無可挑剔。▶ **flaw·less·ly** *adv.*

flax /flæks/ *noun* [U] **1** a plant with blue flowers, grown for its STEM that is used to make thread and its seeds that are used to make LINSEED OIL 亞麻 **2** threads from the STEM of the flax plant, used to make LINEN 亞麻纖維

flax·en /ˈflæksn/ *adj.* (*literary*) (of hair 毛髮) pale yellow 淺黃色的；亞麻色的 SYN **blonde**

flax·seed /ˈflækssiːd/ *noun* [U, C] the seeds of the flax plant, eaten as a health food or used to make LINSEED OIL 亞麻籽

ˈ**flaxseed oil** *noun* [U] = LINSEED OIL

F

flay /fleɪ/ *verb* **1 ~ sth/sb** to remove the skin from an animal or person, usually when they are dead 剝（死人或動物的皮）**2 ~ sb** to hit or WHIP sb very hard so that some of their skin comes off 毒打，狠狠鞭打（直至皮開肉綻）**3 ~ sb/yourself** (*formal*) to criticize sb/yourself severely 嚴厲批評

flea /fliː/ *noun* a very small jumping insect without wings, that bites animals and humans and sucks their blood 蚤：*The dog has fleas.* 這條狗有跳蚤。

IDM **with a ˈflea in your ear** if sb sends a person away **with a flea in their ear**, they tell them angrily to go away 以氣憤的言語，以責難（把人轟走）➲ VISUAL VOCAB page V13

flea·bag /ˈfliːbæg/ *noun* (*informal*) **1** a person who looks poor and does not take care of their appearance 邋遢的人 **2** an animal that is in poor condition 骯髒的動物 **3** (*especially NAmE*) a hotel that is cheap and dirty 廉價低級旅館

ˈ**flea-bitten** *adj.* (*informal*) in poor condition and with an unpleasant appearance 邋遢的

ˈ**flea market** *noun* an outdoor market that sells SECOND-HAND (= old or used) goods at low prices 跳蚤市場（廉價出售舊物的露天市場）

flea·pit /ˈfliːpɪt/ *noun* (*old-fashioned, BrE, informal*) an old and dirty cinema or theatre 破舊骯髒的電影院（或劇院）

fleck /flek/ *noun, verb*

■ *noun* [usually pl.] **~ (of sth)** **1** a very small area of a particular colour 色斑；斑點：*His hair was dark, with flecks of grey.* 他的黑髮間有縷縷銀絲。**2** a very small piece of sth 微粒；小片：*flecks of dust/foam/dandruff* 灰塵微粒；泡沫；頭皮屑

■ *verb* [usually passive] **~ sth (with sth)** to cover or mark sth with small areas of a particular colour or with small pieces of sth 使有斑點；使斑駁：*The fabric was red, flecked with gold.* 織物是紅色的，帶有金黃色的斑點。◇ *His hair was flecked with paint.* 他的頭髮上粘有點點油漆。

flec·tion = FLEXION

fled *past tense, past part.* of FLEE

fledged /fledʒd/ *adj.* (of birds 鳥) able to fly 能飛翔的；羽翼已豐的 ➲ see also FULLY FLEDGED

fledg·ling (*BrE* also **fledge·ling**) /ˈfledʒlɪŋ/ *noun* **1** a young bird that has just learnt to fly（剛會飛的）幼鳥 **2** (usually before another noun 通常置於另一名詞前) a person, an organization or a system that is new and without experience 初出茅廬的人；無經驗的組織；新體系：*fledgling democracies* 新興的民主國家

flee /fliː/ *verb* (**fled**, **fled** /fled/) [I, T, no passive] to leave a person or place very quickly, especially because you are afraid of possible danger 迅速離開；（尤指害怕有危險而）逃避，逃跑：*She burst into tears and fled.* 她突然哭了起來，跑開了。◇ **~ from sb/sth** *a camp for refugees fleeing from the war* 收留戰爭難民的難民營 ◇ **~ to …/into …** *He fled to London after an argument with his family.* 他與家人爭吵以後離家去了倫敦。◇ **~ sth** *He was caught trying to flee the country.* 他企圖逃離該國時被抓住了。➲ compare FLY *v.* (1), (3)

fleece /fliːs/ *noun, verb*

■ *noun* **1** [C] the wool coat of a sheep; this coat when it has been removed from a sheep (by SHEARING) 羊毛；（一隻羊一次剪下的）毛 **2** [U, C] a type of soft warm cloth that feels like sheep's wool; a jacket or SWEATSHIRT that is made from this cloth 羊毛狀織物；絨頭織物短上衣；絨頭織物運動衫：*a fleece lining* 絨頭織物襯裏 ◇ *a bright red fleece* 鮮紅的絨頭織物

■ *verb* **~ sb** (*informal*) to take a lot of money from sb by charging them too much 敲詐；敲竹槓：*Some local shops have been fleecing tourists.* 當地有些商店一直在敲遊客的竹槓。

fleecy /ˈfliːsi/ *adj.* [usually before noun] made of soft material, like the wool coat of a sheep; looking like this 軟如羊毛的；羊毛似的：*a fleecy sweatshirt* 絨毛長袖運動衫 ◇ *a blue sky with fleecy clouds* 飄浮着朵朵白雲的藍色天空

fleet /fliːt/ *noun, adj.*

■ *noun* **1** [C] a group of military ships commanded by the same person 艦隊 **2** [C] a group of ships fishing together 捕魚船隊：*a **fishing/whaling fleet*** 捕魚／捕鯨船隊 **3 the fleet** [sing.] all the military ships of a particular country（一國的）全部軍艦，海軍：*a reduction in the size of the British fleet* 英國海軍的裁減 **4** [C] **~ (of sth)** a group of planes, buses, taxis, etc. travelling together or owned by the same organization（同一機構或統一調度的）機群，車隊：*the company's new fleet of vans* 公司的新客貨車隊

■ *adj.* (*literary*) able to run fast 跑得快的；快速的：*fleet of foot* 跑得快 ◇ *fleet-footed* 跑得快

ˌ**Fleet ˈAdmiral** (*US*) (*BrE* ˌ**Admiral of the ˈFleet**) *noun* an admiral of the highest rank in the navy（英國）海軍元帥；（美國）海軍五星上將：*Fleet Admiral William Hunter* 海軍五星上將威廉 • 亨特

fleet·ing /ˈfliːtɪŋ/ *adj.* [usually before noun] lasting only a short time 短暫的；閃現的 SYN **brief**：*a **fleeting glimpse/smile*** 短暫的一瞥；一閃即逝的微笑 ◇ *a **fleeting moment** of happiness* 轉瞬即逝的幸福時刻 ◇ *We paid a **fleeting visit** to Paris.* 我們短暫遊覽了巴黎。▶ **fleet·ing·ly** *adv.*

ˈ**Fleet Street** *noun* [U] a street in central London where many national newspapers used to have their offices (now used to mean British newspapers and journalists in general) 艦隊街，弗利特街（位於倫敦中心的一條街道，曾是全國性大報社所在地）；（統稱）英國新聞界

Flem·ish /ˈflemɪʃ/ *noun* [U] the Dutch language as spoken in northern Belgium 佛蘭芒語（比利時北部的荷蘭語）

flesh 0-w /fleʃ/ *noun, verb*

■ *noun* **1** 0-w [U] the soft substance between the skin and bones of animal or human bodies（動物或人的）肉：*The trap had cut deeply into the rabbit's flesh.* 捕夾深深嵌入了兔子的肉裏。◇ *Tigers are **flesh-eating** animals.* 虎是食肉動物。◇ *the smell of rotting flesh* 腐肉的氣味 **2** [U] the skin of the human body（人體的）皮膚：*His fingers closed around the soft flesh of her arm.* 他握住了她柔軟的手臂。◇ ***flesh-coloured*** (= a light brownish pink colour) 肉色的 **3** 0-w [U] the soft part of fruit and vegetables, especially when it is eaten 蔬菜的可食部份；果肉 ➲ VISUAL VOCAB page V30 **4 the flesh** [sing.] (*literary*) the human body when considering its physical and sexual needs, rather than the mind or soul 肉體；肉慾；情慾：*the pleasures/sins of the flesh* 肌膚之樂；肉慾之罪

IDM ˌ**flesh and ˈblood** when you say that sb is **flesh and blood**, you mean that they are a normal human with needs, emotions and weaknesses 血肉之軀（有常人的需要、感情和缺點）：*Listening to the cries was more than flesh and blood could stand.* 聽這種哭喊非常人所能忍受。 **your (ˌown) ˌflesh and ˈblood** a person that you are related to 親骨肉；親人 **in the ˈflesh** if you see sb **in the flesh**, you are in the same place as them and actually see them rather than just seeing a picture of them 活生生地；親自；本人 **make your ˈflesh creep** to make you feel afraid or full of disgust 使起雞皮疙瘩；令人毛骨悚然；使人十分厭惡 **put flesh on (the bones of) sth** to develop a basic idea, etc. by giving more details to make it more complete 充實；加細節於：*The strength of the book is that it puts flesh on the bare bones of this argument.* 本書的優點是對這個論

點的基本事實有翔實的論述。➲ more at POUND *n.*, PRESS *v.*, SPIRIT *n.*, THORN, WAY *n.*

■ *verb*

PHR V ˌ**flesh sth**↔ˈ**out** to add more information or details to a plan, an argument, etc. 充實（計劃、論據等的內容）：*These points were fleshed out in the later parts of the speech.* 這幾點在演講的後面部份已得到充實。

flesh·ly /ˈfleʃli/ *adj.* [only before noun] (*literary*) connected with physical and sexual desires 肉慾的；性慾的：***fleshly temptations/pleasures*** 情慾的誘惑；性快感

flesh·pots /ˈfleʃpɒts; *NAmE* -pɑːts/ *noun* [pl.] (*humorous*) places supplying food, drink and sexual entertainment 滿足肉慾的場所，紅燈區（指提供飲食及性娛樂的場所）

ˈ**flesh wound** *noun* an injury in which the skin is cut but the bones and organs inside the body are not damaged 皮肉之傷（指未傷及骨頭和器官）

fleshy /ˈfleʃi/ *adj.* **1** (of parts of the body or people 人體部位或人) having a lot of flesh 多肉的；肥胖的：*fleshy arms/lips* 肥胖的胳膊；厚嘴唇 ◇ *a large fleshy man* 大個子胖男人 **2** (of plants or fruit 植物或水果) thick and soft 肉質的：***fleshy fruit/leaves*** 肉質水果／葉子

fleur-de-lis (also **fleur-de-lys**) /ˌflɜː də ˈliː; -ˈliːs; *NAmE* ˌflɜːr/ *noun* (*pl.* **fleurs-de-lis** /ˌflɜː də ˈliː; -ˈliːs; *NAmE* ˌflɜːr/) (from *French*) a design representing a flower with three PETALS joined together at the bottom, often used in COATS OF ARMS 鳶尾花飾，百合花飾（常用作紋章）

flew *past tense* of FLY

flex /fleks/ *verb, noun*

■ *verb* [T, I] **~ (sth)** to bend, move or stretch an arm or a leg, or contract a muscle, especially in order to prepare for a physical activity 屈伸，活動（四肢或肌肉，尤指為準備體力活動）：*to flex your fingers/feet/legs* 活動手指／雙腳／雙腿 ◇ *He stood on the side of the pool flexing his muscles.* 他站在游泳池旁活動肌肉。

IDM **flex your ˈmuscles** to show sb how powerful you are, especially as a warning or threat 顯示實力，炫耀力量（尤指作為警告或威脅）

■ *noun* (*BrE*) (also **cord** *NAmE, BrE*) [C, U] a piece of wire that is covered with plastic, used for carrying electricity to a piece of equipment 花線；皮線：*an electric flex* 一根導電花線 ◇ *a length of flex* 一段花線 ➲ picture at CORD

flex·ible AW /ˈfleksəbl/ *adj.* **1** (*approving*) able to change to suit new conditions or situations 能適應新情況的；靈活的；可變動的：*a more **flexible approach*** 更靈活的方法 ◇ *flexible working hours* 彈性工作時間 ◇ *Our plans need to be flexible enough to cater for the needs of everyone.* 我們的計劃必須能夠變通，以滿足每個人的需要。◇ *You need to be more flexible and imaginative in your approach.* 你的方法必須更加靈活，更富有想像力。 **2** able to bend easily without breaking 柔韌的；可彎曲的；有彈性的：*flexible plastic tubing* 撓性塑料管 OPP **inflexible** ▸ **flexi·bil·ity** AW /ˌfleksəˈbɪləti/ *noun* [U]：*Computers offer a much greater degree of flexibility in the way work is organized.* 利用計算機，工作安排可以靈活得多。◇ *exercises to develop the flexibility of dancers' bodies* 增加舞蹈者身體柔軟度的訓練動作 **flex·ibly** *adv.*

flex·ion (also **flec·tion**) /ˈflekʃn/ *noun* [U] the action of bending sth 彎曲；屈曲

flexi·time /ˈfleksitaɪm/ (*especially BrE*) (*NAmE* usually **flex·time** /ˈflekstaɪm/) *noun* [U] a system in which employees work a particular number of hours each week or month but can choose when they start and finish work each day 彈性工作時間制：*She works flexi-time.* 她的上班時間是彈性的。

flex·or /ˈfleksə(r); *NAmE* also ˈfleksɔːr/ (also ˈ**flexor muscle**) *noun* (*anatomy* 解) a muscle that allows you to bend part of your body 屈肌 ➲ compare EXTENSOR

flib·ber·ti·gib·bet /ˈflɪbətidʒɪbɪt; ˌflɪbətiˈdʒɪbɪt; *NAmE* -bər-/ *noun* (*informal*) a person who is not serious enough or talks a lot about silly things 輕浮的人；饒舌的人

flick /flɪk/ *verb, noun*

■ *verb* **1** [T] **~ sth + adv./prep.** to hit sth with a sudden quick movement, especially using your finger and thumb together, or your hand（尤指用手指或手快速地）輕擊，輕拍，輕拂，輕彈：*She flicked the dust off her collar.* 她輕輕彈掉了衣領上的灰塵。◇ *The horse was flicking flies away with its tail.* 馬輕輕甩動尾巴把蒼蠅趕走。◇ *James flicked a peanut at her.* 詹姆斯朝她輕輕彈一顆花生。◇ *Please don't flick ash on the carpet!* 請勿把煙灰彈在地毯上！ **2** [I, T] to move or make sth move with sudden quick movements（使）突然快速移動：**+ adv./prep.** *The snake's tongue flicked out.* 蛇伸吐着舌頭。◇ *Her eyes flicked from face to face.* 她的眼光掃過人們的臉。◇ **~ sth (+ adv./prep.)** *He lifted his head, flicking his hair off his face.* 他抬起頭，拂開了臉上的頭髮。◇ *The horse moved off, flicking its tail.* 馬甩着尾巴走開了。 **3** [T] to smile or look at sb suddenly and quickly 向…笑了一下（或瞥了一眼等）：**~ a smile/look, etc. at sb** *She flicked a nervous glance at him.* 她緊張不安地瞟了他一眼。◇ **~ sb a smile/look, etc.** *She flicked him a nervous glance.* 她緊張不安地瞟了他一眼。 **4** [T] to press a button or switch quickly in order to turn a machine, etc. on or off（快速地）按開關，按鍵 SYN **flip**：**~ sth** *He flicked a switch and all the lights went out.* 他啪的一聲按了下開關，燈全熄了。◇ **~ sth on/off** *She flicked the TV on.* 她輕輕一按打開了電視機。 **5** [T] to move sth up and down with a sudden movement so that the end of it hits sth（用…）輕揮，輕打：**~ A (with B)** *He flicked me with a wet towel.* 他用濕毛巾輕打我。◇ **~ B (at A)** *He flicked a wet towel at me.* 他用濕毛巾輕打我。◇ *to flick a whip* 用鞭子抽打

PHR V ˌ**flick ˈthrough sth** (*especially BrE*) **1** to turn the pages of a book, etc. quickly and look at them without reading everything 瀏覽；草草翻閱 SYN **flip through**：*I've only had time to flick through your report but it seems to be fine.* 我的時間不多，只是草草翻閱了一下你的報告，但似乎還不錯。 **2** to keep changing television channels quickly to see what programmes are on 快速瀏覽，不停地變換（電視頻道）SYN **flip through**：*Flicking through the channels, I came across an old war movie.* 我快速瀏覽電視頻道，發現有一部老的戰爭片在播放。

■ *noun* **1** [C, usually sing.] a small sudden, quick movement or hit, for example with a WHIP or part of the body（用鞭子等的）輕打；（身體部份的）小快動作：*Bell's flick into the penalty area helped to create the goal.* 貝爾迅速插進罰球區助攻，製造了這次進球的機會。◇ *All this information is available **at the flick of a switch*** (= by simply turning on a machine). 這所有的信息只需按一下開關便可到手。◇ *He threw the ball back with a quick **flick of the wrist**.* 他手腕一抖把球傳了回來。 **2** [sing.] **a ~ through sth** a quick look through the pages of a book, magazine, etc. 瀏覽；草草翻閱 SYN **flip**：*I had a flick through the catalogue while I was waiting.* 我等待時瀏覽了目錄。 **3** [C] (*old-fashioned, informal*) a film/movie 電影 **4 the flicks** [pl.] (*old-fashioned, BrE, informal*) a cinema 電影院

flicker /ˈflɪkə(r)/ *verb, noun*

■ *verb* **1** [I] (of a light or a flame 燈光或火焰) to keep going on and off as it shines or burns 閃爍；閃現；忽隱忽現；搖曳：*The lights flickered and went out.* 燈光閃了閃就熄了。◇ *the flickering screen of the television* 圖像在抖動的電視熒光屏 **2** [I] **+ adv./prep.** (of an emotion, a thought, etc. 情緒、思想等) to be expressed or appear somewhere for a short time 閃現；一閃而過：*Anger flickered in his eyes.* 他眼中閃現出一股怒火。 **3** [I] to move with small quick movements 快速擺動；顫動；抖動；拍動：*Her eyelids flickered as she slept.* 她睡覺時眼瞼不停地眨動。

■ *noun* [usually sing.] **~ (of sth) 1** a light that shines in an unsteady way（光）搖曳，閃爍，忽隱忽現：*the flicker of a television/candle* 電視畫面的閃動；燭光的搖曳 **2** a small, sudden movement with part of the body（身體部位的）小而快的動作：*the flicker of an eyelid* 眼瞼的跳動 **3** a feeling or an emotion that lasts for only a very short time（情感、情緒的）閃現，一閃而過：***a flicker of hope/doubt/interest*** 希望／懷疑／興趣的閃現 ◇ *A flicker of a smile crossed her face.* 她臉上閃過一絲微笑。

F

'**flick knife** (*BrE*) (also **switch·blade** *NAmE, BrE*) *noun* a knife with a blade inside the handle that jumps out quickly when a button is pressed 彈簧刀

flier *noun* = FLYER

flies /flaɪz/ *noun* [pl.] **1** *pl.* of FLY **2** (*BrE*) = FLY *n.* (3) **3 the flies** the space above the stage in a theatre, used for lights and for storing SCENERY（舞台上方）懸吊佈景的空間，吊景區

flight /flaɪt/ *noun, verb*

■ *noun*

▸ **JOURNEY BY AIR** 空中航行 **1** [C] a journey made by air, especially in a plane（尤指乘飛機的）空中航行，航程：*a* ***smooth/comfortable/bumpy flight*** 平穩／舒適／顛簸的空中航行 ◇ ***a domestic/an international flight*** 國內／國際航班 ◇ *a hot-air balloon flight* 熱氣球航行 ◇ *We met on a flight from London to Paris.* 我們在從倫敦到巴黎的飛行途中相遇。➲ see also IN-FLIGHT

▸ **PLANE** 飛機 **2** [C] a plane making a particular journey 航班飛機；班機：*We're booked on the same flight.* 我們訂了同一班機的機票。◇ *Flight BA 4793 is now boarding at Gate 17.* * BA 4793 航班現在正在 17 號登機口登機。◇ *If we leave now, I can catch the earlier flight.* 我們要是現在動身，我就可以趕上早一點的航班。◇ ***mercy/relief flights*** (= planes taking help to countries where there is a war) 急救／救援班機（運送救援物資至發生戰爭的國家）➲ COLLOCATIONS at TRAVEL

▸ **FLYING** 飛 **3** [U] the act of flying 飛行；飛翔：*the age of supersonic flight* 超音速飛行時代 ◇ *flight safety* 飛行安全 ◇ *The bird is easily recognized* ***in flight*** (= when it is flying) *by the black band at the end of its tail.* 這種鳥尾部末端有一條黑帶，飛翔時很容易認出來。

▸ **MOVEMENT OF OBJECT** 物體的運動 **4** [U] the movement or direction of an object as it travels through the air（物體的）飛行，飛行方向：*the flight of a ball* 球的飛行

▸ **OF STEPS** 台階 **5** [C] a series of steps between two floors or levels 一段樓梯；一段階梯：*She fell down* ***a flight of stairs/steps*** *and hurt her back.* 她從一段樓梯上跌了下來，摔傷了背。

▸ **RUNNING AWAY** 逃走 **6** [U, sing.] the act of running away from a dangerous or difficult situation（從危險或困境中的）逃避，躲避：*the flight of refugees from the advancing forces* 難民躲避挺進的軍隊 ◇ *The main character is a journalist in flight from a failed marriage.* 主角是一個逃避失敗婚姻的記者。

▸ **OF FANCY/IMAGINATION** 幻想；想像 **7** [C] **~ of fancy/imagination** an idea or a statement that shows a lot of imagination but is not practical or sensible 異想天開；奇思怪想；天花亂墜

▸ **GROUP OF BIRDS/AIRCRAFT** 鳥／機群 **8** [C] a group of birds or aircraft flying together（一起飛行的）鳥群（或機群）：*a flight of geese* 一隊飛雁 ◇ *an aircraft of the Queen's flight* 女王專機機隊中的一架飛機

IDM **in the first/top 'flight** among the best of a particular group 名列前茅；佼佼者 ➲ see also TOP-FLIGHT **put sb to 'flight** (*old-fashioned*) to force sb to run away 迫使逃竄 **take 'flight** to run away 逃走：*The gang took flight when they heard the police car.* 這夥歹徒聽見警車聲就逃走了。

■ *verb* [usually passive] **~ sth** (*BrE, sport* 體) to kick, hit or throw a ball through the air in a skilful way（熟練地踢、擊或擲）使球在空中飛行：*He equalized with a beautifully flighted shot.* 他漂亮一擊把比分扳平。

'**flight attendant** *noun* a person whose job is to serve and take care of passengers on an aircraft（客機的）乘務員；空服員

'**flight crew** *noun* [C+sing./pl. v.] the people who work on a plane during a flight（統稱）機組人員

'**flight deck** *noun* **1** an area at the front of a large plane where the pilot sits to use the controls and fly the plane（飛機的）駕駛艙 ➲ VISUAL VOCAB page V53 **2** a long flat surface on top of a ship that carries aircraft (= an AIRCRAFT CARRIER) where they take off and land（航空母艦上的）飛行甲板

'**flight jacket** (*US*) (*BrE* '**flying jacket**) *noun* a short leather jacket with a warm LINING and COLLAR, originally worn by pilots 飛行夾克；翻領皮夾克

flight·less /'flaɪtləs/ *adj.* [usually before noun] (of birds or insects 鳥或昆蟲) unable to fly 不能飛的

,**flight lieu'tenant** *noun* (*abbr.* **Flt. Lt.**) an officer of fairly high rank in the British AIR FORCE（英國空軍）上尉：*Flight Lieutenant Richard Clarkson* 理查德•克拉克森空軍上尉

'**flight path** *noun* the route taken by an aircraft through the air（飛機的）飛行路線，航跡

'**flight recorder** *noun* = BLACK BOX (1)

'**flight sergeant** *noun* a member of the British AIR FORCE, just below the rank of an officer（英國空軍）上士：*Flight Sergeant Bob Andrews* 鮑勃•安德魯斯空軍上士

'**flight simulator** *noun* a device that reproduces the conditions that exist when flying an aircraft, used for training pilots 飛行模擬裝置；飛行練習器

flighty /'flaɪti/ *adj.* (*informal*) a **flighty** woman is one who cannot be relied on because she is always changing activities, ideas and partners without treating them seriously（女子）反覆無常的，輕浮的

flim·flam /'flɪmflæm/ *noun* [U] (*old-fashioned, informal*) nonsense 廢話；無聊話

flimsy /'flɪmzi/ *adj.* (**flim·sier**, **flim·si·est**) **1** badly made and not strong enough for the purpose for which it is used 劣質的；不結實的 SYN **rickety**：*a flimsy table* 不結實的桌子 **2** (of material 材料) thin and easily torn 薄而易損壞的：*a flimsy piece of paper/fabric/plastic* 薄薄的一張紙／一塊織物／一片塑料 **3** difficult to believe 不足信的 SYN **feeble**：*a flimsy excuse/explanation* 站不住腳的藉口／解釋 ◇ *The evidence against him is pretty flimsy.* 對他不利的證據很難站住腳。▸ **flim·sily** *adv.* **flim·si·ness** *noun* [U]

flinch /flɪntʃ/ *verb* [I] to make a sudden movement with your face or body as a result of pain, fear, surprise, etc.（突然）退縮；畏縮：*He met my gaze without flinching.* 他毫不畏縮，跟我對視着。◇ **~ at sth** *He flinched at the sight of the blood.* 他一見到血就往後退。◇ **~ away** *She flinched away from the dog.* 她一下子避開了那條狗。➲ see also UNFLINCHING

PHR V '**flinch from sth** | '**flinch from doing sth** (often used in negative sentences 常用於否定句) to avoid thinking about or doing sth unpleasant 不想，不做（不愉快的事）；畏縮不前：*He never flinched from facing up to trouble.* 他敢於面對困難，從不退縮。

fling /flɪŋ/ *verb, noun*

■ *verb* (**flung**, **flung** /flʌŋ/) **1 ~ sb/sth + adv./prep.** to throw sb/sth somewhere with force, especially because you are angry（尤指生氣地）扔，擲，拋，丟 SYN **hurl**：*Someone had flung a brick through the window.* 有人把一塊磚扔進了窗戶。◇ *He flung her to the ground.* 他把她推倒在地。◇ *The door was suddenly flung open.* 門突然被推開了。◇ *He had his enemies* ***flung into prison.*** 他把敵人投進了監獄。➲ SYNONYMS at THROW **2 ~ yourself/sth + adv./prep.** to move yourself or part of your body suddenly and with a lot of force 猛動（身體或身體部位）：*She flung herself onto the bed.* 她撲倒在牀上。◇ *He flung out an arm to stop her from falling.* 他猛伸手臂扶她，她才沒有跌倒。**3 ~ sth (at sb)** | **+ speech** to say sth to sb in an aggressive way 粗暴地（向某人）說；氣勢洶洶地（對某人）說 SYN **hurl**：*They were flinging insults at each other.* 他們互相辱罵。➲ see also FAR-FLUNG

PHR V '**fling yourself at sb** (*informal, disapproving*) to make it too obvious to sb that you want to have a sexual relationship with them（太露骨地）向某人求愛；向（異性）獻殷勤 '**fling yourself into sth** to start to do sth with a lot of energy and enthusiasm 投身於；一心撲在…上：*They flung themselves into the preparations for the party.* 他們一心一意地準備聚會。,**fling sth↔'off/'on** (*informal*) to take off or put on clothing in a quick and careless way 匆匆脫下（或穿上）：*He flung off his coat and collapsed on the sofa.* 他隨手脫掉大衣，倒在沙發上。,**fling sb↔'out** (*BrE, informal*) to make sb leave a place suddenly 逐出；開除 SYN **throw out**

ˌ**fling sth↔'out** (*BrE, informal*) to get rid of sth that you do not want any longer 扔掉；丟掉 SYN **throw out**

■ ***noun*** [usually sing.] (*informal*) **1** a short period of enjoyment when you do not allow yourself to worry or think seriously about anything 一陣盡情歡樂；一時的放縱：*He was determined to have one last fling before retiring.* 他決心在退休前最後來一次痛痛快快的玩樂。**2 ~ (with sb)** a short sexual relationship with sb 短暫的風流韻事 ➲ see also HIGHLAND FLING

flint /flɪnt/ *noun* **1** [U, C] a type of very hard grey stone that can produce a SPARK when it is hit against steel 燧石；火石：*prehistoric flint implements* 史前燧石工具 ◇ *His eyes were as hard as flint.* 他的眼神冷酷無情。**2** [C] a piece of flint or hard metal that is used to produce a SPARK 打火石

flint·lock /'flɪntlɒk; *NAmE* -lɑːk/ *noun* a gun used in the past that produced a SPARK from a flint when the TRIGGER was pressed（舊時的）燧發槍，明火槍

flinty /'flɪnti/ *adj.* **1** showing no emotion 冷冷的：*a **flinty** look/gaze/stare* 冷冷的目光／凝視／盯視 **2** containing flint 含燧石的：***flinty** pebbles/soils* 含燧石的卵石／土壤

flip /flɪp/ *verb, noun, adj.*

■ ***verb*** (-pp-) **1** [I, T] to turn over into a different position with a sudden quick movement; to make sth do this（使）快速翻轉，迅速翻動：*The plane flipped and crashed.* 飛機猛地翻轉，撞毀了。◇ (*figurative*) *She felt her heart flip* (= with excitement, etc.). 她感到心潮澎湃。◇ **~ sth (+ adj.)** *He flipped the lid open and looked inside the case.* 他猛然開蓋，朝箱裏看。➲ see also FLIP OVER **2** [T] to press a button or switch in order to turn a machine, etc. on or off 按（開關）；按（按鈕）；開（或關）（機器等）SYN **flick**：**~ sth** *to flip a switch* 按開關 ◇ **~ sth on/off** *She reached over and flipped off the light.* 她伸過手去關掉了燈。**3** [T] to throw sth somewhere using your thumb and/or fingers（用手指）輕拋，輕擲 SYN **toss**：**~ a coin** *They flipped a coin to decide who would get the ticket.* 他們擲幣決定誰得這張票。◇ **~ sth + adv./prep.** *He flipped the keys onto the desk.* 他把鑰匙輕拋到桌上。**4** [I] **~ (out)** (*informal*) to become very angry, excited or unable to think clearly 十分氣憤；異常激動；神志不清：*She finally flipped under the pressure.* 她在這種壓力下終於發瘋了。

IDM ˌ**flip your 'lid** (*informal*) to become very angry and lose control of what you are saying or doing 發火；氣得喪失自制力；氣得發瘋 SYN **go mad**

PHR V ˌ**flip 'over** to turn onto the other side or upside down 翻倒；翻轉：*The car hit a tree and flipped over.* 汽車撞上一棵樹，翻倒了。◇ *He flipped over and sat up.* 他翻了一個身坐了起來。ˌ**flip sth↔'over** to turn sth onto the other side or upside down 使翻倒；使翻轉：*The wind flipped over several cars.* 大風吹翻了幾輛汽車。'**flip through sth** **1** to turn the pages of a book, etc. quickly and look at them without reading everything 瀏覽；草草翻閱 SYN **flick through**：*She flipped through the magazine looking for the letters page.* 她瀏覽雜誌尋找讀者來信頁。**2** (*especially NAmE*) to keep changing television channels quickly to see what shows are on 不斷轉換（電視頻道）SYN **flick through**：*Flipping through the channels, I came across an old war movie.* 我不停地轉換電視頻道，偶然發現了一部舊戰爭片。

■ ***noun*** **1** [C] a small quick hit with a part of the body that causes sth to turn over 輕拋；捻擲：*The whole thing was decided on the **flip of a coin**.* 整個事情都是由擲幣決定的。**2** [C] a movement in which the body turns over in the air 空翻 SYN **somersault**：*The handstand was followed by a back flip.* 先倒立，接着後空翻。◇ (*figurative*) *Her heart did a flip.* 她心裏咯噔了一下子。**3** [sing.] **~ through sth** a quick look through the pages of a book, magazine, etc. 瀏覽；草草翻閱 SYN **flick**：*I had a quick flip through the report while I was waiting.* 我等待時迅速瀏覽了一下報告。

■ ***adj.*** (*informal*) = FLIPPANT：*a flip answer/comment* 輕率的答覆；輕浮的話 ◇ *Don't be flip with me.* 不要對我油腔滑舌。

'**flip chart** *noun* large sheets of paper fixed at the top to a stand so that they can be turned over, used for presenting information at a talk or meeting 活動掛圖；配套掛圖 ➲ VISUAL VOCAB page V69

'**flip-flop** *noun, verb*

■ ***noun*** (*NAmE* also **thong**) a type of SANDAL (= open shoe) that has a piece of leather, etc. that goes between the big toe and the toe next to it 人字拖鞋；夾腳指拖鞋：*a pair of flip-flops* 一雙人字拖鞋 ➲ VISUAL VOCAB page V64

■ ***verb*** (-pp-) [I] **~ (on sth)** (*informal, especially NAmE*) to change your opinion about sth, especially when you then hold the opposite opinion 改變觀點；（尤指）轉持相反觀點，來一個 180 度的大轉彎：*The vice-president was accused of flip-flopping on several major issues.* 副總統受到譴責，說他在幾個重大問題上出爾反爾。

'**flip-flopper** /'flɪpflɒpə(r); *NAmE* -flɑːpər/ *noun* (*informal, especially NAmE*) a person, especially a politician, who suddenly changes his or her opinion or policy 出爾反爾的人（尤指政客）➲ see also U-TURN (2)

flip·pant /'flɪpənt/ (also *informal* **flip**) *adj.* showing that you do not take sth as seriously as other people think you should 輕率的：*a **flippant** answer/attitude* 輕率的回答；輕浮的態度 ◇ *Sorry, I didn't mean to sound flippant.* 對不起，我並不是故意油嘴滑舌的。▶ **flip·pancy** /-ənsi/ *noun* [U] **flip·pant·ly** *adv.*

flip·per /'flɪpə(r)/ *noun* [usually pl.] **1** a flat part of the body of some sea animals such as SEALS and TURTLES, used for swimming（海豹、海龜等的）鰭肢，鰭足 ➲ VISUAL VOCAB page V13 **2** a long flat piece of rubber or plastic that you wear on your foot to help you swim more quickly, especially below the surface of the water（潛水、游泳用的）腳蹼，蛙鞋，鴨腳板，橡皮腳掌 ➲ VISUAL VOCAB page V40

'**flip phone** *noun* a small mobile/cell phone with a cover that opens upwards 摺疊式手機；翻蓋式手機

flip·ping /'flɪpɪŋ/ *adj., adv.* (*BrE, informal*) used as a mild swear word by some people to emphasize sth or to show that they are annoyed 該死；真討厭；糟透：*I hate this flipping hotel!* 我討厭這個該死的旅館！◇ *Flipping kids!* 這些孩子真討厭！◇ *It's flipping cold today!* 今天冷得要命！

'**flip side** *noun* [usually sing.] **~ (of/to sth)** **1** different and less welcome aspects of an idea, argument or action（想法、論點或行動的）反面，負面 **2** (*old-fashioned*) the side of a record that does not have the main song or piece of music on it 唱片反面（尤指沒有主要歌曲或樂曲的一面）

flirt /flɜːt; *NAmE* flɜːrt/ *verb, noun*

■ ***verb*** [I] **~ (with sb)** to behave towards sb as if you find them sexually attractive, without seriously wanting to have a relationship with them 調情

PHR V '**flirt with sth** **1** to think about or be interested in sth for a short time but not very seriously 玩兒似地想做某事：*She flirted with the idea of becoming an actress when she was younger.* 她年輕時曾鬧着玩似地想過當演員。**2** to take risks or not worry about a dangerous situation that may happen 冒險；不顧危險後果：*to flirt with danger/death/disaster* 冒險；玩命兒；不把災禍當回事

■ ***noun*** [usually sing.] a person who flirts with a lot of people 與多人調情的人：*She's a real flirt.* 她是個打情罵俏的老手。

flir·ta·tion /flɜː'teɪʃn; *NAmE* flɜːr't-/ *noun* **1** [C, U] **~ with sth** a short period of time during which sb is involved or interested in sth, often not seriously 不認真對待；一時的參與；一時興起；逢場作戲：*a brief and unsuccessful flirtation with the property market* 對房地產市場一時興起、並不成功的介入 **2** [U] behaviour that shows you find sb sexually attractive but are not serious about them 調情：*Frank's efforts at flirtation had become tiresome to her.* 弗蘭克一個勁地打情罵俏使得她非常厭倦。**3** [C] **~ (with sb)** a short sexual relationship with sb that is not taken seriously 短暫的風流韻事

flir·ta·tious /flɜː'teɪʃəs; *NAmE* flɜːr't-/ (also *informal* **flirty**) *adj.* behaving in a way that shows a sexual attraction to sb that is not serious 賣弄風情的；打情罵

F

俏的：*a flirtatious young woman* 賣弄風情的年輕女子 ◇ *a flirtatious smile* 賣弄風情的一笑 ▸ **flir·ta·tious·ly** *adv.* **flir·ta·tious·ness** *noun* [U]

flit /flɪt/ *verb, noun*

■ *verb* (-tt-) **1** [I] to move lightly and quickly from one place or thing to another 輕快地從一處到另一處；掠過：**~ from A to B** *Butterflies flitted from flower to flower.* 蝴蝶在花叢中飛來飛去。◇ *He flits from one job to another.* 他頻繁跳槽。◇ **+ adv./prep.** *A smile flitted across his face.* 他臉上笑容一閃而過。◇ *A thought flitted through my mind.* 我腦海中掠過一個念頭。**2** [I] (*ScotE*) to change the place where you live 遷移；遷居；搬家：*I had to change schools every time my parents flitted.* 我父母每次遷居，我都得換學校。

F

■ *noun*

IDM **do a moonlight/midnight 'flit** (*BrE, informal*) to leave a place suddenly and secretly at night, usually in order to avoid paying money that you owe to sb（通常為了躲債）夜間偷偷逃走

float 0→ /fləʊt; *NAmE* floʊt/ *verb, noun*

■ *verb*

▸ ON WATER/IN AIR 水上；空中 **1** 0→ [I] **+ adv./prep.** to move slowly on water or in the air 浮動；漂流；飄動；飄移 SYN **drift**：*A group of swans floated by.* 一群天鵝緩緩游過。◇ *The smell of new bread floated up from the kitchen.* 廚房裏飄出新鮮麪包的香味。◇ *Beautiful music came floating out of the window.* 美妙的樂聲從窗口傳出。◇ (*figurative*) *An idea suddenly floated into my mind.* 我腦海裏突然浮現出一個想法。◇ (*figurative*) *People seem to float in and out of my life.* 不同的人在我的生命中出現和消失。**2** 0→ [I] to stay on or near the surface of a liquid and not sink 浮；漂浮：*Wood floats.* 木頭能浮起來。◇ **~ in/on sth** *A plastic bag was floating in the water.* 一個塑料袋在水中漂浮。◇ *Can you float on your back?* 你能仰浮嗎？**3** [T] to make sth move on or near the surface of a liquid 使浮動；使漂流：**~ sth** *There wasn't enough water to float the ship.* 水不夠深，船浮動不起來。◇ **~ sth + adv./prep.** *They float the logs down the river to the towns.* 他們把原木沿河漂流至城鎮。

▸ WALK LIGHTLY 飄然走動 **4** [I] **+ adv./prep.** (*literary*) to walk or move in a smooth and easy way 輕盈走動；飄然移動 SYN **glide**：*She floated down the steps to greet us.* 她輕盈地下樓來迎接我們。

▸ SUGGEST IDEA 提出想法 **5** [T] **~ sth** to suggest an idea or a plan for other people to consider 提出，提請考慮（想法或計劃）：*They floated the idea of increased taxes on alcohol.* 他們建議提高酒稅。

▸ BUSINESS/ECONOMICS 商業；經濟學 **6** [T] **~ sth** (*business* 商) to sell shares in a company or business to the public for the first time（公司或企業）發行（股票）上市：*The company was floated on the stock market in 2007.* 這家公司於 2007 年上市。◇ *Shares were floated at 585p.* 股票最初上市價為 5 英鎊 85 便士。**7** [T, I] **~ (sth)** (*economics* 經) if a government **floats** its country's money or allows it to **float**, it allows its value to change freely according to the value of the money of other countries（使貨幣匯率）自由浮動

IDM **float sb's 'boat** (*informal*) to be what sb likes 為某人所喜歡：*You can listen to whatever kind of music floats your boat.* 無論你喜歡哪種音樂，你都可以聽。➲ more at AIR *n.*

PHR V **,float a'bout/a'round** (usually used in the progressive tenses 通常用於進行時) if an idea, etc. is **floating around**, it is talked about by a number of people or passed from one person to another（思想等）傳播，流傳

■ *noun*

▸ VEHICLE 車輛 **1** a large vehicle on which people dressed in special COSTUMES are carried in a festival 彩車：*a carnival float* 狂歡節彩車

▸ IN FISHING 釣魚 **2** a small light object attached to a FISHING LINE that stays on the surface of the water and moves when a fish has been caught 魚漂；浮子

▸ FOR SWIMMING 游泳 **3** a light object that floats in the water and is held by a person who is learning to swim to stop them from sinking（學游泳用的）浮板

▸ DRINK 飲料 **4** (*NAmE*) a drink with ice cream floating in it 加冰淇淋的飲料：*a Coke float* 一杯加冰淇淋的可口可樂

▸ MONEY 錢 **5** (*especially BrE*) a sum of money consisting of coins and notes of low value that is given to sb before they start selling things so that they can give customers change（商店的）備用零錢

▸ BUSINESS 商業 **6** = FLOTATION (1)

float·er /'fləʊtə(r); *NAmE* 'floʊt-/ *noun* (*medical* 醫) a very small object inside a person's eye which they see moving up and down（眼睛中的）浮動物

float·ing /'fləʊtɪŋ; *NAmE* 'floʊt-/ *adj.* [usually before noun] not fixed permanently in one particular position or place 不固定的；流動的；浮動的：***floating exchange rates*** 浮動匯率 ◇ *a **floating population*** (= one in which people frequently move from one place to another) 流動人口 ◇ (*medical* 醫) *a floating kidney* 游走腎

,floating 'rib (also **,false 'rib**) *noun* (*anatomy* 解) any of the lower RIBS which are not attached to the BREASTBONE 浮肋；浮動弓肋

,floating 'voter (*BrE*) (*NAmE* **'swing voter**) *noun* a person who does not always vote for the same political party and who has not decided which party to vote for in an election 游離選民（不認定投某一政黨的票）

floaty /'fləʊti; *NAmE* 'floʊti/ *adj.* (of cloth or clothing 布料或衣服) very light and thin 十分輕薄的

flock /flɒk; *NAmE* flɑːk/ *noun, verb*

■ *noun* **1** [C+sing./pl. v.] **~ (of sth)** a group of sheep, GOATS or birds of the same type（羊或鳥）群 ➲ compare HERD (1) **2** [C+sing./pl. v.] **~ (of sb)** a large group of people, especially of the same type（尤指同類人的）一大群：*a flock of children/reporters* 一大群兒童／記者 ◇ *They came in flocks to see the procession.* 他們成群結隊來看遊行隊伍。**3** [C+sing./pl. v.] (*literary*) the group of people who regularly attend the church of a particular priest, etc.（常跟隨某聖職人員等學習的）信眾 **4** [U] small pieces of soft material used for filling CUSHIONS, chairs, etc.（填充墊子、椅子等的）小塊軟填料 **5** [U] small pieces of soft material on the surface of paper or cloth that produce a raised pattern（植絨用的）短絨，絨屑：*flock wallpaper* 植絨牆紙

■ *verb* [I] to go or gather together somewhere in large numbers 群集；聚集；蜂擁：**+ adv./prep.** *Thousands of people flocked to the beach this weekend.* 這個週末有好幾千人蜂擁到了海灘。◇ *Huge numbers of birds had flocked together by the lake.* 成群的鳥聚集在湖邊。◇ **~ to do sth** *People flocked to hear him speak.* 人們成群結隊地去聽他演講。IDM see BIRD *n.*

floe /fləʊ; *NAmE* floʊ/ *noun* = ICE FLOE

flog /flɒg; *NAmE* flɑːg/ *verb* (-gg-) **1** [often passive] **~ sb** to punish sb by hitting them many times with a WHIP or stick 鞭笞，棒打（作為懲罰）：*He was publicly flogged for breaking the country's alcohol laws.* 他因違犯國家的酒法而被當眾處以鞭刑。**2** (*BrE, informal*) to sell sth to sb 出售（某物給某人）：**~ sth (to sb)** *She flogged her guitar to another student.* 她把吉他賣給另一個同學。◇ **~ sth (off)** *We buy them cheaply and then flog them off at a profit.* 我們低價買下這些，然後賣出獲利。◇ **~ sb sth** *I had a letter from a company trying to flog me insurance.* 我收到了一家公司的信，向我推銷保險。

IDM **,flog a dead 'horse** (*BrE, informal*) to waste your effort by trying to do sth that is no longer possible 鞭策死馬；做徒勞無益的事 **,flog sth to 'death** (*BrE, informal*) to use an idea, a story, etc. so often that it is no longer interesting 多次重複（想法、故事等）而使人失去興趣

flog·ging /'flɒgɪŋ; *NAmE* 'flɑːg-/ *noun* [C, U] a punishment in which sb is hit many times with a WHIP or stick（作為懲罰的）鞭笞，棒打：*a public flogging* 當眾處以鞭刑

flood 0→ /flʌd/ *noun, verb*

■ *noun*

▸ WATER 水 **1** 0→ [C, U] a large amount of water covering an area that is usually dry 洪水；水災：*The heavy rain has caused floods in many parts of the country.* 大雨使全國許多地方泛濫成災。◇ *flood damage* 洪澇災害 ◇ *Police have issued **flood warnings** for Nevada.* 警方已經發佈

了內華達州的水災警告。◇ *The river is* ***in flood*** (= has more water in it than normal and has caused a flood). 河水泛濫。➲ see also FLASH FLOOD

▸ **LARGE NUMBER** 大量 **2** [C] **~ (of sth)** a very large number of things or people that appear at the same time 大批，大量（的人或事物）：*a flood of complaints* 大量投訴 ◇ *a flood of refugees* 難民潮 ◇ *The child was* ***in floods of tears*** (= crying a lot). 小孩哭得淚人兒似的。

■ ***verb***

▸ **FILL WITH WATER** 灌滿水 **1** [I, T] if a place **floods** or sth **floods** it, it becomes filled or covered with water（使）灌滿水；淹沒：*The cellar floods whenever it rains heavily.* 只要一下大雨地窖就淹水。◇ **~ sth** *If the pipe bursts it could flood the whole house.* 要是水管破裂整座房子就會灌滿水。

▸ **OF RIVER** 河 **2** [I, T] to become so full that it spreads out onto the land around it 泛濫；淹沒：*When the Ganges floods, it causes considerable damage.* 恆河泛濫時造成嚴重損害。◇ **~ sth** *The river flooded the valley.* 河水泛濫淹沒了河谷。

▸ **LARGE NUMBERS** 大量 **3** [I] **~ in/into/out of sth** to arrive or go somewhere in large numbers 大量湧入；蜂擁而出 **SYN** **pour**：*Refugees continue to flood into neighbouring countries.* 難民不斷湧入鄰國。◇ *Telephone calls* ***came flooding in*** *from all over the country.* 全國各地的電話像潮水般打來。 **4** [T, usually passive] **~ sb/sth with sth** to send sth somewhere in large numbers 大量送至；擠滿；擁滿：*The office was flooded with applications for the job.* 辦公室堆滿了應徵該職的求職信。 **5** [T] to become or make sth become available in a place in large numbers（使）充斥，充滿：**~ sth** *Cheap imported goods are* ***flooding the market.*** 廉價進口商品充斥着市場。◇ **~ sth with sth** *A man who planned to flood Britain with cocaine was jailed for 15 years.* 一個企圖在英國大量銷售可卡因的男人被判刑 15 年。

▸ **OF FEELING/THOUGHT** 思想；感情 **6** [I, T] to affect sb suddenly and strongly 使大受感動；充滿：**+ adv./prep.** *A great sense of relief flooded over him.* 他深感寬慰。◇ *Memories of her childhood* ***came flooding back.*** 她童年的往事湧上心頭。◇ **~ sb with sth** *The words flooded him with self-pity.* 這些話使他充滿了自憐。

▸ **OF LIGHT/COLOUR** 光；顏色 **7** [I, T] to spread suddenly into sth; to cover sth 照進；覆蓋：**+ adv./prep.** *She drew the curtains and the sunlight flooded in.* 她拉開窗簾，陽光灑了進來。◇ **~ sth** *She looked away as the colour flooded her cheeks.* 她雙頰泛出紅暈，視線轉向別處。◇ **be flooded with sth** *The room was flooded with evening light.* 室內一片暮色。

▸ **ENGINE** 發動機 **8** [I, T] **~ (sth)** if an engine **floods** or if you **flood** it, it becomes so full of petrol/gas that it will not start（使）溢流

▸ **flood·ed** *adj.*：*flooded fields* 淹沒的田地 **flood·ing** *noun* [U]：*There will be heavy rain with flooding in some areas.* 將有大雨，有些地方會泛濫成災。

PHR V **,flood sb↔'out** [usually passive] to force sb to leave their home because of a flood 洪水迫使某人背井離鄉

flood·gate /ˈflʌdɡeɪt/ *noun* [usually pl.] a gate that can be opened or closed to control the flow of water on a river 防洪閘門；泄水閘門：(*figurative*) *If the case is successful, it may* ***open the floodgates*** *to more damages claims against the industry* (= start sth that will be difficult to stop). 如果本案勝訴，就可能有更多的人向這個產業提出損害索賠，從而一發不可收拾。

flood·light /ˈflʌdlaɪt/ *noun, verb*

■ ***noun*** [usually pl.] a large powerful lamp, used for lighting sports grounds, theatre stages and the outside of buildings 泛光燈，泛光照明燈（運動場、舞台和建築物外牆等用）：*a match played* ***under floodlights*** 泛光燈下進行的比賽 ▸ **flood·light·ing** *noun* [U]：*The floodlighting had been turned off.* 泛光燈照明已關閉。

■ ***verb*** (**flood·lit**, **flood·lit** /-lɪt/) [usually passive] **~ sth** to light a place or a building using floodlights 用泛光燈照明：*The swimming pool is floodlit in the evenings.* 游泳池晚間有泛光燈照明。◇ *floodlit tennis courts* 泛光燈照明的網球場

ˈflood·plain /ˈflʌdpleɪn/ *noun* an area of flat land beside a river that regularly becomes flooded when there is too much water in the river 洪泛區；泛濫平原

ˈflood tide *noun* a very high rise in the level of the sea as it moves in towards the coast 漲潮 ➲ compare HIGH TIDE

flood·water /ˈflʌdwɔːtə(r); *NAmE* also -wɑːtər/ *noun* [U] (also **floodwaters** [pl.]) water that covers land after there has been a flood 洪水：*The floodwaters have now receded.* 洪水現已消退。

Synonyms 同義詞辨析

floor

ground • land • earth

These are all words for the surface that you walk on. 以上各詞均指地面。

floor the surface of a room that you walk on 指室內地板、地面：*She was sitting on the floor watching TV.* 她坐在地板上看電視。

ground (often **the ground**) the solid surface of the earth that you walk on（常作 the ground）指室外地、地面：*I found her lying on the ground.* 我發現她躺在地上。◇ *The rocket crashed a few seconds after it left the ground.* 火箭離開地面幾秒鐘便墜毀了。

land the surface of the earth that is not sea 指陸地、大地：*It was good to be back on dry land again.* 回到陸地上真好。◇ *They fought both at sea and on land.* 他們在海上和陸上都打過仗。

earth (often **the earth**) the solid surface of the world that is made of rock, soil, sand, etc（常作 the earth）指大地、陸地、地面：*You could feel the earth shake as the truck came closer.* 卡車開近時可感覺到地面在震動。

GROUND, LAND OR EARTH? 用 ground、land 還是 earth？

Ground is the normal word for the solid surface that you walk on when you are not in a building or vehicle. You can use **earth** if you want to draw attention to the rock, soil etc. that the ground is made of. **Land** is only used when you want to contrast it with the sea.
* ground 常指樓房或車輛外的地面。如果關注的是構成大地的岩石、土壤等可用 earth。land 只在與海相對照時使用：~~the land beneath our feet~~ ◇ ~~feel the land shake~~ ◇ ~~sight ground/earth~~ ◇ ~~travel by ground/earth~~

PATTERNS

- **on/under** the floor/ground/earth
- **bare** floor/ground/earth
- to **drop/fall to** the floor/the ground/(the) earth
- to **reach** the floor/the ground/land

floor /flɔː(r)/ *noun, verb*

■ ***noun***

▸ **OF ROOM** 房間 **1** [C, usually sing.] the surface of a room that you walk on 地板；地面：*a* ***wooden/concrete/marble, etc. floor*** 木質、水泥、大理石等地板 ◇ *ceramic floor tiles* 陶瓷地板磚 ◇ *The body was lying on the kitchen floor.* 屍體躺在廚房的地上。◇ *The alterations should give us extra floor space.* 這些改動應該使我們有更大的居住面積。

▸ **OF VEHICLE** 車輛 **2** (*NAmE* also **floor·board**) [C, usually sing.] the bottom surface of a vehicle 車廂內的）底板：*The floor of the car was covered in cigarette ends.* 小轎車內底板上滿是煙蒂。

▸ **LEVEL OF BUILDING** 樓層 **3** [C] all the rooms that are on the same level of a building 樓層：*Her office is* ***on the second floor.*** 她的辦公室在第二層。◇ *the Irish guy who lives two floors above* 住在兩層樓上面的愛爾蘭人 ◇ *There is a lift to all floors.* 有電梯通往各層樓。◇ *Their house is* ***on three floors*** (= it has three floors). 他們的房子有三層。➲ note at STOREY ➲ see also GROUND FLOOR

▸ **OF THE SEA/FORESTS** 海；森林 **4** [C, usually sing.] the ground at the bottom of the sea, a forest, etc.（海等

的）底；（森林等的）地面： *the **ocean/valley/cave/forest floor*** 海底；谷底；洞底；森林的地面

‣ IN PARLIAMENT, ETC. 議會等 **5 the floor** [sing.] the part of a building where discussions or debates are held, especially in a parliament; the people who attend a discussion or debate 議員席；全體議員；全體與會者： *Opposition politicians registered their protest on the floor of the House.* 反對黨從政者在議院的議員席提出了抗議。◇ *We will now take any questions from the floor.* 現在我們將接受會眾席上的任何提問。

‣ AREA FOR WORK 工作區 **6** [C, usually sing.] an area in a building that is used for a particular activity（建築物內的）場地： *on the floor of the Stock Exchange* (= where trading takes place) 在證券交易所的交易廳 ➲ see also DANCE FLOOR, FACTORY FLOOR, SHOP FLOOR (1)

F

‣ FOR WAGES/PRICES 工資；物價 **7** [C, usually sing.] the lowest level allowed for wages or prices（工資或物價的）最低額，底價： *Prices have **gone through the floor*** (= fallen to a very low level). 物價已經探底。➲ compare CEILING (2)

IDM **get/be given/have the 'floor** to get/be given/have the right to speak during a discussion or debate（討論或辯論中）取得發言權 **,hold the 'floor** to speak during a discussion or debate, especially for a long time so that nobody else is able to say anything 發言；長篇大論地發言（尤指使他人無法發言） **,take (to) the 'floor** to start dancing on a DANCE FLOOR（在舞池）開始跳舞： *Couples took the floor for the last dance of the evening.* 雙雙對對開始跳晚會的最後一輪舞。 **wipe/mop the 'floor with sb** (*informal*) to defeat sb completely in an argument or a competition（在辯論或競賽中）徹底打敗對手，把對手打得一敗塗地 ➲ more at GROUND FLOOR

■ *verb*

‣ SURPRISE/CONFUSE 驚奇；困惑 **1 ~ sb** to surprise or confuse sb so that they are not sure what to say or do 使驚奇；使困惑

‣ HIT 擊中 **2** [usually passive] **~ sb** to make sb fall down by hitting them, especially in a sport（尤指體育運動中）擊倒，打倒

‣ BUILDING/ROOM 建築物；房間 **3** [usually passive] **~ sth** to provide a building or room with a floor 給…安裝地板；給…鋪設地面

‣ DRIVING 駕駛 **4 ~ the accelerator** to press the ACCELERATOR pedal of a car hard 把（汽車的油門踏板）踩到底

British/American 英式/美式英語

floor

- In *BrE* the floor of a building at street level is the **ground floor**, the one above it is the **first floor** and the one below it is the **basement**, or **lower ground floor** in a public building. 在英式英語中，地面的樓層叫 ground floor，上面一層叫 first floor，下面一層叫 basement 或在公共建築中叫 lower ground floor。
- In *NAmE* the floor at street level is usually called the **first floor**, the one above it is the **second floor** and the one below it is the **basement**. In public buildings the floor at street level can also be called the **ground floor**. 在美式英語中，地面的一層通常叫 first floor，上面一層叫 second floor，下面一層叫 basement。在公共建築中，地面的一層亦可稱為 ground floor。

➲ note at STOREY

floor·board /ˈflɔːbɔːd; *NAmE* ˈflɔːrbɔːrd/ *noun* **1** a long flat piece of wood in a wooden floor 木質地板條： *bare/polished floorboards* 素面／打了蠟的地板 ➲ VISUAL VOCAB page V21 **2** [usually sing.] (*NAmE*) = FLOOR (2)： *a car floorboard* 汽車底板 ◇ *He had his foot to the floorboard* (= was going very fast). 他猛踩油門飛速駕駛。

floor·cloth /ˈflɔːklɒθ; *NAmE* ˈflɔːrklɔːθ/ *noun* (*BrE*) a cloth for cleaning floors 擦地布

floor·ing /ˈflɔːrɪŋ/ *noun* [U] material used to make the floor of a room 鋪室內地面的材料： *vinyl/wooden flooring* 乙烯基塑料／木地板 ◇ *kitchen/bathroom flooring* 廚房／浴室地磚

ˈfloor lamp (*BrE* also **ˈstandard lamp**) *noun* a tall lamp that stands on the floor 落地燈 ➲ VISUAL VOCAB page V21

ˈfloor manager *noun* the person responsible for the lighting and other technical arrangements for a television production（電視節目的）現場指導

ˈfloor plan *noun* (*technical* 術語) a drawing of the shape of a room or building, as seen from above, showing the position of the furniture, etc. 樓層平面圖

ˈfloor show *noun* a series of performances by singers, dancers, etc. at a restaurant or club（旅館或夜總會的）系列表演

floozy (also **flooz·ie**) /ˈfluːzi/ *noun* (*pl.* **-ies**) (*old-fashioned, informal, disapproving*) a woman who has sexual relationships with many different men 蕩婦

flop /flɒp; *NAmE* flɑːp/ *verb, noun*

■ *verb* (**-pp-**) **1** [I] **~ into/on sth** | **~ (down/back)** to sit or lie down in a heavy and sudden way because you are very tired（因疲憊而）猛然坐下，沉重地躺下： *Exhausted, he flopped down into a chair.* 他筋疲力盡，一屁股坐到椅子上。 **2** [I] **+ adv./prep.** to fall, move or hang in a heavy or awkward way, without control（沉重、笨拙或不自主地）落下，移動，懸掛： *Her hair flopped over her eyes.* 她的頭髮耷拉下來遮住了眼睛。◇ *The young man flopped back, unconscious.* 那年輕人仰面倒下，不省人事。◇ *The fish were flopping around in the bottom of the boat.* 魚在船底撲騰。 **3** [I] (*informal*) to be a complete failure 砸鍋；完全失敗： *The play flopped on Broadway.* 這齣戲在百老匯砸了鍋。

■ *noun* (*informal*) a film/movie, play, party, etc. that is not successful（電影、戲劇、聚會等）失敗，不成功 OPP hit ➲ see also BELLYFLOP

flop·house /ˈflɒphaʊs; *NAmE* ˈflɑːp-/ (*NAmE*) (*BrE* **doss-house**) *noun* (*informal*) a cheap place to stay for people who have no home（供流浪者投宿的）廉價客店

floppy /ˈflɒpi; *NAmE* ˈflɑːpi/ *adj.* (**flop·pier, flop·piest**) hanging or falling loosely; not hard and stiff 鬆散下垂的；耷拉的；鬆軟的： *a floppy hat* 耷拉着的帽子

,floppy ˈdisk (also **floppy** *pl.* **-ies**) (also **disk·ette**) *noun* a flat disk inside a plastic cover, that is used to store data in the form that a computer can read, and that can be removed from the computer 軟（磁）盤；軟碟 ➲ compare HARD DISK

flora /ˈflɔːrə/ *noun* [U] (*technical* 術語) the plants of a particular area, type of environment or period of time（某地區、環境或時期的）植物群： *alpine flora* 高山植物群 ◇ *rare species of **flora and fauna*** (= plants and animals) 動植物的罕見物種

floral /ˈflɔːrəl/ *adj.* [usually before noun] **1** consisting of pictures of flowers; decorated with pictures of flowers 繪有花的；飾以花的： *wallpaper with a **floral design/pattern*** 有花卉圖案的牆紙 ◇ *a floral dress* 有花卉圖案的連衣裙 **2** made of flowers 花的： *a **floral arrangement/display*** 插花；花展 ◇ ***Floral tributes** were sent to the church.* 敬獻的鮮花已送往教堂。

flor·en·tine /ˈflɒrəntaɪn; -tiːn; *NAmE* ˈflɔːrəntiːn; -tɪn/ *adj., noun*

■ *adj.* (of food 食物) served on SPINACH 佛羅倫薩式的；（上菜時）放在菠菜上的： *eggs florentine* 佛羅倫薩式雞蛋

■ *noun* a biscuit/cookie containing nuts and fruit, half covered in chocolate（一面有巧克力的）乾果餅乾

floret /ˈflɒrət; *NAmE* ˈflɔː-/ *noun* a flower part of some vegetables, for example BROCCOLI and CAULIFLOWER. Each vegetable has several florets coming from one main STEM.（花椰菜等的）花部 ➲ VISUAL VOCAB page V31

flori·bunda /ˌflɒrɪˈbʌndə; *NAmE* ˌflɔːr-/ *noun* (*technical* 術語) a plant, especially a ROSE, with flowers that grow very close together in groups 多花植物

florid /ˈflɒrɪd; *NAmE* ˈflɔː-; ˈflɑː-/ *adj.* **1** (of a person's face 人臉) red 紅潤的： *a florid complexion* 紅潤的臉色

2 (usually *disapproving*) having too much decoration or detail 過分裝飾的；過多修飾的：*florid language* 辭藻堆砌的言語 ▸ **florid·ly** *adv.*

florin /ˈflɒrɪn; *NAmE* ˈflɔː-; ˈflɑː-/ *noun* an old British coin worth two SHILLINGS (= now 10p) 弗羅林（英國舊時價值兩先令的硬幣，相當於現在的 10 便士）

flor·ist /ˈflɒrɪst; *NAmE* ˈflɔː-/ *noun* **1** a person who owns or works in a shop/store that sells flowers and plants 花商 **2** **flor·ist's** (*pl.* **flor·ists**) a shop/store that sells flowers and plants 花店：*I've ordered some flowers from the florist's.* 我向花店訂購了一些花。

floss /flɒs; *NAmE* flɔːs; flɑːs/ *noun, verb*

■ *noun* [U] **1** = DENTAL FLOSS **2** thin silk thread 絲線 ➲ see also CANDYFLOSS

■ *verb* [I, T] **~** (sth) to clean between your teeth with DENTAL FLOSS 用牙線剔牙縫

flo·ta·tion /fləʊˈteɪʃn; *NAmE* floʊ-/ *noun* **1** (also **float**) [C, U] (*business* 商) the process of selling shares in a company to the public for the first time in order to raise money（公司的）發行股份：*plans for (a) flotation on the stock exchange* 在證券市場上發行股份的計劃 ◇ *a stock-market flotation* 在股票市場上市 **2** [U] the act of floating on or in water 浮；漂浮

floˈtation ˌtank *noun* a container filled with salt water in which people float in the dark as a way of relaxing 鹽水浮力池（解乏用）

flo·tilla /fləˈtɪlə; *NAmE* floʊˈt-/ *noun* a group of boats or small ships sailing together 船隊；小型艦隊

flot·sam /ˈflɒtsəm; *NAmE* ˈflɑːt-/ *noun* [U] **1** parts of boats, pieces of wood or rubbish/garbage, etc. that are found on land near the sea or floating on the sea; any kind of rubbish/garbage（沖上岸或漂浮水面的）船隻殘骸，碎木，零碎雜物；廢料：*The beaches are wide and filled with interesting* ***flotsam and jetsam.*** 海灘寬闊，到處是有趣的被沖上岸的零碎雜物。➲ compare JETSAM **2** people who have no home or job and who move from place to place, often rejected by society 無家可歸者；失業流浪者：*the human flotsam of inner cities* 市中心貧民區無家可歸、失業流浪的人

flounce /flaʊns/ *verb, noun*

■ *verb* [I] (**+ adv./prep.**) to move somewhere in a way that draws attention to yourself, for example because you are angry or upset（因憤怒或煩躁等而）走動，急動，驟動，扭轉：*She flounced out of the room.* 她憤憤地衝出房間。

■ *noun* **1** a strip of cloth that is sewn around the edge of a skirt, dress, curtain, etc.（衣、裙、窗簾等的）荷葉邊 **2** a quick and exaggerated movement that you make when you are angry or want people to notice you（因氣憤而猛然做出的）動作；故作誇張的動作：*She left the room with a flounce.* 她氣沖沖地衝出房間。▸ **flounced** *adj.*：*a flounced skirt* 鑲荷葉邊的裙子

floun·der /ˈflaʊndə(r)/ *verb, noun*

■ *verb* **1** [I, T] (**+ speech**) to struggle to know what to say or do or how to continue with sth 不知所措；撓頭；支吾：*His abrupt change of subject left her floundering helplessly.* 他突然改變話題，使她茫然不知所措。**2** [I] to have a lot of problems and to be in danger of failing completely 困難重重；艱苦掙扎：*At that time the industry was floundering.* 那時這個行業舉步維艱。**3** [I] (**+ adv./prep.**) to struggle to move or get somewhere in water, mud, etc.（在水、泥等中）掙扎：*She was floundering around in the deep end of the swimming pool.* 她在游泳池深水區掙扎着。

■ *noun* (*pl.* **floun·der** or **floun·ders**) a small flat sea fish that is used for food 偏口魚

flour 🔑 /ˈflaʊə(r)/ *noun, verb*

■ *noun* 🔑 [U] a fine white or brown powder made from grain, especially WHEAT, and used in cooking for making bread, cakes, etc.（尤指小麥的）麵粉；（穀物磨成的）粉 ➲ see also PLAIN FLOUR, SELF-RAISING FLOUR

■ *verb* [usually passive] **~ sth** to cover sth with a layer of flour 在…上撒（或覆以）麵粉：*Roll the dough on a lightly floured surface.* 揉生麵糰時，案板上要撒點麵粉。

flour·ish /ˈflʌrɪʃ; *NAmE* ˈflɜːrɪʃ/ *verb, noun*

■ *verb* **1** [I] to develop quickly and be successful or common 繁榮；昌盛；興旺 SYN **thrive**：*Few businesses are flourishing in the present economic climate.* 在目前的經濟氣候下，很少有企業興旺發達。**2** [I] to grow well; to be healthy and happy 茁壯成長；健康幸福 SYN **thrive**：*These plants flourish in a damp climate.* 這些植物在潮濕的氣候下長勢茂盛。◇ (*especially BrE*) *I'm glad to hear you're all flourishing.* 聽說你們都健康幸福，我感到高興。**3** [T] **~ sth** to wave sth around in a way that makes people look at it（為引起注意）揮舞

■ *noun* **1** [usually sing.] an exaggerated movement that you make when you want sb to notice you（為引起注意的）誇張動作：*He opened the door for her with a flourish.* 他做了一個誇張動作為她開了門。**2** [usually sing.] an impressive act or way of doing sth 給人深刻印象的行動；令人難忘的方式：*The season ended with a flourish for Rooney, when he scored in the final minute of the match.* 魯尼本賽季華麗收關：他在比賽最後一分鐘射進一球。**3** details and decoration that are used in speech or writing（講話或文章的）華麗辭藻，修飾：*a speech full of rhetorical flourishes* 滿篇華麗辭藻的演講 **4** a curved line, that is used as decoration, especially in writing（尤指手寫體的）裝飾曲線；花彩字 **5** [usually sing.] a loud short piece of music, that is usually played to announce an important person or event 花彩號聲：*a flourish of trumpets* 小號齊鳴

floury /ˈflaʊəri/ *adj.* **1** covered with flour 覆有麵粉的：*floury hands* 粘滿麵粉的雙手 **2** like flour; tasting of flour 麵粉似的；味道像麵粉的：*a floury texture* 粉質 **3** (of potatoes 土豆) soft and light when they are cooked（煮後）很麵的

flout /flaʊt/ *verb* **~ sth** to show that you have no respect for a law, etc. by openly not obeying it 公然藐視，無視（法律等）SYN **defy**：*Motorists regularly* ***flout the law.*** 駕車者經常無視法律。◇ *to* ***flout authority/convention*** 公然藐視權威／慣例

flow 🔑 /fləʊ; *NAmE* floʊ/ *noun, verb*

■ *noun* [C, usually sing., U]

▸ CONTINUOUS MOVEMENT 流動 **1** 🔑 **~ (of sth/sb)** the steady and continuous movement of sth/sb in one direction 流；流動：*She tried to stop the flow of blood from the wound.* 她試圖止住傷口流血。◇ *an endless flow of refugees into the country* 難民源源不斷流入這個國家 ◇ *to improve traffic flow* (= make it move faster) 改善交通流量 ◇ *to control the direction of flow* 控制流向

▸ PRODUCTION/SUPPLY 生產；供應 **2** 🔑 **~ (of sth)** the continuous production or supply of sth 持續生產；不斷供應：*the flow of goods and services to remote areas* 商品和服務對邊遠地區源源不斷的供應 ◇ *to encourage the free flow of information* 鼓勵信息自由交流 ◇ *data flow* 數據流 ➲ see also CASH FLOW

▸ OF SPEECH/WRITING 言語；文字 **3** continuous talk by sb 滔滔不絕：*You've interrupted my flow—I can't remember what I was saying.* 你打斷了我的話，我記不得我在說什麼了。◇ *As usual, Tom was* ***in full flow.*** 湯姆如常地口若懸河。**4** **~ of sth** the way that words and ideas are linked together in speech or writing 連貫；流暢：*Too many examples can interrupt the smooth flow of the text.* 例子太多會使行文不流暢。

▸ OF THE SEA 海 **5** the movement of the sea towards the land 漲潮：*the* ***ebb and flow*** *of the tide* 潮漲潮落

IDM **go with the ˈflow** (*informal*) to be relaxed and not worry about what you should do 隨遇而安 ➲ more at EBB *n.*

■ *verb*

▸ MOVE CONTINUOUSLY 不斷移動 **1** 🔑 [I] (of liquid, gas or electricity 液體、氣體或電) to move steadily and continuously in one direction 流；流動：*She lost control and the tears began to flow.* 她禁不住淚如泉湧。◇ **+ adv./prep.** *It's here that the river flows down into the ocean.* 這條河就在這裏匯入海洋。◇ *Blood flowed from a cut on her head.* 血從她頭上的傷口處流出來。◇ *This can prevent air from flowing freely to the lungs.* 這可以防止空氣任意流入肺部。**2** 🔑 [I] (**+ adv./prep.**) (of people or things 人或事物) to move or pass continuously from one place or person to another, especially in large numbers or amounts 湧流；流動：*Constant streams of traffic flowed past.* 車流不斷通過。◇ *Election results flowed in throughout the night.* 整夜不斷傳來選舉的結果。

▸ OF IDEAS/CONVERSATION 思想；交談 **3** [I] to develop or be produced in an easy and natural way 流暢：*Conversation flowed freely throughout the meal.* 席間大家一直談笑甚歡。

▸ BE AVAILABLE EASILY 有的是 **4** [I] to be available easily and in large amounts 有的是；大量供應：*It was obvious that money flowed freely in their family.* 顯然他們家族有的是錢。◇ *The party got livelier as the drink began to flow.* 開始盡興暢飲時，聚會的氣氛活躍起來。

▸ OF FEELING 感覺 **5** [I] **+ adv./prep.** to be felt strongly by sb 強烈感到：*Fear and excitement suddenly flowed over me.* 我突然感到又恐懼又興奮。

▸ OF CLOTHES/HAIR 衣服；頭髮 **6** [I] **~ (down/over sth)** to hang loosely and freely 飄垂；飄拂：*Her hair flowed down over her shoulders.* 她的頭髮垂到肩上。◇ *long flowing skirts* 飄逸長裙

▸ OF THE SEA 海 **7** [I] (of the TIDE in the sea/ocean 海潮) to come in towards the land 漲；漲潮 OPP **ebb**

PHR V **ˈflow from sth** (*formal*) to come or result from sth 來自；由…引起

ˈflow chart (also **ˈflow diagram**) *noun* a diagram that shows the connections between the different stages of a process or parts of a system 流程圖

flower /ˈflaʊə(r)/ *noun, verb*

▪ ***noun* 1** the coloured part of a plant from which the seed or fruit develops. Flowers usually grow at the end of a STEM and last only a short time. 花；花朵：*The plant has a beautiful bright red flower.* 這株植物開了一朵美麗鮮紅的花。◇ *The roses are **in flower** early this year.* 今年玫瑰花開得早。◇ *The crocuses are late **coming into flower**.* 番紅花開得遲。➲ COLLOCATIONS at LIFE ➲ VISUAL VOCAB page V11 **2** a plant grown for the beauty of its flowers 開花植物：*a garden full of flowers* 種滿花的花園 ◇ *a **flower garden/show*** 花園／展 **3** a flower with its STEM that has been picked as a decoration（已摘）帶梗的花：*I **picked some flowers**.* 我摘了一些花。◇ *a **bunch of flowers*** 一束花 ◇ *a **flower arrangement*** 一組插花 ➲ see also BOUQUET (1)

IDM **the flower of sth** (*literary*) the finest or best part of sth（某事物的）最佳部份，精華；精英

▪ ***verb* 1** [I] (of a plant or tree 花草樹木) to produce flowers 開花 SYN **bloom**：*This particular variety flowers in July.* 這個品種七月開花。◇ *early-flowering spring bulbs* 早開花的春季鱗莖植物 **2** [I] (*literary*) to develop and become successful 成熟；繁榮；興旺 SYN **blossom**

ˈflower arranging *noun* [U] the art of arranging cut flowers in an attractive way 插花

ˈflower bed *noun* a piece of ground in a garden/yard or park where flowers are grown 花壇 ➲ VISUAL VOCAB page V19

flowered /ˈflaʊəd; *NAmE* ˈflaʊərd/ *adj.* [usually before noun] decorated with patterns of flowers 飾有花卉圖案的

flower·ing /ˈflaʊərɪŋ/ *noun* **1** [U] the time when a plant has flowers 開花時節 **2** [C, usually sing.] **~ of sth** the time when sth, especially a period of new ideas in art, music, science, etc., reaches its most complete and successful stage of development（新思想、藝術、音樂、科學等的）繁榮時期，鼎盛時期

flower·pot /ˈflaʊəpɒt; *NAmE* ˈflaʊərpɑːt/ *noun* a container made of plastic or CLAY for growing plants in 花盆 ➲ VISUAL VOCAB page V19

ˈflower power *noun* [U] the culture connected with young people of the 1960s and early 1970s who believed in love and peace and were against war 權力歸花兒（20 世紀 60 年代和 70 年代初期年輕人信奉愛與和平、反對戰爭的文化取向）

flowery /ˈflaʊəri/ *adj.* [usually before noun] **1** covered with flowers or decorated with pictures of flowers 覆蓋着花的；飾以花卉圖形的 **2** smelling or tasting of flowers 花香的；花味的 **3** (*usually disapproving*) (of speech or writing 言語文字) too complicated; not expressed in a clear and simple way 過分複雜費解的；華而不實的

flown *past part.* of FLY

ˈflow-on *noun, adj.* (*AustralE, NZE*)

▪ ***noun*** an increase in pay or an improvement in working conditions that is made because one has already been given in a similar job 順勢加薪，順勢改善工作條件（因大勢所趨）

▪ ***adj.*** **flow-on** effects, etc. are ones that happen as a result of sth else（效應等）順勢的

fl oz *abbr.* (*pl.* **fl oz**) (in writing) FLUID OUNCE（書寫形式）液量盎司：*Add 8 fl oz water.* 加 8 液量盎司水。

flu /fluː/ (often **the flu**) (also *formal* **in·flu·enza**) *noun* [U] an infectious disease like a very bad cold, that causes fever, pains and weakness 流行性感冒；流感：*The whole family has the flu.* 全家都患流感。◇ (*BrE*) *She's got flu.* 她患上了流感。➲ COLLOCATIONS at ILL

flub /flʌb/ *verb* (**-bb-**) [T, I] **~ (sth)** (*NAmE, informal*) to do sth badly or make a mistake 搞壞；搞糟；犯錯誤 SYN **fluff, bungle**：*She flubbed the first line of the song.* 她把第一行歌詞唱錯了。▸ **flub** *noun*

fluc·tu·ate AW /ˈflʌktʃueɪt/ *verb* [I] to change frequently in size, amount, quality, etc., especially from one extreme to another（大小、數量、質量等）波動；（在…之間）起伏不定 SYN **vary**：*fluctuating prices* 波動的價格 ◇ **~ between A and B** *During the crisis, oil prices fluctuated between $20 and $40 a barrel.* 在危機時期，每桶石油價格在 20 元至 40 元之間波動。◇ **+ adv./prep.** *Temperatures can fluctuate by as much as 10 degrees.* 溫差可達 10 度之多。◇ *My mood seems to fluctuate from day to day.* 我的情緒似乎天天在變。▸ **fluc·tu·ation** AW /ˌflʌktʃuˈeɪʃn/ *noun* [C, U]：**~ (in/of sth)** *wild fluctuations in interest rates* 利率的瘋狂波動

flue /fluː/ *noun* a pipe or tube that takes smoke, gas or hot air away from a fire, a HEATER or an oven 煙道

flu·ency /ˈfluːənsi/ *noun* [U, sing.] **1** the quality of being able to speak or write a language, especially a foreign language, easily and well（尤指外語）流利，流暢：*Fluency in French is required for this job.* 這個工作要求法語熟練自如。**2** the quality of doing sth in a smooth and skilful way 熟練自如；流暢：*The team lacked fluency during the first half.* 該隊在上半場打得不夠流暢。

flu·ent /ˈfluːənt/ *adj.* **1 ~ (in sth)** able to speak, read or write a language, especially a foreign language, easily and well（尤指外語）流利，文字流暢：*She's fluent in Polish.* 她的波蘭語很流利。◇ *a **fluent speaker/reader*** 說話流利的人；閱讀熟練的人 **2** (of a language, especially a foreign language 語言，尤指外語) expressed easily and well 流利的；通暢的：*He speaks fluent Italian.* 他說一口流利的意大利語。**3** (of an action 動作) done in a smooth and skilful way 流暢熟練的：*fluent handwriting* 優美熟練的筆跡 ◇ *fluent movements* 優美流暢的動作 ▸ **flu·ent·ly** *adv.*

fluff /flʌf/ *noun, verb*

▪ ***noun*** [U] **1** (*BrE*) (also **lint** *NAmE, BrE*) small pieces of wool, cotton, etc. that gather on clothes and other surfaces（衣服等上的）絨毛，蓬鬆毛團，塵團 **2** soft animal fur or bird feathers, that is found especially on young animals or birds（禽獸，尤指幼者的）絨毛 **3** (*informal, especially NAmE*) entertainment that is not serious and is not considered to have great value 沒多大意義的娛樂

▪ ***verb* 1 ~ sth** (*informal*) to do sth badly or to fail at sth 搞糟；弄砸 SYN **bungle**：*He completely fluffed an easy shot* (= in sport). 一個唾手可得的進球機會被他搞砸了。◇ *Most actors fluff their lines occasionally.* 多數演員都會偶爾唸錯台詞。**2 ~ sth (out/up)** to shake or brush sth so that it looks larger and/or softer 抖鬆；使鬆散：*The female sat on the eggs, fluffing out her feathers.* 母鳥抖開羽毛孵蛋。◇ *Let me fluff up your pillows for you.* 我來把你的枕頭拍鬆。

fluffy /ˈflʌfi/ *adj.* (**fluf·fier**, **fluf·fiest**) **1** like fluff; covered in fluff 絨毛般的；覆有絨毛的：*a little fluffy kitten* 毛茸茸的小貓 **2** (of food 食物) soft, light and containing air 鬆軟的：*Beat the butter and sugar until soft and fluffy.* 攪打奶油和糖直到鬆軟為止。 **3** looking as if it is soft and light 輕軟狀的：*fluffy white clouds* 輕飄飄的白雲 **4** (*informal, disapproving*) light and not serious; having no substance, depth or power 輕浮的；空洞的；淺薄的；無説服力的：*a fluffy film/movie* 內容空洞的影片 ◇ *a fluffy argument* 一個無説服力的論據

flu·gel·horn /ˈfluːɡlhɔːn; *NAmE* -hɔːrn/ *noun* a BRASS musical instrument like a small TRUMPET 夫呂號，富魯格號（銅管樂器，類似小號）

fluid /ˈfluːɪd/ *noun, adj.*

■ ***noun*** [C, U] (*formal* or *technical* 術語) a liquid; a substance that can flow 液體；流體；液：*body fluids* (= for example, blood) 體液（如血液）◇ *The doctor told him to drink plenty of fluids.* 醫生要他多喝流質。◇ *cleaning fluid* 清洗液

■ ***adj.*** **1** (*formal*) (of movements, designs, music, etc. 動作、設計、音樂等) smooth and elegant 流暢優美的 SYN **flowing**：*a loose, fluid style of dancing* 靈活流暢優美的跳舞風格 ◇ *fluid guitar playing* 流暢優美的吉他演奏 ◇ *the fluid lines of the drawing* 圖畫的流暢線條 **2** (*formal*) (of a situation 形勢) likely to change; not fixed 易變的；不穩定的：*a fluid political situation* 不穩定的政治局勢 **3** (*technical* 術語) that can flow freely, as gases and liquids do 流動的；流體的：*a fluid consistency* 流體黏稠度

flu·id·ity /fluˈɪdəti/ *noun* [U] **1** (*formal*) the quality of being smooth and elegant 流暢優美：*She danced with great fluidity of movement.* 她跳舞的動作十分流暢優美。 **2** (*formal*) the quality of being likely to change 易變（性）；不穩定（性）：*the fluidity of human behaviour* 人的行為的易變性 ◇ *social fluidity* 社會的不穩定性 **3** (*technical* 術語) the quality of being able to flow freely, as gases and liquids do 流動（性）

ˌfluid ˈounce *noun* (*abbr.* **fl oz**) a unit for measuring liquids. There are 20 fluid ounces in a British pint and 16 in an American pint. 液量盎司（液量單位，英制等於 1/20 品脱，美制等於 1/16 品脱）

fluke /fluːk/ *noun* [usually sing.] (*informal*) a lucky or unusual thing that happens by accident, not because of planning or skill 僥幸；偶然；意外：*They are determined to show that their last win was no fluke.* 他們決心證明上一次的勝利絕非僥幸。◇ *a fluke goal* 偶然的進球 ▸ **fluky** (also **flukey**) /ˈfluːki/ *adj.*

flume /fluːm/ *noun* **1** a narrow channel made to carry water for use in industry（工業用）引水槽，放水溝 **2** a water CHUTE (= a tube for sliding down) at an AMUSEMENT PARK or a swimming pool（遊樂園或游泳池的）水滑道

flum·mery /ˈflʌməri/ *noun* [U] nonsense, especially praise that is silly or not sincere 廢話；（尤指）無聊（或虛假）的恭維話：*She hated the flummery of public relations.* 她討厭公關工作中的虛誇恭維。

flum·mox /ˈflʌməks/ *verb* [usually passive] (not used in the progressive tenses 不用於進行時) **~ sb** (*informal*) to confuse sb so that they do not know what to say or do 使困惑；使糊塗：*I was flummoxed by her question.* 她的問題把我弄糊塗了。 ▸ **flum·moxed** *adj.*

flung *past tense, past part.* of FLING

flunk /flʌŋk/ *verb* (*informal, especially NAmE*) **1** [T, I] **~ (sth)** to fail an exam, a test or a course（考試、測驗等）失敗，不及格：*I flunked math in second grade.* 我二年級時數學不及格。 **2** [T] **~ sb** to make sb fail an exam, a test, or a course by giving them a low mark/grade 給某人不及格：*She's flunked 13 of the 18 students.* * 18 個學生她就給了 13 個不及格。

PHR V **ˌflunk ˈout (of sth)** (*NAmE, informal*) to have to leave a school or college because your marks/grades are not good enough（因不及格而）離（校），給開除（學籍），退學

flun·key (also **flunky**) /ˈflʌŋki/ *noun* (*pl.* **-eys** or **-ies**) **1** (*disapproving*) a person who tries to please sb who is important and powerful by doing small jobs for them 阿諛奉承者；勢利小人；馬屁精 **2** (*old-fashioned*) a servant in uniform（穿制服的）男僕

fluor·es·cent /ˌflɔːˈresnt; ˌflʊəˈr-; *NAmE* also ˌflʊˈr-/ *adj.* **1** (of substances 物質) producing bright light by using some forms of RADIATION 發熒光的：*a fluorescent lamp* (= one that uses such a substance) 熒光燈 ◇ *fluorescent lighting* 熒光照明 **2** (of a colour, material, etc. 顏色、材料等) appearing very bright when light shines on it; that can be seen in the dark 強烈反光的；發亮的：*fluorescent armbands worn by cyclists* 騎自行車者戴的發亮臂章 ➲ compare PHOSPHORESCENT (1) ▸ **fluor·es·cence** *noun* [U]

fluorid·ation /ˌflɔːrɪˈdeɪʃn; *BrE* also ˌflʊər-; *NAmE* also ˌflʊr-/ *noun* [U] the practice of adding fluoride to drinking water to prevent tooth decay 飲用水氟化（以防止牙齒蛀蝕）

fluor·ide /ˈflɔːraɪd; *BrE* also ˈflʊər-; *NAmE* also ˈflʊr-/ *noun* a chemical containing fluorine that protects teeth from decay and is often added to TOOTHPASTE and sometimes to drinking water 氟化物

fluor·ine /ˈflɔːriːn; *BrE* also ˈflʊər-; *NAmE* also ˈflʊr-/ *noun* [U] (*symb.* **F**) a chemical element. Fluorine is a poisonous pale yellow gas and is very REACTIVE. 氟

flur·ried /ˈflʌrid; *NAmE* ˈflɜːrid/ *adj.* nervous and confused, especially because there is too much to do（尤指因事情過多而）慌亂的 SYN **flustered**

flurry /ˈflʌri; *NAmE* ˈflɜːri/ *noun* (*pl.* **-ies**) **1** [usually sing.] an occasion when there is a lot of activity, interest, excitement, etc. within a short period of time 一陣忙亂（或激動、興奮等）：*a sudden **flurry of activity*** 突然的頻繁活動 ◇ *Her arrival caused a **flurry of excitement**.* 她的到來引起了一陣哄動。◇ ***A flurry of shots** rang out in the darkness.* 黑暗中突然發出一陣槍聲。 **2** a small amount of snow, rain, etc. that falls for a short time and then stops 小陣雪（或雨等）：***snow flurries*** 小雪陣陣 ◇ *flurries of snow* 陣陣小雪 **3** a sudden short movement of paper or cloth, especially clothes（紙張、織物，尤指衣服）窸窣：*The ladies departed in a flurry of silks and satins.* 女士們在一片綢緞窸窣聲中離去。

flush /flʌʃ/ *verb, noun, adj.*

■ ***verb*** **1** [I, T] (of a person or their face 人或臉) to become red, especially because you are embarrassed, angry or hot 發紅；臉紅：*She flushed with anger.* 她氣得漲紅了臉。◇ **+ adj.** *Sam felt her cheeks flush red.* 薩姆感覺她滿臉通紅。◇ **~ sth** *A rosy blush flushed her cheeks.* 她面若桃花。 **2** [I, T] **~ (sth)** when a toilet **flushes** or you **flush** it, water passes through it to clean it, after a handle, etc. has been pressed 沖洗（抽水馬桶） **3** [T] to clean sth by causing water to pass through it（用水）沖洗淨，沖洗：**~ sth out (with sth)** *Flush the pipe out with clean water.* 用淨水沖洗管子。◇ **~ sth through sth** *Flush clean water through the pipe.* 用淨水沖洗管子。 **4** [T] **+ adv./prep.** to get rid of sth with a sudden flow of water（用水）沖走：*They flushed the drugs down the toilet.* 他們從馬桶沖走了毒品。◇ *Drinking lots of water will help to flush toxins out of the body.* 大量飲水有助於清除體內毒素。

PHR V **ˌflush sb/sth ˈout (of sth)** | **ˌflush sb/sth↔ˈout** to force a person or an animal to leave the place where they are hiding 把（人或動物從隱蔽處）驅趕出來

■ ***noun*** **1** [C, usually sing.] a red colour that appears on your face or body because you are embarrassed, excited or hot 臉紅；潮紅：*A pink flush spread over his cheeks.* 他滿臉通紅。➲ see also HOT FLUSH **2** [C, usually sing.] a sudden strong feeling; the hot feeling on your face or body caused by this 一陣突如其來的強烈情感；（流露出的）一陣激情：***a flush of anger/embarrassment/enthusiasm/guilt*** 一陣憤怒／尷尬／熱情／內疚 **3** [sing.] the act of cleaning a toilet with a sudden flow of water 沖洗（抽水馬桶）：*Give the toilet a flush.* 沖洗抽水馬桶。 **4** [C] (in card games 紙牌遊戲) a set of cards that a player has that are all of the same SUIT 同花的一手牌

IDM **(in) the first flush of sth** (*formal*) (at) a time when sth is new, exciting and strong（在）新鮮興奮時刻，初期強盛階段：*in the first **flush of youth/enthusiasm/***

romance 在青春活力旺盛時期；在熱情高漲階段；在熱戀的初期

■ **adj.** [not before noun] **1** (*informal*) having a lot of money, usually for a short time 富有，很有錢（通常為短期的） **2 ~ with sth** (of two surfaces 兩個表面) completely level with each other 完全齊平：*Make sure the paving stones are flush with the lawn.* 務必要使鋪路石和草坪齊平。

flushed /flʌʃt/ *adj.* (of a person 人) red; with a red face 臉紅的：*flushed cheeks* 發紅的雙頰 ◇ *Her face was flushed with anger.* 她的臉氣紅了。◇ (*figurative*) *He was **flushed with success*** (= very excited and pleased) *after his first novel was published.* 他的第一部小說發表以後，他志得意滿。

F

flus·ter /ˈflʌstə(r)/ *verb, noun*

■ **verb** [often passive] **~ sb** to make sb nervous and/or confused, especially by giving them a lot to do or by making them hurry 使忙亂；使慌亂；使緊張 ▸ **flus·tered** *adj.* SYN **flurried**：*She arrived late, looking hot and flustered.* 她遲到了，顯得火急火燎，局促不安。

■ **noun** [sing.] (*BrE*) a state of being nervous and confused 慌亂；慌張

flute /fluːt/ *noun* **1** a musical instrument of the WOODWIND group, shaped like a thin pipe. The player holds it sideways and blows across a hole at one end. 長笛 ➲ **VISUAL VOCAB** page V34 **2 champagne ~** a tall narrow glass used for drinking CHAMPAGNE 細長香檳杯（形似長笛） ➲ **VISUAL VOCAB** page V22

fluted /ˈfluːtɪd/ *adj.* (especially of a round object 尤指圓物體) with a pattern of curves cut around the outside 外部有凹槽紋的：*fluted columns* 飾有凹槽紋的柱子 ▸ **flut·ing** *noun* [U]

flut·ist /ˈfluːtɪst/ (*NAmE*) (*BrE* **flaut·ist**) *noun* a person who plays the FLUTE 長笛手

flut·ter /ˈflʌtə(r)/ *verb, noun*

■ **verb** **1** [I, T] to move lightly and quickly; to make sth move in this way （使）飄動，揮動，顫動：*Flags fluttered in the breeze.* 旗幟在微風中飄揚。◇ *Her eyelids fluttered but did not open.* 她的眼皮動了一下，但沒有睜開眼。◇ **~ sth** *He fluttered his hands around wildly.* 他拚命揮舞着雙手。◇ *She **fluttered her eyelashes** at him* (= tried to attract him in order to persuade him to do sth). 她向他使了個眼色。 **2** [I, T] **~ (sth)** when a bird or an insect **flutters** its wings, or its wings **flutter**, the wings move lightly and quickly up and down （鳥或昆蟲）拍（翅），振（翅），鼓（翼） **3** [I] **+ adv./prep.** (of a bird or an insect 鳥或昆蟲) to fly somewhere moving the wings quickly and lightly 飛來飛去；翩翩飛舞：*The butterfly fluttered from flower to flower.* 蝴蝶在花叢中飛來飛去。 **4** [I] (of your heart, etc. 心臟等) to beat very quickly and not regularly 怦怦亂跳；撲騰：*I could feel a fluttering pulse.* 我感到脈搏跳動。◇ (*figurative*) *The sound of his voice in the hall made her heart flutter.* 他在大廳中講話的聲音使她的心怦怦直跳。

■ **noun** **1** [C, usually sing.] a quick, light movement 振動；飄動；揮動；顫動：*the flutter of wings* 翅膀的拍動 ◇ *with a flutter of her long, dark eyelashes* 她那長長的黑睫毛眨了一下 ◇ (*figurative*) *to feel a flutter of panic in your stomach* 胸中感到一陣恐慌 **2** [C, usually sing.] **~ (on sth)** (*BrE, informal*) a small bet 小賭注：*to have a flutter on the horses* 賽馬中下小賭注 **3** [sing.] a state of nervous or confused excitement 緊張興奮；慌亂：*Her sudden arrival caused quite a flutter.* 她的突然來到引起一片慌亂。 **4** [C] a very fast HEARTBEAT, caused when sb is nervous or excited （心臟的）怦怦亂跳，撲騰：*Her heart gave a flutter when she saw him.* 她見到他時心怦怦亂跳。 **5** [U] (*medical* 醫) a medical condition in which you have a fast, unsteady HEARTBEAT 撲動；快速的顫動（或搏動） **6** [U] (*technical* 術語) rapid changes in the PITCH or volume of recorded sound （重放錄音的）顫振 ➲ compare WOW (2)

flu·vial /ˈfluːviəl/ *adj.* (*technical* 術語) connected with rivers 河流的；與河流有關的

flux /flʌks/ *noun* **1** [U] continuous movement and change 不斷的變動；不停的變化：*Our society is **in a state of flux**.* 我們的社會在不斷演變。 **2** [C, usually sing., U] (*technical* 術語) a flow; an act of flowing 通量；流動：*a flux of neutrons* 一個中子通量

fly 🔑 /flaɪ/ *verb, noun, adj.*

■ **verb** (**flies**, **fly·ing**, **flew** /fluː/, **flown** /fləʊn; *NAmE* floʊn/)

HELP In sense 15 **flied** is used for the past tense and past participle. 作第 15 義時過去時和過去分詞用 flied。

▸ **OF BIRD/INSECT** 鳥；昆蟲 **1** 🔑 [I] (**+ adv./prep.**) to move through the air, using wings 飛；飛翔：*A stork flew slowly past.* 一隻鸛緩緩飛過。◇ *A wasp had flown in through the window.* 一隻黃蜂從窗口飛了進來。

▸ **AIRCRAFT/SPACECRAFT** 飛行器；航天器 **2** 🔑 [I] (**+ adv./prep.**) (of an aircraft or a SPACECRAFT 航空器或航天器) to move through air or space （在空中或宇宙）飛行，航行：*They were on a plane flying from London to New York.* 他們在從倫敦飛往紐約的飛機上。◇ *to fly at the speed of sound* 以音速飛行 ◇ *Lufthansa fly to La Paz from Frankfurt.* 漢莎航空公司的飛機從法蘭克福飛往拉巴斯。 **3** 🔑 [I] to travel in an aircraft or a SPACECRAFT （乘飛行器或航天器）航行，飛行：*Is this the first time that you've flown?* 這是你第一次乘飛機嗎？◇ **~ (from …) (to …)** *I'm flying to Hong Kong tomorrow.* 明天我要乘飛機去香港。◇ **+ noun** *I always fly business class.* 我搭飛機總是坐商務艙。◇ *We're flying KLM.* 我們乘坐荷蘭皇家航空公司的飛機。 **4** 🔑 [T, I] **~ (sth)** to control an aircraft, etc. in the air 駕駛（飛機等）；操縱（飛行器等）：*a pilot trained to fly large passenger planes* 受過駕駛大型客機訓練的飛行員 ◇ *children flying kites* 放風箏的兒童 ◇ *He's learning to fly.* 他在學習駕駛飛機。 **5** [T] **+ adv./prep.** to transport goods or passengers in a plane 空運（貨物或乘客）：*The stranded tourists were finally flown home.* 滯留的遊客終於由飛機送返家園。◇ *He had flowers specially flown in for the ceremony.* 他特地為這個典禮空運鮮花來。 **6** [T] **~ sth** to travel over an ocean or area of land in an aircraft 乘飛行器飛越（海洋或陸地）：*to fly the Atlantic* 飛越大西洋

▸ **MOVE QUICKLY/SUDDENLY** 快速／突然移動 **7** 🔑 [I] (**+ adv./prep.**) to go or move quickly 疾馳；疾行；快速移動：*The train was flying along.* 火車飛馳着。◇ *She gasped and her hand flew to her mouth.* 她大口喘氣，連忙用手掩着嘴。◇ *It's late—I must fly.* 已經晚了，我得趕快走。 **8** 🔑 [I] (**+ adv./prep.**) to move suddenly and with force 猛然移動：(**+ adv./prep.**) *A large stone came flying in through the window.* 一塊大石頭飛進了窗戶。◇ *Several people were hit by flying glass.* 有幾個人被飛濺的玻璃擊中。◇ **+ adj.** *David gave the door a kick and it flew open.* 戴維踢了門一腳，門一下子開了。

▸ **OF TIME** 時間 **9** 🔑 [I] to seem to pass very quickly 飛逝：*Doesn't time fly?* 時間過得真快！◇ **~ by/past** *Summer has just flown by.* 夏天一晃就過去了。

▸ **FLAG** 旗幟 **10** [I, T] if a flag **flies**, or if you **fly** it, it is displayed, for example on a long pole （旗）飄揚；升，懸掛（旗）：*Flags were flying at half mast on all public buildings.* 所有的公共建築都降半旗。◇ **~ sth** *to fly the Stars and Stripes* 懸掛美國國旗

▸ **MOVE FREELY** 自由移動 **11** [I] to move around freely 自由移動：*hair flying in the wind* 隨風飄拂的頭髮

▸ **OF STORIES/RUMOURS** 故事；傳聞 **12** [I] to be talked about by many people 流傳；四處傳播

▸ **ESCAPE** 逃跑 **13** [T, I] **~ (sth)** (*formal*) to escape from sb/sth （從…）逃走，逃跑：*Both suspects have flown the country.* 兩個嫌疑犯都逃到國外了。 ➲ compare FLEE

▸ **OF PLAN** 計劃 **14** [I] (*NAmE*) to be successful 成功：*It remains to be seen whether his project will fly.* 他的計劃能否成功尚需拭目以待。

▸ **IN BASEBALL** 棒球 **15** (**flies**, **flying**, **flied**, **flied**) [I, T] **~ (sth)** to hit a ball high into the air 擊（球）騰空

IDM **fly the ˈcoop** (*informal, especially NAmE*) to escape from a place 逃走 **fly ˈhigh** to be successful 成功 **fly in the face of ˈsth** to oppose or be the opposite of sth that is usual or expected 悍然不顧；公然違抗；與…相悖：*Such a proposal is flying in the face of common sense.* 這個建議違反常識。 **fly into a ˈrage, ˈtemper, etc.** to become suddenly very angry 勃然大怒 **(go) fly a/your ˈkite** (*NAmE, informal*) used to tell sb to go away and stop annoying you or INTERFERING 走開；別煩人；別打擾人 **ˌfly the ˈnest** **1** (of a young bird 幼鳥) to become able to fly and leave its nest 羽翼已豐可離巢 **2** (*informal*) (of sb's child 子女) to leave home and live somewhere else 另立門戶 **fly off the ˈhandle** (*informal*) to suddenly become very angry 大發雷霆 **go 'flying** (*BrE, informal*) to fall, especially as a result of not seeing sth under your feet 跌倒；（尤指）絆了一跤：*Someone's going to go flying if you don't pick up these toys.* 你要是不撿起這些玩具，就會絆倒別人。 **let 'fly (at sb/sth) (with sth)** to attack sb by hitting them or speaking angrily to them （用…）打；（向某人）大發雷霆：*He let fly at me with his fist.* 他揮拳打我。◇ *She let fly with a stream of abuse.* 她破口大罵了一通。➲ more at BIRD *n.*, CROW *n.*, FLAG *n.*, PIG *n.*, SEAT *n.*, TANGENT, TIME *n.*, WINDOW

PHR V **'fly at sb** (of a person or an animal 人或動物) to attack sb suddenly 撲向；猛烈攻擊

■ ***noun*** (*pl.* **flies**)

▸ **INSECT** 昆蟲 **1** 🔑 [C] a small flying insect with two wings. There are many different types of fly. 蠅；蒼蠅：*A fly was buzzing against the window.* 一隻蒼蠅嗡嗡地飛着，直撞窗子。◇ *Flies rose in thick black swarms.* 蒼蠅黑壓壓地成群飛起。

▸ **IN FISHING** 釣魚 **2** [C] a fly or sth made to look like a fly, that is put on a hook and used as BAIT to catch fish （作釣餌的）蒼蠅，假蠅：*fly fishing* 用假蠅作餌釣魚

▸ **ON TROUSERS/PANTS** 褲子 **3** [sing.] (*BrE* also **flies**) an opening down the front of a pair of trousers/pants that fastens with a ZIP or buttons and is usually covered over by a strip of material （褲子的）前襠開口：*Your fly is undone!* 你的褲子前襠沒拉上！◇ *Your flies are undone!* 你的褲子前襠開着呢！➲ VISUAL VOCAB page V63

▸ **ON TENT** 帳篷 **4** [C] a piece of material that covers the entrance to a tent 門簾 ➲ see also FLIES

IDM **die/fall/drop like 'flies** (*informal*) to die or fall down in very large numbers 大批死亡；大批倒下：*People were dropping like flies in the intense heat.* 酷暑中人們成批死去。 **a/the fly in the 'ointment** a person or thing that spoils a situation or an occasion that is fine in all other ways 掃興的人；煞風景的事物 **a fly on the 'wall** a person who watches others without being noticed 不為人覺察的觀察者：*I'd love to be a fly on the wall when he tells her the news.* 他把這消息告訴她時，我想悄悄在旁觀看。◇ *fly-on-the-wall documentaries* (= in which people are filmed going about their normal lives as if the camera were not there) 紀實影片 **(there are) no flies on 'sb** (*informal*) the person mentioned is clever and not easily tricked 某人精明得不會上當 **not harm/hurt a 'fly** to be kind and gentle and unwilling to cause unhappiness 連一隻蒼蠅都不肯傷害；心地善良 **on the 'fly** (*informal*) if you do sth **on the fly**, you do it quickly while sth else is happening, and without thinking about it very much 趕緊地；匆忙中

■ ***adj.*** (*informal*) **1** (*BrE*) clever and showing good judgement about people, especially so that you can get an advantage for yourself 機靈的；機警的；不會上當的 **2** (*NAmE*) fashionable and attractive 時髦迷人的；漂亮的

fly agaric /ˌflaɪ ˈæɡərɪk; ˌflaɪ əˈɡɑːrɪk/ *noun* [U] a poisonous MUSHROOM with a red top with white spots 撲蠅蕈，毒蠅傘（有毒蘑菇）

fly·away /ˈflaɪəweɪ/ *adj.* (especially of hair 尤指毛髮) soft and fine; difficult to keep tidy 細軟的；凌亂的；飄拂的

'fly ball *noun* (in BASEBALL 棒球) a ball that is hit high into the air 高飛球；騰空球

fly·blown /ˈflaɪbləʊn; *NAmE* -bloʊn/ *adj.* (*BrE*) dirty and in bad condition; not fit to eat 不潔淨的；沾有蒼蠅卵的；不能食用的

'fly boy *noun* (*NAmE, informal*) a pilot, especially one in the AIR FORCE （尤指空軍）飛行員

'fly-by *noun* (*pl.* **fly-bys**) **1** the flight of a SPACECRAFT near a planet to record data （航天器的）近天體探測飛行 **2** (*NAmE*) (also **'flyover**) (both *NAmE*) (*BrE* **'fly-past**) a special flight by a group of aircraft, for people to watch at an important ceremony （飛機編隊的）檢閱飛行

'fly-by-night *adj.* [only before noun] (of a person or business 人或企業) dishonest and only interested in making money quickly 無信用（或不可靠）而唯利是圖的 ▸ **'fly-by-night** *noun*

fly·catch·er /ˈflaɪkætʃə(r)/ *noun* a small bird that catches insects while it is flying 翔食雀（能躍飛空中捕捉昆蟲）

'fly-drive *adj.*, *noun* (*BrE*)

■ ***adj.*** [only before noun] (of a holiday/vacation 假期) organized by a travel company at a fixed price that includes your flight to a place, a car to drive while you are there and somewhere to stay 飛行駕車之旅的（由旅行社組織，費用包含航班、自行駕車以及住宿）：*a fly-drive break* 飛行駕車之旅休假

■ ***noun*** a fly-drive holiday 飛行駕車之旅假期

flyer (also **flier**) /ˈflaɪə(r)/ *noun* **1** (*informal*) a person who flies an aircraft (usually a small one, not a passenger plane) （常指駕駛小飛機而非客機的）飛行員 **2** a person who travels in a plane as a passenger 飛機乘客：*frequent flyers* 常坐飛機的人 **3** a person who operates sth such as a model aircraft or a KITE from the ground 地面操縱飛行器者（如玩模型或放風箏的人） **4** a thing, especially a bird or an insect, that flies in a particular way 飛行物（尤指飛鳥或昆蟲）：*Butterflies can be strong flyers.* 蝴蝶的飛翔力強。 **5** a small sheet of paper that advertises a product or an event and is given to a large number of people 小（廣告）傳單 **6** (*informal*) a person, an animal or a vehicle that moves very quickly 能飛跑的人（或動物）；能疾馳的車輛：*Ford's flashy new flyer* 福特牌新型高速轎車 **7** = FLYING START ➲ see also HIGH-FLYER

'fly fishing *noun* [U] the sport of fishing in a river or lake using an artificial fly at the end of the line to attract and catch the fish 用假蠅釣魚；甩竿釣

ˌfly 'half *noun* = STAND-OFF HALF

fly·ing 🔑 /ˈflaɪɪŋ/ *adj.*, *noun*

■ ***adj.*** 🔑 [only before noun] able to fly 能飛的：*flying insects* 能飛的昆蟲

IDM **with ˌflying 'colours** very well; with a very high mark/grade 很好；成績優異：*She passed the exam with flying colours.* 她以優異成績通過了考試。 **ORIGIN** In the past, a ship returned to port after a victory in battle decorated with flags (= colours). 源自舊時戰船凱旋回港用彩旗裝飾。

■ ***noun*** [U] **1** 🔑 travelling in an aircraft 乘飛機：*I'm terrified of flying.* 我十分害怕坐飛機。 **2** 🔑 operating the controls of an aircraft 飛行；飛行器駕駛：*flying lessons* 飛行駕駛課

'flying boat *noun* a large plane that can take off from and land on water 水上飛機

ˌflying 'buttress *noun* (*architecture* 建) a half ARCH of brick or stone that supports the outside wall of a large building such as a church 拱扶垛

ˌflying 'doctor *noun* (especially in Australia) a doctor who travels in an aircraft to visit patients who live far from a town （尤指澳大利亞乘飛機出診的）飛行醫生：*A **flying doctor service** operates in remote regions.* 在偏遠地區有飛行醫生服務。

ˌflying 'fish *noun* a tropical sea fish that can rise and move forwards above the surface of the water, using its FINS (= flat parts that stick out from its body) as wings 飛魚（分佈於暖水海洋，有翼狀鰭）

ˌflying 'fox *noun* a large BAT (= an animal like a mouse with wings) that lives in hot countries and eats fruit 狐蝠；飛狐

'flying jacket (*BrE*) (*US* **'flight jacket**) *noun* a short leather jacket with a warm LINING and COLLAR, originally worn by pilots 飛行夾克；翻領皮夾克

ˌflying 'leap *noun* a long high jump made while you are running quickly （奔跑途中的）騰空跳遠：*to take a flying leap into the air* 騰空向前一跳

'flying machine *noun* an aircraft, especially one that is unusual or was built a long time ago （尤指非同尋常或很久以前造的）飛機，航空器

'flying officer *noun* an officer of lower rank in the British AIR FORCE （英國）皇家空軍中尉：*Flying Officer Ian Wall* 伊恩 • 沃爾皇家空軍中尉

ˌflying 'picket *noun* (*BrE*) a worker on strike who can go quickly to other factories, etc. to help persuade the workers there to join the strike 流動罷工鼓動員

ˌflying ˈsaucer *noun* a round SPACECRAFT that some people claim to have seen and that some people believe comes from another planet 飛碟 ➲ compare UFO

ˈflying squad *noun* (usually **the Flying Squad**) a group of police officers in Britain who are ready to travel very quickly to the scene of a serious crime （英國）機動警察隊，快速特警隊

ˌflying ˈsquirrel *noun* a small animal like a SQUIRREL which travels through the air between trees, spreading out the skin between its front and back legs to stop itself from falling too quickly 飛鼠

ˌflying ˈstart (also *less frequent* **flyer**) *noun* [sing.] a very fast start to a race, competition, etc. （賽跑、競賽等的）快速起動
IDM **get off to a ˌflying ˈstart | get off to a ˈflyer** to make a very good start; to begin sth well 有很好的開端；有良好的起步；開門紅

ˈflying suit *noun* a piece of clothing that covers the whole body, worn by the pilot and CREW of a military or light aircraft （連體）飛行服

ˌflying ˈvisit *noun* (*BrE*) a very short visit 短暫訪問；閃電式訪問

fly·leaf /ˈflaɪliːf/ *noun* (*pl.* **fly·leaves**) an empty page at the beginning or end of a book （書籍前後的）空白頁，襯頁

fly·over /ˈflaɪəʊvə(r); *NAmE* -oʊvər/ *noun* **1** (*BrE*) (*NAmE* **over·pass**) a bridge that carries one road over another one 跨線橋；立交橋；立體交叉道 **2** (*NAmE*) = FLY-BY (2)

ˈflyover country *noun* [U] (also **the ˈflyover states** [pl.]) (*informal, disapproving*) (in the US) the area in the middle of the country between the states on the coasts 飛越之地（指位於美國東、西海岸各州之間的中部地區）：*It's an area most New Yorkers know as flyover country.* 那個地區被大多數紐約人稱之為飛越之地。

fly·paper /ˈflaɪpeɪpə(r)/ *noun* [C, U] a strip of sticky paper that you hang in a room to catch flies 捕蠅紙

ˈfly-past (*BrE*) (*NAmE* **ˈfly-by**, **ˈflyover**) *noun* a special flight by a group of aircraft, for people to watch at an important ceremony 檢閱飛行

ˈfly-post *verb* [I, T] **~ (sth)** (*BrE*) to put up pieces of paper that advertise sth in public places, without official permission （未經正式許可）張貼小廣告 ▸ **ˈfly-posting** *noun* [U] **ˈfly-poster** *noun*

fly·sheet /ˈflaɪʃiːt/ *noun* (*BrE*) an extra sheet of material on the outside of a tent that keeps the rain out （帳篷外層防雨的）篷蓋

ˈfly-tip *verb* (**-pp-**) [I] (*BrE*) to leave waste somewhere illegally 亂倒垃圾 ▸ **ˈfly-tipping** *noun* [U] **ˈfly-tipper** *noun*

fly·weight /ˈflaɪweɪt/ *noun* a BOXER, WRESTLER, etc. of the lightest class, usually weighing between 48 and 51 kilograms 特輕量級拳擊手，次最輕量級拳擊手，最輕量級摔跤手，蠅量級拳擊手（體重 48 至 51 公斤之間）

fly·wheel /ˈflaɪwiːl/ *noun* a heavy wheel in a machine or an engine that helps to keep it working smoothly and at a steady speed 飛輪；慣性輪

FM *abbr.* **1** /ˌef ˈem/ frequency modulation (a method of broadcasting high-quality sound by radio) 調頻；頻率調制：*Radio 1 FM* 無線電調頻 1 台 **2** (in writing) FIELD MARSHAL （書寫形式）陸軍元帥

foal /fəʊl; *NAmE* foʊl/ *noun, verb*
■ *noun* a very young horse or DONKEY 駒子；小馬駒；小驢子
IDM **in foal** (of a female horse 母馬) pregnant 懷孕的，懷駒的
■ *verb* [I] to give birth to a foal 產駒

foam /fəʊm; *NAmE* foʊm/ *noun, verb*
■ *noun* **1** (also ˌ**foam ˈrubber**) [U] a soft light rubber material, full of small holes, that is used for seats, MATTRESSES, etc. 泡沫橡膠；海綿橡膠：*a foam mattress* 泡沫橡膠牀墊 ◇ *foam packaging* 泡沫橡膠包裝材料 **2** [U] a mass of very small air bubbles on the surface of a liquid 泡沫 **SYN** froth：*a glass of beer with a good head of foam* 一杯表面有厚厚一層泡沫的啤酒 ◇ *The breaking waves left the beach covered with foam.* 浪花四濺，海灘上滿是泡沫。 ➲ VISUAL VOCAB page V4, V5 **3** [U, C] a chemical substance that forms or produces a soft mass of very small bubbles, used for washing, shaving, or putting out fires, for example 泡沫劑（用於洗滌、剃鬚、滅火等）：*shaving foam* 剃鬚泡沫膏 ➲ picture at FROTH
■ *verb* [I] (of a liquid 液體) to have or produce a mass of small bubbles 有泡沫；起泡沫 **SYN** froth
IDM **foam at the ˈmouth** **1** (especially of an animal 尤指動物) to have a mass of small bubbles in and around its mouth, especially because it is sick or angry 口吐白沫（尤指因發病或暴怒） **2** (*informal*) (of a person 人) to be very angry 大發雷霆

foamy /ˈfəʊmi; *NAmE* ˈfoʊmi/ *adj.* consisting of or producing a mass of small bubbles; like foam 泡沫的；起泡沫的；泡沫般的

FOB /ˌef əʊ ˈbiː; *NAmE* oʊ/ *noun* (becoming *old-fashioned, informal, offensive, especially NAmE*) the abbreviation for 'fresh off the boat' (a person who has recently come to a country as an IMMIGRANT and does not speak or behave like people who have lived there a long time) 新移民（全寫為 fresh off the boat，指其不諳當地語言以及尚未融入當地社會）

fob /fɒb; *NAmE* fɑːb/ *verb, noun*
■ *verb* (**-bb-**)
PHR V ˌ**fob sb↔ˈoff (with sth)** **1** to try to stop sb asking questions or complaining by telling them sth that is not true （用不實之詞）搪塞，欺騙：*Don't let him fob you off with any more excuses.* 別讓他再以任何藉口哄騙你了。◇ *She wouldn't be fobbed off this time.* 這次她一定不會上當受騙了。 **2** to give sb sth that is not what they want or is of worse quality than they want （把劣質的或不想要的商品）騙售給：*He was unaware that he was being fobbed off with out-of-date stock.* 他沒有意識到對方向他騙售過期存貨。
■ *noun* **1** a short chain that is attached to a watch that is carried in a pocket 懷錶短鏈 **2** (also **ˈfob watch**) a watch that is attached to a fob 帶錶鏈的懷錶 **3** a small decorative object that is attached to a KEY RING, etc. （鑰匙環等上的）小飾物

f.o.b. *abbr.* (in writing) FREE ON BOARD （書寫形式）船上交貨價，離岸價格

focal /ˈfəʊkl; *NAmE* ˈfoʊkl/ *adj.* [only before noun] central; very important; connected with or providing a focus 中心的；很重要的；焦點的；有焦點的

fo·cal·ize (*BrE* also **-ise**) /ˈfəʊkəlaɪz; *NAmE* ˈfoʊ-/ *verb* **~ sth** (*formal*) to make sth focus or concentrate on a particular thing 使聚焦；使集中 ▸ **fo·cal·iza·tion, -isa·tion** /ˌfəʊkəlaɪˈzeɪʃn; *NAmE* ˌfoʊ-/ *noun* [U, C]

ˌfocal ˈlength *noun* (*physics* 物) the distance between the centre of a mirror or a LENS and its FOCUS 焦距

ˈfocal point *noun* **1** a thing or person that is the centre of interest or activity 集中點，焦點（指人或事物）；活動中心：*In rural areas, the school is often the focal point for the local community.* 在農村，學校常常是當地社區的活動中心。◇ *He quickly became the focal point for those who disagreed with government policy.* 他迅速成為不同意政府政策者的中心人物。 **2** (*technical* 術語) = FOCUS *n.* (3)

fo'c'sle = FORECASTLE

focus 🔑 **AW** /ˈfəʊkəs; *NAmE* ˈfoʊ-/ *verb, noun*
■ *verb* (**-s-** or **-ss-**) **1** 🔑 [I, T] to give attention, effort, etc. to one particular subject, situation or person rather than another 集中（注意力、精力等）於：**~ (on/upon sb/sth)** *The discussion focused on three main problems.* 討論集中在三個主要問題上。◇ *Each exercise focuses on a different grammar point.* 每個練習各有不同的語法重點。◇ **~ sth (on/upon sb/sth)** *The visit helped to focus world attention on the plight of the refugees.* 這次訪問促使全世界關注難民的困境。 **2** 🔑 [I, T] (of your eyes, a camera, etc. 眼睛、攝影機等) to adapt or be adjusted so that things can be seen clearly; to adjust sth so that you can see things clearly （使）調節焦距：*It took a few moments for her eyes to focus in the dark.* 過了一會兒她的眼睛才適應了黑暗。◇ **~ on sb/sth** *Let your eyes focus on objects that*

are further away from you. 睜大眼睛看清楚離你較遠的物體。◇ *In this scene, the camera focuses on the actor's face.* 在這個鏡頭中，攝影機對準演員的臉部。◇ **~ sth (on sb/sth)** *He focused his blue eyes on her.* 他那藍色的眼睛注視着她。◇ *I quickly focused the camera on the children.* 我迅速把照相機的鏡頭對準孩子們。 **3** [T] **~ sth (on sth)** (*technical* 術語) to aim light onto a particular point using a LENS 集中光束（於）；聚焦（於）

■ ***noun*** (*pl.* **fo·cuses** or **foci** /ˈfəʊsaɪ; *NAmE* ˈfoʊ-/) **1** [U, C, usually sing.] the thing or person that people are most interested in; the act of paying special attention to sth and making people interested in it 中心點（指人或事物）；關注；引起關注：*It was the main* ***focus of attention*** *at the meeting.* 這是會議上關注的主要焦點。◇ **~ for sth** *His comments provided a focus for debate.* 他的評論提供了辯論的重點。◇ **~ on sth** *We shall maintain our focus on the needs of the customer.* 我們將繼續重點關注顧客的需要。◇ *In today's lecture the focus will be on tax structures within the European Union.* 今天講課的重點是歐洲聯盟內部的稅制結構。◇ *The incident* ***brought*** *the problem of violence in schools* ***into*** *sharp* ***focus***. 這次事件使校園暴力成為焦點問題。◇ *What we need now is a* ***change of focus*** (= to look at things in a different way). 我們現在需要的是改變對事物的看法。 **2** [U] a point or distance at which the outline of an object is clearly seen by the eye or through a LENS（眼睛或鏡頭的）焦距，調焦：*The children's faces are badly* ***out of focus*** (= not clearly shown) *in the photograph.* 照片上孩子們的臉模糊不清。◇ *The binoculars were not* ***in focus*** (= were not showing things clearly). 這副雙筒望遠鏡的焦距不對。 **3** (also **ˈfocal point**) [C] (*physics* 物) a point at which waves of light, sound, etc. meet after REFLECTION or REFRACTION; the point from which waves of light, sound, etc. seem to come（光、聲等的）焦點，中心點，源 **4** [C] (*geology* 地) the point at which an EARTHQUAKE starts to happen（地震的）震源

fo·cused (also **fo·cussed**) /ˈfəʊkəst; *NAmE* ˈfoʊ-/ *adj.* with your attention directed to what you want to do; with very clear aims 注意力集中的；目標明確的：*She should do well in her studies this year—she's very focused.* 今年她的功課應該學得好，她的注意力很集中。

ˈfocus group *noun* a small group of people, specially chosen to represent different social classes, etc., who are asked to discuss and give their opinions about a particular subject. The information obtained is used by people doing MARKET RESEARCH, for example about new products or for a political party. 焦點小組（選自各階層，討論某專項問題；所得信息常為市場研究者或某政黨所用）

fod·der /ˈfɒdə(r); *NAmE* ˈfɑːd-/ *noun* [U] **1** food for horses and farm animals（馬等家畜的）飼料，秣 **2** (*disapproving*) (often after a noun 常置於名詞後) people or things that are considered to have only one use（人或東西）只能是…的料：*Without education, these children will end up as factory fodder* (= only able to work in a factory). 不受教育，這些孩子將來只能到工廠幹活。◇ *This story will be more fodder for the gossip columnists.* 這個傳聞會是閒談專欄作家的又一素材。➲ see also CANNON FODDER

foe /fəʊ; *NAmE* foʊ/ *noun* (*old-fashioned* or *formal*) an enemy 敵人；仇敵

foehn = FÖHN

foe·tal (*BrE*) (also **fetal** *NAmE, BrE*) /ˈfiːtl/ *adj.* [only before noun] connected with a foetus; typical of a foetus 胎兒的；胎的：*foetal abnormalities* 胎兒異常 ◇ *She lay curled up in a* ***foetal position***. 她像胎兒一樣蜷曲地躺着。

foe·tid = FETID

foe·tus (*BrE*) (also **fetus** *NAmE, BrE*) /ˈfiːtəs/ *noun* a young human or animal before it is born, especially a human more than eight weeks after FERTILIZATION 胎兒；胎

fog /fɒg; *NAmE* fɔːg; fɑːg/ *noun, verb*

■ ***noun*** [U, C] **1** a thick cloud of very small drops of water in the air close to the land or sea, that is very difficult to see through 霧：***Dense/thick fog*** *is affecting roads in the north and visibility is poor.* 濃霧影響了北部的公路，能見度很低。◇ ***freezing fog*** 寒霧 ◇ ***Patches of fog*** *will clear by mid-morning.* 上午十時左右，部份地區的霧將散去。◇ *We get heavy fogs on this coast in winter.* 冬天這片海岸霧氣很重。◇ *The town was covered in a thick* ***blanket of fog***. 大霧籠罩了這個城鎮。◇ *The fog finally* ***lifted*** (= disappeared). 霧終於散了。➲ COLLOCATIONS at WEATHER ➲ compare MIST *n.* (1) **2** a state of confusion, in which things are not clear 迷惘；困惑：*He went through the day with his mind* ***in a fog***. 整整一天，他的頭腦都是昏昏沉沉的。

■ ***verb*** (**-gg-**) **1** [I, T] **~ (sth) (up)** if a glass surface **fogs** or **is fogged** up, it becomes covered in steam or small drops of water so that you cannot see through（使）霧氣籠罩 **2** [T] **~ sth** to make sb/sth confused or less clear 使迷惘；使困惑：*I tried to clear the confusion that was fogging my brain.* 我試圖解除使我迷茫的困惑。◇ *The government was trying to* ***fog the*** *real* ***issues*** *before the election.* 政府企圖在選舉前混淆實質問題。

fog·bound /ˈfɒgbaʊnd; *NAmE* ˈfɔːg-; ˈfɑːg-/ *adj.* unable to operate because of fog; unable to travel or to leave a place because of fog 因霧不能運行的；因霧滯留的：*a fogbound airport* 因霧關閉的機場 ◇ *fogbound passengers* 因霧受阻的旅客 ◇ *She spent hours fogbound in Brussels.* 她因霧在布魯塞爾滯留了好幾個小時。

fogey (also **fogy**) /ˈfəʊgi; *NAmE* ˈfoʊgi/ *noun* (*pl.* **fogeys, fo·gies**) a person with old-fashioned ideas that he or she is unwilling to change 老頑固；守舊落伍的人：*He sounds like such an* ***old fogey!*** 他說話聽起來真是個老頑固！

foggy /ˈfɒgi; *NAmE* ˈfɔːgi; ˈfɑːgi/ *adj.* (**fog·gier, fog·gi·est**) not clear because of FOG 有霧的；霧茫茫的：*foggy conditions* 有霧的狀況 ◇ *a foggy road* 霧茫茫的道路

IDM **not have the ˈfoggiest (idea)** (*informal*) to not know anything at all about sth 完全不知道；一無所知；茫無頭緒：*'Do you know where she is?' 'Sorry, I haven't the foggiest.'* "你知道她在哪兒嗎？" "對不起，我一點也不知道。"

fog·horn /ˈfɒghɔːn; *NAmE* ˈfɔːghɔːrn; ˈfɑːg-/ *noun* an instrument that makes a loud noise to warn ships of danger in FOG 霧角，霧喇叭（向霧中的船隻發警告）：*He's got a voice like a foghorn* (= a loud unpleasant voice). 他那大嗓門像霧角一樣刺耳。

ˈfog lamp (*BrE*) (also **ˈfog light** *NAmE, BrE*) *noun* a very bright light on the front or back of a car to help the driver to see or be seen in FOG 霧燈（在車頭或尾）

fogy = FOGEY

föhn (also **foehn**) /fɜːn/ *noun* (usually **the föhn**) [sing.] a hot wind that blows in the Alps（阿爾卑斯山脈的）焚風

foi·ble /ˈfɔɪbl/ *noun* a silly habit or a strange or weak aspect of a person's character, that is considered harmless by other people（性格上無傷大雅的）怪癖，弱點，小缺點 SYN **idiosyncrasy**：*We have to tolerate each other's little foibles.* 我們得互相容忍對方的小缺點。

ˌfoie ˈgras *noun* [U] ➲ PÂTÉ DE FOIE GRAS

foil /fɔɪl/ *noun, verb*

■ ***noun*** **1** (*BrE* also **ˌsilver ˈfoil**) [U] metal made into very thin sheets that is used for covering or wrapping things, especially food（尤指包裝食物等用的）箔：(*BrE*) *aluminium foil* 鋁箔 ◇ (*NAmE*) *aluminum foil* 鋁箔 ➲ see also TINFOIL **2** [U] paper that is covered in very thin sheets of metal 箔紙（覆有箔的紙）：*The chocolates are individually wrapped in gold foil.* 巧克力用金箔紙一顆顆獨立包裝。 **3** [C] **~ (for sb/sth)** a person or thing that contrasts with, and therefore emphasizes, the qualities of another person or thing 陪襯者；陪襯物：*The pale walls provide a perfect foil for the furniture.* 淺色的牆壁完全襯托出傢具的特色。 **4** [C] a long thin light SWORD used in the sport of FENCING（擊劍運動用的）花劍，鈍劍 ➲ VISUAL VOCAB page V47

■ ***verb*** [often passive] to stop sth from happening, especially sth illegal; to prevent sb from doing sth 挫敗，阻止，制止（非法活動等）SYN **thwart**：**~ sth** *to foil* ***a plan/crime/plot*** 挫敗計劃 / 犯罪 / 陰謀 ◇ *Customs officials foiled an attempt to smuggle the paintings out of* *the country.* 海關關員阻截了一次企圖走私畫作出境的陰謀。◇ **~ sb (in sth)** *They were foiled in their attempt to smuggle the paintings.* 他們走私繪畫作品的企圖給偵破了。

foist /fɔɪst/ *verb*

PHR V **'foist sb/sth on/upon sb** to force sb to accept sb/sth that they do not want 強迫接受；把…強加於：*The title for her novel was foisted on her by the publishers.* 她的小說書名是出版商強加給她的。

fold 🔑 /fəʊld; *NAmE* foʊld/ *verb, noun*

■ **verb** **1** 🔑 [T] to bend sth, especially paper or cloth, so that one part lies on top of another part 摺疊，對摺（紙、織物等）：**~ sth (up)** *He folded the map up and put it in his pocket.* 他把地圖摺疊起來，放進了口袋。◇ *First,* ***fold*** *the paper* ***in half/in two.*** 首先，把紙對摺起來。◇ **~ sth (back, down, over, etc.)** *The blankets had been folded down.* 毛毯已摺疊起來。◇ *a pile of neatly folded clothes* 一摞摺疊整齊的衣服 ◇ *The bird folded its wings.* 那隻鳥收起了翅膀。**OPP** **unfold** ➲ see also FOLD-UP **2** 🔑 [T, I] to bend sth so that it becomes smaller or flatter and can be stored or carried more easily; to bend or be able to bend in this way 摺小，疊平，可摺小，可疊平（以便貯存或攜帶）：**~ sth (away/down/up)** *The bed can be folded away during the day.* 這張牀在白天可以摺疊收起。◇ **~ (away/up)** *The table folds up when not in use.* 這桌子不用時可以摺疊起來。◇ (*figurative*) *When she heard the news, her legs just folded under her* (= she fell). 她聽到這消息時雙腿發軟（倒在地上）。◇ **+ adj.** *The ironing board folds flat for easy storage.* 燙衣板能夠摺起來，便於存放。**3** [T] to wrap sth around sb/sth 包；裹：**~ A in B** *She gently folded the baby in a blanket.* 她輕輕地把嬰兒裹在毯子裏。◇ **~ B round/over A** *She folded a blanket around the baby.* 她用毯子把嬰兒裹了起來。**4** [I] (of a company, a play, etc. 公司、戲劇等) to close because it is not successful 倒閉；停演；結束

IDM **fold sb in your 'arms** (*literary*) to put your arms around sb and hold them against your body 擁抱；摟住 **fold your 'arms** to put one of your arms over the other one and hold them against your body 雙臂交叉在胸前 **fold your 'hands** to bring or hold your hands together 十指交叉合攏交疊：*She kept her hands folded in her lap.* 她雙手合攏，放在腿上。

PHR V **ˌfold sth↔'in** | **ˌfold sth 'into sth** (in cooking 烹飪) to add one substance to another and gently mix them together 把…調入；拌入：*Fold in the beaten egg whites.* 調入打好的蛋白。

■ **noun** **1** 🔑 [C] a part of sth, especially cloth, that is folded or hangs as if it had been folded 褶；褶層；摺疊部份：*the folds of her dress* 她的連衣裙上的褶 ◇ *loose folds of skin* 皮膚鬆垮的褶皺 **2** [C] a mark or line made by folding sth, or showing where sth should be folded 褶痕；褶縫；褶線 **3** [C] an area in a field surrounded by a fence or wall where sheep are kept for safety 羊欄；羊圈 **4** **the fold** [sing.] a group of people with whom you feel you belong or who share the same ideas or beliefs 志趣相同的人們；同一信仰的人們：*He called on former Republican voters to return to the fold.* 他號召昔日擁護共和黨的選民重新回到支持共和黨的行列。**5** [C] (*geology* 地) a curve or bend in the line of the layers of rock in the earth's CRUST（地殼岩石層的）褶皺 **6** [C] (*BrE*) a hollow place among hills or mountains 山坳；山窪；山谷

IDM **aˌbove/beˌlow the 'fold** in/not in a position where you see it first, for example in the top/bottom part of a newspaper page or web page（報紙或網頁）最上／下面部份，最顯眼／不顯眼部份：*Your ad will be placed above the fold for prominent exposure.* 你們的廣告將放在頁面上端的醒目位置。➲ compare ABOVE-THE-FOLD, BELOW-THE-FOLD

-fold *suffix* (in adjectives and adverbs 構成形容詞和副詞) multiplied by; having the number of parts mentioned 乘以；…倍；由…部份組成：*to increase tenfold* 增加到十倍

fold·away /'fəʊldəweɪ; *NAmE* 'foʊld-/ *adj.* = FOLDING

fold·er /'fəʊldə(r); *NAmE* 'foʊld-/ *noun* **1** a cardboard or plastic cover for holding loose papers, etc. 文件夾；紙夾 ➲ VISUAL VOCAB page V69 **2** (in some computer systems) a way of organizing and storing computer files（某些計算機系統中的）文件夾，頁面叠

fold·ing 🔑 /'fəʊldɪŋ; *NAmE* 'foʊ-/ (also *less frequent* **fold·away**) *adj.* [only before noun] (of a piece of furniture, a bicycle, etc. 傢具、自行車等) that can be folded, so that it can be carried or stored in a small space 摺疊式的；可摺疊的：*a folding chair* 摺椅 ◇ *a foldaway bed* 摺疊牀

'fold-up *adj.* [only before noun] (of an object 物件) that can be made smaller by closing or folding so that it takes up less space 可收攏的；可摺疊的

fo·li·age /'fəʊliɪdʒ; *NAmE* 'foʊ-/ *noun* [U] the leaves of a tree or plant; leaves and branches together（植物的）葉；枝葉：*dense green foliage* 茂密的綠葉 ➲ VISUAL VOCAB page V10

fo·liar /'fəʊliə(r); *NAmE* 'foʊ-/ *adj.* (*technical* 術語) relating to leaves 葉的；葉狀的：*foliar colour* 葉子的顏色

folic acid /ˌfɒlɪk 'æsɪd; ˌfəʊ-; *NAmE* ˌfoʊ-/ *noun* [U] a VITAMIN found in green vegetables, LIVER and KIDNEY, needed by the body for the production of red blood cells 葉酸（見於綠色蔬菜、肝、腎的一種維生素，用於造紅血球）

folio /'fəʊliəʊ; *NAmE* 'foʊlioʊ/ *noun* (*pl.* **-os**) **1** a book made with large sheets of paper, especially as used in early printing（尤指早期印刷的）對開本 **2** (*technical* 術語) a single sheet of paper from a book（書籍的）一頁

folk /fəʊk; *NAmE* foʊk/ *noun, adj.*

■ **noun** **1** (also **folks** especially in *NAmE*) [pl.] (*informal*) people in general 人們：*ordinary working-class folk* 普通勞動大眾 ◇ *I'd like a job working with* ***old folk*** *or kids.* 我喜歡與老人或小孩打交道的工作。◇ *the folks back home* (= from the place where you come from) 家鄉的鄉親父老 **2** **folks** [pl.] (*informal*) a friendly way of addressing more than one person 各位；大夥兒：*Well, folks, what are we going to do today?* 喂，夥計們，我們今天要幹什麼？**3** **folks** [pl.] (*informal, especially NAmE*) the members of your family, especially your parents 親屬；家屬；（尤指）爹媽：*How are your folks?* 你爸媽好嗎？**4** [pl.] people from a particular country or region, or who have a particular way of life（某國、某地區或某生活方式的）普通百姓：*country folk* 鄉下人 ◇ *townsfolk* 城裏人 ◇ *farming folk* 農民 **5** (also **'folk music**) [U] music in the traditional style of a country or community 民間音樂：*a* ***folk festival/concert*** 民間音樂節／會

■ **adj.** [only before noun] **1** (of art, culture, etc. 藝術、文化等) traditional and typical of the ordinary people of a country or community 傳統民間的；民俗的：*folk art* 民間藝術 ◇ *a folk museum* 民俗博物館 **2** based on the beliefs of ordinary people 流傳民間的；普通百姓的：*folk wisdom* 民間智慧 ◇ *Garlic is widely used in Chinese folk medicine.* 大蒜廣泛應用於中國民間醫藥。

'folk dance *noun* [C, U] a traditional dance of a particular area or country; a piece of music for such a dance 土風舞；民間舞蹈；民間舞曲

'folk etymology (also **ˌpopular ety'mology**) *noun* [U, C] a process by which a word is changed, for example because of a mistaken belief that it is related to another word, or to make a foreign word sound more familiar 民間詞源；通俗詞源：*Folk etymology has created the cheeseburger and the beanburger, but the first hamburgers were in fact named after the city of Hamburg.* 民間詞源創造了 cheeseburger 和 beanburger，但原始 hamburger 一詞實際上是以德國漢堡市命名的。

'folk hero *noun* a person that people in a particular place admire because of sth special he or she has done 民間英雄

folk·lore /'fəʊklɔː(r); *NAmE* 'foʊk-/ *noun* [U] the traditions and stories of a country or community 民間傳統；民俗；民間傳說：*Irish/Indian folklore* 愛爾蘭／印度民俗 ◇ *The story rapidly became part of family folklore.* 這個故事很快就成為家族傳說的一部份。

folk·lor·ist /ˈfəʊklɔːrɪst; *NAmE* ˈfoʊk-/ *noun* a person who studies folklore, especially as an academic subject 民俗學家；民俗學研究者

ˌfolk ˈmemory *noun* [C, U] a memory of sth in the past that the people of a country or community never forget 民間共同記憶（一個國家或社區的人不會忘記的事）

ˈfolk music *noun* [U] = FOLK *n.* (5)

ˌfolk ˈrock *noun* [U] a style of music that combines elements of folk music and rock 民歌搖滾樂

ˈfolk singer *noun* a person who sings folk songs 民歌手；唱民歌者

ˈfolk song *noun* **1** a song in the traditional style of a country or community 民歌；民謠 **2** a type of song that became popular in the US in the 1960s, played on a GUITAR and often about political topics 仿民歌歌曲（美國 20 世紀 60 年代盛行，吉他伴奏，常以政治為題材）

folksy /ˈfəʊksi; *NAmE* ˈfoʊksi/ *adj.* **1** (*especially NAmE*) simple, friendly and informal 淳樸友好自然的；樸實熱情隨意的：*They wanted the store to have a folksy small-town image.* 他們希望這家商店具有小城鎮那種樸實熱情的形象。 **2** (*sometimes disapproving*) done or made in a traditional style that is typical of simple customs in the past 有民間傳統的；有民間風味的；土裏土氣的：*a folksy ballad* 有民間風味的歌謠

ˈfolk tale *noun* a very old traditional story from a particular place that was originally passed on to people in a spoken form 民間故事；民間傳說

fol·licle /ˈfɒlɪkl; *NAmE* ˈfɑːl-/ *noun* one of the very small holes in the skin which hair grows from （毛）囊

fol·low 0-w /ˈfɒləʊ; *NAmE* ˈfɑːloʊ/ *verb*

▸ **GO AFTER** 跟隨 **1** 0-w [T, I] **~ (sb/sth)** to come or go after or behind sb/sth 跟隨；跟着：*He followed her into the house.* 他跟隨她走進房屋。◇ *Follow me please. I'll show you the way.* 請跟我走。我來給你指路。◇ *I think we're being followed.* 我認為有人跟踪我們。◇ (*figurative*) *She followed her mother into the medical profession.* 她走她母親的路，從事醫務工作。◇ *Wherever she led, they followed.* 她引向哪裏，他們就跟到哪裏。◇ *Sam walked in, with the rest of the boys following closely behind.* 薩姆走了進來，其他男孩緊跟其後。

▸ **HAPPEN/DO AFTER** 在…後發生 / 做 **2** 0-w [T, I] **~ (sth/sb)** to come after sth/sb else in time or order; to happen as a result of sth else （時間或順序上）在…後發生；因…而發生：*The first two classes are followed by a break of ten minutes.* 上完頭兩節課，有十分鐘的課間休息。◇ *I remember little of the days that followed the accident.* 那次事故以後的日子我記不大清楚了。◇ *A period of unrest followed the president's resignation.* 總統辭職之後有一段時期的動盪。◇ *A detailed news report will follow shortly.* 下面緊接着是詳細的新聞報道。◇ ***There followed** a short silence.* 接着沉默了一會兒。◇ *The opening hours are **as follows** …* 營業時間如下…◇ *A new proposal followed on from the discussions.* 討論之後，出了一個新提案。 **3** 0-w [T] to do sth after sth else 在…後做：**~ sth with sth** *Follow your treatment with plenty of rest.* 你治療以後要多休息。◇ **~ sth up with sth** *They follow up their March show with four UK dates next month.* 他們在三月演出以後，下個月在英國就有四場演出。

▸ **BE RESULT** 結果 **4** 0-w [I, T] (not usually used in the progressive tenses 通常不用於進行時) to be the logical result of sth 是…的必然結果：**~ (from sth)** *I don't see how that follows from what you've just said.* 根據你剛才所說的，我不明白怎麼會產生那樣的結果。◇ **it follows that …** *If a = b and b = c it follows that a = c.* 設 a = b，b = c，則 a = c。

▸ **OF PART OF MEAL** 一餐的部份 **5** 0-w [T, I] **~ (sth)** to come or be eaten after another part 接着是；然後是；下一道是：*The main course was followed by fresh fruit.* 主菜以後是新鮮水果。 HELP This pattern is usually used in the passive. 此句型通常用於被動語態：*I'll have soup and fish **to follow**.* 我要湯，然後要魚。

▸ **ROAD/PATH** 道路；小徑 **6** 0-w [T] **~ sth** to go along a road, path, etc. 沿着（道路、小徑等）：*Follow this road until you get to the school, then turn left.* 沿着這條路走到學校，然後向左拐。 **7** 0-w [T] **~ sth** (of a road, path, etc. 道路、小徑等) to go in the same direction as sth or parallel to sth 沿着…伸延；與…平行：*The lane follows the edge of a wood for about a mile.* 小路沿樹林邊延伸約一英里。

▸ **ADVICE/INSTRUCTIONS** 忠告；指示 **8** 0-w [T] **~ sth** to accept advice, instructions, etc. and do what you have been told or shown to do 接受，遵循，聽從（忠告、指示等）：*to **follow a diet/recipe*** 按照規定飲食；採用規定食譜 ◇ *He has trouble **following** simple **instructions**.* 簡單的指示他都難以照辦。◇ *Why didn't you **follow** my **advice**?* 你為什麼不聽我的勸告？

▸ **ACCEPT/COPY** 接受；效仿 **9** 0-w [T] **~ sth** to accept sb/sth as a guide, a leader or an example; to copy sb/sth 接受…為指導（或領導、榜樣）；追隨；擁護；仿效：*They followed the teachings of Buddha.* 他們信佛教。◇ *He always followed the latest fashions* (= dressed in fashionable clothes). 他總是緊跟着服裝潮流。◇ *I don't want you to follow my example and rush into marriage.* 我不希望你走我的老路，匆忙結婚。◇ *The movie follows the book faithfully.* 這部電影忠於原著。

▸ **UNDERSTAND** 理解 **10** 0-w [I, T] to understand an explanation or the meaning of sth 理解，明白（說明或意思）：**~ (sb)** *Sorry, I don't follow.* 對不起，我不明白。◇ *Sorry, I don't follow you.* 對不起，我聽不懂你的話。◇ **~ sth** *The plot is almost impossible **to follow**.* 故事情節幾乎叫人看不懂。 ⇨ SYNONYMS at UNDERSTAND

▸ **WATCH/LISTEN** 注視；聽 **11** 0-w [T] **~ sb/sth** to watch or listen to sb/sth very carefully 密切注視；傾聽：*The children were following every word of the story intently.* 孩子們一字不漏地專心聽故事。◇ *Her eyes followed him everywhere* (= she was looking at him all the time). 她一直在注視着他。

▸ **BE INTERESTED IN** 興趣 **12** 0-w [T] **~ sth** to take an active interest in sth and be aware of what is happening 對…產生濃厚興趣而關注：*Have you been following the basketball championships?* 你是否一直在注意籃球錦標賽的賽程？◇ *Millions of people followed the trial on TV.* 幾百萬人饒有興趣地收看了電視轉播的審判。

▸ **OF BOOK/MOVIE** 書籍；電影 **13** [T] **~ sth** to be concerned with the life or development of sb/sth 涉及…生活；有關…發展：*The novel follows the fortunes of a village community in Scotland.* 小說敘述了蘇格蘭一個村落的變遷。

▸ **PATTERN/COURSE** 模式；進展 **14** [T] **~ sth** to develop or happen in a particular way 按…方式（或方向）發展；以…方式發生：*The day followed the usual pattern.* 這一天和平常過得一樣。

IDM **follow in sb's ˈfootsteps** to do the same job, have the same style of life, etc. as sb else, especially sb in your family 仿效某人：*She works in television, following in her father's footsteps.* 她步父親的後塵，在電視台工作。 **follow your ˈnose 1** to be guided by your sense of smell 憑嗅覺指引 **2** to go straight forward 一直向前走：*The garage is a mile ahead up the hill—just follow your nose.* 汽車修理站在前面一英里處的山坡上，一直往前走就可以到。 **3** to act according to what seems right or reasonable, rather than following any particular rules 憑感覺行事；憑直覺辦事 **follow ˈsuit 1** (in card games 紙牌遊戲) to play a card of the same SUIT that has just been played 跟牌（跟着別人出同花色的牌） **2** to act or behave in the way that sb else has just done 跟着某人做；仿效某人；照着做 ⇨ more at ACT *n.*

PHR V **ˌfollow sb aˈround/aˈbout** to keep going with sb wherever they go 到處跟隨；跟踪：*Will you stop following me around!* 你不要再到處跟着我了！ **ˌfollow ˈon** to go somewhere after sb else has gone there 跟着走；接着來；隨後去：*You go to the beach with the kids and I'll follow on when I've finished work.* 你和孩子們去海濱，我辦完事隨後就去。 **ˌfollow ˈthrough** (in TENNIS, GOLF, etc. 網球、高爾夫球等) to complete a stroke by continuing to move the club, RACKET, etc. after hitting the ball（擊球後球拍、球棒等）完成順勢動作 ⇨ related noun FOLLOW-THROUGH (1) **ˌfollow ˈthrough (with sth)** | **ˌfollow sth↔ˈthrough** to finish sth that you have started 把…進行到底；完成（開了頭的事） ⇨ related noun FOLLOW-THROUGH (2) **ˌfollow sth↔ˈup 1** 0-w to add to sth that you have just done by doing sth else 對…採取進一步行動；…後接着：*You should follow up your phone call with an email or a letter.* 你打電話後應

該接着發一封電子郵件或寫封信。 **2** to find out more about sth that sb has told you or suggested to you 追查更多情況 SYN **investigate**: *The police are following up several leads after their TV appeal for information.* 警方在電視上呼籲提供信息後正沿着幾條線索繼續追查。 ➲ related noun FOLLOW-UP

fol·low·er /ˈfɒləʊə(r); NAmE ˈfɑːloʊ-/ *noun* **1** a person who supports and admires a particular person or set of ideas 擁護者；追隨者；信徒: *the followers of Mahatma Gandhi* 聖雄甘地的擁護者 **2** a person who is very interested in a particular activity and follows all the recent news about it 愛好者: *keen followers of football* 足球迷 ◇ *a follower of fashion* 趕時髦者 **3** a person who does things after sb else has done them first 仿效者；追隨者: *She is a leader, not a follower.* 她是領導者，不是追隨者。

F

fol·low·ing 🔑 /ˈfɒləʊɪŋ; NAmE ˈfɑːloʊɪŋ/ *adj., noun, prep.*

■ *adj.* **the following ...** **1** 🔑 next in time (時間上) 接着的: *the following afternoon/month/year/week* 第二天下午；第二個月；第二年；第二週 ◇ *They arrived on Monday evening and we got there the following day.* 他們是星期一晚上到的，我們次日也抵達那裏。 **2** 🔑 that is/are going to be mentioned next 下述的；下列的: *Answer the following questions.* 回答下列問題。 ➲ LANGUAGE BANK at FIRST

IDM **a ˌfollowing ˈwind** a wind blowing in the same direction as a ship or other vehicle that helps it move faster 順風

■ *noun* **1** 🔑 [usually sing.] a group of supporters (統稱) 擁護者，追隨者: *The band has a huge following in Italy.* 這個樂隊在意大利有一大批熱心的觀眾。 **2** 🔑 **the following** (used with either a singular or a plural verb, depending on whether you are talking about one thing or person or several things or people 動詞用單數還是複數取決於後面談及人、事物的單複數) the thing or things that you will mention next; the person or people that you will mention next 下述；下列；如下: *The following is a summary of events.* 現將重大事件綜述如下。 ◇ *The following have been chosen to take part: Watts, Hodges and Lennox.* 已選定下列人員參加：沃茨、霍奇斯和倫諾克斯。

■ *prep.* 🔑 after or as a result of a particular event 在 (某事) 以後；由於: *He took charge of the family business following his father's death.* 父親死後他就接管了家族企業。

ˌfollow-ˈon *noun* [sing.] (in CRICKET 板球) a second INNINGS (= a period during which a team is BATTING) that a team is made to play immediately after its first, if it fails to reach a particular score (一局未得分後的) 二局繼續擊球 ▸ **ˌfollow-ˈon** *verb* [I]

ˌfollow-the-ˈleader (also **ˌfollow-my-ˈleader**) *noun* [U] a children's game in which people follow the person in front of them in a line, going wherever they go 學樣遊戲 (參加者模仿領頭人的動作)

ˌfollow-ˈthrough *noun* **1** [U, sing.] (in TENNIS, GOLF, etc. 網球、高爾夫球等) the final part of a stroke after the ball has been hit (擊球後的) 隨球動作，順勢動作 **2** [U] the actions that sb takes in order to complete a plan (為完成某計劃所採取的) 後續行動: *The project could fail if there is inadequate follow-through.* 如果缺少恰當的後續行動，該項目可能失敗。

ˈfollow-up *noun* [C, U] an action or a thing that continues sth that has already started or comes after sth similar that was done earlier 後續行動；後續事物: *The book is a follow-up to her excellent television series.* 這本書是繼她的優秀電視系列片之後的又一力作。 ▸ **ˈfollow-up** *adj.* [only before noun]: *a follow-up study* 進一步的研究

folly /ˈfɒli; NAmE ˈfɑːli/ *noun* (*pl.* **-ies**) **1** [U, C] a lack of good judgement; the fact of doing sth stupid; an activity or idea that shows a lack of judgement 愚蠢；愚笨；愚蠢的想法 (或事情、行為) SYN **stupidity**: *an act of sheer folly* 純粹是愚蠢的行動 ◇ *Giving up a secure job seems to be the height of folly.* 放棄一份安定的工作似乎愚蠢至極。 ◇ **~ (to do sth)** *It would be folly to turn the offer down.* 拒絕這個建議是愚蠢之舉。 ◇ *the follies of youth* 青年時期的愚蠢行為 **2** [C] a building that has no practical purpose but was built in the past for decoration, often in the garden of a large country house (常見於舊時鄉間豪宅花園中的) 裝飾性建築

fo·ment /fəʊˈment; NAmE foʊ-/ *verb* **~ sth** (*formal*) to create trouble or violence or make it worse 挑起，激起，煽動 (事端或暴力) SYN **incite**: *They accused him of fomenting political unrest.* 他們指控他煽動政治動亂。

fond /fɒnd; NAmE fɑːnd/ *adj.* (**fond·er**, **fond·est**) **1 ~ of sb** feeling affection for sb, especially sb you have known for a long time 喜愛 (尤指認識已久的人): *Over the years, I have **grown quite fond of** her.* 經過這麼多年，我已相當喜歡她了。 ➲ SYNONYMS at LOVE **2 ~ of (doing) sth** finding sth pleasant or enjoyable, especially sth you have liked or enjoyed for a long time 喜愛 (尤指長期喜愛的事物): *fond of music/cooking* 喜好音樂 / 烹飪 ◇ *We had **grown fond of** the house and didn't want to leave.* 我們已經喜歡上了這座房子，不想搬家。 ➲ SYNONYMS at LIKE **3 ~ of (doing) sth** liking to do sth which other people find annoying or unpleasant, and doing it often 喜歡 (做令人不快的事): *Sheila's very fond of telling other people what to do.* 希拉好對別人指手畫腳。 ◇ *He's rather too fond of the sound of his own voice* (= he talks too much). 他太愛講話了。 **4** [only before noun] kind and loving 深情的；溫情的；慈愛的 SYN **affectionate**: *a **fond look/embrace/farewell*** 慈愛的目光；溫情的擁抱；深情的告別 ◇ *I have very **fond memories** of my time in Spain* (= I remember it with affection and pleasure). 我十分懷念從前在西班牙的時光。 **5** [only before noun] **~ hope** a hope about sth that is not likely to happen (指希望) 難以實現的；痴想的: *I waited all day **in the fond hope that** she would change her mind.* 我整天等待，痴迷地希望她會回心轉意。 ▸ **fond·ness** *noun* [U, sing.]: *He will be remembered by the staff with great fondness.* 全體人員將深摯地懷念他。 ◇ **~ for sb/sth** *a fondness for animals* 喜愛動物 IDM see ABSENCE

fon·dant /ˈfɒndənt; NAmE ˈfɑːn-/ *noun* **1** [U] a thick sweet soft mixture made from sugar and water, used especially to cover cakes 軟糖料 (尤用於裝飾糕點): *fondant icing* 軟糖料糖霜 **2** [C] a soft sweet/candy that melts in the mouth, made of fondant 方旦軟糖

fon·dle /ˈfɒndl; NAmE ˈfɑːndl/ *verb* **~ sb/sth** to touch and move your hand gently over sb/sth, especially in a sexual way, or in order to show love (尤指示愛或兩性間) 愛撫，撫摸 SYN **caress**

fond·ly /ˈfɒndli; NAmE ˈfɑːndli/ *adv.* **1** in a way that shows great affection 深情地；溫情地；慈愛地 SYN **affectionately**: *He looked at her fondly.* 他深情地望着她。 ◇ *I fondly remember my first job as a reporter.* 我深深地記得我初次工作當記者時的情景。 **2** in a way that shows hope that is not reasonable or realistic 天真地；想當然地；一廂情願地: *I fondly imagined that you cared for me.* 我天真地以為你很喜歡我。

fon·due /ˈfɒndjuː; NAmE fɑːnˈduː/ *noun* [C, U] **1** a Swiss dish of melted cheese and wine into which pieces of bread are DIPPED 奶酪火鍋 (瑞士特色菜，蘸麵包片吃) **2** a dish of hot oil into which small pieces of meat, vegetables, etc. are DIPPED 熱油火鍋 (在熱油中涮肉片、蔬菜等)

font /fɒnt; NAmE fɑːnt/ *noun* **1** a large stone bowl in a church that holds water for the ceremony of BAPTISM 聖洗池 (設於教堂中，常為石造) **2** (*technical* 術語) the particular size and style of a set of letters that are used in printing, etc. (同樣字體和字號的) 一副鉛字，字模，字型

fon·ta·nelle (*US* usually **fon·ta·nel**) /ˌfɒntəˈnel; NAmE ˌfɑːn-/ *noun* (*anatomy* 解) a space between the bones of a baby's SKULL, which makes a soft area on the top of the baby's head 囟，囟門 (嬰兒頭頂骨未合縫處)

food 🔑 /fuːd/ *noun*

1 🔑 [U] things that people or animals eat 食物: ***a shortage of food/food shortages*** 糧食短缺 ◇ *food and drink* 飲食 ◇ *the food industry* 食品工業 **2** 🔑 [C, U] a particular type of food (某種) 食物: *Do you like Italian food?* 你喜歡意大利食物嗎？ ◇ ***frozen foods*** 冷凍食品

◇ *a can of* **dog food** (= for a dog to eat) 一罐狗糧 ◇ *He's* **off his food** (= he does not want to eat anything). 他不想吃東西。➲ see also CONVENIENCE FOOD, FAST FOOD, FUNCTIONAL FOOD, HEALTH FOOD, JUNK FOOD, SEAFOOD, SOUL FOOD, WHOLEFOOD

IDM **food for 'thought** an idea that makes you think seriously and carefully 引人深思的想法

'food bank *noun* (in the US) a place where poor people can go to get free food（美國）食物賑濟處

'food chain *noun* (usually **the food chain**) a series of living creatures in which each type of creature feeds on the one below it in the series 食物鏈：*Insects are fairly low down (on) the food chain.* 在食物鏈中，昆蟲是相當低的一級生物。

foodie /'fuːdi/ *noun* (*informal*) a person who is very interested in cooking and eating different kinds of food 美食家

'food mile *noun* a measurement of the distance food has to be transported from the producer to the consumer and the fuel that this uses 食物里程（指食物從產地運送到消費者手中的距離及油耗）：*We keep food miles to a minimum by sourcing products locally.* 我們在當地採購產品，從而將食物里程控制在最低。

'food poisoning *noun* [U] an illness of the stomach caused by eating food that contains harmful bacteria 食物中毒

'food processor *noun* a piece of equipment that is used to mix or cut up food 食物加工器 ➲ VISUAL VOCAB page V25

'food science *noun* [U] the scientific study of food, for example what it is made of, the effects it has on our body, and how to prepare it and store it safely 食品科學（研究食品成分、對身體的作用及加工和貯存方法等）

'food stamp *noun* (*US*) a piece of paper that is given by the government to poor people, for them to buy food with（政府發給貧民的）食物券

food·stuff /'fuːdstʌf/ *noun* [usually pl.] (*technical* 術語) any substance that is used as food 食物；食品：*basic foodstuffs* 基本食物

'food web *noun* (*technical* 術語) a system of FOOD CHAINS that are related to and depend on each other 食物網（即相互關聯和依存的食物鏈體系）

fool /fuːl/ *noun, verb, adj.*

■ *noun* **1** [C] a person who you think behaves or speaks in a way that lacks intelligence or good judgement 蠢人；傻瓜 **SYN** **idiot**：*Don't be such a fool!* 別這麼傻了！◇ *I* **felt a fool** *when I realized my mistake.* 我意識到了自己的錯誤，覺得自己是個傻瓜。◇ *He told me he was an actor and I* **was fool enough to** *believe him.* 他告訴我他是演員，而我真傻，竟相信了他的話。**2** [C] (in the past) a man employed by a king or queen to entertain people by telling jokes, singing songs, etc.（舊時國王或王后豢養供人娛樂的）小丑，弄臣 **SYN** **jester** **3** [U, C] (*BrE*) (usually in compounds 通常構成複合詞) a cold light DESSERT (= a sweet dish) made from fruit that is cooked and crushed and mixed with cream or CUSTARD 奶油果泥，蛋奶果泥（甜食）：*rhubarb fool* 奶油大黃泥

IDM **act/play the 'fool** to behave in a stupid way in order to make people laugh, especially in a way that may also annoy them 裝傻，扮醜相（以逗人笑，但往往惹人惱怒）：*Quit playing the fool and get some work done!* 別再裝傻了，幹點實事吧！**any fool can/could ...** (*informal*) used to say that sth is very easy to do 任何人都能；容易得很：*Any fool could tell she was lying.* 任何人都可以看出她在撒謊。**be ˌno/ˌnobody's 'fool** to be too intelligent or know too much about sth to be tricked by other people 精明機智；不易上當：*She's nobody's fool when it comes to dealing with difficult patients.* 她對付難纏的病人很有辦法。**a ˌfool and his ˌmoney are soon 'parted** (*saying*) a person who is not sensible usually spends money too quickly or carelessly, or is cheated by others 傻瓜口袋漏，有錢留不住；蠢人不積財 **fools rush 'in (where angels fear to 'tread)** (*saying*) people with little experience try to do the difficult or dangerous things which more experienced people would not consider doing（智者卻步處）愚者獨敢闖 **make a 'fool of sb** to say or do sth deliberately so that people will think that sb is stupid 愚弄某人：*Can't you see she's making a fool of you?* 難道你不明白她是在愚弄你？➲ SYNONYMS at CHEAT **make a 'fool of yourself** to do sth stupid which makes other people think that you are a fool 出醜：*I made a complete fool of myself in front of everyone!* 我當眾出了大醜了！**ˌmore fool 'sb (for doing sth)** (*informal*) used to say that you think that sb was stupid to do sth, especially when it causes them problems 蠢極了；犯傻：*'He's not an easy person to live with.' 'More fool her for marrying him!'* "和他共同生活很難。" "她和他結婚真傻！" **(there's) ˌno fool like an 'old fool** (*saying*) an older person who behaves in a stupid way is worse than a younger person who does the same thing, because experience should have taught him or her not to do it 糊塗莫過老糊塗；老糊塗最糊塗 ➲ more at SUFFER

■ *verb* **1** [T] to trick sb into believing sth that is not true 欺騙；愚弄：**~ sb** *You don't fool me!* 不要騙我！◇ *She certainly* **had me fooled**—*I really believed her!* 她確實把我騙了，我真的相信了她的話！◇ **~ yourself** *You're fooling yourself if you think none of this will affect you.* 你要是認為此事一點也不會影響你，那就是欺騙自己。◇ **~ sb into doing sth** *Don't be fooled into thinking they're going to change anything.* 別上當受騙，以為他們打算作出任何改變。**2** [I] to say or do stupid or silly things, often in order to make people laugh 說蠢話，幹傻事（常為逗樂）：**~ (about/around)** *Stop fooling around and sit down!* 別幹傻事了，坐下來！◇ **~ (about/around) with sth** *If you fool about with matches, you'll end up getting burned.* 如果你擺弄火柴，最後可能燒到自己。

IDM **you could have fooled 'me** (*informal*) used to say that you do not believe sth that sb has just told you（表示不相信別人的話）休想騙我，說得像真的一樣：*'I'm trying as hard as I can!' 'You could have fooled me!'* "我要盡力而為！" "說得像真的似的！"

PHR V **ˌfool a'round** **1** (*BrE* also **ˌfool a'bout**) to waste time instead of doing sth that you should be doing 閒耍；虛度光陰 **SYN** **mess around** **2 ~ (with sb)** to have a sexual relationship with another person's partner; to have a sexual relationship with sb who is not your partner（和某人）亂搞男女關係 **SYN** **mess around**：*She's been fooling around with a married man.* 她一直和一個有婦之夫鬼混。

■ *adj.* [only before noun] (*informal*) showing a lack of intelligence or good judgement 傻的；愚蠢的 **SYN** **silly, stupid, foolish**：*That was a damn fool thing to do!* 幹那種事真蠢！

fool·hardy /'fuːlhɑːdi; *NAmE* -hɑːrdi/ *adj.* (*disapproving*) taking unnecessary risks 莽撞的；有勇無謀的 **SYN** **reckless**：*It would be foolhardy to sail in weather like this.* 這種天氣出航就是瞎冒險。▶ **fool·hardi·ness** *noun* [U]

fool·ish /'fuːlɪʃ/ *adj.* **1** (of actions or behaviour 作為或行為) not showing good sense or judgement 愚蠢的；傻的 **SYN** **silly, stupid**：*She's just a vain, foolish woman.* 她不過是個愚蠢虛榮的女人。◇ *I was foolish enough to believe what Jeff told me.* 我真蠢，竟相信傑夫和我說的話。◇ *The accident was my fault—***it would be foolish** *to pretend otherwise.* 這次事故是我的過失——裝作沒有責任那才傻呢。◇ *How could she have been so foolish as to fall in love with him?* 她怎麼這麼傻，竟愛上了他？◇ *a foolish idea/dream/mistake* 荒唐的想法／夢／錯誤 ◇ *It was a very foolish thing to do.* 幹那種事很蠢。**2** [not usually before noun] made to feel or look silly and embarrassed 不知所措；出醜；顯得尷尬 **SYN** **silly, stupid**：*I felt foolish and a failure.* 我自覺是個愚蠢的失敗者。◇ *He's afraid of looking foolish in front of his friends.* 他怕在朋友面前出醜。▶ **fool·ish·ly** *adv.*：*We foolishly thought that everyone would speak English.* 我們真蠢，竟以為人人都會說英語。◇ *Foolishly, I allowed myself to be persuaded to enter the contest.* 我竟傻乎乎地讓人說服去參加比賽。**fool·ish·ness** *noun* [U]：*Jenny had to laugh at her own foolishness.* 珍妮只好拿自己的愚蠢解嘲了。

fool·proof /'fuːlpruːf/ *adj.* (of a plan, machine, method, etc. 計劃、機器、方法等) very well designed and easy to use so that it cannot fail and you cannot use it wrongly

F

使用簡便的；完全可靠的；萬無一失的 SYN infallible：*This recipe is foolproof—it works every time.* 這個食譜絕對管用，每次都萬無一失。

fools·cap /ˈfuːlskæp/ *noun* [U] (*BrE*) a large size of paper for writing on（書寫紙規格）大裁，大頁紙

ˌfool's ˈerrand *noun* [sing.] a task that has no hope of being done successfully 徒勞無益的差事：*He sent me* ***on a fool's errand.*** 他派我去幹白費力的事。

ˌfool's ˈgold *noun* [U] **1** a yellow mineral found in rock, which looks like gold but is not valuable, also called **iron pyrites** 愚人金（指黃鐵礦）➲ see also PYRITES **2** something that you think is valuable or will earn you a lot of money, but which has no chance of succeeding 虛幻的搖錢樹

ˌfool's ˈparadise *noun* [usually sing.] a state of happiness that is based on sth that is false or cannot last although the happy person does not realize it 虛幻的幸福

foos·ball /ˈfuːzbɔːl/ (*NAmE*) (*BrE* **ˈtable football**) *noun* [U] an indoor game for two people or teams, played by moving rows of small models of football (SOCCER) players in order to move a ball on a board that has marks like a football (SOCCER) field 桌上足球；桌式手動足球；足球機

foot 0→ /fʊt/ *noun, verb*

■ ***noun*** (*pl.* **feet** /fiːt/)

▸ PART OF BODY 身體部位 **1** 0→ [C] the lowest part of the leg, below the ankle, on which a person or an animal stands（人或動物的）腳，足：*My feet are aching.* 我的腳疼。◇ *to get/rise* ***to your feet*** (= stand up) 起立 ◇ *I've been* ***on my feet*** (= standing or walking around) *all day.* 我一整天沒歇腳。◇ *We came* ***on foot*** (= we walked). 我們是走來的。◇ *walking around the house* ***in bare feet*** (= not wearing shoes or socks) 赤腳在房子四處走來走去 ◇ *Please* ***wipe your feet*** (= your shoes) *on the mat.* 請在墊子上蹭一蹭腳。◇ *a* ***foot pump*** (= operated using your foot, not your hand) 腳踏泵 ◇ *a* ***foot passenger*** (= one who travels on a FERRY without a car) 步行旅客（無車上渡船者）➲ SYNONYMS at STAND ➲ COLLOCATIONS at PHYSICAL ➲ VISUAL VOCAB page V59 ➲ see also ATHLETE'S FOOT, BAREFOOT, CLUB FOOT, UNDERFOOT

▸ -FOOTED …腳 **2** (in adjectives and adverbs 構成形容詞和副詞) having or using the type or number of foot/feet mentioned 有…腳（或足的）；有…隻腳（的）；用…腳（或足的）：*bare-footed* 赤腳 ◇ *four-footed* 四足的 ◇ *a left-footed shot into the corner* 踢入球門死角的左腳一記抽射 ➲ see also FLAT-FOOTED, SURE-FOOTED

▸ PART OF SOCK 襪子部份 **3** [C, usually sing.] the part of a sock, STOCKING, etc. that covers the foot（襪子的）足部

▸ BASE/BOTTOM 基礎；底部 **4** 0→ [sing.] **the ~ of sth** the lowest part of sth; the base or bottom of sth 最下部；基礎；底部：*the* ***foot of the stairs/page/mountain*** 樓梯底部；頁末；山腳 ◇ *The nurse hung a chart at the* ***foot of the bed*** (= the part of the bed where your feet normally are when you are lying in it). 護士在牀腳上掛了一張表。➲ SYNONYMS at BOTTOM

▸ MEASUREMENT 計量 **5** 0→ (*pl.* **feet** or **foot**) (*abbr.* **ft**) a unit for measuring length equal to 12 inches or 30.48 centimetres 英尺（＝12 英寸或 30.48 厘米）：*a 6-foot high wall* * 6 英尺高的牆 ◇ *We're flying at 35 000 feet.* 我們在 35 000 英尺高空飛行。◇ *'How tall are you?' 'Five foot nine'* (= five feet and nine inches). "你多高？" "五英尺九英寸。"

▸ -FOOTER …英尺高（或長）者 **6** (in compound nouns 構成複合名詞) a person or thing that is a particular number of feet tall or long …英尺高的人（或東西）；…英尺長的東西：*His boat is an eighteen-footer.* 他的小船長十八英尺。

▸ IN POETRY 詩歌 **7** [sing.] (*technical* 術語) a unit of rhythm in a line of poetry containing one stressed syllable and one or more syllables without stress. Each of the four divisions in the following line is a foot. 音步（詩行中的節奏單位，每個音步中有一個重讀音節）：*For ˈmen/may ˈcome/and ˈmen/may ˈgo.*（此詩行四個部份有四個音步）

IDM **be rushed/run off your ˈfeet** to be extremely busy; to have too many things to do 忙得不可開交；要做太多的事 **fall/land on your ˈfeet** to be lucky in finding yourself in a good situation, or in getting out of a difficult situation 特別走運；安然脱離困境；幸免於難 **feet ˈfirst 1** with your feet touching the ground before any other part of your body 腳先着地：*He landed feet first.* 他落地時雙腳先着地。**2** (*humorous*) if you leave a place **feet first**, you are carried out after you are dead 伸腿離開某地（指死去）：*You'll have to carry me out feet first!* 想把我攆走，除非讓我橫着出去！ **get/have a/your ˌfoot in the ˈdoor** to manage to enter an organization, a field of business, etc. that could bring you success 設法加入，涉足（某組織、行業等）：*I always wanted to work in TV but it took me two years to get a foot in the door.* 我一直想做電視工作，但花了兩年才進了這個圈子。 **get/start off on the right/wrong ˈfoot (with sb)** (*informal*) to start a relationship well/badly 開始時關係良好／不好：*I seem to have got off on the wrong foot with the new boss.* 看來我和新老闆的關係一開頭就不好。 **get your ˈfeet wet** (*especially NAmE, informal*) to start doing sth that is new for you 初次涉足；開始做（新鮮的事情）：*At that time he was a young actor, just getting his feet wet.* 那時他還是個年輕演員，才初出茅廬。 **have feet of ˈclay** to have a fault or weakness in your character 品格上有缺陷（或弱點） **have/keep your ˈfeet on the ground** to have a sensible and realistic attitude to life 實事求是；腳踏實地 **have/keep a foot in both ˈcamps** to be involved in or connected with two different or opposing groups 腳踩兩隻船 **have ˌone foot in the ˈgrave** (*informal*) to be so old or ill/sick that you are not likely to live much longer 行將就木；命不久矣；大去之期不遠 **… my ˈfoot!** (*informal, humorous*) a strong way of saying that you disagree completely with what has just been said（完全不同意對方所説）胡説八道：*'Ian can't come because he's tired.' 'Tired my foot! Lazy more like!'* "伊恩不能來，因為他累了。" "累個屁！説懶還差不多！" **on your ˈfeet** completely well or in a normal state again after an illness or a time of trouble（困境後）恢復，完全復原；（病後）痊癒：*Sue's back on her feet again after her operation.* 蘇手術後又恢復健康了。◇ *The new chairman hopes to get the company back on its feet within six months.* 新董事長希望在六個月以內使公司恢復元氣。➲ note at STAND **put your best foot ˈforward** to make a great effort to do sth, especially if it is difficult or you are feeling tired 竭盡全力；全力以赴 **put your ˈfeet up** to sit down and relax, especially with your feet raised and supported（尤指擱起雙腿）坐下休息：*After a hard day's work, it's nice to get home and put your feet up.* 辛勞一天後回家擱起雙腿休息是很愜意的。 **put your ˈfoot down 1** to be very strict in opposing what sb wishes to do 堅決制止；執意反對：*You've got to put your foot down and make him stop seeing her.* 你得堅決制止他再見她。**2** (*BrE*) to drive faster 踩油門；加速行駛：*She put her foot down and roared past them.* 她猛踩油門，從他們旁邊呼嘯而過。 **put your ˈfoot in it** (*BrE*) (also **put your foot in your ˈmouth** *NAmE, BrE*) to say or do sth that upsets, offends or embarrasses sb（在語言或行為上）使人不安，冒犯別人，使人尷尬：*I really put my foot in it with Ella—I didn't know she'd split up with Tom.* 我真的冒犯了埃拉，我不知道她和湯姆分手了。 **put a foot ˈwrong** (usually used in negative sentences 通常用於否定句) to make a mistake 犯錯誤；做錯事：*In the last two games he has hardly put a foot wrong.* 他在上兩局比賽中幾乎一點錯都沒有出。 **set ˈfoot in/on sth** to enter or visit a place 進入，訪問，參觀（某地）：*the first man to set foot on the moon* 第一個登上月球的人 ◇ *I vowed never to set foot in the place again.* 我發誓再不去那個地方了。 **set sb/sth on their/its ˈfeet** to make sb/sth independent or successful 使獨立；使成功：*His business sense helped set the club on its feet again.* 他的經營意識使俱樂部又重振雄風。 **stand on your own (two) ˈfeet** to be independent and able to take care of yourself 自立；獨立：*When his parents died he had to learn to stand on his own two feet.* 他的父母去世後他不得不學會自立。 **under your ˈfeet** in the way; stopping you from working, etc. 阻礙，妨礙（工作等）；礙手礙腳：*I don't want you kids under my feet while I'm cooking.* 我做飯時不希望你們這些孩子在我這兒礙手礙腳的。➲ more at BOOT *n.*, COLD *adj.*, DRAG *v.*,

FIND *v.*, GRASS *n.*, GROUND *n.*, HAND *n.*, HEAD *n.*, ITCHY, LEFT *adj.*, PATTER *n.*, PULL *v.*, SHOE *n.*, SHOOT *v.*, SIT, STOCKING, SWEEP *v.*, THINK *v.*, VOTE *v.*, WAIT *v.*, WALK *v.*, WEIGHT *n.*, WORLD

■ *verb*

IDM **foot the 'bill** (*informal*) to be responsible for paying the cost of sth 負擔費用：*Once again it will be the taxpayer who has to foot the bill.* 這一次掏腰包的又得是納稅人。

foot·age /'fʊtɪdʒ/ *noun* [U] part of a film showing a particular event（影片中的）連續鏡頭，片段：*old film footage of the moon landing* 一段登月的老影片

ˌfoot-and-'mouth disˌease (*NAmE* also **ˌhoof-and-'mouth disease**) *noun* [U] a disease of cows, sheep, etc., which causes sore places on the mouth and feet 口蹄疫（牛羊等的疾病，引起口、蹄潰瘍）

foot·ball 🔑 /'fʊtbɔːl/ *noun*
1 🔑 [U] (also *formal* **Asˌsociation 'football**) (both *BrE*) (also **soc·cer** *NAmE*, *BrE*) (also *BrE informal* **footy**, **footie**) a game played by two teams of 11 players, using a round ball which players kick up and down the playing field. Teams try to kick the ball into the other team's goal. 足球運動：*to* **play football** 踢足球 ◇ *a* **football match/team/stadium** 足球比賽／隊；足球比賽專用體育場 ➲ VISUAL VOCAB page V44 ➲ see also GAELIC FOOTBALL **2** 🔑 [U] (*NAmE*) = AMERICAN FOOTBALL ➲ VISUAL VOCAB page V44 **3** 🔑 [C] a large round or OVAL ball made of leather or plastic and filled with air 足球；橄欖球 ➲ VISUAL VOCAB page V44 **4** [C] (always used with an adjective 常與形容詞連用) an issue or a problem that frequently causes argument and disagreement 屢起爭議的課題；被踢來踢去的難題：*Health care should not become a political football.* 保健問題不應該成為被踢來踢去的政治皮球。

'football boot *noun* (*BrE*) a leather shoe with pieces of rubber on the bottom to stop it slipping, worn for playing football (SOCCER) 足球鞋（鞋底有防滑橡膠釘）➲ compare CLEAT (3)

foot·baller /'fʊtbɔːlə(r)/ *noun* (*BrE*) a person who plays football (SOCCER), especially as a profession（職業）足球運動員

foot·ball·ing /'fʊtbɔːlɪŋ/ *adj.* [only before noun] (*BrE*) connected with the game of football (SOCCER) 足球的；與足球比賽有關的：*footballing skills* 足球技巧

'football pools (also **the pools**) *noun* [pl.] a form of gambling in Britain in which people try to win money by saying what the results of football (SOCCER) matches will be 賭球，足球普爾（猜足球賽輸贏的賭博）：*They've had a big win on the football pools.* 他們在賭球中贏了一大筆錢。

foot·brake /'fʊtbreɪk/ *noun* a BRAKE in a vehicle which is operated using your foot 腳剎車

foot·bridge /'fʊtbrɪdʒ/ *noun* a narrow bridge used only by people who are walking 人行橋；步行橋 ➲ VISUAL VOCAB pages V2, V3

foot·er /'fʊtə(r)/ *noun* **1** a line or block of text that is automatically added to the bottom of every page that is printed from a computer（計算機打印的每頁的）頁腳，頁尾 ➲ compare HEADER (2) **2** a line at the bottom of a page on the Internet（網頁的）頁腳：*a website footer* 一個網站頁腳

foot·fall /'fʊtfɔːl/ *noun* **1** [C] (*literary*) the sound of the steps made by sb walking 腳步聲 **2** [U] (*BrE*, *business* 商) the number of people that visit a particular shop/store, shopping centre, etc. over a period of time 客流，人流（商店、購物中心在一段時間內的訪客人數）：*a campaign to increase footfall* 旨在增加客流的活動

'foot fault *noun* (in TENNIS 網球) a mistake that is made by not keeping behind the line when SERVING 腳部犯規（發球踏線）

foot·hill /'fʊthɪl/ *noun* [usually pl.] a hill or low mountain at the base of a higher mountain or range of mountains 山麓小丘：*the foothills of the Himalayas* 喜馬拉雅山脈山麓丘陵 ➲ VISUAL VOCAB page V5

foot·hold /'fʊthəʊld; *NAmE* -hoʊld/ *noun* **1** a crack, hole or branch where your foot can be safely supported when climbing 立足處（攀登時足可踩的縫、洞、樹枝等）**2** [usually sing.] a strong position in a business, profession, etc. from which sb can make progress and achieve success（可以此發展或取得成功的）穩固地位，立足點：*The company is eager to* **gain a foothold** *in Europe.* 這家公司急於在歐洲取得一席之地。

footie /'fʊti/ *noun* [U] (*BrE*, *informal*) = FOOTBALL (1)

foot·ing /'fʊtɪŋ/ *noun* [sing.] **1** the position of your feet when they are safely on the ground or some other surface 站穩：*She* **lost her footing** (= she slipped or lost her balance) *and fell backwards into the water.* 她腳未站穩，向後一仰掉進水中。◇ *I slipped and struggled to regain my footing.* 我滑了一下，但掙扎着站穩了腳跟。**2** the basis on which sth is established or organized 立足點；基礎：*The company is now* **on a sound** *financial* **footing**. 該公司現在已是資金穩健。◇ *The country has been* **on a war footing** (= prepared for war) *since March.* 自三月份起這個國家就準備要打仗。**3** the position or status of sb/sth in relation to others; the relationship between two or more people or groups 地位；人際關係：*The two groups must meet* **on an equal footing**. 這兩個集團必須以平等地位會談。◇ *They were demanding to be treated* **on the same footing** *as the rest of the teachers.* 他們要求得到和其他老師同等的待遇。

foot·lights /'fʊtlaɪts/ *noun* [pl.] a row of lights along the front of the stage in a theatre 腳燈（舞台前面的一排燈）

foot·ling /'fuːtlɪŋ/ *adj.* (*old-fashioned*, *informal*) not important and likely to make you annoyed 無足輕重的；無聊（而煩人）的

foot·loose /'fʊtluːs/ *adj.* free to go where you like or do what you want because you have no responsibilities 行動無拘無束的；自由自在的：*Bert was a footloose, unemployed actor.* 伯特是不受雇於任何人的自由演員。◇ *Ah, I was still* **footloose and fancy-free** (= free to enjoy myself) *in those days.* 啊，那些日子我還是自由自在、無憂無慮的。

foot·man /'fʊtmən/ *noun* (*pl.* **-men** /-mən/) a male servant in a house in the past, who opened the door to visitors, served food at table, etc.（舊時宅院的）男僕，門房，侍者

foot·note /'fʊtnəʊt; *NAmE* -noʊt/ *noun* **1** an extra piece of information that is printed at the bottom of a page in a book 腳註；註腳 ➲ WRITING TUTOR page WT18 **2** (of an event or a person 事情或人) that may be remembered but only as sth/sb that is not important 次要者

foot·path /'fʊtpɑːθ; *NAmE* -pæθ/ *noun* **1** (*BrE*) a path that is made for people to walk along, especially in the country（尤指鄉間的）人行小道：*a public footpath* 人行道 ➲ VISUAL VOCAB pages V2, V3 **2** (*AustralE*, *NZE*) = PAVEMENT

foot·plate /'fʊtpleɪt/ *noun* (*BrE*) the part of a steam train's engine where the driver stands（蒸汽機車司機站立的）平台

foot·print /'fʊtprɪnt/ *noun* **1** [usually pl.] a mark left on a surface by a person's foot or shoe or by an animal's foot 腳印；足跡：*footprints in the sand* 沙地足跡 ◇ *muddy footprints on the kitchen floor* 廚房地板上的泥腳印 **2** the amount of space that sth fills, for example the amount of space that a computer takes up on a desk（某物所佔的）空間量 **3** the area on the earth in which a signal from a communications SATELLITE can be received（通信衛星）覆蓋區

foot·rest /'fʊtrest/ *noun* a support for your foot or feet, for example on a motorcycle or when you are sitting down 擱腳物

the Foot·sie™ /'fʊtsi/ *noun* = FTSE INDEX

foot·sie /'fʊtsi/ *noun* (*informal*)

IDM **play 'footsie with sb** to touch sb's feet lightly with your own feet, especially under a table, as an expression of affection or sexual interest（在桌下）與某人腳碰腳調情，腳挨腳愛撫

F

F

'foot soldier *noun* **1** a soldier who fights on foot, not on a horse or in a vehicle 步兵 **2** a person in an organization who does work that is important but boring, and who has no power or responsibility （組織中從事乏味而不擔責任，但又不可或缺的）群眾員工

foot·sore /ˈfʊtsɔː(r)/ *adj.* (*formal*) having sore or tired feet, especially after walking a long way （因走遠路）腳痛，腳疲

foot·step /ˈfʊtstep/ *noun* [usually pl.] the sound or mark made each time your foot touches the ground when you are walking or running 腳步聲；足跡：*the sound of footsteps on the stairs* 樓梯上的腳步聲 ◇ *footsteps in the snow* 雪地上的足跡 IDM ▸ see FOLLOW

foot·stool /ˈfʊtstuːl/ *noun* a low piece of furniture used for resting your feet on when you are sitting 腳凳（坐時擱腳的矮凳）➲ VISUAL VOCAB page V21

foot·sure /ˈfʊtʃʊə(r); -ʃɔː(r); *NAmE* -ʃʊr/ *adj.* = SURE-FOOTED

foot·way /ˈfʊtweɪ/ *noun* (*BrE, formal*) a flat part at the side of a road for people to walk on（馬路邊的）人行道 SYN **pavement, sidewalk**

foot·wear /ˈfʊtweə(r); *NAmE* -wer/ *noun* [U] things that people wear on their feet, for example shoes and boots 鞋類（如鞋和靴）：*Be sure to wear the correct footwear to prevent injuries to your feet.* 一定要穿合適的鞋，以免腳受傷。

foot·work /ˈfʊtwɜːk; *NAmE* -wɜːrk/ *noun* [U] **1** the way in which a person moves their feet when playing a sport or dancing （體育、舞蹈的）步法，腳步動作 **2** the ability to react quickly and skilfully to a difficult situation （應付困境的）策略，應變能力：*It was going to take some deft political footwork to save the situation.* 當時得採取一些巧妙的政治手段以挽回局勢。

footy /ˈfʊti/ *noun* [U] (*BrE, informal*) = FOOTBALL (1)

fop /fɒp; *NAmE* fɑːp/ *noun* (*old-fashioned*) a man who is too interested in his clothes and the way he looks 紈袴子弟；花花公子 ▸ **fop·pish** *adj.*

for 🔑 /fə(r); *strong form* fɔː(r)/ *prep., conj.*

■ *prep.* HELP For the special uses of **for** in phrasal verbs, look at the entries for the verbs. For example **fall for sb** is in the phrasal verb section at **fall**. * for 在短語動詞中的特殊用法見有關動詞詞條。如 fall for sb 在詞條 fall 的短語動詞部份。 **1** 🔑 used to show who is intended to have or use sth or where sth is intended to be put （表示對象、用途等）給，對，供：*There's a letter for you.* 有你一封信。◇ *It's a book for children.* 這是本兒童讀物。◇ *We got a new table for the dining room.* 我們給飯廳添了一張新桌子。◇ *This is the place for me* (= I like it very much). 這裏很適合我。 **2** 🔑 in order to help sb/sth 以幫助；為了：*What can I do for you* (= how can I help you)? 有什麼事我可以為你效勞？◇ *Can you translate this letter for me?* 你能為我翻譯這封信嗎？◇ *I took her classes for her while she was sick.* 她生病時我為她代課。◇ *soldiers fighting for their country* 為祖國出征的軍人 **3** 🔑 concerning sb/sth 關於：*They are anxious for her safety.* 他們為她的安全擔心。◇ *Fortunately for us, the weather changed.* 我們運氣好，天氣變了。 **4** 🔑 as a representative of 代表：*I am speaking for everyone in this department.* 我代表這個部門全體人員講話。 **5** 🔑 employed by 受雇於：*She's working for IBM.* 她在國際商用機器公司工作。 **6** 🔑 meaning 意思是：*Shaking your head for 'No' is not universal.* 以搖頭表示“不”，並非放諸四海而皆準。 **7** 🔑 in support of sb/sth 支持；擁護：*Are you for or against the proposal?* 你支持還是反對這個建議？◇ *They voted for independence in a referendum.* 他們在全民公決投票中贊成獨立。◇ *There's a strong case for postponing the exam.* 有充分理由推遲考試。◇ *I'm* **all for** *people having fun.* 我完全贊成人們盡情享樂。 ➲ compare AGAINST (2) **8** 🔑 used to show purpose or function （表示目的或功能）：*a machine for slicing bread* 切麪包片機 ◇ *Let's go for a walk.* 咱們去散散步。◇ *Are you learning English for pleasure or for your work?* 你學英語是出於消遣還是為了工作？◇ *What did you do that for* (= Why did you do that)? 你為什麼幹那件事？ **9** 🔑 used to show a reason or cause 因為；由於：*The town is famous for its cathedral.* 這個城鎮以大教堂著名。◇ *She gave me a watch for my birthday.* 她送給我一塊手錶作為生日禮物。◇ *He got an award for bravery.* 他因英勇受獎。◇ *I couldn't speak for laughing.* 我笑得說不出話來。 **10** 🔑 in order to obtain sth 為得到；為獲取：*He came to me for advice.* 他來徵求我的意見。◇ *For more information, call this number.* 欲知詳情，請撥打此電話號碼。◇ *There were over fifty applicants for the job.* 有五十多人申請這個工作。 **11** 🔑 in exchange for sth 換取：*Copies are available for two dollars each.* 兩元一份。◇ *I'll swap these two bottles for that one.* 我要拿這兩瓶換那一瓶。 **12** 🔑 considering what can be expected from sb/sth 就…而言：*The weather was warm for the time of year.* 在一年的這個時節這天氣算是暖和的了。◇ *She's tall for her age.* 從她這個年齡看她個子算是高的。◇ *That's too much responsibility for a child.* 對於一個孩子來說，這責任是太重了。 **13 better, happier, etc. ~ sth** better, happier, etc. following sth …後（更好、更快樂等）：*You'll feel better for a good night's sleep.* 你晚上睡個好覺就會覺得好些。◇ *This room would look more cheerful for a spot of paint.* 這個房間油漆一下就會顯得更加悅目。 **14** 🔑 used to show where sb/sth is going （表示去向）往，向：*Is this the bus for Chicago?* 這輛公共汽車是去芝加哥的嗎？◇ *She knew she was destined for a great future.* 她知道她注定要成大器。 **15** 🔑 used to show a length of time（表示一段時間）：*I'm going away for a few days.* 我要離開幾天。◇ *That's all the news there is* **for now**. 目前新聞就這麼多。 **16** 🔑 used to show that sth is arranged or intended to happen at a particular time （安排或預定）在…時：*an appointment for May 12* * 5 月 12 日的一次約見 ◇ *We're invited for 7.30.* 我們受到邀請，7 點 30 分出席。 **17** 🔑 used to show the occasion when sth happens （表示場合）：*I'm warning you for the last time—stop talking!* 我最後一次警告你 —— 閉嘴！ **18** 🔑 used to show a distance （表示距離）：*The road went on for miles and miles.* 這條道路綿延數英里。 **19** 🔑 used to say how difficult, necessary, pleasant, etc. sth is that sb might do or has done 對（某人）來說（困難、必需、愉快等）：*It's useless* **for** *us* **to** *continue.* 我們繼續做下去也無用。◇ *There's no need* **for** *you* **to** *go.* 你不必走。◇ *For her to have survived such an ordeal was remarkable.* 她經歷了那樣的苦難活下來了，真不簡單。◇ *The box is* **too** *heavy* **for** *me* **to** *lift.* 這隻箱子太沉，我搬不動。◇ *Is it clear* **enough for** *you* **to** *read?* 這個你讀起來清不清楚？ **20** used to show who can or should do sth （表示誰可以或應該做某事）：*It's not for me to say why he left.* 不適宜由我說出他離開的原因。◇ *How to spend the money is for you to decide.* 怎樣花這筆錢由你決定。

IDM ▸ **be ˈin for it** (*BrE* also **be ˈfor it**) (*informal*) to be going to get into trouble or be punished 會惹出麻煩；要受懲罰：*We'd better hurry or we'll be in for it.* 我們最好趕快，不然要受罰的。 **for ˈall 1** despite 儘管；雖然：*For all its clarity of style, the book is not easy reading.* 這本書雖然文體清晰，但讀起來並不容易。 **2** used to say that sth is not important or of no interest or value to you/sb （表示對某人不重要、無價值或無所謂）：*For* **all I know** *she's still living in Boston.* 說不定她還住在波士頓。◇ *You can do what you like, for all I care.* 你想幹什麼就可以幹什麼，我才不管呢。◇ *For all the good it's done we might as well not have bothered.* 那件事帶來的好處不多，我們本不該操心的。 **there's/that's … for you** (often *ironic*) used to say that sth is a typical example of its kind …的典型；…就是這樣：*She might at least have called to explain. There's gratitude for you.* 她本來至少可以來電話解釋一下。她就這麼表示感謝。

■ *conj.* (*old-fashioned* or *literary*) used to introduce the reason for sth mentioned in the previous statement 因為；由於：*We listened eagerly, for he brought news of our families.* 我們急不可待地聽着，因為他帶來了我們家人的消息。◇ *I believed her—for surely she would not lie to me.* 我相信她的話，因為她肯定不會向我撒謊。

for·age /ˈfɒrɪdʒ; *NAmE* ˈfɔː-; ˈfɑː-/ *verb, noun*

■ *verb* **1** [I] **~ (for sth)** (especially of an animal 尤指動物) to search for food 覓（食） **2** [I] **~ (for sth)** (of a person 人) to search for sth, especially using the hands （尤指用手）搜尋（東西） SYN **rummage**

■ *noun* [U] food for horses and cows（牛馬的）飼料：*forage crops/grass* 飼料作物；飼草

foray /ˈfɒreɪ; *NAmE* ˈfɔː-; ˈfɑː-/ *noun* **1 ~ (into sth)** an attempt to become involved in a different activity or profession（改變職業、活動的）嘗試：*the company's first foray into the computer market* 該公司的初次涉足計算機市場 **2 ~ (into sth)** a short sudden attack made by a group of soldiers 突襲；閃電式襲擊 **3 ~ (to/into …)** a short journey to find a particular thing or to visit a new place 短途（尋物）；短暫訪問（新地方）**SYN expedition**：*weekend shopping forays to France* 週末赴法國購物

for·bade *past tense* of FORBID

for·bear *verb, noun*

■ *verb* /fɔːˈbeə(r); *NAmE* fɔːrˈber/ (**for·bore** /fɔːˈbɔː(r); *NAmE* fɔːrˈb-/, **for·borne** /fɔːˈbɔːn; *NAmE* fɔːrˈbɔːrn/) [I, T] (*formal*) to stop yourself from saying or doing sth that you could or would like to say or do 克制；自制；忍住（不說話或不做某事）：**~ (from sth/from doing sth)** *He wanted to answer back, but he forbore from doing so.* 他想頂嘴，但是忍住了。◇ **~ to do sth** *She forbore to ask any further questions.* 她克制自己，不再進一步提問。

■ *noun* = FOREBEAR

for·bear·ance /fɔːˈbeərəns; *NAmE* fɔːrˈber-/ *noun* [U] (*formal*) the quality of being patient and sympathetic towards other people, especially when they have done sth wrong 寬容

for·bear·ing /fɔːˈbeərɪŋ; *NAmE* fɔːrˈber-/ *adj.* (*formal*) showing forbearance 寬容的 **SYN patient**：*Thank you for being so forbearing.* 感謝您如此寬宏大量。

for·bid /fəˈbɪd; *NAmE* fərˈb-/ *verb* (**for·bade** /fəˈbæd; fəˈbeɪd; *NAmE* fərˈb-/, **for·bid·den** /fəˈbɪdn; *NAmE* fərˈb-/) **1** to order sb not to do sth; to order that sth must not be done 禁止；不准：**~ sb (from doing sth)** *He forbade them from mentioning the subject again.* 他不准他們再提到這個問題。◇ **~ sth** *Her father forbade the marriage.* 她的父親不允許這樁婚事。◇ **~ sb to do sth** *You are all forbidden to leave.* 你們都不准離開。◇ **~ sb sth** *My doctor has forbidden me sugar.* 醫生禁止我吃糖。◇ **~ (sb) doing sth** *She knew her mother would forbid her going.* 她知道她媽媽是不會讓她去的。**OPP allow, permit** **2 ~ sth | ~ sb to do sth** (*formal*) to make it difficult or impossible to do sth 妨礙；阻礙；阻止 **SYN prohibit**：*Lack of space forbids further treatment of the topic here.* 由於篇幅所限，這裏不能深入闡述這個問題。

IDM **God/Heaven forˈbid (that …)** (*informal*) used to say that you hope that sth will not happen 但願這事不發生：*'Maybe you'll end up as a lawyer, like me.' 'God forbid!'* "也許你會像我一樣，最終成為律師。" "但願不會這樣！" **HELP** Some people find this use offensive. 有人認為此用法含冒犯意。

for·bid·den /fəˈbɪdn; *NAmE* fərˈb-/ *adj.* not allowed 禁止的；不准的：*Photography is **strictly forbidden** in the museum.* 博物館內禁止攝影。◇ *The conversation was in danger of wandering into forbidden territory* (= topics that they were not allowed to talk about). 談話很可能離題而涉及禁止討論的領域。

IDM **forˌbidden ˈfruit** a thing that is not allowed and that therefore seems very attractive 禁果（唯其禁止，故特別誘人）

for·bid·ding /fəˈbɪdɪŋ; *NAmE* fərˈb-/ *adj.* seeming unfriendly and frightening and likely to cause harm or danger 冷峻的；令人生畏的：***a forbidding appearance/look/manner*** 冷峻的樣子／面孔／態度 ◇ *The house looked dark and forbidding.* 房子黑森森的，令人望而生畏。▶ **for·bid·ding·ly** *adv.*

for·bore *past tense* of FORBEAR

for·borne *past part.* of FORBEAR

force 🔑 /fɔːs; *NAmE* fɔːrs/ *noun, verb*

WORD FAMILY
force *noun, verb*
forceful *adj.*
forcefully *adv.*
forced *adj.* (≠ unforced)
forcible *adj.*
forcibly *adv.*
enforce *verb*

■ *noun*

▸ **VIOLENT ACTION** 暴力行動 **1** 🔑 [U] violent physical action used to obtain or achieve sth 武力；暴力：*The release of the hostages could not be achieved without the use of force.* 不使用武力不可能使人質獲釋。◇ *The rioters were taken away **by force**.* 聚眾鬧事者被強行帶走。◇ *The ultimatum contained the threat of military force.* 這份最後通牒含有武力威脅。◇ *We will achieve much more by persuasion than by **brute force**.* 我們通過說服會比使用暴力更有成效。

▸ **PHYSICAL STRENGTH** 力 **2** 🔑 [U] the physical strength of sth that is shown as it hits sth else 力；力量：***the force of the blow/explosion/collision*** 打擊／爆炸／碰撞力 ◇ *The shopping centre took the **full force** of the blast.* 購物中心承受了全部爆炸力。

▸ **STRONG EFFECT** 強大效力 **3** 🔑 [U] the strong effect or influence of sth 強大效力；巨大影響：*They realized the force of her argument.* 他們領悟到了她那論據的威力。◇ *He controlled himself by **sheer force of will**.* 他全憑意志力控制住了自己。◇ *She spoke with force and deliberation.* 她講話鏗鏘有力，字斟句酌。

▸ **SB/STH WITH POWER** 具有力量的人／事物 **4** 🔑 [C] a person or thing that has a lot of power or influence 力量大的人（或事物）；影響大的人（或事物）：***economic/market forces*** 經濟／市場力量 ◇ ***the forces of good/evil*** 善／惡的力量 ◇ *Ron is **the driving force*** (= the person who has the most influence) *behind the project.* 羅恩是這個計劃的主心骨。◇ *She's **a force to be reckoned with*** (= a person who has a lot of power and influence and should therefore be treated seriously). 她是個有影響力的人物，需要認真對待。◇ *The expansion of higher education should be a powerful **force for change**.* 高等教育的發展對變革應該是一個強大的推動力。

▸ **AUTHORITY** 權威 **5** [U] the authority of sth 權力；效力：*These guidelines do not have **the force of law**.* 這些指導原則不具有法律效力。◇ *The court ruled that these standards have force in English law.* 法院裁定，這些標準在英國法律中有效。

▸ **GROUP OF PEOPLE** 一群人 **6** 🔑 [C+sing./pl. v.] a group of people who have been organized for a particular purpose（為某目的組織起來的）一群人：*a member of **the sales force*** 推銷人員中的一員 ◇ *A large proportion of **the labour force*** (= all the people who work in a particular company, area, etc.) *is unskilled.* 很大一部份勞動力是非技術工人。➲ see also WORKFORCE

▸ **MILITARY** 武裝力量 **7** 🔑 [C+sing./pl. v.] a group of people who have been trained to protect other people, usually by using weapons 武裝部隊；部隊：*a member of the security forces* 保安部隊成員 ◇ ***rebel/government forces*** 反叛／政府武裝力量 ◇ *a peace-keeping force* 維和部隊 ➲ see also AIR FORCE, POLICE FORCE, TASK FORCE **8 the forces** [pl.] (*BrE*) the army, navy and AIR FORCE 兵力，武裝力量（陸海空三軍）：*allied forces* 盟軍 ➲ see also THE ARMED FORCES **9 forces** [pl.] the weapons and soldiers that an army, etc. has, considered as things that may be used 武裝力量：*strategic nuclear forces* 戰略核部隊

▸ **POLICE** 警察 **10 the force** [sing.] (*BrE*) the police force 警察部門：*He joined the force twenty years ago.* 他二十年前加入了警隊。

▸ **PHYSICS** 物理 **11** 🔑 [C, U] an effect that causes things to move in a particular way 力：*The moon exerts a force on the earth.* 月球對地球有引力。◇ *the force of gravity* 重力 ◇ *magnetic/centrifugal force* 磁力；離心力

▸ **OF WIND** 風 **12** [C, usually sing.] a unit for measuring the strength of the wind 風力；風力等級：*a force 9 gale* * 9 級大風 ◇ *a gale force wind* 一場大風級的風 ➲ see also TOUR DE FORCE

IDM **bring sth into ˈforce** to cause a law, rule, etc. to start being used（使法律、規則等）開始生效，開始實施：*They are hoping to bring the new legislation into force before the end of the year.* 他們希望在年底前實施新法。**come/enter into ˈforce** 🔑 (of a law, rule, etc. 法律、規則等) to start being used 開始生效；開始實施：*When do the new regulations come into force?* 新規章什麼時候開始執行？**force of ˈhabit** if you do sth from or out of **force of habit**, you do it automatically and in a particular way because you have always done it that way in the past 習慣力量 **the forces of ˈnature** the power of the wind, rain, etc., especially when it causes damage or harm（尤指造成損害的）自然力；大自然的

F

力量 **in 'force** **1** (of people 人) in large numbers 大量；眾多：*Protesters turned out in force.* 有很多抗議者出席。**2** (of a law, rule, etc. 法律、規則等) being used 已生效；在實施中：*The new regulations are now in force.* 新規章已生效。**join/combine 'forces (with sb)** to work together in order to achieve a shared aim （同…）聯合；（與…）合作：*The two firms joined forces to win the contract.* 兩家公司聯合起來爭取合同。➲ more at SPENT

■ *verb*

▸ **MAKE SB DO STH** 使做某事 **1** [often passive] to make sb do sth that they do not want to do 強迫，迫使（某人做某事）SYN **compel**：**~ sb into doing sth** *The President was forced into resigning.* 總統被迫辭職。◇ **~ sb/yourself to do sth** *The President was forced to resign.* 總統被迫辭職。◇ *I* **was forced to** *take a taxi because the last bus had left.* 最後一班公共汽車已經開走，所以我只好叫了一輛出租汽車。◇ *She forced herself to be polite to them.* 她對他們強裝客氣。◇ **~ sb into sth** *Ill health forced him into early retirement.* 他由於健康不佳不得不提前退休。◇ **~ sb** *He didn't force me—I wanted to go.* 他沒有逼迫我，是我想去的。◇ **~ yourself** (*informal, humorous*) *'I shouldn't really have any more.' 'Go on—force yourself!'* "我確實不應該再吃了。" "接着吃，再努力努力！" ◇ **~ sth** *Public pressure managed to force a change in the government's position.* 公眾的壓力成功地迫使政府改變了立場。

▸ **USE PHYSICAL STRENGTH** 用體力 **2** to use physical strength to move sb/sth into a particular position 用力，強行（把…移動）：**~ sth** *to* ***force a lock/window/door*** (= to break it open using force) 強行打開鎖／窗／門 ◇ *to* ***force an entry*** (= to enter a building using force) 強行進入建築物 ◇ **~ sth + adv./prep.** *She* ***forced her way*** *through the crowd of reporters.* 她在記者群中擠出一條通路。◇ *He tried to force a copy of his book into my hand.* 他硬要把他的一本書往我手裏塞。◇ **~ sth + adj.** *The door had been* ***forced open***. 門被強行打開了。

▸ **MAKE STH HAPPEN** 使發生 **3** to make sth happen, especially before other people are ready 使發生（尤指趁他人尚未準備）：**~ sth** *He was in a position where he had to force a decision.* 他當時的處境是，不得不強行通過一項決定。◇ **~ sth + adv./prep.** *Building a new road here will force house prices down.* 在這裏修建一條新道路將使房價下跌。

▸ **A SMILE/LAUGH** 微笑；大笑 **4 ~ sth** to make yourself smile, laugh, etc. rather than doing it naturally 強作笑顏；強裝歡笑：*She managed to force a smile.* 她勉強笑笑。

▸ **FRUIT/PLANTS** 果實；植物 **5 ~ sth** to make fruit, plants, etc. grow or develop faster than normal by keeping them in special conditions 人工催長；加速（水果、植物等）生長；催熟：*forced rhubarb* 人工催長的大黃 ◇ (*figurative*) *It is unwise to force a child's talent.* 對兒童的才能拔苗助長是不明智的。

IDM **force sb's 'hand** to make sb do sth that they do not want to do or make them do it sooner than they had intended 迫使某人做某事（或提前行動） **'force the issue** to do sth to make people take a decision quickly 迫使從速決定 **force the 'pace** (*especially BrE*) **1** to run very fast in a race in order to make the other people taking part run faster 迫使（賽跑對手）加速 **2** to make sb do sth faster than they want to 迫使（某人）加快速度：*The demonstrations have succeeded in forcing the pace of change.* 示威成功地促使改革進程加快。➲ more at THROAT

PHR V ˌ**force sth↔'back** to make yourself hide an emotion 強忍（不表露情感）：*She swallowed hard and forced back her tears.* 她使勁嚥了一下口水，強忍住了眼淚。ˌ**force sth↔'down** **1** to make yourself eat or drink sth that you do not really want 強迫嚥下（食物或飲料）**2** to make a plane, etc. land, especially by threatening to attack it 迫使（飛機等）降落 **'force sb/sth on/upon sb** to make sb accept sth that they do not want 強迫接受；把…強加給：*to force your attentions/opinions/company on sb* 強行對（某人）獻殷勤；把意見強加給（某人）；硬要陪伴（某人）ˌ**force sth 'out of sb** to make sb tell you sth, especially by threatening them 強使說出（尤其通過威脅）：*I managed to force the truth out of him.* 我設法迫使他說出了真情。

forced /fɔːst; *NAmE* fɔːrst/ *adj.* **1** happening or done against sb's will 被迫的；不得已的：*forced relocation to a job in another city* 不得已遷移至另一城市工作 ◇ *a forced sale of his property* 強制變賣他的財產 **2** not sincere; not the result of genuine emotions 勉強的；不真誠的：*She said she was enjoying herself but her smile was forced.* 她說自己很快活，但是她的笑容很勉強。➲ see also UNFORCED

ˌ**forced 'entry** *noun* [U, C] an occasion when sb enters a building illegally, using force 強行闖入（建築物）

ˌ**forced 'labour** (*especially US* ˌ**forced 'labor**) *noun* [U] **1** hard physical work that sb, often a prisoner or SLAVE, is forced to do （對囚犯、奴隸等實施的）強制勞動 **2** prisoners or SLAVES who are forced to work 強制勞工（如囚犯或奴隸）：*The mines were manned by forced labour from conquered countries.* 這些礦由來自被征服國家的強制勞工開採。

ˌ**forced 'landing** *noun* an act of having to land an aircraft unexpectedly in order to avoid a crash（飛行器的）迫降，強迫着陸：*to make a forced landing* 強迫着陸

ˌ**forced 'march** *noun* a long march, usually made by soldiers in difficult conditions 強行軍

ˌ**force-'feed** *verb* **~ sb** to use force to make sb, especially a prisoner, eat or drink, by putting food or drink down their throat 強迫進食（尤指把飲食灌進囚犯等口中）

'force field *noun* (often used in stories about space travel 常用於有關太空旅行的小說) a barrier that you cannot see（無形的）力障礙區

force·ful /ˈfɔːsfl; *NAmE* ˈfɔːrsfl/ *adj.* **1** (of people 人) expressing opinions firmly and clearly in a way that persuades other people to believe them 強有力的；堅強的 SYN **assertive**：*a forceful woman/speaker* 強有力的婦女；說話有說服力的人 ◇ *a forceful personality* 堅強的個性 **2** (of opinions, etc. 意見等) expressed firmly and clearly so that other people believe them 有說服力的：*a forceful argument/speech* 有說服力的論據／演講 **3** using force 強迫的；使用武力的：*the forceful suppression of minorities* 對少數族群的武力鎮壓 ▸ **force·ful·ly** /-fəli/ *adv.*：*He argued his case forcefully.* 他雄辯地闡述了他的立場。 **force·ful·ness** *noun* [U]

force ma·jeure /ˌfɔːs mæˈʒɜː(r); *NAmE* ˌfɔːrs/ *noun* [U] (from *French*, *law* 律) unexpected circumstances, such as war, that can be used as an excuse when they prevent sb from doing sth that is written in a contract 不可抗力（如戰爭，常指未能履行合約的原因）

force·meat /ˈfɔːsmiːt; *NAmE* ˈfɔːrs-/ *noun* [U] a mixture of meat or vegetables cut into very small pieces, which is often placed inside a chicken, etc. before it is cooked to give it flavour（常作烹飪填料用的）碎肉，菜末

'force-out *noun* (in BASEBALL 棒球) a situation in which a player running to a BASE is out because a FIELDER is holding the ball at the base 封殺；封殺出局

for·ceps /ˈfɔːseps; *NAmE* ˈfɔːrs-/ *noun* [pl.] an instrument used by doctors, with two long thin parts for picking up and holding things（醫生用的）鑷子，鉗子：*a pair of forceps* 一把鑷子 ◇ ***a forceps delivery*** (= a birth in which the baby is delivered with the help of forceps) 產鉗分娩

for·cible /ˈfɔːsəbl; *NAmE* ˈfɔːrs-/ *adj.* [only before noun] involving the use of physical force 強行的；用暴力的：*forcible repatriation* 強行遣返 ◇ *The police checked all windows and doors for signs of forcible entry.* 警察檢查了所有的門窗以尋找強行闖入的痕跡。

for·cibly /ˈfɔːsəbli; *NAmE* ˈfɔːrs-/ *adv.* **1** in a way that involves the use of physical force 用強力；用武力：*Supporters were forcibly removed from the court.* 支持者都被強行從法庭驅走。**2** in a way that makes sth very clear 明白地；清楚地：*It struck me forcibly how honest he'd been.* 我猛然醒悟他是多麼的正直。

ford /fɔːd; *NAmE* fɔːrd/ *noun, verb*

■ *noun* a shallow place in a river where it is possible to drive or walk across（可涉過或駛過的）河流淺水處

■ ***verb*** **~ sth** to walk or drive across a river or stream 涉過，駛過（淺水）

fore /fɔː(r)/ *noun, adj., adv.*

■ ***noun***

IDM **be/come to the 'fore** (*BrE*) (*NAmE* **be at the 'fore**) to be/become important and noticed by people; to play an important part 變得重要（或突出）；起重要作用：*She has always been to the fore at moments of crisis.* 在危急時刻她總是挺身而出。◇ *The problem has come to the fore again in recent months.* 近幾個月來這個問題又成為熱點。 **bring sth to the 'fore** to make sth become noticed by people 使處於顯要地位；使突出

■ ***adj.*** [only before noun] (*technical* 術語) located at the front of a ship, an aircraft or an animal 在（船、飛行器或動物）前部的；在頭部的 ➲ compare AFT, HIND

■ ***adv.*** **1** at or towards the front of a ship or an aircraft 在（或向）船頭；在（或向）飛行器頭部 ➲ compare AFT **2 Fore!** used in the game of GOLF to warn people that they are in the path of a ball that you are hitting 前方注意，看球（打高爾夫球時警告前面球路中的人以免被擊中）

fore- /fɔː(r)/ *combining form* (in nouns and verbs 構成名詞和動詞) **1** before; in advance 先於；預先：*foreword* 前言 ◇ *foretell* 預言 **2** in the front of 在…的前部：*the foreground of the picture* 圖畫的前景

fore·arm¹ /ˈfɔːrɑːm; *NAmE* -ɑːrm/ *noun* the part of the arm between the elbow and the wrist 前臂 ➲ VISUAL VOCAB page V59

fore·arm² /ˌfɔːrˈɑːm; *NAmE* -ˈɑːrm/ *verb* IDM see FOREWARN

fore·bear (also **for·bear**) /ˈfɔːbeə(r); *NAmE* ˈfɔːrber/ *noun* [usually pl.] (*formal* or *literary*) a person in your family who lived a long time ago 祖先；祖宗 SYN **ancestor**

fore·bod·ing /fɔːˈbəʊdɪŋ; *NAmE* fɔːrˈboʊ-/ *noun* [U, C] a strong feeling that sth unpleasant or dangerous is going to happen（對不祥或危險事情的）強烈預感：*She had **a sense of foreboding** that the news would be bad.* 她預感到這會是壞消息。◇ *He knew from her face that his forebodings had been justified.* 他從她的臉上看出，自己不祥的預感是正確的。 ▸ **fore·bod·ing** *adj.*：*a foreboding feeling that something was wrong* 出了問題的不祥預感

fore·brain /ˈfɔːbreɪn; *NAmE* ˈfɔːr-/ *noun* (*anatomy* 解) the front part of the brain 前腦

fore·cast 🔑 /ˈfɔːkɑːst; *NAmE* ˈfɔːrkæst/ *noun, verb*

■ ***noun*** 🔑 a statement about what will happen in the future, based on information that is available now 預測；預報：*sales forecasts* 銷售預測 ◇ *The forecast said there would be sunny intervals and showers.* 預報間晴，有陣雨。➲ see also WEATHER FORECAST

■ ***verb*** 🔑 (**fore·cast, fore·cast** or **fore·cast·ed, fore·cast·ed**) to say what you think will happen in the future based on information that you have now 預測；預報 SYN **predict**：**~ sth** *Experts are forecasting a recovery in the economy.* 專家預測經濟將復蘇。◇ *Snow is forecast for tomorrow.* 預報明天有雪。◇ **~ sth to do sth** *Temperatures were forecast to reach 40°C.* 預報溫度將達 40 攝氏度。◇ **~ that …** *The report forecasts that prices will rise by 3% next month.* 報告預測下月物價將上漲 3%。◇ **~ how, what, etc. …** *It is difficult to forecast how the markets will react.* 很難預測市場會有什麼樣的反應。 ➲ COLLOCATIONS at WEATHER ➲ LANGUAGE BANK at EXPECT

fore·cast·er /ˈfɔːkɑːstə(r); *NAmE* ˈfɔːrkæstər/ *noun* a person who says what is expected to happen, especially sb whose job is to forecast the weather 預測者；（尤指）天氣預報員，氣象預報員：*a weather forecaster* 天氣預報員 ◇ *an economic forecaster* 經濟預測專家

fore·castle (also **fo'c'sle**) /ˈfəʊksl; *NAmE* ˈfoʊksl/ *noun* the front part of a ship below the DECK, where the sailors live（前甲板下面的）水手艙

fore·close /fɔːˈkləʊz; *NAmE* fɔːrˈkloʊz/ *verb* **1** [I, T] **~ (on sb/sth)** | **~ sth** (*finance* 財) (especially of a bank 尤指銀行) to take control of sb's property because they have not paid back money that they borrowed to buy it（因抵押人未如期還貸）取消贖回權 ➲ COLLOCATIONS at HOUSE **2** [T] **~ sth** (*formal*) to reject sth as a possibility 排除…的可能 SYN **exclude**

fore·clos·ure /fɔːˈkləʊʒə(r); *NAmE* fɔːrˈkloʊ-/ *noun* [U, C] (*finance* 財) the act of foreclosing on money that has been borrowed; an example of this 抵押品贖回權的取消

fore·court /ˈfɔːkɔːt; *NAmE* ˈfɔːrkɔːrt/ *noun* (*BrE*) a large open space in front of a building, for example a PETROL/GAS STATION or hotel, often used for parking cars on 大片空地（在建築物如加油站或旅館前面，常用作停車）

fore·doomed /fɔːˈduːmd; *NAmE* fɔːrˈd-/ *adj.* **~ (to sth)** (*formal*) that will not be successful, as if FATE has decided this from the beginning 注定（失敗）的：*Any attempt to construct an ideal society is foredoomed to failure.* 任何構建理想社會的努力都注定要失敗。

fore·father /ˈfɔːfɑːðə(r); *NAmE* ˈfɔːrf-/ *noun* [usually pl.] (*formal* or *literary*) a person (especially a man) in your family who lived a long time ago 祖先，祖宗（尤指男性） SYN **ancestor**

fore·fend = FORFEND (1)

fore·fin·ger /ˈfɔːfɪŋgə(r); *NAmE* ˈfɔːrf-/ *noun* the finger next to the thumb 食指 SYN **index finger**

fore·foot /ˈfɔːfʊt; *NAmE* ˈfɔːrfʊt/ *noun* (*pl.* **forefeet** /-fiːt/) either of the two front feet of an animal that has four feet（四足動物的）前足

fore·front /ˈfɔːfrʌnt; *NAmE* ˈfɔːrf-/ *noun* [sing.]

IDM **at/in/to the 'forefront (of sth)** in or into an important or leading position in a particular group or activity 處於最前列；進入重要地位（或主要地位）：*Women have always been at the forefront of the Green movement.* 婦女總是在環境保護運動的最前列。◇ *The new product took the company to the forefront of the computer software field.* 該新產品使這家公司躋身計算機軟件業的前列。◇ *The court case was constantly in the forefront of my mind* (= I thought about it all the time). 這個訴訟案件一直縈繫在我的心頭。

fore·gather (also **for·gather**) /ˌfɔːˈgæðə(r); *NAmE* ˌfɔːrˈg-/ *verb* [I] (*formal*) to meet together in a group（一群人）聚會，集合

fore·go = FORGO

fore·going /ˈfɔːgəʊɪŋ; *NAmE* ˈfɔːrgoʊɪŋ/ *adj.* [only before noun] (*formal*) **1** used to refer to sth that has just been mentioned 上述的；前述的：*the foregoing discussion* 上述討論 **2 the foregoing** *noun* [sing.+sing./pl. v.] what has just been mentioned 前面所提到的事物；以上所述 OPP **following**

fore·gone /ˈfɔːgɒn; *NAmE* ˈfɔːrgɔːn/ *adj.*

IDM **a ˌforegone conˈclusion** if you say that sth is **a foregone conclusion**, you mean that it is a result that is certain to happen 預料中的必然結局

fore·ground /ˈfɔːgraʊnd; *NAmE* ˈfɔːrg-/ *noun, verb*

■ ***noun*** **the foreground 1** [C, usually sing.] the part of a view, picture, etc. that is nearest to you when you look at it（景物、圖畫等的）前景：*The figure **in the foreground** is the artist's mother.* 圖畫前景中的人是畫家的母親。 **2** [sing.] an important position that is noticed by people 矚目地位；重要位置：*Inflation and interest rates will be very much **in the foreground of** their election campaign.* 通貨膨脹和利率將很可能是他們競選的重點問題。➲ compare BACKGROUND (3), (4)

IDM **in the 'foreground** (*computing* 計) (of a computer program 計算機程序) being used at the present time and appearing in front of any other programs on the screen 在前台；在前景中 ➲ compare IN THE BACKGROUND at BACKGROUND

■ ***verb*** **~ sth** to give particular importance to sth 強調；突出：*The play foregrounds the relationship between father and daughter.* 這部戲劇凸顯了父女之間的關係。

fore·hand /ˈfɔːhænd; *NAmE* ˈfɔːrh-/ *noun* [usually sing.] (in TENNIS, etc. 網球等) a way of hitting a ball in which the inner part of the hand (= the PALM) faces the ball as it is hit 正手擊球；正手；正拍：*She has a strong forehand.* 她正手擊球強勁有力。◇ *a forehand volley* 正手

截擊球◇*He served to his opponent's forehand.* 他把球發向對方的正手方向。➲ compare BACKHAND

fore·head /ˈfɔːhed; ˈfɒrɪd; *NAmE* ˈfɔːrhed; ˈfɔːred/ *noun* the part of the face above the eyes and below the hair 額；前額 SYN **brow** ➲ COLLOCATIONS at PHYSICAL ➲ VISUAL VOCAB page V59

for·eign /ˈfɒrən; *NAmE* ˈfɔːrən; ˈfɑːrən/ *adj.* **1** in or from a country that is not your own 外國的：*a foreign accent/language/student* 外國口音／語言／學生◇*a foreign-owned company* 外資公司◇*foreign holidays* 外國假日◇*You could tell she was foreign by the way she dressed.* 從她的穿着就可以看出她是外國人。**2** [only before noun] dealing with or involving other countries 涉外的；外交的：***foreign affairs/news/policy/trade*** 外交事務；外國新聞；對外政策／貿易◇***foreign aid*** 外援◇*a* ***foreign correspondent*** (= one who reports on foreign countries in newspapers or on television) 駐外記者 OPP **domestic**, **home** **3 ~ to sb/sth** (*formal*) not typical of sb/sth; not known to sb/sth and therefore seeming strange 非典型的；陌生的：*Dishonesty is foreign to his nature.* 弄虛作假並非他的本性。**4 ~ object/body** (*formal*) an object that has entered sth by accident and should not be there 異物；異體：*Tears help to protect the eye from potentially harmful foreign bodies.* 眼淚有助於保護眼睛去除可能有害的異物。

the ˌForeign and ˈCommonwealth Office *noun* [sing.+sing./pl. v.] (*abbr.* **FCO**) the British government department that deals with relations with other countries. It used to be called **the Foreign Office** and it is still often referred to as this. 外交和聯邦事務部（英國政府部門，舊稱 the Foreign Office，現在有時仍見此說法）

for·eign·er /ˈfɒrənə(r); *NAmE* ˈfɔːr-; ˈfɑːr-/ *noun* (sometimes *offensive*) **1** a person who comes from a different country 外國人：*The fact that I was a foreigner was a big disadvantage.* 我是外國人這事實對我十分不利。**2** a person who does not belong in a particular place 外來人；外地人：*I have always been regarded as a foreigner by the local folk.* 當地人總把我視為外地人。

ˌforeign exˈchange *noun* **1** [U, C] the system of exchanging the money of one country for that of another country; the place where money is exchanged 國際匯兑；外匯市場；外幣兑換處：*The euro fell on the foreign exchanges yesterday.* 歐元匯價昨天下跌。**2** [U] money that is obtained using this system 外匯：*our largest source of foreign exchange* 我們外匯的最主要來源

the ˈForeign Office *noun* [sing.+sing./pl. v.] = THE FOREIGN AND COMMONWEALTH OFFICE

ˌforeign-reˈturned *adj.* (*IndE, informal*) (of a person 人) educated or trained in a foreign country, and having returned to India 學成歸國的；海歸的

the ˌForeign ˈSecretary *noun* the British government minister in charge of the FOREIGN AND COMMONWEALTH OFFICE（英國）外交大臣

ˈForeign Service *noun* (*NAmE*) = DIPLOMATIC SERVICE

fore·know·ledge /fɔːˈnɒlɪdʒ; *NAmE* fɔːrˈnɑːl-/ *noun* [U] (*formal*) knowledge of sth before it happens 預知；事先知道

fore·land /ˈfɔːlənd; *NAmE* ˈfɔːr-/ *noun* [sing., U] **1** an area of land which lies in front of sth 前陸；前沿地；前方地 **2** an area of land which sticks out into the sea 岬；陸岬

fore·leg /ˈfɔːleg; *NAmE* ˈfɔːrleg/ (also **fore·limb** /ˈfɔːlɪm; *NAmE* ˈfɔːr-/) *noun* either of the two front legs of an animal that has four legs（四足動物的）前足，前腿

fore·lock /ˈfɔːlɒk; *NAmE* ˈfɔːrlɑːk/ *noun* **1** a piece of hair that grows at the front of the head and hangs down over the FOREHEAD 額髮 **2** a part of a horse's MANE that grows forwards between its ears（馬的）額毛，門鬃
IDM **touch/tug your ˈforelock (to sb)** (*BrE, disapproving*) to show too much respect for sb, especially because you are anxious about what they think of you（對某人）必恭必敬 ORIGIN In the past people of the lower classes either took off their hats or pulled on their forelocks to show respect. 源自舊時下層人或者脱掉帽子，或者緊拽額髮，以示恭敬。

fore·man /ˈfɔːmən; *NAmE* ˈfɔːrmən/, **fore·woman** /ˈfɔːwʊmən; *NAmE* ˈfɔːrw-/ *noun* (*pl.* **-men** /-mən/, **-women** /-wɪmɪn/) **1** a worker who is in charge of a group of other factory or building workers 領班；工頭 **2** a person who acts as the leader of a JURY in court 陪審團團長 ➲ note at GENDER

fore·most /ˈfɔːməʊst; *NAmE* ˈfɔːrmoʊst/ *adj., adv.*
■ ***adj.*** the most important or famous; in a position at the front 最重要的；最著名的；最前的：*the world's foremost authority on the subject* 該學科全世界首屈一指的權威◇*The Prime Minister was foremost among those who condemned the violence.* 首相帶頭譴責暴力行為。◇*This question has been foremost in our minds recently.* 近來在我們的心目中這一直是個最重要的問題。
■ ***adv.*** IDM see FIRST *adv.*

fore·name /ˈfɔːneɪm; *NAmE* ˈfɔːrn-/ *noun* (*formal*) a person's first name rather than the name that they share with the other members of their family (= their SURNAME) 名：*Please check that your surname and forenames have been correctly entered.* 請核對你的姓名已正確輸入。

fore·noon /ˈfɔːnuːn; *NAmE* ˈfɔːr-/ *noun* (*NAmE, ScotE*) the morning 上午；午前

fo·ren·sic /fəˈrensɪk; -ˈrenzɪk/ *adj.* [only before noun] **1** connected with the scientific tests used by the police when trying to solve a crime 法醫的：***forensic evidence/medicine/science/tests*** 法醫證據／學／科學／檢驗◇*the forensic laboratory* 法醫檢驗室◇*a forensic pathologist* 法醫病理學家 ➲ COLLOCATIONS at CRIME **2** connected with or used in court 法庭的；與法庭有關的；用於法庭的：*a forensic psychiatrist* (= one who examines people who have been accused of a crime) 司法精神病學家

fore·play /ˈfɔːpleɪ; *NAmE* ˈfɔːrp-/ *noun* [U] sexual activity, such as touching the sexual organs and kissing, that takes place before people have sex（性交的）前戲

fore·run·ner /ˈfɔːrʌnə(r)/ *noun* **~ (of sb/sth)** a person or thing that came before and influenced sb/sth else that is similar; a sign of what is going to happen 先驅；先行者；預兆；前兆：*Country music was undoubtedly one of the forerunners of rock and roll.* 鄉村音樂無疑是搖滾樂的先導之一。

fore·sail /ˈfɔːseɪl; ˈfɔːsl; *NAmE* ˈfɔːrseɪl; ˈfɔːrsl/ *noun* [usually sing.] the main sail on the MAST of a ship which is nearest the front (called the **foremast**) 前桅帆；前帆

fore·see /fɔːˈsiː; *NAmE* fɔːrˈsiː/ *verb* (**fore·saw** /fɔːˈsɔː; *NAmE* fɔːrˈsɔː/, **fore·seen** /fɔːˈsiːn; *NAmE* fɔːrˈsiːn/) to think sth is going to happen in the future; to know about sth before it happens 預料；預見；預知 SYN **predict**：**~ sth** *We do not foresee any problems.* 我們預料不會出任何問題。◇*The extent of the damage could not have been foreseen.* 損害的程度是無法預見到的。◇**~ (that) ...** *No one could have foreseen (that) things would turn out this way.* 誰都沒有預料到事情的結果會這樣。◇**~ how, what, etc. ...** *It is impossible to foresee how life will work out.* 不可能預知生命將如何發展。◇**~ sb/sth doing sth** *I just didn't foresee that happening.* 我只是沒預料到會發生那種事。➲ compare UNFORESEEN

fore·see·able /fɔːˈsiːəbl; *NAmE* fɔːrˈs-/ *adj.* that you can predict will happen; that can be foreseen 可預料的；可預見的；可預知的：***foreseeable risks/consequences*** 可預料的危險／後果 OPP **unforeseeable**
IDM **for/in the foreseeable ˈfuture** for/in the period of time when you can predict what is going to happen, based on the present circumstances（在）可預見的將來：*The statue will remain in the museum for the foreseeable future.* 短期內這座雕像將留在博物館。◇*It's unlikely that the hospital will be closed in the foreseeable future* (= soon). 這所醫院不大可能很快就關閉。

fore·shadow /fɔːˈʃædəʊ; *NAmE* fɔːrˈʃædoʊ/ *verb* **~ sth** (*formal*) to be a sign of sth that will happen in the future 預示；是…的預兆

fore·shore /ˈfɔːʃɔː(r); *NAmE* ˈfɔːrʃ-/ *noun* [C, usually sing., U] **1** (on a beach or by a river) the part of the SHORE between the highest and lowest levels reached by the water（海灘上或河邊最高水位和最低水位之間的）灘頭，

前灘，灘地 **2** the part of the SHORE between the highest level reached by the water and the area of land that has buildings, plants, etc. on it（最高水位與建築物或樹木等之間的）海濱，水邊土地

fore·short·en /fɔːˈʃɔːtn; *NAmE* fɔːrˈʃɔːrtn/ *verb* **1** **~ sth/sb** (*technical* 術語) to draw, photograph, etc. objects or people so that they look smaller or closer together than they really are（繪畫、攝影等）用透視法縮小（或縮短） **2** **~ sth** (*formal*) to end sth before it would normally finish 提前結束；縮短；節略 **SYN** **curtail**： *a foreshortened education* 縮短了的教育

fore·sight /ˈfɔːsaɪt; *NAmE* ˈfɔːrs-/ *noun* [U] (*approving*) the ability to predict what is likely to happen and to use this to prepare for the future 深謀遠慮；先見之明： *She had had the foresight to prepare herself financially in case of an accident.* 她有先見之明，經濟上作了準備以防萬一發生事故。 ➲ compare HINDSIGHT

fore·skin /ˈfɔːskɪn; *NAmE* ˈfɔːrs-/ *noun* the loose piece of skin that covers the end of a man's PENIS 包皮

for·est 0-w /ˈfɒrɪst; *NAmE* ˈfɔːr-; ˈfɑːr-/ *noun* **1** 0-w [C, U] a large area of land that is thickly covered with trees 森林；林區： *a tropical forest* 熱帶森林 ◇ *a forest fire* 森林火災 ◇ *Thousands of hectares of forest are destroyed each year.* 每年都有幾千公頃的森林遭到破壞。 ➲ see also RAINFOREST ➲ **VISUAL VOCAB** pages V4, V5 **2** [C] **~ (of sth)** a mass of tall narrow objects that are close together（森林似的）一叢，一片： *a forest of television aerials* 林立的電視天線

IDM **not see the ˌforest for the ˈtrees** (*NAmE*) (*BrE* **not see the ˌwood for the ˈtrees**) to not see or understand the main point about sth, because you are paying too much attention to small details 見樹不見林

fore·stall /fɔːˈstɔːl; *NAmE* fɔːrˈs-/ *verb* **~ sth/sb** (*formal*) to prevent sth from happening or sb from doing sth by doing sth first 預先阻止；在（他人）之前行動；先發制人： *Try to anticipate what your child will do and forestall problems.* 盡量預見你的孩子會幹什麼，並預先阻止問題發生。

for·ested /ˈfɒrɪstɪd; *NAmE* ˈfɔːr-; ˈfɑːr-/ *adj.* covered in forest 滿是森林的；林木覆蓋的： ***thickly forested** hills* 森林密佈的丘陵 ◇ *The province is **heavily forested** and sparsely populated.* 該省森林茂密，人煙稀少。

for·est·er /ˈfɒrɪstə(r); *NAmE* ˈfɔːr-; ˈfɑːr-/ *noun* a person who works in a forest, taking care of the trees, planting new ones, etc. 林務員；護林人

for·est·ry /ˈfɒrɪstri; *NAmE* ˈfɔːr-; ˈfɑːr-/ *noun* [U] the science or practice of planting and taking care of trees and forests 林學；林業

fore·taste /ˈfɔːteɪst; *NAmE* ˈfɔːrt-/ *noun* [sing.] **a ~ (of sth)** a small amount of a particular experience or situation that shows you what it will be like when the same thing happens on a larger scale in the future 預先的體驗；預示；徵象： *They were unaware that the street violence was just a foretaste of what was to come.* 他們沒有意識到，這起街頭暴力預示着未來大規模的暴力行為。

fore·tell /fɔːˈtel; *NAmE* fɔːrˈtel/ *verb* (**fore·told**, **fore·told** /fɔːˈtəʊld; *NAmE* fɔːrˈtoʊld/) (*literary*) to know or say what will happen in the future, especially by using magic powers（尤指用魔力）預知，預言： **~ sth** *to foretell the future* 預言未來 ◇ **~ that ...** *The witch foretold that she would marry a prince.* 女巫預言她將嫁給王子。 ◇ **~ what, when, etc. ...** *None of us can foretell what lies ahead.* 我們誰都不能預知未來。

fore·thought /ˈfɔːθɔːt; *NAmE* ˈfɔːrθ-/ *noun* [U] careful thought to make sure that things are successful in the future 深謀遠慮： *Some forethought and preparation are necessary before you embark on the project.* 你着手進行這個項目之前必須有所考慮，有所準備。 **IDM** see MALICE

fore·told *past tense, past part.* of FORETELL

for·ever 0-w /fərˈevə(r)/ *adv.* **1** 0-w (*BrE* also **for ever**) used to say that a particular situation or state will always exist 永遠： *I'll love you forever!* 我永遠愛你！ ◇ *After her death, their lives changed forever.* 她死後他們的生活從此改變了。 ◇ *Just keep telling yourself that it won't last forever.* 要不停地提醒自己，這不會永世長存的。 **2** 0-w (*BrE* also **for ever**) (*informal*) a very long time 長久地： *It takes her forever to get dressed.* 她穿衣打扮要用好長的時間。 **3** (*informal*) used with verbs in the progressive tenses to say that sb does sth very often and in a way that is annoying to other people（與動詞進行時連用）老是，沒完沒了地： *She's forever going on about how poor they are.* 她老是沒完沒了地講他們有多窮。

fore·warn /fɔːˈwɔːn; *NAmE* fɔːrˈwɔːrn/ *verb* [often passive] **~ sb (of sth)** | **~ sb that ...** (*formal*) to warn sb about sth bad or unpleasant before it happens 預先警告；事先告誡： *The commander had been forewarned of the attack.* 指揮官預先得到敵人要發動襲擊的警報。 ▸ **fore·warn·ing** *noun* [U, C]

IDM **foreˌwarned is foreˈarmed** (*saying*) if you know about problems, dangers, etc. before they happen, you can be better prepared for them 預警即預備；有備無患

fore·woman *noun* ➲ FOREMAN

fore·word /ˈfɔːwɜːd; *NAmE* ˈfɔːrwɜːrd/ *noun* a short introduction at the beginning of a book（書的）前言，序言 ➲ compare PREFACE *n.*

for·feit /ˈfɔːfɪt; *NAmE* ˈfɔːrfət/ *verb, noun, adj.*

■ ***verb*** **~ sth** to lose sth or have sth taken away from you because you have done sth wrong（因犯錯）喪失，被沒收： *If you cancel your flight, you will forfeit your deposit.* 乘客取消航班訂位，訂金概不退還。 ◇ *He has forfeited his right to be taken seriously.* 他被取消了需要認真對待的權利。

■ ***noun*** something that a person has to pay, or sth that is taken from them, because they have done sth wrong 罰金；沒收物

■ ***adj.*** [not before noun] (*formal*) taken away from sb as a punishment 被罰；被沒收

for·feit·ure /ˈfɔːfɪtʃə(r); *NAmE* ˈfɔːrfətʃər/ *noun* [U] (*law* 律) the act of forfeiting sth 喪失；沒收： *the forfeiture of property* 財產的喪失

for·fend /fɔːˈfend; *NAmE* fɔːr-/ *verb* **1** (also **fore·fend**) **~ sth** (*NAmE*) to prevent sth 防止；阻止 **2** **~ sth** (*old use*) to prevent sth or keep sth away 防止；擋開

IDM **Heaven/God forˈfend (that) ...** (*humorous* or *old use*) used to say that you are frightened of the idea of sth happening 但願不要…；千萬別…： *Heaven forfend that students are encouraged to think!* 千萬不要鼓勵學生思考！

for·gather *verb* [I] = FOREGATHER

for·gave *past tense* of FORGIVE

forge /fɔːdʒ; *NAmE* fɔːrdʒ/ *verb, noun*

■ ***verb*** **1** [T] **~ sth** to put a lot of effort into making sth successful or strong so that it will last 艱苦幹成；努力加強： *a move to forge new links between management and workers* 努力建立勞資新關係的措施 ◇ *Strategic alliances are being forged with major European companies.* 正與歐洲主要公司設法結成戰略同盟。 ◇ *She forged a new career in the music business.* 她在樂壇上另創一番新事業。 **2** [T] **~ sth** to make an illegal copy of sth in order to cheat people 偽造；假冒： *to forge a passport/banknote/cheque* 偽造護照／鈔票／支票 ◇ *He's getting good at forging his mother's signature.* 他把母親的簽名偽造得越來越維妙維肖了。 ➲ **COLLOCATIONS** at CRIME ➲ compare COUNTERFEIT *v.* **3** [T] **~ sth (from sth)** to shape metal by heating it in a fire and hitting it with a hammer; to make an object in this way 鍛造；製作： *swords forged from steel* 用鋼鍛造的刀劍 **4** [I] **+ adv./prep.** (*formal*) to move forward in a steady but powerful way 穩步前進： *He forged through the crowds to the front of the stage.* 他擠過人群穩步走到台前。 ◇ *She forged into the lead* (= in a competition, race, etc.). 她（在比賽、賽跑等中）穩步領先。

PHR V **ˌforge aˈhead (with sth)** to move forward quickly; to make a lot of progress quickly 迅速向前；進步神速： *The company is forging ahead with its plans for expansion.* 公司的拓展計劃正順利進行。

■ ***noun*** **1** a place where objects are made by heating and shaping pieces of metal, especially one where a BLACKSMITH works 鐵匠鋪 **2** a large piece of equipment used

F

for heating metals in; a building or part of a factory where this is found 鍛鐵爐；鍛造車間；鍛造工廠

for·ger /ˈfɔːdʒə(r); *NAmE* ˈfɔːrdʒ-/ *noun* a person who makes illegal copies of money, documents, etc. in order to cheat people 偽造者；犯偽造罪的人 ➲ compare COUNTERFEITER

for·gery /ˈfɔːdʒəri; *NAmE* ˈfɔːrdʒ-/ *noun* **1** [U] the crime of copying money, documents, etc. in order to cheat people 偽造；偽造罪 SYN **fake** **2** [C] something, for example a document, piece of paper money, etc., that has been copied in order to cheat people 偽造品；贋品：*Experts are dismissing claims that the painting is a forgery.* 專家排除了這幅畫是贋品的說法。➲ compare COUNTERFEIT *adj.*

F

for·get 0-w /fəˈget; *NAmE* fərˈg-/ *verb* (**for·got** /fəˈgɒt; *NAmE* fərˈgɑːt/, **for·got·ten** /fəˈgɒtn; *NAmE* fərˈgɑːtn/)

▸ **EVENTS/FACTS** 事情；事實 **1** 0-w [I, T] (not usually used in the progressive tenses 通常不用於進行時) to be unable to remember sth that has happened in the past or information that you knew in the past 忘記；遺忘：**~ (about sth)** *I'd completely forgotten about the money he owed me.* 我完全記不得他欠我的錢了。◇ *Before I forget, there was a call from Italy for you.* 趁我還記得，有一個從意大利打來的電話找你。◇ **~ sth** *I never forget a face.* 見過的面孔我從不忘記。◇ *Who could forget his speech at last year's party?* 誰能忘記他去年在聚會上的講話呢？◇ **~ (that) …** *She keeps forgetting (that) I'm not a child any more.* 她老是忘了我不再是個小孩子了。◇ ***I was forgetting*** (= I had forgotten) *(that) you've been here before.* 我忘了你以前來過這裏。◇ **~ where, how, etc. …** *I've forgotten where they live exactly.* 我忘記了他們的確切住址。◇ *I forget how much they paid for it.* 我忘了他們用多少錢買的這東西。◇ **~ (sb) doing sth** *I'll never forget hearing this piece of music for the first time.* 我永遠不會忘記第一次聽到這首曲子的情景。◇ **it is forgotten that …** ***It should not be forgotten that*** *people used to get much more exercise.* 不應忘記的是，人們過去的鍛煉要多得多。

▸ **TO DO STH** 做某事 **2** 0-w [I, T] to not remember to do sth that you ought to do, or to bring or buy sth that you ought to bring or buy 忘記做（或帶、買等）：**~ (about sth)** *'Why weren't you at the meeting?' 'Sorry—I forgot.'* "你為什麼沒有參加會議？" "對不起，我忘了。" ◇ **~ to do sth** *Take care, and don't forget to write.* 要保重，別忘了寫信。◇ *I forgot to ask him for his address.* 我忘記向他要地址。◇ **~ sth/sb** *I forgot my purse* (= I did not remember to bring it). 我忘了帶錢包。◇ *'Hey, don't forget me!'* (= don't leave without me) "喂，走時別落下我！" ◇ ***Aren't you forgetting something?*** (= I think you have forgotten to do sth) 你難道沒有忘記要做的事嗎？HELP You cannot use **forget** if you want to mention the place where you have left something. 把東西忘在某處不用 forget：*I've left my book at home.* ◇ ~~*I've forgotten my book at home.*~~

▸ **STOP THINKING ABOUT STH** 不再想 **3** 0-w [I, T] to deliberately stop thinking about sb/sth 不再想；不再把…放在心上：**~ (about sb/sth)** *Try to forget about what happened.* 盡量不再想發生過的事情。◇ *Could you possibly forget about work for five minutes?* 你能不能勻出五分鐘來不去想工作？◇ **~ sb/sth** *Forget him!* 別把他放在心上！◇ *Let's forget our differences and be friends.* 咱們別把分歧放在心上，做個朋友吧。◇ **~ (that) …** *Forget (that) I said anything!* 不要把我說的話放在心上！ **4** [I, T] to stop thinking that sth is a possibility 不再考慮…的可能：**~ about sth** *If I lose this job, we can forget about buying a new car.* 要是我丟掉這份工作，我們就別想買新車。◇ **~ sth** *'I was hoping you might be able to lend me the money.' 'You can forget that!'* "我希望你能借錢給我。" "打消這個念頭吧！"

▸ **YOURSELF** 自己 **5** [T] **~ yourself** to behave in a way that is not socially acceptable（舉止）不得體：*I'm forgetting myself. I haven't offered you a drink yet!* 我真是不成體統。還沒有讓您喝點什麼呢！

IDM **and don't (you) for'get it** (*informal*) used to tell sb how they should behave, especially when they have been behaving in a way you do not like 可別忘了；你可給我記住；你給我老實點：*You're a suspect, not a detective, and don't you forget it.* 你是嫌疑犯，不是偵探，給我記住了。**for'get it** (*informal*) **1** used to tell sb that sth is not important and that they should not worry about it 沒關係；不必在意：*'I still owe you for lunch yesterday.' 'Forget it.'* "昨天午飯我還欠着你呢。" "算了吧！" **2** used to tell sb that you are not going to repeat what you said（表示不想重複說過的話）別提它了：*'Now, what were you saying about John?' 'Forget it, it doesn't matter.'* "嗳，你剛才說約翰什麼來着？" "別提了，那無關緊要。" **3** used to emphasize that you are saying 'no' to sth 休想；不可能：*'Any chance of you helping out here?' 'Forget it, I've got too much to do.'* "這兒你能幫個忙嗎？" "不可能，我還有一大堆活要幹呢。" **4** used to tell sb to stop talking about sth because they are annoying you 住嘴；別再煩人地說下去了：*Just forget it, will you!* 閉上嘴，行不行！ **not forgetting …** (*BrE*) used to include sth in the list of things that you have just mentioned 還包括：*I share the house with Jim, Ian and Sam, not forgetting Spike, the dog.* 我和吉姆、伊恩、薩姆共住一所房子，還有這條狗斯派克。➲ more at FORGIVE

for·get·ful /fəˈgetfl; *NAmE* fərˈg-/ *adj.* **1** often forgetting things 健忘的；好忘事的 SYN **absent-minded**：*She has become very forgetful in recent years.* 近年來她變得十分健忘。 **2 ~ of sb/sth** (*formal*) not thinking about sb/sth that you should be thinking about 疏忽的；不經心的 ▸ **for·get·ful·ly** /-fəli/ *adv.* **for·get·ful·ness** *noun* [U]

for'get-me-not *noun* a small wild plant with light blue flowers 勿忘我，勿忘草（野生，開藍花）

for·get·table /fəˈgetəbl; *NAmE* fərˈg-/ *adj.* not interesting or special and therefore easily forgotten（因平淡無奇）易被忘記的，容易遺忘的：*an instantly forgettable tune* 轉瞬即忘的曲調 OPP **unforgettable**

for·giv·able /fəˈgɪvəbl; *NAmE* fərˈg-/ *adj.* that you can understand and forgive 可原諒的；可寬恕的 SYN **excusable**：*His rudeness was forgivable in the circumstances.* 他當時的無理情有可原。OPP **unforgivable**

for·give 0-w /fəˈgɪv; *NAmE* fərˈgɪv/ *verb* (**for·gave** /fəˈgeɪv; *NAmE* fərˈg-/, **for·given** /fəˈgɪvn; *NAmE* fərˈg-/)
1 0-w [T, I] to stop feeling angry with sb who has done sth to harm, annoy or upset you; to stop feeling angry with yourself 原諒；寬恕：**~ sb/yourself (for sth/for doing sth)** *I'll never forgive her for what she did.* 我絕不會原諒她做的事。◇ *I'd never forgive myself if she heard the truth from someone else.* 如果她從別人那裏聽到了真相，我永遠不會原諒自己。◇ **~ (sth)** *I can't forgive that type of behaviour.* 我不能寬恕那種行為。◇ *We all have to learn to forgive.* 我們都得學會寬恕。◇ **~ sb sth** *She'd forgive him anything.* 無論他做了什麼，她都會原諒他。 **2** 0-w [T] used to say in a polite way that you are sorry if what you are doing or saying seems rude or silly 對不起；請原諒：**~ me** *Forgive me, but I don't see that any of this concerns me.* 對不起，我就看不出這與我有啥關係。◇ **~ me for doing sth** *Forgive me for interrupting, but I really don't agree with that.* 請原諒我打岔，不過我確實不同意那一點。◇ **~ my …** *Forgive my ignorance, but what exactly does the company do?* 請原諒我的無知，這家公司到底是幹什麼的？◇ **~ my doing sth** *Forgive my interrupting but I really don't agree with that.* 請原諒我打岔，不過我確實不同意那一點。 **3** [T] **~ (sb) sth** (*formal*) (of a bank, country, etc. 銀行、國家等) to say that sb does not need to pay back money that they have borrowed 免除（債務）：*The government has agreed to forgive a large part of the debt.* 政府同意免除一大部份債務。

IDM **sb could/might be forgiven for doing sth** used to say that it is easy to understand why sb does or thinks sth, although they are wrong 某人的做法雖錯卻是可以理解的：*Looking at the crowds out shopping, you could be forgiven for thinking that everyone has plenty of money.* 見到人們成群結隊地外出購物，難怪你會以為人人都很富有。 **for,give and for'get** to stop feeling angry with sb for sth they have done to you and to behave as if it had not happened 不念舊惡；不記仇

for·give·ness /fəˈgɪvnəs; *NAmE* fərˈg-/ *noun* [U] the act of forgiving sb; willingness to forgive sb 原諒；寬恕；寬宏大量：*to pray for God's forgiveness* 祈求上帝寬恕 ◇ *the* *forgiveness of sins* 對罪的寬恕 ◇ *He begged forgiveness for what he had done.* 他乞求饒恕他的所作所為。

for·giv·ing /fəˈɡɪvɪŋ; *NAmE* fərˈɡ-/ *adj.* willing to forgive 寬宏大量的；寬容的：*She had not inherited her mother's forgiving nature.* 她沒有承襲她母親的寬厚天性。◇ **~ of sth** *The public was more forgiving of the president's difficulties than the press and fellow politicians.* 公眾比報界和總統的政界同事更能體諒他的難處。

forgo (also **forego**) /fɔːˈɡəʊ; *NAmE* fɔːrˈɡoʊ/ *verb* (**for·went** /fɔːˈwent; *NAmE* fɔːrˈwent/, **for·gone** /fɔːˈɡɒn; *NAmE* fɔːrˈɡɔːn/) **~ sth** (*formal*) to decide not to have or do sth that you would like to have or do 放棄，棄絕（想做的事或想得之物）：*No one was prepared to forgo their lunch hour to attend the meeting.* 誰都不願意放棄午餐時間出席會議。

for·got *past tense* of FORGET

for·got·ten *past part.* of FORGET

fork 🔑 /fɔːk; *NAmE* fɔːrk/ *noun, verb*

■ ***noun*** **1** 🔑 a tool with a handle and three or four sharp points (called PRONGS), used for picking up and eating food 餐叉：*to eat with a **knife and fork*** 用刀叉吃東西 ➲ VISUAL VOCAB page V22 **2** a garden tool with a long or short handle and three or four sharp metal points, used for digging 叉（挖掘用的園藝工具）➲ VISUAL VOCAB page V19 ➲ see also PITCHFORK **3** a place where a road, river, etc. divides into two parts; either of these two parts（道路、河流等的）分岔處，分流處，岔口，岔路：*Shortly before dusk they reached a fork and took the left-hand track.* 快到黃昏時，他們來到一個岔路口，沿着左邊的小徑走去了。◇ *Take the right fork.* 走右邊的岔路。**4** a thing shaped like a fork, with two or more long parts 叉狀物：*a jagged fork of lightning* 鋸齒狀閃電 ➲ see also TUNING FORK **5** either of two metal supporting pieces into which a wheel on a bicycle or motorcycle is fitted（自行車或摩托車的）車叉子 ➲ VISUAL VOCAB page V51

■ ***verb*** **1** [I] (not used in the progressive tenses 不用於進行時) (**+ adv./prep.**) (of a road, river, etc. 道路、河流等) to divide into two parts that lead in different directions 分岔；岔開兩條分支：*The path forks at the bottom of the hill.* 小徑在山丘腳下分岔。◇ *The road forks right after the bridge.* 這條路過橋後岔開分成兩條。**2** [I] **+ adv./prep.** (not used in the progressive tenses 不用於進行時) (of a person 人) to turn left or right where a road, etc. divides into two 走岔路中的一條：*Fork right after the bridge.* 過橋後走右邊那條岔路。**3** [T] (**+ adv./prep.**) to move, carry or dig sth using a fork 叉運；叉掘：*Clear the soil of weeds and fork in plenty of compost.* 清除土中的雜草，然後叉入大量堆肥。

PHR V **ˌfork ˈout (for sth)** | **ˌfork ˈout sth (for/on sth)** (*informal*) to spend a lot of money on sth, especially unwillingly（尤指不情願地）大量花錢，大把掏錢：*Why fork out for a taxi when there's a perfectly good bus service?* 有挺好的公共汽車，幹嗎要多掏錢坐出租汽車？◇ *We've forked out a small fortune on their education.* 我們在他們的教育上可花了不少錢。

forked /fɔːkt; *NAmE* fɔːrkt/ *adj.* with one end divided into two parts, like the shape of the letter 'Y' 叉狀的（形如字母 Y）：*a bird with a forked tail* 有叉形尾羽的鳥 ◇ *the forked tongue of a snake* 蛇的叉形舌 ➲ VISUAL VOCAB page V13

ˌforked ˈlightning *noun* [U] the type of LIGHTNING that is like a line that divides into smaller lines near the ground 叉狀閃電 ➲ compare SHEET LIGHTNING

fork·ful /ˈfɔːkfʊl; *NAmE* ˈfɔːrk-/ *noun* the amount that a fork holds 一叉子（的量）

fork·lift truck /ˌfɔːklɪft ˈtrʌk; *NAmE* ˌfɔːrk-/ (also **ˈfork-lift**) *noun* a vehicle with special equipment on the front for moving and lifting heavy objects 叉車；叉式裝卸車；堆高機 ➲ VISUAL VOCAB page V57

for·lorn /fəˈlɔːn; *NAmE* fərˈlɔːrn/ *adj.* **1** (of a person 人) appearing lonely and unhappy 孤苦伶仃的；孤獨淒涼的：*She looked so forlorn, standing there in the rain.* 她站在雨中，顯得孤苦伶仃。**2** (of a place 地方) not cared for and with no people in it 淒涼的；荒蕪的：*Empty houses quickly take on a forlorn look.* 空無一人的房屋很快就顯得淒涼。**3** unlikely to succeed, come true, etc. 不大可能成功的；難以實現的：*She waited **in the forlorn hope** that he would one day come back to her.* 她幾乎毫無指望地等待他有一天會回到她的身邊。◇ *His father smiled weakly **in a forlorn attempt** to reassure him that everything was all right.* 他父親淡淡地一笑，枉然地試圖要他放心，一切都安然無恙。▶ **for·lorn·ly** *adv.*

form 🔑 /fɔːm; *NAmE* fɔːrm/ *noun, verb*

■ ***noun***

▸ TYPE 類型 **1** 🔑 [C] a type or variety of sth 類型；種類：*forms of transport/government/energy* 運輸種類；政體類型；能源種類 ◇ *one of the most common forms of cancer* 最普通的一種癌症 ◇ *all the millions of different life forms on the planet today* 當今地球上所有的幾百萬生命種類 ➲ see also ART FORM

▸ WAY STH IS/LOOKS 形式 **2** 🔑 [C, U] the particular way sth is, seems, looks or is presented 形式；外表；樣子：*The disease can take several different forms.* 這種疾病可能有幾種不同的形式。◇ *Help **in the form of** money will be very welcome.* 以錢的形式資助將十分受歡迎。◇ *Help arrived **in the form of** two police officers.* 來支援的是兩名警察。◇ *The training programme **takes the form of** a series of workshops.* 培訓課程採取一系列研討會的形式。◇ *Most political questions involve morality **in some form or other**.* 多數政治問題牽涉到這樣或那樣的道義性。◇ *We need to come to **some form of** agreement.* 我們需要達成某種形式的協議。◇ *I'm opposed to censorship **in any shape or form**.* 我反對任何形式的審查。◇ *This dictionary is also available in electronic form.* 這部詞典也有電子版本的。

▸ DOCUMENT 文件 **3** 🔑 [C] an official document containing questions and spaces for answers 表格：*an **application/entry/order form*** 申請 / 報名表；訂貨單 ◇ (*especially BrE*) *to **fill in a form*** 填表 ◇ (*especially NAmE*) *to **fill out a form*** 填表 ◇ *I filled in/out a form on their website.* 我在他們的網站上填了一張表。◇ *to complete a form* 填表 ◇ (*BrE*) *a **booking form*** 預訂單 ◇ (*NAmE*) *a **reservation form*** 預訂單

▸ SHAPE 形狀 **4** 🔑 [C] the shape of sb/sth; a person or thing of which only the shape can be seen 形狀；體形：*her slender form* 她苗條的身段 ◇ *The human form has changed little over the last 30 000 years.* * 3 萬多年以來，人的體形沒有多大變化。◇ *They made out a shadowy form in front of them.* 他們隱約認出了前面的模糊人影。

▸ ARRANGEMENT OF PARTS 結構 **5** [U] the arrangement of parts in a whole, especially in a work of art or piece of writing（尤指藝術作品或文章的）結構，形式：*In a novel, form and content are equally important.* 小說的形式和內容同樣重要。➲ SYNONYMS at STRUCTURE

▸ BEING FIT/HEALTHY 健壯；健康 **6** [U] (*BrE*) how fit and healthy sb is; the state of being fit and healthy 體能；良好的健康狀態：*After six months' training the whole team is in superb form.* 經過半年的訓練，全隊狀態極佳。◇ *I really need to get back **in form**.* 我實在需要恢復狀態。◇ *The horse was clearly **out of form**.* 這匹馬顯然狀態不佳。

▸ PERFORMANCE 表現 **7** [U] how well sb/sth is performing; the fact that sb/sth is performing well 表現狀態；良好表現：*Midfielder Elliott has shown disappointing form recently.* 中場隊員埃利奧特近來表現令人失望。◇ ***On current/present form** the party is heading for another election victory.* 就該黨目前情況來看，下屆選舉又會勝利。◇ *She signalled her return to form with a convincing victory.* 她令人信服的勝利顯示她已恢復狀態。◇ *He's right **on form*** (= performing well) *as a crazy science teacher in his latest movie.* 他在最近的一部電影中扮演瘋狂的理科教師，表現出色。◇ *The whole team was **on good form** and deserved the win.* 全隊表現良好，獲勝是理所當然的。◇ *She was **in great form*** (= happy and cheerful and full of energy) *at the wedding party.* 在婚宴上她歡欣雀躍。

▸ WAY OF DOING THINGS 做事方式 **8** [U, C] (*especially BrE*) the usual way of doing sth 慣常做法；常規；習俗：*What's the form when you apply for a research grant?* 申請科研補助金按常規應該怎麼辦？◇ *conventional social forms* 常規社會習俗 ◇ ***True to form*** (= as he usually does) *he arrived an hour late.* 他和往常一樣遲到了一小

F

時。◇ *Partners of employees are invited* ***as a matter of form***. 按慣例，雇員的配偶受到了邀請。 **9** [U] **good/bad ~** (*old-fashioned, BrE*) the way of doing things that is socially acceptable/not socially acceptable 禮貌；禮節

▸ **OF WORD 單詞 10** [C] a way of writing or saying a word that shows, for example, if it is plural or in a particular tense 詞形；形式： *the infinitive form of the verb* 動詞不定式

▸ **IN SCHOOL 學校 11** (*BrE, old-fashioned*) a class in a school 年級： *Who's your form teacher?* 你們的年級老師是誰？ ➲ see also SIXTH FORM **12 -former** (in compounds 構成複合詞) (*BrE, old-fashioned*) a student in the form mentioned at school …年級學生： *a third-former* 三年級學生 ➲ see also SIXTH-FORMER

F

IDM **take 'form** (*formal*) to gradually form into a particular shape; to gradually develop 逐漸成形；漸漸發展： *In her body a new life was taking form.* 一個新的生命在她的體內逐漸形成。 ➲ more at SHAPE *n.*

■ *verb*

▸ **START TO EXIST 開始存在 1** 🔑 [I, T] (especially of natural things 尤指自然事物) to begin to exist and gradually develop into a particular shape; to make sth begin to exist in a particular shape （使）出現，產生： *Flowers appeared, but fruits failed to form.* 開了花，但沒有結果。◇ *Storm clouds are forming on the horizon.* 天邊出現了暴雨雲。◇ **~ sth** *These hills were formed by glaciation.* 這些山丘是冰川作用形成的。 **2** 🔑 [I, T] to start to exist and develop; to make sth start to exist and develop （使）形成： *A plan formed in my head.* 一個計劃在我的頭腦中形成。◇ **~ sth** *I formed many close friendships at college.* 我大學時結交了許多密友。◇ *I didn't see enough of the play to form an opinion about it.* 我對這部戲劇瞭解得不夠，說不出什麼意見。 ➲ SYNONYMS at MAKE

▸ **MAKE SHAPE/FORM 使成形 3** 🔑 [T, often passive] to produce sth in a particular way or make it have a particular shape （使）成形，組成；製作： **~ sth** *Bend the wire so that it forms a 'V'.* 把鐵絲彎成 V 形。◇ *Rearrange the letters to form a new word.* 重新排列字母，組成另一單詞。◇ *Games can help children learn to form letters.* 遊戲可以幫助兒童學會組合字母。◇ *Do you know how to form the past tense?* 你知道怎樣構成過去時嗎？◇ **~ sth into sth** *Form the dough into balls with your hands.* 用手把生麪糰揉成一些球團。◇ **~ sth from/of sth** *The chain is formed from 136 links.* 這根鏈條由 136 個環組成。 **4** 🔑 [T, I] to move or arrange objects or people so that they are in a group with a particular shape; to become arranged in a group like this （使）排列成，排成： **~ sb/sth (up) (into sth)** ***to form a line/queue/circle*** 排成一行／長列／圈 ◇ *First get students to form groups of four.* 首先讓學生分成四人一組。◇ **~ (up) (into sth)** *Queues were already forming outside the theatre.* 劇院外已經在排隊了。◇ *The teams formed up into lines.* 各隊已整好了隊。

▸ **HAVE FUNCTION/ROLE 功能；作用 5** 🔑 [T] **~ sth** to have a particular function or pattern 有…功能；有…模式： *The trees form a natural protection from the sun's rays.* 樹木起天然的保護作用，遮擋了陽光的照射。 **6** *linking verb* **+ noun** to be sth 是；成為： *The castle forms the focal point of the city.* 這座城堡是城市的中心。◇ *The survey* ***formed part of*** *a larger programme of research.* 這個調查是研究計劃的一部份。◇ *These drawings will* ***form the basis of*** *the exhibition.* 這些畫作將成為展覽的基本部份。

▸ **ORGANIZATION 組織 7** 🔑 [T, I] **~ (sth)** to start a group of people, such as an organization, a committee, etc.; to come together in a group of this kind 組織；建立： *They hope to form the new government.* 他們希望組建新政府。◇ *He formed a band with some friends from school.* 他和來自學校的一些朋友組成一支樂隊。◇ *a newly-formed political party* 新建立的政黨 ◇ *The band formed in 2007.* 這支樂隊成立於 2007 年。

▸ **HAVE INFLUENCE ON 影響 8** [T] **~ sth** to have an influence on the way that sth develops 對…的發展有影響 SYN **mould** : *Positive and negative experiences form a child's character.* 正反兩方面的經歷都影響兒童性格的形成。

for·mal 🔑 /ˈfɔːml; *NAmE* ˈfɔːrml/ *adj.* **1** 🔑 (of a style of dress, speech, writing, behaviour, etc. 穿着、言語、行為等) very correct and suitable for official or important occasions 適合正式場合的；正規的；莊重的： *formal evening dress* 晚禮服 ◇ *The dinner was a formal affair.* 這是正式宴會。◇ *He kept the tone of the letter formal and businesslike.* 他使這封信保持正式公文的語氣。◇ *She has a very formal manner, which can seem unfriendly.* 她的舉止很是鄭重其事，有可能會顯得不友好。 OPP **informal 2** 🔑 official; following an agreed or official way of doing things 正式的；合乎規矩的： *formal legal processes* 正式法律程序 ◇ *to make a* ***formal apology/complaint/request*** 正式道歉／投訴／要求 ◇ *Formal diplomatic relations between the two countries were re-established in December.* 兩國於十二月重新建立了正式外交關係。◇ *It is time to put these arrangements on a slightly more formal basis.* 是應該把這些安排做得略為正式一點的時候了。 **3** 🔑 (of education or training 學校教育或培訓) received in a school, college or university, with lessons, exams, etc., rather than gained just through practical experience 正規的： *He has no formal teaching qualifications.* 他沒有正規的教學資歷證明。◇ *Young children are beginning their formal education sometimes as early as four years old.* 幼兒有時早在四歲時就開始接受正規教育。 **4** concerned with the way sth is done rather than what is done 方式上的；做法上的；形式上的： *Getting approval for the plan is a purely formal matter; nobody will seriously oppose it.* 尋求計劃獲得批准純粹是一個形式上的問題，沒有人會認真反對的。◇ *Critics have concentrated too much on the formal elements of her poetry, without really looking at what it is saying.* 評論家過多地集中評論她詩歌的形式，而沒有真正看其內容。 **5** (of a garden, room or building 花園、房間、建築物) arranged in a regular manner, according to a clear, exact plan 整齊的；佈置井然的： *delightful formal gardens, with terraced lawns and an avenue of trees* 精心佈置的有片片草坪和林蔭道的宜人花園 OPP **informal** ▸ **for·mal·ly** 🔑 /-məli/ *adv.* : *'How do you do?' she said formally.* "你好！" 她拘謹地說。◇ *The accounts were formally approved by the board.* 賬目已由董事會正式批准。◇ *Although not formally trained as an art historian, he is widely respected for his knowledge of the period.* 雖然他不是科班出身的藝術史學家，但他對這一時期的知識卻普遍為人尊重。

for·mal·de·hyde /fɔːˈmældɪhaɪd; *NAmE* fɔːrˈm-/ *noun* [U] **1** (*symb.* **CH_2O**) a gas with a strong smell 甲醛 **2** (also *technical* 術語 **for·mal·in** /ˈfɔːməlɪn; *NAmE* ˈfɔːrm-/) a liquid made by mixing formaldehyde and water, used for preserving BIOLOGICAL SPECIMENS, making plastics and as a DISINFECTANT 福爾馬林；甲醛水溶液

for·mal·ism /ˈfɔːməlɪzəm; *NAmE* ˈfɔːrm-/ *noun* [U] a style or method in art, music, literature, science, etc. that pays more attention to the rules and the correct arrangement and appearance of things than to inner meaning and feelings 形式主義 ▸ **for·mal·ist** /ˈfɔːməlɪst; *NAmE* ˈfɔːrm-/ *noun* **for·mal·ist** *adj.* [usually before noun] : *formalist theory* 形式主義理論

for·mal·ity /fɔːˈmæləti; *NAmE* fɔːrˈm-/ *noun* (*pl.* **-ies**) **1** [C, usually pl.] a thing that you must do as a formal or official part of a legal process, a social situation, etc. 正式手續： *to go through all the formalities necessary in order to get a gun licence* 辦理取得持槍執照的全部必要手續 ◇ *Let's skip the formalities and get down to business.* 咱們省去繁文縟節，開始討論實質問題吧。 **2** [C, usually sing.] a thing that you must do as part of an official process, but which has little meaning and will not affect what happens 例行公事： *He already knows he has the job so the interview is a mere formality.* 他已知道得到了這個工作，所以面試僅僅是走走過場。 **3** [U] correct and formal behaviour 遵守禮節： *Different levels of formality are appropriate in different situations.* 不同程度的注重禮節適用於不同場合。◇ *She greeted him with stiff formality.* 她拘謹地按禮節向他致意。

for·mal·ize (*BrE* also **-ise**) /ˈfɔːməlaɪz; *NAmE* ˈfɔːrm-/ *verb* **1 ~ sth** to make an arrangement, a plan or a relationship official 使（安排、計劃、關係）成為正式的： *They decided to formalize their relationship by getting married.* 他們決定結婚，正式確定關係。 **2 ~ sth**

to give sth a fixed structure or form by introducing rules（通過規則）使有固定體系，使定形： *The college has a highly formalized system of assessment.* 這所學院有一套十分固定的評估體系。 ▸ **for·mal·iza·tion, -isa·tion** /ˌfɔːməlaɪˈzeɪʃn; *NAmE* ˌfɔːrmələˈz-/ *noun* [U]

for·mat AW /ˈfɔːmæt; *NAmE* ˈfɔːrmæt/ *noun, verb*

■ ***noun*** **1** the general arrangement, plan, design, etc. of sth 總體安排；計劃；設計： *The format of the new quiz show has proved popular.* 新的智力競賽節目的總體安排結果證明很受歡迎。 **2** the shape and size of a book, magazine, etc.（出版物的）版式，開本： *They've brought out the magazine in a new format.* 他們用新的版式出版這雜誌。 **3** (*computing* 計) the way in which data is stored or held to be worked on by a computer 格式

■ ***verb*** (-tt-) **1 ~ sth** to prepare a computer disk so that data can be recorded on it 格式化 **2 ~ sth** (*technical* 術語) to arrange text in a particular way on a page or a screen 安排版式

for·ma·tion /fɔːˈmeɪʃn; *NAmE* fɔːrˈm-/ *noun* **1** [U] the action of forming sth; the process of being formed 組成；形成： *the formation of a new government* 組成新政府 ◇ *evidence of recent star formation in the galaxy* 銀河系新恒星形成的證據 **2** [C] a thing that has been formed, especially in a particular place or in a particular way 組成物；形成物： *rock formations* 岩層 **3** [U, C] a particular arrangement or pattern 編隊；隊形： *aircraft flying **in formation*** 編隊飛行的飛機 ◇ *formation flying* 編隊飛行 ◇ *The team usually plays in a 4-4-2 formation.* 這支球隊比賽通常排出的是 4–4–2 陣形。

for·ma·tive /ˈfɔːmətɪv; *NAmE* ˈfɔːrm-/ *adj.* [only before noun] having an important and lasting influence on the development of sth or of sb's character（對某事物或性格的發展）有重大影響的： *the **formative years** of childhood* 童年性格形成的時期

for·mer 🔑 /ˈfɔːmə(r); *NAmE* ˈfɔːrm-/ *adj.* [only before noun]

1 🔑 that used to exist in earlier times 以前的： *in former times* 從前 ◇ *the countries of the former Soviet Union* 前蘇聯國家 ◇ *This beautiful old building has been restored to **its former glory**.* 這座美麗的老建築物已恢復了昔日的壯觀。 **2** 🔑 that used to have a particular position or status in the past 昔日的；前： *the former world champion* 前世界冠軍 ◇ *my former boss/colleague/wife* 以前的老闆／同事；前妻 **3** 🔑 **the former ...** used to refer to the first of two things or people mentioned（兩者中）前者的： *The former option would be much more sensible.* 前一種選擇要明智得多。 ⊃ compare LATTER *adj.* (1) **4** 🔑 **the former** *pron.* the first of two things or people mentioned（兩者中的）前者： *He had to choose between giving up his job and giving up his principles. He chose the former.* 他得在放棄工作和放棄原則二者中擇其一。他選擇了前者。 ⊃ compare LATTER *n.*

IDM **be a shadow/ghost of your former ˈself** to not have the strength, influence, etc. that you used to have 失去昔日的力量（或影響等）；威風不再；不如當年

for·mer·ly 🔑 /ˈfɔːməli; *NAmE* ˈfɔːrmərli/ *adv.* in earlier times 以前；從前 SYN **previously**： *Namibia, formerly known as South West Africa* 納米比亞，舊稱西南非洲 ◇ *I learnt that the house had formerly been an inn.* 我得知這座房子以前是家客棧。 ◇ *John Marsh, formerly of London Road, Leicester, now living in France* 約翰 • 馬什，以前家在萊斯特市倫敦路，現居住在法國

For·mica™ /fɔːˈmaɪkə; *NAmE* fɔːrˈm-/ *noun* [U] a hard plastic that can resist heat, used for covering work surfaces, etc. 福米加（商標，用作貼面板等的抗熱硬塑料）

for·mic acid /ˌfɔːmɪk ˈæsɪd; *NAmE* ˌfɔːrmɪk/ *noun* [U] (*chemistry* 化) an acid made from CARBON MONOXIDE and steam. It is also present in a liquid produced by some ANTS. 甲酸；蟻酸

for·mid·able /ˈfɔːmɪdəbl; fəˈmɪd-; *NAmE* ˈfɔːrm-; fərˈm-/ *adj.* if people, things or situations are **formidable**, you feel fear and/or respect for them, because they are impressive or powerful, or because they seem very difficult 可怕的；令人敬畏的；難對付的： *In debate he was a formidable opponent.* 在辯論中他是位難應付的對手。 ◇ *She has a formidable list of qualifications.* 她有一長串令人敬畏的資歷。 ◇ *The two players together make a formidable combination.* 這兩個隊員配對兒，難以對付。 ◇ *The task was a formidable one.* 這任務非常艱巨。 ◇ *They had to overcome formidable obstacles.* 他們得克服重重障礙。 ▸ **for·mid·ably** /-əbli/ *adv.*： *He now has the chance to prove himself in a formidably difficult role.* 現在他的任務十分艱巨，有機會證明自己的能力。 ◇ *She's formidably intelligent.* 她聰明絕頂。

form·less /ˈfɔːmləs; *NAmE* ˈfɔːrm-/ *adj.* without a clear or definite shape or structure 無明確形狀的；無定形的；結構不清的： *formless dreams* 雜亂的夢 ▸ **form·less·ness** *noun* [U]

F

for·mula 🔑 AW /ˈfɔːmjələ; *NAmE* ˈfɔːrm-/ *noun* (*pl.* **for·mu·las** or, especially in scientific use, 科技用語常作 **for·mu·lae** /-liː/)

1 🔑 [C] (*mathematics* 數) a series of letters, numbers or symbols that represent a rule or law 公式；方程式；計算式： *This formula is used to calculate the area of a circle.* 這個公式用於計算圓的面積。 **2** 🔑 [C] (*chemistry* 化) letters and symbols that show the parts of a chemical COMPOUND, etc. 分子式： *CO is the formula for carbon monoxide.* * CO 是一氧化碳的分子式。 **3** 🔑 [C] a particular method of doing or achieving sth 方案；方法： *They're trying to work out a **peace formula** acceptable to both sides in the dispute.* 他們正在設法制訂出一個爭執雙方都可以接受的和平方案。 ◇ **~ for sth/for doing sth** *There's no **magic formula** for a perfect marriage.* 沒有一個達到完美婚姻的神奇方法。 **4** 🔑 [C] a list of the things that sth is made from, giving the amount of each substance to use 配方；處方；藥方： *the secret formula for the blending of the whisky* 調配威士忌的秘方 **5** (also **ˈformula milk**) [U, C] (*especially NAmE*) a type of liquid food for babies, given instead of breast milk 配方奶（母乳的替代品） **6** [C] a class of racing car, based on engine size, etc. 方程式（按發動機大小等對賽車的分級）： *Formula One racing™* 一級方程式賽車 **7** [C] a fixed form of words used in a particular situation（特定場合的）慣用詞語，套話： *legal formulae* 法律慣用詞語 ◇ *The minister keeps coming out with the same tired formulas.* 這個牧師開口便是千篇一律、使人厭倦的套話。

for·mu·la·ic /ˌfɔːmjuˈleɪɪk; *NAmE* ˌfɔːrm-/ *adj.* (*formal*) made up of fixed patterns of words or ideas 由固定套話堆砌的；公式化構思的： *Traditional stories make use of formulaic expressions like 'Once upon a time ...'.* 傳統故事採用"從前…"一類的套語。

for·mu·late AW /ˈfɔːmjuleɪt; *NAmE* ˈfɔːrm-/ *verb* **1** to create or prepare sth carefully, giving particular attention to the details 制訂；規劃；構想；準備： **~ sth** *to **formulate a policy/theory/plan/proposal*** 制訂政策；創立理論；構想計劃；準備建議 ◇ *The compost is specially formulated for pot plants.* 此混合肥料專門用於盆栽植物。 ◇ **~ sth to do sth** *This new kitchen cleaner is formulated to cut through grease and dirt.* 這種新的廚房清潔劑能去除油漬和污垢。 **2 ~ sth** to express your ideas in carefully chosen words 確切表達；認真闡述： *She has lots of good ideas, but she has difficulty formulating them.* 她有很多好主意，但就是不善於表達。 ▸ **for·mu·la·tion** AW /ˌfɔːmjuˈleɪʃn; *NAmE* ˌfɔːrm-/ *noun* [U, C]： *the formulation of new policies* 新政策的制訂

for·ni·cate /ˈfɔːnɪkeɪt; *NAmE* ˈfɔːrn-/ *verb* [I] (*formal, disapproving*) to have sex with sb that you are not married to 私通；通姦 ▸ **for·ni·ca·tion** /ˌfɔːnɪˈkeɪʃn; *NAmE* ˌfɔːrn-/ *noun* [U] **for·ni·ca·tor** *noun*

for·sake /fəˈseɪk; *NAmE* fərˈs-/ *verb* (**for·sook** /fəˈsʊk; *NAmE* fərˈs-/, **for·saken** /fəˈseɪkən; *NAmE* fərˈs-/) (*literary*) **1 ~ sb/sth (for sb/sth)** to leave sb/sth, especially when you have a responsibility to stay 拋棄，遺棄，離開（尤指不履行責任） SYN **abandon**： *He had made it clear to his wife that he would never forsake her.* 他明確地向妻子說，永遠不離開她。 **2 ~ sth (for sb/sth)** to stop doing sth, or leave sth, especially sth that you enjoy 摒棄，離開（尤指喜愛的事物） SYN **renounce**： *She forsook the glamour of the city and went to live in the* *wilds of Scotland.* 她拋開城市的絢爛，去蘇格蘭荒原居住。➲ see also GODFORSAKEN

for·sooth /fəˈsuːθ; *NAmE* fərˈ-/ *adv.* (*old use* or *humorous*) used to emphasize a statement, especially in order to show surprise（用以強調，尤為表示驚訝）實在，確實

for·swear /fɔːˈsweə(r); *NAmE* fɔːrˈswer/ *verb* (**for·swore** /fɔːˈswɔː(r); *NAmE* fɔːrˈs-/, **for·sworn** /fɔːˈswɔːn; *NAmE* fɔːrˈswɔːrn/) **~ sth** (*formal* or *literary*) to stop doing or using sth; to make a promise that you will stop doing or using sth 放棄；發誓戒除 **SYN** **renounce**: *The group forswears all worldly possessions.* 這個團體放棄一切塵世財物。◇ *The country has not forsworn the use of chemical weapons.* 該國並未保證禁用化學武器。

for·sythia /fɔːˈsaɪθiə; *NAmE* fərˈsɪθiə/ *noun* [U, C] a bush that has small bright yellow flowers in the early spring 連翹，金鐘花（灌木，早春開小黃花）

fort /fɔːt; *NAmE* fɔːrt/ *noun* **1** a building or buildings built in order to defend an area against attack 要塞；堡壘；城堡 ➲ VISUAL VOCAB page V15 **2** (*NAmE*) a place where soldiers live and have their training 兵營；軍營；營地：*Fort Drum* 德魯姆堡

IDM **hold the ˈfort** (*BrE*) (*NAmE* **hold down the ˈfort**) (*informal*) to have the responsibility for sth or care of sb while other people are away or out 代為負責（某事）；代為照看（某人）：*Why not have a day off? I'll hold the fort for you.* 幹嗎不休息一天？我來為你代管。

forte /ˈfɔːteɪ; *NAmE* ˈfɔːrt-/ *noun, adv.*

■ ***noun*** /*NAmE* also fɔːrt/ [sing.] a thing that sb does particularly well 專長；特長：*Languages were never my forte.* 語言從來就不是我的強項。

■ ***adv.*** (*music* 音) played or sung loudly（演奏或歌唱）強，強有力 **OPP** **piano** ▸ **forte** *adj.*

For·tean /ˈfɔːtiən; *NAmE* ˈfɔːrt-/ *adj.* involving or relating to things that cannot be explained by science 福庭現象的；無法用科學解釋的；超自然的；神秘莫測的 **SYN** **paranormal**

forth /fɔːθ; *NAmE* fɔːrθ/ *adv.* (*literary* except in particular idioms and phrasal verbs 文學用語，但在某些習語和短語動詞中例外) **1** away from a place; out 離去；外出：*They set forth at dawn.* 他們在黎明時出發。◇ *Huge chimneys belched forth smoke and grime.* 巨大的煙囱冒出煙和灰塵。**2** towards a place; forwards 向前；向某處：*Water gushed forth from a hole in the rock.* 水從岩洞裏湧出。➲ see also BRING FORTH at BRING *v.*

IDM **from that day/time ˈforth** (*literary*) beginning on that day; from that time 從那天起；從那時以後 ➲ more at BACK *adv.*, SO *adv.*

the ˌForth ˈBridge *noun*

IDM **like painting the Forth ˈBridge** (*BrE*) used to describe a job that never seems to end because by the time you get to the end you have to start at the beginning again 永無止境的工作（快完成時又得重新開始）**ORIGIN** From the name of a very large bridge over the river Forth in Scotland. 源自蘇格蘭福斯河（river Forth）上巨型的福斯橋。

forth·com·ing **AW** /ˌfɔːθˈkʌmɪŋ; *NAmE* ˌfɔːrθ-/ *adj.* **1** [only before noun] going to happen, be published, etc. very soon 即將發生（或出版等）的：*the forthcoming elections* 即將舉行的選舉 ◇ *a list of forthcoming books* 近期將出版書籍的目錄 ◇ *the band's forthcoming UK tour* 樂隊即將在英國的巡迴演出 **2** [not before noun] ready or made available when needed 現成；隨要隨有：*Financial support was not forthcoming.* 財政支援尚未到手。**3** [not before noun] willing to give information about sth 樂於提供信息：*She's never very forthcoming about her plans.* 她一直不很願意說出自己的計劃。**OPP** **unforthcoming**

forth·right /ˈfɔːθraɪt; *NAmE* ˈfɔːrθ-/ *adj.* direct and honest in manner and speech 直率的；直截了當的；坦誠的 **SYN** **frank**: *a woman of forthright views* 觀點明確的女子 ▸ **forth·right·ly** *adv.* **forth·right·ness** *noun* [U]

forth·with /ˌfɔːθˈwɪθ; -ˈwɪð; *NAmE* ˌfɔːrθ-/ *adv.* (*formal*) immediately; at once 立即；馬上；立刻：*The agreement between us is terminated forthwith.* 我們之間的協議立即終止。

for·ti·eth ➲ FORTY

for·ti·fi·ca·tion /ˌfɔːtɪfɪˈkeɪʃn; *NAmE* ˌfɔːrt-/ *noun* **1** [C, usually pl.] a tower, wall, gun position, etc. built to defend a place against attack 碉堡；圍牆；炮台；防禦工事：*the ramparts and fortifications of the Old Town* 舊城區的城牆和城堡 **2** [U] the act of fortifying or making sth stronger 築城；設防；加強：*plans for the fortification of the city* 城市設防計劃

for·tify /ˈfɔːtɪfaɪ; *NAmE* ˈfɔːrt-/ *verb* (**for·ti·fies**, **for·ti·fy·ing**, **for·ti·fied**, **for·ti·fied**) **1 ~ sth** (**against sb/sth**) to make a place more able to resist attack, especially by building high walls 築防禦工事；（尤指）築城防禦：*a fortified town* 設防的城鎮 **2 ~ sb/yourself** (**against sb/sth**) to make sb/yourself feel stronger, braver, etc.（在物質或精神上）加強，增強：*He fortified himself against the cold with a hot drink.* 他喝了一杯熱飲禦寒。**3** to make a feeling or an attitude stronger 增強（感覺或態度）：*The news merely fortified their determination.* 這消息僅僅增強了他們的決心。**4 ~ sth** (**with sth**) to increase the strength or quality of food or drink by adding sth to it（加入某物）強化（食品或飲料）；提高營養價值：*Sherry is **fortified wine*** (= wine with extra alcohol added). 雪利酒是添加了酒精的葡萄酒。◇ *cereal fortified with extra vitamins* 添加維生素的穀類食物

for·ti·ori ➲ A FORTIORI

for·tis·simo /fɔːˈtɪsɪməʊ; *NAmE* fɔːrˈtɪsɪmoʊ/ *adv.* (*abbr.* **ff**) (*music* 音) played or sung very loudly（演奏或歌唱）很強 **OPP** **pianissimo**

for·ti·tude /ˈfɔːtɪtjuːd; *NAmE* ˈfɔːrtətuːd/ *noun* [U] (*formal*) courage shown by sb who is suffering great pain or facing great difficulties（在巨大痛苦或困難面前表現出的）勇氣，膽量，剛毅 **SYN** **bravery, courage**

Fort Knox /ˌfɔːt ˈnɒks; *NAmE* ˌfɔːrt ˈnɑːks/ *noun*

IDM **be like/as safe as Fort ˈKnox** (of a building 建築物) to be strongly built, often with many locks, strong doors, guards, etc., so that it is difficult for people to enter and the things kept there are safe 堅固且戒備森嚴；固若金湯：*This home of yours is like Fort Knox.* 你這所房子可以說是固若金湯。**ORIGIN** From the name of the military base in Kentucky where most of the US's store of gold is kept. 源自美國肯塔基州存放美國大部份黃金儲備的軍事基地名。

fort·night /ˈfɔːtnaɪt; *NAmE* ˈfɔːrt-/ *noun* [usually sing.] (*BrE*) two weeks 兩星期：*a fortnight's holiday* 兩週的假期 ◇ *a fortnight ago* 兩星期以前 ◇ *in a fortnight's time* 在兩週的時間內 ◇ *He's had three accidents in the past fortnight.* 在過去兩週他出了三次事故。

fort·night·ly /ˈfɔːtnaɪtli; *NAmE* ˈfɔːrt-/ *adj.* (*BrE*) happening once a fortnight 兩星期一次的：*Meetings take place at fortnightly intervals.* 每兩週開一次會。▸ **fort·night·ly** *adv.*: *The committee meets fortnightly.* 委員會兩星期開一次會。

fort·ress /ˈfɔːtrəs; *NAmE* ˈfɔːrt-/ *noun* a building or place that has been made stronger and protected against attack 城堡；堡壘；要塞；設防的地方：*a fortress town enclosed by four miles of ramparts* 由四英里長的城牆圍着的設防城鎮 ◇ *Fear of terrorist attack has turned the conference centre into a fortress.* 由於害怕恐怖分子襲擊，會議中心已變成了堡壘。

for·tuit·ous /fɔːˈtjuːɪtəs; *NAmE* fɔːrˈtuː-/ *adj.* (*formal*) happening by chance, especially a lucky chance that brings a good result 偶然發生的；（尤指）巧合的 ▸ **for·tuit·ous·ly** *adv.*

for·tu·nate /ˈfɔːtʃənət; *NAmE* ˈfɔːrtʃ-/ *adj.* having or bringing an advantage, an opportunity, a piece of good luck, etc. 幸運的；交好運的；吉利的 **SYN** **lucky**: **~ (to do sth)** *I have been fortunate enough to visit many parts of the world as a lecturer.* 我很有福氣，去過世界許多地方作演講。◇ **~ (in having ...)** *I was fortunate in having a good teacher.* 我很幸運，有位好老師。◇ *Remember those less fortunate than yourselves.* 要記住那些不如你們幸運的人。◇ **~ (for sb) (that ...)** *It was very **fortunate** for him that I arrived on time.* 算他運氣好，我準時到了。**OPP** **unfortunate**

for·tu·nate·ly /ˈfɔːtʃənətli; *NAmE* ˈfɔːrtʃ-/ *adv.* by good luck 幸運地；交好運地；吉利地 SYN **luckily**：*I was late, but fortunately the meeting hadn't started.* 我遲到了，不過幸好會議還沒有開始。◇ *Fortunately for him, he was very soon offered another job.* 他運氣好，很快就有人聘請他做另一個工作。OPP **unfortunately**

for·tune /ˈfɔːtʃuːn; *NAmE* ˈfɔːrtʃən/ *noun*
1 [U] chance or luck, especially in the way it affects people's lives（尤指影響人生的）機會，運氣：*I have **had the good fortune to** work with some brilliant directors.* 我有幸與一些卓越的主管人員共事。◇ ***By a stroke of fortune** he found work almost immediately.* 他運氣好，幾乎立刻找到了工作。◇ ***Fortune smiled on me*** (= I had good luck). 我交了好運。 **2** [C] a large amount of money 大筆的錢；巨款：*He **made a fortune** in real estate.* 他在房地產上發了財。◇ *She inherited a share of the family fortune.* 她繼承了家庭的一份財產。◇ *A car like that costs **a small fortune**.* 像這樣的轎車要花一大筆錢。◇ *You don't have to **spend a fortune** to give your family tasty, healthy meals.* 讓家裏人吃味道好又健康的餐食並不需要花許多錢。◇ *She is hoping her US debut will be the first step on the road to **fame and fortune**.* 她希望她在美國的首次演出將是她走上名利雙收之路的第一步。◇ *That ring must be **worth a fortune**.* 那隻戒指肯定要值好多錢。 **3** [C, usually pl., U] the good and bad things that happen to a person, family, country, etc.（個人、家庭、國家等的）發展變化的趨勢，命運，際遇：*the changing fortunes of the film industry* 電影業的變遷 ◇ *the fortunes of war* 戰爭的局勢 ◇ *a reversal of fortune(s)* 命運的扭轉 **4** [C] a person's FATE or future（個人的）命運，前途：*She can **tell your fortune** by looking at the lines on your hand.* 她可憑看手紋替你算命。IDM see HOSTAGE, SEEK ➲ see also SOLDIER OF FORTUNE

ˈfortune cookie *noun* a thin hollow biscuit/cookie, served in Chinese restaurants, containing a short message that predicts what will happen to you in the future 籤語餅，幸運餅乾（中國餐館提供的薄脆餅，內有預測命運的小紙條）

ˈfortune hunter *noun* a person who tries to become rich by marrying sb with a lot of money（企圖通過跟有錢人結婚）獵財的人，攀龍附鳳的人

ˈfortune-teller *noun* a person who claims to have magic powers and who tells people what will happen to them in the future 給人算命的人；算命先生

forty /ˈfɔːti; *NAmE* ˈfɔːrti/
1 *number* 40 四十 **2** *noun* **the for·ties** [pl.] numbers, years or temperatures from 40 to 49 四十幾；四十年代
▸ **fortieth** /ˈfɔːtiəθ; *NAmE* ˈfɔːrt-/ *ordinal number, noun* HELP There are examples of how to use ordinal numbers at the entry for **fifth**. 序數詞用法示例見 fifth 條。
IDM **in your forties** between the ages of 40 and 49 * 40 多歲

the ˌforty-ninth ˈparallel *noun* the line on a map that is 49° north of the EQUATOR, thought of as forming the border between western Canada and the US 北緯 49 度緯線（據認為形成加拿大西部和美國之間的邊境線）

ˌforty ˈwinks *noun* [pl.] (*informal*) a short sleep, especially during the day（尤指白天）打盹，小睡，午睡：*I'll feel much better when I've had forty winks.* 我打個盹就會感到好得多。

forum /ˈfɔːrəm/ *noun* **1** ~ (**for sth**) a place where people can exchange opinions and ideas on a particular issue; a meeting organized for this purpose 公共討論場所；論壇；討論會：*Television is now an important forum for political debate.* 電視現在成了政治辯論的重要平台。◇ *an Internet forum* 互聯網論壇 ◇ *to hold an international forum on drug abuse* 舉行藥物濫用問題國際論壇 ➲ COLLOCATIONS at EMAIL **2** (in ancient Rome) a public place where meetings were held（古羅馬）公共集會場所

for·ward /ˈfɔːwəd; *NAmE* ˈfɔːrwərd/ *adv., adj., verb, noun*
■ *adv.* **1** (also **for·wards** especially in *BrE*) towards a place or position that is in front 向前：*She leaned forward and kissed him on the cheek.* 她傾身向前，吻了他的面頰。◇ *He took two steps forward.* 他向前走了兩步。◇ *They ran forward to welcome her.* 他們跑向前去歡迎她。OPP **back, backward(s)** **2** towards a good result 進展；前進：*We consider this agreement to be an important **step forward**.* 我們認為，這項協定是向前邁出了重要的一步。◇ *Cutting our costs is the only **way forward**.* 降低成本是我們發展的唯一途徑。◇ *We are not getting any **further forward** with the discussion.* 我們的討論沒有取得任何進展。◇ *The project will **go forward*** (= continue) *as planned.* 這個項目將按計劃繼續進行。OPP **backward(s)** **3** towards the future; ahead in time 向將來；往後：***Looking forward**, we hope to expand our operations in several of our overseas branches.* 展望未來，我們希望拓展其中幾家海外分公司的業務。◇ *The next scene takes the story forward five years.* 下一個場面是描述故事中五年後的情況。◇ (*old use*) *from this day forward* 從今天起 **4** earlier; sooner 提前：*It was decided to bring the meeting forward two weeks.* 已決定把會議提前兩週。 **5** (*technical* 術語) in or towards the front part of a ship or plane 在（或向）船頭；在（或向）機首：*The main cabin is situated forward of* (= in front of) *the mast.* 主艙在桅杆的前面。➲ see also LOOK FORWARD at LOOK *v.*, PUT FORWARD at PUT *v.*
IDM **ˌgoing/ˌmoving ˈforward** (*formal* or *business* 商) in the future, starting from now 將來；以後；從現在起：*We have a very solid financial position going forward.* 今後我們會有非常穩健的財務狀況。➲ more at BACKWARD(S), CLOCK *n.*, FOOT *n.*
■ *adj.* **1** [only before noun] directed or moving towards the front 向前的；前進的：*The door opened, blocking his **forward movement**.* 門開了，擋住他前進的路。◇ *a **forward pass*** (= in a sports game) 向前傳球 **2** [only before noun] (*technical* 術語) located in front, especially on a ship, plane or other vehicle（尤指船、飛機或其他交通工具）前部的，前面的：*the forward cabins* 前部艙室 ◇ *A bolt may have fallen off the plane's forward door.* 飛機前艙門的一個門閂可能脫落了。 **3** relating to the future 未來的；將來的：*the forward movement of history* 歷史的向前發展 ◇ *A little **forward planning** at the outset can save you a lot of expense.* 一開始就為未來作點打算能節約很多開支。◇ *The plans are still **no further forward** than they were last month.* 計劃無絲毫進展，仍是上個月的老樣子。 **4** behaving towards sb in a manner which is too confident or too informal 魯莽的；冒失的；無禮的：*I hope you don't think I'm being too forward.* 我希望你不要認為我太冒失。➲ compare BACKWARD
■ *verb* **1** (*formal*) to send or pass goods or information to sb 發送，寄（商品或信息）：**~ sth to sb** *We will be forwarding our new catalogue to you next week.* 我們將於下星期給你寄上新的商品目錄。◇ **~ sb sth** *We will be forwarding you our new catalogue next week.* 我們將於下星期給你寄上新的商品目錄。◇ **~ sth** *to forward a request/complaint/proposal* 提出要求／投訴／建議 **2** to send a letter, etc. received at the address a person used to live at to their new address（按新地址）轉寄，轉投，轉交 SYN **send on**：**~ sth (to sb)** *Could you forward any mail to us in New York?* 你能不能把所有信件轉寄到紐約給我們？◇ **~ (sth)** *I put 'please forward' on the envelope.* 我在信封上寫了"請轉遞"。 **3 ~ sth** (*formal*) to help to improve or develop sth 促進；有助於…的發展；增進 SYN **further**：*He saw the assignment as a way to forward his career.* 他把這項任務看作事業發展的途徑。➲ see also FAST-FORWARD
■ *noun* an attacking player whose position is near the front of a team in some sports（運動隊的）前鋒 ➲ compare BACK *n.* (8)

ˈforwarding address *noun* a new address to which letters should be sent on from an old address that sb has moved away from（信件應轉遞的）新地址

ˈforward-looking *adj.* (*approving*) planning for the future; willing to consider modern ideas and methods 向前看的；有遠見的；有進步思想的

F

for·ward·ness /ˈfɔːwədnəs; *NAmE* ˈfɔːrwərd-/ *noun* [U] behaviour that is too confident or too informal 魯莽；冒失；無禮；孟浪

ˈforward slash *noun* the symbol (/) used in computer commands and in Internet addresses to separate the different parts 正斜槓（用於計算機命令和互聯網地址）➲ compare BACKSLASH

for·went *past tense* of FORGO

fos·sick /ˈfɒsɪk; *NAmE* ˈfɑːs-/ *verb* (*AustralE, NZE, informal*) **1** [I] **~ (through sth)** to search through sth（在…中）搜尋，查找：*He spent ages fossicking through the documents.* 他花了老半天時間在那些文件中搜尋。**2** [I] to search for gold in mines that are no longer used（在廢礦中）淘金

F

fos·sil /ˈfɒsl; *NAmE* ˈfɑːsl/ *noun* **1** the remains of an animal or a plant which have become hard and turned into rock 化石：*fossils over two million years old* 兩百多萬年的化石 **2** (*informal, disapproving*) an old person, especially one who is unable to accept new ideas or adapt to changes 老人；（尤指）老頑固，老古董

ˈfossil fuel *noun* [C, U] fuel such as coal or oil, that was formed over millions of years from the remains of animals or plants 礦物燃料（如煤或石油）➲ compare BIOMASS (2) ➲ **VISUAL VOCAB** page V6

fos·sil·ize (*BrE* also **-ise**) /ˈfɒsəlaɪz; *NAmE* ˈfɑːs-/ *verb* **1** [T, usually passive, I] **~ (sth)** to become or make sth become a fossil（使）變成化石，石化：*fossilized bones* 成為化石的骨骼 **2** [I, T] **~ (sb/sth)** (*disapproving*) to become, or make sb/sth become, fixed and unable to change or develop（使人或物）僵化 ▸ **fos·sil·iza·tion**, **-isa·tion** /ˌfɒsəlaɪˈzeɪʃn; *NAmE* ˌfɑːsələˈz-/ *noun* [U]

fos·ter /ˈfɒstə(r); *NAmE* ˈfɔːs-; ˈfɑːs-/ *verb, adj.*

■ *verb* **1** [T] **~ sth** to encourage sth to develop 促進；助長；培養；鼓勵 **SYN** **encourage, promote**：*The club's aim is to foster better relations within the community.* 俱樂部的宗旨是促進團體內部的關係。**2** [T, I] **~ (sb)** (*especially BrE*) to take another person's child into your home for a period of time, without becoming his or her legal parents 代養，撫育，照料（他人子女一段時間）：*They have fostered over 60 children during the past ten years.* 在過去十年間，他們撫育了 60 多個兒童。◇ *We couldn't adopt a child, so we decided to foster.* 我們不能領養孩子，所以決定代養一個。➲ **COLLOCATIONS** at CHILD ➲ compare ADOPT (1)

■ *adj.* [only before noun] used with some nouns in connection with the fostering of a child（與某些代養有關的名詞連用）：*a* ***foster mother/father/family*** 代養母親／父親；代養的家庭 ◇ ***foster parents*** 代養父母 ◇ *a* ***foster child*** 代養的小孩 ◇ *a* ***foster home*** 寄養家庭 ◇ ***foster care*** 寄養照管

fought *past tense, past part.* of FIGHT

foul /faʊl/ *adj., verb, noun*

■ *adj.* (**foul·er**, **foul·est**) **1** dirty and smelling bad 骯髒惡臭的；難聞的：***foul air/breath*** 污濁難聞的空氣／氣息 ◇ *a* ***foul-smelling*** *prison* 臭烘烘的監獄 ➲ **SYNONYMS** at DISGUSTING **2** (*especially BrE*) very unpleasant; very bad 很令人不快的；很壞的：*She's in a* ***foul mood.*** 她的情緒很糟。◇ *His boss has a* ***foul temper.*** 他的老闆脾氣很壞。◇ *This tastes foul.* 這個味道難吃。**3** (of language 語言) including rude words and swearing 充滿髒話的；辱罵性的；下流的 **SYN** **offensive**：***foul language*** 髒話 ◇ *I'm sick of her* ***foul mouth*** (= habit of swearing). 我討厭她一開口就罵人的那張臭嘴。◇ *He called her the foulest names imaginable.* 他用最下流的話辱罵她。**4** (of weather 天氣) very bad, with strong winds and rain 惡劣的；風雨交加的：*a foul night* 風雨交加的夜晚 **5** (*literary*) very evil or cruel 邪惡的；殘忍的 **SYN** **abominable**：*a* ***foul crime/murder*** 邪惡的罪行；惡毒的謀殺 ▸ **foul·ly** /ˈfaʊlli/ *adv.*：*He swore foully.* 他惡毒地詛咒。◇ *She had been foully murdered during the night.* 她在夜間被殘忍地謀殺了。**foul·ness** *noun* [U]：*The air was heavy with the stink of damp and foulness.* 空氣中有一股潮濕的惡臭味。

IDM **fall foul of ˈsb/ˈsth** to get into trouble with a person or an organization because of doing sth wrong or illegal（因做錯事或不法行為）與…發生麻煩，與…產生糾葛，冒犯：*to fall foul of the law* 觸犯了法律 ➲ more at CRY *v.*, FAIR *adj.*

■ *verb* **1** [T] **~ sb** (in sport 體育運動) to do sth to another player that is against the rules of the game（對對手）犯規：*He was fouled inside the penalty area.* 在罰球區內對方隊員對他犯規。**2** [I, T] **~ (sth)** (in BASEBALL 棒球) to hit the ball outside the playing area 擊球出界 **3** [T] **~ sth** to make sth dirty, especially with waste matter from the body（尤指用糞便）弄髒，污染：*Do not permit your dog to foul the grass.* 禁止狗在草地便溺。**4** [T, I] to become caught or twisted in sth and stop it working or moving（被）纏住：**~ sth (up)** *The rope fouled the propeller.* 繩索纏住了螺旋槳。◇ **~ (up)** *A rope fouled up* (= became twisted) *as we pulled the sail down.* 我們收帆時有一根繩索纏住了。

PHR V **ˌfoul ˈup** (*informal*) to make a lot of mistakes; to do sth badly 大量出錯；搞糟：*I've fouled up badly again, haven't I?* 我又搞砸了，是不是？➲ related noun FOUL-UP **ˌfoul sth↔ˈup** (*informal*) to spoil sth, especially by doing sth wrong 把…搞糟；弄亂 ➲ related noun FOUL-UP

■ *noun* (in sport 體育運動) an action that is against the rules of the game 犯規：*It was a clear foul by Ford on the goalkeeper.* 這明顯是福特對守門員犯規。◇ (*NAmE*) *to hit a foul* (= in BASEBALL, a ball that is too far left or right, outside the lines that mark the side of the field)（棒球）擊球出界 ➲ see also PROFESSIONAL FOUL

ˈfoul ball *noun* (in BASEBALL 棒球) a hit that goes outside the allowed area 界外球

ˈfoul line *noun* **1** (in BASEBALL 棒球) either of two lines that show the area inside which the ball must be hit 邊線 **2** (in BASKETBALL 籃球) a line from which a player is allowed to try to throw the ball into the BASKET after a foul 罰球線

ˌfoul-ˈmouthed *adj.* using rude, offensive language 說下流話的；口出惡言的：*a foul-mouthed racist* 口出惡言的種族主義分子

ˌfoul ˈplay *noun* [U] **1** criminal or violent activity that causes sb's death 謀殺罪行；暴力致死行為：*Police immediately began an investigation, but did not suspect foul play* (= did not suspect that the person had been murdered). 警方立即開始調查，但沒有懷疑謀殺。**2** (*BrE*) dishonest or unfair behaviour, especially during a sports game（尤指體育比賽中的）犯規動作，不公平行為

ˈfoul-up *noun* (*informal*) a problem caused by bad organization or a stupid mistake（因組織不當或愚蠢錯誤而引起的）混亂，差錯

found 0-w **AW** /faʊnd/ *verb*

1 0-w **~ sth** to start sth, such as an organization or an institution, especially by providing money 創建，創辦（組織或機構，尤指提供資金）**SYN** **establish**：*to found a club/company* 創辦俱樂部／公司 ◇ *Her family founded the college in 1895.* 她的家族於 1895 年創辦了這所學院。**2** 0-w **~ sth** to be the first to start building and living in a town or country 建立，興建（城鎮或國家）：*The town was founded by English settlers in 1790.* 這座城鎮是英格蘭移民於 1790 年建立的。**3** [usually passive] **~ sth (on sth)** to base sth on sth 把…基於；把…建立在：*Their marriage was founded on love and mutual respect.* 他們的婚姻建立在愛情和互相尊重的基礎上。➲ see also ILL-FOUNDED, UNFOUNDED, WELL FOUNDED **4** **~ sth** (*technical* 術語) to melt metal and pour it into a MOULD; to make objects using this process 熔鑄；鑄造 ➲ see also FIND *v.*

foun·da·tion 0-w **AW** /faʊnˈdeɪʃn/ *noun*

1 0-w [C, usually pl.] a layer of bricks, concrete, etc. that forms the solid underground base of a building 地基；房基；基礎：*The builders are now beginning* ***to lay the foundations*** *of the new school.* 建築工人正開始給新校舍打地基。◇ *The explosion shook the foundations of the houses nearby.* 爆炸震撼了附近房屋的地基。➲ **SYNONYMS** at BOTTOM **2** 0-w [C, U] a principle, an idea or a fact that sth is based on and that it grows from 基本原理；根據；基礎：*Respect and friendship provide a* ***solid foundation*** *for marriage.* 尊重和友愛是婚姻的牢固基礎。◇ *The rumour is totally* ***without foundation*** (= not based on any facts). 這謠傳毫無事實根據。◇ *These stories have* *no foundation* (= are not based on any facts). 這些故事純屬虛構。➲ SYNONYMS at BASIS **3** 🔑 [C] an organization that is established to provide money for a particular purpose, for example for scientific research or charity 基金會：*The money will go to the San Francisco AIDS Foundation.* 這筆錢將交給舊金山艾滋病基金會。 **4** 🔑 [U] the act of starting a new institution or organization（機構或組織的）創建，創辦 SYN **establishment**：*The organization has grown enormously since its foundation in 1955.* 該組織自 1955 年創建以來已有重大的發展。 **5** [U] a skin-coloured cream that is put on the face underneath other make-up（化妝打底用的）粉底霜 ➲ VISUAL VOCAB page V60

IDM **shake/rock the 'foundations of sth | shake/rock sth to its 'foundations** to cause people to question their basic beliefs about sth 從根本上動搖：*This issue has shaken the foundations of French politics.* 這個問題從根本上動搖了法國的政治。

foun'dation course *noun* (*BrE*) a general course at a college that prepares students for longer or more difficult courses 基礎課程

foun'dation stone *noun* a large block of stone that is put at the base of an important new public building in a special ceremony 基石，奠基石（重要公共建築奠基典禮時放置）：*to lay the foundation stone of the new museum* 為新建博物館奠基

foun·der /'faʊndə(r)/ *noun, verb*

▪ ***noun*** a person who starts an organization, institution, etc. or causes sth to be built（組織、機構等的）創建者，創辦者，發起人：*the founder and president of the company* 公司的創辦人和總裁

▪ ***verb*** (*formal*) **1** [I] **~ (on sth)** (of a plan, etc. 計劃等) to fail because of a particular problem or difficulty 失敗；破產：*The peace talks foundered on a basic lack of trust.* 由於缺乏基本信任，和平談判擱淺。 **2** [I] **~ (on sth)** (of a ship 船) to fill with water and sink 沉沒：*Our boat foundered on a reef.* 我們的船觸礁沉沒。

ˌfounder 'member (*BrE*) (*NAmE* **ˌcharter 'member**) *noun* one of the first members of a society, an organization, etc., especially one who helped start it（社團、組織等的）創辦人之一，發起人之一，創建人之一

ˌfounding 'father *noun* **1** (*formal*) a person who starts or develops a new movement, institution or idea（運動、機構或思想的）創建人，發起人，元勳 **2 Founding Father** a member of the group of people who wrote the Constitution of the US in 1787（1787 年參加制訂美國憲法的）制憲元勳

found·ling /'faʊndlɪŋ/ *noun* (*old-fashioned*) a baby who has been left by its parents and who is found and taken care of by sb else 棄嬰；棄兒

foun·dry /'faʊndri/ *noun* (*pl.* **-ies**) a factory where metal or glass is melted and made into different shapes or objects 鑄造廠；玻璃廠：*an iron foundry* 鑄鐵廠 ◇ *foundry workers* 鑄造工人 ➲ SYNONYMS at FACTORY

fount /faʊnt/ *noun* **~ (of sth)** (*literary* or *humorous*) the place where sth important comes from（重要事物的）來源，根源，源泉 SYN **source**：*She treats him as if he were **the fount of all knowledge**.* 她把他當成無所不曉。

foun·tain /'faʊntən; *NAmE* 'faʊntn/ *noun* **1** a structure from which water is sent up into the air by a PUMP, used to decorate parks and gardens/yards 人工噴泉；噴水池 ➲ VISUAL VOCAB pages V2, V3 ➲ see also DRINKING FOUNTAIN **2** a strong flow of liquid or of another substance that is forced into the air 噴泉；（液體或其他物質的）噴射，湧流：*The amplifier exploded in a fountain of sparks.* 放大器爆炸，噴射出火星。 **3** a rich source or supply of sth 豐富來源；源泉：*Tourism is a fountain of wealth for the city.* 旅遊業是該市的重要收入來源。

foun·tain·head /'faʊntənhed; *NAmE* -tnhed/ *noun* (*literary*) a source or origin 泉源；根源；來源

'fountain pen *noun* a pen with a container that you fill with ink that flows to a NIB 自來水筆 ➲ VISUAL VOCAB page V69

four 🔑 /fɔː(r)/

1 🔑 *number* 4 四 HELP There are examples of how to use numbers at the entry for **five**. 數詞用法示例見 five 條。 **2** *noun* a group of four people or things 四個人（或事物）的一組：*to **make up a four** at tennis* 湊成四個人打網球 ◇ *a coach and four* (= four horses) 四匹馬拉的四輪大馬車 **3** *noun* (in CRICKET 板球) a shot that scores four RUNS 得四分的一擊 **4** *noun* a team of four people who ROW a long narrow boat in races; the boat that they row 四人賽艇的全體成員；四人賽艇

IDM **on all 'fours** (of a person 人) bent over with hands and knees on the ground 匍匐着；趴着：*We were crawling around on all fours.* 我們匍匐着四處爬行。 **these four 'walls** used when you are talking about keeping sth secret（用於叮囑保守秘密）到此為止：*Don't let this go further than these four walls* (= Don't tell anyone else who is not in the room now). 走出屋外這事就不要再談了。

ˌfour-by-'four (also **4x4**) *noun* a vehicle with FOUR-WHEEL DRIVE (= a system in which power is given to all four wheels) 四輪驅動汽車

ˌfour-colour 'process *noun* (*technical* 術語) a way of reproducing natural colours in photographs and printing using COLOUR SEPARATION 四色印刷

ˌfour-di'mension·al *adj.* having four DIMENSIONS, usually length, width, depth, and time 四維的（包括長、寬、高和時間）；四度空間的

four·fold /'fɔːfəʊld; *NAmE* 'fɔːrfoʊld/ *adj., adv.* ➲ -FOLD

ˌfour-letter 'word *noun* a short word that is considered rude or offensive, especially because it refers to sex or other functions of the body（字母少的）粗俗下流詞 SYN **swear word**

ˌfour-poster 'bed (also **ˌfour-'poster**) *noun* a large bed with a tall post at each of the four corners, a cover over the top and curtains around the sides 四帷柱大牀 ➲ VISUAL VOCAB page V23

four·some /'fɔːsəm; *NAmE* 'fɔːrsəm/ *noun* [C+sing./pl. v.] a group of four people taking part in a social activity or sport together 四人一組，四人參加的活動（指社交活動或體育活動）：*Can you **make up a foursome** for tennis tomorrow?* 你們明天能湊足四人打網球嗎？

ˌfour-'square *adj.* **1** (of a building 建築物) square in shape, solid and strong 方形堅固的；方方正正的 **2** (of a person 人) firm, steady and determined 堅決果斷的；堅定不移的 ▸ **ˌfour-'square** *adv.*：*I stand four-square with the President on this issue.* 在這個問題上我堅定不移地和總統站在一起。

'four-star *adj.* [usually before noun] **1** having four stars in a system that measures quality. The highest quality is shown by either four or five stars. 四星級的（表示優質）：*a four-star hotel* 四星級賓館 **2** (*NAmE*) having the second-highest military rank, and wearing a uniform that has four stars on it（軍階）四星級的：*a four-star general* 四星上將

'four-stroke *adj.* (*technical* 術語) (of an engine or vehicle 發電機或機動車) with a PISTON that makes four up and down movements in each power CYCLE 四衝程的 ➲ compare TWO-STROKE

four·teen 🔑 /ˌfɔː'tiːn; *NAmE* ˌfɔːr't-/ *number* 14 十四 ▸ **four·teenth** 🔑 /ˌfɔː'tiːnθ; *NAmE* ˌfɔːr't-/ *ordinal number, noun* HELP There are examples of how to use ordinal numbers at the entry for **fifth**. 序數詞用法示例見 fifth 條。

the ˌFourteenth A'mendment *noun* [sing.] a change made to the US Constitution in 1866 that gave all Americans equal rights and allowed former SLAVES to become citizens 第十四次修正案（1866 年對美國憲法進行的修正，授予所有美國人平等權利並讓此前奴隸成為公民）

fourth 🔑 /fɔːθ; *NAmE* fɔːrθ/ *ordinal number, noun*

▪ ***ordinal number*** 🔑 4th 第四 HELP There are examples of how to use ordinal numbers at the entry for **fifth**. 序數詞用法示例見 fifth 條。

▪ ***noun*** 🔑 (*especially NAmE*) = QUARTER (1)

the ˌfourth di'mension *noun* [sing.] **1** (used by scientists and writers of SCIENCE FICTION) time 第四維，第四

度空間（科學家和科幻小說作家用語，即時間） **2** an experience that is outside normal human experience 非常人的體驗

the ˌfourth eˈstate *noun* [sing.] newspapers and journalists in general and the political influence that they have 第四等級（指報界及其政治影響） SYN **the press**

fourth·ly /ˈfɔːθli; *NAmE* ˈfɔːrθ-/ *adv.* used to introduce the fourth of a list of points you want to make in a speech or piece of writing（用於列舉）第四

the ˌFourth of Juˈly *noun* [sing.] a national holiday in the US when people celebrate the anniversary of the Declaration of Independence in 1776 美國獨立紀念日（紀念美國於 1776 年 7 月 4 日獨立） ➲ see also INDEPENDENCE DAY

F

ˌfour-way ˈstop *noun* (*SAfrE*) a place where two roads cross each other, at which there are signs indicating that vehicles must stop before continuing 停車前行路口，四叉停車路口（有路標提示車輛先停後開）

ˌfour-wheel ˈdrive (*especially NAmE* **ˌall-wheel ˈdrive**) *noun* [U, C] a system in which power is applied to all four wheels of a vehicle, making it easier to control; a vehicle with this system（車輛）四輪驅動；四輪驅動汽車：*a car with four-wheel drive* 四輪驅動轎車 ◇ *We rented a four-wheel drive to get around the island.* 我們租了一輛四輪驅動車作環島旅遊。 ➲ VISUAL VOCAB page V52 ➲ see also FOUR-BY-FOUR

ˌfour-ˈwheeler (*NAmE*) (*BrE* **ˈquad bike**) *noun* a motorcycle with four large wheels, used for riding over rough ground, often for fun 四輪摩托車（常用於娛樂） ➲ see also ATV

fowl /faʊl/ *noun* **1** [C, U] (*pl.* **fowl** or **fowls**) a bird that is kept for its meat and eggs, for example a chicken 家禽：*fowl such as turkeys and ducks* 諸如火雞和鴨之類的家禽 **2** [C] (*old use*) any bird 鳥 ➲ see also GUINEAFOWL, WATERFOWL, WILDFOWL IDM see FISH *n.*

fox /fɒks; *NAmE* fɑːks/ *noun, verb*

■ ***noun*** **1** [C] a wild animal of the dog family, with reddish-brown fur, a pointed face and a thick heavy tail 狐；狐狸 ➲ see also FLYING FOX, VIXEN (1) **2** [U] the skin and fur of the fox, used to make coats, etc. 狐皮 **3** [C] (often *disapproving*) a person who is clever and able to get what they want by influencing or tricking other people 狡猾的人；老狐狸；老滑頭：*He's a wily old fox.* 他是個詭計多端的老狐狸。 **4** [C] (*informal*) an attractive young woman 漂亮的年輕女子

■ ***verb* ~ sb** (*informal, especially BrE*) to be too difficult for sb to understand or solve; to trick or confuse sb 使猜不透；把…難住；使上當；使迷惑：*The last question foxed even our panel of experts.* 最後這個問題甚至把我們的專家小組都難倒了。

foxed /fɒkst; *NAmE* fɑːkst/ *adj.* **1** unable to understand or solve sth 困惑的；迷惑不解的：*I must admit I'm completely foxed.* 我得承認我一點都不懂。 **2** (of the paper of old books or prints 舊書書頁或圖片) covered with brown spots 佈滿褐色斑點的

fox·glove /ˈfɒksglʌv; *NAmE* ˈfɑːks-/ *noun* [C, U] a tall plant with purple or white flowers shaped like bells growing up its STEM 洋地黃，毛地黃（高棵植物，開紫色或白色鐘狀花朵）

fox·hole /ˈfɒkshəʊl; *NAmE* ˈfɑːkshoʊl/ *noun* a hole in the ground that soldiers use as a shelter against the enemy or as a place to fire back from 散兵坑 ➲ compare HOLE *n.* (3)

fox·hound /ˈfɒkshaʊnd; *NAmE* ˈfɑːks-/ *noun* a dog with a very good sense of smell, that is trained to hunt FOXES 狐猩；獵狐狗

ˈfox-hunting (*BrE* also **hunt·ing**) *noun* [U] a sport in which FOXES are hunted by specially trained dogs and by people on horses. Fox-hunting with dogs is now illegal in the UK. 獵狐（如今在英國用狗獵狐是違法的）：*to go fox-hunting* 去獵狐 ▸ **ˈfox hunt** *noun*：*a ban on fox hunts* 禁止獵狐令

ˌfox ˈterrier *noun* a small dog with short hair 獵狐㹴狗

fox·trot /ˈfɒkstrɒt; *NAmE* ˈfɑːkstrɑːt/ *noun* a formal dance for two people together, with both small fast steps and longer slow ones; a piece of music for this dance 狐步舞；狐步舞曲

foxy /ˈfɒksi; *NAmE* ˈfɑːksi/ *adj.* **1** like a FOX in appearance 貌似狐狸的 **2** (*informal, especially NAmE*) (of a woman 女子) sexually attractive 性感的；狐媚的 SYN **sexy** **3** clever at tricking others 狡猾的；奸詐的 SYN **cunning**

foyer /ˈfɔɪeɪ; *NAmE* ˈfɔɪər/ *noun* **1** a large open space inside the entrance of a theatre or hotel where people can meet or wait（劇院或旅館的）門廳，休息廳 SYN **lobby** **2** (*NAmE*) an entrance hall in a private house or flat/apartment（私宅或公寓的）前廳，門廳

Fr (also **Fr.** especially in *NAmE*) *abbr.* Father (used in front of the name of some Christian priests) 神父（用於姓名前）：*Fr (Paul) O'Connor*（保祿）奧康納神父

fra·cas /ˈfrækɑː; *NAmE* ˈfreɪkəs/ *noun* (*pl.* **fra·cas** /-kɑːz/, *NAmE* **fra·cases**) [usually sing.] a noisy argument or fight, usually involving several people（通常有好幾個人的）高聲爭吵，打鬥

frac·tal /ˈfræktl/ *noun* (*mathematics* 數, *physics* 物) a curve or pattern that includes a smaller curve or pattern which has exactly the same shape 分形；碎形

frac·tion /ˈfrækʃn/ *noun* **1** a small part or amount of sth 小部份；少量；一點兒：*Only a small fraction of a bank's total deposits will be withdrawn at any one time.* 任何時候，一家銀行的總存款只有少量會被提取。◇ *She hesitated for the merest fraction of a second.* 她略微猶豫了一下。 HELP If **fraction** is used with a plural noun, the verb is usually plural. 如 fraction 與複數名詞連用，則動詞用複數：*Only a fraction of cars in the UK* **use** *leaded petrol.* If it is used with a singular noun that represents a group of people, the verb can be singular or plural in *BrE*, but is usually singular in *NAmE*. 如與表示一群人的單數名詞連用，在英式英語中動詞用單複數均可，但在美式英語中動詞通常用單數：*A tiny fraction of the population never* **vote/votes**. **2** a division of a number, for example ⅝ 分數；小數 ➲ LANGUAGE BANK at PROPORTION ➲ compare INTEGER ➲ see also VULGAR FRACTION

frac·tion·al /ˈfrækʃənl/ *adj.* **1** (*formal*) very small; not important 很小的；很少的；微不足道的 SYN **minimal**：*a fractional decline in earnings* 利潤微降 **2** (*mathematics* 數) of or in fractions 分數的；小數的：*a fractional equation* 分式方程

ˌfractional distilˈlation *noun* [U] (*chemistry* 化) the process of separating the parts of a liquid mixture by heating it. As the temperature goes up, each part in turn becomes a gas, which then cools as it moves up a tube and can be collected as a liquid. 分餾

frac·tion·al·ly /ˈfrækʃənəli/ *adv.* to a very small degree 很小；很少：*He was just fractionally ahead at the finishing line.* 在終點線他只是稍微領先。

frac·tious /ˈfrækʃəs/ *adj.* (*especially BrE*) **1** bad-tempered or easily upset, especially by small things 暴躁的；易怒的；動輒煩躁的 SYN **irritable**：*Children often get fractious and tearful when tired.* 孩子們疲倦時易煩躁好哭。 **2** (*formal*) making trouble and complaining 搗亂的；表示不滿的：*The six fractious republics are demanding autonomy.* 這六個鬧分裂的加盟共和國要求自治。

frac·ture /ˈfræktʃə(r)/ *noun, verb*

■ ***noun*** **1** [C] a break in a bone or other hard material（指狀態）骨折，斷裂，折斷，破裂：*a fracture of the leg/skull* 腿骨／顱骨骨折 ◇ *a* ***compound/simple fracture*** (= one in which the broken bone comes/does not come through the skin) 複合（開放）骨折；單純（閉合）骨折 ➲ COLLOCATIONS at INJURY **2** [U] the fact of sth breaking, especially a bone（指事實）骨折，斷裂，折斷，破裂：*Old people's bones are more prone to fracture.* 老人更易骨折。

■ ***verb*** **1** [I, T] to break or crack; to make sth break or crack（使）斷裂，折斷，破裂：*His leg fractured in two places.* 他的一條腿有兩處骨折。◇ **~ sth** *She fell and fractured her skull.* 她跌倒摔裂了顱骨。◇ *a fractured pipeline* 破裂的管道 **2** [I, T] (*formal*) (of a society, an organization, etc. 團體、組織等) to split into several parts so that it no longer functions or exists; to split a society or an organization, etc. in this way（使）分裂： *Many people predicted that the party would fracture and split.* 很多人預言該黨將分崩離析。◇ **~ sth (into sth)** *The company was fractured into several smaller groups.* 這家公司被支解成幾家小公司。▸ **frac·tured** *adj.* [usually before noun]： *He suffered a badly fractured arm.* 他的手臂嚴重骨折。◇ (*figurative*) *They spoke a sort of fractured German.* 他們講德語結結巴巴。

frae·nu·lum (*BrE*) = FRENULUM

fra·gile /ˈfrædʒaɪl; *NAmE* -dʒl/ *adj.* **1** easily broken or damaged 易碎的；易損的： *fragile china/glass/bones* 易碎的瓷器／玻璃製品／骨骼 **2** weak and uncertain; easily destroyed or spoilt 不牢固的；脆弱的： *a* ***fragile alliance/ceasefire/relationship*** 不牢固的聯盟；不確定的停火／關係 ◇ *The economy remains extremely fragile.* 經濟仍然極其脆弱。 **3** delicate and often beautiful 纖巧的；精細的；纖巧美麗的： *fragile beauty* 纖美 ◇ *The woman's fragile face broke into a smile.* 那面孔秀麗的女子粲然一笑。 **4** not strong and likely to become ill/sick 虛弱的： *Her father is now 86 and in fragile health.* 她的父親現在 86 歲，身體虛弱。◇ (*BrE, informal*) *I'm feeling a bit fragile after last night* (= not well, perhaps because of drinking too much alcohol). 昨夜以後我覺得身子有點發虛（可能是縱酒所致）。▸ **fra·gil·ity** /frəˈdʒɪləti/ *noun* [U]： *the fragility of the human body* 人體的脆弱

frag·ment *noun, verb*

▪ ***noun*** /ˈfræɡmənt/ a small part of sth that has broken off or comes from sth larger 碎片；片段： *Police found fragments of glass near the scene.* 警方在現場附近發現了玻璃碎片。◇ *The shattered vase lay in fragments on the floor.* 打碎的花瓶在地上成了一堆碎片。◇ *I overheard a fragment of their conversation.* 我無意中聽到他們談話的片段。

▪ ***verb*** /fræɡˈment/ [I, T] **~ (sth)** to break or make sth break into small pieces or parts（使）碎裂，破裂，分裂 ▸ **frag·men·ta·tion** /ˌfræɡmenˈteɪʃn/ *noun* [U]： *the fragmentation of the country into small independent states* 該國分裂成一些獨立的小國家 **frag·ment·ed** *adj.*： *a fragmented society* 一個四分五裂的社會

frames 框架；構架

window frame 窗框
picture frame 畫框
frames 眼鏡框
bicycle frame 自行車架
cold frame （保護育種或幼苗抗寒的）冷牀
climbing frame (*BrE*) **jungle gym** (*NAmE*) 攀爬架
Zimmer frame™ (*BrE*) **walker** (*NAmE*) 齊默式助行架

frag·men·tary /ˈfræɡməntri; *NAmE* -teri/ *adj.* (*formal*) made of small parts that are not connected or complete 殘缺不全的；不完整的： *There is only fragmentary evidence to support this theory.* 只有零零星星的證據證實這個理論。

ˌfragmenˈtation grenade (also **ˌfragmenˈtation bomb**) *noun* a bomb that breaks into very small pieces when it explodes 高爆手雷（爆炸時迸射出大量碎片）

fra·grance /ˈfreɪɡrəns/ *noun* **1** [C, U] a pleasant smell 香氣；香味；芳香： *The bath oil comes in various fragrances.* 這種沐浴油有不同的香味。 **2** [C] a liquid that you put on your skin in order to make yourself smell nice 香水 SYN **perfume**： *an exciting new fragrance from Dior* 迪奧新推出的一款令人驚喜的香水

fra·grant /ˈfreɪɡrənt/ *adj.* having a pleasant smell 香的；芳香的： *fragrant herbs/flowers/oils* 芳草；香花／油 ◇ *The air was fragrant with scents from the sea and the hills.* 空氣中盪漾着山和海的芬芳氣息。▸ **fra·grant·ly** *adv.*

fraidy cat /ˈfreɪdi kæt/ *noun* (*US, informal, disapproving*) = SCAREDY-CAT

frail /freɪl/ *adj.* (**frail·er, frail·est**) **1** (especially of an old person 尤指老人) physically weak and thin 瘦弱的： *Mother was becoming too frail to live alone.* 母親已逐漸衰弱到無法獨居。 **2** weak; easily damaged or broken 弱的；易損的；易碎的： *the frail stems of the flowers* 柔弱的花莖 ◇ *Human nature is frail.* 人性脆弱。

frailty /ˈfreɪlti/ *noun* (*pl.* **-ies**) **1** [U] weakness and poor health 虛弱；衰弱： *Increasing frailty meant that she was more and more confined to bed.* 日益衰弱意味着她愈來愈需要臥牀。 **2** [U, C] (*formal*) weakness in a person's character or moral standards（性格或道德上的）弱點，懦弱，軟弱： *human frailty* 人性的弱點 ◇ *the frailties of human nature* 人性的種種弱點

frame 🗝 /freɪm/ *noun, verb*

▪ ***noun***

▸ **BORDER** 邊框 **1** 🗝 [C] a strong border or structure of wood, metal, etc. that holds a picture, door, piece of glass, etc. in position（圖畫、門、玻璃等的）框架： *a picture frame* 畫框 ◇ *aluminium window frames* 鋁窗框 ➲ picture at EDGE

▸ **STRUCTURE** 結構 **2** 🗝 [C] the supporting structure of a piece of furniture, a building, a vehicle, etc. that gives it its shape（傢具、建築物、車輛等的）構架，支架，骨架： *the frame of an aircraft/a car/a bicycle* 飛機／汽車／自行車構架 ➲ **VISUAL VOCAB** page V51 ➲ see also CLIMBING FRAME

▸ **OF GLASSES** 眼鏡 **3** [C, usually pl.] a structure of plastic or metal that holds the LENSES in a pair of glasses 眼鏡框： *gold-rimmed frames* 金邊眼鏡框

▸ **PERSON/ANIMAL'S BODY** 人／動物的身體 **4** [C, usually sing.] the form or structure of a person or animal's body 體形；身材；骨架： *to have a* ***small/slender/large frame*** 小的／苗條的／大的體形

▸ **GENERAL IDEAS** 總的思想 **5** [sing.] the general ideas or structure that form the background to sth（構成某事物背景的）總的思想，體系，體制，模式： *In this course we hope to look at literature in the frame of its social and historical context.* 在本課程中，我們希望從社會和歷史背景的整體結構來看文學。➲ see also TIME FRAME

▸ **OF FILM/MOVIE** 電影 **6** [C] one of the single photographs that a film or video is made of 鏡頭；畫面

▸ **OF PICTURE STORY** 連環畫 **7** [C] a single picture in a COMIC STRIP（連環漫畫中的）一幅畫

▸ **COMPUTING** 計算機技術 **8** [C] one of the separate areas on an Internet page that you can SCROLL through (= read by using the mouse to move the text up or down) 幀；頁幀（框）；圖文框

▸ **IN GARDEN** 花園 **9** [C] = COLD FRAME

▸ **IN SNOOKER/BOWLING** 斯諾克；保齡球 **10** [C] a single section of play in the game of SNOOKER, etc., or in BOWLING 一輪；一回；一局

IDM **be in/out of the ˈframe** be taking part/not taking part in sth 參加；不參加： *We won our match, so we're still in the frame for the championship.* 我們贏了比賽，所以仍可參加錦標賽。

F

■ ***verb***
▸ MAKE BORDER 做邊框 **1** [usually passive] **~ sth** to put or make a frame or border around sth 給…做框；給…鑲邊：*The photograph had been framed.* 照片已鑲了框。◇ *Her blonde hair framed her face.* 她的金髮襯着面龐。◇ *He stood there, head back, framed against the blue sky.* 他站在那裏，頭向後仰，襯托在藍天下。
▸ PRODUCE FALSE EVIDENCE 作偽證 **2** [usually passive] **~ sb (for sth)** to produce false evidence against an innocent person so that people think he or she is guilty 作偽證陷害 SYN **fit up**：*He says he was framed.* 他說他是被誣陷的。
▸ DEVELOP PLAN/SYSTEM 擬訂計劃／體系 **3 ~ sth** (*formal*) to create and develop sth such as a plan, a system or a set of rules 制訂；擬訂
▸ EXPRESS STH 表達 **4 ~ sth** to express sth in a particular way（以某種方式）表達：*You'll have to be careful how you frame the question.* 如何提出這個問題，你得慎重。
▸ **framed** *adj.* (often in compounds 常構成複合詞)：*a framed photograph* 裝在相框裏的相片 ◇ *a timber-framed house* (= with a supporting structure of wood) 木結構房屋

ˌframe of ˈmind *noun* [sing.] the way you feel or think about sth at a particular time 心態；心緒：*We'll discuss this when you're in a better frame of mind.* 你心情好些時我們再討論這件事。

ˌframe of ˈreference *noun* (*pl.* **frames of reference**) a particular set of beliefs, ideas or experiences that affects how a person understands or judges sth（影響人理解和判斷事物的）信仰和準則

ˈframe tent (*BrE*) (*NAmE* **ˈwall tent**) *noun* a large tent with a roof and walls that do not slope much 框架式大帳篷（篷頂和篷壁形成的坡度很小）➲ compare DOME TENT, RIDGE TENT

ˈframe-up *noun* (*informal*) a situation in which false evidence is produced in order to make people think that an innocent person is guilty of a crime 誣陷；陷害

frame·work AW /ˈfreɪmwɜːk; *NAmE* -wɜːrk/ *noun* **1** the parts of a building or an object that support its weight and give it shape（建築物或物體的）構架，框架，結構 ➲ SYNONYMS at STRUCTURE **2 ~ (of/for sth)** a set of beliefs, ideas or rules that is used as the basis for making judgements, decisions, etc.（作為判斷、決定等基礎的）信念，觀點，準則：*The report provides a framework for further research.* 報告提供了進一步研究的原則。➲ COLLOCATIONS at SCIENTIFIC **3** the structure of a particular system（體系的）結構，機制：*We need to establish a legal framework for the protection of the environment.* 我們需要建立一個法律體制來保護環境。◇ *the basic framework of society* 社會的基本結構

franc /fræŋk/ *noun* the unit of money in Switzerland and several other countries (replaced in 2002 in France, Belgium and Luxembourg by the euro) 法郎（瑞士等國的貨幣單位，在法國、比利時和盧森堡於 2002 年為歐元所取代）

fran·chise /ˈfræntʃaɪz/ *noun, verb*
■ ***noun*** **1** [C, U] formal permission given by a company to sb who wants to sell its goods or services in a particular area; formal permission given by a government to sb who wants to operate a public service as a business（公司授予的）特許經銷權；（國家授予的）特別經營權，特許：*a **franchise agreement/company*** 特許經銷權協議；特約代銷公司 ◇ *a catering/rail franchise* 餐飲／鐵路經營權 ◇ *In the reorganization, Southern Television lost their franchise.* 在改組過程中南方電視公司失去了特許經營權。◇ *to operate a business **under franchise*** 根據特許經營權經營 ➲ COLLOCATIONS at BUSINESS **2** [C] a business or service run under franchise 獲特許權的商業機構（或服務）：*They operate franchises in London and Paris.* 他們在倫敦和巴黎經營專賣店。◇ *a burger franchise* 漢堡包特許經銷店 **3** [U] (*formal*) the right to vote in a country's elections（公民）選舉權：*universal adult franchise* 成年人普選權 ➲ see also ENFRANCHISE
■ ***verb*** [usually passive] **~ sth (out) (to sb/sth)** to give or sell a franchise (1) to sb 授予（或出售）特許經銷權（或經營權）：*Catering has been franchised (out) to a private company.* 餐飲特許經營權已授予一家私人公司。◇ *franchised restaurants* 獲經營權的餐廳 ▸ **fran·chis·ing** *noun* [U]

fran·chisee /ˌfræntʃaɪˈziː/ *noun* a person or company that has been given a franchise 獲特許權的人（或公司）；特許經營人（或公司）

fran·chiser (also **fran·chisor**) /ˈfræntʃaɪzə(r)/ *noun* a company or an organization that gives sb a franchise 授予（他人）特許權的公司（或組織）

Fran·cis·can /frænˈsɪskən/ *noun, adj.*
■ ***noun*** a member of a religious organization started in 1209 by St Francis of Assisi in Italy 方濟各會修士（方濟各會於 1209 年由聖方濟各創辦）
■ ***adj.*** relating to St Francis or to this organization 聖方濟各的；方濟各會的：*a Franciscan monk* 方濟各會修士

fran·cium /ˈfrænsiəm/ *noun* [U] (*symb.* **Fr**) a chemical element. Francium is a RADIOACTIVE metal. 鈁（放射性化學元素）

Franco- /ˈfræŋkəʊ; *NAmE* ˈfræŋkoʊ/ *combining form* (in nouns and adjectives 構成名詞和形容詞) French; France 法國的；法國人的；法國：*the Franco-Prussian War* 普法戰爭 ◇ *Francophile* 親法的人

franco·phone /ˈfræŋkəfəʊn; *NAmE* -foʊn/ *adj.* [only before noun] speaking French as the main language 說法語的 ▸ **franco·phone** *noun*：*Canadian francophones* 說法語的加拿大人

fran·gi·pani /ˌfrændʒiˈpæni; -ˈpɑːni/ *noun* **1** [U, C] a tropical American tree or bush with groups of white, pink, or yellow flowers 雞蛋花樹（或灌木）（產於美洲熱帶）**2** [U] a PERFUME that is made from the frangipani plant 雞蛋花香水

frank /fræŋk/ *adj., verb*
■ ***adj.*** (**frank·er**, **frank·est**) HELP **More frank** is also common. * more frank 也常用。) honest and direct in what you say, sometimes in a way that other people might not like 坦率的；直率的：*a full and frank discussion* 坦誠的充分討論 ◇ *a frank admission of guilt* 坦率承認心裏有愧 ◇ *He was very frank about his relationship with the actress.* 他對自己和那位女演員的關係直言不諱。◇ ***To be frank with you**, I think your son has little chance of passing the exam.* 坦誠相告，我認為你的兒子不大可能通過考試。➲ SYNONYMS at HONEST ▸ **frank·ness** *noun* [U]：*They outlined their aims with disarming frankness.* 他們友好坦誠地簡述了他們的宗旨。
■ ***verb*** [often passive] **~ sth** to stamp a mark on an envelope, etc. to show that the cost of posting it has been paid or does not need to be paid（在信件上）蓋郵資已付印記，蓋免付郵資印記

Fran·ken·food /ˈfræŋkənfuːd/ (also **ˈFrankenstein food**) *noun* [C, U] (*informal, disapproving*) food that has been GENETICALLY MODIFIED 轉基因食物；基因改造食品

Fran·ken·stein /ˈfræŋkənstaɪn/ *noun* (also **ˌFranken·stein's ˈmonster**, **ˌFrankenstein ˈmonster**) used to talk about sth that sb creates or invents that goes out of control and becomes dangerous, often destroying the person who created it 失控的受造物（常毀滅創造者）ORIGIN From the novel *Frankenstein* by Mary Shelley in which a scientist called Frankenstein makes a creature from pieces of dead bodies and brings it to life. 源自瑪麗•雪萊的小說《科學怪人》，其中的科學家弗蘭肯斯坦用屍體部位拼成了一個怪物並使之復活。

frank·furt·er /ˈfræŋkfɜːtə(r); *NAmE* -fɜːrt-/ (*NAmE* also **wie·ner**, *informal* **wee·nie**) *noun* a long thin smoked SAUSAGE with a reddish-brown skin, often eaten in a long bread roll as a HOT DOG 法蘭克福熏腸（常用於做熱狗）

frank·in·cense /ˈfræŋkɪnsens/ *noun* [U] a substance that is burnt to give a pleasant smell, especially during religious ceremonies 乳香（點燃時散發出香味，尤用於宗教禮儀）

ˈfranking machine (*especially BrE*) (*NAmE* usually **ˈpostage meter**) *noun* a machine that prints an official mark on a letter to show that the cost of posting it has been paid, or does not need to be paid 郵資機（加蓋郵資已付印記）

frank·ly /ˈfræŋkli/ *adv.* **1** in an honest and direct way that people might not like 坦率地；直率地：*He spoke frankly about the ordeal.* 他直率地講出了苦難的經歷。◇ *They frankly admitted their responsibility.* 他們坦率地承認了責任。 **2** used to show that you are being honest about sth, even though people might not like what you are saying（表示直言）老實說：*Frankly, I couldn't care less what happens to him.* 說實話，我才不管他出什麼事呢。◇ ***Quite frankly**, I'm not surprised you failed.* 老實說，我對你的失敗不感到意外。

fran·tic /ˈfræntɪk/ *adj.* **1** done quickly and with a lot of activity, but in a way that is not very well organized 緊張忙亂的；手忙腳亂的 SYN **hectic**：*a frantic dash/search/struggle* 不顧一切的猛衝；瘋狂的搜查 / 鬥爭 ◇ *They made **frantic attempts** to revive him.* 他們拚命地努力讓他蘇醒過來。◇ *Things are frantic in the office right now.* 現在辦公室裏忙作一團。 **2** unable to control your emotions because you are extremely frightened or worried about sth（由於恐懼或擔心）無法控制感情的，發狂似的 SYN **beside yourself**：*frantic with worry* 憂慮得要命 ◇ *Let's go back. Your parents must be **getting frantic** by now.* 咱們回家吧。你的父母現在肯定快要急死了。◇ *The children are driving me frantic* (= making me very annoyed). 孩子們快要使我發瘋了。 ▸ **fran·tic·al·ly** /-kli/ *adv.*：*They worked frantically to finish on time.* 他們拚命工作以按時完成。

frappé /ˈfræpeɪ; *NAmE* fræˈpeɪ/ *adj.*, *noun* (from French)
■ ***adj.*** [after noun] (of drinks 飲料) served cold with a lot of ice 加冰（的）；冰鎮：*coffee frappé* 加冰咖啡
■ ***noun*** a drink or sweet food served cold with very small pieces of ice 冰鎮飲料（或甜食）；碎冰飲料

frat /fræt/ *noun* (*NAmE, informal*) = FRATERNITY (2)：*a frat boy* (= a member of a fraternity)（美國）男大學生聯誼會會員

fra·ter·nal /frəˈtɜːnl; *NAmE* -ˈtɜːrnl/ *adj.* [usually before noun] **1** connected with the relationship that exists between people or groups that share the same ideas or interests（指志趣相投者）兄弟般的，親如手足的：*a fraternal organization/society* 兄弟會組織；共濟會 **2** connected with the relationship that exists between brothers 兄弟間的：*fraternal rivalry* 兄弟鬩牆 ▸ **fra·ter·nal·ly** *adv.*

fraˌternal ˈtwin (also ˌ**non-iˌdentical ˈtwin**) (*technical* 術語 ˌ**dizyˌgotic ˈtwin**) *noun* either of two children or animals born from the same mother at the same time but not from the same egg 雙卵性雙胞胎之一 ➲ compare IDENTICAL TWIN, MONOZYGOTIC TWIN

fra·ter·nity /frəˈtɜːnəti; *NAmE* -ˈtɜːrn-/ *noun* (*pl.* **-ies**) **1** [C+sing./pl. v.] a group of people sharing the same profession, interests or beliefs（有相同職業、愛好或信仰的）群體，同仁；同好：*members of **the medical/banking/racing, etc. fraternity*** 醫務界、銀行界、賽馬圈等同仁 **2** (also *NAmE informal* **frat**) [C] a club for a group of male students at an American college or university（美國男大學生的）聯誼會，兄弟會 ➲ compare SORORITY **3** [U] (*formal*) a feeling of friendship and support that exists between the members of a group（團體內的）情誼，兄弟般友誼，博愛：*the ideals of liberty, equality and fraternity* 自由、平等和博愛的理想

frat·er·nize (*BrE* also **-ise**) /ˈfrætənaɪz; *NAmE* -tərn-/ *verb* [I] **~ (with sb)** to behave in a friendly manner, especially towards sb that you are not supposed to be friendly with（與尤指不該親善者）親善：*She was accused of fraternizing with the enemy.* 她被指責親敵。 ▸ **frat·er·niza·tion, -isa·tion** /ˌfrætənaɪˈzeɪʃn; *NAmE* -tərnəˈz-/ *noun* [U]

frat·ri·cide /ˈfrætrɪsaɪd/ *noun* [U, C] **1** (*formal*) the crime of killing your brother or sister; a person who is guilty of this crime 殺害兄弟（或姐妹）罪；殺害兄弟（或姐妹）者 ➲ compare MATRICIDE, PARRICIDE, PATRICIDE **2** the crime of killing people of your own country or group; a person who is guilty of this crime 殺害同胞罪；殺害同胞者 ▸ **frat·ri·cidal** /ˌfrætrɪˈsaɪdl/ *adj.*：*to be engaged in a fratricidal struggle* 進行自相殘殺的鬥爭

fraud /frɔːd/ *noun* **1** [U, C] the crime of cheating sb in order to get money or goods illegally 欺詐罪；欺騙罪：*She was charged with credit card fraud.* 她被控告信用卡欺騙罪。◇ *property that has been obtained by fraud* 欺詐所得的財產 ◇ *a $100 million fraud* * 1 億元數額的詐騙罪 ➲ COLLOCATIONS at CRIME **2** [C] a person who pretends to have qualities, abilities, etc. that they do not really have in order to cheat other people 騙子；行騙的人：*He's nothing but a liar and a fraud.* 他只不過是個撒謊者和騙子。◇ *She felt a fraud accepting their sympathy* (= because she was not really sad). 她接受他們的同情時感到自己是在騙人。 **3** [C] something that is not as good, useful, etc. as people claim it is 偽劣品；冒牌貨

ˈfraud squad *noun* [sing.+sing./pl. v.] (*BrE*) part of a police force that investigates fraud（警方的）詐騙案調查小組

fraud·ster /ˈfrɔːdstə(r)/ *noun* (*BrE*) a person who commits fraud 犯欺詐罪者；犯欺騙罪者

fraudu·lent /ˈfrɔːdjələnt; *NAmE* -dʒə-/ *adj.* (*formal*) intended to cheat sb, usually in order to make money illegally 欺騙的；欺詐的：*fraudulent advertising* 虛假不實的廣告 ◇ *fraudulent insurance claims* 詐騙性的保險索賠 ▸ **fraudu·lence** /ˈfrɔːdjələns; *NAmE* -dʒə-/ *noun* [U] **fraudu·lent·ly** /ˈfrɔːdjələntli; *NAmE* -dʒə-/ *adv.*

fraught /frɔːt/ *adj.* **1 ~ with sth** filled with sth unpleasant 充滿（不愉快事物）的：*a situation **fraught with danger/difficulty/problems*** 充滿危險 / 困難重重 / 問題成堆的局面 **2** (*especially BrE*) causing or feeling worry and anxiety 焦慮的；憂慮的；擔心的 SYN **tense**：*She looked/sounded fraught.* 她愁容滿面；她的話音顯出憂慮。◇ *There was a fraught silence.* 有一陣令人焦慮的沉默。◇ *Things are as fraught as ever in the office.* 辦公室的情況和往常一樣令人擔心。

fray /freɪ/ *verb*, *noun*
■ ***verb*** **1** [I, T] if cloth **frays** or sth **frays** it, the threads in it start to come apart（使織物邊沿）磨損，磨散：*The cuffs of his shirt were fraying.* 他襯衣的袖口磨破了。◇ *This material frays easily.* 這布料容易磨損。◇ **~ sth** *It was fashionable to fray the bottoms of your jeans.* 曾經時興把牛仔褲磨毛。 **2** [I, T] **~ (sth)** if sb's nerves or TEMPER **frays** or sth **frays** them, the person starts to get irritated or annoyed（使）煩躁，惱火：*As the debate went on, tempers began to fray.* 隨着辯論的繼續，火氣就上來了。 ▸ **frayed** *adj.*：*frayed denim shorts* 磨損的牛仔短褲 ◇ *Tempers were getting very frayed.* 脾氣變得暴躁起來。
IDM ˌ**fray at/around the ˈedges/ˈseams** to start to come apart or to fail 開始捲邊；脫線腳；分崩離析；失敗：*Support for the leader was fraying at the edges.* 對這位領導人的擁護已開始瓦解。
■ ***noun* the fray** [sing.] a fight, a competition or an argument, especially one that is exciting or seen as a test of your ability 打鬥，競爭，爭辯（尤指激烈或視為檢驗能力的）：*They were ready for the fray.* 他們準備好了爭鬥。◇ *to **enter/join the fray*** 加入爭辯 ◇ *At 71, he has now retired from the political fray.* 他現年 71 歲，已經退出了政治角逐。

fraz·zle /ˈfræzl/ *noun*
IDM **be burnt, worn, etc. to a ˈfrazzle** (*informal*) to be completely burnt/extremely tired 被燒成灰燼；筋疲力盡

fraz·zled /ˈfræzld/ *adj.* (*informal*) tired and easily annoyed 疲憊而煩躁的：*They finally arrived home, hot and frazzled.* 他們終於回到家，又熱又累。

freak /friːk/ *noun*, *adj.*, *verb*
■ ***noun*** **1** (*informal*) a person with a very strong interest in a particular subject 狂熱愛好者：*a **health/fitness/jazz, etc. freak*** 對健康、健身等着迷的人；爵士樂迷 ➲ see also CONTROL FREAK **2** (*disapproving*) a person who is considered to be unusual because of the way they behave, look or think（行為、外表、想法）怪異的人；怪人：*She was treated like a freak because she didn't want children.* 她因為不要孩子而被當作怪人。◇ *He's going out with a real freak.* 他和一個真正的怪人在談戀愛。 **3** (also ˌ**freak of ˈnature**) (sometimes *offensive*) a person, an animal, a plant or a thing that is not physically normal（指人、動植物和東西）畸形 **4** a very unusual and unexpected event 怪異的事；不尋常的事：

F

*By some **freak of fate** they all escaped without injury.* 由於命運之神的奇特安排，他們全都死裏逃生，毫髮未損。

■ **adj.** [only before noun] (of an event or the weather 事情或天氣) very unusual and unexpected 不正常的；怪異的：*a **freak accident/storm/occurrence*** 反常的事故／暴風雨／事變 ◇ *freak weather conditions* 反常的天氣狀況

■ **verb** [I, T] (*informal*) if sb **freaks** or if sth **freaks** them, they react very strongly to sth that makes them suddenly feel shocked, surprised, frightened, etc. （使）強烈反應，震驚，畏懼：**~ (out)** *My parents really freaked when they saw my hair.* 我父母看見我的頭髮時大驚失色。◇ **~ sb (out)** *Snakes really freak me out.* 我一看見蛇便渾身發麻。

F

freak·ing /ˈfriːkɪŋ/ *adv., adj.* [only before noun] (*NAmE, taboo, slang*) a swear word that many people find offensive, used to emphasize a comment or an angry statement to avoid saying 'fucking'（加強語氣，用以替代 fucking）該死的，他媽的

freak·ish /ˈfriːkɪʃ/ *adj.* very strange, unusual or unexpected 怪異的；反常的；意外的：*freakish weather/behaviour* 反常的天氣；怪異的行為 ▸ **freak·ish·ly** *adv.*

ˈfreak show *noun* **1** a small show at a FAIR, where people pay to see people or animals with strange physical characteristics 畸種（人或動物）展覽 **2** (*disapproving*) an event that people watch because it is very strange 人們享受觀看的怪事

freaky /ˈfriːki/ *adj.* (*informal*) very strange or unusual 怪異的；反常的

freckle /ˈfrekl/ *noun* [usually pl.] a small, pale brown spot on a person's skin, especially on their face, caused by the sun 雀斑；小斑點 ➲ compare MOLE (2) ▸ **freckled** /ˈfrekld/ *adj.*：*a freckled face/schoolgirl* 有雀斑的臉／女學生

free 🔑 /friː/ *adj., verb, adv.*

■ **adj.** (**freer** /ˈfriːə(r)/, **freest** /ˈfriːɪst/)

▸ NOT CONTROLLED 不受控制 **1** 🔑 not under the control or in the power of sb else; able to do what you want 能隨自己意願的；隨心所欲的：*I have no ambitions other than to have a happy life and be free.* 我沒有雄心大志，只求自由自在地過幸福生活。◇ *Students have a **free choice** of courses in their final year.* 學生在最後一學年可以自由選修課程。◇ **~ to do sth** *You are free to come and go as you please.* 你來去自由。◇ (*informal*) *'Can I use the phone?' 'Please, **feel free*** (= of course you can use it).' "我能用一下電話嗎？" "請便吧。" **2** 🔑 not restricted or controlled by anyone else; able to do or say what you want 不受限制的；不受約束的；言行自由的：*A true democracy complete with **free speech** and a free press was called for.* 人們呼籲要有包括言論自由和新聞自由在內的真正民主。◇ *the country's first free election* 該國的第一次自由選舉 ◇ *They gave me free access to all the files.* 他們讓我自由查閱所有檔案資料。

▸ NOT PRISONER 非囚犯 **3** 🔑 (of a person 人) not a prisoner or SLAVE 自由的（不是囚犯或奴隸）：*He walked out of jail **a free man**.* 他獲釋出獄，成為自由人。

▸ ANIMAL/BIRD 動物；鳥 **4** 🔑 not tied up or in a CAGE 未拴住的；非關在籠中的：*The researchers **set** the birds **free**.* 研究人員把鳥放了。

▸ NO PAYMENT 不用付款 **5** 🔑 costing nothing 不收費的：*Admission is free.* 免費入場。◇ ***free samples/tickets/advice*** 免費樣品／票／咨詢 ◇ *We're offering a fabulous **free gift** with each copy you buy.* 購買一冊就可以得到一份免費好禮。◇ *You can't expect people to work **for free*** (= without payment). 你不能指望人工作不要報酬。

▸ NOT BLOCKED 無阻礙 **6** 🔑 clear; not blocked 無阻礙的；暢通的：*Ensure there is a free flow of air around the machine.* 要確保機器周圍空氣暢通。

▸ WITHOUT STH 沒有 **7** 🔑 **~ from/of sth** not containing or affected by sth harmful or unpleasant 不含有害物的；不受…傷害（或影響等）的：*free from difficulty/doubt/fear* 沒有困難；不懷疑／害怕 ◇ *free from artificial colours and flavourings* 不含人工色素和人工調味料 ◇ *It was several weeks before he was completely free of pain.* 過了幾星期他的疼痛才完全消除。 **8** 🔑 **-free** (in adjectives 構成形容詞) without the thing mentioned 沒有…的：*virtually fat-free yogurt* 幾乎無脂的酸奶 ◇ *tax-free earnings* 免稅收入 ◇ *a trouble-free life* 無憂無慮的生活

▸ NOT ATTACHED/TRAPPED 未固定／縛住 **9** 🔑 **~ (of sth)** not attached to sth or trapped by sth 未固定的；未縛住的：*Pull gently on the free end of the rope.* 輕拉繩索鬆開的一端。◇ *They had to be **cut free** from their car after the accident.* 事故後，得破開汽車把他們救出來。◇ *She finally managed to pull herself free.* 她終於設法掙脫了。

▸ NOT BEING USED 未使用 **10** 🔑 not being used 未使用的；空着的：*He held out his free hand and I took it.* 他伸出空着的一隻手，我就抓住了。◇ *Is this seat free?* 這個座位空着嗎？

▸ NOT BUSY 不忙 **11** 🔑 **~ (for sth)** (of a person or time 人或時間) without particular plans or arrangements; not busy 沒有安排活動的；空閒的：*If Sarah is free for lunch I'll take her out.* 如果薩拉有空吃午飯，我就請她出去吃。◇ *Keep Friday night free for my party.* 把星期五晚上空出來，參加我的晚會。◇ *What do you like to do in your **free time*** (= when you are not working)? 你閒暇時喜歡幹什麼？

▸ READY TO GIVE 樂於給予 **12** **~ with sth** (often *disapproving*) ready to give sth, especially when it is not wanted 隨便給出的：*He's too free with his opinions.* 他太隨便發表意見了。

▸ TRANSLATION 翻譯 **13** a **free** translation is not exact but gives the general meaning 不拘泥原文的；（翻譯）根據大意的；意譯的 ➲ compare LITERAL (2)

IDM **free and ˈeasy** informal; relaxed 隨便；無拘束；輕鬆；自由自在：*Life was never going to be so free and easy again.* 生活絕不會再那樣無拘無束了。 **get, have, etc. a free ˈhand** to get, have, etc. the opportunity to do what you want to do and to make your own decisions 可以全權處理；有自主權：*I was given a free hand in designing the syllabus.* 我獲准全權制訂教學大綱。 **get, take, etc. a free ˈride** to get or take sth without paying because sb else is paying for it 白白得到好處（因他人已代付款） **it's a free ˈcountry** (*informal*) used as a reply when sb suggests that you should not do sth（有人建議不應做某事時用於回答）這是個自由的國家：*It's a free country; I'll say what I like!* 這是個自由的國家，我想說什麼就說什麼！ **there's no such ˌthing as a free ˈlunch** (*informal*) used to say that it is not possible to get sth for nothing（表示白得東西是不可能的）沒有免費的午餐 ➲ more at HOME *adv.*, REIN *n.*

■ **verb**

▸ PRISONER 囚犯 **1** 🔑 **~ sb (from sth)** to allow sb to leave prison or somewhere they have been kept against their will 釋放；使自由 SYN **release**：*By the end of May nearly 100 of an estimated 2 000 political prisoners had been freed.* 至五月底，估計 2 000 名政治犯中有近 100 人已經獲釋。◇ *The hijackers agreed to free a further ten hostages.* 劫持者已同意再釋放十名人質。

▸ SB/STH TRAPPED 被困住的人／物 **2** 🔑 **~ sb/sth/yourself (from sth)** to move sb/sth that is caught or fixed on sth 釋放；使擺脫 SYN **release**：*Three people were freed from the wreckage.* 有三人被救出殘骸。◇ *She struggled to free herself.* 她掙扎着以求脱身。

▸ REMOVE STH 去除某物 **3** 🔑 **~ sb/sth of/from sb/sth** to remove sth that is unpleasant or not wanted from sb/sth 解除（或去除、清除）SYN **rid**：*These exercises help free the body of tension.* 這些鍛煉可使緊張的身體放鬆。◇ *The police are determined to free the town of violent crime.* 警方決心消滅該城鎮的暴力犯罪。◇ *The centre aims to free young people from dependency on drugs.* 這個中心的宗旨是使年輕人解除對毒品的依賴。

▸ MAKE AVAILABLE 使現成可用 **4** **~ sb/sth (up)** to make sb/sth available for a particular purpose 使可用（於某目的）：*We freed time each week for a project meeting.* 我們每週都騰出時間開一次項目會議。◇ *The government has promised to free up more resources for education.* 政府保證調撥更多資源用於教育。 **5** **~ sb to do sth** to give sb the extra time to do sth that they want to do 使能騰出時間：*Winning the prize freed him to paint full-time.* 獲獎使他能騰出時間整天作畫。

■ **adv.**

▸ WITHOUT PAYMENT 不需付款 **1** 🔑 (also **ˌfree of ˈcharge**) without payment 免費：*Children under five travel free.* 五歲以下兒童免費乘坐。

▸ NOT TRAPPED 未困住 **2** ⊶ away from or out of a position in which sb/sth is stuck or trapped 脫離束縛：*The wagon broke free from the train.* 這節貨車車廂脫離了列車。➲ see also SCOT-FREE

IDM **make free with 'sth** (*disapproving*) to use sth a lot, even though it does not belong to you 任意使用他人物品 **run 'free** (of an animal 動物) to be allowed to go where it likes; not tied to anything or kept in a CAGE 四處自由走動；自由自在 ➲ more at WALK *v.*

,free 'agent *noun* a person who can do whatever they want because they are not responsible to or for anyone else 有自主權的人；行動自由的人

free·base /'fri:beɪs/ *noun* [U] (*slang*) a specially prepared form of the powerful illegal drug COCAINE 精煉可卡因

free·bas·ing /'fri:beɪsɪŋ/ *noun* [U] (*slang*) the activity of smoking freebase 吸食精煉可卡因

free·bie /'fri:bi/ *noun* (*informal*) something that is given to sb without payment, usually by a company（常指公司提供的）免費品：*He took all the freebies that were on offer.* 他取了可得的全部免費品。◇ *a freebie holiday* 免費度假

free·boot·er /'fri:bu:tə(r)/ *noun* a person who takes part in a war in order to steal goods and money 戰爭掠奪者 ▸ **free·boot·ing** *adj., noun* [U]

free·born /'fri:bɔ:n; *NAmE* -bɔ:rn/ *adj.* [only before noun] (*formal*) not born as a SLAVE 生來自由的；生為自由民的

,Free 'Church *noun* a Christian Church that does not belong to the established Church in a particular country 自由教會（不屬於國教）

free·dom ⊶ /'fri:dəm/ *noun*

1 ⊶ [U, C] **~ (of sth)** the right to do or say what you want without anyone stopping you（指權利）自由：***freedom of speech/thought/expression/worship*** 言論／思想／表達／信仰自由 ◇ *a threat to* ***press/academic, etc. freedom*** 對新聞、學術等自由的威脅 ◇ *rights and freedoms guaranteed by the constitution* 憲法保障的權利和自由 **2** ⊶ [U, sing.] the state of being able to do what you want, without anything stopping you（指狀態）自由：**~ (of sth)** ***freedom of action/choice*** 行動／選擇自由 ◇ *Thanks to the automobile, Americans soon had a freedom of movement previously unknown.* 由於有了汽車，美國人很快就獲得了前所未有的行動自由。◇ **~ (to do sth)** *complete freedom to do as you wish* 按照自己意願行事的絕對自由 **3** ⊶ [U] the state of not being a prisoner or SLAVE 自由民地位（不是囚犯或奴隸）：*He finally won his freedom after twenty years in jail.* 他蹲了二十年監獄以後終於獲得了自由。 **4** ⊶ [U] **~ from sth** the state of not being affected by the thing mentioned 沒有…的情況；不受…影響的狀態：***freedom from fear/pain/hunger, etc.*** 免於恐懼、痛苦、飢餓等 **5** [sing.] **the ~ of sth** permission to use sth without restriction 自由使用權：*I was given the freedom of the whole house.* 我獲得全座房子的自由使用權。

IDM **the freedom of the 'city** (in Britain) an honour that is given to sb by a city as a reward for work they have done（英國）榮譽市民稱號 ➲ see also FREEMAN (1)

IDM see MANOEUVRE *n.*

'freedom fighter *noun* a name used to describe a person who uses violence to try to remove a government from power, by people who support this 自由鬥士（支持者用以稱呼使用暴力推翻政府的人）➲ compare GUERRILLA *n.*

,freedom of as'sembly *noun* [U] the right to have public meetings which is guaranteed by law in the US 集會自由（受美國法律保障的公開集會權利）

,freedom of associ'ation *noun* [U] the right to meet people and to form organizations without needing permission from the government 結社自由（無須政府批准成立組織的權利）

,freedom of infor'mation *noun* [U] the right to see any information that a government has about people and organizations 信息自由，資訊自由（查閱政府所掌握有關人民及組織的信息的權利）

,free 'enterprise *noun* [U] an economic system in which private businesses compete with each other without much government control 自由企業（原則）➲ compare PRIVATE ENTERPRISE

,free 'fall *noun* [U] **1** the movement of an object or a person falling through the air without engine power or a PARACHUTE（人或物的）自由下落：*a free fall display* 自由下落表演 **2** a sudden drop in the value of sth that cannot be stopped 價值突降不止：*Share prices have gone into free fall.* 股價猛跌不止。

,free-'floating *adj.* not attached to or controlled by anything 自由浮動的：*a free-floating exchange rate* 自由浮動匯率

Free·fone™ *noun* [U] = FREEPHONE

'free-for-all *noun* [sing.] **1** a situation in which there are no rules or controls and everyone acts for their own advantage 不加管制；自由放任：*The lowering of trade barriers has led to a free-for-all among exporters.* 降低貿易壁壘導致出口商各自為政。**2** a noisy fight or argument in which a lot of people take part 混戰；眾人激烈爭辯；大吵大鬧

'free form (also **,free 'morpheme**) *noun* (*linguistics* 語言) a unit of language that can be used by itself 自由語素；自由形素；自由形位：*The plural 's' is not a free form, as it must always be attached to a noun.* 表示複數的 s 不是自由語素，必須附着於名詞。

'free-form *adj.* [only before noun] (of art or music 美術或音樂) not created according to standard forms or structures 不按傳統格式的；獨創的：*a free-form jazz improvisation* 自由創作的爵士樂即興演出

free·gan /'fri:gən/ *noun* a person who only eats food that they can get for free and that would otherwise be thrown out or wasted 免費素食主義者（只吃不要錢的、將要扔掉或浪費的食物）

free·hand /'fri:hænd/ *adj.* [only before noun] drawn without using a ruler or other instruments 徒手畫的；不用儀器畫的：*a freehand drawing* 一幅徒手畫 ▸ **free·hand** *adv.*：*to draw freehand* 徒手作畫

free·hold /'fri:həʊld; *NAmE* -hoʊld/ *noun* [C, U] (*law* 律) (*especially BrE*) the fact of owning a building or piece of land for a period of time that is not limited（房地產）自由保有，完全保有，終身保有 ▸ **free·hold** *adj.*：*a freehold property* 終身保有的財產 **free·hold** *adv.*：*to buy a house freehold* 購買自由保有的房子 ➲ compare LEASEHOLD

free·hold·er /'fri:həʊldə(r); *NAmE* -hoʊld-/ *noun* (*law* 律) (*especially BrE*) a person who owns the freehold of a building or piece of land（房地產的）終身保有者，自由保有者，完全保有者 ➲ compare LEASEHOLDER

,free 'house *noun* (in Britain) a pub that can sell different types of beer because it is not owned and controlled by one particular BREWERY (= a company producing beer)（英國，不受某個酒廠約束的）酒吧，酒店 ➲ compare TIED HOUSE

,free 'kick *noun* (in football (SOCCER) and RUGBY 足球和橄欖球) an opportunity to kick the ball without any opposition, that is given to one team when the other team does sth wrong 任意球；自由球：*to take a free kick* 發任意球

free·lance /'fri:lɑ:ns; *NAmE* -læns/ *adj., verb*

▪ *adj.* earning money by selling your work or services to several different organizations rather than being employed by one particular organization 特約的；自由職業（者）的：*a freelance journalist* 自由新聞工作者 ◇ *freelance work* 特約工作 ➲ COLLOCATIONS at JOB ▸ **free·lance** *adv.*：(*especially BrE*) *I work freelance from home.* 我是在家中工作的自由職業者。

▪ *verb* [I] to earn money by selling your work to several different organizations 做特約工作；從事自由職業

free·lancer /'fri:lɑ:nsə(r); *NAmE* -lænsər/ (also **free·lance**) *noun* a person who works freelance 特約人員；自由職業者

free·load·er /'fri:ləʊdə(r); *NAmE* -loʊd-/ *noun* (*informal, disapproving*) a person who is always accepting free food and accommodation from other people without giving them anything in exchange 白吃白佔的人；寄生蟲；愛佔便宜的人 ▸ **free·load** *verb* [I] **free·load·ing** *adj.*, *noun* [U]

ˌfree ˈlove *noun* [U] (*old-fashioned*) the practice of having sex without being married or having several sexual relationships at the same time（無婚約的）自由性愛

free·ly 🔑 /ˈfriːli/ *adv.*
1 🔑 without anyone trying to prevent or control sth 不受限制地；無拘無束地；自由地：*the country's first freely elected president* 該國第一次自由選舉出的總統 ◇ *EU citizens can now travel freely between member states.* 歐盟國家的公民現在可以在成員國之間自由旅行。 **2** 🔑 without anything stopping the movement or flow of sth 無阻礙地；暢通地：*When the gate is raised, the water can flow freely.* 閘門提起時水就可以暢流。◇ *Traffic is now moving more freely following an earlier accident.* 早些時候的交通事故過後，現在交通順暢些了。◇ *The book is now* ***freely available*** *in the shops* (= it is not difficult to get a copy). 現在這本書在商店可以隨時買到。◇ (*figurative*) *The wine flowed freely* (= there was a lot of it to drink). 葡萄酒無限量供應。 **3** 🔑 without trying to avoid the truth even though it might be unpleasant or embarrassing 自願地；甘心情願地：*I freely admit that I made a mistake.* 我爽快地承認我犯了錯誤。 **4** 🔑 in an honest way without worrying about what people will say or do 直率地；坦率地：*For the first time he was able to speak freely without the fear of reprisals against his family.* 他第一次能夠直言不諱而不怕家人遭到報復。 **5** 🔑 in a willing and generous way 慷慨地；大方地：*Millions of people gave freely in response to the appeal for the victims of the earthquake.* 為響應救濟地震災民的呼籲，幾百萬人慷慨相助。 **6** a piece of writing that is translated **freely** is not translated exactly but the general meaning is given 以意譯方法；不拘於原文

free·man /ˈfriːmən/ *noun* (*pl.* **-men** /-mən/) **1** (*BrE*) a person who has been given the FREEDOM of a particular city as a reward for the work that they have done 榮譽市民 **2** a person who is not a SLAVE 自由民（非奴隸）

ˌfree ˈmarket *noun* an economic system in which the price of goods and services is affected by supply and demand rather than controlled by a government 自由市場：*She was a supporter of the* ***free market economy***. 她是自由市場經濟的擁護者。

ˌfree ˌmarkeˈteer *noun* a person who believes that prices should be allowed to rise and fall according to supply and demand and not be controlled by the government 主張自由市場者

Free·mason /ˈfriːmeɪsn/ (also **Mason**) *noun* a man belonging to a secret society whose members help each other and communicate using secret signs 共濟會成員

Free·mason·ry /ˈfriːmeɪsnri/ *noun* [U] **1** the system and practices of Freemasons 共濟會制 **2** **freemasonry** the friendship that exists between people who have the same profession or interests 同行情誼；志趣相投：*the freemasonry of actors* 演員的志趣相投

ˌfree ˈmorpheme *noun* (*linguistics* 語言) = FREE FORM

ˌfree on ˈboard *adj.* (*abbr.* **f.o.b.**) (*business* 商) including the cost of putting goods onto a ship in the price 船上交貨的；離岸價格的

ˌfree ˈpardon *noun* (*BrE*, *law* 律) = PARDON *n.* (1)

ˌfree ˈperiod *noun* (*BrE*) a period of time in a school day when a student or teacher does not have a class 空課，空課時間（學生或教師沒有課的時候）

Free·phone (also **Free·fone™**) /ˈfriːfəʊn; *NAmE* -foʊn/ *noun* [U] (in Britain) a system in which the cost of a telephone call is paid for by the organization being called, rather than by the person making the call（英國）受話方付費電話 ➲ compare TOLL-FREE

ˌfree ˈport *noun* a port at which tax is not paid on goods that have been brought there temporarily before being sent to a different country 自由港

Free·post /ˈfriːpəʊst; *NAmE* -poʊst/ *noun* [U] (in Britain) a system in which the cost of sending a letter is paid for by the organization receiving it, rather than by the person sending it（英國）受方付費郵遞

ˌfree ˈradical *noun* (*chemistry* 化) an atom or group of atoms that has an ELECTRON that is not part of a pair, causing it to take part easily in chemical reactions. Free radicals in the body are thought to be one of the causes of diseases such as cancer. 自由基；游離基 ➲ see also ANTIOXIDANT (1)

ˌfree-ˈrange *adj.* [usually before noun] connected with a system of farming in which animals are kept in natural conditions and can move around freely（動物）放養的：*free-range chickens* 放養的雞 ◇ *free-range eggs* 放養的雞產的蛋 ➲ compare BATTERY (4), BATTERY FARM

free·ride /ˈfriːraɪd/ (also **ˈfreeride board**) *noun* a type of SNOWBOARD used for riding on all types of snow 全能滑雪板（在各種雪上使用）

freeˈrunning *noun* [U] the activity or art of moving through a city by running, jumping and climbing under, around and through things in a way that is as elegant as possible 自由跑（指在城市中以儘量優美的方式奔跑、跳躍、攀爬、環繞、穿越的行為或藝術）➲ compare PARKOUR

ˌfree ˈsafety *noun* (in AMERICAN FOOTBALL 美式足球) a defending player who can try to stop any attacking player rather than one particular attacking player 自由後衛（沒有特定防守對象）

free·sia /ˈfriːʒə; ˈfriːziə/ *noun* a plant with yellow, pink, white or purple flowers with a sweet smell, which are also called freesias 小蒼蘭（花有香味，呈黃、粉紅、白或紫色）

ˌfree ˈspirit *noun* a person who is independent and does what they want instead of doing what other people do 獨立自主的人；有主見的人

ˌfree-ˈstanding *adj.* **1** not supported by or attached to anything 自力支撐的；無依附的；獨立的：*a free-standing sculpture* 獨立的雕塑 **2** not a part of sth else 單獨的；獨立的：*a free-standing adult education service* 自成體系的成人教育服務

free·style /ˈfriːstaɪl/ *noun*, *verb*
■ ***noun*** [U] **1** a swimming race in which people taking part can use any stroke they want (usually CRAWL) 自由式游泳競賽（泳式不限，參加者常選擇爬泳）：*the men's 400 m freestyle* 男子 400 米自由泳 **2** (often used as an adjective 常用作形容詞) a sports competition in which people taking part can use any style that they want 自由式體育比賽：*freestyle skiing* 自由式滑雪
■ ***verb*** [I] to RAP, play music, dance, etc. by inventing it as you do it, rather than by planning it in advance or following fixed patterns 即興說唱（或奏樂、舞蹈等）**SYN** **improvise**

free·think·er /ˌfriːˈθɪŋkə(r)/ *noun* a person who forms their own ideas and opinions rather than accepting those of other people, especially in religious teaching（尤指宗教教義的）自由思想者，思想自由的人 ▸ **ˌfree-ˈthink·ing** *adj.* [only before noun]

ˌfree ˈthrow *noun* (in BASKETBALL 籃球) an attempt to throw a ball into the BASKET without any player trying to stop you, that you are allowed after a FOUL 罰球

ˌfree-to-ˈair (*BrE*) *adj.* [usually before noun] (of television programmes 電視節目) that you do not have to pay to watch 免費收視的：*The company provides more than 20 free-to-air channels.* 本公司提供 20 多個免費收視頻道。

ˌfree ˈtrade *noun* [U] a system of international trade in which there are no restrictions or taxes on imports and exports 自由貿易（制度）➲ **COLLOCATIONS** at INTERNATIONAL

ˌfree ˈverse *noun* [U] (*technical* 術語) poetry without a regular rhythm or RHYME（無固定格律的）自由詩 ➲ compare BLANK VERSE

ˌfree ˈvote *noun* (in Britain) a vote by members of parliament in which they can vote according to their own beliefs rather than following the policy of their political party 自由投票（根據個人信念而非政黨政策）

free·ware /ˈfriːweə(r); *NAmE* -wer/ *noun* [U] (*computing* 計) computer software that is offered free for anyone to use 免費軟件；免費軟體 ➲ compare SHAREWARE

free·way /ˈfriːweɪ/ (also **ex·press·way**) *noun* (in the US) a wide road, where traffic can travel fast for long distances. You can only enter and leave freeways at special RAMPS. （美國）高速公路：*a freeway exit* 高速公路出口 ◇ *an accident on the freeway* 高速公路事故

free·wheel /ˌfriːˈwiːl/ *verb* [I] (+ **adv./prep.**) to ride a bicycle without using the PEDALS （騎自行車）滑行：*I freewheeled down the hill to the village.* 我從山上騎自行車一路滑行至村莊。

free·wheel·ing /ˌfriːˈwiːlɪŋ/ *adj.* [only before noun] (*informal*) not concerned about rules or the possible results of what you do 隨心所欲的；無拘無束的：*a free-wheeling lifestyle* 自由放縱的生活方式

ˌfree ˈwill *noun* [U] the power to make your own decisions without being controlled by God or FATE 自由意志

IDM **of your own free ˈwill** because you want to do sth rather than because sb has told or forced you to do it 自願：*She left of her own free will.* 她是自願離開的。

freeze /friːz/ *verb, noun*

■ **verb** (**froze** /frəʊz; *NAmE* froʊz/, **fro·zen** /ˈfrəʊzn; *NAmE* ˈfroʊzn/)

▸ **BECOME ICE** 結冰 **1** [I, T] to become hard, and often turn to ice, as a result of extreme cold; to make sth do this （使）凍結，結冰：*Water freezes at 0°C.* 水在 0 攝氏度時結冰。◇ *It's so cold that even the river has frozen.* 天氣冷得河都封凍了。◇ **~ sth** *The cold weather had frozen the ground.* 寒冷的天氣使地面都凍硬了。◇ **+ adj.** *The clothes **froze solid** on the washing-line.* 衣服在曬衣繩上凍成了硬塊。**OPP** **thaw**

▸ **OF PIPE/LOCK/MACHINE** 管子；鎖；機器 **2** [I, T] if a pipe, lock or machine **freezes**, or sth **freezes** it, it becomes blocked with frozen liquid and therefore cannot be used （使）凍住，凍堵：**~ (up)** *The pipes have frozen, so we've got no water.* 水管已經結冰堵住了，我們接不到水。◇ **~ sth (up)** *Ten degrees of frost had frozen the lock on the car.* 零下十攝氏度把轎車上的鎖凍住了。

▸ **OF WEATHER** 天氣 **3** [I] when **it freezes**, the weather is at or below 0° Celsius 冰凍；嚴寒：*It may freeze tonight, so bring those plants inside.* 今夜可能有霜凍，把花草搬進屋來吧。

▸ **BE VERY COLD** 很冷 **4** [I, T] to be very cold; to be so cold that you die 極冷；（使）凍死：*Every time she opens the window we all freeze.* 每次她開窗戶，我們都冷得要死。◇ *Two men **froze to death** on the mountain.* 兩個男子在山上凍死了。◇ **~ sb** *Two men were frozen to death on the mountain.* 兩個男子在山上凍死了。

▸ **FOOD** 食物 **5** [T] **~ sth** to keep food at a very low temperature in order to preserve it 冷凍貯藏；冷藏：*Can you freeze this cake?* 你能不能把這個蛋糕冷藏起來？◇ *These meals are ideal for home freezing.* 這些飯食很適合家庭冷藏。**6** [I] to be able to be kept at a very low temperature 能冷凍貯藏的：*Some fruits freeze better than others.* 有些水果比其他的適宜於冷藏。

▸ **STOP MOVING** 停住 **7** [I] to stop moving suddenly because of fear, etc. （因害怕等）不動，停住；驚呆；嚇呆：*I froze with terror as the door slowly opened.* 門慢慢開啟時我嚇呆了。◇ (*figurative*) *The smile froze on her lips.* 她保持着微笑的表情。◇ *The police officer shouted 'Freeze!' and the man dropped the gun.* 警察大喊"不准動！"那個男人便放下了槍。

▸ **COMPUTER** 計算機 **8** [I] when a computer screen **freezes**, you cannot move any of the images, etc. on it, because there is a problem with the system （熒幕）凍結

▸ **FILM/MOVIE** 電影 **9** [T] **~ sth** to stop a film/movie or video in order to look at a particular picture 使定格：*Freeze the action there!* 把這個畫面定格在那裏！➲ see also FREEZE-FRAME

▸ **WAGES/PRICES** 工資；物價 **10** [T] **~ sth** to hold wages, prices, etc. at a fixed level for a period of time 使固定不動 **SYN** **peg**：*Salaries have been frozen for the current year.* 今年的工資已凍結。

▸ **MONEY/BANK ACCOUNT** 現金賬；銀行賬戶 **11** [T] **~ sth** to prevent money, a bank account, etc. from being used by getting a court order which bans it 凍結（資金、銀行賬戶等）：*The company's assets have been frozen.* 這家公司的資產已被凍結。

IDM **freeze your ˈblood** | **make your ˈblood freeze** to make you extremely frightened or shocked 使人恐怖萬分；令人毛骨悚然 ➲ more at TRACK *n.*

PHR V **ˌfreeze sb↔ˈout (of sth)** (*informal*) to be deliberately unfriendly to sb, creating difficulties, etc. in order to stop or DISCOURAGE them from doing sth or taking part in sth 排擠，排斥（使不能參與…） **ˌfreeze ˈover** to become completely covered by ice 冰封：*The lake freezes over in winter.* 這個湖冬天全讓冰封住。

■ **noun**

▸ **OF WAGES/PRICES** 工資；價格 **1** the act of keeping wages, prices, etc. at a particular level for a period of time 凍結：*a wage/price freeze* 工資／物價的凍結

▸ **STOPPING STH** 停止 **2** [usually sing.] **~ (on sth)** the act of stopping sth 停止：*a freeze on imports* 停止進口

▸ **COLD WEATHER** 寒冷天氣 **3** [usually sing.] (*BrE*) an unusually cold period of weather during which temperatures stay below 0° Celsius 冰凍期；嚴寒期：*Farmers still talk about the **big freeze** of '99.* 農民至今還在談論 1999 年的大嚴寒。 **4** (*NAmE*) a short period of time, especially at night, when the temperature is below 0° Celsius 霜凍：*A freeze warning was posted for Thursday night.* 據警報星期四夜間有霜凍。

ˈfreeze-dry *verb* [usually passive] **~ sth** to preserve food or drink by freezing and drying it very quickly 冷凍乾燥保存（食物）

ˈfreeze-frame *noun* [U] the act of stopping a moving film at one particular FRAME (= picture) 定格；定幀

freezer /ˈfriːzə(r)/ (*BrE* also **ˌdeep ˈfreeze**) (*US* also **Deepfreeze™**, **ˌdeep ˈfreezer**) *noun* a large piece of electrical equipment in which you can store food for a long time at a low temperature so that it stays frozen 冷凍櫃；冰櫃 ➲ see also FRIDGE-FREEZER

freez·ing /ˈfriːzɪŋ/ *adj.* **1** extremely cold 極冷的：*It's freezing in here!* 這兒冷得不得了！◇ *I'm freezing!* 我要凍僵了！ ➲ **SYNONYMS** at COLD **2** [only before noun] having temperatures that are below 0° Celsius 冰凍的；冰點以下的：*freezing fog* 冰霧 ◇ *freezing temperatures* 凍結溫度 ➲ **SYNONYMS** at COLD ▸ **freez·ing** *adv.*：(*informal*) *It's freezing cold outside.* 外面極為寒冷。

ˈfreezing point *noun* **1** (also **freez·ing**) [U] 0° Celsius, the temperature at which water freezes 冰點：*Tonight temperatures will fall well below freezing (point).* 今夜溫度將遠降至冰點以下。 **2** [C, usually sing.] the temperature at which a particular liquid freezes 凍結點；凝固點：*the freezing point of polar sea water* 極地海水的凍結點

freight /freɪt/ *noun, verb*

■ **noun** [U] goods that are transported by ships, planes, trains or lorries/trucks; the system of transporting goods in this way （海運、空運或陸運的）貨物；貨運：*to send goods by air freight* 空運貨物 ◇ *a freight business* 貨運公司 ◇ *passenger and freight transportation services* 客貨運業務

■ **verb 1** **~ sth** to send or carry goods by air, sea or train 寄送，運送（貨物）；貨運 **2** [usually passive] **~ sth with sth** (*literary*) to fill sth with a particular mood or tone 使充滿（某種心情或口氣）：*Each word was freighted with anger.* 字字充滿憤怒。

ˈfreight car (*NAmE*) (*BrE* **wagon**) *noun* a railway/railroad truck for carrying goods （鐵路）貨車車廂，車皮

freight·er /ˈfreɪtə(r)/ *noun* a large ship or plane that carries goods 貨船；運輸飛機

ˈfreight train (*BrE* also **ˈgoods train**) *noun* a train that carries only goods 貨運列車 ➲ **VISUAL VOCAB** page V58

French /frentʃ/ *adj., noun*

■ **adj.** of or connected with France, its people or its language 法國的；法國人的；法語的

IDM **take French ˈleave** (*BrE*) to leave work without asking permission first 擅離職守

■ **noun** the language of France and some other countries 法語

IDM **excuse/pardon my 'French** (*informal*) used to say that you are sorry for swearing 請原諒我說髒話了；不好意思，我罵人了

ˌFrench ˈbean *noun* (*BrE*) = GREEN BEAN

ˌFrench ˈbraid (*NAmE*) (*BrE* **ˌFrench ˈplait**) *noun* a HAIRSTYLE for women in which all the hair is gathered into one large PLAIT/BRAID down the back of the head 法式辮子（腦後的一根大辮） ➲ **VISUAL VOCAB** page V60

ˌFrench ˈbread *noun* [U] white bread in the shape of a long thick stick 法式麵包棒

ˌFrench ˈCanada *noun* [U] the part of Canada where most French-speaking Canadians live, especially Quebec 加拿大法語區（尤指魁北克省，講法語的人聚居）

ˌFrench Caˈnadian *noun* a Canadian whose first language is French 母語為法語的加拿大人；法裔加拿大人 ► **ˌFrench Caˈnadian** *adj.*

ˌFrench ˈdoor *noun* (*especially NAmE*) a glass door, often one of a pair, that leads to a room, a garden/yard or a BALCONY 落地窗 ➲ **VISUAL VOCAB** page V17

ˌFrench ˈdressing *noun* [U, C] a mixture of oil, VINEGAR, etc. used to add flavour to a salad 法式色拉調料 **SYN** **vinaigrette**

ˌFrench ˈfry (also **fry**) (both *especially NAmE*) (*BrE* also **chip**) *noun* [usually pl.] a long thin piece of potato fried in oil or fat 油炸土豆條；炸薯條

ˌFrench ˈhorn (also **horn** especially in *BrE*) *noun* a BRASS musical instrument that consists of a long tube curled around in a circle with a wide opening at the end（銅管樂器）法國號，圓號 ➲ **VISUAL VOCAB** page V34

ˌFrench ˈkiss *noun* a kiss during which people's mouths are open and their tongues touch 法式接吻（接觸舌頭）

ˌFrench ˈletter *noun* (*old-fashioned, BrE, informal*) = CONDOM

ˌFrench ˈloaf *noun* = BAGUETTE (1)

ˌFrench ˈplait (*BrE*) (*NAmE* **ˌFrench ˈbraid**) *noun* a HAIRSTYLE for women in which all the hair is gathered into one large PLAIT/BRAID down the back of the head 法式辮子（腦後的一根大辮） ➲ **VISUAL VOCAB** page V60

ˌFrench ˈpleat (*BrE*) (*NAmE* **ˌFrench ˈtwist**) *noun* a HAIRSTYLE for women in which all the hair is lifted up at the back of the head, twisted and held in place（婦女的）捲筒型髮式；法式盤髮

ˌFrench ˈpolish *noun* [U] (*BrE*) a type of VARNISH (= transparent liquid) that is painted onto wooden furniture to give it a hard shiny surface 罩光漆；拋光漆 ► **ˌFrench ˈpolish** *verb* **~ sth**

ˌFrench ˈpress (*NAmE*) (*BrE* **cafe·tière**) *noun* a special glass container for making coffee with a metal FILTER that you push down 法式咖啡壺（有活動金屬過濾網） ➲ **VISUAL VOCAB** page V25

ˌFrench ˈstick *noun* = BAGUETTE (1) ➲ picture at STICK

ˌFrench ˈtoast *noun* [U] slices of bread that have been covered with a mixture of egg and milk and then fried 法國吐司（用麪包片蘸蛋奶油炸而成）

ˌFrench ˈtwist (*NAmE*) (*BrE* **ˌFrench ˈpleat**) *noun* a HAIRSTYLE for women in which all the hair is lifted up at the back of the head, twisted and held in place（婦女的）捲筒型髮式；法式盤髮 ➲ **VISUAL VOCAB** page V60

ˌFrench ˈwindow *noun* [usually pl.] a glass door, usually one of a pair, that leads to a garden/yard or BALCONY 落地窗 ➲ **VISUAL VOCAB** page V17

fre·net·ic /frəˈnetɪk/ *adj.* involving a lot of energy and activity in a way that is not organized 發狂似的；狂亂的：*a scene of frenetic activity* 瘋狂活動的場面 ► **fre·net·ic·al·ly** /-kli/ *adv.*

frenu·lum /ˈfrenjələm; *BrE* also ˈfriːn-/ (*BrE* also **frae·nu·lum**) /ˈfriːn-/ *noun* (*anatomy* 解) a small fold of skin that prevents an organ from moving too much, for example the fold of skin under the tongue 繫帶

fren·zied /ˈfrenzid/ *adj.* [usually before noun] involving a lot of activity and strong emotions in a way that is often violent or frightening and not under control 瘋狂的；狂暴的：*a frenzied attack* 瘋狂的進攻 ◇ *frenzied activity* 狂暴的活動 ► **fren·zied·ly** *adv.*

frenzy /ˈfrenzi/ *noun* [C, usually sing., U] (*pl.* **-ies**) **~ (of sth)** a state of great activity and strong emotion that is often violent or frightening and not under control 瘋狂；狂亂；狂暴：*in a **frenzy of activity/excitement/violence*** 瘋狂的活動／興奮／暴力 ◇ *The speaker worked the crowd up **into a frenzy**.* 演講者把聽眾煽動得瘋狂起來。◇ *an outbreak of patriotic frenzy* 愛國狂熱的迸發 ◇ *a killing frenzy* 使人精疲力竭的瘋狂 ➲ see also FEEDING FRENZY

fre·quency /ˈfriːkwənsi/ *noun* (*pl.* **-ies**) **1** [U, C] the rate at which sth happens or is repeated 發生率；出現率；重複率：*Fatal road accidents have decreased in frequency over recent years.* 近年來致命交通事故發生率已經下降。◇ *a society with a **high/low frequency*** (= happening often/not very often) *of stable marriages* 婚姻穩定率高／低的社會 ◇ *The program can show us **word frequency*** (= how often words occur in a language). 這個程序可給我們顯示詞頻。 **2** [U] the fact of sth happening often 頻繁：*the alarming frequency of computer errors* 計算機出錯的情況驚人的多 ◇ *Objects like this turn up at sales with surprising frequency.* 這樣的東西在拍賣會上出人意料地頻繁出現。 **3** [C, U] (*technical* 術語) the rate at which a sound or ELECTROMAGNETIC wave VIBRATES (= moves up and down)（聲波或電磁波振動的）頻率：*a **high/low frequency*** 高頻；低頻 **4** [C, U] (*technical* 術語) the number of radio waves for every second of a radio signal 頻率（無線電信號每秒電波數）：*a frequency band* 頻帶 ◇ *There are only a limited number of broadcasting frequencies.* 廣播頻率的數量有限。

fre·quent 🔑 *adj., verb*

■ ***adj.*** 🔑 /ˈfriːkwənt/ happening or doing sth often 頻繁的；經常發生的：*He is a frequent visitor to this country.* 他常常訪問這個國家。◇ *Her calls became less frequent.* 她打電話的次數減少了。◇ *There is a frequent bus service into the centre of town.* 公共汽車有很多班次開往市中心區。◇ *How frequent is this word* (= how often does it occur in the language)? 這個單詞出現的頻率如何？ **OPP** **infrequent**

■ ***verb*** /friˈkwent/ **~ sth** (*formal*) to visit a particular place often 常去，常到（某處）：*We met in a local bar much frequented by students.* 我們在學生經常去的一家酒吧裏相遇。

fre·quent·ly 🔑 /ˈfriːkwəntli/ *adv.* often 頻繁地；經常：*Buses run frequently between the city and the airport.* 公共汽車頻繁地來往於市區與機場之間。◇ *some of the most frequently asked questions about the Internet* 有關互聯網的最常見的提問 **OPP** **infrequently**

fresco /ˈfreskəʊ; *NAmE* -koʊ/ *noun* (*pl.* **-oes** or **-os**) [C, U] a picture that is painted on a wall while the PLASTER is still wet; the method of painting in this way 濕壁畫（牆壁灰泥未乾時繪）；濕壁畫技法 ➲ **COLLOCATIONS** at ART ➲ see also AL FRESCO

fresh 🔑 /freʃ/ *adj., adv.*

■ ***adj.*** (**fresh·er**, **fresh·est**)

► FOOD 食物 **1** 🔑 (usually of food 通常指食物) recently produced or picked and not frozen, dried or preserved in tins or cans 新鮮的；新產的；剛摘的：*Is this milk fresh?* 這是鮮牛奶嗎？◇ *fresh bread/flowers* 剛出爐的麪包；鮮花 ◇ *Eat plenty of fresh fruit and vegetables.* 多吃新鮮水果和蔬菜。◇ *vegetables fresh from the garden* 剛從菜園摘的蔬菜 ◇ *Our chefs use only the freshest produce available.* 我們的廚師只用現有最新鮮的農產品。

► NEW 新 **2** 🔑 made or experienced recently 新近的；新近出現的；新近體驗的：*fresh tracks in the snow* 雪地上的新腳印 ◇ *Let me write it down while it's still **fresh in my mind**.* 趁記憶猶新，我來把它寫下來。 **3** 🔑 [usually before noun] new or different in a way that adds to or replaces sth 新的；不同的：*fresh evidence* 新證據 ◇ *I think it's time we tried a fresh approach.* 我認為是嘗試新方法的時候了。◇ *a fresh coat of paint* 剛塗的一道油漆 ◇ *Could we order some fresh coffee?* 我們能點新煮的咖啡嗎？◇ *This is the opportunity he needs to **make a fresh start*** (= to try sth new after not being successful at sth else). 這是他所需要的重振旗鼓的機會。

▸ CLEAN/COOL 清潔；涼爽 **4** 🗝 [usually before noun] pleasantly clean, pure or cool 清新的；涼爽的： *a toothpaste that leaves a nice fresh taste in your mouth* 在口中留下舒適清涼味道的牙膏 ◇ *Let's go and get some* ***fresh air*** (= go outside where the air is cooler). 咱們出去呼吸點新鮮空氣。

▸ WATER 水 **5** 🗝 [usually before noun] containing no salt 淡的；無鹽的： *There is a shortage of fresh water on the island.* 島上缺少淡水。 ➲ see also FRESHWATER

▸ WEATHER 天氣 **6** 🗝 (of the wind 風) quite strong and cold 涼颼颼的 SYN **brisk**： *a fresh breeze* 清新的微風 **7** (*BrE*) quite cold with some wind 清涼的；清爽的： *It's fresh this morning, isn't it?* 今天早上涼颼颼的，是不是？

▸ CLEAR/BRIGHT 潔淨；鮮明 **8** 🗝 looking clear, bright and attractive 潔淨的；明淨的；亮麗的： *He looked fresh and neat in a clean white shirt.* 他穿上乾淨的白襯衫顯得清爽利落。 ◇ *a collection of summer dresses in fresh colours* 一系列色彩鮮豔的女夏裝 ◇ *a fresh complexion* 白淨的膚色

▸ FULL OF ENERGY 精力充沛 **9** [not usually before noun] full of energy 精力充沛： *Regular exercise will help you feel fresher and fitter.* 經常鍛煉會使你感覺更加精力充沛，身體健康。 ◇ *I managed to sleep on the plane and arrived feeling* ***as fresh as a daisy***. 我總算在飛機上睡了覺，到達時精神煥發。

▸ JUST FINISHED 剛結束 **10** **~ from sth** having just come from a particular place; having just had a particular experience 剛從…來；剛有過…經歷： *students fresh from college* 剛剛畢業的大學生 ◇ *fresh from her success at the Olympic Games* 剛從奧運會凱旋歸來的她

▸ RUDE/CONFIDENT 粗魯；自信 **11** [not before noun] **~ (with sb)** (*informal*) rude and too confident in a way that shows a lack of respect for sb or a sexual interest in sb 粗魯；無禮；（對異性）放肆： *Don't get fresh with me!* 別對我無禮！ ▸ **fresh·ness** *noun* [U]： *We guarantee the freshness of all our produce.* 我們保證我們的農產品都是新鮮的。 ◇ *the cool freshness of the water* 水的清涼 ◇ *I like the freshness of his approach to the problem.* 我喜歡他對這個問題新穎的處理方法。 IDM see BLOOD *n.*, BREATH, HEART

■ *adv.*

IDM **fresh out of sth** (*informal, especially NAmE*) having recently finished a supply of sth 剛用完（或售完等）： *Sorry, we're fresh out of milk.* 對不起，牛奶我們剛賣完。

fresh·en /ˈfreʃn/ *verb* **1** [T] **~ sth (up)** to make sth cleaner, cooler, newer or more pleasant 使潔淨（或涼爽、新鮮、宜人）： *The walls need freshening up with white paint.* 牆壁需要用白漆刷新。 ◇ *The rain had freshened the air.* 下雨使空氣變得清新了。 ◇ *Using a mouthwash freshens the breath.* 使用漱口液可以使口氣清新。 **2** [T] **~ sth (up)** (*especially NAmE*) to add more liquid to a drink, especially an alcoholic one 添加液體於（飲料，尤指酒）之中 ➲ see also TOP UP at TOP *v.* **3** [I] (of the wind 風) to become stronger and colder 增強變冷： *The wind will freshen tonight.* 今夜風力將加大，氣溫下降。

PHR V **ˌfreshen ˈup** | **ˌfreshen yourself ˈup** to wash and make yourself look clean and tidy 梳洗打扮： *I'll just go and freshen up before supper.* 晚飯前我要去梳洗打扮一番。

fresh·ener /ˈfreʃnə(r)/ *noun* [U, C] (often in compounds 常構成複合詞) a thing that makes sth cleaner, purer or more pleasant 使清潔（或純淨、清新、涼爽）之物： *air freshener* 空氣淨化劑

fresh·er /ˈfreʃə(r)/ *noun* (*BrE, informal*) a student who has just started his or her first term at a university 大學一年級新生

ˈfresh-faced *adj.* having a young, healthy-looking face 青春容光煥發的： *fresh-faced kids* 容光煥發的少年

fresh·ly 🗝 /ˈfreʃli/ *adv.*
usually followed by a past participle showing that sth has been made, prepared, etc. recently（通常後接過去分詞）剛剛，新近： *freshly brewed coffee* 剛煮的咖啡

fresh·man /ˈfreʃmən/ *noun* (*pl.* **-men** /-mən/) **1** (*especially NAmE*) a student who is in his or her first year at a university or college, or in the ninth grade at school（大學）一年級新生；（中學）九年級學生： *high school/college freshmen* 中學 / 大學一年級新生 ◇ *during my freshman year* 在我一年級期間 ➲ compare SOPHOMORE **2** (*CanE*) a first-year student at a university or college 大學一年級新生

fresh·water /ˈfreʃwɔːtə(r)/ *adj.* [only before noun] **1** living in water that is not the sea and is not salty 淡水中生長的： *freshwater fish* 淡水魚 **2** having water that is not salty 淡水的： *freshwater lakes* 淡水湖 ➲ compare SALT WATER

fret /fret/ *verb, noun*

■ *verb* **(-tt-)** [I, T] **~ (about/over sth)** | **~ (that ...)** (*especially BrE*) to be worried or unhappy and not able to relax 苦惱；煩躁；焦慮不安： *Fretting about it won't help.* 苦惱於事無補。 ◇ *Her baby starts to fret as soon as she goes out of the room.* 她一走出房間，嬰兒就躁動起來。

■ *noun* **1** one of the bars on the long thin part of a GUITAR, etc. Frets show you where to press the strings with your fingers to produce particular sounds.（吉他等指板上定音的）品 ➲ VISUAL VOCAB page V36 **2** (also **ˈsea fret**) (*NEngE*) MIST or FOG that comes in from the sea（從海上飄來的）霧氣，薄霧，霧

fret·ful /ˈfretfl/ *adj.* behaving in a way that shows you are unhappy or uncomfortable 煩躁的；苦惱的；不舒適的 SYN **restless** ▸ **fret·ful·ly** *adv.*

fret·saw /ˈfretsɔː/ *noun* a SAW with a thin blade that is used for cutting patterns in wood, metal, etc. 線鋸

fret·ted /ˈfretɪd/ *adj.* (*technical* 術語) (especially of wood or stone 尤指木頭或石頭) decorated with patterns 迴紋裝飾的；迴紋雕飾的

fret·work /ˈfretwɜːk; *NAmE* -wɜːrk/ *noun* [U] patterns cut into wood, metal, etc. to decorate it; the process of making these patterns 迴紋飾；迴紋飾工序

Freud·ian /ˈfrɔɪdiən/ *adj.* **1** connected with the ideas of Sigmund Freud about the way the human mind works, especially his theories of unconscious sexual feelings 弗洛伊德學說的，與弗洛伊德學說有關的（關於人的內心活動方式，尤指對潛在性感情的理論） **2** (of sb's speech or behaviour 語言或行為) showing your secret thoughts or feelings, especially those connected with sex（尤指性方面）表示出內心思想感情的

ˌFreudian ˈslip *noun* something you say by mistake but which is believed to show your true thoughts 漏嘴，失言（無意中泄露內心思想） ORIGIN This expression is named after Sigmund Freud and his theories of unconscious thought. 源自西格蒙德 • 弗洛伊德及其潛意識理論。

fri·able /ˈfraɪəbl/ *adj.* (*technical* 術語) easily broken up into small pieces 脆的；易碎的；易粉碎的： *friable soil* 鬆散土壤

friar /ˈfraɪə(r)/ *noun* a member of one of several Roman Catholic religious communities of men who in the past travelled around teaching people about Christianity and lived by asking other people for food (= by BEGGING)（天主教）托鉢會士 ➲ compare MONK

fri·ary /ˈfraɪəri/ *noun* (*pl.* **-ies**) a building in which friars live 托鉢修院；會院

fric·as·see /ˈfrɪkəsiː/ *noun* [C, U] a hot dish consisting of small pieces of meat and vegetables that are cooked and served in a thick white sauce 濃汁肉菜丁；白汁燉肉

frica·tive /ˈfrɪkətɪv/ (*BrE*) (*NAmE* **spir·ant**) *noun* (*phonetics* 語音) a speech sound made by forcing breath out through a narrow space in the mouth with the lips, teeth or tongue in a particular position, for example /f/ and /ʃ/ in *fee* and *she* 摩擦音 ▸ **frica·tive** *adj.* ➲ compare PLOSIVE

fric·tion /ˈfrɪkʃn/ *noun* **1** [U] the action of one object or surface moving against another 摩擦： *Friction between moving parts had caused the engine to overheat.* 活動部件的摩擦使發動機過熱。 **2** [U] (*physics* 物) the RESISTANCE (= the force that stops sth moving) of one surface to another surface or substance moving over or through it 摩擦力： *The force of friction slows the spacecraft down as it re-enters the earth's atmosphere.* 太空船重返地球

F

大氣層時因有摩擦力而減慢速度。 **3** [U, C] **~ (between A and B)** disagreement or a lack of friendship among people who have different opinions about sth 爭執；分歧；不和 **SYN** **tension**： *conflicts and frictions that have still to be resolved* 仍有待解決的衝突和摩擦

'friction tape *noun* [U] (*US*) = INSULATING TAPE

Fri·day /'fraɪdeɪ; -di/ *noun* [C, U] (*abbr.* **Fri.**) the day of the week after Thursday and before Saturday 星期五 **HELP** To see how **Friday** is used, look at the examples at **Monday**. * Friday 的用法見詞條 Monday 下的示例。 **ORIGIN** Originally translated from the Latin for 'day of the planet Venus' *Veneris dies* and named after the Germanic goddess *Frigga*. 譯自拉丁文 Veneris dies，原意為 day of the planet Venus（金星日），以日耳曼女神 Frigga（弗麗嘉）命名。

F

fridge /frɪdʒ/ (*BrE*) (*NAmE* or *formal* **re·friger·ator**) (*US* also *old-fashioned* **ice·box**) *noun* a piece of electrical equipment in which food is kept cold so that it stays fresh 冰箱： *This dessert can be served straight from the fridge.* 這種甜食從冰箱裏拿出來就可以吃。 ⊃ VISUAL VOCAB page V25

,fridge-'freezer *noun* (*BrE*) a piece of kitchen equipment that consists of a fridge/refrigerator and a FREEZER together（有冷藏室和冷凍室的）立式冰箱；雙門冰箱

fried *past tense, past part.* of FRY

friend /frend/ *noun*

▸ PERSON YOU LIKE 喜歡的人 **1** a person you know well and like, and who is not usually a member of your family 朋友；友人：*This is my friend Tom.* 這是我的朋友湯姆。◇ *Is he* ***a friend of yours?*** 他是你的朋友嗎？◇ *She's an* ***old friend*** (= I have known her a long time). 她是我的老朋友。◇ *He's one of my* ***best friends.*** 他是我最要好的朋友之一。◇ *a* ***close/good friend*** 密友；好友◇ *a* ***childhood/family/lifelong friend*** 兒時／家庭／終生朋友◇ *I heard about it through* ***a friend of a friend.*** 我通過朋友的朋友聽到這事的。◇ *She has a wide* ***circle of friends.*** 她交遊很廣。 ⊃ see also BEFRIEND, BOYFRIEND, FAIR-WEATHER, FALSE FRIEND (1), GIRLFRIEND, PENFRIEND, SCHOOL FRIEND

▸ SUPPORTER 支持者 **2** a person who supports an organization, a charity, etc., especially by giving or raising money; a person who supports a particular idea, etc. 贊助者；支持者：*the Friends of St Martin's Hospital* 聖馬丁醫院的贊助者◇ *a friend of democracy* 維護民主的人

▸ NOT ENEMY 不是敵人 **3** a person who has the same interests and opinions as yourself, and who will help and support you 自己人；同志；同夥；同盟者： *You're among friends here—you can speak freely.* 這兒都是自己人，有話直說吧。

▸ SILLY/ANNOYING PERSON 愚蠢的／討厭的人 **4** (*ironic*) used to talk about sb you do not know who has done sth silly or annoying（指做傻事或煩人的事而說話者不認識的人）： *I wish our friend at the next table would shut up.* 但願我們鄰桌那位仁兄閉嘴。

▸ IN PARLIAMENT/COURT 議會；法庭 **5** (in Britain 英國) used by a member of parliament to refer to another member of parliament or by a lawyer to refer to another lawyer in a court of law（議員間或律師間的一種稱呼）朋友，閣下，同仁： *my* ***honourable friend,*** *the member for Henley* (= in the House of Commons) 我尊敬的朋友亨利區議員（下院用語）◇ *my* ***noble friend*** (= in the House of Lords) 我尊貴的朋友（上院用語）◇ *my* ***learned friend*** (= in a court of law) 我博學的同仁（法庭用語）

▸ IN RELIGION 宗教 **6 Friend** a member of the Society of Friends（新教）公誼會成員 **SYN** **Quaker**

IDM **be/make 'friends (with sb)** to be/become a friend of sb 是／成為（某人的）朋友：*We've been friends for years.* 我們是多年的朋友了。◇ *They had a quarrel, but they're friends again now.* 他們吵過架，不過現在又和好了。◇ *Simon finds it hard to make friends with other children.* 西蒙感到難以和其他孩子交朋友。 **be (just) good 'friends** used to say that two friends are not having a romantic relationship with each other（無戀愛關係）（只）是好朋友 **a ,friend in 'need (is a ,friend in'deed)** (*saying*) a friend who gives you help when you need it (is a true friend) 患難的朋友（才是真正的朋友）；患難之交（見真情） **have ,friends in high 'places** to know important people who can help you 有位高權重的朋友；有貴人相助 ⊃ more at MAN *n.*

friend·less /'frendləs/ *adj.* without any friends 沒有朋友的

friend·ly /'frendli/ *adj., noun*

■ *adj.* (**friend·lier, friend·li·est**) **1** behaving in a kind and pleasant way because you like sb or want to help them 友愛的；友好的：*a warm and friendly person* 熱情友好的人◇ **~ to/toward(s) sb** *Everyone was very friendly towards me.* 每個人都對我十分友好。 **OPP** **unfriendly** **2** showing kindness; making you feel relaxed and as though you are among friends 善意的；親切的；和藹可親的： *a* ***friendly smile/welcome*** 親切的微笑；友好的歡迎◇ *a small hotel with a friendly atmosphere* 賓至如歸的小旅館 **OPP** **unfriendly** **3** **~ (with sb)** treating sb as a friend 朋友似的： *We soon became friendly with the couple next door.* 我們很快就和隔壁的夫婦友好相處了。◇ *She was* ***on friendly terms*** *with most of the hospital staff.* 她和醫院大多數工作人員關係融洽。 **4** (especially of the relationship between countries 尤指國與國之間的關係) not treating sb/sth as an enemy 友好的；和睦的： *to maintain* ***friendly relations*** *with all countries* 與所有國家保持友好關係 **OPP** **hostile** **5** (often in compound adjectives 常構成複合形容詞) that is helpful and easy to use; that helps sb/sth or does not harm it 好用的；有用的；無害的： *This software is much friendlier than the previous version.* 這個軟件比之前的版本好用得多。◇ *environmentally-friendly farming methods* 環保耕作法◇ *ozone-friendly cleaning materials* 對臭氧無害的清潔材料 ⊃ see also USER-FRIENDLY **6** in which the people, teams, etc. taking part are not seriously competing against each other（比賽）為增進友誼的；非對抗性的： *a friendly argument* 友好的辯論◇ *friendly rivalry* 友好競爭◇ (*BrE*) *It was only a friendly match.* 這僅是一場友誼賽。 ▸ **friend·li·ness** *noun* [U]

■ *noun* (*pl.* **-ies**) (also **'friendly match**) (both *BrE*) a game of football (SOCCER) etc. that is not part of an important competition（足球等的）友誼賽

,friendly 'fire *noun* [U] in a war, if people are killed or injured by **friendly fire**, they are hit by a bomb or weapon that is fired by their own side 誤殺，誤傷（戰爭中由己方或友軍造成的死傷）

'friendly society *noun* (in Britain) an organization that people pay regular amounts of money to, and which gives them money when they are ill/sick or old（英國）友愛社（會員定期交費以備生病或年老之用）

friend·ship /'frendʃɪp/ *noun*

1 [C] a relationship between friends 友誼；朋友關係： *a* ***close/lasting/lifelong friendship*** 親密的／持久的／終生的友誼◇ *friendships formed while she was at college* 她在大學時建立的友誼◇ **~ with sb** *He seemed to have already* ***struck up*** (= begun) ***a friendship*** *with Jo.* 他似乎已經開始和喬交朋友了。◇ **~ between A and B** *It's the story of an extraordinary friendship between a boy and a seal.* 這是一個關於男孩和海豹之間非凡友誼的故事。 **2** [U] the feeling or relationship that friends have; the state of being friends 友情；友誼；友好： *Your friendship is very important to me.* 你的友情對我非常重要。◇ *a conference to promote international friendship* 促進國際友好關係的會議

frier = FRYER

Frie·sian /'friːʒn/ (*BrE*) (*NAmE* **Hol·stein**) *noun* a type of black and white cow that produces a lot of milk 黑白花乳牛，荷蘭牛（產奶量很大）

frieze /friːz/ *noun* **1** a border that goes around the top of a room or building with pictures or CARVINGS on it 飾帶，帶狀裝飾 **2** a long narrow picture, usually put up in a school, that children have made or that teaches them sth 長條橫幅圖畫（通常校內展示的學生習作或有教育意義的圖畫）

frig·ate /'frɪɡət/ *noun* a small fast ship in the navy that travels with other ships in order to protect them（小型）護衛艦

frig·ging /ˈfrɪɡɪŋ/ *adv., adj.* [only before noun] (*taboo, slang*) a swear word that many people find offensive, used to emphasize a comment or an angry statement to avoid saying 'fucking'（避免使用 fucking 而說的粗話）該死地（的），他媽地（的）：*It's frigging cold outside.* 外面真他媽的冷。◇ *Mind your own frigging business!* 別他媽多管閒事！

fright /fraɪt/ *noun* **1** [U] a feeling of fear 驚嚇；恐怖：*to cry out **in fright*** 嚇得大聲叫喊 ◇ *He was shaking **with fright**.* 他嚇得發抖。➲ SYNONYMS at FEAR ➲ see also STAGE FRIGHT **2** [C] an experience that makes you feel fear 使人驚嚇的經歷；恐怖的經歷：*You **gave me a fright** jumping out at me like that.* 你這樣跳起來撲向我，把我嚇了一大跳。◇ *I got the **fright of my life**.* 我嚇得要命。
IDM **look a ˈfright** (*old-fashioned, BrE*) to look ugly or ridiculous 模樣醜陋；像醜八怪；樣子古怪 **take ˈfright (at sth)** (*formal*) to be frightened by sth（因某事）受驚嚇：*The birds took fright and flew off.* 鳥受驚飛走了。

fright·en 🗝 /ˈfraɪtn/ *verb*
[T, I] **~ (sb)** | **~ sb to do sth** to make sb suddenly feel afraid 使驚嚇；使驚恐：*Sorry, I didn't mean to frighten you.* 對不起，我沒有嚇唬你的意思。◇ *She's not easily frightened.* 她不是輕易嚇倒的。◇ *She **doesn't frighten easily*** (= it is not easy to make her afraid). 她不是輕易嚇倒的。**IDM** see DAYLIGHTS, DEATH, LIFE
PHR V **ˌfrighten sb/sth↔aˈway/ˈoff** | **ˌfrighten sb/sth aˈway from sth** **1** 🗝 to make a person or an animal go away by making them feel afraid 把…嚇走（或嚇跑）：*He threatened the intruders with a gun and frightened them off.* 他用槍威脅闖入者，把他們嚇跑了。**2** 🗝 to make sb afraid or nervous so that they no longer want to do sth 把…嚇得不敢（做某事）：*The high prices have frightened off many customers.* 高價使許多顧客卻步。**ˈfrighten sb into sth/into doing sth** to make sb do sth by making them afraid 把…嚇得做某事

Synonyms 同義詞辨析

frighten
scare • alarm • terrify

These words all mean to make sb afraid. 以上各詞均含使害怕、使恐懼之意。

frighten to make sb feel afraid, often suddenly 指（常為突如其來地）使驚嚇、使驚恐：*He brought out a gun and frightened them off.* 他掏出一把槍，把他們嚇跑了。

scare to make sb feel afraid 指使害怕、使恐懼：*They managed to scare the bears away.* 他們設法把那些熊嚇跑了。

alarm to make sb anxious or afraid 指使驚恐、使害怕、使擔心：*It alarms me that nobody takes this problem seriously.* 誰都不認真對待這個問題，我非常擔心。**NOTE** **Alarm** is used when sb has a feeling that sth unpleasant or dangerous might happen in the future; the feeling is often more one of worry than actual fear. * alarm 指令人擔心不好的事情或危險可能發生，多為憂慮而非真的害怕。

terrify to make sb feel extremely afraid 指使恐懼、使十分害怕、使驚嚇：*Flying terrified her.* 她害怕坐飛機。

FRIGHTEN OR SCARE? 用 frighten 還是 scare？

Scare is slightly more informal than **frighten**. * scare 較 frighten 稍非正式。

PATTERNS

- to frighten/scare sb/sth **away/off**
- to frighten/scare/terrify sb **into** doing sth
- **It** frightens/scares/alarms/terrifies me **that** …
- **It** frightens/scares/alarms/terrifies me **to** think, see, etc.

fright·ened 🗝 /ˈfraɪtnd/ *adj.*
afraid; feeling fear 驚嚇的；受驚的；害怕的：*a frightened child* 受了驚嚇的小孩 ◇ *Don't be frightened.* 別害怕。◇ *He sounded frightened.* 他聽起來受了驚。◇ **~ of sth** *What are you frightened of?* 你怕什麼？◇ **~ of doing sth** *I'm frightened of walking home alone in the dark.* 我害怕在黑夜單獨走路回家。◇ **~ to do sth** *I'm too frightened to ask him now.* 現在我嚇得不敢問他了。◇ **~ that …** *She was frightened that the plane would crash.* 她害怕飛機會墜毀。◇ **~ for sb** *I'm frightened for him* (= that he will be hurt, etc.). 我為他的安全擔驚受怕。◇ (*informal*) *I'd never do that. I'd be **frightened to death**.* 我絕不會幹。我會嚇死的。➲ SYNONYMS at AFRAID **IDM** see SHADOW *n.*, WIT

fright·en·ers /ˈfraɪtnəz; *NAmE* -nərz/ *noun*
IDM **put the ˈfrighteners on sb** (*BrE, slang*) to threaten sb in order to make them do what you want 威逼，脅迫（某人做某事）

fright·en·ing 🗝 /ˈfraɪtnɪŋ/ *adj.*
making you feel afraid 引起恐懼的；使驚恐的；駭人的：*a frightening experience/prospect/thought* 可怕的經歷／景象／想法 ◇ ***It's frightening** to think it could happen again.* 想到此事可能再次發生就使人不寒而慄。▸ **fright·en·ing·ly** *adv.*

fright·ful /ˈfraɪtfl/ *adj.* (*old-fashioned, especially BrE*) **1** (*informal*) used to emphasize how bad sth is 極壞的；很糟的 **SYN** **awful, terrible**：*It was absolutely frightful!* 簡直糟透了！◇ *This room's in a frightful mess.* 房間裏亂七八糟。**2** very serious or unpleasant 十分嚴重的；令人很不愉快的 **SYN** **awful, terrible**：*a frightful accident* 十分嚴重的事故

fright·ful·ly /ˈfraɪtfəli/ *adv.* (*old-fashioned, especially BrE*) very; extremely 十分；極其 **SYN** **awfully**：*I'm frightfully sorry.* 我非常抱歉。

ˈfright wig *noun* a WIG with the hair standing up or sticking out, especially worn by a CLOWN（尤指小丑戴的髮絲豎立或四散的）滑稽假髮

fri·gid /ˈfrɪdʒɪd/ *adj.* **1** (of a woman 女子) not able to enjoy sex 性冷淡的；達不到性高潮的；性冷感的 **2** very cold 寒冷的；嚴寒的：*frigid air* 冰冷的空氣 **3** not showing any feelings of friendship or kindness 冷淡的 **SYN** **frosty**：*a frigid voice* 冷冰冰的聲音 ◇ *There was a frigid atmosphere in the room.* 房間裏一片冷淡的氣氛。▸ **fri·gid·ly** *adv.*

fri·gid·ity /frɪˈdʒɪdəti/ *noun* [U] (in a woman) the lack of the ability to enjoy sex（女子）性冷淡，性感缺失，性冷感

ˈfrigid zone *noun* [C, usually sing.] (*technical* 術語) the area inside the Arctic Circle or Antarctic Circle（南、北極圈內的）寒帶 ➲ compare TEMPERATE ZONE, TORRID ZONE

frill /frɪl/ *noun* **1** (*BrE*) [C] a narrow strip of cloth with a lot of folds that is attached to the edge of a dress, curtain, etc. to decorate it（衣服、窗簾等的）飾邊，褶邊，荷葉邊：*a white blouse with frills at the cuffs* 袖口上有褶邊的女襯衫 **SYN** **ruffle** **2** **frills** [pl.] things that are not necessary but are added to make sth more attractive or interesting 不實用的裝飾；虛飾：*a simple meal with no frills* 簡單的一頓便飯 ➲ see also NO-FRILLS

frilled /frɪld/ *adj.* (*BrE*) decorated with 帶飾邊的；有褶邊的 frills **SYN** **ruffled**

frilly /ˈfrɪli/ *adj.* having a lot of frills 多飾邊的；多褶邊的：*a frilly blouse* 多褶邊的女襯衫

fringe /frɪndʒ/ *noun, verb*
■ **noun** **1** [C, usually sing.] (*BrE*) (*NAmE* **bangs** [pl.]) the front part of sb's hair that is cut so that it hangs over their FOREHEAD 額前短垂髮；劉海兒 ➲ VISUAL VOCAB page V60 **2** [C] a strip of hanging threads attached to the edge of sth to decorate it（某物的）穗，緣飾，流蘇 **3** [C] a narrow strip of trees, buildings, etc. along the edge of sth（沿…邊緣的）一排（樹木、房屋等）：*a fringe of woodland* 一條林帶 ◇ *Along the coast, an industrial fringe had already developed.* 沿海岸一片帶狀

F

工業區已發展起來。**4** [C] (*BrE*) the outer edge of an area or a group （地區或群體的）邊緣：*on the northern fringe of the city* 該市的北部邊緣 ◇ *the urban/rural fringe* 市區 / 農村邊緣 ◇ *the fringes of society* 社會的邊緣 ◇ *Nina remained on the fringe of the crowd.* 尼娜仍然在人群的邊上。**5** [sing.] (usually **the fringe**) groups of people, events and activities that are not part of the main group or activity （指群體、事情或活動）次要部份，外圍：*Street musicians have been gathering as part of the festival fringe.* 街頭音樂人正聚集起來，為會演作助興演出。◇ *fringe meetings at the party conference* 黨會議的一些分組會議 **IDM** see LUNATIC *adj.*

■ *verb* [usually passive] **~ sth** to form a border around sth 形成…的邊緣：*The beach was fringed by coconut palms.* 沿海岸邊長着椰子樹。▸ **fringed** *adj.*：*a carpet with a fringed edge* 四邊有穗子的地毯

ˈfringe benefit *noun* [usually pl.] extra things that an employer gives you as well as your wages（工資外的）額外補貼，附加福利：*The fringe benefits include free health insurance.* 附加福利包括免費健康保險。

ˌfringe ˈmedicine *noun* [U] any type of treatment which is not accepted by many people as being part of Western medicine, for example one using plants instead of artificial drugs 邊緣療法（不為多數人所接受的非西醫療法）

ˌfringe ˈtheatre *noun* [U, C] (*BrE*) plays, often by new writers, that are unusual and question the way people think; a theatre where such plays are performed 邊緣戲劇（常由新作家寫）；邊緣劇院 ➲ compare OFF-BROADWAY

frip·pery /ˈfrɪpəri/ *noun* [C, usually pl., U] (*pl.* **-ies**) (*disapproving, especially BrE*) objects, decorations and other items that are considered unnecessary and expensive 不必要的昂貴飾品（或物件）

Fris·bee™ /ˈfrɪzbi/ *noun* a light plastic object, shaped like a plate, that is thrown from one player to another in a game 弗里斯比飛盤（投擲遊戲用的飛碟）➲ VISUAL VOCAB page V37

fri·sée /ˈfriːzeɪ; *NAmE* friːˈzeɪ/ *noun* = CHICORY (2)

Fris·ian /ˈfriːʒn/ *noun* [U] the traditional language of the region of Frisia in NW Europe, closely related to German, Dutch and English 弗里西亞語

frisk /frɪsk/ *verb* **1** [T] **~ sb** to pass your hands over sb's body to search them for hidden weapons, drugs, etc. 搜（某人）的身 **2** [I] **~ (around)** (of animals 動物) to run and jump in a lively and happy way 活蹦亂跳 **SYN** **gambol, skip**：*Lambs frisked in the fields.* 羊羔在田野裏活蹦亂跳。

frisky /ˈfrɪski/ *adj.* (**frisk·ier**, **friski·est**) **1** (of people or animals 人或動物) full of energy; wanting to play 活潑的；活蹦亂跳的；愛玩耍的：*a frisky puppy* 活潑的小狗 **2** (*informal*) wanting to enjoy yourself in a sexual way 有性要求的；動手動腳的

fris·son /ˈfriːsɒ̃; *NAmE* friːˈsoʊn/ *noun* [usually sing.] (from *French*) a sudden strong feeling, especially of excitement or fear 強烈興奮感；恐懼感；震顫

fri·til·lary /frɪˈtɪləri; *NAmE* ˈfrɪtleri/ *noun* (*pl.* **fri·til·lar·ies**) **1** a plant with flowers shaped like bells 貝母（花鐘狀）**2** a BUTTERFLY with orange-brown and black wings 豹紋蝶

frit·ter /ˈfrɪtə(r)/ *verb, noun*

■ *verb*

PHR V **ˌfritter sth↔aˈway (on sth)** to waste time or money on things that are not important 浪費（時間、金錢）；揮霍：*He frittered away the millions his father had left him.* 他揮霍掉了父親留給他的數百萬錢財。

■ *noun* (usually in compounds 通常構成複合詞) a piece of fruit, meat or vegetable that is covered with BATTER and fried 油炸餡餅

fritz /frɪts/ *noun*

IDM **on the ˈfritz** (*NAmE, informal*) not working 出故障：*The TV is on the fritz again.* 電視機又出故障了。

fri·vol·ity /frɪˈvɒləti; *NAmE* -ˈvɑːl-/ *noun* (*pl.* **-ies**) (often *disapproving*) [U, C] behaviour that is silly or amusing, especially when this is not suitable 愚蠢的行為；可笑的表現；輕浮的舉止：*It was just a piece of harmless frivolity.* 這僅是無惡意的愚蠢行為。◇ *I can't waste time on such frivolities.* 我不能把時間浪費在這種無聊的活動上。

frivo·lous /ˈfrɪvələs/ *adj.* (*disapproving*) **1** (of people or their behaviour 人或行為) silly or amusing, especially when such behaviour is not suitable 愚蠢的；可笑的：***frivolous comments/suggestions*** 愚蠢的話；可笑的建議 ◇ *Sorry, I was being frivolous.* 對不起，我失態了。**2** having no useful or serious purpose 無聊的；不嚴肅的：***frivolous pastimes/pleasures*** 無聊的消遣 / 娛樂 ▸ **frivo·lous·ly** *adv.*

frizz /frɪz/ *verb, noun*

■ *verb* [I, T] **~ (sth)** (*informal*) (of hair 頭髮) to curl very tightly; to make hair do this （使）鬈曲，捲緊 ▸ **frizzy** *adj.* (**friz·zi·er**, **friz·zi·est**)：*frizzy hair* 鬈髮

■ *noun* [U] (*disapproving*) hair that is very tightly curled 鬈髮；鬈毛

friz·zle /ˈfrɪzl/ *verb* **~ sth** to heat sth until it forms curls or until it burns 把…燙捲曲；把…烤焦：*frizzled hair* 鬈髮 ◇ *frizzled bacon* 烤熏豬肉

fro /frəʊ; *NAmE* froʊ/ *adv.* **IDM** see TO *adv.*

frock /frɒk; *NAmE* frɑːk/ *noun* (*old-fashioned, especially BrE*) a dress 連衣裙；女裝：*a party frock* 女式禮服

ˈfrock coat *noun* a long coat worn in the past by men, now worn only for special ceremonies 男長禮服；佛若克男禮服大衣

frog /frɒg; *NAmE* frɔːg; frɑːg/ *noun* **1** a small animal with smooth skin, that lives both on land and in water (= is an AMPHIBIAN). Frogs have very long back legs for jumping, and no tail. 蛙；青蛙：*the croaking of frogs* 蛙鳴 ➲ VISUAL VOCAB page V13 **2** **Frog** (*informal*) an offensive word for a French person （對法國人的蔑稱）

IDM **have, etc. a ˈfrog in your throat** to lose your voice or be unable to speak clearly for a short time （暫時）失音，嗓音嘶啞

frog·ging /ˈfrɒgɪŋ; *NAmE* ˈfrɔːg-; ˈfrɑːg-/ *noun* [U] a decorative fastening on a coat consisting of a long wooden button and a LOOP 盤花鈕扣

frog·let /ˈfrɒglət; *NAmE* ˈfrɔːg-; ˈfrɑːg-/ *noun* **1** a type of small frog 小青蛙 **2** a small frog that has recently changed from being a TADPOLE 幼蛙

frog·man /ˈfrɒgmən; *NAmE* ˈfrɔːg-; ˈfrɑːg-/ *noun* (*pl.* **-men** /-mən/) (*BrE*) a person who works underwater, wearing a rubber suit, FLIPPERS, and special equipment to help them breathe 蛙人：*Police frogmen searched the lake for the murder weapon.* 警方的蛙人搜索這個湖，尋找謀殺兇器。➲ compare DIVER (1)

frog·march /ˈfrɒgmɑːtʃ; *NAmE* ˈfrɔːgmɑːrtʃ; ˈfrɑːg-/ *verb* **~ sb + adv./prep.** (*BrE*) to force sb to go somewhere by holding their arms tightly so they have to walk along with you 緊抓雙臂押送；挾持而行：*He was grabbed by two men and frogmarched out of the hall.* 他被兩個男人緊抓雙臂押出大廳。

frog·spawn /ˈfrɒgspɔːn; *NAmE* ˈfrɔːg-; ˈfrɑːg-/ *noun* [U] an almost transparent substance that looks like jelly and contains the eggs of a FROG 蛙卵；蛙的卵塊 ➲ VISUAL VOCAB page V13

fro·ing /ˈfrəʊɪŋ; *NAmE* ˈfroʊɪŋ/ *noun* **IDM** see TOING

frolic /ˈfrɒlɪk; *NAmE* ˈfrɑːl-/ *verb, noun*

■ *verb* (**-ck-**) [I] to play and move around in a lively, happy way 嬉戲；嬉鬧：*children frolicking on the beach* 在海灘上嬉戲的兒童

■ *noun* [C, U] (*old-fashioned*) a lively and enjoyable activity during which people forget their problems and responsibilities 歡樂的活動：*It was just a harmless frolic.* 那不過是個無害的嬉鬧遊戲。

frolic·some /ˈfrɒlɪksəm; *NAmE* ˈfrɑːl-/ *adj.* (especially *literary*) playing in a lively happy way 嬉戲的；歡鬧的：*frolicsome lambs* 嬉戲的羔羊

from 0-π /frəm; *strong form* frɒm; *NAmE* frʌm; frɑːm/ *prep.*

HELP For the special uses of **from** in phrasal verbs, look at the entries for the verbs. For example **keep sth from sb** is in the phrasal verb section at **keep**. * from 在短語動詞中的特殊用法見有關動詞詞條。如 keep sth from sb 在詞條 keep 的短語動詞部份。 **1** 0-π used to show where sb/sth starts（表示起始點）從…起，始於：*She began to walk away from him.* 她開始離他而去。◇ *Has the train from Bristol arrived?* 從布里斯托爾開來的火車到了沒有？ **2** 0-π used to show when sth starts（表示開始的時間）從…開始：*We're open from 8 a.m. to 7 p.m. every day.* 我們每天從早 8 點至晚 7 點營業。◇ *He was blind from birth.* 他天生失明。 **3** 0-π used to show who sent or gave sth/sb（表示由某人發出或給出）寄自，得自：*a letter from my brother* 我哥哥來的信 ◇ *information from witnesses* 證人提供的信息 ◇ *the man from* (= representing) *the insurance company* 保險公司的人 **4** 0-π used to show what the origin of sb/sth is（表示來源）來自，源於，出自，從…來：*I'm from Italy.* 我是意大利人。◇ *documents from the sixteenth century* * 16 世紀的文獻 ◇ *quotations from Shakespeare* 莎士比亞語錄 ◇ *heat from the sun* 太陽熱 **5** 0-π used to show the material that sth is made of（表示所用的原料）由…（製成）：*Steel is made from iron.* 鋼是由鐵煉成的。 **6** 0-π used to show how far apart two places are（表示兩地的距離）離：*100 metres from the scene of the accident* 離事故現場 100 米 **7** 0-π used to show sb's position or point of view（表示位置或觀點）從：*You can see the island from here.* 從這裏可以看見那海島。◇ *From a financial point of view the project was a disaster.* 從經濟觀點看，這個項目徹底失敗了。 **8** 0-π **~ sth (to sth)** used to show the range of sth（表示幅度或範圍）從…（到）：*The temperature varies from 30 degrees to minus 20.* 溫度在 30 度至零下 20 度之間變化。◇ *The store sells everything from shoelaces to computers.* 這家商店出售的商品從鞋帶到計算機應有盡有。◇ *Conditions vary from school to school.* 各所學校的情況不同。 **9** 0-π **~ sth (to sth)** used to show the state or form of sth/sb before a change（表示改變前的狀態或形式）從…（到）：*Things have gone **from bad to worse**.* 情況越來越糟。◇ *translating from English to Spanish* 從英語譯成西班牙語 ◇ *You need a break from routine.* 你需要從日常工作中解脱出來去休息一下。 **10** 0-π used to show that sb/sth is separated or removed（表示分離或去除）：*The party was ousted from power after eighteen years.* 該黨執政十八年後被趕下台。 **11** 0-π used to show that sth is prevented（表示防止）使免遭，使免受：*She saved him from drowning.* 她救了他一命，使他免遭淹死。 **12** 0-π used to show the reason for sth（表示原因）由於，因為：*She felt sick from tiredness.* 她累得渾身不對勁。 **13** 0-π used to show the reason for making a judgement（表示進行判斷的原因）根據，從…來看：*You can tell a lot about a person from their handwriting.* 根據一個人的筆跡可以瞭解很多有關他的情況。◇ *From what I heard the company's in deep trouble.* 就我所聽到的，這家公司已深陷困境。 **14** 0-π used when distinguishing between two people or things（區別二者時用）與…（不同）：*Is Portuguese very different from Spanish?* 葡萄牙語與西班牙語區別很大嗎？◇ *I can't tell one twin from the other.* 我分不出雙胞胎中誰是誰。

IDM **from ... on** 0-π starting at the time mentioned and continuously after that 從…時起：***From now on** you can work on your own.* 從現在起你可以獨自工作。◇ *She never spoke to him again from that day on.* 從那天起她就再沒和他說話。

from·age frais /ˌfrɒmɑːʒ ˈfreɪ; *NAmE* frəˈmɑːʒ/ *noun* [U] (from *French*) a type of very soft cheese, similar to YOGURT 新鮮軟乾酪（類似酸乳酪）

frond /frɒnd; *NAmE* frɑːnd/ *noun* **1** a long leaf of some plants or trees, especially PALMS or FERNS. Fronds are often divided into parts along the edge.（尤指棕櫚類或蕨類的）葉；蕨葉 **2** a long piece of SEAWEED that looks like one of these leaves（海藻長條形的）植物體，葉狀體

front 0-π /frʌnt/ *noun, adj., verb*

■ *noun*

▸ **FORWARD PART/POSITION** 前部；前部位置 **1** 0-π [C, usually sing.] (usually **the front**) the part or side of sth that faces forward; the side of sth that you look at first 正面：*The front of the building was covered with ivy.* 大樓的正面爬滿了常春藤。◇ *The book has a picture of Rome **on the front**.* 書的封面有一張羅馬的照片。◇ *The front of the car was badly damaged.* 轎車的頭部嚴重損壞。➲ see also SHOPFRONT, Y-FRONTS **2** 0-π **the front** [sing.] the position that is in the direction that sb/sth is facing 前面；正前方：*Keep your eyes to the front and walk straight ahead.* 兩眼看着正前方逕直往前走。◇ *There's a garden **at the front of** the house.* 房子的前面有一座花園。 **3** 0-π **the front** [sing.] the part of sth that is furthest forward 前部：*I prefer to travel **in the front of** the car* (= next to the driver). 我喜歡坐在轎車的前座。◇ *The teacher made me move my seat to the front of the classroom.* 老師要我把座位移到課室前方。◇ *Write your name in the front of the book* (= the first few pages). 在前面的書頁寫上你的名字。

▸ **CHEST** 胸部 **4** 0-π **sb's front** [sing.] the part of sb's body that faces forwards; sb's chest 身體前部；胸部：*She was lying on her front.* 她俯卧着。◇ *I spilled coffee down my front.* 我把咖啡濺到前襟上。

▸ **SIDE OF BUILDING** 建築物的面 **5** [C] **the west, north, south, east, etc. ~** the side of a large building, especially a church, that faces west, north, etc.（建築物，尤指教堂朝西、北、東、南等的）面：*the west front of the cathedral* 大教堂朝西的一面

▸ **EDGE OF SEA/LAKE** 海／湖邊 **6** **the front** [sing.] (*BrE*) the road or area of land along the edge of the sea, a lake or a river 海濱；湖畔；河邊；沿海（或湖、河）道路：*Couples walked hand in hand along the front.* 對對情侶手牽手沿河邊散步。➲ see also SEAFRONT

▸ **IN WAR** 戰爭 **7** [C, usually sing.] an area where fighting takes place during a war 前線；前方：*More British troops have been sent to the front.* 更多的英國部隊已派往前線。◇ *to serve at the front* 在前方服役 ◇ *fighting a war on two fronts* 在兩條戰線上戰鬥 ➲ see also FRONT LINE, HOME FRONT

▸ **AREA OF ACTIVITY** 活動領域 **8** [C] a particular area of activity 活動領域；陣線：*Things are looking unsettled on the economic front.* 經濟戰線上的情況顯得不穩定。◇ *Progress has been made **on all fronts**.* 各方面都取得了進展。

▸ **HIDING TRUE FEELINGS** 隱藏感情 **9** [sing.] behaviour that is not genuine, done in order to hide your true feelings or opinions 表面；外表：*Rudeness is just a front for her shyness.* 她的粗魯只是為了掩飾羞怯。◇ *It's not always easy to **put on a** brave **front** for the family.* 常為家人裝出勇敢的樣子並不容易。◇ *The prime minister stressed the need to **present a united front*** (= show people that all members of the group have the same opinion about things). 首相強調必須表現出團結一致。

▸ **HIDING STH ILLEGAL** 掩蓋非法活動 **10** [C, usually sing.] **~ (for sth)** a person or an organization that is used to hide an illegal or secret activity 非法（或秘密）活動掩護者：*The travel company is just a front for drug trafficking.* 這家旅行社不過是毒品交易的掩護場所。

▸ **POLITICAL ORGANIZATION** 政治組織 **11** **Front** [sing.] used in the names of some political organizations（用於政治組織的名稱）陣線：*the Animal Liberation Front* 動物解放陣線 ➲ see also POPULAR FRONT

▸ **WEATHER** 天氣 **12** [C] the line where a mass of cold air meets a mass of warm air（冷暖空氣團接觸的）鋒：*a **cold/warm front*** 冷／暖鋒

IDM **ˌfront and ˈcenter** (*NAmE*) in or into the most important position 在（或進入）最重要位置 **in ˈfront** *adv.* **1** 0-π in a position that is further forward than sb/sth but not very far away 在前面：*Their house is the one with the big garden in front.* 他們的房子是前面有大花園的那一座。 **2** 0-π in first place in a race or competition（賽跑或比賽）領先：*The blue team is currently in front with a lead of six points.* 藍隊目前以六分領先。 **in ˈfront of** *prep.* **1** 0-π in a position that is further forward than sb/sth but not very far away 在…前面：*The car in front of me stopped suddenly and I had to brake.* 我前面那輛車突然停下來，我也只好剎車。◇ *The bus stops right in front of our house.* 公共汽車就停在我們的房子前面。◇ *He was standing in front of me in the line.* 在隊列中他

站在我的前面。◇ *She spends all day* ***sitting in front of*** (= working at) *her computer.* 她整天坐在計算機前工作。**2** if you do sth **in front of** sb, you do it when they are there 當着…的面；在…面前：*Please don't talk about it in front of the children.* 請不要當着孩子們的面談那件事。**3 ~ sb** (of time 時間) still to come; not yet passed 未來；在…前面：*Don't give up. You still have your whole life in front of you.* 不要放棄，你的前面還有一輩子呢。
out 'front 1 in the part of a theatre, restaurant, etc. where the public sits（劇院等）觀眾席；（餐廳等）座席：*There's only a small audience out front tonight.* 今夜觀眾席上人很少。**2** (also *BrE informal* **out the 'front**) in the area near to the entrance to a building 在（建築物）大門外：*I'll wait for you out (the) front.* 我在大門外等你。 **up 'front** (*informal*) **1** as payment in advance 預付；先付：*We'll pay you half up front and the other half when you've finished the job.* 我們先付一半給你，工作完成後再付另一半。**2** (in sports 體育運動) in a forward position 在前鋒位置：*to play up front* 踢前鋒 ➲ see also UPFRONT (2) ➲ more at BACK *n.*, CASH *n.*, EYE *n.*, LEAD[1] *v.*

■ **adj.** [only before noun] **1** on or at the front of sth 前面的；前部的；在前的；正面的：*front teeth* 門牙 ◇ *the front wheels of the car* 汽車的前輪 ◇ *We had seats in the front row.* 我們坐在前排座位。◇ *an animal's front legs* 動物的前腿 ◇ *Let's go through to the* ***front room*** (= the main room in a house where people sit and entertain guests). 咱們穿過去直到客廳。◇ *a front-seat passenger* 前排座位的一個乘客 ➲ compare BACK *adj.* (1), HIND *adj.* **2** (*phonetics* 語音) (of a vowel 元音) produced with the front of the tongue in a higher position than the back, for example /iː/ in English 舌前位發的；舌前的 ➲ compare BACK *adj.* (4), CENTRAL (5)

IDM **on the 'front burner** (*informal, especially NAmE*) (of an issue, a plan, etc. 問題、計劃等) being given a lot of attention because it is considered important 處於前列重要地位；受到重視；為當務之急：*Anything that keeps education on the front burner is good.* 任何重視教育的事都是好事。 ➲ compare ON THE BACK BURNER at BACK *adj.*

■ **verb**

▸ FACE STH 面向 **1** [T, I] to face sth or be in front of sth; to have the front pointing towards sth 面向；在…前面；朝；向：**~ sth** *The cathedral fronts the city's main square.* 大教堂面向城市的主廣場。◇ **~ onto sth** *The line of houses fronted straight onto the road.* 這排房子正對着馬路。

▸ COVER FRONT 覆蓋正面 **2** [T, usually passive] **~ sth** to have the front covered with sth 用…作正面；用…覆蓋正面：*a glass-fronted bookcase* 正面是玻璃的書櫃

▸ LEAD GROUP 領導團體 **3** [T] **~ sth** to lead or represent an organization, a group, etc. 領導，代表（團體、組織等）：*He fronts a multinational company.* 他領導一家跨國公司。◇ *A former art student fronted the band* (= was the main singer). 樂隊的主音歌手曾是一位藝術院校學生。

▸ PRESENT TV PROGRAMME 主持電視節目 **4** [T] **~ sth** (*especially BrE*) to present a television programme, a show, etc. 主持（電視節目、演出等）

▸ GRAMMAR 語法 **5** [T] **~ sth** (*linguistics* 語言) to give more importance to a part of a sentence by placing it at or near the beginning of the sentence, as in 'That I would like to see.'（為強調而將句子某一部份）前置

PHR V **'front for sb/sth** to represent a group or an organization and try to hide its secret or illegal activities 為…掩護（秘密、非法活動）：*He fronted for them in several illegal property deals.* 他為他們在幾次非法房地產交易中作了掩護。

front·age /ˈfrʌntɪdʒ/ *noun* **1** [C, U] the front of a building, especially when this faces a road or river（建築物，尤指臨街或臨河的）正面：*the baroque frontage of Milan Cathedral* 米蘭大教堂巴羅克風格的正面 **2** [U] (*especially NAmE*) land that is next to a building, a street or an area of water 臨街（或河等的）土地：*They bought two miles of river frontage along the Colorado.* 他們買了兩英里科羅拉多河沿河的土地。

Which Word? 詞語辨析

in front of / in the front of

- **In front of** can mean the same as **outside**, but not **opposite**. * in front of 可表示 outside 的詞義，但不能表示 opposite 的詞義：*I'll meet you in front of/ outside your hotel.* 我在你的旅館前面 / 外面接你。◇ *There's a bus stop in front of the house* (= on the same side of the road). 房子前面有一個公共汽車站（在公路的這面）。◇ *There's a bus stop opposite the house* (= on the other side of the road). 房子對面有一個公共汽車站（在公路的對面）。
- **In/at the front (of sth)** means 'in the most forward part of something'. * in / at the front (of sth) 表示在某物的最前部份：*The driver sits at the front of the bus.* 駕駛員坐在公共汽車的前端。◇ *Put the shortest flowers in the front (of the bunch).* 把最短的花放在花束的靠前位置。

'frontage road *noun* (*NAmE*) = SERVICE ROAD

front·al /ˈfrʌntl/ *adj.* [only before noun] **1** connected with the front of sth 正面的；前部的：*Airbags protect the driver in the event of a severe frontal impact.* 汽車若遇到正面猛烈撞擊，安全氣囊可以保護駕車者。**2** (also **ˌfull-'frontal**) a **frontal** attack or a criticism is very strong and direct 正面的，劈頭蓋臉的，直截了當的（攻擊或批評）：*They launched a frontal attack on company directors.* 他們向公司董事發起了正面攻擊。**3** connected with a weather FRONT（天氣）鋒的：*a cold frontal system* 冷鋒系 **4** (*medical* 醫) connected with the front part of the head 前額的：*the frontal lobes of the brain* 大腦額葉 ▸ **front·al·ly** /-təli/ *adv.*

ˌfrontal 'lobe *noun* (*anatomy* 解) either of the two parts at the front of the brain that are concerned with behaviour, learning and personality 額葉（與行為、學習和個性有關）

the ˌfront 'bench *noun* [C+sing./pl. v.] the most important members of the government and the opposition in the British parliament, who sit in the front rows of seats 前座議員（英國議會中坐在前排座位的政府和反對黨要員的總稱）：*an Opposition front-bench spokesman on defence* 一位談論國防事務的反對黨前座議員發言人 ➲ compare BACK BENCH

front·bench·er /ˌfrʌntˈbentʃə(r)/ *noun* an important member of the government or the opposition in the British parliament, who sits in the front rows of seats（英國議會中的）前座議員 ➲ compare BACKBENCHER

ˌfront 'desk *noun* the desk inside the entrance of a hotel, an office building, etc. where guests or visitors go when they first arrive（旅館等處的）前枱，總枱 ➲ compare RECEPTION (1)

ˌfront 'door *noun* the main entrance to a house, usually at the front 正門；前門：*There's someone at the front door.* 前門有個人。➲ **VISUAL VOCAB** page V17

'front-end *adj.* [only before noun] (*computing* 計) (of a device or program 器件或程序) directly used by a user, and allowing the user to use other devices or programs 前端的；前置的；用戶直接調用的 ➲ compare BACK-END (2)

ˌfront-ˌend 'loader *noun* (*especially NAmE*) a large vehicle with machinery for digging worked by a system of HYDRAULICS 正鏟鏟斗車

fron·tier /ˈfrʌntɪə(r); *NAmE* frʌnˈtɪr/ *noun* **1** (*BrE*) [C] a line that separates two countries, etc.; the land near this line 國界；邊界；邊境：**~ (between A and B)** *the frontier between the land of the Saxons and that of the Danes* 撒克遜人土地和古斯堪的納維亞人土地的邊界 ◇ **~ (with sth)** *a customs post on the frontier with Italy* 與意大利交界的邊境上的海關關卡 ◇ ***a frontier town/zone/ post*** 邊陲小鎮；邊疆地帶；邊防站 ➲ **SYNONYMS** at BORDER **2 the frontier** [sing.] the edge of land where people live and have built towns, beyond which the country is wild and unknown, especially in the western US in the 19th century（尤指 19 世紀美國西部的）開發地區邊緣地帶，邊遠地區：*a remote frontier settlement*

邊遠地區定居點 **3** [C, usually pl.] **~ (of sth)** the limit of sth, especially the limit of what is known about a particular subject or activity（學科或活動的）尖端，邊緣：*to **push back the frontiers** of science* (= to increase knowledge of science) 開拓科學新領域 ◇ *to **roll back the frontiers** of government* (= to limit the powers of the government) 限制政府權力

fron·tiers·man /ˈfrʌntɪəzmən; NAmE frʌnˈtɪrz-/ *noun* (*pl.* **-men** /-mən/) a man living on the frontier especially one who lived in the western US during the 19th century（尤指 19 世紀美國西部的）開拓者，拓荒者，邊遠地區居民

fron·tis·piece /ˈfrʌntɪspiːs/ *noun* [usually sing.] a picture at the beginning of a book, on the page opposite the page with the title on it（與書名頁相對一頁上的）卷首插圖

the ˌfront ˈline *noun* [sing.] an area where the enemies are facing each other during a war and where fighting takes place 前線：*Tanks have been deployed all along the front line.* 沿整個前線已部署了坦克。◇ *front-line troops* 前線部隊

IDM **in the front line (of sth)** doing work that will have an important effect on sth 在最重要的崗位上；在第一線：*a life spent in the front line of research* 在研究的第一線度過的一生

ˌfront-ˈload *verb* **1 ~ sth** (*business* 商) to spread the costs of a project so that more of the money is spent in the earlier stages 將（成本）的大頭提前花費；提前負載：*a need to front-load budget spending* 前期花費大部份預算支出的需要 ◇ *the positive effects of front-loading funds* 前期投入大部份資金的好處 **2 ~ sth** to organize work on a project or information in a document so that the more important work or information is done or placed first 將（項目或文章）的重點前置：*Teach your students to front-load their research.* 教學生從事研究時學會前緊後鬆。

front·man /ˈfrʌntmæn/ *noun* (*pl.* **-men** /-men/) **1** a person who represents an organization and tries to make its activities seem acceptable to the public, although in fact they may be illegal（某組織的）代表，頭面人物；（非法活動的）掩護者：*He acted as a frontman for a drugs cartel.* 他給一個毒品集團當掩護。**2** the leader of a group of musicians 樂隊領銜者 **3** (*BrE*) a person who presents a television programme 電視節目主持人

ˌfront ˈoffice *noun* [sing.] (*especially NAmE*) the part of a business concerned with managing things or dealing with the public（企業的）管理部門，與公眾打交道的部門

ˌfront-of-ˈhouse *noun* [U] (*BrE*) **1** the parts of a theatre that are used by the audience（劇院的）觀眾席 **2** (often used as an adjective 常用作形容詞) the business of dealing with an audience at a theatre, for example selling tickets and programmes（劇院的）前台事務，劇場服務

ˌfront ˈpage *noun* the first page of a newspaper, where the most important news is printed（報紙的）頭版：*The story was on the front pages of all the tabloids.* 所有小報都在頭版報道了這件事。▸ **ˈfront-page** *adj.* [only before noun]：*The divorce made **front-page news**.* 這樁離婚成了頭版新聞。

ˌfront ˈrunner *noun* a person, an animal or an organization that seems most likely to win a race or competition（賽跑或競賽中）最可能獲勝者，領先者

ˌfront-wheel ˈdrive *noun* [U] a system in which power from the engine is sent to the front wheels of a vehicle 前輪驅動系統 ➲ compare REAR-WHEEL DRIVE

frost /frɒst; NAmE frɔːst/ *noun, verb*

■ ***noun*** **1** [U, C] a weather condition in which the temperature drops below 0°C (= FREEZING POINT) so that a thin white layer of ice forms on the ground and other surfaces, especially at night 嚴寒天氣；霜凍；冰點以下的溫度：*It will be a clear night with some **ground frost**.* 今夜晴，部份地面有霜凍。◇ *a **sharp/hard/severe frost*** 酷寒 ◇ *There were ten degrees of frost* (= the temperature dropped to -10°C) *last night.* 昨夜零下 10 攝氏度。◇ *frost damage* 霜凍害 **2** [U] the thin white layer of ice that forms when the temperature drops below 0°C 霜：*The car windows were covered with frost.* 車窗玻璃結了霜。➲ see also HOAR FROST

■ ***verb*** **1** [T, I] to cover sth or to become covered with a thin white layer of ice（使）蒙上霜，結霜：**~ sth (over/up)** *The mirror was frosted up.* 鏡子蒙了一層霜。◇ **~ (over/up)** *The windows had frosted over.* 窗子結滿了霜。**2** [T] **~ sth** (*especially NAmE*) to cover a cake with ICING/FROSTING 給（糕餅）覆上糖霜

frost·bite /ˈfrɒstbaɪt; NAmE ˈfrɔːst-/ *noun* [U] a medical condition in which parts of the body, especially the fingers and toes, become damaged as a result of extremely cold temperatures 凍傷；凍瘡 ▸ **frost·bit·ten** /ˈfrɒstbɪtn; NAmE ˈfrɔːst-/ *adj.*

frost·ed /ˈfrɒstɪd; NAmE ˈfrɔːstɪd/ *adj.* **1** [only before noun] (of glass 玻璃) that has been given a rough surface, so that it is difficult to see through 毛面的；磨砂的 **2** (*especially NAmE*) (of cakes, etc. 糕餅等) covered with ICING/FROSTING 覆有（或撒有）糖霜的 **3** covered with FROST 結霜的：*the frosted garden* 寒霜覆蓋的花園 **4** containing very small shiny pieces 含有閃光小顆粒的：*frosted eyeshadow* 閃光點眼影

frost·ing /ˈfrɒstɪŋ; NAmE ˈfrɔːst-/ *noun* [U] **1** (*NAmE*) = ICING **2** [U] (*BrE*) the crime of stealing a vehicle that has been left with the engine running in cold weather so that the engine warms up（冷天趁發動機預熱車輛無人看管時下手的）盜竊車輛罪

frosty /ˈfrɒsti; NAmE ˈfrɔːsti/ *adj.* (**frost·ier**, **frosti·est**) **1** (of the weather 天氣) extremely cold; cold with FROST 嚴寒的；霜凍的：*a frosty morning* 嚴寒的早晨 ◇ *He breathed in the frosty air.* 他吸進冰冷的空氣。**2** covered with FROST 結霜的：*frosty fields* 結霜的田地 **3** unfriendly, in a way that suggests that sb does not approve of sth 冷淡的；冷若冰霜的：***a frosty look/reply*** 冷冰冰的樣子；冷淡的答覆 ◇ *The latest proposals were given a frosty reception.* 對最新的建議反應冷淡。▸ **frost·ily** /-ɪli/ *adv.*：*'No, thank you,' she said frostily.* "不，謝謝你。" 她冷冰冰地説。

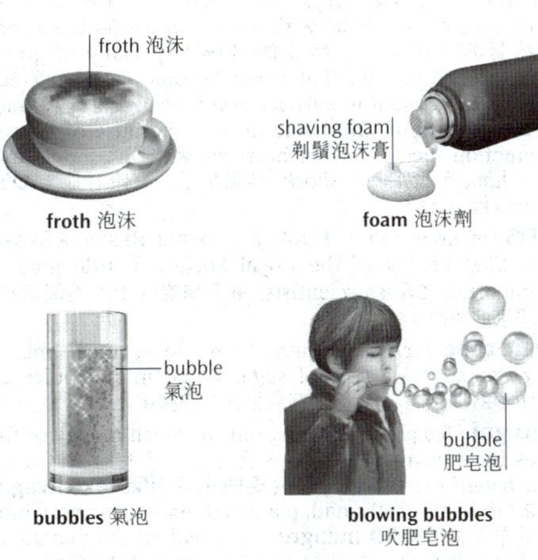

froth 泡沫 foam 泡沫劑 bubbles 氣泡 blowing bubbles 吹肥皂泡

froth /frɒθ; NAmE frɔːθ/ *noun, verb*

■ ***noun*** **1** [U] a mass of small bubbles, especially on the surface of a liquid（尤指液體表面的）泡沫，泡 **SYN** **foam**：*a glass of beer with thick froth on top* 上面有厚厚一層泡沫的一杯啤酒 **2** [U] ideas, activities, etc. that seem attractive and enjoyable but have no real value 華而不實的思想（或活動等） **3** [sing.] **~ of sth** something that looks like a mass of small bubbles on liquid 泡沫狀物：*a froth of black lace* 起泡狀的黑色花邊

■ ***verb*** **1** [I, T] **~ (sth)** if a liquid **froths**, or if sb/sth **froths** it, a mass of small bubbles appears on the surface（使）起泡沫：*a cup of frothing coffee* 一杯起泡的咖啡 **2** [I] to produce a lot of SALIVA (= liquid in your mouth)

F

（口）吐白沫：*The dog was* ***frothing at the mouth.*** 這條狗口吐白沫。◇ (*figurative*) *He* ***frothed at the mouth*** (= was very angry) *when I asked for more money.* 我還要錢時他氣得七竅生煙。

frothy /ˈfrɒθi; *NAmE* ˈfrɔːθi/ *adj.* **1** (of liquids 液體) having a mass of small bubbles on the surface 有泡沫的；起泡沫的：*frothy coffee* 泡沫咖啡 **2** seeming attractive and enjoyable but having no real value 華而不實的；夸夸其談的；花架子的：*frothy romantic novels* 輕浮淺薄的浪漫小說 **3** (of clothes or cloth 衣服或布料) light and delicate 輕薄精巧的

frown /fraʊn/ *verb, noun*

■ ***verb*** [I, T] to make a serious, angry or worried expression by bringing your EYEBROWS closer together so that lines appear on your FOREHEAD 皺眉；蹙額：**~ (at sb/sth)** *What are you frowning at me for?* 你為什麼朝我皺眉頭？◇ **+ speech** *'I don't understand,' she frowned.* "我不懂。" 她皺着眉說。

PHR V **'frown on/upon sb/sth** to disapprove of sb/sth 不贊成；不同意；不許可：*In her family, any expression of feeling was frowned upon.* 她家裏對任何感情的流露都不以為然。

■ ***noun*** [usually sing.] a serious, angry or worried expression on a person's face that causes lines on their FOREHEAD 皺眉；蹙額：*She looked up* ***with a*** *puzzled* ***frown*** *on her face.* 她抬頭望着，滿臉困惑，雙眉緊鎖。◇ *a slight* ***frown of disapproval/concentration, etc.*** 略顯不贊成的臉色、全神貫注地微皺眉頭等

frow·sty /ˈfraʊsti/ *adj.* (*BrE*) smelling bad because there is no fresh air 悶熱的；不通風的；霉臭的 **SYN** **fusty, musty**：*a small frowsty office* 狹小憋氣的辦公室

froze *past tense of* FREEZE

fro·zen 0‑m /ˈfrəʊzn; *NAmE* ˈfroʊzn/ *adj.*

1 0‑m [usually before noun] (of food 食物) kept at a very low temperature in order to preserve it 冷凍的；冷藏的：*frozen peas* 冷凍豌豆 **2** 0‑m [not usually before noun] (of people or parts of the body 人或身體部位) extremely cold 凍僵；極冷：*I'm absolutely frozen!* 我簡直凍僵了！◇ *You look* ***frozen stiff.*** 你看來凍僵了。 **3** 0‑m (of rivers, lakes, etc. 河、湖等) with a layer of ice on the surface 冰封的；封凍的；結冰的 **4** 0‑m (especially of ground 尤指地面) so cold that it has become very hard 凍硬的：*The ground was* ***frozen solid.*** 地面凍得硬邦邦的。 **5** 0‑m **~ with/in sth** unable to move because of a strong emotion such as fear or horror 嚇呆；驚呆：*She stared at him, frozen with shock.* 她驚呆了，直瞪着他。➲ see also FREEZE *v.*

FRS /ˌef ɑːr ˈes/ *abbr.* **1** (*NAmE*) FEDERAL RESERVE SYSTEM **2** (*BrE*) Fellow of the Royal Society (a title given to important British scientists) 皇家學院院士（英國傑出科學家的頭銜）

fruc·tose /ˈfrʌktəʊs; -təʊz; *NAmE* -toʊs; -toʊz/ *noun* [U] (*chemistry* 化) a type of sugar found in fruit juice and HONEY 果糖，左旋糖（存於果汁、蜂蜜中）

fru·gal /ˈfruːɡl/ *adj.* **1** using only as much money or food as is necessary（對金錢、食物等）節約的，節儉的：*a* ***frugal existence/life*** 儉樸的生活 **OPP** **extravagant** **2** (of meals 飯菜) small, plain and not costing very much 簡單廉價的 **SYN** **meagre**：*a frugal lunch of bread and cheese* 麵包夾奶酪的簡單午餐 ▸ **fru·gal·ity** /fruˈɡæləti/ *noun* [U] **fru·gal·ly** /-ɡəli/ *adv.*：*to* ***live/eat frugally*** 生活/吃飯節儉

fruit 0‑m /fruːt/ *noun, verb*

■ ***noun*** **1** 0‑m [C, U] the part of a plant that consists of one or more seeds and flesh, can be eaten as food and usually tastes sweet 水果：*tropical fruits, such as bananas and pineapples* 熱帶水果，如香蕉和菠蘿 ◇ *Eat plenty of fresh fruit and vegetables.* 要多吃新鮮水果和蔬菜。◇ *a* ***piece of fruit*** (= an apple, an orange, etc.) 一個水果 ◇ *fruit juice* 果汁 ◇ *fruit trees* 果樹 ➲ VISUAL VOCAB page V30 ➲ compare VEGETABLE (1) ➲ see also DRIED FRUIT, FIRST FRUIT, SOFT FRUIT **2** [C] (*technical* 術語) a part of a plant or tree that is formed after the flowers have died and in which seeds develop 果實 **3** [C, usually pl.] (*literary*) all the natural things that the earth produces（大地的）產物；農產品 **4** [C] (*offensive*) an offensive word for a HOMOSEXUAL man 男同性戀者

IDM **the fruit/fruits of sth** the good results of an activity or a situation 成果；成效；結果：*to enjoy the fruits of your labours* (= the rewards for your hard work) 享受你艱苦勞動的成果 ◇ *The book is the fruit of years of research.* 這本書是多年研究的成果。➲ more at BEAR *v.*, FORBIDDEN

■ ***verb*** [I] (*technical* 術語) (of a tree or plant 樹或花草) to produce fruit 結果

fruit·ar·ian /fruːˈteəriən; *NAmE* -ˈter-/ *noun* a person who eats only fruit 只吃水果的人；果素者 ➲ compare VEGETARIAN

ˈfruit bat *noun* a BAT (= an animal like a mouse with wings) that lives in hot countries and eats fruit 果蝠（熱帶大蝙蝠，以水果為食）

ˈfruit cake *noun* **1** [C, U] a cake containing dried fruit 乾果蛋糕 **2** **fruitcake** [C] (*informal*) a person who behaves in a strange or crazy way 怪人；瘋子：*She's* ***nutty as a fruitcake.*** 她古怪得很。

ˌfruit ˈcocktail *noun* [U] a mixture of pieces of fruit in liquid, sold in tins（罐裝）什錦水果

ˌfruit ˈcup *noun* [U, C] **1** (*BrE*) a drink consisting of fruit juices and pieces of fruit 什錦水果杯（用多種果汁和水果混合的飲料） **2** (*NAmE*) = FRUIT SALAD

fruit·er·er /ˈfruːtərə(r)/ *noun* (*old-fashioned, especially BrE*) a person who owns or manages a shop/store selling fruit 水果商 ➲ compare GREENGROCER (1)

ˈfruit fly *noun* a small fly that eats plants that are decaying, especially fruit 果蠅；實蠅

fruit·ful /ˈfruːtfl/ *adj.* **1** producing many useful results 成果豐碩的；富有成效的 **SYN** **productive**：*a fruitful collaboration/discussion* 富有成效的合作/討論 **OPP** **fruitless** **2** (*literary*) (of land or trees 土地或樹木) producing a lot of crops 富饒的；豐產的 ▸ **fruit·ful·ly** /ˈfruːtfəli/ *adv.* **fruit·ful·ness** /ˈfruːtfəlnəs/ *noun* [U]

fruiti·ness /ˈfruːtinəs/ *noun* [U] (especially of wine 尤指果酒) the quality of tasting or smelling strongly of fruit 果味濃郁

fru·ition /fruˈɪʃn/ *noun* [U] (*formal*) the successful result of a plan, a process or an activity（計劃、過程或活動的）完成，實現，取得成果：*After months of hard work, our plans finally* ***came to fruition.*** 經過幾個月的艱苦工作，我們的計劃終於完成了。◇ *His extravagant ideas were never* ***brought to fruition.*** 他不切實際的想法永遠沒有實現。

fruit·less /ˈfruːtləs/ *adj.* producing no useful results 沒有成果的；無成效的；徒然的 **SYN** **unproductive**：*a* ***fruitless attempt/search*** 徒然的嘗試/搜查 ◇ *Our efforts to persuade her proved fruitless.* 我們努力說服她，但毫無成效。**OPP** **fruitful** ▸ **fruit·less·ly** *adv.*

ˈfruit machine (*BrE*) (also **ˌone-armed ˈbandit, ˈslot machine** *NAmE, BrE*) *noun* a gambling machine that you put coins into and that gives money back if particular pictures appear together on the screen 吃角子老虎賭博機；老虎機

ˌfruit ˈsalad (*NAmE* also **ˌfruit ˈcup**) *noun* [U, C] a cold DESSERT (= a sweet dish) consisting of small pieces of different types of fruit 水果色拉

fruity /ˈfruːti/ *adj.* (**fruit·ier, fruiti·est**) **1** smelling or tasting strongly of fruit 果香味濃的：*The wine from this region is rich and fruity.* 這個地區產的葡萄酒濃郁醇香。**2** (of a voice or laugh 嗓音或笑聲) deep and pleasant in quality 圓潤的 **3** (*NAmE, informal*) (of people 人) slightly crazy 有點瘋瘋癲癲的；古怪的

frump /frʌmp/ *noun* (*disapproving*) a woman who wears clothes that are not fashionable 衣着老式的女子 ▸ **frumpy** (also *less frequent* **frump·ish**) *adj.*：*frumpy clothes* 過時的衣服 ◇ *a frumpy housewife* 穿着過時的家庭主婦

frus·trate /frʌˈstreɪt; *NAmE* ˈfrʌstreɪt/ *verb* **1** **~ sb** to make sb feel annoyed or impatient because they cannot do or achieve what they want 使懊喪；使懊惱；使沮喪：*What frustrates him is that there's too little money to spend on the project.* 使他懊惱的是可用於這個項目的資

金太少。 **2 ~ sb/sth** to prevent sb from doing sth; to prevent sth from happening or succeeding 阻止；防止；挫敗 SYN **thwart**： *The rescue attempt was frustrated by bad weather.* 拯救行動因天氣惡劣受阻。

frus·trated /frʌˈstreɪtɪd; *NAmE* ˈfrʌstreɪtɪd/ *adj.* **1** feeling annoyed and impatient because you cannot do or achieve what you want 懊喪；懊惱；沮喪：*It's very easy to get frustrated in this job.* 這個工作很容易令人懊惱。◇ **~ at/with sth** *They felt frustrated at the lack of progress.* 沒有進展，他們感到懊喪。**2** (of an emotion 情感) having no effect; not being satisfied 無效的；沒有得到滿足的：*He stamped his foot in frustrated rage.* 他怒氣難消，氣得跺腳。◇ *frustrated desires* 沒有得到滿足的慾望 **3** [only before noun] unable to be successful in a particular career 失意的；不得志的： *a frustrated artist* 不得志的藝術家 **4** not satisfied sexually 性慾沒有得到滿足的

frus·trat·ing /frʌˈstreɪtɪŋ; *NAmE* ˈfrʌstreɪtɪŋ/ *adj.* causing you to feel annoyed and impatient because you cannot do or achieve what you want 令人懊惱的；令人沮喪的： *It's frustrating to have to wait so long.* 要等這麼長時間，真令人懊惱。 ▶ **frus·trat·ing·ly** *adv.*： *Progress was frustratingly slow.* 進展慢得使人沮喪。

frus·tra·tion /frʌˈstreɪʃn/ *noun* **1** [U] the feeling of being frustrated 懊喪；懊惱；沮喪： *Dave thumped the table* ***in frustration***. 戴夫懊惱得捶打桌子。◇ *She couldn't stand the frustration of not being able to help.* 她幫不上忙，懊喪得不行。◇ *sexual frustration* 性挫敗 **2** [C, usually pl.] something that causes you to feel frustrated 令人懊喪（或懊惱、沮喪）的事物： *Every job has its difficulties and frustrations.* 每個工作都有困難和令人懊惱之處。◇ *Inevitably she took out her frustrations on the children.* 她不可避免地把氣出在孩子們身上。 **3** [U] **~ of sth** (*formal*) the fact that sth is preventing sth/sb from succeeding 受阻；受挫；阻止；挫敗： *the frustration of all his ambitions* 對他所有抱負的打擊

fry 🔑 /fraɪ/ *verb, noun*

■ ***verb*** (**fries**, **fry·ing**, **fried**, **fried**) **1** 🔑 [T, I] **~ (sth)** to cook sth in hot fat or oil; to be cooked in hot fat or oil 油炸；油煎；油炒： *fried fish* 炸魚 ◇ *the smell of bacon frying* 煎熏鹹肉的氣味 ➲ related noun FRY-UP ➲ **COLLOCATIONS** at COOKING ➲ **VISUAL VOCAB** page V27 ➲ see also STIR-FRY **2** [I] (*informal*) to be burnt by the sun（被陽光）灼傷，曬傷： *You'll fry on the beach if you're not careful.* 你在海灘上若不小心會被太陽灼傷的。

IDM see FISH *n.*

■ ***noun*** **1** [pl.] very small young fish 魚苗；魚秧子 ➲ see also SMALL FRY **2** [C] (usually **fries** [pl.]) (*especially NAmE*) = FRENCH FRY： *Would you like ketchup with your fries?* 你吃炸薯條要番茄醬嗎？

fryer (also **frier**) /ˈfraɪə(r)/ *noun* **1** a large deep pan used for frying food in（深底）油炸鍋：*a deep-fat fryer* 深油炸鍋 **2** (*NAmE*) a young chicken that is suitable for frying（適於炸食的）仔雞，雛雞

ˈfrying pan (*NAmE* also **fry·pan**, **skil·let**) *noun* a large shallow pan with a long handle, used for frying food in 長柄平底煎鍋 ➲ **VISUAL VOCAB** page V27

IDM **out of the ˈfrying pan into the ˈfire** (*saying*) from a bad situation to one that is worse 跳出油鍋又落火坑；逃出虎口又入狼窩；每況愈下

ˈfry-up *noun* (*BrE, informal*) a meal of fried food, such as BACON and eggs 一份油煎食物（如熏鹹肉和雞蛋）

FT (also **F/T**) *abbr.* (in writing) FULL-TIME（書寫形式）全日（制），全職的，全日的： *The course is 1 year FT, 2 years PT.* 該課程全日制學習一年，非全日制學習兩年。 ➲ compare PT (2)

Ft (also **Ft.** especially in *NAmE*) *abbr.* FORT 兵營；軍營；營地： *Ft William* 威廉堡

ft (*BrE*) (also **ft.** *NAmE, BrE*) *abbr.* (in writing measurements) feet; foot（書寫形式）英尺： *The room is 12ft × 9ft.* 房間面積是 12 英尺 × 9 英尺。

the FTC /ˌef tiː ˈsiː/ *abbr.* the Federal Trade Commission (the US government organization that is responsible for making sure that there is fair competition in business) 聯邦貿易委員會（美國負責確保公平商業競爭的政府機構）

FTP /ˌef tiː ˈpiː/ *abbr.* file transfer protocol (a set of rules for sending files from one computer to another on the Internet) 文件傳輸協議，檔案傳輸協定（計算機通過互聯網傳輸文件的一系列規則）

the FTSE index™ /ˈfʊtsi ɪndeks/ (also **the FT index** /ˌef ˈtiː/, **the Fiˌnancial Times ˈindex**, **the Foot·sie™**) *noun* [sing.] a figure that shows the relative price of shares on the London Stock Exchange《金融時報》指數（顯示倫敦證券交易所的相對股票價格）

fuch·sia /ˈfjuːʃə/ *noun* [C, U] a small bush with flowers in two colours of red, purple or white, that hang down 倒掛金鐘（灌木，花吊掛，呈紅、紫或白色）

fuck /fʌk/ *verb, noun*

■ ***verb*** (*taboo, slang*) **1** [I, T] **~ (sb)** to have sex with sb 與…性交；肏 **2** [I, T] a swear word that many people find offensive that is used to express anger, disgust or surprise（表示氣憤、厭惡、驚奇的粗話）他媽的，見他媽的鬼，滾他媽的蛋： *Oh, fuck! I've lost my keys.* 噢，他媽的！我把鑰匙丟了。◇ **~ sb/sth** *Fuck it! We've missed the train.* 真他媽的見鬼！我們錯過了這趟火車。◇ *Fuck you—I'm leaving.* 滾你媽的蛋，我要走了。

IDM **ˌfuck ˈme** used to express surprise（表示驚奇）我他媽的見鬼了

PHR V **ˌfuck aˈround** (*BrE* also **ˌfuck aˈbout**) to waste time by behaving in a silly way 胡混；瞎混 HELP A more polite, informal way of saying this is **mess about** (*BrE*) or **mess around** (*NAmE* , *BrE*). 較禮貌和非正式的說法是 mess about（英式英語）或 mess around（美式英語、英式英語）。 **ˌfuck sb aˈround** (*BrE* also **ˌfuck sb aˈbout**) to treat sb in a way that is deliberately not helpful to them or wastes their time 瞎胡弄；故意浪費某人的時間 HELP A more polite, informal way of saying this is **mess sb about/around** (*BrE*). 較禮貌和非正式的說法是 mess sb about/around（英式英語）。**ˌfuck ˈoff** (usually used in orders 通常用於命令) to go away 滾開；走開： *Why don't you just fuck off?* 你幹嗎不這就滾開？ **ˌfuck ˈup** to do sth badly or make a bad mistake 弄糟；搞壞；出了大錯： *You've really fucked up this time!* 你這次確實搞得一塌糊塗！ HELP A more polite way to express this is **mess up**. 較禮貌的說法是 mess up。 **ˌfuck sb↔ˈup** to upset or confuse sb so much that they are not able to deal with problems in their life 使某人的感情受到創傷；完全打亂了某人的生活： *My parents' divorce really fucked me up.* 父母離婚真把我的生活全擾亂了。 HELP A more polite way to express this is **mess sb up**. 較禮貌的說法是 mess sb up。**ˌfuck sth↔ˈup** to do sth badly or spoil sth 弄糟；搞壞：*I completely fucked up my exams.* 我完全考砸了。 HELP A more polite, informal way of saying this is **mess sth up**. 較禮貌和非正式的說法是 mess sth up。 **ˈfuck with sb** to treat sb badly in a way that makes them annoyed 虧待，惡待（使某人惱怒）：*Don't fuck with him.* 不要激怒他。 HELP A more polite way to express this is **mess with sb**. 較禮貌的說法是 mess with sb。

■ ***noun*** (*taboo, slang*) **1** [C, usually sing.] an act of sex 性交；肏 **2 the fuck** [sing.] used for emphasis, or to show that you are angry, annoyed or surprised（用於強調或表示氣憤、厭惡或驚奇）他媽的： *What the fuck are you doing?* 你他媽的在幹啥？◇ *Let's get the fuck out of here!* 咱們他媽的走吧！

IDM **not give a ˈfuck (about sb/sth)** to not care at all about sb/sth 毫不在乎；毫不關心 ➲ see also F-WORD

ˌfuck ˈall *noun* [U] (*BrE, taboo, slang*) a phrase that many people find offensive, used to mean 'none at all' or 'nothing at all'（冒犯語）他媽的一點沒有，他媽的絲毫沒有： *You've done fuck all today.* 你他媽的今天啥也沒幹。◇ *These instructions make fuck all sense to me.* 這些指示我他媽的一點也看不懂。

fuck·er /ˈfʌkə(r)/ *noun* (*taboo, slang*) a very offensive word used to insult sb（冒犯語）笨蛋，渾蛋

fuck·ing /ˈfʌkɪŋ/ *adj., adv.* (*taboo, slang*) a swear word that many people find offensive that is used to emphasize a comment or an angry statement（加強語氣）該死的，他媽的： *I'm fucking sick of this fucking rain!* 這該死的雨真他媽的讓我心煩！◇ *He's a fucking good player.* 他是個他媽的優秀球員。

F

IDM 'fucking well (*especially BrE*) used to emphasize an angry statement or an order（強調憤怒或命令）: *You're fucking well coming whether you want to or not.* 不管你想不想來你他媽的給我過來。

fud·dled /ˈfʌdld/ *adj.* unable to think clearly, usually as a result of being old or drinking alcohol 頭腦糊塗的，思路不清的（常因年老或飲酒）

fuddy-duddy /ˈfʌdi dʌdi/ *noun* (*pl.* **fuddy-duddies**) (*informal*) a person who has old-fashioned ideas or habits 守舊的人；老頑固；老古董；老古板 ▸ **fuddy-duddy** *adj.*

F

fudge /fʌdʒ/ *noun, verb*

■ *noun* **1** [U] a type of soft brown sweet/candy made from sugar, butter and milk 法奇軟糖，乳脂軟糖（用糖、黃油和牛奶製成） **2 a fudge** [sing.] (*especially BrE, rather informal*) a way of dealing with a situation that does not really solve the problems but is intended to appear to do so 敷衍，裝模作樣（沒有真正解決問題）: *This solution is a fudge rushed in to win cheers at the party conference.* 這個解決方案是為了贏得黨的會議的讚譽而倉促搞出來的表面文章。

■ *verb* [T, I] **~ (on) sth** (*rather informal*) to avoid giving clear and accurate information, or a clear answer 含混其詞；迴避: *I asked how long he was staying, but he fudged the answer.* 我問他要待多久，但他含混其詞。◇ *Politicians are often very clever at* ***fudging the issue.*** 從政者都常常巧妙地迴避問題。

fuel 🔑 /ˈfjuːəl/ *noun, verb*

■ *noun* **1** 🔑 [U, C] any material that produces heat or power, usually when it is burnt 燃料: ***solid fuel*** (= wood, coal, etc.) 固體燃料 ◇ *nuclear fuels* 核燃料 ◇ *a car with high* ***fuel consumption*** 耗油量大的汽車 ➲ see also FOSSIL FUEL **2** [U] a thing that is said or done that makes sth, especially an argument, continue or get worse（尤指使爭論等繼續或更加激烈的）刺激性言行: *The new information adds fuel to the debate over safety procedures.* 新信息對於有關安全程序的辯論是火上澆油。◇ *The revelations gave new fuel to angry opponents of the proposed law.* 新披露的情況使反對該法律提案的人更為激憤。◇ *His remarks simply* ***added fuel to the fire/flames*** *of her rage.* 他的話只是給她的憤怒火上澆油。

■ *verb* (**-ll-**, *US* **-l-**) **1** [T] **~ sth** to supply sth with material that can be burnt to produce heat or power 給…提供燃料: *Uranium is used to fuel nuclear plants.* 鈾用作核電廠的燃料。◇ *oil-fuelled power stations* 燃油發電廠 **2** [T, I] **~ (sth) (up)** to put petrol/gas into a vehicle 給（交通工具）加油: *The helicopter was already fuelled (up) and ready to go.* 直升機已加好油，準備起飛。**3** [T] **~ sth** to increase sth; to make sth stronger 增加；加強；刺激 SYN **stoke**: *to* ***fuel speculation/rumours/fears*** 引起猜測／謠傳／恐懼 ◇ *Higher salaries helped to fuel inflation.* 工資提高刺激通貨膨脹。

ˈfuel cell *noun* a device that produces electricity directly from a fuel, such as HYDROGEN, by its reaction with another chemical, such as OXYGEN, without any burning, in order to supply power to a vehicle or machine 燃料電池

ˈfuel injection *noun* [U] a system of putting fuel into the engine of a car under pressure as a way of improving its performance（向汽車發動機的）燃料噴射，噴油

ˈfuel rod *noun* (*technical* 術語) a long thin piece of fuel used in a nuclear power station（核電站的）燃料棒

fufu /ˈfuːfuː/ *noun* [U] (*WAfrE*) a smooth white food often eaten with soups or STEWS and made by boiling and crushing the roots of plants such as COCOYAMS and CASSAVA 馥馥白糕（將煮熟的芋頭或木薯等碾碎製成，常與湯或燉菜一起吃）

fug /fʌg/ *noun* [sing.] (*BrE, informal*) air in a room that is hot and smells unpleasant because there are too many people in the room or because people are smoking（室內）悶熱污濁的空氣

fugal /ˈfjuːgl/ *adj.* (*music* 音) similar to or related to a FUGUE 賦格式的；賦格曲的

fu·gi·tive /ˈfjuːdʒətɪv/ *noun, adj.*

■ *noun* **~ (from sb/sth)** a person who has escaped or is running away from somewhere and is trying to avoid being caught 逃亡者；逃跑者；亡命者: *a fugitive from justice* 逃犯

■ *adj.* [only before noun] **1** trying to avoid being caught 逃亡的；逃跑的: *a fugitive criminal* 逃犯 **2** (*literary*) lasting only for a very short time 短暫的；易逝的 SYN **fleeting**: *a* ***fugitive idea/thought*** 轉瞬即逝的想法／思想

fugue /fjuːg/ *noun* a piece of music in which one or more tunes are introduced and then repeated in a complicated pattern 賦格曲

-ful *suffix* **1** (in adjectives 構成形容詞) full of; having the qualities of; tending to 充滿…的；有…性質（或傾向）的: *sorrowful* 悲傷 ◇ *masterful* 專橫 ◇ *forgetful* 健忘 **2** (in nouns 構成名詞) an amount that fills sth 充滿…的量: *handful* 一把 ◇ *spoonful* 一匙

ful·crum /ˈfʊlkrəm; ˈfʌlk-/ *noun* (*pl.* **ful·crums** or **ful·cra** /ˈfʊlkrə; ˈfʌlk-/) **1** (*physics* 物) the point on which a LEVER turns or is supported（槓桿的）支點，支軸 **2** [usually sing.] the most important part of an activity or a situation（活動、情況的）最重要部份，支柱

ful·fil (*BrE*) (*NAmE* **ful·fill**) /fʊlˈfɪl/ *verb* (**ful·fill·ing, ful·filled, ful·filled**) **1 ~ sth** to do or achieve what was hoped for or expected 實現: *to* ***fulfil*** *your* ***dream/ambition/potential*** 實現夢想／抱負；發揮潛力 **2 ~ sth** (*formal*) to do or have what is required or necessary 履行；執行；符合；具備: *to* ***fulfil a duty/an obligation/a promise*** 履行職責／義務／諾言 ◇ *to* ***fulfil the terms/conditions*** *of an agreement* 執行協定條款／條件 ◇ *No candidate fulfils all the criteria for this position.* 沒有候選人完全符合這個職位要求的標準。**3 ~ sth** to have a particular role or purpose 起…作用；目的是: *Nursery schools should* ***fulfil the function*** *of preparing children for school.* 幼兒園應該起到為兒童進小學作準備的作用。**4 ~ sb/yourself** to make sb feel happy and satisfied with what they are doing or have done 使高興；使滿意: *I need a job that really fulfils me.* 我需要一份真正令我感到滿足的工作。◇ *He was able to fulfil himself through his painting.* 他以繪畫充分發揮了自己的才能。▸ **ful·fil·ment** (*BrE*) (*NAmE* **ful·fill·ment**) *noun* [U]: *the fulfilment of a dream* 夢想的實現 ◇ *to find personal fulfilment* 尋求個人的滿足 ➲ SYNONYMS at SATISFACTION

ful·filled /fʊlˈfɪld/ *adj.* feeling happy and satisfied that you are doing sth useful with your life 感到滿足的；覺得滿意的；滿足的: *He doesn't feel fulfilled in his present job.* 目前的工作未能讓他感到滿足。OPP **unfulfilled**

ful·fil·ling /fʊlˈfɪlɪŋ/ *adj.* causing sb to feel satisfied and useful 讓人感覺有意義的；令人滿足的: *a fulfilling experience* 有成就感的經歷 OPP **unfulfilling** ➲ SYNONYMS at SATISFYING

full 🔑 /fʊl/ *adj., adv.*

■ *adj.* (**full·er, fullest**)

▸ WITH NO EMPTY SPACE 滿 **1** 🔑 **~ (of sth)** containing or holding as much or as many as possible; having no empty space 滿的；充滿的；滿是…的: *a full bottle of wine* 一滿瓶葡萄酒 ◇ *She could only nod, because her mouth was full.* 她只能點點頭，因為她嘴裏塞滿了東西。◇ *My suitcase was full of books.* 我的提箱裝滿了書。◇ *There were cardboard boxes* ***stuffed full of*** *clothes.* 有塞滿衣服的一個個紙箱。◇ (*BrE*) *Sorry, the hotel is* ***full up*** *tonight.* 對不起，今晚旅館客滿。

▸ HAVING A LOT 大量 **2** 🔑 **~ of sth** having or containing a large number or amount of sth（有）大量的；（有）許多的；豐富的: *The sky was full of brightly coloured fireworks.* 滿天一片色彩絢麗的煙火。◇ ***Life is full of*** *coincidences.* 生活中巧合很多。◇ *Our new brochure is* ***crammed full of*** *inspirational ideas.* 我們新的小冊子中振奮人心的妙計比比皆是。◇ *animals* ***pumped full of*** *antibiotics* 注入大量抗生素的動物 ◇ *She was full of admiration for the care she had received.* 她對所受到的關懷照顧讚不絕口。◇ *He smiled, his eyes full of laughter.* 他露出了笑容，雙眼也滿含着笑意。

▸ TALKING A LOT 話多 **3 ~ of sth** (of a person 人) thinking or talking a lot about a particular thing（關於某事物）想得很多，談得很多: *He was full of his new job and* *everything he'd been doing.* 他滔滔不絕地談他的新工作和所做的一切。

▸ **WITH FOOD 食物 4** [usually before noun] (*BrE* also **ˌfull ˈup**) having had enough to eat 吃飽了的：*No more for me, thanks—I'm full up.* 謝謝，我不要了，我已經飽了。◇ *The kids still weren't full, so I gave them an ice cream each.* 孩子們還沒有吃飽，所以我給他們每人一份冰淇淋。◇ *You can't run* ***on a full stomach.*** 飽餐之後不能跑步。

▸ **COMPLETE 完全 5** [usually before noun] complete; with nothing missing 完全的；完整的；詳盡的：*Full details are available on request.* 詳情備索。◇ *I still don't think we've heard* ***the full story.*** 我還是認為我們未瞭解全部情況。◇ *a full English breakfast* 全份英式早餐 ◇ *A full refund will be given if the item is faulty.* 如貨有瑕疵將退回全部貨款。◇ *Fill in your full name and address.* 填寫全名和地址。◇ *The country applied for full membership of the European Union.* 這個國家申請成為歐洲聯盟的正式成員。

▸ **AS MUCH AS POSSIBLE 盡量 6** [usually before noun] to the highest level or greatest amount possible 最高級的；盡量多的；最大量的 SYN **maximum**：*Many people don't use their computers to their* ***full potential.*** 很多人沒有充分利用他們計算機的全部潛在功能。◇ *measures to achieve* ***full employment*** 力求充分就業的措施 ◇ *Students should* ***take full advantage of*** *the university's facilities.* 學生應該充分利用大學的設施。◇ *She came round the corner* ***at full speed.*** 她全速拐過彎道。

▸ **BUSY 忙碌 7** busy; involving a lot of activities 忙的；有很多活動的：*He'd had a very* ***full life.*** 他度過了一個豐富的人生。◇ *Her life was too full to find time for hobbies.* 她的生活太忙，沒有業餘愛好的時間。

▸ **FOR EMPHASIS 強調 8** [only before noun] used to emphasize an amount or a quantity（強調數量）足足的，整整的：*She is a full four inches shorter than her sister.* 她比姐姐足足矮四英寸。

▸ **MOON 月亮 9** appearing as a complete circle 圓的；滿的：*The moon was full, the sky clear.* 圓月碧空。⮊ see also FULL MOON

▸ **FAT 肥胖 10** (of a person or part of the body 人或身體部份) large and round. 'Full' is sometimes used to avoid saying 'fat'. 豐滿的；圓鼓鼓的（有時用 full 以避免用 fat）：*He kissed her full sensual lips.* 他吻了她那豐滿性感的嘴唇。◇ *They specialize in clothes for women with a fuller figure.* 他們專為體形較豐滿的女士做衣服。

▸ **CLOTHES 衣服 11** made with plenty of cloth; fitting loosely 寬鬆的；肥大的：*a full skirt* 寬裙

▸ **TONE/VOICE/FLAVOUR 音調；嗓音；味道 12** deep, strong and rich 圓渾的；圓潤的；濃郁的：*He draws a unique full sound from the instrument.* 他用樂器奏出了獨特圓渾的音調。◇ *the full fruity flavour of the wine* 這葡萄酒濃郁的水果味

IDM Most idioms containing **full** are at the entries for the nouns and verbs in the idioms, for example **full of the joys of spring** is at **joy**. 大多數含 full 的習語，都可在該等習語中的名詞及動詞相關詞條找到，如 full of the joys of spring 在詞條 joy 下。 **ˈfull of it** (*informal, disapproving, especially NAmE*) (of a person 指人) not telling the truth; tending to exaggerate things 亂說；誇大其詞：*'You are so full of it!' she retorted furiously.* "你胡說！" 她生氣地反駁道。 **ˈfull of yourself** (*disapproving*) very proud; thinking only of yourself 自滿；自視甚高；只顧自己 **in full** including the whole of sth 整個；全部：*The address must be printed in full.* 地址必須以正體詳盡填寫。 **to the full** (*NAmE* usually **to the fullest**) to the greatest possible degree 達到最大程度；充分：*I've always believed in living life to the full.* 我總是相信生活要盡量充實。

■ ***adv.*** **~ in/on sth** directly 直接地；逕直地：*She looked him full in the face.* 她逕直望着他的臉。

full·back /ˈfʊlbæk/ *noun* **1** [C] one of the defending players in football (SOCCER), HOCKEY or RUGBY whose position is near the goal they are defending（足球、曲棍球或橄欖球）後衛 **2** [C] the attacking player in AMERICAN FOOTBALL whose position is behind the QUARTERBACK and beside the HALFBACKS（美式足球）進攻後衛，殿衛 **3** [U] the position a fullback plays at 後衛位置：*Hunter is at fullback.* 亨特擔任後衛。

ˌfull ˈbeam *noun* [U] (*BrE*) the brightest light that a vehicle's HEADLIGHTS can give, usually used when there are no street lights and no other traffic（車前燈的）最強亮度，最強光：*Even with the lights on full beam I couldn't see very far.* 即使把燈打到了最強光我還是看不了多遠。

ˌfull-ˈblooded *adj.* [only before noun] **1** involving very strong feelings or actions; done in an enthusiastic way 感情強烈的；猛烈的；精力旺盛的；熱情的：*a full-blooded attack* 猛烈攻擊 **2** having parents, grandparents, etc. from only one race or country 全血緣的；純血統的：*a full-blooded Scotsman* 純血統的蘇格蘭人

ˌfull-ˈblown *adj.* [only before noun] having all the characteristics of sb/sth; fully developed 具所有特徵的；成熟的：*full-blown AIDS* 完全型艾滋病 ◇ *The border dispute turned into a full-blown crisis.* 邊境爭端已演變成全面性的危機。

ˌfull ˈboard (*BrE*) (*NAmE* **Aˌmerican ˈplan**) *noun* [U] a type of accommodation in a hotel, etc. that includes all meals（旅館的）全食宿：*Do you require full or half board?* 你要全食宿還是半食宿？⮊ compare BED AND BREAKFAST (1), EUROPEAN PLAN, HALF BOARD

ˌfull-ˈbodied *adj.* having a pleasantly strong taste or sound（味道）濃郁的，濃烈的；（聲音）圓潤的，圓渾的：*a full-bodied red wine* 濃郁的紅葡萄酒 ◇ *a full-bodied string section* 圓潤悅耳的弦樂部

ˌfull-ˈcolour (*especially US* **ˌfull-ˈcolor**) *adj.* [only before noun] printed using colours rather than just black and white 彩色的；全色的

ˌfull-court ˈpress *noun* [sing.] (*NAmE*) **1** (in BASKETBALL 籃球) a way of attacking in which the members of a team stay close to their opponents over the whole area of play 全場緊逼 **2** (*informal*) a strong effort to influence sb or a group of people by putting pressure on them 全面攻勢；全面出擊

ˌfull-ˈcream *adj.* (*BrE*) (of milk 牛奶) with none of the fat taken away 全脂的

full·er's earth /ˌfʊləz ˈɜːθ; *NAmE* ˌfʊlərz ˈɜːrθ/ *noun* [U] a type of CLAY used for cleaning cloth and making it thicker 漂白土；漂布泥

ˌfull ˈface *adj., adv.* showing the whole of sb's face; not in PROFILE 臉正面的（地）；正臉的（地）：*a full-face* ***view/portrait*** 正面面孔／肖像

ˌfull-ˈfat *adj.* [usually before noun] (*especially BrE*) (of milk, cheese, etc. 牛奶、奶酪等) without any of the fat removed 全脂的

ˌfull-ˈfledged (*especially NAmE*) (*BrE* also **ˌfully ˈfledged**) *adj.* completely developed; with all the qualifications necessary for sth 成熟的；完全合格的

ˌfull ˈforward *noun* (in AUSTRALIAN RULES football 澳式橄欖球) an attacking player who plays near the opposing team's goal（站在進攻方得分線前的）大前鋒

ˌfull-ˈfrontal *adj., noun*

■ ***adj.*** [only before noun] **1** showing the whole of the front of a person's body 裸露正面的：*full-frontal nudity* 正面全裸 **2** = FRONTAL (2)

■ ***noun*** a picture or a scene in a film/movie which shows the naked body of a person from the front 正面全裸的照片（或電影鏡頭）

ˌfull-ˈgrown *adj.* (of people, animals or plants 人或動植物) having reached the greatest size to which they can grow and stopped growing 長足了的；長成的；成熟的

ˌfull ˈhouse *noun* **1** an occasion in a theatre, cinema/movie theater, etc. when there are no empty seats（劇院、電影院等）滿座，客滿：*They played to a full house.* 他們的演出座無虛席。 **2** (in the card game of POKER) three cards of one kind and two of another kind 滿堂紅（撲克牌遊戲中三張點數相同，另兩張點數相同的一手牌）

ˌfull-ˈlength *adj., adv.*

■ ***adj.*** [only before noun] **1** (of a mirror or picture 鏡子或相片) showing the whole of a person's body 全身的：*a full-length portrait* 全身肖像 **2** (of a book, play, etc. 書、劇本等) not made shorter; of the usual length 足本的：*a full-length novel* 足本小說 **3** (of curtains or a window 窗簾或窗子) reaching the ground 長及地面的；落地的 **4** (of clothing 衣服) reaching a person's ankles 長及腳踝的：*a full-length skirt* 拖地長裙

■ ***adv.*** a person who is lying **full-length** is lying flat with their legs straight（身體）伸展開，伸直：*He was sprawled full-length across the bed.* 他手腳攤開橫躺在牀上。

ˌfull ˈmarks *noun* [pl.] (*BrE*) the highest mark/grade in a test, etc. (when you get nothing wrong)（成績）滿分：*She got full marks in the exam.* 她考試得了滿分。◇ (*figurative*) ***Full marks to** Bill for an excellent idea!* (= he deserves praise) 比爾的主意極妙，值得讚揚！

F

ˌfull ˈmoon *noun* [C, usually sing., U] the moon when it appears as a full circle; a time when this happens 滿月；望月；望日 ➲ compare HALF-MOON (1), HARVEST MOON, NEW MOON

full·ness /ˈfʊlnəs/ *noun* [U, sing.] **1** (of the body or part of the body 身體或身體部份) the quality of being large and round 豐滿：*the fullness of her lips* 她豐滿的雙唇 **2** (of colours, sounds and flavours 顏色、聲音和味道) the quality of being deep and rich（顏色）深濃；（聲音）圓渾，圓潤；（味道）濃郁 **3** the quality of being complete and satisfying 完美；完全：*the fullness of life* 生命的圓滿

IDM **in the fullness of ˈtime** when the time is appropriate, usually after a long period 在適當時候，時機成熟時（尤指久待之後）

ˌfull-ˈon *adj.* (*informal*) used to say that sth is done to the greatest possible degree（表示最大程度）完全的；最強烈的：*It was a full-on night out with the boys.* 這是與男孩們外出玩得最盡興的一個晚上。

ˌfull-ˈpage *adj.* [only before noun] filling a complete page of a newspaper or magazine（報紙）整版的；（雜誌）全頁的：*a full-page ad* 整版廣告

ˌfull ˈpoint *noun* = FULL STOP

ˈfull professor *noun* (*NAmE*) = PROFESSOR (1)

ˌfull-ˈscale *adj.* [only before noun] **1** that is as complete and thorough as possible 全面的；完全的；徹底的：*a full-scale attack* 全面攻擊 **2** that is the same size as sth that is being copied 原尺寸的；和實物同樣大小的：*a full-scale model* 原尺寸模型

ˌfull-ˈsize (also **ˌfull-ˈsized**) *adj.* [usually before noun] not made smaller; of the usual size 原尺寸的；和通常大小一樣的：*a full-size model* 原尺寸模型 ◇ *a full-size snooker table* 標準尺寸的斯諾克球枱

ˌfull ˈstop *noun, adv.*

■ ***noun*** (also *less frequent* **stop**) (also **ˌfull ˈpoint**) (all *BrE*) (*NAmE* **period**) the mark (.) used at the end of a sentence and in some abbreviations, for example *e.g.* 句點；句號

IDM **come to a full ˈstop** to stop completely 完全停止

■ ***adv.*** (*BrE*) (also **period** *NAmE, BrE*) (*informal*) used at the end of a sentence to emphasize that there is nothing more to say about a subject（用於句末，強調不再多說）到此為止，就是這話：*I've already told you—we can't afford it, full stop!* 我已經告訴過你，我們負擔不起，不再說了！

ˌfull-ˈterm *adj.* (*technical* 術語) **1** (of a PREGNANCY 懷胎) lasting the normal length of time 足月的 **2** (of a baby 嬰兒) born after a PREGNANCY lasting the normal length of time 足月生的

ˌfull ˈtime *noun* [U] (*BrE*) the end of a sports game（體育運動的）全場比賽結束時間，終場：*The referee blew his whistle for full time.* 裁判吹響了比賽結束的哨音。◇ *The full-time score was 1-1.* 全場比賽結果為 1:1。➲ compare HALF-TIME

ˌfull-ˈtime *adj., adv.* (*abbr.* FT) for all the hours of a week during which people normally work or study, rather than just for a part of it 全日（制）；全職的；全日的：*students in full-time education* 全日制學生 ◇ *a full-time employee* 全職雇員 ◇ *a full-time job* 一份全職工作 ◇ *Looking after a child is a full-time job* (= hard work that takes a lot of time). 照管小孩是一天忙到晚的活兒。◇ *She works full-time and still manages to run a home.* 她做全職工作，仍能照管好家庭。➲ compare PART-TIME

ˌfull-ˈtimer *noun* a person who works full-time 全日制工作者；全職人員

ˌfull ˈtoss *noun* (in CRICKET 板球) a ball that reaches the BATSMAN without touching the ground and is easy to hit 未着地的直線球

fully 0ꟷ /ˈfʊli/ *adv.*

1 0ꟷ completely 完全地；全部地；充分地：*She had **fully recovered** from the accident.* 事故後她已經完全恢復過來。◇ *We are **fully aware** of the dangers.* 我們充分意識到危險。◇ *I **fully understand** your motives.* 我完全理解你的動機。 **2** (*formal*) (used to emphasize an amount 強調數量) the whole of; as much as 整整；足足：*The disease affects fully 30 per cent of the population.* 這種病感染了足足 30% 的人口。

ˌfully ˈfledged (*BrE*) (also **ˌfull-ˈfledged** *NAmE, BrE*) *adj.* [usually before noun] completely developed; with all the qualifications necessary for sth 成熟的；完全合格的：*the emergence of a fully fledged market economy* 成熟市場經濟的出現 ◇ *She was now a fully fledged member of the teaching profession.* 她現在是完全合格的教師。

ful·mar /ˈfʊlmə(r)/ *noun* a grey and white bird that lives near the sea 暴風鸌（海鳥）

ful·min·ate /ˈfʊlmɪneɪt; ˈfʌl-/ *verb* [I] **~ against (sb/sth)** (*formal*) to criticize sb/sth angrily 憤怒譴責；怒斥 ▶ **ful·min·ation** /ˌfʊlmɪˈneɪʃn; ˌfʌl-/ *noun* [C, U]

ful·some /ˈfʊlsəm/ *adj.* (*disapproving*) too generous in praising or thanking sb, or in saying sorry, so that you do not sound sincere 過分恭維的；諂媚的；感謝過頭的：*a fulsome apology* 低三下四的道歉 ◇ *He was fulsome in his praise of the Prime Minister.* 他稱讚首相時有溢美之詞。▶ **ful·some·ly** *adv.*

fum·ble /ˈfʌmbl/ *verb, noun*

■ ***verb*** **1** [I, T] to use your hands in an awkward way when you are doing sth or looking for sth 笨手笨腳地做（某事）；笨拙地摸找（某物）：**~ (at/with/in sth) (for sth)** *She fumbled in her pocket for a handkerchief.* 她在口袋裏胡亂摸找手帕。◇ *He fumbled with the buttons on his shirt.* 他笨手笨腳地擺弄襯衣上的鈕扣。◇ **~ around** *She was fumbling around in the dark looking for the light switch.* 她摸黑找電燈開關。◇ **~ sth (+ adv./prep.)** *He fumbled the key into the ignition.* 他笨拙地把鑰匙插進汽車點火開關。◇ **~ to do sth** *I fumbled to zip up my jacket.* 我笨手笨腳地拉上夾克的拉鏈。 **2** [I, T] to have difficulty speaking clearly or finding the right words to say 笨嘴拙舌地說話；支支吾吾地說：**~ (for sth)** *During the interview, she fumbled helplessly for words.* 面試時她支支吾吾找不出適當的話語。◇ **~ sth** *to fumble an announcement* 結結巴巴地宣告 **3** [T] **~ sth** (especially in sport 尤用於體育運動) to drop a ball or to fail to stop or kick it 失球；接球失誤；漏接

■ ***noun*** **1** [sing.] (also **fum·bling** [C, usually pl.]) an awkward action using the hands 笨拙的手部動作；亂摸 **2** [C] (*NAmE*) the action of dropping the ball while it is in play in AMERICAN FOOTBALL（美式足球）失球，接球失誤，漏接

fum·bling /ˈfʌmblɪŋ/ *adj.* awkward, uncertain or hesitating 笨拙的；遲疑的：*a fumbling schoolboy* 笨拙的男生

fume /fjuːm/ *verb* **1** [I, T] to be very angry about sth（對…）大為生氣，十分惱火：**~ (at/over/about sb/sth)** *She sat in the car, silently fuming at the traffic jam.* 她坐在汽車裏，心中對交通堵塞感到十分惱火。◇ **~ (with sth)** *He was fuming with indignation.* 他憤憤不平。◇ **+ speech** *'This is intolerable!' she fumed.* "這真讓人不可容忍！" 她怒氣沖沖地說。 **2** [I] to produce smoke or fumes 冒煙；冒氣

fumes /fjuːmz/ *noun* [pl.] (also *less frequent* **fume** [U]) smoke, gas, or sth similar that smells strongly or is dangerous to breathe in（濃烈的或有害的）煙，氣，汽：***diesel/petrol/exhaust fumes*** 強烈的柴油味／汽油味／廢氣 ➲ VISUAL VOCAB page V6：*to be overcome by smoke and fumes* 被濃煙熏倒 ◇ *Clouds of toxic fumes escaped in a huge chemical factory blaze.* 從化工廠熊熊

烈火中泄漏出團團有毒氣體。◇ *The body of a man was found in a **fume-filled** car yesterday.* 昨天在一輛充滿煙的汽車中發現了一具男屍。

fu·mi·gate /ˈfjuːmɪɡeɪt/ *verb* **~ sth** to use special chemicals, smoke or gas to destroy the harmful insects or bacteria in a place 煙熏，熏蒸（以滅蟲或消毒）：*to fumigate a room* 用熏蒸的方法給房間消毒 ▸ **fu·mi·ga·tion** /ˌfjuːmɪˈɡeɪʃn/ *noun* [U, C]

Synonyms 同義詞辨析

fun

pleasure • (a) good time • enjoyment • (a) great time

These are all words for the feeling of enjoying yourself, or activities or time that you enjoy. 以上各詞均表示愉快、快樂的事、歡樂的時光。

fun (*rather informal*) the feeling of enjoying yourself; activities that you enjoy 指享樂、樂趣、享樂的事：*We had a lot of fun at Sarah's party.* 我們在薩拉的聚會上玩得很開心。◇ *Sailing is **good/great fun**.* 帆船運動很／極有樂趣。

pleasure (*rather formal*) the feeling of enjoying yourself or being satisfied 指高興、快樂、愉快、滿意：*Reading for pleasure and reading for study are not the same.* 讀書以自娛和讀書以學習是不相同的。

(a) good time (*rather informal*) a time that you spend enjoying yourself 指歡樂、愉快的時光：*We had a good time in Spain.* 我們在西班牙過得很愉快。

enjoyment (*rather formal*) the feeling of enjoying yourself 指愉快、快樂、樂趣：*I get a lot of enjoyment from music.* 我從音樂中獲得很多樂趣。

PLEASURE OR ENJOYMENT? 用 pleasure 還是 enjoyment？

Enjoyment usually comes from an activity that you do; **pleasure** can come from sth that you do or sth that happens. * enjoyment 通常源於活動；pleasure 既可源於所做的事也可源於發生的事：*He beamed with pleasure at seeing her.* 他看到她時喜不自勝。◇ ~~*He beamed with enjoyment at seeing her.*~~

(a) great time (*rather informal*) a time that you spend enjoying yourself very much 指非常歡樂、愉快的時光：*We had a really great time together.* 我們一起度過了非常快樂的時光。

PATTERNS

- to do sth **for** fun/pleasure/enjoyment
- **great** fun/pleasure/enjoyment
- to **have** fun/a good time/a great time
- to **get** pleasure/enjoyment **from** sth
- to **spoil** the fun/sb's pleasure/sb's enjoyment

fun 🔑 /fʌn/ *noun, adj.*
■ ***noun*** [U] **1** 🔑 enjoyment; pleasure; a thing that gives enjoyment or pleasure and makes you feel happy 享樂；樂趣；快樂；享樂的事：*We had a lot of fun at Sarah's party.* 我們在薩拉的聚會上玩得很開心。◇ *Sailing is **good fun**.* 帆船運動很有樂趣。◇ ***Have fun!*** (= Enjoy yourself) 盡情地玩吧！◇ *I decided to learn Spanish, just **for fun**.* 我決定學西班牙語只是為了好玩。◇ *I didn't do all that work just **for the fun of it**.* 我做這一切並不僅僅是為了好玩。◇ *It's not much fun going to a party on your own.* 獨自一人參加聚會沒什麼意思。◇ *'What fun!' she said with a laugh.* "真開心呀！" 她笑着說。◇ *Walking three miles in the pouring rain is **not my idea of fun**.* 頂着傾盆大雨走三英里路，我可不認為是好玩的事。◇ *'What do you say to a weekend in New York?' 'Sounds like fun.'* "在紐約度週末怎麼樣？" "聽起來很愜意。" **2** 🔑 behaviour or activities that are not serious but come from a sense of enjoyment 嬉戲；逗樂；玩笑：*She's very lively and **full of fun**.* 她很活潑，挺有趣的。◇ *We didn't mean to hurt him. It was just **a bit of fun**.* 我們並非有意要傷害他，只不過是開個玩笑罷了。◇ *It wasn't serious - it was all done **in fun**.* 那不是認真的，全是鬧着玩的。➲ SYNONYMS at ENTERTAINMENT

IDM **fun and 'games** (*informal*) activities that are not serious and that other people may disapprove of 嬉戲；歡鬧；尋歡作樂 **make 'fun of sb/sth** 🔑 to laugh at sb/sth or make other people laugh at them, usually in an unkind way 嘲弄；取笑；拿…開玩笑：*It's cruel to make fun of people who stammer.* 嘲笑口吃的人是很不人道的。➲ more at FIGURE *n.*, POKE *v.*
■ ***adj.*** 🔑 amusing or enjoyable 逗樂的；有趣的；使人快樂的：*She's really fun to be with.* 和她在一起真開心。◇ *This game looks fun!* 這個遊戲看來好玩！◇ *There are lots of fun things for young people to do here.* 這裏有許多供年輕人玩樂的東西。

func·tion 🔑 AW /ˈfʌŋkʃn/ *noun, verb*
■ ***noun*** **1** 🔑 [C, U] a special activity or purpose of a person or thing 作用；功能；職能；機能：*to **fulfil/perform a function*** 發揮功能 ◇ ***bodily functions*** (= for example eating, sex, using the toilet) 身體機能 ◇ *The function of the heart is to pump blood through the body.* 心臟的功能就是把血液輸往全身。◇ *This design aims for harmony of form and function.* 這個設計旨在使形式和功能協調一致。**2** 🔑 [C] a social event or official ceremony 社交聚會；典禮；宴會：*The hall provided a venue for weddings and other functions.* 大廳可以舉辦婚禮和其他公開活動。**3** [C] (*mathematics* 數) a quantity whose value depends on the varying values of others. In the statement 2x=y, y is a function of x. 函數：(*figurative*) *Salary is **a function of** age and experience.* 工資視乎年齡和經驗而定。**4** [C] (*computing* 計) a part of a program, etc. that performs a basic operation 子程序；例程
■ ***verb*** 🔑 [I] **(+ adv./prep.)** (rather *formal*) to work in the correct way 起作用；正常工作；運轉 SYN **operate**：*Despite the power cuts, the hospital continued to function normally.* 儘管供電中斷，醫院繼續照常運作。◇ *We now have a functioning shower.* 現在我們有一個功能正常的淋浴器。◇ *Many children can't function effectively in large classes.* 許多孩子在大夥兒上課時學習效果不好。

PHR V **'function as sb/sth** 🔑 to perform the action or the job of the thing or person mentioned 起…作用；具有…功能：*The sofa also functions as a bed.* 這沙發還可當牀用。

func·tion·al AW /ˈfʌŋkʃənl/ *adj.* **1** practical and useful; with little or no decoration 實用的 SYN **utilitarian**：*Bathrooms don't have to be purely functional.* 浴室不必完全只為了實用。◇ *The office was large and functional rather than welcoming.* 這個辦公室大而實用，但不怎麼宜人。**2** having a special purpose; making it possible for sb to do sth or for sth to happen 作用的；功能的；機能的；職能的：*a functional disorder* (= an illness caused when an organ of the body fails to perform its function) 功能紊亂 ◇ *a functional approach to language learning* 功能語言學習法 ◇ *These units played a key functional role in the military operation.* 這些單位在軍事行動中起到了主要的職能作用。**3** (especially of a machine, an organization or a system 尤指機器、組織、機構或體系) working; able to work (能)起作用的，工作的，運轉的：*The hospital will soon be fully functional.* 這家醫院將很快全面運作。▸ **func·tion·al·ly** AW /-ʃənəli/ *adv.*

ˌfunctional 'food *noun* [C, U] (also **nutra·ceut·ical**) food that has had substances that are good for your health specially added to it 功能食品；保健食品

ˌfunctional 'grammar *noun* [U] (*linguistics* 語言) grammar that analyses how language is used to communicate 功能語法（分析語言如何用於交際的語法）

func·tion·al·ism /ˈfʌŋkʃənəlɪzəm/ *noun* [U] the idea or belief that the most important thing about the style or design of a building or object is how it is going to be used, not how it will look 功能主義，實用建築主義（主張建築或物品設計首要的是用途而不是外觀）▸ **func·tion·al·ist** /-ʃənəlɪst/ *noun* **func·tion·al·ist** *adj.* [usually before noun]

func·tion·al·ity /ˌfʌŋkʃəˈnæləti/ *noun* (*pl.* **-ies**) **1** [U] the quality in sth of being very suitable for the purpose it was designed for 實用；符合實際 SYN **practicality** **2** [U] the purpose that sth is designed for or expected to perform 設計目的；設計功能：*Manufacturing processes* *may be affected by the functionality of the product.* 生產過程可能要受到產品設計目的的影響。 **3** [U, C] (*computing* 計) the range of functions that a computer or other electronic system can perform（計算機或電子系統的）功能：*new software with additional functionality* 有附加功能的新軟件

func·tion·ary /ˈfʌŋkʃənəri; *NAmE* -neri/ *noun* (*pl.* **-ies**) (often *disapproving*) a person with official duties 公職人員；官員 **SYN** **official**：***party/state/government functionaries*** 政黨／國家／政府的官員

ˈfunction key *noun* (*computing* 計) one of several keys on a computer keyboard, each marked with 'F' and a number, that can be used to do sth, such as save a file or get to the 'help' function in a program 功能鍵

F

ˈfunction word (also **func·tor**) *noun* (*grammar* 語法) a word that is important to the grammar of a sentence rather than its meaning, for example 'do' in 'we do not live here' 功能詞，虛詞（如 we do not live here 中的 do 一詞）➲ compare CONTENT WORD

func·tor /ˈfʌŋktə(r)/ *noun* **1** (*mathematics* 數) a FUNCTION or a symbol such as + or × 函子 **2** (*grammar* 語法) = FUNCTION WORD

fund 🗝 **AW** /fʌnd/ *noun, verb*

▪ ***noun*** **1** 🗝 [C] an amount of money that has been saved or has been made available for a particular purpose 基金；專款：*a disaster relief fund* 賑災專款 ◇ *the company's pension fund* 公司的退休基金 ◇ *the International Monetary Fund* 國際貨幣基金組織 **2** 🗝 **funds** [pl.] money that is available to be spent 資金；現款：*government funds* 政府資金 ◇ *The hospital is trying to raise funds for a new kidney machine.* 這家醫院正設法募集資金購買一台新的血液透析器。◇ *The project has been cancelled because of lack of funds.* 這個項目因缺乏資金已經撤銷。◇ *I'm* ***short of funds*** *at the moment—can I pay you back next week?* 我目前缺錢，下週還你行嗎？ ➲ COLLOCATIONS at FINANCE **3** [sing.] **~ of sth** an amount or a supply of sth（相當）數量；儲備：*a fund of knowledge* 豐富的知識

▪ ***verb*** 🗝 **~ sth** to provide money for sth, usually sth official 提供資金；撥款：*a dance festival funded by the Arts Council* 由藝術委員會資助的舞蹈節 ◇ *The museum is privately funded.* 這家博物館由私人提供資金。◇ *a government-funded programme* 政府資助項目

fun·da·men·tal 🗝 **AW** /ˌfʌndəˈmentl/ *adj., noun*

▪ ***adj.*** **1** 🗝 serious and very important; affecting the most central and important parts of sth 十分重大的；根本的 **SYN** **basic**：*There is a* ***fundamental difference*** *between the two points of view.* 這兩個觀點有根本區別。◇ *A* ***fundamental change*** *in the organization of health services was required.* 公共醫療在組織上需要一個根本性的變革。◇ *a question of fundamental importance* 首要問題 **2** 🗝 **~ (to sth)** central; forming the necessary basis of sth 基礎的；基本的 **SYN** **essential**：*Hard work is fundamental to success.* 勤奮工作是成功的基礎。 **3** [only before noun] (*physics* 物) forming the source or base from which everything else is made; not able to be divided any further 基本的；不能再分的：*a fundamental particle* 基本粒子

▪ ***noun*** [usually pl.] a basic rule or principle; an essential part 基本規律；根本法則；基本原理；基礎：*the fundamentals of modern physics* 現代物理學的基本原理 ◇ *He taught me the fundamentals of the job.* 他教給了我這工作的基本知識。

ˌfundamental ˈforce *noun* (*technical* 術語) a force that is a property (= characteristic) of everything in the universe. There are four fundamental forces including GRAVITY and ELECTROMAGNETISM. 基本力（宇宙萬物所具有的特性，包括引力和電磁力等四種）

fun·da·men·tal·ism /ˌfʌndəˈmentəlɪzəm/ *noun* [U] **1** the practice of following very strictly the basic rules and teachings of any religion 原教旨主義（認為應嚴格奉行宗教原則和教義） **2** (in Christianity) the belief that everything that is written in the Bible is completely true（基督教的）基要主義，原教旨主義（強調直解《聖經》）▸ **fun·da·men·tal·ist** /-ɪst/ *noun* **fun·da·men·tal·ist** /-ɪst/ *adj.*

fun·da·men·tal·ly **AW** /ˌfʌndəˈmentəli/ *adv.* **1** in every way that is important; completely 根本上；完全地：*The two approaches are fundamentally different.* 這兩個處理方法完全不同。◇ *By the 1960s the situation had changed fundamentally.* 到 20 世紀 60 年代形勢已發生了根本的變化。◇ *They remained fundamentally opposed to the plan.* 他們依然從根本上反對這項計劃。 **2** used when you are introducing a topic and stating sth important about it（引入話題時說）從根本上說，基本上 **SYN** **basically**：*Fundamentally, there are two different approaches to the problem.* 從根本上說，這個問題有兩種不同的處理方法。 **3** used when you are saying what is the most important thing about sb/sth（表示最重要的方面）根本上，基本上 **SYN** **basically**：*She is fundamentally a nice person, but she finds it difficult to communicate.* 她基本上是個好人，但她覺得難以和人溝通。

fun·der **AW** /ˈfʌndə(r)/ *noun* a person or an organization that provides money for a particular purpose 基金贊助者；提供資金者

fund·holding /ˈfʌndhəʊldɪŋ; *NAmE* -hoʊ-/ *noun* [U] a system in Britain in which the government gives GPs (= family doctors) an amount of money with which they can buy some hospital services 費用負責制（英國政府發給家庭醫生支付某些醫院服務費用的制度）▸ **ˈfund·holder** *noun*

fundi /ˈfʊndiː/ *noun* (*SAfrE*) a person who is very skilled at sth or who has gained a lot of knowledge about a particular subject 匠人；行家；專家：*a computer fundi* 電腦高手 ◇ *He's become quite a fundi on wine.* 他對葡萄酒很在行。

fund·ing **AW** /ˈfʌndɪŋ/ *noun* [U] money for a particular purpose; the act of providing money for such a purpose 基金；資金；提供基金；提供資金：*There have been large cuts in government funding for scientific research.* 政府提供的科研資金已大幅度削減。

ˈfund-raiser *noun* **1** a person who collects money for a charity or an organization 募集資金者；募捐者 **2** a social event or an entertainment held in order to collect money for a charity or an organization 募捐活動；募捐會；義演 ▸ **ˈfund-raising** *noun* [U]

fu·neral 🗝 /ˈfjuːnərəl/ *noun* a ceremony, usually a religious one, for burying or CREMATING (= burning) a dead person 葬禮；喪禮；出殯：*Hundreds of people attended the funeral.* 數百人參加了葬禮。◇ *a funeral procession* 送葬隊伍 ◇ *a funeral march* (= a sad piece of music suitable for funerals) 喪禮進行曲

IDM **it's ˈyour funeral** (*informal*) used to tell sb that they, and nobody else, will have to deal with the unpleasant results of their own actions 這是你自作自受

ˈfuneral director *noun* (*formal*) = UNDERTAKER

ˈfuneral parlour (*especially US* **ˈfuneral parlor**) (also **ˈfuneral home** *NAmE, BrE*) (*NAmE* also **mor·tu·ary**) *noun* a place where dead people are prepared for being buried or CREMATED (= burned) and where visitors can see the body 殯儀館

fu·ner·ary /ˈfjuːnərəri; *NAmE* -reri/ *adj.* [only before noun] (*formal*) of or used at a funeral（用於）葬禮的，喪葬的：***funerary monuments/rites*** 墓碑；喪葬儀式

fu·ner·eal /fjuˈnɪəriəl; *NAmE* -ˈnɪr-/ *adj.* (*formal*) suitable for a funeral; sad 適於葬禮的；悲傷的：*a funereal atmosphere* 悲哀肅穆的氣氛

fun·fair /ˈfʌnfeə(r); *NAmE* -fer/ *noun* (*BrE*) = FAIR *n.* (1)

fung·al /ˈfʌŋgl/ *adj.* of or caused by FUNGUS 真菌的；真菌引起的：*a fungal infection* 真菌感染

fun·gi·cide /ˈfʌŋgɪsaɪd; ˈfʌndʒɪ-/ *noun* [C, U] a substance that kills fungus 殺真菌劑

fun·goid /ˈfʌŋgɔɪd/ *adj.* (*technical* 術語) like a FUNGUS 似真菌的；真菌式的：*a fungoid growth* 真菌式生長

fun·gus /ˈfʌŋgəs/ *noun* (*pl.* **fungi** /ˈfʌŋgiː; -gaɪ; ˈfʌndʒaɪ/) **1** [C] any plant without leaves, flowers or green colouring, usually growing on other plants or on decaying matter. MUSHROOMS and MILDEW are both fungi. 真菌（如蘑菇和黴） ➲ COLLOCATIONS at LIFE **2** [U, C] a covering of MOULD or a similar fungus, for example on a plant or wall 黴；黴菌： *fungus infections* 黴菌感染

fun·house /ˈfʌnhaʊs/ *noun* (*especially NAmE*) a building at an AMUSEMENT PARK containing mirrors that produce strange images, moving floors, and other devices for scaring and amusing people 奇幻屋，歡樂屋（內設哈哈鏡、活動地板等驚險有趣的設施）

fu·nicu·lar /fjuːˈnɪkjələ(r)/ (also **fu,nicular ˈrailway**) *noun* a railway on a steep slope, used to transport passengers up and down in special cars by means of a moving cable 纜索鐵道 ➲ VISUAL VOCAB page V58

Synonyms 同義詞辨析

funny

amusing • entertaining • witty • humorous • comic • hilarious

These words all describe sb/sth that makes you laugh or smile. 以上各詞均用以形容人或事好笑的、滑稽的。

funny that makes you laugh 指好笑的、滑稽的： *a funny story* 滑稽的故事 ◇ *He was a very funny guy.* 他這個人很滑稽。

amusing funny and enjoyable 指逗人笑的、有樂趣的、好笑的： *It's a very amusing game to play.* 這種遊戲玩起來非常有趣。

entertaining amusing and interesting 指有趣的、令人開心的、使人愉快的： *It was a very entertaining evening.* 那是一場非常令人開心的晚會。

witty clever and amusing; able to say or write clever and amusing things 指機智的、巧妙的、妙趣橫生的、言辭詼諧的： *a witty remark* 機智的話 ◇ *a witty public speaker* 語言幽默的公開演講人

humorous funny and entertaining; showing a sense of humour 指滑稽有趣的、有幽默感的： *a humorous look at the world of fashion* 對時裝界幽默的審視

comic that makes you laugh 指滑稽的、使人發笑的： *Many of the scenes in the book are richly comic.* 這本書裏的許多情節都非常滑稽可笑。

hilarious extremely funny 指極其滑稽的

FUNNY, AMUSING, HUMOROUS OR COMIC? 用 funny、amusing、humorous 還是 comic？

Amusing is the most general of these words because it includes the idea of being enjoyable as well as making people laugh and can be used to describe events, activities and occasions. * amusing 在這組詞中最通用，既表示逗人笑，也表示好笑、有樂趣，可用以形容事情、活動和場合： *an amusing party/game/evening* 充滿樂趣的聯歡會／遊戲／晚會 ◇ ~~*a funny/humorous/comic party/game/evening*~~ **Humorous** is more about showing that you see the humour in a situation, than actually making people laugh out loud. **Comic** is used especially to talk about writing and drama or things that are funny in a deliberate and theatrical way. It is not used to describe people (except for *comic writers*). **Funny** can describe people, jokes and stories, things that happen, or anything that makes people laugh. * humorous 更多表示明白情景中的有趣之處，而非實際使人大笑。comic 尤指作品、戲劇、事物等故意營造的戲劇性的滑稽可笑，但不用以描述人（comic writers 除外）。funny 可形容人、笑話、故事、發生的事情以及任何使人發笑的事物。

PATTERNS

- a(n) funny/amusing/entertaining/witty/humorous/comic **story**
- a(n) funny/amusing/entertaining/witty/humorous **speech**
- a(n) funny/entertaining/witty/humorous/comic **writer**
- a(n) funny/amusing/hilarious **joke**
- to **find sth** funny/amusing/entertaining/witty/humorous/hilarious

funk /fʌŋk/ *noun, verb*

■ ***noun*** **1** [U] a type of dance music with a strong rhythm, developed by African American musicians in the 1960s（20 世紀 60 年代美國黑人音樂家創造的節奏感很強的）放克音樂 **2** (also **,blue ˈfunk**) [sing.] (*old-fashioned, informal*) a state of fear or anxiety 恐懼；憂慮 **3** [C, usually sing.] (*NAmE*) a strong unpleasant smell 濃烈臭味；惡臭

■ ***verb* ~ sth** (*BrE, informal*) to avoid doing sth because you are afraid to or find it difficult（因畏懼而）逃避，迴避

funky /ˈfʌŋki/ *adj.* (**funk·ier**, **funki·est**) (*informal*) **1** (of pop music 流行音樂) with a strong rhythm that is easy to dance to 節奏強適宜跳舞的： *a funky disco beat* 適宜跳舞的迪斯科強節奏 **2** (*approving*) fashionable and unusual 時髦獨特的： *She wears really funky clothes.* 她穿的衣服真是時髦又獨特。 **3** (*NAmE*) having a strong unpleasant smell 惡臭的

ˈfun-loving *adj.* (of people 人) liking to enjoy themselves 喜歡玩樂的

fun·nel /ˈfʌnl/ *noun, verb*

■ ***noun*** **1** a device that is wide at the top and narrow at the bottom, used for pouring liquids or powders into a small opening 漏斗 ➲ VISUAL VOCAB page V70 **2** (*BrE*) (also **smoke·stack** *NAmE, BrE*) a metal CHIMNEY, for example on a ship or an engine, through which smoke comes out（蒸汽機車或輪船上的）煙囱

■ ***verb*** (**-ll-**, *especially US* **-l-**) [I, T] to move or make sth move through a narrow space, or as if through a funnel（使）流經狹窄空間，經過漏斗形口子： **(+ adv./prep.)** *Wind was funnelling through the gorge.* 風吹過峽谷。 ◇ **~ sth (+ adv./prep.)** *Huge pipes funnel the water down the mountainside.* 巨大的管道把水沿山坡輸送下山。 ◇ *Barricades funnelled the crowds towards the square.* 設置的路障控制了人流湧向廣場的方向。 ◇ (*figurative*) *Some $10 million in aid was funnelled into the country through government agencies.* 約 1 000 萬元援助款已通過政府各部門發放到農村。

the fun·nies /ˈfʌniz/ *noun* [pl.] (*NAmE, informal*) the part of a newspaper where there are several COMIC STRIPS (= series of drawings that tell a funny story)（報章的）滑稽連環漫畫

fun·nily /ˈfʌnəli/ *adv.* in a strange way 奇怪地
IDM **funnily eˈnough** used to show that you expect people to find a particular fact surprising 真奇怪；說來也巧： *Funnily enough, I met her only yesterday.* 說來也巧，昨天我才碰見了她。

funny 🔑 /ˈfʌni/ *adj.* (**fun·nier**, **fun·ni·est**)

▸ **AMUSING** 好笑 **1** 🔑 making you laugh; amusing 滑稽的；好笑的： *a funny story* 滑稽的故事 ◇ *That's the funniest thing I've ever heard.* 那是我聽過的最滑稽可笑的事。 ◇ *It's not funny! Someone could have been hurt.* 這沒什麼好玩的！可能有人會受到傷害。 ◇ *I was really embarrassed, but then I **saw the funny side of it**.* 我確實感到尷尬，但接着我發現了事情好笑的一面。 ◇ (*ironic*) *Oh **very funny**! You expect me to believe that?* 哦，真滑稽！你認為我相信那個嗎？ ◇ ***'What's so funny?'** she demanded.* "什麼事這麼好笑？" 她問道。 HELP Note that **funny** does not mean 'enjoyable'. 注意 funny 不表示 enjoyable 的意思： *The party was great fun.* ◇ ~~*The party was very funny.*~~

▸ **STRANGE** 奇怪 **2** 🔑 difficult to explain or understand 奇怪的；難以解釋的；難理解的 SYN **strange, peculiar**： *A funny thing happened to me today.* 今天我碰上了一件奇怪的事。 ◇ ***It's funny how** things never happen the way you expect them to.* 真是不懂，事情總是出人意表的。 ◇ ***That's funny**—he was here a moment ago and now he's gone.* 真怪，他剛才還在這兒，現在就沒影了。 ◇ ***The funny thing is** it never happened again after that.* 奇怪的是從那以後這事再也沒有發生過。 ◇ *The engine's making a very funny noise.* 發動機發出一種很怪的聲音。 ◇ *I'm pleased I didn't get that job, in a funny sort of way.* 我沒有得到那份工作，但我有一種說不清楚的高興。

▸ **SUSPICIOUS/ILLEGAL** 可疑；非法 **3** (*informal*) suspicious and probably illegal or dishonest 可疑的；非法的；不誠實的： *I suspect there may be something funny going* on. 我懷疑可能有某種非法勾當在進行中。◇ *If there has been any **funny business**, we'll soon find out.* 如果有任何非法的事，我們會很快發現的。

▸ WITHOUT RESPECT 不尊重 **4** (*BrE*) humorous in a way that shows a lack of respect for sb 嬉皮笑臉的；放肆的 SYN **cheeky**：*Don't you **get funny** with me!* 你不要對我放肆！

▸ ILL/SICK 有病；不適 **5** (*informal*) slightly ill/sick 小病的；微恙的；稍有不適的：*I feel a bit funny today—I don't think I'll go to work.* 我今天感到有點不舒服，應該不去上班了。

▸ CRAZY 瘋癲 **6** (*BrE, informal*) slightly crazy; not like other people 瘋瘋癲癲的；不很正常的 SYN **strange, peculiar**：*That Dave's a funny chap, isn't he?* 那個戴夫瘋瘋癲癲的，是不是？◇ *She went a bit funny after her husband died.* 丈夫死後她神志就有點不大正常了。

▸ MACHINE 機器 **7** (*informal*) not working as it should 出故障的：*My computer keeps **going funny**.* 我的計算機老出故障。

F

IDM ,**funny ha-'ha** (*informal*) used to show that 'funny' is being used with the meaning of 'amusing' 滑稽可笑 ,**funny pe'culiar** (*BrE*) (*US* ,**funny 'weird/'strange**) (*informal*) used to show that 'funny' is being used with the meaning of 'strange' 稀奇古怪

'funny bone *noun* [usually sing.] (*informal*) the part of the elbow containing a very sensitive nerve that is painful if you hit it against sth 麻筋兒，麻嘴突，肘的尺骨端（肘端神經敏感部位）

'funny farm *noun* (*informal, offensive*) a hospital for people who are mentally ill 精神病院

,**funny 'money** *noun* [U] (*informal, disapproving*) **1** a CURRENCY (= the money used in one country) which is not worth much and whose value can change quickly 幣值低（或不穩定）的貨幣 **2** money that has been FORGED (= is not real) or stolen or that has come from illegal activities 假幣；來路不明的錢；黑錢

'fun run *noun* (*especially BrE*) an event in which people run a long distance, for fun, and to collect money for charity 募捐公益長跑

fur 0┳ /fɜː(r)/ *noun*

1 0┳ [U] the soft thick mass of hair that grows on the body of some animals（動物濃厚的）軟毛 **2** 0┳ [U] the skin of an animal with the fur still on it, used especially for making clothes（動物的）毛皮：*a fur coat* 毛皮大衣 ◇ *the fur trade* 毛皮貿易 ◇ *a fur farm* (= where animals are bred and killed for their fur) 毛皮動物飼養場 ◇ *The animal is hunted for its fur.* 狩獵這種動物是為了獲取其毛皮。◇ *fur-lined gloves* 毛皮襯裏手套 **3** 0┳ [U] an artificial material that looks and feels like fur 人造毛皮 **4** 0┳ [C] a piece of clothing, especially a coat or jacket, made of real or artificial fur 毛皮衣服，裘皮衣服（尤指大衣或短上衣）：*elegant ladies in furs* 穿着裘皮衣服的高雅貴婦 **5** (*BrE*) = SCALE *n.* (9) **6** [U] a greyish-white layer that forms on a person's tongue, especially when they are ill/sick 舌苔 ➲ see also FURRED

furi·ous /ˈfjʊəriəs; *NAmE* ˈfjʊr-/ *adj.* **1** very angry 狂怒的；暴怒的：**~ (at sth/sb)** *She was absolutely furious at having been deceived.* 她受了騙，怒不可遏。◇ **~ (with sb/yourself)** *He was furious with himself for letting things get so out of control.* 他對自己很惱火，怪自己竟讓事情變得如此不可收拾。◇ **~ (that ...)** *I'm furious that I wasn't told about it.* 這事沒有跟我說，我十分氣憤。**2** with great energy, speed or anger 激烈的；猛烈的；高速的；盛怒的：*a furious debate* 激烈的辯論 ◇ *She drove off at a furious pace.* 她駕車飛馳而去。➲ see also FURY ▸ **furi·ous·ly** *adv.*：*furiously angry* 大發雷霆 ◇ *'Damn!' he said furiously.* "該死的！"他十分憤怒地說。◇ *They worked furiously all weekend, trying to get it finished on time.* 整個週末他們拚命工作，以求按時完成這項任務。IDM see FAST *adj.*

furl /fɜːl; *NAmE* fɜːrl/ *verb* **~ sth** to roll and fasten sth such as a sail, a flag or an umbrella 捲起，收攏（帆、旗或傘）

fur·long /ˈfɜːlɒŋ; *NAmE* ˈfɜːrlɔːŋ; ˈfɜːrlɑːŋ/ *noun* (especially in horse racing 尤指賽馬) a unit for measuring distance, equal to 220 yards or 201 metres; one eighth of a mile 弗隆，浪（長度單位，相當於 220 碼、201 米或 ⅛ 英里）

fur·lough /ˈfɜːləʊ; *NAmE* ˈfɜːrloʊ/ *noun* [U, C] **1** permission to leave your duties for a period of time, especially for soldiers working in a foreign country（尤指在國外服役士兵的）休假（許可）**2** (*NAmE*) permission for a prisoner to leave prison for a period of time（犯人的）准假 **3** (*NAmE*) a period of time during which workers are told not to come to work, usually because there is not enough money to pay them（通常因發不出工資而給的）准假 ▸ **fur·lough** *verb* **~ sb**

fur·nace /ˈfɜːnɪs; *NAmE* ˈfɜːrnɪs/ *noun* **1** a space surrounded on all sides by walls and a roof for heating metal or glass to very high temperatures 熔爐：*It's like **a furnace*** (= very hot) *in here!* 這裏熱得像火爐！➲ see also BLAST FURNACE **2** (*especially NAmE*) = BOILER

fur·nish /ˈfɜːnɪʃ; *NAmE* ˈfɜːrnɪʃ/ *verb* **1 ~ sth** to put furniture in a house, room, etc. 佈置傢具：*The room was furnished with antiques.* 房間裏擺放了古董。➲ COLLOCATIONS at DECORATE **2 ~ sb/sth with sth | ~ sth** (*formal*) to supply or provide sb/sth with sth; to supply sth to sb 向（某人或某事物）供應，提供：*She furnished him with the facts surrounding the case.* 她向他提供了與案件有關的真實情況。

fur·nished /ˈfɜːnɪʃt; *NAmE* ˈfɜːrnɪʃt/ *adj.* (of a house, room, etc. 房屋、房間等) containing furniture 配備傢具的：*furnished accommodation* (= to rent complete with furniture) 連傢具出租房 ◇ *The house was simply furnished.* 這房子陳設簡單。

fur·nish·ings /ˈfɜːnɪʃɪŋz; *NAmE* ˈfɜːrn-/ *noun* [pl.] the furniture, carpets, curtains, etc. in a room or house 傢具陳設：*soft furnishings* 織物製成的室內陳設 ◇ *The wallpaper should match the furnishings.* 牆紙應和傢具陳設諧調。

fur·ni·ture 0┳ /ˈfɜːnɪtʃə(r); *NAmE* ˈfɜːrn-/ *noun* [U] objects that can be moved, such as tables, chairs and beds, that are put into a house or an office to make it suitable for living or working in（可移動的）傢具：*a **piece of furniture*** 一件傢具 ◇ ***garden/office, etc. furniture*** 花園、辦公室等處的傢具 ◇ *We need to buy some new furniture.* 我們需要買一些新傢具。➲ see also DOOR FURNITURE, STREET FURNITURE IDM see PART *n.*

'furniture van *noun* (*BrE*) = REMOVAL VAN

fur·ore /fjuˈrɔːri; ˈfjʊərɔː(r); *NAmE* ˈfjʊr-/ (also **furor** /ˈfjʊərɔː(r); *NAmE* ˈfjʊr-/ especially in *NAmE*) *noun* [sing.] great anger or excitement shown by a number of people, usually caused by a public event 群情激憤；騷動；轟動：**~ (among sb)** *His novel about Jesus caused a furore among Christians.* 他關於耶穌的小說激起了基督教徒的公憤。◇ **~ (about/over sth)** *the recent furore over the tax increases* 近來因增稅引起的騷動 SYN **uproar**

furphy /ˈfɜːfi; *NAmE* ˈfɜːrfi/ *noun* (*pl.* **-ies**) (*AustralE*) a piece of information or a story, that people talk about but that may not be true 傳聞；傳言 SYN **rumour**

fur·red /fɜːd; *NAmE* fɜːrd/ *adj.* covered with fur or with sth that looks like fur 覆蓋毛皮的；穿戴毛皮衣物的；長舌苔的：*a furred tongue* 長苔的舌頭

fur·rier /ˈfʌriə(r)/ *noun* a person who prepares or sells clothes made from fur 毛皮加工者；皮貨商

fur·row /ˈfʌrəʊ; *NAmE* ˈfɜːroʊ/ *noun, verb*

■ ***noun*** **1** a long narrow cut in the ground, especially one made by a PLOUGH for planting seeds in 犁溝；溝；車轍 ➲ VISUAL VOCAB pages V2, V3 **2** a deep line in the skin of the face（臉上的）皺紋 IDM see PLOUGH *v.*

■ ***verb*** **1** [T] **~ sth** to make a furrow in the earth 犁：*furrowed fields* 犁過的田地 **2** [I, T] **~ (sth)** (*formal*) if your BROWS OR EYEBROWS **furrow** or **are furrowed**, you pull them together, usually because you are worried, and so produce lines on your face（使）皺（眉），蹙（額）

furry /ˈfɜːri/ *adj.* (**fur·rier**, **fur·ri·est**) **1** covered with fur 覆蓋毛皮的；穿戴毛皮衣物的：*small furry animals* 毛茸茸的小動物 **2** like fur 毛皮似的；毛一般的：*The moss was soft and furry to the touch.* 苔蘚柔軟，摸起來像絨毛。

fur·ther /ˈfɜːðə(r); *NAmE* ˈfɜːrð-/ *adv., adj., verb*

■ ***adv.*** **1** (comparative of *far* * far 的比較級) (*especially BrE*) at or to a greater distance (空間距離)較遠，更遠 **SYN** **farther**：*We had walked further than I had realized.* 在我不知不覺中我們已走得很遠。◇ *Two miles further on we came to a small town.* 我們又走了兩英里，來到了一座小鎮。◇ *The hospital is further down the road.* 沿這條路走下去就是醫院。◇ *Can you stand a bit further away?* 你能不能站遠一點？ **2** a longer way in the past or the future (過去或未來)較遠，更久遠：*Think further back into your childhood.* 再往前回想你的童年。◇ *How will the company be doing ten years further on?* 十年以後公司的情況將如何呢？ **3** to a greater degree or extent 進一步；在更大程度上；在更大範圍內：*The police decided to investigate further.* 警方決定作進一步調查。◇ *My life is further complicated by having to work such long hours.* 我得工作這麼長的時間，因此生活中的麻煩事就更多了。◇ *Nothing could be* ***further from the truth.*** 絕不是那回事。 **4** (*formal*) in addition to what has just been said 此外；而且 **SYN** **furthermore**：*Further, it is important to consider the cost of repairs.* 此外，重要的是要考慮修理費用。➲ note at FARTHER

IDM **go ˈfurther 1** to say more about sth, or make a more extreme point about it 進一步說；提出更極端的意見：*I would go even further and suggest that the entire government is corrupt.* 我甚至進而想要說，整個政府都是腐敗的。**2** to last longer; to serve more people 更經久；為更多人服務：*They watered down the soup to make it go further.* 他們在湯裏摻水，好讓更多的人喝。 **go no ˈfurther | not go any ˈfurther** if you tell sb that a secret will **go no further**, you promise not to tell it to anyone else 到此為止；不再傳下去 **take sth ˈfurther** to take more serious action about sth or speak to sb at a higher level about it 採取進一步行動；把…向上級反映：*I am not satisfied with your explanation and intend to take the matter further.* 我對你的解釋不滿意，打算進一步探討這個問題。➲ more at AFIELD

■ ***adj.*** (comparative of *far* * far 的比較級) more; additional 更多的；更進一步的；附加的：*Cook for a further 2 minutes.* 再煮兩分鐘。◇ *Have you any further questions?* 你還有問題嗎？◇ *For further details call this number.* 欲知詳情，請撥打這個電話號碼。◇ *We have decided to take no further action.* 我們決定不採取進一步行動。◇ *The museum is closed* ***until further notice*** (= until we say that it is open again). 博物館現在閉館，開館時間另行通知。➲ LANGUAGE BANK at ADDITION

■ ***verb*** **~ sth** to help sth to develop or be successful 促進；增進：*They hoped the new venture would further the cause of cultural cooperation in Europe.* 他們希望這個新項目將促進歐洲文化合作事業。◇ *She took the new job to further her career.* 她接受了這項新工作以進一步發展她的事業。

fur·ther·ance /ˈfɜːðərəns; *NAmE* ˈfɜːrð-/ *noun* [U] (*formal*) the process of helping sth to develop or to be successful 促進；增進 **SYN** **advancement**：*He took these actions purely* ***in (the) furtherance of*** *his own career.* 他採取這些行動純粹是為了促進自己的事業發展。

ˌfurther eduˈcation *noun* [U] (*abbr.* **FE**) (*BrE*) education that is provided for people after leaving school, but not at a university 繼續教育，進修教育(為中學畢業後的人舉辦，但非大學) ➲ compare HIGHER EDUCATION

fur·ther·more **AW** /ˌfɜːðəˈmɔː(r); *NAmE* ˌfɜːrðərˈmɔːr/ *adv.* (*formal*) in addition to what has just been stated. Furthermore is used especially to add a point to an argument. 此外；而且；再者 **SYN** **moreover**：*He said he had not discussed the matter with her. Furthermore, he had not even contacted her.* 他說他沒有和她討論過這個問題。而且，甚至沒有和她聯繫過。➲ LANGUAGE BANK at ADDITION

fur·ther·most /ˈfɜːðəməʊst; *NAmE* ˈfɜːrðərmoʊst/ *adj.* (*formal*) located at the greatest distance from sth 最遠的：*at the furthermost end of the street* 在街尾

ˈfurther to *prep.* (*formal*) used in letters, emails, etc. to refer to a previous letter, email, conversation, etc. (用於書信、電郵等)關於，至於，考慮到：*Further to our conversation of last Friday, I would like to book the conference centre for 26 June.* 按我們上星期五說過的，我想預約 6 月 26 日使用會議中心。

fur·thest /ˈfɜːðɪst; *NAmE* ˈfɜːrð-/ *adj., adv.* = FARTHEST

fur·tive /ˈfɜːtɪv; *NAmE* ˈfɜːrtɪv/ *adj.* (*disapproving*) behaving in a way that shows that you want to keep sth secret and do not want to be noticed 偷偷摸摸的；鬼鬼祟祟的；遮遮掩掩的 **SYN** **stealthy**：*She cast a* ***furtive glance*** *over her shoulder.* 她偷偷往背後瞥了一下。◇ *He looked sly and furtive.* 他顯得偷偷摸摸，鬼鬼祟祟。▸ **fur·tive·ly** *adv.* **fur·tive·ness** *noun* [U]

fury /ˈfjʊəri; *NAmE* ˈfjʊri/ *noun* **1** [U] extreme anger that often includes violent behaviour 狂怒；暴怒；狂暴；大發雷霆 **SYN** **rage**：*Her eyes blazed with fury.* 她的雙眼迸發出暴怒之火。◇ *Fury over tax increases* (= as a newspaper HEADLINE). 對增稅極端憤怒(作報紙標題)。◇ (*figurative*) *There was no shelter from the fury of the storm.* 那時沒有地方可以躲避狂風暴雨。 **2** [sing.] a state of being extremely angry about sth 狂怒；暴怒 **SYN** **rage**：*He flew into a fury when I refused.* 我拒絕他就勃然大怒。 **3 the Furies** [pl.] (in ancient Greek stories) three GODDESSES who punish people for their crimes (古希臘神話)復仇三女神 ➲ see also FURIOUS

IDM **like fury** (*informal*) with great effort, power, speed, etc. 拚命；猛烈；迅猛 ➲ more at HELL

furze /fɜːz; *NAmE* fɜːrz/ *noun* [U] (*BrE*) = GORSE

fuse /fjuːz/ *noun, verb*

■ ***noun*** **1** a small wire or device inside a piece of electrical equipment that breaks and stops the current if the flow of electricity is too strong 保險絲；熔絲：*to change a fuse* 換保險絲 ◇ *Check whether a fuse has blown.* 檢查一下保險絲是否燒斷了。 **2** a long piece of string or paper which is lit to make a bomb or a FIREWORK explode 導火線；導火索 **3** (*NAmE* also **fuze**) a device that makes a bomb explode when it hits sth or at a particular time 引信；信管；雷管：*He set the fuse to three minutes.* 他把引信設定為三分鐘起爆。◇ *The bombs inside were on a one-hour fuse.* 炸彈內裝有一小時起爆的引信。 **IDM** see BLOW *v.*, SHORT *adj.*

■ ***verb*** **1** [I, T] (*formal* or *technical* 術語) when one thing **fuses** with another, or two things **fuse** or **are fused**, they are joined together to form a single thing (使)融合，熔接，結合：**~ (together)** *As they heal, the bones will fuse together.* 骨頭癒合時將會連接在一起。◇ **~ (into sth)** *Our different ideas fused into a plan.* 我們不同的想法融合成一項計劃。◇ **~ with sth** *The sperm fuses with the egg to begin the process of fertilization.* 精子與卵子結合開始受精過程。◇ **~ sth (into sth)** *The two companies have been fused into a single organization.* 兩家公司合併成一個機構。◇ *Atoms of hydrogen are fused to make helium.* 氫原子可熔合成氦。 **2** [I, T] **~ (sth)** (*technical* 術語) when a substance, especially metal, **fuses**, or you **fuse** it, it is heated until it melts (使)熔化 **3** [I, T] **~ (sth)** (*BrE*) to stop working or to make sth stop working because a fuse melts (使保險絲熔斷而)停止工作：*The lights have fused.* 保險絲燒斷，燈都滅了。◇ *I've fused the lights.* 我把照明保險絲燒斷了。 **4** [T, usually passive] **~ sth** to put a fuse in a CIRCUIT or in a piece of equipment 在(電路或電器)中安裝保險絲：*Is this plug fused?* 這個插頭有沒有安裝保險絲？

ˈfuse box *noun* a small box or cupboard that contains the fuses of the electrical system of a building 保險絲盒；熔絲盒

fu·sel·age /ˈfjuːzəlɑːʒ; *NAmE* ˈfjuːs-/ *noun* the main part of an aircraft in which passengers and goods are carried (飛機的)機身 ➲ VISUAL VOCAB page V53

ˈfuse wire *noun* [U] thin wire used in an electrical FUSE 熔絲；保險絲

fu·si·lier /ˌfjuːzəˈlɪə(r)/ *noun* (in the past) a soldier who carried a light gun (舊時的)燧發槍士兵，明火槍士兵

fu·sil·lade /ˌfjuːzəˈleɪd; *NAmE* -sə-/ *noun* a rapid series of shots fired from one or more guns; a rapid series of objects that are thrown (槍炮的)連發，連續齊射；(某物的)連續投擲 **SYN** **barrage**：*a* ***fusillade of bullets/stones*** 槍林彈雨；雨點般投擲的石頭 ◇ (*figurative*) *He faced a fusillade of questions from the waiting journalists.* 正在等候的記者們向他發出連珠炮似的提問。

F

F

fu·sion /ˈfjuːʒn/ *noun* **1** [U, sing.] the process or result of joining two or more things together to form one 融合；熔接；結合：*the fusion of copper and zinc to produce brass* 銅與鋅熔合成黃銅 ◇ *The movie displayed a perfect fusion of image and sound.* 這部電影展示了影像與音響的完美結合。 **2** (also ˌ**nuclear** ˈ**fusion**) [U] (*physics* 物) the act or process of combining the NUCLEI (= central parts) of atoms to form a heavier NUCLEUS, with energy being released 核聚變；熱核反應 ➲ compare FISSION (1) **3** [U] music that is a mixture of different styles, especially JAZZ and ROCK 合成音樂，混合音樂（尤指爵士樂和搖滾樂） **4** [U] cooking that is a mixture of different styles（各種方式的）混合烹調：*French–Thai fusion* 法泰式混合烹飪

ˈ**fusion bomb** *noun* a bomb that gets its energy from nuclear FUSION, especially a HYDROGEN BOMB 聚變彈；熱核彈；（尤指）氫彈

fu·sion·ist /ˈfjuːʒənɪst/ *noun* a musician who plays FUSION music 合成音樂演奏者

fuss /fʌs/ *noun, verb*

■ ***noun*** **1** [U, sing.] unnecessary excitement, worry or activity 無謂的激動（或憂慮、活動）；大驚小怪：*He does what he's told without any fuss.* 他不聲不響地按照吩咐辦事。◇ *All that fuss over a few pounds!* 為幾英鎊就那麼大驚小怪的！◇ *It's a very ordinary movie—I don't know* ***what all the fuss is about*** (= why other people think it is so good). 這是部很普通的電影，我不懂為什麼就轟動一時。◇ *It was all* ***a fuss about nothing.*** 這完全是無謂地自尋煩惱。◇ *We'd like a quiet wedding without any fuss.* 我們喜歡靜靜舉行婚禮，不大事鋪張。 **2** [sing.] anger or complaints about sth, especially sth that is not important（為小事）大吵大鬧，大發牢騷：*I'm sorry for* ***making such a fuss*** *about the noise.* 對不起，我為吵鬧聲發了這麼大的牢騷。◇ *Steve* ***kicks up a fuss*** *every time I even suggest seeing you.* 每次只要我提議看望你，史蒂夫就大吵大鬧。

IDM **make a fuss of/over sb** to pay a lot of attention to sb, usually to show how much you like them 關愛備至；過分愛護：*They made a great fuss of the baby.* 他們對嬰兒呵護備至。◇ *The dog loves being made a fuss of.* 這狗喜歡受到寵愛。

■ ***verb*** **1** [I] to do things, or pay too much attention to things, that are not important or necessary 瞎忙一氣；過分關心（枝節小事）：**~ (around)** *Stop fussing around and find something useful to do!* 別瞎忙活了，找點有用的事幹！◇ **~ (with/over sth)** *Don't fuss with your hair!* 不要老在擺弄你的頭髮了！ **2** [I] **~ (about sth)** to worry about things that are not very important（為小事）煩惱，憂慮：*Don't fuss, Mum, everything is all right.* 別瞎操心了，媽媽，一切都好。

IDM **not be fussed (about sb/sth)** (*BrE, informal*) to not mind about sth; to not have feelings about sth 不在意；無所謂；不關心 **SYN** **not be bothered**：*It'd be good to be there, but I'm not that fussed.* 去那裏當然好，不過我無所謂。

PHR V ˈ**fuss over sb** to pay a lot of attention to sb 對…關愛備至；過分關心

fuss·pot /ˈfʌspɒt; *NAmE* -pɑːt/ (*BrE*) (*NAmE* **fuss·budget** /ˈfʌsbʌdʒɪt/) *noun* (*informal*) a person who is often worried about unimportant things and is difficult to please 大驚小怪的人；好挑剔的人；愛吹毛求疵的人

fussy /ˈfʌsi/ *adj.* (**fuss·ier, fussi·est**) **1** too concerned or worried about details or standards, especially unimportant ones 無謂憂慮（或擔心）的；大驚小怪的；挑剔的：*fussy parents* 瞎操心的父母 ◇ **~ (about sth)** *Our teacher is very fussy about punctuation.* 我們老師對標點符號十分挑剔。◇ *She's such a fussy eater.* 她太挑食。◇ *'Where do you want to go for lunch?' 'I'm not fussy* (= I don't mind).' "你想去哪兒吃午餐？" "我無所謂。" **2** doing sth with small, quick, nervous movements 緊張不安的：*a fussy manner* 局促不安的舉止 ◇ *the quick, fussy movements of her small hands* 她的一雙小手快捷而緊張不安的動作 **3** having too much detail or decoration 過分瑣碎的；裝飾太多的：*The costume designs are too fussy.* 這些服裝設計過於花哨。 ▸ **fuss·ily** *adv.* **fussi·ness** *noun* [U]

fus·tian /ˈfʌstiən; *NAmE* -tʃən/ *noun* [U] **1** a thick strong cotton cloth with a slightly rough surface, used in the past for making clothes 緯起絨布（舊時用作衣料） **2** (*literary*) language that sounds impressive but does not mean much 浮誇的言語

fusty /ˈfʌsti/ *adj.* (*disapproving*) **1** smelling old, damp or not fresh 腐臭的；霉濕味的 **SYN** **musty**：*a dark fusty room* 陰暗霉濕的房間 **2** old-fashioned 過時的；守舊的：*fusty ideas* 守舊的思想 ◇ *a fusty old professor* 古板的老教授

fu·tile /ˈfjuːtaɪl; *NAmE* -tl/ *adj.* having no purpose because there is no chance of success 徒然的；徒勞的；無效的 **SYN** **pointless**：*a* ***futile attempt/exercise/gesture*** 徒然的嘗試／練習／姿態 ◇ *Their efforts to revive him were futile.* 他們努力使他蘇醒，但失敗了。◇ ***It would be futile to*** *protest.* 抗議也無用。◇ *My appeal proved futile.* 我的申訴白費了。 ▸ **fu·tile·ly** *adv.* **fu·til·ity** /fjuːˈtɪləti/ *noun* [U]：*a sense of futility* 徒勞感 ◇ *the futility of war* 戰爭的徒然無益

fu·ton /ˈfuːtɒn; *NAmE* -tɑːn/ *noun* a Japanese MATTRESS, often on a wooden frame, that can be used for sitting on or rolled out to make a bed 日本牀墊（摺疊時可坐，鋪開時可臥） ➲ VISUAL VOCAB page V23

fu·ture 🔑 /ˈfjuːtʃə(r)/ *noun, adj.*

■ ***noun*** **1** 🔑 **the future** [sing.] the time that will come after the present or the events that will happen then 將來；未來：*We need to plan for the future.* 我們需要為將來作好打算。◇ *What will the cities of the future look like?* 未來的城市會是什麼樣子呢？◇ *The movie is set in the future.* 這部電影以未來為背景。◇ *The exchange rate is likely to fall* ***in the near future*** (= soon). 匯率可能不久就要下跌。◇ *What does the future hold?* 未來將會如何？ **2** 🔑 [C] what will happen to sb/sth at a later time 未來的事；將來發生的事；前景：*Her future is uncertain.* 她前途未卜。◇ *This deal could safeguard the futures of the 2 000 employees.* 這個協議可以保障 2 000 名雇員今後的生活。 **3** 🔑 [sing., U] the possibility of being successful or surviving at a later time 前途；前程：*She has* ***a great future*** *ahead of her.* 她前程遠大。◇ *I can't see any future in this relationship.* 我看不出這個關係會有什麼前途。 **4** **futures** [pl.] (*finance* 財) goods or shares that are bought at agreed prices but that will be delivered and paid for at a later time 期貨：*oil futures* 石油期貨 ◇ *the futures market* 期貨市場 **5** **the future** [sing.] (*grammar* 語法) (also **the** ˌ**future** ˈ**tense**) the form of a verb that expresses what will happen after the present（動詞的）將來時，將來式，未來式

IDM **in future** 🔑 (*BrE*) (*NAmE* **in the future**) from now on 今後；從今以後：*Please be more careful in future.* 今後請多加小心。◇ *In future, make sure the door is never left unlocked.* 從今以後，千萬別忘記鎖好門戶。 ➲ more at DISTANT, FORESEEABLE

■ ***adj.*** 🔑 [only before noun] taking place or existing at a time after the present 將來的；未來的；將來發生的：*future generations* 子孫後代 ◇ *at a future date* 將來某個時候 ◇ *future developments in computer software* 計算機軟件的未來發展 ◇ *He met his future wife at law school.* 他在法學院結識了他未來的妻子。

the ˌ**future** ˈ**perfect** (also **the** ˌ**future** ˌ**perfect** ˈ**tense**) *noun* [sing.] (*grammar* 語法) the form of a verb that expresses an action completed before a particular point in the future, formed in English with *will have* or *shall have* and the past participle 將來完成時；未來完成式

ˈ**future-proof** *adj., verb*

■ ***adj.*** (*business* 商 or *technical* 術語) designed to continue working or to be effective after changes that may happen in the future 不會過時的：*future-proof website design* 常青而實用的網站設計

■ ***verb*** **~ sth** to make sth future-proof 使不過時：*The firm claims that it future-proofs its software.* 這家公司聲稱其軟件不會被時間淘汰。

fu·tur·ism /ˈfjuːtʃərɪzəm/ *noun* [U] a movement in art and literature in the 1920s and 30s that did not try to show realistic figures and scenes but aimed to express confidence in the modern world, particularly in modern machines 未來主義（20 世紀 20 和 30 年代的文藝運動，強調對技術時代的讚歎）▸ **fu·tur·ist** *noun* **fu·tur·ist** *adj.*：*futurist poets* 未來主義詩人

fu·tur·is·tic /ˌfjuːtʃəˈrɪstɪk/ *adj.* **1** extremely modern and unusual in appearance, as if belonging to a future time 極其現代的；未來派的：*futuristic design* 極其新潮的設計 **2** imagining what the future will be like 幻想未來的；想像未來情況的：*a futuristic novel* 幻想未來的小說

fu·tur·ity /fjuˈtjʊərəti; *NAmE* -ˈtʊr-/ *noun* [U] (*formal*) the time that will come after the present and what will happen then 將來；未來：*a vision of futurity* 夢幻中的未來

fu·tur·olo·gist /ˌfjuːtʃəˈrɒlədʒɪst; *NAmE* -ˈrɑːl-/ *noun* a person who is an expert in futurology 未來學家

fu·tur·ology /ˌfjuːtʃəˈrɒlədʒi; *NAmE* -ˈrɑːl-/ *noun* [U] the study of how people will live in the future 未來學

fuze (*NAmE*) = FUSE *n.* (3)

fuzz /fʌz/ *noun* **1** [U] short soft fine hair or fur that covers sth, especially a person's face or arms 茸毛，絨毛（尤指人臉或手臂的）SYN **down** **2** [sing.] a mass of hair in tight curls 鬈髮：*a fuzz of blonde hair* 一團金色鬈髮 **3 the fuzz** [sing.+sing./pl. v.] (*old-fashioned, slang*) the police 警方 **4** something that you cannot see clearly 模糊的東西 SYN **blur**：*I saw it as a dim fuzz through the binoculars.* 我從雙筒望遠鏡看只見一團模模糊糊的東西。

fuzz·box /ˈfʌzbɒks; *NAmE* -bɑːks/ *noun* a device that is used to change the sound of an electric GUITAR or other instrument by making the notes sound noisier and less clear（電吉他等的）模糊音裝置

fuzzy /ˈfʌzi/ *adj.* (**fuzz·ier**, **fuzzi·est**) **1** covered with short soft fine hair or fur 覆有絨毛的；毛茸茸的 SYN **downy** **2** (of hair 毛髮) in a mass of tight curls 緊鬈的；拳曲的 **3** not clear in shape or sound（形狀或聲音）模糊不清的 SYN **blurred**：*a fuzzy image* 模糊的形象 ◇ *The soundtrack is fuzzy in places.* 這電影聲帶有些地方模糊不清。**4** confused and not expressed clearly 糊塗的；含混不清的：***fuzzy ideas/thinking*** 糊塗的想法／思想 ▸ **fuzz·ily** *adv.* **fuzzi·ness** *noun* [U]

ˌfuzzy ˈlogic *noun* [U] (*computing* 計) a type of logic that is used to try to make computers behave like the human brain 模糊邏輯（嘗試使計算機模擬人腦）

FWIW *abbr.* (*informal*) used in writing to mean 'for what it's worth' 不論真偽；不論好壞

ˈF-word *noun* [sing.] (*informal*) used to replace a word beginning with F that you do not want to say, especially the offensive swear word 'fuck' * F 開頭的詞（用以替代不想說出口以 F 開頭的冒犯性髒話，尤其是粗俗的罵人話 fuck）：*He was shocked at how often she used the F-word.* 她出口髒言之頻密使他感到震驚。➲ compare C-WORD

FX /ˌef ˈeks/ *abbr.* **1** a short way of writing SPECIAL EFFECTS（電影、電視的）特技效果 **2** a short way of writing FOREIGN EXCHANGE 外匯（全寫為 foreign exchange）

-fy ➲ -IFY

FYI *abbr.* used in writing to mean 'for your information' 供參考（for your information 的書寫形式）

Gg

G /dʒiː/ *noun, abbr.*

▪ ***noun*** (also **g**) [C, U] (*pl.* **Gs, G's, g's** /dʒiːz/) **1** the 7th letter of the English alphabet 英語字母表的第 7 個字母：*'Gold' begins with (a) G/'G'.* * gold 一詞以字母 g 開頭。 **2 G** (*music* 音) the fifth note in the SCALE of C MAJOR * G 音（C 大調的第 5 音或音符）➲ see also G AND T, G-STRING

▪ ***abbr.*** **1** (*NAmE*) general audience (a label for a film/movie that is suitable for anyone, including children) * G 級，老少咸宜（影片分級用語，表示適合包括兒童在內的任何人觀看）**2** (*NAmE, informal*) $1 000 * 1 000 元

g *abbr.* **1** gram(s) 克：*400g flour* * 400 克麪粉 **2** /dʒiː/ (*technical* 術語) GRAVITY or a measurement of the force with which sth moves faster through space because of GRAVITY 重力；地球引力：*Spacecraft which are re-entering the earth's atmosphere are affected by g forces.* 重返大氣層的航天器受到重力的作用。

gab /ɡæb/ *verb, noun*

▪ ***verb*** (**-bb-**) (*informal*) [I] to talk for a long time about things that are not important 喋喋不休；囉唆；嘮叨

▪ ***noun*** IDM see GIFT *n.*

gab·ar·dine (also **gab·er·dine**) /ˌɡæbəˈdiːn; ˈɡæbədiːn; *NAmE* -bərd-/ *noun* **1** [U] a strong material used especially for making RAINCOATS 華達呢，軋別丁（結實織物，尤用於製雨衣）**2** [C] a coat, especially a RAINCOAT, made of gabardine 華達呢外衣；華達呢雨衣

gab·ble /ˈɡæbl/ *verb, noun*

▪ ***verb*** [I, T] (*informal*) to talk quickly so that people cannot hear you clearly or understand you 急促而含混不清地說：*She was nervous and started to gabble.* 她緊張得話都說不清了。◇ **~ on/away** *They were gabbling on about the past.* 他們喋喋不休地談論過去。◇ **~ sth** *He was gabbling nonsense.* 他在嘴里咕嚕說廢話。◇ **+ speech** *'No, no, not all,' she gabbled.* "不，不，不是所有。" 她急促而含糊地說。

▪ ***noun*** [sing.] fast speech that is difficult to understand, especially when a lot of people are talking at the same time（尤指許多人同時說話時）急促不清的話

gabby /ˈɡæbi/ *adj.* (*informal, disapproving*) talking a lot, especially about things that are not important 貧嘴的；饒舌的；聒噪的

gab·fest /ˈɡæbfest/ *noun* (*NAmE, informal*) an informal meeting to talk and exchange news; a long conversation 雜談會；長時間的交談

ga·bion /ˈɡeɪbiən/ *noun* a large square container made of wire in which rocks are packed. Gabions are used for building structures outdoors, for example to support pieces of ground or control a flow of water. 石籠（築堤等用的鐵絲網）

gable /ˈɡeɪbl/ *noun* the upper part of the end wall of a building, between the two sloping sides of the roof, that is shaped like a triangle 三角牆；山牆 ➲ VISUAL VOCAB page V17

gabled /ˈɡeɪbld/ *adj.* having one or more gables 有三角牆的；有山牆的：*a* ***gabled house/roof*** 有山牆的房子／屋頂

ga·boon /ɡəˈbuːn/ (also **gaˌboon maˈhogany**) *noun* [U] the hard wood of a tropical African tree, used especially for making parts of musical instruments or small pieces of decoration 加蓬桃花心木（非洲熱帶硬質木材，尤用於製作樂器部件或小飾物）

gad /ɡæd/ *verb* (**-dd-**)

PHR V **ˌgad aˈbout/aˈround** (*informal, especially BrE*) to visit different places and have fun, especially when you should be doing sth else 閒逛；遊蕩

gad·about /ˈɡædəbaʊt/ *noun* (*informal*, often *humorous*) a person who is always going out socially or travelling for pleasure 好社交者；好旅遊者

gad·fly /ˈɡædflaɪ/ *noun* (*pl.* **-ies**) (usually *disapproving*) a person who annoys or criticizes other people in order to make them do sth（為使別人做某事而對其進行騷擾或批評的）討人厭者

gadget /ˈɡædʒɪt/ *noun* a small tool or device that does sth useful 小器具；小裝置

gadget·ry /ˈɡædʒɪtri/ *noun* [U] (sometimes *disapproving*) a collection of modern tools and devices（統稱）小器具，小裝置：*His desk is covered with electronic gadgetry.* 他的書桌上擺滿了各種電子裝置。

gado·lin·ium /ˌɡædəˈlɪniəm/ *noun* [U] (*symb.* **Gd**) a chemical element. Gadolinium is a soft silver-white metal. 釓

gad·zooks /ɡædˈzuːks/ *exclamation* (*old use*) used in the past to show that sb is surprised or annoyed（舊時用語，表示驚訝或惱怒）天哪，哎呀，該死

Gael·ic *noun* [U] **1** /ˈɡælɪk; ˈɡeɪlɪk/ the Celtic language of Scotland（蘇格蘭的）蓋爾語 ➲ compare SCOTS **2** /ˈɡeɪlɪk/ (also **ˌIrish ˈGaelic**) the Celtic language of Ireland（愛爾蘭的）蓋爾語 ➲ compare ERSE, IRISH *n.* (1) ▸ **Gael·ic** *adj.*

ˌGaelic ˈfootball *noun* [U] a game played mainly in Ireland between two teams of 15 players. The players of one team try to kick or hit a round ball into or over the other team's goal. 蓋利克足球，愛爾蘭式足球（兩隊各 15 人，將球踢進球門或越過門梁得分）

the Gael·tacht /ˈɡeɪltæxt/ *noun* the parts of Ireland and Scotland where Gaelic is spoken by a large part of the population（愛爾蘭和蘇格蘭的）蓋爾語地區

gaff /ɡæf/ *noun* **1** a pole with a hook on the end used to pull large fish out of the water（將大魚拉出水的）挽鉤，手鉤 **2** (*BrE, slang*) the house, flat/apartment, etc. where sb lives 住所；安樂窩 IDM see BLOW *v.*

gaffe /ɡæf/ *noun* a mistake that a person makes in public or in a social situation, especially sth embarrassing 失禮；失態；失言 SYN **faux pas**

gaf·fer /ˈɡæfə(r)/ *noun* **1** (*BrE, informal*) a person who is in charge of a group of people, for example, workers in a factory, a sports team, etc.（工廠的）工頭，領班；（運動隊等的）領隊，負責人 SYN **boss 2** the person who is in charge of the electrical work and the lights when a film/movie or television programme is being made（拍電影或電視節目的）照明電工

ˈgaffer tape *noun* [U] (*BrE*) strong sticky tape with cloth on the back 電工膠布；厚膠布

gag /ɡæɡ/ *noun, verb*

▪ ***noun*** **1** a piece of cloth that is put over or in sb's mouth to stop them speaking（使人不能說話的）塞口物 **2** an order that prevents sth from being publicly reported or discussed 禁刊令（阻止公開報道或討論某事的法令）：*a press gag* 新聞禁刊令 ◇ *a* ***gag rule/order*** (= one given by a court of law) 禁止發言規則；限制言論令 **3** (*informal*) a joke or a funny story, especially one told by a professional COMEDIAN（尤指專業喜劇演員的）插科打諢，笑話，噱頭 SYN **joke**：*to* ***tell/crack a gag*** 講／說笑話 ◇ *a* ***running gag*** (= one that is regularly repeated during a performance) 重複出現的笑話橋段 **4** (*especially NAmE*) a trick you play on sb 惡作劇；詭計；花招：*It was just a gag—we didn't mean to upset anyone.* 這只是逗着玩，我們並未想使任何人不高興。

▪ ***verb*** (**-gg-**) **1** [T] **~ sb** to put a piece of cloth in or over sb's mouth to prevent them from speaking or shouting 捂住，塞住（某人的嘴）：*The hostages were* ***bound and gagged.*** 人質被綁起來並被人用東西塞住了嘴。 **2** [T] **~ sb/sth** to prevent sb from speaking freely or expressing their opinion 壓制…的言論自由；使緘默：*The new laws are seen as an attempt to gag the press.* 人們認為新法律企圖壓制新聞界的言論自由。◇ *a* ***gagging order*** (= one given by a court of law) 司法限制言論令 **3** [I] **~ (on sth)** to have the unpleasant feeling in your mouth and stomach as if you are going to VOMIT 作嘔 SYN **retch**：*She gagged on the blood that filled her mouth.* 她因嘴裏含滿了血而作嘔。

IDM **be gagging for sth/to do sth** (*BrE, slang*) to want sth or want to do sth very much 渴求（某物）；迫切想

做（某事） **be 'gagging for it** (*BrE, slang*) to want very much to have sex 慾火中燒

gaga /ˈɡɑːɡɑː/ *adj.* [not usually before noun] (*informal*) **1** (*offensive*) confused and not able to think clearly, especially because you are old 迷糊；（尤因年老）糊塗：*He has gone completely gaga.* 他完全老糊塗了。**2** slightly crazy because you are very excited about sb/sth, or very much in love 狂熱；着迷：*The fans went totally gaga over the band.* 樂迷們對這個樂隊完全着迷了。

gage (*US*) = GAUGE

gag·gle /ˈɡæɡl/ *noun* **1** a group of noisy people 一群（吵鬧的人）：*a* ***gaggle of tourists/schoolchildren*** 一群喧鬧的遊客 / 嘰嘰喳喳的小學生 **2** a group of GEESE 一群（鵝）；（鵝）群

Gaia /ˈɡaɪə/ *noun* [sing.] the Earth, considered as a single natural system which organizes and controls itself 蓋婭（被視為能進行自我組織與控制的單一自然體系的地球）

gai·ety /ˈɡeɪəti/ *noun* [U] (*old-fashioned*) the state of being cheerful and full of fun 快樂；愉快；高興：*The colourful flags added to the gaiety of the occasion.* 彩旗增添了盛會的歡樂氣氛。➲ compare GAYNESS ➲ see also GAILY, GAY

gaily /ˈɡeɪli/ *adv.* **1** in a bright and attractive way 花哨地；艷麗地；華麗地：*a gaily decorated room* 裝飾華麗的房間 **2** in a cheerful way 快樂地；歡樂地；喜氣洋洋地：*gaily laughing children* 喜笑顏開的孩子 ◇ *She waved gaily to the little crowd.* 她高興地向這一小群人揮手。**3** without thinking or caring about the effect of your actions on other people 欠思索地；毫無顧忌地；輕率地：*She gaily announced that she was leaving the next day.* 她不假思索地宣佈說她第二天要離開。➲ see also GAIETY, GAY

gain 🔑 /ɡeɪn/ *verb, noun*

■ ***verb***

▸ **OBTAIN/WIN 獲得；贏得** **1** 🔑 [T] to obtain or win sth, especially sth that you need or want 獲得；贏得；博得；取得：**~ sth** *to* ***gain entrance/entry/access*** *to sth* 得以進入 / 接近某物 ◇ *The country gained its independence ten years ago.* 這個國家十年前就贏得了獨立。◇ *The party gained over 50% of the vote.* 該黨獲得超過 50% 的選票。◇ **~ sb sth** *Her unusual talent gained her worldwide recognition.* 她非凡的才能舉世公認。**2** 🔑 [T, I] to obtain an advantage or benefit from sth or from doing sth（從…中）受益，獲益；得到（好處）：**~ sth (by/from sth)** *There is* ***nothing to be gained*** *from delaying the decision.* 推遲決定沒有任何好處。◇ **~ (by/from sth)** *Who* ***stands to gain from*** *this decision?* 誰會從這一決定中受益呢？

▸ **GET MORE 增加** **3** 🔑 [T] **~ sth** to gradually get more of sth 增加；增添；增進；增長：*to* ***gain confidence/strength/experience*** 增加信心 / 力量 / 經驗 ◇ *I've* ***gained weight*** *recently.* 最近我的體重增加了。**OPP** lose

▸ **OF WATCH/CLOCK 鐘錶** **4** [T, I] **~ (sth)** to go too fast 走得太快；快：*My watch gains two minutes every 24 hours.* 我的錶每 24 小時快兩分鐘。**OPP** lose

▸ **OF CURRENCIES/SHARES 貨幣；股票** **5** [T, I] to increase in value 增值；升值：**~ sth** *The shares gained 14p to 262p.* 股價上升了 14 便士，收報 262 便士。◇ **~ against sth** *The euro gained against the dollar again today.* 今天歐元兑美元的匯率又上升了。

▸ **REACH PLACE 到達某地** **6** [T] **~ sth** (*formal*) to reach a place, usually after a lot of effort（經過努力）到達：*At last she gained the shelter of the forest.* 她終於到達了森林中的隱蔽處。

IDM **gain 'ground** to become more powerful or successful 變得更強大（或更有成效、更成功）；有進步；獲得進展：*Sterling continues to gain ground against the dollar.* 英鎊兑美元繼續走高。**gain 'time** to delay sth so that you can have more time to make a decision, deal with a problem, etc.（通過拖延）贏得時間 ➲ more at VENTURE *v.*

PHR V **'gain in sth** to get more of a particular quality 增加；增長：*to gain in confidence* 增加信心 ◇ *His books have gained in popularity in recent years.* 近年來他的書越來越受歡迎。**'gain on sb/sth** to get closer to sb/sth that you are chasing 接近，逼近（所追逐的人或物）

■ ***noun***

▸ **INCREASE 增加** **1** 🔑 [C, U] an increase in the amount of sth, especially in wealth or weight（尤指財富、重量的）增值，增加：*a £3 000 gain from our investment* 從我們的投資中獲取的 3 000 英鎊的收益 ◇ *Regular exercise helps prevent weight gain.* 經常鍛煉有助於防止體重增加。

▸ **ADVANTAGE 好處** **2** 🔑 [C] an advantage or improvement 好處；利益；改進：*efficiency gains* 效率提高 ◇ *These policies have resulted in great gains in public health.* 這些政策使公共衛生得到極大改進。◇ *Our loss is their gain.* 我們之所失即他們之所得。**OPP** loss

▸ **PROFIT 利潤** **3** [U] (often *disapproving*) financial profit 利潤；經濟收益：*He only seems to be interested in personal gain.* 他似乎只在乎個人的收益。◇ *It's amazing what some people will do* ***for gain.*** 有的人為一己之利而幹出的事令人驚訝。**IDM** see PAIN *n.*

gain·ful /ˈɡeɪnfl/ *adj.* (*formal*) used to describe useful work that you are paid for 有收益的；有報酬的；有利可圖的：*gainful employment* 有酬的工作 ▸ **gain·ful·ly** /-fəli/ *adv.*：*gainfully employed* 有酬雇用

gain·say /ˌɡeɪnˈseɪ/ *verb* (**gain·says** /-ˈsez/, **gain·said**, **gain·said** /-ˈsed/) **~ sth** (*formal*) (often used in negative sentences 常用於否定句) to say that sth is not true; to disagree with or deny sth 反駁；反對；否認 **SYN** **deny**：*Nobody can gainsay his claims.* 沒人能夠反駁他的說法。

gait /ɡeɪt/ *noun* [sing.] a way of walking 步態；步法：*He walked with a rolling gait.* 他走起路來搖搖晃晃。

gai·ter /ˈɡeɪtə(r)/ *noun* [usually pl.] a cloth or leather covering for the leg between the knee and the ankle. Gaiters were worn by men in the past and are now mainly worn by people who go walking or climbing. 綁腿，護腿（舊時為男士所穿，現主要為徒步者或登山者所穿）：*a pair of gaiters* 一副綁腿

gal /ɡæl/ *noun* (*old-fashioned, informal, especially NAmE*) a girl or woman 女孩；姑娘；女子

gal. *abbr.* (in writing) gallon(s)（書寫形式）加侖

gala /ˈɡɑːlə; *NAmE* ˈɡeɪlə/ *noun* **1** a special public celebration or entertainment 慶典；盛會；演出：*a charity gala* 慈善義演 ◇ *a* ***gala dinner/night*** 盛宴；晚會 **2** (*BrE*) a sports competition, especially in swimming 體育運動會，體育競賽（尤指游泳）：*a swimming gala* 游泳比賽

ga·lac·tic /ɡəˈlæktɪk/ *adj.* relating to a galaxy 銀河的；星系的

galah /ɡəˈlɑː/ *noun* (*AustralE, informal*) a stupid person 蠢人；傻瓜

gal·axy /ˈɡæləksi/ *noun* (*pl.* **-ies**) **1** [C] any of the large systems of stars, etc. in outer space 星系 **2** **the Galaxy** (also **the ˌMilky 'Way**) [sing.] the system of stars that contains our sun and its planets, seen as a bright band in the night sky 銀河；銀河系 **3** [C] (*informal*) a group of famous people, or people with a particular skill 群英；人才薈萃：*a galaxy of Hollywood stars* 好萊塢影星的薈萃

gale /ɡeɪl/ *noun* an extremely strong wind 大風；颶風：*The gale blew down hundreds of trees.* 大風吹倒了數百棵樹。◇ ***gale-force winds*** 七級以上的大風 ◇ (*BrE*) *It's* ***blowing a gale*** *outside* (= a strong wind is blowing). 外面在颳大風。➲ COLLOCATIONS at WEATHER

IDM **gale(s) of laughter** the sound of people laughing very loudly 一陣大笑聲：*His speech was greeted with gales of laughter.* 人們對他的演講報以陣陣笑聲。

gall /ɡɔːl/ *noun, verb*

■ ***noun*** **1** rude behaviour showing a lack of respect that is surprising because the person behaving badly is not embarrassed 魯莽；厚顏無恥 **SYN** **impudence**：*Then they* ***had the gall to*** *complain!* 那時他們居然還有臉抱怨！**2** (*formal*) a bitter feeling full of hatred 怨恨；怨憤 **SYN** **resentment** **3** a swelling on plants and trees caused by insects, disease, etc. 癭，蟲癭（植物因受病原刺激或蟲害而出現的局部增生）**4** (*old-fashioned*) = BILE

■ ***verb*** **~ sb** | **it galls sb to do sth** | **it galls sb that …** to make sb feel upset and angry, especially because sth is unfair 使煩惱，使憤怒（尤指因不公平引起）：*It galls me*

G

to have to apologize to her. 非得向她道歉使我感到惱火。 ➲ see also GALLING

gal·lant *adj., noun*

■ ***adj.*** /ˈɡælənt/ **1** (*old-fashioned* or *literary*) brave, especially in a very difficult situation（尤指在困境中）勇敢的，英勇的 **SYN heroic**：*gallant soldiers* 勇敢的軍人 ◇ *She made a gallant attempt to hide her tears.* 她強掩住淚水。 **2** (of a man 男子) giving polite attention to women 對女子殷勤的 ▸ **gal·lant·ly** *adv.*：*She gallantly battled on alone.* 她單槍匹馬繼續英勇頑強地戰鬥。◇ *He bowed and gallantly kissed my hand.* 他鞠了一躬，殷勤地吻了吻我的手。

■ ***noun*** /ɡəˈlænt; ˈɡælənt/ (*old-fashioned*) a fashionable young man, especially one who gives polite attention to women（尤指對女子殷勤的）時髦男子

G

gal·lant·ry /ˈɡæləntri/ *noun* [U] (*formal*) **1** courage, especially in a battle（尤指在戰場上）勇敢，英勇頑強：*a medal for gallantry* 英勇勳章 **2** polite attention given by men to women（男子對女子的）殷勤

ˈgall bladder *noun* an organ attached to the LIVER in which BILE is stored 膽囊 ➲ **VISUAL VOCAB** page V59

gal·leon /ˈɡæliən/ *noun* a large Spanish sailing ship, used between the 15th and the 17th centuries（15–17 世紀使用的）西班牙大帆船

gal·ler·ied /ˈɡælərid/ *adj.* (of a building 建築物) having a gallery (3) 有樓座的

gal·lery /ˈɡæləri/ *noun* (*pl.* **-ies**) **1** a room or building for showing works of art, especially to the public（藝術作品的）陳列室，展覽館；畫廊：***an art/a picture gallery*** 美術館；繪畫陳列室 ◇ *the National Gallery* 國家美術館 ➲ **COLLOCATIONS** at ART ➲ see also ART GALLERY **2** a small private shop/store where you can see and buy works of art 私家畫店 **3** an upstairs area at the back or sides of a large hall where people can sit（大廳的）樓座，樓上旁聽席：*Relatives of the victim watched from the public gallery as the murder charge was read out in court.* 法庭宣讀謀殺指控時受害者的親屬在公共旁聽席觀看。➲ see also PRESS GALLERY **4** the highest level in a theatre where the cheapest seats are（劇場中票價最低的）頂層樓座 **5** a long narrow room, especially one used for a particular purpose 長廊；走廊；柱廊 ➲ see also SHOOTING GALLERY **6** a level passage under the ground in a mine or CAVE（礦坑或洞穴中的）水平巷道

IDM **play to the ˈgallery** to behave in an exaggerated way to attract people's attention 譁眾取寵；行為惹人注目

gal·ley /ˈɡæli/ *noun* **1** a long flat ship with sails, usually ROWED by SLAVES or criminals, especially one used by the ancient Greeks or Romans in war（常由奴隸或囚犯划槳的）槳帆船；（古希臘和古羅馬的）戰艦 **2** the kitchen on a ship or plane（船或飛機上的）廚房

Gal·lic /ˈɡælɪk/ *adj.* connected with or considered typical of France or its people 法國的；法國人的；高盧的；高盧人的：*Gallic charm* 法國人的魅力

gall·ing /ˈɡɔːlɪŋ/ *adj.* [not usually before noun] (of a situation or fact 境況或事實) making you angry because it is unfair 令人惱怒；使人煩惱；使人感到屈辱：*It was galling to have to apologize to a man she hated.* 令人惱火的是得向她憎惡的男人道歉。

gal·lium /ˈɡæliəm/ *noun* [U] (*symb.* **Ga**) a chemical element. Gallium is a soft silver-white metal. 鎵

gal·li·vant /ˈɡælɪvænt/ *verb* [I] (usually used in the progressive tenses 通常用於進行時) **~ (about/around)** (*old-fashioned, informal*) to go from place to place enjoying yourself 遊玩；遊覽；閒逛 **SYN gad**：*You're too old to go gallivanting around Europe.* 你年紀太大，不能到歐洲各地遊逛去了。

gal·lon 🔑 /ˈɡælən/ *noun* (*abbr.* **gal.**) a unit for measuring liquid. In the UK, Canada and other countries it is equal to about 4.5 litres; in the US it is equal to about 3.8 litres. There are four QUARTS in a gallon. 加侖（液量單位，在英國、加拿大及其他一些國家約等於 4.5 升，在美國約等於 3.8 升，一加侖為四夸脫）

gal·lop /ˈɡæləp/ *verb, noun*

■ ***verb*** **1** [I] (**+ adv./prep.**) when a horse or similar animal **gallops**, it moves very fast and each STRIDE includes a stage when all four feet are off the ground together（馬等）飛奔，奔馳，疾馳 ➲ compare CANTER **2** [I, T] to ride a horse very fast, usually at a gallop 騎馬奔馳；使（馬）飛奔：(**+ adv./prep.**) *Jo galloped across the field towards him.* 喬騎馬穿過田野向他奔去。◇ **~ sth** (**+ adv./prep.**) *He galloped his horse home.* 他騎着馬飛奔回家。➲ compare CANTER **3** [I] (**+ adv./prep.**) (*informal*) (of a person 人) to run very quickly 飛跑；奔跑 **SYN charge**：*She came galloping down the street.* 她沿街飛奔而來。

■ ***noun*** **1** [sing.] the fastest speed at which a horse can run, with a stage in which all four feet are off the ground together（馬的）飛奔，奔馳，疾馳：*He rode off **at a gallop**.* 他騎馬疾馳而去。◇ *My horse suddenly **broke into a gallop**.* 我的馬突然飛奔起來。 **2** [C] a ride on a horse at its fastest speed 騎馬奔馳：*to go for a gallop* 去騎馬奔馳一番 **3** [sing.] an unusually fast speed 飛快；高速度

gal·lop·ing /ˈɡæləpɪŋ/ *adj.* [only before noun] increasing or spreading rapidly 迅速增加（或蔓延）的：*galloping inflation* 急劇的通貨膨脹

gal·lows /ˈɡæləʊz; *NAmE* -loʊz/ *noun* (*pl.* **gal·lows**) a structure on which people, for example criminals, are killed by hanging 絞刑架；絞台：*to send a man to the gallows* (= to send him to his death by hanging) 把一名男子送上絞刑架

ˌgallows ˈhumour (*especially US* **ˌgallows ˈhumor**) *noun* [U] jokes about unpleasant things like death 面臨大難的幽默

gall·stone /ˈɡɔːlstəʊn; *NAmE* -stoʊn/ *noun* a hard painful mass that can form in the GALL BLADDER 膽（結）石

Gal·lup poll™ /ˈɡæləp pəʊl; *NAmE* poʊl/ *noun* a way of finding out public opinion by asking a typical group of people questions 蓋洛普民意調查 **ORIGIN** From G H Gallup, who invented it. 源自創始人蓋洛普（Gallup）的名字。

gal·ore /ɡəˈlɔː(r)/ *adj.* [after noun] (*informal*) in large quantities 大量；很多：*There will be games and prizes galore.* 將有很多遊戲和獎品。

gal·oshes /ɡəˈlɒʃɪz; *NAmE* -ˈlɑːʃ-/ *noun* [pl.] rubber shoes (no longer very common) that are worn over normal shoes in wet weather 橡膠套鞋（雨天套在平常穿的鞋上，現已不常見）：*a pair of galoshes* 一雙橡膠套鞋

gal·umph /ɡəˈlʌmf/ *verb* [I] **+ adv./prep.** (*informal*) to move in an awkward, careless or noisy way 笨拙（或懶散）地挪動；腳步聲嘈雜地行進

gal·van·ic /ɡælˈvænɪk/ *adj.* **1** (*technical* 術語) producing an electric current by the action of a chemical on metal（以化學作用）產生電流的 **2** (*formal*) making people react in a sudden and dramatic way 令人一下子產生強烈反應的；使人激動的

gal·van·ize (*BrE* also **-ise**) /ˈɡælvənaɪz/ *verb* **1 ~ sb (into sth/into doing sth)** to make sb take action by shocking them or by making them excited 使震驚；使振奮；激勵；刺激：*The urgency of his voice **galvanized them into action**.* 他急迫的聲音激勵他們行動起來。 **2 ~ sth** (*technical* 術語) to cover metal with ZINC in order to protect it from RUST 電鍍；給（金屬）鍍鋅：*a galvanized bucket* 鍍鋅桶 ◇ *galvanized steel* 鍍鋅鋼

gam·bit /ˈɡæmbɪt/ *noun* **1** a thing that sb does, or sth that sb says at the beginning of a situation or conversation, that is intended to give them some advantage 開頭一招；開局；開場白：*an **opening gambit*** (= the first thing you say) 開場白 **2** a move or moves made at the beginning of a game of CHESS in order to gain an advantage later（國際象棋中為獲得優勢而採取的）開局讓棋法

gam·ble 🔑 /ˈɡæmbl/ *verb, noun*

■ ***verb*** **1** 🔑 [I, T] to risk money on a card game, horse race, etc.（牌戲、賽馬等中）賭博，打賭：**~ (at/on sth)** *to **gamble at cards*** 賭紙牌 ◇ *to **gamble on the horses*** 賭馬 ◇ **~ sth (at/on sth)** *I gambled all my winnings on the last race.* 我把贏了的錢全壓在最後一場比賽上了。 **2** 🔑 [T, I] to risk losing sth in the hope of being successful 冒風

險；碰運氣；以…為賭注：**~ sth (on sth)** *He's gambling his reputation on this deal.* 他在以自己的聲譽為這筆交易作賭注。◇ **~ with/on sth** *It was wrong to gamble with our children's future.* 拿我們孩子的未來冒險是錯誤的。
▸ **gam·bler** /ˈɡæmblə(r)/ *noun*：*He was a* ***compulsive gambler*** (= found it difficult to stop). 他嗜賭成癖。

PHR V **ˌgamble sth↔aˈway** to lose sth such as money, possessions, etc. by gambling 賭掉；賭光 **ˈgamble on sth/on doing sth** to take a risk with sth, hoping that you will be successful 冒…的風險；碰…的運氣：*He gambled on being able to buy a ticket at the last minute.* 他碰運氣看能否在最後一刻買到票。

■ ***noun*** 🔑 [sing.] an action that you take when you know there is a risk but when you hope that the result will be a success 賭博；打賭；冒險：*She knew she was* ***taking a gamble*** *but decided it was worth it.* 她知道是在冒險，但她認為冒這個險值得。◇ *They invested money in the company right at the start and* ***the gamble paid off*** (= brought them success). 他們一開始就把資金投到這家公司，結果這一冒險獲得了成功。

gam·bling 🔑 /ˈɡæmblɪŋ/ *noun* [U] the activity of playing games of chance for money and of betting on horses, etc. 賭博；打賭；賭錢：*heavy gambling debts* 沉重的賭債

gam·bol /ˈɡæmbl/ *verb* (**-ll-**, *US* also **-l-**) [I] (**+ adv./prep.**) to jump or run about in a lively way 跳躍；嬉戲：*lambs gambolling in the meadow* 在草地上蹦蹦跳跳的小羊羔

game 🔑 /ɡeɪm/ *noun, adj.*

■ ***noun***

▸ **ACTIVITY/SPORT 活動；體育運動** **1** 🔑 [C] an activity or a sport with rules in which people or teams compete against each other（有規則的）遊戲，運動，比賽項目：*card games* 紙牌遊戲 ◇ *board games* 棋類遊戲 ◇ *a* ***game of chance/skill*** 靠運氣決定勝負 / 憑技巧取勝的遊戲 ◇ ***ball games****, such as football or tennis* 諸如足球或網球等球類運動 ◇ (*NAmE*) *We're going to the* ***ball game*** (= BASEBALL game). 我們要去看棒球比賽。➲ VISUAL VOCAB pages V37, V38 ➲ see also WAR GAME **2** 🔑 [C] an occasion of playing a game（一項）遊戲，運動，比賽：*to* ***play a game of*** *chess* 下一盤國際象棋 ◇ *Saturday's League game against Swansea* 聯賽中星期六對斯旺西隊的比賽 ◇ *Let's* ***have a game of*** *table tennis.* 咱們來打場乒乓球賽吧。◇ *They're in training for the big game.* 他們正在為大賽進行訓練。 **3** [sing.] **sb's ~** the way in which sb plays a game 比賽時用的手法；比賽技巧：*Maguire* ***raised his game*** *to collect the £40 000 first prize.* 馬圭爾的比賽技巧有所提高，得到了 4 萬英鎊的頭等獎。◇ *Stretching exercises can help you avoid injury and improve your game.* 伸展運動有助於防止身體受傷，並能提高比賽技巧。

▸ **SPORTS 體育運動** **4** 🔑 **games** [pl.] a large organized sports event 運動會：*the Olympic Games* 奧運會 **5** **games** [pl.] (*old-fashioned, BrE*) sport as a lesson or an activity at school（學校的）體育課，體育活動：*I always hated games at school.* 我唸書的時候一直不喜歡體育活動。

▸ **PART OF SPORTS MATCH 體育比賽的一部份** **6** 🔑 [C] a section of some games, such as TENNIS, which forms a unit in scoring（網球等比賽的）一局，一場：*two games all* (= both players have won two games) 各贏兩局

▸ **CHILDREN'S ACTIVITY 兒童活動** **7** 🔑 [C] a children's activity when they play with toys, pretend to be sb else, etc. 兒童遊戲：*a game of cops and robbers* 警察抓強盜的遊戲 ➲ SYNONYMS at INTEREST

▸ **FUN 娛樂** **8** [C] an activity that you do to have fun 娛樂；消遣；玩耍：*He was* ***playing games*** *with the dog.* 他在逗着狗玩。➲ SYNONYMS at INTEREST

▸ **ACTIVITY, BUSINESS 活動；行業** **9** [C] a type of activity or business 行當；行業；職業：*How long have you been in this game?* 你幹這行當多長時間了？◇ *the game of politics* 政治活動 ◇ *I'm* ***new to this game*** *myself.* 我個人對這一範疇不熟悉。◇ *Getting dirty was* ***all part of the game*** *to the kids.* 對孩子來説弄髒是很正常的事。➲ see also WAITING GAME

▸ **SECRET PLAN 秘密計劃** **10** [C] (*informal*) a secret and clever plan; a trick 詭計；策略；花招：*So* ***that's his game*** (= now I know what he has been planning). 原來這就是他的鬼把戲。

▸ **WILD ANIMALS/BIRDS 野生鳥獸** **11** [U] wild animals or birds that people hunt for sport or food 獵物；野禽；野味 ➲ VISUAL VOCAB page V12 ➲ see also BIG GAME, FAIR GAME

IDM **be a ˈgame** to not be considered to be serious 不當一回事；當兒戲；鬧着玩：*For her the whole project was* ***just a game****.* 對她來説，整個計劃不過是場兒戲而已。 **be on the ˈgame** (*BrE, slang*) to be a PROSTITUTE 賣淫；當"野雞" **be ˌout of the ˈgame** to no longer have a chance of winning a game or succeeding in an activity that you are taking part in 退出比賽；被淘汰出局 **be ˌstill/ˌback in the ˈgame** to still/once again have a good chance of winning a game or succeeding in an activity that you are taking part in 沒有出局；仍有獲勝（或成功）的機會：*The team was still in the game, just one goal down.* 這個隊還沒出局，只落後一球。 **the game is ˈup** (*BrE, informal*) said to sb who has done sth wrong, when they are caught and the crime or trick has been discovered（對做壞事被抓或罪行敗露者説的話）戲該收場了，別再演戲了 **game ˈon** (*informal*) used after sth has happened that makes it clear that a contest is not yet decided and anyone could still win（賽場局勢發生變化後表明）勝負難料：*We were losing 2–0 with ten minutes to go, and then we scored. It was game on!* 離終場還有十分鐘，我們以 0:2 落後，隨後我們進球了。誰輸誰贏還説不定呢！ **give the ˈgame away** to tell a secret, especially by accident; to show sth that should be kept hidden 不慎泄露；露餡；露馬腳 **the only game in ˈtown** (*informal*) the most important thing of a particular type, or the only thing that is available 同類中最重要的事物；唯一的選擇 **play the ˈgame** to behave in a fair and honest way 辦事公道；為人誠實 **play sb's ˈgame** to do sth which helps sb else's plans, especially by accident, when you did not intend to help them（無意中）促成某人的計劃 **play (silly) ˈgames (with sb)** not to treat a situation seriously, especially in order to cheat sb（與某人）耍花招，玩鬼把戲：*Don't play silly games with me; I know you did it.* 別跟我兜圈子，我知道是你幹的。 **ˈtwo can play at ˈthat game** (*saying*) used to tell sb who has played a trick on you that you can do the same thing to them（表示也會對方耍的花招）這一套你會我也會 **what's sb's/your ˈgame?** (*BrE, informal*) used to ask why sb is behaving as they are 在幹什麼；怎麼啦 ➲ more at BEAT *v.*, CAT, FUN *n.*, MUG *n.*, NAME *n.*, NUMBER *n.*, RULE *n.*, TALK *v.*, WORTH *adj.*

■ ***adj.*** **~ (for sth/to do sth)** ready and willing to do sth new, difficult or dangerous 甘願嘗試；有冒險精神：*She's game for anything.* 她什麼事都敢試。◇ *We need a volunteer for this exercise. Who's game to try?* 我們需要有人自告奮勇來做這個練習，誰願意來試試？

ˈgame bird *noun* a bird that people hunt for sport or food 可捕獵的鳥；野禽；野味

ˈgame-changer *noun* (*NAmE*) a person, an idea or an event that completely changes the way a situation develops 遊戲規則改變者（指徹底改變事態發展的人、理念或事件）

game·keep·er /ˈɡeɪmkiːpə(r)/ *noun* a person whose job is to take care of and breed wild animals and birds that are kept on private land in order to be hunted（私有獵場的）獵物看守人 **IDM** see POACHER

game·lan /ˈɡæməlæn/ *noun* a traditional group of Indonesian musicians, playing instruments such as XYLOPHONES and GONGS 加美蘭樂隊，佳美蘭，甘美朗（以木琴、大吊鑼等樂器為主的印度尼西亞傳統樂隊）

game·ly /ˈɡeɪmli/ *adv.* in a way that seems brave, although a lot of effort is involved 頑強勇敢地；勇於承擔地：*She tried gamely to finish the race.* 她頑強地努力跑完比賽。

ˈgame plan *noun* a plan for success in the future, especially in sport, politics or business（尤指體育運動、政治或商業方面的）行動計劃，方案，對策

game·play /ˈɡeɪmpleɪ/ *noun* [U] the features of a computer game, such as its story or the way it is played, rather than the images or sounds it uses 電腦遊戲情節

G

G

,game 'point *noun* (especially in TENNIS 尤指網球) a point that, if won by a player, will win them the game (一局的)決勝分；局點

gamer /'geɪmə(r)/ *noun* (*informal*) **1** a person who likes playing computer games 喜歡玩電腦遊戲的人 **2** (*NAmE*) (in sports 體育運動) a player who is enthusiastic and works hard 堅毅的運動員

'game reserve (also **'game park**) (both *BrE*) (*NAmE* **'game preserve**) *noun* a large area of land where wild animals can live in safety 禁獵區；野生動物保護區

'game show *noun* a television programme in which people play games or answer questions to win prizes (電視)遊戲表演，競賽節目

games·man·ship /'geɪmzmənʃɪp/ *noun* [U] the ability to win games by making your opponent less confident and using rules to your advantage 比賽的戰術；比賽策略

gam·ete /'gæmiːt/ *noun* (*biology* 生) a male or female cell that joins with a cell of the opposite sex to form a ZYGOTE (= a single cell that develops into a person, animal or plant) 配子(形成受精卵的精子或卵子)

'game theory *noun* [U] the part of mathematics that deals with situations in which people compete with each other, for example war or business 博弈論；對策論；賽局理論

'game warden *noun* a person whose job is to manage and take care of the wild animals in a GAME RESERVE (野生動物保護區的)看守人，管理員

gamey (also **gamy**) /'geɪmi/ *adj.* (of meat that has been hunted 野味) having a strong flavour or smell as a result of being kept for some time before cooking 有變質味道的；有羶味的

gam·ine /gæ'miːn/ *adj.* (*formal*) (of a young woman 年輕女子) thin and attractive; looking like a boy 嬌小迷人的；男孩子氣的 ▸ **gam·ine** *noun*

gam·ing /'geɪmɪŋ/ *noun* [U] **1** (*old-fashioned* or *law* 律) = GAMBLING : *He spent all night at the gaming tables.* 他通宵賭博。 **2** playing computer games 玩電腦遊戲 ➲ see also WAR GAMING

gamma /'gæmə/ *noun* the third letter of the Greek alphabet (Γ, γ) 希臘字母表的第 3 個字母

gamma globulin /,gæmə 'glɒbjʊlɪn; *NAmE* 'glɑːb-/ *noun* (*biology* 生) [U] a type of PROTEIN in the blood that gives protection against some types of diseases 丙種球蛋白；γ 球蛋白

,gamma radi'ation *noun* [U] (also **'gamma rays** [pl.]) (*physics* 物) high-energy RAYS of very short WAVELENGTH sent out by some RADIOACTIVE substances * γ 輻射；伽馬輻射；γ 射線；伽馬射線

gam·mon /'gæmən/ *noun* [U] (*BrE*) meat from the back leg or side of a pig that has been CURED (= preserved using salt or smoke), usually served in thick slices 醃豬後腿；熏腿；熏豬肋肉 ➲ compare BACON, HAM *n.* (1), PORK

gammy /'gæmi/ *adj.* [usually before noun] (*old-fashioned, BrE, informal*) (of a leg or knee 腿或膝) injured 受傷的；受損的

the gamut /'gæmət/ *noun* [sing.] the complete range of a particular kind of thing 全部；全範圍： *The network will provide the gamut of computer services to your home.* 這個網絡將為家庭提供全方位的計算機服務。◇ *She felt she had* ***run the (whole) gamut of*** *human emotions from joy to despair.* 她感到自己嚐遍了從喜到悲的七情六慾。

gamy = GAMEY

Gan /gæn/ *noun* [U] a form of Chinese, spoken mainly in Jiangxi 贛語；贛方言

gan·der /'gændə(r)/ *noun* a male GOOSE (= a bird like a large DUCK) 公鵝

IDM **have/take a 'gander (at sth)** (*informal*) to look at sth 看一看；看一眼 ➲ more at SAUCE

G and T /,dʒiː ən 'tiː/ *noun* a drink consisting of GIN mixed with TONIC WATER 摻奎寧水的杜松子酒

gang /gæŋ/ *noun, verb*

■ ***noun*** [C+sing./pl. v.] **1** an organized group of criminals 一幫，一夥(罪犯)： *criminal gang members and drug dealers* 犯罪集團成員和毒品販子 ◇ *a gang of pickpockets* 扒手集團 ◇ *A four-man gang carried out the robbery.* 這起搶劫是一個四人團夥所為。 **2** a group of young people who spend a lot of time together and often cause trouble or fight against other groups 一幫，一群，一夥(鬧事、鬥毆的年輕人)： *a gang of youths* 一幫小混混 ◇ *a street gang* 街頭流氓團夥 **3** (*informal*) a group of friends who meet regularly 一夥(經常聚在一起的朋友)： *The whole gang will be there.* 大夥兒都將在那兒。 **4** an organized group of workers or prisoners doing work together 一隊，一組(一起幹活的工人或囚犯) ➲ see also CHAIN GANG

■ ***verb***

PHR V **,gang to'gether** (*informal*) to join together in a group in order to have more power or strength 結成一夥；拉幫結夥 **,gang 'up (on/against sb)** (*informal*) to join together in a group to hurt, frighten or oppose sb 結夥，聯合起來，拉幫結派(傷害、恐嚇或反對某人)： *At school the older boys ganged up on him and called him names.* 在學校讀書時那些大男孩聯合起來欺負他，辱罵他。

'gang bang *noun* (*slang*) **1** an occasion when a number of people have sex with each other in a group 集體淫亂活動 **2** the RAPE of a person by a number of people one after the other 輪姦 ▸ **'gang-bang** *verb* **~ sb**

gang·bust·ers /'gæŋbʌstəz; *NAmE* -ərz/ *noun*

IDM **like 'gangbusters** (*NAmE, informal*) with a lot of energy and enthusiasm 精力充沛；熱情洋溢

gang·land /'gæŋlænd/ *noun* [sing.] the world of organized and violent crime 盜匪世界；黑社會： *gangland killings* 犯罪集團間的殺戮

gan·gling /'gæŋglɪŋ/ (also **gan·gly** /'gæŋgli/) *adj.* (of a person 人) tall, thin and awkward in their movements 又高又瘦且動作笨拙的 **SYN** **lanky** : *a* ***gangling youth/adolescent*** 高瘦而笨拙的青年 / 青少年

gan·glion /'gæŋgliən/ *noun* (*pl.* **gan·glia** /-liə/) (*medical* 醫) **1** a mass of nerve cells 神經節 **2** a swelling in a TENDON, often at the back of the hand 腱鞘囊腫(經常出現在手背)

gang·mas·ter /'gæŋmɑːstə(r); *NAmE* -mæs-/ *noun* (*BrE*) a person or company that organizes groups of workers on a temporary basis to do MANUAL work (= physical work using their hands), especially work on farms 非法雇主(大批雇用臨時工人從事體力勞動，尤其是農場工作)

gang·plank /'gæŋplæŋk/ *noun* a board placed between the side of a boat and land so people can get on and off (上下船用的)跳板，步橋

'gang rape *noun* [U, C] the RAPE of a person by a number of people one after the other 輪姦 ▸ **'gang-rape** *verb* **~ sb**

gan·grene /'gæŋgriːn/ *noun* [U] the decay that takes place in a part of the body when the blood supply to it has been stopped because of an illness or injury 壞疽： *Gangrene set in and he had to have his leg amputated.* 他的腿生了壞疽，必須截除。▸ **gan·gren·ous** /'gæŋgrɪnəs/ *adj.*

gang·sta /'gæŋstə/ *noun* **1** [C] (*NAmE, slang*) a member of a street GANG 街頭流氓；地痞；痞子 **2** (also **,gangsta 'rap**) [U] a type of RAP music, typically with words about violence, guns, drugs and sex 岡斯特說唱樂，岡斯特快板歌(歌詞內容通常與暴力、槍殺、吸毒和色情有關)

gang·ster /'gæŋstə(r)/ *noun* a member of a group of violent criminals 匪徒；歹徒；土匪： *Chicago gangsters* 芝加哥的歹徒

gang·way /'gæŋweɪ/ *noun* **1** (*BrE*) a passage between rows of seats in a theatre, an aircraft, etc. (劇場、飛機等的)座間通道 ➲ compare AISLE **2** a bridge placed between the side of a ship and land so people can get on and off (上下船用的)舷門，舷梯，步橋，跳板

ganja /ˈgændʒə; ˈgɑːn-/ *noun* [U] (*slang*) = MARIJUANA

gan·net /ˈgænɪt/ *noun* **1** a large bird that lives near the sea which catches fish by diving 塘鵝（潛水捕魚的大海鳥） **2** (*BrE, informal*) a person who eats a lot 大胃王；吃得多的人

gan·try /ˈgæntri/ *noun* (*pl.* **-ies**) a tall metal frame that is used to support a CRANE, road signs, a SPACECRAFT while it is still on the ground, etc. （起重的）龍門架；（道路的）路標架；（發射航天器的）豎架

Gantt chart /ˈgænt tʃɑːt; *NAmE* tʃɑːrt/ *noun* (*business* 商) a chart used for managing the tasks involved in a project that shows when each stage should start and end and compares the amount of work done with the amount planned 甘特圖（用於項目任務管理，顯示各階段的起迄時間，並將已完成和計劃工作量進行對比）

gaol, **gaoler** (*BrE*) = JAIL, JAILER

gap 0➡ /gæp/ *noun*

~ (in/between sth) **1** 0➡ a space between two things or in the middle of sth, especially because there is a part missing 開口；豁口；缺口；裂口：*a gap in a hedge* 樹籬的豁口 ◇ *Leave a gap between your car and the next.* 在車與車之間留條道。 **2** 0➡ a period of time when sth stops, or between two events 間斷；間隔；間隙：*a gap in the conversation* 談話的間隙 ◇ *They met again after a gap of twenty years.* 他們闊別二十年後又見面了。◇ *There's a big **age gap** between them* (= a big difference in their ages). 他們之間年齡差距很大。 **3** 0➡ a difference that separates people, or their opinions, situation, etc. 分歧；隔閡；差距：*the gap between rich and poor* 貧富之間的差距 ◇ *the gap between theory and practice* 理論與實踐的脱節 ➲ see also CREDIBILITY GAP at CREDIBILITY, GENERATION GAP **4** 0➡ a space where sth is missing 缺口；空白；漏洞：*His death left an enormous gap in my life.* 他去世給我的生活留下巨大的空白。◇ *There were several gaps in my education.* 我受的教育有幾個欠缺之處。◇ *We think we've identified **a gap in the market*** (= a business opportunity to make or sell sth that is not yet available). 我們認為已經發現了市場上一個尚待填補的空白。
IDM see BRIDGE *v.*

gape /geɪp/ *verb* **1** [I] **~ (at sb/sth)** to stare at sb/sth with your mouth open because you are shocked or surprised 張口結舌地看；目瞪口呆地凝視 **2** [I] to be or become wide open 張開；裂開；豁開：*a **gaping hole/mouth/wound*** 豁開的洞；張大的嘴；裂開的傷口 ◇ **~ open** *He stood yawning, his pyjama jacket gaping open.* 他敞開睡衣站着打哈欠。 ▸ **gape** *noun*

gap·per /ˈgæpə(r)/ *noun* (*BrE*) a young person who is spending a year working or travelling after leaving school and before going to university 空缺年休假者（中學畢業後到上大學前用一年時間實習或旅遊）

ˌgap-ˈtoothed *adj.* [usually before noun] having wide spaces between your teeth 齒縫很大的；有齒縫的

ˈgap year *noun* (*BrE*) a year that a young person spends working and/or travelling, often between leaving school and starting university 空缺年（常指中學畢業後上大學前所休的一年假期，用於實習或旅遊）：*I'm planning to take a gap year and go backpacking in India.* 我準備休假一年去印度背包旅行。

gar·age 0➡ /ˈgærɑːʒ; -rɑːdʒ; -rɪdʒ; *NAmE* gəˈrɑːʒ; -ˈrɑːdʒ/ *noun, verb*

■ *noun* **1** 0➡ [C] a building for keeping one or more cars or other vehicles in 停車房；車庫：(*BrE*) *a house with a built-in garage* 內設車庫的房子 ◇ (*NAmE*) *a house with an attached garage* 旁設車庫的房子 ◇ *a double garage* (= one for two cars) 停放兩輛車的車房 ◇ *a bus garage* 公共汽車車庫 ◇ *an underground garage* (= for example under an office building) 地下停車庫 ➲ VISUAL VOCAB page V17 **2** 0➡ [C] a place where vehicles are repaired and where you can buy a car or buy petrol/gas and oil （兼營汽車銷售、修理及加油的）汽車修理廠：*a garage mechanic* 汽車修理廠的機修工 ➲ see also PETROL STATION **3** [U] a type of HOUSE MUSIC 車庫音樂，加拉奇音樂（貨倉音樂的一種）

■ *verb* **~ sth** to put or keep a vehicle in a garage 把…送入車庫（或修車廠）

ˌgarage ˈrock *noun* [U] a type of rock music played with a lot of energy, often by musicians who are not professionals 車庫搖滾樂（充滿活力，常為業餘樂手演奏）

ˈgarage sale *noun* a sale of used clothes, furniture, etc., held in the garage of sb's house （在私人住宅的車庫裏進行的）舊物銷售

garam masala /ˌgʌrəm məˈsɑːlə; *NAmE* ˌgɑːrɑːm/ *noun* [U] a mixture of spices with a strong flavour, used in S Asian cooking （用於南亞烹飪的）辛辣香料粉

garb /gɑːb; *NAmE* gɑːrb/ *noun* [U] (*formal* or *humorous*) clothes, especially unusual clothes or those worn by a particular type of person（尤指某類人穿的特定）服裝，衣服；制服：*prison garb* 囚服

gar·bage 0➡ /ˈgɑːbɪdʒ; *NAmE* ˈgɑːrb-/ *noun* [U]

1 0➡ (*especially NAmE*) waste food, paper, etc. that you throw away （生活）垃圾；廢物：*garbage collection* 垃圾收集 ◇ *Don't forget to take out the garbage.* 別忘了把垃圾拿出去。 ➲ COLLOCATIONS at ENVIRONMENT **2** 0➡ (*especially NAmE*) a place or container where waste food, paper, etc. can be placed 垃圾場；垃圾箱；垃圾桶：*Throw it in the garbage.* 把它扔到垃圾箱裏去。 **3** 0➡ (*informal*) something stupid or not true 廢話；無聊的東西 **SYN** **rubbish** ➲ note at RUBBISH
IDM **garbage ˌin, garbage ˈout** (*abbr.* **GIGO**) used to express the idea that if wrong or poor quality data is put into a computer, wrong or poor quality data will come out of it （用於計算機）廢料輸入廢料輸出，無用輸入無用輸出

ˈgarbage can (also **ˈtrash can**) (both *NAmE*) (*BrE* **dust·bin**) *noun* a large container with a lid, used for putting rubbish/garbage in, usually kept outside the house （常置於房外的）垃圾桶，垃圾箱 ➲ note at RUBBISH

ˈgarbage dis·posal *noun* (*NAmE*) = WASTE-DISPOSAL UNIT

ˈgarbage man (also *formal* **ˈgarbage collector**) (both *NAmE*) (*BrE* **dust·man**, *informal* **bin·man**, *formal* **ˈrefuse collector**) *noun* a person whose job is to remove waste from outside houses, etc. 垃圾工 ➲ note at RUBBISH

ˈgarbage truck (*NAmE*) (*BrE* **dust·cart**) *noun* a vehicle for collecting rubbish/garbage from outside houses, etc. 垃圾車

gar·banzo /gɑːˈbænzəʊ; *NAmE* gɑːrˈbɑːnzoʊ; -ˈbæn-/ (also **garˈbanzo ˌbean**) (both *NAmE*) *noun* (*pl.* **-os**) = CHICKPEA

garbed /gɑːbd; *NAmE* gɑːrbd/ *adj.* [not before noun] (*formal*) **~ (in sth)** dressed in a particular way 以…方式穿着：*brightly garbed* 穿着鮮豔

gar·bled /ˈgɑːbld; *NAmE* ˈgɑːrbld/ *adj.* (of a message or story 信息或敍述) told in a way that confuses the person listening, usually by sb who is shocked or in a hurry 混亂不清的，引起誤解的（常因講述者驚慌或匆忙所致） **SYN** **confused**：*He gave a garbled account of what had happened.* 他對所發生事情的敍述含混不清。◇ *There was a garbled message from her on my voicemail.* 我的語音信箱裏有她含混不清的留言。

garbo /ˈgɑːbəʊ; *NAmE* ˈgɑːrboʊ/ *noun* (*pl.* **-os**) (*AustralE, informal*) a person whose job is to remove waste from outside houses, etc. 垃圾工 **SYN** **dustman**, **garbage collector**

Garda /ˈgɑːdə; *NAmE* ˈgɑːrdə/ *noun* **1** **the Garda** [U] the police force of the Republic of Ireland （愛爾蘭共和國的）警察部門，警察機關 **2** [C] (also **garda**) (*pl.* **gardai** /ˈgɑːdiː; *NAmE* ˈgɑːrdiː/) a police officer of the Republic of Ireland （愛爾蘭共和國的）警察

gar·den 0➡ /ˈgɑːdn; *NAmE* ˈgɑːrdn/ *noun, verb*

■ *noun* **1** 0➡ [C] (*BrE*) (*NAmE* **yard**) a piece of land next to or around your house where you can grow flowers, fruit, vegetables, etc., usually with a LAWN (= an area of grass) （住宅旁或周圍的）庭園，花園，果園，菜園：*a **front/back garden*** 前 / 後花園 ◇ *children playing in the garden* 在花園裏玩耍的孩子 ◇ ***garden flowers/plants*** 園藝花卉 / 植物 ◇ *out in the garden* 在戶外的花園裏 ◇ *a rose garden* (= where only roses are grown) 玫瑰園

G

➲ see also KITCHEN GARDEN, MARKET GARDEN, ROCK GARDEN, ROOF GARDEN **2** [C] (*NAmE*) an area in a yard where you grow flowers or plants 庭園；園子 **3** [C] (usually **gardens**) a public park 公園：*the botanical gardens in Edinburgh* 愛丁堡的植物園 ➲ see also ZOOLOGICAL GARDEN **4 gardens** [sing.] (*abbr.* **Gdns**) (*BrE*) used in the name of streets（用於街名）園，街，廣場：*39 Belvoir Gardens* 貝爾沃街 39 號

IDM **everything in the garden is 'rosy** (*BrE, saying*) everything is fine 一切都好；事事如意 ➲ more at COMMON *adj.*, LEAD[1] *v.*

■ *verb* [I] to work in a garden 做園藝工作；種植花木 ▸ **gar·den·er** /ˈɡɑːdnə(r); *NAmE* ˈɡɑːrd-/ *noun*：*My wife's a keen gardener.* 我的妻子是個熱衷園藝的人。◇ *We employ a gardener two days a week.* 我們雇了個花匠，每週工作兩天。 **gar·den·ing** /ˈɡɑːdnɪŋ; *NAmE* ˈɡɑːrd-/ *noun* [U]：*organic gardening* 有機種植花木 ◇ *gardening gloves* 園藝用手套 ◇ *a gardening programme on TV* 電視上的園藝節目 ➲ VISUAL VOCAB page V41

ˈgarden centre *noun* (*BrE*) a place that sells plants, seeds, garden equipment, etc. 園藝品店

ˌgarden ˈcity, ˌgarden ˈsuburb *nouns* (*BrE*) a city or part of a city that has been specially designed to have a lot of open spaces, parks and trees 花園城市（園林化都市或市區）

ˈgarden egg *noun* [C, U] (*WAfrE*) a type of AUBERGINE/EGGPLANT with purple, white or greenish-yellow skin 彩茄；觀賞茄子

gar·denia /ɡɑːˈdiːniə; *NAmE* ɡɑːrˈd-/ *noun* a bush with shiny leaves and large white or yellow flowers with a sweet smell, also called gardenias 梔子

ˈgardening leave *noun* [U] (*BrE*) a period during which sb does not work but remains employed by a company in order to prevent them working for another company 園藝假（離職後繼續受薪但不用上班，以免受雇於另一公司的一段時期）：*She handed in her resignation and was put on three months' gardening leave.* 她遞了辭呈，但要休三個月的園藝假。

the ˌGarden of ˈEden *noun* [sing.] = EDEN

ˈgarden party *noun* a formal social event that takes place in the afternoon in a large garden 遊園會，園遊會（下午在大花園舉行）

ˌgarden ˈsalad [U, C] (*NAmE*) a salad containing a variety of raw vegetables, especially LETTUCE 田園色拉（包括各種生食蔬菜，特別是生菜）

ˈgarden-variety (*NAmE*) (*BrE* **ˌcommon or ˈgarden**) *adj.* [only before noun] ordinary; with no special features 普通的；平常的；一般的：*He is not one of your garden-variety criminals.* 他不是個普通的罪犯。

gar·gan·tuan /ɡɑːˈɡæntʃuən; *NAmE* ɡɑːrˈɡ-/ *adj.* [usually before noun] extremely large 巨大的；龐大的 SYN **enormous**：*a gargantuan appetite/meal* 食慾極佳；豐盛的大餐

gar·gle /ˈɡɑːɡl; *NAmE* ˈɡɑːrɡl/ *verb, noun*

■ *verb* [I] ~ (**with sth**) to wash inside your mouth and throat by moving a liquid around at the back of your throat and then SPITTING it out 含漱；漱喉

■ *noun* **1** [C, U] a liquid used for gargling（含）漱液：*an antiseptic gargle* 消毒含漱液 **2** [sing.] an act of gargling or a sound like that made when gargling 含漱；漱口；含漱聲：*to have a gargle with salt water* 用鹽水含漱

gar·goyle /ˈɡɑːɡɔɪl; *NAmE* ˈɡɑːrɡ-/ *noun* an ugly figure of a person or an animal that is made of stone and through which water is carried away from the roof of a building, especially a church（建築物，尤指教堂頂上石頭怪人或怪獸狀的）滴水嘴；滴水獸 ➲ VISUAL VOCAB page V14

gar·ish /ˈɡeərɪʃ; *NAmE* ˈɡerɪʃ/ *adj.* very brightly coloured in an unpleasant way 俗豔的；花哨的；炫目的 SYN **gaudy**：*garish clothes/colours* 花裏胡哨的衣服；過於豔麗的色彩 ▸ **gar·ish·ly** *adv.*：*garishly decorated/lit/painted* 裝飾得花裏胡哨；照得燈火輝煌；油漆得過於鮮豔

gar·land /ˈɡɑːlənd; *NAmE* ˈɡɑːrl-/ *noun, verb*

■ *noun* a circle of flowers and leaves that is worn on the head or around the neck or is hung in a room as decoration 花環；花冠；環狀花飾

■ *verb* [usually passive] ~ **sb/sth** (*literary*) to decorate sb/sth with a garland or garlands 用花環裝飾；給…飾以花環（或戴上花冠）

gar·lic /ˈɡɑːlɪk; *NAmE* ˈɡɑːrlɪk/ *noun* [U] a vegetable of the onion family with a very strong taste and smell, used in cooking to give flavour to food 蒜；大蒜：*a clove of garlic* (= one section of it) 一瓣蒜 ➲ VISUAL VOCAB page V31 ▸ **gar·licky** *adj.*：*garlicky breath/food* 帶大蒜味的氣息；加有大蒜的食物

ˌgarlic ˈbread *noun* [U] bread, usually in the shape of a stick, containing melted butter and garlic 蒜蓉麪包

gar·ment /ˈɡɑːmənt; *NAmE* ˈɡɑːrm-/ *noun* (*formal*) a piece of clothing（一件）衣服：*a strange shapeless garment that had once been a jacket* 用夾克衫改成的不成形的一件怪衣服 ◇ *woollen/winter/outer garments* 毛衣；冬裝；外衣 ➲ SYNONYMS at CLOTHES ➲ see also UNDERGARMENT

gar·ner /ˈɡɑːnə(r); *NAmE* ˈɡɑːrn-/ *verb* ~ **sth** (*formal*) to obtain or collect sth such as information, support, etc. 獲得，得到，收集（信息、支持等）SYN **gather, acquire**

gar·net /ˈɡɑːnɪt; *NAmE* ˈɡɑːrn-/ *noun* a clear dark red SEMI-PRECIOUS STONE that is fairly valuable 石榴子石

gar·nish /ˈɡɑːnɪʃ; *NAmE* ˈɡɑːrnɪʃ/ *verb, noun*

■ *verb* ~ **sth** (**with sth**) to decorate a dish of food with a small amount of another food（用菜）為（食物）加裝飾；加飾菜於 ➲ COLLOCATIONS at COOKING

■ *noun* [C, U] a small amount of food that is used to decorate a larger dish of food（食物上的）裝飾菜

gar·otte (*BrE*) = GARROTTE

gar·ret /ˈɡærət/ *noun* a room, often a small dark unpleasant one, at the top of a house, especially in the roof 閣樓；頂樓小屋 ➲ compare ATTIC ➲ see also LOFT *n.* (1)

gar·rison /ˈɡærɪsn/ *noun, verb*

■ *noun* [C+sing./pl. v.] a group of soldiers living in a town or FORT to defend it; the buildings these soldiers live in 衞戍部隊；守備部隊；衞戍區；駐防地：*a garrison of 5 000 troops* 有 5 000 士兵駐守的防地 ◇ *a garrison town* 有駐防的城鎮 ◇ *Half the garrison is/are on duty.* 衞戍部隊有半數人在執勤。

■ *verb* to put soldiers in a place in order to defend it from attack 駐防；派（兵）駐守：~ **sth** *Two regiments were sent to garrison the town.* 派了兩個團駐守在那個城鎮。◇ ~ **sb + adv./prep.** *100 soldiers were garrisoned in the town.* 派了 100 名士兵在城裏駐防。

gar·rotte (*BrE* also **gar·otte**) (*US* also **gar·rote**) /ɡəˈrɒt; *NAmE* ɡəˈrɑːt/ *verb, noun*

■ *verb* ~ **sb** to kill sb by putting a piece of wire, etc. around their neck and pulling it tight（用金屬絲等）勒死，絞殺，扼殺

■ *noun* a piece of wire, etc. used for garrotting sb 用於絞殺的金屬絲（或繩索等）；絞刑刑具

gar·ru·lous /ˈɡærələs; *BrE* also -rjʊl-/ *adj.* talking a lot, especially about unimportant things（尤指在瑣事上）饒舌的，嘮叨的，喋喋不休的 SYN **talkative** ▸ **gar·rul·ous·ly** *adv.*

gar·ter /ˈɡɑːtə(r); *NAmE* ˈɡɑːrt-/ *noun* **1** a band, usually made of ELASTIC, that is worn around the leg to keep up a sock or STOCKING（通常為彈性的）襪帶 **2** (*NAmE*) (*BrE* **sus·pend·er**) a short circle of ELASTIC for holding up a sock or STOCKING 吊襪帶 IDM see GUT *n.*

ˈgarter belt (*NAmE*) (*BrE* **susˈpender belt**) *noun* a piece of women's underwear like a belt, worn around the waist, used for holding STOCKINGS up（女用）吊襪腰帶

ˈgarter snake *noun* a harmless American snake with coloured lines along its back 襪帶蛇（見於美洲，無害）

gas /ɡæs/ *noun, verb*

■ *noun* (*pl.* **gases** *or less frequent* **gas·ses**)

▸ NOT SOLID/LIQUID 非固體／液體 **1** [C, U] any substance like air that is neither a solid nor a liquid, for example HYDROGEN and OXYGEN are both gases 氣體：*Air is a* mixture of gases. 空氣為混合氣體。◇ *CFC gases* 含氯氟烴氣體 ◇ *a **gas bottle/cylinder*** (= for storing gas) 氣瓶／罐 ➲ see also GREENHOUSE GAS **2** 0┳ [U] a particular type of gas or mixture of gases used as fuel for heating and cooking 氣體燃料；煤氣；天然氣：*a gas cooker/fire/furnace/oven/ring/stove* 煤氣灶；煤氣取暖器；煤氣鍋爐；煤氣烤箱；煤氣灶火圈；煤氣爐 ◇ *a gas explosion/leak* 氣體爆炸；煤氣泄漏 ◇ *gas central heating* 燃氣中央供暖系統 ◇ (*BrE*) *Preheat the oven to gas mark 5* (= a particular temperature of a gas oven) 把烤爐預熱至 5 擋。➲ see also CALOR GAS, COAL GAS, NATURAL GAS **3** [U] a particular type of gas used during a medical operation, to make the patient sleep or to make the pain less（外科手術用）麻醉氣：*an anaesthetic gas* 麻醉氣體 ◇ *During the birth she was given gas and air.* 她分娩時醫生給她吸了麻醉氣。➲ see also LAUGHING GAS **4** [U] a particular type of gas used in war to kill or injure people, or used by the police to control people（戰爭用）毒氣；（警察用）瓦斯：*a gas attack* 毒氣攻擊 ➲ see also CS GAS, NERVE GAS, TEAR GAS

▸ IN VEHICLE 車輛 **5** 0┳ (also **gas·oline**) (both *NAmE*) (*BrE* **pet·rol**) [U] a liquid obtained from PETROLEUM, used as fuel in car engines, etc. 汽油：*a gas station* 加油站 ◇ *a gas pump* 加（汽）油泵 ◇ *to fill up the gas tank* 加滿油箱 **6 the gas** [sing.] (*especially NAmE*) = GAS PEDAL：***Step on the gas**, we're late.* 加大油門，我們要遲到了。

▸ FUN 樂趣 **7** [sing.] (*especially NAmE*) a person or an event that is fun 有趣的人（或事物）：*The party was a real gas.* 這次聚會真有趣。

▸ IN STOMACH 胃 **8** (*NAmE*) (*BrE* **wind**) [U] air that you swallow with food or drink; gas that is produced in your stomach or INTESTINES that makes you feel uncomfortable（隨食物或飲料）吞下的氣；胃氣；腸氣 **IDM** see COOK *v.*

■ *verb* (-ss-)

▸ KILL/HARM WITH GAS 用毒氣殺死／傷害 **1** [T] **~ sb/yourself** to kill or harm sb by making them breathe poisonous gas 用毒氣殺傷；使吸入毒氣

▸ TALK 談論 **2** [I] (usually used in the progressive tenses 通常用於進行時) (*old-fashioned, informal*) to talk for a long time about things that are not important 閒聊；空談；瞎扯 **SYN** chat

gas·bag /ˈɡæsbæɡ/ *noun* (*informal, humorous*) a person who talks a lot 夸夸其談的人；貧嘴子；聒噪的人

ˈgas chamber *noun* a room that can be filled with poisonous gas for killing animals or people 毒氣室（用於毒死動物或人）

ˈgas-cooled *adj.* [only before noun] using gas to keep the temperature cool 氣冷的；用氣體冷卻的：*gas-cooled nuclear reactors* 氣冷核反應堆

gas·eous /ˈɡæsiəs; ˈɡeɪsiəs/ *adj.* [usually before noun] like or containing gas 似氣體的；含氣體的：*a gaseous mixture* 氣體混合物 ◇ *in gaseous form* 處於氣態

ˌgas-ˈfired *adj.* [usually before noun] (*BrE*) using gas as a fuel 燃氣的；以煤氣為燃料的：*gas-fired central heating* 燃氣中央供暖系統

ˌgas ˈgiant *noun* (*astronomy* 天) a large planet made mostly of the gases HYDROGEN and HELIUM, for example Jupiter or Saturn 氣體巨星（主要由氫氣和氦氣構成，如木星或土星）

ˈgas guzzler (also **guz·zler**) *noun* (*informal, especially NAmE*) a car that needs a lot of petrol/gas 高油耗汽車；油老虎 ▸ **ˈgas-guzzling** *adj.* [only before noun]

gash /ɡæʃ/ *noun, verb*

■ *noun* **~ (in/on sth)** a long deep cut in the surface of sth, especially a person's skin 深長的切口（或傷口、劃傷）

■ *verb* **~ sth/sb** to make a long deep cut in sth, especially a person's skin 劃傷，砍傷（尤指人的皮膚）：*He gashed his hand on a sharp piece of rock.* 他的手在一塊尖石頭上劃了一個大口子。

gas·hold·er /ˈɡæshəʊldə(r); *NAmE* -hoʊl-/ *noun* = GASOMETER

gas·ket /ˈɡæskɪt/ *noun* a flat piece of rubber, etc. placed between two metal surfaces in a pipe or an engine to prevent steam, gas or oil from escaping 墊圈；襯墊；密封墊：*The engine had **blown a gasket*** (= had allowed steam, etc. to escape). 發動機的密封圈漏氣了。◇ (*figurative, informal*) *He **blew a gasket** at the news* (= became very angry). 他聽到這消息勃然大怒。

ˈgas lamp (also **gas·light**) *noun* a lamp in the street or in a house, that produces light from burning gas 煤氣燈

gas·light /ˈɡæslaɪt/ *noun* **1** [U] light produced from burning gas 煤氣燈光：*In the gaslight she looked paler than ever.* 在煤氣燈光下她顯得比以往任何時候都蒼白。**2** [C] = GAS LAMP

gas·man /ˈɡæsmæn/ *noun* (*pl.* **-men** /-men/) (*informal*) a man whose job is to visit people's houses to see how much gas they have used, or to fit and check gas equipment 煤氣抄表員；煤氣收費員；煤氣設備安裝（或檢修）工

ˈgas mantle *noun* = MANTLE *n.* (4)

ˈgas mask *noun* a piece of equipment worn over the face as protection against poisonous gas 防毒面具

gaso·hol /ˈɡæsəhɒl; *NAmE* -hɔːl; -hɑːl/ *noun* [U] (*NAmE*) a mixture of petrol/gas and alcohol which can be used in cars（汽車用）汽油和酒精混合燃料

ˈgas oil *noun* [U] a type of oil obtained from PETROLEUM which is used as a fuel 粗柴油；瓦斯油

gas·oline 0┳ (also **gas·olene**) /ˈɡæsəliːn/ *noun* [U] (*NAmE*) = GAS (5)：*I **fill up** the tank **with gasoline** about once a week.* 我大約一個星期加滿一箱汽油。◇ ***leaded/unleaded gasoline*** 含鉛／無鉛汽油

gas·om·eter /ɡæˈsɒmɪtə(r); *NAmE* -ˈsɑːm-/ (also **gas·hold·er**) *noun* a very large round container or building in which gas is stored and from which it is sent through pipes to other buildings（大型）貯燃氣罐，貯氣庫

gasp /ɡɑːsp; *NAmE* ɡæsp/ *verb, noun*

■ *verb* **1** [I, T] to take a quick deep breath with your mouth open, especially because you are surprised or in pain（尤指由於驚訝或疼痛而）喘氣，喘息，倒抽氣：**~ (at sth)** *She gasped at the wonderful view.* 如此美景使她驚訝得屏住了呼吸。◇ *They gasped in astonishment at the news.* 他們聽到這消息驚訝得倒抽了一口氣。◇ **+ speech** *'What was that noise?' he gasped.* "那是什麼聲音？"他喘着氣問。**2** [I, T] to have difficulty breathing or speaking 透不過氣；氣喘吁吁地說：**~ (for sth)** *He came to the surface of the water gasping for air.* 他浮出水面急促地喘着氣。◇ **~ (sth) (out)** *She managed to gasp out her name.* 她終於氣喘吁吁地說出了她的名字。◇ **+ speech** *'Can't breathe,' he gasped.* "透不過氣來了。"他氣喘吁吁地說。**3 be gasping (for sth)** [I] (*BrE, informal*) to want or need sth very badly, especially a drink or a cigarette 渴望，很想要（尤指飲料或香煙）

■ *noun* a quick deep breath, usually caused by a strong emotion（常指由強烈情感引起的）深吸氣，喘息，倒抽氣：*to give a **gasp of horror/surprise/relief*** 驚恐得／吃驚得倒抽一口氣；如釋重負地鬆一口氣 ◇ *His breath came in short gasps.* 他急促地喘着氣。**IDM** see LAST[1] *det.*

ˈgas pedal (*especially NAmE*) (*BrE* also **ac·cel·er·ator**) *noun* the PEDAL in a car or other vehicle that you press with your foot to control the speed of the engine（汽車等的）加速裝置，油門踏板 ➲ VISUAL VOCAB page V52

ˌgas-ˈpermeable *adj.* allowing gases to pass through 透氣的：*gas-permeable contact lenses* 透氣隱形眼鏡

ˈgas ring *noun* (*especially BrE*) a round piece of metal with holes in it on the top of a gas cooker/stove, where the gas is lit to produce the flame for cooking 煤氣灶火圈 ➲ picture at RING[1] ➲ VISUAL VOCAB page V25

ˈgas station (*NAmE*) (*BrE* **ˈpetrol station**) (also **ˈfilling station**, **ˈservice station** *NAmE, BrE*) *noun* a place at the side of a road where you take your car to buy petrol/gas, oil, etc. 汽車加油站

gassy /ˈɡæsi/ *adj.* **1** (*BrE*) (of drinks 飲料) containing too much gas in the form of bubbles 充滿氣泡的 **2** (*NAmE*) (of people 人) having a lot of gas in your stomach, etc.（腸胃）脹氣的

gas·tric /ˈɡæstrɪk/ *adj.* [only before noun] (*medical* 醫) connected with the stomach 胃的；胃部的：*a gastric*

G

ulcer 胃潰瘍 ◇ *gastric juices* (= the acids in your stomach that help you to DIGEST food) 胃液（有助於消化的胃酸）

ˌgastric ˈflu *noun* [U] an illness affecting the stomach, which does not last long and is thought to be caused by a virus 胃流感（一種被認為是由病毒引起的短期胃病）

gas·tri·tis /gæˈstraɪtɪs/ *noun* [U] (*medical* 醫) an illness in which the inside of the stomach becomes swollen and painful 胃炎

gastro·enter·itis /ˌgæstrəʊˌentəˈraɪtɪs; *NAmE* ˌgæstroʊ-/ *noun* [U] (*medical* 醫) an illness of the stomach and other food passages that causes DIARRHOEA and VOMITING 胃腸炎；腸胃炎

gas·tro·intest·inal /ˌgæstrəʊɪnˈtestɪnl; *NAmE* -roʊ-; *BrE* also ˌgæstrəʊɪnteˈstaɪnl/ *adj.* (*medical* 醫) of or related to the stomach and INTESTINES 胃腸的

G

gas·tro·nom·ic /ˌgæstrəˈnɒmɪk; *NAmE* -ˈnɑːm-/ *adj.* [only before noun] connected with cooking and eating good food 烹飪的；美食的 ▸ **gas·tro·nom·ic·al·ly** /-kli/ *adv.*

gas·tron·omy /gæˈstrɒnəmi; *NAmE* -ˈstrɑːn-/ *noun* [U] (*formal*) the art and practice of cooking and eating good food 烹飪法；美食學

gas·tro·pod /ˈgæstrəpɒd; *NAmE* -pɑːd/ *noun* (*biology* 生) a MOLLUSC such as a SNAIL or SLUG, that moves on one large foot 腹足類；腹足綱軟體動物 ➲ VISUAL VOCAB page V13

gas·tro·pub /ˈgæstrəʊpʌb; *NAmE* -troʊ-/ *noun* (*BrE*) a pub which is well known for serving good food 美食酒吧

gas·works /ˈgæswɜːks; *NAmE* -wɜːrks/ *noun* (*pl.* **gas·works**) [C+sing./pl. v.] a factory where gas for lighting and heating is made from coal 煤氣廠

gate 🔑 /geɪt/ *noun*

1 🔑 [C] a barrier like a door that is used to close an opening in a fence or a wall outside a building 大門；柵欄門；圍牆門：*an iron gate* 鐵門 ◇ *He pushed open the garden gate.* 他推開了花園的門。◇ *A crowd gathered at the factory gates.* 一群人聚集在工廠的大門口。◇ *the gates of the city* 城門 ➲ VISUAL VOCAB page V19 ➲ see also LYCHGATE, STARTING GATE **2** 🔑 [C] an opening that can be closed by a gate or gates 大門口：*We drove through the palace gates.* 我們驅車駛過重重宮門。 **3** [C] a barrier that is used to control the flow of water on a river or CANAL 閘門；閥門：*a lock/sluice gate* 船閘閘門；水閘 **4** 🔑 [C] a way out of an airport through which passengers go to get on their plane 登機門；登機口：*BA flight 726 to Paris is now boarding at gate 16.* 飛往巴黎的英航 726 號班機在 16 號門登機。 **5** [C] the number of people who attend a sports event（體育比賽的）觀眾人數：*Tonight's game has attracted the largest gate of the season.* 今晚比賽吸引的觀眾人數創本賽季之最。 **6** (also **ˈgate money**) [U] the amount of money made by selling tickets for a sports event（體育比賽的）門票收入：*Today's gate will be given to charity.* 今天的門票收入將捐獻給慈善事業。 **7 -gate** (forming nouns from the names of people or places; used especially in newspapers 與人名或地名構成名詞，尤用於報刊) a political SCANDAL connected with the person or place mentioned（與所提到的人或地方有關的）政治醜聞 ORIGIN From **Watergate**, the scandal in the United States that brought about the resignation of President Nixon in 1974. 源自美國的"水門事件"（Watergate），此醜聞導致 1974 年尼克松總統辭職。 **8** (*computing* 計) = LOGIC GATE

gat·eau /ˈgætəʊ; *NAmE* gæˈtoʊ/ *noun* [C, U] (*pl.* **gat·eaux** /ˈgætəʊ; *NAmE* gæˈtoʊ/) a large cake filled with cream and usually decorated with fruit, nuts, etc. 奶油水果大蛋糕：*a strawberry gateau* 草莓奶油大蛋糕 ◇ *Is there any gateau left?* 奶油水果大蛋糕有剩的嗎？

gate·crash /ˈgeɪtkræʃ/ (also *informal* **crash**) *verb* [T, I] **~ (sth)** to go to a party or social event without being invited 未獲邀請而參加（或出席）；做（聚會等的）不速之客 ▸ **gate·crash·er** *noun*

gated /ˈgeɪtɪd/ *adj.* [usually before noun] (of a road 道路) having gates that need to be opened and closed by drivers 有門的

ˌgated comˈmunity *noun* a group of houses surrounded by a wall or fence, with an entrance that is guarded 住宅小區（四周有圍牆或柵欄，入口有門衛）

gate·fold /ˈgeɪtfəʊld; *NAmE* -foʊld/ *noun* a large page folded to fit a book or magazine that can be opened out for reading（書籍、雜誌的）大張摺疊插頁，大摺頁

gate·house /ˈgeɪthaʊs/ *noun* a house built at or over a gate, for example at the entrance to a park or castle 門房；門樓

gate·keep·er /ˈgeɪtkiːpə(r)/ *noun* **1** a person whose job is to check and control who is allowed to go through a gate 看門人；守門人；門衛 **2** a person, system, etc. that decides whether sb/sth will be allowed, or allowed to reach a particular place or person 看門人；把關系統：*His secretary acts as a gatekeeper, reading all mail before it reaches her boss.* 老闆的秘書負責把關，所有郵件都由她先過目再呈送給老闆。

gate·leg table /ˌgeɪtleg ˈteɪbl/ *noun* a table with extra sections that can be folded out to make it larger, supported on legs that swing out from the centre 摺疊活腿桌；摺疊桌

ˈgate money *noun* [U] = GATE (6)

gate·post /ˈgeɪtpəʊst; *NAmE* -poʊst/ *noun* a post to which a gate is attached or against which it is closed 門柱

IDM **between you, me and the ˈgatepost** (*BrE*, *informal*) used to show that what you are going to say next is a secret（引出秘密）你我私下說，別對外人講

gate·way /ˈgeɪtweɪ/ *noun* **1** an opening in a wall or fence that can be closed by a gate 大門口；門道；出入口：*They turned through the gateway on the left.* 他們穿過出入口向左轉去。 **2** [usually sing.] **~ to/into …** a place through which you can go to reach another larger place（通往其他地區的）門戶：*Perth, the gateway to Western Australia* 珀斯——通向西澳大利亞的門戶 **3** [usually sing.] **~ to sth** a means of getting or achieving sth 途徑；方法；手段：*A good education is the gateway to success.* 良好的教育是通往成功之路。 **4** (*computing* 計) a device that connects two computer networks that cannot be connected in any other way 網關；網間連接器

gather 🔑 /ˈgæðə(r)/ *verb*

▸ COME/BRING TOGETHER 聚集；集合 **1** 🔑 [I, T] to come together, or bring people together, in one place to form a group 聚集；集合；召集：*A crowd soon gathered.* 很快就聚集起了一群人。◇ **+ adv./prep.** *His supporters gathered in the main square.* 他的支持者聚集在主廣場上。◇ *Can you all **gather round**? I've got something to tell you.* 你們都圍過來好嗎？我有事要告訴你們。◇ *The whole family **gathered together** at Ray's home.* 全家人聚集在雷的家中。◇ **be gathered + adv./prep.** *They were all **gathered round** the TV.* 他們都圍到電視機旁。◇ *A large crowd was gathered outside the studio.* 召集了一大群人在製片廠外面。◇ *The kids were **gathered together** in one room.* 孩子們被聚集在一個房間裏。 **2** 🔑 [T] to bring things together that have been spread around 收攏，歸攏（分散的東西）：**~ sth** *People slowly gathered their belongings and left the hall.* 人們慢慢地收起他們的隨身物離開了大廳。◇ **~ sth together/up** *I waited while he gathered up his papers.* 他整理文件時我就在一旁等待。 ➲ SYNONYMS at COLLECT

▸ COLLECT 收集 **3** 🔑 [T] **~ sth** to collect information from different sources 搜集，收集（情報）：*Detectives have spent months gathering evidence.* 偵探們花了數月時間搜集證據。 ➲ SYNONYMS at COLLECT **4** 🔑 [T] **~ sth** to collect plants, fruit, etc. from a wide area 採集（植物、水果等）：*to gather wild flowers* 採集野花

▸ CROPS/HARVEST 莊稼；收成 **5** [T] **~ sth (in)** (*formal* or *literary*) to pick or cut and collect crops to be stored 收割；收穫：*It was late August and the harvest had been safely gathered in.* 已是八月下旬，莊稼都妥善收割完畢。

▸ BELIEVE/UNDERSTAND 相信；理解 **6** [T, I] (not used in the progressive tenses 不用於進行時) to believe or understand that sth is true because of information or evidence you have 認為；猜想；推斷；理解：**~ (that)** … *I gather (that) you wanted to see me.* 我猜想你想要見我。◇ *I gather from your letter that you're not enjoying your job.* 我從信中瞭解到你並不喜歡你的工作。◇ **~ (sth)** *'There's been a delay.' 'I gathered that.'* "已經耽擱了。" "那是我預料中的事。" ◇ *'She won't be coming.' 'So I gather.'* "她不會來了。" "我也這麼認為。" ◇ *You're self-employed, I gather.* 我想你是個體經營吧。◇ ***As far as I can gather****, he got involved in a fight.* 據我瞭解，他捲入了一場爭鬥之中。◇ ***From what I can gather****, there's been some kind of problem.* 從我瞭解的情況看還存在某種問題。

▸ INCREASE 增加 **7** [T] **~ sth** to increase in speed, force, etc. 增加（速度、力量等）：*The truck* ***gathered speed****.* 卡車加快了速度。◇ *During the 1980s the green movement* ***gathered momentum****.* * 20 世紀 80 年代期間綠色運動的勢頭開始增強。◇ *Thousands of these machines are* ***gathering dust*** (= not being used) *in stockrooms.* 數千台這樣的機器都塵封在倉庫裏。

▸ OF CLOUDS/DARKNESS 雲層；黑暗 **8** [I] to gradually increase in number or amount 逐漸增加；積聚：*The storm clouds were gathering.* 暴風雨烏雲正在聚集。◇ *the gathering gloom of a winter's afternoon* 天色越來越暗的一個冬日下午

▸ CLOTHING 衣服 **9** [T] to pull a piece of clothing tighter to your body 收緊，攏起（衣服）：**~ sth around you/sth** *He gathered his cloak around him.* 他用披風把身子裹緊。◇ **~ sth up** *She gathered up her skirts and ran.* 她提起裙襬就跑。 **10** [T] **~ sth (in)** to pull parts of a piece of clothing together in folds and sew them in place 給…打褶子：*She wore a skirt gathered (in) at the waist.* 她穿了一條腰部打褶的裙子。

▸ HOLD SB 拉住某人 **11** [T] **~ sb + adv./prep.** to pull sb towards you and put your arms around them 拉近；擁抱：*She gathered the child in her arms and held him close.* 她把孩子拉過來緊緊抱在懷裏。◇ *He gathered her to him.* 他把她拉到身邊。

▸ PREPARE YOURSELF 做好準備 **12** [T] **~ sth/yourself** to prepare yourself to do sth that requires effort 攢（勁）；使做好準備：*I sat down for a moment to gather my strength.* 我坐下片刻積蓄力量。◇ *She was still trying to gather her thoughts together when the door opened.* 門打開時她還努力讓自己集中精神。◇ *Fortunately the short delay gave him time to gather himself.* 幸運的是這短暫的拖延給了他喘息的時間。 IDM see ROLL *v.*

gath·er·er /ˈɡæðərə(r)/ *noun* a person who collects sth 收集者；採集者：*prehistoric hunters and gatherers* 史前的狩獵者和採集者

gath·er·ing /ˈɡæðərɪŋ/ *noun* **1** [C] a meeting of people for a particular purpose 聚集；聚會；集會：*a* ***social/family gathering*** 社交 / 家庭聚會 ◇ *a gathering of religious leaders* 宗教領袖的集會 **2** [U] the process of collecting sth 收集；採集；搜集：*methods of information gathering* 信息採集的各種方法

gathers /ˈɡæðəz; *NAmE* ˈɡæðərz/ *noun* [pl.] small folds that are sewn into a piece of clothing 皺襉；褶襉

ga·tor /ˈɡeɪtə(r)/ *noun* (*NAmE, informal*) = ALLIGATOR

GATT /ɡæt/ *noun* the General Agreement on Tariffs and Trade (in the past, an international organization that tried to encourage international trade and reduce taxes on imports; the agreement by which this organization was created. GATT was replaced by the WTO in 1994.) 關稅及貿易總協定組織（1994 年由世貿組織取代）；關稅及貿易總協定

gauche /ɡəʊʃ; *NAmE* ɡoʊʃ/ *adj.* awkward when dealing with people and often saying or doing the wrong thing 笨拙的；不善社交的；不老練的：*a gauche schoolgirl/manner* 不善社交的女生；笨拙的舉止 ▸ **gauche·ness** (also **gauch·erie** /ˈɡəʊʃəri; *NAmE* ˌɡoʊʃəˈriː/) *noun* [U]：*the gaucheness of youth* 青年人的不老練

gau·cho /ˈɡaʊtʃəʊ; *NAmE* -tʃoʊ/ *noun* (*pl.* **-os**) a S American COWBOY 南美牛仔

gaudy /ˈɡɔːdi/ *adj.* (**gaud·ier**, **gaudi·est**) (*disapproving*) too brightly coloured in a way that lacks taste 俗豔的；花哨的 SYN garish：*gaudy clothes/colours* 過於花哨的衣服 / 色彩 ▸ **gaud·ily** /ˈɡɔːdɪli/ *adv.*：*gaudily dressed/painted* 穿着 / 塗飾得太俗豔 **gaudi·ness** /ˈɡɔːdinəs/ *noun* [U]

gauge (*US* also **gage**) /ɡeɪdʒ/ *noun, verb*

■ ***noun*** **1** (often in compounds 常構成複合詞) an instrument for measuring the amount or level of sth 測量儀器（或儀表）；計量器：*a* ***fuel/petrol/temperature, etc.*** *gauge* 燃料表、汽油量表、溫度計等 ➲ VISUAL VOCAB page V52 **2** a measurement of the width or thickness of sth 寬度；厚度：*What gauge of wire do we need?* 我們需要多大直徑的金屬絲？ **3** (also **bore** especially in *BrE*) a measurement of the width of the BARREL of a gun（槍管的）口徑，碼：*a 12-gauge shotgun* * 12 號獵槍 **4** the distance between the rails of a railway/railroad track or the wheels of a train（鐵道的）軌距；（火車的）輪距：***standard gauge*** (= 56½ inches in Britain) 標準軌距（在英國為 56.5 英寸）◇ *a* ***narrow gauge*** (= narrower than standard) *railway* 窄軌鐵路 **5** [usually sing.] **~ (of sth)** a fact or an event that can be used to estimate or judge sth（用於估計或判斷的）事實，依據，尺度，標準：*Tomorrow's game against Arsenal will be a good gauge of their promotion chances.* 明天與阿森納隊的比賽是衡量他們能否升級的很好依據。

■ ***verb*** **1** to make a judgement about sth, especially people's feelings or attitudes 判定，判斷（尤指人的感情或態度）：**~ sth** *They interviewed employees to gauge their reaction to the changes.* 他們與雇員面談以判定他們的應變能力。◇ *He tried to gauge her mood.* 他試圖揣摩她的心情。◇ **~ whether, how, etc. …** *It was difficult to gauge whether she was angry or not.* 很難判斷她是否在生氣。**2 ~ sth** to measure sth accurately using a special instrument（用儀器）測量：*precision instruments that can gauge the diameter to a fraction of a millimetre* 可測出直徑為若干分之一毫米的精密儀器 **3 ~ sth | ~ how, what, etc. …** to calculate sth approximately 估計；估算：*We were able to gauge the strength of the wind from the movement of the trees.* 我們可根據樹的搖動估計風力。

gaunt /ɡɔːnt/ *adj.* **1** (of a person 人) very thin, usually because of illness, not having enough food, or worry 瘦削憔悴的（常因疾病、飢餓或憂慮）：*a gaunt face* 憔悴的面容 **2** (of a building 建築物) not attractive and without any decoration 寒磣的；破敗的 ▸ **gaunt·ness** *noun* [U]

gaunt·let /ˈɡɔːntlət/ *noun* **1** a metal glove worn as part of a suit of ARMOUR by soldiers in the Middle Ages（中世紀武士鎧甲的）金屬手套，鐵手套 **2** a strong glove with a wide covering for the wrist, used for example when driving（駕駛等用的）長手套，防護手套：*motorcyclists with leather gauntlets* 戴着皮護手套的摩托車手

IDM **run the ˈgauntlet** to be criticized or attacked by a lot of people, especially a group of people that you have to walk through 受嚴厲譴責；受夾道攻擊：*Some of the witnesses had to run the gauntlet of television cameras and reporters.* 一些目擊者不得不在眾多電視攝像機和記者的圍堵下穿行。 ORIGIN This phrase refers to an old army punishment where a man was forced to run between two lines of soldiers hitting him. 此短語源自古老的軍中懲罰，受罰者從兩排夾擊他的士兵中間跑過。 **take up the ˈgauntlet** to accept sb's invitation to fight or compete 接受挑戰；應戰 ORIGIN In the Middle Ages a knight threw his gauntlet at the feet of another knight as a challenge to fight. If he accepted the challenge, the other knight would pick up the glove. 在中世紀，一個騎士把鐵手套扔在另一個騎士的腳下，以示挑戰。如果對方接受挑戰，就會撿起鐵手套。 **throw down the ˈgauntlet** to invite sb to fight or compete with you 發出挑戰

gauze /ɡɔːz/ *noun* **1** [U] a type of light transparent cloth, usually made of cotton or silk 薄紗，紗羅（通常由棉或絲織成） **2** [U] a type of thin cotton cloth used for covering and protecting wounds 紗布（包紮傷口用）：*a gauze dressing* 紗布敷料 **3** [U, C] material made of a network of wire; a piece of this（金屬絲製的）網紗，網：*wire gauze* 金屬網紗 ➲ VISUAL VOCAB page V70 ▸ **gauzy** *adj.* [usually before noun]：*a gauzy material* 薄紗料

gave *past tense of* GIVE

gavel /ˈɡævl/ *noun* a small hammer used by a person in charge of a meeting or an AUCTION, or by a judge in court, in order to get people's attention（會議主席、拍賣商或法官用的）小槌

ga·vial /ˈɡeɪviəl/ *noun* = GHARIAL

ga·votte /ɡəˈvɒt; *NAmE* ɡəˈvɑːt/ *noun* a French dance that was popular in the past; a piece of music for this dance 加沃特舞，加沃特舞曲（舊時流行於法國）

Gawd /ɡɔːd/ *noun, exclamation* (*informal*) used in written English to show that the word 'God' is being pronounced in a particular way to express surprise, anger or fear（書面語中代表發音特別的 God，表示吃驚、氣憤或恐懼）上帝，老天爺：*For Gawd's sake hurry up!* 看在上帝的分上快點吧！

G

gawk /ɡɔːk/ *verb* [I] **~ (at sb/sth)** (*informal*) to stare at sb/sth in a rude or stupid way 無禮地瞪眼看；呆頭呆腦地盯着 SYN **gape**

gawky /ˈɡɔːki/ *adj.* (especially of a tall young person 尤指高個子的年輕人) awkward in the way they move or behave 笨拙的；笨手笨腳的 ▸ **gawk·ily** /ˈɡɔːkɪli/ *adv.* **gawki·ness** /ˈɡɔːkinəs/ *noun* [U]

gawp /ɡɔːp/ *verb* [I] **~ (at sb/sth)** (*BrE, informal*) to stare at sb/sth in a rude or stupid way 無禮地瞪眼看；呆頭呆腦地盯着 SYN **gape**

gay /ɡeɪ/ *adj., noun*

▪ *adj.* **1** (of people, especially men 人，尤指男性) sexually attracted to people of the same sex 同性戀的 SYN **homosexual**：*gay men* 同性戀的男人 ◇ *I didn't know he was gay.* 我不知道他是同性戀者。◇ *Is she gay?* 她是同性戀者嗎？ OPP **straight** **2** [only before noun] connected with people who are gay 與同性戀者有關的：*a gay club/bar* 同性戀者俱樂部／酒吧 ◇ *the lesbian and gay community* 男女同性戀者群落 **3** [not before noun] (*slang, disapproving*, sometimes *offensive*) (used especially by young people 尤為年輕人用語) boring and not fashionable or attractive 無聊的；不時尚的；沒吸引力的：*She didn't like the ringtone—said it was gay.* 她不喜歡那個手機鈴聲，說它不時尚。◇ *That is so gay!* 那太無聊了！ **4** (**gayer, gayest**) (*old-fashioned*) happy and full of fun 愉快的；快樂的；充滿樂趣的：*gay laughter* 歡快的笑聲 **5** (*old-fashioned*) brightly coloured 鮮豔的；豔麗的：*The garden was gay with red geraniums.* 花園裏紅色的天竺葵花色彩豔麗。➲ see also GAIETY, GAILY

IDM **with ˈgay abandon** without thinking about the results or effects of a particular action 不考慮後果；輕率

▪ *noun* a person who is HOMOSEXUAL, especially a man 同性戀者（尤指男性）

gay·dar /ˈɡeɪdɑː(r)/ *noun* [U] (*informal*) the ability that a HOMOSEXUAL person is supposed to have to recognize other people who are homosexual 同性戀雷達（同性戀者識別其他同性戀者的能力）

gay·ness /ˈɡeməs/ *noun* [U] the state of being HOMOSEXUAL 同性戀 ➲ compare GAIETY

ˌgay ˈpride *noun* [U] the feeling that HOMOSEXUAL people should not be ashamed of telling people that they are homosexual and should feel proud of themselves 同性戀者尊嚴

gaze /ɡeɪz/ *verb, noun*

▪ *verb* [I] **+ adv./prep.** to look steadily at sb/sth for a long time, either because you are very interested or surprised, or because you are thinking of sth else 凝視；注視；盯着 SYN **stare**：*She gazed at him in amazement.* 她驚異地注視着他。◇ *He sat for hours just **gazing into space**.* 他一連幾個小時坐在那裏茫然地看着前面。➲ SYNONYMS at STARE

▪ *noun* [usually sing.] a long steady look at sb/sth 凝視；注視：*He **met her gaze*** (= looked at her while she looked at him). 他與她凝視的目光相遇。◇ *She **dropped her gaze*** (= stopped looking). 她目光低垂，不再凝視。➲ SYNONYMS at LOOK

gazebo 觀景亭；涼亭

gaz·ebo /ɡəˈziːbəʊ; *NAmE* -boʊ/ *noun* (*pl.* **-os**) a small building with open sides in a garden/yard, especially one with a view 觀景亭；涼亭；眺台

gaz·elle /ɡəˈzel/ *noun* (*pl.* **gaz·elle** or **gaz·elles**) a small ANTELOPE 羚羊

gaz·ette /ɡəˈzet/ *noun* **1** an official newspaper published by a particular organization containing important information about decisions that have been made and people who have been employed（某一組織的）公報 **2** **Gazette** used in the titles of some newspapers（用於報刊名）報，報紙：*the Evening Gazette*《晚報》

gaz·et·teer /ˌɡæzəˈtɪə(r); *NAmE* -ˈtɪr/ *noun* a list of place names published as a book or at the end of a book 地名詞典；（書末的）地名索引

ga·zil·lion /ɡəˈzɪljən/ *noun* (*NAmE, informal*) a very large number 很大的數目：*gazillion-dollar houses* 高價房子 ◇ *gazillions of copies* 無數冊書

gaz·pa·cho /ɡæzˈpætʃəʊ; *NAmE* ɡəzˈpɑːtʃoʊ/ *noun* [U] a cold Spanish soup made with tomatoes, peppers, CUCUMBERS, etc. 西班牙冷菜湯（用番茄、青椒、黃瓜等製成）

gaz·ump /ɡəˈzʌmp/ *verb* [usually passive] **~ sb** (*BrE*) when sb who has made an offer to pay a particular price for a house and who has had this offer accepted is **gazumped**, their offer is no longer accepted by the person selling the house, because sb else has made a higher offer（房價議定後因有人出價更高而向買主）食言毀約 ▸ **gaz·ump·ing** /ɡəˈzʌmpɪŋ/ *noun* [U] ➲ compare GAZUNDER

gaz·un·der /ɡəˈzʌndə(r)/ *verb* [often passive] **~ sb** (*BrE*) to offer a lower price for a house that you have already agreed to buy at a higher price, before the contract is signed（簽合同前）壓低房價：*The vendors were gazundered at the last minute.* 賣主在最後一刻被要求降低房價。▸ **gaz·un·der·ing** *noun* [U] ➲ compare GAZUMP

GB *abbr.* **1** /ˌdʒiː ˈbiː/ Great Britain 大不列顛 **2** (in writing 書寫形式) GIGABYTE：*a 750GB hard drive* * 750 千兆字節的硬盤

Gb (also **Gbit**) *abbr.* (in writing 書寫形式) GIGABIT

GBH /ˌdʒiː biː ˈeɪtʃ/ *abbr.* (*BrE, law* 律) GRIEVOUS BODILY HARM 嚴重人體傷害（罪）

GCE /ˌdʒiː siː ˈiː/ *noun* [C, U] the abbreviation for 'General Certificate of Education' (a British exam taken by students in England and Wales and some other countries in any of a range of subjects. GCE O levels were replaced in 1988 by GCSE exams.)（英國）普通教育證書（全寫為 General Certificate of Education，其中的普通證書考試於 1988 年為普通中等教育證書所取代）➲ compare O LEVEL, A LEVEL

GCSE /ˌdʒiː siː es ˈiː/ *noun* [C, U] the abbreviation for 'General Certificate of Secondary Education' (a British exam taken by students in England and Wales and some other countries, usually around the age of 16. GCSE can be taken in any of a range of subjects.)（英國）普通中等教育證書（全寫為 General Certificate of Secondary Education）：*She's got 10 GCSEs.* 她已獲得 10 門學科的普通中等教育證書。◇ *He's doing German at GCSE.* 他在學習普通中等教育證書的德語課程。➲ compare A LEVEL

g'day /ɡəˈdeɪ/ *exclamation* (*AustralE, NZE*) hello 喂；你好

Gdns *abbr.* (*BrE*) (used in written addresses) Gardens（用於書面地址）園，街，廣場：*7 Windsor Gdns* 溫莎街 7 號

GDP /ˌdʒiː diː ˈpiː/ *noun* the abbreviation for 'gross domestic product' (the total value of all the goods and services produced by a country in one year) 國內生產總值，國內生產毛額（全寫為 gross domestic product）➲ compare GNP

GDR /ˌdʒiː diː ˈɑː(r)/ *abbr.* German Democratic Republic 德意志民主共和國（前東德）

gear 🔑 /ɡɪə(r); *NAmE* ɡɪr/ *noun, verb*

■ ***noun***

▸ **IN VEHICLE** 車輛 **1** 🔑 [C, usually pl.] machinery in a vehicle that turns engine power (or power on a bicycle) into movement forwards or backwards 排擋；齒輪；傳動裝置：*Careless use of the clutch may damage the gears.* 離合器使用不慎可能會損壞傳動裝置。➲ VISUAL VOCAB page V51 **2** 🔑 [U, C] a particular position of the gears in a vehicle that gives a particular range of speed and power 擋：***first/second, etc. gear*** 一擋、二擋等 ◇ ***reverse gear*** 倒擋 ◇ ***low/high gear*** 低速／高速擋 ◇ (*BrE*) ***bottom/top gear*** 最低／最高擋 ◇ (*BrE*) ***to change gear*** 換擋 ◇ (*NAmE*) ***to shift gear*** 換擋 ◇ *When parking on a hill, leave the car* ***in gear***. 在斜坡停車時把汽車掛上擋。◇ *What gear are you in?* 你掛的是幾擋？◇ *He drove wildly, crashing through the gears like a maniac.* 他開車很野，發瘋似的啪啦啪啦地換擋。➲ COLLOCATIONS at DRIVING

▸ **EQUIPMENT/CLOTHES** 設備；衣服 **3** 🔑 [U] the equipment or clothing needed for a particular activity（某種活動的）設備，用具，衣服：***climbing/fishing/sports, etc. gear*** 爬山、釣魚、運動等用具 ➲ see also HEADGEAR, RIOT GEAR ➲ SYNONYMS at EQUIPMENT **4** [U] (*informal*) clothes 衣服：*wearing the latest gear* 穿着最新款式的衣服 ➲ SYNONYMS at CLOTHES

▸ **POSSESSIONS** 所有物 **5** [U] (*informal*) the things that a person owns 所有物；財物：*I've left all my gear at Dave's house.* 我把我所有的東西都留在戴夫家了。

▸ **MACHINERY** 機器 **6** [U] (often in compounds 常構成複合詞) a piece of machinery used for a particular purpose（特定用途的）器械，裝置：***lifting/towing/winding, etc. gear*** 起重、牽引、捲揚等裝置 ➲ see also LANDING GEAR

▸ **SPEED/EFFORT** 速度／努力 **7** [U, C] used to talk about the speed or effort involved in doing sth（做事的）速度，努力：(*BrE*) *The party organization is* ***moving into top gear*** *as the election approaches.* 隨着選舉的臨近，這個政黨的組織工作正在緊鑼密鼓地進行。◇ (*NAmE*) ***to move into high gear*** 進入高速發展 ◇ *Coming out of the final bend, the runner* ***stepped up a gear*** *to overtake the rest of the pack.* 那名賽跑選手繞過最後一個彎道後開始加速，以圖超越同組的其他選手。

▸ **DRUGS** 毒品 **8** [U] (*slang*) illegal drugs 毒品

IDM **get into 'gear** | **get sth into 'gear** to start working, or to start sth working, in an efficient way（使）開始工作，進入有效工作狀態 **(slip/be thrown) out of 'gear** (of emotions or situations 情緒或形勢) (to become) out of control 失去控制：*She said nothing in case her temper slipped out of gear.* 她什麼都沒說，免得按捺不住情緒。**IDM** see ASS

■ ***verb***

PHR V **'gear sth to/towards sth** [usually passive] to make, change or prepare sth so that it is suitable for a particular purpose 使與…相適應；使適合於：*The course had been geared towards the specific needs of its members.* 課程已作調整，以滿足學員的特別需要。**ˌgear 'up (for/to sth)** | **ˌgear sb/sth↔'up (for/to sth)** to prepare yourself/sb/sth to do sth（使）為…做好準備：*Cycle organizations are gearing up for National Bike Week.* 自行車組織正在為全國自行車週活動做準備。➲ see also GEARED

gear·box /ˈɡɪəbɒks; *NAmE* ˈɡɪrbɑːks/ *noun* the part containing the gears of a vehicle 變速箱；齒輪箱

geared /ɡɪəd; *NAmE* ɡɪrd/ *adj.* [not before noun] **1 ~ to/towards sth** | **~ to do sth** designed or organized to achieve a particular purpose, or to be suitable for a particular group of people 旨在；適合於：*The programme is geared to preparing students for the world of work.* 本計劃旨在為學生開始就業做準備。◇ *The resort is geared towards children.* 這個旅遊勝地適合兒童玩耍。**2 ~ up (for sth)** | **~ up (to do sth)** prepared and ready for sth（為…）做好準備，準備好：*We have people on board geared up to help with any problems.* 我們已讓船上的人做好準備幫助解決任何問題。

gear·head /ˈɡɪəhed; *NAmE* ˈɡɪrhed/ *noun* (*informal*) a person who is very enthusiastic about cars or new technical devices and equipment 設備發燒友（指對汽車或新科技設備着迷者）：*He's a total gearhead—can't keep away from the race track.* 他是個十足的賽車迷，一刻也離不開賽車道。

gear·ing /ˈɡɪərɪŋ; *NAmE* ˈɡɪrɪŋ/ *noun* [U] **1** (*BrE*) (*NAmE* **le·ver·age**) (*finance* 財) the relationship between the amount of money that a company owes and the value of its shares 資本與負債比率；聯動比率 **2** a particular set or arrangement of gears in a machine or vehicle 齒輪裝置；傳動裝置

'gear lever (also **'gear·stick**) (both *BrE*) (*NAmE* **'gear shift**, **'stick shift**) *noun* a handle used to change the gears of a vehicle 變速桿；換擋桿 ➲ VISUAL VOCAB page V52

gecko /ˈɡekəʊ; *NAmE* ˈɡekoʊ/ *noun* (*pl.* **-os** or **-oes**) a small LIZARD (= a type of REPTILE) that lives in warm countries 壁虎

GED /ˌdʒiː iː ˈdiː/ *noun* (in the US and Canada) the abbreviation for 'general equivalency diploma' or 'general educational development' (an official certificate that people who did not finish high school can get, after taking classes and passing an examination)（美國和加拿大）普通高中同等學歷證書（全寫為 general equivalency diploma 或 general educational development，為修完課程並通過考試的高中未畢業者頒發的官方證書）

ged·dit? /ˈɡedɪt/ *abbr.* (*informal*) Do you get it? (= Do you understand the joke?)（指笑話）明白了嗎

gee /dʒiː/ *exclamation, verb*

■ ***exclamation*** (*especially NAmE*) a word that some people use to show that they are surprised, impressed or annoyed（表示驚奇、感動或氣惱）哇，啊，哎呀：*Gee, what a great idea!* 哇，多好的主意！

■ ***verb*** (*BrE*)

PHR V **ˌgee sb↔'up** | **ˌgee sb↔'on** to encourage sb to work harder, perform better, etc. 激勵，鼓勵（某人更努力、更好地工作等）**ˌgee 'up** used to tell a horse to start moving or to go faster（用以吆喝馬起行或快走）嘰駕，快跑

'gee-gee *noun* (*BrE, informal*) (used especially by and to young children 尤為兒語或對兒童說話時用) a horse 馬兒

geek /ɡiːk/ *noun* (*informal*) a person who is boring, wears clothes that are not fashionable, does not know how to behave in social situations, etc. 悶蛋；土包子 **SYN** nerd：*a computer geek* 電腦迷 ▸ **geeky** *adj.*

geese *pl.* of GOOSE

gee whiz /ˌdʒiː ˈwɪz/ *exclamation* (*old-fashioned, especially NAmE*) = GEE

gee·zer /ˈɡiːzə(r)/ *noun* (*informal*) **1** (*BrE*) a man 男人；傢伙：*Some geezer called Danny did it.* 這事是個叫丹尼的傢伙幹的。**2** (*NAmE*) an old man, especially one who is rather strange 怪老頭；老傢伙

Gei·ger count·er /ˈɡaɪɡə kaʊntə(r); *NAmE* ˈɡaɪɡər/ *noun* a device used for finding and measuring RADIOACTIVITY 蓋革計數器（用以探測和測量放射）

gei·sha /ˈɡeɪʃə/ (also **'geisha girl**) *noun* a Japanese woman who is trained to entertain men with conversation, dancing and singing 藝伎（陪男子聊天、表演歌舞的日本女子）

gel /dʒel/ *noun, verb*

■ ***noun*** [U, C] a thick substance like jelly, especially one used in products for the hair or skin 凝膠，凍膠，膠滯體（尤指用於頭髮或護膚的產品）：***hair/shower gel*** 髮膠；沐浴凝膠

■ ***verb*** (**-ll-**) **1** [I] (*BrE*) (also **jell** *NAmE, BrE*) (of two or more people 二人或以上) to work well together; to form a successful group 聯手共事；結為一體：*We just didn't gel as a group.* 我們就是不能成為一個集體。**2** [I] (*BrE*) (also **jell** *NAmE, BrE*) (of an idea, a thought, a plan, etc. 主意、想法、計劃等) to become clearer and more definite; to work well 變得更清楚；顯得更明確；有效；起作用：*Ideas were beginning to gel in my mind.* 各種想法在我頭腦裏逐漸明朗起來。◇ *That day, everything gelled.* 那天，一切都很順利。**3** [I] (also **jell** especially in *NAmE*) (*technical* 術語) (of a liquid 液體) to become thicker and more solid; to form a gel 膠凝；膠化；形成膠體 **4** [T, usually passive] **~ sth** to put gel on your hair 上髮膠

gel·atin /ˈdʒelətɪn/ (also **gel·atine** /ˈdʒeləti:n/) *noun* [U] a clear substance without any taste that is made from boiling animal bones and is used to make jelly, film for cameras, etc. 明膠；骨膠；凝膠

G

gel·at·in·ous /dʒəˈlætɪnəs/ *adj.* thick and sticky, like a jelly 明膠的；膠狀的：*a gelatinous substance* 膠狀物質

ˈgelatin paper *noun* [U] paper covered with gelatin, used in photography（照相）明膠相紙

geld /geld/ *verb* **~ sth** (*technical* 術語) to remove the TESTICLES of a male animal, especially a horse 閹割（雄性動物，尤指馬）；給（動物）去勢 SYN **castrate**

geld·ing /ˈgeldɪŋ/ *noun* a horse that has been CASTRATED 閹割的馬；去勢的馬 ➲ compare STALLION

gel·ig·nite /ˈdʒelɪgnaɪt/ *noun* [U] a powerful EXPLOSIVE 葛里炸藥；硝銨炸藥；炸膠

gem /dʒem/ *noun* **1** (also *less frequent* **gem·stone** /ˈdʒemstəʊn; *NAmE* -stoʊn/) a PRECIOUS STONE that has been cut and polished and is used in jewellery（經切割打磨的）寶石 SYN **jewel, precious stone**：*a crown studded with gems* 鑲有寶石的皇冠 **2** a person, place or thing that is especially good 難能可貴的人；風景優美的地方；美妙絕倫的事物：*This picture is the gem* (= the best) *of the collection.* 這幅畫是收藏中的極品。◇ *a gem of a place* 勝地 ◇ *She's a real gem!* 她真是難能可貴！➲ compare JEWEL

gemin·ate /ˈdʒemɪneɪt; -nət/ *adj.* (*phonetics* 語音) (of a speech sound 語音) consisting of the same consonant pronounced twice, for example /kk/ in the middle of the word *backcomb* 雙音的，雙輔音的（如 backcomb 中的 /kk/）

Gem·ini /ˈdʒemɪnaɪ; -ni/ *noun* **1** [U] the third sign of the ZODIAC, the TWINS 黃道第三宮；雙子宮；雙子（星）座 **2** [C] a person born when the sun is in this sign, that is between 22 May and 21 June 屬雙子座的人（約出生於 5 月 22 日至 6 月 21 日）

Gen. *abbr.* (in writing) GENERAL（書寫形式）將軍：*Gen. (Stanley) Armstrong*（斯坦利）阿姆斯特朗將軍

gen /dʒen/ *noun, verb*

■ ***noun*** [U] **~ (on sth)** (*old-fashioned, BrE, informal*) information 消息；情報；資料

■ ***verb*** (-nn-)

PHR V **ˌgen ˈup (on sth)** | **ˌgen sb/yourself ˈup (on sth)** (*old-fashioned, BrE, informal*) to find out or give sb information about sth 瞭解情況；知道詳情；向（某人）提供情報

gen·darme /ˈʒɒndɑ:m; *NAmE* ˈʒɑ:ndɑ:rm/ *noun* (from *French*) a member of the French police force（法國的）警察，憲兵

gen·der AW /ˈdʒendə(r)/ *noun* **1** [C, U] the fact of being male or female, especially when considered with reference to social and cultural differences, not differences in biology 性別（尤指社會和文化差異，而非生理差異）：*issues of class, race and gender* 階級、種族和性別問題 ◇ *traditional concepts of gender* 傳統的性別觀念 ◇ ***gender differences/relations/roles*** 性別差異；性別關係；性別角色 ➲ compare SEX *n.* (1) **2** [C, U] (*grammar* 語法) (in some languages 用於某些語言) each of the classes (MASCULINE, FEMININE and sometimes NEUTER) into which nouns, pronouns and adjectives are divided; the division of nouns, pronouns and adjectives into these different genders. Different genders may have different endings, etc. 性（陽性、陰性和中性，不同的性有不同的詞尾等）：*In French the adjective must agree with the noun in number and gender.* 法語中形容詞必須在數和性上與名詞一致。

ˈgender bender *noun* (*informal*) a person who dresses and behaves like a member of the opposite sex 穿着舉止像異性的人；假小子；假娘們

ˌgender reasˈsignment *noun* [U] the act of changing a person's sex by a medical operation in which parts of their body are changed so that they become like a person of the opposite sex 性別再造手術；變性手術

ˈgender-specific *adj.* connected with women only or with men only 女（或男）性特有的；與某一性別有關的：*The report was redrafted to remove gender-specific language.* 重新起草這個報告，刪除帶有性別特點的語言。

gene /dʒi:n/ *noun* (*biology* 生) a unit inside a cell which controls a particular quality in a living thing that has been passed on from its parents 基因：***a dominant/recessive gene*** 顯性／隱性基因 ◇ *genes that code for the colour of the eyes* 為眼睛的顏色編碼的基因 ➲ see also GENETIC

IDM **be in the ˈgenes** to be a quality that your parents have passed on to you 基因使然；是遺傳的：*I've always enjoyed music—it's in the genes.* 我向來喜歡音樂，這是拜父母所賜。

ge·neal·ogist /ˌdʒi:niˈælədʒɪst/ *noun* a person who studies family history 家譜學者；系譜學家；宗譜學家

ge·neal·ogy /ˌdʒi:niˈælədʒi/ *noun* (*pl.* **-ies**) **1** [U] the study of family history, including the study of who the ANCESTORS of a particular person were 家譜學；系譜學；宗譜學 **2** [C] a particular person's line of ANCESTORS; a diagram that shows this 家譜（圖）；系譜（圖）；宗譜（圖）▸ **ge·nea·logic·al** /ˌdʒi:niəˈlɒdʒɪkl; *NAmE* -ˈlɑ:dʒ-/ *adj.* [only before noun]：***a genealogical chart/table/tree*** (= a chart with branches that shows a person's ANCESTORS) 系譜圖；家譜表；家系樹狀圖

ˈgene pool *noun* (*biology* 生) all of the GENES that are available within breeding populations of a particular SPECIES of animal or plant 基因庫（某物種的全部基因）

gen·era *pl.* of GENUS

gen·eral 🔑 /ˈdʒenrəl/ *adj., noun*

■ ***adj.***

▸ **AFFECTING ALL** 涉及全部 **1** 🔑 affecting all or most people, places or things 全體的；普遍的；總的：*The **general opinion** is that the conference was a success.* 普遍認為這次會議是成功的。◇ *the **general belief/consensus*** 普遍的信念／共識 ◇ *books of **general interest*** (= of interest to most people) 普遍感興趣的書籍 ◇ *The bad weather has been fairly general* (= has affected most areas). 壞天氣影響到的範圍相當大。

▸ **USUAL** 通常 **2** 🔑 [usually before noun] normal; usual 正常的；一般的；常規的：*There is one exception to this general principle.* 這個一般性原則有一例外。◇ ***As a general rule*** (= usually) *he did what he could to be helpful.* 一般情況下他都盡力給予幫助。◇ *This opinion is common among the general population* (= ordinary people). 這是人們普遍的看法。

▸ **NOT EXACT** 籠統 **3** 🔑 including the most important aspects of sth; not exact or detailed 概括性的；大體的；籠統的 SYN **overall**：*I check the bookings to get a **general idea** of what activities to plan.* 我核查預訂情況以便對計劃安排些什麼活動有個大體的想法。◇ *I know how it works **in general terms**.* 我大致知道其中的運作原理。◇ *They gave a general description of the man.* 他們對這個男人作了大致的描述。**4 the ~ direction/area** approximately, but not exactly, the direction/area mentioned 大致的，大概的（方向或地區）：*They fired in the general direction of the enemy.* 他們向敵軍大致的方向開了槍。

▸ **NOT LIMITED** 未限定 **5** 🔑 not limited to a particular subject, use or activity 非專門的；一般性的；普通的：*a general hospital* 綜合醫院 ◇ *general education* 普通教育 ◇ *We shall at this stage keep the discussion fairly general.* 我們在此階段應保持相當廣泛的討論。**6** not limited to one part or aspect of a person or thing 整體的；全身的；全面的：*a general anaesthetic* 全身麻醉 ◇ *The building was in a general state of disrepair.* 整座建築處於失修狀態。

▸ HIGHEST IN RANK 最高級別 **7** [only before noun] (also **General**) [after noun] highest in rank; chief 首席的；總管的：*the general manager* 總經理 ◇ *the Inspector General of Police* 警察總監 ➲ see also ATTORNEY GENERAL, DIRECTOR GENERAL, GOVERNOR GENERAL, SECRETARY GENERAL, SOLICITOR GENERAL, SURGEON GENERAL

IDM **in 'general 1** ⊶ usually; mainly 通常；大體上：*In general, Japanese cars are very reliable and breakdowns are rare.* 日本汽車通常是很可靠的，發生故障的情況極少。 ➲ LANGUAGE BANK at CONCLUSION, GENERALLY **2** ⊶ as a whole 總的說來；從總體上看：*This is a crucial year for your relationships in general and your love life in particular.* 這一年總體上對你們的關係，特別是你們的愛情生活是非常關鍵的。

■ ***noun*** (*abbr.* **Gen.**) an officer of very high rank in the army and the US AIR FORCE; the officer with the highest rank in the MARINES 將軍；（陸軍、海軍陸戰隊或美國空軍）上將：*a four-star general* 四星上將 ◇ *General Tom Parker* 湯姆 • 帕克將軍 ➲ see also BRIGADIER GENERAL, MAJOR GENERAL

ˌGeneral Aˈmerican *noun* [U] the way people speak English in most parts of the US, not including New England, New York, and the South 通用美式英語（除新英格蘭、紐約和南方等之外通用於美國大部份地區）

ˌGeneral Cerˌtificate of Eduˈcation *noun* = GCE

ˌGeneral Cerˌtificate of ˌSecondary Eduˈcation *noun* = GCSE

ˌgeneral ˈcounsel *noun* (in the US) the main lawyer who gives legal advice to a company（美國）公司法律總顧問

ˌgeneral deˈlivery (*NAmE*) (*BrE* **poste restˑante**) *noun* [U] an arrangement in which a post office keeps a person's mail until they go to collect it, used especially when sb is travelling 郵件寄存服務，存局候領（郵局暫為保管以候收件人上門自取）

ˌgeneral eˈlection *noun* an election in which all the people of a country vote to choose a government 大選；普選 ➲ compare BY-ELECTION

ˌgeneral headˈquarters *noun* [U+sing./pl. v.] = GHQ

gen·er·al·ist /ˈdʒenrəlɪst/ *noun* a person who has knowledge of several different subjects or activities 多面手；全才；通才 OPP **specialist**

gen·er·al·ity /ˌdʒenəˈræləti/ *noun* (*pl.* **-ies**) **1** [C, usually pl.] a statement that discusses general principles or issues rather than details or particular examples 概述；概論；通則：*to speak in broad generalities* 泛泛地說 ◇ *As usual, he confined his comments to generalities.* 他和往常一樣，只作了籠統的評論。 **2 the generality** [sing.+sing./pl. v.] (*formal*) most of a group of people or things 主體；大多數；大部份：*This view is held by the generality of leading scholars.* 大多數知名學者都持這種觀點。 **3** [U] (*formal*) the quality of being general rather than detailed or

G

More About 補充說明

gender

Ways of talking about men and women
表示男女的說法

■ When you are writing or speaking English it is important to use language that includes both men and women equally. Some people may be very offended if you do not. 說寫英語時，重要的是用詞要把男女都包括在內，否則可能會冒犯某些人。

The human race 人類

■ **Man** and **mankind** have traditionally been used to mean 'all men and women'. Many people now prefer to use **humanity**, **the human race**, **human beings** or **people**. * man 和 mankind 傳統上用以指所有男性和女性，不過，現在許多人喜歡用 humanity、the human race、human beings 或 people。

Jobs 職業

■ The suffix **-ess** in names of occupations such as **actress**, **hostess** and **waitress** shows that the person doing the job is a woman. Many people now avoid these. Instead you can use **actor** or **host**, (although **actress** and **hostess** are still very common) or a neutral word, such as **server** for *waiter* and *waitress*. 後綴 -ess 在職業的名稱如 actress、hostess 和 waitress 中表明從事此職業的是女性。目前，許多人避免用這些詞。取而代之的是 actor 或 host（儘管 actress 和 hostess 仍然很常見）或用中性詞如 server 取代 waiter 和 waitress。

■ Neutral words like **assistant**, **worker**, **person** or **officer** are now often used instead of *-man* or *-woman* in the names of jobs. For example, you can use **police officer** instead of *policeman* or *policewoman*, and **spokesperson** instead of *spokesman* or *spokeswoman*. Neutral words are very common in newspapers, on television and radio and in official writing, in both *BrE* and *NAmE*. 現在職業名稱常用中性詞如 assistant、worker、person 或 officer 取代 -man 或 -woman。例如可用 police officer 代替 policeman 或 policewoman，用 spokesperson 代替 spokesman 或 spokeswoman。在報刊、電視、廣播和公文中，英式英語和美式英語都常用中性詞。

■ When talking about jobs that are traditionally done by the other sex, some people say: **a male secretary/nurse/model** (NOT **man**) or **a woman/female doctor/barrister/driver**. However this is now not usually used unless you need to emphasize which sex the person is, or it is still unusual for the job to be done by a man/woman. 談及傳統上由另一性別幹的工作時，有人用 male secretary/nurse/model（不用 man）或 woman/female doctor/barrister/driver 表示。不過現在這種用法不常見，除非要強調此人的性別，或由某性別幹此工作仍然少見：*My daughter prefers to see a woman doctor.* 我的女兒喜歡讓女醫生看病。◇ *They have a male nanny for their kids.* 他們有個男保母照料孩子。◇ *a female racing driver* 女賽車手

Pronouns 代詞

■ **He** used to be considered to cover both men and women. * he 過去被認為既指男性也指女性：*Everyone needs to feel he is loved.* 人人都需要有被愛的感覺。This is not now acceptable. Instead, after **everybody**, **everyone**, **anybody**, **anyone**, **somebody**, **someone**, etc. one of the plural pronouns **they**, **them**, and **their** is often used. 現在此用法不獲認同。取而代之的是在 everybody、everyone、anybody、anyone、somebody、someone 等之後常用複數代詞 they、them 和 their：*Does everybody know what they want?* 人人都知道自己需要什麼嗎？◇ *Somebody's left their coat here.* 有人把外衣丟在這兒了。◇ *I hope nobody's forgotten to bring their passport with them.* 希望沒人忘了隨身帶上護照。

■ Some people prefer to use **he or she**, **his or her**, or **him or her** in speech and writing. 有人在口語和書面語中喜歡用 he or she、his or her 或 him or her：*Everyone knows what's best for him or herself.* 人人都知道對自己來說什麼是最好的。 **He/she** or **(s)he** can also be used in writing. * he/she 或 (s)he 亦可用於書面語中：*If in doubt, ask your doctor. He/she can give you more information.* 如有疑問請向你的醫生咨詢，他／她會給你更多的信息。 (You may find that some writers just use 'she'. 有些人只用 she。) These uses can seem awkward when they are used a lot. It is better to try to change the sentence, using a plural noun. 這種用法太多可能顯得彆扭。最好盡量改動句子，用複數名詞。 Instead of saying 避免說：*A baby cries when he or she is tired.* you can say 可以說：*Babies cry when they are tired.* 嬰兒疲倦時會哭。

exact 一般性；普遍性；籠統：*An account of such generality is of little value.* 這種一般性描述沒有什麼價值。

gen·er·al·iza·tion (*BrE* also **-isa·tion**) /ˌdʒenrəlaɪˈzeɪʃn; *NAmE* -ləˈz-/ *noun* [C, U] a general statement that is based on only a few facts or examples; the act of making such statements 概括；歸納；泛論：*a speech full of* ***broad/sweeping generalizations*** 滿是概而論之話語的發言 ◇ *to* ***make generalizations about*** *sth* 對某事做出歸納 ◇ *Try to avoid generalization.* 盡量避免泛泛而論。

gen·er·al·ize (*BrE* also **-ise**) /ˈdʒenrəlaɪz/ *verb* **1** [I] **~ (from sth)** to use a particular set of facts or ideas in order to form an opinion that is considered valid for a different situation 概括；歸納：*It would be foolish to generalize from a single example.* 僅從一個事例進行歸納的做法是愚蠢的。 **2** [I] **~ (about sth)** to make a general statement about sth and not look at the details 籠統地講；概括地談論：*It is dangerous to generalize about the poor.* 對窮人一概而論是危險的。 **3** [T, often passive] **~ sth (to sth)** (*formal*) to apply a theory, idea, etc. to a wider group or situation than the original one 擴大…的運用；類推到（較大的範圍）：*These conclusions cannot be generalized to the whole country.* 這些結論不可能推及全國。

gen·er·al·ized (*BrE* also **-ised**) /ˈdʒenrəlaɪzd/ *adj.* [usually before noun] not detailed; not limited to one particular area 籠統的；普遍的；概括性的；全面的：*a generalized discussion* 籠統的討論 ◇ *a* ***generalized disease/rash*** (= affecting the whole body) 全身性疾病 / 疹子

ˌgeneral ˈknowledge *noun* [U] knowledge of facts about a lot of different subjects 一般知識；常識：*a general knowledge quiz* 常識問答比賽

Language Bank 用語庫

generally

Ways of saying 'in general' "通常"的表達方式

- Women **generally** earn less than men. 女人通常比男人掙錢少。
- **Generally speaking**, jobs traditionally done by women are paid at a lower rate than those traditionally done by men. 一般來說，傳統上由婦女幹的工作比傳統上由男人幹的工作報酬低。
- **In general/By and large**, women do not earn as much as men. 總的說來，女人不如男人掙錢多。
- Certain jobs, like nursing and cleaning, are still **mainly** carried out by women. 有些工作仍然主要由女性做，比如護理和清潔。
- Senior management posts are **predominantly** held by men. 高層管理職位大多由男性擔任。
- Most senior management posts **tend to** be held by men. 大多數高層管理職位通常由男性擔任。
- Women are, **for the most part**, still paid less than men. 女人的薪水多半仍比男人低。
- Economic and social factors are, **to a large extent**, responsible for women being concentrated in low-paid jobs. 經濟和社會因素在很大程度上導致女性集中於低報酬工作。

➲ Language Banks at CONCLUSION, EXCEPT, SIMILARLY

gen·er·al·ly 🔑 /ˈdʒenrəli/ *adv.* **1** 🔑 by or to most people 普遍地；廣泛地：*The plan was generally welcomed.* 這個計劃受到普遍的歡迎。◇ *It is now generally accepted that …* 目前，人們普遍認為…◇ *The new drug will be generally available from January.* 這種新藥從一月份開始將可廣泛使用。◇ *He was a generally unpopular choice for captain.* 人們普遍不歡迎他成為隊長的人選。 **2** 🔑 in most cases 一般地；通常；大體上 **SYN** **as a rule**：*I generally get up at six.* 我一般六點鐘起牀。◇ *The male is generally larger with a shorter beak.* 雄鳥通常體形較大，喙較短。 **3** 🔑 without discussing the details of sth 籠統地；概括地；大概：*Let's talk just about investment generally.* 咱們只大概談談投資吧。

ˌgeneral ˈpractice *noun* [U, C] **1** (*especially BrE*) the work of a doctor who treats people in the community rather than at a hospital and who is not a specialist in one particular area of medicine; a place where a doctor like this works （醫院以外的）綜合醫療，全科診療；全科診所：*to be in general practice* 從事普通診療 ◇ *She runs a general practice in Hull.* 她在赫爾開了家全科診所。 **2** (*especially NAmE*) the work of a lawyer who deals with all kinds of legal cases and who is not a specialist in one particular area of law; the place where a lawyer like this works 普通律師業務；普通律師事務所

ˌgeneral pracˈtitioner (also **ˌfamily pracˈtitioner**) (*abbr.* **GP**) (also *informal* **ˌfamily ˈdoctor**) (*especially BrE*) *noun* a doctor who is trained in general medicine and who treats patients in a local community rather than at a hospital （醫院以外的）全科醫生，普通醫師

the ˌgeneral ˈpublic *noun* [sing.+sing./pl. v.] ordinary people who are not members of a particular group or organization 普通百姓；公眾：*At that time, the general public was/were not aware of the health risks.* 那時，公眾對各種危及健康的因素尚不瞭解。◇ *The exhibition is not open to the general public.* 這次展覽不對公眾開放。

ˌgeneral-ˈpurpose *adj.* [only before noun] having a wide range of different uses 多用途的；多功能的：*a general-purpose farm vehicle* 多功能農用機動車

gen·er·al·ship /ˈdʒenrəlʃɪp/ *noun* [U] the skill or practice of leading an army during a battle 指揮作戰；將軍職能

ˌgeneral ˈstaff (often **the general staff**) *noun* [sing.+sing./pl. v.] officers who advise a military leader and help to plan a military operation （軍事）參謀

ˌgeneral ˈstore *noun* (*BrE* also **ˌgeneral ˈstores** [pl.]) a shop/store that sells a wide variety of goods, especially one in a small town or village （尤指小城鎮或鄉村的）雜貨店

ˌgeneral ˈstrike *noun* a period of time when most or all of the workers in a country go on strike 總罷工

gen·er·ate 🔑 **AW** /ˈdʒenəreɪt/ *verb* **~ sth** to produce or create sth 產生；引起：*to* ***generate electricity/heat/power*** 發電；產生熱 / 動力 ◇ *to* ***generate income/profit*** 產生收益 / 利潤 ◇ *We need someone to generate new ideas.* 我們需要有人出新主意。◇ *The proposal has generated a lot of interest.* 這項建議引起眾多的關注。 ➲ SYNONYMS at MAKE

gen·er·ation 🔑 **AW** /ˌdʒenəˈreɪʃn/ *noun* **1** 🔑 [C+sing./pl. v.] all the people who were born at about the same time （統稱）一代人，同代人，同輩人：*the* ***younger/older generation*** 年輕的一代；老一輩 ◇ *My generation have grown up without the experience of a world war.* 我這一代人在成長過程中沒有經歷過世界大戰。◇ *I often wonder what* ***future generations*** *will make of our efforts.* 我常常想，後代將怎樣評價我們所作出的努力。 **2** 🔑 [C] the average time in which children grow up, become adults and have children of their own, (usually considered to be about 30 years) 代，一代，一輩（通常認為大約 30 年）：*a generation ago* 一代人以前 ◇ *My family have lived in this house* ***for generations***. 我家祖祖輩輩都住在這房子裏。 **3** 🔑 [C, U] a single stage in the history of a family （家史中的）一代，一輩：*stories passed down from generation to generation* 世代相傳的故事 ◇ *a* ***first-/second-generation*** *American* (= a person whose family has lived in America for one/two generations) 第一 / 第二代美國人（家人在美國居住了一、二代者） **4** 🔑 [C, usually sing.] a group of people of similar age involved in a particular activity 一批，一屆（從事特定活動的同齡人）：*She has inspired a whole generation of fashion school graduates.* 她激勵了整整一屆時裝學校的畢業生。 **5** [C, usually sing.] a stage in the development of a product, usually a technical one （產品發展，尤指技術方面的）代：*fifth-generation computing* 第五代計算機技術 ◇ *a* ***new generation of*** *vehicle* 新一代交通運輸工具 **6** [U] the production of sth, especially electricity, heat, etc. （尤指電、熱等的）

產生：*the generation of electricity* 發電 ◇ *methods of income generation* 產生收益的方法

gen·er·ation·al /ˌdʒenəˈreɪʃənl/ *adj.* [usually before noun] connected with a particular generation or with the relationship between different generations 一代的；代與代之間的：*generational conflict* 兩代人之間的衝突

the gene'ration gap *noun* [sing.] the difference in attitude or behaviour between young and older people that causes a lack of understanding 代溝；兩代人之間的隔閡：*a movie that is sure to bridge the generation gap* 肯定能彌合代溝的一部電影

Gene,ration 'X *noun* [U] the group of people who were born between the early 1960s and the middle of the 1970s, who seem to lack a sense of direction in life and to feel that they have no part to play in society * X 一代（20 世紀 60 年代初至 70 年代中期出生，缺乏人生目標和感到失落的人）

gen·era·tive /ˈdʒenərətɪv/ *adj.* (*formal*) that can produce sth 有生產力的；能生產的；有生殖力的：*generative processes* 生產過程

,generative 'grammar *noun* [C, U] (*linguistics* 語言) a type of grammar which describes a language by giving a set of rules which can be used to produce all the possible sentences in that language 生成語法

gen·er·ator /ˈdʒenəreɪtə(r)/ *noun* **1** a machine for producing electricity 發電機：*The factory's emergency generators were used during the power cut.* 工廠應急發電機在停電期間用上了。◇ *a wind generator* (= a machine that uses the power of the wind to produce electricity) 風力發電機 **2** a machine for producing a particular substance 發生器；生成器：*The museum uses smells and smoke generators to create atmosphere.* 博物館利用氣味和煙霧生成器製造氣氛。◇ (*figurative*) *The company is a major generator of jobs.* 這家公司創造了相當多的就業機會。 **3** (*BrE*) a company that produces electricity to sell to the public 電力公司：*the UK's major electricity generator* 英國主要的電力公司

gen·er·ic /dʒəˈnerɪk/ *adj.* **1** shared by, including or typical of a whole group of things; not specific 一般的；普通的；通用的：*'Vine fruit' is the* ***generic term*** *for currants and raisins.* * vine fruit 是有核和無核葡萄乾的通稱。**2** (of a product, especially a drug 產品，尤指藥物) not using the name of the company that made it 無廠家商標的；無商標的：*The doctor offered me a choice of a branded or a generic drug.* 醫生讓我選擇用有商標的還是沒有商標的藥物。 ▸ **gen·er·ic·al·ly** /dʒəˈnerɪkli/ *adv.*

gen·er·os·ity /ˌdʒenəˈrɒsəti; *NAmE* -ˈrɑːs-/ *noun* [U, sing.] **~ (to/towards sb)** the fact of being generous (= willing to give sb money, gifts, time or kindness freely) 慷慨；大方；寬宏大量：*He treated them with generosity and thoughtfulness.* 他待他們寬容大度、體貼周到。

gen·er·ous 🔑 /ˈdʒenərəs/ *adj.* (*approving*)
1 🔑 giving or willing to give freely; given freely 慷慨的；大方的；慷慨給予的：*a generous benefactor* 慷慨的捐助者 ◇ **~ (with sth)** *to be generous with your time* 不吝惜時間 ◇ *to be generous in giving help* 樂於助人 ◇ *a generous* ***gift/offer*** 豐厚的禮物；慷慨的提議 ◇ *It was* ***generous of him*** *to offer to pay for us both.* 他主動為我們倆付錢，真是大方。 OPP **mean 2** 🔑 more than is necessary; large 豐富的；充足的；大的 SYN **lavish**：*a generous helping of meat* 一大份肉 ◇ *The car has a generous amount of space.* 這輛汽車的空間很大。 **3** 🔑 kind in the way you treat people; willing to see what is good about sb/sth 寬厚的；寬宏大量的；仁慈的：*a generous mind* 寬闊的胸懷 ◇ *He wrote a very generous assessment of my work.* 他給我寫的工作評價多有讚譽之詞。 ▸ **gen·er·ous·ly** 🔑 *adv.*：*Please give generously.* 請慷慨施與。◇ *a dress that is generously cut* (= uses plenty of material) 用料多的連衣裙

gen·esis /ˈdʒenəsɪs/ *noun* [sing.] (*formal*) the beginning or origin of sth 開端；創始；起源

genet /ˈdʒenɪt/ *noun* a wild animal similar to a cat but with a longer tail and body and a pointed head. Genets are found in Africa, southern Europe and Asia and eat insects and small animals. 獛（棲息於非洲、歐洲南部和亞洲）

'gene therapy *noun* [U] (*medical* 醫) a treatment in which normal GENES are put into cells to replace ones that are missing or not normal 基因療法；基因治療

gen·et·ic /dʒəˈnetɪk/ *adj.* connected with GENES (= the units in the cells of a living thing that control its physical characteristics) or GENETICS (= the study of genes) 基因的；遺傳學的：*genetic and environmental factors* 遺傳和環境因素 ◇ *genetic abnormalities* 基因異常 ▸ **gen·et·ic·al·ly** /-kli/ *adv.*：*genetically engineered/determined/transmitted* 轉基因的；由基因決定的；遺傳的

ge,netically 'modified *adj.* (*abbr.* **GM**) (of a plant, etc. 植物等) having had its genetic structure changed artificially, so that it will produce more fruit or not be affected by disease 轉基因的；基因改造的：*genetically modified foods* (= made from plants that have been changed in this way) 轉基因食品 ➲ COLLOCATIONS at FARMING

ge,netic 'code *noun* the arrangement of GENES that controls how each living thing will develop 遺傳密碼

ge,netic ,engi'neering *noun* [U] the science of changing how a living creature or plant develops by changing the information in its GENES 遺傳工程（學）

ge,netic 'fingerprinting (also **,DNA 'fingerprinting**) *noun* [U] the method of finding the particular pattern of GENES in an individual person, particularly to identify sb or find out if sb has committed a crime 基因指紋鑒定；遺傳指紋法 ▸ **ge,netic 'fingerprint** *noun*

gen·eti·cist /dʒəˈnetɪsɪst/ *noun* a scientist who studies genetics 遺傳學家

gen·et·ics /dʒəˈnetɪks/ *noun* [U] the scientific study of the ways in which different characteristics are passed from each generation of living things to the next 遺傳學

Geneva Convention /dʒəˌniːvə kənˈvenʃn/ *noun* [sing.] an international agreement which states how PRISONERS OF WAR should be treated 日內瓦公約（有關戰俘待遇的國際協定）

Gen·ghis Khan /ˌgeŋgɪs ˈkɑːn; ˌdʒeŋ-/ *noun* [usually sing.] a person who is very cruel or has very RIGHT-WING political opinions 非常殘酷的人；極右分子：*Her politics are somewhere to the right of Genghis Khan.* 她的政治觀點屬於極右。 ORIGIN From the name of the first ruler of the Mongol empire, who was born in the 12th century. 源自出生於 12 世紀的蒙古帝國開國君主成吉思汗。

gen·ial /ˈdʒiːniəl/ *adj.* friendly and cheerful 友好的；親切的；歡快的 SYN **affable**：*a genial person* 和藹可親的人 ◇ *a genial smile* 親切的微笑 ▸ **geni·al·ity** /ˌdʒiːniˈæləti/ *noun* [U]：*an atmosphere of warmth and geniality* 熱情友好的氣氛 **geni·al·ly** /ˈdʒiːniəli/ *adv.*：*to smile genially* 親切地微笑

genie /ˈdʒiːni/ *noun* (*pl.* **gen·ies** or **genii** /ˈdʒiːniaɪ/) (in Arabian stories) a spirit with magic powers, especially one that lives in a bottle or a lamp （阿拉伯故事中，尤指瓶子或燈裏的）傑尼，鎮尼，精靈 SYN **djinn**

geni·tal /ˈdʒenɪtl/ *adj.* [only before noun] connected with the outer sexual organs of a person or an animal 生殖的；生殖器的：*the genital area* 生殖區 ◇ *genital infections* 生殖器傳染病

geni·tals /ˈdʒenɪtlz/ (also **geni·talia** /ˌdʒenɪˈteɪliə/) *noun* [pl.] a person's sex organs that are outside their body 外生殖器

geni·tive /ˈdʒenətɪv/ *noun* (*grammar* 語法) (in some languages 用於某些語言) the special form of a noun, a pronoun or an adjective that is used to show possession or close connection between two things 屬格；所有格 ➲ compare ABLATIVE, ACCUSATIVE, DATIVE, NOMINATIVE, POSSESSIVE, VOCATIVE ▸ **geni·tive** *adj.*

ge·nius /ˈdʒiːniəs/ *noun* (*pl.* **ge·niuses**) **1** [U] unusually great intelligence, skill or artistic ability 天才；天資；天賦：*the genius of Shakespeare* 莎士比亞的天才 ◇ *a statesman of genius* 天才的政治家 ◇ *Her idea was* ***a stroke of genius.*** 她的主意是聰明的一着。 **2** [C] a person who is

G

G

unusually intelligent or artistic, or who has a very high level of skill, especially in one area 天才人物；（某領域的）天才：*a **mathematical/comic, etc. genius*** 數學、喜劇等天才 ◇ *He's a genius at organizing people.* 他是人員組織方面的天才。◇ *You don't have to be a genius to see that they are in love!* 傻子也能看出他們相愛了！ **3** [sing.] **~ for sth/for doing sth** a special skill or ability（特別的）才能，本領：*He had a genius for making people feel at home.* 他有一種能夠使人感覺輕鬆自在的本領。

IDM **sb's good/evil ˈgenius** (*especially BrE*) a person or spirit who is thought to have a good/bad influence over you 給人以好（或壞）影響的人；保護（或毀滅）人的神魔

geno·cide /ˈdʒenəsaɪd/ *noun* [U] the murder of a whole race or group of people 種族滅絕；大屠殺 ➲ COLLOCATIONS at WAR ▸ **geno·cidal** *adj.*

gen·ome /ˈdʒiːnəʊm; *NAmE* -oʊm/ *noun* (*biology* 生) the complete set of GENES in a cell or living thing 基因組；染色體組：*the human genome* 人體基因組

geno·type /ˈdʒenətaɪp; ˈdʒiːn-/ *noun* (*biology* 生) the combination of GENES that a particular living thing carries, some of which may not be noticed from its appearance 基因型 ➲ compare PHENOTYPE

genre /ˈʒɒ̃rə; ˈʒɒnrə; *NAmE* ˈʒɑːnrə/ *noun* (*formal*) a particular type or style of literature, art, film or music that you can recognize because of its special features（文學、藝術、電影或音樂的）體裁，類型

ˈgenre painting *noun* [U, C] (*art* 美術) a style of painting showing scenes from ordinary life that is associated with 17th century Dutch and Flemish artists; a painting done in this style 風俗畫（與 17 世紀荷蘭和佛蘭德斯畫家有關，取材於日常生活的繪畫風格）；風俗畫作品

gent /dʒent/ *noun* (*BrE*) **1** (*old-fashioned* or *humorous*) a man; a gentleman 男士；紳士；先生：*a gent's hairdresser* 男賓理髮師 ◇ *This way please, ladies and gents!* 女士們，先生們，請這邊走！ **2** **a/the gents**, **a/the Gents** [sing.] (*informal*) a public toilet/bathroom for men 男廁所；男衛生間；男盥洗室：*Is there a gents near here?* 附近有男廁所嗎？◇ *Where's the gents?* 男廁所在哪兒？

gen·teel /dʒenˈtiːl/ *adj.* (sometimes *disapproving*) **1** (of people and their way of life 人和生活方式) quiet and polite, often in an exaggerated way; from, or pretending to be from, a high social class 顯得彬彬有禮的；假斯文的；上流社會的；裝體面的；裝出紳士派頭的：*a genteel manner* 彬彬有禮 ◇ *Her genteel accent irritated me.* 她那矯揉造作的腔調使我感到惱火。◇ *He lived in genteel poverty* (= trying to keep the style of a high social class, but with little money). 他擺出一副紳士派頭，過的卻是窮酸的生活。 **2** (of places 地方) quiet and old-fashioned and perhaps slightly boring 幽靜的；古樸單調的 ▸ **gen·teel·ly** /dʒenˈtiːlli/ *adv.*

gen·tian /ˈdʒenʃn/ *noun* [C, U] a small plant with bright blue flowers that grows in mountain areas 龍膽；龍膽草

gen·tile /ˈdʒentaɪl/ (also **Gentile**) *noun* a person who is not Jewish 非猶太人；外邦人（猶太人對非猶太人的通稱）▸ **gen·tile** (also **Gentile**) *adj.* [only before noun]

gen·til·ity /dʒenˈtɪləti/ *noun* [U] (*formal*) **1** very good manners and behaviour; the fact of belonging to a high social class 文雅；彬彬有禮；高貴的身分：*He took her hand with discreet gentility.* 他溫文爾雅地牽着她的手。◇ *She thinks expensive clothes are a mark of gentility.* 她認為昂貴的服裝是身分高貴的標誌。 **2** the fact of being quiet and old-fashioned 幽靜古樸：*the faded gentility of the town* 已失去古樸風貌的城鎮

gen·tle 🔑 /ˈdʒentl/ *adj.* (**gent·ler** /ˈdʒentlə(r)/, **gent·lest** /ˈdʒentlɪst/)

1 🔑 calm and kind; doing things in a quiet and careful way 文靜的；慈祥的；溫柔的；小心的：*a quiet and gentle man* 溫文爾雅的男士 ◇ *a gentle voice/laugh/touch* 溫柔的聲音／笑聲／觸摸 ◇ *She was the gentlest of nurses.* 她是個極其和藹的護士。◇ *He lived in a gentler age than ours.* 他生活的時代比我們這個時代更平靜祥和。◇ *Be gentle with her!* 待她溫柔些！◇ *She agreed to come, after a little **gentle persuasion**.* 經過一陣細心勸說，她表示願意來。◇ *He looks scary but he's really a **gentle giant**.* 他看上去可怕，實際卻是個性格溫和的巨人。 **2** 🔑 (of weather, temperature, etc. 天氣、溫度等) not strong or extreme 溫和的；徐緩的：*a gentle breeze* 和風 ◇ *the gentle swell of the sea* 緩慢起伏的海浪 ◇ *Cook over a gentle heat.* 要用文火煮。 **3** 🔑 having only a small effect; not strong or violent 平和的；柔和的：*We went for a gentle stroll.* 我們遛達去了。◇ *a little **gentle exercise*** 少量溫和的運動 ◇ *This soap is very gentle on the hands.* 這肥皂擦在手上非常柔和。 **4** 🔑 not steep or sharp 平緩的：*a **gentle slope/curve/angle*** 平緩的斜坡／彎道／角度 ➲ see also GENTLY ▸ **gentle·ness** /ˈdʒentlnəs/ *noun* [U]

gentle·folk /ˈdʒentlfəʊk; *NAmE* -foʊk/ *noun* [pl.] (*old-fashioned*) (in the past) people belonging to respected families of the higher social classes（舊時）出身名門世家的人

gentle·man 🔑 /ˈdʒentlmən/ *noun* (*pl.* **-men** /-mən/)

1 🔑 [C] a man who is polite and well educated, who has excellent manners and always behaves well 彬彬有禮的人；有教養的人；君子：*Thank you—you're a real gentleman.* 謝謝您，您是個真正的君子。◇ *He's no gentleman!* 他可不是正人君子！ ➲ compare LADY (2) **2** 🔑 [C, usually pl.] (*formal*) used to address or refer to a man, especially sb you do not know（稱呼或指男子，尤其是不認識的）先生：***Ladies and gentlemen!*** *Can I have your attention, please?* 女士們，先生們，請大家注意！◇ *Gentlemen of the jury!* 陪審團諸位先生！◇ *Can I help you, gentlemen?* 諸位先生，你們要點什麼？◇ *There's a gentleman to see you.* 有位先生要見你。 **HELP** In more informal speech, you could say 在非正式談話中可說：*Can I help you?* ◇ *There's someone to see you.* **3** (*NAmE*) used to address or refer to a male member of a LEGISLATURE, for example the House of Representatives（對立法機構男議員的稱呼）先生，閣下 **4** (*old-fashioned*) a man from a high social class, especially one who does not need to work 有身分的人；紳士；富紳：*a country gentleman* 鄉紳 ◇ *a gentleman farmer* (= one who owns a farm for pleasure, not as his main job) 鄉紳（以擁有農場為樂趣，而不作為主業） **IDM** see LEISURE

gentle·man·ly /ˈdʒentlmənli/ *adj.* (*approving*) behaving very well and showing very good manners; like a gentleman 彬彬有禮的；紳士風度的；紳士派頭的：*gentlemanly behaviour* 紳士般的舉止 ◇ *So far, the election campaign has been a very gentlemanly affair.* 到目前為止，競選活動都秩序良好。

ˌgentleman's aˈgreement (also **ˌgentlemen's aˈgreement**) *noun* an agreement made between people who trust each other, which is not written down and which has no legal force 君子協定；紳士協定

gentle·woman /ˈdʒentlwʊmən/ *noun* (*pl.* **-women** /-wɪmɪn/) **1** (*old use*) a woman who belongs to a high social class; a woman who is well educated and has excellent manners 貴婦人；有教養的婦女；淑女 **2** (*NAmE*) used to address or refer to a female member of a LEGISLATURE, for example the House of Representatives（對立法機構女議員的稱呼）女士，夫人

gent·ly 🔑 /ˈdʒentli/ *adv.*

1 🔑 in a gentle way 溫柔地；溫和地；文靜地；和緩地：*She held the baby gently.* 她輕輕地抱着嬰兒。◇ *'You miss them, don't you?' he asked gently.* "你想念他們，是嗎？"他溫和地問道。◇ *Simmer the soup gently for 30 minutes.* 用文火把湯燉 30 分鐘。◇ *Massage the area **gently but firmly**.* 推拿此部位要柔中帶勁。◇ *leaves moving gently in the breeze* 在微風中緩緩飄動的樹葉 ◇ *The path ran gently down to the sea.* 這條小路平緩地向大海延伸。 **2** **Gently!** (*BrE, informal*) used to tell sb to be careful 注意點；小心點；慢點：*Gently! You'll hurt the poor thing!* 小心點，你會弄痛這可憐的傢伙的！◇ *Don't go too fast—**gently does it!*** 別走太快，慢點吧！

gen·tri·fy /ˈdʒentrɪfaɪ/ *verb* (**gen·tri·fies**, **gen·tri·fy·ing**, **gen·tri·fied**, **gen·tri·fied**) [usually passive] **~ sth/sb** to change an area, a person, etc. so that they are suitable for, or can mix with, people of a higher social class than before 使（地區、人等）貴族化；對（地區、人等）進行改造以適應較高階層的人：*Old working-class areas of the city are being gentrified.* 這個城市工人居

住的老城區正在進行改造，以供較高階層人士居住。 ▸ **gen·tri·fi·ca·tion** *noun* [U]

gen·try /ˈdʒentri/ *noun* [pl.] (usually **the gentry**) (*old-fashioned*) people belonging to a high social class 紳士階層；上流社會人士：*the local gentry* 當地的紳士階層◇ *the landed gentry* (= those who own a lot of land) 鄉紳

genu·flect /ˈdʒenjuflekt/ *verb* (*formal*) **1** [I] to move your body into a lower position by bending one or both knees, as a sign of respect during worship in a church （在教堂）跪拜，單膝跪拜 **2** [I] ~ (**to sth**) (*disapproving*) to show too much respect to sb/sth 卑躬屈膝 ▸ **genu·flec·tion** (*BrE* also **genu·flex·ion**) /ˌdʒenjuˈflekʃn/ *noun* [C, U]

genu·ine 🗝 /ˈdʒenjuɪn/ *adj.*
1 🗝 real; exactly what it appears to be; not artificial 真的；名副其實的 SYN **authentic**：*Is the painting a genuine Picasso?* 這幅畫是畢加索的真跡嗎？◇ *Fake designer watches are sold at a fraction of the price of* ***the genuine article.*** 偽造的名牌手錶以真品若干分之一的價格出售。◇ *Only genuine refugees can apply for asylum.* 只有真正的難民才能申請政治避難。 **2** 🗝 sincere and honest; that can be trusted 真誠的；誠實的；可信賴的：*He made a genuine attempt to improve conditions.* 他真心實意地努力改善環境。◇ *genuine concern for others* 對他人真誠的關心◇ *a very genuine person* 非常誠實可信的人 ▸ **genu·ine·ly** 🗝 *adv.*：*genuinely sorry* 真遺憾 **genu·ine·ness** *noun* [U]

genus /ˈdʒiːnəs/ *noun* (*pl.* **gen·era** /ˈdʒenərə/) (*biology* 生) a group into which animals, plants, etc. that have similar characteristics are divided, smaller than a family and larger than a SPECIES（動植物等分類的）屬 ➲ compare CLASS *n.* (11), KINGDOM (4), ORDER *n.* (11), PHYLUM ➲ see also GENERIC

geo- *combining form* (in nouns, adjectives and adverbs 構成名詞、形容詞和副詞) of the earth 地球的：*geochemical* 地球化學的◇ *geoscience* 地球科學

geo·cen·tric /ˌdʒiːəʊˈsentrɪk; *NAmE* ˌdʒiːoʊ-/ *adj.* (*technical* 術語) with the earth as the centre 以地球為中心的

geo·des·ic /ˌdʒiːəʊˈdesɪk; -ˈdiːsɪk; *NAmE* ˌdʒiːoʊ-/ *adj.* (*technical* 術語) relating to the shortest possible line between two points on a curved surface（連接兩點的）曲面最短線的；測地線的

ˌgeoˌdesic ˈdome *noun* (*architecture* 建) a DOME which is built from panels whose edges form geodesic lines 網格球形穹頂 ➲ VISUAL VOCAB page V14

geog·raph·er /dʒiˈɒɡrəfə(r); *NAmE* -ˈɑːɡ-/ *noun* a person who studies geography; an expert in geography 地理學研究者；地理學家

geog·raphy 🗝 /dʒiˈɒɡrəfi; *NAmE* -ˈɑːɡ-/ *noun*
1 🗝 [U] the scientific study of the earth's surface, physical features, divisions, products, population, etc. 地理（學）：***human/physical/economic/social geography*** 人文／自然／經濟／社會地理學◇ *a* ***geography lesson/department/teacher/textbook*** 地理課／系／教師／課本◇ *a degree in geography* 地理學學位 **2** 🗝 [sing.] the way in which the physical features of a place are arranged 地形；地貌；地勢：*the geography of New York City* 紐約市的地勢◇ *Kim knew the geography of the building and strode along the corridor.* 金熟悉這棟建築物的佈局，大步流星地走在走廊上。 **3** [sing.] the way in which a particular aspect of life or society is influenced by geography or varies according to geography 地理環境：*The geography of poverty and the geography of voting are connected.* 貧窮人口的地理分佈與選票的地理分佈是相聯繫的。 ▸ **geo·graph·ic·al** /ˌdʒiːəˈɡræfɪkl/ (also **geo·graph·ic** /ˌdʒiːəˈɡræfɪk/) *adj.*：*The survey covers a wide* ***geographical area.*** 此項調查覆蓋的地理區域非常廣闊。◇ *The importance of the town is due to its* ***geographical location.*** 這座城鎮的重要性在於它的地理位置。 **geo·graph·ic·al·ly** /-kli/ *adv.*：*geographically remote areas* 地理上的邊遠地區

geolo·gist /dʒiˈɒlədʒɪst; *NAmE* -ˈɑːl-/ *noun* a scientist who studies geology 地質學家

geol·ogy /dʒiˈɒlədʒi; *NAmE* -ˈɑːl-/ *noun* **1** [U] the scientific study of the earth, including the origin and history of the rocks and soil of which the earth is made 地質學 **2** [sing.] the origin and history of the rocks and soil of a particular area（某地區的）地質：*the geology of the British Isles* 不列顛群島的地質 ▸ **geo·logic·al** /ˌdʒiːəˈlɒdʒɪkl; *NAmE* -ˈlɑːdʒ-/ (also **geo·logic** /ˌdʒiːəˈlɒdʒɪk; *NAmE* -ˈlɑːdʒ-/) *adj.*：*a geological survey* 地質勘察 **geo·logic·al·ly** /ˌdʒiːəˈlɒdʒɪkli; *NAmE* -ˈlɑːdʒ-/ *adv.*

geo·mag·net·ism /ˌdʒiːəʊˈmæɡnətɪzəm; *NAmE* ˌdʒiːoʊ-/ *noun* [U] (*geology* 地) the study of the MAGNETIC characteristics of the earth 地磁學 ▸ **geo·mag·net·ic** /ˌdʒiːəʊmæɡˈnetɪk; *NAmE* ˌdʒiːoʊ-/ *adj.*

geo·mancy /ˈdʒiːəʊmænsi; *NAmE* ˈdʒiːoʊ-/ *noun* [U] **1** the art of arranging buildings and areas in a good or lucky position 地相術；風水 **2** a method of saying what will happen in the future using patterns on the ground 地卜，泥土占卜（根據地面所呈圖跡占卜）

geo·met·ric /ˌdʒiːəˈmetrɪk/ (also *less frequent* **geo·met·ric·al** /-ɪkl/) *adj.* of GEOMETRY; of or like the lines, shapes, etc. used in GEOMETRY, especially because of having regular shapes or lines 幾何（學）的；（似）幾何圖形的：*a geometric design* 幾何圖形設計 ▸ **geo·met·ric·al·ly** /ˌdʒiːəˈmetrɪkli/ *adv.*

geoˌmetric ˈmean *noun* the central number in a geometric progression 幾何平均；等比中項

geoˌmetric proˈgression (also **geoˌmetric ˈseries**) *noun* a series of numbers in which each is multiplied or divided by a fixed number to produce the next, for example 1, 3, 9, 27, 81 幾何數列；等比數列 ➲ compare ARITHMETIC PROGRESSION

geom·etry /dʒiˈɒmətri; *NAmE* -ˈɑːm-/ *noun* **1** [U] the branch of mathematics that deals with the measurements and relationships of lines, angles, surfaces and solids 幾何（學） **2** [sing.] the measurements and relationships of lines, angles, etc. in a particular object or shape 幾何形狀；幾何圖形；幾何結構：*the geometry of a spider's web* 蜘蛛網的幾何形狀

geo·phys·ics /ˌdʒiːəʊˈfɪzɪks; *NAmE* ˌdʒiːoʊ-/ *noun* [U] the scientific study of the earth's atmosphere, oceans and climate 地球物理學 ▸ **geo·phys·ic·al** /-ˈfɪzɪkl/ *adj.*：*geophysical data* 地球物理資料 **geo·physi·cist** /-ˈfɪzɪsɪst/ *noun*

geo·pol·it·ics /ˌdʒiːəʊˈpɒlətɪks; *NAmE* ˌdʒiːoʊˈpɑːl-/ *noun* [U+sing./pl. v.] the political relations between countries and groups of countries in the world; the study of these relations 地緣政治；地理政治學 ▸ **geo·pol·it·ical** /ˌdʒiːəʊpəˈlɪtɪkl; *NAmE* ˌdʒiːoʊ-/ *adj.*

Geor·die /ˈdʒɔːdi; *NAmE* ˈdʒɔːrdi/ *noun* (*BrE, informal*) **1** [C] a person from Tyneside in NE England（英格蘭東北部的）泰恩賽德人 **2** [U] a way of speaking, typical of people from Tyneside in NE England（英格蘭東北部的）泰恩賽德口音；喬的語 ▸ **Geor·die** *adj.*：*a Geordie accent* 泰恩賽德人的口音

geor·gette /dʒɔːˈdʒet; *NAmE* ˌdʒɔːrˈdʒet/ *noun* [U] a type of thin silk or cotton cloth, used for making clothes 喬其紗（薄絲或棉織品，用作衣料）

Geor·gian /ˈdʒɔːdʒən; *NAmE* ˈdʒɔːrdʒən/ *adj.* (especially of ARCHITECTURE and furniture 尤指建築和傢具) from the time of the British kings George I–IV (1714–1830) 喬治王朝時期的，喬治一世至四世時代的（1714–1830）：*a fine Georgian house* 優雅的喬治王朝時期的房屋

geo·ther·mal /ˌdʒiːəʊˈθɜːml; *NAmE* ˌdʒiːoʊˈθɜːrml/ *adj.* (*geology* 地) connected with the natural heat of rock deep in the ground 地熱的：*geothermal energy* 地熱能

ge·ra·nium /dʒəˈreɪniəm/ *noun* a garden plant with a mass of red, pink or white flowers on the end of each STEM 天竺葵；老鸛草

ger·bil /ˈdʒɜːbɪl; *NAmE* ˈdʒɜːrbɪl/ *noun* a small desert animal like a mouse, that is often kept as a pet 沙鼠

geri·at·ric /ˌdʒeriˈætrɪk/ *noun* **1** **geriatrics** [U] the branch of medicine concerned with the diseases and care of old people 老年醫學 **2** [C] (*informal, offensive*) an old person, especially one with poor physical or mental health 老年人；老頭子；老婆子；老年病人：*I'm not a* *geriatric yet, you know!* 要知道我還沒有老朽！ ▶ **geri·at·ric** *adj.*：*the geriatric ward* (= in a hospital) 老年人病房 ◇ *a geriatric vehicle* (= old and in bad condition) 老爺車

geria·tri·cian /ˌdʒeriəˈtrɪʃn/ *noun* a doctor who studies and treats the diseases of old people 老年病科醫師；老年病學專家

germ /dʒɜːm; *NAmE* dʒɜːrm/ *noun* **1** [C, usually pl.] a very small living thing that can cause infection and disease 微生物；細菌；病菌：*Disinfectant kills germs.* 消毒劑可殺菌。◇ *Dirty hands can be a breeding ground for germs.* 髒手可能滋生病菌。 **2** [sing.] **~ of sth** an early stage of the development of sth 起源；發端；萌芽：*Here was the germ of a brilliant idea.* 一個絕妙的主意就是從這裏萌發的。 **3** [C] (*biology* 生) the part of a plant or an animal that can develop into a new one 胚芽；胚原基；芽孢；胚胎 ➲ see also WHEATGERM

Ger·man /ˈdʒɜːmən; *NAmE* ˈdʒɜːrmən/ *adj., noun*
▪ ***adj.*** from or connected with Germany 德國的
▪ ***noun*** **1** [C] a person from Germany 德國人 **2** [U] the language of Germany, Austria and parts of Switzerland 德語（德國、奧地利和瑞士部份地區的語言）

ger·mane /dʒɜːˈmeɪn; *NAmE* dʒɜːrˈm-/ *adj.* [not usually before noun] **~ (to sth)** (*formal*) (of ideas, remarks, etc. 想法、言語等) connected with sth in an important or appropriate way 與…有密切關係；貼切；恰當 **SYN** **relevant**：*remarks that are germane to the discussion* 與這次討論密切相關的談話

Ger·man·ic /dʒɜːˈmænɪk; *NAmE* dʒɜːrˈm-/ *adj.* **1** connected with or considered typical of Germany or its people 德國的；德國人的；有德國（或德國人）特點的：*She had an almost Germanic regard for order.* 她簡直像德國人一樣講究條理。 **2** connected with the language family that includes German, English, Dutch and Swedish among others 日耳曼語（族）的

ger·ma·nium /dʒɜːˈmeɪniəm; *NAmE* dʒɜːr-/ *noun* [U] (*symb.* **Ge**) a chemical element. Germanium is a shiny grey element that is similar to a metal (= is a METALLOID). 鍺

ˌ**German** ˈ**measles** (also **ru·bella**) *noun* [U] a mild infectious disease that causes a sore throat and red spots all over the body. It can seriously affect babies born to women who catch it soon after they become pregnant. 德國麻疹；風疹

ˌ**German** ˈ**shepherd** (*especially NAmE*) (*BrE* also **Al·sa·tian**) *noun* a large dog, often trained to help the police, to guard buildings or (especially in the US) to help blind people find their way 德國牧羊犬（常訓練成警犬，看家護院，尤其在美國用作導盲犬）

ger·mi·cide /ˈdʒɜːmɪsaɪd; *NAmE* ˈdʒɜːrm-/ *noun* [C, U] a substance which destroys bacteria, etc. 殺菌劑 ▶ **ger·mi·cidal** /ˌdʒɜːmɪˈsaɪdl; *NAmE* ˌdʒɜːrm-/ *adj.*

ger·min·ate /ˈdʒɜːmɪneɪt; *NAmE* ˈdʒɜːrm-/ *verb* [I, T] **~ (sth)** when the seed of a plant **germinates** or is **germinated**, it starts to grow （使）發芽，萌芽，開始生長：(*figurative*) *An idea for a novel began to germinate in her mind.* 一部小說的構思已經在她的腦海中萌發。 ▶ **ger·min·ation** /ˌdʒɜːmɪˈneɪʃn; *NAmE* ˌdʒɜːrm-/ *noun* [U]

ˌ**germ** ˈ**warfare** *noun* [U] = BIOLOGICAL WARFARE

ger·on·toc·racy /ˌdʒerənˈtɒkrəsi; *NAmE* -ˈtɑːk-/ *noun* (*pl.* **-ies**) [C, U] a state, society, or group governed by old people; government by old people 老人統治的國家（或社會、組織）；老人統治 ▶ **ger·on·to·crat·ic** /dʒəˌrɒntəˈkrætɪk; *NAmE* -ˌrɑːntə-/ *adj.*

ger·ont·olo·gist /ˌdʒerɒnˈtɒlədʒɪst; *NAmE* -rənˈtɑːl-/ *noun* (*especially NAmE*) a person who studies the process of people growing old 老年學專家

ge·ron·tol·ogy /ˌdʒerɒnˈtɒlədʒi; *NAmE* -rənˈtɑːl-/ *noun* [U] the scientific study of OLD AGE and the process of growing old 老年學

ger·ry·man·der (also **jer·ry·man·der**) /ˈdʒerimændə(r)/ *verb* **~ sth** (*disapproving*) to change the size and borders of an area for voting in order to give an unfair advantage to one party in an election 不公正地改劃選區，不公正地劃分選區（旨在使某政黨獲得優勢） ▶ **ger·ry·man·der·ing** (also **jer·ry·man·der·ing**) *noun* [U]

ger·und /ˈdʒerənd/ *noun* (*grammar* 語法) a noun in the form of the present participle of a verb (that is, ending in *-ing*) for example *travelling* in the sentence *I preferred travelling alone.* 動名詞

ge·stalt /gəˈʃtælt; *NAmE* also -ˈʃtɑːlt/ *noun* (*psychology* 心) (from *German*) a set of things, such as a person's thoughts or experiences, that is considered as a single system which is different from the individual thoughts, experiences, etc. within it 格式塔，完形（即有別於其內部個體單位、作為單一體系的一系列思想、經驗等）

ges·tate /dʒeˈsteɪt; *NAmE* ˈdʒesteɪt/ *verb* **~ sth** (*biology* 生 or *medical* 醫) to carry a young human or animal inside the WOMB until it is born 懷孕；妊娠

ges·ta·tion /dʒeˈsteɪʃn/ *noun* **1** [U, sing.] the time that the young of a person or an animal develops inside its mother's body until it is born; the process of developing inside the mother's body 妊娠（期）；懷孕（期）：*a baby born at 38 weeks' gestation* 懷孕 38 週時出生的嬰兒 ◇ *The* ***gestation period*** *of a horse is about eleven months.* 馬的懷孕期大約為十一個月。 **2** [U] (*formal*) the process by which an idea or a plan develops （想法、計劃的）構思，醞釀，孕育 **SYN** **development**

ges·ticu·late /dʒeˈstɪkjuleɪt/ *verb* [I] to move your hands and arms about in order to attract attention or make sb understand what you are saying 做手勢；用手勢表達；用動作示意：*He* ***gesticulated wildly*** *at the clock.* 他使勁指着鐘打手勢。 ▶ **ges·ticu·la·tion** /dʒeˌstɪkjuˈleɪʃn/ *noun* [C, U]：***wild/frantic gesticulations*** 發狂似的手勢

ges·ture /ˈdʒestʃə(r)/ *noun, verb*
▪ ***noun*** **1** [C, U] a movement that you make with your hands, your head or your face to show a particular meaning 手勢；姿勢；示意動作：*He* ***made a*** *rude* ***gesture*** *at the driver of the other car.* 他向另外那輛汽車的司機做了個粗野的手勢。◇ *She finished what she had to say with a gesture of despair.* 她用絕望的姿勢結束了她不得不講的話。◇ *They communicated entirely by gesture.* 他們完全用手勢交流。 **2** [C] something that you do or say to show a particular feeling or intention （表明感情或意圖的）姿態，表示：*They sent some flowers as a gesture of sympathy to the parents of the child.* 他們送了一些花表示對孩子父母的同情。◇ *It was a nice gesture* (= it was kind) *to invite his wife too.* 把他的妻子也請來是友好的表示。◇ *We do not accept responsibility but we will refund the money as a* ***gesture of goodwill.*** 我們不承擔責任，不過我們願意退款以表示我們的善意。◇ *The government has made a gesture towards public opinion* (= has tried to do sth that the public will like). 政府已做出順應民意的姿態。
▪ ***verb*** [I, T] to move your hands, head, face, etc. as a way of expressing what you mean or want 做手勢；用手勢表示；用動作示意：**(+ adv./prep.)** *'I see you read a lot,' he said, gesturing at the wall of books.* "看來你讀很多書。" 他指着那一牆的書說道。◇ **~ to sb (to do sth)** | **~ for sb to do sth** *She gestured for them to come in.* 她示意讓他們進來。◇ **~ (to sb) (that) …** *He gestured (to me) that it was time to go.* 他示意（我）該走了。◇ *They gestured that I should follow.* 他們示意讓我跟在後面。

ge·sund·heit /gəˈzʊndhaɪt/ *exclamation* (*NAmE*, from *German*) used when sb has SNEEZED to wish them good health （別人打噴嚏時說）祝你健康

get 🔑 /get/ *verb* (**getting**, **got**, **got** /gɒt; *NAmE* gɑːt/)
HELP In spoken *NAmE* the past participle **got·ten** /ˈgɒtn/ /ˈgɑːtn/ is almost always used. 美式英語口語中過去分詞幾乎都用 gotten。

▸ **RECEIVE/OBTAIN** 接到；得到 **1** 🔑 [T, no passive] **~ sth** to receive sth 收到；接到：*I got a letter from Dave this morning.* 今天早上我收到戴夫的一封來信。◇ *What* (= What presents) *did you get for your birthday?* 你收到什麼生日禮物了？◇ *He gets* (= earns) *about $40 000 a year.* 他一年掙 4 萬元左右。◇ *This room gets very little sunshine.* 這個房間幾乎照不進陽光。◇ ***I got a shock*** *when I saw the bill.* 我看到賬單時大吃一驚。◇ ***I get the impression*** *that he is bored with his job.* 我的印象是他厭倦他的工作。 **2** 🔑 [T, no passive] to obtain sth 獲得；得到：**~ sth** *Where did you get* (= buy) *that skirt?* 你在

哪兒買的那條裙子？◇ *Did you manage to get tickets for the concert?* 你弄到音樂會的票了嗎？◇ *She opened the door wider to get a better look.* 她把門開大些以便看得更清楚。◇ *Try to get some sleep.* 盡量睡會兒吧。◇ *He has just got a new job.* 他剛找到一份新工作。◇ **~ sth for sb** *Did you get a present for your mother?* 給你母親買禮物了嗎？◇ **~ sb/yourself sth** *Did you get your mother a present?* 給你母親買禮物了嗎？◇ *Why don't you get yourself a car?* 你為什麼不買輛汽車呢？ **3** 🔑 [T, no passive] **~ sth (for sth)** to obtain or receive an amount of money by selling sth （賣某物）掙得，獲得： *How much did you get for your car?* 你的汽車賣了多少錢？

▸ **BRING** 帶來 **4** 🔑 [T] to go to a place and bring sb/sth back 去取（或帶來） **SYN** **fetch**： **~ sb/sth** *Quick—go and get a cloth!* 快，去拿塊布來！◇ *Somebody get a doctor!* 誰去叫個醫生來吧！◇ *I have to go and get my mother from the airport* (= collect her). 我得去機場接我的母親。◇ **~ sth for sb** *Get a drink for John.* 給約翰拿杯飲料來。◇ **~ sb/yourself sth** *Get John a drink.* 給約翰拿杯飲料來。

▸ **PUNISHMENT** 懲罰 **5** [T, no passive] **~ sth** to receive sth as a punishment 受到；遭到；被判（刑）： *He got ten years* (= was sent to prison for ten years) *for armed robbery.* 他因持槍搶劫被判刑十年。

▸ **BROADCASTS** 廣播 **6** [T, no passive] **~ sth** to receive broadcasts from a particular television or radio station 接收到；收聽到；收看到： *We can't get Channel 5 in our area.* 我們地區收不到 5 頻道的節目。

▸ **BUY** 買 **7** [T, no passive] **~ sth** to buy sth, for example a newspaper or magazine, regularly （定期）買，購買 **SYN** **take**： *Which newspaper do you get?* 你訂閱什麼報紙？

▸ **MARK/GRADE** 分數；等級 **8** 🔑 [T, no passive] **~ sth** to achieve or be given a particular mark/grade in an exam （考試）獲得，達到： *He got a 'C' in Chemistry and a 'B' in English.* 他化學考試得中，英語考試得良。

▸ **ILLNESS** 疾病 **9** 🔑 [T, no passive] **~ sth** to become infected with an illness; to suffer from a pain, etc. 感染上；患上；遭受…之苦： *I got this cold off* (= from) *you!* 我這感冒是被你傳染的！◇ *She gets* (= often suffers from) *really bad headaches.* 她經常頭痛得厲害。

▸ **CONTACT** 聯繫 **10** [T, no passive] **~ sb** to be connected with sb by telephone 與（某人）電話聯繫；與（某人）通電話： *I wanted to speak to the manager but I got his secretary instead.* 我想與經理談話，可接電話的卻是他的秘書。

▸ **STATE/CONDITION** 狀態；情況 **11** 🔑 *linking verb* to reach a particular state or condition; to make sb/sth/yourself reach a particular state or condition （使）達到，處於： **+ adj.** *to get angry/bored/hungry/fat* 發怒；生厭；飢餓；發胖 ◇ *You'll soon* **get used to** *the climate here.* 你會很快習慣這兒的氣候的。◇ *We ought to go; it's getting late.* 我們該走了，天色越來越晚了。◇ *to* **get dressed/undressed** (= to put your clothes on/take your clothes off) 穿上／脫下衣服 ◇ *They plan to* **get married** *in the summer.* 他們打算夏天結婚。◇ *She's upstairs getting ready.* 她在樓上做準備。◇ *I wouldn't go there alone; you might get* (= be) *mugged.* 我不會一個人去那兒，說不準會碰上搶劫的。◇ *My car got* (= was) *stolen at the weekend.* 我的汽車週末被偷了。◇ **~ sb/sth + adj.** *Don't get your dress dirty!* 別把你的連衣裙弄髒了！◇ *He got his fingers caught in the door.* 他的手指給門夾了。◇ *She soon got the children ready for school.* 她很快幫孩子們做好了上學的準備。 ➲ SYNONYMS at BECOME **12** 🔑 [I] **~ to do sth** to reach the point at which you feel, know, are, etc. sth 開始（感覺到、認識到、成為）；達到…地步（或程度）： *After a time you get to realize that these things don't matter.* 過段時間你會明白這些事情並不要緊。◇ *You'll like her once you* **get to know** *her.* 你一旦瞭解了她就會喜歡她的。◇ *His drinking is getting to be a problem.* 他的酗酒越來越成問題了。◇ *She's getting to be an old lady now.* 她現在都快是個老太婆了。

▸ **MAKE/PERSUADE** 使；讓；說服 **13** 🔑 [T] to make, persuade, etc. sb/sth to do sth 使，讓（某人或物做某事）；說服（某人做某事）： **~ sb/sth to do sth** *I couldn't get the car to start this morning.* 我今天早上沒法讓這汽車發動起來。◇ *He got his sister to help him with his homework.* 他讓姐姐幫助他做家庭作業。◇ *You'll never get him to understand.* 你永遠不會使他明白的。◇ **~ sb/sth doing sth** *Can you really get that old car going again?* 你真能讓那老爺車再跑起來嗎？◇ *It's not hard to get him talking—the problem is stopping him!* 讓他談話並不難，難的是讓他住口！

▸ **GET STH DONE** 使完成某事 **14** 🔑 [T] **~ sth done** to cause sth to happen or be done 使（某事）發生；使完成（某事）： *I must get my hair cut.* 我得理髮了。◇ *I'll never get all this work finished.* 這麼多的工作我怎麼也幹不完。

▸ **START** 開始 **15** [T] **~ doing sth** to start doing sth 開始；開始做： *I got talking to her.* 我開始與她談起來。◇ *We need to get going soon.* 我們需要馬上出發。

▸ **OPPORTUNITY** 機會 **16** [I] **~ to do sth** (*informal*) to have the opportunity to do sth 有機會（做某事）；得到（做某事的）機會： *He got to try out all the new software.* 他得以試用了所有的新軟件。◇ *It's not fair—I never get to go first.* 這不公平，我從來沒有機會先走。

▸ **ARRIVE** 到達 **17** 🔑 [I] **+ adv./prep.** to arrive at or reach a place or point 抵達，到達（某地或某點）： *We got to San Diego at 7 o'clock.* 我們 7 點鐘到達了聖迭戈。◇ *You got in very late last night.* 你昨晚回來得很晚。◇ *What time did you get here?* 你什麼時候到達這兒的？◇ *I haven't got very far with the book I'm reading.* 我那本書還沒讀多少呢。

▸ **MOVE/TRAVEL** 移動；旅行 **18** 🔑 [I, T] to move to or from a particular place or in a particular direction, sometimes with difficulty; to make sb/sth do this （使）到達，離開，沿…移動，艱難地移動： **+ adv./prep.** *The bridge was destroyed so we couldn't get across the river.* 大橋已經毀壞，我們無法過河了。◇ *She got into bed.* 她上牀睡覺了。◇ *He got down from the ladder.* 他從梯子上下來了。◇ *We didn't* **get** (= go) **to bed** *until 3 a.m.* 我們直到凌晨 3 點才上牀睡覺。◇ *Where do we* **get on** *the bus?* 我們在哪兒上公共汽車？◇ *I'm* **getting off** (= leaving the train) *at the next station.* 我在下一站下車。◇ *Where have they* **got to** (= where are they)? 他們到什麼地方去了？◇ *We must be* **getting home;** *it's past midnight.* 我們得回家了，已過半夜了。◇ **~ sb/sth + adv./prep.** *The general had to get his troops across the river.* 將軍必須讓部隊過河。◇ *We couldn't get the piano through the door.* 我們無法將鋼琴搬過這道門。◇ *We'd better call a taxi and get you home.* 我們最好叫輛出租車送你回家。◇ *I can't get the lid off.* 我打不開蓋子。 **19** 🔑 [T, no passive] **~ sth** to use a bus, taxi, plane, etc. 搭乘，乘坐（公共汽車、出租車、飛機等）： *We're going to be late—let's get a taxi.* 我們要遲到了，咱們坐出租車吧。◇ *I usually get the bus to work.* 我通常坐公共汽車上班。

▸ **MEAL** 飯菜 **20** [T] (*especially BrE*) to prepare a meal 準備，做（飯）： **~ sth** *Who's getting the lunch?* 誰來做午飯？◇ **~ sth for sb/yourself** *I must go home and get tea for the kids.* 我得回家為孩子們準備茶點。◇ **~ sb/yourself sth** *I must go home and get the kids their tea.* 我得回家為孩子們準備茶點。

▸ **TELEPHONE/DOOR** 電話；門 **21** [T] **~ sth** (*informal*) to answer the telephone or a door when sb calls, knocks, etc. 接（電話）；應（門）： *Will you get the phone?* 你去接一下電話好嗎？

▸ **CATCH/HIT** 抓住；擊中 **22** [T] **~ sb** to catch or take hold of sb, especially in order to harm or punish them（尤指為傷害或懲罰）抓住，捉住，逮住： *He was on the run for a week before the police got him.* 他逃跑一週後警方才將他逮住。◇ *to get sb by the arm/wrist/throat* 抓住某人的胳膊／手腕；掐住某人的喉嚨 ◇ *She fell overboard and the sharks got her.* 她從船上跌入水中被鯊魚咬了。◇ *He thinks everybody is* **out to get him** (= trying to harm him). 他認為所有人都想害他。◇ (*informal*) ***I'll get you*** *for that!* 這事我跟你沒完！ **23** [T] **~ sb + adv./prep.** to hit or wound sb 擊中；使受傷： *The bullet got him in the neck.* 子彈擊中了他的頸部。

▸ **UNDERSTAND** 理解 **24** [T, no passive] **~ sb/sth** (*informal*) to understand sb/sth 理解；明白： *I don't get you.* 我搞不懂你的意思。◇ *She didn't get the joke.* 她不明白那笑話的含義。◇ ***I don't get it****—why would she do a thing like that?* 我不明白，她怎麼會幹那種事？◇ ***I get the message****—you don't want me to come.* 我明白這意思，你是不希望我來。 ➲ SYNONYMS at UNDERSTAND

▸ **HAPPEN/EXIST** 發生；存在 **25** [T, no passive] **~ sth** (*informal*) used to say that sth happens or exists （表示

G

發生或存在）：*You* **get** (= There are) *all these kids hanging around in the street.* 所有這些孩子都在街上閒逛。◇ *They still get cases of typhoid there.* 他們那兒仍有傷寒病發生。

▸ CONFUSE/ANNOY 使困惑／煩惱 **26** [T, no passive] **~ sb** (*informal*) to make sb feel confused because they do not understand sth 使困惑；使迷惑；把…難住 SYN **puzzle**：*'What's the capital of Bhutan?' 'You've got me there!'* (= I don't know) "不丹的首都在什麼地方？""你可把我難倒了！" **27** [T, no passive] **~ sb** (*informal*) to annoy sb 使煩惱；使惱火：***What gets me*** *is having to do the same thing all day long.* 使我感到煩惱的是整天都得幹同樣的事。HELP **Get** is one of the most common words in English, but some people try to avoid it in formal writing. * get 是英語中最常用的單詞之一，但有的人在正式文體中盡量避免使用。

G

IDM Most idioms containing **get** are at the entries for the nouns and adjectives in the idioms, for example **get sb's goat** is at **goat**. 大多數含 get 的習語，都可在該等習語中的名詞及形容詞相關詞條找到，如 get sb's goat 在詞條 goat 下。**be getting 'on** (*informal*) **1** (of a person 人) to be becoming old 變老；上年紀 **2** (of time 時間) to be becoming late 漸晚；漸遲：*The time's getting on—we ought to be going.* 時間越來越晚了，我們該走了。**be getting on for …** (*especially BrE*) to be nearly a particular time, age or number 接近（某時刻、年齡或數目）：*It must be getting on for midnight.* 一定快到半夜了。◇ *He's getting on for eighty.* 他近八十歲了。**can't get 'over sth** (*informal*) used to say that you are shocked, surprised, amused, etc. by sth 因…而感到震驚（或驚訝、好笑等）：*I can't get over how rude she was.* 她這麼粗魯真使我感到驚訝。**get a'way from it all** (*informal*) to have a short holiday/vacation in a place where you can relax（到他處度短假）躲清靜 **,get it 'on (with sb)** (*slang, especially NAmE*) to have sex with sb（與某人）性交 **'get it** (also **catch 'hell**) (both *NAmE*) (*BrE* **'catch it**) (*informal*) to be punished or spoken to angrily about sth 受罰；受斥責 **,get it 'up** (*slang*) (of a man 男人) to have an ERECTION 勃起 **get sb 'going** (*BrE, informal*) to make sb angry, worried or excited 激怒某人；使某人擔憂（或激動）**get sb nowhere/not get sb anywhere** to not help sb make progress or succeed 使無所進展（或成就）；徒勞：*This line of investigation is getting us nowhere.* 這種調查方式不會使我們得到任何結果。◇ *Being rude to me won't get you anywhere.* 你對我撒野也沒有用。**get somewhere/anywhere/nowhere** to make some progress/no progress 有所（或無所）進展：*After six months' work on the project, at last I feel I'm getting somewhere.* 那個項目幹了六個月之後我終於感到有了一些進展。◇ *I don't seem to be getting anywhere with this letter.* 這封信似乎對我沒有什麼幫助。**'get there** to achieve your aim or complete a task 達到目的；完成任務；獲得成功：*I'm sure you'll get there in the end.* 我相信你最終會成功的。◇ *It's not perfect but **we're getting there*** (= making progress). 雖然這並非完美無瑕，但我們正朝着目標前進。**,get 'this!** (*informal, especially NAmE*) used to say that you are going to tell sb sth that they will find surprising or interesting 聽好了（用於表示要告訴大家令人吃驚或有趣的事情）：*OK, get this guys—there are only two left!* 好吧，聽好了，夥計們，只剩兩個了！**how selfish, stupid, ungrateful, etc. can you 'get?** (*informal*) used to express surprise or disapproval that sb has been so selfish, etc.（表示驚奇或不贊成）你怎麼這麼自私（或愚蠢、忘恩負義等）**there's no getting a'way from sth | you can't get a'way from sth** you have to admit that sth unpleasant is true 不容否認，只好承認（不愉快的事實）**what are you, was he, etc. 'getting at?** (*informal*) used to ask, especially in an angry way, what sb is/was suggesting（尤指氣憤地問）你（或他等）這話是什麼意思，你（或他等）用意何在：*I'm partly to blame? What exactly are you getting at?* 我應負部份責任？你究竟是什麼意思？**what has got into sb?** (*informal*) used to say that sb has suddenly started to behave in a strange or different way（表示某人突然行為反常起來）…怎麼啦：*What's got into Alex? He never used to worry like that.* 亞歷克斯怎麼啦？他以前從未那樣愁過。

PHR V **,get a'bout** (*BrE*) = GET AROUND
,get a'bove yourself (*especially BrE*) to have too high an opinion of yourself 自以為了不起；自高自大；自視甚高
,get a'cross (to sb) | ,get sth↔a'cross (to sb) to be communicated or understood; to succeed in communicating sth 被傳達；被理解；把…講清楚：*Your meaning didn't really get across.* 你的意思並未真正為別人理解。◇ *He's not very good at getting his ideas across.* 他不太善於清楚地表達自己的思想。
,get a'head (of sb) to make progress (further than others have done) 走在（某人的）前面；領先；勝過（某人）：*She wants to get ahead in her career.* 她想在事業上脫穎而出。◇ *He soon got ahead of the others in his class.* 他很快就在班上名列前茅了。
,get a'long 1 (usually used in the progressive tenses 通常用於進行時) to leave a place 離開；離去：*It's time we were getting along.* 我們該離開了。**2** = GET ON
,get a'round 1 (*BrE* also **,get a'bout**) to move from place to place or from person to person 傳播；流傳；各處走動：*She gets around with the help of a stick.* 她拄着拐杖四處走動。◇ *News soon got around that he had resigned.* 他已辭職的消息很快傳開了。**2** (*especially NAmE*) = GET ROUND
'get at sb (usually used in the progressive tenses 通常用於進行時) to keep criticizing sb 一再批評，不斷指責，老是數落（某人）：*He's always getting at me.* 他老是責備我。◇ *She feels she's being got at.* 她感到自己總是受人數落。**'get at sb/sth** to reach sb/sth; to gain access to sb/sth 到達某處；接近某人（或某物）；夠得着某物：*The files are locked up and I can't get at them.* 文件資料鎖起來了，我取不出來。**'get at sth** to learn or find out sth 獲悉；瞭解；查明；發現：*The truth is sometimes difficult to get at.* 有時真相很難查明。
,get a'way 1 to have a holiday/vacation 度假；休假：*We're hoping to get away for a few days at Easter.* 我們期待着復活節出去休幾天假。➲ related noun GETAWAY **2** (*BrE, informal*) used to show that you do not believe or are surprised by what sb has said（表示不相信或驚奇）別胡扯：*'These tickets didn't cost me a thing.' 'Get away!'* "這些票我一分錢也沒花。""胡說！" **,get a'way (from …)** to succeed in leaving a place（得以）離開，脫身：*I won't be able to get away from the office before 7.* 我 7 點鐘之前無法離開辦公室。**,get a'way (from sb/ …)** 0‑w to escape from sb or a place 擺脫（某人）；逃離（某地）**,get a'way with sth 1** 0‑w to steal sth and escape with it 偷攜某物潛逃；偷走：*Thieves got away with computer equipment worth $30 000.* 盜賊偷走了價值 3 萬元的計算機設備。➲ related noun GETAWAY **2** 0‑w to receive a relatively light punishment 受到從輕發落（輕微懲罰）：*He was lucky to get away with only a fine.* 他算是萬幸，只被罰款了事。**3** 0‑w to do sth wrong and not be punished for it 做（壞事）而未受懲罰：*Don't be tempted to cheat—you'll never get away with it.* 別想着作弊，作弊者一定會受到嚴懲。◇ **~ doing sth** *Nobody gets away with insulting me like that.* 那樣侮辱我的人我決不會善罷甘休。**4** to manage with less of sth than you might expect to need 以（比預期少的事物）就能應付：*After the first month, you should be able to get away with one lesson a week.* 第一個月之後，每週上一次課就可以了。
,get 'back 0‑w to return, especially to your home 返回；回去；回家：*What time did you get back last night?* 你昨晚什麼時候回家的？➲ SYNONYMS at RETURN **,get sth↔'back** 0‑w to obtain sth again after having lost it 尋回，找回，重新獲得（丟失的東西）：*She's got her old job back.* 她已恢復原職。◇ *I never lend books—you never get them back.* 我的書從不外借，借出去就收不回來。**,get 'back (in)** (of a political party 政黨) to win an election after having lost the previous one 重新上台；東山再起 **,get 'back at sb** (*informal*) to do sth bad to sb who has done sth bad to you; to get REVENGE on sb 向某人報復：*I'll find a way of getting back at him!* 我會想法報復他的！**,get 'back to sb** (*informal*) to speak or write to sb again later, especially in order to give a reply 以後再答覆（或回覆）某人：*I'll find out and get back to you.* 我查明之後再答覆你。**,get 'back to sth** to return to sth 回到某事上：*Could we get back to the question of funding?* 我們回到資金問題上來好嗎？**,get back to'gether (with sb)** to start a relationship with sb again, especially a

romantic relationship, after having finished a previous relationship with the same person（與某人，尤指戀人）重歸於好，重修舊好：*I just got back together with my ex-girlfriend.* 我剛和前女友重修舊好。

ˌget beˈhind (with sth) to fail to make enough progress or to produce sth at the right time 落後；拖延；拖欠：*I'm getting behind with my work.* 我的工作拖延了。◇ *He got behind with the payments for his car.* 他拖欠了買汽車的車款。

ˌget ˈby (on/in/with sth) 🔑 to manage to live or do a particular thing using the money, knowledge, equipment, etc. that you have（靠…）維持生計，設法過活，勉強應付：*How does she get by on such a small salary?* 她靠這點微薄的工資怎麼過活？◇ *I can just about get by in German* (= I can speak basic German). 我用德語只能勉強應付。

ˌget ˈdown (of children 兒童) (*BrE*) to leave the table after a meal 飯後離開餐桌 **ˌget sb ˈdown** (*informal*) to make sb feel sad or depressed 使悲傷；使沮喪；使憂鬱 **ˌget sth↔ˈdown** **1** to swallow sth, usually with difficulty（困難地）吞下，嚥下 **2** to make a note of sth 記錄；記下；寫下 SYN **write down**：*Did you get his number down?* 你記下他的號碼了嗎？ **ˌget ˈdown to sth** to begin to do sth; to give serious attention to sth 開始做某事；開始認真注意（或對待）某事：*Let's **get down to business**.* 咱們開始幹正事吧。◇ *I like to **get down to work** by 9.* 我喜歡在 9 點之前開始工作。◇ **~ doing sth** *It's time I got down to thinking about that essay.* 我該認真思考一下那篇論文了。

ˌget ˈin | ˌget ˈinto sth **1** 🔑 to arrive at a place 到達：*The train got in late.* 火車晚點到達。◇ *What time do you get into Heathrow?* 你什麼時候到達希思羅機場？ **2** 🔑 to win an election 當選：*The Republican candidate stands a good chance of getting in.* 共和黨候選人很可能當選。◇ *She first got into Parliament* (= became an MP) *in 2005.* 她 2005 年第一次當選為議員。 **3** 🔑 to be admitted to a school, university, etc. 被錄取；被接受入學：*She's got into Durham to study law.* 她被錄取到達勒姆大學攻讀法律。 **ˌget sb↔ˈin** to call sb to your house to do a job 請某人來家裏做事 **ˌget sth↔ˈin** **1** to collect or gather sth 收集；收割：*to **get the crops/harvest in*** 收穫作物／莊稼 **2** to buy a supply of sth 購買；買進：*Remember to get in some beers for this evening.* 記住為今天的晚會買些啤酒。 **3** to manage to do or say sth 設法做（或說）：*I got in an hour's work while the baby was asleep.* 我趁孩子睡覺抽空幹了一小時的活。◇ *She talks so much it's impossible to get a word in.* 她說起話來滔滔不絕，讓人一句話都插不進去。 **ˌget ˈin on sth** to take part in an activity 參加（活動）：*He's hoping to get in on any discussions about the new project.* 他盼望着參加有關新計劃的任何討論。 **ˌget ˈin with sb** (*informal*) to become friendly with sb, especially in order to gain an advantage（尤指為撈取好處與某人）成為朋友，拉關係，套近乎

ˌget ˈinto sth **1** 🔑 to put on a piece of clothing, especially with difficulty（尤指費力地）穿上：*I can't get into these shoes—they're too small.* 這雙鞋太小，我穿不進去。 **2** 🔑 to start a career in a particular profession 開始從事（某職業）：*What's the best way to get into journalism?* 進入新聞界的最佳途徑是什麼？ **3** 🔑 to become involved in sth; to start sth 參與，開始（某事）：*I got into conversation with an Italian student.* 我與一位意大利學生談了起來。◇ *to get into a fight* 參與鬥毆 **4** 🔑 to develop a particular habit 養成某種習慣；習慣於：*Don't let yourself get into bad habits.* 別讓自己染上惡習。◇ *You should get into the routine of saving the document you are working on every ten minutes.* 你應該養成每十分鐘將正在編輯的文件存盤一次的習慣。◇ *How did she get into* (= start taking) *drugs?* 她是怎麼染上毒品的？ **5** 🔑 (*informal*) to become interested in sth 對…產生興趣：*I'm really getting into jazz these days.* 我最近真的開始喜歡爵士樂了。 **6** to become familiar with sth; to learn sth 開始熟悉；學會：*I haven't really got into my new job yet.* 我還未真正熟悉我的新工作。 **ˌget ˈinto sth | ˌget yourself/sb ˈinto sth** 🔑 to reach a particular state or condition; to make sb reach a particular state or condition（使）陷入，處於，達到：*He got into trouble with the police while he was still at school.* 他還在上學時就與警方發生過糾葛。◇ *Three people were rescued from a yacht which got into difficulties.* 從遇險的快艇中營救出了三人。◇ *She got herself into a real state* (= became very anxious) *before the interview.* 她面試前格外地焦慮不安。

ˌget ˈoff | ˌget ˈoff sb used especially to tell sb to stop touching you or another person（尤用於告訴別人）別碰，走遠點：*Get off me, that hurts!* 別碰我，好痛喲！ **ˌget ˈoff | ˌget sb ˈoff** **1** to leave a place or start a journey; to help sb do this（使某人）離開，出發，動身：*We got off straight after breakfast.* 我們早飯後就立即動身了。◇ *He got the children off to school.* 他打發孩子們上學去了。 **2** (*BrE*) to fall asleep; to make sb do this（使）入睡：*I had great difficulty getting off to sleep.* 我很難入睡。◇ *They couldn't get the baby off till midnight.* 他們直到半夜才把嬰孩哄入睡。 **ˌget ˈoff | ˌget ˈoff sth** to leave work with permission 經允許離開工作；下班：*Could you get off* (*work*) *early tomorrow?* 你明天可以提早下班嗎？ **ˌget ˈoff sth | ˌget sb ˈoff sth** to stop discussing a particular subject; to make sb do this（使）停止討論，不再談論：*Please can we get off the subject of dieting?* 我們別再談論節食這個話題行嗎？◇ *I couldn't get him off politics once he had started.* 他一談起政治我就沒法讓他停下。 **ˌget sth ˈoff** to send sth by post/mail 郵寄某物：*I must get these letters off first thing tomorrow.* 我明天首先得把這些信件寄出去。 **ˌget ˈoff on sth** (*informal*) to be excited by sth, especially in a sexual way 因…而興奮，因…而激動（尤指性興奮） **ˌget ˈoff (with sth)** to have no or almost no injuries in an accident（在事故中）幸免於難，並無大恙：*She was lucky to get off with just a few bruises.* 她幸免於難，只有幾處碰傷。 **ˌget ˈoff (with sth) | ˌget sb ˈoff (with sth)** 🔑 to receive no or almost no punishment; to help sb do this（使）免受處罰，逃脫懲罰：*He was lucky to get off with a small fine.* 他僥幸逃脫懲罰，交了一小筆罰款就了事。◇ *A good lawyer might be able to get you off.* 請位好律師或許能使你脫罪。 **ˌget ˈoff with sb** (*informal, especially BrE*) to have a sexual or romantic experience with sb; to start a sexual relationship with sb（與某人）發生性關係，談戀愛，開始性關係：*Steve got off with Tracey at the party.* 史蒂夫在聚會上就與特蕾西親熱起來。

ˌget ˈon **1** 🔑 (also **ˌget aˈlong**) used to talk or ask about how well sb is doing in a particular situation（談及或問及某人）進展，進步：*He's getting on very well at school.* 他在學校學得很好。◇ ***How did you get on** at the interview?* 你面試的情況怎麼樣？ **2** 🔑 to be successful in your career, etc. 獲得成功；事業有成：*Parents are always anxious for their children to get on.* 父母總是急切地盼望孩子們事業有成。◇ *I don't know how he's going to **get on in life**.* 我不知道他將如何出人頭地。 **3** 🔑 (also **ˌget aˈlong**) to manage or survive 對付；應付；活下來；過活：*We can get on perfectly well without her.* 沒有她我們也能過得很好。◇ *I just can't get along without a secretary.* 沒有秘書我簡直寸步難行。 **ˌget ˈon to sb** **1** to contact sb by telephone, letter or email（用電話、書信或電子郵件）與某人聯繫：*The heating isn't working; I'll get on to the landlord about it.* 暖氣不熱，我得與房東聯繫一下。 **2** to become aware of sb's activities, especially when they have been doing sth bad or illegal 覺察，察覺，識破（某人的不法行為）：*He had been stealing money from the company for years before they got on to him.* 他一直竊取公司的錢，多年後他們才發覺。 **ˌget ˈon to sth** to begin to talk about a new subject 開始討論，轉而談論（新課題）：*It's time we got on to the question of costs.* 我們該討論成本問題了。 **ˌget ˈon with sb | ˌget ˈon (together)** 🔑 (both *BrE*) (also **ˌget aˈlong with sb**, **ˌget aˈlong (together)** *NAmE, BrE*) to have a friendly relationship with sb（與某人）和睦相處，關係良好：*She's never really got on with her sister.* 她從未與妹妹真正和睦相處過。◇ *She and her sister have never really got on.* 她與妹妹一直合不來。◇ *We get along just fine together.* 我們相處得很融洽。 **ˌget ˈon with sth** **1** 🔑 (also **ˌget aˈlong with sth**) used to talk or ask about how well sb is doing a task（談及或問及工作情況）進展，進步：*I'm not getting on very fast with this job.* 我這個工作進展不太快。 **2** 🔑 to continue doing sth, especially after an interruption（尤指中斷後）繼

續做某事：*Be quiet and get on with your work.* 安靜下來，繼續幹你的事。◇ (*informal*) *Get on with it! We haven't got all day.* 繼續幹吧！我們的時間並不多。 **ˌget ˈout** to become known 泄露；被人知道：*If this gets out there'll be trouble.* 這事要是被人知道就麻煩了。 **ˌget sth↔ˈout** **1** to produce or publish sth 生產；發表；出版：*Will we get the book out by the end of the year?* 我們這本書將在年底前出版嗎？ **2** to say sth with difficulty 困難地說出；勉強地說：*She managed to get out a few words of thanks.* 她終於勉強說了幾句道謝的話。 **ˌget ˈout (of sth)** to leave or go out of a place 離開（某地）；從…出來：*You ought to get out of the house more.* 你應該多到戶外去走走。◇ *She screamed at me to get out.* 她衝着我大聲喊，讓我出去。 **ˌget ˈout of sth** **1** 🗝 to avoid a responsibility or duty 逃避，規避，擺脫（責任或義務）：*We promised we'd go—we can't get out of it now.* 我們答應過要去的，現在我們不能食言。◇ **~ doing sth** *I wish I could get out of going to that meeting.* 但願我能不去參加那個會。 **2** 🗝 to stop having a particular habit 放棄，戒除，拋棄（習慣）：*I can't get out of the habit of waking at six in the morning.* 我早上六點鐘醒的習慣改不了。 **ˌget sth ˈout of sb** to persuade sb to tell or give you sth, especially by force（尤指強行）盤問出，獲取：*The police finally got a confession out of her.* 警方最終逼迫她招了供。 **ˌget sth ˈout of sb/sth** to gain or obtain sth good from sb/sth 從…中獲得（有益的東西）：*She seems to get a lot out of life.* 她似乎從生活中獲益良多。◇ *He always gets the best out of people.* 他總能使人發揮最大的潛力。

ˌget ˈover sth 🗝 to deal with or gain control of sth 解決；克服；控制 **SYN** **overcome**：*She can't get over her shyness.* 她無法克服羞怯心理。◇ *I think the problem can be got over without too much difficulty.* 我認為這個問題不太難解決。 **ˌget ˈover sth/sb** 🗝 to return to your usual state of health, happiness, etc. after an illness, a shock, the end of a relationship, etc. 從疾病（或震驚、斷絕關係等）中恢復常態：*He was disappointed at not getting the job, but he'll get over it.* 他沒得到這份工作非常失望，不過他會想得開的。 **ˌget ˈover yourself** (*informal*) to stop thinking that you are so important; to stop being so serious 別自以為是；別太當真了：*Just get over yourself and stop moaning!* 別太當真了，停止抱怨吧！◇ *He needs to grow up a bit and get over himself.* 他需要更成熟一點，不再那麼自以為是。 **ˌget sth↔ˈover (to sb)** to make sth clear to sb 向（某人）講清某事；讓（某人）明白某事：*He didn't really get his meaning over to the audience.* 他沒能把他的意思清楚傳遞給觀眾。 **ˌget sth ˈover (with)** (*informal*) to complete sth unpleasant but necessary 完成，結束（令人不快但免不了的事）：*I'll be glad to* **get** *the exam* **over and done with**. 考試結束後我就高興了。

ˌget ˈround/aˈround sb to persuade sb to agree or to do what you want, usually by doing nice things for them（常用討好賣乖的手段）說服某人同意，哄騙某人依順，籠絡某人：*She knows how to get round her dad.* 她知道怎樣討她爸爸的歡心。 **ˌget ˈround/aˈround sth** 🗝 to deal with a problem successfully 成功地對付；解決；克服 **SYN** **overcome**：*A clever lawyer might find a way of getting round that clause.* 高明的律師也許能找到繞過那個條款的辦法。 **ˌget ˈround/aˈround to sth** 🗝 to find the time to do sth 抽出時間來做某事：*I meant to do the ironing but I didn't get round to it.* 我本想熨衣服的，可就是抽不出時間。◇ **~ doing sth** *I hope to get around to answering your letter next week.* 我希望下週能抽出時間給你回信。

ˈget through sth **1** 🗝 to use up a large amount of sth 消耗掉；用完；耗盡：*We got through a fortune while we were in New York!* 我們在紐約時花掉了一大筆錢！ **2** to manage to do or complete sth（設法）處理，完成：*Let's start—there's a lot to get through.* 咱們開始吧，有很多事要處理呢。 **ˌget ˈthrough (sth)** (*BrE*) to be successful in an exam, etc. 順利通過（考試等） **ˌget sb ˈthrough sth** to help sb to be successful in an exam 幫助某人順利通過考試：*She got all her students through the exam.* 她幫助她所有的學生順利通過了考試。 **ˌget ˈthrough (sth)** | **ˌget sth ˈthrough (sth)** to be officially accepted; to make sth be officially accepted（使）正式通過，獲得採納：*They got the bill through Congress.* 他們使此議案在國會獲得通過。 **ˌget ˈthrough (to sb)** **1** 🗝 to reach sb 到達（某人處）：*Thousands of refugees will die if these supplies don't get through to them.* 如果這些生活用品運不到，數以千計的難民就會死去。 **2** 🗝 to make contact with sb by telephone（用電話）接通，打通，聯繫上：*I tried calling you several times but I couldn't get through.* 我試着給你打了幾次電話，但都沒打通。 **ˌget ˈthrough (to sth)** (of a player or team 選手或隊) to reach the next stage of a competition 進入（下階段比賽）：*Moya has got through to the final.* 莫亞已進入決賽。 **ˌget ˈthrough to sb** to make sb understand or accept what you say, especially when you are trying to help them（尤指在努力幫助某人時）使某人理解，使某人接受（所講的話）：*I find it impossible to get through to her.* 我發覺根本無法讓她聽懂。 **ˌget ˈthrough with sth** to finish or complete a task 結束；完成

ˈget to sb (*informal*) to annoy or affect sb 使煩惱；使生氣；對某人產生影響：*The pressure of work is beginning to get to him.* 工作的壓力使他煩惱起來。

ˌget sb/sth toˈgether to collect people or things in one place 召集；聚集；收集；彙集：*I'm trying to get a team together for Saturday.* 我正設法召集一幫人過週六呢。 **ˌget toˈgether (with sb)** (*informal*) to meet with sb socially or in order to discuss sth 舉行社交聚會；開會：*We must get together for a drink sometime.* 我們什麼時候得聚在一起喝一杯。◇ *Management should get together with the union.* 資方應與工會在一起開個會。 ➲ related noun GET-TOGETHER

ˌget ˈup **1** 🗝 to stand up after sitting, lying, etc. 站起；起來；起身 **SYN** **rise**：*The class got up when the teacher came in.* 老師進來時全班起立。 ➲ **SYNONYMS** at STAND **2** if the sea or wind **gets up**, it increases in strength and becomes violent（海浪或風）增強，變猛烈 **ˌget ˈup** | **ˌget sb ˈup** 🗝 to get out of bed; to make sb get out of bed（使）起牀：*He always gets up early.* 他一向起得早。◇ *Could you get me up at 6.30 tomorrow?* 明天你 6:30 叫我起牀行嗎？ **ˌget yourself/sb ˈup as sth** [often passive] (*BrE*) to dress yourself/sb as sb/sth else（將…）打扮成，化裝成，裝扮成：*She was got up as an Indian princess.* 她被打扮成了印度公主。 ➲ related noun GET-UP **ˌget sth↔ˈup** to arrange or organize sth 安排；組織：*We're getting up a party for her birthday.* 我們正在籌備她的生日聚會。 **ˌget ˈup to sth** **1** to reach a particular point 到達某一點：*We got up to page 72 last lesson.* 我們上一課學到第 72 頁。 **2** to be busy with sth, especially sth surprising or unpleasant 忙於，從事（尤指令人吃驚或不快的事）：*What on earth will he get up to next?* 他下一步究竟要幹什麼？◇ *She's been getting up to her old tricks again!* 她又在故伎重演了！

get·away /ˈgetəweɪ/ *noun* [usually sing.] **1** an escape from a difficult situation, especially after committing a crime（尤指犯罪後的）逃跑，逃走：*to* ***make a quick getaway*** 迅速逃跑 ◇ *a getaway car* 逃跑用的汽車 **2** (*informal*) a short holiday/vacation; a place that is suitable for a holiday/vacation 短假；假日休閒地；適合度假的地方：*a romantic weekend getaway in New York* 在紐約度過的浪漫週末 ◇ *the popular island getaway of Penang* 深受人們喜愛的度假島檳城

ˈget-out *noun* [usually sing.] (*BrE, informal*) a way of avoiding sth, especially a responsibility or duty 迴避（責任或義務）的辦法；藉口：*He said he'd come but he's looking for a get-out.* 他說過他會來，但眼下他又在找藉口。◇ *a* ***get-out clause*** *in the contract* 合約裏的規避條款

get·ting /ˈgetɪŋ/ *noun* [sing.]
IDM **while the ˌgetting is ˈgood** (*NAmE*) (*BrE* **while the ˌgoing is ˈgood**) before a situation changes and it is no longer possible to do sth 趁形勢還未變化時；趁情況還有利時

ˈget-together *noun* (*informal*) an informal meeting; a party（非正式的）聚會；聯歡會

ˈget-up *noun* (*old-fashioned, informal*) a set of clothes, especially strange or unusual ones（尤指奇特的）一套衣服，穿戴，裝束

ˌget-up-and-ˈgo *noun* [U] (*informal*) energy and determination to get things done 幹勁；進取心；魄力；膽量

gew·gaw /'gjuːɡɔː; *NAmE* also 'guː-/ *noun* an object that attracts attention but has no value or use 花哨無用的物品；徒有其表的東西

gey·ser /'giːzə(r); *NAmE* 'ɡaɪzər/ *noun* **1** a natural SPRING that sometimes sends hot water or steam up into the air 間歇泉 **2** (*BrE*) a piece of equipment in a kitchen or bathroom that heats water, usually by gas （廚房或浴室的）煤氣熱水器，熱水鍋爐 **3** (*SAfrE*) a large container in which water is stored and heated, usually by electricity, in order to provide hot water in a building （建築物的）電熱水器，熱水鍋爐

ghagra /'ɡʌɡrɑː/ *noun* a long skirt, worn by women in S Asia （南亞婦女穿的）筒裙

gha·rara /ɡʌ'rɑːrə/ *noun* loose wide trousers, worn with a KAMEEZ and DUPATTA by women in S Asia （南亞婦女配克米茲和圍巾穿的）加格拉喇叭褲

ghar·ial /'ɡæriɑːl; ˌɡʌri'ɑːl; *NAmE* 'ɡeriəl/ (also **ga·vial**) *noun* a S Asian CROCODILE 恆河鱷（棲於南亞）

ghastly /'ɡɑːstli; *NAmE* 'ɡæstli/ *adj.* (**ghast·lier**, **ghast·li·est**) **1** (of an event 事情) very frightening and unpleasant, because it involves pain, death, etc. （因有關疼痛、死亡等而）恐怖的，可怕的，令人毛骨悚然的 **SYN** horrible：*a ghastly crime/murder* 可怕的罪行／謀殺 **2** (*informal*) (of an experience or a situation 經歷或形勢) very bad; unpleasant 糟透的；令人不快的 **SYN** terrible：*The weather was ghastly.* 天氣糟透了。◇ *It's all been a ghastly mistake.* 這是個極其惡劣的錯誤。**3** (*informal*) (of a person or thing 人或物) that you find unpleasant and dislike very much 令人噁心的；令人反感的；討厭的 **SYN** horrible：*her ghastly husband* 她那討厭的丈夫 ◇ *This lipstick is a ghastly colour.* 這唇膏的顏色令人噁心。**4** [not usually before noun] ill/sick or upset 有病；不適；苦惱 **SYN** terrible：*I felt ghastly the next day.* 我第二天感到身體很不舒服。**5** (*literary*) very pale in appearance, like a dead person 死人般蒼白的：*His face was ghastly white.* 他的臉色慘白。

ghat /ɡɑːt/ *noun* (*IndE*) **1** [C] steps leading down to a river or lake 河堤（或湖邊）的台階 **2** [C] a road or way over or through mountains 山路；山道 **3 Ghats** [pl.] the mountains near the eastern and western coasts of India 高止山脈（在印度東、西海岸附近）

ghee /giː/ *noun* [U] a type of butter used in S Asian cooking 印度酥油（用牛乳製成）

gher·kin /'ɡɜːkɪn; *NAmE* 'ɡɜːrkɪn/ *noun* **1** (*BrE*) (*NAmE* **pickle**) a small CUCUMBER that has been preserved in VINEGAR before being eaten 醋泡小黃瓜 **2** (*NAmE*) a small CUCUMBER 小黃瓜

ghetto /'ɡetəʊ; *NAmE* 'ɡetoʊ/ *noun* (*pl.* **-os** or **-oes**) **1** an area of a city where many people of the same race or background live, separately from the rest of the population. Ghettos are often crowded, with bad living conditions. （相同種族或背景人的）聚居區；貧民區：*a poor kid growing up in the ghetto* 在貧民區長大的窮孩子 ◇ *The south coast of Spain has become something of a tourist ghetto.* 西班牙南海岸可以說已經成為旅遊者的聚居區。**2** the area of a town where Jews were forced to live in the past （昔日城鎮中的）猶太人居住區：*the Warsaw ghetto* 華沙的猶太人居住區

'ghetto blaster (also **'boom box** especially in *NAmE*) *noun* (*informal*) a large radio and CD or CASSETTE player that can be carried around, especially to play loud music in public 大型手提式收錄機（音量大）

ghil·lie *noun* = GILLIE

ghost /ɡəʊst; *NAmE* ɡoʊst/ *noun, verb*

■ *noun* **1** [C] the spirit of a dead person that a living person believes they can see or hear 鬼；鬼魂；幽靈：*Do you believe in ghosts* (= believe that they exist)? 你相信有鬼嗎？◇ *the ghost of her father that had come back to haunt her* 回來纏繞她的她父親的幽靈 ◇ *He looked as if he had seen a ghost* (= looked very frightened). 他那副樣子就像是見到鬼一樣。**2** [C] the memory of sth, especially sth bad （尤指可怕事物的）記憶，回憶：*The ghost of anti-Semitism still haunts Europe.* 反猶主義在歐洲仍然陰魂不散。**3** [sing.] **~ of sth** a very slight amount of sth that is left behind or that you are not sure really exists 隱約的一點點；（某物殘留的）一絲，一點：*There was a ghost of a smile on his face.* 他臉上露出隱隱的一絲微笑。◇ *You don't have a ghost of a chance* (= you have no chance). 你一點兒機會都沒有。**4** [sing.] a second image on a television screen that is not as clear as the first, caused by a fault （電視屏幕上的）重影

IDM **give up the 'ghost** **1** to die 死 **2** (*humorous*) (of a machine 機器) to stop working 報廢；不能運轉；完蛋：*My car finally gave up the ghost.* 我的汽車終於報廢了。➲ more at FORMER

■ *verb* **1** = GHOSTWRITE **2** [I] + **adv./prep.** (*literary*) to move without making a sound 悄悄地行進：*They ghosted up the smooth waters of the river.* 他們悄悄地航行在平靜的河水上。

ghost·ing /'ɡəʊstɪŋ; *NAmE* 'ɡoʊ-/ *noun* [U] the appearance of a faint second image next to an image on a television screen, computer screen, etc. （電視、電腦等屏幕上的）重像

ghost·ly /'ɡəʊstli; *NAmE* 'ɡoʊstli/ *adj.* (**ghost·lier**, **ghost·li·est**) looking or sounding like a ghost; full of ghosts 鬼似的；幽靈般的；鬼魂縈繞的：*a ghostly figure* 鬼影 ◇ *ghostly footsteps* 幽靈般的腳步聲 ◇ *the ghostly churchyard* 鬼魂縈繞的教堂墓地

'ghost story *noun* a story about ghosts that is intended to frighten you （用來嚇唬人的）鬼故事

'ghost town *noun* a town that used to be busy and have a lot of people living in it, but is now empty （曾一度繁華的）被廢棄的城鎮

'ghost train *noun* (*BrE*) a small train at a FUNFAIR that goes through a dark tunnel full of frightening things （遊樂場的）遊鬼城小火車

ghost·write /'ɡəʊstraɪt; *NAmE* 'ɡoʊst-/ (also **ghost**) *verb* [T, often passive, I] **~ (sth)** to write a book, an article, etc. for another person who publishes it as their own work 代人寫作；為人捉刀；代寫：*Her memoirs were ghostwritten.* 她的回憶錄是由別人代寫的。

ghost·writer /'ɡəʊstraɪtə(r); *NAmE* 'ɡoʊst-/ *noun* a person who writes a book, etc. for another person, under whose name it is then published 代人寫作者；代筆者；捉刀人

ghoul /ɡuːl/ *noun* **1** (in stories) an evil spirit that opens graves and eats the dead bodies in them （傳說中的）盜墓食屍鬼 **2** (*disapproving*) a person who is too interested in unpleasant things such as death and disaster 對兇殘之事興趣濃厚的人 ▶ **ghoul·ish** /'ɡuːlɪʃ/ *adj.*：*ghoulish laughter* 獰笑

GHQ /ˌdʒiː eɪtʃ 'kjuː/ *noun* [U] the abbreviation for 'general headquarters' (the main centre of a military organization) 總司令部，統帥部（全寫為 general headquarters）：*He was posted to GHQ Cairo.* 他被派往開羅總司令部。

GHz *abbr.* (in writing 書寫形式) GIGAHERTZ

GI /ˌdʒiː 'aɪ/ *noun, abbr.*

■ *noun* (*pl.* **GIs**) a soldier in the US armed forces 美國兵

■ *abbr.* GLYCAEMIC INDEX (= a system for measuring the effect of foods containing CARBOHYDRATES on the level of sugar in the blood) 升糖指數；血糖指數：*The diet is based mainly on low GI foods.* 這種飲食方式主要是以升糖指數低的食物為主。

giant 0→ /'dʒaɪənt/ *noun, adj.*

■ *noun* **1** 0→ (in stories) a very large strong person who is often cruel and stupid （故事中常為殘酷而愚蠢的）巨人 ➲ see also GIANTESS **2** 0→ an unusually large person, animal or plant 巨人；巨獸；巨型植物：*He's a giant of a man.* 他是個巨人。**3** a very large and powerful organization 大公司；強大的組織：*the multinational oil giants* 跨國大石油公司 **4** a person who is very good at sth 偉人；卓越人物：*literary giants* 大文豪

■ *adj.* 0→ [only before noun] very large; much larger or more important than similar things usually are 巨大的；特大的；偉大的：*a giant crab* 巨蟹 ◇ *a giant-size box of tissues* 一盒特大紙巾 ◇ *a giant step towards achieving independence* 朝着獨立邁出的巨大的一步

G

giant·ess /ˌdʒaɪənˈtes/ *noun* (in stories) a female giant （故事中的）女巨人

giant·ism /ˈdʒaɪəntɪzəm/ *noun* [U] = GIGANTISM

ˈgiant-killer *noun* (*BrE*) (especially in sports 尤用於體育運動) a person or team that defeats another much stronger opponent 打敗強大對手的人（或隊）；強手（或強隊）的剋星

ˌgiant ˈpanda *noun* = PANDA (1)

ˌgiant ˈslalom *noun* a SLALOM, SKIING competition over a long distance, with wide fast turns 大迴轉長程滑雪賽；大曲道滑雪賽

GiB *abbr.* (in writing 書寫形式) GIBIBYTE

Gib (also **Gibit**) *abbr.* (in writing 書寫形式) GIBIBIT

G

gib·ber /ˈdʒɪbə(r)/ *verb* [I, T] (+ **speech**) to speak quickly in a way that is difficult to understand, often because of fear （常因害怕而）急促不清地說，語無倫次地說：*He cowered in the corner, gibbering with terror.* 他蜷縮在角落裏，嚇得語無倫次。◇ *By this time I was a* ***gibbering wreck***. 到這時我已是話也說不清的廢人了。

gib·ber·ish /ˈdʒɪbərɪʃ/ *noun* [U] (*informal*) words that have no meaning or are impossible to understand 莫名其妙的話；胡話；令人費解的話 **SYN** **nonsense**：*You were talking gibberish in your sleep.* 你在睡夢裏講着囈語。

gib·bet /ˈdʒɪbɪt/ *noun* (*old-fashioned*) a vertical wooden structure on which criminals used to be hanged 絞刑架；絞台 **SYN** **gallows**

gib·bon /ˈɡɪbən/ *noun* a small APE (= an animal like a large MONKEY without a tail) with long arms, that lives in SE Asia 長臂猿（棲息於東南亞）

gib·bous /ˈɡɪbəs/ *adj.* (*technical* 術語) (of the moon 月球) with the bright part bigger than a SEMICIRCLE and smaller than a circle 光亮部份大於半圓的；盈凸的

gibe = JIBE

gibi·bit /ˈɡɪbibɪt/ *noun* (*abbr.* **Gib**, **Gibit**) (*computing* 計) = GIGABIT (2)

gibi·byte /ˈɡɪbibaɪt/ *noun* (*abbr.* **GiB**) (*computing* 計) = GIGABYTE (2)

gib·lets /ˈdʒɪbləts/ *noun* [pl.] the inside parts of a chicken or other bird, including the heart and LIVER, that are usually removed before it is cooked （禽類的）內臟

giddy /ˈɡɪdi/ *adj.* (**gid·dier**, **gid·di·est**) **1** [not usually before noun] feeling that everything is moving and that you are going to fall 頭暈；眩暈 **SYN** **dizzy**：*When I looked down from the top floor, I felt giddy.* 我從頂樓朝下看時感到頭暈目眩。 **2** [not usually before noun] **~ (with sth)** so happy and excited that you cannot behave normally （高興或激動得）發狂，舉止反常：*She was giddy with happiness.* 她高興得忘乎所以。 **3** [usually before noun] making you feel as if you were about to fall 令人眩暈的；使人頭昏眼花的：*The kids were pushing the roundabout at a giddy speed.* 孩子們推動着旋轉平台快得令人眩暈。◇ (*figurative*) ***the giddy heights of success*** 令人目眩的巨大成功 **4** (*old-fashioned*) (of people 人) not serious 輕率的；輕浮的；不穩重的 **SYN** **silly**：*Isabel's giddy young sister* 伊莎貝爾輕浮的小妹 ▸ **gid·di·ly** /ˈɡɪdɪli/ *adv.*：*She swayed giddily across the dance floor.* 她飛快地飄過舞池，看得人眼暈。 **gid·di·ness** /ˈɡɪdinəs/ *noun* [U]：*Symptoms include nausea and giddiness.* 症狀有惡心和頭暈。

ˌgiddy-ˈup *exclamation* used as a command to a horse to make it go faster （趕馬的吆喝）駕

GIF™ /ɡɪf/ *noun* (*computing* 計) the abbreviation for 'Graphic Interchange Format' (a type of computer file that contains images and is used a lot on the Internet) * GIF 文件，圖形交換格式文件（全寫為 Graphic Interchange Format）：*Send it as a GIF.* 把它以 GIF 文件發送。

gift 🔑 /ɡɪft/ *noun, verb*

■ *noun* **1** 🔑 a thing that you give to sb, especially on a special occasion or to say thank you 禮物；贈品 **SYN** **present**：*The watch was a gift from my mother.* 這塊錶是母親給我的禮物。◇ *Thank you for your generous gift.* 感謝你豐厚的禮物。◇ *a* ***free gift*** *for every reader* 給每位讀者的贈品 ◇ *the gift of life* 生命的給予 ◇ (*formal*) *The family* ***made a gift of*** *his paintings to the gallery.* 家人把他的畫作贈送給了美術館。◇ *gifts of toys for the children* 送給孩子們的玩具禮物 **2** 🔑 a natural ability 天賦；天才；才能 **SYN** **talent**：**~ (for sth)** *She has a great gift for music.* 她極有音樂天賦。◇ **~ (for doing sth)** *He has the gift of making friends easily.* 他天生善交朋友。◇ *She can pick up a tune instantly on the piano. It's a gift.* 她聽到曲子就能馬上用鋼琴彈出來，這是天分。 **3** [usually sing.] (*informal*) a thing that is very easy to do or cheap to buy 輕而易舉的事；極便宜的東西：*Their second goal was an absolute gift.* 他們第二個進球簡直不費吹灰之力。◇ *At £500 it's a gift.* 只賣 500 英鎊，真便宜。

IDM **be in the gift of sb | be in sb's ˈgift** (*especially BrE*) if sth such as an important job or a special right or advantage is **in sb's gift**, that person can decide who to give it to 由某人決定；某人有權決定：*All such posts are in the gift of the managing director* (= only given by the managing director). 所有這些崗位都由總經理決定。 **the gift of the ˈgab** (*BrE*) (*US* **a gift for/of ˈgab**) (*informal*, sometimes *disapproving*) the ability to speak easily and to persuade other people with your words 口才；辯才 **look a gift horse in the ˈmouth** (usually with negatives 通常與否定詞連用) (*informal*) to refuse or criticize sth that is given to you for nothing 拒受饋贈；白送的馬還看牙口；對禮物吹毛求疵 ➲ more at GOD

■ *verb* (*BrE*) (used especially in JOURNALISM 尤用於新聞報道) to give sth to sb without their having to make any effort to get it 白送；白給：**~ sb sth** *They gifted their opponents a goal.* 他們白送給對方一分。◇ **~ sth to sb** *They gifted a goal to their opponents.* 他們白送給對方一分。

ˈgift certificate (*NAmE*) (*BrE* **ˈgift voucher**, **ˈgift token**) *noun* a piece of paper that is worth a particular amount of money and that can be exchanged for goods in a shop/store （購物）禮券

gift·ed /ˈɡɪftɪd/ *adj.* **1** having a lot of natural ability or intelligence 有天才的；有天賦的；天資聰慧的：***a gifted musician/player, etc.*** 天才的音樂家、運動員等 ◇ *gifted children* 天資聰慧的孩子 **2** **~ with sth** having sth pleasant 具有（令人愉快的東西）：*He was gifted with a charming smile.* 他有一副迷人的微笑。

ˈgift shop *noun* a shop/store that sells goods that are suitable for giving as presents 禮品店

ˈgift voucher (also **ˈgift token**) (both *BrE*) (*NAmE* **ˈgift certificate**) *noun* a piece of paper that is worth a particular amount of money and that can be exchanged for goods in a shop/store （購物）禮券

ˈgift wrap *noun* [U] attractive coloured or patterned paper used for wrapping presents 禮品包裝紙

ˈgift-wrap *verb* (**-pp-**) [often passive] **~ sth** to wrap sth as a present for sb, especially in a shop/store （尤指商店裏）將…包裝成禮品：*Would you like the chocolates gift-wrapped?* 你需要我們把巧克力包裝成禮品嗎？◇ *The store offers a gift-wrapping service.* 這家商店提供禮品包裝服務。

gig /ɡɪɡ/ *noun* **1** a performance by musicians playing popular music or JAZZ in front of an audience; a similar performance by a COMEDIAN （流行音樂或爵士樂）現場演奏會，現場演唱會；現場喜劇表演：*to do a gig* 舉行流行音樂演唱會 ◇ *a White Stripes gig* 白條紋樂隊演奏會 ➲ COLLOCATIONS at MUSIC **2** (*NAmE, informal*) a job, especially a temporary one （尤指臨時的）工作：*a gig as a basketball coach* 臨時籃球教練 **3** (*informal*) = GIGABYTE **4** a small light CARRIAGE with two wheels, pulled by one horse 單馬雙輪輕便馬車

giga- /ˈɡɪɡə; ˈdʒɪɡə/ *combining form* (in nouns; used in units of measurement 構成名詞，用於計量單位) **1** 10^9, or 1 000 000 000 十億（吉）（咖），千兆（十進制，等於 1 000 000 000）：*gigahertz* 千兆赫 **2** 2^{30}, or 1 073 741 824 吉（咖），千兆（二進制，等於 1 073 741 824）

giga·bit /ˈɡɪɡəbɪt/ *noun* (*abbr.* **Gb**, **Gbit**) (*computing* 計) **1** a unit of computer memory or data, equal to 10^9, or

1 000³, (= 1 000 000 000) BITS 十億比特，吉比特，千兆比特（十進制計算機內存或數據單位，等於 1 000 000 000 比特） **2** (also **gibi·bit**) a unit of computer memory or data, equal to 2^{30}, or $1\ 024^3$, (= 1 073 741 824) BITS 吉比特，千兆比特（二進制計算機內存或數據單位，等於 1 073 741 824 比特）

giga·byte /ˈɡɪɡəbaɪt/ (also *informal* **gig**) *noun* (*abbr.* **GB**) (*computing* 計) **1** a unit of computer memory or data, equal to 10^9, or $1\ 000^3$, (= 1 000 000 000) BYTES 十億字節，吉字節，千兆字節（十進制計算機內存或數據單位，等於 1 000 000 000 字節） **2** (also **gibi·byte**) a unit of computer memory or data, equal to 2^{30}, or $1\ 024^3$, (= 1 073 741 824) BYTES 吉字節，千兆字節（二進制計算機內存或數據單位，等於 1 073 741 824 字節）

giga·hertz /ˈɡɪɡəhɜːts; ˈdʒɪ-; *NAmE* -hɜːrts/ *noun* (*pl.* **giga·hertz**) (*abbr.* **GHz**) (*computing* 計, *physics* 物) a unit for measuring radio waves and the speed at which a computer operates; 1 000 000 000 HERTZ 十億赫，吉赫，千兆赫（無線電波頻率和計算機運作速度單位，等於 1 000 000 000 赫）

gi·gan·tic /dʒaɪˈɡæntɪk/ *adj.* extremely large 巨大的；龐大的 **SYN** **enormous, huge**

gi·gant·ism /dʒaɪˈɡæntɪzəm; ˈdʒaɪɡæntɪzəm/ (also **giant·ism**) *noun* [U] (*medical* 醫) a condition in which sb grows to an unusually large size 巨人症

gig·gle /ˈɡɪɡl/ *verb, noun*

■ ***verb*** [I, T] **~ (at/about sb/sth)** | (**+ speech**) to laugh in a silly way because you are amused, embarrassed or nervous（因感到有趣、窘迫或緊張而）咯咯地笑，傻笑：*The girls giggled at the joke.* 女孩子們給這笑話逗得咯咯笑。◇ *They giggled nervously as they waited for their turn.* 他們排隊等候時緊張地傻笑着。

■ ***noun*** **1** [C] a slight silly repeated laugh 咯咯笑；傻笑：*She gave a nervous giggle.* 她發出緊張的傻笑。◇ *Matt collapsed into giggles and hung up the phone.* 馬特突然咯咯笑起來，然後掛斷了電話。 **2** [sing.] (*BrE, informal*) a thing that you think is amusing 趣事；玩笑；可笑的事：*We only did it **for a giggle**.* 我們做那件事只是開個玩笑而已。 **3 the giggles** [pl.] (*informal*) continuous giggling that you cannot control or stop 止不住的咯咯笑：*I **get the giggles** when I'm nervous.* 我緊張時就不停地咯咯大笑。◇ *She had a **fit of the giggles** and had to leave the room.* 她突然咯咯笑了起來，不得不走出房間。

gig·gly /ˈɡɪɡli/ *adj.* laughing a lot in a silly, nervous way 咯咯傻笑的；緊張得咯咯笑的

GIGO /ˈɡaɪɡəʊ; *NAmE* -ɡoʊ/ ➲ GARBAGE

gig·olo /ˈʒɪɡələʊ; ˈdʒɪ-; *NAmE* -loʊ/ *noun* (*pl.* **-os**) a man who is paid to be the lover of an older woman, usually one who is rich 舞男；面首

gild /ɡɪld/ *verb* **1 ~ sth** (*literary*) to make sth look bright, as if covered with gold 使如金子般生光（或生輝、生色）：*The golden light gilded the sea.* 金色的陽光使大海如金子般閃閃發光。 **2 ~ sth** to cover sth with a thin layer of gold or gold paint 給…鍍金；塗金於

IDM **gild the ˈlily** to spoil sth that is already good or beautiful by trying to improve it 畫蛇添足；多此一舉

gild·ed /ˈɡɪldɪd/ *adj.* [only before noun] **1** covered with a thin layer of gold or gold paint 鍍金的；塗金色的 **2** (*literary*) rich and belonging to the upper classes 富貴的；上層階級的：*the **gilded youth*** (= rich, upper-class young people) *of the Edwardian era* 愛德華時代富貴的年輕人

gild·ing /ˈɡɪldɪŋ/ *noun* [U] a layer of gold or gold paint; the surface that this makes 鍍金層；金色塗層；鍍金飾面

gilet /ˈʒɪleɪ; ˈʒiː-/ *noun* a light thick jacket without sleeves 厚夾克背心

gill[1] /ɡɪl/ *noun* [usually pl.] one of the openings on the side of a fish's head that it breathes through 鰓 ➲ VISUAL VOCAB page V12

IDM **to the ˈgills** (*informal*) completely full（完全）滿了，飽了；滿滿當當：*I was stuffed to the gills with chocolate cake.* 我吃巧克力蛋糕都撐到嗓子眼兒了。

gill[2] /dʒɪl/ *noun* a unit for measuring liquids. There are four gills in a pint. 及耳（液量單位，一品脫為四及耳）

gil·lie (also **ghil·lie**) /ˈɡɪli/ *noun* (*ScotE*) a man or boy who helps sb who is shooting or fishing for sport in Scotland（蘇格蘭漁獵運動者的）隨從，侍童，男僕

gilt /ɡɪlt/ *noun* **1** [U] a thin layer of gold, or sth like gold that is used on a surface for decoration 鍍金；金色塗層：*gilt lettering* 燙印的金字 **2 gilts** [pl.] (*BrE, finance* 財) gilt-edged investments 金邊證券；績優證券 **3** [C] (*especially NAmE*) a young female pig 小母豬

IDM **take the gilt off the ˈgingerbread** (*BrE*) to do or be sth that makes a situation or achievement less attractive or impressive 使失去吸引力；令人掃興；煞風景

ˌgilt-ˈedged *adj.* (*finance* 財) very safe 金邊的；安全的；高度可靠的：***gilt-edged securities/shares/stocks*** (= investments that are considered safe because they have been sold by the government) 金邊證券 / 股份 / 股票（由政府發行，安全可靠）

gim·crack /ˈdʒɪmkræk/ *adj.* [only before noun] badly made and of little value 粗製濫造的；劣質的；無價值的 **SYN** **shoddy**

gim·let /ˈɡɪmlət/ *noun* a small tool for making holes in wood to put screws in 螺絲錐；手錐；手鑽；木鑽：(*figurative*) *eyes like gimlets* (= looking very hard at things and noticing every detail) 銳利如錐的目光

gimme /ˈɡɪmi/ *short form, noun* (*informal*)

■ a way of writing the way that the words 'give me' are sometimes spoken（give me 的一種書寫形式，表示此短語某些時候的讀法）給我：*Gimme back my bike!* 把自行車還給我！

■ ***noun*** [usually sing.] something that is very easy to do or achieve 輕而易舉的事；容易獲得的事物

gim·mick /ˈɡɪmɪk/ *noun* (often *disapproving*) an unusual trick or unnecessary device that is intended to attract attention or to persuade people to buy sth（為引人注意或誘人購買而搞的）花招，把戲，噱頭：*a **promotional/publicity/sales gimmick*** 以推銷 / 宣傳 / 銷售為目的的花招 ▸ **gim·micky** /ˈɡɪmɪki/ *adj.*：*a gimmicky idea* 鬼主意

gim·mick·ry /ˈɡɪmɪkri/ *noun* [U] (*disapproving*) the use of gimmicks in selling, etc. 玩弄銷售伎倆；耍花招

gin /dʒɪn/ *noun* **1** [U] an alcoholic drink made from grain and flavoured with JUNIPER BERRIES. Gin is usually drunk mixed with TONIC WATER or fruit juice. 杜松子酒 ➲ see also PINK GIN **2** [C] a glass of gin 一杯杜松子酒：*I'll have a gin and tonic, please.* 請來一杯加奎寧水的杜松子酒。 **3** = COTTON GIN

gin·ger /ˈdʒɪndʒə(r)/ *noun, adj., verb*

■ ***noun*** [U] **1** the root of the ginger plant used in cooking as a spice 薑：*a teaspoon of ground ginger* 一茶匙薑粉 ◇ (*BrE*) *ginger biscuits* 薑味餅乾 ➲ VISUAL VOCAB page V32 **2** a light brownish-orange colour 薑黃色

■ ***adj.*** (*BrE*) light brownish-orange in colour 薑黃色的：*ginger hair* 薑黃色的頭髮 ◇ *a ginger cat* 薑黃色的貓

■ ***verb***

PHR V **ˌginger sth/sb↔ˈup** (*BrE*) to make sth/sb more active or exciting 使有活力；使活躍；使興奮 **SYN** **liven up**

ˌginger ˈale *noun* **1** [U] a clear FIZZY drink (= with bubbles) that does not contain alcohol, flavoured with ginger, and often mixed with alcoholic drinks 薑味汽水 **2** [C] a bottle or glass of ginger ale 一瓶（或一杯）薑味汽水

ˌginger ˈbeer *noun* **1** [U] a FIZZY drink (= with bubbles) with a very small amount of alcohol in, flavoured with ginger 薑汁啤酒 **2** [C] a bottle or glass of ginger beer 一瓶（或一杯）薑汁啤酒

gin·ger·bread /ˈdʒɪndʒəbred; *NAmE* -dʒərb-/ *noun* [U] a sweet cake or soft biscuit/cookie flavoured with GINGER 薑餅；薑味餅乾：*a gingerbread man* (= a gingerbread biscuit/cookie in the shape of a person) 人形薑餅 **IDM** see GILT

ˈginger group *noun* (*BrE*) a group of people within a political party or an organization, who work to

G

persuade other members to accept their policies or ideas（政黨或組織中的）活躍分子集團，骨幹小組

gin·ger·ly /ˈdʒɪndʒəli; *NAmE* -dʒərli/ *adv.* in a careful way, because you are afraid of being hurt, of making a noise, etc. 謹慎的；小心翼翼的；輕手輕腳的：*He opened the box gingerly and looked inside.* 他小心翼翼地打開盒子朝裏看。

ˈginger nut (*BrE*) (also **ˈginger snap** *NAmE, BrE*) *noun* a hard sweet biscuit/cookie flavoured with GINGER 薑味硬餅乾

gin·gery /ˈdʒɪndʒəri/ *adj.* like GINGER in colour or flavour 薑色的；薑味的

ging·ham /ˈɡɪŋəm/ *noun* [U] a type of cotton cloth with a pattern of white and coloured squares 格子棉布：*a blue and white gingham dress* 藍白格子布連衣裙

G

gin·gi·vitis /ˌdʒɪndʒɪˈvaɪtəs/ *noun* [U] (*medical* 醫) a condition in which the GUMS around the teeth become painful, red and swollen 牙齦炎

ginkgo /ˈɡɪŋkɡəʊ; *NAmE* -ɡoʊ/ (also **gingko** /ˈɡɪŋkəʊ; *NAmE* -koʊ/) *noun* (*pl.* **-os** or **-oes**) a Chinese tree with yellow flowers 銀杏（原產中國）**SYN** **maidenhair tree**

gi·nor·mous /dʒaɪˈnɔːməs; *NAmE* -ˈnɔːrm-/ *adj.* (*BrE, informal*) extremely large 極大的；巨大的

ˌgin ˈrummy *noun* [U] a card game in which players try to get HANDS (= sets of cards) that add up to ten 金拉米紙牌戲（玩牌者爭取使手中牌加起來不超過 10 點）

gin·seng /ˈdʒɪnseŋ/ *noun* [U] a medicine obtained from a plant root that some people believe helps you stay young and healthy 人參；西洋參

ˈgin trap *noun* a device for trapping small wild animals or birds（捕小野獸或鳥的）齒夾；捕獸夾

gippy tummy (also **gyppy tummy**) /ˌdʒɪpi ˈtʌmi/ *noun* (*old-fashioned, BrE, informal*) DIARRHOEA (= an illness in which waste matter is emptied from the body in liquid form) that affects visitors to hot countries 熱帶腹瀉

Gipsy = GYPSY

gir·affe /dʒəˈrɑːf; *NAmE* -ˈræf/ *noun* (*pl.* **gir·affe** or **gir·affes**) a tall African animal with a very long neck, long legs, and dark marks on its coat 長頸鹿

gird /ɡɜːd; *NAmE* ɡɜːrd/ *verb* **~ sth (with sth)** to surround sth with sth; to fasten sth around sb/sth 束；捆上；纏上

IDM **gird (up) your ˈloins** (*literary* or *humorous*) to get ready to do sth difficult 準備從事（艱苦的工作）；準備行動：*The company is girding its loins for a plunge into the overseas market.* 公司正準備打入海外市場。

PHR V **gird (yourself/sb/sth) (up) for sth** (*literary*) to prepare for sth difficult, especially a fight, contest, etc. 為（戰鬥、比賽等艱苦工作）做好準備

gird·er /ˈɡɜːdə(r); *NAmE* ˈɡɜːrd-/ *noun* a long strong iron or steel bar used for building bridges and the FRAMEWORK of large buildings（橋或建築物的）大梁，承重梁

gir·dle /ˈɡɜːdl; *NAmE* ˈɡɜːrdl/ *noun, verb*

■ *noun* **1** a piece of women's underwear that fits closely around the body from the waist to the top of the legs, designed to make a woman look thinner（女子的）緊身褡 **2** (*literary*) a thing that surrounds sth else 圍繞物：*carefully tended lawns set in a girdle of trees* 樹木環繞、精心修整的草坪 **3** (*old-fashioned*) a belt or thick string fastened around the waist to keep clothes in position 腰帶

■ *verb* **~ sth** (*literary*) to surround sth 圍繞；環繞：*A chain of volcanoes girdles the Pacific.* 環繞太平洋的是一連串的火山。

girl 🔑 /ɡɜːl; *NAmE* ɡɜːrl/ *noun*

1 🔑 [C] a female child 女孩：***a baby girl*** 女嬰 ◇ ***a little girl*** *of six* 六歲的小女孩 ◇ *Hello, girls and boys!* 孩子們好！ ➲ see also POSTER CHILD **2** 🔑 [C] a daughter 女兒：*Our youngest girl is at college.* 我們的小女兒在大學讀書。 **3** 🔑 [C] (sometimes *offensive*) a young woman 年輕女子；女郎：*Alex is not interested in girls yet.* 亞歷克斯對女孩子還不感興趣。◇ *He married the girl next door.* 他與隔壁的女孩結婚了。 **4** [C] (usually in compounds 通常構成複合詞) (*old-fashioned, offensive*) a female worker 女工；女職員：*an office girl* 女辦事員 **5** [C] (*old-fashioned*) a man's girlfriend（男人的）女朋友 **6 girls** [pl.] (used especially as a form of address by women 女性尤用於稱呼) a woman's female friends（女子的）女伴，女友：*I'm having a night out with the girls.* 我今晚要和女友們外出。◇ *Good morning, girls!* 姑娘們，早上好！ **7** [sing.] **old ~** (often *offensive*) an old woman, especially sb's wife or mother 老婆；老母親；老婦人：*How is the old girl these days?* 老母親近來好嗎？ **IDM** see BIG *adj.*

ˈgirl band (also **ˈgirl group**) *noun* a group of attractive young women who sing pop music and dance（演唱流行歌曲和表演舞蹈的）少女組合

ˌgirl ˈFriday *noun* a girl or a woman who is employed in an office to do several different jobs, helping other people 女助手；女秘書；女助理

girl·friend 🔑 /ˈɡɜːlfrend; *NAmE* ˈɡɜːrl-/ *noun*

1 🔑 a girl or a woman that sb is having a romantic relationship with 女朋友；女情人 **2** 🔑 (*especially NAmE*) a woman's female friend（女子的）女伴，女友：*I had lunch with a girlfriend.* 我同女友一起吃了午飯。

ˌGirl ˈGuide *noun* (*old-fashioned, BrE*) = GUIDE *n.* (6)

ˌGirl Guider *noun* (*BrE*) = GUIDER

girl·hood /ˈɡɜːlhʊd; *NAmE* ˈɡɜːrl-/ *noun* [U] (*old-fashioned*) the time when sb is a girl; the fact of being a girl 少女時期；少女時代；少女

girlie /ˈɡɜːli; *NAmE* ˈɡɜːrli/ *adj., noun* (*informal*)

■ *adj.* [only before noun] **1** containing photographs of naked or nearly naked women, that are intended to make men sexually excited 有裸體或半裸體女人照片的：*girlie magazines* 有女子豔照的雜誌 **2** (*disapproving*) suitable for or like girls, not boys 適合少女的；像姑娘一樣的：*girlie games* 女孩子的遊戲

■ *noun* a way of referring to a girl or young woman, that many women find offensive 小妞兒；小娘們兒

girl·ish /ˈɡɜːlɪʃ; *NAmE* ˈɡɜːrlɪʃ/ *adj.* like a girl; of a girl 像女孩子的；女孩子似的；女孩子的：*a girlish giggle* 女孩子氣的咯咯笑 ◇ *a girlish figure* 女孩兒的體形

ˌgirl ˈpower *noun* [U] the idea that women should take control of their careers and lives 女權（認為女性應主宰自己的事業和生活的觀念）

ˌGirl ˈScout (*US*) (*BrE* **Guide**, *old-fashioned* **ˌGirl ˈGuide**) *noun* a member of an organization (called **the Guides** or **the Girl Scouts**) which is similar to the SCOUTS and which trains girls in practical skills and does a lot of activities with them, for example camping 女童子軍

girn = GURN

giro /ˈdʒaɪrəʊ; *NAmE* -roʊ/ *noun* (*pl.* **-os**) (*BrE*) **1** [U] (*finance* 財) a system in which money can be moved from one bank or post office account to another by a central computer（銀行或郵局）直接轉賬：*to pay by giro* 用直接轉賬支付 ◇ ***a giro credit/payment/transfer*** 直接轉賬信貸/支付；直接轉賬 **2** (also **ˈgiro cheque**) [C] a cheque that the government pays through the giro system to people who are unemployed or sick, or who have a very small income（政府支付給失業者、病人或低收入者的）直接轉賬救濟支票：*It is easy for families to run out of money before the weekly giro arrives.* 每週直接轉賬救濟支票還未到之前，錢便花光的情況許多家庭都容易出現。

girth /ɡɜːθ; *NAmE* ɡɜːrθ/ *noun* **1** [U, C] the measurement around sth, especially a person's waist 圍長；幹圍；腰圍：*a man of enormous girth* 腰圍很粗的男人 ◇ *a tree one metre in girth/with a girth of one metre* 幹圍一米的樹 **2** [C] a narrow piece of leather or cloth that is fastened around the middle of a horse to keep the seat (called a SADDLE) or a load in place（固定馬鞍或馱載的）肚帶，腹帶

gismo = GIZMO

gist /dʒɪst/ *noun* (usually **the gist**) [sing.] **~ (of sth)** the main or general meaning of a piece of writing, a speech or a conversation 要點；主旨；大意：*to get* (= understand) *the gist of an argument* 理解辯論的主旨 ◇ *I missed the beginning of the lecture—can you give me the gist of what he said?* 我錯過了講座的開頭，給我講講他說話

的要點好嗎？◇ *I'm afraid I don't quite follow your gist* (= what you really mean). 對不起，我還不太明白你的意思。

git /gɪt/ *noun* (*BrE, slang*) a stupid or unpleasant man 蠢貨；飯桶；討厭鬼

give /gɪv/ *verb, noun*

■ *verb* (**gave** /geɪv/, **given** /'gɪvn/)

▸ **HAND/PROVIDE** 交給；提供 **1** [T] to hand sth to sb so that they can look at it, use it or keep it for a time 給；交給：**~ sth to sb** *Give the letter to your mother when you've read it.* 信看完後交給你母親。◇ *She gave her ticket to the woman at the check-in desk.* 她把票遞給了登機手續服務枱上的女服務員。◇ **~ sb sth** *Give your mother the letter.* 把信給你母親。◇ *They were all given a box to carry.* 給了他們每人一個箱子讓他們搬。 **2** [T, I] to hand sth to sb as a present; to allow sb to have sth as a present 贈送；贈與；送給：**~ sb sth** *What are you giving your father for his birthday?* 你打算送給你父親什麼生日禮物？◇ *She was given a huge bunch of flowers.* 有人給她送了一大束花。◇ *Did you give the waiter a tip?* 你給服務員小費了嗎？◇ **~ sth to sb** *We don't usually give presents to people at work.* 我們一般不給在職員工送禮。◇ **~ (sth)** *They say it's better to give than to receive.* 人們説施比受有福。 **3** [T] to provide sb with sth （為某人）提供，供給，供應：**~ sb sth** *They were all thirsty so I gave them a drink.* 他們都口渴了，所以我給了他們一杯飲料。◇ *Give me your name and address.* 把你的名字和地址報給我。◇ *We've been given a 2% pay increase.* 我們獲得了 2% 的加薪。◇ *I was hoping you would give me a job.* 我還盼望着你能給我份工作呢。◇ *He was given a new heart in a five-hour operation.* 經過五個小時的手術給他移植了一顆新的心臟。◇ *She wants a job that gives her more responsibility.* 她想得到一份責任更大的工作。◇ *Can I give you a ride to the station?* 你搭我的便車去車站好嗎？◇ *They couldn't give me any more information.* 他們不可能給我提供更多的信息。◇ *I'll give you* (= allow you to have) *ten minutes to prepare your answer.* 我會給你十分鐘時間準備回答。◇ *Don't give me any of that backchat* (= don't be rude). 別跟我頂嘴。◇ **~ sth to sb** *He gives Italian lessons to his colleagues.* 他給同事們上意大利語課。◇ *The reforms should give a better chance to the less able children.* 這些改革應該給予能力較低的兒童更好的機會。

▸ **MONEY** 金錢 **4** [I, T] to pay money to a charity, etc., to help people 捐助；捐贈；捐款：*We need your help—please give generously.* 我們需要您的幫助，請慷慨解囊吧。◇ **~ to sth** *They both gave regularly to charity.* 他倆定期為慈善事業捐款。◇ **~ sth (to sth)** *I gave a small donation.* 我給了一點微薄的捐助。 **5** [T] to pay in order to have or do sth（為獲得某物或做某事而）支付，付款：**~ sb sth (for sth)** *How much will you give me for the car?* 你肯出多少錢買我這輛汽車？◇ **~ sth** *I'd give anything to see him again.* 只要能再見他一面我出多少錢都願意。◇ **~ sth for sth** *I gave £50 for the lot.* 我出 50 英鎊一下全買了。

▸ **TREAT AS IMPORTANT** 視為重要 **6** [T] to use time, energy, etc. for sb/sth 將（時間、精力等）用於：**~ sb/sth sth** *I gave the matter a lot of thought.* 我反複思考過這個問題。◇ **~ sth to sb/sth** *I gave a lot of thought to the matter.* 我反複思考過這個問題。◇ *The government has given top priority to reforming the tax system.* 政府優先致力於稅制改革。

▸ **PUNISHMENT** 懲罰 **7** [T] to make sb suffer a particular punishment 使受…懲罰：**~ sb sth** *The judge gave him a nine-month suspended sentence.* 法官判處他有期徒刑九個月，緩期執行。◇ **~ sth to sb** *We discussed what punishment should be given to the boys.* 我們討論了該如何懲罰這些男孩。

▸ **ILLNESS** 疾病 **8** [T] to infect sb with an illness 把（疾病）傳染給：**~ sb sth** *You've given me your cold.* 你把感冒傳染給我了。◇ **~ sth to sb** *She'd given the bug to all her colleagues.* 她把這種病毒傳染給了所有的同事。

▸ **PARTY/EVENT** 聚會；活動 **9** [T] **~ sth** if you **give** a party, you organize it and invite people 舉辦；舉行 **10** [T] **~ sth** to perform sth in public 表演；公開進行：*She gave a reading from her latest volume of poetry.* 她朗誦了她最近出版的詩集裏的一首詩。◇ *The President will be giving a press conference this afternoon.* 總統今天下午將舉行記者招待會。

▸ **DO/PRODUCE STH** 做；產生 **11** [T] used with a noun to describe a particular action, giving the same meaning as the related verb（與名詞連用描述某一動作，意義與該名詞相應的動詞相同）：**~ sth** *She gave a shrug of her shoulders* (= she shrugged). 她聳了聳肩。◇ *He turned to us and gave a big smile* (= smiled broadly). 他轉身對着我們咧開嘴笑。◇ *She looked up from her work and gave a yawn* (= yawned). 她停下工作抬起頭來打了個哈欠。◇ *He gave a loud cry* (= cried out loudly) *and fell to the floor.* 他大叫了一聲倒在地板上。◇ *Her work has given pleasure to* (= pleased) *millions of readers.* 她的著作給數百萬讀者帶來了歡樂。◇ **~ sb sth** *He gave her a kiss* (= kissed her). 他吻了她一下。◇ *I have to admit that the news gave us a shock* (= shocked us). 我不得不承認這個消息讓我們大為震驚。◇ *We'll give you all the help we can* (= help you in every way we can). 我們將盡力幫助你。 **HELP** For other similar expressions, look up the nouns in each. For example, you will find **give your approval** at **approval**. 其他類似詞組見有關名詞詞條。如 give your approval 在詞條 approval 下可以查到。 **12** [T] **~ sb sth** to produce a particular feeling in sb 使產生（某種感覺）：*All that driving has given me a headache.* 這一路開車讓我頭都痛了。◇ *Go for a walk. It'll give you an appetite.* 去散散步，你就有食慾了。

▸ **TELEPHONE CALL** 電話 **13** [T] **~ sb sth** to make a telephone call to sb 給（某人）打（電話）：*Give me a call tomorrow.* 明天給我打個電話。◇ (*BrE*) *I'll give you a ring.* 我會給你打電話的。

▸ **MARK/GRADE** 分數；等級 **14** [T] **~ sb/sth sth** | **~ sth (to sb/sth)** to judge sb/sth to be of a particular standard 給…評定（等級）：*She had given the assignment an A.* 她給這份作業打了個優。◇ *I give it ten out of ten for originality.* 因其創意我給它打滿分。

▸ **PREDICT HOW LONG** 預計多長時間 **15** [T] **~ sb/sth sth** to predict that sth will last a particular length of time 預計將持續（…時間）：*That marriage won't last. I'll give them two years, at the outside.* 那樁婚姻不會持久，我看最多兩年。

▸ **IN SPORT** 體育運動 **16** [T] **~ sb/sth + adj.** to say that a player or the ball is in a particular position 裁定，判（球員或球所處位置）：*The umpire gave the ball out.* 裁判員判球出界。

▸ **BEND** 彎曲 **17** [I] to bend or stretch under pressure（在壓力下）彎曲，伸長，支撐不住：*The branch began to give under his weight.* 他身體的重量把樹枝都壓彎了。◇ (*figurative*) *We can't go on like this—**something's got to give**.* 我們不能繼續這樣了，肯定會出事的。 **18** [I] to agree to change your mind or give up some of your demands 讓步；妥協：*You're going to have to give a little.* 你可能非得稍為讓步不可。

IDM Most idioms containing **give** are at the entries for the nouns and adjectives in the idioms, for example, **give rise to sth** is at **rise** *n.* 大多數含 give 的習語，都可在該等習語中的名詞及形容詞相關詞條找到，如 give rise to sth 在詞條 rise 的名詞部份。 **don't give me 'that** (*informal*) used to tell sb that you do not accept what they say（表示不相信對方説的話）別跟我來這一套，別以為我會相信你：*'I didn't have time to do it.' 'Oh, don't give me that!'* "我沒有時間做這事。" "哦，別以為我會相信你的鬼話！" **,give and 'take** to be willing, in a relationship, to accept what sb else wants and to give up some of what you want 互相讓步；雙方遷就：*You're going to have to learn to give and take.* 你們必須學會互相遷就。 **give as good as you 'get** to react with equal force when sb attacks or criticizes you 回敬；回擊；以牙還牙：*She can give as good as she gets.* 她能夠給以回擊。 **give it up (for sb)** (*informal*) to show your approval of sb by clapping your hands 鼓掌表示支持（某人）：*Give it up for Eddie Murphy!* 給艾迪•墨菲以掌聲鼓勵！ **'give me sth/sb (any day/time)** (*informal*) used to say that you prefer a particular thing or person to the one that has just been mentioned 我寧願；我更喜歡；我寧可選擇：*We don't go out much. Give me a quiet night in front of the TV any day!* 我們不常出去。我寧願坐在電視機前安安靜靜地過一夜！ **give or 'take (sth)** if sth is correct **give or take** a particular amount, it is approximately correct 相差不到；出入至多：*It'll*

G

take about three weeks, give or take a day or so. 這要花大約三週時間，出入不過一天左右。 **give sb to believe/understand (that)** … [often passive] (*formal*) to make sb believe/understand sth 使某人相信；使某人理解： *I was given to understand that she had resigned.* 我得知她已經辭職了。 **I give you** … used to ask people to drink a TOAST to sb 我提議為（某人）乾杯： *Ladies and gentlemen, I give you Geoff Ogilby!* 女士們，先生們，我提議為傑夫 • 奧格爾比乾杯！ **I/I'll give you 'that** (*informal*) used when you are admitting that sth is true 我承認這事有理；我承認這是事實 **what 'gives?** (*informal*) what is happening?; what is the news? 發生了什麼事；有什麼消息

PHR V **,give sb a'way** (in a marriage ceremony 在婚禮上) to lead the BRIDE to the BRIDEGROOM and formally allow her to marry him 將新娘交給新郎： *The bride was given away by her father.* 新娘由父親交給新郎。 **,give sth↔a'way** **1** to give sth as a gift 贈送；捐贈： *He gave away most of his money to charity.* 他把他的大部份錢都捐贈給了慈善事業。◇ (*informal*) *Check out the prices of our pizzas—we're virtually giving them away!* 查看一下我們的比薩餅的價格吧，我們實際上是在白送！ ➲ related noun GIVEAWAY **2** to present sth 頒發；分發： *The mayor gave away the prizes at the school sports day.* 市長在學校運動會那天頒發了獎項。 **3** to carelessly allow sb to have an advantage（粗心地）失去，喪失，錯失（優勢）： *They've given away two goals already.* 他們已白送對手兩分了。 **,give sth/sb↔a'way** to make known sth that sb wants to keep secret 泄露；暴露 **SYN** betray： *She gave away state secrets to the enemy.* 她把國家機密泄露給了敵人。◇ *It was supposed to be a surprise but the children* ***gave the game away.*** 這原本想給人一個驚喜，可孩子們把計劃泄露了。◇ *His voice gave him away* (= showed who he really was). 他的聲音使他露餡了。 ➲ related noun GIVEAWAY

,give sb 'back sth | ,give sth↔'back (to sb) **1** to return sth to its owner 歸還；送回： *Could you give me back my pen?* 把鋼筆還給我好嗎？◇ *Could you give me my pen back?* 把鋼筆還給我好嗎？◇ *I picked it up and gave it back to him.* 我把它撿起來還給了他。◇ (*informal*) *Give it me back!* 把它還給我！ **2** to allow sb to have sth again 使恢復；使重新獲得： *The operation gave him back the use of his legs.* 手術使他雙腿恢復了功能。

,give 'in (to sb/sth) **1** to admit that you have been defeated by sb/sth 屈服；認輸；投降： *The rebels were forced to give in.* 叛亂分子被迫投降了。 **2** to agree to do sth that you do not want to do 讓步；勉強同意： *The authorities have shown no signs of giving in to the kidnappers' demands.* 當局對綁架者的要求沒有絲毫讓步的跡象。 **,give sth 'in (to sb)** (*BrE*) (also **,hand sth↔'in (to sb)** *BrE, NAmE*) to hand over sth to sb in authority 呈上；交上： *Please give your work in before Monday.* 請在星期一之前把作業交上來。

,give 'off sth to produce sth such as a smell, heat, light, etc. 發出，放出（氣味、熱、光等）： *The flowers gave off a fragrant perfume.* 花兒散發出芳香。

'give on to/onto sth [no passive] (*BrE*) to have a view of sth; to lead directly to sth 朝向；面向；通向： *The bedroom windows give on to the street.* 卧室的窗戶面向街道。◇ *This door gives onto the hall.* 這道門通往大廳。

,give 'out **1** to come to an end; to be completely used up 用完；耗盡： *After a month their food supplies gave out.* 一個月以後他們的食物儲備消耗殆盡。◇ *Her patience finally gave out.* 她最終忍無可忍了。 **2** to stop working 停止運行；停止運轉： *One of the plane's engines gave out in mid-air.* 飛機在高空中飛行時一個發動機失靈了。◇ *Her legs gave out and she collapsed.* 她腿一軟倒了下去。 **,give sth↔'out** to give sth to a lot of people 分發；散發： *The teacher gave out the exam papers.* 老師分發了試卷。 **,give 'out sth** **1** to produce sth such as heat, light, etc. 發出，放出（熱、光等）： *The radiator gives out a lot of heat.* 散熱器釋放出大量的熱。 **2** [often passive] (*especially BrE*) to tell people about sth or broadcast sth 公佈；宣佈；播放

,give 'over (*BrE, informal*) used to tell sb to stop doing sth 別再…了；到此為止吧；住手： *Give over, Chris! You're hurting me.* 住手，克里斯！你把我弄痛了。◇ **~ doing sth** *Give over complaining!* 別抱怨了！ **,give yourself 'over to sth** (also **,give yourself 'up to sth**) to spend all your time doing sth or thinking about sth; to allow sth to completely control your life 致力於；沉溺於 **,give sth↔'over to sth** [usually passive] to use sth for one particular purpose 把…專用作（某種用途）： *The gallery is given over to British art.* 此陳列室專門用於陳列英國藝術品。

,give 'up to stop trying to do sth 投降；認輸；放棄： *They gave up without a fight.* 他們不戰而降。◇ *She doesn't give up easily.* 她決不輕易認輸。◇ *I give up—tell me the answer.* 我猜不着了，把答案告訴我吧。 **,give sb 'up** **1** (also **,give 'up on sb** especially in *NAmE*) to believe that sb is never going to arrive, get better, be found, etc. 對某人的到來（或康復、能否找到等）不再抱有希望： *There you are at last! We'd given you up.* 你終於來了！我們都以為你不來了呢。◇ *We hadn't heard from him for so long, we'd* ***given him up for dead.*** 我們這麼長時間沒有他的音信，都以為他死了。 **2** to stop having a relationship with sb 與某人斷絕關係；不再與某人交往： *Why don't you give him up?* 你為什麼不與他一刀兩斷呢？ **,give sth↔'up** **1** [no passive] to stop doing or having sth 停止；中止；放棄；拋棄： *She didn't give up work when she had the baby.* 她有孩子後並未放棄工作。◇ *We'd* ***given up hope*** *of ever having children.* 我們已放棄生孩子的希望。◇ **~ doing sth** *You ought to give up smoking.* 你應該戒煙。 **2** to spend time on a task that you would normally spend on sth else 把（本該做其他事的時間）耗費於： *I gave up my weekend to help him paint his apartment.* 我耗費了一個週末幫他粉刷寓所。 **,give sth↔'up (to sb)** to hand sth over to sb else 把…交給（或讓與）： *We had to give our passports up to the authorities.* 我們得把護照交給當局。◇ *He gave up his seat to a pregnant woman* (= stood up to allow her to sit down). 他把座位讓給了一名孕婦。 **,give yourself/sb 'up (to sb)** to offer yourself/sb to be captured 自首；投案；投降： *After a week on the run he gave himself up to the police.* 他逃跑一週後向警方投案自首了。 **,give yourself 'up to sth** = GIVE YOURSELF OVER TO STH **,give 'up on sb** **1** to stop hoping or believing that sb will change, get better, etc. 對某人不再抱希望（或不再相信）： *His teachers seem to have given up on him.* 他的老師似乎不再對他抱有希望。 **2** (*especially NAmE*) = GIVE SB UP (1)

▪ **noun** [U] the ability of sth to bend or stretch under pressure 伸展性；彈性： *The shoes may seem tight at first, but the leather has plenty of give in it.* 這鞋剛開始穿時可能顯得緊，但皮子的伸展性很好。

IDM **,give and 'take** **1** willingness in a relationship to accept what sb else wants and give up some of what you want 雙方遷就；相互讓步；互相忍讓 **2** an exchange of words or ideas 交談；思想交流： *to encourage a lively give and take* 鼓勵活躍的思想交流

give·away /ˈɡɪvəweɪ/ *noun, adj.*

▪ **noun** (*informal*) **1** something that a company gives free, usually with sth else that is for sale（公司為推銷產品搭送的）隨贈品 **2** something that makes you guess the real truth about sth/sb 使真相暴露的事物： *She pretended she wasn't excited but the expression on her face was a* ***dead*** (= obvious) ***giveaway.*** 她假裝不為所動，可臉上的表情卻將她的心緒暴露無遺。

▪ **adj.** [only before noun] (*informal*) (of prices 價格) very low 低廉的

give·back /ˈɡɪvbæk/ *noun* (*NAmE*) a situation in which workers agree to accept lower wages or fewer benefits at a particular time, in return for more money or benefits later 福利歸還（工人同意在某段時間接受較低工資或較少福利以待日後獲得更多償還）

given /ˈɡɪvn/ *adj., prep., noun*

▪ **adj.** [usually before noun] **1** already arranged 已經安排好的；規定的： *They were to meet at a given time and place.* 他們要在規定的時間和地點會晤。 **2** that you have stated and are discussing; particular 指定的；所述的；特定的： *We can find out how much money is spent on food in any given period.* 我們可以查明在特定時間內花在食物上的錢有多少。

IDM **be given to sth/to doing sth** (*formal*) to do sth often or regularly 經常做；習慣於： *He's given to going for long walks on his own.* 他有獨自長距離步行的習慣。

■ ***prep.*** when you consider sth 考慮到；鑒於：*Given his age* (= considering how old he is)*, he's remarkably active.* 考慮到他的年齡，他已是相當活躍的了。◇ *Given her interest in children, teaching seems the right job for her.* 考慮到她喜歡孩子，教書看來是很適合她的工作。
▶ **given that** *conj.*：*It was surprising the government was re-elected, given that they had raised taxes so much.* 令人驚奇的是政府把稅收提高這麼多仍再次當選了。
■ ***noun*** something that is accepted as true, for example when you are discussing sth, or planning sth 假設事實

'given name *noun* (*especially NAmE*) = FIRST NAME

giver /'gɪvə(r)/ *noun* (often in compounds 常構成複合詞) a person or an organization that gives 給予者；贈與者；捐助機構：*They are very generous givers to charity.* 他們是慈善事業的慷慨捐助者。

gizmo (also **gismo**) /'gɪzməʊ; *NAmE* -moʊ/ *noun* (*informal*) (*pl.* **-os**) a general word for a small piece of equipment, often one that does sth in a new and clever way 小玩意兒；小裝置

giz·zard /'gɪzəd; *NAmE* -zərd/ *noun* the part of a bird's stomach in which food is broken up into smaller pieces before being DIGESTED （鳥的）砂囊，胗，肫

glacé /'glæseɪ; *NAmE* glæ'seɪ/ *adj.* [only before noun] (of fruit 水果) preserved in sugar 糖漬的；蜜餞的：*glacé fruits* 蜜餞果 ◇ *glacé cherries* 蜜餞櫻桃

gla·cial /'gleɪʃl; 'gleɪsiəl/ *adj.* **1** [usually before noun] (*geology* 地) connected with the Ice Age 冰河時代的；冰河期的；冰川期的：*the glacial period* (= the time when much of the northern half of the world was covered by ice) 冰期 **2** (*technical* 術語) caused or made by glaciers; connected with glaciers 冰川造成的；由冰河形成的；冰河的；冰川的：*a glacial landscape* 由冰河形成的自然景觀 ◇ *glacial deposits/erosion* 冰川沉積；冰蝕作用 **3** (*formal*) very cold; like ice 冰冷的；冰一般的 **SYN** **icy**：*glacial winds/temperatures* 刺骨的寒風；極低的溫度 **4** (*formal*) (of people 人) cold and unfriendly; not showing feelings 冷若冰霜的；冷冰冰的 **SYN** **icy**：*Her expression was glacial.* 她表情冷淡。◇ *Relations between the two countries had always been glacial.* 這兩國間關係一直不好。

gla·ci·ation /ˌgleɪsi'eɪʃn/ *noun* [U] (*geology* 地) the process or result of land being covered by glaciers 冰川作用；冰蝕

gla·cier /'glæsiə(r); *NAmE* 'gleɪʃər/ *noun* a large mass of ice, formed by snow on mountains, that moves very slowly down a valley 冰川 ➲ VISUAL VOCAB page V4, V5

glad 0┳ /glæd/ *adj.*
1 0┳ [not before noun] pleased; happy 高興；愉快：*'I passed the test!' 'I'm so glad (for you).'* "我測驗合格了！" "我真（為你）高興。" ◇ *She was glad when the meeting was over.* 會議結束時她很高興。◇ **~ about sth** *'He doesn't need the pills any more.' 'I'm glad about that.'* "他不再需要服那些藥片了。" "這真讓我高興。" ◇ **~ to know, hear, see ...** *I'm glad to hear you're feeling better.* 聽說你感覺好些了，我很高興。◇ **~ (that) ...** *I'm glad (that) you're feeling better.* 你感覺好些了我很高興。◇ *He was glad he'd come.* 他很高興他來了。◇ *I'm so glad (that) you're safe!* 你安然無恙我真高興！◇ **~ to do sth** *I'm glad to meet you. I've heard a lot about you.* 很高興見到你。久聞大名。◇ *I've never been so glad to see anyone in my life!* 我一生中見到誰都未如此高興過！ **2** grateful for sth 感激；感謝：**~ of sth** *She was very glad of her warm coat in the biting wind.* 在刺骨的寒風中她有暖融融的大衣真是謝天謝地。◇ *I'd be glad of your help.* 你若能幫助我，我會非常感激。◇ **~ if ...** *I'd be glad if you could help me.* 你若能幫助我，我會非常感激。 **3 ~ to do sth** very willing to do sth 樂意；情願；願意：*I'd be glad to lend you the money.* 我很樂意借給你錢。◇ *If you'd like me to help you, I'd* ***be only too glad to.*** 你若要我幫忙，我非常願意效勞。 **4** [only before noun] (*old-fashioned*) bringing

Synonyms 同義詞辨析

glad

happy • pleased • delighted • proud • relieved • thrilled

These words all describe people feeling happy about sth that has happened or is going to happen. 以上各詞均形容人對已經發生或將要發生的事感到高興、愉快。

glad [not usually before noun] happy about sth or grateful for it 指高興、愉快、感激：*He was glad he'd come.* 他很高興他來了。◇ *She was glad when the meeting was over.* 會議結束時她很高興。

happy pleased about sth nice that you have to do or sth that has happened to sb 指對必須做的或發生於某人身上的事感到高興、快樂：*We are happy to announce the engagement of our daughter.* 我們高興地宣佈，我們的女兒訂婚了。

pleased [not before noun] happy about sth that has happened or sth that you have to do 指對已經發生或必須做的事感到高興、愉快、滿意：*She was very pleased with her exam results.* 她對考試成績非常滿意。◇ *You're coming? I'm so pleased.* 你要來呀？我太高興了。

GLAD, HAPPY OR PLEASED? 用 glad、happy 還是 pleased？

Feeling **pleased** can suggest that you have judged sb/sth and approve of them. Feeling **glad** can be more about feeling grateful for sth. You cannot be 'glad with sb'. * pleased 表明對人或事有所評價並表示贊同，glad 多表示為某事的感激，但不說 glad with sb：~~*The boss should be glad with you.*~~ **Happy** can mean glad, pleased or satisfied. * happy 表示高興、愉快、滿意。

delighted very pleased about sth; very happy to do sth; showing your delight 指高興的、樂意的、愉快的：*I'm delighted at your news.* 聽到你的消息我非常高興。 **NOTE** **Delighted** is often used to accept an invitation. * delighted 常用於接受邀請：*'Can you stay for dinner?' 'I'd be delighted (to).'* "留下來吃晚飯好嗎？" "我非常樂意。"

proud pleased and satisfied about sth that you own or have done, or are connected with 指驕傲的、自豪的、得意的、滿足的：*proud parents* 自豪的父母 ◇ *He was* ***proud of*** *himself for not giving up.* 他為自己沒有放棄而自豪。

relieved feeling happy because sth unpleasant has stopped or has not happened; showing this 指感到寬慰的、放心的、顯得開心的：*You'll be relieved to know your jobs are safe.* 現在你們知道工作保住了，可以放心了。

thrilled [not before noun] (*rather informal*) extremely pleased and excited about sth 指非常興奮、極為激動：*I was thrilled to be invited.* 我獲得邀請，感到非常興奮。

DELIGHTED OR THRILLED? 用 delighted 還是 thrilled？

Thrilled may express a stronger feeling than **delighted**, but **delighted** can be made stronger with *absolutely, more than* or *only too*. **Thrilled** can be made negative and ironic with *not exactly* or *less than*. * thrilled 比 delighted 的情感更強烈，但 delighted 可與 absolutely、more than 或 only too 連用以增強語氣。thrilled 與 not exactly 或 less than 連用可變為否定或含諷刺意味：*She was* ***not exactly thrilled*** *at the prospect of looking after her niece.* 想到要照料她的姪女，她就高興不起來了。

PATTERNS

- glad/happy/pleased/delighted/relieved/thrilled **about** sth
- pleased/delighted/relieved/thrilled **at** sth
- glad/happy/pleased/delighted/thrilled **for** sb
- glad/happy/pleased/delighted/proud/relieved/thrilled **that .../to see/hear/find/know ...**
- **very** glad/happy/pleased/proud/relieved
- **absolutely** delighted/thrilled

joy; full of joy 令人愉快的；使人高興的；充滿歡樂的： *glad news/tidings* 令人愉快的消息；喜訊

IDM **I'm glad to say (that ...)** (*informal*) used when you are commenting on a situation and saying that you are happy about it （表示對某種情況感到高興）我很高興地說： *Most teachers, I'm glad to say, take their jobs very seriously.* 我很高興地說，多數老師工作都很認真。

glad·den /ˈɡlædn/ *verb* (*old-fashioned*) to make sb feel pleased or happy 使高興；使愉快；使喜悅： **~ sth** *The sight of the flowers* ***gladdened her heart.*** 看到這些花她心花怒放。◇ **it gladdens sb to do sth** *It gladdened him to see them all enjoying themselves.* 見他們都玩得很開心，他非常高興。

glade /ɡleɪd/ *noun* (*literary*) a small open area of grass in a wood or a forest 林中空地 ➲ VISUAL VOCAB page V4, V5

G

ˈ**glad-hand** *verb* [I, T] **~ (sb)** (especially of a politician 尤指政客) to say hello to sb in a friendly way, especially when this is not sincere 熱情招呼；尤指假意歡迎 ▸ ˈ**glad-handing** *noun* [U]

gladi·ator /ˈɡlædieɪtə(r)/ *noun* (in ancient Rome) a man trained to fight other men or animals in order to entertain the public （古羅馬）角鬥士 ▸ **gladia·tor·ial** /ˌɡlædiəˈtɔːriəl/ *adj.*： *gladiatorial combat* 角鬥士的格鬥

gladi·olus /ˌɡlædiˈəʊləs; *NAmE* -ˈoʊləs/ *noun* (*pl.* **gladi·oli** /-laɪ/) a tall garden plant with long thin leaves and brightly coloured flowers growing up the STEM 唐菖蒲；菖蘭；劍蘭

glad·ly /ˈɡlædli/ *adv.* **1** willingly 樂意地；情願地： *I would gladly pay extra for a good seat.* 我情願額外付費坐好座位。 **2** happily; with thanks 高興地；欣然地；感激地： *When I offered her my seat, she accepted it gladly.* 我把座位讓給她時，她欣然接受了。 IDM see SUFFER

glad·ness /ˈɡlædnəs/ *noun* [U] (*literary*) joy; happiness 高興；愉快；快樂

ˈ**glad rags** *noun* [pl.] (*old-fashioned, informal*) a person's best clothes, worn on a special occasion（某人在特殊場合穿的）最考究的衣服，禮服，盛裝

glam·or·ize (*BrE* also **-ise**) /ˈɡlæməraɪz/ *verb* **~ sth** (usually *disapproving*) to make sth bad appear attractive or exciting 使有魅力；使有刺激性；美化： *Television tends to glamorize violence.* 電視往往渲染暴力。

glam·or·ous /ˈɡlæmərəs/ (also *informal* **glam**) *adj.* especially attractive and exciting, and different from ordinary things or people 特別富有魅力的；富於刺激的；獨特的： *glamorous movie stars* 富有魅力的影星 ◇ *a glamorous job* 令人嚮往的工作 OPP **unglamorous** ▸ **glam·or·ous·ly** *adv.*： *glamorously dressed* 衣着華麗

glam·our (*NAmE* also **glamor**) /ˈɡlæmə(r)/ *noun* [U] **1** the attractive and exciting quality that makes a person, a job or a place seem special, often because of wealth or status 吸引力，魅力，誘惑力（常因財富或地位所致）： *hopeful young actors and actresses dazzled by the glamour of Hollywood* 為好萊塢的魅力神魂顛倒時刻懷抱希望的年輕演員 ◇ *Now that she's a flight attendant, foreign travel has lost its glamour for her.* 她現在是空中乘務員了，去國外旅行對她已失去魅力。 **2** physical beauty that also suggests wealth or success（暗示財富或成功的）迷人的美，魅力： *Add a cashmere scarf under your jacket for a touch of glamour.* 在夾克衫裏面圍一條開司米圍巾會使你更有魅力。

ˈ**glamour model** *noun* (*especially BrE*) a person, especially a woman, who is photographed wearing very few or no clothes in order to sexually excite the person looking at the photographs（衣着暴露的）魅力模特；性感女郎

glam rock /ˌɡlæm ˈrɒk; *NAmE* ˈrɑːk/ *noun* [U] a style of music popular in the 1970s, in which male singers wore unusual clothes and make-up 魅惑搖滾（流行於 20 世紀 70 年代，男歌手穿着打扮怪異）

glance /ɡlɑːns; *NAmE* ɡlæns/ *verb, noun*

■ *verb* **1** [I] **+ adv./prep.** to look quickly at sth/sb 瞥一眼；匆匆一看；掃視： *She glanced at her watch.* 她匆匆看了看錶。◇ *He glanced around the room.* 他環視了一下房間。◇ *I glanced up quickly to see who had come in.* 我迅速抬頭瞥了一眼看是誰進來了。 **2** [I] **~ at/down/over/through sth** to read sth quickly and not thoroughly 瀏覽；粗略地看 SYN **scan**： *I only had time to glance at the newspapers.* 我只來得及瀏覽了一下報紙。◇ *He glanced briefly down the list of names.* 他草草看了一遍名單。◇ *She glanced through the report.* 她瀏覽了一下報告。

PHR V ˈ**glance on/off sth** (of light 光) to flash on a surface or be reflected off it 在…上閃爍（或閃耀）；從…中反射 ˌ**glance ˈoff (sth)** to hit sth at an angle and move off it in a different direction 擊中（某物）後改變方向： *The ball glanced off the post into the net.* 球擊中門柱後反彈入網。

■ *noun* **~ (at sb/sth)** a quick look 匆匆一看；一瞥；掃視： *to* ***take/have a glance*** *at the newspaper headlines* 匆匆看一眼報紙的大標題 ◇ *a* ***cursory/brief/casual/furtive glance*** 草草的／短暫的／不經意的／偷偷的一瞥 ◇ *The sisters* ***exchanged glances*** (= looked at each other). 姐妹倆相互對視了一下。◇ *She shot him a* ***sideways glance.*** 她從眼角瞥了他一眼。◇ *He walked away* ***without a backward glance.*** 他頭也不回地揚長而去。◇ *She* ***stole a glance*** (= looked secretly) *at her watch.* 她偷偷看了看錶。 ➲ SYNONYMS at LOOK

IDM **at a (single) ˈglance** immediately; with only a quick look 立刻；一眼；（只）看一眼： *He could tell at a glance what was wrong.* 他一眼就看出了問題所在。 **at first ˈglance** when you first look at or think about sth, often rather quickly 乍一看；乍看之下： *At first glance the problem seemed easy.* 乍一看問題似乎很簡單。

glan·cing /ˈɡlɑːnsɪŋ; *NAmE* ˈɡlænsɪŋ/ *adj.* [only before noun] hitting sth/sb at an angle, not with full force 斜擦而過的；擊偏的： *to strike somebody a* ***glancing blow*** 從側面給某人一擊

gland /ɡlænd/ *noun* an organ in a person's or an animal's body that produces a substance for the body to use. There are many different glands in the body. 腺： *a snake's poison glands* 蛇的毒腺 ◇ *Her glands are swollen.* 她的腺體腫脹。 ➲ see also PITUITARY ▸ **glan·du·lar** /ˈɡlændjələ(r); *NAmE* -dʒə-/ *adj.* [usually before noun]： *glandular tissue* 腺體組織

ˌ**glandular ˈfever** *noun* [U] (*BrE*) = MONONUCLEOSIS

glans /ɡlænz/ (*pl.* **glan·des** /ˈɡlændiːz/) *noun* (*anatomy* 解) the round part at the end of a man's PENIS or a woman's CLITORIS 陰莖頭；龜頭；陰蒂

glare /ɡleə(r); *NAmE* ɡler/ *verb, noun*

■ *verb* **1** [I] **~ (at sb/sth)** to look at sb/sth in an angry way 怒目而視 SYN **glower**： *He didn't shout, he just glared at me silently.* 他沒有喊叫，只是默默地怒視着我。 **2** [I] to shine with a very bright unpleasant light 發出刺眼的光

■ *noun* **1** [U, sing.] a very bright, unpleasant light 刺眼的光： *the glare of the sun* 炫目的陽光 ◇ *The rabbit was caught in the glare of the car's headlights.* 兔子被耀眼的汽車前燈照射着。◇ *These sunglasses are designed to reduce glare.* 這些太陽鏡是為減少刺眼的強光而設計的。◇ (*figurative*) *The divorce was conducted* ***in the full glare of publicity*** (= with continuous attention from newspapers and television). 這樁離婚案是在媒體的密切關注下進行的。 **2** [C] a long, angry look（長久的）怒視，瞪眼： *to give sb a hostile glare* 含敵意地瞪着某人 ➲ SYNONYMS at LOOK, STARE

glar·ing /ˈɡleərɪŋ; *NAmE* ˈɡler-/ *adj.* **1** [usually before noun] (of sth bad 負面的事物) very easily seen 顯眼的；明顯的；易見的 SYN **blatant**： *a* ***glaring error/omission/inconsistency/injustice*** 明顯的錯誤／疏漏／不一致／不公正 ◇ *the most* ***glaring example*** *of this problem* 此問題最明顯的事例 **2** (of a light 光) very bright and unpleasant 刺眼的；炫目的 **3** angry; aggressive 生氣的；憤怒的；富於攻擊性的： *glaring eyes* 憤怒的目光 ▸ **glar·ing·ly** *adv.*： *glaringly obvious* 顯而易見的

glass 0ᵏ /ɡlɑːs; *NAmE* ɡlæs/ *noun, verb*

■ *noun*

▸ TRANSPARENT SUBSTANCE 透明物質 **1** 0ᵏ [U] a hard, usually transparent, substance used, for example, for making windows and bottles 玻璃： *a* ***sheet/pane of glass*** 一片玻璃；一塊窗玻璃 ◇ ***frosted/toughened glass*** 磨砂／鋼化玻璃 ◇ *a* ***glass bottle/dish/roof*** 玻璃瓶／盤／

屋頂◇*I cut myself on a piece of* ***broken glass****.* 我被一塊碎玻璃劃傷了。◇*The vegetables are grown* ***under glass*** (= in a GREENHOUSE). 這些蔬菜是在玻璃溫室種植的。➲ see also CUT GLASS, PLATE GLASS, STAINED GLASS, GLAZIER

▸ **FOR DRINKING** 飲用 **2** [C] (often in compounds 常構成複合詞) a container made of glass, used for drinking out of 玻璃杯；酒杯：*a sherry glass* 雪利酒杯◇*a wine glass* 葡萄酒杯 ➲ **VISUAL VOCAB** page V22 **3** [C] the contents of a glass 一杯（的量）：*a* ***glass of sherry/wine/water, etc.*** 一杯雪利酒、葡萄酒、水等◇*He drank three whole glasses.* 他喝了滿滿三杯。

▸ **GLASS OBJECTS** 玻璃製品 **4** [U] objects made of glass 玻璃製品；玻璃器皿：*We keep all our glass and china in this cupboard.* 我們把所有玻璃器皿和瓷器都放在這個櫥裏。◇*She has a fine collection of Bohemian glass.* 她收藏了一批做工精細的波希米亞玻璃製品。**5** [sing.] a protecting cover made of glass on a watch, picture or photograph frame, FIRE ALARM, etc. 玻璃保護面；玻璃（鏡）框；（火災警報器的）玻璃罩：*In case of emergency, break the glass and press the button.* 如遇緊急情況，擊碎玻璃罩按下按鈕。

▸ **FOR EYES** 眼睛 **6** **glasses** (*NAmE* also **eye·glasses**) (also *old-fashioned* or *formal* **spec·tacles**, *informal* **specs** especially in *BrE*) [pl.] two LENSES in a frame that rests on the nose and ears. People wear glasses in order to be able to see better or to protect their eyes from bright light. 眼鏡：***a pair of glasses*** 一副眼鏡◇*dark glasses* 墨鏡◇***I wear glasses*** *for driving.* 我開車時戴眼鏡。➲ see also FIELD GLASSES, MAGNIFYING GLASS, SUNGLASSES

▸ **MIRROR** 鏡子 **7** [C, usually sing.] (*old-fashioned*) a mirror 鏡子 ➲ see also LOOKING GLASS

▸ **BAROMETER** 氣壓表 **8** **the glass** [sing.] a BAROMETER 氣壓表；晴雨表 **IDM** see PEOPLE *n.*, RAISE *v.*

■ **verb ~ sb** (*BrE, informal*) to hit sb in the face with a glass 用玻璃杯擊（某人的）臉部

PHR V ˌ**glass sth ˈin/ˈover** [usually passive] to cover sth with a roof or wall made of glass 給…裝玻璃；用玻璃把…蓋（或罩、圍）住：*a glassed-in pool* 裝有玻璃屋頂的游泳池 ➲ compare GLAZE *v.* (2)

ˈ**glass-blowing** *noun* [U] the art or activity of blowing hot glass into shapes using a special tube 玻璃吹製（術）；吹玻璃 ▸ ˈ**glass-blower** *noun*

ˌ**glass ˈceiling** *noun* [usually sing.] the way in which unfair attitudes can stop women, or other groups, from getting the best jobs in a company, etc. although there are no official rules to prevent them from getting these jobs 玻璃天花板，無形頂障（雖無明文規定卻實際存在的對婦女等在職務升遷上的無形限制）

ˌ**glass ˈfibre** (*BrE*) (*NAmE* ˌ**glass ˈfiber**) *noun* [U] = FIBRE-GLASS

glass·ful /ˈɡlɑːsfʊl; *NAmE* ˈɡlæs-/ *noun* the amount that a drinking glass will hold 一玻璃杯（的量）

glass·house /ˈɡlɑːshaʊs; *NAmE* ˈɡlæs-/ *noun* (*BrE*) **1** a building with glass sides and a glass roof, for growing plants in; a type of large GREENHOUSE 玻璃暖房；溫室 ➲ **VISUAL VOCAB** page V15 **2** (*slang*) a military prison 軍事監獄

glass·ware /ˈɡlɑːsweə(r); *NAmE* ˈɡlæswer/ *noun* [U] objects made of glass 玻璃器皿；玻璃製品；料器

glassy /ˈɡlɑːsi; *NAmE* ˈɡlæsi/ *adj.* (**glass·ier**, **glassi·est**) **1** like glass; smooth and shiny 像玻璃一樣的；光滑的；光亮透明的：*a glassy lake* 平靜清澈的湖水◇*a glassy material* 玻璃狀材料 **2** showing no feeling or emotion 無表情的；木然的；呆滯的：*glassy eyes* 目光呆滯的眼睛◇*a* ***glassy look/stare*** 呆滯的神色／盯視◇*He looked flushed and* ***glassy-eyed****.* 他顯得滿臉通紅，目光呆滯。

Glas·we·gian /ɡlæzˈwiːdʒən/ *noun* a person from Glasgow in Scotland（蘇格蘭的）格拉斯哥人 ▸ **Glas·we·gian** *adj.*

glau·coma /ɡlɔːˈkəʊmə; *NAmE* ɡlaʊˈkoʊmə; ɡlɔː-/ *noun* [U] an eye disease that causes gradual loss of sight 青光眼

glaze /ɡleɪz/ *verb, noun*

■ **verb 1** [I] **~ (over)** if a person's eyes **glaze** or **glaze over**, the person begins to look bored or tired（眼睛）變呆滯，發呆：*A lot of people's eyes glaze over if you say you are a feminist.* 如果你說你是女權主義者，好多人都會愣住。◇*'I'm feeling rather tired,' he said, his eyes glazing.* "我有點累了。"他目光呆滯地說。**2** [T] **~ sth** to fit sheets of glass into sth 給…安裝玻璃：*to glaze a window/house* 給窗戶／房子安裝玻璃◇*a glazed door* 鑲着玻璃的門 ➲ compare GLASS *v.* ➲ see also DOUBLE GLAZING **3** [T] **~ sth (with sth)** to cover sth with a glaze to give it a shiny surface 給…上釉；使光滑；使光亮：*Glaze the pie with beaten egg.* 在餅的表面刷上打勻的蛋液使它有光澤。◇*glazed tiles* 釉面磚◇(*NAmE*) *a glazed doughnut* 掛糖漿的炸麪圈

■ **noun** [C, U] **1** a thin clear liquid put on CLAY objects such as cups and plates before they are finished, to give them a hard shiny surface 釉；釉料 **2** a thin liquid, made of egg, milk or sugar, for example, that is put on cake, bread, etc. to make it look shiny（澆在糕點上增加光澤的）蛋漿，奶漿，糖漿

glazed /ɡleɪzd/ *adj.* (especially of the eyes 尤指眼睛) showing no feeling or emotion; dull 木然的；呆滯的：*eyes glazed with boredom* 厭倦無神的眼睛

glaz·ier /ˈɡleɪziə(r); *NAmE* -ʒər/ *noun* a person whose job is to fit glass into the frames of windows, etc. 鑲玻璃的工人

gleam /ɡliːm/ *verb, noun*

■ **verb 1** [I] to shine with a pale clear light 發微光；隱約閃光；閃爍：*The moonlight gleamed on the water.* 月光照在水面上泛起粼粼波光。◇*Her eyes gleamed in the dark.* 她的眼睛在黑暗中閃爍。➲ **SYNONYMS** at SHINE **2** [I] to look very clean or bright 顯得光潔明亮：**~ (with sth)** *The house was gleaming with fresh white paint.* 房子剛刷過白漆，顯得光潔明亮。◇**+ adj.** *Her teeth gleamed white against the tanned skin of her face.* 她的牙齒在褐色臉膛映襯下顯得潔白明亮。**3** [I] if a person's eyes **gleam** with a particular emotion, or an emotion **gleams** in a person's eyes, the person shows that emotion（眼睛）表露出，流露出；（在眼中）閃現：**~ (with sth)** *His eyes gleamed with amusement.* 他眼睛裏流露出愉悅的神情。◇**~ (in sth)** *Amusement gleamed in his eyes.* 他眼睛裏流露出愉悅的神情。

■ **noun** [usually sing.] **1** a pale clear light, often reflected from sth 微光（常指反光）：*the gleam of moonlight on the water* 水面上盪漾的月光◇*A few gleams of sunshine lit up the gloomy afternoon.* 幾線陽光使陰暗的下午亮了起來。◇*I saw the gleam of the knife as it flashed through the air.* 我看見了刀在空中劃過時的閃光。**2** a small amount of sth 少量；一絲；一線：*a faint gleam of hope* 微弱的一線希望◇*a serious book with an occasional gleam of humour* 偶有一絲幽默的嚴肅的書 **3** an expression of a particular feeling or emotion that shows in sb's eyes（感情在眼中的）表露，閃現 **SYN** **glint**：*a gleam of triumph in her eyes* 她眼裏閃爍着勝利的光芒◇*a mischievous gleam in his eye* 他淘氣的眼神◇*The gleam in his eye made her uncomfortable* (= as if he was planning sth secret or unpleasant). 他閃爍的眼神令她感到不舒服。

gleam·ing /ˈɡliːmɪŋ/ *adj.* shining brightly 閃耀的；明亮的：*gleaming white teeth* 皓齒

glean /ɡliːn/ *verb* **~ sth (from sb/sth)** to obtain information, knowledge etc., sometimes with difficulty and often from various different places 費力地收集，四處搜集（信息、知識等）：*These figures have been gleaned from a number of studies.* 這些數據是通過多次研究收集得來的。

glean·ings /ˈɡliːnɪŋz/ *noun* [pl.] information, knowledge etc., that you obtain from various different places, often with difficulty（費力從多處）收集的信息（或知識等）

glebe /ɡliːb/ *noun* (*old use*) **1** [C] a piece of land that provided an income for a priest（舊時）作為牧師俸祿來源的土地 **2** [U] land; fields 土地；田地

glee /ɡliː/ *noun* [U] a feeling of happiness, usually because sth good has happened to you, or sth bad has happened to sb else 歡喜；高興；幸災樂禍 **SYN** **delight**：*He rubbed his hands* ***in glee*** *as he thought of all the money he would make.* 他想到自己將賺到那麼多

G

錢就高興得直搓手。◇ *She couldn't disguise her glee at their embarrassment.* 看到他們難堪的樣子她不禁喜形於色。

glee·ful /ˈgliːfl/ *adj.* happy because of sth good you have done or sth bad that has happened to sb else 歡喜的；高興的；幸災樂禍的： *a gleeful laugh* 歡快的笑聲 ▸ **glee·ful·ly** /-fəli/ *adv.*

glen /glen/ *noun* a deep narrow valley, especially in Scotland or Ireland（尤指蘇格蘭或愛爾蘭的）峽谷

glib /glɪb/ *adj.* (*disapproving*) (of speakers and speech 演講者或演講) using words that are clever, but are not sincere, and do not show much thought 油腔滑調的；不誠懇的；未經思考的；膚淺的： *a glib salesman* 油嘴滑舌的推銷員 ◇ *glib answers* 未經思考的回答 ▸ **glib·ly** *adv.*

G

glide /glaɪd/ *verb, noun*

■ *verb* **1** [I] (+ **adv./prep.**) to move smoothly and quietly, especially as though it takes no effort 滑行；滑動；掠過： *Swans went gliding past.* 天鵝滑行而過。◇ *The skaters were gliding over the ice.* 滑冰者在冰上滑行。 **2** [I] (+ **adv./prep.**) (of birds or aircraft 鳥或飛機) to fly using air currents, without the birds moving their wings or the aircraft using the engine 滑翔： *An eagle was gliding high overhead.* 一隻鷹在頭頂上空翱翔。◇ *The plane managed to glide down to the runway.* 飛機終於成功地滑翔降落在跑道上。

■ *noun* **1** [sing.] a continuous smooth movement 滑行；滑動；滑翔： *the graceful glide of a skater* 滑冰者優美的滑行動作 **2** [C] (*phonetics* 語音) a speech sound made while moving the tongue from one position to another 滑音；音渡；過渡音 ➲ compare DIPHTHONG

glider /ˈglaɪdə(r)/ *noun* a light aircraft that flies without an engine 滑翔機 ➲ VISUAL VOCAB page V53

glid·ing /ˈglaɪdɪŋ/ *noun* [U] the sport of flying in a glider 滑翔運動

glim·mer /ˈglɪmə(r)/ *noun, verb*

■ *noun* **1** a faint unsteady light 微弱的閃光；閃爍的微光： *We could see a glimmer of light on the far shore.* 我們可以看到對岸遠處微微閃爍的燈光。 **2** (also **glim·mer·ing**) a small sign of sth 微弱的跡象；一絲；一線： ***a glimmer of hope*** 一線希望 ◇ *I caught the **glimmer of a smile** in his eyes.* 我看到他眼裏閃現出一絲笑意。◇ *the **glimmering of an idea*** 初露端倪的想法

■ *verb* [I] to shine with a faint unsteady light 隱約地閃爍；發出微弱的閃光： *The candles glimmered in the corner.* 燭光在角落裏忽明忽暗地閃爍。◇ (*figurative*) *Amusement glimmered in his eyes.* 他眼裏隱約露出愉悅的神情。

glimpse /glɪmps/ *noun, verb*

■ *noun* [usually sing.] **1 ~ (of sb/sth)** | **~ (at sb/sth)** a look at sb/sth for a very short time, when you do not see the person or thing completely 一瞥；一看： *He **caught a glimpse** of her in the crowd.* 他一眼瞥見她在人群裏。◇ *I came up on deck to get my first glimpse of the island.* 我登上甲板第一次看這島。 ➲ SYNONYMS at LOOK, SEE **2** a short experience of sth that helps you to understand it 短暫的感受（或體驗、領會）： **~ (into sth)** *a fascinating glimpse into life in the ocean* 對海洋生物的一次短暫而動人心魄的感受 ◇ **~ (of sth)** *The programme gives us a rare glimpse of a great artist at work.* 這個節目使我們難得地認識到偉大藝術家工作時的情況。

■ *verb* **1 ~ sb/sth** to see sb/sth for a moment, but not very clearly 瞥見；看一眼 SYN **catch sight of**, **spot**： *He'd glimpsed her through the window as he passed.* 他路過時透過窗戶瞥見了她。 **2 ~ sth** to start to understand sth 開始領悟；開始認識到： *Suddenly she glimpsed the truth about her sister.* 她突然開始瞭解到她姐姐的真實情況。

glint /glɪnt/ *verb, noun*

■ *verb* **1** [I] (+ **adv./prep.**) to produce small bright flashes of light 閃光；閃亮： *The sea glinted in the moonlight.* 月色中海面上波光粼粼。◇ *The sun glinted on the windows.* 太陽照在窗戶上閃閃發光。 ➲ SYNONYMS at SHINE **2** [I] + **adv./prep.** if a person's eyes **glint** with a particular emotion, or an emotion **glints** in a person's eyes, the person shows that emotion, which is usually a strong one（眼睛）流露出（強烈情感）；（強烈情感在眼中）閃現： *Her eyes glinted angrily.* 她眼睛裏閃射着憤怒的目光。◇ *Hostility glinted in his eyes.* 他眼睛裏流露出敵意。

■ *noun* **1** a sudden flash of light or colour shining from a bright surface 閃光；閃亮： *the glint of the sun on the water* 太陽照在水上的閃光 ◇ *golden glints in her red hair* 她的紅髮上閃着的金光 ◇ *She saw a glint of silver in the grass.* 她看到草地上銀光閃亮。 **2** an expression in sb's eyes showing a particular emotion, often a negative one（眼睛裏某種感情，常指負面感情的）閃現： *He had a wicked glint in his eye.* 他眼睛裏閃着邪惡的神色。◇ *a glint of anger* 憤怒的目光

glis·sando /glɪˈsændəʊ; *NAmE* -doʊ/ *noun* (*pl.* **glis·san·dos** or **glis·sandi** /-diː/) (from *Italian*) a way of playing a series of notes so that each one slides into the next, making a smooth continuous sound 滑奏

glis·ten /ˈglɪsn/ *verb* [I] (of sth wet 濕物) to shine 閃光；閃亮： *Her eyes were glistening with tears.* 她眼裏閃着晶瑩的淚珠。◇ *Sweat glistened on his forehead.* 他額頭上的汗珠晶瑩發亮。◇ **+ adj.** *The road glistened wet after the rain.* 雨後的道路潤澤閃亮。 ➲ SYNONYMS at SHINE IDM see GOLD *n.*

glis·ter /ˈglɪstə; *NAmE* ˈglɪstər/ *verb* [I] (*literary*) to shine brightly with little flashes of light, like a diamond 閃耀；閃亮；熠熠生輝 SYN **glitter**

glitch /glɪtʃ/ *noun* (*informal*) a small problem or fault that stops sth working successfully 小故障；小毛病；小差錯

glit·ter /ˈglɪtə(r)/ *verb, noun*

■ *verb* **1** [I] to shine brightly with little flashes of light, like a diamond 閃亮；閃耀；光彩奪目 SYN **sparkle**： *The ceiling of the cathedral glittered with gold.* 大教堂的天花板金光閃閃。◇ *The water glittered in the sunlight.* 水面在陽光下閃閃發光。 ➲ SYNONYMS at SHINE **2** [I] **~ (with sth)** (of the eyes 眼睛) to shine brightly with a particular emotion, usually a strong one 閃現（某種強烈情感）： *His eyes glittered with greed.* 他眼睛裏閃現出貪婪的神色。 IDM see GOLD *n.*

■ *noun* **1** [U] bright light consisting of many little flashes 燦爛的光輝；閃爍；閃耀： *the glitter of diamonds* 鑽石的光彩 **2** [sing.] a bright expression in sb's eyes showing a particular emotion（眼睛裏某種感情的）閃現，流露 SYN **glint**： *There was a triumphant glitter in his eyes.* 他眼睛裏閃爍着勝利的光輝。 **3** [U] the attractive, exciting qualities that sb/sth, especially a rich and famous person or place, seems to have 吸引力；魅力；誘惑力 SYN **glamour**： *the superficial glitter of show business* 表面上光彩迷人的演藝業 **4** [U] very small shiny pieces of thin metal or paper that are stuck to things as a decoration（裝飾用的）小發光物： ***gold/silver glitter*** 金色的／銀色的閃光裝飾物

glit·ter·ati /ˌglɪtəˈrɑːti/ *noun* [pl.] (used in newspapers 報章用語) fashionable, rich and famous people 時髦人物；風雲人物；知名人士

glit·ter·ing /ˈglɪtərɪŋ/ *adj.* [usually before noun] **1** very impressive and successful 輝煌的；成功的： *He has a glittering career ahead of him.* 他前程似錦。 **2** very impressive and involving rich and successful people 盛大的；華麗的；眾星雲集的： ***a glittering occasion/ceremony*** 盛會；盛典 ◇ *a glittering array of stars* 眾星雲集的盛大場面 **3** shining brightly with many small flashes of light 燦爛奪目的；閃閃發光的 SYN **sparkling**： *glittering jewels* 璀璨的寶石

glit·tery /ˈglɪtəri/ *adj.* shining brightly with many little flashes of light 燦爛奪目的；閃閃發光的；華麗的： *a glittery suit* 一套華麗的服裝

glitz /glɪts/ *noun* [U] (sometimes *disapproving*) the quality of appearing very attractive, exciting and impressive, in a way that is not always genuine 耀眼；華麗；浮華： *the glitz and glamour of the music scene* 表面光輝燦爛的樂壇 ▸ **glitzy** *adj.*： *a glitzy, Hollywood-style occasion* 好萊塢式的盛大場面

the gloam·ing /ˈgləʊmɪŋ; *NAmE* ˈgloʊ-/ *noun* [sing.] (*ScotE* or *literary*) the faint light after the sun sets 朦朧的暮色 SYN **twilight**, **dusk**

gloat /ɡləʊt; *NAmE* ɡloʊt/ *verb* [I] **~ (about/at/over sth)** to show that you are happy about your own success or sb else's failure, in an unpleasant way 揚揚得意；沾沾自喜；幸災樂禍 SYN **crow**： *She was still gloating over her rival's disappointment.* 她仍在為對手的失望而幸災樂禍。 ▸ **gloat·ing** *adj.*： *a gloating look* 揚揚得意的樣子

glob /ɡlɒb; *NAmE* ɡlɑːb/ *noun* (*informal*) a small amount of a liquid or substance in a round shape 一小滴；一小團： *thick globs of paint on the floor* 地板上一滴滴黏稠的油漆

global 0⊶ AW /ˈɡləʊbl; *NAmE* ˈɡloʊbl/ *adj.* [usually before noun]

1 0⊶ covering or affecting the whole world 全球的；全世界的： *global issues* 全球性問題 ◇ *The commission is calling for a global ban on whaling.* 委員會要求全球禁止捕鯨。 ◇ *the company's domestic and global markets* 這家公司在國內外的銷售市場 ➲ COLLOCATIONS at INTERNATIONAL **2** considering or including all parts of sth 整體的；全面的；總括的： *We need to take a more global approach to the problem.* 我們需要更全面地看這個問題。 ◇ *global searches on the database* 在數據庫中的全程檢索 ◇ *They sent a global email to all staff.* 他們向全體職員發了一封統一的電郵。 ▸ **glob·al·ly** AW /-bəli/ *adv.*： *We need to start thinking globally.* 我們需着手全面考慮。

glob·al·iza·tion (*BrE* also **-isa·tion**) AW /ˌɡləʊbəlaɪˈzeɪʃn; *NAmE* ˌɡloʊbələˈz-/ *noun* [U] the fact that different cultures and economic systems around the world are becoming connected and similar to each other because of the influence of large MULTINATIONAL companies and of improved communication 全球化，全世界化（世界各地的文化和經濟體系日益關聯） ➲ COLLOCATIONS at INTERNATIONAL

glob·al·ize (*BrE* also **-ise**) /ˈɡləʊbəlaɪz; *NAmE* ˈɡloʊ-/ *verb* [I, T] **~ (sth)** (*economics* 經) if sth, for example a business company, **globalizes** or **is globalized**, it operates all around the world （使）全球化，全世界化

ˌ**global ˈvillage** *noun* [sing.] the whole world, looked at as a single community that is connected by electronic communication systems 地球村（指整個世界作為一個由電子通信系統連接的單一集體）

ˌ**global ˈwarming** *noun* [U] the increase in temperature of the earth's atmosphere, that is caused by the increase of particular gases, especially CARBON DIOXIDE 全球（氣候）變暖；地球大氣層變暖 ➲ COLLOCATIONS at ENVIRONMENT ➲ compare CLIMATE CHANGE ➲ see also GREENHOUSE EFFECT

globe AW /ɡləʊb; *NAmE* ɡloʊb/ *noun* **1** [C] an object shaped like a ball with a map of the world on its surface, usually on a stand so that it can be turned 地球儀 **2 the globe** [sing.] the world (used especially to emphasize its size) 地球，世界（尤用以強調其大）： *tourists from every corner of the globe* 來自世界各地的遊客 **3** [C] a thing shaped like a ball 球體；球狀物

ˌ**globe ˈartichoke** *noun* = ARTICHOKE (1)

globe·trot·ting /ˈɡləʊbtrɒtɪŋ; *NAmE* ˈɡloʊbtrɑːtɪŋ/ *adj.* (*informal*) travelling in many countries all over the world 環球旅行的；周遊世界的： *a globetrotting journalist* 環球工作的記者 ▸ **globe·trot·ter** *noun* **globe·trot·ting** *noun* [U]

globu·lar /ˈɡlɒbjələ(r); *NAmE* ˈɡlɑːb-/ *adj.* shaped like a ball, GLOBE or globule; consisting of globules 球形的；球體的；小球狀的；由小球組成的

glob·ule /ˈɡlɒbjuːl; *NAmE* ˈɡlɑːb-/ *noun* a very small drop or ball of a liquid or of a solid that has been melted （液體或熔化了的固體的）小滴，小球體： *a globule of fat* 一滴油

gloc·al·iza·tion (*BrE* also **-isa·tion**) /ˌɡləʊkəlaɪˈzeɪʃn; *NAmE* ˌɡloʊ-/ *noun* [U] the fact of adapting products or services that are available all over the world to make them suitable for local needs 全球本土化，全球地域一體化，全球地方化（使世界各地的產品或服務適合本地需求）

glock·en·spiel /ˈɡlɒkənʃpiːl; *NAmE* ˈɡlɑːk-/ *noun* a musical instrument made of a row of metal bars of different lengths, that you hit with two small HAMMERS 鐘琴 ➲ VISUAL VOCAB page V35 ➲ compare XYLOPHONE

glom /ɡlɒm; *NAmE* ɡlɑːm/ *verb* (**-mm-**) **~ sth** (*NAmE*, *informal*) to steal 盜竊；竊取

PHR V ˌ**glom ˈonto sth** **1** to develop a strong interest in sth 對…產生強烈的興趣： *Kids soon glom onto the latest trend.* 年輕人很快就迷上了最新的款式。 **2** to become attached or stuck to sth 粘住

gloom /ɡluːm/ *noun* **1** [U, sing.] a feeling of being sad and without hope 憂鬱；愁悶；無望 SYN **depression**： *The gloom deepened as the election results came in.* 選舉結果陸續傳來，失落的情緒越來越重。 **2** [U] (*literary*) almost total DARKNESS 幽暗；黑暗；昏暗： *We watched the boats come back in the gathering gloom.* 我們注視着船隻在朦朧暮色中返航。 IDM see DOOM *n.*, PILE *v.*

gloomy /ˈɡluːmi/ *adj.* (**gloom·ier**, **gloomi·est**) **1** nearly dark, or badly lit in a way that makes you feel sad 黑暗的；陰暗的；幽暗的 SYN **depressing**： *a gloomy room/atmosphere* 昏暗的房間；陰沉沉的氣氛 ◇ *It was a wet and gloomy day.* 那一天下着雨，陰沉沉的。 **2** sad and without hope 憂鬱的；沮喪的；無望的 SYN **glum**： *a gloomy expression* 沮喪的表情 ◇ *We sat in gloomy silence.* 我們鬱鬱不樂地默默坐着。 **3** without much hope of success or happiness in the future 前景黯淡的；悲觀的 SYN **depressing**： *a* ***gloomy picture*** *of the country's economic future* 該國經濟前景的黯淡景象 ◇ *Suddenly, the future didn't look so gloomy after all.* 突然感到前途似乎並非如此黯淡。 ▸ **gloom·ily** /-ɪli/ *adv.*： *He stared gloomily at the phone.* 他滿臉愁容地盯着電話。 **gloomi·ness** *noun* [U]

gloop /ɡluːp/ (*BrE*) (*NAmE* **glop** /ɡlɒp; *NAmE* ɡlɑːp/) *noun* [U] (*informal*) a thick wet substance that looks, tastes or feels unpleasant （難看、味道差或令人噁心的）黏稠物 ▸ **gloopy** (*BrE*) (*NAmE* **gloppy**) *adj.*

glop /ɡlɒp; *NAmE* ɡlɑːp/ *noun* [U] (*informal*, *especially NAmE*) a thick wet substance that looks, tastes or feels unpleasant （難看、味道差或令人噁心的）黏稠物

glori·fied /ˈɡlɔːrɪfaɪd/ *adj.* [only before noun] making sb/sth seem more important or better than they are 吹捧的；吹噓的；美化的： *The restaurant was no more than a glorified fast-food cafe.* 這地方美其名曰餐館，其實只不過是個快餐店而已。

glor·ify /ˈɡlɔːrɪfaɪ/ *verb* (**glori·fies**, **glori·fy·ing**, **glori·fied**, **glori·fied**) **1 ~ sth** (often *disapproving*) to make sth seem better or more important than it really is 吹捧；吹噓；美化： *He denies that the movie glorifies violence.* 他否認這部影片美化暴力。 **2 ~ sb** (*formal*) to praise and worship God 頌揚，讚美，崇拜（上帝） ▸ **glori·fi·ca·tion** /ˌɡlɔːrɪfɪˈkeɪʃn/ *noun* [U]： *the glorification of war* 對戰爭的頌揚

glori·ous /ˈɡlɔːriəs/ *adj.* **1** (*formal*) deserving or bringing great fame and success 值得稱道的；光榮的；榮耀的： *a glorious victory* 輝煌的勝利 ◇ *a glorious chapter in our country's history* 我國歷史上光輝的一頁 ➲ compare INGLORIOUS **2** (*formal*) very beautiful and impressive 壯麗的；輝煌的；光輝燦爛的 SYN **splendid**： *a glorious sunset* 瑰麗的晚霞 **3** extremely enjoyable 極其令人愉快的；極為宜人的 SYN **wonderful**： *a glorious trip to Rome* 極為享受的羅馬之行 **4** (of weather 天氣) hot, with the sun shining 熱的；陽光燦爛的；晴朗的： *They had three weeks of glorious sunshine.* 他們度過了三週陽光燦爛的日子。 ▸ **glori·ous·ly** *adv.*

glory /ˈɡlɔːri/ *noun*, *verb*

▪ ***noun*** **1** [U] fame, praise or honour that is given to sb because they have achieved sth important 榮譽；光榮；桂冠： *Olympic glory in the 100 metres* 奧林匹克 100 米賽跑的桂冠 ◇ *I do all the work and he gets all the glory.* 活兒都是我幹，榮譽都是他得。 ◇ *She wanted to enjoy her moment of glory.* 她希望盡情享受自己的光榮時刻。 ◇ *He came home a rich man,* ***covered in glory***. 他發跡還鄉，榮歸故里。 **2** [U] praise and worship of God （對上帝的）讚頌，讚美，崇拜： *'Glory to God in the highest'* "榮耀歸於至高無上的上帝" **3** [U] great beauty 壯麗；輝煌；燦爛： *The city was spread out beneath us* ***in all its glory***. 這座城市絢麗多彩地展現在我們下方。 ◇ *The house has now been restored to its* ***former glory***. 這棟房子又恢復了

G

它往日的輝煌。 **4** [C] a special cause for pride, respect or pleasure 產生驕傲（或崇敬、愉快）的理由：*The temple is one of the glories of ancient Greece.* 這座廟宇是古希臘的一大驕傲。◇ *Her long black hair is her* ***crowning glory*** (= most impressive feature). 她長長的黑髮是她的無上榮耀。➲ see also REFLECTED GLORY
■ *verb* (**glor·ies, glory·ing, glor·ied, glor·ied**)
PHR V **'glory in sth** to get great pleasure or enjoyment from sth 因某事而喜悅；為某事而欣喜 **SYN** **revel**：*She gloried in her new-found independence.* 她為自己剛剛獲得的獨立而欣喜。

'glory days *noun* [pl.] a time in the past which people look back on as being better than the present 往日的美好時光；昔日的輝煌

gloss /ɡlɒs; *NAmE* ɡlɑːs; ɡlɔːs/ *noun, verb*
■ *noun* **1** [U, sing.] a shine on a smooth surface（平滑表面上的）光澤，光亮：*paper with a high gloss on one side* 單面上光紙 ◇ *The gel gives your hair a gloss.* 髮膠使你的頭髮有光澤。◇ *You can have the photos with either a gloss or a matt finish.* 你可選擇用光面或布面相紙洗印這些照片。 **2** [U] (often in compounds 常構成複合詞) a substance designed to make sth shiny 用以產生光澤的物質：*lip gloss* 唇彩 **3** (also ,**gloss 'paint**) [U] paint which, when dry, has a hard shiny surface 光澤塗料；亮光漆：*two coats of gloss* 兩層亮光漆 **4** [U, sing.] an attractive appearance that is only on the surface and hides what is not so attractive 虛假的外表；虛飾：*Beneath the gloss of success was a tragic private life.* 在成功的外表下面卻隱藏着悲慘的私人生活。◇ *This scandal has taken the gloss off the occasion.* 這醜聞使這次盛會黯然失色。 **5** [C] **~ (on sth)** a way of explaining sth to make it seem more attractive or acceptable 精彩的解釋（或闡述）：*The director puts a Hollywood gloss on the civil war.* 導演對內戰作了一番好萊塢式的精彩闡述。 **6** [C] **~ (on sth)** a note or comment added to a piece of writing to explain a difficult word or phrase 註釋；評註
■ *verb* **~ sth (as sth)** to add a note or comment to a piece of writing to explain a difficult word or idea 在…上作註釋（或評註）
PHR V ,**gloss 'over sth** to avoid talking about sth unpleasant or embarrassing by not dealing with it in detail 掩飾；掩蓋；把…搪塞過去：*to gloss over a problem* 表面上應付問題 ◇ *He glossed over any splits in the party.* 他掩飾了黨內出現的任何分裂現象。

gloss·ary /ˈɡlɒsəri; *NAmE* ˈɡlɑːs-; ˈɡlɔːs-/ *noun* (*pl.* **-ies**) a list of technical or special words, especially those in a particular text, explaining their meanings 術語彙編；詞彙表

glossy /ˈɡlɒsi; *NAmE* ˈɡlɑːsi; ˈɡlɔːsi/ *adj., noun*
■ *adj.* (**gloss·ier, glossi·est**) **1** smooth and shiny 光滑的；光彩奪目的；有光澤的：*glossy hair* 光亮的頭髮 ◇ *a* ***glossy brochure/magazine*** (= printed on shiny paper) 用亮光紙印刷的小冊子／雜誌 **2** giving an appearance of being important and expensive 浮華的；虛有其表的；虛飾的：*the glossy world of fashion* 浮華的時裝界
■ *noun* (*pl.* **-ies**) (*BrE, informal*) an expensive magazine printed on glossy paper, with a lot of colour photographs, etc. 用亮光紙印刷的雜誌

glot·tal /ˈɡlɒtl; *NAmE* ˈɡlɑːtl/ *noun* (*phonetics* 語音) a speech sound produced by the glottis 聲門音；喉音 ▸ **glot·tal** *adj.*

,**glottal 'stop** *noun* (*phonetics* 語音) a speech sound made by closing and opening the glottis, which in English sometimes takes the place of a /t/, for example in *butter* 喉塞音；聲門閉塞音

glot·tis /ˈɡlɒtɪs; *NAmE* ˈɡlɑːt-/ *noun* (*anatomy* 解) the part of the throat that contains the VOCAL CORDS and the narrow opening between them 聲門

glove 🔑 /ɡlʌv/ *noun*
a covering for the hand, made of wool, leather, etc. with separate parts for each finger and the thumb（分手指的）手套：*a pair of gloves* 一副手套 ◇ ***rubber gloves*** 膠皮手套 ◇ *gardening gloves* 園藝用手套 ➲ VISUAL VOCAB pages V20, V44, V47, V65 ➲ compare MITTEN ➲ see also BOXING, OVEN GLOVE
IDM **the gloves are off** used to say that sb is ready for a fight or an argument 準備動手打架；做好戰鬥（或辯論）準備 ➲ more at FIT *v.*, HAND *n.*, IRON *adj.*, KID *n.*

'glove compartment (also **'glove box**) *noun* a small space or shelf facing the front seats of a car, used for keeping small things in（汽車前排座位前放小物件的）雜物箱 ➲ VISUAL VOCAB page V52

gloved /ɡlʌvd/ *adj.* [usually before noun] (of a hand 手) wearing a glove 戴着手套的

'glove puppet (*BrE*) (*NAmE* **'hand puppet**) *noun* a type of PUPPET that you put over your hand and move using your fingers 手偶（套在手上用手指操縱）➲ VISUAL VOCAB page V37

glow /ɡləʊ; *NAmE* ɡloʊ/ *verb, noun*
■ *verb* **1** [I] (especially of sth hot or warm 尤指熱或微溫的物體) to produce a dull, steady light 發出微弱而穩定的光；發出暗淡的光：*The embers still glowed in the hearth.* 餘燼仍在爐膛裏發出暗淡的光。◇ *The strap has a fluorescent coating that* ***glows in the dark***. 皮帶面上有一層熒光在黑暗中微微發光。◇ **+ adj.** *A cigarette end glowed red in the darkness.* 一個煙頭在黑暗中發着紅光。➲ SYNONYMS at SHINE **2** [I] (of a person's body or face 人體或臉) to look or feel warm or pink, especially after exercise or because of excitement, embarrassment, etc.（尤指運動後或因情緒激動、尷尬等而）發紅，發熱，顯得紅，感覺熱：*Her cheeks were glowing.* 她雙頰緋紅。◇ **~ with sth** *His face glowed with embarrassment.* 他窘得滿臉通紅。 **3** [I] **~ (with sth)** to look very pleased or satisfied 喜形於色；心滿意足：*She was positively glowing with pride.* 她一副躊躇滿志的樣子。◇ *He gave her a warm glowing smile.* 他給了她一個熱情洋溢的微笑。 **4** [I] to appear a strong, warm colour 色彩鮮豔；絢麗奪目：**~ (with sth)** *The countryside glowed with autumn colours.* 鄉村裏秋色絢爛。◇ **+ adj.** *The brick walls glowed red in the late afternoon sun.* 磚牆在夕陽的照耀下閃着紅色的光芒。
■ *noun* [sing.] **1** a dull steady light, especially from a fire that has stopped producing flames 微弱穩定的光；暗淡的光：*The city was just a red glow on the horizon.* 城市看上去只是地平線上的一片紅光。◇ *There was no light except for the occasional glow of a cigarette.* 除偶爾有香煙的微弱紅光外沒有一點亮光。 **2** the pink colour in your face when you have been doing exercise or feel happy and excited（運動、高興或激動時）滿面紅光，容光煥發，滿臉通紅：*The fresh air had brought a healthy glow to her cheeks.* 新鮮空氣使她兩頰紅潤、精神煥發。 **3** a gold or red colour 金色；紅色：*the glow of autumn leaves* 秋葉紅似火 **4** a feeling of pleasure and satisfaction 喜悅；滿足的心情：*When she looked at her children, she felt a glow of pride.* 看見自己的孩子，她就感到由衷的自豪。

glow·er /ˈɡlaʊə(r)/ *verb* [I] **~ (at sb/sth)** to look in an angry, aggressive way 怒視；虎視眈眈；咄咄逼人地盯着 **SYN** **glare** ▸ **glow·er** *noun*

glow·ing /ˈɡləʊɪŋ; *NAmE* ˈɡloʊɪŋ/ *adj.* giving enthusiastic praise 熱烈讚揚的；熱情洋溢的：*a* ***glowing account/report/review*** 熱情洋溢的敘述／報道／評論 ◇ *He spoke of her performance in the film* ***in glowing terms*** (= praising her highly). 他熱烈讚揚了她在影片中的表演。▸ **glow·ing·ly** *adv.*

glow·stick /ˈɡləʊstɪk; *NAmE* ˈɡloʊ-/ (also **'light stick**) *noun* a plastic tube filled with chemicals that shines like a lamp when you bend it 熒光棒

'glow-worm *noun* a type of insect. The female has no wings and produces a green light at the end of the tail. 發光蟲

glu·cose /ˈɡluːkəʊs; -kəʊz; *NAmE* -koʊs; -koʊz/ *noun* [U] a simple type of sugar that is an important energy source in living things and which is a part of many CARBOHYDRATES 葡萄糖；右旋糖

glue 🔑 /ɡluː/ *noun, verb*
■ *noun* 🔑 [U, C] a sticky substance that is used for joining things together 膠；膠水：*a tube of glue* 一管膠水 ◇ *He sticks to her like glue* (= never leaves her). 他形影不離地跟着她。➲ VISUAL VOCAB page V69
■ *verb* 🔑 to join two things together using glue（用膠水）粘合，粘牢，粘貼 **SYN** **stick**：**~ A (to/onto B)** *She*

glued the label onto the box. 她把標籤貼在箱子上。◇ **~ A and B** (**together**) *Glue the two pieces of cardboard together.* 把這兩張硬紙板粘在一起。◇ *Make sure the edges are glued down.* 一定要把邊緣粘牢。

IDM **be ˈglued to sth** (*informal*) to give all your attention to sth; to stay very close to sth 全神貫注看着某物；離某物很近：*He spends every evening glued to the TV.* 他每天晚上都泡電視。◇ *Her eyes were glued to the screen* (= she did not stop watching it). 她目不轉睛地盯着屏幕。 **ˌglued to the ˈspot** not able to move, for example because you are frightened or surprised 動彈不得；嚇呆了；驚呆了

ˌglue ˈear *noun* [U] (*BrE*) a medical condition in which the tubes going from the nose to the ear are blocked with MUCUS 膠着耳（咽鼓管由黏液阻塞所致）

ˈglue-sniffing *noun* [U] the habit of breathing in the gases from some kinds of glue in order to produce a state of excitement; a type of SOLVENT ABUSE 吸膠毒，吸膠（為產生興奮而吸入某些類膠中氣體的習慣）

gluey /ˈgluːi/ *adj.* sticky like glue; covered with glue 膠黏的；塗滿膠的

glug /glʌg/ *verb, noun* (*informal*)
- *verb* (**-gg-**) **1** [I] **+ adv./prep.** (of liquid 液體) to pour out quickly and noisily, especially from a bottle （尤指從瓶中）汩汩地倒出來 **2** [T] **~ sth** (**down**) to drink sth quickly 大口喝：*She glugged down a glass of water* 她大口喝下一杯水。
- *noun* a small amount of a drink or liquid poured out 倒出的少量飲料（或液體）

glum /glʌm/ *adj.* sad, quiet and unhappy 憂鬱的；死氣沉沉的；悶悶不樂的 **SYN** **gloomy**：*The players sat there with glum looks on their faces.* 隊員們愁眉苦臉地坐在那兒。 ▸ **glum·ly** *adv.*：*The three of us sat glumly looking out to sea.* 我們三人面向大海悶悶不樂地坐着。

glut /glʌt/ *noun, verb*
- *noun* [usually sing.] **~** (**of sth**) a situation in which there is more of sth than is needed or can be used 供應過剩；供過於求 **SYN** **surfeit**：*a glut of cheap DVDs on the market* 市場上供過於求的廉價 DVD **OPP** **shortage**
- *verb* (**-tt-**) [usually passive] **~ sth** (**with sth**) to supply or provide sth with too much of sth 超量供應；充斥：*The market has been glutted with foreign cars.* 外國汽車充斥市場。

glu·ten /ˈgluːtn/ *noun* [U] a sticky substance that is a mixture of two PROTEINS and is left when STARCH is removed from flour, especially WHEAT flour 穀蛋白；麵筋：*We sell a range of* ***gluten-free*** *products* (= not containing gluten). 我們出售各種無穀蛋白產品。

glutes /gluːts/ *noun* [pl.] (*informal*) the muscles in the BUTTOCKS that move the top of the leg 臀大肌

glu·teus /ˈgluːtiəs; *NAmE* also gluːˈtiəs/ (also **ˈgluteus muscle**) *noun* (*anatomy* 解) any of the three muscles in each BUTTOCK 臀大肌

glu·tin·ous /ˈgluːtənəs/ *adj.* sticky 黏的；膠質的：*glutinous rice* 糯米

glut·ton /ˈglʌtn/ *noun* **1** (*disapproving*) a person who eats too much 貪吃者；吃得過多的人；饕餮 **2** **~ for punishment/work** a person who enjoys doing difficult or unpleasant tasks 吃苦耐勞的人；任勞任怨的人 ▸ **glut·ton·ous** /ˈglʌtənəs/ *adj.* **SYN** **greedy**

glut·tony /ˈglʌtəni/ *noun* [U] the habit of eating and drinking too much 暴食；暴飲；貪食 **SYN** **greed**

gly·caem·ic index (*BrE*) (*NAmE* **gly·cem·ic index**) /glaɪˌsiːmɪk ˈɪndeks/ *noun* = GI *abbr.*

gly·cer·ine /ˈglɪsəriːn; -rɪn; *NAmE* -rən/ (*especially BrE*) (*US* usually **gly·cerin** /-rɪn; *NAmE* -rən/) *noun* [U] a thick sweet clear liquid made from fats and oils and used in medicines, beauty products and EXPLOSIVES 甘油，丙三醇（用於藥物、美容產品和炸藥）

glyph /glɪf/ *noun* a symbol CARVED out of stone, especially one from an ancient writing system 石雕符號；象形文字

GM /ˌdʒiː ˈem/ *abbr.* **1** (*BrE*) GENETICALLY MODIFIED：*GM foods or 'Frankenstein foods' as they are popularly called* 轉基因食品或人們常說的"弗蘭肯斯坦食品" **2** grant-maintained (used in Britain to describe schools that receive money from central, not local, government) （英國學校）由中央政府出資的，中央政府撥款的

gm (*BrE*) (also **gm.** *US, BrE*) *abbr.* (*pl.* **gm** or **gms**) gram(s) 克

GMAT /ˈdʒiːmæt/ *abbr.* Graduate Management Admissions Test (a test taken by GRADUATE students in the US who want to study for a degree in Business) （美國）企業管理研究生入學考試

GMO /ˌdʒiː em ˈəʊ; *NAmE* ˈoʊ/ *noun* (*pl.* **GMOs**) the abbreviation for 'genetically modified organism' (a plant, etc. that has had its genetic structure changed artificially, so that it will produce more fruit or not be affected by disease) 遺傳修飾生物體，基因改造生物（全寫為 genetically modified organism，人為改變基因結構以求產量更高或抗病的生物）

GMT /ˌdʒiː em ˈtiː/ *noun* [U] the abbreviation for 'Greenwich Mean Time' (the time at Greenwich in England on the line of 0° LONGITUDE, used in the past for calculating time everywhere in the world) 格林尼治平時，世界時（全寫為 Greenwich Mean Time）

gnarled /nɑːld; *NAmE* nɑːrld/ *adj.* **1** (of trees 樹木) twisted and rough; covered with hard lumps 扭曲的；多節瘤的；疙疙瘩瘩的：*a gnarled oak/branch/trunk* 多節瘤的橡樹／樹枝／樹幹 **2** (of a person or part of the body 人或身體部位) bent and twisted because of age or illness （因年老或疾病）彎曲的，扭曲的：*gnarled hands* 扭曲的手

gnarly /ˈnɑːli; *NAmE* ˈnɑːrli/ *adj.* (*NAmE, slang*) **1** very good; excellent 呱呱叫的；極好的：*Wow, man! That's totally gnarly!* 哇，老兄，那真是太好了！ **2** not very good 不太好

gnash /næʃ/ *verb*

IDM **gnash your ˈteeth** to feel very angry and upset about sth, especially because you cannot get what you want （尤因不獲所求而氣得）咬牙切齒：*He'll be gnashing his teeth when he hears that we lost the contract.* 他要是聽說我們丟了這份合同，準會氣得咬牙切齒。

gnash·ers /ˈnæʃəz; *NAmE* -ʃərz/ *noun* [pl.] (*BrE, informal*) teeth 牙齒

gnat /næt/ *noun* a small fly with two wings, that bites 叮人小蟲；蚋；蠓

gnaw /nɔː/ *verb* [T, I] to keep biting sth or chewing it hard, so that it gradually disappears 咬；啃；齧：**~ sth** *The dog was gnawing a bone.* 那狗在啃骨頭。◇ **~ through sth** *Rats had gnawed through the cable* 老鼠把電纜咬斷了。◇ **~ at/on sth** *She gnawed at her fingernails.* 她咬手指甲。◇ **~ away at/on sth** (*figurative*) *Self-doubt began to gnaw away at her confidence.* 對自己的懷疑漸漸吞噬了她的自信心。

PHR V **ˈgnaw at sb** to make sb feel anxious, frightened or uncomfortable over a long period of time （長時間）折磨某人：*The problem had been gnawing at him for months.* 幾個月來這個問題一直折磨着他。

gnaw·ing /ˈnɔːɪŋ/ *adj.* [only before noun] making you feel worried over a period of time （長時間）折磨人的，令人痛苦的，使人苦惱的：*gnawing doubts* 令人痛苦的疑慮

gneiss /naɪs/ *noun* [U] (*geology* 地) a type of METAMORPHIC rock formed at high pressure and temperature deep in the ground 片麻岩（地層深處在高壓高溫下形成的變質岩）

gnoc·chi /ˈnjɒki; *NAmE* ˈnjɑːki/ *noun* [pl.] an Italian dish consisting of small balls of potato mixed with flour and boiled, usually eaten with a sauce 意大利糰子（用麵粉和馬鈴薯做成）

gnome /nəʊm; *NAmE* noʊm/ *noun* **1** (in stories) a creature like a small man with a pointed hat, who lives under the ground and guards gold and TREASURE （神話故事中的）地下寶藏守護神 **2** a plastic or stone figure of a gnome, used to decorate a garden （裝飾花園的）守護精靈像

gno·mic /ˈnəʊmɪk; *NAmE* ˈnoʊ-/ *adj.* (*formal*) (of a person or a remark 人或言語) clever and wise but sometimes difficult to understand 喜用格言的；精闢的；深奧的

GNP /ˌdʒiː en ˈpiː/ *noun* the abbreviation for 'gross national product' (the total value of all the goods and services produced by a country in one year, including the total income from foreign countries) 國民生產總值，國民生產毛額（全寫為 gross national product）➲ compare GDP

gnu /nuː; njuː/ *noun* (*pl.* **gnu** or **gnus**) = WILDEBEEST

GNVQ /ˌdʒiː en viː ˈkjuː/ *noun* the abbreviation for 'General National Vocational Qualification' (a qualification which until 2007 was taken in British schools by students aged 15–18 to prepare them for university or work) 全國普通職業證書（全寫為 General National Vocational Qualification，2007 年前英國學校 15 至 18 歲學生為進入大學或就業的資格證書）➲ compare A LEVEL

G

go 🗝 /ɡəʊ; *NAmE* ɡoʊ/ *verb, noun*

■ *verb* (**goes** /ɡəʊz; *NAmE* ɡoʊz/, **went** /went/, **gone** /ɡɒn; *NAmE* ɡɔːn/) **HELP** **Been** is used as the past participle of **go** when sb has gone somewhere and come back. 表示去過某地並已回來時，用 been 作 go 的過去分詞。

▸ **MOVE/TRAVEL** 移動；行走 **1** 🗝 [I] to move or travel from one place to another 去；走：**+ adv./prep.** *She went into her room and shut the door behind her.* 她走進自己的房間，把門關上。◇ *He goes to work by bus.* 他乘公共汽車去上班。◇ *I have to go to Rome on business.* 我得去羅馬出差。◇ *She has gone to China* (= is now in China or is on her way there). 她到中國去了。◇ *She has been to China* (= she went to China and has now returned). 她去過中國。◇ *I think you should go to the doctor's.* 我認為你該去看看醫生。◇ *Are you going home for Christmas?* 你打算回家過聖誕節嗎？◇ **~ to do sth** *She has gone to see her sister this weekend.* 她本週末看她姐姐去了。**HELP** In spoken English **go** can be used with **and** plus another verb to show purpose or to tell sb what to do. 英語口語中，go 可與 and 連用加上另一動詞，表示目的或讓某人做某事：*I'll go and answer the door.* ◇ ***Go and get*** *me a drink!* The **and** is sometimes left out, especially in *NAmE*. * and 有時可省略，尤其是美式英語：***Go ask*** *your mom!* **2** 🗝 [I] **~ (to sth) (with sb)** to move or travel, especially with sb else, to a particular place or in order to be present at an event（尤指與某人）去（某處或出席某項活動）：*Are you going to Dave's party?* 你要去參加戴夫的聚會嗎？◇ *Who else is going?* 還有誰要去？◇ *His dog goes everywhere with him.* 他的狗總是跟着他。**3** 🗝 [I] to move or travel in a particular way or over a particular distance 移動，行走（指方式或距離）：**+ adv./prep.** *He's going too fast.* 他走得太快。◇ **+ noun** *We had gone about fifty miles when the car broke down.* 我們行駛了約莫五十英里，汽車突然拋錨了。**4** 🗝 [I] **~ flying, skidding, etc. (+ adv./prep.)** to move in a particular way or while doing sth else（以某種方式）移動；在移動中做：*The car went skidding off the road into a ditch.* 汽車打滑衝出公路跌進溝裏。◇ *She went sobbing up the stairs.* 她嗚咽着上樓去了。◇ *She crashed into a waiter and his tray of drinks went flying.* 她一下子撞到侍者身上，弄得他托盤裏的飲料四處飛濺。

▸ **LEAVE** 離去 **5** 🗝 [I] to leave one place in order to reach another 離開；離去；出發 **SYN** **depart**：*I must be going now.* 我現在得走了。◇ *They came at six and went at nine.* 他們是六點鐘來的，九點鐘走的。◇ *Has she gone yet?* 她走了嗎？◇ *He's been gone an hour* (= he left an hour ago). 他離開一小時了。◇ *When does the train go?* 火車什麼時候開？**6** 🗝 [I] **~ on sth** to leave a place and do sth different 去做（某事）：*to **go on a journey/a tour/a trip/a cruise*** 去旅行／觀光遊覽／短途旅行／乘船旅遊 ◇ *Richard has gone on leave for two weeks.* 理查德休假兩週了。

▸ **VISIT/ATTEND** 訪問；出席 **7** 🗝 [I] **~ to sth** to visit or attend a place for a particular purpose（為某目的）去（某處）：(*BrE*) *I have to go to hospital for an operation.* 我得去醫院動手術。◇ (*NAmE*) *I have to go to the hospital.* 我得到醫院去。◇ *to go to prison* (= to be sent there as punishment for a crime) 進監獄 ◇ *Do you go to church* (= regularly attend church services)? 你去教堂嗎？

▸ **SWIMMING/FISHING/JOGGING, ETC.** 游泳、釣魚、慢跑等 **8** 🗝 [I] **~ (for) sth** to leave a place or travel to a place in order to take part in an activity or a sport 去參加，去從事（某項活動或運動）：*to **go for a walk/drive/swim/run*** 去散步／兜風／游泳／跑步 ◇ *Shall we go for a drink* (= at a pub or bar) *after work?* 我們下班後去（酒吧）喝一杯好嗎？◇ *I have to go shopping this afternoon.* 我今天下午得去商店買東西。◇ *We're going sailing on Saturday.* 我們打算星期六乘帆船出遊。

▸ **BE SENT** 被發送 **9** 🗝 [I] (**+ adv./prep.**) to be sent or passed somewhere 被發送；被傳遞：*I want this memo to go to all managers.* 我想讓這份備忘錄送交到所有經理手中。

▸ **LEAD** 通向 **10** 🗝 [I] **~ (from ...) (to ...)** to lead or extend from one place to another（從…）通向，延伸到：*I want a rope that will go from the top window to the ground.* 我想要一根可從頂樓窗戶垂到地面的繩子。◇ *Where does this road go?* 這條路通到哪裏？

▸ **PLACE/SPACE** 地方；空處 **11** 🗝 [I] **+ adv./prep.** to have as a usual or correct position; to be placed 被放置，被置於，被安放（在通常或合適的位置）：*This dictionary goes on the top shelf.* 這部詞典放在書架最上層。◇ *Where do you want the piano to go* (= be put)? 你想把鋼琴放在什麼地方？**12** 🗝 [I] **will/would not ~ (in/into sth)** used to say that sth does/did not fit into a particular place or space（不）適合；放（不）進：*My clothes won't all go in that one suitcase.* 一個手提箱裝不下我所有的衣服。◇ *He tried to push his hand through the gap but it wouldn't go.* 他試着把手伸進豁口，可就是伸不進去。

▸ **NUMBERS** 數字 **13** [I] if a number will **go into** another number, it is contained in that number an exact number of times 除盡；除：(**+ adj.**) *3 into 12 goes 4 times.* * 3 除 12 得 4。◇ *7 into 15 won't go.* * 7 除 15 除不盡。◇ (*NAmE*) *7 into 15 doesn't go.* * 7 除 15 除不盡。◇ **~ into sth** *7 won't go into 15.* * 7 除不盡 15。

▸ **PROGRESS** 進展 **14** 🗝 [I] **+ adv./prep.** used to talk about how well or badly sth makes progress or succeeds（事情）進展，進行：*'How did your interview go?' 'It went very well, thank you.'* "你面試的情況如何？" "非常順利，謝謝。" ◇ *Did everything go smoothly?* 一切進行得都順利嗎？◇ *How's it going* (= is your life enjoyable, successful, etc. at the moment)? 近況可好？◇ *The way things are going the company will be bankrupt by the end of the year.* 從事態發展的情況看，到年底公司就得破產。

▸ **STATE/CONDITION** 狀態；狀況 **15** 🗝 [I] used in many expressions to show that sb/sth has reached a particular state/is no longer in a particular state 進入…狀態；處於…狀況；脫離…狀態：**~ to/into sth** *She went to sleep.* 她睡着了。◇ **~ out of sth** *That colour has gone out of fashion.* 那種顏色已不時興了。**16** 🗝 *linking verb* **+ adj.** to become different in a particular way, especially a bad way 變成，變為，變得（尤指朝壞的方面）：*to **go bald/blind/mad/bankrupt, etc.*** 謝頂、失明、發瘋、破產等 ◇ *Her hair is **going grey**.* 她的頭髮日漸花白。◇ *This milk has **gone sour**.* 這牛奶餿了。◇ *The children **went wild** with excitement.* 孩子們欣喜若狂。➲ SYNONYMS at BECOME **17** [I] **+ adj.** to live or move around in a particular state（在某種狀態下）生活，過活，移動：*to **go naked/barefoot*** 光着身子；赤着腳 ◇ *She cannot bear the thought of children going hungry.* 想到孩子們捱餓她就受不了。**18** [I] **~ unnoticed, unreported, etc.** to not be noticed, reported, etc. 未被（注意到、報告等）：*Police are worried that many crimes go unreported.* 警方感到不安的是許多罪行發生後無人報案。

▸ **SONG/STORY** 歌曲；故事 **19** [I, T] used to talk about what tune or words a song or poem has or what happens in a story（詩或歌中詞、調）唱，說；（故事）發生情況如何：**+ adv./prep.** *How does that song go?* 那首歌怎麼唱？◇ *I forget how the next line goes.* 我忘記下一行怎麼說了。◇ **~ that ...** *The story goes that she's been married five times.* 據傳她結過五次婚。

▸ **SOUND/MOVEMENT** 聲音；動作 **20** 🗝 [I] to make a particular sound or movement 發出（某種聲音）；做（某種動作）：**+ noun** *The gun went 'bang'.* 槍"砰"的一聲響了。◇ **+ adv./prep.** *She went like this with her* hand. 她用手這樣比畫着。 **21** 🔑 [I] to be sounded as a signal or warning 發出信號（或警告）: *The whistle went for the end of the game.* 比賽結束的哨聲響了。

▸ **SAY** 説 **22** [T] **+ speech** (*informal*) (used when telling a story 講故事時説) to say 説: *I asked 'How much?' and he goes, 'Fifty' and I go, 'Fifty? You must be joking!'* 我問："多少錢？"他回答説："五十。"我又説："五十？你是在開玩笑吧！"

▸ **START** 開始 **23** [I] to start an activity 開始（活動）: *I'll say 'One, two, three, go!' as a signal for you to start.* 我喊"一、二、三，開始！"作為你開始的信號。◇ *As soon as he gets here we're ready to go.* 他一到我們就可以開始。

▸ **MACHINE** 機器 **24** 🔑 [I] if a machine **goes**, it works 運行；運轉；工作: *This clock doesn't go.* 這鐘不走了。

▸ **DISAPPEAR** 消失 **25** 🔑 [I] to stop existing; to be lost or stolen 不復存在；不見了；丟失；失竊 SYN **disappear**: *Has your headache gone yet?* 你還頭痛嗎？◇ *I left my bike outside the library and when I came out again it had gone.* 我把自行車放在圖書館外面，出來時它就不翼而飛了。

▸ **BE THROWN OUT** 被扔掉 **26** [I] **sb/sth must/has to/can ~** used to talk about wanting to get rid of sb/sth（必須或可以）辭掉（或扔掉、廢棄）: *The old sofa will have to go.* 那舊沙發該扔掉了。◇ *He's useless—he'll have to go.* 他毫無用處，得辭掉他。

▸ **NOT WORK** 不起作用 **27** [I] to get worse; to become damaged or stop working correctly 變壞；損壞；不起作用: *Her sight is beginning to go.* 她的視力開始下降。◇ *His mind is going* (= he is losing his mental powers). 他心智日衰。◇ *I was driving home when my brakes went.* 我正開車回家，突然剎車失靈了。

▸ **DIE** 死 **28** [I] to die. People say 'go' to avoid saying 'die'. 走（委婉説法，與 die 同義）: *You can't take your money with you when you go.* 你不可能把錢帶進棺材。

▸ **MONEY** 錢 **29** [I] when money **goes**, it is spent or used for sth 用於；花掉: *I don't know where the money goes!* 我不知道錢都花到什麼地方去了！◇ **~ on sth** *Most of my salary goes on the rent.* 我大部份工資都花在房租上了。◇ **~ to do sth** *The money will go to finance a new community centre.* 這筆錢將用於資助新的社區活動中心。 **30** [I] **~ (to sb) (for sth)** to be sold 被賣掉；被出售: *We won't let the house go for less than $200 000.* 這房子低於 20 萬元我們是不會賣的。◇ *There was usually some bread **going cheap** (= being sold cheaply) at the end of the day.* 在收市前常常有些麪包降價出售。 **31** [I] **+ adv./prep.** to be willing to pay a particular amount of money for sth 願出價購買: *He's offered £3 000 for the car and I don't think he'll go any higher.* 他出價 3 000 英鎊買這輛汽車，我看他不會願意再多付了。◇ *I'll go to $1 000 but that's my limit.* 我願意出 1 000 元，這可是最大限度了。

▸ **HELP** 有助於 **32** [I] **~ to do sth** to help; to play a part in doing sth 有助於；促成；起作用: *This all goes to prove my theory.* 這一切都有助於證明我的説法是對的。◇ *It (= what has just happened) **just goes to show** you can't always tell how people are going to react.* 這正好説明你不可能總是知道人們會如何反應。

▸ **BE AVAILABLE** 可得到 **33** **be going** [I] (*informal*) to be available 可得到；可買到；現成可用: *There just aren't any jobs going in this area.* 此地幾乎沒有工作可找。

▸ **TIME** 時間 **34** 🔑 [I] **+ adv./prep.** used to talk about how quickly or slowly time seems to pass 流逝；消逝；過去: *Hasn't the time gone quickly?* 時光過得真快，是不是？◇ *Half an hour went past while we were sitting there.* 我們坐在那裏，半個小時就這樣過去了。

▸ **USE TOILET** 用廁所 **35** [I] (*informal*) to use a toilet 用廁所；上廁所: *Do you need to go, Billy?* 你要上廁所嗎，比利？

IDM Most idioms containing **go** are at the entries for the nouns and adjectives in the idioms, for example **go it alone** is at **alone**. 大多數含 go 的習語，都可在該等習語中的名詞及形容詞相關詞條找到，如 go it alone 在詞條 alone 下。 **anything goes** (*informal*) anything that sb says or does is accepted or allowed, however shocking or unusual it may be 無奇不有；什麼事都不新鮮: *Almost anything goes these days.* 這個年月幾乎是無奇不有。 **as people, things, etc. go** in comparison with the average person, thing, etc. 和一般人（或事物等）相比: *As teachers go, he's not bad.* 和一般教師相比，他是不錯的。 **be going on (for) sth** (*BrE*) to be nearly a particular age, time or number 接近（或將近、快到）某一年齡（或時間、數字）: *It was going on (for) midnight.* 快半夜了。 **be going to do sth 1** 🔑 used to show what sb intends to do in the future 打算做某事: *We're going to buy a house when we've saved enough money.* 我們打算攢夠錢後買所房子。 **2** 🔑 used to show that sth is likely to happen very soon or in the future 快要發生某事；某事將要發生: *I think I'm going to faint.* 我看我快昏倒了。◇ *If the drought continues there's going to be a famine.* 如果旱災繼續下去很可能要發生饑荒。 **don't go doing sth** (*informal*) used to tell or warn sb not to do sth（告訴或警告某人）別做某事: *Don't go getting yourself into trouble.* 別自惹麻煩。 **enough/something to be going 'on with** (*BrE*) something that is enough for a short time 暫且夠用；足以應付一時: *£50 should be enough to be going on with.* * 50 英鎊該夠應付一時半會兒的了。 **go all 'out for sth | go all out to 'do sth** to make a very great effort to get sth or do sth 竭力獲取某物；全力以赴做某事；鼓足幹勁做某事 **go and do sth** used to show that you are angry or annoyed that sb has done sth stupid（對某人做了蠢事感到憤怒或煩惱）竟然幹出某事，居然幹出某事: *Trust him to go and mess things up!* 就知道他會把事情弄得一團糟！◇ *Why did you have to go and upset your mother like that?* 你幹嗎非得讓你母親那樣傷心呢？◇ ***You've really gone and done it** now!* (= done sth very stupid) 你竟然幹出這樣的事來！ **go 'off on one** (*BrE, informal*) to suddenly become very angry 突然大怒；暴跳如雷 **go 'on (with you)** (*old-fashioned*) used to express the fact that you do not believe sth, or that you disapprove of sth（表示不相信或不贊同）去你的，我才不信呢 **(have) a lot, nothing, etc. 'going for you** (to have) many/not many advantages 有（或沒有）很多有利條件: *You're young, intelligent, attractive—you have a lot going for you!* 你年輕、聰明、漂亮，有利條件可多啦！ **,no 'go** (*informal*) not possible or allowed 不可能；不行；不允許: *If the bank won't lend us the money it's no go, I'm afraid.* 如果銀行不願貸款給我們，這恐怕就行不通了。 ➲ see also NO-GO AREA **not (even) 'go there** (*informal*) used to say that you do not want to talk about sth in any more detail because you do not even want to think about it 不想細談；甚至不願想起: *Don't ask me to choose. I don't want to go there.* 別讓我挑選。我連想都不願想。◇ *'There was a problem with his parents, wasn't there?' 'Don't even go there!'* "他的父母有問題，是不是？""別往下説了！" **to 'go 1** remaining; still left 剩下的；還有的: *I only have one exam to go.* 我只剩一門考試了。 **2** (*NAmE, informal*) if you buy cooked food **to go** in a restaurant or shop/store, you buy it to take away and eat somewhere else（食品）外賣的；帶出餐館（或商店）吃的: *Two pizzas to go.* 來兩份比薩餅，帶走。 **what ,goes around 'comes around** (*saying*) **1** the way sb behaves towards other people will affect the way those people behave towards them in the future 你怎麼待人，人就怎麼待你 **2** something that is not fashionable now will become fashionable again in the future 現在過時的還會再時興起來；三十年河東，三十年河西 **,where does sb ,go from 'here?** used to ask what action sb should take, especially in order to improve the difficult situation that they are in（尤指為了改變困境而詢問）下一步該怎麼辦，往下怎麼做呢 **,who goes 'there?** used by a soldier who is guarding a place to order sb to say who they are（哨兵喝問對方身分用語）誰，什麼人: *Halt, who goes there?* 站住，什麼人？

PHR V **,go a'bout** (*BrE*) = GO AROUND (3) **'go about sth** to continue to do sth; to keep busy with sth 繼續做某事；忙於某事: *Despite the threat of war, people went about their business as usual.* 雖然戰爭在即，人們照常忙着自己的事。 **,go a'bout sth** to start working on sth 着手做某事；開始做某事 SYN **tackle**: *You're not going about the job in the right way.* 你做這事的方法不對。◇ **~ doing sth** *How should I go about finding a job?* 我該怎樣着手找工作呢？

,go 'after sb to chase or follow sb 追趕某人；跟在某人後面: *He went after the burglars.* 他追趕那些竊賊。◇ *She left the room in tears so I went after her.* 她流着淚離

開了房間，於是我跟着追了出去。**ˌgo ˈafter sb/sth** to try to get sb/sth 追求某人；謀求某事（或某物）：*We're both going after the same job.* 我們倆都在謀求同一份工作。

ˌgo aˈgainst sb to not be in sb's favour or not to their advantage 對某人不利；不利於某人：*The jury's verdict went against him.* 陪審團的裁定對他不利。**ˌgo aˈgainst sb/sth** to resist or oppose sb/sth 反抗（或反對）某人（或某事）；與…相背：*He would not go against his parents' wishes.* 他不會違背父母的意願。**ˌgo aˈgainst sth** to be opposed to sth; to not fit or agree with sth 違反；與…不符（或相反）：*Paying for hospital treatment goes against her principles.* 拿錢到醫院治病有違她的原則。◇ *His thinking goes against all logic.* 他的想法完全不合情理。

ˌgo aˈhead 1 ⊶ to travel in front of other people in your group and arrive before them 走在前面；先走：*I'll go ahead and tell them you're on the way.* 我要先走一步，告訴他們你在路上。**2** ⊶ to happen; to be done 發生；進行 SYN **proceed**：*The building of the new bridge will go ahead as planned.* 新橋的修建將按計劃進行。➲ related noun GO-AHEAD **ˌgo aˈhead (with sth)** ⊶ to begin to do sth, especially when sb has given permission or has expressed doubts or opposition（尤指經某人允許，或有人表示懷疑或反對後）開始做，着手幹：*'May I start now?' 'Yes, go ahead.'* "我現在可以開始了嗎？" "可以，開始吧。" ◇ *The government intends to go ahead with its tax cutting plans* 政府擬開始實施減稅計劃。

ˌgo aˈlong 1 to continue with an activity 繼續：*He made up the story* ***as he went along.*** 這個故事是他現編現講的。**2** to make progress; to develop 進展；發展：*Things are going along nicely.* 情況進展良好。**ˌgo aˈlong with sb/sth** to agree with sb/sth 和某人觀點一致；贊同某事：*I don't go along with her views on private medicine.* 在私人行醫的問題上，我不敢苟同她的觀點。➲ SYNONYMS at AGREE

ˌgo aˈround/ˈround 1 ⊶ to spin or turn 旋轉；轉動：*to go round in a circle* 轉圈 **2** ⊶ to be enough for everyone to have one or some 足夠分給每個人；夠每人一份：*There aren't enough chairs to go around.* 椅子不夠坐。**3** ⊶ (BrE also **ˌgo aˈbout**) to often be in a particular state or behave in a particular way 習慣於（某種狀態或行動方式）：*She often goes around barefoot.* 她常常光着腳到處跑。◇ **~ doing sth** *It's unprofessional to go round criticizing your colleagues.* 總是指責同事，這不符合職業道德。**4** to spread from person to person 流傳；傳播：*There's a rumour going around that they're having an affair.* 謠傳他們之間關係曖昧。**ˌgo aˈround/ˈround (to …)** ⊶ to visit sb or a place that is near 拜訪（某人）；訪問，參觀（附近某處）：*I went round to the post office.* 我到郵局去了一趟。◇ *I'm going around to my sister's* (= her house) *later.* 我打算稍後到姐姐家去看看。

ˈgo at sb to attack sb 攻擊某人：*They went at each other furiously.* 他們相互猛烈攻擊。**ˈgo at sth** to make great efforts to do sth; to work hard at sth 拚命幹；賣力幹：*They went at the job as if their lives depended on it.* 他們幹起活來好像性命攸關似的。

ˌgo aˈway 1 ⊶ to leave a person or place 走開；離開：*Just go away!* 走開！◇ *Go away and think about it, then let me know.* 到一邊去想一想，然後再告訴我。**2** ⊶ to leave home for a period of time, especially for a holiday/vacation 離家外出（尤指度假）：*They've gone away for a few days.* 他們已外出幾天了。◇ *I'm going away on business.* 我要出趟差。**3** ⊶ to disappear 消失：*The smell still hasn't gone away.* 氣味還沒散盡。

ˌgo ˈback if two people **go back** a period of time (usually a long time), they have known each other for that time 相識，已認識（一段時間）：*Dave and I go back twenty years.* 我和戴夫相識有二十年了。**ˌgo ˈback (to …)** to return to a place 回到，返回（某地）：*She doesn't want to go back to her husband* (= to live with him again). 她不想回到丈夫的身邊了。◇ *This toaster will have to go back* (= be taken back to the shop/store where it was bought)—*it's faulty.* 這烤麪包機得退回去，它有毛病。◇ *Of course we want to go back some day—it's our country, our real home.* 我們當然希望有一天能回去，那是我們的祖國，我們真正的家。➲ SYNONYMS at RETURN **ˌgo ˈback (to sth) 1** ⊶ to consider sth that happened or was said at an earlier time 回憶起；回到（原來的話題）：*Can I go back to what you said at the beginning of the meeting?* 我想回到你在會議開始時所提的話題，行嗎？◇ *Once you have made this decision, there will be* ***no going back*** (= you will not be able to change your mind). 你一旦作出這個決定就不能改變。**2** ⊶ to have existed since a particular time or for a particular period 追溯到；回溯到：*Their family goes back to the time of the Pilgrim Fathers.* 他們家族的淵源可追溯到清教徒前輩移民時代。**ˌgo ˈback on sth** to fail to keep a promise; to change your mind about sth 違約；食言；改變主意：*He never* ***goes back on his word*** (= never fails to do what he has said he will do). 他從不食言。**ˌgo ˈback to sth** ⊶ to start doing sth again that you had stopped doing 重新開始；重操舊業：*The kids go back to school next week.* 孩子們下週開學。◇ **~ doing sth** *She's decided to go back to teaching.* 她已決定重新執教。

ˌgo beˈfore to exist or happen in an earlier time 居先；先前存在；以往發生：*The present crisis is worse than any that have gone before.* 目前的危機比以往任何一次危機都嚴重。**ˈgo before sb/sth** to be presented to sb/sth for discussion, decision or judgement 提交給…討論（或決定、裁決）：*My application goes before the planning committee next week.* 我的申請下週提交計劃委員會審批。

ˌgo beˈyond sth to be more than sth 超過（或超出）某事 SYN **exceed**：*This year's sales figures go beyond all our expectations* (= are much better than we thought they would be). 今年的銷售額大大超過我們的預計。

ˌgo ˈby ⊶ (of time 時間) to pass 流逝；過去：*Things will get easier* ***as time goes by.*** 隨着時間的推移情況會有所改善。◇ *The weeks went slowly by.* 時間一週週慢慢地過去了。**ˈgo by sth** to be guided by sth; to form an opinion from sth 遵循（或依照）某事；以某事來判斷：*That's a good rule to go by.* 那是要遵守的好規則。◇ ***If past experience is anything to go by,*** *they'll be late.* 憑以往的經驗看，他們會遲到的。

ˌgo ˈdown 1 to fall to the ground 倒下；落下；倒在地上：*She tripped and went down with a bump.* 她絆了一下，重重地倒在地上。**2** if a ship, etc. **goes down**, it disappears below the water（船等）下沉，沉沒 SYN **sink 3** ⊶ when the sun or moon **goes down**, it disappears below the HORIZON（日、月）落到地平線下，落下 SYN **set 4** if food or drink will/will not **go down**, it is easy/difficult to swallow（食物、飲料）被吞下，被咽下，被喝下：*A glass of wine would go down very nicely* (= I would very much like one). 喝一杯葡萄酒就太痛快了。**5** ⊶ if the price of sth, the temperature, etc. **goes down**, it becomes lower（物價等）下跌；（溫度等）下降 SYN **fall**：*The price of oil is going down.* 油價正在下跌。◇ *Oil is going down in price.* 石油正在跌價。OPP **go up 6** (*informal*) to get worse in quality（質量）下降：*The neighbourhood has gone down a lot recently.* 近來這一帶地方已遠不如從前了。**7** (*computing* 計) to stop working temporarily 暫停作業；暫停運行：*The system is going down in ten minutes.* 這個系統十分鐘後要暫停運行。**8** (*NAmE, informal*) to happen 發生：*You really don't know what's going down?* 你真的不知道發生了什麼事？**ˌgo ˈdown (from …)** (*BrE, formal*) to leave a university, especially Oxford or Cambridge, at the end of a term or after finishing your studies（大學學期結束或畢業時）離校（尤指牛津或劍橋）OPP **go up (to …)** **ˌgo ˈdown (in sth)** to be written in sth; to be recorded or remembered in sth 被寫下；被記下；載入：*It all goes down* (= she writes it all) *in her notebook.* 那些東西全記在她的筆記本上。◇ *He will* ***go down in history*** *as a great statesman.* 他將以偉大的政治家名垂青史。**ˌgo ˈdown (on sb)** (*slang*) to perform ORAL sex on sb (= to use the mouth to give sb sexual pleasure)（為某人）進行口交 **ˌgo ˈdown (to sb)** to be defeated by sb, especially in a game or competition（尤指遊戲或比賽中）被擊敗：*Italy went down to Brazil by three goals to one.* 意大利隊以一比三輸給了巴西隊。**ˌgo ˈdown (to …) (from …)** to go from one place to another, especially further south or from a city or large town to a smaller place（從一處）到（另一處）（尤指南下或從城

市、大城鎮到小地方）：*They've gone down to Brighton for a couple of days.* 他們已南下到布賴頓去待幾天。**OPP** go up **,go 'down (with sb)** to be received in a particular way by sb 受到（某人的…）對待；被接受：*The suggestion didn't go down very well with her boss.* 她的老闆對這個建議不太感興趣。**,go 'down with sth** (*especially BrE*) to become ill/sick with sth 患…病；感染上…病 **SYN** **catch**：*Our youngest boy has gone down with chickenpox.* 我們的小兒子染上了水痘。

'go for sb to attack sb 襲擊某人；抨擊（或攻擊）某人：*She went for him with a knife.* 她手持尖刀向他刺去。**'go for sb/sth** **1** to apply to sb/sth 適用於某人（或某事物）：*What I said about Peter goes for you, too.* 我說的關於彼得的話也適用於你。◇ *They have a high level of unemployment—but* ***the same goes for*** *many other countries.* 他們的失業率很高，不過，其他許多國家也是如此。**2** to go to a place and bring sb/sth back 去帶回某人；去取回某物：*She's gone for some milk.* 她買些牛奶去了。**3** (*informal*) to be attracted by sb/sth; to like or prefer sb/sth 被…所吸引；（更）喜歡某人（或某事物）：*She goes for tall slim men.* 她喜歡瘦高個子的男人。◇ *I don't really go for modern art.* 我並不是很喜歡現代藝術。**'go for sth** **1** to choose sth 選擇某物：*I think I'll go for the fruit salad.* 我想要水果色拉。➲ SYNONYMS at CHOOSE **2** to put a lot of effort into sth, so that you get or achieve sth 努力爭取某事物：***Go for it****, John! You know you can beat him.* 努力爭取吧，約翰！你知道你是可以打敗他的。◇ *It sounds a great idea.* ***Go for it!*** 這聽起來是個極好的主意。努力去實現吧！

,go 'in **1** to enter a room, house, etc. 進入室內；進去：*Let's go in, it's getting cold.* 我們進屋去吧，天冷了。**2** if the sun or moon **goes in**, it disappears behind a cloud（日、月）被烏雲遮住 **,go 'in for sth** **1** (*BrE*) to take an exam or enter a competition 參加考試（或競賽）：*She's going in for the Cambridge First Certificate.* 她打算參加劍橋初級證書考試。**2** to have sth as an interest or a hobby 對某事物有興趣；愛好：*She doesn't go in for team sports.* 她不喜歡團體運動。**,go 'in with sb** to join sb in starting a business 與某人合夥；與某人聯合辦企業：*My brothers are opening a garage and they want me to go in with them.* 我的幾個兄弟要開辦一個汽車修理廠，想讓我與他們合夥幹。

,go 'into sth **1** 🔑 (of a vehicle 交通工具) to hit sth violently 猛烈地撞上某物：*The car skidded and went into a tree.* 汽車打滑，猛地撞到樹上。**2** (of a vehicle or driver 交通工具或駕駛員) to start moving in a particular way 開始某種動作：*The plane went into a nosedive.* 飛機開始俯衝。**3** 🔑 to join an organization, especially in order to have a career in it 加入某組織；從事某職業：*to go into the Army/the Church/Parliament* 參軍；加入教會；當議會議員 ◇ *to go into teaching* 執教 **4** to begin to do sth or behave in a particular way（以某種方式）開始做某事；開始某種表現：*He went into a long explanation of the affair.* 他開始長篇大論地解釋起那件事來。**5** to examine sth carefully 詳細調查（或研究）某事：*We need to go into the question of costs.* 我們需要研究一下費用問題。**6** (of money, time, effort, etc. 金錢、時間、精力等) to be spent on sth or used to do sth 投入某事；用於某事：*More government money needs to go into the project.* 政府需對此工程投入更多的資金。◇ **~ doing sth** *Years of work went into researching the book.* 多年的工夫全花在對這本書的研究上了。

,go 'off **1** to leave a place, especially in order to do sth 離開（尤指去做某事）：*She went off to get a drink.* 她拿飲料去了。**2** 🔑 to be fired; to explode 開火；爆炸：*The gun went off by accident.* 槍走火了。◇ *The bomb went off in a crowded street.* 炸彈在擠滿人群的大街上爆炸了。➲ SYNONYMS at EXPLODE **3** 🔑 if an alarm, etc. **goes off**, it makes a sudden loud noise（警報器等）突然發出巨響 **4** 🔑 if a light, the electricity, etc. **goes off**, it stops working（電燈）熄滅；（電）中斷；停止運行：*Suddenly the lights went off.* 燈突然熄滅了。◇ *The heating goes off at night.* 暖氣夜間停止供熱。**OPP** go on **5** (*BrE, informal*) to fall asleep 入睡；睡着：*Hasn't the baby gone off yet?* 孩子還沒睡着嗎？**6** 🔑 (*BrE*) if food or drink **goes off**, it becomes bad and not fit to eat or drink（食物、飲料）變質，變壞 **7** (*BrE*) to get worse in quality（質量）下降：*Her books have gone off in recent years.* 她近年寫的書質量下降了。**8** to happen in a particular way（以某種方式）發生：*The meeting* ***went off well****.* 會議進行得很好。**,go 'off (on sb)** (*NAmE, informal*) to suddenly become angry with sb 突然生（某人的）氣 **,go 'off sb/sth** (*BrE, informal*) to stop liking sb/sth or lose interest in them 不再喜歡某人（或某事物）；失去對…的興趣：*Jane seems to be going off Paul.* 簡好像不再喜歡保羅了。◇ *I've gone off beer.* 我對啤酒已不感興趣。**,go 'off with sb** to leave your husband, wife, partner, etc. in order to have a relationship with sb else 拋棄原有伴侶等而與另外的某人相好；與某人私奔：*He went off with his best friend's wife.* 他和最要好的朋友的妻子走了。**,go 'off with sth** to take away from a place sth that does not belong to you 攜他人之物而去：*He went off with $10 000 of the company's money.* 他捲走了公司 1 萬元錢。

,go 'on **1** when a performer **goes on**, they begin their performance（演員）上場，出場：*She doesn't go on until Act 2.* 她要到第 2 幕才出場。**2** (in sport 體育運動) to join a team as a SUBSTITUTE during a game（比賽中）以替補隊員身分上場：*Walcott went on in place of Rooney just before half-time.* 就在上半場結束前沃爾科特上場替下了魯尼。**3** 🔑 when a light, the electricity, etc. **goes on**, it starts to work（燈）亮；通（電）；開始運行：*Suddenly all the lights went on.* 突然所有的燈都亮了。**OPP** **go off 4** 🔑 (of time 時間) to pass 流逝；過去：*She became more and more talkative as the evening went on.* 夜漸深，她的話越來越多。**5** 🔑 (usually **be going on**) to happen 發生：***What's going on*** *here?* 這兒出了什麼事？**6** 🔑 if a situation **goes on**, it continues without changing（情況、形勢）繼續下去，持續：*This cannot be allowed to go on.* 決不允許這種情況繼續下去。◇ *How much longer will this hot weather go on for?* 這樣炎熱的天氣還會持續多久？◇ ***We can't go on like this****—we seem to be always arguing.* 我們不能這樣繼續下去，我們似乎老是爭吵不休。**7** 🔑 to continue speaking, often after a short pause（常指短暫停頓後）繼續說：*She hesitated for a moment and then went on.* 她猶豫了一會兒，然後繼續往下說。◇ **+ speech** *'You know,' he went on, 'I think my brother could help you.'* "嗯，"他接着說，"我想我哥哥可以幫助你。" **8** 🔑 used to encourage sb to do sth（用於鼓勵）來吧：*Go on! Have another drink!* 來吧！再喝一杯！◇ *Go on—jump!* 來呀，跳吧！**,go 'on (ahead)** to travel in front of sb else 先走一步；先行：*You go on ahead—I'll catch you up in a few minutes.* 你先走，我一會兒就趕上來。**'go on sth** (used in negative sentences and questions 用於否定句和疑問句) to base an opinion or a judgement on sth 以…為依據；根據…來判斷：*The police don't have much to go on.* 警方沒多少依據。**,go 'on (about sb/sth)** (*informal*) to talk about sb/sth for a long time, especially in a boring or complaining way 嘮叨；沒完沒了地抱怨：*He* ***went on and on*** *about how poor he was.* 他沒完沒了地哭窮。◇ *She does go on sometimes!* 她有時就是嘮叨個沒完！**,go 'on (at sb)** (*informal, especially BrE*) to complain to sb about their behaviour, work, etc. 埋怨；數落；指責 **SYN** **criticize**：*She goes on at him continually.* 她老是責備他。**,go 'on (with sth)** 🔑 to continue an activity, especially after a pause or break（尤指停頓或中斷之後）繼續做（某事）：*That's enough for now—let's go on with it tomorrow.* 現在就到這裏，咱們明天再繼續吧。**,go 'on doing sth** 🔑 to continue an activity without stopping 不停地做某事：*He said nothing but just went on working.* 他什麼都不說，只是不停地幹活。**,go 'on to sth** to pass from one item to the next 進而轉入另外一件事；接着開始另一個項目：*Let's go on to the next item on the agenda.* 咱們接着討論下一項議程吧。**,go 'on to do sth** to do sth after completing sth else（完成某事後）接着做另一事：*The book goes on to describe his experiences in the army.* 本書繼而描述了他在部隊的經歷。

,go 'out **1** 🔑 to leave your house to go to a social event 出門參加社交活動；外出交際；外出娛樂：*She goes out a lot.* 她經常外出參加社交活動。◇ **~ doing sth** *He goes out drinking most evenings.* 他晚上多半在外喝酒。**2** when the TIDE **goes out**, it moves away from the land 退潮；落潮 **SYN** **ebb** **OPP** **come in 3** to be sent 送出；發出；派出：*Have the invitations gone out yet?* 請柬發出去了嗎？**4** (*BrE*) when a radio or television programme

goes out, it is broadcast（廣播或電視節目）播放，播出 **5** when news or information **goes out**, it is announced or published（新聞或消息）發佈，公佈，發表：**~ that ...** *Word went out that the director had resigned* 局長已經辭職的消息公開了。 **6** 🔑 if a fire or light **goes out**, it stops burning or shining（火或燈光）熄滅 **,go 'out (of sth) 1** to fail to reach the next stage of a competition, etc.（競賽等中）被淘汰，出局：*She went out of the tournament in the first round.* 她在錦標賽的第一輪比賽中就被淘汰了。 **2** to be no longer fashionable or generally used 過時；不再流行：*Those skirts went out years ago.* 那些裙子多年前就不時興了。 **,go 'out of sb/sth** (of a quality or a feeling 品質或情感) to be no longer present in sb/sth; to disappear from sb/sth 在…中不復存在；從…中消失：*All the fight seemed to go out of him.* 他身上的所有鬥志似乎都已喪失殆盡。 **,go 'out to sb** if your thoughts, etc. **go out to sb**, you think about them in a kind way and hope that the difficult situation that they are in will get better 對某人產生同情（及寄予良好的祝願）： **go 'out with sb | ,go 'out (together)** 🔑 (especially of young people 尤指年輕人) to spend time with sb and have a romantic or sexual relationship with them 與某人談戀愛（或有性關係）：*Tom has been going out with Lucy for six weeks.* 湯姆與露西相戀六週了。◇ *How long have Tom and Lucy been going out together?* 湯姆和露西相戀多久了？

,go 'over sth 1 🔑 to examine or check sth carefully 仔細檢查（或審查、查閱）某事：*Go over your work before you hand it in.* 把作業仔細檢查後再交。 ➲ SYNONYMS at CHECK **2** to study sth carefully, especially by repeating it 反複研究；仔細琢磨：*He went over the events of the day in his mind* (= thought about them carefully). 他心裏反複琢磨白天發生的事。 **,go 'over (to ...)** to move from one place to another, especially when this means crossing sth such as a room, town or city 從一處到（另一處）：*He went over and shook hands with his guests.* 他走過去與客人們握手。◇ *Many Irish people went over to America during the famine.* 許多愛爾蘭人在饑荒時期遷徙到美國。 **,go 'over to sb/sth** (in broadcasting 廣播) to change to a different person or place for the next part of a broadcast 切換到另一人物（或地點）：*We are now going over to the news desk for an important announcement.* 我們現在轉換到新聞部宣佈一則重要消息。 **,go 'over to sth** to change from one side, opinion, habit, etc. to another 轉向另一立場（或見解、習慣等）：*Two Conservative MPs have gone over to the Liberal Democrats.* 兩名保守黨議員已轉向自由民主黨人一邊。 **,go 'over (with sb)** (*NAmE*) to be received in a particular way by sb 受到（某人的…）對待：*The news of her promotion went over well with her colleagues.* 她晉升的消息一傳開，同事都為她高興。

,go 'round = GO AROUND **,go 'round (to ...)** = GO AROUND (TO ...)

,go 'through if a law, contract, etc. **goes through**, it is officially accepted or completed（法律、合同等正式）通過，接受，達成：*The deal did not go through.* 這筆交易未談成。 **go through sth 1** 🔑 to look at or examine sth carefully, especially in order to find sth 仔細察看某事物；檢查某事物；審查某事物：*I always start the day by going through my email.* 我每天第一件事就是要查閱電子郵件。◇ *She went through the company's accounts, looking for evidence of fraud.* 她仔細審查公司的賬目，尋找詐騙的證據。 **2** 🔑 to study or consider sth in detail, especially by repeating it（尤指反複地）詳細研究，仔細琢磨：*Let's go through the arguments again.* 咱們再詳細研究一下這些論據吧。◇ *Could we go through* (= practise) *Act 2 once more?* 我們把第 2 幕戲再串一次好嗎？ **3** 🔑 to perform a series of actions; to follow a method or procedure 執行某行動；實行某方法；履行某程序：*Certain formalities have to be gone through before you can emigrate.* 必須辦理一定的手續方能移居他國。 **4** 🔑 to experience or suffer sth 經歷；遭受：*She's been going through a bad patch recently.* 她最近很不走運。◇ *He's amazingly cheerful considering all he's had to go through.* 經歷了種種磨難，他還那麼樂觀，令人驚歎。 **5** to use up or finish sth completely 用完；耗盡：*The boys went through two whole loaves of bread.* 這些男孩把整整兩條麵包吃得精光。 **,go 'through with sth** 🔑 to do what is necessary to complete a course of action, especially one that is difficult or unpleasant 完成艱難（或令人不快）的事：*She decided not to go through with* (= not to have) *the operation.* 她決定不動手術。

'go to sb/sth 🔑 to be given to sb/sth 由…得到；被授予某人：*Proceeds from the concert will go to charity.* 音樂會的收入將捐贈給慈善事業。◇ *All her property went to her eldest son* (= when she died).（她死後）全部財產由她的長子繼承了。

,go to'gether = GO WITH STH (3), (4)

'go towards sth to be used as part of the payment for sth 用於支付…的部份款項；作為對…的部份付款：*The money will go towards a new car.* 這筆錢將用於支付新車的部份款項。◇ **~ doing sth** *Part of my pay cheque went towards buying an MP3 player.* 我的部份工資用於買 MP3 播放器了。

,go 'under 1 (of sth that floats 漂浮的東西) to sink below the surface 沉下去；沉沒 **2** (*informal*) to become BANKRUPT (= be unable to pay what you owe) 破產：*The firm will go under unless business improves.* 生意若無起色，這家公司將會倒閉。

,go 'up 1 to be built 被興建；被建造：*New office buildings are going up everywhere.* 到處都在興建新辦公樓。 **2** when the curtain across the stage in a theatre **goes up**, it is raised or opened（劇院幕布）升起 **3** to be destroyed by fire or an explosion 被燒燬；被炸毀：*The whole building went up in flames.* 整座樓房在大火中焚燬。 **4** 🔑 if the price of sth, the temperature, etc. **goes up**, it becomes higher（物價等）上漲；（溫度等）上升 SYN **rise**：*The price of cigarettes is going up.* 香煙價格在上漲。◇ *Cigarettes are going up in price.* 香煙在漲價。 OPP **go down** **,go 'up (to ...)** (*BrE, formal*) to arrive at a university, especially Oxford or Cambridge, at the beginning of a term or in order to begin your studies（大學開學時）到校上學（尤指牛津和劍橋） OPP **go down (from ...)** **,go 'up (to ...) (from ...)** to go from one place to another, especially further north or to a city or large town from a smaller place（從一處）到（另一處）（尤指北上或從小地方到城市或大城鎮）：*When are you next going up to Scotland?* 你下次什麼時候北上蘇格蘭？◇ *We went up to London last weekend.* 我們上週末上倫敦去了。 OPP **go down**

'go with sb 1 (*old-fashioned, informal*) to have a sexual or romantic relationship with sb 與某人有性關係；與某人談戀愛 **2** (*informal*) to have sex with sb 與某人性交 **'go with sth 1** to be included with or as part of sth 是…的一部份；附屬於：*A car goes with the job.* 這份工作配有一輛汽車。 **2** to agree to accept sth, for example a plan or an offer 同意，接受（計劃、報價等）：*You're offering £500? I think we can go with that.* 你出價 500 英鎊？我想我們可以接受。 **3** 🔑 (also **go (together)**) to combine well with sth 與某物相配（或協調、和諧） SYN **match**：*Does this jacket go with this skirt?* 這件上衣與這條裙子相配嗎？◇ *Those colours don't really go (together).* 那些顏色並不十分協調。 **4** 🔑 (also **,go to'gether**) to exist at the same time or in the same place as sth; to be found together 與某事同時（或同地）存在；與某事相伴而生：*Disease often goes with poverty.* 疾病與貧窮常常相伴而生。◇ *Disease and poverty often go together.* 疾病與貧窮常常相伴而生。

,go wi'thout (sth) 🔑 to manage without sth that you usually have or need 沒有…而勉強應付；沒有…也行：*There wasn't time for breakfast, so I had to go without.* 沒有時間吃早飯，我也只好不吃了。◇ *How long can a human being go* (= survive) *without sleep?* 人不睡覺能活多久？◇ **~ doing sth** *She went without eating for three days.* 她三天沒吃東西。

■ ***noun*** (*pl.* **goes** /ɡəʊz; *NAmE* ɡoʊz/) **1** [C] (*BrE*) (also **turn** *NAmE, BrE*) a person's turn to move or play in a game or an activity（遊戲或活動中）輪到的機會：*Whose go is it?* 輪到誰了？◇ *It's your go.* 輪到你啦。◇ *'How much is it to play?' 'It's 50p a go.'* "玩這遊戲多少錢？" "50 便士一回。" ◇ *Can I* ***have a go on*** *your new bike?* 我能騎騎你的新自行車嗎？ **2** [C] (*BrE*) (also **try** *NAmE, BrE*) an attempt at doing sth（做某事的）嘗試，一番努力：*It took three goes to get it right.* 試了三次才把它弄好。◇ *I doubt if he'll listen to advice from me, but* ***I'll give it a go*** (= I'll try but I don't think I will succeed). 我懷疑

他是不是會聽我勸，不過我想試試看。 **3** [U] (*BrE*) energy and enthusiasm 精力；活力；熱情；幹勁：*Mary's always got plenty of go.* 瑪麗總是精力充沛。➲ see also GET-UP-AND-GO

IDM **at one 'go** (*BrE*) in one single attempt or try 一下子；一舉；一口氣：*She blew out the candles at one go.* 她一口氣把蠟燭全吹滅了。 **be a 'go** (*NAmE, informal*) to be planned and possible or allowed 可行；得到允許：*I'm not sure if Friday's trip is a go.* 我說不準星期五是否能成行。 **be all 'go** (*BrE, informal*) to be very busy or full of activity 忙得要命；事兒特別多；手忙腳亂：*It was all go in the office today.* 今天辦公室裏忙得要死。 **be on the 'go** (also **be on the 'move**) (*informal*) to be very active and busy 十分活躍；非常忙碌：*I've been on the go all day.* 我一整天忙得馬不停蹄。◇ *Having four children keeps her on the go.* 她那四個孩子把她忙得不可開交。 **first, second, etc. 'go** (*BrE*) at the first, second, etc. attempt 第一次（或第二次等）嘗試：*I passed my driving test first go.* 我考駕照一次就通過了。 **have a 'go** (*informal, especially BrE*) to attack sb physically（對身體）攻擊，襲擊：*There were about seven of them standing round him, all waiting to have a go.* 他們大約有七個人把他團起來，個個都等着下手。 **have a 'go (at sth/at doing sth)** to make an attempt to do sth 嘗試，試圖（做某事）：*'I can't start the engine.' 'Let me have a go.'* "這發動機我發動不起來了。" "讓我來試試。" ◇ *I'll have a go at fixing it tonight.* 我今晚來試修一下。 **have a 'go at sb** (*informal, BrE*) to criticize sb or complain about sb 指責，剋（某人）：*The boss had a go at me for being late for work.* 我上班遲到，老闆剋了我一頓。 **have sth on the 'go** (*BrE, informal*) to be in the middle of an activity or a project 正忙於（活動或計劃）：*The award-winning novelist often has three or four books on the go at once.* 那位獲獎小說家經常是三四部小說同時寫的。 **in one 'go** (*informal*) all together on one occasion 一舉；一下子：*I'd rather do the journey in one go, and not stop on the way.* 我寧願一次走完全程，中途不停。◇ *They ate the packet of biscuits all in one go.* 他們一下子把那包餅乾全吃光了。 **make a 'go of sth** (*informal*) to be successful in sth 在…方面成功（或有所成就）：*We've had a few problems in our marriage, but we're both determined to make a go of it.* 我們的婚姻有過一些問題，但現在我們倆都決心好好過日子。➲ more at LEAVE *v.*, LET *v.*

goad /ɡəʊd; *NAmE* ɡoʊd/ *verb, noun*

■ ***verb*** to keep irritating or annoying sb/sth until they react（不斷地）招惹，激怒，刺激：**~ sb/sth** *Goaded beyond endurance, she turned on him and hit out.* 她被氣得忍無可忍，於是轉身向他猛擊。◇ **~ sb/sth into sth/into doing sth** *He finally goaded her into answering his question.* 他終於激得她回答了他的問題。

PHR V **,goad sb↔'on** to drive or encourage sb to do sth 驅使（或慫恿、激勵）某人：*The boxers were goaded on by the shrieking crowd.* 拳擊運動員聽見觀眾的喊叫就來勁兒了。

■ ***noun*** **1** a pointed stick used for making cows, etc. move forwards（趕牛等牲畜用的）尖頭棒 **2** something that makes sb do sth, usually by annoying them 刺激；激勵

'go-ahead *noun, adj.*

■ ***noun* the go-ahead** [sing.] (*informal*) permission for sb to start doing sth 批准；許可：*The council has **given the go-ahead** to start building.* 委員會已批准破土動工。

■ ***adj.*** [usually before noun] willing to try new ideas, methods, etc. and therefore likely to succeed 有進取心的；有開拓精神的：*a go-ahead company* 開拓型公司

goal 🔑 AW /ɡəʊl; *NAmE* ɡoʊl/ *noun*

1 🔑 (in sports 體育運動) a frame with a net into which players must kick or hit the ball in order to score a point 球門：*He headed the ball into an open goal* (= one that had nobody defending it). 他把球頂進了空門。◇ *Who is **in goal** (= is the goalkeeper) for Arsenal?* 阿森納隊的守門員是誰？➲ VISUAL VOCAB page V44 **2** 🔑 the act of kicking or hitting the ball into the goal; a point that is scored for this 射門；進球得分：*The **winning goal** was scored by Hill.* 希爾踢進了致勝的一球。◇ *Liverpool won by three goals to one.* 利物浦隊以三比一獲勝。◇ *United conceded two goals in the first half.* 聯隊在上半場被攻入了兩球。◇ *a penalty goal* 點球罰中 ➲ see also DROP GOAL, GOLDEN GOAL, OWN GOAL **3** 🔑 something that you hope to achieve 目標；目的 SYN **aim**：*to work towards a goal* 爭取達到目標 ◇ *to **achieve/attain a goal*** 達到目標 ◇ *You need to **set yourself** some long-term **goals**.* 你得為自己訂一些長期目標。◇ *Our **ultimate goal** must be the preservation of the environment.* 我們的最終目的必須是環境保護。➲ SYNONYMS at TARGET

goal·keep·er /ˈɡəʊlkiːpə(r); *NAmE* ˈɡoʊl-/ (also *informal* **goalie** /ˈɡəʊli; *NAmE* ˈɡoʊli/) (*NAmE* also **goal·tend·er**) (also *BrE informal* **keeper**) *noun* (in football (SOCCER), HOCKEY, etc. 足球、曲棍球等) a player whose job is to stop the ball from going into his or her own team's goal 守門員 ➲ VISUAL VOCAB page V44 ▸ **goal·keep·ing** *noun* [U]：*goalkeeping techniques* 守門的技巧

'goal kick *noun* (in football (SOCCER) 足球) a kick taken by one team after the ball has been kicked over their GOAL LINE by the other team without a goal being scored 球門球

goal·less /ˈɡəʊlləs; *NAmE* ˈɡoʊl-/ *adj.* [usually before noun] without either team scoring a goal 零比零的：(*BrE*) *The match ended in a goalless draw.* 比賽以零比零結束。

'goal line *noun* (in football, HOCKEY, etc. 足球、曲棍球等) the line at either end of a sports field on which the goal stands or which the ball must cross to score a goal or TOUCHDOWN 球門線

goal·mouth /ˈɡəʊlmaʊθ; *NAmE* ˈɡoʊl-/ *noun* the area directly in front of a goal 球門口

'goal poacher *noun* = POACHER (3)

goal·post /ˈɡəʊlpəʊst; *NAmE* ˈɡoʊlpoʊst/ (also **post**) *noun* one of the two vertical posts that form part of a goal 球門柱

IDM **move, etc. the 'goalposts** (*BrE, informal, disapproving*) to change the rules for sth, or conditions under which it is done, so that the situation becomes more difficult for sb 改變規則，改變條件（使某人為難）

goal·scorer /ˈɡəʊlskɔːrə(r); *NAmE* ˈɡoʊl-/ *noun* a player in a sports game who scores a goal（體育比賽的）得分隊員，得分射手，得分者

goal·tend·er /ˈɡəʊltendə(r); *NAmE* ˈɡoʊl-/ *noun* (*NAmE*) = GOALKEEPER

'go-around (also **'go-round**) *noun* **1** (*technical* 術語) a path taken by a plane after an unsuccessful attempt at landing, in order to get into a suitable position to try to land again（飛機降落失敗後的）復飛路線 **2** (*NAmE, informal*) a disagreement or argument 爭論；爭吵

goat /ɡəʊt; *NAmE* ɡoʊt/ *noun* **1** an animal with horns and a coat of hair, that lives wild in mountain areas or is kept on farms for its milk or meat 山羊：*a mountain goat* 山羊 ◇ ***goat's milk/cheese*** 羊奶；羊奶酪 ➲ see also BILLY GOAT, KID *n.* (2), NANNY GOAT **2 old ~** (*informal*) an unpleasant old man who is annoying in a sexual way 老色鬼；色狼；好色之徒

IDM **get sb's 'goat** (*informal*) to annoy sb very much 使某人惱怒 ➲ more at SHEEP

goatee /ɡəʊˈtiː; *NAmE* ɡoʊ-/ *noun* a small pointed beard (= hair growing on a man's face) that is grown only on the chin（男子下巴的）山羊鬍子 ➲ VISUAL VOCAB page V60

goat·herd /ˈɡəʊthɜːd; *NAmE* ˈɡoʊthɜːrd/ *noun* a person whose job is to take care of a group of goats 牧羊人；羊倌

goat·skin /ˈɡəʊtskɪn; *NAmE* ˈɡoʊt-/ *noun* [U] leather made from the skin of a goat 山羊皮革

gob /ɡɒb; *NAmE* ɡɑːb/ *noun, verb*

■ ***noun*** (*slang*) **1** (*BrE*) a rude way of referring to a person's mouth 嘴（粗俗說法）：*Shut your gob!* (= a rude way of telling sb to be quiet) 閉嘴！ **2** a small amount of a thick wet substance 少許（黏濕的物質）：*Gobs of spittle ran down his chin.* 一滴滴口水順着他的下巴往下流。 **3** [usually pl.] (*NAmE*) a large amount of sth 大量：*great gobs of cash* 大量現金

■ ***verb*** (**-bb-**) [I] (*BrE, slang*) to blow SALIVA out of your mouth 吐，啐（唾液） SYN **spit**

G

G

gob·bet /ˈɡɒbɪt; *NAmE* ˈɡɑːb-/ *noun* (*old-fashioned*) **~ (of sth)** a small amount of sth 少量；一點點：*gobbets of food* 一點點食物

gob·ble /ˈɡɒbl; *NAmE* ˈɡɑːbl/ *verb* **1** [T, I] to eat sth very fast, in a way that people consider rude or GREEDY 狼吞虎嚥；貪婪地吃 **SYN** **wolf**：**~ (sth)** *Don't gobble your food like that!* 別那麼狼吞虎嚥地吃東西！◇ **~ sth up/down** *They gobbled down all the sandwiches.* 他們幾口就把三明治全吃光了。**2** [I] when a TURKEY **gobbles**, it makes a noise in its throat（火雞）咯咯叫
PHR V ˌ**gobble sth↔ˈup** (*informal*) **1** to use sth very quickly 很快耗掉某物：*Hotel costs gobbled up most of their holiday budget.* 旅館住宿的費用耗掉他們度假預算的一大部份。**2** if a business company, etc. **gobbles up** a smaller one, it takes control of it（企業等）吞併較小的公司

gobble·de·gook (also **gobble·dy·gook**) /ˈɡɒbldiɡuːk; *NAmE* ˈɡɑːbl-/ *noun* [U] (*informal*) complicated language that is difficult to understand, especially when used in official documents（尤指用於正式文件中的）令人費解的文字，官樣文章：*It's all gobbledegook to me.* 這對我來說完全是天書。

ˈ**go-between** *noun* [C, U] a person who takes messages between one person or group and another 中間人：*to act as (a) go-between* 做中間人

gob·let /ˈɡɒblət; *NAmE* ˈɡɑːb-/ *noun* a cup for wine, usually made of glass or metal, with a STEM and base but no handle（玻璃或金屬製）高腳酒杯

gob·lin /ˈɡɒblɪn; *NAmE* ˈɡɑːb-/ *noun* (in stories) a small ugly creature that likes to trick people or cause trouble（傳說中的）小妖精，醜妖怪

gob·shite /ˈɡɒbʃaɪt; *NAmE* ˈɡɑːb-/ *noun* (*BrE, taboo, slang*) a stupid person who talks nonsense 胡說八道的傻瓜；無聊的蠢人

gob·smacked /ˈɡɒbsmækt; *NAmE* ˈɡɑːb-/ *adj.* (*BrE, informal*) so surprised that you do not know what to say 瞠目結舌的；目瞪口呆的

gob·stop·per /ˈɡɒbstɒpə(r); *NAmE* ˈɡɑːbstɑːpər/ (*BrE*) (*NAmE* **jaw·break·er**) *noun* a very large hard round sweet/candy 大塊圓硬糖

goby /ˈɡəʊbi; *NAmE* ˈɡoʊ-/ *noun* (*pl.* **goby** or **gob·ies**) a small sea fish with a SUCKER underneath 鰕虎魚（腹部帶吸盤的小海魚）

ˈ**go-cart** *noun* (*especially NAmE*) = GO-KART

god 🔑 /ɡɒd; *NAmE* ɡɑːd/ *noun*
1 🔑 **God** [sing.] (not used with *the* 不與定冠詞連用) (in Christianity, Islam and Judaism 基督教、伊斯蘭教和猶太教) the BEING or spirit that is worshipped and is believed to have created the universe 上帝；天主；真主：*Do you **believe in God**?* 你信仰上帝嗎？◇ *Good luck and **God bless you**.* 祝你好運，願上帝保佑你。◇ *the Son of God* (= Christ) 聖子（耶穌基督）➲ COLLOCATIONS at RELIGION **2** 🔑 [C] (in some religions) a BEING or spirit who is believed to have power over a particular part of nature or who is believed to represent a particular quality（某些宗教中主宰某個領域的）神：*Mars was the Roman god of war.* 馬爾斯是古羅馬戰神。◇ *the rain god* 雨神 ◇ *Greek gods* 希臘諸神 ➲ see also GODDESS (1) **3** [C] a person who is loved or admired very much by other people 極受崇拜的人；被崇拜的偶像：*To her fans she's a god.* 對她的狂熱崇拜者來說，她就是偶像。➲ see also GODDESS (2) **4** [C] something to which too much importance or attention is given 受到過分崇尚（或推崇）的事物：*Money is his god.* 錢就是他的命。**5 the gods** [pl.] (*BrE, informal*) the seats that are high up at the back of a theatre（劇院中的）頂層樓座，最高樓座
IDM **by ˈGod!** (*old-fashioned, informal*) used to emphasize a feeling of determination or surprise（強調決心或驚異）老天作證 **HELP** Some people find this use offensive. 有人認為此用法含冒犯意。**God | God alˈmighty | God in ˈheaven | good ˈGod | my ˈGod | oh (dear) ˈGod** 🔑 (*informal*) used to emphasize what you are saying when you are surprised, shocked or annoyed（驚訝、震驚或煩惱時說）天哪，啊喲，主啊：*God, what a stupid thing to do!* 天啊，這事幹得太蠢了！**HELP** Some people find this use offensive. 有人認為此用法含冒犯意。**God ˈbless** used when you are leaving sb, to say that you hope they will be safe, etc.（離別時的祝願語）願上帝保佑，祝一路平安：*Goodnight, God bless.* 晚安，上帝保佑。**God ˌrest his/her ˈsoul | God ˈrest him/her** (*old-fashioned, informal*) used to show respect when you are talking about sb who is dead（對死者表示敬意）魂歸天國，安息主懷 **God's gift (to sb/sth)** (*ironic*) a person who thinks that they are particularly good at sth or who thinks that sb will find them particularly attractive 上帝（對…）的恩寵；上帝恩賜的人（或物）：*He seems to think he's God's gift to women.* 他似乎認為自己是上帝賜給女人的禮物。**God ˈwilling** (*informal*) used to say that you hope that things will happen as you have planned and that there will be no problems（希望事情能按計劃順利進行）如係天意，如上帝許可，如一切順利：*I'll be back next week, God willing.* 如一切順利，我下星期就回來。**play ˈGod** to behave as if you control events or other people's lives 儼然如主宰一切的上帝：*It is unfair to ask doctors to play God and end someone's life.* 讓醫生擔當上帝的角色去結束一個人的生命並不公平。**to ˈGod/ˈgoodness/ˈHeaven** used after a verb to emphasize a particular hope, wish, etc.（用於動詞之後，強調希望、願望等）的確，真：*I wish to God you'd learn to pay attention!* 我真希望你能學會集中注意力！**HELP** Some people find this use offensive. 有人認為此用法含冒犯意。**ye ˈgods!** (*old-fashioned, informal*) used to show surprise, lack of belief, etc.（表示驚訝、不相信等）我的天哪，好傢伙 ➲ more at ACT *n.*, FEAR *n.*, FORBID, GRACE *n.*, HELP *v.*, HONEST, KNOW *v.*, LAP *n.*, LOVE *n.*, MAN *n.*, NAME *n.*, PLEASE *v.*, THANK

ˈ**God-awful** *adj.* [usually before noun] (*informal*) extremely bad 糟糕透頂的；令人憎惡的：*He made a God-awful mess of it!* 他把事情弄得一塌糊塗！**HELP** Some people find this use offensive. 有人認為此用法含冒犯意。

god·child /ˈɡɒdtʃaɪld; *NAmE* ˈɡɑːd-/ *noun* (*pl.* **god·chil·dren** /ˈɡɒdtʃɪldrən; *NAmE* ˈɡɑːd-/) a child that a GODPARENT at a Christian BAPTISM ceremony promises to be responsible for and to teach about the Christian religion 教子（或女）；代子（或女）

god·dam (also **god·damn**) /ˈɡɒdæm; *NAmE* ˈɡɑːd-/ (also **god·damned** /ˈɡɒdæmd; *NAmE* ˈɡɑːd-/) *adj., adv.* (*taboo, slang*) a swear word that many people find offensive, used to show that you are angry or annoyed（表示氣憤或煩惱的詛咒語，許多人認為此用法含冒犯意）該死，討厭，十足，極其：*There's no need to be so goddam rude!* 沒必要如此粗魯！◇ *Where's that goddamned pen?* 那該死的筆哪兒去了？

ˈ**god-daughter** *noun* a female GODCHILD 教女；代女

god·dess /ˈɡɒdes; -əs; *NAmE* ˈɡɑːdəs/ *noun* **1** a female god 女神：*Diana, the goddess of hunting* 狩獵女神狄安娜 **2** a woman who is loved or admired very much by other people 極受崇拜（或敬慕）的女人：*a screen goddess* (= a female film/movie star) 銀幕女神

god·father /ˈɡɒdfɑːðə(r); *NAmE* ˈɡɑːd-/ *noun* **1** a male GODPARENT 教父；代父 **2** (often **Godfather**) a very powerful man in a criminal organization, especially the Mafia（犯罪組織，尤指黑手黨的）頭面人物，首領 **3 ~ of sth** a person who began or developed sth 發起者；開拓者：*He's the godfather of punk.* 他是朋客搖滾樂的創始人。

ˈ**God-fearing** *adj.* [usually before noun] (*old-fashioned*) living a moral life based on religious principles 虔誠的；敬畏上帝的

god·for·saken /ˈɡɒdfəseɪkən; *NAmE* ˈɡɑːdfər-/ *adj.* [only before noun] (of places 地方) boring, depressing and ugly 乏味的；沉悶的；醜陋的：*I can't stand living in this godforsaken hole.* 住在這麼個破地方，我受不了。

ˈ**God-given** *adj.* [usually before noun] given or created by God 天賦的；天賜的；上帝創造的：*a God-given talent* 天賦的才能 ◇ *What gives you **a God-given right** to know all my business?* 誰給你權力過問我所有的事了？

god·head /ˈɡɒdhed; *NAmE* ˈɡɑːd-/ *noun* **the Godhead** [sing.] (*formal*) used in the Christian religion to mean

God, including the Father, Son and HOLY SPIRIT（基督教中指上帝，包括聖父、聖子和聖靈）上帝

god·less /ˈɡɒdləs; *NAmE* ˈɡɑːd-/ *adj.* [usually before noun] not believing in or respecting God 不信神的；不敬上帝的：*a godless generation/world* 無宗教信仰的一代；不信神的世界 ▸ **god·less·ness** *noun* [U]

god·like /ˈɡɒdlaɪk; *NAmE* ˈɡɑːd-/ *adj.* like God or a god in some quality 上帝般的；如神的；神聖的：*his godlike beauty* 他那天仙般的美麗

godly /ˈɡɒdli; *NAmE* ˈɡɑːdli/ *adj.* [usually before noun] (*old-fashioned*) living a moral life based on religious principles 虔誠的；敬畏上帝的；高尚的：*a godly man* 虔誠的人 ▸ **god·li·ness** *noun* [U]

god·mother /ˈɡɒdmʌðə(r); *NAmE* ˈɡɑːd-/ *noun* a female GODPARENT 教母；代母 ➲ see also FAIRY GODMOTHER

go·down /ˈɡəʊdaʊn; *NAmE* ˈɡoʊ-/ *noun* (*IndE*) a WAREHOUSE (= building where goods are stored) 倉庫

god·par·ent /ˈɡɒdpeərənt; *NAmE* ˈɡɑːdperənt/ *noun* a person who promises at a Christian BAPTISM ceremony to be responsible for a child (= his or her GODCHILD) and to teach them about the Christian religion 教父（或母）；代父（或母）

ˌGod ˌSave the ˈKing/ˈQueen *noun* [U] the British national ANTHEM (= song)（英國國歌）天祐吾王

ˈGod's country *noun* (*NAmE*) a beautiful and peaceful area that people love. Americans often use the expression to mean the US, especially the western states. 人間天堂，樂土（美國人常用以指美國，尤指西部各州）

god·send /ˈɡɒdsend; *NAmE* ˈɡɑːd-/ *noun* [sing.] **~ (for sb/sth)** | **~ (to sb/sth)** something good that happens unexpectedly and helps sb/sth when they need help 天賜之物；意外的好運；及時雨：*This new benefit has come as a godsend for low-income families.* 這項新的救濟金是低收入家庭的及時雨。

god·son /ˈɡɒdsʌn; *NAmE* ˈɡɑːd-/ *noun* a male GODCHILD 教子；代子

the ˈGod squad *noun* [sing.] (*informal, disapproving*) Christians, especially ones who try to make people share their beliefs 上帝部隊（指基督教徒，尤指着意傳教者）

goer /ˈɡəʊə(r); *NAmE* ˈɡoʊər/ *noun* **1** **-goer** (in compounds 構成複合詞) a person who regularly goes to the place or event mentioned 常去…的人：*a cinema-goer* 常去看電影的人 ◇ *a moviegoer* 常去看電影的人 **2** (*BrE, informal*) a woman who enjoys having sex frequently, especially with different men 放蕩的女人；騷貨；破鞋

ˌgo-faster ˈstripes *noun* [pl.] (*informal*) **1** coloured lines that can be stuck on the sides of cars（可貼於車身側面的）加速彩條 **2** (*disapproving*) features that are added to a product to attract attention but which actually have no practical use（產品的）華而不實的裝飾

gofer (also **go·pher**) /ˈɡəʊfə(r); *NAmE* ˈɡoʊ-/ *noun* (*informal*) a person whose job is to do small boring tasks for other people in a company 勤雜員；跑腿的辦事員 SYN **dogsbody**：*They call me the gofer—go for this, go for that …* 他們稱我為跑腿的，得一會兒去拿這，一會兒去拿那…

ˈgo-getter *noun* (*informal*) a person who is determined to succeed, especially in business（尤指商業上的）實幹家，志在必得的人

gogga /ˈxɒxə; ˈxɒxɒ; *NAmE* ˈxɑː-; ˈxɔːxɔː/ *noun* (*SAfrE, informal*) an insect 蟲子；昆蟲

gog·gle /ˈɡɒɡl; *NAmE* ˈɡɑːɡl/ *verb* [I] **~ (at sb/sth)** (*old-fashioned, informal*) to look at sb/sth with your eyes wide open, especially because you are surprised or shocked（尤指由於驚恐而）瞪大眼睛看

ˈgoggle-box *noun* (*BrE, old-fashioned, informal*) a television 電視機

ˌgoggle-ˈeyed *adj.* with your eyes wide open, staring at sth, especially because you are surprised（尤指由於驚恐而）瞪大眼睛的，瞪着眼的

gog·gles /ˈɡɒɡlz; *NAmE* ˈɡɑːɡlz/ *noun* [pl.] a pair of glasses that fit closely to the face to protect the eyes from wind, dust, water, etc. 護目鏡；風鏡；游泳鏡：*a pair of swimming/ski/safety goggles* 一副游泳／滑雪／安全護目鏡 ➲ VISUAL VOCAB page V48

ˈgo-go *adj.* **1** connected with a style of dancing to pop music in which women dance wearing very few clothes 歌歌舞的（跳舞的女子衣着暴露）：*a go-go dancer* 歌歌舞舞女 **2** (*NAmE, informal*) of a period of time when businesses are growing and people are making money fast 生意興隆的；賺大錢的：*the go-go years of the 1990s* * 20 世紀 90 年代經濟繁榮的歲月

gogo /ˈɡɔːɡɔː/ *noun* (*SAfrE*) **1** a grandmother 祖母；外婆 **2** the title for an older woman that is polite and shows affection（稱呼有禮貌、有愛心的老年女士）老婆婆，大娘

going /ˈɡəʊɪŋ; *NAmE* ˈɡoʊɪŋ/ *noun, adj.*

■ *noun* **1** [sing.] (*formal*) an act of leaving a place 離去；去；離開 SYN **departure**：*We were all sad at her going.* 我們對她的離去都很難過。 **2** [U] (used with an adjective 與形容詞連用) the speed with which sb does sth; how difficult it is to do sth 進展速度；難度：*Walking four miles in an hour is pretty* ***good going*** *for me.* 一小時走四英里對我來說是相當不錯了。◇ *She had her own company by 25—not* ***bad going!*** 她 25 歲時就有了自己的公司，真了不起！◇ *It was* ***hard going*** *getting up at five every morning.* 每天早上五點鐘起牀太難了。 **3** [U] the condition of the ground, especially in horse racing（尤指賽馬場的）地面狀況：*The going is good to firm.* 賽馬場的地面稍偏硬。 ➲ see also OUTGOINGS

IDM **when the ˌgoing gets ˈtough (the ˌtough get ˈgoing)** (*saying*) when conditions or progress become difficult (strong and determined people work even harder to succeed) 當條件變得艱苦時，當進展變得困難時（隱含有志者更勇往直前之意） **while the ˌgoing is ˈgood** (*BrE*) (*NAmE* **while the ˌgetting is ˈgood**) before a situation changes and it is no longer possible to do sth 趁形勢還未變化時；趁情況還有利時：*Don't you think we should quit while the going is good?* 你不認為我們應該及早脫身嗎？ ➲ more at COMING *n.*, HEAVY *adj.*

■ *adj.* **-going** (in compounds 構成複合詞) going regularly to the place or event mentioned 常去…的：*the theatre-going public* 常去劇院看戲的觀眾 ➲ see also OCEAN-GOING, ONGOING, OUTGOING

IDM **a ˌgoing conˈcern** a business or an activity that is making a profit and is expected to continue to do well 生意興隆的業務；發展中的事業：*He sold the cafe* ***as a going concern.*** 他把經營得正紅火的咖啡館賣掉了。 **the ˌgoing ˈrate (for sth)** the usual amount of money paid for goods or services at a particular time 現行價格；現行收費標準；現行酬金標準：*They pay slightly more than the going rate.* 他們支付的酬金略高於現行標準。

ˌgoing-ˈover *noun* [sing.] (*informal*) **1** a thorough examination of sb/sth 徹底檢查；仔細審查：*The garage gave the car a thorough going-over.* 修車廠對這輛汽車進行了徹底檢修。 **2** a serious physical attack on sb 痛打：*The gang gave him a real going-over.* 那幫流氓把他着實毒打了一頓。

ˌgoings-ˈon *noun* [pl.] (*informal*) activities or events that are strange, surprising or dishonest 異常情況；令人吃驚的活動（或事情）；見不得人的勾當：*There were some strange goings-on next door last night.* 昨天夜裏隔壁有些異常情況。

goitre (*especially US* **goi·ter**) /ˈɡɔɪtə(r)/ *noun* [U, C] a swelling of the throat caused by a disease of the THYROID GLAND 甲狀腺腫

go-kart (*BrE*) (also **go-cart** *NAmE, BrE*) /ˈɡəʊ kɑːt; *NAmE* ˈɡoʊ kɑːrt/ *noun* a vehicle like a small low car with no roof or doors, used for racing（無篷無門的）微型賽車

gold 0➡ /ɡəʊld; *NAmE* ɡoʊld/ *noun, adj.*

■ *noun* **1** 0➡ [U] (*symb.* **Au**) a chemical element. Gold is a yellow PRECIOUS METAL used for making coins, jewellery, decorative objects, etc. 金：***a gold bracelet/ring/watch, etc.*** 金手鐲、金戒指、金錶等 ◇ *18-carat gold* * 18 開金 ◇ *the country's gold reserves* 這個國家的黃金儲備 ◇ *made of* ***solid/pure gold*** 足金／純金製造 ➲ see also FOOL'S GOLD **2** [U] money, jewellery, etc. that is made of gold 金幣；金飾品；黃金製品：*His wife was dripping*

G

with (= wearing a lot of) *gold.* 他的妻子披金戴銀。 **3** [U, C] the colour of gold 金色；金黃色： *I love the reds and golds of autumn.* 我喜歡秋天的火紅色和金黃色。 **4** [U, C] = GOLD MEDAL： *The team look set to win Olympic gold.* 這個隊看來可能會拿奧運會金牌。◇ *He won three golds and a bronze.* 他獲得三枚金牌和一枚銅牌。

IDM **,all that ,glitters/,glistens is not 'gold** (*saying*) not everything that seems good, attractive, etc. is actually good, etc. 閃閃發光的未必都是金子；中看未必中用 **a crock/pot of 'gold** a large prize or reward that sb hopes for but is unlikely to get 不太可能得到的大筆獎賞（或報償） **(as) good as 'gold** (*informal*) behaving in a way that other people approve of 規規矩矩；很乖；表現好： *The kids have been as good as gold all day.* 孩子們一整天都很乖。 ➲ more at HEART, STREET *n.*, STRIKE *v.*, WORTH *adj.*

G

▪ ***adj.*** [only before noun] bright yellow in colour, like gold 金色的： *The company name was spelled out in gold letters.* 該公司的名稱用燙金字母拼成。

'gold brick *noun* (*US, informal*) a person who is lazy and tries to avoid work by pretending to be ill/sick 偷懶的人；（裝病）逃避工作的人

gold·brick /ˈɡəʊldbrɪk; *NAmE* ˈɡoʊld-/ *verb* [I] (*US, informal*) to be lazy and try to avoid work by pretending to be ill/sick 偷懶；（裝病）逃避工作

'gold card *noun* a type of credit card that enables a person to buy more goods and services than a normal card does 信用金卡（信用額度大於普通卡）

gold·crest /ˈɡəʊldkrest; *NAmE* ˈɡoʊld-/ *noun* a very small bird with yellow feathers sticking up from the top of its head 金冠戴菊鳥（頭頂有直立的黃羽毛）

'gold-digger *noun* (*informal, disapproving*) a person who uses the fact that he or she is attractive to get money from a relationship with sb 以色相騙取錢財的人

,gold 'disc *noun* a gold record that is given to a singer or group that sells a particularly high number of records 金唱片（頒發給唱片銷售量特別大的歌手或樂隊）

'gold dust *noun* [U] gold in the form of powder 金粉；砂金；金末

IDM **like 'gold dust** (*BrE*) difficult to find or obtain 難以找到；很難得到： *Tickets for the final are like gold dust.* 決賽票很難弄到。

gold·en /ˈɡəʊldən; *NAmE* ˈɡoʊldən/ *adj.* **1** (especially *literary*) made of gold 金質的；金的： *a golden crown* 金冕 **2** bright yellow in colour like gold 金色的；金黃色的： *golden hair* 金髮 ◇ *miles of golden beaches* 數英里長的金色沙灘 **3** special; wonderful 特別的；美好的： *golden memories* 美好的記憶 ◇ *Businesses have a* ***golden opportunity*** *to expand into new markets.* 商界有開拓新市場的良機。◇ *Hollywood's* ***golden boy*** 好萊塢的金牌男星

IDM **be 'golden** (*NAmE, informal*) in a situation where you are successful or do not have any problems 大功告成；大獲成功；一帆風順： *He thinks once he gets the money he'll be golden.* 他認為只要拿到錢就萬事大吉了。 ➲ more at KILL *v.*, MEAN *n.*, SILENCE *n.*

'golden age *noun* [usually sing.] **~ (of sth)** a period during which sth is very successful, especially in the past（尤指過去的）黃金時代，鼎盛時期： *the golden age of cinema* 電影的鼎盛時期

,golden 'ager *noun* (*informal*) an old person 老人

,golden anni'versary *noun* (*US*) **1** (*BrE* **,golden 'jubilee**) the 50th anniversary of an important event * 50 週年紀念 **2** (*BrE* **,golden 'wedding**) (also **,golden 'wedding anniversary** *NAmE, BrE*) the 50th anniversary of a wedding 金婚紀念（結婚 50 週年）

,golden 'eagle *noun* a large BIRD OF PREY (= a bird that kills other creatures for food) of the EAGLE family, with brownish feathers, that lives in northern parts of the world 金雕（猛禽，羽毛呈棕色，分佈於北半球） ➲ VISUAL VOCAB page V12

,golden 'goal *noun* (in some football (SOCCER) competitions 某些足球比賽) the first goal scored during EXTRA TIME, which ends the game and gives victory to the team that scores the goal 金球，黃金入球（打平後加時賽中第一個進球，進球球隊即贏得比賽）

,golden 'goose *noun* something that provides sb with a lot of money, that they must be very careful with in order not to lose it 產金蛋的鵝（指帶來財富但須小心對待以免失去的事物）： *An increase in crime could kill the golden goose of tourism.* 犯罪率的上升可能會扼殺旅遊業這隻產金蛋的鵝。

,golden 'handcuffs *noun* [pl.] a large sum of money and other financial benefits that are given to sb to persuade them to continue working for a company rather than leaving to work for another company 金手銬（誘人安於現職而不他覓高就的一大筆津貼或其他福利）

,golden 'handshake *noun* a large sum of money that is given to sb when they leave their job, or to persuade them to leave their job（一大筆）退職金，解雇費

,golden hel'lo *noun* a large sum of money that is given to sb for accepting a job 見面厚禮（給新員工的厚遇）

,golden 'jubilee (*BrE*) (*US* **,golden anni'versary**) *noun* the 50th anniversary of an important event * 50 週年紀念： *Queen Victoria's Golden Jubilee celebrations* 維多利亞女王登基 50 週年慶典 ◇ *a party to mark the company's golden jubilee* 慶祝該公司 50 週年的紀念會 ➲ compare DIAMOND JUBILEE, SILVER JUBILEE

,golden 'oldie *noun* (*informal*) **1** a song or film/movie that is quite old but still well known and popular 經久不衰的歌曲（或影片）；經典歌曲；經典影片 **2** a person who is no longer young but still successful in their particular career, sport, etc.（在職業、運動生涯等中）老當益壯者；老將

,golden 'parachute *noun* (*informal*) part of a work contract in which a business person is promised a large amount of money if they have to leave their job "金降落傘"條款（規定員工如被解職即可獲得大筆補償金的聘約條款）

,golden 'raisin (*NAmE*) (*BrE* **sul·tana**) *noun* a small dried GRAPE without seeds, used in cakes, etc. 無核小葡萄乾（用於糕點等）

,golden re'triever *noun* a large dog with thick yellow hair 金毛拾獚，金毛尋回犬，黃金獵犬（一種有濃密黃毛的大犬）

,golden 'rule *noun* [usually sing.] an important principle that should be followed when doing sth in order to be successful 成功之重要原則；指導原則： *The golden rule in tennis is to keep your eye on the ball.* 打好網球的重要原則是眼要緊盯着球。

,golden 'section *noun* (*technical* 術語) the proportion that is considered to be the most attractive to look at when a line is divided into two 黃金分割

,golden 'syrup (also **trea·cle**) (both *BrE*) *noun* [U] a very sweet thick yellow liquid made from sugar 金黃色糖漿

,golden 'wedding (*BrE*) (*US* **,golden anni'versary**) (also **,golden 'wedding anniversary** *NAmE, BrE*) *noun* the 50th anniversary of a wedding 金婚紀念（結婚 50 週年）： *The couple celebrated their golden wedding in January.* 這對夫婦一月份舉行了他們的金婚大慶。 ➲ compare DIAMOND WEDDING, RUBY WEDDING, SILVER WEDDING

gold·field /ˈɡəʊldfiːld; *NAmE* ˈɡoʊld-/ *noun* an area where gold is found in the ground 金礦區；採金地

gold·finch /ˈɡəʊldfɪntʃ; *NAmE* ˈɡoʊld-/ *noun* a small brightly coloured European bird of the FINCH family, with yellow feathers on its wings 紅額金翅雀

gold·fish /ˈɡəʊldfɪʃ; *NAmE* ˈɡoʊld-/ *noun* (*pl.* **gold·fish**) a small orange or red fish. Goldfish are kept as pets in bowls or PONDS. 金魚

'goldfish bowl (also **fish·bowl**) *noun* **1** a glass bowl for keeping fish in as pets 金魚缸 **2** a situation in which people can see everything that happens and nothing is private 金魚缸（指眾目睽睽之下毫無遮掩的局面）： *Living in this goldfish bowl of publicity would crack the strongest marriage.* 生活在這種全無隱私可言的環境之下，最牢固的婚姻也會破裂。

ˌgold ˈleaf (also **ˌgold ˈfoil**) *noun* [U] gold that has been made into a very thin sheet and is used for decoration 金箔；金葉

ˌgold ˈmedal *noun* (also **gold**) a MEDAL made of gold that is given to the winner of a race or competition 金牌；金質獎章：*an Olympic gold medal winner* 奧運會金牌得主 ➲ compare BRONZE MEDAL, SILVER MEDAL ▸ **ˌgold ˈmedallist** (*BrE*) (*NAmE* **ˌgold ˈmedalist**) *noun*：*an Olympic gold medallist* 奧運會金牌得主

ˈgold mine *noun* **1** a place where gold is dug out of the ground 金礦 **2** a business or an activity that makes a large profit 財源；寶庫：*This restaurant is a potential gold mine.* 這家餐館很可能是棵搖錢樹。

ˌgold ˈplate *noun* [U] **1** dishes, etc. made of gold 金質餐具 **2** a thin layer of gold used to cover another metal; objects made in this way 鍍金層；鍍金器具

ˌgold-ˈplated *adj.* covered with a thin layer of gold 鍍金的：*gold-plated earrings* 鍍金耳環

ˈgold reserve *noun* [usually pl.] an amount of gold kept by a country's bank in order to support the supply of money（國家銀行維持貨幣供應量的）黃金儲備

ˈgold rush *noun* a situation in which a lot of people suddenly go to a place where gold has recently been discovered 淘金熱

gold·smith /ˈɡəʊldsmɪθ; *NAmE* ˈɡoʊld-/ *noun* a person who makes, repairs or sells articles made of gold 金匠；金器商

ˈgold standard *noun* **1** (usually **the gold standard**) [sing.] an economic system in which the value of money is based on the value of gold 金本位制 **2** [usually sing.] a high level of quality that others try to copy 黃金標準；典範：*Articles like his are the gold standard of news reporting.* 類似他寫的文章就是新聞報道的典範。

golem /ˈɡəʊləm; ˈɡɔɪ-; *NAmE* ˈɡoʊ-/ *noun* **1** (in Jewish stories 猶太傳說) a figure made of CLAY that comes to life 有生命的泥人 **2** a machine that behaves like a human 機器人

golf /ɡɒlf; *NAmE* ɡɑːlf; ɡɔːlf/ *noun* [U] a game played over a large area of ground using specially shaped sticks to hit a small hard ball (a **golf ball**) into a series of 9 or 18 holes, using as few strokes as possible 高爾夫球運動：*He enjoyed a* ***round of golf*** *on a Sunday morning.* 他喜歡星期天的上午打一場高爾夫球。 ➲ see also CRAZY GOLF, MINIGOLF ➲ VISUAL VOCAB page V40

ˈgolf club *noun* **1** (also **club**) a long metal stick with a piece of metal or wood at one end, used for hitting the ball in golf 高爾夫球棒：*a set of golf clubs* 一套高爾夫球棒 ➲ VISUAL VOCAB page V40 **2** an organization whose members play golf; the place where these people meet and play golf 高爾夫球俱樂部（指組織或所在地）：*Pine Ridge Golf Club* 派恩里奇高爾夫球俱樂部 ◇ *We're going for lunch at the golf club.* 我們會在高爾夫球俱樂部吃午餐。

ˈgolf course (also **course**) *noun* a large area of land that is designed for playing golf on 高爾夫球場 ➲ VISUAL VOCAB page V40

golf·er /ˈɡɒlfə(r); *NAmE* ˈɡɑːl-; ˈɡɔːl-/ *noun* a person who plays golf 高爾夫球運動員 ➲ VISUAL VOCAB page V40

golf·ing /ˈɡɒlfɪŋ; *NAmE* ˈɡɑːlf-; ˈɡɔːlf-/ *adj.* [only before noun] playing golf; connected with golf 打高爾夫球的；與高爾夫球有關的：*a golfing holiday* 打高爾夫球的假期 ▸ **golf·ing** *noun* [U]：*a week's golfing with friends* 與朋友一起打高爾夫球的一週

ˈgolf links (also **links**) *noun* (*pl.* **golf links**) a golf course, especially one by the sea（尤指海邊的）高爾夫球場

Gol·iath /ɡəˈlaɪəθ/ *noun* a person or thing that is very large or powerful 巨人；強大的人（或物）：*a Goliath of a man* 巨人一般高大的男子 ◇ *a Goliath of the computer industry* 計算機行業的鉅頭 **ORIGIN** From **Goliath**, a giant in the Bible who is killed by the boy David with a stone. 源自《聖經》中被男孩大衛用石子射殺的巨人歌利亞（Goliath）。

gol·li·wog /ˈɡɒliwɒɡ; *NAmE* ˈɡɑːliwɑːɡ/ (also *informal* **golly** /ˈɡɒli; *NAmE* ˈɡɑːli/ *pl.* **-ies**) *noun* a DOLL (= a model of a person for a child to play with) made of cloth with a black face and short black hair, now often considered offensive to black people 黑臉短髮布娃娃（現在常被認為會冒犯黑人）

golly /ˈɡɒli; *NAmE* ˈɡɑːli/ *exclamation* (*old-fashioned*, *informal*) used to express surprise（表示驚奇）天哪，啊：*Golly, you're early!* 天哪，你好早喲！

gonad /ˈɡəʊnæd; *NAmE* ˈɡoʊ-/ *noun* (*anatomy* 解) a male sex organ that produces SPERM; a female sex organ that produces eggs 性腺；睾丸；卵巢

gon·dola /ˈɡɒndələ; *NAmE* ˈɡɑːn-; ɡɑːnˈdoʊlə/ *noun* **1** a long boat with a flat bottom and high parts at each end, used on CANALS in Venice 威尼斯小划船；貢多拉；鳳尾船 ➲ VISUAL VOCAB page V55 **2** the part on a CABLE CAR or SKI LIFT where the passengers sit 纜車車廂；纜車座椅 **3** (*especially NAmE*) the part of a hot air BALLOON or AIRSHIP where the passengers sit（熱氣球、飛船上的）吊艙，吊籃

gon·do·lier /ˌɡɒndəˈlɪə(r); *NAmE* ˌɡɑːndəˈlɪr/ *noun* a person whose job is to move and steer a gondola in Venice 威尼斯小划船船夫 ➲ VISUAL VOCAB page V55

Gon·dwana /ɡɒnˈdwɑːnə; *NAmE* ɡɑːn-/ (also **Gon·dwana·land** /ɡɒnˈdwɑːnəlænd; *NAmE* ɡɑːn-/) *noun* [sing.] (*geology* 地) a very large area of land that existed in the southern HEMISPHERE millions of years ago. It was made up of the present Arabia, S America, Antarctica, Australia and India. 岡瓦納古大陸（數百萬年前存在於南半球的大片陸地，由如今的阿拉伯、南美洲、南極洲、澳大利亞和印度組成）

gone /ɡɒn; *NAmE* ɡɔːn/ *adj.*, *prep.* ➲ see also GO *v.*

■ ***adj.*** [not before noun] **1** (of a thing 物品) used up 用完了；用光了：*'Where's the coffee?' 'It's all gone.'* "咖啡在哪兒？" "喝光了。" **2** (of a person 人) having left a place; away from a place 走了；離開了；不在：*'Is Tom here?' 'No, he was gone before I arrived.'* "湯姆在這兒嗎？" "不在，我來之前他就走了。" **3** (*formal*) used to say that a particular situation no longer exists 不復存在；一去不復返：*The days are gone when you could leave your door unlocked at night.* 夜不閉戶的時代已經一去不復返了。 **4** (*BrE*, *informal*) having been pregnant for the length of time mentioned 懷孕…時間了：*She's seven months gone.* 她懷孕七個月了。◇ *How far gone are you?* 你懷孕多久了？

IDM **ˌgoing, ˌgoing, ˈgone** (*BrE*) (also **going ˈonce, going ˈtwice, ˈsold** *NAmE*, *BrE*) said by an AUCTIONEER to show that an item has been sold（拍賣商用語）一次，二次，成交 ➲ more at DEAD *adj.*

■ ***prep.*** (*BrE*, *informal*) later than the time mentioned 晚於；已過 **SYN** **past**：*It's gone six already.* 已經過六點了。

goner /ˈɡɒnə(r); *NAmE* ˈɡɔːn-/ *noun* (*informal*) a person who is going to die soon or who cannot be saved from a dangerous situation 垂死的人；快完蛋的人；無法挽救的人：*We were frantic. We thought you were a goner.* 我們急死了，以為你快完蛋了。

gong /ɡɒŋ; *NAmE* ɡɑːŋ; ɡɔːŋ/ *noun* **1** a round piece of metal that hangs in a frame and makes a loud deep sound when it is hit with a stick. Gongs are used as musical instruments or to give signals, for example that a meal is ready. 鑼 **2** (*BrE*, *informal*) an award or MEDAL given to sb for the work they have done 獎章；勳章

gonna /ˈɡənə; ˈɡɒnə; *NAmE* ˈɡɔːnə/ (*informal*, *non-standard*) a way of saying or writing 'going to' in informal speech, when it refers to the future 即將，將要（非正式用語，即 going to）：*What's she gonna do now?* 她現在要幹什麼？ **HELP** You should not write this form unless you are copying somebody's speech. 只用於記錄講話。

go·nor·rhoea (*BrE*) (*NAmE* **go·nor·rhea**) /ˌɡɒnəˈrɪə; *NAmE* ˌɡɑːnəˈriːə/ *noun* [U] a disease of the sexual organs, caught by having sex with an infected person 淋病 ➲ see also VENEREAL DISEASE

gonzo journalism /ˈɡɒnzəʊ dʒɜːnəlɪzəm; *NAmE* ˈɡɑːnzoʊ dʒɜːrn-/ *noun* [U] (*NAmE*, *informal*) reporting in newspapers that tries to shock or excite readers rather than to give true information 譁眾取寵的新聞報道；新聞炒作

G

goo /ɡuː/ *noun* [U] (*informal*) any unpleasant sticky wet substance（令人不舒服的）黏稠物質 ➲ see also GOOEY

Vocabulary Building 詞彙擴充

Good and very good

Instead of saying that something is **good** or **very good**, try to use more precise and interesting adjectives to describe things. 事物好或非常好，除了用 good 或 very good 外，可盡量用更貼切、更有意思的形容詞。

- **delicious/tasty** food 可口的／美味的食物
- an **exciting/entertaining/absorbing** movie 激動人心的／有趣的／引人入勝的影片
- an **absorbing**/a **fascinating**/an **informative** book 引人入勝的／使人着迷的／內容豐富的書
- a **pleasant**/an **enjoyable** trip 令人愉快的旅行
- a **skilful/talented/fine** player 嫻熟的／有天分的／優秀的運動員
- **impressive/high-quality** acting 令人讚歎的／高質量的表演
- **useful/helpful** advice 有益的／有用的忠告

In conversation you can use words like **great**, **super**, **wonderful**, **lovely** and **excellent**. 對話中可用 great、super、wonderful、lovely 和 excellent 等詞。

➲ note at NICE

good 🔑 /ɡʊd/ *adj., noun, adv.*
■ *adj.* (**bet·ter** /ˈbetə(r)/, **best** /best/)
‣ HIGH QUALITY 高質量 **1** 🔑 of high quality or an acceptable standard 好的；優質的；符合標準的；可接受的：*a good book* 一本好書 ◊ *good food* 符合標準的食品 ◊ *The piano was in good condition.* 這台鋼琴狀況良好。◊ *Your work is just not good enough.* 你的工作就是不夠好。◊ *The results were pretty good.* 結果相當不錯。◊ *Sorry, my English is not very good.* 對不起，我的英語不太好。◊ *This is* **as good a** *place* **as any** *to spend the night.* 有這麼個地方過夜就很好了。◊ *You'll never marry her—she's much too good for you.* 你永遠娶不到她，她對你來說高不可攀。
‣ PLEASANT 令人愉快 **2** 🔑 pleasant; that you enjoy or want 令人愉快的；令人滿意的：*Did you have a* **good time** *in London?* 你在倫敦過得愉快嗎？◊ *It's good to see you again.* 再次見到你真高興。◊ *This is very* **good news**. 這消息真叫人高興。◊ *Let's hope we have good weather tomorrow.* 希望明天是個好天。◊ *We are still friends, though, which is good.* 不過我們仍然是朋友，這令人感到欣慰。◊ ***It's a good thing*** (= it's lucky) *you came early.* 幸好你來得早。
‣ SENSIBLE/STRONG 合情理；有說服力 **3** 🔑 sensible, logical or strongly supporting what is being discussed 合情理的；有說服力的；有充分根據的：*Thank you,* **good question**. 謝謝，問題提得好。◊ *Yes, that's a* **good point**. 是的，那是個有說服力的論據。◊ *I have* **good reason** *to be suspicious.* 我的懷疑有充分理由。◊ *What a* **good idea**! 多好的主意啊！
‣ FAVOURABLE 贊同 **4** 🔑 showing or getting approval or respect 贊同的；贏得讚許的；令人尊敬的：*The play had good reviews.* 這部戲受到好評。◊ *The hotel has a good reputation.* 這家旅館聲譽良好。◊ *He comes from a good family.* 他出身名門。
‣ SKILFUL 熟練 **5** 🔑 able to do sth well 能幹的；精通的；嫻熟的；擅長於…的：*to be a good actor/cook* 是優秀的演員／出色的廚師 ◊ **~ at sth** *to be good at languages/your job* 精通多種語言；工作熟練 ◊ **~ at doing sth** *Nick has always been good at finding cheap flights.* 尼克總能找到價格便宜的航班。 **6** 🔑 **~ with sth/sb** able to use sth or deal with people well 靈巧的；精明的；善於應付…的：*She's good with her hands* (= able to make things, etc.). 她手很巧。◊ *He's very good with children.* 他對孩子很有一套。
‣ MORALLY RIGHT 合乎道德 **7** 🔑 morally right; behaving in a way that is morally right 符合道德的；正派的；高尚的：*She has tried to lead a* **good life**. 她努力規規矩矩地生活。◊ *a* **good deed** 高尚的行為 ◊ *Giving her that money was a good thing to do.* 把那筆錢給她是做了一件善事。◊ *He is a very good man.* 他是個非常高尚的人。
‣ FOLLOWING RULES 遵守規矩 **8** 🔑 following strictly a set of rules or principles 循規蹈矩的；守規矩的：*It is* **good practice** *to supply a written report to the buyer.* 向買主提供書面報告是誠信的做法。◊ *She was a good Catholic girl.* 她是個虔誠的天主教徒。
‣ KIND 善良 **9** 🔑 willing to help; showing kindness to other people 助人為樂的；心地善良的；好心的：**~ (to sb)** *He was very good to me when I was ill.* 我生病時他對我關懷備至。◊ **~ (of sb) (to do sth)** *It was very good of you to come.* 你能來真是太好了。◊ **~ (about sth)** *I had to take a week off work but my colleagues were very good about it.* 我得請一週的假，同事們對此非常諒解。
‣ CHILD 孩子 **10** 🔑 behaving well or politely 溫順的；乖的；有禮貌的：*You can stay up late if you're good.* 你要是聽話就可以晚一點睡覺。◊ *Get dressed now, there's a good girl.* 現在把衣服穿好，乖孩子。
‣ HEALTHY 健康 **11** 🔑 healthy or strong 健康的；強健的；健壯的：*Can you speak into my good ear?* 對着我這隻沒毛病的耳朵說好嗎？◊ *I don't feel too good today.* 我今天感覺不太舒服。◊ *'How are you?' 'I'm good.'* (= used as a general reply to a greeting) "你好嗎？" "我很好。"
‣ USEFUL/HELPFUL 有用；有益 **12** 🔑 **~ (for sb/sth)** having a useful or helpful effect on sb/sth（對…）有用，有好處：*Too much sun isn't good for you.* 曬太陽太多對你並沒有好處。◊ *It's probably good for you to get some criticism now and then.* 偶爾受點批評或許對你還有好處。◊ (*informal*) *Shut your mouth,* ***if you know what's good for you*** (= used as a threat). 你不想找麻煩就把嘴閉上。 **13** 🔑 **no ~ doing sth** | **no ~ to sb** not having a useful or helpful effect 沒有用處（或益處）：*It's no good complaining—they never listen.* 抱怨毫無用處，他們根本不聽。◊ *This book is no good to me: I need the new edition.* 這本書對我沒用，我需要新版本的。
‣ SUITABLE 合適 **14** 🔑 suitable or appropriate 合適的；適宜的；恰當的；適合…的：*Now is a good time to buy a house.* 現在買房子正是時候。◊ **~ for sth/to do sth** *She would be good for the job.* 她幹這工作很合適。◊ **~ for sb** *Can we change our meeting? Monday isn't good* (= convenient) *for me.* 我們把見面時間改改吧，星期一我不方便。
‣ SHOWING APPROVAL 表示贊同 **15** 🔑 (*informal*) used to show that you approve of or are pleased about sth that has been said or done, or to show that you want to move on to a new topic of conversation（表示贊同、滿意或轉向新的話題）：*'Dinner's ready.' 'Good—I'm starving.'* "晚飯好了。" "太好了，我正餓得很。" ◊ *'I got the job.' 'Oh, good.'* "我得到這工作了。" "啊，太好了。" ◊ *Good, I think we've come to a decision.* 好的，我們就這樣決定吧。 **16** 🔑 [only before noun] (*informal*) used as a form of praise（用作讚語）：*Good old Jack!* 好心的傑克！◊ *'I've ordered some drinks.' 'Good man!'* "我叫了些飲料。" "真是好人！"
‣ IN EXCLAMATIONS 感歎 **17** (*informal*) used in exclamations（用於感歎句）：*Good heavens!* 天啊！◊ *Good God!* 上帝呀！
‣ LARGE 大 **18** [only before noun] great in number, amount or degree（數量或程度）相當大的，相當多的：*a good many people* 相當多的人 ◊ *The kitchen is a good size.* 這廚房相當大。◊ *We spent a good while* (= quite a long time) *looking for the house.* 我們花了好長時間找這房子。◊ *He devoted* ***a good deal of*** (= a lot of) *attention to the problem.* 他在這個問題上花了相當多的精力。◊ *There's* ***a good chance*** (= it is likely) *that I won't be here next year.* 我明年很可能不在這兒。
‣ AT LEAST 至少 **19** not less than; rather more than 不少於；稍多於：*We waited for a good hour.* 我們等了整整一小時。◊ *It's a good three miles to the station.* 到車站至少有三英里。
‣ THOROUGH 徹底 **20** [only before noun] thorough; complete 徹底的；完全的：*We had a good laugh about it afterwards.* 我們後來對此笑了個痛快。◊ *You'll feel better after a good sleep.* 好好睡上一覺你會感覺好些。
‣ AMUSING 有趣 **21** [usually before noun] amusing 有趣的；逗笑的：*a* **good story/joke** 有趣的故事／笑話 ◊ (*informal*) *That's a good one!* 那真有意思！

▸ **FOR PARTICULAR TIME/DISTANCE** 特定的時間／距離 **22 ~ for sth** having enough energy, health, strength, etc. to last for a particular length of time or distance（精力、健康、力量等）足以維持…的，能持續…的：*You're good for* (= you will live) *a few years yet.* 你還可以活上幾年。 **23 ~ for sth** valid for sth 有效的：*The ticket is good for three months.* 這張票三個月內有效。

▸ **LIKELY TO PROVIDE** 可能提供 **24 ~ for sth** likely to provide sth 能提供…的：*He's always good for a laugh.* 他總能逗人發笑。◇ *Bobby should be good for a few drinks.* 博比喝上幾杯應該是沒問題的。

IDM Most idioms containing **good** are at the entries for the nouns and verbs in the idioms, for example **(as) good as gold** is at **gold**. 大多數含 good 的習語，都可在該等習語中的名詞及動詞相關詞條找到，如 (as) good as gold 在詞條 gold 下。 **as 'good as** very nearly 與…幾乎一樣；幾乎；簡直是：*The matter is as good as settled.* 這事實際上可以說解決了。◇ *He as good as called me a coward* (= suggested that I was a coward without actually using the word 'coward'). 他就差說我是懦夫了。 **as ˌgood as it 'gets** used when you are saying that a situation is not going to get any better（形勢）不會有什麼好轉，還是老樣子 **good and ...** (*informal*) completely 完全；徹底：*I won't go until I'm good and ready.* 我要完全準備就緒後才走。 **a good 'few** several 好幾個；一些：*There are still a good few empty seats.* 還有好幾個空座位。 **ˌgood for 'you, 'sb, 'them, etc.** (*especially AustralE* **good 'on you, etc.**) (*informal*) used to praise sb for doing sth well（稱讚某人）真行，真棒：*'I passed first time.' 'Good for you!'* "我第一次就過了。" "你真行！"

■ ***noun*** ➲ see also GOODS

▸ **MORALLY RIGHT** 合乎道德 **1** 🔑 [U] behaviour that is morally right or acceptable 合乎道德的行為；正直的行為；善行：*the difference between good and evil* 善與惡的區別 ◇ *Is religion always a force for good?* 宗教一向是誨人行善的力量嗎？ **2 the good** [pl.] people who live a moral life; people who are admired for the work they do to help other people 有道德的人；高尚的人；好人：*a gathering of the great and the good* 群賢薈萃

▸ **STH HELPFUL** 益處 **3** 🔑 [U] something that helps sb/sth 用處；好處；益處：*Cuts have been made* ***for the good of*** ***the company.*** 實行裁減是為了公司的利益。◇ *I'm only telling you this* ***for your own good.*** 我把這事告訴你只是為你好。◇ ***What's the good of*** (= how does it help you) *earning all that money if you don't have time to enjoy it?* 要是沒時間去享受，賺那麼多錢有什麼用？◇ ***What good is it*** *redecorating if you're thinking of moving?* 如果你打算搬走，那重新裝飾有什麼用呢？ ➲ see also DO-GOODER

IDM **ˌall to the 'good** used to say that if sth happens, it will be good, even if it is not exactly what you were expecting 不失為好事：*If these measures also reduce unemployment, that is all to the good.* 要是這些措施也能降低失業率，那就不失為好事。 **be no 'good | not be any/much 'good 1** 🔑 to not be useful; to have no useful effect 沒（或沒什麼、沒多大）用處（或好處）：*This gadget isn't much good.* 這小玩意兒沒多大用處。◇ *It's no good trying to talk me out of leaving.* 想說服我不要離開是沒用的。◇ *Was his advice ever any good?* 他的建議有過用處嗎？ **2** 🔑 to not be interesting or enjoyable 沒（或沒什麼、沒多大）樂趣：*His latest film isn't much good.* 他最近拍攝的影片沒多大意思。 **do 'good | do sb 'good** 🔑 to have a useful effect; to help sb（對某人）有好處，有用處，有益：*Do you think these latest changes will do any good?* 你認為最近這些變化有什麼作用嗎？◇ *Don't you think talking to her would do some good?* 你不覺得和她談一談會有用嗎？◇ *I'm sure a few days off would do you* ***a power of good*** (= improve your health). 休息幾天肯定對你的身體大有好處。 **for 'good** (*BrE* also **for ˌgood and 'all**) permanently 永遠；永久：*This time she's leaving for good* (= she will never return). 她這次走是再也不會回來了。 **to the 'good** used to say that sb now has a particular amount of money that they did not have before 淨賺；盈餘：*We are £500 to the good.* 我們淨賺 500 英鎊。 **up to no 'good** (*informal*) doing sth wrong or dishonest 做壞事；做不光彩的事：*Those kids are always up to no good.* 那些孩子儘會惡作劇。 ➲ more at ILL *adj.*, POWER *n.*, WORLD

■ ***adv.*** (*especially NAmE, informal*) well 好：*'How's it going?' 'Pretty good.'* "事情進展如何？" "非常好。" ◇ (*non-standard*) *Now, you listen to me good!* 喂，好好聽我說！

> **Which Word? 詞語辨析**
>
> **good / goodness**
>
> ■ The noun **good** means actions and behaviour that are morally right. You can talk about a person doing **good**. 名詞 good 指有道德的行為，指人做好事可用 do good：*The charity does a lot of good.* 這家慈善機構做很多善事。◇ *the difference between good and evil* 善惡之分
>
> ■ **Goodness** is the quality of being good. You can talk about a person's **goodness** * goodness 意為善良，可指人的美德：*Her goodness shone through.* 她顯然非常善良。

ˌgood after'noon *exclamation* used to say hello politely when people first see each other in the afternoon; in informal use people often just say *Afternoon.*（下午見面時用語）下午好，你（們）好（非正式場合常說 Afternoon）

good·bye 🔑 /ˌɡʊdˈbaɪ/ *exclamation, noun* used when you are leaving sb or when sb else is leaving 再見；再會：*Goodbye! It was great to meet you.* 再見！認識你很高興。◇ *She didn't even* ***say goodbye*** *to her mother.* 她甚至沒有向母親道個別。◇ *We* ***waved*** *them* ***goodbye.*** 我們向他們揮手告別。◇ *We've already said our goodbyes.* 我們已經道別了。◇ ***Kiss*** *me* ***goodbye!*** 向我吻別吧！◇ (*figurative*) *Take out our service contract and say goodbye to costly repair bills.* 接受我們的服務合同，告別昂貴的修理費吧。 ➲ compare BYE **IDM** see KISS *v.*

ˌgood 'day *exclamation* (*old-fashioned, BrE*) used to say hello or goodbye politely when people first see each other or leave each other during the day（白天見面或分手時用語）白天好，你（們）好，再見：*Good day to you.* 你好。

ˌgood 'evening *exclamation* used to say hello politely when people first see each other in the evening; in informal use people often just say *Evening.*（晚上見面時用語）晚上好，你（們）好（非正式場合常說 Evening）

good 'faith *noun* [U] the intention to be honest and helpful 真誠；善意：*a gesture of good faith* 善意的表示 ◇ *He acted* ***in good faith.*** 他這樣做是出於真心誠意的。

'good-for-nothing *noun* (*informal*) a person who is lazy and has no skills 懶人；無用之人：*an idle good-for-nothing* 遊手好閒的懶蟲 ▸ **'good-for-nothing** *adj.* [usually before noun]：*Where's that good-for-nothing son of yours?* 你那沒出息的兒子在哪兒？

Good 'Friday *noun* [U, C] the Friday before Easter, the day when Christians remember the Crucifixion of Christ 耶穌受難日（復活節前的星期五）

ˌgood-'hearted *adj.* kind; willing to help other people 善良的；好心的；樂於助人的

ˌgood 'humour (*especially US* **ˌgood 'humor**) *noun* [U, sing.] a cheerful mood 愉快的心情；好脾氣：*Everyone admired her patience and unfailing good humour.* 人人都佩服她的耐心和永不衰減的好脾氣。 **OPP** **ill humour** ▸ **ˌgood-'humoured** (*especially US* **ˌgood-'humored**) *adj.*：*a good-humoured atmosphere* 令人愉快的氣氛 **ˌgood-'humoured·ly** (*especially US* **ˌgood-'humored·ly**) *adv.*

goodie = GOODY

good·ish /ˈɡʊdɪʃ/ *adj.* [only before noun] (*BrE, informal*) **1** quite good rather than very good 尚好的；不錯的：*'Is the salary good?' 'Goodish.'* "工資還行吧？" "還可以。" **2** quite large in size or amount 相當大的；相當多的：*It'll be a goodish while yet before I've finished.* 我還得花很長時間才能完成。

G

ˌgood-ˈlooking *adj.* (especially of people 尤指人) physically attractive 漂亮的；好看的 **OPP** **ugly**：*a good-looking man/couple* 俊美的男子；漂亮的一對 ◇ *She's strikingly good-looking.* 她非常漂亮。➲ SYNONYMS at BEAUTIFUL

ˌgood ˈlooks *noun* [pl.] the physical beauty of a person 漂亮的外表；美貌：*an actor famous for his rugged good looks* 以其粗獷美而出名的男演員

good·ly /ˈɡʊdli/ *adj.* [only before noun] **1** (*old-fashioned, formal*) quite large in size or amount 相當大的；相當多的：*a goodly number* 相當大的數目 **2** (*old use*) physically attractive; of good quality 漂亮的；好看的；高質量的

G

ˌgood ˈmorning *exclamation* used to say hello politely when people first see each other in the morning (in informal use people often just say *Morning* in this case); sometimes also used formally when people leave each other in the morning（上午見面時用語，非正式場合常說 Morning）早上好，上午好，你（們）好，你早；（有時用作正式告別語）再見

ˌgood ˈname *noun* [sing.] the good opinion that people have of sb/sth 好名聲；好聲譽 **SYN** **reputation**：*He told the police he didn't know her, to protect her good name.* 為了維護她的好名聲，他對警察說他不認識她。◇ *My election chances are not as important as the good name of the party.* 黨的聲譽比我當選的機會更重要。

ˌgood ˈnature *noun* [U] the quality of being kind, friendly and patient when dealing with people 善良的品性；和善的本性；溫和的性情

ˌgood-ˈnatured *adj.* kind, friendly and patient when dealing with people 本性善良的；和藹可親的；友好的：*a good-natured person/discussion* 和藹可親的人；友好的討論 ▸ **ˌgood-ˈnatured·ly** *adv.*：*to smile good-naturedly* 和善地微笑

ˌgood-ˈneighbour·li·ness *noun* [U] (*BrE*) good relations that exist between people who live in the same area or between countries that are near each other 睦鄰關係

good·ness /ˈɡʊdnəs/ *noun* [U] **1** the quality of being good 善良；優良；美德：*the essential goodness of human nature* 人性善良的本質 ◇ *evidence of God's goodness* 上帝仁慈的明證 ◇ (*formal*) *At least* **have the goodness** (= good manners) *to look at me when I'm talking to you.* 我對你說話，你至少也應該看着我。➲ note at GOOD **2** the part of sth that has a useful effect on sb/sth, especially sb's health（尤指有益健康的）精華，營養，養分：*These vegetables have had all the goodness boiled out of them.* 這些蔬菜的營養都被煮掉了。

IDM **Goodness!** | **ˌGoodness ˈme!** | **ˌMy ˈgoodness!** | **ˌGoodness ˈgracious!** (*informal*) used to express surprise（表示驚訝）天哪，啊呀：*Goodness, what a big balloon!* 啊，好大的氣球呀！◇ *My goodness, you have been busy!* 天哪，你還在忙！◇ *Goodness me, no!* 天啊，不！ **out of the goodness of your ˈheart** from feelings of kindness, without thinking about what advantage there will be for you 出於好心（不從中撈取好處）：*You're not telling me he offered to lend you the money out of the goodness of his heart?* 你該不是說他是純粹出於好心才主動借錢給你的吧？➲ more at GOD, HONEST, KNOW *v.*, THANK

good·night /ˌɡʊdˈnaɪt/ *exclamation* used when you are saying goodbye to sb late in the evening, or when they or you are going to bed; in informal use people often just say *Night.*（晚間道別時或睡前用語）晚安（非正式場合說 Night）

goodo /ˈɡʊdəʊ; *NAmE* -oʊ/ *adj.* (*AustralE, NZE, informal*) good 好的；令人滿意的

ˌgood old ˈboy *noun* (*NAmE, informal*) a man who is considered typical of white men in the southern states of the US 好老弟（美國南方各州的典型白人男子）

goods 🗝 /ɡʊdz/ *noun* [pl.]
1 🗝 things that are produced to be sold 商品；貨品：*cheap/expensive goods* 便宜的／昂貴的商品 ◇ *leather/cotton/paper goods* 皮革／棉織／紙質商品 ◇ *electrical/sports goods* 電器商品；體育器材 ◇ *perishable/durable goods* 易腐／耐用商品 ◇ *increased tax on* **goods and services** 增加了的商品及勞務稅 ➲ see also CONSUMER GOODS ➲ SYNONYMS at PRODUCT **2** 🗝 possessions that can be moved 動產；私人財產：**stolen goods** 贓物 ◇ *The plastic bag contained all his* **worldly goods** (= everything he owned). 這塑料袋裏裝着他的全部家當。➲ SYNONYMS at THING **3** (*BrE*) things (not people) that are transported by rail or road（鐵路或公路）運載的貨物：*a goods train* 貨運列車 ◇ *a heavy goods vehicle* 重型貨車 ➲ compare FREIGHT

IDM **be the ˈgoods** (*BrE, informal*) to be very good or impressive 非常好；給人以深刻印象 **deliver the ˈgoods** | **come up with the ˈgoods** (*informal*) to do what you have promised to do or what people expect or want you to do 履行諾言；不負所望：*We expected great things of the England team, but on the day they simply failed to deliver the goods.* 我們本指望英格蘭隊大獲全勝，可那天他們真是有負眾望。

ˌgoods and ˈchattels *noun* [pl.] (*BrE, law* 律) personal possessions that are not land or buildings 私人財物；有形動產

ˌgood ˈsense *noun* [U] **~** (**to do sth**) the ability to make the right decision about sth; good judgement 正確的決策力（或判斷力）；理智：*a man of honour and good sense* 品德高尚而有頭腦的男人 ◇ *Keeping to a low-fat diet* **makes** *very* **good sense** (= is a sensible thing to do). 堅持低脂飲食是明智的做法。

ˈgoods train *noun* (*BrE*) = FREIGHT TRAIN

ˌgood-ˈtempered *adj.* cheerful and not easily made angry 脾氣好的；快活的；和藹的

ˈgood-time *adj.* [only before noun] only interested in pleasure, and not in anything serious or important 一味追求享樂的；只顧玩樂的：*I was too much of a good-time girl to do any serious studying.* 我過去是個很貪玩的女孩，從來不知道認真學習。

good·will /ˌɡʊdˈwɪl/ *noun* [U] **1** friendly or helpful feelings towards other people or countries 友善；友好；善意；親善：*a spirit of goodwill in international relations* 國際關係中的親善精神 ◇ *a* **goodwill gesture/a gesture of goodwill** 友好的表示 **2** the good relationship between a business and its customers that is calculated as part of its value when it is sold 信譽；商譽

goody /ˈɡʊdi/ *noun, exclamation*
■ *noun* (also **goodie**) [usually pl.] (*pl.* **-ies**) (*informal*)
1 a thing that is very nice to eat 好吃的東西：*a basket of goodies for the children* 給孩子們的一籃好吃的東西
2 anything that is attractive and that people want to have 誘人的東西；人們渴望得到的東西：*We're giving away lots of free goodies—T-shirts, hats and DVDs!* 我們在贈送大量精美禮品：T 恤衫，帽子，還有 DVD！
3 a good person, especially in a book or a film/movie（尤指書和電影中的）正面人物，主人公，好人：*It's sometimes difficult to tell who are the goodies and who are the baddies.* 好人和壞人有時很難分清。**OPP** **baddy**
■ *exclamation* (becoming *old-fashioned*) a word children use when they are excited or pleased about sth（孩童用語）好哇，太好了

ˈgoody bag (also **ˈgoodie bag**) *noun* **1** a bag containing sweets/candy and small presents, given to children to take home at the end of a party 糖果禮品袋（聚會結束時送給小孩）**2** a bag containing examples of a company's products, given away in order to advertise them 樣品袋（為促銷產品而免費贈送）

ˈgoody-goody *noun* (*pl.* **goody-goodies**) (*informal, disapproving*) (used especially by and about children 尤為兒語) a person who behaves very well to please people in authority such as parents or teachers 善於討好賣乖的人

ˌgoody-ˈtwo-shoes *noun* (*pl.* **goody-two-shoes**) (*informal, disapproving*) a person who always behaves well, and perhaps has a disapproving attitude to people who do not 潔身自好的人；嚴於律己責他的人

gooey /ˈɡuːi/ *adj.* (*informal*) soft and sticky 軟而黏的；黏黏糊糊的：*a gooey mess* 黏糊糊的一團 ◇ *gooey cakes* 黏性甜糕點

goof /ɡuːf/ *verb, noun*
■ ***verb*** [I] (*informal, especially NAmE*) to make a stupid mistake 犯愚蠢的錯誤：*Sorry, guys. I goofed.* 對不起，各位。我搞砸了。
PHR V **,goof a'round** (*informal, especially NAmE*) to spend your time doing silly or stupid things 把時間浪費在荒謬無聊的事情上 SYN **mess around** **,goof 'off** (*NAmE, informal*) to spend your time doing nothing, especially when you should be working 閒蕩；混日子；偷懶
■ ***noun*** (*informal, especially NAmE*) **1** a stupid mistake 愚蠢的錯誤 **2** a silly or stupid person 傻瓜；蠢人

goof·ball /ˈɡuːfbɔːl/ *noun* (*NAmE, informal*) a stupid person 傻瓜；蠢人 ▸ **goof·ball** *adj.* [only before noun]：*This is just another of his goofball ideas.* 這不過是他的又一個愚蠢想法。

'goof-off *noun* (*NAmE, slang*) a person who avoids work or responsibility 逃避工作（或責任）的人；懶漢

goofy /ˈɡuːfi/ *adj.* (*informal, especially NAmE*) silly; stupid 愚蠢的；傻的：*a goofy grin* 齜牙咧嘴的傻笑

goog /ɡuːɡ/ *noun* (*AustralE, NZE, informal*) an egg 蛋

google /ˈɡuːɡl/ *verb* [T, I] **~ (sb/sth)** (*computing* 計) to type words into the SEARCH ENGINE Google® in order to find information about sb/sth 用谷歌搜索引擎搜索（字、詞等）：*You can google someone you've recently met to see what information is available about them on the Internet.* 你可以把最近見過的某人鍵入搜索引擎，看看在互聯網上能查到什麼相關信息。◇ *I tried googling but couldn't find anything relevant.* 我試過用搜索引擎檢索，但找不到任何相關信息。

googly /ˈɡuːɡli/ *noun* (*pl.* **-ies**) (in CRICKET 板球) a ball that is BOWLED so that it looks as if it will turn in one direction, but that actually turns the opposite way 變向曲線球：(*figurative*) *He bowled the prime minister a googly* (= asked him a difficult question). 他問了首相一個很棘手的問題。

goo·gol /ˈɡuːɡɒl; *NAmE* -ɡɔːl/ *noun* (*mathematics* 數) the number 10^{100}, or 1 followed by 100 zeros 古戈爾（= 10^{100}）；大數

gook /ɡuːk/ *noun* **1** [U] (*informal*) any unpleasant sticky wet substance 黏乎乎的髒東西 **2** [C] (*NAmE, taboo, slang*) an offensive word for a person from SE Asia （蔑稱）東南亞人

goolie (also **gooly**) /ˈɡuːli/ *noun* [usually pl.] (*pl.* **-ies**) (*BrE, slang*) a rude word for a man's TESTICLE 睾丸

goon /ɡuːn/ *noun* (*informal*) **1** (*especially NAmE*) a criminal who is paid to frighten or injure people （受人雇用的）打手，殺手，暴徒 **2** (*old-fashioned, especially BrE*) a stupid or silly person 傻瓜；蠢人

goose /ɡuːs/ *noun, verb*
■ ***noun*** (*pl.* **geese** /ɡiːs/) **1** [C] a bird like a large DUCK with a long neck. Geese either live wild or are kept on farms. 鵝 **2** [U] meat from a goose 鵝肉：*roast goose* 烤鵝 **3** [C] a female goose 雌鵝 ➲ compare GANDER **4** [C] (*old-fashioned, informal*) a silly person 傻瓜；笨蛋 ➲ see also WILD GOOSE CHASE IDM see COOK *v.*, KILL *v.*, SAUCE, SAY *v.*
■ ***verb*** (*informal*) **1 ~ sb** to touch or squeeze sb's bottom 觸摸（或捏）某人的臀部 **2 ~ sth (along/up)** (*NAmE*) to make sth move or work faster 推動；促進；激勵

goose·berry /ˈɡʊzbəri; *NAmE* ˈɡuːsberi/ *noun* (*pl.* **-ies**) a small green fruit that grows on a bush with THORNS. Gooseberries taste sour and are usually cooked to make jam, PIES, etc. Children are sometimes told that babies come from 'under the gooseberry bush'. 醋栗：*a gooseberry bush* 醋栗灌木 ➲ VISUAL VOCAB page V30
IDM **play 'gooseberry** (*BrE*) to be a third person with two people who have a romantic relationship and want to be alone together 當電燈泡（夾在兩個情侶之間的不知趣者）

goose·bumps /ˈɡuːsbʌmps/ *noun* [pl.] (*especially NAmE*) = GOOSE PIMPLES

'goose egg *noun* (*NAmE, informal*) a score of zero in a game （比賽中的）零分，鴨蛋

'goose pimples *noun* [pl.] (also *less frequent* **goose-flesh** [U]) (both *especially BrE*) (also **goose·bumps** especially in *NAmE*) a condition in which there are raised spots on your skin because you feel cold, frightened or excited （由於寒冷、恐懼或激動而起的）雞皮疙瘩：*It gave me **goose pimples** just to think about it.* 一想到它我就起雞皮疙瘩。

'goose-step *noun* [sing.] (often *disapproving*) a way of marching, used by soldiers in some countries, in which the legs are raised high and straight 正步 ▸ **'goose-step** *verb* (**-pp-**) [I]

GOP /ˌdʒiː əʊ ˈpiː; *NAmE* oʊ/ *abbr.* Grand Old Party (the Republican political party in the US) 老大黨（美國共和黨）

go·pher /ˈɡəʊfə(r); *NAmE* ˈɡoʊ-/ *noun* **1** (also **'ground squirrel**) a N American animal like a RAT, that lives in holes in the ground 囊地鼠；囊鼠 **2** = GOFER

gora /ˈɡɔːrə/ *noun* (*pl.* **goras** or **goray** /ˈɡɔːreɪ/) a word used by people from S Asia for a white person （南亞用語）白人

Gor·dian knot /ˌɡɔːdiən ˈnɒt; *NAmE* ˌɡɔːrdiən ˈnɑːt/ *noun* a very difficult or impossible task or problem 戈爾迪烏姆結；難解的結；難辦的事；棘手的問題：*to **cut/untie the Gordian knot*** (= to solve a problem by taking action) 採取行動解決問題 ORIGIN From the legend in which King Gordius tied a very complicated knot and said that whoever undid it would become the ruler of Asia. Alexander the Great cut through the knot with his sword. 源自傳說：戈爾迪烏斯國王打了一個十分難解的結，並稱誰能解開便會成為亞洲的統治者，結果亞歷山大大帝揮劍將結斬斷。

Gor·don Ben·nett /ˌɡɔːdn ˈbenət; *NAmE* ˌɡɔːrd-/ *exclamation* (*BrE*) people sometimes say **Gordon Bennett!** when they are annoyed or surprised about sth （表示惱怒或驚訝）天哪，哎呀 ORIGIN From James Gordon Bennett, an American newspaper owner and financial supporter of sports events. 源自美國報業老闆和體育比賽贊助人詹姆斯•戈登•貝內特（James Gordon Bennett）。

gore /ɡɔː(r)/ *verb, noun*
■ ***verb* ~ sb/sth** (of an animal 動物) to wound a person or another animal with a horn or TUSK （用角或長牙）頂傷，戳傷：*He was gored by a bull.* 他被公牛頂傷。
■ ***noun*** [U] thick blood that has flowed from a wound, especially in a violent situation （尤指在暴力情況下）傷口流出的血，凝固的血：*The movie is not just **blood and gore*** (= scenes of violence)*; it has a thrilling story.* 這部影片不光是血淋淋的暴力場面，還有扣人心弦的情節。➲ see also GORY

Gore·tex™ /ˈɡɔːteks; *NAmE* ˈɡɔːrt-/ *noun* [U] a light material that does not let water through but that allows air and water VAPOUR through, used for making outdoor and sports clothes 戈特克斯防水透氣布料（用於製作戶外和運動服裝）

gorge /ɡɔːdʒ; *NAmE* ɡɔːrdʒ/ *noun, verb*
■ ***noun*** a deep narrow valley with steep sides 峽；峽谷 SYN **canyon**：*the Rhine Gorge* 萊茵峽谷 ➲ VISUAL VOCAB page V4, V5
IDM **sb's 'gorge rises** (*formal*) somebody feels so angry about sth that they feel physically sick 感到煩心（或厭惡）；作嘔
■ ***verb*** [T, I] **~ (yourself) (on sth)** (sometimes *disapproving*) to eat a lot of sth, until you are too full to eat any more 貪婪地吃；狼吞虎嚥 SYN **stuff yourself**

gor·geous /ˈɡɔːdʒəs; *NAmE* ˈɡɔːrdʒəs/ *adj.* **1** (*informal*) very beautiful and attractive; giving pleasure and enjoyment 非常漂亮的；美麗動人的；令人愉快的 SYN **lovely**：*a gorgeous girl/man* 漂亮的女郎；美男子 ◇ *a gorgeous view* 美麗的景色 ◇ *gorgeous weather* (= warm and with a lot of sun) 宜人的天氣 ◇ *You **look gorgeous**!* 你真漂亮！◇ *It was **absolutely gorgeous**.* 那真是美麗絕倫。➲ SYNONYMS at BEAUTIFUL **2** [usually before noun] (of colours, clothes, etc. 顏色、衣服等) with very deep colours; impressive 絢麗的；燦爛的；華麗的：*exotic birds with feathers of gorgeous colours* 長着絢麗羽毛的異國的鳥 ▸ **gor·geous·ly** *adv.*

G

gor·gon /ˈɡɔːɡən; NAmE ˈɡɔːrɡən/ *noun* **1** (in ancient Greek stories) one of three sisters with snakes on their heads instead of hair, who can change anyone that looks at them into stone 戈耳工蛇髮女怪（古希臘神話中三個蛇髮女怪之一，人見之即化為石頭） **2** an ugly woman who behaves in an aggressive and frightening way 醜陋兇惡的女人

Gor·gon·zola /ˌɡɔːɡənˈzəʊlə; NAmE ˌɡɔːrɡənˈzoʊlə/ *noun* [U] a type of Italian cheese with blue marks and a strong flavour 戈爾貢佐拉乾酪（意大利乾酪，味濃，有藍紋）

gor·illa /ɡəˈrɪlə/ *noun* **1** a very large powerful African APE (= an animal like a large MONKEY without a tail) covered with black or brown hair 大猩猩（產於非洲） **2** (*informal*) a large aggressive man 高大兇惡的人

G

gorm·less /ˈɡɔːmləs; NAmE ˈɡɔːrm-/ *adj.* (*BrE, informal*) stupid 愚蠢的；傻的；沒頭沒腦的：*a gormless boy* 呆小子 ◇ *Don't just stand there looking gormless—do something!* 別只是傻乎乎地站在那兒，幹點事吧！

ˈgo-round *noun* = GO-AROUND

gorp /ɡɔːp; NAmE ɡɔːrp/ *noun* [U] (*NAmE*) a mixture of nuts, dried fruit, etc. eaten between meals to provide extra energy, especially by people on camping trips, etc. 什錦乾果果仁

gorse /ɡɔːs; NAmE ɡɔːrs/ (*BrE* also **furze**) *noun* [U] a bush with thin leaves with sharp points and small yellow flowers. Gorse often grows on land that is not used or cared for. 荊豆（開小黃花，長於荒野）

gory /ˈɡɔːri/ *adj.* (**gor·ier**, **gori·est**) **1** (*informal*) involving a lot of blood or violence; showing or describing blood and violence 血淋淋的；殘暴的；描述流血和暴力的：*a gory accident* 流血事件 ◇ *the gory task of the pathologist* 病理學家經常接觸血的工作 ◇ *a gory movie* 充滿流血和暴力鏡頭的電影 ◇ (*humorous*) *He insisted on telling us all the* ***gory details*** *about their divorce* (= the unpleasant facts). 他堅持要給我們講他們離婚的種種慘痛經歷。 **2** (*literary*) covered with blood 沾滿血污的；血跡斑斑的 SYN **bloodstained**：*a gory figure* 血跡斑斑的人

gosh /ɡɒʃ; NAmE ɡɑːʃ/ *exclamation* (*old-fashioned, informal*) people say **'Gosh!'** when they are surprised or shocked （驚奇或驚訝時說）天哪，啊呀：*Gosh, is that the time?* 啊呀，都這會兒啦？

gos·hawk /ˈɡɒshɔːk; NAmE ˈɡɑːs-/ *noun* a large HAWK with short wings 蒼鷹

gos·ling /ˈɡɒzlɪŋ; NAmE ˈɡɑːz-/ *noun* a young GOOSE (= a bird like a large DUCK) 小鵝；幼鵝

ˌgo-ˈslow (*BrE*) (*NAmE* **slow·down**) *noun* a protest that workers make by doing their work more slowly than usual 怠工 ➲ compare WORK-TO-RULE

gos·pel /ˈɡɒspl; NAmE ˈɡɑːspl/ *noun* **1** [C] (also **Gospel**) one of the four books in the Bible about the life and teaching of Jesus 福音（《聖經》中關於耶穌生平和教誨的四福音書之一）：*the Gospel according to St John* 約翰福音 ◇ *St Mark's Gospel* 《馬可福音》 **2** [sing.] (also **the Gospel**) the life and teaching of Jesus as explained in the Bible 福音（耶穌的事跡和教誨）：***preaching/spreading the gospel*** 宣講／傳佈福音 ➲ COLLOCATIONS at RELIGION **3** [C, usually sing.] a set of ideas that sb believes in and tries to persuade others to accept （個人的）信念，信仰：*He preached a gospel of military strength.* 他鼓吹軍事實力主義。 **4** (also **ˌgospel ˈtruth**) [U] (*informal*) the complete truth 絕對真理：*Is that gospel?* 那是絕對真理嗎？◇ *Don't take his word as gospel.* 別把他的話當作絕對真理。 **5** (also **ˈgospel music**) [U] a style of religious singing developed by African Americans 福音音樂（最初在非洲裔美國人中間傳唱的宗教音樂）：*a gospel choir* 福音唱詩班

gos·samer /ˈɡɒsəmə(r); NAmE ˈɡɑːs-/ *noun* [U] **1** the very fine thread made by spiders 蛛絲 **2** (*literary*) any very light delicate material 薄紗；精細織物：*a gown of gossamer silk* 絲綢女裙服 ◇ *the gossamer wings of a dragonfly* 薄如輕紗的蜻蜓翅膀

gos·sip /ˈɡɒsɪp; NAmE ˈɡɑːsɪp/ *noun, verb*

■ ***noun*** **1** [U] (*disapproving*) informal talk or stories about other people's private lives, that may be unkind or not true 流言蜚語；閒言碎語：*Don't believe all the gossip you hear.* 別對那些道聽途說都信以為真。◇ *Tell me all the* ***latest gossip!*** 把最新的小道消息都講給我聽聽吧！◇ *The gossip was that he had lost a fortune on the stock exchange.* 有小道消息說他在股票交易中賠了一大筆錢。◇ *It was* ***common gossip*** (= everyone said so) *that they were having an affair.* 大家議論紛紛說他們之間關係曖昧。◇ *She's a great one for* ***idle gossip*** (= she enjoys spreading stories about other people that are probably not true). 她是有名的長舌婦。 **2** [C, usually sing.] a conversation about other people and their private lives 張家長，李家短；閒聊：*I love a good gossip.* 我喜歡閒聊天。➲ SYNONYMS at DISCUSSION **3** [C] (*disapproving*) a person who enjoys talking about other people's private lives 喜歡傳播流言蜚語的人；愛說長道短（或說三道四）的人 ➲ SYNONYMS at SPEAKER ▸ **gos·sipy** /ˈɡɒsɪpi; NAmE ˈɡɑːs-/ *adj.*：*a gossipy letter/neighbour* 閒聊式的信；愛說三道四的鄰居

■ ***verb*** [I] to talk about other people's private lives, often in an unkind way 傳播流言蜚語；說三道四；說長道短：*I can't stand here gossiping all day.* 我不能整天站在這兒閒聊啊。◇ **~ about sb/sth** *She's been gossiping about you.* 她一直在說你的閒話。

ˈgossip column *noun* a piece of writing in a newspaper about social events and the private and personal lives of famous people 漫談欄，茶話欄（報刊有關社交活動和名人私生活的專欄） ▸ **ˈgossip columnist** *noun*

got *past tense, past part.* of GET

gotcha /ˈɡɒtʃə; NAmE ˈɡɑːtʃə/ *exclamation* (*non-standard*) the written form of the way some people pronounce 'I've got you', which is not considered to be correct （對 I've got you 發音的書寫形式，此用法被視為不正確）：*'Gotcha!' I yelled as I grabbed him by the arm.* (= used when you have caught sb, or have beaten them at sth). "逮住你了！"我抓住他的胳膊大聲喊道。◇ *'Don't let go.' 'Yeah, gotcha.'* (= Yes, I understand.) "別鬆手。""是，我明白。" HELP You should not write this form unless you are copying somebody's speech. 這種寫法只用於引述別人的話。

goth /ɡɒθ; NAmE ɡɑːθ/ *noun* **1** [U] a style of rock music, popular in the 1980s, that developed from PUNK music. The words often expressed ideas about the end of the world, death or the DEVIL. 哥特搖滾樂（由朋客搖滾樂發展而來，流行於 20 世紀 80 年代，歌詞通常涉及世界末日、死亡或魔鬼） **2** [C] a member of a group of people who listen to goth music and wear black clothes and black and white MAKE-UP 哥特派中的一員（聽哥特搖滾樂、穿黑色衣服和黑白裝扮） ▸ **goth** (also **gothic**) *adj.*

Gotham /ˈɡɒθəm; NAmE ˈɡɑːθ-/ *noun* (*informal*) New York City 傻子村（紐約市的綽號）

Goth·ic /ˈɡɒθɪk; NAmE ˈɡɑːθ-/ *adj., noun*

■ ***adj.*** **1** connected with the Goths (= a Germanic people who fought against the Roman Empire) 哥特人的，哥特族的，哥特語的（指反對羅馬帝國的一支日耳曼民族） **2** (*architecture* 建) built in the style that was popular in western Europe from the 12th to the 16th centuries, and which has pointed ARCHES and windows and tall thin PILLARS 哥特式的，哥特風格的（12 至 16 世紀流行於西歐的建築風格，以尖拱、尖窗和細長柱為特色）：*a Gothic church* 哥特式教堂 **3** (of a novel, etc. 小說等) written in the style popular in the 18th and 19th centuries, which described romantic adventures in mysterious or frightening surroundings 哥特派的，哥特風格的（流行於 18 至 19 世紀，描述神秘或恐怖氣氛中的愛情故事） **4** (of type and printing 字體和印刷字體) having pointed letters with thick lines and sharp angles. German books used to be printed in this style. 哥特體黑體字的（舊時德語書籍常用） **5** connected with goths 哥特派的

■ ***noun*** [U] **1** the Gothic style of ARCHITECTURE 哥特式建築；尖拱式建築 **2** Gothic printing type or printed letters 哥特體黑體字

ˈgo-to *adj.* [only before noun] (*especially NAmE*) used to refer to the person or place that sb goes to for help, advice or information（指對象）尋求協助的，徵詢意見的：*He's the president's go-to guy on Asian politics.* 他是總統的亞洲政治智囊。

gotta /ˈɡɒtə; NAmE ˈɡɑːtə/ (*informal, non-standard*) the written form of the word some people use to mean 'have got to' or 'have got a', which is not considered to be correct（有人用作 have got to 和 have got a 的書寫形式，此用法被視為不正確）：*He's gotta go.* 他得走了。◇ *Gotta cigarette?* 有煙嗎？ **HELP** You should not write this form unless you are copying somebody's speech. 只用於記錄講話。

got·ten (*NAmE*) *past part.* of GET

gou·ache /ɡuˈɑːʃ; ɡwɑːʃ/ *noun* **1** [U] a method of painting using colours that are mixed with water and made thick with a type of glue; the paints used in this method 廣告色畫法；廣告色畫顏料 **2** [C] a picture painted using this method 廣告色畫

Gouda /ˈɡaʊdə; NAmE ˈɡuːdə/ *noun* [U] a type of Dutch cheese that is covered with yellow WAX 豪達奶酪（荷蘭奶酪，外塗黃色石蠟）

gouge /ɡaʊdʒ/ *verb, noun*

■ *verb* **1 ~ sth (in sth)** to make a hole or cut in sth with a sharp object in a rough or violent way 鑿：*The lion's claws had gouged a wound in the horse's side.* 獅爪在馬身一側抓了一道深口。◇ *He had gouged her cheek with a screwdriver.* 他用螺絲起子戳她的臉頰。**2 ~ sb/sth** (*NAmE*) to force sb to pay an unfairly high price for sth; to raise prices unfairly 敲（某人）的竹槓；詐騙錢財；漫天要價：*Price gouging is widespread.* 漫天要價的情況普遍存在。

PHR V **ˌgouge sth↔ˈout (of sth)** to remove or form sth by digging into a surface 摳出某物；挖出某物：*The man's eyes had been gouged out.* 這男人的雙眼已被挖了出來。◇ *Glaciers gouged out valleys from the hills.* 冰川把丘陵地帶沖出一條條山谷。

■ *noun* **1** a sharp tool for making hollow areas in wood 鑿子 **2** a deep, narrow hole or cut in a surface 鑿成的槽（或孔、洞）

gou·jons /ˈɡuːdʒənz; ˈɡuːʒ-/ *noun* [pl.] (*BrE*, from *French*) small pieces of fish or chicken fried in oil 油炸魚丁（或雞丁）

gou·lash /ˈɡuːlæʃ/ *noun* [C, U] a hot spicy Hungarian dish of meat that is cooked slowly in liquid with PAPRIKA 匈牙利紅燴牛肉；匈牙利的辣椒燉肉；菜燉牛肉

gourd /ɡʊəd; ɡɔːd; NAmE ɡʊrd; ɡɔːrd/ *noun* a type of large fruit with hard skin and soft flesh. Gourds are often dried and used as containers. 葫蘆科植物，葫蘆（晾乾後常作容器）➲ see also CALABASH (1)

gour·mand /ˈɡʊəmənd; NAmE ˈɡʊrmɑːnd/ *noun* (*often disapproving*) a person who enjoys eating and eats large amounts of food 大肚子；大肚漢；喜歡吃喝的人

gour·met /ˈɡʊəmeɪ; NAmE ˈɡʊrm-/ *noun* a person who knows a lot about good food and wines and who enjoys choosing, eating and drinking them 美食家；講究飲食的人；美酒美食品嚐家 ▸ **gour·met** *adj.* [only before noun]：*gourmet food* (= of high quality and often expensive) 美味佳肴

gout /ɡaʊt/ *noun* [U] a disease that causes painful swelling in the joints, especially of the toes, knees and fingers 痛風（病）

gov·ern 0‒ /ˈɡʌvn; NAmE ˈɡʌvərn/ *verb*

1 0‒ [T, I] **~ (sth)** to legally control a country or its people and be responsible for introducing new laws, organizing public services, etc. 統治；控制；管理；治理：*The country is governed by elected representatives of the people.* 這個國家由民選代表統治。◇ *He accused the opposition party of being unfit to govern.* 他指責反對黨無力治理國事。 **2** [T, often passive] **~ sth** to control or influence sb/sth or how sth happens, functions, etc. 控制；影響；支配：*Prices are governed by market demand.* 價格的高低取決於市場的需求。◇ *All his decisions have been entirely governed by self-interest.* 他的所有決定都受利己之心的支配。◇ *We need changes in the law governing school attendance.* 我們需要對影響就學率的法規做些改動。 **3** [T] **~ sth** (*grammar* 語法) if a word **governs** another word or phrase, it affects how that word or phrase is formed or used 支配（詞或短語的形式或用法）

gov·ern·ance /ˈɡʌvənəns; NAmE -vərn-/ *noun* [U] (*technical* 術語) the activity of governing a country or controlling a company or an organization; the way in which a country is governed or a company or institution is controlled 統治；管理；治理；統治方式；管理方法

gov·ern·ess /ˈɡʌvənəs; NAmE -vərn-/ *noun* (especially in the past), a woman employed to teach the children of a rich family in their home and to live with them（尤指舊時的）家庭女教師 ➲ compare TUTOR

gov·ern·ing /ˈɡʌvənɪŋ; NAmE -vərn-/ *adj.* [only before noun] having the right and the authority to control sth such as a country or an institution 統治的；控制的；管理的；治理的：*The Conservatives were then the **governing party**.* 那時是保守黨當政。◇ *The school's **governing body*** (= the group of people who control the organization of the school) *took responsibility for the decision.* 學校行政機構對這個決定負責。

gov·ern·ment 0‒ /ˈɡʌvənmənt; NAmE -vərn-/ *noun*

1 0‒ [C+sing./pl. v.] (often **the Government**) (*abbr.* **govt**) the group of people who are responsible for controlling a country or a state 政府；內閣：*to **lead/form a government*** 領導政府；組成內閣 ◇ *the last Conservative government* 上屆保守黨政府 ◇ *the government of the day* 當時的政府 ◇ *Foreign governments have been consulted about this decision.* 這一決定曾徵求過他國政府的意見。◇ *She has resigned from the Government.* 她已辭去內閣職位。◇ *The Government has/have been considering further tax cuts.* 政府一直在考慮進一步減稅的問題。◇ ***government policies/officials/ministers*** 政府政策；內閣官員／部長 ◇ *a **government department/agency/grant*** 政府部門／機構／撥款 ◇ ***government expenditure/intervention*** 政府開支／干預 ➲ COLLOCATIONS at POLITICS **2** 0‒ [U] a particular system or method of controlling a country 政體；國家體制：***coalition/communist/democratic/totalitarian, etc.** government* 聯合、共產主義、民主、極權主義等政體 ◇ *Democratic government has now replaced military rule.* 民主政體現已取代軍事統治。◇ ***central/federal government*** 中央／聯邦政府 **3** 0‒ [U] the activity or the manner of controlling a country（一國的）統治，治理，統治方式，管理方法：*strong government* 強有力的統治 ◇ *The Democrats are now **in government** in the US.* 美國目前是民主黨人執政。➲ see also BIG GOVERNMENT

gov·ern·men·tal /ˌɡʌvnˈmentl; NAmE ˌɡʌvərn-/ *adj.* connected with government; of a government 統治的；政體的；政府的：*governmental agencies* 政府機構 ◇ *governmental actions* 政府行動

ˌgovernment and ˈbinding theory (also **ˈbinding theory**) *noun* [U] (*linguistics* 語言) a theory of grammar based on the idea that a series of conditions relate the parts of a sentence together 支配約束理論，管約理論，管轄約束理論（即基於一系列條件連接起句子各部份的理念的語法理論）

ˌgovernment ˈhealth warning *noun* **1** (in Britain) a notice that must by law appear on a product, especially a pack of cigarettes, that warns people that it is dangerous to their health（在英國於香煙等產品上的）政府健康忠告 **2** (also **ˈhealth warning**) (*BrE*) a warning that sth should be treated carefully because it may cause problems 需謹慎對待的警告：*These figures should come with a government health warning.* 這些數字該附以謹慎對待的警告。

gov·ern·or 0‒ /ˈɡʌvənə(r); NAmE -vərn-/ *noun*

1 0‒ (also **Governor**) a person who is the official head of a country or region that is governed by another country 統治者；管轄者；總督：*the former governor of the colony* 該殖民地的前總督 ◇ *a provincial governor* 省長 **2** 0‒ (also **Governor**) a person who is chosen to be in charge of the government of a state in the US（美國的）州長：*the governor of Arizona* 亞利桑那州州長 ◇ *the Arizona governor* 亞利桑那州州長 ◇ *Governor Bev Perdue*

G

貝福・普爾杜州長 **3** (*especially BrE*) a member of a group of people who are responsible for controlling an institution such as a school, a college or a hospital（學校、學院、醫院等機構的）董事，理事：*a school governor* 學校董事 ◇ *the board of governors of the college* 學院董事會 **4** (*BrE*) a person who is in charge of an institution 主管；機構負責人；總裁：*a prison governor* 監獄長 ◇ *the governor of the Bank of England* 英格蘭銀行總裁 ◇ (*informal*) *I can't decide. I'll have to ask the governor* (= the man in charge, who employs sb). 我做不了主，我得問問老闆。➲ see also GUV'NOR

ˌGovernor ˈGeneral *noun* (*pl.* **Governors General** or **Governor Generals**) the official representative in a country of the country that has or had political control over it, especially the representative of the British King or Queen in a Commonwealth country 總督（派駐政治統轄國的官方代表，尤指英國國王或女王派駐英聯邦國家的代表）

G

govt (also **govt.** especially in *NAmE*) *abbr.* (in writing) government（書寫形式）政府

ˌgo ˈwell *exclamation* (*SAfrE*) used to say goodbye to sb 再見；再會：*I hope you enjoy your holiday. Go well!* 祝你假期玩得愉快。再見！

gown /ɡaʊn/ *noun* **1** a woman's dress, especially a long one for special occasions（尤指特別場合穿的）女裙，女長服，女禮服：*an **evening/wedding gown*** 女晚禮服；新娘的結婚禮服 **2** a long loose piece of clothing that is worn over other clothes by judges and (in Britain) by other lawyers, and by members of universities (at special ceremonies)（法官、英國律師、大學學生在特別儀式上穿的）長袍，長外衣：*a graduation gown* 畢業禮服 **3** a piece of clothing that is worn over other clothes to protect them, especially in a hospital（尤指在醫院穿的）罩衣，外罩：*a surgeon's gown* 外科醫生穿的罩衣 ➲ see also DRESSING GOWN

gowned /ɡaʊnd/ *adj.* wearing a gown 穿着長袍（或長服、禮服）的

goy /ɡɔɪ/ *noun* (*pl.* **goy·im** /ˈɡɔɪɪm/ or **goys**) (*informal*, often *offensive*) a word used by Jewish people for a person who is not Jewish（猶太人用語，含冒犯意）非猶太人，外邦人

GP /ˌdʒiː ˈpiː/ *noun* (*BrE*) the abbreviation for 'general practitioner' (a doctor who is trained in general medicine and who works in the local community, not in a hospital) 全科醫生，普通醫師（全寫為 general practitioner，在社區而非在醫院工作）：*Go and see your GP as soon as possible.* 儘早去看你的全科醫生。◇ *There are four GPs in our local practice.* 在我們地區診所有四個全科醫生。

GPA /ˌdʒiː piː ˈeɪ/ *abbr.* (*NAmE*) GRADE POINT AVERAGE：*He graduated with a GPA of 3.8.* 他畢業時各科成績的平均積分點為 3.8。

Gp Capt *abbr.* GROUP CAPTAIN

GPRS /ˌdʒiː piː ɑːr ˈes/ *abbr.* general packet radio services (a way of sending electronic data as radio signals, used especially between mobile phones/cell phones and the Internet) 通用分組無線業務；通用封包無線服務

GPS /ˌdʒiː piː ˈes/ *abbr.* global positioning system (a system by which signals are sent from SATELLITES to a special device, used to show the position of a person or thing on the surface of the earth very accurately) 全球（衛星）定位系統：*The drivers all have GPS in the van.* 這些司機的廂式貨車裏都裝有全球定位系統。➲ compare SATNAV

grab /ɡræb/ *verb, noun*

■ *verb* (-bb-) **1** [T, I] to take or hold sb/sth with your hand suddenly, firmly or roughly 抓住；攫取 SYN **seize**：~ (sth) *She grabbed the child's hand and ran.* 她抓住孩子的手就跑。◇ *He **grabbed hold of** me and wouldn't let go.* 他抓住我不鬆手。◇ *Don't grab—there's plenty for everyone.* 別搶，多着呢，人人都有。◇ **~ sth from sb/sth** *Jim grabbed a cake from the plate.* 吉姆從盤子裏抓了一塊蛋糕。 **2** [I] to try to take hold of sth（試圖）抓住，奪得：**~ at sth** *She grabbed at the branch, missed and fell.* 她抓樹枝，可沒抓着，就跌倒了。◇ **~ for sth** *Kate grabbed for the robber's gun.* 凱特拚命去奪搶劫者的槍。 **3** [T, I] to take advantage of an opportunity to do or have sth 利用，抓住（機會）SYN **seize**：**~ sth** *This was my big chance and I grabbed it with both hands.* 這是我的大好機會，我緊緊抓住。◇ **~ at sth** *He'll grab at any excuse to avoid doing the dishes.* 他會隨便找個藉口來逃避洗碗。 **4** [T] **~ sth** to have or take sth quickly, especially because you are in a hurry（尤指匆忙地）取，拿，吃，喝：*Let's grab a sandwich before we go.* 咱們趕快吃個三明治就走吧。◇ *I managed to grab a couple of hours' sleep on the plane.* 我在飛機上抓緊時間睡了幾個鐘頭。◇ ***Grab a seat**, I won't keep you a moment.* 趕緊找個座位吧，我不耽誤你的工夫了。 **5** [T] **~ sth** to take sth for yourself, especially in a selfish or GREEDY way（尤指自私、貪婪地）撈取，賺取，搶佔：*By the time we arrived, someone had grabbed all the good seats.* 我們到達時，所有的好位子都給人佔了。 **6** [T] **~ sb/sth** to get sb's attention 引人注意；吸引：*I'll see if I can grab the waitress and get the bill.* 我要看能不能引起服務員的注意，讓她拿賬單來。◇ *Glasgow's drugs problem has **grabbed the headlines tonight*** (= been published as an important story in the newspapers). 格拉斯哥的毒品問題成了今晚報紙的頭條新聞。

IDM **how does ... grab you?** (*informal*) used to ask sb whether they are interested in sth or in doing sth 你對…有興趣嗎；你喜歡…嗎；你認為…如何：*How does the idea of a trip to Rome grab you?* 你認為去趟羅馬這個主意如何？

■ *noun* **1** [usually sing.] **~ (at/for sb/sth)** a sudden attempt to take or hold sb/sth 猛然的抓取；突然的搶奪：*He **made a grab for** her bag.* 他突然去搶她的手提包。➲ see also SMASH-AND-GRAB **2** (*computing* 計) a picture taken from a television or video film, stored as an image on a computer 抓取（或截獲、採集）的圖像：*a screen grab from Wednesday's programme* 從星期三的節目中抓取的熒屏圖像 **3** a piece of equipment which lifts and holds goods, for example the equipment that hangs from a CRANE 抓具；抓斗

IDM **up for ˈgrabs** (*informal*) available for anyone who is interested 提供的；可供爭奪的：*There are £25 000 worth of prizes up for grabs in our competition!* 在我們的比賽中有價值 25 000 英鎊的獎品供人爭奪！

ˈgrab bag *noun* (*NAmE*) **1** (*BrE* **ˌlucky ˈdip**) a game in which people choose a present from a container of presents without being able to see what it is going to be 摸彩遊戲 **2** (*informal*) a mixed collection of things（各種事物的）混雜，聚合：*He offered a grab bag of reasons for his decision.* 他為自己所作的決定提出了各種理由。

grace /ɡreɪs/ *noun, verb*

■ *noun*

▸ OF MOVEMENT 動作 **1** [U] an attractive quality of movement that is smooth, elegant and controlled 優美；優雅：*She moves with the natural grace of a ballerina.* 她的動作具有芭蕾舞演員自然優雅的丰姿。

▸ BEHAVIOUR 行為 **2** [U] a quality of behaviour that is polite and pleasant and deserves respect 文雅；高雅：*He conducted himself with grace and dignity throughout the trial.* 在整個審訊過程中他表現得文雅而有尊嚴。 **3 graces** [pl.] (*especially BrE*) ways of behaving that people think are polite and acceptable 風度；體面：*He was not particularly well versed in the **social graces**.* 他對社交禮節並不特別熟悉。

▸ EXTRA TIME 額外時間 **4** [U] extra time that is given to sb to enable them to pay a bill, finish a piece of work, etc. 寬限期；延緩期：*They've given me a month's grace to get the money.* 他們寬限我一個月弄到這筆錢。

▸ OF GOD 上帝 **5** [U] the kindness that God shows towards the human race 恩寵；恩典：*It was only by the grace of God that they survived.* 承蒙天恩，他們才幸免於難。➲ COLLOCATIONS at RELIGION

▸ PRAYER 祈禱 **6** [U, C] a short prayer that is usually said before a meal to thank God for the food（飯前的）謝恩祈禱：*Let's **say grace**.* 我們做飯前禱告吧。

▸ TITLE 稱呼 **7 His/Her/Your Grace** [C] used as a title of respect when talking to or about an ARCHBISHOP, a DUKE or a DUCHESS（對大主教、公爵、公爵夫人、女

公爵的尊稱）大人，閣下，夫人：*Good Morning, Your Grace.* 早上好，閣下。◇ *Their Graces the Duke and Duchess of Kent.* 肯特公爵及公爵夫人閣下。➲ see also COUP DE GRÂCE, SAVING GRACE

IDM **be in sb's good 'graces** (*formal*) to have sb's approval and be liked by them 為某人所贊同（或喜愛）；得到某人的歡心 **,fall from 'grace** to lose the trust or respect that people have for you, especially by doing sth wrong or immoral（尤指因做了錯事或不道德之事而）失去信任，失去尊重，失去恩寵 **sb's ,fall from 'grace** a situation in which sb loses the trust or respect that people have for them, especially because of sth wrong or immoral that they have done（尤指因做了錯事或不道德之事的）失信 **have the (good) grace to do sth** to be polite enough to do sth, especially when you have done sth wrong（尤指犯錯後）知趣地做某事，通情達理地做某事：*He didn't even have the grace to look embarrassed.* 他甚至連一絲尷尬的神色都沒有。 **there but for the grace of 'God (go 'I)** (*saying*) used to say that you could easily have been in the same difficult or unpleasant situation that sb else is in 若非天助，區區豈能幸免 **with (a) bad 'grace** in an unwilling and/or rude way 勉強地；不情願地；無禮地：*He handed over the money with typical bad grace.* 他照常不情願地把錢交出來。 **with (a) good 'grace** in a willing and pleasant way 心甘情願地；樂意地；高高興興地：*You must learn to accept defeat with good grace.* 你必須學會欣然承認失敗。➲ more at AIR *n.*, STATE *n.*, YEAR

■ ***verb*** (*formal*) **1 ~ sth** to make sth more attractive; to decorate sth 為…增色；為…錦上添花；裝飾：*The table had once graced a duke's drawing room.* 這張桌子曾一度為公爵的起居室增色不少。 **2** (usually *ironic*) to bring honour to sb/sth; to be kind enough to attend or take part in sth 使榮耀；使生輝；承蒙光臨：**~ sb/sth** *She is one of the finest players ever to have graced the game.* 她是曾使這場比賽生輝的最傑出的運動員之一。◇ **~ sb/sth with sth** *Will you be* ***gracing*** *us* ***with your presence*** *tonight?* 請問您今晚能否賞光？

,grace and 'favour *adj.* [only before noun] (*BrE*) used to describe a house or flat/apartment that a king, queen or government has allowed sb to use（房屋或公寓）君主（或政府當局）准予使用的，欽賜的

grace·ful /ˈɡreɪsfl/ *adj.* **1** moving in a controlled, attractive way or having a smooth, attractive form 優美的；優雅的；雅致的：*The dancers were all tall and graceful.* 這些舞蹈演員都個子高高的，動作十分優雅。◇ *He gave a graceful bow to the audience.* 他優雅地向觀眾鞠了一躬。◇ *the graceful curves of the hills* 連綿起伏的丘陵美景 **2** polite and kind in your behaviour, especially in a difficult situation（尤指在困境中）得體的，有風度的：*His father had always taught him to be graceful in defeat.* 他父親總是教導他輸了也要有風度。▸ **grace·ful·ly** /-fəli/ *adv.*：*The cathedral's white towers climb gracefully into the sky.* 大教堂白色的塔樓優雅莊重地聳入雲霄。◇ *I think we should just* ***give in gracefully.*** 我認為我們應該大大方方地認輸。 **grace·ful·ness** *noun* [U]

grace·less /ˈɡreɪsləs/ *adj.* **1** not knowing how to be polite and pleasant to other people 不懂禮貌的；粗魯的；無禮的：*a graceless, angry young man* 粗魯、憤怒的年輕人 **2** not pleasing or attractive to look at 不優美的；不雅致的；難看的：*the graceless architecture of the 1960s* * 20 世紀 60 年代的醜陋建築 **3** moving in an awkward way 笨拙的：*She swam with a graceless stroke.* 她游泳的姿勢很難看。 **OPP** graceful ▸ **grace·less·ly** *adv.*

'grace note *noun* (*music* 音) an extra note which is not a necessary part of a tune, but which is played before one of the notes of the tune as decoration 裝飾音

gra·cious /ˈɡreɪʃəs/ *adj.* **1** (of people or behaviour 人或行為) kind, polite and generous, especially to sb of a lower social position（尤指對社會地位較低者）和藹的，慈祥的，有禮貌的，寬厚的：*a gracious lady* 好心的女士 ◇ *a gracious smile* 慈祥的微笑 ◇ *He has not yet learned how to be gracious in defeat.* 他還沒有學會怎樣豁達大度地面對失敗。 **2** [usually before noun] showing the comfort and easy way of life that wealth can bring 富貴安逸的：*gracious living* 豪華安逸的生活 **3** [only before noun] (*BrE, formal*) used as a very polite word for royal people or their actions（對王族及其行為的敬語）仁慈的，寬厚的：*her gracious Majesty the Queen* 仁慈的女王陛下 **4 ~ (to sb)** (of God 上帝) showing kindness and MERCY 仁慈的；慈悲的；寬大的：*a gracious act of God* 上帝的慈悲 **5** (becoming *old-fashioned*) used for expressing surprise（表示驚異）天哪，老天爺，啊呀：*Goodness gracious!* 老天爺啊！◇ *'I hope you didn't mind my phoning you.' 'Good gracious, no, of course not.'* "我希望你不會介意我給你打電話。" "啊呀，當然不會。" ▸ **gra·cious·ly** *adv.*：*She graciously accepted our invitation.* 她落落大方地接受了我們的邀請。 **gra·cious·ness** *noun* [U]

grad /ɡræd/ *noun* (*informal, especially NAmE*) = GRADUATE

grad·able /ˈɡreɪdəbl/ *adj.* (*grammar* 語法) (of an adjective 形容詞) that can be used in the comparative and superlative forms or be used with words like 'very' and 'less' 可分級的；可分程度的 **OPP** **non-gradable** ▸ **grad·abil·ity** /ˌɡreɪdəˈbɪləti/ *noun* [U]

grad·ation /ɡrəˈdeɪʃn/ *noun* **1** [C, U] (*formal*) any of the small changes or levels which sth is divided into; the process or result of sth changing gradually 逐漸的變化；層次；階段；等級：*gradations of colour* 各種層次的顏色 ◇ *gradation in size* 大小等級 **2** (also **gradu·ation**) [C] a mark showing a division on a scale 刻度：*the gradations on a thermometer* 溫度計上的刻度

G

grade 🔑 **AW** /ɡreɪd/ *noun, verb*

■ ***noun*** **1** 🔑 the quality of a particular product or material（產品、材料的）等級，品級：*All the materials used were of the highest grade.* 使用的材料全是優質品。 **2** 🔑 a level of ability or rank that sb has in an organization（官銜的）級別；職別：*salary grades* (= levels of pay) 工資級別 ◇ *She's still only on a secretarial grade.* 她的職別仍然只是秘書。 **3** 🔑 a mark given in an exam or for a piece of school work 成績等級；評分等級：(*BrE*) *She got good grades in her exams.* 她考試成績優良。◇ (*NAmE*) *She got good grades on her exams.* 她考試成績優良。◇ *70% of pupils got Grade C or above.* * 70% 的小學生成績都在 C 級或以上。 **4** 🔑 (in the US school system) one of the levels in a school with children of similar age（美國學制）年級：*Sam is in (the) second grade.* 薩姆讀二年級。 **5** (*technical* 術語) how serious an illness is（疾病的）程度，階段：***low/high grade*** *fever* 低燒；高燒 **6** (*especially NAmE*) = GRADIENT (1) **7** (*BrE*) a level of exam in musical skill（音樂考試的）級別，水平

IDM **make the 'grade** (*informal*) to reach the necessary standard; to succeed 達到必要標準；符合要求；成功：*About 10% of trainees fail to make the grade.* 接受培訓的人大約有 10% 未達標。

■ ***verb*** **1** 🔑 [often passive] to arrange people or things in groups according to their ability, quality, size, etc.（按能力、質量、大小等）分級，分等，分類：**~ sth/sb (by/according to sth)** *The containers are graded according to size.* 這些容器按大小分類。◇ **~ sth/sb from … to …** *Eggs are graded from small to extra large.* 雞蛋從小號到特大號分成不同等級。◇ *Responses were graded from 1 (very satisfied) to 5 (not at all satisfied).* 回答按 1（非常滿意）到 5（完全不滿意）分類。◇ **~ sth (as) sth** *Ten beaches were graded as acceptable.* 有十個沙灘屬於可接受的那一類。 **2** 🔑 (*especially NAmE*) to give a mark/grade to a student or to a piece of their written work 給…評分；給…分數：**~ sb/sth** *I spent all weekend grading papers.* 我整個週末都在評閱試卷。◇ **~ sb/sth + noun** *The best students are graded A.* 最優秀的學生評為甲等。➲ compare MARK *v.* (6)

graded **AW** /ˈɡreɪdɪd/ *adj.* arranged in order or in groups according to difficulty, size, etc.（按難度、大小等）分級的：*graded tests for language students* 語言學習者的分級測驗 ◇ *graded doses of a drug* 藥物的分級劑量

'grade point average *noun* [usually sing.] (*abbr.* **GPA**) the average of a student's marks/grades over a period of time in the US education system（美國教育體制中學生在某一時期內的）各科成績的平均積分點

grader /ˈɡreɪdə(r)/ *noun* (*NAmE*) **1 first, second, etc. ~** a student who is in the grade mentioned …年級學生：

The play is open to all seventh and eighth graders. 所有七、八年級的學生均可觀看此劇。 **2** (*BrE* **mark·er**) a person who marks/grades students' work or exam papers 閱卷人；給作業打分的人

ˈgrade school *noun* (*informal*) = ELEMENTARY SCHOOL

gra·di·ent /ˈɡreɪdiənt/ *noun* **1** (also **grade** especially in *NAmE*) the degree to which the ground slopes, especially on a road or railway（尤指公路或鐵路的）坡度，斜率，傾斜度： *a steep gradient* 陡峭的坡度 ◇ *a hill with a gradient of 1 in 4 (or 25%)* 傾斜度為 1:4（或 25%）的小山 **2** (*technical* 術語) the rate at which temperature, pressure, etc. changes, or increases and decreases, between one region and another（溫度、壓力等的）變化率，梯度變化曲線

G

grad·ing /ˈɡreɪdɪŋ/ *noun* [U] (*NAmE*) = MARKING (3)

gra·dio·meter /ˌɡreɪdiˈɒmɪtə(r); *NAmE* -ˈɑːm-/ *noun* **1** (*technical* 術語) an instrument for measuring the angle of a slope 坡度測量儀 **2** (*physics* 物) an instrument for measuring the changes in an energy field 重力梯度儀

ˈgrad school *noun* (*NAmE, informal*) = GRADUATE SCHOOL

grad·ual 🔑 /ˈɡrædʒuəl/ *adj.*
1 🔑 happening slowly over a long period; not sudden 逐漸的；逐步的；漸進的： *a gradual change in the climate* 氣候的逐漸變化 ◇ *Recovery from the disease is very gradual.* 這種疾病的康復過程緩慢。 OPP **sudden**
2 (of a slope 斜坡) not steep 平緩的；不陡的

grad·ual·ism /ˈɡrædʒuəlɪzəm/ *noun* [U] a policy of gradual change in society rather than sudden change or revolution（社會改革上的）漸進主義，漸進主義政策 ▸ **grad·ual·ist** *noun*

grad·ual·ly 🔑 /ˈɡrædʒuəli/ *adv.*
slowly, over a long period of time 逐漸地；逐步地；漸進地： *The weather gradually improved.* 天氣逐漸好轉。 ◇ *Gradually, the children began to understand.* 孩子們漸漸開始明白。

gradu·ate *noun, verb*
■ *noun* /ˈɡrædʒuət/ (also *informal* **grad** especially in *NAmE*) **1 ~ (in sth)** a person who has a university degree 大學畢業生；學士學位獲得者： *a graduate in history* 歷史學學士 ◇ *a science graduate* 理學士 ◇ *a graduate of Yale/a Yale graduate* 耶魯大學畢業生 ◇ *a graduate student/course* 研究生；研究生課程 **2** (*NAmE*) a person who has completed their school studies 畢業生： *a high school graduate* 中學畢業生 ➲ SYNONYMS at STUDENT
■ *verb* /ˈɡrædʒueɪt/ **1** [I, T] to get a degree, especially your first degree, from a university or college 獲得學位（尤指學士）；大學畢業： **~ (in sth)** *Only three students graduated in Czech studies last year.* 去年只有三名學生獲得捷克研究學士學位。 ◇ **~ (from …)** *She graduated from Harvard this year.* 她今年畢業於哈佛大學。 ◇ *He graduated from York with a degree in Psychology.* 他畢業於約克大學，獲心理學學士學位。 ◇ **~ sth** (*NAmE*) *She graduated college last year.* 她去年大學畢業。 **2** [I, T] (*NAmE*) to complete a course in education, especially at HIGH SCHOOL 畢業（尤指中學）： **~ (from …)** *Martha graduated from high school two years ago.* 馬莎兩年前高中畢業。 ◇ **~ sth** *Martha graduated high school two years ago.* 馬莎兩年前高中畢業。 **3** [T] **~ sb (from sth)** (*NAmE*) to give a degree, DIPLOMA, etc. to sb 授予（某人）學位（或畢業文憑等）： *The college graduated 50 students last year.* 去年這所學院有 50 名畢業生。 **4** [I] **~ (from sth) to sth** to start doing sth more difficult or important than what you were doing before 逐漸發展（或變化、進展、上升）： *She recently graduated from being a dancer to having a small role in a movie.* 她最近從一個舞蹈演員逐步過渡到在電影裏扮演小角色。 ➲ COLLOCATIONS at EDUCATION

gradu·ated /ˈɡrædʒueɪtɪd/ *adj.* **1** divided into groups or levels on a scale 分等級的；分層次的： *graduated lessons/tests* 分級教程／測驗 **2** (of a container or measure 容器或量具) marked with lines to show measurements 標有刻度的 SYN **calibrated**： *a graduated jar* 標有刻度的廣口瓶

ˌGraduate ˌManagement Adˈmissions Test ➲ GMAT

ˈgraduate school (also *informal* **ˈgrad school**) (both *NAmE*) *noun* a part of a college or university where you can study for a second or further degree 研究生院；研究所

gradu·ation /ˌɡrædʒuˈeɪʃn/ *noun* **1** [U] the act of successfully completing a university degree, or studies at an American HIGH SCHOOL（大學或美國高中的）畢業： *It was my first job after graduation.* 那是我畢業後的第一個工作。 **2** [U, C] a ceremony at which degrees, etc. are officially given out 畢業典禮： *graduation day* 畢業典禮日 ◇ *My whole family came to my graduation.* 我的家人都來參加了我的畢業典禮。 **3** [C] = GRADATION (2)： *The graduations are marked on the side of the flask.* 燒瓶側面標有刻度。

Graeco- (*NAmE* usually **Greco-**) /ˈɡriːkəʊ-; *NAmE* -koʊ/ *combining form* (in adjectives 構成形容詞) Greek 希臘的；希臘人的；希臘語的

graf·fiti /ɡrəˈfiːti/ *noun* [U, pl.] drawings or writing on a wall, etc. in a public place（公共場所牆上等處的）塗鴉，胡寫亂畫： *The subway was covered in graffiti.* 過街地道裏塗滿了亂七八糟的圖畫和文字。

graft /ɡrɑːft; *NAmE* ɡræft/ *noun, verb*
■ *noun* **1** [C] a piece cut from a living plant and fixed in a cut made in another plant, so that it grows there; the process or result of doing this 接穗；嫁接 **2** [C] a piece of skin, bone, etc. removed from a living body and placed in another part of the body which has been damaged; the process or result of doing this 移植的皮膚（或骨骼等）；移植： *a skin graft* 皮移植片 **3** [U] (*BrE, informal*) hard work 艱苦的工作： *Their success was the result of years of* **hard graft**. 他們的成功是多年艱苦奮鬥的結果。 **4** [U] (*especially NAmE*) the use of illegal or unfair methods, especially BRIBERY, to gain advantage in business, politics, etc.; money obtained in this way 行賄；賄賂；受賄；贓款
■ *verb* **1** [T] **~ sth (onto/to/into sth)** | **~ sth (on) (from sth)** to take a piece of skin, bone, etc. from one part of the body and attach it to a damaged part 移植（皮膚、骨骼等）： *newly grafted tissue* 新移植的組織 ◇ *New skin had to be grafted on from his back.* 需從他的背部移植新皮膚。 **2** [T] **~ sth (onto sth)** to cut a piece from a living plant and attach it to another plant 嫁接 **3** [T] **~ sth (onto sth)** to make one idea, system, etc. become part of another one 使（思想、制度等）成為（…的一部份）；植根： *Old values are being grafted onto a new social class.* 舊的價值觀念正植根於新的社會階層。 **4** [I] (*BrE, informal*) to work hard 賣力地工作

graham cracker /ˈɡreɪəm krækə(r)/ *noun* (*NAmE*) a slightly sweet RECTANGULAR biscuit/cookie made with WHOLEMEAL flour（格雷厄姆）全麥粉餅乾

grail /ɡreɪl/ (also **the ˌHoly ˈGrail**) *noun* **1** [sing.] the cup or bowl believed to have been used by Jesus Christ before he died, that became a holy thing that people wanted to find 聖杯（據信為耶穌離世前所用） **2** [C] a thing that you try very hard to find or achieve, but never will 渴望但永遠得不到的東西；努力追求但永遠不可能實現的目標（或理想）

grain 🔑 /ɡreɪn/ *noun*
1 🔑 [U, C] the small hard seeds of food plants such as WHEAT, rice, etc.; a single seed of such a plant 穀物；穀粒： *America's grain exports* 美國的穀物出口 ◇ *a few grains of rice* 幾粒大米 ➲ see also WHOLEGRAIN ➲ VISUAL VOCAB page V32 **2** 🔑 [C] a small hard piece of particular substances 顆粒；細粒： *a* **grain of salt/sand/sugar** 一粒鹽／沙／砂糖 **3** [C] (used especially in negative sentences 尤用於否定句) a very small amount 少量；微量；一點兒 SYN **iota**： *There isn't* **a grain of truth** *in those rumours.* 那些謠傳一點也不可靠。 **4** [C] a small unit of weight, equal to 0.00143 of a pound or 0.0648 of a gram, used for example for weighing medicines 格令（重量單位，等於 0.00143 磅或 0.0648 克，用於稱量藥物等） **5** [U] the natural direction of lines in wood, cloth, etc. or of layers of rock; the pattern of lines that you can see（木、織物或石頭等的）紋理： *to cut a piece of wood* **along/across the grain** 順着紋路劈木頭；

橫對紋路把木頭攔腰截斷 **6** [U, C] how rough or smooth a surface feels（表面的）質地；觸感：*wood of coarse/fine grain* 質地粗 / 細的木頭

IDM **be/go against the 'grain** to be or do sth different from what is normal or natural 違反常理；不正常；不合常情；與…格格不入：*It really goes against the grain to have to work on a Sunday.* 星期天還得上班的確不合常情。

grained /greɪnd/ *adj.* (of wood, stone, etc. 木、石等) **1** having noticeable lines or a pattern on the surface 有紋理的 **2 -grained** having a TEXTURE of the type mentioned 質地…的：*fine-grained stone* 質地細的石頭

grainy /'greɪni/ *adj.* (**grain·ier**, **graini·est**) **1** (especially of photographs 尤指照片) not having completely clear images because they look as if they are made of a lot of small dots and marks 有顆粒的；粒狀的；有紋的：*The film is shot in grainy black and white.* 這部電影拍成有顆粒狀的黑白片。 **2** having a rough surface or containing small bits, seeds, etc. 表面粗糙的；粒面的：*grainy texture* 粒面質地

gram /græm/ *noun*
1 (*BrE* also **gramme**) (*abbr.* **g**, **gm**) a unit for measuring weight. There are 1 000 grams in one kilogram. 克（重量單位，1 公斤為 1 000 克） **2 -gram** a thing that is written or drawn 寫（或畫）的東西：*telegram* 電報 ◇ *hologram* 全息圖

'gram flour (also **besan**, **'chickpea flour**) *noun* [U] flour made from CHICKPEAS 鷹嘴豆粉

gram·mar /'græmə(r)/ *noun*
1 [U] the rules in a language for changing the form of words and joining them into sentences 語法；文法：*the basic rules of grammar* 基本語法規則 ◇ *English grammar* 英語語法 ➲ see also GENERATIVE GRAMMAR **2** [U] a person's knowledge and use of a language（人的）語言知識及運用能力：*His grammar is appalling.* 他運用語言的能力糟透了。◇ *bad grammar* 極差的語言運用能力 **3** [C] a book containing a description of the rules of a language 語法書：*a French grammar* 法語語法書

gram·mar·ian /grə'meəriən; *NAmE* -'mer-/ *noun* a person who is an expert in the study of grammar 語法學家

'grammar school *noun* **1** (in Britain, especially in the past) a school for young people between the ages of 11 and 18 who are good at academic subjects（尤指舊時英國的）文法學校 **2** (*old-fashioned*) = ELEMENTARY SCHOOL

the ˌgrammar trans'lation method *noun* [sing.] (*linguistics* 語言) a traditional way of teaching a foreign language, in which the study of grammar is very important and very little teaching is in the foreign language 語法翻譯法（一種傳統外語教學方法）

gram·mat·ical /grə'mætɪkl/ *adj.* **1** connected with the rules of grammar 語法的；文法的：*a grammatical error* 語法錯誤 **2** correctly following the rules of grammar 符合語法規則的；合乎文法的：*That sentence is not grammatical.* 那個句子不合語法。 ▶ **gram·mat·ical·ly** /-kli/ *adv.*：*a grammatically correct sentence* 語法上正確的句子

gramme (*BrE*) = GRAM (1)

Grammy /'græmi/ (*pl.* **Gram·mies** or **Grammys**) one of the awards for achievement in the music industry given every year by the US National Academy of Recording Arts and Sciences 格萊美獎；葛萊美獎（美國國家錄音藝術與科學學會頒發的音樂界年度獎之一）

gramo·phone /'græməfəʊn; *NAmE* -foʊn/ *noun* (*old-fashioned*) = RECORD PLAYER

gran /græn/ *noun* (*BrE, informal*) grandmother 奶奶；姥姥：*Do you want to go to your gran's?* 你想去奶奶家嗎？◇ *Gran, can I have some more?* 奶奶，我再吃點兒行嗎？

Gran·ary™ /'grænəri/ *adj.* [only before noun] (*BrE*) (of bread 麪包) containing whole grains of WHEAT 穀倉牌的（全麥的）

gran·ary /'grænəri/ *noun* (*pl.* **-ies**) a building where grain is stored 穀倉；糧倉

grand /grænd/ *adj.*, *noun*
■ *adj.* (**grand·er**, **grand·est**) **1** impressive and large or important 壯麗的；堂皇的；重大的：*It's not a very grand house.* 這房子並不是十分富麗堂皇。◇ *The wedding was a very grand occasion.* 婚禮場面非常隆重。 **2 Grand** [only before noun] used in the names of impressive or very large buildings, etc.（用於大建築物等的名稱）大：*the Grand Canyon* 大峽谷 ◇ *We stayed at the Grand Hotel.* 我們住在格蘭酒店。 **3** needing a lot of effort, money or time to succeed but intended to achieve impressive results 宏大的；宏偉的；有氣派的：*a grand design/plan/strategy* 宏偉的藍圖；宏大的計劃；重大的策略 ◇ *New Yorkers built their city* ***on a grand scale.*** 紐約人大規模地建造自己的城市。 **4** (of people 人) behaving in a proud way because they are rich or from a high social class 傲慢的；高高在上的 **5** (*dialect* or *informal*) very good or enjoyable; excellent 極好的；快樂的；美妙的；出色的：*I had a grand day out at the seaside.* 我在海邊痛痛快快玩了一天。◇ *Thanks. That'll be grand!* 謝謝。那太棒了！◇ *Fred did a grand job of painting the house.* 弗雷德粉刷房子幹得很出色。 **6 Grand** used in the titles of people of very high social rank（對上層社會的人的稱呼）大：*the Grand Duchess Elena* 大公夫人埃琳娜 ➲ see also GRANDEUR ▶ **grand·ly** *adv.*：*He described himself grandly as a 'landscape architect'.* 他自封為"景觀建築師"。 **grand·ness** *noun* [U]

IDM **a/the ˌgrand old 'age (of ...)** a great age 高齡：*She finally learned to drive at the grand old age of 70.* 她終於在 70 歲高齡學會了開車。 **a/the ˌgrand old 'man (of sth)** a man who is respected in a particular profession that he has been involved in for a long time 元老；資深前輩；老前輩：*James Lovelock, the grand old man of environmental science* 詹姆斯 • 洛夫洛克，環境科學的元老

■ *noun* **1** (*pl.* **grand**) (*informal*) $1 000; £1 000 * 1 000 元；1 000 英鎊：*It'll cost you five grand!* 這要花去你 5 000 塊錢！ **2** = GRAND PIANO ➲ see also CONCERT GRAND

gran·dad (also **grand·dad** especially in *NAmE*) /'grændæd/ *noun* (*informal*) grandfather 爺爺；姥爺

ˌGrand ˌCentral 'Station *noun* (*US*) used to describe a place that is very busy or crowded 非常繁忙（或擁擠）的地方：*My hospital room was like Grand Central Station with everybody coming and going.* 我的病房就像紐約的中央火車站，整天人來人往。 **ORIGIN** From the name of a very busy train station in New York City. 源自紐約市一個繁忙的火車站站名。 ➲ compare PICCADILLY CIRCUS

grand·child /'græntʃaɪld/ *noun* (*pl.* **grand·chil·dren**) a child of your son or daughter（外）孫子；（外）孫女

grand·daddy (also **gran·daddy**) /'grændædi/ *noun* (*pl.* **-ies**) (*NAmE, informal*) **1** = GRANDFATHER **2 the grand-daddy** the first or greatest example of sth（某事物的）老祖宗，祖師爺

grand·daugh·ter /'grændɔːtə(r)/ *noun* a daughter of your son or daughter（外）孫女 ➲ compare GRANDSON

ˌgrand 'duchess *noun* **1** the wife of a grand duke 大公夫人 **2** (in some parts of Europe, especially in the past), a female ruler of a small independent state（尤指舊時歐洲某些地方的）女大公 **3** (in Russia in the past) a daughter of the TSAR（舊時俄國的）公主

ˌgrand 'duke *noun* **1** (in some parts of Europe, especially in the past), a male ruler of a small independent state（尤指舊時歐洲某些地方的）大公：*The Grand Duke of Tuscany* 托斯卡納大公 **2** (in Russia in the past), a son of the TSAR（舊時俄國的）王子 ➲ compare ARCHDUKE

gran·dee /græn'diː/ *noun* **1** (in the past) a Spanish or Portuguese NOBLEMAN of high rank（舊時西班牙或葡萄牙的）大公 **2** a person of high social rank and importance 大人物；顯要人物

G

grand·eur /ˈgrændʒə(r); -djə(r)/ *noun* [U] **1** the quality of being great and impressive in appearance 宏偉；壯麗；堂皇 SYN **splendour**: *the grandeur and simplicity of Roman architecture* 古羅馬建築的雄偉和簡樸 ◇ *The hotel had an air of faded grandeur.* 這家旅館給人一種繁華已逝的感覺。**2** the importance or social status sb has or thinks they have 高貴；顯赫；偉大：*He has a sense of grandeur about him.* 他覺得自己很了不起。◇ *She is clearly suffering from* **delusions of grandeur** (= thinks she is more important than she really is). 她顯然是犯了妄自尊大的毛病。➲ see also GRAND

grand·father /ˈgrænfɑːðə(r)/ *noun* the father of your father or mother （外）祖父；爺爺；外公 ➲ see also GRANDAD, GRANDDADDY, GRANDPA ➲ compare GRANDMOTHER

G

ˌgrandfather ˈclock *noun* an old-fashioned type of clock in a tall wooden case that stands on the floor （置於高木匣中的）落地擺鐘 ➲ picture at CLOCK

grand·ilo·quent /grænˈdɪləkwənt/ *adj.* (*formal, disapproving*) using long or complicated words in order to impress people 賣弄辭藻的；言辭浮誇的 SYN **pompous** ▶ **grand·ilo·quence** /-əns/ *noun* [U]

gran·di·ose /ˈgrændiəʊs; *NAmE* -oʊs/ *adj.* (*disapproving*) seeming very impressive but too large, complicated, expensive, etc. to be practical or possible 華而不實的；浮誇的；不切實際的：*The grandiose scheme for a journey across the desert came to nothing.* 不切實際的穿越沙漠計劃已成泡影。◇ *a grandiose opera house* 華而不實的歌劇院

ˌgrand ˈjury *noun* (*law* 律) (in the US) a JURY which has to decide whether there is enough evidence against an accused person for a trial in court （美國）大陪審團

grand·ma /ˈgrænmɑː/ *noun* (*informal*) grandmother （外）祖母；奶奶；外婆

grand mal /ˌgrɒ̃ ˈmæl; *NAmE* ˌgræn ˈmɑːl; ˈmæl/ *noun* [U] (from *French, medical* 醫) a serious form of EPILEPSY in which sb becomes unconscious for fairly long periods 癲癇大發作

ˌgrand ˈmaster *noun* a CHESS player of the highest standard 國際象棋大師；西洋棋大師；棋王；棋聖

grand·mother /ˈgrænmʌðə(r)/ *noun* the mother of your father or mother （外）祖母；奶奶；外婆 ➲ see also GRAN, GRANDMA, GRANNY ➲ compare GRANDFATHER IDM see TEACH

ˌgrandmother ˈclock *noun* a clock similar to a GRANDFATHER CLOCK but smaller 小型落地擺鐘

ˌgrand ˈopera *noun* [U, C] OPERA in which everything is sung and there are no spoken parts 大歌劇（無唸白）

grand·pa /ˈgrænpɑː/ *noun* (*informal*) grandfather （外）祖父；爺爺；姥爺；外公 ➲ see also GRANDAD

grand·par·ent /ˈgrænpeərənt; *NAmE* -perənt/ *noun* [usually pl.] the father or mother of your father or mother 祖父；祖母；外祖父；外祖母：*The children are staying with their grandparents.* 孩子們與祖父母住在一起。

ˌgrand ˈpiano (also **grand**) *noun* a large piano in which the strings are horizontal 大鋼琴；三角鋼琴 ➲ VISUAL VOCAB page V36 ➲ compare UPRIGHT PIANO

Grand Prix /ˌgrɒ̃ ˈpriː; *NAmE* ˌgrɑ̃ː/ *noun* (*pl.* **Grands Prix** /ˌgrɒ̃ ˈpriː; *NAmE* ˌgrɑ̃ː/) one of a series of important international races for racing cars or motorcycles 大獎賽（汽車或摩托車的國際系列大賽中的一場比賽）

ˌgrand ˈslam *noun* **1** (also **Grand Slam**) a very important sports event, contest, etc. 大賽；大獎賽：*a Grand Slam* ***tournament/cup/title*** 錦標大賽；大賽獎杯／冠軍 **2** the winning of every part of a sports contest or all the main contests in a year for a particular sport 全勝，大滿貫（每場皆勝或在全年主要比賽上每戰皆勝）：*Will France win the grand slam this year?* (= in RUGBY) 法國隊在今年的橄欖球比賽中會大獲全勝嗎？**3** (also **grand ˌslam home ˈrun**) (in BASEBALL 棒球) a HOME RUN that is worth four points 四分本壘打 **4** (in card games, especially BRIDGE 紙牌遊戲，尤指橋牌) the winning of all the TRICKS in a single game 大滿貫

grand·son /ˈgrænsʌn/ *noun* a son of your son or daughter 孫子；外孫 ➲ compare GRANDDAUGHTER

grand·stand /ˈgrænstænd/ *noun* a large covered structure with rows of seats for people to watch sports events 大看台：*The game was played to a packed grandstand.* 比賽時大看台上座無虛席。◇ *From her house, we had a* ***grandstand view*** (= very good view) *of the celebrations.* 從她的住所望去，我們把整個慶祝活動盡收眼底。

ˌgrandstand ˈfinish *noun* (*BrE*) (in sport 體育運動) a close or exciting finish to a race or competition 比分接近的結局

grand·stand·ing /ˈgrænstændɪŋ/ *noun* [U] (*NAmE*) (especially in business, politics, etc. 尤指在商業、政治等方面) the fact of behaving or speaking in a way that is intended to make people impressed in order to gain some advantage for yourself 譁眾取寵；炫耀

ˌgrand ˈtotal *noun* the final total when a number of other totals have been added together 總計；共計

ˌgrand ˈtour *noun* **1** (often *humorous*) a visit around a building or house in order to show it to sb 參觀，巡視（房屋、住所）：*Steve took us on a grand tour of the house and garden.* 史蒂夫帶我們參觀了這棟住宅和花園。**2** (also **Grand Tour**) a visit to the main cities of Europe made by rich young British or American people as part of their education in the past 遊學旅行（舊時英美富家子弟在歐洲大陸主要城市的觀光旅行，是其教育的一部份）

ˌgrand ˌunified ˈtheory *noun* (*physics* 物) a single theory that tries to explain all the behaviour of SUBATOMIC PARTICLES 大統一理論（試圖解釋亞原子粒子的所有活動方式的單一理論）

grange /greɪndʒ/ *noun* (*BrE*) (often as part of a name 常作名稱的一部份) a country house with farm buildings 農莊；莊園：*Thrushcross Grange* 思拉什克羅斯莊園

gran·ita /grəˈniːtə/ *noun* [U, C] (from *Italian*) a drink or sweet dish made with crushed ice 碎冰飲料；沙冰

gran·ite /ˈgrænɪt/ *noun* [U] a type of hard grey stone, often used in building 花崗岩；花崗石

granny (also *less frequent* **gran·nie**) /ˈgræni/ *noun* (*pl.* **-ies**) (*informal*) grandmother 奶奶；姥姥 ➲ see also GRANDMA ▶ **granny** (also *less frequent* **gran·nie**) *adj.*: *a pair of granny glasses* 一副老花眼鏡

ˈgranny flat *noun* (*BrE*) (also **ˈin-law apartment**, **ˈmother-in-law apartment**, **ˈin-law suite** all *NAmE*) (*informal*) a set of rooms for an old person, especially in a relative's house （尤指親戚家中的）老人套間

ˈgranny knot *noun* an untidy double knot 老奶奶結（不整齊的雙環結）➲ compare REEF KNOT

gran·ola /grəˈnəʊlə; *NAmE* -ˈnoʊ-/ *noun, adj.*

■ ***noun*** [U] (*especially NAmE*) a type of breakfast CEREAL made of grains, nuts, etc. that have been TOASTED 格蘭諾拉麥片（用烘烤過的穀類、堅果等製成的早餐食品）

■ ***adj.*** [only before noun] (*NAmE, informal*) (of a person 人) eating healthy food, supporting the protection of the environment and having LIBERAL views 講求身心健康的（吃得健康、支持環保、思想開明）

grant AW /grɑːnt; *NAmE* grænt/ *verb, noun*

■ ***verb*** **1** [often passive] to agree to give sb what they ask for, especially formal or legal permission to do sth （尤指正式地或法律上）同意，准予，允許：**~ sth** *My request was granted.* 我的請求得到批准。◇ **~ sb sth** *I was granted permission to visit the palace.* 我獲准參觀宮殿。◇ *She was granted a divorce.* 她獲准離婚。◇ *The bank finally granted me a £500 loan.* 銀行終於同意給我貸款 500 英鎊。◇ **~ sth to sb/sth** *The bank finally granted a £500 loan to me.* 銀行終於同意給我貸款 500 英鎊。**2** to admit that sth is true, although you may not like or agree with it （勉強）承認，同意：**~ sb** *She's a smart woman, I grant you, but she's no genius.* 我同意你的觀點，她是一個很聰明的女人，但絕不是天才。◇ **~ (sb) (that)** ... *I grant you (that) it looks good, but it's not* *exactly practical.* 我承認你說的，它好看，可並不是很實用。

IDM **take it for 'granted (that ...)** to believe sth is true without first making sure that it is 認為…是理所當然：*I just took it for granted that he'd always be around.* 我還想當然地以為他總能隨叫隨到呢。 **take sb/sth for 'granted** to be so used to sb/sth that you do not recognize their true value any more and do not show that you are grateful（因習以為常）對…不予重視；（因視為當然而）不把…當回事：*Her husband was always there and she just took him for granted.* 她丈夫隨時都在身邊，她只是認為他理應如此。◇ *We take having an endless supply of clean water for granted.* 我們想當然地認為潔淨水的供應無窮無盡而不予以珍惜。

■ ***noun*** **~ (to do sth)** a sum of money that is given by the government or by another organization to be used for a particular purpose（政府、機構的）撥款：*student grants* (= to pay for their education) 學生助學金 ◇ *He has been awarded a research grant.* 他得到一筆研究經費。

'grant aid *noun* [U] (*BrE*) money given by the government to organizations or local areas（政府對機構或地方的）撥款，資助款 ▶ **,grant-'aided** *adj.*：*a grant-aided school* 受公費補助的學校

grant·ed **AW** /ˈɡrɑːntɪd; *NAmE* ˈɡræn-/ *adv., conj.*

■ ***adv.*** used to show that you accept that sth is true, often before you make another statement about it（表示肯定屬實，然後再作另一番表述）不錯，的確：*'You could have done more to help.' 'Granted.'* "你本可以多給點幫助的。" "我承認。" ◇ *Granted, it's not the most pleasant of jobs but it has to be done.* 的確，這不是最令人愉快的工作，但也得做呀。

■ ***conj.*** **~ (that ...)** because of the fact that 因為：*Granted that it is a simple test to perform, it should be easy to get results quickly.* 因為這化驗做起來簡單，所以應該不難很快得出結果。

,grant-in-'aid *noun* (*pl.* **,grants-in-'aid**) a sum of money given to a local government or an institution, or to a particular person to allow them to study sth（給地方政府、機構或學者的）撥款，研究資助

,grant-main'tained *adj.* (*abbr.* **GM**) (of a school in Britain 英國學校) receiving financial support from central government rather than local government 由中央政府出資的；中央政府撥款的

granu·lar /ˈɡrænjələ(r)/ *adj.* consisting of small GRANULES; looking or feeling like a collection of GRANULES 由顆粒構成的；含顆粒的；似顆粒狀的

granu·lated sugar /ˌɡrænjuleɪtɪd ˈʃʊɡə(r)/ *noun* [U] white sugar in the form of small grains 白砂糖

gran·ule /ˈɡrænjuːl/ *noun* [usually pl.] a small, hard piece of sth; a small grain 顆粒狀物；微粒；細粒：*instant coffee granules* 速溶咖啡顆粒

grape /ɡreɪp/ *noun* a small green or purple fruit that grows in bunches on a climbing plant (called a VINE). Wine is made from grapes. 葡萄：*a bunch of grapes* 一串葡萄 ◇ ***black/white grapes*** (= grapes that are actually purple/green in colour) 紫/綠葡萄 ➲ VISUAL VOCAB page V30 **IDM** see SOUR *adj.*

grape·fruit /ˈɡreɪpfruːt/ *noun* (*pl.* **grapefruit** or **grape·fruits**) [C, U] a large round yellow CITRUS fruit with a lot of slightly sour juice 葡萄柚；柚子；西柚 ➲ VISUAL VOCAB page V30

grape·shot /ˈɡreɪpʃɒt; *NAmE* -ʃɑːt/ *noun* [U] a number of small iron balls that are fired together from a CANNON（大炮發射的）葡萄彈

grape·vine /ˈɡreɪpvaɪn/ *noun* a climbing plant that produces GRAPES 葡萄藤；葡萄樹

IDM **on/through the 'grapevine** by talking in an informal way to other people 小道消息；傳聞：*I heard on the grapevine that you're leaving.* 我聽小道消息說你要離開。

graph /ɡræf; *BrE* also ɡrɑːf/ *noun* a planned drawing, consisting of a line or lines, showing how two or more sets of numbers are related to each other 圖；圖表；曲線圖：*Plot a graph of height against age.* 繪製一張身高與年齡對照的曲線圖。◇ *The graph shows how house prices have risen since the 1980s.* 此圖表明了自 20 世紀 80 年代以來房價上漲的情況。➲ LANGUAGE BANK at ILLUSTRATE ➲ WRITING TUTOR page WT25

graph·eme /ˈɡræfiːm/ *noun* (*linguistics* 語言) the smallest unit that has meaning in a writing system 字位，書寫位（語言書寫系統的最小有意義單位）➲ compare PHONEME

graph·ic /ˈɡræfɪk/ *adj., noun*

■ ***adj.*** **1** [only before noun] connected with drawings and design, especially in the production of books, magazines, etc. 繪畫的；書畫的；圖樣的；圖案的：*graphic design* 平面設計 ◇ *a graphic designer* 平面設計人員 **2** (of descriptions, etc. 描述等) very clear and full of details, especially about sth unpleasant（尤指令人不快的事物）形象的，生動的，逼真的 **SYN** **vivid**：*a **graphic account/description** of a battle* 對戰鬥的生動敘述/描述 ◇ *He kept telling us about his operation, in the most **graphic detail**.* 他不停地向我們繪聲繪色地講述他動手術的詳細情況。

■ ***noun*** a diagram or picture, especially one that appears on a computer screen or in a newspaper or book（尤指電腦熒屏或報紙、書籍上的）圖表，圖形，圖畫 ➲ compare GRAPHICS

graph·ic·al /ˈɡræfɪkl/ *adj.* **1** [only before noun] connected with art or computer graphics 圖形的；計算機圖形的：*The system uses an impressive graphical interface.* 這一系統用特別好的圖形界面。 **2** in the form of a diagram or graph 用圖表示的；圖表顯示的：*a graphical presentation of results* 所得結果的圖演

graph·ic·al·ly /ˈɡræfɪkli/ *adv.* **1** in the form of drawings or diagrams 以書畫（或圖表）形式：*This data is shown graphically on the opposite page.* 對頁以圖表顯示這些數據。 **2** very clearly and in great detail 形象地；生動地；逼真地 **SYN** **vividly**：*The murders are graphically described in the article.* 這篇文章對幾起兇殺案作了血淋淋的描述。

,graphic 'arts *noun* [U] art based on the use of lines and shades of colour 圖像藝術；繪畫藝術 ▶ **,graphic 'artist** *noun*

,graphic 'equalizer *noun* (*technical* 術語) an electronic device or computer program that allows you to control the strength and quality of particular sound FREQUENCIES separately 圖示均衡器，圖形等化器（用以調節聲頻大小及音質）

,graphic 'novel *noun* a novel in the form of a COMIC STRIP 連環畫小說；漫畫小說

graph·ics /ˈɡræfɪks/ *noun* [pl.] designs, drawings or pictures, that are used especially in the production of books, magazines, etc. 圖樣；圖案；繪圖；圖像：*computer graphics* 計算機製圖 ◇ *Text and graphics are prepared separately and then combined.* 文字和圖分別編排後再合成。

'graphics adapter *noun* (*computing* 計) = VIDEO CARD

'graphics card *noun* (*computing* 計) a CIRCUIT BOARD that allows a computer to show images on its screen 圖形卡；圖像適配卡；顯示卡

graph·ite /ˈɡræfaɪt/ *noun* [U] a soft black mineral that is a form of CARBON. Graphite is used to make pencils, to LUBRICATE machinery, and in nuclear REACTORS. 石墨

graph·ology /ɡræˈfɒlədʒi; *NAmE* -ˈfɑːl-/ *noun* [U] the study of HANDWRITING, for example as a way of learning more about sb's character 筆體學，筆跡學（根據筆體推斷人的性格）

'graph paper *noun* [U] paper with small squares of equal size printed on it, used for drawing GRAPHS and other diagrams 方格紙；坐標紙；標繪紙

-graphy *combining form* (in nouns 構成名詞) **1** a type of art or science 某種藝術（或科學）：*choreography* 編舞藝術 ◇ *geography* 地理學 **2** a method of producing images 產生影像的方法：*radiography* 射線照相術 **3** a form of writing or drawing 寫（或畫）的形式：*calligraphy* 書法 ◇ *biography* 傳記

grappa /ˈɡræpə/ *noun* [U, C] a strong alcoholic drink from Italy, made from GRAPES （意大利）葡萄果渣白蘭地

grap·ple /ˈɡræpl/ *verb* **1** [I, T] to take a firm hold of sb/sth and struggle with them 扭打；搏鬥：**~ (with sb/sth)** *Passers-by grappled with the man after the attack.* 襲擊之後過路人便與這男人扭打起來。◇ **~ sb/sth (+ adv./prep.)** *They managed to grapple him to the ground.* 他們終於把他摔倒在地。**2** [I] to try hard to find a solution to a problem 努力設法解決：**~ with sth** *The new government has yet to grapple with the problem of air pollution.* 新政府還需盡力解決空氣污染問題。◇ **~ to do sth** *I was grappling to find an answer to his question.* 我正在努力想辦法解決他的問題。

ˈgrappling iron (also **ˈgrappling hook**) *noun* a tool with several hooks attached to a long rope, used for dragging sth along or holding a boat still 多爪鉤；多爪錨

grasp /ɡrɑːsp; *NAmE* ɡræsp/ *verb, noun*

■ *verb* **1 ~ sb/sth** to take a firm hold of sb/sth 抓緊；抓牢 SYN **grip**：*He grasped my hand and shook it warmly.* 他熱情地抓住我的手握了起來。◇ *Kay grasped him by the wrist.* 凱緊緊抓住他的手腕。➲ SYNONYMS at HOLD **2** to understand sth completely 理解；領會；領悟；明白：**~ sth** *They failed to grasp the importance of his words.* 他們沒有理解他的話的重要性。◇ **~ how, why, etc. …** *She was unable to grasp how to do it.* 她弄不明白這事該怎麼做。◇ **~ that …** *It took him some time to grasp that he was now a public figure.* 他過了些時候才意識到自己已是個公眾人物了。➲ SYNONYMS at UNDERSTAND **3 ~ a chance/an opportunity** to take an opportunity without hesitating and use it 急忙抓住，毫不猶豫地抓住（機會）：*I grasped the opportunity to work abroad.* 我毫不猶豫地抓住了去國外工作的機會。

IDM **grasp the ˈnettle** (*BrE*) to deal with a difficult situation firmly and without hesitating 果斷地處理棘手問題 ➲ more at STRAW

PHR V **ˈgrasp at sth 1** to try to take hold of sth in your hands 盡力抓住某物：*She grasped at his coat as he rushed past her.* 他從她身邊衝過去時，她使勁地向他的外衣抓去。**2** to try to take an opportunity 抓住機會

■ *noun* [usually sing.] **1** a firm hold of sb/sth or control over sb/sth 緊抓；緊握；控制 SYN **grip**：*I grabbed him, but he slipped from my grasp.* 我緊抓着他，可他還是從我手裏溜掉了。◇ *She felt a firm grasp on her arm.* 她感到手臂被緊緊地抓住了。◇ *Don't let the situation escape from your grasp.* 別讓局面失去控制。**2** a person's understanding of a subject or of difficult facts 理解（力）；領會：*He has **a good grasp of** German grammar.* 他德語語法掌握得很好。◇ *These complex formulae are **beyond the grasp of** the average pupil.* 這些複雜的公式是一般小學生不能理解的。**3** the ability to get or achieve sth 能力所及：*Success was **within her grasp**.* 她有把握獲得成功。

grasp·ing /ˈɡrɑːspɪŋ; *NAmE* ˈɡræs-/ *adj.* (*disapproving*) always trying to get money, possessions, power, etc. for yourself 一味攫取的；貪婪的；貪心的 SYN **greedy**：*a grasping landlord* 貪婪的地主

grass 0‑ᵂ /ɡrɑːs; *NAmE* ɡræs/ *noun, verb*

■ *noun* **1** 0‑ᵂ [U] a common wild plant with narrow green leaves and STEMS that are eaten by cows, horses, sheep, etc. 草；青草；牧草：*a **blade of grass*** 一片草葉 ◇ *The dry grass caught fire.* 乾草着火了。**2** [C] any type of grass 禾本科植物：*ornamental grasses* 觀賞性草 **3** 0‑ᵂ [sing., U] (usually **the grass**) an area of ground covered with grass 草地；草坪；草場；牧場：*to **cut/mow the grass*** 割／刈草 ◇ *Don't walk **on the grass**.* 勿踐踏草地。◇ ***Keep off the grass.*** (= on a sign) 請勿踐踏草地。**4** [U] (*slang*) MARIJUANA 大麻 **5** [C] (*BrE, informal*, usually *disapproving*) a person, usually a criminal, who tells the police about sb's criminal activities and plans 向警方告密的人（通常指罪犯）➲ compare SUPERGRASS

IDM **the grass is (always) greener on the other side (of the fence)** (*saying*) said about people who never seem happy with what they have and always think that other people have a better situation than they have 草是那邊綠；這山望着那山高 **not let the grass grow under your feet** to not delay in getting things done （做事）不拖拉，不磨洋工 **put sb out to ˈgrass** (*informal*) to force sb to stop doing their job, especially because they are old 迫使（年老者）退休；讓某人離職 ➲ more at KICK *v.*, SNAKE *n.*

■ *verb* [I] **~ (on sb)** (also ˌ**grass sb↔ˈup**) (both *BrE, informal*) to tell the police about sb's criminal activities （向警方）告密，告發

PHR V ˌ**grass sth↔ˈover** to cover an area with grass 用草覆蓋某物；使長滿草；在…上種草

ˌ**grass ˈcourt** *noun* a TENNIS COURT with a grass surface 草地網球場

ˈgrass-cutter /ˈɡrɑːskʌtə(r); *NAmE* ˈɡræs-/ (also **ˈcutting grass**) *noun* a name used in W Africa for a CANE RAT (= type of large RODENT that is used for food) （西非用語）蔗鼠

grassed /ɡrɑːst; *NAmE* ɡræst/ *adj.* covered with grass 長滿草的；被草覆蓋的

grass·hop·per /ˈɡrɑːshɒpə(r); *NAmE* ˈɡræshɑːp-/ *noun* an insect with long back legs, that can jump very high and that makes a sound with its legs 蝗蟲；蚱蜢；螞蚱 ➲ VISUAL VOCAB page V13 IDM see KNEE-HIGH

grass·land /ˈɡrɑːslænd; *NAmE* ˈɡræs-/ *noun* [U] (also **grasslands** [pl.]) a large area of open land covered with wild grass 草原；草地；草場

ˌ**grass ˈroots** (*BrE*) *noun* [pl.] (often **the grass roots**) ordinary people in society or in an organization, rather than the leaders or people who make decisions 基層民眾；平民百姓：*the grass roots of the party* 黨的基層成員 ◇ *We need support at grass-roots level.* 我們需要基層的支持。

ˌ**grass ˈskirt** *noun* a skirt made of long grass, worn by dancers in the Pacific islands （太平洋島嶼上的跳舞者穿的）草裙

ˈgrass snake *noun* a small harmless snake 遊蛇，青草蛇（無毒小蛇）

ˌ**grass ˈwidow** *noun* a woman whose husband is away from home for long periods of time 活寡婦；守活寡的女子

grassy /ˈɡrɑːsi; *NAmE* ˈɡræsi/ *adj.* (**grass·ier**, **grassi·est**) covered with grass 長滿草的；被草覆蓋的

grate /ɡreɪt/ *noun, verb*

■ *noun* **1** a metal frame for holding the wood or coal in a FIREPLACE 爐條；爐箅 ➲ VISUAL VOCAB page V21 **2** (also **ˈsewer grate**) (both *US*) (*BrE* **drain**) a frame of metal bars over the opening to a DRAIN in the ground 下水道孔蓋 ➲ see also GRATING

■ *verb* **1** [T] **~ sth** to rub food against a GRATER in order to cut it into small pieces 擦碎，磨碎（食物）：***grated apple/carrot/cheese, etc.*** 擦成細絲的蘋果、胡蘿蔔、乾酪等 ➲ COLLOCATIONS at COOKING ➲ VISUAL VOCAB page V28 **2** [I] to irritate or annoy sb 使人煩躁；使人煩惱；使人難受：**~ (on sb)** *Her voice really grates on me.* 她的聲音真叫我難受。◇ **~ (with sb)** *It grated with him when people implied he wasn't really British.* 當有人暗示他不是地道的英國人時，他很是惱火。**3** [I, T] when two hard surfaces **grate** as they rub together, they make a sharp unpleasant sound; sb can also make one thing **grate** against another （使）發出刺耳的聲音，發出吱吱嘎嘎的摩擦聲：*The rusty hinges grated as the gate swung back.* 大門蕩了回去，生銹的鉸鏈發出吱嘎吱嘎的刺耳聲。◇ **~ sth (+ adv./prep.)** *He grated his knife across the plate.* 他用刀子劃過盤子時發出刺耳的聲音。

grate·ful 0‑ᵂ /ˈɡreɪtfl/ *adj.*

> **WORD FAMILY**
> **grateful** *adj.* (≠ ungrateful)
> **gratefully** *adv.*
> **gratitude** *noun* (≠ ingratitude)

1 0‑ᵂ feeling or showing thanks because sb has done sth kind for you or has done as you asked 感激的；表示感謝的：**~ (to sb) (for sth)** *I am extremely grateful to all the teachers for their help.* 我非常感謝所有老師的幫助。◇ *We would be grateful for any information you can give us.* 如能提供信息我們將感激不盡。◇ **~ (to do sth)** *She seems to think I should be grateful to have a job at all.* 她似乎認為我有份工作就該謝天謝地了。◇

~ (**that** …) *He was grateful that she didn't tell his parents about the incident.* 他感到慶幸的是她未將此事告訴他父母。◇ *Grateful thanks are due to the following people for their help …* 向下列給予過幫助的人表示衷心的感謝…◇ *Kate gave him a grateful smile.* 凱特感激地對他笑了笑。 **2** used to make a request, especially in a letter or in a formal situation（尤用於書信或正式場合提出請求）感激不盡，請： *I **would be grateful if you could** send the completed form back as soon as possible.* 如能儘快把表格填好寄回，將不勝感激。 ▸ **grate·ful·ly** /-fəli/ *adv.*： *He nodded gratefully.* 他感激地點了點頭。◇ *All donations will be gratefully received.* 如蒙捐助，定將報以衷心的感謝。 IDM see SMALL *adj.*

grater /ˈɡreɪtə(r)/ *noun* a kitchen UTENSIL (= a tool) with a rough surface, used for GRATING food into very small pieces 礤牀兒，磨碎器（廚房用具）： *a **cheese/nutmeg grater*** 奶酪磨碎器；擦肉豆蔻的礤牀兒 ➲ VISUAL VOCAB pages V23, V25

grat·ifi·ca·tion /ˌɡrætɪfɪˈkeɪʃn/ *noun* [U, C] (*formal*) the state of feeling pleasure when sth goes well for you or when your desires are satisfied; sth that gives you pleasure 滿足；滿意；快感；令人喜悅的事物 SYN **satisfaction**： *sexual gratification* 性滿足◇ *A feed will usually provide instant gratification to a crying baby.* 餵食通常可使正在哭鬧的嬰兒立即得到滿足。

grat·ify /ˈɡrætɪfaɪ/ *verb* (**grati·fies**, **grati·fy·ing**, **grati·fied**, **grati·fied**) **1** (*formal*) to please or satisfy sb 使高興；使滿意： **it gratifies sb to do sth** *It gratified him to think that it was all his work.* 他想到這都是他的工作成果，感到十分欣慰。◇ **~ sb** *I was gratified by their invitation.* 收到他們的邀請，我感到很高興。 **2 ~ sth** (*formal*) to satisfy a wish, need, etc. 滿足（願望、需要等）： *He only gave his consent in order to gratify her wishes.* 他只是為滿足她的願望才同意的。 ▸ **grati·fied** *adj.* [not usually before noun]： **~ (at sth)** | **~ (to find, hear, see, etc.)** *She was gratified to find that they had followed her advice.* 她看到他們聽從了自己的建議，感到很欣慰。

grati·fy·ing /ˈɡrætɪfaɪɪŋ/ *adj.* (*formal*) pleasing and giving satisfaction 令人高興的；使人滿意的： ***It is gratifying** to see such good results.* 看到這麼好的結果真令人欣慰。 ➲ SYNONYMS at SATISFYING ▸ **grati·fy·ing·ly** *adv.*

gra·tin /ˈɡrætæn; *NAmE* ˈɡrætn/ *noun* [U] (from *French*) a cooked dish which is covered with a crisp layer of cheese or BREADCRUMBS 脆皮烙菜（表面為乾酪或麪包屑）

grat·ing /ˈɡreɪtɪŋ/ *noun, adj.*
▪ **noun** a flat frame with metal bars across it, used to cover a window, a hole in the ground, etc.（窗戶、地溝口等的）柵欄，格柵，格子 ➲ see also GRATE *n.* (2)
▪ **adj.** (of a sound or sb's voice 響聲或人的聲音) unpleasant to listen to 刺耳的

gra·tis /ˈɡrætɪs; ˈɡreɪtɪs/ *adv.* done or given without having to be paid for 免費的；無償的 SYN **free of charge**： *I knew his help wouldn't be given gratis.* 我知道他的幫助不會是無償的。 ▸ **gra·tis** *adj.*： *a gratis copy of a book* 一本贈書

grati·tude /ˈɡrætɪtjuːd; *NAmE* -tuːd/ *noun* [U] the feeling of being grateful and wanting to express your thanks 感激之情；感謝： *He smiled at them **with gratitude**.* 他向他們笑了笑表示謝意。◇ **~ (to sb) (for sth)** *I would like to express my gratitude to everyone for their hard work.* 我要對所有辛勤勞動的人表示感謝。◇ *She was presented with the gift **in gratitude for** her long service.* 這禮物贈送給她以表達對她長期服務的感激之情。◇ *a deep sense of gratitude* 深深的謝意◇ *I **owe** you a great **debt of gratitude*** (= feel extremely grateful). 我對你感激不盡。 OPP **ingratitude**

gra·tuit·ous /ɡrəˈtjuːɪtəs; *NAmE* -ˈtuː-/ *adj.* (*disapproving*) done without any good reason or purpose and often having harmful effects 無正當理由（或目的）的；無謂的 SYN **unnecessary**： *gratuitous violence on television* 電視上無謂的暴力鏡頭 ▸ **gra·tuit·ous·ly** *adv.*

gra·tu·ity /ɡrəˈtjuːəti; *NAmE* -ˈtuː-/ *noun* (*pl.* **-ies**) **1** (*formal*) money that you give to sb who has provided a service for you 小費；賞錢；報酬 SYN **tip** **2** (*BrE*) money that is given to employees when they leave their job 退職金；遣散費；退休金

grave¹ /ɡreɪv/ *noun, adj.* ➲ see also GRAVE²
▪ **noun** **1** a place in the ground where a dead person is buried 墳墓；墓穴；墳頭： *We visited Grandma's grave.* 我們給祖母掃了墓。◇ *There were flowers on the grave.* 墳上有些花。 **2** [sing.] (often **the grave**) (usually *literary*) death; a person's death 死亡；去世；逝世： *Is there life beyond the grave* (= life after death)? 人死後有來生嗎？◇ *He followed her to the grave* (= died soon after her). 他緊跟着她離開了人世。◇ *She smoked herself into an early grave* (= died young as a result of smoking). 她因抽煙而早逝。
IDM **turn in his/her ˈgrave** (*BrE*) (*NAmE* **roll in his/her ˈgrave**) (of a person who is dead 亡者) likely to be very shocked or angry 九泉之下不得安寧： *My father would turn in his grave if he knew.* 我父親知道的話在九泉之下也會不得安寧的。 ➲ more at CRADLE *n.*, DIG *v.*, FOOT *n.*
▪ **adj.** (**graver**, **grav·est**) (*formal*) **1** (of situations, feelings, etc. 形勢、感情等) very serious and important; giving you a reason to feel worried 嚴重的；重大的；嚴峻的；深切的： *The police have expressed grave concern about the missing child's safety.* 警方對失踪孩子的安全深表關注。◇ *The consequences will be very grave if nothing is done.* 如果不採取任何措施後果將會是非常嚴重的。◇ *We were in grave danger.* 我們處於極大的危險之中。 **2** (of people 人) serious in manner, as if sth sad, important or worrying has just happened 嚴肅的；莊嚴的；表情沉重的： *He looked very grave as he entered the room.* 他進入房間時表情非常嚴肅。 ➲ see also GRAVITY ➲ SYNONYMS at SERIOUS ▸ **grave·ly** *adv.*： *She is gravely ill.* 她病得很重。◇ *Local people are gravely concerned.* 當地人都深感不安。◇ *He nodded gravely as I poured out my troubles.* 我傾訴我的苦惱時他心情沉重地點了點頭。

grave² /ɡrɑːv/ (also **ˌgrave ˈaccent**) *noun* a mark placed over a vowel in some languages to show how it should be pronounced, as over the *e* in the French word *père* 鈍重音符，沉音符，抑音符（標在元音上面表發音） ➲ compare ACUTE ACCENT, CIRCUMFLEX, TILDE (1), UMLAUT ➲ see also GRAVE¹

grave·dig·ger /ˈɡreɪvdɪɡə(r)/ *noun* a person whose job is to dig graves 掘墓人

gravel /ˈɡrævl/ *noun* [U] small stones, often used to make the surface of paths and roads 沙礫；礫石；石子： *a gravel path* 石子路◇ *a **gravel pit*** (= a place where gravel is taken from the ground) 礫石採掘場

grav·elled (*US* **grav·eled**) /ˈɡrævld/ *adj.* (of a road, etc. 道路等) covered with gravel 礫石鋪的

grav·el·ly /ˈɡrævəli/ *adj.* **1** full of or containing many small stones 沙礫多的；含沙礫的；含碎石的： *a dry gravelly soil* 多沙礫的乾土 **2** (of a voice 嗓音) deep and with a rough sound 低沉沙啞的

gra·ven image /ˌɡreɪvn ˈɪmɪdʒ/ *noun* (*disapproving*) a statue or image which people worship as a god or as if it were a god 神像；偶像

grave·stone /ˈɡreɪvstəʊn; *NAmE* -stoʊn/ *noun* a stone that is put on a grave in a vertical position, showing the name, etc. of the person buried there 墓碑 SYN **headstone** ➲ compare TOMBSTONE

grave·yard /ˈɡreɪvjɑːd; *NAmE* -jɑːrd/ *noun* **1** an area of land, often near a church, where people are buried 墓地，墳場（常在教堂附近） ➲ compare CEMETERY, CHURCHYARD **2** a place where things or people that are not wanted are sent or left 垃圾場；廢物堆積處；收容所

ˈgraveyard shift *noun* (*especially NAmE*) a period of time working at night or in the very early morning 大夜班；凌晨班

gravid /ˈɡrævɪd/ *adj.* (*technical* 術語) pregnant 懷孕的

grav·itas /ˈɡrævɪtɑːs; -tæs/ *noun* [U] (*formal*) the quality of being serious 嚴肅；莊嚴 SYN **seriousness**： *a book of extraordinary gravitas* 一本非常嚴肅的書

gravi·tate /ˈɡrævɪteɪt/ *verb* (*formal*)
PHR V **ˈgravitate to/toward(s) sb/sth** to move towards sb/sth that you are attracted to 被吸引到；受吸引而轉

G

向：*Many young people gravitate to the cities in search of work.* 許多年輕人被吸引到城裏找工作。

gravi·ta·tion /ˌɡrævɪˈteɪʃn/ *noun* [U] (*physics* 物) a force of attraction that causes objects to move towards each other 引力

gravi·ta·tion·al /ˌɡrævɪˈteɪʃənl/ *adj.* connected with or caused by the force of gravity 引力的；重力引起的：*a gravitational field* 引力場 ◇ *the gravitational pull of the moon* 月球的引力

grav·ity /ˈɡrævəti/ *noun* [U] **1** (*abbr.* **g**) the force that attracts objects in space towards each other, and that on the earth pulls them towards the centre of the planet, so that things fall to the ground when they are dropped 重力；地球引力：*Newton's law of gravity* 牛頓萬有引力定律 ➲ see also CENTRE OF GRAVITY **2** (*formal*) extreme importance and a cause for worry 嚴重性 **SYN seriousness**：*I don't think you realise the gravity of the situation.* 我認為你沒有意識到形勢的嚴重性。◇ *Punishment varies according to the gravity of the offence.* 處罰根據罪行的嚴重程度而有所不同。**3** (*formal*) serious behaviour, speech or appearance 嚴肅；莊嚴：*They were asked to behave with the gravity that was appropriate in a court of law.* 他們被要求在法庭上表現出應有的嚴肅態度。➲ see also GRAVE[1] *adj.*

gravy /ˈɡreɪvi/ *noun* [U] **1** a brown sauce made by adding flour to the juices that come out of meat while it is cooking （調味）肉汁 **2** (*NAmE, informal*) something, especially money, that is obtained when you do not expect it 意外之財；飛來福

ˈgravy boat *noun* a long low JUG used for serving and pouring gravy at a meal 船形肉汁盤 ➲ VISUAL VOCAB page V22

ˈgravy train *noun* (*informal*) a situation where people seem to be making a lot of money without much effort 輕鬆賺大錢的機會；美差

gray /ɡreɪ/ (*especially NAmE*) = GREY

gray·beard (*especially NAmE*) = GREYBEARD

gray·ish /ˈɡreɪɪʃ/ *adj.* (*especially NAmE*) = GREYISH

gray·scale (*especially NAmE*) = GREYSCALE

graze /ɡreɪz/ *verb, noun*

■ *verb* **1** [I, T] (of cows, sheep, etc. 牛、羊等) to eat grass that is growing in a field （在草地上）吃青草：*There were cows grazing beside the river.* 有些牛在河邊吃青草。◇ **~ on sth** *The horses were grazing on the lush grass.* 馬群正在啃食茂盛的青草。◇ **~ sth** *The field had been grazed by sheep.* 這塊地羊已經啃過了。**2** [T] **~ sth** to put cows, sheep, etc. in a field so that they can eat the grass there 放牧；放牛；放羊：*The land is used by local people to graze their animals.* 這塊地當地人用來放牧。➲ COLLOCATIONS at FARMING **3** [I] **~ (on sth)** (*informal*) to eat small amounts of food many times during the day, often while doing other things, instead of eating three meals 吃零食（代替正餐）：*I have this really bad habit of grazing on junk food.* 我有個特別不好的習慣，就是吃垃圾食品。**4** [T] **~ sth (on sth)** to break the surface of your skin by rubbing it against sth rough 擦傷，擦破（皮膚）：*I fell and grazed my knee.* 我摔了一跤擦傷了膝蓋。➲ COLLOCATIONS at INJURY **5** [T] **~ sth** to touch sth lightly while passing it （經過時）輕擦，輕觸，蹭：*The bullet grazed his cheek.* 子彈從他的臉頰擦過。

■ *noun* a small injury where the surface of the skin has been slightly broken by rubbing against sth （表皮）擦傷：*Adam walked away from the crash with just **cuts and grazes**.* 亞當在撞車事故中平安脫險，只受了點劃傷和擦傷。

gra·zier /ˈɡreɪziə(r)/ *noun* a farmer who keeps animals that eat grass 牧場主；放牧者

graz·ing /ˈɡreɪzɪŋ/ *noun* [U] land with grass that cows, sheep, etc. can eat 牧場；草場

GRE /ˌdʒiː ɑː ˈiː/ *abbr.* Graduate Record Examination (an examination taken by students who want to study for a further degree in the US) （美國）研究生入學資格考試

grease /ɡriːs/ *noun, verb*

■ *noun* [U] **1** any thick OILY substance, especially one that is used to make machines run smoothly 油脂；潤滑油：*Grease marks can be removed with liquid detergent.* 用洗滌液可除去油漬。◇ *Her hands were covered with oil and grease.* 她滿手油垢。◇ *the grease in his hair* 他頭髮上的油 ➲ see also ELBOW GREASE **2** animal fat that has been made softer by cooking or heating （煉過的）動物油脂：*plates covered with grease* 油膩的盤子

■ *verb* **~ sth** to rub grease or fat on sth 給…加潤滑油；在…上塗油（或抹油、擦油）：*to grease a cake tin/pan* 在蛋糕烤模／烤盤上抹油

IDM **grease sb's ˈpalm** (*old-fashioned, informal*) to give sb money in order to persuade them to do sth dishonest 向某人行賄；用金錢收買 **SYN bribe** **grease the ˈwheels** (*NAmE*) (*BrE* **oil the ˈwheels**) to help sth to happen easily and without problems, especially in business or politics （尤指在商業上或政治上）起促進作用

grease·ball /ˈɡriːsbɔːl/ *noun* (*NAmE, taboo, slang*) a very offensive word for a person from southern Europe or Latin America 油脂球（指南歐人或拉丁美洲人，極具侮慢性）

ˈgrease gun *noun* a tool for applying GREASE to moving parts of a machine, etc. 滑脂槍；注油槍

ˈgrease monkey *noun* (*informal*) an offensive or humorous word for a person whose job is repairing cars 油猢猻，黑手（指汽車修理工，含侮慢意或幽默）

grease·paint /ˈɡriːspeɪnt/ *noun* [U] a thick substance used by actors as make-up （演員化妝用的）油彩

grease·proof paper /ˌɡriːspruːf ˈpeɪpə(r)/ (*BrE*) (*NAmE* **ˈwax paper**) *noun* [U] paper that does not let GREASE, oil, etc. pass through it, used in cooking and for wrapping food in 防油紙，耐脂紙（烹調和包裹食物用）

greasy /ˈɡriːsi; ˈɡriːzi/ *adj.* (**greas·ier**, **greasi·est**) **1** covered in a lot of GREASE or oil 多油的；油污的；沾油脂的：*greasy fingers/marks/overalls* 沾滿油脂的手指；油漬；滿是油污的工作服 **2** (*disapproving*) (of food 食物) cooked with too much oil 油膩的：*greasy chips* 油膩的炸薯條 **3** (*disapproving*) (of hair or skin 頭髮或皮膚) producing too much natural oil 油性的；多脂的：*long greasy hair* 油性長髮 **4** (*informal, disapproving*) (of people or their behaviour 人或其行為) friendly in a way that does not seem sincere 圓滑的；滑頭的；虛情假意的 **SYN smarmy**

IDM **the greasy ˈpole** (*informal*) used to refer to the difficult way to the top of a profession 塗油杆（到達專業之巔的艱難道路）；險峻的職業階梯

ˌgreasy ˈspoon *noun* (*informal, often disapproving*) a small cheap restaurant, usually one that is not very clean or attractive （不衛生且廉價的）低級餐館；邋遢的小飯館

great 🔑 /ɡreɪt/ *adj., noun, adv.*

■ *adj.* (**great·er**, **great·est**)

▸ LARGE 大 **1** 🔑 [usually before noun] very large; much bigger than average in size or quantity 大的；巨大的；數量大的；眾多的：*A great crowd had gathered.* 一大群人聚集在一起。◇ *People were arriving in great numbers.* 人們大批到來。◇ *The **great majority of** (= most) people seem to agree with this view.* 大多數人似乎都同意這種觀點。◇ *He must have fallen from a great height.* 他肯定是從很高的地方摔下來的。◇ *She lived to a great age.* 她活了很大歲數。**2** 🔑 [only before noun] (*informal*) used to emphasize an adjective of size or quality （強調尺寸、體積或質量）很：*There was a **great big** pile of books on the table.* 桌上有很大一摞書。◇ *He cut himself a great thick slice of cake.* 他給自己切了厚厚的一大片蛋糕。**3** 🔑 much more than average in degree or quantity 非常的；很多的；極大的：*a matter of great importance* 非常重要的事 ◇ *The concert had been a great success.* 音樂會非常成功。◇ *Her death was a great shock to us all.* 她的死使我們所有人都感到非常震驚。◇ *It gives me great pleasure to welcome you here today.* 今天能在這裏歡迎您是我極大的榮幸。◇ *Take great care of it.* 對此要多加小心。◇ *You've been a great help.* 你幫了大忙。◇ *We are all **to a great extent** the products of our culture.* 我們在很大程度上都是所屬文化的產物。➲ SYNONYMS at BIG

▸ **ADMIRED** 受讚賞 **4** extremely good in ability or quality and therefore admired by many people 偉大的；優秀的；傑出的；卓越的：*He has been described as the world's greatest violinist.* 他被稱為世界上最傑出的小提琴手。◇ *Sherlock Holmes, the great detective* 赫赫有名的偵探福爾摩斯 ◇ *Great art has the power to change lives.* 偉大藝術品的力量可以改變人們的生活。

▸ **GOOD** 好 **5** (*informal*) very good or pleasant 美妙的；好極的；使人快樂的：*He's a great bloke.* 他是個大好人。◇ *It's great to see you again.* 很高興再次見到你。◇ *What a great goal!* 這球進得真妙！◇ *We had a great time in Madrid.* 我們在馬德里玩得很開心。◇ *'I'll pick you up at seven.' 'That'll be great, thanks.'* "我七點鐘來接你。" "太好了，謝謝。" ◇ (*ironic*) *Oh great, they left without us.* 啊，真絕，他們撇下我們走了。◇ *You've been a great help, I must say* (= no help at all). 依我看，你真是幫了個大忙啊（指幫倒忙）。

▸ **IMPORTANT/IMPRESSIVE** 重要；給人深刻印象 **6** [only before noun] important and impressive 重要的；重大的；給人深刻印象的：*The wedding was a great occasion.* 這婚禮可是一大盛典。◇ *As the great day approached, she grew more and more nervous.* 隨着這重大日子的臨近她心情越來越緊張。◇ ***The great thing** is to get it done quickly.* 重要的是儘快將它完成。◇ *One great advantage of this metal is that it doesn't rust.* 這金屬最大的一個優點就是不生銹。

▸ **WITH INFLUENCE** 有影響 **7** having high status or a lot of influence 地位高的；位高權重的；影響大的：*the great powers* (= important and powerful countries) 大國 ◇ *We can make this country great again.* 我們可以使這個國家再次強大起來。◇ *Alexander the Great* 亞歷山大大帝

▸ **IN GOOD HEALTH** 健康 **8** in a very good state of physical or mental health 身心健康的；心情愉快的：*She seemed in great spirits* (= very cheerful). 她好像心情很不錯。◇ *I **feel great** today.* 我今天感覺特別好。◇ *Everyone's in great form.* 每個人的狀態都很好。

▸ **SKILLED** 熟練 **9** [not usually before noun] **~ at (doing) sth** (*informal*) able to do sth well 擅長；精通：*She's great at chess.* 她國際象棋下得很好。

▸ **USEFUL** 有用 **10 ~ for (doing) sth** (*informal*) very suitable or useful for sth 適合的；（對…）有用的：*This gadget's great for opening jars.* 這小玩意兒開廣口瓶挺好。◇ *Try this cream—it's great for spots.* 試試這種乳霜吧，對皮膚斑點挺有效。

▸ **FOR EMPHASIS** 強調 **11** [only before noun] used when you are emphasizing a particular description of sb/sth（強調某種描述）：*We are great friends.* 我們是最要好的朋友。◇ *I've never been a great reader* (= I do not read much). 我從來都看書不多。◇ *She's a great talker, isn't she?* 她是個話匣子，對不對？

▸ **FAMILY** 家庭 **12 great-** added to words for family members to show a further stage in relationship（冠於家庭成員的稱呼前，表示更高或更低一輩的親屬關係）：*my great-aunt* (= my father's or mother's aunt) 我的姑婆／姨婆 ◇ *her great-grandson* (= the grandson of her son or daughter) 她的曾孫 ◇ *my great-great-grandfather* (= the grandfather of my grandfather) 我的高祖

▸ **LARGER ANIMALS/PLANTS** 較大的動物／植物 **13** [only before noun] used in the names of animals or plants which are larger than similar kinds（用於相似動植物中較大者的名稱前）大：*the great tit* 大山雀

▸ **CITY NAME** 城市名 **14 Greater** used with the name of a city to describe an area that includes the centre of the city and a large area all round it（與城市名連用，指包括市區和周圍廣大地區在內的區域）大：*Greater London* 大倫敦

▸ **great·ness** *noun* [U]

IDM **be going great 'guns** (*informal*) to be doing sth quickly and successfully 做得快；順利；成功：*Work is going great guns now.* 目前工作很順利。 **be a 'great one for (doing) sth** to do sth a lot; to enjoy sth 老做，總是做，喜歡做（某事）：*I've never been a great one for writing letters.* 我向來不喜歡寫信。◇ *You're a great one for quizzes, aren't you?* 你是智力競賽老手，不是嗎？ **be no great 'shakes** (*informal*) to be not very good, efficient, suitable, etc. 不太出色；不太有效；不怎麼合適；不怎麼樣 **ˌgreat and 'small** of all sizes or types 大小；高低；貴賤：*all creatures great and small* 所有大小生物 **great ˌminds think a'like** (*informal, humorous*) used to say that you and another person must both be very clever because you have had the same idea or agree about sth 英雄所見略同 **the great ... in the 'sky** (*humorous*) used to refer to where a particular person is imagined to go when they die or a thing when it is no longer working, similar to the place they were connected with on earth（人死後回到）天上的老家，天國，西天；（東西壞了進）博物館：*Their pet rabbit had gone to the great rabbit hutch in the sky.* 他們的寵兔已回到西天的兔宮了。 ➲ more at OAK, PAINS, SUM *n.*

■ *noun* [usually pl.] (*informal*) a very well-known and successful person or thing 名人；偉人；偉大的事物：*He was one of boxing's all-time greats.* 他是一位空前的拳擊好手。

■ *adv.* (*informal, non-standard*) very well 很好地；極好地；很棒地：*Well done. You did great.* 幹得好。你幹得真棒。

G

Synonyms 同義詞辨析

great

cool • fantastic • fabulous • terrific • brilliant • awesome

These are all informal words that describe sb/sth that is very good, pleasant, enjoyable, etc. 以上各詞均為非正式用語，表示美妙的、使人快樂的、令人愉快的。

great (*informal*) very good; giving a lot of pleasure 指美妙的、好極的、使人快樂的：*We had a great time in Madrid.* 我們在馬德里玩得很開心。

cool (*informal*) used to show that you admire or approve of sth, often because it is fashionable, attractive or different 指因時髦、漂亮或與眾不同而令人欽佩的、絕妙的、頂呱呱的：*I think their new song's really cool.* 我認為他們的新歌棒極了。

fantastic (*informal*) extremely good; giving a lot of pleasure 指極好的、了不起的、非常愉快的：*'How was your holiday?' 'Fantastic!'* "你假期過得好嗎？" "棒極了！"

fabulous (*informal*) extremely good 指極好的、絕妙的：*Jane's a fabulous cook.* 簡的烹飪技巧堪稱一絕。(**Fabulous** is slightly more old-fashioned than the other words in this set. * fabulous 較這組詞中的其他詞稍顯過時。)

terrific (*informal*) extremely good; wonderful 指極好的、絕妙的、了不起的：*She's doing a terrific job.* 她活兒幹得真棒。

brilliant (*BrE, informal*) extremely good; wonderful 指極好的、絕妙的、了不起的：*'How was the show?' 'Brilliant!'* "演出怎麼樣？" "棒極了！"

awesome (*informal, especially NAmE*) very good, impressive, or enjoyable 指極好的、令人驚歎的、極好玩的：*The show was just awesome.* 演出實在棒極了。

PATTERNS

- to have a(n) great/cool/fantastic/fabulous/terrific/brilliant/awesome **time**
- to **look/sound** great/cool/fantastic/fabulous/terrific/brilliant/awesome
- **really** great/cool/fantastic/fabulous/terrific/brilliant/awesome
- **absolutely** great/fantastic/fabulous/terrific/brilliant/awesome

ˌgreat 'ape *noun* [usually pl.] one of the large animals which are most similar to humans (CHIMPANZEES, GORILLAS, and ORANG-UTANS) 猩猩科動物

ˌgreat 'auk *noun* a large bird similar to a PENGUIN, that no longer exists 大海雀（類似企鵝，已滅絕）

the ˌGreat 'Bear *noun* [sing.] (*astronomy* 天) = URSA MAJOR

G

ˌGreat ˈBritain *noun* [U] England, Scotland and Wales, when considered as a unit 大不列顛（包括英格蘭、蘇格蘭和威爾士）HELP Sometimes 'Great Britain' (or 'Britain') is wrongly used to refer to the political state, officially called the 'United Kingdom of Great Britain and Northern Ireland' or the 'UK'. 有時 Great Britain 或 Britain 被錯誤地用來指稱政治意義上的英國，其實官方稱呼應作 United Kingdom of Great Britain and Northern Ireland（大不列顛及北愛爾蘭聯合王國）或簡寫作 UK。

great·coat /ˈgreɪtkəʊt; *NAmE* -koʊt/ *noun* a long heavy coat, especially one worn by soldiers（尤指士兵穿的）厚長大衣

Great Dane /ˌgreɪt ˈdeɪn/ *noun* a very large dog with short hair 丹麥大狗；大丹狗

great·ly 0━ /ˈgreɪtli/ *adv.* (*formal*) (usually before a verb or participle 常用於動詞或分詞前) very much 非常；很；大大地：*People's reaction to the film has varied greatly.* 人們對這部影片的反應大不一樣。◇ *a greatly increased risk* 大大增加了的風險 ◇ *Your help would be greatly appreciated.* 如蒙幫助，感激不盡。

the ˌGreat ˈWar *noun* [sing.] (*old-fashioned*) = THE FIRST WORLD WAR

ˌgreat white ˈshark *noun* a large aggressive SHARK with a brown or grey back, found in warm seas 大白鯊，噬人鯊（棲居於溫熱海域）

the ˌGreat White ˈWay *noun* (*informal*) a name for Broadway in New York City that refers to the many bright lights of its theatres 燈光大道，不夜街（指紐約市百老匯）

grebe /griːb/ *noun* a bird like a DUCK, that can also swim underwater 鸊鷉（潛水鳥）：*a great crested grebe* 鳳頭鸊鷉

Gre·cian /ˈgriːʃn/ *adj.* from ancient Greece or like the styles of ancient Greece 來自古希臘的；古希臘風格的；古希臘式的：*Grecian architecture* 古希臘式建築

ˌGrecian ˈnose *noun* a straight nose that continues the line of the FOREHEAD 希臘式鼻子（鼻梁和額部成一直線）

ˌGreco- *combining form* (*NAmE*) = GRAECO-

greed /griːd/ *noun* [U] (*disapproving*) **1** a strong desire for more wealth, possessions, power, etc. than a person needs 貪婪；貪心；貪慾：*His actions were motivated by greed.* 他的作為是貪婪之心所驅使的。◇ **~ for sth** *Nothing would satisfy her greed for power.* 她對權力貪得無厭。**2** a strong desire for more food or drink when you are no longer hungry or thirsty 貪食；貪吃：*I had another helping of ice cream out of pure greed.* 我純粹是因為嘴饞貪吃，又吃了一份冰淇淋。

greedy /ˈgriːdi/ *adj.* (**greed·ier**, **greedi·est**) wanting more money, power, food, etc. than you really need 貪婪的；貪心的；貪吃的；渴望的：*You greedy pig! You've already had two helpings!* 你這個饞嘴！你已經吃了兩份了！◇ *He stared at the diamonds with greedy eyes.* 他眼巴巴地盯着這些鑽石。◇ **~ for sth** *The shareholders are greedy for profit.* 股東們都利慾熏心。▸ **greed·ily** *adv.*：*She ate noisily and greedily.* 她吧嗒着嘴狼吞虎嚥地吃。

IDM **ˈgreedy guts** (*BrE*, *informal*) used to refer to sb who eats too much 貪吃的傢伙

Greek /griːk/ *noun* **1** [C] a person from modern or ancient Greece 希臘人；古希臘人 **2** [U] the language of modern or ancient Greece 希臘語 **3** [C] (*NAmE*) a member of a FRATERNITY or a SORORITY at a college or university（大學的）學生聯誼會會員，女生聯誼會會員

IDM **it's all ˈGreek to me** (*informal*, *saying*) I cannot understand it 我全然不懂；我一竅不通：*She tried to explain how the system works, but it's all Greek to me.* 她努力解釋系統如何運作，可我就是怎麼也弄不明白。

ˌGreek ˈcross *noun* a cross with all arms of the same length 希臘式十字架（四臂等長）

ˌGreek ˈsalad *noun* [C, U] a salad that is made with tomatoes, OLIVES and FETA CHEESE 希臘風味色拉（用番茄、橄欖和羊奶乾酪調製而成）

green 0━ /griːn/ *adj.*, *noun*, *verb*

■ *adj.* (**green·er**, **green·est**)

▸ COLOUR 顏色 **1** 0━ having the colour of grass or the leaves of most plants and trees 綠色的；草綠色的：*green beans* 青豆 ◇ *Wait for the light to turn green* (= on traffic lights). 等綠燈亮了再走。

▸ COVERED WITH GRASS 青草覆蓋 **2** 0━ covered with grass or other plants 長滿青草的；綠油油的；青葱的：***green fields/hills*** 綠油油的農田；青葱翠綠的山丘 ◇ *After the rains, the land was green with new growth.* 雨天過後，大地一片新綠。

▸ FRUIT 果實 **3** 0━ not yet ready to eat 未成熟的：*green tomatoes* 青西紅柿

▸ POLITICS 政治 **4** 0━ concerned with the protection of the environment; supporting the protection of the environment as a political principle 環境保護的；贊成環保的：*green politics* 主張環保的政見 ◇ *Try to adopt a greener lifestyle.* 盡量採取更環保的生活方式。◇ *the Green Party* 綠黨

▸ PERSON 人 **5** (*informal*) (of a person 人) young and lacking experience 不成熟的；缺乏經驗的；幼稚的：*The new trainees are still very green.* 這些受培訓的新學員還很不成熟。**6** (of a person or their skin 人或其皮膚) being a pale colour, as if the person is going to VOMIT 蒼白的；發青的；無血色的：*It was a rough crossing and most of the passengers looked distinctly green.* 渡海時風浪很大，多數乘客看上去臉色發青。

▸ **green·ness** *noun* [U]：*the greenness of the countryside* 鄉村的青葱翠綠 ◇ *Supermarkets have started proclaiming the greenness of their products.* 超市已開始宣傳他們的產品是綠色環保的。

IDM **ˌgreen with ˈenvy** very jealous（十分）妒忌的，嫉妒的，眼紅的 ➲ more at GRASS *n.*

■ *noun*

▸ COLOUR 顏色 **1** 0━ [U, C] the colour of grass and the leaves of most plants and trees 綠色；草綠色：*the green of the countryside in spring* 春天鄉村的青葱翠綠 ◇ *The room was decorated in a combination of greens and blues.* 這房間是把不同的綠色和藍色搭配起來裝飾的。◇ *She was dressed all in green.* 她全身綠裝。

▸ VEGETABLES 蔬菜 **2** **greens** [pl.] (*especially BrE*) green vegetables 綠色蔬菜；綠葉蔬菜：*Eat up your greens.* 把你那份青菜都吃了吧。

▸ AREA OF GRASS 草地 **3** [C] (*BrE*) an area of grass, especially in the middle of a town or village（尤指城鎮或村莊中心的）草地，草坪，公共綠地：*Children were playing on the village green.* 孩子們在村中心的草地上玩耍。➲ VISUAL VOCAB page V3 **4** [C] (in GOLF 高爾夫球) an area of grass cut short around a hole on a GOLF COURSE 球穴區，果嶺（高爾夫球洞口附近草修得很平整的地區）：*the 18th green* 第 18 輕擊區 ◇ *Did the ball land on the green?* 球落在果嶺了嗎？➲ VISUAL VOCAB page V40 ➲ see also BOWLING GREEN, PUTTING GREEN

▸ POLITICS 政治 **5** **the Greens** [pl.] the Green Party (= the party whose main aim is the protection of the environment) 綠黨（以保護環境為主要目標）

■ *verb*

▸ CREATE PARKS 綠化 **1** **~ sth** to create parks and other areas with trees and plants in a city 綠化：*projects for greening the cities* 綠化城市的方案

▸ POLITICS 政治 **2** **~ sb/sth** to make sb more aware of issues connected with the environment; to make sth appear friendly towards the environment 使增強環境保護意識；使善待環境：*an attempt to green industry bosses* 使企業老闆重視環境保護的努力

▸ **green·ing** *noun* [U]：*the greening of British politics* 使英國政界增加環保意識的過程

ˌgreen ˈaudit *noun* an official examination of the effect of a company's business on the environment 綠色審計，環保審計（就某一公司對環境的影響作出的評估）

green·back /ˈgriːnbæk/ *noun* (*NAmE*, *informal*) an American dollar note 美鈔

ˌgreen ˈbean (*BrE* also **ˌFrench ˈbean**) (*NAmE* also **ˌstring ˈbean**) *noun* a type of BEAN which is a long thin green POD, cooked and eaten whole as a vegetable 青刀豆；四季豆 ➲ VISUAL VOCAB page V31

ˌgreen ˈbelt *noun* [U, C, usually sing.] (*especially BrE*) an area of open land around a city where building is strictly controlled（城市周圍的）綠化地帶：*New roads are cutting into the green belt.* 一條條新路在逐漸吞噬着綠化地帶。

ˌGreen Beˈret *noun* a member of the US army Special Forces 綠色貝雷帽（指美國陸軍特種部隊成員）

ˌgreen ˈcard *noun* **1** a document that legally allows sb from another country to live and work in the US 綠卡（允許外國人在美國居住和工作的法律證件） **2** (*BrE*) an insurance document that you need when you drive your car in another country（在國外開車所需的）綠色保險證

green·ery /ˈɡriːnəri/ *noun* [U] attractive green leaves and plants 青枝綠葉；青葱的草木；綠色植物：*The room was decorated with flowers and greenery.* 房間裏裝點着花卉和綠葉植物。

the ˌgreen-eyed ˈmonster *noun* (*informal*) used as a way of talking about JEALOUSY 綠眼怪獸；嫉妒；妒忌

green·field /ˈɡriːnfiːld/ *adj.* [only before noun] (*BrE*) used to describe an area of land that has not yet had buildings on it, but for which building development may be planned 未開發地區的；地產發展規劃區的；綠色開發區的：*a greenfield site* 綠色開發區

ˌgreen ˈfingers *noun* [pl.] (*BrE*) (*NAmE* **ˌgreen ˈthumb**) if you have **green fingers**, you are good at making plants grow 園藝技能；種植技能 ▸ **ˌgreen-ˈfingered** *adj.* (*BrE*)

green·fly /ˈɡriːnflaɪ/ *noun* [U, C] (*pl.* **green·flies** or **green·fly**) a small flying insect that is harmful to plants 蚜蟲：*The roses have got greenfly.* 這些玫瑰花上有蚜蟲。

green·gage /ˈɡriːnɡeɪdʒ/ *noun* a small soft green fruit that is a type of PLUM 西洋李；青梅子；青李子：*a greengage tree* 青梅子樹

green·gro·cer /ˈɡriːnɡrəʊsə(r); *NAmE* -ɡroʊ-/ *noun* (*especially BrE*) **1** a person who owns, manages or works in a shop/store selling fruit and vegetables 果菜商 ➲ compare FRUITERER **2** **green·gro·cer's** (*pl.* **green·gro·cers**) a shop/store that sells fruit and vegetables 蔬菜水果店

green·horn /ˈɡriːnhɔːn; *NAmE* -hɔːrn/ *noun* (*informal, especially NAmE*) a person who has little experience and can be easily tricked 新手 SYN **tenderfoot**

green·house /ˈɡriːnhaʊs/ *noun* a building with glass sides and a glass roof for growing plants in 溫室；暖房 ➲ **VISUAL VOCAB** page V19

the ˈgreenhouse effect *noun* [sing.] the problem of the gradual rise in temperature of the earth's atmosphere, caused by an increase of gases such as CARBON DIOXIDE in the air surrounding the earth, which trap the heat of the sun 溫室效應 ➲ **COLLOCATIONS** at ENVIRONMENT ➲ see also GLOBAL WARMING

ˌgreenhouse ˈgas *noun* any of the gases that are thought to cause the greenhouse effect, especially CARBON DIOXIDE 溫室氣體（尤指二氧化碳） ➲ **COLLOCATIONS** at ENVIRONMENT

green·ing /ˈɡriːnɪŋ/ *noun* [U] ➲ GREEN *v.*

green·ish /ˈɡriːnɪʃ/ *adj.* fairly green in colour 帶綠色的；淺綠色的

green·keep·er /ˈɡriːnkiːpə(r)/ (*NAmE* also **greens·keep·er**) *noun* a person whose job is to take care of a GOLF COURSE 高爾夫球場看管人

ˌgreen ˈlight *noun* [sing.] permission for a project, etc. to start or continue 准許；許可；綠燈 SYN **go-ahead**：*The government has decided to **give the green light** to the plan.* 政府已決定為這項計劃開綠燈。

ˌgreen maˈnure *noun* [U, C] plants that are dug into the soil in order to improve its quality 綠肥

ˌgreen ˈonion (also **scal·lion**) (both *NAmE*) (*BrE* **ˌspring ˈonion**) *noun* a type of small onion with a long green STEM and leaves. Green onions are often eaten raw in salads. 大葱 ➲ **VISUAL VOCAB** page V31

ˌGreen ˈPaper *noun* (in Britain) a document containing government proposals on a particular subject, intended for general discussion 綠皮書（英國供討論的政府提案文件） ➲ compare WHITE PAPER

ˌgreen ˈpepper *noun* a hollow green fruit that is eaten, raw or cooked, as a vegetable 青椒；甜椒；燈籠椒

ˈgreen roof (also **ˈliving roof**) *noun* a type of roof that has plants growing on it that help to keep the building cool in summer and warm in winter 綠屋頂，綠化屋頂（種植植物以保持房屋冬暖夏涼）

ˈgreen room *noun* a room in a theatre, television studio, etc. where the performers can relax when they are not performing（劇場、電視演播室等的）演員休息室

ˌgreen ˈsalad *noun* [C, U] (*BrE*) a salad that is made with raw green vegetables, especially LETTUCE 綠色拉；生菜色拉：*Serve with a green salad.* 上菜的時候配一份生菜色拉。

greens·keep·er /ˈɡriːnzkiːpə(r)/ *noun* (*NAmE*) = GREENKEEPER

greens·ward /ˈɡriːnswɔːd; *NAmE* -swɔːrd/ *noun* [U] (*literary*) a piece of ground covered with grass 草坪；草地

ˌgreen ˈtea *noun* [U] a pale tea made from leaves that have been dried but not FERMENTED 綠茶

ˌgreen ˈthumb (*NAmE*) (*BrE* **ˌgreen ˈfingers**) *noun* [sing.] if you have a **green thumb**, you are good at making plants grow 園藝技能；種植技能

ˌgreen ˈvegetable *noun* [C, usually pl.] (*BrE* also **greens** [pl.]) a vegetable with dark green leaves, for example CABBAGE or SPINACH 綠葉蔬菜

green·wash /ˈɡriːnwɒʃ; *NAmE* -wɔːʃ/ *noun* [U] (*disapproving*) activities by a company or an organization that are intended to make people think that it is concerned about the environment, even if its real business actually harms the environment 綠色外衣，綠色粉飾，環保幌子，漂綠（指公司或機構假借環保之名進行宣傳）

the ˌgreen ˈwelly brigade *noun* [sing.+sing./pl. v.] (*BrE, humorous, disapproving*) rich people who live in or like to visit the countryside 綠色長筒靴一族（指住在鄉下或熱衷於到鄉下觀光的富人） ORIGIN From the green wellington boots that they often wear. 源自這些人經常穿的綠色威靈頓長筒靴。

Green·wich Mean Time /ˌɡrenɪtʃ ˈmiːn taɪm; -nɪdʒ/ ➲ GMT

greet /ɡriːt/ *verb* **1** to say hello to sb or to welcome them 和（某人）打招呼（或問好）；歡迎；迎接：**～ sb** *He greeted all the guests warmly as they arrived.* 客人到達時他都熱情接待。◇ **～ sb with sth** *She greeted us with a smile.* 她微笑着向我們打招呼。➲ see also MEET-AND-GREET **2** [usually passive] to react to sb/sth in a particular way（以某種方式）對…作出反應：**～ sb/sth** *Loud cheers greeted the news.* 這消息受到熱烈歡呼。◇ **～ sb/sth with sth** *The changes were greeted with suspicion.* 這些變革受到人們的懷疑。◇ **～ sb/sth as sth** *The team's win was greeted as a major triumph.* 這個隊獲勝被看成是一個重大的勝利。 **3** [usually passive] **～ sb** (of sights, sounds or smells 景象、聲音或氣味) to be the first thing that you see, hear or smell at a particular time 映入…的眼簾；傳入…的耳中（或鼻中）：*When she opened the door she was greeted by a scene of utter confusion.* 她打開門，一片混亂不堪的景象呈現在她的眼前。

greet·er /ˈɡriːtə(r)/ *noun* (*especially NAmE*) a person whose job is to meet and welcome people in a public place such as a restaurant or shop/store（餐館、商店等處的）門迎，迎賓

greet·ing /ˈɡriːtɪŋ/ *noun* **1** [C, U] something that you say or do to greet sb 問候；招呼；迎接；致意：*She waved a friendly greeting.* 她友好地揮手致意。◇ *They **exchanged greetings** and sat down to lunch.* 他們相互致意後便坐下吃午飯。◇ *He raised his hand **in greeting**.* 他舉手致意。 **2** **greetings** [pl.] a message of good wishes for sb's health, happiness, etc. 問候的話；祝辭；賀辭：***Christmas/birthday, etc.** greetings* 聖誕、生日等祝辭 ◇ *My mother sends her greetings to you all.* 我母親向你們各位問好。IDM see SEASON *n.*

'greetings card (*BrE*) (*NAmE* **'greeting card**) *noun* a card with a picture on the front and a message inside that you send to sb on a particular occasion such as their birthday 賀卡

gre·gari·ous /grɪ'geəriəs; *NAmE* -'ger-/ *adj.* **1** liking to be with other people 交際的；合群的 SYN **sociable** **2** (*biology* 生) (of animals or birds 動物或鳥) living in groups 群居的 ▶ **gre·gari·ous·ly** *adv.* **gre·gari·ous·ness** *noun* [U]

Gre·gor·ian calendar /grɪˌgɔːriən 'kælɪndə(r)/ *noun* [sing.] the system used since 1582 in Western countries of arranging the months in the year and the days in the months and of counting the years from the birth of Christ 公曆，陽曆，格列高利曆（自 1582 年以來西方國家使用的曆法）➲ compare JULIAN CALENDAR

G

Greˌgorian 'chant *noun* [U, C] a type of church music for voices alone, used since the Middle Ages 格列高利聖歌（自中世紀以來教堂演唱的無伴奏聖歌）

grem·lin /'gremlɪn/ *noun* an imaginary creature that people blame when a machine suddenly stops working（機器停止運轉時人們所責怪假想的）小精靈

gren·ade /grə'neɪd/ *noun* a small bomb that can be thrown by hand or fired from a gun 榴彈；手榴彈；槍榴彈 ➲ see also HAND GRENADE

grena·dier /ˌgrenə'dɪə(r); *NAmE* -'dɪr/ *noun* a soldier in the part of the British army known as the **Grenadiers** or **Grenadier Guards** 英國近衛步兵團的士兵

grena·dine /'grenədiːn/ *noun* [U] a sweet red liquid that is made from POMEGRANATES (= a tropical fruit with many seeds). It is drunk mixed with water or alcoholic drinks. 石榴汁飲料（飲用時摻水或酒）

Gretna Green /ˌgretnə 'griːn/ *noun* a village in Scotland near the border with England, famous in the past as a place where English couples used to go to get married when they were not allowed to get married in England 格雷特納格林（臨近英格蘭邊境的蘇格蘭村莊，舊時一些英格蘭情侶因被禁止在本地結婚而跑到此地成婚，因而聞名）

grew *past tense* of GROW

grey 🔑 (*especially BrE*) (*NAmE* usually **gray**) /greɪ/ *adj.*, *noun*, *verb*

■ ***adj.*** **1** 🔑 having the colour of smoke or ASHES 灰色的；煙灰色的；灰白色的：*grey eyes/hair* 灰色的眼睛；灰白的頭髮 ◇ *wisps of grey smoke* 一縷縷灰色的煙霧 ◇ *a grey suit* 一套灰色西裝 **2** 🔑 [not usually before noun] having grey hair 頭髮花白；頭髮灰白：*He's gone very grey.* 他已滿頭銀絲。**3** 🔑 (of the sky or weather 天空或天氣) dull; full of clouds 昏暗的；陰沉的：*grey skies* 昏暗的天空 ◇ *I hate these grey days.* 我討厭這陰沉沉的天氣。**4** (of a person's skin colour 人的膚色) pale and dull, because they are ill/sick, tired or sad 蒼白的 **5** without interest or variety; making you feel sad 單調乏味的；憂鬱的；沉悶的：*Life seems grey and pointless without him.* 沒有他，生活就顯得沉悶而無意義。**6** (*disapproving*) not interesting or attractive 沒趣味的；毫無吸引力的：*The company was full of faceless grey men who all looked the same.* 公司裏全是些缺乏個性、毫無吸引力的男人。**7** [only before noun] connected with old people 老年人的：*the grey vote* 老年人的投票總數 ◇ *grey power* 長者對社會的影響力 ▶ **grey·ness** (*especially BrE*) (*NAmE* usually **gray·ness**) *noun* [U, sing.]

■ ***noun*** **1** 🔑 [U, C] the colour of smoke or ASHES 灰色；煙灰色；灰白色：*the dull grey of the sky* 暗灰色的天空 ◇ *dressed in grey* 身着灰色衣服 **2** [C] a grey or white horse 灰馬；白馬：*She's riding the grey.* 她騎着一匹灰馬。

■ ***verb*** [I] (of hair 頭髮) to become grey 變灰白；變花白：*His hair was greying at the sides.* 他的兩鬢已漸漸斑白。◇ *a tall woman with greying hair* 頭髮漸白的高個子女人

ˌgrey 'area (*especially BrE*) (*NAmE* usually **ˌgray 'area**) *noun* an area of a subject or situation that is not clear or does not fit into a particular group and is therefore difficult to define or deal with 灰色地帶，中間區域（界線不明、不易歸類、難以界定或處理的領域或形勢）：*Exactly what can be called an offensive weapon is still a grey area.* 究竟什麼可稱作攻擊性武器仍然難以界定。

grey·beard (*especially BrE*) (*NAmE* usually **gray·beard**) /'greɪbɪəd; *NAmE* -bɪrd/ *noun* (*informal*) an old man 老頭兒；老翁：*the greybeards of the art world* 藝術界的老人們

ˌgrey-'haired (*especially BrE*) (*NAmE* usually **ˌgray-'haired**) *adj.* with grey hair 頭髮灰白的；頭髮花白的

grey·hound /'greɪhaʊnd/ *noun* a large thin dog with smooth hair and long thin legs, that can run very fast and is used in the sport of **greyhound racing** 靈猩（身細長、腿長、毛滑、善跑的大賽狗）

grey·ish (*especially BrE*) (*NAmE* usually **gray·ish**) /'greɪɪʃ/ *adj.* fairly grey in colour 帶灰色的；淺灰色的：*greyish hair* 灰白的頭髮

ˌgrey 'market (*NAmE* usually **ˌgray 'market**) *noun* [usually sing.] **1** a system in which products are imported into a country and sold without the permission of the company that produced them 灰市，水貨市場（未經公司授權而進口並銷售其產品的體制）**2** (*BrE*) old people, when they are thought of as customers for goods（統稱）老年顧客，老年客戶

'grey matter (*especially BrE*) (*NAmE* usually **'gray matter**) *noun* [U] (*informal*) a person's intelligence（人的）頭腦，腦子

grey·scale (*especially BrE*) (*NAmE* usually **gray·scale**) /'greɪskeɪl/ *adj.* (*technical* 術語) **1** (of an image 圖像) produced using only shades of grey, not colour 灰度的；灰色調的：*I've printed out the pictures* ***in greyscale***. 我已經用灰色調打印出圖片。**2** (of a printer or SCANNER 打印機或掃描儀) producing images using only shades of grey, not colour 灰度的

grid /grɪd/ *noun* **1** a pattern of straight lines, usually crossing each other to form squares 網格；方格：*New York's grid of streets* 紐約棋盤式的街道佈局 **2** a frame of metal or wooden bars that are parallel or cross each other（金屬或木製的）格子，格柵，柵欄 ➲ see also CATTLE GRID **3** a pattern of squares on a map that are marked with letters or numbers to help you find the exact position of a place（地圖上的）坐標方格：*The* ***grid reference*** *is C8.* 地圖上的坐標方格數字為 C8。**4** (*especially BrE*) a system of electric wires or pipes carrying gas, for sending power over a large area（輸電線路、天然氣管道的）系統網絡；輸電網；煤氣輸送網：*the national grid* (= the electricity supply in a country) 國家輸電網 **5** (in motor racing 汽車比賽) a pattern of lines marking the starting positions for the racing cars 賽車起跑線 **6** (often **the Grid**) [sing.] (*computing* 計) a number of computers that are linked together using the Internet so that they can share power, data, etc. in order to work on difficult problems（利用互聯網的）聯網，聯機

IDM **ˌoff the 'grid** (*especially NAmE*) not using the public supplies of electricity, gas, water, etc. 不用水電等公共設施：*The mountain cabin is entirely off the grid.* 這山中小屋完全不用水電等公共設施。➲ see also OFF-THE-GRID

grid·dle /'grɪdl/ *noun* a flat round iron plate that is heated on a stove or over a fire and used for cooking 鏊子（圓形平底鐵鍋）

grid·iron /'grɪdaɪən; *NAmE* -aɪərn/ *noun* **1** a frame made of metal bars that is used for cooking meat or fish on, over an open fire（烤肉或魚的）烤架，鐵絲格子，鐵箅子 **2** (*NAmE*) a field used for AMERICAN FOOTBALL marked with a pattern of parallel lines（標有平行線的）美式足球球場

grid·lock /'grɪdlɒk; *NAmE* -lɑːk/ *noun* [U] **1** a situation in which there are so many cars in the streets of a town that the traffic cannot move at all 市區交通大堵塞 **2** (usually in politics 通常用於政治) a situation in which people with different opinions are not able to agree with each other and so no action can be taken 僵局（因意見分歧而無法採取行動）：*Congress is in gridlock.* 國會因意見分歧而陷入僵局。▶ **grid·locked** *adj.*

grief /griːf/ *noun* **1** [U, C] **~ (over/at sth)** a feeling of great sadness, especially when sb dies（尤指因某人去世引起的）悲傷，悲痛，傷心：*She was overcome with grief when her husband died.* 丈夫去世時她悲痛欲絕。◇ *They* *were able to share their common joys and griefs.* 他們做到了同甘共苦。 **2** [C, usually sing.] something that causes great sadness 傷心事；悲痛事： *It was a grief to them that they had no children.* 沒有孩子是他們的一塊心病。 **3** [U] (*informal*) problems and worry 擔心；憂慮： *He caused his parents a lot of grief.* 他沒少讓父母操心。

IDM **come to 'grief** (*informal*) **1** to end in total failure 以徹底失敗而告終；慘遭失敗 **2** to be harmed in an accident 受傷；遭到不幸；出事故： *Several pedestrians came to grief on the icy pavement.* 好幾個人都在結了冰的人行道上摔傷了。 **give sb 'grief (about/over sth)** (*informal*) to be annoyed with sb and criticize their behaviour 對某人很生氣（或煩惱）；指責某人 **good 'grief!** (*informal*) used to express surprise or shock （表示驚奇或震驚）哎呀，天哪： *Good grief! What a mess!* 天哪！好亂喲！

'grief-stricken *adj.* feeling extremely sad because of sth that has happened, especially the death of sb（尤因某人的去世而）極度悲傷的，悲痛欲絕的

griev·ance /ˈɡriːvəns/ *noun* ~ (**against sb**) something that you think is unfair and that you complain or protest about 不平的事；委屈；抱怨；牢騷： *Parents were invited to* ***air their grievances*** (= express them) *at the meeting.* 家長們應邀在會上訴說他們的苦衷。◇ *He had been* ***nursing a grievance*** *against his boss for months.* 他幾個月來一直對老闆心懷不滿。◇ *Does the company have a formal* ***grievance procedure*** (= a way of telling sb your complaints at work)? 公司有正式投訴程序嗎？

grieve /ɡriːv/ *verb* **1** [I, T] to feel very sad, especially because sb has died（尤指因某人的去世而）悲傷，悲痛，傷心： ~ (**for/over sb/sth**) *They are still grieving for their dead child.* 他們還在為死去的孩子傷心。◇ *grieving relatives* 悲痛欲絕的親戚 ◇ ~ **sb/sth** *She grieved the death of her husband.* 她為丈夫的去世而悲傷。 **2** [T] (*formal*) to make you feel very sad 使悲傷；使悲痛；使傷心 SYN **pain** : **it grieves sb that ...** *It grieved him that he could do nothing to help her.* 他因無法幫助她而傷心。◇ ~ **sb** *Their lack of interest grieved her.* 他們不感興趣使她很痛心。◇ **it grieves sb to do sth** *It grieved her to leave.* 她要走了，心裏很難過。 IDM see EYE *n.*

griev·ous /ˈɡriːvəs/ *adj.* (*formal*) very serious and often causing great pain or suffering 極嚴重的；使人痛苦的；令人傷心的： *He had been the victim of a grievous injustice.* 他曾遭受極不公正的待遇。▶ **griev·ous·ly** *adv.* : ***grievously hurt/wounded*** 受到嚴重傷害；傷勢嚴重

ˌgrievous ˌbodily 'harm *noun* [U] (*abbr.* **GBH**) (*BrE, law* 律) the crime of causing sb serious physical injury 嚴重人體傷害（罪） ➲ compare ACTUAL BODILY HARM

grif·fin /ˈɡrɪfɪn/ (also **grif·fon**, **gry·phon** /ˈɡrɪfən/) *noun* (in stories) a creature with a LION's body and an EAGLE's wings and head（神話故事中的）獅身鷹首獸

grift·er /ˈɡrɪftə(r)/ *noun* (*especially US*) a person who tricks people into giving them money, etc.（騙取錢財等的）騙子

grill /ɡrɪl/ *noun, verb*

■ **noun** **1** (*BrE*) the part of a cooker that directs heat downwards to cook food that is placed underneath it（炊具、烤爐內的）烤架 ➲ VISUAL VOCAB page V22 ➲ compare BROILER (2) **2** a flat metal frame that you put food on to cook over a fire（置於火上的）烤架 ➲ see also BARBECUE *n.* (1) **3** a dish of grilled food, especially meat 一盤燒烤食物（尤指烤肉） ➲ see also MIXED GRILL **4** (especially in names 尤用於名稱) a restaurant serving grilled food 烤肉餐館；燒烤店： *Harry's Bar and Grill* 哈里烤肉酒吧 **5** = GRILLE

■ **verb** **1** ~ **sth** (*BrE*) to cook food under or over a very strong heat（在高溫下方或上方）燒烤，炙烤： *Grill the sausages for ten minutes.* 把香腸烤十分鐘。◇ *grilled bacon* 烤鹹肉 ➲ compare BROIL (1) ➲ COLLOCATIONS at COOKING **2** ~ **sth** (*NAmE*) to cook food over a fire, especially outdoors（在火上，尤指戶外）燒，烤，焙： *grilled meat and shrimp* 烤肉和烤蝦 **3** ~ **sb** (**about sth**) to ask sb a lot of questions about their ideas, actions, etc., often in an unpleasant way 盤問；追問；審問；責問： *They grilled her about where she had been all night.* 他們盤問她整個夜晚待在什麼地方。 ➲ see also GRILLING

grille (also **grill**) /ɡrɪl/ *noun* a screen made of metal bars or wire that is placed in front of a window, door or piece of machinery in order to protect it（置於窗、門、機器前面的）鐵柵欄，金屬網罩： *a radiator grille* (= at the front of a car)（汽車前的）散熱器面罩 ◇ *a security grille* 安全保護格柵

grill·ing /ˈɡrɪlɪŋ/ *noun* [usually sing.] a period of being questioned closely about your ideas, actions, etc. 盤問，責問，審問（的一段時間）： *The minister faced a tough grilling at today's press conference.* 部長在今天的記者招待會上受到了嚴厲的盤問。

grilse /ɡrɪls/ *noun* a SALMON (= a type of fish) that has returned to a river or lake after spending one winter in the sea（海裏度冬後）洄游的鮭魚

grim /ɡrɪm/ *adj.* (**grim·mer**, **grim·mest**) **1** looking or sounding very serious 嚴肅的；堅定的；陰冷的： *a grim* ***face/look/smile*** 嚴肅的面孔／表情；冷笑 ◇ *She looked grim.* 她表情嚴肅。◇ *with a look of* ***grim determination*** *on his face* 他臉上帶有的堅定不移的神態 ◇ ***grim-faced*** *policemen* 表情嚴肅的警察 **2** unpleasant and depressing 令人不快的；令人沮喪的： *grim news* 令人沮喪的消息 ◇ *We face the grim prospect of still higher unemployment.* 我們面臨着失業率進一步上升的暗淡前景。◇ *The outlook is pretty grim.* 前景令人甚感憂慮。◇ *Things are* ***looking grim*** *for workers in the building industry.* 對建築業的工人來說形勢看來很不樂觀。 **3** (of a place or building 地方或建築物) not attractive; depressing 無吸引力的；陰森的；淒涼的： *The house looked grim and dreary in the rain.* 這房子在雨中顯得陰鬱淒涼。◇ *the grim walls of the prison* 令人抑鬱的監獄四壁 **4** [not before noun] (*BrE, informal*) ill/sick 生病的；不舒服的： *I feel grim this morning.* 我今天早上感到不舒服。 **5** [not usually before noun] (*BrE, informal*) of very low quality 質量低劣；糟糕： *Their performance was fairly grim, I'm afraid!* 很遺憾，他們的表現真不怎麼樣！ ▶ **grim·ly** *adv.* : *'It won't be easy,' he said grimly.* "那不會很容易。" 他嚴肅地說。◇ *grimly determined* 堅定不移 **grim·ness** *noun* [U]

IDM **hang/hold on for/like grim 'death** (*BrE*) (also **hang/hold on for dear 'life** *NAmE, BrE*) (*informal*) to hold sb/sth very tightly because you are afraid（害怕得）死死抓住不放，緊緊抓住不鬆手

grim·ace /ɡrɪˈmeɪs; ˈɡrɪməs/ *verb, noun*

■ **verb** [I] ~ (**at sb/sth**) to make an ugly expression with your face to show pain, disgust, etc.（因痛苦、厭惡等）做鬼臉，做怪相： *He grimaced at the bitter taste.* 他一嚐那苦味，做了個怪相。◇ *She grimaced as the needle went in.* 針扎進去痛得她齜牙咧嘴。

■ **noun** an ugly expression made by twisting your face, used to show pain, disgust, etc. or to make sb laugh 怪相；鬼臉；臉部扭曲： *to* ***make/give a grimace*** *of pain* 做出／露出痛苦的表情 ◇ *'What's that?' she asked with a grimace.* "那是什麼？" 她皺着眉頭問道。

grime /ɡraɪm/ *noun* [U] dirt that forms a layer on the surface of sth 一層污垢；塵垢；積垢 SYN **dirt** : *a face covered with grime and sweat* 滿是污垢和汗水的臉

the ˌGrim 'Reaper *noun* an imaginary figure who represents death. It looks like a SKELETON, wears a long CLOAK and carries a SCYTHE. 猙獰的收割者（指骷髏狀死神，身披斗篷，手持長柄大鐮刀）

grimy /ˈɡraɪmi/ *adj.* (**grimi·er**, **grimi·est**) covered with dirt 沾滿污垢的；滿是灰塵的 SYN **dirty** : *grimy hands/windows* 沾滿污垢的手；滿是灰塵的窗戶

grin /ɡrɪn/ *verb, noun*

■ **verb** (-nn-) [I, T] to smile widely 露齒而笑；咧着嘴笑；粲然而笑： *They grinned with delight when they heard our news.* 他們得知我們的消息時高興得直咧着嘴笑。◇ *He was* ***grinning from ear to ear.*** 他笑得合不攏嘴。◇ ~ **at sb** *She grinned amiably at us.* 她咧着嘴向我們親切地微笑。◇ ~ **sth** *He grinned a wide grin.* 他粲然一笑。

IDM **grin and 'bear it** (only used as an infinitive and in orders 只用作不定式和用於命令中) to accept pain, disappointment or a difficult situation without complaining 默默忍受；苦笑着忍受： *There's nothing we can do about*

G

G

it. We'll just have to grin and bear it. 對此我們無能為力，只好默默地忍受。➲ more at EAR

■ **noun** a wide smile 露齒的笑；咧着嘴笑：*She gave a* ***broad grin****.* 她露出大大的笑容。◇ *a* ***wry/sheepish grin*** 咧嘴苦笑；尷尬的笑◇ *'No,' he said* ***with a grin****.* "不。"他咧嘴笑了笑說。◇ ***Take that grin off your face!*** 別嬉皮笑臉的！

grind /graɪnd/ *verb, noun*

■ **verb** (**ground, ground** /graʊnd/)

▸ **FOOD/FLOUR/COFFEE** 食物；麵粉；咖啡 **1** [T] **~ sth (down/up)** | **~ sth (to/into sth)** to break or crush sth into very small pieces between two hard surfaces or using a special machine 磨碎；碾碎；把…磨成粉：*to grind coffee/corn* 將咖啡 / 穀粒磨成粉 ➲ see also GROUND *adj.* **2** [T] **~ sth** to produce sth such as flour by crushing 磨（粉）：*The flour is ground using traditional methods.* 這麵粉是用傳統方法磨製而成。 **3** [T] **~ sth** (*NAmE*) = MINCE *v.* (1)

▸ **MAKE SHARP/SMOOTH** 使鋒利 / 光滑 **4** [T] **~ sth** to make sth sharp or smooth by rubbing it against a hard surface 使鋒利；磨快；磨光：*a special stone for grinding knives* 專門磨刀用的石頭

▸ **PRESS INTO SURFACE** 擠壓進表層 **5** [T] to press or rub sth into a surface 用力擠壓，用力擦（入表層）：**~ sth into sth** *He ground his cigarette into the ashtray.* 他把香煙按在煙灰缸裏捻滅。◇ **~ sth in** *The dirt on her hands was ground in.* 她手上的泥漬住了。

▸ **RUB TOGETHER** 磨擦 **6** [I, T] to rub together, or to make hard objects rub together, often producing an unpleasant noise 磨擦（發出刺耳聲）：**~ (together)** *Parts of the machine were grinding together noisily.* 機器零件摩擦發出刺耳的聲音。◇ **~ sth (together)** *She* ***grinds her teeth*** *when she is asleep.* 她睡覺時磨牙。◇ *He ground the gears on the car.* 他把汽車排擋踩得嘎嘎作響。

▸ **MACHINE** 機器 **7** [T] **~ sth** to turn the handle of a machine that grinds sth 搖動手柄（操縱機器）：*to grind a pepper mill* 搖動胡椒磨

IDM **bring sth to a grinding 'halt** to make sth gradually go slower until it stops completely 使漸漸停下來 **grind to a 'halt | come to a grinding 'halt** to go slower gradually and then stop completely 慢慢停下來：*Production ground to a halt during the strike.* 罷工期間生產漸漸陷入癱瘓。➲ more at AXE *n.*

PHR V **,grind sb↔'down** to treat sb in a cruel unpleasant way over a long period of time, so that they become very unhappy（長時間）虐待，欺壓，折磨（某人）：*Don't let them grind you down.* 別讓他們欺壓你。◇ *Years of oppression had ground the people down.* 人民年復一年地遭受着壓迫。 **,grind 'on** to continue for a long time, when this is unpleasant 令人厭煩地繼續下去：*The argument ground on for almost two years.* 這場爭論拖拖拉拉持續了近兩年。 **,grind sth↔'out** to produce sth in large quantities, often sth that is not good or interesting 大量生產（常指粗製濫造）**SYN** **churn out**：*She grinds out romantic novels at the rate of five a year.* 她以一年五部的速度胡亂拼湊低劣的愛情小說。

■ **noun**

▸ **BORING ACTIVITY** 乏味的活動 **1** [sing.] (*informal*) an activity that is tiring or boring and takes a lot of time 令人疲勞（或厭倦）的工作；苦差事：*the* ***daily grind*** *of family life* 家庭生活中繁重的家務勞動◇ *It's a long grind to the top of that particular profession.* 爬到那種行業的最高位置要經過漫長的艱苦奮鬥。

▸ **OF MACHINES** 機器 **2** [sing.] the unpleasant noise made by machines 刺耳的摩擦聲

▸ **SWOT** 刻苦用功的人 **3** (*US*) (*BrE* **swot**) [C] (*informal*) a person who spends too much time studying 只知一味用功學習的人；書呆子

grind·er /'graɪndə(r)/ *noun* **1** a machine or tool for grinding a solid substance into a powder 碾磨器械：*a coffee grinder* 磨咖啡機 **2** a person whose job is to make knives sharper; a machine which does this 磨刀匠；磨工；磨牀 ➲ see also ORGAN-GRINDER

grind·ing /'graɪndɪŋ/ *adj.* [only before noun] (of a difficult situation 困難的形勢) that never ends or improves 沒完沒了的；無休止的；無改進的：*grinding poverty* 貧困不堪

grind·stone /'graɪndstəʊn; *NAmE* -stoʊn/ *noun* a round stone that is turned like a wheel and is used to make knives and other tools sharp 磨石；砂輪 **IDM** see NOSE *n.*

gringo /'grɪŋgəʊ; *NAmE* -goʊ/ *noun* (*pl.* **-os**) (*informal, disapproving*) used in Latin American countries to refer to a person from the US 美國佬（在拉丁美洲國家使用）

griot /'gri:əʊ; *NAmE* 'gri:oʊ/ *noun* (in W Africa, especially in the past) a person who sings or tells stories about the history and traditions of their people and community（西非，尤指舊時的）部族史（或傳統）說唱藝人

grip /grɪp/ *noun, verb*

■ **noun**

▸ **HOLDING TIGHTLY** 緊握 **1** [C, usually sing.] **~ (on sb/sth)** an act of holding sb/sth tightly; a particular way of doing this 緊握；緊抓 **SYN** **grasp**：*Keep a tight grip on the rope.* 緊緊抓住繩索不放。◇ *to* ***loosen/release/relax your grip*** 鬆手◇ *She tried to* ***get a grip on*** *the icy rock.* 她盡力抓住那冰冷的石頭。◇ *The climber slipped and* ***lost her grip****.* 登山女子滑了一下鬆開了手。◇ *She struggled from his grip.* 他緊拉住她不放，她奮力掙脫。◇ *Try adjusting your grip on the racket.* 試着調整一下你握球拍的方法。

▸ **CONTROL/POWER** 控制力；影響力 **2** [sing.] **~ (on sb/sth)** control or power over sb/sth（對…的）控制，影響力：*The home team took a firm grip on the game.* 主隊牢牢控制着比賽的局面。◇ *We need to tighten the grip we have on the market.* 我們得加強對市場的控制力。

▸ **UNDERSTANDING** 理解 **3** [sing.] **~ (on sth)** an understanding of sth 理解；瞭解 **SYN** **grasp**：*I couldn't get a grip on what was going on.* 我無法理解正在發生的事情。◇ *You need to keep a good grip on reality in this job.* 做這個工作你需要充分瞭解實際情況。

▸ **MOVING WITHOUT SLIPPING** 不打滑 **4** [U] the ability of sth to move over a surface without slipping 不打滑；走得穩：*These tyres give the bus better grip in slippery conditions.* 這些輪胎可使公共汽車在路滑時行駛得平穩一些。

▸ **PART OF OBJECT** 物體部位 **5** [C] a part of sth that has a special surface so that it can be held without the hands slipping 把手；手柄；握柄：*the grip on a golf club* 高爾夫球棒的握柄

▸ **FOR HAIR** 頭髮 **6** [C] (*BrE*) = HAIRGRIP

▸ **JOB IN THE MOVIES** 影業工作 **7** [C] a person who prepares and moves the cameras, and sometimes the lighting equipment, when a film/movie is being made（拍攝電影時）攝影機和燈光設備管理人員

▸ **BAG** 包 **8** [C] (*old-fashioned*) a large soft bag, used when travelling 旅行袋；手提包

IDM **come/get to 'grips with sth** to begin to understand and deal with sth difficult 開始理解並着手處理難題：*I'm slowly getting to grips with the language.* 我慢慢開始掌握這種語言。 **get/take a 'grip (on yourself)** to improve your behaviour or control your emotions after being afraid, upset or angry 使（自己）鎮定下來；控制住（自己的）情緒：*I have to take a grip on myself, he told himself firmly.* 我一定要控制住自己的情緒，他堅定地對自己說。◇ (*informal*) ***Get a grip!*** (= make an effort to control your emotions) 鎮靜點！ **in the 'grip of sth** experiencing sth unpleasant that cannot be stopped 處於不快卻無法制止的境遇；受制於某事：*a country in the grip of recession* 陷入衰退的國家 **lose your 'grip (on sth)** to become unable to understand or control a situation 失去（對…的）理解（或控制）；駕馭不住：*Sometimes I feel I'm losing my grip.* 有時我感到自己無能為力。

■ **verb** (**-pp-**)

▸ **HOLD TIGHTLY** 緊握 **1** [T, I] to hold sth tightly 緊握；緊抓 **SYN** **grasp**：**~ sth** *'Please don't go,' he said, gripping her arm.* "請別走。"他緊緊抓住她的手臂說。◇ **~ on to sth** *She gripped on to the railing with both hands.* 她雙手緊緊抓住欄杆。➲ SYNONYMS at HOLD

▸ **INTEREST/EXCITE** 使感興趣；使激動 **2** [T] **~ sb** to interest or excite sb; to hold sb's attention 使感興趣；使激動；吸引住（某人）的注意：*The book grips you from start to finish.* 這本書從頭至尾扣人心弦。◇ *I was totally gripped* by the story. 我完全被這故事吸引住了。 ➲ see also GRIPPING

▸ **HAVE POWERFUL EFFECT 具有強烈的影響力 3** [T] **~ sb/sth** (of an emotion or a situation 情緒或形勢) to have a powerful effect on sb/sth 對…產生強有力的影響：*I was gripped by a feeling of panic.* 我驚恐萬狀。◇ *Terrorism has gripped the country for the past two years.* 兩年來恐怖主義一直籠罩着這個國家。

▸ **MOVE/HOLD WITHOUT SLIPPING 不打滑；抓牢 4** [T, I] **~ (sth)** to hold onto or to move over a surface without slipping 抓牢：*tyres that grip the road* 在公路上不打滑的車胎

gripe /ɡraɪp/ *noun, verb*

■ ***noun*** (*informal*) a complaint about sth 抱怨；怨言；牢騷：*My only gripe about the hotel was the food.* 我對這家旅館唯一不滿的是食物。

■ ***verb*** [I] **~ (about sb/sth)** (*informal*) to complain about sb/sth in an annoying way 抱怨；發牢騷：*He's always griping about the people at work.* 他老是抱怨共事的人。

ˈGripe Water™ *noun* [U] (*BrE*) medicine that is given to babies when they have stomach pains （緩解嬰兒腹痛的）止痛水

grip·ing /ˈɡraɪpɪŋ/ *adj.* [only before noun] a **griping** pain is a sudden strong pain in your stomach 腸（或胃）絞痛的

grip·ping /ˈɡrɪpɪŋ/ *adj.* exciting or interesting in a way that keeps your attention 激動人心的；吸引人的；扣人心弦的 ➲ SYNONYMS at INTERESTING

grisly /ˈɡrɪzli/ *adj.* [usually before noun] (**gris·lier**, **gris·li·est**) extremely unpleasant and frightening and usually connected with death and violence 令人厭惡的；恐怖的；可怕的：*a grisly crime* 可憎的罪行

grist /ɡrɪst/ *noun*

IDM **(all) grist to the/sb's ˈmill** (*BrE*) (*NAmE* **(all) grist for the/sb's ˈmill**) something that is useful to sb for a particular purpose 對…有用的東西（或有利的事）：*Political sex scandals are all grist to the mill of the tabloid newspapers.* 政界的性醜聞對通俗小報總是多多益善。

gris·tle /ˈɡrɪsl/ *noun* [U] a hard substance in meat that is unpleasant to eat （肉中的）軟骨：*a lump of gristle* 一塊軟骨

grit /ɡrɪt/ *noun, verb*

■ ***noun*** [U] **1** very small pieces of stone or sand 沙粒；沙礫；細沙：*I had a piece of grit in my eye.* 我眼睛裏進了一粒沙子。◇ *They were spreading grit and salt on the icy roads.* 他們在結冰的路上撒沙子和鹽。 **2** the courage and determination that makes it possible for sb to continue doing sth difficult or unpleasant 勇氣；毅力

■ ***verb*** (**-tt-**) **~ sth** to spread grit, salt or sand on a road that is covered with ice （在結冰的路上）撒沙礫，撒鹽，撒沙子

IDM **grit your ˈteeth 1** to bite your teeth tightly together 咬緊牙關：*She gritted her teeth against the pain.* 她咬牙忍痛。◇ *'Stop it!' he said through gritted teeth.* "住手！" 他咬牙切齒地說。 **2** to be determined to continue to do sth in a difficult or unpleasant situation 下定決心；鼓起勇氣：*It started to rain harder, but we gritted our teeth and carried on.* 雨開始大起來，可我們鼓起勇氣繼續下去。

grits /ɡrɪts/ *noun* [pl.] CORN (MAIZE) that is partly crushed before cooking, often eaten for breakfast or as part of a meal in the southern US （美國南部吃的）粗玉米粉，玉米糝

grit·ter /ˈɡrɪtə(r)/ (*BrE*) (*US* **ˈsalt truck**) *noun* a large vehicle used for putting salt, sand or GRIT on the roads in winter when there is ice on them 鋪沙機，撒鹽車，撒沙車（在結冰的路面上使用）

gritty /ˈɡrɪti/ *adj.* (**grit·ier**, **grit·ti·est**) **1** containing or like GRIT 含沙礫的；沙礫般的：*a layer of gritty dust* 一層沙塵 **2** showing the courage and determination to continue doing sth difficult or unpleasant 有勇氣的；堅定的；堅毅的：*gritty determination* 堅定的決心 ◇ *a gritty performance from the British player* 這位英國運動員的勇敢表現 **3** showing sth unpleasant as it really is （對不好事物的描述）逼真的，真實的，活生生的：*a gritty description of urban violence* 對城市暴力的真實描述 ◇ *gritty realism* 活生生的現實 ➲ see also NITTY-GRITTY

▸ **grit·tily** *adv.* **grit·ti·ness** *noun* [U]

griz·zle /ˈɡrɪzl/ *verb* [I] (*BrE, informal*) (especially of a baby or child 尤指嬰兒或小孩) to cry or complain continuously in a way that is annoying 不斷地啼哭；哭哭啼啼地纏人

griz·zled /ˈɡrɪzld/ *adj.* (*literary*) having hair that is grey or partly grey （頭髮）灰白的，花白的

griz·zly bear /ˌɡrɪzli ˈbeə(r); *NAmE* ˈber/ (also **ˈgriz·zly** *pl.* **-ies**) *noun* a large aggressive brown BEAR that lives in N America and parts of Russia 灰熊，銀尖熊（生活在北美和俄國部份地區的大型棕熊）

groan /ɡrəʊn; *NAmE* ɡroʊn/ *verb, noun*

■ ***verb*** **1** [I, T] to make a long deep sound because you are annoyed, upset or in pain, or with pleasure 呻吟；歎息；哼哼 SYN **moan**：*He lay on the floor groaning.* 他躺在地板上呻吟。◇ **~ with sth** *to groan with pain/pleasure* 痛苦地呻吟；高興得直哼哼 ◇ **~ at sth** *We all groaned at his terrible jokes.* 他講的笑話很糟糕，我們都發出不滿的抱怨聲。◇ **~ about sth** *They were all* ***moaning and groaning*** (= complaining) *about the amount of work they had.* 他們對工作量都怨聲載道。◇ **+ speech** *'It's a complete mess!' she groaned.* "這簡直是一團糟！" 她歎息道。 **2** [I] to make a sound like a person groaning 發出似呻吟的聲音 SYN **moan**：*The trees creaked and groaned in the wind.* 樹在風中嘎吱作響。

IDM **groan under the weight of sth** (*formal*) used to say that there is too much of sth 在某物的折磨（或重壓）下呻吟；被某物壓得喘不過氣來（或無法忍受）

PHR V **ˈgroan with sth** (*formal*) to be full of sth 被某物堆滿（或擺滿、裝滿、充滿）：*tables groaning with food* 擺滿食物的桌子

■ ***noun*** a long deep sound made when sb/sth groans 呻吟聲；歎息聲；哼哼聲；嘎吱聲 SYN **moan**：*She let out a groan of dismay.* 她發出沮喪的歎息聲。◇ *He fell to the floor with a groan.* 他哼了一聲倒在地板上。◇ *The house was filled with the cello's dismal squeaks and groans.* 房子裏迴盪着大提琴低沉而淒厲的聲音。

groat /ɡrəʊt; *NAmE* ɡroʊt/ *noun* a silver coin used in Europe in the past 格羅特（歐洲舊時銀幣）

gro·cer /ˈɡrəʊsə(r); *NAmE* ˈɡroʊ-/ *noun* **1** a person who owns, manages or works in a shop/store selling food and other things used in the home 食物雜貨商 **2 gro·cer's** (*pl.* **gro·cers**) a shop/store that sells these things 食物雜貨店

gro·cery 0‑w /ˈɡrəʊsəri; *NAmE* ˈɡroʊ-/ *noun* (*pl.* **-ies**)
1 0‑w (*especially BrE*) (*NAmE* usually **ˈgrocery store**) [C] a shop/store that sells food and other things used in the home. In American English 'grocery store' is often used to mean 'supermarket'. 食品雜貨店（在美式英語中 grocery store 常用以指 supermarket） **2** 0‑w **groceries** [pl.] food and other goods sold by a grocer or at a supermarket 食品雜貨 ➲ COLLOCATIONS at SHOPPING

▸ **gro·cery** *adj.* [only before noun]：*the grocery bill* 食品雜貨賬單

grog /ɡrɒɡ; *NAmE* ɡrɑːɡ/ *noun* [U] **1** a strong alcoholic drink, originally RUM, mixed with water 格洛格酒（用朗姆酒兑水製成的烈酒） **2** (*informal, AustralE, NZE*) any alcoholic drink, especially beer 酒（尤指啤酒）

groggy /ˈɡrɒɡi; *NAmE* ˈɡrɑːɡi/ *adj.* [not usually before noun] (**grog·gier**, **grog·gi·est**) (*informal*) weak and unable to think or move well because you are ill/sick or very tired （因疾病或疲勞而）昏昏沉沉，眩暈無力，踉踉蹌蹌

groin /ɡrɔɪn/ *noun* **1** the part of the body where the legs join at the top including the area around the GENITALS (= sex organs) 腹股溝；大腿根兒：*She kicked her attacker in the groin.* 她朝襲擊者的下身踢了一腳。◇ *He's been off all season with a groin injury.* 他因腹股溝傷痛休息了整個賽季。 ➲ VISUAL VOCAB page V59 **2** (*especially US*) = GROYNE

grok /ɡrɒk; *NAmE* ɡrɑːk/ (**-kk-**) *verb* **~ sth** (*US, slang*) to understand sth completely using your feelings rather than considering the facts 通過感覺意會：*Children grok this show immediately but their parents take longer to* *get it.* 孩子很快就通過感覺理解了這一演出，他們的父母卻花了更長的時間才理解。

grom·met /ˈɡrɒmɪt; *NAmE* ˈɡrɑːm-/ *noun* **1** a small metal ring placed around a hole in cloth or leather, to make it stronger（織物或皮革上用以加固扣眼的）金屬環，金屬圈 **2** (*BrE*) (*NAmE* **tube**) a small tube placed in a child's ear in order to DRAIN liquid from it 鼓室通氣管；中耳引流管

groom /ɡruːm/ *verb, noun*

■ *verb* **1 ~ sth** to clean or brush an animal（給動物）擦洗，刷洗：*to groom a horse/dog/cat* 刷洗馬／狗／貓 ◇ *The horses are all well fed and groomed.* 這些馬都餵得飽飽的，刷洗得乾乾淨淨。 **2 ~ sth** (of an animal 動物) to clean the fur or skin of another animal or itself（給自己或其他動物）理毛，梳毛：*a female ape grooming her mate* 為同伴梳毛的母猿 **3** to prepare or train sb for an important job or position 使做好準備；培養；訓練：**~ sb (for/as sth)** *Our junior employees are being groomed for more senior roles.* 我們的初級雇員正在接受培訓以承擔更重要的職責。◇ **~ sb to do sth** *The eldest son is being groomed to take over when his father dies.* 長子正在接受培養，以在父親過世後接手父業。 **4 ~ sb** (of a person who is sexually attracted to children 對兒童有性興趣的人) to prepare a child for a meeting, especially using an Internet CHAT ROOM, with the intention of performing an illegal sexual act 為約會（兒童）做準備，引誘（尤指利用互聯網聊天室進行非法性活動）

■ *noun* **1** a person whose job is to feed and take care of horses, especially by brushing and cleaning them 馬夫；馬倌；馬匹飼養員 **2** = BRIDEGROOM

groomed /ɡruːmd/ *adj.* (usually following an adverb 通常用於副詞之後) used to describe the way in which a person cares for their clothes and hair（描述穿着打扮情況）：*She is always perfectly groomed.* 她總是打扮得乾淨利落。➲ see also WELL GROOMED

groom·ing /ˈɡruːmɪŋ/ *noun* [U] **1** the things that you do to keep your clothes and hair clean and neat, or to keep an animal's fur or hair clean 打扮；裝束；刷洗；（給動物）梳毛：*You should always pay attention to personal grooming.* 你應隨時注意個人衣着整潔。 **2** the process in which an adult develops a friendship with a child, particularly through the Internet, with the intention of having a sexual relationship 勾引幼童（尤指通過網絡與兒童交友以達到發生性關係的目的）

grooms·man /ˈɡruːmzmən/ *noun* (*pl.* **-men** /-mən/) (*NAmE*) a friend of the BRIDEGROOM at a wedding, who has special duties 男儐相；伴郎

groove /ɡruːv/ *noun* **1** a long narrow cut in the surface of sth hard 溝；槽；轍；紋 **2** (*informal*) a particular type of musical rhythm（某種）音樂節奏：*a jazz groove* 爵士樂節奏

IDM **be (stuck) in a ˈgroove** (*BrE*) to be unable to change sth that you have been doing the same way for a long time and that has become boring 墨守成規；照慣例行事

grooved /ɡruːvd/ *adj.* having a groove or grooves 有溝的；有槽的

groovy /ˈɡruːvi/ *adj.* (*old-fashioned, informal*) fashionable, attractive and interesting 時髦的；吸引人的；有趣的

grope /ɡrəʊp; *NAmE* ɡroʊp/ *verb, noun*

■ *verb* **1** [I] **~ (around)(for sth)** to try and find sth that you cannot see, by feeling with your hands 摸索；摸索；搜尋；探尋：*He groped around in the dark for his other sock.* 他在黑暗中到處瞎摸找另一隻襪子。◇ (*figurative*) *'It's so ..., so ...' I was groping for the right word to describe it.* "它是那麼…，那麼…"我想找一個恰當的字眼來描述它。 **2** [T, I] to try and reach a place by feeling with your hands because you cannot see clearly（用手）摸索着往前走：**~ your way + adv./prep.** *He groped his way up the staircase in the dark.* 他摸黑走上樓梯。◇ **+ adv./prep.** *She groped through the darkness towards the doors.* 她摸黑朝門口走去。 **3** [T] **~ sb** (*informal*) to touch sb sexually, especially when they do not want you to 猥褻；摸（某人）

■ *noun* (*informal*) an act of groping sb (= touching them sexually) 猥褻；摸

gross /ɡrəʊs; *NAmE* ɡroʊs/ *adj., adv., verb, noun*

■ *adj.* (**gross·er**, **gross·est**) **1** [only before noun] being the total amount of sth before anything is taken away 總的；毛的：***gross weight*** (= including the container or wrapping) 毛重 ◇ ***gross income/wage*** (= before taxes, etc. are taken away)（稅前）總收益／工資 ◇ *Investments showed a **gross profit** of 26%.* 投資毛利為 26%。➲ compare NET *adj.* (1) **2** [only before noun] (*formal* or *law* 律) (of a crime, etc. 罪行等) very obvious and unacceptable 嚴重的：***gross indecency/negligence/misconduct*** 嚴重猥褻／過失／瀆職 ◇ *a **gross violation** of human rights* 嚴重違反人權 **3** (*informal*) very unpleasant 令人不快的；令人噁心的；使人厭惡的 **SYN** **disgusting**：*'He ate it with mustard.' 'Oh, gross!'* "他用芥末拌着吃。""啊，真噁心！" ➲ SYNONYMS at DISGUSTING **4** very rude 粗魯的；不雅的 **SYN** **crude**：*gross behaviour* 粗魯的行為 **5** very fat and ugly 肥胖而醜陋的：*She's not just fat, she's positively gross!* 她不只是胖，她簡直是五大三粗！▸ **gross·ness** *noun* [U]

■ *adv.* in total, before anything is taken away 總共；全部：*She earns £25 000 a year gross.* 她一年總收入為 25 000 英鎊。➲ compare NET *adj.*

■ *verb* **~ sth** to earn a particular amount of money before tax has been taken off it 總收入為；總共賺得：*It is one of the biggest grossing movies of all time.* 這是票房收入創歷史之最的影片之一。

PHR V **ˌgross sb ˈout** (*NAmE, informal*) to be very unpleasant and make sb feel disgusted 使人噁心；令人憎惡；令人作嘔 **SYN** **disgust**：*His bad breath really grossed me out.* 他的口臭實在使我噁心。

■ *noun* **1** (*pl.* **gross**) a group of 144 things 一羅（144 個）：*two gross of apples* 兩羅蘋果 ◇ *to sell sth by the gross* 按羅出售某物 **2** (*pl.* **grosses**) (*especially US*) a total amount of money earned by sth, especially a film/movie, before any costs are taken away（尤指影片的）毛收入，總收入

ˌgross doˌmestic ˈproduct *noun* [sing., U] = GDP

gross·ly /ˈɡrəʊsli; *NAmE* ˈɡroʊsli/ *adv.* (*disapproving*) (used to describe unpleasant qualities 形容令人不快的事物) extremely 極度地；極其；非常：***grossly overweight/unfair/inadequate*** 極胖／不公平／不充分 ◇ *Press reports have been grossly exaggerated.* 新聞報道過於誇張。

ˌgross ˌnational ˈproduct *noun* [sing., U] = GNP

ˈgross-out *noun* (*especially NAmE, informal*) something disgusting 令人厭惡的東西；倒胃口的東西：*They eat flies? What a gross-out!* 他們吃蒼蠅？真噁心！▸ **ˈgross-out** *adj.* [only before noun]：*gross-out movie scenes* 令人作嘔的電影鏡頭

grot /ɡrɒt; *NAmE* ɡrɑːt/ *noun* [U] (*BrE, informal*) something unpleasant, dirty or of poor quality 討厭（或骯髒、劣質）的東西

gro·tesque /ɡrəʊˈtesk; *NAmE* ɡroʊ-/ *adj., noun*

■ *adj.* **1** strange in a way that is unpleasant or offensive 怪誕的；荒唐的；荒謬的：*a grotesque distortion of the truth* 對事實的荒誕歪曲 ◇ *It's grotesque to expect a person of her experience to work for so little money.* 想讓她那樣有經驗的人為這點錢工作真是荒唐。 **2** extremely ugly in a strange way that is often frightening or amusing 醜陋奇異的；奇形怪狀的：*a grotesque figure* 奇形怪狀的人像 ◇ *tribal dancers wearing grotesque masks* 戴着奇異面具的部落跳舞者 ▸ **gro·tesque·ly** *adv.*

■ *noun* **1** [C] a person who is extremely ugly in a strange way, especially in a book or painting（尤指書畫中的）奇形怪狀的人，醜陋的人 **2 the grotesque** [sing.] a style of art using grotesque figures and designs 奇異藝術風格

grotto /ˈɡrɒtəʊ; *NAmE* ˈɡrɑːtoʊ/ *noun* (*pl.* **-oes** or **-os**) a small CAVE, especially one that has been made artificially, for example in a garden 洞穴；（尤指園林等中的）人工洞穴

grotty /ˈɡrɒti; *NAmE* ˈɡrɑːti/ *adj.* (*BrE, informal*) (**grot·tier**, **grot·ti·est**) unpleasant or of poor quality 令人討厭的；令人不悅的；低劣的：*a grotty little hotel* 條件惡劣的小

旅店 ◇ *I'm feeling pretty grotty* (= ill). 我感到身體很不舒服。

grouch /graʊtʃ/ *noun* (*informal*) **1** a person who complains a lot 好抱怨（或發牢騷）的人 **2** a complaint about sth unimportant （對小事的）抱怨，牢騷 ▸ **grouch** *verb* [I]

grouchy /ˈgraʊtʃi/ *adj.* (*informal*) bad-tempered and often complaining 脾氣不好並常發牢騷的；好抱怨的

ground /graʊnd/ *noun, verb, adj.* ➲ see also GRIND *v.*

■ ***noun***

▸ **SURFACE OF EARTH 地面** **1** (often **the ground**) [U] the solid surface of the earth 地；地面：*I found her lying* ***on the ground.*** 我發現她躺在地上。◇ *He lost his balance and fell* ***to the ground.*** 他失去平衡摔倒在地上。◇ *2 metres* ***above/below ground*** 地上／地下 2 米 ◇ *Most of the monkeys' food is found* ***at ground level.*** 猴子的食物大多可在地面找到。◇ ***ground forces*** (= soldiers that fight on land, not in the air or at sea) 地面部隊 ◇ *Houses and a luxury tourist hotel were* ***burned to the ground*** (= completely destroyed, so that there is nothing left). 多間房屋和一家豪華旅館被大火焚燒殆盡。➲ SYNONYMS at FLOOR

▸ **SOIL 土壤** **2** [U] soil on the surface of the earth 土；土地；土壤：*fertile ground for planting crops* 種植農作物的肥沃土壤 ➲ SYNONYMS at SOIL

▸ **AREA OF LAND 場地** **3** [U] an area of open land 開闊地；空曠地：*The kids were playing on* ***waste ground*** *behind the school.* 孩子們在學校後面的荒地上玩耍。**4** [C] (often in compounds 常構成複合詞) (*BrE*) an area of land that is used for a particular purpose, activity or sport（特定用途的）場地：*a* ***football/recreation/ sports, etc. ground*** 足球場、娛樂場地、運動場等 ◇ *ancient burial grounds* 古代墓地 ➲ see also BREEDING GROUND, DUMPING GROUND, PARADE GROUND, STAMPING GROUND, TESTING GROUND ➲ SYNONYMS at LAND **5** **grounds** [pl.] a large area of land or sea that is used for a particular purpose （某種用途的）地域，水域：*fishing grounds* 漁場 ◇ *feeding grounds for birds* 禽類飼養場

▸ **GARDENS 花園** **6** **grounds** [pl.] the land or gardens around a large building （大建築物周圍的）場地，庭院，花園：*the hospital grounds* 醫院的院子

▸ **AREA OF KNOWLEDGE/IDEAS 知識／思想領域** **7** [U] an area of interest, knowledge or ideas （興趣、知識或思想的）範圍，領域：*He managed to* ***cover a lot of ground*** *in a short talk.* 他在簡短的談話中涵蓋了許多領域。◇ *We had to* ***go over the same ground*** (= talk about the same things again) *in class the next day.* 我們得在第二天的課上討論同樣的話題。◇ *You're* ***on dangerous ground*** (= talking about ideas that are likely to offend sb or make people angry) *if you criticize his family.* 你要是批評他的家人可就惹麻煩了。◇ *I thought I was* ***on safe ground*** (= talking about a suitable subject) *discussing music with her.* 我以為與她一起討論音樂是穩妥的。◇ *He was back* ***on familiar ground,*** *dealing with the customers.* 他又幹起了與顧客打交道的老本行。◇ *They are fighting the Conservatives* ***on their own ground.*** 他們以保守黨人自己的邏輯在和他們鬥爭。➲ see also COMMON GROUND, MIDDLE GROUND

▸ **GOOD REASON 充分的理由** **8** [C, usually pl.] **~ for sth/for doing sth** a good or true reason for saying, doing or believing sth 充分的理由；根據：*You have no grounds for complaint.* 你沒有理由抱怨。◇ *What were his grounds for wanting a divorce?* 他要離婚的理由是什麼？◇ *The case was dismissed* ***on the grounds that*** *there was not enough evidence.* 此案因缺乏足夠的證據被駁回。◇ *He retired from the job* ***on health grounds.*** 他因健康原因退職。◇ *Employers cannot discriminate* ***on grounds of*** *age.* 雇主不得有年齡歧視。➲ SYNONYMS at REASON

▸ **IN LIQUID 液體** **9** **grounds** [pl.] the small pieces of solid matter in a liquid that have fallen to the bottom 渣滓；沉澱物：*coffee grounds* 咖啡渣子

▸ **ELECTRICAL WIRE 電線** **10** (*NAmE*) (*BrE* **earth**) [C, usually sing.] a wire that connects an electric CIRCUIT with the ground and makes it safe （接）地線

▸ **BACKGROUND 背景** **11** [C] a background that a design is painted or printed on （繪畫或印刷的）背景，底子：*pink roses on a white ground* 白底粉紅玫瑰

IDM **cut the ground from under sb's 'feet** to suddenly spoil sb's idea or plan by doing sth to stop them from continuing with it 挖某人的牆腳；破壞某人的計劃；拆某人的台 **gain/make up 'ground (on sb/sth)** to gradually get closer to sb/sth that is moving or making progress in an activity 逼近（正在向前的人或物）：*The police car was gaining ground on the suspects.* 警車漸漸逼近犯罪嫌疑人。◇ *They needed to make up ground on their competitors.* 他們必須窮追猛趕競爭對手。**get (sth) off the 'ground** to start happening successfully; to make sth start happening successfully （使）順利開始，開始發生：*Without more money, the movie is unlikely to get off the ground.* 沒有更多的資金，這部影片難以順利開拍。◇ *to get a new company off the ground* 使新公司順利開張 **give/lose 'ground (to sb/sth)** to allow sb to have an advantage; to lose an advantage for yourself 退讓；讓步；失利：*They are not prepared to give ground on tax cuts.* 他們不打算在減稅方面讓步。◇ *The Conservatives lost a lot of ground to the Liberal Democrats at the election.* 在選舉中保守黨大大失利於自由民主黨。**go to 'ground** (*BrE*) to hide, especially to escape sb who is chasing you 躲藏起來；潛伏起來 **hold/stand your 'ground** **1** to continue with your opinions or intentions when sb is opposing you and wants you to change 堅持主張；堅持意圖；堅持立場；不讓步：*Don't let him persuade you—stand your ground.* 別聽他的，堅持自己的主張吧。**2** to face a situation and refuse to run away 堅守陣地；不撤退；不退卻：*It is not easy to hold your ground in front of someone with a gun.* 面對持槍者而不退縮並不容易。**on the 'ground** in the place where sth is happening and among the people who are in the situation, especially a war 當場；在現場；（尤指）戰火中的人之中：*On the ground, there are hopes that the fighting will soon stop.* 戰火中的人都希望戰鬥儘快結束。◇ *There's a lot of support for the policy on the ground.* 很多在場的人支持這一政策。**run/drive/work yourself into the 'ground** to work so hard that you become extremely tired 把自己弄得精疲力竭；把自己累垮 **run sb/sth into the 'ground** to use sth so much that it is broken; to make sb work so hard that they are no longer able to work 耗盡某物；過度使用某物；使某人精疲力竭 **thick/thin on the 'ground** (*BrE*) if people or things are **thick/thin on the ground,** there are a lot/not many of them in a place 為數眾多（或不多）；數目巨大（或微小）；眾多（或稀少）：*Customers are thin on the ground at this time of year.* 一年裏這個時節顧客很少。➲ more at EAR, FIRM *adj.*, FOOT *n.*, GAIN *v.*, HIT *v.*, MORAL *adj.*, NEUTRAL *adj.*, NEW, PREPARE, RIVET *v.*, SHIFT *v.*, STONY, SUIT *v.*

■ ***verb***

▸ **BOAT 船** **1** [T, I] **~ (sth)** when a boat **grounds** or sth **grounds** it, it touches the bottom of the sea and is unable to move （使）擱淺，觸海底：*The fishing boat had been grounded on rocks off the coast of Cornwall.* 漁船在康沃爾海岸外礁石上擱淺了。

▸ **AIRCRAFT 飛行器** **2** [T, often passive] **~ sth** to prevent an aircraft from taking off 使停飛；阻止…起飛：*The balloon was grounded by strong winds.* 熱氣球因強風停飛。◇ *All planes out of Heathrow have been grounded by the strikes.* 所有由希思羅機場起飛的飛機均因罷工而停飛。

▸ **CHILD 孩子** **3** [T, usually passive] **~ sb** to punish a child or young person by not allowing them to go out with their friends for a period of time 罰（兒童）不准出去玩：*You're grounded for a week!* 罰你一週不准出門！

▸ **ELECTRICITY 電** **4** (*NAmE*) (*BrE* **earth**) [T, usually passive] **~ sth** to make electrical equipment safe by connecting it to the ground with a wire 把（電器）接地線 ➲ see also GROUNDED, GROUNDING

■ ***adj.*** [only before noun] (of food 食物) cut, chopped or crushed into very small pieces or powder 磨細的；剁碎的：*ground coffee* 咖啡粉 ◇ (*US*) *ground pork* 豬肉糜 ➲ see also HAMBURGER (2)

'ground ball *noun* = GROUNDER

,ground 'beef *noun* [U] (*NAmE*) = HAMBURGER (2)

G

ground·break·ing /ˈɡraʊndbreɪkɪŋ/ *adj.* [only before noun] making new discoveries; using new methods 開創性的；創新的；革新的： *a groundbreaking piece of research* 富有開拓性的一項研究

ˈ**ground cloth** (*US*) (*BrE* **ground·sheet**) *noun* a large piece of material that does not let water through that is placed on the ground inside a tent（帳篷內鋪地用的）防潮布

ˈ**ground control** *noun* [U] the people and equipment on the ground that make sure that planes or SPACECRAFT take off and land safely（統稱）地面導航人員，地面制導設備

ˈ**ground cover** *noun* [U] plants that cover the soil 地被植物；植被

G

ˈ**ground crew** (also ˈ**ground staff**) *noun* [C+sing./pl. v.] the people at an airport whose job is to take care of aircraft while they are on the ground（統稱）地勤人員

ground·ed /ˈɡraʊndɪd/ *adj.* having a sensible and realistic attitude to life（對生活）持有現實態度的： *Away from Hollywood, he relies on his family and friends to keep him grounded.* 離開好萊塢之後，他靠家人和朋友使自己保持心態平衡。

IDM **(be) ˈgrounded in/on sth** (to be) based on sth 以…為基礎；基於： *His views are grounded on the assumption that all people are equal.* 他的觀點建立在人人平等的假設之上。

ground·er /ˈɡraʊndə(r)/ (also ˈ**ground ball**) *noun* (in BASEBALL 棒球) a ball that runs along the ground after it has been hit 地滾球；地面球

ˌ**ground ˈfloor** (*BrE*) (*NAmE* ˌ**first ˈfloor**) *noun* the floor of a building that is at the same level as the ground outside 底層，底樓，一樓（建築物與外面地面相平的一層）： *a ground-floor window* 一樓窗戶 ◇ *I live on the ground floor.* 我住在一樓。 ➲ note at FLOOR

IDM **be/get in on the ground ˈfloor** to become involved in a plan, project, etc. at the beginning 在開始時參與

ground·hog /ˈɡraʊndhɒɡ; *NAmE* -hɑːɡ; -hɔːɡ/ *noun* = WOODCHUCK

ˈ**Groundhog Day** *noun* **1** (in N America 北美) February 2, when it is said that the groundhog comes out of its hole at the end of winter. If the sun shines and the groundhog sees its shadow, it is said that there will be another six weeks of winter. 土撥鼠日（2月2日，據說是冬末土撥鼠出洞的日子，如果土撥鼠在晴天出洞看到自己的影子，就表示冬天還將持續六個星期） **2** an event that is repeated without changing 原樣重複的事情；重複不變的事情： *The Government lost the vote then and it can expect a Groundhog Day next time.* 政府在投票表決中失利，下一次也會是同樣的結果。 ORIGIN From the film/movie *Groundhog Day* about a man who lives the same day many times. 源自電影《偷天情緣》，其中的男主人公多次重複同一天的生活。

ground·ing /ˈɡraʊndɪŋ/ *noun* **1** [sing.] **~ (in sth)** the teaching of the basic parts of a subject 基礎訓練；基礎教學： *a good grounding in grammar* 扎實的語法基本功訓練 **2** [U, C] the act of keeping a plane on the ground or a ship in a port, especially because it is not in a good enough condition to travel（尤指因機件故障等）（飛機的）留地停飛，（船的）留港停航

ground·less /ˈɡraʊndləs/ *adj.* not based on reason or evidence 無理由的；無根據的 SYN **unfounded**： *groundless allegations* 毫無根據的指控 ◇ *Our fears proved groundless.* 我們的擔心證明是毫無道理的。 ▸ **ground·less·ly** *adv.*

ground·nut /ˈɡraʊndnʌt/ *noun* (*BrE*) = PEANUT (1)

ground·out /ˈɡraʊndaʊt/ *noun* (in BASEBALL 棒球) a situation in which a player hits the ball along the ground but a FIELDER touches first BASE with it before the player reaches the base（擊球員擊出地滾球後的）被殺出局

ˈ**ground plan** *noun* **1** a plan of the ground floor of a building（建築物的）底層平面圖 ➲ compare PLAN *n.* (4) **2** a plan for future action 計劃；大綱

ˈ**ground rent** *noun* [U, C] (in Britain 英國) rent paid by the owner of a building to the owner of the land on which it is built（房產主付給地產主的）地租

ˈ**ground rule** *noun* **1** **ground rules** [pl.] the basic rules on which sth is based 基本原則；基本準則： *The new code of conduct lays down the ground rules for management-union relations.* 新的行為規範確定了資方與工會關係的基本原則。 **2** [C] (*NAmE*, *sport* 體) a rule for the playing of a game on a particular field, etc.（某一體育運動場地等的）比賽規則

ground·sel /ˈɡraʊnsl/ *noun* [U] a wild plant with yellow flowers, sometimes used as food for animals and birds 千里光，緣葉菊（開黃花，有時用作動物和鳥的飼料）

ground·sheet /ˈɡraʊndʃiːt/ (*BrE*) (*US* ˈ**ground cloth**) *noun* a large piece of material that does not let water through that is placed on the ground inside a tent（帳篷內鋪地用的）防潮布

grounds·man /ˈɡraʊndzmən/ *noun* (*pl.* **-men** /-mən/) (*especially BrE*) a man whose job is to take care of a sports ground or large garden 運動場地（或大花園）管理員

ˈ**ground speed** *noun* the speed of an aircraft relative to the ground 地速（飛機相對於地面的速度） ➲ compare AIRSPEED

ˈ**ground squirrel** *noun* = GOPHER (1)

ˈ**ground staff** *noun* [C+sing./pl. v.] **1** (*BrE*) the people at a sports ground whose job it is to take care of the grass, equipment, etc. 運動場管理員 **2** = GROUND CREW

ground·stroke /ˈɡraʊndstrəʊk; *NAmE* -stroʊk/ *noun* (in TENNIS 網球) a hit that is made after the ball has BOUNCED 落地球（球落地彈起之後的一擊）

ground·swell /ˈɡraʊndswel/ *noun* [sing.] **~ (of sth)** (*formal*) the sudden increase of a particular feeling among a group of people（群體情緒的）迅速高漲： *a groundswell of support* 擁護的情緒迅速高漲 ◇ *There was a groundswell of opinion that he should resign.* 要求他辭職的呼聲越來越高。

ground·water /ˈɡraʊndwɔːtə(r)/ *noun* [U] water that is found under the ground in soil, rocks, etc. 地下水

ground·work /ˈɡraʊndwɜːk; *NAmE* -wɜːrk/ *noun* [U] **~ (for sth)** work that is done as preparation for other work that will be done later 基礎工作；準備工作： *Officials are* ***laying the groundwork*** *for a summit conference of world leaders.* 官員們正在為世界首腦峰會做準備工作。

ˌ**ground ˈzero** *noun* [U] **1** the point on the earth's surface where a nuclear bomb explodes（核彈的）爆心投影點 **2** **Ground Zero** the site of the World Trade Center in New York, destroyed on 11 September 2001 歸零地（2001年9月11日炸毀的紐約世界貿易中心遺址） **3** the beginning; a starting point for an activity 開始；起點

group 0‑ᴡ /ɡruːp/ *noun, verb*

■ *noun* [C+sing./pl. v.] **1** 0‑ᴡ a number of people or things that are together in the same place or that are connected in some way 組；群；批；類；簇： *a group of girls/trees/houses* 一群姑娘；一片樹林；一排房子 ◇ *A group of us is/are going to the theatre this evening.* 我們有一幫人今晚要去看戲。 ◇ *Students stood around* ***in groups*** *waiting for their results.* 學生們成群地站在周圍等待成績。 ◇ *The residents formed a community action group.* 居民組成了社區行動組。 ◇ *English is a member of the Germanic group of languages* 英語是日耳曼語系中的一種語言。 ◇ *The proportion of single parent families varies between different income groups.* 單親家庭比例在不同收入群中各不相同。 ◇ *a minority group* 少數群體 ◇ *ethnic groups* 族群 ◇ *a* ***group activity*** (= done by a number of people working together) 小組活動 ◇ *She asked her students to* ***get into groups*** *of four.* 她讓學生每四人分為一小組。 ◇ *to work* ***in groups*** 分組工作 ➲ see also SUBGROUP HELP There are many other compounds ending in **group**. You will find them at their place in the alphabet. 以 group 結尾的複合詞還有

很多，可在各字母中的適當位置查到。 **2** (*business* 商) a number of companies that are owned by the same person or organization 集團： *a newspaper group* 報業集團 ◇ *the Burton group* 伯頓集團 ◇ *the group sales director* 集團銷售董事 **3** (rather *old-fashioned*) a number of musicians who perform together, especially to play pop music （尤指流行音樂的）演奏組，樂團，樂隊： *She sings in a rock group.* 她是搖滾樂隊的歌手。

■ *verb* **1** [T, I] to gather into a group; to make sb/sth form a group （使）成群，成組，聚集： **~ sb/sth/yourself (round/around sb/sth)** *The children grouped themselves around their teacher.* 孩子們聚集在老師周圍。◇ **~ round/around sb/sth** *We all grouped around the tree for a photograph.* 我們全體圍着這棵樹照了張相。◇ **~ (sb/sth) together** *The colleges grouped together to offer a wider range of courses.* 這些學院聯合在一起，以開設範圍更廣的課程。 **2** [T] **~ sb/sth (together)** to divide people or things into groups of people or things that are similar in some way 將…分類；把…分組： *The books are grouped together by subject.* 這些書按科目分類。◇ *Contestants were grouped according to age and ability.* 參賽者按年齡和能力分組。

ˌgroup ˈcaptain *noun* (*abbr.* **Gp Capt**) an officer of high rank in the British AIR FORCE （英國）空軍上校： *Group Captain (Jonathan) Sutton* （喬納森）薩頓空軍上校

groupie /ˈɡruːpi/ *noun* a person, especially a young woman, who follows pop or rock musicians or other famous people around and tries to meet them 流行歌手迷，追星族（尤指少女）

group·ing /ˈɡruːpɪŋ/ *noun* **1** [C] a number of people or organizations that have the same interests, aims or characteristics and are often part of a larger group 小集團；小團體；小圈子： *These small nations constitute an important grouping within the EU.* 這些小國家是歐盟中的一個重要小集團。 **2** [U] the act of forming sth into a group 分組；歸類

ˌgroup ˈpractice *noun* a group of several doctors or other medical workers who work together in the community and use the same building to see patients （社區醫務工作者）聯合醫療，集體行醫

ˌgroup ˈtherapy *noun* [U] a type of PSYCHIATRIC treatment in which people with similar personal problems meet together to discuss them 群體治療；集體心理治療

group·ware /ˈɡruːpweə(r); *NAmE* -wer/ *noun* [U] (*computing* 計) software that is designed to help a group of people on different computers to work together 群件，協同件，組件，小組軟體（協調網絡小組工作的軟件平台）

ˈgroup work *noun* [U] (*BrE*) work done by a group of people working together, for example students in a classroom 團體工作；小組工作；（課堂的）小組討論

grouse /ɡraʊs/ *noun, verb*

■ *noun* **1** [C, U] (*pl.* **grouse**) a bird with a fat body and feathers on its legs, which people shoot for sport and food; the meat of this bird 松雞類；松雞肉： *grouse shooting* 獵捕松雞 ◇ *grouse moors* 松雞棲息區 ◇ *roast grouse* 烤松雞肉 **2** [C] (*informal*) a complaint 怨言；牢騷

■ *verb* [I, T] **~ (about sb/sth)** | (+ **speech**) (*informal*) to complain about sb/sth in a way that other people find annoying 抱怨；發牢騷 SYN **grumble**

grout /ɡraʊt/ (also **grout·ing**) *noun* [U] a substance that is used between the TILES on the walls of kitchens, bathrooms, etc. （用於牆上瓷磚間抹縫的）勾縫劑，薄膠泥 ▸ **grout** *verb* **~ sth**

grove /ɡrəʊv; *NAmE* ɡroʊv/ *noun* **1** (*literary*) a small group of trees 樹叢；小樹林： *a grove of birch trees* 白樺樹叢 **2** a small area of land with fruit trees of particular types on it 果樹林；果園： *an olive grove* 橄欖園 **3** used in the names of streets （用於街道名）街，路： *Elm Grove* 埃爾姆街

grovel /ˈɡrɒvl; *NAmE* ˈɡrɑːvl/ *verb* (**-ll-**, *especially US* **-l-**) **1** [I] **~ (to sb) (for sth)** (*disapproving*) to behave in a very HUMBLE way towards sb who is more important than you or who can give you sth you want 卑躬屈膝；俯首貼耳；奴顏婢膝 SYN **crawl** **2** [I] + **adv./prep.** to move along the ground on your hands and knees, especially because you are looking for sth 爬行，匍匐（尤指找東西） ▸ **grov·el·ling** (*especially US* **grov·el·ing**) *adj.* [only before noun]： *a grovelling letter of apology* 一封低聲下氣的道歉信

grow 🔑 /ɡrəʊ; *NAmE* ɡroʊ/ *verb* (**grew** /ɡruː/, **grown** /ɡrəʊn; *NAmE* ɡroʊn/)

▸ INCREASE 增加 **1** 🔑 [I] to increase in size, number, strength or quality 擴大；增加；增強： *The company profits grew by 5% last year.* 去年公司的利潤增加了5%。◇ *Fears are growing for the safety of a teenager who disappeared a week ago.* 大家對那一週前失踪少年的安危越來越擔憂。◇ **~ in sth** *The family has grown in size recently.* 這家人最近添丁進口了。◇ *She is growing in confidence all the time.* 她的信心在不斷增強。◇ **+ adj.** *The company is growing bigger all the time.* 這家公司在不斷地擴大。

▸ OF PERSON/ANIMAL 人；動物 **2** 🔑 [I] to become bigger or taller and develop into an adult 長大；長高；發育；成長： *You've grown since the last time I saw you!* 自從我上次見到你後，你又見長了！◇ *Nick's grown almost an inch in the last month.* 尼克這一個月來長高了差不多一英寸。◇ **+ adj.** *to grow bigger/taller* 長大 / 高了

▸ OF PLANT 植物 **3** 🔑 [I, T] to exist and develop in a particular place; to make plants grow （使）生長，發育： *The region is too dry for plants to grow.* 這地區乾燥得草木不生。◇ *Tomatoes grow best in direct sunlight.* 西紅柿在陽光直射下長得最好。◇ **~ sth** *I didn't know they grew rice in France.* 我本來不知道法國也種稻子。 ➲ see also HOME-GROWN

▸ OF HAIR/NAILS 頭髮；指甲 **4** 🔑 [I, T] to become longer; to allow sth to become longer by not cutting it （使）留長，蓄長： *I've decided to let my hair grow.* 我已決定留長髮。◇ **~ sth** *I've decided to grow my hair.* 我已決定留長髮。◇ *I didn't recognize him—he's grown a beard.* 我沒認出他來，他留鬍子了。

▸ BECOME/BEGIN 變成；開始 **5** 🔑 *linking verb* **+ adj.** to begin to have a particular quality or feeling over a period of time 逐漸變得；逐漸成為： *to grow old/bored/calm* 變老；膩煩起來；平靜下來 ◇ *As time went on he grew more and more impatient.* 時間長了，他越來越沒有耐心。◇ *The skies grew dark and it began to rain.* 天漸漸黑了，又下起雨來。 **6** [I] **~ to do sth** to gradually begin to do sth 逐漸開始： *I'm sure you'll grow to like her in time.* 我肯定你慢慢就會喜歡她了。

▸ DEVELOP SKILLS 培養技能 **7** [I] **~ (as sth)** (of a person 人) to develop and improve particular qualities or skills 提升品質；培養技能： *She continues to grow as an artist.* 她作為藝術家不斷有所提高。

▸ BUSINESS 業務 **8** [T] **~ sth** to increase the size, quality or number of sth 擴大；擴展；增加： *We are trying to grow the business.* 我們正在努力擴展業務。

IDM **it/money doesn't grow on ˈtrees** (*saying*) used to tell sb not to use sth or spend money carelessly because you do not have a lot of it 樹上長不出錢來，那東西（或錢）來之不易（告誡人不要隨便亂用） ➲ more at ABSENCE, GRASS *n.*

PHR V **ˌgrow aˈpart (from sb)** to stop having a close relationship with sb over a period of time （與某人）逐漸疏遠，漸漸產生隔閡 **ˌgrow aˈway from sb** [no passive] to become less close to sb; to depend on sb or care for sb less 逐漸疏遠某人；對某人的依賴（或關心）減少： *When she left school she grew away from her mother.* 她中學畢業後就不再那麼依賴母親了。 **ˌgrow ˈback** to begin growing again after being cut off or damaged （砍掉或毀壞後）又生長起來 **ˌgrow ˈinto sth** [no passive] **1** to gradually develop into a particular type of person over a period of time 逐漸成長為，變為，長成（某種類型的人） **2** (of a child 孩子) to grow big enough to fit into a piece of clothing that used to be too big 長大可以穿以前嫌大的衣服： *The dress is too long for her now but she'll grow into it.* 這件連衣裙她現在穿太長，不過她長大了可以穿。 **3** to become more confident in a new job, etc. and learn to do it better 對（新工作等）更有信心；學着做得更好： *She's still growing into her new role as a mother.* 她仍在學着適應她作為母親的新角色。 **ˈgrow on sb** [no passive] if sb/sth **grows on** you, you start to like them or it more and more 逐漸為某人所喜愛

ˌ**grow 'out** (of a HAIRSTYLE, etc. 髮式等) to disappear as your hair grows 因頭髮長長而消失：*I had a perm a year ago and it still hasn't grown out.* 我一年前燙的髮，現在髮型依舊。ˌ**grow sth↔'out** to allow your hair to grow in order to change the style 讓頭髮長長以變換髮型：*I've decided to grow my layers out.* 我決定留長髮好讓層次消失。ˌ**grow 'out of sth** [no passive] **1** (of a child 孩子) to become too big to fit into a piece of clothing 長得太大而穿不上衣服 SYN **outgrow**：*He's already grown out of his school uniform.* 他已長得穿不上他的校服了。**2** to stop doing sth as you become older 因長大而改掉（或革除、戒除）某習慣 SYN **outgrow**：*Most children suck their thumbs but they grow out of it.* 大多數孩子都吮拇指，大了就好了。**3** to develop from sth 產生於，源於（某事物）：*The idea for the book grew out of a visit to India.* 這本書的構思源於到印度的一次訪問。ˌ**grow 'up 1** 🗝 (of a person 人) to develop into an adult 長大；成熟；成長：*She grew up in Boston* (= lived there as a child). 她在波士頓長大。◇ *Their children have all grown up and left home now.* 他們的孩子都已長大成人離開家了。◇ **~ to do sth** *He grew up to become a famous pianist.* 他長大後成了著名的鋼琴家。➲ related noun GROWN-UP² **2** 🗝 used to tell sb to stop behaving in a silly way 別那麼幼稚；別耍小孩子脾氣；變得老成些：*Why don't you grow up?* 你怎麼就長不大呢？◇ *It's time you grew up.* 你該懂事了。**3** to develop gradually 逐漸發展；形成：*A closeness grew up between the two girls.* 這兩個女孩的關係越來越親密。IDM see OAK

grow·bag (also **Gro-bag™**) /'grəʊbæg; *NAmE* 'groʊ-/ *noun* a large plastic bag full of soil, used for growing plants 栽培袋，植物生長袋（盛滿泥土的大塑料袋）

grow·er /'grəʊə(r); *NAmE* 'groʊ-/ *noun* **1** a person or company that grows plants, fruit or vegetables to sell 栽培者；種植商；種植公司：*a tobacco grower* 煙草種植商 ◇ *All our vegetables are supplied by local growers.* 我們所有的蔬菜均由當地菜農供應。**2** a plant that grows in the way mentioned （以…方式）生長的植物：*a **fast/slow grower*** 生長快的 / 慢的植物

grow·ing /'grəʊɪŋ; *NAmE* 'groʊɪŋ/ *adj.* [only before noun] increasing in size, amount or degree 增加的；增長的；增強的：*A **growing number** of people are returning to full-time education.* 越來越多的人重返學校接受全日制教育。◇ *one of the country's **fastest growing** industries* 這個國家增長最快的行業之一 ◇ *There is growing concern over the safety of the missing teenager.* 人們對這個失踪少年的安全越來越擔心。

ˈ**growing pains** *noun* [pl.] **1** pains that some children feel in their arms and legs when they are growing （兒童）生長痛，發育期痛 **2** emotional anxieties felt by young people as they grow up 青春期的感情焦慮 **3** problems that are experienced by a company when it begins operating but that are not likely to last （企業）發展初期的困難

ˈ**growing season** *noun* [usually sing.] the period of the year during which the weather conditions are right for plants to grow （植物的）生長季節

growl /graʊl/ *verb, noun*

■ *verb* **1** [I] **~ (at sb/sth)** (of animals, especially dogs 動物，尤指狗) to make a low sound in the throat, usually as a sign of anger 低聲吼叫 **2** [T] to say sth in a low angry voice 發出低沉的怒吼；咆哮：**+ speech (at sb)** *'Who are you?' he growled at the stranger.* "你是誰？"他向陌生人怒吼道。◇ **~ sth (at sb)** *She growled a sarcastic reply.* 她以譏諷的口吻咬牙切齒地回答。

■ *noun* a deep angry sound made when sb/sth growls 怒吼聲；咆哮

grown /grəʊn; *NAmE* groʊn/ *adj.* [only before noun] (of a person 人) mentally and physically an adult 成熟的；成年的；長大的：*It's pathetic that grown men have to resort to violence like this.* 成年人還得這樣訴諸暴力，真可悲。➲ see also FULL-GROWN, HOME-GROWN, GROW *v.*

ˌ**grown-'up¹** *adj.* **1** (of a person 人) mentally and physically an adult 成熟的；成年的；長大成人的 SYN **adult**：*What do you want to be when you're grown-up?* 你長大成人後想做什麼？◇ *She has a grown-up son.* 她有個已成年的兒子。**2** suitable for or typical of an adult 適合成人的；成人特有的：*The child was clearly puzzled at being addressed in such a grown-up way.* 聽到別人用這種成人的方式跟自己說話，那個孩子顯然感到不知所措。

ˈ**grown-up²** *noun* (used especially by and to children 尤為兒語或對兒童說話時用) an adult person 大人 SYN **adult**：*If you're good you can eat with the grown-ups.* 你如果乖一點就可以和大人同桌吃飯。

growth 🗝 /grəʊθ; *NAmE* groʊθ/ *noun*

1 🗝 [U] (of people, animals or plants 人、動物或植物) the process of growing physically, mentally or emotionally 發育；成長；生長：*Lack of water will stunt the plant's growth.* 缺水會妨礙植物生長。◇ *Remove dead leaves to encourage new growth.* 去掉枯葉以促進新葉生長。◇ *a concern with personal* (= mental and emotional) *growth and development* 對個人成長和發展的重視 ◇ *growth hormones* (= designed to make sb/sth grow faster) 生長激素 **2** 🗝 [U] **~ (in/of sth)** an increase in the size, amount or degree of sth 增加；增長；增強：*population growth* 人口增長 ◇ *the rapid growth in violent crime* 暴力犯罪的迅速增加 **3** 🗝 [U] an increase in economic activity 經濟增長；經濟發展：*a disappointing year of little growth in Britain and America* 英美經濟增長無幾令人沮喪的一年 ◇ *policies aimed at sustaining economic growth* 旨在保持經濟增長的政策 ◇ *an annual growth rate of 10%* * 10% 的年增長率 ◇ *a **growth area/industry*** 經濟增長的領域 / 行業 ➲ COLLOCATIONS at ECONOMY **4** [C] a lump caused by a disease that forms on or inside a person, an animal or a plant 贅生物：*a **malignant/cancerous growth*** 惡性 / 癌性腫瘤 **5** [U, C] something that has grown 生長物；長成物；產物：*The forest's dense growth provides nesting places for a wide variety of birds.* 森林裏茂密的植物為各種各樣的鳥兒提供了築巢的地方。◇ *several days' growth of beard* 長了幾天的鬍鬚

ˈ**growth ring** *noun* a layer of wood, shell or bone developed in one year, or in another regular period of growth, that an expert can look at to find out how old sth is （可推斷樹木等年齡的）生長輪，年輪

groyne (*especially US* **groin**) /grɔɪn/ *noun* a low wall built out into the sea to prevent it from washing away sand and stones from the beach 防波堤，折流壩（防止海浪侵蝕海灘沙石的矮牆）

grub /grʌb/ *noun, verb*

■ *noun* **1** [C] the young form of an insect, that looks like a small fat WORM （昆蟲的）幼蟲；蛆；蠐螬 **2** [U] (*informal*) food 食物：*Grub's up!* (= the meal is ready) 飯好了！◇ *They serve good pub grub there.* 他們那兒供應上好的酒吧食物。

■ *verb* (**-bb-**) [I] **~ (around/about) (for sth)** to look for sth, especially by digging or by looking through or under other things 翻找；搜尋；挖掘尋找：*birds grubbing for worms* 刨蟲子的鳥

PHR V ˌ**grub sth↔'up/'out** to dig sth out of the ground 掘出，挖出（某物）

grub·ber /'grʌbə(r)/ *noun* (in CRICKET 板球) a ball that is BOWLED along the ground 地滾球

grubby /'grʌbi/ *adj.* (**grub·bier**, **grub·bi·est**) **1** rather dirty, usually because it has not been washed or cleaned 骯髒的；邋遢的；污穢的：*grubby hands/clothes* 髒手 / 衣服 ➲ SYNONYMS at DIRTY **2** unpleasant because it involves activities that are dishonest or immoral 卑鄙的；可鄙的 SYN **sordid**：*a grubby scandal* 醜聞 ▸ **grubbi·ness** *noun* [U]

ˈ**Grub Street** *noun* used to refer to poor writers and journalists as a group, or the life they live 格拉布街（統稱潦倒的文人）；潦倒文人的生活 ORIGIN From the name of a street in London where many poor writers lived in the 17th century. 源自 17 世紀倫敦居住着很多窮困作家的格拉布街。

grudge /grʌdʒ/ *noun, verb*

■ *noun* **~ (against sb)** a feeling of anger or dislike towards sb because of sth bad they have done to you in the past 積怨；怨恨；嫌隙：*I **bear** him **no grudge**.* 我對他不懷任何積怨。◇ *He **has a grudge against** the world.* 他對世人心存不滿。◇ *I don't **hold any grudges** now.* 我現在沒

有任何怨恨。◇ *He's a man with a grudge.* 他是一個心懷怨恨的人。◇ *England beat New Zealand in a* ***grudge match*** (= a match where there is strong dislike between the teams). 英格蘭隊在一場勢不兩立的比賽中打敗了新西蘭隊。

▪ *verb* **1** to do or give sth unwillingly 勉強做；不情願地給；吝惜 SYN **begrudge**：**~ doing sth** *I grudge having to pay so much tax.* 得付這麼多的稅我很不情願。◇ **~ sth** *He grudges the time he spends travelling to work.* 他不情願上班花這麼多時間在路上。 **2 ~ sb sth** to think that sb does not deserve to have sth 認為…不應得到 SYN **begrudge**：*You surely don't grudge her her success?* 她獲得成功，你沒有不以為然吧？

grudg·ing /ˈgrʌdʒɪŋ/ *adj.* [usually before noun] given or done unwillingly 勉強的；不情願的 SYN **reluctant**：*He could not help feeling a grudging admiration for the old lady.* 他不禁感到不得不欽佩這位老太太。 ▸ **grudg·ing·ly** (also *less frequent* **be·grudg·ing·ly**) *adv.*：*She grudgingly admitted that I was right.* 她勉強承認我是對的。

gruel /ˈgruːəl/ *noun* [U] a simple dish made by boiling OATS in milk or water, eaten especially in the past by poor people（尤指舊時窮人吃的）稀粥，燕麥粥

gruel·ling (*especially BrE*) (*NAmE* usually **gruel·ing**) /ˈgruːəlɪŋ/ *adj.* very difficult and tiring, needing great effort for a long time 使人筋疲力盡的；折磨人的 SYN **punishing**：*a* ***gruelling journey/schedule*** 使人筋疲力盡的旅程；累人的日程 ◇ *I've had a gruelling day.* 我一天下來累得筋疲力盡。

grue·some /ˈgruːsəm/ *adj.* very unpleasant and filling you with horror, usually because it is connected with death or injury 令人厭惡的；恐怖的；可怕的：*a gruesome murder* 駭人聽聞的謀殺案 ◇ *gruesome pictures of dead bodies* 恐怖的死人照片 ◇ (*humorous*) *We spent a week in a gruesome apartment in Miami.* 我們在邁阿密一套糟糕透頂的公寓裏住了一星期。 ▸ **grue·some·ly** *adv.*

gruff /grʌf/ *adj.* **1** (of a voice 聲音) deep and rough, and often sounding unfriendly 低沉沙啞的；生硬的 **2** (of a person's behaviour 人的行為) unfriendly and impatient 冷淡的；態度生硬的：*Beneath his gruff exterior, he's really very kind-hearted.* 他外表冷漠，心地卻十分善良。 ▸ **gruff·ly** *adv.*

grum·ble /ˈgrʌmbl/ *verb, noun*

▪ *verb* **1** [I, T] to complain about sb/sth in a bad-tempered way 咕噥；嘟囔；發牢騷：**~ (at/to sb) (about/at sb/sth)** *She's always grumbling to me about how badly she's treated at work.* 她總是向我抱怨她在工作中如何受虧待。◇ **+ speech** *'I'll just have to do it myself,' he grumbled.* "我只好自己動手了。" 他咕噥着說。◇ **~ that …** *They kept grumbling that they were cold.* 他們不停地嘟囔着說冷。 ➲ SYNONYMS at COMPLAIN **2** [I] to make a deep continuous sound 咕隆；發轟隆聲 SYN **rumble**：*Thunder grumbled in the distance.* 遠處雷聲隆隆。 ▸ **grum·bler** /ˈgrʌmblə(r)/ *noun*

▪ *noun* **1 ~ (about sth)** | **~ (that …)** something that you complain about because you are not satisfied 嘟囔；牢騷：*My main grumble is about the lack of privacy.* 我最大的抱怨是缺乏隱私。 **2** a long low sound 咕隆聲；隆隆聲 SYN **rumble**：*a distant grumble of thunder* 遠處隆隆的雷聲

grum·bling /ˈgrʌmblɪŋ/ *noun* **1** [U] the act of complaining about sth 咕噥；嘟囔；發牢騷：*We didn't hear any grumbling about the food.* 我們沒聽到過對食物的抱怨。 **2 grumblings** [pl.] protests about sth that come from a number of people but that are not expressed very clearly（集體的）隱隱的不滿

grump /grʌmp/ *noun* (*informal*) a bad-tempered person 脾氣壞的人

grumpy /ˈgrʌmpi/ *adj.* (**grump·ier**, **grumpi·est**) (*informal*) bad-tempered 脾氣壞的；性情暴躁的 ▸ **grump·ily** /ˈgrʌmpɪli/ *adv.*

grunge /grʌndʒ/ *noun* [U] **1** (*informal*) dirt of any kind 髒東西 SYN **grime** **2** (also ˈ**grunge rock**) a type of loud rock music, which was popular in the early 1990s 垃圾搖滾樂（流行於 20 世紀 90 年代初） **3** a style of fashion worn by people who like grunge music, usually involving clothes that look untidy 垃圾搖滾風格，垃圾搖滾款式（指迷戀垃圾搖滾樂者的時尚服式，常穿着邋遢的衣服）

grungy /ˈgrʌndʒi/ *adj.* (*informal*) dirty in an unpleasant way 邋遢的；髒的；齷齪的

grunt /grʌnt/ *verb, noun*

▪ *verb* **1** [I] (of animals, especially pigs 動物，尤指豬) to make a short low sound in the throat 發出呼嚕聲 **2** [I, T] (of people 人) to make a short low sound in your throat, especially to show that you are in pain, annoyed or not interested; to say sth using this sound 發出哼聲；咕噥；嘟噥：*He pulled harder on the rope, grunting with the effort.* 他邊用力邊哼聲，使出更大的力氣拉繩子。◇ *When I told her what had happened she just grunted and turned back to her book.* 我告訴她出了什麼事，她只哼了一聲就又看起書來了。◇ **~ sth** *He grunted something about being late and rushed out.* 他嘟噥着說要遲到了便匆匆跑了出去。◇ **+ speech** *'Thanks,' he grunted.* "謝謝。" 他咕噥着說。

▪ *noun* **1** a short, low sound made by a person or an animal (especially a pig) 哼聲；咕噥聲；嘟噥聲；（尤指豬的）呼嚕聲：*to give a* ***grunt of effort/pain*** 發出費力／痛苦的哼聲 **2** (*NAmE, informal*) a worker who does boring tasks for low pay 工作乏味收入低的工人 **3** (*NAmE, informal*) a soldier of low rank 步兵；士兵；大兵

ˈ**grunt work** *noun* [U] (*informal*) hard boring work 乏味的重活：*She has assistants to do the grunt work like research and proofreading.* 她有助手做搜集資料和校對之類的苦差事。

Gruy·ère /ˈgruːjɜː(r); *NAmE* -jər; ˈgriːjər/ *noun* [U] a type of Swiss cheese with a strong flavour 格呂耶爾乾酪（瑞士濃味乾酪）

gryphon /ˈgrɪfən/ *noun* = GRIFFIN

GSM /ˌdʒiː es ˈem/ *abbr.* Global System/Standard for Mobile Communication(s) (an international system for DIGITAL communication by mobile/cell phone) 全球移動通信系統

GSOH *abbr.* good sense of humour (used in personal advertisements) 豐富的幽默感（用於個人廣告中）

ˈ**G spot** *noun* a sensitive area inside a woman's VAGINA that is thought to give great sexual pleasure when touched * G 點（女性的性敏感部位）

GST /ˌdʒiː es ˈtiː/ *noun* [U] (*CanE*) goods and services tax (a tax that is added to the price of goods and services) 商品及服務稅（附加於價格上）

ˈ**G-string** *noun* a narrow piece of cloth that covers the sexual organs and is held up by a string around the waist * G 帶，遮羞布，兜襠布（用繩繫於腰部作三角褲用）

Gt (also **Gt.** especially in *NAmE*) *abbr.* (in names of places) Great（用於地名）大：*Gt Britain* 大不列顛 ◇ *Gt Yarmouth* 大雅茅斯

gua·ca·mole /ˌgwækəˈməʊleɪ; -li; *NAmE* -ˈmoʊ-/ *noun* [U] (from *Spanish*) a Mexican dish of crushed AVOCADO mixed with onion, tomatoes, CHILLIES, etc. 墨西哥油梨醬（用碾碎的油梨加洋葱、番茄、辣椒等調製而成）

guano /ˈgwɑːnəʊ; *NAmE* -noʊ/ *noun* [U] the waste substance passed from the bodies of birds that live near the sea, used to make plants and crops grow well 鳥獸積糞，海鳥糞（用作肥料）

guar·an·tee 🔑 AW /ˌgærənˈtiː/ *noun, verb*

▪ *noun* **1** 🔑 a firm promise that you will do sth or that sth will happen 保證；擔保 SYN **assurance**：*to give a guarantee of good behaviour* 保證行為端正 ◇ *He gave me a guarantee that it would never happen again.* 他向我保證這種事情絕不會再發生。◇ *They are demanding certain guarantees before they sign the treaty.* 他們要求得到某些保證後才簽署條約。 **2** 🔑 a written promise given by a company that sth you buy will be replaced or repaired without payment if it goes wrong within a particular period 保修單；保用證書 SYN **warranty**：*We provide a 5-year guarantee against rust.* 我們保證 5 年不生銹。◇ *The watch is still* ***under guarantee***. 這隻手錶仍在保修期內。◇ *The television comes with a year's guarantee.* 這電

視機有一年的保修期。◇ *a money-back guarantee* 退貨保證 **3** 🔑 something that makes sth else certain to happen 起保證作用的事物： **~ (of sth)** *Career success is no guarantee of happiness.* 事業成功並不是幸福的保證。◇ **~ (that …)** *There's no guarantee that she'll come* (= she may not come). 不能保證她一定會來。 **4** money or sth valuable that you give or promise to a bank, for example, to make sure that you will do what you have promised 保證金；抵押品： *We had to offer our house as a guarantee when getting the loan.* 我們在貸款時不得不拿房子作抵押。 **5** a written promise to pay back money that sb else owes, or do sth that sb else promised to do, if they cannot do it themselves 擔保書： *A close relative, usually a parent, can provide a guarantee for the loan.* 近親屬，通常為父母，可為貸款作擔保。

■ ***verb*** **1** 🔑 to promise to do sth; to promise sth will happen 保證；擔保；保障： **~ sth** *Basic human rights, including freedom of speech, are now guaranteed.* 現在，包括言論自由在內的基本人權已有了保障。◇ **~ (that) …** *We cannot guarantee (that) our flights will never be delayed.* 我們不能保證我們的所有航班均不誤點。◇ **~ sb sth** *The ticket will guarantee you free entry.* 這張票可保證你免費入場。◇ **~ to do sth** *We guarantee to deliver your goods within a week.* 我們保證一週內交貨。 **2** 🔑 **~ sth (against sth)** to give a written promise to replace or repair a product free if it goes wrong 出具保單（免費掉換或修理有問題的產品）： *This iron is guaranteed for a year against faulty workmanship.* 這種熨斗如有工藝缺陷可保修一年。 **3** 🔑 to make sth certain to happen 使必然發生；確保： **~ sth** *Tonight's victory guarantees the team's place in the final.* 今晚的勝利確保這個隊能進入決賽。◇ **~ sb sth** *These days getting a degree doesn't guarantee you a job.* 如今獲得學位並不能保證你有工作。 **4 ~ (that) …** to be certain that sth will happen 肯定…必然發生： *You can guarantee (that) the children will start being naughty as soon as they have to go to bed.* 可以肯定孩子一到上牀睡覺時就不聽話了。 **5** to agree to be legally responsible for sth or for doing sth, especially for paying back money that sb else owes if they cannot pay it back themselves 承諾對…負法律責任；為…作擔保： **~ sth** *to guarantee a bank loan* 為銀行貸款作保◇ **~ to do sth** *to guarantee to pay sb's debts* 為償還某人的債務作保◇ **~ that …** *I guarantee that he will appear in court.* 我保證他會出庭。

IDM **be guaran'teed to do sth** to be certain to have a particular result 肯定會；必定會： *If we try to keep it a secret, she's guaranteed to find out.* 如果我們試圖保密，她肯定會發現。◇ *That kind of behaviour is guaranteed to make him angry.* 那樣的行為肯定會讓他生氣。 ➲ SYNONYMS at CERTAIN

guar·an·tor /ˌɡærənˈtɔː(r)/ *noun* (*formal* or *law* 律) a person who agrees to be responsible for sb or for making sure that sth happens or is done 擔保人；保證人： *The United Nations will act as guarantor of the peace settlement.* 聯合國將充當和平協議的保證人。

guard 🔑 /ɡɑːd; *NAmE* ɡɑːrd/ *noun, verb*

■ ***noun***

▸ **PEOPLE WHO PROTECT** 警衛 **1** 🔑 [C] a person, such as a soldier, a police officer or a prison officer, who protects a place or people, or prevents prisoners from escaping 衛兵；警衛員；看守： *a* ***security guard*** 安全警衛◇ ***border guards*** 邊防衛士◇ *The prisoner slipped past the guards on the gate and escaped.* 犯人從門衛身旁溜出去逃走了。◇ *A guard was posted outside the building.* 建築物外駐了一名警衛。 ➲ compare WARDER ➲ see also BODYGUARD, COASTGUARD, LIFEGUARD **2** [C+sing./pl. v.] a group of people, such as soldiers or police officers, who protect sb/sth（統稱）衛兵，警衛，看守： *the captain of the guard* 衛隊長◇ *the changing of the guard* (= when one group replaces another) 衛隊換崗◇ *The guard is/are being inspected today.* 今天衛隊接受檢閱。◇ *Fellow airmen provided a* ***guard of honour*** *at his wedding.* 空軍戰友們為他的婚禮充當儀仗隊。◇ *The President always travels with an* ***armed guard***. 總統出行總有武裝衛隊保駕。 ➲ see also NATIONAL GUARD, OLD GUARD, REARGUARD **3** 🔑 [U] the act or duty of protecting property, places or people from attack or danger; the act or duty of preventing prisoners from escaping 警戒；保衛；保護；看守： *a sentry* ***on guard*** (= at his or her post, on duty) 執勤哨兵◇ *to do* ***guard duty*** 擔任警戒任務◇ *The escaped prisoner was brought back* ***under armed guard***. 越獄逃犯由武裝警衛押回。◇ *The terrorist was kept* ***under*** *police* ***guard***. 這名恐怖分子當時在警方的看管之下。◇ *One of the men* ***kept guard***, *while the other broke into the house.* 一人放哨，另一人則闖進了房子裏。 **4 the Guards** [pl.] (in Britain and some other countries) special REGIMENTS of soldiers whose original duty was to protect the king or queen（英國和其他一些國家的）禁軍，御林軍，近衛軍

▸ **AGAINST INJURY** 防止受傷 **5** [C] (often in compounds 常構成複合詞) something that covers a part of a person's body or a dangerous part of a machine to prevent injury 防護罩；防護裝置；防護用品： *Ensure the guard is in place before operating the machine.* 一定要在防護裝置到位後才開機器。 ➲ see also FIREGUARD, MOUTHGUARD, MUDGUARD, SAFEGUARD, SHIN GUARD ➲ VISUAL VOCAB page V47

▸ **ON TRAIN** 火車 **6** [C] (*BrE*, becoming *old-fashioned*) = CONDUCTOR (2)

▸ **IN BOXING/FENCING** 拳擊；擊劍 **7** [U] a position you take to defend yourself, especially in a sport such as BOXING or FENCING 防禦姿勢： *to drop/keep up your guard* 放棄／保持防禦姿勢◇ (*figurative*) *In spite of the awkward questions the minister never let his guard fall for a moment.* 儘管遇到些令人尷尬的問題，部長從沒有絲毫退縮。

▸ **IN BASKETBALL** 籃球 **8** [C] one of the two players on a BASKETBALL team who are mainly responsible for staying close to opposing players to stop them from scoring 後衛

▸ **IN AMERICAN FOOTBALL** 美式足球 **9** [C] one of the two players on an AMERICAN FOOTBALL team who play either side of the CENTRE FORWARD 側衛；翼衛

IDM **be on your 'guard** to be very careful and prepared for sth difficult or dangerous 警惕；提防；警戒 **mount/stand/keep 'guard (over sb/sth)** to watch or protect sb/sth 守衛；看守；保衛： *Four soldiers stood guard over the coffin.* 有四名士兵守護靈柩。 **off (your) 'guard** not careful or prepared for sth difficult or dangerous 不警惕；不提防；不警戒： *The lawyer's apparently innocent question was designed to* ***catch*** *the witness* ***off*** *(****his****)* ***guard***. 律師看似不經意的問題是為了使證人措手不及。

■ ***verb*** **1** 🔑 **~ sb/sth** to protect property, places or people from attack or danger 警衛；守衛；保衛： *The dog was guarding its owner's luggage.* 狗守護着主人的行李。◇ *political leaders guarded by the police* 由警方保衛的政界領袖們◇ *You can't get in; the whole place is guarded.* 你進不去，整個地區都戒備森嚴。◇ (*figurative*) *a closely guarded secret* 嚴守的秘密 **2** 🔑 **~ sb** to prevent prisoners from escaping 看守，監視（囚犯）： *The prisoners were guarded by soldiers.* 犯人由士兵看守。

PHR V **'guard against sth** to take care to prevent sth or to protect yourself from sth 防止，防範，提防（某事）： *to guard against accidents/disease* 防止事故；預防疾病

'guard dog *noun* a dog that is kept to guard a building 看門狗

guard·ed /ˈɡɑːdɪd; *NAmE* ˈɡɑːrdɪd/ *adj.* (of a person or a remark they make 人或其言語) careful; not showing feelings or giving much information 謹慎的；有保留的；不明確表態的 **SYN** **cautious**： *a guarded reply* 謹慎的回答◇ *You should be more guarded in what you say to reporters.* 你對記者說話應更謹慎些。◇ *They gave the news a guarded welcome* (= did not show great enthusiasm about it). 他們對這消息表示謹慎的歡迎。 **OPP** **unguarded** ▸ **guard·ed·ly** *adv.*

guard·house /ˈɡɑːdhaʊs; *NAmE* ˈɡɑːrd-/ *noun* a building for soldiers who are guarding the entrance to a military camp or for keeping military prisoners in 衛兵室；禁閉室

guard·ian /ˈɡɑːdiən; *NAmE* ˈɡɑːrd-/ *noun* **1** a person who protects sth 保護者；守衛者；保衛者 **SYN** **custodian**： *Farmers should be guardians of the countryside.* 農民應是農村的保衛者。◇ *The police are guardians of law and order.* 警察是法律和治安的護衛者。 **2** a person who is legally responsible for the care of another person, especially a child whose parents have died （尤指雙親已故孩子的）監護人

ˌguardian ˈangel *noun* a spirit that some people believe protects and guides them, especially when they are in danger 守護天使：(*figurative*) *A delightful guide was my guardian angel for the first week of the tour.* 令人愉快的導遊是我第一週旅行的守護神。

guard·ian·ship /ˈɡɑːdiənʃɪp; *NAmE* ˈɡɑːrd-/ *noun* [U] (*formal* or *law* 律) the state or position of being responsible for sb/sth 監護；監護地位；監護人的身分

ˈguard rail *noun* **1** a rail placed on the edge of a path, a CLIFF or a boat to protect people and prevent them falling over the edge 護欄；扶欄 **2** (*NAmE*) (*BrE* **ˈcrash barrier**) a strong low fence or wall at the side of a road or between the two halves of a major road such as a MOTORWAY or INTERSTATE（高速公路或州際公路上的）防撞護欄，防撞牆

guard·room /ˈɡɑːdruːm; -rʊm; *NAmE* ˈɡɑːrd-/ *noun* a room for soldiers who are guarding the entrance to a building or for keeping military prisoners in 衛兵室；禁閉室

guards·man /ˈɡɑːdzmən; *NAmE* ˈɡɑːrd-/ *noun* (*pl.* **-men** /-mən/) a soldier in the Guards or in the National Guard in the US 禁衛軍士兵；（美國）國民警衛隊士兵

ˈguard's van *noun* (*BrE*) the part of a train where the person who is in charge of the train rides 列車車長室；守車

guava /ˈɡwɑːvə/ *noun* the fruit of a tropical American tree, with yellow skin and pink flesh 番石榴（熱帶美洲水果，黃皮，果肉呈粉紅色）

gub·bins /ˈɡʌbɪnz/ *noun* [U] (*old-fashioned, BrE, informal*) various things that are not important 零碎東西：*All the gubbins that came with the computer is still in the box.* 這台電腦的所有零星配件還在盒子裏。

gu·ber·na·tor·ial /ˌɡuːbənəˈtɔːriəl; *NAmE* -bərnə-/ *adj.* (*formal*) connected with the job of state governor in the US （美國）州長的，州長職位的：*a gubernatorial candidate* 州長候選人 ◇ *gubernatorial duties* 州長的職責

Guern·sey /ˈɡɜːnzi; *NAmE* ˈɡɜːrnzi/ *noun* **1** a type of cow kept for its rich milk 根西牛（產奶量大） **2** **guernsey** a thick sweater made with dark blue wool that has been specially treated so that it does not let water through, worn originally by FISHERMEN 格恩西防水羊毛衫（深藍色，原為漁民所穿） **3** **guernsey** (*AustralE*) a football sweater, especially one of the type without sleeves worn by Australian Rules players 足球運動衫；（尤指澳大利亞式的）足球運動背心

IDM **get a ˈguernsey** (*AustralE, informal*) to be recognized as being good (originally meaning to be chosen for a football team) 獲得認可；得到承認

guer·rilla (also **guer·illa**) /ɡəˈrɪlə/ *noun, adj.*

▪ ***noun*** a member of a small group of soldiers who are not part of an official army and who fight against official soldiers, usually to try to change the government 游擊隊員：*urban guerrillas* (= those who fight in towns) 城市游擊隊員 ◇ ***guerrilla war/warfare*** (= fought by guerrillas on one or both sides) 游擊戰 ◇ *a guerrilla movement* 游擊運動 ➲ compare FREEDOM FIGHTER

▪ ***adj.*** [only before noun] organized in an informal way and without official permission or approval 游擊的；非正式的；沒有官方認可的：*Guerrilla actors took to the streets in army fatigues to protest against the war.* 非正式演員穿着軍服走上街頭舉行反戰示威。◇ *guerrilla marketing* (= marketing that uses unusual methods in order to achieve the greatest effect for the smallest amount of money) 游擊營銷（用不一般的方式以最少金錢取得最大成效）

guess 🔑 /ɡes/ *verb, noun*

▪ ***verb*** **1** 🔑 [I, T] to try and give an answer or make a judgement about sth without being sure of all the facts 猜測；估計：*I don't really know. I'm just guessing.* 我並不知道，我只是猜測。◇ **~ at sth** *We can only guess at her reasons for leaving.* 對她離去的原因我們只能猜測。◇ **+ adj.** *He **guessed** right/wrong.* 他猜對／錯了。◇ **~ (that)** … *I'd guess that she's about 30.* 我估計她大約 30 歲。◇ **~ where, who, etc.** … *Can you guess where I've been?* 你能猜出我去什麼地方了嗎？◇ **~ sth** *Can you guess his age?* 你能猜出他的年齡嗎？ **2** 🔑 [T] to find the right answer to a question or the truth without knowing all the facts 猜對；猜中；猜到：**~ sth** *She guessed the answer straight away.* 她一下子就猜中了答案。◇ **~ what, where, etc.** … ***You'll never guess*** *what she told me.* 你永遠猜不到她對我說了什麼。◇ **~ (that)** … *You would never guess (that) she had problems. She's always so cheerful.* 你怎麼也猜不到她有難以解決的問題。她總是那麼樂觀。➲ see also SECOND-GUESS **3** 🔑 **I guess** [T, I] **~ (that)** … (*informal, especially NAmE*) to suppose that sth is true or likely 想；以為：*I guess (that) you'll be looking for a new job now.* 我想你現在要找新工作了吧。◇ *'He didn't see me, I guess.'* "我想他沒看見我。" ◇ *'Are you ready to go?' 'Yeah, **I guess so**.'* "你準備好出發了嗎？" "是的，應該可以了。" ◇ *'They aren't coming, then?' '**I guess not**.'* "這麼說，他們不來了？" "我想是吧。" **4** 🔑 **guess …!** [T] used to show that you are going to say sth surprising or exciting（引出令人驚奇或激動的事）你猜：**~ sth** *Guess what! He's asked me out!* 你猜怎麼着！他約我出去了！◇ **~ who, where, etc.** … *Guess who I've just seen!* 你猜我剛才見到誰了！

IDM **keep sb ˈguessing** (*informal*) to not tell sb about your plans or what is going to happen next 讓某人捉摸不定（或猜不透）：*It's the kind of book that keeps you guessing right to the end.* 這種書讓你不看到最後都猜不透。

▪ ***noun*** 🔑 an attempt to give an answer or an opinion when you cannot be certain if you are right 猜測；猜想：**~ (at sth)** (*BrE*) *to **have/make a guess** (at sth)*（對某事）作猜測 ◇ (*NAmE*) *to **take a guess*** 推測 ◇ *Go on! Have a guess!* 來呀！猜猜看！◇ **~ (about sth)** *The article is based on guesses about what might happen in the future.* 這篇文章的依據是對未來可能發生什麼事情的猜測。◇ *They might be here by 3—but that's just a **rough guess*** (= not exact). 他們可能 3 點鐘到，不過這只是一個大致的猜測。◇ **~ (that …)** ***My guess is that*** *we won't hear from him again.* 我想我們再不會收到他的消息了。◇ ***At a guess****, there were forty people at the party.* 估計有四十人參加了聚會。◇ *If I might **hazard a guess**, I'd say she was about thirty.* 讓我來猜的話，我說她大約三十歲。◇ *Who do you think I saw yesterday? **I'll give you three guesses**.* 你猜我昨天碰到誰了？我讓你猜三次。

IDM **ˈanybody's/ˈanyone's guess** (*informal*) something that nobody can be certain about 誰也拿不準的事：*What will happen next is anybody's guess.* 下一步會發生什麼事，誰也說不準。 **your ˌguess is as good as ˈmine** (*informal*) used to tell sb that you do not know any more about a subject than the person that you are talking to does 我和你一樣不知道；我和你一樣心中無數：*'Who's going to win?' 'Your guess is as good as mine.'* "誰會贏？" "我和你一樣不知道。" ➲ more at EDUCATED, MISS *v.*

ˈguessing game *noun* **1** a game in which you have to guess the answers to questions 猜謎遊戲 **2** a situation in which you do not know what is going to happen or what sb is going to do 捉摸不定的局面

guess·ti·mate (also **gues·ti·mate**) /ˈɡestɪmət/ *noun* (*informal*) an attempt to calculate sth that is based more on guessing than on information 瞎猜；大致估計

guess·work /ˈɡeswɜːk; *NAmE* -wɜːrk/ *noun* [U] the process of trying to find an answer by guessing when you do not have enough information to be sure 猜想；猜測：*It was pure guesswork on our part.* 這純屬我們的猜測。➲ see also CONJECTURE *n.* (2)

guest 🔑 /ɡest/ *noun, verb*

▪ ***noun*** **1** 🔑 a person that you have invited to your house or to a particular event that you are paying for 客人；賓客：*We have guests staying this weekend.* 這週末我家有客人來住。◇ *more than 100 wedding guests* * 100 多位出席婚禮的賓客 ◇ *I went to the theatre club as Helen's guest.* 海倫請我去戲劇俱樂部看戲了。◇ *He was the **guest of honour*** (= the most important person invited to an event). 他是貴賓。◇ *Liz was not on the **guest list**.* 利茲不在邀請之列。 **2** 🔑 a person who is staying at a hotel, etc. 旅客；房客：*We have accommodation for 500 guests.* 我們有可供 500 位客人住宿的房間。◇ *a* ***paying guest*** (= a person who is living in a private house, but paying as if they were in a hotel) 寄宿客（付費住在私人家中的人）◇ *Guests should vacate their rooms by 10.30 a.m.* 旅客應在上午 10:30 以前騰出房間。 **3** a famous person or performer who takes part in a television show or concert 特別嘉賓；客串演員：*a* ***guest artist/star/singer*** 特約藝人 / 明星 / 歌手 ◇ *Our special guest tonight is …* 今晚我們的特別嘉賓是…◇ *He* ***made a guest appearance*** *on the show.* 他在這個節目裏是客串出場。 **4** a person who is invited to a particular place or organization, or to speak at a meeting 特邀嘉賓：*The scientists are here as guests of our government.* 出席的科學家是我國政府的貴賓。◇ *a* ***guest speaker*** 特邀演講人

G

IDM **be my 'guest** (*informal*) used to give sb permission to do sth that they have asked to do 請便；隨便：*'Do you mind if I use the phone?' 'Be my guest.'* "可以用一下電話嗎？""請便。"

■ **verb** [I] **~ (on sth)** to take part in a television or radio show, a concert, a game, etc. as a visiting or temporary performer or player 做特邀嘉賓；做客串；做特約演員：*She guested on several chat shows while visiting Britain.* 她訪問英國時做過幾個訪談節目的特邀嘉賓。

'guest beer *noun* [U, C] (*BrE*) a beer that is not usually available in a particular pub, but which is served there for a limited period, often at a specially reduced price（酒吧裏常折價限時供應的）款待啤酒

'guest house *noun* **1** (*BrE*) a small hotel 小旅館 **2** (*NAmE*) a small house built near a large house, for guests to stay in（大房子旁供客人居住的）客房

gues·ti·mate = GUESSTIMATE

'guest room *noun* a bedroom that is kept for guests to use 客房；留給客人住的寢室

'guest worker *noun* a person, usually from a poor country, who comes to another richer country in order to work there（通常指來自窮國的）客籍工人，外籍工作人員；外勞

guff /gʌf/ *noun* [U] (*informal*) ideas or talk that you think are stupid 胡思亂想；胡說八道；愚蠢的想法；蠢話 SYN **nonsense**

guf·faw /gəˈfɔː/ *verb* [I, T] (**+ speech**) to laugh noisily 大笑；哄笑；狂笑：*They all guffawed at his jokes.* 他們聽了他的笑話都一陣狂笑。 ► **guf·faw** *noun*：*She let out a loud guffaw.* 她嘎嘎大笑起來。

GUI /ˌdʒiː juː ˈaɪ; ˈguːi/ *abbr.* (*computing* 計) graphical user interface (a way of giving instructions to a computer using things that can be seen on the screen such as symbols and menus) 圖形用戶界面

guid·ance /ˈgaɪdns/ *noun* [U] **1 ~ (on sth)** help or advice that is given to sb, especially by sb older or with more experience 指導；引導；咨詢：*guidance for teachers on how to use video in the classroom* 對教師提供的課堂錄像教學指導 ◇ *Activities all take place* ***under the guidance of*** *an experienced tutor.* 所有活動都在經驗豐富的導師指導下進行。◇ (*NAmE*) *a guidance counselor* (= sb who advises students)（學生）咨詢顧問 ➲ see also MARRIAGE GUIDANCE **2** the process of controlling the direction of a ROCKET, etc., using electronic equipment（火箭等的）制導，導航：*a missile guidance system* 導彈制導系統

guide 🔑 /gaɪd/ *noun, verb*

■ **noun**

► BOOK/MAGAZINE 書刊 **1** 🔑 **~ (to sth)** a book, magazine, etc. that gives you information, help or instructions about sth 指南；手冊：*a Guide to Family Health* 家庭健康指南 ◇ *Let's have a look at the TV guide and see what's on.* 咱們看一下節目表，好知道電視上在放些什麼。 **2** 🔑 (also **guide·book**) **~ (to sth)** a book that gives information about a place for travellers or tourists 旅遊指南（或手冊）：*a guide to Italy* 意大利旅遊指南 ◇ *travel guides* 旅行手冊

► PERSON 人 **3** 🔑 a person who shows other people the way to a place, especially sb employed to show tourists around interesting places 導遊；嚮導：*a tour guide* 導遊 ◇ *We hired a local guide to get us across the mountains.* 我們雇了一名當地人做嚮導帶領我們翻山越嶺。 **4** a person who advises you on how to live and behave 指導者；指引者：*a spiritual guide* 神修指導者

► STH THAT HELPS YOU DECIDE 指導的事物 **5** something that gives you enough information to be able to make a decision about sth or form an opinion 有指導意義的事物；指導的事物：***As a rough guide,*** *allow half a cup of rice per person.* 大致定個標準，就是每人半杯米。◇ *I let my feelings be my guide.* 我是跟着感覺走。

► GIRL 女孩 **6 Guide** (also *old-fashioned* **ˌGirl 'Guide**) (both *BrE*) (*US* **ˌGirl 'Scout**) a member of an organization (called **the Guides** or **the Girl Scouts**) which is similar to the SCOUTS and which trains girls in practical skills and does a lot of activities with them, for example camping 女童子軍 ➲ compare BROWNIE (2), (3)

■ **verb**

► SHOW THE WAY 指路 **1** 🔑 **~ sb (to/through/around sth)** to show sb the way to a place, often by going with them; to show sb a place that you know well 給某人領路（或導遊）；指引：*She guided us through the busy streets to the cathedral.* 她帶領我們穿過繁忙的街道去大教堂。◇ *We were guided around the museums.* 我們在導遊的帶領下參觀了博物館。 ➲ SYNONYMS at TAKE

► INFLUENCE BEHAVIOUR 影響行為 **2** 🔑 **~ sb** to direct or influence sb's behaviour 指導，影響（某人的行為）：*He was always guided by his religious beliefs.* 他的言行總是以自己的宗教信仰作為依歸。

► EXPLAIN 闡明 **3** 🔑 **~ sb (through sth)** to explain to sb how to do sth, especially sth complicated or difficult（向某人）解釋，闡明：*The health and safety officer will guide you through the safety procedures.* 健康安全官員將向你把安全規程解釋一遍。

► HELP SB MOVE 幫助挪動 **4** 🔑 **~ sb/sth (+ adv./prep.)** to help sb to move in a particular direction; to move sth in a particular direction 攙扶（某人朝…方向）走；（朝…方向）移動（某物）：*She took her arm and guided her across the busy road.* 她挽着她的手臂領她穿過繁忙的公路。◇ *He guided her hand to his face.* 他拉起她的手放到他臉上。 ➲ see also GUIDING

guide·book /ˈgaɪdbʊk/ *noun* = GUIDE *n.* (2)

guided /ˈgaɪdɪd/ *adj.* [usually before noun] that is led by sb who works as a guide 有指導的；有嚮導的；有導遊的：***a guided tour/walk*** 有導遊的觀光 / 步行觀光

ˌguided 'missile *noun* a MISSILE that can be controlled while in the air by electronic equipment 導彈

'guide dog (*NAmE* also **ˌSeeing 'Eye dog™**) *noun* a dog trained to guide a blind person 導盲犬；領路狗

guide·line AW /ˈgaɪdlaɪn/ *noun* **1 guidelines** [pl.] rules or instructions that are given by an official organization telling you how to do sth, especially sth difficult 指導方針；指導原則；行動綱領；準則：*The government has* ***drawn up guidelines*** *on the treatment of the mentally ill.* 政府制訂了對待精神病人的指導方針。 **2** [C] something that can be used to help you make a decision or form an opinion 參考：*The figures are a useful guideline when buying a house.* 買房時這些數據很有參考價值。

Gui·der /ˈgaɪdə(r)/ (also *old-fashioned* **ˌGirl 'Guider**) *noun* (*BrE*) an adult leader in the Guides 女童子軍指導員

guid·ing /ˈgaɪdɪŋ/ *adj.* [only before noun] giving advice and help; having a strong influence on people 給予指導的；有影響的：*She was inexperienced and needed a* ***guiding hand.*** 她缺乏經驗，需要有人指導。◇ *a guiding force* 有影響的力量

guild /gɪld/ *noun* [C+sing./pl. v.] **1** an organization of people who do the same job or who have the same interests or aims（同一行業、志趣或目的的）協會：*the Screen Actors' Guild* 影視演員協會 **2** an association of skilled workers in the Middle Ages（中世紀的）行會，同業公會

guil·der /ˈgɪldə(r)/ *noun* the former unit of money in the Netherlands (replaced in 2002 by the euro) 荷蘭盾（荷蘭以前的貨幣單位，2002 年為歐元所取代）

guild·hall /ˈgɪldhɔːl/ *noun* (*BrE*) a building in which the members of a GUILD used to meet, now often used for meetings and performances（行會或同業公會的）會館；會議廳；演出大廳

guile /gaɪl/ *noun* [U] (*formal*) the use of clever but dishonest behaviour in order to trick people 狡詐；欺詐；奸詐 SYN **deceit**

guile·less /ˈgaɪlləs/ *adj.* (*formal*) behaving in a very honest way; not knowing how to trick people 厚道的；老實的；不奸猾的 ▸ **guile·less·ly** *adv.*

guil·le·mot /ˈgɪlɪmɒt; *NAmE* -mɑːt/ *noun* a black and white bird with a long narrow beak that lives near the sea 海鴿（黑白色，喙細長）

guil·lo·tine /ˈgɪlətiːn/ *noun, verb*

▪ *noun* **1** [sing.] a machine, originally from France, for cutting people's heads off. It has a heavy blade that slides down a wooden frame. 斷頭台（源於法國）**2** (*BrE*) (*US* ˈ**paper cutter**) [C] a device with a long blade for cutting paper 裁切機；切紙機 **3** [sing.] (*BrE, politics* 政) the setting of a time limit on a debate in Parliament（議會中）規定截止辯論的時限

▪ *verb* **1 ~ sb** to kill sb by cutting off their head with a guillotine 把（某人）送上斷頭台 **2 ~ sth** (*BrE*) to cut paper using a guillotine（用切紙機）切，切斷 **3 ~ sth** (*BrE, politics* 政) to limit the amount of time spent discussing a new law in Parliament（議會中）限制辯論時間：*to guillotine a bill* 限制議案的辯論時間

guilt /gɪlt/ *noun, verb*

▪ *noun* [U] **1 ~ (about sth)** the unhappy feelings caused by knowing or thinking that you have done sth wrong 內疚；悔恨：*She had feelings of guilt about leaving her children and going to work.* 她因離開自己的孩子去工作而感到內疚。◇ *Many survivors were left with **a sense of guilt**.* 許多幸存者都有內疚感。◇ *a **guilt complex*** (= an exaggerated sense of guilt) 內疚情結 **2** the fact that sb has done sth illegal 犯罪；罪行；有罪：*His guilt was proved beyond all doubt by the prosecution.* 他的罪行已被原告證實確鑿無疑。◇ *an admission of guilt* 承認有罪 OPP **innocence 3** blame or responsibility for doing sth wrong or for sth bad that has happened 罪責；責任；罪過：*The investigation will try to find out where the guilt for the disaster really lies.* 此調查將盡力查出災難的真正責任所在。▸ **guilt·less** *adj.*

IDM **a** ˈ**guilt trip** (*informal*) things you say to sb in order to make them feel guilty about sth 使人內疚的責備：*Don't **lay a guilt trip** on your child about schoolwork.* 別讓你孩子對學業自責不迭。

▪ *verb*

PHR V ˈ**guilt sb into sth/into doing sth** (*informal*) to make sb do sth by persuading them that it is wrong not to do it 誘導某人做某事（使其認為不做不對）：*I only went because she guilted me into it.* 我是受到她的蠱惑才去的。

guilty ⊶ /ˈgɪlti/ *adj.* (**guilt·ier, guilti·est**) HELP **More guilty** and **most guilty** are more common. * more guilty 和 most guilty 更常見。

1 ⊶ **~ (about sth)** feeling ashamed because you have done sth that you know is wrong or have not done sth that you should have done 感到內疚的；感到慚愧的：*I felt guilty about not visiting my parents more often.* 我因沒有常去看望父母而感到內疚。◇ *John had a guilty look on his face.* 約翰臉上顯出慚愧的表情。◇ *I had a **guilty conscience** and could not sleep.* 我問心有愧，睡不着覺。**2** ⊶ **~ (of sth)** having done sth illegal; being responsible for sth bad that has happened 犯了罪；有過失的；有罪責的：*The jury **found** the defendant **not guilty** of the offence.* 陪審團裁決被告無罪。◇ *He **pleaded guilty** to murder.* 他承認犯有謀殺罪。◇ ***the guilty party*** (= the person responsible for sth bad happening) 有罪的一方當事人 ◇ *We've all been guilty of selfishness at some time in our lives.* 我們每個人一生中都有過自私自利的過失。OPP **innocent** ➲ COLLOCATIONS at JUSTICE ▸ **guilt·ily** /-ɪli/ *adv.*

IDM **a guilty** ˈ**secret** a secret that sb feels ashamed about 見不得人的秘密

guinea /ˈgɪni/ *noun* an old British gold coin or unit of money worth 21 SHILLINGS (= now £1.05). Prices are sometimes still given in guineas, for example when buying or selling horses. 幾尼（英國舊時金幣或貨幣單位，價值 21 先令，現值 1.05 英鎊。現時有些價格仍用幾尼計算，如馬匹買賣）

guinea·fowl /ˈgɪnifaʊl/ *noun* [C, U] (*pl.* **guinea·fowl**) a bird of the PHEASANT family, that has dark grey feathers with white spots, and is often used for food; the meat of this bird 珠雞；珠雞肉：*roast guineafowl* 烤珠雞肉

ˈ**guinea pig** *noun* **1** a small animal with short ears and no tail, often kept as a pet 天竺鼠，豚鼠（耳小無尾，常作寵物飼養）**2** a person used in medical or other experiments 實驗對象：*Students in fifty schools are to act as guinea pigs for these new teaching methods.* 五十所學校的學生將作為這些新教學法的試驗對象。

Guin·ness™ /ˈgɪnɪs/ *noun* [U, C] a type of very dark brown beer, with a white HEAD (= top) on it 健力士黑啤酒（帶白色頭沫）

guise /gaɪz/ *noun* a way in which sb/sth appears, often in a way that is different from usual or that hides the truth about them/it 表現形式；外貌；偽裝；外表：*His speech presented racist ideas **under the guise of** nationalism.* 他的講話以民族主義為幌子宣揚種族主義思想。◇ *The story appears in different guises in different cultures.* 這個故事以不同的形式出現在不同的文化中。

gui·tar /gɪˈtɑː(r)/ *noun* a musical instrument that usually has six strings, that you play with your fingers or with a PLECTRUM 吉他：***an acoustic/an electric/a classical, etc. guitar*** 原聲吉他、電吉他、古典吉他等 ◇ *a guitar player* 吉他彈奏者 ◇ *Do you **play the guitar**?* 你會彈吉他嗎？◇ *She plays guitar in a band.* 她在樂隊裏彈奏吉他。◇ *As he sang, he strummed his guitar.* 他邊唱邊撥着吉他。➲ VISUAL VOCAB page V36 ➲ see also AIR GUITAR, BASS[1] *n.* (4)

gui·tar·ist /gɪˈtɑːrɪst/ *noun* a person who plays the guitar 吉他彈奏者；吉他手

Gu·ja·rati (also **Gu·je·rati**) /ˌguːdʒəˈrɑːti/ *noun* **1** [C] a person from the state of Gujarat in western India（印度西部的）古吉拉特人 **2** [U] the language of Gujarat 古吉拉特語 ▸ **Gu·ja·rati** (also **Gu·je·rati**) *adj.*

gulch /gʌltʃ/ *noun* (*especially NAmE*) a narrow valley with steep sides, that was formed by a fast stream flowing through it（兩邊陡峭的）急流峽谷

gulf /gʌlf/ *noun* **1** [C] a large area of sea that is partly surrounded by land 海灣：*the Gulf of Mexico* 墨西哥灣 **2 the Gulf** [sing.] the Persian Gulf, the area of sea between the Arabian PENINSULA and Iran 波斯灣：*the Gulf States* (= the countries with coasts on the Gulf) 海灣國家 **3** [C, usually sing.] **~ (between A and B)** a large difference between two people or groups in the way that they think, live or feel 分歧；鴻溝；隔閡：*The gulf between rich and poor is enormous.* 貧富懸殊。**4** [C] a wide deep crack in the ground（地面的）裂口，深坑，溝壑 IDM see BRIDGE *v.*

the ˈ**Gulf Stream** *noun* [sing.] a warm current of water flowing across the Atlantic Ocean from the Gulf of Mexico towards Europe 墨西哥灣流

gull /gʌl/ (also **sea·gull**) *noun* a bird with long wings and usually white and grey or black feathers that lives near the sea. There are several types of gull. 海鷗 ➲ VISUAL VOCAB page V12 ➲ see also HERRING GULL

Gul·lah /ˈgʌlə/ *noun* [U] a language spoken by black people living on the coast of South Carolina, that is a combination of English and various W African languages 古勒語（居住在美國南卡羅來納州沿海地區的黑人所操的一種語言，為英語與多種西非語言的結合）

gul·let /ˈgʌlɪt/ *noun* the tube through which food passes from the mouth to the stomach 食管；食道 SYN **oesophagus** ➲ VISUAL VOCAB page V59

gul·lible /ˈgʌləbl/ *adj.* too willing to believe or accept what other people tell you and therefore easily tricked 輕信的；易受騙的；易上當的 SYN **naive** ▸ **gul·li·bil·ity** /ˌgʌləˈbɪləti/ *noun* [U]

G

G

gully (also **gul·ley**) /ˈɡʌli/ *noun* (*pl.* **gul·lies**, **gul·leys**) **1** a small, narrow channel, usually formed by a stream or by rain 溪谷；沖溝 **2** a deep DITCH 深溝；溝壑

gulp /ɡʌlp/ *verb, noun*

■ *verb* **1** [T, I] **~ (sth)** | **~ sth down** to swallow large amounts of food or drink quickly 狼吞虎嚥；大口吞嚥；匆匆吞下：*He gulped down the rest of his tea and went out.* 他把剩下的茶一飲而盡便出去了。 **2** [I, T] (+ speech) to swallow, but without eating or drinking anything, especially because of a strong emotion such as fear or surprise（尤因害怕或驚訝而）倒吸氣：*She gulped nervously before trying to answer.* 她緊張地倒吸了一口氣才設法回答。 **3** [I, T] to breathe quickly and deeply, because you need more air 深呼吸；喘大氣；大口大口地吸氣：**~ (for sth)** *She came up **gulping for air**.* 她氣喘吁吁地走上前來。◇ **~ sth (in)** *He leant against the car, gulping in the cold air.* 他倚着汽車大口大口地呼吸冷空氣。

PHR V **ˌgulp sth↔ˈback** to stop yourself showing your emotions by swallowing hard 嚥下…（以防止感情的流露）：*She gulped back her tears and forced a smile.* 她忍住淚水，強作笑容。

■ *noun* **1 ~ (of sth)** an amount of sth that you swallow or drink quickly 吞飲的量；一大口：*He **took a gulp** of coffee.* 他喝了一大口咖啡。 **2** an act of breathing in or of swallowing sth 吸入；吞嚥：*'Can you start on Monday?' Amy gave a gulp. 'Of course,' she said.* "你星期一開始可以嗎？"埃米吸了一口氣。"當然可以。"她說。◇ *He drank the glass of whisky **in one gulp**.* 他將整杯威士忌一飲而盡。

gum /ɡʌm/ *noun, verb*

■ *noun* **1** [C, usually pl.] either of the firm areas of flesh in the mouth to which the teeth are attached 牙齦；齒齦；牙牀：*gum disease* 牙齦病 ➲ VISUAL VOCAB page V59 **2** [U] a sticky substance produced by some types of tree 樹膠；樹脂 **3** [U] a type of glue used for sticking light things together, such as paper 黏膠，膠質物（用以粘輕東西，如紙等） **4** [U] = CHEWING GUM **5** [C] a firm transparent fruit-flavoured sweet/candy that you chew 透明果味糖：*fruit gums* 水果軟糖

IDM **by gum!** (*old-fashioned, BrE, informal*) used to show surprise（表示驚訝）天啊，老天，啊呀

■ *verb* (-mm-) **~ A to B** | **~ sth (down)** (rather *old-fashioned*) to spread glue on the surface of sth; to stick two things together with glue 在…上塗膠；用黏膠粘：*A large address label was gummed to the package.* 包裝袋上貼着一大張地址籤條。

PHR V **ˌgum sth↔ˈup** [usually passive] (*BrE, informal*) to cover or fill sth with a sticky substance so that it stops moving or working as it should 用黏膠將某物粘牢

gum·ball /ˈɡʌmbɔːl/ *noun* (*NAmE*) a small ball of CHEWING GUM that looks like a sweet/candy 球形口香糖

gumbo /ˈɡʌmbəʊ; *NAmE* -boʊ/ *noun* [U] a thick chicken or SEAFOOD soup, usually made with the vegetable OKRA 秋葵湯（用秋葵莢做的濃雞湯或海鮮湯）

gum·boil /ˈɡʌmbɔɪl/ *noun* a small swelling on the GUM in a person's mouth, over an infected area on the root of a tooth 齦膿腫

gum·boot /ˈɡʌmbuːt/ *noun* (*old-fashioned, BrE*) = WELLINGTON

gum·drop /ˈɡʌmdrɒp; *NAmE* -drɑːp/ *noun* a sweet/candy that is like a small firm lump of jelly 膠姆糖；橡皮糖

gummed /ɡʌmd/ *adj.* [usually before noun] (of stamps, paper, etc. 郵票、紙張等) covered with a type of glue that will become sticky when water is put on it 塗膠的；帶黏膠的

gummy /ˈɡʌmi/ *adj.* (*informal*) **1** sticky or covered in gum (3) 黏性的；塗有黏膠的 **2** a **gummy** smile shows your teeth and gums（微笑時）露齒齦的

gump·tion /ˈɡʌmpʃn/ *noun* [U] (*old-fashioned, informal*) **1** the intelligence needed to know what to do in a particular situation 機智；老練；精明 **2** courage and determination 勇氣；膽力；決心

gum·shield /ˈɡʌmʃiːld/ (*BrE*) (*NAmE* **mouth·guard**) *noun* a cover that a sports player wears in his or her mouth to protect the teeth and GUMS（運動員口中所含的）護齒

gum·shoe /ˈɡʌmʃuː/ *noun* (*old-fashioned, NAmE, informal*) = DETECTIVE (1)

ˈgum tree *noun* a EUCALYPTUS tree 桉樹；樹膠樹

IDM **be up a ˈgum tree** (*BrE, informal*) to be in a very difficult situation 陷入困境；一籌莫展

gun 0→ /ɡʌn/ *noun, verb*

■ *noun* **1** 0→ [C] a weapon that is used for firing bullets or SHELLS 槍；炮：*to **fire a gun** at sb* 向某人開火 ◇ *a toy gun* 玩具槍 ◇ *anti-aircraft guns* 高射炮 ◇ *Look out, he's got a gun!* 小心，他有槍！◇ *Should police officers **carry guns**?* 警察應該佩槍嗎？◇ *He **pointed/aimed the gun** at her head.* 他用槍對準／瞄準了她的頭。◇ *The police officers **drew their guns*** (= took them out so they were ready to use). 警察拔槍。◇ *She **pulled a gun** on me* (= took out a gun and aimed it at me). 她掏出槍來對準了我。◇ *The **gun went off** by accident.* 槍走火了。◇ *a **gun battle** between rival gangs* 對立幫派間的槍戰 ➲ see also AIRGUN, HANDGUN, MACHINE GUN, SHOTGUN, STUN GUN, SUB-MACHINE GUN, TOMMY GUN **2** [C] a tool that uses pressure to send out a substance or an object 噴射器；噴槍：*a staple gun* * U 形釘槍 ➲ see also SPRAY GUN **3 the gun** [sing.] the signal to begin a race, that is made by firing a special gun, called a STARTING PISTOL, into the air 起跑信號；發令槍聲 **4** [C] (*informal, especially NAmE*) a person who is paid to shoot sb 受雇殺人的槍手：*a hired gun* 雇用的槍手 ➲ see also FLASHGUN, SON OF A GUN

IDM **hold/put a gun to sb's ˈhead** to force sb to do sth that they do not want to do, by making threats 威脅某人；脅迫某人就範 **under the ˈgun** (*NAmE, informal*) experiencing a lot of pressure 承受很大壓力：*I'm really under the gun today.* 我今天的壓力真大。 **(with) all/both guns ˈblazing** (*informal*) with a lot of energy and determination 充滿活力；精神抖擻：*The champions came out (with) all guns blazing.* 優勝者們神采奕奕地登場亮相。➲ more at GREAT *adj.*, JUMP *v.*, SPIKE *v.*, STICK *v.*

■ *verb* (-nn-) **1** [I] (*NAmE*) (of an engine 發動機) to run very quickly 快速運轉：*a line of motorcycles with their engines gunning* 引擎狂轉的一隊摩托車 **2** [T] **~ sth + adv./prep.** (*NAmE*) to start driving a vehicle very fast 使（車輛）加速：*He gunned the cab through the red light.* 他猛踩油門，開着出租汽車闖過了紅燈。

PHR V **be ˈgunning for sb** (*informal*) to be looking for an opportunity to blame or attack sb 伺機指責（或攻擊）某人 **be ˈgunning for sth** to be competing for or trying hard to get sth 竭力謀求，力圖獲取，尋求（某物）：*She's gunning for the top job.* 她正竭力謀取最高職位。 **ˌgun sb↔ˈdown** [usually passive] to shoot sb, especially killing or seriously injuring them 槍殺，開槍傷害（某人）

gun·boat /ˈɡʌnbəʊt; *NAmE* -boʊt/ *noun* a small ship that is fitted with large guns 炮艇；炮艦

ˌgunboat diˈplomacy *noun* [U] a way of making another country accept your demands by using the threat of force 炮艦外交（以武力相威脅）

ˈgun carriage *noun* a support on wheels for a large heavy gun 炮架

ˈgun control *noun* [U] (*especially NAmE*) laws that restrict the sale and use of guns 槍支管制（法）

ˈgun dog *noun* a dog trained to help in the sport of shooting, for example by finding birds that have been shot 獵犬

gun·fight /ˈɡʌnfaɪt/ *noun* a fight between people using guns 槍戰；炮戰 ▸ **gun·fight·er** *noun*

gun·fire /ˈɡʌnfaɪə(r)/ *noun* [U] the repeated firing of guns; the sound of guns firing（接連不斷的）炮火，炮火聲：*an exchange of gunfire with the police* 與警方的交火 ◇ *I could hear gunfire.* 我可以聽到炮聲。

gunge /gʌndʒ/ (*BrE*) (also **gunk** *NAmE, BrE*) *noun* [U] (*informal*) any unpleasant, sticky or dirty substance 骯髒討厭的黏性物質；黏糊糊的東西 ▸ **gungy** *adj.*

gung-ho /ˌɡʌŋ ˈhəʊ; *NAmE* ˈhoʊ/ *adj.* (*informal, disapproving*) too enthusiastic about sth, without thinking seriously about it, especially about fighting and war（尤指對戰鬥和戰爭）偏激的，狂熱的，莽撞的

gunk /ɡʌŋk/ (*especially NAmE*) (*BrE* also **gunge**) *noun* [U] (*informal*) any unpleasant, sticky or dirty substance 骯髒討厭的黏性物質；黏糊糊的東西 ▸ **gunky** *adj.*

gun·man /ˈɡʌnmən/ *noun* (*pl.* **-men** /-mən/) a man who uses a gun to steal from or kill people 持槍歹徒；持槍殺人者

gun·metal /ˈɡʌnmetl/ *noun* [U] **1** a metal that is a mixture of COPPER, tin and ZINC 炮銅，G 合金（銅、錫和鋅的合金） **2** a dull blue-grey colour 炮銅色；暗藍灰色；鐵灰色

gun·nel = GUNWALE

gun·ner /ˈɡʌnə(r)/ *noun* **1** a member of the armed forces who is trained to use large guns 炮手；炮兵 **2** a soldier in the British ARTILLERY (= the part of the army that uses large guns)（英國炮兵部隊的）士兵；炮兵

gun·nery /ˈɡʌnəri/ *noun* [U] (*technical* 術語) the operation of large military guns 槍炮操作

gunny /ˈɡʌni/ *noun* [U] a type of rough cloth used for making SACKS 黃麻袋布；粗麻布

gun·ny·sack /ˈɡʌnisæk/ *noun* (*NAmE*) a large bag made from rough material and used to store flour, potatoes, etc.（裝麵粉、土豆等的）黃麻袋

gun·point /ˈɡʌnpɔɪnt/ *noun*
IDM **at ˈgunpoint** while threatening sb or being threatened with a gun 用槍威脅；在槍口威脅下：*The driver was robbed at gunpoint.* 司機遭持槍搶劫。

gun·pow·der /ˈɡʌnpaʊdə(r)/ (also **pow·der**) *noun* [U] EXPLOSIVE powder used especially in bombs or FIREWORKS 火藥

gun·run·ner /ˈɡʌnrʌnə(r)/ *noun* a person who secretly and illegally brings guns into a country 私運軍火者；軍火走私者 ▸ **gun·run·ning** *noun* [U]

gun·ship /ˈɡʌnʃɪp/ *noun* an armed military HELICOPTER or other aircraft 武裝直升機；武裝飛機

gun·shot /ˈɡʌnʃɒt; *NAmE* -ʃɑːt/ *noun* **1** [U] the bullets that are fired from a gun（射出的）炮彈，槍彈：*gunshot wounds* 槍傷 **2** [C] the firing of a gun; the sound of it being fired 槍炮射擊；槍炮聲：*I heard the sound of gunshots out in the street.* 我聽到外面街上有槍炮聲。 **3** [U] the distance that a bullet from a gun can travel（槍炮的）射程：*He was* ***out of/within gunshot.*** 他在射程之外 / 內。

gun·sight /ˈɡʌnsaɪt/ *noun* a part of a gun that you look through in order to aim it accurately（槍炮的）瞄準器 ➲ see also SIGHT *n.* (7)

gun·sling·er /ˈɡʌnslɪŋə(r)/ *noun* (*NAmE*) a person who is paid to kill people, especially in films/movies about the American Wild West（尤指美國西部電影中受人雇用的）殺手

gun·smith /ˈɡʌnsmɪθ/ *noun* a person who makes and repairs guns 造槍工；修槍匠；軍械工人

gun·wale (also **gun·nel**) /ˈɡʌnl/ *noun* the upper edge of the side of a boat or small ship 船舷的上緣；舷緣

guppy /ˈɡʌpi/ *noun* (*pl.* **-ies**) a small FRESHWATER fish, commonly kept in AQUARIUMS 虹鱂，孔雀魚（小型淡水觀賞魚）

gur·dwa·ra /ɡɜːˈdwɑːrə; *NAmE* ɡɜːr-/ *noun* a building in which Sikhs worship 謁師所（錫克教禮拜場所）

gur·gle /ˈɡɜːɡl; *NAmE* ˈɡɜːrɡl/ *verb, noun*
■ ***verb*** **1** [I] to make a sound like water flowing quickly through a narrow space 發汩汩聲；發潺潺流水聲：*Water gurgled through the pipes.* 水汩汩地從管道中流過。◇ *a gurgling stream* 潺潺溪流 **2** [I] if a baby **gurgles**, it makes a noise in its throat when it is happy（嬰兒高興時）發出咯咯聲
■ ***noun*** **1** a sound like water flowing quickly through a narrow space 汩汩聲；潺潺聲 **2** the sound that babies make in the throat, especially when they are happy（嬰兒高興時發出的）咯咯聲

Gur·kha /ˈɡɜːkə; *NAmE* ˈɡɜːrkə/ *noun* one of a group of people from Nepal who are known as good soldiers. Some Gurkhas are members of a REGIMENT in the British army. 廓爾喀士兵（善戰的尼泊爾人，有些人服役於英國的一個陸軍團）

gurn (also **girn**) /ɡɜːn; *NAmE* ɡɜːrn/ *verb* [I] (*especially BrE*) to make a ridiculous or unpleasant face 做俏皮相；扮鬼臉 ▸ **gurn·er** /ˈɡɜːnə(r); *NAmE* ˈɡɜːrn-/ *noun*

gur·ney /ˈɡɜːni; *NAmE* ˈɡɜːrni/ *noun* (*NAmE*) a type of TROLLEY which is used for moving patients in a hospital（醫院中推送病人用的）輪牀

guru /ˈɡʊruː/ *noun* **1** a Hindu or Sikh religious teacher or leader 古魯（印度教或錫克教的宗教導師或領袖） **2** (*informal*) a person who is an expert on a particular subject or who is very good at doing sth 專家；權威；大師：***a management/health/fashion, etc. guru*** 管理、保健、時裝等專家

gush /ɡʌʃ/ *verb, noun*
■ ***verb*** **1** [I] **~ out of/from/into sth | ~ out/in** to flow or pour suddenly and quickly out of a hole in large amounts（從…中）噴出，湧出，冒出：*blood gushing from a wound* 從傷口冒出的血 ◇ *Water gushed out of the pipe.* 水從管子中湧出。 **2** [T] **~ sth** (of a container/vehicle etc. 容器、車輛等) to suddenly let out large amounts of a liquid 大量湧出，大量泄出（液體）：*The tanker was gushing oil.* 油箱在大量噴油。◇ (*figurative*) *She absolutely gushed enthusiasm.* 她真是熱情奔放。 **3** [T, I] (+ **speech**) (*disapproving*) to express so much praise or emotion about sb/sth that it does not seem sincere 過分稱讚；誇張地表現對…的感情；裝腔作勢：*'You are clever,' she gushed.* "你好聰明。" 她誇張地稱讚說。
■ ***noun*** [usually sing.] **1 ~** (**of sth**) a large amount of liquid suddenly and quickly flowing or pouring out of sth（液體的）噴出，湧出，冒出：*a gush of blood* 血的湧出 **2 ~** (**of sth**) a sudden strong expression of feeling（感情的）迸發，爆發，發作：*a gush of emotion* 感情的迸發

gush·er /ˈɡʌʃə(r)/ *noun* **1** (*NAmE*) an OIL WELL where the oil comes out quickly and in large quantities 噴油井；自噴井 **2** a person who gushes (3) 過分表露感情的人；言不由衷的人

gush·ing /ˈɡʌʃɪŋ/ *adj.* (*disapproving*) expressing so much enthusiasm, praise or emotion that it does not seem sincere 過分熱情的；過分讚揚的；誇張地表現感情的 ▸ **gush·ing·ly** *adv.*

gus·set /ˈɡʌsɪt/ *noun* an extra piece of cloth sewn into a piece of clothing to make it wider, stronger or more comfortable（縫在衣服上以放大、加固等的）襯料

gussy /ˈɡʌsi/ *verb* (**gus·sies**, **gussy·ing**, **gus·sied**, **gus·sied**)
PHR V **ˌgussy ˈup** (*NAmE, informal*) to dress yourself in an attractive way 把自己打扮得漂漂亮亮（或花枝招展） SYN **dress up**：*Even the stars get tired of gussying up for the awards.* 連明星們也厭煩了把自己打扮起來去領獎。

gust /ɡʌst/ *noun, verb*
■ ***noun*** **1** a sudden strong increase in the amount and speed of wind that is blowing 一陣強風；一陣狂風：*A* ***gust of wind*** *blew his hat off.* 一陣狂風把他的帽子颳掉了。◇ *The wind was blowing in gusts.* 狂風陣陣颳着。 **2** a sudden strong expression of emotion（感情的）迸發，爆發，發作：*a* ***gust of laughter*** 一陣笑聲
■ ***verb*** [I] (of the wind 風) to suddenly blow very hard 猛颳；勁吹：*winds gusting up to 60 mph* 風速達每小時 60 英里的狂風

gusto /ˈɡʌstəʊ; *NAmE* -toʊ/ *noun* [U] enthusiasm and energy in doing sth（做某事的）熱情，興致，精力：*They sang* ***with gusto.*** 他們興致勃勃地唱歌。

gusty /ˈɡʌsti/ *adj.* [usually before noun] with the wind blowing in GUSTS 有陣風在吹的；颳風的：*a gusty morning* 颳風的早晨 ◇ *gusty winds* 陣陣大風

G

G

gut /gʌt/ *noun, verb, adj.*

■ ***noun*** **1** [C] the tube in the body through which food passes when it leaves the stomach 消化道；腸道 **SYN** **intestine** **2 guts** [pl.] the organs in and around the stomach, especially in an animal（尤指動物的）內臟：*I'll only cook fish if the guts have been removed.* 我只燒先去掉內臟的魚。**3** [C] (*informal*) a person's stomach, especially when it is large（尤指大的）胃，肚子 **SYN** **belly**：*Have you seen the gut on him!* 你看到他那大肚子了吧！◇ *a* ***beer gut*** (= caused by drinking beer) 啤酒肚 **4 guts** [pl.] (*informal*) the courage and determination that it takes to do sth difficult or unpleasant 勇氣；膽量；決心；毅力：*He* ***doesn't have the guts*** *to walk away from a well-paid job.* 他沒膽量辭去一份報酬優厚的工作。**5** [C, usually pl.] the place where your natural feelings that make you react in a particular way are thought to be 內心；直覺；本能：*I had a feeling* ***in my guts*** *that something was wrong.* 我內裏感到出了事。**6 guts** [pl.] the most important part of sth 核心；實質；要點：*the guts of the problem* 問題的實質 **7** [U] = CATGUT

IDM **have sb's ˌguts for ˈgarters** (*BrE, informal*) to be very angry with sb and punish them severely for sth they have done 恨死，嚴懲（某人） **slog/sweat/work your ˈguts out** (*informal*) to work very hard to achieve sth 拚命工作；拚命幹活：*I slogged my guts out for the exam.* 我為這次考試命都豁出去了。➲ more at BUST *v.*, GREEDY *adj.*, HATE *v.*, SPILL *v.*

■ ***verb*** (**-tt-**) **1** [usually passive] **~ sth** to destroy the inside or contents of a building or room 損毀（建築物或房屋的）內部：*a factory gutted by fire* 內部被火焚燬的工廠 ◇ *The house was completely gutted.* 這房子裏的東西全部被毀。**2 ~ sth** to remove the organs from inside a fish or an animal to prepare it for cooking 取出…的內臟（以便烹飪）

■ ***adj.*** [only before noun] based on feelings and emotions rather than thought and reason 以感情為基礎的；非理性的；本能的：*a* ***gut feeling/reaction*** 本能的感覺 / 反應 ◇ *You have to work on* ***gut instinct****.* 你得憑藉你的直覺工作。

gut·less /ˈgʌtləs/ *adj.* lacking courage or determination 缺乏勇氣的；怯懦的；無毅力的

gut·ser /ˈgʌtsə(r)/ *noun* (*AustralE, NZE, informal*) an occasion when sb/sth falls or knocks into sth 摔跤；跌倒；撞擊

IDM **come a ˈgutser** to fail or be defeated 失敗；遭挫敗

gutsy /ˈgʌtsi/ *adj.* (*informal*) **1** showing courage and determination 勇敢的；有膽量的；有決心的；堅毅的：*a* ***gutsy fighter/win*** 勇敢的戰士；用堅強的毅力取得的勝利 **2** having strong and unusual qualities 強勁的；熱烈而與眾不同的：*a gutsy red wine* 烈性紅葡萄酒 ◇ *a gutsy song* 滿懷激情的歌

gut·ted /ˈgʌtɪd/ *adj.* [not before noun] (*BrE, informal*) extremely sad or disappointed 十分傷心；極度失望；非常沮喪：*Disappointed? I was gutted!* 失望？我是傷心透了！

gut·ter /ˈgʌtə(r)/ *noun, verb*

■ ***noun*** **1** [C] a long curved channel made of metal or plastic that is fixed under the edge of a roof to carry away the water when it rains 簷溝；天溝：***a blocked/ leaking gutter*** 堵塞了的 / 漏水的簷溝 ➲ VISUAL VOCAB page V17 **2** [C] a channel at the edge of a road where water collects and is carried away to DRAINS 路旁排水溝；陰溝 **3 the gutter** [sing.] the bad social conditions or low moral standards sometimes connected with the lowest level of society 惡劣的社會環境；（社會最低階層的）道德淪落：*She rose from the gutter to become a great star.* 她從貧民區一躍而成為大明星。◇ *the language of the gutter* (= used when swearing) 粗鄙的語言（詛咒時用）

■ ***verb*** [I] (*literary*) (of a flame or CANDLE 火焰或蠟燭) to burn in an unsteady way 忽明忽暗；搖曳不定

gut·ter·ing /ˈgʌtərɪŋ/ *noun* [U] the system of gutters on a building; the material used to make gutters（建築物天溝的）排水系統；用於建築物排水系統的材料：*a length of guttering* 一節溝槽

the ˌgutter ˈpress *noun* [sing.] (*BrE, disapproving*) newspapers that print a lot of shocking stories about people's private lives rather than serious news 低級趣味的報紙

gut·ter·snipe /ˈgʌtəsnaɪp; *NAmE* -tərs-/ *noun* (*informal, disapproving*) a poor and dirty child 骯髒的窮孩子；流浪兒

gut·tur·al /ˈgʌtərəl/ *adj.* (of a sound 聲音) made or seeming to be made at the back of the throat（似）喉間發出的：*guttural consonants* 腭輔音 ◇ *a low guttural growl* 從喉嚨裏發出的低沉的吼聲

ˈgut-wrench·ing *adj.* (*informal*) very unpleasant; making you feel very upset 倒胃口的；非常討厭的；令人厭煩的

guv /gʌv/ *exclamation* (*BrE, informal*) used by a man to address another man who is a customer, etc., meaning 'sir'（男人對男顧客等的稱呼）先生

guv'nor /ˈgʌvnə(r)/ *noun* (*BrE, informal*) (often used as a way of addressing sb 常用作稱呼) a man who is in a position of authority, for example your employer 老闆；頭兒：*Do you want me to ask the guv'nor about it?* 你想讓我就這事問問老闆嗎？➲ see also GOVERNOR

guy 0┳ /gaɪ/ *noun*

1 0┳ [C] (*informal*) a man 男人；小伙子；傢伙：*a big/ nice/tough guy* 大個子男人；好小伙子；硬漢 ◇ *a Dutch guy* 荷蘭男人 ◇ *At the end of the film the bad guy gets shot.* 這壞蛋在影片結尾時被擊斃。➲ see also FALL GUY, WISE GUY **2 guys** [pl.] (*informal, especially NAmE*) a group of people of either sex 一群男人（或女人）；夥計們；兄弟（或姐妹）們：*Come on, you guys, let's get going!* 快點，夥計們，咱們走吧！**3** [C] (in Britain) a model of a man dressed in old clothes that is burned on a BONFIRE on 5 November during the celebrations for Bonfire Night 蓋伊模擬像（英國每年 11 月 5 日慶祝篝火之夜焚燒的身着古裝的人體模型）**4** (also **ˈguy rope**) [C] a rope used to keep a pole or tent in a vertical position（立竿子或架帳篷用的）支索，牽索，拉索 **IDM** see MR *abbr.*

Guy Fawkes night /ˈgaɪ fɔːks naɪt/ *noun* [U, C] Bonfire Night 篝火之夜

guz·zle /ˈgʌzl/ *verb* [T, I] **~ (sth)** (*informal, usually disapproving*) to drink sth quickly and in large amounts. In British English it also means to eat food quickly and in large amounts. 狂飲；猛喝；暴飲；（英式英語）狼吞虎嚥：*The kids seem to be guzzling soft drinks all day.* 孩子們似乎整天都在猛喝汽水。◇ (*figurative*) *My car guzzles fuel.* 我的汽車很耗油。

guz·zler /ˈgʌzlə(r)/ *noun* (*informal, especially NAmE*) = GAS GUZZLER

gweilo /ˈgweɪləʊ; *NAmE* -loʊ/ *noun* (*pl.* **-os**) (*SEAsianE*) used in SE Asia to refer to a person from a foreign country, especially sb from the West（東南亞用語，尤指西方人）外國佬，鬼佬

gybe (*especially BrE*) (*NAmE* usually **jibe**) /dʒaɪb/ *verb, noun*

■ ***verb*** [I] to change direction when sailing with the wind behind you, by swinging the sail from one side of the boat to the other（順風時使船帆從一舷轉至另一舷以）改變方向，轉帆

■ ***noun*** an act of gybing 船帆從一舷轉至另一舷；轉帆

gym /dʒɪm/ *noun* (*informal*) **1** (also *formal* **gym·na·sium**) [C] a room or hall with equipment for doing physical exercise, for example in a school 健身房；體育館：*to play basketball in the gym* 在體育館打籃球 ◇ *The school has recently built a new gym.* 學校最近新建了一個體育館。**2** [U] physical exercises done in a gym, especially at school（尤指學校的）體育活動，健身：*I don't enjoy gym.* 我不喜歡做健身鍛煉。◇ *gym shoes* 運動鞋 **3** [C] = HEALTH CLUB：*I just joined a gym.* 我剛加入了健身俱樂部。◇ *I work out at the gym most days.* 我多數日子都在健身俱樂部鍛煉身體。➲ COLLOCATIONS at DIET

gym·khana /dʒɪmˈkɑːnə/ *noun* (*BrE*) an event in which people riding horses take part in various competitions 賽馬會；馬術比賽

gym·na·sium /dʒɪm'neɪziəm/ *noun* (*pl.* **gym·na·siums** or **gym·na·sia** /-ziə/) (*formal*) = GYM (1)

gym·nast /'dʒɪmnæst/ *noun* a person who performs gymnastics, especially in a competition 體操運動員

gym·nas·tics /dʒɪm'næstɪks/ *noun* [U] physical exercises that develop and show the body's strength and ability to move and bend easily, often done as a sport in competitions 體操；體操訓練：*a gymnastics competition* 體操比賽 ◇ (*figurative*) ***mental/verbal gymnastics*** (= quick or clever thinking or use of words) 智力 / 表達能力訓練 ➲ VISUAL VOCAB page V47 ▸ **gym·nas·tic** *adj.* [only before noun]

'gym shoe *noun* (*BrE* also **plim·soll**, **pump**) a light simple sports shoe made of CANVAS (= strong cotton cloth) with a rubber SOLE 橡膠底帆布鞋；體操鞋

gym·slip /'dʒɪmslɪp/ *noun* (*BrE*) a dress without sleeves worn over a shirt as a school uniform for girls, especially in the past 吉姆無袖衫；（尤指舊時女生穿的）體操衫

gy·nae·colo·gist (*BrE*) (*NAmE* **gyne·colo·gist**) /ˌgaɪnə'kɒlədʒɪst; *NAmE* -'kɑːl-/ *noun* a doctor who studies and treats the medical conditions and diseases of women 婦科醫生；婦科學家

gy·nae·col·ogy (*BrE*) (*NAmE* **gyne·cology**) /ˌgaɪnə'kɒlədʒi; *NAmE* -'kɑːl-/ *noun* [U] the scientific study and treatment of the medical conditions and diseases of women, especially those connected with sexual REPRODUCTION 婦科學；婦科 ▸ **gy·nae·co·logic·al** (*BrE*) (*NAmE* **gyne-**) /ˌgaɪnəkə'lɒdʒɪkl; *NAmE* -'lɑːdʒ-/ *adj.*：*a gynaecological examination* 婦科檢查

gyp /dʒɪp/ *noun, verb*

■ ***noun*** [sing.] (*NAmE, informal*) an act of charging too much money for sth 敲竹槓：*That meal was a real gyp.* 那頓飯簡直是敲竹槓。

IDM **give sb 'gyp** (*BrE, informal*) to cause sb a lot of pain 折磨某人；使某人很痛苦：*My back's been giving me gyp lately.* 最近我的後背疼得要命。

■ ***verb*** (**-pp-**) **~ sb** (*especially NAmE*) to cheat or trick sb, especially by taking their money 敲詐；詐取；詐騙

gyp·sum /'dʒɪpsəm/ *noun* [U] a soft white mineral like CHALK that is found naturally and is used in making PLASTER OF PARIS 石膏

Gypsy (also **Gipsy**) /'dʒɪpsi/ *noun* (*pl.* **-ies**) (sometimes *offensive*) **1** a member of a race of people, originally from Asia, who traditionally travel around and live in CARAVANS. Many people prefer to use the name Roma or Romani. 吉卜賽人（許多人更喜歡用 Roma 或 Romani） **2** = TRAVELLER (2)

gyr·ate /dʒaɪ'reɪt; *NAmE* 'dʒaɪreɪt/ *verb* [I, T] to move around in circles; to make sth, especially a part of your body, move around 旋轉；使（身體部位）旋轉，轉動：*They began gyrating to the music.* 他們隨着音樂的節奏旋轉起來。◇ *The leaves gyrated slowly to the ground.* 樹葉旋轉着慢慢飄落到地上。◇ **~ sth** *As the lead singer gyrated his hips, the crowd screamed wildly.* 當主唱歌手扭擺臀部時，觀眾發狂似地尖叫起來。 ▸ **gyr·ation** /dʒaɪ'reɪʃn/ *noun* [C, usually pl., U]

gyro·scope /'dʒaɪrəskəʊp; *NAmE* -skoʊp/ (also *informal* **gyro** /'dʒaɪrəʊ; *NAmE* -roʊ/) *noun* a device consisting of a wheel that spins rapidly inside a frame and does not change position when the frame is moved. Gyroscopes are often used to keep ships and aircraft steady. 陀螺儀；迴轉儀 ▸ **gyro·scop·ic** /ˌdʒaɪrə'skɒpɪk; *NAmE* -'skɑːpɪk/ *adj.*

G

H h

H (also **h**) /eɪtʃ/ *noun, abbr.*

■ **noun** [C, U] (*pl.* **Hs, H's, h's** /ˈeɪtʃɪz/) the 8th letter of the English alphabet 英語字母表的第 8 個字母：*'Hat' begins with (an) H/'H'.* * hat 一詞以字母 h 開頭。➲ compare AITCH ➲ see also H-BOMB

■ **abbr.** (in writing) HENRY（書寫形式）亨利（電感單位）

ha¹ /hɑː/ *exclamation* **1** (also **hah**) the sound that people make when they are surprised or pleased or when they have discovered sth（驚奇、高興或有所發現時用）哈：*Ha! It serves you right!* 哈！你活該！◇ *Ha! I knew he was hiding something.* 哈！我就知道他在隱瞞什麼。**2** (also **ha! ha!**) the word for the sound that people make when they laugh（笑聲）哈 **3** (also **ha! ha!**) (*informal, ironic*) used to show that you do not think that sth is funny（認為某事並不可笑）：*Ha! Ha! Very funny! Now give me back my shoes.* 哈！哈！真有意思！把我的鞋還給我。

ha² *abbr.* (in writing) HECTARE（書寫形式）公頃

haar /hɑː(r)/ *noun* [sing.] a cold sea FOG on the east coast of England or Scotland 哈霧（英格蘭或蘇格蘭東海岸的冷海霧）

hab·eas cor·pus /ˌheɪbiəs ˈkɔːpəs; *NAmE* ˈkɔːrpəs/ *noun* [U] (from *Latin, law* 律) a law that states that a person who has been arrested should not be kept in prison longer than a particular period of time unless a judge in court has decided that it is right 人身保護法（對被拘禁者的羈押期予以限制）

hab·er·dash·er /ˈhæbədæʃə(r); *NAmE* ˈhæbərd-/ *noun* **1** (*old-fashioned, BrE*) a person who owns or works in a shop/store selling small articles for sewing, for example, needles, pins, cotton and buttons 縫紉用品店店主（或店員）**2** **hab·er·dash·er's** (*pl.* **hab·er·dash·ers**) a shop/store that sells these things 縫紉用品店 **3** (*NAmE*) a person who owns, manages or works in a shop/store that makes and sells men's clothes 男裝店店主（或店員等）

hab·er·dash·ery /ˌhæbəˈdæʃəri; *NAmE* ˈhæbərd-/ *noun* (*pl.* **-ies**) **1** [U] (*old-fashioned, BrE*) small articles for sewing, for example needles, pins, cotton and buttons 縫紉用品 **2** [U] (*old-fashioned, NAmE*) men's clothes 男子服裝 **3** [C] a shop/store or part of a shop/store where haberdashery is sold 縫紉用品店（或櫃枱）；男子服裝店（或櫃枱）

habit 🔑 /ˈhæbɪt/ *noun*

1 🔑 [C] a thing that you do often and almost without thinking, especially sth that is hard to stop doing 習慣：*You need to change your eating habits.* 你得改變你的飲食習慣。◇ ***good/bad habits*** 良好習慣；惡習 ◇ *He has the irritating habit of biting his nails.* 他有咬指甲的討厭習慣。◇ *It's all right to borrow money occasionally, but don't* ***let it become a habit.*** 偶爾借點錢倒沒關係，但不要養成習慣。◇ *I'd prefer you not to* ***make a habit*** *of it.* 我希望你不要習以為常。◇ *I'm not* ***in the habit of*** *letting strangers into my apartment.* 我不習慣讓陌生人進我家。◇ *I've* ***got into the habit of*** *turning on the TV as soon as I get home.* 我習慣了一回家就打開電視。◇ *I'm trying to* ***break the habit*** *of staying up too late.* 我正試圖改掉熬夜的習慣。**2** 🔑 [U] usual behaviour 慣常行為；習性：*I only do it* ***out of habit.*** 我這麼做只是出於習慣。◇ *I'm a* ***creature of habit*** (= I have a fixed and regular way of doing things). 我這人做事總是憑習慣。**3** [C] (*informal*) a strong need to keep using drugs, alcohol or cigarettes regularly（吸毒、喝酒、抽煙的）癮：*He began to finance his habit through burglary.* 他開始靠盜竊來獲取可滿足他毒癮的金錢。◇ *She's tried to give up smoking but just can't* ***kick the habit.*** 她戒過煙，但就是戒不掉。◇ *a 50-a-day habit* 每天抽 50 根煙的煙癮 **4** [C] a long piece of clothing worn by a MONK or NUN（修道士或修女穿的）長袍；道袍；道服 **IDM** see FORCE *n.*

hab·it·able /ˈhæbɪtəbl/ *adj.* suitable for people to live in 適合居住的：*The house should be habitable by the new year.* 房子到新年時應該就可以住進去了。**OPP** **uninhabitable**

habi·tat /ˈhæbɪtæt/ *noun* [C, U] the place where a particular type of animal or plant is normally found（動植物的）生活環境，棲息地：*The panda's* ***natural habitat*** *is the bamboo forest.* 大熊貓的天然棲息地是竹林。◇ *the destruction of wildlife habitat* 野生動植物生存環境的破壞 ➲ **COLLOCATIONS** at ENVIRONMENT

habi·ta·tion /ˌhæbɪˈteɪʃn/ *noun* **1** [U] the act of living in a place 居住：*They looked around for any signs of habitation.* 他們四處尋找有人居住的跡象。◇ *The houses were* ***unfit for human habitation*** (= not clean or safe enough for people to live in). 那些房子不適合人居住。**2** [C] (*formal*) a place where people live 住處；住所；聚居地：*The road serves the scattered habitations along the coast.* 這條路連接着海岸線上分散各處的聚落。

ˈhabit-forming *adj.* a **habit-forming** activity or drug is one that makes you want to continue doing it or taking it 使成習慣的；使上癮的

ha·bit·ual /həˈbɪtʃuəl/ *adj.* **1** [only before noun] usual or typical of sb/sth 慣常的；典型的：*They waited for his habitual response.* 他們等待着他的一貫反應。◇ (*formal*) *a person's place of habitual residence* 某人通常居住的地方 **2** (of an action 行為) done, often in a way that is annoying or difficult to stop 討厭的；上癮的：*habitual complaining* 沒完沒了的抱怨 ◇ *the habitual use of heroin* 服用海洛因上癮 **3** [only before noun] (of a person 人) doing sth that has become a habit and is therefore difficult to stop 習慣性的；積習很深的：*a* ***habitual criminal/drinker/liar, etc.*** 慣犯、嗜酒成性者、習以為常的撒謊者等 **HELP** Some speakers do not pronounce the 'h' at the beginning of **habitual** and use 'an' instead of 'a' before it. This now sounds old-fashioned. 有人說 habitual 時不發 h 音，前面用 an 而不用 a，現在聽起來過時了。▸ **ha·bit·ual·ly** /-tʃuəli/ *adv.*：*the dark glasses he habitually wore* 他慣常戴的墨鏡

ha·bitu·ated /həˈbɪtʃueɪtɪd/ *adj.* **~ (to sth)** (*formal*) familiar with sth because you have done it or experienced it often 熟悉（某事）的；習慣（於某事）的 **SYN** **accustomed**

ha·bi·tué /(h)æˈbɪtʃueɪ/ *noun* (from *French, formal*) a person who goes regularly to a particular place or event 常客：*a(n) habitué of upmarket clubs* 高級俱樂部的常客 **SYN** **regular**

ha·ci·enda /ˌhæsiˈendə/ *noun* a large farm in a Spanish-speaking country（講西班牙語國家的）大莊園，大農場

hack /hæk/ *verb, noun*

■ **verb** **1** [T, I] to cut sb/sth with rough, heavy blows 砍；劈：**~ sb/sth + adv./prep.** *I hacked the dead branches off.* 我把枯樹枝砍掉了。◇ *They were hacked to death as they tried to escape.* 他們企圖逃走時被砍死了。◇ *We had to* ***hack our way*** *through the jungle.* 我們不得不在叢林中闢路穿行。◇ **+ adv./prep.** *We hacked away at the bushes.* 我們劈開灌木叢。**2** [T] **~ sb/sth + adv./prep.** to kick sth roughly or without control 猛踢：*He hacked the ball away.* 他把球一腳踢開。**3** (*computing* 計) [I, T] to secretly find a way of looking at and/or changing information on sb else's computer system without permission 非法侵入（他人的計算機系統）：**~ into sth** *He hacked into the bank's computer.* 他侵入了這家銀行的計算機。◇ **~ sth** *They had hacked secret data.* 他們竊取了保密數據。**4** [T] **can/can't hack it** (*informal*) to be able/not able to manage in a particular situation 能 / 不能應付（某情形）：*Lots of people leave this job because they can't hack it.* 很多人由於應付不了這項工作而放棄了。**5** [I] (usually **go hacking**) (*especially BrE*) to ride a horse for pleasure 騎馬消遣 **6** [I] (*NAmE, informal*) to drive a taxi 開出租車；開計程車

■ **noun** **1** (*disapproving*) a writer, especially of newspaper articles, who does a lot of low quality work and does not get paid much 雇傭文人（尤指廉價受雇撰寫報紙庸俗文章者）**2** (*disapproving*) a person who does the hard and often boring work for an organization, especially a politician（受雇於組織，尤其是政客）從事艱苦乏味工作的人；雜務人員：*a party hack* 政黨雜務人員 **3** a horse for ordinary riding or one that can be hired 供人騎的馬；可出租的馬 **4** (*NAmE, informal*) a taxi 出租車；計程車

5 an act of hitting sth, especially with a cutting tool 砍；劈

ˌhacked ˈoff *adj.* [not before noun] (*BrE, informal*) extremely annoyed 極其惱怒：*I'm really hacked off.* 我真是很惱火。SYN **fed up**

hack·er /ˈhækə(r)/ *noun* a person who secretly finds a way of looking at and/or changing information on sb else's computer system without permission 黑客，駭客（秘密窺視或改變他人計算機系統信息）

ˌhacking ˈcough *noun* [sing.] a dry painful cough that is repeated often 頻咳

ˈhacking jacket *noun* a short jacket worn for horse riding 騎馬短上裝；賽馬服

hackles /ˈhæklz/ *noun* [pl.] the hairs on the back of the neck of a dog, cat, etc. that rise when the animal is afraid or angry（狗、貓等害怕或發怒時豎起的）後頸毛

IDM **make sb's ˈhackles rise | raise sb's ˈhackles** to make sb angry 激怒某人 **sb's ˈhackles rise** to become angry 發火；發怒：*Ben felt his hackles rise as the speaker continued.* 隨着那人不斷地講下去，本不禁怒火中燒。

hack·ney car·riage /ˈhækni kærɪdʒ/ (also **ˈhack·ney cab**) *noun* (*BrE*) a word used in official language for a taxi. In the past hackney carriages were carriages pulled by horses that were used as taxis. 出租車（正式用語，源於舊時的出租馬車）

hack·neyed /ˈhæknid/ *adj.* used too often and therefore boring 陳腐的 SYN **clichéd**：*a hackneyed phrase/subject* 陳詞濫調；老生常談的話題

hack·saw /ˈhæksɔː/ *noun* a tool with a narrow blade in a frame, used for cutting metal 鋼鋸，弓鋸（用以切割金屬）➲ VISUAL VOCAB page V20

had /həd; əd; *strong form* hæd/ ➲ HAVE

had·dock /ˈhædək/ *noun* (*pl.* **had·dock**) [C, U] a sea fish like a COD but smaller, with white flesh that is used for food 黑線鱈（肉白色，可食用）：*smoked haddock* 熏黑線鱈

Hades /ˈheɪdiːz/ *noun* [U] (in ancient Greek stories 古希臘故事) the land of the dead 陰間；冥府 SYN **hell**

Had·ith /hæˈdiːθ/ *noun* (*pl.* **Had·ith** or **Had·iths**) (in Islam 伊斯蘭教) **1** [sing.] a text containing things said by Muhammad and descriptions of his daily life, used by Muslims as a spiritual guide 聖訓，哈底斯（穆罕默德言行錄） **2** [C] one of the things said by Muhammad, recorded in this text（聖訓中的）穆罕默德訓詞

hadn't /ˈhædnt/ *short form* had not

haem·atite (*BrE*) (*NAmE* **hema·tite**) /ˈhiːmətaɪt/ *noun* [U] (*geology* 地) a dark red rock from which iron is obtained 赤鐵礦

haema·tol·ogy (*BrE*) (*NAmE* **hema·tol·ogy**) /ˌhiːməˈtɒlədʒi; *NAmE* -ˈtɑːl-/ *noun* [U] the scientific study of the blood and its diseases 血液學 ▸ **haem·ato·logic·al** (*BrE*) (*NAmE* **hem-**) /ˌhiːmətəˈlɒdʒɪkl; *NAmE* -ˈlɑːdʒ-/ *adj.* **haema·tolo·gist** (*BrE*) (*NAmE* **hem-**) /ˌhiːməˈtɒlədʒɪst; *NAmE* -ˈtɑːl-/ *noun*

haem·atoma (*BrE*) (*NAmE* **hema·toma**) /ˌhiːməˈtəʊmə; *NAmE* -ˈtoʊmə/ *noun* (*medical* 醫) a swollen area on the body consisting of blood that has become thick 血腫

haemo- (*BrE*) (*NAmE* **hemo-**) /ˈhiːməʊ; *NAmE* -moʊ/ *combining form* (in nouns and adjectives 構成名詞和形容詞) connected with blood（有關）血液的：*haemophilia* 血友病

haemo·globin (*BrE*) (*NAmE* **hemo·globin**) /ˌhiːməˈɡləʊbɪn; *NAmE* -ˈɡloʊ-/ *noun* [U] a red substance in the blood that carries OXYGEN and contains iron 血紅蛋白

haemo·philia (*BrE*) (*NAmE* **hemo·philia**) /ˌhiːməˈfɪliə/ *noun* [U] a medical condition that causes severe loss of blood from even a slight injury because the blood fails to CLOT normally. It usually affects only men although it can be passed on by women. 血友病

haemo·phil·iac (*BrE*) (*NAmE* **hemo·phil·iac**) /ˌhiːməˈfɪliæk/ *noun* a person who suffers from haemophilia 血友病患者

haem·or·rhage (*BrE*) (*NAmE* **hem·or·rhage**) /ˈhemərɪdʒ/ *noun, verb*

■ *noun* **1** [C, U] a medical condition in which there is severe loss of blood from inside a person's body 體內（大）出血：*a massive* ***brain/cerebral haemorrhage*** 重度腦溢血 ◇ *He was checked for any signs of haemorrhage.* 他接受檢查，以確定是否有出血跡象。 **2** [C, usually sing.] **~ (of sb/sth)** a serious loss of people, money, etc. from a country, a group or an organization（人、資金等的）大量流失：*Poor working conditions have led to a steady haemorrhage of qualified teachers from our schools.* 工作條件欠佳導致各校大量合格教師不斷流失。

■ *verb* **1** [I] to lose blood heavily, especially from the inside of the body; to have a haemorrhage（尤指體內）大出血 **2** [T] **~ sb/sth** to lose money or people in large amounts at a fast rate 大量快速流失（資金、人等）

haem·or·rhagic (*BrE*) (*NAmE* **hem·or·rhagic**) /ˌheməˈrædʒɪk/ *adj.* (*medical* 醫) happening with or caused by haemorrhage 體內出血的；出血引起的：*a haemorrhagic fever* 出血熱

haem·or·rhoids (*BrE*) (*NAmE* **hem·or·rhoids**) /ˈhemərɔɪdz/ *noun* [pl.] (*medical* 醫) painful swollen VEINS at or near the ANUS 痔 SYN **piles**

haf·nium /ˈhæfniəm/ *noun* [U] (*symb.* **Hf**) a RADIOACTIVE chemical element. Hafnium is a hard silver-grey metal. 鉿（放射性化學元素）

haft /hɑːft; *NAmE* hæft/ *noun* the handle of a knife or weapon（刀或武器的）柄

hag /hæɡ/ *noun* (*offensive*) an ugly and/or unpleasant old woman 醜陋（或討厭）的老女人 ➲ see also FAG HAG

hag·gard /ˈhæɡəd; *NAmE* -ɡərd/ *adj.* looking very tired because of illness, worry or lack of sleep（由於生病、焦慮或睡眠不足）憔悴的，疲憊的 SYN **drawn**

hag·gis /ˈhæɡɪs/ *noun* [C, U] a Scottish dish that looks like a large round SAUSAGE made from the heart, lungs and LIVER of a sheep that are finely chopped, mixed with OATS, HERBS, etc. and boiled in a bag that is traditionally made from part of a sheep's stomach（蘇格蘭）羊雜碎肚（用剁碎的羊的心、肺、肝和燕麥、香草等調成餡，通常包在羊肚中煮成）

hag·gle /ˈhæɡl/ *verb* [I] **~ (with sb) (over sth)** to argue with sb in order to reach an agreement, especially about the price of sth 爭論；（尤指）講價：*I left him in the market haggling over the price of a shirt.* 我扔下他自己在市場上就一件襯衫討價還價。

hagi·og·raph·er /ˌhæɡiˈɒɡrəfə(r); *NAmE* -ˈɑːɡ-/ *noun* (*formal*) **1** a person who writes the life story of a SAINT 聖賢傳記作者；聖徒傳記作者 **2** a person who writes about another person's life in a way that praises them too much, and does not criticize them 偶像化傳記的作者

hagi·og·raphy /ˌhæɡiˈɒɡrəfi; *NAmE* -ˈɑːɡ-/ *noun* (*pl.* **-ies**) [C, U] (*formal*) a book about the life of a person that praises them too much; this style of writing 吹捧性的傳記；偶像化（或理想化）傳記

hah = HA[1] (1)

haiku /ˈhaɪkuː/ *noun* (*pl.* **haiku** or **haikus**) (from *Japanese*) a poem with three lines and usually 17 syllables, written in a style that is traditional in Japan 俳句（日本傳統詩體，三行為一首，通常有 17 個音節）

hail /heɪl/ *verb, noun*

■ *verb* **1** [T, usually passive] to describe sb/sth as being very good or special, especially in newspapers, etc. 讚揚（或稱頌）…為（尤用於報章等）：**~ sb/sth as sth** *The conference was hailed as a great success.* 會議被稱頌為一次巨大的成功。◇ **~ sb/sth + noun** *Teenager Matt Brown is being hailed a hero for saving a young child from drowning.* 因救起一名溺水兒童，少年馬特 • 布朗被譽為英雄。 **2** [T] **~ sth** to signal to a taxi or a bus, in order to get the driver to stop 招手（請出租車或公共汽車停下）：*to* ***hail a taxi/cab*** 打手勢叫出租車 **3** [T] **~ sb** (*literary*) to call to sb in order to say hello to them or attract their attention 跟…打招呼；向…喊：*A voice hailed us from the other side of the street.* 街對面有個聲音招呼我們。 **4** [I] when **it hails**, small balls of ice fall like rain from the sky 下雹：*It's hailing!* 正下着冰雹！

PHR V **'hail from ...** *(formal)* to come from or have been born in a particular place 來自；出生於：*His father hailed from Italy.* 他父親出生於意大利。

■ ***noun*** **1** [U] small balls of ice that fall like rain 雹；冰雹：*We drove through hail and snow.* 我們頂着冰雹和大雪開車。**2** [sing.] **a ~ of sth** a large number or amount of sth that is aimed at sb in order to harm them 一陣像冰雹般襲來的事物；雹子般的一陣：*a **hail of arrows/bullets*** 一陣亂箭／彈雨 ◇ *a hail of abuse* 一頓痛罵

Hail Mary /ˌheɪl ˈmeəri; *NAmE* ˈmeri/ *noun* (*pl.* **Hail Marys**) a Roman Catholic prayer to Mary, the mother of Jesus 萬福瑪利亞（天主教祈禱文）

hail·stone /ˈheɪlstəʊn; *NAmE* -stoʊn/ *noun* [usually pl.] a small ball of ice that falls like rain 雹塊；雹子

hail·storm /ˈheɪlstɔːm; *NAmE* -stɔːrm/ *noun* a storm during which hail falls from the sky 雹暴

H

hair 0┳ /heə(r); *NAmE* her/ *noun*
1 0┳ [U, C] the substance that looks like a mass of fine threads growing especially on the head; one of these threads growing on the body of people and some animals 毛髮；（尤指）頭髮：***fair/dark hair*** 淺色頭髮；黑髮 ◇ ***straight/curly/wavy hair*** 直／鬈／波浪髮 ◇ *to **comb/brush** your **hair*** 梳頭 ◇ *(informal) I'll be down in a minute. I'm **doing*** (= brushing, arranging, etc.) ***my hair.*** 我馬上就下來。我在梳頭呢。◇ *I'm **having my hair cut** this afternoon.* 我今天下午要去理髮。◇ ***body/facial/pubic hair*** 體毛；臉毛；陰毛 ◇ *There's a hair in my soup.* 我的湯裏有根毛。◇ *The rug was covered with cat hairs.* 地毯上淨是貓毛。➲ COLLOCATIONS at FASHION, PHYSICAL ➲ VISUAL VOCAB pages V59, V60 ➲ see also CAMEL HAIR, HORSEHAIR **2 -haired** (in adjectives 構成形容詞) having the type of hair mentioned 有…毛髮（或頭髮）的：*dark-haired* 黑髮的 ◇ *long-haired* 長髮的 **3** [C] a thing that looks like a fine thread growing on the leaves and STEMS of some plants（植物葉莖上的）茸毛

IDM **get in sb's 'hair** *(informal)* to annoy sb by always being near them, asking them questions, etc. 煩擾某人；纏着（提問等） **the hair of the 'dog (that 'bit you)** *(informal)* alcohol that you drink in order to make you feel better when you have drunk too much alcohol the night before 用於解宿醉的酒 **keep your 'hair on** *(BrE, informal)* used to tell sb to stop shouting and become calm when they are angry 冷靜下來，別發脾氣 **let your 'hair down** *(informal)* to relax and enjoy yourself, especially in a lively way 放鬆；輕鬆一下 **make sb's 'hair stand on end** to shock or frighten sb 驚嚇某人；使某人毛骨悚然：*a chilling tale that will make your hair stand on end* 令人毛骨悚然的故事 **not harm/touch a hair of sb's 'head** to not hurt sb physically in any way 不動某人一根頭髮；絲毫不傷害某人 **not have a 'hair out of place** (of a person 人) to look extremely clean and neat 顯得非常整潔 **not turn a 'hair** to show no emotion when sth surprising, shocking, etc. happens 面不改色；鎮定自若 ➲ more at HANG *v.*, HIDE *n.*, SPLIT *v.*, TEAR[1] *v.*

hair·band /ˈheəbænd; *NAmE* ˈherb-/ *noun* a strip of cloth or curved plastic worn by women in their hair, that fits closely over the top of the head and behind the ears 束髮帶；髮箍

hair·brush /ˈheəbrʌʃ; *NAmE* ˈherb-/ *noun* a brush for making the hair tidy or smooth 髮刷；毛刷 ➲ VISUAL VOCAB page V24

hair·cut /ˈheəkʌt; *NAmE* ˈherkʌt/ *noun* **1** the act of sb cutting your hair 理髮：*You need a haircut.* 你該理髮了。◇ *I see you've had a haircut.* 我看得出你理髮了。**2** the style in which sb's hair is cut 髮型；髮式：*What do you think of my new haircut?* 你覺得我的新髮型怎麼樣？◇ *a trendy haircut* 流行髮式 ➲ COLLOCATIONS at FASHION

hair·do /ˈheəduː; *NAmE* ˈherduː/ *noun* (*pl.* **-os**) *(old-fashioned, informal)* the style in which a woman's hair is arranged（女子）髮式，髮型 **SYN** **hairstyle**

hair·dress·er 0┳ /ˈheədresə(r); *NAmE* ˈherd-/ *noun* **1** 0┳ a person whose job is to cut, wash and shape hair 理髮師；美髮師；髮型師 **2** 0┳ **hairdresser's** (*pl.* **hair·dress·ers**) a place where you can get your hair cut, washed and shaped 理髮店；美髮店 ➲ compare BARBER
▸ **hair·dress·ing** *noun* [U]

hair·dryer (also **hair·drier**) /ˈheədraɪə(r); *NAmE* ˈherd-/ *noun* a small machine used for drying your hair by blowing hot air over it（吹乾頭髮的）吹風機

hair·grip /ˈheəgrɪp; *NAmE* ˈherg-/ (also **grip**, **'kirby grip**) (all *BrE*) (*NAmE* **'bobby pin**) *noun* a small thin piece of metal or plastic folded in the middle, used by women for holding their hair in place 髮夾 ➲ compare HAIRPIN (1)

hair·less /ˈheələs; *NAmE* ˈherləs/ *adj.* without hair 無髮的；無毛的；禿的

hair·line /ˈheəlaɪn; *NAmE* ˈherl-/ *noun* **1** the edge of a person's hair, especially at the front（尤指前額的）髮際線：*a receding hairline* 漸禿的前額 **2** (often used as an adjective 常用作形容詞) a very thin crack or line 很細的裂紋；極細的線：*a **hairline crack/fracture*** 細小的裂紋／裂縫

hair·net /ˈheənet; *NAmE* ˈhernet/ *noun* a net worn over the hair to keep it in place 髮網

hair·piece /ˈheəpiːs; *NAmE* ˈherp-/ *noun* a piece of false hair worn to make your own hair look longer or thicker（使頭髮看上去更長或更濃密的）假髮

hair·pin /ˈheəpɪn; *NAmE* ˈherpɪn/ *noun* **1** a small thin piece of wire that is folded in the middle, used by women for holding their hair in place 髮夾 ➲ compare HAIRGRIP **2** = HAIRPIN BEND

ˌhairpin 'bend *(BrE)* (*NAmE* **ˌhairpin 'curve**, **ˌhairpin 'turn**) (also **hair·pin** *BrE, NAmE*) *noun* a very sharp bend in a road, especially a mountain road（尤指山路的）急轉彎

'hair-raising *adj.* extremely frightening but often exciting 令人寒毛直豎的；驚險的：*a **hair-raising adventure/story*** 緊張刺激的歷險／故事

'hair's breadth *noun* [sing.] a very small amount or distance 細微；極短的距離；毫釐之差：*We won by a hair's breadth.* 我們以些微之差贏了對手。◇ *They were within a hair's breadth of being killed.* 他們險些喪命。

ˌhair 'shirt *noun* a shirt made of rough cloth containing hair, worn in the past by people who wished to punish themselves for religious reasons 苦衣，剛毛襯衫（舊時苦修者所穿）

hair·slide /ˈheəslaɪd; *NAmE* ˈhers-/ (also **slide**) (both *BrE*) (*NAmE* **bar·rette**) *noun* a small decorative piece of metal or plastic used by women for holding their hair in place（裝飾性）小髮夾

'hair-splitting *noun* [U] *(disapproving)* the act of giving too much importance to small and unimportant differences in an argument 過於強調微不足道的分歧；吹毛求疵 **SYN** **quibbling** **IDM** see SPLIT *v.*

hair·spray /ˈheəspreɪ; *NAmE* ˈhers-/ *noun* [U, C] a substance sprayed onto the hair to hold it in a particular style 髮膠；定型劑

hair·style /ˈheəstaɪl; *NAmE* ˈhers-/ *noun* the style in which sb's hair is cut or arranged 髮型；髮式 ➲ COLLOCATIONS at FASHION

hair·styl·ist /ˈheəstaɪlɪst; *NAmE* ˈhers-/ *noun* a person whose job is to cut, wash and shape hair 理髮師；美髮師；髮型師

hairy /ˈheəri; *NAmE* ˈheri/ *adj.* (**hair·ier**, **hairi·est**) **1** covered with a lot of hair 多毛的：*a **hairy chest/monster*** 多毛的胸脯；長滿毛的怪獸 ◇ *plants with hairy stems* 莖部有絨毛的植物 **2** *(informal)* dangerous or frightening but often exciting 驚險的；可怕（但刺激）的：*Driving on icy roads can be pretty hairy.* 在結冰的道路上開車很驚險。◇ *a hairy experience* 令人毛骨悚然的經歷 ▸ **hairi·ness** *noun* [U]

hajj (also **haj**) /hædʒ/ *noun* (usually **the Hajj**) [sing.] the religious journey to Mecca that all Muslims try to make at least once in their lives（伊斯蘭教徒去麥加的）朝覲

haka /ˈhɑːkə/ *noun* a traditional Maori war dance with singing. New Zealand RUGBY teams perform a version of it before games. 哈卡舞（傳統毛利伴歌戰舞，新西蘭橄欖球隊在比賽前跳這種舞）

hake /heɪk/ *noun* [C, U] (*pl.* **hake**) a large sea fish that is used for food 無鬚鱈（海產魚，可食用）

ha·kim /hæˈkiːm/ *noun* a doctor in India and Muslim countries who uses HERBS and other traditional ways of treating illnesses（印度和伊斯蘭國家的）草藥醫生，郎中

Hakka /ˈhækə/ (also **Kejia**) *noun* [U] a form of Chinese spoken by a group of people in SE China 客家話（中國東南部的一種方言）

halal /ˈhælæl/ *adj.* [only before noun] (of meat 肉) from an animal that has been killed according to Muslim law 按伊斯蘭教教規宰殺牲畜的：*halal meat* 伊斯蘭教的合法畜肉 ◇ *a halal butcher* (= one who sells halal meat) 售賣伊斯蘭教合法畜肉的肉商

hal·berd /ˈhælbɜːd; *NAmE* -bərd/ *noun* a weapon used in the past which is a combination of a SPEAR and an AXE 戟（舊時結合長矛和斧頭的武器）

hal·cyon /ˈhælsiən/ *adj.* [usually before noun] (*literary*) peaceful and happy 平安幸福的：*the halcyon days of her youth* 她年輕時幸福安寧的日子

hale /heɪl/ *adj.*
IDM **ˌhale and ˈhearty** (especially of an old person 尤指老年人) strong and healthy 健壯的；硬朗的

half 🔑 /hɑːf; *NAmE* hæf/ *noun, det., pron., adv.*
■ *noun* (*pl.* **halves** /hɑːvz; *NAmE* hævz/) **1** 🔑 either of two equal parts into which sth is or can be divided 一半；半：*two and a half kilos* (2½) 兩公斤半 ◇ *One and a half hours are allowed for the exam.* 考試時間為一個半小時。◇ *An hour and a half is allowed for the exam.* 考試時間為一個半小時。◇ *The second half of the book is more exciting.* 書的後半部份比較刺激有趣。◇ *I've divided the money* **in half**. 我把錢平均分成了兩半。◇ *We'll need to reduce the weight* **by half**. 我們得把重量減輕一半。➲ see also HALVE **2** 🔑 either of two periods of time into which a sports game, concert, etc. is divided（比賽、音樂會等的）半場，半局：*No goals were scored in the first half.* 上半場沒有得分。 **3** = HALFBACK ➲ see also CENTRE HALF, SCRUM HALF **4** (*BrE, informal*) half a pint of beer or a similar drink（啤酒等飲料的）半品脫：*Two halves of bitter, please.* 請來兩杯半品脫的苦啤酒。
IDM **and a ˈhalf** (*informal*) bigger, better, more important, etc. than usual 更大（或好、重要等）的；非同尋常的；出色的：*That was a game and a half!* 那場比賽真棒！ **do nothing/not do anything by ˈhalves** to do whatever you do completely and thoroughly 做任何事情都完全徹底；善始善終；不半途而廢：*You're expecting twins? Well, you never did do anything by halves.* 你要生對雙胞胎？唔，你做事倒從來不會只做一半。 **go half and ˈhalf | go ˈhalves (with sb)** to share the cost of sth equally with sb（和某人）平均分攤費用：*We go halves on all the bills.* 我們平均分攤所有的費用。 **the ˈhalf of it** used in negative sentences to say that a situation is worse or more complicated than sb thinks（用於否定句）比想像的更糟糕（或更複雜）的部份：*'It sounds very difficult.' '***You don't know the half of it.***'*"這事聽起來很難。""你還未瞭解更困難的一面呢。" **how the other half ˈlives** the way of life of a different social group, especially one much richer than you 另一類人的生活方式（尤指比自己富有得多的） **too clever, etc. by ˈhalf** (*BrE, informal, disapproving*) clever, etc. in a way that annoys you or makes you suspicious 聰明（等）過頭 ➲ more at MIND *n.*, SIX, TIME *n.*
■ *det., pron.* **1** 🔑 an amount equal to half of sth/sb 半數：*half an hour* 半小時 ◇ *Half (of) the fruit was bad.* 水果壞了一半。◇ *Half of the money was mine.* 那些錢有一半是我的。◇ *He has a half share in the company.* 他擁有該公司的一半股份。◇ *Out of 36 candidates, half passed.* * 36 名考生中有半數及格。➲ LANGUAGE BANK at PROPORTION **2 ~ the time, fun, trouble, etc.** the largest part of sth 絕大部份（時間、樂趣、麻煩等）：*Half the fun of gardening is never knowing exactly what's going to come up.* 園藝的最大樂趣是誰也不知道到底會長出什麼。◇ *Half the time you don't even listen to what I say.* 你大部份時間甚至沒聽我說的話。
IDM **half a ˌloaf is better than no ˈbread** (*saying*) you should be grateful for sth, even if it is not as good, much, etc. as you really wanted; something is better than nothing 半塊麪包比沒有麪包強；聊勝於無 **half a ˈminute, ˈsecond, etc.** (*informal*) a short time 短時間；一會兒：*Hang on. I'll be ready in half a minute.* 等一下。我馬上就準備好了。 **half past ˈone, ˈtwo, etc.** 🔑 (*US* also **half after ˈone, ˈtwo, etc.**) (also *BrE informal* **half ˈone, ˈtwo, etc.**) 30 minutes after any hour on the clock 一點（或兩點）半等
■ *adv.* **1** 🔑 to the extent of half 到一半程度；半：*The glass was half full.* 玻璃杯半滿。 **2** 🔑 partly 部份地：*The chicken was only half cooked.* 雞只煮了半熟。◇ *half-closed eyes* 半睜半閉的眼 ◇ *I'm half inclined to agree.* 我不十分同意。
IDM **ˌhalf as ˌmany, ˌmuch, etc. aˈgain** (*BrE*) (*US* **half aˈgain as much**) an increase of 50% of the existing number or amount * 50% 的增長：*Spending on health is half as much again as it was in 2009.* 衞生保健方面的開銷比 2009 年增加了一半。 **ˌnot ˈhalf** (*BrE, informal*) used to emphasize a statement or an opinion 很；非常：*It wasn't half good* (= it was very good). 這很好。◇ *'Was she annoyed?' 'Not half!'* (= she was extremely annoyed) "她生氣了嗎？""非常生氣！" **not ˈhalf as | not ˈhalf such a** not nearly 遠非；差得多：*He is not half such a fool as they think.* 他遠不是他們以為的那麼傻。 **not half ˈbad** (*informal*) (used to show surprise 表示吃驚) not bad at all; good 一點不壞；很好：*It really isn't half bad, is it?* 這的確很不錯，對嗎？

Grammar Point 語法說明

half / whole / quarter

- **Quarter**, **half** and **whole** can all be nouns. * quarter、half 和 whole 均可作名詞：*Cut the apple into quarters.* 把蘋果切成四等份。◇ *Two halves make a whole.* 兩個一半構成一個整體。
- **Whole** is also an adjective. * whole 亦作形容詞：*I've been waiting here for a whole hour.* 我在這兒等了整整一個小時。
- **Half** is also a determiner. * half 亦作限定詞：*Half (of) the work is already finished.* 工作已經完成了一半。◇ *They spent half the time looking for a parking space.* 他們花了一半的時間尋找停車位。◇ *Her house is half a mile down the road.* 她的房子在這條路上前面半英里遠的地方。Note that you do not put *a* or *the* in front of **half** when it is used in this way. 注意在此用法中 half 前面不加 a 或 the：*I waited for half an hour.* 我等了半個小時。◇ ~~*I waited for a half an hour.*~~
- **Half** can also be used as an adverb. * half 亦可作副詞：*This meal is only half cooked.* 這頓飯只煮了個半熟。

ˌhalf-and-ˈhalf *adj., adv., noun*
■ *adj.* being half one thing and half another 兩種事物各半的：*I was in that half-and-half land where you are not completely asleep nor completely awake.* 我當時半睡半醒。 ▸ **ˌhalf-and-ˈhalf** *adv.*
■ *noun* [U] (*NAmE*) a mixture of milk and cream that is used in tea and coffee 咖啡伴侶，茶伴侶（一種牛奶與奶油的混合物）

ˌhalf-ˈarsed (*BrE*) (*NAmE* **ˈhalf-assed**) *adj.* (*slang*) **1** done without care or effort; not well planned 馬虎的；草草了事的 **2** stupid 愚蠢的；糊塗的

half·back /ˈhɑːfbæk; *NAmE* ˈhæf-/ (also **half**) *noun* **1** [C] one of the defending players in HOCKEY or RUGBY whose position is between those who play at the front of a team and those who play at the back（曲棍球或橄欖球的）前衞 **2** (also **tail·back**) [C] one of the two attacking players in AMERICAN FOOTBALL whose position is behind the QUARTERBACK and beside the FULLBACKS（美式足球的）前衞 **3** (also **tail·back**) [U] the position a halfback plays at 前衞的位置；中場

ˌhalf-ˈbaked *adj.* [usually before noun] (*informal*) not well planned or considered 計劃不完善的；考慮不周的：*a half-baked idea* 不成熟的想法

'half-bath *noun* (*NAmE*) a small room in a house, containing a WASHBASIN and a toilet 小盥洗室（內設洗臉盆和抽水馬桶） SYN **powder room**

,half 'board *noun* [U] (*BrE*) a type of accommodation at a hotel, etc. that includes breakfast and an evening meal 半膳宿（旅館等包括早、晚餐的住宿） ➲ compare AMERICAN PLAN, EUROPEAN PLAN, BED AND BREAKFAST (1), FULL BOARD

'half-breed *noun* (*taboo, offensive*) a person whose parents are from different races, especially when one is white and the other is a Native American（尤指白人和美洲土著人的）混血兒 ▸ **'half-breed** *adj.* (*taboo, offensive*) HELP It is more acceptable to talk about 'a person **of mixed race**'. 說 a person of mixed race 比較容易讓人接受。

'half-brother *noun* a person's **half-brother** is a boy or man with either the same mother or the same father as they have 同母異父（或同父異母）的兄弟 ➲ compare STEPBROTHER

'half-caste *noun* (*taboo, offensive*) a person whose parents are from different races（不同人種的）混血兒 ▸ **'half-caste** *adj.* (*taboo, offensive*) HELP It is more acceptable to talk about 'a person **of mixed race**'. 說 a person of mixed race 比較容易讓人接受。

,half-'century *noun* **1** a period of 50 years 半個世紀；50 年 **2** (in CRICKET 板球) a score of 50 * 50 分

,half-'cock *noun*
IDM **go off at ,half-'cock** (*BrE, informal*) to start before preparations are complete, so that the effect or result is not as it should be 沒準備好就開始幹，操之過急（而效果或結果不好）

,half-'crown (also **,half a 'crown**) *noun* an old British coin worth 2½ SHILLINGS (= now 12½ pence) * 2 先令 6 便士硬幣（英國舊制硬幣，相當於現在 12½ 便士）

,half 'day *noun* a day on which people work only in the morning or in the afternoon 半工作日（只在上午或下午工作）：*Tuesday is her half day.* 星期二她只工作半天。

,half 'dollar *noun* a US coin worth 50 cents（美國的）50 分硬幣

,half-'hearted *adj.* done without enthusiasm or effort 不熱心的；不盡力的；冷淡的：*He made a **half-hearted attempt** to justify himself.* 他沒有盡力證明自己有理。 ▸ **,half-'heart·ed·ly** *adv.*

,half-'hour (also **,half an 'hour**) *noun* a period of 30 minutes 半小時；30 分鐘：*He should arrive within the next half-hour.* 他應該會在半小時內到達。◇ *a half-hour drive* 半小時的車程

,half-'hourly *adj.* happening every 30 minutes 每半小時的：*a half-hourly bus service* 每半小時一班的公共汽車 ▸ **,half-'hourly** *adv.*：*The buses run half-hourly.* 公共汽車每半小時一班。

'half-life *noun* [C] **1** (*physics* 物) the time taken for the RADIOACTIVITY of a substance to fall to half its original value（放射性物質的）半衰期 **2** (*chemistry* 化) the time taken for the concentration of a REACTANT to fall to half of its original value in a chemical reaction 半反應期

'half-light *noun* [sing., U] a dull light in which it is difficult to see things 昏暗的光線：*in the grey half-light of dawn* 在黎明的灰暗光線中

,half 'mast *noun*
IDM **at ,half 'mast** (of a flag 旗) flown at the middle of the MAST as a sign of respect for a person who has just died 降半旗，下半旗（以示哀悼）：*Flags were flown at half mast on the day of his funeral.* 在他葬禮那天降了半旗。

,half 'measures *noun* [pl.] a policy or plan of action that is weak and does not do enough 不強硬的折衷政策；不徹底的行動計劃：*There are **no half measures** with this company.* 這家公司做事決不會半途而廢。

,half-'moon *noun* **1** the moon when only half of it can be seen from the earth; the time when this happens 半月；出現半月的時候 ➲ compare FULL MOON, HARVEST MOON, NEW MOON **2** a thing that is shaped like a half-moon 半月形的東西

'half note (*NAmE*) (*BrE* **minim**) *noun* (*music* 音) a note that lasts twice as long as a CROTCHET/QUARTER NOTE 二分音符；半音符 ➲ picture at MUSIC

'half pants *noun* [pl.] (*IndE, informal*) short trousers/pants 短褲 SYN **shorts**

half·penny *noun* (*pl.* **-ies**) **1** (also **ha'penny**) /ˈheɪpni/ a British coin in use until 1971, worth half a penny. There were 480 halfpennies in a pound. 半便士硬幣（1971 年前使用的英國硬幣，480 半便士硬幣為一英鎊） **2** /ˈhɑːfpeni/ (also **half·pence** /ˌhɑːfˈpens/) a British coin in use between 1971 and 1984, worth half a penny. There were 200 halfpennies in a pound. 半便士硬幣（1971 至 1984 年間使用的英國硬幣，200 半便士硬幣為一英鎊） IDM see SPOIL *v.*

'half-pipe *noun* a U-shaped structure or a U-shaped channel cut into snow, used for performing complicated movements in SKATEBOARDING, ROLLERBLADING and SNOWBOARDING（滑板、輪滑、滑雪等運動中供人完成複雜動作的）U 型滑道

,half-'price *adj.* costing half the usual price 半價的：*a half-price ticket* 半票 ▸ **,half-'price** *adv.*：*Children aged under four go half-price.* 四歲以下兒童半票。 **,half 'price** *noun* [U]：*Many items are at half price.* 許多商品都以半價出售。

'half-sister *noun* a person's **half-sister** is a girl or woman who has either the same mother or the same father as them 同母異父（或同父異母）的姐妹 ➲ compare STEPSISTER

'half step (also **'half-tone**) (both *NAmE*) (*BrE* **semi·tone**) *noun* (*music* 音) half a TONE on a musical SCALE, for example the INTERVAL between C and C♯ or between E and F 半音 ➲ compare STEP *n.* (10)

,half-'term *noun* (in British schools) a short holiday/vacation in the middle of each term（英國學校的）期中假：*the **half-term break/holiday*** 期中假 ◇ *What are you doing **at half-term**?* 你期中假打算幹什麼？

,half-'timbered *adj.* [usually before noun] (of a building 建築物) having walls that are made from a wooden frame filled with brick, stone, etc. so that the FRAMEWORK can still be seen 露明木架的

,half-'time *noun* [U] a short period between the two halves of a sports game during which the players rest（體育比賽上下半場之間的）中場休息時間：*The score at half-time was two all.* 上半場比分為二平。◇ *the half-time score* 上半場比分 ➲ compare FULL TIME

'half-tone *noun* **1** (*technical* 術語) a print of a black and white photograph in which the different shades of grey are produced from small and large black dots 網目（凸）版；網版畫 **2** (*NAmE, music* 音) = HALF STEP

'half-truth *noun* a statement that gives only part of the truth, especially when it is intended to cheat sb 半真半假的陳述（尤指為欺騙人）：*The newspaper reports are a mixture of gossip, lies and half-truths.* 報紙的這些報道盡是些流言蜚語、謊言和真假參半的內容。

'half-volley *noun* (in TENNIS and football (SOCCER) 網球和足球) a stroke or kick immediately after the ball has BOUNCED（球反彈當即的）半截擊，反彈球，凌空抽射

half·way /ˌhɑːfˈweɪ; *NAmE* ˌhæf-/ *adv.* **1** at an equal distance between two points; in the middle of a period of time 在…的中間；在中途；到一半：*It's about halfway between London and Bristol.* 它大約位於倫敦和布里斯托爾的中間。◇ *He left halfway through the ceremony.* 他在儀式進行到一半時離開了。◇ *I'm afraid we're not even **halfway there** yet.* 恐怕我們連一半的路都還沒走完。 **2 ~ to/towards sth | ~ to/towards doing sth** part of the way towards doing or achieving sth 部份地做（或達到）…：*This only goes halfway to explaining what really happened.* 這只是部份地解釋了實際發生的事。 **3 ~ decent** (*informal*) fairly, but not very, good 還不錯的；過得去的：*Any halfway decent map will give you that information.* 任何一張還算像樣的地圖都能提供那些信息。 ▸ **half·way** *adj.*：*the **halfway point/stage*** 中間點／階段 IDM see MEET *v.*

ˌhalfway ˈhouse *noun* **1** [sing.] (*BrE*) something that combines the features of two very different things（兩種迥然不同事物特徵的）折衷，妥協 **2** [C] a place where prisoners, mental patients, etc. can stay for a short time after leaving a prison or hospital, before they start to live on their own again 重返社會訓練所，中途之家，中途宿舍（為出獄者及離開精神病院的病人而設）

ˈhalfway line *noun* a line across a sports field at an equal distance between the ends（球場等的）中線，中場線

half·wit /ˈhɑːfwɪt; *NAmE* ˈhæf-/ *noun* (*informal*) a stupid person 傻瓜；笨蛋 SYN **idiot** ▸ **ˌhalf-ˈwitted** *adj.*

ˌhalf-ˈyearly *adj.* [only before noun] happening every six months; happening after the first six months of the year 每半年一次的；半年度的：*a half-yearly meeting* 每半年舉行一次的會議◇*the half-yearly sales figures* 上半年的銷售額 ▸ **ˌhalf-ˈyearly** *adv.*：*Interest will be paid half-yearly in June and December.* 利息將每半年一次於六月份和十二月份支付。

hali·but /ˈhælɪbət/ *noun* [C, U] (*pl.* **hali·but**) a large flat sea fish that is used for food 聖日比目魚，大比目魚（可食用）

hali·tosis /ˌhælɪˈtəʊsɪs; *NAmE* -ˈtoʊ-/ *noun* [U] (*medical* 醫) a condition in which the breath smells unpleasant 口臭 SYN **bad breath**

hall 0-w /hɔːl/ *noun*

1 0-w (also **hall·way**) (*NAmE* also **entry**) a space or passage inside the entrance or front door of a building 門廳；正門過道：*She ran into the hall and up the stairs.* 她跑進門廳，衝上樓梯。➲ see also ENTRANCE HALL **2** 0-w (*NAmE* also **hall·way**) a passage in a building with rooms down either side（大樓內的）走廊 SYN **corridor**：*I headed for Scott's office down the hall.* 我沿着走廊直奔斯科特的辦公室。 **3** 0-w a building or large room for public meetings, meals, concerts, etc. 禮堂；大廳：*a **concert/banqueting/sports/exhibition, etc. hall*** 音樂廳、宴會廳、體育館、展廳等◇*There are three dining halls on campus.* 校園裏有三個餐廳。◇*The Royal Albert Hall* 皇家艾伯特廳◇(*BrE*) *A jumble sale will be held in the village hall on Saturday.* 星期六將在村禮堂舉行義賣。➲ see also CITY HALL, DANCE HALL, GUILDHALL, MUSIC HALL, TOWN HALL **4** (*BrE*) = HALL OF RESIDENCE：*She's living **in hall**(s).* 她住在學生宿舍。 **5** (*BrE*) (often as part of a name 常作名稱的一部份) a large country house 大莊園府邸：*Haddon Hall* 哈登府

hal·le·lu·jah /ˌhælɪˈluːjə/ (also **al·le·luia**) *noun* a song or shout of praise to God 哈利路亞（意為讚美上帝）▸ **hal·le·lu·jah** *exclamation*

hall·mark /ˈhɔːlmɑːk; *NAmE* -mɑːrk/ *noun, verb*

■ ***noun*** **1** a feature or quality that is typical of sb/sth 特徵；特點：*Police said the explosion **bore all the hallmarks of** a terrorist attack.* 警方稱這次爆炸具有恐怖分子襲擊的所有特徵。 **2** a mark put on gold, silver and PLATINUM objects that shows the quality of the metal and gives information about when and where the object was made 金銀純度印記（打在金、銀、鉑製品上，表示純度、生產日期及產地）

■ ***verb*** **~ sth** to put a hallmark on metal goods 給…打金銀純度印記

hallo (*BrE*) = HELLO

ˌHall of ˈFame *noun* (*pl.* **ˌHalls of ˈFame**) (*especially NAmE*) **1** a place for people to visit, like a museum, with things connected with famous people from a particular sport or activity 名人紀念館；名人堂：*the Country Music Hall of Fame* 鄉村音樂名人堂 **2** [sing.] the group of people who have done a particular activity or sport particularly well（統稱體育運動等領域的）代表人物，出類拔萃者，佼佼者

ˌhall of ˈresidence (also **hall**) *noun* (*pl.* **halls of residence, halls**) (both *BrE*) (*NAmE* **dor·mi·tory**) a building for university or college students to live in（大學）學生宿舍

hal·loo /həˈluː/ *exclamation* **1** used to attract sb's attention（用以引起注意）嘿，喂 **2** used in hunting to tell the dogs to start chasing an animal（打獵時令狗出發追逐獵物）嘿，上 ▸ **hal·loo** *verb* [T, I] **~ (sb)**

hal·lowed /ˈhæləʊd; *NAmE* -loʊd/ *adj.* [only before noun] **1** (especially of old things 尤指古老的事物) respected and important 受崇敬的 SYN **sacred**：*one of the theatre's most hallowed traditions* 戲院最受尊崇的傳統之一 **2** that has been made holy 神聖（化）的：*to be buried in hallowed ground* 被安葬在神聖的土地上 SYN **sacred**

Hal·low·een (also **Hal·low·e'en**) /ˌhæləʊˈiːn; *NAmE* -loʊ-/ *noun* [C, U] the night of 31st October when it was believed in the past that dead people appeared from their graves, and which is now celebrated in the US, Canada and Britain by children who dress as GHOSTS, WITCHES, etc. 萬聖節前夕（10 月 31 號晚，過去認為死人此時會從墳墓中走出來，如今兒童會裝鬼玩鬧）➲ see also TRICK OR TREAT at TRICK *n.*

hal·lu·cin·ate /həˈluːsɪneɪt/ *verb* [I] to see or hear things that are not really there because of illness or drugs（由於生病、吸毒）幻視，幻聽，產生幻覺

hal·lu·cin·ation /həˌluːsɪˈneɪʃn/ *noun* **1** [C, U] the fact of seeming to see or hear sb/sth that is not really there, especially because of illness or drugs 幻覺，幻視，幻聽（尤指生病或毒品所致）：*to have hallucinations* 產生幻覺◇*High temperatures can cause hallucination.* 高燒可使人產生幻覺。 **2** [C] something that is seen or heard when it is not really there 幻視（或幻聽）到的東西；幻覺；幻象：*Was the figure real or just a hallucination?* 那個人影是真的呢，還是幻象？ HELP Some speakers do not pronounce the 'h' at the beginning of **hallucination** and use 'an' instead of 'a' before it. This now sounds old-fashioned. 有人說 hallucination 時不發 h 音，前面用 an 而不用 a，現在聽起來過時了。

hal·lu·cin·atory /həˈluːsɪnətri; həˌluːsɪˈneɪtəri; *NAmE* həˈluːsənətɔːri/ *adj.* [only before noun] connected with or causing hallucinations 幻覺的；引起幻覺的：*a hallucinatory experience* 一次幻覺經歷◇*hallucinatory drugs* 致幻藥

hal·lu·cino·gen /həˈluːsɪnədʒən/ *noun* a drug, such as LSD, that affects people's minds and makes them see and hear things that are not really there 致幻劑；幻覺劑 ▸ **hal·lu·cino·gen·ic** /həˌluːsɪnəˈdʒenɪk/ *adj.*：***hallucinogenic drugs/effects*** 致幻藥；致幻作用

hall·way /ˈhɔːlweɪ/ *noun* **1** (*especially BrE*) = HALL (1) **2** (*NAmE*) = HALL (2)

halo /ˈheɪləʊ; *NAmE* -loʊ/ *noun* (*pl.* **-oes** or **-os**) **1** (in paintings, etc.) a circle of light shown around or above the head of a holy person（繪畫等中環繞聖人頭上的）光環，光輪：*She played the part of an angel, complete with wings and a halo.* 她扮演天使，身上的雙翼和頭上的光輪一應俱全。◇(*figurative*) *a halo of white frizzy hair* 一圈白色鬈髮 **2** (*informal*) = CORONA

halo·gen /ˈhælədʒən/ *noun* (*chemistry* 化) any of a set of five chemical elements, including FLUORINE, CHLORINE and IODINE, that react with HYDROGEN to form acids from which simple salts can be made. Halogens, in the form of gas, are used in lamps and cookers/stoves. 鹵素

halon /ˈheɪlɒn; *NAmE* -lɑːn/ *noun* (*chemistry* 化) a gas that is made up of CARBON and one or more halogens, used especially to stop fires 鹵化烷（尤用以滅火）

halt /hɔːlt; *BrE* also hɒlt/ *verb, noun*

■ ***verb*** [I, T] to stop; to make sb/sth stop（使）停止，停下：*She walked towards him and then halted.* 她向他走去，然後停下。◇*'Halt!' the Major ordered* (= used as a command to soldiers). "立定！"少校發出命令。◇ **~ sb/sth** *The police were halting traffic on the parade route.* 警察正阻止遊行路線上的車輛前行。◇*The trial was halted after the first week.* 第一週結束後，審判暫停。 IDM see TRACK *n.*

■ ***noun*** **1** [sing.] an act of stopping the movement or progress of sb/sth 停止；阻止；暫停：*Work **came to a halt** when the machine broke down.* 機器一壞，工作便停了下來。◇*The thought **brought her to an** abrupt **halt**.* 她一想到這個便猛地停下了。◇*The car skidded to a halt.*

H

汽車打滑一段後停了下來。◇ *Strikes have led to **a halt in** production.* 罷工已經使生產陷於停頓。◇ *They decided it was time to **call a halt to** the project* (= stop it officially). 他們決定該叫停這項工程了。 **2** [C] (*BrE*) a small train station in the country that has a platform but no buildings 鄉間小火車站（只有站台） **IDM** see GRIND *v.*

hal·ter /ˈhɔːltə(r); *BrE* also ˈhɒlt-/ *noun* **1** a rope or narrow piece of leather put around the head of a horse for leading it with （馬的）籠頭，繮繩 **2** (usually used as an adjective 通常用作形容詞) a narrow piece of cloth around the neck that holds a woman's dress or shirt in position, with the back and shoulders not covered （女式露背裝的）繞頸繫帶： *She was dressed in a halter top and shorts.* 她穿着三角背心和短褲。

halt·ing /ˈhɔːltɪŋ; *BrE* also ˈhɒlt-/ *adj.* [usually before noun] (especially of speech or movement 尤指講話或動作) stopping and starting often, especially because you are not certain or are not very confident 斷斷續續的；結結巴巴的 **SYN** **hesitant**： *a halting conversation* 斷斷續續的談話 ◇ *a toddler's first few halting steps* 學步幼兒的蹣跚腳步 ▸ **halt·ing·ly** *adv.*： *'Well ... ' she began haltingly.* "唔…"她開始結結巴巴地講話。

halve /hɑːv; *NAmE* hæv/ *verb* **1** [I, T] to reduce by a half; to make sth reduce by a half （使）減半： *The shares have **halved in value**.* 股價已經跌了一半。◇ **~ sth** *The company is halving its prices.* 該公司正將產品半價出售。 **2** [T] **~ sth** to divide sth into two equal parts 把…對半分 **IDM** see TROUBLE *n.*

halves *pl.* of HALF

halwa /ˈhælwɑː/ *noun* [U] a sweet food from S Asia, made from SEMOLINA or carrots, with ALMONDS and CARDAMOM 哈瓦（用粗麵粉或胡蘿蔔加杏仁和豆蔻乾籽製成的南亞甜食）

hal·yard /ˈhæljəd; *NAmE* -jərd/ *noun* (*technical* 術語) a rope used for raising or taking down a sail or flag （帆或旗的）升降索

ham /hæm/ *noun, verb*

■ ***noun*** **1** [C, U] the top part of a pig's leg that has been CURED (= preserved using salt or smoke) and is eaten as food; the meat from this 火腿；火腿肉： *The hams were cooked whole.* 這些火腿是整條烹製的。◇ *a slice of ham* 一片火腿 ◇ *a ham sandwich* 火腿三明治 ➲ compare BACON, GAMMON, PORK **2** [C] a person who sends and receives radio messages as a hobby rather than as a job 無線電通訊愛好者： *a radio ham* 無線電通訊愛好者 **3** [C] (*informal*) (often used as an adjective 常用作形容詞) an actor who performs badly, especially by exaggerating emotions 拙劣演員（尤指表演過火者）： *a ham actor* 表演過火的演員 **4** [C, usually pl.] (*informal*) the back part of a person's leg above the knee （人的）大腿後部 ➲ see also HAMSTRING

■ ***verb*** (**-mm-**)

IDM ˌ**ham it ˈup** (*informal*) (especially of actors 尤指演員) when people **ham it up**, they deliberately exaggerate their emotions or movements 有意誇張表情（或動作）；表演過火

ham·burg·er /ˈhæmbɜːɡə(r); *NAmE* -bɜːrɡ-/ (also **bur·ger**) *noun* **1** (*BrE* also **beef·burg·er**) [C] finely chopped beef made into a flat round shape that is then fried, often served in a bread roll 漢堡包；漢堡牛肉餅 **2** (also ˈ**hamburger meat**) (both *US*) (*NAmE* also ˌ**ground ˈbeef**) (*BrE* **mince**) [U] beef that has been finely chopped in a special machine 絞碎的牛肉；牛肉末

ˌ**ham-ˈfisted** (*NAmE* also ˈ**ham-handed**) *adj.* (*informal*) lacking skill when using your hands or when dealing with people 笨手笨腳的；愚笨的 **SYN** **clumsy**： *his ham-fisted efforts to assist her* 他為了幫她做出的笨手笨腳的努力

ham·let /ˈhæmlət/ *noun* a very small village 小村莊

ham·mer 0ꟷ /ˈhæmə(r)/ *noun, verb*

■ ***noun***

▸ **TOOL** 工具 **1** 0ꟷ [C] a tool with a handle and a heavy metal head, used for breaking things or hitting nails 錘子；榔頭：(*figurative*) *The decision is a hammer blow for the steel industry.* 這一決定對於鋼鐵業是一個沉重的打擊。 ➲ VISUAL VOCAB page V20 ➲ see also SLEDGEHAMMER **2** [C] a tool with a handle and a wooden head, used by a person in charge of an AUCTION (= a sale at which things are sold to the person who offers the most money) in order to get people's attention when sth is just being sold （拍賣用的）木槌： *to come/go **under the hammer*** (= to be sold at AUCTION) 被拍賣

▸ **IN PIANO** 鋼琴 **3** [C] a small wooden part inside a piano, that hits the strings to produce a sound 音槌

▸ **IN GUN** 槍炮 **4** [C] a part inside a gun that makes the gun fire 擊鐵

▸ **SPORT** 體育運動 **5** [C] a metal ball attached to a wire, thrown as a sport 鏈球 **6** **the hammer** [sing.] the event or sport of throwing the hammer 擲鏈球（運動） ➲ VISUAL VOCAB page V46

IDM ˌ**hammer and ˈtongs** if two people are **at it hammer and tongs** or **go at it hammer and tongs**, they argue or fight with a lot of energy and noise 激烈爭吵（或打鬥）

■ ***verb***

▸ **HIT WITH TOOL** 用工具錘打 **1** [I, T] to hit sth with a hammer （用錘子）敲，錘打： *I could hear somebody hammering next door.* 我聽到隔壁有人在錘打東西。◇ **~ sth (in/into/onto sth)** *She hammered the nail into the wall.* 她把釘子釘到牆上。◇ **~ sth + adj.** *He was hammering the sheet of copper flat.* 他正把銅片錘平。

▸ **HIT MANY TIMES** 連續敲打 **2** [I, T] to hit sth hard many times, especially so that it makes a loud noise 反複敲打，連續擊打（尤指發出大聲） **SYN** **pound**： *Someone was hammering at the door.* 有人在砰砰地打門。◇ *Hail was hammering down onto the roof.* 冰雹砸得屋頂咚咚響。◇ (*figurative*) *I was so scared my heart was hammering* (= beating very fast) *in my chest.* 我嚇得心裏怦怦直跳。◇ **~ sth** *He hammered the door with his fists.* 他不斷地用拳頭擂門。 ➲ SYNONYMS at BEAT

▸ **KICK/HIT BALL** 踢／擊球 **3** [T] **~ sth (+ adv./prep.)** (*informal*) to kick or hit a ball very hard 猛踢；猛擊： *He hammered the ball into the net.* 他一記猛射，將球踢進網。

▸ **DEFEAT EASILY** 輕易打敗 **4** [T] **~ sb** (*informal*) to defeat sb very easily 輕易打敗（對方）： *Our team was hammered 5-1.* 我隊以 1:5 的懸殊比分敗北。

PHR V ˌ**hammer aˈway at sth** to work hard in order to finish or achieve sth; to keep repeating sth in order to get the result that you want 努力幹；孜孜以求 ˌ**hammer sth↔ˈhome 1** to emphasize a point, an idea, etc. so that people fully understand it 反複講透，重點講清（要點、想法等） **2** to kick a ball hard and score a goal 用力踢球得分；把球猛踢進球門 ˌ**hammer sth ˈinto sb** to make sb learn or remember sth by repeating it many times 反複灌輸 ˌ**hammer ˈout sth 1** to discuss a plan, an idea, etc. until everyone agrees or a decision is made 反複討論出（一致意見）；充分研討出（決定）： *to hammer out a compromise* 反複討論達成妥協 **2** to play a tune, especially on a piano, loudly and not very well （在鋼琴等上）敲打出

ˌ**hammer and ˈsickle** *noun* [sing.] tools representing the people who work in industry and farming, used on the flag of the former Soviet Union and as a symbol of Communism 錘子和鐮刀（代表工人農民，前蘇聯國旗用以象徵共產主義）

ham·mered /ˈhæməd; *NAmE* -ərd/ *adj.* [not before noun] (*slang*) very drunk 爛醉

ham·mer·head /ˈhæməhed; *NAmE* -mər-/ (also ˌ**hammerhead ˈshark**) *noun* a SHARK with flat parts sticking out from either side of its head with eyes at the ends 錘頭鯊；雙髻鯊

ham·mer·ing /ˈhæmərɪŋ/ *noun* **1** [U, sing.] the sound of sb hitting sth with a hammer or with their FISTS （錘子或拳頭的）敲打聲，捶打聲： *the sound of hammering from the next room* 隔壁傳來的敲打聲 **2** [C, usually sing.] (*BrE*, *informal*) an act of defeating or criticizing sb severely 挫敗；嚴厲批評： *Our team took a real hammering in the first half.* 上半場我隊吃了個大敗仗。

ˈ**hammer price** *noun* the last and highest amount offered for sth at an AUCTION which is the price for which it is sold （拍賣）成交價，擊槌價

ham·mock /'hæmək/ *noun* a type of bed made from a net or from a piece of strong material, with ropes at each end that are used to hang it between two trees, posts, etc. 吊牀 ➲ **VISUAL VOCAB** page V23

Hammond organ™ /ˌhæmənd 'ɔːɡən; *NAmE* 'ɔːrɡ-/ *noun* a type of electronic organ 哈蒙德（電）風琴

hammy /'hæmi/ *adj.* (**ham·mier**, **ham·mi·est**) (*informal*) (of a style of acting 演出風格) artificial or exaggerated 做作的；過火的

ham·per /'hæmpə(r)/ *verb, noun*

■ ***verb*** [often passive] **~ sb/sth** to prevent sb from easily doing or achieving sth 妨礙；阻止；阻礙 **SYN** **hinder**

■ ***noun*** **1** a large BASKET with a lid, especially one used to carry food in （尤指用於盛食物的）帶蓋大籃子：*a picnic hamper* 野餐籃 ➲ picture at BASKET **2** (*especially BrE*) a box or package containing food, sent as a gift（作為禮品的）盒裝食物，袋裝食物：*a Christmas hamper* 聖誕禮品盒 **3** (*NAmE*) a large BASKET that you keep your dirty clothes in until they are washed 盛髒衣服的大籃子

ham·ster /'hæmstə(r)/ *noun* an animal like a large mouse, with large cheeks for storing food. Hamsters are often kept as pets. 倉鼠（有頰囊可存放食物，常作寵物）

ham·string /'hæmstrɪŋ/ *noun, verb*

■ ***noun*** **1** one of the five TENDONS behind the knee that connect the muscles of the upper leg to the bones of the lower leg 膕繩肌腱：*a hamstring injury* 膕繩肌腱受傷 ◇ *She's pulled a hamstring.* 她拉傷了一條膕繩肌腱。 **2** a TENDON behind the middle joint (= HOCK) of the back leg of a horse and some other animals（馬等跗關節後部的）後腿肌腱，大肌腱

■ ***verb*** (**ham·strung**, **ham·strung** /'hæmstrʌŋ/) [often passive] **~ sb/sth** to prevent sb/sth from working or taking action in the way that is needed 妨礙；使不能正常工作（或行動）

hand 🔑 /hænd/ *noun, verb*

■ ***noun***

▸ **PART OF BODY** 身體部位 **1** 🔑 [C] the part of the body at the end of the arm, including the fingers and thumb 手：*Ian placed a hand on her shoulder.* 伊恩把一隻手搭在她的肩上。◇ ***Put your hand up*** *if you know the answer.* 知道答案就舉手。◇ *Keep both hands on the steering wheel at all times.* 雙手要始終握住方向盤。◇ *She was* ***on*** *(****her****)* ***hands and knees*** (= CRAWLING on the floor) *looking for an earring.* 她正趴在地板上到處尋找耳環。◇ *Couples strolled past* ***holding hands.*** 一對對戀人手拉手漫步經過。◇ ***Give me your hand*** (= hold my hand) *while we cross the road.* 過馬路時拉着我的手。◇ *The crowd* ***threw up their hands*** (= lifted them into the air) *in dismay.* 群眾沮喪地舉起雙手。◇ *He killed the snake* ***with his bare hands*** (= using only his hands). 他徒手殺死了那條蛇。◇ *a* ***hand towel*** (= a small towel for drying your hands on) 擦手的小毛巾 ◇ *a* ***hand drill*** (= one that is used by turning a handle rather than powered by electricity) 手搖鑽 ➲ **COLLOCATIONS** at PHYSICAL ➲ **VISUAL VOCAB** page V59 ➲ see also LEFT-HAND, RIGHT-HAND

▸ **-HANDED** …手 **2** (in adjectives 構成形容詞) using the hand or number of hands mentioned 用…手的；用…隻手的：*a one-handed catch* 單手抓接 ◇ *left-handed scissors* (= intended to be held in your left hand) 供左手使用的剪刀

▸ **HELP** 幫助 **3** 🔑 **a hand** [sing.] (*informal*) help in doing sth 幫助；協助：*Let me* ***give you a hand*** *with those bags* (= help you to carry them). 我來幫你拎那些包吧。◇ *Do you* ***need a hand*** *with those invoices?* 要不要我幫你處理那些發票？◇ *The neighbours are always willing to* ***lend a hand.*** 鄰居們總是樂於幫忙。

▸ **ROLE IN SITUATION** 角色 **4** [sing.] **~ in sth** the part or role that sb/sth plays in a particular situation; sb's influence in a situation 角色；作用；影響：*Early reports suggest the hand of rebel forces in the bombings.* 早期的報道暗示叛亂武裝插手了爆炸案。◇ *Several of his colleagues* ***had a hand in*** *his downfall.* 他的幾個同事促使了他下台。◇ *This appointment was an attempt to* ***strengthen her hand*** *in policy discussions.* 這次任命旨在加強她在政策討論中的作用。

▸ **ON CLOCK/WATCH** 鐘錶 **5** [C] (usually in compounds 通常構成複合詞) a part of a clock or watch that points to the numbers 指針 ➲ picture at CLOCK ➲ see also HOUR HAND, MINUTE HAND, SECOND HAND

▸ **WORKER** 工人 **6** [C] a person who does physical work on a farm or in a factory（農場或工廠的）體力勞動者，工人 ➲ see also CHARGEHAND, FARMHAND, HIRED HAND, STAGEHAND

▸ **SAILOR** 船員 **7** [C] a sailor on a ship 船員：*All hands on deck!* 全體船員到甲板上集合！➲ see also DECKHAND

▸ **HAND-** 手工 **8** (in compounds 構成複合詞) by a person rather than a machine 手工：*hand-painted pottery* 手繪陶器 ◇ *hand-knitted* 手工編織的 ◇ *This item should be hand washed.* 這件物品要用手洗。➲ see also HAND-MADE

▸ **IN CARD GAMES** 紙牌遊戲 **9** [C] a set of PLAYING CARDS given to one player in a game（分給遊戲者的）一手牌：*to be dealt a* ***good/bad hand*** 拿到一手好牌／壞牌 ➲ **VISUAL VOCAB** page V37 **10** [C] one stage of a game of cards（紙牌遊戲的）一盤：*I'll have to leave after this hand.* 這一盤打完後我必須走了。

▸ **WRITING** 書寫 **11** [sing.] (*old use*) a particular style of writing 筆跡 ➲ see also FREEHAND

▸ **MEASUREMENT FOR HORSE** 馬的測量 **12** [C] a unit for measuring the height of a horse, equal to 4 inches or 10.16 centimetres 一手之寬（測量馬的高度的單位，等於 4 英寸或 10.16 厘米）➲ see also DAB HAND, OLD HAND, SECOND-HAND, UNDERHAND

IDM **all ˌhands on 'deck** (also **all ˌhands to the 'pump**) (*saying, humorous*) everyone helps or must help, especially in a difficult situation 總動員；全民皆兵：*There are 30 people coming to dinner tonight, so it's all hands on deck.* 今天晚上有 30 人來吃飯，要全體動員了。 **(close/near) at 'hand** close to you in time or distance（在時間或距離上）接近：*Help was at hand.* 援助近在咫尺。◇ *The property is ideally located with all local amenities close at hand.* 這處房地產的位置很理想，離當地的福利設施都近。 **at the hands of sb** | **at sb's hands** (*formal*) if you experience sth **at the hands of sb**, they are the cause of it 某人導致；出自某人之手 **be good with your 'hands** to be skilful at making or doing things with your hands 技術嫻熟 **bind/tie sb hand and 'foot 1** to tie sb's hands and feet together so that they cannot move or escape 捆綁住某人的手腳 **2** to prevent sb from doing what they want by creating rules, restrictions, etc. 用條條框框限制某人 **by 'hand 1** 🔑 by a person rather than a machine 手工：*The fabric was painted by hand.* 這個織品是手染的。 **2** 🔑 if a letter is delivered **by hand**, it is delivered by the person who wrote it, or sb who is sent by them, rather than by post/mail（信件）親手交付，由專人遞送 **fall into sb's 'hands/the 'hands of sb** (*formal*) to become controlled by sb 受制於某人；被某人控制：*The town fell into enemy hands.* 那個小鎮落入敵人手裏了。◇ *We don't want this document* ***falling into the wrong hands.*** 我們不想使這份文件落入不當的人手中。 **(at) first 'hand** by experiencing, seeing, etc. sth yourself rather than being told about it by sb else 第一手；親自：*The President visited the area to see the devastation at first hand.* 總統親臨該地區視察受損情況。 **get your 'hands dirty** to do physical work 做體力工作；體力勞動：*He's not frightened of getting his hands dirty.* 他不怕體力勞動。 **sb's 'hand (in marriage)** (*old-fashioned*) permission to marry sb, especially a woman 答應求婚（尤指女方）：*He asked the general for his daughter's hand in marriage.* 他請求將軍把女兒許配給他。 **ˌhand in 'glove (with sb)** working closely with sb, especially in a secret and/or illegal way 同某人密切合作（尤指勾結） **ˌhand in 'hand 1** if two people are **hand in hand**, they are holding each other's hand 手拉手 **2** if two things **go hand in hand**, they are closely connected and one thing causes the other 密切關聯；相連帶：*Poverty and poor health often go hand in hand.* 貧困和健康不良常有連帶關係。 **ˌhands 'down** (*informal*) easily and without any doubt 容易地；易如反掌地；毋庸置疑地：*They* ***won hands down.*** 他們輕鬆取勝。◇ *It is hands down the best movie this year.* 這無疑是今年最好的電影。➲ see also HANDS-DOWN *adj.* **(get/take your) ˌhands 'off (sth/sb)** (*informal*) used to tell sb not to touch sth/sb（命令）別動某物／某人：

Get your hands off my wife! 不許碰我妻子！◇ *Hey, hands off! That's my drink!* 嘿，別動！那是我的飲料！ **,hands 'up!** (*informal*) **1** used to tell a group of people to raise one hand in the air if they know the answer to a question, etc. 舉手（答問）：*Hands up all those who want to go swimming.* 想去游泳的人舉手。 **2** used by sb who is threatening people with a gun to tell them to raise both hands in the air 舉手（投降） **have your 'hands full** to be very busy or too busy to do sth else 忙得不可開交；應接不暇：*She certainly has her hands full with four kids in the house.* 家裏養着四個孩子，她當然忙得團團轉。 **have your 'hands tied** to be unable to do what you want to do because of rules, promises, etc. 受到制約：*I really wish I could help but my hands are tied.* 我的確想幫忙，但卻多有不便。 **hold sb's 'hand** to give sb support in a difficult situation（困難時）給某人支持；拉某人一把：*Do you want me to come along and hold your hand?* 你想讓我過去幫你一把嗎？ **in sb's capable, safe, etc. 'hands** being taken care of or dealt with by sb that you think you can rely on 由可信任的人負責（或處理等）：*Can I leave these queries in your capable hands?* 我能否請你這個能手來解答這些疑問？ **in 'hand 1** if you have time or money **in hand**, it is left and available to be used 在手頭；可供使用 **2** if you have a particular situation **in hand**, you are in control of it 在掌握中；在控制中 **3** the job, question, etc. **in hand** is the one that you are dealing with 正在處理中 **4** if sb works a week, month, etc. **in hand**, they are paid for the work a week, etc. after they have completed it（按星期、月等）領取工資 **in the hands of sb | in sb's 'hands** 🔑 being taken care of or controlled by sb 受某人照料；受某人控制：*The matter is now in the hands of my lawyer.* 這件事現在正由我的律師處理。◇ *At that time, the castle was in enemy hands.* 那時城堡在敵人手中。 **keep your 'hand in** to occasionally do sth that you used to do a lot so that you do not lose your skill at it 偶爾操練某事以保持熟練：*She retired last year but still teaches the odd class to keep her hand in.* 她去年退休了，但偶爾還上課，以免技巧生疏。 **lay/get your 'hands on sb** to catch sb that you are annoyed with 捉住使你不快的人：*Wait till I get my hands on him!* 等着我抓住他吧！ **lay/get your 'hands on sth** to find or get sth 找到 / 得到某物：*I know their address is here somewhere, but I can't lay my hands on it right now.* 我知道他們的地址就放在這塊兒，但我一時找不到。 **many hands make light 'work** (*saying*) used to say that a job is made easier if a lot of people help 人多好辦事；眾人拾柴火焰高 **not do a hand's 'turn** (*old-fashioned*) to do no work 什麼活也不幹：*She hasn't done a hand's turn all week.* 她閒了整整一星期。 **off your 'hands** no longer your responsibility 不再由某人負責 **on either/every 'hand** (*literary*) on both/all sides; in both/all directions 在雙方面 / 各個方面；在兩個 / 各個方向 **on 'hand** available, especially to help 現有（尤指幫助）：*The emergency services were on hand with medical advice.* 隨時都有急診服務，並提供醫療咨詢。 **on your 'hands** if you have sb/sth **on your hands**, you are responsible for them or it 由某人負責（某人、某事）：*Let me take care of the invitations—you've enough on your hands with the caterers.* 讓我來負責發邀請吧，你負責治辦酒席就夠忙了。 **(on the 'one hand ...) on the 'other (hand) ...** used to introduce different points of view, ideas, etc., especially when they are opposites（引出不同的，尤指對立的觀點、思想等）一方面…另一方面…：*On the one hand they'd love to have kids, but on the other, they don't want to give up their freedom.* 一方面，他們想要孩子，但另一方面，他們又不想放棄自由自在的生活。 ➲ LANGUAGE BANK at CONTRAST **out of 'hand 1** difficult or impossible to control 難以（或無法）控制：*Unemployment is getting out of hand.* 失業問題越來越難以控制。 **2** if you reject, etc. sth **out of hand**, you do so immediately without thinking about it fully or listening to other people's arguments 不假思索（拒絕等）：*All our suggestions were dismissed out of hand.* 我們的建議均遭到了草率的拒絕。 **,out of your 'hands** no longer your responsibility 不再由某人負責：*I'm afraid the matter is now out of my hands.* 恐怕這件事現已不歸我管。 **,play into sb's 'hands** to do exactly what an enemy, opponent, etc. wants so that they gain the advantage in a particular situation 幹敵人（或對手等）所希望的事；做有利於敵人（或對手等）的事；授人以可乘之機：*If we get the police involved, we'll be playing right into the protesters' hands.* 如果出動警察，那將正中抗議者的下懷。 **put your ,hand in your 'pocket** (*BrE*) to spend money or give it to sb 掏腰包；出錢；付款：*I've heard he doesn't like putting his hand in his pocket.* 我聽說他手很緊。 **(at) second, third, etc. 'hand** by being told about sth by sb else who has seen it or heard about it, not by experiencing, seeing, etc. it yourself 經過二手三手地；間接地；非親身經歷：*I'm fed up of hearing about these decisions third hand!* 我厭倦了從別人那裏聽說這些決定！ **,take sb in 'hand** to deal with sb in a strict way in order to improve their behaviour 管教某人 **take sth into your own 'hands** to deal with a particular situation yourself because you are not happy with the way that others are dealing with it 親自處理某事 **throw your 'hand in** (*informal*) to stop doing sth or taking part in sth, especially because you are not successful（尤指不成功而）放棄，退出 **to 'hand** that you can reach or get easily 在手邊；隨時可得到：*I'm afraid I don't have the latest figures to hand.* 恐怕我手頭沒有最新的數據。 **turn your 'hand to sth** to start doing sth or be able to do sth, especially when you do it well（尤指成功、順利地）着手做，能夠做：*Jim can turn his hand to most jobs around the house.* 吉姆能擔當起家裏的大部份雜活。 ➲ more at BIG *adj.*, BIRD, BITE *v.*, BLOOD *n.*, CAP *n.*, CASH *n.*, CHANGE *v.*, CLOSE² *adv.*, COURAGE, DEAD *adj.*, DEVIL, EAT, FIRM *adj.*, FOLD *v.*, FORCE *v.*, FREE *adj.*, HAT, HEAVY, HELP *v.*, IRON *adj.*, JOIN *v.*, KNOW *v.*, LAW, LIFE, LIFT *v.*, LIVE¹, MONEY, OFFER *v.*, OVERPLAY, PAIR *n.*, PALM *n.*, PUTTY, RAISE *v.*, SAFE *adj.*, SHOW *n.*, SHOW *v.*, SLEIGHT at SLEIGHT OF HAND, STAY *v.*, TIME *n.*, TRY *v.*, UPPER *adj.*, WAIT *v.*, WASH *v.*, WHIP *n.*, WIN *v.*, WRING

■ ***verb*** 🔑 to pass or give sth to sb 交；遞；給：**~ sth to sb** *She handed the letter to me.* 她把信交給我。◇ **~ sb sth** *She handed me the letter.* 她把信交給我。

IDM **hand sth to sb on a 'plate** (*informal*) to give sth to sb without the person concerned making any effort 把某事物拱手送給某人：*Nobody's going to hand you success on a plate.* 沒有人會把勝利白白地送給你的。 **have (got) to 'hand it to sb** (*informal*) used to say that sb deserves praise for sth（表示某人值得稱讚）：*You've got to hand it to her—she's a great cook.* 你沒法不佩服她，她的廚藝的確了不起。

PHR V **,hand sth↔a'round/'round** 🔑 to offer or pass sth, especially food or drinks, to all the people in a group 傳遞，分發（尤指食物或飲料） **,hand sth 'back (to sb)** 🔑 to give or return sth to the person who owns it or to where it belongs 歸還某物 **,hand sth↔'down (to sb) 1** 🔑 [usually passive] to give or leave sth to sb who is younger than you 把某事物傳下去；傳給（後代） **SYN** **pass down**：*These skills used to be handed down from father to son.* 這些技藝以往都是父子相傳。➲ related noun HAND-ME-DOWN **2** to officially give a decision/statement, etc. 正式宣佈；公佈 **SYN** **announce**：*The judge has handed down his verdict.* 法官已經宣佈了裁決結果。 **,hand sth↔'in (to sb)** 🔑 (*BrE* also **,give sth 'in (to sb)**) to give sth to a person in authority, especially a piece of work or sth that is lost 提交，呈交，上交（尤指書面材料或失物）：*You must all hand in your projects by the end of next week.* 你們都必須在下週末前交出研究報告。◇ *I handed the watch in to the police.* 我把那塊錶交給了警察。◇ *to* ***hand in your notice/resignation*** (= formally tell your employer that you want to stop working for them) 遞交辭呈 **,hand sb↔'off** (*BrE*) (also **,straight-'arm, ,stiff-'arm** both *NAmE*) (in sport 體育運動) to push away a player who is trying to stop you, with your arm straight 伸直手臂擋開（對手） **,hand sth↔'on (to sb)** to give or leave sth for another person to use or deal with 把某事物交給或留給（某人）使用（或處理） **SYN** **pass on** **,hand sth↔'out (to sb) 1** 🔑 to give a number of things to the members of a group 分發某物 **SYN** **distribute**：*Could you hand these books out, please?* 請把這些書發給大家好嗎？ ➲ related noun HANDOUT **2** (*informal*) to give advice, a punishment, etc. 提出，給予（建議、懲罰等）: *He's always handing out advice to people.* 他總是喜歡給人講大道理。 **,hand 'over (to sb)** | **,hand sth↔'over (to sb)** to give sb else your position of power or the responsibility for sth 把（權力或責任）移交給（某人）: *She resigned and handed over to one of her younger colleagues.* 她辭職了，由一位比她年輕的同事接任。◇ *He finally handed over his responsibility for the company last year.* 他終於在去年交出了公司的職務。➲ related noun HANDOVER **,hand sb 'over to sb** to let sb listen or speak to another person, especially on the telephone or in a news broadcast （尤指打電話或在新聞廣播中）讓某人聽另一個人講話或同其談話: *I'll hand you over to my boss.* 我把這通電話接給我的老闆。 **,hand sb/sth↔'over (to sb)** 🔑 to give sth/sb officially or formally to another person 把某事物／某人正式交給（某人）: *He handed over a cheque for $200 000.* 他交出了一張 20 萬元的支票。◇ *They handed the weapons over to the police.* 他們把武器交給了警方。➲ related noun HANDOVER

Vocabulary Building 詞彙擴充

Using your hands 用手

Touch 接觸

These verbs describe different ways of touching things.
下列動詞表示用手接觸東西的不同方式：

feel（用手）摸，觸摸	*I felt the bag to see what was in it.* 我摸了摸提包，看裏面有什麼東西。
finger（用手指）摸，觸摸	*She fingered the silk delicately.* 她用手指輕輕地摸了摸絲綢。
handle 觸碰；拿	*Handle the fruit with care.* 拿水果時小心點。
rub 揉；搓；擦	*She rubbed her eyes wearily.* 她疲倦地揉了揉眼睛。
stroke 輕撫；撫摩	*The cat loves being stroked.* 這貓喜歡別人摩挲。
pat 輕拍	*He patted my arm and told me not to worry.* 他輕輕地拍了拍我手臂，叫我別擔心。
tap 輕擊；輕敲	*Someone was tapping lightly at the door.* 有人在輕輕敲門。
squeeze 擠；捏	*I took his hand and squeezed it.* 我抓住他的手捏了捏。

Hold 拿住

You can use these verbs to describe taking something quickly. 可用下列動詞表示迅速抓住：

grab 抓；搶	*I grabbed his arm to stop myself from falling.* 我抓住他的手臂以免自己摔倒。
snatch 一手抓起；一下奪過	*She snatched the letter out of my hand.* 她一把將信從我手上搶走。

These verbs describe holding things tightly.
下列動詞表示緊緊握住：

clasp 握緊；抱緊	*Her hands were clasped behind her head.* 她雙手緊緊抱住後腦勺。
clutch 抱緊；抓緊	*The child was clutching a doll in her hand.* 女孩手裏緊緊抱着一個玩具娃娃。
grasp 抓住	*Grasp the rope with both hands and pull.* 雙手抓住繩子拉。
grip 緊抓；緊握	*He gripped his bag tightly and wouldn't let go.* 他緊緊抓住包不鬆手。

hand·bag /'hændbæg/ (*NAmE* also **purse**) *noun* a small bag for money, keys, etc., carried especially by women 小手提包；（尤指）坤包 ➲ VISUAL VOCAB page V64

'hand baggage *noun* [U] (*especially NAmE*) = HAND LUGGAGE

hand·ball *noun* **1** /'hændbɔːl/ [U] (*US* also **'team hand-ball**) a team game for two teams of seven players, usually played indoors, in which players try to score goals by throwing a ball with their hand 手球（比賽兩隊各七人，通常在室內進行，用手擊球或擲球） **2** /'hændbɔːl/ [U] (*NAmE*) a game in which players hit a small ball against a wall with their hand 牆手球（兩人比賽，用手或拳把小球擊向牆） **3** /,hænd'bɔːl/ [C, U] (in football (SOCCER) 足球) the offence of touching the ball with your hands 手球（用手觸球的犯規動作）: *a penalty for handball* 因手球犯規而罰點球

hand·basin /'hændbeɪsn/ *noun* (*BrE*) a small bowl that has taps/faucets and is fixed to the wall, used for washing your hands in （固定在牆上有水龍頭的）洗手盆

hand·bas·ket /'hændbɑːskɪt; *NAmE* -bæs-/ *noun*
IDM **go to hell in a 'handbasket** (*NAmE*) = GO TO THE DOGS at DOG *n.*

hand·bell /'hændbel/ *noun* a small bell with a handle, especially one of a set used by a group of people to play tunes 手搖鈴（常指成套搖鈴之一，用於小組演奏）

hand·bill /'hændbɪl/ *noun* a small printed advertisement that is given to people by hand 傳單

hand·book /'hændbʊk/ *noun* a book giving instructions on how to use sth or information about a particular subject 手冊；指南 ➲ compare MANUAL

hand·brake /'hændbreɪk/ (*especially BrE*) (*NAmE* usually **'emergency brake**, **'parking brake**) *noun* a BRAKE in a vehicle that is operated by hand, used especially when the vehicle is not moving （車輛的）手閘，手刹車: *to put the handbrake on* 拉上手閘 ◇ *to take the handbrake off* 放開手閘 ◇ *Is the handbrake on?* 手閘扳上了嗎？ ➲ COLLOCATIONS at DRIVING ➲ VISUAL VOCAB page V52

hand·cart /'hændkɑːt; *NAmE* -kɑːrt/ *noun* = CART *n.* (2)

hand·craft /'hændkrɑːft; *NAmE* -kræft/ *noun* (*NAmE*) = HANDICRAFT

hand·craf·ted /'hændkrɑːftɪd; *NAmE* -kræft-/ *adj.* skilfully made by hand, not by machine 手工製作的: *a handcrafted chair* 手工做成的椅子

'hand cream *noun* [U] cream that you put on your hands to prevent dry skin 護手霜；潤手霜

hand·cuff /'hændkʌf/ *verb* [usually passive] **~ sb** to put handcuffs on sb or to fasten sb to sth/sb with handcuffs 用手銬銬住（某人）；把（某人）銬在（某物、某人）上

hand·cuffs /'hændkʌfs/ (also *informal* **cuffs**) *noun* [pl.] a pair of metal rings joined by a chain, used for holding the wrists of a prisoner together 手銬: *a pair of handcuffs* 一副手銬 ◇ *She was led away* **in handcuffs**. 她被銬住雙手帶走了。➲ see also GOLDEN HANDCUFFS

hand·ful /'hændfʊl/ *noun* **1** [C] **~ (of sth)** the amount of sth that can be held in one hand 一把（的量）；用手抓起的數量: *a handful of rice* 一把米 **2** [sing.] **~ (of sb/sth)** a small number of people or things 少數人（或物）: *Only a handful of people came.* 只有少數幾個人來了。 **3 a ~** [sing.] (*informal*) a person or an animal that is difficult to control 難以控制的人（或動物）: *Her children can be a real handful.* 她的孩子們有時很難管教。

'hand grenade *noun* a small bomb that is thrown by hand 手榴彈

hand·grip /'hændgrɪp/ *noun* **1** a handle for holding sth 把手；柄 **2** a soft bag with handles for carrying things while you are travelling 手提袋

hand·gun /'hændgʌn/ *noun* a small gun that you can hold and fire with one hand 手槍

,hand-'held *adj.* [usually before noun] small enough to be held in the hand while being used 便攜式的；手提式的 ▸ **'hand-held** *noun*: *I prefer to consult a dictionary on a hand-held.* 我比較喜歡查電子詞典。

hand·hold /'hændhəʊld; *NAmE* -hoʊld/ *noun* something on the surface of a steep slope, wall, etc. that a person can hold when climbing up it 攀緣時手可抓的東西（或地方）

ˈhand-hot *adj.* water that is **hand-hot** is hot, but not too hot to put your hand into（水）熱但不燙手的

handi·cap /ˈhændikæp/ *noun, verb*

■ *noun* **1** [C, U] (becoming *old-fashioned*, sometimes *offensive*) a permanent physical or mental condition that makes it difficult or impossible to use a particular part of your body or mind 生理缺陷；弱智；殘疾 SYN **disability**：*Despite her handicap, Jane is able to hold down a full-time job.* 儘管有生理缺陷，卻能夠保住一份全職工作。◇ ***mental/physical/visual handicap*** 智力／生理／視力缺陷 ➲ note at DISABLED **2** [C] something that makes it difficult for sb to do sth 障礙；阻礙 SYN **obstacle**：*Not speaking the language proved to be a bigger handicap than I'd imagined.* 事實證明不會講這種語言造成的障礙比我所想像的大。 **3** [C] (*sport* 體) a race or competition in which the most skilful must run further, carry extra weight, etc. in order to give all those taking part an equal chance of winning; the disadvantage that is given to sb you are competing against in such a race or competition 讓步賽（使參賽者中的優勢方跑得較遠、增加負重等）；（讓步賽中給優勢方施加的）障礙，不利條件 **4** [C] (in GOLF 高爾夫球) an advantage given to a weaker player so that competition is more equal when they play against a stronger player. It is expressed as a number related to the number of times a player hits the ball and gets lower as he/she improves. 給弱者增加的杆數（按擊球次數計算，並隨參賽者的進步而減少）

■ *verb* (**-pp-**) [usually passive] **~ sb/sth** to make sth more difficult for sb to do 妨礙；阻礙：*British exports have been handicapped by the strong pound.* 英鎊強勢影響了英國的出口。

handles 柄；把手

knobs 球形把手；旋鈕

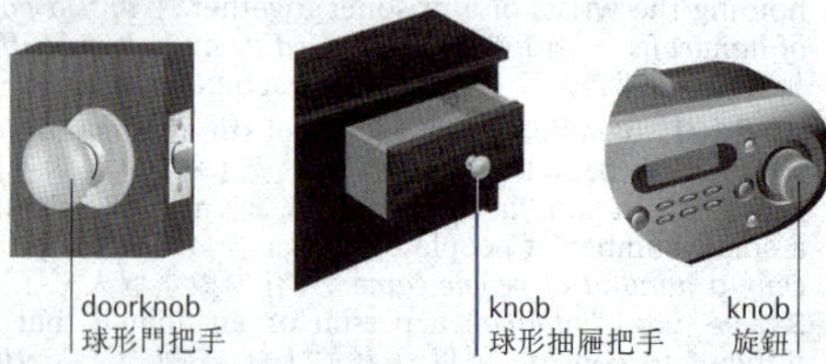

buttons 按鈕；鍵

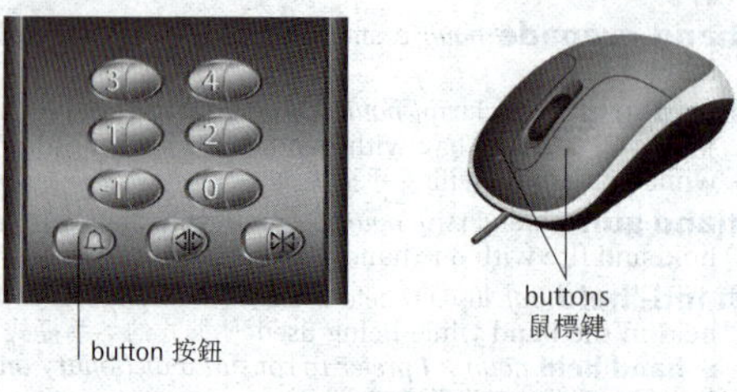

handi·capped /ˈhændikæpt/ *adj.* (becoming *old-fashioned*, sometimes *offensive*) **1** suffering from a mental or physical handicap 有生理缺陷的；殘疾的；弱智的 SYN **disabled**：*a visually handicapped child* 弱視兒童 ◇ *The accident left him physically handicapped.* 那次事故使他落下了殘疾。➲ see also MENTALLY HANDICAPPED **2 the handicapped** *noun* [pl.] people who are handicapped 殘疾人；弱智者：*a school for the physically handicapped* 殘疾人學校 ➲ note at DISABLED

han·di·craft /ˈhændikrɑːft; *NAmE* -kræft/ (*NAmE* also **hand·craft**) *noun* [C, usually pl., U] **1** activities such as sewing and making cloth that use skill with your hands and artistic ability to make things 手工藝：*to teach handicrafts* 傳授手工藝 ◇ *Her hobbies are music, reading and handicraft.* 她的愛好是音樂、讀書和手工。 **2** things made in this way 手工藝品：*traditional handicrafts bought by tourists* 旅遊者購買的傳統手工藝品

hand·ily /ˈhændɪli/ *adv.* **1** in a way that is HANDY (= convenient) 方便地；便利地：*We're handily placed for the train station.* 我們被安置在去火車站近便的地方。 **2** (*especially NAmE*) easily 容易地；輕鬆地：*He handily defeated his challengers.* 他輕而易舉地打敗了向他挑戰的人。

han·di·work /ˈhændiwɜːk; *NAmE* -wɜːrk/ *noun* [U] **1** work that you do, or sth that you have made, especially using your artistic skill 手工（藝）；手工（藝）製品：*We admired her exquisite handiwork.* 我們欣賞她精緻的手工藝品。 **2** a thing done by a particular person or group, especially sth bad 某人（或團夥）之所為（尤指壞事）：*This looks like the handiwork of an arsonist.* 這看上去像是縱火犯幹的。

hand·job /ˈhænddʒɒb; *NAmE* -dʒɑːb/ *noun* (*taboo, slang*) the act of a person rubbing a man's PENIS with their hand to give sexual pleasure（對男性的）手淫

hand·ker·chief /ˈhæŋkətʃɪf; -tʃiːf; *NAmE* -kərtʃ-/ *noun* (*pl.* **hand·ker·chiefs** or **hand·ker·chieves** /-tʃiːvz/) (also *informal* **hanky**, **han·kie**) a small piece of material or paper that you use for blowing your nose, etc. 手帕；紙巾

han·dle 🔑 /ˈhændl/ *verb, noun*

■ *verb*

▸ DEAL WITH 處理 **1** 🔑 [T] to deal with a situation, a person, an area of work or a strong emotion 處理，應付（局勢、人、工作或感情）：**~ sth/sb** *A new man was appointed to handle the crisis.* 新指派了一個人來處理這場危機。◇ *She's very good at handling her patients.* 她對待病人很有辦法。◇ *The sale was handled by Adams Commercial.* 亞當斯公司經營這筆買賣。◇ *We can handle up to 500 calls an hour at our new offices.* 我們的新辦公室每小時可處理 500 通電話。◇ *We all have to learn to handle stress.* 我們都得學會調節壓力。◇ *This matter has been handled very badly.* 這件事處理得很糟糕。◇ (*informal*) *'Any problems?' 'Nothing **I can't handle**.'* "有問題嗎？" "沒有什麼我不能對付的。" ◇ (*informal*) *I've got to go. I can't **handle it** any more* (= deal with a difficult situation). 我得走了，我已無計可施。◇ **~ yourself** (*informal*) *You have to know how to handle yourself in this business* (= know the right way to behave). 你必須知道在這行業上如何自處。

▸ TOUCH WITH HANDS 用手觸摸 **2** 🔑 [T] **~ sth** to touch, hold or move sth with your hands（用手）觸，拿，搬動：*Our cat hates being handled.* 我們的貓不喜歡被人摸弄。◇ *The label on the box said: 'Fragile. **Handle with care**.'* 箱子上的標籤寫着："易碎品，小心輕放。"

▸ CONTROL 控制 **3** 🔑 [T] **~ sth** to control a vehicle, an animal, a tool, etc. 控制，操縱（車輛、動物、工具等）：*I wasn't sure if I could handle such a powerful car.* 我沒有把握是否能駕駛功率這樣大的車。◇ *She's a difficult horse to handle.* 那是匹桀驁不馴的母馬。 **4** [I] **~ well/badly** to be easy/difficult to drive or control（容易／難以）駕駛，操縱：*The car handles well in any weather.* 這輛車在任何天氣下開起來都很靈便。

▸ BUY/SELL 買賣 **5** [T] **~ sth** to buy or sell sth 買；賣 SYN **deal in**：*They were arrested for **handling stolen goods**.* 他們因收受贓物而遭逮捕。

■ *noun*

▸ OF DOOR/DRAWER/WINDOW 門窗；抽屜 **1** 🔑 the part of a door, drawer, window, etc. that you use to open it 把手；拉手：*She turned the handle and opened the door.* 她轉動把手，打開了門。➲ VISUAL VOCAB page V52

▸ **OF CUP/BAG/TOOL** 杯子；包；工具 **2** 🔑 the part of an object, such as a cup, a bag, or a tool that you use to hold it, or carry it 柄；把；提梁；把手：*the handle of a knife* 刀柄 ◇ *a broom handle* 掃帚把 ➲ **VISUAL VOCAB** pages V22, V26, V64 ➲ see also LOVE HANDLES
▸ **-HANDLED** 有…柄 **3** (in adjectives 構成形容詞) having the number or type of handle mentioned 有…個柄的；有…柄的：*a long-handled spoon* 一把長柄匙

IDM **get/have a 'handle on sb/sth** (*informal*) to understand or know about sb/sth, especially so that you can deal with it or them later 弄懂；理解；搞明白：*I can't get a handle on these sales figures.* 我搞不懂這些銷售數字。 **give sb a 'handle (on sth)** (*informal*) to give sb enough facts or knowledge for them to be able to deal with sth（使）弄懂，理解，明白 ➲ more at FLY *v.*

handle·bar /'hændlbɑː(r)/ *noun* [C] (also **handlebars** [pl.]) a metal bar, with a handle at each end, that you use for steering a bicycle or motorcycle （自行車或摩托車的）把手：*to hold onto the handlebars* 抓緊把手 ➲ **VISUAL VOCAB** page V51 ➲ see also DROP HANDLEBARS

ˌhandlebar mous'tache *noun* a MOUSTACHE that is curved upwards at each end 翹八字鬍

hand·ler /'hændlə(r)/ *noun* (especially in compounds 尤用於構成複合詞) **1** a person who trains and controls animals, especially dogs 馴獸員；（尤指）馴犬員 **2** a person who carries or touches sth as part of their job 搬運工；操作者：*airport baggage handlers* 機場行李員 ◇ *food handlers* 食品處理者 **3** (*especially NAmE*) a person who organizes sth or advises sb 組織者；顧問：*the President's campaign handlers* 總統的競選智囊

hand·ling /'hændlɪŋ/ *noun* [U] **1** the way that sb deals with or treats a situation, a person, an animal, etc.（對形勢、人、動物等的）處理，對付，對待：*I was impressed by his handling of the affair.* 他對此事的處理方式我甚感佩服。◇ *This horse needs firm handling.* 這匹馬需要嚴加訓練。 **2** the action of organizing or controlling sth 組織；控制；管理：*data handling on computer* 計算機的數據處理 **3** the action of touching, feeling or holding sth with your hands （手的）觸摸，觸摸感覺，握，拿：*toys that can stand up to rough handling* 經得起摔打的玩具 **4** the cost of dealing with an order, delivering goods, booking tickets, etc.（訂貨、送貨、訂票等的）費用，手續費：*a small handling charge* 少許的手續費 **5** the way in which a vehicle can be controlled by the driver （車輛的）駕駛，操縱：*a car designed for easy handling* 為駕駛簡便而設計的汽車 **6** (also *BrE* **car·riage**) (*formal*) the act or cost of transporting goods from one place to another 運輸；運費

'hand luggage (*especially BrE*) (also **'hand baggage**, **'carry-on baggage** especially in *NAmE*) *noun* [U] small bags that you can keep with you on an aircraft 手提行李（可隨身帶到飛機上）

hand·made /ˌhænd'meɪd/ *adj.* made by a person using their hands rather than by machines 手工製作的 ➲ compare MACHINE-MADE

hand·maiden /'hændmeɪdn/ (also **hand·maid** /'hændmeɪd/) *noun* **1** (*old-fashioned*) a female servant 女傭人；侍女 **2** (*formal*) something that supports and helps sth else 根基；基礎：*Mathematics was once dubbed the handmaiden of the sciences.* 數學曾一度被視為各門科學的基礎。

'hand-me-down *noun* [usually pl.] (*especially NAmE*) = CAST-OFF：*She hated having to wear her sister's hand-me-downs.* 她討厭穿她姐姐穿過的舊衣服。 ▸ **'hand-me-down** *adj.* (*especially NAmE*) = CAST-OFF

'hand-me-up *noun* an item that sb gives to an older member of their family because they no longer use it or because they have bought sth better to replace it（送給年長親屬的）舊東西，替換下的東西

hand·off /'hændɒf; *NAmE* -ɔːf; -ɑːf/ *noun* **1** (especially in RUGBY 尤指橄欖球) an act of preventing an opponent from TACKLING you by blocking them with your hand while keeping your arm straight 伸手阻擋對手 **2** (in AMERICAN FOOTBALL 美式足球) an act of giving the ball to another player on your team 給球；傳球

hand·out /'hændaʊt/ *noun* **1** (sometimes *disapproving*) food, money or clothes that are given to a person who is poor 捐贈品；救濟品 **2** (often *disapproving*) money that is given to a person or an organization by the government, etc., for example to encourage commercial activity 政府撥款（為促進商業活動） **3** a free document that gives information about an event or a matter of public interest, or that states the views of a political party, etc. 傳單 ➲ see also PRESS RELEASE **4** a document that is given to students in class or people attending a talk, etc. and that contains a summary of the lesson/talk, a set of exercises, etc.（發給學生或參與討論者等的）講義，文字材料

hand·over /'hændəʊvə(r); *NAmE* -oʊvər/ *noun* [C, U] **1** the act of moving power or responsibility from one person or group to another; the period during which this is done （權力、責任等的）移交，移交期：*the smooth handover of power from a military to a civilian government* 從軍政府到文人政府的權力的順利移交 **2** the act of giving a person or thing to sb in authority （某人或某物的）交出，上交：*the handover of the hostages* 人質的交出

hand·phone /'hændfəʊn; *NAmE* -foʊn/ *noun* used in SE Asia as the word for a mobile/cell phone （東南亞用語）手機，移動電話

ˌhand-'picked *adj.* carefully chosen for a special purpose 仔細挑選的；精選的

hand·print /'hændprɪnt/ *noun* a mark left by the flat part of someone's hand on a surface 手印

'hand puppet (*NAmE*) (*BrE* **'glove puppet**) *noun* a type of PUPPET that you put over your hand and move using your fingers 手偶（套在手上用手指操縱） ➲ **VISUAL VOCAB** page V37

hand·rail /'hændreɪl/ *noun* a long narrow bar that you can hold onto for support, for example when you are going up or down stairs （樓梯等的）扶手 ➲ picture at STAIRCASE

hand·saw /'hændsɔː/ *noun* a SAW (= a tool with a long blade with sharp teeth along one edge) that is used with one hand only 手鋸 ➲ **VISUAL VOCAB** page V20

ˌhands-'down *adj.* [only before noun] **~ winner/favourite/choice** (*informal*) easily the winner of a contest; definitely the one that people prefer 輕易取勝的；首選無疑的：*These kits were hands-down favourites with our testers.* 這套工具絕對是我們的測試者一見傾心的首選。 **IDM** see HAND *n.*

hand·set /'hændset/ *noun* **1** the part of a telephone that you hold close to your mouth and ear to speak into and listen 電話聽筒 ➲ compare RECEIVER (1) **2** a mobile/cell phone or SMARTPHONE, especially the main part of the phone not including the battery or SIM CARD 手機，智能手機（尤指電話的主體部份，不包括電池或 SIM 卡）：*mobile handsets* 移動電話 ◇ *handset manufacturers* 手機生產商 **3** a device that you hold in your hand to operate a television, etc. （電視等的）遙控器 ➲ see also REMOTE CONTROL (2)

'hands-free *adj.* (of a telephone, etc. 電話等) able to be used without needing to be held in the hand 免提的

hand·shake /'hændʃeɪk/ *noun* an act of shaking sb's hand with your own, used especially to say hello or goodbye or when you have made an agreement 握手 ➲ see also GOLDEN HANDSHAKE

ˌhands-'off *adj.* [usually before noun] dealing with people or a situation by not becoming involved and by allowing people to do what they want to 不介入的；放手的：*a hands-off approach to staff management* 不干涉的職員管理方法 ➲ compare HANDS-ON

hand·some /'hænsəm/ *adj.* (**hand·somer**, **hand·som·est**) **HELP** More handsome and most handsome are more common. * more handsome 和 most handsome 更常見。 **1** (of men 男子) attractive 英俊的；漂亮的；有魅力的 **SYN** **good-looking**：*a handsome face* 英俊的相貌 ◇ *He's the most handsome man I've ever met.* 他是我見過的最俊美的男子。◇ *He was aptly described as* ***'tall, dark, and handsome'.*** 他被恰如其分地描述為"高大黝黑、相貌堂堂"。 ➲ **SYNONYMS** at BEAUTIFUL **2** (of women 女子)

H

attractive, with large strong features rather than small delicate ones 健美的：*a tall, handsome woman* 一位高個頭的健美女子 ➲ SYNONYMS at BEAUTIFUL **3** beautiful to look at 美觀的；悅目的：*a handsome horse/house/city* 漂亮的馬／房子／城市 ◇ *The two of them made a **handsome couple**.* 這對夫妻男俊女靚。**4** large in amount or quantity 數量大的：*a **handsome profit*** 一大筆利潤 ◇ *He was elected by a handsome majority* (= a lot of people voted for him). 他以高票當選。**5** generous 大方的；慷慨的；氣量大的：*She paid him a handsome compliment.* 她讚揚了他一番。▸ **hand·some·ly** *adv.*：*a handsomely dressed man* 穿著瀟灑的男子 ◇ *a handsomely produced book* 印刷精美的書 ◇ *to be **paid/rewarded handsomely*** 得到可觀的工資／報酬 **hand·some·ness** *noun* [U]

ˌhands-ˈon *adj.* [usually before noun] doing sth rather than just talking about it 動手的；實際操作的：*hands-on computer training* 計算機操作培訓 ◇ *to gain **hands-on experience** of industry* 獲得勤勞工作的實際經驗 ◇ *a hands-on style of management* 事必躬親的管理方式 ➲ compare HANDS-OFF

hand·spring /ˈhændsprɪŋ/ *noun* a movement in gymnastics in which you jump through the air landing on your hands, then again landing on your feet（體操動作）手翻

hand·stand /ˈhændstænd/ *noun* a movement in which you balance on your hands and put your legs straight up in the air 倒立（動作）

ˌhand-to-ˈhand *adj.* **hand-to-hand** fighting involves physical contact with your opponent 交手的；白刃的；肉搏的

ˌhand-to-ˈmouth *adj.* [usually before noun] if you have a **hand-to-mouth** life, you spend all the money you earn on basic needs such as food and do not have anything left 僅夠餬口的；勉強維持生計的 IDM see LIVE[1]

hand·writ·ing /ˈhændraɪtɪŋ/ *noun* [U] **1** writing that is done with a pen or pencil, not printed or typed 手寫；書寫 **2** a person's particular style of writing in this way 筆跡：*I can't read his handwriting.* 我看不懂他寫的字。

IDM **the ˌhandwriting on the ˈwall** (*NAmE*) = THE WRITING ON THE WALL at WRITING

hand·writ·ten /ˌhændˈrɪtn/ *adj.* written by hand, not printed or typed 手寫的：*a handwritten note* 手寫的便條

handy /ˈhændi/ *adj.* (**hand·ier**, **handi·est**) (*informal*) **1** easy to use or to do 易使用的；容易做的；便利的 SYN **useful**：*a handy little tool* 好用的小工具 ◇ ***handy hints/tips** for removing stains* 清除污漬的妙招／竅門兒 **2** [not before noun] located near to sb/sth; located or stored in a convenient place 近便的；便利的：*Always keep a first-aid kit handy.* 要常備急救箱。◇ *Have you got a pen handy?* 你手頭有筆嗎？◇ **~ (for sth/for doing sth)** (*BrE*) *Our house is very handy for the station.* 我們家離車站很近。**3** [not before noun] skilful in using your hands or tools to make or repair things 手巧；有手藝：*to be handy around the house* 對家裏敲打修理的雜事很在行 ➲ see also HANDILY ▸ **handi·ness** *noun* [U]

IDM **ˌcome in ˈhandy** (*informal*) to be useful 有用處：*The extra money came in very handy.* 這筆額外的錢正好派上了用場。◇ *Don't throw that away—it might come in handy.* 別把它扔了，它或許有用。

handy·man /ˈhændimæn/ *noun* (*pl.* **-men** /-men/) a man who is good at doing practical jobs inside and outside the house, either as a hobby or as a job 善於做室內外雜活的人；雜活工

hang 0-w /hæŋ/ *verb*, *noun*

■ ***verb*** (**hung**, **hung** /hʌŋ/ HELP In sense 4, **hanged** is used for the past tense and past participle. 作第 4 義時過去時和過去分詞用 hanged。)

▸ **ATTACH FROM TOP** 懸掛 **1** 0-w [T, I] to attach sth, or to be attached, at the top so that the lower part is free or loose 懸掛；吊：**~ sth + adv./prep.** *Hang your coat on the hook.* 把你的大衣掛在衣鉤上。◇ **~ sth up** *Shall I hang your coat up?* 我把你的大衣掛起來好嗎？◇ **~ sth (out)** (*BrE*) *Have you hung out the washing?* 你把洗好的衣服晾在外面了嗎？◇ (*NAmE*) *Have you hung the wash?* 你把洗好的衣服晾了嗎？◇ **~ adv./prep.** *There were several expensive suits hanging in the wardrobe.* 衣櫃裏掛着幾套昂貴的套裝。

▸ **FALL LOOSELY** 垂落 **2** 0-w [I] **~ adv./prep.** when sth **hangs** in a particular way, it falls in that way 垂下；垂落：*Her hair hung down to her waist.* 她的長髮垂及腰際。◇ *He had lost weight and the suit hung loosely on him.* 他體重減輕了，這套衣服他穿在身上鬆鬆垮垮的。

▸ **BEND DOWNWARDS** 下垂 **3** 0-w [I, T] to bend or let sth bend downwards（使）低垂，下垂：**~ adv./prep.** *The dog's tongue was hanging out.* 狗的舌頭耷拉在外面。◇ *Children hung (= were leaning) over the gate.* 孩子們趴在門上。◇ *A cigarette hung from her lips.* 她嘴唇上叼着香煙。◇ **~ sth** *She **hung her head** in shame.* 她羞愧得垂下了頭。

▸ **KILL SB** 殺人 **4** 0-w (**hanged**, **hanged**) [T, I] **~ (sb/yourself)** to kill sb, usually as a punishment, by tying a rope around their neck and allowing them to drop; to be killed in this way（被）絞死，施以絞刑：*He was the last man to be hanged for murder in this country.* 他是這個國家中最後一個被處以絞刑的謀殺犯。◇ *She had committed suicide by hanging herself from a beam.* 她懸梁自盡了。◇ *At that time you could hang for stealing.* 那時犯盜竊罪可被絞死。

▸ **PICTURES** 圖畫 **5** 0-w [T, I] **~ (sth)** to attach sth, especially a picture, to a hook on a wall; to be attached in this way（使）掛在牆上：*We hung her portrait above the fireplace.* 我們把她的畫像掛在壁爐上方。◇ *Several of his paintings hang in the Tate Gallery.* 他的幾幅油畫掛在塔特美術館。**6** [T, usually passive] **~ sth with sth** to decorate a place by placing paintings, etc. on a wall 掛圖畫等裝飾（某處）：*The rooms were hung with tapestries.* 這些房間裝飾着掛毯。

▸ **WALLPAPER** 壁紙 **7** [T] **~ sth** to stick WALLPAPER to a wall（在牆上）貼壁紙

▸ **DOOR/GATE** 門 **8** [T] **~ sth** to attach a door or gate to a post so that it moves freely 把（門）裝在門柱上；裝（門）

▸ **STAY IN THE AIR** 懸在空中 **9** [I] **+ adv./prep.** to stay in the air 懸浮（在空中）：*Smoke hung in the air above the city.* 城市上空煙霧瀰漫。

IDM **ˈhang sth** (*BrE*, *informal*) used to say that you are not going to worry about sth 不在乎；不管：*Oh, let's get two and hang the expense!* 哎呀，我們買兩份吧，管它多少錢！ **hang a ˈleft/ˈright** (*NAmE*) to take a left/right turn 向左／向右轉 **hang by a ˈhair/ˈthread** (of a person's life 人的生命) to be in great danger 命懸一線；氣若游絲；危在旦夕 **hang (on) ˈin there** (*informal*) to remain determined to succeed even when a situation is difficult 保持信心；堅持下去；不氣餒 **hang on sb's ˈwords/on sb's every ˈword** to listen with great attention to sb you admire 專心致志地聽所崇拜的人講話；洗耳恭聽某人的話 **hang ˈtough** (*NAmE*) to be determined and refuse to change your attitude or ideas 立場堅定；態度堅決 **let it all hang ˈout** (*informal*) to express your feelings freely 宣泄情感 ➲ more at BALANCE *n.*, FIRE *n.*, GRIM, HEAVY *adv.*, LOOSE *adj.*, PEG *n.*, WELL *adv.*

PHR V **ˌhang aˈbout** (*BrE*, *informal*) **1** 0-w to wait or stay near a place, not doing very much（在某處附近）等待，逗留，閒蕩：*kids hanging about in the streets* 在街上到處閒晃的少年 **2** to be very slow doing sth 慢悠悠：*I can't hang about—the boss wants to see me.* 我可不能磨磨蹭蹭了，老闆要見我。**3** (*informal*) used to tell sb to stop what they are doing or saying for a short time 停一下；等一等：*Hang about! There's something not quite right here.* 且慢！這兒有點不對頭。 **ˌhang aˈbout with sb** 0-w (*BrE*) (*NAmE* **ˈhang with sb**) (*informal*) to spend a lot of time with sb（和某人）長時間待在一起，泡在一塊兒 **ˌhang aˈround (...)** 0-w (*informal*) to wait or stay near a place, not doing very much（在某處附近）等待，逗留，閒蕩：*You hang around here in case he comes, and I'll go on ahead.* 你在這附近等着以防萬一他來了；我繼續往前走。 **ˌhang aˈround with sb** 0-w (*informal*) to spend a lot of time with sb（和某人）長時間待在一起，泡在一塊兒 **ˌhang ˈback** to remain in a place after all the other people have left 留下；繼續留在原處 **ˌhang ˈback (from sth)** to hesitate because you are nervous about doing or saying sth 猶豫；畏縮；吞吞吐吐：*I was sure she knew the answer but for some reason she hung back.* 我敢保證她知道答案，但不知為什麼她不敢說出來。 **ˌhang ˈon 1** to hold sth tightly 抓緊：*Hang on tight—we're off!* 抓緊了，我們出發了！ ➲ SYNONYMS at HOLD **2** (*informal*) used to ask sb to wait for a short time or to stop what they are doing 等一下；停一下：*Hang on—I'm not quite ready.* 等一等，我還沒準備好呢。◇ *Now hang on a minute—you can't really believe what you just said!* 等一下，你不可能真的相信你剛才說的話吧！ **3** to wait for sth to happen 等待某事發生；等候：*I haven't heard if I've got the job yet—they've kept me hanging on for days.* 我是否得到了那份工作的事還沒消息，他們讓我等了好幾天了。 **4** (*informal*) used on the telephone to ask sb who is calling to wait until they can talk to the person they want 別掛電話，等一下：*Hang on—I'll just see if he's here.* 等一下，我這就看看他在不在。**5** to continue doing sth in difficult circumstances（在逆境中）堅持，不放棄：*The team hung on for victory.* 這個隊為了勝利堅持不懈。 **ˈhang on sth** to depend on sth 有賴於，取決於（某事物）：*A lot hangs on this decision.* 很多事情都取決於這一決定。 **ˌhang ˈon to sth 1** to hold sth tightly 抓緊某物：*Hang on to that rope and don't let go.* 抓緊那根繩子，別鬆手。 **2** (*informal*) to keep sth, not sell it or give it away 保留；不賣掉；不放棄：*Let's hang on to those old photographs—they may be valuable.* 咱們留着那些舊照片吧，它們或許有價值。 **ˌhang ˈout** (*informal*) to spend a lot of time in a place 常去某處；泡在某處：*The local kids hang out at the mall.* 當地的孩子常在商場閒蕩。 ➲ related noun HANG-OUT **ˌhang sth↔ˈout** (*especially BrE*) to attach things that you have washed to a piece of thin rope or wire, etc. outside so that they can dry; to attach sth such as a flag outside a window or in the street（把洗好的東西）掛在外面晾乾；（把旗子等）掛在外面 **ˌhang ˈover sb** if sth bad or unpleasant is **hanging over** you, you think about it and worry about it a lot because it is happening or might happen 使憂心忡忡；擔心可能發生：*The possibility of a court case is still hanging over her.* 可能被告上法庭的陰影依然籠罩在她的心頭。 **ˌhang toˈgether 1** to fit together well; to be the same as or CONSISTENT with each other 相符；一致；連貫：*Their accounts of what happened don't hang together.* 他們各人對事情的描述不吻合。 **2** (of people 人) to support or help one another 相互支持；互相幫助；同心協力 **ˌhang ˈup** 🗝 to end a telephone conversation by putting the telephone RECEIVER down or switching the telephone off 掛斷電話：*After I hung up I remembered what I'd wanted to say.* 我掛斷電話之後才想起來原本想說的話。 **ˌhang sth↔ˈup** (*informal*) to finish using sth for the last time 終止使用某物：*Ruth has hung up her dancing shoes.* 魯思已掛起舞鞋退出舞台了。 **ˌhang ˈup on sb** (*informal*) to end a telephone call by suddenly and unexpectedly putting the telephone down 突然掛斷某人的電話：*Don't hang up on me—we must talk!* 別掛斷電話，我們一定得談談！ ➲ see also HUNG UP **ˈhang with sb** (*NAmE*) (*BrE* **ˌhang aˈbout with sb**) (*informal*) to spend a lot of time with sb 和某人長時間待在一起；和某人一起消磨時間

■ *noun* [sing.] the way in which a dress, piece of cloth, etc. falls or moves（衣服、織物等的）懸掛方式，下垂

IDM **get the ˈhang of sth** (*informal*) to learn how to do or to use sth; to understand sth 掌握…的要領；瞭解…的用法；找到了訣竅：*It's not difficult once you get the hang of it.* 你掌握了要領就不難了。

hangar /ˈhæŋə(r); ˈhæŋɡə(r)/ *noun* a large building in which aircraft are kept 飛機庫

hang·dog /ˈhæŋdɒɡ; *NAmE* -dɔːɡ; -dɑːɡ/ *adj.* [only before noun] if a person has a **hangdog** look, they look sad or ashamed 顯得難過的；羞愧的

hanger /ˈhæŋə(r)/ (also **ˈcoat hanger**, **ˈclothes hanger**) *noun* a curved piece of wood, plastic or wire, with a hook at the top, that you use to hang clothes up on 衣架 ➲ VISUAL VOCAB pages V23, V63

ˌhanger-ˈon *noun* (*pl.* **ˌhangers-ˈon**) (often *disapproving*) a person who tries to be friendly with a famous person or who goes to important events, in order to get some advantage 逢迎者；攀附權貴者

ˈhang-glider *noun* **1** the frame used in hang-gliding 懸掛式滑翔機 **2** a person who goes hang-gliding 懸掛式滑翔機運動員

ˈhang-gliding *noun* [U] a sport in which you fly while hanging from a frame like a large KITE which you control with your body movements 懸掛式滑翔運動：*to go hang-gliding* 進行懸掛式滑翔運動 ➲ VISUAL VOCAB page V49

hang·ing /ˈhæŋɪŋ/ *noun* **1** [U, C] the practice of killing sb as a punishment by putting a rope around their neck and hanging them from a high place; an occasion when this happens 絞死；絞刑：*to sentence sb to death by hanging* 判處某人絞刑 ◇ *public hangings* 公開執行的絞刑 **2** [C, usually pl.] a large piece of material that is hung on a wall for decoration 牆幔；帷幔：*wall hangings* 掛在牆上的裝飾織物

ˌhanging ˈbasket *noun* a BASKET or similar container with flowers growing in it, that is hung from a building by a short chain or rope 吊花籃；吊花盆 ➲ picture at BASKET ➲ VISUAL VOCAB page V17

ˌhanging ˈvalley *noun* (*technical* 術語) a valley which joins a deeper valley, often with a WATERFALL where the two valleys join 懸谷（下接更深的溪谷，連接處常有瀑布）

hang·man /ˈhæŋmən/ *noun* (*pl.* **-men** /-mən/) **1** [C] a man whose job is to hang criminals 執行絞刑的人；劊子手 **2** [U] a game in which one player chooses a word and the other players try to guess it, letter by letter. Each time they guess wrongly, the first person draws one part of a man being hanged. The other players have to guess the word before the drawing is complete. 猜詞畫人遊戲（一個玩家選一個單詞，其他玩家設法猜出，每猜錯一個字母就畫一部份吊着的人的身體，其他玩家須在全部身體畫完之前猜出該詞。）

hang·nail /ˈhæŋneɪl/ *noun* a piece of skin near the bottom or at the side of your nail that is loose and sore（指甲根部或兩側的）倒刺

ˈhang-out *noun* (*informal*) a place where sb lives or likes to go often 住所；經常去的地方 SYN **haunt**

hang·over /ˈhæŋəʊvə(r); *NAmE* -oʊvər/ *noun* **1** the headache and sick feeling that you have the day after drinking too much alcohol 宿醉（過量喝酒後第二天的頭痛以及惡心反應）：*She woke up with a terrible hangover.* 她醒來時宿醉反應很厲害。 **2** [usually sing.] **~ (from sth)** a feeling, custom, idea, etc. that remains from the past, although it is no longer practical or suitable 遺留的感覺；沿襲下來的風俗（或思想等）：*the insecure feeling that was a hangover from her childhood* 她兒時留下的不安全感 ◇ *hangover laws from the previous administration* 從上屆政府沿襲下來的法律 ➲ see also HOLDOVER

the Hang Seng Index /ˌhæŋ ˈseŋ ɪndeks/ *noun* a figure that shows the relative price of shares on the Hong Kong Stock Exchange（香港股票交易所的）恒生指數

ˈhang-up *noun* (*informal*) **1 ~ (about sth)** an emotional problem about sth that makes you embarrassed or worried 苦惱；難堪；焦慮：*He's got a real hang-up about his height.* 他為他的身高很是苦惱。 **2** (*NAmE*) a problem that delays sth being agreed or achieved（拖延協議等達成的）難題，障礙

hank /hæŋk/ *noun* a long piece of wool, thread, rope, etc. that is wound into a large loose ball（毛線、棉線、繩等的）團

han·ker /ˈhæŋkə(r)/ *verb* [I] to have a strong desire for sth 渴望，渴求（某事物）：**~ after/for sth** *He had hankered after fame all his life.* 他一生追求名望。◇ **~ to do sth** *She hankered to go back to Australia.* 她渴望回到澳大利亞。

han·ker·ing /ˈhæŋkərɪŋ/ *noun* [usually sing.] **~ (for/after sth)** | **~ (to do sth)** a strong desire（對或做某事的）強烈慾望：*a hankering for a wealthy lifestyle* 渴望過富裕生活

hanky (also **han·kie**) /ˈhæŋki/ *noun* (*pl.* **-ies**) (*informal*) = HANDKERCHIEF

hanky-panky /ˌhæŋki ˈpæŋki/ *noun* [U] (*old-fashioned, informal*) **1** sexual activity that is not considered acceptable 不得體的性行為；調戲；不正當性活動 **2** dishonest behaviour 欺騙行為；花招

Han·sard /ˈhænsɑːd; *NAmE* -sɑːrd/ *noun* [U] (in the British, Canadian, Australian, New Zealand or South African parliaments) the official written record of everything that is said in the parliament（英國、加拿大、澳大利亞、新西蘭或南非議會的）議會議事錄

han·som /ˈhænsəm/ (also **ˈhansom cab**) *noun* a CARRIAGE with two wheels, pulled by one horse, used in the past to carry two passengers（舊時由一匹馬拉的）雙輪雙座馬車

Ha·nuk·kah (also **Cha·nuk·kah**, **Cha·nuk·ah**) /ˈhænʊkə/ *noun* an eight-day Jewish festival and holiday in November or December when Jews remember the occasion when the TEMPLE in Jerusalem was DEDICATED again in 165 BC 修殿節（歷時八天的猶太人光明節，紀念公元前 165 年重獻耶路撒冷聖殿）

H

ha'·penny = HALFPENNY (1)

hap·haz·ard /hæpˈhæzəd; *NAmE* -zərd/ *adj.* (*disapproving*) with no particular order or plan; not organized well 無秩序的；無計劃的；組織混亂的： *The books had been piled on the shelves in a haphazard fashion.* 書架上的書堆放得雜亂無序。◇ *The government's approach to the problem was haphazard.* 政府解決這一問題的方法缺乏計劃。▶ **hap·haz·ard·ly** *adv.*

hap·less /ˈhæpləs/ *adj.* [only before noun] (*formal*) not lucky; unfortunate 倒運的；不幸的： *the hapless victims of exploitation* 受到剝削的不幸犧牲品

hap·loid /ˈhæplɔɪd/ *adj.* (*biology* 生) (of a cell 細胞) containing the set of CHROMOSOMES from one parent only 單倍體的 ➲ compare DIPLOID

ha'p'orth /ˈheɪpəθ; *NAmE* -pərθ/ *noun* [sing.] (*old-fashioned, BrE, informal*) a very small amount (in the past, an amount that could be bought for a HALFPENNY) 很少的量，微量（舊時半便士可購買的量） **IDM** see SPOIL *v.*

hap·pen 🔑 /ˈhæpən/ *verb*
1 🔑 [I] to take place, especially without being planned（尤指偶然）發生，出現： *You'll never guess what's happened!* 你根本猜不到出了什麼事！◇ *Accidents like this happen all the time.* 此類事故經常發生。◇ *Let's see what happens next week.* 咱們等着瞧下一週會怎麼樣。◇ *I'll be there* ***whatever happens***. 不管發生什麼事我都會到那兒的。◇ *I don't know how this happened.* 我不知道這事怎麼發生的。 **2** 🔑 [I] to take place as the result of sth（作為結果）出現，發生： *She pressed the button but nothing happened.* 她按下按鈕，但什麼反應也沒有。◇ *What happens if nobody comes to the party?* 要是沒有人來參加聚會，會怎麼樣呢？◇ *Just plug it in and* ***see what happens***. 就把插頭插上，看看會怎麼樣。 **3** *linking verb* to do or be sth by chance 碰巧；恰好： **~ to be/do sth** *She happened to be out when we called.* 我們打電話時她剛巧不在家。◇ *You don't happen to know his name, do you?* 你不會碰巧知道他的名字吧？◇ **it happens that …** *It happened that she was out when we called.* 我們打電話時她剛巧不在家。 **4** [T] **~ to be/do sth** used to tell sb sth, especially when you are disagreeing with them or annoyed by what they have said（向對方表示異議或不悅等）： *That happens to be my mother you're talking about!* 你們談論的是我母親！

IDM **anything can/might ˈhappen** used to say that it is not possible to know what the result of sth will be 什麼事都可能發生；結果難以預料 **as it happens/happened** used when you say sth that is surprising, or sth connected with what sb else has just said 令人驚奇的是；恰恰： *I agree with you, as it happens.* 我恰恰和你意見一致。◇ *As it happens, I have a spare set of keys in my office.* 碰巧我在辦公室有一套備用鑰匙。 **it (just) so happens that …** by chance 碰巧；恰好： *It just so happened they'd been invited too.* 他們碰巧也獲得邀請。 **ˌthese things ˈhappen** used to tell sb not to worry about sth they have done 這類事在所難免；別為做過的事擔憂： *'Sorry—I've spilt some wine.' 'Never mind. These things happen.'* "對不起，我弄灑了些酒。" "沒關係。這種事在所難免。" ➲ more at ACCIDENT, EVENT, SHIT *n.*, WAIT *v.*

PHR V **ˈhappen on sth** (*old-fashioned*) to find sth by chance 偶然發現某物 **ˈhappen to sb/sth** 🔑 to have an effect on sb/sth 遭到；遇到： *I hope nothing (= nothing unpleasant) has happened to them.* 我希望他們沒出事。◇ *It's the best thing that has ever happened to me.* 這是我所遇到的最好的事。◇ *What's happened to your car?* 你的車出什麼毛病了？◇ *Do you know what happened to Gill Lovecy (= have you any news about her)?* 你有吉爾•洛夫西的消息嗎？

hap·pen·ing /ˈhæpənɪŋ/ *noun, adj.*
■ ***noun*** **1** [usually pl.] an event; something that happens, often sth unusual 事件；發生的事情（常指不尋常的）： *There have been strange happenings here lately.* 這兒最近發生了一些怪事。 **2** an artistic performance or event that is not planned 即興藝術表演
■ ***adj.*** [only before noun] (*informal*) where there is a lot of exciting activity; fashionable 熱鬧的；時髦的： *a happening place* 時髦的地方

hap·pen·stance /ˈhæpənstæns; *BrE* also -stɑːns/ *noun* [U, C] (*literary*) chance, especially when it results in sth good 偶然情況；（尤指）機遇

hap·pily 🔑 /ˈhæpɪli/ *adv.*
1 🔑 in a cheerful way; with feelings of pleasure or satisfaction 快樂地；高興地；滿足地： *children playing happily on the beach* 在海灘上嬉戲的孩子們 ◇ *to be happily married* 美滿地結婚 ◇ *I think we can manage quite happily on our own.* 我想我們自己完全能夠應付。◇ ***And they all lived happily ever after*** (= used as the end of a FAIRY TALE). 從此他們都過着幸福美滿的生活（用作童話故事的結尾）。 **2** 🔑 by good luck 幸運地 **SYN** **fortunately**： *Happily, the damage was only slight.* 所幸的是，損傷不大。 **3** willingly 欣然；情願地： *I'll happily help, if I can.* 如果我能幫忙，我倒很樂意。 **4** (*formal*) in a way that is suitable or appropriate 合適地；恰當地：*This suggestion did not fit very happily with our existing plans.* 這個建議與我們目前的計劃不十分契合。

happy 🔑 /ˈhæpi/ *adj.* (**hap·pier**, **hap·pi·est**)

> **WORD FAMILY**
> **happy** *adj.* (≠ unhappy)
> **happily** *adv.* (≠ unhappily)
> **happiness** *noun* (≠ unhappiness)

▸ **FEELING/GIVING PLEASURE** 感到／給予快樂 **1** 🔑 feeling or showing pleasure; pleased 感到（或顯得）快樂的；高興的： *a happy smile/face* 快活的微笑／面容 ◇ *You don't look very happy today.* 你今天好像不太高興。◇ **~ to do sth** *We are happy to announce the engagement of our daughter.* 我們高興地宣佈，我們的女兒已訂婚。◇ **~ for sb** *I'm very happy for you.* 我真為你感到高興。◇ **~ (that) …** *I'm happy (that) you could come.* 我很高興你能來。 ➲ **SYNONYMS** at GLAD **2** 🔑 giving or causing pleasure 給予（或帶來）快樂的；使人高興的；幸福的： *a happy marriage/memory/childhood* 幸福的婚姻／回憶／童年 ◇ *The story has a* ***happy ending***. 故事的結局很圓滿。◇ *Those were the happiest days of my life.* 那是我一生中最幸福的一段時光。

▸ **AT CELEBRATION** 祝賀 **3** 🔑 if you wish sb a **Happy Birthday**, **Happy New Year**, etc. you mean that you hope they have a pleasant celebration（表示祝願，如 Happy Birthday 生日快樂、Happy New Year 新年好等）

▸ **SATISFIED** 滿意 **4** 🔑 satisfied that sth is good or right; not anxious（對事物）滿意的，放心的： **~ (with sb/sth)** *Are you happy with that arrangement?* 你對這一安排感到滿意嗎？◇ *I'm not happy with his work this term.* 我對他這學期的表現不滿意。◇ *She was happy enough with her performance.* 她對於自己的表現還算滿意。◇ **~ (about sb/sth)** *If there's anything you're not happy about, come and ask.* 你如果有什麼不滿意的，來説一聲。◇ *I'm not too happy about her living alone.* 我不太放心讓她一個人住。◇ *I said I'd go just to* ***keep him happy***. 我説過我要走只是為了讓他高興。

▸ **WILLING** 情願 **5** 🔑 **~ to do sth** (*formal*) willing or pleased to do sth 情願，樂意（做某事）：*I'm happy to leave it till tomorrow.* 我願意把它留到明天再做。◇ *He will be* ***more than happy*** *to come with us.* 他巴不得和我們一起來。

▸ **LUCKY** 幸運 **6** lucky; successful 幸運的；成功的 **SYN** **fortunate**： *By a* ***happy coincidence****, we arrived* *at exactly the same time.* 碰巧運氣好，我們恰恰同時到達。◇ *He is* ***in the happy position of*** *never having to worry about money.* 他運氣真好，從來不用為金錢操心。

▸ SUITABLE 合適 **7** (*formal*) (of words, ideas or behaviour 言語、思想或行為) suitable and appropriate for a particular situation 合適的；恰當的：*That wasn't the happiest choice of words.* 那樣的措辭並不是十分恰當。

▸ **hap·pi·ness** noun [U]：*to* ***find*** *true* ***happiness*** 尋找真正的幸福 ◇ *Her eyes shone with happiness.* 她雙眼閃爍着幸福的光芒。➲ SYNONYMS at SATISFACTION

IDM **a ˌhappy eˈvent** the birth of a baby（生孩子）喜事 **a/the happy ˈmedium** something that is in the middle between two choices or two ways of doing sth 折衷辦法 **not a ˌhappy ˈbunny** (*BrE*) (*NAmE* **not a ˌhappy ˈcamper**) (*informal*) not pleased about a situation 對境況不滿意：*She wasn't a happy bunny at all.* 她一點兒都不滿意。 **many happy reˈturns (of the ˈday)** used to wish sb a happy and pleasant birthday（生日祝福）生日快樂，長命百歲 ➲ more at MEAN *n.*

Synonyms 同義詞辨析

happy

satisfied • content • contented • joyful • blissful

These words all describe feeling, showing or giving pleasure or satisfaction. 以上各詞均表示快樂、愉快、滿意。

happy feeling, showing or giving pleasure; satisfied with sth or not worried about it 指快樂的、滿意的、放心的：*a happy marriage/memory/childhood* 幸福的婚姻／回憶／童年 ◇ *I said I'd go, just to* ***keep him happy***. 我說過我要去只是為了讓他高興。

satisfied pleased because you have achieved sth or because sth has happened as you wanted it to; showing this satisfaction 指滿意的、滿足的、欣慰的：*She's never satisfied with what she's got.* 她對自己所得到的從不感到滿足。◇ *a satisfied smile* 滿意的微笑

content [not before noun] happy and satisfied with what you have 指滿意、滿足：*I'm perfectly* ***content just to*** *lie in the sun.* 我在陽光下躺着就感到非常滿足。

contented happy and comfortable with what you have; showing this 指滿意的、滿足的、愜意的：*a contented baby* 心滿意足的小寶貝 ◇ *a long contented sigh* 愜意的長歎

CONTENT OR CONTENTED? 用 content 還是 contented？

Being **contented** depends more on having a comfortable life; being **content** can depend more on your attitude to your life: you can *have to be content* or *learn to be content*. People or animals can be **contented** but only people can be **content**.
* contented 多指因生活舒適而愜意；content 多指對生活的態度，可以用 have to be content（只好知足）或 learn to be content（學會知足）。人和動物均可用 contented，但只有人才能用 content。

joyful (*rather formal*) very happy; making people very happy 指高興的、快樂的、令人愉快的

blissful making people very happy; showing this happiness 指令人愉快的、極樂的、幸福的：*three blissful weeks away* 無憂無慮的三週假期

JOYFUL OR BLISSFUL? 用 joyful 還是 blissful？

Joy is a livelier feeling; **bliss** is more peaceful. * joy 較活躍和富活力，bliss 則較平和。

PATTERNS

- happy/satisfied/content/contented **with** sth
- a happy/satisfied/contented/blissful **smile**
- a happy/joyful **occasion/celebration**
- to **feel** happy/satisfied/content/contented/joyful
- **very/perfectly/quite** happy/satisfied/content/contented

happy-clappy /ˌhæpi ˈklæpi/ *adj.* (*BrE*, often *disapproving*) connected with a Christian group which worships in a very loud and enthusiastic way, showing a lot of feeling（基督教祈禱儀式等）熱情過頭的

ˌhappy ˈfamilies noun [U] a children's card game played with special cards with pictures of family members on them. The aim is to get as many whole families as possible. 快樂家庭紙牌遊戲（用家庭成員照片進行，贏得最多完整家庭紙牌者獲勝）

IDM **ˌplay happy ˈfamilies** to do things that normal happy families do, especially when you want it to appear that your family is happy 做快樂家庭所做的事：*I'm not going to play happy families just for the benefit of your parents.* 我不會僅僅為了顧全你父母而裝出合家歡的假象。

ˌhappy-go-ˈlucky *adj.* not caring or worrying about the future 無憂無慮的；樂天的：*a happy-go-lucky attitude* 無憂無慮的態度 ◇ *a happy-go-lucky sort of person* 樂天派的人

ˈhappy hour noun [usually sing.] (*informal*) a time, usually in the early evening, when a pub or a bar sells alcoholic drinks at lower prices than usual 歡樂時光（酒吧的減價時段）

ˈhappy slapping noun (*BrE*) [U] the practice of several people attacking sb while another person in the group makes a film of the attack 開心掌摑（指幾人圍毆一人，由同夥將襲擊畫面拍下）

hap·tic /ˈhæptɪk/ *adj.* (*technical* 術語) relating to or involving the sense of touch 觸覺的；與觸覺有關的：*Players use a haptic device such as a joystick to control the game.* 遊戲者用遊戲桿之類的觸覺設備玩遊戲。

hara-kiri /ˌhærə ˈkɪri; *NAmE* ˌherə ˈkeri/ noun [U] (from *Japanese*) an act of killing yourself by cutting open your stomach with a SWORD, performed especially by the SAMURAI in Japan in the past, to avoid losing honour 切腹，剖腹自盡（尤指舊時日本武士為免受屈辱而自殺的行為）

har·am·bee /həˈræmbiː/ noun (*EAfrE*) **1** [C] a meeting that is held in order to collect money for sth, for example a community project（為社區項目等舉行的）募捐會，籌款會：*They held a harambee meeting to raise funds for a new classroom.* 他們為籌款建新教室而辦了個募捐會。 **2** [U] the act of joining with other people to achieve a difficult task 齊心協力：*the spirit of harambee* 眾志成城的精神

har·angue /həˈræŋ/ verb, noun

- **verb ~ sb** to speak loudly and angrily in a way that criticizes sb/sth or tries to persuade people to do sth 呵斥；大聲譴責；慷慨激昂地勸說
- **noun** a long loud angry speech that criticizes sb/sth or tries to persuade people to do sth 義憤填膺的譴責；慷慨激昂的勸說

har·ass /ˈhærəs; həˈræs/ verb **1** [often passive] **~ sb** to annoy or worry sb by putting pressure on them or saying or doing unpleasant things to them 侵擾；騷擾：*He has complained of being harassed by the police.* 他投訴受到警方侵擾。◇ *She claims she has been* ***sexually harassed*** *at work.* 她聲稱在工作中受到性騷擾。 **2 ~ sb/sth** to make repeated attacks on an enemy 不斷攻擊（敵人） SYN **harry** ▸ **har·ass·ment** noun [U]：***racial/sexual harassment*** 種族侵擾；性騷擾

har·assed /ˈhærəst; həˈræst/ *adj.* tired and anxious because you have too much to do 疲憊焦慮的：*a harassed-looking waiter* 愁眉苦臉的服務員 ◇ *harassed mothers with their children* 帶着孩子的疲憊不堪的母親們

har·bin·ger /ˈhɑːbɪndʒə(r); *NAmE* ˈhɑːrb-/ noun **~ (of sth)** (*formal* or *literary*) a sign that shows that sth is going to happen soon, often sth bad（常指壞的）預兆，兆頭

har·bour (*especially US* **har·bor**) /ˈhɑːbə(r); *NAmE* ˈhɑːrb-/ noun, verb

- **noun** [C, U] an area of water on the coast, protected from the open sea by strong walls, where ships can shelter

H

（海）港；港口；港灣：*Several boats lay at anchor in the harbour.* 港灣裏停泊着幾條船。◇ *to **enter/leave harbour*** 進入／離開港口 ➲ VISUAL VOCAB page V5
■ **verb 1 ~ sb** to hide and protect sb who is hiding from the police 窩藏，庇護（罪犯等）：*Police believe someone must be harbouring the killer.* 警方相信一定有人窩藏了殺人犯。**2 ~ sth** to keep feelings or thoughts, especially negative ones, in your mind for a long time 懷有，心懷（尤指反面感情或想法）：*The arsonist may **harbour a grudge** against the company.* 縱火犯可能對公司懷恨在心。◇ *She began to harbour doubts about the decision.* 她開始對這個決定產生懷疑。**3 ~ sth** to contain sth and allow it to develop 包含；藏有：*Your dishcloth can harbour many germs.* 洗碗布中可能藏有很多病菌。

ˈharbour master (*especially US* **har·bor·mas·ter**) *noun* an official in charge of a harbour 港務長

hard 🔑 /hɑːd; *NAmE* hɑːrd/ *adj., adv.*

H

■ **adj.** (**hard·er, hard·est**)
▸ **SOLID/STIFF** 堅固；堅硬 **1** 🔑 solid, firm or stiff and difficult to bend or break 堅固的；堅硬的；結實的：*Wait for the concrete to go hard.* 等待混凝土凝結。◇ *a hard mattress* 硬牀墊 ◇ *Diamonds are the hardest known mineral.* 鑽石是已知的最堅硬的礦石。**OPP** soft
▸ **DIFFICULT** 不易 **2** 🔑 difficult to do, understand or answer 難做的；難懂的；難以回答的：*a hard choice/question* 為難的選擇；難以回答的問題 ◇ **~ to do sth** *It is **hard to believe** that she's only nine.* 很難相信她只有九歲。◇ *It's **hard to see** how they can lose.* 很難理解他們怎麼會輸。◇ *'When will the job be finished?' 'It's **hard to say**.'* (= it is difficult to be certain) "這項工作什麼時候能完成？" "難說。" ◇ *I find his attitude very **hard to take*** (= difficult to accept). 他的態度讓我難以接受。◇ *We're finding reliable staff **hard to come by*** (= difficult to get). 我們覺得難以找到可靠的職員。◇ **~ for sb (to do sth)** *It's hard for old people to change their ways.* 老年人難以改變他們的習慣。◇ *It must be hard for her, bringing up four children on her own.* 她一個人撫養四個孩子一定很艱難。**OPP** easy **3** 🔑 full of difficulty and problems, especially because of a lack of money 困苦的；艱苦的；艱難的 **SYN** tough：*Times were hard at the end of the war.* 戰爭後期生活很艱苦。◇ *She's had a hard life.* 她一生艱苦。**OPP** easy
▸ **NEEDING/USING EFFORT** 費力；用力 **4** 🔑 needing or using a lot of physical strength or mental effort 耗費體力（或腦力）的；辛苦的：*It's **hard work** shovelling snow.* 鏟雪是個苦活兒。◇ *I've had a long hard day.* 我度過了漫長辛苦的一天。➲ SYNONYMS at DIFFICULT **5** 🔑 (of people 人) putting a lot of effort or energy into an activity 努力的；勤勞的：*She's a very hard worker.* 她工作很賣力。◇ *He's **hard at work** on a new novel.* 他正努力忙着寫一本新小說。◇ *When I left they were all still **hard at it*** (= working hard). 我離開的時候他們都還在努力工作。➲ SYNONYMS at DIFFICULT **6** 🔑 done with a lot of strength or force 用力的；猛烈的：*He gave the door a good hard kick.* 他狠狠踢了一下門。◇ *a hard punch* 砰的一拳
▸ **WITHOUT SYMPATHY** 缺乏同情心 **7** 🔑 showing no sympathy or affection 冷酷無情的；硬心腸的；苛刻的：*My father was a hard man.* 我父親是個不講情面的人。◇ *She gave me a hard stare.* 她狠狠地看了我一眼。◇ *He said some very hard things to me.* 他對我說了些很不近人情的話。
▸ **NOT AFRAID** 不畏懼 **8** (*informal*) (of people 人) ready to fight and showing no signs of fear or weakness 準備戰鬥的；不軟弱退縮的：*Come and get me if you think you're hard enough.* 你要是覺得自己有種，就衝着我來吧。◇ *You think you're really hard, don't you?* 你是不是以為自己真的很勇猛？
▸ **FACTS/EVIDENCE** 事實；證據 **9** [only before noun] definitely true and based on information that can be proved 確鑿的；可證實的；可靠的：*Is there any **hard evidence** either way?* 不管正反，有什麼確鑿證據嗎？◇ *The newspaper story is based on **hard facts**.* 報紙的這篇報道有可靠的事實根據。
▸ **WEATHER** 天氣 **10** very cold and severe 寒冷的；凜冽的：*It had been a **hard winter**.* 那年的冬天特別冷。◇ *There was a **hard frost** that night.* 那天晚上寒冷多霜。➲ compare MILD *adj.* (2)
▸ **DRINK** 飲料 **11** [only before noun] strongly alcoholic 酒精濃度高的；烈性的：***hard liquor*** 烈酒 ◇ (*informal*) *a drop of **the hard stuff*** (= a strong alcoholic drink) 少許烈酒 ➲ compare SOFT DRINK
▸ **WATER** 水 **12** containing CALCIUM and other mineral salts that make mixing with soap difficult 硬的（含鈣及鎂鹽較多）：*a **hard water** area* 硬水區 ◇ *Our water is very hard.* 我們的水很硬。**OPP** soft
▸ **CONSONANTS** 輔音 **13** (*phonetics* 語音) used to describe a letter *c* or *g* when pronounced as in 'cat' or 'go', rather than as in 'city' or 'giant' 硬音的（如字母 c 或 g 在 cat 或 go 等詞中的發音）**OPP** soft
▸ **hard·ness** *noun* [U]：*water hardness* 水的硬度 ◇ *hardness of heart* 硬心腸

IDM **be ˈhard on sb/sth 1** 🔑 to treat or criticize sb in a very severe or strict way 嚴厲對待，嚴格批評（某人或某事）：*Don't be too hard on him—he's very young.* 別對他太苛刻了，他還很小呢。**2** 🔑 to be difficult for or unfair to sb/sth 使…為難；對…不公平：*It's hard on people who don't have a car.* 對於沒有車的人來說，這不公平。**3** to be likely to hurt or damage sth 可能損傷，可能損壞（某物）：*Looking at a computer screen all day can be very hard on the eyes.* 成天盯着計算機屏幕可能會對眼睛造成嚴重損害。**drive/strike a hard ˈbargain** to argue in an aggressive way and force sb to agree on the best possible price or arrangement 狠狠地殺價 **give sb a hard ˈtime** to deliberately make a situation difficult and unpleasant for sb 給某人找茬兒；使某人不好過：*They really gave me a hard time at the interview.* 面試時他們確實是在難為我。**ˌhard and ˈfast** (especially after a negative 尤用於否定詞後) that cannot be changed in any circumstances 板上釘釘；不容更改：*There are **no hard and fast rules** about this.* 這事沒有什麼硬性的規定。**(as) ˌhard as ˈnails** showing no sympathy, kindness or fear 冷酷無情；鐵石心腸；毫無懼色 **ˌhard ˈcheese** (*BrE, informal*) used as a way of saying that you are sorry about sth, usually IRONICALLY (= you really mean the opposite)（常作反話）太不幸了，真夠倒霉 **ˌhard ˈgoing** difficult to understand or needing a lot of effort 難懂；費力：*I'm finding his latest novel very hard going.* 我覺得他最近的這部小說很晦澀。**ˌhard ˈluck/ˈlines** (*BrE*) used to tell sb that you feel sorry for them（表示惋惜）真遺憾，太不幸了：*'Failed again, I'm afraid.' 'Oh, hard luck.'* "恐怕我又失敗了。" "哦，太不幸了。" **the ˈhard way** by having an unpleasant experience or by making mistakes 通過痛苦的經歷；通過出錯：*She won't listen to my advice so she'll just have to **learn the hard way**.* 她不肯聽我的忠告，所以只好吃了苦頭才知道厲害。**make hard ˈwork of sth** to use more time or energy on a task than is necessary 在某事上耗費過多時間（或精力）；費冤枉力 **no hard ˈfeelings** used to tell sb you have been arguing with or have beaten in a contest that you would still like to be friendly with them（向爭論或打敗的對方表示繼續友好）別往心裏去，別記恨：*It looks like I'm the winner again. No hard feelings, Dave, eh?* 看來我又贏了。你不會不高興吧，戴夫？**play hard to ˈget** (*informal*) to make yourself seem more attractive or interesting by not immediately accepting an invitation to do sth 故作姿態；故意擺譜；佯裝拿架子 **too much like hard ˈwork** needing too much effort 太費力：*I can't be bothered making a hot meal—it's too much like hard work.* 我懶得做熱飯熱菜，太麻煩了。➲ more at ACT *n.*, JOB, LONG *adj.*, NUT *n.*, ROCK *n.*

■ **adv.** (**hard·er, hard·est**)
▸ **WITH EFFORT** 努力 **1** 🔑 with great effort; with difficulty 努力地；費力地；艱難地：*to **work hard*** 努力工作 ◇ *You must **try harder**.* 你得更加努力。◇ *She **tried her hardest** not to show how disappointed she was.* 她竭力不流露出自己有多失望。◇ *Don't hit it so hard!* 別這麼用力打！◇ *He was still breathing hard after his run.* 他跑完步，現在還氣喘吁吁的。◇ *Our victory was hard won* (= won with great difficulty). 我們的勝利來之不易。
▸ **WITH FORCE** 猛力 **2** 🔑 with great force 猛力地；猛烈地：(*figurative*) *Small businesses have been **hit hard/hard hit** by the recession.* 小企業受到了經濟衰退的沉重打擊。

▸ CAREFULLY 仔細 **3** very carefully and thoroughly 徹底認真地： *to think hard* 認真思考 ◇ *We thought **long and hard** before deciding to move house.* 我們經過長久慎重的考慮之後才決定搬家。

▸ A LOT 大量 **4** heavily; a lot or for a long time 沉重地；大量地；長時間地： *It was **raining hard** when we set off.* 我們出發時正下着大雨。

▸ LEFT/RIGHT 左；右 **5** at a sharp angle to the left/right 向左（或右）急轉彎： *Turn hard right at the next junction.* 在下個路口處向右急轉彎。

IDM **be/feel hard 'done by** (*informal*) to be or feel unfairly treated 受到不公平待遇；感到委屈： *She has every right to feel hard done by—her parents have given her nothing.* 她覺得委屈完全合理，她父母什麼都沒給她。 **be ˌhard 'pressed/'pushed to do sth | be hard 'put (to it) to do sth** to find it very difficult to do sth 很難做某事： *He was hard put to it to explain her disappearance.* 他覺得她的消失很難解釋得通。 **be hard 'up for sth** to have too few or too little of sth 某物匱乏： *We're hard up for ideas.* 我們再想不出主意了。 ➲ see also HARD UP **'hard on sth** very soon after 緊接着： *His death followed hard on hers.* 她死後不久，他也死了。 **take sth 'hard** to be very upset by sth 為某事很苦惱（或難受）： *He took his wife's death very hard.* 他對妻子的死感到很難過。 ➲ more at DIE *v.*, HEEL *n.*

Which Word? 詞語辨析

hard / hardly

- The adverb from the adjective **hard** is **hard**. 形容詞 hard 的副詞為 hard： *I have to work hard today.* 今天我得努力工作。◇ *She has thought very hard about her future plans.* 她曾經悉心思考她未來的計劃。◇ *It was raining hard outside.* 外面雨下得很大。
- **Hardly** is an adverb meaning 'almost not'. * hardly 為副詞，意為幾乎不、幾乎沒有： *I hardly ever go to concerts.* 我很少去聽音樂會。◇ *I can hardly wait for my birthday.* 我迫切等待着我的生日。 It cannot be used instead of **hard**. 該詞不能代替 hard： ~~*I've been working hardly today.*~~ ◇ ~~*She has thought very hardly about her future plans.*~~ ◇ ~~*It was raining hardly outside.*~~

➲ note at HARDLY

hard·back /'hɑːdbæk; *NAmE* 'hɑːrd-/ (also **hard·cover** especially in *NAmE*) *noun* [C, U] a book that has a stiff cover 精裝書： *What's the price of the hardback?* 精裝本多少錢？◇ *It was published **in hardback** last year.* 這書去年以精裝本出版。◇ ***hardback books/editions*** 精裝書；精裝本 ➲ compare PAPERBACK

hard·ball /'hɑːdbɔːl; *NAmE* 'hɑːrd-/ *noun* (*NAmE*) **1** the game of BASEBALL (when contrasted with SOFTBALL) 棒球運動（與壘球運動相對） **2** used to refer to a way of behaving, especially in politics, that shows that a person is determined to get what they want 果敢，果決（尤指政治手段）： *I want us to **play hardball** on this issue.* 我希望我們在這個問題上不手軟。◇ *hardball politics* 強硬政治

hard·bit·ten /ˌhɑːd'bɪtn; *NAmE* ˌhɑːrd-/ *adj.* not easily shocked and not showing emotion, because you have experienced many unpleasant things 久經磨練而堅強的

hard·board /'hɑːdbɔːd; *NAmE* 'hɑːrdbɔːrd/ *noun* [U] a type of stiff board made by crushing very small pieces of wood together into thin sheets 硬質纖維板（由碎木壓成）

ˌhard-'boiled *adj.* **1** (of an egg 雞蛋) boiled until the inside is hard 煮老的；煮硬的 ➲ compare SOFT-BOILED **2** (of people 人) not showing much emotion 不動感情的；不流露情感的

ˌhard 'by *prep.* (*old-fashioned*) very near sth 很接近；臨近 ▸ **ˌhard 'by** *adv.*

ˌhard 'candy (*NAmE*) (*BrE* **ˌboiled 'sweet**) *noun* [U] a hard sweet/candy made from boiled sugar, often with fruit flavours 硬糖（常有水果味）

ˌhard 'cash (*BrE*) (*NAmE* **ˌcold 'cash**) *noun* [U] money, especially in the form of coins and notes, that you can spend 現金（尤指硬幣和紙幣）

ˌhard-'charging *adj.* [only before noun] working or performing with a lot of energy and skill 熟練且有幹勁的；全力進取的： *He changed from a goofy kid to a hard-charging soldier.* 他從傻乎乎的孩子變成了勇猛幹練的士兵。

'hard cider (*NAmE*) (*BrE* **cider**) *noun* [U, C] an alcoholic drink made from the juice of apples 蘋果酒

ˌhard-'code *verb* **~ sth** (*computing* 計) to write data so that it cannot easily be changed 編寫硬代碼，硬編碼（編碼不能被輕易更改）

ˌhard 'copy *noun* [U, C] (*computing* 計) information from a computer that has been printed on paper 硬拷貝，打印件（打印出的計算機資料） ➲ VISUAL VOCAB page V69

ˌhard 'core *noun* (*BrE*) **1** [sing.+sing./pl. v.] the small central group in an organization, or in a particular group of people, who are the most active or who will not change their beliefs or behaviour 核心力量；骨幹；中堅力量： *It's really only the hard core that bother(s) to go to meetings.* 也只有那些骨幹分子願意去開會。◇ *A hard core of drivers ignores the law.* 部份頑固的駕車人無視這項法律。 **2** [U] (usually **'hardcore**) small pieces of stone, brick, etc. used as a base for building roads on 路基碎磚石；路基墊層

ˌhard-'core *adj.* **1** having a belief or a way of behaving that will not change 中堅的；骨幹的： *hard-core party members* 核心黨員 **2** showing or describing sexual activity in a detailed or violent way （關於性愛）露骨的，赤裸裸的： *They sell **hard-core pornography**.* 他們出售赤裸裸的色情物品。 ➲ compare SOFT-CORE

ˌhard 'court *noun* an area with a hard surface for playing TENNIS on, not grass 硬地網球場

hard·cover /'hɑːdkʌvə(r); *NAmE* 'hɑːrd-/ *noun* (*especially NAmE*) = HARDBACK

ˌhard 'currency *noun* [U, C] money that is easy to exchange for money from another country, because it is not likely to lose its value 硬通貨（幣值穩定，容易兌換）

ˌhard 'disk *noun* a disk inside a computer that stores data and programs 硬盤；硬碟 ➲ VISUAL VOCAB page V66 ➲ compare FLOPPY DISK

ˌhard 'disk recorder *noun* a DIGITAL recording system that records sound or video directly to a hard disk, without using tape 硬盤錄製系統；硬碟錄製器（直接將數字音頻或視頻錄製到硬盤）

'hard-drinking *adj.* drinking a lot of alcohol 大量飲酒的；海量的

'hard drive *noun* (*computing* 計) a part of a computer that reads data on a HARD DISK 硬盤驅動器；硬碟驅動器

ˌhard 'drug *noun* [usually pl.] a powerful illegal drug, such as HEROIN, that some people take for pleasure and can become ADDICTED to 硬性毒品（容易成癮） ➲ compare SOFT DRUG

ˌhard-'earned *adj.* that you get only after a lot of work and effort 辛勤掙來的；來之不易的： *hard-earned cash* 用汗水換來的錢 ◇ *We finally managed a hard-earned draw.* 我們終於追成了平局。

ˌhard-'edged *adj.* powerful, true to life and not affected by emotion 客觀逼真的： *the movie's hard-edged realism* 那部電影逼真的現實主義

hard·en /'hɑːdn; *NAmE* 'hɑːrdn/ *verb* **1** [I, T] to become or make sth become firm, stiff or solid （使）變硬，硬化： *The varnish takes a few hours to harden.* 清漆需要幾個小時才能乾透。◇ **~ sth** *a method for hardening and preserving wood* 硬化和保存木料的方法 **2** [I, T] if your voice, face, etc. **hardens**, or you **harden** it, it becomes more serious or severe （使聲音、面孔等）更嚴肅，更嚴厲： *Her face hardened into an expression of hatred.*

H

她的臉沉下來，面帶恨意。◇ **~ sth** *He hardened his voice when he saw she wasn't listening.* 看到她沒在聽他講話，他聲音嚴厲起來。 **3** [I, T] if sb's feelings or attitudes **harden** or sb/sth **hardens** them, they become more fixed and determined （使）更堅定，更強硬：*Public attitudes to the strike have hardened.* 公眾對這次罷工所持的態度已強硬起來。◇ *Their suspicions hardened into certainty.* 他們由懷疑變成肯定。◇ **~ sth** *The incident hardened her resolve to leave the company.* 這件事使她更加堅定了離開公司的決心。 **4** [T, usually passive] **~ sb/sth/yourself** to make sb less kind or less affected by extreme situations 使變得無情；使不被打動：*Joe sounded different, hardened by the war.* 喬讓人覺得變了，因戰爭變得冷酷無情了。◇ *They were* ***hardened criminals*** (= they showed no regret for their crimes). 他們都是死不悔改的罪犯。◇ *In this job you have to* ***harden your heart*** *to pain and suffering.* 做這項工作面對傷痛和病患時你得保持沉着冷靜。 ▶ **hard·en·ing** *noun* [U, sing.]：*hardening of the arteries* 動脈硬化 ◇ *a hardening of attitudes towards one-parent families* 對單親家庭態度的冷漠化

ˌhard-ˈfaced *adj.* (*disapproving*) (of a person 人) showing no feeling or sympathy for other people 缺乏同情心的；麻木不仁的

ˌhard-ˈfought *adj.* that involves fighting very hard 艱苦鬥爭的；激烈戰鬥的：***a hard-fought battle/win/victory*** 激烈的戰鬥；來之不易的勝利

ˌhard ˈhat *noun* a hat worn by building workers, etc. to protect their heads 安全帽（建築工人等戴）➲ VISUAL VOCAB page V65

ˌhard-ˈheaded *adj.* determined and not allowing your emotions to affect your decisions 堅定而不感情用事的；精明冷靜的

ˌhard-ˈhearted *adj.* giving no importance to the feelings or problems of other people 鐵石心腸的；無情的 ➲ compare SOFT-HEARTED

ˌhard-ˈhitting *adj.* not afraid to talk about or criticize sb/sth in an honest and very direct way 直言不諱的；單刀直入的：*a hard-hitting speech* 直言不諱的講話

ˌhard ˈlabour (*especially US* **ˌhard ˈlabor**) *noun* [U] punishment in prison that involves a lot of very hard physical work 勞役；苦役

ˌhard ˈleft *noun* [sing.+sing./pl. v.] (*especially BrE*) the members of a LEFT-WING political party who have the most extreme opinions 極左派：*hard-left policies* 極左派政策

ˌhard ˈline *noun* [sing.] a strict policy or attitude 強硬政策（或態度）：*the judge's hard line against drug dealers* 法官對待毒品販子的堅定態度 ◇ *The government* ***took a hard line on*** *the strike.* 政府對罷工採取了強硬態度。

ˌhard-ˈline *adj.* [usually before noun] **1** (of a person 人) having very fixed beliefs and being unlikely or unwilling to change them 有堅定信仰的；不妥協的：*a hard-line conservative* 鐵杆的保守黨支持者 **2** (of ideas 思想) very fixed and unlikely to change 堅定的；堅決的：*a hard-line attitude* 堅定的態度 ▶ **hard·liner** /ˌhɑːdˈlaɪnə(r); *NAmE* ˌhɑːrd-/ *noun*：*a Republican hardliner* 一名共和黨的忠實黨員

ˌhard-ˈluck story *noun* a story about yourself that you tell sb in order to get their sympathy or help（為博得他人同情或幫助而訴說的）不幸的遭遇

hard·ly 🗝 /ˈhɑːdli; *NAmE* ˈhɑːrd-/ *adv.*
1 🗝 almost no; almost not; almost none 幾乎不；幾乎沒有：*There's* ***hardly any*** *tea left.* 沒有剩什麼茶了。◇ *Hardly anyone has bothered to reply.* 幾乎沒人開口回答。◇ *She* ***hardly ever*** *calls me* (= almost never). 她幾乎從未給我來過電話。◇ *We hardly know each other.* 我們彼此還不大認識呢。◇ ***Hardly a day goes by without*** *my thinking of her* (= I think of her almost every day). 我幾乎天天想着她。 **2** 🗝 used especially after 'can' or 'could' and before the main verb, to emphasize that it is difficult to do sth（尤用於 can 或 could 之後，主要動詞之前，強調做某事很難）：*I can hardly keep my eyes open* (= I'm almost falling asleep). 我睏得都快睜不開眼了。◇ ***I could hardly believe*** *it when I read the letter.* 讀到那封信時，我簡直不敢相信。 **3** 🗝 used to say that sth has just begun, happened, etc. 剛剛；才：*We can't stop for coffee now, we've hardly started.* 現在不能停下來喝咖啡，我們剛剛才開始工作呢。◇ *We had hardly sat down to supper when the phone rang.* 我們剛坐下用晚餐，電話就響了。◇ (*formal*) *Hardly had she spoken than she regretted it bitterly.* 話剛出口，她就後悔不迭。 **4** 🗝 used to suggest that sth is unlikely or unreasonable or that sb is silly for saying or doing sth（表示不大可能、不合理或愚蠢）：*He is hardly likely to admit he was wrong.* 他不大可能承認自己錯了。◇ *It's* ***hardly surprising*** *she was fired; she never did any work.* 她被解雇了不足為怪；她從來沒幹過任何工作。◇ *It's* ***hardly the time*** *to discuss it now.* 現在並不是討論的時候。◇ *You* ***can hardly*** *expect her to do it for free.* 你不可能指望她無償地做這事。◇ *'Couldn't you have just said no?' 'Well, hardly* (= of course not), *she's my wife's sister.'* "你不能就說聲不嗎？" "喔，不可能，她是我小姨子。" ➲ note at HARD

Grammar Point 語法說明

hardly / scarcely / barely / no sooner

- **Hardly**, **scarcely** and **barely** can all be used to say that something is only just true or possible. They are used with words like *any* and *anyone*, with adjectives and verbs, and are often placed between *can*, *could*, *have*, *be*, etc. and the main part of the verb.
  * hardly、scarcely 和 barely 均可指幾乎不，與 any 和 anyone 等詞以及形容詞和動詞連用，常置於 can、could、have、be 等和主要動詞之間：*They have sold scarcely any copies of the book.* 這書他們幾乎沒賣出幾本。◇ *I barely recognized her.* 我幾乎認不出她了。◇ *His words were barely audible.* 他的話勉強聽得見。◇ *I can hardly believe it.* 我幾乎不敢相信。◇ ~~*I hardly can believe it.*~~
- **Hardly**, **scarcely** and **barely** are negative words and should not be used with *not* or other negatives.
  * hardly、scarcely 和 barely 為否定詞，不應與 not 或其他否定詞連用：~~*I can't hardly believe it.*~~
- You can also use **hardly**, **scarcely** and **barely** to say that one thing happens immediately after another.
  亦可用 hardly、scarcely 和 barely 表示剛…就…：*We had hardly/scarcely/barely sat down at the table, when the phone rang.* 我們剛在桌子旁坐下電話鈴就響了。 In formal, written English, especially in a literary style, these words can be placed at the beginning of the sentence and then the subject and verb are turned around. 在正式的書面英語中，尤其在文學體中，上述各詞可置於句首，然後將主語和動詞的位置倒裝：*Hardly/Scarcely had we sat down at the table, when the phone rang.* 我們剛在桌子旁坐下電話鈴就響了。 Note that you usually use *when* in these sentences, not *than*. You can also use *before*. 注意：在這類句子中通常用 when 而非 than，亦可用 before：*I scarcely had time to ring the bell before the door opened.* 我剛一按門鈴，門就開了。
  No sooner can be used in the same way, but is always used with *than*. * no sooner 與上述詞用法相同，但總與 than 連用：*No sooner had we sat down at the table than the phone rang.* 我們剛在桌子旁坐下電話鈴就響了。
- **Hardly** and **scarcely** can be used to mean 'almost never', but **barely** is not used in this way. * hardly 和 scarcely 可表示幾乎從不、難得，但 barely 不這樣用：*She hardly (ever) sees her parents these days.* 這些日子她難得見到她父母。◇ ~~*She barely sees her parents these days.*~~

ˌhard-ˈnosed *adj.* not affected by feelings when trying to get what you want 頑強的；不屈不撓的；不講情面的：*a hard-nosed journalist* 不屈不撓的記者

ˌhard of ˈhearing *adj.* [not before noun] **1** unable to hear very well 聽力弱；耳背 **2** **the hard of hearing** *noun* [pl.] people who are unable to hear very well 聽力

弱的人；耳背的人：*subtitles for the deaf and the hard of hearing* 為耳聾和聽力不佳者打出的字幕

ˈhard-on *noun* (*taboo, slang*) an ERECTION (1) 陰莖勃起

ˌhard ˈporn *noun* [U] (*informal*) films/movies, pictures, books, etc. that show sexual activity in a very detailed and sometimes violent way 色情電影（或圖片、書刊等） ➲ compare SOFT PORN

ˌhard-ˈpressed *adj.* **1** having a lot of problems, especially too much work, and too little time or money 處於強大壓力下的（尤指工作重、時間緊迫、資金少） **2 ~ to do sth** finding sth very difficult to do 很難（做某事）：*You would be hard-pressed to find a better secretary.* 找一位更好的秘書很難。

ˌhard ˈright *noun* [sing.+sing./pl. v.] (*especially BrE*) the members of a RIGHT-WING political party who have the most extreme opinions 極右派：*hard-right opinions* 極右派觀點

ˌhard ˈrock *noun* [U] a type of loud rock music with a very strong beat, played on electric GUITARS 硬搖滾樂（用電吉他演奏，節奏強勁）

ˌhard ˈscience *noun* **1** [U] science that is based on the objective measurement and observation of physical facts or events 硬科學（以客觀量度和觀察物質數據為準） **2** [C] a science that involves the objective measurement and observation of physical facts or events, such as physics and chemistry 硬科學學科（如物理、化學）

hard·scrab·ble /ˌhɑːdˈskræbl; *NAmE* ˌhɑːrd-/ *adj.* (*NAmE*) not having enough of the basic things you need to live 艱難困苦的；貧困的；勉強維持的：*a* ***hardscrabble life/upbringing*** 貧困的生活；艱苦的成長

ˌhard ˈsell *noun* [sing.] a method of selling that puts a lot of pressure on the customer to buy 強行推銷 ➲ compare SOFT SELL

hard·ship /ˈhɑːdʃɪp; *NAmE* ˈhɑːrd-/ *noun* [U, C] a situation that is difficult and unpleasant because you do not have enough money, food, clothes, etc. 艱難；困苦；拮据：***economic/financial, etc. hardship*** 經濟、財政等困難 ◇ *People suffered many hardships during that long winter.* 在那個漫長的冬季，人們吃了很多苦頭。◇ *It was* ***no hardship*** *to walk home on such a lovely evening.* 在這麼一個宜人的傍晚步行回家一點也不辛苦。

ˌhard ˈshoulder (*BrE*) (*US* **ˈbreakdown lane**) *noun* [sing.] a strip of ground with a hard surface beside a major road such as a MOTORWAY or INTERSTATE where vehicles can stop in an emergency 硬質路肩（在高速公路旁，可供緊急停車）：*to pull over onto the hard shoulder/into the breakdown lane* 把車開到硬質路肩 / 故障檢修道

hard·top /ˈhɑːdtɒp; *NAmE* ˈhɑːrdtɑːp/ *noun* a car with a metal roof 硬頂小汽車

ˌhard ˈup *adj.* (*informal*) **1** having very little money, especially for a short period of time 拮据的，缺錢的（尤指暫時性的） ➲ note at POOR **2 ~ (for sth)** lacking in sth interesting to do, talk about, etc. 無所事事的；無聊的：*'You could always go out with Steve.' 'I'm not that hard up!'* "你總可以和史蒂夫出去玩玩吧。" "我還沒無聊到那個地步呢！"

hard·ware /ˈhɑːdweə(r); *NAmE* ˈhɑːrdwer/ *noun* [U] **1** (*computing* 計) the machinery and electronic parts of a computer system 硬件；硬體 ➲ compare SOFTWARE **2** (*BrE* also **iron·mon·gery**) tools and equipment that are used in the house and garden/yard （家庭及園藝用）工具，設備，五金製品：*a hardware shop* 五金店 **3** the equipment, machinery and vehicles used to do sth 硬件設備；機器；車輛：*tanks and other military hardware* 坦克和其他軍事裝備

ˈhardware dealer *noun* (*NAmE*) **1** (*BrE*, becoming *old-fashioned* **iron·mon·ger**) a person who owns or works in a shop/store selling tools and equipment for the house and garden/yard 五金商人 **2** (*BrE* **ironmonger's**) a shop that sells tools and equipment for the house and garden/yard 五金商店

ˌhard-ˈwearing *adj.* (*BrE*) that lasts a long time and remains in good condition 經久耐用的：*a hard-wearing carpet* 耐磨的地毯

ˌhard-ˈwired *adj.* **1** (*technical* 術語) (of computer functions 計算機功能) built into the permanent system and not provided by software 硬（佈）線的；硬接連的 **2** (of a skill, quality or type of behaviour) present when you are born and not changing during your life （某種技能、品質或行為等）與生俱來的，固有的：*Many aspects of morality appear to be hard-wired in the brain.* 道德的許多觀念似乎是人們與生俱來便根植在腦中的。

ˌhard-ˈwon *adj.* [usually before noun] that you only get after fighting or working hard for it 經奮鬥（或努力）得到的；來之不易的：*She was not going to give up her hard-won freedom so easily.* 她不會這麼輕易地放棄得來不易的自由。

hard·wood /ˈhɑːdwʊd; *NAmE* ˈhɑːrd-/ *noun* [U, C] hard heavy wood from a BROADLEAVED tree 硬材（硬木闊葉樹種的木材） ➲ compare SOFTWOOD

ˌhard-ˈworking *adj.* putting a lot of effort into a job and doing it well 工作努力的；辛勤的：*hard-working nurses* 辛勤的護士

hardy /ˈhɑːdi; *NAmE* ˈhɑːrdi/ *adj.* (**har·dier**, **har·di·est**) **1** strong and able to survive difficult conditions and bad weather 能吃苦耐勞的；適應力強的：*a hardy breed of sheep* 適應力強的綿羊品種 **2** (of a plant 植物) that can live outside through the winter 耐寒的；能越冬的 ▸ **hardi·ness** *noun* [U]

hare /heə(r); *NAmE* her/ *noun, verb*

■ ***noun*** an animal like a large RABBIT with very strong back legs, that can run very fast 野兔 ➲ picture at RABBIT **IDM** see MAD

■ ***verb*** [I] **+ adv./prep.** (*BrE*) to run or go somewhere very fast 飛跑；疾走

hare·bell /ˈheəbel; *NAmE* ˈherbel/ (*ScotE* **blue·bell**) *noun* a wild plant with delicate blue flowers shaped like bells 圓葉風鈴草

ˈhare-brained *adj.* (*informal*) crazy and unlikely to succeed 瘋狂的；輕率的：*a* ***hare-brained scheme/idea/theory*** 輕率的計劃 / 想法 / 理論

Hare Krishna /ˌhɑːreɪ ˈkrɪʃnə; ˌhæri/ *noun* **1** [U] a religious group whose members wear orange ROBES and use the name of the Hindu god Krishna in their worship 國際黑天覺悟會，哈里 • 克里希那（宗教派別，崇信印度教黑天神） **2** [C] a member of this religious group 國際黑天覺悟會成員；克里希那教徒

hare·lip /ˈheəlɪp; *NAmE* ˈherlɪp/ *noun* an old-fashioned and now offensive word for CLEFT LIP 兔唇，唇裂（舊式用語，含冒犯意，現稱 cleft lip）

harem /ˈhɑːriːm; -rəm; *NAmE* ˈhærəm/ *noun* **1** the women or wives belonging to a rich man, especially in some Muslim societies in the past 哈來姆（尤指舊時某些穆斯林社會中富人的女眷） **2** the separate part of a traditional Muslim house where the women live （穆斯林傳統住宅中的）閨閣，閨房 **3** (*technical* 術語) a group of female animals that share the same male for reproducing 繁殖群（和同一雄性動物交配的一群雌性動物）

hari·cot /ˈhærɪkəʊ; *NAmE* -koʊ/ (also **ˌharicot ˈbean**) (both *BrE*) (*NAmE* **ˈnavy bean**) *noun* a type of small white BEAN that is usually dried before it is sold and then left in water before cooking 菜豆；芸豆；扁豆

hark /hɑːk; *NAmE* hɑːrk/ *verb* [I] (*old use*) used only as an order to tell sb to listen （用於命令）聽着，聽

PHR V **ˈhark at sb** (*BrE, informal*) used only as an order to draw attention to sb who has just said sth stupid or who is showing too much pride （僅用作命令）聽聽某人的蠢話，看某人的傲慢樣子：*Just hark at him! Who does he think he is?* 瞧他那副德行！他以為他是誰呀？ **ˌhark ˈback (to sth)** **1** to remember or talk about sth that happened in the past 回憶起，重提（過去的事）：*She's always harking back to how things used to be.* 她總是念叨以前的世道。 **2** to remind you of, or to be like, sth in the past 使想起；和（過去的事物）相似：*The newest styles hark back to the clothes of the Seventies.* 最新的款式使人想起 70 年代的服裝。

har·ken = HEARKEN

Har·le·quin /ˈhɑːləkwɪn; *NAmE* ˈhɑːrl-/ *noun* an amusing character in some traditional plays, who wears special brightly coloured clothes with a diamond pattern（傳統戲劇中穿色彩斑斕菱形花紋服裝的）滑稽角色

Har·ley Street /ˈhɑːli striːt; *NAmE* ˈhɑːrli/ *noun* a street in central London in which many private doctors have their offices where they talk to and examine patients 哈利街（倫敦市中心街道，很多私人醫生在此設門診）：*a Harley Street doctor* 哈利街的醫生

har·lot /ˈhɑːlət; *NAmE* ˈhɑːrlət/ *noun* (*old use, disapproving*) a PROSTITUTE, or a woman who looks and behaves like one 妓女；蕩婦

harm 0‑ /hɑːm; *NAmE* hɑːrm/ *noun, verb*

■ **noun** 0‑ [U] damage or injury that is caused by a person or an event 傷害；損害：*He would never frighten anyone or* **cause** *them* **any harm**. 他永遠不會嚇唬或傷害任何人。◇ *He may look fierce, but he* **means no harm**. 他可能看上去很兇，但並無惡意。◇ *The court case will* **do serious harm to** *my business.* 這起訴訟案件將嚴重損害我的生意。◇ *The accident could have been much worse; luckily* **no harm was done**. 這次事故本來可能糟糕得多；所幸沒有造成傷害。◇ *Don't worry, we'll see that the children* **come to no harm**. 別擔心，我們會保證孩子們安然無恙的。◇ *I can't say I like Mark very much, but I don't* **wish him any harm**. 我不能說我很喜歡馬克，但我並不願他遭到傷害。◇ *Hard work* **never did anyone any harm**. 努力工作對任何人都絕無害處。◇ *Look, we're just going out for a few drinks,* **where's the harm in that?** 瞧，我們只不過要出去喝幾杯，這有什麼壞處？◇ *The treatment they gave him did him* **more harm than good**. 他們的治療對他弊多於利。

IDM **it wouldn't do sb any harm (to do sth)** used to suggest that it would be a good idea for sb to do sth（做某事）不會對某人有壞處；不妨：*It wouldn't do you any harm to smarten yourself up.* 你不妨打扮一下。 **ˌno ˈharm done** (*informal*) used to tell sb not to worry because they have caused no serious damage or injury 沒造成嚴重損害（或傷害） **out of harm's ˈway** in a safe place where sb/sth cannot be hurt or injured or do any damage to sb/sth 在安全的地方；被隔離 **there is no harm in (sb's) doing sth | it does no harm (for sb) to do sth** used to tell sb that sth is a good idea and will not cause any problems 做某事是個好主意（或沒有壞處）：*He may say no, but there's no harm in asking.* 他可能拒絕，但問一問也無妨。◇ *It does no harm to ask.* 問一問也無妨。

■ **verb** 0‑ **~ sb/sth** to hurt or injure sb or to damage sth 傷害；損害：*He would never harm anyone.* 他永遠不會傷害任何人。◇ *Pollution can harm marine life.* 污染會危及海洋生物。◇ *These revelations will harm her chances of winning the election.* 這些揭露的事實將不利於她贏得選舉。 IDM see FLY *n.*, HAIR ➲ **SYNONYMS** at DAMAGE

harm·ful 0‑ /ˈhɑːmfl; *NAmE* ˈhɑːrmfl/ *adj.* (*rather formal*) causing damage or injury to sb/sth, especially to a person's health or to the environment（尤指對健康或環境）有害的，導致損害的：*the harmful effects of alcohol* 酒精的害處 ◇ *the sun's harmful ultra-violet rays* 太陽的有害紫外線 ◇ *Many household products are potentially harmful.* 很多家用產品有潛在的危害。◇ **~ to sb/sth** *Fruit juices can be harmful to children's teeth.* 果汁可能損壞兒童的牙齒。 ▸ **harm·fully** /-fəli/ *adv.* **harm·ful·ness** *noun* [U]

harm·less 0‑ /ˈhɑːmləs; *NAmE* ˈhɑːrm-/ *adj.*
1 0‑ **~ (to sb/sth)** unable or unlikely to cause damage or harm 無害的；不會導致損傷的：*The bacteria is harmless to humans.* 這種細菌對人類無害。 **2** 0‑ unlikely to upset or offend anyone 不會引起不快的；無惡意的 SYN **innocuous**：*It's just a bit of harmless fun.* 開個小玩笑罷了，並無惡意的。 ▸ **harm·less·ly** *adv.*：*The missile fell harmlessly into the sea.* 導彈落到了海裏，沒有造成任何傷害。 **harm·less·ness** *noun* [U]

har·mon·ic /hɑːˈmɒnɪk; *NAmE* hɑːrˈmɑːn-/ *adj., noun*

■ **adj.** [usually before noun] (*music* 音) relating to the way notes are played or sung together to make a pleasing sound 和聲的

■ **noun** [usually pl.] (*music* 音) **1** a note that sounds together with the main note being played and is higher and quieter than that note 泛音 **2** a high quiet note that can be played on some instruments like the VIOLIN by touching the string very lightly 和聲

har·mon·ica /hɑːˈmɒnɪkə; *NAmE* hɑːrˈmɑːn-/ (*BrE* also **ˈmouth organ**) *noun* a small musical instrument that you hold near your mouth and play by blowing or sucking air through it 口琴

har·mo·ni·ous /hɑːˈməʊniəs; *NAmE* hɑːrˈmoʊ-/ *adj.* **1** (of relationships, etc. 關係等) friendly, peaceful and without any disagreement 友好和睦的；和諧的 **2** arranged together in a pleasing way so that each part goes well with the others 協調的；和諧的 SYN **pleasing**：*a harmonious combination of colours* 協調的色彩搭配 **3** (of sounds 聲音) very pleasant when played or sung together 和諧的；諧調的 ▸ **har·mo·ni·ous·ly** *adv.*：*They worked very harmoniously together.* 他們合作得十分融洽。

har·mo·nium /hɑːˈməʊniəm; *NAmE* hɑːrˈmoʊ-/ *noun* a musical instrument like a small organ. Air is forced through metal pipes to produce the sound and the different notes are played on the keyboard. 簧風琴（鍵盤樂器，以氣流使簧片振動發聲）

har·mon·ize (*BrE* also **-ise**) /ˈhɑːmənaɪz; *NAmE* ˈhɑːrm-/ *verb* **1** [I] **~ (with sth)** if two or more things **harmonize** with each other or one thing **harmonizes** with the other, the things go well together and produce an attractive result（和某事物）協調，和諧：*The new building does not harmonize with its surroundings.* 那棟新樓與周圍環境不協調。 **2** [T] **~ sth** to make systems or rules similar in different countries or organizations 使（不同國家或組織的體制或規則）相一致；使協調：*the need to harmonize tax levels across the European Union* 使歐盟各國的稅收標準相一致的必要 **3** [I] **~ (with sb/sth)** to play or sing music that combines with the main tune to make a pleasing sound 為（主調）配和聲 ▸ **har·mon·iza·tion, -isa·tion** /ˌhɑːmənaɪˈzeɪʃn; *NAmE* ˌhɑːrmənəˈz-/ *noun* [U, C]

har·mony /ˈhɑːməni; *NAmE* ˈhɑːrm-/ *noun* (*pl.* **-ies**) **1** [U] a state of peaceful existence and agreement 融洽；和睦：*the need to* **be in harmony with** *our environment* 同我們的環境協調的必要 ◇ *to live together in perfect harmony* 十分和睦地一同生活 ◇ ***social/racial harmony*** 社會 / 種族融洽 ➲ compare DISCORD (1) **2** [U, C] (*music* 音) the way in which different notes that are played or sung together combine to make a pleasing sound 和聲：*to sing in harmony* 用和聲唱 ◇ *to study four-part harmony* 研究四部和聲 ◇ *passionate lyrics and stunning vocal harmonies* 充滿激情的歌詞和絕妙的和聲演唱 ➲ compare DISCORD (2) **3** [C, U] a pleasing combination of related things 和諧；協調：*the harmony of colour in nature* 自然界色彩的協調

har·ness /ˈhɑːnɪs; *NAmE* ˈhɑːrnɪs/ *noun, verb*

■ **noun** **1** a set of strips of leather and metal pieces that is put around a horse's head and body so that the horse can be controlled and fastened to a CARRIAGE, etc. 馬具；挽具 **2** a set of strips of leather, etc. for fastening sth to a person's body or to keep them from moving off or falling（防止人移動或墜落的）背帶，保護帶：*a safety harness* 安全帶

IDM **in ˈharness** (*BrE*) doing your normal work, especially after a rest or a holiday（尤指休息或假期結束後）做正常工作 **in harness (with sb)** (*BrE*) working closely with sb in order to achieve sth（同某人）聯手；密切合作

■ **verb** **1** to put a harness on a horse or other animal; to attach a horse or other animal to sth with a harness 給（馬等）上挽具；用挽具把…套到…上：**~ sth** *to harness a horse* 給馬上挽具 ◇ **~ sth to sth** *We harnessed two ponies to the cart.* 我們把兩匹矮種馬套到了車上。◇ (*figurative*) *In some areas, the poor feel harnessed to their jobs.* 有些地區的窮人感覺終身被套牢在他們的工作上。 **2 ~ sth** to control and use the force or strength of sth to produce power or to achieve sth 控制，利用（以產生能量等）：*attempts to harness the sun's rays as a source of energy* 利用日光作為能源的嘗試 ◇ *We must harness the skill and creativity of our workforce.* 我們必須盡量發揮全體職工的技能和創造力。

harp /hɑːp; *NAmE* hɑːrp/ *noun, verb*
■ ***noun*** a large musical instrument with strings stretched on a vertical frame, played with the fingers 豎琴 ➲ VISUAL VOCAB page V34 ➲ see also JEW'S HARP
■ ***verb***
PHR V **ˌharp ˈon (about sth)** | **ˈharp on sth** to keep talking about sth in a boring or annoying way 喋喋不休地談論；嘮叨

harp·ist /ˈhɑːpɪst; *NAmE* ˈhɑːrp-/ *noun* a person who plays the harp 豎琴演奏者

har·poon /hɑːˈpuːn; *NAmE* hɑːrˈp-/ *noun, verb*
■ ***noun*** a weapon like a SPEAR that you can throw or fire from a gun and is used for catching large fish, WHALES, etc. 漁獵標槍；魚叉
■ ***verb* ~ sth** to hit sth with a harpoon 用魚叉叉

harp·si·chord /ˈhɑːpsɪkɔːd; *NAmE* ˈhɑːrpsɪkɔːrd/ *noun* an early type of musical instrument similar to a piano, but with strings that are PLUCKED (= pulled), not hit 撥弦鍵琴；羽管鍵琴

harp·si·chord·ist /ˈhɑːpsɪkɔːdɪst; *NAmE* ˈhɑːrpsɪkɔːrd-/ *noun* a person who plays the harpsichord 撥弦鍵琴演奏者

harpy /ˈhɑːpi; *NAmE* ˈhɑːrpi/ *noun* (*pl.* **-ies**) **1** (in ancient Greek and Roman stories) a cruel creature with a woman's head and body and a bird's wings and feet 鳥身女妖，哈比（古希臘和羅馬神話中的怪物） **2** a cruel woman 兇殘的女子

har·ri·dan /ˈhærɪdən/ *noun* (*old-fashioned* or *literary*) a bad-tempered unpleasant woman 脾氣暴躁的討厭女人；潑婦

har·rier /ˈhæriə(r)/ *noun* a BIRD OF PREY (= a bird that kills other creatures for food) of the HAWK family 鷂（鷹科猛禽）

har·row /ˈhærəʊ; *NAmE* -roʊ/ *noun* a piece of farming equipment that is pulled over land that has been PLOUGHED to break up the earth before planting 耙 ▶ **har·row** *verb* **~ sth**

har·row·ing /ˈhærəʊɪŋ; *NAmE* -roʊ-/ *adj.* very shocking or frightening and making you feel very upset 恐怖的；令人腸斷的；使人十分難過的

har·rumph /həˈrʌmf/ *verb* [I] (*informal*) to express disagreement or disapproval, especially by making a sound in your throat like a cough（表示不同意而）乾咳 ▶ **har·rumph** *noun* [sing.]

harry /ˈhæri/ *verb* (**har·ries**, **harry·ing**, **har·ried**, **har·ried**) (*formal*) **1 ~ sb** to annoy or upset sb by continuously asking them questions or for sth（不斷）煩擾；折磨 SYN **harass**：*She has been harried by the press all week.* 整個星期她都受到新聞界的不斷煩擾。 **2 ~ sb/sth** to make repeated attacks on an enemy 反複進攻；不斷襲擊 SYN **harass**

harsh /hɑːʃ; *NAmE* hɑːrʃ/ *adj.* (**harsh·er**, **harsh·est**) **1** cruel, severe and unkind 殘酷的；嚴酷的；嚴厲的：*The punishment was harsh and unfair.* 處罰很重而且不公平。◇ *The minister received some* ***harsh criticism***. 部長受到了嚴厲的批評。◇ *the harsh treatment of slaves* 對奴隸的虐待 ◇ *He regretted his harsh words.* 他對自己的刻薄言辭感到後悔。◇ *We had to face up to the* ***harsh realities*** *of life sooner or later.* 我們遲早都得正視生活的嚴酷現實。 **2** (of weather or living conditions 天氣或生活環境) very difficult and unpleasant to live in 惡劣的；艱苦的：*a* ***harsh winter/wind/climate*** 寒冷的冬天；凜冽的風；惡劣的氣候 ◇ *the harsh conditions of poverty which existed for most people at that time* 那時大多數人所面對的艱苦境況 **3** too strong and bright; ugly or unpleasant to look at 強烈刺眼的；醜陋的：*harsh colours* 扎眼的色彩 ◇ *She was caught in the harsh glare of the headlights.* 她遭到車前燈的強光照射。◇ *the harsh lines of concrete buildings* 混凝土建築物的粗陋線條 OPP **soft 4** unpleasant to listen to 刺耳的；難聽的：*a harsh voice* 刺耳的嗓音 **5** too strong and rough and likely to damage sth 粗糙的；毛糙的；刺激性強的：*harsh detergents* 刺激性強的洗滌劑 ▶ **harsh·ly** *adv.*：*She was treated very harshly.* 她受到了苛刻的對待。◇ *Alec laughed harshly.* 亞歷克刺耳地大笑。 **harsh·ness** *noun* [U]

hart /hɑːt; *NAmE* hɑːrt/ *noun* a male DEER, especially a RED DEER; a STAG 雄鹿（尤指雄赤鹿） ➲ compare BUCK *n.* (2), HIND *n.*

harum-scarum /ˌheərəm ˈskeərəm; *NAmE* ˌherəm ˈskerəm; ˌhærəm ˈskærəm/ *adj.* (*old-fashioned*) behaving in a wild and sometimes careless way 魯莽的；莽撞的

har·vest /ˈhɑːvɪst; *NAmE* ˈhɑːrv-/ *noun, verb*
■ ***noun* 1** [C, U] the time of year when the crops are gathered in on a farm, etc.; the act of cutting and gathering crops 收穫季節；收割；收穫：*harvest time* 收穫季節 ◇ *Farmers are extremely busy during the harvest.* 農民在收穫季節裏十分忙碌。 **2** [C] the crops, or the amount of crops, cut and gathered 收成；收穫量：*the grain harvest* 穀物的收成 ◇ *a* ***good/bad harvest*** (= a lot of crops or few crops) 豐收；歉收 ◇ (*figurative*) *The appeal produced a rich harvest of blankets, medicines and clothing.* 呼籲的成果頗豐，收到了大批毛毯、藥物和衣服。 IDM see REAP
■ ***verb* 1** [I, T] **~ (sth)** to cut and gather a crop; to catch a number of animals or fish to eat 收割（莊稼）；捕獵（動物、魚） ➲ COLLOCATIONS at FARMING **2** [T] **~ sth** (*medical* 醫) to collect cells or TISSUE from sb's body for use in medical experiments or operations 採集（人體的細胞或組織，以供醫學實驗等）：*She had her eggs harvested and frozen for her own future use.* 她的卵子已經採集下來，冷凍後以備她將來使用。

har·vest·er /ˈhɑːvɪstə(r); *NAmE* ˈhɑːrv-/ *noun* **1** a machine that cuts and gathers grain 收割機 ➲ see also COMBINE HARVESTER at COMBINE *n.* (1) **2** (*old-fashioned*) a person who helps to gather in the crops 收割莊稼的人

ˌharvest ˈfestival *noun* a service held in Christian churches when people thank God for the crops that have been gathered 秋收感恩節 ➲ compare THANKSGIVING (1)

ˌharvest ˈmoon *noun* [sing.] a full moon in the autumn/fall nearest the time when day and night are of equal length 穫月（最接近秋分的滿月） ➲ compare FULL MOON, HALF-MOON (1)

has /həz; əz; *strong form* hæz/ ➲ HAVE

has-been /ˈhæz biːn/ *noun* (*informal, disapproving*) a person who is no longer as famous, successful or important as they used to be 一度有名（或成功、重要）的人物；曾紅極一時的人物；過氣名人

hash /hæʃ/ *noun, verb*
■ ***noun* 1** [U, C] a hot dish of cooked meat and potatoes that are cut into small pieces and mixed together 肉丁土豆泥 **2** [U] (*informal*) = HASHISH **3** (also **ˈhash sign**) (both *BrE*) (*NAmE* **ˈpound sign**) [C] the symbol (#), especially one on a telephone（尤指電話上的）井號 (#)
IDM **make a ˈhash of sth** (*informal*) to do sth badly 把某事弄糟：*I made a real hash of the interview.* 我的面試糟透了。
■ ***verb***
PHR V **ˌhash sth↔ˈout** (*informal, especially NAmE*) to discuss sth thoroughly in order to reach an agreement or decide sth 充分討論（以達成協議或決定）

ˌhash ˈbrowns *noun* [pl.] (*NAmE*) a dish of chopped potatoes and onions, fried until they are brown 洋蔥土豆煎餅

hash·ish /ˈhæʃiːʃ; hæˈʃiːʃ/ (also *informal* **hash**) *noun* [U] a drug made from the RESIN of the HEMP plant, which gives a feeling of being relaxed when it is smoked or chewed. Use of the drug is illegal in many countries. 哈希什，大麻麻醉劑（吸食或咀嚼時有放鬆感。很多國家的法律禁止服用該毒品） SYN **cannabis**

Has·id·ism (also **Has·sid·ism**) /ˈhæsɪdɪzəm/ *noun* [U] a form of the Jewish religion which has very strict beliefs 哈西德教派（猶太教的一支，有嚴格教義） ▶ **Hasid** (also **Has·sid**) /ˈhæsɪd/ *noun* **Has·id·ic** (also **Has·sid·ic**) /hæˈsɪdɪk/ *adj.*

hasn't /ˈhæznt/ *short form* has not

hasp /hɑːsp; *NAmE* hæsp/ *noun* a flat piece of metal with a long narrow hole in it, used with a PADLOCK to fasten doors, boxes, etc.（門、箱子等掛鎖的）搭扣

Has·sid·ism = HASIDISM

has·sium /ˈhæsiəm/ *noun* [U] (*symb.* **Hs**) a chemical element. Hassium is produced when atoms COLLIDE (= crash into each other). 𨭆（化學元素）

has·sle /ˈhæsl/ *noun, verb*

▪ ***noun*** [C, U] (*informal*) **1** a situation that is annoying because it involves doing sth difficult or complicated that needs a lot of effort 困難；麻煩：*Send them an email—it's a lot less hassle than phoning.* 給他們發個電郵吧，這比打電話省事多了。◇ *legal hassles* 法律程序的繁複 **2** a situation in which people disagree, argue or annoy you 分歧；爭論；煩惱：*Do as you're told and don't give me any hassle!* 告訴你怎麼做就怎麼做，別跟我頂嘴！

▪ ***verb*** **~ sb (for sth/to do sth)** (*informal*) to annoy sb or cause them trouble, especially by asking them to do sth many times （不斷）煩擾，麻煩 **SYN** **bother**：*Don't keep hassling me! I'll do it later.* 別老煩我！我晚一點會做的。

has·sock /ˈhæsək/ *noun* **1** a thick firm CUSHION on which you rest your knees when saying prayers in a church 跪墊（在教堂祈禱時用） **2** (*NAmE*) (*BrE* **pouffe**) a large thick CUSHION used as a seat or for resting your feet on（厚實的）坐墊，腳墊

hast /hæst/ **thou hast** (*old use*) a way of saying 'you have'（you have 的意思）

haste /heɪst/ *noun* [U] (*formal*) speed in doing sth, especially because you do not have enough time 急速；匆忙；倉促 **SYN** **hurry**：*In her haste to complete the work on time, she made a number of mistakes.* 她急急忙忙想按時完工，結果出了不少錯。◇ *The letter had clearly been written* ***in haste***. 這封信明顯是在匆忙中寫的。◇ *After his first wife died, he married again with almost indecent haste.* 他的第一任妻子死後，他幾乎是迫不及待地就再婚了。◇ (*old-fashioned*) *She* ***made haste*** *to open the door.* 她急忙打開門。

IDM **ˌmore ˈhaste, ˌless ˈspeed** (*BrE, saying*) you will finish doing sth sooner if you do not try to do it too quickly because you will make fewer mistakes 欲速則不達 ➲ more at MARRY

has·ten /ˈheɪsn/ *verb* **1** [I] **~ to do sth** to say or do sth without delay 急忙進行；趕緊說（或做）：*She saw his frown and hastened to explain.* 看到他皺起眉頭，她趕緊解釋。◇ *He has been described as a 'charmless bore'—not by me, **I hasten to add**.* 他被說成是"無聊的囉嗦鬼"——不是我說的，我趕忙加了一句。 **2** [T] **~ sth** (*formal*) to make sth happen sooner or more quickly 促進；使加快：*The treatment she received may, in fact, have hastened her death.* 實際上，她所接受的治療可能加快了她的死亡。◇ *News of the scandal certainly hastened his departure from office.* 這一醜聞肯定加速了他的離任。 **3** [I] **+ adv./prep.** (*literary*) to go or move somewhere quickly 趕往（某地） **SYN** **hurry**

hasty /ˈheɪsti/ *adj.* (**hasti·er, hasti·est**) **1** said, made or done very quickly, especially when this has bad results 匆忙的；倉促而就的；草率的 **SYN** **hurried**：*a hasty departure/meal/farewell* 急急忙忙的離去／用餐／辭別 ◇ *Let's not make any hasty decisions.* 我們不要匆忙做決定。 **2 ~ in doing sth** (of a person 人) acting or deciding too quickly, without enough thought 倉促行事；草率做出決定；考慮不周密：*Perhaps I was too hasty in rejecting his offer.* 我拒絕他的提議也許過於草率了。 **IDM** see BEAT *v.* ▸ **hasti·ly** /-ɪli/ *adv.*：*Perhaps I spoke too hastily.* 或許我說話太急了些。◇ *She hastily changed the subject.* 她匆匆換了個話題。

hat 0⊸ /hæt/ *noun*

1 0⊸ a covering made to fit the head, often with a BRIM, (= a flat edge that sticks out) and worn out of doors （常指帶簷的）帽子：*a straw/woolly, etc. hat* 草帽、毛線帽等 ◇ *to **put on/take off a hat*** 戴／脫帽子 ➲ VISUAL VOCAB page V65 **2** (*informal*) a position or role, especially an official or professional role, when you have more than one such role（雙重的）職位，角色（尤指官職或職業角色）：*I'm wearing two hats tonight—parent and teacher.* 我今晚身兼兩職，既是家長又是老師。◇ *I'm telling you this with my lawyer's hat on, you understand.* 你要明白，我是以律師的身分告訴你這事。➲ see also OLD HAT

IDM **go hat in ˈhand (to sb)** (*NAmE*) (*BrE* **go cap in ˈhand (to sb)**) to ask sb for sth, especially money, in a very polite way that makes you seem less important 謙卑地要，恭敬地討（尤指錢） **keep sth under your ˈhat** (*informal*) to keep sth secret and not tell anyone else 將某事保密 **ˌmy ˈhat** (*old-fashioned, BrE*) used to express surprise（表示驚奇） **out of a/the ˈhat** if sth such as a name is picked **out of a/the hat**, it is picked at RANDOM from a container into which all the names are put, so that each name has an equal chance of being picked, in a competition, etc. 隨機抽出 **I take my ˈhat off to sb | hats off to sb** (both *especially BrE*) (*NAmE* usually **I tip my ˈhat to sb**) (*informal*) used to say that you admire sb very much for sth they have done（表示敬佩） **throw your ˈhat into the ring** to announce officially that you are going to compete in an election, a competition, etc. 正式宣佈參加競選（或比賽等）➲ more at DROP *n.*, EAT, KNOCK *v.*, PASS *v.*, PULL *v.*, TALK *v.*

hat·band /ˈhætbænd/ *noun* a band of cloth placed around a hat as decoration 帽帶（圍着帽作裝飾）

hat·box /ˈhætbɒks; *NAmE* -bɑːks/ *noun* a round box used for keeping a hat in, to stop it from being crushed or damaged 帽盒

hatch /hætʃ/ *verb, noun*

▪ ***verb*** **1** [I] **~ (out)** (of a young bird, fish, insect, etc. 小鳥、小魚、小蟲等) to come out of an egg 孵出；出殼：*Ten chicks hatched (out) this morning.* 今早有十隻小雞出殼了。 **2** [I] **~ (out)** (of an egg 蛋) to break open so that a young bird, fish, insect, etc. can come out 孵化；破殼：*The eggs are about to hatch.* 這些蛋就要孵化了。➲ COLLOCATIONS at LIFE **3** [T] **~ sth** to make a young bird, fish, insect, etc. come out of an egg 使（小鳥、小魚、小蟲等）孵出：*The female must find a warm place to hatch her eggs.* 母的必須找個温暖的地方孵蛋。 **4** [T] **~ sth (up)** to create a plan or an idea, especially in secret 策劃；（尤指）密謀：*Have you been hatching up a deal with her?* 你是不是在和她密謀什麼交易？ **IDM** see COUNT *v.*

▪ ***noun*** **1** (also **hatch·way**) an opening or a door in the DECK of a ship or the bottom of an aircraft, through which goods to be carried are passed（船甲板或飛機底部裝貨物的）艙口 **2** an opening in a wall between two rooms, especially a kitchen and a DINING ROOM, through which food can be passed（尤指廚房和餐廳之間供傳遞食物的）兩室之間的小窗口：*a serving hatch* 傳遞飯菜的窗口 **3** a door in an aircraft or a SPACECRAFT（飛機或宇宙飛船的）艙門：*an escape hatch* 緊急出口 **4** an opening or a door in a floor or ceiling（地面或天花板的）開口，門，蓋子：*a hatch to the attic* 通閣樓的門

IDM **ˌdown the ˈhatch** (*informal, saying*) used before drinking sth, especially to express good wishes before drinking alcohol 乾杯（尤作祝酒辭）➲ more at BATTEN *v.*

hatch·back /ˈhætʃbæk/ *noun* a car with a sloping door at the back that opens upwards 掀背式汽車 ➲ VISUAL VOCAB page V52

hatch·ery /ˈhætʃəri/ *noun* (*pl.* **-ies**) a place for HATCHING eggs as part of a business 孵化處；孵化場：*a trout hatchery* 鱒魚孵化場

hatchet /ˈhætʃɪt/ *noun* a small AXE (= a tool with a heavy blade for chopping things) with a short handle 短柄小斧 ➲ picture at AXE **IDM** see BURY

ˈhatchet-faced *adj.* (*disapproving*) (of a person 人) having a long thin face and sharp features 臉瘦削而五官尖細的

ˈhatchet job *noun* [usually sing.] **~ (on sb/sth)** (*informal*) strong criticism that is often unfair and is intended to harm sb/sth 惡毒攻擊；誹謗；詆譭：*The press did a very effective hatchet job on her last movie.* 新聞界對她新近拍攝的電影大加詆譭。

'hatchet man *noun* (*informal*) a person employed by an organization to make changes that are not popular with the other people who work there "刀斧手"(受雇進行不受歡迎的改革的人)

hatch·ling /ˈhætʃlɪŋ/ *noun* a baby bird or animal which has just come out of its shell 剛出殼的雛鳥(或小動物)

hatch·way /ˈhætʃweɪ/ *noun* = HATCH *n.* (1)

Synonyms 同義詞辨析

hate

dislike • can't stand • despise • can't bear • loathe • detest

These words all mean to have a strong feeling of dislike for sb/sth. 以上各詞均含厭惡、討厭、憎惡之義。

hate to have a strong feeling of dislike for sb/sth 指厭惡、討厭、憎惡 NOTE Although **hate** is generally a very strong verb, it is also commonly used in spoken or informal English to talk about people or things that you dislike in a less important way, for example a particular type of food. 儘管 hate 通常為語氣很強的動詞，但亦常用於口語或非正式英語中，談論不太喜歡的人或物，如某種食物等：*He hates violence in any form.* 他憎惡任何形式的暴力。◇ *I've always hated cabbage.* 我從來都討厭吃捲心菜。

dislike (*rather formal*) to not like sb/sth 指不喜歡、厭惡 NOTE **Dislike** is a rather formal word; it is less formal, and more usual, to say that you *don't like* sb/sth, especially in spoken English. * dislike 為相當正式的用語，don't like 則較非正式，而且較常用，尤其在英語口語中：*I don't like it when you phone me so late at night.* 我不喜歡你夜裏這麼晚給我打電話。

can't stand (*rather informal*) used to emphasize that you really do not like sb/sth 強調不喜歡、受不了、不能容忍：*I can't stand his brother.* 他弟弟讓我受不了。◇ *She couldn't stand being kept waiting.* 叫她等着，她會受不了。

despise to dislike and have no respect for sb/sth 指鄙視、蔑視、看不起：*He despised himself for being so cowardly.* 他為自己如此怯懦而自慚形穢。

can't bear used to say that you dislike sth so much that you cannot accept or deal with it 指無法承受、應付不了：*I can't bear having cats in the house.* 家裏有貓我可受不了。

CAN'T STAND OR CAN'T BEAR? 用 can't stand 還是 can't bear？

In many cases you can use either word, but **can't bear** is slightly stronger and slightly more formal than **can't stand**. 在許多情況下，兩個短語可通用，但 can't bear 比 can't stand 語氣稍強，而且較正式。

loathe to hate sb/sth very much 指極不喜歡、厭惡：*They loathe each other.* 他們相互討厭。NOTE **Loathe** is generally an even stronger verb than **hate**, but it can also be used more informally to talk about less important things, meaning 'really don't like'. * loathe 通常比 hate 語氣還強，但亦可用於非正式場合指不太重要的事情，意為確實不喜歡：*Whether you love or loathe their music, you can't deny their talent.* 無論你是否喜歡他們的音樂，你都無法否認他們的才能。

detest (*rather formal*) to hate sb/sth very much 指厭惡、憎恨、討厭：*They absolutely detest each other.* 他們完全是相互憎恨。

PATTERNS

- I hate/dislike/can't stand/can't bear/loathe/detest **doing sth**.
- I hate/can't bear **to do sth**.
- I hate/dislike/can't stand/can't bear **it when** ...
- I **really** hate/dislike/can't stand/despise/can't bear/detest sb/sth
- I **absolutely** hate/can't stand/loathe/detest sb/sth

hate 🔑 /heɪt/ *verb, noun*

■ ***verb*** (not used in the progressive tenses 不用於進行時) **1** 🔑 to dislike sth very much 厭惡，討厭，憎惡(某事物)：**~ sth** *I hate spinach.* 我討厭菠菜。◇ *I hate Monday mornings.* 我討厭星期一早晨。◇ *I **hate it** when people cry.* 我厭煩別人哭。◇ *He **hated it** in France* (= did not like the life there). 他對法國的生活感到厭惡。◇ *I **hate the way** she always criticizes me.* 我對她不斷批評我很反感。◇ **~ doing sth** *She hates making mistakes.* 她討厭出錯。◇ **~ to do sth** *He hated to be away from his family.* 他很不願意離開家。◇ *She's a person who hates to make mistakes.* 她是個討厭出錯的人。◇ *I **hate to think** what would have happened if you hadn't been there.* 我真不敢想要是你不在那裏會出什麼事。◇ **~ sb/sth doing sth** *He hates anyone parking in his space.* 他討厭別人佔他的車位停車。◇ **~ sb/sth to do sth** *She would have hated him to see how her hands shook.* 她會很不願意讓他看到她的雙手抖得厲害。◇ *I'd hate anything to happen to him.* 但願他平安無事。**2** 🔑 to dislike sb very much 憎恨，憎惡，仇恨(某人)：**~ sb/yourself** *The two boys hated each other.* 那兩個男孩相互仇視。◇ *He was her most hated enemy.* 他是她最恨的人。◇ **~ sb/yourself for sth/for doing sth** *I hated myself for feeling jealous.* 我恨自己的嫉妒心。**3** [no passive] **~ to do sth** used when saying sth that you would prefer not to have to say, or when politely asking to do sth (表示不願說某事，或客氣地請求)不願，不想：*I **hate to say it**, but I don't think their marriage will last.* 我不願這麼說，但我覺得他們的婚姻不會長久。◇ *I hate to trouble you, but could I use your phone?* 我不願麻煩你，但我能用一下你的電話嗎？

▸ **hater** *noun*：*I'm not a woman hater, I just don't like Joan.* 我並非憎恨女人，只是不喜歡瓊。

IDM **hate sb's 'guts** (*informal*) to dislike sb very much 對某人恨之入骨

■ ***noun*** **1** 🔑 [U] a very strong feeling of dislike for sb 憎恨；厭惡；仇恨 SYN **hatred**：*a look of hate* 憎恨的目光 ◇ *a hate campaign* (= cruel comments made about sb over a period of time in order to damage their reputation) 對某人名譽的詆譭 ◇ ***hate mail*** (= letters containing cruel comments) 詆譭信件 **2** [C] (*informal*) a person or thing that you hate 所憎惡的人(或事物)：*Plastic flowers have always been a particular hate of mine.* 我一向特別厭惡塑料花。IDM see PET *adj.*

Which Word? 詞語辨析

hate / hatred

- These two words have a similar meaning. **Hatred** is more often used to describe a very strong feeling of dislike for a particular person or thing. 這兩個詞意義相似。hatred 較常用以指對某人或某事物的強烈仇恨、憎恨：*Her deep hatred of her sister was obvious.* 一眼便能看出她對姐姐恨之入骨。◇ *a cat's hatred of water* 貓對水的憎恨 **Hate** is more often used when you are talking about this feeling in a general way. * hate 較常用以泛指仇恨、憎恨、厭惡：*a look of pure hate* 充滿憎恨的目光 ◇ *people filled with hate* 充滿仇恨的人們

'hate crime *noun* **1** [U] violent acts that are committed against people because they are of a different race, because they are HOMOSEXUAL, etc. (因種族、同性戀等歧視引起的)仇恨犯罪，仇恨罪 **2** [C] a single act of this type 仇恨犯罪行為：*the victim of a hate crime* 仇恨犯罪的受害人

hate·ful /ˈheɪtfl/ *adj.* very unkind or unpleasant 可惡的；十分討厭的：*a hateful person/place/face* 可惡的人／地方／面孔 ◇ **~ to sb** *The idea of fighting against men of their own race was hateful to them.* 一想到要跟本族人交戰他們就十分難受。

hath /hæθ/ (*old use*) = HAS

hat·pin /ˈhætpɪn/ *noun* a long pin used for fastening a hat to your hair, especially in the past (尤指舊時的)女帽飾針，帽針

hat·red 0-n /ˈheɪtrɪd/ *noun* [U, C] a very strong feeling of dislike for sb/sth 仇恨；憎恨；厭惡：*He looked at me with intense hatred.* 他滿懷敵意地看着我。◇ *There was fear and hatred in his voice.* 他的聲音裏透露着恐懼和仇恨。◇ **~ (for/of sb/sth)** *She felt nothing but hatred for her attacker.* 她對攻擊她的人只有恨。◇ *a profound hatred of war* 對戰爭的深惡痛絕 ◇ **~ (towards sb)** *feelings of hatred towards the bombers* 對轟炸機的痛恨 ◇ *racial hatred* (= between people from different races) 種族仇恨 ◇ *The debate simply revived old hatreds.* 這一辯論不過是再次挑起了夙仇。➲ note at HATE

hat·stand /ˈhætstænd/ *noun* a vertical pole with large hooks around the top, for hanging hats and coats on 立式衣帽架

hat·ter /ˈhætə(r)/ *noun* (*old-fashioned*) a person who makes and sells hats 製帽者；帽商 IDM see MAD

H

ˈhat-trick *noun* three points, goals, etc. scored by the same player in a particular match or game; three successes achieved by one person （比賽或遊戲中）一人連得三分，一人連續三次取勝；帽子戲法：*to score a hat-trick* 上演帽子戲法

haughty /ˈhɔːti/ *adj.* (**haught·ier**, **haught·iest**) behaving in an unfriendly way towards other people because you think that you are better than them 傲慢的；高傲自大的 SYN **arrogant**：*a* ***haughty face/look/manner*** 自負的面容／神態／態度 ◇ *He replied with haughty disdain.* 他的回答充滿了不屑。▸ **haught·ily** /-ɪli/ *adv.* **haughti·ness** *noun* [U]

haul /hɔːl/ *verb, noun*

■ ***verb*** **1** to pull sth/sb with a lot of effort （用力）拖，拉，拽：**~ sth/sb** *The wagons were hauled by horses.* 那些貨車是馬拉的。◇ **~ sth/sb + adv./prep.** *He reached down and hauled Liz up onto the wall.* 他俯身把利茲拉上牆頭。➲ SYNONYMS at PULL **2 ~ yourself up/out of, etc.** to move yourself somewhere slowly and with a lot of effort 用力緩慢挪動到（某處）：*She hauled herself out of bed.* 她費勁地下了牀。**3 ~ sb + adv./prep.** to force sb to go somewhere they do not want to go 強迫（某人）去某處：*A number of suspects have been hauled in for questioning.* 一批嫌疑犯被拘捕接受訊問。**4** [usually passive] **~ sb (up) before sb/sth** to make sb appear in court in order to be judged 使某人出庭受審；把某人提交法庭：*He was hauled up before the local magistrates for dangerous driving.* 他因危險駕駛而被移交地方法庭審判。

IDM **haul sb over the ˈcoals** (*BrE*) (*NAmE* **rake sb over the ˈcoals**) to criticize sb severely because they have done sth wrong 嚴厲訓斥（或斥責）某人

■ ***noun*** **1** a large amount of sth that has been stolen or that is illegal 大批贓物；大量非法物品：*a haul of weapons* 大批非法武器 ◇ *a drugs haul* 一大批毒品 **2** (especially in sport 尤用於體育運動) a large number of points, goals, etc. 很高的得分：*His haul of 40 goals in a season is a record.* 他在一個賽季中得了 40 分，創下了紀錄。**3** [usually sing.] the distance covered in a particular journey 旅行的距離；旅程：*They began the long slow haul to the summit.* 他們踏上了攀登頂峰的漫長行程。◇ *Our camp is only a short haul from here.* 我們的營地離這裏很近。◇ *Take the coast road—it'll be less of a haul* (= an easier journey). 走海岸線吧，這樣會好走一些。➲ see also LONG HAUL, SHORT-HAUL **4** a quantity of fish caught at one time 一次捕獲的魚；一網魚

haul·age /ˈhɔːlɪdʒ/ *noun* [U] (*BrE*) the business of transporting goods by road or railway; money charged for this （公路或鐵路的）貨運，貨運費：*the road haulage industry* 公路貨運業 ◇ *a* ***haulage firm/contractor*** 陸路貨運公司／承包人 ◇ *How much is haulage?* 運費是多少？

haul·ier /ˈhɔːliə(r)/ (*BrE*) (*NAmE* **haul·er** /ˈhɔːlə(r)/) *noun* a person or company whose business is transporting goods by road or railway/railroad 陸路運輸業者；陸路貨運承運人；貨運公司

haunch /hɔːntʃ/ *noun* **1 haunches** [pl.] the tops of the legs and BUTTOCKS; the similar parts at the back of the body of an animal that has four legs 臀胯部；（四足動物的）腰腿：*to crouch/squat* ***on your haunches*** 蹲着 **2** [C] a back leg and LOIN of an animal that has four legs, eaten as food （四足動物可食用的）腰腿肉：*a haunch of venison* 一條鹿腰腿肉

haunt /hɔːnt/ *verb, noun*

■ ***verb*** **1 ~ sth/sb** if the GHOST of a dead person **haunts** a place, people say that they have seen it there （鬼魂）出沒：*A headless rider haunts the country lanes.* 一個無頭騎士常出沒於鄉間的小路上。**2 ~ sb** if sth unpleasant **haunts** you, it keeps coming to your mind so that you cannot forget it （不快的事情）縈繞於腦際，難以忘卻：*The memory of that day still haunts me.* 我的腦海中常常回想起那天的情景。◇ *For years she was haunted by guilt.* 多年來她一直感到愧疚。**3 ~ sb** to continue to cause problems for sb for a long time 長期不斷地纏擾（某人）：*That decision* ***came back to haunt him.*** 那個決定對他造成無法擺脫的困擾。

■ ***noun*** a place that sb visits often or where they spend a lot of time 常去的場所；消磨時光的去處：*The pub is a favourite haunt of artists.* 這家酒吧是藝術家最愛光顧的地方。

haunt·ed /ˈhɔːntɪd/ *adj.* **1** (of a building 建築物) believed to be visited by GHOSTS （被認為）鬧鬼的，有鬼魂出沒的：*a haunted house* 鬧鬼的房子 **2** (of an expression on sb's face 面部表情) showing that sb is very worried 憂心忡忡的；滿面愁容的：*There was a haunted look in his eyes.* 他眼中透露出憂慮的神色。

haunt·ing /ˈhɔːntɪŋ/ *adj.* beautiful, sad or frightening in a way that cannot be forgotten 縈繞心頭的；使人難忘的：*a* ***haunting melody/experience/image*** 難以忘懷的優美樂曲；痛苦難忘的經歷；嚇人難忘的形象 ▸ **haunt·ing·ly** *adv.*

Hausa /ˈhaʊsə; -zə/ *noun* [U] a language spoken by the Hausa people of W Africa, especially in Nigeria and Niger, and also used in other parts of W Africa as a language of communication between different peoples 豪薩語（現通用於尼日利亞、尼日爾和其他一些西非地區）

haute cou·ture /ˌəʊt kuˈtjʊə(r); *NAmE* ˌoʊt kuˈtʊr/ *noun* [U] (from *French*) the business of making fashionable and expensive clothes for women; the clothes made in this business 高檔女子時裝業；高檔女子時裝

haute cuis·ine /ˌəʊt kwɪˈziːn; *NAmE* ˌoʊt/ *noun* [U] (from *French*) cooking of a very high standard 高級烹飪

haut·eur /əʊˈtɜː(r); *NAmE* hɔːˈtɜːr; oʊˈt-/ *noun* [U] (*formal*) an unfriendly way of behaving towards other people suggesting that you think that you are better than they are 傲慢；高傲自大

have 0-n /həv; əv; *strong form* hæv/ *verb, auxiliary verb* ➲ IRREGULAR VERBS at page R5

■ ***verb*** (In some senses **have got** is also used, especially in British English. 作某些意義時也用 have got，尤其是英式英語。)

▸ **OWN/HOLD 擁有；持有 1** 0-n (also **have got**) **~ sth** (not used in the progressive tenses 不用於進行時) to own, hold or possess sth 有；持有；佔有：*He had a new car and a boat.* 他有一輛新車和一條船。◇ *Have you got a job yet?* 你有工作了嗎？◇ *I don't have that much money on me.* 我身上沒帶那麼多錢。◇ *She's got a BA in English.* 她有英語學士學位。

▸ **CONSIST OF 由…組成 2** 0-n (also **have got**) **~ sth** (not used in the progressive tenses 不用於進行時) be made up of 由…組成：*In 2008 the party had 10 000 members.* 這個黨在 2008 年時擁有 1 萬名黨員。

▸ **QUALITY/FEATURE 性質；特徵 3** 0-n (also **have got**) (not used in the progressive tenses 不用於進行時) to show a quality or feature 顯示出，帶有（性質、特徵）：**~ sth** *The ham had a smoky flavour.* 這火腿散發着一種煙熏的香味。◇ *The house has gas-fired central heating.* 這所房子有燃氣中央供暖系統。◇ *They have a lot of courage.* 他們勇氣十足。◇ **~ sth + adj.** *He's got a front tooth missing.* 他有一顆門牙掉了。**4** 0-n (also **have got**) **~ sth to do sth** (not used in the progressive tenses 不用於進行時) to show a particular quality by your actions （通過行動）表現出（品質）：*Surely she didn't have the nerve to say that to him?* 她一定沒有膽量跟他這樣說吧？

▸ **RELATIONSHIP** 關係 **5** ⊶ (also **have got**) **~ sb/sth** (not used in the progressive tenses 不用於進行時) used to show a particular relationship（表示關係）有： *He's got three children.* 他有三個孩子。◇ *Do you have a client named Peters?* 你們有一位名叫彼得斯的客戶嗎？

▸ **STH AVAILABLE** 可利用 **6** ⊶ (also **have got**) **~ sth** (not used in the progressive tenses 不用於進行時) to be able to make use of sth because it is available 能用： *Have you got time to call him?* 你有時間給他打電話嗎？◇ *We have no choice in the matter.* 我們在這件事上別無選擇。

▸ **SHOULD/MUST** 應該；必須 **7** ⊶ (also **have got**) **~ sth** (not used in the progressive tenses 不用於進行時) to be in a position where you ought to do sth 有責任（或義務）： *We have a duty to care for the refugees.* 我們有義務關懷這些難民。 **8** ⊶ (also **have got**) (not used in the progressive tenses 不用於進行時) to be in a position of needing to do sth 須要，有必要（做某事）： **~ sth** *I've got a lot of homework tonight.* 我今晚有很多家庭作業要做。◇ **~ sth to do** *I must go—I have a bus to catch.* 我必須走了，我得去趕公共汽車。

▸ **HOLD** 抓住 **9** ⊶ (also **have got**) (not used in the progressive tenses 不用於進行時) **~ sb/sth + adv./prep.** to hold sb/sth in the way mentioned 抓住；握着；支承： *She'd got him by the collar.* 她抓住了他的衣領。◇ *He had his head in his hands.* 他雙手抱着腦袋。

▸ **PUT/KEEP IN A POSITION** 放／保持在某位置 **10** ⊶ (also **have got**) **~ sth + adv./prep.** (not used in the progressive tenses 不用於進行時) to place or keep sth in a particular position 使放在；使保持（在）： *Mary had her back to me.* 瑪麗背對着我。◇ *I soon had the fish in a net.* 我不一會就網住了那條魚。

▸ **FEELING/THOUGHT** 感覺；思想 **11** ⊶ (also **have got**) (not used in the progressive tenses 不用於進行時) **~ sth** to let a feeling or thought come into your mind 感到；想到： *He had the strong impression that someone was watching him.* 他強烈地感覺到有人在監視他。◇ *We've got a few ideas for the title.* 關於名稱，我們有幾種想法。◇ (*informal*) ***I've got it!*** *We'll call it 'Word Magic'.* 我想到了！我們就叫它"文字魔術"吧。

▸ **ILLNESS** 病 **12** ⊶ (also **have got**) **~ sth** (not used in the progressive tenses 不用於進行時) to suffer from an illness or a disease 患病；得病；染病： *I've got a headache.* 我頭痛。

▸ **EXPERIENCE** 經歷 **13** ⊶ **~ sth** to experience sth 經受；經歷；經驗： *I went to a few parties and had a good time.* 我參加了幾次聚會，過得很愉快。◇ *I was having difficulty in staying awake.* 我正睏得睜不開眼。◇ *She'll have an accident one day.* 她總有一天會出事的。

▸ **EVENT** 活動 **14** ⊶ **~ sth** to organize or hold an event 組織；舉辦： *Let's have a party.* 我們辦一次聚會吧。

▸ **EAT/DRINK/SMOKE** 飲食；吸煙 **15** ⊶ **~ sth** to eat, drink or smoke sth 吃；喝；吸（煙等）： *to* ***have breakfast/lunch/dinner*** 吃早飯／午飯／正餐◇ *I'll have the salmon* (= for example, in a restaurant). 我要一份鮭魚。◇ *I had a cigarette while I was waiting.* 我等候時抽了一支煙。

▸ **DO STH** 做某事 **16** ⊶ **~ sth** to perform a particular action 進行（活動）： *I had a swim to cool down.* 我游了泳，涼快涼快。◇ (*BrE*) *to* ***have a wash/shower/bath*** 洗一下；沖淋浴；洗澡

▸ **GIVE BIRTH** 生 **17** ⊶ **~ sb/sth** to give birth to sb/sth 生；生產： *She's going to have a baby.* 她快生孩子了。

▸ **EFFECT** 效果 **18** ⊶ **~ sth** to produce a particular effect 產生（效果）： *His paintings had a strong influence on me as a student.* 我當學生時，他的畫對我產生過強烈的影響。◇ *The colour green has a restful effect.* 綠色使人感到寧靜。

▸ **RECEIVE** 接收 **19** ⊶ **~ sth** (not usually used in the progressive tenses 通常不用於進行時) to receive sth from sb 收到；接到： *I had a letter from my brother this morning.* 我今天早晨收到了弟弟的一封信。◇ ***Can I have*** *the bill, please?* 請給我賬單。 **20** ⊶ **~ sth** to be given sth; to have sth done to you 得到；接受；受到： *I'm having treatment for my back problem.* 我正接受背部疾患的治療。◇ *How many driving lessons have you had so far?* 你到目前為止上過多少節駕駛課了？ **21** ⊶ (also **have got**) (not used in the progressive tenses 不用於進行時) **~ sth doing sth** to experience the effects of sb's actions 接受（某人行為的效果）：*We have orders coming in from all over the world.* 我們接到來自世界各地的訂單。

▸ **HAVE STH DONE** 讓某事做成 **22** ⊶ (used with a past participle 與過去分詞連用) **~ sth done** to suffer the effects of what sb else does to you 蒙受（他人所為的後果）：*She had her bag stolen.* 她的包被偷了。**23** ⊶ (used with a past participle 與過去分詞連用) **~ sth done** to cause sth to be done for you by sb else 讓（他人）為你做（某事）：*You've had your hair cut!* 你理髮了！◇ *We're having our car repaired.* 我們的車正在修理。 **24** to tell or arrange for sb to do sth for you 要（或安排）（某人）做（某事）： **~ sb do sth** *He had the bouncers throw them out of the club.* 他叫保安人員把他們轟出了俱樂部。◇ (*informal*) ***I'll have you know*** (= I'm telling you) *I'm a black belt in judo.* 你聽着，我可是柔道黑帶級高手。◇ **~ sb + adv./prep.** *She's always having the builders in to do something or other.* 她總是讓建築工人到家裏來幹這幹那。

▸ **ALLOW** 允許 **25** (used in negative sentences, especially after *will not*, *cannot*, etc. 用於否定句，尤置於 will not、cannot 等之後) to allow sth; to accept sth without complaining 允許；容忍： **~ sth** *I'm sick of your rudeness—I won't have it any longer!* 你的無禮我已經受夠了，我不會再容忍下去了！◇ **~ sb/sth doing sth** *We can't have people arriving late all the time.* 我們不能允許有人總是遲到。

▸ **PUT SB/STH IN A CONDITION** 使處於某狀況 **26** ⊶ to cause sb/sth to be in a particular state; to make sb react in a particular way 使處於（某狀態）；使做出（某種反應）： **~ sb/sth + adj.** *I want to have everything ready in good time.* 我要求一切都得準時備妥。◇ **~ sb/sth doing sth** *He had his audience listening attentively.* 他抓住了聽眾的注意力。

▸ **IN ARGUMENT** 辯論 **27** (also **have got**) **~ sb** (*informal*) (not used in the progressive tenses 不用於進行時) to put sb at a disadvantage in an argument 辯過；勝過： ***You've got me there.*** *I hadn't thought of that.* 你把我問住了。我沒想過這個。

▸ **SEX** 性 **28** **~ sb** (*slang*) to have sex with sb 同（某人）性交： *He had her in his office.* 他在他的辦公室裏和她搞上了。

▸ **TRICK** 欺騙 **29** [usually passive] **~ sb** (*informal*) to trick or cheat sb 欺騙；矇騙： *I'm afraid you've been had.* 恐怕你上當了。

▸ **GUESTS** 客人 **30** ⊶ [no passive] **~ sb/sth** to take care of sb/sth in your home, especially for a limited period（尤指短期在自己家中）照料，照看： *We're having the kids for the weekend.* 這個週末孩子們要到我們家來由我們照料。 **31** ⊶ [no passive] **~ sb + adv./prep.** to entertain sb in your home（在家中）招待，款待： *We had some friends to dinner last night.* 我們昨晚請了幾位朋友來家裏吃飯了。

▸ **BE WITH** 在一起 **32** ⊶ (also **have got**) **~ sb with you** (not used in the progressive tenses 不用於進行時) to be with sb 同（某人）在一起： *She had some friends with her.* 她和幾個朋友在一起。

▸ **FOR A JOB** 工作 **33** [no passive] **~ sb as sth** to take or accept sb for a particular role 讓，接受（某人承擔任務）： *Who can we have as treasurer?* 我們讓誰來主管財務？

IDM Most idioms containing **have** are at the entries for the nouns and adjectives in the idioms, for example **have your eye on sb** is at **eye** *n.* 大多數含 have 的習語，都可在該等習語中的名詞及形容詞相關詞條找到，如 have your eye on sb 在詞條 eye 的名詞部份。 **have 'done with sth** (*especially BrE*) to finish sth unpleasant so that it does not continue 結束（不愉快的事）： *Let's have done with this silly argument.* 我們結束這場無聊的爭辯吧。 **have 'had it** (*informal*) **1** to be in a very bad condition; to be unable to be repaired 情形很糟；不能修復： *The car had had it.* 這輛車無法修復了。 **2** to be extremely tired 極度疲乏： *I've had it! I'm going to bed.* 我太睏了！我要去睡覺了。 **3** to have lost all chance of surviving sth 毫無幸存機會；完蛋： *When the truck smashed into me, I thought I'd had it.* 那輛卡車撞上我時，我想這下完了。 **4** to be going to experience sth unpleasant 將吃苦頭： *Dad saw you scratch the car—you've had it now!* 爸爸看見你把車身劃了，這下可有你好受的了！**5** to be unable to accept a situation any longer

H

無法繼續容忍：*I've had it (up to here) with him—he's done it once too often.* 我受夠他了，這次我不會放過他的。 **have it 'off/a'way (with sb)** (*BrE, slang*) to have sex with sb 同（某人）性交 **'have it (that …)** to claim that it is a fact that … 稱…屬實；說…是真的：*Rumour has it that we'll have a new manager soon.* 據傳我們即將有一位新經理。 **have (got) it/that 'coming (to you)** to be likely to suffer the unpleasant effects of your actions and to deserve to do so 活該；罪有應得：*It was no surprise when she left him—everyone knew he had it coming to him.* 她離開了他，這絲毫不奇怪。大家都知道是他自己造成的。 **have it 'in for sb** (*informal*) to not like sb and be unpleasant to them 跟某人過不去 **have it 'in you (to do sth)** (*informal*) to be capable of doing sth 有能力（做某事）：*Everyone thinks he has it in him to produce a literary classic.* 大家都認為他有能力寫出一部文學名著。◇ *You were great. I didn't know you had it in you.* 你真了不起。我不知道你有這本事。 **have (got) 'nothing on sb/sth** (*informal*) to be not nearly as good as sb/sth 不如；比不上 ➲ see also HAVE (GOT) STH ON SB **not 'having any** (*informal*) not willing to listen to or believe sth 不願聽，不願相信（某事）：*I tried to persuade her to wait but she wasn't having any.* 我竭力勸她等一下，可她不肯聽。 **what 'have you** (*informal*) other things, people, etc. of the same kind 諸如此類的事物（或人等）：*There's room in the cellar to store old furniture and what have you.* 地下室有地方存放舊傢具之類的東西。

H

PHR V **,have (got) sth a'gainst sb/sth** (not used in the progressive tenses 不用於進行時) to dislike sb/sth for a particular reason 因…而討厭某人／某事：*What have you got against Ruth? She's always been good to you.* 你為什麼不喜歡魯思？她一直對你很好。 **,have sb↔'back** to allow a husband, wife or partner that you are separated from to return 允許分手的丈夫（或妻子、伴侶）回頭；願與某人重修舊好 **,have sth 'back** 🔑 to receive sth that sb has borrowed or taken from you 收回被借走（或拿走）的東西：*You can have your files back after we've checked them.* 我們核對完你的文件之後就還給你。 **,have (got) sth 'in** (not used in the progressive tenses 不用於進行時) to have a supply of sth in your home, etc. 存有某物：*Have we got enough food in?* 我們家裏存有足夠的食物嗎？ **,have sb 'on** (*informal*) to try to make sb believe sth that is not true, usually as a joke 哄騙，欺騙（通常作為玩笑）：*You didn't really, did you? You're not having me on, are you?* 你真的沒有幹吧？你不是在哄我吧？ **,have (got) sth 'on** (not used in the progressive tenses 不用於進行時) **1** 🔑 to be wearing sth 穿着；戴着：*She had a red jacket on.* 她穿着件紅夾克。◇ *He had nothing (= no clothes) on.* 他沒穿衣服。 **2** to leave a piece of equipment working 讓設備運轉着：*She has her TV on all day.* 她一整天都開着電視機。 **3** 🔑 to have arranged to do sth 安排（做某事）：*I can't see you this week—I've got a lot on.* 我這個星期不能見你，我安排得很滿。 **,have (got) sth 'on sb** [no passive] (*informal*) (not used in the progressive tenses 不用於進行時) to know sth bad about sb, especially sth that connects them with a crime 有某人的把柄，掌握某人的證據（尤指與犯罪有關的）：*I'm not worried—they've got nothing on me.* 我不擔心，他們沒抓住我什麼把柄。 **,have sth 'out** to cause sth, especially a part of your body, to be removed 去除，切除（身體部位等）：*I had to have my appendix out.* 我只好把盲腸切除了。 **,have sth 'out (with sb)** to try to settle a disagreement by discussing or arguing about it openly（與某人）辯論出個結果，把某事講個明白：*I need to have it out with her once and for all.* 我有必要跟她公開徹底地把話說清楚。 **,have sb 'up (for sth)** (*BrE, informal*) [usually passive] to cause sb to be accused of sth in court（為某事）把某人告上法庭：*He was had up for manslaughter.* 他因誤殺罪被送上法庭。

■ ***auxiliary verb*** 🔑 used with the past participle to form perfect tenses（與過去分詞連用構成完成時）：*I've finished my work.* 我幹完我的活兒了。◇ *He's gone home, hasn't he?* 他回家去了，對嗎？◇ *'Have you seen it?' 'Yes, I have/No, I haven't.'* "你看見了嗎？" "是的，看見了／沒有，沒看見。" ◇ *She'll have had the results by now.* 她現在應該知道結果了。◇ *Had they left before you got there?* 你到那裏時他們已經離開了嗎？◇ *If I hadn't seen it with my own eyes I wouldn't have believed it.* 要不是親眼看見了，我不會相信的。◇ (*formal*) *Had I known that* (= if I had known that) *I would never have come.* 要是早知道，我絕不會來的。

British/American 英式／美式英語

have you got? / do you have?

- **Have got** is the usual verb in *BrE* to show possession, etc. in positive statements in the present tense, in negative statements and in questions. 在英式英語中，動詞 have got 常用於現在時的肯定句、否定句和疑問句中，表示擁有等：*They've got a wonderful house.* 他們有一所漂亮的房子。◇ *We haven't got a television.* 我們沒有電視機。◇ *Have you got a meeting today?* 你今天有會嗎？ Questions and negative statements formed with **do** are also common. 以 do 構成疑問句和否定句亦常見：*Do you have any brothers and sisters?* 你有兄弟姐妹嗎？◇ *We don't have a car.* 我們沒有汽車。
- **Have** is also used but is more formal. 亦可用 have 構成疑問句和否定句，但較正式：*I have no objection to your request.* 我不反對你的請求。◇ *Have you an appointment?* 你有約會嗎？ Some expressions with **have** are common even in informal language. 非正式用語中也常見一些帶 have 的短語：*I'm sorry, I haven't a clue.* 對不起，我一無所知。
- In the past tense **had** is used in positive statements. In negatives and questions, forms with **did have** are usually used. 在過去時中 had 用於肯定句，而否定句和疑問句通常用 did have：*They had a wonderful house.* 他們曾有一所漂亮的房子。◇ *We didn't have much time.* 我們沒有多少時間。◇ *Did she have her husband with her?* 她那時與丈夫在一起嗎？
- In *NAmE* **have** and forms with **do/does/did** are the usual way to show possession, etc. in positive statements, negatives and questions. 美式英語通常用 have，以及 have 和 do/does/did 構成的各種形式表示擁有等，用於肯定句、否定句和疑問句：*They have a wonderful house.* 他們有一所漂亮的房子。◇ *We don't have a television.* 我們沒有電視機。◇ *Do you have a meeting today?* 你今天有會嗎？ **Have got** is not used in questions, but is used in positive statements, especially to emphasize that somebody has one thing rather than another. * have got 不用於疑問句，而用於肯定句中，着重強調某人有某物而非另一物：*'Does your brother have brown hair?' 'No, he's got blond hair.'* "你弟弟的頭髮是棕色的嗎？" "不，他有一頭金髮。"
- In both *BrE* and *NAmE* **have** and forms with **do/does** and **did** are used when you are referring to a habit or routine. 英式英語和美式英語均用 have，以及 have 和 do/does/did 構成的各種形式表示習慣或常規：*We don't often have time to talk.* 我們一般沒有時間談話。

haven /'heɪvn/ *noun* a place that is safe and peaceful where people or animals are protected 安全的地方；保護區：*The hotel is a haven of peace and tranquility.* 這家旅館是一處安寧的去處。◇ *The river banks are a haven for wildlife.* 河的兩岸是野生動物的自然棲息地。➲ see also SAFE HAVEN, TAX HAVEN

the ,have-'nots *noun* [pl.] people who do not have money and possessions 一無所有的人；窮人 ➲ compare THE HAVES

haven't /'hævnt/ *short form* have not

hav·er·sack /'hævəsæk; *NAmE* -vərs-/ *noun* (*old-fashioned, BrE*) a bag that is carried on the back or over the shoulder, especially when walking in the country（尤指野外步行背的）背包，褡褳

the 'haves *noun* [pl.] people who have enough money and possessions 有錢人；富人：*the division between the haves and the have-nots* 富人和窮人之間的差異 ➲ compare THE HAVE-NOTS

have to /ˈhæv tə; ˈhæf/ *modal verb* (**has to** /ˈhæz tə; ˈhæs/, **had to**, **had to** /ˈhæd tə; ˈhæt/)
1 (also **have got to**) used to show that you must do sth 必須；不得不：*Sorry, I've got to go.* 對不起，我必須走了。◇ *Did she have to pay a fine?* 她非得交罰款嗎？◇ *You don't have to knock—just walk in.* 不必敲門，進來就是了。◇ *I haven't got to leave till seven.* 我可以等到七點鐘才離開。◇ *First, you have to think logically about your fears.* 首先，你得對你擔憂的理由好好地想想。◇ ***I have to admit**, the idea of marriage scares me.* 我不得不承認，一想到結婚我就害怕。◇ *Do you have to go?* 你非得走嗎？◇ (*especially BrE*) *Have you got to go?* 你非得走嗎？ **2** (also **have got to** especially in *BrE*) used to give advice or recommend sth（勸告或建議時用）：*You simply have to get a new job.* 你就是得找份新工作。◇ *You've got to try this recipe—it's delicious.* 你得試試這種烹調法，味道很不錯。 **3** (also **have got to** especially in *BrE*) used to say that sth must be true or must happen（表示一定真實或肯定發生）：*There has to be a reason for his strange behaviour.* 他的古怪行為一定事出有因。◇ *This war has got to end soon.* 這場戰爭必將很快結束。 **4** used to suggest that an annoying event happens in order to annoy you, or that sb does sth in order to annoy you（用以暗示麻煩的事或某人有意搗蛋）：*Of course, it had to start raining as soon as we got to the beach.* 可惡的雨，我們一到海灘它就非得下起來。◇ ***Do you have to** hum so loudly?* (= it is annoying) 你非得用這麼大嗓門哼唱不可嗎？ ➲ note at MODAL, MUST

havoc /ˈhævək/ *noun* [U] a situation in which there is a lot of damage, destruction or confusion 災害；禍患；浩劫：*The floods caused havoc throughout the area.* 洪水給整個地區帶來了災害。◇ *Continuing strikes are beginning to **play havoc with** the national economy.* 持續的罷工開始嚴重破壞國家經濟。◇ *These insects can **wreak havoc on** crops.* 這些昆蟲可嚴重危害農作物。

haw /hɔː/ *verb* IDM see HUM *v.*

Ha·wai·ian shirt /həˌwaɪən ˈʃɜːt; *NAmE* ˈʃɜːrt/ (also **aˈloha shirt**) *noun* a loose cotton shirt with a brightly coloured pattern and short sleeves 夏威夷衫，夏威夷襯衫（圖案豔麗，短袖）

hawk /hɔːk/ *noun, verb*
■ *noun* **1** a strong fast BIRD OF PREY (= a bird that kills other creatures for food) 鷹；隼：*He waited, **watching her like a hawk*** (= watching her very closely). 他等待着，用鷹一樣銳利的目光緊盯着她。 ➲ see also SPARROWHAWK **2** a person, especially a politician, who supports the use of military force to solve problems 鷹派分子；主戰分子 OPP **dove** IDM see EYE *n.*
■ *verb* **1** [T] **~ sth** to try to sell things by going from place to place asking people to buy them 沿街叫賣 SYN **peddle** **2** [I, T] **~ (sth)** to get PHLEGM in your mouth when you cough 咳痰

hawk·er /ˈhɔːkə(r)/ *noun* a person who makes money by hawking goods 沿街叫賣者；小販

ˌhawk-ˈeyed *adj.* (of a person 人) watching closely and carefully and noticing small details 嚴密注視的；目光犀利的 SYN **eagle-eyed**

hawk·ish /ˈhɔːkɪʃ/ *adj.* preferring to use military action rather than peaceful discussion in order to solve a political problem 鷹派的；主戰的；強硬的 OPP **dovish**

haw·ser /ˈhɔːzə(r)/ *noun* (*technical* 術語) a thick rope or steel cable used on a ship（船上用的）纜索，鋼纜

haw·thorn /ˈhɔːθɔːn; *NAmE* -θɔːrn/ *noun* [U, C] a bush or small tree with THORNS, white or pink flowers and small dark red BERRIES 山楂

hay /heɪ/ *noun* [U] **1** grass that has been cut and dried and is used as food for animals（用作飼料的）乾草，草料：*a bale of hay* 一大捆乾草 ➲ compare STRAW (1) ➲ VISUAL VOCAB pages V2, V3 **2** (*NAmE, informal*) a small amount of money 少量的錢
IDM **make hay while the ˈsun shines** (*saying*) to make good use of opportunities, good conditions, etc. while they last 趁有太陽時曬乾草；抓緊時機；打鐵趁熱 ➲ more at HIT *v.*, ROLL *n.*

ˈhay fever *noun* [U] an illness that affects the nose, eyes and throat and is caused by POLLEN from plants that is breathed in from the air 枯草熱，花粉病（由於吸入空氣中的花粉而引起的鼻、眼、喉部的過敏症）

hay·loft /ˈheɪlɒft; *NAmE* -lɔːft/ *noun* a place at the top of a farm building used for storing HAY（農舍頂部的）乾草棚；乾草頂閣

hay·mak·ing /ˈheɪmeɪkɪŋ/ *noun* [U] the process of cutting and drying grass to make HAY 製乾草

hay·ride /ˈheɪraɪd/ *noun* (*NAmE*) a ride for pleasure on a CART filled with HAY, pulled by a horse or TRACTOR 乘坐（由馬或拖拉機拉的）乾草車出遊

hay·stack /ˈheɪstæk/ (also *less frequent* **hay·rick** /ˈheɪrɪk/) *noun* a large pile of HAY, used as a way of storing it until it is needed 乾草堆；乾草垛 IDM see NEEDLE *n.* ➲ VISUAL VOCAB pages V2, V3

hay·wire /ˈheɪwaɪə(r)/ *adj.*
IDM **go ˈhaywire** (*informal*) to stop working correctly or become out of control 出故障；紊亂；失去控制：*After that, things started to go haywire.* 此後事情開始失去控制。

H

haz·ard /ˈhæzəd; *NAmE* -ərd/ *noun, verb*
■ *noun* a thing that can be dangerous or cause damage 危險；危害：*a **fire/safety hazard*** 火災／安全隱患 ◇ **~ (to sb/sth)** *Growing levels of pollution represent a serious **health hazard** to the local population.* 日益嚴重的污染對當地人民的健康構成了重大威脅。◇ **~ (of sth/of doing sth)** *Everybody is aware of the hazards of smoking.* 大家都明白吸煙的危害。◇ ***hazard lights*** (= flashing lights on a car that warn other drivers of possible danger)（汽車上的）危險示警燈
■ *verb* **1** to make a suggestion or guess which you know may be wrong 試着提出；大膽猜測：**~ sth** *Would you like to **hazard a guess**?* 你想猜猜看嗎？◇ **+ speech** *'Is it Tom you're going with?' she hazarded.* "你要和湯姆一起去嗎？" 她大膽猜測道。◇ **~ that ...** *I would hazard that she is the sole reason we are here.* 我猜想我們來這兒全是因為她。 **2 ~ sth** (*formal*) to risk sth or put it in danger 冒…的風險；使處於危險 SYN **endanger**：*Careless drivers hazard other people's lives as well as their own.* 粗心大意的駕駛者拿他人和自己的生命冒險。

haz·ard·ous /ˈhæzədəs; *NAmE* -ərdəs/ *adj.* involving risk or danger, especially to sb's health or safety 危險的；有害的：***hazardous waste/chemicals*** 有害廢物／化學製品 ◇ *a hazardous journey* 危險的旅程 ◇ *It would be hazardous to invest so much.* 投資這麼多會有風險。◇ *a list of products that are potentially hazardous to health* 對健康有潛在危害的產品清單

ˈhazard pay (also **ˈdanger pay**) (both *US*) (*BrE* **ˈdanger money**) *noun* [U] extra pay for doing work that is dangerous 危險工作津貼

haze /heɪz/ *noun, verb*
■ *noun* **1** [C, U] air that is difficult to see through because it contains very small drops of water, especially caused by hot weather（尤指熱天引起的）薄霧，霧靄：*a heat haze* 熱天的霧氣 **2** [sing.] air containing sth that makes it difficult to see through it（煙塵等的）霧靄，煙霧：*a **haze of smoke/dust/steam*** 煙霧；塵霧；蒸汽霧 **3** [sing.] a mental state in which your thoughts, feelings, etc. are not clear 迷蒙；迷糊：*an alcoholic haze* 喝醉酒的迷糊
■ *verb* **1** [I, T] **~ (sth)** to become covered or to cover sth in a HAZE（使）籠罩在薄霧中 **2 ~ sb** (*NAmE*) to play tricks on sb, especially a new student, or to give them very unpleasant things to do, sometimes as a condition for entering a FRATERNITY or SORORITY 戲弄，欺凌（新生等，有時作為加入美國大學生聯誼會的條件）

hazel /ˈheɪzl/ *noun, adj.*
■ *noun* [C, U] a small tree that produces small nuts (called hazelnuts) that can be eaten 榛樹（其果實榛子可食）
■ *adj.* (of eyes 眼睛) greenish-brown or reddish-brown in colour 淡綠褐色的；淺赤褐色的

hazel·nut /ˈheɪzlnʌt/ (also **fil·bert** especially in *NAmE*) *noun* the small brown nut of the HAZEL tree 榛子 ➲ VISUAL VOCAB page V32

hazy /ˈheɪzi/ *adj.* (**hazi·er**, **hazi·est**) **1** not clear because of HAZE 朦朧的；薄霧濛濛的：*a **hazy afternoon/sky***

霧濛濛的下午 / 天空 ◇ **hazy light/sunshine** 曚曨的光線 / 陽光 ◇ *The mountains were hazy in the distance.* 遠處的山巒在薄霧中若隱若現。 **2** not clear because of a lack of memory, understanding or detail 記不清的；模糊的 **SYN** **vague**： *a **hazy memory/idea*** 模糊不清的記憶 / 概念 ◇ *What happened next is all very hazy.* 接下來發生的事都記不清楚了。 **3** (of a person 人) uncertain or confused about sth 主意不定的；困惑的： *I'm a little hazy about what to do next.* 我還有點拿不準下一步要做什麼。 ▸ **haz·ily** *adv.*： *'Why now?' she wondered hazily.* "為什麼是現在？" 她困惑地思忖。

'H-bomb *noun* = HYDROGEN BOMB

HCF /ˌeɪtʃ siː ˈef/ *abbr.* (*mathematics* 數) HIGHEST COMMON FACTOR

HCFC /ˌeɪtʃ siː ef ˈsiː/ *noun* (*chemistry* 化) the abbreviation for 'hydrochlorofluorocarbon' (a type of gas used especially in AEROSOLS (= types of container that release liquid in the form of a spray) instead of CFC, as it is less harmful to the layer of the gas OZONE in the earth's atmosphere) 氫氯氟烴（全寫為 hydrochlorofluorocarbon）

HD /ˌeɪtʃ ˈdiː/ *abbr.* high-definition (used of television, film or video images that are extremely high quality, with very clear, sharp outlines and details)（電視、電影或錄像圖像）高清晰度，高畫質： *The film was shot in HD.* 這部影片是用高清技術拍攝的。

HDTV /ˌeɪtʃ diː tiː ˈviː/ *noun* [U] (*technical* 術語) the abbreviation for 'high definition television' (technology that produces extremely clear images on a television screen) 高清晰度電視（技術），高畫質電視（技術）（全寫為 high definition television）

HE (*BrE*) (also **H.E.** *US, BrE*) *abbr.* **1** Her/His EXCELLENCY 閣下： *HE the Australian Ambassador* 澳大利亞大使閣下 **2** HIGHER EDUCATION 高等教育

he 🔑 /hi; iː; i; *strong form* hiː/ *pron., noun*

■ ***pron.*** (used as the subject of a verb 用作動詞主語) **1** 🔑 a male person or animal that has already been mentioned or is easily identified 他；它（指雄性動物）： *Everyone liked my father—he was the perfect gentleman.* 大家都喜歡我父親，他是真正的紳士。◇ *He* (= the man we are watching) *went through that door.* 他進了那道門。 **2** (becoming *old-fashioned*) a person, male or female, whose sex is not stated or known, especially when referring to sb mentioned earlier or to a group in general 人（指性別未說明或不知道的男性或女性，尤指曾提過的人或泛指某群體時）： *Every child needs to know that he is loved.* 每個孩子都需要知道自己是有人愛的。◇ (*saying*) *He who* (= anyone who) *hesitates is lost.* 優柔寡斷者坐失良機。 ➲ note at GENDER **3 He** used when referring to God 祂（指上帝） ➲ compare HIM

■ ***noun*** /hiː/ **1** [sing.] (*informal*) a male 雄性： *What a nice dog—is it a he or a she?* 多好看的狗，它是公的還是母的？ **2 he-** (in compound nouns 構成複合名詞) a male animal 雄性動物： *a he-goat* 一頭公山羊

head 🔑 /hed/ *noun, verb*

■ ***noun***

▸ **PART OF BODY 身體部位 1** 🔑 [C] the part of the body on top of the neck containing the eyes, nose, mouth and brain 頭；頭部： *She **nodded her head** in agreement.* 她點頭表示同意。◇ *He **shook his head** in disbelief.* 他搖頭表示不信。◇ *The boys **hung their heads** in shame.* 男孩子們羞愧地低着頭。◇ *The driver suffered head injuries.* 司機頭部受傷。◇ *She always **has her head in a book*** (= is always reading). 她總是埋頭讀書。◇ *He still has a **good head of hair*** (= a lot of hair). 他的頭髮依然很多。 ➲ **COLLOCATIONS** at PHYSICAL ➲ **VISUAL VOCAB** page V59 ➲ see also DEATH'S HEAD

▸ **MIND 頭腦 2** 🔑 [C] the mind or brain 頭腦；腦筋： *I sometimes wonder what goes on in that head of yours.* 我有時不明白你腦子裏想些什麼。◇ *I wish you'd **use your head*** (= think carefully before doing or saying sth). 我希望你凡事多用用腦筋。◇ *The thought **never entered my head**.* 我從未有過那種想法。◇ *I **can't work it out in my head**—I need a calculator.* 我沒法心算出來，我得用計算器。◇ *I **can't get** that tune **out of my head**.* 我忘不掉那個曲調。◇ *When will you **get it into your head*** (= understand) *that I don't want to discuss this any more!* 你何時才能明白我不想再談論這件事了！◇ *For some reason, she's **got it into her head*** (= believes) *that the others don't like her.* 由於某種原因，她有一種感覺，認為其他人都不喜歡她。◇ *Who's been **putting** such weird ideas **into your head*** (= making you believe that)? 是誰讓你產生這種怪念頭的？◇ *Try to **put** the exams **out of your head*** (= stop thinking about them) *for tonight.* 今晚盡量別想考試的事了。 ➲ see also HOTHEAD

▸ **MEASUREMENT 量度 3 a head** [sing.] the size of a person's or animal's head, used as a measurement of distance or height（人或動物的）一頭長，一頭高： *She's a good head taller than her sister.* 她比妹妹足足高出了一個頭。◇ *The favourite won **by a short head*** (= a distance slightly less than the length of a horse's head). 最被看好的那匹馬以不足一馬頭之差的優勢獲勝。

▸ **PAIN 疼痛 4** [C, usually sing.] (*informal*) a continuous pain in your head（持續的）頭痛 **SYN** **headache**： *I woke up with a really bad head this morning.* 我今天早晨醒來時頭痛得厲害。

▸ **OF GROUP/ORGANIZATION 團體；組織 5** 🔑 [C, U] the person in charge of a group of people or an organization 負責人；領導人： *the **heads of government/state*** 政府首腦；國家元首 ◇ *She resigned as **head of department**.* 她辭去了部門主管的職務。◇ *the **crowned heads*** (= the kings and queens) *of Europe* 歐洲各國君主 ◇ *the **head gardener/waiter, etc.*** 園藝主管、餐館服務員領班等 ◇ (*BrE*) *the **head boy/girl*** (= a student who is chosen to represent the school) 學校男生 / 女生代表

▸ **OF SCHOOL/COLLEGE 學校；學院 6** [C] (often **Head**) (*BrE*) the person in charge of a school or college 校長；院長 **SYN** **headmaster, headmistress, head teacher**： *I've been called in to see the Head.* 我接到通知去見校長。◇ *the deputy head* 副校長

▸ **SIDE OF COIN 硬幣的面 7 heads** [U] the side of a coin that has a picture of the head of a person on it, used as one choice when a coin is TOSSED to decide sth 硬幣正面（有人頭像） ➲ compare TAIL *n.* (7)

▸ **END OF OBJECT 物體一端 8** [C, usually sing.] **~ (of sth)** the end of a long narrow object that is larger or wider than the rest of it 較寬大的一端；頭： *the head of a nail* 釘子的頭 ➲ **VISUAL VOCAB** page V20 ➲ see also BEDHEAD

▸ **TOP 頂 9** [sing.] **~ of sth** the top or highest part of sth 頂端；上端： *at the head of the page* 在頁眉處 ◇ *They finished the season at the head of their league.* 賽季結束時他們在聯賽中排名榜首。

▸ **OF RIVER 河 10** [sing.] **the ~ of the river** the place where a river begins（河流）源頭 **SYN** **source**

▸ **OF TABLE 桌子 11** [sing.] **the ~ of the table** the most important seat at a table 上座（桌子旁最重要的座位）： *The President sat at the head of the table.* 總統坐在桌子的上首。

▸ **OF LINE OF PEOPLE 人的行列 12** [sing.] **the ~ of sth** the position at the front of a line of people 領頭位置；排頭： *The prince rode at the head of his regiment.* 王子騎馬走在衛隊的前頭。

▸ **OF PLANT 植物 13** [C] **~ (of sth)** the mass of leaves or flowers at the end of a STEM（莖梗頂端的）葉球，頭狀花序： *Remove the dead heads to encourage new growth.* 把枯萎了的殘花除掉以促使新芽生長。

▸ **ON BEER 啤酒 14** [sing.] the mass of small bubbles on the top of a glass of beer 啤酒泡沫；酒頭

▸ **OF SPOT 斑 15** [C] the part of a spot on your skin that contains a thick yellowish liquid (= PUS) 膿頭 ➲ see also BLACKHEAD

▸ **IN TAPE/VIDEO RECORDER 錄音 / 錄像機 16** [C] the part of a TAPE RECORDER or VIDEO RECORDER that touches the tape and changes the electrical signals into sounds and/or pictures 磁頭

▸ **NUMBER OF ANIMALS 動物數量 17 ~ of sth** [pl.] used to say how many animals of a particular type are on a farm, in a HERD, etc.（表示農場或牧群等的牲畜的數目）頭： *200 head of sheep* * 200 頭綿羊

▸ **OF STEAM 蒸汽 18 a ~ of steam** [sing.] the pressure produced by steam in a confined space 蒸汽壓力

▸ **SEX 性 19** [U] (*taboo, slang*) ORAL sex (= using the mouth to give sb sexual pleasure) 口交： *to give head* 進行口交

▸ **LINGUISTICS 語言學 20** [C] the central part of a phrase, which has the same GRAMMATICAL function as the whole phrase. In the phrase 'the tall man in a suit', *man* is the head. （短語的）中心成分，中心詞，主導詞

IDM **a/per 'head** for each person 每人：*The meal worked out at $20 a head.* 這餐飯算下來每人 20 元。 **bang/knock your/their 'heads together** (*informal*) to force people to stop arguing and behave in a sensible way 強行制止人們爭吵並使之恢復理智 **be banging, etc. your head against a brick 'wall** (*informal*) to keep trying to do sth that will never be successful 用頭撞牆；徒勞無益；枉費心機：*Trying to reason with them was like banging my head against a brick wall.* 試圖和他們講道理只是白費口舌。 **be/stand head and 'shoulders above sb/sth** to be much better than other people or things 比其他人（或事物）好得多；出類拔萃；鶴立雞群 **bite/snap sb's 'head off** (*informal*) to shout at sb in an angry way, especially without reason 氣憤地對某人大喊大叫；（尤指毫無道理地）呵斥某人 **bring sth to a 'head | come to a 'head** if you **bring** a situation **to a head** or if a situation **comes to a head**, you are forced to deal with it quickly because it suddenly becomes very bad （使）事情達到緊要關頭，需要當機立斷 **bury/hide your head in the 'sand** to refuse to admit that a problem exists or refuse to deal with it 採取鴕鳥政策；不正視現實；迴避問題 **can't make head nor 'tail of sth** to be unable to understand sth 不理解某事；不明白某事：*I couldn't make head nor tail of what he was saying.* 我弄不懂他在說些什麼。 **do sb's 'head in** (*BrE, informal*) to make you feel confused, upset and/or annoyed 使某人困惑（或煩惱、生氣）：*Shut up! You're doing my head in.* 閉嘴！你讓我煩死了。 **do sth standing on your 'head** (*informal*) to be able to do sth very easily and without having to think too much 做某事不費吹灰之力 **from ˌhead to 'foot/'toe** covering your whole body 從頭到腳；遍佈全身：*We were covered from head to foot in mud.* 我們渾身是泥。 **get your 'head down** (*informal*) **1** (*BrE*) to sleep 睡覺：*I managed to get my head down for an hour.* 我將就着睡了一小時。 **2** = KEEP/GET YOUR HEAD DOWN **get your 'head round sth** (*BrE, informal*) to be able to understand or accept sth 能夠理解；接受得了：*She's dead. I can't get my head round it yet.* 她死了。我仍然無法相信這事。 **give sb their 'head** to allow sb to do what they want without trying to stop them 讓某人隨心所欲 **go head to 'head (with sb)** to deal with sb in a very direct and determined way （與某人）面對面直接談判 **go to sb's 'head 1** (of alcohol 酒精) to make you feel drunk 上頭；使醉：*That glass of wine has gone straight to my head.* 那杯酒一下子就把我弄得頭暈腦脹。 **2** (of success, praise, etc. 成功、讚揚等) to make you feel too proud of yourself in a way that other people find annoying 使人過於驕傲；沖昏頭腦 **have a good 'head on your shoulders** to be a sensible person 頭腦清醒；理智 **have a head for sth 1** to be good at sth 擅長某事：*to have* ***a head for figures/business*** 長於算術；有生意頭腦 **2** if sb does not **have a head for heights**, they feel nervous and think they are going to fall when they look down from a high place 不懼（高）；無恐（高）症 **have your head in the 'clouds 1** to be thinking about sth that is not connected with what you are doing 心不在焉；走神 **2** to have ideas, plans, etc. that are not realistic 有不切實際的想法（或計劃等）；想入非非 **have your 'head screwed on (the right way)** (*informal*) to be a sensible person 頭腦清醒；理智 **ˌhead 'first 1** moving forwards or downwards with your head in front of the rest of your body 頭在前；頭朝下：*He fell head first down the stairs.* 他倒栽葱摔下樓梯。 **2** without thinking carefully about sth before acting 未經深思；輕率；魯莽：*She got divorced and rushed head first into another marriage.* 她離婚後又倉促再婚了。 **SYN** **headlong** **head over heels in 'love** loving sb very much 深深愛着某人；迷戀：*He's fallen head over heels in love with his boss.* 他深深迷戀上了他的上司。 **heads or 'tails?** used to ask sb which side of a coin they think will be facing upwards when it is TOSSED in order to decide sth by chance（擲硬幣做決定時說）正面還是反面 **'heads will roll (for sth)** (*informal, usually humorous*) used to say that some people will be punished because of sth that has happened 有些人將（為某事）受到懲罰 **hold your 'head high | hold up your 'head** to be proud of or not feel ashamed about sth that you have done 昂首挺胸；抬起頭來：*She managed to hold her head high and ignore what people were saying.* 她勉力昂首挺胸，不理會人家的閒言碎語。 **in over your 'head** involved in sth that is too difficult for you to deal with 捲入棘手的事：*After a week in the new job, I soon realized that I was in over my head.* 新工作剛做了一個星期，我便意識到自己做不了。 **keep/get your 'head down** to avoid attracting attention to yourself 避免引起注意；保持低姿態 **keep your 'head | keep a clear/cool 'head** to remain calm in a difficult situation （在困境中）保持冷靜 **keep your 'head above water** to deal with a difficult situation, especially one in which you have financial problems, and just manage to survive 勉強逃脱困境；設法不舉債；掙扎求存 **laugh, scream, etc. your 'head off** (*informal*) to laugh, etc. a lot and very loudly 大笑（或大叫等） **lose your 'head** to become unable to act in a calm or sensible way 慌亂；昏了頭；失去理智 **on your (own) head 'be it** used to tell sb that they will have to accept any unpleasant results of sth that they decide to do 你（自己）必須承擔任何後果：*Tell him the truth if you want to, but on your own head be it!* 你想把真相告訴他就告訴他吧，但後果自負！ **out of/off your 'head** (*BrE, informal*) **1** crazy 發瘋 **2** not knowing what you are saying or doing because of the effects of alcohol or drugs（酒後或使用藥物後）胡言亂語，行為乖張，神志不清 **over sb's 'head 1** too difficult or complicated for sb to understand 超過某人理解力；過於複雜：*A lot of the jokes went* (= were) *right over my head.* 那些笑話有很多我完全聽不懂。 **2** to a higher position of authority than sb 職位比某人高；超過某人：*I couldn't help feeling jealous when she was promoted over my head.* 她受到提拔職位超過了我，我不由得感到嫉妒。 **put our/your/their 'heads together** to think about or discuss sth as a group 集體思考（或討論）；集思廣益 **stand/turn sth on its 'head** to make people think about sth in a completely different way 使人完全改變思路；使人從反面思考 **take it into your head to do sth** to suddenly decide to do sth, especially sth that other people think is stupid 忽發奇想；心血來潮 **take it into your head that ...** to suddenly start thinking sth, especially sth that other people think is stupid 忽發奇想；突然開始想某事 **turn sb's 'head** (of success, praise, etc. 成功、讚揚等) to make a person feel too proud in a way that other people find annoying 使某人得意忘形 **two heads are better than 'one** (*saying*) used to say that two people can achieve more than one person working alone 兩人智慧勝一人 ➲ more at BEAR *n.*, BLOCK *n.*, BOTHER *v.*, DRUM *v.*, EYE *n.*, GUN *n.*, HAIR, HEART, HIT *v.*, IDEA, KNOCK *v.*, LAUGH *v.*, NEED *v.*, OLD, PRICE *n.*, REAR *v.*, RING² *v.*, ROOF *n.*, SCRATCH *v.*, THICK *adj.*, TOP *n.*

■ ***verb***

▸ **MOVE TOWARDS 移向 1** [I] (also **be headed** especially in *NAmE*) **+ adv./prep.** to move in a particular direction 朝（某方向）行進：*Where are we heading?* 我們要往哪兒去？◇ *Where are you two headed?* 你們兩個去哪兒？◇ *Let's head back home.* 咱們回家吧。◇ *She headed for the door.* 她朝着門走去。◇ (*figurative*) *Can you forecast where the economy is heading?* 你能預測經濟的發展方向嗎？

▸ **GROUP/ORGANIZATION 團體；機構 2** [T] **~ sth** (also **ˌhead sth↔'up**) to lead or be in charge of sth 領導；主管：*She has been appointed to head the research team.* 她受命領導研究小組。

▸ **LIST/LINE OF PEOPLE 名單；隊列 3** [T] **~ sth** to be at the top of a list of names or at the front of a line of people 位於排行之首；排在前頭：*Italy heads the table after two games.* 兩場比賽之後意大利隊排名榜首。◇ *to* ***head a march/procession*** 在遊行隊伍 / 隊伍前列

▸ **BE AT TOP 在頂端 4** [T, usually passive] **~ sth** to put a word or words at the top of a page or section of a book as a title 在（頁或篇章的）頂端加標題：*The chapter was headed 'My Early Life'.* 這一章的標題是"我的早年生活"。

▸ FOOTBALL 足球 **5** [T] **~ sth** to hit a football with your head 用頭頂（球）: *Walsh headed the ball into an empty goal.* 沃爾什把球頂進了空門。 **PHR V** **be 'heading for sth** (also **be 'headed for sth** especially in *NAmE*) to be likely to experience sth bad 很可能遭受（不幸）；會招致: *They look as though they're heading for divorce.* 他們看樣子會離婚。 **,head sb↔'off** to get in front of sb in order to make them turn back or change direction 攔擋某人；使改變方向 **SYN** **intercept**: *We'll head them off at the bridge!* 我們將在橋頭攔截他們！ **,head sth↔'off** to take action in order to prevent sth from happening 阻止，防止（某事發生）: *He headed off efforts to replace him as leader.* 他挫敗了要取代他的領導地位的企圖。 **,head sth↔'up** to lead or be in charge of a department, part of an organization, etc. 領導，主管（某部門或機構分支等） ➲ see also HEAD *v.* (2)

-head /hed/ *suffix* (*informal*) (in nouns) a person who is very enthusiastic about a particular thing or is addicted to a particular drug（構成名詞）…迷，…癮君子: *The cybercafe was a nethead's dream.* 網吧是網迷的樂園。◇ *a gearhead* 技術設備發燒友 ◇ *a crackhead* 強效可卡因癮君子 ◇ *a smackhead* 吸白粉成癮的人 ◇ *a pothead* 大麻癮君子

head·ache 🔑 /'hedeɪk/ *noun*
1 🔑 a continuous pain in the head 頭痛: *to suffer from headaches* 頭痛 ◇ *Red wine gives me a headache.* 我喝紅酒會頭痛。◇ *I have **a splitting headache*** (= a very bad one). 我頭痛欲裂。➲ COLLOCATIONS at ILL **2** (*informal*) a person or thing that causes worry or trouble 令人頭痛的人（或事物）；麻煩: *The real headache will be getting the bank to lend you the money.* 真正的麻煩將是設法讓銀行貸款給你。

head·band /'hedbænd/ *noun* a strip of cloth worn around the head, especially to keep hair or sweat out of your eyes when playing sports 頭帶（運動時常用以固定頭髮或吸汗）

head·bang·er /'hedbæŋə(r)/ *noun* (*informal*) **1** a person who likes to shake their head violently up and down while listening to rock music（聽搖滾樂時）拚命搖頭者 **2** a stupid or crazy person 愚蠢的人；瘋狂的人 ▸ **head·banging** *noun* [U]

head·board /'hedbɔːd; *NAmE* -bɔːrd/ *noun* the vertical board at the end of a bed where you put your head 牀頭板 ➲ VISUAL VOCAB page V23

,head 'boy *noun* (in some British schools) the boy who is chosen each year to represent his school（某些英國學校每年挑選的）男生代表

head·butt /'hedbʌt/ *verb* **~ sb** (*especially BrE*) to deliberately hit sb hard with your head 故意用頭撞（人） ▸ **head·butt** *noun*

head·case /'hedkeɪs/ *noun* (*BrE, informal*) a person who behaves in a strange way and who seems to be mentally ill 怪人；神經兮兮的人

head·cheese /'hedtʃiːz/ (*NAmE*) (*BrE* **brawn**) *noun* [U] meat made from the head of a pig or CALF that has been boiled and pressed into a container, served cold in thin slices（罐裝）豬頭肉，牛犢頭肉

head·count /'hedkaʊnt/ *noun* an act of counting the number of people who are at an event, employed by an organization, etc.; the number of people that have been counted in this way 人數統計；統計出的人數: *to do a headcount* 統計人數 ◇ *What's the latest headcount?* 最新統計的人數是多少？

head·dress /'heddres/ *noun* a covering worn on the head on special occasions（特殊場合戴的）頭巾，頭飾

head·ed /'hedɪd/ *adj.* **1** (of writing paper 信紙) having the name and address of a person, an organization, etc. printed at the top 頂端印有名稱和地址的；有信頭的: *headed notepaper* 有信頭的便箋紙 **2** **-headed** (in adjectives 構成形容詞) having the type of head or number of heads mentioned 有…頭的；有…個頭的: *a bald-headed man* 禿頂男子 ◇ *a three-headed monster* 三頭怪獸 ➲ see also BIG-HEADED, CLEAR-HEADED, COOL-HEADED, EMPTY-HEADED, HARD-HEADED, LEVEL-HEADED, LIGHT-HEADED, PIG-HEADED, WRONG-HEADED

head·er /'hedə(r)/ *noun* **1** (in football (SOCCER) 足球) an act of hitting the ball with your head 用頭頂球；頭球 **2** a line or block of text that is automatically added to the top of every page that is printed from a computer（計算機打印時自動加在各頁頂端的）標頭，首標 ➲ compare FOOTER (1)

head·gear /'hedgɪə(r); *NAmE* -gɪr/ *noun* [U] anything worn on the head, for example a hat 頭戴之物；帽子: *protective headgear* 安全帽

,head 'girl *noun* (in some British schools) the girl who is chosen each year to represent her school（某些英國學校每年挑選的）女生代表

head·hunt /'hedhʌnt/ *verb* **~ sb** to find sb who is suitable for a senior job and persuade them to leave their present job 獵頭（物色、延攬高層人員）: *I was headhunted by a marketing agency.* 我被一家銷售代理公司物色上了。 ▸ **head·hunt·ing** *noun* [U]

head·hunt·er /'hedhʌntə(r)/ *noun* **1** a person whose job is to find people with the necessary skills to work for a particular company and to persuade them to join this company 獵頭者（專門負責延攬人才） **2** a member of a people that collects the heads of the people they kill 獵頭部落成員（收集所殺者的人頭）

head·ing /'hedɪŋ/ *noun* **1** a title printed at the top of a page or at the beginning of a section of a book（頁首或章節開頭的）標題: *chapter headings* 篇章標題 **2** the subject of each section of a speech or piece of writing（講話或作品各章節的）主題: *The company's aims can be grouped under three main headings.* 公司的目標可分成三大類。

head·lamp /'hedlæmp/ *noun* (*especially BrE*) = HEADLIGHT

head·land /'hedlənd; -lænd/ *noun* a narrow piece of high land that sticks out from the coast into the sea 岬，岬角（突入海中的狹長高地） **SYN** **promontory** ➲ VISUAL VOCAB pages V4, V5

head·less /'hedləs/ *adj.* [usually before noun] without a head 無頭的: ***a headless body/corpse*** 無頭屍體 **IDM** **run around like a ,headless 'chicken** to be very busy and active trying to do sth, but not very organized, with the result that you do not succeed 茫無頭緒地瞎忙一通

head·light /'hedlaɪt/ *noun* (also **head·lamp** especially in *BrE*) a large light, usually one of two, at the front of a vehicle; the BEAM from this light（車輛的）前燈，頭燈，前燈的光束: *He dipped his headlights* (= directed the light downwards) *for the oncoming traffic.* 考慮到迎面而來的車輛，他把自己的前燈調為近光。➲ VISUAL VOCAB page V52

head·line /'hedlaɪn/ *noun, verb*

■ ***noun*** **1** [C] the title of a newspaper article printed in large letters, especially at the top of the front page（報紙的）大字標題: *They ran the story under the headline 'Home at last!'.* 報紙刊登這個報道的大標題為"終於回家了！"。◇ *The scandal was in the headlines for several days.* 這一醜聞連續幾天都刊登在頭版頭條。◇ *headline news* 頭條新聞 ➲ see also BANNER HEADLINE **2** **the headlines** [pl.] a short summary of the most important items of news, read at the beginning of a news programme on the radio or television（電台或電視的）新聞摘要 **IDM** **grab/hit/make the 'headlines** to be an important item of news in newspapers or on the radio or television 成為重要新聞

■ ***verb*** **1** [T, usually passive] **~ sth + noun** to give a story or article a particular headline 給（報道、文章）加標題: *The story was headlined 'Back to the future'.* 報道的標題是"回到未來"。 **2** [T, I] **~ (sth)** to be the main performer in a concert or show 是（音樂會或演出的）主角: *The concert is to be headlined by Steve Earle.* 音樂會的主角將是史蒂夫•厄爾。

head·lock /'hedlɒk; *NAmE* -lɑːk/ *noun* (in WRESTLING 摔跤運動) a way of holding an opponent's head so that they cannot move 夾頭: *He had him in a headlock.* 他夾住了他的頭。

head·long /ˈhedlɒŋ; *NAmE* -lɔːŋ; -lɑːŋ/ *adv.* **1** with the head first and the rest of the body following 頭朝前 **SYN** **head first**：*She fell headlong into the icy pool.* 她倒栽葱掉進了冰冷的水池中。 **2** without thinking carefully before doing sth 輕率地：*The government is taking care not to **rush headlong into** another controversy.* 政府現在很謹慎，以防不慎陷入另一場爭端。 **3** quickly and without looking where you are going 莽撞地；慌慌張張地：*He ran headlong into a police car.* 他一頭撞上了一輛警車。 ▸ **head·long** *adj.* [only before noun]：*a headlong dive/rush* 頭先入水的跳水；莽撞的向前衝

head·man /ˈhedmæn; -mən/ *noun* (*pl.* **-men** /-men; -mən/) the leader of a community （群體的）頭人，首領，酋長 **SYN** **chief**：*the village headman* 村長

head·mas·ter /ˌhedˈmɑːstə(r); *NAmE* -ˈmæs-/, **head·mis·tress** /ˌhedˈmɪstrəs/ *noun* (*NAmE* usually **prin·ci·pal**) a teacher who is in charge of a school, especially a private school （尤指私立學校的）校長 ➲ see also HEAD TEACHER

ˌ**head ˈoffice** *noun* [C, U+sing./pl. v.] the main office of a company; the managers who work there 總公司；總部：*Their head office is in New York.* 他們的總部在紐約。◇ *I don't know what head office will think about this proposal.* 我不知道總公司對此提案會有何想法。

ˌ**head of ˈstate** *noun* (*pl.* **heads of state**) the official leader of a country who is sometimes also the leader of the government 國家元首

ˌ**head-ˈon** *adj.* [only before noun] **1** in which the front part of one vehicle hits the front part of another vehicle 迎頭相撞的；正面相撞的：*a **head-on crash/collision*** 迎面碰撞／相撞 **2** in which people express strong views and deal with sth in a direct way 正面反對的；迎頭的：*There was a **head-on confrontation** between management and unions.* 資方與工會之間發生了正面衝突。 ▸ ˌ**head-ˈon** *adv.*：*The cars **crashed head-on**.* 汽車迎頭相撞。◇ *We hit the tree head-on.* 我們迎面撞到了樹上。◇ *to **tackle a problem head-on*** (= without trying to avoid it) 正面處理問題

head·phones /ˈhedfəʊnz; *NAmE* -foʊnz/ (also **ear·phones**) *noun* [pl.] a piece of equipment worn over or in the ears that makes it possible to listen to music, the radio, etc. without other people hearing it 耳機；頭戴式受話器：*a **pair/set of headphones*** 一副耳機

head·quar·tered /ˌhedˈkwɔːtəd; *NAmE* ˈhedkwɔːrtərd/ *adj.* [not before noun] having headquarters in a particular place 總部在某地：*News Corporation is headquartered in New York.* 新聞集團的總部設在紐約。

head·quar·ters /ˌhedˈkwɔːtəz; *NAmE* ˈhedkwɔːrtərz/ *noun* [U+sing./pl. v., C] (*pl.* **head·quar·ters**) (*abbr.* **HQ**) a place from which an organization or a military operation is controlled; the people who work there 總部；總公司；大本營；司令部：*The firm's headquarters is/are in London.* 公司總部設在倫敦。◇ *Several companies have their headquarters in the area.* 有幾家公司總部設在這個地區。◇ *I'm now based at headquarters.* 我現在在總公司工作。◇ *police headquarters* 警察總局 ◇ *Headquarters in Dublin has/have agreed.* 都柏林總部已經同意了。

head·rest /ˈhedrest/ *noun* the part of a seat or chair that supports a person's head, especially on the front seat of a car （尤指汽車前排座位的）頭枕，頭墊 ➲ VISUAL VOCAB page V52

head·room /ˈhedruːm; -rʊm/ *noun* [U] **1** the amount of space between the top of a vehicle and an object it drives under （機動車車頂與其上方橋梁等之間的）淨空 **2** the amount of space between the top of your head and the roof of a vehicle （機動車內的）頭上空間：*There's a lot of headroom for such a small car.* 這麼小的一輛汽車的頭上空間蠻大的。

ˈ**head rush** *noun* a thing or an experience that you find very exciting 令人興奮的事（或經歷）：*the physical head rush of being in love* 談戀愛這一引發身心躁動的經歷

head·scarf /ˈhedskɑːf; *NAmE* -skɑːrf/ *noun* (*pl.* **head·scarves**) a square piece of cloth tied around the head by women or girls, usually with a knot under the chin （女用）方頭巾

head·set /ˈhedset/ *noun* a pair of HEADPHONES, especially one with a MICROPHONE attached to it （尤指帶麥克風的）頭戴式受話器，耳機 ➲ VISUAL VOCAB page V66

head·ship /ˈhedʃɪp/ *noun* ~ (**of sth**) **1** the position of being in charge of an organization 主管職位：*the headship of the department* 部門領導的職位 **2** (*BrE*) the position of being in charge of a school 校長職位

head·stand /ˈhedstænd/ *noun* a position in which a person has their head on the ground and their feet straight up in the air 頭倒立

ˌ**head ˈstart** *noun* [sing.] ~ (**on/over sb**) an advantage that sb already has before they start doing sth 起步前的優勢：*Being able to speak French gave her a head start over the other candidates.* 會説法語使她比其他候選人佔優勢。

head·stone /ˈhedstəʊn; *NAmE* -stoʊn/ *noun* a piece of stone placed at one end of a grave, showing the name, etc. of the person buried there 墓碑 **SYN** **gravestone** ➲ compare TOMBSTONE

head·strong /ˈhedstrɒŋ; *NAmE* -strɔːŋ/ *adj.* (*disapproving*) a **headstrong** person is determined to do things their own way and refuses to listen to advice 固執的；倔強任性的

ˈ**heads-up** *noun* (*pl.* **heads-up** or **heads-ups**) ~ (**about sth**) (*especially NAmE*) a piece of information given in advance of sth or as advice 預先通知；預先勸告：*Send everyone a heads-up about the changes well in advance.* 把這些變化早早通知每個人。

ˌ**head ˈtable** (*NAmE*) (*BrE* ˌ**top ˈtable**) *noun* the table at which the most important guests sit at a formal dinner （正式宴會上的）主桌

ˌ**head ˈteacher** *noun* (*BrE*) (*NAmE* **prin·ci·pal**) a teacher who is in charge of a school 校長

ˌ**head-to-ˈhead** *adj.* [only before noun] in which two people or groups face each other directly in order to decide the result of a disagreement or competition 正面交鋒的；面對面的：*a **head-to-head battle/clash/contest*** 正面戰鬥／衝突／競爭 ▸ ˌ**head-to-ˈhead** *adv.*：*They are set to meet head-to-head in next week's final.* 他們將在下個星期的決賽中正面交鋒。

head·waters /ˈhedwɔːtəz; *NAmE* -tərz/ *noun* [pl.] streams forming the source of a river 河源；上游

head·way /ˈhedweɪ/ *noun* [U]
IDM **make ˈheadway** to make progress, especially when this is slow or difficult 取得（緩慢的或艱難的）進展：*We are making little headway with the negotiations.* 我們的談判沒有取得什麼進展。◇ *The boat was unable to make much headway against the tide.* 船逆着潮水沒法開快。

head·wind /ˈhedwɪnd/ *noun* a wind that is blowing towards a person or vehicle, so that it is blowing from the direction in which the person or vehicle is moving 逆風；頂風 ➲ compare TAILWIND

head·word /ˈhedwɜːd; *NAmE* -wɜːrd/ *noun* (*technical* 術語) a word that forms a HEADING in a dictionary, under which its meaning is explained （詞典中的）詞目，首詞

heady /ˈhedi/ *adj.* (**head·ier**, **headi·est**) **1** [usually before noun] having a strong effect on your senses; making you feel excited and confident 強烈作用於感官的；使興奮的；使有信心的 **SYN** **intoxicating**：*the heady days of youth* 令人陶醉的年輕時代 ◇ *the heady scent of hot spices* 辣味香料的刺鼻氣味 ◇ *a heady mixture of desire and fear* 既期待又害怕的複雜心情 ➲ SYNONYMS at EXCITING **2** [not before noun] (of a person 人) excited in a way that makes you do things without worrying about the possible results 衝動；冒失：*She felt heady with success.* 成功使她得意忘形。

heal 0→ /hiːl/ *verb*
1 0→ [I, T] to become healthy again; to make sth healthy again （使）康復，復原：*It took a long time for the wounds to heal.* 傷口過了很長時間才痛合。◇ ~ **up** *The cut healed up without leaving a scar.* 傷口痛合沒留下疤痕。◇ ~ **sth** *This will help to heal your cuts and scratches.*

H

這個會有助於治好割傷和擦傷。◇ (*figurative*) *It was a chance to* ***heal the wounds*** *in the party* (= to repair the damage that had been done). 那是個彌合黨內創傷的機會。 **2** [T] **~ sb (of sth)** (*old use* or *formal*) to cure sb who is ill/sick; to make sb feel happy again 治療（病人）；使又愉快起來：*the story of Jesus healing ten lepers of their disease* 耶穌治癒十個麻風病人的故事 ◇ *I felt healed by his love.* 他的愛使我又快樂了起來。 **3** [T, I] **~ (sth)** to put an end to sth or make sth easier to bear; to end or become easier to bear （使）結束，較容易忍受：*She was never able to heal the rift between herself and her father.* 她一直未能填平和她父親之間的鴻溝。◇ *The breach between them never really healed.* 他們之間的裂痕從來沒有真正彌合。

heal·er /ˈhiːlə(r)/ *noun* **1** a person who cures people of illnesses and disease using natural powers rather than medicine 用自然力（而非藥物）治療別人者：*a faith/spiritual healer* 醫治信仰 / 心靈的人 **2** something that makes a bad situation easier to deal with 緩解情勢的事物：*Time is a great healer.* 時間是良藥。

heal·ing /ˈhiːlɪŋ/ *noun* [U] the process of becoming or making sb/sth healthy again; the process of getting better after an emotional shock 康復；治療；（情感創傷的）癒合：*the healing process* 康復過程 ◇ *emotional healing* 感情上的癒合 ➲ see also FAITH HEALING

health 🔑 /helθ/ *noun* [U]

1 🔑 the condition of a person's body or mind 人的身體（或精神）狀況；健康：*Exhaust fumes are bad for your health.* 廢氣對健康有害。◇ ***to be in poor/good/excellent/the best of health*** 健康狀況不好 / 好 / 極好 / 好極 ◇ *Smoking can seriously* ***damage your health.*** 吸煙會嚴重損害健康 ◇ ***mental health*** 心理健康 ➲ see also ILL HEALTH **2** 🔑 the state of being physically and mentally healthy 健康：*He was nursed back to health by his wife.* 他在妻子的照料下恢復了健康。◇ *She was glowing with health and clearly enjoying life.* 她容光煥發，顯然生活得很快活。◇ *As long as you have your health, nothing else matters.* 只要身體健康，其他任何事都無關緊要。 **3** 🔑 the work of providing medical services 醫療；保健；衞生：*All parties are promising to increase spending on health.* 各政黨都在許諾增加醫療開支。◇ *the Health Minister* 衞生部長 ◇ *the Department of Health* 衞生部 ◇ ***health insurance*** 健康保險 ◇ ***health and safety regulations*** (= laws that protect the health of people at work) 健康和安全規則 **4** how successful sth is 狀況；牢靠性：*the health of your marriage/finances* 婚姻 / 財政狀況 IDM see CLEAN *adj.*, DRINK *v.*, PROPOSE, RUDE

ˈ**health care** *noun* [U] the service of providing medical care 醫療（服務）：*the costs of health care for the elderly* 老年人的醫療費用 ◇ ***health care workers/professionals*** 醫療工作人員 / 專家

ˈ**health centre** (*BrE*) (*especially US* ˈ**health ˌcenter**) *noun* a building where a group of doctors see their patients and where some local medical services have their offices 衞生院；保健中心

ˈ**health club** *noun* (also **gym**) a private club where people go to do physical exercise in order to stay or become healthy and fit 健身俱樂部

ˈ**health farm** *noun* (*especially BrE*) = HEALTH SPA

ˈ**health food** *noun* [U, C, usually pl.] food that does not contain any artificial substances and is therefore thought to be good for your health 保健食物；綠色食物

health·ful /ˈhelθfl/ *adj.* [usually before noun] (*formal* or *NAmE*) good for your health 有益於健康的 ▸ **health·ful·ly** *adv.*

ˈ**health service** *noun* a public service providing medical care 公共醫療保健服務 ➲ see also NATIONAL HEALTH SERVICE

ˈ**health spa** (also ˈ**health farm** especially in *BrE*) *noun* a place where people can stay for short periods of time in order to try to improve their health by eating special food, doing physical exercise, etc. 健身莊，休閒健身中心（提供特定飲食、身體鍛煉等短期休養服務）

ˈ**health visitor** *noun* (in Britain) a trained nurse whose job is to visit people in their homes, for example new parents, and give them advice on some areas of medical care （英國）家訪護士

healthy 🔑 /ˈhelθi/ *adj.* (**health·ier**, **healthi·est**)

1 🔑 having good health and not likely to become ill/sick 健康的；健壯的：*a healthy child/animal/tree* 健康的孩子 / 動物 / 樹 ◇ ***Keep healthy*** *by eating well and exercising regularly.* 通過良好飲食和經常性鍛煉保持健康。 OPP **unhealthy** ➲ SYNONYMS at WELL **2** 🔑 [usually before noun] good for your health 有益於健康的：*a* ***healthy diet/climate/lifestyle*** 對健康有益的飲食 / 氣候 / 生活方式 OPP **unhealthy** **3** 🔑 [usually before noun] showing that you are in good health 反映健康的：*to have a healthy appetite* 胃口好 ◇ *a shampoo that keeps hair looking healthy* 護髮洗髮劑 **4** normal and sensible 正常合理的：*The child showed a healthy curiosity.* 這孩子的好奇心很正常。◇ *She has a healthy respect for her rival's talents.* 她很有風度地尊重對手的才能。◇ *It's not healthy the way she clings to the past.* 她那種沉湎於過去的態度不明智。 OPP **unhealthy** **5** successful and working well 興旺的；發達的；順利的：*a healthy economy* 繁榮的經濟 ◇ *Your car doesn't sound very healthy.* 你的車聽聲音好像不很正常。 **6** [usually before noun] large and showing success 大而顯得成功的；可觀的：*a healthy bank balance* 一大筆銀行結餘 ◇ *a healthy profit* 豐厚的利潤 ▸ **health·ily** *adv.*：*to eat healthily* 吃得健康 **healthi·ness** *noun* [U]

heap /hiːp/ *noun, verb*

■ ***noun*** **1 ~ (of sth)** an untidy pile of sth （凌亂的）一堆：*The building was reduced to a heap of rubble.* 大樓變成了一片殘垣斷壁。◇ *a compost heap* 一堆堆肥 ◇ *His clothes lay* ***in a heap*** *on the floor.* 他的衣服堆在地板上。◇ *Worn-out car tyres were stacked* ***in heaps.*** 汽車廢輪胎散亂地堆放着。 ➲ see also SCRAPHEAP, SLAG HEAP **2** [usually pl.] (*informal*) a lot of sth 許多；大量：(*BrE*) *There's heaps of time before the plane leaves.* 離飛機起飛還有很多時間。◇ (*NAmE*) *I've got a heap of things to do.* 我有一大堆事情要做。 **3** (*informal, humorous*) a car that is old and in bad condition 破舊的汽車；老爺車

IDM **at the top/bottom of the ˈheap** high up/low down in the structure of an organization or a society 在（機構或社會的）頂層 / 底層：*These workers are at the bottom of the economic heap.* 這些工人處在經濟結構的底層。 **collapse, fall, etc. in a ˈheap** to fall down heavily and not move 重重地倒下（不能動） **heaps ˈbetter, ˈmore, ˈolder, etc.** (*BrE, informal*) a lot better, etc. 好（或多、老等）得多：*Help yourself—there's heaps more.* 請隨便取用，還多着呢。◇ *He looks heaps better than when I last saw him.* 他看上去比我上回見他時好多了。

■ ***verb*** **1 ~ sth (up)** to put things in an untidy pile 堆積（東西）；堆置：*Rocks were heaped up on the side of the road.* 路邊堆積着石頭。 **2** to put a lot of sth in a pile on sth 在…上放很多（東西）：**~ A on B** *She heaped food on my plate.* 她往我的盤子裏夾了很多食物。◇ **~ B with A** *She heaped my plate with food.* 她往我的盤子裏夾了很多食物。 **3** to give a lot of sth such as praise or criticism to sb 對（某人）大加讚揚（或批評等）：**~ A on B** *He* ***heaped praise*** *on his team.* 他高度讚揚了他的隊。◇ **~ B with A** *He heaped his team with praise.* 他高度讚揚了他的隊。 IDM see SCORN *n.*

heap·ed /hiːpt/ (*especially BrE*) (*NAmE* usually **heap·ing**) *adj.* used to describe a spoon, etc. that has as much in it or on it as it can hold 滿滿的（一匙等）：*a heaped teaspoon of sugar* 滿滿一茶匙糖 ◇ *heaping plates of scrambled eggs* 盛得滿滿的一盤盤炒雞蛋 ➲ compare LEVEL *adj.* (1)

hear 🔑 /hɪə(r); *NAmE* hɪr/ *verb* (**heard**, **heard** /hɜːd; *NAmE* hɜːrd/)

1 🔑 [I, T] (not used in the progressive tenses 不用於進行時) to be aware of sounds with your ears 聽見；聽到：*I can't hear very well.* 我聽覺不太好。◇ **~ sth/sb** *She heard footsteps behind her.* 她聽到背後有腳步聲。◇ **~ sb/sth doing sth** *He could hear a dog barking.* 他聽得到狗叫。◇ **~ sb/sth do sth** *Did you hear him go out?* 你聽到他出去了嗎？◇ **~ what …** *Didn't you hear what I said?* 難道你沒有聽到我的話？◇ **sb/sth is heard to do**

sth *She has been heard to make threats to her former lover.* 有人聽見她威脅她先前的戀人。 **2** 🔑 [T] (not used in the progressive tenses 不用於進行時) to listen or pay attention to sb/sth 聽；注意聽；傾聽： **~ sth** *Did you hear that play on the radio last night?* 你昨晚收聽了那齣廣播劇嗎？◇ **~ sb/sth/yourself do sth** *Be quiet—**I can't hear myself think!*** (= it is so noisy that I can't think clearly) 安靜點，我都給吵昏頭了！◇ **~ what ...** *We'd better hear what they have to say.* 我們最好還是聽聽他們有什麼話要說。◇ ***I hear what you're saying*** (= I have listened to your opinion), *but you're wrong.* 我已經聽到你的意見了，但你錯了。 **3** 🔑 [I, T] (not usually used in the progressive tenses 通常不用於進行時) to be told about sth 聽說；得知： *Haven't you heard? She resigned.* 你還沒聽說嗎？她辭職了。◇ *'I'm getting married.' **'So I've heard.'*** "我要結婚了。" "我聽說了。" ◇ *Things are going well **from what I hear**.* 從我所聽到的來看，事情進展不錯。◇ **~ about sb/sth** *I was sorry to hear about your accident.* 獲悉你遇到意外，我很難過。◇ *I've heard about people like you.* 我聽說過像你這樣的人。◇ **~ sth** *We had heard nothing for weeks.* 我們好幾個星期都沒得到任何消息了。◇ **~ (that) ...** *I was surprised to hear (that) he was married.* 聽說他結婚了，我很驚訝。◇ *I hear you've been away this weekend.* 我聽說你這個週末外出了。◇ **~ it said (that) ...** *I've heard it said (that) they met in Italy.* 我聽說他們是在意大利認識的。◇ **~ what, how, etc. ...** *Did you hear what happened?* 你聽說發生什麼事了嗎？ **4** [T] **~ sth** to listen to and judge a case in court 審理；聽審： *The appeal was heard in private.* 這件上訴案不公開審理。◇ *Today the jury began to hear the evidence.* 今天陪審團開始聽證。

IDM **have you heard the one about ...?** used to ask sb if they have heard a particular joke before 你聽說過（某笑話）嗎？ **ˌhear! ˈhear!** used to show that you agree with or approve of what sb has just said, especially during a speech（表示贊同，尤指在聽演講時）對！對！ **hear ˈtell (of sth)** (*old-fashioned* or *formal*) to hear people talking about sth 聽到人談論（某事）；聽說： *I've often heard tell of such things.* 我常聽到人談起這種事。 **I've heard it all beˈfore** (*informal*) used to say that you do not really believe sb's promises or excuses because they are the same ones you have heard before（表示不相信某人的許諾或辯解）這種話我聽得多了 **let's hear it for ...** (*informal*) used to say that sb/sth deserves praise（表示值得稱讚）咱們為…鼓掌，讓我們為…喝彩： *Let's hear it for the teachers, for a change.* 咱們變換一下，這回為老師們鼓鼓掌。 **not/never hear the ˈend of it** to keep being reminded of sth because sb is always talking to you about it 被人不斷糾纏，沒完沒了： *If we don't get her a dog we'll never hear the end of it.* 我們要是不給她弄條狗來，這事就沒完沒了。 **you could hear a ˈpin drop** it was extremely quiet 鴉雀無聲；萬籟俱寂：*The audience was so quiet you could have heard a pin drop.* 觀眾安靜得連針落地的聲音也聽得見。 **(do) you ˈhear (me)?** (*informal*) used to tell sb in an angry way to pay attention and obey you（生氣地要某人聽從）聽到我的話沒有： *You can't go—do you hear me?* 你不能走，聽清楚了嗎？ ➲ more at LAST[1] *n.*, THING, VOICE *n.*

PHR V **ˈhear from sb | ˈhear sth from sb** 🔑 to receive a letter, email, phone call, etc. from sb 收到某人的信件（或電子郵件、電話等）；得到某人的消息： *I look forward to hearing from you.* 盼望着收到你的信。◇ *I haven't heard anything from her for months.* 我好幾個月都沒有她的音信了。 **ˈhear of sb/sth | ˈhear sth of sb/sth** 🔑 to know about sb/sth because you have been told about them 聽說，得知（某人或某事）： *I've never heard of the place.* 我從來沒聽說過這個地方。◇ *She disappeared and was never heard of again.* 她消失了，再也沒人聽到過她的消息。◇ ***The last I heard of** him he was living in Glasgow.* 我最後一次聽到他的消息時，他住在格拉斯哥。◇ *This is **the first I've heard of** it!* 這可是我第一次聽說這件事！ **not ˈhear of sth** to refuse to let sb do sth, especially because you want to help them 出於善意拒絕（或不允許）某事： *She wanted to walk home but I wouldn't hear of it.* 她想步行回家，但我就是不允許。◇ **~ sb doing sth** *He wouldn't hear of my walking home alone.* 他不讓我獨自一人走回家。 ➲ see also UNHEARD-OF **ˌhear sb ˈout** to listen until sb has finished saying what they want to say 聽某人把話說完

hear·er /ˈhɪərə(r); *NAmE* ˈhɪr-/ *noun* a person who hears sth or who is listening to sb 受話人；聽者 **SYN** **listener**

hear·ing 🔑 /ˈhɪərɪŋ; *NAmE* ˈhɪr-/ *noun* **1** 🔑 [U] the ability to hear 聽力；聽覺： *Her hearing is poor.* 她的聽覺不靈。◇ *He's **hearing-impaired*** (= not able to hear well). 他聽覺受損。 ➲ see also HARD OF HEARING **2** [C] an official meeting at which the facts about a crime, complaint, etc. are presented to the person or group of people who will have to decide what action to take 審訊；審理；聽審；聽證會： *a **court/disciplinary hearing*** 庭審；紀律聆訊 ➲ COLLOCATIONS at JUSTICE **3** [sing.] an opportunity to explain your actions, ideas or opinions（行為、思想或意見的）解釋機會，申辯機會： *to get/give sb **a fair hearing*** 得到／給予某人公正的申辯機會◇ *His views may be unfashionable but he deserves a hearing.* 他的觀點可能不合潮流，但應該給他機會解釋。

IDM **in/within (sb's) ˈhearing** near enough to sb so that they can hear what is said 在（某人）聽得見的範圍內 **SYN** **within earshot**： *She shouldn't have said such things in your hearing.* 她不應該在你面前說這種事情。◇ *I had no reason to believe there was anyone within hearing.* 我不相信周圍會有人聽得見。 **out of ˈhearing** too far away to hear sb/sth or to be heard 離得太遠聽不見；在聽力範圍外： *She had moved out of hearing.* 她走遠了，已經聽不到。

ˈhearing aid *noun* a small device that fits inside the ear and makes sounds louder, used by people who cannot hear well 助聽器： *to **have/wear a hearing aid*** 有／戴助聽器

ˈhearing dog *noun* a dog trained to make a deaf person (= person who cannot hear well) aware of sounds such as the ringing of a telephone or a DOORBELL 導聾犬（經訓練用來提醒耳聾者如電話鈴、門鈴等聲響）

heark·en (also **hark·en**) /ˈhɑːkən; *NAmE* ˈhɑːrkən/ *verb* [I] **~ (to sb/sth)** (*old use*) to listen to sb/sth 傾聽；聆聽

hear·say /ˈhɪəseɪ; *NAmE* ˈhɪrseɪ/ *noun* [U] things that you have heard from another person but do not (definitely) know to be true 道聽途說；傳聞： *We can't make a decision based on hearsay and guesswork.* 我們不能根據傳言和猜測做決定。◇ *hearsay evidence* 傳聞的證據

hearse /hɜːs; *NAmE* hɜːrs/ *noun* a long vehicle used for carrying the coffin (= the box for the dead body) at a funeral 靈車；柩車

heart 🔑 /hɑːt; *NAmE* hɑːrt/ *noun*
▸ PART OF BODY 身體部位 **1** 🔑 [C] the organ in the chest that sends blood around the body, usually on the left in humans 心；心臟： *The patient's heart stopped beating for a few seconds.* 病人的心跳停頓了幾秒鐘。◇ ***heart trouble/failure*** 心臟病；心力衰竭◇ *to have a weak heart* 心臟不好◇ *I could feel my heart pounding in my chest* (= because of excitement, etc.). 我能感覺到我的心在胸腔裏怦怦直跳。 ➲ VISUAL VOCAB page V59 ➲ see also CORONARY (HEART) DISEASE at CORONARY, OPEN-HEART SURGERY **2** [C] (*literary*) the outside part of the chest where the heart is 胸部心臟的部位： *She clasped the photo to her heart.* 她把相片緊緊地抱在懷裏。
▸ FEELINGS/EMOTIONS 感情；心情 **3** 🔑 [C] the place in a person where the feelings and emotions are thought to be, especially those connected with love 內心；心腸；（尤指）愛心： *She has a kind heart.* 她有一顆善良的心。◇ *Have you no heart?* 你沒有一點同情心嗎？◇ *He returned with a **heavy heart*** (= sad). 他心情沉重地回來了。◇ *Her novels tend to deal with **affairs of the heart**.* 她的小說往往是有關愛情故事的。◇ *The story captured **the hearts and minds** of a generation.* 這部小說準確地傳達了一代人的感情和思想。 ➲ see also BROKEN HEART
▸ -HEARTED 有…心 **4** (in adjectives 構成形容詞) having the type of character or personality mentioned 有…性格（或品格）的： *cold-hearted* 冷酷無情的◇ *kind-hearted* 好心腸的

H

▸ **IMPORTANT PART 重要部份 5** [sing.] **~ (of sth)** the most important part of sth 重點；核心；要點：*the heart of the matter/problem* 事情／問題的核心 ◇ *The committee's report* ***went to the heart of*** *the government's dilemma.* 委員會的報告直指政府兩難困境的要害。◇ *The distinction between right and wrong* ***lies at the heart of*** *all questions of morality.* 是非界限是所有道德問題的核心。

▸ **CENTRE 中心 6** [C, usually sing.] **~ (of sth)** the part that is in the centre of sth 中心；中央：*a quiet hotel* ***in the very heart of*** *the city* 一家位於市中心的安靜的旅館

▸ **OF CABBAGE 捲心菜 7** [C] the smaller leaves in the middle of a CABBAGE, LETTUCE, etc. 菜心

▸ **SHAPE 形狀 8** [C] a thing shaped like a heart, often red and used as a symbol of love; a symbol shaped like a heart used to mean the verb 'love' 心形物；（常指象徵愛的）紅心；心形（表示動詞"愛"）：*The words 'I love you' were written inside a big red heart.* "我愛你"這幾個字寫在一個大紅心裏。◇ (*informal*) *I ♥ New York.* 我愛紐約。

H

▸ **IN CARD GAMES 紙牌遊戲 9 hearts** [pl., U] one of the four sets of cards (called SUITS) in a PACK/DECK of cards, with red heart symbols on them（統稱）紅桃牌，紅心牌：*the queen of hearts* 紅桃王后 ◇ *Hearts is/are trumps.* 紅桃是主。➲ **VISUAL VOCAB** page V37 **10** [C] one card from the set of hearts（一張）紅桃牌，紅心牌：*Who played that heart?* 誰打出那張紅桃？

IDM **at 'heart** used to say what sb is really like even though they may seem to be sth different 內心裏；本質上：*He's still a socialist at heart.* 他本質上還是個社會主義者。 **break sb's 'heart** to make sb feel very unhappy 使某人很難過；使心碎：*She broke his heart when she called off the engagement.* 她取消婚約使他為之心碎。◇ *It breaks my heart to see you like this.* 看到你這個樣子我很難過。 **by 'heart** (*BrE* also **off by 'heart**) using only your memory 單憑記憶；能背誦：*I've dialled the number so many times I know it by heart.* 這個號碼我撥了很多次，都記住了。◇ *She's learnt the whole speech off by heart.* 她把整篇講話都背熟了。 **close/dear/near to sb's 'heart** having a lot of importance and interest for sb 為某人所重視關心；為某人所愛 **from the (bottom of your) 'heart** in a way that is sincere 真誠地；從內心（深處）：*I beg you, from the bottom of my heart, to spare his life.* 我誠心誠意地懇求你饒他一命吧。◇ *It was clearly an offer that came from the heart.* 那很明顯是由衷的提議。 **give sb (fresh) 'heart** to make sb feel positive, especially when they thought that they had no chance of achieving sth 激勵某人；使某人振作 **give your 'heart to sb** to give your love to one person 愛上某人；傾心 **have a 'heart!** (*informal*) used to ask sb to be kind and/or reasonable 發發善心吧；講點情理吧 **have a heart of 'gold** to be a very kind person 有金子般的心；心腸很好 **have a heart of 'stone** to be a person who does not show others sympathy or pity 鐵石心腸；冷酷無情 **heart and 'soul** with a lot of energy and enthusiasm 滿腔熱忱幹勁十足；全心全意：*They threw themselves heart and soul into the project.* 他們全心全意地投入了這個項目。 **your heart goes 'out to sb** used to say that you feel a lot of sympathy for sb 十分同情；憐憫：*Our hearts go out to the families of the victims.* 我們很同情那些受害者的家人。 **sb's heart is in their 'mouth** somebody feels nervous or frightened about sth 提心吊膽；心慌意亂 **sb's heart is in the right 'place** used to say that sb's intentions are kind and sincere even though they sometimes do the wrong thing 本意是好的；心眼是好的 **your 'heart is not in sth** used to say that you are not very interested in or enthusiastic about sth 對某事不很感興趣（或不熱衷） **sb's heart 'leaps** used to say that sb has a sudden feeling of happiness or excitement 心花怒放 **sb's heart misses a 'beat** used to say that sb has a sudden feeling of fear, excitement, etc.（表示突然感到恐懼、興奮等）心裏咯噔一下 **sb's heart 'sinks** used to say that sb suddenly feels sad or depressed about sth（表示突然感到悲傷或沮喪）心裏一沉：*My heart sank when I saw how much work there was left.* 我看到還有那麼多活沒幹時，心頓時沉了下去。◇ *She watched him go* ***with a sinking heart.*** 她心情沉重地看着他走了。 **in good 'heart** (*BrE*) happy and cheerful 心情舒暢；興高采烈 **in your 'heart (of 'hearts)** if you know sth **in your heart**, you have a strong feeling that it is true 在內心深處；內心強烈地感覺到：*She knew in her heart of hearts that she was making the wrong decision.* 她心底裏明白她在做出錯誤的決定。 **it does sb's 'heart good (to do sth)** it makes sb feel happy when they see or hear sth（看到或聽到某事時）使人感到高興，使人心曠神怡：*It does my heart good to see the old place being taken care of so well.* 看到故居被照管得這麼好，真叫人高興。 **let your ˌheart rule your 'head** to act according to what you feel rather than to what you think is sensible 感情用事 **lose 'heart** to stop hoping for sth or trying to do sth because you no longer feel confident 喪失信心；泄氣 **lose your 'heart (to sb/sth)** (*formal*) to fall in love with sb/sth 愛上（某人或某事物） **a man/woman after your own 'heart** a man/woman who likes the same things or has the same opinions as you 趣味相投者；情投意合者 **my heart 'bleeds (for sb)** (*ironic*) used to say that you do not feel sympathy or pity for sb（表示不同情或憐憫）真可憐：*'I have to go to Brazil on business.' 'My heart bleeds for you!'* "我要出差去巴西。" "真夠可憐的！" **not have the 'heart (to do sth)** to be unable to do sth because you know that it will make sb sad or upset 不忍心（做某事） **off by 'heart** (*BrE*) = BY HEART **pour out/open your 'heart to sb** to tell sb all your problems, feelings, etc. 向某人敞開心扉；傾訴衷腸 **set your 'heart on sth | have your heart 'set on sth** to want sth very much 渴望；一心想要 **take 'heart (from sth)** to feel more positive about sth, especially when you thought that you had no chance of achieving sth（由於某事）增強信心；重新振作起來：*The government can take heart from the latest opinion polls.* 政府可以從最近的民意測驗中找回信心。 **take sth to 'heart** to be very upset by sth that sb says or does 對某事感到煩惱；十分介意（某人的話或行為）；耿耿於懷 **ˌtear/ˌrip the 'heart out of sth** to destroy the most important part or aspect of sth 摧毀…的核心 **to your heart's con'tent** as much as you want 盡情地；心滿意足：*a supervised play area where children can run around to their heart's content* 一處能讓孩子們盡情遊玩且有人看管的地方 **with all your 'heart/your whole 'heart** completely 完全地；全心全意：*I hope with all my heart that things work out for you.* 我衷心希望你一切順利。➲ more at ABSENCE, CHANGE *n.*, CROSS *v.*, EAT, ETCH, EYE *n.*, FIND *v.*, GOODNESS, HOME *n.*, INTEREST *n.*, SICK *adj.*, SOB *v.*, STEAL *v.*, STRIKE *v.*, TEAR[1] *v.*, WARM *v.*, WAY *n.*, WEAR *v.*, WIN *v.*, YOUNG *adj.*

heart·ache /'hɑːteɪk; *NAmE* 'hɑːrt-/ *noun* [U, C] a strong feeling of sadness or worry 痛心；傷心；憂慮：*The relationship caused her a great deal of heartache.* 這段戀情使她非常傷心。◇ *the heartaches of being a parent* 為人父母的煩惱

'heart attack *noun* a sudden serious medical condition in which the heart stops working normally, sometimes causing death 心臟病發作 ➲ **COLLOCATIONS** at ILL ➲ compare CORONARY THROMBOSIS

heart·beat /'hɑːtbiːt; *NAmE* 'hɑːrt-/ *noun* **1** [C, U] the movement or sound of the heart as it sends blood around the body 心跳；心搏；心跳聲：*a* ***rapid/regular heartbeat*** 急速／正常的心跳 **2** [sing.] **the ~ of sth** (*NAmE*) an important feature of sth, that is responsible for making it what it is 重要特徵；中心：*The candidate said that he understood the heartbeat of the Hispanic community in California.* 這位候選人說他瞭解加利福尼亞州的西班牙語裔美國人社區的特點。

IDM **a 'heartbeat away (from sth)** very close to sth（離…）很近；近在咫尺 **in a 'heartbeat** very quickly, without thinking about it 瞬間；隨即：*If I was offered another job, I'd leave in a heartbeat.* 如果能找到另外一份工作，我馬上就走。

heart·break /'hɑːtbreɪk; *NAmE* 'hɑːrt-/ *noun* [U, C] a strong feeling of sadness 強烈的悲痛感；心碎：*They suffered the heartbreak of losing a child through cancer.* 他們因癌症奪去了一個孩子而肝腸寸斷。▸ **'heart·break·ing** *adj.*：*a heartbreaking story* 令人心碎的故事 ◇ *It's heartbreaking to see him wasting his life like this.* 看到他如此糟蹋自己的生命真讓人心碎。

heart·broken /ˈhɑːtbrəʊkən; *NAmE* ˈhɑːrtbroʊkən/ *adj.* extremely sad because of sth that has happened 極為悲傷的；心碎的 SYN **broken-hearted**

heart·burn /ˈhɑːtbɜːn; *NAmE* ˈhɑːrtbɜːrn/ *noun* [U] a pain that feels like sth burning in your chest caused by INDIGESTION（消化不良引起的）胃灼熱，燒心

heart·en /ˈhɑːtn; *NAmE* ˈhɑːrtn/ *verb* [usually passive] **~ sb** to give sb encouragement or hope 激勵；鼓勵 OPP **dishearten** ▸ **heart·en·ing** *adj.*: *It is heartening to see the determination of these young people.* 看到這些年輕人如此堅決真令人鼓舞。

ˈ**heart failure** *noun* [U] a serious medical condition in which the heart does not work correctly 心力衰竭

heart·felt /ˈhɑːtfelt; *NAmE* ˈhɑːrt-/ *adj.* [usually before noun] showing strong feelings that are sincere 衷心的；真誠的 SYN **sincere**: *a **heartfelt apology/plea/sigh*** 真切的道歉／懇求／歎息 ◇ ***heartfelt sympathy/thanks*** 由衷的同情／感謝

hearth /hɑːθ; *NAmE* hɑːrθ/ *noun* **1** the floor at the bottom of a FIREPLACE (= the space for a fire in the wall of a room); the area in front of this 壁爐爐牀；壁爐前的地面：*A log fire roared in the open hearth.* 柴火在敞開着的壁爐裏熊熊燃燒。◇ *The cat dozed in its favourite spot on the hearth.* 貓躺在壁爐前它最喜歡的地方打盹。➲ VISUAL VOCAB page V21 **2** (*literary*) home and family life 家和家庭生活：*a longing for **hearth and home*** 對溫暖家庭的渴望

hearth·rug /ˈhɑːθrʌg; *NAmE* ˈhɑːrθ-/ *noun* a RUG (= a small carpet) placed on the floor in front of a FIREPLACE 壁爐前的地毯

heart·ily /ˈhɑːtɪli; *NAmE* ˈhɑːrt-/ *adv.* **1** with obvious enjoyment and enthusiasm 盡情地；關懷地；勁頭十足地：*to laugh/sing/eat heartily* 開懷大笑；放聲歌唱；大吃 **2** in a way that shows that you feel strongly about sth 強烈地；堅定地：*I heartily agree with her on this.* 在這一點上我十分贊同她。**3** extremely 極為；極其：*heartily glad/relieved* 極為高興；愁雲盡掃

heart·land /ˈhɑːtlænd; *NAmE* ˈhɑːrt-/ *noun* (also **heart·lands** [pl.]) **1** the central part of a country or an area（國家或地區的）腹地，中心區域：*the great Russian heartlands* 廣袤的俄羅斯中心地帶 **2** an area that is important for a particular activity or political party（活動或政黨的）重要場所，核心區域：*the industrial heartland of Germany* 德國的中心工業區 ◇ *the traditional Tory heartland of Britain's boardrooms* 保守黨的傳統領地：英國的各董事會

heart·less /ˈhɑːtləs; *NAmE* ˈhɑːrt-/ *adj.* feeling no pity for other people 無情的；狠心的 SYN **cruel**: *What a heartless thing to say!* 這麼說話太無情了！▸ **heart·less·ly** *adv.* **heart·less·ness** *noun* [U]

ˌ**heart-ˈlung machine** *noun* a machine that replaces the functions of the heart and lungs, for example during a medical operation on the heart 心肺機（手術等時發揮心肺功能）

ˈ**heart-rending** *adj.* [usually before noun] causing feelings of great sadness 令人悲痛的 SYN **heartbreaking**: *a heart-rending story* 令人心痛的故事

ˈ**heart-searching** *noun* [U] the process of examining carefully your feelings or reasons for doing sth 反省；自我檢討

heart·sick /ˈhɑːtsɪk; *NAmE* ˈhɑːrt-/ *adj.* [not usually before noun] (*literary*) extremely unhappy or disappointed 悲痛；傷心失望

ˈ**heart-stopping** *adj.* [usually before noun] causing feelings of great excitement or worry 使人非常興奮的；令人十分擔憂的：*For one heart-stopping moment she thought they were too late.* 一時間她十分擔心他們已經太晚了。

heart·strings /ˈhɑːtstrɪŋz; *NAmE* ˈhɑːrt-/ *noun* [pl.] strong feelings of love or pity 深切的愛（或同情）；心弦：*to **tug/pull at sb's heartstrings*** (= to cause such feelings in sb) 動人心弦

ˈ**heart-throb** *noun* (used especially in newspapers) a famous man, usually an actor or a singer, that a lot of women find attractive（尤用於報章，常指男性演員或歌手）萬人迷，大眾情人

ˌ**heart-to-ˈheart** *noun* [usually sing.] a conversation in which two people talk honestly about their feelings and personal problems 坦誠親切的交談；談心：*to have a heart-to-heart with sb* 和某人談心 ▸ ˌ**heart-to-ˈheart** *adj.*: *a heart-to-heart talk* 坦誠親切的交談

ˈ**heart-warming** *adj.* causing feelings of happiness and pleasure 使人幸福愉快的

heart·wood /ˈhɑːtwʊd; *NAmE* ˈhɑːrt-/ *noun* [U] the hard older inner layers of the wood of a tree（樹木的）心材 ➲ compare SAPWOOD

hearty /ˈhɑːti; *NAmE* ˈhɑːrti/ *adj.*, *noun*

■ ***adj.*** (**heart·ier**, **hearti·est**) **1** [usually before noun] showing friendly feelings for sb 親切的；友好的：*a hearty welcome* 熱情的歡迎 **2** (sometimes *disapproving*) loud, cheerful and full of energy 喧鬧而活潑的；吵鬧快活且精力充沛的：*a hearty and boisterous fellow* 活潑愛吵鬧的傢伙 ◇ *a hearty voice* 響亮的嗓子 **3** [only before noun] (of a meal or sb's APPETITE 飯菜或胃口) large; making you feel full 大的；豐盛的：*a hearty breakfast* 豐盛的早餐 ◇ *to have a hearty appetite* 胃口極好 **4** [usually before noun] showing that you feel strongly about sth 強烈的；盡情的：*He nodded his head in hearty agreement.* 他十分贊同地點了點頭。◇ *Hearty congratulations to everyone involved.* 謹向所有有關人員表示熱烈的祝賀。◇ *a hearty dislike of sth* 對某事物的強烈反感 IDM see HALE ▸ **hearti·ness** *noun* [U]

■ ***noun*** (*pl.* **-ies**) (*BrE*, sometimes *disapproving*) a person who is loud, cheerful and full of energy, especially one who plays a lot of sport 喧鬧、快活而且精力充沛的人（尤指好體育運動的人）

heat 🔑 /hiːt/ *noun*, *verb*

■ ***noun***

▸ **BEING HOT/TEMPERATURE** 熱；高溫 **1** 🔑 [U, sing.] the quality of being hot 熱：*He could feel the heat of the sun on his back.* 他感覺到太陽照射在背上的熱力。◇ *Heat rises.* 熱空氣向上升。◇ *The fire gave out a fierce heat.* 火焰散發出熾熱。➲ see also WHITE HEAT **2** 🔑 [U, C, usually sing.] the level of temperature 溫度：*to **increase/reduce the heat*** 提高／降低溫度 ◇ *Test the heat of the water before getting in.* 入水之前先試一試水溫。◇ *Set the oven to a **low/high/moderate** heat.* 把烤箱的溫度設定為低／高／中擋。➲ see also BLOOD HEAT **3** 🔑 [U] hot weather; the hot conditions in a building/vehicle, etc. 炎熱天氣；（建築物、車輛等中的）高溫，熱的環境：*You should not go out in **the heat of the day*** (= at the hottest time). 你不應該在天最熱的時候外出。◇ *to suffer from the heat* 受暑熱之苦 ◇ *the **afternoon/midday heat*** 午後／正午時分的熱浪 ◇ *The heat in the factory was unbearable.* 工廠裏的高溫令人無法忍受。➲ see also PRICKLY HEAT

▸ **FOR COOKING** 燒煮食物 **4** 🔑 [U] a source of heat, especially one that you cook food on 爐灶；灶眼；爐火：*Return the pan to the heat and stir.* 把鍋放回灶上再攪拌。

▸ **IN BUILDING/ROOM** 建築物；房間 **5** 🔑 [U] (*especially NAmE*) = HEATING: *The heat wasn't on and the house was freezing.* 暖氣沒有開，房子裏冰冷。

▸ **STRONG FEELINGS** 強烈感情 **6** [U] strong feelings, especially of anger or excitement 強烈感情；（尤指）憤怒，激動：*'No, I won't,' he said with heat in his voice.* "不，我絕不。" 他怒氣沖沖地說。◇ *The chairman tried to take the heat out of the situation* (= to make people calmer). 主席盡力平息人們的激憤情緒。◇ ***In the heat of the moment*** *she forgot what she wanted to say* (= because she was so angry or excited). 她因為過於激動而忘記了要說的話。◇ *In the heat of the argument he said a lot of things he regretted later.* 他在激烈爭吵時說了許多他後來感到後悔的話。

▸ **PRESSURE** 壓力 **7** [U] pressure on sb to do or achieve sth 壓力；逼迫：***The heat is on*** *now that the election is only a week away.* 離選舉只有一個星期了，因此大家開始感覺到有壓力了。◇ *United turned up the heat on their opponents with a second goal.* 聯隊進了第二個球，這使對手感到的壓力更大了。◇ *Can she **take the heat** of this level of competition?* 她承受得了這種水平的比賽的壓力嗎？

▸ **RACE** 比賽 **8** [C] one of a series of races or competitions, the winners of which then compete against each other

H

in the next part of the competition 預賽；分組賽：*a qualifying heat* 資格賽 ◇ *She won her heat.* 她在預賽中獲勝。◇ *He did well in **the heats**; hopefully he'll do as well in the final.* 他在預賽中成績很好，且有望在決賽中也有同樣出色的表現。➲ see also DEAD HEAT

IDM **be on 'heat** (*BrE*) (*NAmE* **be in 'heat**) (of a female MAMMAL 雌性哺乳動物) to be in a sexual condition ready to reproduce 處於發情期 **if you can't stand the 'heat (get out of the 'kitchen)** (*informal*) used to tell sb to stop trying to do sth if they find it too difficult, especially in order to suggest that they are less able than other people 如果感到太困難（就別幹了）

■ ***verb*** ⊶ [T, I] **~ (sth)** to make sth hot or warm; to become hot or warm 加熱；變熱；（使）變暖：*Heat the oil and add the onions.* 把油燒熱後加入洋蔥。◇ *The system produced enough energy to heat several thousand homes.* 系統產生的能量足以給幾千戶人家供暖。➲ COLLOCATIONS at COOKING

PHR V **,heat 'up 1** ⊶ to become hot or warm 變熱；變暖 SYN **warm up**：*The oven takes a while to heat up.* 烤箱得過會兒才能熱起來。**2** (*especially NAmE*) (*BrE* also **,hot 'up**) to become more exciting or to show an increase in activity 激烈起來；更加活躍：*The election contest is heating up.* 選舉競爭正趨於白熱化。**,heat sth↔'up** ⊶ to make sth hot or warm 使變熱；使變暖 SYN **warm up**：*Just heat up the food in the microwave.* 把食物放在微波爐裏熱熱就行了。

heat·ed /'hi:tɪd/ *adj.* **1** (of a person or discussion 人或討論) full of anger and excitement 憤怒的；激烈的；十分激動的：*a **heated argument/debate*** 激烈的爭論 / 辯論 ◇ *She became very heated.* 她不禁怒火中燒。**2** (of a room, building, etc. 房間、建築物等) made warmer using a heater（用加熱器）加熱了的：*a heated swimming pool* 温水游泳池 OPP **unheated** ▸ **heat·ed·ly** *adv.*：*'You had no right!' she said heatedly.* "你沒有權利！"她憤怒地說。

heat·er /'hi:tə(r)/ *noun* a machine used for making air or water warmer 加熱器；爐子；熱水器：*a gas heater* 煤氣爐 ◇ *a water heater* 熱水器 ➲ see also IMMERSION HEATER, STORAGE HEATER

'heat exchanger *noun* (*technical* 術語) a device for making heat pass from one liquid to another without allowing the liquids to mix 熱交換器（使熱從熱流體傳遞給冷流體）

heath /hi:θ/ *noun* a large area of open land that is not used for farming and is covered with rough grass and other small wild plants（雜草和灌木叢生的）荒地，荒野

hea·then /'hi:ðn/ *noun, adj.*

■ ***noun*** (*old-fashioned, offensive*) **1** used by people who have a strong religious belief as a way of referring to a person who has no religion or who believes in a religion that is not one of the world's main religions 無宗教信仰者；異教徒 **2** used to refer to a person who shows lack of education 未開化的人；不文明的人

■ ***adj.*** (*old-fashioned, offensive*) connected with heathens 無宗教信仰的；異教徒的；不文明的：*heathen gods* 異教的神祇 ◇ *He set out to convert **the heathen*** (= people who are heathens). 他決心要使異教徒皈依。

hea·ther /'heðə(r)/ *noun* [U] a low wild plant with small purple, pink or white flowers, that grows on hills and areas of wild open land (= MOORLAND) 帚石楠（低矮野生，開紫、粉紅或白色小花）

heath·land /'hi:θlənd; *NAmE* -lænd/ *noun* [U] **heath·lands** [pl.] a large area of heath 歐石楠叢生的大片地方

Heath Rob·in·son /,hi:θ 'rɒbɪnsən; *NAmE* 'rɑ:b-/ (*BrE*) (*NAmE* **,Rube 'Gold·berg**) *adj.* [only before noun] (*humorous*) (of machines and devices 機器和裝置) having a very complicated design, especially when used to perform a very simple task; not practical 結構過於複雜的；不實用的：*a Heath Robinson contraption* 複雜而不實用的裝置

heat·ing ⊶ /'hi:tɪŋ/ *noun* [U] (*especially BrE*) (also **heat** especially in *NAmE*) the process of supplying heat to a room or building; a system used to do this 供暖；供暖系統；暖氣設備：*Who turned the heating off?* 誰把暖氣關掉了？◇ *What type of heating do you have?* 你們用什麼供暖？◇ *a gas heating system* 燃氣供暖系統 ◇ *heating bills* 暖氣開銷 ➲ see also CENTRAL HEATING

heat·proof /'hi:tpru:f/ *adj.* that cannot be damaged by heat 隔熱的；抗熱的；耐高温的：*a heatproof dish* 耐高温的盤子

'heat-resist·ant *adj.* not easily damaged by heat 抗熱的；耐熱的

'heat-seeking *adj.* [only before noun] (of a weapon 武器) that moves towards the heat coming from the aircraft, etc. that it is intended to hit and destroy 熱自導引的；跟踪熱源的：*heat-seeking missiles* 熱自導引導彈

heat·stroke /'hi:tstrəʊk; *NAmE* -stroʊk/ *noun* [U] an illness with fever and often loss of CONSCIOUSNESS, caused by being in too great a heat for too long 中暑

heat·wave /'hi:tweɪv/ *noun* a period of unusually hot weather 酷熱期；熱浪

heave /hi:v/ *verb, noun*

■ ***verb*** **1** [T, I] to lift, pull or throw sb/sth very heavy with one great effort（用力）舉起，拖，拉，拋：**~ sth/sb/yourself + adv./prep.** *I managed to heave the trunk down the stairs.* 我用力把箱子弄下樓梯。◇ *They heaved the body overboard.* 他們使勁把屍體從船上拋入水中。◇ **+ adv./prep.** *We all heaved on the rope.* 我們大家一起用力拉繩子。**2** [I] to rise up and down with strong, regular movements（強烈而有節奏地）起伏：*The boat heaved beneath them.* 小船在他們腳下顛簸着。◇ **~ with sth** *Her shoulders heaved with laughter.* 她笑得雙肩抖動。**3** [T] **~ a sigh, etc.** to make a sound slowly and often with effort（常指吃力地）緩慢發出（聲音）：*We all **heaved a sigh of relief**.* 我們都如釋重負地舒了一口氣。**4** [I] to experience the tight feeling in your stomach that you get before you VOMIT 惡心：*The thought of it makes me heave.* 一想到那事我就惡心。

IDM **,heave into 'sight/'view** (*formal*) (especially of ships 尤指船) to appear, especially when moving gradually closer from a long way off 從遠處出現；進入視野：*A ship hove into sight.* 遠處出現了一條船。HELP **Hove** is usually used for the past tense and past participle in this idiom. 這個習語通常用 hove 作過去時及過去分詞。

PHR V **,heave 'to** (*technical* 術語) if a ship or its CREW (= the people sailing it) **heave to**, the ship stops moving 停船 HELP **Hove** is usually used for the past tense and past participle in this phrasal verb. 這個短語動詞通常用 hove 作過去時及過去分詞。

■ ***noun*** **1** [C] an act of lifting, pulling or throwing 舉；拖；拉；拋：*With a mighty heave he lifted the sack onto the truck.* 他用勁一舉，把大麻袋扔到卡車上。**2** [U] (especially *literary*) a rising and falling movement 起伏：*the steady heave of the sea* 大海洶湧不斷的波濤

heave-ho /,hi:v 'həʊ; *NAmE* 'hoʊ/ *noun* [sing.]

IDM **give sb the (old) heave-'ho** (*informal*) to dismiss sb from their job; to end a relationship with sb 解雇某人；同某人斷絕關係

heaven ⊶ /'hevn/ *noun*

1 ⊶ (also **Heaven**) [U] (used without *the* 不與 the 連用) (in some religions 某些宗教) the place believed to be the home of God where good people go when they die 天堂；天國：*the kingdom of heaven* 天國 ◇ *I feel like I've died and gone to heaven.* 我彷彿覺得自己已經死了，進了天堂。**2** ⊶ [U, C] (*informal*) a place or situation in which you are very happy 極樂之地；極樂：*This isn't exactly my idea of heaven!* 這可不太像我所想像的那麼美妙！◇ *It was heaven being away from the office for a week.* 一個星期遠離辦公室真是快活極了。◇ *The island is truly a **heaven on earth**.* 那個島堪稱人間天堂。**3 the heavens** [pl.] (*literary*) the sky 天空：*Four tall trees stretched up to the heavens.* 四棵大樹參天而立。

IDM **(Good) 'Heavens!** | **,Heavens a'bove!** (*informal*) used to show that you are surprised or annoyed（表示驚奇或氣惱）天哪，我的天：*Good heavens, what are you doing?* 天哪，你在幹什麼？**the heavens 'opened** it began to rain heavily 下起了傾盆大雨 **made in 'heaven** (especially of a marriage or other relationship 尤指婚姻或其他關係) seeming to be perfect 天作之合；

天造地設 ➲ more at FORBID, GOD, HELP *v.*, HIGH *adj.*, KNOW *v.*, MOVE *v.*, NAME *n.*, SEVENTH *ordinal number*, THANK

heav·en·ly /ˈhevnli/ *adj.* **1** [only before noun] connected with heaven 天國的；天堂的：*our heavenly Father* (= God) 上帝 ◇ *the heavenly kingdom* 天國 **2** [only before noun] connected with the sky 天空的：***heavenly bodies*** (= the sun, moon, stars and planets) 天體 **3** (*informal*) very pleasant 十分舒適的；很愉快的；美好的 SYN **wonderful**：*a heavenly morning/feeling* 愉快的早晨／感覺 ◇ *This place is heavenly.* 這個地方好極了。

ˌheaven-ˈsent *adj.* [usually before noun] happening unexpectedly and at exactly the right time 天賜的；正合時宜的

heav·en·ward /ˈhevnwəd; *NAmE* -wərd/ (also **heav·en·wards**) *adv.* (*literary*) towards heaven or the sky 朝天上；向天空：*to* ***cast/raise your eyes heavenward*** (= to show you are annoyed or impatient) 翻白眼（表示生氣或不耐煩）

heav·ily 🔑 /ˈhevɪli/ *adv.*
1 🔑 to a great degree; in large amounts 在很大程度上；大量地：*It was raining heavily.* 雨下得很大。◇ *to drink/smoke heavily* 喝酒／抽煙很兇 ◇ ***heavily armed*** *police* (= carrying a lot of weapons) 全副武裝的警察 ◇ *a* ***heavily pregnant*** *woman* (= one whose baby is nearly ready to be born) 臨產的孕婦 ◇ *They are both* ***heavily involved*** *in politics.* 他們倆都深深捲入政治中。◇ *He* ***relies heavily*** *on his parents.* 他極度依賴父母。◇ *She has been* ***heavily criticized*** *in the press.* 她受到報界的猛烈抨擊。 **2** with a lot of force or effort 以猛力；沉重地：*She fell heavily to the ground.* 她重重地摔倒在地。 **3 ~ built** (of a person 人) with a large, solid and strong body 身材壯實 **4** slowly and loudly 緩慢又高聲地：*She was now breathing heavily.* 她喘着粗氣。◇ *He was snoring heavily.* 他發着粗重的鼾聲。 **5** in a slow way that sounds as though you are worried or sad 緩慢而憂鬱地；悲傷地：*He sighed heavily.* 他長歎了一聲。 **6** in a way that makes you feel uncomfortable or anxious 令人心情沉重：*Silence hung heavily in the room.* 房間裏寂若死灰。◇ *The burden of guilt weighed heavily on his mind.* 愧疚之情壓得他透不過氣來。 **7 ~ loaded/laden** full of or loaded with heavy things 裝滿（或裝載）重物的；重載的：*a heavily loaded van* 滿載重物的貨車

heav·ing /ˈhiːvɪŋ/ *adj.* [not before noun] **~ (with sb/sth)** full of sb/sth 充滿（人或事物）：*The place was heaving with journalists.* 那個地方擠滿了記者。

heavy 🔑 /ˈhevi/ *adj.*, *noun*, *adv.*
■ ***adj.*** (**heav·ier**, **heavi·est**)
▸ WEIGHING A LOT 重量大 **1** 🔑 weighing a lot; difficult to lift or move 重的；沉的：*She was struggling with a heavy suitcase.* 她正費力地拎着一隻沉重的手提箱。◇ *My brother is much heavier than me.* 我弟弟比我重得多。◇ *He tried to push the heavy door open.* 他試圖推開那扇沉重的門。◇ ***How heavy*** *is it* (= how much does it weigh)? 這東西有多重？◇ (*especially NAmE*) *Many young people today are too heavy* (= fat). 現今許多青年人都過於肥胖。◇ (*figurative*) *Her father carried a* ***heavy burden*** *of responsibility.* 她父親肩負着重大責任。 OPP **light**
▸ WORSE THAN USUAL 比一般嚴重 **2** 🔑 more or worse than usual in amount, degree, etc. （在數量、程度等方面）超出一般的，比一般嚴重的：*the noise of* ***heavy traffic*** 繁忙交通的噪音 ◇ ***heavy frost/rain/snow*** 嚴重霜凍；暴雨；大雪 ◇ *the effects of* ***heavy drinking*** 過量飲酒的後果 ◇ *There was heavy fighting in the capital last night.* 昨晚首都發生了激烈戰鬥。◇ *The penalty for speeding can be a* ***heavy fine.*** 超速駕駛可能會被處以高額罰款。◇ *She spoke with* ***heavy irony.*** 她的話充滿了諷刺。 OPP **light**
▸ NOT DELICATE 不精緻 **3** 🔑 (of sb/sth's appearance or structure 人或物的外表或構造) large and solid; not delicate 大而結實的；不精緻的：*big, dark rooms full of heavy furniture* 裝滿厚實傢具，又大又暗的房間 ◇ *He was tall and strong, with heavy features.* 他長得高大壯實，濃眉大眼。
▸ MATERIAL 材料 **4** 🔑 (of the material or substance that sth is made of 原材料或原料) thick 厚的：*heavy curtains* 厚窗簾 ◇ *a heavy coat* 厚外套 OPP **light**
▸ FULL OF STH 充滿 **5 ~ with sth** (*literary*) full of or loaded with sth 充滿，滿載（某物）：*trees heavy with apples* 掛滿蘋果的樹 ◇ *The air was heavy with the scent of flowers.* 空氣中瀰漫着濃郁的花香。◇ *His voice was heavy with sarcasm.* 他的語氣帶着十足的諷刺意味。
▸ MACHINES 機器 **6** [usually before noun] (of machines, vehicles or weapons 機器、車輛或武器) large and powerful 重型的；大型的：*a wide range of engines and* ***heavy machinery*** 各種各樣的發動機和重型機器 ◇ ***heavy lorries/trucks*** 重型卡車
▸ BUSY 繁忙 **7** 🔑 [usually before noun] involving a lot of work or activity; very busy 工作（或活動）多的；繁忙的：*a* ***heavy schedule*** 安排很緊的日程 ◇ *She'd had a heavy day.* 她忙了一天。
▸ WORK 工作 **8** 🔑 hard, especially because it requires a lot of physical strength 辛苦的；費力的：***heavy digging/lifting*** 費力的挖掘／提舉
▸ FALL/HIT 落下；打擊 **9** 🔑 falling or hitting sth with a lot of force 沉重的；猛烈的：*a* ***heavy fall/blow*** 重重的跌落／一擊
▸ MEAL/FOOD 餐食；食物 **10** 🔑 large in amount or very solid 量大的；厚實的：*a* ***heavy lunch/dinner*** 豐盛的午餐／正餐 ◇ *a heavy cake* 厚實的餅 OPP **light**
▸ DRINKER/SMOKER/SLEEPER 喝酒／抽煙／睡覺的人 **11** 🔑 [only before noun] (of a person 人) doing the thing mentioned more, or more deeply, than usual （做某事）過量的，超出一般的，過度的：*a* ***heavy drinker/smoker*** 酒癮／煙癮大的人 ◇ *a heavy sleeper* 睡得很死的人
▸ SOUND 聲音 **12** 🔑 (of a sound that sb makes 人聲) loud and deep 響而深沉的：***heavy breathing/snoring*** 沉重的呼吸聲／鼾聲 ◇ *a* ***heavy groan/sigh*** 深沉的呻吟／歎息
▸ USING A LOT 用很多 **13 ~ on sth** (*informal*) using a lot of sth 使用很多…的；耗費…的：*Older cars are heavy on gas.* 老舊的汽車耗油多。◇ *Don't go so heavy on the garlic.* 別用這麼多蒜。
▸ SERIOUS/DIFFICULT 嚴肅；困難 **14** (usually *disapproving*) (of a book, programme, style, etc. 書、節目、風格等) serious; difficult to understand or enjoy 嚴肅的；難懂的；艱澀的：*We found the play very heavy.* 我們覺得這部戲很艱澀。◇ *The discussion got a little heavy.* 討論變得有點嚴肅。
▸ SEA/OCEAN 海；洋 **15** dangerous because of big waves, etc. 危險的；洶湧的：*strong winds and heavy seas* 風急浪高
▸ AIR/WEATHER 空氣；天氣 **16** hot and lacking fresh air, in a way that is unpleasant 悶熱的；沉悶的：*It's very heavy—I think there'll be a storm.* 天氣很悶熱，我覺得暴風雨要來了。
▸ SOIL 泥土 **17** wet, sticky and difficult to dig or to move over 泥濘難挖（或難挪動）的
▸ STRICT 嚴厲 **18** (of a person 人) very strict and severe 苛刻的；嚴厲的：*Don't be so heavy on her—it wasn't her fault.* 別對她這麼苛刻，這不是她的過錯。
▸ **heavi·ness** *noun* [U]

IDM **get ˈheavy** (*informal*) to become very serious, because strong feelings are involved 變得嚴重；變得激烈：*They started shouting at me. It got very heavy.* 他們開始對我大喊大叫，情勢變得很激烈。 **ˌheavy ˈgoing** used to describe sb/sth that is difficult to deal with or understand 難以打交道；難以處理；難以理解：*She's a bit heavy going.* 她有點難纏。◇ *I found the course rather heavy going.* 我覺得這門課相當難。 **heavy ˈhand** a way of doing sth or of treating people that is much stronger and less sensitive than it needs to be 嚴厲手段；粗暴方式；暴虐方式：*the heavy hand of management* 粗暴的管理方式 **a heavy ˈheart** a feeling of great sadness 悲哀的心情：*She left her children behind with a heavy heart.* 她十分難過地丟下了她的孩子們。 **the ˈheavy mob/brigade** (*BrE*, *informal*) a group of strong, often violent people employed to do sth such as protect sb （雇傭的）打手隊，保鏢團 **a heavy ˈsilence/ˈatmosphere** a situation when people do not say anything, but feel embarrassed or uncomfortable 令人尷尬（或不安）的沉默（或氣氛） **make heavy ˈweather of sth** to seem to find sth more difficult or complicated than it needs to be 小題大做 ➲ more at CROSS *n.*, TOLL *n.*

■ ***noun*** (*pl.* **-ies**) **1** [C] (*informal*) a large strong man whose job is to protect a person or place, often using violence

H

保鏢；打手 **2** [U] (*ScotE*) strong beer, especially bitter 烈性啤酒；（尤指）苦啤酒：*a pint of heavy* 一品脫烈性啤酒

■ *adv.*

IDM **hang/lie 'heavy 1 ~ (on/in sth)** (of a feeling or sth in the air 感情或空氣中的東西) to be very noticeable in a particular place in a way that is unpleasant 明顯地懸浮於；明顯積鬱着：*Smoke lay heavy on the far side of the water.* 水面對岸懸浮着黑沉沉的煙霧。◇ *Despair hangs heavy in the stifling air.* 絕望的感覺積壓在憋悶的空氣中。 **2 ~ on sb/sth** to cause sb/sth to feel uncomfortable or anxious 使不安；使擔憂：*The crime lay heavy on her conscience.* 那件罪行使她內疚不安。

,heavy 'breather *noun* a person who gets sexual pleasure from calling sb on the telephone and not speaking to them 濁重呼吸者（給人打電話又不說話，從中得到性快感）▶ **,heavy 'breathing** *noun* [U]

,heavy-'duty *adj.* [only before noun] **1** not easily damaged and therefore suitable for hard physical work or to be used all the time 結實的；重型的；耐用的：*a heavy-duty carpet* 耐磨的地毯 **2** (*informal, especially NAmE*) very serious or great in quantity 嚴重的；嚴肅的；大量的：*I think you need some heavy-duty advice.* 我想你需要一些有分量的意見。

,heavy 'goods vehicle *noun* (*BrE*) = HGV

,heavy-'handed *adj.* **1** not showing a sympathetic understanding of the feelings of other people 缺乏同情心的；冷酷的：*a heavy-handed approach* 冷酷無情的方法 **2** using unnecessary force 強暴的；高壓的：*heavy-handed police methods* 警察的高壓手段 **3** (of a person 人) using too much of sth in a way that can cause damage 用某物過多的；大手大腳的：*Don't be too heavy-handed with the salt.* 別放太多的鹽。

,heavy 'hitter *noun* (*informal, especially NAmE*) a person with a lot of power, especially in business or politics（尤指商業或政界的）大亨，要員，大人物

,heavy 'industry *noun* [U, C] industry that uses large machinery to produce metal, coal, vehicles, etc. 重工業 ➲ compare LIGHT INDUSTRY

,heavy 'metal *noun* **1** [U] a type of rock music with a very strong beat played very loud on electric GUITARS 重金屬搖滾樂 **2** [C] (*technical* 術語) a metal that has a very high DENSITY (= the relation of its weight to its volume), such as gold or LEAD 重金屬

,heavy 'petting *noun* [U] sexual activity that does not involve full SEXUAL INTERCOURSE 性愛撫

,heavy-'set *adj.* having a broad heavy body 敦實的；壯碩的 **SYN** THICKSET

'heavy water *noun* [U] (*chemistry* 化) water in which HYDROGEN is replaced by DEUTERIUM, used in nuclear reactions 重水，氧化氘（用於核反應）

heavy·weight /'heviweɪt/ *noun* **1** a BOXER of the heaviest class in normal use, weighing 79.5 kilograms or more 重量級拳擊手（體重 79.5 公斤或以上）：*a heavyweight champion* 重量級拳擊冠軍 **2** a person or thing that weighs more than is usual 特別重的人（或物） **3** a very important person, organization or thing that influences others 有影響力的人（或組織、事物）：*a political heavyweight* 政界要人 ◇ *a heavyweight journal* 有影響力的刊物

Heb·raic /hi'breɪɪk/ *adj.* of or connected with the Hebrew language or people 希伯來語的；希伯來人的：*Hebraic poetry* 希伯來語詩歌

Heb·rew /'hi:bru:/ *noun* **1** a member of an ancient race of people living in what is now Israel and Palestine. Their writings and traditions form the basis of the Jewish religion. 希伯來人 **2** the language traditionally used by the Hebrew people 希伯來語 **3** a modern form of the Hebrew language which is the official language of modern Israel 現代希伯來語（現代以色列的官方語言）➲ compare YIDDISH ▶ **Heb·rew** *adj.*

heck /hek/ *exclamation, noun* (*informal*) used to show that you are slightly annoyed or surprised（表示略微煩惱或吃驚）：*Oh heck, I'm going to be late!* 見鬼，我要遲到了！◇ *We had to wait **a heck of a** long time!* 我們只好等了很長時間！◇ *Who **the heck** are you?* 你究竟是誰？

IDM **for the 'heck of it** (*informal*) just for pleasure rather than for a reason 只是鬧着玩；不為什麼 **what the 'heck!** (*informal*) used to say that you are going to do sth that you know you should not do（表示明知不應做某事，卻偏要做）：*It means I'll be late for work but what the heck!* 那意味着我上班會遲到，不過管它的呢！

heckle /'hekl/ *verb* [T, I] **~ (sb)** to interrupt a speaker at a public meeting by shouting out questions or rude remarks（對演說者）責問，詰問，起鬨 **SYN** **barrack**：*He was booed and heckled throughout his speech.* 他的演說自始至終都遭到喝倒彩起鬨。▶ **heck·ler** /'heklə(r)/ *noun* **heck·ling** *noun* [U]

hec·tare /'hekteə(r); *NAmE* -ter; *BrE* also 'hektɑ:(r)/ *noun* (*abbr.* **ha**) a unit for measuring an area of land; 10 000 square metres or about 2.5 ACRES 公頃（土地丈量單位，等於 1 萬平方米或約 2.5 英畝）

hec·tic /'hektɪk/ *adj.* very busy; full of activity 忙碌的；繁忙的：*to lead a hectic life* 生活十分忙碌 ◇ *a hectic schedule* 安排很滿的日程表

hecto·litre (*especially US* **hecto·liter**) /'hektəli:tə(r)/ *noun* (*abbr.* **hl**) a unit for measuring volume; 100 litres 百升（容量單位）

hec·tor /'hektə(r)/ *verb* **~ sb** | **+ speech** (*formal*) to try to make sb do sth by talking or behaving in an aggressive way 威逼；威嚇 **SYN** **bully** ▶ **hec·tor·ing** *adj.*：*a hectoring tone of voice* 威逼的口氣

he'd /hi:d/ *short form* **1** he had **2** he would

hedge /hedʒ/ *noun, verb*

■ *noun* **1** a row of bushes or small trees planted close together, usually along the edge of a field, garden/yard or road 樹籬：*a privet hedge* 女貞樹籬 ➲ VISUAL VOCAB pages V2, V19 **2 ~ against sth** a way of protecting yourself against the loss of sth, especially money 防止損失（尤指金錢）的手段：*to buy gold as a hedge against inflation* 購買黃金以抵消通貨膨脹造成的損失

■ *verb* **1** [I] to avoid giving a direct answer to a question or promising to support a particular idea, etc. 避免正面回答；不直接許諾；拐彎抹角：*Just answer 'yes' or 'no'—and stop hedging.* 只要回答"是"或"不是"，別再閃爍其詞了。 **2** [T] **~ sth** to put a hedge around a field, etc. 在（田地等周圍）植樹籬；用樹籬圍住 **3** [T, usually passive] **~ sb/sth (about/around) (with sth)** (*formal*) to surround or limit sb/sth 包圍；限制：*His religious belief was always hedged with doubt.* 他的宗教信仰一直受到心不誠的局限。◇ *Their offer was hedged around with all sorts of conditions.* 他們的建議附帶了各種各樣的限制條件。

IDM **,hedge your 'bets** to reduce the risk of losing or making a mistake by supporting more than one side in a competition, an argument, etc., or by having several choices available to you（為防止損失或出錯）幾面下注，有幾項選擇可選取

PHR V **'hedge against sth** to do sth to protect yourself against problems, especially against losing money 採取保護措施（尤指為避免損失金錢）：*a way of hedging against currency risks* 避免貨幣風險的保值措施 **,hedge sb/sth↔'in** to surround sb/sth with sth 包圍；環繞 **SYN** **hem sb/sth in**：*The cathedral is now hedged in by other buildings.* 大教堂現在被其他建築物包圍着。◇ (*figurative*) *Married life made him feel hedged in and restless.* 婚姻生活使他感覺受到束縛而且心煩。

hedge·hog /'hedʒhɒg; *NAmE* -hɔ:g; -hɑ:g/ *noun* a small brown European animal with stiff parts like needles (called SPINES) covering its back. Hedgehogs are NOCTURNAL (= active mostly at night) and can roll into a ball to defend themselves when they are attacked. 刺猬

hedge·row /'hedʒrəʊ; *NAmE* -roʊ/ *noun* (especially in Britain) a line of bushes planted along the edge of a field or road（尤指英國田邊或路邊的）樹籬 ➲ VISUAL VOCAB pages V2, V3

he·don·ism /ˈhiːdənɪzəm/ *noun* [U] the belief that pleasure is the most important thing in life 享樂主義 ▸ **he·don·is·tic** /ˌhiːdəˈnɪstɪk/ *adj.*

he·don·ist /ˈhiːdənɪst/ *noun* a person who believes that pleasure is the most important thing in life 享樂主義者

the heebie-jeebies /ˌhiːbi ˈdʒiːbiz/ *noun* [pl.] (*old-fashioned, informal*) a feeling of nervous fear or worry 忐忑不安；坐立不安

heed /hiːd/ *verb, noun*

■ **verb** **~ sb/sth** (*formal*) to pay careful attention to sb's advice or warning 留心，注意，聽從（勸告或警告） SYN **take notice of**

■ **noun** [U]

IDM **give/pay ˈheed (to sb/sth) | take ˈheed (of sb/sth)** (*formal*) to pay careful attention to sb/sth 留心；注意；聽從

heed·ful /ˈhiːdfl/ *adj.* **~ (of sb/sth)** (*formal*) paying careful attention to sb/sth 留心的；注意的

heed·less /ˈhiːdləs/ *adj.* [not usually before noun] **~ (of sb/sth)** (*formal*) not paying careful attention to sb/sth 不加注意；掉以輕心 ▸ **heed·less·ly** *adv.*

hee-haw /ˈhiː hɔː/ *noun* the way of writing the sound made by a DONKEY 驢叫聲

heel 🔑 /hiːl/ *noun, verb*

■ **noun**

▸ PART OF FOOT 腳的部位 **1** 🔑 [C] the back part of the foot below the ankle 足跟；腳後跟 ➲ VISUAL VOCAB page V59

▸ PART OF SOCK/SHOE 襪子／鞋的部份 **2** [C] the part of a sock, etc. that covers the heel （襪子等的）後跟 **3** 🔑 [C] the raised part on the bottom of a shoe, boot, etc. that makes the shoe, etc. higher at the back （鞋、靴子等的）後跟： *shoes with a* ***low/high heel*** 低／高跟鞋 ◇ *a stiletto heel* 細高跟 ◇ *The sergeant clicked his heels and walked out.* 中士將鞋跟咔嚏一併，走了出去。 ➲ VISUAL VOCAB page V64 ➲ compare SOLE *n.* (2)

▸ -HEELED 後跟…的 **4** (in adjectives 構成形容詞) having the type of heel mentioned 有…後跟的： *high-heeled shoes* 高跟鞋 ➲ see also WELL HEELED

▸ SHOES 鞋 **5 heels** [pl.] a pair of women's shoes that have high heels 女高跟鞋： *She doesn't often wear heels.* 她不常穿高跟鞋。 ➲ see also KITTEN HEELS

▸ PART OF HAND 手的部位 **6** [C] **~ of your hand/palm** the raised part of the inside of the hand where it joins the wrist 手掌根（手掌靠近腕部的隆起部份） ➲ VISUAL VOCAB page V59

▸ UNPLEASANT MAN 可惡的人 **7** [C] (*old-fashioned, informal*) a man who is unpleasant to other people and cannot be trusted 卑鄙的傢伙；渾蛋 ➲ see also ACHILLES HEEL, DOWN AT HEEL

IDM **at/on sb's ˈheels** following closely behind sb 緊跟某人： *He fled from the stadium with the police at his heels.* 他逃離了運動場，警察在後面緊追不捨。 **bring sb/sth to ˈheel** **1** to force sb to obey you and accept discipline 使某人就範；迫使某人服從（紀律） **2** to make a dog come close to you 讓狗靠近；喚狗來到身邊 **come to ˈheel** **1** (of a person 人) to agree to obey sb and accept their orders 願意聽從（某人）；順從 **2** (of a dog 狗) to come close to the person who has called it 走近喚狗人 **(hard/hot) on sb's/sth's ˈheels** very close behind sb/sth; very soon after sth 緊跟；緊接在後： *News of rising unemployment followed hard on the heels of falling export figures.* 出口數字下降之後緊接着就是失業率上升的消息。 **ˌtake to your ˈheels** to run away from sb/sth 逃走；溜掉 **ˌturn/ˌspin on your ˈheel** to turn around suddenly so that you are facing in the opposite direction 急向後轉；突然轉身 **under the ˈheel of sb** (*literary*) completely controlled by sb 完全受某人控制 ➲ more at COOL *v.*, DIG *v.*, DRAG *v.*, HEAD *n.*, KICK *v.*, TREAD *v.*

■ **verb**

▸ REPAIR SHOE 修鞋 **1** [T] **~ sth** to repair the heel of a shoe, etc. 給（鞋等）修理後跟

▸ OF BOAT 船 **2** [I] **~ (over)** to lean over to one side 傾側；傾斜： *The boat heeled over in the strong wind.* 船在狂風中傾側了。

Heely™ /ˈhiːli/ *noun* (*pl.* **Heelys**) (*especially BrE*) (also **ˈskate shoe** especially in *NAmE*) a sports shoe that has one or more wheels underneath it 赫利滑輪鞋；暴走鞋；飛行鞋；犀利鞋

heft /heft/ *verb, noun*

■ **verb** **1 ~ sth (+ adv./prep.)** to lift or carry sth heavy from one position to another 舉起，搬動（重物）： *The two men hefted the box into the car.* 兩個男子把箱子搬進了汽車。 **2 ~ sth** to lift or hold sth in order to estimate its weight 掂…的重量： *Anna took the old sword and hefted it in her hands.* 安娜拿起那把古劍掂了掂分量。

■ **noun** [U] (*NAmE*) the weight of sb/sth 重量： *She was surprised by the sheer heft of the package.* 就那包裹沉甸甸的分量夠她吃驚的了。

hefty /ˈhefti/ *adj.* (**heft·ier, hefti·est**) **1** (of a person or an object 人或物體) big and heavy 大而重的： *Her brothers were both hefty men in their forties.* 她的兩個兄弟都是四十多歲，身高體壯。 **2** (of an amount of money 錢的數額) large; larger than usual or expected 很大的；超出一般的；可觀的： *They sold it easily and made a hefty profit.* 他們毫不費力地賣掉了它，得到了一筆可觀的利潤。 **3** using a lot of force 用力的；猛烈的： *He gave the door a hefty kick.* 他猛踢了一下門。 ▸ **heft·ily** *adv.*

he·gem·ony /hɪˈdʒeməni; -ˈge-; ˈhedʒɪməni; *NAmE* -moʊni/ *noun* [U, C] (*pl.* **-ies**) (*formal*) control by one country, organization, etc. over other countries, etc. within a particular group 支配權；霸權 ▸ **hege·mon·ic** /ˌhedʒɪˈmɒnɪk; ˌhegɪ-; *NAmE* -ˈmɑːnɪk/ *adj.*： *hegemonic control* 霸權統治

He·gi·ra (also **He·ji·ra**) /ˈhedʒɪrə; hɪˈdʒaɪrə/ (also **Hijra**) *noun* [sing.] **1** (usually **the Hegira**) the occasion when Muhammad left Mecca to go to Medina in AD 622 希吉拉（意為遷徙，指公元 622 年穆罕默德從麥加前往麥地那） **2** the period which began at this time; the Muslim ERA 伊斯蘭紀元，回教紀元（從公元 622 年開始）

heifer /ˈhefə(r)/ *noun* a young female cow, especially one that has not yet had a CALF （尤指未生育過的）小母牛

height 🔑 /haɪt/ *noun*

▸ MEASUREMENT 量度 **1** 🔑 [U, C] the measurement of how tall a person or thing is （人或物的）身高，高度： *Height: 210 mm. Width: 57 mm. Length: 170 mm.* 高：210 毫米；寬：57 毫米；長：170 毫米。◇ *Please state your height and weight.* 請說明身高和體重。◇ *It is almost 2 metres* ***in height.*** 它差不多有 2 米高。◇ *She is the same height as her sister.* 她和她姐姐一樣高。◇ *to be of* ***medium/average height*** 中等身材 ◇ *You can adjust the height of the chair.* 你可以調節椅子的高度。◇ *The table is available in several different heights.* 這款桌子有幾種不同的高度供選擇。

▸ BEING TALL 高 **2** 🔑 [U] the quality of being tall or high 高： *She worries about her height* (= that she is too tall). 她為個子太高而煩惱。◇ *The height of the mountain did not discourage them.* 山高並沒有使他們泄氣。

▸ DISTANCE ABOVE GROUND 高度 **3** 🔑 [C, U] a particular distance above the ground（離地面的）高度： *The plane flew* ***at a height of*** *3 000 metres.* 飛機在 3 000 米的高空飛行。◇ *The stone was dropped* ***from a great height.*** 那塊石頭是從很高的地方掉落下來的。◇ *The aircraft was gaining height.* 飛機在爬高。◇ *to be at* ***shoulder/chest/waist height*** 齊肩／胸／腰高

▸ HIGH PLACE 高處 **4** 🔑 [C, usually pl.] (often used in names 常用於名稱) a high place or position 高地；高處；高位： *Brooklyn Heights* 布魯克林高地 ◇ *He doesn't have* ***a head for heights*** (= is afraid of high places). 他懼高。◇ *a fear of heights* 恐高 ◇ *We looked out over the city from the heights of Edinburgh Castle.* 我們從愛丁堡城堡所在的高處俯視整個城市。◇ *The pattern of the ancient fields is clearly visible* ***from a height.*** 古戰場的佈局從高處清晰可見。

▸ STRONGEST POINT/LEVEL 最強點；最高水平 **5** 🔑 [sing.] the point when sth is at its best or strongest 最佳點；最強點；頂點： *He is at the height of his career.* 他正處於事業的巔峰。◇ *She is still at the* ***height of her powers.*** 她仍然處於最佳狀態。◇ *I wouldn't go there* ***in the height of summer.*** 我不會在盛夏時節去那裏。◇ *The fire* ***reached its height*** *around 2 a.m.* 大火在半夜兩點鐘左右燒得

H

最猛。◇ *The crisis was* **at its height** *in May.* 危機在五月份到了最嚴重的關頭。 **6 heights** [pl.] a better or greater level of sth; a situation where sth is very good 更好；更高水平；極佳狀況： *Their success had reached* **new heights**. 他們的成就達到新高水平。 IDM see DIZZY

▸ EXTREME EXAMPLE 極端例子 **7** [sing.] **~ of sth** an extreme example of a particular quality 極端；極度： *It would be* **the height of folly** (= very stupid) *to change course now.* 現在改變方向可謂愚蠢至極。◇ *She was dressed in the* **height of fashion**. 她穿着最時髦的衣服。

IDM **draw yourself up/rise to your full 'height** to stand straight and tall in order to show your determination or high status 昂首挺胸地站立（以示決心或地位高）

height·en /ˈhaɪtn/ *verb* [I, T] if a feeling or an effect **heightens**, or sth **heightens** it, it becomes stronger or increases （使）加強，提高，增加 SYN **intensify**： *Tension has heightened after the recent bomb attack.* 最近的炸彈襲擊之後，情勢更加緊張。◇ **~ sth** *The campaign is intended to heighten public awareness of the disease.* 這場運動的目的是使公眾更加瞭解這種疾病。

hein·ous /ˈheɪnəs/ *adj.* [usually before noun] (*formal*) morally very bad 極惡毒的；道德敗壞的： *a heinous crime* 十惡不赦的罪行 ▸ **hein·ous·ly** *adv.* **hein·ous·ness** *noun* [U]

heir /eə(r); *NAmE* er/ *noun* **~ (to sth)** | **~ (of sb)** **1** a person who has the legal right to receive sb's property, money or title when that person dies 繼承人；後嗣： *to be heir to a large fortune* 是大筆財產的繼承人 ◇ *the heir to the throne* (= the person who will be the next king or queen) 王位繼承人 **2** a person who is thought to continue the work or a tradition started by sb else（工作或傳統的）繼承者，承襲者，傳人： *the president's political heirs* 總統的政治繼承者 HELP Use **an**, not **a**, before **heir**. * heir 之前用 an，不用 a。

ˌheir apˈparent *noun* (*pl.* **heirs apparent**) **~ (to sth)** **1** an HEIR whose legal right to receive sb's property, money or title cannot be taken away because it is impossible for sb with a stronger claim to be born 當然繼承人；法定繼承人 **2** a person who is expected to take the job of sb when that person leaves（職位的）確定接替者；確定接班者

heir·ess /ˈeəres; -rəs; *NAmE* ˈer-/ *noun* **~ (to sth)** a female heir, especially one who has received or will receive a large amount of money 女繼承人；嗣女 HELP Use **an**, not **a**, before **heiress**. * heiress 之前用 an，不用 a。

heir·loom /ˈeəluːm; *NAmE* ˈerl-/ *noun, adj.*

▪ *noun* a valuable object that has belonged to the same family for many years 傳家寶；世代相傳之物： *a family heirloom* 傳家寶 HELP Use **an**, not **a**, before **heirloom**. * heirloom 之前用 an，不用 a。

▪ *adj.* [only before noun] (*NAmE*) **heirloom** plants are varieties which were commonly grown in the past but are no longer grown as commercial crops 稀罕的，稀有的（通常指過去大量種植，但再不作為經濟作物而種植的植物）

ˌheir preˈsumptive *noun* (*pl.* **heirs presumptive**) an HEIR who may lose his or her legal right to receive sb's property, money or title if sb with a stronger claim is born 假定繼承人（其繼承權會因有血統更近的繼承人出生而喪失）

heist /haɪst/ *noun, verb*

▪ *noun* (*informal, especially NAmE*) an act of stealing sth valuable from a shop/store or bank（對商店、銀行貴重物、錢的）盜竊 SYN **robbery**： *a bank heist* 銀行盜竊案

▪ *verb* **~ sth** (*informal, especially NAmE*) to steal sth valuable from a shop/store or bank（在商店、銀行）盜竊（貴重物品）

Hej·ira = HEGIRA

held *past tense, past part.* of HOLD

hel·ic·al /ˈhelɪkl; ˈhiːl-/ *adj.* (*technical* 術語) like a HELIX 螺旋的；螺旋形的

heli·cop·ter /ˈhelɪkɒptə(r); *NAmE* -kɑːp-/ (also *informal* **cop·ter**, **chop·per**) *noun* an aircraft without wings that has large blades on top that go round. It can fly straight up from the ground and can also stay in one position in the air 直升機： *He was rushed to the hospital* **by helicopter**. 他由直升機火速送到醫院。◇ *a police helicopter* 警用直升機 ◇ *a helicopter pilot* 直升機駕駛員 ➲ VISUAL VOCAB page V53

ˈhelicopter view (*business* 商) a broad general view or description of a problem（鳥瞰式的）概況，概述 SYN **10 000-foot view, overview**

he·lio·cen·tric /ˌhiːliəˈsentrɪk/ *adj.* (*astronomy* 天) with the sun as the centre 日心的： *the heliocentric model of the solar system* 太陽系的日心模型

he·lio·graph /ˈhiːliəɡrɑːf; *NAmE* -ɡræf/ *noun* **1** a device which gives signals by reflecting flashes of light from the sun 日光反射信號器；回光信號器；日光儀 **2** (also **he·lio·gram** /ˈhiːliəɡræm/) a message which is sent using signals from a heliograph 日光反射信號；回光信號 **3** a special camera which takes photographs of the sun（拍攝太陽用的）太陽照相儀

he·lio·trope /ˈhiːliətrəʊp; *NAmE* -troʊp/ *noun* **1** [C, U] a garden plant with pale purple flowers with a sweet smell 天芥菜（開芳香淡紫色花） **2** [U] a pale purple colour 淡紫色

heli·pad /ˈhelipæd/ (also **ˈhelicopter pad**) *noun* a small area where HELICOPTERS can take off and land 直升機停機坪

heli·port /ˈhelipɔːt; *NAmE* -pɔːrt/ *noun* a place where HELICOPTERS take off and land 直升機機場

heli-skiing /ˈheliskiːɪŋ/ *noun* [U] the sport of flying in a HELICOPTER to a place where there is a lot of snow on a mountain in order to SKI there 直升機滑雪

he·lium /ˈhiːliəm/ *noun* [U] (*symb.* **He**) a chemical element. Helium is a very light gas that does not burn, often used to fill BALLOONS and to freeze food. 氦；氦氣

helix 螺旋（形）

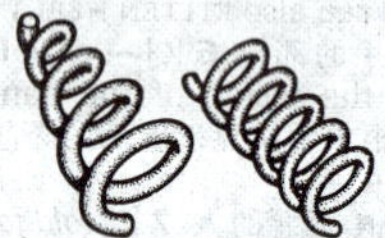

helix /ˈhiːlɪks/ *noun* (*pl.* **heli·ces** /ˈhiːlɪsiːz/) a shape like a SPIRAL or a line curved around a CYLINDER or CONE 螺旋（形） ➲ see also DOUBLE HELIX

hell 🔑 /hel/ *noun*

1 🔑 [sing.] (usually **Hell**) (used without *a* or *the* 不與 a 或 the 連用) in some religions, the place believed to be the home of DEVILS and where bad people go after death 地獄 **2** 🔑 [U, sing.] a very unpleasant experience or situation in which people suffer very much 苦難的經歷；悲慘的境況： *The last three months have been hell.* 過去的三個月真受罪。◇ *He went* **through hell** *during the trial.* 審訊期間他吃盡了苦頭。◇ *Her parents made her life hell.* 她的父母使她生活得很痛苦。◇ *Being totally alone is my idea of* **hell on earth**. 完全的孤獨對我而言就是置身人間地獄。 **3** 🔑 [U] a swear word that some people use when they are annoyed or surprised or to emphasize sth. Its use is offensive to some people.（有人認為含冒犯意）該死，見鬼： *Oh hell, I've burned the pan.* 真該死，我把鍋燒煳了。◇ *What the hell do you think you are doing?* 你到底知不知道自己在幹什麼？◇ *Go to hell!* 去死吧！◇ *I can't really afford it, but, what the hell* (= it doesn't matter), *I'll get it anyway.* 實在說我是買不起，但管它呢，無論如何我買定了。◇ *He's as guilty as hell.* 他罪孽深重。◇ (*NAmE*) *'Do you understand?' 'Hell, no. I don't.'* "你懂了嗎？" "懂個鬼。我根本不懂。"

IDM **all ˈhell broke loose** (*informal*) suddenly there was a lot of noise, arguing, fighting or confusion 突然喧鬧（或爭辯、打鬥）起來；頓時亂作一團： *There was a* *loud bang and then all hell broke loose.* 一聲巨響之後頓時一片混亂。 **beat/kick (the) 'hell out of sb/sth | knock 'hell out of sb/sth** (*informal*) to hit sb/sth very hard 猛擊；狠打： *He was a dirty player and loved to kick hell out of the opposition.* 他是個不講體育道德的球員，喜歡猛力衝撞對方。 **(just) for the 'hell of it** (*informal*) just for fun; for no real reason 只是鬧着玩；沒有真正動機： *They stole the car just for the hell of it.* 他們偷這輛汽車只是為了尋求刺激。 **from 'hell** (*informal*) used to describe a very unpleasant person or thing; the worst that you can imagine 十分討厭；最壞： *They are the neighbours from hell.* 這些鄰居太可惡了。 **get the hell 'out (of ...)** (*informal*) to leave a place very quickly 迅速離開： *Let's get the hell out of here.* 我們馬上離開這裏吧。**give sb 'hell** (*informal*) **1** to make life unpleasant for sb 讓某人受罪；使某人不好受： *He used to give his mother hell when he was a teenager.* 他十幾歲時常常給他母親惹麻煩。◇ *My new shoes are giving me hell* (= are hurting me). 我的新鞋磨得我腳疼死了。 **2** to shout at or speak angrily to sb 呵斥；申斥： *Dad will give us hell when he sees that mess.* 爸爸要是看見那亂糟糟的樣子會罵我們的。**go to hell in a 'handbasket** (*NAmE, informal*) = GO TO THE DOGS at DOG *n.* **hell for 'leather** (*old-fashioned, BrE, informal*) as quickly as possible 儘快： *to ride hell for leather* 拚命快騎 **hell hath no 'fury (like a woman 'scorned)** (*BrE*) used to refer to sb, usually a woman, who has reacted very angrily to sth, especially the fact that her husband or lover has been UNFAITHFUL（尤指女人因丈夫或情人不忠而）大發雷霆；醋勁大發 **(come) hell or high 'water** despite any difficulties 無論有什麼困難： *I was determined to go, come hell or high water.* 我決心要去，不管有什麼困難。 **Hell's 'teeth** (*old-fashioned, BrE, informal*) used to express anger or surprise（表示氣憤或吃驚）可惡，天哪 **like 'hell 1** (*informal*) used for emphasis 非常；極其： *She worked like hell for her exams.* 她為了考試而拚命複習。◇ *My broken finger hurt like hell.* 我的手指骨折，痛得要命。 **2** (*informal*) used when you are refusing permission or saying that sth is not true 絕不；不對： *'I'm coming with you.' 'Like hell you are.'* (= you certainly are not) "我要和你一起去。" "鬼才信呢。" **a/one hell of a ... | a/one helluva ...** /'heləvə/ (*slang*) used to give emphasis to what a person is saying 極其；非常： *The firm was in a hell of a mess when he took over.* 他接手時公司一團糟。◇ *It must have been one hell of a party.* 那肯定是一次很棒的聚會。◇ *That's one helluva big house you've got.* 你的房子真是大極了。 **play (merry) 'hell with sth/sb** (*BrE, informal*) to affect sth/sb badly 對⋯造成嚴重影響；嚴重損害⋯ **scare, annoy, etc. the 'hell out of sb** (*informal*) to scare, annoy, etc. sb very much 使某人十分恐懼（或惱怒等） **to 'hell and back** (*informal*) used to say that sb has been through a difficult situation 經歷過困境；歷劫歸來： *We'd been to hell and back together and we were still good friends.* 我們曾經患難與共，現在依然是好友。 **to 'hell with sb/sth** (*informal*) used to express anger or dislike and to say that you no longer care about sb/sth and will take no notice of them（表示憤怒或厭惡，不再在乎）見鬼去吧，隨便： *'To hell with him,' she thought, 'I'm leaving.'* "讓他見鬼去吧，" 她想，"我走了。" ➲ more at BAT *n.*, BUG *v.*, CAT, CATCH *v.*, HOPE *n.*, PAY *v.*, RAISE *v.*, ROAD, SNOWBALL *n.*

he'll /hiːl/ *short form* he will

ˌhell-'bent *adj.* **~ on sth/on doing sth** determined to do sth even though the results may be bad 不顧一切地（做某事）： *He seems hell-bent on drinking himself to death.* 他一個勁地喝酒，似乎命都不要了。

hel·le·bore /'helɪbɔː(r)/ *noun* a poisonous plant with divided leaves and large green, white or purple flowers 鹿食草（有毒）

Hel·lene /'heliːn/ *noun* a person from Greece, especially ancient Greece 希臘人；（尤指）古希臘人

Hel·len·ic /he'lenɪk; -'liːn-/ *adj.* of or connected with ancient or modern Greece 希臘的；古希臘的

Hel·len·is·tic /ˌhelɪ'nɪstɪk/ *adj.* of or connected with the Greek history, language and culture of the 4th–1st centuries BC（公元前 4 至前 1 世紀）希臘化（時期）的

hell·fire /'helfaɪə(r)/ *noun* [U] the fires which are believed by some religious people to burn in hell, where bad people go to be punished after they die 地獄之火

hell·hole /'helhəʊl; *NAmE* -hoʊl/ *noun* (*informal*) a very unpleasant place 非常討厭的地方

hel·lion /'heliən/ *noun* (*NAmE*) a badly behaved child who annoys other people 調皮搗蛋的孩子

hell·ish /'helɪʃ/ *adj.* (*informal, especially BrE*) extremely unpleasant 極不愉快的

hello 🔑 (also **hullo** especially in *BrE*) (*BrE* also **hallo**) /hə'ləʊ; *NAmE* hə'loʊ/ *exclamation, noun* (*pl.* **-os**) **1** 🔑 used as a GREETING when you meet sb, when you answer the telephone or when you want to attract sb's attention（用於問候、接電話或引起注意）哈囉，喂，你好： *Hello John, how are you?* 哈囉，約翰，你好嗎？◇ *Hello, is there anybody there?* 喂，那裏有人嗎？◇ ***Say hello*** *to Liz for me.* 替我向利茲問好。◇ *They exchanged* ***hellos*** (= said hello to each other) *and forced smiles.* 他們相互打個招呼，勉強笑笑。 **2** (*BrE*) used to show that you are surprised by sth（表示驚訝）嘿： *Hello, hello, what's going on here?* 嘿，嘿，這是在幹嗎？ **3** (*informal*) used to show that you think sb has said sth stupid or is not paying attention（認為別人說了蠢話或分心）喂，嘿： *Hello? You didn't really mean that, did you?* 嘿？你不會真是那個意思吧？◇ *I'm like, 'Hello! Did you even listen?'* 我說："嘿！你到底有沒有聽我說話？" ➲ see also GOLDEN HELLO

More About 補充說明

greetings 打招呼

- **Hello** is the most usual word and is used in all situations, including answering the telephone. * Hello 最為常用，用於所有場合，包括接電話。
- **Hi** is more informal and is now very common. * Hi 較非正式，現在使用很普遍。
- **How are you?** or **How are you doing?** (*very informal*) often follow **Hello** and **Hi**. * How are you? 或 How are you doing?（非常口語化）常用於 Hello 和 Hi 之後： *'Hello, Mark.' 'Oh, hi, Kathy! How are you?'* "馬克，你好。" "噢，凱西，你好！最近好嗎？"
- **Good morning** is often used by members of a family or people who work together when they see each other for the first time in the day. It can also be used in formal situations and on the telephone. In informal speech, people may just say **Morning**. * Good morning 常在家庭成員或同事之間一天中第一次見面時說，亦可用於正式場合和電話中。在非正式談話中，可只說 Morning。
- **Good afternoon** and **Good evening** are much less common. **Good night** is not used to greet somebody, but only to say goodbye late in the evening or when you are going to bed. * Good afternoon 和 Good evening 少用得多。Good night 只在晚上說再見或上牀睡覺前說，不用以打招呼。
- If you are meeting someone for the first time, you can say **Pleased to meet you** or **Nice to meet you** (*less formal*). Some people use **How do you do?** in formal situations. The correct reply to this is **How do you do?**. 第一次與人見面時可說 Pleased to meet you 或 Nice to meet you（較非正式）。在正式場合有些人用 How do you do?，正確的回答是 How do you do?。

hell·rais·er /'helreɪzə(r)/ *noun* a person who causes trouble by behaving loudly and often violently, especially when they have drunk too much alcohol 吵鬧搗蛋的人；胡打瞎鬧的人；（尤指）耍酒瘋的人

ˌHell's 'Angel *noun* a member of a group of people, usually men, who ride powerful motorcycles, wear leather clothes and used to be known for their wild and violent behaviour 地獄天使（穿皮衣、騎大馬力摩托車橫衝直撞，通常為男性）

H

hel·luva ➲ HELL

helm /helm/ *noun* a handle or wheel used for steering a boat or ship 舵柄；舵輪 ➲ compare TILLER

IDM **at the 'helm** **1** in charge of an organization, project, etc. 負責；掌管 **2** steering a boat or ship 掌舵 **take the 'helm** **1** to take charge of an organization, project, etc. 擔任領導人；掌管 **2** to begin steering a boat or ship 開始掌舵

hel·met /'helmɪt/ *noun* a type of hard hat that protects the head, worn, for example, by a police officer, a soldier or a person playing some sports 頭盔；防護帽 ➲ VISUAL VOCAB pages V44, V47, V51 ➲ see also CRASH HELMET

hel·met·ed /'helmɪtɪd/ *adj.* [only before noun] wearing a helmet 戴着頭盔（或防護帽）的

helms·man /'helmzmən/ *noun* (*pl.* **-men** /-mən/) a person who steers a boat or ship 舵手

help 🔑 /help/ *verb, noun*

■ *verb*

▸ MAKE EASIER/BETTER 使更容易／更好 **1** 🔑 [I, T] to make it easier or possible for sb to do sth by doing sth for them or by giving them sth that they need 幫助；協助；援助：*Help, I'm stuck!* 救命，我被卡住了！◇ **~ with sth** *He always helps with the housework.* 他總是幫着做家務。◇ **~ sb** *We must all try and help each other.* 我們都必須努力互相幫助。◇ **~ sb with sth** *Jo will help us with some of the organization.* 喬將幫我們做一部份組織工作。◇ **~ (sb) in doing sth** *I need contacts that could help in finding a job.* 我需要能幫我找到工作的社會關係。◇ **~ sb (to) do sth** *The college's aim is to help students (to) achieve their aspirations.* 大學的目標是幫助學生實現他們的抱負。◇ *This charity aims to help people (to) help themselves.* 這個慈善機構的宗旨是幫助人自力更生。◇ *Come and help me lift this box.* 來幫我抬這個箱子。◇ **~ (to) do sth** *She helped (to) organize the party.* 她協助籌備了晚會。**HELP** In verb patterns with a **to** infinitive, the 'to' is often left out, especially in informal or spoken English. 帶 to 的不定式動詞結構常省略 to，非正式英語和英語口語中尤其如此。 **2** 🔑 [I, T] to improve a situation; to make it easier for sth to happen 改善狀況；促進；促使：*It **helped** being able to talk about it.* 能談談這件事很有好處。◇ **~ sth** *It doesn't really **help matters** knowing that everyone is talking about us.* 知道大家都在議論我們也於事無補。◇ **~ (to) do sth** *This should help (to) reduce the pain.* 這個應有助於減輕痛楚。

▸ SB TO MOVE 移動某人 **3** 🔑 [T] **~ sb + adv./prep.** to help sb move by letting them lean on you, guiding them, etc. 攙扶；帶領：*She helped him to his feet.* 她扶他站了起來。◇ *We were helped ashore by local people.* 我們被當地人救上岸。

▸ GIVE FOOD/DRINK 給食物／飲料 **4** 🔑 [T] to give yourself/sb food, drinks, etc. 為（自己或某人）取用：**~ yourself** *If you want another drink, just help yourself.* 你要是想再喝一杯就請自便。◇ **~ yourself/sb to sth** *Can I help you to some more salad?* 再給你來點色拉好嗎？

▸ STEAL 偷竊 **5** [T] **~ yourself to sth** (*informal, disapproving*) to take sth without permission 擅自拿走；竊取 **SYN** **steal**：*He'd been helping himself to the money in the cash register.* 他一直在偷現金出納機中的錢。

IDM **sb can (not) help (doing) sth | sb can not help but do sth** 🔑 used to say that it is impossible to prevent or avoid sth 某人忍不住（或無法抑制）做某事；不可能避免某事：*I can't help thinking he knows more than he has told us.* 我總覺得他沒把他知道的事全告訴我們。◇ *She couldn't help but wonder what he was thinking.* 她不禁琢磨着他在想些什麼。◇ ***It couldn't be helped*** (= there was no way of avoiding it and we must accept it). 這是不可避免的。◇ *I always end up having an argument with her, I don't know why, I just **can't help it**.* 我總是和她意見不合，鬧得不歡而散，我不知道為什麼，我就是忍不住。◇ *I couldn't help it if the bus was late* (= it wasn't my fault). 公共汽車晚點了，我沒辦法。◇ *She burst out laughing—she **couldn't help herself*** (= couldn't stop herself). 她突然大笑起來，無法自抑。 **give/lend a ˌhelping 'hand** to help sb 幫助；伸出援助之手 **God/Heaven 'help sb** (*informal*) used to say that you are afraid sb will be in danger or that sth bad will happen to them（表示擔心某人將有危險或有難）：*God help us if this doesn't work.* 如果這個行不通，那就要靠上帝了。**HELP** Some people find this use offensive. 有人認為此用法含冒犯意。 **so 'help me (God)** used to swear that what you are saying is true, especially in a court of law 我發誓，上帝作證（尤用於法庭）

PHR V **ˌhelp sb 'off/'on with sth** to help sb take off/put on a piece of clothing 幫某人脱（或穿）衣服：*Let me help you off with your coat.* 我來幫你脱大衣吧。 **ˌhelp 'out | ˌhelp sb↔'out** 🔑 to help sb, especially in a difficult situation 幫助某人擺脱（困境）：*He's always willing to help out.* 他總是急人之難。◇ *When I bought the house, my sister helped me out with a loan.* 我買這所房子時，我姐姐借給了我一筆錢解了急。

■ *noun*

▸ MAKING EASIER/BETTER 使較容易／較好 **1** 🔑 [U] the act of helping sb to do sth 幫助；協助；援助：*Thank you for all your help.* 感謝你的一切幫助。◇ **~ (with sth)** *Do you need any help with that?* 這事你需要幫忙嗎？◇ *Can I be **of any help** to you?* 我能幫你什麼忙嗎？◇ *None of this would have been possible without their help.* 如果沒有他們的協助，這事沒有一樣能辦成。◇ *She stopped smoking **with the help** of her family and friends.* 她在家人和朋友的幫助下戒了煙。

▸ ADVICE/MONEY 忠告；錢 **2** 🔑 [U] advice, money, etc. that is given to sb in order to solve their problems 有助益的東西（如忠告、錢等）：*to **seek financial/legal/medical, etc. help*** 尋求經濟、法律、醫療等援助◇ **~ in doing sth** *The organization offers practical help in dealing with paperwork.* 這個機構提供文件處理方面的實際幫助。◇ **~ with sth** *You should qualify for help with the costs of running a car.* 你應該符合條件獲取養車補助。◇ *a **help key/screen*** (= a function on a computer that provides information on how to use the computer) 幫助鍵／屏幕（計算機中提供計算機使用信息的功能）

▸ BEING USEFUL 有用 **3** 🔑 [U] the fact of being useful 有用：*The map wasn't **much help**.* 這張地圖沒多大用處。◇ ***With the help of** a ladder, neighbours were able to rescue the children from the blaze.* 鄰居們借助一把梯子把孩子們從大火中救了出來。◇ *Just shouting at him isn't going to be a lot of help.* 光是對他大喊大叫不會有多大用處。

▸ FOR SB IN DANGER 對處於危險中的人 **4** 🔑 [U] the act of helping sb who is in danger 救助：*Quick, get help!* 快，找人援救！◇ *She screamed for help.* 她高聲喊救命。

▸ PERSON/THING 人；事物 **5** [sing.] **a ~ (to sb)** a person or thing that helps sb 有幫助的人（或事物）：*She was more of a hindrance than a help.* 她非但沒幫上忙，反而礙事。◇ *Your advice was a big help.* 你的建議很有幫助。◇ (*ironic*) *You're a great help, I must say!* 我得說，你可沒少幫忙！

▸ IN HOUSE 住宅 **6 the help** [U+sing./pl. v.] (*especially NAmE*) the person or people who are employed by sb to clean their house, etc. 僕人 ➲ see also HOME HELP

IDM **there is no 'help for it** (*especially BrE*) it is not possible to avoid doing sth that may harm sb in some way 沒辦法；別無選擇：*There's no help for it. We shall have to call the police.* 沒法子了。我們只得叫警察了。

'help desk *noun* a service, usually in a business company, that gives people information and help, especially if they are having problems with a computer（商業公司的）咨詢服務，咨詢枱；（尤指有關電腦問題的）技術支援服務

help·er /'helpə(r)/ *noun* a person who helps sb to do sth 幫手；助手：*a willing helper* 自願幫忙者

help·ful 🔑 /'helpfl/ *adj.*

1 🔑 able to improve a particular situation 有用的；有益的；有幫助的 **SYN** **useful**：***helpful advice/information/suggestions*** 有用的勸告／信息／建議 ◇ *Sorry I can't be more helpful.* 對不起，我幫不上更多的忙。◇ **~ (for sb) (to do sth)** *It would be helpful for me to see the damage for myself.* 要能親眼看看造成的破壞會對我有所幫助。◇ **~ in doing sth** *Role-play is helpful in developing communication skills.* 角色扮演有助於提高溝通技巧。◇ **~ to sb** *The booklet should be very helpful to parents of disabled children.* 這本小冊子對於殘疾兒童的父母會很有用。 **2** 🔑 (of a person 人) willing to help sb 願意幫忙的：*I called the police but they weren't very* *helpful.* 我叫了警察，但他們不太肯幫忙。◇ *The staff couldn't have been more helpful.* 職員們十分願意幫忙。 **OPP** **unhelpful** ▸ **help·ful·ly** /-fəli/ *adv.*： *She helpfully suggested that I try the local library.* 她很熱心地建議我試試本地的圖書館。 **help·ful·ness** *noun* [U]

help·ing /ˈhelpɪŋ/ *noun* **~** (**of sth**) an amount of food given to sb at a meal（進餐時的）一份食物，一客食物 **SYN** **serving**： *a small/generous helping* 一小份／一大份食物 ◇ *We all had a* ***second helping*** *of pie.* 我們又都吃了一份餡餅。

help·less /ˈhelpləs/ *adj.* **1** unable to take care of yourself or do things without the help of other people 無自理能力的；不能自立的；無助的： *the helpless victims of war* 無助的戰爭受害者 ◇ *a helpless gesture/look* 無可奈何的姿勢／表情 ◇ *He lay helpless on the floor.* 他無力地躺在地板上。◇ *It's natural to feel helpless against such abuse.* 對這種虐待感到無能為力是自然的。◇ *The worst part is being helpless to change anything.* 最糟糕的是沒有能力改變任何事情。 **2** unable to control a strong feeling 無法抑制的： ***helpless panic/rage*** 抑制不住的恐慌／憤怒 ◇ **~ with sth** *The audience was* ***helpless with laughter.*** 觀眾情不自禁地大笑。 ▸ **help·less·ly** *adv.*： *They watched helplessly as their home went up in flames.* 他們無奈地看着自己的家被大火吞沒。 **help·less·ness** *noun* [U]： *a* ***feeling/sense of helplessness*** 無能為力的感覺

help·line /ˈhelplaɪn/ *noun* (*BrE*) a telephone service that provides advice and information about particular problems（提供咨詢和信息的電話）服務熱線

help·mate /ˈhelpmeɪt/ (also **help·meet** /ˈhelpmiːt/) *noun* (*formal* or *literary*) a helpful partner, especially a wife 得力的伴侶；（尤指）妻子

helter-skelter /ˌheltə ˈskeltə(r); *NAmE* ˌheltər/ *noun, adj.*

▪ ***noun*** (*BrE*) a tall tower at a FAIRGROUND that has a path twisting around the outside of it from the top to the bottom for people to slide down（遊樂場的）螺旋滑梯

▪ ***adj.*** [only before noun] done in a hurry and in a way that lacks organization 忙亂的；倉促的： *a helter-skelter dash to meet the deadline* 最後期限到來前的匆忙趕工 ▸ **helter-skelter** *adv.*

hem /hem/ *noun, verb*

▪ ***noun*** the edge of a piece of cloth that has been folded over and sewn, especially on a piece of clothing（衣服等的）褶邊，捲邊： *to take up the hem of a dress* (= to make the dress shorter) 把連衣裙改短

▪ ***verb*** (**-mm-**) **~ sth** to make a hem on sth（給某物）縫邊，鑲邊： *to hem a skirt* 給裙子縫邊

IDM **ˌhem and ˈhaw** (*NAmE*) (*BrE* **ˌhum and ˈhaw**) (*informal*) to take a long time to make a decision or before you say sth 猶豫不决；支支吾吾；嗯嗯呃呃

PHR V **ˌhem sb/sth↔ˈin** to surround sb/sth so that they cannot move or grow easily 包圍，限制（某人或某事物） **SYN** **hedge sb/sth in**： *The village is hemmed in on all sides by mountains.* 村子四面環山。◇ (*figurative*) *She felt hemmed in by all their petty rules and regulations.* 她覺得受到他們那些瑣碎的規章制度的束縛。

ˈhe-man *noun* (*pl.* **he-men**) (often *humorous*) a strong man with big muscles, especially one who likes to show other people how strong he is 強健的男子（尤指好顯示其體魄者）

hema·tite (*NAmE*) (*BrE* **haem·atite**) /ˈhiːmətaɪt/ *noun* [U] (*geology* 地) a dark red rock from which iron is obtained 赤鐵礦

hema·tol·ogy (*NAmE*) (*BrE* **haema·tol·ogy**) /ˌhiːməˈtɒlədʒi; *NAmE* -ˈtɑːl-/ *noun* [U] the scientific study of the blood and its diseases 血液學 ▸ **hema·to·logic·al** (*NAmE*) (*BrE* **haem-**) /ˌhiːmətəˈlɒdʒɪkl; *NAmE* -ˈlɑːdʒ-/ *adj.* **hema·tolo·gist** (*NAmE*) (*BrE* **haem-**) /ˌhiːməˈtɒlədʒɪst; *NAmE* -ˈtɑːl-/ *noun*

hema·toma (*NAmE*) (*BrE* **haem·atoma**) /ˌhiːməˈtəʊmə; *NAmE* -ˈtoʊmə/ *noun* (*medical* 醫) a swollen area on the body consisting of blood that has become thick 血腫

hemi·sphere /ˈhemɪsfɪə(r); *NAmE* -sfɪr/ *noun* **1** one half of the earth, especially the half above or below the EQUATOR（地球的）半球；（尤指）北半球，南半球： *the* ***northern/southern hemisphere*** 北半球；南半球 **2** either half of the brain（大腦的）半球： *the* ***left/right cerebral hemisphere*** 大腦左半球／右半球 **3** one half of a SPHERE (= a round solid object)（球體的）半球

hemi·spher·ic·al /ˌhemɪˈsferɪkl; *NAmE* also -ˈsfɪr-/ *adj.* shaped like a hemisphere 半球形的

hem·line /ˈhemlaɪn/ *noun* the bottom edge of a dress or skirt; the length of a dress or skirt（衣裙的）底邊，下襬；衣裙長度： *Shorter hemlines are back in this season.* 本季又重新時興較短的衣裙。

hem·lock /ˈhemlɒk; *NAmE* -lɑːk/ *noun* **1** [U, C] a poisonous plant with a mass of small white flowers growing at the end of a STEM that is covered in spots 毒芹 **2** [U] poison made from hemlock 從毒芹提煉的毒藥

hemo- (*NAmE*) (*BrE* **haemo-**) /ˈhiːməʊ; *NAmE* -moʊ/ *combining form* (in nouns and adjectives 構成名詞和形容詞) connected with blood（有關）血液的： *hemophilia* 血友病

hemp /hemp/ *noun* [U] a plant which is used for making rope and cloth, and also to make the drug CANNABIS 大麻

hen /hen/ *noun* **1** a female chicken, often kept for its eggs or meat 母雞： *a small flock of laying hens* 一小群下蛋的母雞 ◇ *battery hens* 層架式雞籠飼養的母雞 **2** (especially in compounds 尤用於構成複合詞) any female bird 雌禽： *a hen pheasant* 雌雉 ➲ compare COCK *n.* (1), (2) ➲ see also MOORHEN

hence **AW** /hens/ *adv.* (*formal*) for this reason 因此；由此： *We suspect they are trying to hide something, hence the need for an independent inquiry.* 我們懷疑他們在企圖隱瞞什麼事，因此有必要進行獨立調查。 ➲ LANGUAGE BANK at THEREFORE

IDM **... days, weeks, etc. ˈhence** (*formal*) a number of days, etc. from now（從現在開始）…天、星期等之後： *The true consequences will only be known several years hence.* 真正的後果只有在幾年之後才能知道。

hence·forth /ˌhensˈfɔːθ; *NAmE* -ˈfɔːrθ/ (also **hence·for·ward** /ˌhensˈfɔːwəd; *NAmE* -ˈfɔːrwərd/) *adv.* (*formal*) starting from a particular time and at all times in the future 此後；從此以後： *Friday 31 July 1925 henceforth became known as 'Red Friday'.* * 1925 年 7 月 31 日這個星期五從此以後就稱為"紅色星期五"。

hench·man /ˈhentʃmən/ *noun* (*pl.* **-men** /-mən/) a faithful supporter of a powerful person, for example a political leader or criminal, who is prepared to use violence or become involved in illegal activities to help that person（政治領袖人物或罪犯等的）忠實支持者，親信，心腹，追隨者

hen·deca·syl·lable /ˌhendekəˈsɪləbl/ *noun* (*technical* 術語) a line of poetry with eleven syllables 十一音節的詩句 ▸ **hen·deca·syl·lab·ic** /ˌhendekəsɪˈlæbɪk/ *adj.*

hen·dia·dys /henˈdaɪədɪs/ *noun* [U] (*grammar* 語法) the use of two words joined with 'and' to express a single idea, for example 'nice and warm' 二詞一義，重言法（用 and 連接兩個詞表達一個意思，如 nice and warm）

henge /hendʒ/ *noun* a circle of large vertical wooden or stone objects built in PREHISTORIC times（史前的）環狀直立木（或石）結構

henna /ˈhenə/ *noun* [U] a reddish-brown DYE (= a substance used to change the colour of sth), used especially on the hair and skin 散沫花染劑（棕紅色，尤用於染髮和塗飾皮膚）

ˈhen party (also **ˈhen night**) *noun* (*BrE, informal*) a party for women only, especially one held for a woman who will soon get married 準新娘聚會（只有女性參與） ➲ compare STAG NIGHT

hen·pecked /ˈhenpekt/ *adj.* (*informal*) a man who people say is **henpecked** has a wife who is always telling him what to do, and is too weak to disagree with her 怕老婆的；懼內的

henry /ˈhenri/ *noun* (*pl.* **hen·ries** or **henrys**) (*abbr.* **H**) a unit for measuring the INDUCTANCE in an electric CIRCUIT 亨利（電感單位）

H

hep·at·ic /hɪˈpætɪk/ *adj.* (*biology* 生) connected with the LIVER 肝的

hepa·titis /ˌhepəˈtaɪtɪs/ *noun* [U] a serious disease of the LIVER. There are three main forms: **hepatitis A** (the least serious, caused by infected food), **hepatitis B** and **hepatitis C** (both very serious and caused by infected blood). 肝炎

hepta·gon /ˈheptəgən; *NAmE* -gɑːn/ *noun* (*geometry* 幾何) a flat shape with seven straight sides and seven angles 七邊形；七角形 ▸ **hept·agon·al** /hepˈtægənl/ *adj.*

hept·ath·lon /hepˈtæθlən/ *noun* a sporting event, especially one for women, in which people compete in seven different sports（尤指女子）七項全能（運動）➲ compare BIATHLON, DECATHLON, PENTATHLON, TRIATHLON

her 🔑 /hə(r); ɜː(r); ə(r); *strong form* hɜː(r)/ *pron., det.*

H

■ ***pron.*** 🔑 used as the object of a verb, after the verb *be* or after a preposition to refer to a woman or girl who has already been mentioned or is easily identified（用作動詞或介詞的賓語，或作表語）她：*We're going to call her Sophie.* 我們將給她起名索菲。◇ *Please give her my regards.* 請代我問候她。◇ *The manager will be free soon—you can wait for her here.* 經理很快就有空了，你可以在這裏等她。◇ *That must be her now.* 這會兒一定是她了。➲ compare SHE *pron.* ➲ note at GENDER

■ ***det.*** 🔑 (the possessive form of *she* * she 的所有格形式) of or belonging to a woman or girl who has already been mentioned or is easily identified 她的：*Meg loves her job.* 梅格熱愛她的工作。◇ *She broke her leg skiing.* 她滑雪時摔斷了腿。➲ see also HERS

her·ald /ˈherəld/ *verb, noun*

■ ***verb*** (*formal*) **1 ~ sth** to be a sign that sth is going to happen 是（某事）的前兆；預示：*These talks could herald a new era of peace.* 這些談判可能預示着新的和平時代的來臨。**2 ~ sb/sth (as sth)** [often passive] to say in public that sb/sth is good or important 宣稱（…是好的或重要的）：*The report is being heralded as a blueprint for the future of transport.* 這份報告被宣稱是未來運輸的藍圖。

■ ***noun*** **1** something that shows that sth else is going to happen soon 預兆：*The government claims that the fall in unemployment is the herald of economic recovery.* 政府宣稱失業人數減少是經濟復蘇的先兆。**2** (in the past) a person who carried messages from a ruler（舊時的）信使，傳令官，使者

her·ald·ry /ˈherəldri/ *noun* [U] the study of the COATS OF ARMS and the history of old families 紋章學 ▸ **her·al·dic** /heˈrældɪk/ *adj.*

herb /hɜːb; *NAmE* ɜːrb; hɜːrb/ *noun* **1** a plant whose leaves, flowers or seeds are used to flavour food, in medicines or for their pleasant smell. PARSLEY, MINT and OREGANO are all herbs. 藥草；香草：*a herb garden* 芳草園 ◇ (*NAmE*) *an herb garden* 芳草園 ➲ **VISUAL VOCAB** page V32 **2** (*technical* 術語) a plant with a soft STEM that dies down after flowering 草本植物

herb·aceous /hɜːˈbeɪʃəs; *NAmE* ɜːrˈb-; hɜːrˈb-/ *adj.* (*technical* 術語) connected with plants that have soft STEMS 草本的：*a herbaceous plant* 草本植物

her,baceous 'border *noun* a piece of ground in a garden/yard containing plants that produce flowers every year without being replaced（花園、庭院中）種植多年生花草的花壇

herb·age /ˈhɜːbɪdʒ; *NAmE* ˈɜːrb-; ˈhɜːrb-/ *noun* [U] (*technical* 術語) plants in general, especially grass that is grown for cows, etc. to eat（統稱）草本植物；（尤指）牧草

herb·al /ˈhɜːbl; *NAmE* ˈɜːrbl; ˈhɜːrbl/ *adj., noun*

■ ***adj.*** connected with or made from HERBS 藥草的；香草的：***herbal medicine/remedies*** 草藥；草藥療法

■ ***noun*** a book about HERBS, especially those used in medicines 草本植物誌；（尤指）草藥誌

herb·al·ism /ˈhɜːblɪzəm; *NAmE* ˈɜːrbl-; ˈhɜːrbl-/ *noun* [U] the medical use of plants, especially as a form of ALTERNATIVE MEDICINE 草藥療法（尤指作為另類療法）

herb·al·ist /ˈhɜːbəlɪst; *NAmE* ˈɜːrb-; ˈhɜːrb-/ *noun* a person who grows, sells or uses HERBS for medical purposes 藥草栽培者；藥草商；草藥醫生

,herbal 'tea *noun* [U, C] a drink made from dried HERBS and hot water 草藥茶

herbi·cide /ˈhɜːbɪsaɪd; *NAmE* ˈɜːrb-; ˈhɜːrb-/ *noun* [C, U] a chemical that is poisonous to plants, used to kill plants that are growing where they are not wanted 除莠劑；除草劑 ➲ see also INSECTICIDE, PESTICIDE

herbi·vore /ˈhɜːbɪvɔː(r); *NAmE* ˈɜːrb-; ˈhɜːrb-/ *noun* any animal that eats only plants 食草動物；草食動物 ➲ compare CARNIVORE, INSECTIVORE, OMNIVORE, VEGETARIAN ▸ **herb·iv·or·ous** /hɜːˈbɪvərəs; *NAmE* ɜːrˈb-; hɜːrˈb-/ *adj.*：*herbivorous dinosaurs* 食草恐龍

Her·cu·lean /ˌhɜːkjuˈliːən; *NAmE* ˌhɜːrk-/ *adj.* [usually before noun] needing a lot of strength, determination or effort 費力的；需要決心的；艱巨的：*a Herculean task* 艱巨的任務 **ORIGIN** From the Greek myth in which **Hercules** proved his courage and strength by completing twelve very difficult tasks (called the Labours of Hercules). 源自希臘神話。赫拉克勒斯（Hercules）完成了十二項十分艱巨的任務（"赫拉克勒斯的功績"），由此證明了他的勇氣和力量。

herd /hɜːd; *NAmE* hɜːrd/ *noun, verb*

■ ***noun*** **1** a group of animals of the same type that live and feed together 獸群；牧群：***a herd of cows/deer/elephants*** 一群牛／鹿／象 ◇ ***a beef/dairy herd*** 肉牛群；奶牛群 ➲ compare FLOCK *n.* (1) **2** (usually *disapproving*) a large group of people of the same type 人群；芸芸眾生：*She pushed her way through a herd of lunchtime drinkers.* 她從一群午餐時飲酒的人中間擠了過去。◇ *the **common herd*** (= ordinary people) 普通百姓 ◇ *Why **follow the herd*** (= do and think the same as everyone else)? 為什麼隨大溜呢？ **IDM** see RIDE *v.*

■ ***verb*** **1** [I, T] to move or make sb/sth move in a particular direction（使）向…移動：**+ adv./prep.** *We all herded on to the bus.* 我們全都擁上了公共汽車。◇ **~ sb/sth + adv./prep.** *They were herded together into trucks and driven away.* 他們被一起趕上卡車拉走了。**2** [T] **~ sth** to make animals move together as a group 牧放（牲畜、獸群）：*a shepherd herding his flock* 正在放羊的羊倌

herd·er /ˈhɜːdə(r); *NAmE* ˈhɜːrder/ *noun* a person whose job is to take care of a group of animals such as sheep and cows in the countryside 放牧人；牧工

'herd instinct *noun* [sing.] the natural tendency in people or animals to behave or think like other people or animals 群體本能（人或動物在行為或思維上從眾的自然趨勢）

herds·man /ˈhɜːdzmən; *NAmE* ˈhɜːrd-/ *noun* (*pl.* **-men** /-mən/) a man whose job is to take care of a group of animals such as sheep and cows in the countryside 牧人

here 🔑 /hɪə(r); *NAmE* hɪr/ *adv., exclamation*

■ ***adv.*** **1** 🔑 used after a verb or preposition to mean 'in, at or to this position or place'（用於動詞或介詞之後）在這裏，向這裏：*I live here.* 我住這兒。◇ *Put the box here.* 把箱子放在這裏。◇ *Let's get out of here.* 我們離開這裏吧。◇ *Come over here.* 過來吧。**2** 🔑 now; at this point 現在；在這一點上：*The countdown to Christmas **starts here**.* 現在開始聖誕節倒計時。◇ *Here the speaker paused to have a drink.* 講到這裏，演講人停下來喝了口水。**3** 🔑 used when you are giving or showing sth to sb（給某人東西或指出某物時說）：*Here's the money I promised you.* 這是我答應給你的錢。◇ *Here's a dish that is simple and quick to make.* 這是一道簡單易做的菜。◇ *Here is your opportunity.* 你的機會來了。◇ ***Here comes** the bus.* 公共汽車來了。◇ *I can't find my keys. Oh, **here they are**.* 我找不到我的鑰匙。哦，原來在這裏。◇ ***Here we are*** (= we've arrived). 我們到了。**4** 🔑 **~ to do sth** used to show your role in a situation（表示某人的作用）：*I'm here to help you.* 我是來幫助你的。**5** (used after a noun, for emphasis 用於名詞之後，表示強調)：*My friend here saw it happen.* 我的這位朋友目睹了事情的經過。

IDM **by 'here** (*WelshE*) here; to here 在這裏；到這裏：*Come by here now!* 現在到這兒來！ **,here and 'there** in various places 在各處；到處：*Papers were scattered here and there on the floor.* 地板上到處散落着文件。 **,here 'goes** (*informal*) used when you are telling people that you are just going to do sth exciting, dangerous, etc. （宣稱即將開始令人興奮或危險的活動）看我的 **here's to sb/sth** used to wish sb health or success, as you lift a glass and drink a TOAST （祝酒辭）為…的健康（或勝利）乾杯：*Here's to your future happiness!* 為你今後的幸福乾杯！ **,here, ,there and 'everywhere** in many different places; all around 在很多地方；四處 **,here we 'go** (*informal*) said when sth is starting to happen（某事）開始了：*'Here we go,' thought Fred, 'she's sure to say something.'* "這就開始了。" 弗雷德想，"她肯定有話要說。" **,here we go a'gain** (*informal*) said when sth is starting to happen again, especially sth bad（尤指壞事）又開始了，又一次發生了 **,here you 'are** (*informal*) used when you are giving sth to sb 給你：*Here you are. This is what you were asking for.* 給你。這就是你一直要的東西。 **,here you 'go** (*informal*) used when you are giving sth to sb 給你：*Here you go. Four copies, is that right?* 給你，四本，對嗎？ **neither 'here nor 'there** not important 不重要 **SYN** **irrelevant**：*What might have happened is neither here nor there.* 曾經發生過什麼事已經都不重要了。 ➲ more at OUT *adv., prep.*

■ ***exclamation*** **1** (*BrE*) used to attract sb's attention（用以引起注意）喂，嘿：*Here, where are you going with that ladder?* 嘿，你要把梯子搬到哪裏？ **2** used when offering sth to sb（主動提議時說）：*Here, let me carry that for you.* 來，讓我幫你搬吧。

here·abouts /ˌhɪərəˈbaʊts; *NAmE* ˌhɪr-/ (*NAmE* also **here·about**) *adv.* near this place 在這附近：*There aren't many houses hereabouts.* 這一帶房子不多。

here·after /ˌhɪərˈɑːftə(r); *NAmE* ˌhɪrˈæf-/ *adv., noun*

■ ***adv.*** **1** (also **here·in·after**) (*law* 律) (in legal documents, etc. 用於法律文件等) in the rest of this document 在本文件其餘部份；以下 **2** (*formal*) from this time; in future 此後；今後；將來 ➲ compare THEREAFTER **3** (*formal*) after death 死後：*Do you believe in a life hereafter?* 你相信有來世嗎？

■ ***noun*** **the hereafter** [sing.] a life believed to begin after death 死後的生命；陰世

here·by /ˌhɪəˈbaɪ; *NAmE* ˌhɪrˈbaɪ/ *adv.* (in legal documents, etc. 用於法律文件等) as a result of this statement, and in a way that makes sth legal 特此；以此

her·edi·tary /həˈredɪtri; *NAmE* -teri/ *adj.* **1** (especially of illnesses 尤指疾病) given to a child by its parents before it is born 遺傳的；遺傳性的：*a* ***hereditary illness/disease/condition/problem*** 遺傳的疾病／問題 ◇ *Epilepsy is hereditary in her family.* 癲癇是她家的遺傳病。 **2** that is legally given to sb's child, when that person dies 世襲的：*a* ***hereditary title/monarchy*** 世襲的頭銜／君主制 **3** holding a rank or title that is hereditary 有世襲身分（或頭銜）的：***hereditary peers/rulers*** 世襲的貴族／統治者

her·ed·ity /həˈredəti/ *noun* [U] the process by which mental and physical characteristics are passed by parents to their children; these characteristics in a particular person 遺傳（過程）；遺傳特徵：*the debate over the effects of heredity and environment* 有關遺傳與環境影響的辯論

here·in /ˌhɪərˈɪn; *NAmE* ˌhɪrˈɪn/ *adv.* (*formal* or *law* 律) in this place, document, statement or fact 在此處；於此文件（或聲明、事實）中：*Neither party is willing to compromise and herein lies the problem.* 雙方都不願意妥協，問題就在這裏。

here·in·after /ˌhɪərɪnˈɑːftə(r); *NAmE* ˌhɪrɪnˈæf-/ *adv.* (*law* 律) = HEREAFTER (1)

here·of /ˌhɪərˈɒv; *NAmE* ˌhɪrˈʌv; -ˈɑːv/ *adv.* (*law* 律) of this 關於這個；在本文件中：*a period of 12 months from the date hereof* (= the date of this document) 從本文件日期起的 12 個月的時間

her·esy /ˈherəsi/ *noun* [U, C] (*pl.* **-ies**) **1** a belief or an opinion that is against the principles of a particular religion; the fact of holding such beliefs 宗教異端；信奉邪說：*He was burned at the stake for heresy.* 他因為信奉異端思想而以火刑處死。◇ *the heresies of the early Protestants* 早期新教徒的異端邪說 ➲ COLLOCATIONS at RELIGION **2** a belief or an opinion that disagrees strongly with what most people believe 離經叛道的信念（或觀點）：*The idea is heresy to most employees of the firm.* 這種想法有悖於公司大多數員工的意見。

her·et·ic /ˈherətɪk/ *noun* a person who is guilty of heresy 犯異端罪者；離經叛道者 ▸ **her·et·ical** /həˈretɪkl/ *adj.*：*heretical beliefs* 異端信仰

here·to /ˌhɪəˈtuː; *NAmE* ˌhɪrˈtuː/ *adv.* (*law* 律) to this 到此為止；至此；於此

here·to·fore /ˌhɪətuˈfɔː(r); *NAmE* ˌhɪrt-/ *adv.* (*law* 律 or *formal*) before this time 在這之前

here·upon /ˌhɪərəˈpɒn; *NAmE* ˌhɪrəˈpɑːn/ *adv.* (*literary*) after this; as a direct result of this situation 此後；於是；隨即

here·with /ˌhɪəˈwɪð; -ˈwɪθ; *NAmE* ˌhɪrˈw-/ *adv.* (*formal*) with this letter, book or document 隨同此信（或書、文件）：*I enclose herewith a copy of the policy.* 我隨信附上一份保險單。

her·it·able /ˈherɪtəbl/ *adj.* (*law* 律) (of property 財產) that can be passed from one member of a family to another 可繼承的；可傳承的

heri·tage /ˈherɪtɪdʒ/ *noun* [usually sing.] the history, traditions and qualities that a country or society has had for many years and that are considered an important part of its character 遺產（指國家或社會長期形成的歷史、傳統和特色）：*Spain's rich cultural heritage* 西班牙的豐富文化遺產 ◇ *The building is part of our national heritage.* 這個建築是我們民族遺產的一部份。

'heritage centre *noun* (*BrE*) a place where there are exhibitions that people visit to learn about life in the past 文化遺產展覽館；原貌館

herm·aph·ro·dite /hɜːˈmæfrədaɪt; *NAmE* hɜːrˈm-/ *noun* a person, an animal or a flower that has both male and female sexual organs or characteristics 雌雄同體的人（或動物、植物） ▸ **herm·aph·ro·dite** *adj.*

her·men·eut·ic /ˌhɜːməˈnjuːtɪk; *NAmE* ˌhɜːrməˈnjuːtɪk; -ˈnuː-/ *adj.* (*technical* 術語) relating to the meaning of written texts（對書面文本）解釋的，闡釋的；解經的

her·men·eut·ics /ˌhɜːməˈnjuːtɪks; *NAmE* ˌhɜːrməˈnjuːtɪks; -ˈnuː-/ *noun* [pl.] (*technical* 術語) the area of study that analyses and explains written texts（對書面文本等的）解釋學，闡釋學；解經原則

her·met·ic /hɜːˈmetɪk; *NAmE* hɜːrˈm-/ *adj.* **1** (*technical* 術語) tightly closed so that no air can escape or enter 密封的；不透氣的 **SYN** **airtight** **2** (*formal, disapproving*) closed and difficult to become a part of 封閉的；不受外界影響的：*the strange, hermetic world of the theatre* 神秘、與世隔絕的戲劇世界 ▸ **her·met·ic·al·ly** /-kli/ *adv.*：*a hermetically sealed container* 密封的容器

her·mit /ˈhɜːmɪt; *NAmE* ˈhɜːrmɪt/ *noun* a person who, usually for religious reasons, lives a very simple life alone and does not meet or talk to other people 隱士；隱修者；遁世者

her·mit·age /ˈhɜːmɪtɪdʒ; *NAmE* ˈhɜːrm-/ *noun* a place where a hermit lives or lived 隱居處；修道院

'hermit crab *noun* a CRAB (= a sea creature with eight legs and, usually, a hard shell) that has no shell of its own and has to use the empty shells of other sea creatures 寄居蟹

her·nia /ˈhɜːniə; *NAmE* ˈhɜːrniə/ *noun* [C, U] a medical condition in which part of an organ is pushed through a weak part of the body wall 疝；突出

hero /ˈhɪərəʊ; *NAmE* ˈhɪroʊ; ˈhiː-/ *noun* (*pl.* **-oes**)
1 a person, especially a man, who is admired by many people for doing sth brave or good 英雄，豪傑（尤指男性）：*a* ***war hero*** (= sb who was very brave during a war) 抗戰英雄 ◇ *The Olympic team were given* ***a hero's welcome*** *on their return home.* 奧運代表隊回國時受到了英雄般的歡迎。◇ *one of the country's* ***national heroes*** 這個國家的一位民族英雄 **2** the main male

H

character in a story, novel, film/movie, etc.（故事、小說、電影等的）男主人公，男主角：*The hero of the novel is a ten-year old boy.* 這部小說的主人公是個十歲的男孩。 **3** a person, especially a man, that you admire because of a particular quality or skill that they have 崇拜的對象，偶像（尤指男性）：*my childhood hero* 我孩提時的偶像 **4** (*NAmE*) = SUBMARINE (2) ➲ see also HEROINE

hero·ic /hə'rəʊɪk; *NAmE* -'roʊ-/ *adj.* **1** showing extreme courage and admired by many people 英勇的；英雄的 SYN **courageous**：*a heroic figure* 英雄人物 ◇ *Rescuers made* ***heroic efforts*** *to save the crew.* 救援人員不畏艱險努力營救全體船員。 **2** showing great determination to succeed or to achieve sth, especially sth difficult 有必勝決心的；不畏艱難的：*We watched our team's heroic struggle to win back the cup.* 我們目睹了我隊為贏回獎杯所付出的不懈努力。 **3** that is about or involves a hero（關於）英雄的：*a* ***heroic story/poem*** 英雄故事 / 頌詩 ◇ ***heroic deeds/myths*** 英雄事跡 / 神話故事 **4** very large or great 非常大的；巨大的：*This was foolishness on a* ***heroic scale.*** 這簡直是天大的蠢事。 ▶ **hero·ic·al·ly** /-kli/ *adv.*

he,roic 'couplet *noun* (*technical* 術語) two lines of poetry one after the other that RHYME and usually contain ten syllables and five stresses 英雄體偶句詩（相互押韻的含有五個抑揚格的二行詩）

hero·ics /hə'rəʊɪks; *NAmE* -'roʊ-/ *noun* [pl.] **1** (*disapproving*) talk or behaviour that is too brave or dramatic for a particular situation 譁眾取寵的言語（或行為）：*Remember, no heroics, we just go in there and do our job.* 記住，不要大肆宣揚，我們只要到那兒去幹我們的活兒就行了。 **2** actions that are brave and determined 勇敢果斷的行為：*Thanks to Bateman's heroics in the second half, the team won 2–0.* 由於貝特曼在下半場的英勇表現，球隊以 2:0 獲勝。

her·oin /'herəʊɪn; *NAmE* -roʊ-/ *noun* [U] a powerful illegal drug made from MORPHINE, that some people take for pleasure and can become ADDICTED to 海洛因：*a heroin addict* 吸海洛因上癮的人

hero·ine /'herəʊɪn; *NAmE* -roʊ-/ *noun* **1** a girl or woman who is admired by many for doing sth brave or good 女英雄；女豪傑：*the heroines of the revolution* 那場革命中的各位女英雄 **2** the main female character in a story, novel, film/movie, etc.（故事、小說、電影等中的）女主人公，女主角：*The heroine is played by Demi Moore.* 女主角由黛米 • 穆爾扮演。 **3** a woman that you admire because of a particular quality or skill that she has 崇拜的女人；女偶像：*Madonna was her teenage heroine.* 麥當娜是她十幾歲時的偶像。

hero·ism /'herəʊɪzəm; *NAmE* -roʊ-/ *noun* [U] very great courage 英勇表現；英雄精神

heron /'herən/ *noun* a large bird with a long neck and long legs, that lives near water 鷺

'hero worship *noun* [U] great admiration for sb because you think they are extremely beautiful, intelligent, etc. 英雄崇拜；個人崇拜

'hero-worship *verb* (-pp-) **~ sb** to admire sb very much because you think they are extremely beautiful, intelligent, etc. 崇拜（某人）

her·pes /'hɜːpiːz; *NAmE* 'hɜːrp-/ *noun* [U] one of a group of infectious diseases, caused by a virus, that cause painful spots on the skin, especially on the face and sexual organs 疱疹

herpes zoster /ˌhɜːpiːz 'zɒstə(r); *NAmE* ˌhɜːrpiːz 'zɑːstər/ *noun* [U] (*medical* 醫) **1** = SHINGLES **2** a virus which causes SHINGLES and CHICKENPOX 帶狀疱疹病毒

her·ring /'herɪŋ/ *noun* (*pl.* **her·ring** or **her·rings**) [U, C] a N Atlantic fish that swims in very large groups and is used for food 鯡（產於北大西洋，成大群游動，可食）：*shoals of herring* 鯡魚群 ◇ *fresh herring fillets* 新鮮鯡魚片 ◇ *pickled herrings* 醃製的鯡魚 ➲ see also RED HERRING

her·ring·bone /'herɪŋbəʊn; *NAmE* -boʊn/ *noun* [U] a pattern used, for example, in cloth consisting of lines of V-shapes that are parallel to each other（織物等的）人字形平行花紋

'herring gull *noun* a large N Atlantic bird of the GULL family, with black tips to its wings 銀鷗（產於北大西洋，體大，翼端為黑色）

hers 0→ /hɜːz; ɜːz; *NAmE* hɜːrz; ɜːrz/ *pron.* of or belonging to her 她的；屬於她的：*His eyes met hers.* 他的目光和她的相遇了。 ◇ *The choice was hers.* 那個選擇是她做出的。 ◇ *a friend of hers* 她的一位朋友 ➲ note at GENDER

her·self 0→ /hɜː'self; *NAmE* hɜːr's-; *weak form* hə'self; *NAmE* hər's-/ *pron.* **1** 0→ (the reflexive form of *she* * she 的反身形式) used when the woman or girl who performs an action is also affected by it（用作女性的反身代詞）她自己，自己：*She hurt herself.* 她弄傷了自己。 ◇ *She must be very proud of herself.* 她一定非常自豪。 **2** 0→ used to emphasize the female subject or object of a sentence（強調句中的女性主語或賓語）：*She told me the news herself.* 是她本人告訴我這個消息的。 ◇ *Jane herself was at the meeting.* 簡親自參加了會議。

IDM **be, seem, etc. her'self** (of a woman or girl 女性) to be in a normal state of health or happiness; not influenced by other people 身體或心情狀況正常；如平時一樣；沒有受他人影響：*She didn't seem quite herself this morning.* 她今天早上好像有點不太對勁。 ◇ *She needed space to be herself.* 她需要自己的獨立空間。 **(all) by her'self** **1** alone; without anyone else（她）獨自，單獨：*She lives by herself.* 她獨自一人生活。 **2** without help（她）獨立地：*She runs the business by herself.* 她自己經營這項生意。 **(all) to her'self** for only her to have or use 歸她自己一人佔有（或使用）：*She wants a room all to herself.* 她想要一個完全屬於自己的房間。

hertz /hɜːts; *NAmE* hɜːrts/ *noun* (*pl.* **hertz**) (*abbr.* **Hz**) a unit for measuring the FREQUENCY of sound waves 赫，赫茲（聲波頻率單位）

he's *short form* **1** /hiːz; hiz; ɪz/ he is **2** /hiːz/ he has

hesi·tancy /'hezɪtənsi/ *noun* [U] the state or quality of being slow or uncertain in doing or saying sth 猶豫；躊躇；遲疑不決：*I noticed a certain hesitancy in his voice.* 我注意到他的聲音有點猶豫。

hesi·tant /'hezɪtənt/ *adj.* slow to speak or act because you feel uncertain, embarrassed or unwilling 猶豫的；躊躇的；不情願的：*a hesitant smile* 勉強的微笑 ◇ *the baby's first few hesitant steps* 嬰兒遲疑地邁出的最初幾步 ◇ **~ about sth** *She's hesitant about signing the contract.* 她對是否簽這個合同還猶豫不決。 ◇ **~ to do sth** *Doctors are hesitant to comment on the new treatment.* 醫生們不願對新療法作出評論。 ▶ **hesi·tant·ly** *adv.*

hesi·tate 0→ /'hezɪteɪt/ *verb* **1** 0→ [I, T] to be slow to speak or act because you feel uncertain or nervous（對某事）猶豫，遲疑不決：*She hesitated before replying.* 她猶豫了一下才回答。 ◇ **~ about/over sth** *I didn't hesitate for a moment about taking the job.* 我毫不猶豫地接受了那份工作。 ◇ **+ speech** *'I'm not sure,' she hesitated.* "我不確定。" 她猶豫不決地說。 **2** 0→ [I] **~ to do sth** to be worried about doing sth, especially because you are not sure that it is right or appropriate 顧慮；疑慮：*Please do not hesitate to contact me if you have any queries.* 如果有疑問就請儘管和我聯繫。 ▶ **hesi·ta·tion** /ˌhezɪ'teɪʃn/ *noun* [U, C]：*She agreed* ***without*** *the slightest* ***hesitation.*** 她毫不猶豫地同意了。 ◇ *I* ***have no hesitation in*** *recommending her for the job.* 我毫不猶豫地推薦她做這項工作。 ◇ *He spoke fluently and without unnecessary hesitations.* 他說得很流暢，毫不支吾。

IDM **he who 'hesitates (is 'lost)** (*saying*) if you delay in doing sth you may lose a good opportunity 當斷不斷（，反受其亂）；優柔寡斷者坐失良機

hes·sian /'hesiən; *NAmE* 'heʃn/ (*especially BrE*) (*NAmE* usually **bur·lap**) *noun* [U] a type of strong rough brown cloth, used especially for making SACKS 棕色粗麻布

hetero- /'hetərəʊ-; *NAmE* -roʊ/ *combining form* (in nouns, adjectives and adverbs 構成名詞、形容詞和副詞) other; different 其他；不同的：*heterogeneous* 由很多種類組成的 ◇ *heterosexual* 異性戀者 ➲ compare HOMO-

het·ero·dox /ˈhetərədɒks; *NAmE* -dɑːks/ *adj.* (*formal*) not following the usual or accepted beliefs and opinions 異端的；非正統的 ➲ compare ORTHODOX (1), UNORTHODOX ▸ **het·ero·doxy** *noun* [U, C] (*pl.* **-ies**)

het·ero·ge·neous /ˌhetərəˈdʒiːniəs/ *adj.* (*formal*) consisting of many different kinds of people or things 由很多種類組成的；各種各樣的：*the heterogeneous population of the United States* 由不同族裔組成的美國人口 OPP **homogeneous** ▸ **het·ero·gen·eity** /-dʒəˈniːəti/ *noun* [U]

het·ero·nym /ˈhetərənɪm/ *noun* (*linguistics* 語言) **1** one of two or more words that have the same spelling but different meanings and pronunciation, for example 'tear' meaning 'rip' and 'tear' meaning 'liquid from the eye' 同形異音異義詞（如表示 "撕裂" 的 tear 與表示 "眼淚" 的 tear） **2** one of two or more words that refer to the same thing, for example 'lift' and 'elevator' 異形同義詞（如 lift 和 elevator）

het·ero·sex·ual /ˌhetərəˈsekʃuəl/ *noun* a person who is sexually attracted to people of the opposite sex 異性戀者 ➲ compare BISEXUAL, HOMOSEXUAL ▸ **het·ero·sex·ual** *adj.*：*a heterosexual relationship* 異性戀關係 **het·ero·sexu·al·ity** /ˌhetərəˌsekʃuˈæləti/ *noun* [U]

het·ero·zy·gote /ˌhetərəˈzaɪɡəʊt; *NAmE* -ɡoʊt/ *noun* (*biology* 生) a living thing that has two varying forms of a particular GENE, and whose young may therefore vary in a particular characteristic 雜合子（基因有兩種不同形式的生物） ▸ **het·ero·zy·gous** /-ɡəs/ *adj.*

het up /ˌhet ˈʌp/ *adj.* [not before noun] ~ (**about/over sth**) (*BrE, informal*) anxious, excited or slightly angry 焦慮；興奮；生氣：*What are you getting so het up about?* 什麼事讓你這麼激動？

heur·is·tic /hjuˈrɪstɪk/ *adj.* (*formal*) **heuristic** teaching or education encourages you to learn by discovering things for yourself（教學或教育）啟發式的

heur·is·tics /hjuˈrɪstɪks/ *noun* [U] (*formal*) a method of solving problems by finding practical ways of dealing with them, learning from past experience 探索法；啟發式

hew /hjuː/ *verb* (**hewed, hewed** or **hewn** /hjuːn/) **1** ~ **sth** (*old-fashioned*) to cut sth large with a tool 砍，劈（大的物體）：*to hew wood* 劈木頭 **2** ~ **sth** (**out of sth**) (*formal*) to make or shape sth large by cutting 砍成，劈出（某種形狀、某物）：*roughly hewn timber frames* 粗劈成的木架子 ◇ *The statues were hewn out of solid rock.* 這些雕像是在實心岩石上鑿出來的。

hex /heks/ *verb* ~ **sb** (*NAmE*) to use magic powers in order to harm sb 施魔法以加害（某人） ▸ **hex** *noun*：*to put a hex on sb* 施魔法使某人遭殃 ➲ compare CURSE *v.* (3)

hexa- /ˈheksə/ (also **hex-**) *combining form* (in nouns, adjectives and adverbs 構成名詞、形容詞和副詞) six; having six 六；有六個的

hexa·deci·mal /ˌheksəˈdesɪml/ (also **hex** /heks/) *adj.* (*computing* 計) a system for representing pieces of data using the numbers 0-9 and the letters A-F 十六進制的：*The number 107 is represented in hexadecimal as 6B.* * 107 這個數用十六進制表示為 6B。

hexa·gon /ˈheksəɡən; *NAmE* -ɡɑːn/ *noun* (*geometry* 幾何) a flat shape with six straight sides and six angles 六邊形；六角形 ➲ VISUAL VOCAB page V71 ▸ **hex·agon·al** /heksˈæɡənl/ *adj.*

hexa·gram /ˈheksəɡræm/ *noun* (*geometry* 幾何) a shape made by six straight lines, especially a star made from two triangles with equal sides 六角星形；六角形

hex·am·eter /hekˈsæmɪtə(r)/ *noun* (*technical* 術語) a line of poetry with six stressed syllables 六音步詩行

hey /heɪ/ *exclamation* (*informal*) **1** used to attract sb's attention or to express interest, surprise or anger（用以引起注意或表示興趣、驚訝或生氣）嘿，喂：*Hey, can I just ask you something?* 嘿，問你點事好嗎？◇ *Hey, leave my things alone!* 喂，別碰我的東西！ **2** used to show that you do not really care about sth or that you think it is not important（表示不真正在意或認為不重要）嘿：*That's the third time I've been late this week—but hey!—who's counting?* 那是我這個星期第三次遲到了。不過，嘿，管它多少次呢。 **3** (*SAfrE*) used at the end of a statement, to show that you have finished speaking, or to form a question or invite sb to reply（用於陳述末尾，表示話已說完，或構成問題或請求回答）就這樣，怎麼樣，你說呢：*Thanks for your help, hey.* 謝謝你的幫助啦。◇ *My new bike's nice, hey?* 我的新自行車挺好，你說呢？

IDM **what the ˈhey!** (*NAmE, informal*) used to say that sth does not matter or that you do not care about it 那有什麼要緊；沒什麼；管它呢：*This is probably a bad idea, but what the hey!* 這大概是個餿主意，但管它呢！

hey·day /ˈheɪdeɪ/ *noun* [usually sing.] the time when sb/sth had most power or success, or was most popular 最為強大（或成功、繁榮）的時期 SYN **prime**：*In its **heyday**, the company ran trains every fifteen minutes.* 公司在最興隆時期每隔十五分鐘就開出一列火車。◇ *a fine example from the heyday of Italian cinema* 意大利電影業全盛期的一部優秀代表作 ◇ *a picture of Brigitte Bardot in her heyday* 碧姬 • 芭鐸事業鼎盛時的一張照片

ˌhey ˈpresto *exclamation* (*BrE*) (*NAmE* **presto**) **1** something that people say when they have just done sth so quickly and easily that it seems to have been done by magic 嘿，瞧（變魔術般迅速輕鬆地做完某事時所說）：*You just press the button and, hey presto, a perfect cup of coffee!* 只要按下按鈕，嘿，馬上就出來一杯上好的咖啡！ **2** something that people say just before they finish a magic trick 變（變戲法完成之前所說）

HFC /ˌeɪtʃ ef ˈsiː/ *noun* [C, U] the abbreviation for 'hydrofluorocarbon' (a type of gas used especially in AEROSOLS (= types of container that release liquid in the form of a spray). HFCs are not harmful to the layer of the gas OZONE in the earth's atmosphere.) 氟烷，氟代烷烴，氫氟碳化合物（全寫為 hydrofluorocarbon，尤用於氣霧劑中，對臭氧層無害）

HGV /ˌeɪtʃ dʒiː ˈviː/ *abbr.* (*BrE*) heavy goods vehicle (a large vehicle such as a lorry/truck) 重型貨車；大型貨運卡車：*You need an HGV licence for this job.* 從事這項工作得有重型貨車駕駛執照。

HHS /ˌeɪtʃ eɪtʃ ˈes/ *abbr.* Department of Health and Human Services (the US government department responsible for national health programmes and the SOCIAL SERVICES ADMINISTRATION)（美國）健康與社會服務部

hi 🔑 /haɪ/ *exclamation* (*informal*) used to say hello（用於打招呼）喂，嗨：*Hi guys!* 嗨，夥計們！◇ ***Hi, there!** How're you doing?* 喂！你好嗎？

hia·tus /haɪˈeɪtəs/ *noun* [sing.] (*formal*) **1** a pause in activity when nothing happens 間斷；停滯 **2** a space, especially in a piece of writing or in a speech, where sth is missing 空隙；（尤指文章或說話中的）缺漏，漏字，漏句

hi·ber·nate /ˈhaɪbəneɪt; *NAmE* -bərn-/ *verb* [I] (of animals 動物) to spend the winter in a state like deep sleep 冬眠；蟄伏 ➲ COLLOCATIONS at LIFE ▸ **hi·ber·na·tion** /ˌhaɪbəˈneɪʃn; *NAmE* -bərˈn-/ *noun* [U]

hi·bis·cus /hɪˈbɪskəs; haɪ-/ *noun* [U, C] (*pl.* **hi·bis·cus**) a tropical plant or bush with large brightly coloured flowers 木槿

hic·cup (also **hic·cough**) /ˈhɪkʌp/ *noun, verb*

■ ***noun*** **1** [C] a sharp, usually repeated, sound made in the throat, that is caused by a sudden movement of the DIAPHRAGM and that you cannot control 嗝；呃逆：*She gave a loud hiccup.* 她打了一個響嗝。 **2** **(the) hiccups** [pl.] a series of hiccups 一連串的打嗝：*I ate too quickly and got hiccups.* 我吃得太快，結果不斷地打嗝。◇ *He had the hiccups.* 他接連打嗝。 **3** [C] (*informal*) a small problem or temporary delay 小問題；暫時性耽擱：*There was a slight hiccup in the timetable.* 時間安排上出了點小問題。

■ ***verb*** [I] to have hiccups or a single hiccup 打嗝；打呃

hick /hɪk/ *noun* (*informal, especially NAmE*) a person from the country who is considered to be stupid and to have little experience of life 鄉巴佬；土裏土氣的人：*I was*

H

just a hick from Texas then. 那時我不過是從得克薩斯州來的土包子。▶ **hick** *adj.*：*a hick town* 小鄉鎮

hickey /ˈhɪki/ (*NAmE*) (*BrE* **ˈlove bite**) *noun* a red mark on the skin that is caused by sb biting or sucking their partner's skin when they are kissing 愛痕（在皮膚上吻或咬出的紅色印跡）

hick·ory /ˈhɪkəri/ *noun* [U] the hard wood of the N American **hickory tree** 山核桃木（產於北美）

HICP /ˌeɪtʃ aɪ siː ˈpiː/ *abbr.* harmonized index of consumer prices (a list of the prices of some ordinary goods and services which shows how much these prices change each month. It is used by the European Central Bank and began to be used in the UK in 2003, where it is called the 'Consumer Price Index'.) 消費者物價調和指數（歐洲中央銀行用以顯示普通商品每月價格變化情況，英國於 2003 年開始使用並稱之為"消費物價指數"）

H

ˌhidden aˈgenda *noun* (*disapproving*) the secret intention behind what sb says or does（言語或行為背後的）隱秘意圖，秘密目的：*There are fears of a hidden agenda behind this new proposal.* 人們擔心這一新提議的背後有不可告人的目的。

Synonyms 同義詞辨析

hide

conceal • cover • disguise • mask • camouflage

These words all mean to put or keep sb/sth in a place where they/it cannot be seen or found, or to keep the truth or your feelings secret. 以上各詞均含藏、隱藏、掩蓋、隱瞞之意。

hide to put or keep sb/sth in a place where they/it cannot be seen or found; to keep sth secret, especially your feelings 指藏、隱藏、掩蓋（尤指感情）：*He hid the letter in a drawer.* 他把信藏在抽屜裏。◇ *She managed to hide her disappointment.* 她設法掩藏了自己的失望。

conceal (*formal*) to hide sb/sth; to keep sth secret 指隱藏、隱瞞、掩蓋：*The paintings were concealed beneath a thick layer of plaster.* 那些畫藏在厚厚的灰泥層下面。◇ *Tim could barely conceal his disappointment.* 蒂姆幾乎掩飾不住自己的失望。

NOTE When it is being used to talk about emotions, **conceal** is often used in negative statements.
* conceal 指掩藏感情時常用於否定句。

cover to place sth over or in front of sth in order to hide it 指掩蔽、遮蓋：*She covered her face with her hands.* 她雙手掩面。

disguise to hide or change the nature of sth, so that it cannot be recognized 指掩蔽、掩飾、偽裝，以免被認出：*He tried to disguise his accent.* 他竭力掩飾自己的口音。

mask to hide a feeling, smell, fact, etc. so that it cannot be easily seen or noticed 指掩飾、掩藏（情感、氣味、事實等），以免被看出或注意到：*She masked her anger with a smile.* 她用微笑來掩飾她的憤怒。

camouflage to hide sb/sth by making them/it look like the things around, or like sth else 指通過使人或事物與周圍環境或其他事物相似而達到偽裝、掩飾的目的：*The soldiers camouflaged themselves with leaves and twigs.* 士兵用樹葉和樹枝來偽裝自己。

PATTERNS

- to hide/conceal/disguise/mask/camouflage sth **behind** sth
- to hide/conceal sth **under** sth
- to hide/conceal sth **from** sb
- to hide/conceal/disguise/mask **the truth/the fact that** ...
- to hide/conceal/disguise/mask **your feelings**

hide 0→ /haɪd/ *verb, noun*

■ *verb* (**hid** /hɪd/, **hid·den** /ˈhɪdn/) **1** 0→ [T] to put or keep sb/sth in a place where they/it cannot be seen or found 藏；隱蔽 SYN **conceal**：**~ sb/sth** *He hid the letter in a drawer.* 他把信藏在抽屜裏。◇ *I keep my private papers hidden.* 我藏起了我的私人文件。◇ **~ sb/sth from sth** *They hid me from the police in their attic.* 他們把我藏在他們的閣樓上躲避警察。**2** 0→ [I, T] to go somewhere where you hope you will not be seen or found 躲避；隱匿：*Quick, hide!* 快，躲起來！◇ **+ adv./prep.** *I hid under the bed.* 我躲在牀底下。◇ (*figurative*) *He hid behind a false identity.* 他隱姓埋名。◇ **~ yourself** (**+ adv.prep.**) *She hides herself away in her office all day.* 她成天躲在辦公室裏。**3** 0→ [T] to cover sth so that it cannot be seen 遮住；遮擋 SYN **conceal**：**~ sth + adv./prep.** *He hid his face in his hands.* 他用手捂住了臉。◇ **~ sth** *The house was hidden by trees.* 那所房子被樹叢遮住了。◇ *No amount of make-up could hide her age.* 再多的化妝品也遮掩不住她的年齡。**4** 0→ [T] **~ sth** to keep sth secret, especially your feelings 掩蓋，隱瞞（尤指感情）SYN **conceal**：*She struggled to hide her disappointment.* 她竭力掩飾她的失望。◇ *I have never tried to hide the truth about my past.* 我從未設法隱瞞我的過去。◇ *They claim that they* ***have nothing to hide*** (= there was nothing wrong or illegal about what they did). 他們聲稱他們沒什麼可隱瞞的。◇ *She felt sure the letter had some* ***hidden meaning***. 她確信那封信中有言外之意。

IDM **hide your light under a ˈbushel** (*BrE*) to not let people know that you are good at sth 不顯露才能；不露鋒芒 ➲ more at HEAD *n.*, MULTITUDE

■ *noun* **1** [C] (*BrE*) a place from which people can watch wild animals or birds, without being seen by them（觀看野生動物的）隱蔽處，藏身處 **2** [C, U] an animal's skin, especially when it is bought or sold or used for leather（尤指買賣或用作皮革的）皮，毛皮：*boots made from buffalo hide* 用水牛皮做的靴子 **3** [sing.] (*informal, especially NAmE*) used to refer to sb's life or safety when they are in a difficult situation（困境中的）生命，人身安全：*All he's worried about is his own hide* (= himself). 他所擔心的只是他自己的生命安全。

IDM **have/tan sb's ˈhide** (*old-fashioned, informal* or *humorous*) to punish sb severely 嚴懲某人 **not see hide nor ˈhair of sb/sth** (*informal*) not to see sb/sth for some time（一段時間）不見某人（或某物）的蹤影：*I haven't seen hide nor hair of her for a month.* 我有一個月沒見過她了。IDM see SAVE *v.*

hide-and-seek /ˌhaɪd n ˈsiːk/ *noun* [U] a children's game in which one player covers his or her eyes while the other players hide, and then tries to find them 捉迷藏遊戲

hide·away /ˈhaɪdəweɪ/ *noun* a place where you can go to hide or to be alone 藏身處；退隱處

hide·bound /ˈhaɪdbaʊnd/ *adj.* (*disapproving*) having old-fashioned ideas, rather than accepting new ways of thinking 守舊的；迂腐的 SYN **narrow-minded**

hid·eous /ˈhɪdiəs/ *adj.* very ugly or unpleasant 十分醜陋的；令人厭惡的 SYN **revolting**：*a hideous face/building/dress* 醜陋的面孔／建築物／衣服 ◇ *Their new colour scheme is hideous!* 他們新的顏色搭配難看極了！◇ *a hideous crime* 駭人聽聞的罪行 ◇ *The whole experience had been like some hideous nightmare.* 整個經歷就像一場可怕的噩夢。▶ **hid·eous·ly** *adv.*：*His face was hideously deformed.* 他的臉嚴重變形。

hide·out /ˈhaɪdaʊt/ *noun* a place where sb goes when they do not want anyone to find them 藏身處；隱蔽所

hidey-hole (also **hidy-hole**) /ˈhaɪdi həʊl; *NAmE* -hoʊl/ *noun* (*informal*) a place where sb hides, especially in order to avoid being with other people 躲藏處；隱藏處；獨居處

hid·ing /ˈhaɪdɪŋ/ *noun* **1** [U] the state of being hidden 隱藏；躲藏：*After the trial, she had to* ***go into hiding*** *for several weeks.* 審訊後她不得不躲藏了幾個星期。◇ *He only* ***came out of hiding*** *ten years after the war was over.* 戰爭結束十年之後他才露面。◇ *We spent months* ***in hiding***. 我們躲藏了好幾個月。**2** [C, usually sing.] (*informal, especially BrE*) a physical punishment, usually involving being hit hard many times 體罰；痛打 SYN **beating**：

to give sb/get a (*good*) *hiding* 給某人／遭到一頓（狠）揍 ◊ (*figurative*) *The team got a hiding in their last game.* 那支球隊在最後一場比賽中被打得一敗塗地。

IDM **on a ˌhiding to ˈnothing** (*BrE, informal*) having no chance of success, or not getting much advantage even if you do succeed 毫無成功機會；（即使成功了）也得不到多大好處

ˈhiding place *noun* a place where sb/sth can be hidden 隱藏處；藏身地

hie /haɪ/ *verb* (**hies**, **hying**, **hied**) [I] **+ adv./prep.** (*old use*) to go quickly 快走；急行

hier·arch·ic·al **AW** /ˌhaɪəˈrɑːkɪkl; *NAmE* -ˈrɑːrk-/ *adj.* arranged in a hierarchy 按等級劃分的；等級制度的：*a* ***hierarchical society/structure/organization*** 分等級的社會／結構／組織 ▸ **hier·arch·ic·al·ly** /-kli/ *adv.*

hier·archy **AW** /ˈhaɪərɑːki; *NAmE* -rɑːrki/ *noun* (*pl.* **-ies**) **1** [C, U] a system, especially in a society or an organization, in which people are organized into different levels of importance from highest to lowest 等級制度（尤指社會或組織）：*the* ***social/political hierarchy*** 社會／政治等級制度 ◊ *She's quite high up in the management hierarchy.* 她位居管理層要職。 **2** [C+sing./pl. v.] the group of people in control of a large organization or institution 統治集團 **3** [C] (*formal*) a system that ideas or beliefs can be arranged into 層次體系：*a hierarchy of needs* 不同層次的需要

hiero·glyph /ˈhaɪərəglɪf/ *noun* a picture or symbol of an object, representing a word, syllable or sound, especially as used in ancient Egyptian and other writing systems 象形文字，象形符號（尤指古埃及等所用的文字） ▸ **hiero·glyph·ic** /ˌhaɪərəˈglɪfɪk/ *adj.*

hieroglyphics 象形文字；象形符號

hiero·glyph·ics /ˌhaɪərəˈglɪfɪks/ *noun* [pl.] writing that uses hieroglyphs 用象形文字書寫的東西

hi-fi /ˈhaɪ faɪ/ *noun* [C, U] equipment for playing recorded music that produces high-quality STEREO sound 高保真音響設備 ▸ **hi-fi** *adj.* [usually before noun]：*a hi-fi system* 高保真系統 ➲ VISUAL VOCAB page V21

higgledy-piggledy /ˌhɪgldi ˈpɪgldi/ *adv.* (*informal*) in an untidy way that lacks any order 雜亂無章；混亂：*Files were strewn higgledy-piggledy over the floor.* 文件亂七八糟地扔了一地。 ▸ **higgledy-piggledy** *adj.*：*a higgledy-piggledy collection of houses* 一片錯落雜亂的房屋

high 🔑 /haɪ/ *adj.*, *noun*, *adv.*

WORD FAMILY
high *adj., noun, adv.*
highly *adv.*
height *noun*
heighten *verb*

■ *adj.* (**high·er**, **high·est**)

▸ FROM BOTTOM TO TOP 從底到頂 **1** 🔑 measuring a long distance from the bottom to the top 高的：*What's the highest mountain in the US?* 美國哪座山最高？◊ *The house has a high wall all the way round it.* 這棟房子的四周圍着高牆。◊ *shoes with high heels* 高跟鞋 ◊ *He has a round face with a high forehead.* 他圓臉、高額頭。 **OPP** low **2** 🔑 used to talk about the distance that sth measures from the bottom to the top 有某高度的：*How high is Everest?* 珠穆朗瑪峰有多高？◊ *It's only a low wall—about a metre high.* 那只不過是一堵矮牆，約一米高。◊ *The grass was waist-high.* 那片草齊腰高。

▸ FAR ABOVE GROUND 離地面遠 **3** 🔑 at a level which is a long way above the ground or above the level of the sea（離地面）很高的；海拔很高的：*a high branch/shelf/window* 高處的樹枝／擱板／窗 ◊ *The rooms had high ceilings.* 那些房間的天花板很高。◊ *They were flying at high altitude.* 他們正在高空飛行。◊ *the grasslands of the high prairies* 高地草原 **OPP** low

▸ GREATER THAN NORMAL 超出常規 **4** 🔑 greater or better than normal in quantity or quality, size or degree（數量、質量、體積或程度）高的，超乎尋常的：*a high temperature/speed/price* 高溫；高速；高價 ◊ *a high rate of inflation* 高通貨膨脹率 ◊ *Demand is high at this time of year.* 一年的這個時期需求很大。◊ *a* ***high level*** *of pollution* 嚴重的污染 ◊ *a* ***high standard*** *of craftsmanship* 高水平的手工藝 ◊ ***high-quality*** *goods* 優質商品 ◊ *A* ***high degree*** *of accuracy is needed.* 需要高度的準確性。◊ *The tree blew over in the* ***high winds***. 樹被大風颳倒了。◊ *We had* ***high hopes*** *for the business* (= we believed it would be successful). 我們對這項生意寄予了很大希望。◊ *The cost in terms of human life was high.* 付出了很大的生命代價。 ➲ compare LOW *adj.* (4)

▸ CONTAINING A LOT 含量多 **5** 🔑 **~ (in sth)** containing a lot of a particular substance 含某物多 **OPP** low：*foods which are high in fat* 高脂肪食物 ◊ *a high potassium content* 高鉀含量 ◊ *a* ***high-fat*** *diet* 高脂肪的飲食

▸ RANK/STATUS 等級；地位 **6** (usually before noun 通常用於名詞前) near the top in rank or status 上層的；地位高的：*She has held* ***high office*** *under three prime ministers.* 她曾在三任首相手下任過要職。◊ *He has friends* ***in high places*** (= among people of power and influence). 他有位高權重的朋友。 **OPP** low

▸ VALUABLE 有價值 **7** of great value 價值高的：*to play for high stakes* 豪賭 ◊ *My highest card is ten.* 我最大的牌是十。

▸ IDEALS/PRINCIPLES 理想；準則 **8** (usually before noun 通常用於名詞前) morally good 高尚的；崇高的：*a man of* ***high ideals/principles*** 有崇高理想／道德準則的人

▸ APPROVING 贊同 **9** (usually before noun 通常用於名詞前) showing a lot of approval or respect for sb 十分贊同的；非常尊敬的：*She is held in very high regard by her colleagues.* 她很受同事們的敬重。◊ *You seem to have a* ***high opinion*** *of yourself!* 你似乎自我評價很高嘛！ **OPP** low

▸ SOUND 聲音 **10** at the upper end of the range of sounds that humans can hear; not deep or low 高音的：*She has a high voice.* 她嗓音很尖。◊ *That note is definitely too high for me.* 那個音對我來說絕對太高了。 **OPP** low

▸ OF PERIOD OF TIME 時段 **11** [only before noun] used to describe the middle or the most attractive part of a period of time 中間的；全盛的：*high noon* 正午 ◊ *high summer* 盛夏

▸ FOOD 食物 **12** (of meat, cheese, etc. 肉、奶酪等) beginning to go bad and having a strong smell 開始變質的；開始發餿的

▸ ON ALCOHOL/DRUGS 喝酒；吸毒 **13** [not before noun] **~ (on sth)** (*informal*) behaving in an excited way because of the effects of alcohol or drugs 有醉意；表現興奮

▸ PHONETICS 語音學 **14** (*phonetics* 語音) = CLOSE² *adj.* (16)

IDM **be/get on your high ˈhorse** (*informal*) to behave in a way that shows you think you are better than other people 趾高氣揚；自命不凡；自以為了不起 **have a ˈhigh old time** (*old-fashioned, informal*) to enjoy yourself very much 玩得很開心 **high and ˈdry** **1** (of a boat, etc. 小船等) in a position out of the water 高出水面；擱淺：*Their yacht was left high and dry on a sandbank.* 他們的帆船擱淺在沙丘上了。 **2** in a difficult situation, without help or money 處境艱難；無依無靠；身無分文 **high and ˈmighty** (*informal*) behaving as though you think you are more important than other people 趾高氣揚；神氣活現；自高自大 **high as a ˈkite** (*informal*) behaving in a very excited way, especially because of being strongly affected by alcohol or drugs（尤指因酗酒或吸毒）異常興奮，神情恍惚 **in high ˈdudgeon** (*old-fashioned, formal*) in an angry or offended mood, and showing other people that you are angry 憤然；怒沖沖：*He stomped out of the room in high dudgeon.* 他憤怒地噔噔走出了屋子。 **smell, stink, etc. to high ˈheaven** (*informal*)

H

1 to have a strong unpleasant smell 發出難聞氣味；難聞透頂 **2** to seem to be very dishonest or morally unacceptable 很不誠實；不道德 ➲ more at HELL, MORAL *adj.*, ORDER *n.*, PROFILE *n.*, TIME *n.*

■ ***noun***

▸ **LEVEL/NUMBER 水平；數量 1** the highest level or number 最高水平；最大數量：*Profits reached an **all-time high** last year.* 去年的利潤空前地高。

▸ **WEATHER 天氣 2** an area of high air pressure; an ANTICYCLONE 高氣壓區；反氣旋：*A high over southern Europe is bringing fine, sunny weather to all parts.* 歐洲南部上空的高氣壓正給各地帶來陽光燦爛的好天氣。**3** the highest temperature reached during a particular day, week, etc.（某天、某星期等的）最高氣温：*Highs today will be in the region of 25°C.* 今天的最高氣温將為25攝氏度左右。

▸ **FROM DRUGS 毒品引起 4** (*informal*) the feeling of extreme pleasure and excitement that sb gets after taking some types of drugs（毒品引致的）快感：*The high lasted all night.* 那種快感持續了一整夜。

▸ **FROM SUCCESS/ENJOYMENT 來自成功／樂趣 5** (*informal*) the feeling of extreme pleasure and excitement that sb gets from doing sth enjoyable or being successful at sth 極大歡樂；極度高興；樂不可支：*He was **on a real high** after winning the competition.* 他贏了那場比賽後高興極了。◇ *the **highs and lows** of her acting career* 她的演員生涯的大起大落

▸ **SCHOOL 學校 6** used in the name of a high school（用於中學校名）：*He graduated from Little Rock High in 1982.* 他1982年畢業於小石城中學。

IDM **on 'high 1** (*formal*) in a high place 在高處：*We gazed down into the valley from on high.* 我們從高處向下眺望山谷。**2** (*humorous*) the people in senior positions in an organization 高層人員：*An order came down from on high that lunchbreaks were to be half an hour and no longer.* 上頭指示說午餐休息時間不得超過半小時。**3** in heaven 在天上：*The disaster was seen as a judgement from on high.* 這場災難被視作上天的懲罰。

■ ***adv.*** (**high·er**, **high·est**)

▸ **FAR FROM GROUND/BOTTOM 遠離地面／底部 1** 🔑 at or to a position or level that is a long way up from the ground or from the bottom 在高處；向高處；高：*An eagle circled high overhead.* 一隻鷹在頭頂上空盤旋。◇ *I can't jump any higher.* 我沒法跳得更高了。◇ *She never got very high in the company.* 她在公司裏從未坐到很高的位置。◇ *His desk was **piled high** with papers.* 他的桌子上擺着高高的一堆文件。◇ *She's **aiming high*** (= hoping to be very successful) *in her exams.* 她期望考出優異成績。

▸ **VALUE/AMOUNT 價值；數量 2** 🔑 at or to a large cost, value or amount（成本、價值）高；（數量）大：*Prices are expected to rise even higher this year.* 預計今年的價格將漲得更高。

▸ **SOUND 聲音 3** 🔑 at a high PITCH 音調高：*I can't sing that high.* 我唱不了那麼高的調子。**OPP** **low**

IDM **,high and 'low** everywhere 到處；各地：*I've searched high and low for my purse.* 我到處找我的錢包。**run 'high** (especially of feelings 尤指情緒) to be strong and angry or excited 激憤；激昂：*Feelings ran high as the election approached.* 選舉臨近，大家情緒都很激動。➲ more at FLY *v.*, HEAD *n.*, RIDE *v.*

,high and 'tight *noun* (*US*) a military HAIRSTYLE in which the sides of the head are shaved and the top is cut very short（一種只留頭頂寸髮的）軍人髮型

high·ball /'haɪbɔːl/ *noun, verb* (*NAmE*)

■ ***noun*** a strong alcoholic drink, such as WHISKY or GIN, mixed with FIZZY water (= with bubbles) or GINGER ALE, etc. and served with ice 開波酒，冰威士忌蘇打（用烈酒摻入汽水等加冰）

■ ***verb*** (*informal*) **1** [I] + **adv./prep.** to go somewhere very quickly 高速行進：*They highballed out of town.* 他們急匆匆地出了城。**2** [T] **~ sth** to deliberately make an estimate of the cost, value, etc. of sth that is too high 故意高估價值（或成本）：*He thought she was highballing her salary requirements.* 他認為她的薪金要求過高。**OPP** **lowball**

Which Word? 詞語辨析

high / tall

■ **High** is used to talk about the measurement from the bottom to the top of something. * high 用以指從底部到頂部的高度：*The fence is over five metres high.* 這圍欄有五米多高。◇ *He has climbed some of the world's highest mountains.* 他攀登過幾座世界最高峰。You also use **high** to describe the distance of something from the ground. 亦可用 high 表示離地面的距離：*How high was the plane when the engine failed?* 發動機出故障時飛機離地面多高？

■ **Tall** is used instead of **high** to talk about people. 指人用 tall，不用 high：*My brother's much taller than me.* 我哥哥比我高多了。**Tall** is also used for things that are high and narrow such as trees. * tall 亦可指高而窄的事物，如樹木：*She ordered cold beer in a tall glass.* 她叫了一杯高玻璃杯裝的冰鎮啤酒。◇ *tall factory chimneys* 工廠的高煙囱 Buildings can be **high** or **tall**. 建築物用 high 或 tall 均可。

'high beams *noun* [pl.] (*NAmE*) the lights on a car when they are pointing a long way ahead, not down at the road（汽車的）遠光燈

,high-'born *adj.* (*old-fashioned* or *formal*) having parents who are members of the highest social class 出身高貴的 **SYN** **aristocratic** **OPP** **low-born**

high·boy /'haɪbɔɪ/ (*NAmE*) (*BrE* **tall·boy**) *noun* a tall piece of furniture with drawers, used for storing clothes in（帶抽屜的）高腳衣櫃

high·brow /'haɪbraʊ/ *adj.* (sometimes *disapproving*) concerned with or interested in serious artistic or cultural ideas 關於正統藝術（或文化）思想的；對正統的藝術（或文化）感興趣的 **SYN** **intellectual**：*highbrow newspapers* 格調高雅的報紙 ◇ *highbrow readers* 趣味高雅的讀者 **OPP** **lowbrow** ➲ compare MIDDLEBROW

'high chair *noun* a special chair with long legs and a little seat and table, for a small child to sit in when eating 高腳椅（幼兒進食時坐的，帶小飯桌）➲ VISUAL VOCAB page V22

,High 'Church *adj.* connected with the part of the Anglican Church that is most similar to the Roman Catholic Church in its beliefs and practices 高派教會的（聖公會的一派，在信仰和禮儀方面與羅馬天主教最相似）

,high-'class *adj.* **1** excellent; of good quality 極好的；高級的：*a high-class restaurant* 一家高級餐廳 ◇ *to stay in high-class accommodation* 住在上好的住所 **2** connected with a high social class 上流社會的：*to come from a high-class background* 出身於上層社會 **OPP** **low-class**

,high com'mand *noun* [usually sing.] the senior leaders of the armed forces of a country（全國武裝力量的）統帥部，最高指揮部

,high com'mission *noun* **1** the office and the staff of an EMBASSY that represents the interests of one Commonwealth country in another（英聯邦國家相互派駐的）高級專員公署 **2** a group of people who are working for a government or an international organization on an important project（政府或國際組織的）重大項目工作組；特別事務公署：*the United Nations High Commission for Refugees* 聯合國難民事務高級專員公署

,High Com'missioner *noun* **1** a person who is sent by one Commonwealth country to live in another, to protect the interests of their own country（英聯邦國家之間互派的）高級專員 **2** a person who is head of an important international project 重大國際項目負責人；高級專員：*the United Nations High Commissioner for Refugees* 聯合國難民事務高級專員

,High 'Court (also **,High Court of 'Justice**) *noun* **1** a court in England and Wales that deals with the most serious CIVIL cases (= not criminal cases) 高等法院（在英格蘭和威爾士審理最嚴重的民事案件）**2** = SUPREME COURT

'high day *noun* (*old-fashioned, BrE*) the day of a religious festival 宗教節日

IDM **ˌhigh days and ˈholidays** festivals and special occasions 節日和假日；節慶日

ˌhigh-defiˈnition *adj.* (*abbr.* **HD**) [only before noun] (*technical* 術語) using or produced by a system that gives very clear detailed images 高清晰度的；高分辨率的：*high-definition television* 高清晰度電視機 ◇ *high-definition displays* 高清晰度顯像 ➲ see also HDTV

ˌhigh-ˈend *adj.* (*NAmE*) expensive and of high quality 高檔的；高端的；價高質優的

High·er /ˈhaɪə(r)/ *noun* (in Scotland) an exam in a particular subject at a higher level than STANDARD GRADE. Highers are usually taken around the age of 17 to 18. （蘇格蘭）學生高級證書考試（應試年齡一般在 17 至 18 歲）

high·er /ˈhaɪə(r)/ *adj.* [only before noun] at a more advanced level; greater in rank or importance than others 高等級的；級別較高的；較重要的：*The case was referred to a higher court.* 案件轉到了上級法院。◇ *higher mathematics* 高等數學 ◇ *My mind was on higher things.* 我那時想着更重要的事。

ˌhigher ˈanimals, ˌhigher ˈplants *noun* [pl.] (*technical* 術語) animals and plants that have reached an advanced stage of development 高等動物，高等植物（發展到高等進化程度的動植物）

ˌhigher eduˈcation *noun* [U] (*abbr.* **HE**) education and training at college and university, especially to degree level （尤指達到學位水平的）高等教育 ➲ compare FURTHER EDUCATION

ˌhigher-ˈup *noun* (*informal*) a person who has a higher rank or who is more senior than you 上級；上司；長官

ˌhighest common ˈfactor *noun* (*abbr.* **HCF**) (*mathematics* 數) the highest number that can be divided exactly into two or more numbers 最大公約數

ˌhigh exˈplosive *noun* [C, U] a very powerful substance that is used in bombs and can damage a very large area 高爆炸藥；烈性炸藥

high·fa·lu·tin /ˌhaɪfəˈluːtɪn/ *adj.* (*informal*) trying to be serious or important, but in a way that often appears silly and unnecessary 裝模作樣的；浮誇的；做作的 **SYN** **pretentious**

ˌhigh fiˈdelity *noun* [U] (*old-fashioned*) = HI-FI

ˌhigh ˈfive *noun* (*especially NAmE*) an action to celebrate victory or to express happiness in which two people raise one arm each and hit their open hands together 相互高舉胳膊擊掌（以示慶祝或高興）：*Way to go! High five!* 好樣的！祝賀！

ˌhigh-ˈflown *adj.* (usually *disapproving*) (of language and ideas 語言和思想) very grand and complicated 浮誇的；故弄玄虛的；說大話的 **SYN** **bombastic**：*His high-flown style just sounds absurd today.* 他的浮誇風格如今聽起來真是荒謬。

ˌhigh-ˈflyer (also **ˌhigh-ˈflier**) *noun* a person who has the desire and the ability to be very successful in their job or their studies 有抱負有能力的人；有能耐的人：*academic high-flyers* 有學術抱負的人

ˌhigh-ˈflying *adj.* [only before noun] **1** very successful 十分成功的：*a high-flying career woman* 事業成功的職業女性 **2** that flies very high in the air 在高空飛行的

ˌhigh-ˈgrade *adj.* [usually before noun] of very good quality 優質的；高級的：*high-grade petrol* 高級汽油

ˈhigh ground *noun* (usually **the high ground**) [sing.] the advantage in a discussion or an argument, etc. （討論或爭論中的）優勢，有利條件：*The government is claiming the high ground in the education debate.* 政府在教育辯論中處於有利地位。**IDM** see MORAL *adj.*

ˌhigh-ˈhanded *adj.* (of people or their behaviour 人或行為) using authority in an unreasonable way, without considering the opinions of other people 專橫的；高壓的 **SYN** **overbearing**

ˈhigh-hat *noun* = HI-HAT ➲ VISUAL VOCAB page V35

ˌhigh ˈheels *noun* [pl.] shoes that have very high heels, usually worn by women （女）高跟鞋 ► **ˌhigh-ˈheeled** *adj.* [only before noun]：*high-heeled shoes/boots* 高跟鞋；高跟靴

ˌhigh ˈjinks (*NAmE* also **hi·jinks**) *noun* [pl.] (*old-fashioned, informal*) lively and excited behaviour 狂歡作樂；喧鬧 **SYN** **fun**

the ˈhigh jump *noun* [sing.] a sporting event in which people try to jump over a high bar that is gradually raised higher and higher 跳高：*She won a silver medal in the high jump.* 她跳高得了銀牌。➲ VISUAL VOCAB page V46

IDM **be for the ˈhigh jump** (*BrE, informal*) to be going to be severely punished 將遭到嚴厲懲罰

high·land /ˈhaɪlənd/ *adj., noun*

■ ***adj.*** [only before noun] **1** connected with an area of land that has hills or mountains 高地的；高原的；山區的：*highland regions* 高原地區 **2** **Highland** connected with the Highlands of Scotland 蘇格蘭高地的 ➲ compare LOWLAND

■ ***noun*** **1** [C, usually pl.] an area of land with hills or mountains 高地；高原 **2** **the Highlands** [pl.] the high mountain region of Scotland 蘇格蘭高地 ➲ compare LOWLAND

ˌHighland ˈcattle *noun* [pl.] cows of a breed with long rough hair and large horns. An individual animal is a **Highland cow**. （統稱）高原牛（毛長而粗糙，角長）

ˌHighland ˈdress *noun* [U] traditional clothing worn by men in the Scottish Highlands, which includes a KILT and a SPORRAN (= a small decorated bag worn around the waist that hangs down at the front) 蘇格蘭高地男裝（包括格子呢短裙和毛皮袋）

high·land·er /ˈhaɪləndə(r)/ *noun* **1** a person who comes from an area where there are a lot of mountains 高原地區的人；山地人 **2** **High·land·er** a person who comes from the Scottish Highlands 蘇格蘭高地人 ➲ compare LOWLANDER

ˌHighland ˈfling *noun* a fast Scottish dance that is danced by one person 高地舞（輕快蘇格蘭單人舞）

ˌHighland ˈGames *noun* [pl.] a Scottish event with traditional sports, dancing and music 蘇格蘭高地運動會（包括傳統體育運動、跳舞和音樂）

ˌhigh-ˈlevel *adj.* [usually before noun] **1** involving senior people 級別高的；高層的：***high-level talks/negotiations*** 高層會談／談判 ◇ *high-level staff* 高級職員 **2** in a high position or place 位置高的；在高處的：*a high-level walk in the hills* 在山地徒步旅行 **3** advanced 高級的；高等的：*a high-level course* 高級課程 **4** (*computing* 計) (of a computer language 計算機語言) similar to an existing language such as English, making it fairly simple to use 高級的 **OPP** **low-level**

ˈhigh life *noun* (also **the high life**) [sing., U] (also **ˌhigh ˈliving** [U]) (sometimes *disapproving*) a way of life that involves going to parties and spending a lot of money on food, clothes, etc. 豪華的生活；燈紅酒綠的生活

high·life /ˈhaɪlaɪf/ *noun* [U] a style of dance and music from W Africa influenced by rock and JAZZ and popular especially in the 1950s and 1960s 強節奏爵士舞，強節奏爵士樂（尤指 20 世紀 50 年代和 60 年代受搖滾樂、爵士樂和流行音樂影響的源於西非的舞蹈和音樂風格）

high·light 🔑 **AW** /ˈhaɪlaɪt/ *verb, noun*

■ ***verb*** **1** 🔑 **~ sth** to emphasize sth, especially so that people give it more attention 突出；強調：*The report highlights the major problems facing society today.* 報告特別強調了當今社會所面臨的主要問題。➲ LANGUAGE BANK at EMPHASIS **2** **~ sth** to mark part of a text with a special coloured pen, or to mark an area on a computer screen, to emphasize it or make it easier to see 將（文本的某部份）用彩筆做標記；將（計算機屏幕的某區域）增強亮度；使醒目：*I've highlighted the important passages in yellow.* 我用黃色標出了重要段落。**3** **~ sth** to make some parts of your hair a lighter colour than the rest by using a chemical substance on them 挑染（將部份頭髮染成淺色）

■ ***noun*** **1** 🔑 the best, most interesting or most exciting part of sth 最好（或最精彩、最激動人心）的部份：*One of the highlights of the trip was seeing the Taj Mahal.* 這次旅行中的最精彩的一件事是參觀泰姬陵。◇ *The*

H

highlights of the match will be shown later this evening. 比賽最精彩的片段將於今晚播出。**2 highlights** [pl.] areas of hair that are lighter than the rest, usually because a chemical substance has been put on them 挑染的頭髮 ➲ compare LOWLIGHTS **3 highlights** [pl.] (*technical* 術語) the light or bright part of a picture or photograph（圖畫或照片的）強光部份

high·light·er /ˈhaɪlaɪtə(r)/ *noun* **1** (also **ˈhighlighter pen**) a special pen used for marking words in a text in bright colours（顏色鮮亮的）標記筆；熒光筆 ➲ VISUAL VOCAB page V69 **2** a coloured substance that you put above your eyes or on your cheeks to make yourself more attractive（勾畫臉、眼的）彩妝

high·ly /ˈhaɪli/ *adv.*
1 very 很；非常：*highly successful/skilled/intelligent* 十分成功／熟練／聰明 ◊ *highly competitive/critical/sensitive* 非常有競爭力／關鍵／敏感 ◊ *It is **highly unlikely** that she'll be late.* 她不大可能會遲到。**2** at or to a high standard, level or amount 高標準地；高級地；大量地：***highly trained/educated*** 受過高級培訓／高等教育 ◊ *a **highly paid** job* 高薪工作 **3** with admiration or praise 欽佩地；讚賞地：*His teachers **think very highly of him*** (= have a very good opinion of him). 老師們很欣賞他。◊ *She **speaks highly of you.*** 她對你大加稱讚。◊ *Her novels are very highly regarded.* 她的小說受到很高的評價。

ˌhighly ˈstrung (*BrE*) (*NAmE* **ˌhigh-ˈstrung**) *adj.* (of a person or an animal 人或動物) nervous and easily upset 緊張不安的：*a sensitive and highly-strung child* 敏感而脆弱的孩子 ◊ *Their new horse is very highly strung.* 他們的新馬很容易受驚。➲ compare NERVOUS (2)

ˌhigh-ˈmainten·ance *adj.* needing a lot of attention or effort 耗費精力的；費神費力的：*a high-maintenance girlfriend* 需要操心呵護的女朋友 OPP **low-maintenance**

ˌhigh-ˈminded *adj.* (of people or ideas 人或思想) having strong moral principles 高尚的；高潔的 ▸ **ˌhigh-ˈminded·ness** *noun* [U]

High·ness /ˈhaɪnəs/ *noun* **His/Her/Your Highness** a title of respect used when talking to or about a member of the royal family（對王室成員的尊稱）殿下，閣下 ➲ see also ROYAL HIGHNESS

ˌhigh ˈnoon *noun* **1** exactly twelve o'clock in the middle of the day 中午十二點整；正午 **2** (*formal*) the most important stage of sth, when sth that will decide the future happens 最重要的階段；決定性時刻

ˌhigh-ˈoctane *adj.* [only before noun] **1** (of fuel used in engines 發動機燃料) of very good quality and very efficient 優質的；高辛烷值的 **2** (*informal*) full of energy; powerful 充滿活力的；強有力的：*a high-octane athlete* 體力充沛的運動員

ˌhigh-perˈform·ance *adj.* [only before noun] that can go very fast or do complicated things 高速的；高性能的；功能複雜的：***a high-performance car/computer, etc.*** 高性能的汽車、計算機等

ˌhigh-ˈpitched *adj.* (of sounds 聲音) very high 很高的；尖利的：*a high-pitched voice/whistle* 尖嗓子；尖銳的口哨聲 OPP **low-pitched**

ˈhigh point (*BrE* also **ˈhigh spot**) *noun* the most interesting, enjoyable or best part of sth 最有意思（或最令人愉快、最好）的部份：*It was the high point of the evening.* 那是晚會最精彩的部份。OPP **low point**

ˌhigh-ˈpowered *adj.* **1** (of people 人) having a lot of power and influence; full of energy 有權勢的；精力旺盛的：*high-powered executives* 勁頭十足的行政人員 **2** (of activities 活動) important; with a lot of responsibility 重要的；責任重大的：*a high-powered job* 位高權重的工作 **3** (also **ˌhigh-ˈpower**) (of machines 機器) very powerful 大功率的：***a high-powered car/computer, etc.*** 大馬力的汽車、高性能的計算機等

ˌhigh ˈpressure *noun* [U] **1** the condition of air, gas, or liquid that is kept in a small space by force 高壓：*Water is forced through the pipes at **high pressure**.* 水在高壓下流過水管。**2** a condition of the air which affects the weather, when the PRESSURE is higher than average 高氣壓 ➲ compare LOW PRESSURE

ˌhigh-ˈpressure *adj.* [only before noun] **1** that involves aggressive ways of persuading sb to do sth or to buy sth 強力勸說的：*high-pressure sales techniques* 強行推銷術 **2** that involves a lot of worry and anxiety 令人焦慮的；非常緊張的；壓力大的 SYN **stressful**：*a high-pressure job* 壓力很大的工作 **3** using or containing a great force of a gas or a liquid（氣體或液體產生的）高壓：*a high-pressure water jet* 高壓水噴

ˌhigh-ˈpriced *adj.* [usually before noun] expensive 昂貴的；高價的：*high-priced housing/cars* 昂貴的住房／汽車 OPP **low-priced**

ˌhigh ˈpriest *noun* **1** the most important priest in the Jewish religion in the past（舊時猶太教的）祭司長 **2** (*feminine* **ˌhigh ˈpriestess**) an important priest in some other non-Christian religions（某些非基督教的）大祭司：(*figurative*) *Janis Joplin was known as the High Priestess of Rock.* 賈尼斯・喬普林就是眾所周知的搖滾樂大師。

ˌhigh-ˈprofile *adj.* [usually before noun] receiving or involving a lot of attention and discussion on television, in newspapers, etc. 經常出鏡（或見報）的；高姿態的：*a high-profile campaign* 廣受關注的運動 ➲ see also PROFILE

ˌhigh-ˈranking *adj.* senior; important 職位高的；顯要的：***a high-ranking officer/official*** 高級軍官／官員 ◊ *a high-ranking post* 顯要崗位 OPP **low-ranking**

ˌhigh-resoˈlution (also **hi-res**, **high-res**) *adj.* (of a photograph or an image on a computer or television screen 照片、計算機或電視屏幕的圖像) showing a lot of clear sharp detail 高清晰度的；高分辨率的：*a high-resolution scan* 高清晰度掃描 OPP **low-resolution**

ˈhigh-rise *adj.* [only before noun] (of a building 建築物) very tall and having a lot of floors 高層的：*high-rise housing* 高層住宅 ▸ **ˈhigh-rise** *noun*: *to live in a high-rise* 住在高層樓房裏 ➲ compare LOW-RISE *adj.* (1)

ˌhigh-ˈrisk *adj.* [usually before noun] involving a lot of danger and the risk of injury, death, damage, etc. 有高風險的；高危的：*a high-risk sport* 高風險的運動 ◊ *high-risk patients* (= who are very likely to get a particular illness) 高危病人 ➲ compare LOW-RISK

ˈhigh road *noun* [usually sing.] **1** (*old-fashioned*, *BrE*) a main or important road 公路幹線；交通要道 **2 ~ (to sth)** the most direct way 最直接的方式：*This is the high road to democracy.* 這是通向民主的直接途徑。
IDM **take the ˈhigh road (in sth)** (*NAmE*) to take the most positive course of action 採取最積極的行動方針：*He took the high road in his campaign.* 他在競選活動中採取了最積極的方針。

ˌhigh ˈroller *noun* (*NAmE*, *informal*) a person who spends a lot of money, especially on gambling 揮霍的人；（尤指）豪賭者

ˈhigh school *noun* [C, U] **1** (in the US and some other countries) a school for young people between the ages of 14 and 18（美國和其他一些國家 14 到 18 歲青年的）中學，高中 **2** often used in Britain in the names of schools for young people between the ages of 11 and 18 中學，完全中學（英國常用於為 11 到 18 歲青年開辦的學校名稱中）：*Worthing High School* 沃辛高中 ➲ compare SECONDARY SCHOOL ➲ COLLOCATIONS at EDUCATION

the ˌhigh ˈseas *noun* [pl.] (*formal* or *literary*) the areas of sea that are not under the legal control of any one country 公海

ˌhigh ˈseason *noun* [U, sing.] (*especially BrE*) the time of year when a hotel or tourist area receives most visitors（旅館或旅遊地區的）旺季 ➲ compare LOW SEASON

ˌhigh-seˈcurity *adj.* [only before noun] **1** (of buildings and places 建築或地方) very carefully locked and guarded 戒備森嚴的；警戒嚴密的：*a high-security prison* 警備森嚴的監獄 **2** (of prisoners 囚犯) kept in a prison that is very carefully locked and guarded 關押在警備森嚴的監獄裏的

ˈhigh-sounding *adj.* (*especially BrE*, often *disapproving*) (of language or ideas 語言或思想) complicated and intended to sound important 誇張的；高調的 **SYN** **pretentious**

ˌhigh-ˈspeed *adj.* [only before noun] that travels, works or happens very fast 高速的；高效率的；迅速的：*a high-speed train* 高速列車 ◇ *a high-speed car chase* 高速汽車追逐

ˌhigh-ˈspirit·ed *adj.* **1** (of people 人) very lively and active 興致勃勃的；興高采烈的：*a high-spirited child* 興高采烈的孩子 ◇ *high-spirited behaviour* 朝氣蓬勃 **2** (of animals, especially horses 動物，尤指馬) lively and difficult to control 烈性的；歡蹦亂跳的 **OPP** **placid** ➲ see also SPIRIT

ˈhigh spot *noun* (*BrE*) = HIGH POINT

ˈhigh street (*BrE*) (*NAmE* **ˈmain street**) *noun* (especially in names 尤用於名稱) the main street of a town, where most shops/stores, banks, etc. are 大街（城鎮的主要街道）：*Peckham High Street* 佩卡姆大街 ◇ *106 High Street, Peckham* 佩卡姆，商業大街 106 號 ◇ ***high-street banks/shops*** 商業區大街上的銀行 / 商店 ➲ **VISUAL VOCAB** page V3

ˌhigh-ˈstrung (*NAmE*) (*BrE* **ˌhighly ˈstrung**) *adj.* (of a person or an animal 人或動物) nervous and easily upset 緊張不安的 ➲ **SYNONYMS** at NERVOUS

ˌhigh ˈtable *noun* [C, U] (*BrE*) a table on a raised platform, where the most important people at a formal dinner sit to eat 高台餐桌（正式宴會上為顯要人士設在高平台上的餐桌）

high·tail /ˈhaɪteɪl/ *verb*
IDM **ˈhightail it** (*informal, especially NAmE*) to leave somewhere very quickly 迅速離開

ˌhigh ˈtea *noun* (*BrE*) a meal consisting of cooked food, bread and butter and cakes, usually with tea to drink, eaten in the late afternoon or early evening instead of dinner 傍晚茶（傍晚前後吃的膳食，通常有茶，代替晚上正餐）

ˌhigh-ˈtech (also **ˌhi-ˈtech**) *adj.* (*informal*) **1** using the most modern methods and machines, especially electronic ones 高技術的，高科技的（尤指電子方面）：*high-tech industries* 高科技產業 **2** (of designs, objects, etc. 圖案、物體等) very modern in appearance; using modern materials 樣式新穎的；用高新技術材料的：*a high-tech table made of glass and steel* 用玻璃和鋼製成的現代化桌子 ➲ compare LOW-TECH

ˌhigh techˈnology *noun* [U] the most modern methods and machines, especially electronic ones; the use of these in industry, etc. 高科技，高技術（尤指電子技術）；高科技的運用

ˌhigh-ˈtension *adj.* [only before noun] carrying a very powerful electric current 高（電）壓的：***high-tension wires/cables*** 高壓電線 / 電纜

ˌhigh ˈtide *noun* [U, C] the time when the sea has risen to its highest level; the sea at this time （海的）高潮時期，高潮，滿潮：*You can't walk along this beach **at high tide**.* 高潮時你不能在這個海灘散步。 ➲ compare FLOOD TIDE, HIGH WATER **OPP** **low tide**

ˈhigh-tops *noun* [pl.] (*especially NAmE*) sports shoes that cover the ankle, worn especially for playing BASKETBALL 高幫運動鞋（尤用於籃球運動） ▸ **ˈhigh-top** *adj.* [usually before noun]：*high-top sneakers* 高幫運動鞋

ˌhigh ˈtreason *noun* [U] = TREASON

ˈhigh-up *noun* (*BrE, informal*) an important person with a high rank 高官；要員

ˌhigh ˈwater *noun* [U] the time when the sea or the water in a river has risen to its highest level （海、河的）高潮，滿潮；高水位：*Fishing is good at high water.* 高水位有利於釣魚。 ➲ compare HIGH TIDE **IDM** see HELL

ˌhigh-ˈwater mark *noun* a line or mark showing the highest point that the sea or FLOODWATER has reached 高水位線（海水或洪水所達到的最高水位）：(*figurative*) *the high-water mark of Parisian fashion* (= the most successful time) 巴黎時裝最流行的時期 ➲ compare LOW-WATER MARK

high·way 🗝 /ˈhaɪweɪ/ *noun*
1 🗝 (*especially NAmE*) a main road for travelling long distances, especially one connecting and going through cities and towns （尤指城鎮間的）公路，幹道，交通要道：*an interstate highway* （美國）州際公路 ◇ *Highway patrol officers closed the road.* 公路巡警關閉了這條路。 **2** (*BrE, formal*) a public road 公用通道：*A parked car was obstructing the highway.* 一輛停放的汽車堵住了通道。
IDM **ˌhighway ˈrobbery** (*informal, especially NAmE*) = DAYLIGHT ROBBERY at DAYLIGHT ➲ more at WAY *n.*

the ˌHighway ˈCode *noun* [sing.] (in Britain) the official rules for drivers and other users of public roads; the book that contains these rules （英國）公用通道法規，公用通道法規彙編

high·way·man /ˈhaɪweɪmən/ *noun* (*pl.* **-men** /-mən/) a man, usually on a horse and carrying a gun, who stole from travellers on public roads in the past （舊時常騎馬持槍的）攔路強盜

ˌhigh ˈwire *noun* [usually sing.] a rope or wire that is stretched high above the ground, and used by CIRCUS performers （雜技演員使用的）高空繩索，空中鋼絲 **SYN** **tightrope**

ˈhi-hat (also **ˈhigh-hat**) *noun* a pair of CYMBALS on a set of drums, operated by the foot 踩鈸（通過踏板控制） ➲ **VISUAL VOCAB** page V35

hi·jab /hɪˈdʒɑːb/ *noun* **1** [C] a head covering worn in public by some Muslim women（穆斯林婦女出門戴的）頭巾，蓋頭 **2** [U] the religious system which controls the wearing of such clothing 頭巾制度（規定戴頭巾的宗教制度）

hi·jack /ˈhaɪdʒæk/ *verb* **1** **~ sth** to use violence or threats to take control of a vehicle, especially a plane, in order to force it to travel to a different place or to demand sth from a government 劫持（交通工具，尤指飛機）：*The plane was hijacked by two armed men on a flight from London to Rome.* 飛機在從倫敦飛往羅馬途中遭到兩名持械男子劫持。 ➲ **COLLOCATIONS** at CRIME **2** **~ sth** (*disapproving*) to use or take control of sth, especially a meeting, in order to advertise your own aims and interests 操縱（會議等，以推銷自己的意圖） ▸ **hi·jack·ing** (also **hi·jack**) *noun* [C, U]：*There have been a series of hijackings recently in the area.* 這個地區最近發生了一連串劫持事件。 ◇ *an unsuccessful hijack* 劫持未遂 ➲ compare CARJACKING

hi·jack·er /ˈhaɪdʒækə(r)/ *noun* a person who hijacks a plane or other vehicle 劫機者；劫持交通工具者；劫持者

hi·jinks (*NAmE*) = HIGH JINKS

Hijra /ˈhɪdʒrə/ *noun* = HEGIRA

hike /haɪk/ *noun, verb*
■ ***noun*** **1** a long walk in the country 遠足；徒步旅行：*They went on a ten-mile hike through the forest.* 他們進行了一次穿越森林的十英里徒步旅行。 ◇ *We could go into town but it's a real hike* (= a long way) *from here.* 我們本可以進城去，但走到那兒實在太遠。 **2** (*informal*) a large or sudden increase in prices, costs, etc. （價格、花費等的）大幅度提高，猛增：*a **tax/price hike*** 稅額 / 價格的大幅度增長 ◇ **~ in sth** *the latest hike in interest rates* 新近利率的大幅上揚
IDM **take a ˈhike** (*NAmE, informal*) a rude way of telling sb to go away 滾開；走開
■ ***verb*** **1** [I, T] to go for a long walk in the country, especially for pleasure 去…遠足；做徒步旅行：*strong boots for hiking over rough country* 適合在崎嶇不平的山路徒步旅行用的結實靴子 ◇ **~ sth** (*NAmE*) *to hike the Rockies* 去落基山脈徒步旅行 **2** [I] **go hiking** to spend time hiking for pleasure 遠足；徒步旅行：*If the weather's fine, we'll go hiking this weekend.* 如果天氣好，我們這個週末就去遠足。 **3** [T] **~ sth (up)** to increase prices, taxes, etc. suddenly by large amounts 把（價格、稅率等）大幅提高：*The government hiked up the price of milk by over 40%.* 政府把牛奶的價格提高了四成多。
PHR V **ˌhike sth↔ˈup** (*informal*) to pull or lift sth up, especially your clothing 拉起，提起（衣服等）

H

SYN hitch up : *She hiked up her skirt and waded into the river.* 她提起裙子走進河水中。

hiker /ˈhaɪkə(r)/ *noun* a person who goes for long walks in the country for pleasure 遠足者；徒步旅行者 ➲ see also HITCHHIKER

hik·ing /ˈhaɪkɪŋ/ *noun* [U] the activity of going for long walks in the country for pleasure 遠足；徒步旅行：*to go hiking* 徒步旅行 ◇ *hiking boots* （徒步）旅行靴 ➲ VISUAL VOCAB page V64

hil·ari·ous /hɪˈleəriəs; *NAmE* -ˈler-/ *adj.* extremely funny 極其滑稽的：*a hilarious joke/story* 令人捧腹的笑話 / 故事 ◇ *Lynn found the whole situation hilarious.* 林恩覺得這一切都非常滑稽。◇ *Do you know Pete? He's hilarious.* 你認識皮特嗎？他風趣得很。➲ SYNONYMS at FUNNY ▸ **hil·ari·ous·ly** *adv.* : *hilariously funny* 滑稽可笑

hil·ar·ity /hɪˈlærəti/ *noun* [U] a state of great AMUSEMENT which makes people laugh 歡鬧；狂歡

H

hill 🔑 /hɪl/ *noun*

1 🔑 [C] an area of land that is higher than the land around it, but not as high as a mountain 山丘；小山：*a region of gently rolling hills* 緩緩起伏的丘陵地區 ◇ *a* **hill** *farm/town/fort* 小山上的農場 / 城鎮 / 城堡 ◇ *The house is built* **on the side of a hill** *overlooking the river.* 房子建在可俯視河流的小山坡上。◇ *I love walking* **in the hills** (= in the area where there are hills). 我喜歡在山中散步。➲ VISUAL VOCAB pages V2, V3 ➲ see also ANTHILL, FOOTHILL, MOLEHILL **2** 🔑 [C] a slope on a road （道路的）斜坡：*Always take care when driving down* **steep hills**. 下陡坡時一定要小心駕駛。◇ *a* **hill start** (= the act of starting a vehicle on a slope) 汽車爬坡起步 ➲ see also DOWNHILL, UPHILL **3 the Hill** [sing.] (*NAmE, informal*) = CAPITOL HILL

IDM **a ˌhill of ˈbeans** (*old-fashioned, NAmE, informal*) something that is not worth much 沒有多大價值的東西 **ˌover the ˈhill** (*informal*) (of a person 人) old and therefore no longer useful or attractive 老而不中用的；人老珠黃的 ➲ more at OLD

hill·billy /ˈhɪlbɪli/ *noun* (*pl.* **-ies**) (*NAmE, disapproving*) a person who lives in the mountains and is thought to be stupid by people who live in the towns 山區鄉巴佬

hil·lock /ˈhɪlək/ *noun* a small hill 小丘

hill·side /ˈhɪlsaɪd/ *noun* the side of a hill 小山坡：*The crops will not grow on exposed hillsides.* 在裸露的山坡上莊稼沒法生長。◇ *Our hotel was on the hillside overlooking the lake.* 我們的旅館位於可俯瞰湖水的小山坡上。

ˈhill station *noun* a small town in the hills, especially in S Asia, where people go to find cooler weather in summer （尤指南亞的）山區避暑小鎮

hill·top /ˈhɪltɒp; *NAmE* -tɑːp/ *noun* the top of a hill 小山頂：*the hilltop town of Urbino* 建在小山頂上的烏爾比諾鎮

hill·walk·ing /ˈhɪlwɔːkɪŋ/ *noun* [U] the activity of walking on or up hills in the countryside for pleasure 丘陵地帶徒步旅行；丘陵遠足

hilly /ˈhɪli/ *adj.* (**hill·ier**, **hilli·est**) having a lot of hills 多小山的；多丘陵的：*a* **hilly** *area/region* 丘陵地區

hilt /hɪlt/ *noun* the handle of a SWORD, knife, etc. 刀（或劍等的）柄 ➲ picture at SWORD

IDM **(up) to the ˈhilt** as much as possible 盡量；盡可能：*We're mortgaged up to the hilt.* 我們已經把什麼都抵押了。◇ *They have promised to back us to the hilt.* 他們保證全力支持我們。

him 🔑 /hɪm; ɪm/ *pron.*

1 🔑 used as the object of a verb, after the verb *be* or after a preposition to refer to a male person or animal that has already been mentioned or is easily identified 他，它（用作動詞或介詞的賓語，或作表語）：*When did you see him?* 你什麼時候見到他的？◇ *He took the children with him.* 他帶着孩子。◇ *I'm taller than him.* 我比他高。◇ *It's him.* 是他。➲ compare HE *pron.* ➲ note at GENDER **2 Him** used when referring to God 祂（指上帝）

him·self 🔑 /hɪmˈself/ *pron.*

1 🔑 (the reflexive form of *he* * he 的反身形式) used when the man or boy who performs an action is also affected by it （用作男性的反身代詞）他自己，自己：*He introduced himself.* 他作了自我介紹。◇ *Peter ought to be ashamed of himself.* 彼得應為自己感到羞恥。 **2** 🔑 used to emphasize the male subject or object of a sentence （強調句中的男性主語或賓語）：*The doctor said so himself.* 是醫生本人這麼說的。◇ *Did you see the manager himself?* 你見到經理本人了嗎？

IDM **be, seem, etc. himˈself** (of a man or boy 男性) to be in a normal state of health or happiness; not influenced by other people 一切正常；如平時一般；未受他人影響：*He didn't seem quite himself this morning.* 他今天上午似乎有點不對勁。◇ *He needed space to be himself.* 他需要自己的獨立的空間。 **(all) by himˈself 1** alone; without anyone else （他）獨自，單獨：*He lives all by himself.* 他獨自一人生活。**2** without help （他）獨立地：*He managed to repair the car by himself.* 他自己設法修了汽車。 **(all) to himˈself** for only him to have or use 歸自己一人佔有（或使用）：*He has the house to himself during the week.* 一週之中除週末外他可以一人住這座房子。

hind /haɪnd/ *adj., noun*

■ ***adj.*** [only before noun] the **hind** legs or feet of an animal with four legs are those at the back （四足動物的腿、蹄）後面的：*The horse reared up on its hind legs.* 那匹馬後腿直立，站了起來。 OPP **fore**, **front** IDM see TALK *v.*

■ ***noun*** a female DEER, especially a RED DEER; a DOE 雌鹿（尤指雌赤鹿）➲ compare HART

hind·brain /ˈhaɪndbreɪn/ *noun* (*anatomy* 解) the part of the brain near the base of the head 後腦

hin·der /ˈhɪndə(r)/ *verb* to make it difficult for sb to do sth or for sth to happen 阻礙；妨礙；阻擋 SYN **hamper** : **~ sb/sth** *a political situation that hinders economic growth* 妨礙經濟發展的政治局面 ◇ *Some teachers felt hindered by a lack of resources.* 有些教師因資源不足而感到困難重重。◇ **~ sb/sth from sth/from doing sth** *An injury was hindering him from playing his best.* 受傷後他無法發揮出最高水平。➲ see also HINDRANCE

Hindi /ˈhɪndi/ *noun* [U] one of the official languages of India, spoken especially in northern India 印地語（印度官方語言之一，尤通用於印度北部）▸ **Hindi** *adj.*

hind·limb /ˈhaɪndlɪm/ *noun* one of the legs at the back of an animal's body （動物的）後肢，後腿

hind·quar·ters /ˌhaɪndˈkwɔːtəz; *NAmE* -ˈkwɔːrtərz/ *noun* [pl.] the back part of an animal that has four legs, including its two back legs （四腿動物的）臀部及後腿

hin·drance /ˈhɪndrəns/ *noun* **1** [C, usually sing.] a person or thing that makes it more difficult for sb to do sth or for sth to happen 造成妨礙的人（或事物）：*To be honest, she was more of a hindrance than a help.* 說實在的，她沒幫上忙，反而成了累贅。◇ **~ to sth/sb** *The high price is a major hindrance to potential buyers.* 價格高是使潛在買主卻步的主要因素。 **2** [U] (*formal*) the act of making it more difficult for sb to do sth or for sth to happen 妨礙；阻撓：*They were able to complete their journey without further hindrance.* 剩下的旅程他們沒再受到阻礙。➲ see also HINDER IDM see LET *n.*

hind·sight /ˈhaɪndsaɪt/ *noun* [U] the understanding that you have of a situation only after it has happened and that means you would have done things in a different way 事後聰明；事後的領悟：**With hindsight** *it is easy to say they should not have released him.* 事後才說他們本不應該釋放他，這倒容易。◇ *What looks obvious in hindsight was not at all obvious at the time.* 事後一目瞭然的事在當時根本看不清。◇ *It's easy to criticize* **with the benefit of hindsight**. 事後明白了再評價，這自然容易。➲ compare FORESIGHT

Hindu /ˈhɪnduː; ˌhɪnˈduː/ *noun* a person whose religion is Hinduism 印度教教徒 ▸ **Hindu** *adj.* : *a Hindu temple* 印度教廟宇

Hin·du·ism /ˈhɪnduːɪzəm/ *noun* [U] the main religion of India and Nepal which includes the worship of one or more gods and belief in REINCARNATION 印度教（印度

和尼泊爾的主要宗教，敬拜一位或多位神衹，相信輪迴轉世）

hinge 鉸鏈

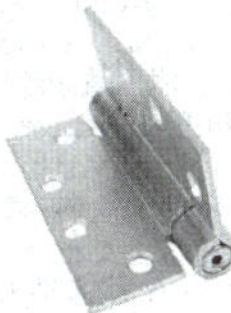

hinge /hɪndʒ/ *noun, verb*

■ ***noun*** a piece of metal, plastic, etc. on which a door, lid or gate moves freely as it opens or closes 鉸鏈；合葉：*The door had been pulled off its hinges.* 門從鉸鏈上扯下來了。

■ ***verb*** [usually passive] **~ sth** to attach sth with a hinge 給（某物）裝鉸鏈 ▸ **hinged** *adj.*：*a hinged door/lid* 鉸接的門／蓋

PHR V **ˈhinge on/upon sth** (of an action, a result, etc. 行動、結果等) to depend on sth completely 有賴於；取決於：*Everything hinges on the outcome of these talks.* 一切都取決於這幾次會談的結果。◇ **~ how, what, etc. …** *His success hinges on how well he does at the interview.* 他能否成功要看他在面試中的表現。

Hing·lish /ˈhɪŋglɪʃ/ *noun* [U] (*informal*) language which is a mixture of ENGLISH and HINDI, especially a type of English that includes many Hindi words 印地英語；印度英語

hint /hɪnt/ *noun, verb*

■ ***noun*** **1** something that you say or do in an indirect way in order to show sb what you are thinking 暗示；提示；示意：*He gave a **broad hint*** (= one that was obvious) *that he was thinking of retiring.* 他幾乎明示他正在考慮退休。◇ *Should I **drop a hint*** (= give a hint) *to Matt?* 我應該給馬特一點暗示嗎？ **2** something that suggests what will happen in the future 徵兆；跡象 **SYN** **sign**：*At the first hint of trouble, they left.* 他們一發現有點不妙的跡象就離開了。 **3** [usually sing.] **~ (of sth)** a small amount of sth 少許；少量 **SYN** **suggestion, trace**：*a hint of a smile* 一絲笑意 ◇ *There was more than a hint of sadness in his voice.* 他的聲音中流露出了深切的悲傷。◇ *The walls were painted white with a hint of peach.* 牆壁粉刷成了略呈桃紅的白色。 **4** [usually pl.] **~ (on sth)** a small piece of practical information or advice 秘訣；竅門 **SYN** **tip**：*handy hints on saving money* 省錢妙訣

IDM **take a/the ˈhint** to understand what sb wants you to do even though they tell you in an indirect way 領會某人的暗示：*I thought they'd never go—some people just can't take a hint.* 我以為他們永遠也不會走的，有些人就是不會看眼色。◇ *Sarah hoped he'd take the hint and leave her alone.* 薩拉希望他能明白她的意思，不來打擾她。

■ ***verb*** [I, T] to suggest sth in an indirect way 暗示；透露；示意：**~ at sth** *What are you hinting at?* 你在暗示什麼？ ◇ **~ (that) …** *They hinted (that) there might be more job losses.* 他們暗示說可能會有更多人失業。◇ **+ speech** *'I might know something about it,' he hinted.* "這事我也許知道一些。"他暗示道。

hin·ter·land /ˈhɪntəlænd; *NAmE* -tərl-/ *noun* [usually sing.] the areas of a country that are away from the coast, from the banks of a large river or from the main cities 內陸；腹地；內地：*the rural/agricultural hinterland* 內陸鄉下；內地農村

hip /hɪp/ *noun, adj., exclamation*

■ ***noun*** **1** the area at either side of the body between the top of the leg and the waist; the joint at the top of the leg 臀部；髖：*She stood with her hands on her hips.* 她雙手叉腰站着。◇ *These jeans are too tight around the hips.* 這條牛仔褲的臀部太窄。◇ *a hip replacement operation* 髖部復位手術 ◇ *the hip bone* 髖骨 ◇ *She broke her hip in the fall.* 她摔倒時折斷了髖骨。 ➲ COLLOCATIONS at PHYSICAL ➲ VISUAL VOCAB page V59 **2 -hipped** (in adjectives 構成形容詞) having hips of the size or shape mentioned 臀部…的：*large-hipped* 臀部大的 ◇ *slim-hipped* 臀部窄的 **3** (also **ˈrose hip**) the red fruit that grows on some types of wild ROSE bush 野薔薇果

IDM see SHOOT *v.*

■ ***adj.*** (**hip·per**, **hip·pest**) (*informal*) following or knowing what is fashionable in clothes, music, etc. （衣服、音樂等方面）時髦的，趕時髦的

■ ***exclamation***

IDM **hip, hip, hooˈray!** (also *less frequent* **hip, hip, hurˈrah/hurˈray!**) used by a group of people to show their approval of sb. One person in the group says 'hip, hip' and the others then shout 'hooray'. 嘿，嘿，烏拉（或萬歲）（集體歡呼聲。其中一人說 hip，hip，其他人隨後喊 hooray）：*'Three cheers for the bride and groom: Hip, hip …' 'Hooray!'* "向新娘和新郎歡呼三聲：嘿嘿…" "好哪！"

ˈhip bath *noun* a small bath/BATHTUB that you sit in rather than lie down in 坐浴盆

ˈhip flask (*BrE*) (also **flask** *NAmE, BrE*) *noun* a small flat bottle made of metal or glass and often covered with leather, used for carrying alcohol 小扁酒瓶（用金屬或玻璃製成，常帶皮套，隨身攜帶）

ˈhip hop *noun* [U] **1** a type of popular music with spoken words and a steady beat played on electronic instruments, originally played by young African Americans 嘻哈音樂（由美國黑人興起，包括說唱和電子樂器演奏） **2** the culture of the young African Americans and others who enjoy this type of music, including special styles of art, dancing, dress, etc. 嘻哈文化，嬉蹦文化（包括藝術、舞蹈、裝束等）

ˈhip-huggers (*NAmE*) (*BrE* **hip·sters**) *noun* [pl.] trousers/pants that cover the hips but not the waist 低腰長褲（褲腰低及臀部） ▸ **ˈhip-hugger** *adj.* [only before noun]

ˈhip joint *noun* the joint that connects the leg to the body, at the top of the THIGH bone 髖關節

hip·pie (also **hippy**) /ˈhɪpi/ *noun* (*pl.* **-ies**) a person who rejects the way that most people live in Western society, often having long hair, wearing brightly coloured clothes and taking illegal drugs. The hippie movement was most popular in the 1960s. 嬉皮士（拒絕西方主流生活方式的人，常留長髮、衣着鮮豔、吸毒。嬉皮士運動在 20 世紀 60 年代最盛行）

hippo /ˈhɪpəʊ; *NAmE* ˈhɪpoʊ/ *noun* (*pl.* **-os**) (*informal*) = HIPPOPOTAMUS

hippo·cam·pus /ˌhɪpəˈkæmpəs/ *noun* (*pl.* **hippo·campi** /-paɪ; -pi/) (*anatomy* 解) either of the two areas of the brain thought to be the centre of emotion and memory 海馬體（大腦中被認為是感情和記憶中心的部份）

ˌhip ˈpocket *noun* a pocket at the back or the side of a pair of trousers/pants or a skirt（褲子或裙子的）後口袋，側口袋

the Hippo·crat·ic oath /ˌhɪpəkrætɪk ˈəʊθ; *NAmE* ˈoʊθ/ *noun* [sing.] the promise that doctors make to keep to the principles of the medical profession 希波克拉底誓言（醫生保證遵守醫生職業道德的誓言）

hip·po·drome /ˈhɪpədrəʊm; *NAmE* -droʊm/ *noun* **1** (*BrE*) used in the names of some theatres and concert halls（用於名稱）劇院，音樂廳 **2** (*NAmE*) an ARENA, especially one used for horse shows 競技場；（尤指）馬術表演場 **3** a track in ancient Greece or Rome on which horse races or CHARIOT races took place（古希臘或羅馬的）賽馬場，戰車競技場

hippo·pot·amus /ˌhɪpəˈpɒtəməs; *NAmE* -ˈpɑːtə-/ (also *informal* **hippo**) *noun* (*pl.* **hippo·pot·amuses** /-məsɪz/ or **hip·po·pot·ami** /-maɪ/) a large heavy African animal with thick dark skin and short legs, that lives in rivers and lakes 河馬

hippy = HIPPIE

hip·sters /ˈhɪpstəz; *NAmE* -stərz/ (*BrE*) (*NAmE* **ˈhip-huggers**) *noun* [pl.] trousers/pants that cover the hips but not the waist 低腰長褲（褲腰低及臀部）：*a pair of*

H

hipsters 一條低腰長褲 ▸ **hip·ster** *adj.* [only before noun]：*hipster jeans* 低腰牛仔褲

hira·gana /ˌhɪrəˈɡɑːnə/ *noun* [U] (from *Japanese*) a set of symbols used in Japanese writing （日語中的）平假名 ➲ compare KATAKANA

hire 🔑 /ˈhaɪə(r)/ *verb, noun*

■ ***verb*** **1** 🔑 [T] **~ sth** (*especially BrE*) to pay money to borrow sth for a short time 租用；租借：*to hire a car/room/video* 租汽車；租房間；租錄像帶 ➲ note at RENT **2** 🔑 [T, I] **~ (sb)** (*especially NAmE*) to give sb a job 聘用；錄用；雇用：*She was hired three years ago.* 她是三年前錄用的。◇ *He does the* ***hiring and firing*** *in our company.* 他在我們公司負責員工的聘用和辭退。➲ COLLOCATIONS at JOB **3** 🔑 [T] **~ sb/sth** to employ sb for a short time to do a particular job 臨時雇用：*to hire a lawyer* 聘請律師 ◇ *They hired a firm of consultants to design the new system.* 他們請了一家咨詢公司來設計新的系統。

PHR V ˌ**hire sth↔ˈout** 🔑 to let sb use sth for a short time, in return for payment 出租某物 ˌ**hire yourself ˈout (to sb)** to arrange to work for sb 為（某人）工作；受聘於；受雇於：*He hired himself out to whoever needed his services.* 他以前接受任何人雇用。

■ ***noun*** **1** 🔑 [U] (*especially BrE*) the act of paying to use sth for a short time 租借；租用；租賃：*bicycles* ***for hire****, £2 an hour* 自行車出租，每小時 2 英鎊 ◇ *a* ***hire car*** 供租用的汽車 ◇ *a* ***car hire*** *firm* 汽車出租公司 ◇ *The price includes the hire of the hall.* 費用包括禮堂租金。◇ *The costumes are* ***on hire from*** *the local theatre.* 戲裝可向本地劇院租用。➲ note at RENT **2** [C] (*especially NAmE*) a person who has recently been given a job by a company 新雇員；新員工 IDM see PLY *v.*

ˌ**hired ˈhand** *noun* (*NAmE*) a person who is paid to work on a farm 農場雇工

hire·ling /ˈhaɪəlɪŋ; *NAmE* ˈhaɪərlɪŋ/ *noun* (*disapproving*) a person who is willing to do anything or work for anyone as long as they are paid 給錢就什麼都願幹的人；有奶就叫娘的人

ˌ**hire ˈpurchase** *noun* [U] (*BrE*) (*abbr.* **h.p.**, **HP**) (*NAmE* **inˈstallment plan**) a method of buying an article by making regular payments for it over several months or years. The article only belongs to the person who is buying it when all the payments have been made. 分期付款購買：*a hire purchase agreement* 分期付款協議 ◇ *We're buying a new cooker* ***on hire purchase****.* 我們以分期付款方式購買一座新爐具。➲ compare CREDIT *n.* (1)

hi-res (also **high-res**) /ˌhaɪ ˈrez/ *adj.* (*informal*) = HIGH-RESOLUTION

hir·sute /ˈhɜːsjuːt; *NAmE* ˈhɜːrsuːt/ *adj.* (*literary* or *humorous*) (especially of a man 尤指男子) having a lot of hair on the face or body 滿臉鬍鬚的；體毛多的 SYN **hairy**

his 🔑 /hɪz; ɪz/ *det., pron.*

■ ***det.*** (the possessive form of *he* * he 的所有格形式) **1** 🔑 of or belonging to a man or boy who has already been mentioned or is easily identified 他的：*James has sold his car.* 詹姆斯把他的車賣了。◇ *He broke his leg skiing.* 他滑雪時摔斷了腿。 **2 His** of or belonging to God 上帝的；屬於上帝的

■ ***pron.*** 🔑 of or belonging to him 他的；屬於他的：*He took my hand in his.* 他握住我的手。◇ *The choice was his.* 選擇由他做出。◇ *a friend of his* 他的一位朋友 ➲ note at GENDER

His·pan·ic /hɪˈspænɪk/ *adj., noun*

■ ***adj.*** of or connected with Spain or Spanish-speaking countries, especially those of Latin America 西班牙的；西班牙語國家（尤指拉丁美洲）的

■ ***noun*** a person whose first language is Spanish, especially one from a Latin American country living in the US or Canada 母語為西班牙語的人（尤指住在美國或加拿大的拉丁美洲人）

His·pan·o- /hɪˈspænəʊ; *NAmE* -noʊ/ *combining form* (in nouns and adjectives 構成名詞和形容詞) Spanish 西班牙的：*the Hispano-French border* 西班牙與法國邊境 ◇ *Hispanophile* 親西班牙的

hiss /hɪs/ *verb, noun*

■ ***verb*** **1** [I] **~ (at sb/sth)** to make a sound like a long 's' 發嘶嘶聲：*The steam escaped with a loud hissing noise.* 蒸汽冒了出來，發出很響的嘶嘶聲。◇ *The snake lifted its head and hissed.* 蛇昂起頭發出嘶嘶聲。 **2** [T, I] **~ (sb/sth)** | **~ (sb/sth + adv./prep.)** to make a sound like a long 's' to show disapproval of sb/sth, especially an actor or a speaker 發噓聲（表示不滿，尤指對演員或演講人）：*He was booed and hissed off the stage.* 他在一片倒彩聲和噓聲中被轟下台。 **3** [I, T] to say sth in a quiet angry voice 帶怒氣地低聲說出（某事）：**~ at sb** *He hissed at them to be quiet.* 他生氣地低聲要他們安靜點。◇ **+ speech** *'Leave me alone!' she hissed.* "別煩我！" 她生氣地低聲說。

■ ***noun*** a sound like a long 's'; this sound used to show disapproval of sb 嘶嘶聲；噓聲：*the hiss of the air brakes* 氣閘的嘶嘶聲 ◇ *the snake's hiss* 蛇發出的嘶嘶聲 ◇ *The performance was met with boos and hisses.* 演出換來一片倒彩聲和噓聲。

ˈ**hissy fit** *noun* [C, usually sing.] (*informal*) a state of being bad-tempered and unreasonable 壞脾氣 SYN **tantrum**：*She* ***threw a hissy fit*** *because her dressing room wasn't painted blue.* 她發脾氣是因為她的梳妝室沒有漆成藍色。

his·ta·mine /ˈhɪstəmiːn/ *noun* [U] (*medical* 醫) a chemical substance that is given out in the body in response to an injury or an ALLERGY 組胺（遇組織受傷或過敏時釋放）➲ see also ANTIHISTAMINE

histo·gram /ˈhɪstəɡræm/ *noun* (*technical* 術語) a diagram which uses RECTANGLES (= bars) of different heights (and sometimes different widths) to show different amounts, so that they can be compared 條形圖，柱形圖（以不同長度的粗線條表示不同數量以作比較）➲ compare BAR CHART

his·tolo·gy /hɪˈstɒlədʒi; *NAmE* -ˈstɑːl-/ *noun* [U] the scientific study of the extremely small structures that form living TISSUE 組織學 ▸ **his·tolo·gist** /hɪˈstɒlədʒɪst; *NAmE* -ˈstɑːl-/ *noun*

histo·path·ology /ˌhɪstəʊpəˈθɒlədʒi; *NAmE* ˌhɪstoʊpəˈθɑːl-/ *noun* [U] the study of changes in cells where disease is present 組織病理學

his·tor·ian /hɪˈstɔːriən/ *noun* a person who studies or writes about history; an expert in history 史學工作者；歷史學家 HELP Some speakers do not pronounce the 'h' at the beginning of **historian** and use 'an' instead of 'a' before it. This now sounds old-fashioned. 有人說 historian 時不發 h 音，前面用 an 而不用 a，現在聽起來過時了。

Which Word? 詞語辨析

historic / historical

■ **Historic** is usually used to describe something that is so important that it is likely to be remembered. * historic 通常用以表示具有重要歷史意義：*Today is a historic occasion for our country.* 今天是我國具有歷史意義的日子。 **Historical** usually describes something that is connected with the past or with the study of history, or something that really happened in the past. * historical 通常涉及歷史、史學、過去的事實：*I have been doing some historical research.* 我一直在進行史學研究。◇ *Was Robin Hood a historical figure?* 羅賓漢是歷史人物嗎？

his·tor·ic /hɪˈstɒrɪk; *NAmE* -ˈstɔːr-; -ˈstɑːr-/ *adj.* [usually before noun] **1** important in history; likely to be thought of as important at some time in the future 歷史上著名（或重要）的；可名垂青史的：*a historic building/monument* 有歷史意義的建築／紀念碑 ◇ *The area is of special historic interest.* 這個地區有特別歷史意義。◇ *a historic occasion/decision/day/visit/victory* 歷史性的時刻／決定／日子／訪問／勝利 **2** of a period during which history was recorded 有史時期的：*in historic times* 在有史時期 ➲ compare PREHISTORIC HELP Some speakers do not pronounce the 'h' at the beginning of **historic** and use 'an' instead of 'a' before it. This now sounds old-fashioned. 有人説 historic 時不發 h 音，前面用 an 而不用 a，現在聽起來過時了。

his·tor·ic·al /hɪ'stɒrɪkl; *NAmE* -'stɔːr-; -'stɑːr-/ *adj.* [usually before noun] **1** connected with the past（有關）歷史的：*the historical background to the war* 這次戰爭的歷史背景 ◇ *You must place these events in their **historical context**.* 必須把這些事件同它們的歷史環境聯繫起來看。 **2** connected with the study of history 有關歷史研究的；歷史學的：***historical documents/records/research*** 史學文獻／檔案／研究 ◇ *The building is of **historical importance**.* 這棟建築有重要的歷史研究價值。 **3** (of a book, film/movie, etc. 書、電影等) about people and events in the past 歷史題材的：*a historical novel* 歷史小説 **HELP** Some speakers do not pronounce the 'h' at the beginning of **historical** and use 'an' instead of 'a' before it. This now sounds old-fashioned. 有人説 historical 時不發 h 音，前面用 an 而不用 a，現在聽起來過時了。 ▸ **his·tor·ic·al·ly** /-kli/ *adv.*：*The book is historically inaccurate.* 這本書與史實不符。◇ *Historically, there has always been a great deal of rivalry between the two families.* 這兩個家族世世代代對立鬥爭。

his·tori·cism /hɪ'stɒrɪsɪzəm; *NAmE* -'stɔːr-; -'stɑːr-/ *noun* [U] the theory that cultural and social events and situations can be explained by history 歷史決定論

the his,toric 'present *noun* [sing.] (*grammar* 語法) the simple present tense used to describe events in the past in order to make the description more powerful 歷史現在時，歷史現在式（為了表述的生動，用一般現在時描述過去的事情）

his·tor·iog·raphy /hɪ,stɒri'ɒgrəfi; *NAmE* -,stɔːri'ɑːg-; -,stɑːr-/ *noun* [U] the study of writing about history 編史；撰史；歷史編纂學 ▸ **his·tori·og·raph·ical** /hɪ,stɒriə'græfɪkl; *NAmE* -,stɔːr-; -,stɑː-/ *adj.*

his·tory /'hɪstri/ *noun* (*pl.* **-ies**)
1 [U] all the events that happened in the past 歷史（指過去發生的所有事情）：*a turning point in human history* 人類歷史的一個轉折點 ◇ *one of the worst disasters in **recent history*** 近代史上最大的災難之一 ◇ *a people with no **sense of history*** 一個沒有歷史感的民族 ◇ *Many people throughout history have dreamt of a world without war.* 歷史上有很多人夢想過沒有戰爭的世界。◇ *The area was inhabited long before the dawn of **recorded history*** (= before people wrote about events). 早在有歷史記載之前很久這個地區就有人居住了。◇ *These events changed the **course of history**.* 這些事件改變了歷史的進程。 **2** [sing., U] the past events concerned in the development of a particular place, subject, etc.（有關某個地方、主題等的）發展史，歷史：*the history of Ireland/democracy/popular music* 愛爾蘭／民主／流行音樂的歷史 ◇ *The **local history** of the area is fascinating.* 這個地區的歷史很有意思。◇ *The school traces its history back to 1865.* 這個學校的歷史可以追溯到 1865 年。 **3** [U] the study of past events as a subject at school or university 歷史課；歷史學：*a **history teacher*** 歷史科老師 ◇ *a degree in History* 歷史學學位 ◇ ***social/economic/political history*** 社會／經濟／政治史 ◇ ***ancient/medieval/modern history*** 古代／中世紀／近代史 ◇ *She's studying **art history**.* 她正在研讀藝術史。 ➲ see also NATURAL HISTORY **4** [C] a written or spoken account of past events 歷史（指歷史記載或歷史傳説）：*She's writing a new history of Europe.* 她正在寫一部新的歐洲史。◇ *She went on to catalogue a long history of disasters.* 接下來她列舉了一長串災難。 **5** [sing.] ~ (**of sth**) a record of sth happening frequently in the past life of a person, family or place; the set of facts that are known about sb's past life（某人的）履歷，經歷；家族史；（某地的）沿革：*He has a history of violent crime.* 他有暴力犯罪的前科。◇ *There is a history of heart disease in my family.* 我家有家族心臟病史。◇ *a patient's **medical history*** 病人的病歷 ➲ see also CASE HISTORY, LIFE HISTORY
IDM **be 'history** (*informal*) to be dead or no longer important 完蛋；已過去了；不再重要；成為歷史：*Another mistake like that and you're history.* 要是再犯那種錯誤你就完了。◇ *We won't talk about that—that's history.* 我們不會談論那件事的，那都已經過去了。◇ *That's **past history** now.* 那是以前的事了。 **the 'history books** the record of great achievements in history 歷史上重大成就的記載：*She has earned her place in the history books.* 她名垂青史。 **history re'peats itself** used to say that things often happen later in the same way as before 歷史時常重演 **make 'history | go down in 'history** to be or do sth so important that it will be recorded in history 載入史冊；青史留名；創造歷史：*a discovery that made medical history* 載入醫學史冊的一項重大發現 ➲ more at REST *n.*

his·tri·on·ic /,hɪstri'ɒnɪk; *NAmE* -'ɑːnɪk/ *adj.* [usually before noun] (*formal, disapproving*) **histrionic** behaviour is very emotional and is intended to attract attention in a way that does not seem sincere 矯揉造作的；裝腔作勢的 ▸ **his·tri·on·ic·al·ly** /-kli/ *adv.* **his·tri·on·ics** *noun* [pl.]：*She was used to her mother's histrionics.* 她習慣了母親裝腔作勢的樣子。

hit /hɪt/ *verb, noun*
■ ***verb*** (**hit·ting, hit, hit**)
▸ **TOUCH SB/STH WITH FORCE** 打 **1** [T] to bring your hand, or an object you are holding, against sb/sth quickly and with force（用手或器具）擊，打：**~ sb/sth** *My parents never used to hit me.* 我的父母以前從來不打我。◇ **~ sb/sth with sth** *He hit the nail squarely on the head with the hammer.* 他用錘子正對着釘子敲下去。◇ *She hit him on the head with her umbrella.* 她用雨傘打他的頭。 **2** [T] **~ sth/sb** to come against sth/sb with force, especially causing damage or injury 碰撞；撞擊（造成損傷）：*The bus hit the bridge.* 公共汽車撞到了橋上。◇ *I was hit by a falling stone.* 我被一塊墜落的石頭擊中。 **3** [T] **~ sth** (**on/against sth**) to knock a part of your body against sth 使（身體部位）碰上（某物）：*He hit his head on the low ceiling.* 他的頭碰了低矮的天花板。 **4** [T, often passive] **~ sb/sth** (of a bullet, bomb, etc. or a person using them 子彈、炸彈或射擊者、拋擲者) to reach and touch a person or thing suddenly and with force 擊中；命中：*The town was hit by bombs again last night.* 這個鎮子昨晚又一次遭到了轟炸。◇ *He was hit by a sniper.* 他被狙擊手擊中。
▸ **BALL** 球 **5** [T] **~ sth** (**+ adv./prep.**) to bring a BAT, etc. against a ball and push it away with force 擊（球）：*She hit the ball too hard and it went out of the court.* 她用力過猛，把球打出了場外。◇ *We've hit our ball over the fence!* 我們把球擊過圍欄去了！ **6** [T] **~ sth** (*sport* 體) to score points by hitting a ball 擊球得分：*to hit a home run* 打出本壘打
▸ **HAVE BAD EFFECT** 有壞影響 **7** [T, I] **~ (sb/sth)** to have a bad effect on sb/sth 產生不良影響；打擊；危害：*The tax increases will certainly hit the poor.* 增稅肯定會加重窮人的負擔。◇ *His death didn't really hit me at first.* 他的死起初並沒有對我產生影響。◇ *Rural areas have been worst hit by the strike.* 這次罷工對農村地區的打擊最沉重。◇ *Spain was one of the **hardest hit** countries.* 西班牙是遭受打擊最嚴重的國家之一。◇ *A tornado hit on Tuesday night.* 星期二晚上發生一次龍捲風。
▸ **ATTACK** 攻擊 **8** [T, I] **~ (sb/sth)** to attack sb/sth 攻擊；進攻；襲擊：*We hit the enemy when they least expected it.* 我們在敵人最意想不到的時候發動了進攻。
▸ **REACH** 到達 **9** [T] **~ sth** (*informal*) to reach a place 到達（某地）：*Follow this footpath and you'll eventually hit the road.* 沿着這條小路走，終會走上大路。◇ *The President **hits town** tomorrow.* 總統明天到鎮子上來。 **10** [T] **~ sth** to reach a particular level 達到（某水平）：*Temperatures hit 40° yesterday.* 昨天氣溫高達 40 度。◇ *The euro hit a record low in trading today.* 今天歐元的兑換價降到了歷史最低水平。
▸ **PROBLEM/DIFFICULTY** 問題；困難 **11** [T] **~ sth** (*informal*) to experience sth difficult or unpleasant 遇到（困難）；經歷（不愉快的事情）：*We seem to have hit a problem.* 我們似乎遇到了問題。◇ *Everything was going well but then we hit trouble.* 原本一切都進行得很順利，但後來我們遇到了麻煩。
▸ **SUDDENLY REALIZE** 突然意識到 **12** [T] **~ sb** (*informal*) to come suddenly into your mind 使突然想起：*I couldn't remember where I'd seen him before, and then it suddenly hit me.* 起初我想不起以前在哪裏見過他，後來猛然記起來了。

▸ **PRESS BUTTON** 按鈕 **13** [T] **~ sth** (*informal*) to press sth such as a button to operate a machine, etc. 按，壓（按鈕等）: *Hit the brakes!* 踩刹車！

IDM **hit (it) 'big** (*informal*) to be very successful 很成功: *The band has hit big in the US.* 樂隊在美國一炮打響。 **hit the 'buffers** (*informal*) if a plan, sb's career, etc. **hits the buffers**, it suddenly stops being successful（計劃、事業等）突然受挫 **hit the 'ceiling/'roof** (*informal*) to suddenly become very angry 勃然大怒；怒氣沖天 **hit the 'deck** (*informal*) to fall to the ground 摔倒在地；落到地上 **ˌhit the ground 'running** (*informal*) to start doing sth and continue very quickly and successfully 迅速而順利地投入某事；一炮打響；一舉成功 **hit the 'hay/'sack** (*informal*) to go to bed 上牀睡覺 **hit a/the 'wall** to reach a point when you cannot continue or make any more progress 筋疲力盡；陷入絕境；遇到不可逾越的障礙: *We hit a wall and we weren't scoring.* 我們已經筋疲力盡，得不到分了。 **hit sb (straight/right) in the 'eye** to be very obvious to sb 很顯然；一目瞭然 **'hit it** (*informal*) used to tell sb to start doing sth, such as playing music（要某人開始做某事，如演奏音樂）開始吧: *Hit it, Louis!* 開始吧，路易斯！ **hit it 'off (with sb)** (*informal*) to have a good friendly relationship with sb（和某人）投緣: *We hit it off straight away.* 我們一見如故。 **hit the 'jackpot** to make or win a lot of money quickly and unexpectedly 突然意外賺大錢（或贏大錢）；發大財 **hit the nail on the 'head** to say sth that is exactly right 說到點子上；正中要害 **hit the 'road/'trail** (*informal*) to start a journey/trip 出發；上路 **hit the 'roof** = GO THROUGH THE ROOF (2) at ROOF *n.* **hit the 'spot** (*informal*) if sth **hits the spot** it does exactly what it should do 發揮正當作用；適得其用；恰到好處 **hit the 'streets | hit the 'shops/'stores** (*informal*) to become widely available for sale 大量上市: *The new magazine hits the streets tomorrow.* 新的雜誌明天發行。 **hit sb when they're 'down** to continue to hurt sb when they are already defeated 落井下石；乘人之危 **hit sb where it 'hurts** to affect sb where they will feel it most 刺着某人痛處；擊中要害 ➲ more at HEADLINE *n.*, HOME *adv.*, KNOW *v.*, MARK *n.*, NERVE *n.*, NOTE *n.*, PAY DIRT, SHIT *n.*, SIX, STRIDE *n.*

PHR V **ˌhit 'back (at sb/sth)** to reply to attacks or criticism 回擊；反擊 **SYN** **retaliate**: *In a TV interview she hit back at her critics.* 她在電視採訪中反駁了那些批評者。 **'hit on sb** (*NAmE, slang*) to start talking to sb to show them that you are sexually attracted to them 開始與某人調情 **'hit on/upon sth** [no passive] (rather *informal*) to think of a good idea suddenly or by chance 突然有個好主意；偶然想到妙點子: *She hit on the perfect title for her new novel.* 她靈機一動，為自己的新小說找到了一個理想的書名。 **ˌhit 'out (at sb/sth)** to attack sb/sth violently by fighting them or criticizing them 猛烈攻擊；狠狠抨擊: *I just hit out blindly in all directions.* 我只是漫無目的地四處出擊。◇ *In a rousing speech the minister hit out at racism in the armed forces.* 在一次激勵人心的講話中，部長嚴厲抨擊了軍中的種族主義。 **ˌhit sb 'up for sth | 'hit sb for sth** (*NAmE, informal*) to ask sb for money 向某人要錢: *Does he always hit you up for cash when he wants new clothes?* 他要買新衣服時是不是總找你要錢？ **'hit sb with sth** (*informal*) to tell sb sth, especially sth that surprises or shocks them（把嚇人的事等）告訴某人: *How much is it going to cost, then? Come on, hit me with it!* 那麼它究竟要花費多少錢？快點告訴我吧！

■ ***noun***

▸ **ACT OF HITTING** 打 **1** ⊶ an act of hitting sb/sth with your hand or with an object held in your hand 打；擊: *Give it a good hit.* 用力打它一下。◇ *He made the winning hit.* 他擊出了致勝的一球。 **2** ⊶ an occasion when sth that has been thrown, fired, etc. at an object reaches that object 命中；擊中: *The bomber scored a **direct hit** on the bridge.* 轟炸機直接炸中了那座橋。◇ *We finished the first round with a score of two hits and six misses.* 我們在第一輪結束時的分數是兩次擊中，六次未中。

▸ **STH POPULAR** 受歡迎的事物 **3** ⊶ a person or thing that is very popular 很受歡迎的人（或事物）: *The duo were a real hit in last year's show.* 這一對搭檔在去年的演出中大出風頭。◇ *a hit musical* 風靡一時的音樂劇 ◇ *Her new series is a **smash hit**.* 她的新系列節目極為成功，引起轟動。

▸ **POP MUSIC** 流行音樂 **4** ⊶ a successful pop song or record 風行一時的流行歌曲（或唱片）: *They are about to release an album of their greatest hits.* 他們即將發行收錄他們最熱門歌曲的專輯。◇ *She played all her old hits.* 她演奏了她所有曾轟動一時的老曲子。◇ *a **hit record/single*** 風靡一時的唱片／單曲唱片

▸ **OF DRUG** 毒品 **5** (*slang*) an amount of an illegal drug that is taken at one time 一劑毒品

▸ **MURDER** 兇殺 **6** (*slang, especially NAmE*) a violent crime or murder 暴力犯罪；兇殺 ➲ see also HIT MAN

▸ **COMPUTING** 計算機技術 **7** a result of a search on a computer, for example on the Internet（在計算機或互聯網上搜索的）查詢結果: *How many hits did you get?* 你在網上搜到了多少個結果？

IDM **be/make a 'hit (with sb)** to be liked very much by sb when they first meet you 給（某人）留下很好的第一印象；使（某人）一見鍾情 **take a 'hit** to be damaged or badly affected by sth 遭到破壞；受到嚴重影響: *The airline industry took a hit last year.* 去年航空業受到了嚴重衝擊。

Synonyms 同義詞辨析

hit

knock • bang • strike • bump • bash

These words all mean to come against sth with a lot of force. 以上各詞均含用力撞擊、擊打之義。

hit to come against sth with force, especially causing damage or injury 指碰撞、撞擊，尤指造成損傷: *The boy was hit by a speeding car.* 男孩被超速行駛的汽車撞倒了。

knock to hit sth so that it moves or breaks; to put sb/sth into a particular state or position by hitting them/it 指打掉、敲動、打破、撞成…: *Someone had knocked a hole in the wall.* 有人在牆上打了個洞。

bang to hit sth in a way that makes a loud noise 指大聲地猛敲、砸: *The baby was banging the table with his spoon.* 嬰兒用調羹敲打着桌子。

strike (*formal*) to hit sb/sth hard 指猛烈地撞、碰、撞擊、碰撞: *The ship struck a rock.* 船觸礁了。

bump to hit sb/sth accidentally 指無意地碰、撞: *In the darkness I bumped into a chair.* 我在黑暗中撞上了一把椅子。

bash (*informal*) to hit against sth very hard 指猛擊、猛撞: *I braked too late, bashing into the car in front.* 我剎車太晚，撞上了前面的車。

PATTERNS

- to hit/knock/bang/bump/bash **against** sb/sth
- to knock/bang/bump/bash **into** sb/sth
- to hit/strike the **ground/floor/wall**

ˌhit-and-'miss (also **ˌhit-or-'miss**) *adj.* not done in a careful or planned way and therefore not likely to be successful 粗製濫造的；時好時壞的

ˌhit-and-'run *adj.* [only before noun] **1** (of a road accident 交通事故) caused by a driver who does not stop to help 駕駛人肇事後逃逸的: *a **hit-and-run accident/death*** 駕駛人肇事後逃離現場的交通事故／引起的死亡 ◇ *a **hit-and-run driver*** (= one who causes an accident but drives away without helping) 肇事後逃走的駕駛人 **2** (of a military attack 軍事進攻) happening suddenly and unexpectedly so that the people attacking can leave quickly without being hurt 突襲後迅速撤離的: *hit-and-run raids* 打了就撤的襲擊 ▸ **ˌhit-and-'run** *noun*: *He was killed in a hit-and-run.* 他被車撞死，車主肇事後不顧而去。

hitch /hɪtʃ/ *verb, noun*

■ ***verb*** **1** [T, I] to get a free ride in a person's car; to travel around in this way, by standing at the side of the road and trying to get passing cars to stop 免費搭車；搭便車：**~ sth** *They **hitched a ride** in a truck.* 他們搭乘了一輛路過的貨車。◇ (*BrE* also) *They **hitched a lift**.* 他們搭了便車。◇ (**+ adv./prep.**) *We spent the summer hitching around Europe.* 我們藉搭便車在歐洲各地旅行了一個夏天。➲ see also HITCHHIKE **2** [T] **~ sth (up)** to pull up a piece of your clothing 提起，拉起（衣服）**SYN** **hike up**：*She hitched up her skirt and waded into the river.* 她提起裙子，蹚進河裏。 **3** [T] **~ yourself (up, etc.)** to lift yourself into a higher position, or the position mentioned 攀上；躍上：*She hitched herself up.* 她爬了上去。◇ *He hitched himself onto the bar stool.* 他一躍坐上酒吧高腳凳上。 **4** [T] **~ sth (to sth)** to fix sth to sth else with a rope, a hook, etc. 拴住；套住；鉤住：*She hitched the pony to the gate.* 她把小馬拴在大門上。

IDM **get 'hitched** (*informal*) to get married 結婚

■ ***noun*** **1** a problem or difficulty that causes a short delay 暫時的困難（或問題）；故障；障礙：*The ceremony went off **without a hitch**.* 儀式進行得很順利。◇ *a technical hitch* 技術故障 **2** a type of knot （某種）結：*a clove hitch* 捲結

hitch·hike /ˈhɪtʃhaɪk/ *verb* [I] to travel by asking for free rides in other people's cars, by standing at the side of the road and trying to get passing cars to stop 免費搭便車；搭順風車：*They hitchhiked around Europe.* 他們一路搭便車周遊歐洲。➲ see also HITCH *v.* (1) ▸ **hitch·hiker** (also **hitch·er** /ˈhɪtʃə(r)/) *noun*：*He picked up two hitchhikers on the road to Bristol.* 他在前往布里斯托爾的路上捎帶了兩個搭便車的人。

ˌhi-ˈtech = HIGH-TECH

hither /ˈhɪðə(r)/ *adv.* (*old use*) to this place 到此處；向此地

IDM **ˌhither and ˈthither** | **ˌhither and ˈyon** (especially *literary*) in many different directions 各處；四處

hith·er·to /ˌhɪðəˈtuː; *NAmE* ˌhɪðərˈtuː/ *adv.* (*formal*) until now; until the particular time you are talking about 迄今；直到某時：*a hitherto unknown species of moth* 迄今仍屬未知品種的蛾

ˈhit list *noun* (*informal*) a list of people, organizations, etc. against whom some unpleasant action is being planned 打擊對象名單：*Which services are on the government's hit list?* 哪些部門被列入了政府要整頓的機構名單？◇ *She was at the top of the terrorists' hit list for over two years.* 她被恐怖分子列為頭號謀殺對象長達兩年。

ˈhit man *noun* (*informal*) a criminal who is paid to kill sb 受雇充當刺客的人；職業殺手

ˌhit-or-ˈmiss *adj.* = HIT-AND-MISS

ˈhit-out *noun* (in AUSTRALIAN RULES football 澳式橄欖球) a hit of the ball towards a player from your team after it has been BOUNCED by the UMPIRE 反彈後擲球（在裁判擲地反彈之後投向同隊隊員的球）

the ˈhit parade *noun* (*old-fashioned*) a list published every week that shows which pop records have sold the most copies （每週）最暢銷流行唱片榜

ˈhit squad *noun* a group of criminals who are paid to kill a person 職業殺手團夥；受雇殺人小集團

hit·ter /ˈhɪtə(r)/ *noun* (often in compounds 常構成複合詞) **1** (in sports 體育運動) a person who hits the ball in the way mentioned 擊球手：*a **big/long/hard hitter*** 很棒的／善於長打的／打擊力強的擊球手 **2** (in politics or business 政治或商業) a person who is powerful 要員；大亨：*the **heavy hitters** of Japanese industry* 日本的工業鉅子

HIV /ˌeɪtʃ aɪ ˈviː/ *noun* [U] the abbreviation for 'human immunodeficiency virus' (the virus that can cause AIDS) 人體免疫缺損病毒，艾滋病病毒（全寫為 human immunodeficiency virus）：*to be infected with HIV* 染上艾滋病病毒 ◇ *to be **HIV-positive/HIV-negative*** (= to have had a medical test which shows that you are/are not infected with HIV) 人體免疫缺損病毒檢測呈陽性／陰性反應

hive /haɪv/ *noun, verb*

■ ***noun*** **1** (also **bee·hive**) [C] a structure made for BEES to live in 蜂房；蜂箱 **2** [C] the BEES living in a hive 一箱蜜蜂；蜂群 **3** [C, usually sing.] **a ~ of activity/industry** a place full of people who are busy 忙碌的場所；繁忙的地方 **4 hives** [U] = URTICARIA

■ ***verb***

PHR V **ˌhive sth↔ˈoff (to/into sth)** [often passive] (*especially BrE*) to separate one part of a group from the rest; to sell part of a business 把一部份分拆出來；賣掉公司的一部份：*The IT department is being hived off into a new company.* 信息技術部正被分拆出來，成立新公司。

hiya /ˈhaɪjə/ *exclamation* used to say hello to sb in an informal way （非正式招呼語）嗨，你好

hl *abbr.* HECTOLITRE(S) 百升

HM (*BrE*) (also **H.M.** *US, BrE*) *abbr.* Her/His MAJESTY('s) 陛下：*HM the Queen* 女王陛下 ◇ *HM Customs* 英國海關

HMG *abbr.* (*BrE*) Her Majesty's Government 女王陛下政府；英國政府

hmm (also **hm**, **h'm**) /m; hm/ *exclamation* used in writing to show the sound that you make to express doubt or when you are hesitating （書寫形式，表示有疑慮或猶豫時發出的聲音）呣，嗯，唔，哼

HMRC /ˌeɪtʃ em ɑː ˈsiː; *NAmE* -ɑːr-/ *abbr.* HM Revenue and Customs 英國稅務海關總署

ˌHM ˌRevenue and ˈCustoms *noun* [U] (*abbr.* **HMRC**) the government department in Britain that is responsible for collecting taxes. It replaced the INLAND REVENUE and HM CUSTOMS AND EXCISE in 2005. 英國稅務海關總署（於 2005 年取代了稅務局和海關與貨物稅務署）➲ compare INTERNAL REVENUE SERVICE

HMS /ˌeɪtʃ em ˈes/ *abbr.* Her/His Majesty's Ship (used before the name of a ship in the British navy) 皇家海軍艦艇（用於英國海軍艦艇名前）：*HMS Apollo* 皇家海軍阿波羅號

HNC /ˌeɪtʃ en ˈsiː/ *noun* the abbreviation for 'Higher National Certificate' (a British university or college qualification, especially in a technical or scientific subject) 國家高級證書（全寫為 Higher National Certificate，尤指英國大學科技學科的）：*to do an HNC in electrical engineering* 攻讀電機工程國家高級證書

HND /ˌeɪtʃ en ˈdiː/ *noun* the abbreviation for 'Higher National Diploma' (a British university or college qualification, especially in a technical or scientific subject) 國家高級文憑（全寫為 Higher National Diploma，尤指英國大學科技學科的）：*to do an HND in fashion design* 攻讀時裝設計國家高級文憑

ho /həʊ; *NAmE* hoʊ/ *noun* (*pl.* **hos** or **hoes**) (*NAmE, taboo, slang*) **1** a female PROSTITUTE 娼妓；妓女 **2** an offensive word used about a woman, especially one who you think has sex with a lot of men 破鞋 **ORIGIN** Short form of *whore*. 源自 whore 一詞的簡約式。

hoagie /ˈhəʊgi; *NAmE* ˈhoʊ-/ *noun* (*NAmE*) **1** a long piece of bread filled with meat, cheese and salad （在長條麪包中夾肉、乾酪、色拉等做成的）大型三明治 **2** a piece of bread used to make a hoagie（用以做大型三明治的）長條麪包

hoard /hɔːd; *NAmE* hɔːrd/ *noun, verb*

■ ***noun*** **~ (of sth)** a collection of money, food, valuable objects, etc., especially one that sb keeps in a secret place so that other people will not find or steal it （錢、食物、貴重物品等的）貯存，聚藏；（尤指）秘藏

■ ***verb*** [I, T] **~ (sth)** to collect and keep large amounts of food, money, etc., especially secretly 貯藏；囤積；（尤指）秘藏 ▸ **hoard·er** *noun*

hoard·ing /ˈhɔːdɪŋ; *NAmE* ˈhɔːrd-/ *noun* **1** (*BrE*) (also **bill·board** *NAmE, BrE*) [C] a large board on the outside of a building or at the side of the road, used for putting advertisements on 大幅廣告牌 ➲ VISUAL VOCAB pages V2, V3 **2** [C] (*BrE*) a temporary fence made of boards that is placed around an area of land until a building has been built （建築工地用木板搭起的）臨時圍欄 **3** [U] the act of hoarding things 貯存；聚藏；（尤指）秘藏

hoar frost /ˈhɔː frɒst; *NAmE* ˈhɔːr frɔːst/ *noun* [U] a layer of small pieces of ice that look like white needles and that form on surfaces outside when temperatures are very low 霜；冰霜

hoarse /hɔːs; *NAmE* hɔːrs/ *adj.* (of a person or voice 人或嗓音) sounding rough and unpleasant, especially because of a sore throat 嘶啞的；沙啞的：*He shouted himself hoarse.* 他把嗓子喊啞了。◇ *a* ***hoarse cough/cry/scream*** 粗啞的咳嗽；嘶啞的哭聲 / 尖叫聲 ▸ **hoarse·ly** *adv.* **hoarse·ness** *noun* [U]

hoary /ˈhɔːri/ *adj.* [usually before noun] **1** (*old-fashioned*) very old and well known and therefore no longer interesting 陳腐的；老掉牙的；陳舊的：*a hoary old joke* 老掉牙的笑話 **2** (*literary*) (especially of hair 尤指頭髮) grey or white because a person is old（因年老）灰白的，花白的

hoax /həʊks; *NAmE* hoʊks/ *noun, verb*

■ ***noun*** an act intended to make sb believe sth that is not true, especially sth unpleasant 騙局；惡作劇：*a bomb hoax* 炸彈騙局 ◇ *hoax calls* 惡作劇的電話

■ ***verb* ~ sb** to trick sb by making them believe sth that is not true, especially sth unpleasant 作弄；欺騙 ▸ **hoax·er** *noun*

H

hob /hɒb; *NAmE* hɑːb/ *noun* **1** (*BrE*) (*NAmE* **stove·top**) the top part of a cooker where food is cooked in pans; a similar surface that is built into a kitchen unit and is separate from the oven 爐盤；爐頭：*an electric/a gas hob* 電爐 / 煤氣爐爐盤 ➲ VISUAL VOCAB page V25 **2** a metal shelf at the side of a fire, used in the past for heating pans, etc. on（舊時放在爐側用於加熱鍋等的）火爐擱架，壁爐擱架

hob·ble /ˈhɒbl; *NAmE* ˈhɑːbl/ *verb* **1** [I] (**+ adv./prep.**) to walk with difficulty, especially because your feet or legs hurt 蹣跚；跛行 SYN **limp**：*The old man hobbled across the road.* 老人一瘸一拐地穿過馬路。 **2** [T] **~ sth** to tie together two legs of a horse or other animal in order to stop it from running away 捆綁（馬等的）兩腿（以防其走失） **3** [T] **~ sth** to make it more difficult for sb to do sth or for sth to happen 阻止；妨礙

hobby 0‑π /ˈhɒbi; *NAmE* ˈhɑːbi/ *noun* (*pl.* **-ies**) an activity that you do for pleasure when you are not working 業餘愛好：*Her hobbies include swimming and gardening.* 她愛好游泳和園藝。◇ *I only play jazz as a hobby.* 我彈奏爵士樂只是一種業餘愛好。 ➲ SYNONYMS at INTEREST ➲ VISUAL VOCAB pages V40, V41

ˈhobby horse *noun* **1** (sometimes *disapproving*) a subject that sb feels strongly about and likes to talk about 熱衷談論的話題：*to* ***get on your hobby horse*** (= talk about your favourite subject) 談論自己喜愛的話題 **2** a toy made from a long stick that has a horse's head at one end. Children pretend to ride on it. 馬頭長桿玩具；竹馬

hob·by·ist /ˈhɒbiɪst; *NAmE* ˈhɑːb-/ *noun* (*formal*) a person who is very interested in a particular hobby（業餘）愛好者

hob·gob·lin /hɒbˈɡɒblɪn; ˈhɒbɡɒblɪn; *NAmE* ˈhɑːbɡɑːb-/ *noun* (in stories) a small ugly creature that likes to trick people or cause trouble（傳說中的）淘氣的小妖精

hob·nail boot /ˌhɒbneɪl ˈbuːt; *NAmE* ˌhɑːb-/ (also **hob·nailed boot** /-neɪld/) *noun* [usually pl.] a heavy shoe whose SOLE is attached to the upper part with short heavy nails 平頭釘靴子

hob·nob /ˈhɒbnɒb; *NAmE* ˈhɑːbnɑːb/ *verb* (**-bb-**) [I] **~ (with sb)** (*informal*) to spend a lot of time with sb, especially sb who is rich and/or famous（尤指同有錢有名望的人）過從甚密，親近；巴結

hobo /ˈhəʊbəʊ; *NAmE* ˈhoʊboʊ/ *noun* (*pl.* **-os**) (*old-fashioned, especially NAmE*) **1** a person who travels from place to place looking for work, especially on farms 流浪的季節工人；（尤指農場）季節工人，零工 **2** = TRAMP *n.* (1)

Hob·son's choice /ˌhɒbsnz ˈtʃɔɪs; *NAmE* ˌhɑːb-/ *noun* [U] a situation in which sb has no choice because if they do not accept what is offered, they will get nothing 無選擇餘地的局面；不得已的選擇 ORIGIN From Tobias Hobson, a man who hired out horses in the 17th century. He gave his customers the choice of the horse nearest the stable door or none at all. 源自 17 世紀做馬匹出租生意的托拜厄斯 • 霍布森。他根本不容主顧選擇，只讓其租離廄門最近的馬。

hock /hɒk; *NAmE* hɑːk/ *noun, verb*

■ ***noun* 1** [C] the middle joint of an animal's back leg（動物後腿的）跗關節 **2** [U, C] (*BrE*) a German white wine 萊茵白葡萄酒 **3** [U, C] (*especially NAmE*) = KNUCKLE (2) **4** [U] (*informal*) if sth that you own is in **hock**, you have exchanged it for money but hope to buy it back later 典當；抵押

IDM **be in ˈhock (to sb)** to owe sb sth 欠（某人某物）：*I'm in hock to the bank for £6 000.* 我欠銀行 6 000 英鎊。

■ ***verb* ~ sth** (*informal*) to leave a valuable object with sb in exchange for money that you borrow 典當；抵押 SYN **pawn**

hockey /ˈhɒki; *NAmE* ˈhɑːki/ *noun* [U] **1** (*BrE*) (*NAmE* **ˈfield hockey**) a game played on a field by two teams of 11 players, with curved sticks and a small hard ball. Teams try to hit the ball into the other team's goal. 曲棍球：*to play hockey* 打曲棍球 ◇ ***a hockey stick/player/team*** 曲棍球球棍 / 球員 / 球隊 **2** (*NAmE*) (*BrE* **ˈice hockey**) a game played on ice, in which players use long sticks to hit a hard rubber disc (called a PUCK) into the other team's goal 冰球運動；冰上曲棍球 ➲ VISUAL VOCAB page V44

hocus-pocus /ˌhəʊkəs ˈpəʊkəs; *NAmE* ˌhoʊkəs ˈpoʊkəs/ *noun* [U] language or behaviour that is nonsense and is intended to hide the truth from people 騙人的鬼話；花招；騙術

hod /hɒd; *NAmE* hɑːd/ *noun* an open box attached to a pole, used by building workers for carrying bricks on the shoulder（建築工人扛磚用的長柄）磚斗

hodge·podge /ˈhɒdʒpɒdʒ; *NAmE* ˈhɑːdʒpɑːdʒ/ *noun* [sing.] (*NAmE*) = HOTCHPOTCH

Hodg·kin's dis·ease /ˈhɒdʒkɪnz dɪziːz; *NAmE* ˈhɑːdʒ-/ *noun* [U] a serious disease of the LYMPH NODES, LIVER and SPLEEN 霍奇金氏病；淋巴網狀細胞瘤

hoe /həʊ; *NAmE* hoʊ/ *noun, verb*

■ ***noun*** a garden tool with a long handle and a blade, used for breaking up soil and removing WEEDS (= plants growing where they are not wanted) 鋤頭 ➲ VISUAL VOCAB page V19

■ ***verb*** (**hoe·ing**, **hoed**, **hoed**) [T, I] **~ (sth)** to break up soil, remove plants, etc. with a hoe 用鋤頭鋤地（或除草）：*to hoe the flower beds* 用鋤頭給花壇除草鬆土

PHR V **hoe ˈin** (*AustralE, NZE, informal*) to eat with enthusiasm 痛快地吃

hoe·down /ˈhəʊdaʊn; *NAmE* ˈhoʊ-/ *noun* (*NAmE*) **1** a social occasion when lively dances are performed 熱烈的民間舞舞會 **2** a lively dance 熱烈的民間舞蹈

hog /hɒɡ; *NAmE* hɔːɡ; hɑːɡ/ *noun, verb*

■ ***noun* 1** (*especially NAmE*) a pig, especially one that is kept and made fat for eating（尤指餵肥供食用的）豬 **2** (*BrE*) a male pig that has been CASTRATED (= had part of its sex organs removed) and is kept for its meat（供食用的）閹公豬 ➲ compare BOAR (2), SOW² ➲ see also ROAD HOG, WARTHOG

IDM **go the whole ˈhog** (*informal*) to do sth thoroughly or completely 徹底地做某事；貫徹到底

■ ***verb*** (**-gg-**) **~ sth** (*informal*) to use or keep most of sth yourself and stop others from using or having it 多佔；獨佔：*to hog the road* (= to drive so that other vehicles cannot pass) 佔着馬路中間開車 ◇ *to hog the bathroom* (= to spend a long time in it so that others cannot use it) 長時間佔用浴室

Hog·ma·nay /ˈhɒɡməneɪ; ˌhɒɡməˈneɪ; *NAmE* hɑːɡ-/ *noun* [U] (in Scotland) New Year's Eve (31 December) and the celebrations that happen on that day（蘇格蘭 12 月 31 日的）除夕以及除夕歡慶活動

hog·wash /ˈhɒɡwɒʃ; *NAmE* ˈhɔːɡwɑːʃ; ˈhɑːɡ-; -wɔːʃ/ *noun* [U] (*informal*) an idea, argument, etc. that you think is stupid 愚蠢的想法（或論點等）；胡言亂語

ho ho /ˌhəʊ ˈhəʊ; *NAmE* ˌhoʊ ˈhoʊ/ *exclamation* **1** used to show the sound of a deep laugh（表示深沉的笑聲） **2** used to show surprise（表示驚訝）：*Ho, ho! What have we here?* 嗬嗬！這是什麼？

ho-hum /ˌhəʊ ˈhʌm; *NAmE* ˌhoʊ/ *exclamation* used to show that you are bored（表示厭倦）

hoick /hɔɪk/ *verb* **~ sth (+ adv./prep.)** (*BrE, informal*) to lift or pull sth in a particular direction, especially with a quick sudden movement 猛提；猛拉 SYN **jerk**

the hoi pol·loi /ˌhɔɪ pəˈlɔɪ/ *noun* [pl.] (*disapproving* or *humorous*) an insulting word for ordinary people 尋常百姓；草民；烏合之眾

hoist /hɔɪst/ *verb, noun*

■ ***verb*** **~ sth (+ adv./prep.)** to raise or pull sth up to a higher position, often using ropes or special equipment 吊起；提升；拉高：*He hoisted himself onto a high stool.* 他抬身坐上了一張高凳子。◇ *The cargo was hoisted aboard by crane.* 貨物由起重機吊上了船。◇ *to* ***hoist a flag/sail*** 升旗；升帆

IDM **be hoist/hoisted by/with your own peˈtard** to be hurt or to have problems as a result of your own plans to hurt or trick others 害人反害己；自食其果

■ ***noun*** a piece of equipment used for lifting heavy things, or for lifting people who cannot stand or walk 起重機；吊車；（殘疾人用）升降機

hoity-toity /ˌhɔɪti ˈtɔɪti/ *adj.* (*old-fashioned, informal*) behaving in a way that suggests that you think you are more important than other people 大模大樣的；自命不凡的

hokey /ˈhəʊki; *NAmE* ˈhoʊki/ *adj.* (*NAmE, informal*) expressing emotions in a way that seems exaggerated or silly 矯揉造作的；誇張可笑的

hoki /ˈhəʊki; *NAmE* ˈhoʊki/ *noun* (*pl.* **hoki**) a fish found in the seas off New Zealand 福氣魚（見於新西蘭附近海域）

hokum /ˈhəʊkəm; *NAmE* ˈhoʊ-/ *noun* [U] (*informal, especially NAmE*) **1** a film/movie, play, etc. that is not realistic and has no artistic qualities 做作的電影（或戲劇等）**2** an idea, argument, etc. that you think is stupid 愚蠢的想法（或論點等）：*What a bunch of hokum!* 真是一派胡言！

hold 🔑 /həʊld; *NAmE* hoʊld/ *verb, noun*

■ ***verb*** (**held, held** /held/)

▸ **IN HAND/ARMS** 手；雙臂 **1** 🔑 [T] **~ sb/sth (+ adv./prep.)** to carry sth; to have sb/sth in your hand, arms, etc. 拿着；抓住；抱住；托住；夾着：*She was holding a large box.* 她提着一隻大箱子。◇ *I held the mouse by its tail.* 我抓着耗子的尾巴倒提起來。◇ *The girl held her father's hand tightly.* 女孩緊緊地拉着她父親的手。◇ *He was holding the baby in his arms.* 他抱着嬰兒。◇ *The winning captain held the trophy in the air.* 獲勝隊的隊長把獎杯高舉到空中。◇ *We were* ***holding hands*** (= holding each other's hands). 我們手拉着手。◇ *The lovers held each other close.* 這對戀人緊緊相擁着。**2** 🔑 [T] **~ sth** to put your hand on part of your body, usually because it hurts 抱住，捂住，按住（受傷的身體部位等）：*She groaned and held her head.* 她呻吟一聲，用手抱住頭。

▸ **IN POSITION** 位置 **3** 🔑 [T] to keep sb/sth in a particular position 使保持（在某位置）：**~ sth (+ adv./prep.)** *Hold your head up.* 抬起頭來。◇ *Hold this position for a count of 10.* 保持這個姿勢別動，數到 10。◇ *The wood is held in position by a clamp.* 這木頭用夾鉗固定住了。◇ *I had to hold my stomach in* (= pull the muscles flat) *to zip up my jeans.* 我得把肚皮收緊才能拉上牛仔褲的拉鏈。◇ **~ sth + adj.** *I'll hold the door open for you.* 我會把門給你開着的。

▸ **SUPPORT** 支撐 **4** 🔑 [T] **~ sb/sth** to support the weight of sb/sth 支撐…的重量：*I don't think that branch will hold your weight.* 我覺得那根樹枝撐不住你的重量。

▸ **CONTAIN** 容納 **5** 🔑 [T] **~ sb/sth** to have enough space for sth/sb; to contain sth/sb 容納；包含：*This barrel holds 25 litres.* 這隻桶能盛 25 升。◇ *The plane holds about 300 passengers.* 這架飛機可容納大約 300 名乘客。

▸ **SB PRISONER** 監禁 **6** 🔑 [T] to keep sb and not allow them to leave 監禁；拘留：**~ sb** *Police are holding two men in connection with last Thursday's bank raid.* 警方拘留了兩名與上星期四的銀行搶劫案有關的男子。◇ **~ sb + noun** *He was* ***held prisoner*** *for two years.* 他被囚禁了兩年。

▸ **CONTROL** 控制 **7** [T] **~ sth** to defend sth against attack; to have control of sth 守衛；控制：*The rebels held the radio station.* 叛亂者佔據了電台。

▸ **REMAIN** 保持 **8** [I] to remain strong and safe or in position 承受住；堅持住；保持原位：*They were afraid the dam wouldn't hold.* 他們擔心大壩會承受不住。**9** [I] to remain the same 保持不變：*How long will the fine weather hold?* 好天氣會持續多久？◇ *If their luck holds, they could still win the championship.* 如果他們的好運持續下去，他們仍能贏得冠軍。

▸ **KEEP** 使持續 **10** 🔑 [T] **~ sth** to keep sb's attention or interest 使（注意力或興趣）持續不減；吸引住：*There wasn't much in the museum to hold my attention.* 博物館中沒有很多讓我感興趣的東西。**11** [T] **~ sth (at sth)** to keep sth at the same level, rate, speed, etc. 使保持同樣程度（或比率、速度等）：*Hold your speed at 70.* 保持 70 邁的速度。**12** 🔑 [T] **~ sth** to keep sth so that it can be used later 保存；存貯：*records held on computer* 存在計算機中的記錄 ◇ *Our solicitor holds our wills.* 律師保存着我們的遺囑。◇ *We can hold your reservation for three days.* 您的預訂我們可以保留三天。

▸ **OWN** 擁有 **13** 🔑 [T] **~ sth** (rather *formal*) to own or have sth 擁有；持有：*Employees hold 30% of the shares.* 雇員持有 30% 的股份。

▸ **JOB** 工作 **14** 🔑 [T] **~ sth** to have a particular job or position 擔任；任職：*How long has he held office?* 他任職有多久了？

▸ **RECORD/TITLE** 紀錄；稱號 **15** 🔑 [T] **~ sth** to have sth you have gained or achieved 獲得；贏得：*Who holds the world record for the long jump?* 跳遠世界紀錄的保持者是誰？◇ *She held the title of world champion for three years.* 她保持了三年的世界冠軍頭銜。

▸ **OPINION** 意見 **16** [T] to have a belief or an opinion about sb/sth 懷有，持有（信念、意見）：**~ sth** *He holds strange views on education.* 他對教育的看法不同尋常。◇ **~ sb/sth + adv./prep./adj.** *She is* ***held in high regard*** *by her students* (= they have a high opinion of her). 學生對她評價很高。◇ *firmly-held beliefs* 堅定的信念 **17** [T] (*formal*) to consider that sth is true 認為；相信：**~ that …** *I still hold that the government's economic policies are mistaken.* 我仍然認為政府的經濟政策是錯誤的。◇ **~ sb/sth + adj.** *Parents will be* ***held responsible*** *for their children's behaviour.* 父母將要對孩子的行為負責。◇ **be held to be sth** *These vases are held to be the finest examples of Greek art.* 這些花瓶被視為希臘藝術的最佳典範。

▸ **MEETING** 會議 **18** 🔑 [T, usually passive] **~ sth** to have a meeting, competition, conversation, etc. 召開；舉行；進行：*The meeting will be held in the community centre.* 會議將在社區活動中心舉行。◇ *It's impossible to hold a conversation with all this noise.* 噪音這麼大，根本沒法進行交談。

▸ **ROAD/COURSE** 道路；路線 **19** [T] **~ the road** (of a vehicle 機動車) to be in close contact with the road and easy to control, especially when driven fast（尤指高速行駛時）平穩行駛 **20** [T] **~ a course** (of a ship or an aircraft 船或飛機) to continue to move in a particular direction 保持航線

▸ **IN MUSIC** 音樂 **21** [T] **~ sth** to make a note continue for a particular time 延長，繼續唱（某音符）

▸ **ON TELEPHONE** 電話 **22** [I, T] to wait until you can speak to the person you have telephoned（打電話時）等待，不掛斷：*That extension is busy right now. Can you hold?* 分機現在佔線。您能等一會嗎？◇ **~ the line** *She asked me to hold the line.* 她要我別掛斷電話。

▸ **STOP** 停止 **23** [T] **~ sth** used to tell sb to stop doing sth or not to do sth 停下；不要做：*Hold your fire!* (= don't shoot) 別開槍！◇ *Hold the front page!* (= don't print it until a particular piece of news is available) 把頭版給我預留着！◇ (*NAmE, informal*) *Give me a hot dog, but hold the* (= don't give me any) *mustard.* 給我來份熱狗，但別加芥末。

IDM Most idioms containing **hold** are at the entries for the nouns and adjectives in the idioms, for example **hold the fort** is at **fort**. 大多數含 hold 的習語，都可在該等習語中的名詞及形容詞相關詞條找到，如 hold the fort 在詞條 fort 下。**hold ˈgood** to be true 正確；適用：*The same argument does not hold good in every case.* 同樣的論點並非在所有的情況下都適用。**ˈhold it** (*informal*) used to ask sb to wait, or not to move 稍等；別動：

Hold it a second—I don't think everyone's arrived yet. 請稍候，我想人還沒有到齊。 **there is no 'holding sb** a person cannot be prevented from doing sth 阻攔不住某人：*Once she gets on to the subject of politics there's no holding her.* 她一談起政治就滔滔不絕。

PHR V **,hold sth a'gainst sb** to allow sth that sb has done to make you have a lower opinion of them 因某人的所為而對其評價低：*I admit I made a mistake—but don't hold it against me.* 我承認我做錯了，但別因此而記恨我。

,hold sb/sth↔'back **1** to prevent sb/sth from moving forward or crossing sth 攔阻；阻擋：*The police were unable to hold back the crowd.* 警察阻攔不住人群。 **2** to prevent the progress or development of sb/sth 妨礙進展：*Do you think that mixed-ability classes hold back the better students?* 你認為把能力參差的學生混在一班會妨礙高水平學生進步嗎？ **,hold sth↔'back** **1** to not tell sb sth they want or need to know 不向（某人）透露情況；隱瞞：*to hold back information* 隱瞞信息 **2** to stop yourself from expressing how you really feel 抑制，控制（感情等）；不露聲色：*She just managed to hold back her anger.* 她勉強壓住了自己的怒火。◇ *He bravely held back his tears.* 他勇敢地沒讓眼淚流出來。 **,hold 'back (from doing sth)** | **,hold sb 'back (from doing sth)** to hesitate to act or speak （使）猶豫，躊躇：*She held back, not knowing how to break the terrible news.* 她躊躇着，不知如何說出這一可怕的消息。◇ *I wanted to tell him the truth, but something held me back.* 我本想告訴他真實情況，但又開不了口。

,hold sb↔'down **1** to prevent sb from moving, using force 按住某人：*It took three men to hold him down.* 三個人才把他制伏了。 **2** to prevent sb from having their freedom or rights 剝奪某人的自由（或權利）：*The people are held down by a repressive regime.* 人民受到了專制政權的壓迫。 **,hold sth↔'down** **1** to keep sth at a low level 使保持低水平：*The rate of inflation must be held down.* 通貨膨脹率必須控制在低水平。 **2** [no passive] to keep a job for some time 保住（工作、職位）：*He was unable to hold down a job after his breakdown.* 他精神崩潰以後就沒能保住工作。 **3** [no passive] (*NAmE, informal*) to limit sth, especially a noise 限制（尤指噪音）：*Hold it down, will you? I'm trying to sleep!* 小點聲行嗎？我要睡覺！

,hold 'forth to speak for a long time about sth in a way that other people might find boring 喋喋不休；大發議論

,hold sth↔'in to not express how you really feel 克制，忍住（真實感情）：*to hold in your feelings/anger* 不流露感情；忍住怒火 OPP **let sth out**

,hold 'off **1** (of rain or a storm 雨或風暴) to not start 不開始；延遲：*The rain held off just long enough for us to have our picnic.* 雨還好，等到我們用完野餐才下起來。 **2** to not do sth immediately 推遲：*We could get a new computer now or hold off until prices are lower.* 我們現在就可以買新計算機，不然就等到降價再說。◇ **~ doing sth** *Could you hold off making your decision for a few days?* 你能推遲幾天再做決定嗎？ **,hold sb/sth↔'off** to stop sb/sth defeating you 戰勝；克服：*She held off all the last-minute challengers and won the race in a new record time.* 她最後一刻甩掉了所有對手，以新的紀錄贏得了賽跑冠軍。

,hold 'on **1** (*informal*) used to tell sb to wait or stop 等着；停住 SYN **wait**：*Hold on a minute while I get my breath back.* 稍等一下，讓我喘口氣。◇ *Hold on! This isn't the right road.* 等一下！這條路不對。 **2** to survive in a difficult or dangerous situation （在困境或危險中）堅持住，挺住：*They managed to hold on until help arrived.* 他們勉強堅持到救援到來。 **3** (*informal*) used on the telephone to ask sb to wait until they can talk to the person they want （電話用語）別掛斷，等一下：*Can you hold on? I'll see if he's here.* 等一下行嗎？我去看看他在不在。 **,hold sth↔'on** to keep sth in position 固定：*These nuts and bolts hold the wheels on.* 這些螺母和螺栓把輪子固定住了。◇ *The knob is only held on by sticky tape.* 這個旋鈕只是用膠帶粘住的。 **,hold 'on (to sth/sb)** | **,hold 'on to sth/sb** [no passive] to keep holding sth/sb 抓緊；不放開：*Hold on and don't let go until I say so.* 握緊，等我讓你鬆手時再鬆開。◇ *He held on to the back of the chair to stop himself from falling.* 他扶住椅子後背，以免摔倒。 ➲ SYNONYMS at HOLD **,hold 'on to sth** | **,hold 'onto sth** **1** to keep sth that is an advantage for you; to not give or sell sth to sb else 保住（優勢）；不送（或不賣）某物：*You should hold on to your oil shares.* 你應該繼續保留住你的石油股份。◇ *She took an early lead in the race and held on to it for nine laps.* 賽跑一開始她便衝到了前面，並一直保持領先了九圈。 **2** to keep sth for sb else or for longer than usual （替別人或更長時間地）保存某物：*I'll hold on to your mail for you until you get back.* 你回來之前我將一直替你保管郵件。

,hold 'out **1** to last, especially in a difficult situation 維持；堅持：*We can stay here for as long as our supplies hold out.* 我們可以在這裏一直待到我們的貯備品用完。 **2** to resist or survive in a dangerous or difficult situation 抵抗；幸存：*The rebels held out in the mountains for several years.* 反叛分子在山區頑抗了幾年。 **,hold 'out sth** to offer a chance, hope or possibility of sth 提供機會；給予希望；使有可能：*Doctors hold out little hope of her recovering.* 醫生對她的痊癒不抱很大的希望。 **,hold sth↔'out** to put your hand or arms, or sth in your hand, towards sb, especially to give or offer sth 伸出手（或胳膊）；遞出東西：*I held out my hand to steady her.* 我伸出手扶住她。◇ *He held out the keys and I took them.* 他伸手把鑰匙遞過來，我接了。 **,hold 'out for sth** [no passive] to cause a delay in reaching an agreement because you hope you will gain sth （為得到利益）拖延達成協議：*The union negotiators are holding out for a more generous pay settlement.* 工會談判代表拖延着，以期達成較優厚的薪酬協議。 **,hold 'out on sb** (*informal*) to refuse to tell or give sb sth 拒絕告訴（或給予）某人

,hold sth↔'over [usually passive] **1** to not deal with sth immediately; to leave sth to be dealt with later 擱置；推遲 SYN **postpone**：*The matter was held over until the next meeting.* 這件事被推遲到下次會議。 **2** to show a film/movie, play, etc. for longer than planned 延長（電影、戲劇等）的上演期：*The movie proved so popular it was held over for another week.* 這部電影十分受歡迎，因此又繼續上演了一週。 **,hold sth 'over sb** to use knowledge that you have about sb to threaten them or make them do what you want 以某事要挾（或威逼）某人

'hold sb to sth **1** to make sb keep a promise 要求某人遵守諾言 **2** to stop an opposing team scoring more points, etc. than you 壓住對方；不讓對方的（得分等）超過己方：*The league leaders were held to a 0–0 draw.* 在聯賽中領先的隊伍打成了 0:0 的平局。

,hold to'gether | **,hold sth↔to'gether** **1** to remain, or to keep sth, united （使）保持團結：*A political party should hold together.* 一個政黨應當團結一致。◇ *It's the mother who usually holds the family together.* 使全家人凝聚在一起的通常是母親。 **2** (of an argument, a theory or a story 論點、理論或故事) to be logical or CONSISTENT 合乎邏輯；連貫：*Their case doesn't hold together when you look at the evidence.* 你看一下證據就知道他們的論點前後不一致。 ➲ compare HANG TOGETHER at HANG *v.* **3** if a machine or an object **holds together** or sth **holds it together**, the different parts stay together so that it does not break （機器、物品）完好無損

,hold 'up to remain strong and working effectively 支持住；承受住；支撐得住：*She's holding up well under the pressure.* 她承受住了壓力。 **,hold sb/sth↔'up** [often passive] **1** to support sb/sth and stop them from falling 攙扶；支撐；舉起；抬起 **2** to delay or block the movement or progress of sb/sth 延遲；阻礙：*An accident is holding up traffic.* 一場事故造成了交通阻塞。◇ *My application was held up by the postal strike.* 我的申請因郵政部門罷工而耽擱了。 ➲ related noun HOLD-UP (1) **3** to use or present sb/sth as an example 舉出（例子）；提出（作為榜樣）：*She's always holding up her children as models of good behaviour.* 她總是舉例說自己的孩子表現如何好。◇ *His ideas were held up to ridicule.* 他的想法被當成了笑料。 **,hold up 'sth** to steal from a bank, shop/store, etc. using a gun 持槍搶劫（銀行、商店等） ➲ related noun HOLD-UP (2)

'hold with sth [no passive] (used in negative sentences or in questions 用於否定句或疑問句) to agree with sth

同意；贊成 SYN **approve of**： *I don't hold with the use of force.* 我不贊成使用武力。◇ **~ doing sth** *They don't hold with letting children watch as much TV as they want.* 他們不贊成讓孩子隨心所欲地看太多電視。

■ ***noun***

▸ **WITH HAND 用手** **1** [sing., U] the action of holding sb/sth; the way you are holding sb/sth 抓；握；拿；支撐 SYN **grip**： *His hold on her arm tightened.* 他把她的胳膊抓得更緊了。◇ *She tried to **keep hold of** the child's hand.* 她盡力拉住那孩子的手不放。◇ *Make sure you've got a steady hold on the camera.* 一定要拿穩相機。

▸ **IN SPORT 體育運動** **2** [C] a particular way of holding sb, especially in a sport such as WRESTLING or in a fight 持；握；抓；抱；（尤指摔跤、拳擊中的）擒拿法： *The wrestler put his opponent into a head hold.* 那位摔跤手給對手來了個頭部擒拿。

▸ **POWER/CONTROL 權力；控制** **3** [sing.] **~ (on/over sb/sth)** influence, power or control over sb/sth 影響；左右力；控制：*What she knew about his past gave her a hold over him.* 她知道他的過去，所以能夠控制他。◇ *He struggled to get a hold of his anger.* 他竭力壓制自己的怒火。➲ see also STRANGLEHOLD

▸ **IN CLIMBING 攀登** **4** [C] a place where you can put your hands or feet when climbing 支撐點（可手攀或腳踏的地方）➲ see also FOOTHOLD, HANDHOLD, TOEHOLD

▸ **ON SHIP/PLANE 船；飛機** **5** [C] the part of a ship or plane where the goods being carried are stored 貨艙 ➲ **VISUAL VOCAB** page V53

IDM **catch, get, grab, take, etc. (a) 'hold of sb/sth** to have or take sb/sth in your hands 抓住；拿着；握着；握住： *He caught hold of her wrists so she couldn't get away.* 他抓住她的手腕，使她無法掙脫。◇ *Lee got hold of the dog by its collar.* 李拉住了狗的項圈。◇ *Quick, grab a hold of that rope.* 快，抓住那條繩子。◇ *Gently, she took hold of the door handle and turned it.* 她輕輕地握住門把手扭動了它。 **get 'hold of sb** to contact or find sb 和某人聯繫；找到某人： *Where have you been? I've been trying to get hold of you all day.* 你去哪了？我一整天都在找你。 **get 'hold of sth** **1** to find sth that you want or need 找到所需要的東西： *I need to get hold of Tom's address.* 我需要找到湯姆的地址。◇ *It's almost impossible to get hold of tickets for the final.* 幾乎不可能搞到決賽的門票。 **2** to learn or understand sth 學會；理解 **,no ,holds 'barred** with no rules or limits on what sb is allowed to do 不加約束；沒有限制 **on 'hold** **1** delayed until a later time or date 推遲；中斷： *She **put** her career **on hold** to have a baby.* 她中斷了事業以便生孩子。◇ *The project is on hold until more money is available.* 這項工程暫停，等到有更多的資金時再進行。 **2** if a person on the telephone is put **on hold**, they have to wait until the person that they want to talk to is free （電話接通後）等某人接電話 **take (a) 'hold** to begin to have complete control over sb/sth; to become very strong 開始完全控制；變得十分強大： *Panic took hold of him and he couldn't move.* 他突然驚慌得動彈不得。◇ *They got out of the house just before the flames took hold.* 他們就在大火吞噬房子之前逃了出來。◇ *It is best to treat the disease early before it takes a hold.* 最好還是病向淺中醫。➲ more at WRONG *adj.*

hold·all /'həʊldɔːl; *NAmE* 'hoʊ-/ (*BrE*) (*NAmE* **'duffel bag**) *noun* a large bag made of strong cloth or soft leather, used when you are travelling for carrying clothes, etc. 大旅行袋（用帆布或軟皮製造）➲ **VISUAL VOCAB** page V64

hold·er /'həʊldə(r); *NAmE* 'hoʊ-/ *noun* (often in compounds 常構成複合詞) **1** a person who has or owns the thing mentioned 持有者；擁有者： *a licence holder* 執照持有人◇ *a season ticket holder* 有季票的人◇ *the current holder of the world record* 目前的世界紀錄保持者◇ *holders of high office* 高級官員◇ *the holder of a French passport* 持有法國護照者 ➲ see also RECORD HOLDER, TITLE-HOLDER **2** a thing that holds the object mentioned 支托（或握持）…之物： *a pen holder* 筆筒 ➲ **VISUAL VOCAB** pages V22, V25, V69 ➲ see also CIGARETTE HOLDER

hold·ing /'həʊldɪŋ; *NAmE* 'hoʊ-/ *noun* **1 ~ (in sth)** a number of shares that sb has in a company 股份： *She has a 40% holding in the company.* 她持有公司 40% 的股份。➲ see also FUNDHOLDING **2** an amount of property that is owned by a person, museum, library, etc. 私有財產；（博物館、圖書館等的）館藏： *one of the most important private holdings of Indian art* 印度藝術最重大的私人館藏之一。 **3** a piece of land that is rented by sb and used for farming 租種的土地 ➲ see also SMALL-HOLDING

'holding company *noun* a company that is formed to buy shares in other companies which it then controls 控股公司

'holding operation *noun* a course of action that is taken so that a particular situation stays the same or does not become any worse 維持現狀的行動；使局勢不致惡化的做法

Synonyms 同義詞辨析

hold

hold on • cling • clutch • grip • grasp • clasp • hang on

These words all mean to have sb/sth in your hands or arms. 以上各詞均表示抓住、抱住。

hold to have sb/sth in your hand or arms 指抓住、抱住、托住、夾住： *She was holding a large box.* 她提着一隻大箱子。◇ *I held the baby gently in my arms.* 我把嬰兒輕輕地抱在懷裏。

hold on (to sb/sth) to continue to hold sb/sth; to put your hand on sb/sth and not take your hand away 指抓緊、不放開： *Hold on and don't let go until I say so.* 握緊，我讓你鬆手時才鬆開。

cling to hold on to sb/sth tightly, especially with your whole body 尤指用身體緊抱、緊握、抓緊：*Survivors **clung to** pieces of floating debris.* 生還者緊緊抱住一塊塊漂浮在水面上的殘骸。

clutch to hold sb/sth tightly, especially in your hand; to take hold of sth suddenly 尤指用手抓緊、緊握、抱緊、突然抓住： *She stood there, the flowers still clutched in her hand.* 她站在那裏，手裏仍然緊握着花束。◇ *He felt himself slipping and **clutched at** a branch.* 他感到自己滑了一下便一把抓住一根樹枝。

grip to hold on to sth very tightly with your hand 指用手緊握、緊抓： *Grip the rope as tightly as you can.* 盡可能緊緊抓住繩子。

grasp to take hold of sth firmly 指抓緊、抓牢： *He grasped my hand and shook it warmly.* 他熱情地抓着我的手握了起來。 NOTE The object of **grasp** is often sb's *hand* or *wrist*. * grasp 的賓語通常為 hand 或 wrist。

clasp (*formal*) to hold sb/sth tightly in your hand or in your arms 指緊握、攥緊、抱緊：*They clasped hands* (= held each other's hands). 他們相互緊握着對方的手。◇ *She clasped the children in her arms.* 她把孩子緊緊地摟在懷裏。 NOTE The object of **clasp** is often your *hands*, sb else's *hand* or another person. * clasp 的賓語通常為 hand 或另一個人。

hang on (to sth) to hold on to sth very tightly, especially in order to support yourself or stop yourself from falling 尤指為支撐自己或防止跌倒而緊緊抓住某物： *Hang on tight. We're off!* 抓緊，我們出發了！

PATTERNS

- to hold/clutch/grip/clasp sth **in your hand/hands**
- to hold/catch/clasp sb/sth **in your arms**
- to hold/clutch/grip/grasp/clasp/hang **on to** sth
- to hold/cling/hang **on**
- to hold/clutch/clasp sb/sth **to** you
- to hold/hold on to/cling to/clutch/grip/grasp/clasp/hang on to sb/sth **tightly**
- to hold/hold on to/cling to/clutch/grip/grasp/clasp sb/sth **firmly**
- to hold/hold on to/clutch/grip/clasp/hang on to sb/sth **tight**

H

'holding pattern *noun* the route that a plane travels while it is flying above an airport waiting for permission to land 等待航線（飛機在機場上空待降時的飛行路線）

hold·over /'həʊldəʊvə(r); *NAmE* 'hoʊldoʊvər/ *noun* (*NAmE*) a person who keeps a position of power, for example sb who had a particular position in one ADMINISTRATION and who still has it in the next（在下屆政府中）留任的官員

'hold-up *noun* **1** a situation in which sth is prevented from happening for a short time 停頓；阻滯；阻礙 SYN **delay**：*What's the hold-up?* 遇到什麼障礙了？◇ *We should finish by tonight, barring hold-ups.* 倘若沒有延誤，我們應該在今晚完工。◇ (*BrE*) *Sorry I'm late. There was a hold-up on the motorway.* 抱歉，我來晚了。公路上堵車了。 **2** (also **'stick-up** especially in *NAmE*) an act of stealing from a bank, etc. using a gun 持槍搶劫

H

hole 🔑 /həʊl; *NAmE* hoʊl/ *noun, verb*

■ ***noun***

▸ HOLLOW SPACE 空的空間 **1** 🔑 [C] a hollow space in sth solid or in the surface of sth 洞；孔；坑：*He **dug** a deep **hole** in the garden.* 他在花園裏挖了個深坑。◇ *The bomb blew a huge hole in the ground.* 炸彈在地上炸了一個大坑。◇ *Water had collected in the holes in the road.* 水積聚在道路的坑窪處。

▸ OPENING 裂口 **2** 🔑 [C] a space or opening that goes all the way through sth 裂口；開口；孔眼：*to **drill/bore/punch/kick a hole** in sth* 把某物鑽／挖／衝／踢穿◇ *There were holes in the knees of his trousers.* 他褲子的膝部有破洞。◇ *The children climbed through a hole in the fence.* 孩子們從柵欄的缺口處爬了過去。◇ *a **bullet hole*** 槍眼◇ *the hole in the ozone layer* 臭氧層空洞 ➲ see also OZONE HOLE

▸ ANIMAL'S HOME 動物住處 **3** 🔑 [C] the home of a small animal 洞穴；巢穴：*a **rabbit/mouse, etc. hole*** 兔窩、老鼠洞等 ➲ compare FOXHOLE, PIGEONHOLE ➲ see also BOLT-HOLE

▸ UNPLEASANT PLACE 糟糕的地方 **4** [C, usually sing.] (*informal, disapproving*) an unpleasant place to live or be in 糟糕的住所（或處所） SYN **dump**：*I am not going to bring up my child in this hole.* 我不會在這個鬼地方養育孩子的。 ➲ see also HELLHOLE

▸ IN GOLF 高爾夫球 **5** [C] a hollow in the ground that you must get the ball into; one of the sections of a GOLF COURSE with the TEE at the beginning and the hole at the end 球洞；球座到球洞的區域：*The ball rolled into the hole and she had won.* 球滾進了洞，她贏了。◇ *an eighteen-hole golf course* 有十八個洞的高爾夫球場◇ *He liked to play a few holes after work.* 他下班後喜歡打幾杆高爾夫球。◇ *She won the first hole.* 她在第一洞時領先。 ➲ VISUAL VOCAB page V40

▸ FAULT/WEAKNESS 錯誤；缺陷 **6** [C, usually pl.] a fault or weakness in sth such as a plan, law or story（計劃、法律或報道等的）錯誤，缺陷，漏洞：*He was found not guilty because of holes in the prosecution case.* 由於起訴案情有破綻，他被判無罪。◇ *I don't believe what she says—her story is full of holes.* 我不相信她的話，她的說法漏洞百出。 ➲ see also LOOPHOLE

▸ EMPTY PLACE/POSITION 空缺的地方／位置 **7** [sing.] a place or position that needs to be filled because sb/sth is no longer there 空缺的地方（或位置）：*After his wife left, there was a gaping hole in his life.* 妻子離開後，他的人生中出現了一大片空洞。◇ *Buying the new equipment left a big hole in the company's finances.* 購買新設備給公司的財政造成了一個大洞。 HELP There are many other compounds ending in **hole**. You will find them at their place in the alphabet. 以 hole 結尾的複合詞還有很多，可在各字母中的適當位置查到。

IDM **in a 'hole** (*informal*) in a difficult situation 處於困境：*He had got himself into a hole and it was going to be difficult to get out of it.* 他使自己陷入了困境，難以擺脫。 **in the 'hole** (*NAmE, informal*) owing money 負債；欠錢；虧空 SYN **in debt**：*We start the current fiscal year $30 million in the hole.* 我們今年的財政年度一開始便負着 3 000 萬元的債。 **make a 'hole in sth** to use up a large amount of sth that you have, especially money 大量耗費（尤指錢）：*School fees can make a big hole in your savings.* 學費可以花掉一大筆的儲蓄。 ➲ more at ACE *n.*, BURN *v.*, DIG *v.*, PICK *v.*, SQUARE *adj.*

■ ***verb***

▸ MAKE A HOLE 打洞／孔 **1** [T, usually passive] **~ sth** to make a hole or holes in sth, especially a boat or ship（尤指在船上）打洞，造成破洞

▸ IN GOLF 高爾夫球 **2** [T, I] to hit a GOLF ball into the hole 擊球入洞：**~ sth** *She holed a 25 foot putt.* 她打了一個 25 英尺遠的推杆進洞。◇ **~ (out)** *She holed out from 25 feet.* 她在 25 英尺處把球推進洞中。

PHR V **,hole 'up | be ,holed 'up** (*informal*) to hide in a place 躲藏：*He'll hole up now and move again tomorrow, after dark.* 他現在將躲起來，等明天天黑以後再動身。◇ *We believe the gang are holed up in the mountains.* 我們認為那幫匪徒躲藏在山裏。

,hole-and-'corner *adj.* done in secret because you want to avoid being noticed 暗地裏的；秘密的：*a hole-and-corner wedding* 悄悄舉行的婚禮

hole-in-'one *noun* (*pl.* **holes-in-one**) an occasion in GOLF when a player hits the ball from the TEE into the hole using only one shot（高爾夫球）一杆進洞

,hole in the 'heart *noun* (*medical* 醫) a condition in which a baby is born with a problem with the wall dividing the parts of its heart, so that it does not get enough OXYGEN in its blood 先天性心膜缺損

,hole in the 'wall *noun* [sing.] (*informal*) **1** (*BrE*) = CASH MACHINE **2** (*NAmE*) a small dark shop/store or restaurant 陰暗小店（或餐館） ▸ **,hole-in-the-'wall** *adj.* [only before noun]：*hole-in-the-wall cash machines/restaurants* 自動提款機；狹小餐館

holey /'həʊli; *NAmE* 'hoʊ-/ *adj.* a **holey** piece of clothing or material has a lot of holes in it 多洞的

British/American 英式／美式英語

holiday / vacation

- You use **holiday** (or **holidays**) in *BrE* and **vacation** in *NAmE* to describe the regular periods of time when you are not at work or school, or time that you spend travelling or resting away from home. * holiday 或 holidays（英式英語）和 vacation（美式英語）均表示休息日、假日、外出休假期：*I get four weeks' holiday/vacation a year.* 我一年有四週休假。◇ *He's on holiday/vacation this week.* 他本週休假。◇ *I like to take my holiday/vacation in the winter.* 我喜歡在冬天休假。◇ *the summer holidays/vacation* 暑假
- In *NAmE* a **holiday** (or a **public holiday**) is a single day when government offices, schools, banks and businesses are closed. 在美式英語中，holiday 或 public holiday 指政府機關、學校、銀行和商業機構關門休息的公共假日：*The school will be closed Monday because it's a holiday.* 星期一是公共假日，所以學校不上課。 This is called a **bank holiday** in *BrE*. 在英式英語中，公共假日叫做 bank holiday。
- **The holidays** is used in *NAmE* to refer to the time in late December and early January that includes Christmas, Hanukkah and the New Year. 在美式英語中，the holidays 指十二月下旬至一月上旬，包括聖誕節、修殿節和新年在內的這段時間。
- **Vacation** in *BrE* is used mainly to mean one of the periods when universities are officially closed for the students. 在英式英語中，vacation 主要指大學的休假時期。

holi·day 🔑 /'hɒlədeɪ; *NAmE* 'hɑːl-; *BrE* also -di/ *noun, verb*

■ ***noun* 1** 🔑 [U] (also **holidays** [pl.]) (both *BrE*) (*NAmE* **vac·ation**) a period of time when you are not at work or school 假期：*the **school/summer/Christmas, etc. holidays*** 學校假期、暑假、聖誕節等假期◇ *I'm afraid Mr Walsh is away **on holiday** this week.* 很抱歉，沃爾什先生這個星期休假去了。◇ *The package includes 20 days'* *paid holiday a year.* 這一攬子福利包括每年 20 天的帶薪假。◇ ***holiday pay*** 假日薪金 ◇ *a* ***holiday job*** (= done by students during the school holidays)（學生在學校放假時做的）假期工作 **2** [C] (*BrE*) (*NAmE* **vac·ation**) a period of time spent travelling or resting away from home（外出旅遊或休閒的）度假：*a* ***camping/skiing/walking, etc. holiday*** 露營、滑雪、遠足等度假 ◇ *a* ***family holiday*** 合家度假 ◇ *a* ***foreign holiday*** 國外度假 ◇ *a* ***holiday cottage/home/resort*** 度假別墅 / 住所 / 勝地 ◇ *the holiday industry* 度假服務業 ◇ *Where are you going* ***for your holidays*** *this year?* 你今年要到哪裏休假？◇ *They met while* ***on holiday*** *in Greece.* 他們是在希臘度假時認識的。◇ *We* ***went on holiday*** *together last summer.* 去年夏天我們一起去度假了。➲ COLLOCATIONS at TRAVEL ➲ see also BUSMAN'S HOLIDAY, PACKAGE TOUR **3** [C] a day when most people do not go to work or school, especially because of a religious or national celebration 假日，節日（尤指宗教節日或國家慶典日）：*a national holiday* 全國假日 ◇ *Today is a holiday in Wales.* 在威爾士今天是假日。➲ see also BANK HOLIDAY, PUBLIC HOLIDAY **4** **holidays** [pl.] (*NAmE*) the time in December and early January that includes Christmas, Hanukkah and New Year 節日假期（從十二月到一月上旬，包括聖誕節、修殿節和新年）：*Happy Holidays!* 節日愉快！

■ ***verb*** (*BrE*) (*NAmE* **vac·ation**) [I] (**+ adv./prep.**) to spend a holiday somewhere 度假；休假：*She was holidaying with her family in Ireland.* 她當時正和家人在愛爾蘭度假。

ˈholiday camp *noun* (*BrE*) a place that provides accommodation and entertainment for large numbers of people who are on holiday/vacation 度假營地（提供膳宿和娛樂活動）

holi·day·maker /ˈhɒlədeɪmeɪkə(r); *NAmE* ˈhɑːl-; *BrE* also -dimeɪ-/ *noun* (*BrE*) (*NAmE* **vac·ation·er**) a person who is visiting a place on holiday/vacation 度假者

holier-than-thou /ˌhəʊliə ðən ˈðaʊ; *NAmE* ˌhoʊliər/ *adj.* (*disapproving*) showing that you think that you are morally better than other people 自命清高的 SYN **self-righteous**：*I can't stand his holier-than-thou attitude.* 我無法忍受他那種自命不凡的態度。

holi·ness /ˈhəʊlinəs; *NAmE* ˈhoʊ-/ *noun* **1** [U] the quality of being holy 神聖 **2 His/Your Holiness** [C] a title of respect used when talking to or about the Pope and some other religious leaders 聖座，宗座（對教皇及其他宗教領袖的尊稱）：*His Holiness Pope Benedict XVI* 教皇聖座本篤十六世

hol·ism /ˈhəʊlɪzəm; ˈhɒl-; *NAmE* ˈhoʊl-; ˈhɑːl-/ *noun* [U] **1** the idea that the whole of sth must be considered in order to understand its different parts 整體論（即必須通過整體理解各部份）➲ compare ATOMISM **2** the idea that the whole of a sick person, including their body, mind and way of life, should be considered when treating them, and not just the SYMPTOMS (= effects) of the disease 整體觀念（治病應全面考量個人的身體、思想和生活方式等）

hol·is·tic /həʊˈlɪstɪk; hɒˈl-; *NAmE* hoʊˈl-; hɑːˈl-/ *adj.* **1** (*informal*) considering a whole thing or being to be more than a collection of parts 整體的；全面的：*a holistic approach to life* 對生命的全面探討 **2** (*medical* 醫) treating the whole person rather than just the SYMPTOMS (= effects) of a disease 功能整體性的：*holistic medicine* 整體醫學 ▸ **hol·is·tic·al·ly** /-kli/ *adv.*

hol·land·aise sauce /ˌhɒləndeɪz ˈsɔːs; *NAmE* ˌhɑːl-/ *noun* [U] a sauce made with butter, egg YOLKS (= yellow parts) and VINEGAR 荷蘭酸醬（由黃油、蛋黃、醋等製成）

hol·ler /ˈhɒlə(r); *NAmE* ˈhɑːl-/ *verb* [I, T] (*informal, especially NAmE*) to shout loudly 叫喊 SYN **yell**：**~ (at sb)** *Don't holler at me!* 別對我大喊大叫的！◇ **+ speech** *'Look out!' I hollered.* "當心！" 我大喊一聲。◇ **~ sth** *He hollered something I couldn't understand.* 他大聲嚷了一些我不明白的話。

hol·low /ˈhɒləʊ; *NAmE* ˈhɑːloʊ/ *adj., noun, verb*

■ ***adj.*** **1** having a hole or empty space inside 中空的；空心的：*a hollow ball/centre/tube* 中空的球 / 中心部位 / 管子 ◇ *The tree trunk was hollow inside.* 這樹幹裏面是空的。◇ *Her stomach felt hollow with fear.* 她嚇得魂不附體。**2** (of parts of the face 臉上的部位) sinking deeply into the face 凹陷的：***hollow eyes/cheeks*** 凹陷的雙眼 / 雙頰 ◇ *hollow-eyed from lack of sleep* 因缺乏睡眠而雙眼凹陷的 **3** [usually before noun] (of sounds 聲音) making a low sound like that made by an empty object when it is hit 沉悶迴盪的；空響的：*a hollow groan* 低沉的呻吟 **4** [usually before noun] not sincere 無誠意的；虛偽的：***hollow promises/threats*** 空洞的許諾；虛張聲勢的威脅 ◇ *a hollow laugh* 乾笑 ◇ *Their appeals for an end to the violence had a* ***hollow ring****.* 他們要求停止使用暴力的呼籲並不真切。**5** [usually before noun] without real value 無真正價值的：*to win a* ***hollow victory*** 取得表面勝利 IDM see RING² *v.* ▸ **hol·low·ly** *adv.*：*to laugh hollowly* 發出乾笑 **hol·low·ness** *noun* [U]：*the hollowness of the victory* 那場勝利的了無意義

■ ***noun*** **1** an area that is lower than the surface around it, especially on the ground 凹陷處；坑窪處：*muddy hollows* 泥濘的窪地 ◇ *The village lay secluded in a hollow of the hills* (= a small valley). 村子坐落在一個幽靜的小山谷中。◇ *She noticed the slight hollows under his cheekbones.* 她注意到他顴骨下面的輕微凹陷。**2** a hole or a confined space in sth 洞；孔；圍起來的空間：*The squirrel disappeared into a hollow at the base of the tree.* 松鼠鑽進了樹根處的一個洞。

■ ***verb*** [usually passive] **~ sth** to make a flat surface curve in 挖

PHR V **ˌhollow sth↔ˈout** **1** to make a hole in sth by removing part of it 挖空（某物）；挖出（孔、洞）：*Hollow out the cake and fill it with cream.* 在蛋糕上挖個洞，填入奶油。**2** to form sth by making a hole in sth else 挖洞（成某物）：*The cave has been hollowed out of the mountainside.* 窰洞是在半山腰挖成的。

holly /ˈhɒli; *NAmE* ˈhɑːli/ *noun* (*pl.* **-ies**) [U, C] a bush or small tree with hard shiny leaves with sharp points and bright red BERRIES in winter, often used as a decoration at Christmas 冬青：*a sprig of holly* 冬青樹枝

hol·ly·hock /ˈhɒlihɒk; *NAmE* ˈhɑːlihɑːk/ *noun* a tall garden plant with white, yellow, red or purple flowers growing up its STEM 蜀葵

Hol·ly·wood /ˈhɒliwʊd; *NAmE* ˈhɑːl-/ *noun* [U] the part of Los Angeles where the film/movie industry is based (used to refer to the US film/movie industry and the way of life that is associated with it) 好萊塢；美國電影業；好萊塢生活方式 ➲ COLLOCATIONS at CINEMA

ˌHollywood ˈending *noun* (usually *disapproving*) an ending in a film/movie, novel, etc., which happens in the way you expect, is full of exaggerated happiness, pity or love, and may not be very realistic 好萊塢式結尾（指電影、小說等過分渲染的、不太真實的結局）：*The film refuses to sell out and provide a Hollywood ending.* 這部影片拒絕背棄題旨採用好萊塢式的結尾。

hol·mium /ˈhəʊlmiəm; *NAmE* ˈhoʊl-/ *noun* [U] (*symb.* **Ho**) a chemical element. Holmium is a soft silver-white metal. 鈥

holo·caust /ˈhɒləkɔːst; *NAmE* ˈhɑːlə-; ˈhoʊlə-/ *noun* **1** [C] a situation in which many things are destroyed and many people killed, especially because of a war or a fire（尤指戰爭或火災引起的）大災難，大毀滅：*a nuclear holocaust* 核災難 **2 the Holocaust** [sing.] the killing of millions of Jews by the Nazis in the 1930s and 1940s（20 世紀 30 年代和 40 年代納粹對數百萬猶太人的）大屠殺

holo·gram /ˈhɒləgræm; *NAmE* ˈhɑːl-; ˈhoʊl-/ *noun* a special type of picture in which the objects seem to be THREE-DIMENSIONAL (= solid rather than flat) 全息圖

holo·graph /ˈhɒləgrɑːf; *NAmE* ˈhɑːləgræf; ˈhoʊl-/ *noun* (*technical* 術語) a piece of writing that has been written by hand by its author 親筆文件；手書

holo·graph·ic /ˌhɒləˈgræfɪk; *NAmE* ˌhɑːl-; ˌhoʊl-/ *adj.* [usually before noun] connected with holograms 全息圖的：*a holographic picture* 全息圖片

holo·phra·sis /ˌhɒləˈfreɪsɪs; *NAmE* həˈlɑːfrəsɪs/ *noun* [U] (*linguistics* 語言) the expression of a whole idea in a single word, for example a baby saying 'up' for 'I want you to pick me up' 獨詞表達，單詞句（以一個單詞表達整

H

句意思，如嬰兒用 up 一詞表達 I want you to pick me up 的意思） ▸ **holo·phras·tic** /ˌhɒləˈfræstɪk; *NAmE* ˌhɑːlə-; ˌhoʊlə-/ *adj.*

hols /hɒlz; *NAmE* hɑːlz/ *noun* [pl.] (*old-fashioned, BrE, informal*) holidays 假期

Hol·stein /ˈhɒlstaɪn; -stiːn; *NAmE* ˈhoʊl-/ (*NAmE*) (*BrE* **Frie·sian**) *noun* a type of black and white cow that produces a lot of milk 黑白花乳牛，荷蘭牛（產奶量很大）

hol·ster /ˈhəʊlstə(r); *NAmE* ˈhoʊ-/ *noun, verb*
■ ***noun*** a leather case worn on a belt or on a narrow piece of leather under the arm, used for carrying a small gun 手槍皮套（掛在腰帶或腋下皮帶上）
■ ***verb*** **~ sth** to put a gun in a holster 把（槍）放在手槍皮套裏

holy /ˈhəʊli; *NAmE* ˈhoʊli/ *adj.* (**holi·er**, **holi·est**)
1 [usually before noun] connected with God or a particular religion 與神（或宗教）有關的；神聖的：*the **Holy Bible/Scriptures*** 《聖經》◇ *holy ground* 聖地 ◇ *a holy war* (= one fought to defend the beliefs of a particular religion) 聖戰 ◇ *the holy city of Mecca* 聖城麥加 ◇ *Islam's holiest shrine* 伊斯蘭教最神聖的聖地 OPP **unholy** ➲ see also HOLY ORDERS **2** good in a moral and religious way 聖潔的：*a holy life/man* 聖潔的生活／人 OPP **unholy** **3** [only before noun] (*informal*) used to emphasize that you are surprised, afraid, etc.（強調驚訝、害怕等）：*Holy cow! What was that?* 天哪！那是什麼？➲ see also HOLIER-THAN-THOU, HOLINESS

ˌHoly Comˈmunion *noun* [U] = COMMUNION (1)

the ˌHoly ˈFather *noun* [sing.] the POPE 教宗

the ˌHoly ˈGhost *noun* [sing.] = THE HOLY SPIRIT

the ˌHoly ˈGrail *noun* [sing.] = GRAIL

the ˌholy of ˈholies *noun* [sing.] **1** the most holy part of a religious building 至聖所 **2** (*humorous*) a special room or building that can only be visited by important people 貴賓室；貴賓樓

ˌholy ˈorders *noun* [pl.] the official position of being a priest 聖秩；聖品：*to take holy orders* (= to become a priest) 領受聖秩

Holy·rood /ˈhɒliruːd; *NAmE* ˈhɑːl-/ *noun* [U] the Scottish parliament and government 蘇格蘭議會和政府；荷里路德：*elections to Holyrood* 蘇格蘭議會選舉 ORIGIN From the name of the part of Edinburgh where the parliament building is. 源自愛丁堡議會大廈所在地的名稱。

the ˌHoly ˈSee *noun* [sing.] **1** the job or authority of the Pope 聖座，宗座（指教宗的職位或權力） **2** the Roman Catholic court at the Vatican in Rome 羅馬教廷（設在梵蒂岡）

the ˌHoly ˈSpirit (also **the ˌHoly ˈGhost**) *noun* [sing.] (in Christianity 基督教) God in the form of a spirit 聖靈；聖神

ˌholy ˈwater *noun* [U] water that has been BLESSED by a priest 聖水

ˈHoly Week *noun* in the Christian Church, the week before Easter Sunday 聖週（基督教指復活節前的一週）

ˌHoly ˈWrit *noun* [U] (*old-fashioned*) the Bible《聖經》：(*figurative*) *You shouldn't take what he says as Holy Writ* (= accept that it is true without questioning it). 你不應該把他的話當作聖經。

hom·age /ˈhɒmɪdʒ; *NAmE* ˈhɑːm-/ *noun* [U, C, usually sing.] **~ (to sb/sth)** (*formal*) something that is said or done to show respect for sb 敬辭；表示敬意的舉動：*The kings of France **paid homage** to no one.* 法國國王不向任何人致敬。◇ *He describes his book as 'a homage to my father'.* 他說他的書是"獻給父親"的。◇ *They stood in silent homage around the grave.* 他們恭敬地站在墳墓周圍致默哀禮。

hom·bre /ˈɒmbreɪ; *NAmE* ˈɑːmb-/ *noun* (from *Spanish*, *NAmE, informal*) a man, especially one of a particular type（尤指某類）男人：*Their quarterback is one tough hombre.* 他們的四分衛是個壯漢。

hom·burg /ˈhɒmbɜːg; *NAmE* ˈhɑːmbɜːrg/ *noun* a man's soft hat with a narrow, curled BRIM 洪堡氈帽（男用軟帽，帽邊狹窄捲曲）

home /həʊm; *NAmE* hoʊm/ *noun, adj., adv., verb*
■ ***noun***
▸ **HOUSE, ETC.** 房子等 **1** [C, U] the house or flat/apartment that you live in, especially with your family 家；住所：*We are not far from my home now.* 我們現在離我家不遠了。◇ *Old people prefer to stay in their own homes.* 老年人喜歡待在自己家中。◇ *She leaves home at 7 every day.* 她每天 7 點鐘離家。◇ *the family home* 家庭住宅 ◇ *While travelling she missed the comforts of home.* 旅行期間她想念家裏的舒適。◇ *He **left home*** (= left his parents and began an independent life) *at sixteen.* 他十六歲時離家獨立生活。◇ *Nowadays a lot of people **work from home**.* 如今有很多人在家工作。◇ *I'll call you from home later.* 我過會兒從家裏給你打電話。◇ (*figurative*) *We haven't found a home for all our books yet* (= a place where they can be kept). 我們還沒找到存放全部書籍的地方。◇ *stray dogs needing new homes* 需要新家的流浪狗 ➲ see also STAY-AT-HOME **2** [C] a house or flat/apartment, etc., when you think of it as property that can be bought and sold（可買賣的）房子，住宅，寓所：*a **holiday/summer home*** 假日／消夏寓所 ◇ *A lot of new homes are being built on the edge of town.* 小鎮外圍正在興建很多新房屋。◇ *Private **home ownership** is increasing faster than ever.* 私有房產正以前所未有的速度增長。◇ *They applied for a home improvement loan.* 他們申請了房屋修繕貸款。➲ COLLOCATIONS at DECORATE, HOUSE ➲ VISUAL VOCAB page V16 ➲ see also MOBILE HOME, SECOND HOME, STATELY HOME
▸ **TOWN/COUNTRY** 城鎮；國家 **3** [C, U] the town, district, country, etc. that you come from, or where you are living and that you feel you belong to 家鄉；故鄉；定居地：*I often think about my friends **back home**.* 我常常想起老家的朋友。◇ *Jane left England and made Greece her home.* 簡離開了英國，在希臘安了家。◇ *Jamaica is home to over two million people.* 牙買加是兩百多萬人的家鄉。
▸ **FAMILY** 家庭 **4** [C] used to refer to a family living together, and the way it behaves 家庭：*She came from a violent home.* 她出身於一個有暴力行為的家庭。◇ *He had always wanted a real home with a wife and children.* 他一直想要一個有妻子和孩子的真正的家庭。➲ see also BROKEN HOME
▸ **FOR OLD PEOPLE/CHILDREN** 老年人；孩子 **5** [C] a place where people who cannot care for themselves live and are cared for by others 養老院；養育院：*a **children's home*** 兒童之家 ◇ *an **old people's home*** 養老院 ◇ *a **retirement home*** 退休療養院 ◇ *a home for the mentally ill* 精神病院 ◇ *She has lived **in a home** since she was six.* 她從六歲起就在保育院生活。➲ see also NURSING HOME, REST HOME
▸ **FOR PETS** 寵物 **6** [C] a place where pets with no owner are taken care of 收養所：*a **dogs'/cats' home*** 狗／貓之家
▸ **OF PLANT/ANIMAL** 動植物 **7** [sing., U] the place where a plant or animal usually lives; the place where sb/sth can be found 生息地；棲息地；產地：*This region is the home of many species of wild flower.* 這個地區有很多種類的野花。◇ *The tiger's home is in the jungle.* 老虎棲息在叢林裏。◇ *The Rockies are home to bears and mountain lions.* 落基山脈中有熊和美洲獅棲息。
▸ **WHERE STH FIRST DONE** 發祥地 **8** [sing.] **the ~ of sth** the place where sth was first discovered, made or invented 發源地；發祥地：*New Orleans, the home of jazz* 新奧爾良，爵士樂的發源地 ◇ *Greece, the home of democracy* 希臘，民主的發祥地

IDM **at ˈhome 1** in a person's own house, flat/apartment, etc. 在家裏：*I phoned you last night, but you weren't at home.* 我昨晚給你打電話了，但你不在家。◇ *Oh no, I left my purse at home.* 糟了，我把錢包落在家裏了。◇ *He lived at home* (= with his parents) *until he was thirty.* 他一直和父母同住到三十歲。**2** comfortable and relaxed 舒適自在；無拘無束：*Sit down and **make yourself at home**.* 坐下，別拘束。◇ *Simon feels very at home on a horse.* 西蒙騎馬得心應手。**3** (used especially in JOURNALISM 尤用於報刊新聞) in sb's own country, not in a foreign country 在本國；在國內：*The* *president is not as popular at home as he is abroad.* 總統在國內不如在國外受歡迎。 **4** if a sports team plays **at home**, it plays in the town, etc. that it comes from (比賽隊)在主場：*Leeds are playing at home this weekend.* 本週末利茲隊將在主場進行比賽。◇ *Is the match on Saturday at home or away?* 星期六的比賽是在主場還是在客場？ **away from 'home** **1** away from a person's own house, flat/apartment, etc. 離開家：*He works away from home during the week.* 他除了週末都在外工作。◇ *I don't want to be away from home for too long.* 我不想離家時間太長。 **2** (*BrE*) if a sports team plays **away from home**, it plays in the town, etc. that its opponent comes from (比賽隊)在客場 **a ˌhome from 'home** (*BrE*) (*NAmE* **a ˌhome away from 'home**) a place where you feel relaxed and comfortable as if you were in your own home 像家一樣舒適自在的地方 **ˌhome is where the 'heart is** (*saying*) a home is where the people you love are 家乃心之所繫 **home sweet 'home** (often *ironic*) used to say how pleasant your home is (especially when you really mean that it is not pleasant at all) 可愛的家；家總是家(有時有反諷意思，指並不愉快) **set up 'home** (*BrE*) (used especially about a couple) to start living in a new place (尤指夫婦)建立家庭，成家：*They got married and set up home together in Hull.* 他們結婚了，一同在赫爾建立了新家。 **when he's, it's, etc. at 'home** (*BrE*, *humorous*) used to emphasize a question about sb/sth (加強疑問語氣)到底，究竟：*Who's she when she's at home?* (= I don't know her) 她到底是誰？ ➲ more at CHARITY, CLOSE² *adj.*, EAT, ENGLISHMAN, SPIRITUAL *adj.*

■ ***adj.*** [only before noun]

▸ **WHERE YOU LIVE** 家 **1** connected with the place where you live 家的；家庭的：***home life*** (= with your family) 家庭生活 ◇ *a person's* ***home address/town*** 家庭地址；家鄉 ◇ *We offer customers a free* ***home delivery*** *service.* 我們為客戶提供免費送貨上門的服務。

▸ **MADE/USED AT HOME** 家裏做／用 **2** made or used at home 在家裏做的；家用的：*home movies* 家庭電影 ◇ *home cooking* 家常飯菜 ◇ *a home computer* 家用電腦

▸ **OWN COUNTRY** 本國 **3** (*especially BrE*) connected with your own country rather than foreign countries 本國的；國內的 **SYN** **domestic**：*products for the home market* 為國內市場生產的產品 ◇ ***home news/affairs*** 國內新聞／事件 **OPP** **foreign, overseas**

▸ **IN SPORT** 體育運動 **4** connected with a team's own sports ground 主場的：*a* ***home match/win*** 主場比賽／勝利 ◇ *the* ***home team*** 主隊 ◇ *Rangers were playing in front of their* ***home crowd.*** 流浪隊在主場觀眾面前比賽。 ➲ compare AWAY (6)

■ ***adv.***

▸ **WHERE YOU LIVE** 居住地 **1** 🔑 to or at the place where you live 到家；向家；在家：*Come on, it's time to* ***go home.*** 快點，該回家了。◇ *What time did you* ***get home*** *last night?* 你昨晚什麼時間到家的？◇ *The trip has been exhausting and I'll be glad to* ***be home.*** 這個旅程令人疲憊不堪，要是能回家就好了。◇ *After a month, they went* ***back home*** *to America.* 一個月之後，他們返回了美國。◇ *It was a lovely day so I walked home.* 那天天氣很好，所以我走路回家了。◇ *Anna will drive me home after work.* 下班後安娜會開車送我回家。◇ *Hopefully the doctors will allow her home tomorrow.* 明天醫生可望會允許她回家。◇ (*NAmE*) *I like to* ***stay home*** *in the evenings.* 我喜歡晚上待在家裏。

▸ **INTO CORRECT POSITION** 正確位置 **2** into the correct position 到正確的位置：*She leaned on the door and pushed the bolt home.* 她倚在門上，上好了門閂。◇ *He drove the ball home* (= scored a goal) *from 15 metres.* 他從 15 米遠處勁射破門得分。◇ *The torpedo struck home on the hull of the ship.* 魚雷正擊中船身。

IDM **be home and 'dry** (*BrE*) (*NAmE* **be home 'free**) to have done sth successfully, especially when it was difficult 做成某事(尤指難事)：*I could see the finish line and thought I was home and dry.* 我能看見終點線了，我想我終於成功了。 **bring home the 'bacon** (*informal*) to be successful at sth; to earn money for your family to live on 成功；掙到養家餬口的錢 **bring sth 'home to sb** to make sb realize how important, difficult or serious sth is 使某人瞭解某事的重要性(或艱難、嚴重程度)：*The television pictures brought home to us the full horror of the attack.* 電視畫面使我們充分地瞭解這次襲擊有多麼恐怖。 **come 'home to sb** to become completely clear to sb, often in a way that is painful 使人(痛苦地)完全明白：*It suddenly came home to him that he was never going to see Julie again.* 他突然明白他再也見不到朱莉了。 **sth comes home to 'roost** (also **the chickens come home to 'roost**) used to say that if sb says or does sth bad or wrong, it will affect them badly in the future 自食惡果；報應到自己身上 **hit/strike 'home** if a remark, etc. **hits/strikes home**, it has a strong effect on sb, in a way that makes them realize what the true facts of a situation are (言語等)正中要害，說到點子上：*Her face went pale as his words hit home.* 他的話切中要害，她的臉變白了。 ➲ more at COW *n.*, DRIVE *v.*, LIGHT *n.*, PRESS *v.*, RAM *v.*, ROMP *v.*, WRITE

■ ***verb***

PHR V **ˌhome 'in on sth** **1** to aim at sth and move straight towards it 朝向，移向，導向(目標)：*The missile homed in on the target.* 導彈正向目標飛去。 **2** to direct your thoughts or attention towards sth 把(思想、注意力)集中於：*I began to feel I was really homing in on the answer.* 我開始覺得我快找到答案了。

ˌhome 'base *noun* [sing., U] **1** = HOME PLATE **2** the place where sb/sth usually lives, works or operates from 基地；大本營

home·body /ˈhəʊmbɒdi; *NAmE* ˈhoʊmbɑːdi/ *noun* (*pl.* **-ies**) (*informal*, *especially NAmE*) a person who enjoys spending time at home 喜歡待在家裏的人；戀家的人

home·boy /ˈhəʊmbɔɪ; *NAmE* ˈhoʊm-/ (also **homie**) *noun* (*NAmE*, *informal*) a male friend from the same town as you; a member of your GANG (= a group of young people who go around together) (男)老鄉，夥伴，同夥

ˌhome 'brew *noun* [U] **1** beer that sb makes at home 家釀啤酒 **2** something that sb makes at home rather than buying it 自己製作的東西：*The security software he uses is home brew.* 他用的安全軟件是自己編寫的。 ▸ **ˌhome-'brew** (also **ˌhome-'brewed**) *adj.*

home·buy·er /ˈhəʊmbaɪə(r); *NAmE* ˈhoʊm-/ *noun* a person who buys a house, flat/apartment, etc. 購房者

ˌhome 'cinema (*BrE*) (*NAmE* **ˌhome 'theater**) *noun* [U] television and video equipment designed to give a similar experience to being in a cinema/movie theater, with high-quality pictures and sound and a large screen 家庭影院

home·com·ing /ˈhəʊmkʌmɪŋ; *NAmE* ˈhoʊm-/ *noun* **1** [C, U] the act of returning to your home after being away for a long time (長時間離家後的)回家，返家，回國 **2** [C] (*NAmE*) a social event that takes place every year at a HIGH SCHOOL, college or university for people who used to be students there (一年一度的)校友返校活動

the ˌHome 'Counties *noun* [pl.] the counties around London 倫敦周圍各郡

ˌhome eco'nomics *noun* [U] cooking and other skills needed at home, taught as a subject in school 家政學

ˌhome 'front *noun* [sing.] the people who do not go to fight in a war but who stay in a country to work (戰時的)後方民眾，大後方

IDM **on the 'home front** happening at home, or in your own country 發生在家鄉(或本國)

home·girl /ˈhəʊmɡɜːl; *NAmE* ˈhoʊmɡɜːrl/ (also **homie**) *noun* (*NAmE*, *informal*) a female friend from the same town as you; a member of your GANG (= a group of young people who go around together) 女同鄉；(女)玩伴

ˌhome 'ground *noun* [sing., U] **1** (*BrE*) a sports ground that a team regularly plays on in their own area or town 主場場地；主隊運動場 **2** a place where sb lives or works and where they feel confident, rather than a place that is not familiar to them 自己的家；熟悉的工作地方；自己的地盤：*I'd rather meet him here on my own home ground.* 我寧願在我自己的地盤上見他。

H

ˌhome-ˈgrown *adj.* **1** (of plants, fruit and vegetables 植物、水果和蔬菜) grown in a person's garden 自家園子裏產的：*home-grown tomatoes* 自家種的西紅柿 **2** made, trained or educated in your own country, town, etc. 本國（或本地）製造的（或培養的、教育的）：*The team has a wealth of home-grown talent.* 該隊有很多自己培養的人才。

ˌhome ˈhelp *noun* (*BrE*) a person whose job is to help old or sick people with cooking, cleaning, etc.（給老人或病人料理家務的）傭人

ˌhome imˈprovement *noun* [C, U] changes that are made to a house, that increase its value（為增值進行的）房屋修繕，家居裝修：*They've spent a lot of money on home improvements.* 他們花了很多錢裝修家居。◇ *home-improvement products* 家居裝修產品 ➲ COLLOCATIONS at DECORATE

H

home·land /ˈhəʊmlænd; *NAmE* ˈhoʊm-/ *noun* **1** [usually sing.] the country where a person was born 祖國；家鄉：*Many refugees have been forced to flee their homeland.* 很多難民被迫逃離了祖國。 **2** (in the Republic of South Africa under the APARTHEID system in the past) one of the areas with some SELF-GOVERNMENT that were intended for a group of black African people to live in（南非共和國過去在種族隔離制度下設立、有一定自治權的）黑人定居地：*the Transkei homeland* 特蘭斯凱黑人定居地

ˌHomeland Seˈcurity *noun* [U] the activities and organizations whose aim is to prevent TERRORIST attacks in the US 國土安全（美國防止恐怖襲擊的行動及機構）：*the Department of Homeland Security* 國土安全部

home·less /ˈhəʊmləs; *NAmE* ˈhoʊm-/ *adj.* **1** having no home 無家的：*The scheme has been set up to help homeless people.* 這個計劃的目的是幫助無家可歸的人。 **2 the homeless** *noun* [pl.] people who have no home 無家可歸的人們：*helping the homeless* 幫助無家可歸者 ▸ **home·less·ness** *noun* [U]

ˌhome ˈloan *noun* (*informal*) = MORTGAGE

home·ly /ˈhəʊmli; *NAmE* ˈhoʊm-/ *adj.* (**home·lier, home·li·est**) **1** (*BrE, approving*) (of a place 地方) making you feel comfortable, as if you were in your own home 在家一樣舒適的；猶如在自家一樣的：*The hotel has a lovely homely feel to it.* 那家旅館給人一種賓至如歸的感覺。 **2** (*approving, especially BrE*) simple and good 簡單且好的；家常的：*homely cooking* 家常烹調 **3** (*BrE, approving*) (of a woman 女人) warm and friendly and enjoying the pleasures of home and family 熱情友好並熱衷家庭生活的；親切喜家的：*His landlady was a kind, homely woman.* 他的房東太太心地善良，待人親切。 **4** (*NAmE, disapproving*) (of a person's appearance 人的外表) not attractive 相貌平平的 SYN **plain**：*a homely child* 相貌普通的孩子

ˌhome-ˈmade *adj.* made at home, rather than produced in a factory and bought in a shop/store 自製的；家裏做的

home·maker /ˈhəʊmmeɪkə(r); *NAmE* ˈhoʊm-/ *noun* (*especially NAmE*) a person who works at home and takes care of the house and family 料理家務者；操持家務者 ▸ **home·making** *noun* [U]

the ˈHome Office *noun* [sing.+sing./pl. v.] the British government department that deals with the law, the police and prisons, and with decisions about who can enter the country（英國）內政部

ˌhome ˈoffice *noun* a room in sb's home that is used for work 家庭辦公室

homeo·path (*BrE* also **hom·oeo-**) /ˈhəʊmiəpæθ; ˈhɒmi-; *NAmE* ˈhoʊ-; ˈhɑːm-/ *noun* a person who treats illness using homeopathic methods 順勢療法醫生

hom·eop·athy (*BrE* also **hom·oeo-**) /ˌhəʊmiˈɒpəθi; ˌhɒm-; *NAmE* ˌhoʊmiˈɑːp-; ˌhɑːm-/ *noun* [U] a system of treating diseases or conditions using very small amounts of the substance that causes the disease or condition 順勢療法 ▸ **homeo·path·ic** (*BrE* also **hom·oeo-**) /ˌhəʊmiəˈpæθɪk; ˌhɒm-; *NAmE* ˌhoʊm-; ˌhɑːm-/ *adj.*: *homeopathic medicines/remedies/treatments* 順勢療法藥物；順勢療法；順勢治療

homeo·stasis (*BrE* also **hom·oeo-**) /ˌhəʊmiəˈsteɪsɪs; ˌhɒm-; *NAmE* ˌhoʊm-/ *noun* [U] (*biology* 生) the process by which the body reacts to changes in order to keep conditions inside the body, for example temperature, the same 自穩態，內環境穩定（身體對變化作出自我調整）

home·own·er /ˈhəʊməʊnə(r); *NAmE* ˈhoʊmoʊ-/ *noun* a person who owns their house or flat/apartment 房主

ˈhome page *noun* (*computing* 計) **1** the main page created by a company, an organization, etc. on the Internet from which connections to other pages can be made（網站）主頁，首頁 ➲ VISUAL VOCAB page V68 **2** a page on the Internet that you choose to appear first on your screen whenever you make a connection to the Internet 主頁，起始頁（上網時首先登錄的網頁）

ˈhome plate (also **ˌhome ˈbase**) (*NAmE* also **plate**) *noun* (in BASEBALL 棒球) the place where the person hitting the ball stands and where they must return to after running around all the bases 本壘板

homer /ˈhəʊmə(r); *NAmE* ˈhoʊm-/ *noun* (*NAmE, informal*) = HOME RUN：*He hit a homer.* 他擊出了一記本壘打。

home·room /ˈhəʊmruːm; -rʊm; *NAmE* ˈhoʊm-/ *noun* [C, U] (*NAmE*) a room in a school where students go at the beginning of each school day, so that teachers can check who is in school; the time spent in this room 進行課前點名的教室；課前點名教室集合時間

ˌhome ˈrule *noun* [U] the right of a country or region to govern itself, especially after another country or region has governed it（尤指受其他國家或地區統治之後的）地方自治權

ˌhome ˈrun (also *NAmE informal* **homer**) *noun* (in BASEBALL 棒球) a hit that allows the person hitting the ball to run around all the bases without stopping 本壘打

home·school·ing /ˌhəʊmˈskuːlɪŋ; *NAmE* ˌhoʊm-/ *noun* [U] the practice of educating children at home, not in schools（兒童）在家受教育，家學 ▸ **home·school** /ˌhəʊmˈskuːl; *NAmE* ˌhoʊm-/ *verb* **~ sb**

ˌHome ˈSecretary *noun* the British government minister in charge of the Home Office（英國）內政大臣

ˌhome ˈshopping *noun* [U] the practice of ordering goods by phone or by email and having them delivered to your home 家居購物（通過電話或電子郵件購買）

home·sick /ˈhəʊmsɪk; *NAmE* ˈhoʊm-/ *adj.* sad because you are away from home and you miss your family and friends 思鄉的；想家的；患懷鄉病的：*I felt homesick for Scotland.* 我思念故鄉蘇格蘭。 ▸ **home·sick·ness** *noun* [U]

home·spun /ˈhəʊmspʌn; *NAmE* ˈhoʊm-/ *adj.* **1** (especially of ideas 尤指思想) simple and ordinary; not coming from an expert 樸素的；平常的 **2** (of cloth 布) made at home 家紡的；家裏製作的

home·stay /ˈhəʊmsteɪ; *NAmE* ˈhoʊm-/ *noun* [C, U] an arrangement that provides accommodation for students or tourists in the home of a family in exchange for payment（為學生或遊客提供的）家庭寄宿：*The trip includes a homestay in a traditional village.* 這次旅行包括在一個傳統村莊的家庭住宿。◇ *Live with an American family in homestay and learn the language and customs.* 住在美國家庭，學習他們的語言與習俗。

home·stead /ˈhəʊmsted; *NAmE* ˈhoʊm-/ *noun, verb*

■ *noun* **1** a house with the land and buildings around it, especially a farm（包括周圍土地和附屬房屋的）家宅；（尤指）農莊 **2** (in the US in the past) a piece of land given to sb by the government on condition that they lived on it and grew crops on it 宅地（美國舊時由國家分給個人居住並開墾的土地）

■ *verb* [I] (*old-fashioned, NAmE*) to live and work on a homestead (2) 在分到的土地上居住並勞作 ▸ **home·stead·er** *noun*

the ˌhome ˈstraight (*especially BrE*) (also **the ˌhome ˈstretch** especially in *NAmE*) *noun* [sing.] **1** the last part of a race（賽跑的）最後階段，衝刺階段 **2** the last part of an activity, etc. when it is nearly completed（活動等的）最後部份，接近完成的階段

ˌ**home ˈtheater** (*NAmE*) (*BrE* ˌ**home ˈcinema**) *noun* [U] television and video equipment designed to give a similar experience to being in a cinema/movie theater, with high-quality pictures and sound and a large screen 家庭影院

home·town /ˈhəʊmtaʊn; *NAmE* ˈhoʊm-/ *noun* the place where you were born or lived as a child 家鄉；故鄉

ˌ**home ˈtruth** *noun* [usually pl.] a true but unpleasant fact about a person, usually told to them by sb else 使人不愉快的事實（通常由別人告知）；（關於某人的）大實話：*It's time you told him a few home truths.* 現在你該給他講點實話了。

ˈ**home unit** *noun* (*AustralE, NZE*) = UNIT (9)

home·ward /ˈhəʊmwəd; *NAmE* ˈhoʊmwərd/ *adj.* going towards home 回家的；回國的：*the homeward journey* 歸家的旅程 ▶ **home·ward** (also **home·wards** especially in *BrE*) *adv.*：*Commuters were heading homeward at the end of the day.* 一天結束時下班的人們正趕着回家。◇ *We drove homewards in silence.* 我們默默地開車回家。◇ *We were* ***homeward bound*** *at last.* 我們終於要回家了。

home·work 🔑 /ˈhəʊmwɜːk; *NAmE* ˈhoʊmwɜːrk/ *noun* [U]
1 🔑 work that is given by teachers for students to do at home（學生的）家庭作業：*I still haven't done my geography homework.* 我還沒做完地理科家庭作業呢。◇ *How much homework do you get?* 你有多少家庭作業？◇ *I have to write up the notes* ***for homework***. 我得整理筆記寫成家庭作業。➲ COLLOCATIONS at EDUCATION **2** (*informal*) work that sb does to prepare for sth 準備工作：*You could tell that he had really* ***done his homework*** (= found out all he needed to know). 你能看得出他確實做了充分準備。

home·work·er /ˈhəʊmwɜːkə(r); *NAmE* ˈhoʊmwɜːrk-/ *noun* a person who works at home, often doing jobs that are not well paid such as making clothes for shops/stores 在家工作的人（常做報酬低微的工作）▶ **home·work·ing** *noun* [U]

homey (also **homy**) /ˈhəʊmi; *NAmE* ˈhoʊmi/ *adj., noun*
■ ***adj.*** (*informal, especially NAmE*) pleasant and comfortable, like home 愉快舒適的；像家一樣的：*The hotel had a nice, homey atmosphere.* 這旅館有一種舒適美好、賓至如歸的氣氛。
■ ***noun*** = HOMIE

homi·cidal /ˌhɒmɪˈsaɪdl; *NAmE* ˌhɑːm-/ *adj.* likely to kill another person; making sb likely to kill another person（使）可能會殺人的：*a homicidal maniac* 殺人狂 ◇ *He had clear homicidal tendencies.* 他有明顯的殺人傾向。

homi·cide /ˈhɒmɪsaɪd; *NAmE* ˈhɑːm-/ *noun* [C, U] (*especially NAmE, law* 律) the crime of killing sb deliberately（蓄意）殺人罪 SYN **murder** ➲ compare CULPABLE HOMICIDE, MANSLAUGHTER

homie (also **homey**) /ˈhəʊmi; *NAmE* ˈhoʊmi/ *noun* (*NAmE, informal*) a HOMEBOY or HOMEGIRL 老鄉；同鄉；玩伴

hom·ily /ˈhɒməli; *NAmE* ˈhɑːm-/ (*pl.* **-ies**) *noun* (*formal, often disapproving*) a speech or piece of writing giving advice on the correct way to behave, etc.（有關規矩等的）說教，說教作品：*She delivered a homily on the virtues of family life.* 她進行了一場家庭生活美德方面的說教。

hom·ing /ˈhəʊmɪŋ; *NAmE* ˈhoʊm-/ *adj.* [only before noun]
1 (of a bird or an animal 鳥或動物) trained, or having a natural ability, to find the way home from a long distance away 經訓練能返回原地的；有返回原地本能的：*Many birds have a remarkable* ***homing instinct***. 很多鳥類具有了不起的返回原地的本能。 **2** (of a MISSILE, etc. 導彈等) fitted with an electronic device that enables it to find and hit the place or object it is aimed at 自動尋向的；自導引的：*a* ***homing device*** 自動導引的裝置

ˈ**homing pigeon** *noun* a PIGEON (= a type of bird) that has been trained to find its way home from a long distance away, and that people race against other pigeons for sport 信鴿；賽鴿

hom·in·id /ˈhɒmɪnɪd; *NAmE* ˈhɑːm-/ *noun* (*technical* 術語) a human, or a creature that lived in the past which humans developed from 人科動物

hom·in·oid /ˈhɒmɪnɔɪd; *NAmE* ˈhɑːm-/ *noun* (*technical* 術語) a human, or a creature related to humans 類人動物

hom·iny /ˈhɒmɪni; *NAmE* ˈhɑːm-/ *noun* [U] dried CORN (MAIZE), boiled in water or milk, eaten especially in the southern states of the US 玉米糝兒（美國南方各州常用水或牛奶煮後食用）

Homo /ˈhɒməʊ; ˈhəʊməʊ; *NAmE* ˈhoʊmoʊ/ *noun* (from *Latin, technical* 術語) the GENUS (= group) of PRIMATES that includes early and modern humans 人屬（靈長目人科的一屬，包括早期和現代人）

homo- /ˈhɒməʊ-; ˈhəʊm-; *NAmE* ˈhoʊmoʊ-/ *combining form* (in nouns, adjectives and adverbs 構成名詞、形容詞和副詞) the same 同樣；相同 ➲ compare HETERO-

hom·oe·op·ath (*BrE*) = HOMEOPATH

hom·oe·op·athy (*BrE*) = HOMEOPATHY

hom·oeo·stasis (*BrE*) = HOMEOSTASIS

Homo erectus /ˌhɒməʊ ɪˈrektəs; ˌhəʊməʊ; *NAmE* ˌhoʊmoʊ/ *noun* [U] (from *Latin, technical* 術語) an early form of human which was able to walk on two legs 直立人（能用腿行走的早期人科成員）

homo·erot·ic /ˌhɒməʊɪˈrɒtɪk; ˌhəʊm-; *NAmE* ˌhoʊmoʊɪˈrɑːtɪk/ *adj.* relating to HOMOSEXUAL sex and sexual desire 同性戀性行為的；同性戀性慾的

homo·gen·eity /ˌhɒmədʒəˈniːəti; *NAmE* ˌhɑːm-/ *noun* [U] (*formal*) the quality of being homogeneous 同種；同質

homo·ge·neous /ˌhɒməˈdʒiːniəs; *NAmE* ˌhoʊm-/ *adj.* (*formal*) consisting of things or people that are all the same or all of the same type 由同類事物（或人）組成的；同種類的：*a homogeneous group/mixture/population* 相同成分組成的群體／混合物；同類人口 OPP **heterogeneous**

hom·ogen·ized (*BrE* also **-ised**) /həˈmɒdʒənaɪzd; *NAmE* həˈmɑːdʒ-/ *adj.* (of milk 牛奶) treated so that the cream is mixed in with the rest 經過均質處理的

homo·graph /ˈhɒməɡrɑːf; *NAmE* ˈhɑːməɡræf/ *noun* (*grammar* 語法) a word that is spelt like another word but has a different meaning from it, and may have a different pronunciation, for example *bow* /baʊ/, *bow* /bəʊ/, /boʊ/ 同形異義詞（拼寫相同，意義不同，讀音可能不同）

Homo habilis /ˌhɒməʊ ˈhæbɪlɪs; ˌhəʊməʊ; *NAmE* ˌhoʊmoʊ/ *noun* [U] (from *Latin, technical* 術語) an early form of human which was able to use tools 能人（能用手準確把握器物的早期人科成員）

hom·olo·gous /həˈmɒləɡəs; *NAmE* hoʊˈmɑːl-; he-/ *adj.* ~ **(with sth)** (*technical* 術語) similar in position, structure, etc. to sth else（位置、結構等）相應的，類似的；同源的：*The seal's flipper is homologous with the human arm.* 海豹的鰭肢與人類的手臂同源。

homo·nym /ˈhɒmənɪm; *NAmE* ˈhɑːm-; ˈhoʊm-/ *noun* (*grammar* 語法) a word that is spelt like another word (or pronounced like it) but which has a different meaning, for example *can* meaning 'be able' and *can* meaning 'put sth in a container' 同形（同音）異義詞（寫法或讀音相同，但意義不同）

homo·pho·bia /ˌhɒməˈfəʊbiə; ˌhəʊm-; *NAmE* ˌhoʊməˈfoʊ-/ *noun* [U] a strong dislike and fear of HOMOSEXUAL people 對同性戀者的厭惡和恐懼 ▶ **homo·pho·bic** *adj.*

homo·phone /ˈhɒməfəʊn; *NAmE* ˈhɑːməfoʊn/ *noun* (*grammar* 語法) a word that is pronounced like another word but has a different spelling or meaning, for example *some, sum* /sʌm/ 同音異形詞，同音異義詞（讀音相同，寫法或意義不同）

hom·oph·onous /həˈmɒfənəs; *NAmE* -ˈmɑːf-/ *adj.* (*linguistics* 語言) (of a word 詞語) having the same pronunciation as another word but a different meaning or spelling 同音異義的；同音異形的：*'Bear' and 'bare' are homophonous.* * bear 和 bare 是同音異形詞。

Homo sa·pi·ens /ˌhɒməʊ ˈsæpienz; ˌhəʊm-; *NAmE* ˌhoʊmoʊ ˈseɪp-; ˈsæp-/ *noun* [U] (from *Latin, technical* 術語) the kind or SPECIES of human that exists now 智人（全部現代人的屬和種）

H

homo·sex·ual /ˌhəʊməˈsekʃuəl; ˌhɒm-; *NAmE* ˌhoʊm-/ *noun* a person, usually a man, who is sexually attracted to people of the same sex 同性戀者（通常指男性）：*a practising homosexual* 有同性戀行為的人 ⊃ compare BISEXUAL, GAY, HETEROSEXUAL, LESBIAN ▶ **homo·sex·ual** *adj.*：*a homosexual act/relationship* 同性戀行為／關係 **homo·sexu·al·ity** /ˌhəʊməˌsekʃuˈæləti; ˌhɒm-; *NAmE* ˌhoʊm-/ *noun* [U]

homo·zy·gote /ˌhɒməˈzaɪgəʊt; *NAmE* ˌhɑːməˈzaɪgoʊt/ *noun* (*biology* 生) a living thing that has only one form of a particular GENE, and whose young are more likely to share a particular characteristic 純合子（只有某基因的一種形式的生物體）▶ **homo·zy·gous** /-gəs/ *adj.*

homy = HOMEY

Hon (also **Hon.** especially in *NAmE*) /ɒn; *NAmE* ɑːn/ *abbr.* **1** (*BrE*) HONORARY (used in official titles of jobs)（用於官方職位頭銜）名譽的，義務的：*Hon Treasurer: D Shrimpton* 名譽司庫：D・施林普頓 **2** HONOURABLE 閣下：*the Hon Member for Bolsover* 博爾索弗區議員閣下

hon·cho /ˈhɒntʃəʊ; *NAmE* ˈhɑːntʃoʊ/ *noun* (*pl.* **-os**) (*informal, especially NAmE*) the person who is in charge 主管；老闆；頭兒 SYN **boss**：*Claude is the studio's* ***head honcho***. 克勞德是電影公司的老闆。

hone /həʊn; *NAmE* hoʊn/ *verb* **1** to develop and improve sth, especially a skill, over a period of time 磨練，訓練（尤指技藝）：**~ sth** *She honed her debating skills at college.* 她在大學時便練就了辯論技巧。◇ *It was a finely honed piece of writing.* 那是一篇經過仔細推敲寫成的文章。◇ **~ sth to sth** *His body was honed to perfection.* 他的身體鍛煉得十全十美。**2 ~ sth (to sth)** to make a blade sharp or sharper 磨（刀）；把（刀）磨快 SYN **sharpen**

hon·est 0-π /ˈɒnɪst; *NAmE* ˈɑːn-/ *adj.*
1 0-π always telling the truth, and never stealing or cheating 誠實的；老實的；正直的：*an honest man/woman* 誠實的男人／女人 OPP **dishonest** **2** 0-π not hiding the truth about sth 坦率的；坦誠的：*an honest answer* 坦率的回答 ◇ **~ (about sth)** *Are you being completely honest about your feelings?* 你絲毫沒有隱瞞你的感情嗎？◇ **~ (with sb)** *Thank you for being so honest with me.* 感謝你對我這麼坦誠。◇ *Give me your honest opinion.* 告訴我你的真實意見。◇ ***To be honest*** (= what I really think is), *it was one of the worst books I've ever read.* 說實在的，那是我讀過的最差的書之一。◇ ***Let's be honest***, *she's only interested in Mike because of his money.* 坦率地說吧，她對邁克有好感只不過是因為他有錢。**3** 0-π showing an honest mind or attitude 真誠的；顯示內心誠意的；表示態度誠懇的：*She's got an honest face.* 她有一張真誠的面孔。**4** (of work or wages 工作或工資) earned or resulting from hard work 辛勤掙得的；勤勞的：*He hasn't done* ***an honest day's work*** *in his life.* 他一輩子從未努力認真幹過一天活兒。◇ *It's quite a struggle to make* ***an honest living***. 要踏實地過日子，總是十分辛苦的。HELP Use **an**, not **a**, before **honest**. * honest 之前用 an，不用 a。

IDM **honest!** (*informal*) used to emphasize that you are not lying 真的；我發誓：*I didn't mean it, honest!* 我不是有意的，真的！**honest to 'God/'goodness** used to emphasize that what you are saying is true 老天爺作證；說實話：*Honest to God, Mary, I'm not joking.* 老天爺作證，瑪麗，我不是開玩笑。HELP Some people find this use offensive. 有人認為此用法含冒犯意。**make an honest 'woman of sb** (*old-fashioned, humorous*) to marry a woman after having had a sexual relationship with her 與跟自己有過性關係的女人結婚

ˌhonest 'broker *noun* a person or country that tries to get other people or countries to reach an agreement or to solve a problem, without getting involved with either side（人際或國際糾紛中的）公正調解者，調停者

hon·est·ly 0-π /ˈɒnɪstli; *NAmE* ˈɑːn-/ *adv.*
1 0-π in an honest way 誠實地；正當地：*I can't believe he got that money honestly.* 我不相信他是靠正當手段弄到那筆錢的。OPP **dishonestly** **2** 0-π used to emphasize that what you are saying is true, however surprising it may seem 真的；確實：*I didn't tell anyone, honestly!* 我確實沒告訴過任何人！◇ *I honestly can't remember a thing about last night.* 我實在想不起昨晚的事了。◇ *You can't honestly expect me to believe that!* 你休想指望我相信那種事！**3** (*informal*) used to show that you disapprove of sth and are irritated by it（表示不贊成並且生氣）：*Honestly! Whatever will they think of next?* 真是的！他們接下來還會想出什麼？

ˌhonest-to-'goodness *adj.* [only before noun] (*approving*) simple and good 實實在在的；真正的；地道的：*honest-to-goodness country food* 真正的鄉下食物

Synonyms 同義詞辨析

honest

frank • direct • open • outspoken • straight • blunt

These words all describe people saying exactly what they mean without trying to hide feelings, opinions or facts. 以上各詞均形容人坦率、坦誠。

honest not hiding the truth about sth 指坦率的、坦誠的：*Thank you for being so honest with me.* 感謝你對我這麼坦誠。

frank honest in what you say, sometimes in a way that other people might not like 指坦率的、直率的（有時可能不討人喜歡）：*To be frank with you, I think your son has little chance of passing the exam.* 坦白說，我認為你的兒子不大可能通過考試。

direct saying exactly what you mean in a way that nobody can pretend not to understand 指直接的、直率的、坦率的：*You'll have to get used to his direct manner.* 你得慢慢習慣他這種直率的方式。
NOTE Being **direct** is sometimes considered positive but sometimes it is used as a 'polite' way of saying that sb is rude. * direct 有時被認為含褒義，但有時是以禮貌的方式表示某人有些無禮。

open (*approving*) (of a person) not keeping thoughts and feelings hidden 指為人誠懇的、坦誠的、直率的：*He was quite open about his reasons for leaving.* 他對離開的原因完全未加隱瞞。

outspoken saying exactly what you think, even if this shocks or offends people 指直率的、坦誠的、直言不諱的：*She was outspoken in her criticism of the plan.* 她對該計劃的批評直言不諱。

straight honest and direct 指坦誠的、直率的：*I don't think you're being straight with me.* 我覺得你沒跟我坦誠相見。

blunt saying exactly what you think without trying to be polite 指嘴直的、直言不諱的：*She has a reputation for blunt speaking.* 她說話出了名的直截了當。

WHICH WORD? 詞語辨析

Honest and **frank** refer to *what* you say as much as *how* you say it. * honest 和 frank 既指說話方式，也指說話內容：*a(n) honest/frank admission of guilt* 坦承有罪 They are generally positive words, although it is possible to be *too* frank in a way that other people might not like. 這兩個詞通常用作褒義詞，但有時也可能指過於直率而使人不快。**Direct**, **outspoken** and **blunt** all describe sb's manner of saying what they think. **Outspoken** suggests that you are willing to shock people by saying what you believe to be right. **Blunt** and **direct** often suggest that you think honesty is more important than being polite. **Open** is positive and describes sb's character. * direct、outspoken 和 blunt 都表示說話方式直率，其中 outspoken 表示寧可冒犯他人也要直抒己見；blunt 和 direct 常表示說話人認為誠實比客套重要；open 含褒義，用來形容人的性格：*I'm a very open person.* 我這個人非常坦誠直率。

PATTERNS

- honest/frank/direct/open/outspoken/straight **about** sth
- honest/frank/direct/open/straight/blunt **with** sb
- a(n) honest/direct/straight/blunt **answer**
- a frank/direct/blunt **manner**

hon·esty /ˈɒnəsti; *NAmE* ˈɑːn-/ *noun* [U] the quality of being honest 誠實；老實；正直：*She answered all my questions with her usual honesty.* 她像平常一樣老老實實地回答了我的所有問題。◇ *His honesty is not in question.* 他的誠實是毋庸置疑的。

IDM **in all ˈhonesty** used to state a fact or an opinion which, though true, may seem disappointing 說實話；其實：*The book isn't, in all honesty, as good as I expected.* 說實話，這本書並沒有我預期的那麼好。

honey /ˈhʌni/ *noun* **1** [U] a sweet sticky yellow substance made by BEES that is spread on bread, etc. like jam 蜂蜜 **2** [C] (*informal*) a way of addressing sb that you like or love （愛稱）親愛的，寶貝：*Have you seen my keys, honey?* 你見到我的鑰匙了嗎，寶貝？ **3** [C] (*informal*) a person that you like or love and think is very kind 可愛的人：*He can be a real honey when he wants to be.* 他高興的時候挺招人喜歡的。**IDM** see LAND *n.*

honey·bee /ˈhʌnibiː/ *noun* a BEE that makes honey 蜜蜂

honey·comb /ˈhʌnikəʊm; *NAmE* -koʊm/ (also **comb**) *noun* [C, U] a structure of cells with six sides, made by BEES for holding their honey and their eggs 蜂巢

honey·combed /ˈhʌnikəʊmd; *NAmE* -koʊmd/ *adj.* **~ (with sth)** filled with holes, tunnels, etc. 蜂窩狀的；多洞的；多孔道的

honey·dew melon /ˌhʌnidjuː ˈmelən; *NAmE* -duː/ *noun* a type of MELON with a pale skin and green flesh 蜜瓜；白蘭瓜

hon·eyed /ˈhʌnid/ *adj.* (*literary*) **1** (of words 言辭) soft and intended to please, but often not sincere 柔順討好的；甜言蜜語的 **2** tasting or smelling like honey, or having the colour of honey 蜂蜜味的；蜂蜜色的

honey·moon /ˈhʌnimuːn/ *noun, verb*

■ ***noun*** [usually sing.] **1** a holiday/vacation taken by a couple who have just got married 蜜月：*We went to Venice for our honeymoon.* 我們去了威尼斯度蜜月。◇ *They're **on their honeymoon**.* 他們正在度蜜月。 **2** the period of time at the start of a new activity when nobody is criticized and people feel enthusiastic （新活動之初的）和諧時期：*The **honeymoon period** for the government is now over.* 這屆政府的蜜月期現在已經過去了。

■ ***verb*** [I] **+ adv./prep.** to spend your honeymoon somewhere （去某處）度蜜月 ▸ **honey·moon·er** *noun*

honey·pot /ˈhʌnipɒt; *NAmE* -pɑːt/ *noun* [usually sing.] (*BrE*) a place, thing or person that a lot of people are attracted to 富有吸引力的地方（或事物、人）

honey·suckle /ˈhʌnisʌkl/ *noun* [U, C] a climbing plant with white, yellow or pink flowers with a sweet smell 忍冬（蔓生，開白色、黃色或粉紅色花，氣味芬芳）

hongi /ˈhɒŋi; *NAmE* ˈhɑːŋi/ *noun* (*NZE*) a traditional Maori GREETING in which people press their noses together 摩擦鼻子（毛利人表示歡迎的方式）

honk /hɒŋk; *NAmE* hɑːŋk; hɔːŋk/ *noun, verb*

■ ***noun*** **1** the noise made by a GOOSE 鵝叫聲 **2** the noise made by a car horn 汽車喇叭聲

■ ***verb*** **1** [I, T] if a car horn **honks** or you **honk** or **honk the horn**, the horn makes a loud noise （使汽車喇叭）鳴響 **SYN** **hoot**：*honking taxis* 喇叭聲大作的出租車 ◇ **~ at sb/sth** *Why did he honk at me?* 他為什麼衝我按喇叭？◇ **~ sth** *People honked their horns as they drove past.* 人們開車經過時大按喇叭。 **2** [I] when a GOOSE **honks**, it makes a loud noise （鵝）叫

honky /ˈhɒŋki; *NAmE* ˈhɑːŋ-; ˈhɔːŋ-/ *noun* (*pl.* **-ies**) (*NAmE, slang*) an offensive word for a white person, used by black people （黑人對白人的冒犯稱呼）白鬼

honky-tonk /ˈhɒŋki tɒŋk; *NAmE* ˈhɑːŋki tɑːŋk; ˈhɔːŋki tɔːŋk/ *noun* **1** [C] (*NAmE*) a cheap, noisy bar or dance hall 低級嘈雜的酒吧（或舞廳） **2** [U] a type of lively JAZZ played on a piano 杭基湯克音樂，酒吧爵士樂（用鋼琴演奏的活潑爵士樂）

honor, **hon·or·able** (*especially US*) = HONOUR, HONOURABLE

hon·or·arium /ˌɒnəˈreəriəm; *NAmE* ˌɑːnəˈrer-/ *noun* (*pl.* **hon·or·aria** /-riə/) (*formal*) a payment made for sb's professional services 酬金；謝禮 **HELP** Use **an**, not **a**, before **honorarium**. * honorarium 之前用 an，不用 a。

hon·or·ary /ˈɒnərəri; *NAmE* ˈɑːnəreri/ *adj.* (*abbr.* **Hon**) **1** (of a university degree, a rank, etc. 大學學位、級別等) given as an honour, without the person having to have the usual qualifications 榮譽的：*an **honorary doctorate/degree*** 榮譽博士學位；榮譽學位 **2** (of a position in an organization 機構中的職位) not paid 無報酬的；義務的：*the honorary president* 名譽校長 ◇ *The post of treasurer is a purely honorary position.* 司庫的職位純屬義務性質。 **3** treated like a member of group without actually belonging to it 被待作…成員的：*She was treated as an honorary man.* 她得到了男子般的待遇。**HELP** Use **an**, not **a**, before **honorary**. * honorary 之前用 an，不用 a。

hon·or·ee (*BrE* also **hon·our·ee**) /ˌɒnəˈriː; *NAmE* ˌɑːnəˈriː/ *noun* (*especially NAmE*) a person or thing that wins an award 獲獎者；獲獎作品：*The author is a Pulitzer Prize honoree.* 這名作者是普利策獎獲得者。**HELP** Use **an**, not **a**, before **honoree**. * honoree 前用 an，不用 a。

hon·or·if·ic /ˌɒnəˈrɪfɪk; *NAmE* ˌɑːnə-/ *adj.* (*formal*) showing respect for the person you are speaking to 表示尊敬的：*an honorific title* 尊稱 **HELP** Use **an**, not **a**, before **honorific**. * honorific 之前用 an，不用 a。

hon·oris causa /ɒˌnɔːrɪs ˈkaʊzɑː; *NAmE* əˌnɔːrəs ˈkɔːzə/ *adv.* (from *Latin*) (especially of a degree 尤指學位) given to a person as a sign of honour and respect, without their having to take an exam 作為榮譽；名譽上：*She was awarded a degree honoris causa.* 她獲授予名譽學位。

ˈhonor roll *noun* (*especially US*) **1** (*BrE* **ˌroll of ˈhonour**) [usually sing.] a list of people who are being praised officially for sth they have done 榮譽名冊；光榮榜 **2** a list of the best students in a college or HIGH SCHOOL （大、中學的）優秀生名單，光榮榜

ˈhonor society *noun* (in the US) an organization for students with the best grades at school or college （美國學校或大學的）優等生聯合會

ˈhonor system *noun* [sing.] (*NAmE*) an agreement in which people are trusted to obey rules 誠信制度（信賴人能自動守規則的制度）

hon·our 🔑 (*especially US* **honor**) /ˈɒnə(r); *NAmE* ˈɑːnər/ *noun, verb*

■ ***noun*** **HELP** Use **an**, not **a**, before **honour**. * honour 前用 an，不用 a。

▸ **RESPECT** 尊敬 **1** 🔑 [U] great respect and admiration for sb 尊敬；尊重；崇敬：*the **guest of honour*** (= the most important one) 貴賓 ◇ *the **seat/place of honour*** (= given to the most important guest) 上座／席 ◇ *They stood in silence as a mark of honour to her.* 他們肅立以示對她的敬意。➲ see also MAID OF HONOUR, MATRON OF HONOUR

▸ **PRIVILEGE** 榮幸 **2** 🔑 [sing.] something that you are very pleased or proud to do because people are showing you great respect 榮幸；光榮：*It was a great honour to be invited here today.* 今天承蒙邀請到此，深感榮幸。 **SYN** **privilege** ➲ SYNONYMS at PLEASURE

▸ **MORAL BEHAVIOUR** 道德品行 **3** 🔑 [U] the quality of knowing and doing what is morally right 正義感；道義；節操：*a man of honour* 品德高尚的人 ◇ *Proving his innocence has become a matter of honour.* 證實他的清白已經成了一件道義上的事。

▸ **REPUTATION** 名譽 **4** 🔑 [U] a good reputation; respect from other people 榮譽；名譽；他人的尊敬：*upholding the honour of your country* 捍衛祖國的榮譽 ◇ *The family honour is at stake.* 家族名譽岌岌可危。➲ compare DISHONOUR **5** [sing.] **~ to sth/sb** a person or thing that causes others to respect and admire sth/sb 引起尊敬（或尊重，崇敬）的人（或事物）：*She is an honour to the profession.* 她是這一行業的光榮。

▸ **AWARD** 獎勵 **6** 🔑 [C] an award, official title, etc. given to sb as a reward for sth that they have done （為表揚某人的）獎勵，榮譽稱號，頭銜：*the New Year's Honours list* (= in Britain, a list of awards and titles given on January 1 each year) （英國）元旦受勳者名冊 ◇ *to win the highest honour* 贏得最高榮譽 ◇ *He was buried **with full military honours*** (= with a special military service as a sign of respect). 他以隆重的軍葬禮下葬。 ➲ see also ROLL OF HONOUR

▸ AT UNIVERSITY/SCHOOL 大學；學校 **7 honours, honors** [pl.] (*abbr.* **Hons**) (often used as an adjective 常用作形容詞) a university course that is of a higher level than a basic course (in the US also used to describe a class in school which is at a higher level than other classes) 大學榮譽學位課程；（美國的）學校優等班： *an* ***honours degree/course*** 榮譽學位／課程 ◇ *a First Class Honours degree* 一級榮譽學位 ◇ (*NAmE*) *I took an honors class in English.* 我選了一個英語優等班課程。 **8 honours, honors** [pl.] if you pass an exam or GRADUATE from a university or school **with honours**, you receive a special mark/grade for having achieved a very high standard 優異成績

▸ JUDGE/MAYOR 法官；市長 **9 His/Her/Your Honour** [C] a title of respect used when talking to or about a judge or a US MAYOR 法官大人；（美國）市長閣下： *No more questions, Your Honour.* 沒有其他問題了，法官大人。

▸ IN CARD GAMES 紙牌遊戲 **10** [C, usually pl.] the cards that have the highest value 最大點數的牌

IDM **do sb an 'honour | do sb the 'honour (of doing sth)** (*formal*) to do sth to make sb feel very proud and pleased 使增光；賞光；給…帶來榮譽： *Would you do me the honour of dining with me?* 你能賞光和我一塊吃飯嗎？ **do the 'honours** to perform a social duty or ceremony, such as pouring drinks, making a speech, etc. 履行社交責任；執行儀式： *Would you do the honours and draw the winning ticket?* 能勞駕為我們抽出獲獎的票嗎？ **have the 'honour of sth/of doing sth** (*formal*) to be given the opportunity to do sth that makes you feel proud and happy 得到某殊榮；有幸做某事： *May I have the honour of the next dance?* 能賞光和我跳下一支舞嗎？ **(there is) honour among 'thieves** (*saying*) used to say that even criminals have standards of behaviour that they respect 盜亦有道 **(feel) honour-'bound to do sth** (*formal*) to feel that you must do sth because of your sense of moral duty （感到）道義上應做某事： *She felt honour-bound to attend as she had promised to.* 她覺得既然答應了就應該出席。 ➲ compare DUTY-BOUND **the honours are 'even** no particular person, team, etc. is doing better than the others in a competition, an argument, etc. 勢均力敵；不分勝負 **in 'honour of sb/sth | in sb's/sth's 'honour** in order to show respect and admiration for sb/sth 為向…表示敬意： *a ceremony in honour of those killed in the explosion* 為紀念爆炸中的死難者所舉行的儀式 ◇ *A banquet was held in her honour.* 為歡迎她而設宴。 **on your 'honour** (*old-fashioned*) **1** used to promise very seriously that you will do sth or that sth is true 用人格擔保；以名譽擔保： *I swear on my honour that I knew nothing about this.* 我以人格擔保我根本不知道這件事。 **2** to be trusted to do sth 受到信任；被信賴： *You're on your honour not to go into my room.* 依你的人格，相信你不會進我的房間。 ➲ more at POINT *n.*

■ *verb*

▸ SHOW RESPECT 表示敬意 **1 ~ sb (with sth)** to do sth that shows great respect for sb/sth 尊敬，尊重（某人）： *The President honoured us with a personal visit.* 總統親臨，使我們感到榮幸。 ◇ *our honoured guests* 我們的貴賓 ◇ (*ironic*) *I'm glad to see that you've decided to* ***honour us with your presence!*** 很高興看到你已決定大駕光臨！

▸ GIVE AWARD 頒獎 **2 ~ sb/sth (with sth) (for sth)** to give public praise, an award or a title to sb for sth they have done 給予表揚（或獎勵、頭銜、稱號）： *He has been honoured with a knighthood for his scientific work.* 他因科研成就而獲授予爵士頭銜。

▸ KEEP PROMISE 遵守諾言 **3 ~ sth** (*formal*) to do what you have agreed or promised to do 信守，執行（承諾）： *I have every intention of honouring our contract.* 我完全願意執行我們的合約。 ◇ *to honour a cheque* (= to keep an agreement to pay it) 承兑支票

IDM **be/feel honoured (to do sth)** to feel proud and happy （做某事）感到榮幸： *I was honoured to have been mentioned in his speech.* 他在講話中提到了我，真是榮幸。

hon·our·able (*especially US* **hon·or·able**) /ˈɒnərəbl; *NAmE* ˈɑːnə-/ *adj.* **1** deserving respect and admiration 可敬的；值得欽佩的： *a long and honourable career in government* 長期光榮的從政生涯 ◇ *They managed an honourable 2–2 draw.* 他們奮力打成了 2:2 平局，值得敬佩。 ◇ ***With a few honourable exceptions****, the staff were found to be incompetent.* 除了幾個優秀的人以外，其他職員都不能勝任工作。 **2** showing high moral standards 品格高尚的： *an honourable man* 高尚的人 **3** allowing sb to keep their good name and the respect of others 保護聲譽的；體面的： *an honourable compromise* 體面的妥協 ◇ *They urged her to* ***do the honourable thing*** *and resign.* 他們力勸她辭職以保全名節。 ◇ *He received an honourable discharge from the army.* 他獲准體面退伍。 **OPP** **dishonourable** **4 the Honourable** (*abbr.* **Hon**) [only before noun] (in Britain) a title used by a child of some ranks of the NOBILITY（英國某些貴族子女的頭銜） **5 the/my Honourable …** (*abbr.* **Hon**) [only before noun] (in Britain) a title used by Members of Parliament when talking about or to another Member during a debate （英國議會議員辯論時相互間的尊稱）： *If my Honourable Friend would give me a chance to answer, …* 如果我的朋友閣下能給我答辯的機會… **6** (*abbr.* **Hon**) a title of respect used by an official of high rank （高級官員的尊稱）： *the Honorable Alan Simpson, US senator* 美國參議員艾倫•辛普森 ➲ compare RIGHT HONOURABLE **HELP** Use **an**, not **a**, before **honourable.** * honourable 之前用 an，不用 a。 ▸ **hon·our·ably** (*especially US* **hon·or·ably**) /-əbli/ *adv.*： *to behave honourably* 行為光明磊落

hon·our·ee (*especially US* **hon·or·ee**) /ˌɒnəˈriː; *NAmE* ˌɑːnəˈriː/ *noun* (*especially NAmE*) a person or thing that wins an award 獲獎者： *The author is a Pulitzer Prize honouree.* 這名作者是普利策獎獲得者。

Hons /ɒnz; *NAmE* ɑːnz/ *abbr.* (*BrE*) HONOURS (used after the name of a university degree) 榮譽學位（用於大學學位名稱之後）： *Tim Smith BA (Hons)* （榮譽）文學士蒂姆•史密斯

hooch /huːtʃ/ *noun* [U] (*informal, especially NAmE*) strong alcoholic drink, especially sth that has been made illegally（尤指非法釀造的）烈酒

hood /hʊd/ *noun* **1** a part of a coat, etc. that you can pull up to cover the back and top of your head 風帽，兜帽（外衣的一部份，可拉起蒙住頭頸）： *a jacket with a detachable hood* 有拆除式風帽的夾克 ➲ VISUAL VOCAB pages V61, V65 **2** a piece of cloth put over sb's face and head so that they cannot be recognized or so that they cannot see （布質）面罩 **3** a piece of coloured silk or fur worn over an academic GOWN to show the kind of degree held by the person wearing it 學位連領帽（表示學位種類） **4** (*especially BrE*) a folding cover over a car, etc. （汽車等的）摺疊式車篷： *We drove all the way with the hood down.* 我們一路上敞着車篷開車。 ➲ picture at PUSHCHAIR **5** (*NAmE*) (*BrE* **bon·net**) the metal part over the front of a vehicle, usually covering the engine（車輛的）引擎蓋 ➲ VISUAL VOCAB page V52 **6** a cover placed over a device or machine, for example, to protect it （設備或機器的）防護罩，罩： *a lens hood* 鏡頭遮光罩 ◇ *an extractor hood* (= one that removes cooking smells from a kitchen) （廚房）排氣罩 ➲ VISUAL VOCAB page V25 **7** (*slang, especially NAmE*) = HOODLUM (1) **8** (also **'hood**) (*slang, especially NAmE*) a neighbourhood, especially a person's own neighbourhood 街區；鄰里；左鄰右舍

-hood *suffix* (in nouns 構成名詞) **1** the state or quality of …的狀態（或性質）： *childhood* 兒童時期 ◇ *falsehood* 虛假 **2** a group of people of the type mentioned （某類人的）集體： *the priesthood* 司祭團

hood·ed /ˈhʊdɪd/ *adj.* **1** having or wearing a hood 有（或戴）兜帽的： *a hooded jacket* 有兜帽的夾克 ◇ *A hooded figure waited in the doorway.* 一個戴兜帽的人在門口等候。 **2** (of eyes 眼睛) having large EYELIDS that always look as if they are partly closed 眼皮耷拉（而狀似半睜半閉）的

hood·lum /ˈhuːdləm/ *noun* (*informal*) **1** (also *slang* **hood** especially in *NAmE*) a violent criminal, especially one who is part of a GANG 暴徒，惡棍（尤指屬於某團夥者）

2 a violent and noisy young man 小阿飛；小流氓 SYN hooliganism

hoo·doo /'huːduː/ *noun* (*pl.* **-oos**) (*especially US*) a person or thing that brings or causes bad luck 帶來厄運的人；不祥之物

hood·wink /'hʊdwɪŋk/ *verb* **~ sb (into doing sth)** to trick sb 欺詐，欺騙（某人）：*She had been hoodwinked into buying a worthless necklace.* 她受騙買了條一文不值的項鏈。

hoody (also **hoodie**) /'hʊdi/ *noun* (*pl.* **-ies**) (*informal*) a jacket or a SWEATSHIRT with a HOOD 帶兜帽短上衣，連帽短上衣（或運動衫）➲ VISUAL VOCAB page V63

hooey /'huːi/ *noun* [U] (*informal, especially NAmE*) nonsense; stupid talk 廢話；胡說八道

hoof /huːf/ *noun, verb*

■ ***noun*** (*pl.* **hoofs** or **hooves** /huːvz/) the hard part of the foot of some animals, for example horses （馬等動物的）蹄 ➲ VISUAL VOCAB page V12

IDM **on the 'hoof** **1** meat that is sold, transported, etc. **on the hoof** is sold, etc. while the cow or sheep is still alive （牲畜等）活着的，待宰的 **2** (*BrE, informal*) if you do sth **on the hoof**, you do it quickly and without giving it your full attention because you are doing sth else at the same time 草草地；順便

■ ***verb*** **~ sth** (*informal*) to kick a ball very hard or a long way 猛踢（球）；把（球）踢出很遠

IDM **'hoof it** (*informal*) to go somewhere on foot; to walk somewhere 步行（到某處）：*We hoofed it all the way to 42nd Street.* 我們一路步行到了第 42 街。

,hoof-and-'mouth disease *noun* [U] (*NAmE*) = FOOT-AND-MOUTH DISEASE

hoo-ha /'huː hɑː/ *noun* [U, sing.] (*BrE, informal*) noisy excitement, especially about sth unimportant 鬧嚷；激動；（尤指）小題大做，大驚小怪 SYN **fuss**

hooks 鈎子；鈎拳

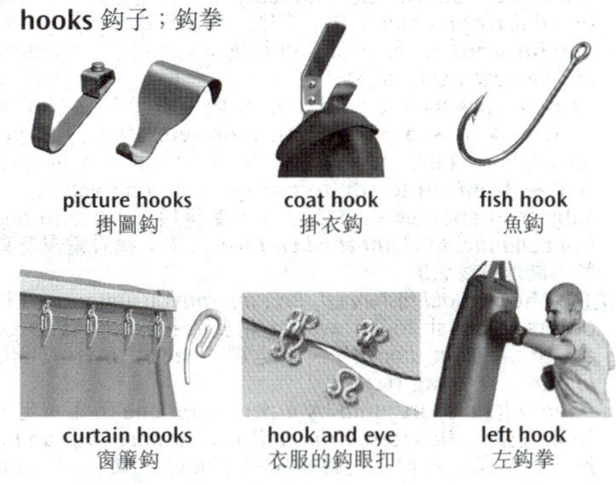

picture hooks 掛圖鈎 | coat hook 掛衣鈎 | fish hook 魚鈎 | curtain hooks 窗簾鈎 | hook and eye 衣服的鈎眼扣 | left hook 左鈎拳

hook 0→ /hʊk/ *noun, verb*

■ ***noun*** **1** 0→ a curved piece of metal, plastic or wire for hanging things on, catching fish with, etc. 鈎；釣鈎；掛鈎；魚鈎：*a **picture/curtain/coat hook*** 掛圖鈎；窗簾鈎；掛衣鈎 ◇ *a fish hook* 魚鈎 ◇ *Hang your towel **on the hook**.* 把你的毛巾掛在鈎上。➲ VISUAL VOCAB page V41 ➲ see also BOATHOOK **2** (in boxing 拳擊運動) a short hard blow that is made with the elbow bent 鈎拳：*a left hook to the jaw* 擊向下頜的一記左鈎拳 **3** (in CRICKET and GOLF 板球及高爾夫球) a way of hitting the ball so that it curves sideways instead of going straight ahead 曲線球 **4** a thing that is used to make people interested in sth 吸引人的事物；誘餌：*The images are used as a hook to get children interested in science.* 這些圖像用以吸引孩子們對科學產生興趣。

IDM **by ,hook or by 'crook** using any method you can, even a dishonest one 想方設法；不擇手段 **get (sb) off the 'hook | let sb off the 'hook** to free yourself or sb else from a difficult situation or a punishment（使）擺脫困境，逃避懲罰 **hook, line and 'sinker** completely 完全地；毫無保留：*What I said was not true, but he fell for it* (= believed it) *hook, line and sinker.* 我的話並非實

話，但他完全相信了。**off the 'hook** if you leave or take the telephone **off the hook**, you take the RECEIVER (= the part that you pick up) off the place where it usually rests, so that nobody can call you （為防止電話打進來而使聽筒）不掛上 ➲ more at RING² *v.*, SLING *v.*

■ ***verb*** **1** [T, I] to fasten or hang sth on sth else using a hook; to be fastened or hanging in this way （使）鈎住，掛住：**~ sth + adv./prep.** *We hooked the trailer to the back of the car.* 我們把拖車掛在汽車尾部。◇ **+ adv./prep.** *a dress that hooks at the back* 從後背用鈎扣的連衣裙 **2** [T, I] to put sth, especially your leg, arm or finger, around sth else so that you can hold onto it or move it; to go around sth else in this way （尤指用腿、胳膊、手指等）鈎住，箍住：**~ sth + adv./prep.** *He hooked his foot under the stool and dragged it over.* 他用腳從底下鈎住凳子，把它拖了過去。◇ *Her thumbs were hooked into the pockets of her jeans.* 她的雙手拇指鈎在牛仔褲袋裏。◇ **+ adv./prep.** *Suddenly an arm hooked around my neck.* 突然有一條胳臂箍住了我的脖子。 **3** [T] **~ sth** to catch a fish with a hook 釣（魚）：*It was the biggest pike I ever hooked.* 那是我釣到的最大的狗魚。◇ (*figurative*) *She had managed to hook a wealthy husband.* 她成功地嫁到了一個有錢的丈夫。 **4** [T] **~ sth** (especially in GOLF, CRICKET or football (SOCCER) 尤指高爾夫球、板球或足球) to hit or kick a ball so that it goes to one side instead of straight ahead 打曲線球；踢弧線球

PHR V **,hook 'up (to sth) | ,hook sb/sth↔'up (to sth)** to connect sb/sth to a piece of electronic equipment, to a power supply or to the Internet 連接到電子設備（或電源、互聯網）；接通：*She was then hooked up to an IV drip.* 接着就給她接上了靜脈滴注。◇ *Check that the computer is hooked up to the printer.* 檢查一下計算機是否與打印機接通。◇ *A large proportion of the nation's households are hooked up to the Internet.* 全國大部份家庭都接通了互聯網。**,hook 'up with sb** (*informal*) **1** to meet sb and spend time with them 與某人來往 **2** to start working with sb 搭檔工作 **,hook sb 'up with sb/sth** (*informal*) to put sb in contact with sb who can help them; to get sth for sb that they want 把某人介紹給某人；讓某人與某人拉上關係；幫某人搞到某物：*Can you hook me up with someone with a car?* 你能幫我聯繫到一個有車的人嗎？

hoo·kah /'hʊkə/ *noun* a long pipe for smoking that passes smoke through a container of water to cool it 水煙袋；水煙筒

,hook and 'eye *noun* (*pl.* **hooks and eyes**) a device for fastening clothes, consisting of a small thin piece of metal curved round, and a hook that fits into it （衣服的）鈎眼扣 ➲ picture at HOOK ➲ VISUAL VOCAB page V63

hooked /hʊkt/ *adj.* **1** curved; shaped like a hook 彎曲的；鈎形的：*a **hooked nose/beak/finger*** 鷹鈎鼻子；鈎喙；屈指 **2** [not before noun] **~ (on sth)** (*informal*) needing sth that is bad for you, especially a drug 上癮；（尤指）有毒癮 **3** [not before noun] **~ (on sth)** (*informal*) enjoying sth very much, so that you want to do it, see it, etc. as much as possible （對某事）着迷 **4** having one or more hooks 有鈎的

hook·er /'hʊkə(r)/ *noun* **1** the player in a RUGBY team, whose job is to pull the ball out of the SCRUM with his foot （橄欖球並列爭球時的）鈎球隊員，鈎射 **2** (*informal, especially NAmE*) a PROSTITUTE 賣淫者

hookey = HOOKY

'hook shot *noun* **1** (in BASKETBALL 籃球) a shot in which a player throws the ball towards the BASKET in a wide curve, by stretching their arm out to the side and throwing over their head 鈎手投籃 **2** (in CRICKET 板球) a shot in which a player hits the ball to the side by swinging the BAT across their chest 側飛球

'hook-up *noun* a connection between two pieces of equipment, especially electronic equipment used in broadcasting, or computers （廣播等的）聯播；（計算機之間的）聯機：*a satellite hook-up between the major European networks* 歐洲各主要電視網通過衛星的聯播

hook·worm /'hʊkwɜːm; *NAmE* -wɜːrm/ *noun* **1** [C] a WORM that lives in the INTESTINES of humans and

H

animals 鉤蟲（寄生於人或動物腸道）**2** [U] a disease caused by hookworms 鉤蟲病

hooky (also **hookey**) /ˈhʊki/ (*old-fashioned, NAmE*)
IDM **play ˈhooky** (*informal*) (*BrE* **play ˈtruant**) to stay away from school without permission 曠課；逃學

hooli·gan /ˈhuːlɪɡən/ *noun* a young person who behaves in an extremely noisy and violent way in public, usually in a group（通常結夥的）阿飛，小流氓：*English football hooligans* 英國足球流氓 ▸ **hooli·gan·ism** /-ɪzəm/ *noun* [U]

hoon /huːn/ *noun* (*AustralE, NZE, informal*) a man who behaves in a rude and aggressive way, especially one who drives in a dangerous way 莽漢；（尤指）危險駕駛的男子，橫衝直撞的駕駛員 ▸ **hoon** *verb* [I]

hoop /huːp/ *noun* **1** a large ring of plastic, wood or iron 箍；環；圈：*a barrel bound with iron hoops* 用鐵箍箍緊的桶 ◇ *hoop earrings* (= in the shape of a hoop) 耳環 ➲ VISUAL VOCAB page V65 **2** the ring that the players throw the ball through in the game of BASKETBALL in order to score points（籃球）籃圈；籃框：*Let's shoot some hoops.* 我們投幾下籃吧。➲ VISUAL VOCAB page V44 **3** a large ring that was used as a children's toy in the past, or for animals or riders to jump through at a CIRCUS（舊時兒童玩的）大環子；（馬戲團用的）大圈 **4** = HULA HOOP **5** a small ARCH made of metal or plastic, put into the ground（兩端埋在地裏的）小鐵弓，小塑料弓：*croquet hoops* 槌球戲中的拱門 ◇ *Grow lettuces under plastic stretched over wire hoops.* 在鐵弓撐起的塑料棚下種植生菜。**IDM** see JUMP *v.*

hooped /huːpt/ *adj.* shaped like a hoop 環形的：*hooped earrings* 圈狀耳環

hoopla /ˈhuːplɑː/ *noun* **1** [U, sing.] (*informal, especially NAmE*) excitement about sth which gets a lot of public attention 大吹大擂；喧鬧 **2** [U] (*BrE*) (*NAmE* **ring·toss**) a game in which players try to throw rings over objects in order to win them as prizes 投環套物

hoo·poe /ˈhuːpuː; -pəʊ; *NAmE* -poʊ/ *noun* an orange-pink bird with a long beak that curves downwards, black and white wings and a CREST on its head 戴勝（一種鳥，粉紅褐色，喙長而下彎，有冠，翅有黑白相間的條斑）

hoo·ray /huˈreɪ/ *exclamation* **1** (also **hur·rah**, **hur·ray**) used to show that you are happy or that you approve of sth（表示快樂或贊同）好極了，好哇 **2** (also **hoo·roo**) (*AustralE, NZE*) goodbye 再見 **IDM** see HIP *exclam.*

Hoo·ray Hen·ry /ˌhuːreɪ ˈhenri/ *noun* (*pl.* **Hoo·ray Hen·rys** or **Hoo·ray Hen·ries**) (*BrE, informal, disapproving*) a young upper-class man who enjoys himself in a loud and silly way 愛喧鬧和幹蠢事的上流社會年輕人；紈絝子弟

hoo·roo /həˈruː; hʌˈruː/ *exclamation* (*AustralE*) = HOORAY (2)

hoot /huːt/ *verb, noun*

■ *verb* **1** [I] to make a loud noise 發出大聲；喊叫：*He had the audience **hooting with laughter**.* 他令觀眾哄堂大笑。◇ *Some people hooted in disgust.* 有些人厭惡地大聲嚷嚷。**2** [I, T] (*BrE*) if a car horn **hoots** or you **hoot** or **hoot the horn**, the horn makes a loud noise（使汽車喇叭）鳴響 **SYN** **honk**：*hooting cars* 喇叭聲大作的汽車 ◇ **~ at sb/sth** *Why did he hoot at me?* 他為什麼對着我按喇叭？◇ **~ sth** *Passing motorists hooted their horns.* 路過的駕駛者按響了汽車喇叭。◇ *The train hooted a warning* (= the driver sounded the horn to warn people). 火車鳴笛示警。**3** [I] when an OWL **hoots**, it makes a long calling sound（貓頭鷹）鳴叫

■ *noun* **1** [C] (*especially BrE*) a short loud laugh or shout 大笑；大喊：*The suggestion was greeted by **hoots of laughter**.* 這個建議引起了陣陣哄笑。**2** [sing.] (*informal*) a situation or a person that you find very funny 可笑的事情（或人）：*You ought to meet her—she's a hoot!* 你應該見見她，她笑料十足！**3** the loud sound made by the horn of a vehicle（車輛的）喇叭聲 **4** the cry of an OWL（貓頭鷹的）鳴叫聲

IDM **not care/give a ˈhoot | not care/give two ˈhoots** (*informal*) not to care at all 絲毫不在乎

hoote·nanny /ˈhuːtnæni/ *noun* (*pl.* **-ies**) (*especially US*) an informal social event at which people play FOLK MUSIC, sing and sometimes dance 民歌演唱會；民間歌舞會

hoot·er /ˈhuːtə(r)/ *noun* **1** (*BrE*, rather *old-fashioned*) the device in a vehicle, or a factory, that makes a loud noise as a signal（車輛的）喇叭；（工廠的）汽笛 **2** (*BrE, slang*) a person's nose, especially a large one（尤指大的）鼻子 **3** [usually pl.] (*NAmE, slang*) a woman's breast（女人的）乳房

Hoo·ver™ /ˈhuːvə(r)/ *noun* (*BrE*) = VACUUM CLEANER

hoo·ver /ˈhuːvə(r)/ *verb* [T, I] **~ (sth)** (*BrE*) to clean a carpet, floor, etc. with a vacuum cleaner 用真空吸塵器清掃（地毯、地板等的灰塵）**SYN** **vacuum**：*to hoover the carpet* 用吸塵器清掃地毯

PHR V **ˌhoover sth↔ˈup** **1** to remove sth from a carpet, floor, etc. with a VACUUM CLEANER 用真空吸塵器把…清除掉：*to hoover up all the dust* 用吸塵器清除所有的灰塵 **2** (*informal*) to get or collect sth in large quantities 獲得大量的（某物）：*The US and Canada usually hoover up most of the gold medals.* 美國和加拿大通常奪得大部份的金牌。▸ **hoo·ver·ing** *noun* [U]：*It's your turn to **do the hoovering**.* 該你做吸塵清潔了。

hooves *pl.* of HOOF

hop /hɒp; *NAmE* hɑːp/ *verb, noun*

■ *verb* (**-pp-**) **1** [I] (**+ adv./prep.**) (of a person 人) to move by jumping on one foot 單腳跳行：*I couldn't put my weight on my ankle and had to hop everywhere.* 我一隻腳的腳踝使不上勁，不得不單腳跳來跳去。◇ *kids hopping over puddles* 單足跳過水坑的孩子們 **2** [I] **+ adv./prep.** (of an animal or a bird 動物或鳥) to move by jumping with all or both feet together 齊足（或雙足）跳行：*A robin was hopping around on the path.* 一隻知更鳥在小路上跳來跳去。**3** [I] **+ adv./prep.** (*informal*) to go or move somewhere quickly and suddenly 突然快速去某處：*Hop in, I'll drive you home.* 快上車吧，我開車送你回家。◇ *to **hop into/out of** bed* 一頭鑽進被窩；猛然起牀 ◇ *I hopped on the next train.* 我跳上了下一列火車。◇ *We hopped over to Paris for the weekend.* 我們衝到巴黎去過了個週末。**4** [T] **~ a plane, bus, train, etc.** (*NAmE*) to get on a plane, bus, etc. 登上（飛機、汽車、火車等）**5** [I] **~ (from sth to sth)** to change from one activity or subject to another 換來換去；不斷更換：*I like to hop from channel to channel when I watch TV.* 我看電視時喜歡不斷地轉換頻道。

IDM **ˈhop it** (*old-fashioned, BrE, informal*) usually used in orders to tell sb to go away（用於命令）走開 **SYN** **go away**：*Go on, hop it!* 快點走開！ **hop ˈto it** (*NAmE, informal*) = JUMP TO IT

■ *noun* **1** [C] a short jump by a person on one foot 單足短距離跳躍：*He crossed the hall with a hop, skip and a jump.* 他來了一個三級跳遠穿過了大廳。**2** [C] a short jump by an animal or a bird with all or both feet together（動物或鳥的）齊足（或雙足）短距離跳躍 **3** [C] a short journey, especially by plane（尤指乘飛機的）短途旅行 **4** [C] a tall climbing plant with green female flowers that are shaped like CONES 忽布；啤酒花 **5** **hops** [pl.] the green female flowers of the hop plant that have been dried, used for making beer（乾的）忽布花，啤酒花 **6** [C] (*old-fashioned, informal*) a social event at which people dance in an informal way（非正式）舞會 ➲ see also HIP HOP **IDM** see CATCH *v.*

hope 🔑 /həʊp; *NAmE* hoʊp/ *verb, noun*

■ *verb* 🔑 [I, T] to want sth to happen and think that it is possible 希望，期望（某事發生）：**~ (for sth)** *We are hoping for good weather on Sunday.* 我們盼望着星期天天氣好。◇ *All we can do now is wait and hope.* 我們現在所能做的就是等候和期待。◇ *'Do you think it will rain?' '**I hope not.**'* "你覺得會下雨嗎？" "但願不會。" ◇ *'Will you be back before dark?' '**I hope so, yes.**'* "你天黑之前能回來嗎？" "但願吧。" ◇ **~ (that)** … *I hope (that) you're okay.* 我希望你平安無事。◇ ***Let's hope** we can find a parking space.* 希望咱們能找到個停車位。◇ **it is hoped (that)** … *It is hoped that over £10 000 will be raised.* 希望籌款能超過 1 萬英鎊。◇ **~ to do sth** *She is hoping to win the gold medal.* 她希望贏得金牌。◇ *We hope to arrive* *around two.* 我們希望能在兩點鐘左右到達。**HELP** **Hope** can be used in the passive in the form **it is hoped that ...** . **For** must always be used with **hope** in other passive sentences. * hope 可用於 it is hoped that ... 這一句型的被動句，其他被動句中 hope 必須與 for 連用：*The improvement that had been hoped for never came.* ◇ *The hoped-for improvement never came.*

IDM **ˌhope against ˈhope (that ...)** to continue to hope for sth although it is very unlikely to happen（尤指某事希望渺茫但）依舊抱一線希望 **ˌhope for the ˈbest** to hope that sth will happen successfully, especially where it seems likely that it will not 希望某事順利；寄予最大的希望 **I should hope so/not | so I should hope** (*informal*) used to say that you feel very strongly that sth should/should not happen 希望如此 / 不如此；但願如此 / 不如此：*'Nobody blames you.' 'I should hope not!'* "沒有人責怪你呀。" "但願沒有！" ➲ more at CROSS *v.*

■ ***noun*** **1** 🗝 [U, C] a belief that sth you want will happen 希望；期望：**~ (of sth)** *There is now hope of a cure.* 現在有望治癒了。◇ **~ (for sb/sth)** *Hopes for the missing men are fading.* 找到失踪者的希望逐漸渺茫。◇ **~ (that ...)** *There is **little hope that** they will be found alive.* 活着找到他們的希望很渺茫。◇ **~ (of doing sth)** *They have **given up hope** of finding any more survivors.* 他們已不抱希望再找到幸存者了。◇ *She **has high hopes** of winning* (= is very confident about it). 她抱着必勝的信念。◇ *The future is not without hope.* 未來並非沒有希望。◇ *Don't **raise your hopes** too high, or you may be disappointed.* 不要希望過高，否則你可能會失望的。◇ *I'll do what I can, but don't **get your hopes up**.* 我會盡力而為的，但別抱太大希望。◇ *There is still a **glimmer of hope**.* 仍有一線希望。◇ *The situation is not good but we **live in hope** that it will improve.* 情況不好，但我們依然希望會好轉。 **2** 🗝 [C] **~ (of/for sth) | ~ (for sb) | ~ (that ...) | ~ (of doing sth)** something that you wish for 希望的東西；期望的事情：*She told me all her hopes, dreams and fears.* 她把一切希望、夢想和擔心都告訴了我。◇ *They **have high hopes** for their children.* 他們對自己的孩子們寄予厚望。 **3** [C, usually sing.] **~ (of sth) | ~ (for sb)** a person, a thing or a situation that will help you get what you want 被寄予希望的人（或事物、情況）：*He turned to her in despair and said, 'You're my **last hope**.'* 他絕望地向她求助說："你是我最後的希望。" ◇ *The operation was Kelly's **only hope of** survival.* 那次手術是凱利生存的唯一希望。

IDM **be beyond ˈhope (of sth)** to be in a situation where no improvement is possible 毫無希望 **hold out little, etc. ˈhope (of sth/that ...) | not hold out any, much, etc. ˈhope (of sth/that ...)** to offer little, etc. reason for believing that sth will happen 不大相信某事會發生：*The doctors did not hold out much hope for her recovery.* 醫生們對她的痊癒不抱什麼希望。 **ˌhope springs eˈternal** (*saying*) people never stop hoping 人生永遠充滿希望 **in the hope of sth | in the hope that ...** (*NAmE* also **in hopes that ...**) because you want sth to happen 抱着…的希望：*I called early in the hope of catching her before she went to work.* 我很早就打了個電話，希望在她上班之前找到她。◇ *He asked her again **in the vain hope** that he could persuade her to come* (= it was impossible). 他又問了她一次，徒然指望着能說服她來。 **not have a ˈhope (in ˈhell) (of doing sth)** (*informal*) to have no chance at all 毫無機會；不抱希望：*She doesn't have a hope of winning.* 她根本無望取勝。 **ˌsome ˈhope!** (*BrE, informal*) used to say that there is no chance at all that sth will happen 毫無希望；妄想 ➲ more at DASH *v.*, PIN *v.*

ˈhope chest *noun* (*NAmE*) items for the house collected by a woman, especially in the past, in preparation for her marriage (and often kept in a large CHEST)（尤指過去未婚女子的）嫁妝 ➲ compare BOTTOM DRAWER

ˈhoped-for *adj.* [only before noun] wanted and thought possible 期待的；所希望的：*The new policy did not bring the hoped-for economic recovery.* 新政策並沒有帶來所期待的經濟復蘇。

hope·ful /ˈhəʊpfl; *NAmE* ˈhoʊp-/ *adj., noun*

■ ***adj.*** **1** [not usually before noun] (of a person 人) believing that sth you want will happen 抱有希望；滿懷希望 **SYN** **optimistic**：**~ (that ...)** *I feel hopeful that we'll find a suitable house very soon.* 我對很快找到合適的房子抱有希望。◇ **~ (about sth)** *He is not very hopeful about the outcome of the interview.* 他對面試的結果不抱很大希望。◇ **~ (of doing sth)** (*BrE*) *She is hopeful of returning to work soon.* 她希望很快回去工作。**OPP** **pessimistic** **2** [only before noun] (of a person's behaviour 人的行為) showing hope 表現出希望的：*a hopeful smile* 充滿希望的微笑 **3** (of a thing 事物) making you believe that sth you want will happen; bringing hope 給人以希望的 **SYN** **promising**：*The latest trade figures are a hopeful sign.* 最新貿易數字令人鼓舞。◇ *The future did not seem very hopeful.* 前景似乎不太樂觀。▸ **hope·ful·ness** *noun* [U]

■ ***noun*** a person who wants to succeed at sth 希望成功的人；雄心勃勃的人：*50 young hopefuls are trying for a place in the England team.* * 50 名雄心勃勃的年輕人亟欲躋身英格蘭隊。

hope·ful·ly /ˈhəʊpfəli; *NAmE* ˈhoʊp-/ *adv.* **1** used to express what you hope will happen 有希望地；可以指望：*Hopefully, we'll arrive before dark.* 我們有望在天黑前到達。**HELP** Although this is the most common use of **hopefully**, it is a fairly new use and some people think it is not correct. 儘管這是 hopefully 最常見的用法，但算是相當新的用法，有人認為並不正確。 **2** showing hope 抱有希望的：*'Are you free tonight?' she asked hopefully.* "你今晚有空嗎？" 她抱着希望地問。

hope·less /ˈhəʊpləs; *NAmE* ˈhoʊp-/ *adj.* **1** if sth is **hopeless**, there is no hope that it will get better or succeed 沒有好轉（或成功）希望的；無望的：*a hopeless situation* 無可挽救的局勢 ◇ ***It's hopeless** trying to convince her.* 想說服她簡直是徒勞。◇ *Most of the students are making good progress, but Michael is **a hopeless case**.* 大多數學生都很有進步，唯有邁克爾不可救藥。◇ *He felt that his life was a hopeless mess.* 他覺得他生活得狼狽不堪。 **2** (*BrE, informal*) extremely bad 極差的；糟糕透頂的 **SYN** **terrible**：*The buses are absolutely hopeless these days!* 如今的公共汽車簡直糟透了。 **3** (*especially BrE*) (of people 人) very bad (at sth); with no ability or skill 不能勝任的；無能的；缺乏技能的 **SYN** **terrible**：*a hopeless driver* 無用的司機 ◇ **~ at sth** *I'm hopeless at science.* 我對理科一竅不通。 **4** feeling or showing no hope 感到（或顯得）無望的：*She felt lonely and hopeless.* 她感到孤獨絕望。 ▸ **hope·less·ly** *adv.*：*hopelessly outnumbered* 數量上被遠遠超過 ◇ *They were hopelessly lost.* 他們徹底失敗了。◇ *to be hopelessly in love* 愛得不能自拔 ◇ *'I'll never manage it,' he said hopelessly.* "我永遠也搞不定。" 他絕望地說。 **hope·less·ness** *noun* [U]：*a **sense/feeling of hopelessness*** 絕望感

Hopi /ˈhəʊpi; *NAmE* ˈhoʊpi/ *noun* (*pl.* **Hopi** or **Hopis**) a member of a Native American people, many of whom live in the US state of Arizona 霍皮人（美洲土著，很多居於美國亞利桑那州）

hop·per /ˈhɒpə(r); *NAmE* ˈhɑːp-/ *noun* a container shaped like a V, that holds grain, coal, or food for animals, and lets it out through the bottom * V 形送料斗；漏斗

hop·ping /ˈhɒpɪŋ; *NAmE* ˈhɑːp-/ *adj., adv.*

■ ***adj.*** (*NAmE, informal*) very lively or busy 很活躍的；忙忙碌碌的：*The clubs in town are really hopping.* 城裏的俱樂部真夠熱鬧的。

■ ***adv.***

IDM **ˌhopping ˈmad** (*informal*) very angry 憤怒；暴跳如雷

hop·scotch /ˈhɒpskɒtʃ; *NAmE* ˈhɑːpskɑːtʃ/ *noun* [U] a children's game played on a pattern of squares marked on the ground. Each child throws a stone into a square then HOPS (= jumps on one leg) and jumps along the empty squares to pick up the stone again. 跳房子（兒童單足跳石子的遊戲）

horde /hɔːd; *NAmE* hɔːrd/ *noun* (sometimes *disapproving*) a large crowd of people 一大群人：*There are always hordes of tourists here in the summer.* 夏天這裏總有成群結隊的遊客。◇ *Football fans turned up **in hordes**.* 來了大批大批的足球迷。

hori·zon /həˈraɪzn/ *noun* **1** **the horizon** [sing.] the furthest that you can see, where the sky seems to meet the land or the sea 地平線：*The sun sank below the horizon.* 太陽落到了地平線下。◇ *A ship appeared on the horizon.* 一艘船出現在地平線上。➲ VISUAL VOCAB pages

H

V4, V5 **2** [C, usually pl.] the limit of your desires, knowledge or interests（欲望、知識或興趣的）範圍，眼界：*She wanted to travel to* **broaden her horizons**. 她想旅行，以開闊眼界。◇ *The company needs new horizons now.* 公司現在需要開拓新的領域。

IDM **on the ho'rizon** likely to happen soon 很可能即將發生；已露端倪：*There's trouble looming on the horizon.* 可能快要出事了。

hori·zon·tal /ˌhɒrɪˈzɒntl; *NAmE* ˌhɔːrəˈzɑːntl; ˌhɑːr-/ *adj., noun*

■ **adj.** flat and level; going across and parallel to the ground rather than going up and down 水平的；與地面平行的；橫的：*horizontal lines* 橫線 ⇨ compare VERTICAL *adj.* (1) ▸ **hori·zon·tal·ly** /-təli/ *adv.*：*Cut the cake in half horizontally and spread jam on one half.* 把蛋糕橫切成兩半，把果醬塗在半面上。

■ **noun** **1** **the hori·zon·tal** [U] a horizontal position 水平位置：*He shifted his position from the horizontal.* 他從水平姿勢變換成其他姿勢。**2** [C] a horizontal line or surface 水平線；水平面；橫線；橫切面

H

Hor·licks™ /ˈhɔːlɪks; *NAmE* ˈhɔːrl-/ *noun* **1** [U] powder that contains MALT that you mix with hot milk to make a drink 好立克粉（含麥乳精，可與熱牛奶混合製作飲料）**2** [U, C] a drink made by mixing Horlicks powder with hot milk 好立克熱飲

IDM **make a 'horlicks of sth** (*old-fashioned, BrE, informal*) to do sth badly 弄得一團糟

hor·mone /ˈhɔːməʊn; *NAmE* ˈhɔːrmoʊn/ *noun* a chemical substance produced in the body or in a plant that encourages growth or influences how the cells and TISSUES function; an artificial substance that has similar effects 激素；荷爾蒙：*growth hormones* 生長激素 ◇ *a hormone imbalance* 激素失調 ◇ *Oestrogen is a female sex hormone.* 雌激素是一種雌性荷爾蒙。▸ **hor·mo·nal** /hɔːˈməʊnl; *NAmE* hɔːrˈmoʊnl/ *adj.* [usually before noun]：*the hormonal changes occurring during pregnancy* 妊娠期間的激素變化

ˌhormone re'placement therapy *noun* [U] = HRT

horn /hɔːn; *NAmE* hɔːrn/ *noun, verb*

■ **noun** **1** [C] a hard pointed part that grows, usually in pairs, on the heads of some animals, such as sheep and cows. Horns are often curved.（羊、牛等動物的）角 ⇨ VISUAL VOCAB page V12 **2** [U] the hard substance of which animal horns are made 角質物 **3** [C] a simple musical instrument that consists of a curved metal tube that you blow into（樂器）號：*a hunting horn* 獵號 **4** [C] (*especially BrE*) = FRENCH HORN：*a horn concerto* 法國號協奏曲 **5** [C] a device in a vehicle for making a loud sound as a warning or signal（車輛的）喇叭：*to* **honk your car horn** 按響汽車喇叭 ◇ (*BrE*) *to* **sound/toot your horn** 鳴喇叭 ⇨ VISUAL VOCAB page V52 ⇨ see also FOGHORN

IDM **blow/toot your own 'horn** (*NAmE, informal*) = BLOW YOUR OWN TRUMPET at BLOW *v.* **draw/pull your 'horns in** to start being more careful in your behaviour, especially by spending less money than before 行為檢點；（尤指）減少開支 **on the horns of a di'lemma** in a situation in which you have to make a choice between things that are equally unpleasant 進退兩難；左右為難 ⇨ more at BULL, LOCK *v.*

■ **verb**

PHR V **ˌhorn 'in (on sb/sth)** (*NAmE, informal*) to involve yourself in a situation that does not concern you 干預，介入，插手（與己無關的事）：*I'm sure she doesn't want us horning in on her business.* 我肯定她不希望我們插手她的事。

horn·beam /ˈhɔːnbiːm; *NAmE* ˈhɔːrn-/ *noun* [C, U] a tree with smooth grey BARK and hard wood 鵝耳櫪（樹皮平滑呈灰色，木質堅韌）

horn·bill /ˈhɔːnbɪl; *NAmE* ˈhɔːrn-/ *noun* a tropical bird with a very large curved beak 犀鳥（熱帶鳥類）

horned /hɔːnd; *NAmE* hɔːrnd/ *adj.* having horns or having sth that looks like horns 有角的；有角狀物的

hor·net /ˈhɔːnɪt; *NAmE* ˈhɔːrnɪt/ *noun* a large WASP (= a black and yellow flying insect) that has a very powerful sting 大黃蜂；馬蜂

IDM **a 'hornets' nest** a difficult situation in which a lot of people get very angry 引起公憤的狀況；困境：*His letter to the papers* **stirred up a real hornets' nest**. 他給報界寫的信着實引發了眾怒。

ˌhorn of 'plenty *noun* = CORNUCOPIA (1)

horn·pipe /ˈhɔːnpaɪp; *NAmE* ˈhɔːrn-/ *noun* a fast dance for one person, traditionally performed by sailors; the music for the dance 號笛舞（水手傳統單人舞）；號笛舞樂

'horn-rimmed *adj.* (of a pair of glasses 眼鏡) with frames made of material that looks like horn 角質鏡架的

horny /ˈhɔːni; *NAmE* ˈhɔːrni/ *adj.* **1** (*informal*) sexually excited 性興奮的：*to feel horny* 慾火中燒 **2** (*informal*) sexually attractive 性感的；妖媚的：*to look horny* 外表性感 **3** made of a hard substance like horn 角質的；角質物製的：*the bird's horny beak* 鳥的角質喙 **4** (of skin, etc. 皮膚等) hard and rough 粗硬的；粗糙的：*horny hands* 粗糙的雙手

hor·ol·ogy /hɒˈrɒlədʒi; *NAmE* həˈrɑːl-/ *noun* [U] **1** the study and measurement of time 鐘錶學；計時學 **2** the art of making clocks and watches 鐘錶製造術

horo·scope /ˈhɒrəskəʊp; *NAmE* ˈhɔːrəskoʊp; ˈhɑːr-/ *noun* a description of what is going to happen to sb in the future, based on the position of the stars and the planets when the person was born 占星預言

hor·ren·dous /hɒˈrendəs; *NAmE* hɔːˈr-; hɑːˈr-/ *adj.* **1** extremely shocking 令人震驚的；駭人的 **SYN** **horrific**, **horrifying**：*horrendous injuries* 可怕的傷勢 **2** (*informal*) extremely unpleasant and unacceptable 討厭得難以容忍的 **SYN** **terrible**：*horrendous traffic* 糟透了的交通 **HELP** Some speakers do not pronounce the 'h' at the beginning of **horrendous** and use 'an' instead of 'a' before it. This now sounds old-fashioned. 有人說 horrendous 時不發 h 音，前面用 an 而不用 a，現在聽起來過時了。⇨ SYNONYMS at TERRIBLE ▸ **hor·ren·dous·ly** *adv.*：*horrendously expensive* 貴得離譜

hor·rible /ˈhɒrəbl; *NAmE* ˈhɔːr-; ˈhɑːr-/ *adj.* **1** (*informal*) very bad or unpleasant; used to describe sth that you do not like 極壞的；十分討厭的；可惡的：*horrible weather/children/shoes* 糟透了的天氣／孩子／鞋 ◇ *The coffee tasted horrible.* 這種咖啡難喝極了。◇ *I've got a horrible feeling she lied to us.* 我有種不快的感覺，覺得她對我們說了謊。⇨ SYNONYMS at TERRIBLE **2** making you feel very shocked and frightened 令人震驚的；恐怖的 **SYN** **terrible**：*a horrible crime/nightmare* 駭人聽聞的罪行；可怕的噩夢 **3** (*informal*) (of people or their behaviour 人或行為) unfriendly, unpleasant or unkind 不友善的；討厭的；不厚道的 **SYN** **nasty**, **obnoxious**：*a horrible man* 討厭的人 ◇ *My sister was being horrible to me all day.* 我姐姐一整天都對我很兇。◇ *What a horrible thing to say!* 講這話太不近人情啦！▸ **hor·ribly** /-əbli/ *adv.*：*It was horribly painful.* 疼極了。◇ *The experiment went horribly wrong.* 實驗弄得一塌糊塗。

hor·rid /ˈhɒrɪd; *NAmE* ˈhɔːr-; ˈhɑːr-/ *adj.* (*old-fashioned* or *informal, especially BrE*) very unpleasant or unkind 非常討厭的；很不友好的 **SYN** **horrible**：*a horrid child* 很討人厭的孩子 ◇ *a horrid smell* 惡臭 ◇ *Don't be so horrid to your brother.* 別對你弟弟那麼兇。

hor·rif·ic /həˈrɪfɪk/ *adj.* **1** extremely bad and shocking or frightening 極壞的；令人震驚的；令人驚恐的 **SYN** **horrifying**：*a horrific murder/accident/attack, etc.* 駭人聽聞的謀殺、事故、攻擊等 ◇ *Her injuries were horrific.* 她的傷勢極為嚴重。**2** (*informal*) very bad or unpleasant 極差的；很不愉快的 **SYN** **horrendous**：*We had a horrific trip.* 我們的旅行糟糕透頂。**HELP** Some speakers do not pronounce the 'h' at the beginning of **horrific** and use 'an' instead of 'a' before it. This now sounds old-fashioned. 有人說 horrific 時不發 h 音，前面用 an 而不用 a，現在聽起來過時了。▸ **hor·rif·ic·al·ly** /-kli/ *adv.*

hor·rify /ˈhɒrɪfaɪ; *NAmE* ˈhɔːr-; ˈhɑːr-/ *verb* (**hor·ri·fies**, **hor·ri·fy·ing**, **hor·ri·fied**, **hor·ri·fied**) to make sb feel extremely shocked, disgusted or frightened 驚嚇；使厭

惡；恐嚇 SYN **appal**： **~ sb** *The whole country was horrified by the killings.* 全國都對這些兇殺案感到大為震驚。◇ **it horrifies sb to do sth** *It horrified her to think that he had killed someone.* 一想到他殺過人，她就感到毛骨悚然。◇ **it horrifies sb that …** *It horrified her that he had actually killed someone.* 他確實殺過人，這件事使她感到毛骨悚然。 ▸ **hor·ri·fied** *adj.*： *He was horrified when he discovered the conditions in which they lived.* 看到他們的生活狀況時，他很震驚。◇ *She gazed at him in horrified disbelief.* 她既驚愕又難以置信地盯着他。

hor·ri·fy·ing /ˈhɒrɪfaɪɪŋ; *NAmE* ˈhɔːr-; ˈhɑːr-/ *adj.* making you feel extremely shocked, disgusted or frightened 令人極其震驚的（或厭惡的、恐懼的） SYN **horrific**： *a* ***horrifying sight/experience/story*** 恐怖的景象／經歷／故事◇ *It's horrifying to see such poverty.* 看到這種貧困狀況令人震驚。 ▸ **hor·ri·fy·ing·ly** *adv.*

hor·ror 0━ /ˈhɒrə(r); *NAmE* ˈhɔːr-; ˈhɑːr-/ *noun*
1 0━ [U] a feeling of great shock, fear or disgust 震驚；恐懼；厭惡： *People watched* ***in horror*** *as the plane crashed to the ground.* 人們驚恐地看着飛機墜落到地面上。◇ *With a look of horror, he asked if the doctor thought he had cancer.* 他驚恐失色地問醫生是否認定他患了癌症。◇ *The thought of being left alone filled her with horror.* 想到被孤零零地留下，她就不寒而慄。◇ *She recoiled in horror at the sight of an enormous spider.* 看到一隻巨大的蜘蛛，她嚇得直退。◇ ***To his horror,*** *he could feel himself starting to cry* (= it upset him very much). 他很恐懼，感到自己都快哭了。◇ *Her eyes were wide with horror.* 她嚇得目瞪口呆。 **2** 0━ [sing.] a great fear or hatred of sth 對某事物的強烈畏懼（或憎恨）： **~ of sth** *a horror of deep water* 恐懼深水◇ **~ of doing sth** *Most people have a horror of speaking in public.* 大多數人都十分害怕當眾講話。 **3** 0━ [U] **the ~ of sth** the very unpleasant nature of sth, especially when it is shocking or frightening （某事物）令人厭惡的性質；（尤指）震驚性，恐怖性： ***The full horror of*** *the accident was beginning to become clear.* 這次悲慘事故的真相已開始逐漸清晰了。◇ *In his dreams he relives the horror of the attack.* 那次襲擊的恐怖景象在他的夢中一再重現。 **4** 0━ [C, usually pl.] a very unpleasant or frightening experience 極其不愉快的（或可怕的）經歷： *the horrors of war* 戰爭的恐怖經歷 **5** 0━ [U] a type of book, film/movie, etc. that is designed to frighten people 恐怖故事（或電影等）： *In this section you'll find horror and science fiction.* 你可以在這一部份找到恐怖和科幻小說。◇ *a* ***horror film/movie*** 恐怖片 ➲ see also HORROR STORY **6** [C] (*BrE, informal*) a child who behaves badly 調皮搗蛋的孩子： *Her son is a little horror.* 她的兒子是個小搗蛋鬼。
IDM **ˌhorror of ˈhorrors** (*BrE, humorous* or *ironic*) used to emphasize how bad a situation is 極其糟糕： *I stood up to speak and—horror of horrors—realized I had left my notes behind.* 我站起來講話，可是，可怕的是，我發現自己忘了帶講稿。 ➲ more at SHOCK *n.*

ˈhorror story *noun* **1** a story about strange and frightening things that is designed to entertain people 恐怖故事 **2** (*informal*) a report that describes an experience of a situation as very unpleasant 可怕經歷的描述；嚇人報道： *horror stories about visits to the dentist* 有關看牙醫的種種嚇人說法

ˈhorror-struck (also **ˈhorror-stricken**) *adj.* suddenly feeling very shocked, frightened or disgusted 突然感到震驚的（或驚恐的、厭惡的）

hors de com·bat /ˌɔː də ˈkɒ̃bɑː; *NAmE* ˌɔːr də koʊmˈbɑː/ *adj.* (from *French, formal*) unable to fight or to take part in an activity, especially because you are injured （尤指因傷）喪失戰鬥力的，無法參加的

hors d'oeuvre /ˌɔː ˈdɜːv; *NAmE* ˌɔːr ˈdɜːrv/ *noun* [C, U] (*pl.* **hors d'oeuvres** /ˌɔː ˈdɜːv; *NAmE* ˌɔːr ˈdɜːrv/) (from *French*) a small amount of food, usually cold, served before the main part of a meal 開胃小吃；開胃冷盤 ➲ compare STARTER (1)

horse 0━ /hɔːs; *NAmE* hɔːrs/ *noun, verb*
■ ***noun*** **1** 0━ a large animal with four legs, a MANE (= long thick hair on its neck) and a tail. Horses are used for riding on, pulling CARRIAGES, etc. 馬： *He mounted his horse and rode off.* 他跨上馬騎走了。◇ *a horse and cart* 一輛馬車 ➲ see also COLT (1), FILLY, FOAL, GELDING, MARE, STALLION **2** **the horses** [pl.] (*informal*) horse racing 賽馬： *He lost a lot of money on the horses* (= by gambling on races). 他賭賽馬輸了很多錢。 **3** = VAULTING HORSE ➲ see also CLOTHES HORSE, HOBBY HORSE, QUARTER HORSE, ROCKING HORSE, SEA HORSE, STALKING HORSE, TROJAN HORSE, WHITE HORSES
IDM **(straight) from the horse's ˈmouth** (*informal*) (of information 信息) given by sb who is directly involved and therefore likely to be accurate 直接的；可靠的 **hold your ˈhorses** (*informal*) used to tell sb that they should wait a moment and not be so excited that they take action without thinking about it first 且慢；請三思 **ˌhorses for ˈcourses** (*BrE*) the act of matching people with suitable jobs or tasks 知人善任 ORIGIN This expression refers to the fact that horses race better on a track that suits them. 含義來自馬在合適的跑道上跑得更快。 **a one, two, three, etc. horse ˈrace** a competition or an election in which there are only one, two, etc. teams or candidates with a chance of winning 只有一個（或兩個、三個）隊（或候選人）有獲勝機會的比賽（或競選） **you can ˌlead/ˌtake a horse to ˌwater, but you ˌcan't make it ˈdrink** (*saying*) you can give sb the opportunity to do sth, but you cannot force them to do it if they do not want to 牽馬近水易，逼馬飲水難；機會可以給，做不做由人；老牛不飲水，不能強按頭 ➲ more at BACK *v.*, BARN, CART *n.*, CHANGE *v.*, DARK *adj.*, DRIVE *v.*, EAT, FLOG, GIFT *n.*, HIGH *adj.*, STABLE DOOR, WILD *adj.*, WISH *n.*
■ ***verb***
PHR V **ˌhorse aˈbout/aˈround** (*informal*) to play in a way that is noisy and not very careful so that you could hurt sb or damage sth 胡鬧；瞎鬧 SYN **fool around**

horse·back /ˈhɔːsbæk; *NAmE* ˈhɔːrs-/ *noun, adj.*
■ ***noun***
IDM **on ˈhorseback** sitting on a horse; using horses 騎着馬；駕馭着馬： *a soldier on horseback* 騎着馬的士兵
■ ***adj.*** [only before noun] sitting on a horse 騎着馬的： *a horseback tour* 騎馬旅行 ▸ **horse·back** *adv.*： *to ride horseback* 騎馬

ˈhorseback riding *noun* [U] (*NAmE*) = RIDING (1)

horse·box /ˈhɔːsbɒks; *NAmE* ˈhɔːrsbɑːks/ *noun* (*BrE*) a vehicle for transporting horses in, sometimes pulled behind another vehicle 運馬車；運馬拖車 ➲ see also HORSE TRAILER

ˌhorse ˈchestnut *noun* **1** a large tall tree with spreading branches, white or pink flowers and nuts that grow inside cases which are covered with SPIKES 七葉樹；馬栗 ➲ **VISUAL VOCAB** page V10 ➲ see also CHESTNUT **2** the smooth brown nut of the horse chestnut tree 七葉樹的堅果 ➲ compare CONKER (1)

ˈhorse-drawn *adj.* [only before noun] (of a vehicle 車輛) pulled by a horse or horses 馬拉的

horse·flesh /ˈhɔːsfleʃ; *NAmE* ˈhɔːrs-/ *noun* [U] horses, especially when being bought or sold （尤指買賣的）馬匹

horse·fly /ˈhɔːsflaɪ; *NAmE* ˈhɔːrs-/ *noun* (*pl.* **-ies**) a large fly that bites horses and cows 虻

horse·hair /ˈhɔːsheə(r); *NAmE* ˈhɔːrsher/ *noun* [U] hair from the MANE or tail of a horse, used, in the past, for filling MATTRESSES, chairs, etc. 馬鬃，馬尾毛（舊時用作牀墊、椅子等的填料）

horse·man /ˈhɔːsmən; *NAmE* ˈhɔːrs-/ *noun* (*pl.* **-men** /-mən/) a rider on a horse; a person who can ride horses 騎手；騎馬的人： *a good horseman* 優秀騎手 ➲ see also HORSEWOMAN

horse·man·ship /ˈhɔːsmənʃɪp; *NAmE* ˈhɔːrs-/ *noun* [U] skill in riding horses 馬術；騎術

horse·play /ˈhɔːspleɪ; *NAmE* ˈhɔːrs-/ *noun* [U] rough noisy play in which people push or hit each other for fun 打鬧嬉戲；玩鬧

horse·power /ˈhɔːspaʊə(r); *NAmE* ˈhɔːrs-/ *noun* [C, U] (*pl.* **horse·power**) (*abbr.* **h.p.**) a unit for measuring the power of an engine 馬力（功率單位）： *a powerful car* *with a 170 horsepower engine* 發動機為 170 馬力的大功率汽車

'horse race *noun* a race between horses with riders 賽馬

'horse racing *noun* [U] a sport in which horses with riders race against each other 賽馬運動 ➲ VISUAL VOCAB page V46

horse·rad·ish /ˈhɔːsrædɪʃ; *NAmE* ˈhɔːrs-/ *noun* [U] **1** a hard white root vegetable that has a taste like pepper 辣根 **2** (*BrE* also ˌ**horseradish 'sauce**) a sauce made from horseradish, that is eaten with meat 辣根沙司： *roast beef and horseradish* 烤牛肉加辣根沙司

'horse riding *noun* [U] (*BrE*) = RIDING (1)

horse·shoe /ˈhɔːsʃuː; ˈhɔːʃʃuː; *NAmE* ˈhɔːrʃ-; ˈhɔːrs-/ *noun* (also **shoe**) **1** a piece of curved iron that is attached with nails to the bottom of a horse's foot. A horseshoe is often used as a symbol of good luck. 馬蹄鐵，馬掌（常用來象徵好運）**2** anything shaped like a horseshoe 馬蹄鐵形物： *a horseshoe bend in the river* 河道中的馬蹄形彎曲

H

'horse-trading *noun* [U] the activity of discussing business with sb using clever or secret methods in order to reach an agreement that suits you 精明的交易；留有一手的交易

'horse trailer *noun* (*NAmE*) a vehicle for transporting horses in, pulled by another vehicle 運馬車；運馬拖車 ➲ see also HORSEBOX

horse·whip /ˈhɔːswɪp; *NAmE* ˈhɔːrs-/ *noun, verb*

■ ***noun*** a long stick with a long piece of leather attached to the end that is used to control or train horses 馬鞭

■ ***verb*** (**-pp-**) **~ sb** to beat sb with a horsewhip 用馬鞭抽打（人）

horse·woman /ˈhɔːswʊmən; *NAmE* ˈhɔːrs-/ *noun* (*pl.* **-women** /-wɪmɪn/) a woman rider on a horse; a woman who can ride horses well 騎馬的女子；女騎手；女騎師： *a good horsewoman* 優秀女騎手

horsey (also **horsy**) /ˈhɔːsi; *NAmE* ˈhɔːrsi/ *adj.* **1** interested in and involved with horses or horse racing 愛馬的；愛賽馬的 **2** connected with horses; like a horse 與馬有關的；像馬的： *She had a long, horsey face.* 她有一張長長的馬臉。

horti·cul·ture /ˈhɔːtɪkʌltʃə(r); *NAmE* ˈhɔːrt-/ *noun* [U] the study or practice of growing flowers, fruit and vegetables 園藝學；園藝： *a college of agriculture and horticulture* 農藝和園藝學院 ➲ compare GARDENING at GARDEN *v.* ▶ **horti·cul·tural** /ˌhɔːtɪˈkʌltʃərəl; *NAmE* ˌhɔːrt-/ *adj.*： *a horticultural show* 園藝展覽 **horti·cul·tur·al·ist**, **horti·cul·tur·ist** *noun*

hos·anna (also **hos·annah**) /həʊˈzænə; *NAmE* hoʊ-/ *exclamation* used in worship to express praise, joy and love for God, especially in the Christian and Jewish religions（尤指在基督教和猶太教中對上帝的）歡呼之聲；賀三納 ▶ **hos·anna** *noun*

hose /həʊz; *NAmE* hoʊz/ *noun, verb*

■ ***noun*** **1** (also **hose·pipe** /ˈhəʊzpaɪp; *NAmE* ˈhoʊz-/) [C, U] (*BrE*) a long tube made of rubber, plastic, etc., used for putting water onto fires, gardens, etc.（滅火、澆花等用的）橡皮管，塑料管，水龍帶： *a garden hose* 澆花園的軟管 ◇ *a length of hose* 一段軟管 ➲ VISUAL VOCAB page V19 ➲ see also FIRE HOSE **2** [pl.] = HOSIERY **3** [pl.] trousers/pants that fit tightly over the legs, worn by men in the past（舊時的）男式緊身褲： *doublet and hose* 緊身上衣和緊身褲

■ ***verb*** **~ sth** to wash or pour water on sth using a hose 用軟管輸水沖洗（或澆水）： *Firemen hosed the burning car.* 消防隊員用水龍向燃燒的汽車噴水。

PHR V ˌ**hose sth↔'down** to wash sth using a hose 用噴水軟管沖洗某物

ho·siery /ˈhəʊziəri; *NAmE* ˈhoʊʒəri/ (also **hose**) *noun* [U] used especially in shops/stores as a word for TIGHTS, STOCKINGS and socks（尤用於商店）襪類： *the hosiery department* 襪類部

hos·pice /ˈhɒspɪs; *NAmE* ˈhɑːs-/ *noun* a hospital for people who are dying 臨終安養院： *an AIDS hospice* 艾滋病患者安養院

hos·pit·able /hɒˈspɪtəbl; ˈhɒspɪtəbl; *NAmE* hɑːˈs-; ˈhɑːs-/ *adj.* **1 ~ (to/towards sb)** (of a person 人) pleased to welcome guests; generous and friendly to visitors 好客的；熱情友好的；殷勤的 **SYN** **welcoming**： *The local people are very hospitable to strangers.* 當地人對外來客人十分友好熱情。 **2** having good conditions that allow things to grow; having a pleasant environment（作物生長條件）適宜的；（環境）舒適的： *a hospitable climate* 宜人的氣候 **OPP** **inhospitable** ▶ **hos·pit·ably** /-əbli/ *adv.*

hos·pital 🔑 /ˈhɒspɪtl; *NAmE* ˈhɑːs-/ *noun* a large building where people who are ill/sick or injured are given medical treatment and care 醫院： (*BrE*) *He had to go* ***to hospital*** *for treatment.* 他得到醫院接受治療。◇ (*NAmE*) *He had to go* ***to the hospital*** *for treatment.* 他得到醫院接受治療。◇ *to* ***be admitted to*** (*the*) ***hospital*** 被接受入院 ◇ *to* ***be discharged from*** (*the*) ***hospital*** 獲准出院 ◇ *The injured were* ***rushed to*** (*the*) ***hospital*** *in an ambulance.* 救護車把傷員火速送往醫院。◇ *He died in (the) hospital.* 他在醫院裏去世。◇ *I'm going to the hospital to visit my brother.* 我要去醫院探望我弟弟。◇ *a* ***psychiatric/mental hospital*** 精神病院 ◇ ***hospital doctors/nurses/staff*** 醫院醫生／護士／職工 ◇ *There is an urgent need for more hospital beds.* 醫院牀位急需增加。 ➲ see also COTTAGE HOSPITAL

British/American 英式／美式英語

hospital

- In *BrE* you say **to hospital** or **in hospital** when you talk about somebody being there as a patient. 在英式英語中，去醫院看病或住院診治用 to hospital 或 in hospital： *I had to go to hospital.* 我得去醫院看病。◇ *She spent two weeks in hospital.* 她住院兩週。
- In *NAmE* you need to use **the**. 美式英語要用定冠詞 the： *I had to go to the hospital.* 我得去醫院看病。◇ *She spent two weeks in the hospital.* 她住院兩週。

ˌ**hospital 'corners** *noun* [pl.] a way of folding the sheets at the corners of a bed tightly and neatly, in a way that they are often folded in a hospital 醫院牀單摺角法（整齊緊摺四角）

hos·pi·tal·ity /ˌhɒspɪˈtæləti; *NAmE* ˌhɑːs-/ *noun* [U] **1** friendly and generous behaviour towards guests 好客；殷勤： *Thank you for your kind hospitality.* 感謝你的友好款待。 **2** food, drink or services that are provided by an organization for guests, customers, etc.（款待客人、顧客等的）食物，飲料，服務；款待： *We were entertained in the company's* ***hospitality suite.*** 公司款待我們住進他們的迎賓套間。◇ *the hospitality industry* (= hotels, restaurants, etc.) 招待性行業（如旅館、飯店等）

hos·pi·tal·ize (*BrE* also **-ise**) /ˈhɒspɪtəlaɪz; *NAmE* ˈhɑːs-/ *verb* [usually passive] **~ sb** to send sb to a hospital for treatment 送（某人）入院治療 ▶ **hos·pi·tal·iza·tion**, **-isa·tion** /ˌhɒspɪtəlaɪˈzeɪʃn; *NAmE* ˌhɑːspɪtələˈz-/ *noun* [U]： *a long period of hospitalization* 長期住院

host 🔑 /həʊst; *NAmE* hoʊst/ *noun, verb*

■ ***noun*** **1** 🔑 [C] a person who invites guests to a meal, a party, etc. or who has people staying at their house 主人： *Ian, our host, introduced us to the other guests.* 主人伊恩把我們介紹給了其他客人。 ➲ see also HOSTESS **2** 🔑 [C] a country, a city or an organization that holds and arranges a special event 東道主；主辦國（或城市、機構）： *The college is* ***playing host to*** *a group of visiting Russian scientists.* 學院正在接待一批來訪的俄羅斯科學家。 **3** 🔑 [C] a person who introduces a television or radio show, and talks to guests（電視或廣播的）節目主持人 **SYN** **compère**： *a TV game show host* 電視遊戲節目主持人 ➲ see also ANNOUNCER (1), PRESENTER **4** [C] (*technical* 術語) an animal or a plant on which another animal or plant lives and feeds（寄生動植物的）寄主，宿主 **5** [C] **~ of sb/sth** a large number of people or things 許多；大量：*a host of possibilities* 多種可能性 **6** [C] the main computer in a network that controls or supplies information to other computers that are connected to it（計算機網絡的）主機，服務機：*transferring files from the host to your local computer* 從主機向你的本地機傳送文件 **7 the Host** [sing.] the bread that is used in the Christian service of COMMUNION, after it has been BLESSED 聖餅（基督教聖餐儀式中經過祝謝的麪包）

■ *verb* **1** ~ **sth** to organize an event to which others are invited and make all the arrangements for them 主辦，主持（活動）：*South Africa hosted the World Cup finals.* 南非主辦了世界杯決賽。 **2** ~ **sth** to introduce a television or radio programme, a show, etc. 主持（電視或廣播節目等） SYN **compère 3** ~ **sth** to organize a party that you have invited guests to 作為主人組織（聚會）；做東：*to host a dinner* 設宴招待客人 **4** ~ **sth** to store a website on a computer connected to the Internet, usually in return for payment（通常收費在與互聯網連接的計算機上）存貯網站：*a company that builds and hosts e-commerce sites* 在互聯網上建立並存貯電子商務網站的公司

hos·tage /ˈhɒstɪdʒ; *NAmE* ˈhɑːs-/ *noun* a person who is captured and held prisoner by a person or group, and who may be injured or killed if people do not do what the person or group is asking 人質：*Three children were **taken hostage** during the bank robbery.* 在銀行搶劫案中有三名兒童被扣為人質。◇ *He was **held hostage** for almost a year.* 他被扣為人質幾近一年。◇ *The government is negotiating the release of the hostages.* 政府正就釋放人質進行談判。

IDM **a ˌhostage to ˈfortune** something that you have, or have promised to do, that could cause trouble or worry in the future 可能招惹麻煩（或擔憂）的東西（或許諾）；造成後患的事物

ˈhostage-taker *noun* a person, often one of a group, who captures sb and holds them prisoner, and who may injure or kill them if people do not do what the person is asking 劫持人質者 ▸ **ˈhostage-taking** *noun* [U]

hos·tel /ˈhɒstl; *NAmE* ˈhɑːstl/ *noun* **1** a building that provides cheap accommodation and meals to students, workers or travellers 宿舍，招待所（提供廉價服務） ➲ see also YOUTH HOSTEL **2** (*BrE*) (also **shel·ter** *NAmE*, *BrE*) a building, usually run by a charity, where people who have no home can stay for a short time 臨時收容所；慈善收容所：*a hostel for the homeless* 流浪者之家

hos·tel·ry /ˈhɒstəlri; *NAmE* ˈhɑːs-/ (*pl.* **-ies**) *noun* (*old use* or *humorous*) a pub or hotel 酒吧；旅店

host·ess /ˈhəʊstəs; -es; *NAmE* ˈhoʊstəs/ *noun* **1** a woman who invites guests to a meal, a party, etc.; a woman who has people staying at her home 女主人；女房東：*Mary was always the perfect hostess.* 瑪麗總是最殷勤的女主人。 **2** a woman who is employed to welcome and entertain men at a NIGHTCLUB（夜總會的）女招待 **3** a woman who introduces and talks to guests on a television or radio show（電視或廣播節目的）女主持人 SYN **compère** ➲ note at GENDER **4** (*NAmE*) a woman who welcomes the customers in a restaurant（餐館的）女迎賓，女門迎 ➲ see also HOST

hos·tile /ˈhɒstaɪl; *NAmE* ˈhɑːstl; -taɪl/ *adj.* **1** very unfriendly or aggressive and ready to argue or fight 敵意的；敵對的：*The speaker got a hostile reception from the audience.* 演講人遭到了聽眾喝倒彩。◇ ~ **to/towards sb/sth** *She was openly hostile towards her parents.* 她公然對抗她的父母。 **2** ~ (**to sth**) strongly rejecting sth 堅決否定；強烈反對 SYN **opposed to**：*hostile to the idea of change* 強烈反對變革 **3** making it difficult for sth to happen or to be achieved 有阻礙的；不利的：*hostile conditions for plants to grow in* 不利於植物生長的環境 **4** belonging to a military enemy 敵軍的；敵人的：*hostile territory* 敵方領土 **5** (*business* 商) (of an offer to buy a company, etc. 收購公司等的建議) not wanted by the company that is to be bought 不受（被購公司）歡迎的；敵意的：*a hostile takeover bid* 出價敵意收購

hos·til·ity /hɒˈstɪləti; *NAmE* hɑːˈs-/ *noun* **1** [U] unfriendly or aggressive feelings or behaviour 敵意；對抗：~ (**to/towards sb/sth**) *feelings of hostility towards people from other backgrounds* 對其他不同背景的人的敵視情緒 ◇ ~ (**between A and B**) *There was **open hostility** between the two schools.* 這兩所學校公開相互敵對。 **2** [U] ~ (**to/towards sth**) strong and angry opposition towards an idea, a plan or a situation（對思想、計劃或情形的）憤怒反對，憤怒反抗：*public hostility to nuclear power* 公眾對核動力的憤然反對 **3 hostilities** [pl.] (*formal*) acts of fighting in a war 戰爭行為：*the **start/outbreak of hostilities** between the two sides* 雙方之間敵對行為的爆發 ◇ *a **cessation of hostilities*** (= an end to fighting) 戰爭停止 ➲ COLLOCATIONS at WAR

host·ler /ˈhɒslə(r); *NAmE* ˈhɑːs-/ *noun* (*NAmE*) = OSTLER

hot /hɒt; *NAmE* hɑːt/ *adj.*, *verb*

■ *adj.* (**hot·ter**, **hot·test**)

▸ **TEMPERATURE** 溫度 **1** having a high temperature; producing heat 溫度高的；熱的：*Do you like this hot weather?* 你喜歡這種炎熱的天氣嗎？◇ *It's hot today, isn't it?* 今天很熱，對嗎？◇ *It was hot and getting hotter.* 天氣很熱，而且氣溫在不斷升高。◇ *It was the hottest July on record.* 那是歷史記載中最熱的七月。◇ *a hot dry summer* 炎熱乾燥的夏天 ◇ *Be careful—the plates are hot.* 當心，盤子燙手。◇ *All rooms have hot and cold water.* 所有的房間都有冷、熱水。◇ *a hot bath* 熱水浴 ◇ *a hot meal* (= one that has been cooked) 熱的飯菜 ◇ *I couldn't live in a hot country* (= one which has high average temperatures). 我無法在炎熱的國家生活。◇ *Cook in a very hot oven.* 放在烤箱裏用高溫烤。◇ *Eat it while it's hot.* 趁熱吃了它吧。◇ *I touched his forehead. He felt hot and feverish.* 我摸了摸他的前額，感到很燙，是在發燒。 ➲ see also BAKING HOT at BAKING *adj.*, BOILING HOT at BOILING, PIPING HOT, RED-HOT, WHITE-HOT **2** (of a person 人) feeling heat in an unpleasant or uncomfortable way 覺得悶（或燥、濕）熱：*Is anyone too hot?* 有人覺得太熱了嗎？◇ *I feel hot.* 我覺得很熱。◇ *Her cheeks were hot with embarrassment.* 她的雙頰窘得發燙。 **3** making you feel hot 使人感到熱的：*London was hot and dusty.* 倫敦很熱而且灰塵多。◇ *a long hot journey* 又遠又熱的旅行

▸ **FOOD WITH SPICES** 辣的食物 **4** containing pepper and spices and producing a burning feeling in your mouth 辣的；辛辣的：*hot spicy food* 辛辣的食物 ◇ *You can make a curry hotter simply by adding chillies.* 你只需加辣椒就能增加咖喱菜的辣味。◇ *hot mustard* 辣芥末 OPP **mild**

▸ **CAUSING STRONG FEELINGS** 引起強烈感情 **5** involving a lot of activity, argument or strong feelings 活躍的；激烈的；強烈的：*Today we enter the hottest phase of the election campaign.* 今天我們進入了競選活動最激烈的階段。◇ *The environment has become a very hot issue.* 環境已成為很熱門的話題。◇ *Competition is getting hotter day by day.* 競爭日趨白熱化。

▸ **DIFFICULT/DANGEROUS** 艱難；危險 **6** difficult or dangerous to deal with and making you feel worried or uncomfortable 艱難的；棘手的；危險的：*When things got too hot most journalists left the area.* 事態發展到過於嚴峻時，大多數記者便撤離了這個地區。◇ *They're making life hot for her.* 他們使得她日子難過。

▸ **POPULAR** 流行 **7** (*informal*) new, exciting and very popular 風行的；風靡一時的；走紅的：*This is one of the hottest clubs in town.* 這是市裏一家最受歡迎的夜總會。◇ *They are one of this year's hot new bands.* 他們是今年走紅的新樂隊之一。◇ *The couple are Hollywood's **hottest property**.* 這對夫妻是好萊塢最炙手可熱的人物。

▸ **NEWS** 新聞 **8** fresh, very recent and usually exciting 最新的，新近的（通常令人興奮）：*I've got some hot gossip for you!* 我要告訴你一些最新的傳聞！◇ *a story that is **hot off the press*** (= has just appeared in the newspapers) 剛剛出爐的報道

▸ **TIP/FAVOURITE** 熱門 **9** [only before noun] likely to be successful 有望成功的：*She seems to be the **hot favourite** for the job.* 她似乎是這份工作最熱門的人選。◇ *Do you have any **hot tips** for today's race?* 你可有今天賽馬的內部消息嗎？

▸ **GOOD AT STH/KNOWING A LOT** 擅長；熟識 **10** [not before noun] ~ **at/on sth** (*informal*) very good at doing sth; knowing a lot about sth 善於（做某事）；（對某事）

瞭解很多：*Don't ask me—I'm* ***not too hot on*** *British history.* 別問我，我不大瞭解英國歷史。

▸ **ANGER 憤怒** **11** if sb has a **hot temper** they become angry very easily 易發怒的；暴躁的（脾氣）

▸ **SEXUAL EXCITEMENT 性激動** **12** feeling or causing sexual excitement 感到（或引起）性激動的：*You were as hot for me as I was for you.* 當時你想要我，我也想要你。◇ *I've got a* ***hot date*** *tonight.* 我今晚有一場令人激動的約會。

▸ **SHOCKING/CRITICAL 驚人；嚴重** **13** containing scenes, statements, etc. that are too shocking or too critical and are likely to cause anger or disapproval（場面、說話等）過激的，過火的：*Some of the nude scenes were regarded as too hot for Broadway.* 有些裸露場面被認為太過火了，不適合在百老匯上演。◇ *The report was highly critical of senior members of the Cabinet and was considered too hot to publish.* 報道中對內閣高級官員的批評被認為過於激烈，不宜發表。➲ see also HOT STUFF (4)

H

▸ **STRICT 嚴格** **14** [not before noun] **~ on sth** thinking that sth is very important and making sure that it always happens or is done 重視，確保（某事發生或完成）：*They're very hot on punctuality at work.* 他們很重視工作守時。

▸ **MUSIC 音樂** **15** (of music, especially JAZZ 音樂，尤指爵士樂) having a strong and exciting rhythm 節奏強的

▸ **GOODS 貨物** **16** stolen and difficult to get rid of because they can easily be recognized 偷來（因容易識別）而難以銷贓的：*I'd never have touched those CDs if I'd known they were hot.* 早知道那些光盤是偷來的，我絕不會碰的。

▸ **IN CHILDREN'S GAMES 兒童遊戲** **17** [not before noun] used in children's games to say that the person playing is very close to finding a person or thing, or to guessing the correct answer 快找到了；快猜中了：*You're getting hot!* 你快猜中了！

IDM **be ˌhot to ˈtrot** (*informal*) **1** to be very enthusiastic about starting an activity 期待（某活動）**2** to be excited in a sexual way 慾火中燒；性慾高漲 **be in/get into hot ˈwater** (*informal*) to be in or get into trouble 有麻煩；惹上麻煩 **go hot and ˈcold** to experience a sudden feeling of fear or anxiety 突然感到害怕（或焦慮）：*When the phone rang I just went hot and cold.* 電話鈴響時我嚇得一陣冷一陣熱。 **go/sell like hot ˈcakes** to sell quickly or in great numbers 暢銷 **(all) hot and ˈbothered** (*informal*) in a state of anxiety or confusion because you are under too much pressure, have a problem, are trying to hurry, etc.（因壓力過大、有難題、時間緊迫等）焦灼不安，心慌意亂 **hot on sb's/sth's ˈheels** following sb/sth very closely 緊跟着；接踵而至：*He turned and fled with Peter hot on his heels.* 他轉身逃跑，彼得窮追不捨。◇ *Further successes came hot on the heels of her first best-selling novel.* 她的第一部暢銷小說之後是接二連三的成功。 **hot on sb's/sth's ˈtracks/ˈtrail** (*informal*) close to catching or finding the person or thing that you have been chasing or searching for 快要抓到，即將找到（某人或物）**hot under the ˈcollar** (*informal*) angry or embarrassed 憤怒的；窘迫的：*He got very hot under the collar when I asked him where he'd been all day.* 我問他一整天到哪裏去了，他很尷尬。 **in hot purˈsuit (of sb)** following sb closely and determined to catch them（對某人）窮追不捨：*She sped away in her car with journalists in hot pursuit.* 她開車迅速離去，記者們則在後面窮追不捨。 **not so/too ˈhot** **1** not very good in quality 質量不大好：*Her spelling isn't too hot.* 她的拼字不太好。 **2** not feeling well 不舒服：*'How are you today?' 'Not so hot, I'm afraid.'* "你今天怎麼樣了？""很遺憾，不怎麼樣。" ➲ more at BLOW *v.*, CAT, HEEL *n.*, STRIKE *v.*

■ ***verb*** (-tt-)

PHR V **ˌhot ˈup** (*BrE*) (also **ˌheat ˈup** *NAmE, BrE*) (*informal*) to become more exciting or to show an increase in activity 激烈起來；更加活躍：*Things are really hotting up in the election campaign.* 競選活動的確日益激烈了。

ˌhot ˈair *noun* [U] (*informal*) claims, promises or statements that sound impressive but have no real meaning or truth 夸夸其談；大話；空話

ˌhot-ˈair balloon *noun* = BALLOON (2) ➲ VISUAL VOCAB page V53

hot·bed /ˈhɒtbed; *NAmE* ˈhɑːt-/ *noun* [usually sing.] **~ of sth** a place where a lot of a particular activity, especially sth bad or violent, is happening（壞事、暴力等的）溫牀：*The area was a hotbed of crime.* 這個地區是犯罪活動的溫牀。

ˌhot-ˈblooded *adj.* (of a person 人) having strong emotions and easily becoming very excited or angry 情感強烈的；血氣方剛的；易怒的 **SYN** **passionate** ➲ compare WARM-BLOODED

ˈhot button *noun* (*NAmE, informal*) a subject or issue that people have strong feelings about and argue about a lot 熱點話題：*Race has always been a hot button in this country's history.* 種族一直是這個國家歷史上爭論不休的問題。◇ *the hot-button issue of nuclear waste disposal* 核廢料處理這個熱門話題

ˌhot ˈchocolate (*BrE* also **choc·olate**) *noun* [U, C] a drink made by mixing chocolate powder with hot water or milk; a cup of this drink 巧克力熱飲；一杯巧克力熱飲：*Two coffees and a hot chocolate, please.* 請來兩杯咖啡和一杯熱巧克力。

hotch·potch /ˈhɒtʃpɒtʃ; *NAmE* ˈhɑːtʃpɑːtʃ/ (*especially BrE*) (*NAmE* usually **hodge·podge**) *noun* [sing.] (*informal*) a number of things mixed together without any particular order or reason 雜亂無章的一堆東西；大雜燴

ˌhot cross ˈbun *noun* a small sweet bread roll that contains CURRANTS and has a pattern of a cross on top, traditionally eaten in Britain around Easter 十字麪包

ˌhot-ˈdesking *noun* [U] the practice in an office of giving desks to workers when they are required, rather than giving each worker their own desk 辦公桌輪用（非固定分配）

ˈhot dog (*BrE* also **ˌhot ˈdog**) *noun* **1** a hot SAUSAGE served in a long bread roll 熱狗（香腸麪包）**2** (*NAmE*) a person who performs clever or dangerous tricks while SKIING, SNOWBOARDING or SURFING（滑雪、滑雪板運動或衝浪的）動作靈巧表演者，高難動作表演者：*He's a real hot dog.* 他是個十足的驚險動作運動員。

ˈhot-dog *verb* (-gg-) [I] (*NAmE, informal*) to perform clever or dangerous tricks while SKIING, SNOWBOARDING or SURFING（在滑雪、滑雪板運動或衝浪中）表演技巧，表演高難動作

hotel 🔑 /həʊˈtel; *NAmE* hoʊ-/ *noun*

1 🔑 a building where people stay, usually for a short time, paying for their rooms and meals 旅館；旅社：*We stayed at/in a hotel.* 我們住在旅館裏。◇ ***hotel rooms/guests*** 旅館的房間 / 客人 ◇ *a* ***two-star/five-star, etc. hotel*** 兩星級、五星級等旅館 ◇ *a* ***luxury hotel*** 豪華旅館 ◇ *a friendly, family-run hotel* 一家親切隨和、家庭經營的旅店 ➲ COLLOCATIONS at TRAVEL **2** (*AustralE, NZE*) a pub 酒吧；酒館 **3** (*IndE*) a restaurant 餐館 **HELP** Some speakers do not pronounce the 'h' at the beginning of **hotel** and use 'an' instead of 'a' before it. This now sounds old-fashioned. 有人說 hotel 時不發 h 音，前面用 an 而不用 a，現在聽起來過時了。

ho·tel·ier /həʊˈteliə(r); -lier; *NAmE* hoʊˈteljər; ˌoʊtelˈjeɪ/ *noun* a person who owns or manages a hotel 旅館老闆；旅館經理

hot·fix /ˈhɒtfɪks; *NAmE* ˈhɑːt-/ *noun* (*computing* 計) a file that is used to correct a fault in a computer program（電腦的）補丁程序，補丁程式

ˌhot ˈflush (*BrE*) (*NAmE* **ˌhot ˈflash**) *noun* a sudden hot and uncomfortable feeling in the skin, especially experienced by women during the MENOPAUSE 熱潮紅（皮膚的灼熱陣感，尤見於更年期女性）

hot·foot /ˈhɒtfʊt; *NAmE* ˈhɑːt-/ *adv., verb*

■ ***adv.*** moving quickly and in a hurry 急匆匆地；匆忙地：*He had just arrived hotfoot from London.* 他剛從倫敦匆匆趕來。

■ ***verb***

IDM **ˈhotfoot it** (*informal*) to walk or run somewhere quickly 急走，快跑（到某地）：*When the police arrived, they hotfooted it out of there.* 警察到達時，他們匆忙逃離了那裏。

hot·head /ˈhɒthed; *NAmE* ˈhɑːt-/ *noun* a person who often acts too quickly, without thinking of what might happen 莽撞的人；急躁的人 ▸ ˌ**hot-ˈheaded** *adj.*

hot·house /ˈhɒthaʊs; *NAmE* ˈhɑːt-/ *noun* **1** a heated building, usually made of glass, used for growing delicate plants in 温室；暖房：*hothouse flowers* 温室花卉 **2** a place or situation that encourages the rapid development of sb/sth, especially ideas and emotions 有利於迅速發展的地方（或環境）；（尤指有利於思想感情發展的）温牀

ˈ**hot key** *noun* (*computing* 計) a key on a computer keyboard that you can press to perform a set of operations quickly, rather than having to press a number of different keys 熱鍵，快捷鍵（按下後可迅速進行一系列操作）

hot·line /ˈhɒtlaɪn; *NAmE* ˈhɑːt-/ *noun* **1** a special telephone line that people can use in order to get information or to talk about sth 電話咨詢服務專線；熱線 **2** a direct telephone line between the heads of government in different countries（各國政府首腦之間通話的）熱線

hot·link /ˈhɒtlɪŋk; *NAmE* ˈhɑːt-/ *noun* = HYPERLINK

hot·list /ˈhɒtlɪst; *NAmE* ˈhɑːt-/ *noun* **1** a list of popular, fashionable or important people or things 熱點（或重要）人物名單；熱點（或重要）事物清單 **2** (*computing* 計) a personal list of your favourite or most frequently visited websites that you store on your computer 熱表；熱門網頁列表

hotly /ˈhɒtli; *NAmE* ˈhɑːtli/ *adv.* **1** done in an angry or excited way or with a lot of strong feeling 憤怒地；激動地；強烈地：*a hotly debated topic* 激烈辯論的話題 ◇ *Recent reports in the press have been hotly denied.* 新聞界最近的報道遭到了堅決否認。◇ *'Nonsense!' he said hotly.* "廢話！"他怒氣沖沖地説。◇ *The results were hotly disputed.* 結果引起了極大爭議。 **2** done with a lot of energy and determination 起勁地；堅決地 SYN **closely**：*hotly contested elections* 競爭激烈的選舉 ◇ *She ran out of the shop, **hotly pursued** by the store detective.* 她衝出商店，商店偵探在後面猛追。

ˈ**hot pants** *noun* [pl.] very short, tight women's SHORTS 女式緊身超短褲；熱褲

hot·plate /ˈhɒtpleɪt; *NAmE* ˈhɑːt-/ *noun* a flat, heated metal surface, for example on a cooker/stove, that is used for cooking food or for keeping it hot 烤盤，加熱板（置於爐灶等的上面，用於烹調或使食物保温）

hot·pot /ˈhɒtpɒt; *NAmE* ˈhɑːtpɑːt/ *noun* **1** [C, U] (*BrE*) a hot dish of meat, potato, onion, etc. cooked slowly in liquid in the oven 燜罐（內裝燉的肉、土豆、洋蔥等） **2** [C] (*NAmE*) a small electric pot that you can use to heat water or food 小電熱鍋（可燒水或熱飯）

ˌ**hot poˈtato** *noun* [usually sing.] (*informal*) a problem, situation, etc. that is difficult and unpleasant to deal with 棘手的問題（或情況等）；燙手山芋

ˈ**hot rod** *noun* a car that has been changed and improved to give it extra power and speed 改裝而成的高速汽車

hots /hɒts; *NAmE* hɑːts/ *noun* [pl.]
IDM **get/have the ˈhots for sb** (*informal*) to be sexually attracted to sb 對某人有情慾

the ˈhot seat *noun* [sing.] (*informal*) if sb is **in the hot seat**, they have to take responsibility for important or difficult decisions and actions 責任重大的位置

hot·shot /ˈhɒtʃɒt; *NAmE* ˈhɑːtʃɑːt/ *noun* (*informal*) a person who is extremely successful in their career or at a particular sport 很有成就的人；運動高手 ▸ **hot·shot** *adj.* [only before noun]：*a hotshot lawyer* 業績非凡的律師

ˈ**hot spot** *noun* (*informal*) **1** a place where fighting is common, especially for political reasons 多事之地；（尤指政治原因的）熱點地區 **2** a place where there is a lot of activity or entertainment 活動多的地方；熱鬧的娛樂場所 **3** (*NAmE*) a place that is very hot and dry, where a fire has been burning or is likely to start 火災多發地區 **4** (*computing* 計) an area on a computer screen that you can click on to start an operation such as loading a file（屏幕上點擊後即可啟動程序的）熱點區，點選處 **5** a place in a hotel, restaurant, airport, etc. that is fitted with a special device that enables you to connect a computer to the Internet without using wires 熱點（旅館、飯店、機場等安裝設備可無線上網的地方）

ˌ**hot ˈstuff** *noun* [U] (*informal, especially BrE*) **1** a person who is sexually attractive 性感的人：*She's pretty hot stuff.* 她很性感。 **2** a film/movie, book, etc. which is exciting in a sexual way 豔情電影（或書籍等） **3 ~ (at sth)** a person who is very skilful at sth 技藝很高的人；高手：*She's really hot stuff at tennis.* 她的確是網球高手。 **4** something that is likely to cause anger or disagreement 很可能惹人生氣（或引起爭執）的事物：*These new proposals are proving to be hot stuff.* 這些新的建議結果證明是有爭議性的。

ˌ**hot-ˈtempered** *adj.* (*especially BrE*) tending to become very angry easily 易怒的；暴躁的

hot·tie (also **hotty**) /ˈhɒti; *NAmE* ˈhɑːti/ *noun* (*informal*) a person who is very sexually attractive 熱辣性感的人；辣哥；辣妹

ˈ**hot tub** *noun* a heated bath/BATHTUB, often outside, that several people can sit in together to relax 熱水浴池（常置於室外，可供數人坐在裏面休息）

ˌ**hot-ˈwater bottle** *noun* a rubber container that is filled with hot water and put in a bed to make it warm 熱水袋

ˈ**hot-wire** *verb* **~ sth** (*informal*) to start the engine of a vehicle by using a piece of wire instead of a key 熱線發動，短路點火（不用鑰匙而用電線短路方法發動汽車）

Hou·dini /huːˈdiːni/ *noun* a person or an animal that is very good at escaping 善於逃脱的人（或動物）
ORIGIN From Harry Houdini, a famous performer in the US who escaped from ropes, chains, boxes, etc. 源自美國著名的脱身魔術演員哈里・烏丹尼（Harry Houdini）。

hou·mous = HUMMUS

hound /haʊnd/ *noun, verb*
▪ ***noun*** a dog that can run fast and has a good sense of smell, used for hunting 獵犬；獵狗 ➲ see also AFGHAN HOUND, BLOODHOUND, FOXHOUND, GREYHOUND, WOLFHOUND
▪ ***verb*** **~ sb** to keep following sb and not leave them alone, especially in order to get sth from them or ask them questions 追踪；追逐；糾纏 SYN **harass**：*They were hounded day and night by the press.* 他們日夜遭到新聞界的跟踪。
PHR V ˌ**hound sb ˈout (of sth)** | ˈ**hound sb from sth** [usually passive] to force sb to leave a job or a place, especially by making their life difficult and unpleasant 逼迫某人離職（或離開某地）

ˈ**hound dog** *noun* (*NAmE*) (especially in the southern US) a dog used in hunting（尤指美國南部）獵犬

hounds·tooth /ˈhaʊndztuːθ/ *noun* [U] a type of large pattern with pointed shapes, often in black and white, used especially in cloth for jackets and suits 犬牙織紋；犬牙花紋

hour 0-w /ˈaʊə(r)/ *noun*
HELP Use **an**, not **a**, before **hour**. * hour 之前用 an，不用 a。 **1** 0-w [C] (*abbr.* **hr**, **hr.**) 60 minutes; one of the 24 parts that a day is divided into 小時：*It will take about an hour to get there.* 到那裏大約需要一小時。◇ *The interview lasted half an hour.* 會見持續了半小時。◇ *It was a three-hour exam.* 那是三小時的考試。◇ *I waited **for an hour** and then I left.* 我等了一個小時，然後就走了。◇ *He'll be back **in an hour**.* 他一小時後回來。◇ *We're paid **by the hour**.* 我們是論小時獲得報酬的。◇ *The minimum wage was set at £5.80 **an hour**.* 最低工資定為每小時 5.80 英鎊。◇ *Top speed is 120 miles **per hour**.* 最高時速為 120 英里。◇ *York was within an hour's drive.* 開車到約克不會超過一小時。◇ *Chicago is two hours away* (= it takes two hours to get there). 到芝加哥需要兩小時。◇ *We're four hours ahead of New York* (= referring to the time difference). 我們比紐約早四個小時。◇ *We hope to be there **within the hour*** (= in less than an hour). 我們希望一小時內到達那裏。 **2** 0-w [C, usually sing.] a period of about an hour, used for a particular purpose

約一小時的時間：*I use the Internet at work, during my **lunch hour**.* 我上班時在午餐時間使用互聯網。➲ see also HAPPY HOUR, RUSH HOUR **3** **hours** [pl.] a fixed period of time during which people work, an office is open, etc.（工作、辦公等的）固定時間：***Opening hours** are from 10 to 6 each day.* 開放時間為每天 10 點到 6 點。◇ *Most people in this kind of job tend to work **long hours**.* 很多從事這種工作的人往往工作時間很長。◇ *What are your **office hours**?* 你的辦公時間是幾點到幾點？◇ *a hospital's **visiting hours*** 醫院的探視時間 ◇ *Britain's **licensing hours*** (= when pubs are allowed to open) *used to be very restricted.* 英國的酒吧營業時間從前受到很嚴格的限制。◇ *This is the only place to get a drink **after hours*** (= after the normal closing time for pubs). 這是酒吧正常關門時間之後唯一能喝一杯的地方。◇ *Clients can now contact us by email **out of hours*** (= when the office is closed). 現在於辦公時間以外顧客可以用電郵和我們聯繫。**4** **hours** [pl.] a long time 長時間：*It took hours getting there.* 花了好長時間才到達那裏。◇ *I've been waiting **for hours**.* 我等了很久了。◇ *'How long did it last?' 'Oh, **hours and hours**.'* "持續了多久？" "噢，很久很久。" **5** [sing.] a particular point in time 某個時間：*You can't turn him away at this hour of the night.* 天這麼晚了，你不能把他趕走。**6** [C, usually sing.] the time when sth important happens 重要時刻：*This was often thought of as the country's **finest hour**.* 一般認為這是該國家最美好的一段時光。◇ *She thought her **last hour** had come.* 她以為她生命的最後時刻到了。◇ *Don't desert me in my **hour of need**.* 不要在我困難的時候離開我。**7** **the hour** [sing.] the time when it is exactly 1 o'clock, 2 o'clock, etc. 整點：*There's a bus every hour **on the hour**.* 每小時整點有一班公共汽車。◇ *The clock **struck the hour**.* 鐘敲過整點了。**8** **hours** [pl.] used when giving the time according to the 24-hour clock, usually in military or other official language（按 24 小時制給出的時間，通常用於軍事或其他官方用語）點鐘：*The first missile was launched at 2300 hours* (= at 11 p.m.). 首枚導彈是在 23 點（晚上 11 點）發射的。**HELP** This is pronounced '23 hundred hours'. 這要讀作 23 hundred hours。

IDM **'all hours** any time, especially a time which is not usual or suitable 任何時間（尤指非正常或不合適的時間）：*He's started staying out **till all hours*** (= until very late at night). 他已經開始在外面待得很晚了。◇ *She thinks she can call me **at all hours of the day and night**.* 她以為她可以不分晝夜隨時給我打電話。**keep ... 'hours** if you keep regular, strange, etc. **hours**, the times at which you do things (especially getting up or going to bed) are regular, strange, etc. 做事（尤指作息）時間有規律（或怪異等）**the 'small/'early hours** (also **the wee small 'hours** *ScotE*, *NAmE* also **the wee 'hours**) the period of time very early in the morning, soon after midnight 午夜剛過的一段時間；凌晨時分：*We worked well into the small hours.* 我們一直工作到了午夜之後。◇ *The fighting began in the early hours of Saturday morning.* 戰鬥在星期六凌晨打響了。➲ more at ELEVENTH at ELEVEN, EVIL *adj.*, KILL *v.*, UNEARTHLY, UNGODLY

hour·glass /ˈaʊəɡlɑːs; *NAmE* ˈaʊərɡlæs/ *noun*, *adj.*

■ ***noun*** a glass container holding sand that takes exactly an hour to pass through a small opening between the top and bottom sections 沙漏（上部的沙子經一小孔漏到下部，全部漏完正好一小時）➲ compare EGG TIMER

■ ***adj.*** [only before noun] a woman who has an **hourglass** figure, shape, etc. has large breasts and hips and a small waist（女人身材）豐乳肥臀的，上凸下翹的

'hour hand *noun* the small hand on a clock or watch that points to the hour（鐘錶的）時針 ➲ picture at CLOCK

hour·ly /ˈaʊəli; *NAmE* ˈaʊərli/ *adj.*, *adv.* **HELP** Use **an**, not **a**, before **hourly**. * hourly 之前用 an，不用 a。

■ ***adj.*** [only before noun] **1** done or happening every hour 每小時（一次）的：*an hourly bus service* 每小時一班的公共汽車 ◇ *Trains leave at hourly intervals.* 火車每一小時發出一列。**2** an **hourly wage, fee, rate, etc.** is the amount that you earn every hour or pay for a service every hour（工資、酬金、費用等）按鐘點計算的，論小時的：*an hourly rate of $30 an hour* 每小時 30 元的收費率

■ ***adv.*** every hour 每小時（一次）地：*Reapply sunscreen hourly and after swimming.* 每小時以及游泳後抹一次防曬霜。◇ *Dressings are changed four hourly* (= every four hours) *to help prevent infection.* 每四小時更換一次敷料，以防感染。

house *noun*, *verb*

■ ***noun*** /haʊs/ (*pl.* **houses** /ˈhaʊzɪz/)

▸ **BUILDING 建築** **1** [C] a building for people to live in, usually for one family 房屋；房子；住宅：*He went into the house.* 他進了房子。◇ *a two-bedroom house* 兩居室的住宅 ◇ *Let's have the party **at my house**.* 我們在我家裏聚會吧。◇ *house prices* 房價 ◇ *What time do you leave the house in the morning* (= to go to work)? 你早晨幾點出門去上班？◇ (*BrE*) *We're **moving house*** (= leaving our house and going to live in a different one). 我們要搬家了。➲ COLLOCATIONS at DECORATE ➲ VISUAL VOCAB page V17 ➲ see also PENTHOUSE, SAFE HOUSE, SHOW HOUSE **2** [sing.] all the people living in a house 住在一所房子裏的人；全家人 **SYN** **household**：*Be quiet or you'll wake the whole house!* 安靜點，別把全家人都吵醒！**3** [C] (in compounds 構成複合詞) a building used for a particular purpose, for example for holding meetings in or keeping animals or goods in 某種用途的建築物：*an opera house* 歌劇院 ◇ *a henhouse* 雞舍 ➲ see also DOGHOUSE, DOSSHOUSE, HALFWAY HOUSE, HOTHOUSE, LIGHTHOUSE, MADHOUSE, OUTHOUSE, STOREHOUSE, WAREHOUSE **4** **House** [sing.] (*BrE*) used in the names of office buildings（用於辦公樓名稱）大廈，大樓：*Their offices are on the second floor of Chester House.* 他們的辦公室在切斯特大廈三樓。

▸ **COMPANY/INSTITUTION 公司；機構** **5** [C] (in compounds 構成複合詞) a company involved in a particular kind of business; an institution of a particular kind（從事某種生意的）公司，機構：*a **fashion/banking/publishing, etc. house*** 時裝公司、銀行、出版社等 ◇ *a religious house* (= a CONVENT or a MONASTERY) 會院 ◇ *I work **in house*** (= in the offices of the company that I work for, not at home). 我在公司裏上班。➲ see also CLEARING HOUSE, IN-HOUSE

▸ **RESTAURANT 餐館** **6** [C] (in compounds 構成複合詞) a restaurant 餐館；餐廳：*a steakhouse* 牛排餐館 ◇ *a coffee house* 咖啡館 ◇ *a bottle of **house wine*** (= the cheapest wine available in a particular restaurant, sometimes not listed by name) 一瓶本店特價酒 ➲ see also FREE HOUSE, PUBLIC HOUSE, ROADHOUSE, TIED HOUSE

▸ **PARLIAMENT 議院** **7** [C] (often **House**) a group of people who meet to discuss and make the laws of a country 議院；議會；國會：*Legislation requires approval by both houses of parliament.* 立法須要得到議會兩院的一致通過。➲ see also LOWER HOUSE, UPPER HOUSE **8** **the House** [sing.] the House of Commons or the House of Lords in Britain; the House of Representatives in the US（英國）下議院，上議院；（美國）眾議院

▸ **IN DEBATE 辯論** **9** **the house** [sing.] a group of people discussing sth in a formal debate（統稱）參與辯論的人：*I urge the house to vote against the motion.* 我呼籲參加辯論的諸位投票反對這項動議。

▸ **IN THEATRE 劇院** **10** [C] the part of a theatre where the audience sits; the audience at a particular performance 觀眾席；（統稱）觀眾：*playing to a **full/packed/empty house*** (= to a large/small audience) 演出座無虛席／滿座／觀眾寥寥無幾 ◇ *The spotlight faded and the house lights came up.* 聚光燈漸漸熄滅，觀眾席的燈亮了。➲ see also FRONT-OF-HOUSE, FULL HOUSE (1)

▸ **IN SCHOOL 學校** **11** [C] (in some British schools) an organized group of students of different ages who compete against other groups in sports competitions, etc. and who may, in BOARDING SCHOOLS, live together in one building（英國某些學校為進行體育比賽或按宿舍將學生分成的）社，舍

▸ **FAMILY 家庭** **12** [C] (usually **the House of ...**) an old and famous family 名門世家；望族：*the House of Windsor* (= the British royal family) 温莎王室

▸ **MUSIC 音樂** **13** [U] = HOUSE MUSIC ➲ see also ACID HOUSE, ART-HOUSE, OPEN HOUSE, POWERHOUSE **HELP** There are many other compounds ending in **house**. You will find them at their place in the alphabet. 以 house 結尾的複合詞還有很多，可在各字母中的適當位置查到。

IDM **bring the 'house down** to make everyone laugh or CHEER, especially at a performance in the theatre（尤指劇院的演出）博得滿堂大笑（或喝彩） **get on like a 'house on fire** (*BrE*) (*NAmE* **get along like a 'house on fire**) (*informal*) (of people 人) to become friends quickly and have a very friendly relationship 很快就打得火熱；一見如故；一拍即合 **go all round the 'houses** (*BrE, informal*) to do sth or ask a question in a very complicated way instead of in a simple, direct way 繞圈子；拐彎抹角；不直截了當 **keep 'house** to cook, clean and do all the other jobs around the house 操持家務 **on the 'house** drinks or meals that are **on the house** are provided free by the pub/bar or restaurant and you do not have to pay（酒吧或飯店）免費提供的 **put/set your (own) 'house in order** to organize your own business or improve your own behaviour before you try to criticize sb else 先管好自己的事；律人先律己 **set up 'house** to make a place your home（在某處）建立家庭： *They set up house together in a small flat in Brighton.* 他們一同在布賴頓的一個小公寓裏建立了家庭。 ➲ more at CLEAN *v.*, DRY *adj.*, EAT, PEOPLE *n.*, SAFE *adj.*

■ *verb* /haʊz/

▸ PROVIDE HOME 提供住所 **1 ~ sb** to provide a place for sb to live 給（某人）提供住處： *The government is committed to housing the refugees.* 政府承諾收容難民。

▸ KEEP STH 保存 **2 ~ sth** to be the place where sth is kept or where sth operates from 是（某物）的貯藏處（或安置處）；收藏；安置： *The gallery houses 2 000 works of modern art.* 美術館收藏了 2 000 件現代藝術作品。◇ *The museum is housed in the Old Court House.* 博物館設在舊法院大樓裏。

'house arrest *noun* [U] the state of being a prisoner in your own house rather than in a prison 軟禁： *to be under house arrest* 遭到軟禁 ◇ *She was* ***placed under house arrest***. 她遭到了軟禁。

house·boat /'haʊsbəʊt; *NAmE* -boʊt/ *noun* a boat that people can live in, usually kept at a particular place on a river or CANAL 供居住的船；水上住宅 ➲ VISUAL VOCAB page V16

house·bound /'haʊsbaʊnd/ *adj.* **1** unable to leave your house because you cannot walk very far as a result of being ill/sick or old（因病或年邁）不能離家的，出不了門的 **2 the housebound** *noun* [pl.] people who are housebound 出不了門的人

house·boy /'haʊsbɔɪ/ *noun* a young male servant in a house 年輕男僕

house·break·ing /'haʊsbreɪkɪŋ/ *noun* [U] (*especially BrE*) the crime of entering a house illegally by using force, in order to steal things from it 入室行竊 SYN **burglary** ▸ **house·break·er** /'haʊsbreɪkə(r)/ *noun*

'house-broken (*NAmE*) (*BrE* **'house-trained**) *adj.* (of pet cats or dogs 寵物貓或狗) trained to DEFECATE and URINATE outside the house or in a special box 經訓練在戶外（或專用盒子裏）便溺的；養成良好衞生習慣的

house·coat /'haʊskəʊt; *NAmE* -koʊt/ *noun* a long loose piece of clothing, worn in the house by women（女式）家居袍

'house dust mite *noun* = DUST MITE

house·fly /'haʊsflaɪ/ *noun* (*pl.* **-ies**) a common fly that lives in houses 家蠅

house·ful /'haʊsfʊl/ *noun* [sing.] a large number of people in a house 一大家人；滿屋子人： *He grew up in a houseful of women.* 他在一個滿是女人的家庭裏長大。◇ *They had a houseful so we didn't stay.* 他們滿屋子都是人，所以我們沒有留下來。

H

Collocations 詞語搭配

Moving house 搬家

Renting 租房子

- **live in** a rented/(*especially NAmE*) rental property 住在租來的住所裏
- **rent/share/move into** a furnished house/(*BrE*) flat/(*especially NAmE*) apartment 租用／合住／搬進配有傢具的房屋／公寓
- **rent** a studio/(*BrE*) a studio flat/(*especially NAmE*) a studio apartment/(*BrE*) a bedsit 租一個單間公寓
- **find/get** a housemate/(*BrE*) a flatmate/(*NAmE*) a roommate 找／找到一個室友
- **sign/break** the lease/rental agreement/contract 簽署／違反租約／租賃協議／合同
- **extend/renew/terminate** the lease/(*BrE*) tenancy 延長租賃期限；續簽／終止租約
- **afford/pay** the rent/the bills/(*NAmE*) the utilities 付得起／支付租金／賬單／水電氣等雜費
- (*especially BrE*) **fall behind with**/(*especially NAmE*) **fall behind on** the rent 拖欠租金
- **pay/lose/return** a damage deposit/(*NAmE*) security deposit 支付／失去／退還損壞押金／保證金
- **give/receive** a month's/two-weeks' notice to leave/vacate the property 提前一個月／兩週發出／收到離開／騰空住房的通知

Being a landlord 做房東

- **have a flat/apartment/room** (*BrE*) to let/(*especially NAmE*) for rent 有一間公寓／一個房間要出租
- **rent (out)/lease (out)**/(*BrE*) **let (out)/sublet** a flat/apartment/house/property 出租／轉租公寓／房屋／房產
- **collect/increase/raise** the rent 收取／增加／提高房租
- **evict** the existing tenants 趕走現有房客
- **attract/find** new/prospective tenants 吸引／尋找新的／可能的房客
- **invest in** rental property/(*BrE*) property to let/(*BrE*) the buy-to-let market 投資購房用於出租

Buying 購買房子

- **buy/acquire/purchase** a house/(a) property/(*especially NAmE*) (a piece of) prime real estate 購置一棟房子／一處房產／（一塊）優質房地產
- **call/contact/use** (*BrE*) an estate agent/(*NAmE*) a Realtor™/(*NAmE*) a real estate agent/broker 電話聯繫／聯繫／任用房地產經紀人
- **make/**(*BrE*) **put in** an offer on a house 提供房子的報價
- **put down/save for** (*BrE*) a deposit on a house 支付／存錢付房屋訂金
- **make/put/save for** (*especially NAmE*) a down payment on a house/home 支付／攢錢支付買房的首付金
- **apply for/arrange/take out** a mortgage/home loan 申請／商定／取得按揭／住房貸款
- **(struggle to) pay** the mortgage （竭力）支付按揭貸款
- **make/meet/keep up/cover** the monthly mortgage payments/(*BrE also*) repayments 支付每月的按揭貸款
- (*BrE*) **repossess**/(*especially NAmE*) **foreclose on** sb's home/house 收回某人的房子；終止某人的房屋贖回權

Selling 出售房子

- **put your house/property** on the market/up for sale/up for auction 將房屋／房產投放市場／出售／拍賣
- **increase/lower** your price/the asking price 提高／降低價格／要價
- **have/hold/hand over** the deed/(*especially BrE*) deeds of/to the house, land, etc. 持有／移交房屋、土地等契約

'house guest *noun* a person who is staying in your house for a short time 在家小住的客人

house·hold 0-w /'haʊshəʊld; *NAmE* -hoʊld/ *noun* all the people living together in a house or flat/apartment 一家人；家庭；同住一所（或一套）房子的人：*Most households now own at least one car.* 大多數家庭現在至少有一輛汽車。◇ ***low-income/one-parent, etc. households*** 低收入、單親等家庭 ◇ ***the head of the household*** 戶主 ▸ **house·hold** 0-w *adj.* [only before noun]：***household bills/chores/goods*** (= connected with looking after a house and the people living in it) 家庭賬單／雜務／用品

house·hold·er /'haʊshəʊldə(r); *NAmE* -hoʊld-/ *noun* (*formal*) a person who owns or rents the house that they live in 房主；住戶

ˌhousehold 'name (also *less frequent* **ˌhousehold 'word**) *noun* a name that has become very well known 家喻戶曉的名字：*She became a household name in the 1960s.* 她在 20 世紀 60 年代成為家喻戶曉的人物。

'house-hunting *noun* [U] the activity of looking for a house to buy 找房子，看房子（以便購買）▸ **'house-hunter** *noun*

'house husband *noun* a man who stays at home to cook, clean, take care of the children, etc. while his wife or partner goes out to work 操持家務的丈夫；"家庭主夫" ➲ compare HOUSEWIFE

house·keep·er /'haʊski:pə(r)/ *noun* **1** a person, usually a woman, whose job is to manage the shopping, cooking, cleaning, etc. in a house or an institution 管家，雜務主管（通常為女性）**2** a person whose job is to manage the cleaning of rooms in a hotel（旅館的）房間清潔工

house·keep·ing /'haʊski:pɪŋ/ *noun* [U] **1** the work involved in taking care of a house, especially shopping and managing money 家務（尤指採購和管理開支）**2** the department in a hotel, a hospital, an office building, etc. that is responsible for cleaning the rooms, etc.（旅館、醫院、寫字樓等的）總務處，後勤部：*Call housekeeping and ask them to bring us some clean towels.* 給總務處打電話，讓他們給我們送些乾淨的毛巾來。**3** (also **'housekeeping money** especially in *BrE*) the money used to buy food, cleaning materials and other things needed for taking care of a house 家務開支 **4** jobs that are done to enable an organization or computer system to work well 內務處理：*Most large companies now use computers for accounting and housekeeping operations.* 多數大公司現在用計算機進行會計運算和內務操作。

house·maid /'haʊsmeɪd/ *noun* (*old-fashioned*) a female servant in a large house who cleans the rooms, etc. and often lives there（家庭的）女僕，女傭

house·man /'haʊsmən/ *noun* (*pl.* **-men** /-mən/) **1** (*old-fashioned, BrE*) = HOUSE OFFICER **2** (*NAmE*) a man employed to do general jobs in a house, hotel, etc.（家庭或旅館等的）男勤雜工，男僕

'house martin *noun* a small black and white European bird like a SWALLOW 家馬丁鳥（歐洲燕子）

house·mas·ter /'haʊsmɑ:stə(r); *NAmE* -mæs-/, **house·mis·tress** /'haʊsmɪstrəs/ *noun* (*especially BrE*) a teacher in charge of a group of children (called a HOUSE) in a school, especially a private school（尤指私立學校的）舍監

house·mate /'haʊsmeɪt/ *noun* a person that you share a house with, but who is not one of your family 同屋（指同住一所房子但非家庭成員的人）

'house music (also **house**) *noun* [U] a type of electronic dance music with a fast beat 浩室音樂（一種快節奏電子舞曲）

ˌhouse of 'cards *noun* [sing.] **1** a plan, an organization, etc. that is so badly arranged that it could easily fail 不可靠的計劃；搖搖欲墜的組織 **2** a structure built out of PLAYING CARDS 用紙牌搭成的房子

the ˌHouse of 'Commons (also **the Com·mons**) *noun* **1** [sing.+sing./pl. v.] (in Britain and Canada) the part of Parliament whose members are elected by the people of the country（英國）下議院；（加拿大）眾議院 **2** [sing.] the building where the members of the House of Commons meet 下議院大樓 ➲ compare THE HOUSE OF LORDS

'house officer *noun* (in Britain) a doctor who has finished medical school and who is working at a hospital to get further practical experience（英國的）見習醫生；實習醫生 ➲ compare INTERN *n.* (1)

ˌhouse of 'God *noun* [usually sing.] (*pl.* **houses of God**) (*literary*) a church or other religious building 教堂；宗教建築

the ˌHouse of 'Lords (also **the Lords**) *noun* **1** [sing.+sing./pl. v.] (in Britain) the part of Parliament whose members are not elected by the people of the country（英國）上議院，貴族院 **2** [sing.] the building where members of the House of Lords meet 上議院大樓 ➲ compare THE HOUSE OF COMMONS

the ˌHouse of Repre'sentatives *noun* [sing.] the largest part of Congress in the US, or of the Parliament in Australia, whose members are elected by the people of the country（美國國會或澳大利亞議會的）眾議院 ➲ compare SENATE (1)

'house party *noun* a party held at a large house in the country where guests stay for a few days; the guests at this party 鄉村府邸聚會，鄉村府邸聚會的全體賓客（常留宿幾天）

'house plant (*BrE* also **'pot plant**) *noun* a plant that you grow in a pot and keep indoors 室內盆栽植物 ➲ VISUAL VOCAB page V21

'house-proud *adj.* spending a lot of time making your house look clean and attractive, and thinking that this is important 熱衷於收拾家的

house·room /'haʊsru:m; -rʊm/ *noun* [U] space in a house for sb/sth 家裏的容納空間；家裏放東西的地方
IDM **not give sth 'houseroom** (*BrE*) to not like sth and not want it in your house 不喜歡把某物放在家裏

'house-sit *verb* (-tt-) [I] to live in sb's house while they are away in order to take care of it for them（屋主外出時）代為照看房子

the ˌHouses of 'Parliament *noun* [pl.] (in Britain 英國) the Parliament that consists of both the HOUSE OF COMMONS and the HOUSE OF LORDS; the buildings in London where the British Parliament meets（包括上、下議院的）議會；（倫敦）議會大廈

ˌhouse 'style *noun* [U, C] the way a company such as a PUBLISHER prefers its written materials to be expressed and arranged（出版社等書面材料的）出版樣式

ˌhouse-to-'house *adj.* [only before noun] visiting every house in a particular area 挨家挨戶的：*a house-to-house collection/search* 挨家收集／搜查 ◇ *The police are making house-to-house enquiries.* 警察正在逐戶調查。

'house-trained (*BrE*) (*NAmE* **'house-broken**) *adj.* (of pet cats or dogs 作寵物的貓或狗) trained to DEFECATE and URINATE outside the house or in a special box 經訓練在戶外（或專用盒子裏）便溺的；養成良好衛生習慣的

house·wares /'haʊsweəz; *NAmE* -werz/ *noun* [pl.] (*NAmE*) (in shops/stores 商店) small items used in the house, especially kitchen equipment 家用器皿；（尤指）廚房用具

'house-warming *noun* a party given by sb who has just moved into a new house 喬遷聚會

house·wife /'haʊswaɪf/ *noun* (*pl.* **-wives** /-waɪvz/) a woman who stays at home to cook, clean, take care of the children, etc. while her husband or partner goes out to work 主婦；家庭婦女 ➲ compare HOUSE HUSBAND ▸ **house·wife·ly** *adj.*

house·work /'haʊswɜ:k; *NAmE* -wɜ:rk/ *noun* [U] the work involved in taking care of a home and family, for example cleaning and cooking 家務勞動；家務事：*to do the housework* 做家務

hous·ing 0-w /'haʊzɪŋ/ *noun*
1 0-w [U] houses, flats/apartments, etc. that people live

in, especially when referring to their type, price or condition（統稱，尤指住房類型、價格、條件）住房，住宅：*public/private housing* 公共／私人住房 ◇ *poor housing conditions* 惡劣的居住條件 ◇ *the housing shortage* 住房短缺 ◇ *the* ***housing market*** (= the activity of buying and selling houses, etc.) 住房市場 **2** 🔑 [U] the job of providing houses, flats/apartments, etc. for people to live in 住房供給：*the housing department* 住房建設部門 ◇ *the council's housing policy* 市政住房政策 **3** [C] a hard cover that protects part of a machine（機器的）外殼，套：*a car's rear axle housing* 汽車的後軸套

'housing association *noun* (in Britain) an organization that owns houses, flats/apartments, etc. and helps people to rent or buy them at a low price（英國）房屋協會（以低價出租或出售房屋）

'housing benefit *noun* [U, C] (in Britain) money given by the government to people who do not earn much, to help them pay for a place to live in（英國）住房補貼

'housing estate (*BrE*) (also **'housing development** *NAmE, BrE*) *noun* an area in which a large number of houses or flats/apartments are planned and built together at the same time（統建的）住宅區，住宅群：*They live on a housing estate.* 他們住在一個住宅區裏。

'housing project (also **pro·ject**) (both *NAmE*) *noun* a group of houses or flats/apartments built for poor families, usually with government money 住宅區，居民村（常由政府為貧困家庭營造）

hove *past tense, past part.* of HEAVE

hovel /ˈhɒvl; *NAmE* ˈhʌvl/ *noun* (*disapproving*) a house or room that is not fit to live in because it is dirty or in very bad condition（不適於居住的）骯髒簡陋的住所

hover /ˈhɒvə(r); *NAmE* ˈhʌvər/ *verb* **1** [I] (**+ adv./prep.**) (of birds, HELICOPTERS, etc. 鳥、直升機等) to stay in the air in one place 翱翔；盤旋：*A hawk hovered over the hill.* 一隻鷹在小山的上空翱翔。 **2** [I] (**+ adv./prep.**) (of a person 人) to wait somewhere, especially near sb, in a shy or uncertain manner 躊躇，彷徨（尤指在某人身邊）：*He hovered nervously in the doorway.* 他在門口緊張地來回踱步。 **3** [I] **+ adv./prep.** to stay close to sth, or to stay in an uncertain state 靠近（某事物）；處於不穩定狀態：*Temperatures hovered around freezing.* 氣溫在冰點上下徘徊。◇ *He hovered on the edge of consciousness.* 他似醒非醒。◇ *A smile hovered on her lips.* 她的嘴上掛着一絲笑容。

hov·er·craft /ˈhɒvəkrɑːft; *NAmE* ˈhʌvərkræft/ *noun* a vehicle that travels just above the surface of water or land, held up by air being forced downwards 氣墊船；氣墊運載工具 ➲ **VISUAL VOCAB** page V54 ➲ compare HYDROFOIL

ˌHO'V lane /ˌeɪtʃ əʊ ˈviː leɪn; *NAmE* oʊ/ *noun* (*especially NAmE*) high-occupancy vehicle lane (a part of the road that may only be used by vehicles that are carrying two or more people) 高乘載率汽車專用車道，多乘員汽車車道（僅供搭載兩人以上的車輛通行）

how 🔑 /haʊ/ *adv.*

1 🔑 in what way or manner 怎樣；如何：*How does it work?* 它是如何運作的？◇ *He did not know how he ought to behave.* 他不知道自己應該怎樣表現。◇ *I'll show you how to load the software.* 我給你演示一下如何裝入這套軟件。◇ *'Her behaviour was very odd.'* ***'How so?'*** "她的舉止非常奇怪。" "如何奇怪呢？" ◇ *It's funny how* (= that) *people always remember him.* 有趣的是人們總是忘不了他。◇ *Do you* ***remember how*** (= that) *the kids always loved going there?* 你記得孩子們總喜歡去那裏嗎？◇ ***How ever*** *did you get here so quickly?* 你怎麼這麼快就過來了？ ➲ compare HOWEVER **2** 🔑 used to ask about sb's health（詢問健康狀況）：*How are you?* 你（身體）好嗎？◇ *How are you feeling now?* 你現在感覺怎麼樣？ **3** 🔑 used to ask whether sth is successful or enjoyable（詢問是否成功或愉快）：*How was your trip?* 你旅行愉快嗎？◇ *How did they play?* 他們的比賽表現怎樣？ **4** 🔑 used before an adjective or adverb to ask about the amount, degree, etc. of sth, or about sb's age（後接形容詞或副詞）多少，多麼，多大：***How often*** *do you go swimming?* 你多久去游泳一次？◇ *I didn't know how much to bring.* 我不知道該帶多少。◇ ***How much*** *are those earrings* (= What do they cost)? 那對耳環多少錢？◇ ***How many*** *people were there?* 有多少人？◇ *How old is she?* 她有多大了？ **5** 🔑 used to express surprise, pleasure, etc.（表示驚奇、高興等）：*How kind of you to help!* 你來幫忙，真是太好了！◇ *How he wished he had been there!* 他多麼希望當時自己也在場！ **6** 🔑 in any way in which 以任何方式；無論用什麼方法 **SYN** **however**：*I'll dress how I like in my own house!* 我在自己家裏愛怎麼穿就怎麼穿！

IDM ***how about ... ?*** **1** 🔑 used when asking for information about sb/sth（詢問信息）…怎麼樣，…情況如何：*I'm not going. How about you?* 我不打算去。你呢？ **2** 🔑 used to make a suggestion（提出建議）…怎麼樣，…行不行，…好嗎：*How about a break?* 休息一下好嗎？◇ *How about going for a meal?* 去吃飯好不好？◇ (*especially NAmE*) *How about we go for a meal?* 我們去吃飯好不好？ **how 'can/'could you!** (*informal*) used to show that you strongly disapprove of sb's behaviour or are very surprised by it（表示很不贊同或吃驚）你怎麼能：*Ben! How could you? After all they've done for us!* 本！他們為我們做了這麼多，你怎麼能這樣！◇ *Ugh! How can you eat that stuff?* 啊！你怎麼吃得下那種東西？ **how 'come?** 🔑 (*informal*) used to ask the reason for sth 為什麼；怎麼會：*'I think you owe me some money.' 'How come?'* "我想你欠我一些錢呢。" "怎麼會呢？" **ˌhow do you 'do** 🔑 (becoming *old-fashioned*) used as a formal GREETING when you meet sb for the first time. The usual reply is also *How do you do?*（首次見面時的問候語。通常的回答也是 How do you do?）你好 **ˌhow's 'that?** (*informal*) **1** used to ask the reason for sth 為什麼；那是怎麼回事：*'I left work early today.' 'How's that* (= Why)?' "我今天提前下班了。" "為什麼？" **2** used when asking sb's opinion of sth（你認為）怎麼樣，如何：*I'll tuck your sheets in for you. How's that? Comfortable?* 我給你把被單掖在墊褥下面吧。怎麼樣？舒服嗎？◇ *Two o'clock on the dot!* ***How's that for*** *punctuality!* 兩點整！夠守時吧！

how·dah /ˈhaʊdə/ *noun* a seat for riding on the back of an ELEPHANT or a CAMEL, often for more than one person 象轎，駝轎（大象或駱駝背上的鞍座，常常可坐多於一人）

howdy /ˈhaʊdi/ *exclamation* (*NAmE, informal*, often *humorous*) used to say hello（招呼語）你好：*Howdy, partner.* 你好，夥計。

how·ever 🔑 /haʊˈevə(r)/ *adv.*

1 🔑 used with an adjective or adverb to mean 'to whatever degree'（與形容詞或副詞連用）無論到什麼程度，不管多麼：*He wanted to take no risks, however small.* 他再小的險也不想冒。◇ *She has the window open, however cold it is outside.* 不管外面多冷她都開着窗戶。◇ *However carefully I explained, she still didn't understand.* 無論我解釋得多麼仔細，她還是沒弄懂。 **HELP** When **ever** is used to emphasize **how**, meaning 'In what way or manner?', it is usually written as a separate word. 用 ever 來強調 how（意為"以何種方式"）時 ever 通常要寫作單獨的一個詞：***How ever*** *did you get here so quickly?* **2** 🔑 in whatever way 不管怎樣；無論如何：*However you look at it, it's going to cost a lot.* 不管你怎麼看，它都要花很多錢。 **3** 🔑 used to introduce a statement that contrasts with sth that has just been said 然而；不過；仍然：*He was feeling bad. He went to work, however, and tried to concentrate.* 他感覺不舒服，但他仍然去上班，並且努力集中精神工作。◇ *We thought the figures were correct. However, we have now discovered some errors.* 我們原以為這些數據正確，不過我們現在發現了一些錯誤。 ➲ **LANGUAGE BANK** at next page

how·itz·er /ˈhaʊɪtsə(r)/ *noun* a heavy gun that fires SHELLS high into the air for a short distance 榴彈炮

howl /haʊl/ *verb, noun*

■ ***verb*** **1** [I] (of a dog, WOLF, etc. 狗、狼等) to make a long, loud cry 長嚎；嗥叫 **2** [I] **~ (in/with sth)** to make a loud cry when you are in pain, angry, amused, etc.（因疼痛、憤怒、開心等）大聲叫喊：*to howl in pain* 疼得直叫喊 ◇ *We howled with laughter.* 我們放聲大笑。◇ *The baby was howling* (= crying loudly) *all the time I was there.* 我在那裏時孩子一直哭得很厲害。 **3** [I] (of the wind 風) to

H

blow hard and make a long loud noise 怒號；呼嘯：*The wind was howling around the house.* 狂風在房子四周呼嘯。**4** [T] **~ sth | + speech** to say sth loudly and angrily 怒吼：*The crowd howled its displeasure.* 群眾不滿地怒吼着。

PHR V ,howl sb↔'down to prevent a speaker from being heard by shouting angrily 以怒吼聲壓倒講演者的聲音 **SYN shout sb down**

■ *noun* **1** a long loud cry made by a dog, WOLF, etc.（狗、狼等的）嗥叫，長嚎 **2** a loud cry showing that you are in pain, angry, amused, etc.（因疼痛、憤怒、高興等發出的）喊叫聲：*to let out a howl of anguish* 發出痛苦的喊叫聲 ◇ *The suggestion was greeted with* ***howls of laughter****.* 這個建議引起了陣陣大笑。**3** a long loud sound made when the wind is blowing strongly（狂風的）嘯鳴，怒號：*They listened to the howl of the wind through the trees.* 他們聽着風在林間呼嘯的聲音。

H

howl·er /ˈhaʊlə(r)/ *noun* (*informal, especially BrE*) a stupid mistake, especially in what sb says or writes（尤指言談或行文中的）愚蠢的錯誤 **SYN glaring error**：*The report is full of howlers.* 這份報告錯漏百出。➲ SYNONYMS at MISTAKE

howl·ing /ˈhaʊlɪŋ/ *adj.* [only before noun] **1** (of a storm, etc. 風暴等) very violent, with strong winds 怒號的；猛烈的：*a* ***howling gale/storm/wind*** 怒吼着的大風 / 風暴 / 風 **2** (*informal*) very great or extreme 很大的；極端的：*a howling success* 轟動的成就 ◇ *She flew into a howling rage.* 她暴跳如雷。

ˈhow-to *adj.* [only before noun] providing detailed instructions or advice on how to do sth 指導的；指南的：*how-to books on computing* 計算機操作説明書 ▸ **ˈhow-to** *noun* (*pl.* **-os**)：*Visit our downloads page for free how-tos and tutorials.* 可到我們網頁的下載區獲取免費指南和教程。

how·zat /ˌhaʊˈzæt/ *exclamation* used in CRICKET to tell the UMPIRE that you think the other team's BATSMAN is out 怎麼回事（責問板球裁判員何以擊球手未判出局）

how·zit /ˈhaʊzɪt/ *exclamation* (*SAfrE, informal*) used to say hello when you meet sb（打招呼用語）你好：*Howzit Mandla, how's it going?* 你好，曼德拉，怎麼樣啊？◇ *Please say howzit to Nicki for me.* 請代我向尼基問好。

h.p. /ˌeɪtʃ ˈpiː/ *abbr.* **1** HORSEPOWER 馬力 **2** (also **HP**) (*BrE*) HIRE PURCHASE 分期付款購買

Language Bank 用語庫

however

Ways of saying 'but'“但是”的表達方式

- Politicians have promised to improve road safety. So far, **however**, little has been achieved. 政客們承諾要提高道路安全。但是，迄今為止成效微乎其微。
- **Despite** clear evidence from road safety studies, no new measures have been introduced. 儘管道路安全研究已得出確切依據，但仍未實施任何新措施。
- Politicians have promised to improve road safety. **In spite of this/Despite this**, little has been achieved so far. 政客們承諾要提高道路安全。儘管如此，迄今為止成效微乎其微。
- **Although** politicians have promised to improve road safety, little has been achieved so far. 儘管政客們承諾要提高道路安全，但是迄今為止成效微乎其微。
- Some politicians claim that the new transport policy has been a success. **In fact**, it has been a total disaster. 一些政客宣稱新的交通政策非常成功，實際上卻是徹頭徹尾的失敗。
- Government campaigns have had a measure of success, **but the fact remains that** large numbers of accidents are still caused by careless drivers. 政府的宣傳活動取得了一定的成功，但實際情況是大量的交通事故仍然是由於駕駛者疏忽造成的。

➲ Language Bank at NEVERTHELESS

HQ /ˌeɪtʃ ˈkjuː/ *abbr.* HEADQUARTERS 總部：*See you back at HQ.* 回總部見。◇ *police HQ* 警察總局

HR /ˌeɪtʃ ˈɑː(r)/ *abbr.* HUMAN RESOURCES

hr (also **hr.** especially in *NAmE*) *abbr.* (*pl.* **hrs** or **hr**) (in writing) hour（書寫形式）小時：*Cover and chill for 1 hr.* 蓋上蓋子冷卻 1 小時。

HRH /ˌeɪtʃ ɑːr ˈeɪtʃ/ *abbr.* His/Her ROYAL HIGHNESS（他稱）殿下：*HRH Prince Harry* 哈里王子殿下

HRT /ˌeɪtʃ ɑː ˈtiː; *NAmE* ɑːr/ *noun* [U] the abbreviation for 'hormone replacement therapy' (medical treatment for women going through the MENOPAUSE in which HORMONES are added to the body) 激素替代療法（全寫為 hormone replacement therapy，為更年期女性注射激素以提高體內雌激素水平）

Hsiang /ʃiːˈæŋ/ *noun* [U] = XIANG

HTML /ˌeɪtʃ tiː em ˈel/ *abbr.* (*computing* 計) Hypertext Mark-up Language (a system used to mark text for World Wide Web pages in order to obtain colours, style, pictures, etc.) 超文本置標語言

HTTP (also **http**) /ˌeɪtʃ tiː tiː ˈpiː/ *abbr.* (*computing* 計) Hypertext Transfer Protocol (the set of rules that control the way data is sent and received over the Internet) 超文本傳送協議

hua·rache /wəˈrɑːtʃi; wəˈr-/ *noun* a type of SANDAL (= open shoe) made of many narrow strips of leather twisted together 皮條編織的涼鞋

hub /hʌb/ *noun* **1** [usually sing.] **~ (of sth)** the central and most important part of a particular place or activity（某地或活動的）中心，核心：*the commercial hub of the city* 城市的商業中心 ◇ *to be at the hub of things* (= where things happen and important decisions are made) 在核心部門 ◇ *a hub airport* (= a large important one where people often change from one plane to another) 樞紐機場 **2** the central part of a wheel 輪轂 ➲ VISUAL VOCAB page V51

hub·bub /ˈhʌbʌb/ *noun* [sing., U] **1** the loud sound made by a lot of people talking at the same time 喧鬧聲；嘈雜聲：*It was difficult to hear what he was saying over the hubbub.* 聲音太嘈雜，難以聽清楚他的講話。**2** a situation in which there is a lot of noise, excitement and activity 喧鬧；騷亂；混亂：*the hubbub of city life* 鬧哄哄的城市生活

hubby /ˈhʌbi/ *noun* (*pl.* **-ies**) (*informal*) = HUSBAND

hub·cap /ˈhʌbkæp/ *noun* a round metal cover that fits over the HUB of a vehicle's wheel（輪）轂蓋 ➲ VISUAL VOCAB page V52

hu·bris /ˈhjuːbrɪs/ *noun* [U] (*literary*) the fact of sb being too proud. In literature, a character with this pride ignores warnings and laws and this usually results in their DOWNFALL and death. 傲慢；狂妄

huckle·berry /ˈhʌklbəri; *NAmE* -beri/ *noun* (*pl.* **-ies**) a small soft round purple N American fruit. The bush it grows on is also called a huckleberry. 美洲越橘漿果（或灌木）；黑美洲越橘

huck·ster /ˈhʌkstə(r)/ *noun* (*old-fashioned, NAmE*) **1** (*disapproving*) a person who uses aggressive or annoying methods to sell sth 強行推銷的人 **2** a person who sells things in the street or by visiting people's houses 沿街叫賣的小販；上門推銷員

HUD /ˌeɪtʃ juː ˈdiː/ *abbr.* Department of Housing and Urban Development (the US government department in charge of financial programmes to build houses and to help people buy their own homes)（美國）住房與城市發展部

hud·dle /ˈhʌdl/ *verb, noun*

■ *verb* **1** [I] **~ (up/together)** (**+ adv./prep.**) (of people or animals 人或動物) to gather closely together, usually because of cold or fear（通常因寒冷或害怕）擠在一起：*We huddled together for warmth.* 我們擠在一塊取暖。◇ *They all huddled around the fire.* 他們都聚集在火堆周圍。**2** [I] **~ (up)** (**+ adv./prep.**) to hold your arms and legs close to your body, usually because you are cold or frightened（通常因寒冷或害怕）蜷縮，縮成一團：*I huddled under a blanket on the floor.* 我在地板上蓋着毯子縮成一團。▸ **hud·dled** *adj.*：*People were huddled* *together around the fire.* 人們圍攏着火堆。◇ *huddled figures in shop doorways* 商店門口蜷縮着的人影 ◇ *We found him huddled on the floor.* 我們發現他蜷縮在地板上。

■ ***noun*** **1** a small group of people, objects or buildings that are close together, especially when they are not in any particular order （尤指雜亂地）擠在一起的人（或物品、建築）: *People stood around in huddles.* 人們三五成群地到處聚集着。◇ *The track led them to a huddle of outbuildings.* 那條小路把他們帶到了一片雜亂擁擠的棚子。 **2** (in AMERICAN FOOTBALL 美式足球) a time when the players gather round to hear the plan for the next part of the game 隊員靠攏（磋商戰術）

IDM **get/go into a 'huddle (with sb)** to move close to sb so that you can talk about sth without other people hearing 湊近（某人）說悄悄話；交頭接耳

hue /hju:/ *noun* **1** (*literary* or *technical* 術語) a colour; a particular shade of a colour 顏色；色度；色調: *His face took on an unhealthy whitish hue.* 他的臉上透出一絲病態的蒼白。◇ *Her paintings capture the subtle hues of the countryside in autumn.* 她的油畫捕捉住了秋天鄉村的微妙色調。 ➲ SYNONYMS at COLOUR **2** (*formal*) a type of belief or opinion 信仰；觀點: *supporters of every political hue* 各種政治信仰的擁護者

IDM **,hue and 'cry** strong public protest about sth 公眾的強烈抗議

huff /hʌf/ *verb, noun*

■ ***verb*** [T, I] (**+ speech**) to say sth or make a noise in a way that shows you are offended or annoyed 生氣地說；怒氣沖沖: *'Well, nobody asked you,' she huffed irritably.* "哼，誰問你了。" 她怒氣沖沖地說。

IDM **,huff and 'puff** (*informal*) **1** to breathe in a noisy way because you are very tired 氣喘吁吁；上氣不接下氣: *Jack was huffing and puffing to keep up with her.* 傑克氣喘吁吁地跟着她。 **2** to make it obvious that you are annoyed about sth without doing anything to change the situation 發脾氣；憤然不理；生悶氣；氣呼呼: *After much huffing and puffing, she finally agreed to help.* 她生了好一陣悶氣之後才終於同意幫忙。

■ ***noun***

IDM **in a 'huff** (*informal*) in a bad mood, especially because sb has annoyed or upset you 怒氣沖沖；生氣: *She went off in a huff.* 她怒氣沖沖地走了。

huffy /'hʌfi/ *adj.* (*informal*) in a bad mood, especially because sb has annoyed or upset you 生氣的；發怒的 ▸ **huff·ily** *adv.*

hug /hʌg/ *verb, noun*

■ ***verb*** (**-gg-**) **1** [T, I] **~ (sb)** to put your arms around sb and hold them tightly, especially to show that you like or love them 擁抱；摟抱 **SYN** **embrace**: *They hugged each other.* 他們相互擁抱。◇ *She hugged him tightly.* 她緊緊地摟住他。◇ *They put their arms around each other and hugged.* 他們伸出雙臂彼此擁抱。 **2** [T] **~ sth** to put your arms around sth and hold it close to your body 抱緊: *She sat in the chair, hugging her knees.* 她雙臂抱膝坐在椅子上。◇ *He hugged the hot-water bottle to his chest.* 他把熱水袋緊捂在胸口。 **3** [T] **~ sth** (of a path, vehicle, etc. 小路、車輛等) to keep close to sth for a distance 有一段距離地挨着（某物）: *The track hugs the coast for a mile.* 那條小徑有一英里緊靠海岸。 **4** [T] **~ sth** to fit tightly around sth, especially a person's body 纏緊，縛緊（某物，尤指人體）: *figure-hugging jeans* 緊身牛仔褲

■ ***noun*** an act of putting your arms around sb and holding them tightly, especially to show that you like or love them 擁抱；摟抱: *She gave her mother a big hug.* 她熱烈地擁抱了她的母親。◇ *He stopped to receive* ***hugs and kisses*** *from the fans.* 他停下來接受追隨者的擁抱親吻。 ➲ see also BEAR HUG

huge 🔑 /hju:dʒ/ *adj.*

1 🔑 extremely large in size or amount; great in degree 巨大的；極多的；程度高的 **SYN** **enormous, vast**: *a huge crowd* 龐大的人群 ◇ *He gazed up at her with huge brown eyes.* 他睜着棕色的大眼睛盯着她。◇ *huge debts* 巨債 ◇ *huge amounts of data* 超大量的數據 ◇ *The sums of money involved are potentially huge.* 涉及的金額可能很大。◇ *The party was a huge success.* 聚會辦得非常成功。◇ *This is going to be a huge problem for us.* 這將是我們的一大難題。 **2** (*informal*) very successful 非常成功的；走紅的: *I think this band is going to be huge.* 我想這個樂隊要走紅了。

huge·ly /'hju:dʒli/ *adv.* **1** extremely 極度；極其: *hugely entertaining/important/popular/successful* 極其有趣／重要／受歡迎／成功 **2** very much 非常；深深地；大大地: *They intended to invest hugely in new technology.* 他們打算在新技術方面投入大量資金。◇ *He turned around, grinning hugely.* 他轉過身來，咧着嘴樂。

huh /hʌ/ *exclamation* **1** people use **Huh?** at the end of questions, suggestions, etc., especially when they want sb to agree with them （用於問題、建議等之後，尤希望對方同意）: *So you won't be coming tonight, huh?* 那麼你今晚就不來了嗎，嗯？◇ *Let's get out of here, huh?* 我們離開這裏吧，嗯？ **2** people say **Huh!** to show anger, surprise, disagreement, etc. or to show that they are not impressed by sth （表示憤怒、驚奇、異議等，或認為沒有什麼了不起）: *Huh! Is that all you've done?* 噢！你做的就是這麼多了嗎？ **3** (*NAmE*) (*BrE* **eh**) people say **Huh?** to show that they have not heard what sb has just said （表示沒有聽清楚）: *'Are you feeling OK?' 'Huh?'* "你感覺好嗎？" "啊？"

hula hoop (*US* **Hula-Hoop™**) /'hu:lə hu:p/ *noun* a large plastic ring that you spin around your waist by moving your hips 呼啦圈

hulk /hʌlk/ *noun* **1** the main part of an old vehicle, especially a ship, that is no longer used （車、船等的）殘骸: *the hulk of a wrecked ship* 遇難輪船的殘骸 **2** a very large person, especially one who moves in an awkward way 高大的人；（尤指）高大粗笨的人: *a great hulk of a man* 粗笨的大漢 **3** a very large object, especially one that causes you to feel nervous or afraid （尤指令人緊張或害怕的）龐然大物

hulk·ing /'hʌlkɪŋ/ *adj.* [only before noun] very large or heavy, often in a way that causes you to feel nervous or afraid 很大的；很沉重的；大得嚇人的: *a hulking figure crouching in the darkness* 黑暗中蹲伏着的一個龐大身影 ◇ *I don't want that hulking great computer in my office.* 我不要把那台又笨又大的計算機放在我的辦公室。

hull /hʌl/ *noun, verb*

■ ***noun*** the main, bottom part of a ship, that goes in the water 船身；船體: *a* ***wooden/steel hull*** 木質／鋼質船體 ◇ *They climbed onto the upturned hull and waited to be rescued.* 他們爬上了傾覆的船體，等候救援。 ➲ VISUAL VOCAB page V54

■ ***verb*** **~ sth** to remove the outer covering of PEAS, BEANS, etc. or the ring of leaves attached to STRAWBERRIES 剝去（豌豆、大豆等的）外殼；摘掉（草莓的）花萼

hul·la·ba·loo /ˌhʌləbə'lu:/ *noun* [sing.] a lot of loud noise, especially made by people who are annoyed or excited about sth 嘈雜；喧鬧；吵鬧聲 **SYN** **commotion, uproar**

hullo (*especially BrE*) = HELLO

hum /hʌm/ *verb, noun*

■ ***verb*** (**-mm-**) **1** [I, T] to sing a tune with your lips closed 哼（曲子）: *She was humming softly to herself.* 她在輕聲哼着曲子。◇ **~ sth** *What's that tune you're humming?* 你哼的是什麼曲子？ ➲ COLLOCATIONS at MUSIC **2** [I] to make a low continuous sound 發嗡嗡聲: *The computers were humming away.* 計算機在嗡嗡作響。 **3** [I] to be full of activity 活躍；繁忙: *The streets were beginning to hum with life.* 街道開始熱鬧起來。

IDM **,hum and 'haw** (*BrE*) (*NAmE* **,hem and 'haw**) (*informal*) to take a long time to make a decision or before you say sth 猶豫不決；支支吾吾；嗯嗯呃呃

■ ***noun*** [sing.] **~ (of sth)** a low continuous sound 嗡嗡聲；嘈雜聲: *the* ***hum of bees/traffic/voices*** 蜜蜂的嗡嗡聲；車輛的嗚嗚聲；人的嘈雜聲 ◇ *The room filled with the hum of conversation.* 房間裏充滿了嘈雜的談話聲。

human 🔑 /'hju:mən/ *adj., noun*

■ ***adj.*** **1** 🔑 [only before noun] of or connected with people rather than animals, machines or gods 人的: *the* ***human body/brain*** 人體；人腦 ◇ ***human anatomy/activity/behaviour/experience*** 人體解剖學；人的活動／行為／

H

經歷 ◇ *a terrible loss of **human life*** 生命的慘重損失 ◇ *Contact with other people is a basic **human need.*** 和他人接觸是人的基本需要。◇ *This food is not fit for **human consumption.*** 這種食物不適合人食用。◇ ***human geography*** (= the study of the way different people live around the world) 人文地理學 ◇ *The hostages were used as a **human shield*** (= a person or group of people that is forced to stay in a particular place where they would be hurt or killed if their country attacked it). 人質被當成了人體盾牌。◇ *Firefighters formed a **human chain*** (= a line of people) *to carry the children to safety.* 消防隊員組成人鏈把孩子們救到了安全的地方。◇ ***Human remains*** (= the body of a dead person) *were found inside the house.* 在房子裏發現了屍體。**2** showing the weaknesses that are typical of people, which means that other people should not criticize the person too much 顯示人類特有弱點的；人本性的：***human weaknesses/failings*** 人性的弱點／缺點 ◇ *We must allow for **human error.*** 我們必須考慮到人為的失誤。◇ ***It's only human** to want the best for your children.* 為自己的孩子謀求最好的條件是人之常情。**3** having the same feelings and emotions as most ordinary people 有人情味的；通人情的：*He's really very human when you get to know him.* 你若瞭解他，就知道他確實很有人情味。◇ *The public is always attracted to politicians who have **the human touch*** (= the ability to make ordinary people feel relaxed when they meet them). 公眾總是對平易近人的政治人物有好感。➲ compare INHUMAN, NON-HUMAN

IDM **the ˈhuman face of …** a person who is involved in a subject, issue, etc. and makes it easier for ordinary people to understand and have sympathy with it（某主題、話題等的）標誌性人物：*He is the human face of party politics.* 他是政黨政治的標誌性人物。**with a human ˈface** that considers the needs of ordinary people 考慮老百姓需要的；有人情味的；有人性的：*This was science with a human face.* 這是大眾需要的科學。➲ more at MILK *n.*

■ *noun* (also **ˌhuman ˈbeing**) a person rather than an animal or a machine 人：*Dogs can hear much better than humans.* 狗的聽覺比人靈敏得多。◇ *That is no way to treat another human being.* 那絕不是對待他人的方式。

hu·mane /hjuːˈmeɪn/ *adj.* showing kindness towards people and animals by making sure that they do not suffer more than is necessary 善良的；仁慈的；人道的：*a caring and humane society* 充滿關懷和人道的社會 ◇ *the humane treatment of refugees* 人道地對待難民 ◇ *the humane killing of animals* 對動物的人道毀滅 **OPP** **inhumane** ▶ **hu·mane·ly** *adv.*：*to treat sb humanely* 仁慈地對待某人 ◇ *meat that has been humanely produced* 通過無痛屠宰法生產的肉 ◇ *The dog was humanely destroyed.* 那條狗被人道毀滅了。

ˌhuman ˈinterest *noun* [U] the part of a story in a newspaper, etc. that people find interesting because it describes the experiences, feelings, etc. of the people involved（新聞報道等中的）人情味

hu·man·ism /ˈhjuːmənɪzəm/ *noun* [U] a system of thought that considers that solving human problems with the help of reason is more important than religious beliefs. It emphasizes the fact that the basic nature of humans is good. 人文主義 ▶ **hu·man·is·tic** /ˌhjuːməˈnɪstɪk/ *adj.*：*humanistic ideals* 人文主義理想

hu·man·ist /ˈhjuːmənɪst/ *noun* a person who believes in humanism 人文主義者

hu·mani·tar·ian /hjuːˌmænɪˈteəriən; *NAmE* -ˈter-/ *adj.* [usually before noun] concerned with reducing suffering and improving the conditions that people live in 人道主義的（主張減輕人類苦難、改善人類生活）；慈善的：*to provide **humanitarian aid** to the war zone* 給戰區提供人道主義援助 ◇ *humanitarian issues* 人道主義問題 ◇ *a humanitarian organization* 慈善機構 ◇ *They are calling for the release of the hostages on **humanitarian grounds.*** 他們站在人道主義立場要求釋放人質。◇ *The expulsion of thousands of people represents a humanitarian catastrophe of enormous proportions.* 驅逐成千上萬人意味着人道主義的巨大災難。▶ **hu·mani·tar·ian** *noun* **hu·mani·tar·ian·ism** /-ɪzəm/ *noun* [U]

hu·man·ity /hjuːˈmænəti/ *noun* **1** [U] people in general（統稱）人；人類：*crimes against humanity* 危害人類罪 ➲ note at GENDER **2** [U] the state of being a person rather than a god, an animal or a machine 人性：*The story was used to emphasize the humanity of Jesus.* 人們用這個故事來強調耶穌人性的一面。◇ *united by a sense of common humanity* 因一種同是人的情感而團結在一起 **3** [U] the quality of being kind to people and animals by making sure that they do not suffer more than is necessary; the quality of being HUMANE 人道；仁慈：*The judge was praised for his courage and humanity.* 法官的勇氣和人道受到稱讚。**OPP** **inhumanity** **4** **(the) humanities** [pl.] the subjects of study that are concerned with the way people think and behave, for example literature, language, history and philosophy 人文學科 ➲ compare SCIENCE (3)

hu·man·ize (*BrE* also **-ise**) /ˈhjuːmənaɪz/ *verb* **~ sth** to make sth more pleasant or suitable for people; to make sth more HUMANE 使更適合人；使更人道：*These measures are intended to humanize the prison system.* 這些措施的目的是使監獄體制更人道。

hu·man·kind /ˌhjuːmənˈkaɪnd/ *noun* [U] people in general（統稱）人；人類 ➲ see also MANKIND

hu·man·ly /ˈhjuːmənli/ *adv.* within human ability; in a way that is typical of human behaviour, thoughts and feelings 在人力所能及的範圍內；以人特有的方式：*The doctors did all that was **humanly possible.*** 醫生們盡了人力所及的最大努力。◇ *He couldn't humanly refuse to help her.* 從人道角度，他不能拒絕幫助她。

ˌhuman ˈnature *noun* [U] the ways of behaving, thinking and feeling that are shared by most people and are considered to be normal 人性：*Her kindness has restored my faith in human nature* (= the belief that people are good). 她的善良使我重新燃起了對人性的信心。◇ ***It's only human nature** to be worried about change.* 對變革有憂慮不過是人之常情。

hu·man·oid /ˈhjuːmənɔɪd/ *noun* a machine or creature that looks and behaves like a human 人形機器人；類人動物 ▶ **hu·man·oid** *adj.*

the ˌhuman ˈrace *noun* [sing.] all people, considered together as a group 人類

ˌhuman reˈsources *noun* **1** [pl.] people's skills and abilities, seen as sth a company, an organization, etc. can make use of 人力資源 **2** (*abbr.* **HR**) [U+sing./pl. v.] the department in a company that deals with employing and training people（公司的）人事部，人力資源部 **SYN** **personnel**：*the human resources director* 人事部主管

ˌhuman ˈright *noun* [usually pl.] one of the basic rights that everyone has to be treated fairly and not in a cruel way, especially by their government 人權：*The country has a poor record on human rights.* 這個國家人權記錄不佳。◇ *to campaign for human rights* 爭取人權的運動 ◇ ***human rights abuses/violations*** 對人權的侵犯

hum·ble /ˈhʌmbl/ *adj., verb*

■ *adj.* (**hum·bler** /ˈhʌmblə(r)/, **hum·blest** /ˈhʌmblɪst/)
1 showing you do not think that you are as important as other people 謙遜的；虛心的 **SYN** **modest**：*Be humble enough to learn from your mistakes.* 要虛心地從自己的錯誤中學習。◇ *my humble tribute to this great man* 鄙人對這位偉人表示敬意 ➲ see also HUMILITY **2** (*ironic* or *humorous*) used to suggest that you are not as important as other people, but in a way that is not sincere or not very serious（表示謙遜，但不夠誠摯或認真）：***In my humble opinion,** you were in the wrong.* 依拙見，你錯了。◇ ***My humble apologies.** I did not understand.* 對不起。我沒有弄懂。**3** having a low rank or social position（級別或地位）低下的，卑微的：*a man of **humble birth/origins*** 出身低微的人 ◇ *a humble occupation* 卑下職業 ◇ *the daughter of a humble shopkeeper* 一位小店主的女兒 **4** (of a thing 事物) not large or special in any way 不大的；沒有特別之處的 **SYN** **modest**：*a humble farmhouse* 小農舍 ◇ *The company has worked its way up from humble beginnings to become the market leader.* 公司已從創業期的微不足道發展成了市場的主導

者。▶ **hum·bly** /ˈhʌmbli/ *adv.*：*I would humbly suggest that there is something wrong here.* 愚以為這裏有點錯誤。◇ *'Sorry,' she said humbly.* "對不起。" 她謙遜地說。**IDM** see EAT

■ *verb* **1 ~ sb** to make sb feel that they are not as good or important as they thought they were 貶低；使感到卑微：*He was humbled by her generosity.* 她的大度使他覺得自己渺小。◇ *a humbling experience* 一次令人慚愧的經歷 **2** [usually passive] **~ sb** to easily defeat an opponent, especially a strong or powerful one 輕鬆打敗（尤指強大的對手）：*The world champion was humbled last night in three rounds.* 這位世界冠軍昨晚三個回合就被輕鬆擊敗。**3 ~ yourself** to show that you are not too proud to ask for sth, admit that you have been wrong, etc. 低聲下氣；謙遜；虛心 ➲ see also HUMILITY

hum·bug /ˈhʌmbʌɡ/ *noun* **1** [U] (*old-fashioned*) dishonest language or behaviour that is intended to trick people 謊言；騙人的把戲；欺騙行為：*political humbug* 政治騙術 **2** [C] (*old-fashioned*) a person who is not sincere or honest 虛偽的人 **3** [C] (*BrE*) a hard sweet/candy made from boiled sugar, especially one that tastes of PEPPERMINT 硬糖；（尤指）薄荷糖

hum·ding·er /ˌhʌmˈdɪŋə(r)/ *noun* [sing.] (*informal*) something that is very exciting or impressive 令人興奮的事物；出色的事物：*It turned into a real humdinger of a game.* 那場比賽變得扣人心弦。

hum·drum /ˈhʌmdrʌm/ *adj.* boring and always the same 乏味的；單調的 **SYN** **dull, tedious**：*a* ***humdrum existence/job/life*** 平淡的生活；乏味的工作 / 生活

hu·mec·tant /hjuːˈmektənt; *NAmE* also juː-/ *noun* (*technical* 術語) **1** a substance added to foods to stop them from becoming dry （保藏食物用的）濕潤劑 **2** a substance added to skin cream to stop your skin from being dry （護膚霜中的）保濕劑

hu·merus /ˈhjuːmərəs/ *noun* (*pl.* **hu·meri** /ˈhjuːməraɪ/) (*anatomy* 解) the large bone in the top part of the arm between the shoulder and the elbow 肱骨 ➲ **VISUAL VOCAB** page V59

humid /ˈhjuːmɪd/ *adj.* (of the air or climate 空氣或氣候) warm and damp 溫暖潮濕的；濕熱的：*These ferns will grow best in a humid atmosphere.* 這些蕨類植物在濕熱的環境中長得最旺。◇ *The island is hot and humid in the summer.* 這個島在夏季又熱又潮濕。

humi·dex /ˈhjuːmɪdeks/ *noun* [sing.] (*CanE*) a scale that measures how unpleasant hot and HUMID weather feels to people 濕熱指數（測量濕熱天氣使人不舒服的程度）

hu·midi·fier /hjuːˈmɪdɪfaɪə(r)/ *noun* a machine used for making the air in a room less dry 增濕器；加濕器 ➲ see also DEHUMIDIFIER

hu·mid·ity /hjuːˈmɪdəti/ *noun* [U] **1** the amount of water in the air（空氣中的）濕度：***high/low humidity*** 高 / 低濕度 ◇ *70% humidity* * 70% 的濕度 **2** conditions in which the air is very warm and damp 濕熱；高溫潮濕：*These plants need heat and humidity to grow well.* 這些植物在高溫潮濕的環境中才能生長得旺盛。◇ *The humidity was becoming unbearable.* 這種潮濕使人越來越難以忍受了。

hu·mili·ate /hjuːˈmɪlieɪt/ *verb* **~ sb/yourself/sth** to make sb feel ashamed or stupid and lose the respect of other people 羞辱；使喪失尊嚴：*I didn't want to humiliate her in front of her colleagues.* 我不想當着她同事們的面令她難堪。◇ *I've never felt so humiliated.* 我從未感到如此羞辱。◇ *The party was humiliated in the recent elections.* 該黨在新近的選舉中恥辱地失敗了。▶ **hu·mili·at·ing** *adj.*：*a humiliating defeat* 恥辱的失敗 **hu·mili·ation** /hjuːˌmɪliˈeɪʃn/ *noun* [U, C]：*She suffered the humiliation of being criticized in public.* 她當眾受到指責，丟了面子。

hu·mil·ity /hjuːˈmɪləti/ *noun* [U] the quality of not thinking that you are better than other people; the quality of being humble 謙遜；謙虛：*Her first defeat was an early lesson in humility.* 她的第一次失敗使她很早便懂得了謙遜。◇ *an act of genuine humility* 真正謙虛的舉動

Hum·int /ˈhjuːmɪnt/ *noun* [U] the activity or job of collecting secret information about people or governments （針對人或政府的）情報收集，諜報工作

ORIGIN A combination of *human* and *intelligence*. 源自 human 和 intelligence 的組合。

hum·ming·bird /ˈhʌmɪŋbɜːd; *NAmE* -bɜːrd/ *noun* a small brightly coloured bird that lives in warm countries and that can stay in one place in the air by beating its wings very fast, making a continuous low sound (= a HUMMING sound) 蜂鳥（快速扇動翅膀發出聲音，能原位停留）

hum·mock /ˈhʌmək/ *noun* (*BrE*) a small hill or pile of earth 小山；小丘

hum·mus (also **hou·mous**) /ˈhʊməs; ˈhuːməs/ *noun* [U] a type of food, originally from the Middle East, that is a soft mixture of CHICKPEAS, SESAME seeds, oil, lemon juice and GARLIC 鷹嘴豆泥（中東食品，將鷹嘴豆、芝麻、油、檸檬汁和大蒜搗碎而成）

hu·mon·gous (also **hu·mun·gous**) /hjuːˈmʌŋɡəs/ *adj.* (*informal*) very big 巨大的；龐大的 **SYN** **enormous**

humor, humor·less (*especially US*) = HUMOUR, HUMOURLESS

hu·mor·ist /ˈhjuːmərɪst/ *noun* a person who is famous for writing or telling amusing stories 幽默作家；詼諧風趣的人

hu·mor·ous 0-w /ˈhjuːmərəs/ *adj.* funny and entertaining; showing a sense of humour 滑稽有趣的；有幽默感的：*He gave a humorous account of their trip to Spain.* 他饒有風趣地講述了他們的西班牙之行。◇ *He had a wide mouth and humorous grey eyes.* 他有一張大嘴巴和一雙滑稽的灰眼睛。➲ **SYNONYMS** at FUNNY ▶ **hu·mor·ous·ly** *adv.*：*The poem humorously describes local characters and traditions.* 那首詩幽默地描述了當地的人物和傳統。

hu·mour 0-w (*especially US* **hu·mor**) /ˈhjuːmə(r)/ *noun, verb*

■ *noun* **1** 0-w [U] the quality in sth that makes it funny or amusing; the ability to laugh at things that are amusing 幽默；幽默感：*a story full of gentle humour* 充滿輕鬆幽默的故事 ◇ *She ignored his feeble attempt at humour.* 她沒理他想表現卻又差勁的幽默。◇ *They failed to see the humour of the situation.* 他們沒有看出這情景的滑稽之處。◇ *I can't stand people with no* ***sense of humour***. 我無法忍受毫無幽默感的人。◇ *She smiled with a rare flash of humour.* 她以少有的一絲詼諧微笑了。◇ *She has her very own brand of humour.* 她的幽默很獨特。◇ *The film is only funny if you appreciate French humour* (= things that cause French people to laugh). 只有能理解法國式的幽默才會領略這部電影的趣味。 **2** [C, U] (*formal*) the state of your feelings or mind at a particular time 感覺；心情；精神狀態：*to be in the best of humours* 情緒極好 ◇ *The meeting dissolved in* ***ill humour***. 會議不歡而散。◇ *to be* ***out of humour*** (= in a bad mood) 心情不好 ➲ see also GOOD HUMOUR, GOOD-HUMOURED at GOOD HUMOUR, ILL-HUMOURED at ILL HUMOUR **3** [C] (*old use*) one of the four liquids that were thought in the past to be in a person's body and to influence health and character 體液（舊時認為存在人體內，有四種，可影響健康和性格）

■ *verb* **~ sb** to agree with sb's wishes, even if they seem unreasonable, in order to keep the person happy 遷就；順應：*She thought it best to humour him rather than get into an argument.* 她想最好是順他的意，而不和他爭吵。

hu·mour·less (*especially US* **hu·mor·less**) /ˈhjuːmələs; *NAmE* -ərləs/ *adj.* not having or showing the ability to laugh at things that other people think are amusing 無幽默感的 ▶ **hu·mour·less·ly** (*especially US* **hu·mor·less·ly**) *adv.*

hump /hʌmp/ *noun, verb*

■ *noun* **1** a large lump that sticks out above the surface of sth, especially the ground （平面上的）大隆起物；（尤指）土墩，丘，岡：*the dark hump of the mountain in the distance* 遠處高大的黑魆魆的山 ◇ (*BrE*) *a* ***road/speed/traffic hump*** (= a hump on a road that forces traffic to drive more slowly) 公路上的限速路墩 **2** a large lump on the back of some animals, especially CAMELS （某些動物的）峰；（尤指）駝峰 **3** a large lump on the

H

back of a person, caused by an unusual curve in the SPINE (= the row of bones in the middle of the back)（人的）駝背

IDM **be over the 'hump** to have done the most difficult part of sth 完成最困難的部份；渡過最困難階段 **get/take the 'hump** (*BrE, informal*) to become annoyed or upset about sth 對某事惱怒（或煩惱）：*Fans get the hump when the team loses.* 球隊失利時，球迷們感到沮喪。

■ *verb* **1 ~ sth (+ adv./prep.)** (*BrE*) to carry sth heavy 背負（重物）：*I've been humping furniture around all day.* 我扛了一整天的傢具。 **2 ~ sb** (*taboo, slang*) to have sex with sb 與（某人）性交

hump·back /ˈhʌmpbæk/ *noun* **1** = HUMPBACK WHALE **2** = HUNCHBACK

,humpback 'bridge (also **,humpbacked 'bridge**) *noun* (*BrE*) a small bridge that slopes steeply on both sides 拱橋；弓形橋 ➲ VISUAL VOCAB page V14

,humpback 'whale (also **hump·back**) *noun* a large WHALE (= a very large sea animal) with a back shaped like a HUMP 駝背鯨；座頭鯨

humped /hʌmpt/ *adj.* having a HUMP or HUMPS; shaped like a HUMP 有隆起物的；似駝峰的：*a humped back* 駝背 ◇ *He was tall and broad with humped shoulders.* 他身高體寬，雙肩隆起。

humph *exclamation* the way of writing the sound /həmf/ that people use to show they do not believe sth or do not approve of it（書寫中代表 /həmf/ 的音，表示懷疑或不贊成）哼

hu·mun·gous = HUMONGOUS

humus /ˈhjuːməs/ *noun* [U] a substance made from dead leaves and plants, added to soil to help plants grow 腐殖質

Hun /hʌn/ *noun* (*pl.* **Huns** or **the Hun**) (*informal*) an offensive word for a German person, used especially during the First and Second World Wars（蔑稱，尤用於第一次和第二次世界大戰）德國佬

hunch /hʌntʃ/ *verb, noun*

■ *verb* [I, T] to bend the top part of your body forward and raise your shoulders and back 弓身；弓背；聳肩：**(+ adv./prep.)** *She leaned forward, hunching over the desk.* 她身體前傾，伏在寫字枱上。◇ **~ sth** *He hunched **his shoulders** and thrust his hands deep into his pockets.* 他聳着肩，雙手深深地插進衣袋。 ▸ **hunched** *adj.*：*a hunched figure* 弓着背的人形 ◇ *He sat hunched over his breakfast.* 他弓着背吃早飯。

■ *noun* a feeling that sth is true even though you do not have any evidence to prove it 預感；直覺：*It seemed that the doctor's hunch had been right.* 看起來醫生的直覺是對的。◇ *I had a hunch (that) you'd be back.* 我有預感你會回來。◇ *to follow/back your hunches* 憑直覺做事

hunch·back /ˈhʌntʃbæk/ (also **hump·back**) *noun* (*offensive*) a person who has a HUMP on their back 駝背的人 ▸ **hunch·backed** /ˈhʌntʃbækt/ *adj.*

hun·dred 🔑 /ˈhʌndrəd/ *number* (*plural verb* 複數動詞)

1 🔑 100 一百：*One hundred (of the children) have already been placed with foster families.* 有一百名（兒童）已經獲安排領養。◇ *There were just a hundred of them there.* 他們那裏只有一百人。◇ *This vase is worth several hundred dollars.* 這隻花瓶值幾百元。◇ *She must be over a hundred (= a hundred years old).* 她肯定有一百多歲了。◇ *Hundreds of thousands of people are at risk.* 有幾十萬人正處於危險中。◇ *a hundred-year lease* 一百年的租約 HELP You say **a, one, two, several, etc. hundred** without a final 's' on 'hundred'. **Hundreds (of ...)** can be used if there is no number or quantity before it. Always use a plural verb with **hundred** or **hundreds**, except when an amount of money is mentioned. 說 a, one, two, several, etc. hundred 時，hundred 後面不加 s。若前面沒有數目或數量，可用 hundreds (of ...)。除指金額外，hundred 和 hundreds 均用複數動詞：*Four hundred (people) are expected to attend.* 預期有四百人出席。◇ *Two hundred (pounds) was withdrawn from the account.* 從賬戶裏提取了二百英鎊。 **2** 🔑 **a hundred** or **hundreds (of ...)** (usually *informal*) a large amount 許多；數量大：*hundreds of miles away* 數百里之遙 ◇ *for hundreds of years* 幾百年來 ◇ *If I've said it once, I've said it a hundred times.* 這事我曾經說過，而且是說過很多次了。◇ *I have **a hundred and one** things to do.* 我有一大堆事情要做。◇ (*formal*) *Men died in their hundreds.* 大批的人死亡。 **3 the hundreds** [pl.] the numbers from 100 to 999 * 100 到 999 間的數目；百位數：*We're talking about a figure in the low hundreds.* 我們談論的是一個兩三百的數字。 **4 the ... hundreds** [pl.] the years of a particular century 某個世紀的年代：*the early nineteen hundreds* (= written 'early 1900s') * 20 世紀早期 **5 one, two, three, etc. ~ hours** used to express whole hours in the 24-hour system（表示 24 小時制的整點）一點、兩點、三點等整：*twelve hundred hours* (= 12.00, midday) 十二點整

IDM **a/one 'hundred per cent** **1** in every way 在各方面；百分之百；完全 SYN **completely**：*I'm not a hundred per cent sure.* 我不能百分之百肯定。◇ *My family supports me one hundred per cent.* 我的家人全力支持我。 **2** (*BrE*) completely fit and healthy 十分健康：*I still don't feel a hundred per cent.* 我還是覺得有些不舒服。 **give a 'hundred (and ten) per cent** to put as much effort into sth as you can 全力以赴；竭盡全力：*Every player gave a hundred per cent tonight.* 今天晚上所有的運動員都盡了最大的努力。 ➲ more at NINETY

,hundreds and 'thousands (*BrE*) (*NAmE* **sprinkles**) *noun* [pl.] extremely small pieces of coloured sugar, used to decorate cakes, etc. 着色珠子糖（裝飾糕點等用）

hun·dredth 🔑 /ˈhʌndrədθ; -ətθ/ *ordinal number, noun*

■ *ordinal number* 🔑 100th 第一百：*her hundredth birthday* 她的百歲誕辰

■ *noun* 🔑 each of one hundred equal parts of sth 百分之一：*a/one hundredth of a second* 百分之一秒

hun·dred·weight /ˈhʌndrədweɪt/ *noun* (*pl.* **hun·dred·weight**) (*abbr.* **cwt**) a unit for measuring weight equal to 112 pounds in the UK and 100 pounds in the US. There are 20 hundredweight in a ton. 英擔（在英國等於 112 磅，在美國等於 100 磅。一噸為 20 英擔）

hung /hʌŋ/ *adj.* [only before noun] **1** (of a parliament or council 上下議院或市郡議會) (*BrE*) in which no political party has more elected members than all the other parties added together 任何政黨都不佔多數席位的 **2** (of a JURY 陪審團) unable to agree about whether sb is guilty of a crime 不能取得一致意見的 ➲ see also HANG *v.*

hun·ger /ˈhʌŋɡə(r)/ *noun, verb*

■ *noun* **1** [U] the state of not having enough food to eat, especially when this causes illness or death 飢餓；饑荒 SYN **starvation**：*Around fifty people die of hunger every day in the camp.* 集中營裏每天大約有五十人餓死。◇ *The organization works to alleviate world hunger and disease.* 這個機構致力於減少世界上的飢餓和疾病。 **2** [U] the feeling caused by a need to eat 飢餓感；食慾；胃口：*hunger pangs* 飢餓引起的胃痛 ◇ *I felt faint with hunger.* 我當時餓得發昏。 **3** [sing.] **~ (for sth)** (*formal*) a strong desire for sth（對某事物的）渴望，渴求：*a hunger for knowledge* 對知識的渴求 ◇ *Nothing seemed to satisfy their hunger for truth.* 似乎沒有什麼能滿足他們對真理的渴求。

■ *verb*

PHR V **'hunger for/after sth/sb** (*literary*) to have a strong desire or need for sth/sb 渴望得到；渴求

'hunger strike *noun* [C, U] the act of refusing to eat for a long period of time in order to protest about sth 絕食（抗議）：*to **be on /go on hunger strike*** 進行絕食抗議 ▸ **'hunger striker** *noun*

hung·over /,hʌŋˈəʊvə(r)/ *adj.* [not usually before noun] a person who is **hungover** is feeling ill/sick because they drank too much alcohol the night before 宿醉 ➲ see also HANGOVER

hun·gry 🔑 /ˈhʌŋɡri/ *adj.* (**hun·grier**, **hun·gri·est**)

1 🔑 feeling that you want to eat sth 感到餓的：*I'm really hungry.* 我真是餓了。◇ *Is anyone getting hungry?* 有人覺得餓嗎？◇ *All this talk of food is making me hungry.* 老這麼談吃的勾起我的食慾了。◇ *I have a hungry family to feed.* 我得養活嗷嗷待哺的一家人。 **2** 🔑 not having enough food to eat 飢餓的；捱餓的：*Thousands are **going hungry** because of the failure of this year's harvest.* 由於今年糧食歉收，成千上萬的人將捱餓。**3 the hungry** *noun* [pl.] people who do not have enough food to eat（統稱）餓民 **4** [only before noun] causing you to feel that you want to eat sth 使人飢餓的；引起食慾的：*All this gardening is hungry work.* 這些園藝活兒讓人幹了肚子餓。 **5** ~ **(for sth)** having or showing a strong desire for sth 渴望得到；渴求：*Both parties are hungry for power.* 兩黨都渴望掌權。◇ *power-hungry* 渴求權力 ◇ *The child is simply hungry for affection.* 這個孩子只不過是渴望得到愛。◇ *His eyes had a wild hungry look in them.* 他的目光裏有一種強烈的渴望神情。▸ **hun·grily** /ˈhʌŋɡrəli/ *adv.*：*They gazed hungrily at the display of food.* 他們飢腸轆轆地盯着那些擺放着的食物。◇ *He kissed her hungrily.* 他如飢似渴地親吻她。

ˌhung ˈup *adj.* [not before noun] ~ **(on/about sth/sb)** (*informal, disapproving*) very worried about sth/sb; thinking about sth/sb too much 十分擔憂；想得過多：*You're not still hung up on that girl?* 你不是還在念念不忘那個女孩吧？◇ *He's too hung up about fitness.* 他對健身過於憂心忡忡。

hunk /hʌŋk/ *noun* **1** a large piece of sth, especially food, that has been cut or broken from a larger piece（尤指食物切下或掰下的）大塊，大片：*a hunk of bread/cheese/meat* 一大塊麵包／乾酪／肉 **2** (*informal*) a man who is big, strong and sexually attractive 魁梧性感的男子；猛男：*He's a real hunk.* 他身材真結實。

hun·ker /ˈhʌŋkə(r)/ *verb*

PHR V **ˌhunker ˈdown** **1** (*especially NAmE*) to sit on your heels with your knees bent up in front of you 蹲；蹲坐；蹲下 SYN **squat**：*He hunkered down beside her.* 他挨着她蹲下。**2** to prepare yourself to stay somewhere, keep an opinion, etc. for a long time 準備長期待在某處（或堅持某觀點等） **3** to refuse to change an opinion, way of behaving, etc. 拒絕改變觀點（或習性等）

hun·kers /ˈhʌŋkəz; *NAmE* -kərz/ *noun* [pl.]

IDM **on your ˈhunkers** sitting on your heels with your knees bent up in front of you 蹲着；蹲坐 SYN **haunches**

hunky /ˈhʌŋki/ *adj.* (**hunk·ier**, **hunk·iest**) (of a man 男子) big, strong and sexually attractive 結實性感的

hunky-dory /ˌhʌŋki ˈdɔːri/ *adj.* [not before noun] (*informal*) if you say that **everything is hunky-dory**, you mean that there are no problems and that everyone is happy 平安無事；皆大歡喜

hunt /hʌnt/ *verb, noun*

■ *verb* **1** [I, T] to chase wild animals or birds in order to catch or kill them for food, sport or to make money 打獵；獵取；獵殺：*Lions sometimes hunt alone.* 獅子有時單獨獵食。◇ ~ **sth** *Whales are still being hunted and killed in the Arctic.* 北冰洋的鯨類仍然遭到獵殺。**2** [I] to look for sth that is difficult to find 搜尋；搜索 SYN **search**：*I've hunted everywhere but I can't find it.* 我到處都搜遍了，就是找不到它。◇ ~ **for sth** *She is still hunting for a new job.* 她還在找新工作。 **3** [T, I] to look for sb in order to catch them or harm them 追踪；追捕：~ **sb** *Police are hunting an escaped criminal.* 警察正在追捕一名逃犯。◇ ~ **for sb** *Detectives are hunting for thieves who broke into a warehouse yesterday.* 偵探正在追踪昨天侵入倉庫的竊賊。 **4** [I, T] ~ **(sth)** (in Britain) to chase and kill FOXES as a sport, riding horses and using dogs. FOX-HUNTING with dogs has been illegal in the UK since 2005.（英國）獵狐（作為運動，自 2005 年起用狗獵狐是違法的）

PHR V **ˌhunt sb↔ˈdown** to search for sb until you catch or find them, especially in order to punish or harm them 追捕，緝捕（某人） **ˌhunt sth↔ˈdown/ˈout** to search for sth until you find it 搜尋，尋找（某物）

■ *noun* **1** [C, usually sing.] ~ **(for sb/sth)** an act of looking for sb/sth that is difficult to find 搜尋；搜索；尋找：***The hunt is on** for a suitable candidate.* 正在物色合適的人選。◇ *Hundreds have joined a police hunt for the missing teenager.* 已有幾百人和警方一同搜尋那名失踪的少年。◇ (*BrE*) *a **murder hunt*** (= to find the person who has killed sb) 追捕殺人犯 ➲ see also TREASURE HUNT, WITCH-HUNT **2** [C] (often in compounds 常構成複合詞) an act of chasing wild animals to kill or capture them 打獵：*a tiger hunt* 獵虎 **3** [C] (in Britain) an event at which people ride horses and hunt FOXES with dogs as a sport, illegal in the UK since 2005（英國）獵狐（作為運動，自 2005 年起用狗獵狐是違法的）：*There will be a hunt on Boxing Day.* 節禮日將有獵狐活動。◇ *a hunt meeting* 獵狐大會 **4** [C+sing./pl. v.] (in Britain) a group of people who regularly hunt FOXES as a sport（英國經常舉行獵狐運動的）獵狐隊伍：*There are several different hunts in the area.* 這個地區有幾支不同的獵狐隊。

IDM **be in the ˈhunt** to have a chance of winning 有機會（贏）：*The team are back in the hunt for the league title.* 這支隊伍又有機會贏得聯賽冠軍了。

hunt·ed /ˈhʌntɪd/ *adj.* (of an expression on sb's face 面部表情) showing that sb is very worried or frightened, as if they are being followed or chased 惴惴不安的；驚恐萬分的：*His eyes had a hunted look.* 他雙眼透露出恐慌的神態。

hunt·er /ˈhʌntə(r)/ *noun* **1** a person who hunts wild animals for food or sport; an animal that hunts its food 獵人；狩獵者；（獵食其他動物的）獵獸 **2** (usually in compounds 通常構成複合詞) a person who looks for and collects a particular kind of thing 搜集某種東西的人：*a bargain hunter* 四處尋找便宜貨的人 ➲ see also HEADHUNTER **3** (*BrE*) a fast strong horse used in hunting FOXES 獵狐馬 **4** (*NAmE*) a dog used in hunting 獵犬

ˌhunter-ˈgather·er *noun* a member of a group of people who do not live in one place but move around and live by hunting, fishing and gathering plants 遊獵採集部族成員

hunt·ing /ˈhʌntɪŋ/ *noun* [U]

1 chasing and killing wild animals and birds as a sport or for food 狩獵運動；打獵：*to go hunting* 去打獵 ◇ *Since 1977 otter hunting has been illegal.* 捕獵水獺 1977 年以後就被列為非法了。 **2** (*BrE*) = FOX-HUNTING **3** (in compounds 構成複合詞) the process of looking for sth 找；尋找：*We're going house-hunting at the weekend.* 週末我們去找房子。◇ *How's the job-hunting going?* 工作找得怎麼樣了？

ˈhunting ground *noun* **1** a place where people with a particular interest can easily find what they want 可以找到所需要的東西的地方：*Crowded markets are a **happy hunting ground** for pickpockets.* 擁擠的市場是扒手大展身手的好地方。 **2** a place where wild animals are hunted 獵場

hunt·ress /ˈhʌntrəs/ *noun* (*literary*) a woman who hunts wild animals 女獵人；女狩獵者

hunts·man /ˈhʌntsmən/ *noun* (*pl.* **-men** /-mən/) a man who hunts wild animals 獵人；狩獵者

hur·dle /ˈhɜːdl; *NAmE* ˈhɜːrdl/ *noun, verb*

■ *noun* **1** each of a series of vertical frames that a person or horse jumps over in a race（供人或馬在賽跑中跨越的）欄架，跨欄：*His horse fell at the final hurdle.* 他騎的馬在最後一個跨欄倒下了。◇ *to **clear a hurdle*** (= jump over it successfully) 跨過欄架 **2 hurdles** [pl.] a race in which runners or horses have to jump over hurdles 跨欄賽：*the 300 m hurdles* * 300 米跨欄賽 ➲ VISUAL VOCAB page V47 **3** a problem or difficulty that must be solved or dealt with before you can achieve sth 難關；障礙 SYN **obstacle**：*The next hurdle will be getting her parents' agreement.* 下一個難關是徵得她父母的同意。

■ *verb* **1** [T, I] to jump over sth while you are running（奔跑中）跳越（某物）：~ **sth** *He hurdled two barriers to avoid reporters.* 他跳過了兩個障礙物以躲避記者。◇ ~ **over sth** *to hurdle over a fence* 跳過一道柵欄 **2** [I] to run in a hurdles race 參加跨欄賽

hurd·ler /ˈhɜːdlə(r); *NAmE* ˈhɜːrd-/ *noun* a person or horse that runs in races over hurdles 跨欄運動員；參加跨欄賽的馬

hurd·ling /ˈhɜːdlɪŋ; *NAmE* ˈhɜːrd-/ *noun* [U] the sport of racing over HURDLES 跨欄賽 ➲ VISUAL VOCAB page V47

hurdy-gurdy /ˈhɜːdi ɡɜːdi; *NAmE* ˈhɜːrdi ɡɜːrdi/ *noun* (*pl.* **-ies**) a small musical instrument that is played by turning a handle with one hand and pressing keys with

H

the other 手搖弦琴，輪擦提琴（通過搖動琴尾曲柄，使連接的木輪旋轉摩擦琴弦發聲）

hurl /hɜːl; *NAmE* hɜːrl/ *verb* **1** [T] **~ sth/sb + adv./prep.** to throw sth/sb violently in a particular direction 猛扔；猛投；猛摔：*He hurled a brick through the window.* 他往窗戶裏扔了塊磚。➲ **SYNONYMS** at THROW **2** [T] **~ abuse, accusations, insults, etc. (at sb)** to shout insults, etc. at sb 大聲說出（辱罵或斥責等）：*Rival fans hurled abuse at each other.* 兩幫對立的球迷相互高聲辱罵。**3** [I] (*NAmE, slang*) to VOMIT 嘔吐

hurl·ing /ˈhɜːlɪŋ; *NAmE* ˈhɜːrlɪŋ/ *noun* [U] an Irish ball game similar to HOCKEY played by two teams of 15 boys or men 愛爾蘭曲棍球（兩隊比賽，各 15 人）

hurly-burly /ˈhɜːli bɜːli; *NAmE* ˈhɜːrli bɜːrli/ *noun* [U] a very noisy and busy activity or situation 騷動；喧鬧：*He enjoys the hurly-burly of political debate.* 他喜歡政治辯論時的喧鬧。

H

hur·rah /həˈrɑː/ (*BrE* **hur·ray** /həˈreɪ/) *exclamation* = HOORAY (1)

hur·ri·cane /ˈhʌrɪkən; *NAmE* ˈhɜːrəkən; -keɪn/ *noun* a violent storm with very strong winds, especially in the western Atlantic Ocean （尤指西大西洋的）颶風：*hurricane-force winds* 颶風級大風 ◇ *Hurricane Betty is now approaching the coast of Florida.* 颶風貝蒂正在逼近佛羅里達州海岸。➲ **COLLOCATIONS** at WEATHER ➲ compare CYCLONE, TYPHOON

ˈhurricane lamp *noun* a type of lamp with glass sides to protect the flame inside from the wind 防風燈

hur·ried /ˈhʌrid; *NAmE* ˈhɜːr-/ *adj.* [usually before noun] done too quickly because you do not have enough time 匆忙完成的；倉促而就的：*I ate a hurried breakfast and left.* 我匆匆忙忙吃完早飯就離開了。**SYN** **rushed** **OPP** **unhurried** ▸ **hur·ried·ly** *adv.*：*I hurriedly got up and dressed.* 我急忙起牀穿好衣服。

hurry 0-π /ˈhʌri; *NAmE* ˈhɜːri/ *verb, noun*

■ *verb* (**hur·ries, hurry·ing, hur·ried, hur·ried**) **1** 0-π [I] to do sth more quickly than usual because there is not much time 趕快，匆忙，急忙（做某事）**SYN** **rush**：*You'll have to hurry if you want to catch that train.* 如果你想趕上那趟火車就得抓緊時間了。◇ *The kids hurried to open their presents.* 孩子們急忙打開禮物。**HELP** In spoken English **hurry** can be used with **and** plus another verb, instead of with **to** and the infinitive, especially to tell somebody to do something quickly. 英語口語中 hurry 可與 and 及所連接的另一個動詞連用，而不和 to 所引導的不定式連用，尤用於告訴某人快點幹某事：*Hurry and open your present—I want to see what it is!* **2** 0-π [I] **+ adv./prep.** to move quickly in a particular direction （朝某方向）迅速移動 **SYN** **rush**：*He picked up his bags and hurried across the courtyard.* 他拎起提包匆匆穿過院子。◇ *She hurried away without saying goodbye.* 她連聲再見都沒說就急忙離開了。**3** 0-π [T] to make sb do sth more quickly 催促（某人）**SYN** **rush**：**~ sb** *I don't want to hurry you but we close in twenty minutes.* 我並不想催你，但我們再過二十分鐘就要關門。◇ **~ sb into doing sth** *She was hurried into making an unwise choice.* 她在催逼之下作出了不明智的選擇。**4** [T] **~ sth + adv./prep.** to deal with sth quickly 迅速處理 **SYN** **rush**：*Her application was hurried through.* 她的申請很快得到了處理。**5** [T, usually passive] **~ sth** to do sth too quickly 倉促（做某事）**SYN** **rush**：*A good meal should never be hurried.* 美餐絕不能狼吞虎嚥。

PHR V **ˌhurry ˈon** to continue speaking without giving anyone else time to say anything 喋喋不休；囉嗦得沒完沒了 **ˌhurry ˈup (with sth)** 0-π to do sth more quickly because there is not much time 趕快，急忙（做某事）：*I wish the bus would hurry up and come.* 我希望公共汽車能快點來。◇ *Hurry up! We're going to be late.* 快點！我們要遲到了。◇ *Hurry up with the scissors. I need them.* 快點用剪刀。我需要用。**ˌhurry sb/sth↔ˈup** to make sb do sth more quickly; to make sth happen more quickly 催促（某人）；使早些發生：*Can you do anything to hurry my order up?* 你能不能設法讓我點的東西快點送來？

■ *noun* 0-π [U, sing.] the need or wish to get sth done quickly 匆忙；急忙：*Take your time—there's no hurry.* 悠着點——不用急。◇ ***In my hurry to leave,*** *I forgot my passport.* 我匆忙動身，忘了帶護照。◇ ***What's the hurry?*** *The train doesn't leave for an hour.* 慌什麼？火車還有一個小時才開呢。

IDM **in a ˈhurry** **1** 0-π very quickly or more quickly than usual 迅速；趕快：*He had to leave in a hurry.* 他不得不趕快離開了。**2** 0-π not having enough time to do sth 倉促；匆忙：*Sorry, I haven't got time to do it now—I'm in a hurry.* 對不起，我現在沒時間管這個，我忙着呢。◇ *Alice was* ***in a tearing hurry*** *as usual.* 艾麗斯一如往常地來去匆匆。**in a ˈhurry to do sth** impatient to do sth 急於做某事：*My daughter is in such a hurry to grow up.* 我女兒恨不得一下子就長大。◇ *Why are you in such a hurry to sell?* 你為什麼如此迫不及待地要賣出？**in no ˈhurry (to do sth) | not in a/any ˈhurry (to do sth)** **1** having plenty of time 有足夠的時間，不着急（做某事）：*I don't mind waiting—I'm not in any particular hurry.* 我可以等，我沒什麼特別急的事。**2** not wanting or not willing to do sth 不想，不情願（做某事）：*We were in no hurry to get back to work after the holiday.* 假期結束後我們不想急着回去工作。**sb will not do sth again in a ˈhurry** (*informal*) used to say that sb does not want to do sth again because it was not enjoyable 某人再不願做某事：*I won't be going there again in a hurry—the food was terrible.* 我再不願去那裏了，那裏吃的東西糟透了。

hurt 0-π /hɜːt; *NAmE* hɜːrt/ *verb, adj., noun*

■ *verb* (**hurt, hurt**) **1** 0-π [T, I] **~ (sb/sth/yourself)** to cause physical pain to sb/yourself; to injure sb/yourself （使）疼痛，受傷：*He hurt his back playing squash.* 他打壁球時背部受傷了。◇ *Did you hurt yourself?* 你傷着自己了嗎？◇ *Stop it. You're hurting me.* 住手。你弄疼我了。◇ *My back is really hurting me today.* 我今天背疼得厲害。◇ *My shoes hurt—they're too tight.* 我的鞋子太緊，穿着夾腳。➲ **SYNONYMS** at INJURE ➲ **COLLOCATIONS** at INJURY **2** 0-π [I] to feel painful 感到疼痛：*My feet hurt.* 我腳疼。◇ *Ouch! That hurt!* 哎喲！好疼！◇ ***It hurts*** *when I bend my knee.* 我的膝蓋一彎就疼。**3** 0-π [I, T] to make sb unhappy or upset 使不快；使煩惱：*What really hurt was that he never answered my letter.* 真正讓我傷心的是他從不給我回信。◇ **~ sb/sth** *I'm sorry, I didn't mean to hurt you.* 對不起，我不是故意傷害你的。◇ *I didn't want to* ***hurt his feelings.*** 我並沒有想傷害他的感情。◇ **it hurts (sb) to do sth** *It hurt me to think that he would lie to me.* 一想到他會對我說謊，我就很傷心。**4** [I] **be hurting** (*informal*) to feel unhappy or upset 感到不高興（或煩惱）：*I know you're hurting and I want to help you.* 我知道你心煩，我想幫助你。**5** [T] **~ sb/sth** to have a bad effect on sb/sth 對…有不良影響：*Many people on low incomes will be hurt by the government's plans.* 很多低收入的人將受到政府這些方案的打擊。➲ **SYNONYMS** at DAMAGE **6** [I] **be hurting (for sth)** (*NAmE*) to be in a difficult situation because you need sth, especially money 處於困境；手頭拮据：*His campaign is already hurting for money.* 他從事的社會運動已經因缺乏經費而難以為繼了。

IDM **it won't/wouldn't ˈhurt (sb/sth) (to do sth)** used to say that sb should do a particular thing （做某事）不會有什麼損害；（某人）應該做某事：*It wouldn't hurt you to help with the housework occasionally.* 你應該偶爾幫忙做做家務。➲ more at FLY *n.*, HIT *v.*

■ *adj.* **1** 0-π injured physically （身體上）受傷的：*None of the passengers were* ***badly hurt.*** 乘客中沒有人嚴重受傷。**OPP** **unhurt** **2** 0-π upset and offended by sth that sb has said or done （感情上）受傷的：***a hurt look/expression*** 傷心的眼神／表情 ◇ *She was* ***deeply hurt*** *that she had not been invited.* 她未被邀請，感到十分難過。◇ *Martha's hurt pride showed in her eyes.* 從瑪莎的眼神可以看出她的自尊受到了傷害。

■ *noun* [U, sing.] (rather *informal*) a feeling of unhappiness because sb has been unkind or unfair to you 心靈創傷；委屈：*There was hurt and real anger in her voice.* 她的聲音顯得既難過又憤怒。◇ *It was a hurt that would take a long time to heal.* 那是需要很長時間才能癒合的創傷。

Synonyms 同義詞辨析

hurt

ache • burn • sting • tingle • itch • throb

These are all words that can be used when part of your body feels painful. 以上各詞均可指身體部位感到疼痛。

hurt (of part of your body) to feel painful; (of an action) to cause pain 指（身體部位）感到疼痛、（某一動作）引起疼痛：*My feet hurt.* 我腳疼。◇ *Ouch! That hurt!* 哎喲！好疼！

ache to feel a continuous dull pain 指疼痛、隱痛：*I'm aching all over.* 我周身疼痛。

burn (of part of your body) to feel very hot and painful 指（身體部位）火辣辣地痛、發燙：*Our eyes were burning from the chemicals in the air.* 空氣中瀰漫的化學物質熏得我們的眼睛火辣辣地痛。

sting to make sb feel a sharp burning pain or uncomfortable feeling in part of their body; (of part of your body) to feel this pain 指（使）身體部位感覺刺痛、灼痛：*My eyes were stinging from the smoke.* 煙熏得我眼睛痛。

tingle (of part of your body) to feel as if a lot of small sharp points are pushing into the skin there 指（身體部位）感到刺痛：*The cold air made her face tingle.* 冷空氣凍得她的臉發痛。

itch to have an uncomfortable feeling on your skin that makes you want to scratch; to make your skin feel like this 指（使）皮膚發癢：*I itch all over.* 我渾身癢。◇ *Does the rash itch?* 皮疹癢嗎？

throb (of part of your body) to feel pain as a series of regular beats 指（身體部位）有規律地抽動、抽痛：*His head throbbed painfully.* 他的頭一抽一跳地痛。

PATTERNS

- your **eyes** hurt/ache/burn/sting/itch
- your **skin** hurts/burns/stings/tingles/itches
- your **flesh** hurts/burns/stings/tingles
- your **head** hurts/aches/throbs
- your **stomach** hurts/aches
- to **really** hurt/ache/burn/sting/tingle/itch/throb
- to hurt/ache/sting/itch **badly/a lot**
- **It** hurts/stings/tingles/itches.

hurt·ful /ˈhɜːtfl; *NAmE* ˈhɜːrtfl/ *adj.* (of comments 評論) making you feel upset and offended 傷感情的；傷害自尊的 SYN **unkind**：*I cannot forget the hurtful things he said.* 我無法忘記他的那些傷感情的話。◇ **~ to sb** *The bad reviews of her new book were very hurtful to her.* 對她的新書的負面評論使她很難過。▸ **hurt·ful·ly** /-fəli/ *adv.*：*He said, rather hurtfully, that he had better things to do than come and see me.* 他相當刻薄地說來看我還不如去幹別的事。

hur·tle /ˈhɜːtl; *NAmE* ˈhɜːrtl/ *verb* [I] **+ adv./prep.** to move very fast in a particular direction（向某個方向）飛馳，猛衝：*A runaway car **came hurtling** towards us.* 一輛失控的汽車朝我們飛馳而來。

hus·band 🔑 /ˈhʌzbənd/ *noun, verb*

■ *noun* 🔑 (also *informal* **hubby**) the man that a woman is married to; a married man 丈夫：*This is my husband, Steve.* 這位是我的丈夫，史蒂夫。➲ COLLOCATIONS at MARRIAGE

IDM ˌ**husband and ˈwife** a man and woman who are married to each other 夫婦：*They lived together as husband and wife* (= as if they were married) *for years.* 他們像夫妻一樣共同生活了很多年。◇ *a husband-and-wife team* 夫妻隊

■ *verb* **~ sth** (*formal*) to use sth very carefully and make sure that you do not waste it 節儉使用

hus·band·ry /ˈhʌzbəndri/ *noun* **1** farming, especially when done carefully and well（尤指精心經營的）農牧業：***animal/crop husbandry*** 畜牧業；種植業 **2** (*old-fashioned*) the careful use of food, money and supplies 節儉使用；精打細算

hush /hʌʃ/ *verb, noun*

■ *verb* **1** [I] (used especially in orders 尤用於命令) to be quiet; to stop talking or crying 安靜；別說話；別叫喊：*Hush now and try to sleep.* 別出聲了，睡吧。**2** [T] **~ sb/sth** to make sb/sth become quieter; to make sb stop talking, crying, etc. 使安靜下來；使停止說話（或叫喊等）

PHR V ˌ**hush sth↔ˈup** to hide information about a situation because you do not want people to know about it 掩蓋，蒙蔽（事實）：*He claimed that the whole affair had been hushed up by the council.* 他聲稱整個事件都被議會一手捂住了。

■ *noun* [sing., U] a period of silence, especially following a lot of noise, or when people are expecting sth to happen 寂靜；鴉雀無聲：*There was **a deathly hush** in the theatre.* 戲院裏一片寂靜。◇ ***A hush descended** over the waiting crowd.* 等候着的人群變得鴉雀無聲。◇ (*BrE, informal*) ***Can we have a bit of hush?*** (= please be quiet) 大家能安靜一點嗎？

hushed /hʌʃt/ *adj.* **1** (of a place 地方) quiet because nobody is talking; much quieter than usual 寂靜的；寧靜的：*A hushed courtroom listened as the boy gave evidence.* 那個男孩作證時法庭裏的人都屏息傾聽。**2** [usually before noun] (of voices 噪音) speaking very quietly 輕的；低聲的：*a hushed whisper* 低聲耳語

ˌ**hush-ˈhush** *adj.* (*informal*) secret and not known about by many people 秘密的；不公開的：*Their wedding was very hush-hush.* 他們的婚禮非常秘密。

ˈ**hush money** *noun* [U] money that is paid to sb to prevent them from giving other people information that could be embarrassing or damaging 封嘴錢（用於防止某人透露令人尷尬或有損害的消息）

ˈ**hush puppy** *noun* a small fried cake made of CORNMEAL, eaten especially in the southern US 炸玉米餅（美國南方食品）

husk /hʌsk/ *noun, verb*

■ *noun* the dry outer covering of nuts, fruits and seeds, especially of grain（尤指穀類、果實和種子的）外殼，外皮

■ *verb* **~ sth** to remove the husks from grain, seeds, nuts, etc. 去皮；去殼；去莢

husky /ˈhʌski/ *adj., noun*

■ *adj.* (**husk·ier**, **husk·iest**) **1** (of a person or their voice 人或噪音) sounding deep, quiet and rough, sometimes in an attractive way 深沉沙啞的：*She spoke in a husky whisper.* 她低沉沙啞地輕聲說話。**2** (*NAmE*) (of a man 男子) big, strong and sexually attractive 粗壯有魅力的；高大威猛的 ▸ **husk·ily** *adv.* **huski·ness** *noun* [U]

■ *noun* (*NAmE* also **huskie**) (*pl.* **-ies**) a large strong dog with thick hair, used for pulling SLEDGES across snow 愛斯基摩狗（高大強壯，毛厚，用來拉雪橇）

hus·sar /həˈzɑː(r)/ *noun* (in the past) a CAVALRY soldier who carried light weapons（舊時的）輕騎兵

hussy /ˈhʌsi/ *noun* (*pl.* **-ies**) (*old-fashioned, disapproving*) a girl or woman who behaves in a way that is considered shocking or morally wrong 粗野女子；淫蕩女子；蕩婦

hust·ings /ˈhʌstɪŋz/ *noun* **the hustings** [pl.] (*especially BrE*) the political meetings, speeches, etc. that take place in the period before an election 競選活動（競選前進行的政治集會、演講等）：*Most candidates will be **out on the hustings** this week.* 大多數候選人本星期將進行競選活動。

hus·tle /ˈhʌsl/ *verb, noun*

■ *verb* **1** [T] **~ sb + adv./prep.** to make sb move quickly by pushing them in a rough aggressive way 推搡；猛推：*He grabbed her arm and hustled her out of the room.* 他抓住她的胳膊把她推出房間。**2** [T] **~ sb (into sth)** to force sb to make a decision before they are ready or sure 催促（某人做決定）**3** [T, I] **~ (sth)** (*informal, especially NAmE*) to sell or obtain sth, often illegally（常指非法地）兜售，取得：*to hustle dope* 兜售麻醉品 ◇ *They survive by hustling on the streets.* 他們靠沿街兜售為生。**4** [I] (*NAmE, informal*) to act in an aggressive way or with

H

a lot of energy 強行；強迫；硬幹 **5** [I] (*NAmE*) to work as a PROSTITUTE 當妓女

■ ***noun*** [U] busy noisy activity of a lot of people in one place 忙碌喧囂：*We escaped from the* ***hustle and bustle*** *of the city for the weekend.* 我們週末時躲開了城市的擁擠喧囂。

hust·ler /ˈhʌslə(r)/ *noun* (*informal*) **1** (*especially NAmE*) a person who tries to trick sb into giving them money 耍詭計騙錢的人 **2** (*NAmE*) a PROSTITUTE 妓女

hut /hʌt/ *noun* a small, simply built house or shelter 簡陋的小房子（或棚、舍）：*a beach hut* 海灘棚屋◇ *a wooden hut* 小木屋 ➲ VISUAL VOCAB page V15

hutch /hʌtʃ/ *noun* **1** a wooden box with a front made of wire, used for keeping RABBITS or other small animals in（養兔子等小動物的）籠子 **2** (*NAmE*) a large piece of wooden furniture with shelves in the top part and cupboards below, used for displaying and storing cups, plates, etc. 廚櫃，餐具櫃（上部為擱架，下部為櫃子）

hwyl /hɔɪl/ *noun* [U] (*WelshE*) a strong feeling of emotion and enthusiasm 強烈感情；激情

hya·cinth /ˈhaɪəsɪnθ/ *noun* a plant with a mass of small blue, white or pink flowers with a sweet smell that grow closely together around a thick STEM 風信子

hy·aena = HYENA

hy·brid /ˈhaɪbrɪd/ *noun* **1** an animal or plant that has parents of different SPECIES or varieties 雜種動物；雜交植物；雜種：*A mule is a hybrid of a male donkey and a female horse.* 騾子是公驢和母馬交配而生的雜種動物。➲ compare CROSS-BREED **2 ~ (between/of A and B)** something that is the product of mixing two or more different things（不同事物的）混合物，合成物 SYN **mixture**：*The music was a hybrid of Western pop and traditional folk song.* 這種音樂融合了西方流行音樂和傳統民歌。 **3** a vehicle that uses two different types of power, especially petrol/gas or DIESEL and electricity 混合動能車（使用兩種不同能源，尤指汽油或柴油與電混合使用）▸ **hy·brid** *adj.*：*a hybrid car/vehicle* 混合動力車

hy·brid·ize (*BrE* also **-ise**) /ˈhaɪbrɪdaɪz/ *verb* [I, T] **~ (sth)** (*technical* 術語) if an animal or a plant **hybridizes** or **is hybridized** with an animal or a plant of another SPECIES, they join together to produce a hybrid（使）產生雜交品種，雜交 ▸ **hy·brid·iza·tion, -isa·tion** /ˌhaɪbrɪdaɪˈzeɪʃn; *NAmE* -dəˈzeɪ-/ *noun* [U]

hydel /ˈhaɪdel/ *abbr.* (*IndE*) HYDROELECTRIC 水力發電的

hydra /ˈhaɪdrə/ *noun* **1 Hydra** (in ancient Greek stories 古希臘故事) a snake with several heads. As one head was cut off, another one grew. In the end it was killed by Hercules. 許德拉，多頭蛇（砍去一個頭即長出新頭，後為大力神赫拉克勒斯所殺） **2** (*formal*) a thing that is very difficult to deal with, because it continues for a long time or because it has many different aspects 棘手的複雜事物；難以根絕的禍患 **3** (*biology* 生) an extremely small water creature with a tube-shaped body and TENTACLES around its mouth 水螅

hy·dran·gea /haɪˈdreɪndʒə/ *noun* a bush with white, pink or blue flowers that grow closely together in the shape of a large ball 繡球花

hy·drant /ˈhaɪdrənt/ *noun* = FIRE HYDRANT

hy·drate /ˈhaɪdreɪt; haɪˈdreɪt/ *verb* **~ sth** (*technical* 術語) to make sth absorb water 使吸入水分；使水合；使成水合物 ▸ **hy·dra·tion** /haɪˈdreɪʃn/ *noun* [U] ➲ compare DEHYDRATE

hy·draul·ic /haɪˈdrɔːlɪk; *BrE* also -ˈdrɒl-/ *adj.* [usually before noun] **1** (of water, oil, etc. 水、油等) moved through pipes, etc. under pressure（通過水管等）液壓的，水力的：*hydraulic fluid* 液壓液體 **2** (of a piece of machinery 機器) operated by liquid moving under pressure 液壓驅動的：*hydraulic brakes* 液壓制動器 **3** connected with hydraulic systems 與水利（或液壓）系統有關的：*hydraulic engineering* 水利工程 ▸ **hy·draul·ic·al·ly** /-kli/ *adv.*：*hydraulically operated doors* 液壓傳動門

hy·draul·ics /haɪˈdrɔːlɪks; *BrE* also -ˈdrɒl-/ *noun* **1** [pl.] machinery that works by the use of liquid moving under pressure 液壓裝置 **2** [U] the science of the use of liquids moving under pressure 水力學

hydr(o)- /ˈhaɪdr(əʊ); *NAmE* -dr(oʊ)/ *combining form* (in nouns, adjectives and adverbs 構成名詞、形容詞和副詞) **1** connected with water 與水有關的；水的 **2** (*chemistry* 化) combined with HYDROGEN 含氫的；氫化的

hydro /ˈhaɪdrəʊ; *NAmE* -droʊ/ *noun* [U] (*CanE*) electricity 電：*to pay your hydro bill* 付電費

hydro·car·bon /ˌhaɪdrəˈkɑːbən; *NAmE* -ˈkɑːrb-/ *noun* (*chemistry* 化) a chemical made up of HYDROGEN and CARBON only. There are many different hydrocarbons found in petrol/gas, coal and natural gas. 烴；碳氫化合物

hydro·chlor·ic acid /ˌhaɪdrəˌklɒrɪk ˈæsɪd; *NAmE* -ˌklɔːr-/ *noun* [U] (*chemistry* 化) (*symb.* **HCl**) an acid containing HYDROGEN and CHLORINE 鹽酸

hydro·chloro·fluoro·carbon /ˌhaɪdrəʊklɒrəʊˈflʊərəkɑːbən; *NAmE* ˌhaɪdroʊklɔːroʊˈflʊrəkɑːrbən/ *noun* (*chemistry* 化) = HCFC

hydro·cor·ti·sone /ˌhaɪdrəˈkɔːtɪzəʊn; *NAmE* -ˈkɔːrtɪzoʊn/ *noun* [U] a HORMONE produced in the body that is used in drugs to help with diseases of the skin and muscles 皮質醇，氫化可的松（體內分泌的荷爾蒙，用於治療皮膚和肌肉疾病）

hydro·elec·tric /ˌhaɪdrəʊɪˈlektrɪk; *NAmE* ˌhaɪdroʊ-/ *adj.* using the power of water to produce electricity; produced by the power of water 使用水力發電的；水力產生的：*a hydroelectric plant* 水力發電站◇ *hydroelectric power* 水力發出的電 ➲ VISUAL VOCAB page V8 ▸ **hydro·elec·tri·city** /-ɪˌlekˈtrɪsəti/ *noun* [U]

hydro·fluoro·car·bon /ˌhaɪdrəʊˈflʊərəʊkɑːbən; *NAmE* ˌhaɪdroʊˈflʊroʊkɑːrbən/ *noun* (*chemistry* 化) = HFC

hydro·foil /ˈhaɪdrəfɔɪl/ *noun* a boat which rises above the surface of the water when it is travelling fast 水翼船 ➲ VISUAL VOCAB page V54 ➲ compare HOVERCRAFT

hydro·gen /ˈhaɪdrədʒən/ *noun* [U] (*symb.* **H**) a chemical element. Hydrogen is a gas that is the lightest of all the elements. It combines with OXYGEN to form water. 氫；氫氣

hy·dro·gen·ated /haɪˈdrɒdʒəneɪtɪd; *NAmE* -ˈdrɑːdʒ-/ *adj.* (*chemistry* 化) **hydrogenated** oils have had hydrogen added to them（油類）氫化的，加氫的

ˈ**hydrogen bomb** (also ˈ**H-bomb**) *noun* a very powerful nuclear bomb 氫彈

ˌ**hydrogen peˈroxide** *noun* [U] (*symb.* H_2O_2) (*chemistry* 化) = PEROXIDE

hy·drol·ogy /haɪˈdrɒlədʒi; *NAmE* -ˈdrɑːl-/ *noun* [U] (*technical* 術語) the scientific study of the earth's water, especially its movement in relation to land 水文學；水文地理學

hy·droly·sis /haɪˈdrɒlɪsɪs; *NAmE* -ˈdrɑːl-/ *noun* [U] (*chemistry* 化) a reaction with water which causes a COMPOUND to separate into its parts 水解（化合物的加水分解）

hydro·pho·bia /ˌhaɪdrəˈfəʊbiə; *NAmE* -ˈfoʊbiə/ *noun* [U] extreme fear of water, which happens with RABIES infection in humans（狂犬病患者的）恐水，畏水 ▸ **hydro·pho·bic** /ˌhaɪdrəˈfəʊbɪk; *NAmE* -ˈfoʊ-/ *adj.*

hydro·plane /ˈhaɪdrəpleɪn/ *noun, verb*

■ ***noun*** **1** a light boat with an engine and a flat bottom, designed to travel fast over the surface of water 水上滑行艇 **2** (*NAmE*) = SEAPLANE

■ ***verb*** **1** (*NAmE*) (*BrE* **aqua·plane**) (of a motor vehicle 機動車輛) to slide out of control on a wet road 在潮濕路面上打滑失控 **2** (of a boat 船) to travel fast over the surface of the water 飛掠過水面

hydro·plan·ing /ˈhaɪdrəpleɪnɪŋ/ (*NAmE*) (*BrE* **aqua·plan·ing**) *noun* [U] the fact of a vehicle sliding on a wet surface, so that it is out of control（汽車在潮濕路面上的）打滑

hydro·pon·ics /ˌhaɪdrəˈpɒnɪks; *NAmE* -ˈpɑːn-/ *noun* [U] the process of growing plants in water or sand, rather than in soil 溶液栽培；水培

hydro·speed /ˈhaɪdrəʊspiːd; *NAmE* -droʊ-/ (*BrE* also **hydro·speed·ing**) *noun* [U] the sport of jumping into a river that is flowing fast, wearing equipment that allows you to float 急流跳水漂流

hydro·ther·apy /ˌhaɪdrəʊˈθerəpi; *NAmE* ˌhaɪdroʊ-/ *noun* [U] the treatment of disease or injury by doing physical exercises in water 水療法

hy·drox·ide /haɪˈdrɒksaɪd; *NAmE* -ˈdrɑːks-/ *noun* (*chemistry* 化) a chemical consisting of a metal and a combination of OXYGEN and HYDROGEN 氫氧化物

hyena (also **hy·aena**) /haɪˈiːnə/ *noun* a wild animal like a dog, that eats the meat of animals that are already dead and has a cry like a human laugh. Hyenas live in Africa and Asia. 鬣狗（分佈於非洲和亞洲，以動物屍體為食）

hy·giene /ˈhaɪdʒiːn/ *noun* [U] the practice of keeping yourself and your living and working areas clean in order to prevent illness and disease 衞生：*food hygiene* 食物衞生 ◇ *personal hygiene* 個人衞生 ◇ *In the interests of hygiene, please wash your hands.* 為了衞生，請洗手。

hy·gien·ic /haɪˈdʒiːnɪk; *NAmE* usually -ˈdʒen-/ *adj.* clean and free of bacteria and therefore unlikely to spread disease 衞生的：*Food must be prepared in hygienic conditions.* 食物必須在衞生的環境中製作。 OPP **unhygienic**
▸ **hy·gien·ic·al·ly** /-kli/ *adv.*：*Medical supplies are disposed of hygienically.* 醫療用品經衞生方法處理掉。

hy·gien·ist /haɪˈdʒiːnɪst/ (also **ˈdental hygienist** especially in *NAmE*) *noun* a person who works with a dentist and whose job is to clean people's teeth and give them advice about keeping them clean 牙科保健員；牙科潔治員

hymen /ˈhaɪmən/ *noun* (*anatomy* 解) a piece of skin that partly covers the opening of the VAGINA in women who have never had sex 處女膜

hymn /hɪm/ *noun* **1** a song of praise, especially one praising God and sung by Christians 讚美詩，聖歌（尤指基督徒唱的頌揚上帝的歌） **2** [usually sing.] if a film/movie, book, etc. is a **hymn to sth**, it praises it very strongly 歌頌某事物的電影（或書等） IDM see SING

ˈhymn book (also *old-fashioned* **hym·nal** /ˈhɪmnəl/) *noun* a book of hymns 讚美詩集

hype /haɪp/ *noun, verb*
■ *noun* [U] (*informal, disapproving*) advertisements and discussion on television, radio, etc. telling the public about a product and about how good or important it is（電視、廣播等中言過其實的）促銷廣告，促銷討論：*marketing/media hype* 誇張的促銷 / 媒體廣告 ◇ *Don't believe all the hype—the book isn't that good.* 別相信那些天花亂墜的宣傳，那本書沒那麼好。
■ *verb* (*informal, disapproving*) to advertise sth a lot and exaggerate its good qualities, in order to get a lot of public attention for it 誇張地宣傳（某事物）：**~ sth** *This week his much hyped new movie opens in London.* 本週他那部被大肆炒作的新電影在倫敦上映。◇ **~ sth up** *The meeting was hyped up in the media as an important event.* 這次會議被媒體吹成一件大事。

ˌhyped ˈup *adj.* (*informal*) (of a person 人) very worried or excited about sth that is going to happen 十分擔憂的；很激動的；十分興奮的

hyper /ˈhaɪpə(r)/ *adj.* (*informal*) excited and nervous; having too much nervous energy 既興奮又緊張的；精力過旺的

hyper- /ˈhaɪpə(r)/ *prefix* (in adjectives and nouns 構成形容詞和名詞) more than normal; too much 過度；過多：*hypercritical* 批評苛刻的 ◇ *hypertension* 高血壓 ➲ compare HYPO-

hyper·active /ˌhaɪpərˈæktɪv/ *adj.* (especially of children and their behaviour 尤指兒童及其行為) too active and only able to keep quiet and still for short periods 過分活躍的；多動的 ▸ **hyper·activ·ity** /ˌhaɪpərækˈtɪvəti/ *noun* [U]

hyper·bar·ic /ˌhaɪpəˈbærɪk; *NAmE* ˌhaɪpər-/ *adj.* (*physics* 物) (of gas 氣體) at a higher pressure than normal 高氣壓的；高壓的

hyper·bola /haɪˈpɜːbələ; *NAmE* -ˈpɜːr-/ *noun* (*pl.* **hyper·bolas** or **hyper·bolae** /-liː/) a SYMMETRICAL open curve 雙曲線 ➲ VISUAL VOCAB page V71

hyper·bole /haɪˈpɜːbəli; *NAmE* -ˈpɜːrb-/ *noun* [U, C, usually sing.] a way of speaking or writing that makes sth sound better, more exciting, dangerous, etc. than it really is 誇張 SYN **exaggeration**

hyper·bol·ic /ˌhaɪpəˈbɒlɪk; *NAmE* -pərˈbɑːl-/ *adj.* **1** (*mathematics* 數) of or related to a hyperbola 雙曲線的 **2** (of language 言語) deliberately exaggerated; using hyperbole 誇張的；誇張法的

hyper·cor·rec·tion /ˌhaɪpəkəˈrekʃn; *NAmE* -pərk-/ *noun* [U, C] (*linguistics* 語言) the use of a wrong form or pronunciation of a word by sb who is trying to show that they can use language correctly. For example, the use of *I* instead of *me* in the sentence 'They invited my husband and I to dinner'. 矯枉過正；改正過頭

hyper·gly·caemia (*BrE*) (*NAmE* **hyper·gly·cemia**) /ˌhaɪpəglaɪˈsiːmiə; *NAmE* -pərg-/ *noun* [U] (*medical* 醫) the condition of having too high a level of blood sugar 高血糖

hyper·in·fla·tion /ˌhaɪpərɪnˈfleɪʃn/ *noun* [U] a situation in which prices rise very fast, causing damage to a country's economy 惡性通貨膨脹；超通貨膨脹；過度通貨膨脹

hyper·link /ˈhaɪpəlɪŋk; *NAmE* -pərl-/ (also **hot·link**) *noun* a place in an electronic document on a computer that is linked to another electronic document 超級鏈接；超連結：*Click on the hyperlink.* 點擊超級鏈接。

hyper·mar·ket /ˈhaɪpəmɑːkɪt; *NAmE* -pərmɑːrk-/ *noun* (*BrE*) a very large shop located outside a town, that sells a wide range of goods 特大型商店（坐落在城外，商品種類繁多）

hyper·media /ˌhaɪpəˈmiːdiə; *NAmE* -pərˈm-/ *noun* [U] (*computing* 計) a system that links text to files containing images, sound or video 超媒體（連接文本與圖像、聲音或影像文件的系統）

hyper·nym /ˈhaɪpənɪm; *NAmE* -pərn-/ *noun* (*linguistics* 語言) = SUPERORDINATE ➲ compare HYPONYM

hyper·sen·si·tive /ˌhaɪpəˈsensətɪv; *NAmE* -pərˈs-/ *adj.* **~ (to sth) 1** very easily offended 非常敏感的；很容易生氣的：*He's hypersensitive to any kind of criticism.* 他對任何批評都受不了。 **2** extremely physically sensitive to particular substances, medicines, light, etc.（對某些物質、藥物、光等）過敏的：*Her skin is hypersensitive.* 她的皮膚過敏。 ▸ **hyper·sen·si·tiv·ity** /ˌhaɪpəˌsensəˈtɪvəti; *NAmE* -pərˌs-/ *noun* [U]

hyper·space /ˈhaɪpəspeɪs; *NAmE* -pərs-/ *noun* [U] **1** (*technical* 術語) space which consists of more than three DIMENSIONS 超空間；多維空間 **2** (in stories 小說) a situation in which it is possible to travel faster than light 超光速狀態

hyper·ten·sion /ˌhaɪpəˈtenʃn; *NAmE* -pərˈt-/ *noun* [U] (*medical* 醫) blood pressure that is higher than is normal 高血壓

hyper·text /ˈhaɪpətekst; *NAmE* -pərt-/ *noun* [U] text stored in a computer system that contains links that allow the user to move from one piece of text or document to another 超文本 ➲ see also HTML

hyper·thy·roid·ism /ˌhaɪpəˈθaɪrɔɪdɪzəm; *NAmE* -pərˈθ-/ *noun* [U] (*medical* 醫) a condition in which the THYROID is too active, making the heart and other body systems function too quickly 甲狀腺功能亢進

hyper·trophy /haɪˈpɜːtrəfi; *NAmE* -ˈpɜːrt-/ *noun* [U] (*biology* 生) an increase in the size of an organ or TISSUE because its cells grow in size（器官或組織的）肥大，過度生長

hyper·ven·ti·late /ˌhaɪpəˈventɪleɪt; *NAmE* -pərˈv-/ *verb* [I] (*technical* 術語) to breathe too quickly because you

H

are very frightened or excited 換氣過度；通氣增強 ▸hyper·ven·ti·la·tion /ˌhaɪpəˌventɪˈleɪʃn; NAmE -pərˌven-/ noun [U]

hy·phen /ˈhaɪfn/ *noun* the mark (-) used to join two words together to make a new one, as in *back-up*, or to show that a word has been divided between the end of one line and the beginning of the next 連字符 ➲ compare DASH *n.* (4)

hy·phen·ate /ˈhaɪfəneɪt/ *verb* **~ sth** to join two words together using a hyphen; to divide a word between two lines of text using a hyphen 用連字符連接；用連字符分割（詞語）：*Is your name hyphenated?* 你的名字有用連字符嗎？▸ **hy·phen·ation** /ˌhaɪfəˈneɪʃn/ *noun* [U]：*hyphenation rules* 連字符使用規則

H

hyp·no·sis /hɪpˈnəʊsɪs; NAmE -ˈnoʊ-/ *noun* [U] **1** an unconscious state in which sb can still see and hear and can be influenced to follow commands or answer questions 催眠狀態：*She only remembered details of the accident* ***under hypnosis****.* 她只有在催眠狀態下才能記起那次事故的細節。 **2** = HYPNOTISM：*He uses hypnosis as part of the treatment.* 他用催眠術作為治療的一部份。◇ *Hypnosis helped me give up smoking.* 催眠幫助我戒了煙。

hypno·ther·apy /ˌhɪpnəʊˈθerəpi; NAmE ˌhɪpnoʊ-/ *noun* [U] a kind of treatment that uses HYPNOSIS to help with physical or emotional problems 催眠療法

hyp·not·ic /hɪpˈnɒtɪk; NAmE -ˈnɑːt-/ *adj., noun*

■ ***adj.*** **1** making you feel as if you are going to fall asleep, especially because of a regular, repeated noise or movement 有催眠作用的；使人昏昏欲睡的 SYN **mesmerizing, soporific**：*hypnotic music* 引人昏昏欲睡的音樂 ◇ *His voice had an almost hypnotic effect.* 他的聲音有一種近乎催眠的作用。 **2** [only before noun] connected with or produced by hypnosis 催眠狀態的；催眠狀態引起的：*a* ***hypnotic trance/state*** 催眠迷睡／狀態 **3** (of a drug 藥物) making you sleep 安眠的

■ ***noun*** (*technical* 術語) a drug that makes you sleep; a SLEEPING PILL 安眠藥

hyp·no·tism /ˈhɪpnətɪzəm/ (also **hyp·no·sis**) *noun* [U] the practice of HYPNOTIZING a person (= putting them into an unconscious state) 催眠術；催眠

hyp·no·tist /ˈhɪpnətɪst/ *noun* a person who hypnotizes people 催眠術專家

hyp·no·tize (*BrE* also **-ise**) /ˈhɪpnətaɪz/ *verb* **1 ~ sb** to produce a state of HYPNOSIS in sb 對（某人）施催眠術 **2** [usually passive] **~ sb** (*formal*) to interest sb so much that they can think of nothing else 使（某人）着迷；迷住 SYN **mesmerize**

hypo- /ˈhaɪpəʊ; NAmE -poʊ/ (also **hyp-**) *prefix* (in adjectives and nouns 構成形容詞和名詞) under; below normal 在…下；低於；次於：*hypodermic* 皮下注射的 ◇ *hypothermia* 體溫過低 ➲ compare HYPER-

hypo·allergen·ic /ˌhaɪpəʊˌæləˈdʒenɪk; NAmE ˌhaɪpoʊˌælər-/ *adj.* (*technical* 術語) **hypoallergenic** substances and materials are unlikely to cause an ALLERGIC reaction in the person who uses them 不致過敏的；低過敏原的

hypo·chon·dria /ˌhaɪpəˈkɒndriə; NAmE -ˈkɑːn-/ *noun* [U] a state in which sb worries all the time about their health and believes that they are ill/sick when there is nothing wrong with them 疑病（症）

hypo·chon·driac /ˌhaɪpəˈkɒndriæk; NAmE -ˈkɑːn-/ *noun* a person who suffers from hypochondria 疑病患者：*Don't be such a hypochondriac!—there's nothing wrong with you.* 別這麼憂心忡忡的了！你根本沒病。▸ **hypo·chon·driac** (also **hypo·chon·driacal** /ˌhaɪpəˌkɒnˈdraɪəkl; NAmE -ˌkɑːnˈd-/) *adj.*

hyp·oc·risy /hɪˈpɒkrəsi; NAmE hɪˈpɑːk-/ *noun* (*pl.* **-ies**) [U, C] (*disapproving*) behaviour in which sb pretends to have moral standards or opinions that they do not actually have 偽善；虛偽：*He condemned the hypocrisy of those politicians who do one thing and say another.* 他譴責了那些說一套做一套的政客的虛偽。

hypo·crite /ˈhɪpəkrɪt/ *noun* (*disapproving*) a person who pretends to have moral standards or opinions that they do not actually have 偽君子；偽善者；虛偽的人 ▸ **hypo·crit·ical** /ˌhɪpəˈkrɪtɪkl/ *adj.*：*It would be hypocritical of me to have a church wedding when I don't believe in God.* 我不信上帝卻到教堂舉行婚禮，那就是我的虛偽了。 **hypo·crit·ic·al·ly** /-kli/ *adv.*

hypo·der·mic /ˌhaɪpəˈdɜːmɪk; NAmE -ˈdɜːrm-/ (also **ˌhypodermic ˈneedle**, **ˌhypodermic syˈringe**) *noun* a medical instrument with a long thin needle that is used to give sb an INJECTION under their skin 皮下注射器 ▸ **hypo·der·mic** *adj.*：*a hypodermic injection* (= one under the skin) 皮下注射

hypo·gly·caemia (*BrE*) (*NAmE* **hypo·gly·cemia**) /ˌhaɪpəʊglaɪˈsiːmiə; NAmE -poʊg-/ *noun* [U] (*medical* 醫) the condition of having too low a level of blood sugar 低血糖

hypo·nym /ˈhaɪpənɪm/ *noun* (*linguistics* 語言) a word with a particular meaning that is included in the meaning of a more general word, for example 'dog' and 'cat' are **hyponyms** of 'animal' 下義詞，下位詞（如 dog 和 cat 是 animal 的下義詞）➲ compare SUPERORDINATE

hypo·taxis /ˌhaɪpəʊˈtæksɪs; NAmE -poʊ-/ *noun* [U] (*grammar* 語法) the use of SUBORDINATE CLAUSES 從句的使用；從屬關係；主從結構 ➲ compare PARATAXIS

hypot·en·use /haɪˈpɒtənjuːz; NAmE -ˈpɑːtənuːs; -njuːz/ *noun* (*geometry* 幾何) the side opposite the RIGHT ANGLE of a RIGHT-ANGLED triangle （直角三角形的）斜邊，弦 ➲ VISUAL VOCAB page V71

hypo·thal·amus /ˌhaɪpəˈθæləməs/ *noun* (*anatomy* 解) an area in the central lower part of the brain that controls body temperature, HUNGER, and the release of HORMONES 下丘腦（有調節體溫、攝食、內分泌等的功能）

hypo·ther·mia /ˌhaɪpəˈθɜːmiə; NAmE -ˈθɜːrm-/ *noun* [U] a medical condition in which the body temperature is much lower than normal 體溫過低

hy·poth·esis AW /haɪˈpɒθəsɪs; NAmE -ˈpɑːθ-/ *noun* (*pl.* **hy·poth·eses** /-siːz/) **1** [C] an idea or explanation of sth that is based on a few known facts but that has not yet been proved to be true or correct （有少量事實依據但未被證實的）假說，假設 SYN **theory**：*to* ***formulate/confirm a hypothesis*** 提出／證實假設 ◇ *a hypothesis about the function of dreams* 關於夢的作用的假說 ➲ COLLOCATIONS at SCIENTIFIC **2** [U] guesses and ideas that are not based on certain knowledge （憑空的）猜想，猜測 SYN **speculation**：*It would be pointless to engage in hypothesis before we have the facts.* 在我們還沒掌握事實之前瞎猜是毫無意義的。

hy·pothe·size (*BrE* also **-ise**) AW /haɪˈpɒθəsaɪz; NAmE -ˈpɑːθ-/ *verb* [T, I] **~ (sth)** | **~ that ...** (*formal*) to suggest a way of explaining sth when you do not definitely know about it; to form a hypothesis 假設；假定：*The causes can be hypothesized but not proved.* 原因能夠被假定，但不能被證實。◇ *We can only hypothesize that the cases we know about are typical.* 我們只能假設我們知道的案例是典型的。

hypo·thet·ic·al AW /ˌhaɪpəˈθetɪkl/ *adj.* based on situations or ideas which are possible and imagined rather than real and true 假設的；假定的：*a* ***hypothetical question/situation/example*** 假定的問題／情況／例子 ◇ *Let us take the hypothetical case of Sheila, a mother of two ...* 我們且舉關於希拉這個假定的例子，她是一位有兩個孩子的母親… ◇ *I wasn't asking about anybody in particular—it was a* ***purely hypothetical*** *question.* 我並沒有問到具體某個人，那不過是個純粹假設性的問題。 ▸ **hypo·thet·ic·al·ly** AW /-kli/ *adv.*

hypo·thy·roid·ism /ˌhaɪpəʊˈθaɪrɔɪdɪzəm; NAmE -poʊ-/ *noun* [U] (*medical* 醫) a condition in which the THYROID is not active enough, making growth and mental development slower than normal 甲狀腺功能減退

hyp·ox·aemia (*BrE*) (*NAmE* **hyp·ox·emia**) /ˌhaɪpɒkˈsiːmiə; NAmE -pɑːk-/ *noun* [U] (*medical* 醫) a lower than normal amount of OXYGEN in the blood 低氧血；低血氧

hyp·oxia /haɪˈpɒksiə; *NAmE* -ˈpɑːk-/ *noun* [U] (*medical* 醫) a condition in which not enough OXYGEN reaches the body's TISSUES 缺氧；低氧

hys·ter·ec·tomy /ˌhɪstəˈrektəmi/ *noun* (*pl.* **-ies**) [C, U] a medical operation to remove a woman's WOMB 子宮切除（術）

hys·teria /hɪˈstɪəriə; *NAmE* -ˈstɪr-/ *noun* [U] **1** a state of extreme excitement, fear or anger in which a person, or a group of people, loses control of their emotions and starts to cry, laugh, etc. 歇斯底里；情緒失控：*There was* ***mass hysteria*** *when the band came on stage.* 樂隊登台時觀眾一片瘋狂。◇ *A note of hysteria crept into her voice.* 她的聲音聽來有點歇斯底里。 **2** (*disapproving*) an extremely excited and exaggerated way of behaving or reacting to an event 大肆鼓吹；狂熱誇張；大驚小怪：*the usual media hysteria that surrounds royal visits* 媒體對於王室成員訪問的慣常的大肆渲染 ◇ *public hysteria about AIDS* 公眾對艾滋病談虎色變 **3** (*medical* 醫) a condition in which sb experiences violent or extreme emotions that they cannot control, especially as a result of shock 癔病；歇斯底里

hys·ter·ic·al /hɪˈsterɪkl/ *adj.* **1** in a state of extreme excitement, and crying, laughing, etc. in an uncontrolled way 歇斯底里的；情緒狂暴不可抑止的：*hysterical screams* 歇斯底里的尖叫 ◇ *a hysterical giggle* 無法控制的傻笑 ◇ *He became almost hysterical when I told him.* 我告訴他時，他幾乎要發瘋了。◇ *Let's not get hysterical.* 咱們別太激動。◇ (*disapproving*) *He thought I was being a hysterical female.* 他覺得我當時像個歇斯底里的女人。 **2** (*informal*) extremely funny 極其可笑的 SYN **hilarious**：*She seemed to find my situation absolutely hysterical.* 她好像覺得我的處境極端可笑。 HELP Some speakers do not pronounce the 'h' at the beginning of **hysterical** and use 'an' instead of 'a' before it. This now sounds old-fashioned. 有人說 hysterical 時不發 h 音，前面用 an 而不用 a，現在聽起來過時了。 ▸ **hys·ter·ic·al·ly** /-kli/ *adv.*：*to laugh/cry/scream/sob hysterically* 歇斯底里地大笑／大哭／尖叫／哭泣 ◇ *hysterically funny* 極其可笑

hys·ter·ics /hɪˈsterɪks/ *noun* [pl.] **1** an expression of extreme fear, excitement or anger that makes sb lose control of their emotions and cry, laugh, etc. 歇斯底里的表現：*He went into hysterics when he heard the news.* 他聽到這個消息時變得歇斯底里。 **2** (*informal*) wild LAUGHTER 狂笑：*She had the audience* ***in hysterics***. 她令觀眾捧腹大笑。

IDM **have hysterics** (*informal*) to be extremely upset and angry 極其憤怒：*My mum'll have hysterics when she sees the colour of my hair.* 我媽媽看到我的頭髮的顏色會火冒三丈的。

Hz *abbr.* (in writing) HERTZ（書寫形式）赫，赫茲

H

Ii

I /aɪ/ *noun, pron., symbol, abbr.*
■ ***noun*** (also **i**) [C, U] (*pl.* **Is, I's, i's** /aɪz/) the 9th letter of the English alphabet 英語字母表的第 9 個字母：*'Island' begins with (an) I/'I'.* * island 一詞以字母 i 開頭。 **IDM** see DOT *v.*
■ ***pron.*** used as the subject of a verb when the speaker or writer is referring to himself/herself（指稱自己，作動詞的主語）我：*I think I'd better go now.* 我想我最好現在就走。◇ *He and I are old friends.* 他和我是老朋友。◇ *When they asked me if I wanted the job, I said yes.* 他們問我是否想要那份工作，我說想。◇ *I'm not going to fall, am I?* 我不會摔倒的，對吧？◇ *I'm taller than her, aren't I?* 我比她高，是吧？ ➲ see also ME
■ ***symbol*** (also **i**) the number 1 in ROMAN NUMERALS（羅馬數字）1
■ ***abbr.*** (also **I.**) (especially on maps) Island(s); ISLE(S)（尤用於地圖）島，群島

i- /aɪ/ *combining form* (in the names of products 構成產品名稱) (*computing* 計) INTERACTIVE (= allowing information to be passed continuously and in both directions between a computer and the person who uses it)（人與計算機）交互的，互動的：*The i-writer teaches you how to plan and write essays.* 交互式寫作程序教你如何構思與撰寫文章。

I-9 form /ˌaɪ ˈnaɪn fɔːm; *NAmE* fɔːrm/ *noun* (*US*) an official document that an employer must have which shows that an employee has the right to work in the US * I-9 表，雇員雇傭資格證明（雇主必須持有，證明雇員有權在美國工作）

-ial *suffix* (in adjectives 構成形容詞) typical of 有…特性的：*dictatorial* 獨裁的 ▸ **-ially** (in adverbs 構成副詞)：*officially* 正式地

iam·bic /aɪˈæmbɪk/ *adj.* (*technical* 術語) (of rhythm in poetry 詩的韻步) in which one weak or short syllable is followed by one strong or long syllable 抑揚格的（每一短或弱音節後接一長或強音節）：*a poem written in **iambic pentameters*** (= in lines of ten syllables, five short and five long) 抑揚格五音步詩

iam·bus /aɪˈæmbəs/ *noun* (*pl.* **iambi** /-baɪ/, **iam·buses**) (also **iamb** /ˈaɪæm; ˈaɪæmb/) (*technical* 術語) a unit of sound in poetry consisting of one weak or short syllable followed by one strong or long syllable（詩歌的）抑揚格

-ian, -an *suffix* **1** (in nouns and adjectives 構成名詞和形容詞) from; typical of 來自；有…特徵的：*Bostonian* 波士頓人 ◇ *Brazilian* 巴西人 ◇ *Shakespearian* 莎士比亞的 ◇ *Libran* 屬天秤座的 **2** (in nouns 構成名詞) a specialist in 專長於…的人；…專家：*mathematician* 數學家

-iana, -ana *suffix* (in nouns 構成名詞) a collection of objects, facts, stories, etc. connected with the person, place, period, etc. mentioned 集；彙編；收藏品：*Mozartiana* 莫扎特作品集 ◇ *Americana* 美國資料彙編 ◇ *Victoriana* 維多利亞時代的收藏品

IB /ˌaɪ ˈbiː/ *abbr.* INTERNATIONAL BACCALAUREATE 國際中學畢業會考：*to do the IB* 參加國際中學畢業會考

Iber·ian /aɪˈbɪəriən; *NAmE* -ˈbɪr-/ *adj.* relating to Spain and Portugal 伊比利亞的；西班牙和葡萄牙的：*the Iberian peninsula* 伊比利亞半島

ibex /ˈaɪbeks/ *noun* (*pl.* **ibex**) a mountain GOAT with long curved horns 北山羊，羱羊（角長而彎曲）

ibid. (also **ib.**) *abbr.* in the same book or piece of writing as the one that has just been mentioned (from Latin 'ibidem')（源自拉丁語 ibidem，指在同一書或作品中）同前，同上

-ibility ➲ -ABLE, -IBLE

ibis /ˈaɪbɪs/ *noun* (*pl.* **ibises**) a bird with a long neck, long legs and a long beak that curves downwards, that lives near water 鸛（涉禽，長頸長腿，喙長而向下彎曲）

-ible, -ibly ➲ -ABLE, -ABLY

Ibo /ˈiːbəʊ; *NAmE* ˈiːboʊ/ *noun* = IGBO

ibu·profen /ˌaɪbjuːˈprəʊfen; *NAmE* -ˈproʊ-/ *noun* [U] a drug used to reduce pain and INFLAMMATION 布洛芬，異丁苯丙酸（鎮痛消炎藥）

-ic *suffix* **1** (in adjectives and nouns 構成形容詞和名詞) connected with 與…有關；…的：*scenic* 風景優美的 ◇ *economic* 經濟的 ◇ *Arabic* 阿拉伯語 **2** (in adjectives 構成形容詞) that performs the action mentioned 動作（或行為）…的：*horrific* 恐怖的 ◇ *specific* 獨特的 ▸ **-ical** (in adjectives 構成形容詞)：*comical* 滑稽的 **-ically** (in adverbs 構成副詞)：*physically* 身體上

ice /aɪs/ *noun, verb*
■ ***noun*** **1** [U] water that has frozen and become solid 冰：*There was ice on the windows.* 窗戶上有冰花。◇ *The lake was covered with a **sheet of ice**.* 湖面上覆蓋着一層冰。◇ *My hands are as cold as ice.* 我的雙手冰冷。 ➲ VISUAL VOCAB pages V4, V5 ➲ see also ICY, BLACK ICE, DRY ICE **2** [sing.] (usually **the ice**) a frozen surface that people SKATE on 冰場；溜冰場：*The dancers came out onto the ice.* 舞蹈表演者出場來到滑冰場上。◇ *Both teams are on the ice, waiting for the whistle.* 兩支參賽隊伍都在冰場上等待着哨音。 **3** [U] a piece of ice used to keep food and drinks cold 冰塊：*I'll have lemonade please—no ice.* 請給我來杯檸檬汽水，不要加冰塊。 **4** [C] (*old-fashioned, especially BrE*) an ice cream 一份冰淇淋 **5** [U] (*NAmE*) a type of sweet food that consists of ice that has been crushed and flavoured 冰凍甜食
IDM **break the ˈice** to say or do sth that makes people feel more relaxed, especially at the beginning of a meeting, party, etc.（尤指聚會等開始時，用言語或行動）打破隔閡；打頭說話 ➲ see also ICEBREAKER (2) **cut no ˈice (with sb)** to have no influence or effect on sb（對某人）無影響，不起作用：*His excuses cut no ice with me.* 他的申辯絲毫不能説服我。 **on ˈice** **1** (of wine, etc. 果酒等) kept cold by being surrounded by ice 冰鎮 **2** (of a plan, etc. 計劃等) not being dealt with now; waiting to be dealt with at a later time 被擱置；留待考慮：*We've had to **put** our plans **on ice** for the time being.* 我們不得不把計劃暫時擱置。 **3** (of entertainment, etc. 娛樂等) performed by SKATERS on an ICE RINK 冰上表演的：*Cinderella on ice*《灰姑娘》冰上演出 ➲ more at THIN *adj.*
■ ***verb*** **~ sth** to cover a cake with ICING 在（糕餅上）加糖霜
PHR V **ˌice ˈover/ˈup** | **ˌice sth↔ˈover/ˈup** to cover sth with ice; to become covered with ice（使）結上一層冰，覆蓋着冰

ˈice age (often **the Ice Age**) *noun* one of the long periods of time, thousands of years ago, when much of the earth's surface was covered in ice 冰期；冰川期；冰河時代

ˈice axe (*BrE*) (*US* usually **ˈice ax**) *noun* a tool used by people climbing mountains for cutting steps into ice 冰鎬（登山用） ➲ picture at AXE

ice·berg /ˈaɪsbɜːɡ; *NAmE* -bɜːrɡ/ *noun* an extremely large mass of ice floating in the sea 冰山（浮在海上的巨大冰塊） **IDM** see TIP *n.*

ˌiceberg ˈlettuce *noun* a type of LETTUCE (= a salad vegetable) with crisp pale green leaves that form a tight ball 捲心萵苣

ice·block /ˈaɪsblɒk; *NAmE* -blɑːk/ *noun* (*AustralE, NZE*) a piece of flavoured ice on a stick 棒冰；冰棍；冰棒

ˌice-ˈblue *adj.* (especially of eyes 尤指眼睛) very pale blue in colour 淡藍色的

ˈice-bound *adj.* surrounded by or covered in ice 被冰圍封的；冰封的

ice·box /ˈaɪsbɒks; *NAmE* -bɑːks/ *noun* (*old-fashioned, especially US*) = FRIDGE

ice·break·er /ˈaɪsbreɪkə(r)/ *noun* **1** a strong ship designed to break a way through ice, for example in the Arctic or Antarctic 破冰船 **2** a thing that you do or say, like a game or a joke, to make people feel less nervous when they first meet（初次見面時）消除隔閡的行動，活躍氣氛的話

ˈice bucket *noun* a container filled with ice and used for keeping bottles of wine, etc. cold 冰桶（冰鎮用）

ˈice cap *noun* a layer of ice permanently covering parts of the earth, especially around the North and South Poles（尤指北極和南極的）冰冠

ˌice-ˈcold *adj.* **1** as cold as ice; very cold 冰凍的；冰涼的：*ice-cold beer* 冰鎮啤酒 ◊ *My hands were ice-cold.* 我的手冰冷。**2** not having or showing any emotion 冷漠無情的；冷淡的：*His eyes had grown ice-cold.* 他的目光變得冷酷無情。

ˌice ˈcream 0‑ᵂ (also **ˈice cream** especially in *NAmE*) *noun* [U, C]
a type of sweet frozen food made from milk fat, flavoured with fruit, chocolate, etc. and often eaten as a DESSERT; a small amount of this food intended for one person, often served in a container made of biscuit that is shaped like a CONE（一份）冰淇淋，冰激凌：*Desserts are served with cream or ice cream.* 甜點上加奶油或冰淇淋。◊ *Who wants an ice cream?* 誰要冰淇淋？

ˈice cube *noun* a small, usually square, piece of ice used for making drinks cold 小冰塊（用於冷飲）

iced /aɪst/ *adj.* **1** (of drinks 飲料) made very cold; containing ice 冰鎮的；加冰塊的：*iced coffee/tea* 冰咖啡；冰茶 **2** (of a cake, etc. 糕餅等) covered with ICING 加糖霜的：*an iced cake* 加糖霜的蛋糕

ˈice dancing (also **ˈice dance**) *noun* [U] the sport of dancing on ice 冰上舞蹈；冰舞 ▸ **ˈice dancer** *noun*

ˌiced ˈwater (*BrE*) (*NAmE* **ˈice water**) *noun* water with ice in it for drinking 冰水（飲料）

ˈice field *noun* a large area of ice, especially one near the North or South Pole 冰原（尤指南、北極附近）

ˈice floe (also **floe**) *noun* a large area of ice, floating in the sea（海上的）大片浮冰

ˈice hockey (*BrE*) (*NAmE* **hockey**) *noun* [U] a game played on ice, in which players use long sticks to hit a hard rubber disc (called a PUCK) into the other team's goal 冰球運動；冰上曲棍球 ➲ VISUAL VOCAB page V44

ˈice house *noun* a building for storing ice in, especially in the past, usually underground or partly underground（尤指舊時的）藏冰窖，藏冰庫

ˌice ˈlolly (also *informal* **lolly**) (both *BrE*) (*NAmE* **Pop·sicle™**) *noun* a piece of ice flavoured with fruit, served on a stick 冰棍；冰棒

ˈice pack *noun* a plastic container filled with ice that is used to cool parts of the body that are injured, etc. 冰袋（用於受傷等部位降溫）

ˈice pick *noun* a tool with a very sharp point for breaking ice with 碎冰錐

ˈice rink (also **ˈskating rink**, **rink**) *noun* a specially prepared flat surface of ice, where you can ice-skate; a building where there is an ice rink 溜冰場；溜冰館 ➲ VISUAL VOCAB pages V40, V44

ˈice sheet *noun* (*technical* 術語) a layer of ice that covers a large area of land for a long period of time 冰原；冰蓋

ˈice shelf *noun* (*technical* 術語) a layer of ice that is attached to land and covers a large area of sea 冰架，冰棚（與陸地相接的厚層浮動冰體）

ˈice skate (also **skate**) *noun* a boot with a thin metal blade on the bottom, that is used for SKATING on ice 冰鞋；溜冰鞋 ➲ VISUAL VOCAB page V44

ˈice-skate *verb* [I] to SKATE on ice 滑冰；溜冰 ▸ **ˈice skater** *noun*

ˈice skating *noun* [U] = SKATING：*to go ice skating* 去溜冰 ➲ VISUAL VOCAB page V40

ˈice water (*NAmE*) (*BrE* **ˌiced ˈwater**) *noun* water with ice in it for drinking 冰水（飲料）

icicle /ˈaɪsɪkl/ *noun* a pointed piece of ice that is formed when water freezes as it falls down from sth such as a roof（屋簷等處滴水形成的）冰錐，冰柱

icily /ˈaɪsɪli/ *adv.* said or done in a very unfriendly way（態度）冷冰冰地：*'I have nothing to say to you,' she said icily.* "我對你沒什麼可說的。" 她冷冷地說。

icing /ˈaɪsɪŋ/ (*especially BrE*) (*NAmE* usually **frost·ing**) *noun* [U] a sweet mixture of sugar and water, milk, butter or egg white that is used to cover and decorate cakes 糖霜（用以裝飾糕餅等）➲ see also ROYAL ICING

IDM **the icing on the ˈcake** (*US* also **the frosting on the ˈcake**) something extra and not essential that is added to an already good situation or experience and that makes it even better 錦上添花

ˈicing sugar (*BrE*) (*US* **conˈfectioner's sugar**, **ˈpow·dered sugar**) *noun* [U] fine white powder made from sugar, that is mixed with water to make icing（製糖霜用的）糖粉

icky /ˈɪki/ *adj.* (**ick·ier**, **icki·est**) (*informal*) unpleasant (used especially about sth that is wet and sticky) 黏糊糊（令人不舒服）的

icon /ˈaɪkɒn; *NAmE* -kɑːn/ *noun* **1** (*computing* 計) a small symbol on a computer screen that represents a program or a file 圖標；圖符；圖示：*Click on the printer icon with the mouse.* 用鼠標點擊打印機圖標。➲ VISUAL VOCAB page V68 **2** a famous person or thing that people admire and see as a symbol of a particular idea, way of life, etc. 崇拜對象；偶像：*Madonna and other pop icons of the 1980s* 麥當娜以及其他 20 世紀 80 年代的流行音樂偶像 ◊ *a **feminist/gay icon*** (= sb that feminists/gay people admire) 女權主義者的／同性戀者的偶像 **3** (also **ikon**) (in the Orthodox Church 東正教) a painting or statue of a holy person that is also thought of as a holy object 聖像

icon·ic /aɪˈkɒnɪk; *NAmE* -ˈkɑːnɪk/ *adj.* acting as a sign or symbol of sth 符號的；圖標的；圖符的；偶像的

icono·clast /aɪˈkɒnəklæst; *NAmE* -ˈkɑːnə-/ *noun* (*formal*) a person who criticizes popular beliefs or established customs and ideas 批評傳統信仰（或習俗、思想）的人；反傳統者

icono·clas·tic /aɪˌkɒnəˈklæstɪk; *NAmE* ˌkɑːnə-/ *adj.* (*formal*) criticizing popular beliefs or established customs and ideas 批評傳統信仰（或習俗思想）的 ▸ **icono·clasm** /aɪˈkɒnəklæzəm; *NAmE* -ˈkɑːnə-/ *noun* [U]：*the iconoclasm of the early Christians* 早期基督徒廢除聖像的主張

icon·og·raphy /ˌaɪkəˈnɒɡrəfi; *NAmE* -ˈnɑːɡ-/ *noun* [U] the use or study of images or symbols in art 圖示法；象徵手法；圖像學

icon·ology /ˌaɪkəˈnɒlədʒi; *NAmE* -ˈnɑːl-/ *noun* [U] the fact of a work of art being an image or symbol of sth（藝術上的）象徵手法

-ics *suffix* (in nouns 構成名詞) the science, art or activity of …的科學（或藝術、活動）：*physics* 物理學 ◊ *dramatics* 戲劇表演藝術 ◊ *athletics* 田徑運動

ICT /ˌaɪ siː ˈtiː/ *noun* [U] (*BrE*) the abbreviation for 'information and communications technology' (the study of the use of computers, the Internet, video, and other technology as a subject at school) 信息與通信技術（全寫為 information and communications technology，學科）

ICU /ˌaɪ siː ˈjuː/ *abbr.* intensive care unit (in a hospital) 特別護理病房；重症監護室；加護病房；深切治療部

icy /ˈaɪsi/ *adj.* (**icier**, **ici·est**) **1** very cold 冰冷的；冰凍的 SYN **freezing**：*icy winds/water* 凜冽的風；冰冷的水 ◊ *My feet were **icy cold**.* 我雙腳冰冷。**2** covered with ice 覆蓋着冰的；結滿冰的：*icy roads* 結滿冰的路 **3** (of a person's voice, manner, etc. 嗓音、態度等) not friendly or kind; showing feelings of dislike or anger 冷冰冰的；冷峻的：*My eyes met his icy gaze.* 我的雙眼迎視他冰冷的目光。➲ see also ICILY ▸ **ici·ness** *noun* [U]

ID /ˌaɪ ˈdiː/ *noun, verb*
▪ *noun* **1** [U, C] the abbreviation for 'identity' or 'identification' (an official way of showing who you are, for example a document with your name, date of birth and often a photograph on it) 身分證明（全寫為 identity 或 identification）：*You must carry ID at all times.* 你必須隨身攜帶身分證。◊ *The police checked IDs at the gate.* 警察在大門口查看身分證。◊ *an ID card* 身分證 **2** [C] IDENTIFICATION：*The police need a witness to make a positive ID.* 警方需要有目擊者加以確認。➲ see also CALLER ID
▪ *verb* (**ID's**, **ID'ing**, **ID'd**, **ID'd**) (*informal*) = IDENTIFY

Id = EID

id /ɪd/ *noun* (*psychology* 心) the part of the unconscious mind where many of a person's basic needs, feelings and desires are supposed to exist 本我，伊德（指人的潛意識中其基本需求、感情和慾望假定存在的部份） ➲ compare EGO, SUPEREGO

I'd /aɪd/ *short form* **1** I had **2** I would

I'D card *noun* = IDENTITY CARD

-ide *suffix* (*chemistry* 化) (in nouns 構成名詞) a COMPOUND of …化合物： *chloride* 氯化物

idea /aɪˈdɪə; *NAmE* -ˈdiːə/ *noun*
▸ **PLAN/THOUGHT 計劃；思想 1** [C] a plan, thought or suggestion, especially about what to do in a particular situation 想法；構思；主意： *It would be **a good idea** to call before we leave.* 我們出發之前打個電話是個好主意。◇ **~ (of sth/of doing sth)** *I like the idea of living on a boat.* 我喜歡在船上居住的構想。◇ **~ (for sth)** *He already had an idea for his next novel.* 他已經構思好了下一部小說。◇ *Her family expected her to go to college, but she had **other ideas**.* 她的家人希望她上大學，但她另有打算。◇ *The surprise party was Jane's idea.* 那次驚喜聚會是簡的主意。◇ ***It might be an idea*** (= it would be sensible) *to try again later.* 稍後再試或許是明智的。◇ *We've been toying with the idea of* (= thinking about) *getting a dog.* 我們一直有意無意地想着養條狗。◇ ***It seemed like a good idea at the time**, and then it all went horribly wrong.* 那在當時似乎是個好主意，但後來卻鑄成大錯。◇ *The latest **big idea** is to make women more interested in sport.* 最近的流行思想是促進婦女對體育的興趣。
▸ **IMPRESSION 印象 2** [U, sing.] **~ (of sth)** a picture or an impression in your mind of what sb/sth is like 印象；概念： *The brochure should give you **a good idea of** the hotel.* 這本小冊子詳細介紹這家旅館。◇ *I had **some idea of** what the job would be like.* 我對於這份工作有了一些瞭解。◇ *She doesn't seem to have any idea of what I'm talking about.* 她對我所說的似乎一點也不懂。◇ *I don't want anyone **getting the wrong idea*** (= getting the wrong impression about sth). 我不希望任何人有所誤會。◇ *An evening at home watching TV is not my idea of a good time.* 晚上待在家裏看電視，我不認為是什麼賞心樂事。
▸ **OPINION 意見 3** [C] **~ (about sth)** an opinion or a belief about sth 意見；看法；信念： *He has some very strange ideas about education.* 他對教育有些非常奇怪的看法。
▸ **FEELING 感覺 4** [sing.] **~ (that …)** a feeling that sth is possible（認為某事可能發生的）感覺： *What gave you the idea that he'd be here?* 是什麼讓你想到他會來這裏？◇ *I have a pretty good idea where I left it—I hope I'm right.* 我記得很清楚把它落在哪兒了——但願我是對的。
▸ **AIM 目標 5 the idea** [sing.] **~ of sth/of doing sth** the aim or purpose of sth 目標；意圖： *You'll soon **get the idea*** (= understand). 你很快就會明白的。◇ ***What's the idea of the game?*** 這個遊戲的目的是什麼？ ➲ **SYNONYMS** at PURPOSE

IDM **give sb i'deas | put i'deas into sb's head** to give sb hopes about sth that may not be possible or likely; to make sb act or think in an unreasonable way 使某人抱有空想（或做不切實際的事）： *Who's been putting ideas into his head?* 是誰一直在讓他想入非非的？ **have no i'dea | not have the faintest, first, etc. idea** (*informal*) used to emphasize that you do not know sth 絲毫不知道： *'What's she talking about?' 'I've no idea.'* "她在講什麼？" "我一點也不瞭解。" ◇ *He hasn't the faintest idea how to manage people.* 他根本不懂得人事管理。 **have the right i'dea** to have found a very good or successful way of living, doing sth, etc. 找到好的（或成功的）方式；找對路： *He's certainly got the right idea—retiring at 55.* 他真的想通了——打算在 55 歲時退休。 **'that's an idea!** (*informal*) used to reply in a positive way to a suggestion that sb has made 好主意！： *Hey, that's an idea! And we could get a band, as well.* 嘿，好主意！而且我們還可以找支樂隊。 **'that's the idea!** (*informal*) used to encourage people and to tell them that they are doing sth right 幹得好；做得對： *That's the idea! You're doing fine.* 對啦！你做得不錯。 **you have no i'dea …** (*informal*) used to show that sth is hard for sb else to imagine 你難以想像⋯： *You've no idea how much traffic there was tonight.* 你難以想像今晚的交通有多擁擠。 ➲ more at BUCK *v.*

ideal /aɪˈdiːəl/ *adj., noun*
■ ***adj.* 1** **~ (for sth)** perfect; most suitable 完美的；理想的；最合適的： *This beach is ideal for children.* 這個海灘是孩子的理想去處。◇ *She's the ideal candidate for the job.* 她是這項工作最合適的人選。◇ *The trip to Paris will be an **ideal opportunity** to practise my French.* 去巴黎旅行將是我練習法語的絕好機會。 **2** [only before noun] existing only in your imagination or as an idea; not likely to be real 想像的；不切實際的： *the search for ideal love* 對理想中的愛的尋求 ◇ ***In an ideal world** there would be no poverty and disease.* 在理想的世界裏沒有貧窮和疾病。 **IDM** see WORLD ▸ **ideal·ly** /aɪˈdiːəli/ *adv.*： *She's **ideally suited** for this job.* 她最適合這項工作。◇ *Ideally, I'd like to live in New York, but that's not possible.* 按理想來說，我希望住在紐約，但那是不可能的。
■ ***noun* 1** [C] an idea or standard that seems perfect, and worth trying to achieve or obtain 理想；看似完美的思想（或標準）： *political ideals* 政治理想 ◇ *She found it hard to live up to his high ideals.* 她覺得很難做到他的高標準要求。 **2** [C, usually sing.] **~ (of sth)** a person or thing that you think is perfect 完美的人（或事物）： *It's my ideal of what a family home should be.* 這是我心目中完美的家庭住宅。

ideal·ism /aɪˈdiːəlɪzəm/ *noun* [U] **1** the belief that a perfect life, situation, etc. can be achieved, even when this is not very likely 理想主義： *He was full of youthful idealism.* 他滿腦子都是年輕人的理想主義。 **2** (*philosophy* 哲) the belief that our ideas are the only things that are real and that we can know about 唯心主義；唯心論；觀念論；理念論 ➲ compare MATERIALISM, REALISM ▸ **ideal·ist** *noun*： *He's too much of an idealist for this government.* 在現政府的眼中，他是一個過度的理想主義者。

ideal·is·tic /ˌaɪdiəˈlɪstɪk/ *adj.* having a strong belief in perfect standards and trying to achieve them, even when this is not realistic 理想主義的；空想的： *She's still young and idealistic.* 她還年輕並且耽於空想。 ▸ **ideal·is·tic·al·ly** /ˌaɪdiəˈlɪstɪkli/ *adv.*

ideal·ize (*BrE* also **-ise**) /aɪˈdiːəlaɪz/ *verb* **~ sb/sth** to consider or represent sb/sth as being perfect or better than they really are 將⋯視為理想；將⋯理想化： *It is tempting to idealize the past.* 人都愛把過去的日子說得很美好。◇ *an idealized view of married life* 對於婚姻生活的理想化的看法 ▸ **ideal·iza·tion, -isa·tion** /aɪˌdiːəlaɪˈzeɪʃn; *NAmE* -ləˈz-/ *noun* [U, C]

ide·ate /ˈaɪdieɪt/ *verb* (*formal*) **1** [T] **~ sth** to form an idea of sth; to imagine sth 對⋯形成概念；想像 **2** [I] to form ideas; to think 形成概念；想 ▸ **idea·tion** /ˌaɪdiˈeɪʃn/ *noun* [U]

idée fixe /ˌiːdeɪ ˈfiːks/ *noun* (*pl.* **idées fixes** /ˌiːdeɪ ˈfiːks/) (from *French*) an idea or a desire which is so strong that you cannot think about anything else 執著的想法（或慾望）；固有觀念

idem /ˈɪdem/ *adv.* (from *Latin*) from the same book, article, author, etc. as the one that has just been mentioned（指出自同一書、文章、作者等）同前，同上

ident /ˈaɪdent/ *noun* (*BrE*) a piece of music or a short film that is broadcast between programmes so that people can recognize a radio station or television channel（電台或電視節目之間插播的）標誌曲，標誌短片

iden·ti·cal **AW** /aɪˈdentɪkl/ *adj.* **1** similar in every detail 完全同樣的；相同的： *a row of identical houses* 完全一樣的一排房子 ◇ *The two pictures are similar, although not identical.* 這兩幅畫很相似，雖然不完全相同。◇ **~ to sb/sth** *Her dress is almost identical to mine.* 她的連衣裙和我的幾乎一模一樣。◇ **~ with sb/sth** *The number on the card should be identical with the one on the chequebook.* 卡上的號碼應該和支票簿上的相同。 ➲ **LANGUAGE BANK** at SIMILARLY **2 the identical** [only before noun] the same 同一的： *This is the identical room we stayed in last* *year.* 這就是我們去年住的那個房間。 ▸ **iden·ti·cal·ly** AW /-kli/ *adv.* : *The children were dressed identically.* 孩子們的穿着完全一樣。

i,dentical 'twin (also *technical* 術語 **monozy,gotic 'twin**) *noun* either of two children or animals born from the same mother at the same time who have developed from a single egg. Identical twins are of the same sex and look very similar. 單卵性雙胞胎之一（性別相同，外貌相似） ➲ compare DIZYGOTIC TWIN, FRATERNAL TWIN

iden·ti·fi·able AW /aɪˌdentɪˈfaɪəbl/ *adj.* that can be recognized 可識別的；可辨認的： *identifiable characteristics* 可識別的特徵 ◇ *The house is easily identifiable by the large tree outside.* 這房子很容易從外面的這棵大樹辨認出來。 OPP **unidentifiable**

iden·ti·fi·ca·tion AW /aɪˌdentɪfɪˈkeɪʃn/ *noun* **1** (*abbr.* **ID**) [U, C] the process of showing, proving or recognizing who or what sb/sth is 鑒定；辨認： *The identification of the crash victims was a long and difficult task.* 辨認墜機意外傷亡者的工作費時而且困難重重。◇ *Each product has a number for easy identification.* 每件產品都有號碼以便於識別。◇ *an identification number* 識別號碼 ◇ *Only one witness could make a positive identification.* 只有一位目擊者能夠直接確認。 **2** [U] the process of recognizing that sth exists, or is important 確認；確定： *The early identification of children with special educational needs is very important.* 早期確認兒童有特殊教育需求很重要。 **3** (*abbr.* **ID**) [U] official papers or a document that can prove who you are 身分證明： *Can I see some identification, please?* 請出示任何身分證件好嗎？ **4** [U, C] **~ (with sb/sth)** a strong feeling of sympathy, understanding or support for sb/sth 強烈的同情感（或諒解、支持）： *her emotional identification with the play's heroine* 她與劇中女主人公在情感上的共鳴 ◇ *their increasing identification with the struggle for independence* 他們對爭取獨立的鬥爭越來越大的支持 **5** [U, C] **~ (of sb) (with sb/sth)** the process of making a close connection between one person or thing and another 密切關聯；緊密聯繫： *the voters' identification of the Democrats with high taxes* 選民把民主黨和高稅收畫上等號

i,dentifi'cation parade *noun* (also *informal* **i'dentity parade**) (both *BrE*) (also **'line-up** *NAmE, BrE*) a row of people, including one person who is suspected of a crime, who are shown to a witness to see if he or she can recognize the criminal 辨認行列，列隊認人（把嫌疑犯同其他人排在一起，讓目擊者辨認）

iden·ti·fier /aɪˈdentɪfaɪə(r)/ *noun* (*computing* 計) a series of characters used to refer to a program or set of data within a program 標識符，標識號，識別字（可用以進入程序或其中的數據集）

iden·tify 🔑 AW /aɪˈdentɪfaɪ/ *verb* (**iden·ti·fies, iden·ti·fy·ing, iden·ti·fied, iden·ti·fied**)

1 🔑 (also *informal* **ID**) to recognize sb/sth and be able to say who or what they are 確認；認出；鑒定： **~ sb/sth as sb/sth** *The bodies were identified as those of two suspected drug dealers.* 那兩具屍體被辨認出原是兩名販毒嫌疑犯。◇ **~ sb/sth** *She was able to identify her attacker.* 她認出了襲擊她的人。◇ *Passengers were asked to identify their own suitcases before they were put on the plane.* 乘客被要求先確認自己的旅行箱再送上飛機。◇ *Many of those arrested refused to* ***identify themselves*** (= would not say who they were). 很多被逮捕的人拒不透露身分。◇ *First of all we must identify the problem areas.* 首先我們必須找出問題所在。 **2** 🔑 to find or discover sb/sth 找到；發現： **~ sth** *Scientists have identified a link between diet and cancer.* 科學家發現了飲食與癌症之間的關聯。◇ *As yet they have not identified a buyer for the company.* 迄今為止他們還沒有為公司找到買主。◇ **~ what, which, etc. …** *They are trying to identify what is wrong with the present system.* 他們正試圖弄清現行制度的弊端所在。 **3 ~ sb/sth (as sb/sth)** to make it possible to recognize who or what sb/sth is 顯示；說明身分： *In many cases, the clothes people wear identify them as belonging to a particular social class.* 很多情況下，人們的穿着顯示出他們的社會階級。

PHR V **i'dentify with sb** 🔑 to feel that you can understand and share the feelings of sb else 與某人產生共鳴；諒解；同情 SYN **sympathize with** : *I didn't enjoy the book because I couldn't identify with any of the main characters.* 我不喜歡這本書，因為我無法與其中的任何主要角色產生共鳴。 **i'dentify sb with sth** to consider sb to be sth 把某人視為： *He was not the 'tough guy' the public identified him with.* 他並不是公眾所認定的那種硬漢。 **i'dentify sth with sth** to consider sth to be the same as sth else 認為某事物等同於 SYN **equate** : *You should not identify wealth with happiness.* 你不應該認為財富就等於幸福。 **be i'dentified with sb/sth | i'dentify yourself with sb/sth** to support sb/sth; to be closely connected with sb/sth 支持；與…有密切關聯： *The Church became increasingly identified with opposition to the regime.* 教會日益和反對政權的勢力走到一起。

Synonyms 同義詞辨析

identify

know • recognize • name • make sb/sth out

These words all mean to be able to see or hear sb/sth and especially to be able to say who or what they are. 以上各詞均含認出、辨別出之意。

identify to be able to say who or what sb/sth is 指確認、認出、鑒定： *She was able to identify her attacker.* 她認出了襲擊她的人。

know to be able to say who or what sth is when you see or hear it because you have seen or heard it before 指能認出、能辨認出 NOTE **Know** is used especially to talk about sounds that seem familiar and when sb recognizes the quality or opportunity that sb/sth represents. * know 尤指認出熟悉的聲音、辨別出人或事物所表現出的特質以及發現機會： *I couldn't see who was speaking, but I knew the voice.* 我看不到誰在講話，但我能辨別出聲音。◇ *She knows a bargain when she sees one.* 她一看就知道有沒有便宜可撿。

recognize to know who sb is or what sth is when you see or hear them/it, because you have seen or heard them/it before 指認識、認出、辨別出： *I recognized him as soon as he came in the room.* 他一進屋我就認出了他。

name to say the name of sb/sth in order to show that you know who/what they are 指能說出…的名稱、叫出…的名字： *The victim has not yet been named.* 受害人的姓名仍未得知。

make sb/sth out to manage to see or hear sb/sth that is not very clear 指看清、聽清、分清、辨認清楚： *I could just make out a figure in the darkness.* 黑暗中我只看出了一個人的輪廓。

PATTERNS

- to identify/know/recognize sb/sth **by** sth
- to identify/recognize/name sb/sth **as** sb/sth
- to identify/know/recognize/make out **who/what/how …**
- to **easily/barely/just** identify/recognize/make out sb/sth

Iden·ti·kit™ /aɪˈdentɪkɪt/ (*BrE*) (*US* **com·pos·ite, com'posite sketch**) *noun* a set of drawings of different features that can be put together to form the face of a person, especially sb wanted by the police, using descriptions given by people who saw the person; a picture made in this way 艾登蒂基特容貌拼圖（根據目擊者描述拼製出人的面部像，尤指警方要捉拿的人） ➲ compare E-FIT™, PHOTOFIT

iden·tity 🔑 AW /aɪˈdentəti/ *noun* (*pl.* **-ies**)

1 🔑 [C, U] (*abbr.* **ID**) who or what sb/sth is 身分；本身；本體： *The police are trying to discover the identity of the killer.* 警方正努力調查殺人兇手的身分。◇ *Their identities were kept secret.* 他們的身分保密。◇ *She is innocent; it was* ***a case of mistaken identity.*** 她是無辜的；那是身分判斷錯誤。◇ *Do you have any proof of identity?* 你有身分證明嗎？◇ *The thief used a false identity.* 竊賊使用的

I

是假身分。◇ *She went through an **identity crisis** in her teens* (= was not sure of who she was or of her place in society). 她在十多歲時經歷了一次自我認同的危機。**2** 🔑 [C, U] the characteristics, feelings or beliefs that distinguish people from others 特徵；特有的感覺（或信仰）：*a sense of **national/cultural/personal/group identity*** 民族／文化／個人／群體特性的認同感 ◇ *a plan to strengthen the **corporate identity** of the company* 加強公司的企業形象的計劃 **3** [U] **~ (with sb/sth)** | **~ (between A and B)** the state or feeling of being very similar to and able to understand sb/sth 同一性；相同；一致：*an identity of interests* 利益一致 ◇ *There's a close identity between fans and their team.* 球迷和他們的球隊之間有密切的同一性。

i'dentity card (also **I'D card**) *noun* a card with a person's name, date of birth, photograph, etc. on it that proves who they are 身分證；身分卡

i'dentity parade *noun* (*BrE, informal*) = IDENTIFICATION PARADE

I

i'dentity theft *noun* [U] using sb else's name and personal information in order to obtain credit cards and other goods or to take money out of the person's bank accounts 身分盜竊（利用別人的名字、個人信息等獲得信用卡、其他物品或從別人的賬戶中提取現金等）

ideograms 表意文字；表意符號

Chinese character for soil
漢字的土

Roman numeral three
羅馬數字 3

wheelchair access sign
輪椅通道標誌

biohazard sign
有害生物物質標誌

ideo·gram /'ɪdiəgræm/ (also **ideo·graph** /'ɪdiəgrɑːf; *NAmE* -græf/) *noun* **1** a symbol that is used in a writing system, for example Chinese, to represent the idea of a thing, rather than the sounds of a word 表意文字（或符號） **2** (*technical* 術語) a sign or a symbol for sth 表意標誌；表意符號

ideo·logue /'aɪdiəlɒg; 'ɪd-; *NAmE* -lɔːg; -lɑːg/ (also **ideolo·gist** /ˌaɪdi'ɒlədʒɪst; *NAmE* -'ɑːl-/) *noun* (*formal*, sometimes *disapproving*) a person whose actions are influenced by belief in a set of principles (= by an ideology) 理論家；思想家；空想家

ideol·ogy AW /ˌaɪdi'ɒlədʒi; *NAmE* -'ɑːl-/ *noun* [C, U] (*pl.* **-ies**) (sometimes *disapproving*) **1** a set of ideas that an economic or political system is based on 思想（體系）；思想意識：***Marxist/capitalist ideology*** 馬克思主義／資本主義思想體系 **2** a set of beliefs, especially one held by a particular group, that influences the way people behave 意識形態；觀念形態：*the ideology of gender roles* 性別角色的觀念形態 ◇ *alternative ideologies* 非傳統的意識形態 ▶ **ideo·logic·al** AW /ˌaɪdiə'lɒdʒɪkl; *NAmE* -'lɑːdʒ-/ *adj.*：*ideological differences* 意識形態上的差別 **ideo·logic·al·ly** AW /-kli/ *adv.*：*ideologically correct* 意識上正確

ides /aɪdz/ *noun* [pl.] the middle day of the month in the ancient Roman system, from which other days were calculated 月中日（古羅馬曆每月居中的一天）：*the ides of March* * 3 月 15 日

idi·ocy /'ɪdiəsi/ *noun* (*pl.* **-ies**) (*formal*) **1** [U] very stupid behaviour; the state of being very stupid 愚蠢行為；愚昧 SYN **stupidity 2** [C] a very stupid act, remark, etc. 愚蠢的行動（或言論等）：*the idiocies of bureaucracy* 官僚體系所做的蠢事

idio·lect /'ɪdiəlekt/ *noun* [C, U] (*linguistics* 語言) the way that a particular person uses language 個人語型；個人言語方式 ➲ compare DIALECT

idiom /'ɪdiəm/ *noun* **1** [C] a group of words whose meaning is different from the meanings of the individual words 習語；成語；慣用語：*'Let the cat out of the bag' is an idiom meaning to tell a secret by mistake.* "讓貓從袋子裏跑出來"是慣用語，意思是無意中泄露秘密。➲ SYNONYMS at WORD **2** [U, C] (*formal*) the kind of language and grammar used by particular people at a particular time or place（某時期或某地區的人的）語言和語法 **3** [U, C] (*formal*) the style of writing, music, art, etc. that is typical of a particular person, group, period or place（寫作、音樂、藝術等的）典型風格：*the **classical/contemporary/popular idiom*** 古典／當代／通俗風格

idiom·at·ic /ˌɪdiə'mætɪk/ *adj.* **1** containing expressions that are natural to a NATIVE SPEAKER of a language 表達方式地道的；符合（某一）語言習慣的：*She speaks fluent and idiomatic English.* 她講一口流利地道的英語。**2** containing an idiom 包含習語的：*an idiomatic expression* 慣用語 ▶ **idiom·at·ic·al·ly** /-kli/ *adv.*

idio·syn·crasy /ˌɪdiə'sɪŋkrəsi/ *noun* [C, U] (*pl.* **-ies**) a person's particular way of behaving, thinking, etc., especially when it is unusual; an unusual feature（個人特有的）習性；特徵；癖好 SYN **eccentricity**：*The car has its little idiosyncrasies.* 這輛車有它的一些小小脾氣。▶ **idio·syn·crat·ic** /ˌɪdiəsɪŋ'krætɪk/ *adj.*：*His teaching methods are idiosyncratic but successful.* 他的教學方法很奇特，但很成功。

idiot /'ɪdiət/ *noun* **1** (*informal*) a very stupid person 蠢人；笨蛋 SYN **fool**：*When I lost my passport, I felt such an idiot.* 我丟了護照時覺得自己像個大傻瓜。◇ *Not that switch, you idiot!* 不是那個開關，你這個蠢貨！**2** (*old-fashioned, offensive*) a person with very low intelligence who cannot think or behave normally 白痴

idi·ot·ic /ˌɪdi'ɒtɪk; *NAmE* -'ɑːtɪk/ *adj.* very stupid 十分愚蠢的；白痴般的 SYN **ridiculous**：*an idiotic question* 很愚蠢的問題 ◇ *Don't be so idiotic!* 別這麼傻了！▶ **idi·ot·ic·al·ly** /-kli/ *adv.*

idiot sav·ant /ˌiːdjəʊ sæ'vɒ̃; *NAmE* ˌiːdjoʊ sæ'vɑ̃ː/ *noun* (*pl.* **idiot sav·ants** or **idiots sav·ants** /ˌiːdjəʊ sæ'vɒ̃; *NAmE* ˌiːdjoʊ sæ'vɑ̃ː/) (from *French*) a person who has severe LEARNING DIFFICULTIES, but who has an unusually high level of ability in a particular skill, for example in art or music, or in remembering things 弱能特才，低能特才（有嚴重的學習障礙，但在藝術、音樂或記憶等方面有超常能力）

idle /'aɪdl/ *adj.*, *verb*

■ ***adj.*** **1** (of people 人) not working hard 懈怠的；懶惰的 SYN **lazy**：*an idle student* 懶散的學生 **2** (of machines, factories, etc. 機器、工廠等) not in use 閒置的：*to **lie/stand/remain idle*** 閒置着 **3** (of people 人) without work 沒有工作的；閒散的 SYN **unemployed**：*Over ten per cent of the workforce is now idle.* 現在有超過百分之十的勞動力閒置。**4** [usually before noun] with no particular purpose or effect; useless 漫無目的的；無效的；無用的：***idle chatter/curiosity*** 無聊的嘮叨／好奇 ◇ *It was just an **idle threat*** (= not serious). 那只不過是嚇唬嚇唬而已。◇ ***It is idle to** pretend that their marriage is a success.* 佯稱他們的婚姻有多美滿是無意義的。**5** [usually before noun] (of time 時間) not spent doing work or sth particular 空閒的：*In idle moments, he carved wooden figures.* 他空閒時就刻木雕。IDM see DEVIL ▶ **idle·ness** *noun* [U]：*After a period of enforced idleness, she found a new job.* 她在被迫閒散了一段時間之後找到了份新工作。

■ ***verb*** **1** [T, I] to spend time doing nothing important 混時間；閒蕩；無所事事：**~ sth** (+ **adv./prep.**) *They idled the days away, talking and watching television.* 他們天天在閒聊和看電視中消磨時光。◇ (+ **adv./prep.**) *They idled along by the river* (= walked slowly and with no particular purpose). 他們沿着河邊閒逛。 **2** [I] (of an engine 發動機) to run slowly while the vehicle is not moving 空轉；掛空擋；未熄火 **SYN** **tick over**： *She left the car idling at the roadside.* 她把汽車掛空擋停在路邊。 **3** [T] **~ sb/sth** (*NAmE*) to close a factory, etc. or stop providing work for the workers, especially temporarily（尤指暫時地）關閉工廠，使（工人）閒着： *The strikes have idled nearly 4 000 workers.* 罷工使近 4 000 名工人閒着沒事幹。

idler /ˈaɪdlə(r)/ *noun* a person who is lazy and does not work 懶漢；無所事事的人 **SYN** **loafer**

idli /ˈɪdliː/ *noun* an Indian rice cake cooked using steam 印度蒸米糕

idly /ˈaɪdli/ *adv.* without any particular reason, purpose or effort; doing nothing 毫無目的地；漫不經心地；閒散地： *She sat in the sun, idly sipping a cool drink.* 她坐在陽光下懶洋洋地抿着冷飲。◇ *He wondered idly what would happen.* 他漫不經心地幻想着會發生什麼事。◇ *We can't* ***stand idly by*** (= do nothing) *and let people starve.* 我們不能袖手旁觀，讓一些人捱餓。

idol /ˈaɪdl/ *noun* **1** a person or thing that is loved and admired very much 受到熱愛和崇拜的人（或物）；偶像： *a* ***pop/football/teen, etc. idol*** 流行音樂偶像、足球明星、青少年的偶像等 ◇ *the idol of countless teenagers* 無數青少年崇拜的偶像 ◇ *a* ***fallen idol*** (= sb who is no longer popular) 隕落的明星 **2** a statue that is worshipped as a god 神像

idol·atry /aɪˈdɒlətri; *NAmE* -ˈdɑːl-/ *noun* [U] **1** the practice of worshipping statues as gods 神像崇拜；偶像崇拜 **2** (*formal*) too much love or admiration for sb/sth 盲目崇拜： *football fans whose support for their team borders on idolatry* 對球隊幾乎到了盲目崇拜地步的足球迷 ▸ **idol·atrous** /aɪˈdɒlətrəs; *NAmE* -ˈdɑːl-/ *adj.*

idol·ize (*BrE* also **-ise**) /ˈaɪdəlaɪz/ *verb* **~ sb** to admire or love sb very much 崇拜；熱愛 **SYN** **worship**： *a pop star idolized by millions of fans* 受數百萬歌迷崇拜的流行音樂歌星 ◇ *They idolize their kids.* 他們溺愛自己的孩子。 ▸ **idol·iza·tion**, **-isa·tion** /ˌaɪdəlaɪˈzeɪʃn; *NAmE* -əˈzeɪʃn/ *noun* [U]

Language Bank 用語庫

i.e.

Explaining what you mean 解釋意思

- Some poems are mnemonics, **i.e.** they are designed to help you remember something. 有些詩歌是記憶代碼，即是說，其目的是幫助人們記起某事。
- Some poems are mnemonics, **that is to say**, they are designed to help you remember something. 有些詩歌是記憶代碼，就是說，其目的是幫助人們記起某事。
- Mnemonic poems, **that is** poems designed to help you remember something, are an excellent way to learn lists. 記事詩，即幫助人記起事情的詩歌，是記住一系列事物的極佳方式。
- A limerick's rhyme scheme is A–A–B–B–A. **In other words**, the first, second, and fifth lines all rhyme with one another, while the third and fourth lines have their own rhyme. 五行打油詩的韻律是 A-A-B-B-A。就是說，第一行、第二行和第五行押一個韻，而第三行和第四行押另一個韻。
- In this exercise the reader is encouraged to work out the meaning, **or rather** the range of meanings, of the poem. 這個練習鼓勵讀者弄清這首詩的意思，更確切地說是弄清其幾種涵義。
- This is a poem about death, **or, more precisely**, dying. 這是一首關於死亡的詩，更確切地說是關於臨終的詩。
- He says his poems deal with 'the big issues', **by which he means** love, loss, grief and death. 他說他的詩涉及一些"重大問題"，這些問題是指愛、失去、痛苦和死亡。

➲ Language Bank at ABOUT

idyll /ˈɪdɪl; *NAmE* ˈaɪdl/ *noun* **1** (*literary*) a happy and peaceful place, event or experience, especially one connected with the countryside（尤指鄉下的）愉快恬靜的地方（或事情、經歷） **2** a short poem or other piece of writing that describes a peaceful and happy scene 描述恬靜愉快情景的短詩（或短文）；田園詩

idyl·lic /ɪˈdɪlɪk; *NAmE* aɪˈd-/ *adj.* peaceful and beautiful; perfect, without problems 平和美麗的；完美無瑕的： *a house set in idyllic surroundings* 在田園風光的環境中的房子 ◇ *to lead an idyllic existence* 過着詩情畫意的生活 ◇ *The cottage sounds idyllic.* 小屋看來恬靜宜人。 ▸ **idyl·lic·al·ly** /-kli/ *adv.* : *a house idyllically set in wooded grounds* 詩情畫意般的林蔭中的房子

i.e. 🔑 /ˌaɪ ˈiː/ *abbr.* used to explain exactly what the previous thing that you have mentioned means (from Latin 'id est') 也就是，亦即（源自拉丁文 id est）： *the basic essentials of life, i.e. housing, food and water* 生活的基本需要，即住房、食物和水

-ie ➲ -Y (4)

IED /ˌaɪ iː ˈdiː/ *abbr.* improvised explosive device (a bomb made and used by people who are not members of the military forces of a country) 臨時爆炸裝置

IELTS /ˈaɪelts/ *noun* [U] the abbreviation for 'International English Language Testing System' (a test that measures a person's ability to speak and write English at the level that is necessary to go to university in the UK, Ireland, Australia, Canada, South Africa and New Zealand) 國際英語測試系統考試，雅思考試（全寫為 International English Language Testing System，英國、愛爾蘭、澳大利亞、加拿大、南非和新西蘭大學入學水平的英語運用能力考試）

if 🔑 /ɪf/ *conj.*, *noun*

■ ***conj.*** **1** 🔑 used to say that one thing can, will or might happen or be true, depending on another thing happening or being true 如果；假若；倘若： *If you see him, give him this note.* 你要是見到他，就把這個便條給他。◇ *I'll only stay if you offer me more money.* 你給我更多的錢我才會留下。◇ *If necessary I can come at once.* 如果有必要，我可以馬上來。◇ *You can stay for the weekend if you like.* 你如果願意就留在這裏過週末吧。◇ *If anyone calls, tell them I'm not at home.* 要是有人打電話來，就說我不在家。◇ *If he improved his IT skills, he'd* (= he would) *easily get a job.* 他如果提高了自己的信息技術技能，就會容易找到工作。◇ *You would know what was going on if you'd* (= you had) *listened.* 你若是注意聽了就會知道發生什麼事了。◇ *They would have been here by now if they'd caught the early train.* 假若他們趕上了早班火車，現在就該到這裏了。◇ *If I was in charge, I'd do things differently.* 假若由我負責，我不會這樣辦事的。◇ (rather *formal*) *If I were in charge …* 假若由我負責… ◇ ***Even if*** (= although) *you did see someone, you can't be sure it was him.* 即使你確實看見有個人，也不能保證那就是他。 **2** 🔑 when; whenever; every time 當；無論何時；每次： *If metal gets hot it expands.* 金屬受熱就膨脹。◇ *She glares at me if I go near her desk.* 我一走近她的辦公桌，她就對我瞪眼。 **3** (*formal*) used with *will* or *would* to ask sb politely to do sth（與 will 或 would 連用，表示客氣地請求）： *If you will sit down for a few moments, I'll tell the manager you're here.* 請稍坐，我這就告訴經理說您來了。◇ *If you would care to leave your name, we'll contact you as soon as possible.* 麻煩您留下姓名，我們會儘快與您聯繫的。 **4** 🔑 used after *ask*, *know*, *find out*, *wonder*, etc. to introduce one of two or more possibilities（用於 ask、know、find out、wonder 等之後，引出兩個或以上的可能性之一）是否 **SYN** **whether**： *Do you know if he's married?* 你知道他是否結婚了？◇ *I wonder if I should wear a coat or not.* 我不知道該不該穿外套。◇ *He couldn't tell if she was laughing or crying.* 他弄不清楚她是在笑還是在哭。◇ *Listen to the tune and see if you can remember the words.* 聽聽曲調，看你能否記起歌詞。 **5** 🔑 used after verbs or adjectives expressing feelings（用於表示情感的動詞或形容詞之後）： *I am sorry if I disturbed you.* 很抱歉，打攪您了。◇ *I'd be grateful if you would keep it a secret.* 你如

I

果能對此保密，我將不勝感激。◇ *Do you mind if I turn the TV off?* 我關上電視可以嗎？ **6** 🔑 used to admit that sth is possible, but to say that it is not very important（承認某事可能，但不很重要）即使，雖然：*If she has any weakness, it is her Italian.* 如果要說她有什麼缺點，那就是她的意大利語不大行。◇ ***So what if** he was late. Who cares?* 他就是遲到了又怎麼樣。誰在乎？ **7** used before an adjective to introduce a contrast（置於形容詞之前，引出對比）雖然，儘管：*He's a good driver, if a little over-confident.* 他是個好司機，雖然有點過於自信。◇ *We'll only do it once— **if at all**.* 我們就是幹也只會幹一次。 **8** 🔑 used to ask sb to listen to your opinion（請對方聽自己的意見）：*If you ask me, she's too scared to do it.* 依我看，她被嚇得不敢做了。◇ *If you think about it, those children must be at school by now.* 想想吧，那些孩子現在一定在學校了。◇ *If you remember, Mary was always fond of animals.* 記得吧，瑪麗總是喜歡動物。 **9** used before *could, may* or *might* to suggest sth or to interrupt sb politely（置於 could、may 或 might 之前，以提出建議或客氣地打斷別人的話）：*If I may make a suggestion, perhaps we could begin a little earlier next week.* 我來提個建議吧，或許我們下個星期可以早一點開始。

IDM **ˌif and ˈwhen** used to say sth about an event that may or may not happen（談及可能發生或不發生的事時說）：*If and when we ever meet again I hope he remembers what I did for him.* 倘若我們再次見面，我希望他還記得我為他做的事。 **if ˈanything** used to express an opinion about sth, or after a negative statement to suggest that the opposite is true（表達看法，或用在否定句之後表示反面意見才對）：*I'd say he was more like his father, if anything.* 依我看，如果一定要說他像誰的話，他比較像他的父親。◇ *She's not thin—if anything she's on the plump side.* 她並不瘦，其實她還有點胖呢。 **if ˌI were ˈyou** 🔑 used to give sb advice（提出勸告時說）：*If I were you I'd start looking for another job.* 我要是你，就會去另找工作了。 **if ˈnot** **1** 🔑 used to introduce a different suggestion, after a sentence with *if*（用在 if 引導的句子之後）不然，要不：*I'll go if you're going. If not (= if you are not) I'd rather stay at home.* 你去我就去。不然的話，我寧願待在家裏。 **2** 🔑 used after a *yes/no* question to say what will or should happen if the answer is 'no'（用於 yes/no 疑問句之後，表示如果答案是 no，將會或應該發生什麼）：*Are you ready? If not, I'm going without you.* 你準備好了嗎？否則我就自己去了。◇ *Do you want that cake? If not, I'll have it.* 你要那塊蛋糕嗎？不然我就要了。 **3** used to suggest that sth may be even larger, more important, etc. than was first stated（表示可能更大或更重要等）：*They cost thousands if not millions of pounds to build.* 建設要耗費數千英鎊，甚至可能是數百萬英鎊。 **if ˈonly** 🔑 used to say that you wish sth was true or that sth had happened 但願：*If only I were rich.* 但願我很富有。◇ *If only I knew her name.* 我要是知道她的名字就好了。◇ *If only he'd remembered to send that letter.* 要是他沒忘記發那封信就好了。◇ *If only I had gone by taxi.* 我要是乘出租車去就好了。 **it's not as if** used to say that sth that is happening is surprising（表示所發生的事情令人驚訝）：*I'm surprised they've invited me to their wedding—it's not as if I know them well.* 我很驚訝他們居然請我參加他們的婚禮，我跟他們似乎並不熟。 **ˈonly if** (rather *formal*) used to state the only situation in which sth can happen 只有：*Only if a teacher has given permission is a student allowed to leave the room.* 學生只有得到老師的許可才能離開教室。◇ *Only if the red light comes on is there any danger to employees.* 只有紅燈閃亮時才有危及職工的險情。

■ ***noun*** (*informal*) a situation that is not certain 不確定的情況：*If he wins—and **it's a big if**—he'll be the first Englishman to win for fifty years.* 假設他贏了，不過這還是個很大的疑問，他將成為五十年以來第一個獲勝的英國人。◇ *There are still a lot of **ifs and buts** before everything's settled.* 在一切得以解決之前還有很多不定因素。

Grammar Point 語法說明

if / whether

- Both **if** and **whether** are used in reporting questions which expect 'yes' or 'no' as the answer * if 和 whether 均用於要求以 yes 或 no 作答的轉述疑問句中：*She asked if/whether I wanted a drink.* 她問我要不要喝點什麼。 although **whether** sounds more natural with particular verbs such as **discuss**, **consider** and **decide**. When a choice is offered between alternatives **if** or **whether** can be used. 不過 whether 與 discuss、consider 和 decide 等動詞連用聽起來更自然。提供選擇時用 if 或 whether 均可：*We didn't know if/whether we should write or phone.* 我們不知道是寫信好還是打電話好。 In this last type of sentence, **whether** is usually considered more formal and more suitable for written English. 在最後這一句型中，一般認為 whether 較正式，更適用於書面英語。

iff /ɪf/ *conj.* (*mathematics* 數) an expression used in mathematics to mean 'if and only if' 當且僅當；在而且只有在…時

iffy /ˈɪfi/ *adj.* (*informal*) **1** (*especially BrE*) not in perfect condition; bad in some way 不完美的；有點壞的：*That meat smells a bit iffy to me.* 那塊肉聞起來有點變質了。 **2** not certain 未確定的：*The weather looks slightly iffy.* 看來天氣有些不穩定。

-ify, **-fy** *suffix* (in verbs 構成動詞) to make or become 使得；變成：*purify* 淨化 ◇ *solidify* 使凝固

Igbo (also **Ibo**) /ˈiːbəʊ; *NAmE* ˈiːboʊ/ *noun* [U] a language spoken by the Igbo people of W Africa, especially in SE Nigeria 伊格博語，伊博語（西非伊格博族語言，尤指尼日利亞東南部方言）

igloo /ˈɪɡluː/ *noun* (*pl.* **-oos**) a small round house or shelter built from blocks of hard snow by the Inuit people of northern N America（北美北部因努伊特人的拱形圓頂）冰屋

ig·ne·ous /ˈɪɡniəs/ *adj.* (*geology* 地) (of rocks 岩石) formed when MAGMA (= melted or liquid material lying below the earth's surface) becomes solid, especially after it has poured out of a VOLCANO 火成的（尤指火山噴出的）

ig·nite /ɪɡˈnaɪt/ *verb* [I, T] (*formal*) to start to burn; to make sth start to burn（使）燃燒，着火；點燃：*Gas ignites very easily.* 汽油易燃。◇ (*figurative*) *Tempers ignited when the whole family spent Christmas together.* 全家湊到一起度聖誕節，大家心裏都十分激動。◇ **~ sth** *Flames melted a lead pipe and ignited leaking gas.* 火焰熔化了一段鉛管，燃着了漏出來的煤氣。◇ (*figurative*) *His words ignited their anger.* 他的話引發了他們的怒火。

ig·ni·tion /ɪɡˈnɪʃn/ *noun* **1** [C, usually sing.] the electrical system of a vehicle that makes the fuel begin to burn to start the engine; the place in a vehicle where you start this system 點火裝置；點火開關：*to **turn the ignition on/off*** 打開／關上點火開關 ◇ *to put the key **in the ignition*** 把鑰匙插進點火開關 ➲ COLLOCATIONS at DRIVING ➲ VISUAL VOCAB page V42 **2** [U] (*technical* 術語) the action of starting to burn or of making sth burn 着火；點火；點燃：*The flames spread to all parts of the house within minutes of ignition.* 着火後只有幾分鐘火焰就蔓延到房子的各個部份。

ig·noble /ɪɡˈnəʊbl; *NAmE* -ˈnoʊ-/ *adj.* (*formal*) not good or honest; that should make you feel shame 卑劣的；不誠實的；不光彩的 **SYN** **base**：*ignoble thoughts* 可恥的想法 ◇ *an ignoble person* 卑鄙的人 **OPP** **noble**

ig·no·mini·ous /ˌɪɡnəˈmɪniəs/ *adj.* (*formal*) that makes, or should make, you feel ashamed 恥辱的；可恥的；不光彩的 **SYN** **disgraceful**, **humiliating**：*an ignominious defeat* 可恥的失敗 ◇ *He made one mistake and his career came to an ignominious end.* 他犯了一個錯誤，他的事業就很不體面地結束了。 ▸ **ig·no·mini·ous·ly** *adv.*

ig·no·miny /ˈɪɡnəmɪni/ *noun* [U] (*formal*) public shame and loss of honour 公開的恥辱；不名譽 **SYN** **disgrace**：*They suffered the ignominy of defeat.* 他們蒙受了失敗的恥辱。

ig·nor·amus /ˌɪɡnəˈreɪməs/ *noun* (usually *humorous*) a person who does not have much knowledge 無知識的人：*When it comes to music, I'm a complete ignoramus.* 說到音樂，我完全是個門外漢。

ig·nor·ance AW /ˈɪɡnərəns/ *noun* [U] **~ (of/about sth)** a lack of knowledge or information about sth 無知：*widespread* ***ignorance of/about*** *the disease* 對這種疾病的普遍不瞭解 ◇ *They fought a long battle against prejudice and ignorance.* 他們同偏見與無知進行了長期的鬥爭。◇ *She was kept* ***in ignorance of*** *her husband's activities.* 關於丈夫的活動，她一直蒙在鼓裏。◇ *Children often behave badly* ***out of/through ignorance.*** 兒童往往出於無知而不守規矩。

IDM ˌ**ignorance is** ˈ**bliss** (*saying*) if you do not know about sth, you cannot worry about it 無知是福；不知道心不煩：*Some doctors believe ignorance is bliss and don't give their patients all the facts.* 有些醫生認為無知是福，因此不向病人透露全部病情。

ig·nor·ant AW /ˈɪɡnərənt/ *adj.* **1** lacking knowledge or information about sth; not educated （對某事物）不瞭解的；無知的；愚昧的；無學識的：*an ignorant person/question* 無知的人／提問 ◇ *Never make your students feel ignorant.* 千萬別讓你的學生感到無知。◇ **~ about sth** *He's ignorant about modern technology.* 他對現代科技一無所知。◇ **~ of sth** *At that time I was ignorant of events going on elsewhere.* 那時我並不瞭解其他地方發生的事情。 **2** (*informal*) with very bad manners 很無禮的；十分不懂規矩的 SYN **uncouth**：*a rude, ignorant person* 粗魯無禮的人 ▶ **ig·nor·ant·ly** *adv.*

ig·nore 0-π AW /ɪɡˈnɔː(r)/ *verb*
1 0-π **~ sth** to pay no attention to sth 忽視；對…不予理會 SYN **disregard**：*He ignored all the 'No Smoking' signs and lit up a cigarette.* 他無視所有"禁止吸煙"的警示，點了香煙。◇ *I made a suggestion but they chose to ignore it.* 我提了個建議，但他們不予理會。◇ *We cannot afford to ignore their advice.* 我們不能不考慮他們的勸告。 **2** 0-π **~ sb** to pretend that you have not seen sb or that sb is not there 佯裝未見；不予理睬 SYN **take no notice of**：*She ignored him and carried on with her work.* 她沒理他，繼續幹她的活。

igu·ana /ɪˈɡwɑːnə/ *noun* a large tropical American LIZARD (= a type of REPTILE) 鬣鱗蜥，鬣蜥（美洲熱帶大蜥蜴）

iguan·odon /ɪˈɡwɑːnədɒn; *NAmE* -dɑːn/ *noun* a large DINOSAUR 禽龍

ike·bana /ˌɪkɪˈbɑːnə; ˌɪkeɪ-/ *noun* [U] (from *Japanese*) Japanese flower arranging, that has strict formal rules （日本）插花藝術，花道

ikon = ICON (3)

il- *prefix* ➲ IN- (1)

ileum /ˈɪliəm/ *noun* (*pl.* **ilea** /ˈɪliə/) (*anatomy* 解) the third part of the small INTESTINE 迴腸 ➲ compare DUODENUM, JEJUNUM ▶ **ileal** /ˈɪliəl/ *adj.*

ilk /ɪlk/ *noun* [usually sing.] (sometimes *disapproving*) type; kind 類型；種類：*the world of media people* ***and their ilk*** 新聞媒體一類人等 ◇ *I can't stand him, or any others* ***of that ilk.*** 我無法忍受他或他這類的人。

ill 0-π /ɪl/ *adj., adv., noun*
■ ***adj.*** **1** 0-π (*especially BrE*) (*NAmE* usually **sick**) [not usually before noun] suffering from an illness or disease; not feeling well 有病；不舒服：*Her father is* ***seriously ill*** *in St Luke's hospital.* 她父親住在聖路加醫院，病情很重。◇ *She* ***was taken ill*** *suddenly.* 她突然病倒了。◇ *We both started to* ***feel ill*** *shortly after the meal.* 我們倆飯後不

Collocations 詞語搭配

Illnesses 疾病

Becoming ill 生病

- **catch** a cold/an infectious disease/the flu/(*BrE*) flu/pneumonia/a virus/(*informal*) a bug 染上感冒／傳染病／流感／肺炎／病毒／小毛病
- **get** (*BrE*) ill/(*NAmE*) sick/a disease/AIDS/breast cancer/a cold/the flu/(*BrE*) flu/a migraine 患病／艾滋病／乳腺癌／感冒／流感／偏頭痛
- **come down with** a cold/the flu/(*BrE*) flu 得了感冒／流感
- **contract** a deadly disease/a serious illness/HIV/AIDS 感染致命疾病／嚴重疾病／艾滋病病毒／艾滋病
- **be infected with** a virus/a parasite/HIV 受病毒／寄生蟲／艾滋病病毒感染
- **develop** cancer/diabetes/a rash/an ulcer/symptoms of hepatitis 患上癌症／糖尿病／皮疹／潰瘍；出現肝炎症狀
- **have** a heart attack/a stroke 心臟病／中風發作
- **provoke/trigger/produce** an allergic reaction 引起／產生過敏反應
- **block/burst/rupture** a blood vessel 使血管阻塞／破裂
- **damage/sever** a nerve/an artery/a tendon 損傷／切斷神經／動脈／肌腱

Being ill 病了

- **feel** (*BrE*) ill/sick/nauseous/queasy 感到不適／想吐／噁心
- **be running** (*BrE*) a temperature/(*NAmE*) a fever 發燒
- **have** a head cold/diabetes/heart disease/lung cancer/a headache/(*BrE*) a high temperature/(*NAmE*) a fever 患傷風感冒／糖尿病／心臟病／肺癌；頭痛；發高燒
- **suffer from** asthma/malnutrition/frequent headaches/bouts of depression/a mental disorder 患哮喘／營養不良症／經常性頭痛／多發性抑鬱症／精神錯亂
- **be laid up with**/(*BrE*) **be in bed with** a cold/the flu/(*BrE*) flu/a migraine 因感冒／流感／偏頭痛而臥牀休息
- **nurse** a cold/a headache/a hangover 調治感冒／頭痛／宿醉
- **battle/fight** cancer/depression/addiction/alcoholism 與癌症／抑鬱症作鬥爭；戒癮／酒

Treatments 治療

- **examine** a patient 給病人做檢查
- **diagnose** a condition/disease/disorder 診斷疾病
- **be diagnosed with** cancer/diabetes/schizophrenia 診斷為癌症／糖尿病／精神分裂症
- **prescribe/be given/be on/take** drugs/medicine/medication/pills/painkillers/antibiotics 開／獲開／服用藥／藥片／止痛藥／抗生素
- **treat sb for** cancer/depression/shock 治療某人的癌症／抑鬱症／休克
- **have/undergo** an examination/an operation/surgery/a kidney transplant/therapy/chemotherapy/treatment for cancer 做檢查／手術／外科手術／腎移植手術／治療／化療／癌症治療
- **have/be given** an injection/(*BrE*) a flu jab/(*NAmE*) a flu shot/a blood transfusion/a scan/an X-ray 打針；接種流感疫苗；接受輸血；做掃描檢查；照 X 光
- **cure** a disease/an ailment/cancer/a headache/a patient 治療疾病／病痛／癌症／頭痛／病人
- **prevent** the spread of disease/further outbreaks/damage to the lungs 防止疾病擴散／疾病進一步爆發／對肺部造成傷害
- **be vaccinated against** the flu/(*BrE*) flu/the measles/(*BrE*) measles/polio/smallpox 接種流感／麻疹／小兒麻痹症／天花疫苗
- **enhance/boost/confer/build** immunity to a disease 增加對疾病的免疫力

久就都開始感到不適。◇ *Uncle Harry is **terminally ill** with cancer* (= he will die from his illness). 哈里叔叔癌症已到了末期。◇ *the **mentally ill*** (= people with a mental illness) 精神病患者 ◇ (*formal*) *He **fell ill** and died soon after.* 他病倒不久便去世了。➲ see also ILLNESS **2** [usually before noun] bad or harmful 壞的；不良的；有害的：*He resigned because of **ill health*** (= he was often ill). 他因健康狀況不佳而辭職。◇ *She suffered no **ill effects** from the experience.* 這次經歷沒有使她受到不良影響。◇ *a woman of **ill repute*** (= considered to be immoral) 名聲不好的女人 **3** (*formal*) that brings, or is thought to bring, bad luck 不吉利的；不祥的：*a bird of ill omen* 不祥之鳥

IDM **ˌill at ˈease** feeling uncomfortable and embarrassed 局促不安的：*I **felt ill at ease** in such formal clothes.* 我穿着這樣正式的衣服覺得很拘謹。 **it's an ˌill ˈwind (that blows nobody any good)** (*saying*) no problem is so bad that it does not bring some advantage to sb 沒有絕對的壞事；任何壞事都會有利於某些人 ➲ more at FEELING

■ **adv.** **1** (especially in compounds 尤用於構成複合詞) badly or in an unpleasant way 惡劣地；討厭地：*The animals had been grossly ill-treated.* 那些動物受到了恣意虐待。 **2** (*formal*) badly; not in an acceptable way 差勁；不足：*They live in an area ill served by public transport.* 他們住在公共交通條件很差的地區。 **3** (*formal*) only with difficulty 困難地：*We're wasting valuable time, time we can ill afford.* 我們是在浪費寶貴的時間，我們浪費不起的時間。

IDM **speak/think ˈill of sb** (*formal*) to say or think bad things about sb 說…的壞話；把…往壞處想：*Don't speak ill of the dead.* 勿議已故者之短。

■ **noun** **1** [usually pl.] (*formal*) a problem or harmful thing; an illness 問題；弊端；疾病：*social/economic ills* 社會/經濟弊病 ◇ *the ills of the modern world* 現代世界的弊端 **2** [U] (*literary*) harm; bad luck 傷害；厄運：*I may not like him, but I wish him no ill.* 我雖然不喜歡他，但我並不希望他倒運。

I'll /aɪl/ *short form* **1** I shall **2** I will

ˌill-adˈvised *adj.* not sensible; likely to cause difficulties in the future 不明智的；考慮不全面的；會造成困難的：*Her remarks were ill-advised, to say the least.* 她的話不夠謹慎，至少可以這麼說。◇ *You **would be ill-advised to** travel on your own.* 你要獨自旅行是不明智的。➲ compare WELL ADVISED ▸ **ˌill-adˈvised·ly** *adv.*

ˌill-asˈsort·ed *adj.* (of a group of people or things 人或事物) not seeming suited to each other 不相配的；不相稱的：*They seem an ill-assorted couple.* 他倆似乎不般配。

ˌill-ˈbred *adj.* rude or badly behaved, especially because you have not been taught how to behave well 粗魯的；沒禮貌的；（尤指）沒教養的 **OPP** **well bred**

ˌill-conˈcealed *adj.* (*formal*) (of feelings or expressions of feeling 感情或感情的流露) not hidden well from other people 不加掩飾的；外露的

ˌill-conˈceived *adj.* badly planned or designed 考慮不周的；構想拙劣的

ˌill-conˈsid·ered *adj.* not carefully thought about or planned 考慮欠周的；計劃不嚴密的

ˌill-deˈfined *adj.* **1** not clearly described 不清楚的；含混的：*an ill-defined role* 不明確的角色 **2** not clearly marked or easy to see 輪廓不清的；不明顯的：*an ill-defined path* 若隱若現的小徑 **OPP** **well defined**

ˌill-disˈposed *adj.* ~ (**towards sb**) (*formal*) not feeling friendly towards sb 不友好的；無好感的 **OPP** **well disposed**

il·legal **AW** /ɪˈliːɡl/ *adj.*, *noun*

■ **adj.** not allowed by the law 不合法的；非法的；違法的：*illegal immigrants/aliens* 非法移民/外僑 ◇ *It's illegal to drive through a red light.* 開車闖紅燈是違章行為。 **OPP** **legal** ▸ **il·legal·ly** **AW** /-ɡəli/ *adv.*：*an illegally parked car* 違章停放的汽車 ◇ *He entered the country illegally.* 他通過非法途徑進入了這個國家。

■ **noun** (*NAmE*) a person who lives or works in a country illegally 非法移民；非法勞工

il·legal·ity **AW** /ˌɪliˈɡæləti/ *noun* (*pl.* **-ies**) **1** [U] the state of being illegal 不合法；違法：*No illegality is suspected.* 未懷疑有違法之事。 **2** [C] an illegal act 非法行為 ➲ compare LEGALITY

il·legible /ɪˈledʒəbl/ (also **un·read·able**) *adj.* difficult or impossible to read 難以辨認的；無法辨識的；字跡模糊的：*an illegible signature* 難以辨認的簽名 **OPP** **legible** ▸ **il·legibly** *adv.* /-əbli/

il·legit·im·ate /ˌɪləˈdʒɪtəmət/ *adj.* **1** born to parents who are not married to each other 私生的；非婚生的 **2** (*formal*) not allowed by a particular set of rules or by law 不符合規定的；非法的 **SYN** **unauthorized**：*illegitimate use of company property* 不正當使用公司財產 **OPP** **legitimate** ▸ **il·legit·im·acy** /ˌɪləˈdʒɪtəməsi/ *noun* [U] **il·legit·im·ate·ly** *adv.*

ˌill-eˈquipped *adj.* ~ (**for sth**) | ~ (**to do sth**) not having the necessary equipment or skills 裝備不完善的；技術不夠的

ˌill-ˈfated (also **fated**) *adj.* (*formal*) not lucky and ending sadly, especially in death or failure 注定要倒霉的；時運不濟的；（尤指）結局悲慘的：*an ill-fated expedition* 注定不會成功的探險

ˌill-ˈfitting *adj.* not the right size or shape （大小或形狀）不合適的：*ill-fitting clothes* 不合身的衣服

ˌill-ˈfounded *adj.* (*formal*) not based on fact or truth 憑空的；無根據的；毫無理由的：*All our fears proved ill-founded.* 我們所有的擔心結果都證明是杞人憂天。 **OPP** **well founded**

ˌill-ˈgotten *adj.* (*old-fashioned* or *humorous*) obtained dishonestly or unfairly 非法得到的；來路不正的：***ill-gotten gains*** (= money that was not obtained fairly) 不義之財

ˌill ˈhealth *noun* [U] the poor condition of a person's body or mind （身心）健康狀況差；生病：*He retired early **on grounds of ill health**.* 他由於身體不好而提早退休。➲ SYNONYMS at ILLNESS

ˌill ˈhumour (*especially US* **ˌill ˈhumor**) *noun* [U, C] (*literary*) a bad mood 壞心情；壞脾氣 **OPP** **good humour** ▸ **ˌill-ˈhumoured** (*especially US* **ˌill-ˈhumored**) *adj.*

il·lib·eral /ɪˈlɪbərəl/ *adj.* (*formal*) not allowing much freedom of opinion or action 不容言論（或行動）自由的；不開明的 **SYN** **intolerant**：*illiberal policies* 限制言行自由的政策

il·licit /ɪˈlɪsɪt/ *adj.* **1** not allowed by the law 非法的；違法的 **SYN** **illegal**：*illicit drugs* 違禁藥物 **2** not approved of by the normal rules of society 違背社會常規的；不正當的：*an illicit love affair* 不正當的風流韻事 ▸ **illicit·ly** *adv.*

ˌill-inˈformed *adj.* having or showing little knowledge of sth 瞭解不夠的；信息不足的 **OPP** **well informed**

il·lit·er·ate /ɪˈlɪtərət/ *adj.*, *noun*

■ **adj.** **1** (of a person 人) not knowing how to read or write 不會讀寫的；不識字的；文盲的 **OPP** **literate** **2** (of a document or letter 文件或信函) badly written, as if by sb without much education 行文拙劣的；不通順的 **3** (usually after a noun or adverb 通常在名詞或副詞之後) not knowing very much about a particular subject area （對某學科）瞭解不多的，外行的：*computer illiterate* 計算機盲 ◇ *musically illiterate* 音樂盲 ▸ **il·lit·er·acy** /ɪˈlɪtərəsi/ *noun* [U]

■ **noun** a person who is illiterate 文盲；無知識的人

ˌill-ˈjudged *adj.* (*formal*) that has not been carefully thought about; not appropriate in a particular situation 考慮不周的；判斷不當的；不合實際情況的

ˌill-ˈmannered *adj.* (*formal*) not behaving well or politely in social situations 舉止粗魯的；不禮貌的 **SYN** **rude** **OPP** **well mannered**

ill·ness /ˈɪlnəs/ *noun*

1 [U] the state of being physically or mentally ill （身體或精神上的）疾病，病：*mental illness* 精神病 ◇ *I missed a lot of school through illness last year.* 我去年因病耽誤了很多功課。 **2** [C] a type or period of illness （某種）病；患病期：***minor/serious illnesses*** 小/重病 ◇ *childhood illnesses* 兒童患的各種病 ◇ *He died after a*

long illness. 他久病不痛而亡。➲ SYNONYMS at DISEASE
➲ COLLOCATIONS at ILL

Synonyms 同義詞辨析

illness

sickness • ill health • trouble

These are all words for the state of being physically or mentally ill. 以上各詞均指身體或精神上的不適、疾病。

illness the state of being physically or mentally ill 指身體或精神上的疾病

sickness illness; bad health 指疾病、不健康：*I recommend you get insurance against sickness and unemployment.* 我建議你辦個疾病和失業保險。

ILLNESS OR SICKNESS? 用 illness 還是 sickness？

Sickness is used especially in contexts concerning work and insurance. It is commonly found with words such as *pay*, *leave*, *absence* and *insurance*. **Illness** has a wider range of uses and is found in more general contexts. * sickness 尤用於與工作和保險有關的語境中，通常與 pay、leave、absence 和 insurance 等詞連用。illness 的用法較廣，用於較一般的語境中。

ill health (*rather formal*) the state of being physically ill or having lots of health problems 指健康狀況不佳：*She resigned because of ill health.* 她因健康狀況不佳而辭職。NOTE **Ill health** often lasts a long period of time. * ill health 常持續較長時間。

trouble illness or pain 指疾病、疼痛：*heart trouble* 心臟病 NOTE When **trouble** is used with this meaning, it is necessary to say which part of the body is affected. * trouble 用於此義時須說明疾病或疼痛所在的身體部位。

PATTERNS

- **chronic** illness/sickness/ill health
- **to suffer from** illness/sickness/ill health/heart, etc. trouble

il·logic·al AW /ɪˈlɒdʒɪkl; NAmE -ˈlɑːdʒ-/ *adj.* not sensible or thought out in a logical way 悖理的；不合邏輯的；乖戾的：*illogical behaviour/arguments* 乖戾的行為；不合邏輯的論點 ◇ *She has an illogical fear of insects.* 她毫無道理地害怕昆蟲。OPP **logical** ▸ **il·logic·al·ity** /ɪˌlɒdʒɪˈkæləti; NAmE -ˌlɑːdʒ-/ *noun* [U, C] **il·logic·al·ly** AW /-kli/ *adv.*

ˌill-ˈomened *adj.* (*formal*) (of an event or activity 事情或活動) seeming likely to be unlucky or unsuccessful because there are a lot of unlucky signs relating to it 凶多吉少的；不吉利的

ˌill-preˈpared *adj.* **1 ~ (for sth)** not ready, especially because you were not expecting sth to happen 未準備好的；（尤指）想不到的，猝不及防的：*The team was ill-prepared for a disaster on that scale.* 這樣的慘敗全隊根本就沒有料到。**2** badly planned or organized 規劃不周的；組織不嚴密的：*an ill-prepared speech* 準備不周全的講話

ˌill-ˈstarred *adj.* (*formal*) not lucky and likely to bring unhappiness or to end in failure 注定要倒霉（或失敗）的；時運不濟的：*an ill-starred marriage* 注定要失敗的婚姻

ˌill-ˈtempered *adj.* (*formal*) angry and rude or irritated, especially when this seems unreasonable 脾氣暴躁的；動輒發怒的

ˌill-ˈtimed *adj.* done or happening at the wrong time 不適時的；不合時宜的：*an ill-timed visit* 不適時的來訪 OPP **well timed**

ˌill-ˈtreat *verb* **~ sb** to treat sb in a cruel or unkind way 虐待 ▸ **ˌill-ˈtreatment** *noun* [U]：*the ill-treatment of prisoners* 對犯人的虐待

il·lu·min·ate /ɪˈluːmɪneɪt/ (also *less frequent* **il·lu·mine**) *verb* **1 ~ sth** (*formal*) to shine light on sth 照明；照亮；照射：*Floodlights illuminated the stadium.* 泛光燈照亮了體育場。◇ *The earth is illuminated by the sun.* 太陽照亮地球。**2 ~ sth** (*formal*) to make sth clearer or easier to understand 闡明；解釋 SYN **clarify**：*This text illuminates the philosopher's early thinking.* 這篇文章解釋了這位哲學家的早期思想。**3 ~ sth** to decorate a street, building, etc. with bright lights for a special occasion 用彩燈裝飾 **4 ~ sth** (*literary*) to make a person's face, etc. seem bright and excited 使容光煥發 SYN **light up**：*Her smile illuminated her entire being.* 微笑使她整個人神采奕奕。

il·lu·min·ated /ɪˈluːmɪneɪtɪd/ *adj.* [usually before noun] **1** lit with bright lights 被照明的；被照亮的：*the illuminated city at night* 夜幕中萬家燈火的城市 **2** (of books, etc. 書等) decorated with gold, silver and bright colours in a way that was done in the past, by hand 用鮮明色彩手工裝飾的；裝飾古樸華美的：*illuminated manuscripts* 裝飾華麗的手稿

il·lu·min·at·ing /ɪˈluːmɪneɪtɪŋ/ *adj.* helping to make sth clear or easier to understand 富於啟發性的：*We didn't find the examples he used particularly illuminating.* 我們覺得他採用的那些例證啟發性不是特別大。

il·lu·min·ation /ɪˌluːmɪˈneɪʃn/ *noun* **1** [U, C] light or a place that light comes from 照明；光源：*The only illumination in the room came from the fire.* 屋子裏唯一的光亮來自爐火。**2 illuminations** [pl.] (*BrE*) bright coloured lights used to decorate a town or building for a special occasion 彩燈；燈飾：*Christmas illuminations* 聖誕節的彩燈 **3** [C, usually pl.] a coloured decoration, usually painted by hand, in an old book（舊時書上通常用手工繪製的）彩飾，彩圖 **4** [U] (*formal*) understanding or explanation of sth 啟示；啟迪；闡明：*spiritual illumination* 精神上的啟發

il·lu·mine /ɪˈluːmɪn/ *verb* (*formal*) = ILLUMINATE

ˌill-ˈused *adj.* (*old-fashioned* or *formal*) badly treated 受虐待的；被糟蹋的

il·lu·sion /ɪˈluːʒn/ *noun* **1** [C, U] a false idea or belief, especially about sb or about a situation 錯誤的觀念；幻想：*She's **under the illusion that*** (= believes wrongly that) *she'll get the job.* 她存有幻想，認為她會得到那份工作。◇ *The new president **has no illusions** about the difficulties facing her country* (= she knows that the country has serious problems). 新任總統清楚地知道她的國家面臨的困難。◇ *He could no longer distinguish between illusion and reality.* 他再也分不清幻想與現實之間的區別了。**2** [C] something that seems to exist but in fact does not, or seems to be sth that it is not 幻想的事物；錯覺：*Mirrors in a room often give an illusion of space.* 房間裏的鏡子常給人一種空間增大的錯覺。◇ *The idea of absolute personal freedom is an illusion.* 絕對個人自由的觀念是一種幻想。➲ picture at OPTICAL ILLUSION

il·lu·sion·ist /ɪˈluːʒənɪst/ *noun* an entertainer who performs tricks that seem strange or impossible to believe 幻術師；魔術師

il·lu·sive /ɪˈluːsɪv/ *adj.* (*literary, rare*) not real although seeming to be 虛幻的；虛假的；迷惑人的 SYN **illusory**：*There is an illusive sense of depth.* 有一種仿真的縱深感。HELP *Illusive* is sometimes confused with *elusive* which has a different meaning. * illusive 有時與 elusive 混淆，兩者詞義不同。

il·lu·sory /ɪˈluːsəri/ *adj.* (*formal*) not real, although seeming to be 虛假的；幻覺的；迷惑人的：*an illusory sense of freedom* 虛幻的自由感

il·lus·trate 🔑 AW /ˈɪləstreɪt/ *verb* **1** 🔑 [usually passive] to use pictures, photographs, diagrams, etc. in a book, etc. 加插圖於；給（書等）做圖表：**~ sth** *an illustrated textbook* 有插圖的課本 ◇ **~ sth with sth** *His lecture was illustrated with photos taken during the expedition.* 他在演講中使用了探險時拍攝的照片。**2** 🔑 to make the meaning of sth clearer by using examples, pictures, etc.（用示例、圖畫等）說明，解釋：**~ sth** *To **illustrate my point**, let me tell you a little story.* 為了說明我的觀點，讓我來給你們講個小故事。◇ *Last year's sales figures are illustrated in Figure 2.* 圖 2 顯示了去年的銷售數字。◇ **~ how, what, etc. …** *Here's an example to illustrate what I mean.* 這兒有個例子可以說

明我的意思。➲ LANGUAGE BANK at PROCESS **3** **~ sth** | **~ how, what, etc. ...** | **~ that ...** to show that sth is true or that a situation exists 表明…真實；顯示…存在 **SYN** **demonstrate**：*The incident illustrates the need for better security measures.* 這次事件説明了加強安全措施的必要。

Language Bank 用語庫

illustrate

Referring to a chart, graph or table 描述圖或表

- This bar chart **illustrates** how many journeys people made on public transport over a three-month period. 這個柱狀圖顯示三個月期間人們乘坐公共交通往來的次數。
- This table **compares** bus, train, and taxi use between April and June. 這個表比較了四月至六月公交車、火車和出租車的使用情況。
- The results **are shown** in the chart below. 結果顯示在下面的圖表中。
- In this pie chart, the survey results **are broken down** by age. 在這個餅分圖中，調查結果按年齡劃分。
- This pie chart **breaks down** the survey results by age. 這個餅分圖按年齡對調查結果進行分類。
- **As can be seen from** these results, younger people use buses more than older people. 從結果可以看出，年輕人比老年人乘坐公交車的頻率更高。
- **According to** these figures, bus travel accounts for 60% of public transport use. 從這些數字看，乘坐公交車出行佔公共交通使用率的 60%。
- **From** the data in the above graph, **it is apparent that** buses are the most widely used form of public transport. 從上圖的數據明顯看出：公交車是公共交通中使用最廣泛的類型。

➲ Language Banks at EVIDENCE, FALL, INCREASE, PROPORTION, SURPRISING

il·lus·tra·tion **AW** /ˌɪləˈstreɪʃn/ *noun* **1** [C] a drawing or picture in a book, magazine, etc. especially one that explains sth （書、雜誌等中的）圖表，插圖：*50 full-colour illustrations* * 50 張全彩色插圖 **2** [U] the process of illustrating sth 圖解；圖示；例釋：*the art of book illustration* 書籍插圖的藝術 **3** [C, U] a story, an event or an example that clearly shows the truth about sth （説明事實的）故事，實例，示例：*The statistics are a clear illustration of the point I am trying to make* 這些統計數字清楚地闡明了我要陳述的要點。◇ *Let me, **by way of illustration**, quote from one of her poems.* 作為説明，讓我援引她的一首詩。➲ SYNONYMS at EXAMPLE

il·lus·tra·tive **AW** /ˈɪləstrətɪv; *NAmE* ɪˈlʌs-/ *adj.* (*formal*) helping to explain sth or show it more clearly 説明的；解釋性的 **SYN** **explanatory**：*an illustrative example* 示例

il·lus·tra·tor /ˈɪləstreɪtə(r)/ *noun* a person who draws or paints pictures for books, etc. （書等的）插圖畫家

il·lus·tri·ous /ɪˈlʌstriəs/ *adj.* (*formal*) very famous and much admired, especially because of what you have achieved 著名的；傑出的；卓越的 **SYN** **distinguished**：*The composer was one of many illustrious visitors to the town.* 那位作曲家是許多造訪過這個城市的傑出人物之一。◇ *a long and illustrious career* 長期卓越的事業

ˌill ˈwill *noun* [U] bad and unkind feelings towards sb 惡意；憎恨；敵意：*I bear Sue no ill will.* 我對蘇沒有敵意。

il·ly·whack·er /ˈɪliwækə(r)/ *noun* (*AustralE, informal*) a person who tricks others into giving him or her money, etc. 騙子（詐騙錢財等）**SYN** **confidence trickster**

ILO /ˌaɪ el ˈəʊ; *NAmE* ˈoʊ/ *abbr.* International Labour Organization (an organization within the United Nations concerned with work and working conditions) 國際勞工組織（全寫為 International Labour Organization，聯合國組織）

I'm /aɪm/ *short form* I am

im- ➲ IN-

image **O‑w** **AW** /ˈɪmɪdʒ/ *noun*

1 **O‑w** [C, U] the impression that a person, an organization or a product, etc. gives to the public 形象；印象；聲譽：*His public image is very different from the real person.* 他在公眾心目中的形象與他真實的本人截然不同。◇ *The advertisements are intended to improve the company's image.* 這些廣告旨在提高公司的形象。◇ *Image is very important in the music world.* 在音樂界，個人形象很重要。◇ *stereotyped images of women in children's books* 兒童圖書中千篇一律的女性形象 **2** **O‑w** [C] a mental picture that you have of what sb/sth is like or looks like（心目中的）形象，印象：*images of the past* 對過去的印象 ◇ *I had a **mental image** of what she would look like.* 我能想像出她的樣貌如何。**3** **O‑w** [C] (*formal*) a copy of sb/sth in the form of a picture or statue 畫像；雕像；塑像：*Images of deer and hunters decorate the cave walls.* 洞穴壁上裝飾着鹿和獵人的畫像。◇ *a wooden image of the Hindu god Ganesh* 印度教神靈象頭神的木雕像 **4** **O‑w** [C] a picture of sb/sth seen in a mirror, through a camera, or on a television or computer 鏡像；影像；映像；圖像：*He stared at his own image reflected in the water.* 他凝視着自己在水中的倒影。◇ *Slowly, an image began to appear on the screen.* 屏幕上慢慢地出現了一幅圖像。➲ see also MIRROR IMAGE **5** **O‑w** [C] a word or phrase used with a different meaning from its normal one, in order to describe sth in a way that produces a strong picture in the mind 比喻；意象：*poetic images of the countryside* 鄉村的詩情畫意景象

IDM **be the image of sb/sth** to look very like sb/sth else 酷似；和…非常相像：*He's the image of his father.* 他酷似他的父親。➲ see also SPITTING IMAGE

im·agery **AW** /ˈɪmɪdʒəri/ *noun* [U] **1** language that produces pictures in the minds of people reading or listening 形象的描述；意象：*poetic imagery* 詩的意象 ➲ COLLOCATIONS at LITERATURE ➲ see also METAPHOR **2** (*formal*) pictures, photographs, etc. 像；畫像；照片：*satellite imagery* (= for example, photographs of the earth taken from space) 衛星影像（如從太空拍攝地球的照片）

im·agin·able /ɪˈmædʒɪnəbl/ *adj.* **1** used with superlatives, and with *all* and *every*, to emphasize that sth is the best, worst, etc. that you can imagine, or includes every possible example（與形容詞最高級或與 all、every 連用，表示強調或概括）想像得到的：*The house has the most spectacular views imaginable.* 從這所房子可以看到所能想像的最壯麗的景色。◇ *They stock every imaginable type of pasta.* 他們備有各種能想到的意大利麵食。**2** possible to imagine 可想像的：*These technological developments were hardly imaginable 30 years ago.* 這些科技新產品在 30 年前幾乎是不可想像的。

im·agin·ary **O‑w** /ɪˈmædʒɪnəri; *NAmE* -neri/ *adj.* existing only in your mind or imagination 想像中的；幻想的；虛構的：*imaginary fears* 想像中的恐懼 ◇ *The equator is an imaginary line around the middle of the earth.* 赤道是一條假想的環繞地球腰部的線。

iˌmaginary ˈnumber *noun* (*mathematics* 數) a number expressed as the SQUARE ROOT of a negative number, especially the square root of -1 虛數 ➲ compare COMPLEX NUMBER, REAL NUMBER

im·agin·ation **O‑w** /ɪˌmædʒɪˈneɪʃn/ *noun*

1 **O‑w** [U, C] the ability to create pictures in your mind; the part of your mind that does this 想像力；想像：*a **vivid/fertile imagination*** 生動的 / 豐富的想像 ◇ *He's got no imagination.* 他缺乏想像力。◇ *It doesn't **take much imagination** to guess what she meant.* 不難猜出她的意思。◇ *I won't tell you his reaction—**I'll leave that to your imagination**.* 我不告訴你他的反應，你自己去想好了。◇ *Don't let your imagination run away with you* (= don't use too much imagination). 不要一味憑空想像。◇ *The new policies appear to have **caught the imagination of the public*** (= they find them interesting and exciting). 新出台的政策似乎恰恰投合了公眾的喜好。◇ *Nobody hates you—it's all **in your imagination**.* 沒人

討厭你，都是你在胡思亂想。◇ *(informal)* ***Use your imagination!*** (= used to tell sb that they will have to guess the answer to the question they have asked you, usually because it is obvious or embarrassing) 你自己動動腦筋嘛！ **2** [U] something that you have imagined rather than sth that exists 想像的事物；幻想物：*She was no longer able to distinguish between imagination and reality.* 她再也不能分清幻想和現實了。◇ *Is it my imagination or have you lost a lot of weight?* 是我的錯覺，還是你確實瘦了許多？ **3** [U] the ability to have new and exciting ideas 創造力；創作力：*His writing lacks imagination.* 他的作品缺乏想像。◇ ***With a little imagination**, you could turn this place into a palace.* 稍微動點腦筋，就能把這個地方變得富麗堂皇。

IDM **leave nothing/little to the imagi'nation** (of clothes 衣服) to allow more of sb's body to be seen than usual（暴露身體）沒有想像的餘地：*Her tight-fitting dress left nothing to the imagination.* 她的緊身連衣裙令身材表露無遺。➲ more at FIGMENT, STRETCH *n.*

im·agina·tive /ɪˈmædʒɪnətɪv/ *adj.* having or showing new and exciting ideas 富於想像力的；創新的 **SYN** **inventive**：*an imaginative approach/idea/child* 有創意的方法／思想／孩子 ◇ *recipes that make **imaginative** use of seasonal vegetables* 妙用時令蔬菜的菜譜 **OPP** **unimaginative** ▶ **im·agina·tive·ly** *adv.*：*The stables have been imaginatively converted into offices.* 馬房被別出心裁地改成了辦公室。

im·agine /ɪˈmædʒɪn/ *verb*
1 [T, I] to form a picture in your mind of what sth might be like 想像；設想：**~ sth** *The house was just as she had imagined it.* 這房子正是她所想像的。◇ *I can't imagine life without the children now.* 我現在無法設想沒有了孩子們的生活。◇ **~ (that)** ... *Close your eyes and imagine (that) you are in a forest.* 閉上眼睛，設想自己在森林裏。◇ **~ what, how, etc.** ... *Can you imagine what it must be like to lose your job after 20 years?* 你能想像得出幹了 20 年之後被辭退會是什麼樣的滋味嗎？◇ **~ doing sth** *She imagined walking into the office and handing in her resignation.* 她想像着自己走進辦公室，遞上辭呈。◇ *Imagine earning that much money!* 想想看，竟賺那麼多的錢！◇ **~ sb/sth doing sth** *I can just imagine him saying that!* 我確實能想到他那麼說！◇ **~ sb/sth to be/do sth** *I had imagined her to be older than that.* 我本來以為她的年齡還要大一些。◇ **~ (sb + adj./noun)** *I can imagine him really angry.* 我可以想像得出他怒氣沖沖的樣子。◇ *(informal) 'He was furious.' '**I can imagine.**'* "他氣瘋了。" "我想像得出。" **2** [T] to believe sth that is not true 誤以為；胡亂猜想；猜測：**~ (that)** ... *He's always imagining (that) we're talking about him behind his back.* 他總是胡亂猜想我們在背後說他的閒話。◇ **~ sth** *There's nobody there. You're **imagining things**.* 那裏根本沒有人。你在胡思亂想。 **3** [I, T] to think that sth is probably true 料想；認為 **SYN** **suppose, assume**：*'Can we still buy tickets for the concert?' 'I imagine so.'* "我們還能買到音樂會的票嗎？" "我想可以吧。" ◇ **~ (that)** ... *I don't imagine (that) they'll refuse.* 我認為他們不會拒絕。

im·agin·eer /ɪˌmædʒɪˈnɪə(r); *NAmE* -ˈnɪr/ *noun, verb*
■ ***noun*** a person who invents sth exciting, especially a machine for people to ride on in a THEME PARK 構想工程師（發明主題公園中的機動遊戲等）
■ ***verb*** **~ sth** to invent sth exciting, especially a machine for people to ride on in a THEME PARK 構想，發明（刺激好玩的東西，如主題公園的機動遊戲等）▶ **im·agin·eer·ing** *noun* [U]

im·aging /ˈɪmɪdʒɪŋ/ *noun* [U] *(computing* 計) the process of capturing, storing and showing an image on a computer screen 成像：*imaging software* 成像軟件

im·agin·ings /ɪˈmædʒɪnɪŋz/ *noun* [pl.] things that you imagine, that exist only in your mind 想像出的事物；幻想物

imago /ɪˈmeɪɡəʊ; ɪˈmɑːɡ-; *NAmE* -ɡoʊ/ *noun* **1** *(psychology* 心) a mental image of sb as being perfect that you do not realize you have and that influences your behaviour 無意識意象（無意識地對他人形成的理想形象） **2** *(pl.* **im·agos** or **im·agi·nes** /ɪˈmeɪdʒɪniːz; ɪˈmɑːdʒ-/) the final and fully developed adult stage of an insect, especially one with wings（尤指有翅昆蟲的）成蟲

Synonyms 同義詞辨析

imagine

think • see • envisage • envision

These words all mean to form an idea in your mind of what sb/sth might be like. 以上各詞均含想像、設想之義。

imagine to form an idea in your mind of what sb/sth might be like 指想像、設想：*The house was just as she had imagined it.* 這房子正如她所想像的。

think to imagine sth that might happen or might have happened 指猜想、想像、試想：*We couldn't think where you'd gone.* 我們猜想不出來你到哪裏去了。◇ ***Just think**—this time tomorrow we'll be lying on a beach.* 想想看，明天這個時候我們就躺在海灘上了。

see to consider sth as a future possibility; to imagine sb as sth 指設想、想像：*I can't see her changing her mind.* 我無法想像她會改變主意。◇ *His colleagues see him as a future director.* 他的同事認為他很可能是未來的負責人。

envisage *(especially BrE)* to imagine what will happen in the future 指想像、設想、展望：*I don't envisage working with him again.* 我想像不出再與他一起工作的可能。 **NOTE** The usual word for this in American English is **envision** (see below). 在美式英語中，這一意義常用 envision（見下）。

envision to imagine what a situation will be like in the future, especially a situation that you intend to work towards 指展望、想像：*They envision an equal society, free from poverty and disease.* 他們嚮往一個沒有貧窮和疾病的平等社會。 **NOTE** **Envision** is used especially in business and political contexts. In North American English it is also used as another form of the word **envisage**. * envision 尤用於商業和政治語境，在美式英語中亦作 envisage 的另一種形式：*I don't envision working with him again.* 我想像不出再與他一起工作的可能。

PATTERNS

- to imagine/see/envisage/envision sb/sth **as** sth
- to imagine/see/envisage/envision (sb) **doing sth**
- to imagine/think/see/envisage/envision **who/what/how** ...
- to imagine/think/envisage/envision **that** ...

imam /ɪˈmɑːm/ *noun* (in Islam 伊斯蘭教) **1** a religious man who leads the prayers in a MOSQUE 伊瑪目（在清真寺內主持禮拜的人） **2 Imam** the title of a religious leader 伊瑪目（伊斯蘭教領袖）

IMAX™ /ˈaɪmæks/ *noun* **1** [U] technology which allows films/movies to be shown on extremely large screens 艾麥克斯寬銀幕技術；IMAX 超大銀幕技術 **2** [C] a cinema/movie theater or screen that uses IMAX 艾麥克斯影院；艾麥克斯寬銀幕；超大銀幕

im·bal·ance /ɪmˈbæləns/ *noun* [C, U] a situation in which two or more things are not the same size or are not treated the same, in a way that is unfair or causes problems 失衡；不平衡；不公平：**~ (in/of sth)** *a global imbalance of/in power* 全球權力的不平衡 ◇ **~ (between A and B)** *Attempts are being made to **redress** (= put right) **the imbalance** between our import and export figures.* 我們正努力糾正進出口的不平衡。

im·be·cile /ˈɪmbəsiːl; *NAmE* -sl/ *noun* **1** a rude way to describe a person that you think is very stupid 笨蛋；蠢貨 **SYN** **idiot**：*They behaved like imbeciles.* 他們表現得像傻瓜。 **2** *(old-fashioned, offensive)* a person who has a very low level of intelligence 低能者；弱智者 ▶ **im·be·cile** (also **im·be·cil·ic**) *adj.* [usually before noun]：*imbecile remarks* 蠢話 **im·be·cil·ity** /ˌɪmbəˈsɪləti/ *noun* [U, C]

imbed = EMBED

im·bibe /ɪmˈbaɪb/ *verb* **1** [I, T] **~ (sth)** (*formal* or *humorous*) to drink sth, especially alcohol 喝，飲（酒等） **2** [T] **~ sth** (*formal*) to absorb sth, especially information 吸收，接受（信息等）

im·bizo /ɪmˈbiːzəʊ; *NAmE* -zoʊ/ *noun* (*pl.* **-os**) (*SAfrE*) a meeting, especially one between politicians and members of the public, that is held in order to discuss general issues or a particular problem 討論會；（尤指政界人士和公眾的）對話會：*a government imbizo on poverty* 政府關於貧困問題的討論會 ◇ *The minister of labour will be holding an imbizo with farmers in the area.* 勞工部長將與這一地區的農民舉行對話會。

im·bro·glio /ɪmˈbrəʊliəʊ; *NAmE* ɪmˈbroʊlioʊ/ *noun* (*pl.* **-os**) (*formal*) a complicated situation that causes confusion or embarrassment, especially one that is political（尤指政治上）混亂複雜的局面，尷尬的處境

imbue /ɪmˈbjuː/ *verb* [often passive] **~ sb/sth (with sth)** (*formal*) to fill sb/sth with strong feelings, opinions or values 使充滿，灌輸，激發（強烈感情、想法或價值） **SYN** **infuse**：*Her voice was imbued with an unusual seriousness.* 她的聲音裏充滿着一種不尋常的嚴肅語氣。◇ *He was imbued with a desire for social justice.* 他滿懷着尋求社會正義的願望。

IMF /ˌaɪ em ˈef/ *abbr.* International Monetary Fund (the organization within the United Nations which is concerned with trade and economic development) 國際貨幣基金組織（聯合國下屬組織，關注貿易和經濟的發展）

im·i·tate /ˈɪmɪteɪt/ *verb* **1 ~ sb/sth** to copy sb/sth 模仿；仿效：*Her style of painting has been imitated by other artists.* 她的繪畫風格為其他畫家所模仿。◇ *Art imitates Nature.* 藝術是對大自然的仿製。◇ *Teachers provide a model for children to imitate.* 教師是孩子仿效的典範。◇ *No computer can imitate the complex functions of the human brain.* 任何計算機都無法模擬人腦的複雜功能。 **2 ~ sb** to copy the way a person speaks or behaves, in order to amuse people 模仿（某人的講話、舉止）；作滑稽模仿 **SYN** **mimic**：*She knew that the girls used to imitate her and laugh at her behind her back.* 她知道那些女孩子過去常在背地裏模仿她、嘲笑她。

imi·ta·tion /ˌɪmɪˈteɪʃn/ *noun* **1** [C] a copy of sth, especially sth expensive 仿製品；贋品：*a* ***poor/cheap imitation*** *of the real thing* 低劣的仿製品 ◇ *This latest production is a* ***pale imitation*** *of the original* (= it is not nearly as good). 最新推出的製作遠不如它所依據的原著精彩。◇ *imitation leather/pearls* 人造革；假珍珠 ➲ SYNONYMS at ARTIFICIAL **2** [U] the act of copying sb/sth 模仿；效仿：*A child learns to talk by imitation.* 小孩子通過模仿學會說話。◇ *Many corporate methods have been adopted by American managers* ***in imitation of*** *Japanese practice.* 美國的營商者採用了很多取法日本的公司經營之道。 **3** [C] an act of copying the way sb talks and behaves, especially to make people laugh 模仿（某人）的言談舉止；（尤指）滑稽模仿 **SYN** **impersonation, impression**：*He* ***does an imitation of*** *Barack Obama.* 他滑稽地模仿巴拉克•奧巴馬。

imi·ta·tive /ˈɪmɪtətɪv; *NAmE* -teɪtɪv/ *adj.* (*formal*, sometimes *disapproving*) that copies sb/sth 模仿的；仿製的；仿效的：*movies that encourage imitative crime* 鼓勵模擬電影中犯罪的電影 ◇ *His work has been criticized for being imitative and shallow.* 他的作品被批評為抄襲而且膚淺。

imi·ta·tor /ˈɪmɪteɪtə(r)/ *noun* a person or thing that copies sb/sth else 模仿者；模擬…的人（或事物）：*The band's success has inspired hundreds of would-be imitators.* 樂隊的成功激勵了數以百計未來的追隨者。

im·macu·late /ɪˈmækjələt/ *adj.* **1** extremely clean and tidy 特別整潔的 **SYN** **spotless**：*She always looks immaculate.* 她總是打扮得乾淨利落。◇ *an immaculate uniform/room* 整潔的制服／房間 **2** containing no mistakes 無誤的；無過失的 **SYN** **perfect**：*an immaculate performance* 完美的演出 ▸ **im·macu·late·ly** *adv.*：*immaculately dressed* 衣着整潔

the Im͵maculate Conˈception *noun* [sing.] (*religion* 宗) the Christian belief that the Virgin Mary's soul was free from ORIGINAL SIN from the moment of her CONCEPTION 聖母無原罪始胎（基督教信條，認為瑪利亞自懷胎耶穌就不再受原罪的影響）

im·man·ent /ˈɪmənənt/ *adj.* (*formal*) present as a natural part of sth; present everywhere 內在的；固有的；無所不在的

im·ma·ter·ial /ˌɪməˈtɪəriəl; *NAmE* -ˈtɪr-/ *adj.* **1** [not usually before noun] not important in a particular situation 不重要；無關緊要 **SYN** **irrelevant**：*The cost is immaterial.* 費用並不重要。◇ **~ to sb/sth** *It is immaterial to me whether he stays or goes.* 他的去留與我無關。 **2** (*formal*) not having a physical form 無形體的；非物質的：*an immaterial God* 無形的上帝 **OPP** **material**

im·ma·ture **AW** /ˌɪməˈtjʊə(r); *NAmE* -ˈtʃʊr; -ˈtʊr/ *adj.* **1** behaving in a way that is not sensible and is typical of people who are much younger（行為）不成熟的，不夠老練的，幼稚的：*immature behaviour* 不成熟的行為 **2** not fully developed or grown 未長成的；發育未全的：*immature plants* 未成長的植物 **OPP** **mature** ▸ **im·ma·tur·ity** **AW** /ˌɪməˈtjʊərəti; *NAmE* -ˈtʃʊr-; -ˈtʊr-/ *noun* [U]

im·meas·ur·able /ɪˈmeʒərəbl/ *adj.* (*formal*) too large, great etc. to be measured 不可估量的；無限的；無窮的：*to cause immeasurable harm* 造成不可估量的損害 ▸ **im·meas·ur·ably** /-bli/ *adv.*：*Housing standards improved immeasurably after the war.* 戰後住房水平大大提高。◇ *Stress has an immeasurably more serious effect on our lives than we realize.* 壓力對我們的生活造成的影響比我們意識到的要嚴重得多。

im·me·di·acy /ɪˈmiːdiəsi/ *noun* [U] (*formal*) **1** the quality in sth that makes it seem as if it is happening now, close to you and is therefore important, urgent, etc. 直接性；即時性；直觀性；迫切性：*the* ***immediacy of*** *threat* 威脅的迫切性 ◇ *Email lacks the immediacy of online chat.* 電子郵件缺乏在線交談的即時性。 **2** lack of delay; speed 立即；迅速：*Our aim is immediacy of response to emergency calls.* 我們的目標是對緊急求救電話立刻作出回應。

im·me·di·ate 🔑 /ɪˈmiːdiət/ *adj.* **1** 🔑 happening or done without delay 立即的；立刻的 **SYN** **instant**：*an* ***immediate reaction/response*** 即時的反應／回應 ◇ *to take* ***immediate action*** 立刻採取行動 **2** 🔑 [usually before noun] existing now and needing urgent attention 目前的；當前的；迫切的：*Our immediate concern is to help the families of those who died.* 我們的當務之急是幫助那些死者的親屬。◇ *The effects of global warming, while not immediate, are potentially catastrophic.* 全球氣溫上升的後果雖然並非即時發生，但可能潛伏着大災難。◇ *The hospital says she's out of* ***immediate danger.*** 醫院說她眼下已沒有危險。 **3** 🔑 [only before noun] next to or very close to a particular place or time 接近的；附近的；緊接的：*in the* ***immediate vicinity*** 近在咫尺 ◇ *The prospects for the* ***immediate future*** *are good.* 短期內前景樂觀。◇ *The director is standing on her immediate right.* 主管就挨在她的右邊站着。◇ *my immediate predecessor in the job* (= the person who had the job just before me) 我的職位的前一任 **4** [only before noun] nearest in relationship or rank（關係或級別）最接近的，直系的，直接的：*The funeral was attended by her* ***immediate family*** (= her parents, children, brothers and sisters) *only.* 只有她的直系親屬參加了葬禮。◇ *He is my* ***immediate superior*** (= the person directly above me) *in the company.* 他在公司裏是我的頂頭上司。 **5** [only before noun] having a direct effect（作用）直接的：*The immediate cause of death is unknown.* 造成死亡的直接原因不明。 **IDM** see EFFECT *n.*

im·me·di·ate·ly 🔑 /ɪˈmiːdiətli/ *adv., conj.*

■ ***adv.*** **1** 🔑 without delay 立即；馬上；即刻 **SYN** **at once**：*She answered almost immediately.* 她幾乎立刻就回答了。◇ *The point of my question may not be immediately apparent.* 我的問題的要點可能不是一下子就能看出來的。 **2** 🔑 (usually with prepositions 通常與介詞連用) next to or very close to a particular place or time 接近；緊接；附近：*Turn right immediately after the church.* 一過教堂就向右拐。◇ *the years immediately before the war* 戰前的最後幾年 **3** 🔑 (usually with past participles

通常與過去分詞連用) closely and directly 緊接地；直接地：*Counselling is being given to those most immediately affected by the tragedy.* 目前正在向慘劇的最直接受害者提供輔導服務。

■ ***conj.*** (*especially BrE*) as soon as 一…就；即刻：*Immediately she'd gone, I remembered her name.* 她剛走開我就想起了她的名字。

im·me·mor·ial /ˌɪməˈmɔːriəl/ *adj.* (*formal* or *literary*) that has existed for longer than people can remember 古老的；遠古的；無法追憶的：*an immemorial tradition* 古老的傳統 ◇ *My family has lived in this area* ***from time immemorial*** (= for hundreds of years). 我的家族在這個地區已經生活了不知有多少年了。

im·mense /ɪˈmens/ *adj.* extremely large or great 極大的；巨大的 **SYN enormous**：*There is still an immense amount of work to be done.* 還有非常非常多的工作要做。◇ *The benefits are immense.* 效益是極大的。◇ *a project of immense importance* 極其重要的工程

im·mense·ly /ɪˈmensli/ *adv.* extremely; very much 極端地；非常；極大地 **SYN enormously**：*immensely popular/difficult/grateful* 非常受歡迎／艱難／感激 ◇ *We enjoyed ourselves immensely.* 我們快活極了。

im·mens·ity /ɪˈmensəti/ *noun* [U] the large size of sth 巨大；廣大：*the immensity of the universe* 宇宙的浩瀚無垠 ◇ *We were overwhelmed by the sheer immensity of the task.* 任務太重，把我們都嚇倒了。

im·merse /ɪˈmɜːs; *NAmE* ɪˈmɜːrs/ *verb* **1 ~ sb/sth (in sth)** to put sb/sth into a liquid so that they or it are completely covered 使浸沒於 **2 ~ yourself/sb in sth** to become or make sb completely involved in sth （使）深陷於，沉浸在：*She immersed herself in her work.* 她埋頭工作。◇ *Clare and Phil were immersed in conversation in the corner.* 克萊爾和菲爾在角落裏深談。

im·mer·sion /ɪˈmɜːʃn; *NAmE* ɪˈmɜːrʃn; -ʒn/ *noun* [U] **1 ~ (in sth)** the act of putting sb/sth into a liquid so that they or it are completely covered; the state of being completely covered by a liquid 浸沒；浸：*Immersion in cold water resulted in rapid loss of heat.* 浸泡在冷水中導致熱量迅速散失。◇ *baptism by total immersion* (= putting the whole body underwater) 浸水式洗禮 **2 ~ (in sth)** the state of being completely involved in sth 沉浸；專心；陷入：*his long immersion in politics* 他的長期潛心從政 ◇ *a two-week immersion course in French* (= in which the student will hear and use only French) 兩週的沉浸式法語課程（學生身處完全的法語環境中）

imˈmersion heater *noun* (*BrE*) a device that provides hot water for a house by heating water in a tank （家用）浸沒式加熱器

im·mer·sive /ɪˈmɜːsɪv; *NAmE* ɪˈmɜːrs-/ *adj.* (*technical* 術語) used to describe a computer system or image that seems to surround the user（計算機系統或圖像）沉浸式虛擬現實的

im·mi·grant **AW** /ˈɪmɪɡrənt/ *noun* a person who has come to live permanently in a country that is not their own （外來）移民；外僑：***immigrant communities/families/workers*** 僑民社區／家庭／勞工 ◇ *illegal immigrants* 非法移民 ➲ COLLOCATIONS at RACE ➲ compare EMIGRANT, MIGRANT (2)

im·mi·grate **AW** /ˈɪmɪɡreɪt/ *verb* [I] **~ (to …) (from …)** (*especially NAmE*) to come and live permanently in a country after leaving your own country （從外地）移居；移民 ➲ compare EMIGRATE

im·mi·gra·tion **AW** /ˌɪmɪˈɡreɪʃn/ *noun* [U] **1** the process of coming to live permanently in a country that is not your own; the number of people who do this 移居（入境）；移民人數：*laws restricting immigration into the US* 美國限制外來移民的法律 ◇ *a rise/fall in immigration* 移民人數的增加／減少 ◇ *immigration officers* 移民局官員 ➲ COLLOCATIONS at RACE ➲ compare EMIGRATION **2** (also **immiˈgration control**) the place at a port, an airport, etc. where the passports and other documents of people coming into a country are checked 移民局檢查站：*to go through immigration* 通過移民局檢查

im·mi·nent /ˈɪmɪnənt/ *adj.* (especially of sth unpleasant 尤指不愉快的事) likely to happen very soon 即將發生的；臨近的：*the imminent threat of invasion* 迫在眉睫的入侵威脅 ◇ *The system is* ***in imminent danger of*** *collapse.* 這個體制面臨着崩潰的危險。◇ *An announcement about his resignation is imminent.* 馬上就要宣佈他的辭職。▶ **im·mi·nence** /-əns/ *noun* [U]：*the imminence of death* 死亡的逼近 **im·mi·nent·ly** *adv.*

im·mis·cible /ɪˈmɪsəbl/ *adj.* (*technical* 術語) (of liquids 液體) that cannot be mixed together 不互溶的；非混相的 **OPP miscible**

im·mo·bile /ɪˈməʊbaɪl; *NAmE* ɪˈmoʊbl/ *adj.* **1** not moving 不動的；靜止的 **SYN motionless**：*She stood immobile by the window.* 她一動不動地靠窗站着。 **2** unable to move 不能移動的；不能活動的：*His illness has left him completely immobile.* 他的病使他完全喪失了活動能力。**OPP mobile** ▶ **im·mo·bil·ity** /ˌɪməˈbɪləti/ *noun* [U]

im·mo·bil·ize (*BrE* also **-ise**) /ɪˈməʊbəlaɪz; *NAmE* ɪˈmoʊ-/ *verb* **~ sth/sb** to prevent sth/sb from moving or from working normally 使不動；使不能正常運作：*a device to immobilize the car engine in case of theft* 遇到有人盜車時使汽車引擎發動不了的裝置 ◇ *Always immobilize a broken leg immediately.* 腿斷了應立即避免挪動。▶ **im·mo·bil·iza·tion**, **-isa·tion** /ɪˌməʊbəlaɪˈzeɪʃn; *NAmE* ɪˌmoʊbələˈz-/ *noun* [U]

im·mo·bil·izer (also **-iser**) /ɪˈməʊbəlaɪzə(r); *NAmE* ɪˈmoʊ-/ *noun* a device that is fitted to a car to stop it moving if sb tries to steal it 汽車防盜器（遇到有人盜車時使汽車開不動的裝置）

im·mod·er·ate /ɪˈmɒdərət; *NAmE* ɪˈmɑːd-/ *adj.* [usually before noun] (*formal, disapproving*) extreme; not reasonable 極端的；不適度的；不合理的；過度的 **SYN excessive**：*immoderate drinking* 無節制的飲酒 **OPP moderate** ▶ **im·mod·er·ate·ly** *adv.*

im·mod·est /ɪˈmɒdɪst; *NAmE* ɪˈmɑːd-/ *adj.* **1** (*disapproving*) having or showing a very high opinion of yourself and your abilities 自負的；傲慢的 **SYN conceited** **2** not considered to be socially acceptable by most people, especially concerning sexual behaviour 不正派的；不合禮儀的；猥褻的：*an immodest dress* 有傷風化的連衣裙 **OPP modest**

im·mol·ate /ˈɪməleɪt/ *verb* **~ sb** (*formal*) to kill sb by burning them 燒死 ▶ **im·mol·ation** /ˌɪməˈleɪʃn/ *noun* [U]

im·moral 🔑 /ɪˈmɒrəl; *NAmE* ɪˈmɔːr-; ɪˈmɑːr-/ *adj.* **1** 🔑 (of people and their behaviour 人及行為) not considered to be good or honest by most people 不道德的；邪惡的：*It's immoral to steal.* 偷盜是不道德的。◇ *There's nothing immoral about wanting to earn more money.* 想多賺點錢沒什麼不道德。 **2** 🔑 not following accepted standards of sexual behaviour 放蕩的；淫蕩的：*an immoral act/life/person* 淫蕩的舉動／生活／人 ◇ *They were charged with living off* ***immoral earnings*** (= money earned by working as a PROSTITUTE). 她們被控靠賣淫為生。➲ compare AMORAL, MORAL ▶ **im·mor·al·ity** /ˌɪməˈræləti/ *noun* [U, C] (*pl.* **-ies**)：*the immorality of war* 戰爭的邪惡 ◇ *a life of immorality* 淫蕩的生活 **im·mor·al·ly** /ɪˈmɒrəli; *NAmE* ɪˈmɔːr-; ɪˈmɑːr-/ *adv.*

im·mor·tal /ɪˈmɔːtl; *NAmE* ɪˈmɔːrtl/ *adj., noun*

■ ***adj.*** **1** that lives or lasts for ever 長生的；永世的；不朽的：*The soul is immortal.* 靈魂不滅。**OPP mortal** **2** famous and likely to be remembered for ever 流芳百世的；名垂千古的：*the immortal Goethe* 名垂千古的歌德 ◇ *In the immortal words of Henry Ford, 'If it ain't broke, don't fix it.'* 按照亨利 • 福特的不朽名言："如果東西沒壞掉，就不要去修理它。"

■ ***noun*** **1** a person who is so famous that they will be remembered for ever 不朽的人物；名垂千古的人物：*She is one of the Hollywood immortals.* 她是一位千古流芳的好萊塢名人。 **2** a god or other BEING who is believed to live for ever 神；永生不滅者

im·mor·tal·ity /ˌɪmɔːˈtæləti; *NAmE* ˌɪmɔːrˈt-/ *noun* [U] the state of being immortal 永生；不朽；不滅：*belief in the immortality of the soul* 靈魂不滅的信念 ◇ *He is well on his way to showbusiness immortality.* 他很快就會成為娛樂界永世流芳的人物。

im·mor·tal·ize (*BrE* also **-ise**) /ɪˈmɔːtəlaɪz; *NAmE* ɪˈmɔːrt-/ *verb* **~ sb/sth (in sth)** to prevent sb/sth from being forgotten in the future, especially by mentioning them in literature, making films/movies about them, painting them, etc. 使不朽，使名垂千古（尤指通過文學藝術作品等）：*The poet fell in love with her and immortalized her in his verse.* 詩人愛上了她，並以詩歌使她名傳後世。

im·mov·able /ɪˈmuːvəbl/ *adj.* **1** [usually before noun] that cannot be moved 不能移動的；固定的：*an immovable object* 固定的物體 **2** (of a person or an opinion, etc. 人、主張等) impossible to change or persuade 不動搖的；無法說服的：*On this issue he is completely immovable.* 他在這個問題上堅定不移。

im·mune /ɪˈmjuːn/ *adj.* [not usually before noun] **1 ~ (to sth)** that cannot catch or be affected by a particular disease or illness 有免疫力：*Adults are often immune to German measles.* 成人往往對風疹有免疫力。 **2 ~ (to sth)** not affected by sth 不受影響：*You'll eventually become immune to criticism.* 你終究會變得不在乎批評了。 **3 ~ (from sth)** protected from sth and therefore able to avoid it 受保護；免除；豁免 SYN **exempt**：*No one should be immune from prosecution.* 任何人都不應免於被起訴。

im,mune res'ponse *noun* (*biology* 生) the reaction of the body to the presence of an ANTIGEN (= a substance that can cause disease) 免疫應答（機體對抗原的應答）

im'mune system *noun* the system in your body that produces substances to help it fight against infection and disease 免疫系統

im·mun·ity /ɪˈmjuːnəti/ *noun* [U, C] (*pl.* **-ies**) **1** the body's ability to avoid or not be affected by infection and disease 免疫力：**~ (to sth)** *immunity to infection* 對傳染病的免疫力 ◇ **~ (against sth)** *The vaccine provides longer immunity against flu.* 這種疫苗對流感的免疫效力時間較長。➲ COLLOCATIONS at ILL **2 ~ (from sth)** the state of being protected from sth 受保護；豁免；免除：*The spies were all granted immunity from prosecution.* 這些間諜都獲得免予公訴。◇ ***parliamentary/congressional immunity*** (= protection against particular laws that is given to politicians) 議會／國會豁免權 ◇ *Officials of all member states receive certain privileges and immunities.* 各成員國的官員均享有某些特權和豁免權。➲ see also DIPLOMATIC IMMUNITY

im·mun·ize (*BrE* also **-ise**) /ˈɪmjunaɪz/ *verb* **~ sb/sth (against sth)** to protect a person or an animal from a disease, especially by giving them an INJECTION of a VACCINE （尤指通過注射疫苗）使免疫 ➲ compare INOCULATE, VACCINATE ▸ **im·mun·iza·tion, -isa·tion** /ˌɪmjunaɪˈzeɪʃn; *NAmE* -nəˈz-/ *noun* [U, C]：*an immunization programme to prevent epidemics* 防止流行病的免疫注射方案

im·muno·defi·ciency /ɪˌmjuːnəʊdɪˈfɪʃnsi; *NAmE* -noʊd-/ (also **im'mune deficiency**) *noun* [U] a medical condition in which your body does not have the normal ability to resist infection 免疫缺陷：*human immunodeficiency virus or HIV* 人體免疫缺陷病毒，即 HIV

im·mun·ology /ˌɪmjuˈnɒlədʒi; *NAmE* -ˈnɑːl-/ *noun* [U] the scientific study of protection against disease 免疫學 ▸ **im·muno·logic·al** /ˌɪmjunəˈlɒdʒɪkl; *NAmE* -ˈlɑːdʒɪkl/ *adj.*

im·muno·sup·pres·sion /ˌɪmjunəʊsəˈpreʃn; *NAmE* -noʊ-/ *noun* [U] (*medical* 醫) the act of stopping the body from reacting against ANTIGENS, for example in order to prevent the body from rejecting a new organ 免疫抑制 ▸ **im·muno·sup·pres·sant** /ˌɪmjunəʊsəˈpresənt; *NAmE* -noʊ-/ *noun*

im·mure /ɪˈmjʊə(r); *NAmE* ɪˈmjʊr/ *verb* **~ sb** (*literary*) to shut sb in a place so that they cannot get out 禁閉；監禁 SYN **imprison**

im·mut·able /ɪˈmjuːtəbl/ *adj.* (*formal*) that cannot be changed; that will never change 不可改變的；永恆不變的 SYN **unchangeable** ▸ **im·mut·abil·ity** /ɪˌmjuːtəˈbɪləti/ *noun* [U]

imp /ɪmp/ *noun* **1** (in stories) a small creature like a little man, that has magic powers and behaves badly （故事中的）小惡魔，小魔鬼 **2** a child who behaves badly, but not in a serious way 小淘氣；頑童

im·pact AW *noun, verb*

■ ***noun*** /ˈɪmpækt/ [C, usually sing., U] **1 ~ (of sth) (on sb/sth)** the powerful effect that sth has on sb/sth 巨大影響；強大作用：*the environmental impact of tourism* 旅遊事業對環境的巨大影響 ◇ *The report assesses the impact of AIDS on the gay community.* 這個報告評估了艾滋病對同性戀群體的影響。◇ *Her speech made a profound impact on everyone.* 她的講話對每個人都有深遠的影響。◇ *Businesses are beginning to feel the full impact of the recession.* 工商企業開始感受到了經濟衰退的全面衝擊。 **2** the act of one object hitting another; the force with which this happens 撞擊；衝撞；衝擊力：*craters made by meteorite impacts* 隕石撞擊而成的隕石坑 ◇ *The impact of the blow knocked Jack off balance.* 這一記猛擊把傑克打了個趔趄。◇ *The bomb explodes **on impact*** (= when it hits something). 炸彈受到撞擊就爆炸。◇ *The car is fitted with **side impact** bars* (= to protect it from a blow from the side). 這輛車的兩側都安裝了保險槓。

■ ***verb*** /ɪmˈpækt/ **1** [I, T] to have an effect on sth （對某事物）有影響，有作用 SYN **affect**：**~ on/upon sth** *Her father's death impacted greatly on her childhood years.* 父親去世對她的童年造成巨大影響。◇ **~ sth** (*business* 商) *The company's performance was impacted by the high value of the pound.* 公司的業績受到了英鎊高值的衝擊。 **2** [I, T] **~ (on/upon/with) sth** (*formal*) to hit sth with great force 衝擊；撞擊

im·pact·ed /ɪmˈpæktɪd/ *adj.* (of a tooth 牙齒) that cannot grow correctly because it is under another tooth 阻生的

im·pair /ɪmˈpeə(r); *NAmE* ɪmˈper/ *verb* **~ sth** (*formal*) to damage sth or make sth worse 損害；削弱 ➲ SYNONYMS at DAMAGE

im·paired /ɪmˈpeəd; *NAmE* ɪmˈperd/ *adj.* **1** damaged or not functioning normally 受損的；損壞的；出毛病的：*impaired vision/memory* 受損的視力／記憶力 **2 -im·paired** having the type of physical or mental problem mentioned 有（身體或智力）缺陷的；有…障礙的：*hearing-impaired children* 聽力受損的兒童 ◇ *Nowadays we say someone is 'speech-impaired', not dumb.* 現在我們說某個人"有語言障礙"，而不說是啞巴。➲ note at DISABLED

im·pair·ment /ɪmˈpeəmənt; *NAmE* -ˈperm-/ *noun* [U, C] (*technical* 術語) the state of having a physical or mental condition which means that part of your body or brain does not work correctly; a particular condition of this sort （身體或智力方面的）缺陷，障礙，損傷；某種缺陷：*impairment of the functions of the kidney* 腎功能障礙 ◇ *visual impairments* 視力受損

im·pala /ɪmˈpɑːlə/ *noun* (*pl.* **im·pala** or **im·palas**) an African ANTELOPE with curled horns 黑斑羚（棲息在非洲，角彎曲）

im·pale /ɪmˈpeɪl/ *verb* **1 ~ sth (on sth)** to push a sharp pointed object through sth（用尖物）刺穿 SYN **spear**：*She impaled a lump of meat on her fork.* 她用叉子戳起一塊肉。 **2 ~ sb/yourself on sth** if you **impale** yourself on sth, or **are impaled** on it, you have a sharp pointed object pushed into you and you may be caught somewhere by it （被）刺中，穿透：*He had fallen and been impaled on some iron railings.* 他摔下去，穿在了鐵欄杆上。

im·palp·able /ɪmˈpælpəbl/ *adj.* (*formal*) **1** that cannot be felt physically 觸摸不到的；感覺不着的 **2** very difficult to understand 難以理解的；難懂的 OPP **palpable**

im·panel (also **em·panel**) /ɪmˈpænl/ *verb* (**-ll-**, *US* **-l-**) **~ sb/sth** (*especially US*) to choose the members of a JURY in a court case; to choose sb as a member of a JURY 選任（陪審員）；選任…為陪審員

im·part /ɪmˈpɑːt; *NAmE* ɪmˈpɑːrt/ *verb* (*formal*) **1 ~ sth (to sb)** to pass information, knowledge, etc. to other people 通知；透露；傳授 SYN **convey** **2 ~ sth (to sth)** to give a particular quality to sth 把（某性質）賦予；將…給予 SYN **lend**：*The spice imparts an Eastern flavour to the dish.* 這種調味品給菜肴添加了一種東方風味。

im·par·tial /ɪmˈpɑːʃl; *NAmE* ɪmˈpɑːrʃl/ *adj.* not supporting one person or group more than another 公正的；不偏不倚的；中立的 SYN **neutral, unbiased**：

*an **impartial** inquiry/observer* 公正的調查／觀察者 ◇ *to give **impartial advice*** 提出不偏不倚的建議 ◇ *As chairman, I must remain impartial.* 作為主席，我必須保持中立。 OPP **partial** ▸ **im·par·ti·al·ity** /ˌɪmˌpɑːʃiˈæləti; NAmE -ˌpɑːrʃi-/ *noun* [U] **im·par·tial·ly** /-ʃəli/ *adv.*

im·pass·able /ɪmˈpɑːsəbl; NAmE -ˈpæs-/ *adj.* (of a road, an area etc. 道路、地區等) impossible to travel on or through, especially because it is in bad condition or it has been blocked by sth 不能通行的（尤指因路況惡劣或被阻斷） OPP **passable**

im·passe /ˈæmpɑːs; NAmE ˈɪmpæs/ *noun* [usually sing.] a difficult situation in which no progress can be made because the people involved cannot agree what to do 僵局；絕境 SYN **deadlock**：*to **break/end the impasse*** 打破／結束僵局 ◇ *Negotiations have **reached an impasse**.* 談判已陷入僵局。

im·pas·sioned /ɪmˈpæʃnd/ *adj.* [usually before noun] (usually of speech 通常指講話) showing strong feelings about sth 充滿激情的；熱烈的 SYN **fervent**：*an **impassioned plea/speech/defence*** 熱切的懇求；充滿激情的講話／辯護

im·pas·sive /ɪmˈpæsɪv/ *adj.* not showing any feeling or emotion 無表情的；無動於衷的；不動聲色的 SYN **emotionless**：*her **impassive expression/face*** 她冷漠的表情／面容 ▸ **im·pas·sive·ly** *adv.*

im·pa·tient 0-ᴡ /ɪmˈpeɪʃnt/ *adj.*
1 0-ᴡ annoyed or irritated by sb/sth, especially because you have to wait for a long time 不耐煩的；沒有耐心的：*I'd been waiting for twenty minutes and I was getting impatient.* 我等了二十分鐘，有點不耐煩了。◇ **~ (with sb/sth)** *Try not to be too impatient with her.* 盡量別對她太沒耐心。◇ **~ (at sth)** *Sarah was becoming increasingly impatient at their lack of interest.* 薩拉對他們的缺乏興趣的情況越來越不能忍耐了。◇ *He waved them away with an impatient gesture.* 他厭煩地揮手把他們打發走了。
2 0-ᴡ wanting to do sth soon; wanting sth to happen soon 急於；熱切期待：**~ to do sth** *She was clearly impatient to leave.* 她顯然是迫不及待地想離開。◇ **~ for sth** *impatient for change* 急於求變 **3 ~ of sb/sth** (*formal*) unable or unwilling to accept sth unpleasant（對不愉快的事）不能容忍，不願接受：*impatient of criticism* 不願接受批評 ▸ **im·pa·tience** /ɪmˈpeɪʃns/ *noun* [U]：*She was bursting with impatience to tell me the news.* 她迫不及待地要告訴我這個消息。 **im·pa·tient·ly** *adv.*：*We sat waiting impatiently for the movie to start.* 我們坐着，焦急地等待電影開演。

im·peach /ɪmˈpiːtʃ/ *verb* **1 ~ sb (for sth)** (of a court or other official body, especially in the US 尤指美國的法庭或其他官方機構) to charge an important public figure with a serious crime 控告（顯要公職人員）犯重大罪行；彈劾 **2 ~ sth** (*formal*) to raise doubts about sth 懷疑 SYN **question**：*to impeach sb's motives* 懷疑某人的動機 ▸ **im·peach·ment** *noun* [U, C]

im·peach·able /ɪmˈpiːtʃəbl/ *adj.* (*especially US*) (of a crime 罪行) for which a politician or a person who works for the government can be impeached 會招致控告（或彈劾）的：*an impeachable offense* 可彈劾的罪行

im·pec·cable /ɪmˈpekəbl/ *adj.* without mistakes or faults 無錯誤的；無瑕疵的；完美的 SYN **perfect**：***impeccable manners/taste*** 無可挑剔的舉止／品味 ◇ *Her written English is impeccable.* 她寫的英語無可挑剔。◇ *He was dressed in a suit and an impeccable white shirt.* 他身穿一套禮服和一件潔白的襯衣。 ▸ **im·pec·cably** /-bli/ *adv.*：*to behave impeccably* 舉止無可挑剔 ◇ *impeccably dressed* 穿着十分得體

im·pe·cu·ni·ous /ˌɪmpɪˈkjuːniəs/ *adj.* (*formal or humorous*) having little or no money 貧窮的；不名一文的 SYN **poor, penniless**

im·ped·ance /ɪmˈpiːdns/ *noun* [U] (*physics* 物) a measurement of the total RESISTANCE of a piece of electrical equipment, etc. to the flow of an ALTERNATING CURRENT 阻抗；全電阻

im·pede /ɪmˈpiːd/ *verb* [often passive] **~ sth** (*formal*) to delay or stop the progress of sth 阻礙；阻止 SYN **hinder, hamper**：*Work on the building was impeded by severe weather.* 樓房的施工因天氣惡劣而停了下來。

im·pedi·ment /ɪmˈpedɪmənt/ *noun* **1 ~ (to sth)** (*formal*) something that delays or stops the progress of sth 妨礙；阻礙；障礙 SYN **obstacle**：*The level of inflation is a serious impediment to economic recovery.* 通貨膨脹是影響經濟復蘇的嚴重障礙。 **2** a physical problem that makes it difficult to speak normally 口吃；結巴：*a speech impediment* 言語障礙

im·pedi·menta /ɪmˌpedɪˈmentə/ *noun* [pl.] (*formal or humorous*) the bags and other equipment that you take with you, especially when travelling, and that are difficult to carry 行囊；妨礙行進的重負（行李）；輜重

impel /ɪmˈpel/ *verb* (**-ll-**) (*formal*) if an idea or feeling **impels** you to do sth, you feel as if you are forced to do it 促使；驅策；迫使：**~ sb to do sth** *He felt impelled to investigate further.* 他覺得有必要作進一步調查。◇ **~ sb (to sth)** *There are various reasons that impel me to that conclusion.* 有各種原因促使我作出那個結論。

im·pend·ing /ɪmˈpendɪŋ/ *adj.* [only before noun] (usually of an unpleasant event 通常指不愉快的事) that is going to happen very soon 即將發生的；迫在眉睫的 SYN **imminent**：*his impending retirement* 他即將到來的退休 ◇ *warnings of **impending danger/disaster*** 對馬上到來的危險／災難的預警

im·pene·trable /ɪmˈpenɪtrəbl/ *adj.* **1** that cannot be entered, passed through or seen through 不可進入的；穿不過的；無法透視的：*an impenetrable jungle* 無法穿越的叢林 ◇ *impenetrable darkness* 漆黑 OPP **penetrable** **2** impossible to understand 不可理解的；高深莫測的 SYN **incomprehensible**：*an impenetrable mystery* 不解之謎 ◇ **~ to sb** *Their jargon is impenetrable to an outsider.* 他們的行話外人聽不懂。 ▸ **im·pene·tra·bil·ity** /ɪmˌpenɪtrəˈbɪləti/ *noun* [U] **im·pene·trably** /-bli/ *adv.*

im·peni·tent /ɪmˈpenɪtənt/ *adj.* (*formal*) not feeling ashamed or sorry about sth bad you have done 不知羞愧的；無悔意的

im·pera·tive /ɪmˈperətɪv/ *adj., noun*
▪ ***adj.*** **1** [not usually before noun] (*formal*) very important and needing immediate attention or action 重要緊急的；迫切的；急需處理的 SYN **vital**：**~ (that ...)** *It is absolutely imperative that we finish by next week.* 我們的當務之急是必須於下週完成。◇ **~ (to do sth)** *It is imperative to continue the treatment for at least two months.* 必須繼續治療至少兩個月。 ⊃ LANGUAGE BANK at VITAL **2** (*formal*) expressing authority 表示權威的：*an imperative tone* 命令的語調 **3** [only before noun] (*grammar* 語法) expressing an order 表示命令的：*an imperative sentence* 祈使句
▪ ***noun*** **1** (*formal*) a thing that is very important and needs immediate attention or action 重要緊急的事；必要的事：*the economic imperative of quality education for all* 向全民提供高質量教育對經濟發展的重要性 **2** (*grammar* 語法) the form of a verb that expresses an order; a verb in this form 祈使語氣；祈使語氣動詞：*In 'Go away!' the verb is **in the imperative**.* * Go away! 中的動詞是祈使語氣動詞。◇ *'Go away!' is an imperative.* * Go away! 是祈使句。

im·per·cept·ible /ˌɪmpəˈseptəbl; NAmE -pərˈs-/ *adj.* (*formal*) very small and therefore unable to be seen or felt（小得）無法察覺的，感覺不到的 OPP **perceptible**：*imperceptible changes in temperature* 難以覺察的氣溫變化 ▸ **im·per·cept·ibly** /-əbli/ *adv.*

im·per·fect /ɪmˈpɜːfɪkt; NAmE -ˈpɜːrf-/ *adj., noun*
▪ ***adj.*** containing faults or mistakes; not complete or perfect 有缺點的；有缺陷的；不完全的；不完美的 SYN **flawed**：*an imperfect world* 不完美的世界 ◇ *an imperfect understanding of English* 對英語的不透徹理解 ◇ *All our sale items are slightly imperfect.* 我們所有的廉價商品都稍有缺陷。 ▸ **im·per·fect·ly** *adv.*
▪ ***noun* the imperfect** (also **the imˌperfect ˈtense**) [sing.] (*grammar* 語法) the verb tense that expresses action in the past that is not complete. It is often called the **past progressive** or **past continuous**. 過去未完成時，未完成式（常稱為過去進行時）：*In 'while I was washing my hair',*

the verb is **in the imperfect**. * while I was washing my hair 中的動詞是過去未完成時。

im·per·fec·tion /ˌɪmpəˈfekʃn; NAmE -pərˈf-/ noun [C, U] a fault or weakness in sb/sth 缺點；瑕疵：*They learned to live with each other's imperfections.* 他們學會了容忍對方的缺點。

im·per·ial /ɪmˈpɪəriəl; NAmE -ˈpɪr-/ adj. [only before noun] **1** connected with an empire 帝國的；皇帝的：*the imperial family/palace/army* 皇室家族；皇宮；皇家陸軍 ◇ *imperial power/expansion* 皇權；帝國的擴張 **2** connected with the system for measuring length, weight and volume using pounds, inches, etc.（度量衡）英制的 ➲ compare METRIC

im·peri·al·ism /ɪmˈpɪəriəlɪzəm; NAmE -ˈpɪr-/ noun [U] (usually disapproving) **1** a system in which one country controls other countries, often after defeating them in a war 帝國統治；帝國主義：*Roman imperialism* 羅馬帝國統治 **2** the fact of a powerful country increasing its influence over other countries through business, culture, etc.（商業、文化等向外國的）擴張；擴張主義：***cultural/economic imperialism*** 文化／經濟擴張 ▶ **im·peri·al·ist** (also **im·peri·al·is·tic** /ɪmˌpɪəriəˈlɪstɪk; NAmE -ˌpɪr-/) adj.：*an imperialist power* 帝國主義國家 ◇ *imperialist ambitions* 帝國主義野心

im·peri·al·ist /ɪmˈpɪəriəlɪst; NAmE -ˈpɪr-/ noun (usually disapproving) a person, such as a politician, who supports imperialism 帝國主義者；帝國統治擁護者

im·peril /ɪmˈperəl/ verb (-ll-, US -l-) ~ **sth/sb** (formal) to put sth/sb in danger 使陷於危險；危及 SYN **endanger**

im·peri·ous /ɪmˈpɪəriəs; NAmE -ˈpɪr-/ adj. (formal) expecting people to obey you and treating them as if they are not as important as you 專橫的；蠻橫的；盛氣凌人的：*an **imperious gesture/voice/command*** 盛氣凌人的姿勢／語調／命令 ▶ **im·peri·ous·ly** adv.：*'Get it now,' she demanded imperiously.* "現在就給我拿來。" 她蠻橫地要求。

im·per·ish·able /ɪmˈperɪʃəbl/ adj. (formal or literary) that will last for a long time or forever 不會腐爛的；不壞的；不朽的 SYN **enduring**

im·per·man·ent /ɪmˈpɜːmənənt; NAmE -ˈpɜːrm-/ adj. (formal) that will not last or stay the same forever 非永久的；短暫的；暫時的 OPP **permanent** ▶ **im·per·man·ence** /-əns/ noun [U]

im·per·me·able /ɪmˈpɜːmiəbl; NAmE -ˈpɜːrm-/ adj. ~ (**to sth**) (technical 術語) not allowing a liquid or gas to pass through 不可滲透的；不透氣的；不透水的 OPP **permeable**

im·per·mis·sible /ˌɪmpɜːˈmɪsəbl; NAmE -pɜːrˈm-/ adj. that cannot be allowed 不允許的；不許可的：*an impermissible invasion of privacy* 對個人隱私的非法侵犯 OPP **permissible**

im·per·son·al /ɪmˈpɜːsənl; NAmE -ˈpɜːrs-/ adj. **1** (usually disapproving) lacking friendly human feelings or atmosphere; making you feel unimportant 缺乏人情味的；冷淡的：*a vast impersonal organization* 龐大而不講人情的組織 ◇ *an impersonal hotel room* 冷冰冰的旅館房間 ◇ *Business letters need not be formal and impersonal.* 商業信函不一定就得刻板而缺乏人情味。◇ *a cold impersonal stare* 冷漠的凝視 **2** not referring to any particular person 非指個人的；客觀的：*Let's keep the criticism general and impersonal.* 讓我們作整體的批評，不要針對個人。**3** (grammar 語法) an **impersonal** verb or sentence has 'it' or 'there' as the subject（動詞或句子）無人稱的，非人稱的 ▶ **im·per·son·al·ity** /ɪmˌpɜːsəˈnæləti; NAmE -ˌpɜːrs-/ noun [U]：*the cold impersonality of some modern cities* 某些現代城市的冷漠無情 **im·per·son·ally** /ɪmˈpɜːsənəli; NAmE -ˈpɜːrs-/ adv.

imˌpersonal ˈpronoun noun (grammar 語法) a pronoun (in English, the pronoun 'it') that does not refer to a person or thing or to any other part of the sentence, for example in 'it was raining' 非人稱代詞（如 it was raining 中的 it）

Language Bank 用語庫

impersonal

Giving opinions using impersonal language
用客觀的語言發表意見

- **It is vital that** more is done to prevent the illegal trade in wild animals. 應進一步阻止非法買賣野生動物的行為，這一點至關重要。◇ (Compare 比較：*We have to do more to stop people trading wild animals illegally.* 我們必須進一步阻止人們非法買賣野生動物。)
- **It is clear that** more needs to be done to protect biodiversity. 顯然，應進一步保護生物多樣性。◇ (Compare 比較：*We clearly need to do more to protect biodiversity.* 很明顯，我們需要進一步保護生物多樣性。)
- **It is unfortunate that** the practice of keeping monkeys as pets still continues. 不幸的是，將猴子當寵物飼養的做法仍在持續。◇ (Compare 比較：*It's absolutely terrible that people still keep monkeys as pets.* 非常糟糕的是有人仍將猴子當寵物飼養。)
- **It is difficult** for many people **to** understand the reasons why certain individuals choose to hunt animals for sport. 許多人都難以理解為什麼有些人選擇捕獵作為消遣。◇ (Compare 比較：*I can't understand why anyone would want to kill animals for fun.* 我不明白為什麼有人會以獵殺動物為樂。)
- Unfortunately, **it would seem that** not enough is being done to support tiger conservation. 遺憾的是，在保護老虎方面給予的支持似乎還不夠。◇ (Compare 比較：*Governments aren't doing enough to help tiger conservation.* 政府沒有採取足夠措施促進對老虎的保護。)
- **There is no doubt that** the greatest threat to polar bears comes from global warming. 毫無疑問，對北極熊的最大威脅是全球變暖。◇ (Compare 比較：*I believe that the greatest threat ...* 我認為最大的威脅…)

➲ Language Banks at OPINION, PERHAPS, VITAL

im·per·son·ate /ɪmˈpɜːsəneɪt; NAmE -ˈpɜːrs-/ verb ~ **sb** to pretend to be sb in order to trick people or to entertain them 冒充；假扮；扮演：*He was caught trying to impersonate a security guard.* 他企圖假扮警衛被抓獲。◇ *They do a pretty good job of impersonating Laurel and Hardy.* 他們扮演勞萊和哈代很成功。▶ **im·per·son·ation** /ɪmˌpɜːsəˈneɪʃn; NAmE -ˌpɜːrs-/ noun [C, U] SYN **impression**：*He did an extremely convincing impersonation of the singer.* 他模仿那位歌手維妙維肖。

im·per·son·ator /ɪmˈpɜːsəneɪtə(r); NAmE -ˈpɜːrs-/ noun a person who copies the way another person talks or behaves in order to entertain people 模仿他人的滑稽演員；扮演他人的人：*The show included a **female impersonator*** (= a man dressed as a woman). 演出中有一位男扮女裝的演員。

im·per·tin·ent /ɪmˈpɜːtɪnənt; NAmE -ˈpɜːrtn-/ adj. rude and not showing respect for sb who is older or more important 粗魯無禮的；不敬的 SYN **impolite**：*an impertinent question/child* 沒有禮貌的提問／孩子 ◇ *Would it be impertinent to ask why you're leaving?* 問一下你為什麼要離開不知是否唐突？➲ SYNONYMS at RUDE ▶ **im·per·tin·ence** /-əns/ noun [U, C, usually sing.]：*She had the impertinence to ask my age!* 她居然探問我的年齡，真沒禮貌！**im·per·tin·ent·ly** adv.

im·per·turb·able /ˌɪmpəˈtɜːbəbl; NAmE -pərˈtɜːrb-/ adj. (formal) not easily upset or worried by a difficult situation; calm 冷靜的；不易生氣的；沉着的 ▶ **im·per·turb·ability** /ˌɪmpəˌtɜːbəˈbɪləti; NAmE -pərˌtɜːrb-/ noun [U] **im·per·turb·ably** /-əbli/ adv.

im·per·vi·ous /ɪmˈpɜːviəs; NAmE -ˈpɜːrv-/ adj. **1** ~ **to sth** not affected or influenced by sth 不受影響的：*impervious to criticism/pain* 能忍受批評／疼痛的 **2** (technical 術語) not allowing a liquid or gas to pass through 不能滲透的；不透氣的；不透水的：*an **impervious rock/***

layer 不透水的岩石 / 地層 ◇ **~ to sth** *impervious to moisture* 防潮的

im·pe·tigo /ˌɪmpɪˈtaɪɡəʊ; *NAmE* -ɡoʊ/ *noun* [U] an infectious disease that causes sore areas on the skin 膿疱病

im·petu·ous /ɪmˈpetʃuəs/ *adj.* acting or done quickly and without thinking carefully about the results 鲁莽的；衝動的；輕率的 SYN **rash, impulsive**： *an impetuous young woman* 莽撞的年輕女子 ◇ *an impetuous decision* 草率的決定 ▸ **im·petu·os·ity** /ɪmˌpetʃuˈɒsəti; *NAmE* -ˈɑːsəti/ *noun* [U] **im·petu·ous·ly** *adv.*

im·petus /ˈɪmpɪtəs/ *noun* **1** [U, sing.] something that encourages a process or activity to develop more quickly 動力；推動；促進；刺激 SYN **stimulus**： *The debate seems to have lost much of its initial impetus.* 辯論會似乎沒有開始時那麼大的衝勁了。◇ **~ to sth/to do sth** *to give (a)* ***new/fresh impetus*** *to sth* 給某事物以新的推進力 ◇ **~ for sth** *His articles provided the main impetus for change.* 他的那些文章是促進變革的主要推動力。 **2** [U] (*technical* 術語) the force or energy with which sth moves 動量；動力；慣性

im·pinge /ɪmˈpɪndʒ/ *verb* [I] **~ (on/upon sth/sb)** (*formal*) to have a noticeable effect on sth/sb, especially a bad one 對…有明顯作用（或影響）；妨礙；侵犯 SYN **encroach**： *He never allowed his work to impinge on his private life.* 他從不讓他的工作妨礙私生活。

im·pious /ˈɪmpiəs; ɪmˈpaɪəs/ *adj.* (*formal*) showing a lack of respect for God and religion （對上帝或宗教）不敬的，不恭的 OPP **pious** ▸ **im·pi·ety** /ɪmˈpaɪəti/ *noun* [U]

imp·ish /ˈɪmpɪʃ/ *adj.* showing a lack of respect for sb/sth in a way that is amusing rather than serious 頑童似的；頑皮的；淘氣的 SYN **mischievous**： *an* ***impish grin/look*** 頑皮的笑臉 / 表情 ➲ see also IMP ▸ **imp·ish·ly** *adv.*

im·plac·able /ɪmˈplækəbl/ *adj.* **1** (of strong negative opinions or feelings 強烈的消極看法或感情) that cannot be changed 不能改變的： *implacable hatred* 難以化解的仇恨 **2** (of a person 人) unwilling to stop opposing sb/sth 不願和解的；不饒人的： *an implacable enemy* 死敵 ▸ **im·plac·ably** /ɪmˈplækəbli/ *adv.*： *to be implacably opposed to the plan* 堅決反對這個計劃

im·plant *verb, noun*

■ ***verb*** /ɪmˈplɑːnt; *NAmE* -ˈplænt/ **1** [T] **~ sth (in/into sth)** to fix an idea, attitude, etc. firmly in sb's mind 灌輸，注入（觀念、看法等）；（在思想上）生根： *Prejudices can easily become implanted in the mind.* 偏見容易在頭腦中扎根。 **2** [T] **~ sth (in/into sth)** to put sth (usually sth artificial) into a part of the body for medical purposes, usually by means of an operation 將（人造器官等）置入；（通常指通過手術）將…植入： *an electrode implanted into the brain* 植入大腦中的電極 ➲ compare TRANSPLANT **3** [I] **~ (in/into sth)** (of an egg or an EMBRYO 卵子或胚胎) to become fixed inside the body of a person or an animal so that it can start to develop 被移植到（人或動物體內發育） ▸ **im·plant·ation** /ˌɪmplɑːnˈteɪʃn; *NAmE* -plæn-/ *noun* [U]

■ ***noun*** /ˈɪmplɑːnt; *NAmE* -plænt/ something that is put into a person's body in a medical operation （植入人體中的）移植物，植入物： *silicone breast implants* 硅酮乳房填充物 ➲ compare TRANSPLANT

im·plaus·ible /ɪmˈplɔːzəbl/ *adj.* not seeming reasonable or likely to be true 似乎不合情理的；不像真實的： *an* ***implausible claim/idea/theory*** 悖於情理的要求 / 思想 / 理論 ◇ *It was all* ***highly implausible.*** 這毫無道理。 OPP **plausible** ▸ **im·plaus·ibly** *adv.*

im·ple·ment AW *verb, noun*

■ ***verb*** /ˈɪmplɪment/ **~ sth** (*formal*) to make sth that has been officially decided start to happen or be used 使生效；貫徹；執行；實施 SYN **carry out**： *to implement* ***changes/decisions/policies/reforms*** 實行變革；執行決議 / 政策；實施改革 ▸ **im·ple·men·ta·tion** AW /ˌɪmplɪmenˈteɪʃn/ *noun* [U]： *the implementation of the new system* 新體制的實施

■ ***noun*** /ˈɪmplɪmənt/ (*formal*) a tool or an instrument, often one that is quite simple and that is used outdoors 工具，器具（常指簡單的戶外用具）： *agricultural implements* 農具

im·pli·cate AW /ˈɪmplɪkeɪt/ *verb* **1 ~ sb (in sth)** to show or suggest that sb is involved in sth bad or criminal 牽涉，涉及（某人） SYN **incriminate**： *He tried to avoid saying anything that would implicate him further.* 他盡力避免說出任何會進一步牽連他的事情。 **2 ~ sth (in/as sth)** to show or suggest that sth is the cause of sth bad 表明（或意指）…是起因： *The results implicate poor hygiene as one cause of the outbreak.* 這些結果說明衛生條件差是疾病爆發的一個原因。

IDM **be implicated in sth** to be involved in a crime; to be responsible for sth bad 與某罪行有牽連；對某壞事有責任： *Senior officials were implicated in the scandal.* 一些高級官員受到這一醜聞的牽連。

im·pli·ca·tion 🔑 AW /ˌɪmplɪˈkeɪʃn/ *noun* **1** 🔑 [C, usually pl.] **~ (of sth) (for sth)** a possible effect or result of an action or a decision 可能的影響（或作用、結果）： *They failed to consider the wider implications of their actions.* 他們沒有考慮到他們的行動會產生更廣泛的影響。◇ *The development of the site will* ***have implications for*** *the surrounding countryside.* 這個地點的開發將會影響周圍的鄉村。 **2** 🔑 [C, U] something that is suggested or indirectly stated (= sth that is implied) 含意；暗指： *The implication in his article is that being a housewife is greatly inferior to every other occupation.* 他那篇文章的含意是，當家庭主婦遠遠不如所有其他職業。◇ *He criticized the Director and,* ***by implication,*** *the whole of the organization.* 他抨擊主管，其實是間接批評了整個機構。 **3** [U] **~ (of sb) (in sth)** the fact of being involved, or of involving sb, in sth, especially a crime （被）牽連，牽涉 SYN **involvement**： *He resigned after his implication in a sex scandal.* 他在涉及一件性醜聞之後辭職了。

im·pli·ca·ture /ˈɪmplɪkətʃə(r)/ *noun* (*technical* 術語) **1** [U] the act of suggesting that you feel or think sth is true, without saying so directly 含蓄行為；含蓄表達 **2** [C] something that you can understand from what is said, but which is not stated directly 隱含意；言外之意： *An implicature of 'Some of my friends came' is 'Some of my friends did not come'.* "我的一些朋友來了"這句話的言外之意是"我的一些朋友沒有來"。

im·pli·cit AW /ɪmˈplɪsɪt/ *adj.* **1 ~ (in sth)** suggested without being directly expressed 含蓄的；不直接言明的： *Implicit in his speech was the assumption that they were guilty.* 他話語中的言外之意是設定他們有罪。◇ *implicit criticism* 含蓄的批評 **2 ~ (in sth)** forming part of sth (although perhaps not directly expressed) 成為一部份的；內含的： *The ability to listen is implicit in the teacher's role.* 教師的角色包括了懂得傾聽。 **3** complete and not doubted 完全的；無疑問的 SYN **absolute**： *She had the implicit trust of her staff.* 她得到了全體職員的絕對信任。 ➲ compare EXPLICIT ▸ **im·pli·cit·ly** AW *adv.*： *It reinforces, implicitly or explicitly, the idea that money is all-important.* 這或暗示或明確地強調了金錢至上這一觀念。◇ *I trust John implicitly.* 我完全相信約翰。

im·plode /ɪmˈpləʊd; *NAmE* ɪmˈploʊd/ *verb* **1** [I] to burst or explode and collapse into the centre 向心聚爆；內爆；向內坍塌 **2** [I] (of an organization, a system, etc. 組織、體制等) to fail suddenly and completely 突然崩潰 ▸ **im·plo·sion** /ɪmˈpləʊʒn; *NAmE* -ˈploʊ-/ *noun* [C, U]

im·plore /ɪmˈplɔː(r)/ *verb* (*formal* or *literary*) to ask sb to do sth in an anxious way because you want or need it very much 懇求；哀求 SYN **beseech, beg**： **~ sb to do sth** *She implored him to stay.* 她懇求他留下。◇ **~ (sb) + speech** *'Help me,' he implored.* "救救我吧。"他哀求道。◇ **~ sb** *Tell me it's true. I implore you.* 告訴我那是真的。求求你。 ▸ **im·plor·ing** *adj.*： *She gave him an imploring look.* 她對他露出哀求的神情。

imply 🔑 AW /ɪmˈplaɪ/ *verb* (**im·plies, im·ply·ing, im·plied, im·plied**)

1 🔑 to suggest that sth is true or that you feel or think sth, without saying so directly 含有…的意思；暗示；暗指： **~ (that)** … *Are you implying (that) I am wrong?* 你的意思是不是說我錯了？◇ **~ sth** *I disliked the implied criticism in his voice.* 我討厭他暗中批評的口吻。◇ **it is implied that** … *It was implied that we were at fault.* 這意味着

我們錯了。➲ note at INFER **2** 🔑 to make it seem likely that sth is true or exists 說明；表明 SYN **suggest**：**~ (that)** … *The survey implies (that) more people are moving house than was thought.* 調查顯示，準備搬家的人口比想像的要多。◇ **it is implied that** … *It was implied in the survey that* … 這次調查表明…◇ **~ sth** *The fact that she was here implies a degree of interest.* 她到場就說明了她有一定程度的興趣。 **3 ~ sth** (of an idea, action, etc. 思想、行為等) to make sth necessary in order to be successful 必然包含；使有必要 SYN **mean**：*The project implies an enormous investment in training.* 這個項目需要在培訓方面做巨大的投資。➲ see also IMPLICATION

im·pol·ite /ˌɪmpəˈlaɪt/ *adj.* not polite 不禮貌的；粗魯的 SYN **rude**：*Some people think it is impolite to ask someone's age.* 有些人認為詢問別人的年齡是不禮貌的。➲ SYNONYMS at RUDE ▸ **im·pol·ite·ly** *adv.* **im·pol·ite·ness** *noun* [U]

im·pol·it·ic /ɪmˈpɒlətɪk; *NAmE* -ˈpɑːl-/ *adj.* (*formal*) not wise 不明智的；不策略的 SYN **unwise**：*It would have been impolitic to refuse his offer.* 當時若拒絕了他的好意就太不明智了。

im·pon·der·able /ɪmˈpɒndərəbl; *NAmE* -ˈpɑːn-/ *noun* [usually pl.] (*formal*) something that is difficult to measure or estimate 難以衡量（或估量）的事物：*We can't predict the outcome. There are too many imponderables.* 我們無法預測結果。難以逆料的情況太多了。▸ **im·pon·der·able** *adj.*

im·port 🔑 *noun, verb*

■ ***noun*** /ˈɪmpɔːt; *NAmE* ˈɪmpɔːrt/ **1** 🔑 [C, usually pl.] a product or service that is brought into one country from another 進口；輸入的產品（或勞務）：*food imports from abroad* 從外國進口的食物 OPP **export** ➲ COLLOCATIONS at ECONOMY **2** 🔑 [U, pl.] the act of bringing a product or service into one country from another（產品、勞務的）進口，輸入，引進：*The report calls for a ban on the import of hazardous waste.* 這篇報道呼籲禁止危險廢棄物的進口。◇ *import controls* 進口管制 ◇ *an import licence* 進口許可證 ◇ *imports of oil* 石油的進口 OPP **export** **3** [U] (*formal*) importance 重要性：*matters of great import* 非常重要的事情 **4 the ~ (of sth)** [sing.] (*formal*) the meaning of sth, especially when it is not immediately clear 意思；含意：*It is difficult to understand the full import of this statement.* 很難理解這份聲明中的全部含意。

■ ***verb*** /ɪmˈpɔːt; *NAmE* ɪmˈpɔːrt/ **1** 🔑 to bring a product, a service, an idea, etc. into one country from another 進口；輸入；引進：**~ sth** *The country has to import most of its raw materials.* 這個國家大多數原料均依賴進口。◇ **~ sth (from …) (into …)** *goods imported from Japan into the US* 從日本輸入到美國的貨品 ◇ *customs imported from the West* 從西方傳入的風俗習慣 **2 ~ sth (from …) (into …)** (*computing* 計) to get data from another program, changing its form so that the program you are using can read it 導入；輸入；移入 OPP **export** ▸ **im·port·ation** /ˌɪmpɔːˈteɪʃn; *NAmE* -pɔːrˈt-/ *noun* [U, C] SYN **import**：*a ban on the importation of ivory* 禁止象牙進口的法令

im·port·ance 🔑 /ɪmˈpɔːtns; *NAmE* -ˈpɔːrt-/ *noun* [U] the quality of being important 重要性；重要；重大：*She **stressed the importance of** careful preparation.* 她強調了認真準備的重要性。◇ *It's a matter **of the greatest importance** to me.* 這對我來說是最重要的事情。◇ *They **attach** great **importance** to the project.* 他們高度重視這個項目。◇ *the relative importance of the two ideas* 這兩種想法的相對重要性 ◇ *State your reasons **in order of importance**.* 按重要性順序陳述你的理由。◇ *He was very aware of his own importance* (= of his status). 他十分清楚自己的重要地位。

im·port·ant 🔑 /ɪmˈpɔːtnt; *NAmE* -ˈpɔːrt-/ *adj.*

1 🔑 having a great effect on people or things; of great value 重要的；有重大影響的；有巨大價值的：*an important decision/factor* 重要決定／因素 ◇ *I have an important announcement to make.* 我要宣佈一件重要的事情。◇ *Money played an important role in his life.* 金錢在他的生活中扮演了重要的角色。◇ *Listening is an important part of the job.* 傾聽是這項工作的一個重要部份。◇ *one of the most important collections of American art* 美國藝術的最有價值的收藏品之一 ◇ ***It is important to** follow the manufacturer's instructions.* 遵照廠家的說明很重要。◇ ***It is important that** he attend every day.* 他每天都要出席，這很重要。◇ (*BrE*) ***It is important that** he should attend every day.* 他每天都要出席，這很重要。◇ ***It is important for** him **to** attend every day.* 他每天都要出席，這很重要。◇ **~ (to sb)** *It's very important to me that you should be there.* 你應該到場，這對我很重要。◇ ***The important thing** is to keep trying.* 重要的是要不斷嘗試。➲ LANGUAGE BANK at EMPHASIS **2** 🔑 (of a person 人) having great influence or authority 影響很大的；權威的：*an important member of the team* 舉足輕重的一位隊員 ◇ *He likes to feel important.* 他喜歡感到自己很重要。 ▸ **im·port·ant·ly** 🔑 *adv.*：*More importantly, can he be trusted?* 更重要的是，他值得信任嗎？◇ *She was sitting importantly behind a big desk.* 她神氣十足地坐在一張大寫字枱後面。➲ LANGUAGE BANK at EMPHASIS

im·port·er /ɪmˈpɔːtə(r); *NAmE* -ˈpɔːrt-/ *noun* a person, company, etc. that buys goods from another country in order to sell them in their own country 從事進口的人（或公司等）；進口商：*a London-based importer of Italian food* 基地設在倫敦的意大利食品進口商 ➲ compare EXPORTER

im·por·tun·ate /ɪmˈpɔːtʃənət; *NAmE* -ˈpɔːrt-/ *adj.* (*formal*) asking for things many times in a way that is annoying 再三要求的；糾纏不休的

im·por·tune /ˌɪmpɔːˈtjuːn; *NAmE* -pɔːrˈtuːn/ *verb* **~ sb (for sth) | ~ sb to do sth** (*formal*) to ask sb for sth many times and in a way that is annoying 再三要求；糾纏 SYN **pester**

im·pose 🔑 AW /ɪmˈpəʊz; *NAmE* ɪmˈpoʊz/ *verb*

1 🔑 [T] **~ sth (on/upon sth/sb)** to introduce a new law, rule, tax, etc.; to order that a rule, punishment, etc. be used 推行，採用（規章制度）；強制實行：*A new tax was imposed on fuel.* 當局開始對燃油徵收一項新稅。 **2** 🔑 [T] **~ sth (on/upon sb/sth)** to force sb/sth to have to deal with sth that is difficult or unpleasant 迫使；把…強加於：*to **impose limitations/restrictions/constraints** on sth* 強行限制／管制／約束某事物 ◇ *This system imposes additional financial burdens on many people.* 這個制度給很多人增加了額外的經濟負擔。 **3** 🔑 [T] **~ sth (on/upon sb)** to make sb accept the same opinions, wishes, etc. as your own 使（別人）接受自己的意見：*She didn't want to impose her values on her family.* 她並不想勉強家人接受自己的價值觀。◇ *It was noticeable how a few people managed to **impose** their **will on** the others.* 顯而易見，有少數幾個人設法把自己的意志強加於別人。 **4** [I] to expect sb to do sth for you or to spend time with you, when it may not be convenient for them 勉強（某人做某事）；硬要…和…在一起：*'You must stay for lunch.' 'Well, thanks, but I don't want to impose …'* "你一定得留下吃午飯。" "唔，謝謝，但我不想添麻煩…" ◇ **~ on/upon sb/sth** *Everyone imposes on Dave's good nature.* 大家都欺負戴夫脾氣好。 **5** [T] **~ yourself (on/upon sb/sth)** to make sb/sth accept or be aware of your presence or ideas 使接受，使意識到（自己的在場或想法）：*European civilization was the first to impose itself across the whole world.* 歐洲文明是最先傳播到全世界的。

im·pos·ing /ɪmˈpəʊzɪŋ; *NAmE* -ˈpoʊz-/ *adj.* impressive to look at; making a strong impression 壯觀的；使人印象深刻的：*a grand and imposing building* 雄偉壯觀的建築物 ◇ *a tall imposing woman* 高大壯碩的女人

im·pos·ition AW /ˌɪmpəˈzɪʃn/ *noun* **1** [U] the act of introducing sth such as a new law or rule, or a new tax（新法律或規則等的）頒佈，實施；（新稅的）徵收：*the imposition of martial law* 戒嚴令的實施 ◇ *the imposition of tax on domestic fuel* 家用燃料稅的徵收 **2** [C] an unfair or unreasonable thing that sb expects or asks you to do 不公平（或不合理）的要求：*I'd like to stay if it's not too much of an imposition.* 如果不會給您增添太多麻煩，我倒願意留下。

im·pos·sible 🔑 /ɪmˈpɒsəbl; *NAmE* -ˈpɑːs-/ *adj.*

1 🔑 that cannot exist or be done; not possible 不可能存在（或做到）的；不可能的：***almost/virtually impossible*** 幾乎／實際上不可能 ◇ ***It's impossible for** me to be* *there before eight.* 我在八點之前不可能趕到那裏。◇ *It's impossible to prove.* 這件事無法證實。◇ *I find it* ***impossible*** *to lie to her.* 我覺得無法對她撒謊。◇ *an* ***impossible dream/goal*** 無法實現的夢想／目標 **OPP possible** **2** very difficult to deal with 難處理的；很難對付的：*I've been placed in an* ***impossible position.*** 我陷入了進退維谷的境地。◇ *Honestly, you're impossible at times!* 說實話，你有時真令人難以忍受。 **3 the impossible** *noun* [sing.] a thing that is or seems impossible（似乎）不可能的事：*to attempt the impossible* 明知不可為而為之 ▸ **im·pos·si·bil·ity** /ɪmˌpɒsəˈbɪləti; *NAmE* -ˌpɑːsə-/ *noun* [U, C, usually sing.] (*pl.* **-ies**)：*the sheer impossibility of providing enough food for everyone* 完全無法給每個人提供足夠的食物 ◇ *a virtual impossibility* 幾乎不可能的事 **im·pos·sibly** /ɪmˈpɒsəbli; *NAmE* -ˈpɑːs-/ *adv.*：*an impossibly difficult problem* (= impossible to solve) 無法解決的難題 ◇ *He was impossibly handsome* (= it was difficult to believe that he could be so handsome). 簡直難以相信他有這麼英俊。

im·pos·tor (*BrE* also **im·pos·ter**) /ɪmˈpɒstə(r); *NAmE* -ˈpɑːs-/ *noun* a person who pretends to be sb else in order to trick people 冒名頂替者；冒名行騙者

im·pos·ture /ɪmˈpɒstʃə(r); *NAmE* -ˈpɑːs-/ *noun* [U, C] (*formal*) an act of tricking people deliberately by pretending to be sb else 冒名行騙

im·po·tent /ˈɪmpətənt/ *adj.* **1** having no power to change things or to influence a situation 無能為力的；不起作用的 **SYN powerless**：*Without the chairman's support, the committee is impotent.* 沒有主席的支持，委員會是無能為力的。◇ *She blazed with impotent rage.* 她勃然大怒，但於事無補。 **2** (of a man 男子) unable to achieve an ERECTION and therefore unable to have full sex 性無能的；陽痿的 ▸ **im·po·tence** /ˈɪmpətəns/ *noun* [U]：*a feeling of impotence in the face of an apparently insoluble problem* 面對顯然無法解決的問題的無力感 ◇ *male impotence* 陽痿 **im·po·tent·ly** *adv.*

im·pound /ɪmˈpaʊnd/ *verb* (*law* 律) **1 ~ sth** (of the police, courts of law, etc. 警察、法庭等) to take sth away from sb, so that they cannot use it 暫時沒收；扣押 **SYN confiscate**：*The car was impounded by the police after the accident.* 那輛車在發生車禍之後被警察扣留了。 **2 ~ sth** to shut up dogs, cats, etc. found on the streets in a POUND, until their owners collect them 收押（待領的狗、貓等）

im·pov·er·ish /ɪmˈpɒvərɪʃ; *NAmE* -ˈpɑːv-/ *verb* **1 ~ sb** to make sb poor 使貧窮：*These changes are likely to impoverish single-parent families even further.* 這些變革很可能使單親家庭更加貧困。 **2 ~ sth** to make sth worse in quality 使貧瘠；使枯竭：*Intensive cultivation has impoverished the soil.* 集約耕作使土壤變得貧瘠。 ▸ **im·pov·er·ish·ment** *noun* [U]

im·pov·er·ished /ɪmˈpɒvərɪʃt; *NAmE* -ˈpɑːv-/ *adj.* **1** very poor; without money 赤貧的；不名一文的：*impoverished peasants* 貧困的農民 ◇ *the impoverished areas of the city* 這個城市的貧民區 ➲ SYNONYMS at POOR **2** poor in quality, because sth is missing 貧乏的；貧瘠的；枯竭的

im·prac·tic·able /ɪmˈpræktɪkəbl/ *adj.* impossible or very difficult to do; not practical in a particular situation 不可行的；不切實際的：*It would be impracticable for each member to be consulted on every occasion.* 不可能每一次都徵求每個成員的意見。 ➲ compare IMPRACTICAL **OPP practicable** ▸ **im·prac·tic·abil·ity** /ɪmˌpræktɪkəˈbɪləti/ *noun* [U]

im·prac·ti·cal /ɪmˈpræktɪkl/ *adj.* **1** not sensible or realistic 不明智的；不現實的：*It was totally impractical to think that we could finish the job in two months.* 認為我們能在兩個月之內完成這項工作，這完全是不切實際的。 **2** (of people 人) not good at doing things that involve using the hands; not good at planning or organizing things 手不靈巧的；不善於規劃（或組織）的 **OPP practical** ➲ compare IMPRACTICABLE ▸ **im·prac·ti·cal·ity** /ɪmˌpræktɪˈkæləti/ *noun* [U]

im·pre·ca·tion /ˌɪmprɪˈkeɪʃn/ *noun* (*formal*) a CURSE (= an offensive word that is used to express extreme anger) 咒語

im·pre·cise **AW** /ˌɪmprɪˈsaɪs/ *adj.* not giving exact details or making sth clear 不確切的；不精確的；不明確的 **SYN inaccurate**：*an imprecise definition* 不確切的定義 ◇ *imprecise information* 不準確的信息 ◇ *The witness's descriptions were too imprecise to be of any real value.* 證人的描述太不明確，沒有任何實際價值。 **OPP precise** ▸ **im·pre·cise·ly** *adv.*：*These terms are often used imprecisely and interchangeably.* 這些詞語的使用常常不夠精確，而且常常交互使用。 **im·pre·ci·sion** /ˌɪmprɪˈsɪʒn/ *noun* [U]：*There is considerable imprecision in the terminology used.* 所用的術語相當不準確。

im·preg·nable /ɪmˈpreɡnəbl/ *adj.* **1** an **impregnable** building is so strongly built that it cannot be entered by force 堅不可摧的；牢不可破的：*an impregnable fortress* 堅不可摧的要塞 **2** strong and impossible to defeat or change 不可戰勝的；難以改變的 **SYN invincible**：*The team built up an impregnable 5–1 lead.* 這個隊以 5:1 的絕對優勢領先。

im·preg·nate /ˈɪmpreɡneɪt; *NAmE* ɪmˈpreɡ-/ *verb* **1** [usually passive] **~ sth (with sth)** to make a substance spread through an area so that the area is full of the substance 使充滿；使遍佈：*The pad is impregnated with insecticide.* 墊子上滿是殺蟲劑。 **2 ~ sb/sth** (*formal*) to make a woman or female animal pregnant 使懷孕；使妊娠 ▸ **im·preg·na·tion** /ˌɪmpreɡˈneɪʃn/ *noun* [U]

im·pres·ario /ˌɪmprəˈsɑːriəʊ; *NAmE* -rioʊ/ *noun* (*pl.* **-os**) a person who arranges plays in the theatre, etc., especially a person who manages a theatre, OPERA or BALLET company（劇院、歌劇或芭蕾舞團的）經理

im·press /ɪmˈpres/ *verb* **1** [T, I] if a person or thing **impresses** you, you feel admiration for them or it 使欽佩；使敬仰；給…留下深刻的好印象：**~ (sb)** *We interviewed a number of candidates but none of them impressed us.* 我們和數名申請人進行了面談，但都沒有給我們留下什麼印象。◇ *The Grand Canyon never fails to impress.* 大峽谷永遠讓人歎為觀止。◇ *His sincerity impressed her.* 他的真誠打動了她。◇ **~ sb with sth/sb** *He impressed her with his sincerity.* 他的真誠打動了她。◇ **it impresses sb that …** *It impressed me that she remembered my name.* 令我佩服的是她記得我的名字。◇ **sb is impressed that …** *I was impressed that she remembered my name.* 令我佩服的是她記得我的名字。 ➲ see also IMPRESSED, IMPRESSIVE **2** [T] **~ sth on/upon sb** (*formal*) to make sb understand how important, serious, etc. sth is by emphasizing it 使意識到（重要性或嚴肅性等）：*He impressed on us the need for immediate action.* 他讓我們認識到立刻採取行動的必要。 **3** [T] **~ sth/itself on/upon sth** (*formal*) to have a great effect on sth, especially sb's mind, imagination, etc. 使銘記；給…留下深刻印象：*Her words impressed themselves on my memory.* 她的話語我銘記在心裏。

im·pressed /ɪmˈprest/ *adj.* feeling admiration for sb/sth because you think they are particularly good, interesting, etc.（對…）欽佩，敬仰，有深刻的好印象：*I must admit I am impressed.* 我得承認我很佩服。◇ **~ by/with sb/sth** *We were all impressed by her enthusiasm.* 我們都被她的熱情打動了。◇ *She was* ***suitably impressed*** (= as impressed as sb had hoped) *with the painting.* 果然不出所料，她對那幅油畫產生了興趣。 ➲ see also UNIMPRESSED

im·pres·sion /ɪmˈpreʃn/ *noun* ▸ **IDEA/OPINION 想法；看法** **1** an idea, a feeling or an opinion that you get about sb/sth, or that sb/sth gives you 印象；感想：***a general/an overall impression*** 總的／整體印象 ◇ ***an initial/a lasting impression*** 初次／持久的印象 ◇ **~ (of sb/sth)** *to get* ***a good/bad impression*** *of sb/sth* 對某人／某事物的印象好／不好 ◇ *My* ***first impression*** *of him was favourable.* 他給我的第一印象不錯。◇ *She* ***gives the impression*** *of being very busy.* 她給人的印象是特別忙。◇ **~ (that …)** *I did not* ***get the impression*** *that they were unhappy about the situation.* 我並不覺得他們不滿於當時的狀況。◇ ***My impression is*** *that there are still a lot of problems.* 依我看問題還是挺多的。◇ *Try and smile. You don't want to* ***give people the wrong***

impression (= that you are not friendly). 盡量微笑。不要讓人誤以為你很冷漠。

▸ **EFFECT 作用 2** the effect that an experience or a person has on sb/sth 影響；效果：*a **big impression*** 大的影響 ◇ **~ (on sb)** *His trip to India **made a** strong **impression** on him.* 他的印度之行對他的觸動很大。◇ *My words **made no impression** on her.* 我的話絲毫沒有對她起作用。◇ *You'll have to play better than that if you really want to **make an impression*** (= to make people admire you). 你如果真的想給人留下好印象，就得表現得更好。

▸ **DRAWING 圖畫 3** a drawing showing what a person looks like or what a place or a building will look like in the future 印象畫：*This is an **artist's impression** of the new stadium.* 這是一位藝術家對未來新運動場作的印象畫。

▸ **AMUSING COPY OF SB 滑稽模仿 4 ~ (of sb)** an amusing copy of the way a person acts or speaks（對某人舉止言談的）滑稽模仿 SYN **impersonation**：*He did an impression of Tom Hanks.* 他滑稽地模仿了湯姆•漢克斯。

▸ **FALSE APPEARANCE 假象 5** an appearance that may be false（虛假的）外觀；假象：*Clever lighting creates an impression of space in a room.* 巧妙的照明會讓人有屋子空間增大的感覺。

▸ **MARK 痕跡 6** a mark that is left when an object is pressed hard into a surface 壓痕

▸ **BOOK 書籍 7** all the copies of a book that are printed at one time, with few or no changes to the contents since the last time the book was printed 重印本；印次 ➲ compare EDITION

IDM **(be) under the im'pression that ...** believing, usually wrongly, that sth is true or is happening 以為…；（通常指）誤認為…：*I was under the impression that the work had already been completed.* 我還以為已經完工了呢。➲ SYNONYMS at THINK

im·pres·sion·able /ɪmˈpreʃənəbl/ *adj.* (of a person, especially a young one 人，尤指年輕人) easily influenced or affected by sb/sth 易受影響的：*children at an impressionable age* 處於易受外界影響的年齡的兒童

Im·pres·sion·ism /ɪmˈpreʃənɪzəm/ *noun* [U] a style in painting developed in France in the late 19th century that uses colour to show the effects of light on things and to suggest atmosphere rather than showing exact details 印象主義，印象派（19 世紀下半葉興起於法國的繪畫風格，主要表現光與色的效果，不着眼於準確的細節）▸ **Im·pres·sion·ist** *adj.* [usually before noun]：*Impressionist landscapes* 印象派風景畫

im·pres·sion·ist /ɪmˈpreʃənɪst/ *noun* **1** (usually **Impressionist**) an artist who paints in the style of Impressionism 印象派畫家：*Impressionists such as Monet and Pissarro* 莫奈和畢沙羅等的印象派畫家 **2** a person who entertains people by copying the way a famous person speaks or behaves 模仿演員（常模仿名人言行）

im·pres·sion·is·tic /ˌɪmpreʃəˈnɪstɪk/ *adj.* giving a general idea rather than particular facts or details 給人以大致印象的；不精確的；憑印象的

im·pres·sive /ɪmˈpresɪv/ *adj.* (of things or people 事物或人) making you feel admiration, because they are very large, good, skilful, etc. 令人讚歎的；令人敬佩的：*an impressive building with a huge tower* 有高塔的壯觀建築 ◇ *an impressive performance* 令人難忘的演出 ◇ *one of the most impressive novels of recent years* 近年來給人印象最深的小說之一 ◇ *She was very impressive in the interview.* 她在面試中表現得十分出色。OPP **unimpressive** ▸ **im·pres·sive·ly** *adv.*：*impressively high* 異常高 ◇ *impressively organized* 組織得有條不紊

im·pri·ma·tur /ˌɪmprɪˈmɑːtə(r)/ *noun* [sing.] (*formal*) official approval of sth, given by a person in a position of authority 正式批准；認可；同意

im·print *verb, noun*

■ *verb* /ɪmˈprɪnt/ **1 ~ A in/on B | ~ B with A** to have a great effect on sth so that it cannot be forgotten, changed, etc. 產生重大影響；銘刻；使銘記：*The terrible scenes were indelibly imprinted on his mind.* 那些恐怖場面深深地銘刻在他的心中。**2 ~ A in/on B | ~ B with A** to print or press a mark or design onto a surface 印；壓印：*clothes imprinted with the logos of sports teams* 印着運動隊標誌的衣服

■ *noun* /ˈɪmprɪnt/ **1 ~ (of sth) (in/on sth)** a mark made by pressing or stamping sth onto a surface 印記；壓印；痕跡：*the imprint of a foot in the sand* 沙灘上的足跡 **2** [usually sing.] **~ (of sth) (on sb/sth)** (*formal*) the lasting effect that a person or an experience has on a place or a situation 持久影響 **3** (*technical* 術語) the name of the PUBLISHER of a book, usually printed below the title on the first page 出版商名稱（通常印在第一頁的書名下面）

im·prison /ɪmˈprɪzn/ *verb* [often passive] **~ sb** to put sb in a prison or another place from which they cannot escape 監禁；關押 SYN **jail**：*They were imprisoned for possession of drugs.* 他們因藏毒品而被監禁。◇ (*figurative*) *Some young mothers feel imprisoned in their own homes.* 有些年輕的母親感到待在家裏如同坐牢。➲ COLLOCATIONS at JUSTICE ▸ **im·pris·on·ment** /-mənt/ *noun* [U]：*to be sentenced to **life imprisonment** for murder* 因犯謀殺罪被判終身監禁

im·prob·able /ɪmˈprɒbəbl; *NAmE* -ˈprɑːb-/ *adj.* **1** not likely to be true or to happen 不大可能真實的（或發生的）；不大可能的 SYN **unlikely**：*an improbable story* 大概不是真實的故事 ◇ *It all sounded **highly improbable**.* 一切聽上去很荒唐。◇ **~ that ...** *It seems improbable that the current situation will continue.* 當前的局勢似乎不大可能繼續下去。OPP **probable 2** seeming strange because it is not what you would expect 奇異的；荒謬的 SYN **unexpected**：*Her hair was an improbable shade of yellow.* 她的頭髮帶有怪怪的黃色。▸ **im·prob·abil·ity** /ɪmˌprɒbəˈbɪləti; *NAmE* -ˌprɑːbə-/ *noun* [U, C]：*the improbability of finding them alive* 找到他們存活的可能性不大 ◇ *statistical improbability* 統計學上來說不太可能的事 **im·prob·ably** /-əbli/ *adv.*：*He claimed, improbably, that he had never been there.* 他聲稱從未去過那裏，令人覺得不可靠。◇ *an improbably happy end* 看似不大可能的圓滿結局

im·promptu /ɪmˈprɒmptjuː; *NAmE* -ˈprɑːmptuː/ *adj.* done without preparation or planning 無準備的；即興的；即席的 SYN **improvised**：*an impromptu speech* 即興講演

im·proper /ɪmˈprɒpə(r); *NAmE* -ˈprɑːp-/ *adj.* (*formal*) **1** dishonest, or morally wrong 不誠實的；不正當的；不道德的：*improper business practices* 不正當的商業手法 ◇ *improper conduct* 不道德的行為 ◇ *There was nothing improper about our relationship* (= it did not involve sex). 我們的關係沒有什麼不正當的。OPP **proper 2** not suited or appropriate to the situation 不合適的；不適當的；不得體的 SYN **inappropriate**：*It would be improper to comment at this stage.* 在這個階段發表評論並不恰當。OPP **proper 3** wrong; not correct 錯誤的；不正確的：*improper use of the drug* 藥物的誤用 ▸ **im·prop·er·ly** *adv.*：*to behave improperly* 表現得沒有分寸 ◇ *He was improperly dressed for the occasion.* 他的衣着不大適合這個場合。◇ *improperly cooked meat* 烹調不當的肉

im,proper 'fraction *noun* (*mathematics* 數) a FRACTION in which the top number is greater than the bottom number, for example 7⁄3 假分數

im·pro·pri·ety /ˌɪmprəˈpraɪəti/ *noun* [U, C] (*pl.* **-ies**) (*formal*) behaviour or actions that are dishonest, morally wrong or not appropriate for a person in a position of responsibility 不誠實（或不正當、不合適）的行為舉止 OPP **propriety**

im·prove /ɪmˈpruːv/ *verb* [I, T] to become better than before; to make sth/sb better than before 改進；改善：*His quality of life has improved dramatically since the operation.* 手術後他的生活質量大大改善了。◇ *The doctor says she should continue to improve* (= after an illness). 醫生說她還會繼續康復。◇ **~ sth** *to improve standards* 提高水平 ◇ *The company needs to improve performance in all these areas.* 公司需要在所有這些方面改善業績。◇ *I need to improve my French.* 我得提高我的法語水平。

PHR V **im'prove on/upon sth** to achieve or produce sth that is of a better quality than sth else 改進；做出比…

更好的成績：*We've certainly improved on last year's figures.* 我們的業績的確超過了去年的數字。

im·prove·ment 🔑 /ɪm'pruːvmənt/ *noun* **1** 🔑 [U] the act of making sth better; the process of sth becoming better 改善；改進：*Sales figures continue to show signs of improvement.* 銷售額持續顯示出增加的跡象。◇ *We expect to see **further improvement** over the coming year.* 我們期望來年會有更進一步的改善。◇ **~ in/on/to sth** *There is still **room for improvement** in your work.* 你的工作尚有改進的餘地。 **2** 🔑 [C] a change in sth that makes it better; sth that is better than it was before 改進處；改善的事物：*a **significant/substantial/dramatic improvement*** 重要的／重大的／巨大的改進 ◇ *a **slight/steady improvement*** 輕微的／穩定的提升 ◇ **~ in/on/to sth** *an improvement in Anglo-German relations* 英德關係的改善 ◇ *This is a great improvement on your previous work.* 你的工作比先前有很大進步。◇ *improvements to the bus service* 公共汽車服務的改善

im·provi·dent /ɪm'prɒvɪdənt; *NAmE* -'prɑːv-/ *adj.* (*formal*) not thinking about or planning for the future; spending money in a careless way 不顧將來的；沒有長遠打算的；揮霍的；不節儉的 **OPP** **provident** ▸ **im·provi·dence** /-əns/ *noun* [U]

im·pro·vise /'ɪmprəvaɪz/ *verb* **1** [I, T] to make or do sth using whatever is available, usually because you do not have what you really need 臨時拼湊；臨時做：*There isn't much equipment. We're going to have to improvise.* 設備不多，我們只能將就着用。◇ **~ sth** *We improvised some shelves out of planks of wood and bricks.* 我們用木板和磚頭臨時搭了些架子。 **2** [I, T] to invent music, the words in a play, a statement, etc. while you are playing or speaking, instead of planning it in advance 即興創作（音樂、台詞、演講詞等）：*'It'll be ready some time next week, I expect,' she said, improvising.* "我估計下個星期內會準備好的。"她隨口說道。◇ **~ on sth** *He improvised on the melody.* 他即興演奏了那首曲子。◇ **~ sth** *an improvised speech* 即席講演 ▸ **im·pro·visa·tion** /ˌɪmprəvaɪ'zeɪʃn; *NAmE* ɪmˌprɑːvə'zeɪʃn/ *noun* [U, C]

im·pru·dent /ɪm'pruːdnt/ *adj.* (*formal*) not wise or sensible 不明智的；不謹慎的 **SYN** **unwise**：*It would be imprudent to invest all your money in one company.* 把所有的錢都投資在一家公司是不明智的。 **OPP** **prudent** ▸ **im·pru·dence** /-ns/ *noun* [U] **im·pru·dent·ly** *adv.*

im·pu·dent /'ɪmpjədənt/ *adj.* (*formal*) rude; not showing respect for other people 粗魯的；不恭的 **SYN** **impertinent**：*an impudent young fellow* 莽撞的年輕人 ◇ *an impudent remark* 粗魯的話 ▸ **im·pu·dence** /-əns/ *noun* [U]

im·pugn /ɪm'pjuːn/ *verb* **~ sth** (*formal*) to express doubts about whether sth is right, honest, etc. 對…表示懷疑；置疑 **SYN** **challenge**

im·pulse /'ɪmpʌls/ *noun* **1** [C, usually sing., U] **~ (to do sth)** a sudden strong wish or need to do sth, without stopping to think about the results 衝動；心血來潮；一時的念頭：*He had a sudden impulse to stand up and sing.* 他突然心血來潮，想站起來歌唱。◇ *I resisted the impulse to laugh.* 我強忍着沒有笑出來。◇ *Her first impulse was to run away.* 她的第一個念頭就是逃走。◇ *The door was open and **on (an) impulse** she went inside.* 門開着，她一時心血來潮就走了進去。◇ *He tends to act **on impulse**.* 他往往憑一時衝動行事。 **2** [C] (*technical* 術語) a force or movement of energy that causes sth else to react 動力；衝力；衝量：***nerve/electrical impulses*** 神經衝動；電路脈衝 **3** [C, usually sing., U] (*formal*) something that causes sb/sth to do sth or to develop and make progress 推動力；刺激：*to give an impulse to the struggling car industry* 給予掙扎中的汽車工業一點刺激

'impulse buying *noun* [U] buying goods without planning to do so in advance, and without thinking about it carefully 即興購買 ▸ **'impulse buy** *noun*：*It was an impulse buy.* 這是一時心血來潮買的。

im·pul·sion /ɪm'pʌlʃn/ *noun* (*formal*) **1** [C] a strong desire to do sth 衝動；強烈慾望 **2** [U] a reason for doing sth 理由；緣由：*Lack of food and water provided much of the impulsion for their speed.* 缺少食物和水促使他們加快了速度。

im·pul·sive /ɪm'pʌlsɪv/ *adj.* (of people or their behaviour 人或行為) acting suddenly without thinking carefully about what might happen because of what you are doing 憑衝動行事的；易衝動的 **SYN** **impetuous, rash**：*an **impulsive decision/gesture*** 衝動的決定／姿態 ◇ *You're so impulsive!* 你太衝動了！◇ *He has an impulsive nature.* 他生性衝動。 ▸ **im·pul·sive·ly** *adv.*：*Impulsively he reached out and took her hand.* 他一時衝動便伸手握住她的手。 **im·pul·sive·ness** *noun* [U]

im·pun·ity /ɪm'pjuːnəti/ *noun* [U] (*formal, disapproving*) if a person does sth bad **with impunity**, they do not get punished for what they have done 免於懲罰；不受懲處；逃過懲罰

im·pure /ɪm'pjʊə(r); *NAmE* ɪm'pjʊr/ *adj.* **1** not pure or clean; not consisting of only one substance but mixed with one or more substances often of poorer quality 不純的；不潔的；有雜質的：*impure gold* 不純的金子 **2** (*old-fashioned* or *formal*) (of thoughts or feelings 思想或感情) morally bad, especially because they are connected with sex 道德敗壞的；（尤指）淫亂的 **OPP** **pure**

im·pur·ity /ɪm'pjʊərəti; *NAmE* -'pjʊr-/ *noun* (*pl.* **-ies**) **1** [C] a substance that is present in small amounts in another substance, making it dirty or of poor quality 雜質：*A filter will remove most impurities found in water.* 過濾器會濾掉水中的大部份雜質。 **2** [U] the state of being dirty or not pure 骯髒；不純；淫穢 **OPP** **purity**

im·pute /ɪm'pjuːt/

PHR V **im'pute sth to sb/sth** (*formal*) to say, often unfairly, that sb is responsible for sth or has a particular quality（常指不公正地把責任等）歸咎於 **SYN** **attribute** ▸ **im·put·ation** /ˌɪmpju'teɪʃn/ *noun* [U, C]

in 🔑 /ɪn/ *prep., adv., adj., noun*

■ ***prep.*** **HELP** For the special uses of **in** in phrasal verbs, look at the entries for the verbs. For example **deal in sth** is in the phrasal verb section at **deal**. * in 在短語動詞中的特殊用法見有關動詞詞條。如 deal in sth 在詞條 deal 的短語動詞部份。 **1** 🔑 at a point within an area or a space 在（某範圍或空間內的）某一點：*a country in Africa* 非洲的一個國家 ◇ *The kids were playing in the street.* 孩子們在街上玩。◇ *It's in that drawer.* 它放在那個抽屜裏。◇ *I read about it in the paper.* 我是在報紙上讀到這事的。 **2** 🔑 within the shape of sth; surrounded by sth 在（某物的形體或範圍）中；在…內；在…中：*She was lying in bed.* 她躺在牀上。◇ *sitting in an armchair* 坐在扶手椅裏 ◇ *Leave the key in the lock.* 把鑰匙留在鎖孔裏。◇ *Soak it in cold water.* 把這東西浸泡在冷水裏。 **3** 🔑 into sth 進入：*He dipped his brush in the paint.* 他把毛刷在塗料裏蘸了蘸。◇ *She got in her car and drove off.* 她鑽進汽車裏，開走了。 **4** 🔑 forming the whole or part of sth/sb; contained within sth/sb 構成…的整體（或部份）；包含在…之內：*There are 31 days in May.* 五月份有 31 天。◇ *all the paintings in the collection* 收藏品中的所有畫作 ◇ *I recognize his father in him* (= his character is similar to his father's). 我在他身上看到了他父親的氣質。 **5** 🔑 during a period of time 在（某段時間）內：*in 2009* 在 2009 年 ◇ *in the 18th century* 在 18 世紀 ◇ *in spring/summer/autumn/winter* 在春天／夏天／秋天／冬天 ◇ *in the fall* 在秋天 ◇ *in March* 在三月 ◇ *in the morning/afternoon/evening* 在上午／下午／晚上 ◇ *I'm getting forgetful in my old age.* 我現在上了年紀，變得健忘了。 **6** 🔑 after a particular length of time 在（某段時間）之後：*to return in a few minutes/hours/days/months.* 幾分鐘／幾小時／幾天／幾個月後回來 ◇ *It will be ready in a week's time* (= one week from now). 只需一週的時間就會準備好。◇ *She learnt to drive in three weeks* (= after three weeks she could drive). 她花了三個星期就學會開車。 **7** 🔑 (used in negative sentences or after *first, last*, etc. 用於否定句或 first、last 等之後) for a particular period of time 在（某段時間）內：*I haven't seen him in years.* 我有好些年沒見過他了。◇ *It's the first letter I've had in ten days.* 這是我十天來收到的第一封信。 **8** 🔑 wearing sth 穿着；戴着：*dressed in their best clothes* 穿着他們最好的衣服 ◇ *the man in the hat* 戴帽子的男子 ◇ *to be in uniform* 穿着制服 ◇ *She was all in black.* 她穿着一身黑。 **9** 🔑 used to describe physical surroundings（用以描述具體的環境）：*We went out in the rain.* 我們冒雨出去了。◇ *He was sitting alone in the* darkness. 他獨自坐在黑暗中。**10** used to show a state or condition（表示狀態或狀況）: *I'm in love!* 我戀愛了！◇ *The house is in good repair.* 這所房子保養得不錯。◇ *I must put my affairs in order.* 我必須整理整理我的事務。◇ *a man in his thirties* 一名三十多歲的男子 ◇ *The daffodils were in full bloom.* 水仙花正盛開。**11** involved in sth; taking part in sth 參與；參加：*to act in a play* 參加演戲 **12** used to show sb's job or profession（顯示工作或職業）: *He is in the army.* 他在軍隊服役。◇ *She's in computers.* 她從事計算機業。◇ *in business* 從商 **13** used to show the form, shape, arrangement or quantity of sth（顯示某物的形式、形狀、安排或數量）: *a novel in three parts* 分為三部的小說 ◇ *Roll it up in a ball.* 把它捲成一個球。◇ *They sat in rows.* 他們一排一排地坐着。◇ *People flocked in their thousands to see her.* 現場聚集了數以千計的人爭相目睹她的丰采。**14** used to show the language, material, etc. used（表示使用的語言、材料等）: *Say it in English.* 用英語說吧。◇ *She wrote in pencil.* 她用鉛筆寫的。◇ *Put it in writing.* 把它寫下來。◇ *I paid in cash.* 我用現金支付的。◇ *He spoke in a loud voice.* 他大聲說話。**15** concerning sth 關於；在…方面：*She was not lacking in courage.* 她並不缺乏勇氣。◇ *a country rich in minerals* 礦藏豐富的國家 ◇ *three metres in length* 三米長 **16** while doing sth; while sth is happening 做…時；…發生時；當…時：*In attempting to save the child from drowning, she nearly lost her own life.* 她在搶救落水的兒童時，自己差點喪命。◇ *In all the commotion I forgot to tell him the news.* 在一陣混亂之中我忘了告訴他那個消息。**17** used to introduce the name of a person who has a particular quality（引出具某種品質的人的名字）: *We're losing a first-rate editor in Jen.* 我們即將失去詹恩這位一流的編輯。**18** used to show a rate or relative amount（顯示比率或相對數量）: *a gradient of one in five* 五分之一的坡度 ◇ *a tax rate of 22 pence in the pound* 每英鎊 22 便士的稅率

IDM **in that** /ɪn ðət/ (*formal*) for the reason that; because 原因是；因為：*She was fortunate in that she had friends to help her.* 她很幸運，有一些朋友幫助她。

■ *adv.* HELP For the special uses of **in** in phrasal verbs, look at the entries for the verbs. For example **fill in (for sb)** is in the phrasal verb section at **fill**. * in 在短語動詞中的特殊用法見有關動詞詞條。如 fill in (for sb) 在詞條 fill 的短語動詞部份。**1** contained within an object, an area or a substance 在裏面；在內：*We were locked in.* 我們被鎖在裏面了。◇ *I can't drink coffee with milk in.* 我不能喝加牛奶的咖啡。**2** into an object, an area or a substance 進入：*She opened the door and went in.* 她打開門進去了。◇ *The kids were playing by the river and one of them fell in.* 孩子們在河邊玩耍時，其中一個突然落水了。**3** (of people 人) at home or at a place of work 在家裏；在工作單位：*Nobody was in when we called.* 我們打電話過去時沒有人在。OPP **out 4** (of trains, buses, etc. 火車、公共汽車等) at the place where people can get on or off, for example the station 在車站；在停靠站：*The bus is due in* (= it should arrive) *at six.* 公共汽車應該在六點鐘到站。**5** (of letters, etc. 信件等) received 收到；被投遞到：*Applications must be in by April 30.* 申請務必於四月三十日之前寄到。**6** (of the TIDE 潮汐) at or towards its highest point on land 上漲；在最高點：*Is the tide coming in or going out?* 現在是漲潮還是落潮？**7** elected 當選：*Several new councillors got in at the last election.* 幾位新政務委員在最近一輪選舉中當選。**8** (in CRICKET, BASEBALL, etc. 板球、棒球等) if a team or team member is **in**, they are BATTING 擊球 **9** (in TENNIS, etc. 網球等) if the ball is **in**, it has landed inside the line（球）落在界內：*Her serve was just in.* 她發的球剛好落在界內。

IDM **be in at sth** to be present when sth happens 某事發生時在場：*They were in at the start.* 開始時他們在場。**be 'in for sth** (*informal*) to be going to experience sth soon, especially sth unpleasant 即將經歷，即將遭受（不愉快的事）: *He's in for a shock!* 他很快就會感到震驚的！◇ *I'm afraid we're in for a storm.* 看來我們就要遇到風暴了。**be/get 'in on sth** (*informal*) to be/become involved in sth; to share or know about sth 參與；瞭解：*I'd like to be in on the plan.* 我很想參與這項計劃。◇ *Is she in on the secret?* 她知道這個秘密嗎？**be (well) 'in with sb** (*informal*) to be (very) friendly with sb, and likely to get an advantage from the friendship 和…（十分）友好（很可能從中得到好處）**,in and 'out (of sth)** going regularly to a place 時常出入：*He was in and out of jail for most of his life.* 他大半生的時間都是監獄的常客。

■ *adj.* [usually before noun] (*informal*) popular and fashionable 流行的；時髦的：*Purple is the in colour this spring.* 紫色是今年春天的流行色。◇ *Exotic pets are the in thing right now.* 奇異的寵物眼下很時髦。◇ *Short skirts are in again.* 現在又時興穿短裙子了。➔ see also IN-JOKE

■ *noun*

IDM **an 'in to sth** = A WAY INTO STH at WAY *n.* **have an 'in with sb** (*especially NAmE*) to have influence with sb 對某人有影響 **the ,ins and 'outs (of sth)** all the details, especially the complicated or difficult ones（尤指複雜或難的）全部細節，詳情：*the ins and outs of the problem* 問題的來龍去脈 ◇ *He quickly learned the ins and outs of the job.* 他很快就掌握了工作的全部訣竅。

in- *prefix* /ɪn/ **1** (also **il-** /ɪl/, **im-** /ɪm/, **ir-** /ɪr/) (in adjectives, adverbs and nouns 構成形容詞、副詞和名詞) not; the opposite of 不；非；相反的：*infinite* 無限的 ◇ *illogical* 不合邏輯的 ◇ *immorally* 不道德 ◇ *irrelevance* 不相關 **2** (also **im-** /ɪm/) (in verbs 構成動詞) to put into the condition mentioned 使置於某狀況：*inflame* 使憤怒 ◇ *imperil* 使處於危險之中

-in *combining form* (in nouns 構成名詞) an activity in which many people take part 很多人參加的活動：*a sit-in* 靜坐示威 ◇ *a teach-in* 研討會

in. *abbr.* (*pl.* **in.** or **ins.**) INCH 英寸：*Height: 6ft 2in.* 高：6 英尺 2 英寸。

in·abil·ity /ˌɪnəˈbɪləti/ *noun* [U, sing.] **~ (to do sth)** the fact of not being able to do sth 無能；無力；不能：*the government's inability to provide basic services* 政府在提供基本服務方面的無能 ◇ *Some families go without medical treatment because of their inability to pay.* 有些家庭因無力支付醫療費用而得不到醫治。OPP **ability**

in ab·sen·tia /ˌɪn æbˈsenʃiə/ *adv.* (from *Latin*) while not present at the event being referred to 缺席：*Two foreign suspects will be tried in absentia.* 兩名外籍嫌疑犯將被缺席審判。

in·access·ible AW /ˌɪnækˈsesəbl/ *adj.* difficult or impossible to reach or to get 難以達到的；不可得到的：*They live in a remote area, inaccessible except by car.* 他們住在一處偏遠地區，只能開車去。◇ **~ to sb/sth** *The temple is now inaccessible to the public.* 這個寺廟現在不對公眾開放了。◇ (*figurative*) *The language of teenagers is often completely inaccessible to* (= not understood by) *adults.* 青少年的語言成人往往聽不懂。OPP **accessible** ▶ **in·access·ibil·ity** /ˌɪnækˌsesəˈbɪləti/ *noun* [U]

in·accur·ate AW /ɪnˈækjərət/ *adj.* not exact or accurate; with mistakes 不精確的；不準確的；有錯誤的：*an inaccurate statement* 不確切的說法 ◇ *inaccurate information* 不準確的信息 ◇ *All the maps we had were wildly inaccurate.* 我們所有的地圖誤差都非常大。OPP **accurate** ▶ **in·accur·acy** AW /ɪnˈækjərəsi/ *noun* [C, U] (*pl.* **-ies**): *The article is full of inaccuracies.* 這篇文章裏的錯誤比比皆是。◇ *The writer is guilty of bias and inaccuracy.* 這位作者失於偏頗，且敍述不實。➔ SYNONYMS at MISTAKE **in·accur·ate·ly** *adv.*

in·action /ɪnˈækʃn/ *noun* [U] (usually *disapproving*) lack of action; the state of doing nothing about a situation or a problem 無行動；不採取措施

in·acti·vate /ɪnˈæktɪveɪt/ *verb* **~ sth** (*technical* 術語) to make sth stop doing sth; to make sth no longer active 使滅活；使停止活動

in·active /ɪnˈæktɪv/ *adj.* **1** not doing anything; not active 無行動的；不活動的；不活躍的：*Some animals are inactive during the daytime.* 有些動物白天不活動。◇ *politically inactive* 對政治不熱衷 ◇ *The volcano has been inactive for 50 years.* 這座火山處於休眠狀態 50 年了。**2** not in use; not working 未使用的；不運轉的：*an inactive oil well* 閒置的油井 **3** having no effect 無作用的；無效的：*an* ***inactive drug/disease*** 失效的藥物；非活動性疾病 OPP **active** ▶ **in·activ·ity** /ˌɪnækˈtɪvəti/ *noun* [U]: *periods of enforced inactivity and boredom* 被迫無

事可做、單調乏味的時期 ◇ *The inactivity of the government was deplorable.* 政府的無所作為受到了譴責。

in·ad·equacy AW /ɪnˈædɪkwəsi/ *noun* (*pl.* **-ies**) **1** [U] **~ (of sth)** the state of not being enough or good enough 不充分；不足；不夠：*the inadequacy of our resources* 我們的資源的貧乏 OPP **adequacy** **2** [U] a state of not being able or confident to deal with a situation 不勝任；缺乏信心：*a* ***feeling/sense of inadequacy*** 不稱職之感 **3** [C, usually pl.] **~ (of/in sth)** a weakness; a lack of sth 弱點；缺陷；某事物的缺乏：*gross inadequacies in the data* 數據資料的極端匱乏 ◇ *He had to face up to his own inadequacies as a father.* 他不得不正視自身作為父親的不足。

in·ad·equate AW /ɪnˈædɪkwət/ *adj.* **1** not enough; not good enough 不充分的；不足的；不夠的：*inadequate supplies* 供應短缺 ◇ **~ for sth** *The system is inadequate for the tasks it has to perform.* 這個系統要完成它的任務還不夠完善。◇ **~ to do sth** *The food supplies are inadequate to meet the needs of the hungry.* 食物供應還不足以應付饑民的需求。OPP **adequate** **2** (of people 人) not able, or not confident enough, to deal with a situation 不勝任的；缺乏信心的 SYN **incompetent**：*I felt totally* ***inadequate*** *as a parent.* 我覺得我作為父親（或母親）完全不稱職。▸ **in·ad·equate·ly** AW *adv.*：*to be inadequately prepared/insured/funded* 準備不充分；保額／資金不足

in·ad·mis·sible /ˌɪnədˈmɪsəbl/ *adj.* (*formal*) that cannot be allowed or accepted, especially in court（尤指法庭上）不允許的，不能採納的：*inadmissible evidence* 不可採納的證據 OPP **admissible**

in·ad·vert·ent·ly /ˌɪnədˈvɜːtəntli; *NAmE* -ˈvɜːrt-/ *adv.* by accident; without intending to 無意地；不經意地 SYN **unintentionally**：*We had inadvertently left without paying the bill.* 我們無意之中未付賬就離開了。▸ **in·ad·vert·ent** *adj.*：*an inadvertent omission* 不經意的疏忽 **in·ad·ver·tence** *noun* [U]

in·ad·vis·able /ˌɪnədˈvaɪzəbl/ *adj.* [not usually before noun] **~ (for sb) (to do sth)** (*formal*) not sensible or wise; that you would advise against 不明智；不可取：***It is inadvisable to*** *bring children on this trip.* 這次旅行帶孩子不妥當。OPP **advisable**

in·ali·en·able /ɪnˈeɪliənəbl/ (also *less frequent* **un·ali·en·able**) *adj.* [usually before noun] (*formal*) that cannot be taken away from you 不可剝奪（或分割）的：*the* ***inalienable right*** *to decide your own future* 不可剝奪的決定自己未來的權利

in·am·or·ata /ɪnˌæməˈrɑːtə/ *noun* (from *Italian*, *formal* or *humorous*) a person's female lover 女情人

inane /ɪˈneɪn/ *adj.* stupid or silly; with no meaning 愚蠢的；無意義的：*an inane remark* 無聊的話語 ▸ **in·ane·ly** *adv.*：*to grin inanely* 咧嘴憨笑 **in·an·ity** /ɪˈnænəti/ *noun* [U, C, usually pl.] (*pl.* **-ies**)

in·ani·mate /ɪnˈænɪmət/ *adj.* **1** not alive in the way that people, animals and plants are 無生命的：*A rock is an inanimate object.* 岩石是無生命的物體。OPP **animate** **2** dead or appearing to be dead 死的；像已死的：*A man was lying inanimate on the floor.* 一個男子躺在地板上，看樣子像是死了。

in·applic·able /ˌɪnəˈplɪkəbl; ɪnˈæplɪkəbl/ *adj.* [not before noun] **~ (to sb/sth)** that cannot be used, or that does not apply, in a particular situation 不適用；不可應用：*These regulations are inapplicable to international students.* 這些規章不適用於外籍學生。OPP **applicable**

in·appro·pri·ate AW /ˌɪnəˈprəʊpriət; *NAmE* -ˈproʊ-/ *adj.* not suitable or appropriate in a particular situation 不適當的；不合適的：*inappropriate behaviour/language* 不恰當的行為／語言 ◇ **~ (for sb/sth) (to do sth)** ***It would be inappropriate for me to*** *comment.* 由我評論並不恰當。◇ **~ to/for sth** *clothes inappropriate to the occasion* 不得體的衣着 OPP **appropriate** ▸ **in·appro·pri·acy** AW *noun* [U] **in·appro·pri·ate·ly** AW *adv.*：*She was inappropriately dressed for a funeral.* 她的穿着不適合參加葬禮。**in·appro·pri·ate·ness** *noun* [U]

in·articu·late /ˌɪnɑːˈtɪkjələt; *NAmE* -ɑːrˈtɪk-/ *adj.* **1** (of people 人) not able to express ideas or feelings clearly or easily 不善於表達的；不善於說話的 **2** (of speech 講話) not using clear words; not expressed clearly 詞不達意的；表達得不清楚的：*an inarticulate reply* 含混不清的回答 OPP **articulate** ▸ **in·articu·late·ly** *adv.*

in·as·much as /ˌɪnəzˈmʌtʃ əz/ *conj.* (*formal*) used to add a comment on sth that you have just said and to say in what way it is true 因為；鑒於；在…範圍內：*He was a very unusual musician inasmuch as he was totally deaf.* 他是完全失聰的，從這點上來說，他是個很了不起的音樂家。

in·atten·tion /ˌɪnəˈtenʃn/ *noun* [U] (usually *disapproving*) lack of attention 不注意；不經心：*The accident was the result of a moment's inattention.* 這次事故是一時不小心造成的。

in·atten·tive /ˌɪnəˈtentɪv/ *adj.* (*disapproving*) not paying attention to sth/sb 不注意的；不經心：*an inattentive pupil* 注意力不集中的學生 ◇ **~ to sth/sb** *inattentive to the needs of others* 漠視他人的需要 OPP **attentive** ▸ **in·atten·tive·ly** *adv.*

in·aud·ible /ɪnˈɔːdəbl/ *adj.* **~ (to sb)** that you cannot hear 聽不見的：*The whistle was inaudible to the human ear.* 這種哨聲人耳聽不到。OPP **audible** ▸ **in·audi·bil·ity** /ɪnˌɔːdəˈbɪləti/ *noun* [U] **in·aud·ibly** /ɪnˈɔːdəbli/ *adv.*

in·aug·ural /ɪˈnɔːgjərəl/ *adj.* [only before noun] (of an official speech, meeting, etc. 正式講話、會議等) first, and marking the beginning of sth important, for example the time when a new leader or parliament starts work, when a new organization is formed or when sth is used for the first time 就職的；開幕的；成立的；創始的：*the President's inaugural address* 總統的就職演說 ◇ *the inaugural meeting of the geographical society* 地理學會的成立大會 ◇ *the inaugural flight of the space shuttle* 航天飛機的首次飛行 ▸ **in·aug·ural** *noun* [C, usually sing.] (*especially NAmE*)：*the presidential inaugural in January* 一月間的總統就職演說

in·aug·ur·ate /ɪˈnɔːgjəreɪt/ *verb* **1** **~ sb (as sth)** | **~ sb + noun** to introduce a new public official or leader at a special ceremony 為（某人）舉行就職典禮：*He will be inaugurated (as) President in January.* 他將於一月份就任總統。**2** **~ sth** to officially open a building or start an organization with a special ceremony 為…舉行落成儀式（或創建儀式）：*The new theatre was inaugurated by the mayor.* 新落成的劇院由市長主持了開幕典禮。**3** **~ sth** (*formal*) to introduce a new development or an important change 引進；開創；開始：*The moon landing inaugurated a new era in space exploration.* 登陸月球開創了太空探索的新紀元。▸ **in·aug·ur·ation** /ɪˌnɔːgjəˈreɪʃn/ *noun* [U, C]：*the President's inauguration* 總統就職典禮 ◇ *an inauguration speech* 就職演說

Iˌnaugu'ration Day *noun* (in the US) 20 January, officially the first day of a new President's period of office 美國總統就職日（1 月 20 日）

in·aus·pi·cious /ˌɪnɔːˈspɪʃəs/ *adj.* (*formal*) showing signs that the future will not be good or successful 預示前景黯淡的；不祥的；不吉利的：*an inauspicious start* 不吉利的開頭 OPP **auspicious** ▸ **in·aus·pi·cious·ly** *adv.*

in·authen·tic /ˌɪnɔːˈθentɪk/ *adj.* not genuine; that you cannot believe or rely on 假的；不可信的；不可靠的 OPP **authentic** ▸ **in·authen·ti·city** /ˌɪnɔːθenˈtɪsəti/ *noun* [U]

in·board /ˈɪnbɔːd; *NAmE* -bɔːrd/ *adj.* (*technical* 術語) located on the inside of a boat, plane or car（船、飛機或汽車）內部的；艙內的：*an inboard motor* 艙內馬達 OPP **outboard** ▸ **in·board** *adv.*

in·born /ˌɪnˈbɔːn; *NAmE* -ˈbɔːrn/ (also *less frequent* **in·bred**) *adj.* an **inborn** quality is one that you are born with 天生的；先天的 SYN **innate**

in·bound /ˈɪnbaʊnd/ *adj.* (*formal*) travelling towards a place rather than leaving it 到達的；入境的：***inbound flights/passengers*** 入境班機／乘客 OPP **outbound**

in·bounds /ˈɪnbaʊndz/ *adj.* (in BASKETBALL 籃球) relating to a throw that puts the ball into play again after it has gone out of play 從界外擲入界內的：*an inbounds pass* 從界外投到界內的傳球

'in box *noun* (*NAmE*) = IN TRAY

in·box /ˈɪnbɒks; *NAmE* -bɑːks/ *noun* (*computing* 計) the place on a computer where new email messages are shown （電子郵件）收件箱：*I have a stack of emails in my inbox.* 我的收件箱裏有很多電郵。➲ COLLOCATIONS at EMAIL

in·bred /ˌɪnˈbred/ *adj.* **1** produced by breeding among closely related members of a group of animals, people or plants 近親繁殖的；同系交配的：*an inbred racehorse* 同系交配的賽馬 **2** = INBORN

in·breed·ing /ˈɪnbriːdɪŋ/ *noun* [U] breeding between closely related people or animals 近親繁殖；同系交配

in·built /ˈɪnbɪlt/ *adj.* [only before noun] an **inbuilt** quality exists as an essential part of sth/sb 內在的；本質的；天生的：*His height gives him an inbuilt advantage over his opponent.* 他的身高成為他相對於對手的先天優勢。➲ compare BUILT-IN

ˌin-ˈbuilt *adj.* = BUILT-IN

Inc. /ɪŋk/ (also **inc**) *abbr.* Incorporated (used after the name of a company in the US) 公司（美國用法，置於公司名稱之後）：*Texaco Inc.* 德士古石油公司

inc. *abbr.* (*BrE*) = INCL.

in·cal·cul·able /ɪnˈkælkjələbl/ *adj.* (*formal*) very large or very great; too great to calculate 極大的；不可計算的；不可估量的：*The oil spill has caused incalculable damage to the environment.* 這次石油泄漏對環境造成了難以估計的損害。➲ compare CALCULABLE ▸ **in·cal·cul·ably** /-əbli/ *adv.*

in·can·des·cent /ˌɪnkænˈdesnt/ *adj.* **1** (*technical* 術語) giving out light when heated 白熱的；白熾的：*incandescent lamps* 白熾燈 **2** (*formal*) very bright 十分明亮的；耀眼的：*incandescent white* 刺眼的白色 **3** (*formal*) full of strong emotion 感情強烈的；激情的：*an incandescent musical performance* 充滿激情的音樂演奏 ◇ *She was incandescent with rage.* 她怒不可遏。▸ **in·can·des·cence** /-sns/ *noun* [U]

in·can·ta·tion /ˌɪnkænˈteɪʃn/ *noun* [C, U] special words that are spoken or sung to have a magic effect; the act of speaking or singing these words 符咒；咒語；唸咒語

in·cap·able AW /ɪnˈkeɪpəbl/ *adj.* **1** not able to do sth 沒有能力（做某事）：**~ of sth** *incapable of speech* 不會說話 ◇ **~ of doing sth** *The children seem to be* ***totally incapable*** *of working by themselves.* 孩子們好像完全不能靠自己做功課。 **2** not able to control yourself or your affairs; not able to do anything well 不能克制自己的；不能自理的；什麼事也做不好的：*He was found lying in the road, drunk and incapable.* 他被發現躺在路上，爛醉如泥。◇ *If people keep telling you you're incapable, you begin to lose confidence in yourself.* 如果人們不斷地對你說你無能，你就開始失去自信心了。OPP **capable**

in·cap·aci·tate AW /ˌɪnkəˈpæsɪteɪt/ *verb* [usually passive] **~ sb/sth** (*formal*) to make sb/sth unable to live or work normally 使失去正常生活（或工作）能力

in·cap·acity /ˌɪnkəˈpæsəti/ *noun* [U] (*formal*) **1 ~ (of sb/sth) (to do sth)** lack of ability or skill 無能力；缺乏技能 SYN **inability**：*their incapacity to govern effectively* 他們缺乏有效治理的能力 **2** the state of being too ill/sick to do your work or take care of yourself 臥病；孱弱：*She returned to work after a long period of incapacity.* 她病了很長一段時間之後回去工作了。

ˌin-ˈcar *adj.* [only before noun] relating to sth that you have or use inside a car, for example a radio or CD player 車內安裝（或使用）的；車內的：*in-car entertainment* 安裝於車內的娛樂系統

in·car·cer·ate /ɪnˈkɑːsəreɪt; *NAmE* -ˈkɑːrs-/ *verb* [usually passive] **~ sb (in sth)** (*formal*) to put sb in prison or in another place from which they cannot escape 監禁；關押；禁閉 SYN **imprison** ▸ **in·car·cer·ation** /ɪnˌkɑːsəˈreɪʃn; *NAmE* -ˌkɑːrs-/ *noun* [U]

in·car·nate *adj.*, *verb*

■ *adj.* /ɪnˈkɑːnət; *NAmE* -ˈkɑːrn-/ (usually after nouns 通常在名詞之後) (*formal*) in human form 人體化的；化身的；擬人化的：*The leader seemed the devil incarnate.* 那個首領猶如魔鬼的化身。

■ *verb* /ˈɪnkɑːneɪt; *NAmE* -kɑːrn-/ **~ sth** (*formal*) to give a definite or human form to a particular idea or quality 將（概念或品質）具體化；使人格化；擬人化 SYN **embody**

in·car·na·tion /ˌɪnkɑːˈneɪʃn; *NAmE* -kɑːrˈn-/ *noun* **1** [C] a period of life in a particular form（某一段時間內的）化身：*one of the incarnations of Vishnu* 守護神毗濕奴的化身之一 ◇ *He believed he had been a prince in a previous incarnation.* 他相信他的前生是個王子。◇ (*figurative*) *I worked for her in her earlier incarnation* (= her previous job) *as a lawyer.* 她先前當律師時我曾受雇於她。 **2** [C] a person who represents a particular quality, for example, in human form 代表某種品質的人；化身 SYN **embodiment**：*the incarnation of evil* 邪惡的化身 **3** [sing., U] (also **the Incarnation**) (in Christianity 基督教) the act of God coming to earth in human form as Jesus 道成肉身（上帝化身為耶穌來到人間）

in·cau·tious /ɪnˈkɔːʃəs/ *adj.* (*formal*) done without thinking carefully about the results; not thinking about what might happen 不慎重的；輕率的；魯莽的 ▸ **in·cau·tious·ly** *adv.*

in·cen·di·ary /ɪnˈsendiəri; *NAmE* -dieri/ *adj.*, *noun*

■ *adj.* [only before noun] **1** designed to cause fires 放火的；縱火的；能引起燃燒的：*an* ***incendiary device/bomb/attack*** 噴火器；燃燒彈；火攻 **2** (*formal*) causing strong feelings or violence 煽動的 SYN **inflammatory**：*incendiary remarks* 煽動性言論

■ *noun* (*pl.* **-ies**) a bomb that is designed to make a fire start burning when it explodes 燃燒彈 SYN **firebomb**

in·cense *noun*, *verb*

■ *noun* /ˈɪnsens/ [U] a substance that produces a pleasant smell when you burn it, used particularly in religious ceremonies 香（尤指宗教禮儀用的）

■ *verb* /ɪnˈsens/ **~ sb** to make sb very angry 激怒；使大怒：*The decision incensed the workforce.* 這個決定激怒了勞工大眾。

in·censed /ɪnˈsenst/ *adj.* very angry 非常憤怒的；大怒的：*They were incensed at the decision.* 他們被這個決定激怒了。

in·cen·tive AW /ɪnˈsentɪv/ *noun* [C, U] **~ (for/to sb/sth) (to do sth)** something that encourages you to do sth 激勵；刺激；鼓勵：*tax incentives to encourage savings* 鼓勵儲蓄的稅收措施 ◇ *There is no incentive for people to save fuel.* 沒有鼓勵人們節約燃料的措施。OPP **disincentive**

in·cen·tiv·ize (*BrE* also **-ise**) /ɪnˈsentɪvaɪz/ *verb* to encourage sb to behave in a particular way by offering them a reward 激勵；獎勵：**~ sth** *ways to incentivize innovation* 獎掖鼓勵創新的途徑 ◇ **~ sb to do sth** *You need to incentivize your existing customers to stay with you.* 你得獎勵並留住現有客戶。

in·cep·tion /ɪnˈsepʃn/ *noun* [sing.] (*formal*) the start of an institution, an organization, etc.（機構、組織等的）開端，創始：*The club has grown rapidly since its inception in 2007.* 這個俱樂部自從 2007 年成立以來發展迅速。

in·ces·sant /ɪnˈsesnt/ *adj.* (usually *disapproving*) never stopping 不停的；持續不斷的 SYN **constant**：*incessant noise/rain/chatter* 不間斷的噪音／陰雨／絮叨 ◇ *incessant meetings* 接二連三的會議 ▸ **in·ces·sant·ly** *adv.*：*to talk incessantly* 滔滔不絕地談話

in·cest /ˈɪnsest/ *noun* [U] sexual activity between two people who are very closely related in a family, for example, a brother and sister, or a father and daughter 亂倫；血親相姦

in·ces·tu·ous /ɪnˈsestjuəs; *NAmE* -tʃuəs/ *adj.* **1** involving sex between two people in a family who are very closely related 亂倫的；血親相姦的：*an incestuous relationship* 亂倫關係 **2** (*disapproving*) involving a group of people who have a close relationship and do not want to include anyone outside the group 小集團的；小團體的；排外的：*The music industry is an incestuous business.* 音樂界是一個封閉的行業。▸ **in·ces·tu·ous·ly** *adv.*

inch 🔑 /ɪntʃ/ *noun*, *verb*

■ *noun* **1** 🔑 (*abbr.* **in.**) a unit for measuring length, equal to 2.54 centimetres. There are 12 inches in a foot. 英寸（長度單位，等於 2.54 厘米，1 英尺等於 12 英寸）：*1.14 inches of rain fell last night.* 昨晚的降雨量為 1.14

英寸。◇ *She's a few inches taller than me.* 她比我高幾英寸。 **2** a small amount or distance 少量；短距離： *He escaped death* ***by an inch.*** 他差點喪了命。◇ *The car missed us* ***by inches.*** 那輛車險些撞到了我們。◇ *He was just inches away from scoring.* 他只差一點兒就得分了。

IDM every inch 1 the whole of sth 整體；全部： *The doctor examined every inch of his body.* 醫生檢查了他全身的每一部份。◇ (*figurative*) *If they try to fire me I'll fight them* ***every inch of the way.*** 他們要是想解雇我，我就和他們抗爭到底。 **2** completely 完全地： *In his first game the young player already looked every inch a winner.* 那位年輕的選手在第一場比賽就已經被認為勝券在握。 **give sb an 'inch (and they'll take a 'mile/'yard)** (*saying*) used to say that if you allow some people a small amount of freedom or power they will see you as weak and try to take a lot more 得寸進尺 **,inch by 'inch** very slowly and with great care or difficulty 緩慢而謹慎地；一步一步： *She crawled forward inch by inch.* 她一點一點地往前爬。 **not budge/give/move an 'inch** to refuse to change your position, decision, etc. even a little 寸步不讓： *We tried to negotiate a lower price but they wouldn't budge an inch.* 我們試圖把價還低一些，但他們寸步不讓。 **within an 'inch of sth/of doing sth** very close to sth/doing sth 差一點；險些： *She was within an inch of being killed.* 她險些喪命。◇ *They beat him (to) within an inch of his life* (= very severely). 他們險些兒把他打死。 ➲ more at TRUST *v.*

■ ***verb*** [I, T] to move or make sth move slowly and carefully in a particular direction （使朝某方向）謹慎移動： **+ adv./prep.** *She moved forward, inching towards the rope.* 她小心翼翼地慢慢向繩子挪過去。◇ **~ sth + adv./prep.** *I inched the car forward.* 我開着車小心地緩緩前行。◇ *He* ***inched his way*** *through the narrow passage.* 他一點一點地穿過狹窄的通道。

in·charge /ˈɪntʃɑːdʒ; *NAmE* -tʃɑːrdʒ/ *noun* (*IndE*) the person who is officially responsible for a department, etc. （部門等的）負責人，主管： *the incharge of the district hospital* 區醫院院長

in·cho·ate /ɪnˈkəʊət; ˈɪnkəʊeɪt; *NAmE* -ˈkoʊ-/ *adj.* (*formal*) just beginning to form and therefore not clear or developed 初期的；雛形的；不成熟的： *inchoate ideas* 初步想法

in·cho·ative /ɪnˈkəʊətɪv; *NAmE* -ˈkoʊə-/ *adj.* (*grammar* 語法) (of verbs 動詞) expressing a change of state that happens on its own. *Opened* in *the door opened* is an example of an inchoative verb. 表始的（表示動作自動開始的，如 the door opened 中的 opened） ➲ compare CAUSATIVE, ERGATIVE

in·ci·dence AW /ˈɪnsɪdəns/ *noun* **1** [C, usually sing.] **~ of sth** (*formal*) the extent to which sth happens or has an effect 發生範圍；影響程度；發生率： *an area with a* ***high incidence*** *of crime* 犯罪率高的地區 **2** [U] (*physics* 物) the way in which light meets a surface 入射（角）： *the angle of incidence* 入射角

in·ci·dent 🔑 AW /ˈɪnsɪdənt/ *noun*

1 🔑 [C] something that happens, especially sth unusual or unpleasant 發生的事情（尤指不尋常的或討厭的）： *His bad behaviour was just an isolated incident.* 他的不良行為只是個別事件。◇ *One particular incident sticks in my mind.* 有一件事我總忘不了。 **2** 🔑 [C, U] a serious or violent event, such as a crime, an accident or an attack 嚴重事件，暴力事件（如犯罪、事故、襲擊等）： *There was a shooting incident near here last night.* 昨夜這附近發生了槍擊事件。◇ *The demonstration passed off* ***without incident.*** 這次示威和平地結束了。 **3** 🔑 [C] a disagreement between two countries, often involving military forces （兩國間的）摩擦，衝突；（常指）軍事衝突： ***a border/diplomatic incident*** 邊境／外交衝突

in·ci·den·tal /ˌɪnsɪˈdentl/ *adj., noun*

■ ***adj.*** **1 ~ (to sth)** happening in connection with sth else, but not as important as it, or not intended 附帶發生的；次要的；非有意的： *The discovery was incidental to their main research.* 這一發現是他們主要研究中的附帶收穫。◇ ***incidental music*** (= music used with a play or a film/movie to give atmosphere) 配樂 ◇ *You may be able to get help with* ***incidental expenses*** (= small costs that you get in connection with sth). 你可以付些錢找人幫忙。 **2 ~ to sth** (*technical* 術語) happening as a natural result of sth 作為自然結果的；伴隨而來的；免不了的： *These risks are incidental to the work of a firefighter.* 這些風險是擔任消防員不可避免的。

■ ***noun*** [usually pl.] something that happens in connection with sth else, but is less important 附帶的次要事情： *You'll need money for incidentals such as tips and taxis.* 你將需要準備好付小費和乘出租車之類的雜項開銷。

in·ci·den·tal·ly AW /ˌɪnsɪˈdentli/ *adv.* **1** used to introduce a new topic, or some extra information, or a question that you have just thought of （引出新話題、附加信息、或臨時想到的問題）順便提一句 SYN **by the way**： *Incidentally, have you heard the news about Sue?* 順便問一句，你聽說過蘇的事了嗎？ **2** in a way that was not planned but that is connected with sth else 偶然；附帶地： *The information was only discovered incidentally.* 這個信息只是偶然得到的。

ˈincident room *noun* (*BrE*) a room near where a serious crime has taken place where the police work to collect evidence and information （設在嚴重罪案現場附近的）案件調查室

in·cin·er·ate /ɪnˈsɪnəreɪt/ *verb* [often passive] **~ sth** (*formal*) to burn sth until it is completely destroyed 把…燒成灰燼；焚燬 ▶ **in·cin·er·ation** /ɪnˌsɪnəˈreɪʃn/ *noun* [U]： *high-temperature incineration plants* 高溫焚化廠

in·cin·er·ator /ɪnˈsɪnəreɪtə(r)/ *noun* a container which is closed on all sides for burning waste at high temperatures （垃圾）焚化爐

in·cipi·ent /ɪnˈsɪpiənt/ *adj.* [usually before noun] (*formal*) just beginning 剛開始的；初始的；早期的： *signs of incipient unrest* 動亂的初期跡象

in·cise /ɪnˈsaɪz/ *verb* **~ sth (in/on/onto sth)** (*formal*) to cut words, designs, etc. into a surface （在表面）雕，刻；切入 ➲ compare ENGRAVE

in·ci·sion /ɪnˈsɪʒn/ *noun* [C, U] a sharp cut made in sth, particularly during a medical operation; the act of making a cut in sth 割口；（尤指手術的）切口；切開： *Make a small incision below the ribs.* 在肋骨下方切開一個小口。

in·ci·sive /ɪnˈsaɪsɪv/ *adj.* (*approving*) **1** showing clear thought and good understanding of what is important, and the ability to express this 鋭利的；透徹的： ***incisive comments/criticism/analysis*** 深刻的評論／批評／分析 ◇ *an incisive mind* 敏鋭的頭腦 **2** showing sb's ability to take decisions and act with force 果斷的；當機立斷的： *an incisive performance* 果敢的表現 ▶ **in·ci·sive·ly** *adv.* **in·ci·sive·ness** *noun* [U]

in·ci·sor /ɪnˈsaɪzə(r)/ *noun* one of the eight sharp teeth at the front of the mouth that are used for biting 切牙；門齒 ➲ compare CANINE (1), MOLAR

in·cite /ɪnˈsaɪt/ *verb* to encourage sb to do sth violent, illegal or unpleasant, especially by making them angry or excited 煽動；鼓動： **~ sth** *to* ***incite crime/racial hatred/violence*** 教唆犯罪；煽動種族仇恨／暴力 ◇ **~ sb (to sth)** *They were accused of inciting the crowd to violence.* 他們被控煽動群眾暴亂。◇ **~ sb to do sth** *He incited the workforce to come out on strike.* 他煽動工人罷工。

in·cite·ment /ɪnˈsaɪtmənt/ *noun* [U, C] **~ (to sth)** the act of encouraging sb to do sth violent, illegal or unpleasant 煽動；鼓動： *incitement to racial hatred* 種族仇恨的挑起

in·civil·ity /ˌɪnsəˈvɪləti/ *noun* [U, C] (*pl.* **-ies**) (*formal*) rude behaviour; rude remarks 粗魯的舉動；無禮的語言；不文明 ➲ see also UNCIVIL

incl. (*BrE* also **inc.**) *abbr.* **1** (in advertisements 廣告用) including; included 包括；連同…在內： *transport not incl.* 不包括運輸 ◇ *£29.53 inc. tax* 連稅在內共 29.53 英鎊 **2** INCLUSIVE 包括提到的所有天數（或月、數目等）： *Open 1 April to 31 October incl.* 從 4 月 1 號到 10 月 31 號每天營業。

in·clem·ent /ɪnˈklemənt/ *adj.* (*formal*) (of the weather 天氣) not pleasant; cold, wet, etc. 惡劣的（指寒冷的、潮濕的等） OPP **clement** ▶ **in·clem·ency** /-ənsi/ *noun* [U]

I

in·cli·nation AW /ˌɪnklɪˈneɪʃn/ *noun* **1** [U, C] a feeling that makes you want to do sth 傾向；意願：**~ (to do sth)** *He did not show the* ***slightest inclination*** *to leave.* 他絲毫沒有表現出要離開的意思。◇ *My* ***natural inclination*** *is to find a compromise.* 我生性易於妥協。◇ *She had neither the time nor the inclination to help them.* 她既沒有時間也不願意幫助他們。◇ **~ (towards/for sth)** *She lacked any inclination for housework.* 她一點都沒有興趣做家務。◇ *He was a loner by nature and* ***by inclination.*** 他天性不喜交際，且自己也無意於此。◇ *You must follow your own inclinations when choosing a career.* 你必須按照自己的意願選擇職業。 **2** [C] **~ to do sth** a tendency to do sth 趨向；趨勢：*There is an inclination to treat geography as a less important subject.* 有一種趨向認為地理是一門次要的學科。 **3** [C, usually sing., U] (*technical* 術語) a degree of sloping 傾斜度：*an inclination of 45°* * 45° 的傾斜度 ◇ *the angle of inclination* 傾角 **4** [C] a small downward movement, usually of the head 向下的輕微動作；（通常指）點頭

I

in·cline AW *verb, noun*

■ ***verb*** /ɪnˈklaɪn/ (*formal*) **1** [I, T] to tend to think or behave in a particular way; to make sb do this（使）傾向於，有…的趨勢：**~ to/towards sth** *I incline to the view that we should take no action at this stage.* 我傾向於認為我們在這個階段不應採取行動。◇ **~ to do sth** *The government is more effective than we incline to think.* 政府的效率比我們所慣常以為的要高。◇ **~ sb to/towards sth** *Lack of money inclines many young people towards crime.* 缺錢使很多年輕人產生了犯罪傾向。◇ **~ sb to do sth** *His obvious sincerity inclined me to trust him.* 他滿臉的真誠，讓我願意相信他。 **2** [T] **~ your head** to bend your head forward, especially as a sign of agreement, welcome, etc. 點頭（尤指以示同意、歡迎等） **3** [I, T] **~ (sth) (to/towards sth)** to lean or slope in a particular direction; to make sth lean or slope（使）傾斜：*The land inclined gently towards the shore.* 地面緩緩向海岸傾斜。

■ ***noun*** /ˈɪnklaɪn/ (*formal*) a slope 斜坡；傾斜；斜度：*a* ***steep/slight incline*** 陡 / 緩坡

in·clined AW /ɪnˈklaɪnd/ *adj.* **1** [not before noun] **~ (to do sth)** wanting to do sth 想（做某事）：*She was inclined to trust him.* 她願意相信他。◇ *He writes only when he feels inclined to.* 他只在想寫作的時候才動筆寫。◇ *There'll be time for a swim if you* ***feel so inclined.*** 你要是想游泳的話，還有時間呢。 **2 ~ to do sth** tending to do sth; likely to do sth 有…傾向；很可能：*He's inclined to be lazy.* 他喜歡偷懶。◇ *They'll be more inclined to listen if you don't shout.* 你要是不大聲嚷叫，他們會更願意傾聽。 **3 ~ to agree, believe, think, etc.** used when you are expressing an opinion but do not want to express it very strongly（溫和地表達意見）傾向於同意（或相信、認為等）：*I'm inclined to agree with you.* 我傾向於同意你的觀點。 **4** (used with particular adverbs 與某些副詞連用) having a natural ability for sth; preferring to do sth 有（某種）天賦的；寧願（做某事）的：***musically/academically inclined*** *children* 有音樂天賦的 / 喜歡讀書的兒童 **5** sloping; at an angle 傾斜的；成某角度的

in·clude 🔑 /ɪnˈkluːd/ *verb*
1 🔑 (not used in the progressive tenses 不用於進行時) if one thing **includes** another, it has the second thing as one of its parts 包括；包含：**~ sth** *The tour included a visit to the Science Museum.* 這次遊覽包括參觀科學博物館。◇ *Does the price include tax?* 這個價錢是否包括稅款？◇ **~ doing sth** *Your duties include typing letters and answering the telephone.* 你的職責包括打信件和接電話。 **2** 🔑 to make sb/sth part of sth 使成為…的一部份：**~ sb/sth (as/in/on sth)** *You should include some examples in your essay.* 你應該在文章裏舉一些例子。◇ *We all went,* ***me included.*** 我們都去了，連我在內。◇ **~ sb/sth as sth** *Representatives from the country were included as observers at the conference.* 這個國家的代表都被列為會議的觀察員。 OPP **exclude**

in·clud·ing 🔑 /ɪnˈkluːdɪŋ/ *prep.* (*abbr.* **incl.**) having sth as part of a group or set 包括…在內：*I've got three days' holiday including New Year's Day.* 包括元旦在內我有三天假。◇ *Six people were killed in the riot, including a policeman.* 暴亂中有六人死亡，包括一名警察。◇ *It's £7.50,* ***not including*** *tax.* 共計 7.50 英鎊，不含稅款。 OPP **excluding** ➲ LANGUAGE BANK at E.G.

in·clu·sion /ɪnˈkluːʒn/ *noun* **1** [U] the fact of including sb/sth; the fact of being included（被）包括，包含：*His inclusion in the team is in doubt.* 他是否能被選入這個隊還未定案。 **2** [C] a person or thing that is included 被包括的人（或事物）：*There were some surprising inclusions in the list.* 名單中包括一些意想不到的人。 OPP **exclusion**

in·clu·sive /ɪnˈkluːsɪv/ *adj.* **1** having the total cost, or the cost of sth that is mentioned, contained in the price 包含全部費用的；包括所提到的費用在內的：*The* ***fully inclusive*** *fare for the trip is £52.* 這次旅行的全部費用是 52 英鎊。◇ **~ of sth** *The rent is inclusive of water and heating.* 租金包括水費和暖氣費。 OPP **exclusive** **2 (from) ... to ... inclusive** (*BrE*) including all the days, months, numbers, etc. mentioned 包括提到的所有的天數（或月、數目等）在內：*We are offering free holidays for children aged two to eleven inclusive.* 我們提供的度假活動，兩歲至十一歲的兒童免費。◇ *The castle is open daily from May to October inclusive.* 這個古堡從五月起每天開放，直至十月尾。 **3** including a wide range of people, things, ideas, etc. 包容廣闊的；範圍廣泛的：*The party must adopt more inclusive strategies and a broader vision.* 這個黨必須採取更廣泛的策略和更遠大的視野。 OPP **exclusive** ▸ **in·clu·sive·ly** *adv.*：*The word 'men' can be understood inclusively* (= including men and women). * men 這個詞可以作概括性的解釋（包括男人和女人）。 **in·clu·sive·ness** *noun* [U]

British/American 英式/美式英語

inclusive / through

- In *BrE* **inclusive** is used to emphasize that you are including the days, months, numbers, etc. mentioned, especially in formal or official situations. 在英式英語中，inclusive 用以強調所提到的日子、月份、數字等均包括在內，尤用於正式場合：*Answer questions 8 to 12 inclusive.* 回答第 8 到第 12 題。◇ *The amusement park is open daily from May to October inclusive.* 遊樂園從五月至十月每天都開放。
- In *NAmE* **through** is used. 美式英語用 through：*Answer questions 8 through 12.* 回答第 8 到第 12 題。◇ *The amusement park is open (from) May through October.* 遊樂園從五月到十月每天都開放。
- **To** can also be used with this meaning in *BrE* and *NAmE*. 英式英語和美式英語都可用 to：*The park is open from 1 May to 31 October.* 公園從 5 月 1 日到 10 月 31 日開放。

in·cog·nito /ˌɪnkɒɡˈniːtəʊ; *NAmE* ˌɪnkɑːɡˈniːtoʊ/ *adv.* in a way that prevents other people from finding out who you are 偽裝；隱姓埋名：*Movie stars often prefer to travel incognito.* 電影明星旅行時常喜歡隱瞞身分。 ▸ **in·cog·nito** *adj.*：*an incognito visit* 化名出訪

in·co·her·ent AW /ˌɪnkəʊˈhɪərənt; *NAmE* ˌɪnkoʊˈhɪr-/ *adj.* **1** (of people 人) unable to express yourself clearly, often because of emotion 口齒不清的；語無倫次的：*She broke off, incoherent with anger.* 她氣得話都說不清了，便住口了。 OPP **coherent** **2** (of sounds 聲音) not clear and hard to understand 不清楚的；難以分辨的；難懂的 SYN **unintelligible**：*Rachel whispered something incoherent.* 雷切爾低聲說了些什麼，聽不清楚。 **3** not logical or well organized 邏輯不清的；不連貫的：*an incoherent policy* 前後不一致的政策 OPP **coherent** ▸ **in·co·her·ence** /-əns/ *noun* [U] **in·co·her·ent·ly** AW *adv.*

in·come 🔑 AW /ˈɪnkʌm; -kəm/ *noun* [C, U] the money that a person, a region, a country, etc. earns from work, from investing money, from business, etc. 收入；收益；所得：*people* ***on high/low incomes*** 高 / 低收入的人 ◇ *a weekly* ***disposable income*** (= the money that you have left to spend after tax, etc.) *of £200* * 200 英鎊的稅後實得週薪 ◇ *a rise in* ***national income*** 國民收

入的增長◇ *They receive a proportion of their income from the sale of goods and services.* 他們一部份的收入來自出售貨品和各種服務所得。◇ *Tourism is a major* ***source of income*** *for the area.* 旅遊業是這個地區的主要收入來源。◇ ***higher/middle/lower income*** *groups* 較高／中等／較低收入階層 ➲ COLLOCATIONS at FINANCE ➲ compare EXPENDITURE (1)

Synonyms 同義詞辨析

income

wage/wages • pay • salary • earnings

These are all words for money that a person earns or receives for their work. 以上各詞均指收入、工資、薪水。

income money that a person receives for their work, or from investments or business 指收入、收益、所得： *people on low incomes* 低收入的人

wage/wages money that employees get for doing their job, usually paid every week 通常指按週領取的工資、工錢： *a weekly wage of £200* 週薪 200 英鎊

pay money that employees earn for doing their job 指工資、薪水： *The job offers good rates of pay.* 這工作報酬高。

salary money that employees earn for doing their job, usually paid every month 通常指按月發放的薪水、薪金

WAGE, PAY OR SALARY? 用 wage、pay 還是 salary？

Pay is the most general of these three words. Employees who work in factories, etc. get their **wages** each week. Employees who work in offices or professional people such as teachers or doctors receive a **salary** that is paid each month, but is usually expressed as an annual figure. * pay 在這組詞中含義最廣。在工廠等工作的雇員按週領取的工錢用 wages。辦公室工作人員、教師、醫生等專業人員按月領取的薪金用 salary，但通常以年薪表示。

earnings money that a person earns from their work 指薪水、工資、收入： *a rise in average earnings for factory workers* 工廠工人平均收入的增加

PATTERNS

- (a) **high/low/basic** income/wage/pay/salary/earnings
- to **earn** an income/a wage/your pay/a salary
- to **be on** a(n) income/wage/salary of …

in·comer /ˈɪnkʌmə(r)/ *noun* (*BrE*) a person who comes to live in a particular place 新來的人；移民

ˌincome supˈport *noun* [U] (in Britain) the money that the government pays to people who have no income or a very low income（英國為無收入或收入很低者提供的）收入補貼

ˈincome tax *noun* [U, C] the amount of money that you pay to the government according to how much you earn（個人）所得税： *The standard rate of income tax was cut to 23p in the pound.* 所得税的標準税率削減到了每英鎊 23 便士。

in·com·ing /ˈɪnkʌmɪŋ/ *adj.* [only before noun] **1** recently elected or chosen 新當選的；新任的： *the* ***incoming government/president/administration*** 新一屆政府／總統／行政當局 OPP **outgoing 2** arriving somewhere, or being received 正到達某地的；剛收到的： ***incoming flights*** 進港航班◇ *the* ***incoming tide*** 漲潮◇ ***incoming calls/mail*** 打進來的電話；寄來的郵件 OPP **outgoing**

in·com·men·sur·able /ˌɪnkəˈmenʃərəbl/ *adj.* **~ (with sth)** (*formal*) if two things are **incommensurable**, they are so completely different from each other that they cannot be compared 不能相比的；無共同尺度的；大相逕庭的

in·com·men·sur·ate /ˌɪnkəˈmenʃərət/ *adj.* **~ (with sth)** (*formal*) not matching sth in size, importance, quality, etc. 不相稱的；不適當的；不匹配的 OPP **commensurate**

in·com·mode /ˌɪnkəˈməʊd; *NAmE* -ˈmoʊd/ *verb* **~ sb** (*formal*) to cause sb difficulties or problems 造成困難；打擾；妨礙： *We are very sorry to have incommoded you.* 很抱歉給您添麻煩了。

in·com·mu·ni·cado /ˌɪnkəˌmjuːnɪˈkɑːdəʊ; *NAmE* -ˈkɑːdoʊ/ *adj.* without communicating with other people, because you are not allowed to or because you do not want to 不允許與他人接觸；不願與他人接觸： *The prisoner has been* ***held incommunicado*** *for more than a week.* 這名囚犯已被單獨囚禁了一個多星期。

in·com·par·able /ɪnˈkɒmprəbl; *NAmE* -ˈkɑːm-/ *adj.* so good or impressive that nothing can be compared to it 不可比擬的；無比的；無雙的 SYN **matchless**： *the incomparable beauty of Lake Garda* 加爾達湖的絕妙美景 ▸ **in·com·par·abil·ity** /ɪnˌkɒmpərəˈbɪləti; *NAmE* -ˌkɑːm-/ *noun* [U] **in·com·par·ably** /ɪnˈkɒmprəbli; *NAmE* -ˈkɑːm-/ *adv.*

in·com·pat·ible AW /ˌɪnkəmˈpætəbl/ *adj.* **1 ~ (with sth)** two actions, ideas, etc. that are **incompatible** are not acceptable or possible together because of basic differences（與某事物）不一致，不相配： *The hours of the job are incompatible with family life.* 這份工作的上班時間和家庭生活有衝突。◇ *These two objectives are* ***mutually incompatible.*** 這兩個目標相互矛盾。 **2** two people who are **incompatible** are very different from each other and so are not able to live or work happily together（與某人）合不來，不能和睦相處 **3 ~ (with sth)** two things that are **incompatible** are of different types so that they cannot be used or mixed together（與某物）不匹配，不兼容，互斥： *New computer software is often incompatible with older computers.* 新的計算機軟件往往和舊式計算機不兼容。◇ *Those two blood groups are incompatible.* 那兩種血型是不相容的。 OPP **compatible** ▸ **in·com·pati·bil·ity** AW /ˌɪnkəmˌpætəˈbɪləti/ *noun* [U, C] (*pl.* **-ies**)

in·com·pe·tence /ɪnˈkɒmpɪtəns; *NAmE* -ˈkɑːm-/ *noun* [U] the lack of skill or ability to do your job or a task as it should be done 無能力；不勝任；不稱職： *professional incompetence* 專業方面不稱職◇ *police incompetence* 警方的無能◇ *He was dismissed for incompetence.* 他因不稱職而被解雇。

in·com·pe·tent /ɪnˈkɒmpɪtənt; *NAmE* -ˈkɑːm-/ *adj.*, *noun*

■ ***adj.*** not having the skill or ability to do your job or a task as it should be done 無能力的；不勝任的；不稱職的： *an incompetent teacher* 不稱職的教師◇ *his incompetent handling of the affair* 他在處理這件事上的無能表現◇ *The Prime Minister was attacked as incompetent to lead.* 首相被抨擊缺乏領導能力。 OPP **competent** ▸ **in·com·pe·tent·ly** *adv.*

■ ***noun*** a person who does not have the skill or ability to do their job or a task as it should be done 不稱職（或不能勝任、無能）的人

in·com·plete /ˌɪnkəmˈpliːt/ *adj.*, *noun*

■ ***adj.*** not having everything that it should have; not finished or complete 不完整的；不完全的；不完善的： *an incomplete set of figures* 一組不完整的數字◇ *Spoken language contains many incomplete sentences.* 口語中有很多不完整的句子。 OPP **complete** ▸ **in·com·plete·ly** *adv.*： *The causes of the phenomenon are still incompletely understood.* 造成這種現象的原因尚未徹底弄清。 **in·com·plete·ness** *noun* [U]

■ ***noun*** (*NAmE*) the grade that a student gets for a course of education when they have not completed all the work for that course（學業成績評分）未修畢，未完成

in·com·pre·hen·sible /ɪnˌkɒmprɪˈhensəbl; *NAmE* -ˌkɑːm-/ *adj.* **~ (to sb)** impossible to understand 無法理解的；難懂的 SYN **unintelligible**： *Some application forms can be incomprehensible to ordinary people.* 有些申請表格一般人可能看不懂。◇ *He found his son's actions totally incomprehensible.* 他感覺他兒子的行為完全理解不了。 OPP **comprehensible** ▸ **in·com·pre·hen·si·bil·ity** /ɪnˌkɒmprɪˌhensəˈbɪləti; *NAmE* -ˌkɑːm-/ *noun* [U] **in·com·pre·hen·sibly** /-səbli/ *adv.*

I

in·com·pre·hen·sion /ˌɪnˌkɒmprɪˈhenʃn; *NAmE* -ˌkɑːm-/ *noun* [U] the state of not being able to understand sb/sth 不理解；不懂：*Anna read the letter with incomprehension.* 安娜茫然不解地讀了那封信。

in·con·ceiv·able AW /ˌɪnkənˈsiːvəbl/ *adj.* impossible to imagine or believe 難以想像的；無法相信的 SYN **unthinkable**：***It is inconceivable that*** *the minister was not aware of the problem.* 令人難以置信的是那位大臣竟然沒有意識到這個問題。OPP **conceivable** ▸ **in·con·ceiv·ably** AW *adv.*

in·con·clu·sive AW /ˌɪnkənˈkluːsɪv/ *adj.* not leading to a definite decision or result 非決定性的；無定論的；不確定的：*inconclusive evidence/results/tests* 沒有說服力的證據；無定論的結果 / 試驗 ◇ *inconclusive discussions* 無結果的討論 OPP **conclusive** ▸ **in·con·clu·sive·ly** AW *adv.*：*The last meeting had ended inconclusively.* 上一次會議沒有結果。

in·con·gru·ous /ɪnˈkɒŋɡruəs; *NAmE* -ˈkɑːŋ-/ *adj.* strange, and not suitable in a particular situation 不合適的；不相稱的；不協調的 SYN **inappropriate**：*Such traditional methods seem incongruous in our technical age.* 此類傳統方法似乎同我們今天的科技時代格格不入。▸ **in·con·gru·ity** /ˌɪnkɒnˈɡruːəti; *NAmE* ˌɪnkɑːn-/ *noun* [U, C] (*pl.* **-ies**)：*She was struck by the incongruity of the situation.* 這一局面煞是怪異，讓她驚愕不已。**in·con·gru·ous·ly** *adv.*：*incongruously dressed* 穿着不協調

in·con·se·quen·tial /ɪnˌkɒnsɪˈkwenʃl; *NAmE* -ˌkɑːn-/ *adj.* not important or worth considering 不重要的；微不足道的；細瑣的 SYN **trivial**：*inconsequential details* 無關緊要的細節 ◇ *inconsequential chatter* 無謂的嘮叨 OPP **consequential** ▸ **in·con·se·quen·tial·ly** /-ʃəli/ *adv.*

in·con·sid·er·able /ˌɪnkənˈsɪdrəbl/ *adj.*
IDM **not inconˈsiderable** (*formal*) large; large enough to be considered important 巨大的；值得重視的：*We have spent a not inconsiderable amount of money on the project already.* 我們已經在這一項目上投入了一筆相當大的資金。

in·con·sid·er·ate /ˌɪnkənˈsɪdərət/ *adj.* (*disapproving*) not giving enough thought to other people's feelings or needs 不為別人着想的；不體諒別人的；考慮不周的 SYN **thoughtless**：*inconsiderate behaviour* 考慮不周的行為 ◇ *It was inconsiderate of you not to call.* 你連個電話也不打，不夠體諒人。OPP **considerate** ▸ **in·con·sid·er·ate·ly** *adv.*

in·con·sist·ent AW /ˌɪnkənˈsɪstənt/ *adj.* **1** [not usually before noun] ~ (**with sth**) if two statements, etc. are **inconsistent**, or one is **inconsistent with** the other, they cannot both be true because they give the facts in a different way 不一致；相矛盾：*The report is inconsistent with the financial statements.* 這個報告與財務報表內容不一致。◇ *The witnesses' statements were inconsistent.* 各證人的證詞相互抵觸。**2** ~ **with sth** not matching a set of standards, ideas, etc. 不符合（某套標準、思想等）：*Her behaviour was clearly inconsistent with her beliefs.* 她的行為顯然違背了她的信仰。**3** (*disapproving*) tending to change too often; not staying the same 反覆無常的；沒有常性的：*inconsistent results* 變幻無常的結果 ◇ *Children find it difficult if a parent is inconsistent.* 如果做父母的不始終如一，孩子會覺得無所適從。OPP **consistent** ▸ **in·con·sis·tency** AW /-ənsi/ *noun* [U, C] (*pl.* **-ies**)：*There is some inconsistency between the witnesses' evidence and their earlier statements.* 證人的證詞與他們先前的陳述有些出入。◇ *I noticed a few minor inconsistencies in her argument.* 我注意到她的論證中有幾處小矛盾。**in·con·sist·ent·ly** *adv.*

in·con·sol·able /ˌɪnkənˈsəʊləbl; *NAmE* -ˈsoʊl-/ (also **un·con·sol·able**) *adj.* very sad and unable to accept help or comfort 悲痛欲絕的；無法慰藉的：*They were inconsolable when their only child died.* 他們唯一的孩子去世時，他們簡直痛不欲生。▸ **in·con·sol·ably** /-əbli/ (also **un·con·sol·ably**) *adv.*：*to weep inconsolably* 悲痛欲絕地哭泣

I

in·con·spicu·ous /ˌɪnkənˈspɪkjuəs/ *adj.* not attracting attention; not easy to notice 不引人注目的；不起眼的 OPP **conspicuous** ▸ **in·con·spicu·ous·ly** *adv.*

in·con·stant /ɪnˈkɒnstənt; *NAmE* -ˈkɑːn-/ *adj.* (*formal*) **1** not faithful in love or friendship（對愛情或友情）不忠的，不專一的 SYN **fickle** **2** that frequently changes 不穩定的；經常變換的 OPP **constant** ▸ **in·con·stancy** AW /-ənsi/ *noun* [U]

in·con·test·able /ˌɪnkənˈtestəbl/ *adj.* (*formal*) that is true and cannot be disagreed with or denied 無可辯駁的；不可否認的；無可置疑的 SYN **indisputable**：*an incontestable right/fact* 無可爭辯的權利；無可置疑的事實 ▸ **in·con·test·ably** /-əbli/ *adv.*

in·con·tin·ence /ɪnˈkɒntɪnəns; *NAmE* -ˈkɑːn-/ *noun* [U] the lack of ability to control the BLADDER and BOWELS 失禁 OPP **continence** ▸ **in·con·tin·ent** /-ənt; *NAmE* -ˈkɑːntnənt/ *adj.*：*Many of our patients are incontinent.* 我們很多病人都有失禁現象。

in·con·tro·vert·ible /ˌɪnkɒntrəˈvɜːtəbl; *NAmE* ˌɪnkɑːntrəˈvɜːrt-/ *adj.* (*formal*) that is true and cannot be disagreed with or denied 無可爭辯的；不能否認的；無可置疑的 SYN **indisputable**：***incontrovertible evidence/proof*** 無可置疑的證據 ▸ **in·con·tro·vert·ibly** /ˌɪnkɒntrəˈvɜːtəbli; *NAmE* ˌɪnkɑːntrəˈvɜːrt-/ *adv.*

in·con·veni·ence /ˌɪnkənˈviːniəns/ *noun, verb*
■ ***noun*** **1** [U] trouble or problems, especially concerning what you need or would like yourself 不便；麻煩；困難：*We apologize for the delay and regret any inconvenience it may have caused.* 我們對此次延誤以及因此有可能造成的所有不便表示道歉。◇ *I have already been put to considerable inconvenience.* 我已經遇到了相當的麻煩了。**2** [C] a person or thing that causes problems or difficulties 帶來不便者；麻煩的人（或事物）SYN **nuisance**：*I can put up with minor inconveniences.* 我能忍受些小的不便。
■ ***verb*** ~ **sb** (*formal*) to cause trouble or difficulty for sb 給（某人）造成不便（或帶來麻煩）：*I hope that we haven't inconvenienced you.* 我希望我們沒有給你添麻煩。

in·con·veni·ent /ˌɪnkənˈviːniənt/ *adj.* causing trouble or problems, especially concerning what you need or would like yourself 不方便的；引起麻煩的；造成困難的：*an* ***inconvenient time/place*** 不方便的時間 / 地點 OPP **convenient** ▸ **in·con·veni·ent·ly** *adv.*

in·corp·or·ate AW /ɪnˈkɔːpəreɪt; *NAmE* -ˈkɔːrp-/ *verb* **1** to include sth so that it forms a part of sth 將…包括在內；包含；吸收；使併入：~ **sth** *The new car design incorporates all the latest safety features.* 新的汽車設計包括了所有最新的安全配備。◇ ~ **sth in/into/within sth** *We have incorporated all the latest safety features into the design.* 我們在設計中納入了所有最新的安全裝置。◇ *Many of your suggestions have been incorporated in the plan.* 你的很多建議已納入計劃中。**2** [often passive] ~ **sth** (*business* 商) to create a legally recognized company 註冊成立：*The company was incorporated in 2008.* 這家公司成立於 2008 年。▸ **in·corp·or·ation** AW /ɪnˌkɔːpəˈreɪʃn; *NAmE* -ˌkɔːrp-/ *noun* [U]：*the incorporation of foreign words into the language* 這一語言對外來詞彙的吸收 ◇ *the articles of incorporation of the company* 有關創建公司的條款

in·corp·or·ated /ɪnˈkɔːpəreɪtɪd; *NAmE* -ˈkɔːrp-/ *adj.* (*abbr.* **Inc.**) (*business* 商) formed into a business company with legal status 組成有法人地位的營業公司的；組成公司的

in·cor·por·eal /ˌɪnkɔːˈpɔːriəl; *NAmE* -kɔːrˈp-/ *adj.* (*formal*) without a body or form 無形體的；無形的

in·cor·rect /ˌɪnkəˈrekt/ *adj.* **1** not accurate or true 不準確的；不正確的；不真實的：*incorrect information/spelling* 失實的信息；錯誤的拼寫 ◇ *His version of what happened is incorrect.* 他對所發生的事情的說法不準確。**2** speaking or behaving in a way that does not follow the accepted standards or rules（說話或舉止）不合規矩的，不當的，不端的 OPP **correct** ➲ see also POLITICALLY CORRECT ▸ **in·cor·rect·ly** *adv.*：*an incorrectly addressed letter* 地址有誤的信件 **in·cor·rect·ness** *noun* [U]

in·cor·ri·gible /ɪnˈkɒrɪdʒəbl; *NAmE* -ˈkɔːr-; -ˈkɑːr-/ *adj.* (*disapproving* or *humorous*) having bad habits which cannot be changed or improved 無法改正的；屢教不改

的 SYN **incurable**： *Her husband is an incorrigible flirt.* 她的丈夫是個積習難改的調情老手。◇ *You're incorrigible!* 你簡直不可救藥！ ▶ **in·cor·ri·gibly** /ɪnˈkɒrɪdʒəbli; *NAmE* -ˈkɔːr-; -ˈkɑːr/ *adv.*

in·cor·rupt·ible /ˌɪnkəˈrʌptəbl/ *adj.* **1** (of people 人) not able to be persuaded to do sth wrong or dishonest, even if sb offers them money 廉潔的；不接受賄賂的 **2** that cannot decay or be destroyed 不會腐蝕的；不可摧毀的 OPP **corruptible** ▶ **in·cor·rupt·ibil·ity** /ˌɪnkəˌrʌptəˈbɪləti/ *noun* [U]

in·crease *verb, noun*

■ ***verb*** /ɪnˈkriːs/ [I, T] to become or to make sth greater in amount, number, value, etc. （使）增長，增多；增加： **~ (from A) (to B)** *The population has increased from 1.2 million to 1.8 million.* 人口已從 120 萬增加到了 180 萬。◇ *increasing levels of carbon dioxide in the earth's atmosphere* 地球大氣層中日益增多的二氧化碳含量 ◇ *The price of oil increased.* 石油價格上漲了。◇ **~ in sth** *Oil increased in price.* 石油價格上漲了。◇ **~ by sth** *The rate of inflation increased by 2%.* 通貨膨脹率增長了 2%。◇ **~ with sth** *Disability increases with age* (= the older sb is, the more likely they are to be disabled). 身體機能隨着年齡退化。◇ **~ sth (from A) (to B)** *We need to increase productivity.* 我們需要提高生產力。◇ **~ sth (by sth)** *They've increased the price by 50%.* 他們已經把價格提高了 50%。 OPP **decrease** ▶ **in·creased** *adj.* [only before noun]： *increased demand* 增加的需求

■ ***noun*** /ˈɪŋkriːs/ [C, U] **~ (in sth)** a rise in the amount, number or value of sth 增長；增多；增加： *an increase in spending* 開支的增長 ◇ *an increase of 2p in the pound on income tax* 所得稅每英鎊增加 2 便士 ◇ *an increase of nearly 20%* 近 20% 的增長 ◇ *a* ***significant/substantial increase*** *in sales* 銷售量的顯著／可觀增長 ◇ ***price/tax/wage increases*** 價格／稅額／工資的上漲 ◇ *Homelessness* ***is on the increase*** (= increasing). 無家可歸者越來越多。 OPP **decrease**

Language Bank 用語庫

increase

Describing an increase 描述增長

- Student numbers in English language schools in this country **increased** from 66 000 in 2008 to just over 84 000 in 2009. 這個國家英語語言學校的學生人數從 2008 年的 66 000 增長到 2009 年的 84 000 多一點。
- The number of students **increased** by almost 30% compared with the previous year. 學生人數與去年相比增長了近 30%。
- Student numbers **shot up/increased dramatically** in 2009. 學生人數在 2009 年急劇增長。
- The proportion of Spanish students **rose sharply** from 5% in 2008 to 14% in 2009. 西班牙學生所佔比例從 2008 年的 5% 猛增到 2009 年的 14%。
- There was a significant **rise** in student numbers in 2009. 學生人數在 2009 年大幅上升。
- The 2009 figure was 84 000, **an increase of** 28% on the previous year. * 2009 年的數據是 84 000，比前一年增長了 28%。
- The 2009 figure was 84 000, 28 per cent **up** on the previous year. * 2009 年的數據是 84 000，比前一年上升了 28%。
- As the chart shows, this can partly be explained by **a dramatic increase** in students from Spain. 如圖所示，這種情況的部份原因是西班牙學生人數的急劇上升。

➲ Language Banks at EXPECT, FALL, ILLUSTRATE, PROPORTION

in·creas·ing·ly /ɪnˈkriːsɪŋli/ *adv.* more and more all the time 越來越多地；不斷增加地： *increasingly difficult/important/popular* 越來越困難／重要／普及 ◇ *It is becoming increasingly clear that this problem will not be easily solved.* 越來越明顯的是，這個問題不會輕易解決。◇ *Increasingly, training is taking place in the office rather than outside it.* 越來越多的職場培訓在工作場所舉行，而不是出外培訓。

in·cred·ible /ɪnˈkredəbl/ *adj.* **1** impossible or very difficult to believe 不能相信的；難以置信的 SYN **unbelievable**： *an incredible story* 不可思議的故事 ◇ *It seemed incredible that she had been there a week already.* 真讓人難以置信，她已經在那裏待了一個星期了。 **2** (*informal*) extremely good or extremely large 極好的；極大的： *The hotel was incredible.* 這家旅館棒極了。◇ *an incredible amount of work* 極大量的工作

in·cred·ibly /ɪnˈkredəbli/ *adv.* **1** extremely 極端地；極其 SYN **unbelievably**： *incredibly lucky/stupid/difficult/beautiful* 極其幸運／愚蠢／困難／美麗 **2** in a way that is very difficult to believe 令人難以置信： *Incredibly, she had no idea what was going on.* 令人難以置信的是，她當時對發生的事一無所知。

in·credu·lous /ɪnˈkredjələs; *NAmE* -dʒəl-/ *adj.* not willing or not able to believe sth; showing an inability to believe sth 不肯相信的；不能相信的；表示懷疑的： *'Here?' said Kate, incredulous.* "這兒？" 凱特表示懷疑地說。◇ *an incredulous look* 懷疑的神色 ➲ compare CREDULOUS ▶ **in·credu·lity** /ˌɪnkrəˈdjuːləti; *NAmE* -ˈduː-/ *noun* [U] SYN **disbelief**： *a look of surprise and incredulity* 驚疑的神色 **in·credu·lous·ly** *adv.*： *He laughed incredulously.* 他滿腹狐疑地大笑起來。

in·cre·ment /ˈɪŋkrəmənt/ *noun* **1** a regular increase in the amount of money that sb is paid for their job 定期的加薪： *a salary of £25 K with annual increments* 薪酬 25 000 英鎊，並逐年增加 **2** (*formal*) an increase in a number or an amount 增量；增加 ▶ **in·cre·men·tal** /ˌɪŋkrəˈmentl/ *adj.*： *incremental costs* 增長的費用 **in·cre·men·tal·ly** /-təli/ *adv.*

in·crim·in·ate /ɪnˈkrɪmɪneɪt/ *verb* **~ sb** to make it seem as if sb has done sth wrong or illegal 使負罪；連累： *They were afraid of answering the questions and incriminating themselves.* 他們擔心因回答這些問題而受到牽連。 ▶ **in·crim·in·at·ing** *adj.* [usually before noun]： *incriminating evidence* 顯示有罪的證據 **in·crim·in·ation** /ɪnˌkrɪmɪˈneɪʃn/ *noun* [U]

ˈin-crowd *noun* [sing.] a small group of people within a larger group who seem to be the most popular or fashionable 最受歡迎（或最時髦）的小團體；時髦一族

in·crust·ation (also **en·crust·ation**) /ˌɪnkrʌˈsteɪʃn/ *noun* [U, C] the process of forming a hard outer covering or layer; the covering or layer that is formed 結殼；形成硬外層；硬殼；硬外層

in·cu·bate /ˈɪŋkjubeɪt/ *verb* **1** [T] **~ sth** (of a bird 鳥) to sit on its eggs in order to keep them warm until they HATCH 孵（卵）；孵化 **2** [T] **~ sth** (*biology* 生) to keep cells, bacteria, etc. at a suitable temperature so that they develop 培養（細胞、細菌等） **3** [T] **be incubating sth** (*medical* 醫) to have an infectious disease developing inside you before SYMPTOMS (= signs of illness) appear 有（傳染病在體內）潛伏 **4** [I] (*medical* 醫) (of a disease 疾病) to develop slowly without showing any signs 潛伏

in·cu·ba·tion /ˌɪŋkjuˈbeɪʃn/ *noun* **1** [U] the HATCHING of eggs 孵（卵）；孵化 **2** [C] (also **incuˈbation period**) (*medical* 醫 or *biology* 生) the time between sb being infected with a disease and the appearance of the first SYMPTOMS (= signs)（傳染病的）潛伏期 **3** [U] (*biology* 生) the development and growth of bacteria, etc. （細菌等的）繁殖

in·cu·ba·tor /ˈɪŋkjubeɪtə(r)/ *noun* **1** a piece of equipment in a hospital which new babies are placed in when they are weak or born too early, in order to help them survive （體弱或早產嬰兒）恒溫箱 **2** a machine like a box where eggs are kept warm until the young birds are born 孵化器

in·cu·bus /ˈɪŋkjʊbəs/ *noun* (*pl.* **in·cu·buses** or **in·cubi** /-baɪ/) **1** (*literary*) a problem that makes you worry a lot 沉重的壓力；巨大的精神負擔 **2** a male evil spirit, supposed in the past to have sex with a sleeping woman 夢淫妖（舊時傳說中與熟睡女子交合的妖魔）➲ compare SUCCUBUS

in·cul·cate /ˈɪnkʌlkeɪt; NAmE ɪnˈkʌl-/ *verb* (*formal*) to cause sb to learn and remember ideas, moral principles, etc., especially by repeating them often 反複灌輸；諄諄教誨：**～ sth (in/into sb)** *to inculcate a sense of responsibility in sb* 諄諄教導某人要有責任感 ◇ **～ sb with sth** *to inculcate sb with a sense of responsibility* 諄諄教導某人要有責任感 ▶ **in·cul·ca·tion** /ˌɪnkʌlˈkeɪʃn/ *noun* [U]

in·cum·bency /ɪnˈkʌmbənsi/ *noun* (*pl.* **-ies**) (*formal*) an official position or the time during which sb holds it 現任職位；任期

in·cum·bent /ɪnˈkʌmbənt/ *noun, adj.*
■ *noun* a person who has an official position 在職者；現任者：*the* **present incumbent** *of the White House* 現任美國總統
■ *adj.* **1** [only before noun] having an official position 在職的；現任的：*the incumbent president* 現任總統 **2** [not before noun] **～ upon/on sb** (*formal*) necessary as part of sb's duties 有責任；必須履行：*It was incumbent on them to attend.* 他們必須出席。

I

incur /ɪnˈkɜː(r)/ *verb* (**-rr-**) (*formal*) **1 ～ sth** if you **incur** sth unpleasant, you are in a situation in which you have to deal with it 招致；遭受；引起：*She had incurred the wrath of her father by marrying without his consent* 她未經父親同意就結婚，使父親震怒。 **2 ～ sth** if you **incur** costs, you have to pay them 引致，帶來（成本、花費等）：*You risk incurring bank charges if you exceed your overdraft limit.* 如果超出了透支限額，就有被銀行加收費用的風險。

in·cur·able /ɪnˈkjʊərəbl; NAmE -ˈkjʊr-/ *adj.* **1** that cannot be cured 不能治癒的：*an* **incurable disease/illness** 不治之症 OPP **curable 2** that cannot be changed 不能改變的；無法矯正的 SYN **incorrigible**：*She's an incurable optimist.* 她是個不可救藥的樂天派。▶ **in·cur·ably** /-əbli/ *adv.*：*incurably ill/romantic* 病入膏肓；浪漫至極

in·curi·ous /ɪnˈkjʊəriəs; NAmE -ˈkjʊr-/ *adj.* (*formal*) having no interest in knowing or discovering things 不感興趣的；不好奇的；漫不經心的 ▶ **in·curi·ous·ly** *adv.*

in·cur·sion /ɪnˈkɜːʃn; NAmE ɪnˈkɜːrʒn/ *noun* **～ (into sth)** (*formal*) **1** a sudden attack on a place by foreign armies, etc. 突然入侵；突然侵犯；襲擊 **2** the sudden appearance of sth in a particular area of activity that is either not expected or not wanted（意外的）攪擾，介入

Ind. *abbr.* (*BrE, politics* 政) INDEPENDENT：*G Green (Ind.)* *G • 格林（獨立候選人）

in·daba /ɪnˈdɑːbə/ *noun* (*SAfrE*) **1** a large meeting at which politicians, professional people, etc. have discussions about an important subject（重要問題）大會，研討會：*a national indaba on land reform* 全國土地改革大會 **2** (*informal*) a difficulty or matter that concerns you 所關心的困難（或事情）；擔心；憂慮：*I don't care what he does. That's his indaba!* 我不在乎他的所作所為。那是他自己的事！

in·debt·ed /ɪnˈdetɪd/ *adj.* **1 ～ (to sb) (for sth)** (*formal*) grateful to sb for helping you 感激的；蒙恩的：*I am* **deeply indebted** *to my family for all their help.* 我深深感激我的家人給我所有的幫助。 **2** (of countries, governments, etc. 國家、政府等) owing money to other countries or organizations 負債的：*a list of the fifteen most* **heavily indebted** *nations* 十五個負債最重的國家的名單 ▶ **in·debt·ed·ness** *noun* [U]

in·decency /ɪnˈdiːsnsi/ *noun* (*pl.* **-ies**) **1** [U] behaviour that is thought to be morally or sexually offensive 下流的行為；猥褻：*an act of* **gross indecency** (= a sexual act that is a criminal offence) 嚴重猥褻（罪） **2** [C, usually sing.] an indecent act, expression, etc. 下流的動作（或表情等）

in·decent /ɪnˈdiːsnt/ *adj.* **1** (of behaviour, talk, etc. 行為、講話等) thought to be morally offensive, especially because it involves sex or being naked 下流的；有傷風化的；猥褻的：*indecent conduct/photos* 下流的行為；淫穢的照片 ➲ compare DECENT (4) **2** (of clothes 衣服) showing parts of the body that are usually covered 過分暴露的：*That skirt of hers is positively indecent.* 她的那條裙子太暴露了。 **3** not done in the appropriate or usual amount of time 不合時宜的；不適當的：*They left the funeral with almost* **indecent haste** (= too quickly). 他們離開葬禮時倉促得近乎失禮。▶ **in·decent·ly** *adv.*：*He was charged with indecently assaulting five women.* 他被控猥褻五名婦女。

inˌdecent asˈsault *noun* [C, U] (*law* 律) a sexual attack on sb but one that does not include RAPE 猥褻（罪）；猥褻侵犯他人身體

inˌdecent exˈposure *noun* [U] (*law* 律) the crime of showing your sexual organs to other people in a public place 猥褻露體（罪）；有傷風化的露體

in·de·cipher·able /ˌɪndɪˈsaɪfrəbl/ *adj.* (of writing or speech 文字或言語) impossible to read or understand 難以辨認（或弄懂）的

in·deci·sion /ˌɪndɪˈsɪʒn/ (also *less frequent* **in·deci·sive·ness**) *noun* [U] the state of being unable to decide 無決斷力；優柔寡斷：*After a moment's indecision, he said yes.* 他猶豫片刻之後答應了。➲ compare DECISION

in·deci·sive /ˌɪndɪˈsaɪsɪv/ *adj.* **1** (of a person 人) unable to make decisions 無決斷力的；優柔寡斷的：*a weak and indecisive man* 軟弱而且不果斷的人 **2** not providing a clear and definite answer or result 模糊不清的；不明確的；無決定性的：*an indecisive battle* 非決定性的一戰 OPP **decisive** ▶ **in·deci·sive·ly** *adv.* **in·deci·sive·ness** *noun* [U] = INDECISION

in·dec·or·ous /ɪnˈdekərəs/ *adj.* (*formal*) (of behaviour 舉止) embarrassing or not socially acceptable 令人難堪的；不得體的；不適當的

in·deed 🔑 /ɪnˈdiːd/ *adv.*
1 🔑 used to emphasize a positive statement or answer（強調肯定的陳述或答覆）：*'Was he very angry?' 'Indeed he was.'* "他很生氣嗎？" "的確很生氣。" ◇ *'Do you agree?' 'Indeed I do/Yes, indeed.'* "你同意嗎？" "當然同意了。" ◇ *'You said you'd help?' 'I did indeed—yes.'* "你說過你要幫忙？" "是的，我的確說過。" ◇ *It is indeed a remarkable achievement.* 這的確是非凡的成就。 **2** 🔑 (*especially BrE*) used after *very* and an adjective or adverb to emphasize a statement, description, etc.（用於 very 和形容詞或副詞之後，強調敘述、描寫等）真正地：*Thank you very much indeed!* 真的很感謝您！◇ *I was very sad indeed to hear of your father's death.* 聽到令尊大人去世，我感到非常難過。 **3** (*formal, especially BrE*) used to add information to a statement 其實；實際上：*I don't mind at all. Indeed, I would be delighted to help.* 我根本不介意。其實，我倒很樂意幫上一把。 **4** (*informal, especially BrE*) used to show that you are surprised at sth or that you find sth ridiculous（表示驚訝或覺得某事物荒謬）：*A ghost indeed! I've never heard anything so silly.* 真是見鬼！我可從沒聽說過這樣無聊的事。 **5** (*informal*) used when you are repeating a question that sb has just asked and showing that you do not know the answer（重複對方的問題，表示不知道答案）：*'Why did he do it?' 'Why indeed?'* "他為什麼那樣做？" "是呀，為什麼呢？" IDM see FRIEND

in·defat·ig·able /ˌɪndɪˈfætɪɡəbl/ *adj.* (*formal, approving*) never giving up or getting tired of doing sth 不屈不撓的；不知疲倦的：*an indefatigable defender of human rights* 不屈不撓的人權捍衛者 ▶ **in·defat·ig·ably** /ˌɪndɪˈfætɪɡəbli/ *adv.*

in·defens·ible /ˌɪndɪˈfensəbl/ *adj.* **1** that cannot be defended or excused because it is morally unacceptable（道德上）無可辯解的，不能原諒的：*indefensible behaviour* 不可原諒的行為 ◇ *The Prime Minister was accused of defending the indefensible.* 首相被指責庇護不可原諒的行為。 **2** (of a place or building 地方或建築) impossible to defend from military attack 無法防守的

in·defin·able /ˌɪndɪˈfaɪnəbl/ *adj.* difficult or impossible to define or explain 難以定義的；無法解釋的：*She has that indefinable something that makes an actress a star.* 她具備了那種使演員成為明星的說不出的特質。▶ **in·defin·ably** /-əbli/ *adv.*

in·def·in·ite AW /ɪnˈdefɪnət/ *adj.* **1** lasting for a period of time that has no fixed end 無限期的；期限不定的：

She will be away for the indefinite future. 她將離開一段時間，期限不定。 **2** not clearly defined 模糊不清的；不明確的 **SYN** **imprecise**： *an indefinite science* 界定不明的科學

in,definite 'article *noun* (*grammar* 語法) the word *a* or *an* in English, or a similar word in another language 不定冠詞（如英語中的 a 或 an） ➲ compare DEFINITE ARTICLE

in·def·in·ite·ly **AW** /ɪnˈdefɪnətli/ *adv.* for a period of time with no fixed limit 無限期地： *The trial was postponed indefinitely.* 審訊無限期延遲。

in,definite 'pronoun *noun* (*grammar* 語法) a pronoun that does not refer to any person or thing in particular, for example 'anything' and 'everyone' 不定代詞（如 anything 和 everyone）

in·del·ible /ɪnˈdeləbl/ *adj.* **1** impossible to forget or remove 無法忘記的；不可磨滅的 **SYN** **permanent**： *The experience made an indelible impression on me.* 那次經歷使我難以忘懷。◇ *Her unhappy childhood left an indelible mark.* 她不幸的童年留下了不可磨滅的痕跡。 **2** (of ink, pens, etc. 墨水、鋼筆等) leaving a mark that cannot be removed （筆跡）無法消除的，擦不掉的 **SYN** **permanent**： *an indelible marker* 筆跡擦不掉的記號筆 ▸ **in·del·ibly** /-əbli/ *adv.*： *That day is stamped indelibly on my memory.* 那一天在我的腦海中留下了不可磨滅的回憶。

in·deli·cate /ɪnˈdelɪkət/ *adj.* (*formal*) likely to be thought rude or embarrassing 不文雅的；頗粗魯的；令人尷尬的： *an indelicate question* 無禮的提問 ▸ **in·deli·cacy** /-kəsi/ *noun* [U]

in·dem·nify /ɪnˈdemnɪfaɪ/ *verb* (**in·dem·ni·fies**, **in·dem·ni·fy·ing**, **in·dem·ni·fied**, **in·dem·ni·fied**) (*law* 律) **1 ~ sb** (**against sth**) to promise to pay sb an amount of money if they suffer any damage or loss 保證賠償 **2 ~ sb** (**for sth**) to pay sb an amount of money because of the damage or loss that they have suffered 賠償；補償 ▸ **in·dem·ni·fi·ca·tion** /ɪnˌdemnɪfɪˈkeɪʃn/ *noun* [U]

in·dem·nity /ɪnˈdemnəti/ *noun* (*pl.* **-ies**) (*formal* or *law* 律) **1** [U] **~** (**against sth**) protection against damage or loss, especially in the form of a promise to pay for any damage or loss that happens 保障；賠償；補償： *an indemnity clause/fund/policy* 賠償條款／基金／保險單◇ *indemnity insurance* 賠償保險 **2** [C] a sum of money that is given as payment for damage or loss 賠款；補償金

in·dent *verb*, *noun*

■ *verb* /ɪnˈdent/ **~ sth** to start a line of print or writing further away from the edge of the page than the other lines 將（印刷或書寫的行）縮進，縮格，縮排： *The first line of each paragraph should be indented.* 每段的第一行應縮格。

■ *noun* /ˈɪndent/ **1 ~** (**for sth**) (*business* 商) (*especially BrE*) an official order for goods or equipment 訂單；訂購 **2** = INDENTATION

in·den·ta·tion /ˌɪndenˈteɪʃn/ *noun* **1** [C] a cut or mark on the edge or surface of sth 缺口；凹陷；凹痕： *The horse's hooves left deep indentations in the mud.* 馬蹄在泥地裏留下了深深的蹄印。 **2** (also **in·dent**) [C] a space left at the beginning of a line of print or writing 行首縮進；行首空格 **3** [U] the action of indenting sth or the process of being indented 造成凹陷（或缺口）；將行首縮進

in·dented /ɪnˈdentɪd/ *adj.* (of an edge or a surface 邊緣或表面) an **indented** edge is not even, because parts of it are missing or have been cut away 鋸齒狀的；參差不齊的： *an indented coastline* 犬牙交錯的海岸線

in·den·ture /ɪnˈdentʃə(r)/ *noun* a type of contract in the past that forced a servant or APPRENTICE to work for their employer for a particular period of time （舊時的）師徒契約 ▸ **in·den·tured** *adj.*

in·de·pend·ence 🔑 /ˌɪndɪˈpendəns/ *noun* [U] **1** 🔑 **~** (**from sb/sth**) (of a country 國家) freedom from political control by other countries 獨立： *Cuba gained independence from Spain in 1898.* 古巴於 1898 年脫離西班牙而獲得獨立。 **2** 🔑 the time when a country gains freedom from political control by another country 獨立（之日）： *independence celebrations* 獨立紀念慶典◇ *the first elections since independence* 獨立之後的第一次選舉 **3** 🔑 the freedom to organize your own life, make your own decisions, etc. without needing help from other people 自主；自立： *He values his independence.* 他珍惜他的獨立自主。◇ *a woman's financial independence* 婦女在經濟上的自立 **OPP** **dependence**

Inde'pendence Day *noun* 4 July, celebrated in the US as the anniversary of the day in 1776 when the Americans declared themselves independent of Britain 美國獨立紀念日（7 月 4 日，美國國慶日，紀念 1776 年美國宣佈脫離英國） ➲ see also THE FOURTH OF JULY

in·de·pend·ent 🔑 /ˌɪndɪˈpendənt/ *adj.*, *noun*

■ *adj.*

▸ COUNTRY 國家 **1** 🔑 **~** (**from/of sth**) (of countries 國家) having their own government 獨立的；自主的；自治的 **SYN** **self-governing**： *Mozambique became independent in 1975.* 莫桑比克於 1975 年獲得獨立。

▸ SEPARATE 分開 **2** 🔑 done or given by sb who is not involved in a situation and so is able to judge it fairly 不相干的人所做的（或提供的）；公正的；無偏見的： *an **independent inquiry/witness*** 獨立的調查；無偏見的證人◇ *She went to a lawyer for some **independent advice**.* 她去找了一位律師尋求獨立意見。 **3** 🔑 **~** (**of sb/sth**) not connected with or influenced by sth; not connected with each other 不相關的；不受影響的；無關聯的： *The police force should be independent of direct government control.* 警方應該不受政府的直接控制。◇ *Two independent research bodies reached the same conclusions.* 兩個彼此不相關的研究部門得出了同樣的結論。

▸ ORGANIZATION 機構 **4** 🔑 supported by private money rather than government money 私營的；獨立： ***independent television/schools*** 私營電視台；私立學校◇ *the independent sector* 私營部門

▸ PERSON 人 **5** 🔑 **~** (**of sb/sth**) confident and free to do things without needing help from other people 自主的；有主見的： *Going away to college has made me much more independent.* 離家上大學使我變得獨立自主得多。◇ *She's a very independent-minded young woman.* 她是個很有主見的年輕女子。◇ *Students should aim to become more independent of their teachers.* 學生應該努力逐漸減少對老師的依賴。 **OPP** **dependent** **6** 🔑 **~** (**of sb/sth**) having or earning enough money so that you do not have to rely on sb else for help 自立的；自食其力的： *It was important to me to be financially independent of my parents.* 在經濟上不依賴父母，這對我很重要。◇ *a man **of independent means*** (= with an income that he does not earn by working) 無需工作便可衣食無憂的人 **OPP** **dependent**

▸ POLITICIAN 從政者 **7** not representing or belonging to a particular political party 無黨派的；獨立的： *an independent candidate* 獨立候選人

▸ **in·de·pend·ent·ly** 🔑 *adv.*： **~** (**of sb/sth**) *The two departments work independently of each other.* 這兩個部門獨立運作。◇ *It was the first time that she had lived independently.* 那是她第一次獨立生活。

■ *noun* (*abbr.* **Ind.**) a member of parliament, candidate, etc. who does not belong to a particular political party 無黨派議員（或候選人等）

inde,pendent 'school *noun* = PRIVATE SCHOOL

inde,pendent 'variable *noun* (*mathematics* 數) a VARIABLE whose value does not depend on another variable 自變量；獨立變量；自變數

,in-'depth *adj.* [usually before noun] very thorough and detailed 徹底的；深入詳盡的： *an **in-depth discussion/study*** 深入徹底的討論／研究 ➲ see also DEPTH

in·des·crib·able /ˌɪndɪˈskraɪbəbl/ *adj.* so extreme or unusual it is almost impossible to describe 難以形容的；無法言傳的： *The pain was indescribable.* 疼痛得無法形容。 ▸ **in·des·crib·ably** /-əbli/ *adv.*： *indescribably beautiful/boring* 無法形容地美麗／乏味

in·des·truct·ible /ˌɪndɪˈstrʌktəbl/ *adj.* that is very strong and cannot easily be destroyed 不可摧毀的；破壞不了的： *plastic containers that are virtually indestructible* 幾乎不可毀壞的塑料容器◇ *an indestructible bond of friendship* 堅不可摧的友誼紐帶

in·de·ter·min·ate /ˌɪndɪˈtɜːmɪnət; *NAmE* -ˈtɜːrm-/ *adj.* that cannot be identified easily or exactly 模糊的；不確定的；難以識別的：*She was a tall woman of indeterminate age.* 她是個看不出年齡的高大女子。▸ **in·de·ter·min·acy** /-nəsi/ *noun* [U]

index 0━ AW /ˈɪndeks/ *noun, verb*

■ *noun* **1** 0━ (*pl.* **in·dexes**) a list of names or topics that are referred to in a book, etc., usually arranged at the end of a book in alphabetical order or listed in a separate file or book 索引：*Look it up in the index.* 在索引中查找。◇ *Author and subject indexes are available on a library database.* 作者索引和學科索引可在圖書館的數據庫中找到。 **2** (*BrE*) = CARD INDEX ➲ **VISUAL VOCAB** page V69 **3** 0━ (*pl.* **in·dexes** or **in·dices** /ˈɪndɪsiːz/) a system that shows the level of prices and wages, etc. so that they can be compared with those of a previous date（物價和工資等的）指數：*the cost-of-living index* 生活費用指數◇ *The Dow Jones index fell 15 points this morning.* 道瓊斯指數今天上午下跌了 15 點。◇ *stock-market indices* 股市指數◇ *house price indexes* 房價指數 **4** (*pl.* **in·dices** /ˈɪndɪsiːz/) a sign or measure that sth else can be judged by 標誌；指標；表徵；量度：*The number of new houses being built is a good index of a country's prosperity.* 新建房屋的數量是國家繁榮的一個可靠指標。 **5** (usually **indices** [pl.]) (*mathematics* 數) the small number written above a larger number to show how many times that number must be multiplied by itself. In the EQUATION $4^2 = 16$, the number 2 is an index. 指數，冪（如在等式 $4^2 = 16$ 中，2 是指數）

■ *verb* **1** ~ **sth** to make an index of documents, the contents of a book, etc.; to add sth to a list of this type 為…編索引；將…編入索引：*All publications are indexed by subject and title.* 所有出版物都按學科和名稱編索引。 **2** [usually passive] ~ **sth** (**to sth**) to link wages, etc. to the level of prices of food, clothing, etc. so that they both increase at the same rate 將（工資等）與（物價水平等）掛鈎；使指數化

in·dex·ation /ˌɪndekˈseɪʃn/ *noun* [U] the linking of increases in wages, etc. to increases in prices（工資等相對於物價的）指數化

ˈ**index card** *noun* a small card that you can write information on and keep with other cards in a box or file 索引卡 ➲ see also CARD INDEX ➲ **VISUAL VOCAB** page V69

ˈ**index finger** (also ˌ**first ˈfinger**) *noun* the finger next to the thumb 食指 SYN **forefinger** ➲ **VISUAL VOCAB** page V59 ➲ compare POINTER FINGER

ˌ**index-ˈlinked** *adj.* (*BrE*) (of wages, etc. 工資等) rising in value according to increases in the cost of living 按生活指數調整的 ▸ ˌ**index-ˈlinking** *noun* [U]

In·dian /ˈɪndiən/ *noun* **1** a person from India 印度人 **2** (*old-fashioned, offensive*) = NATIVE AMERICAN **3** (*CanE*) a Native Canadian who is not Inuit or Metis（非因努伊特人或米提人的）加拿大土著；加拿大印第安人 ▸ **In·dian** *adj.* IDM see CHIEF *n.*, FILE *n.*

ˌ**Indian ˈcorn** *noun* [U] (*especially NAmE*) a type of CORN (MAIZE) with large brown and yellow grains, not usually eaten but sometimes used to make decorations, for example at Thanksgiving 印第安玉米（通常不食用，用於感恩節等裝飾）

ˌ**Indian ˈink** (also ˌ**India ˈink**) *noun* [U] a very black ink used in drawing and technical drawing 印度墨；中國墨

ˌ**Indian ˈsummer** *noun* **1** a period of dry warm weather in the autumn/fall 印第安夏（秋季乾燥溫暖）**2** a pleasant period of success or improvement, especially later in sb's life 興旺時期，進步時期（尤指在一生中較晚的時期）

India rubber /ˌɪndiə ˈrʌbə(r)/ *noun* [U] (*old-fashioned*) natural rubber 天然橡膠

in·di·cate 0━ AW /ˈɪndɪkeɪt/ *verb*

▸ **SHOW** 表明 **1** 0━ [T, I] to show that sth is true or exists 表明；標示；顯示：~ **sth** *Record profits in the retail market indicate a boom in the economy.* 零售市場上有史以來的最高利潤顯示出經濟的突飛猛進。◇ ~ (**that** …) *Research indicates that eating habits are changing fast.* 研究顯示，飲食習慣正迅速改變。◇ *Kingston-upon-Thames, as the name indicates, is situated on the banks of the Thames.* 泰晤士河畔金斯頓區，正如其名稱所示，位於泰晤士河畔。◇ ~ **how, what etc.** … *Our results indicate how misleading it could be to rely on this method.* 我們的結果表明，依賴這種方法可能產生多麼嚴重的誤導。

▸ **SUGGEST** 暗示 **2** 0━ [T] to be a sign of sth; to show that sth is possible or likely 象徵；暗示：~ **sth** *A red sky at night often indicates fine weather the next day.* 夜空呈紅色往往預兆第二天天氣晴朗。◇ ~ **that** … *Early results indicate that the government will be returned to power.* 早期的結果預示這個政府將重新執政。

▸ **MENTION** 提及 **3** 0━ [T] to mention sth, especially in an indirect way 暗示；間接提及；示意：~ (**to sb**) (**that**) … *In his letter he indicated to us (that) he was willing to cooperate.* 他在信中向我們透露他願意合作。◇ ~ **sth** (**to sb**) *He indicated his willingness to cooperate.* 他暗示願意合作。◇ ~ **whether, when, etc.** … *Has she indicated yet whether she would like to be involved?* 她表明了她是否願意參加嗎？➲ **SYNONYMS** at DECLARE

▸ **POINT TO** 指向 **4** 0━ [T] (*formal*) to make sb notice sb/sth, especially by pointing or moving your head 指示；指出：~ **sb/sth** (**to sb**) *She took out a map and indicated the quickest route to us.* 她拿出一張地圖，給我們指出最快捷的路線。◇ ~ **where, which, etc.** … *He indicated where the furniture was to go.* 他指示了傢具要如何擺放。◇ ~ **that** … *She indicated that I was to sit down.* 她示意我坐下。

▸ **GIVE INFORMATION** 提供信息 **5** [T] ~ **sth** (*formal*) to represent information without using words 顯示（信息）；標示：*The results are indicated in Table 2.* 結果列在表 2 中。 **6** [T] (*formal*) to give information in writing 寫明；註出：~ **sth** *You are allowed 20kgs of baggage unless indicated otherwise on your ticket.* 除非票上另有註明，否則可攜帶行李為 20 公斤。◇ ~ **which, where, etc.** … *Please indicate clearly which colour you require.* 請標明您要求的顏色。

▸ **SHOW MEASUREMENT** 顯示量度 **7** [T] ~ **sth** | ~ **how much, how many, etc.** … (of an instrument for measuring things 測量器具) to show a particular measurement 顯示（量度）：*When the temperature gauge indicates 90°F or more, turn off the engine.* 當溫度計顯示 90 華氏度或以上時，關閉發動機。

▸ **IN VEHICLE** 車輛等 **8** [I, T] (*BrE*) to show that your vehicle is going to change direction, by using lights or your arm（用燈光或手臂）打行車轉向信號 SYN **signal**：*Always indicate before moving into another lane.* 開入其他車道前一定要打轉向燈。◇ ~ **sth** *He indicated left and then turned right.* 他打出的是左轉信號，然後卻向右轉了。◇ ~ (**that**) … *She indicated that she was turning right.* 她打開了右轉向燈。

▸ **BE RECOMMENDED** 建議 **9** [T, usually passive] ~ **sth** (*formal*) to be necessary or recommended 有必要；被建議：*A course of chemotherapy was indicated.* 建議進行化療。

in·di·ca·tion 0━ AW /ˌɪndɪˈkeɪʃn/ *noun* [C, U] a remark or sign that shows that sth is happening or what sb is thinking or feeling 表明；標示；顯示；象徵：~ (**of sth**) *They **gave no indication** of how the work should be done.* 他們根本沒說明這項工作該怎樣做。◇ ~ (**of doing sth**) *He shows every indication (= clear signs) of wanting to accept the post.* 他顯然想接受這個職位。◇ ~ (**that** …) *There are clear indications that the economy is improving.* 有明顯的跡象顯示經濟開始好轉。◇ *All the indications are that the deal will go ahead as planned.* 從所有的跡象看，交易將按計劃進行。➲ **SYNONYMS** at SIGN

in·di·ca·tive AW /ɪnˈdɪkətɪv/ *adj., noun*

■ *adj.* **1** [not usually before noun] ~ (**of sth**) (*formal*) showing or suggesting sth 表明；標示；顯示；暗示：*Their failure to act is indicative of their lack of interest.* 他們未採取行動，這表示他們沒有興趣。 **2** [only before noun] (*grammar* 語法) stating a fact 陳述的；指示的

■ *noun* **the indicative** [sing.] (*grammar* 語法) the form of a verb that states a fact 陳述語氣的動詞形式：*In 'Ben likes school', the verb 'like' is in the indicative.* 在 Ben likes school 中，動詞 like 是陳述語氣。

in·di·ca·tor AW /ˈɪndɪkeɪtə(r)/ *noun* **1** a sign that shows you what sth is like or how a situation is changing 指示信號；標誌；跡象：*The economic indicators are better* *than expected.* 經濟指標比預期的好。 ➲ SYNONYMS at SIGN **2** a device on a machine that shows speed, pressure, etc. 指示器；指針： *a depth indicator* 深度指示器 **3** (*BrE*) (*NAmE* **'turn signal**) (also *informal* **blink·er** *NAmE, BrE*) a light on a vehicle that flashes to show that the vehicle is going to turn left or right 轉向燈；方向燈 ➲ VISUAL VOCAB page V52

in·dices *pl.* of INDEX

in·dict /ɪnˈdaɪt/ *verb* [usually passive] **~ sb (for sth)** | **~ sb (on charges/on a charge of sth)** (*especially NAmE, law* 律) to officially charge sb with a crime 控告；起訴： *The senator was indicted for murder.* 那位參議員被控犯謀殺罪。◇ *She was indicted on charges of corruption.* 她被控貪腐，受到起訴。 ➲ COLLOCATIONS at JUSTICE

in·dict·able /ɪnˈdaɪtəbl/ *adj.* (*law* 律) **1** (of a crime 罪行) for which you can be indicted 可提起公訴的： *an indictable offense* 可起訴的犯罪 **2** (of a person 人) able to be indicted 可被控告的；可被起訴的

in·dict·ment /ɪnˈdaɪtmənt/ *noun* **1** [C, usually sing.] **~ (of/on sb/sth)** a sign that a system, society, etc. is very bad or very wrong （制度、社會等的）衰敗跡象，腐敗跡象： *The poverty in our cities is a damning indictment of modern society.* 我們的城市中的貧民苦況是現代社會的一大敗象。 **2** [C] (*especially NAmE*) a written statement accusing sb of a crime 刑事起訴書；公訴書 **3** [U] (*especially NAmE*) the act of officially accusing sb of a crime 控告；起訴： *This led to his indictment on allegations of conspiracy.* 這件事最終使他被控犯有共謀罪。

indie /ˈɪndi/ *adj., noun*

■ ***adj.*** (of a company, person or product 公司、人或產品) not belonging to, working for or produced by a large organization; independent 不屬於大公司的；不是大公司生產的；獨立的： *an indie publisher/newspaper* 獨立發行人；獨立發行的報紙 ◇ *indie music* 獨立音樂 ◇ *an indie band/record label* 不知名的小樂隊 / 唱片公司

■ ***noun*** a small independent company, or sth produced by such a company 獨立小公司；獨立小公司的產品

in·dif·fer·ence /ɪnˈdɪfrəns/ *noun* [U, sing.] **~ (to sb/sth)** a lack of interest, feeling or reaction towards sb/sth 漠不關心；冷淡；不感興趣；無動於衷： *his total indifference to what people thought of him* 他對別人怎麼看他絲毫不在乎的態度 ◇ *What she said is* ***a matter of complete indifference*** *to me.* 她的話對於我來說完全無關緊要。◇ *Their father treated them with indifference.* 他們的父親對他們漠不關心。◇ *an indifference to the needs of others* 對於他人的需要置若罔聞

in·dif·fer·ent /ɪnˈdɪfrənt/ *adj.* **1** [not usually before noun] **~ (to sb/sth)** having or showing no interest in sb/sth 漠不關心；不感興趣： *The government cannot afford to be indifferent to public opinion.* 政府不可不關注輿論。 **2** not very good 不很好的；一般的 SYN **mediocre**： *an indifferent meal* 一般的飯食 ◇ *The festival has the usual mixture of movies—****good, bad and indifferent****.* 電影節的影片一如既往的良莠不齊，有優秀的、低劣的和一般的。 ▸ **in·dif·fer·ent·ly** *adv.*： *He shrugged indifferently.* 他滿不在乎地聳了聳肩。

in·di·gen·ous /ɪnˈdɪdʒənəs/ *adj.* (*formal*) belonging to a particular place rather than coming to it from somewhere else 本地的；當地的；土生土長的 SYN **native**： *the* ***indigenous*** *peoples/languages of the area* 該地區的本地人 / 語言 ◇ **~ to …** *The kangaroo is indigenous to Australia.* 袋鼠原產於澳大利亞。

in·di·gent /ˈɪndɪdʒənt/ *adj.* [usually before noun] (*formal*) very poor 十分貧窮的

in·di·gest·ible /ˌɪndɪˈdʒestəbl/ *adj.* **1** (of food 食物) that cannot easily be DIGESTED in the stomach 不易消化的： *an indigestible meal* 難消化的一餐 **2** (of facts, information, etc. 事實、信息等) difficult to understand, and presented in a complicated way 難解的；複雜難懂的 OPP **digestible**

in·di·ges·tion /ˌɪndɪˈdʒestʃən/ *noun* [U] pain caused by difficulty in DIGESTING food 消化不良（症） SYN **dyspepsia**

in·dig·nant /ɪnˈdɪɡnənt/ *adj.* feeling or showing anger and surprise because you think that you have been treated unfairly 憤慨的；憤怒的；義憤的： *an indignant letter/look* 憤慨的信 / 神情 ◇ **~ at/about sth** *She was very indignant at the way she had been treated.* 她對於自己受到的待遇大為光火。◇ **~ that …** *They were indignant that they hadn't been invited.* 他們因沒有受到邀請而憤憤不平。 ➲ note at ANGRY ▸ **in·dig·nant·ly** *adv.*： *'I'm certainly not asking him!' she retorted indignantly.* "我絕對不是在問他！" 她憤然反駁說。

in·dig·na·tion /ˌɪndɪɡˈneɪʃn/ *noun* [U] **~ (at/about sth)** | **~ (that …)** a feeling of anger and surprise caused by sth that you think is unfair or unreasonable 憤慨；憤怒；義憤： *The rise in train fares has aroused public indignation.* 火車票提價激起了公憤。◇ *Joe quivered* ***with indignation*** *that Paul should speak to him like that.* 喬認為保羅竟然那樣對他說話，氣得直發抖。◇ *Some benefits apply only to men, much* ***to the indignation of*** *working women.* 對職業女性大為不平的是有些福利只提供給男性。◇ *to be full of* ***righteous indignation*** (= the belief that you are right to be angry even though other people do not agree) 義憤填膺

in·dig·nity /ɪnˈdɪɡnəti/ *noun* [U, C] (*pl.* **-ies**) **~ (of sth/of doing sth)** a situation that makes you feel embarrassed or ashamed because you are not treated with respect; an act that causes these feelings 侮辱；輕蔑；侮辱性的行為 SYN **humiliation**： *The chairman* ***suffered the indignity of*** *being refused admission to the meeting.* 主席蒙受了被拒於會議之外的侮辱。◇ *the daily indignities of imprisonment* 身陷囹圄每日所遭受的侮辱

in·digo /ˈɪndɪɡəʊ; *NAmE* -ɡoʊ/ *adj.* very dark blue in colour 靛藍；靛青： *an indigo sky* 靛藍色的天空 ▸ **in·digo** *noun* [U]

in·dir·ect 🔑 /ˌɪndəˈrekt; -daɪˈr-/ *adj.* [usually before noun]

1 🔑 happening not as the main aim, cause or result of a particular action, but in addition to it 間接的；附帶的： *the* ***indirect effects*** *of the war* 戰爭的間接後果 ◇ *to find something out by* ***indirect methods*** 間接地查明某事 ◇ *The building collapsed as an* ***indirect result*** *of the heavy rain.* 大雨間接造成了那座樓房的倒塌。◇ *There would be some benefit, however indirect, to the state.* 國家會得到一些利益，不管有多少。◇ ***indirect costs*** (= costs that are not directly connected with making a product, for example training, heating, rent, etc.) 間接成本 **2** 🔑 avoiding saying sth in a clear and obvious way 閃爍其詞的；拐彎抹角的： *an indirect attack* 影射攻擊 **3** 🔑 not going in a straight line 迂迴的；彎曲的： *an* ***indirect route*** 迂迴的路線 OPP **direct** ▸ **in·dir·ect·ly** 🔑 *adv.*： *The new law will affect us all, directly or indirectly.* 新的法規將直接或間接地影響我們所有的人。 **in·dir·ect·ness** *noun* [U]

ˌindirect ˈobject *noun* (*grammar* 語法) a noun, noun phrase or pronoun in a sentence, used after some verbs, that refers to the person or thing that an action is done to or for 間接賓語；間接受詞： *In 'Give him the money', 'him' is the indirect object and 'money' is the direct object.* 在 give him the money 中，him 是間接賓語，money 是直接賓語。

ˌindirect ˈquestion (also **reˌported ˈquestion**) *noun* (*grammar* 語法) a question in REPORTED SPEECH, for example *She asked where I was going.* 間接疑問句 HELP Do not put a question mark after an indirect question. 間接疑問句不加問號。

ˌindirect ˈspeech *noun* [U] (*grammar* 語法) = REPORTED SPEECH ➲ compare DIRECT SPEECH

ˌindirect ˈtax *noun* [C, U] a tax that is paid as an amount added to the price of goods and services and not paid directly to the government 間接稅 ➲ compare DIRECT TAX ▸ **ˌindirect taxˈation** *noun* [U]

in·dis·cern·ible /ˌɪndɪˈsɜːnəbl; *NAmE* -ˈsɜːrn-/ *adj.* that cannot be seen, heard or understood 隱約的；依稀的；不明顯的

in·dis·cip·line /ɪnˈdɪsɪplɪn/ *noun* [U] (*formal*) a lack of control in the behaviour of a group of people 無紀律；無秩序；缺乏管理

in·dis·creet AW /ˌɪndɪˈskriːt/ *adj.* not careful about what you say or do, especially when this embarrasses or offends sb 不慎重的；不審慎的；魯莽的 OPP discreet ▸ **in·dis·creet·ly** *adv.*

in·dis·cre·tion AW /ˌɪndɪˈskreʃn/ *noun* **1** [C] an act or remark that is indiscreet, especially one that is not morally acceptable 不慎的言行；（尤指道德上）不檢點的言行：*youthful indiscretions* 年輕人的不檢點行為 **2** [U] the act of saying or doing sth without thinking about the effect it may have, especially when this embarrasses or offends sb 輕率；魯莽：*He talked to the press in a moment of indiscretion.* 他一時衝動對新聞界發表了講話。➲ compare DISCRETION

in·dis·crim·in·ate /ˌɪndɪˈskrɪmɪnət/ *adj.* **1** an **indiscriminate** action is done without thought about what the result may be, especially when it causes people to be harmed 隨意的；恣意的；不加選擇的：*indiscriminate attacks on motorists by youths throwing stones* 年輕人亂扔石頭襲擊駕車的人 ◇ *Doctors have been criticized for their indiscriminate use of antibiotics.* 醫生被指責濫用抗生素。**2** acting without careful judgement 不加分析的；不加判斷的：*She's always been indiscriminate in her choice of friends.* 她一向擇友不慎。▸ **in·dis·crim·in·ate·ly** *adv.*：*The soldiers fired indiscriminately into the crowd.* 士兵對着人群胡亂開槍。

in·dis·pens·able /ˌɪndɪˈspensəbl/ *adj.* too important to be without 不可或缺的；必不可少的 SYN **essential**：*Cars have become an indispensable part of our lives.* 汽車已成了我們生活中必不可少的一部份。◇ **~ to sb/sth** *She made herself indispensable to the department.* 她成為這個部門不可缺少的一分子。◇ **~ for sth/for doing sth** *A good dictionary is indispensable for learning a foreign language.* 一本好詞典是學習外語必備的。OPP **dispensable** ➲ SYNONYMS at ESSENTIAL ➲ LANGUAGE BANK at VITAL

in·dis·posed /ˌɪndɪˈspəʊzd; *NAmE* -ˈspoʊzd/ *adj.* (*formal*) **1** [not usually before noun] unable to do sth because you are ill/sick, or for a reason you do not want to give（因病或不願透露的原因）不能做某事 SYN **unwell** **2** [not before noun] **~ to do sth** not willing to do sth 不願（做某事）

in·dis·pos·ition /ˌɪndɪspəˈzɪʃn/ *noun* [C, U] (*formal*) a slight illness that makes you unable to do sth 小病；微恙

in·dis·put·able /ˌɪndɪˈspjuːtəbl/ *adj.* that is true and cannot be disagreed with or denied 不容置疑的；無可爭辯的；不容否認的 SYN **undeniable**：*indisputable evidence* 不可否認的證據 ◇ *an indisputable fact* 不容置疑的事實 ◇ *It is indisputable that the crime rate has been rising.* 毫無疑問，犯罪率一直在上升。➲ compare DISPUTABLE ▸ **in·dis·put·ably** *adv.*：*This painting is indisputably one of his finest works.* 這幅畫無疑是他最好的作品之一。

in·dis·sol·uble /ˌɪndɪˈsɒljəbl; *NAmE* -ˈsɑːl-/ *adj.* (*formal*) (of a relationship 關係) that cannot be ended 牢不可破的；穩定持久的：*an indissoluble friendship* 穩固持久的友誼 ▸ **in·dis·sol·ubly** /ˌɪndɪˈsɒljəbli; *NAmE* -ˈsɑːl-/ *adv.*：*indissolubly linked* 關係牢固

in·dis·tinct AW /ˌɪndɪˈstɪŋkt/ *adj.* that cannot be seen, heard or remembered clearly 模糊不清的；不清楚的 SYN **vague, hazy** ▸ **in·dis·tinct·ly** AW *adv.*

in·dis·tin·guish·able /ˌɪndɪˈstɪŋɡwɪʃəbl/ *adj.* **1 ~ (from sth)** if two things are **indistinguishable**, or one is **indistinguishable from** the other, it is impossible to see any differences between them 無法分辨的；無法區分的：*The male of the species is almost indistinguishable from the female.* 這個物種的雄性和雌性幾乎分辨不出。**2** not clear; not able to be clearly identified 不清楚的；無法識別的：*His words were indistinguishable.* 他說的話聽不清楚。

in·dium /ˈɪndiəm/ *noun* [U] (*symb.* **In**) a chemical element. Indium is a soft silver-white metal. 銦

in·di·vid·ual 0→ AW /ˌɪndɪˈvɪdʒuəl/ *adj., noun*

■ *adj.* **1** 0→ [only before noun] (often used after *each* 常用於 each 之後) considered separately rather than as part of a group 單獨的；個別的：*We interviewed each individual member of the community.* 我們採訪了社區中的每個成員。◇ *The minister refused to comment on individual cases.* 那位部長拒絕對個別情況發表評論。**2** 0→ [only before noun] connected with one person; designed for one person 一個人的；供一人用的：*respect for individual freedom* 對個人自由的尊重 ◇ *an individual pizza* 供一人食用的比薩餅 **3** (usually *approving*) typical of one particular person or thing in a way that is different from others 獨特的；與眾不同的 SYN **distinctive**：*a highly individual style of dress* 十分有個性的衣着風格

■ *noun* **1** 0→ a person considered separately rather than as part of a group 個人：*The competition is open to both teams and individuals.* 團隊和個人均可參加比賽。◇ *Treatment depends on the individual involved.* 治療方式因人而異。◇ *donations from private individuals* (= ordinary people rather than companies, etc.) 私人捐贈 **2** a person who is original and very different from others 與眾不同的人；有個性的人：*She's grown into quite an individual.* 她已經長成了一個相當有個性的人。**3** (*informal*, usually *disapproving*) a person of a particular type, especially a strange one 某種類型的人；（尤指）古怪的人：*an odd-looking individual* 模樣怪異的人 ◇ *So this individual came up and demanded money.* 於是這個怪人就走上前來要錢了。

in·di·vidu·al·ism AW /ˌɪndɪˈvɪdʒuəlɪzəm/ *noun* [U] **1** the quality of being different from other people and doing things in your own way 個性；獨特的氣質 **2** the belief that individual people in society should have the right to make their own decisions, etc., rather than be controlled by the government 個人主義；個人至上：*Capitalism stresses innovation, competition and individualism.* 資本主義強調的是創新、競爭和個人至上。▸ **in·di·vidu·al·ist** AW /-əlɪst/ *noun*：*She's a complete individualist in her art.* 她在藝術創作上完全是個自行其是的人。**in·di·vidu·al·is·tic** AW /ˌɪndɪˌvɪdʒuəˈlɪstɪk/ (also **in·di·vidu·al·ist**) *adj.*：*an individualistic culture* 有特色的文化 ◇ *His music is highly individualistic and may not appeal to everyone.* 他的音樂很獨特，可能不是人人都喜歡的。

in·di·vidu·al·ity AW /ˌɪndɪˌvɪdʒuˈæləti/ *noun* [U] the qualities that make sb/sth different from other people or things 個性；個人（或個體）特徵：*She expresses her individuality through her clothes.* 她從穿着上表現出她的個性。

in·di·vidu·al·ize (*BrE* also **-ise**) /ˌɪndɪˈvɪdʒuəlaɪz/ *verb* **~ sth** to make sth different to suit the needs of a particular person, place, etc. 使個性化；使因人（或因地等）而異：*to individualize children's learning* 對兒童因材施教 ▸ **in·di·vidu·al·iza·tion, -isa·tion** /ˌɪndɪvɪdʒuəlaɪˈzeɪʃn; *NAmE* -əˈzeɪʃn/ *noun* [U]

in·di·vidu·al·ized (*BrE* also **-ised**) /ˌɪndɪˈvɪdʒuəlaɪzd/ *adj.* designed for a particular person or thing; connected with a particular person or thing 個性化的；與個人（或個體）有關的：*individualized teaching* 因材施教 ◇ *a highly individualized approach to management* 很有針對性的管理方法

in·di·vidu·al·ly AW /ˌɪndɪˈvɪdʒuəli/ *adv.* separately, rather than as a group 分別地；單獨地；各別地：*individually wrapped chocolates* 獨立包裝的巧克力 ◇ *The manager spoke to them all individually.* 經理逐一和他們各人談話。◇ *The hotel has 100 individually designed bedrooms.* 這家旅館有 100 個設計各不相同的房間。

in·di·vidu·ate /ˌɪndɪˈvɪdʒueɪt/ *verb* **~ sb/sth** (*formal*) to make sb/sth clearly different from other people or things of the same type 使個性化；使有明顯特色

in·di·vis·ible /ˌɪndɪˈvɪzəbl/ *adj.* that cannot be divided into separate parts 分不開的；不可分割的 OPP **divisible** ▸ **in·di·vis·ibil·ity** /ˌɪndɪˌvɪzəˈbɪləti/ *noun* [U] **in·di·vis·ibly** /ˌɪndɪˈvɪzəbli/ *adv.*

Indo- /ˈɪndəʊ; *NAmE* ˈɪndoʊ/ *combining form* (in nouns and adjectives 構成名詞和形容詞) Indian 印度的；印度人：*the Indo-Pakistan border* 印巴邊境

Indo-Ca'nadian *noun* [C] (*CanE*) a Canadian who was born in S Asia, especially India, or whose family originally came from S Asia 生於南亞（或南亞裔）的加拿大人；（尤指）生於印度（或印度裔）的加拿大人

in·doc·trin·ate /ɪnˈdɒktrɪneɪt; *NAmE* ɪnˈdɑːk-/ *verb* **~ sb (with sth)** | **~ sb (to do sth)** (*disapproving*) to force sb to accept a particular belief or set of beliefs and not allow them to consider any others 強行灌輸（信仰或學說）: *They had been indoctrinated from an early age with their parents' beliefs.* 他們從小就被滿腦子灌入了他們父母的信仰。 ▸ **in·doc·trin·ation** /ɪnˌdɒktrɪˈneɪʃn; *NAmE* -ˌdɑːk-/ *noun* [U]: ***political/religious indoctrination*** 政治思想 / 宗教教義的灌輸

ˌIndo-ˌEuroˈpean *adj.* of or connected with the family of languages spoken in most of Europe and parts of western Asia (including English, French, Latin, Greek, Swedish, Russian and Hindi) 印歐語系的（指歐洲大部份地區和西亞的部份地區的語言譜系，包括英語、法語、拉丁語、希臘語、瑞典語、俄語和印地語）

in·do·lent /ˈɪndələnt/ *adj.* (*formal*) not wanting to work 懶惰的；懶散的；好逸惡勞的 SYN **lazy** ▸ **in·do·lence** /-əns/ *noun* [U]

in·dom·it·able /ɪnˈdɒmɪtəbl; *NAmE* ɪnˈdɑːm-/ *adj.* (*formal, approving*) not willing to accept defeat, even in a difficult situation; very brave and determined 不屈不撓的；勇敢堅定的

in·door 0-w /ˈɪndɔː(r)/ *adj.* [only before noun] located, done or used inside a building （在）室內的；在戶內進行的；在室內用的: *an indoor swimming pool* 室內游泳池 ◇ *indoor games* 室內遊戲 ◇ *the world indoor 200 metres champion* 室內 200 米賽世界冠軍 OPP **outdoor**

in·doors 0-w /ˌɪnˈdɔːz; *NAmE* ˌɪnˈdɔːrz/ *adv.* inside or into a building 在室內；進入戶內: *to* ***go/stay indoors*** 進入 / 留在屋裏 ◇ *Many herbs can be grown indoors.* 很多香草植物能在室內種植。 OPP **outdoors**

in·drawn /ˌɪnˈdrɔːn/ *adj.* (*literary*) **indrawn breath** is air that sb breathes in suddenly and quickly, expressing surprise or shock（驚慌時）吸入的，倒吸的（一口氣）

in·dub·it·ably /ɪnˈdjuːbɪtəbli; *NAmE* -ˈduː-/ *adv.* (*formal*) in a way that cannot be doubted; without question 不容置疑地；毫無疑問地 SYN **undoubtedly**: *He was, indubitably, the most suitable candidate.* 他無疑是最合適的人選。 ▸ **in·dub·it·able** *adj.*: *indubitable proof* 確證

in·duce AW /ɪnˈdjuːs; *NAmE* -ˈduːs/ *verb* **1 ~ sb to do sth** (*formal*) to persuade or influence sb to do sth 勸說；誘使: *Nothing would induce me to take the job.* 沒有什麼能誘使我接受這份工作。 **2 ~ sth** (*formal*) to cause sth 引起；導致: *drugs which induce sleep* 使人昏昏欲睡的藥物 ◇ *a drug-induced coma* 藥物引起的昏迷狀態 **3 ~ sb/sth** (*medical* 醫) to make a woman start giving birth to her baby by giving her special drugs 催產；催生: *an induced labour* 催生 ◇ *We'll have to induce her.* 我們得給她引產。

in·duce·ment /ɪnˈdjuːsmənt; *NAmE* ɪnˈduːsmənt/ *noun* [C, U] **~ (to/for sb) (to do sth)** something that is given to sb to persuade them to do sth 引誘；刺激；誘因 SYN **incentive**: *financial inducements to mothers to stay at home* 促使母親守在家裏的經濟誘因 ◇ *There is little inducement for them to work harder.* 沒有什麼動力能促使他們加把勁工作。 ◇ *Government officials have been accused of accepting inducements* (= BRIBES) *from local businessmen.* 政府官員被指控接受了當地商人的賄賂。

in·duct /ɪnˈdʌkt/ *verb* [often passive] **~ sb (into sth) (as sth)** (*formal*) **1** to formally give sb a job or position of authority, especially as part of a ceremony （尤指在典禮上）使正式就職 **2** to officially introduce sb into a group or an organization, especially the army 正式吸收（為成員）；（尤指）徵召入伍 **3** to introduce sb to a particular area of knowledge 使瞭解；傳授: *They were inducted into the skills of magic.* 他們獲得傳授魔術。

in·duct·ee /ˌɪndʌkˈtiː/ *noun* (*especially NAmE*) a person who is being, or who has just been, introduced into a special group of people, especially sb who has just joined the army 新成員；（尤指）新入伍者

in·duc·tion AW /ɪnˈdʌkʃn/ *noun* **1** [U, C] **~ (into sth)** the process of introducing sb to a new job, skill, organization, etc.; a ceremony at which this takes place 就職；入門；接納會員；就職儀式 **2** [U, C] the act of making a pregnant woman start to give birth, using artificial means such as a special drug 催產；催生 **3** [U] (*technical* 術語) a method of discovering general rules and principles from particular facts and examples 歸納法 ➲ compare DEDUCTION (1) **4** [U] (*physics* 物) the process by which electricity or MAGNETISM passes from one object to another without them touching 電磁感應

inˈduction course *noun* (*BrE*) a training course for new employees, students, etc. that is designed to give them a general introduction to the business, school, etc. 培訓課程；入門課程

inˈduction loop *noun* a system in theatres, etc., which helps people who cannot hear well. A ring of wire around the room produces a signal that can be received directly by HEARING AIDS.（劇院等的）感應環路助聽系統

in·duct·ive /ɪnˈdʌktɪv/ *adj.* **1** (*technical* 術語) using particular facts and examples to form general rules and principles 歸納法的；歸納的: *an inductive argument* 歸納論證 ◇ *inductive reasoning* 歸納推理 ➲ compare DEDUCTIVE **2** (*physics* 物) connected with the INDUCTION of electricity 電感應的 ▸ **in·duct·ive·ly** *adv.*: *a theory derived inductively from the data* 從數據中歸納出的理論

in·dulge /ɪnˈdʌldʒ/ *verb* **1** [I, T] to allow yourself to have or do sth that you like, especially sth that is considered bad for you 沉湎，沉迷，沉溺（於…）: **~ in sth** *They went into town to indulge in some serious shopping.* 他們進城去大肆購物。 ◇ **~ yourself (with sth)** *I indulged myself with a long hot bath.* 我盡情享受了一次長時間的熱水浴。 **2** [T] **~ sth** to satisfy a particular desire, interest, etc. 滿足（慾望、興趣等）: *The inheritance enabled him to indulge his passion for art.* 這筆遺產使他能夠盡情投入他熱愛的藝術。 **3** [T] to be too generous in allowing sb to have or do whatever they like 放縱；聽任: **~ sb (with sth)** *She did not believe in indulging the children with presents.* 她認為不能慣着孩子們要什麼就給什麼。 ◇ **~ sth** *Her father had always* ***indulged her every whim.*** 她的父親總是讓她放任自流。 **4** [I] **~ in sth** to take part in an activity, especially one that is illegal 參加，參與（尤指違法活動）

in·dul·gence /ɪnˈdʌldʒəns/ *noun* **1** [U] (usually *disapproving*) the state or act of having or doing whatever you want; the state of allowing sb to have or do whatever they want 沉溺；放縱；縱容: *to lead a life of indulgence* 過着放縱的生活 ◇ *Avoid excessive indulgence in sweets and canned drinks.* 避免食用過多的甜食和罐裝飲料。 ◇ *There is no limit to the indulgence he shows to his grandchildren.* 他無度地溺愛嬌慣孫子孫女。 **2** [C] something that you allow yourself to have even though it is not essential 嗜好；愛好；享受: *The holiday was an extravagant indulgence.* 那個假期是一次奢華的享受。 ➲ see also SELF-INDULGENCE **3** [U] (*formal*) willingness to ignore the weaknesses in sb/sth 寬容；包涵 SYN **patience**: *They begged the audience's indulgence.* 他們懇求觀眾包涵。

in·dul·gent /ɪnˈdʌldʒənt/ *adj.* **1** (usually *disapproving*) tending to allow sb to have or do whatever they want 縱容的；放縱的: *indulgent parents* 縱容子女的父母 ◇ *an indulgent smile* 遷就的微笑 ➲ see also SELF-INDULGENT **2** willing or too willing to ignore the weaknesses in sb/sth 寬容的；過於寬厚的 SYN **patient**: *to take an indulgent view of sth* 寬宏大量地看待某事 ▸ **in·dul·gent·ly** *adv.*: *to laugh indulgently* 寬容地笑

in·duna /ɪnˈduːnə/ *noun* (*SAfrE*) a senior leader of a TRIBE 族長；酋長

in·dus·trial 0-w /ɪnˈdʌstriəl/ *adj.* [usually before noun] **1** 0-w connected with industry 工業的；產業的: *industrial unrest* 產業工人騷亂 ◇ *industrial output* 工業產量 ◇ *an industrial accident* 工傷事故 ◇ *They had made* ***industrial quantities*** *of food* (= a lot). 他們生產了大量的食品。 **2** 0-w used by industries 用於工業的: *industrial chemicals* 工業用化學製品 **3** 0-w having many industries 有很多產業的；工業發達的: *an industrial town* 工業城市 ◇ *an industrial society* 工業發達的社會 ◇ *the world's leading* ***industrial nations*** 全球主要工業國

▸ **in·dus·tri·al·ly** /-əli/ *adv.*： *industrially advanced countries* 工業發達的國家

in‚dustrial 'action *noun* [U] (*especially BrE*) action that workers take, especially stopping work, to protest to their employers about sth 勞工行動；（尤指）罷工，怠工

in‚dustrial archae'ology *noun* [U] the study of machines, factories, bridges, etc. used in the past in industry 工業考古學

in‚dustrial 'arts (also **shop**, **'shop class**) *noun* [U] (*NAmE*) a school subject in which students learn to make things from wood and metal using tools and machines 工藝課

in‚dustrial e'state (*BrE*) (*NAmE* **in‚dustrial 'park**) *noun* an area especially for factories, on the edge of a town（位於市郊的）工業區 ⊃ compare TRADING ESTATE

in·dus·tri·al·ism /ɪn'dʌstriəlɪzəm/ *noun* [U] (*technical* 術語) an economic and social system based on industry 工業主義；產業主義

in·dus·tri·al·ist /ɪn'dʌstriəlɪst/ *noun* a person who owns or runs a large factory or industrial company 工業家；實業家；工廠主

in·dus·tri·al·ize (*BrE* also **-ise**) /ɪn'dʌstriəlaɪz/ *verb* [T, I] **~ (sth)** if a country or an area **is industrialized** or if it **industrializes**, industries are developed there（使國家或地區）工業化：*The southern part of the country was slow to industrialize.* 這個國家的南部工業化進程緩慢。▸ **in·dus·tri·al·iza·tion**, **-isa·tion** /ɪn‚dʌstriəlaɪ'zeɪʃn; *NAmE* -lə'z-/ *noun* [U]：*the rapid industrialization of Japan* 日本的迅速工業化 **in·dus·tri·al·ized**, **-ised** *adj.*：*an industrialized country* 工業化國家

in‚dustrial 'park (*NAmE*) (*BrE* **in‚dustrial e'state**) *noun* an area especially for factories, on the edge of a town（位於市郊的）工業園區

in‚dustrial re'lations *noun* [pl.] relations between employers and employees 勞資關係

the In‚dustrial Revo'lution *noun* [sing.] the period in the 18th and 19th centuries in Europe and the US when machines began to be used to do work, and industry grew rapidly 工業革命，產業革命（指 18 及 19 世紀歐美使用機器、工業迅速發展的階段）

in'dustrial-strength *adj.* (often *humorous*) very strong or powerful 強勁的；強效的；強大的：*industrial-strength coffee* 特別提神的咖啡

in‚dustrial tri'bunal *noun* (*BrE*) = EMPLOYMENT TRIBUNAL

in·dus·tri·ous /ɪn'dʌstriəs/ *adj.* (*approving*) working hard; busy 勤奮的；勤勞的；忙碌的 SYN **hard-working**：*an industrious student* 勤勉的學生 ▸ **in·dus·tri·ous·ly** *adv.*

in·dus·try 0━ /'ɪndəstri/ *noun* (*pl.* **-ies**)
1 0━ [U] the production of goods from raw materials, especially in factories 工業；生產製造：***heavy/light industry*** 重 / 輕工業 ◇ *the needs of British industry* 英國工業的需求 ◇ *She got a job **in industry**.* 她找了份工廠裏的工作。⊃ COLLOCATIONS at ECONOMY **2** 0━ [C] the people and activities involved in producing a particular thing, or in providing a particular service 行業：*the steel industry* 鋼鐵業 ◇ *the **catering/tourist, etc. industry*** 飲食、旅遊等行業 ◇ *We need to develop local industries.* 我們需要發展地方工業。◇ (*figurative*) *the Madonna industry* (= the large number of people involved in making Madonna successful) 麥當娜策劃集團 ⊃ see also CAPTAIN OF INDUSTRY, COTTAGE INDUSTRY, HEAVY INDUSTRY, SUNRISE INDUSTRY, SUNSET INDUSTRY **3** [U] (*formal*) the quality of working hard 勤奮；勤勞：*We were impressed by their industry.* 他們的勤奮給我們留下深刻印象。

Indy /'ɪndi/ (also **'Indy racing**, **'Indycar**, **'Indy car racing**) *noun* [U] motor racing around a track which is raised at both sides 印第安那波利斯式賽車，印地車賽（跑道為橢圓形，兩旁有護牆）

Indy·car /'ɪndikɑː(r)/ *noun* **1** [U] = INDY **2** [C] a car used in Indy racing 印地車賽賽車

in·ebri·ated /ɪ'niːbrieɪtɪd/ *adj.* (*formal* or *humorous*) drunk 喝醉的 ▸ **in·ebri·ation** /ɪ‚niːbri'eɪʃn/ *noun* [U]

in·ed·ible /ɪn'edəbl/ *adj.* that you cannot eat because it is of poor quality, or poisonous 不能吃的；不宜食用的 OPP **edible**

in·ef·fable /ɪn'efəbl/ *adj.* (*formal*) too great or beautiful to describe in words（美好得）難以形容的，不可言喻的：*ineffable joy* 難以形容的喜悅

in·ef·fect·ive /‚ɪnɪ'fektɪv/ *adj.* not achieving what you want to achieve; not having any effect 無效果的；不起作用的；不奏效的：*The new drug was ineffective.* 新藥不起作用。◇ *ineffective management* 管理不善 ◇ **~ in doing sth** *The law proved ineffective in dealing with the problem.* 事實證明這條法規未能真正解決問題。OPP **effective** ▸ **in·ef·fect·ive·ness** *noun* [U] **in·ef·fect·ive·ly** *adv.*

in·ef·fec·tual /‚ɪnɪ'fektʃuəl/ *adj.* (*formal*) without the ability to achieve much; weak; not achieving what you want to 無能的；軟弱的；達不到目的的：*an ineffectual teacher* 不稱職的教師 ◇ *an ineffectual attempt to reform the law* 改革法律的徒勞無益的嘗試 ▸ **in·ef·fec·tu·al·ly** /-tʃuəli/ *adv.*

in·ef·fi·cient /‚ɪnɪ'fɪʃnt/ *adj.* not doing a job well and not making the best use of time, money, energy, etc. 效率低的；能力差的；浪費的：*an inefficient heating system* 效率不佳的暖氣系統 ◇ *inefficient government* 無能的政府 ◇ *an extremely inefficient secretary* 極不稱職的秘書 ◇ *inefficient use of time and energy* 時間和精力的浪費 OPP **efficient** ▸ **in·ef·fi·ciency** /-ənsi/ *noun* [U, C] (*pl.* **-ies**)：*waste and inefficiency in government* 政府中的浪費與低效能 ◇ *inefficiencies in the system* 這個系統中的低效率現象 **in·ef·fi·cient·ly** *adv.*

in·ele·gant /ɪn'elɪɡənt/ *adj.* not attractive or elegant 不優美的；不優雅的 OPP **elegant** ▸ **in·ele·gant·ly** *adv.*

in·eli·gible /ɪn'elɪdʒəbl/ *adj.* not having the necessary qualifications to have or to do sth 不合格的；不符合資格的：**~ (for sth)** *ineligible for financial assistance* 無資格得到財政援助 ◇ **~ (to do sth)** *ineligible to vote* 無投票資格 OPP **eligible** ▸ **in·eli·gi·bil·ity** /ɪn‚elɪdʒə'bɪləti/ *noun* [U]

in·eluct·able /‚ɪnɪ'lʌktəbl/ *adj.* (*formal*) that you cannot avoid 無可避免的 SYN **unavoidable** ▸ **in·eluct·ably** /-əbli/ *adv.*

inept /ɪ'nept/ *adj.* acting or done with no skill 缺乏技巧的；無能的；笨拙的：*She was left feeling inept and inadequate.* 她被弄得感到笨拙無能。◇ *an inept remark* 笨拙的發言 ▸ **in·ept·ly** *adv.*

in·epti·tude /ɪ'neptɪtjuːd; *NAmE* -tuːd/ *noun* [U] lack of skill 缺乏技巧；無能；笨拙：*the ineptitude of the police in handling the situation* 警方在處理這個局面時的無能

in·equal·ity /‚ɪnɪ'kwɒləti; *NAmE* -'kwɑːl-/ *noun* [U, C] (*pl.* **-ies**) the unfair difference between groups of people in society, when some have more wealth, status or opportunities than others 不平等；不平衡；不平均：*inequality of opportunity* 機會的不均 ◇ *economic inequalities between different areas* 不同地區間的經濟不平衡落差 ◇ *racial inequality* 種族不平等 OPP **equality** ⊃ COLLOCATIONS at RACE ⊃ see also UNEQUAL

in·equit·able /ɪn'ekwɪtəbl/ *adj.* (*formal*) not fair; not the same for everyone 不公正的；不公平的 SYN **unfair**：*inequitable distribution of wealth* 財富的不公平分配 OPP **equitable**

in·equity /ɪn'ekwəti/ *noun* [C, U] (*pl.* **-ies**) (*formal*) something that is unfair; the state of being unfair 不公正的事；不公正；不公平 SYN **injustice**

in·erad·ic·able /‚ɪnɪ'rædɪkəbl/ *adj.* (*formal*) (of a quality or situation 品質或狀況) that cannot be removed or changed 不可除去的；無法改變的

inert /ɪ'nɜːt; *NAmE* ɪ'nɜːrt/ *adj.* **1** (*formal*) without power to move or act 無活動能力的；無行動力的：*He lay inert with half-closed eyes.* 他半睜着雙眼一動不動地躺着。**2** (*chemistry* 化) without active chemical or other properties (= characteristics) 惰性的；不活潑的

i‚nert 'gas *noun* (*chemistry* 化) = NOBLE GAS

in·er·tia /ɪˈnɜːʃə; *NAmE* ɪˈnɜːrʃə/ *noun* [U] **1** (usually *disapproving*) lack of energy; lack of desire or ability to move or change 缺乏活力；惰性；保守：*I can't seem to throw off this feeling of inertia.* 我好像無法擺脱這種無力的感覺。◇ *the forces of institutional inertia in the school system* 學校體制內的惰性 **2** (*physics* 物) a property (= characteristic) of MATTER (= a substance) by which it stays still or, if moving, continues moving in a straight line unless it is acted on by a force outside itself 慣性

in·er·tial /ɪˈnɜːʃl; *NAmE* ɪˈnɜːrʃl/ *adj.* (*technical* 術語) connected with or caused by inertia 慣性的

iˈnertia reel *noun* a round device that one end of a car SEAT BELT is wound around so that it will move freely unless it is pulled suddenly, for example in an accident（汽車安全帶的）慣性捲筒

in·escap·able /ˌɪnɪˈskeɪpəbl/ *adj.* (of a fact or a situation 現實或狀況) that you cannot avoid or ignore 不可避免的；逃避不了的；不能忽視的 SYN **unavoidable**：*an inescapable fact* 不可逃避的現實 ◇ *This leads to the inescapable conclusion that the two things are connected.* 這就必然得出一個結論：這兩件事互有關聯。▸ **in·escap·ably** /-əbli/ *adv.*

in·es·sen·tial /ˌɪnɪˈsenʃl/ *adj.* not necessary 非必需的；無關緊要的：*inessential luxuries* 不必要的奢侈 ▸ **in·es·sen·tial** *noun*：*Few people had spare cash for inessentials.* 很少人有閒錢買那些可有可無的東西。➲ compare ESSENTIAL (1), NON-ESSENTIAL

in·estim·able /ɪnˈestɪməbl/ *adj.* (*formal*) too great to calculate（大得）難以估量的，無法估計的：*The information he provided was **of inestimable value**.* 他提供的信息價值難以估量。

in·ev·it·able 0‑w AW /ɪnˈevɪtəbl/ *adj.*
1 0‑w that you cannot avoid or prevent 不可避免的；不能防止的 SYN **unavoidable**：*It was an inevitable consequence of the decision.* 那是這個決定的必然後果。◇ ***It was inevitable that** there would be job losses.* 裁員已是不可避免的事。◇ *A rise in the interest rates seems inevitable.* 提高利率似乎是不可避免的。 **2** [only before noun] (often *humorous*) so frequent that you always expect it 總會發生的；照例必有的；慣常的：*the English and their inevitable cups of tea* 英國人和他們例行的飲茶 **3 the inevitable** *noun* [sing.] something that is certain to happen 必然發生的事；不可避免的事：*You have to accept the inevitable.* 你得接受必然發生的事。◇ *The inevitable happened—I forgot my passport.* 逃不掉的事情發生了，我忘了帶護照。▸ **in·ev·it·abil·ity** AW /ɪnˌevɪtəˈbɪləti/ *noun* [U, sing.]：*the inevitability of death* 死亡的必然性 ◇ *There was an inevitability about their defeat.* 他們的失敗自有其必然。

in·ev·it·ably 0‑w AW /ɪnˈevɪtəbli/ *adv.*
1 0‑w as is certain to happen 不可避免地；必然地：*Inevitably, the press exaggerated the story.* 新聞界照例又誇大了這件事。 **2** (often *humorous*) as you would expect 意料之中：*Inevitably, it rained on the day of the wedding.* 果然不出所料，婚禮的那天下起了雨。

in·exact /ˌɪnɪɡˈzækt/ *adj.* not accurate or exact 不準確的；不精確的：*an inexact description* 不準確的描述 ◇ *Economics is an inexact science.* 經濟學是一門不精確的科學。

in·exac·ti·tude /ˌɪnɪɡˈzæktɪtjuːd; *NAmE* -tuːd/ *noun* [U] (*formal*) the quality of being not accurate or exact 不精確；不準確

in·ex·cus·able /ˌɪnɪkˈskjuːzəbl/ *adj.* too bad to accept or forgive 不可寬恕的；無法原諒的 SYN **unjustifiable**：*inexcusable rudeness* 不可原諒的粗魯無禮 OPP **excusable** ▸ **in·ex·cus·ably** /-əbli/ *adv.*

in·ex·haust·ible /ˌɪnɪɡˈzɔːstəbl/ *adj.* that cannot be EXHAUSTED (= finished); very great 用之不竭的；無窮無盡的：*an inexhaustible supply of good jokes* 講不完的精彩笑話 ◇ *Her energy is inexhaustible.* 她有無窮的精力。

in·ex·or·able /ɪnˈeksərəbl/ *adj.* (*formal*) (of a process 過程) that cannot be stopped or changed 不可阻擋的；無法改變的 SYN **relentless**：*the inexorable rise of crime* 阻遏不了的犯罪上升趨勢 ▸ **in·ex·or·abil·ity** /ɪnˌeksərəˈbɪləti/ *noun* [U]：*the inexorability of progress* 阻擋不了的進展趨勢 **in·ex·or·ably** /ɪnˈeksərəbli/ *adv.*：*events leading inexorably towards a crisis* 不可避免地導致危機的一些事件

in·ex·pe·di·ent /ˌɪnɪkˈspiːdiənt/ *adj.* [not usually before noun] (*formal*) (of an action 行為) not fair or right 不公正；不正確；不恰當：*It would be inexpedient to raise taxes further.* 進一步加稅就是不合理。OPP **expedient**

in·ex·pen·sive /ˌɪnɪkˈspensɪv/ *adj.* not costing a lot of money 不昂貴的：*a relatively inexpensive hotel* 相對廉價的旅館 OPP **expensive** ➲ SYNONYMS at CHEAP ▸ **in·ex·pen·sive·ly** *adv.*

in·ex·peri·ence /ˌɪnɪkˈspɪəriəns; *NAmE* -ˈspɪr-/ *noun* [U] lack of knowledge and experience 缺乏經驗；經驗不足：*His mistake was due to youth and inexperience.* 他失誤的原因是年輕沒有經驗。

in·ex·peri·enced /ˌɪnɪkˈspɪəriənst; *NAmE* -ˈspɪr-/ *adj.* having little knowledge or experience of sth 缺乏認識（或經驗）的：*inexperienced drivers/staff* 沒有經驗的司機／職員 ◇ *inexperienced in modern methods* 不熟悉現代方法 ◇ *a child too young and inexperienced to recognize danger* 因太年幼無知而意識不到危險的孩子 OPP **experienced**

in·ex·pert /ɪnˈekspɜːt; *NAmE* -pɜːrt/ *adj.* without much skill 不熟練的；缺乏技巧的 ➲ compare EXPERT ▸ **in·ex·pert·ly** *adv.*

in·ex·plic·able /ˌɪnɪkˈsplɪkəbl/ *adj.* that cannot be understood or explained 費解的；無法解釋的 SYN **incomprehensible**：*inexplicable behaviour* 令人費解的行為 ◇ ***For some inexplicable reason** he gave up a fantastic job.* 由於某種莫名其妙的原因，他放棄了一份很不錯的工作。OPP **explicable** ▸ **in·ex·plic·ably** *adv.*：*inexplicably delayed/absent* 令人不解地耽擱／缺席 ◇ *She inexplicably withdrew the offer.* 她不可思議地撤回了提議。

in·ex·press·ible /ˌɪnɪkˈspresəbl/ *adj.* (of feelings 感情) too strong to be put into words（強烈得）難以言傳的，無法形容的：*inexpressible joy* 無法形容的喜悦

in ex·tre·mis /ˌɪn ɪkˈstriːmɪs/ *adv.* (from *Latin*, *formal*) **1** in a very difficult situation when very strong action is needed 在危急關頭；在緊急情況下；在絕境 **2** at the moment of death 臨終；彌留之際

in·ex·tric·able /ˌɪnɪkˈstrɪkəbl; ɪnˈekstrɪkəbl/ *adj.* (*formal*) too closely linked to be separated 無法分開的；分不開的：*an inextricable connection between the past and the present* 過去和現在之間密不可分的關係

in·ex·tric·ably /ˌɪnɪkˈstrɪkəbli; ɪnˈekstrɪkəbli/ *adv.* if two things are **inextricably linked**, etc., it is impossible to separate them 不可分開地；密不可分地：*Europe's foreign policy is inextricably linked with that of the US.* 歐洲的對外政策和美國的緊密相扣。◇ *She had become inextricably involved in the campaign.* 她已陷入這場運動之中，以致無法脱身。

in·fal·lible /ɪnˈfæləbl/ *adj.* **1** never wrong; never making mistakes 永無過失的；一貫正確的：*infallible advice* 絕對正確的忠告 ◇ *Doctors are not infallible.* 醫生並非永不犯錯。OPP **fallible 2** that never fails; always doing what it is supposed to do 絕對可靠的；萬無一失的：*an infallible method of memorizing things* 百試百靈的記憶方法 ▸ **in·fal·li·bil·ity** /ɪnˌfæləˈbɪləti/ *noun* [U]：*papal infallibility* 教宗的絕對正確 **in·fal·libly** /-əbli/ *adv.*

in·fam·ous /ˈɪnfəməs/ *adj.* (*formal*) well known for being bad or evil 臭名遠揚的；聲名狼藉的 SYN **notorious**：*a general who was infamous for his brutality* 因殘忍而惡名昭彰的將軍 ◇ *the most infamous concentration camp* 最惡名遠揚的集中營 ◇ (*humorous*) *the infamous British sandwich* 以難吃著名的英國三明治 ➲ compare FAMOUS

in·famy /ˈɪnfəmi/ *noun* (*pl.* **-ies**) (*formal*) **1** [U] the state of being well known for sth bad or evil 臭名昭著；聲名狼藉：*a day that will live in infamy* 遺臭萬年的一天 **2** [U, C] evil behaviour; an evil act 惡行；罪惡：*scenes of horror and infamy* 恐怖與罪惡的場面

in·fancy /ˈɪnfənsi/ *noun* [U] **1** the time when a child is a baby or very young 嬰兒期；幼兒期：*to die **in infancy*** 嬰兒夭折 **2** the early development of sth 初期；初創期：

I

a time when the cinema was still ***in its infancy*** 電影業尚處於初創的時期

in·fant /ˈɪnfənt/ *noun, adj.*

■ **noun 1** (*formal* or *technical* 術語) a baby or very young child 嬰兒；幼兒： *a nursery for infants under two* 兩歲以下嬰幼兒的託兒所 ◇ *their infant son* 他們幼小的兒子 ◇ *She was seriously ill as an infant.* 她年幼時曾患重病。◇ *the infant mortality rate* 嬰幼兒死亡率 ◇ *Mozart was an* ***infant prodigy*** (= a child with unusual ability). 莫扎特是個神童。 HELP In *NAmE* **infant** is only used for a baby, especially a very young one. 美式英語中 infant 僅指嬰兒，尤指新生兒。 **2** (in British and Australian education 英國和澳大利亞的教育) a child at school between the ages of four and seven 四歲到七歲之間的學童： *an infant school* 幼兒學校 ◇ *infant teachers* 幼兒教師 ◇ *I've known her since we were in the infants* (= at infant school). 從幼兒學校時我就認識她了。

■ **adj.** [only before noun] **1** designed to be used by infants 供嬰幼兒用的： *infant formula* (= milk for babies) 嬰兒配方奶粉 **2** new and not yet developed 初期的；初創期的： *infant industries* 新興工業

I

in·fanti·cide /ɪnˈfæntɪsaɪd/ *noun* (*formal*) **1** [U, C] the crime of killing a baby; a person who is guilty of this crime 殺嬰（罪）；殺嬰犯 **2** [U] (in some cultures) the practice of killing babies that are not wanted, for example because they are girls and not boys 殺嬰（某些文化中殺女嬰等的做法）

in·fant·ile /ˈɪnfəntaɪl/ *adj.* **1** (*disapproving*) typical of a small child (and therefore not suitable for adults or older children) 嬰幼兒特有的；孩子氣的 SYN **childish** **2** [only before noun] (*formal* or *technical* 術語) connected with babies or very young children 嬰兒的；幼兒的

in·fant·il·ism /ɪnˈfæntɪlɪzəm/ *noun* [U] (*psychology* 心) the fact of adults continuing to behave like children, in a way that is not normal（成人的）幼稚病

in·fanti·lize (*BrE* also **-ise**) /ɪnˈfæntɪlaɪz/ *verb* **~ sb** (*formal*) to treat sb as though they are a child 當作幼兒對待

in·fan·try /ˈɪnfəntri/ *noun* [C+sing./pl. v.] soldiers who fight on foot （統稱）步兵： *infantry units* 步兵分隊 ◇ *The infantry was/were guarding the bridge.* 步兵守衛着橋梁。

in·fan·try·man /ˈɪnfəntrimən/ *noun* (*pl.* **-men** /-mən/) a soldier who fights on foot（一名）步兵

in·farc·tion /ɪnˈfɑːkʃn; *NAmE* -ˈfɑːrk-/ *noun* (*medical* 醫) a condition in which the blood supply to an area of TISSUE is blocked and the TISSUE dies 梗塞；梗死

in·fatu·ated /ɪnˈfætʃueɪtɪd/ *adj.* **~ (with sb/sth)** having a very strong feeling of love or attraction for sb/sth so that you cannot think clearly and in a sensible way 熱戀的；痴情的 SYN **besotted**： *She was completely infatuated with him.* 她完全迷戀上了他。

in·fatu·ation /ɪnˌfætʃuˈeɪʃn/ *noun* [C, U] **~ (with/for sb/sth)** very strong feelings of love or attraction for sb/sth, especially when these are unreasonable and do not last long（尤指一時的）熱戀，痴迷： *It isn't love, it's just a passing infatuation.* 那不是愛情，只不過是一時的痴迷。

in·fect /ɪnˈfekt/ *verb*

1 to make a disease or an illness spread to a person, an animal or a plant 傳染；使感染： **~ sb/sth** *It is not possible to infect another person through kissing.* 接吻不可能把這種病傳染給他人。◇ **~ sb/sth with sth** *people infected with HIV* 染上艾滋病病毒的人 **2** **~ sth (with sth)** [usually passive] to make a substance contain harmful bacteria that can spread disease 使攜帶病菌 SYN **contaminate**： *eggs infected with salmonella* 帶沙門氏菌的雞蛋 **3** **~ sth (with sth)** to make a computer virus spread to another computer or program 傳染，使感染（計算機病毒） **4** **~ sb (with sth)** to make sb share a particular feeling 使感染（某種感情）；影響： *She infected the children with her enthusiasm for music.* 她對音樂的熱愛感染了孩子們。

in·fected /ɪnˈfektɪd/ *adj.*

1 containing harmful bacteria 帶菌的；感染病菌的： *The wound from the dog bite had become infected.* 狗咬的傷口感染了。◇ *an infected water supply* 受污染的供水系統 **2** (*computing* 計) affected by a computer virus 感染電腦病毒的： *an infected PC* 中了病毒的電腦

in·fec·tion /ɪnˈfekʃn/ *noun*

1 [U] the act or process of causing or getting a disease 傳染；感染： *to be exposed to infection* 暴露於易受感染的環境 ◇ *to increase the* ***risk of infection*** 增加傳染的危險 ➲ see also CROSS-INFECTION **2** [C] an illness that is caused by bacteria or a virus and that affects one part of the body（身體某部位的）感染；傳染病： *an* ***ear/throat, etc. infection*** 耳部、喉部等感染 ◇ *to spread an infection* 傳染疾病 ➲ **SYNONYMS** at DISEASE ➲ compare CONTAGION

in·fec·tious /ɪnˈfekʃəs/ *adj.*

1 an **infectious** disease can be passed easily from one person to another, especially through the air they breathe 傳染性的，感染的（尤指通過呼吸）： *Flu is highly infectious.* 流感的傳染性很高。◇ (*figurative*) *infectious laughter* 富有感染力的笑聲 **2** [not usually before noun] if a person or an animal is **infectious**, they have a disease that can be spread to others 患有傳染病；有傳染力： *I'm still infectious.* 我還處在傳染期。➲ compare CONTAGIOUS ▸ **in·fec·tious·ly** *adv.*： *to laugh infectiously* 笑得有感染力 **in·fec·tious·ness** *noun* [U]

in·fect·ive /ɪnˈfektɪv/ *adj.* (*medical* 醫) able to cause infection 會傳染的；傳染性的

infer AW /ɪnˈfɜː(r)/ *verb* (**-rr-**) **1** to reach an opinion or decide that sth is true on the basis of information that is available 推斷；推論；推理 SYN **deduce**： **~ sth (from sth)** *Much of the meaning must be inferred from the context.* 大部份含意必須從上下文中推斷。◇ **~ that …** *It is reasonable to infer that the government knew about these deals.* 有理由推想政府知悉這些交易。 **2** **~ (that) … | ~ sth** (*non-standard*) to suggest indirectly that sth is true 間接地提出；暗示；意指： *Are you inferring (that) I'm not capable of doing the job?* 你的言外之意是不是我不能勝任這份工作？

Which Word? 詞語辨析

infer / imply

- **Infer** and **imply** have opposite meanings. The two words can describe the same event, but from different points of view. If a speaker or writer **implies** something, they suggest it without saying it directly. * infer 和 imply 意義相反，兩詞可能描述同一事情，但角度不同。imply 意為暗示、暗指、意味着： *The article implied that the pilot was responsible for the accident.* 文章暗指飛行員應對事故負責。 If you **infer** something from what a speaker or writer says, you come to the conclusion that this is what he or she means. * infer 意為從…中推斷、推論、推定： *I inferred from the article that the pilot was responsible for the accident.* 我從這篇文章推斷，飛行員應對事故負責。
- **Infer** is now often used with the same meaning as **imply**. However, many people consider that a sentence such as *Are you inferring that I'm a liar?* is incorrect, although it is fairly common in speech. 現在 infer 常用以表達與 imply 相同的含義，不過許多人認為 Are you inferring that I'm a liar?（你意思是說我撒謊嗎？）這樣的句子不正確，雖然此用法在口語中相當普遍。

in·fer·ence AW /ˈɪnfərəns/ *noun* **1** [C] something that you can find out indirectly from what you already know 推斷的結果；結論 SYN **deduction**： *to* ***draw/make inferences*** *from the data* 根據資料推論出結果 ◇ *The clear inference is that the universe is expanding.* 顯然結論是宇宙在擴大。➲ **COLLOCATIONS** at SCIENTIFIC **2** [U] the act or process of forming an opinion, based on what you already know 推斷；推理；推論： *If he is guilty then,* ***by inference****, so is his wife* (= it is logical to think so, from the same evidence). 如果他有罪，那麼由此可以推斷他的妻子也同樣有罪。

in·fer·ior /ɪnˈfɪəriə(r); *NAmE* -ˈfɪr-/ *adj., noun*
■ ***adj.* 1** not good or not as good as sb/sth else 較差的；次的；比不上…的：*of inferior quality* 劣質的 ◇ *inferior goods* 劣質商品 ◇ *to make sb* ***feel inferior*** 使某人自慚形穢 ◇ **~ to sb/sth** *Modern music is often considered inferior to that of the past.* 現代音樂常被認為不如過去的。**2** [usually before noun] (*formal*) of lower rank; lower 級別低的；較低的：*an inferior officer* 下級軍官 OPP **superior**
■ ***noun*** a person who is not as good as sb else; a person who is lower in rank or status 不如別人的人；級別（或地位）低的人

in·fer·ior·ity /ɪnˌfɪəriˈɒrəti; *NAmE* -ˌfɪriˈɔːr-; -ˈɑːr-/ *noun* [U] the state of not being as good as sb/sth else 低等；劣等；劣勢：*a sense of inferiority* 自卑感 ◇ *social inferiority* 社會地位低下 OPP **superiority**

inˌferiˈority complex *noun* a feeling that you are not as good, as important or as intelligent as other people 自卑情結；自卑感

in·fer·nal /ɪnˈfɜːnl; *NAmE* ɪnˈfɜːrnl/ *adj.* **1** [only before noun] (*old-fashioned*) extremely annoying 極討厭的；可惡的：*Stop that infernal noise!* 別那麼死命嚷嚷了！**2** (*literary*) connected with hell 地獄的；陰間的 ▸ **in·fer·nal·ly** /-nəli/ *adv.*

in·ferno /ɪnˈfɜːnəʊ; *NAmE* ɪnˈfɜːrnoʊ/ *noun* [usually sing.] (*pl.* **-os**) a very large dangerous fire that is out of control 無法控制的大火：*a* ***blazing/raging inferno*** 熊熊的 / 烈焰衝天的火海

in·fer·tile /ɪnˈfɜːtaɪl; *NAmE* ɪnˈfɜːrtl/ *adj.* **1** (of people, animals and plants 人或動植物) not able to have babies or produce young 不育的；不結果實的：*an infertile couple* 一對不能生育的夫婦 **2** (of land 土地) not able to produce good crops 貧瘠的 OPP **fertile** ▸ **in·fer·til·ity** /ˌɪnfɜːˈtɪləti; *NAmE* -fɜːrˈt-/ *noun* [U]：*an infertility clinic* 醫治不育症的診所 ◇ *infertility treatment for couples* 對不育症夫婦的治療

in·fest /ɪnˈfest/ *verb* [usually passive] **~ sth** (especially of insects or animals such as RATS 尤指昆蟲或老鼠之類的動物) to exist in large numbers in a particular place, often causing damage or disease 大量滋生；大批出沒於：*shark-infested waters* 鯊魚成群的水域 ◇ *The kitchen was infested with ants.* 廚房裏到處是螞蟻。▸ **in·festa·tion** /ˌɪnfeˈsteɪʃn/ *noun* [C, U]：*an infestation of lice* 長滿蝨子

in·fi·del /ˈɪnfɪdəl/ *noun* (*old use*) an offensive way of referring to sb who does not believe in what the speaker considers to be the true religion 異教徒

in·fi·del·ity /ˌɪnfɪˈdeləti/ *noun* [U, C] (*pl.* **-ies**) the act of not being faithful to your wife, husband or partner, by having sex with sb else（夫妻或伴侶間的）不忠行為；通姦 SYN **unfaithfulness**：*marital infidelity* 對婚姻的不忠誠 ◇ *She could not forgive his infidelities.* 她無法原諒他的不忠行為。OPP **fidelity**

in·field /ˈɪnfiːld/ *noun, adv.*
■ ***noun*** [sing.] the inner part of the field in BASEBALL, CRICKET and some other sports（棒球、板球等場地的）內場 ➲ compare OUTFIELD
■ ***adv.*** in or to the infield 在（或向）場中心：*Ronaldo came infield from the right to score.* 羅納爾多從右側切入中場射門。

in·fight·ing /ˈɪnfaɪtɪŋ/ *noun* [U] arguments and disagreements between people in the same group who are competing for power 團體內部的爭權奪利；內訌：*political infighting within the party* 黨內的政治鬥爭

in·fill /ˈɪnfɪl/ *noun* [U] **1** the filling in of a space with sth, especially the building of new houses in spaces between existing ones 填補空間；（尤指）在舊房間隙處建新房：*infill development* 市區空隙處新房的添建 **2** the material used to fill in a space or a hole 填充物；空隙填料：*gravel infill* 沙礫填料 ▸ **in·fill** *verb* [I, T] **~ (sth)**

in·fil·trate /ˈɪnfɪltreɪt/ *verb* **1** [T, I] to enter or make sb enter a place or an organization secretly, especially in order to get information that can be used against it（使）悄悄進入，潛入：**~ sth** *The headquarters had been infiltrated by enemy spies.* 總部混入了敵方特務。◇ **~ sb into sth** *Rebel forces were infiltrated into the country.* 反叛力量潛入了這個國家。◇ **~ into sth** *The CIA agents successfully infiltrated into the terrorist organizations.* 中央情報局的特工人員成功地滲入了恐怖分子組織。**2** [I, T] **~ (into) sth** (*technical* 術語) (especially of liquids or gases 尤指液體或氣體) to pass slowly into sth 滲入；滲透：*Only a small amount of the rainwater actually infiltrates into the soil.* 實際上只有少量雨水滲進了土壤。▸ **in·fil·tra·tion** /ˌɪnfɪlˈtreɪʃn/ *noun* [U]：*the infiltration of terrorists from across the border* 恐怖分子的越境滲透 ◇ *the infiltration of rain into the soil* 雨水滲透土壤

in·fil·tra·tor /ˈɪnfɪltreɪtə(r)/ *noun* a person who secretly becomes a member of a group or goes to a place, to get information or to influence the group 潛入者；滲入者

in·fin·ite AW /ˈɪnfɪnət/ *adj., noun*
■ ***adj.* 1** very great; impossible to measure 極大的；無法衡量的 SYN **boundless**：*an infinite variety of plants* 數不清的植物種類 ◇ *a teacher with infinite patience* 有無比耐心的教師 ◇ (*ironic*) *The company* ***in its infinite wisdom*** *decided to close the staff restaurant* (= they thought it was a good thing to do, but nobody else agreed). 公司以無比的智慧關掉了職工食堂。**2** without limits; without end 無限的；無窮盡的：*an infinite universe* 無垠的宇宙 OPP **finite**
■ ***noun*** [sing.] **1** **the infinite** something that has no end 無限的事物；無窮盡的事物 **2** **the Infinite** God 上帝

in·fin·ite·ly AW /ˈɪnfɪnətli/ *adv.* **1** (used especially in comparisons 尤用於比較) very much 非常：*Your English is infinitely better than my German.* 你的英語比我的德語好太多了。**2** extremely; with no limit 極其；無限地：*Human beings are infinitely adaptable.* 人類的適應力是無限的。

in·fini·tesi·mal /ˌɪnfɪnɪˈtesɪml/ *adj.* (*formal*) extremely small 極小的；微量的 SYN **tiny**：*infinitesimal traces of poison* 微量毒素 ◇ *an infinitesimal risk* 微乎其微的風險 ▸ **in·fini·tesi·mal·ly** /-məli/ *adv.*

in·fini·tive /ɪnˈfɪnətɪv/ *noun* (*grammar* 語法) the basic form of a verb such as *be* or *run*. In English, an infinitive is used by itself, for example *swim* in *She can swim* (this use is sometimes called the **bare infinitive**), or with *to* (the **to-infinitive**) as in *She likes to swim.*（動詞的）不定式，不定詞（英語中的動詞不定式可單獨使用，如 She can swim 中的 swim，或帶 to，如 She likes to swim）IDM see SPLIT *v.*

in·fin·ity /ɪnˈfɪnəti/ *noun* (*pl.* **-ies**) **1** [U] (also **in·fin·it·ies** [pl.]) the state of having no end or limit 無限；無窮：*the infinity/infinities of space* 太空的無垠 **2** [U] a point far away that can never be reached 無限遠的點；無窮遠：*The landscape seemed to stretch into infinity.* 風景似乎延伸到了無窮遠處。**3** (*symb.* ∞) [U, C] (*mathematics* 數) a number larger than any other 無窮大，無限大（的數）**4** [sing.] a large amount that is impossible to count 無法計算的量；無限大的量：*an infinity of stars* 數不清的星星

inˈfinity pool *noun* a swimming pool that is specially designed so that, when you are in it, the pool seems to stretch to the HORIZON (= where the sky seems to meet the land or sea) 無邊際游泳池（經特別設計使游泳者產生水天相連之感）

in·firm /ɪnˈfɜːm; *NAmE* ɪnˈfɜːrm/ *adj.* **1** ill/sick and weak, especially over a long period or as a result of being old 病弱的；年老體弱的 **2** **the infirm** *noun* [pl.] people who are weak and ill/sick for a long period 病弱的人；體弱的人：*care for the elderly and infirm* 對年老體弱者的照顧

in·firm·ary /ɪnˈfɜːməri; *NAmE* -ˈfɜːrm-/ *noun* (*pl.* **-ies**) **1** (often used in names) a hospital（常用於名稱）醫院 **2** a special room in a school, prison, etc. for people who are ill/sick（學校、監獄等的）醫務室

in·firm·ity /ɪnˈfɜːməti; *NAmE* -ˈfɜːrm-/ *noun* [U, C] (*pl.* **-ies**) weakness or illness over a long period（長期的）體弱，生病：*We all fear disability or infirmity.* 我們都害怕傷殘或體弱。◇ *the infirmities of old age* 老年體弱

I

infix /ˈɪnfɪks/ *noun* (*grammar* 語法) a letter or group of letters added to the middle of a word to change its meaning 中綴；中加成分

in fla·grante /ˌɪn fləˈɡrænti/ *adv.* (from *Latin*, *literary* or *humorous*) if sb is found or caught **in flagrante**, they are discovered doing sth that they should not be doing, especially having sex 當場（尤指被捉姦）；在作案現場

in·flame /ɪnˈfleɪm/ *verb* (*formal*) **1 ~ sb/sth** to cause very strong feelings, especially anger or excitement, in a person or in a group of people 激起…的強烈感情；（尤指）使憤怒，使激動：*His comments have inflamed teachers all over the country.* 他的評論激怒了全國教師。**2 ~ sth** to make a situation worse or more difficult to deal with 使（局勢）惡化；使更棘手：*The situation was further inflamed by the arrival of the security forces.* 保安部隊的到達使局勢更加難以控制。

in·flamed /ɪnˈfleɪmd/ *adj.* **1** (of a part of the body 身體部位) red, sore and hot because of infection or injury 發炎的；紅腫的 ➲ SYNONYMS at PAINFUL **2** (of people, feelings, etc. 人、感情等) very angry or excited 憤怒的；非常激動的

I

in·flam·mable /ɪnˈflæməbl/ *adj.* **1** (*especially BrE*) = FLAMMABLE：*inflammable material* 易燃物 **2** full of strong emotions or violence 易激動的；易激怒的

in·flam·ma·tion /ˌɪnfləˈmeɪʃn/ *noun* [U, C] a condition in which a part of the body becomes red, sore and swollen because of infection or injury 發炎；炎症

in·flam·ma·tory /ɪnˈflæmətri; *NAmE* -tɔːri/ *adj.* **1** (*disapproving*) intended to cause very strong feelings of anger 煽動性的；使人發怒的：*inflammatory remarks* 煽動的言語 **2** (*medical* 醫) causing or involving inflammation 發炎的；炎性的

in·flat·able /ɪnˈfleɪtəbl/ *adj.*, *noun*

■ ***adj.*** needing to be filled with air or gas before you use it 需充氣的：*an inflatable mattress* 充氣墊

■ ***noun*** **1** an inflatable boat 充氣小艇 **2** a large object made of plastic or rubber and filled with air or gas, used for children to play on, or as an advertisement for sth 充氣玩具；大型充氣宣傳品

inˌflatable ˈbouncer *noun* (*NAmE*) = BOUNCER (3)

in·flate /ɪnˈfleɪt/ *verb* **1** [T, I] **~ (sth)** to fill sth or become filled with gas or air 使充氣；膨脹：*Inflate your life jacket by pulling sharply on the cord.* 猛拽繩扣使你的救生衣充氣。◇ *The life jacket failed to inflate.* 救生衣未能充氣。**2** [T] **~ sth** to make sth appear to be more important or impressive than it really is 鼓吹；吹捧 **3** [T, I] **~ (sth)** to increase the price of sth; to increase in price（使）漲價：*The principal effect of the demand for new houses was to inflate prices.* 對新住宅需求的主要結果是促使價格上漲。◇ *Food prices are no longer inflating at the same rate as last year.* 食物價格的上漲率已不再像去年那樣高了。➲ compare DEFLATE (3), REFLATE

in·flated /ɪnˈfleɪtɪd/ *adj.* **1** (especially of prices 尤指價格) higher than is acceptable or reasonable 過高的；高得不合理的：*inflated prices/salaries* 過高的價格 / 薪金 **2** (of ideas, claims, etc. 思想、主張等) believing or claiming that sb/sth is more important or impressive than they really are 誇張的；言過其實的：*He has an inflated sense of his own importance.* 他自視過高。

in·fla·tion /ɪnˈfleɪʃn/ *noun* [U] **1** a general rise in the prices of services and goods in a particular country, resulting in a fall in the value of money; the rate at which this happens 通貨膨脹；通脹率：*the fight against **rising inflation*** 對抗不斷升高的通貨膨脹 ◇ *to **control/curb inflation*** 控制 / 抑制通貨膨脹 ◇ *to **reduce/bring down** inflation* 減少 / 降低通貨膨脹 ◇ *a high/low **rate of inflation*** 高 / 低通脹率 ◇ *an **inflation rate** of 3%* 通脹率 3% ◇ *Wage increases must be **in line with inflation**.* 工資的增長必須與通貨膨脹一致。◇ *Inflation is currently running at 3%.* 當前的通貨膨脹率為 3%。➲ COLLOCATIONS at ECONOMY **2** the act or process of filling sth with air or gas 充氣：*life jackets with an automatic inflation device* 有自動充氣裝置的救生衣 OPP **deflation**

in·fla·tion·ary /ɪnˈfleɪʃənri; *NAmE* -neri/ *adj.* [usually before noun] causing or connected with a general rise in the prices of services and goods 通貨膨脹的；引起通脹的：*the inflationary effects of price rises* 物價上漲引起的通貨膨脹 ◇ *Our economy is in an **inflationary spiral** of wage and price increases* (= a continuing situation in which an increase in one causes an increase in the other). 我們的經濟處於工資和物價交互上漲的循環中。

in·flect /ɪnˈflekt/ *verb* [I] (*grammar* 語法) if a word **inflects**, its ending or spelling changes according to its GRAMMATICAL function in a sentence; if a language **inflects**, it has words that do this 屈折變化；詞尾變化 ▸ **in·flect·ed** *adj.* [usually before noun]：*an **inflected language/form/verb*** 有屈折變化的語言；屈折變化形式 / 動詞

in·flec·tion (also **in·flex·ion** especially in *BrE*) /ɪnˈflekʃn/ *noun* [C, U] **1** a change in the form of a word, especially the ending, according to its GRAMMATICAL function in a sentence（尤指詞尾的）屈折變化 **2** a change in how high or low your voice is as you are speaking 語調的抑揚變化

in·flex·ible AW /ɪnˈfleksəbl/ *adj.* **1** (*disapproving*) that cannot be changed or made more suitable for a particular situation 缺乏彈性的；僵化的 SYN **rigid**：*an inflexible attitude/routine/system* 死硬的態度；僵化的常規 / 體制 **2** (*disapproving*) (of people or organizations 人或機構) unwilling to change their opinions, decisions, etc., or the way they do things 固守己見的；死板的；頑固的：*He's completely inflexible on the subject.* 他在這個問題上寸步不讓。**3** (of a material 材料) difficult or impossible to bend 不能彎曲的；硬的 SYN **stiff** OPP **flexible** ▸ **in·flex·ibil·ity** AW /ɪnˌfleksəˈbɪləti/ *noun* [U] **in·flex·ibly** /-əbli/ *adv.*

in·flict /ɪnˈflɪkt/ *verb* to make sb/sth suffer sth unpleasant 使遭受打擊；使吃苦頭：**~ sth on/upon sb/sth** *They inflicted a humiliating defeat on the home team.* 他們使主隊吃了一場很沒面子的敗仗。◇ *Heavy casualties were inflicted on the enemy.* 敵人遭受了慘重傷亡。◇ (*humorous*) *Do you have to inflict that music on us?* 你非得逼我們聽那種音樂嗎？◇ **~ sth** *They surveyed the damage inflicted by the storm.* 他們調查了暴風雨造成的損失。▸ **in·flic·tion** /ɪnˈflɪkʃn/ *noun* [U]：*the infliction of pain* 痛苦的施加

PHR V **inˈflict yourself/sb on sb** (often *humorous*) to force sb to spend time with you/sb, when they do not want to 不請自來；打擾：*Sorry to inflict myself on you again like this!* 對不起，又這麼打擾你了！◇ *She inflicted her nephew on them for the weekend.* 她把姪兒打發到他們那兒去度週末，真是添亂。

ˌin-ˈflight *adj.* [only before noun] provided or happening during a journey on a plane 飛行中供應（或發生）的：*an in-flight meal/movie* 飛行中提供的餐食 / 電影 ◇ *in-flight refuelling* 空中加油

in·flow /ˈɪnfləʊ; *NAmE* -floʊ/ *noun* **1** [C, U] the movement of a lot of money, people or things into a place from somewhere else（資金、人或事物的）流入，湧入 SYN **influx** **2** [sing., U] the movement of a liquid or of air into a place from somewhere else（液體、空氣的）流入，滲入：*an inflow pipe* 注入管道 OPP **outflow**

in·flu·ence 🔑 /ˈɪnfluəns/ *noun*, *verb*

■ ***noun*** **1** 🔑 [U, C] **~ (on/upon sb/sth)** the effect that sb/sth has on the way a person thinks or behaves or on the way that sth works or develops 影響；作用：*to **have/exert a strong influence** on sb* 對某人產生強大的影響 ◇ *the influence of the climate on agricultural production* 氣候對農業生產的影響 ◇ *What exactly is the influence of television on children?* 電視對兒童究竟有什麼影響？**2** 🔑 [U] the power that sb/sth has to make sb/sth behave in a particular way 支配力；控制力；影響力：**~ (over sb/sth)** *Her parents no longer have any real influence over her.* 她的父母對她不再有任何真正的約束力了。◇ **~ (with sb)** *She could probably **exert her influence** with the manager and get you a job.* 她很有可能對經理施展她的影響力，給你弄份工作。◇ *He committed the crime **under the influence of** drugs.* 他是在吸毒後犯罪的。**3** 🔑 [C] a person or thing that affects the way a person behaves and thinks（對…）有影響的人（或事物）：

cultural influences 文化影響 ◇ **~ (on sb/sth)** *Those friends are* ***a bad influence*** *on her.* 那些朋友對她有負面的影響。◇ *His first music teacher was a major influence in his life.* 他的第一位音樂老師是他一生中對他影響非常大的人。

IDM **under the 'influence** having had too much alcohol to drink 喝酒過多；醉酒：*She was charged with driving under the influence.* 她被控酒後駕駛。

■ *verb* **1** 🔑 to have an effect on the way that sb behaves or thinks, especially by giving them an example to follow 影響；對…起作用：**~ sb/sth** *His writings have influenced the lives of millions.* 他的作品影響了千百萬人的一生。◇ *to be* ***strongly influenced*** *by sth* 受到某事物的強烈影響 ◇ *Don't let me influence you either way.* 何去何從都別受我的影響。◇ **~ how, whether, etc. …** *The wording of questions can influence how people answer.* 問題的措辭會影響人們的回答。◇ **~ sb to do sth** *She was influenced to take up voluntary work by her teacher.* 受她老師的影響，她當起義工來了。 **2** 🔑 **~ sth | ~ how, where, etc. …** to have an effect on a particular situation and the way that it develops 支配；左右：*A number of social factors influence life expectancy.* 諸多社會因素左右着人的預期壽命。

'influence peddling *noun* [U] the illegal activity of a politician doing sth for sb in return for payment （從政者的）以權謀利，索賄 SYN **corruption**

in·flu·en·tial /ˌɪnfluˈenʃl/ *adj.* having a lot of influence on sb/sth 有很大影響的；有支配力的：*a highly influential book* 十分有影響力的書 ◇ **~ in sth** *She is one of the most influential figures in local politics.* 她是本地政壇舉足輕重的人物。◇ **~ in doing sth** *The committee was influential in formulating government policy on employment.* 委員會左右着政府就業政策的制訂。

in·flu·enza /ˌɪnfluˈenzə/ *noun* [U] (*formal*) = FLU

in·flux /ˈɪnflʌks/ *noun* [usually sing.] **~ (of sb/sth) (into …)** the fact of a lot of people, money or things arriving somewhere （人、資金或事物的）湧入，流入：*a* ***massive/sudden influx*** *of visitors* 遊客的大量 / 突然湧入 ◇ *the influx of wealth into the region* 財富大量湧入這個地區

info /ˈɪnfəʊ; *NAmE* ˈɪnfoʊ/ *noun* **1** [U] (*informal*) information 信息；消息；資訊：*Have you had any more info about the job yet?* 關於這份工作你有進一步的消息嗎？ **2 info-** (in nouns 構成名詞) connected with information 信息的；消息的；資訊的：*an infosheet* 一頁信息資料 ◇ *We send all potential clients an infopack.* 我們給所有潛在的客戶都發了信息包。

info·bahn /ˈɪnfəʊbɑːn; *NAmE* ˈɪnfoʊ-/ *noun* (*informal*) = INFORMATION SUPERHIGHWAY

info·mer·cial /ˌɪnfəʊˈmɜːʃl; *NAmE* ˌɪnfoʊˈmɜːrʃl/ *noun* (*especially NAmE*) a long advertisement on television that tries to give a lot of information about a subject, so that it does not appear to be an advertisement（電視上的）商業信息片，資訊廣告節目

in·form 🔑 /ɪnˈfɔːm; *NAmE* ɪnˈfɔːrm/ *verb* **1** 🔑 to tell sb about sth, especially in an official way 知會；通知；通告：**~ sb (of/about sth)** *Please inform us of any changes of address.* 地址若有變動請通知我們。◇ **~ sb that …** *I have been* ***reliably informed*** *(= somebody I trust has told me) that the couple will marry next year.* 我得到可靠消息說他們倆明年結婚。◇ **~ sb + speech** *'He's already left,' she informed us.* "他已經走了。" 她告訴我們說。◇ **~ sb when, where, etc. …** *I have not been informed when the ceremony will take place.* 沒人通知我典禮何時舉行。 **2 ~ yourself (of/about sth)** to find out information about sth 瞭解；熟悉：*We need time to inform ourselves thoroughly of the problem.* 我們需要時間對這個問題有個透徹的瞭解。 **3 ~ sth** (*formal*) to have an influence on sth 對…有影響：*Religion informs every aspect of their lives.* 宗教影響着他們生活的各個方面。

PHR V **in'form on sb** to give information to the police or sb in authority about the illegal activities of sb 告發；檢舉：*He informed on his own brother.* 他告發了他的親弟弟。

in·for·mal 🔑 /ɪnˈfɔːml; *NAmE* ɪnˈfɔːrml/ *adj.* **1** 🔑 relaxed and friendly; not following strict rules of how to behave or do sth 不拘禮節的；友好隨便的；非正規的：*an informal atmosphere* 友好輕鬆的氣氛 ◇ *an informal arrangement/meeting/visit* 非正式的安排 / 會議 / 訪問 ◇ *Discussions are held on an informal basis within the department.* 討論限於在本部門內非正式地進行。 **2** 🔑 (of clothes 衣服) suitable for wearing at home or when relaxing rather than for a special or an official occasion 日常的；隨便的 SYN **casual** OPP **formal** **3** 🔑 (of language 語言) suitable for normal conversation and writing to friends rather than for serious speech and letters 非正式的；口語體的：*an informal expression* 非正式用語 ➲ compare FORMAL, SLANG ▶ **in·for·mal·ity** /ˌɪnfɔːˈmæləti; *NAmE* -fɔːrˈm-/ *noun* [U] **in·for·mal·ly** /ɪnˈfɔːməli; *NAmE* -ˈfɔːrm-/ *adv.*：*They told me informally (= not officially) that I had got the job.* 他們非正式地告訴我說，我得到了那份工作。◇ *to dress informally* 穿着便服

in,formal 'settlement *noun* (*SAfrE*) a place where people decide to live and build temporary shelters, often followed by more permanent houses. Sometimes informal settlements are supplied with water, electricity, etc. and people can become owners of individual pieces of land. 非正式居所區；臨時棚屋區

in·form·ant /ɪnˈfɔːmənt; *NAmE* -ˈfɔːrm-/ *noun* **1** a person who gives secret information about sb/sth to the police or a newspaper（向警方或報紙）提供消息的人，告密者，線民 SYN **informer** **2** (*technical* 術語) a person who gives sb information about sth, for example to help them with their research（為研究等）提供資料的人；合作者：*His informants were middle-class professional women.* 他的合作者是中產階級職業婦女。

in·form·at·ics /ˌɪnfəˈmætɪks; *NAmE* ˌɪnfər-/ *noun* [U] = INFORMATION SCIENCE

in·for·ma·tion 🔑 /ˌɪnfəˈmeɪʃn; *NAmE* ˌɪnfərˈm-/ (also *informal* **info**) *noun* [U]

1 🔑 **~ (on/about sb/sth)** facts or details about sb/sth 信息；消息；情報；資料；資訊：*a* ***piece of information*** 一則消息 ◇ *a source of information* 消息來源 ◇ *to* ***collect/gather/obtain/receive information*** 收集 / 搜集 / 獲取 / 接收信息 ◇ *to* ***provide/give/pass on information*** 提供 / 給予 / 傳遞信息 ◇ *For* ***further information*** *on the diet, write to us at this address.* 欲知規定飲食的詳情，請按這個地址給我們寫信。◇ ***Our information is*** *that the police will shortly make an arrest.* 我們得到的情報是，警察不久就要逮捕人了。◇ *This leaflet is produced* ***for the information of*** *(= to inform) our customers.* 這張傳單是為向我們的顧客提供信息而印製的。◇ *an information desk* 問詢處 ◇ *He refused to comment before he had seen all the* ***relevant information.*** 在看到全部相關資料之前他拒絕評論。 **2** (*NAmE, informal*) = DIRECTORY ENQUIRIES ▶ **in·for·ma·tion·al** /-ʃənl/ *adj.* [only before noun]：*the informational content of a book* 書的信息內容 ◇ *the informational role of the media* 新聞媒體的信息功能

IDM **for information 'only** written on documents that are sent to sb who needs to know the information in them but does not need to deal with them（文件）僅供參考 **for your infor'mation** **1** (*abbr.* **FYI**) = FOR INFORMATION ONLY **2** (*informal*) used to tell sb that they are wrong about sth（指出對方弄錯）需要提醒你的是，需要說明的是：*For your information, I don't even have a car.* 你要知道，我連汽車都沒有。➲ more at MINE *n.*

infor,mation 'science (also **in·form·at·ics**) *noun* [U] (*computing* 計) the study of processes for storing and obtaining information 信息科學；資訊科學

infor,mation super'highway (also **super·high·way**, *informal* **info·bahn**) *noun* (*computing* 計) a large electronic network such as the Internet, used for sending information such as sound, pictures and video quickly in DIGITAL form 信息高速公路；資訊高速公路

infor,mation tech'nology *noun* [U] (*abbr.* **IT**) the study or use of electronic equipment, especially computers, for storing and analysing information 信息技術，資訊科技（尤指對計算機等電子設備在存貯、分析信息諸方面的研究和應用）

infor'mation theory *noun* [U] (*mathematics* 數) a theory that is used to calculate the most efficient way

I

to send information over distances in the form of signals or symbols 信息論；資訊理論

in·for·ma·tive /ɪnˈfɔːmətɪv; *NAmE* -ˈfɔːrm-/ *adj.* giving useful information 提供有用信息的；給予知識的：*The talk was both informative and entertaining.* 這次談話既長見識又饒有趣味。**OPP** **uninformative**

in·formed /ɪnˈfɔːmd; *NAmE* ɪnˈfɔːrmd/ *adj.* having or showing a lot of knowledge about a particular subject or situation 有學問的；有見識的：*an informed critic* 有見地的批評家 ◇ *an* ***informed choice/decision/guess/opinion*** 有依據的選擇／決定／猜測／看法 ◇ *They are* ***not fully informed*** *about the changes.* 他們不完全瞭解這些改變。◇ ***Keep me informed*** *of any developments.* 隨時通知我進展情況。**OPP** **uninformed** ➲ see also ILL-INFORMED, WELL INFORMED

in·form·er /ɪnˈfɔːmə(r); *NAmE* -ˈfɔːrm-/ *noun* a person who gives information to the police or other authority （向警方或其他當局的）告密者；線人

info·tain·ment /ˌɪnfəʊˈteɪnmənt; *NAmE* ˌɪnfoʊ-/ *noun* [U] television programmes, etc. that present news and serious subjects in an entertaining way 資訊娛樂節目

I

infra- *prefix* (in adjectives 構成形容詞) below or beyond a particular limit 低於（或超出）某限度的：*infrared* 紅外線的 ➲ compare ULTRA-

in·frac·tion /ɪnˈfrækʃn/ *noun* [C, U] (*formal*) an act of breaking a rule or law 犯規；違法 **SYN** **infringement**：*minor infractions of EU regulations* 對歐盟規定的輕微觸犯

infra dig /ˌɪnfrə ˈdɪɡ/ *adj.* [not before noun] (*old-fashioned, informal*) considered to be below the standard of behaviour appropriate in a particular situation or to sb's social position 有失身分；有失體面

in·fra·red /ˌɪnfrəˈred/ *adj.* (*physics* 物) having or using ELECTROMAGNETIC waves which are longer than those of red light in the SPECTRUM, and which cannot be seen 紅外線的；使用紅外線的：*infrared radiation* 紅外輻射 ◇ *an infrared lamp* 紅外線燈 ➲ compare ULTRAVIOLET

in·fra·struc·ture **AW** /ˈɪnfrəstrʌktʃə(r)/ *noun* [C, U] the basic systems and services that are necessary for a country or an organization to run smoothly, for example buildings, transport and water and power supplies （國家或機構的）基礎設施，基礎建設 ▸ **in·fra·struc·tural** /ˌɪnfrəˈstrʌktʃərəl/ *adj.* [usually before noun]：*infrastructural development* 基礎建設的發展

in·fre·quent /ɪnˈfriːkwənt/ *adj.* not happening often 不常發生的；罕見的 **SYN** **rare**：*her infrequent visits home* 她少有的探望家人 ◇ *Muggings are relatively infrequent in this area.* 在這個地區行兇搶劫事件相對少見。**OPP** **frequent** ▸ **in·fre·quent·ly** *adv.*：*This happens not infrequently* (= often). 這種事常常發生。

in·fringe /ɪnˈfrɪndʒ/ *verb* (*formal*) **1** [T] **~ sth** (of an action, a plan, etc. 行動、計劃等) to break a law or rule 違背，觸犯（法規）：*The material can be copied without infringing copyright.* 這份材料可以複製，不會侵犯版權。**2** [T, I] to limit sb's legal rights 侵犯，侵害（合法權益）：**~ sth** *They said that compulsory identity cards would infringe civil liberties.* 他們說強制辦理身分證會侵犯公民的自由。◇ **~ on/upon sth** *She refused to answer questions that infringed on her private affairs.* 她拒絕回答侵犯她隱私的問題。▸ **in·fringe·ment** /-mənt/ *noun* [U, C]：*copyright infringement* 對版權的侵犯 ◇ *an infringement of liberty* 對自由的侵犯

in·furi·ate /ɪnˈfjʊərieɪt; *NAmE* -ˈfjʊr-/ *verb* to make sb extremely angry 使極為生氣；使大怒；激怒 **SYN** **enrage**：**~ sb** *Her silence infuriated him even more.* 她的沉默使他更加憤怒了。◇ **it infuriates sb that … /to do sth** *It infuriates me that she was not found guilty.* 令我大怒的是她獲判無罪。

in·furi·at·ing /ɪnˈfjʊərieɪtɪŋ; *NAmE* -ˈfjʊr-/ *adj.* making you extremely angry 使人極為生氣（或憤怒）的：*an infuriating child/delay* 令人極為生氣的孩子；使人憤怒的延誤 ◇ *It is infuriating to talk to someone who just looks out of the window.* 和眼睛只看着窗外的人講話很讓人窩火。▸ **in·furi·at·ing·ly** *adv.*：*to smile infuriatingly* 笑得使人惱火 ◇ *Infuriatingly, the shop had just closed.* 真讓人生氣，商店剛剛關門。

in·fuse /ɪnˈfjuːz/ *verb* **1** [T] **~ A into B | ~ B with A** (*formal*) to make sb/sth have a particular quality 使具有，注入（某特性）：*Her novels are infused with sadness.* 她的小說充滿哀傷。**2** [T] **~ sth** (*formal*) to have an effect on all parts of sth 全面影響：*Politics infuses all aspects of our lives.* 政治影響着我們生活的各個方面。**3** [T, I] **~ (sth)** if you **infuse** HERBS, etc. or they **infuse**, you put them in hot water until the flavour has passed into the water 泡製（草藥等）；泡；沏 **4** [T] **~ sth (into sth)** (*medical* 醫) to slowly put a drug or other substance into a person's VEIN 輸注（藥物等）

in·fu·sion /ɪnˈfjuːʒn/ *noun* **1** [C, U] **~ of sth (into sth)** (*formal*) the act of adding sth to sth else in order to make it stronger or more successful 注入；灌輸：*a cash infusion into the business* 對企業的現金注入 ◇ *an infusion of new talent into science education* 理科教育中新人才的注入 ◇ *The company needs an infusion of new blood* (= new employees with new ideas). 公司需要吸收新人。**2** [C] a drink or medicine made by leaving HERBS, etc. in hot water 沏成的飲料；泡製的草藥 **3** [C, U] (*medical* 醫) an act of slowly putting a drug or other substance into a person's VEIN; the drug that is used in this way （藥物等的）輸注；注入用藥物

-ing *suffix* used to make the present participle of regular verbs （用以構成規則動詞的現在分詞）：*hating* 憎恨 ◇ *walking* 步行 ◇ *loving* 愛

in·geni·ous /ɪnˈdʒiːniəs/ *adj.* **1** (of an object, a plan, an idea, etc. 物體、計劃、思想等) very suitable for a particular purpose and resulting from clever new ideas 精巧的；新穎獨特的；巧妙的：*an ingenious device* 精巧的裝置 ◇ *ingenious ways of saving energy* 節約能源的巧妙方法 **2** (of a person 人) having a lot of clever new ideas and good at inventing things 心靈手巧的；機敏的；善於創造發明的：*an ingenious cook* 心靈手巧的廚師 ◇ *She's very ingenious when it comes to finding excuses.* 她很善於找藉口。▸ **in·geni·ous·ly** *adv.*：*ingeniously designed* 設計巧妙

in·génue /ˈænʒemjuː; *NAmE* ˈændʒənuː/ *noun* (from *French*) an innocent young woman, especially in a film/movie or play （尤指電影或戲劇中的）天真少女

in·genu·ity /ˌɪndʒəˈnjuːəti; *NAmE* -ˈnuː-/ *noun* [U] the ability to invent things or solve problems in clever new ways 獨創力；聰明才智；心靈手巧 **SYN** **inventiveness**

in·genu·ous /ɪnˈdʒenjuəs/ *adj.* (*formal*, sometimes *disapproving*) honest, innocent and willing to trust people 單純的；天真的 **SYN** **naive**：*You're too ingenuous.* 你太老實了。◇ *an ingenuous smile* 純真的微笑 ◇ *It is ingenuous to suppose that money did not play a part in his decision.* 如果以為他的決定沒有金錢的因素，那就太天真了。➲ compare DISINGENUOUS ▸ **in·genu·ous·ly** *adv.*

Inger·land /ˈɪŋɡəlænd/ *noun* (*BrE, informal, non-standard, humorous*) a way of writing and saying England used by football fans as a name for the England national football (SOCCER) team 英格蘭（足球迷對 England 的書面或口頭表達方式，用以稱呼英格蘭國家足球隊）

in·gest /ɪnˈdʒest/ *verb* **~ sth** (*technical* 術語) to take food, drugs, etc. into your body, usually by swallowing 攝入；食入；嚥下 ▸ **in·gest·ion** *noun* [U]

ingle·nook /ˈɪŋɡlnʊk/ *noun* a space at either side of a large FIREPLACE where you can sit 壁爐邊（壁爐兩側供人坐的地方）

in·glori·ous /ɪnˈɡlɔːriəs/ *adj.* [usually before noun] (*literary*) causing feelings of shame 令人羞愧的；可恥的；不光彩的 **SYN** **shameful**：*an inglorious chapter in the nation's history* 這個民族歷史上可恥的一頁 ➲ compare GLORIOUS (1) ▸ **in·glori·ous·ly** *adv.*

ˈin-goal area *noun* [sing.] (in RUGBY 橄欖球) the area between the GOAL LINE and the line at the end of the field, inside which a player must put the ball in order to score a TRY 球門後得分區

ingot /ˈɪŋɡət/ *noun* a solid piece of metal, especially gold or silver, usually shaped like a brick（尤指金、銀的）鑄塊，錠

in·grained /ɪnˈɡreɪnd/ *adj.* **1 ~ (in sb/sth)** (of a habit, an attitude, etc. 習慣、態度等) that has existed for a long time and is therefore difficult to change 根深蒂固的；日久難改的 **SYN deep-rooted**：*ingrained prejudices* 很深的成見 **2** (of dirt 灰塵) under the surface of sth and therefore difficult to get rid of 深嵌並難以清除的

in·grati·ate /ɪnˈɡreɪʃieɪt/ *verb* [no passive] **~ yourself (with sb)** (*disapproving*) to do things in order to make sb like you, especially sb who will be useful to you 討好；巴結；迎合：*The first part of his plan was to ingratiate himself with the members of the committee.* 他的計劃的第一步是拉攏委員會的成員。

in·grati·at·ing /ɪnˈɡreɪʃieɪtɪŋ/ *adj.* (*disapproving*) trying too hard to please sb 竭力討好的；巴結的：*an ingratiating smile* 阿諛奉承的微笑 ▶ **in·grati·at·ing·ly** *adv.*

in·grati·tude /ɪnˈɡrætɪtjuːd; *NAmE* -tuːd/ *noun* [U] the state of not feeling or showing that you are grateful for sth 忘恩負義 **OPP gratitude**

in·gre·di·ent 0⊷ /ɪnˈɡriːdiənt/ *noun* **~ (of/in/for sth) 1** 0⊷ one of the things from which sth is made, especially one of the foods that are used together to make a particular dish 成分；（尤指烹飪）材料：*Coconut is a basic ingredient for many curries.* 椰子是多種咖喱菜的基本成分。◇ *Our skin cream contains only natural ingredients.* 我們的護膚霜只含天然成分。**2** 0⊷ one of the things or qualities that are necessary to make sth successful（成功的）因素，要素：*the essential ingredients for success* 成功的基本要素 ◇ *It has* ***all the ingredients*** *of a good mystery story.* 它具備一個好的玄幻故事的所有要素。

in·gress /ˈɪnɡres/ *noun* [U] (*formal*) the act of entering a place; the right to enter a place 進入；進入權；入境權 ➲ compare EGRESS

ˈ**in-group** *noun* (usually *disapproving*) a small group of people in an organization or a society whose members share the same interests, language, etc. and try to keep other people out 小集團；小圈子 **SYN clique**

in·grow·ing /ˈɪnɡrəʊɪŋ; *NAmE* -ɡroʊ-/ (*BrE*) (also **ingrown** *NAmE, BrE*) *adj.* [only before noun] (of the nail of a toe 腳指甲) growing into the skin 長進肉裏的；向內生長的

in·habit /ɪnˈhæbɪt/ *verb* **~ sth** (*formal*) to live in a particular place 居住在；棲居於：*some of the rare species that inhabit the area* 生活在這個地區的一些罕見物種

> **WORD FAMILY**
> **inhabit** *verb*
> **habitable** *adj.* (≠ uninhabitable)
> **inhabited** *adj.* (≠ uninhabited)
> **inhabitant** *noun*

in·hab·it·ant /ɪnˈhæbɪtənt/ *noun* a person or an animal that lives in a particular place（某地的）居民，棲息動物：*the oldest inhabitant of the village* 這個村最早的居民 ◇ *a town of 11 000 inhabitants* 有 11 000 名居民的城鎮

in·hab·ited /ɪnˈhæbɪtɪd/ *adj.* with people or animals living there 有人居住的；有動物棲居的：*The island is no longer inhabited.* 這個島已經沒有人居住了。◇ *The building is now inhabited by birds.* 這所建築物現在有鳥兒棲息。**OPP uninhabited**

in·hal·ant /ɪnˈheɪlənt/ *noun* a drug or medicine that you breathe in 吸入藥；吸入劑

in·hale /ɪnˈheɪl/ *verb* [I, T] (rather *formal*) to take air, smoke, gas, etc. into your lungs as you breathe 吸入；吸氣 **SYN breathe in**：*She closed her eyes and inhaled deeply.* 她合上雙眼，深深吸了一口氣。◇ *He inhaled deeply on another cigarette.* 他又點了一根煙深深地吸了一口。◇ **~ sth** *Local residents needed hospital treatment after inhaling fumes from the fire.* 當地居民吸入了大火的濃煙，需要入院治療。**OPP exhale** ▶ **in·hal·ation** /ˌɪnhəˈleɪʃn/ *noun* [U, C]：*Hundreds of children were treated for smoke inhalation.* 數以百計的兒童因吸入濃煙而接受了治療。

in·haler /ɪnˈheɪlə(r)/ (also *informal* **puff·er**) *noun* a small device containing medicine that you breathe in through your mouth, used by people who have problems with breathing 吸入器（吸藥用）

in·har·mo·ni·ous /ˌɪnhɑːˈməʊniəs; *NAmE* -hɑːrˈmoʊ-/ *adj.* (*formal*) not combining well together or with sth else 不和諧的；不協調的

in·here /ɪnˈhɪə(r); *NAmE* ɪnˈhɪr/ *verb*
PHR V **inˈhere in sth** (*formal*) to be a natural part of sth 是…的內在部份；自然存在於：*the meaning which inheres in words* 詞語中的含義

in·her·ent **AW** /ɪnˈhɪərənt; -ˈher-; *NAmE* -ˈhɪr-/ *adj.* **~ (in sb/sth)** that is a basic or permanent part of sb/sth and that cannot be removed 固有的；內在的 **SYN intrinsic**：*the difficulties inherent in a study of this type* 這類研究本身的困難 ◇ *Violence is inherent in our society.* 在我們的社會中暴力是難免的。◇ *an inherent weakness in the design of the machine* 機器設計中的內在缺陷 ▶ **in·her·ent·ly** **AW** /ɪnˈhɪərəntli; -ˈher-; *NAmE* -ˈhɪr-/ *adv.*：*an inherently unworkable system* 根本行不通的體制

in·herit /ɪnˈherɪt/ *verb* **1** [T, I] **~ (sth) (from sb)** to receive money, property, etc. from sb when they die 繼承（金錢、財產等）：*She inherited a fortune from her father.* 她從她父親那裏繼承了一大筆財富。➲ compare DISINHERIT **2** [T] **~ sth (from sb)** to have qualities, physical features, etc. that are similar to those of your parents, grandparents, etc. 經遺傳獲得（品質、身體特徵等）：*He has inherited his mother's patience.* 這種耐心是母親遺傳給他的。◇ *an inherited disease* 遺傳病 **3** [T] **~ sth (from sb)** if you **inherit** a particular situation from sb, you are now responsible for dealing with it, especially because you have replaced that person in their job 接替（責任等）；繼任：*policies inherited from the previous administration* 因襲上屆政府的政策

in·herit·able /ɪnˈherɪtəbl/ *adj.* (*biology* 生) (of a feature or disease 特徵或疾病) capable of being passed from a parent to a child in the GENES 可遺傳的；有遺傳性的：*inheritable characteristics* 可遺傳的特性

in·her·it·ance /ɪnˈherɪtəns/ *noun* **1** [C, U] the money, property, etc. that you receive from sb when they die; the fact of receiving sth when sb dies 繼承物（如金錢、財產等）；遺產；繼承：*She spent all her inheritance in a year.* 她在一年之內用完了所有繼承的遺產。◇ *The title passes by inheritance to the eldest son.* 這一頭銜按世襲傳給長子。➲ COLLOCATIONS at FINANCE **2** [U, C, usually sing.] something from the past or from your family that affects the way you behave, look, etc. 遺傳特徵；遺產：*our cultural inheritance* 我們的文化遺產 ◇ *Physical characteristics are determined by genetic inheritance.* 身體的特徵取決於基因遺傳。

inˈheritance tax (*NAmE* also **eˈstate tax**) *noun* [U] tax that you must pay on the money or property that you receive from sb when they die 遺產稅

in·heri·tor /ɪnˈherɪtə(r)/ *noun* **1** [usually pl.] **~ of sth** a person who is affected by the work, ideas, etc. of people who lived before them 後繼者；繼承人 **SYN heir**：*We are the inheritors of a great cultural tradition.* 我們是一個偉大文化傳統的繼承者。**2** a person who receives money, property, etc. from sb when they die 遺產繼承人 **SYN heir**

in·hibit **AW** /ɪnˈhɪbɪt/ *verb* **1 ~ sth** (*formal*) to prevent sth from happening or make it happen more slowly or less frequently than normal 阻止；阻礙；抑制：*A lack of oxygen may inhibit brain development in the unborn child.* 缺氧可能阻礙胎兒的大腦發育。**2 ~ sb (from sth/from doing sth)** to make sb nervous or embarrassed so that they are unable to do sth 使拘束；使尷尬：*The managing director's presence inhibited them from airing their problems.* 總經理的在場使他們不便暢談他們的問題。

in·hibit·ed /ɪnˈhɪbɪtɪd/ *adj.* unable to relax or express your feelings in a natural way 拘束的；拘謹的：*Boys are often more inhibited than girls about discussing their problems.* 男孩子往往不如女孩子敢於談論自己的問題。

I

in·hib·ition AW /ˌɪnhɪˈbɪʃn; ˌɪnɪˈb-/ *noun* **1** [C, U] a shy or nervous feeling that stops you from expressing your real thoughts or feelings 拘謹；拘束感：*The children were shy at first, but soon lost their inhibitions.* 孩子們起初很羞澀，但很快就放開了。◇ *She had no inhibitions about making her opinions known.* 她敢於公開地談論自己的想法。 **2** [U] (*formal*) the act of restricting or preventing a process or an action 阻止；抑制；禁止：*the inhibition of growth* 對生長的抑制

in·hibi·tor /ɪnˈhɪbɪtə(r)/ *noun* **1** (*chemistry* 化) a substance which delays or prevents a chemical reaction 抑制劑；阻聚劑 **2** (*biology* 生) a GENE which prevents another gene from being effective 抑制基因

in·hos·pit·able /ˌɪnhɒˈspɪtəbl; *NAmE* ˌɪnhɑːˈs-/ *adj.* **1** (of a place 地方) difficult to stay or live in, especially because there is no shelter from the weather 不適於居住的；（尤指）無遮蔽處的，荒涼的 SYN **unwelcoming**：*inhospitable terrain* 荒涼地帶 ◇ *an inhospitable climate* 不宜人的氣候 **2** (of people 人) not giving a friendly or polite welcome to guests 不殷勤待客的；不好客的 OPP **hospitable**

in-ˈhouse *adj.* [only before noun] existing or happening within a company or an organization （公司或機構）內部存在的，內部進行的：*an in-house magazine* 機構內部發行的雜誌 ◇ *in-house language training* 公司內的語言訓練

in·human /ɪnˈhjuːmən/ *adj.* **1** lacking the qualities of kindness and pity; very cruel 無同情心的；冷酷無情的：*inhuman and degrading treatment* 不人道的羞辱性對待 **2** not human; not seeming to be produced by a human and therefore frightening 非人的；（似非人所為而）恐怖的：*There was a strange inhuman sound.* 有一種不像人發出的奇怪聲音。➲ compare HUMAN, NON-HUMAN, SUBHUMAN

in·humane /ˌɪnhjuːˈmeɪn/ *adj.* not caring about the suffering of other people; very cruel （對他人的疾苦）無動於衷的；殘忍的；不人道的 SYN **callous**：*inhumane treatment of animals/prisoners* 對動物的殘忍行為；對囚犯的非人對待 OPP **humane** ▸ **in·hu·mane·ly** *adv.*

in·human·ity /ˌɪnhjuːˈmænəti/ *noun* [U] cruel behaviour or treatment; the fact of not having the usual human qualities of kindness and pity 殘酷的行為（或待遇）；無人性；不人道：*man's inhumanity to man* 人類相殘 ◇ *the inhumanity of the system* 這個體制的不人道 OPP **humanity**

in·huma·tion /ˌɪnhjuːˈmeɪʃn/ *noun* [U] (*technical* 術語) the act of burying dead people, used especially in relation to ancient times （尤指古代）埋葬，土葬

in·imi·cal /ɪˈnɪmɪkl/ *adj.* (*formal*) **1** ~ **to sth** harmful to sth; not helping sth 對…有害的；不利於…的：*These policies are inimical to the interests of society.* 這些政策有損於社會的利益。 **2** unfriendly 不友好的；敵意的：*an inimical stare* 敵意的注視

in·im·it·able /ɪˈnɪmɪtəbl/ *adj.* too good or individual for anyone else to copy with the same effect 無與倫比的；無法仿效的：*John related in his own* ***inimitable way*** *the story of his trip to Tibet.* 約翰以他自己特有的方式講述了他的西藏之行。

ini·qui·tous /ɪˈnɪkwɪtəs/ *adj.* (*formal*) very unfair or wrong 很不公正的；十分錯誤的；很不正當的 SYN **wicked**：*an iniquitous system/practice* 很不公正的制度/做法

ini·quity /ɪˈnɪkwəti/ *noun* [U, C] (*pl.* **-ies**) (*formal*) the fact of being very unfair or wrong; sth that is very unfair or wrong 很不公正，十分錯誤，很不正當（的事）：*the iniquity of racial prejudice* 種族偏見的罪惡 ◇ *the iniquities of the criminal justice system* 刑事審判體制的不公正之處

ini·tial ⚷ AW /ɪˈnɪʃl/ *adj., noun, verb*

■ **adj.** ⚷ [only before noun] happening at the beginning; first 最初的；開始的；第一的：*an initial payment of £60 and ten instalments of £25* * 60 英鎊的首期付款加十次 25 英鎊的分期付款 ◇ *in the* ***initial stages*** (= at the beginning) *of the campaign* 運動的最初階段 ◇ *My* ***initial reaction*** *was to decline the offer.* 我最初的反應是婉言謝絕這個提議。

■ **noun** **1** ⚷ [C] the first letter of a person's first name （名字的）首字母：*'What initial is it, Mrs Owen?' 'It's J, J for Jane.'* "首字母是什麼，歐文太太？" "是 J，Jane 的 J。" **2** ⚷ **initials** [pl.] the first letters of all of a person's names （全名的）首字母：*John Fitzgerald Kennedy was often known by his initials JFK.* 人們常以姓名的首字母 JFK 稱約翰•菲茨傑拉德•肯尼迪。◇ *Just write your initials.* 寫下你的姓名首字母即可。

■ **verb** (**-ll-**, *especially US* **-l-**) **~ sth** to mark or sign sth with your initials 用姓名的首字母作標記（或簽名）於：*Please initial each page and sign in the space provided.* 請在每一頁寫上姓名首字母並在規定的空白處簽字。

ini·tial·ize (*BrE* also **-ise**) /ɪˈnɪʃəlaɪz/ *verb* **~ sth** (*computing* 計) to make a computer program or system ready for use or FORMAT a disk 初始化（計算機程序或系統）；啟動；格式化（磁盤）▸ **ini·tial·iza·tion**, **-isa·tion** /ɪˌnɪʃəlaɪˈzeɪʃn; *NAmE* -ləˈz-/ *noun* [U]

ini·tial·ly ⚷ AW /ɪˈnɪʃəli/ *adv.* at the beginning 開始；最初；起初：*Initially, the system worked well.* 開始時系統運轉良好。◇ *The death toll was initially reported at around 250, but was later revised to 300.* 最初報道死亡人數約 250，後修訂為 300。

ini·ti·ate AW *verb, noun*

■ **verb** /ɪˈnɪʃieɪt/ **1 ~ sth** (*formal*) to make sth begin 開始；發起；創始 SYN **set in motion**：*to initiate legal proceedings against sb* 對某人提起訴訟 ◇ *The government has initiated a programme of economic reform.* 政府已開始實施經濟改革方案。 **2 ~ sb** (**into sth**) to explain sth to sb and/or make them experience it for the first time 使瞭解；傳授；教…開始嘗試：*Many of them had been initiated into drug use at an early age.* 他們中有很多人在早年就被教會了吸毒。 **3 ~ sb** (**into sth**) to make sb a member of a particular group, especially as part of a secret ceremony （尤指在秘密儀式上）使加入，接納，吸收：*Hundreds are initiated into the sect each year.* 每年有好幾百人被接納到這個教派中。

■ **noun** /ɪˈnɪʃiət/ a person who has been allowed to join a particular group, organization, or religion and is learning its rules and secrets 新加入某組織（或機構、宗教）的人；新入會的人

ini·ti·ation AW /ɪˌnɪʃiˈeɪʃn/ *noun* [U] **1** the act of sb becoming a member of a group, often with a special ceremony; the act of introducing sb to an activity or skill （常指通過特別儀式的）入會；介紹某人初試某活動（或技藝）：*an initiation ceremony* 入會儀式 ◇ **~ into sth** *her initiation into the world of marketing* 她的初次涉足營銷界 **2** (*formal*) the act of starting sth 開始；創始；發起：*the initiation of criminal proceedings* 提起刑事訴訟

ini·tia·tive ⚷ AW /ɪˈnɪʃətɪv/ *noun*

1 ⚷ [C] a new plan for dealing with a particular problem or for achieving a particular purpose 倡議；新方案：*a United Nations peace initiative* 聯合國的和平倡議 ◇ *a government initiative to combat unemployment* 政府應付失業問題的新方案 **2** ⚷ [U] the ability to decide and act on your own without waiting for sb to tell you what to do 主動性；積極性；自發性：*You won't get much help. You'll have to* ***use your initiative.*** 你不會得到多少幫助的。你得自己想辦法。◇ *She did it* ***on her own initiative*** (= without anyone telling her to do it). 她是主動這麼做的。 **3** ⚷ **the initiative** [sing.] the power or opportunity to act and gain an advantage before other people do 掌握有利條件的能力（或機會）；主動權：*to* ***seize/lose the initiative*** 掌握/喪失先機 ◇ *It was up to the US to* ***take the initiative*** *in repairing relations.* 在修復關係方面應由美國採取主動。 **4** [C] (*NAmE, law* 律) (in some states of the US) a process by which ordinary people can suggest a new law by signing a PETITION （美國某些州的）公民立法提案程序

ini·ti·ator AW /ɪˈnɪʃieɪtə(r)/ *noun* (*formal*) the person who starts sth 發起人；創始人

in·ject /ɪnˈdʒekt/ *verb* **1** to put a drug or other substance into a person's or an animal's body using a SYRINGE （給…）注射（藥物等）：**~ sth** (**into yourself/sb/sth**) *Adrenaline was injected into the muscle.* 往肌肉裏注射了

腎上腺素。◇ **~ yourself/sb/sth (with sth)** *She has been injecting herself with insulin since the age of 16.* 她從 16 歲起就開始自行注射胰島素。 **2** to put a liquid into sth using a SYRINGE or similar instrument（給⋯）注射（液體）: **~ A (with B)** *The fruit is injected with chemicals to reduce decay.* 水果注入了化學藥品以防腐壞。◇ **~ B (into A)** *Chemicals are injected into the fruit to reduce decay.* 水果注入了化學藥品以防腐壞。 **3 ~ sth (into sth)** to add a particular quality to sth（給⋯）添加，增加（某品質）: *His comments injected a note of humour into the proceedings.* 他的發言給整個活動增添了一絲幽默的氣氛。 **4 ~ sth (into sth)** to give money to an organization, a project, etc. so that it can function（給⋯）投入（資金）: *They are refusing to inject any more capital into the industry.* 他們拒絕對這一產業投入更多的資金。

in·jec·tion /ɪnˈdʒekʃn/ *noun* **1** [C, U] an act of injecting sb with a drug or other substance 注射: *to* ***give sb an injection*** 給某人打針 ◇ *He was treated with penicillin injections.* 他接受了青黴素注射。◇ *An anaesthetic was administered* ***by injection.*** 麻醉劑已注射入體內。◇ *daily injections of insulin* 每天的胰島素注射 ➲ COLLOCATIONS at ILL **2** [C] a large sum of money that is spent to help improve a situation, business, etc. 大量資金的投入: *The theatre faces closure unless it gets an urgent cash injection.* 劇院面臨着倒閉，除非有大筆救急現金投入。 **3** [U, C] an act of forcing liquid into sth（液體的）注入，噴入: *a fuel injection system* 燃油注入裝置

in,jection ˈmoulding (*BrE*) (*NAmE* **in,jection ˈmolding**) *noun* [U] (*technical* 術語) a way of shaping plastic or rubber by heating it and pouring it into a MOULD 熱壓鑄；（塑膠）射出成型 ▸ **in,jection-ˈmoulded** (*NAmE* **in,jection-ˈmolded**) *adj.*

ˈin-joke *noun* a joke that is only understood by a particular group of people 圈子裏的笑話；行內笑話

in·ju·di·cious /ˌɪndʒuˈdɪʃəs/ *adj.* (*formal*) not sensible or wise; not appropriate in a particular situation 不明智的；不當的 **SYN unwise**: *an injudicious remark* 不當的言語 **OPP judicious** ▸ **in·ju·di·cious·ly** *adv.*

Injun /ˈɪndʒən/ *noun* (*US, taboo, slang*) an offensive word for a Native American（含侮慢意）美洲土著

in·junc·tion /ɪnˈdʒʌŋkʃn/ *noun* **1** an official order given by a court which demands that sth must or must not be done（法院的）強制令，禁制令: *to* ***seek/obtain an injunction*** 請求／得到強制令 ◇ **~ against sb** *The court* ***granted an injunction against*** *the defendants.* 法庭對被告發出了禁制令。 ➲ compare RESTRAINING ORDER **2** (*formal*) a warning or an order from sb in authority 警告；指令；命令

in·jure 🔑 **AW** /ˈɪndʒə(r)/ *verb* **1** 🔑 **~ sb/sth/yourself** to harm yourself or sb else physically, especially in an accident（尤指在事故中）傷害，使受傷: *He injured his knee playing hockey.* 他打曲棍球時膝蓋受傷。◇ *Three people were killed and five injured in the crash.* 撞車事故中有三人死亡，五人受傷。 ➲ COLLOCATIONS at INJURY **2** 🔑 **~ sth** to damage sb's reputation, pride, etc. 損害，傷害（名譽、自尊等）: *This could seriously injure the company's reputation.* 這會嚴重損害公司的聲譽。

in·jured 🔑 **AW** /ˈɪndʒəd; *NAmE* -dʒərd/ *adj.* **1** 🔑 physically hurt; having an injury 受傷的；有傷的: *an injured leg* 受傷的腿 ◇ *Luckily, she isn't injured.* 幸運的是，她沒受傷。◇ *Carter is playing in place of the injured O'Reilly.* 卡特替代受傷的奧賴利上場比賽。 **OPP uninjured** **2 the injured** *noun* [pl.] the people injured in an accident, a battle, etc. 受傷的人；傷員；傷兵: *Ambulances took the injured to a nearby hospital.* 救護車把傷者送到了附近的一所醫院。 **3** 🔑 (of a person or their feelings 人或感情) upset or offended because sth unfair has been done 委屈的；受到傷害的: *an* ***injured look/tone*** 委屈的樣子／語調 ◇ ***injured pride*** 受傷的自尊心

the ˌinjured ˈparty *noun* [sing.] (*law* 律) the person who has been treated unfairly, or the person who claims in court to have been treated unfairly 受害人；受害一方

Synonyms 同義詞辨析

injure

wound • hurt • bruise • sprain • pull • strain

These words all mean to harm yourself or sb else physically, especially in an accident. 以上各詞主要指在事故中傷害、使受傷。

injure to harm yourself or sb else physically, especially in an accident 尤指在事故中傷害、使受傷: *He injured his knee playing hockey.* 他打曲棍球時膝蓋受了傷。◇ *Three people were injured in the crash.* 撞車事故中有三人受傷。

wound [often passive] (*rather formal*) to injure part of the body, especially by making a hole in the skin using a weapon 指使身體受傷，尤指用武器傷害: *50 people were seriously wounded in the attack.* 這次攻擊中有 50 人受重傷。 **NOTE** **Wound** is often used to talk about people being hurt in war or in other attacks which affect a lot of people. * wound 常指在戰爭中或在波及許多人的其他攻擊中受傷。

hurt to cause physical pain to sb/yourself; to injure sb/yourself 指（使）疼痛、受傷: *Did you hurt yourself?* 你傷着自己了嗎？

INJURE OR HURT? 用 injure 還是 hurt？

You can **hurt** or **injure** a part of the body in an accident. **Hurt** emphasizes the physical pain caused; **injure** emphasizes that the part of the body has been damaged in some way. 在事故中身體受傷可用 hurt 或 injure，hurt 強調引起的身體疼痛，injure 強調身體部位受到某種程度的損傷。

bruise to make a blue, brown or purple mark (= a bruise) appear on the skin after sb has fallen or been hit; to develop a bruise 指摔傷、撞傷、（使）出現瘀傷

sprain to injure part of your body, especially your ankle, wrist or knee, by suddenly bending it in an awkward way, causing pain and swelling 指扭傷（踝、腕、膝）

pull to damage a muscle, etc., by using too much force 指拉傷、扭傷（肌肉等）

strain to injure yourself or part of your body by making it work too hard 指損傷、拉傷、扭傷: *Don't strain your eyes by reading in poor light.* 別在光線不足的地方看書把眼睛給傷了。

PATTERNS

- to injure/hurt/strain **yourself**
- to injure/hurt/sprain/pull/strain a **muscle**
- to injure/hurt/sprain your **ankle/foot/knee/wrist/hand**
- to injure/hurt/strain your **back/shoulder/eyes**
- to injure/hurt your **spine/neck**
- to be **badly/severely/slightly** injured/wounded/hurt/bruised/sprained

in·juri·ous /ɪnˈdʒʊəriəs; *NAmE* -ˈdʒʊr-/ *adj.* **~ (to sb/sth)** (*formal*) causing or likely to cause harm or damage 造成傷害的；有害的 **SYN damaging**

in·jury 🔑 **AW** /ˈɪndʒəri/ *noun* (*pl.* **-ies**) **1** 🔑 [C, U] harm done to a person's or an animal's body, for example in an accident（對軀體的）傷害，損傷: ***serious injury/injuries*** 重傷 ◇ ***minor injuries*** 輕傷 ◇ *to* ***sustain injuries/an injury*** 受傷 ◇ *to* ***escape injury*** 險受傷害 ◇ **~ (to sb/sth)** *injury to the head* 頭部受傷 ◇ *a head injury* 頭部受傷 ◇ *Two players are out of the team* ***because of injury.*** 兩名隊員因傷退出了比賽。◇ *There were* ***no injuries*** *in the crash* (= no people injured). 撞車事故中無人受傷。◇ (*BrE, informal*) *Don't do that. You'll* ***do yourself an injury*** (= hurt yourself). 別那樣做。你會把自己弄傷的。 **2** [U] (*law* 律) damage to a person's feelings（對感情的）傷害，挫傷: *Damages may be*

awarded for emotional injury. 可能會判處精神傷害賠償。
IDM see ADD

Collocations 詞語搭配

Injuries 身體損傷

Being injured 受傷

- **have** a fall/an injury 跌了一跤；受傷
- **receive/suffer/sustain** a serious injury/a hairline fracture/(*especially BrE*) whiplash/a gunshot wound 受重傷／輕微骨裂／鞭傷／槍傷
- **hurt/injure** your ankle/back/leg 傷到腳踝／背／大腿
- **damage** the brain/an ankle ligament/your liver/the optic nerve/the skin 損傷大腦／腳踝韌帶／肝臟／視神經／皮膚
- **pull/strain/tear** a hamstring/ligament/muscle/tendon 拉傷膕繩肌腱／韌帶／肌肉／肌腱
- **sprain/twist** your ankle/wrist 扭傷腳踝／手腕
- **break** a bone/your collarbone/your leg/three ribs 骨折；鎖骨／大腿／三根肋骨骨折
- **fracture/crack** your skull 頭蓋骨破裂
- **break/chip/knock out/lose** a tooth 碰斷了一顆牙；使牙齒崩缺了一塊；磕掉／掉了一顆牙
- **burst/perforate** your eardrum 使耳膜破裂；鼓膜穿孔
- **dislocate** your finger/hip/jaw/shoulder 使手指／臀部／下巴／肩膀脫臼
- **bruise/cut/graze** your arm/knee/shoulder 擦傷／割破／擦破手臂／膝蓋／肩膀
- **burn/scald** yourself/your tongue 燒傷／燙傷自己／舌頭
- **bang/bump/hit/**(*informal*) **bash** your elbow/head/knee (on/against sth)（在某物上）撞到肘部／頭／膝蓋

Treating injuries 治療傷病

- **treat sb for** burns/a head injury/a stab wound 給某人治療燒傷／頭部傷／刺傷
- **examine/clean/dress/bandage/treat** a bullet wound 檢查／清洗／包紮／用繃帶包紮／治療槍傷
- **repair** a damaged/torn ligament/tendon/cartilage 修復損傷的／拉傷的韌帶／肌腱／軟骨
- **amputate/cut off** an arm/a finger/a foot/a leg/a limb 截去一隻胳膊／一根手指／一隻腳／一條腿；截肢
- **put on/**(*formal*) **apply/take off** (*especially NAmE*) a Band-Aid™/(*BrE*) a plaster/a bandage 貼上／使用／撕掉創可貼；纏上／使用／解掉繃帶
- **need/require/put in/**(*especially BrE*) **have** (**out**)/(*NAmE*) **get** (**out**) stitches 需要縫針；縫針；拆線
- **put on/rub on/**(*formal*) **apply** cream/ointment/lotion 塗抹護膚霜／藥膏／護膚液
- **have/receive/undergo** (*BrE*) physiotherapy/(*NAmE*) physical therapy 接受物理療法

ˈinjury time *noun* [U] (*BrE*) time added at the end of a game of football (SOCCER), HOCKEY, etc. because the game has been interrupted by injured players needing treatment 傷停補時（足球、曲棍球等比賽為彌補因隊員受傷處理而延遲結束的時間）

in·just·ice /ɪnˈdʒʌstɪs/ *noun* [U, C] the fact of a situation being unfair and of people not being treated equally; an unfair act or an example of unfair treatment 不公正，不公平（的對待或行為）：*fighting against poverty and injustice* 與貧困和不公平鬥爭 ◇ *a burning* **sense of** *injustice* 強烈感覺到遭受不公正待遇 ◇ *social injustice* 社會的不公平 ◇ *She was enraged at the injustice of the remark.* 她被那句話的不公激怒了。◇ *The report exposes the injustices of the system.* 報告揭露了這個制度的種種不公正。 OPP **justice**
IDM **do yourself/sb an inˈjustice** to judge yourself/sb unfairly 待…不公正；冤枉：*We may have been doing him an injustice. This work is good.* 我們可能冤枉他了。這工作幹得不錯。

ink 🔑 /ɪŋk/ *noun, verb*
■ **noun** 🔑 [U, C] coloured liquid for writing, drawing and printing 墨水；墨汁；油墨：*written* **in ink** 用墨水寫的 ◇ *a pen and ink drawing* 鋼筆畫 ◇ *different coloured inks* 各種顏色的墨水 ➲ see also INKY
■ **verb 1 ~ sth** to cover sth with ink so that it can be used for printing 給…上油墨（以供印刷） **2 ~ sth** (*NAmE, informal*) to sign a document, especially a contract 簽署，簽訂（合同等）：*The group has just inked a $10 million deal.* 這個集團剛剛簽訂了一份 1 000 萬元的協議。
PHR V **ˌink sth↔ˈin** to write or draw in ink over sth that has already been written or drawn in pencil 給（鉛筆畫或底線）上墨；用墨水加描：(*figurative*) *The date for the presentation should have been inked in* (= made definite) *by now.* 演出的日期現在應該敲定了。

ˈink-blot test *noun* (*psychology* 心) = RORSCHACH TEST

ink-jet printer /ˈɪŋkdʒet prɪntə(r)/ *noun* a printer that uses very small JETS to blow ink onto paper in order to form letters, numbers, etc. 噴墨打印機；噴墨印表機

ink·ling /ˈɪŋklɪŋ/ *noun* [usually sing.] a slight knowledge of sth that is happening or about to happen（對正在或即將發生的事的）略知 SYN **suspicion**：**~ (of sth)** *He had no inkling of what was going on.* 他對正在發生的事情一無所知。◇ **~ (that …)** *The first inkling I had that something was wrong was when I found the front door wide open.* 我發現前門大開着時就隱約感覺到出了事。

ˈink-pad *noun* a thick piece of soft material full of ink, used with a rubber stamp 印台；打印台 ➲ VISUAL VOCAB page V69

ink·well /ˈɪŋkwel/ *noun* a pot for holding ink that fits into a hole in a desk (used in the past)（舊時嵌入寫字枱的）墨水池

inky /ˈɪŋki/ *adj.* **1** black like ink 墨黑的；漆黑的：*the inky blackness of the cellar* 地窖裏的一片漆黑 **2** made dirty with ink 沾有墨水的；被墨水弄髒的：*inky fingers* 沾滿墨水的手指

in·laid /ˌɪnˈleɪd/ *adj.* (of furniture, floors, etc. 傢具、地板等) decorated with designs of wood, metal, etc. that are set into the surface 鑲嵌着（木質、金屬等）圖案的；嵌飾的：*an inlaid wooden box* 嵌花木盒子 ◇ **~ with sth** *a box inlaid with gold* 鑲金盒子

in·land *adv., adj.*
■ **adv.** /ˌɪnˈlænd/ in a direction towards the middle of a country; away from the coast 向（或在）內陸；向（或在）內地：*The town lies a few kilometres inland.* 這個城鎮位於內陸幾公里處。◇ *We travelled further inland the next day.* 我們第二天繼續向內陸行進。
■ **adj.** /ˈɪnlænd/ [usually before noun] located in or near the middle of a country, not near the edge or on the coast（在）內陸的；（在）內地的：*inland areas* 內陸地區 ◇ *inland lakes* 內陸湖 ➲ compare COASTAL

the ˌInland ˈRevenue *noun* [sing.] the government department in Britain that was responsible for collecting taxes until 2005 when it was replaced by HM REVENUE AND CUSTOMS（英國）國內稅收署，稅務局（2005 年被 HM Revenue and Customs（英國稅務海關總署）所取代）➲ compare THE INTERNAL REVENUE SERVICE

ˈin-law apartment (also **ˈmother-in-law apartment**, **ˈin-law suite**) (all *NAmE*) (*BrE* **ˈgranny flat**) *noun* (*informal*) a set of rooms for an old person, especially in a relative's house（尤指親人家中的）老人套間

ˈin-laws *noun* [pl.] (*informal*) your relatives by marriage, especially the parents of your husband or wife 姻親；（尤指）公婆，岳父母：*We're visiting my in-laws on Sunday.* 我們星期天要去拜訪我的姻親。

inlay *verb, noun*
■ **verb** /ˌɪnˈleɪ/ (**in·lay·ing**, **in·laid**, **in·laid** /ˌɪnˈleɪd/) [often

passive] ~ A (with B) | ~ B (in/into A) to decorate the surface of sth by putting pieces of wood or metal into it in such a way that the surface remains smooth 鑲嵌；把（圖案等）嵌入：*The lid of the box had been inlaid with silver.* 盒蓋上鑲嵌着銀飾。

■ ***noun*** /ˈɪnleɪ/ [C, U] a design or pattern on a surface made by setting wood or metal into it; the material that this design is made of 鑲嵌藝術；鑲嵌裝飾（或圖案）；鑲嵌材料：*The table was decorated with gold inlay.* 桌子裝飾着黃金鑲嵌的圖案。

inlet /ˈɪnlet/ *noun* **1** a narrow strip of water that stretches into the land from the sea or a lake, or between islands（海、湖伸向陸地或島嶼間的）小灣，水灣 **2** (*technical* 術語) an opening through which liquid, air or gas can enter a machine（液體、空氣或氣體進入機器的）入口，進口：*a fuel inlet* 燃料進口 OPP **outlet**

ˌin-line ˈskate (*BrE* also **Roll·er·blade™**) (*NAmE* also **Roller Blade™**) *noun* a type of boot with a line of small wheels attached to the bottom 直排滾軸旱冰鞋；直排輪滑鞋 ➲ VISUAL VOCAB page V40 ▸ **ˌin-line ˈskating** *noun* [U]

in loco par·en·tis /ɪn ˌləʊkəʊ pəˈrentɪs; *NAmE* ˌloʊkoʊ/ *adv.* (from *Latin, formal*) having the same responsibility for a child as a parent has 代人盡父母責任；代替家長責任

in·mate /ˈɪnmeɪt/ *noun* one of the people living in an institution such as a prison or a mental hospital（監獄或精神病院等處）同住者；同獄犯人；同病房者

in med·ias res /ɪn ˌmiːdiæs ˈreɪz/ *adv.* (*formal*, from *Latin*) straight into the main part of a story or account without giving any introduction 直接切入本題；單刀直入：*He began his story in medias res.* 他開門見山地講了起來。

in me·mor·iam /ˌɪn məˈmɔːriəm/ *prep.* (from *Latin*) used to mean 'in memory of', for example on the stone over a grave（用於墓碑等）為紀念

in·most /ˈɪnməʊst; *NAmE* ˈɪnmoʊst/ *adj.* [only before noun] = INNERMOST

inn /ɪn/ *noun* **1** (*old-fashioned, BrE*) a pub, usually in the country and often one where people can stay the night（通常指鄉村的，常可夜宿的）小酒店 **2** (*NAmE*) a small hotel, usually in the country（通常指鄉村的）小旅館，客棧 **3 Inn** used in the names of many pubs, hotels and restaurants（用於客棧、旅館和飯店的名稱中）：*Holiday Inn* 假日酒店

in·nards /ˈɪnədz; *NAmE* ˈɪnərdz/ *noun* [pl.] (*informal*) **1** the organs inside the body of a person or an animal, especially the stomach 內臟；（尤指）胃 SYN **entrails, guts 2** the parts inside a machine（機器的）內部結構

in·nate /ɪˈneɪt/ *adj.* (of a quality, feeling, etc. 品質、感情等) that you have when you are born 天生的；先天的；與生俱來的 SYN **inborn**：*the innate ability to learn* 天生的學習能力 ▸ **in·nate·ly** *adv.*：*He believes that humans are innately violent.* 他相信人性本惡。

inner 0ₙ /ˈɪnə(r)/ *adj.* [only before noun]

1 0ₙ inside; towards or close to the centre of a place 裏面的；向內的；內部的；接近中心的：*an inner courtyard* 內院 ◇ *inner London* 倫敦市中心區 ◇ *the inner ear* 內耳 OPP **outer 2** (of feelings, etc. 感情等) private and secret; not expressed or shown to other people 內心的；未表達出來的；隱藏的：*She doesn't reveal much of her inner self.* 她不大流露她的內心自我。

ˌinner ˈcircle *noun* the small group of people who have a lot of power in an organization, or who control it 核心集團

ˌinner ˈcity *noun* the part near the centre of a large city, which often has social problems 市中心區（常有社會問題）：*There are huge problems in our inner cities.* 我們各個市中心區存在着許多大的問題。◇ *an inner-city **area/school*** 市中心的地區 / 學校

ˌinner ˈear *noun* (*anatomy* 解) the parts of the ear which form the organs of balance and hearing, including the COCHLEA 內耳，內耳迷路（包括聽覺器官和平衡器官）

in·ner·most /ˈɪnəməʊst; *NAmE* ˈɪnərmoʊst/ *adj.* [only before noun] **1** (also *less frequent* **in·most**) most private, personal and secret 內心深處的：*I could not express my innermost feelings to anyone.* 我不能向任何人表達我內心深處的感情。 **2** nearest to the centre or inside of sth 最靠近中心的；最深處的：*the innermost shrine of the temple* 神殿最深處的聖壇 OPP **outermost**

ˈinner tube *noun* a rubber tube filled with air inside a tyre（輪胎的）內胎

in·ning /ˈɪnɪŋ/ *noun* (in BASEBALL 棒球) one of the nine periods of a game in which each team has a turn at BATTING 局；回合

in·nings /ˈɪnɪŋz/ *noun* (*pl.* **in·nings**) (in CRICKET 板球) a period of time in a game during which a team or a single player is BATTING 局；回合

IDM **sb had a good ˈinnings** (*BrE, informal*) used about sb who has died to say that they had a long life（用以指死者）…夠長壽了，終其天年

innit /ˈɪnɪt/ *exclamation* (*BrE, non-standard*) **1** a way of saying 'isn't it'（即 isn't it）是否，是不是：*Cold, innit?* 很冷，是不是？ **2** a way of saying any QUESTION TAG, such as 'don't you?' or 'haven't you?' 是嗎；是不是：*You got it, innit?* 你明白了，是嗎？

inn·keep·er /ˈɪnkiːpə(r)/ *noun* (*old-fashioned*) a person who owns or manages an INN 客棧老闆；（鄉村）酒鋪掌櫃

in·no·cence /ˈɪnəsns/ *noun* [U] **1** the fact of not being guilty of a crime, etc. 清白；無辜；無罪：*She **protested her innocence*** (= said repeatedly that she was innocent). 她一再申明自己是無辜的。◇ *This new evidence will prove their innocence.* 這一新的證據將證明他們的清白。◇ *I asked if she was married **in all innocence*** (= without knowing it was likely to offend or upset her). 我問她結婚了沒有，完全沒有惡意。 OPP **guilt 2** lack of knowledge and experience of the world, especially of evil or unpleasant things 天真；純真；單純：*Children lose their innocence as they grow older.* 兒童隨着年齡的增長而失去其天真。

in·no·cent 0ₙ /ˈɪnəsnt/ *adj.*, *noun*

■ ***adj.*** **1** 0ₙ not guilty of a crime, etc.; not having done sth wrong 無辜的；清白的；無罪的：*They have imprisoned an innocent man.* 他們監禁了一名無辜的男子。◇ ~ (**of sth**) *She was found innocent of any crime.* 她獲判無罪。◇ *He was the **innocent party*** (= person) *in the breakdown of the marriage.* 他們的婚姻破裂，他是無過錯的一方。 OPP **guilty 2** 0ₙ [only before noun] suffering harm or being killed because of a crime, war, etc. although not directly involved in it 無辜受害的；成為犧牲品的：*an innocent bystander* 無辜受害的旁觀者 ◇ *innocent victims of a bomb blast* 炸彈爆炸中的無辜受害者 **3** 0ₙ having little experience of the world, especially of sexual matters, or of evil or unpleasant things 天真無邪的；純真的 SYN **naive**：*an innocent young child* 天真無邪的小孩子 **4** not intended to cause harm or upset sb 無惡意的；無冒犯之意的 SYN **harmless**：*It was all innocent fun.* 那不過是些無惡意的玩笑。◇ *It was a perfectly innocent remark.* 那是一句毫無冒犯之意的話。 ▸ **in·no·cent·ly** *adv.*：*'Oh, Sue went too, did she?' I asked innocently* (= pretending I did not know that this was important). "噢，蘇也去了，是嗎？" 我裝作若無其事地問。

■ ***noun*** an innocent person, especially a young child 無辜者，單純的人（尤指天真無邪的孩子）

in·nocu·ous /ɪˈnɒkjuəs; *NAmE* ɪˈnɑːk-/ *adj.* (*formal*) **1** not intended to offend or upset anyone 無惡意的；無意冒犯的 SYN **harmless**：*It seemed a perfectly innocuous remark.* 那像是一句毫無惡意的話。 **2** not harmful or dangerous 無害的；無危險的 SYN **harmless**：*an innocuous substance* 無害物質

in·nov·ate AW /ˈɪnəveɪt/ *verb* [I, T] to introduce new things, ideas, or ways of doing sth 引入（新事物、思想或方法）；創新；改革：*We must constantly adapt and innovate to ensure success in a growing market.* 我們必須不時地適應並創新，以確保在不斷擴大的市場中取得成功。◇ ~ **sth** *to innovate new products* 創造新產品 ▸ **in·nov·ator** AW /ˈɪnəveɪtə(r)/ *noun*

in·nov·ation AW /ˌɪnəˈveɪʃn/ *noun* **1** [U] **~ (in sth)** the introduction of new things, ideas or ways of doing sth（新事物、思想或方法的）創造；創新；改革：*an age of technological innovation* 技術革新的時代 **2** [C] **~ (in sth)** a new idea, way of doing sth, etc. that has been introduced or discovered 新思想；新方法：*recent innovations in steel-making technology* 新近的煉鋼技術革新

in·nova·tive AW /ˈɪnəveɪtɪv; *BrE* also ˈɪnəvətɪv/ (also *less frequent* **in·nov·atory** /ˌɪnəˈveɪtəri; *NAmE* also ˈɪnəvətɔːri/) *adj.* (*approving*) introducing or using new ideas, ways of doing sth, etc. 引進新思想的；採用新方法的；革新的；創新的：*There will be a prize for the most innovative design.* 將設立一項最具創意設計獎。

in·nu·endo /ˌɪnjuˈendəʊ; *NAmE* -doʊ/ *noun* [C, U] (*pl.* **-oes** or **-os**) (*disapproving*) an indirect remark about sb/sth, usually suggesting sth bad or rude; the use of remarks like this 暗指；影射：*innuendoes about her private life* 對她私生活含沙射影的指責 ◇ *The song is full of sexual innuendo.* 那首歌充滿了性的暗示。

in·nu·mer·able /ɪˈnjuːmərəbl; *NAmE* ɪˈnuː-/ *adj.* too many to be counted; very many 多得數不清的；很多的 SYN **countless**：*Innumerable books have been written on the subject.* 已經有無數書籍寫過這個主題。

in·nu·mer·ate /ɪˈnjuːmərət; *NAmE* ɪˈnuː-/ *adj.* unable to count or do simple mathematics 不會數數的；不會計算的；不懂算術的 OPP **numerate**

in·ocu·late /ɪˈnɒkjuleɪt; *NAmE* ɪˈnɑːk-/ *verb* **~ sb (against sth)** to protect a person or an animal from catching a particular disease by INJECTING them with a mild form of the disease（給…）接種，打預防針 ➲ compare IMMUNIZE, VACCINATE ▸ **in·ocu·la·tion** /ɪˌnɒkjuˈleɪʃn; *NAmE* ɪˌnɑːk-/ *noun* [C, U]

in·offen·sive /ˌɪnəˈfensɪv/ *adj.* not likely to offend or upset anyone 不會冒犯人的；不討人嫌的：*a shy, inoffensive young man* 靦腆温和的青年男子 OPP **offensive**

in·op·er·able /ɪnˈɒpərəbl; *NAmE* ɪnˈɑːp-/ *adj.* **1** (of an illness, especially cancer 疾病，尤指癌) not able to be cured by a medical operation 手術無法治癒的：*an inoperable brain tumour* 不能手術治療的腦瘤 **2** (*formal*) that cannot be used or made to work; not practical 無法使用的；不能實行的；不實用的：*The policy was thought to be inoperable.* 這項政策被認為行不通。 OPP **operable**

in·op·era·tive /ɪnˈɒpərətɪv; *NAmE* ɪnˈɑːp-/ *adj.* (*formal*) **1** (of a rule, system, etc. 規則、體系等) not valid or able to be used 無效的；不能實行的 **2** (of a machine 機器) not working; not functioning correctly 不運轉的；運行不正常的 OPP **operative**

in·op·por·tune /ɪnˈɒpətjuːn; *NAmE* ɪnˌɑːpərˈtuːn/ *adj.* (*formal*) happening at a bad time 不合時宜的；不是時候的 SYN **inappropriate, inconvenient**：*They arrived at an inopportune moment.* 他們到得不是時候。 OPP **opportune**

in·or·din·ate /ɪnˈɔːdɪnət; *NAmE* -ˈɔːrd-/ *adj.* (*formal*) far more than is usual or expected 過度的；過分的；超乎預料的 SYN **excessive** ▸ **in·or·din·ate·ly** *adv.*：*inordinately high prices* 高得離譜的價格

in·or·gan·ic /ˌɪnɔːˈɡænɪk; *NAmE* ˌɪnɔːrˈɡ-/ *adj.* not consisting of or coming from any living substances 無生物的；無機的：*inorganic fertilizers* 無機肥料 OPP **organic**

ˌinorganic ˈchemistry *noun* [U] the branch of chemistry that deals with substances that do not contain CARBON 無機化學 ➲ compare ORGANIC CHEMISTRY

in·pa·tient /ˈɪnpeɪʃnt/ *noun* a person who stays in a hospital while receiving treatment 住院病人 ➲ compare OUTPATIENT

input AW /ˈɪnpʊt/ *noun, verb*

▪ *noun* **1** [C, U] time, knowledge, ideas, etc. that you put into work, a project, etc. in order to make it succeed; the act of putting sth in 投入資源（指時間、知識、思想等）；投入；輸入：**~ (into/to sth)** *Her specialist input to the discussions has been very useful.* 她在這些討論中提供的專家建議很有助益。◇ *I'd appreciate your input on this.* 我將感激你在這方面的投入。◇ **~ (of sth)** *There has been a big input of resources into the project from industry.* 工業界對這個項目投入了大量資源。 **2** [U] (*computing* 計) the act of putting information into a computer; the information that you put in 輸入；輸入的信息：*data input* 數據輸入 ◇ *This program accepts input from most word processors.* 這個程序可接受大多數文字處理系統輸入的信息。 **3** [C] (*technical* 術語) a place or means for electricity, data, etc. to enter a machine or system（電、數據等的）輸入端 ➲ compare OUTPUT (1), (2)

▪ *verb* (**in·put·ting, input, input** or **in·put·ting, in·put·ted, in·put·ted**) **~ sth** to put information into a computer 輸入（信息）：*to* **input** *text/data/figures* 把文本 / 數據 / 數字輸入計算機 ➲ compare OUTPUT

in·quest /ˈɪŋkwest/ *noun* **1** an official investigation to find out the cause of sb's death, especially when it has not happened naturally 死因審理；驗屍；勘驗：*An inquest was held to discover the cause of death.* 對死亡原因進行了調查。◇ **~ (on/into sth)** *a coroner's inquest into his death* 進行驗屍以探究他的死因 **2 ~ (on/into sth)** a discussion about sth that has failed（對失敗的事進行的）討論：*An inquest was held on the team's poor performance.* 對該隊在比賽中的差勁表現進行了檢討。

in·quire, in·quirer, in·quir·ing, in·quiry = ENQUIRE, ENQUIRER, ENQUIRING, ENQUIRY

in·qui·si·tion /ˌɪnkwɪˈzɪʃn/ *noun* **1 the Inquisition** [sing.] the organization set up by the Roman Catholic Church to punish people who opposed its beliefs, especially from the 15th to the 17th century（尤指 15 到 17 世紀天主教的）宗教裁判所，異端審問 **2** [C] (*formal* or *humorous*) a series of questions that sb asks you, especially when they ask them in an unpleasant way 一連串的提問；（尤指）盤問，責難 ➲ see also SPANISH INQUISITION

in·quisi·tive /ɪnˈkwɪzətɪv/ *adj.* **1** (*disapproving*) asking too many questions and trying to find out about what other people are doing, etc. 過分打聽他人私事的 SYN **curious**：*Don't be so inquisitive. It's none of your business!* 別這麼追根問底的。這與你無關！ **2** very interested in learning about many different things 好學的；好奇的；興趣廣泛的 SYN **enquiring**：*an inquisitive mind* 勤學好問的精神 ▸ **in·quisi·tive·ly** *adv.* **in·quisi·tive·ness** *noun* [U]

in·quisi·tor /ɪnˈkwɪzɪtə(r)/ *noun* **1** a person who asks a lot of difficult questions, especially in a way that makes you feel threatened 連續不斷地發問的人；（尤指）盤問者 **2** an officer of the Inquisition of the Roman Catholic Church（天主教異端審問的）裁判人 ▸ **in·quisi·tor·ial** /ɪnˌkwɪzəˈtɔːriəl/ *adj.*：*He questioned her in a cold inquisitorial voice.* 他像個審判官似的冷冷質問她。 **in·quisi·tor·ial·ly** *adv.*

in·quor·ate /ɪnˈkwɔːreɪt; -ət/ *adj.* (*BrE, technical* 術語) a meeting that is **inquorate** does not have enough people present for them to make official decisions by voting（會議）不構成法定人數的 OPP **quorate**

in·road /ˈɪnrəʊd; *NAmE* -roʊd/ *noun* **~ (into sth)** something that is achieved, especially by reducing the power or success of sth else（尤指通過消耗或削弱其他事物取得的）進展：*This deal is their first major inroad into the American market.* 這交易是他們進軍美國市場的首次重大收穫。

IDM **make inroads into/on sth** if one thing **makes inroads into** another, it has a noticeable effect on the second thing, especially by reducing it, or influencing it 消耗，削弱，影響（某事物）：*Tax rises have made some inroads into the country's national debt.* 增加稅收已使國債有所減少。

in·rush /ˈɪnrʌʃ/ *noun* [usually sing.] a sudden flow towards the inside（突然的）流入，湧入，進入：*an inrush of air/water* 空氣 / 水的湧入

in·salu·bri·ous /ˌɪnsəˈluːbriəs/ *adj.* (of a place 地方) dirty and with many things that need to be repaired, cleaned or replaced 骯髒破舊的 OPP **salubrious**

in·sane /ɪnˈseɪn/ *adj.* **1** seriously mentally ill and unable to live in normal society 精神失常的；精神錯亂的：*Doctors certified him as insane.* 醫生證明他精神失常。◇

*The prisoners were slowly **going insane**.* 囚犯正慢慢地變得精神錯亂起來。**OPP** **sane** ➲ SYNONYMS at MENTALLY **2 the insane** *noun* [pl.] people who are insane 精神失常的人；精神錯亂的人：*a hospital for the insane* 精神病院 **3** (*informal*) very stupid, crazy or dangerous 十分愚蠢的；瘋狂的；危險的：*I must have been insane to agree to the idea.* 我肯定是犯傻了，居然同意了這個想法。◇ *This job is **driving me insane*** (= making me feel very angry). 這份工作快要把我逼瘋了。➲ see also INSANITY ▶ **in·sane·ly** *adv.*：*He is insanely jealous.* 他嫉妒得發瘋。

in·sani·tary /ɪn'sænətri; *NAmE* -teri/ (also **un·sani·tary** especially in *NAmE*) *adj.* dirty and likely to spread disease 不衛生的；不潔的 **OPP** **sanitary**

in·san·ity /ɪn'sænəti/ *noun* [U] **1** the state of being INSANE 精神失常；精神錯亂；精神病 **SYN** **madness**：*He was found not guilty, by reason of insanity.* 他以精神失常為理由獲判無罪。**OPP** **sanity** **2** actions that are very stupid and possibly dangerous 十分愚蠢的行為；荒唐的行為 **SYN** **madness, lunacy**：*It would be sheer insanity to attempt the trip in such bad weather.* 天氣這麼糟糕還要去旅行，太荒唐了。

in·sati·able /ɪn'seɪʃəbl/ *adj.* always wanting more of sth; not able to be satisfied 不知足的；無法滿足的：*an **insatiable appetite/curiosity/thirst*** 永不滿足的食慾／好奇心／渴望 ◇ *There seems to be an **insatiable demand** for more powerful computers.* 人們對計算機性能的要求似乎永無止境。▶ **in·sati·ably** /-ʃəbli/ *adv.*

in·scribe /ɪn'skraɪb/ *verb* to write or cut words, your name, etc. onto sth 在…上寫（詞語、名字等）；題；刻：**~ A (on/in B)** *His name was inscribed on the trophy.* 他的名字刻在獎杯上。◇ **~ B (with A)** *The trophy was inscribed with his name.* 獎杯上刻着他的名字。◇ *She signed the book and inscribed the words 'with grateful thanks' on it.* 她在書上簽了名，並在上面寫道"謹致由衷感謝"。

in·scrip·tion /ɪn'skrɪpʃn/ *noun* words written in the front of a book or cut in stone or metal （書首頁的）題辭；（石頭或金屬上）刻寫的文字，銘刻，碑文

in·scrut·able /ɪn'skru:təbl/ *adj.* if a person or their expression is **inscrutable**, it is hard to know what they are thinking or feeling, because they do not show any emotion 難以捉摸的；難以理解的；神秘莫測的 ▶ **in·scrut·abil·ity** /ɪnˌskru:tə'bɪləti/ *noun* [U] **in·scrut·ably** /ɪn'skru:təbli/ *adv.*

in·seam /'ɪnsi:m/ (*NAmE*) (*BrE* ˌ**inside 'leg**) *noun* [sing.] a measurement of the length of the inside of sb's leg, used for making or choosing trousers of the correct size 下落襠（褲腿內側長度的尺寸，用於訂做或選購長褲）

in·sect 🔑 /'ɪnsekt/ *noun*
any small creature with six legs and a body divided into three parts. Insects usually also have wings. ANTS, BEES and flies are all insects. 昆蟲：*insect species* 昆蟲種類 ◇ ***insect repellent*** (= a chemical that keeps insects away) 驅蟲劑 ◇ *an **insect bite*** 昆蟲咬傷 ➲ COLLOCATIONS at LIFE ➲ VISUAL VOCAB page V13 ➲ see also STICK INSECT **HELP** **Insect** is often used to refer to other small creatures, for example spiders, although this is not correct scientific language. * insect 常用以指蜘蛛等其他小動物，但從科學術語來說並不準確。

in·secti·cide /ɪn'sektɪsaɪd/ *noun* [C, U] a chemical used for killing insects 殺蟲劑；殺蟲藥 ➲ see also HERBICIDE, PESTICIDE ▶ **in·secti·cidal** /ɪnˌsektɪ'saɪdl/ *adj.*

in·sect·ivore /ɪn'sektɪvɔ:(r)/ *noun* any animal that eats insects 食蟲動物 ➲ compare CARNIVORE, HERBIVORE, OMNIVORE ▶ **in·sect·iv·or·ous** /ˌɪnsek'tɪvərəs/ *adj.*

in·se·cure **AW** /ˌɪnsɪ'kjʊə(r); *NAmE* -'kjʊr/ *adj.* **1** not confident about yourself or your relationships with other people 缺乏信心的；無把握的：*He's very insecure about his appearance.* 他對自己的長相沒有信心。◇ *She felt nervous and insecure.* 她感到局促不安。**2** not safe or protected 不安全的；無保障的；不牢靠的：*Jobs nowadays are much more insecure than they were ten years ago.* 當今的工作比十年前要不穩固得多了。◇ *As an artist he was always financially insecure.* 作為一名藝術家，他在經濟上總是沒有保障。◇ *Insecure doors and windows* (= for example, without good locks) *make life easy for burglars.* 門窗不牢靠方便了竊賊。**OPP** **secure** ▶ **in·se·cure·ly** *adv.* **in·secur·ity** **AW** /ˌɪnsɪ'kjʊərəti; *NAmE* -'kjʊr-/ *noun* [U, C] (*pl.* **-ies**)：*feelings of insecurity* 不安全感 ◇ *job insecurity* 工作無保障 ◇ *We all have our fears and insecurities.* 我們大家都有各自的恐懼和不安全感。

in·sem·in·ate /ɪn'semɪneɪt/ *verb* **~ sb/sth** (*technical* 術語) to put SPERM into a woman or female animal in order to make her pregnant 使受精；授精：*The cows are **artificially inseminated**.* 這些母牛是人工授精的。▶ **in·sem·in·ation** /ɪnˌsemɪ'neɪʃn/ *noun* [U] ➲ see also ARTIFICIAL INSEMINATION

in·sens·ibil·ity /ɪnˌsensə'bɪləti/ *noun* [U] **1** (*formal*) the state of being unconscious 無知覺；不省人事 **2** the fact of not being able to react to a particular thing （對某事物的）麻木，無反應能力：*insensibility to pain* 對疼痛無感覺

in·sens·ible /ɪn'sensəbl/ *adj.* (*formal*) **1** [not before noun] **~ (to sth)** unable to feel sth or react to it （對某事物）無感覺，無反應能力，麻木：*insensible to pain/cold* 感覺不到疼痛／冷 **2** [not before noun] **~ (of sth)** not aware of a situation or of sth that might happen 未察覺；意識不到 **SYN** **unaware**：*They were not insensible of the risks.* 他們對這些危險並非沒有意識。**OPP** **sensible** **3** unconscious as the result of injury, illness, etc. 失去知覺；昏迷：*He drank himself insensible.* 他喝酒醉得不省人事。▶ **in·sens·ibly** /-əbli/ *adv.*

in·sensi·tive /ɪn'sensətɪv/ *adj.* **1** not realizing or caring how other people feel, and therefore likely to hurt or offend them （對他人的感受）未意識到的，漠不關心的 **SYN** **unsympathetic**：*an insensitive remark* 冷漠的言語 ◇ **~ to sth** *She's completely insensitive to my feelings.* 她全然不顧我的感情。**2 ~ (to sth)** not aware of changing situations, and therefore of the need to react to them （對變化）懵然不知的，麻木不仁的：*The government seems totally insensitive to the mood of the country.* 政府似乎對全國民眾的心情完全懵然不知。**3 ~ (to sth)** not able to feel or react to sth （對某事物）無感覺，無反應：*insensitive to pain/cold* 感覺不到疼痛／寒冷 ◇ *He seems completely insensitive to criticism.* 他似乎對批評麻木不仁。**OPP** **sensitive** ▶ **in·sensi·tive·ly** *adv.* **in·sensi·tiv·ity** /ɪnˌsensə'tɪvəti/ *noun* [U]

in·sep·ar·able /ɪn'seprəbl/ *adj.* **1 ~ (from sth)** not able to be separated （與某事物）不可分離的，分不開的：*Our economic fortunes are inseparable from those of Europe.* 我們的經濟命運和歐洲的息息相關。**2** if people are **inseparable**, they spend most of their time together and are very good friends 形影不離的 ▶ **in·sep·ar·ab·il·ity** /ɪnˌseprə'bɪləti/ *noun* [U] **in·sep·ar·ably** /ɪn'seprəbli/ *adv.*：*Our lives were inseparably linked.* 我們的生活息息相通。

in·sert 🔑 **AW** *verb, noun*

■ *verb* /ɪn'sɜ:t; *NAmE* ɪn'sɜ:rt/ **1** 🔑 **~ sth (in/into/between sth)** to put sth into sth else or between two things 插入；嵌入：*Insert coins into the slot and press for a ticket.* 把硬幣放進投幣口，按鈕取票。◇ *They inserted a tube in his mouth to help him breathe.* 他們在他嘴裏插了根導管幫助他呼吸。**2** 🔑 to add sth to a piece of writing （在文章中）添加，加插：**~ sth** *Position the cursor where you want to insert a word.* 把光標移到你想插入字詞的地方。◇ **~ sth into sth** *Later, he inserted another paragraph into his will.* 後來他在他的遺囑中又加了一段。

■ *noun* /'ɪnsɜ:t; *NAmE* 'ɪnsɜ:rt/ **~ (in sth)** **1** an extra section added to a book, newspaper or magazine, especially to advertise sth （書報的）插頁，廣告附加頁：*an 8-page insert on the new car models* 附加的 8 頁新型汽車廣告 **2** something that is put inside sth else, or added to sth else 插入物；添加物：*These inserts fit inside any style of shoe.* 這些鞋墊適合任何式樣的鞋。

in·ser·tion **AW** /ɪn'sɜ:ʃn; *NAmE* ɪn'sɜ:rʃn/ *noun* **1** [U, C] **~ (in/into sth)** the act of putting sth inside sth else; a thing that is put inside sth else 插入；嵌入；插入物：*An examination is carried out before the insertion of the tube.* 插入導管前先要進行檢查。**2** [C, U] a thing that

I

is added to a book, piece of writing, etc.; the act of adding sth（書、文章等中）添加的東西；添加；插入：*the insertion of an extra paragraph* 插入一個附加段落

ˌin-ˈservice *adj.* [only before noun] (of training, courses of study, etc. 訓練、課程等) done while sb is working in a job, in order to learn new skills 在職進行的；不脫產的：*in-service training* 在職培訓

inset /ˈɪnset/ *noun, verb*

■ **noun** **1** a small picture, map, etc. inside a larger one（套印在大圖片、地圖等中的）小圖，小地圖：*For the Shetland Islands, see inset.* 關於設得蘭群島，見小地圖。**2** something that is added on to sth else, or put inside sth else 嵌入物；附加物：*The windows have beautiful stained glass insets.* 窗戶上鑲着漂亮的彩色玻璃。

■ **verb** (**in·set·ting**, **inset**, **inset**) **1** [usually passive] to fix sth into the surface of sth else, especially as a decoration 嵌入，插入（作為裝飾等）：**~ A (with B)** *The tables were inset with ceramic tiles.* 桌子上鑲嵌着瓷磚。◇ **~ B (into A)** *Ceramic tiles were inset into the tables.* 桌子上鑲嵌着瓷磚。**2 ~ sth (into sth)** to put a small picture, map, etc. inside the borders of a bigger one（在大圖片、地圖等中）套印小圖

I

in·shore /ˈɪnʃɔː(r)/ *adj.* [usually before noun] in the sea but close to the SHORE 近岸的；近海的：*an inshore breeze* 海岸邊的微風 ◇ *an inshore lifeboat* (= that stays close to the land) 近海救生艇 ▸ **ˌin'shore** *adv.*：*The boat came inshore* (= towards the land). 船駛近海岸。➲ compare OFFSHORE (1), (2)

in·side 0- /ˌɪnˈsaɪd/ *prep., adv., noun, adj.*

■ **prep.** (also **in·side of** especially in *NAmE*) **1** 0- on or to the inner part of sth/sb; within sth/sb 在（或向）…內；在（或向）…裏：*Go inside the house.* 進屋裏吧。◇ *Inside the box was a gold watch.* 盒子裏裝着一隻金錶。◇ *For years we had little knowledge of what life was like inside China.* 以往很多年我們對於中國國內的生活情況所知甚少。◇ *You'll feel better with a good meal inside you.* 你肚子飽了感覺就會好些的。◇ (*figurative*) *Inside most of us is a small child screaming for attention.* 我們大多數人的內心都藏着一個呼求關注的小孩。**OPP** **outside 2** in less than the amount of time mentioned 少於（某時間）：*The job is unlikely to be finished inside (of) a year* 這項工作不大可能在一年之內完成。

■ **adv.** **1** 0- on or to the inside 在（或向）裏面：*She shook it to make sure there was nothing inside.* 她把它晃了晃，以確定裏面沒有東西。◇ *We had to move inside* (= indoors) *when it started to rain.* 開始下雨了，我們只好躲進屋裏。◇ (*figurative*) *I pretended not to care but I was screaming inside.* 表面上我佯裝不在乎，但內心卻在高聲喊叫。**OPP** **outside 2** (*informal*) in prison 在監獄裏；被監禁：*He was sentenced to three years inside.* 他被判三年監禁。

■ **noun** **1** 0- [C, usually sing.] (usually **the inside**) the inner part, side or surface of sth 裏面；內部；內側：*The inside of the box was blue.* 盒子的內面呈藍色。◇ *The door was locked from the inside.* 門從裏面鎖上了。◇ *The shell is smooth on the inside.* 貝殼內壁光滑。◇ *the insides of the windows* 窗戶的內側 **OPP** **the outside** **2** **the inside** [sing.] the part of a road nearest the edge, that is used by slower vehicles（靠近路邊的）慢車道：*He tried to overtake* ***on the inside.*** 他試圖從慢車道超車。**OPP** **the outside** **3** **the inside** [sing.] the part of a curved road or track nearest to the middle or shortest side of the curve（道路或跑道拐彎處的）內側，裏道，內圈：*The French runner is coming up fast on the inside.* 法國的賽跑選手正從內圈迅速趕上來。**OPP** **the outside** **4** **insides** [pl.] (*informal*) a person's stomach and BOWELS（人的）腸胃，內臟：*She was so nervous, her insides were like jelly.* 她緊張得六神無主。

IDM **ˌinside ˈout** 0- with the part that is usually inside facing out 裏面朝外：*You've got your sweater on inside out.* 你把毛線衫穿反了。◇ *Turn the bag inside out and let it dry.* 把包翻過來晾乾。➲ compare BACK TO FRONT at BACK *n.* **on the in'side** belonging to a group or an organization and therefore able to get information that is not available to other people 屬於某團夥（或組織）的；知情的：*The thieves must have had someone on the inside helping them.* 這些竊賊肯定有內應。**turn sth ˌinside ˈout** **1** to make a place very untidy when you are searching for sth 把某處翻得亂七八糟：*The burglars had turned the house inside out.* 竊賊把房子翻了個底朝天。**2** to cause large changes 引起巨大變化：*The new manager turned the old systems inside out.* 新任經理對舊體制進行了徹底的改革。➲ more at KNOW *v.*

■ **adj.** [only before noun] **1** 0- forming the inner part of sth; not on the outside 內部的；裏面的：*the inside pages of a newspaper* 報紙的內頁 ◇ *an inside pocket* 裏袋 ◇ (*BrE*) *I was driving in the* ***inside lane*** (= the part nearest the edge, not the middle of the road). 我當時駕車在慢車道上行駛。**2** known or done by sb in a group or an organization 從內部瞭解到的；內線幹的：*inside information* 內部情報 ◇ *Any newspaper would pay big money to get* ***the inside story*** *on her marriage.* 任何一家報紙都願出高價購買她婚姻的內幕消息。◇ *The robbery appeared to have been an* ***inside job.*** 這次搶劫像是內部人幹的。

ˌinside ˈleg (*BrE*) (*NAmE* **inseam**) *noun* [sing.] a measurement of the length of the inside of sb's leg, used for making or choosing trousers of the correct size 下落襠（腿內側長度）

in·sider /ɪnˈsaɪdə(r)/ *noun* a person who knows a lot about a group or an organization, because they are part of it 知內情者；內部的人：*The situation was described by one insider as 'absolute chaos'.* 據一名內部人士說，實情是亂作一團。➲ compare OUTSIDER

inˌsider ˈtrading (also **inˌsider ˈdealing**) *noun* [U] the crime of buying or selling shares in a company with the help of information known only by those connected with the business, before this information is available to everybody 內線交易，內幕交易（根據內線消息買賣股票的違法行為）

ˌinside ˈtrack *noun* [sing.] (*especially NAmE*) a position in which you have an advantage over sb else 有利位置

in·sidi·ous /ɪnˈsɪdiəs/ *adj.* (*formal, disapproving*) spreading gradually or without being noticed, but causing serious harm 潛伏的；隱襲的；隱伏的：*the insidious effects of polluted water supplies* 供水系統污染的潛在惡果 ▸ **in·sidi·ous·ly** *adv.*

in·sight **AW** /ˈɪnsaɪt/ *noun* **1** [U] (*approving*) the ability to see and understand the truth about people or situations 洞察力；領悟：*a writer of great insight* 有深刻洞察力的作家 ◇ *With a flash of insight I realized what the dream meant.* 我突然明白了這個夢意味着什麼。**2** [C, U] **~ (into sth)** an understanding of what sth is like 洞悉；瞭解：*The book gives us fascinating insights into life in Mexico.* 這本書生動地表現了墨西哥的生活。

in·sight·ful **AW** /ˈɪnsaɪtfʊl/ *adj.* (*approving*) showing a clear understanding of a person or situation 有深刻瞭解的；富有洞察力的 **SYN** **perceptive**

in·sig·nia /ɪnˈsɪɡniə/ *noun* [U+sing./pl. v.] the symbol, BADGE or sign that shows sb's rank or that they are a member of a group or an organization（級別或成員的）標記，象徵；徽章；證章：*the royal insignia* 皇家徽章 ◇ *His uniform bore the insignia of a captain.* 他的制服上有上尉徽章。

in·sig·nifi·cant **AW** /ˌɪnsɪɡˈnɪfɪkənt/ *adj.* not big or valuable enough to be considered important 微不足道的；無足輕重的：*an insignificant difference* 微不足道的差別 ◇ *The levels of chemicals in the river are not insignificant.* 河水中的化學物質含量不容忽視。◇ *He made her feel insignificant and stupid.* 他使她感到卑微愚蠢。**OPP** **significant** ▸ **in·sig·nifi·cance** /-kəns/ *noun* [U]：*Her own problems* ***paled into insignificance*** *beside this terrible news.* 跟這個可怕的消息相比，她自己的問題顯得無關緊要了。**in·sig·nifi·cant·ly** **AW** *adv.*

in·sin·cere /ˌɪnsɪnˈsɪə(r); *NAmE* -ˈsɪr/ *adj.* (*disapproving*) saying or doing sth that you do not really mean or believe 不誠懇的；不真心的：*an insincere smile* 虛情假意的微笑 **OPP** **sincere** ▸ **in·sin·cere·ly** *adv.* **in·sin·cer·ity** /ˌɪnsɪnˈserəti/ *noun* [U]：*She accused him of insincerity.* 她指責他缺乏誠意。

in·sinu·ate /ɪnˈsɪnjueɪt/ *verb* **1** to suggest indirectly that sth unpleasant is true 暗示，旁敲側擊地指出（不快的事）**SYN** **imply**：**~ that ...** *The article insinuated that* *he was having an affair with his friend's wife.* 文章含沙射影地點出他和朋友的妻子有染。◇ **~ sth** *What are you trying to insinuate?* 你拐彎抹角想說什麼？◇ *an insinuating smile* 暗示的微笑 **2 ~ yourself into sth** (*formal, disapproving*) to succeed in gaining sb's respect, affection, etc. so that you can use the situation to your own advantage 鑽營；活動：*In the first act, the villain insinuates himself into the household of the man he intends to kill.* 在第一幕中，惡棍混進了他企圖謀殺的男子的家庭。 **3 ~ yourself/sth + adv./prep.** (*formal*) to slowly move yourself or a part of your body into a particular position or place（使）緩慢進入；慢慢伸入：*She insinuated her right hand under his arm.* 她悄悄把右手插到他胳膊底下。

in·sinu·ation /ɪnˌsɪnjuˈeɪʃn/ *noun* **1** [C] something that sb insinuates 旁敲側擊的話；影射；暗示：*She resented the insinuation that she was too old for the job.* 她憎惡暗示她太老不適合這項工作的話。 **2** [U] the act of insinuating sth 旁敲側擊；含沙射影；巧妙進入

in·sipid /ɪnˈsɪpɪd/ *adj.* (*disapproving*) **1** having almost no taste or flavour 無味道的；淡而無味的 SYN **flavourless**：*a cup of insipid coffee* 一杯淡而無味的咖啡 **2** not interesting or exciting 沒有趣味的；枯燥乏味的 SYN **dull**：*After an hour of insipid conversation, I left.* 經過一個小時乏味的談話之後，我離開了。

in·sist 0-w /ɪnˈsɪst/ *verb*
1 0-w [I, T] to demand that sth happens or that sb agrees to do sth 堅決要求；堅持：*I didn't really want to go but he insisted.* 我並不真的想去，但他硬要我去。◇ *'Please come with us.' 'Very well then, **if you insist**.'* "請和我們一起來吧。" "好吧，你一定要我來，我就來。" **~ on sth/sb doing sth** (*formal*) *She insisted on his/him wearing a suit.* 她堅持要他穿西裝。◇ **~ that ...** *He insists that she come.* 他執意要她來。◇ (*BrE* also) *He insists that she should come.* 他執意要她來。➲ SYNONYMS at DEMAND **2** 0-w [I, T] to say firmly that sth is true, especially when other people do not believe you 堅持說；固執己見：**~ on sth** *He insisted on his innocence.* 他堅持說他是無辜的。◇ **~ (that) ...** *He insisted (that) he was innocent.* 他堅持說他是無辜的。◇ **+ speech** *'It's true,' she insisted.* "那是真的。" 她堅持道。

PHR V **in'sist on/upon sth** 0-w to demand sth and refuse to be persuaded to accept anything else 堅決要求：*We insisted on a refund of the full amount.* 我們堅決要求全額退款。◇ **~ doing sth** *They insisted upon being given every detail of the case.* 他們堅持要求說明事情的整個來龍去脈。 **in'sist on doing sth** 0-w to continue doing sth even though other people think it is annoying 執意繼續做：*They insist on playing their music late at night.* 他們執意地在深夜演奏他們的音樂。

in·sist·ence /ɪnˈsɪstəns/ *noun* [U] **~ (on sth/on doing sth)** | **~ (that ...)** an act of demanding or saying sth firmly and refusing to accept any opposition or excuses 堅決要求；堅持；固執：*their insistence on strict standards of behaviour* 他們對嚴格行為規範的堅決主張 ◇ ***At her insistence**, the matter was dropped.* 在她的堅持下，這件事被擱置了。

in·sist·ent /ɪnˈsɪstənt/ *adj.* **1** demanding sth firmly and refusing to accept any opposition or excuses 堅決要求的；堅持的；固執的：**~ (on sth/on doing sth)** *They were insistent on having a contract for the work.* 他們堅持要就這項工作立一份合同。◇ **~ (that ...)** *Why are you so insistent that we leave tonight?* 你為什麼一定要我們今晚離開？◇ *She didn't want to go but her brother was insistent.* 她不想去，但她哥哥非得要她去。 **2** continuing for a long period of time in a way that cannot be ignored 持續不斷的；再三的；反複的：*insistent demands* 再三的要求 ◇ *the insistent ringing of the telephone* 沒完沒了的電話鈴聲 ▸ **in·sist·ent·ly** *adv.*

in situ /ˌɪn ˈsɪtjuː; ˈsaɪt-; *NAmE* ˈsaɪtuː/ *adv.* (from *Latin*) in the original or correct place 在原位；在原地；在合適地方

in·so·bri·ety /ˌɪnsəˈbraɪəti/ *noun* [U] (*formal*) the state of being drunk; wild and noisy behaviour which is typical of this state 醉酒；（酒後）撒野，無節制 OPP **sobriety**

in·so·far as /ˌɪnsəˈfɑːr əz/ = IN SO FAR AS at FAR

in·sole /ˈɪnsəʊl; *NAmE* ˈɪnsoʊl/ *noun* a piece of material shaped like your foot that is placed inside a shoe to make it more comfortable 鞋墊

in·so·lent /ˈɪnsələnt/ *adj.* extremely rude and showing a lack of respect 粗野的；無禮的；侮慢的：*an insolent child/smile* 粗野的孩子；侮慢的微笑 ➲ SYNONYMS at RUDE ▸ **in·so·lence** /-əns/ *noun* [U]：*Her insolence cost her her job.* 她的蠻橫態度使她丟了工作。 **in·so·lent·ly** *adv.*

in·sol·uble /ɪnˈsɒljəbl; *NAmE* -ˈsɑːl-/ *adj.* **1** (*especially BrE*) (*US* usually **in·sol·vable** /ɪnˈsɒlvəbl; *NAmE* -ˈsɑːl-/) (of a problem, mystery, etc. 問題、謎團等) that cannot be solved or explained 無法解決的；不能解釋的 **2 ~ (in sth)** (of a substance 物質) that does not dissolve in a liquid 不能溶解的；不溶的 OPP **soluble**

in·solv·ent /ɪnˈsɒlvənt; *NAmE* -ˈsɑːl-/ *adj.* not having enough money to pay what you owe 無力償付債務的；破產的 SYN **bankrupt**：*The company has been declared insolvent.* 這家公司被宣佈破產了。 OPP **solvent** ▸ **in·solv·ency** /-ənsi/ *noun* [U, C] (*pl.* **-ies**)

in·som·nia /ɪnˈsɒmniə; *NAmE* -ˈsɑːm-/ *noun* [U] the condition of being unable to sleep 失眠（症）：*to suffer from insomnia* 失眠 ➲ see also SLEEPLESSNESS

in·som·niac /ɪnˈsɒmniæk; *NAmE* -ˈsɑːm-/ *noun* a person who finds it difficult to sleep 失眠患者

in·sou·ci·ance /ɪnˈsuːsiəns/ *noun* [U] (*formal*) the state of not being worried about anything 無憂無慮；漫不經心 SYN **nonchalance**：*She hid her worries behind an air of insouciance.* 她掩飾着自己的煩惱，表現得無憂無慮。 ▸ **in·sou·ci·ant** /-siənt/ *adj.*

Insp *abbr.* INSPECTOR (especially in the British police force)（尤指英國警察）巡官：*Chief Insp (Paul) King* 總巡官（保羅）金

in·spect AW /ɪnˈspekt/ *verb* **1** to look closely at sth/sb, especially to check that everything is as it should be 檢查；查看；審視 SYN **examine**：**~ sth/sb** *The teacher walked around inspecting their work.* 老師走來走去檢查他們的作業。◇ *Make sure you inspect the goods before signing for them.* 要確保在簽收貨物之前進行檢驗。◇ **~ sth/sb for sth** *The plants are regularly inspected for disease.* 這些植物定期檢查是否有病害。➲ SYNONYMS at CHECK **2 ~ sth** to officially visit a school, factory, etc. in order to check that rules are being obeyed and that standards are acceptable 視察：*Public health officials were called in to inspect the premises.* 公共衞生官員奉召來視察了建築物。➲ SYNONYMS at CHECK

in·spec·tion AW /ɪnˈspekʃn/ *noun* [U, C] **1** an official visit to a school, factory, etc. in order to check that rules are being obeyed and that standards are acceptable 視察：*Regular **inspections** are **carried out** at the prison.* 經常有人來視察這座監獄。◇ *The head went on a **tour of inspection** of all the classrooms.* 校長巡視了所有教室。 **2** the act of looking closely at sth/sb, especially to check that everything is as it should be 檢查；查看；審視 SYN **examination**：*The documents are available **for inspection**.* 這些文件可供查閱。◇ ***On closer inspection**, the notes proved to be forgeries.* 經進一步檢查發現鈔票都是偽造的。◇ *Engineers **carried out a** thorough **inspection** of the track.* 工程師對軌道進行了徹底檢查。

in·spect·or AW /ɪnˈspektə(r)/ *noun* **1** a person whose job is to visit schools, factories, etc. to check that rules are being obeyed and that standards are acceptable 檢查員；視察員；巡視員：*a **school/health/safety, etc. inspector*** 督學；衞生、安全等檢查員 ➲ see also TAX INSPECTOR **2** (*abbr.* **Insp**) an officer of middle rank in the POLICE FORCE（警察）巡官：*Inspector Maggie Forbes* 瑪吉•福布斯巡官 ➲ see also CHIEF INSPECTOR **3** (in Britain) a person whose job is to check tickets on a bus or train to make sure that they are valid（英國公共汽車或火車上的）查票員 **4** (*NAmE*) (*BrE* **sur·vey·or**) a person whose job is to examine a building to make sure it is in good condition, usually done for sb who is thinking of buying it（建築物）鑒定人

I

in·spect·or·ate /ɪnˈspektərət/ *noun* [C+sing./pl. v.] (*especially BrE*) an official group of inspectors who work together on the same subject or at the same kind of institution 視察團；檢查團：*The schools inspectorate has/have published a report on science teaching.* 督學團發表了關於科學教學的報告。

in,spector of 'taxes (also **'tax inspector**) *noun* (in Britain) a person who is responsible for collecting the tax that people must pay on the money they earn（英國）稅務員，稅務稽查員 ➲ see also TAX COLLECTOR, TAXMAN

in·spir·ation /ˌɪnspəˈreɪʃn/ *noun* **1** [U] **~ (to do sth)** | **~ (for sth)** the process that takes place when sb sees or hears sth that causes them to have exciting new ideas or makes them want to create sth, especially in art, music or literature 靈感：*Dreams can be a rich source of inspiration for an artist.* 夢境有可能是藝術家靈感的豐富源泉。◇ *Both poets* ***drew their inspiration from*** *the countryside.* 兩位詩人都是從鄉村得到他們的靈感。◇ *Looking for inspiration for a new dessert? Try this recipe.* 正在尋找製作新式甜食的靈感嗎？試試這份食譜吧。**2** [C, usually sing.] **~ (for sth)** a person or thing that is the reason why sb creates or does sth 啟發靈感的人（或事物）；使人產生動機的人（或事物）：*He says my sister was the inspiration for his heroine.* 他說我姐姐是他的女主人公的原型。◇ *Clark was the inspiration behind Saturday's victory.* 克拉克是星期六的勝利的靈魂。**3** [C, usually sing.] **~ (to/for sb)** a person or thing that makes you want to be better, more successful, etc. 鼓舞人心的人（或事物）：*Her charity work is an inspiration to us all.* 她的慈善工作激勵着我們所有人。**4** [C, usually sing., U] a sudden good idea（突然想到的）好主意，妙計：*He had an inspiration: he'd give her a dog for her birthday.* 他突然想到一個好主意，他要送她一條狗作為生日禮物。◇ *It came to me in a* ***flash of inspiration****.* 那是我靈機一動想到的。

in·spir·ation·al /ˌɪnspəˈreɪʃənl/ *adj.* providing inspiration 啟發靈感的；鼓舞人心的：*an inspirational leader* 有感召力的領袖

in·spire /ɪnˈspaɪə(r)/ *verb* **1** to give sb the desire, confidence or enthusiasm to do sth well 激勵；鼓舞：**~ sb (with sth)** *The actors inspired the kids with their enthusiasm.* 演員以熱情鼓舞着孩子們。◇ *The actors' enthusiasm inspired the kids.* 演員們的熱情鼓舞着孩子們。◇ **~ sb to sth** *His superb play inspired the team to a thrilling 5–0 win.* 他的出色表現使球隊士氣大振，以5:0 大獲全勝。◇ **~ sb to do sth** *By visiting schools, the actors hope to inspire children to put on their own productions.* 演員希望通過訪問學校鼓勵孩子們演出自己的作品。**2** [usually passive] **~ sth** to give sb the idea for sth, especially sth artistic or that shows imagination 賦予靈感；引起聯想；啟發思考：*The choice of decor was inspired by a trip to India.* 選用這種裝飾格調是從一次印度之行中得到的啟發。**3** to make sb have a particular feeling or emotion 使產生（感覺或情感）：**~ sb (with sth)** *Her work didn't exactly* ***inspire me with confidence****.* 她的工作並沒有真正地使我產生信心。◇ **~ sth (in sb)** *As a general, he inspired great loyalty in his troops.* 作為一位將軍，他得到了部隊的精誠效忠。

in·spired /ɪnˈspaɪəd; *NAmE* ɪnˈspaɪərd/ *adj.* **1** having excellent qualities or abilities; produced with the help of INSPIRATION 品質優秀的；能力卓越的；借助於靈感創作的：*an inspired performance* 優秀的演出 ◇ *an* ***inspired choice/guess*** (= one that is right but based on feelings rather than knowledge) 得自靈感的選擇 / 猜測 **OPP** **uninspired** **2** **-inspired** used with nouns, adjectives and adverbs to form adjectives that show how sth has been influenced（與名詞、形容詞以及副詞構成形容詞）受…影響的：*politically-inspired killings* 政治性的謀殺事件

in·spir·ing /ɪnˈspaɪərɪŋ/ *adj.* exciting and encouraging you to do or feel sth 鼓舞人心的；激勵的；啟發靈感的：*an inspiring teacher* 啟發能力強的教師 ◇ (*informal*) *The book is less than inspiring.* 那本書不大吸引人。**OPP** **uninspiring** ➲ see also AWE-INSPIRING

in·stabil·ity **AW** /ˌɪnstəˈbɪləti/ *noun* [U, C, usually pl.] (*pl.* **-ies**) **1** the quality of a situation in which things are likely to change or fail suddenly 不穩定；不穩固：*political and economic instability* 政治和經濟的不穩定 **2** a mental condition in which sb's behaviour is likely to change suddenly（精神的）不穩定狀態，變化無常：***mental/emotional instability*** 精神 / 情緒的不穩定 **OPP** **stability** ➲ see also UNSTABLE

in·stall 🔑 /ɪnˈstɔːl/ *verb* **1** 🔑 **~ sth** to fix equipment or furniture into position so that it can be used 安裝；設置：*He's getting a phone installed tomorrow.* 他明天要裝電話。◇ *The hotel chain has recently installed a new booking system.* 這家連鎖旅館最近安裝了新的預訂系統。**2** 🔑 **~ sth** to put a new program into a computer 安裝，建立（程序）：*I'll need some help installing the software.* 我得找人幫忙安裝這個軟件。**3** **~ sb (as sth)** to put sb in a new position of authority, often with an official ceremony（常以正式儀式）使就職，任命：*He was installed as President last May.* 他於去年五月份正式就任總統。**4** **~ sb/yourself (+ adv./prep.)** to make sb/yourself comfortable in a particular place or position 安頓；安置：*We installed ourselves in the front row.* 我們舒舒服服地坐進了前排。

in·stal·la·tion /ˌɪnstəˈleɪʃn/ *noun* **1** [U, C] the act of fixing equipment or furniture in position so that it can be used 安裝；設置：*installation costs* 安裝費 ◇ *Installation of the new system will take several days.* 新系統的安裝需要幾天時間。**2** [C] a piece of equipment or machinery that has been fixed in position so that it can be used 安裝的設備（或機器）：*a heating installation* 供暖裝置 **3** [C] a place where specialist equipment is kept and used 設施：*a military installation* 軍事設施 **4** [U] the act of placing sb in a new position of authority, often with a ceremony 就職；就職儀式：*the installation of the new vice chancellor* 新任校長的就職 **5** [C] (*art* 美術) a piece of modern SCULPTURE that is made using sound, light, etc. as well as objects 現代雕塑裝置（除物體外用聲、光等元素）

in'stallment plan (*NAmE*) (*BrE* **,hire 'purchase**) *noun* [U, C] a method of buying an article by making regular payments for it over several months or years. The article only belongs to the person who is buying it when all the payments have been made. 分期付款 ➲ compare CREDIT (1)

in·stal·ment (*especially BrE*) (*NAmE* usually **in·stall·ment**) /ɪnˈstɔːlmənt/ *noun* **1** one of a number of payments that are made regularly over a period of time until sth has been paid for（分期付款的）一期付款：*We paid for the car* ***by/in instalments****.* 我們以分期付款買了這輛車。◇ *The final instalment on the loan is due next week.* 貸款的最後一期付款下個星期到期。◇ *They were unable to keep up* (= continue to pay regularly) *the instalments.* 他們未能繼續按時交付這筆分期付款。➲ **SYNONYMS** at PAYMENT ➲ **COLLOCATIONS** at FINANCE **2** one of the parts of a story that appears regularly over a period of time in a newspaper, on television, etc.（報章連載小說的）一節；（電視連續劇的）一集 **SYN** **episode**

in·stance 🔑 **AW** /ˈɪnstəns/ *noun, verb*

■ ***noun*** 🔑 a particular example or case of sth 例子；事例；實例：*The report highlights a number of instances of injustice.* 這篇報道重點列舉了一些不公正的實例。◇ *In most instances, there will be no need for further treatment.* 多數情況下，不必繼續治療。◇ *I would normally suggest taking time off work, but* ***in this instance*** *I'm not sure that would do any good.* 我通常會建議休假，但就這個情況而言，我不敢保證休假會有什麼好處。➲ **SYNONYMS** at EXAMPLE

IDM **for 'instance** 🔑 for example 例如；比如：*What would you do, for instance, if you found a member of staff stealing?* 比如說，如果你發現有職員偷東西，你該怎麼辦？➲ **LANGUAGE BANK** at E.G. **in the 'first instance** (*formal*) as the first part of a series of actions 第一；首先：*In the first instance, notify the police and then contact your insurance company.* 首先是報警，然後與你的保險公司聯繫。

■ ***verb*** **~ sth** (*formal*) to give sth as an example 舉…為例

in·stant /ˈɪnstənt/ *adj., noun*
■ ***adj.*** **1** [usually before noun] happening immediately 立即的；立刻的 **SYN** **immediate**：*She took an instant dislike to me.* 她立刻就討厭我。◇ *This account gives you instant access to your money.* 這個賬戶讓你隨時調動款項。◇ *The show was an instant success.* 演出一炮打響。 **2** [only before noun] (of food 食物) that can be made quickly and easily, usually by adding hot water 速食的；即食的；速溶的；方便的：*instant coffee* 速溶咖啡
■ ***noun*** [usually sing.] **1** a very short period of time 瞬間；片刻 **SYN** **moment**：*I'll be back in an instant.* 我馬上就回來。◇ *Just for an instant I thought he was going to refuse.* 剎那間我以為他會拒絕。 **2** a particular point in time 某一時刻：*At that (very) instant, the door opened.* 就在那時，門開了。◇ *I recognized her **the instant** (that)* (= as soon as) *I saw her.* 我一眼就認出她了。◇ *Come here **this instant**!* (= immediately) 馬上過來！

in·stant·an·eous /ˌɪnstənˈteɪniəs/ *adj.* happening immediately 立即的；立刻的；瞬間的：*an instantaneous response* 即時的反應 ◇ *Death was almost instantaneous.* 當時生命垂危。▶ **in·stant·an·eous·ly** *adv.*

in·stant·ly /ˈɪnstəntli/ *adv.* immediately 立刻；立即；馬上：*Her voice is instantly recognizable.* 她的聲音一下子就聽出來了。◇ *The driver was killed instantly.* 司機當場死亡。

ˌinstant ˈmessaging *noun* [U] a system on the Internet that allows people to exchange written messages with each other very quickly 即時通信，即時通訊（互聯網的快捷信息傳遞系統）

ˌinstant ˈreplay (*NAmE*) (*BrE* **ˌaction ˈreplay**) *noun* part of sth, for example a sports game on television, that is immediately repeated, often more slowly, so that you can see a goal or another exciting or important moment again（體育比賽等電視畫面的）即時重放，慢鏡頭回放

in·stead 🔑 /ɪnˈsted/ *adv.*
in the place of sb/sth 代替；頂替；反而；卻：*Lee was ill so I went instead.* 李病了，所以我代他去了。◇ *He didn't reply. Instead, he turned on his heel and left the room.* 他沒有回答，反而轉身離開了房間。◇ *She said nothing, preferring instead to save her comments till later.* 她什麼也沒說，而是想稍後再作評論。

inˈstead of 🔑 *prep.*
in the place of sb/sth 代替；作為…的替換：*We just had soup instead of a full meal.* 我們沒有吃全餐，只喝了湯。◇ *Now I can walk to work instead of going by car.* 現在我可以步行去上班，而不必開車了。

in·step /ˈɪnstep/ *noun* **1** the top part of the foot between the ankle and toes 足背；足弓 ⊃ **VISUAL VOCAB** page V59 **2** the part of a shoe that covers the instep 鞋面

in·sti·gate /ˈɪnstɪɡeɪt/ *verb* (*formal*) **1 ~ sth** (*especially BrE*) to make sth start or happen, usually sth official 使（正式）開始；使發生 **SYN** **bring sth about**：*The government has instigated a programme of economic reform.* 政府已實施了經濟改革方案。 **2 ~ sth** to cause sth bad to happen 煽動；唆使；鼓動：*They were accused of instigating racial violence.* 他們被控煽動種族暴力。

in·sti·ga·tion /ˌɪnstɪˈɡeɪʃn/ *noun* [U] the act of causing sth to begin or happen 發起；唆使；煽動：*An appeal fund was launched **at the instigation of** the President.* 總統授意發起了一項救援基金。◇ *It was done **at his instigation**.* 那件事是在他的鼓動下幹的。

in·sti·ga·tor /ˈɪnstɪɡeɪtə(r)/ *noun* **~ (of sth)** a person who causes sth to happen, especially sth bad 發起人；（尤指）唆使者，煽動者，慫恿者：*the instigators of the riots* 煽動騷亂的人

in·stil (*BrE*) (*NAmE* **in·still**) /ɪnˈstɪl/ *verb* (**-ll-**) **~ sth (in/into sb)** to gradually make sb feel, think or behave in a particular way over a period of time 逐漸灌輸，逐步培養（感受、思想或行為）：*to **instil confidence/discipline/fear** into sb* 逐步使某人樹立信心／守紀律／產生恐懼

in·stinct /ˈɪnstɪŋkt/ *noun* [U, C] **1 ~ (for sth/for doing sth)** | **~ (to do sth)** a natural tendency for people and animals to behave in a particular way using the knowledge and abilities that they were born with rather than thought or training 本能；天性：*maternal instincts* 母性 ◇ *Children do not know **by instinct** the difference between right and wrong.* 兒童並非生來就會分辨是非。◇ *His first instinct was to run away.* 他的本能反應就是逃跑。◇ *Horses have a well-developed instinct for fear.* 馬天性易受驚嚇。◇ *Even at school, he showed he **had an instinct for*** (= was naturally good at) *business.* 他早在求學時期就表現出經商的天賦。 **2 ~ (that …)** a feeling that makes you do sth or believe that sth is true, even though it is not based on facts or reason 直覺 **SYN** **intuition**：*Her instincts had been right.* 她當時的直覺是對的。

in·stinct·ive /ɪnˈstɪŋktɪv/ *adj.* based on instinct, not thought or training 本能的；直覺的；天生的：*instinctive knowledge* 本能的知識 ◇ *She's an instinctive player.* 她是個天生的運動員。◇ *My instinctive reaction was to deny everything.* 我的本能反應是否認一切。▶ **in·stinct·ive·ly** *adv.*：*He knew instinctively that something was wrong.* 他憑直覺知道出事了。

in·stinct·ual /ɪnˈstɪŋktʃuəl/ *adj.* (*psychology* 心) based on natural instinct; not learned 本能（而非習得）的

in·sti·tute 🔑 **AW** /ˈɪnstɪtjuːt; *NAmE* -tuːt/ *noun, verb*
■ ***noun*** 🔑 an organization that has a particular purpose, especially one that is connected with education or a particular profession; the building used by this organization（教育、專業等）機構，機構建築：*a research institute* 研究所 ◇ *the Institute of Chartered Accountants*（英國皇家）特許會計師協會 ◇ *institutes of higher education* 高等學校
■ ***verb*** **~ sth** (*formal*) to introduce a system, policy, etc. or start a process 建立，制訂（體系、政策等）；開始；實行：*to institute criminal proceedings against sb* 對某人提起刑事訴訟 ◇ *The new management intends to institute a number of changes.* 新任管理部門打算實行一些改革。

in·sti·tu·tion 🔑 **AW** /ˌɪnstɪˈtjuːʃn; *NAmE* -ˈtuːʃn/ *noun*
1 🔑 [C] a large important organization that has a particular purpose, for example, a university or bank（大學、銀行等規模大的）機構：*an **educational/financial, etc. institution*** 教育、金融等機構 ◇ *the Smithsonian Institution* 史密森學會 **2** [C] (usually *disapproving*) a building where people with special needs are taken care of, for example because they are old or mentally ill 慈善機構；社會福利機構：*a mental institution* 精神病院 ◇ *We want this to be like a home, not an institution.* 我們希望這裏像個家，而不像收容所。 **3** [C] a custom or system that has existed for a long time among a particular group of people（由來已久的）風俗習慣，制度：*the institution of marriage* 婚姻制度 **4** [U] the act of starting or introducing sth such as a system or a law 建立；設立；制訂：*the institution of new safety procedures* 新安全規程的制訂 **5** [C] (*informal, humorous*) a person who is well known because they have been in a particular place or job for a long time（某地或某工作領域）出名的人：*You must know him—he's an institution around here!* 你一定認識他，他是這一帶的知名人物！

in·sti·tu·tion·al **AW** /ˌɪnstɪˈtjuːʃənl; *NAmE* -ˈtuː-/ *adj.* [usually before noun] connected with an institution 機構的；慈善機構的：*institutional investors* 機構投資者 ◇ *institutional care* 慈善機構的照顧 ▶ **in·sti·tu·tion·ally** **AW** /-ʃənəli/ *adv.*

in·sti·tu·tion·al·ize (*BrE* also **-ise**) **AW** /ˌɪnstɪˈtjuːʃənəlaɪz; *NAmE* -ˈtuː-/ *verb* **1 ~ sb** to send sb who is not capable of living independently to live in a special building (= an institution) especially when it is for a long period of time 將（生活不能自理的人）送到收容機構（或社會福利機構） **2 ~ sth** to make sth become part of an organized system, society or culture, so that it is considered normal 使成慣例；使制度化 ▶ **in·sti·tu·tion·al·iza·tion**, **-isa·tion** /ˌɪnstɪˌtjuːʃənəlaɪˈzeɪʃn; *NAmE* -ˌtuːʃənələˈz-/ *noun* [U]

in·sti·tu·tion·al·ized (*BrE* also **-ised**) **AW** /ˌɪnstɪˈtjuːʃənəlaɪzd; *NAmE* -ˈtuː-/ *adj.* **1** (usually *disapproving*) that has happened or been done for so long that it is

I

considered normal 約定俗成的；成慣例的：*institutionalized racism* 由來已久的種族偏見 **2** (of people 人) lacking the ability to live and think independently because they have spent so long in an institution（因長期生活在福利機構）缺乏自理能力的：*institutionalized patients* 失去自理能力的病人

in-'store *adj.* [only before noun] within a large shop/store 大商店內的；大商店所屬的：*an in-store bakery* 設在大商店裏的麵包店

in·struct AW /ɪn'strʌkt/ *verb* **1** (*formal*) to tell sb to do sth, especially in a formal or official way 指示；命令；吩咐 SYN **direct, order**：**~ sb to do sth** *The letter instructed him to report to headquarters immediately.* 那封信指示他立即向總部彙報。◇ **~ sb where, what, etc. …** *You will be instructed where to go as soon as the plane is ready.* 飛機一準備好就會通知你去何處。◇ **~ sb** *She arrived at 10 o'clock **as instructed**.* 她依照指示於 10 點鐘到達。◇ **~ that …** *He instructed that a wall be built around the city.* 他下令在城的周圍築一道城牆。◇ (*BrE* also) *He instructed that a wall should be built around the city.* 他下令在城的周圍築一道城牆。◇ **~ (sb) + speech** *'Put it there,' she instructed (them).* "把它放在那兒。" 她吩咐（他們）道。➲ SYNONYMS at ORDER **2 ~ sb (in sth)** (*formal*) to teach sb sth, especially a practical skill 教授，傳授（技能等）：*All our staff have been instructed in sign language.* 我們的員工都接受過手語訓練。**3** [usually passive] **~ sb that …** (*formal*) to give sb information about sth 告知；通知：*We **have been instructed that** a decision will not be made before the end of the week.* 我們已獲悉週末前不會作出決定。**4 ~ sb (to do sth)** (*law* 律) to employ sb to represent you in a legal situation, especially as a lawyer 委託（律師）；託辦

in·struc·tion 0→ AW /ɪn'strʌkʃn/ *noun, adj.*

■ *noun* **1** 0→ **instructions** [pl.] detailed information on how to do or use sth 用法說明；操作指南 SYN **directions**：***Follow the instructions** on the packet carefully.* 仔細按照包裝上的說明操作。◇ *Always **read the instructions** before you start.* 使用前務請閱讀操作說明。◇ **~ on how to do sth** *The plant comes with **full instructions** on how to care for it.* 這棵植物附有詳盡的護養說明。**2** 0→ [C, usually pl.] **~ (to do sth) | ~ (that …)** something that sb tells you to do 指示；命令；吩咐 SYN **order**：*to **ignore/carry out sb's instructions*** 忽視 / 執行某人的命令 ◇ *I'm **under instructions** to keep my speech short.* 我接到指示講話要簡短。**3** [C] a piece of information that tells a computer to perform a particular operation.（計算機的）指令 **4** [U] **~ (in sth)** (*formal*) the act of teaching sth to sb 教授；教導；傳授：*religious instruction* 教義講授

■ *adj.* [only before noun] giving detailed information on how to do or use sth (= giving instructions) 說明用法的；操作指南的：*an **instruction book/manual*** 說明書；用法指南

in·struc·tion·al /ɪn'strʌkʃənl/ *adj.* [usually before noun] (*formal*) that teaches people sth 教學的；教育的：*instructional materials* 教材

in·struct·ive AW /ɪn'strʌktɪv/ *adj.* giving a lot of useful information 富有教益的；增長知識的：*a most instructive experience* 獲益良多的經歷 ◇ *It is instructive to see how other countries are tackling the problem.* 瞭解別的國家如何處理這個問題是具有啟發性的。▸ **in·struct·ive·ly** *adv.*

in·struct·or AW /ɪn'strʌktə(r)/ *noun* **1** a person whose job is to teach sb a practical skill or sport 教練；導師：*a driving instructor* 駕駛教練 **2** (*NAmE*) a teacher below the rank of ASSISTANT PROFESSOR at a college or university（大學）講師

in·stru·ment 0→ /'ɪnstrəmənt/ *noun*

1 0→ a tool or device used for a particular task, especially for delicate or scientific work 器械；儀器；器具：***surgical/optical/precision, etc. instruments*** 外科器械；光學、精密等儀器 ◇ *instruments of torture* 刑具 **2** 0→ = MUSICAL INSTRUMENT：*Is he learning an instrument?* 他在學習演奏樂器嗎？◇ ***brass/stringed, etc. instruments*** 銅管樂器、弦樂器等 **3** 0→ a device used for measuring speed, distance, temperature, etc. in a vehicle or on a piece of machinery（車輛、機器的）儀器，儀表：*the flight instruments* 飛行儀表 ◇ *the instrument panel* 儀表盤 **4** (*formal*) something that is used by sb in order to achieve sth; a person or thing that makes sth happen 促成某事的人（或事物）；手段：**~ for sth/for doing sth** *The law is not the best instrument for dealing with family matters.* 法律並不是處理家庭問題的最佳方法。◇ **~ of sth** *an instrument of change* 促成變革的措施 **5 ~ of sb/sth** (*formal*) a person who is used and controlled by sb/sth that is more powerful 受利用（或控制）的人；工具：*an instrument of fate* 受命運擺佈的人 **6** (*law* 律) a formal legal document 文據；正式法律文件

in·stru·men·tal /ˌɪnstrə'mentl/ *adj., noun*

■ *adj.* **1 ~ (in sth/in doing sth)** important in making sth happen 起重要作用：*He was instrumental in bringing about an end to the conflict.* 他在終止衝突的過程中起了重要作用。**2** made by or for musical instruments 用樂器演奏的；為樂器譜寫的：*instrumental music* 器樂曲 ▸ **in·stru·men·tal·ly** /-təli/ *adv.*

■ *noun* **1** a piece of music (usually popular music) in which only musical instruments are used with no singing 器樂曲 **2** (*grammar* 語法) (in some languages 用於某些語言) the form of a noun, pronoun or adjective when it refers to a thing that is used to do sth 工具格；工具詞

in·stru·men·tal·ist /ˌɪnstrə'mentəlɪst/ *noun* a person who plays a musical instrument 樂器演奏者 ➲ compare VOCALIST

in·stru·men·ta·tion /ˌɪnstrəmen'teɪʃn/ *noun* [U] **1** a set of instruments used in operating a vehicle or a piece of machinery（一套）儀器，儀表 **2** the way in which a piece of music is written for a particular group of instruments 器樂譜寫

in·sub·or·din·ation /ˌɪnsəˌbɔːdɪ'neɪʃn; *NAmE* -ˌbɔːrd-/ *noun* [U] (*formal*) the refusal to obey orders or show respect for sb who has a higher rank 不服從命令；抗命；犯上 SYN **disobedience** ▸ **in·sub·or·din·ate** /ˌɪnsə'bɔːdɪnət; *NAmE* -'bɔːrd-/ *adj.*

in·sub·stan·tial /ˌɪnsəb'stænʃl/ *adj.* **1** not very large, strong or important 不大的；不堅固的；不重要的：*an insubstantial construction of wood and glue* 用木頭和膠粘合的簡單構造 ◇ *an insubstantial argument* 不充實的論據 **2** (*literary*) not real or solid 非真實的；非實體的；虛幻的：*as insubstantial as a shadow* 虛無縹緲

in·suf·fer·able /ɪn'sʌfrəbl/ *adj.* extremely annoying, unpleasant and difficult to bear 難以忍受的；難以容忍的 SYN **unbearable** ▸ **in·suf·fer·ably** /-əbli/ *adv.*：*insufferably hot* 酷熱難當

in·suf·fi·cient AW /ˌɪnsə'fɪʃnt/ *adj.* **~ (to do sth) | ~ (for sth)** (*formal*) not large, strong or important enough for a particular purpose 不充分的；不足的；不夠重要的 SYN **inadequate**：*insufficient time* 時間不夠 ◇ *His salary is insufficient to meet his needs.* 他的薪水不夠應付需要。OPP **sufficient** ▸ **in·suf·fi·cient·ly** AW *adv.* **in·suf·fi·ciency** /-ʃənsi/ *noun* [U, sing.] (*technical* 術語)：*cardiac insufficiency* 心功能不全

in·su·lar /'ɪnsjələ(r); *NAmE* 'ɪnsələr/ *adj.* **1** (*disapproving*) only interested in your own country, ideas, etc. and not in those from outside 只關心本國利益的；思想褊狹的；保守的：*The British are often accused of being insular.* 英國人常被指責為思想褊狹。**2** (*technical* 術語) connected with an island or islands 海島的；島嶼的：*the coastal and insular areas* 沿海和島嶼區域 ▸ **in·su·lar·ity** /ˌɪnsju'lærəti; *NAmE* -sə'l-/ *noun* [U]

in·su·late /'ɪnsjuleɪt; *NAmE* -səl-/ *verb* **1 ~ sth (from/against sth)** to protect sth with a material that prevents heat, sound, electricity, etc. from passing through 使隔熱；使隔音；使絕緣：*Home owners are being encouraged to insulate their homes to save energy.* 當局鼓勵房主在住房加隔熱裝置以節約能源。➲ COLLOCATIONS at DECORATE **2 ~ sb/sth from/against sth** to protect sb/sth from unpleasant experiences or influences 使免除（不愉快的經歷）；使免受（不良影響）；隔離 SYN **shield**

in·su·lated /ˈɪnsjuleɪtɪd; *NAmE* -səl-/ *adj.* protected with a material that prevents heat, sound, electricity, etc. from passing through 有隔熱（或隔音、絕緣）保護的：*insulated wires* 絕緣線 ◇ *a well-insulated house* 隔熱性能好的房子

in·su·lat·ing /ˈɪnsjuleɪtɪŋ; *NAmE* ˈɪnsəleɪtɪŋ/ *adj.* [only before noun] preventing heat, sound, electricity, etc. from passing through 起隔熱（或隔音、絕緣）作用的：*insulating materials* 絕緣材料

ˈ**insulating tape** (*US* also ˈ**friction tape**) *noun* [U] a strip of sticky material used for covering the ends of electrical wires to prevent the possibility of an electric shock 絕緣膠帶；電線膠布

in·su·la·tion /ˌɪnsjuˈleɪʃn; *NAmE* -səˈl-/ *noun* [U] the act of protecting sth with a material that prevents heat, sound, electricity, etc. from passing through; the materials used for this 隔熱；隔音；絕緣；隔熱（或隔音、絕緣）材料：*Better insulation of your home will help to reduce heating bills.* 加強房子的隔熱性能有助於減少供暖費用。◇ *foam insulation* 泡沫絕緣材料 ➲ COLLOCATIONS at DECORATE

in·su·la·tor /ˈɪnsjuleɪtə(r); *NAmE* -səl-/ *noun* a material or device used to prevent heat, electricity, or sound from escaping from sth 隔熱（或絕緣、隔音等的）材料（或裝置）

in·su·lin /ˈɪnsjəlɪn; *NAmE* -səl-/ *noun* [U] a chemical substance produced in the body that controls the amount of sugar in the blood (by influencing the rate at which it is removed); a similar artificial substance given to people whose bodies do not produce enough naturally 胰島素：*insulin-dependent diabetes* 胰島素依賴型糖尿病

in·sult 0ꞏ *verb, noun*

▪ ***verb*** 0ꞏ /ɪnˈsʌlt/ **~ sb/sth** to say or do sth that offends sb 辱罵；侮辱；冒犯：*I have never been so insulted in my life!* 我一生中從未被如此侮辱過！◇ *She felt insulted by the low offer.* 那麼低的出價使她覺得受到了侮辱。

▪ ***noun*** 0ꞏ /ˈɪnsʌlt/ a remark or an action that is said or done in order to offend sb 辱罵；侮辱；冒犯：*The crowd were shouting insults at the police.* 群眾大聲辱罵着警察。◇ **~ to sb/sth** *His comments were seen as an insult to the president.* 他的評論被看成是對主席的冒犯。◇ *The questions were an* ***insult to our intelligence*** (= too easy). 那些問題（簡單得）有辱我們的智慧。 IDM see ADD

in·sult·ing 0ꞏ /ɪnˈsʌltɪŋ/ *adj.* causing or intending to cause sb to feel offended 侮辱的；有冒犯性的；無禮的：*insulting remarks* 侮辱性的話語 ◇ **~ to sb/sth** *She was really insulting to me.* 她對我實在粗魯無禮。

in·su·per·able /ɪnˈsuːpərəbl; *BrE* also -ˈsjuː-/ *adj.* (*formal*) (of difficulties, problems, etc. 困難、問題等) that cannot be dealt with successfully 無法克服的；不可逾越的 SYN **insurmountable**

in·sup·port·able /ˌɪnsəˈpɔːtəbl; *NAmE* -ˈpɔːrt-/ *adj.* so bad or difficult that you cannot accept it or deal with it 難以接受的；棘手的 SYN **intolerable**

in·sur·ance 0ꞏ /ɪnˈʃʊərəns; -ˈʃɔːr-; *NAmE* -ˈʃʊr-/ *noun* **1** 0ꞏ [U, C] an arrangement with a company in which you pay them regular amounts of money and they agree to pay the costs, for example, if you die or are ill/sick, or if you lose or damage sth 保險：***life/car/travel/household, etc. insurance*** 人壽、汽車、旅行平安、家庭財產等保險 ◇ *to have adequate* ***insurance cover*** 有足夠的保險保障 ◇ **~ (against sth)** *to* ***take out insurance*** *against fire and theft* 辦理火險和盜竊保險 ◇ ***insurance premiums*** (= the regular payments made for insurance) 保險費 ◇ *Can you claim for the loss* ***on your insurance***? 你能向你投保的公司要求賠償這一損失嗎？ ➲ see also NATIONAL INSURANCE **2** 0ꞏ [U] the business of providing people with insurance 保險業：*an* ***insurance broker/company*** 保險經紀／公司 ◇ *He works in insurance.* 他在保險業工作。 **3** [U] money paid by or to an insurance company 保險費；保費：*to pay insurance on your house* 交住房保險金 ◇ *When her husband died, she received £50 000 in insurance.* 她丈夫去世，她得到了一筆 5 萬英鎊的保險金。 **4** [U, C] **~ (against sth)** something you do to protect yourself against sth bad happening in the future（防備不測的）保障措施，安全保證：*At that time people had large families as an insurance against some children dying.* 那時人們養的子女很多，以防有孩子夭折。

inˈ**surance adjuster** (*NAmE*) (*BrE* ˈ**loss adjuster**) *noun* a person who works for an insurance company and whose job is to calculate how much money sb should receive after they have lost sth or had sth damaged（保險公司的）險損估價師，損失理算人，理賠員

inˈ**surance policy** *noun* a written contract between a person and an insurance company 保險單：*a travel insurance policy* 旅行保險單 ◇ (*figurative*) *Always make a backup disk as an insurance policy.* 為保險起見，每次都要做備份磁盤。

in·sure /ɪnˈʃʊə(r); -ˈʃɔː(r); *NAmE* -ˈʃʊr/ *verb* **1** [T, I] to buy insurance so that you will receive money if your property, car, etc. gets damaged or stolen, or if you get ill/sick or die 投保；給…保險：**~ sth/yourself (for sth)** *The painting is insured for $1 million.* 這幅油畫投了 100 萬元的保險。◇ **~ sth/yourself (against sth)** *Luckily he had insured himself against long-term illness.* 幸運的是，他為自己投保了長期病險。◇ (*figurative*) *Having a lot of children is a way of insuring themselves against loneliness in old age.* 養很多孩子是他們預防老年孤寂的一種辦法。◇ **~ against sth** *We strongly recommend insuring against sickness or injury.* 我們強烈建議投傷病保險。 **2** [T] **~ sb/sth** to sell insurance to sb for sth 接受投保；承保：*The company can refuse to insure a property that does not have window locks.* 保險公司可以拒絕為沒有窗鎖的房產提供保險。 **3** (*especially NAmE*) = ENSURE

in·sured /ɪnˈʃʊəd; -ˈʃɔːd; *NAmE* -ˈʃʊrd/ *adj.* **1** having insurance 被保險的：*Was the vehicle insured?* 那輛車上保險了嗎？◇ **~ to do sth** *You're not insured to drive our car.* 你開我們的車不在保險範圍內。◇ **~ against sth** *It isn't insured against theft.* 它沒有買盜竊險。 **2 the insured** *noun* (*pl.* **the insured**) (*law* 律) the person who has made an agreement with an insurance company and who receives money if, for example, they are ill/sick or if they lose or damage sth 受保人

in·surer /ɪnˈʃʊərə(r); -ˈʃɔːr-; *NAmE* -ˈʃʊr-/ *noun* a person or company that provides people with insurance 承保人；保險公司

in·sur·gency /ɪnˈsɜːdʒənsi; *NAmE* -ˈsɜːrdʒ-/ *noun* [U, C] (*pl.* **-ies**) an attempt to take control of a country by force 起義；叛亂；造反 SYN **rebellion** ➲ COLLOCATIONS at WAR ➲ see also COUNTER-INSURGENCY

in·sur·gent /ɪnˈsɜːdʒənt; *NAmE* -ˈsɜːrdʒ-/ *noun* [usually pl.] (*formal*) a person fighting against the government or armed forces of their own country 起義者；叛亂者；造反者 SYN **rebel** ▸ **in·sur·gent** *adj.* SYN **rebellious**

in·sur·mount·able /ˌɪnsəˈmaʊntəbl; *NAmE* -sərˈm-/ *adj.* (*formal*) (of difficulties, problems, etc. 困難、問題等) that cannot be dealt with successfully 無法克服的；難以解決的；不可逾越的 SYN **insuperable**

in·sur·rec·tion /ˌɪnsəˈrekʃn/ *noun* [C, U] a situation in which a large group of people try to take political control of their own country with violence 起義；叛亂；暴動 SYN **uprising** ▸ **in·sur·rec·tion·ary** /ˌɪnsəˈrekʃənri; *NAmE* -neri/ *adj.*

in·tact /ɪnˈtækt/ *adj.* [not usually before noun] complete and not damaged 完好無損；完整 SYN **undamaged**：*Most of the house* ***remains intact*** *even after two hundred years.* 即使過了兩百年，這房子的大部份還保持完好。◇ *He emerged from the trial with his reputation intact.* 他受審獲釋，名譽絲毫未受損害。

in·take /ˈɪnteɪk/ *noun* **1** [U, C] the amount of food, drink, etc. that you take into your body（食物、飲料等的）攝取量，吸入量：*high fluid intake* 高流質攝取量 ◇ *to reduce your daily intake of salt* 減少每天的食鹽量 **2** [C, U] the number of people who are allowed to enter a school, college, profession, etc. during a particular period（一定時期內）納入的人數：*the annual student intake* 每年招收的新生人數 **3** [C] a place where liquid,

I

air, etc. enters a machine（機器上的液體、空氣等的）進口：*the air/fuel intake* 進氣口；加燃料口 **4** [C, usually sing.] an act of taking sth in, especially breath 吸收；吸入；（尤指）吸氣：*a sharp intake of breath* 猛吸一口氣

in·tan·gible /ɪnˈtændʒəbl/ *adj.* **1** that exists but that is difficult to describe, understand or measure 難以形容（或理解）的；不易度量的：*The old building had an intangible air of sadness about it.* 那座舊建築籠罩着一種說不出的悲涼氣氛。◇ *The benefits are intangible.* 好處是難以計算的。**2** (*business* 商) that does not exist as a physical thing but is still valuable to a company 無形的（指不以實體存在的公司資產）：***intangible assets/property*** 無形資產／財產 OPP **tangible** ▸ **in·tan·gible** *noun* [usually pl.]：*intangibles such as staff morale and goodwill* 員工士氣和商譽之類的無形資產

in·te·ger /ˈɪntɪdʒə(r)/ *noun* (*mathematics* 數) a whole number, such as 3 or 4 but not 3.5 整數 ➲ compare FRACTION (2)

in·te·gral AW /ˈɪntɪɡrəl; ɪnˈteɡ-/ *adj.* **1** being an essential part of sth 必需的；不可或缺的：*Music is **an integral part of** the school's curriculum.* 音樂是這所學校的課程中基本的一環。◇ **~ to sth** *Practical experience is integral to the course.* 這門課程不可缺少實踐經驗。**2** [usually before noun] included as part of sth, rather than supplied separately 作為組成部份的：*All models have an integral CD player.* 所有型號都有內置的激光唱片機。**3** [usually before noun] having all the parts that are necessary for sth to be complete 完整的；完備的：*an integral system* 完整的系統 ▸ **in·te·gral·ly** /ˈɪntɪɡrəli; ɪnˈteɡ-/ *adv.*

ˌintegral ˈcalculus *noun* [U] (*mathematics* 數) a type of mathematics that deals with quantities that change in time. It is used to calculate a quantity between two particular moments. 積分學 ➲ compare DIFFERENTIAL CALCULUS

in·te·grate AW /ˈɪntɪɡreɪt/ *verb* **1** [I, T] to combine two or more things so that they work together; to combine with sth else in this way（使）合併，成為一體：**~ into/with sth** *These programs will integrate with your existing software.* 這些程序會和你原有的軟件整合起來。◇ **~ A (into/with B)** | **~ A and B** *These programs can be integrated with your existing software.* 這些程序能和你原有的軟件整合起來。**2** [I, T] to become or make sb become accepted as a member of a social group, especially when they come from a different culture（使）加入，融入群體：**~ (into/with sth)** *They have not made any effort to integrate with the local community.* 他們完全沒有嘗試融入本地社區。◇ **~ sb (into/with sth)** *The policy is to integrate children with special needs into ordinary schools.* 這項政策旨在使有特殊需要的兒童融入普通學校。➲ compare SEGREGATE

in·te·grated AW /ˈɪntɪɡreɪtɪd/ *adj.* [usually before noun] in which many different parts are closely connected and work successfully together 各部份密切協調的；綜合的；完整統一的：*an integrated transport system* (= including buses, trains, taxis, etc.) 綜合聯運體系 ◇ *an integrated school* (= attended by students of all races and religions) 混合學校（招收不同種族和宗教信仰的學生）

ˌintegrated ˈcircuit *noun* (*physics* 物) a small MICROCHIP that contains a large number of electrical connections and performs the same function as a larger CIRCUIT made from separate parts 集成電路；積體電路

in·te·gra·tion AW /ˌɪntɪˈɡreɪʃn/ *noun* **1** [U, C] the act or process of combining two or more things so that they work together (= of integrating them) 結合；整合；一體化：*The aim is to promote closer economic integration.* 目的是進一步促進經濟一體化。◇ *His music is an integration of tradition and new technology.* 他的音樂結合了傳統和新技術。**2** [U] the act or process of mixing people who have previously been separated, usually because of colour, race, religion, etc.（不同膚色、種族、宗教信仰等的人的）混合，融合：*racial integration in schools* 學校招收不同種族的學生 ➲ COLLOCATIONS at RACE

Synonyms 同義詞辨析

intelligent

smart • clever • brilliant • bright

These words all describe people who are good at learning, understanding and thinking about things, and the actions that show this ability. 以上各詞均形容人有才智、悟性強、聰明。

intelligent good at learning, understanding and thinking in a logical way about things; showing this ability 指有才智的、悟性強的、聰明的：*He's a **highly intelligent** man.* 他是一個很有才智的人。◇ *She asked a lot of intelligent questions.* 她問了許多機智的問題。

smart (*especially NAmE*) quick at learning and understanding things; showing the ability to make good business or personal decisions 指聰明的、機敏的、精明的：*She's smarter than her brother.* 她比她哥哥聰明。◇ *That was a smart career move.* 那是個人事業發展上的明智之舉。

clever (*sometimes disapproving, especially BrE*) quick at learning and understanding things; showing this ability 指聰明的、聰穎的：*How clever of you to work it out!* 你解決了這個問題真是太聰明了。◇ *He's **too clever by half**, if you ask me.* 恕我直言，他未免聰明過頭了。NOTE People use **clever** in the phrase *Clever boy/girl!* to tell a young child that they have learnt or done sth well. When used to or about an adult **clever** can be disapproving. * clever 用於短語 Clever boy/girl!（多麼聰明的男孩／女孩！）表示孩子學習悟性強、做事聰明伶俐。clever 用於成年人可能含貶義。

brilliant extremely intelligent or skilful 指聰穎的、技藝高的：*He's a brilliant young scientist.* 他是一個才華橫溢的青年科學家。

bright intelligent; quick to learn 指聰明的、悟性強的：*She's probably the brightest student in the class.* 她大概是班裏最聰明的學生。NOTE **Bright** is used especially to talk about young people. Common collocations of **bright** include *girl, boy, kid, student, pupil*. * bright 主要用於年輕人，常與之搭配的詞有 girl、boy、kid、student、pupil 等。

PATTERNS

- clever/brilliant **at** sth
- a(n) intelligent/smart/clever/brilliant/bright **child/boy/girl/man/woman**
- a(n) intelligent/smart/clever/brilliant **thing to do**

in·teg·rity AW /ɪnˈteɡrəti/ *noun* [U] **1** the quality of being honest and having strong moral principles 誠實正直：***personal/professional/artistic integrity*** 個人的／職業上的／藝術家的誠實正直 ◇ *to behave with integrity* 行為表現誠實正直 **2** (*formal*) the state of being whole and not divided 完整；完好 SYN **unity**：*to respect the territorial integrity of the nation* 尊重該國的領土完整

in·tel·lect /ˈɪntəlekt/ *noun* **1** [U, C] the ability to think in a logical way and understand things, especially at an advanced level; your mind（尤指高等的）智力，思維邏輯領悟力：*a man of considerable intellect* 相當有才智的人 **2** [C] a very intelligent person 智力高的人；才智超群的人：*She was one of the most formidable intellects of her time.* 她是當時的一名蓋世英才。

in·tel·lec·tual /ˌɪntəˈlektʃuəl/ *adj., noun*

■ *adj.* **1** [usually before noun] connected with or using a person's ability to think in a logical way and understand things 智力的；腦力的；理智的 SYN **mental**：*intellectual curiosity* 求知慾 ◇ *an intellectual novel* 推理小說 **2** (of a person 人) well educated and enjoying activities in which you have to think seriously about things 有才智的；智力發達的：*She's very intellectual.* 她很聰慧。▸ **in·tel·lec·tual·ism** /ˌɪntəˈlektʃuəlɪzəm/ *noun* [U] (usually *disapproving*) **in·tel·lec·tu·al·ly** *adv.*：*intellectually challenging* 考驗智慧的

■ ***noun*** a person who is well educated and enjoys activities in which they have to think seriously about things 知識分子；腦力勞動者

ˌintelˌlectual ˈproperty *noun* [U] (*law* 律) an idea, a design, etc. that sb has created and that the law prevents other people from copying 知識財產：*intellectual property rights* 知識產權

in·tel·li·gence 🔑 AW /ɪnˈtelɪdʒəns/ *noun* [U] **1** 🔑 the ability to learn, understand and think in a logical way about things; the ability to do this well 智力；才智；智慧：*a person of* ***high/average/low intelligence*** 智力高的 / 一般的 / 低下的人 ◇ *He didn't even have the intelligence to call for an ambulance.* 他連呼叫救護車的頭腦都沒有。➲ see also ARTIFICIAL INTELLIGENCE, EMOTIONAL INTELLIGENCE **2** 🔑 secret information that is collected, for example about a foreign country, especially one that is an enemy; the people that collect this information（機密）情報；情報人員：*intelligence reports* 情報人員的報告 ◇ *the US Central Intelligence Agency* 美國中央情報局

inˈtelligence quotient *noun* = IQ

inˈtelligence test *noun* a test to measure how well a person is able to understand and think in a logical way about things 智力測驗

in·tel·li·gent 🔑 AW /ɪnˈtelɪdʒənt/ *adj.* **1** 🔑 good at learning, understanding and thinking in a logical way about things; showing this ability 有才智的；悟性強的；聰明的：*a* ***highly intelligent*** *child* 非常聰明的孩子 ◇ *to ask an intelligent question* 問一個機智的問題 OPP **unintelligent** **2** 🔑 (of an animal, a being, etc. 動物、生物等) able to understand and learn things 有智力的；有理解和學習能力的：*a search for intelligent life on other planets* 在其他行星上探索有智力的生命 **3** (*computing* 計) (of a computer, program, etc. 計算機、程序等) able to store information and use it in new situations 智能的：***intelligent software/systems*** 智能軟件 / 系統 ▸ **in·tel·li·gent·ly** AW *adv.*

inˌtelligent deˈsign *noun* [U] the belief that the universe and living things were created by an intelligent being 智創論，智能設計論，智慧設計論（相信宇宙及生物是智能創造的結果）：*the legal battle about the teaching of intelligent design as science* 圍繞將智創論作為科學進行教授的法律戰 ➲ compare CREATIONISM

in·tel·li·gent·sia /ɪnˌtelɪˈdʒentsiə/ (usually **the intelligentsia**) *noun* [sing.+sing./pl. v.] the people in a country or society who are well educated and are interested in culture, politics, literature, etc. 知識界；知識階層

in·tel·li·gible /ɪnˈtelɪdʒəbl/ *adj.* **~ (to sb)** that can be easily understood 易懂的；容易理解的 SYN **understandable**：*His lecture was readily intelligible to all the students.* 他的講課學生們都能輕鬆地聽懂。OPP **unintelligible** ▸ **in·tel·li·gi·bil·ity** /ɪnˌtelɪdʒəˈbɪləti/ *noun* [U] **in·tel·li·gibly** *adv.*

in·tem·per·ate /ɪnˈtempərət/ *adj.* (*formal*) **1** showing a lack of control over yourself 放縱的；無節制的：*intemperate language* 過激的言語 OPP **temperate** **2** (*especially NAmE*) regularly drinking too much alcohol 酗酒的 ▸ **in·tem·per·ance** /-pərəns/ *noun* [U]

in·tend 🔑 /ɪnˈtend/ *verb*

> **WORD FAMILY**
> **intend** *verb*
> **intended** *adj.*
> (≠ unintended)
> **intention** *noun*
> **intentional** *adj.*
> (≠ unintentional)
> **intentionally** *adv.*
> (≠ unintentionally)

1 🔑 [I, T] to have a plan, result or purpose in your mind when you do sth 打算；計劃；想要：*We finished later than we had intended.* 我們完成時已超出原定時間。◇ **~ to do sth** *I* ***fully intended*** (= definitely intended) *to pay for the damage.* 我確實誠心想賠償損失。◇ **~ sb/sth to do sth** *The writer clearly intends his readers to identify with the main character.* 作者顯然想使讀者能與主人公產生共鳴。◇ **~ doing sth** (*BrE*) *I don't intend staying long.* 我不打算長期逗留。◇ **~ sth** *The company intends a slow-down in expansion.* 公司準備放慢擴展速度。◇ **~ sb sth** *He intended her no harm* (= it was not his plan to harm her). 他無意傷害她。◇ **it is intended that ...** *It is intended that production will start next month.* 計劃在下個月開始生產。◇ **~ that ...** *We intend that production will start next month.* 我們計劃下個月開始生產。**2** 🔑 [T] (rather *formal*) to plan that sth should have a particular meaning 意指 SYN **mean**：**~ sth (by sth)** *What exactly did you intend by that remark?* 你那句話到底想說什麼？◇ **~ sth (as sth)** *He intended it as a joke.* 他只想開個玩笑。

in·tend·ed 🔑 /ɪnˈtendɪd/ *adj.* **1** 🔑 [only before noun] that you are trying to achieve or reach 意欲達到的；打算的；計劃的：*the intended purpose* 原來的目的 ◇ *the intended audience* 預期的觀眾 ◇ *The bullet missed its intended target.* 子彈未擊中預定的目標。**2** 🔑 planned or designed for sb/sth 為…打算（或設計）的：**~ for sb/sth** *The book is intended for children.* 這本書是為兒童寫的。◇ **~ as sth** *The notes are intended as an introduction to the course.* 這些筆記的目的是作為對這門課程的介紹。◇ **~ to be/do sth** *This list is not intended to be a complete catalogue.* 這張清單並非要做成一張完整的目錄。➲ see also UNINTENDED

in·tense AW /ɪnˈtens/ *adj.* **1** very great; very strong 很大的；十分強烈的 SYN **extreme**：*intense heat/cold/pain* 酷熱；嚴寒；劇痛 ◇ *The President is under intense pressure to resign.* 總統承受着沉重的辭職壓力。◇ *the intense blue of her eyes* 她眼睛的深藍色 ◇ *intense interest/pleasure/desire/anger* 濃厚的興趣；十分快樂；強烈的慾望；極端憤怒 **2** serious and often involving a lot of action in a short period of time 嚴肅緊張的；激烈的：*intense competition* 激烈的競爭 ◇ *It was a period of intense activity.* 那是活動激烈的時期。**3** (of a person 人) having or showing very strong feelings, opinions or thoughts about sb/sth 有強烈感情（或意見、想法）的；尖銳的；熱切的：*an intense look* 熱切的神情 ◇ *He's very intense about everything.* 他對一切都很熱心。➲ compare INTENSIVE (1), (2) ▸ **in·tense·ly** AW *adv.*：*She disliked him intensely.* 她非常討厭他。

in·ten·si·fier /ɪnˈtensɪfaɪə(r)/ *noun* (*grammar* 語法) a word, especially an adjective or an adverb, for example *so* or *very*, that makes the meaning of another word stronger 強調成分，強化詞（尤指形容詞或副詞，如 so 或 very）

in·ten·sify AW /ɪnˈtensɪfaɪ/ *verb* (**in·ten·si·fies**, **in·ten·si·fy·ing**, **in·ten·si·fied**, **in·ten·si·fied**) [I, T] to increase in degree or strength; to make sth increase in degree or strength （使）加強，增強，加劇 SYN **heighten**：*Violence intensified during the night.* 在夜間暴力活動加劇了。◇ **~ sth** *The opposition leader has intensified his attacks on the government.* 反對派領袖加強了對政府的攻擊。▸ **in·tensi·fi·ca·tion** AW /ɪnˌtensɪfɪˈkeɪʃn/ *noun* [U, sing.]

in·ten·sity AW /ɪnˈtensəti/ *noun* (*pl.* **-ies**) **1** [U, sing.] the state or quality of being intense 強烈；緊張；劇烈：*intensity of light/sound/colour* 光 / 聲音 / 色彩的強度 ◇ *intensity of feeling/concentration/relief* 感情的強烈；高度精神集中；大為寬慰 ◇ *He was watching her with an intensity that was unnerving.* 他用一種令她心慌的專注神情看着她。◇ *The storm resumed with even greater intensity.* 風暴更猛烈地再度肆虐。**2** [U, C] (*technical* 術語) the strength of sth, for example light, that can be measured 強度；烈度：*varying intensities of natural light* 自然光不斷變化的強度

in·ten·sive AW /ɪnˈtensɪv/ *adj.* **1** involving a lot of work or activity done in a short time 短時間內集中緊張進行的；密集的：*an intensive language course* 速成語言課程 ◇ *two weeks of intensive training* 兩週的強化訓練 ◇ *intensive diplomatic negotiations* 緊張的外交談判 **2** extremely thorough; done with a lot of care 徹底的；十分細緻的：*His disappearance has been the subject of intensive investigation.* 他的失踪一直是大力調查的重點。**3** (of methods of farming 農業方法) aimed at producing as much food as possible using as little land or as little money as possible 集約的：*Traditionally reared animals grow more slowly than those reared under intensive farming conditions.* 按傳統方式飼養的家畜比集約飼養的長得慢。◇ *intensive agriculture* 集約農業 ➲ see also CAPITAL-INTENSIVE, LABOUR-INTENSIVE ▸ **in·ten·sive·ly**

I

AW *adv.*：*This case has been intensively studied.* 這一案件已經過深入研究。◇ *intensively farmed land* 集約耕作的農田

in,tensive 'care *noun* [U] **1** continuous care and attention, often using special equipment, for people in hospital who are very seriously ill or injured （醫院裏的）特別護理；重症監護；深切治療：*She needed intensive care for several days.* 她需要幾天的特別護理。◇ *intensive care patients/beds* 特別護理病房的病人／牀位 **2** (also **in,tensive 'care unit** [C]) (*abbr.* **ICU**) the part of a hospital that provides intensive care 特別護理病房；重症監護室；加護病房；深切治療部：*The baby was **in intensive care** for 48 hours.* 嬰兒在加護病房看護了 48 小時。

in·tent /ɪn'tent/ *adj., noun*

■ ***adj.*** **1** showing strong interest and attention 熱切的；專注的：*an **intent gaze/look*** 專注的目光／神情 ◇ *His eyes were suddenly intent.* 他的目光突然專注起來。 **2** (*formal*) determined to do sth, especially sth that will harm other people 決心做（尤指傷害他人的事）：**~ on/upon sth** *They were intent on murder.* 他們存心謀殺。◇ **~ on/upon doing sth** *Are you intent upon destroying my reputation?* 你是不是存心要敗壞我的名譽？ **3 ~ on/upon sth** giving all your attention to sth 專心；專注：*I was so intent on my work that I didn't notice the time.* 我專心工作，以致忘了時間。 ▸ **in·tent·ly** *adv.*：*She looked at him intently.* 她目不轉睛地看着他。

■ ***noun*** [U] **~ (to do sth)** (*formal* or *law* 律) what you intend to do 意圖；意向；目的 **SYN** **intention**：*She denies possessing the drug with intent to supply.* 她否認擁有毒品是為了提供給別人。◇ *a **letter/statement of intent*** 意向書 ◇ *His intent is clearly not to placate his critics.* 他的目的顯然不是要安撫批評他的人。

IDM **to all intents and 'purposes** (*BrE*) (*NAmE* **for all intents and 'purposes**) in the effects that sth has, if not in reality; almost completely 幾乎完全；差不多等於：*By 1981 the docks had, to all intents and purposes, closed.* 到 1981 年，這些碼頭幾乎等於關閉了。◇ *The two items are, to all intents and purposes, identical.* 這兩件物品幾乎完全一樣。

in·ten·tion 🔑 /ɪn'tenʃn/ *noun* [C, U] what you intend or plan to do; your aim 打算；計劃；意圖；目的：**~ (of doing sth)** *I have **no intention** of going to the wedding.* 我無意去參加婚禮。◇ *He left England **with the intention of** travelling in Africa.* 他離開英國，打算去非洲旅行。◇ *I **have every intention** of paying her back what I owe her.* 我一心想把我欠她的還給她。◇ **~ (to do sth)** *He has announced his intention to retire.* 他已經宣佈他打算退休。◇ **~ (that ...)** *It was not my intention that she should suffer.* 我沒有要她吃苦頭的意思。◇ *The original intention was to devote three months to the project.* 最初的計劃是在這個項目上投入三個月的時間。◇ *She's full of **good intentions** but they rarely work out.* 她雖然處處出於善意，卻很少成功。◇ *I did it **with the best (of) intentions*** (= meaning to help), *but I only succeeded in annoying them.* 我的原意是要幫忙，卻惹得他們生氣了。 ➲ SYNONYMS at PURPOSE ➲ see also WELL INTENTIONED **IDM** see ROAD

in·ten·tion·al /ɪn'tenʃənl/ *adj.* done deliberately 故意的；有意的；存心的 **SYN** **deliberate, intended**：*I'm sorry I left you off the list—it wasn't intentional.* 很抱歉沒把你列入名單，我不是有意的。 **OPP** **unintentional** ▸ **in·ten·tion·al·ly** /-ʃənəli/ *adv.*：*She would never intentionally hurt anyone.* 她從來不會故意傷害任何人。◇ *I kept my statement intentionally vague.* 我故意含糊其詞。

inter /ɪn'tɜː(r)/ *verb* (**-rr-**) [usually passive] **~ sb** (*formal*) to bury a dead person 埋葬（遺體） **OPP** **disinter** ➲ see also INTERMENT

inter- /'ɪntə(r)/ *prefix* (in verbs, nouns, adjectives and adverbs 構成動詞、名詞、形容詞和副詞) between; from one to another 在…之間；從此到彼；相互：*interface* 界面 ◇ *interaction* 相互作用 ◇ *international* 國際的 ➲ compare INTRA-

inter·act **AW** /,ɪntər'ækt/ *verb* **1** [I] **~ (with sb)** to communicate with sb, especially while you work, play or spend time with them 交流；溝通；合作：*Teachers have a limited amount of time to interact with each child.* 教師和每個孩子溝通的時間有限。 **2** [I] **~ (with sth)** if one thing **interacts** with another, or if two things **interact**, the two things have an effect on each other 相互影響；相互作用：*Perfume interacts with the skin's natural chemicals.* 香水和皮膚的天然化學物質相互作用。 ▸ **inter·action** **AW** /-'ækʃn/ *noun* [U, C]：**~ (between sb/sth)** *the interaction between performers and their audience* 演員和觀眾之間的互動 ◇ **~ (with sb/sth)** *the interaction of bacteria with the body's natural chemistry* 細菌和身體的天然化學變化的相互作用

inter·active **AW** /,ɪntər'æktɪv/ *adj.* **1** that involves people working together and having an influence on each other 合作的；相互影響的；互相配合的：*The school believes in interactive teaching methods.* 這所學校推崇互動教學法。 **2** (*computing* 計) that allows information to be passed continuously and in both directions between a computer and the person who uses it 交互式的；人機對話的；互動的：***interactive systems/video*** 交互式系統／視頻 ◇ *an **interactive whiteboard*** 交互式電子白板 ➲ VISUAL VOCAB page V70 ▸ **inter·active·ly** **AW** *adv.* **inter·activ·ity** /,ɪntəræk'tɪvəti/ *noun* [U]

inter alia /,ɪntər 'eɪliə/ *adv.* (from *Latin, formal*) among other things 除了其他事物之外

inter·breed /,ɪntə'briːd; *NAmE* -tər'b-/ *verb* [I, T] **~ (sth) (with sth)** if animals from different SPECIES **interbreed**, or sb **interbreeds** them, they produce young together （使）雜交繁殖

inter·cede /,ɪntə'siːd; *NAmE* -tər's-/ *verb* [I] **~ (with sb) (for/on behalf of sb)** (*formal*) to speak to sb in order to persuade them to have pity on sb else or to help settle an argument （為某人）說情；（向某人）求情 **SYN** **intervene**：*They interceded with the authorities on behalf of the detainees.* 他們為被拘留者向當局求情。 ▸ **inter·ces·sion** /,ɪntə'seʃn; *NAmE* -tər's-/ *noun* [U]：*the intercession of a priest* 神父的代禱

inter·cept /,ɪntə'sept; *NAmE* -tər's-/ *verb* **~ sb/sth** to stop sb/sth that is going from one place to another from arriving 攔截；攔阻；截住：*Reporters intercepted him as he tried to leave the hotel.* 他正要離開旅館，記者們把他攔截住了。◇ *The letter was intercepted.* 信被截查了。 ▸ **inter·cep·tion** /,ɪntə'sepʃn; *NAmE* -tər's-/ *noun* [U, C]：*the interception of enemy radio signals* 偵聽敵方無線電信號

inter·cept·or /,ɪntə'septə(r); *NAmE* -tər's-/ *noun* a fast military plane that attacks enemy planes that are carrying bombs 截擊機

inter·change *noun, verb*

■ ***noun*** /'ɪntətʃeɪndʒ; *NAmE* -tərtʃ-/ **1** [C, U] the act of sharing or exchanging sth, especially ideas or information （思想、信息等的）交換，互換：*a continuous interchange of ideas* 不斷的思想交流 ◇ *electronic data interchange* 電子數據交換 **2** [C] a place where a road joins a major road such as a MOTORWAY or INTERSTATE, designed so that vehicles leaving or joining the road do not have to cross other lines of traffic （進出高速公路的）互通式立交，立體交叉道

■ ***verb*** /,ɪntə'tʃeɪndʒ; *NAmE* -tər'tʃ-/ **1** [T] **~ sth** to share or exchange ideas, information, etc. 交換，互換（思想、信息等） **2** [T, I] to put each of two things or people in the other's place; to move or be moved from one place to another in this way 將…交換；（使）互換位置：**~ A and B** *to interchange the front and rear tyres of a car* 將汽車的前後輪胎對調 ◇ **~ (A) (with B)** *to interchange the front tyres with the rear ones* 將前後輪胎對調 ◇ *The front and rear tyres interchange* (= can be exchanged). 前後輪胎可互換。

inter·change·able /,ɪntə'tʃeɪndʒəbl; *NAmE* -tər'tʃ-/ *adj.* that can be exchanged, especially without affecting the way in which sth works 可交換的；可互換的；可交替的：*The two words are virtually interchangeable* (= have almost the same meaning). 這兩個詞大體上可以交換使用。◇ **~ with sth** *The V8 engines are all interchangeable with each other.* * V8 型的發動機都可以相互替換。 ▸ **inter·change·abil·ity** /,ɪntə,tʃeɪndʒə'bɪləti; *NAmE* -tər,tʃ-/ *noun* [U] **inter·change·ably** *adv.*：*These terms are used interchangeably.* 這些詞語互換着使用。

inter·city /ˌɪntəˈsɪti; *NAmE* -tərˈs-/ *adj.* [usually before noun] (of transport 交通運輸) travelling between cities, usually with not many stops on the way 城市間的，城際的（通常中途停站不多）：*an intercity rail service* 一趟城際火車班次 ◇ *intercity travel* 市際旅行

inter·col·le·gi·ate /ˌɪntəkəˈliːdʒiət; *NAmE* ˌɪntərkə-/ *adj.* (*especially NAmE*) involving competition between colleges 學院之間（競賽）的；（大學）校際的：*intercollegiate football* 大學校際足球賽

inter·com /ˈɪntəkɒm; *NAmE* ˈɪntərkɑːm/ *noun* a system of communication by telephone or radio inside an office, plane, etc.; the device you press or switch on to start using this system 內部通話系統（或設備）：*to announce sth **over the intercom*** 通過內部通話系統宣佈 ◇ *They called him on the intercom.* 他們用內部通話系統呼叫他。

inter·com·mu·ni·ca·tion /ˌɪntəkəˌmjuːnɪˈkeɪʃn; *NAmE* -tərkə-/ *noun* [U] the process of communicating between people or groups 相互交流；相互通信；相互溝通

inter·con·nect /ˌɪntəkəˈnekt; *NAmE* -tərkə-/ *verb* [T, I] to connect similar things; to be connected to or with similar things（使類似的事物）相聯繫，相互聯繫，相互連接：**~ A with B** *Bad housing is interconnected with debt and poverty.* 住房條件差與負債以及貧困相關聯。◇ **~ A and B** *Bad housing, debt and poverty are interconnected.* 惡劣的住房條件、負債以及貧困是相互關聯的。◇ **~ (with sth)** *separate bedrooms that interconnect* 相通的獨立臥室 ▸ **inter·con·nec·tion** /-ˈnekʃn/ *noun* [C, U]：*interconnections between different parts of the brain* 大腦各部份間的相互聯繫

inter·con·tin·en·tal /ˌɪntəˌkɒntɪˈnentl; *NAmE* ˌɪntərˌkɑːn-/ *adj.* [usually before noun] between continents 洲際的；洲與洲之間的：***intercontinental flights/missiles/travel/trade*** 洲際航班／導彈／旅行／貿易

inter·cos·tal /ˌɪntəˈkɒstl; *NAmE* ˌɪntərˈkɑːstl/ *adj.* (*anatomy* 解) located between the RIBS (= the curved bones that go around the chest) 肋間的：*intercostal muscles* 肋間肌

inter·course /ˈɪntəkɔːs; *NAmE* ˈɪntərkɔːrs/ *noun* [U] **1** = SEXUAL INTERCOURSE：*The prosecution stated that intercourse had occurred on several occasions.* 控方稱發生過數次性行為。◇ *anal intercourse* 肛門交媾 **2** (*old-fashioned*) communication between people, countries, etc.（人、國家之間的）往來，交往，交際：*the importance of social intercourse between different age groups* 不同年齡段的人之間交往的重要性

inter·cul·tural /ˌɪntəˈkʌltʃərəl; *NAmE* ˌɪntər-/ *adj.* existing or happening between different cultures 跨文化的；各文化之間的

inter·cut /ˌɪntəˈkʌt; *NAmE* ˌɪntər-/ *verb* (**inter·cut·ting, inter·cut, inter·cut**) **~ sth (with sth)** (*technical* 術語) to put a film/movie scene between two parts of a different scene 使鏡頭交切：*Scenes of city life were intercut with interviews with local people.* 城市生活的鏡頭與訪問當地人的畫面相互交切。

inter·de·nom·in·ation·al /ˌɪntədɪˌnɒmɪˈneɪʃənl; *NAmE* ˌɪntərdɪˌnɑːm-/ *adj.* shared by different religious groups (= different DENOMINATIONS) 各教派間共有的

inter·de·part·men·tal /ˌɪntəˌdiːpɑːtˈmentl; *NAmE* ˌɪntərˌdiːpɑːrt-/ *adj.* between departments; involving more than one department 各部門（或系）間的；多個部門（或系）的

inter·de·pend·ent /ˌɪntədɪˈpendənt; *NAmE* -tərdɪ-/ *adj.* that depend on each other; consisting of parts that depend on each other（各部份）相互依存的，相互依賴的：*interdependent economies/organizations/relationships* 相互依賴的經濟體系／機構／關係 ◇ *The world is becoming increasingly interdependent.* 世界正變得越來越需要相互依存。▸ **inter·de·pend·ence** /-əns/ (also *less frequent* **inter·de·pend·ency** *pl.* **-ies**) *noun* [U, C]

inter·dict /ˈɪntədɪkt; *NAmE* ˈɪntərd-/ *noun* **1** (*law* 律) an official order from a court that orders you not to do sth（法庭的）禁令 **2** (*technical* 術語) (in the Roman Catholic Church 羅馬天主教) an order banning sb from taking part in church services, etc. 禁罰；禁行聖事令

inter·dic·tion /ˌɪntəˈdɪkʃn; *NAmE* -tərˈd-/ *noun* [U] (*formal, especially NAmE*) the act of stopping sth that is being transported from one place from reaching another place, especially by using force（強制）禁運，封鎖，阻斷：*the Customs Service's drug interdiction programs* 海關的毒品查禁方案

inter·dis·cip·lin·ary /ˌɪntəˈdɪsəplɪnəri; *NAmE* ˌɪntərˈdɪsəplɪneri/ *adj.* involving different areas of knowledge or study 多學科的；跨學科的：*interdisciplinary research* 跨學科研究 ◇ *an interdisciplinary approach* 跨學科方法

inter·est 0-w /ˈɪntrəst; -trest/ *noun, verb*

■ ***noun***

▸ **WANTING TO KNOW MORE** 求知 **1** 0-w [sing., U] **~ (in sb/sth)** the feeling that you have when you want to know or learn more about sb/sth 興趣；關注：*to **feel/have/show/express** (an) **interest** in sth* 對…感到／表現出／表示關注 ◇ *Do your parents **take an interest in** your friends?* 你的父母有興趣瞭解你的朋友嗎？◇ *By that time I had **lost** (**all**) **interest** in the idea.* 那時我已經對此想法（完全）失去興趣了。◇ *I watched **with interest**.* 我興致勃勃地看着。◇ ***As a matter of interest*** (= I'd like to know), *what time did the party finish?* 我想知道，晚會是什麼時間結束的？◇ ***Just out of interest**, how much did it cost?* 我只是好奇問問，這個花了多少錢？➲ compare DISINTEREST

▸ **ATTRACTION** 吸引力 **2** 0-w [U] the quality that sth has when it attracts sb's attention or makes them want to know more about it 引人關注的性質；吸引力；趣味：*There are many **places of interest** near the city.* 這座城市附近有許多有意思的地方。◇ *The subject **is of no interest** to me at all.* 我對此課題一點也不感興趣。◇ *These plants will add interest to your garden in winter.* 這些植物在冬季會給你的花園增添勝景。◇ *These documents are of great historical interest.* 這些文件具有重要的歷史價值。◇ *to be of cultural/scientific interest* 具有文化／科學價值 ➲ see also HUMAN INTEREST, LOVE INTEREST

▸ **HOBBY** 業餘愛好 **3** 0-w [C] an activity or a subject that you enjoy and that you spend your free time doing or studying 業餘愛好：*Her main interests are music and tennis.* 她的主要愛好是音樂和網球。◇ *He was a man of wide interests outside his work.* 他是個有廣泛業餘愛好的人。➲ compare HOBBY

▸ **MONEY** 錢 **4** 0-w [U] **~ (on sth)** (*finance* 財) the extra money that you pay back when you borrow money or that you receive when you invest money 利息：*to **pay interest** on a loan* 付貸款利息 ◇ *The money was repaid **with interest**.* 這筆錢是帶息償還的。◇ ***interest charges/payments*** 利息；利息的支付 ◇ ***Interest rates** have risen by 1%.* 利率上升了 1%。◇ *high **rates of interest*** 高利率 ➲ see also COMPOUND INTEREST, SIMPLE INTEREST

▸ **ADVANTAGE** 利益 **5** [C, usually pl., U] a good result or an advantage for sb/sth 好處；利益：*to **promote/protect/safeguard** sb's **interests*** 提高／保護／維護某人的利益 ◇ *She was acting entirely **in her own interests**.* 她所做的完全是為了自己的好處。◇ *These reforms were **in the best interests of** local government.* 這些改革對地方政府最有利。◇ *It is **in the public interest** that these facts are made known.* 公開這些真相是為了公眾的利益。➲ see also SELF-INTEREST

▸ **SHARE IN BUSINESS** 企業股份 **6** [C, usually pl.] **~ (in sth)** a share in a business or company and its profits（企業或公司的）股份；權益；股權：*She has business interests in France.* 她在法國擁有企業權益。◇ *American interests in Europe* (= money invested in European countries) 在歐洲的美國權益 ➲ see also CONTROLLING INTEREST

▸ **CONNECTION** 關係 **7** [C, U] **~ (in sth)** a connection with sth which affects your attitude to it, especially because you may benefit from it in some way 利害關係；利益關係：*I should, at this point, **declare my interest**.* 到了這個時候，我應該申明我的利益關係。◇ *Organizations **have an interest in** ensuring that employee motivation is high.* 各機構皆知獲利之道在於確保員工士氣高昂。➲ compare DISINTEREST ➲ see also VESTED INTEREST

▸ **GROUP OF PEOPLE** 團體 **8** [C, usually pl.] a group of people who are in the same business or who share the same aims which they want to protect 同行；同業；利害與共

者；利益團體：*powerful farming interests* 強大的農民團體 ◇ *relationships between local government and business interests* 地方政府和企業團體之間的關係

IDM **do sth (back) with interest** to do the same thing to sb as they have done to you, but with more force, enthusiasm, etc. 加倍回報（或回擊等） **have sb's interests at 'heart** to want sb to be happy and successful even though your actions may not show this 關心…的幸福成功；暗暗地替…着想 **in the interest(s) of sth** in order to help or achieve sth 為了；為幫助（或取得）：*In the interest(s) of safety, smoking is forbidden.* 禁止吸煙，以策安全。 ➲ more at CONFLICT *n.*

■ ***verb*** to attract your attention and make you feel interested; to make yourself give your attention to sth 使感興趣；使關注：**~ sb** *Politics doesn't interest me.* 我對政治不感興趣。 ◇ **~ sb/yourself in sth** *She has always interested herself in charity work.* 她始終關注慈善工作。 ◇ **it interests sb to do sth** *It may interest you to know that Andy didn't accept the job.* 或許你有興趣知道，安迪沒有接受這份工作。

PHR V **'interest sb in sth** to persuade sb to buy, do or eat sth 勸說某人買（或做、吃）：*Could I interest you in this model, Sir?* 先生，請你瞧瞧這個型號好嗎？

Synonyms 同義詞辨析

interest

hobby • game • pastime

These are all words for activities that you do for pleasure in your spare time. 以上各詞均指業餘消遣、閒暇活動。

interest an activity or a subject that you do or study for pleasure in your spare time 指業餘愛好（活動或科目）：*Her main interests are music and gardening.* 她的主要愛好是音樂和園藝。

hobby an activity that you do for pleasure in your spare time 指業餘愛好（活動）：*His hobbies include swimming and cooking.* 他愛好游泳和烹飪。

game a children's activity when they play with toys, pretend to be sb else, etc.; an activity that you do to have fun 指兒童遊戲、玩耍、娛樂：*a game of cops and robbers* 警察抓強盜的遊戲 ◇ *He was playing games with the dog.* 他在逗狗玩。

pastime an activity that people do for pleasure in their spare time 指消遣、休閒活動：*Eating out is the national pastime in France.* 在法國，上館子是全國人普遍的消遣活動。

INTEREST, HOBBY OR PASTIME? 用 interest、hobby 還是 pastime？

A **hobby** is often more active than an **interest**. * hobby 常較 interest 主動、積極：*His main hobby is football* (= he plays football). 他的主要業餘愛好是踢足球（他踢足球）。 ◇ *His main interest is football* (= he watches and reads about football, and may or may not play it). 他的主要業餘愛好是足球（他看足球賽和閱讀有關足球的消息，但不一定踢足球）。**Pastime** is used when talking about people in general; when you are talking about yourself or an individual person it is more usual to use **interest** or **hobby**. * pastime 泛指一般人的消遣活動，指自己或個人的業餘愛好較常用 interest 或 hobby：~~*Eating out is the national interest/hobby in France.*~~ ◇ ~~*Do you have any pastimes?*~~

PATTERNS

- a **popular** interest/hobby/pastime
- to **have/share** interests/hobbies
- to **take up/pursue** a(n) interest/hobby

inter·est·ed /ˈɪntrəstɪd; -trest-/ *adj.*

1 giving your attention to sth because you enjoy finding out about it or doing it; showing interest in sth and finding it exciting 感興趣的；關心的；表現出興趣的：**~ (in sth/sb)** *I'm very interested in history.* 我很喜歡歷史。 ◇ **~ (in doing sth)** *Anyone interested in joining the club should contact us at the address below.* 有意加入俱樂部者請按下面的地址和我們聯繫。 ◇ **~ (to do sth)** *We would be interested to hear your views on this subject.* 我們很想聽聽你對這個課題的看法。 ◇ *an interested audience* 興致勃勃的觀眾 ◇ *There's a talk on Italian art—are you interested* (= would you like to go)? 有個關於意大利藝術的演講 —— 你想去聽嗎？ ◇ *He sounded genuinely interested.* 聽他的口氣，他真的感興趣。 **2** in a position to gain from a situation or be affected by it 有利害關係的；當事人的：*As an **interested party**, I was not allowed to vote.* 作為有利害關係的一方，我不得投票。 ◇ *Interested groups will be given three months to give their views on the new development.* 有關團體將有三個月的時間提出他們對新開發項目的看法。

Which Word? 詞語辨析

interested / interesting / uninterested / disinterested / uninteresting

- The opposite of **interested** is **uninterested** or **not interested**. * interested 的反義詞為 uninterested 或 not interested：*He is completely uninterested in politics.* 他對政治毫無興趣。 ◇ *I am not really interested in politics.* 我並不真正熱衷於政治。
- **Disinterested** means that you can be fair in judging a situation because you do not feel personally involved in it. * disinterested 意為不涉及個人利害關係、公正無私、不偏不倚：*A solicitor can give you disinterested advice.* 律師可給你公正的忠告。However, in speech it is sometimes used instead of **uninterested**, although this is thought to be incorrect. 不過，在口語中有時用此詞代替 uninterested，但一般認為此用法不正確。
- The opposite of **interesting** can be **uninteresting**. * interesting 的反義詞可以是 uninteresting：*The food was dull and uninteresting.* 食物單調無味。It is more common to use a different word such as **dull** or **boring**. 用其他詞如 dull 或 boring 則更普遍。

ˌinterest-ˈfree *adj.* with no interest charged on money borrowed 免息的；不收取利息的：*an interest-free loan* 免息貸款 ◇ *interest-free credit* 免息信貸

ˈinterest group *noun* a group of people who work together to achieve sth that they are particularly interested in, especially by putting pressure on the government, etc.（尤指給政府施加壓力等的）利益集團，利益團體：*a special interest group of US lumber producers* 美國木材生產商特殊利益集團 ➲ compare ADVOCACY GROUP, PRESSURE GROUP

inter·est·ing /ˈɪntrəstɪŋ; -trest-/ *adj.*

attracting your attention because it is special, exciting or unusual 有趣的；有吸引力的：*an interesting question/point/example* 耐人尋味的問題／論點／例子 ◇ *interesting people/places/work* 有趣的人／地方／工作 ◇ **~ (to do sth)** *It would be interesting to know what he really believed.* 瞭解他的真實信仰會很有意思。 ◇ *It is particularly interesting to compare the two versions.* 把兩個版本加以比較特別耐人尋味。 ◇ **~ (that ...)** *I find it interesting that she claims not to know him.* 她聲稱不認識他，我覺得真是耐人尋味。 ◇ *Can't we do something more interesting?* 我們就不能做點更有意義的事情嗎？ ◇ *Her account makes interesting reading.* 她的敍述讀起來趣味橫生。 ▸ **inter·est·ing·ly** *adv.*：*Interestingly, there are very few recorded cases of such attacks.* 有意思的是，記錄在案的此類襲擊事件很少。 ➲ LANGUAGE BANK at SURPRISING

inter·face /ˈɪntəfeɪs; *NAmE* -tərf-/ *noun, verb*

■ ***noun*** **1** (*computing* 計) the way a computer program presents information to a user or receives information from a user, in particular the LAYOUT of the screen and the menus（人機）界面（尤指屏幕佈局和選單）：*the user interface* 用戶界面 **2** (*computing* 計) an electrical CIRCUIT, connection or program that joins one device or system to another 接口；接口程序；連接電路：*the* *interface between computer and printer* 計算機和打印機之間的接口 **3 ~ (between A and B)** the point where two subjects, systems, etc. meet and affect each other（兩學科、體系等的）接合點，邊緣區域：*the interface between manufacturing and sales* 製造和銷售之間的銜接

■ ***verb*** [I, T] **~ (sth) (with sth) | ~ A and B** (*computing* 計) to be connected with sth using an interface; to connect sth in this way（使通過界面或接口）接合，連接：*The new system interfaces with existing telephone equipment.* 新系統與現有的電話設備相連接。

inter·faith /ˈɪntəfeɪθ; *NAmE* -tərf-/ *adj.* [only before noun] between or connected with people of different religions 不同宗教信仰者（間）的；不同宗教團體（間）的：*an interfaith memorial service* 不同宗教團體參加的追悼儀式

inter·fere /ˌɪntəˈfɪə(r); *NAmE* ˌɪntərˈfɪr/ *verb* [I] to get involved in and try to influence a situation that does not concern you, in a way that annoys other people 干涉；干預；介入：*I wish my mother would stop interfering and let me make my own decisions.* 我希望我母親不再干預，讓我自己拿主意。◇ **~ in sth** *The police are very unwilling to interfere in family problems.* 警方很不情願插手家庭問題。

PHR V **interˈfere with sb 1** to illegally try to influence sb who is going to give evidence in court, for example by threatening them or offering them money 干擾證人（企圖威脅或賄賂等）**2** (*BrE*) to touch a child in a sexual way（觸摸兒童）意圖性侵犯 **interˈfere with sth 1** to prevent sth from succeeding or from being done or happening as planned 妨礙；干擾：*She never allows her personal feelings to interfere with her work.* 她從不讓她的個人感情妨礙工作。**2** to touch, use or change sth, especially a piece of equipment, so that it is damaged or no longer works correctly 弄壞（器材等）：*I'd get fired if he found out I'd been interfering with his records.* 要是他發現我把他的唱片搗鼓壞了，我就得被解雇了。

inter·fer·ence /ˌɪntəˈfɪərəns; *NAmE* -tərˈfɪr-/ *noun* [U] **1 ~ (in sth)** the act of interfering 干涉；干預；介入：*They resent foreign interference in the internal affairs of their country.* 他們憎惡對他們國家內政的外來干涉。**2** interruption of a radio signal by another signal on a similar WAVELENGTH, causing extra noise that is not wanted（無線電信號的）干擾

IDM **run interference** (*NAmE*) **1** (in AMERICAN FOOTBALL 美式足球) to clear the way for the player with the ball by blocking players from the opposing team 掩護阻擋（為己方持球隊員讓出道路）**2** (*informal*) to help sb by dealing with problems for them so that they do not need to deal with them（為幫助某人）積極介入

inter·fer·ing /ˌɪntəˈfɪərɪŋ; *NAmE* -tərˈfɪr-/ *adj.* [usually before noun] (*disapproving*) involving yourself in an annoying way in other people's private lives 干涉他人私生活的；管閒事的：*She's an interfering busybody!* 她是個好管閒事的人！

inter·feron /ˌɪntəˈfɪərɒn; *NAmE* ˌɪntərˈfɪrɑːn/ *noun* [U] (*biology* 生) a substance produced by the body to prevent harmful viruses from causing disease 干擾素

inter·gal·act·ic /ˌɪntəɡəˈlæktɪk; *NAmE* -tərɡə-/ *adj.* [only before noun] existing or happening between GALAXIES of stars 星系際的：*intergalactic space/travel* 星系際空間／航行

inter·gov·ern·men·tal /ˌɪntəˌɡʌvənˈmentl; *NAmE* ˌɪntərˌɡʌvərn-/ *adj.* [only before noun] concerning the governments of two or more countries 政府間的：*an intergovernmental conference* 政府對政府的會議

in·terim /ˈɪntərɪm/ *adj., noun*

■ ***adj.*** [only before noun] **1** intended to last for only a short time until sb/sth more permanent is found 暫時的；過渡的：*an interim government/measure/report* 過渡政府；臨時措施／報告 ◇ *The vice-president took power in the* ***interim period*** *before the election.* 在大選之前的過渡階段由副總統執政。**2** (*finance* 財) calculated before the final results of sth are known 期中的 SYN **provisional**：***interim figures/profits/results*** 期中數字／利潤／結果

■ ***noun***

IDM **in the interim** during the period of time between two events; until a particular event happens 在其間；在其前：*Despite everything that had happened in the interim, they had remained good friends.* 不管在此間所發生的一切，他們還是好朋友。◇ *Her new job does not start until May and she will continue in the old job in the interim.* 她的新工作要到五月份才開始，在這期間她將繼續原有的工作。

in·ter·ior 🔑 /ɪnˈtɪəriə(r); *NAmE* -ˈtɪr-/ *noun, adj.*

■ ***noun* 1** 🔑 [C, usually sing.] the inside part of sth 內部；裏面：*the interior of a building/a car* 樓房／汽車的內部 OPP **exterior 2 the interior** [sing.] the central part of a country or continent that is a long way from the coast 內陸；內地；腹地：*an expedition into the interior of Australia* 深入澳大利亞腹地的探險 **3 the Interior** [sing.] a country's own affairs rather than those that involve other countries（國家的）內政，內務：*the* ***Department/Minister of the Interior*** 內政部／大臣

■ ***adj.*** 🔑 [only before noun] connected with the inside part of sth 內部的；裏面的：*interior walls* 內牆 OPP **exterior**

inˌterior ˈdecorator *noun* a person whose job is to design and/or decorate a room or the inside of a house, etc. with paint, paper, carpets, etc. 室內裝飾設計師；室內設計裝潢商（或裝潢工）▶ **inˌterior decoˈration** *noun* [U]：*an interior decoration scheme* 室內裝飾設計

inˌterior deˈsign *noun* [U] the art or job of choosing the paint, carpets, furniture, etc. to decorate the inside of a house 室內設計 ▶ **inˌterior deˈsigner** *noun*

I

Synonyms 同義詞辨析

interesting

fascinating • compelling • stimulating • gripping • absorbing

These words all describe sb/sth that attracts or holds your attention because they are exciting, unusual or full of good ideas. 以上各詞均形容人或事物有吸引力、有趣味。

interesting attracting your attention because it is exciting, unusual or full of good ideas 指有趣的、有吸引力的：*That's an interesting question, Daniel.* 那是個有趣的問題，丹尼爾。

fascinating extremely interesting or attractive 指極有吸引力的、迷人的：*The exhibition tells the fascinating story of the steam age.* 展覽講述了蒸汽時代引人入勝的故事。

compelling (*rather formal*) so interesting or exciting that it holds your attention 指引人入勝的、扣人心弦的：*Her latest book makes compelling reading.* 她新出的書讀起來扣人心弦。

stimulating full of interesting or exciting ideas; making people feel enthusiastic 指趣味盎然的、激勵人的、振奮人心的：*Thank you for a most stimulating discussion.* 感謝你們妙趣橫生的討論。

gripping so exciting or interesting that it holds your attention completely 指激動人心的、吸引人的、扣人心弦的：*His books are always so gripping.* 他的書總是那麼扣人心弦。

absorbing so interesting or enjoyable that it holds your attention 指十分吸引人的、引人入勝的、精彩的：*Chess can be an extremely absorbing game.* 國際象棋有時就是一場引人入勝的遊戲。

PATTERNS

- interesting/fascinating/stimulating **for** sb
- interesting/fascinating **to** sb
- interesting/fascinating **that** …
- interesting/fascinating **to see/hear/find/learn/know** …
- a(n) interesting/fascinating/compelling/gripping **story/read/book**
- a(n) interesting/fascinating/stimulating **experience/discussion/idea**
- **to find sth** interesting/fascinating/compelling/stimulating/gripping/absorbing

in,terior 'monologue *noun* (in literature 文學) a piece of writing that expresses a character's inner thoughts and feelings 內心獨白

inter·ject /ˌɪntəˈdʒekt; *NAmE* -tərˈdʒ-/ *verb* [T, I] **+ speech** | **~ (sth)** (*formal*) to interrupt what sb is saying with your opinion or a remark 打斷（別人的講話）；插話：*'You're wrong,' interjected Susan.* "你錯了。" 蘇珊插嘴說。

inter·jec·tion /ˌɪntəˈdʒekʃn; *NAmE* -tərˈdʒ-/ *noun* (*grammar* 語法) a short sound, word or phrase spoken suddenly to express an emotion. *Oh!*, *Look out!* and *Ow!* are interjections. 感歎詞；感歎語 **SYN exclamation**

inter·lace /ˌɪntəˈleɪs; *NAmE* -tərˈl-/ *verb* [T, I] **~ (sth) (with sth)** (*formal*) to twist things together over and under each other; to be twisted together in this way（使）編結，交錯：*Her hair was interlaced with ribbons and flowers.* 她的頭髮上編紮着緞帶和花。◇ *interlacing branches* 交錯的枝條

inter·lan·guage /ˈɪntəlæŋɡwɪdʒ; *NAmE* -tərl-/ *noun* [U, C] (*linguistics* 語言) a language system produced by sb who is learning a language, which has features of the first language which they are learning and also of their first language 中間語言，中介語言（第二語言學習者在學習過程中形成的語言，具有所學語言和其母語的特徵）

inter·leave /ˌɪntəˈliːv; *NAmE* -tərˈl-/ *verb* **~ sth (with sth)** to put sth, especially thin layers of sth, between things（尤指將片狀物）插入，嵌入

inter·lin·ear /ˌɪntəˈlɪniə(r); *NAmE* -tərˈl-/ *adj.* (*technical* 術語) written or printed between the lines of a text 行間書寫（或印刷）的

inter·lin·gual /ˌɪntəˈlɪŋɡwəl; *NAmE* -tərˈl-/ *adj.* **1** (*linguistics* 語言) using, between, or relating to two different languages 使用兩種語言的；介於兩種語言間的；語際的：*interlingual communication* 語際交流 **2** relating to an INTERLANGUAGE 中間語言的；中介語言的

inter·link /ˌɪntəˈlɪŋk; *NAmE* -tərˈl-/ *verb* [T, usually passive, I] **~ (sth) (with sth)** to connect things; to be connected with other things（使）連接：*The two processes are interlinked.* 這兩個過程是相互連接的。◇ *a series of short interlinking stories* 一系列相互銜接的短篇故事

inter·lock /ˌɪntəˈlɒk; *NAmE* ˌɪntərˈlɑːk/ *verb* [I, T] **~ (sth) (with sth)** to fit or be fastened firmly together（使）連鎖，緊密連接，扣緊：*interlocking shapes/systems/pieces* 緊密相扣的形狀／系統／部件

inter·locu·tor /ˌɪntəˈlɒkjətə(r); *NAmE* ˌɪntərˈlɑːk-/ *noun* (*formal*) **1** a person taking part in a conversation with you 參加談話者；對話者 **2** a person or an organization that talks to another person or organization on behalf of sb else（代表他人的）中間對話者

inter·loper /ˈɪntələʊpə(r); *NAmE* ˈɪntərloʊpər/ *noun* a person who is present in a place or a situation where they do not belong 闖入者；干涉者 **SYN intruder**

inter·lude /ˈɪntəluːd; *NAmE* -tərl-/ *noun* **1** a period of time between two events during which sth different happens（兩事件之間的）間歇；插入事件：*a romantic interlude* (= a short romantic relationship) 短暫的戀愛 ◇ *Apart from a brief interlude of peace, the war lasted nine years.* 除了一段短暫的和平，那場戰爭持續了九年。**2** a short period of time between the parts of a play, film/movie, etc.（戲劇、電影等的）幕間休息：*There will now be a short interlude.* 現在有一段短時間的幕間休息。**3** a short piece of music or a talk, etc. that fills this period of time 幕間樂曲（或節目、表演）：*a musical interlude* 幕間音樂插曲

inter·marry /ˌɪntəˈmæri; *NAmE* -tərˈm-/ *verb* (**inter·mar·ries, inter·marry·ing, inter·mar·ried, inter·mar·ried**) **1** [I] to marry sb of a different race or from a different country or a different religious group 不同種族（或國家、教派）間通婚：*Blacks and whites often intermarried* (= married each other). 黑人和白人時有通婚。◇ **~ with sb** *They were not forbidden to intermarry with the local people.* 他們未被禁止與當地人通婚。**2** [I] to marry sb within your own family or group 近族通婚；近親結婚：*cousins who intermarry* 近親結婚的堂表兄弟姐妹

▸ **inter·mar·riage** /ˌɪntəˈmærɪdʒ/ *noun* [U, C]：*intermarriage between blacks and whites* 黑人和白人之間的通婚

inter·medi·ary /ˌɪntəˈmiːdiəri; *NAmE* ˌɪntərˈmiːdieri/ *noun* (*pl.* **-ies**) **~ (between A and B)** a person or an organization that helps other people or organizations to make an agreement by being a means of communication between them 中間人；調解人 **SYN mediator, go-between**：*Financial institutions act as intermediaries between lenders and borrowers.* 金融機構充當貸方和借方的中間人。◇ *All talks have so far been conducted through an intermediary.* 到目前為止所有的談判都是通過調停人進行的。▸ **inter·medi·ary** *adj.* [only before noun]：*to play an intermediary role in the dispute* 擔任糾紛中的調解人

inter·medi·ate **AW** /ˌɪntəˈmiːdiət; *NAmE* -tərˈm-/ *adj., noun*

■ ***adj.*** **1** [usually before noun] located between two places, things, states, etc.（兩地、兩物、兩種狀態等）之間的，中間的：*an* ***intermediate stage/step*** *in a process* 中間階段／步驟 ◇ **~ between A and B** *Liquid crystals are considered to be intermediate between liquid and solid.* 液晶被認為介於液態和固態之間。**2** having more than a basic knowledge of sth but not yet advanced; suitable for sb who is at this level 中級的；中等的；適合中等程度者的：*an* ***intermediate skier/student, etc.*** 中等程度的滑雪者、學生等 ◇ *an intermediate coursebook* 中級課本 ◇ ***pre-/upper-intermediate*** *classes* 初等／高等中級班

■ ***noun*** a person who is learning sth and who has more than a basic knowledge of it but is not yet advanced 中級學生

intermediate tech'nology *noun* [U] technology that is suitable for use in developing countries as it is cheap and simple and can use local materials 中間技術（因成本低廉、簡便以及可使用當地原料而適用於發展中國家）

in·ter·ment /ɪnˈtɜːmənt; *NAmE* -ˈtɜːrm-/ *noun* [C, U] (*formal*) the act of burying a dead person 埋葬；安葬 **SYN burial** ➲ see also INTER *v.*

inter·mesh /ˌɪntəˈmeʃ; *NAmE* -tərˈm-/ *verb* [I] (of two objects or parts 兩個物體或部份) to fit closely together 互相嚙合；緊密相接：*intermeshing cogs* 相互咬合的輪齒

inter·mezzo /ˌɪntəˈmetsəʊ; *NAmE* ˌɪntərˈmetsoʊ/ *noun* (*pl.* **inter·mezzi** /-ˈmetsiː/ or **inter·mezzos** /-ˈmetsəʊz; *NAmE* -ˈmetsoʊz/) (*music* 音) (from *Italian*) a short piece of music for the ORCHESTRA that is played between two parts in an OPERA or other musical performance 間奏曲，幕間曲（歌劇或其他音樂演出中幕與幕之間的過場音樂）

in·ter·min·able /ɪnˈtɜːmɪnəbl; *NAmE* -ˈtɜːrm-/ *adj.* lasting a very long time and therefore boring or annoying 冗長的；沒完沒了的 **SYN endless**：*an interminable speech/wait/discussion* 無休止的講話／等待／討論 ◇ *The drive seemed interminable.* 這次開車好像沒有盡頭。▸ **in·ter·min·ably** /-əbli/ *adv.*：*The meeting dragged on interminably.* 會議沒完沒了地拖延着。

inter·min·gle /ˌɪntəˈmɪŋɡl; *NAmE* -tərˈm-/ *verb* [T, I] (*formal*) to mix people, ideas, colours, etc. together; to be mixed in this way 使（人、思想、色彩等）混合：**~ A with B** *The book intermingles fact with fiction.* 這本書事實和虛構並存。◇ **~ A and B** *The book intermingles fact and fiction.* 這本書事實和虛構並存。◇ **~ (with sb/sth)** *tourists and local people intermingling in the market square* 聚集在市場廣場上的觀光客和當地人

inter·mis·sion /ˌɪntəˈmɪʃn; *NAmE* -tərˈm-/ *noun* [C, U] **1** (*especially NAmE*) a short period of time between the parts of a play, film/movie, etc.（戲劇、電影等的）幕間休息，中間休息：*Coffee was served during the intermission.* 幕間休息時有咖啡供應。◇ (*NAmE*) *After intermission, the second band played.* 幕間休息後第二支樂隊開始演奏。**HELP** This meaning is only [U] in *NAmE*. 作此義時在美式英語中是不可數的。**2** a period of time during which sth stops before continuing again 間歇；暫停：*This state of affairs lasted without intermission for a hundred years.* 這種局面從未間斷地持續了一百年。

inter·mit·tent /ˌɪntəˈmɪtənt; *NAmE* -tərˈm-/ *adj.* stopping and starting often over a period of time, but not regularly 斷斷續續的；間歇的 **SYN sporadic**：*intermittent bursts of applause* 一陣陣的掌聲 ◇ *intermittent showers*

陣雨 ▸ **inter·mit·tent·ly** *adv.*： *Protests continued intermittently throughout November.* 整個十一月份抗議活動此起彼落。

inter·mix /ˌɪntəˈmɪks; *NAmE* -tərˈm-/ *verb* [T, I] **~ (sth) (with sth)** to mix things together; to be mixed together （使）混合；（使）混雜： *Grass fields were intermixed with areas of woodland.* 草地和林地相互交錯。

in·tern *verb, noun*

■ ***verb*** /ɪnˈtɜːn; *NAmE* ɪnˈtɜːrn/ [often passive] **~ sb (in sth)** to put sb in prison during a war or for political reasons, although they have not been charged with a crime（戰爭期間或由於政治原因未經審訊）拘留，禁閉，關押 ➲ see also INTERNEE ▸ **in·tern·ment** /ɪnˈtɜːnmənt; *NAmE* -ˈtɜːrn-/ *noun* [U]： *the internment of suspected terrorists* 拘留可疑恐怖分子 ◇ *internment camps* 拘留營

■ ***noun*** (also **in·terne**) /ˈɪntɜːn; *NAmE* ˈɪntɜːrn/ (*NAmE*) **1** an advanced student of medicine, whose training is nearly finished and who is working in a hospital to get further practical experience 實習醫生 ➲ compare HOUSE OFFICER **2** a student or new GRADUATE who is getting practical experience in a job, for example during the summer holiday/vacation 實習學生；畢業實習生： *a summer intern at a law firm* 暑假在法律事務所實習的學生 ➲ see also INTERNSHIP

in·tern·al 🔑 **AW** /ɪnˈtɜːnl; *NAmE* ɪnˈtɜːrnl/ *adj.*
1 🔑 [only before noun] connected with the inside of sth 內部的；裏面的： *the internal structure of a building* 大樓的內部結構 ◇ *internal doors* 內門 **OPP** **external** **2** 🔑 [only before noun] connected with the inside of your body 體內的： ***internal organs/injuries*** 內臟；內傷 ◇ *The medicine is not for* ***internal use.*** 這種藥不可內服。 **OPP** **external** **3** 🔑 [usually before noun] involving or concerning only the people who are part of a particular organization rather than people from outside it（機構）內部的： *an internal inquiry* 內部調查 ◇ *the internal workings of government* 政府內部的運作 ◇ *internal divisions within the company* 公司內部的各部門 **OPP** **external** **4** 🔑 [only before noun] connected with a country's own affairs rather than those that involve other countries 內政的；國內的 **SYN** **domestic**： ***internal affairs/trade/markets*** 內政；國內貿易/市場 ◇ *an* ***internal flight*** (= within a country) 國內航班 **OPP** **external** **5** coming from within a thing itself rather than from outside it 本身的；自身的： *a theory which lacks* ***internal consistency*** (= whose parts are not in agreement with each other) 自相矛盾的理論 ◇ *Some photos contain* ***internal evidence*** (= fashions, transport, etc.) *that may help to date them.* 有些照片自身就含有確定拍攝日期的佐證。 **6** happening or existing in your mind 內心的；頭腦中的 **SYN** **inner**： *internal rage* 內心的憤怒 ▸ **in·tern·al·ly** **AW** /-nəli/ *adv.*： *internally connected rooms* 內部連通的房間 ◇ *The new posts were only advertised internally.* 新職位僅限於內部招聘。

inˌternal-comˈbustion engine *noun* a type of engine used in most cars that produces power by burning petrol/gas inside 內燃機

in·tern·al·ize (*BrE* also **-ise**) **AW** /ɪnˈtɜːnəlaɪz; *NAmE* -ˈtɜːrn-/ *verb* **~ sth** (*technical* 術語) to make a feeling, an attitude, or a belief part of the way you think and behave 使（感情、態度或信仰）成為思想行為的一部份；使內在化 ➲ compare EXTERNALIZE ▸ **in·tern·al·iza·tion, -isa·tion** /ɪnˌtɜːnəlaɪˈzeɪʃn; *NAmE* -ˌtɜːrnələˈz-/ *noun* [U]

inˌternal ˈmarket *noun* (*business* 商) a situation in which different departments, countries, etc. in the same organization buy goods and services from each other 內部市場；內部貿易

the Inˌternal ˈRevenue Service *noun* [sing.] (*abbr.* **IRS**) (in the US) the government department that is responsible for collecting most national taxes, for example income tax（美國）國稅局 ➲ compare HM REVENUE AND CUSTOMS

inter·nation·al 🔑 /ˌɪntəˈnæʃnəl; *NAmE* -tərˈn-/ *adj., noun*

■ ***adj.*** 🔑 [usually before noun] connected with or involving two or more countries 國際的： *international trade/law/sport* 國際貿易；國際法；國際體育運動 ◇ *an international airport/school/company* 國際機場/學校/公司 ◇ *international relations* 國際關係 ◇ *a pianist with an international reputation* 飲譽國際的鋼琴家 ▸ **inter·nation·al·ly** /-nəli/ *adv.*： *internationally famous* 國際知名的

■ ***noun*** **1** (*BrE*) a sports competition involving teams from two countries 國際體育比賽： *the France-Scotland rugby international* 法國對蘇格蘭的國際橄欖球賽 **2** (*BrE*) a player who takes part in a sports competition against another country 國際體育比賽選手： *a former swimming international* 前國際游泳選手 **3** (*NAmE*) a person from a foreign country 外國人： *an English course for internationals* 為外國人開設的英語課程 ➲ COLLOCATIONS at next page

the ˌInterˌnational Bacca'laureate™ *noun* [sing.] (*abbr.* **IB**) an exam which is taken by students in many different countries in the world around the age of 18 or 19, and which includes up to six subjects 國際中學畢業會考（考生年齡約為 18 或 19 歲，包括最多六門課程）

the Interˌnational ˈDate Line (also **ˈDate Line**) *noun* [sing.] the imaginary line that goes from north to south through the Pacific Ocean. The date on the west side is different by one day from that on the east side. 國際日界線，日界線，國際換日線（聯結地球南北極的假想線。向東航行越過此線須減去一天，向西須增加一天）

the Inter·nation·ale /ˌɪntənæʃəˈnɑːl; *NAmE* -tərn-/ *noun* [sing.] an international SOCIALIST song written in France that was the official ANTHEM of the USSR until 1944 《國際歌》（創作於法國，1944 年之前為蘇聯國歌）

inter·nation·al·ism /ˌɪntəˈnæʃnəlɪzəm; *NAmE* -tərˈn-/ *noun* [U] the belief that countries should work together in a friendly way 國際主義

inter·nation·al·ist /ˌɪntəˈnæʃnəlɪst; *NAmE* -tərˈn-/ *noun* **1** a person who believes that countries should work together in a friendly way 國際主義者 **2** (*ScotE*) a player who takes part in a sports competition against another country 參加國際比賽的國家隊選手： *a Scottish rugby internationalist* 參加國際比賽的蘇格蘭橄欖球隊隊員 ▸ **inter·nation·al·ist** *adj.*

inter·nation·al·ize (*BrE* also **-ise**) /ˌɪntəˈnæʃnəlaɪz; *NAmE* -tərˈn-/ *verb* **~ sth** to bring sth under the control or protection of many nations; to make sth international 使國際共管；使國際化 ▸ **inter·nation·al·iza·tion, -isa·tion** /ˌɪntəˌnæʃnəlaɪˈzeɪʃn; *NAmE* -tərˌnæʃnələˈz-/ *noun* [U]

the Interˌnational Phoˌnetic ˈAlphabet *noun* [sing.] (*abbr.* **IPA**) an alphabet that is used to show the pronunciation of words in any language 國際音標

in·terne *noun* = INTERN

inter·necine /ˌɪntəˈniːsaɪn; *NAmE* -tərˈn-/ *adj.* [only before noun] (*formal*) happening between members of the same group, country or organization（團體、國家、組織）內部發生的，內訌的： ***internecine struggles/warfare/feuds*** 內部鬥爭；內戰；內部世仇

in·tern·ee /ˌɪntɜːˈniː; *NAmE* ˌɪntɜːrˈniː/ *noun* a person who is put in prison for political reasons, usually without a trial (= who is INTERNED)（通常指未經審訊而關押的）政治犯

Inter·net 🔑 (also **inter·net**) /ˈɪntənet; *NAmE* -tərn-/ *noun* (usually **the Internet**) (also *informal* **the Net**) [sing.] an international computer network connecting other networks and computers from companies, universities, etc.（國際）互聯網；因特網；網路： *I looked it up* ***on the Internet.*** 我在互聯網上查過此事。 ◇ *You can buy our goods* ***over the Internet.*** 可以通過互聯網購買我們的貨品。 ◇ *All the rooms have access to the Internet/* ***Internet access.*** 所有的房間都可以接入互聯網。 ◇ *an* ***Internet service provider*** (= a company that provides you with an Internet connection and services such as email, etc.) 互聯網服務供應商 ➲ COLLOCATIONS at EMAIL ➲ see also INTRANET, WWW

in·tern·ist /ɪnˈtɜːnɪst; *NAmE* -ˈtɜːrn-/ *noun* (*NAmE*) a doctor who is a specialist in the treatment of diseases of the organs inside the body and who does not usually do medical operations 內科醫生

in·tern·ment ➲ INTERN

in·tern·ship /ˈɪntɜːnʃɪp; *NAmE* -tɜːrn-/ *noun* (*NAmE*) **1** a period of time during which a student or new GRADUATE gets practical experience in a job, for example during the summer holiday/vacation（學生或畢業生的）實習期：*an internship at a television station* 在電視台的實習期 ➲ compare PLACEMENT (2), WORK EXPERIENCE **2** a job that an advanced student of medicine, whose training is nearly finished, does in a hospital to get further practical experience 醫科學生的實習工作

inter·oper·able /ˌɪntərˈɒpərəbl; *NAmE* -ˈɑːp-/ *adj.* (*technical* 術語) (of computer systems or programs 計算機系統或程序) able to exchange information 互相操作的；配合動作的；互用的

inter·pene·trate /ˌɪntəˈpenɪtreɪt; *NAmE* -tərˈp-/ *verb* [I, T] **~ (sth)** (*formal*) to spread completely through sth or from one thing to another in each direction（互相）貫穿，滲透 ▸ **inter·pene·tra·tion** /ˌɪntəˌpenɪˈtreɪʃn; *NAmE* -tərˌp-/ *noun* [U, C]

inter·per·son·al /ˌɪntəˈpɜːsənl; *NAmE* -tərˈpɜːrs-/ *adj.* [only before noun] connected with relationships between people 人際關係的；人際的：*interpersonal skills* 人際交往技巧

inter·plan·et·ary /ˌɪntəˈplænɪtri; *NAmE* ˌɪntərˈplænəteri/ *adj.* [only before noun] between planets 行星間的：*interplanetary travel* 星際旅行

inter·play /ˈɪntəpleɪ; *NAmE* -tərp-/ *noun* [U, sing.] **~ (of/between A and B)** (*formal*) the way in which two or more things or people affect each other 相互影響（或作用）SYN **interaction**：*the interplay between*

Collocations 詞語搭配

International relations 國際關係

Trade 貿易

- **facilitate/regulate** trade (with other countries) 促進／規範（與其他國家的）貿易
- **form/join** a trading bloc 建立／加入貿易同盟
- **live in/compete in** a global/the world economy 生存於全球／世界經濟中；參與全球／世界經濟競爭
- **support/promote** free trade 支持／促進自由貿易
- **adopt/call for/oppose** protectionist measures 採取／呼籲／反對保護主義措施
- **erect/impose/reduce/remove** trade barriers 設置／推行／減少／消除貿易壁壘
- **impose/lift/raise/eliminate** import tariffs (on sth) 徵收／取消／提高／廢除（某物的）進口關稅
- **have/run** a huge/large/growing trade surplus/deficit 有巨額／持續增長的貿易順差／逆差
- **embrace/resist/drive** globalization 接受／抵制／推進全球化

Politics and law 政治與法律

- **conduct/handle/talk about/discuss** foreign policy 執行／掌控／談論／討論外交政策
- **pursue** an aggressive/a hawkish foreign policy 執行強硬的外交政策
- **require/use/conduct** diplomacy 需要／使用／實施外交手段
- **establish/break off/sever/restore** diplomatic relations 建立／中斷／斷絕／恢復外交關係
- **foster/promote/strengthen** regional cooperation 促進地區間合作
- **facilitate/achieve** economic/political integration 促進／實現經濟／政治一體化
- **exercise/defend/protect/transfer/restore/regain** national/state/full/limited sovereignty 行使／維護／保護／移交／恢復／重獲民族／國家／全部／部份主權
- **consolidate/extend/lose/retain** your power (in the region) 鞏固／擴張／喪失／保持（區域內的）勢力
- **hold/maintain/change/alter/shift/be a shift in** the balance of power (in the region) 維持／改變（區域內的）勢力均衡
- **cause/create/open/expose/heal/repair** a deep/growing/major/serious rift between X and Y 導致／造成／引發／暴露出／彌合／修復 X 與 Y 之間深層次的／不斷擴大的／主要的／嚴重的分歧

Meetings and agreements 會議與協議

- **have/hold/host/attend** an international conference/an economic forum/a G20 summit 召開／舉行／主辦／出席國際會議／經濟論壇／二十國集團峰會
- **launch** a new round of global/multilateral/world trade negotiations 發起新一輪的全球／多邊／世界貿易談判
- **send/head/lead/meet** a high-level/an official/a trade delegation 派遣／領導／帶領／會見高層／官方／貿易代表團
- **begin/start/continue/resume** peace talks 開始／繼續／重啟和平談判
- **be committed to/be opposed to/disrupt/undermine/derail/sabotage** the peace process 致力於／反對／擾亂／損害／干擾／破壞和平進程
- **negotiate/achieve** a lasting political settlement 達成／取得長期的政治協議
- **broker/sign** a peace deal/agreement/treaty 協商／簽署和平協議

Conflict 衝突

- **be/constitute/pose** a threat to global security 構成對全球安全的一大威脅
- **compromise/endanger/protect** national security 損害／危及／保護國家安全
- **justify/be in favour of/**(*especially US*) **be in favor of/be against** military intervention 證明軍事干預合理；支持／反對軍事干預
- **threaten/authorize/launch/take/support/oppose** unilateral/pre-emptive military action 揚言採取／授權使用／發起／採取／支持／反對單邊的／先發制人的軍事行動
- **impose/enforce/lift/end** economic sanctions/an arms embargo/a naval blockade 強制實行／解除經濟制裁／武器禁運／海上封鎖
- **close/protect/secure/patrol** the border 封鎖／保衛邊境；在邊境地區巡邏
- **lead/be involved in** a peacekeeping operation 領導／參與維和行動

Aid 援助

- **negotiate/announce** a $15 billion aid package/an economic stimulus package 達成／宣佈 150 億元的一套援助計劃／刺激經濟的一攬子計劃
- **send/provide/request/cut off** military aid 派遣／提供／請求／中斷軍事援助
- **bring/provide** emergency/humanitarian relief 帶來／提供緊急／人道主義救助
- **deliver/distribute** medical supplies/(*BrE*) food parcels 運送／分發醫療用品／食品包
- **fund/run** a foreign/a local/an international NGO 資助／管理外國／當地／國際非政府組織
- **reduce/eradicate** child/global/world poverty 減少／根除兒童／全球性／世界性貧困

politics and the environment 政治與環境的相互影響 ◊ *the subtle interplay of colours* 色彩的相互掩映

Inter·pol /ˈɪntəpɒl; *NAmE* ˈɪntərpoːl; ˈɪntərpɑːl/ *noun* [sing.+sing./pl. v.] an international organization that enables the police forces of different countries to help each other to solve crimes 國際刑警組織

in·ter·pol·ate /ɪnˈtɜːpəleɪt; *NAmE* -ˈtɜːrp-/ *verb* (*formal*) **1** + speech | **~ sth** to make a remark that interrupts a conversation 插話；插嘴 SYN **interject**: *'But why?' he interpolated.* "但為什麼？" 他插嘴問。 **2 ~ sth** (**into sth**) to add sth to a piece of writing（在文章中）插入，添加內容 SYN **insert**: *The lines were interpolated into the manuscript at a later date.* 這幾行文字是後來加到稿子中的。 **3 ~ sth** (*mathematics* 數) to add a value into a series by calculating it from surrounding known values 插值；內插 ▸ **in·ter·pol·ation** /ɪnˌtɜːpəˈleɪʃn; *NAmE* -ˌtɜːrp-/ *noun* [U, C]

inter·pose /ˌɪntəˈpəʊz; *NAmE* ˌɪntərˈpoʊz/ *verb* (*formal*) **1** + speech | **~ sth** to add a question or remark into a conversation 插入，插進（問題或話語）: *'Just a minute,' Charles interposed. 'How do you know?'* "且慢，" 查爾斯插話説，"你是怎麼知道的？" **2 ~ sb/sth** (**between A and B**) to place sth between two people or things 將…置於（二者）之間；插入；夾進: *He quickly interposed himself between Mel and the doorway.* 他迅速擋在梅爾和門口之間。

in·ter·pret 🔑 AW /ɪnˈtɜːprɪt; *NAmE* -ˈtɜːrp-/ *verb* **1** 🔑 [T] **~ sth** to explain the meaning of sth 詮釋；説明: *The students were asked to interpret the poem.* 學生們被要求詮釋那首詩的意義。 **2** 🔑 [T] to decide that sth has a particular meaning and to understand it in this way 把…理解為；領會: **~ sth as sth** *I didn't know whether to interpret her silence as acceptance or refusal.* 我不知該把她的沉默看作是接受還是拒絕。◊ **~ sth** *The data can be interpreted in many different ways.* 這份資料可以從多方面解讀。 ➲ compare MISINTERPRET **3** 🔑 [I] **~** (**for sb**) to translate one language into another as you hear it 口譯；傳譯: *She couldn't speak much English so her children had to interpret for her.* 她講不了幾句英語，所以她的孩子們得給她翻譯。 **4** [T] **~ sth** to perform a piece of music, a role in a play, etc. in a way that shows your feelings about its meaning 演繹（按自己的感覺演奏音樂或表現角色）: *He interpreted the role with a lot of humour.* 他把這個角色演得十分幽默。 ▸ **in·ter·pret·able** /ɪnˈtɜːprɪtəbl; *NAmE* -ˈtɜːrp-/ *adj.*: *interpretable data* 可解釋的資料

in·ter·pret·ation 🔑 AW /ɪnˌtɜːprɪˈteɪʃn; *NAmE* -ˌtɜːrp-/ *noun* [C, U] **1** 🔑 the particular way in which sth is understood or explained 理解；解釋；説明: *Her evidence suggests a different interpretation of the events.* 她的證據顯示這些事件可能有另外一種解釋。◊ *It is not possible for everyone to put their own interpretation on the law.* 不可能讓每個人自行闡釋法律。◊ *Dreams are* ***open to interpretation*** (= they can be explained in different ways). 夢可以作各種詮釋。 **2** the particular way in which sb chooses to perform a piece of music, a role in a play, etc. 演繹；演奏方式；表演方式: *a modern interpretation of 'King Lear'* 《李爾王》的現代演繹

in·ter·pret·ative AW /ɪnˈtɜːprɪtətɪv; *NAmE* ɪnˈtɜːrprəteɪtɪv/ (also **in·ter·pret·ive** /ɪnˈtɜːprɪtɪv; *NAmE* -ˈtɜːrp-/ especially in *NAmE*) *adj.* [usually before noun] (*formal*) connected with the particular way in which sth is understood, explained or performed; providing an interpretation 理解的；解釋的；表演的；演繹的: *an interpretative problem* 理解方面的問題 ◊ *an interpretative exhibition* 演示

in·ter·pret·er /ɪnˈtɜːprɪtə(r); *NAmE* -ˈtɜːrp-/ *noun* **1** a person whose job is to translate what sb is saying into another language 口譯工作者；口譯譯員；傳譯員: *Speaking* ***through an interpreter***, *the President said that the talks were going well.* 總統通過口譯員説會談進展良好。◊ *a sign language interpreter* (= a person who translates what sb is saying into sign language for deaf people) 手語翻譯員 ➲ compare TRANSLATOR **2** a person who performs a piece of music or a role in a play in a way that clearly shows their ideas about its meaning 演繹（音樂、戲劇中人物等）的人: *She is one of the finest interpreters of Debussy's music.* 她是將德彪西的音樂演繹得最出色的演奏者之一。 **3** (*computing* 計) a computer program that changes the instructions of another program into a form that the computer can understand and use 解釋程序；解釋程式

inter·racial /ˌɪntəˈreɪʃl/ *adj.* [only before noun] involving people of different races 不同種族的人的；種族間的: *interracial marriage* 種族間的通婚

inter·reg·num /ˌɪntəˈregnəm/ *noun* [usually sing.] (*pl.* **inter·reg·nums**) (*formal*) a period of time during which a country, an organization, etc. does not have a leader and is waiting for a new one（政府改組期間的）政權空白；（機構的）權力空白

inter·relate /ˌɪntərɪˈleɪt/ *verb* [I, T, usually passive] if two or more things **interrelate**, or if they are **interrelated**, they are closely connected and they affect each other 相互關聯（或影響）: *a discussion of how the mind and body interrelate* 關於精神和肉體相互聯繫的討論 ◊ **~ with sth** *a discussion of how the mind interrelates with the body* 關於精神和肉體相互聯繫的討論 ◊ **be interrelated** *a discussion of how the mind and body are interrelated* 關於精神和肉體如何相互聯繫的討論 ▸ **inter·related** *adj.*: *a number of interrelated problems* 一些相互關聯的問題

inter·rela·tion·ship /ˌɪntərɪˈleɪʃnʃɪp/ (also **inter·rela·tion** /ˌɪntərɪˈleɪʃn/) *noun* [C, U] **~** (**of/between A and B**) the way in which two or more things or people are connected and affect each other 相互關聯；相互影響

in·ter·ro·gate /ɪnˈterəgeɪt/ *verb* **1 ~ sb** to ask sb a lot of questions over a long period of time, especially in an aggressive way 訊問；審問；盤問: *He was interrogated by the police for over 12 hours.* 他被警察審問了 12 個多小時。 **2 ~ sth** (*technical* 術語) to obtain information from a computer or other machine（在計算機或其他機器上）查詢，詢問 ▸ **in·ter·ro·ga·tion** /ɪnˌterəˈgeɪʃn/ *noun* [U, C]: *He confessed after four days* ***under interrogation***. 他在受訊問四天之後招認了。◊ *She hated her parents' endless interrogations about where she'd been.* 她討厭父母沒完沒了地盤問她去哪裏了。 ➲ SYNONYMS at INTERVIEW **in·ter·ro·ga·tor** *noun*

inter·roga·tive /ˌɪntəˈrɒgətɪv; *NAmE* -ˈrɑːg-/ *adj.*, *noun*

■ ***adj.*** **1** (*formal*) asking a question; in the form of a question 詢問的；提問的；疑問式的: *an interrogative gesture/remark/sentence* 疑問的手勢／言語；疑問句 **2** (*grammar* 語法) used in questions 用於疑問句的: *interrogative pronouns/determiners/adverbs* (= for example, *who*, *which* and *why*) 疑問代詞／限定詞／副詞 ▸ **inter·roga·tive·ly** *adv.*

■ ***noun*** (*grammar* 語法) a question word, especially a pronoun or a determiner such as *who* or *which* 疑問詞；（尤指）疑問代詞，疑問限定詞

inter·roga·tory /ˌɪntəˈrɒgətri; *NAmE* -ˈrɑːg-/ *adj.*, *noun*

■ ***adj.*** seeming to be asking a question or demanding an answer to sth 疑問的；質問的: *an interrogatory stare* 帶着疑問的注視

■ ***noun*** (*pl.* **-ies**) (*law* 律) a written question, asked by one party in a legal case, which must be answered by the other party（訴訟中一方向另一方提出的）書面質詢

inter·rupt 🔑 /ˌɪntəˈrʌpt/ *verb* **1** 🔑 [I, T] to say or do sth that makes sb stop what they are saying or doing 插嘴；打擾；打岔: *Sorry to interrupt, but there's someone to see you.* 對不起打擾一下，有人要見你。◊ **~ with sth** *Would you mind not interrupting with questions all the time?* 請你別老是插嘴問問題好嗎？◊ **~ sb/sth** (**with sth**) *I hope I'm not interrupting you.* 我希望我沒有打攪你。◊ *They were interrupted by a knock at the door.* 他們被敲門聲打斷了。◊ **~** (**sb**) + speech *'I have a question,' she interrupted.* "我有一個問題。" 她插嘴道。 **2** 🔑 [T] **~ sth** to stop sth for a short time 使暫停；使中斷: *The game was interrupted several times by rain.* 比賽因下雨中斷了幾次。◊ *We interrupt this programme to bring you an important news bulletin.* 我們暫停本節目，插播重要新聞。 **3** [T] **~ sth** to stop a line, surface, view, etc. from being even or continuous 阻斷，遮擋（連續線條、平面、景色等）

inter·rup·tion 0-w /ˌɪntəˈrʌpʃn/ *noun* [C, U] **1** 0-w something that temporarily stops an activity or a situation; a time when an activity is stopped 阻斷物；中斷時間：*The birth of her son was a minor interruption to her career.* 她兒子的出生對她的事業造成一個小小的中斷。◊ *an interruption to the power supply* 停電 ◊ *I managed to work for two hours* ***without interruption.*** 我總算連續工作了兩小時。**2** 0-w the act of interrupting sb/sth and of stopping them from speaking 打擾；插嘴；打岔：*He ignored her interruptions.* 他沒有理會她的打岔。◊ *She spoke for 20 minutes* ***without interruption.*** 她連續講了 20 分鐘。

inter·sect /ˌɪntəˈsekt; *NAmE* -tərˈs-/ *verb* **1** [I, T] (of lines, roads, etc. 線、道路等) to meet or cross each other 相交；交叉：**~ (sth)** *a pattern of intersecting streets* 縱橫交錯的街道圖 ◊ *The lines intersect at right angles.* 線條垂直相交。◊ **~ with sth** *The path intersected with a busy road.* 小路與一條繁忙的大路相交。**2** [T, usually passive] **~ sth (with sth)** to divide an area by crossing it 橫穿；貫穿；橫斷：*The landscape is intersected with spectacular gorges.* 在大地景色中點綴着壯觀的峽谷。

inter·sec·tion /ˌɪntəˈsekʃn; *NAmE* -tərˈs-/ *noun* **1** [C] (*NAmE or formal, BrE*) a place where two or more roads, lines, etc. meet or cross each other 十字路口；交叉路口；交點：*Traffic lights have been placed at all major intersections.* 所有主要的交叉路口都安裝了交通信號燈。**2** [U] the act of intersecting sth 橫斷；交叉；相交

inter·sex /ˈɪntəseks; *NAmE* -tərs-/ *noun* [U] (*medical* 醫) the physical condition of being partly male and partly female 間性；雌雄間性；雌雄間體

inter·sperse /ˌɪntəˈspɜːs; *NAmE* -tərˈspɜːrs/ *verb* **be interspersed with/in sth** to put sth in sth else or among or between other things 散佈；散置；點綴：*Lectures will be interspersed with practical demonstrations.* 講課中將不時插入實際示範。

inter·state /ˈɪntəsteɪt; *NAmE* -tərs-/ *adj., noun*
■ ***adj.*** [only before noun] between states, especially in the US（尤指美國）州與州之間的，州際的：*interstate commerce* 州際貿易
■ ***noun*** (also ˌ**interstate ˈhighway**) (in the US) a wide road, with at least two lanes in each direction, where traffic can travel fast for long distances across many states. You can only enter and leave interstates at special RAMPS.（美國）州際公路 ➲ compare MOTORWAY

inter·stel·lar /ˌɪntəˈstelə(r); *NAmE* -tərˈst-/ *adj.* [only before noun] between the stars in the sky 星際的 ➲ compare STELLAR (1)

in·ter·stice /ɪnˈtɜːstɪs; *NAmE* -ˈtɜːrs-/ *noun* [usually pl.] (*formal*) a small crack or space in sth 裂縫；空隙

inter·sti·tial /ˌɪntəˈstɪʃl; *NAmE* -tərˈs-/ *adj.* (*medical* 醫) in or related to small spaces between the parts of an organ or between groups of cells or TISSUES 間質的；組織間隙的：*interstitial cells* 間質細胞

inter·text·ual·ity /ˌɪntətekstʃuˈæləti; *NAmE* ˌɪntər-/ *noun* [U] (*technical* 術語) the relationship between texts, especially literary texts（尤指文學文本之間的）互文性

inter·twine /ˌɪntəˈtwaɪn; *NAmE* -tərˈtw-/ *verb* [usually passive] **1** [I, T] if two or more things **intertwine** or are **intertwined**, they are twisted together so that they are very difficult to separate（使）纏結，纏繞在一起：*intertwining branches* 纏繞在一起的樹枝 ◊ **~ sth (with sth)** *a necklace of rubies intertwined with pearls* 纏着珍珠的紅寶石項鏈 **2** [T, usually passive, I] **~ (sth)** to be or become very closely connected with sth/sb else 緊密相連：*Their political careers had become* ***closely intertwined.*** 他們的政治生涯已經緊密地結合在一起了。

inter·val 0-w AW /ˈɪntəvl; *NAmE* ˈɪntərvl/ *noun* **1** 0-w a period of time between two events（時間上的）間隔，間隙，間歇：*The interval between major earthquakes might be 200 years.* 大地震之間的間隔時間可能有 200 年。**2** (*BrE*) (also **inter·mis·sion** *NAmE, BrE*) a short period of time separating parts of a play, film/movie or concert（戲劇、電影或音樂會的）幕間休息，休息時間：*There will be an interval of 20 minutes after the second act.* 第二幕結束後將休息 20 分鐘。**3** 0-w [usually pl.] a short period during which sth different happens from what is happening the rest of the time（其他事情）穿插出現的間隙：*She's delirious, but has lucid intervals.* 她神志昏亂，但有時清醒。◊ (*BrE*) *The day should be mainly dry with sunny intervals.* 白天大致乾燥無雨，間有陽光。**4** (*music* 音) a difference in PITCH (= how high or low a note sounds) between two notes 音程：*an interval of one octave* 一個八度音程
IDM **at (...) intervals** **1** 0-w with time between 每隔…時間；間或；不時：*Buses to the city leave* ***at regular intervals.*** 開往城裏的公共汽車每隔一定時間發出一班。◊ *The runners started at 5-minute intervals.* 賽跑的人每隔 5 分鐘出發一批。**2** 0-w with spaces between 每隔…距離；間隔：*Flaming torches were positioned at intervals along the terrace.* 沿台階間隔地插着燃燒着的火炬。

ˈ**interval training** *noun* [U] sports training consisting of different activities which require different speeds or amounts of effort 間歇訓練（包括不同速度或強度的活動）

inter·vene AW /ˌɪntəˈviːn; *NAmE* -tərˈv-/ *verb* **1** [I] to become involved in a situation in order to improve or help it 出面；介入：*She might have been killed if the neighbours hadn't intervened.* 要不是鄰居介入，她可能會沒命了。◊ **~ in sth** *The President intervened personally in the crisis.* 總統親自出面處理這場危機。**2** [T, I] **(+ speech)** to interrupt sb when they are speaking in order to say sth 插嘴；打斷（別人的話）：*'But,' she intervened, 'what about the others?'* "但是，" 她插嘴說，"其他的怎麼辦呢？" **3** [I] to happen in a way that delays sth or prevents it from happening 阻礙；阻撓；干擾：*They were planning to get married and then the war intervened.* 他們正準備結婚，不巧卻因爆發戰事而受阻。**4** [I] (*formal*) to exist between two events or places 介於…之間：*I saw nothing of her during the years that intervened.* 這期間的幾年中我根本沒有見過她。▸ **inter·ven·tion** AW /ˌɪntəˈvenʃn; *NAmE* -tərˈv-/ *noun* [U, C]：**~ (in sth)** *calls for government intervention to save the steel industry* 呼籲政府出面挽救鋼鐵業 ◊ ***armed/military intervention*** 武裝／軍事干涉 ➲ COLLOCATIONS at INTERNATIONAL

inter·ven·ing /ˌɪntəˈviːnɪŋ; *NAmE* -tərˈv-/ *adj.* [only before noun] coming or existing between two events, dates, objects, etc. 發生於其間的；介於中間的：*Little had changed in the intervening years.* 這些年間沒有發生什麼變化。

inter·ven·tion·ism /ˌɪntəˈvenʃənɪzəm; *NAmE* -tərˈv-/ *noun* [U] the policy or practice of a government influencing the economy of its own country, or of becoming involved in the affairs of other countries 政府干預（政策）▸ **inter·ven·tion·ist** /-ʃənɪst/ *adj., noun*：*interventionist policies* 干預政策

inter·view 0-w /ˈɪntəvjuː; *NAmE* -tərv-/ *noun, verb*
■ ***noun*** **1** 0-w a formal meeting at which sb is asked questions to see if they are suitable for a particular job, or for a course of study at a college, university, etc. 面試；面談：*a* ***job interview*** 求職面試 ◊ *to be* ***called for (an) interview*** 獲通知約見 ◊ **~ for a job, etc.** *He* ***has an interview*** *next week for the manager's job.* 他下週要接受一個經理職位的面試。➲ COLLOCATIONS at JOB **2** 0-w a meeting (often a public one) at which a journalist asks sb questions in order to find out their opinions（常指公開的）記者採訪，訪談：*a* ***television/radio/newspaper interview*** 電視／電台／報紙採訪 ◊ **~ (with sb)** *an interview with the new Governor* 對新任州長的訪問 ◊ *to* ***give an interview*** (= to agree to answer questions) 接受採訪 ◊ *Yesterday,* ***in an interview*** *on German television, the minister denied the reports.* 昨天，在德國電視台的採訪中，部長否認了那些報道。◊ *to* ***conduct an interview*** (= to ask sb questions in public) 進行採訪 ◊ *The interview was published in all the papers.* 各家報紙都刊載了這次訪談。**3** 0-w **~ (with sb)** a private meeting between people when questions are asked and answered（私下的）面談，會談，晤談：*an interview with the careers adviser* 和擇業指導員的面談
■ ***verb*** **1** 0-w [T, I] **~ (sb) (for a job, etc.)** to talk to sb and ask them questions at a formal meeting to find out if they are suitable for a job, course of study, etc. 對（某人）

進行面試（或面談）：*Which post are you being interviewed for?* 你參加哪個職位的面試？◇ *We interviewed ten people for the job.* 我們為這份工作面試了十人。**2** [I] (*especially NAmE*) **~ (for a job, etc.)** to talk to sb and answer questions at a formal meeting to get a job, a place on a course of study, etc. 接受面試：*The website gives you tips on interviewing for colleges.* 這個網站為你提供大學面試的竅門。◇ (*BrE, NAmE*) *If you don't interview well you are unlikely to get the job.* 如果面試時表現不好，你很可能不會得到這份工作。**3** [T] to ask sb questions about their life, opinions, etc., especially on the radio or television or for a newspaper or magazine（媒體）採訪，訪問：**~ sb about sth** *Next week, I will be interviewing Spielberg about his latest movie.* 下週我將訪問斯皮爾伯格，談論他的最新電影。◇ **~ sb** *The Prime Minister declined to be interviewed.* 首相婉拒了採訪。**4** [T] **~ sb (about sth)** to ask sb questions at a private meeting（私下）提問，面談：*The police are waiting to interview the injured man.* 警察正等待着向受傷的男子問話。▸ **inter·view·ing** *noun* [U]：*The research involves in-depth interviewing.* 這一調查包括深入的採訪。◇ *interviewing techniques* 面談技巧

Synonyms 同義詞辨析

interview

interrogation • audience • consultation

These are all words for a meeting or occasion when sb is asked for information, opinions or advice. 以上各詞均表示會見、詢問、咨詢。

interview a formal meeting at which sb is asked questions, for example, to see if they are suitable for a particular job or course of study, or in order to find out their opinions about sth 指面試、面談：*a job interview* 求職面試

interrogation the process of asking sb a lot of questions, especially in an aggressive way, in order to get information; an occasion on which this is done 指訊問、審問、盤問：*He confessed after four days **under interrogation**.* 他在受訊問四天之後招認了。

audience a formal meeting with an important person 指與要人的會見、覲見：*The Pope granted her a private audience.* 教宗同意私下接見她。

consultation a meeting with an expert, especially a doctor, to get advice or treatment 指向專家請教的咨詢，尤指就診

PATTERNS

- an **in-depth** interview/consultation
- a **police** interview/interrogation
- to **have/request** a(n) interview/audience/consultation **with** sb
- to **give/grant** sb a(n) interview/audience/consultation
- to **carry out/conduct** an interview/interrogation

inter·view·ee /ˌɪntəvjuːˈiː; *NAmE* -tərv-/ *noun* the person who answers the questions in an interview 參加面試者；接受採訪者

inter·view·er /ˈɪntəvjuːə(r); *NAmE* -tərv-/ *noun* the person who asks the questions in an interview 主持面試者；採訪者

inter·war /ˌɪntəˈwɔː(r); *NAmE* -tərˈw-/ *adj.* [only before noun] happening or existing between the First and the Second World Wars 兩次世界大戰之間的：*the **interwar years/period*** 兩次世界大戰之間的年月 / 時期

inter·weave /ˌɪntəˈwiːv; *NAmE* -tərˈw-/ *verb* (**inter·wove** /-ˈwəʊv; *NAmE* -ˈwoʊv/, **inter·woven** /-ˈwəʊvn; *NAmE* -ˈwoʊvn/) [T, usually passive, I] **~ (sth) (with sth)** to twist together two or more pieces of thread, wool, etc. 交織；交錯編織：*The blue fabric was interwoven with red and gold thread.* 藍布中交織着紅色和金色的線。◇ (*figurative*) *The problems are inextricably interwoven* (= very closely connected). 問題盤根錯節。

in·tes·tate /ɪnˈtesteɪt/ *adj.* (*law* 律) not having made a WILL (= a legal document that says what is to happen to a person's property when they die) 未留遺囑的 ▸ **in·tes·tacy** /ɪnˈtestəsi/ *noun* [U]

inˌtestinal ˈfortitude *noun* (*NAmE*, *formal* or *humorous*) the courage and determination necessary to do sth difficult or unpleasant (used when you want to avoid using the word *guts*) 勇氣，毅力（避免說 guts 時用）：*He did not have the intestinal fortitude to implement the changes.* 他沒有膽量實行變革。

in·tes·tine /ɪnˈtestɪn/ *noun* [usually pl.] a long tube in the body between the stomach and the ANUS. Food passes from the stomach to the **small intestine** and from there to the **large intestine**. 腸 ➲ VISUAL VOCAB page V59 ▸ **in·tes·tinal** /ɪnˈtestɪnl; ˌɪnteˈstaɪnl/ *adj.* [usually before noun]

in·tim·acy /ˈɪntɪməsi/ *noun* (*pl.* **-ies**) **1** [U] the state of having a close personal relationship with sb 親密；密切；關係密切 **2** [C, usually pl.] a thing that a person says or does to sb that they know very well 親密的言語（或行為）**3** [U] (*formal* or *law* 律) sexual activity, especially an act of SEXUAL INTERCOURSE 性行為；（尤指）性交

in·tim·ate *adj., verb, noun*

■ ***adj.*** /ˈɪntɪmət/ **1** (of people 人) having a close and friendly relationship 親密的；密切的：*intimate friends* 密友 ◇ *We're not **on intimate terms with** our neighbours.* 我們和鄰居來往不多。**2** private and personal, often in a sexual way 個人隱私的（常指性方面的）：*The article revealed **intimate details** about his family life.* 文章披露了他的家庭生活中的隱私。◇ *the most intimate parts of her body* 她的身體的最隱私部位 **3** (of a place or situation 地方或情形) encouraging close, friendly relationships, sometimes of a sexual nature 宜於密切關係的；溫馨的；便於有性關係的：*an intimate restaurant* 幽靜溫馨的餐廳 ◇ *He knew an intimate little bar where they would not be disturbed.* 他知道一處適合幽會的小酒吧，他們在那裏不會受到打擾。**4** (of knowledge 知識) very detailed and thorough 詳盡的；精通的：*an intimate knowledge of the English countryside* 對英國鄉村的透徹瞭解 **5** (of a link between things 事物間的聯繫) very close 密切的；緊密的：*an **intimate connection** between class and educational success* 社會階層和優良教育之間的密切聯繫 **6 ~ (with sb)** (*formal* or *law* 律) having a sexual relationship with sb 有性關係的；曖昧的 ▸ **in·tim·ate·ly** *adv.*：***intimately connected/linked/related*** 密切關聯 / 聯繫 / 相關 ◇ *an area of the country that he knew intimately* 他十分熟悉的本國的一個地區 ◇ *She was **intimately involved** in the project.* 她已投到這個項目中去。◇ *They touched each other intimately* (= in a sexual way). 他們相互愛撫。

■ ***verb*** /ˈɪntɪmeɪt/ (*formal*) to let sb know what you think or mean in an indirect way 透露；（間接）表示；暗示 SYN **make known**：**~ sth (to sb)** *He has already intimated to us his intention to retire.* 他已經向我們透露了他要退休的打算。◇ **~ (that) …** *He has already intimated (that) he intends to retire.* 他已經暗示他打算退休。

■ ***noun*** /ˈɪntɪmət/ (*formal*) a close personal friend 密友；至交；知己

in·tim·ation /ˌɪntɪˈmeɪʃn/ *noun* [C, U] (*formal*) the act of stating sth or of making it known, especially in an indirect way 透露；間接表示；暗示：*There was no intimation from his doctor that his condition was serious.* 他的醫生沒有透露他的病情很嚴重。

in·timi·date /ɪnˈtɪmɪdeɪt/ *verb* **~ sb (into sth/into doing sth)** to frighten or threaten sb so that they will do what you want 恐嚇；威脅：*They were accused of intimidating people into voting for them.* 他們被控脅迫選民投他們的票。◇ *She refused to be intimidated by their threats.* 她沒有被他們的威脅嚇倒。▸ **in·timi·da·tion** /ɪnˌtɪmɪˈdeɪʃn/ *noun* [U]：*the intimidation of witnesses* 對目擊證人的恐嚇

in·timi·dated /ɪnˈtɪmɪdeɪtɪd/ *adj.* [not usually before noun] feeling frightened and not confident in a particular situation 膽怯；怯場：*We try to make sure children* *don't feel intimidated on their first day at school.* 我們努力確保孩子們在上學的第一天不膽怯。

in·timi·dat·ing /ɪnˈtɪmɪdeɪtɪŋ/ *adj.* frightening in a way which makes a person feel less confident 嚇人的；令人膽怯的：*an intimidating manner* 使人望而生畏的態度 ◇ **~ for/to sb** *This kind of questioning can be very intimidating to children.* 這種問話的方式可能讓孩子們非常害怕。

in·timi·da·tory /ɪnˌtɪmɪˈdeɪtəri/ *adj.* (*formal*) intended to frighten or threaten sb 恐嚇的；威脅的

into /ˈɪntə; *before vowels* ˈɪntu; *strong form* ˈɪntuː/ *prep.*

HELP For the special uses of **into** in phrasal verbs, look at the entries for the verbs. For example **lay into sb/sth** is in the phrasal verb section at **lay**. * into 在短語動詞中的特殊用法見有關動詞詞條。如 lay into sb/sth 在詞條 lay 的短語動詞部份。 **1** to a position in or inside sth 到…裏面；進入：*Come into the house.* 進屋裏來吧。◇ *She dived into the water.* 她潛入水中。◇ *He threw the letter into the fire.* 他把信扔進了爐火。◇ (*figurative*) *She turned and walked off into the night.* 她轉過身去，走進黑夜裏。 **2** in the direction of sth 朝；向；對着：*Speak clearly into the microphone.* 清楚地對着麥克風講話。◇ *Driving into the sun, we had to shade our eyes.* 面向太陽開車，我們只好遮擋着眼睛。 **3** to a point at which you hit sb/sth 撞上；碰上：*The truck crashed into a parked car.* 卡車撞上了一輛停放着的汽車。 **4** to a point during a period of time 到（一段時間的某一點）：*She carried on working late into the night.* 她一直工作到了深夜。◇ *He didn't get married until he was well into his forties.* 他到四十好幾才結婚。 **5** used to show a change in state（表示狀態的變化）：*The fruit can be made into jam.* 這種水果可以製成果醬。◇ *Can you translate this passage into German?* 你能把這一段文字譯成德語嗎？◇ *They came into power in 2008.* 他們於 2008 年上台掌權。◇ *She was sliding into depression.* 她逐漸消沉下去。 **6** used to show the result of an action（表示行動的結果）：*He was shocked into a confession of guilt.* 他被嚇得認罪了。 **7** about or concerning sth 關於；有關：*an inquiry into safety procedures* 關於安全程序的調查 **8** used when you are dividing numbers（用於除數）除：*3 into 24 is 8.* * 24 除以 3 等於 8。

IDM **be ˈinto sb for sth** (*US, informal*) to owe sb money or be owed money by sb 欠某人（錢）；某人欠（錢）：*By the time he'd fixed the leak, I was into him for $500.* 他補好漏洞時，我就該付給他 500 元。◇ *The bank was into her for $100 000.* 她欠了銀行 10 萬元。 **be ˈinto sth** (*informal*) to be interested in sth in an active way 對…十分感興趣；很喜歡：*He's into surfing in a big way.* 他迷上了衝浪運動。

in·toler·able /ɪnˈtɒlərəbl; *NAmE* -ˈtɑːl-/ *adj.* so bad or difficult that you cannot TOLERATE it; completely unacceptable 無法忍受的；不能容忍的；完全不可接受的 **SYN** **unbearable**：*an intolerable burden/situation* 無法承受的負擔；不能容忍的情況 ◇ *The heat was intolerable.* 炎熱讓人受不了。 ▸ **in·toler·ably** /-əbli/ *adv.*：*intolerably hot* 熱得無法忍受

in·toler·ant /ɪnˈtɒlərənt; *NAmE* -ˈtɑːl-/ *adj.* **1 ~ (of sb/sth)** (*disapproving*) not willing to accept ideas or ways of behaving that are different from your own 不容忍的；褊狹的；不容異說的；偏執的 **OPP** **tolerant** **2** (*technical* 術語) not able to eat particular foods, use particular medicines, etc.（對食物、藥物等）過敏；不耐的：*recipes for people who are gluten intolerant* 穀蛋白過敏人士的食譜 ▸ **in·toler·ance** /-əns/ *noun* [U, C]：*religious intolerance* 宗教上的不寬容 ◇ *an intolerance to dairy products* 對乳製品過敏

in·ton·ation /ˌɪntəˈneɪʃn/ *noun* **1** [U, C] (*phonetics* 語音) the rise and fall of the voice in speaking, especially as this affects the meaning of what is being said 語調：*intonation patterns* 語調類型 ◇ *In English, some questions have a rising intonation.* 英語中有些疑問句使用升調。 ➲ compare STRESS *n.* (4) **2** [U] (*music* 音) the quality of playing or singing exactly in tune（演奏或唱歌中的）音準

in·tone /ɪnˈtəʊn; *NAmE* ɪnˈtoʊn/ *verb* **~ sth** | **+ speech** (*formal*) to say sth in a slow and serious voice without much expression 緩慢莊重地說：*The priest intoned the final prayer.* 神父莊重地唸了最後的禱文。

in toto /ˌɪn ˈtəʊtəʊ; *NAmE* ˈtoʊtoʊ/ *adv.* (from *Latin*, *formal*) completely; including all parts 完全地；完整地；全部地

in·toxi·cant /ɪnˈtɒksɪkənt; *NAmE* -ˈtɑːk-/ *noun* (*technical* 術語) a substance such as alcohol that produces false feelings of pleasure and a lack of control 麻醉劑；毒藥；酒類飲料

in·toxi·cated /ɪnˈtɒksɪkeɪtɪd; *NAmE* -ˈtɑːk-/ *adj.* (*formal*) **1** under the influence of alcohol or drugs 喝醉的；（吸毒後）迷醉的：(*NAmE*) *He was arrested for DWI* (= driving while intoxicated). 他因酒醉駕駛而被拘捕。 **2 ~ (by/with sth)** very excited by sth, so that you cannot think clearly 陶醉的；忘乎所以的；極度興奮的：*intoxicated with success* 被成功沖昏了頭腦 ▸ **in·toxi·cate** *verb* **~ sb**

in·toxi·cat·ing /ɪnˈtɒksɪkeɪtɪŋ; *NAmE* -ˈtɑːk-/ *adj.* (*formal*) **1** (of drink 飲料) containing alcohol 含酒精的；醉人的 **2** making you feel excited so that you cannot think clearly 令人陶醉的；令人頭腦迷糊的：*Power can be intoxicating.* 權力能讓人得意忘形。 ▸ **in·toxi·ca·tion** /ɪnˌtɒksɪˈkeɪʃn; *NAmE* -ˌtɑːk-/ *noun* [U]

intra- *prefix* (in adjectives and adverbs 構成形容詞和副詞) inside; within 在…裏；在…內：*intravenous* 靜脈內的 ◇ *intra-departmental* (= within a department) 部門內的 ➲ compare INTER-

in·tract·able /ɪnˈtræktəbl/ *adj.* (*formal*) (of a problem or a person 問題或人) very difficult to deal with 很難對付（或處理）的 **OPP** **tractable** ▸ **in·tract·abil·ity** /ɪnˌtræktəˈbɪləti/ *noun* [U]

intra·mural /ˌɪntrəˈmjʊərəl; *NAmE* -ˈmjʊrəl/ *adj.* (*especially NAmE*) taking place within a single institution, especially a school or college 機構內部的；（尤指）學校內的，大學內的：*Jeff played intramural basketball in high school.* 傑夫在中學時參加了校內籃球賽。

intra·mus·cu·lar /ˌɪntrəˈmʌskjələ(r)/ *adj.* (*medical* 醫) happening inside a muscle or put into a muscle 肌肉內的；注入肌內的：*intramuscular pain* 肌疼痛 ◇ *an intramuscular injection* 肌內注射

intra·net /ˈɪntrənet/ *noun* (*computing* 計) a computer network that is private to a company, university, etc. but is connected to and uses the same software as the Internet 內聯網，企事業單位內部互聯網（公司、大學等的內部網絡，但與互聯網相接並共享軟件）

in·transi·gent /ɪnˈtrænsɪdʒənt; *NAmE* -ˈtrænz-/ *adj.* (*formal, disapproving*) (of people 人) unwilling to change their opinions or behaviour in a way that would be helpful to others 不妥協的；不願合作的；不肯讓步的 **SYN** **stubborn** ▸ **in·transi·gence** /-əns/ *noun* [U]

in·transi·tive /ɪnˈtrænsətɪv/ *adj.* (*grammar* 語法) (of verbs 動詞) used without a DIRECT OBJECT 不及物的 **OPP** **transitive**：*The verb 'die' as in 'He died suddenly', is intransitive.* * He died suddenly 中的動詞 die 是不及物的。 ▸ **in·transi·tive·ly** *adv.*：*The verb is being used intransitively.* 這個動詞此處作為不及物動詞使用。

intra·uter·ine /ˌɪntrəˈjuːtəraɪn/ *adj.* (*medical* 醫) within the UTERUS 子宮內的

ˌintrauterine deˈvice *noun* = IUD

intra·ven·ous /ˌɪntrəˈviːnəs/ *adj.* (*abbr.* **IV**) (*medical* 醫) (of drugs or food 藥物或食物) going into a VEIN 注入靜脈的；靜脈內的：*intravenous fluids* 靜脈供給液 ◇ *an intravenous injection* 靜脈注射 ◇ *an intravenous drug user* 使用靜脈注射的吸毒者 ▸ **intra·ven·ous·ly** *adv.*

ˈin tray (*NAmE* also **ˈin box**) *noun* (in an office) a container on your desk for letters that are waiting to be read or answered（辦公室中的）收件盤 ➲ compare OUT TRAY ➲ **VISUAL VOCAB** page V69

in·trench = ENTRENCH

in·trepid /ɪnˈtrepɪd/ *adj.* (*formal*, often *humorous*) very brave; not afraid of danger or difficulties 勇敢的；無畏的 **SYN** **fearless**：*an intrepid explorer* 勇敢的探險家

in·tri·cacy /ˈɪntrɪkəsi/ *noun* **1 in·tri·ca·cies** [pl.] **the ~ of sth** the complicated parts or details of sth 錯綜複雜的事物（或細節）：*the intricacies of economic policy* 經濟政策的錯綜複雜 **2** [U] the fact of having complicated parts, details or patterns 錯綜複雜：*the intricacy of the design* 設計的複雜性

in·tri·cate /ˈɪntrɪkət/ *adj.* having a lot of different parts and small details that fit together 錯綜複雜的：*intricate patterns* 複雜的圖案 ◇ *an intricate network of loyalties and relationships* 忠誠與人事的複雜關係 ▸ **in·tri·cate·ly** *adv.*：*intricately carved* 精雕細刻的

in·trigue *verb, noun*

■ *verb* /ɪnˈtriːɡ/ **1** [T, often passive] **~ sb** | **it intrigues sb that …** to make sb very interested and want to know more about sth 激起…的興趣；引發…的好奇心：*You've really intrigued me—tell me more!* 你說的真有意思，再給我講一些吧！ **2** [I] **~ (with sb) (against sb)** (*formal*) to secretly plan with other people to harm sb 秘密策劃（加害他人）；密謀

■ *noun* /ˈɪntriːɡ; ɪnˈtriːɡ/ **1** [U] the activity of making secret plans in order to achieve an aim, often by tricking people 密謀策劃；陰謀：*political intrigue* 政治陰謀 ◇ *The young heroine steps into a web of intrigue in the academic world.* 年輕的女主人公陷入了學術界鉤心鬥角的羅網。 **2** [C] a secret plan or relationship, especially one which involves sb else being tricked 密謀；秘密關係；陰謀詭計：*I soon learnt about all the intrigues and scandals that went on in the little town.* 我很快便知道了小鎮上流傳的種種陰謀與醜聞。 **3** [U] the atmosphere of interest and excitement that surrounds sth secret or important 神秘氣氛；引人入勝的複雜情節

in·trigued /ɪnˈtriːɡd/ *adj.* [not usually before noun] very interested in sth/sb and wanting to know more about it/them 着迷；很感興趣；好奇：*He was intrigued by her story.* 他被她的故事迷住了。◇ **~ to do sth** *I'm intrigued to know what you thought of the movie.* 我很想知道你對這部電影的看法。

in·tri·guing /ɪnˈtriːɡɪŋ/ *adj.* very interesting because of being unusual or not having an obvious answer 非常有趣的；引人入勝的；神秘的：*These discoveries raise intriguing questions.* 這些發現帶來了非常有趣的問題。◇ *an intriguing possibility* 令人不解的可能性 ◇ *He found her intriguing.* 他覺得她很迷人。 ▸ **in·tri·guing·ly** *adv.*

in·trin·sic **AW** /ɪnˈtrɪnsɪk; -zɪk/ *adj.* belonging to or part of the real nature of sth/sb 固有的；內在的；本身的：*the intrinsic value of education* 教育的固有價值 ◇ *These tasks were repetitive, lengthy and lacking any intrinsic interest.* 這些作業重複冗長，本質上缺乏趣味。◇ **~ to sth** *Small local shops are intrinsic to the town's character.* 本地的一些小店鋪是這個鎮的基本特點。 ➲ compare EXTRINSIC ▸ **in·trin·sic·al·ly** **AW** /-kli/ *adv.*：*There is nothing intrinsically wrong with the idea* (= it is good in itself but there may be outside circumstances which mean it is not suitable). 這種想法本身並沒有錯。

intro /ˈɪntrəʊ; *NAmE* ˈɪntroʊ/ *noun* (*pl.* **-os**) (*informal*) an introduction to sth, especially to a piece of music or writing 介紹；（尤指）前奏，前言，導言

intro·duce 🔑 /ˌɪntrəˈdjuːs; *NAmE* -ˈduːs/ *verb*

▸ **PEOPLE** 人 **1** 🔑 to tell two or more people who have not met before what each other's names are; to tell sb what your name is 把…介紹（給）；引見；（自我）介紹：**~ sb** *Can I introduce my wife?* 我來介紹一下我的妻子。◇ **~ A to B (as sth)** *He introduced me to a Greek girl at the party.* 他在聚會上介紹我認識了一位希臘姑娘。◇ **~ A and B** *We've already been introduced.* 我們已經介紹認識了。◇ **~ yourself (to sb)** *Can I introduce myself? I'm Helen Robins.* 讓我來自我介紹一下吧。我叫海倫•羅賓斯。◇ *'Kay, this is Steve.' 'Yes, I know—we've already introduced ourselves.'* "凱，這是史蒂夫。" "是的，我知道，我們已經自己相互介紹了。"

▸ **TV/RADIO SHOW** 電視／電台節目 **2** 🔑 **~ sb/sth** to be the main speaker in a television or radio show, who gives details about the show and who presents the people who are in it; to tell the audience the name of the person who is going to speak or perform 主持（節目）；介紹（講演者或演員）：*The next programme will be introduced by Mary David.* 下一個節目由瑪麗•戴維主持。◇ *May I introduce my first guest on the show tonight …* 請讓我介紹今晚節目的第一位嘉賓…

▸ **NEW EXPERIENCE** 新經歷 **3** 🔑 to make sb learn about sth or do sth for the first time 使初次瞭解；使嘗試：**~ sb to sth** *The first lecture introduces students to the main topics of the course.* 第一堂課是讓學生瞭解這門課的主要內容。◇ **~ sth (to sb)** *It was she who first introduced the pleasures of sailing to me.* 是她最先使我體會到了帆船運動的樂趣。

▸ **NEW PRODUCT/LAW** 新產品／法律 **4** 🔑 to make sth available for use, discussion, etc. for the first time 推行；實施；採用 **SYN** **bring in**：**~ sth** *The company is introducing a new range of products this year.* 公司今年將推出一系列新產品。◇ *The new law was introduced in 2007.* 這項新法律是於 2007 年開始實施的。◇ **~ sth into/to sth** *We want to introduce the latest technology into schools.* 我們想向各學校推介最新的技術。

▸ **PLANT/ANIMAL/DISEASE** 動植物；疾病 **5** 🔑 **~ sth (to/into sth)** to bring a plant, an animal or a disease to a place for the first time 引進（動物或植物）；傳入（疾病）：*Vegetation patterns changed when goats were introduced to the island.* 自從引進山羊之後，這個島上的植被模式改變了。

▸ **START** 開始 **6** 🔑 **~ sth** to be the start of sth new 作為（新事物）的開頭；使開始；創始：*Bands from London introduced the craze for this kind of music.* 倫敦的樂隊引發了對這種音樂的狂熱。◇ *A slow theme introduces the first movement.* 緩慢的主旋律引出了第一樂章。

▸ **IN PARLIAMENT** 議會 **7** **~ sth** to formally present a new law so that it can be discussed 將（法案）提交討論：*to introduce a bill (before Parliament)* （向議會）提交議案

▸ **ADD** 增加 **8** **~ sth (into sth)** (*formal*) to put sth into sth 將…放進；添入：*Particles of glass had been introduced into the baby food.* 這種嬰兒食品中被摻進了玻璃碎屑。

intro·duc·tion 🔑 /ˌɪntrəˈdʌkʃn/ *noun*

▸ **BRINGING INTO USE/TO A PLACE** 採用；引進 **1** 🔑 [U] the act of bringing sth into use or existence for the first time, or of bringing sth to a place for the first time 初次投入使用；採用；引進；推行：*the introduction of new manufacturing methods* 新製造方法的採用 ◇ *the introduction of compulsory military service* 義務兵役制的實行 ◇ *the 1 000th anniversary of the introduction of Christianity to Russia* 基督教傳入俄羅斯 1 000 週年的紀念 **2** 🔑 [C] a thing that is brought into use or introduced to a place for the first time 新採用（或新引進）的事物：*The book lists plants suitable for the British flower garden, among them many new introductions.* 這本書列出了適合英國花園種植的花草，其中有很多新引進的品種。

▸ **OF PEOPLE** 人 **3** 🔑 [C] **~ (to sb)** the act of making one person formally known to another, in which you tell each the other's name （正式的）介紹，引見：*Introductions were made and the conversation started to flow.* 大家相互介紹之後交談就開始了。◇ *Our speaker today **needs no introduction*** (= is already well known). 我們今天的演講者就不必介紹了。◇ *a **letter of introduction*** (= a letter which tells sb who you are, written by sb who knows both you and the person reading the letter) 介紹信

▸ **FIRST EXPERIENCE** 初次經歷 **4** 🔑 [sing.] **~ (to sth)** a person's first experience of sth 初次經歷；首次體驗：*This album was my first introduction to modern jazz.* 這張唱片專輯讓我初次接觸了現代爵士樂。

▸ **OF BOOK/SPEECH** 書；講話 **5** 🔑 [C, U] **~ (to sth)** the first part of a book or speech that gives a general idea of what is to follow 序言；引言；導論：*a brief introduction* 簡短的序言 ◇ *a book with an excellent introduction and notes* 有精彩前言和註釋的書 ◇ ***By way of introduction****, let me give you the background to the story.* 作為引言，我先來介紹一下故事的背景。 ➲ compare PREFACE

▸ **TO SUBJECT** 學科 **6** 🔑 [C] **~ (to sth)** a book or course for people beginning to study a subject 初級讀物；入門課程：*'An Introduction to Astronomy'* 《天文學入門》◇ *It's a useful introduction to an extremely complex subject.* 這是對一門極為複雜的學科的有益入門教程。

I

▸ IN MUSIC 音樂 **7** [C] (*music* 音) a short section at the beginning of a piece of music 前奏： *an eight-bar introduction* 有八個小節的前奏

intro·duc·tory /ˌɪntrəˈdʌktəri/ *adj.* **1** written or said at the beginning of sth as an introduction to what follows 序言的；引導的；介紹的 SYN **opening**：*introductory chapters/paragraphs/remarks* 序篇；引言段；開場白 **2** intended as an introduction to a subject or an activity for people who have never done it before 入門的；初步的：*introductory courses/lectures* 基礎課程／講座 **3** offered for a short time only, when a product is first on sale（新產品）試銷的：*a special* ***introductory price*** *of just $10* 僅 10 元的優惠上市價 ◇ *This* ***introductory offer*** *is for three days only.* 本試銷優惠只為期三天。

intro·spec·tion /ˌɪntrəˈspekʃn/ *noun* [U] the careful examination of your own thoughts, feelings and reasons for behaving in a particular way 內省；反省

intro·spect·ive /ˌɪntrəˈspektɪv/ *adj.* tending to think a lot about your own thoughts, feelings, etc. 好內省的；好反省的

I

intro·vert /ˈɪntrəvɜːt; *NAmE* -vɜːrt/ *noun* a quiet person who is more interested in their own thoughts and feelings than in spending time with other people 內向的人；不喜歡與人交往的人 OPP **extrovert** ▸ **intro·ver·sion** /ˌɪntrəˈvɜːʃn; *NAmE* -ˈvɜːrʒn/ *noun* [U]

intro·vert·ed /ˈɪntrəvɜːtɪd; *NAmE* -vɜːrt-/ (also **intro·vert**) *adj.* more interested in your own thoughts and feelings than in spending time with other people 內向的；不喜歡交往的 OPP **extrovert**

in·trude /ɪnˈtruːd/ *verb* (*formal*) **1** [I] to go or be somewhere where you are not wanted or are not supposed to be 闖入；侵入；打擾：*I'm sorry to intrude, but I need to talk to someone.* 對不起打擾了，不過我有話要找人談。◇ **~ into/on/upon sb/sth** *legislation to stop newspapers from intruding on people's private lives* 禁止報章侵犯他人私生活的立法 **2** [I] **~ (on/into/upon sth)** to disturb sth or have an unpleasant effect on it 擾亂；侵擾：*The sound of the telephone intruded into his dreams.* 電話鈴聲把他從夢中擾醒了。

in·truder /ɪnˈtruːdə(r)/ *noun* **1** a person who enters a building or an area illegally 闖入者；侵入者 **2** a person who is somewhere where they are not wanted 不受歡迎的人；不速之客：*The people in the room seemed to regard her as an unwelcome intruder.* 屋子裏的人似乎把她當成不受歡迎的外人。

in·tru·sion /ɪnˈtruːʒn/ *noun* [U, C] **1** something that affects a situation or people's lives in a way that they do not want 侵擾性的事物；擾亂；侵犯：**~ (on/upon sth)** *They claim the noise from the new airport is an intrusion on their lives.* 他們聲稱新機場的噪音侵擾了他們的生活。◇ **~ (into sth)** *This was another example of press intrusion into the affairs of the royals.* 這是新聞界侵擾王室成員私事的又一實例。 **2 ~ (into/on/upon sth)** (*formal*) the act of entering a place which is private or where you may not be wanted 闖入；侵入：*She apologized for the intrusion but said she had an urgent message.* 她為逕自闖進來道歉，但說她有緊急消息。

in·tru·sive /ɪnˈtruːsɪv/ *adj.* **1** too noticeable, direct, etc. in a way that is disturbing or annoying 侵入的；闖入的；侵擾的；煩擾的：*intrusive questions* 唐突的問題 ◇ *The constant presence of the media was very intrusive.* 媒體一直在場十分令人討厭。 **2** (*phonetics* 語音) (of a speech sound 語音) produced in order to link two words together when speaking, for example the /r/ sound produced at the end of *law* by some English speakers in the phrase 'law and order'. Intrusive 'r' is not considered part of standard English. 添加的；插入的

in·tub·ate /ˈɪntjubeɪt; *NAmE* -tu-/ *verb* [T, I] **~ (sb/sth)** to put a tube into a hollow space in the body, for example to allow a person to breathe（給…）插管；插入喉管：*They managed to intubate the victim inside the wrecked car.* 他們設法為失事汽車裏的受害者插了管。◇ *to intubate the trachea* 給氣管插管 ◇ *We made the decision not to intubate.* 我們決定不用插管的做法。

in·tuit /ɪnˈtjuːɪt; *NAmE* -ˈtuː-/ *verb* **~ that …** | **~ sth** | **~ what, why, etc. …** (*formal*) to know that sth is true based on your feelings rather than on facts, what sb tells you, etc. 憑直覺知道：*She intuited that something was badly wrong.* 她憑直覺感到出了大問題。

in·tu·ition /ˌɪntjuˈɪʃn; *NAmE* -tu-/ *noun* **1** [U] the ability to know sth by using your feelings rather than considering the facts 直覺力 **2** [C] **~ (that …)** an idea or a strong feeling that sth is true although you cannot explain why（一種）直覺：*I had an intuition that something awful was about to happen.* 我直覺感到要出亂子了。

in·tui·tive /ɪnˈtjuːɪtɪv; *NAmE* -ˈtuː-/ *adj.* **1** (of ideas 思想) obtained by using your feelings rather than by considering the facts 憑直覺得到的；直覺的：*He had an intuitive sense of what the reader wanted.* 他能直覺地感到讀者需要什麼。 **2** (of people 人) able to understand sth by using feelings rather than by considering the facts 有直覺力的 **3** (of computer software, etc. 計算機軟件等) easy to understand and to use 易懂的；使用簡便的 ▸ **in·tui·tive·ly** *adv.*：*Intuitively, she knew that he was lying.* 她憑直覺知道他在說謊。

Inuit /ˈɪnjuɪt; ˈɪnuɪt/ *noun* [pl.] (*sing.* **Inuk** /ˈɪnʊk/) a race of people from northern Canada and parts of Greenland and Alaska. The name is sometimes also wrongly used to refer to people from Siberia and S and W Alaska. 因努伊特人（加拿大北部以及格陵蘭和阿拉斯加部份地區的一個種族的人，有時誤指西伯利亞及阿拉斯加南部和西部的人）➲ compare ESKIMO

Inuk·ti·tut /ɪˈnʊktɪtʊt/ *noun* [U] the language of the Inuit people 因努伊特語

in·un·date /ˈɪnʌndeɪt/ *verb* [usually passive] **1 ~ sb (with sth)** to give or send sb so many things that they cannot deal with them all 使不勝負荷；使應接不暇 SYN **overwhelm, swamp**：*We have been inundated with offers of help.* 主動援助多得使我們應接不暇。 **2 ~ sth** (*formal*) to cover an area of land with a large amount of water 淹沒；泛濫 SYN **flood** ▸ **in·un·da·tion** /ˌɪnʌnˈdeɪʃn/ *noun* [U, C]

inure /ɪˈnjʊə(r); *NAmE* ɪˈnjʊr/ *verb*

PHR V **iˈnure sb/yourself to sth** (*formal*) to make sb/yourself get used to sth unpleasant so that they/you are no longer strongly affected by it 使習慣於，使適應於（不愉快的事物）

in·vade /ɪnˈveɪd/ *verb* **1** [I, T] to enter a country, town, etc. using military force in order to take control of it 武裝入侵；侵略；侵犯：*Troops invaded on August 9th that year.* 軍隊是在那年的 8 月 9 日入侵的。◇ **~ sth** *When did the Romans invade Britain?* 古羅馬人是何時侵略英國的？ **2** [T] **~ sth** to enter a place in large numbers, especially in a way that causes damage or confusion（尤指造成損害或混亂地）湧入；侵襲：*Demonstrators invaded the government buildings.* 大批示威者闖進了政府辦公大樓。◇ *As the final whistle blew, fans began invading the field.* 比賽結束的哨聲一響，球迷便開始衝入球場。◇ *The cancer cells may invade other parts of the body.* 癌細胞可能擴散到身體的其他部位。 **3** [T] **~ sth** to affect sth in an unpleasant or annoying way 侵擾；干擾：*Do the press have the right to* ***invade her privacy*** *in this way?* 新聞界有權以這種方式干擾她的私生活嗎？ ➲ see also INVASION, INVASIVE

in·vader /ɪnˈveɪdə(r)/ *noun* an army or a country that enters another country by force in order to take control of it; a soldier fighting in such an army 武裝入侵的軍隊（或國家）；侵略者：*a foreign invader* 外國侵略者 ◇ *They prepared to repel the invaders.* 他們準備趕走侵略軍。◇ (*figurative*) *The white blood cells attack cells infected with an invader.* 白細胞攻擊受到感染的細胞。

in·valid *adj., noun, verb*

▪ ***adj.*** /ɪnˈvælɪd/ **1** not legally or officially acceptable（法律上或官方）不承認的；無效的：*The treaty was declared invalid because it had not been ratified.* 條約還沒得到批准，因此被宣佈無效。◇ *People with invalid papers are deported to another country.* 持無效證件的人被驅逐到別國。 **2** not based on all the facts, and therefore not correct 無充分事實的；站不住腳的：*an invalid argument* 站不住腳的論點 **3** (*computing* 計) of a type that the computer cannot recognize 不能識別的；無效的：*An error code will be displayed if any invalid information has been entered.* 輸入了無效信息將顯示錯誤代碼。◇ *invalid characters* 無效字符 OPP **valid**

■ **noun** /ˈɪnvəlɪd; *BrE* also ˈɪnvəliːd/ a person who needs other people to take care of them, because of illness that they have had for a long time 病弱者；久病衰弱者：*She had been a delicate child and her parents had treated her as an invalid.* 她小時候很虛弱，父母就把她當個病人照料。◇ *his invalid wife* 他的體弱多病的妻子

■ **verb** /ˈɪnvəlɪd; ˈɪnvəliːd/ **~ sb (out) | ~ sb (out of sth)** (*BrE*) to force sb to leave the armed forces because of an illness or injury（因傷病）令…退役：*He was invalided out of the army in 1943.* 他於 1943 年因傷病退役。

in·vali·date AW /ɪnˈvælɪdeɪt/ *verb* **1 ~ sth** to prove that an idea, a story, an argument, etc. is wrong 證明…錯誤；使站不住腳：*This new piece of evidence invalidates his version of events.* 這條新證據推翻了他對事件經過的說法。 **2 ~ sth** if you **invalidate** a document, contract, election, etc., you make it no longer legally or officially valid or acceptable 使無效；使作廢 OPP **validate** ▸ **in·vali·da·tion** /ɪnˌvælɪˈdeɪʃn/ *noun* [U]

in·val·id·ity AW /ˌɪnvəˈlɪdəti/ *noun* [U] **1** (*BrE, technical* 術語) the state of being unable to take care of yourself because of illness or injury 病弱；傷殘；不能自理 **2** (*formal*) the state of not being legally or officially acceptable 無效；失效 ➲ compare VALIDITY

in·valu·able /ɪnˈvæljuəbl/ *adj.* extremely useful 極有用的；極寶貴的 SYN **valuable**：*invaluable information* 寶貴的信息◇ **~ to/for sb/sth** *The book will be invaluable for students in higher education.* 這本書對於高校學生將有重大價值。◇ **~ in sth** *The research should* ***prove invaluable*** *in the study of children's language.* 這項調查對於兒童語言的研究應極有價值。➲ compare VALUABLE

HELP **Invaluable** means 'very valuable or useful'. The opposite of **valuable** is **valueless** or **worthless**. * invaluable 表示十分寶貴或有用，反義詞是 valueless 或 worthless。

in·vari·able AW /ɪnˈveəriəbl; *NAmE* -ˈver-/ *adj.* always the same; never changing 始終如一的；永無變化的 SYN **unchanging**：*Her routine was invariable.* 她的日常生活總是千篇一律。◇ *his invariable courtesy and charm* 他那一貫的彬彬有禮和魅力◇ *an invariable principle* 一貫原則 ➲ compare VARIABLE

in·vari·ably AW /ɪnˈveəriəbli; *NAmE* -ˈver-/ *adv.* always 始終如一地；一貫地 SYN **without fail**：*This acute infection of the brain is almost invariably fatal.* 這種急性大腦傳染病幾乎總是導致死亡。◇ *This is not invariably the case.* 事情並非總是如此。◇ *Invariably the reply came back, 'Not now!'* 答覆無例外地又是："現在不行！"

in·vari·ant /ɪnˈveəriənt; *NAmE* -ˈver-/ *adj.* (*technical* 術語) always the same; never changing 不變的；恆定的 SYN **invariable**

in·va·sion /ɪnˈveɪʒn/ *noun* [C, U] **1** the act of an army entering another country by force in order to take control of it 武裝入侵；侵略；侵犯：*the German invasion of Poland in 1939* 德國於 1939 年對波蘭的侵略◇ *the threat of invasion* 入侵的威脅◇ *an* ***invasion force/fleet*** 侵略軍／艦隊 ➲ COLLOCATIONS at WAR **2** the fact of a large number of people or things arriving somewhere, especially people or things that are disturbing or unpleasant（尤指煩擾的）湧入：*the annual tourist invasion* 一年一度遊客的湧入◇ *Farmers are struggling to cope with an invasion of slugs.* 農民正在努力對付蛞蝓的大肆侵害。 **3** an act or a process that affects sb/sth in a way that is not welcome 侵犯；干預：*The actress described the photographs of her as an* ***invasion of privacy***. 那位女演員認為她的這些照片是對隱私權的侵犯。➲ see also INVADE

in·va·sive /ɪnˈveɪsɪv/ *adj.* (*formal*) **1** (especially of diseases within the body 尤指體內疾病) spreading very quickly and difficult to stop 侵入的；侵襲的：*invasive cancer* 擴散性腫瘤 **2** (of medical treatment 醫療) involving cutting into the body 切入的；開刀的：*invasive surgery* 開刀手術 ➲ see also INVADE OPP **non-invasive**

in·vec·tive /ɪnˈvektɪv/ *noun* [U] (*formal*) rude language and unpleasant remarks that sb shouts when they are very angry 辱罵；咒罵

in·veigh /ɪnˈveɪ/ *verb*
PHR V **inˈveigh against sb/sth** (*formal*) to criticize sb/sth strongly 猛烈抨擊；痛罵

in·vei·gle /ɪnˈveɪgl/ *verb* **~ sb/yourself (into sth/into doing sth)** (*formal*) to achieve control over sb in a clever and dishonest way, especially so that they will do what you want 引誘；哄騙；騙取：*He* ***inveigled himself into her affections*** (= dishonestly made her love him). 他騙取了她的愛。

in·vent 0‑w /ɪnˈvent/ *verb*
1 0‑w **~ sth** to produce or design sth that has not existed before 發明；創造：*Who invented the steam engine?* 誰發明了蒸汽機？ **2** 0‑w **~ sth** to say or describe sth that is not true, especially in order to trick people 編造；捏造；虛構：*What excuse did he invent this time?* 他這次編了什麼藉口？◇ *Many children invent an imaginary friend.* 很多兒童都有一個假想朋友。

in·ven·tion 0‑w /ɪnˈvenʃn/ *noun*
1 0‑w [C] a thing or an idea that has been invented 發明（物）；創造：*Fax machines were a wonderful invention at the time.* 傳真機在當時是一項了不起的發明。 **2** 0‑w [U] the act of inventing sth 發明；創造：*Such changes have not been seen since the invention of the printing press.* 自從發明了印刷機，這種變革再也沒有出現過。 **3** [C, U] the act of inventing a story or an idea and pretending that it is true; a story invented in this way 虛構；編造；虛構的故事：*This story is apparently a complete invention.* 這個故事顯然完全是虛構的。 **4** [U] the ability to have new and interesting ideas 創造力；創意：*John was full of invention—always making up new dance steps and sequences.* 約翰有豐富的創造力——總能編出新的舞步和連續舞步。 IDM see NECESSITY

in·vent·ive /ɪnˈventɪv/ *adj.* **1** (especially of people 尤指人) able to think of new and interesting ideas 善於創新的；有創意的 SYN **imaginative**：*She has a highly inventive mind.* 她的頭腦非常善於創新。 **2** (of ideas 思想) new and interesting 有新意的；有創意的 ▸ **in·vent·ive·ly** *adv.* **in·ven·tive·ness** *noun* [U]

in·vent·or /ɪnˈventə(r)/ *noun* a person who has invented sth or whose job is inventing things 發明者；發明家；創造者

in·ven·tory /ˈɪnvəntri; *NAmE* -tɔːri/ *noun, verb*
■ **noun** (*pl.* **-ies**) **1** [C] a written list of all the objects, furniture, etc. in a particular building（建築物裏的物品、傢具等的）清單；財產清單：*an inventory of the museum's contents* 博物館館藏清單 **2** [U] (*NAmE*) all the goods in a shop（商店的）存貨，庫存 SYN **stock**：*The inventory will be disposed of over the next twelve weeks.* 在未來的十二個星期中將進行清倉處理。◇ *inventory control* 庫存管理 ➲ compare STOCKTAKING (1)
■ **verb** (**in·ven·tor·ies**, **in·ven·tory·ing**, **in·ven·tor·ied**, **in·ven·tor·ied**) **~ sth** (*formal*) to make a complete list of sth 開列清單：*I've inventoried my father's collection of prints.* 我把父親收藏的圖片列成了清單。

in·verse /ˌɪnˈvɜːs; *NAmE* ˌɪnˈvɜːrs/ *adj.* **1** [only before noun] opposite in amount or position to sth else（數量、位置）相反的，反向的：*A person's wealth is often* ***in inverse proportion to*** *their happiness* (= the more money they have, the less happy they are). 一個人的財富常常與他的幸福成反比。◇ *There is often an* ***inverse relationship*** *between the power of the tool and how easy it is to use.* 工具的功能越強大，操作起來往往越費事。
2 the ˈinverse *noun* [sing.] (*technical* 術語) the exact opposite of sth 反面；相反的事物 ▸ **in·verse·ly** /ˌɪnˈvɜːsli; *NAmE* -ˈvɜːrs-/ *adv.*：*We regard health as inversely related to social class.* 我們認為健康狀況與社會地位成相反關係。

in·ver·sion /ɪnˈvɜːʃn; *NAmE* ɪnˈvɜːrʒn; -ʃn/ *noun* [U, C] (*technical* 術語) the act of changing the position or order of sth to its opposite, or of turning sth upside down 倒置；顛倒；倒轉：*the inversion of normal word order* 正常詞序的倒裝◇ *an inversion of the truth* 顛倒是非

I

in·vert /ɪnˈvɜːt; *NAmE* ɪnˈvɜːrt/ *verb* **~ sth** (*formal*) to change the normal position of sth, especially by turning it upside down or by arranging it in the opposite order （使）倒轉，顛倒，倒置： *Place a plate over the cake tin and invert it.* 在蛋糕烤模上蓋一個盤子，然後將其翻倒過來。

in·ver·te·brate /ɪnˈvɜːtɪbrət; *NAmE* -ˈvɜːrt-/ *noun* (*technical* 術語) any animal with no BACKBONE, for example a WORM 無脊椎動物 ➲ compare VERTEBRATE

in͵verted ˈcommas *noun* [pl.] (*BrE*) = QUOTATION MARKS

IDM **in inverted commas** (*informal*) used to show that you think a particular word, description, etc. is not true or appropriate（對正確性或適合性表示置疑）所謂的，加引號的： *The manager showed us to our 'luxury apartment', in inverted commas.* 經理帶我們去看了我們所謂的"豪華單元"。

in͵verted ˈsnobbery *noun* [U] (*BrE, disapproving*) the attitude that disapproves of everything connected with high social status and that is proud of low social status 倒轉勢利眼（反對一切與社會高層有關的事物，而為社會底層感到自豪）

in·vest 🔑 **AW** /ɪnˈvest/ *verb*
1 🔑 [I, T] to buy property, shares in a company, etc. in the hope of making a profit 投資： **~ (in sth)** *Now is a good time to invest in the property market.* 現在是對房地產市場投資的好時機。◇ **~ sth (in sth)** *He invested his life savings in his daughter's business.* 他把一生的積蓄投資到了女兒的企業。 **2** 🔑 [I, T] (of an organization or government, etc. 機構、政府等) to spend money on sth in order to make it better or more successful （把資金）投入： **~ (in/on sth)** *The government has* ***invested heavily*** *in public transport.* 政府已對公共交通投入了大量資金。◇ **~ sth (in/on sth)** *The college is to invest $2 million in a new conference hall.* 這所學院計劃投入 200 萬元建造新的會議大廳。◇ *In his time managing the club he has invested millions on new players.* 他在管理俱樂部期間投入了幾百萬培養新運動員。 **3** [T] **~ sth (in sth)** | **~ sth (in) doing sth** to spend time, energy, effort, etc. on sth that you think is good or useful 投入（時間、精力等）： *She had invested all her adult life in the relationship.* 她把成年後的時間全用於維護那一關係。 **4** [T] (*formal*) to give sb power or authority, especially as part of their job 授予，給予（權力等）： **~ sb (with sth)** *The new position invested her with a good deal of responsibility.* 新職位賦予她重大的責任。◇ **~ sb (as sth)** *The interview was broadcast on the same day he was invested as President.* 這次訪問是在他成為總統的當天播放的。 ➲ see also INVESTITURE

PHR V **inˈvest in sth** (*informal*, often *humorous*) to buy sth that is expensive but useful 購買昂貴有用的東西： *Don't you think it's about time you invested in a new coat?* 你不覺得該花點錢買件新外套了嗎？ **inˈvest sb/sth with sth** (*formal*) to make sb/sth seem to have a particular quality 使似乎具備某性質： *Being a model invests her with a certain glamour.* 當模特兒似乎給她增添了一定的魅力。

in·ves·ti·gate 🔑 **AW** /ɪnˈvestɪɡeɪt/ *verb*
1 🔑 [I, T] to carefully examine the facts of a situation, an event, a crime, etc. to find out the truth about it or how it happened 調查，偵查（某事）： *The FBI has been called in to investigate.* 聯邦調查局奉命進行調查。◇ (*informal*) *'What was that noise?' 'I'll go and investigate.'* "那是什麼聲音？" "我去看一下。" ◇ **~ sth** *Police are investigating possible links between the murders.* 警察正在調查這些謀殺案之間可能存在的關聯。◇ **~ what, how, etc. …** *Police are investigating what happened.* 警察正在調查事情發生的經過。 ➲ **COLLOCATIONS** at CRIME **2** 🔑 [T] **~ sb (for sth)** to try to find out information about sb's character, activities, etc. 調查（某人）： *This is not the first time he has been investigated by the police for fraud.* 這不是警方第一次調查他是否有欺詐行為。 **3** 🔑 [T, I] to find out information and facts about a subject or problem by study or research 研究；調查： **~ (sth)** *Scientists are investigating the effects of diet on fighting cancer.* 科學家正在研究飲食的抗癌作用。◇ **~ how, what, etc. …** *The research investigates how foreign speakers gain fluency.* 這項研究旨在調查講外語的人如何增加流利程度。

in·ves·ti·ga·tion 🔑 **AW** /ɪn͵vestɪˈɡeɪʃn/ *noun* [C, U]
1 🔑 an official examination of the facts about a situation, crime, etc.（正式的）調查，偵查： *a* ***criminal/murder/police investigation*** 刑事／兇案／警方調查 ◇ *She is still* ***under investigation***. 她仍在接受調查。 ◇ **~ into sth** *The police have completed their investigations into the accident.* 警察已完成對這次事故的調查。 ➲ **COLLOCATIONS** at CRIME **2** 🔑 **~ (into sth)** a scientific or academic examination of the facts of a subject or problem 科學研究；學術研究 **SYN** **enquiry**： *an investigation into the spending habits of teenagers* 對十幾歲青少年的消費習慣進行的調查研究

in·ves·ti·ga·tive **AW** /ɪnˈvestɪɡətɪv; *NAmE* -ɡeɪtɪv/ (also *less frequent* **in·ves·ti·ga·tory** /ɪnˈvestɪɡətəri; *NAmE* -ɡətɔːri/) *adj.* [usually before noun] involving examining an event or a situation to find out the truth 調查研究的；偵查的： *The article was an excellent piece of* ***investigative journalism***. 這是一篇優秀的調查研究報道。◇ *The police have full investigatory powers.* 警察擁有調查全權。

in·ves·ti·ga·tor **AW** /ɪnˈvestɪɡeɪtə(r)/ *noun* a person who examines a situation such as an accident or a crime to find out the truth 調查者；偵查員： *air safety investigators* 飛行安全調查人員 ◇ *a* ***private investigator*** (= a DETECTIVE) 私人偵探

in·ves·ti·ture /ɪnˈvestɪtʃə(r)/ *noun* [U, C] a ceremony at which sb formally receives an official title or special powers 授銜儀式；授權儀式

in·vest·ment 🔑 **AW** /ɪnˈvestmənt/ *noun*
1 🔑 [U] the act of investing money in sth 投資： *to* ***encourage foreign investment*** 鼓勵外國投資 ◇ *investment income* 投資收益 ◇ **~ in sth** *This country needs investment in education.* 這個國家需要對教育進行投資。 ➲ **COLLOCATIONS** at ECONOMY **2** 🔑 [C] the money that you invest, or the thing that you invest in 投資額；投資物： *a minimum investment of $10 000* * 1 萬元的最低投資額 ◇ *a high* ***return on my investments*** 我的投資的高收益 ◇ *Our investments are not doing well.* 我們的投資境況不佳。◇ *We bought the house* ***as an investment*** (= to make money). 我們買這所房子作為投資。 ➲ **COLLOCATIONS** at BUSINESS **3** 🔑 [C] a thing that is worth buying because it will be useful or helpful 值得買的東西；有用的投資物： *A microwave is a* ***good investment***. 微波爐值得買。 **4** [U, C] the act of giving time or effort to a particular task in order to make it successful （時間、精力的）投入： *The project has demanded considerable investment of time and effort.* 該項目已讓我們投入了相當多的時間和精力。

inˈvestment bank (*NAmE*) (*BrE* ͵**merchant ˈbank**) *noun* a bank that deals with large businesses 投資銀行 ▸ **in͵vestment ˈbanker** *noun* **in͵vestment ˈbanking** *noun* [U]

in·vest·or **AW** /ɪnˈvestə(r)/ *noun* a person or an organization that invests money in sth 投資者；投資機構： *small investors* (= private people) 小額投資者 ◇ *institutional investors* 機構投資者

in·vet·er·ate /ɪnˈvetərət/ *adj.* [usually before noun] (*formal*, often *disapproving*) **1** (of a person 人) always doing sth or enjoying sth, and unlikely to stop 積習難改的；有…癮的： *an inveterate liar* 積習難改的說謊者 **2** (of a bad feeling or habit 惡感或陋習) done or felt for a long time and unlikely to change 長期形成的；根深蒂固的： *inveterate hostility* 根深蒂固的敵意

in·vidi·ous /ɪnˈvɪdiəs/ *adj.* (*formal*) unpleasant and unfair; likely to offend sb or make them jealous 討厭而不公正的；易引起反感的；招人嫉妒的： *We were* ***in the invidious position*** *of having to choose whether to break the law or risk lives.* 我們處於左右為難的窘境，不知是要違法還是要拿生命冒險。◇ *It would be invidious to single out any one person to thank.* 單獨感謝任何一個人都易引起反感。

in·vigi·late /ɪnˈvɪdʒɪleɪt/ *verb* (*BrE*) (*NAmE* **proc·tor**) [T, I] **~ (sth)** to watch people while they are taking an exam to make sure that they have everything they need, that they keep to the rules, etc. 監(考): *to invigilate an exam* 監考 ▸ **in·vigi·la·tion** /ɪnˌvɪdʒɪˈleɪʃn/ *noun* [U] **in·vigi·la·tor** /ɪnˈvɪdʒɪleɪtə(r)/ (*BrE*) (*NAmE* **proc·tor**) *noun*: *If you have a problem, ask the invigilator.* 有問題就問監考人。

in·vig·or·ate /ɪnˈvɪɡəreɪt/ *verb* **1** [often passive] **~ sb** to make sb feel healthy and full of energy 使生氣勃勃;使精神煥發: *The cold water invigorated him.* 冷水讓他打起了精神。◇ *They felt refreshed and invigorated after the walk.* 散步之後他們感到精神煥發。 **2 ~ sth** to make a situation, an organization, etc. efficient and successful 使蒸蒸日上;使興旺發達: *They are looking into ways of invigorating the department.* 他們正在尋找激發這個部門活力的方法。 ▸ **in·vig·or·at·ing** *adj.*: *an invigorating walk/shower* 令人精神振作的散步/淋浴

in·vin·cible /ɪnˈvɪnsəbl/ *adj.* too strong to be defeated or changed 不可戰勝的;不能改變的 SYN **unconquerable**: *The team seemed invincible.* 這個隊似乎戰無不勝。◇ *an invincible belief in his own ability* 對他自己的能力堅定不移的信念 ▸ **in·vin·ci·bil·ity** /ɪnˌvɪnsəˈbɪləti/ *noun* [U]

in·viol·able /ɪnˈvaɪələbl/ *adj.* (*formal*) that must be respected and not attacked or destroyed 不容褻瀆的;不可侵犯的;不容破壞的: *the inviolable right to life* 不可侵犯的生命權 ◇ *inviolable territory* 不可侵犯的領土 ◇ *an inviolable rule* 不容違背的規則 ▸ **in·viol·abil·ity** /ɪnˌvaɪələˈbɪləti/ *noun* [U]

in·viol·ate /ɪnˈvaɪələt/ *adj.* (*formal*) that has been, or must be, respected and cannot be attacked or destroyed 未受(或不容)侵犯的;未受(或不容)褻瀆的;不容破壞的

in·vis·ible AW /ɪnˈvɪzəbl/ *adj.* **1** that cannot be seen 看不見的;隱形的: *a wizard who could make himself invisible* 能隱身的術士 ◇ *She felt invisible in the crowd.* 她覺得自己淹沒在人群中。◇ **~ to sb/sth** *stars invisible to the naked eye* 肉眼看不見的星球 OPP **visible** **2** (*economics* 經) connected with a service that a country provides, such as banks or TOURISM, rather than goods 無形的(與服務而非商品有關): *invisible earnings* 無形收益 ▸ **in·visi·bil·ity** AW /ɪnˌvɪzəˈbɪləti/ *noun* [U]: *The ink had faded to invisibility.* 墨水已褪色看不見了。 **in·vis·ibly** /ɪnˈvɪzəbli/ *adv.*: *He looked at me and nodded, almost invisibly.* 他看着我點了點頭,幾乎讓人看不出來。

in·vi·ta·tion 🔑 /ˌɪnvɪˈteɪʃn/ *noun*
1 🔑 [C] a spoken or written request to sb to do sth or to go somewhere (口頭或書面的)邀請: *to* ***issue/extend an invitation*** 發出/致送邀請 ◇ *to* ***accept/turn down/decline an invitation*** 接受/拒絕/婉拒邀請 ◇ **~ to sth** *an invitation to the party* 參加晚會的請柬 ◇ **~ to do sth** *I have an* ***open invitation*** (= not restricted to a particular date) *to visit my friend in Japan.* 我在日本的朋友邀請我隨時去看他。 **2** 🔑 [U] the act of inviting sb or of being invited 邀請;獲得邀請: *A concert was held* ***at the invitation of*** *the mayor.* 在市長的邀請下舉辦了一場音樂會。◇ *Admission is* ***by invitation only***. 憑請柬入場。 **3** 🔑 [C] a card or piece of paper that you use to invite sb to sth 請柬;請帖: *Have you ordered the wedding invitations yet?* 你訂製婚禮請帖了嗎? **4** [sing.] **~ to sb (to do sth) | ~ to sth** something that encourages sb to do sth, usually sth bad 鼓勵;(尤指)慫恿,招致: *Leaving the doors unlocked is an* ***open invitation*** *to burglars.* 出門不上鎖無異於開門揖盜。

in·vi·ta·tion·al /ˌɪnvɪˈteɪʃənl/ *noun* (*especially NAmE*) (often used in names 常用於名稱) a sports event that you can take part in only if you are invited 邀請賽 ▸ **in·vi·ta·tion·al** *adj.*

in·vite 🔑 *verb, noun*

▪ ***verb*** /ɪnˈvaɪt/ **1** 🔑 to ask sb to come to a social event 邀請: **~ sb to sth** *Have you been invited to their party?* 你接到參加他們的聚會的邀請了嗎? ◇ **~ sb** *I'd have liked to have gone but I wasn't invited.* 我倒是想去,但我沒接到邀請。◇ **~ sb to do sth** *They have invited me to go to Paris with them.* 他們邀請我和他們一同去巴黎。 **2** 🔑 (*formal*) to ask sb formally to go somewhere or do sth (正式)邀請,請求,要求: **~ sb (to/for sth)** *Successful candidates will be invited for interview next week.* 通過甄別的候選人將獲邀於下週參加面試。◇ **~ sth (from sb)** *He invited questions from the audience.* 他請聽眾提問。◇ **~ sb to do sth** *Readers are invited to email their comments to us.* 歡迎讀者通過電子郵件向我們反饋意見。 **3 ~ sth | ~ sb/sth to do sth** to make sth, especially sth bad or unpleasant, likely to happen 招致(尤指壞事) SYN **ask for**: *Such comments are just inviting trouble.* 這種評論簡直是在惹麻煩。 ➲ see also UNINVITED

PHR V **inˌvite sb aˈlong** to ask sb to go somewhere with you and other people 邀請某人一道去;請某人同行: *I got myself invited along.* 我爭得受邀一同前往。 **inˌvite sb ˈback 1** to ask sb to come to your home after you have been somewhere together (一起相處後)邀請某人回自己家: *After the movie, she invited me back for a drink.* 看完電影後,她請我到她家去喝了一杯。 **2** to ask sb to come to your home a second time, or to ask sb to come to your home after you have been to theirs 邀請再訪(或回訪) **inˌvite sb ˈin/ˈup** to ask sb to come into your home, especially after you have been somewhere together (尤指一起到某處之後)邀請某人到自己家中 **inˌvite sb ˈover/ˈround/aˈround** to ask sb to come to your home 邀請某人到家中

▪ ***noun*** /ˈɪnvaɪt/ (*informal*) an invitation 邀請;請柬: *Thanks for your invite.* 感謝你的邀請。

in·vit·ing /ɪnˈvaɪtɪŋ/ *adj.* making you want to do, try, taste, etc. sth 誘人的;吸引人的 SYN **attractive**: *an inviting smell* 誘人的氣味 ◇ *The water looks really inviting.* 水面看上去真誘人。 ▸ **in·vit·ing·ly** *adv.*

in vitro /ɪn ˈviːtrəʊ; *NAmE* ˈviːtroʊ/ *adj.* (from *Latin, biology* 生) (of processes 過程) taking place outside a living body, in scientific APPARATUS 在生物體外進行的;在科學儀器中進行的: *in vitro experiments* 在儀器中進行的實驗 ◇ *the development of* ***in vitro fertilization*** 體外受精的研究發展 ➲ see also IVF ▸ **in vitro** *adv.*: *an egg fertilized in vitro* 體外受精卵

in vivo /ɪn ˈviːvəʊ; *NAmE* ˈviːvoʊ/ *adj.* (from *Latin, biology* 生) (of processes 過程) taking place in a living body 在生物體內進行的 ▸ **in vivo** *adv.*

in·vo·ca·tion /ˌɪnvəˈkeɪʃn/ *noun* [U, C] **1** (*formal*) the act of asking for help, from a god or from a person in authority; the act of referring to sth or of calling for sth to appear (向神或權威人士的)求助;祈禱 **2** (*computing* 計) the act of making a particular function start 調用;啟用

in·voice /ˈɪnvɔɪs/ *noun, verb*

▪ ***noun*** a list of goods that have been sold, work that has been done etc., showing what you must pay 發票;(發貨或服務)費用清單 SYN **bill**: *to* ***send/issue/settle an invoice*** *for the goods* 送出/開出/結清費用清單 ◇ *an invoice for £250* 一張 250 英鎊的發票 ➲ SYNONYMS at BILL

▪ ***verb*** (*business* 商) to write or send sb a bill for work you have done or goods you have provided 開發票(或清單);發出發票(或清單): **~ sb (for sth)** *You will be invoiced for these items at the end of the month.* 你將於月底收到這些項目的費用清單。◇ **~ sth (to sb/sth)** *Invoice the goods to my account.* 請把貨品的發票開到我的賬上。

in·voke AW /ɪnˈvəʊk; *NAmE* ɪnˈvoʊk/ *verb* **1 ~ sth (against sb)** to mention or use a law, rule, etc. as a reason for doing sth 援引,援用(法律、規則等作為行動理由): *It is unlikely that libel laws will be invoked.* 不大可能訴諸誹謗法。 **2 ~ sb/sth** to mention a person, a theory, an example, etc. to support your opinions or ideas, or as a reason for sth 提及,援引(某人、某理論、實例等作為支持): *She invoked several eminent scholars to back up her argument.* 她援引了幾位赫赫有名的學者來支持她的論點。 **3 ~ sth** to mention sb's name to make people feel a particular thing or act in a particular way 提出(某人的名字,以激發某種感覺或行動): *His name was invoked as a symbol of the revolution.* 他的名字被提出作為那次革命的象徵。 **4 ~ sb** to make a request (for help) to sb, especially a god 向(某人)請求幫助;(尤指)祈求神助 **5 ~ sth** to make sb have a particular feeling or imagine a particular scene 使產生,喚起,引起(感情或想像) SYN **evoke**:

I

The opening paragraph invokes a vision of England in the early Middle Ages. 頭一段的引言描繪出中世紀前期的英格蘭景象。**HELP** Some people think this use is not correct. 有些人認為此用法不正確。 **6 ~ sth** (*computing* 計) to begin to run a program, etc. 調用；激活：*This command will invoke the HELP system.* 這條指令將啟用"幫助"系統。 **7 ~ sb/sth** to make evil appear by using magic 用法術召喚（魔鬼）

in·vol·un·tary /ɪnˈvɒləntri; *NAmE* ɪnˈvɑːlənteri/ *adj.* **1** an **involuntary** movement, etc. is made suddenly, without you intending it or being able to control it 無意識的；不自覺的：*an involuntary cry of pain* 不由自主的痛苦的喊叫 **OPP** **voluntary** **2** happening without the person concerned wanting it to 非自願的；非本意的：*the involuntary repatriation of immigrants* 對移民的強制性遣返 ◇ *involuntary childlessness* 出於無奈的無子女狀況 ▸ **in·vol·un·tar·ily** /ɪnˈvɒləntrəli; *NAmE* ɪnˌvɑːlənˈterəli/ *adv.*

in·volve 0m **AW** /ɪnˈvɒlv; *NAmE* ɪnˈvɑːlv/ *verb* **1** 0m if a situation, an event or an activity **involves** sth, that thing is an important or necessary part or result of it 包含；需要；使成為必然部份（或結果）**SYN** **entail**：**~ sth** *Any investment involves an element of risk.* 任何投資都有一定的風險。◇ *Many of the crimes involved drugs.* 許多罪案都與毒品有關。◇ **~ doing sth** *The test will involve answering questions about a photograph.* 考試將包括回答一些關於一張照片的問題。◇ **~ sb/sth doing sth** *The job involves me travelling all over the country.* 這份工作需要我在全國各地來往。◇ (*formal*) *The job involves my travelling all over the country.* 這份工作需要我在全國各地來往。 **2** 0m **~ sb/sth** if a situation, an event or an activity **involves** sb/sth, they take part in it or are affected by it 牽涉；牽連；影響：*There was a serious incident involving a group of youths.* 有一起涉及一群年輕人的嚴重事件。◇ *How many vehicles were involved in the crash?* 這次撞車事故涉及多少輛汽車？ **3** 0m to make sb take part in sth （使）參加，加入：**~ sb (in sth/in doing sth)** *We want to involve as many people as possible in the celebrations.* 我們希望參加慶典的人越多越好。◇ **~ yourself (in sth)** *Parents should involve themselves in their child's education.* 父母應當參與孩子的教育。 **4 ~ sb (in sth)** to say or do sth to show that sb took part in sth, especially a crime 表明（某人參與了犯罪等）**SYN** **implicate**：*His confession involved a number of other politicians in the affair.* 他的自白供出其他一些政治人物也涉及此事。

PHR V **inˈvolve sb in sth** to make sb experience sth, especially sth unpleasant 把某人牽涉（或牽扯）到某事裏：*You have involved me in a great deal of extra work.* 你害得我添了一大堆額外的工作。

in·volved 0m **AW** /ɪnˈvɒlvd; *NAmE* ɪnˈvɑːlvd/ *adj.* **1** 0m [not before noun] **~ (in sth)** taking part in sth; being part of sth or connected with sth 參與；作為一部份；有關聯：*to* **be/become/get involved** *in politics* 參與政治 ◇ *We need to examine all the costs involved in the project first.* 我們首先應該仔細考慮所有與這一項目有關的費用。◇ *We'll make our decision and contact the people involved.* 我們將作出決定，再與有關人員聯繫。◇ *Some people tried to stop the fight but I didn't want to get involved.* 有人設法阻止打鬥，但我不想牽涉進去。**HELP** In this meaning, **involved** is often used after a noun. * involved 作此義時常用於名詞之後。**OPP** **uninvolved** **2** 0m [not usually before noun] giving a lot of time or attention to sb/sth 付出很多時間；關注：**~ (with sth/sb)** *She was deeply involved with the local hospital.* 她曾全心投入當地醫院。◇ **~ (in sth/sb)** *I was so involved in my book I didn't hear you knock.* 我全神貫注在看書，沒聽到你敲門。◇ *He's a very involved father* (= he spends a lot of time with his children). 他是個很投入的父親。**OPP** **uninvolved** **3** 0m [not usually before noun] having a close personal relationship with sb 關係密切：*They're not romantically involved.* 他們並沒有墮入情網。◇ **~ with sb/sth** *You're too emotionally involved with the situation.* 你在這件事上投入太多感情了。**OPP** **uninvolved** **4** complicated and difficult to understand 複雜難解的 **SYN** **complex**：*an involved plot* 複雜的情節

in·volve·ment 0m **AW** /ɪnˈvɒlvmənt; *NAmE* -ˈvɑːlv-/ *noun* **1** 0m [U] **~ (in/with sth)** the act of taking part in sth 參與；加入；插手 **SYN** **participation**：*US involvement in European wars* 美國對歐洲戰爭的干預 **2** 0m [U, C] **~ (in/with sth)** the act of giving a lot of time and attention to sth you care about 耗費時間；投入；沉迷：*her growing involvement with contemporary music* 她對現代音樂的日益投入 **3** [C, U] **~ (with sb)** a romantic or sexual relationship with sb that you are not married to 戀愛；性愛：*He spoke openly about his involvement with the singer.* 他公開講述了他和那個歌手的私情。

in·vul·ner·able /ɪnˈvʌlnərəbl/ *adj.* that cannot be harmed or defeated; safe 不會受傷害的；打不敗的；安全的：*to be in an invulnerable position* 立於不敗之地 ◇ **~ to sth** *The submarine is invulnerable to attack while at sea.* 潛艇在海上是不會受到攻擊的。**OPP** **vulnerable** ▸ **in·vul·ner·abil·ity** /ɪnˌvʌlnərəˈbɪləti/ *noun* [U]

in·ward /ˈɪnwəd; *NAmE* -wərd/ *adj., adv.*

■ ***adj.*** **1** [only before noun] inside your mind and not shown to other people 內心的；精神的：*an inward smile* 內心的微笑 ◇ *Her calm expression hid her inward panic.* 她平靜的外表掩蓋了內心的恐慌。 **2** towards the inside or centre of sth 向內的；向中心的：*an inward flow* 朝裏的流動 ◇ *an inward curve* 內彎 **OPP** **outward**

■ ***adv.*** (also **in·wards** especially in *BrE*) **1** towards the inside or centre 向內；向中心：*The door opens inwards.* 門向裏開。 **2** towards yourself and your interests 向自己；向內心：*Her thoughts turned inwards.* 她的思想轉向了內省。◇ (*disapproving*) *an inward-looking person* (= one who is not interested in other people) 對他人不感興趣的人 **OPP** **outwards**

ˌ**inward inˈvestment** *noun* [U, C] (*business* 商) money that is invested in a particular country from outside it 對內投資

in·ward·ly /ˈɪnwədli; *NAmE* -wərd-/ *adv.* in your mind; secretly 在內心；秘密地：*She groaned inwardly.* 她在心裏呻吟。◇ *I was inwardly furious.* 我當時怒火中燒。**OPP** **outwardly**

in·ward·ness /ˈɪnwədnəs; *NAmE* -wərd-/ *noun* [U] (*formal* or *literary*) interest in feelings and emotions rather than in the world around 心性；靈性；精神性

in·yanga /ɪnˈjɑːŋə/ *noun* (*pl.* **in·yangas** or **izin·yanga** /ˌɪzɪnˈjɑːŋə/) (*SAfrE*) a person who treats people who are ill/sick using natural materials such as plants, etc. 草藥醫生；郎中 ➲ compare SANGOMA

in-your-ˈface *adj.* (*informal*) used to describe an attitude, a performance, etc. that is aggressive in style and deliberately designed to make people react strongly for or against it （態度、表演等）赤裸裸的，富刺激性的，有意惹人發怒的：*in-your-face action thrillers* 刺激的驚險動作片

iod·ide /ˈaɪədaɪd/ *noun* [C] (*chemistry* 化) a chemical which contains iodine 碘化物

iod·ine /ˈaɪədiːn; *NAmE* -daɪn/ *noun* [U] (*symb.* **I**) a chemical element. Iodine is a substance found in sea water. A liquid containing iodine is sometimes used as an ANTISEPTIC (= a substance used on wounds to prevent infection). 碘

ion /ˈaɪən; *BrE* also ˈaɪɒn; *NAmE* also ˈaɪɑːn/ *noun* (*physics* 物 or *chemistry* 化) an atom or a MOLECULE with a positive or negative electric charge caused by its losing or gaining one or more ELECTRONS 離子

-ion (also **-ation**, **-ition**, **-sion**, **-tion**, **-xion**) *suffix* (in nouns 構成名詞) the action or state of …行為；…狀態：*hesitation* 猶豫 ◇ *competition* 競爭 ◇ *confession* 供認

ionic /aɪˈɒnɪk; *NAmE* -ˈɑːn-/ *adj.* **1** (*chemistry* 化) of or related to ions 離子的 **2** (*chemistry* 化) (of a chemical BOND 化學鍵) using the electrical pull between positive and negative ions 離子的；電價的 ➲ compare COVALENT **3 Ionic** (*architecture* 建) used to describe a style of ARCHITECTURE in ancient Greece that uses a curved decoration in the shape of a SCROLL 愛奧尼亞柱式的（古希臘建築風格，有渦捲飾）

ion·ize (*BrE* also **-ise**) /ˈaɪənaɪz/ *verb* [T, I] **~ (sth)** (*technical* 術語) to change sth or be changed into ions （使）

電離，離子化 ▸ **ion·iza·tion, -isa·tion** /ˌaɪənaɪˈzeɪʃn; *NAmE* -nəˈz-/ *noun* [U]

ion·izer (*BrE* also **-iser**) /ˈaɪənaɪzə(r)/ *noun* a device that is used to make air in a room fresh and healthy by producing negative IONS 負離子發生器；離子化裝置

iono·sphere /aɪˈɒnəsfɪə(r); *NAmE* aɪˈɑːnəsfɪr/ *noun* **the ionosphere** [sing.] a layer of the earth's atmosphere between about 80 and 1 000 kilometres above the surface of the earth, that reflects radio waves around the earth 電離層 ➲ compare STRATOSPHERE

iota /aɪˈəʊtə; *NAmE* aɪˈoʊtə/ *noun* **1** [sing.] (usually used in negative sentences 通常用於否定句) an extremely small amount 微量；極少量：*There is not one iota of truth* (= no truth at all) *in the story.* 這種説法沒有絲毫真實性。◇ *I don't think that would help one iota.* 我認為那樣毫無幫助。**2** the 9th letter of the Greek alphabet (Ι, ι) 希臘字母表的第 9 個字母

IOU /ˌaɪ əʊ ˈjuː; *NAmE* oʊ/ *noun* (*informal*) a written promise that you will pay sb the money you owe them (a way of writing 'I owe you') 借據，欠條（表示 I owe you）：*an IOU for £100* * 100 英鎊的借據

IPA /ˌaɪ piː ˈeɪ/ *abbr.* International Phonetic Alphabet (an alphabet that is used to show the pronunciation of words in any language) 國際音標

IP address /ˌaɪ ˈpiː ədres/ *noun* (*computing* 計) a series of numbers separated by dots that identifies a particular computer connected to the Internet（計算機的）網際協議地址，IP 地址

IPO /ˌaɪ piː ˈəʊ; *NAmE* ˈoʊ/ *abbr.* (*business* 商) initial public offering (the act of selling shares in a company for the first time)（公司股票的）首次公開發行，上市

iPod™ /ˈaɪpɒd; *NAmE* -pɑːd/ *noun* a small piece of equipment that can store information taken from the Internet and that you carry with you, for example so that you can listen to music（便攜式）蘋果播放器

ipso facto /ˌɪpsəʊ ˈfæktəʊ; *NAmE* ˌɪpsoʊ ˈfæktoʊ/ *adv.* (from *Latin*, *formal*) because of the fact that has been mentioned 根據該事實；根據事實本身：*You cannot assume that a speaker of English is ipso facto qualified to teach English.* 你不能假定會説英語的人就有資格教英語。

IQ /ˌaɪ ˈkjuː/ *noun* the abbreviation for 'intelligence quotient' (a measurement of a person's intelligence that is calculated from the results of special tests) 智商（全寫為 intelligence quotient）：*an IQ of 120* 智商 120 ◇ *to have a* ***high/low IQ*** 智商高／低 ◇ *IQ tests* 智商測驗

ir- ➲ IN-

IRA /ˌaɪ ɑːr ˈeɪ/ *abbr.* the abbreviation for 'Irish Republican Army' (an illegal organization which has fought for Northern Ireland to be united with the Republic of Ireland) 愛爾蘭共和軍（全寫為 Irish Republican Army，以武力爭取北愛爾蘭與愛爾蘭共和國統一的非法組織）

iras·cible /ɪˈræsəbl/ *adj.* (*formal*) becoming angry very easily 易怒的；暴躁的 SYN **irritable** ▸ **iras·ci·bil·ity** /ɪˌræsəˈbɪləti/ *noun* [U]

irate /aɪˈreɪt/ *adj.* very angry 極其憤怒的；暴怒的：*irate customers* 憤怒的顧客 ◇ *an irate phone call* 怒氣沖沖的電話 ➲ SYNONYMS at ANGRY

IRC /ˌaɪ ɑː ˈsiː; *NAmE* ɑːr/ *abbr.* Internet Relay Chat (an area of the Internet where users can communicate directly with each other) 互聯網接力聊天室，互聯網接力閒談（用戶可實時聊天）

ire /ˈaɪə(r)/ *noun* [U] (*formal* or *literary*) anger 憤怒 SYN **wrath**：*to* ***arouse/raise/provoke the ire*** *of local residents* 激怒當地居民 ◇ (*US*) *to* ***draw the ire*** *of local residents* 激怒當地居民

iri·des·cent /ˌɪrɪˈdesnt/ *adj.* (*formal*) showing many bright colours that seem to change in different lights 色彩斑斕閃耀的：*a bird with iridescent blue feathers* 藍色羽毛閃爍的鳥 ▸ **iri·des·cence** /-ˈdesns/ *noun* [U]

irid·ium /ɪˈrɪdiəm/ *noun* [U] (*symb.* **Ir**) a chemical element. Iridium is a very hard yellow-white metal, used especially in making ALLOYS. 銥

irio /ˈɪrɪɒ; *NAmE* ˈɪrɪɑː/ *noun* [U] (*EAfrE*) a type of food made from a mixture of some or all of the following: MAIZE (CORN), BEANS, green vegetables and PEAS 依麗什錦菜（用玉米、豆子、青菜和豌豆等拌和而成）

iris /ˈaɪrɪs/ *noun* **1** the round coloured part that surrounds the PUPIL of your eye 虹膜 ➲ VISUAL VOCAB page V59 **2** a tall plant with long pointed leaves and large purple or yellow flowers 鳶尾屬植物 ➲ VISUAL VOCAB page V11

Irish /ˈaɪrɪʃ/ *noun, adj.*

■ ***noun*** **1** (also **ˌIrish ˈGaelic**, **Gaelic**) the Celtic language of Ireland 愛爾蘭語；愛爾蘭蓋爾語 ➲ compare ERSE **2 the Irish** [pl.] the people of Ireland 愛爾蘭人

■ ***adj.*** of or connected with Ireland, its people or its language 愛爾蘭的；愛爾蘭人的；愛爾蘭語的

ˌIrish ˈcoffee *noun* **1** [U] hot coffee mixed with WHISKY and sugar, with thick cream on top 愛爾蘭咖啡（摻威士忌和糖及加奶油的熱飲料）**2** [C] a cup or glass of Irish coffee 一杯愛爾蘭咖啡

ˌIrish ˈstew *noun* [U, C] a hot dish of meat and vegetables boiled together 愛爾蘭燉菜；蔬菜燉肉

irk /ɜːk; *NAmE* ɜːrk/ *verb* **~ sb (to do sth)** | **it irks sb that ...** (*formal* or *literary*) to annoy or irritate sb 使煩惱；激怒：*Her flippant tone irked him.* 她輕佻的語調使他很生氣。

irk·some /ˈɜːksəm; *NAmE* ˈɜːrk-/ *adj.* (*formal*) annoying or irritating 使人煩惱的；令人生氣的 SYN **tiresome**：*I found the restrictions irksome.* 我對那些限制感到很煩。

IRL /ˌaɪ ɑːr ˈel/ *abbr.* in real life; not on the Internet (used in chat on the Internet) 在現實生活中，不在網絡上（互聯網聊天用語）：*If he did that IRL he'd have a bullet in his head.* 他如果在現實生活中那麼幹，腦袋就會捱槍子。

iroko /ɪˈrəʊkəʊ; *NAmE* ɪˈroʊkoʊ/ *noun* (*pl.* **-os**) **1** [C, U] a tall tree found in tropical W Africa that lives for many years. Some people believe that creatures with magic powers live in irokos. 伊羅科樹（西非熱帶的多年生高大樹木，有人認為樹中居住着精靈）**2** [U] the wood from this tree, which is hard and used especially for outdoor building work 伊羅科木（木質堅硬，尤用作戶外建築材料）

iron 🔑 /ˈaɪən; *NAmE* ˈaɪərn/ *noun, verb, adj.*

■ ***noun***

▸ METAL 金屬 **1** 🔑 [U] (*symb.* **Fe**) a chemical element. Iron is a hard strong metal that is used to make steel and is also found in small quantities in blood and food. 鐵：***cast/wrought/corrugated iron*** 鑄鐵；熟鐵；波紋鐵 ◇ ***iron gates/bars/railings*** 鐵門／柵／欄杆 ◇ *an* ***iron and steel*** *works* 鋼鐵廠 ◇ ***iron ore*** (= rock containing iron) 鐵礦石 ◇ *patients with* ***iron deficiency*** (= not enough iron in their blood) 缺鐵型病人 ◇ ***iron tablets*** (= containing iron prepared as a medicine) 含鐵的藥片 ◇ (*figurative*) *She had a* ***will of iron*** (= it was very strong). 她有鋼鐵般的意志。

▸ TOOL 工具 **2** 🔑 [C] a tool with a flat metal base that can be heated and used to make clothes smooth 熨斗：*a steam iron* 蒸汽熨斗 ➲ VISUAL VOCAB page V20 **3** [C] (usually in compounds 通常構成複合詞) a tool made of iron or another metal 鐵器；金屬工具 ➲ see also BRANDING IRON, SOLDERING IRON, TIRE IRON

▸ FOR PRISONERS 囚犯 **4 irons** [pl.] chains or other heavy objects made of iron, attached to the arms and legs of prisoners, especially in the past（尤指舊時的）鐐銬

▸ IN GOLF 高爾夫球 **5** [C] one of the set of CLUBS (= sticks for hitting the ball with) that have a metal head 鐵頭球棒 ➲ compare WOOD

IDM **have several, etc. irons in the ˈfire** to be involved in several activities or areas of business at the same time, hoping that at least one will be successful 分散活動（或經營）；廣泛撒網 ➲ more at PUMP *v.*, RULE *v.*, STRIKE *v.*

■ ***verb*** 🔑 [T, I] **~ (sth)** to make clothes, etc. smooth by using an iron（用熨斗）熨，燙平：*I'll need to iron that dress before I can wear it.* 我得先把那件連衣裙燙平再穿。◇ *He was ironing when I arrived.* 我到的時候他正在熨衣服。➲ see also IRONING

PHR V ˌ**iron sth↔ˈout** **1** to remove the CREASES (= folds that you do not want) from clothes, etc. by using an iron 熨平（衣服等的）皺褶 **2** to get rid of any problems or difficulties that are affecting sth 解決影響…的問題（或困難）: *There are still a few details that need ironing out.* 還有幾處細節問題需要解決。

■ **adj.** [only before noun] very strong and determined 堅強的；強硬堅定的：*She was known as the 'Iron Lady'.* 大家都稱她為"鐵娘子"。◇ *a man of* ***iron will*** 意志堅強的男子

IDM **an iron ˈfist/ˈhand (in a velvet ˈglove)** if you use the words **an iron fist/hand** when describing the way that sb behaves, you mean that they treat people severely. This treatment may be hidden behind a kind appearance (the **velvet glove**).（溫和背後的）鐵拳

the ˈIron Age *noun* [sing.] the historical period about 3 000 years ago when people first used iron tools 鐵器時代

iron·clad /ˈaɪənklæd; *NAmE* ˈaɪərn-/ *adj.* so strong that it cannot be challenged or changed 鐵定的；不容置疑的：*an ironclad alibi/contract/excuse/guarantee* 無懈可擊的不在犯罪現場證據；鐵定的合同；滴水不漏的理由；斬釘截鐵的保證 ◇ *His memo is ironclad proof he was involved.* 他的備忘錄是他參與其中的鐵證。➲ compare CAST-IRON (2)

the ˌIron ˈCurtain *noun* [sing.] the name that people used for the border that used to exist between Western Europe and the COMMUNIST countries of Central and Eastern Europe 鐵幕（指昔日西歐與中東歐共產黨國家之間想像的屏障）

ˌ**iron-ˈgrey** (*especially BrE*) (also ˌ**iron-ˈgray** especially in *NAmE*) *adj.* dark grey in colour 鐵灰色的：*iron-grey hair* 鐵灰色的毛髮

iron·ic /aɪˈrɒnɪk; *NAmE* -ˈrɑːn-/ (also *less frequent* **iron·ic·al** /aɪˈrɒnɪkl; *NAmE* -ˈrɑːn-/) *adj.* **1** showing that you really mean the opposite of what you are saying; expressing IRONY 反語的；諷刺的：*an ironic comment* 譏諷的話 **2** (of a situation 情形) strange or amusing because it is very different from what you expect（因出乎意料而）奇怪的，好笑的：***It's ironic that*** *she became a teacher—she used to hate school.* 令人啼笑皆非的是她成了教師——她過去一向厭惡學校。➲ see also IRONY ▸ **iron·ic·al·ly** /aɪˈrɒnɪkli; *NAmE* -ˈrɑːn-/ *adv.*: *Ironically, the book she felt was her worst sold more copies than any of her others.* 具有諷刺意味的是，那本書她覺得最糟糕，卻比她的其他任何一本書賣得都好。◇ *He smiled ironically.* 他譏諷地微微一笑。

iron·ing /ˈaɪənɪŋ; *NAmE* ˈaɪərnɪŋ/ *noun* [U] **1** the task of pressing clothes, etc. with an iron to make them smooth 熨燙：*to* ***do the ironing*** 熨衣服 **2** the clothes, etc. that you have just ironed or that need to be done 剛熨好的（或待熨燙的）衣物：*a pile of ironing* 一堆待熨燙的衣服

ˈ**ironing board** *noun* a long narrow board covered with cloth, and usually with folding legs, that you iron clothes on 燙衣板 ➲ VISUAL VOCAB page V20

iron·mon·ger /ˈaɪənmʌŋgə(r); *NAmE* ˈaɪərn-/ (*BrE*, becoming *old-fashioned*) (*NAmE* ˈ**hardware dealer**) *noun* **1** a person who owns or works in a shop/store selling tools and equipment for the house and garden/yard 五金商人 **2** **ironmonger's** (*pl.* **iron·mon·gers**) a shop that sells tools and equipment for the house and garden/yard 五金商店 ▸ **iron·mon·gery** /-mʌŋgəri/ *noun* [U] (*BrE*) = HARDWARE (2)

ˌ**iron ˈrations** *noun* [pl.] (often *humorous*) a small amount of food that soldiers and people walking or climbing carry to use in an emergency（戰士、步行者或登山者隨身攜帶的）應急口糧

iron·stone /ˈaɪənstəʊn; *NAmE* ˈaɪərnstoʊn/ *noun* [U] a type of rock that contains iron 鐵礦石

iron·work /ˈaɪənwɜːk; *NAmE* ˈaɪərnwɜːrk/ *noun* [U] things made of iron, such as gates, parts of buildings, etc. 鐵製品；（建築物的）鐵結構

iron·works /ˈaɪənwɜːks; *NAmE* ˈaɪərnwɜːrks/ *noun* (*pl.* **iron·works**) [C+sing./pl. v.] a factory where iron is obtained from ORE (= rock containing metal), or where heavy iron goods are made 鋼鐵廠

irony /ˈaɪrəni/ *noun* (*pl.* **-ies**) **1** [U, C] the amusing or strange aspect of a situation that is very different from what you expect; a situation like this（出乎意料的）奇異可笑之處；有諷刺意味的情況：***The irony is that*** *when he finally got the job, he discovered he didn't like it.* 諷刺的是，當他最終得到那份工作時，他發現自己並不喜歡它。◇ *It was one of life's little ironies.* 那是生活中的一個小小的嘲弄。**2** [U] the use of words that say the opposite of what you really mean, often as a joke and with a tone of voice that shows this 反語；反話：*'England is famous for its food,' she said with* ***heavy irony.*** "英國的食物很有名哪。"她極其諷刺地說道。◇ *There was a note of irony in his voice.* 他的聲音裏有一絲挖苦的味道。◇ *She said it without a* ***hint/trace of irony.*** 她說此話沒有一點嘲諷之意。

ir·radi·ance /ɪˈreɪdiəns/ *noun* [U] (*physics* 物) a measurement of the amount of light that comes from sth 輻照度；輻射通量密度

ir·radi·ate /ɪˈreɪdieɪt/ *verb* **1 ~ sth** (*technical* 術語) to treat food with GAMMA RADIATION in order to preserve it 照射（食物以放射線處理，以便貯存）**2 ~ sth (with sth)** (*literary*) to make sth look brighter and happier 使生輝；使煥發：*faces irradiated with joy* 一張張高興得神采奕奕的面孔 ▸ **ir·radi·ation** /ɪˌreɪdiˈeɪʃn/ *noun* [U]

ir·ration·al **AW** /ɪˈræʃənl/ *adj.* not based on, or not using, clear logical thought 不合邏輯的；沒有道理的 **SYN** **unreasonable**：*an irrational fear* 無端的恐懼 ◇ *You're being irrational.* 你不可理喻。**OPP** **rational** ▸ **ir·ration·al·ity** /ɪˌræʃəˈnæləti/ *noun* [U, C, usually sing.] **ir·ration·al·ly** /ɪˈræʃnəli/ *adv.*：*to behave irrationally* 表現得沒有理性

irˌrational ˈnumber (also **surd**) *noun* (*mathematics* 數) a number, for example π or the SQUARE ROOT of 2, that cannot be expressed as the RATIO of two whole numbers 無理數

ir·re·con·cil·able /ɪˈrekənsaɪləbl; ɪˌrekənˈsaɪləbl/ *adj.* (*formal*) **1** if differences or disagreements are **irreconcilable**, they are so great that it is not possible to settle them 不能調和的；無法化解的 **2** if an idea or opinion is **irreconcilable** with another, it is impossible for sb to have both of them together（思想、觀點）相對立的，相反的，矛盾的：*This view is irreconcilable with common sense.* 這個觀點有悖於常識。**3** people who are **irreconcilable** cannot be made to agree 勢不兩立的：*irreconcilable enemies* 勢不兩立的仇敵

ir·re·cov·er·able /ˌɪrɪˈkʌvərəbl/ *adj.* (*formal*) that you cannot get back; lost 無法挽回的；丟失的；逝去的：*irrecoverable costs* 無法收回的成本 ◇ *irrecoverable loss of sight* 永久的失明 **OPP** **recoverable** ▸ **ir·re·cov·er·ably** /-əbli/ *adv.*

ir·re·deem·able /ˌɪrɪˈdiːməbl/ *adj.* (*formal*) too bad to be corrected, improved or saved 不能改正的；無法改進的；不能挽救的 **SYN** **hopeless** ▸ **ir·re·deem·ably** /-əbli/ *adv.*：*irredeemably spoilt* 嬌慣得不可救藥

ir·re·du·cible /ˌɪrɪˈdjuːsəbl; *NAmE* -ˈduːs-/ *adj.* (*formal*) that cannot be made smaller or simpler 不能再分的；無法簡化的：*to cut staff to an irreducible minimum* 把員工人數削減到最低限度 ◇ *an irreducible fact* 不可化簡的事實 ▸ **ir·re·du·cibly** /-əbli/ *adv.*

ir·re·fut·able /ˌɪrɪˈfjuːtəbl; ɪˈrefjətəbl/ *adj.* (*formal*) that cannot be proved wrong and that must therefore be accepted 無可辯駁的；不能否認的：*irrefutable evidence* 無法推翻的證據 ▸ **ir·re·fut·ably** /-əbli/ *adv.*

ir·regu·lar /ɪˈregjələ(r)/ *adj., noun*

■ **adj.** **1** not arranged in an even way; not having an even, smooth pattern or shape 不整齊的；不平整的；參差不齊的 **SYN** **uneven**：*irregular teeth* 不整齊的牙齒 ◇ *an irregular outline* 不平整的外形 **2** not happening at times that are at an equal distance from each other; not happening regularly 不規則的；無規律的；紊亂的：*irregular meals* 不定時的進食 ◇ *an irregular heartbeat* 心律不齊 ◇ *irregular attendance at school* 斷斷續續的上學 ◇ *He visited his parents* ***at irregular intervals.*** 他不定期

地看望父母。 **3** not normal; not according to the usual rules 不正常的；不合乎常規的 SYN **abnormal**：*an irregular practice* 不合常規的做法 ◇ *His behaviour is highly irregular.* 他的行為很不正常。 **4** (*grammar* 語法) not formed in the normal way （形式）不規則的：*an irregular verb* 不規則動詞 **5** (of a soldier etc. 士兵等) not part of a country's official army 非正規軍的 OPP **regular** ▸ **ir·regu·lar·ly** *adv.*

▪ *noun* a soldier who is not a member of a country's official army 非正規軍軍人

ir·regu·lar·ity /ɪˌregjəˈlærəti/ *noun* (*pl.* **-ies**) **1** [C, U] an activity or a practice which is not according to the usual rules, or not normal 不合乎常規的行為；不正常的做法：*alleged irregularities in the election campaign* 被指稱競選運動中的不正當行為 ◇ *suspicion of financial irregularity* 對財政違規行為的懷疑 **2** [C, U] something that does not happen at regular intervals 不規則（或無規律）的事物：*a slight irregularity in his heartbeat* 他略微的心跳不齊 **3** [U, C] something that is not smooth or regular in shape or arrangement 不整齊的事物；不平整的事物：*The paint will cover any irregularity in the surface of the walls.* 油漆會遮蓋住牆壁上任何不平整的地方。 ➲ compare REGULARITY

ir·rele·vance AW /ɪˈreləvəns/ (also *less frequent* **ir·rele·vancy** /-ənsi/ *pl.* **-ies**) *noun* **1** [U] lack of importance to or connection with a situation 無關緊要；不相關：*the irrelevance of the curriculum to children's daily life* 課程與孩子們日常生活的脫節 OPP **relevance** **2** [C, usually sing.] something that is not important to or connected with a situation 無關緊要的事物；不相關的事物：*His idea was rejected as an irrelevance.* 他的想法被認為離題而遭否定。

ir·rele·vant AW /ɪˈreləvənt/ *adj.* not important to or connected with a situation 無關緊要的；不相關的：***totally/completely/largely irrelevant*** 完全／絕對／基本上無關緊要 ◇ *irrelevant remarks* 不相關的言論 ◇ *Whether I believe you or not is irrelevant now.* 我是否相信你，現在已無關緊要了。◇ **~ to sth/sb** *That evidence is irrelevant to the case.* 那條證據與本案無關。◇ *Many people consider politics irrelevant to their lives.* 許多人認為政治與他們的生活不相干。 OPP **relevant** ▸ **ir·rele·vant·ly** *adv.*

ir·re·li·gious /ˌɪrɪˈlɪdʒəs/ *adj.* (*formal*) without any religious belief; showing no respect for religion 無宗教信仰的；漠視宗教的

ir·re·me·di·able /ˌɪrɪˈmiːdiəbl/ *adj.* (*formal*) too bad to be corrected or cured 無法糾正的；不可治癒的：*an irremediable situation* 無法補救的局面 OPP **remediable** ▸ **ir·re·me·di·ably** /-əbli/ *adv.*

ir·rep·ar·able /ɪˈrepərəbl/ *adj.* (of a loss, injury, etc. 損失、傷害等) too bad or too serious to repair or put right 無法彌補的；不能修復的；不可恢復的：*to cause* ***irreparable damage/harm*** *to your health* 對健康造成不可彌補的損害 ◇ *Her death is an irreparable loss.* 她的死是無法挽回的損失。 OPP **repairable** ▸ **ir·rep·ar·ably** /-əbli/ *adv.*：*irreparably damaged* 受到無法治癒的創傷

ir·re·place·able /ˌɪrɪˈpleɪsəbl/ *adj.* too valuable or special to be replaced （因貴重或獨特）不能替代的 ➲ SYNONYMS at VALUABLE OPP **replaceable**

ir·re·press·ible /ˌɪrɪˈpresəbl/ *adj.* **1** (of a person 人) lively, happy and full of energy 情緒高漲的；勁頭十足的 SYN **ebullient** **2** (of feelings, etc. 感情等) very strong; impossible to control or stop 十分強烈的；無法控制的；難以遏制的：*irrepressible confidence* 十足的信心 ▸ **ir·re·press·ibly** /-əbli/ *adv.*

ir·re·proach·able /ˌɪrɪˈprəʊtʃəbl; *NAmE* -ˈproʊ-/ *adj.* (of a person or their behaviour 人或行為) free from fault and impossible to criticize 無可指責的；無懈可擊的 SYN **blameless**

ir·re·sist·ible /ˌɪrɪˈzɪstəbl/ *adj.* **1** so strong that it cannot be stopped or resisted 不可遏止的；無法抵制的：*I felt an irresistible urge to laugh.* 我禁不住想笑出來。◇ *His arguments were irresistible.* 他的論點無可反駁。 OPP **resistible** **2** so attractive that you feel you must have it 極誘人的；忍不住想要的：*an irresistible bargain* 忍不住想買的便宜貨 ◇ *On such a hot day, the water was irresistible* (= it made you want to swim in it). 這麼一個大熱天，我們見了水便禁不住要下去。◇ **~ to sb** *The bright colours were irresistible to the baby.* 那些鮮豔的色彩逗得嬰兒直想去抓。 ▸ **ir·re·sist·ibly** /-əbli/ *adv.*：*They were irresistibly drawn to each other.* 他們相互傾心。

ir·reso·lute /ɪˈrezəluːt/ *adj.* (*formal*) not able to decide what to do 躊躇的；猶豫不決的 OPP **resolute** ▸ **ir·reso·lute·ly** *adv.* **ir·reso·lu·tion** /ɪˌrezəˈluːʃn/ *noun* [U]

ir·re·spect·ive of /ɪrɪˈspektɪv əv/ *prep.* without considering sth or being influenced by it 不考慮；不管；不受…影響 SYN **regardless of**：*Everyone is treated equally, irrespective of race.* 不分種族，每個人都受到公平對待。◇ *The weekly rent is the same irrespective of whether there are three or four occupants.* 無論三個還是四個人住，週租金不變。

ir·re·spon·sible /ˌɪrɪˈspɒnsəbl; *NAmE* -ˈspɑːn-/ *adj.* (*disapproving*) (of a person 人) not thinking enough about the effects of what they do; not showing a feeling of responsibility 不負責任的；無責任感的：*an irresponsible teenager* 沒有責任感的少年 ◇ *an irresponsible attitude* 不負責任的態度 ◇ ***It would be irresponsible*** *to ignore the situation.* 對這一狀況不聞不問是不負責任。 OPP **responsible** ▸ **ir·re·spon·si·bil·ity** /ˌɪrɪˌspɒnsəˈbɪləti; *NAmE* -ˌspɑːnsə-/ *noun* [U] **ir·re·spon·sibly** /-əbli/ *adv.*

ir·re·triev·able /ˌɪrɪˈtriːvəbl/ *adj.* (*formal*) that you can never make right or get back 不可糾正的；無法挽回的：*an irretrievable situation* 無法挽回的局面 ◇ *the irretrievable breakdown of the marriage* 無法挽救的婚姻破裂 ◇ *The money already paid is irretrievable.* 已經支付的錢是無法收回的。 OPP **retrievable** ▸ **ir·re·triev·ably** /-əbli/ *adv.*：*Some of our old traditions are irretrievably lost.* 我們的一些老傳統已經失傳，無法追溯。

ir·rev·er·ent /ɪˈrevərənt/ *adj.* (usually *approving*) not showing respect to sb/sth that other people usually respect 不敬的；不恭的：*irreverent wit* 失禮的俏皮話 ◇ *an irreverent attitude to tradition* 不把傳統放在眼裏的態度 ▸ **ir·rev·er·ence** /-əns/ *noun* [U] **ir·rev·er·ent·ly** *adv.*

ir·re·vers·ible AW /ˌɪrɪˈvɜːsəbl; *NAmE* -ˈvɜːrs-/ *adj.* that cannot be changed back to what it was before 無法復原（或挽回）的；不能倒轉的：*an irreversible change/decline/decision* 不可逆轉的變化；不能挽救的衰落；不可撤回的決定 ◇ *irreversible brain damage* (= that will not improve) 無法治癒的腦損傷 OPP **reversible** ▸ **ir·re·vers·ibly** /-əbli/ *adv.*

ir·rev·oc·able /ɪˈrevəkəbl/ *adj.* (*formal*) that cannot be changed 無法改變的；不可更改的 SYN **final**：***an irrevocable decision/step*** 最後的決定／一步 ▸ **ir·rev·oc·ably** /-əbli/ *adv.*：*irrevocably committed* 義無反顧地獻身

ir·ri·gate /ˈɪrɪɡeɪt/ *verb* **1 ~ sth** to supply water to an area of land through pipes or channels so that crops will grow 灌溉：*irrigated land/crops* 經過灌溉的土地／農作物 **2 ~ sth** (*medical* 醫) to wash out a wound or part of the body with a flow of water or liquid 沖洗（傷口或身體部位） ▸ **ir·ri·ga·tion** /ˌɪrɪˈɡeɪʃn/ *noun* [U]：*irrigation channels* 灌溉渠

ir·rit·able /ˈɪrɪtəbl/ *adj.* getting annoyed easily; showing your anger 易怒的；暴躁的 SYN **bad-tempered**：*to be tired and irritable* 勞累煩躁 ◇ *an irritable gesture* 急躁的姿勢 ▸ **ir·rit·abil·ity** /ˌɪrɪtəˈbɪləti/ *noun* [U] **ir·rit·ably** /-əbli/ *adv.*

irritable 'bowel syndrome *noun* [U] a condition of the BOWELS that causes pain and DIARRHOEA or CONSTIPATION, often caused by stress or anxiety 過敏性腸綜合症，過敏性結腸綜合症（常由緊張或焦慮引起，表現為腹痛、腹瀉或便秘）

ir·ri·tant /ˈɪrɪtənt/ *noun* **1** (*technical* 術語) a substance that makes part of your body sore 刺激物 **2** something that makes you annoyed or causes trouble 令人煩惱的事物；造成麻煩的事物 ▸ **ir·ri·tant** *adj.* [usually before noun]：*irritant substances* 刺激性物質

ir·ri·tate 0-w /ˈɪrɪteɪt/ *verb*

1 0-w **~ sb** to annoy sb, especially by sth you continuously do or by sth that continuously happens 使煩惱（尤指不斷重複的事情）：*The way she puts on that* *accent really irritates me.* 她故意模那種口音的樣子實在令我惱火。 **2** ⊶ **~ sth** to make your skin or a part of your body sore or painful 刺激（皮膚或身體部位）：*Some drugs can irritate the lining of the stomach.* 有些藥物可能刺激胃內壁。 ▸ **ir·ri·tat·ing** ⊶ *adj.*：*I found her extremely irritating* 我覺得她極其令人惱火。◇ *an irritating habit* 惱人的習慣 ◇ *an irritating cough/rash* 令人痛苦的咳嗽／皮疹 **ir·ri·tat·ing·ly** *adv.* **ir·ri·ta·tion** /ˌɪrɪˈteɪʃn/ *noun* [U, C]：*He noted, with some irritation, that the letter had not been sent.* 他注意到那封信還沒有發出去，有點生氣。◇ *a skin irritation* 皮膚發炎

ir·ri·tated ⊶ /ˈɪrɪteɪtɪd/ *adj.*
~ (at/by/with sth) annoyed or angry 煩惱；惱怒：*She was getting more and more irritated at his comments.* 她對他的評論越來越感到惱火。

ir·rupt /ɪˈrʌpt/ *verb* [I] **+ adv./prep.** (*formal*) to enter or appear somewhere suddenly and with a lot of force 闖入；突然衝進；爆發：*Violence once again irrupted into their peaceful lives.* 他們平靜的生活中再度爆發了暴力衝突。 ▸ **ir·rup·tion** /ɪˈrʌpʃn/ *noun* [U, C]

IRS /ˌaɪ ɑːr ˈes/ *abbr.* Internal Revenue Service （美國）國稅局

Is. *abbr.* (especially on maps) Island(s); ISLE(s) （尤用於地圖）島，群島

is /ɪz/ ➲ BE

ISA¹ /ˈaɪsə/ *noun* the abbreviation for 'Individual Savings Account' (a special account in Britain in which you can invest a limited amount each year without paying tax on the income) 個人儲蓄賬戶（全寫為 Individual Savings Account，英國一種儲蓄賬戶，如年存款低於一定額度可免稅）

ISA² /ˌaɪ es ˈeɪ/ *abbr.* Industry Standard Architecture (the usual international system used for connecting computers and other devices) 工業標準體系結構（連接計算機與其他設備的國際通用體系）

ISBN /ˌaɪ es biː ˈen/ *noun* the abbreviation for 'International Standard Book Number' (a number that identifies an individual book and its PUBLISHER) 國際標準圖書編號（全寫為 International Standard Book Number，用於識別圖書及其出版商）

is·chae·mia (*NAmE* **is·che·mia** /ɪˈskiːmiə/) *noun* [U] (*medical* 醫) the situation when the supply of blood to an organ or part of the body, especially the heart muscles, is less than is needed 缺血（尤指心肌缺血）

ISDN /ˌaɪ es diː ˈen/ *abbr.* integrated services digital network (a system for carrying sound signals, images, etc. along wires at high speed) 綜合業務數字網，ISDN 網，整合服務數位網路（高速傳送聲音信號、圖像等的系統）：*an ISDN Internet connection* * ISDN 互聯網連接

-ise ➲ -IZE

ish /ɪʃ/ *adv.* (*BrE, informal*) used after a statement to make it less definite（用於陳述句之後，以緩和語氣）：*I've finished. Ish. I still need to make the sauce.* 我做好了。還有，我得調些醬料。

-ish ⊶ *suffix* (in adjectives 構成形容詞)
1 ⊶ from the country mentioned …國家的：*Turkish* 土耳其的 ◇ *Irish* 愛爾蘭的 **2** ⊶ (sometimes *disapproving*) having the nature of; like 有…性質的；像…似的：*childish* 孩子氣的 **3** ⊶ fairly; approximately 有點…的；近乎…的：*reddish* 略呈紅色的 ◇ *thirtyish* 三十左右 ▸ **-ishly** (in adverbs 構成副詞)：*foolishly* 傻裏傻氣地

Islam /ˈɪzlɑːm; ɪzˈlɑːm/ *noun* [U] **1** the Muslim religion, based on belief in one God and REVEALED through Muhammad as the Prophet of Allah 伊斯蘭教；回教 **2** all Muslims and Muslim countries in the world（統稱）伊斯蘭教徒，伊斯蘭教國家 ▸ **Is·lam·ic** /ɪzˈlæmɪk; -ˈlɑːm-/ *adj.*：*Islamic law* 伊斯蘭教戒律

Is·lam·ist /ˈɪzləmɪst/ *noun* a person who believes strongly in the teachings of Islam 伊斯蘭教徒 ▸ **Is·lam·ism** /ˈɪzləmɪzəm/ *noun* [U] **Is·lam·ist** *adj.*

is·land ⊶ /ˈaɪlənd/ *noun*
1 ⊶ (*abbr.* **I**, **I.**, **Is.**) a piece of land that is completely surrounded by water 島：*We spent a week on the Greek island of Kos.* 我們在希臘的科斯島上待了一個星期。◇ *a remote island off the coast of Scotland* 一個遠離蘇格蘭海岸的島 ➲ VISUAL VOCAB page V5 ➲ see also DESERT ISLAND **2** (*BrE*) = TRAFFIC ISLAND

is·land·er /ˈaɪləndə(r)/ *noun* a person who lives on an island, especially a small one 島上居民，島民（尤指小島上的）

ˈ**island-hopping** *noun* [U] the activity of travelling from one island to another in an area that has lots of islands, especially as a tourist 列島旅行；列島旅遊

isle /aɪl/ *noun* (*abbr.* **I**, **I.**, **Is.**) used especially in poetry and names to mean 'island'（常用於詩歌和名稱中）島：*the Isle of Skye* 斯凱島 ◇ *the British Isles* 英倫列島

islet /ˈaɪlət/ *noun* a very small island 很小的島；小島

ism /ˈɪzəm/ *noun* (usually *disapproving*) used to refer to a set of ideas or beliefs or behaviour 主義；學說；體系；制度：*You're always talking in isms—sexism, ageism, racism.* 你張口閉口就是各種主義，性別主義、年齡歧視、種族主義。

-ism *suffix* (in nouns 構成名詞) **1** the action or result of …的行為（或結果）：*criticism* 批評 **2** the state or quality of …的狀態（或品質）：*heroism* 英勇 **3** the teaching, system or movement of …的教義（或體系、運動）：*Buddhism* 佛教 **4** unfair treatment or hatred for the reason mentioned 因…的不公平對待（或敵意）：*racism* 種族偏見 **5** a feature of language of the type mentioned …語言特點：*an Americanism* 美式英語用法 ◇ *a colloquialism* 口語體 **6** a medical condition or disease 健康狀況；疾病：*alcoholism* 酒精中毒

isn't /ˈɪznt/ *short form* is not

ISO /ˌaɪ es ˈəʊ; *NAmE* ˈoʊ/ *abbr.* International Organization for Standardization (an organization established in 1946 to make the measurements used in science, industry and business standard throughout the world) 國際標準化組織（成立於 1946 年，制訂世界通用的科學、工業及商業計算標準）

iso- /ˈaɪsəʊ; *NAmE* ˈaɪsoʊ/ *combining form* (in nouns, adjectives and adverbs 構成名詞、形容詞和副詞) equal 相等；相同：*isotope* 同位素 ◇ *isometric* 等距的

iso·bar /ˈaɪsəbɑː(r)/ *noun* (*technical* 術語) a line on a weather map that joins places that have the same air pressure at a particular time（天氣圖上的）等壓線

isol·ate **AW** /ˈaɪsəleɪt/ *verb* **1** to separate sb/sth physically or socially from other people or things（使）隔離，孤立，脫離：**~ sb/yourself/sth** *Patients with the disease should be isolated.* 這種病的患者應予以隔離。◇ **~ sb/yourself/sth from sb/sth** *He was immediately isolated from the other prisoners.* 他被立刻與其他囚犯隔離開來。◇ *This decision will isolate the country from the rest of Europe.* 這一決定會使國家孤立於歐洲其他國家。 **2 ~ sth (from sth)** (*formal*) to separate a part of a situation, problem, idea, etc. so that you can see what it is and deal with it separately 將…剔出（以便看清和單獨處理）：*It is possible to isolate a number of factors that contributed to her downfall.* 可以找出造成她垮台的一些因素。 **3 ~ sth (from sth)** (*technical* 術語) to separate a single substance, cell, etc. from others so that you can study it 使（某物質、細胞等）分離；使離析：*Researchers are still trying to isolate the gene that causes this abnormality.* 研究人員仍然在試圖分離導致這種畸形的基因。

isol·ated **AW** /ˈaɪsəleɪtɪd/ *adj.* **1** (of buildings and places 建築物或地方) far away from any others 偏遠的；孤零零的 **SYN** **remote**：*isolated rural areas* 偏僻的農村地區 **2** without much contact with other people or other countries 孤獨的；孤立的：*I felt very isolated in my new job.* 我在新的工作崗位上覺得很孤獨。◇ *Elderly people easily become socially isolated.* 上了年紀的人很容易變得與社會隔絕。◇ *The decision left the country isolated from its allies.* 這個決定使這個國家在盟國中受到孤立。 **3** single; happening once 單獨的；只出現一次的：*The police said the attack was an isolated incident.* 警方稱這次襲擊只是個別事件。

isol·at·ing /ˈaɪsəleɪtɪŋ/ *adj.* (*linguistics* 語言) = ANALYTIC

isol·ation AW /ˌaɪsəˈleɪʃn/ *noun* [U] **1** the act of separating sb/sth; the state of being separate 隔離；隔離狀態：*geographical isolation* 地理上的隔離 ◇ *an* ***isolation hospital/ward*** (= for people with infectious diseases) 隔離病院／病房 ◇ **~ (from sb/sth)** *The country has been threatened with complete isolation from the international community unless the atrocities stop.* 這個國家受到了被國際社會完全孤立的威脅，除非其暴行得以制止。◇ *He lives in* ***splendid isolation*** (= far from, or in a superior position to, everyone else). 他過着遠離塵世的生活。**2 ~ (from sb/sth)** the state of being alone or lonely 孤獨；孤立狀態：*Many unemployed people experience feelings of isolation and depression.* 很多失業者有孤獨沮喪的感覺。

IDM **in isolation (from sb/sth)** separately; alone 單獨地；孤立地：*To make sense, these figures should not be looked at in isolation.* 這些數據不應孤立起來看，否則就沒有意義。

isol·ation·ism AW /ˌaɪsəˈleɪʃənɪzəm/ *noun* [U] the policy of not becoming involved in the affairs of other countries or groups 孤立主義 ► **isol·ation·ist** /-ʃənɪst/ *adj.*, *noun*：*an isolationist foreign policy* 孤立主義外交政策

iso·mer /ˈaɪsəmə(r)/ *noun* **1** (*chemistry* 化) one of two or more COMPOUNDS which have the same atoms, but in different arrangements 異構體；同分異構體 **2** (*physics* 物) one of two or more NUCLEI that have the same ATOMIC NUMBER, but different energy states 同核異能素；同質異能素 ► **iso·mer·ic** /ˌaɪsəˈmerɪk/ *adj.* **iso·mer·ism** /ˈaɪsəmərɪzəm/ *noun* [U]

iso·met·ric /ˌaɪsəˈmetrɪk/ *adj.* **1** (*technical* 術語) connected with a type of physical exercise in which muscles are made to work without the whole body moving 提高肌張力的，靜力鍛煉的（指肌肉工作但整個身體不動）**2** (*geometry* 幾何) connected with a style of drawing in three DIMENSIONS without PERSPECTIVE（圖畫）無透視三維的；等距的

iso·met·rics /ˌaɪsəˈmetrɪks/ *noun* [pl.] physical exercises in which the muscles work against each other or against a fixed object 靜力鍛煉；肌肉鍛煉 ► **iso·met·ric** *adj.*：*isometric exercises* 肌肉鍛煉運動

iso·prene /ˈaɪsəpriːn/ *noun* [U] a liquid HYDROCARBON obtained from PETROLEUM that is used to make artificial rubber. Isoprene is also found in natural rubber. 異戊二烯（用於製造合成橡膠）

isos·celes tri·angle /aɪˌsɒsəliːz ˈtraɪæŋɡl; *NAmE* -ˌsɑːs-/ *noun* (*geometry* 幾何) a triangle with two of its three sides the same length 等腰三角形 ➲ VISUAL VOCAB page V71

iso·therm /ˈaɪsəθɜːm; *NAmE* -θɜːrm/ *noun* (*technical* 術語) a line on a weather map that joins places that have the same temperature at a particular time （天氣圖上的）等溫線，恆溫線

iso·ton·ic /ˌaɪsəʊˈtɒnɪk; *NAmE* ˌaɪsoʊˈtɑːn-/ *adj.* (of a drink 飲料) with added minerals and salts, intended to replace those lost during exercise 含礦物質和鹽分的；等滲的

iso·tope /ˈaɪsətəʊp; *NAmE* -toʊp/ *noun* (*physics* 物, *chemistry* 化) one of two or more forms of a chemical element which have the same number of PROTONS but a different number of NEUTRONS in their atoms. They have different physical PROPERTIES (= characteristics) but the same chemical ones 同位素：*radioactive isotopes* 放射性同位素 ◇ *the many isotopes of carbon* 碳的諸多同位素

ISP /ˌaɪ es ˈpiː/ *abbr.* Internet Service Provider (a company that provides you with an Internet connection and services such as email, etc.) 互聯網服務供應商；網際網路服務提供商

I-spy /ˌaɪ ˈspaɪ/ *noun* [U] a children's game in which one player gives the first letter of a thing that they can see and the others have to guess what it is 我來猜（兒童遊戲，一人說出所見物名稱的第一個字母，其他人猜所指之物）

Is·rael·ite /ˈɪzrəlaɪt; ˈɪzriə-/ *noun* a member of the ancient Hebrew nation described in the Bible（《聖經》中的）希伯來人，以色列人

issue 0→ AW /ˈɪʃuː; *BrE* also ˈɪsjuː/ *noun*, *verb*

■ ***noun***

► **TOPIC OF DISCUSSION** 議題 **1** 0→ [C] an important topic that people are discussing or arguing about 重要議題；爭論的問題：*a* ***key/sensitive/controversial issue*** 關鍵的／敏感的／有爭議的問題 ◇ *This is a* ***big issue****; we need more time to think about it.* 這是個重大問題，我們需要花較多的時間考慮。◇ *She usually writes about environmental issues.* 她通常寫環境方面的題材。◇ *The union plans to* ***raise the issue*** *of overtime.* 工會打算提出加班的問題。◇ *The party was divided on this issue.* 該黨在這一問題上存在分歧。◇ *You're just* ***avoiding the issue****.* 你只不過是在迴避問題。◇ *Don't* ***confuse the issue****.* 不要把問題弄複雜。

► **PROBLEM/WORRY** 問題；憂慮 **2** 0→ [C] a problem or worry that sb has with sth（有關某事的）問題，擔憂：*Money is* ***not an issue****.* 錢不是問題。◇ *I don't think my private life is the issue here.* 我認為問題並非我的私生活。◇ *I'm not bothered about the cost—you're the one who's* ***making an issue*** *of it.* 我不在乎花錢，是你一直在拿錢大做文章。◇ *Because I grew up in a dysfunctional family, anger is a big issue for me.* 我是在一個不正常的家庭裏長大的，所以亂發脾氣是我的一大問題。◇ *She's always on a diet—she* ***has issues about*** *food.* 她經常節食，她擔心吃得太多。◇ *He still has* ***some issues with*** *women* (= has problems dealing with them). 他在與女性打交道方面仍有些問題。◇ *If you have any issues, please call this number.* 如有問題，請撥打這個電話號碼。

► **MAGAZINE/NEWSPAPER** 報刊 **3** 0→ [C] one of a regular series of magazines or newspapers 一期；期號：*the July issue of 'What Car?'* 汽車雜誌《What car?》的七月號 ◇ *The article appeared in issue 25.* 該文發表在第 25 期。

► **OF STAMPS/COINS/SHARES** 郵票；錢幣；股份 **4** [C] a number or set of things that are supplied and made available at the same time 一次發行額（或一套）：*The company is planning a new* ***share issue****.* 公司正計劃發行新股。◇ *a special issue of stamps* 特別發行的一套郵票

► **MAKING AVAILABLE/KNOWN** 發出；發佈 **5** [U] the act of supplying or making available things for people to buy or use 發行；分發：*I bought a set of the new stamps on the date of issue.* 我在新郵票發行的當天就買了一套。◇ *the issue of blankets to the refugees* 給難民分發毯子 ◇ *the issue of a joint statement by the French and German foreign ministers* 法德兩國外交部長聯合聲明的發佈

► **CHILDREN** 孩子 **6** [U] (*law* 律) children of your own 子女；後嗣：*He died without issue.* 他死後無子嗣。

IDM **be at ˈissue** to be the most important part of the subject that is being discussed 是討論的焦點：*What is at issue is whether she was responsible for her actions.* 議論的焦點是她是否對自己的行為負有責任。 **take ˈissue with sb (about/on/over sth)** (*formal*) to start disagreeing or arguing with sb about sth 向某人提出異議；開始與某人爭論：*I must take issue with you on that point.* 我必須就那一點向你提出異議。➲ more at FORCE *v.*

■ ***verb***

► **MAKE KNOWN** 公佈 **1** 0→ **~ sth (to sb)** to make sth known formally 宣佈；公佈；發出：*They issued a joint statement denying the charges.* 他們發表聯合聲明否認指控。◇ *The police have issued an appeal for witnesses.* 警方發出了尋找目擊證人的呼籲。

► **GIVE** 給 **2** 0→ [often passive] to give sth to sb, especially officially（正式）發給，供給：**~ sth** *to* ***issue passports/visas/tickets*** 發護照／簽證／票 ◇ **~ sb with sth** *New members will be issued with a temporary identity card.* 新成員將獲發臨時身分卡。◇ **~ sth to sb** *Work permits were issued to only 5% of those who applied for them.* 工作許可證只發給了 5% 的申請人。

► **LAW** 法律 **3 ~ sth** to start a legal process against sb, especially by means of an official document（尤指通過正式文件）將…訴諸法律：*to issue a writ against sb*

傳訊某人 ◇ *A warrant has been issued for his arrest.* 已對他發出逮捕令。
▸ **MAGAZINE** 刊物 **4 ~ sth** to produce sth such as a magazine, article, etc. 出版；發表：*We issue a monthly newsletter.* 我們出版一份通訊月刊。
▸ **STAMPS/COINS/SHARES** 郵票；錢幣；股票 **5 ~ sth** to produce new stamps, coins, shares, etc. for sale to the public 發行（新的一批）：*They issued a special set of stamps to mark the occasion.* 他們特別發行了一套紀念郵票。

PHR V **'issue from sth** (*formal*) to come out of sth 從…中出來：*A weak trembling sound issued from his lips.* 他嘴裏發出了微弱顫抖的聲音。 ▸ **is·suer** *noun*：*credit-card issuers* 信用卡發行機構

-ist *suffix* (in nouns and some related adjectives 構成名詞和某些相關的形容詞) **1** a person who believes or practises sth …的信仰者；…的實行者：*atheist* 無神論者 **2** a member of a profession or business activity 專業人員；…專家；從事…的人：*dentist* 牙醫 **3** a person who uses a thing …使用者：*violinist* 小提琴手 **4** a person who does sth 幹…的人：*plagiarist* 剽竊者

I

-ista /ˈɪstə/ *suffix* (in nouns 構成名詞) a person who is very enthusiastic about sth 非常熱衷於…的人：*fashionistas who are slaves to the latest trends* 被潮流拖着鼻子走的趕時髦者

isth·mus /ˈɪsməs/ *noun* a narrow strip of land, with water on each side, that joins two larger pieces of land 地峽

IT /ˌaɪ ˈtiː/ *noun* [U] the abbreviation for 'information technology' (the study and use of electronic processes and equipment to store and send information of all kinds, including words, pictures and numbers) 信息技術，資訊科技（全寫為 information technology，對將電子處理程序及設備應用於貯存和發送各類信息的研究和利用）

it 0┳ /ɪt/ *pron.*
(used as the subject or object of a verb or after a preposition 用作動詞主語或賓語，或置於介詞之後) **1** 0┳ used to refer to an animal or a thing that has already been mentioned or that is being talked about now（指提到過的或正在談論的動物或事物）它：*'Where's your car?' 'It's in the garage.'* "你的汽車在哪兒？" "在車庫裏。" ◇ *Did you see it?* 你看見它了嗎？◇ *Start a new file and put this letter in it.* 建立一個新檔案，把這封信放進去。◇ *Look! It's going up that tree.* 瞧！它正在往那棵樹上爬呢。◇ *We have $500. Will it be enough for a deposit?* 我們有 500 元。夠不夠作押金？ **2** 0┳ used to refer to a baby, especially one whose sex is not known（指嬰兒，尤指性別不詳者）：*Her baby's due next month. She hopes it will be a boy.* 她的孩子該下個月出生。她希望會是個男孩。 **3** 0┳ used to refer to a fact or situation that is already known or happening（指已知或正在發生的事實或情況）：*When the factory closes, it will mean 500 people losing their jobs.* 工廠如果關閉，就意味着 500 人要失業。◇ *Yes, I was at home on Sunday. What about it?* (= Why do you ask?) 是的，我星期天待在家裏。怎麼了？◇ *Stop it, you're hurting me!* 住手，你把我弄疼了！ **4** 0┳ used to identify a person（用以明確身分）：*It's your mother on the phone.* 是你母親來的電話。◇ *Hello, Peter, it's Mike here.* 喂，彼得，我是邁克。◇ *Hi, it's me!* 嗨，是我！◇ *Was it you who put these books on my desk?* 是你把這些書放在我桌子上的嗎？ **5** 0┳ used in the position of the subject or object of a verb when the real subject or object is at the end of the sentence（用作形式主語或形式賓語，而真正的主語或賓語在句末）：*Does it matter what colour it is?* 它是什麼顏色重要嗎？◇ *It's impossible to get there in time.* 不可能及時到達那裏。◇ *It's no use shouting.* 喊也沒有用。◇ *She finds it boring at home.* 她覺得待在家裏無聊。◇ *It appears that the two leaders are holding secret talks.* 看來兩位領導人正在密談。◇ *I find it strange that she doesn't want to go.* 她居然不想去，我覺得奇怪。 ➲ **LANGUAGE BANK** at IMPERSONAL **6** 0┳ used in the position of the subject of a verb when you are talking about time, the date, distance, the weather, etc.（談論時間、日期、距離、天氣等時用作主語）：*It's ten past twelve.* 現在十二點十分。◇ *It's our anniversary.* 今天是我們的週年紀念日。◇ *It's two miles to the beach.* 距離海灘兩英里遠。◇ *It's a long time since they left.* 他們已經離開很久了。◇ *It was raining this morning.* 今天上午在下雨。◇ *It's quite warm at the moment.* 現在天氣相當暖和。 **7** 0┳ used when you are talking about a situation（談論情況時用）：*If it's convenient I can come tomorrow.* 方便的話，我可以明天過來。◇ *It's good to talk.* 談一談很好。◇ *I like it here.* 我喜歡這裏。 **8** 0┳ used to emphasize any part of a sentence（強調句子的某部份）：*It's Jim who's the clever one.* 就數吉姆聰明。◇ *It's Spain that they're going to, not Portugal.* 他們要去的是西班牙，不是葡萄牙。◇ *It was three weeks later that he heard the news.* 三個星期之後他才聽到這個消息。 **9** exactly what is needed 正好是所需的；恰好：*In this business, either you've got it or you haven't.* 在這件事上，你不是成功了就是失敗了。 ➲ see also ITS

IDM **that is 'it** **1** this/that is the important point, reason, etc. 這（或那）是要點（或重要原因等）；正是這樣：*That's just it—I can't work when you're making so much noise.* 問題是，你那麼吵，我沒法工作。 **2** 0┳ this/that is the end 這（或那）就是終結：*I'm afraid that's it—we've lost.* 我看就這樣了，我們輸了。**this is 'it** **1** the expected event is just going to happen（期待的事）就要發生了：*Well, this is it! Wish me luck.* 好了，要來的已經來了！祝我走運吧。 **2** this is the main point 這就是要點：*'You're doing too much.' 'Well, this is it. I can't cope with any more work.'* "你太勞累了。" "哎，你說到點子上了。我什麼事都再也幹不了了。"

Ital·ian·ate /ɪˈtæljəneɪt/ *adj.* in an Italian style 意大利風格的：*a Italianate villa* 意大利式別墅

Ital·ic /ɪˈtælɪk/ *adj.* [only before noun] of or connected with the branch of Indo-European languages that includes Latin and some other ancient languages of Italy, and the Romance languages 意大利語族的（包括拉丁語和其他一些古代意大利語以及羅曼諸語言）

ital·ic /ɪˈtælɪk/ *adj.* (of printed or written letters 印刷或書寫字母) leaning to the right 斜體的：*The example sentences in this dictionary are printed in italic type.* 本詞典中的例句都是用斜體排印的。◇ *Use an italic font.* 用斜體字。 ➲ compare ROMAN (4)

itali·cize (*BrE* also **-ise**) /ɪˈtælɪsaɪz/ *verb* [often passive] **~ sth** to write or print sth in italics 用斜體書寫（或印刷）

ital·ics /ɪˈtælɪks/ *noun* [pl.] (also **italic** [sing.]) printed letters that lean to the right 斜體字：*Examples in this dictionary are in italics.* 本詞典中的例子用斜體顯示。◇ *Use italics for the names of books or plays.* 書名或劇名用斜體。 ➲ compare ROMAN (3)

Italo- /ˈɪtələʊ; ɪˈtæləʊ; *NAmE* -loʊ/ *combining form* (with nouns and adjectives 與名詞和形容詞結合) Italian; Italian and something else 意大利（人）的；意大利和…的：*Italo-Americans* 意裔美國人 ◇ *Italophiles* 親意大利的人

itch /ɪtʃ/ *verb, noun*
■ *verb* **1** [I] to have an uncomfortable feeling on your skin that makes you want to scratch; to make your skin feel like this（使）發癢：*I itch all over.* 我渾身癢。◇ *Does the rash itch?* 皮疹癢嗎？◇ *This sweater really itches.* 這件毛衣真刺癢。 ➲ **SYNONYMS** at HURT **2** [I] (*informal*) (often used in the progressive tenses 常用於進行時) to want to do sth very much 渴望；熱望：**~ for sth** *The crowd was itching for a fight.* 那群人摩拳擦掌地想打架。◇ **~ to do sth** *He's itching to get back to work.* 他巴不得馬上回去工作。
■ *noun* **1** [C, usually sing.] an uncomfortable feeling on your skin that makes you want to scratch yourself 癢：*to get/have an itch* 覺得癢 **2** [sing.] **~ (to do sth)** (*informal*) a strong desire to do sth 渴望；熱望：*She has an itch to travel.* 她渴望旅行。◇ *the creative itch* 創作慾
IDM see SEVEN

itchy /ˈɪtʃi/ *adj.* having or producing an itch on the skin 發癢的：*an itchy nose/rash* 發癢的鼻子／皮疹 ◇ *I feel itchy all over.* 我覺得渾身癢。 ➲ **SYNONYMS** at PAINFUL ▸ **itchi·ness** *noun* [U]

IDM **(get/have) itchy 'feet** (*informal*) to want to travel or move to a different place; to want to do sth different 渴望旅行（或換個地方、做別的事）

it'd /ˈɪtəd/ *short form* **1** it had **2** it would

-ite *suffix* (in nouns 構成名詞) (often *disapproving*) a person who follows or supports sb/sth 追隨者；支持者：*Blairite* 布萊爾的支持者 ◇ *Trotskyite* 托洛茨基分子

item 🔑 AW /ˈaɪtəm/ *noun*
1 🔑 one thing on a list of things to buy, do, talk about, etc. 項目：*What's the next item on the agenda?* 議程的下一項是什麼？ **2** 🔑 a single article or object 一件商品（或物品）：*Can I pay for each item separately?* 我能否一件一件地分別付錢？◇ *The computer was my largest single item of expenditure.* 電腦是我花錢最多的一件東西。◇ *This clock is a **collector's item*** (= because it is rare and valuable). 這座鐘是一件珍藏。 **3** 🔑 a single piece of news in a newspaper, on television, etc. 一則，一條（新聞）：*an item of news/a news item* 一條新聞
IDM **be an item** (*informal*) to be involved in a romantic or sexual relationship 戀愛；有性關係：*Are they an item?* 他們在戀愛嗎？

item·ize (*BrE* also **-ise**) AW /ˈaɪtəmaɪz/ *verb* **~ sth** to produce a detailed list of things 列出清單：*The report itemizes 23 different faults.* 報告列舉了 23 處錯誤。◇ *an itemized phone bill* (= each call is shown separately) 電話明細賬單

it·er·ate /ˈɪtəreɪt/ *verb* [I] to repeat a MATHEMATICAL or COMPUTING process or set of instructions again and again, each time applying it to the result of the previous stage 迭代（數學或計算過程，或一系列指令）

it·er·ation /ˌɪtəˈreɪʃn/ *noun* **1** [U, C] the process of repeating a MATHEMATICAL or COMPUTING process or set of instructions again and again, each time applying it to the result of the previous stage 迭代 **2** [C] a new version of a piece of computer software（計算機）新版軟件，新版軟體

it·in·er·ant /aɪˈtɪnərənt/ *adj.* [usually before noun] (*formal*) travelling from place to place, especially to find work 巡迴的；流動的；（尤指為找工作）四處奔波的：***itinerant workers/musicians*** 流動工人；巡迴樂師 ◇ *to lead an itinerant life* 過漂泊不定的生活 ▸ **it·in·er·ant** *noun*：*homeless itinerants* 無家可歸的流浪者

it·in·er·ary /aɪˈtɪnərəri; *NAmE* aɪˈtɪnəreri/ *noun* (*pl.* **-ies**) a plan of a journey, including the route and the places that you visit 行程；旅行日程 ➲ COLLOCATIONS at TRAVEL

-ition ➲ -ION

-itis *suffix* (in nouns 構成名詞) **1** (*medical* 醫) a disease of …病：*tonsillitis* 扁桃體炎 **2** (*informal*, especially *humorous*) too much of; too much interest in 過度的；沉迷於：*World Cup-itis* 世界杯狂

it'll /ˈɪtl/ *short form* it will

its 🔑 /ɪts/ *det.*
belonging to or connected with a thing, an animal or a baby（指事物、動物或嬰兒）它的，他的，她的：*Turn the box on its side.* 把箱子側着立起來。◇ *Have you any idea of its value?* 你知道它的價值嗎？◇ *The dog had hurt its paw.* 狗弄傷了爪子。◇ *The baby threw its food on the floor.* 嬰兒把食物扔到地板上了。

it's /ɪts/ *short form* **1** it is **2** it has

it·self 🔑 /ɪtˈself/ *pron.*
1 🔑 (the reflexive form of *it* * it 的反身形式) used when the animal or thing that does an action is also affected by it（指施動並受其影響的動物或事物）：*The cat was washing itself.* 貓在清潔自己。◇ *Does the computer turn itself off?* 電腦會自動關機嗎？◇ *The company has got itself into difficulties.* 公司本身陷入了困境。◇ *There's no need for the team to feel proud of itself.* 那支隊伍無須自鳴得意。 **2** 🔑 used to emphasize an animal, a thing, etc.（用以強調某動物、某事物等）：*The village itself is pretty, but the surrounding countryside is rather dull.* 村子本身很美，但周圍的田野相當單調。
IDM **be ˌpatience, ˌhonesty, simˌplicity, etc. itˈself** to be an example of complete patience, etc. 十分有耐心（或誠實、樸素等）：*The manager of the hotel was courtesy itself.* 旅館經理彬彬有禮。 **(all) by itˈself 1** automatically; without anyone doing anything（完全）自動，無人操作：*The machine will start by itself in a few seconds.* 機器將在幾秒鐘後自動啟動。 **2** alone 獨自；單獨：*The house stands by itself in an acre of land.* 房子孤零零地坐落在一大片田野間。 **in itˈself** considered separately from other things; in its true nature 本身；本質上：*In itself, it's not a difficult problem to solve.* 這本身並不是個難解決的問題。 **to itˈself** not shared with others 獨自擁有；獨佔：*It doesn't have the market to itself.* 它未能獨佔市場。

itty-bitty /ˌɪti ˈbɪti/ (also **itsy-bitsy** /ˌɪtsi ˈbɪtsi/) *adj.* [only before noun] (*informal, especially NAmE*) very small 很小的；微小的

ITV /ˌaɪ tiː ˈviː/ *abbr.* Independent Television (a group of British companies that produce programmes that are paid for by advertising) 獨立電視公司（英國集團，播放節目費用由廣告支付）

-ity *suffix* (in nouns 構成名詞) the quality or state of …性質；…狀態：*purity* 純淨 ◇ *oddity* 奇特

IUD /ˌaɪ juː ˈdiː/ (also **coil**) *noun* the abbreviation for 'intrauterine device' (a small plastic or metal object placed inside a woman's UTERUS (= where a baby grows before it is born) to stop her becoming pregnant) 宮內節育器（全寫為 intrauterine device）

IV /ˌaɪ ˈviː/ *abbr., noun*
■ ***abbr.*** INTRAVENOUS, INTRAVENOUSLY 注入靜脈的；靜脈內
■ ***noun*** (*NAmE*) = DRIP (3)

I've /aɪv/ *short form* I have

-ive *suffix* (in nouns and adjectives 構成名詞和形容詞) tending to; having the nature of …傾向（的）；…性質（的）：*explosive* 炸藥 ◇ *descriptive* 描述的

IVF /ˌaɪ viː ˈef/ *noun* [U] (*technical* 術語) the abbreviation for 'in vitro fertilization' (a process which FERTILIZES an egg from a woman outside her body. The egg is then put inside her UTERUS to develop.) 體外受精（全寫為 in vitro fertilization，使卵子在母體外受精後再放回子宮內發育） ➲ see also TEST-TUBE BABY

ivory /ˈaɪvəri/ (*pl.* **-ies**) *noun* **1** [U] a hard yellowish-white substance like bone that forms the TUSKS (= long teeth) of ELEPHANTS and some other animals 象牙；（某些其他動物的）長牙：*a ban on the ivory trade* 象牙貿易禁令 ◇ *an ivory chess set* 一副象牙國際象棋 **2** [C] an object made of ivory 象牙製品 **3** [U] a yellowish-white colour 象牙色；乳白色

ˌivory ˈtower *noun* (*disapproving*) a place or situation where you are separated from the problems and practical aspects of normal life and therefore do not have to worry about or understand them 象牙塔（指遠離問題、脫離現實的小天地）：*academics living in ivory towers* 生活在象牙塔中的學者

ivy /ˈaɪvi/ *noun* [U, C] (*pl.* **-ies**) a climbing plant, especially one with dark green shiny leaves with five points 常春藤：*stone walls covered in ivy* 爬滿常春藤的石牆 ➲ VISUAL VOCAB page V11 ➲ see also POISON IVY

the ˌIvy ˈLeague *noun* [sing.] a group of eight traditional universities in the eastern US with high academic standards and a high social status 常春藤聯盟（指美國東部八所學術和社會地位高的大學） ➲ compare OXBRIDGE ▸ **ˌIvy ˈLeague** *adj.*：*Ivy League colleges* 常春藤大學

iwi /ˈiːwi/ *noun* (*pl.* **iwi**) (*NZE*) a Maori community or people 毛利部落；毛利部族；毛利人

-ize, -ise *suffix* (in verbs 構成動詞) **1** to become, make or make like 成為；使；使像：*privatize* 私有化 ◇ *fossilize* 變成化石 ◇ *Americanize* 美國化 **2** to speak, think, act, treat, etc. in the way mentioned 以…方式說（或想、行動、對待等）：*criticize* 批評 ◇ *theorize* 將…理論化 ◇ *deputize* 代表 ◇ *pasteurize* 用巴氏法消毒 **3** to place in 放在…裏；置於…中：*hospitalize* 送醫院治療 ▸ **-ization, -isation** (in nouns 構成名詞)：*immunization* 免疫作用 **-izationally, -isationally** (in adverbs 構成副詞)：*organizationally* 有組織地

I

Jj

J (also **j**) /dʒeɪ/ *noun* [C, U] (*pl.* **Js, J's, j's** /dʒeɪz/) the 10th letter of the English alphabet 英語字母表的第 10 個字母：*'Jelly' begins with (a) J/'J'.* * jelly 一詞以字母 j 開頭。

ja /jɑː/ *exclamation* (*SAfrE, informal*) yes 是；對

jab /dʒæb/ *verb, noun*

■ **verb** (-bb-) [T, I] to push a pointed object into sb/sth, or in the direction of sb/sth, with a sudden strong movement 戳；刺；捅；猛擊 **SYN prod**：**～ sb/sth (in sth) (with sth)** *She jabbed him in the ribs with her finger.* 她用手指捅了捅他的腰。◇ **～ sth in sth** *She jabbed her finger in his ribs.* 她用手指捅了捅他的腰。◇ **～ (at sb/sth) (with sth)** *He jabbed at the picture with his finger.* 他用手指戳戳那幅畫。◇ *The boxer jabbed at his opponent.* 拳擊手向對手猛擊。

■ **noun 1** a sudden strong hit with sth pointed or with a FIST (= a tightly closed hand) 戳；刺；捅；用拳猛擊：*She gave him a jab in the stomach with her elbow.* 她用胳膊肘猛頂他的肚子。◇ *a boxer's left jab* 拳擊手的左刺拳 **2** (*BrE, informal*) an INJECTION to help prevent you from catching a disease 注射；接種；預防針：*a flu jab* 流感預防針

jab·ber /ˈdʒæbə(r)/ *verb* [I, T] **～ (about sth)** | **+ speech** (*disapproving*) to talk quickly and in an excited way so that it is difficult to understand what you are saying 急促（或激動）而含混不清地說 **SYN gabble**：*What is he jabbering about now?* 他在嘰里咕嚕地說什麼呢？
▸ **jab·ber** *noun* [U]

jaca·randa /ˌdʒækəˈrændə/ *noun* [C, U] a tropical tree with blue flowers and pleasant-smelling wood; the wood of this tree 藍花楹（熱帶樹，木質芳香）；藍花楹木

jack /dʒæk/ *noun, verb, adj.*

■ **noun 1** [C] a device for raising heavy objects off the ground, especially vehicles so that a wheel can be changed 千斤頂，起重器（換車輪時常用）**2** [C] an electronic connection between two pieces of electrical equipment（電）插孔，插座，插口；塞孔 **3** [C] (in a PACK/DECK of cards 紙牌) a card with a picture of a young man on it, worth more than a ten and less than a queen * J 牌；傑克：*the jack of clubs* 梅花傑克 ➲ **VISUAL VOCAB** page V37 **4** [C] (in the game of BOWLS 滾木球遊戲) a small white ball towards which players roll larger balls 靶子球（白色，較其他球小）**5 jacks** [pl.] a children's game in which players BOUNCE a small ball and pick up small metal objects, also called jacks, before catching the ball 拋接子遊戲（兒童遊戲）**6** (also **jack 'shit**, *taboo*) [U] (*NAmE, slang*) (usually used in negative sentences 通常用於否定句) anything or nothing at all 絲毫，根本，一點（不）：*You don't know jack.* 你什麼都不知道。➲ see also BLACKJACK, FLAPJACK, UNION JACK

IDM **a jack of 'all trades** a person who can do many different types of work, but who perhaps does not do them very well 博而不精的人；萬金油；三腳貓 ➲ more at ALL RIGHT *adj.*, WORK *n.*

■ **verb ～ sth | ～ sb (for sth)** (*NAmE, informal*) to steal sth from sb, especially sth small or of low value 偷，悄悄拿走，竊取（尤指小的或不值錢的東西）：*Someone jacked my seat.* 有人偷偷佔了我的座位。

PHR V **ˌjack sb aˈround** (*NAmE, informal*) to treat sb in a way that is deliberately not helpful to them or wastes their time 把某人擺來擺去；故意不合作（或浪費某人的時間）：*Let's go. We're being jacked around here.* 咱們走吧。別在這兒浪費時間了。**ˌjack 'in/'into sth** (*informal*) to connect to a computer system 登錄；聯網；接入（計算機系統）：*I'm jacking into the Internet now.* 我正要接入互聯網。**ˌjack sth↔'in** (*BrE, informal*) to decide to stop doing sth, especially your job 決定結束，決定放棄（工作等）：*After five years, he decided to **jack it all in**.* 五年後，他就決定完全放棄了。**ˌjack 'off** (*taboo, slang*) (of a man 男人) to MASTURBATE 手淫 **ˌjack 'up** (*informal*) to INJECT an illegal drug directly into your blood 注射毒品：*Drug users were jacking up in the stairwells.* 當時癮君子正在樓梯井注射毒品。**ˌjack sth↔'up 1** to lift sth, especially a vehicle, off the ground using a jack 用千斤頂托起（汽車等）**2** (*informal*) to increase sth, especially prices, by a large amount 大幅度增加（或提高、抬高）（價格等）

■ **adj.** [not before noun] **～ of sb/sth** (*AustralE*) tired of or bored with sb/sth（對…）厭倦，厭煩

jackal /ˈdʒækl; -kɔːl/ *noun* a wild animal like a dog, that eats the meat of animals that are already dead and lives in Africa and Asia 豺；胡狼

jacka·napes /ˈdʒækəneɪps/ *noun* (*old use*) a person who is rude in an annoying way 粗魯無禮的人；蠻橫的人

jacka·roo /ˌdʒækəˈruː/ *noun* (*pl.* **-oos**) (*AustralE, NZE, informal*) a young man who is working on a farm in Australia/New Zealand to get experience（澳大利亞或新西蘭的）農場見習青年工人，農場新手 ➲ compare JILLAROO

jack·ass /ˈdʒækæs/ *noun* (*informal, especially NAmE*) a stupid person 蠢人；笨蛋；傻瓜：*Careful, you jackass!* 小心點，你這笨蛋！

jack·boot /ˈdʒækbuːt/ *noun* **1** [C] a tall boot that reaches up to the knee, worn by soldiers, especially in the past 長筒靴；（尤指舊時的）長筒軍靴 **2 the jackboot** [sing.] used to refer to cruel military rule（用以指殘酷的軍事統治）軍事壓迫，暴政：*to be **under the jackboot of** a dictatorial regime* 處在專制制度的鐵蹄之下

'Jack cheese *noun* [U] (*NAmE*) = MONTEREY JACK

jack·daw /ˈdʒækdɔː/ *noun* a black and grey bird of the CROW family 寒鴉

jacket 🔑 /ˈdʒækɪt/ *noun*

1 🔑 a piece of clothing worn on the top half of the body over a shirt, etc. that has sleeves and fastens down the front; a short, light coat 夾克衫；短上衣：*a denim/tweed jacket* 斜紋布 / 花呢夾克衫 ◇ *I have to wear a jacket and tie to work.* 我上班得穿短上衣打領帶。➲ **VISUAL VOCAB** page V61 ➲ see also BOMBER JACKET, DINNER JACKET, DONKEY JACKET, FLAK JACKET, LIFE JACKET, SMOKING JACKET, SPORTS JACKET, STRAITJACKET **2** (also **'dust jacket**) a loose paper cover for a book, usually with a design or picture on it（書籍通常帶有圖案或畫面的）護封，書套 **3** an outer cover around a hot water pipe, etc., for example to reduce loss of heat（熱水管的）保溫套，絕熱罩 **4** (*BrE*) the skin of a baked potato 烤過的土豆的皮：*potatoes baked in their jackets* 帶皮烤的土豆 **5** (*especially NAmE*) = SLEEVE (3)

ˌjacket po'tato *noun* = BAKED POTATO

ˌJack 'Frost *noun* [sing.] FROST, considered as a person（擬人用法）霜：*Jack Frost was threatening to kill the new plants.* 霜降危及新作物的存活。

jack·fruit /ˈdʒækfruːt/ *noun* **1** [C, U] a large tropical fruit 木菠蘿，菠蘿蜜（熱帶大水果）**2** [C] the tree that jackfruits grow on 木菠蘿樹；菠蘿蜜樹

jack·ham·mer /ˈdʒækhæmə(r)/ (*NAmE*) (*BrE* **pneuˌmatic 'drill**) *noun* a large powerful tool, worked by air pressure, used especially for breaking up road surfaces 風鑽

'jack-in-the-box *noun* a toy in the shape of a box with a figure inside on a spring that jumps up when you open the lid 玩偶匣（揭開匣蓋即跳起的玩偶）

jack·knife /ˈdʒæknaɪf/ *noun, verb*

■ **noun** (*pl.* **jack·knives** /-naɪvz/) a large knife with a folding blade 大摺刀

■ **verb** [I] to form a V-shape. For example if a lorry/truck that is in two parts **jackknifes**, the driver loses control and the back part moves towards the front part. 彎成 V 字形（如鉸接貨車失控時的彎折）

jack-o'-lantern /ˌdʒæk ə ˈlæntən; *NAmE* ˈdʒækə læntərn/ *noun* a PUMPKIN (= a large orange vegetable) with a face cut into it and a CANDLE put inside to shine through the holes 南瓜燈

ˈ**jack plug** *noun* a type of plug used to make a connection between the parts of a SOUND SYSTEM, etc. （音響系統等的）插頭，接頭

jack·pot /ˈdʒækpɒt; *NAmE* -pɑːt/ *noun* a large amount of money that is the most valuable prize in a game of chance（在碰運氣遊戲中的）頭獎，最高獎： *to win the jackpot* 得頭獎 ◇ *jackpot winners* 頭獎得主 ◇ (*figurative*) *United* ***hit the jackpot*** (= were successful) *with a 5-0 win over Liverpool.* 聯隊以 5:0 狂勝利物浦隊。

jack·rab·bit /ˈdʒækræbɪt/ *noun* a large N American HARE (= an animal like a large RABBIT) with very long ears 傑克兔（北美野兔）

Jack Robinson /ˌdʒæk ˈrɒbɪnsn; *NAmE* ˈrɑːb-/ *noun*
IDM **before you can say Jack ˈRobinson** (*old-fashioned*) very quickly; very soon 一剎那；一眨眼工夫；突然間

ˌ**jack ˈshit** *noun* [U] (*NAmE, taboo, slang*) = JACK (6)

jack·sie (also **jack·sy**) /ˈdʒæksi/ *noun* (*BrE, informal*) your bottom (= the part of your body that you sit on) 屁股

jack·straw /ˈdʒækstrɔː/ (*NAmE*) (*BrE* **spilli·kins**) *noun* [U] a game in which you remove a small stick from a pile, without moving any of the other sticks 挑棒遊戲（挑出一堆小棒中的一根而不觸動其他的小棒）

ˌ**Jack ˈTar** *noun* (*BrE, old-fashioned, informal*) a sailor 水手；船員

ˌ**Jack the ˈLad** *noun* [sing.] (*BrE, informal*) a young man who is very confident in a rude and noisy way, and enjoys going out with male friends, drinking alcohol and trying to attract women 浪蕩少年

Jaco·bean /ˌdʒækəˈbiːən/ *adj.* connected with the time when James I (1603–25) was King of England 英王詹姆斯一世時期的；具有詹姆斯一世時期風格的： *Jacobean drama* 具有詹姆斯一世時期風格的戲劇

Jaco·bite /ˈdʒækəbaɪt/ *noun* a supporter of King James II of England, Scotland and Ireland, or his son or grandson, after he was removed from power in 1688 詹姆斯黨人（擁護 1688 年被廢的英王詹姆斯二世及其後嗣為帝）

Ja·cuzzi™ /dʒəˈkuːzi/ (also **spa** especially in *NAmE*) *noun* a large bath/BATHTUB with a PUMP that moves the water around, giving a pleasant feeling to your body 極可意渦流式浴缸；按摩浴缸

jade /dʒeɪd/ *noun* [U] **1** a hard stone that is usually green and is used in making jewellery and decorative objects 玉；翡翠；碧玉： *a jade necklace* 翡翠項鏈 **2** objects made of jade 玉製品；玉器： *a collection of Chinese jade* 一批中國玉器 **3** (also ˌ**jade ˈgreen**) a bright green colour 翡翠色；綠玉色

jaded /ˈdʒeɪdɪd/ *adj.* tired and bored, usually because you have had too much of sth 精疲力竭的；厭倦的；膩煩的： *I felt terribly jaded after working all weekend.* 整個週末工作之後我感到疲憊不堪。◇ *It was a meal to tempt even the most jaded palate.* 這頓飯能使最沒胃口的人產生食慾。

jag /dʒæg/ *noun* (*informal, especially NAmE*) a short period of doing sth or of behaving in a particular way, especially in a way that you cannot control（難以控制的）一陣： *a crying jag* 一陣哭泣

jagged /ˈdʒægɪd/ *adj.* with rough, pointed, often sharp edges 凹凸不平的；有尖突的；鋸齒狀的： *jagged rocks/peaks/edges* 高高低低的岩石；嶙峋的山峰；參差不齊的邊緣

jag·uar /ˈdʒægjuə(r)/ *noun* a large animal of the cat family, that has yellowish-brown fur with black rings and spots. Jaguars live in parts of Central and S America. 美洲豹；美洲虎

jail (*BrE* also **gaol**) /dʒeɪl/ *noun, verb*
■ ***noun*** [U, C] a prison 監獄： *She spent a year in jail.* 她坐了一年牢。◇ *He has been released from jail.* 他已從監獄裏放出來了。◇ *a ten-year jail sentence* 十年監禁的判刑 ◇ *Britain's overcrowded jails* 英國過度擁擠的監獄 ➲ COLLOCATIONS at JUSTICE ➲ note at SCHOOL
■ ***verb*** [usually passive] **~ sb** (**for sth**) to put sb in prison 監禁 **SYN** **imprison**： *He was* ***jailed for life*** *for murder.* 他因謀殺罪被終身監禁。

jail·bait /ˈdʒeɪlbeɪt/ *noun* [U] (*informal*) a girl or boy who is too young to have sex with legally 禍水妞（或郎）（指與之發生性關係即構成犯罪的未成年人）

jail·bird /ˈdʒeɪlbɜːd; *NAmE* -bɜːrd/ *noun* (*old-fashioned, informal*) a person who has spent a lot of time in prison 長期坐牢的囚犯

jail·break /ˈdʒeɪlbreɪk/ *noun* (*especially NAmE*) an escape from prison, usually by several people（數人）越獄

jail·er /ˈdʒeɪlə(r)/ (*BrE* also **gaol·er**) *noun* (*old-fashioned*) a person in charge of a prison and the prisoners in it 監獄看守；獄卒

jail·house /ˈdʒeɪlhaʊs/ *noun* (*NAmE*) a prison 監獄

Jain /dʒeɪn/ *noun* a member of an Indian religion whose principles include not harming any living creature and a belief in REINCARNATION 印度耆那教教徒（反對傷害眾生、主張輪迴說） ▶ **Jain** *adj.* **Jain·ism** /ˈdʒeɪnɪzəm/ *noun* [U]

jala·peño /ˌhæləˈpeɪnjəʊ; *NAmE* ˌhɑːləˈpeɪnjoʊ/ (also ˌ**jalaˌpeño ˈpepper**) *noun* (from *Spanish*) the small green fruit of a type of pepper plant, that has a very hot taste and is used in Mexican cooking 青辣椒（墨西哥烹飪常用）

jal·opy /dʒəˈlɒpi; *NAmE* -ˈlɑːpi/ *noun* (*pl.* **-ies**) (*old-fashioned, informal*) an old car that is in bad condition 破舊的汽車

jam 🔑 /dʒæm/ *noun, verb*
■ ***noun***
▸ **SWEET FOOD** 甜食 **1** 🔑 [U, C] a thick sweet substance made by boiling fruit with sugar, often sold in JARS and spread on bread 果醬： *strawberry jam* 草莓醬 ◇ *recipes for jams and preserves* 果醬和蜜餞的製作方法 ◇ (*BrE*) *a jam doughnut* 果醬炸麵圈 ➲ compare JELLY (3), MARMALADE
▸ **MANY PEOPLE/VEHICLES** 多人／車輛 **2** [C] a situation in which it is difficult or impossible to move because there are so many people or vehicles in one particular place 擁擠；堵塞： *The bus was delayed in a five-mile jam.* 公共汽車因長達五英里的交通堵塞而延誤。◇ *As fans rushed to leave, jams formed at all the exits.* 因球迷都急於離開，所有出口都給阻塞了。➲ see also TRAFFIC JAM
▸ **MACHINE** 機器 **3** [C] a situation in which a machine does not work because sth is stuck in one position 卡住（因而發生故障）： *There's a paper jam in the photocopier.* 複印機卡紙了。
IDM **be in a ˈjam** (*informal*) to be in a difficult situation 陷入困境 **jam toˈmorrow** (*BrE, informal*) good things that are promised for the future but never happen 可望而不可即的美好未來；許而不予的好東西： *They refused to settle for a promise of jam tomorrow.* 他們並不滿足於那些美好未來的空話。➲ more at MONEY
■ ***verb*** (**-mm-**)
▸ **PUSH WITH FORCE** 用力推 **1** [T] **~ sth + adv./prep.** to push sth somewhere with a lot of force 使勁（往某處）擠（或壓、塞）： *He jammed his fingers in his ears.* 他用手指使勁堵住耳朵。◇ *A stool had been jammed against the door.* 門被一把凳子頂住了。
▸ **STOP MOVING/WORKING** 停止移動／運轉 **2** [I, T] to become unable to move or work; to make sth do this （使）卡住，不能動彈，不能運轉： **~ (up)** *The photocopier keeps jamming up.* 這台複印機總是卡紙。◇ **~ sth (up)** *There's a loose part that keeps jamming the mechanism.* 有個零件鬆了經常卡住機器。◇ **+ adj.** *The valve has jammed shut.* 閥門給卡住了打不開。◇ **~ sth + adj.** *He jammed the door open with a piece of wood.* 他用一塊木頭卡住門讓它開着。
▸ **PUT INTO SMALL SPACE** 塞進 **3** [T, I] to put sb/sth into a small space where there is very little room to move 塞入；塞進；擠進 **SYN** **squash, squeeze**： **~ sb/sth + adv./prep.** *Six of us were jammed into one small car.* 我們六個人被塞進一輛小汽車裏。◇ *We were jammed together like sardines in a can.* 我們像罐頭裏的沙丁魚一般緊緊擠在一起。◇ *The cupboards were* ***jammed full*** *of old newspapers.* 櫥櫃裏塞滿了舊報紙。◇ **+ adv./prep.**

Nearly 1 000 students jammed into the hall. 近 1 000 名學生擠到禮堂裏。➲ see also JAM-PACKED

▸ FILL WITH PEOPLE/THINGS 擠滿人／物 **4** [T] **~ sth (up) (with sb/sth)** to fill sth with a large number of people or things so that it is unable to function as it should 擠滿；塞緊 SYN **block**：*Viewers jammed the switchboard with complaints.* 打電話投訴的觀眾使總機應接不暇。

▸ RADIO BROADCAST 無線電廣播 **5** [T] **~ sth** (*technical* 術語) to send out radio signals to prevent another radio broadcast from being heard（發射無線電波）干擾

▸ PLAY MUSIC 演奏音樂 **6** [I, T] **~ (sth)** to play music with other musicians in an informal way without preparing or practising first 即興演奏

IDM **jam on the brake(s)** | **jam the brake(s) on** to operate the BRAKES on a vehicle suddenly and with force 猛踩刹車：*The car skidded as he jammed on the brakes.* 他緊急刹車時汽車向前滑了一段路。

jamb /dʒæm/ *noun* a vertical post at the side of a door or window 門窗邊框

jam·ba·laya /ˌdʒæmbəˈlaɪə/ *noun* [U] a spicy dish of rice, SEAFOOD, chicken, etc. from the southern US（美國南部的）什錦飯（用米飯、海鮮、雞肉等加香料製作而成）

jam·bo·ree /ˌdʒæmbəˈriː/ *noun* **1** a large party or celebration 大型聚會；慶祝會：*the movie industry's annual jamboree at Cannes* 在戛納舉行的一年一度的影展 **2** a large meeting of SCOUTS or GUIDES 童子軍大會；女童子軍大會

ˈjam jar *noun* (*BrE*) a glass container for jam, etc. 果醬瓶；果醬罐

jammed /dʒæmd/ *adj.* **1** [not before noun] not able to move 動彈不得；卡住了 SYN **stuck**：*I can't get the door open—it's completely jammed.* 我打不開門 —— 卡死了。 **2** (*especially NAmE*) very full; crowded 擠滿的；塞滿的；擁擠不堪的 SYN **jam-packed**：*Hundreds more people were waiting outside the jammed stadium.* 還有數百人在擁擠不堪的體育場外等候。

jammy /ˈdʒæmi/ *adj.* **1** covered with jam 塗有果醬的；滿是果醬的：*jammy fingers* 滿是果醬的手指 **2** (*BrE, informal*) lucky, especially because sth good has happened to you without you making any effort 幸運的；運氣好的

jam-ˈpacked *adj.* [not usually before noun] **~ (with sb/sth)** (*informal*) very full or crowded 擠滿；擁擠：*The train was jam-packed with commuters.* 火車上擠滿了上下班的乘客。

ˈjam session *noun* an occasion when musicians perform in an informal way without practising first 即興演奏會

Jane Doe /ˌdʒem ˈdəʊ; *NAmE* ˈdoʊ/ *noun* [sing.] (*NAmE*) **1** used to refer to a woman whose name is not known or is kept secret, especially in a court of law 無名女士，某女（不知姓名或在法庭等上隱匿真名的女當事人） **2** an average woman 普通女子 ➲ compare JOHN DOE

jan·gle /ˈdʒæŋgl/ *verb, noun*

■ **verb** **1** [I, T] to make an unpleasant sound, like two pieces of metal hitting each other; to make sth do this（使）發出金屬撞擊聲，發出丁零噹啷的刺耳聲：*The shop bell jangled loudly.* 商店的鐘發出丁零噹啷的巨大響聲。◇ **~ sth** *He jangled the keys in his pocket.* 他把兜裏的鑰匙弄得丁零噹啷亂響。 **2** [I, T] **~ (sth)** if your nerves **jangle**, or if sb/sth **jangles** them, you feel anxious or upset 刺激，煩擾（神經）；（使）煩躁不安：*She was suddenly wide awake, her nerves jangling.* 她突然間清醒過來，神經焦躁不安。

■ **noun** [usually sing.] a hard noise like that of metal hitting metal 金屬撞擊聲；丁零噹啷的刺耳聲

jani·tor /ˈdʒænɪtə(r)/ *noun* (*NAmE, ScotE*) = CUSTODIAN (2)

Janu·ary 🔑 /ˈdʒænjuəri; *NAmE* -jueri/ *noun* [U, C] (*abbr.* **Jan.**) the 1st month of the year, between December and February 一月 HELP To see how **January** is used, look at the examples at **April**. * January 的用法見詞條 April 下的示例。

Jap /dʒæp/ *noun* (*taboo, slang*) an offensive word for a Japanese person 日本佬；日本鬼子

jape /dʒeɪp/ *noun* (*old-fashioned, BrE*) a trick or joke that is played on sb 戲弄；惡作劇；玩笑

ja·pon·ica /dʒəˈpɒnɪkə; *NAmE* -ˈpɑːn-/ *noun* a Japanese bush that is often grown in gardens/yards, and that has red flowers and pale yellow fruit（日本）貼梗海棠

jar /dʒɑː(r)/ *noun, verb*

■ **noun** **1** [C] a round glass container, with a lid, used for storing food, especially jam, HONEY, etc.（玻璃）罐子；廣口瓶：*a storage jar* 廣口貯藏瓶 ➲ VISUAL VOCAB page V33 ➲ see also JAM JAR **2** [C] a jar and what it contains 一罐，一瓶（的量）：*a jar of coffee* 一罐咖啡 **3** [C] a tall container with a wide mouth, with or without handles, used in the past for carrying water, etc. 缸；罎子：*a water jar* 水缸 ➲ see also BELL JAR **4** [C] (*BrE, informal*) a glass of beer 一杯啤酒：*Do you fancy a jar after work?* 你喜歡下班後喝杯啤酒嗎？ **5** [sing.] an unpleasant shock, especially from two things being suddenly shaken or hit 猛然震動；撞擊：*The fall gave him a nasty jar.* 這一跤把他摔得好厲害。

■ **verb** (-rr-) **1** [T, I] to give or receive a sudden sharp painful knock（使）撞擊，受震動而疼痛：**~ sth** *The jolt seemed to jar every bone in her body.* 這震動似乎把她渾身上下每根骨頭都弄疼了。◇ **~ (sth) (on sth)** *The spade jarred on something metal.* 鐵鍬撞在什麼金屬物件上發出刺耳的聲音。 **2** [I, T] **~ (on sth)** | **~ (sth)** to have an unpleasant or annoying effect（對…）產生不快的影響；使煩躁 SYN **grate**：*His constant moaning was beginning to jar on her nerves.* 他不停的呻吟使她焦躁不安起來。◇ *There was a jarring note of triumph in his voice.* 他聲音裏含有一種煩人的揚揚得意的口氣。 **3** [I] **~ (with sth)** to be different from sth in a strange or unpleasant way（與…）不協調，不和諧，相衝突 SYN **clash**：*Her brown shoes jarred with the rest of the outfit.* 她那雙棕色的鞋與她的衣着不協調。

jar·gon /ˈdʒɑːgən; *NAmE* ˈdʒɑːrgən/ *noun* [U] (often *disapproving*) words or expressions that are used by a particular profession or group of people, and are difficult for others to understand 行話；行業術語；切口：***medical/legal/computer, etc. jargon*** 醫學、法律、計算機等術語 ◇ *Try to avoid using too much technical jargon.* 盡量避免使用太多的技術用語。

jar·head /ˈdʒɑːhed; *NAmE* ˈdʒɑːr-/ *noun* (*NAmE, informal*) a member of the US Marine Corps (= American soldiers trained to serve on land or at sea) 鍋蓋頭（指美國海軍陸戰隊士兵）

jas·mine /ˈdʒæzmɪn/ *noun* [U, C] a plant with white or yellow flowers with a sweet smell, sometimes used to make PERFUME and to flavour tea 茉莉；素馨

jaun·dice /ˈdʒɔːndɪs/ *noun* [U] a medical condition in which the skin and the white parts of the eyes become yellow 黃疸

jaun·diced /ˈdʒɔːndɪst/ *adj.* **1** not expecting sb/sth to be good or useful, especially because of experiences that you have had in the past（尤指因以前的經歷）有偏見的，狹隘的：*He had a jaundiced view of life.* 他具有狹隘的人生觀。◇ *She looked on politicians* ***with a jaundiced eye.*** 她對政治家有偏見。 **2** suffering from jaundice 患黃疸病的：*a* ***jaundiced patient/liver*** 黃疸病人；肝內膽紅素過多

jaunt /dʒɔːnt/ *noun* (*old-fashioned* or *humorous*) a short journey that you make for pleasure（短途）遊覽，旅行 SYN **excursion**

jaunty /ˈdʒɔːnti/ *adj.* **1** showing that you are feeling confident and pleased with yourself 得意揚揚的；無憂無慮的；神氣活現的 SYN **cheerful**：*a jaunty smile* 得意揚揚的微笑 **2** lively 輕鬆活潑的：*a jaunty tune* 輕鬆活潑的曲子 ▸ **jaunt·ily** *adv.*：*He set off jauntily, whistling to himself.* 他吹着口哨神氣活現地出發了。 **jaunti·ness** *noun* [U]

jav·elin /ˈdʒævlɪn/ *noun* **1** [C] a light SPEAR (= a long stick with a pointed end) which is thrown in a sporting event 標槍 **2 the javelin** [sing.] the event or sport of throwing a javelin as far as possible 投擲標槍項目（或運動）➲ VISUAL VOCAB page V46

jaw /dʒɔː/ *noun, verb*

■ ***noun*** **1** [C] either of the two bones at the bottom of the face that contain the teeth and move when you talk or eat 頜：*the* ***top/upper jaw*** 上頜 ◇ *the* ***bottom/lower jaw*** 下頜 **2** [sing.] the lower part of the face; the lower jaw 下巴；下頜：*He has a strong square jaw.* 他長着一副結實的方下巴。◇ *The punch broke my jaw.* 這一拳打壞了我的下巴。➲ VISUAL VOCAB page V59 **3 jaws** [pl.] the mouth and teeth of a person or an animal 口部；嘴：*The alligator's jaws snapped shut.* 鈍吻鱷的嘴吧嗒一聲閉上了。 **4 jaws** [pl.] the parts of a tool or machine that are used to hold things tightly（工具或機器的）鉗夾部份，鉗口：*the jaws of a vice* 虎鉗口

IDM **sb's 'jaw dropped/fell/sagged** used to say that sb suddenly looked surprised, shocked or disappointed（突然吃驚或失望得）張口結舌，目瞪口呆，垂頭喪氣 **the jaws of 'death, de'feat, etc.** (*literary*) used to describe an unpleasant situation that almost happens 鬼門關；失敗的險境：*The team snatched victory from the jaws of defeat.* 這個隊翻盤而得險勝。 **the jaws of a tunnel, etc.** the narrow entrance to a tunnel, etc., especially one that looks dangerous（隧道等處尤指看起來危險的）狹窄入口

■ ***verb*** [I] (*informal, often disapproving*) to talk, especially to talk a lot or for a long time 嘮嘮叨叨；喋喋不休

jawan /dʒə'wɑːn/ *noun* (*IndE*) a soldier of low rank 士兵；步兵

jaw·bone /'dʒɔːbəʊn; *NAmE* -boʊn/ *noun* the bone that forms the lower jaw 下頜骨 SYN **mandible** ➲ VISUAL VOCAB page V59

jaw·break·er /'dʒɔːbreɪkə(r)/ (*NAmE*) (*BrE* **gob·stop·per**) *noun* a very large hard round sweet/candy 大塊圓硬糖

'jaw-dropping *adj.* (*informal*) so large or good that it amazes you 令人大驚失色的；令人咋舌的：*a jaw-dropping 5 million dollars* 令人吃驚的 500 萬巨款 ◇ *The production is absolutely jaw dropping.* 這部作品真是令人叫絕。▸ **'jaw-droppingly** *adv.*：*jaw-droppingly beautiful* 美豔得讓人見了合不攏嘴的

jaw·line /'dʒɔːlaɪn/ *noun* the outline of the lower jaw 下頜的輪廓；下巴的外形

jay /dʒeɪ/ *noun* a European bird of the CROW family, with bright feathers and a noisy call 松鴉，樫鳥（見於歐洲，羽毛鮮豔，喜大聲鳴叫）➲ see also BLUEJAY

Jay·cee /'dʒeɪsiː/ *noun* (*NAmE, informal*) a member of the United States Junior Chamber, an organization for people between the ages of 21 and 39 that provides help in local communities in the US and other countries 美國青年商會會員（年齡在 21 至 39 歲之間，為美國和其他國家的當地社區提供援助）

jay·walk /'dʒeɪwɔːk/ *verb* [I] to walk along or across a street illegally or without paying attention to the traffic（無視交通規則）亂穿馬路 ▸ **jay·walk·er** *noun* **jay·walk·ing** *noun* [U]

jazz /dʒæz/ *noun, verb*

■ ***noun*** [U] a type of music with strong rhythms, in which the players often IMPROVISE (= make up the music as they are playing), originally created by African American musicians 爵士樂：*a* ***jazz band/club*** 爵士樂隊／夜總會 ◇ ***traditional/modern jazz*** 傳統／現代爵士樂 ◇ *jazz musicians* 爵士樂師 ➲ COLLOCATIONS at MUSIC ➲ see also ACID JAZZ

IDM **and all that 'jazz** (*informal*) and things like that 以及諸如此類的東西（或事情）：*How's it going? You know—love, life and all that jazz.* 怎麼樣啊？你知道，說的就是愛情、生活以及諸如此類的事情嘛。

■ ***verb***

PHR V **,jazz sth↔'up** (*informal*) **1** to make sth more interesting, exciting or attractive 使某事更有趣；使某事更令人興奮；使某事更有吸引力 **2** to make a piece of music sound more modern, or more like popular music or jazz 使一段音樂聽起來更現代化；使更具有流行音樂（或爵士樂）的風格：*It's a jazzed up version of an old tune.* 這是把一段古老的曲調翻新了。

jazzed /dʒæzd/ *adj.* [not before noun] (*informal*) excited 興奮；激動：*I was jazzed to meet someone so famous.* 和這麼有名的人見面我很激動。

jazzy /'dʒæzi/ *adj.* (*informal*) **1** in the style of jazz 爵士樂風格的：*a* ***jazzy melody/tune*** 爵士樂風格的曲調 **2** (*sometimes disapproving*) brightly coloured and likely to attract attention 絢麗的；花哨的 SYN **snazzy**：*That's a jazzy tie you're wearing.* 你繫的那條領帶太豔麗了。

JCB™ /,dʒeɪ siː 'biː/ *noun* (*BrE*) a powerful vehicle with a long arm for digging and moving earth * JCB 挖掘裝載機

JCL /,dʒeɪ siː 'el/ *abbr.* job control language (a computer language that lets the user state what tasks they want the OPERATING SYSTEM to do) 作業控制語言（讓計算機用戶給操作系統分配作業）

'J-cloth™ *noun* a type of light cloth used for cleaning * J 清潔布；輕軟抹布

JCR /,dʒeɪ siː 'ɑː(r)/ *abbr.* JUNIOR COMMON ROOM

jeal·ous 0-m /'dʒeləs/ *adj.*

1 0-m feeling angry or unhappy because sb you like or love is showing interest in sb else 吃醋的；妒忌的：*a* ***jealous wife/husband*** 好吃醋的妻子／丈夫 ◇ *He's only talking to her to make you jealous.* 他跟她講話只是讓你妒忌。 **2** 0-m **~ (of sb/sth)** feeling angry or unhappy because you wish you had sth that sb else has 妒羨的；忌妒的 SYN **envious**：*She's jealous of my success.* 她忌妒我的成功。◇ *Children often feel jealous when a new baby arrives.* 新生嬰兒出世時孩子常常感到忌妒。 **3 ~ (of sth)** wanting to keep or protect sth that you have because it makes you feel proud 珍惜的；愛惜的；精心守護的：*They are very jealous of their good reputation* (= they do not want to lose it). 他們極為珍惜自己的聲譽。 ▸ **jeal·ous·ly** *adv.*：*She eyed Natalia jealously.* 她妒忌地看着納塔莉亞。◇ *a* ***jealously guarded*** *secret* 嚴守的秘密

jeal·ousy /'dʒeləsi/ *noun* (*pl.* **-ies**) **1** [U] a feeling of being jealous 忌妒；妒羨；羨慕：*I felt sick with jealousy.* 我羨慕得要死。◇ *sexual jealousy* 因愛生妒現象 **2** [C] an action or a remark that shows that a person is jealous 忌妒，妒羨，羨慕（的言行）：*I'm tired of her petty jealousies.* 我厭煩她那小肚雞腸的忌妒。

jeans 0-m /dʒiːnz/ *noun* [pl.]

trousers/pants made of strong cotton, especially DENIM 牛仔褲；粗斜紋棉布褲：*a faded pair of blue jeans* 一條褪了色的藍色牛仔褲 ➲ VISUAL VOCAB page V63 ➲ see also DENIMS at DENIM (2) ORIGIN From **Janne**, the Old French name for Genoa, where the heavy cotton now used for jeans was first made. 源自古法語 Janne，即 Genoa（熱那亞），牛仔褲用的粗棉布始產於此地。

Jeep™ /dʒiːp/ *noun* a small strong vehicle used, especially by the army, for driving over rough ground 吉普車；越野車 ➲ VISUAL VOCAB page V57

jee·pers /'dʒiːpəz; *NAmE* -pərz/ (also **,jeepers 'creepers**) *exclamation* (*especially NAmE, informal*) used to express surprise or shock（表示驚奇或震驚）天哪，哎呀：*Jeepers! That car nearly hit us!* 天哪！那輛車差點撞了我們！

jeer /dʒɪə(r); *NAmE* dʒɪr/ *verb, noun*

■ ***verb*** [I, T] to laugh at sb or shout rude remarks at them to show that you do not respect them 嘲笑；嘲弄；譏諷；奚落 SYN **taunt**：*a jeering crowd* 起鬨的一群人 ◇ **~ at sb** *The police were jeered at by the waiting crowd.* 警方受到在等待的人群的嘲弄。◇ **~ sb** *The players were jeered by disappointed fans.* 球員受到大失所望的球迷奚落。◇ **+ speech** *'Coward!' he jeered.* "懦夫！"他嘲笑道。

■ ***noun*** [usually pl.] a rude remark that sb shouts at sb else to show that they do not respect or like them 嘲笑，嘲弄，譏諷，奚落（的言語）SYN **taunt**：*He walked on to the stage to be greeted with jeers and whistles.* 他登上舞台，結果迎來陣陣嘲笑和口哨噓聲。

Jeez /dʒiːz/ *exclamation* (*informal, especially NAmE*) used to express anger, surprise, etc.（表示憤怒、驚訝等）天哪，哎呀

jehad = JIHAD

Je·ho·vah /dʒɪˈhəʊvə; *NAmE* -ˈhoʊ-/ (also **Yah·weh**) *noun* the name of God that is used in the Old Testament of the Bible 耶和華（《〈聖經〉舊約》中對上帝的稱呼）

Je,hovah's 'Witness *noun* a member of a religious organization based on Christianity, which believes that the end of the world is near and that only its members will be saved from being DAMNED 耶和華見證人（相信世界末日在即，只有其信徒才能免受懲罰）

je·june /dʒɪˈdʒuːn/ *adj.* (*formal*) **1** too simple 太幼稚的；不成熟的；頭腦簡單的 **SYN** **naive 2** (of a speech, etc. 演講等) not interesting 枯燥無味的；單調的；空洞的

je·junum /dʒɪˈdʒuːnəm/ *noun* (*anatomy* 解) the second part of the small INTESTINE 空腸 ➲ compare DUODENUM, ILEUM ▸ **je·junal** /-ˈdʒuːnl/ *adj.*

Jek·yll and Hyde /ˌdʒekl ən ˈhaɪd/ *noun* [sing.] a person who is sometimes very pleasant (*Jekyll*) and sometimes very unpleasant (*Hyde*) or who leads two very separate lives 兩重性格交替出現的人；具有善惡雙重人格的人 **ORIGIN** From the story by Robert Louis Stevenson, *Dr Jekyll and Mr Hyde*, in which Dr Jekyll takes a drug which separates the good and bad sides of his personality into two characters. All the negative aspects go into the character of Mr Hyde. 源自羅伯特・路易斯・史蒂文森的小說《化身博士》，小說中哲基爾醫生服用了一種藥，把他性格中的善與惡分在兩個人物身上，所有的惡念都分給了海德先生。

J

jell (*especially NAmE*) (*BrE* usually **gel**) /dʒel/ *verb* **1** [I] (of two or more people 兩個或更多的人) to work well together; to form a successful group 聯手共事；結為一體：*We just didn't jell as a group.* 我們就是不能成為一個集體。 **2** [I] (of an idea, a thought, a plan, etc. 主意、想法、計劃等) to become clearer and more definite; to work well 變得更清楚；顯得更明確；有效；起作用：*Ideas were beginning to jell in my mind.* 各種想法在我頭腦裏逐漸明朗起來。◇ *That day, everything jelled.* 那天，一切都很順利。 **3** [I] (*technical* 術語) (of a liquid 液體) to become thicker and more solid; to form a GEL 膠凝；膠化；形成膠體

jel·lied /ˈdʒelid/ *adj.* [only before noun] (*especially BrE*) prepared or cooked in jelly 做成膠凍狀的：*jellied eels* 鰻魚凍

jelly 🔑 /ˈdʒeli/ (*pl.* **-ies**) *noun*
1 🔑 [U, C] (*BrE*) (*NAmE* **jello, Jell-O™** [U]) a cold sweet transparent food made from GELATIN, sugar and fruit juice, that shakes when it is moved 果凍：*jelly and ice cream* 果凍冰淇淋 ◇ *a raspberry jelly* 山莓凍 **2** [U] a substance like jelly made from GELATIN and meat juices, served around meat, fish, etc. 肉凍 **SYN** **aspic**：*chicken in jelly* 雞肉凍 **3** 🔑 [U, C] a type of jam that does not contain any pieces of fruit（不含水果塊的）果醬：*blackcurrant jelly* 黑加侖果醬 ➲ compare JAM *n.* (1) **4** 🔑 [U] any thick sticky substance, especially a type of cream used on the skin 膠狀物，膠凝物（尤指護膚霜）➲ see also PETROLEUM JELLY, ROYAL JELLY **5** (also **'jelly shoe**) [C] a light plastic shoe designed for wearing on the beach and in the sea（海灘和海上穿的）輕便塑料鞋 ➲ VISUAL VOCAB page V64
IDM **be/feel like 'jelly | turn to 'jelly** (of legs or knees 雙腿或雙膝) to feel weak because you are nervous 緊張得發軟

'jelly baby *noun* (*BrE*) a small soft sweet/candy in the shape of a baby, made from GELATIN and flavoured with fruit 娃娃膠糖（果味凝膠軟糖）

'jelly bean *noun* a small sweet/candy shaped like a BEAN, with a hard outside and a centre like jelly 軟心豆粒糖

jel·ly·fish /ˈdʒelifɪʃ/ *noun* (*pl.* **jel·ly·fish**) a sea creature with a body like jelly and long thin parts called TENTACLES that can give a sharp sting 水母；海蜇

'jelly roll (*NAmE*) (*BrE* **ˌSwiss 'roll**) *noun* a thin flat cake that is spread with jam, etc. and rolled up 捲筒蛋糕（夾有果醬等）

jembe /ˈdʒembe/ *noun* **1** [C] (*EAfrE*) a farming tool with a long handle and a blade at one end, used for digging, breaking up soil or removing WEEDS (= plants growing where they are not wanted)（長柄）鋤頭 **2** [C] a traditional W African drum 金貝鼓（西非的一種傳統鼓） **3** [U] a type of W African music 西非打擊樂

jemmy /ˈdʒemi/ (*BrE*) (*NAmE* **jimmy**) *noun* (*pl.* **-ies**) a short heavy metal bar used by thieves to force open doors and windows 短撬棍，鐵撬棍（竊賊撬門窗用）

je ne sais quoi /ˌʒə nə seɪ ˈkwɑː/ *noun* [U] (from *French*, often *humorous*) a good quality that is difficult to describe 難以描述的好品質；妙不可言的特性：*He has that je ne sais quoi that distinguishes a professional from an amateur.* 他有那種難以言表的特質，體現出他是專業而非業餘的。

jenny /ˈdʒeni/ *noun* (*pl.* **-ies**) a female DONKEY or ASS 母驢

jeop·ard·ize (*BrE* also **-ise**) /ˈdʒepədaɪz; *NAmE* -pərd-/ *verb* **~ sth/sb** (*formal*) to risk harming or destroying sth/sb 冒…的危險；危及；危害；損害 **SYN** **endanger**：*He would never do anything to jeopardize his career.* 他決不會做任何有損於他事業的事。

jeop·ardy /ˈdʒepədi; *NAmE* -pərdi/ *noun*
IDM **in 'jeopardy** in a dangerous position or situation and likely to be lost or harmed 處於危險境地；受到威脅 ➲ see also DOUBLE JEOPARDY

jere·miad /ˌdʒerɪˈmaɪæd/ *noun* (*formal*) a very long sad complaint or list of complaints 哀訴；訴求清單

jerk /dʒɜːk; *NAmE* dʒɜːrk/ *verb, noun*
▪ *verb* [T, I] to move or to make sth move with a sudden short sharp movement 急拉；猛推；猝然一動：**~ sth (+ adv./prep.)** *He jerked the phone away from her.* 他猛然一下從她那兒把電話搶走。◇ *She jerked her head up.* 她猛然抬起頭來。◇ **+ adv./prep.** *The bus jerked to a halt.* 那輛公共汽車猛地一顛停下了。◇ *He grabbed a handful of hair and jerked at it.* 他抓住一把頭髮猛拉。◇ **~ sth + adj.** *She got to the door and jerked it open.* 她走到門口，猛然一把將門拉開。
PHR V **ˌjerk sb a'round** (*informal, especially NAmE*) to make things difficult for sb, especially by not being honest with them（尤指通過不誠實的手段）給某人出難題，為某人設置障礙，為難某人：*Consumers are often jerked around by big companies.* 消費者經常受大公司的捉弄。 **ˌjerk 'off** (*taboo, slang*) (of a man 男子) to MASTURBATE 手淫 **ˌjerk 'out | ˌjerk sth↔'out** to say sth in a quick and awkward way because you are nervous（緊張得）急促而斷續地說出，結結巴巴地說
▪ *noun* **1** [C] a sudden quick sharp movement 急拉；猛推；猝然一動 **SYN** **jolt**：*She sat up* **with a jerk**. 她猛地坐了起來。 **2** [C] (*informal*) a stupid person who often says or does the wrong thing 蠢人；傻瓜；笨蛋 **3** [U] meat that is MARINATED (= left in a mixture of oil and spices before being cooked) to give it a strong flavour and then cooked over a wood fire 醃製後放在木火上烤的肉：*jerk chicken* 烤雞

jer·kin /ˈdʒɜːkɪn; *NAmE* ˈdʒɜːrkɪn/ *noun* (*BrE*) a short jacket without sleeves, especially one worn by men in the past（尤指舊時男子穿的）坎肩

jerky /ˈdʒɜːki; *NAmE* ˈdʒɜːrki/ *adj., noun*
▪ *adj.* making sudden starts and stops and not moving smoothly 忽動忽停的；顛簸的 ▸ **jerk·ily** /-ɪli/ *adv.*：*The car moved off jerkily.* 汽車顛簸着開走了。
▪ *noun* [U] (*NAmE*) meat that has been cut into long strips and smoked or dried 乾肉條；熏肉條：*beef jerky* 牛肉乾條

jero·boam /ˌdʒerəˈbəʊəm; *NAmE* -ˈboʊ-/ *noun* a wine bottle which holds four or six times as much wine as an ordinary bottle（容量相當於普通酒瓶四倍或六倍的）大酒瓶 ➲ compare METHUSELAH

Jerry /ˈdʒeri/ *noun* (*pl.* **-ies**) (*taboo, BrE, slang*) an offensive word for a person from Germany, used especially during the First and Second World Wars 德國佬，德國鬼子（尤用於第一、二次世界大戰期間）

'jerry-built *noun* (*old-fashioned, disapproving*) built quickly and cheaply without caring about quality or safety 草率建成的；粗製濫造的

jer·ry·can /ˈdʒerikæn/ *noun* (*old-fashioned*) a large metal or plastic container with flat sides, used for carrying petrol/gas or water（運送汽油或水的）大扁平容器

jer·ry·man·der, **jer·ry·man·der·ing** = GERRYMANDER, GERRYMANDERING

jer·sey /ˈdʒɜːzi; *NAmE* ˈdʒɜːrzi/ *noun* **1** [C] a shirt worn by sb playing a sports game 參賽者運動衫 ➲ VISUAL VOCAB page V44 **2** [C] a knitted piece of clothing made of wool or cotton for the upper part of the body, with long sleeves and no buttons; a type of sweater（毛或棉的）針織套頭衫 **3** [U] a type of soft fine knitted cloth used for making clothes 平針織物：*made from 100% cotton jersey* 用 100% 的棉織品做成 **4 Jersey** [C] a type of light brown cow that produces high quality milk 澤西牛（一種產優質奶的淺棕色乳牛）

Je·ru·sa·lem ar·ti·choke /dʒəˌruːsələm ˈɑːtɪtʃəʊk; *NAmE* ˈɑːrtətʃoʊk/ *noun* (*BrE* also **ar·ti·choke**) a light brown root vegetable that looks like a potato 洋薑；菊芋；耶路撒冷洋薊

jes·sie /ˈdʒesi/ (also **jessy**) *noun* (*pl.* **-ies**) (*BrE*, *old-fashioned*, *offensive*) a man or boy who is weak or who seems to behave too much like a woman 軟弱的男子（或男孩）；娘娘腔

jest /dʒest/ *noun*, *verb*

■ *noun* (*old-fashioned* or *formal*) something said or done to amuse people 笑話；俏皮話；打趣；玩笑 SYN **joke**

IDM **in ˈjest** as a joke 開玩笑地；鬧着玩：*The remark was made half in jest.* 這話是半開玩笑説出的。◇ *'Many a true word is spoken in jest,' thought Rosie* (= people often say things as a joke that are actually true). “許多真話都是在玩笑中説出的。”羅西想。

■ *verb* [I, T] **~ (about sth)** | **+ speech** (*formal* or *humorous*) to say things that are not serious or true, especially in order to make sb laugh 開玩笑；説笑話 SYN **joke**：*Would I jest about such a thing?* 這種事我會説着玩嗎？

jest·er /ˈdʒestə(r)/ *noun* a man employed in the past at the COURT of a king or queen to amuse people by telling jokes and funny stories（舊時宮廷中的）逗樂小丑，弄臣：*the court jester* 宮廷弄臣

Jes·uit /ˈdʒezjuɪt; *NAmE* ˈdʒeʒəwət/ *noun* a member of the Society of Jesus, a Roman Catholic religious group（天主教）耶穌會會士：*a Jesuit priest* 耶穌會神父

Jesus /ˈdʒiːzəs/ (also **ˌJesus ˈChrist**) *noun* = CHRIST

jet /dʒet/ *noun*, *verb*

■ *noun* **1** [C] a plane driven by JET ENGINES 噴氣式飛機：***a jet aircraft/fighter/airliner*** 噴氣式飛機 / 戰鬥機 / 客機 ◇ *The accident happened as the jet was about to take off.* 事故是在噴氣式飛機正要起飛時發生的。➲ see also JUMBO (JET), JUMP JET **2** [C] a strong narrow stream of gas, liquid, steam or flame that comes very quickly out of a small opening. The opening is also called a jet. 噴射流；噴射口；噴嘴：*The pipe burst and jets of water shot across the room.* 管子爆裂，一股股水從屋子這頭噴到那頭。◇ *to clean the gas jets on the cooker* 把煤氣灶的氣嘴擦乾淨 **3** [U] a hard black mineral that can be polished and is used in jewellery 煤玉；黑玉；黑色大理石；貝褐碳

■ *verb* (**-tt-**) [I] **+ adv./prep.** (*informal*) to fly somewhere in a plane 乘坐飛機旅行

ˌjet ˈblack *adj.* deep shiny black in colour 烏黑發亮的

ˌjet ˈengine *noun* an engine that drives an aircraft forwards by pushing out a stream of gases behind it 噴氣式發動機 ➲ VISUAL VOCAB page V53

jet·foil /ˈdʒetfɔɪl/ *noun* a passenger boat which rises above the surface of the water when it is travelling fast and has JET ENGINES 水翼噴射船；飛翼船

ˈjet lag *noun* [U] the feeling of being tired and slightly confused after a long plane journey, especially when there is a big difference in the time at the place you leave and that at the place you arrive in 飛行時差綜合症；時差反應 ➲ COLLOCATIONS at TRAVEL ▸ **ˈjet-lagged** *adj.*

jet·liner /ˈdʒetlaɪnə(r)/ *noun* a large plane with a jet engine, that carries passengers（大型）噴氣式客機

ˌjet-proˈpelled *adj.* driven by JET ENGINES 噴氣發動機推進的

ˌjet proˈpulsion *noun* [U] the use of JET ENGINES for power 噴氣推進

jet·sam /ˈdʒetsəm/ *noun* things that are thrown away, especially from a ship at sea and that float towards land（尤指沖到岸邊的）船上投棄物 ➲ compare FLOTSAM (1)

the ˈjet set *noun* [sing.+sing./pl. v.] rich and fashionable people who travel a lot（常乘飛機旅行的）富豪一族

ˈjet-setter *noun* a rich, fashionable person who travels a lot 常乘飛機旅行的富豪 ▸ **ˈjet-setting** *adj.* [usually before noun]：*her jet-setting millionaire boyfriend* 她那位常乘飛機旅行的闊男朋友

ˈJet Ski™ *noun* a vehicle with an engine, like a motorcycle, for riding across water 噴氣式滑艇；吉斯基水上摩托艇 ▸ **ˈjet-skiing** *noun* [U] ➲ VISUAL VOCAB page V50

ˈjet stream *noun* **1** (usually **the jet stream**) [sing.] a strong wind that blows high above the earth and that has an effect on the weather（地球高空的）急流 **2** [C] the flow of gases from a plane's engine（飛機發動機的）噴氣流

jet·ti·son /ˈdʒetɪsn/ *verb* **1 ~ sth** to throw sth out of a moving plane or ship to make it lighter（為減輕重量而從行駛的飛機或船上）扔棄，丟棄，投棄：*to jettison fuel* 投棄燃料 **2 ~ sth/sb** to get rid of sth/sb that you no longer need or want 擺脱；除掉；處理掉 SYN **discard**：*He was jettisoned as team coach after the defeat.* 他因這次失敗被撤銷了運動隊教練職務。**3 ~ sth** to reject an idea, belief, plan, etc. that you no longer think is useful or likely to be successful 放棄，拒絕接受（想法、信念、計劃等）SYN **abandon**

jetty /ˈdʒeti/ *noun* (*pl.* **-ies**) (*NAmE* also **dock**) a wall or platform built out into the sea, a river, etc., where boats can be tied and where people can get on and off boats 突堤；棧橋；登岸碼頭 ➲ VISUAL VOCAB page V5

Jet·way™ /ˈdʒetweɪ/ *noun* a bridge that can be moved and put against the door of an aircraft, so people can get on and off 旅客登機（活動）橋；空橋

Jew /dʒuː/ *noun* a member of the people and cultural community whose traditional religion is Judaism and who come from the ancient Hebrew people of Israel; a person who believes in and practises Judaism 猶太人；猶太教徒

jewel /ˈdʒuːəl/ *noun* **1** a PRECIOUS STONE such as a diamond, RUBY, etc. 寶石 SYN **gem** **2** [usually pl.] pieces of jewellery or decorative objects that contain PRECIOUS STONES 珠寶首飾：*The family jewels are locked away in a safe.* 家裏的珠寶首飾都鎖在保險櫃裏。➲ see also CROWN JEWELS **3** a small PRECIOUS STONE or piece of special glass that is used in the machinery of a watch（手錶的）寶石軸承 **4** (*informal*) a person or thing that is very important or valuable 寶貝；難能可貴的人；珍貴的東西 ➲ compare GEM

IDM **the jewel in the ˈcrown** the most attractive or valuable part of sth 王冠上的寶石；最有吸引力（或珍貴、有價值）的東西

ˈjewel case *noun* a plastic box for holding a CD（塑料）光盤盒

jew·elled (*especially US* **jew·eled**) /ˈdʒuːəld/ *adj.* decorated with jewels 飾以寶石的；鑲有寶石的

jew·el·ler (*especially US* **jew·el·er**) /ˈdʒuːələ(r)/ *noun* **1** a person who makes, repairs or sells jewellery and watches 寶石鐘錶匠；寶石鐘錶商 **2 jeweller's** (*pl.* **jew·el·lers**) a shop/store that sells jewellery and watches 珠寶鐘錶店：*I bought it at the jeweller's near my office.* 我在辦公室附近的珠寶店買的。

jew·el·lery 0‑ (*especially US* **jew·el·ry**) /ˈdʒuːəlri/ *noun* [U]

objects such as rings and NECKLACES that people wear as decoration 珠寶；首飾：***silver/gold jewellery*** 銀 / 金首飾 ◇ *She has some lovely **pieces of jewellery**.* 她有幾件漂亮的首飾。➲ COLLOCATIONS at FASHION ➲ VISUAL VOCAB page V65 ➲ see also COSTUME JEWELLERY

Jew·ess /ˈdʒuːəs/ *noun* (often *offensive*) an old-fashioned word for a Jewish woman 猶太女人（舊時用語）

J

Jew·ish /ˈdʒuːɪʃ/ *adj.* connected with Jews or Judaism; believing in and practising Judaism 猶太人的；有關猶太人的；猶太教的；信猶太教的：*We're Jewish.* 我們是猶太人。◇ *the local Jewish community* 當地的猶太人群體 ▸ **Jew·ish·ness** *noun* [U]

Jewry /ˈdʒʊəri; *NAmE* ˈdʒʊri; ˈdʒuː-/ *noun* [U] (*formal*) Jewish people as a group （統稱）猶太人：*British Jewry* 英國猶太人

ˌJew's ˈharp *noun* a small musical instrument which is held between the teeth and played with a finger 口弦，口簧（演奏者含在齒間用指撥奏的小型樂器）

Jez·ebel /ˈdʒezəbel/ *noun* (*old-fashioned*) a woman who is thought to be sexually immoral 蕩婦 **ORIGIN** From the name of the wife of a king of Israel in the Bible, who wore make-up and was criticized by Elijah for worshipping the god Baal. 源自《聖經》中以色列王之妻的名字，她濃妝豔抹，因崇拜神祇巴力而受到以利亞的指責。

jib /dʒɪb/ *noun, verb*

■ ***noun*** **1** a small sail in front of the large sail on a boat 艏三角帆；主帆前的小帆 ➲ **VISUAL VOCAB** page V56 **2** the arm of a CRANE that lifts things （起重機的）懸臂，挺杆

■ ***verb*** (**-bb-**) [I] **～ (at sth/at doing sth)** (*old-fashioned, informal*) to be unwilling to do or accept sth 不願做；不肯接受：*She agreed to attend but jibbed at making a speech.* 她同意出席但不願發言。

jibe (also **gibe**) /dʒaɪb/ *noun, verb*

■ ***noun*** **1 ～ (at sb/sth)** an unkind or insulting remark about sb 嘲諷；嘲弄；譏諷：*He made several cheap jibes at his opponent during the interview.* 在採訪中他好幾次粗俗地嘲諷對手。**2** (*NAmE*) = GYBE

■ ***verb*** **1** [I, T] **～ (at sth)** | **～ that ...** | **+ speech** to say sth that is intended to embarrass sb or make them look silly 嘲諷；嘲弄；挖苦：*He jibed repeatedly at the errors they had made.* 他一而再、再而三地嘲弄他們所犯的錯誤。**2** [I] **～ (with sth)** (*NAmE, informal*) to be the same as sth or to match it （與…）一致，相符，相匹配：*Your statement doesn't jibe with the facts.* 你的說法與事實不符。**3** (*NAmE*) = GYBE

jiffy /ˈdʒɪfi/ *noun* [usually sing.] (*informal*) (*pl.* **-ies**) a moment 一會兒；瞬間：*I'll be with you **in a jiffy*** (= very soon). 我一會兒就來。

ˈJiffy bag™ *noun* **1** (*BrE*) a thick soft envelope for sending things that might break or tear easily 厚層信封（用於郵寄易碎或易受損物品）**2** (*SAfrE*) a clear plastic bag used for storing things in, especially food 透明塑料袋（貯存物品，尤用於盛裝食物）

jig /dʒɪg/ *noun, verb*

■ ***noun*** **1** a quick lively dance; the music for this dance 吉格舞；吉格舞曲：*an Irish jig* 愛爾蘭吉格舞曲 **2** a device that holds sth in position and guides the tools that are working on it 夾具

■ ***verb*** (**-gg-**) [I, T] **～ (sb/sth)** (**+ adv./prep.**) to move or to make sb/sth move up and down with short quick movements （使）上下急動，蹦跳：*He jigged up and down with excitement.* 他激動得又蹦又跳。

jig·ger /ˈdʒɪgə(r)/ *noun* = CHIGGER

jig·gered /ˈdʒɪgəd; *NAmE* -gərd/ *adj.* [not before noun]
IDM **I'll be jiggered!** (*old-fashioned, BrE, informal*) used to show surprise （表示驚訝）天哪

jiggery-pokery /ˌdʒɪgəri ˈpəʊkəri; *NAmE* ˈpoʊk-/ *noun* [U] (*informal, especially BrE*) dishonest behaviour 欺騙行為；騙局；搗鬼

jig·gle /ˈdʒɪgl/ *verb* [I, T] (*informal*) to move or make sth move up and down or from side to side with short quick movements （使）上下急動，左右搖擺，抖動：(**+ adv./prep.**) *Stop jiggling around!* 別晃來晃去的！◇ *She jiggled with the lock.* 她擺弄着鎖。◇ **～ sth (+ adv./prep.)** *He stood jiggling his car keys in his hand.* 他站在那兒手裏擺弄着汽車鑰匙。

jig·saw /ˈdʒɪgsɔː/ *noun* **1** (also **ˈjigsaw puzzle**) (also **puz·zle** especially in *NAmE*) a picture printed on cardboard or wood, that has been cut up into a lot of small pieces of different shapes that you have to fit together again 拼圖；拼板玩具：*to do a jigsaw* 拼圖畫 ➲ **VISUAL VOCAB** page V39 **2** a mysterious situation in which it is not easy to understand all the causes of what is happening; a complicated problem 神秘莫測的事物；謎團 **3** a SAW (= a type of tool) with a fine blade for cutting designs in thin pieces of wood or metal 線鋸；鏤花鋸；鋼絲鋸

jihad (also **jehad**) /dʒɪˈhɑːd/ *noun* **1** (in Islam 伊斯蘭教) a spiritual struggle within yourself to stop yourself breaking religious or moral laws （個人基於宗教或道德原因的）內心掙扎，心靈鬥爭 **2** a holy war fought by Muslims to defend Islam 聖戰；吉哈德

jiko /ˈdʒiːkɒ; *NAmE* -kɔː/ *noun* (*pl.* **-os**) (*EAfrE*) a container made of metal or CLAY and used for burning CHARCOAL or small pieces of wood. It is used for cooking or to give heat. 繢高爐（用金屬或黏土製作，燒煤炭或小木塊）

jil·bab /ˈdʒɪlbæb/ *noun* a full-length piece of clothing worn over other clothes by Muslim women 吉爾巴布（穆斯林女子穿的罩袍）

jill·aroo /ˌdʒɪləˈruː/ *noun* (*pl.* **-oos**) (*AustralE, informal*) a young woman who is working on a farm in Australia/New Zealand to get experience （澳大利亞或新西蘭的）農場見習青年女工 ➲ compare JACKAROO

jilt /dʒɪlt/ *verb* [often passive] **～ sb** to end a romantic relationship with sb in a sudden and unkind way 拋棄，遺棄（情人）：*He was jilted by his fiancée.* 他被未婚妻拋棄了。◇ *a jilted bride/lover* 被拋棄的新娘／情人

Jim Crow /ˌdʒɪm ˈkrəʊ; *NAmE* ˈkroʊ/ *noun* [U] the former practice in the US of using laws that allowed black people to be treated unfairly and kept separate from white people, for example in schools （美國社會過去對黑人的）種族歧視，種族隔離 **ORIGIN** From the title of a song that was sung by white entertainers who tried to look and sound like African Americans. 源自一首由白人藝人演唱的歌曲名稱，他們演唱時試圖在外表和聲音上模仿美國黑人。

jim-jams /ˈdʒɪm dʒæmz/ *noun* [pl.] (*BrE, informal*) = PYJAMAS

jimmy /ˈdʒɪmi/ (*NAmE*) (*BrE* **jemmy**) *noun* (*pl.* **-ies**) a short heavy metal bar used by thieves to force open doors and windows （竊賊撬門窗用的）短撬棍，鐵撬棍

jin·gle /ˈdʒɪŋgl/ *noun, verb*

■ ***noun*** **1** [sing.] a sound like small bells ringing that is made when metal objects are shaken together （金屬撞擊發出的）叮噹聲：*the jingle of coins in his pocket* 他兜裏硬幣的叮噹聲 **2** [C] a short song or tune that is easy to remember and is used in advertising on radio or television （收音機或電視廣告中易記的）短歌，短曲

■ ***verb*** [I, T] **～ (sth)** to make a pleasant gentle sound like small bells ringing; to make sth do this （使）發出叮噹聲：*The chimes jingled in the breeze.* 風鈴在微風中叮噹作響。◇ *She jingled the coins in her pocket.* 她把兜裏的硬幣弄得叮噹響。

jingo /ˈdʒɪŋgəʊ; *NAmE* -goʊ/ *noun*
IDM **by jingo** (*old-fashioned*) used to show surprise or determination （表示驚訝或決心）天哪，嘿，加油啊

jin·go·ism /ˈdʒɪŋgəʊɪzəm; *NAmE* -goʊ-/ *noun* [U] (*disapproving*) a strong belief that your own country is best, especially when this is expressed in support of war with another country 極端愛國主義；沙文主義 ▸ **jin·go·is·tic** /ˌdʒɪŋgəʊˈɪstɪk; *NAmE* -goʊ-/ *adj.*

jink /dʒɪŋk/ *verb* [I] (**+ adv./prep.**) (*BrE, informal*) to move quickly while changing direction suddenly and often, especially in order to avoid sb/sth 急轉；（尤指）躲閃，閃開

jinks /dʒɪŋks/ *noun* ➲ HIGH JINKS

jinx /dʒɪŋks/ *noun* [sing.] **～ (on sb/sth)** bad luck; sb/sth that is thought to bring bad luck in a mysterious way 厄運；霉運；不祥之人（或物）：*I'm convinced there's a jinx on this car.* 我深信這輛汽車沾上晦氣了。▸ **jinx** *verb* **～ sb/sth**

jinxed /dʒɪŋkst/ *adj.* (*informal*) having or bringing more bad luck than is normal 倒霉的；不走運的：*The whole family seemed to be jinxed.* 全家人似乎都走背字。

jism /ˈdʒɪzəm/ (also **jis·som** /ˈdʒɪsəm/) *noun* [U] (*slang*) a man's SEMEN 精液

JIT /ˌdʒeɪ aɪ ˈtiː/ *abbr.* JUST-IN-TIME

jit·ter·bug /ˈdʒɪtəbʌg; *NAmE* -tər-/ *noun* a fast dance that was popular in the 1940s 吉特巴舞（流行於 20 世紀 40 年代的快節奏舞）

jit·ters /ˈdʒɪtəz; *NAmE* -tərz/ (often **the jitters**) *noun* [pl.] (*informal*) feelings of being anxious and nervous, especially before an important event or before having to do sth difficult （事前的）緊張不安：*I always **get the jitters** before exams.* 我考試前總是很緊張。

jit·tery /ˈdʒɪtəri/ *adj.* (*informal*) anxious and nervous 緊張不安的；心神不寧的 ➲ SYNONYMS at NERVOUS

jiu-jitsu = JU-JITSU

jive /dʒaɪv/ *noun, verb*

■ *noun* **1** [U, sing.] a fast dance to music with a strong beat, especially popular in the 1950s 牛仔舞，捷舞（節奏快而強勁，20 世紀 50 年代尤為流行） **2** [U] (*NAmE, old-fashioned, informal*) nonsense 胡說；廢話；蠢話：*to talk jive* 胡說八道

■ *verb* **1** [I] to dance to JAZZ or ROCK AND ROLL music 跳牛仔舞 **2** [I, T] ~ (sb) (*NAmE, old-fashioned, informal*) to try to make sb believe sth that is not true 欺騙；欺瞞 SYN kid

Jnr *abbr.* = JR

Synonyms 同義詞辨析

job

position • post • vacancy • appointment

These are all words for a position doing work for which you receive regular payment. 以上各詞均表示工作、職位。

job a position doing work for which you receive regular payment 指工作、職業、職位：*He's trying to get a job in a bank.* 他正設法在銀行找一個工作。

position (*rather formal*) a job 指職位、職務：*a senior position in a large corporation* 在一家大公司的高級職務

JOB OR POSITION? 用 job 還是 position？

Position usually refers to a particular job within an organization, especially at a high level, and is not usually used about jobs generally. It is also often used in job applications, descriptions and advertisements.
* position 通常指機構中的職位，尤指高級職位，通常不用以指一般的工作。該詞亦常用於工作申請、職位描述和招聘廣告中。

post a job, especially an important one in a large organization 指職位，尤指大機構的要職：*a key post in the new government* 在新政府中的要職

vacancy a job that is available for sb to do 指空缺的職位、空職：*We have several vacancies for casual workers.* 我們有幾個臨時工的空缺。

appointment (*rather formal, especially BrE*) a job or position of responsibility 指承擔一定責任的職務、職位：*This is a permanent appointment, requiring commitment and hard work.* 這是一個固定職位，需要投入和勤奮工作。

PATTERNS

- a **permanent/temporary** job/position/post/vacancy/appointment
- a **full-time/part-time** job/position/post/vacancy/appointment
- to **have/have got** a(n) job/position/post/vacancy/appointment
- to **apply for/fill** a job/position/post/vacancy
- to **resign from/leave/quit** a job/position/post

Job /dʒəʊb; *NAmE* dʒoʊb/ *noun*

IDM **the patience of ˈJob** the fact of being extremely patient and not complaining 極其耐心；心平氣和：*You need the patience of Job to deal with some of our customers.* 和我們的一些顧客打交道需要有極大的耐心。

ORIGIN From **Job**, a man in the Bible who experienced much suffering, including losing his family, his home and his possessions, but continued to believe in and trust God. 源自《聖經》人物約伯（Job），雖歷經失去家人、家園和財產等磨難，依然堅持信奉上帝。

job 🔑 AW /dʒɒb; *NAmE* dʒɑːb/ *noun*

▸ PAID WORK 有酬工作 **1** 🔑 work for which you receive regular payment 工作；職業；職位：*He's trying to **get a job**.* 他正在找工作。◇ *She **took a job** as a waitress.* 她找了個工作，當餐廳服務員。◇ *His brother's just **lost his job**.* 他的弟弟剛丟了工作。◇ *a **summer/holiday/Saturday/vacation job*** 暑期／假日／週末／假期工作 ◇ *a **temporary/permanent job*** 臨時／固定工作 ◇ *I'm thinking of **applying for a** new **job**.* 我在考慮申請一份新工作。◇ *The takeover of the company is bound to mean more **job losses**.* 公司被接管必然意味着更多人要失業。◇ *Many women are in **part-time jobs**.* 許多婦女都是部份時間工作。◇ *Did they **offer you the job**?* 他們給你這個職位了嗎？◇ *He certainly **knows his job*** (= is very good at his job). 他對自己的工作很在行。◇ *I'm **only doing my job*** (= I'm doing what I am paid to do). 我不過在做我分內的事。◇ *He's been **out of a job*** (= unemployed) *for six months now.* 他已經失業六個月了。◇ *She's never had a **steady job*** (= a job that is not going to end suddenly). 她從未有過穩定的工作。➲ COLLOCATIONS at UNEMPLOYMENT

▸ TASK 任務 **2** 🔑 a particular task or piece of work that you have to do （一項）任務；（一件）工作，活兒，事情：*I've got various jobs around the house to do.* 我在家裏有各種各樣的活兒要幹。◇ *Sorting these papers out is going to be a long job.* 整理這些文件是很費工夫的事。◇ *The builder has a couple of jobs on at the moment.* 目前這家建築商有幾項工程在進行。➲ see also BLOW JOB, NOSE JOB ➲ SYNONYMS at TASK

▸ DUTY 職責 **3** 🔑 [usually sing.] (rather *informal*) a responsibility or duty 責任；職責：*It's not my job to lock up!* 上鎖不是我的事兒！

▸ CRIME 罪行 **4** (*informal*) a crime, especially stealing 犯罪行為（尤指偷竊）：*a bank job* 銀行搶劫案 ◇ *an **inside job*** (= done by sb in the organization where the crime happens) 內部人員作的案

▸ OBJECT 物體 **5** (*informal*) a particular kind of thing 東西；物件：*It's real wood—not one of those plastic jobs.* 這是實木的，不是那種塑料產品。

▸ COMPUTING 計算機技術 **6** an item of work which is done by a computer as a single unit （作為一個單元處理的）作業，工作

IDM **do the ˈjob** (*informal*) to be effective or successful in doing what you want 起作用；有效：*This extra strong glue should do the job.* 這種超黏度膠應該管用。 **do a good, bad, etc. ˈjob (on sth) | make a good, bad, etc. job of sth** to do sth well, badly, etc. 幹得好（或差等）；將…辦好（或壞等）：*They did a very professional job.* 他們幹得非常內行。◇ *You've certainly made an excellent job of the kitchen* (= for example, painting it). 你們把廚房弄得好極了。 **give sb/sth up as a bad ˈjob** (*informal*) to decide to stop trying to help sb or to do sth because there is no hope of success 對…不再抱有希望；因沒有希望而決定放棄 **good ˈjob!** (*especially NAmE, informal*) used to tell sb that they have done well at sth 幹得不錯；辦得好；好呀 **a good ˈjob** (*informal*) used to say that you are pleased about a situation or that sb is lucky that sth happened 令人滿意的狀況；幸運的事；好事：*It's a good job you were there to help.* 幸虧你來幫忙。 **have a (hard/difficult) job doing/to do sth** to have difficulty doing sth 幹某事很困難（或很吃力、很費力）：*You'll have a job convincing them that you're right.* 要讓他們信服你是對的還要費點勁。◇ *He had a hard job to make himself heard.* 他好不容易才使別人聽見他的聲音。 **a job of ˈwork** (*BrE, old-fashioned* or *formal*) work that you are paid to do or

J

that must be done 分內的事；必須幹的工作：*There was a job of work waiting for him that he was not looking forward to.* 有一件他不想幹但又必須完成的工作在等待着他。**jobs for the 'boys** (*BrE, informal, disapproving*) people use the expression **jobs for the boys** when they are criticizing the fact that sb in power has given work to friends or relatives 為親信安排的工作（或職位）；任人唯親 **just the 'job** (*BrE*) (also **just the 'ticket** *NAmE, BrE*) (*informal, approving*) exactly what is needed in a particular situation 正需要的東西；求之不得的東西 **more than your 'job's worth (to do sth)** (*BrE, informal*) not worth doing because it is against the rules or because it might cause you to lose your job 工作所不允許的事；違反原則的事；可能丟飯碗的事：*It's more than my job's worth to let you in without a ticket.* 沒有票就讓你進去，我可能會丟飯碗的。➲ see also JOBSWORTH **on the 'job 1** while doing a particular job 在上班時；在幹活時；在工作崗位上：*No sleeping on the job!* 上班時嚴禁睡覺！◇ *on-the-job training* 在職培訓 **2** (*BrE, slang*) having sex 在交媾；在性交；在幹那事 ➲ more at BEST *n.*, DEVIL, WALK *v.*

job·ber /'dʒɒbə(r); *NAmE* 'dʒɑːb-/ (also **stock·job·ber**) *noun* (*finance* 財) (in Britain in the past) a person who worked on the STOCK EXCHANGE, buying shares, etc. from BROKERS and selling them to other brokers（英國舊時的）股票經紀人，證券交易商 ➲ compare BROKER-DEALER

job·bie /'dʒɒbi; *NAmE* 'dʒɑːbi/ *noun* (*informal*) used to refer to an object of a particular kind （特定一類的）物品，產品：*Her bikini was one of those expensive designer jobbies.* 她的比基尼泳裝是那種價格昂貴的名牌產品。

job·bing /'dʒɒbɪŋ; *NAmE* 'dʒɑːb-/ *adj.* [only before noun] (*BrE*) doing pieces of work for different people rather than a regular job 打零工的；做散工的：*a jobbing actor/builder* 臨時演員；打零工的建築工人

job·centre /'dʒɒbsentə(r); *NAmE* 'dʒɑːb-/ *noun* (*BrE*) a government office where people can get advice in finding work and where jobs are advertised（政府的）就業服務中心，職業介紹所

'job creation *noun* [U] the process of providing opportunities for paid work, especially for people who are unemployed（尤指為失業者）提供就業機會

'job description *noun* a written description of the exact work and responsibilities of a job 工作職責說明；崗位責任說明

'job-hunt *verb* [I] (usually used in the progressive tenses 通常用於進行時) to try to find a job 找工作；求職：*At that time I had been job-hunting for six months.* 那時我找工作已經找了六個月了。

job·less /'dʒɒbləs; *NAmE* 'dʒɑːb-/ *adj.* **1** without a job 無工作的；失業的 SYN **unemployed**：*The closure left 500 people jobless.* 這次倒閉使 500 人失業。 **2 the jobless** *noun* [pl.] people who are unemployed 失業者 ▸ **job·less·ness** *noun* [U]

,job 'lot *noun* (*informal*) a collection of different things, especially of poor quality, that are sold together 搭配成批出售的雜貨（尤指質量低劣的物品）

,job satis'faction *noun* [U] the good feeling that you get when you have a job that you enjoy 工作滿意度

'job seeker *noun* often used in official language in Britain to describe a person without a job who is trying to find one 求職者（英國常見的官方用語）

,Jobseeker's Al'lowance *noun* [U] (in Britain) money paid by the state to unemployed people who are looking for work （英國）求職津貼 ➲ see also UNEMPLOYMENT BENEFIT

'job-sharing *noun* [U] an arrangement for two people to share the hours of work and the pay of one job 工作分擔制（兩人分擔一份全職工作，報酬分攤）▸ **'job-share** *noun*：*The company encourages job-shares and part-time*

Collocations 詞語搭配

Jobs 工作

Getting a job 找工作

- **look for** work 找工作
- **look for/apply for/go for** a job 找工作；申請一個職位；努力爭取工作
- **get/pick up/complete/fill out/**(*BrE*) **fill in** an application (form) 得到／拿到／完成／填寫申請（表）
- **send/email** your (*BrE*) CV/(*NAmE*) résumé/application/application form/covering letter 寄／通過電郵發送簡歷／申請／申請表／附函
- **be called for/have/attend** an interview 被要求參加／有／參加面試
- **offer sb** a job/work/employment/promotion 給某人提供一份工作；雇用某人；提拔某人
- **find/get/land** a job 找到工作
- **employ/**(*especially NAmE*) **hire/recruit/**(*especially BrE*) **take on** staff/workers/trainees 雇用員工／工人／實習生
- **recruit/appoint** a manager 招聘／任命經理

Doing a job 做工作

- **arrive at/get to/leave** work/the office/the factory 上／下班；到辦公室／工廠上班；從辦公室／工廠下班
- **start/finish** work/your shift 開始／結束工作／輪班工作時間
- **do/put in/work** overtime 加班
- **have/gain/get/lack/need** experience/qualifications 擁有／獲得／缺乏／需要經驗／資格
- **do/get/have/receive** training 做／得到／接受培訓
- **learn/pick up/improve/develop** (your) skills 學習／偶然學會／提高／發展技能
- **cope with/manage/share/spread** the workload 應付／勉力完成／分擔／分攤工作量
- **improve your/achieve a better** work-life balance 達到更好的工作與生活的平衡
- **have (no)** job satisfaction/job security 有／沒有工作滿足感／職業保障

Building a career 建立職業生涯

- **have** a job/work/a career/a vocation 有工作／事業／職業
- **find/follow/pursue/**(*especially NAmE*) **live (out)** your vocation 找到／從事／致力於／實踐適合自己的職業
- **enter/go into/join** a profession 加入一個行業
- **choose/embark on/start/begin/pursue** a career 選擇／從事／開始／致力於一種職業
- **change** jobs/profession/career 換工作／行業／職業
- **be/**(*both especially BrE*) **work/go** freelance 做自由職業
- **do/take on** temp work/freelance work 做／開始從事臨時工作／特約工作
- **do/be engaged in/be involved in** voluntary work 做／從事／參與義務性工作

Leaving your job 離職

- **leave/**(*especially NAmE*) **quit/resign from** your job 離職；辭職
- **give up** work/your job/your career 放棄工作／事業
- **hand in** your notice/resignation 遞交辭呈
- **plan to/be due to** retire in June/next year, etc. 計劃／預計六月／明年等退休
- **take** early retirement 提前退休

working. 這家公司鼓勵工作分擔和兼職工作。'**job-share** *verb* [I] ~ (**with sb**)

jobs·worth /ˈdʒɒbzwɜːθ; *NAmE* ˈdʒɑːbzwɜːrθ/ *noun* (*BrE*, *informal*, *disapproving*) a person who follows the rules of a job exactly, even when this causes problems for other people, or when the rules are not sensible 刻板的監工；機械式工作的人

Jock /dʒɒk; *NAmE* dʒɑːk/ *noun* (*informal*) a way of describing a person from Scotland, that can be offensive 蘇格蘭佬；蘇格蘭鬼子

jock /dʒɒk; *NAmE* dʒɑːk/ *noun* **1** (*NAmE*) a man or boy who plays a lot of sport 男運動員；愛好體育的男子（或男孩）**2** (*NAmE*) a person who likes a particular activity 熱衷於…的人；愛好者：*a computer jock* 電腦迷 **3** = DISC JOCKEY ➲ compare SHOCK JOCK

jockey /ˈdʒɒki; *NAmE* ˈdʒɑːki/ *noun*, *verb*

■ ***noun*** a person who rides horses in races, especially as a job（尤指職業的）賽馬騎師 ➲ **VISUAL VOCAB** page V46

■ ***verb*** [I] ~ (**with sb**) (**for sth**) | ~ (**with sb**) (**to do sth**) to try all possible ways of gaining an advantage over other people 耍各種手腕獲取；運用手段謀取：*The runners* ***jockeyed for position*** *at the start.* 賽跑選手一開始就力求搶佔有利位置。◇ *The bands are constantly jockeying with each other for the number one spot.* 這些樂隊經常相互耍手段以謀取榜首位置。

ˈ**jock itch** *noun* (*NAmE*, *informal*) an infectious skin disease that affects the GROIN 股癬

jock·strap /ˈdʒɒkstræp; *NAmE* ˈdʒɑːk-/ (also **athˌletic supˈporter** especially in *NAmE*) *noun* a piece of men's underwear worn to support or protect the sexual organs while playing sports（男運動員用的）下體護身

jo·cose /dʒəˈkəʊs; *NAmE* -ˈkoʊs/ *adj.* (*formal*) humorous 幽默的；滑稽的

jocu·lar /ˈdʒɒkjələ(r); *NAmE* ˈdʒɑːk-/ *adj.* (*formal*) **1** humorous 幽默的；滑稽的；詼諧的：*a jocular comment* 詼諧的評論 **2** (of a person 人) enjoying making people laugh 愛開玩笑的；逗樂的；打趣的 **SYN** **jolly** ➲ see also JOKE ▸ **jocu·lar·ity** /ˌdʒɒkjəˈlærəti; *NAmE* ˌdʒɑːk-/ *noun* [U] **jocu·lar·ly** *adv.*

joc·und /ˈdʒɒkənd; ˈdʒəʊk-; *NAmE* ˈdʒɑːk-; ˈdʒoʊk-/ *adj.* (*formal*) cheerful 高興的；歡樂的；愉快的

jodh·purs /ˈdʒɒdpəz; *NAmE* ˈdʒɑːdpərz/ *noun* [pl.] trousers/pants that are loose above the knee and tight from the knee to the ankle, worn when riding a horse 馬褲：*a pair of jodhpurs* 一條馬褲

Joe Bloggs /ˌdʒəʊ ˈblɒgz; *NAmE* ˌdʒoʊ ˈblɑːgz/ (*BrE*) (*NAmE* ˌ**Joe** ˈ**Blow**, ˌ**John** ˈ**Doe**) *noun* [sing.] (*informal*) a way of referring to a typical ordinary person 普通人；平常人

ˌ**Joe** ˈ**Public** (*BrE*) (*NAmE* ˌ**John** ˌ**Q.** ˈ**Public**) *noun* [U] (*informal*) people in general; the public 老百姓；平民百姓；公眾

Joe Six·pack /ˌdʒəʊ ˈsɪkspæk; *NAmE* ˌdʒoʊ/ *noun* (*US*, *informal*) a man who is considered typical of a person who does MANUAL work 壯漢：*Joe Sixpack doesn't care about that.* 那個壯實的傢伙不在意那事。

joey /ˈdʒəʊi; *NAmE* ˈdʒoʊi/ *noun* a young KANGAROO, WALLABY or POSSUM 幼袋鼠；幼沙袋鼠；幼負鼠 ➲ **VISUAL VOCAB** page V12

jog /dʒɒg; *NAmE* dʒɑːg/ *verb*, *noun*

■ ***verb*** (**-gg-**) **1** (also **go jogging**) [I] to run slowly and steadily for a long time, especially for exercise 慢跑，慢步長跑（尤指鍛煉）：*I go jogging every evening.* 我每天晚上都慢跑鍛煉。**2** [T] ~ **sth/sb** to hit sth lightly and by accident（偶然地）輕擊，輕撞，輕碰 **SYN** **nudge**：*Someone jogged her elbow, making her spill her coffee.* 有人不小心輕輕碰了一下她的胳膊肘兒，把咖啡弄灑了。

IDM **jog sb's** ˈ**memory** to say or do sth that makes sb remember sth 喚起某人的記憶；提醒某人

PHR V ˌ**jog aˈlong** (*BrE*, *informal*) to continue as usual with little or no excitement, change or progress（同往常一樣）緩慢而平穩地進行

■ ***noun*** [sing.] **1** a slow run, especially one done for physical exercise 慢跑（尤指鍛煉）：*I like to go for a jog after work.* 我喜歡在下班後慢跑鍛煉。**2** a light push or knock 輕推；輕碰；輕擊 **SYN** **nudge**

jog·ger /ˈdʒɒgə(r); *NAmE* ˈdʒɑːg-/ *noun* **1** [C] a person who jogs regularly for exercise 慢跑鍛煉者 **2** **joggers** [pl.] (*BrE*) soft loose trousers/pants, with ELASTIC at the waist, that you wear for doing exercise in（柔軟寬鬆、腰間有鬆緊帶的）運動褲，運動短褲

jog·ging /ˈdʒɒgɪŋ; *NAmE* ˈdʒɑːg-/ *noun* [U] the activity of running slowly and steadily as a form of exercise 慢跑鍛煉：*to go jogging* 慢跑鍛煉 ➲ **COLLOCATIONS** at DIET ➲ **VISUAL VOCAB** page V42

ˈ**jogging suit** *noun* = TRACKSUIT

jog·gle /ˈdʒɒgl; *NAmE* ˈdʒɑːgl/ *verb* [I, T] ~ (**sb/sth**) (*informal*) to move or to make sb/sth move quickly up and down or from one side to another（使）快速顛動，快速搖擺

jog·trot /ˈdʒɒgtrɒt; *NAmE* ˈdʒɑːgtrɑːt/ *noun* [sing.] a slow steady run 勻速慢跑

john /dʒɒn; *NAmE* dʒɑːn/ *noun* (*informal*, *especially NAmE*) a toilet 廁所；茅房

ˌ**John** ˈ**Bull** *noun* [U, C] (*old-fashioned*) a word that is used to refer to England or the English people, or to a typical Englishman 約翰牛（指英國或典型的英國人）

ˌ**John** ˈ**Doe** *noun* [usually sing.] (*NAmE*) **1** a name used for a person whose name is not known or is kept secret, especially in a court of law 無名氏，某甲（不知姓名或在法庭等上隱匿真名的當事人）**2** an average man 普通男人 ➲ compare JANE DOE

John Han·cock /ˌdʒɒn ˈhænkɒk; *NAmE* ˌdʒɑːn ˈhænkɑːk/ *noun* (*NAmE*, *informal*) a person's signature 親筆簽名

Johnny-come-lately /ˌdʒɒni kʌm ˈleɪtli; *NAmE* ˌdʒɑːni/ *noun* [sing.] (*disapproving* or *humorous*) a person who has only recently arrived in a place or started an activity, especially sb who is more confident than they should be（尤指自負的）新人，新手

Johnny Reb /ˌdʒɒni ˈreb; *NAmE* ˌdʒɑːni/ *noun* (*NAmE*, *informal*) a name for a soldier who fought for the Confederate States in the American Civil War（美國內戰時期的）南方聯盟士兵

John o'Groats /ˌdʒɒn əˈgrəʊts; *NAmE* ˌdʒɑːn əˈgroʊts/ *noun* a village in Scotland that is further north than any other place on the island of Great Britain 約翰奧格羅茨（位於大不列顛島最北端的蘇格蘭小村莊）➲ compare LAND'S END

ˌ**John** ˌ**Q.** ˈ**Public** (*NAmE*) (*BrE* ˌ**Joe** ˈ**Public**) *noun* [U] (*informal*) people in general; the public 老百姓；平民百姓；公眾

joie de vivre /ˌʒwʌ də ˈviːvrə/ *noun* [U] (from *French*) a feeling of great happiness and enjoyment of life 人生的極大樂趣；生活之樂

join 0➡ /dʒɔɪn/ *verb*, *noun*

■ ***verb***

▸ CONNECT 連接 **1** 0➡ [T, I] to fix or connect two or more things together 連接；接合；聯結：~ **A to B** *Join one section of pipe to the next.* 將一段管子與相鄰的管子連接起來。◇ *The island is joined to the mainland by a bridge.* 這個島有一座橋與大陸相連。◇ ~ (**A and B**) (**together/up**) *Join the two sections of pipe together.* 將這兩段管子連接在一起。◇ *Draw a line joining (up) all the crosses.* 畫條線將所有的十字連接起來。◇ *How do these two pieces join?* 這兩件東西怎樣接合呢？

▸ BECOME ONE 合二為一 **2** 0➡ [I, T] if two things or groups join, or if one thing or group **joins** another, they come together to form one thing or group 結合；聯合；匯合：*the place where the two paths join* 兩條小路匯合的地方 ◇ ~ **sth** *The path joins the road near the trees.* 這條小路在樹林旁與公路匯合。

▸ CLUB/COMPANY 俱樂部；公司 **3** 0➡ [T, I] ~ (**sth**) to become a member of an organization, a company, a club, etc. 成為…的一員；參加；加入：*I've joined an aerobics class.* 我參加了有氧健身班。◇ *She joined the company three months ago.* 她三個月前進了這家公司。◇ (*figurative*) *to join the ranks of the unemployed* 加入失業大軍 ◇ *It costs £20 to join.* 需交 20 英鎊才可參加。

▸ **DO STH WITH SB ELSE 參與 4** 🗝 [T] to take part in sth that sb else is doing or to go somewhere with them 參與；加入到…之中；與…一道去：**~ sb (for sth)** *Will you join us for lunch?* 和我們一起吃午飯好嗎？◇ *Do you mind if I join you?* 我和你們在一起，可以嗎？◇ **~ sth** *Over 200 members of staff joined the strike.* * 200 多名雇員參加了罷工。◇ *Members of the public joined the search for the missing boy.* 許多民眾加入了搜尋失蹤男孩的行動。◇ **~ sb in doing sth** *I'm sure you'll all join me in wishing Ted and Laura a very happy marriage.* 我相信大家會願意與我一起共祝特德和勞拉喜結良緣。

▸ **TRAIN/PLANE 火車；飛機 5** [T] **~ sth** (*BrE*) if you **join** a train, plane, etc. you get on it 上（火車、飛機等）

▸ **ROAD/PATH/LINE 道路；小徑；行列 6** [T] **~ sth** if you **join** a road or a line of people, you start to travel along it, or move into it 上（路）；加入（行列）

IDM **join ˈbattle (with sb)** (*formal*) to begin fighting sb 開始（與某人）交戰：(*figurative*) *Local residents have joined battle with the council over the lack of parking facilities.* 當地居民就缺少停車設施一事與政務委員會展開了鬥爭。 **join the ˈclub** (*informal*) used when sth bad that has happened to sb else has also happened to you 同樣倒霉；別人也一樣倒運；彼此彼此：*So you didn't get a job either? Join the club!* 那麼你也沒找到工作？咱們彼此彼此！ **join ˈhands (with sb) 1** if two people **join hands**, they hold each other's hands （與某人）拉起手，挽手 **2** to work together in doing sth 攜手合作；聯合；合夥：*Education has been reluctant to join hands with business.* 教育界一向不肯與商界聯手發展。➲ more at BEAT *v.*, FORCE *n.*

PHR V **ˌjoin ˈin (sth/doing sth)** | **ˌjoin ˈin (with sb/sth)** 🗝 to take part in an activity with other people 參加，加入（活動）：*She listens but she never joins in.* 她只是聽，但從來不發表意見。◇ *I wish he would join in with the other children.* 但願他能跟別的孩子一塊玩。 **ˌjoin ˈup** (*BrE*) to become a member of the armed forces 入伍；參軍 **SYN** **enlist** **ˌjoin ˈup (with sb)** to combine with sb else to do sth （與某人）聯合，會合：*We'll join up with the other groups later.* 我們以後再與其他小組會合。

■ **noun**

▸ **CONNECTION 連接** a place where two things are fixed together 連接處；接合點：*The two pieces were stuck together so well that you could hardly see the join.* 這兩塊粘合得太好了，幾乎看不出接縫。

ˈjoined-up *adj.* [usually before noun] (*BrE*) **1 joined-up** writing is writing in which the letters in a word are joined to each other（筆體）連寫的；草書的 ➲ compare PRINTING **2** intelligent and involving good communication between different parts so that they can work together effectively 明智而協調的：*We need more* ***joined-up thinking*** *in our approach to the environment.* 在處理環境問題上我們需要更協調的思考。

join·er /ˈdʒɔɪnə(r)/ *noun* **1** (*BrE*) a person whose job is to make the wooden parts of a building, especially window frames, doors, etc. 細木工人 ➲ compare CARPENTER **2** a person who joins an organization, club, etc.（組織、俱樂部等的）參加者，入會者，會員：*All joiners will receive a welcome pack.* 每位入會者都會收到一個迎新包。

join·ery /ˈdʒɔɪnəri/ *noun* [U] the work of a joiner or things made by a joiner 細木工人的工作；細木工的製品

joint 🗝 /dʒɔɪnt/ *adj., noun, verb*

■ **adj.** 🗝 [only before noun] involving two or more people together 聯合的；共同的：*a joint account* (= a bank account in the name of more than one person, for example a husband and wife) 聯合賬戶 ◇ *The report was a* ***joint effort*** (= we worked on it together). 這個報告是大家共同努力的成果。◇ *They finished in joint first place.* 他們獲得並列第一。◇ *They were joint owners of the house* (= they owned it together). 他們共同擁有這棟房子。▸ **joint·ly** 🗝 *adv.*：*The event was organized jointly by students and staff.* 這項活動是由師生共同組織的。

■ **noun 1** 🗝 a place where two bones are joined together in the body in a way that enables them to bend and move 關節：*inflammation of the knee joint* 膝關節發炎 ➲ see also BALL-AND-SOCKET JOINT **2** 🗝 a place where two or more parts of an object are joined together, especially to form a corner （尤指構成拐角的）接頭，接合處，接點 **3** (*BrE*) a piece of ROAST meat 一塊烤肉：*a joint of beef* 一塊烤牛肉 ◇ *the Sunday joint* (= one traditionally eaten on a Sunday) 禮拜天吃的大塊烤肉 **4** (*informal*) a place where people meet to eat, drink, dance, etc., especially one that is cheap 公共場所（尤指價格低廉的飲食和娛樂場所）：*a fast-food joint* 快餐店 **5** (*informal*) a cigarette containing MARIJUANA (= an illegal drug) 大麻煙捲

IDM **out of ˈjoint 1** (of a bone 骨頭) pushed out of its correct position 脫臼；脫位 **2** not working or behaving in the normal way 混亂；無秩序；不正常 ➲ more at CASE *v.*, NOSE *n.*

■ **verb ~ sth** to cut meat into large pieces, usually each containing a bone 把…切成帶骨的大塊肉

ˌJoint ˌChiefs of ˈStaff *noun* [pl.] (in the US) the leaders of the ARMED FORCES who advise the President on military matters（美國）參謀長聯席會議

ˌjoint deˈgree *noun* (in Britain and some other countries) a university course in which you study two subjects to the same standard （英國和其他國家的）雙學位

joint·ed /ˈdʒɔɪntɪd/ *adj.* [usually before noun] having parts that fit together and can move 有關節的；有接縫的；活動接頭的：*a doll with* ***jointed arms/legs*** 手臂／腿關節活動的洋娃娃

ˈjoint family *noun* (*IndE*) a family structure in which grandparents, uncles, aunts and cousins are considered as a single unit living in one house 同堂家庭，聯合家庭（包括祖父母和旁系親屬同居一戶的家庭）

ˌjoint resoˈlution *noun* (in the US) a decision that has been approved by the Senate and the House of Representatives （美國）國會兩院的共同決議

ˌjoint-ˈstock company *noun* (*business* 商) a company that is owned by all the people who have shares in it 合股公司

ˌjoint ˈventure *noun* (*business* 商) a business project or activity that is begun by two or more companies, etc., which remain separate organizations 合營企業；合資企業

joist /dʒɔɪst/ *noun* a long thick piece of wood or metal that is used to support a floor or ceiling in a building 擱柵；托梁

jo·joba /həˈhəʊbə; həʊˈhəʊbə; *NAmE* hoʊˈhoʊbə/ *noun* **1** [U] oil from the seeds of an American plant, often used in COSMETICS 霍霍巴油（用美洲植物霍霍巴樹的蒴果製成，常用於化妝品） **2** [U, C] the plant that produces these seeds 霍霍巴樹

joke 🗝 /dʒəʊk; *NAmE* dʒoʊk/ *noun, verb*

■ **noun 1** 🗝 something that you say or do to make people laugh, for example a funny story that you tell 笑話；玩笑：*I can't* ***tell jokes.*** 我不會講笑話。◇ *She's always* ***cracking jokes.*** 她總愛說笑話。◇ *They often* ***make jokes*** *at each other's expense.* 他們經常相互取笑。◇ *I didn't* ***get the joke*** (= understand it). 我不明白這有什麼好笑的。◇ *I wish he wouldn't tell* ***dirty jokes*** (= about sex). 但願他別開下流的玩笑。◇ *I only did it* ***as a joke*** (= it was not meant seriously). 我只是開個玩笑而已。➲ see also IN-JOKE, PRACTICAL JOKE **2** [sing.] (*informal*) a person, thing or situation that is ridiculous or annoying and cannot be taken seriously 荒唐可笑的人（或事物）；笑料；笑柄：*This latest pay offer is a joke.* 最近這次提出的報酬是個玩笑。➲ see also JOCULAR

IDM **be/get beyond a ˈjoke** to become annoying and no longer acceptable 超出開玩笑的限度（令人惱火或無法接受） **be no ˈjoke** to be difficult or unpleasant 不是輕而易舉的事；不是好玩的：*It's no joke trying to find a job these days.* 這些日子想找工作可不是件容易事。 **the joke's on ˈsb** (*informal*) used to say that sb who tried to make another person look ridiculous now looks ridiculous instead 開玩笑開到自己身上了；作弄別人反而捉弄到自己頭上 **make a ˈjoke of sth** to laugh about sth that is serious or should be taken seriously 拿某事開玩笑；以某事為笑柄 **take a ˈjoke** to be able to laugh at a joke against yourself 經得起玩笑話；開得起玩笑：*The trouble with her is she can't take a joke.* 她的問題在於開不起玩笑。

■ ***verb*** **~** (**with sb**) (**about sth**) **1** [I, T] to say sth to make people laugh; to tell a funny story 說笑話；開玩笑：*She was laughing and joking with the children.* 她同孩子們一起嘻嘻哈哈地說笑話。◇ **~ about sth** *They often joked about all the things that could go wrong.* 凡是可能出錯的事他們都常拿來開玩笑。◇ **+ speech** *'I cooked it myself, so be careful!' he joked.* "我親自下廚做的，所以要小心點喲！"他開玩笑說。 **2** [I, T] to say sth that is not true because you think it is funny 鬧着玩；說着玩：*I didn't mean that—I was **only joking**.* 我並沒有那個意思，我只是說着玩兒的。◇ **~ that ...** *She joked that she only loved him for his money.* 她開玩笑說她只愛他的錢。

IDM **,joking a'part/a'side** (*BrE*) used to show that you are now being serious after you have said sth funny 言歸正傳；說正經的 **you're 'joking | you must be 'joking** (*informal*) used to show that you are very surprised at what sb has just said（對某人所說的話表示吃驚）你一定是在開玩笑吧：*No way am I doing that. You must be joking!* 我決不可能做那樣的事。你一定是在開玩笑吧！◇ *She's going out with Dan? You're joking!* 她在同丹談戀愛？你是在開玩笑吧！

joker /'dʒəʊkə(r); *NAmE* 'dʒoʊk-/ *noun* **1** a person who likes making jokes or doing silly things to make people laugh 愛開玩笑的人；愛說笑話的人 **2** (*informal*) a person that you think is stupid because they annoy you 蠢貨；廢人 **3** an extra PLAYING CARD that is used in some card games, usually as a WILD CARD（某些紙牌遊戲中的）百搭，（大、小）王牌 ➲ **VISUAL VOCAB** page V37

IDM **the ,joker in the 'pack** a person or thing who could change the way that things will happen in a way that cannot be predicted 能以意想不到的方式改變形勢的人（或事）

jokey (also **joky**) /'dʒəʊki; *NAmE* 'dʒoʊki/ *adj.* (*informal*) amusing; making people laugh 逗樂的；可笑的；滑稽的

jok·ing·ly /'dʒəʊkɪŋli; *NAmE* 'dʒoʊk-/ *adv.* in a way that is intended to be amusing and not serious 開玩笑地；鬧着玩地；戲謔地

jol /dʒɔːl/ *noun, verb* (*SAfrE, informal*)

■ ***noun*** a time of having fun; a party 娛樂（或快活）時光；聚會：*Have a jol!* 盡情地玩吧！◇ *a New Year's Eve jol* 除夕晚會

■ ***verb*** (**-ll-**) [I] to have fun 開心地玩：*We jolled all night.* 我們盡情玩了一晚上。

jol·lof rice /'dʒɒləf raɪs; *NAmE* 'dʒɑːləf/ *noun* [U] a type of STEW eaten in W Africa made from rice, CHILLIES and meat or fish 西非辣味燜飯（用大米、辣椒和肉或魚烹煮而成）

jolly /'dʒɒli; *NAmE* 'dʒɑːli/ *adj., adv., verb, noun*

■ ***adj.*** (**jol·lier**, **jol·li·est**) **1** happy and cheerful 愉快的；快樂的；高興的：*a jolly crowd/face/mood* 樂呵呵的一群人；快樂的笑臉；愉快的心情 **2** (*old-fashioned*) enjoyable 令人愉快的；令人快樂的；愜意的：*a jolly evening/party/time* 令人愉快的夜晚／聚會／時光 ▸ **jol·lity** /'dʒɒləti; *NAmE* 'dʒɑːl-/ *noun* [U]：(*old-fashioned*) *scenes of high-spirits and jollity* 興高采烈的歡樂景象

■ ***adv.*** (*old-fashioned, BrE, informal*) very 非常；很：*That's a jolly good idea.* 那是個絕妙的主意。

IDM **jolly 'good!** (*old-fashioned, BrE, informal*) used to show that you approve of sth that sb has just said（贊同別人說的話）非常好，太好了 **'jolly well** (*old-fashioned, BrE*) used to emphasize a statement when you are annoyed about sth（生氣時用以加強語氣）當然，無疑，必然：*If you don't come now, you can jolly well walk home!* 你要是還不來，那就步行回家吧！

■ ***verb*** (**jol·lies**, **jolly·ing**, **jol·lied**, **jol·lied**) (*BrE*)

PHR V **,jolly sb a'long** to encourage sb in a cheerful way（用愉快的方式）鼓勵某人 **,jolly sb 'into sth/into 'doing sth** to persuade or encourage sb to do sth by making them feel happy about it 哄着某人做某事 **,jolly sb/sth 'up** to make sb/sth more cheerful 使更有生氣；使更快活

■ ***noun*** (*BrE*) a trip that you make for enjoyment 旅遊；遊玩

IDM **get your 'jollies** (*informal*) to get pleasure or have fun 玩個痛快；作樂；盡情享樂

the ,Jolly 'Roger *noun* [sing.] a black flag with a white SKULL AND CROSSBONES on it, used in the past by PIRATES（舊時的）海盜旗，骷髏旗（飾有白色骷髏和交叉股骨的黑旗）

jolt /dʒəʊlt; *NAmE* dʒoʊlt/ *verb, noun*

■ ***verb*** **1** [I, T] to move or to make sb/sth move suddenly and roughly（使）震動，搖動，顛簸 **SYN** **jerk**：(**+ adv./prep.**) *The truck jolted and rattled over the rough ground.* 卡車嘎吱嘎吱地在凹凸不平的地面上顛簸而行。◇ *The bus jolted to a halt.* 公共汽車猛地一顛停了下來。◇ (*figurative*) *Her heart jolted when she saw him.* 她看到他時心裏咯噔一下子。◇ **~ sb/sth (+ adv./prep.)** *He was jolted forwards as the bus moved off.* 公共汽車開動時他猛然向前晃了一下。 **2** [T] to give sb a sudden shock, especially so that they start to take action or deal with a situation 使受到震驚（而採取行動）；喚醒；使覺醒：**~ sb/sth** (**into sth**) *His remark jolted her into action.* 他的話使她猛然醒悟而行動起來。◇ **~ sb/sth** (**out of sth**) *a method of jolting the economy out of recession* 使經濟從衰退中復蘇的方法◇ **~ sb/sth + adj.** *I was suddenly jolted awake.* 我猛地一下被驚醒。

■ ***noun*** [usually sing.] **1** a sudden rough movement 顛簸；震動；搖晃 **SYN** **jerk**：*The plane landed with a jolt.* 飛機着陸時顛了一下。 **2** a sudden strong feeling, especially of shock or surprise 一陣強烈的感情（尤指震驚或驚訝）：*a jolt of dismay* 一陣驚詫

Joneses /'dʒəʊnzɪz; *NAmE* 'dʒoʊn-/ *noun* [pl.]

IDM **,keep up with the 'Joneses** (*informal*, often *disapproving*) to try to have all the possessions and social achievements that your friends and neighbours have（與朋友和鄰居在物質和社會成就方面）攀比，比富有，比排場，比闊氣

josh /dʒɒʃ; *NAmE* dʒɑːʃ/ *verb* [I, T] **~** (**sb**) | **+ speech** (*informal*) to gently make fun of sb or talk to them in a joking way 開玩笑；戲弄 **SYN** **tease**

joss stick /'dʒɒstɪk; *NAmE* 'dʒɑːs-/ *noun* a thin wooden stick covered with a substance that burns slowly and produces a sweet smell（燒的）香

jos·tle /'dʒɒsl; *NAmE* 'dʒɑːsl/ *verb* [T, I] **~** (**sb**) to push roughly against sb in a crowd（在人群中）擠，推，撞，搡：*The visiting president was jostled by angry demonstrators.* 到訪的總統受到憤怒的示威者的推搡。◇ *People were jostling, arguing and complaining.* 人們推推搡搡，爭吵着抱怨着。

PHR V **'jostle for sth** to compete strongly and with force with other people for sth 爭奪；爭搶：*People in the crowd were jostling for the best positions.* 這群人在競相搶佔最好的位置。

jot /dʒɒt; *NAmE* dʒɑːt/ *verb, noun*

■ ***verb*** (**-tt-**)

PHR V **,jot sth↔'down** to write sth quickly 草草記下；匆匆記下：*I'll just jot down the address for you.* 我這就把地址給你寫下來。

■ ***noun***

IDM **not a/one 'jot** used to mean 'not even a small amount' when you are emphasizing a negative statement 一點不；絲毫不：*There's not a jot of truth in what he says* (= none at all). 他沒有一句實話。

jot·ter /'dʒɒtə(r); *NAmE* 'dʒɑːt-/ *noun* (*BrE*) **1** a small book used for writing notes in 便箋簿；便條簿；記事簿 **2** (*ScotE*) an exercise book 練習簿；練習本

jot·tings /'dʒɒtɪŋz; *NAmE* 'dʒɑːt-/ *noun* [pl.] short notes that are written down quickly 便條；簡短的筆記

joule /dʒuːl/ *noun* (*abbr.* **J**) (*physics* 物) a unit of energy or work 焦耳（能量或功的單位）

jour·nal **AW** /'dʒɜːnl; *NAmE* 'dʒɜːrnl/ *noun* **1** a newspaper or magazine that deals with a particular subject or profession（某學科或行業的）報紙，刊物，雜誌：*a **scientific/trade journal*** 科學／行業雜誌◇ *the British Medical Journal*《英國醫學雜誌》 **2** used in the title of some newspapers（用於報紙名）…報：*the Wall Street Journal*《華爾街日報》 **3** a written record of the things you do, see, etc. every day 日誌；日記：*He kept a* *journal of his travels across Asia.* 他把自己的亞洲之行記錄下來了。➲ compare DIARY

jour·nal·ese /ˌdʒɜːnəˈliːz; *NAmE* ˌdʒɜːrn-/ *noun* [U] (usually *disapproving*) a style of language that is thought to be typical of that used in newspapers 新聞文體；新聞筆調

jour·nal·ism /ˈdʒɜːnəlɪzəm; *NAmE* ˈdʒɜːrn-/ *noun* [U] the work of collecting and writing news stories for newspapers, magazines, radio or television 新聞業；新聞工作

jour·nal·ist 🗝 /ˈdʒɜːnəlɪst; *NAmE* ˈdʒɜːrn-/ *noun* a person whose job is to collect and write news stories for newspapers, magazines, radio or television 新聞記者；新聞工作者 ➲ compare REPORTER

jour·nal·is·tic /ˌdʒɜːnəˈlɪstɪk; *NAmE* ˌdʒɜːrn-/ *adj.* [usually before noun] connected with the work of a journalist 新聞業的；新聞工作（者）的：*journalistic skills* 新聞工作技巧 ◇ *his journalistic background* 他的新聞工作背景

jour·ney 🗝 /ˈdʒɜːni; *NAmE* ˈdʒɜːrni/ *noun, verb*

■ ***noun*** 🗝 an act of travelling from one place to another, especially when they are far apart（尤指長途）旅行，行程：*They went on a long train journey across India.* 他們乘火車作了一次橫跨印度的長途旅行。◇ (*BrE*) *Did you have a good journey?* 你一路順利嗎？◇ *on the* ***outward/return*** *journey* 在外出／返回途中 ◇ (*BrE*) *We* ***broke our journey*** (= stopped for a short time) *in Madrid.* 我們途中在馬德里作了短暫的停留。◇ (*BrE*) *Don't use the car for short journeys.* 短途旅行就別開車。◇ (*BrE*) *It's a day's journey by car.* 開車的話要走一天。◇ (*BrE*) *I'm afraid you've had a wasted journey* (= you cannot do what you have come to do). 對不起，你白跑一趟了。◇ (*BrE, informal*) *Bye!* ***Safe journey!*** (= used when sb is beginning a journey) 再見！一路平安！◇ (*figurative*) *The book describes a spiritual journey from despair to happiness.* 這本書描述了從絕望到高興的心理變化過程。➲ SYNONYMS at TRIP

■ ***verb*** [I] (+ **adv./prep.**) (*formal* or *literary*) to travel, especially a long distance（尤指長途）旅行：*They journeyed for seven long months.* 他們旅行了七個月之久。

jour·ney·man /ˈdʒɜːnimən; *NAmE* ˈdʒɜːrn-/ *noun* (*pl.* **-men** /-mən/) **1** (in the past) a person who was trained to do a particular job and who then worked for sb else（舊時）學徒期滿的工匠，出師的學徒工 **2** a person who has training and experience in a job but who is only average at it 熟練工；熟手

journo /ˈdʒɜːnəʊ; *NAmE* ˈdʒɜːrnoʊ/ (*pl.* **-os**) *noun* (*BrE, slang*) a journalist 新聞記者；新聞工作者

joust /dʒaʊst/ *verb* **1** [I] to fight on horses using a long stick (= a LANCE) to try to knock the other person off their horse, especially as part of a formal contest in the past（尤指舊時作為正式比賽一部份的）馬上長矛打鬥，騎馬比武 **2** [I] (*formal*) to argue with sb, especially as part of a formal or public debate（尤指作為正式或公開辯論一部份的）辯論，討論，爭論 ▸ **joust** *noun*

Jove /dʒəʊv; *NAmE* dʒoʊv/ *noun*

IDM **by 'Jove** (*old-fashioned, informal, especially BrE*) used to express surprise or to emphasize a statement（表示驚奇或加強語氣）啊，哎呀

jo·vial /ˈdʒəʊviəl; *NAmE* ˈdʒoʊ-/ *adj.* very cheerful and friendly 快樂的；愉快的；友好的 ▸ **jovi·al·ity** /ˌdʒəʊviˈæləti; *NAmE* ˌdʒoʊ-/ *noun* [U] **jo·vial·ly** /-iəli/ *adv.*

jowl /dʒaʊl/ *noun* [usually pl.] the lower part of sb's cheek when it is fat and hangs down below their chin 雙下巴；下頜垂肉：*a man with heavy jowls* 下巴底下一堆肉的男人 IDM see CHEEK *n.*

joy 🗝 /dʒɔɪ/ *noun*

1 🗝 [U] a feeling of great happiness 高興；愉快；喜悅 SYN **delight**：*the sheer joy of being with her again* 與她重逢的無比喜悅之情 ◇ *to dance* ***for/with joy*** 高興得跳起舞來 ◇ *I didn't expect them to* ***jump for joy*** *at the news* (= to be very pleased). 沒想到他們聽到這消息高興得跳了起來。◇ *To his great joy, she accepted.* 使他感到非常高興的是她接受了。➲ SYNONYMS at PLEASURE **2** [C] a person or thing that causes you to feel very happy 令人高興的人（或事）；樂事；樂趣：*the joys of fatherhood* 做父親的樂趣 ◇ *The game was a joy to watch.* 這比賽看起來真開心。**3** [U] (*BrE, informal*) (in questions and negative sentences 用於疑問句和否定句) success or satisfaction 成功；滿意；滿足：*We complained about our rooms but got no joy from the manager.* 我們抱怨房間不好，經理卻不理會。◇ *'Any joy at the shops?' 'No, they didn't have what I wanted.'* "逛商店有收穫嗎？" "沒有，哪裏都沒有我想要的。"

IDM **full of the joys of 'spring** very cheerful 快活極了；非常愉快；活潑愉快 ➲ more at PRIDE *n.*

joy·ful /ˈdʒɔɪfl/ *adj.* very happy; causing people to be happy 高興的；快樂的；令人愉快的 ➲ SYNONYMS at HAPPY ▸ **joy·ful·ly** /-fəli/ *adv.* **joy·ful·ness** *noun* [U]

joy·less /ˈdʒɔɪləs/ *adj.* (*formal*) bringing no happiness; without joy 沒有歡樂的；不快活的：*a joyless childhood* 沒有歡樂的童年

joy·ous /ˈdʒɔɪəs/ *adj.* (*literary*) very happy; causing people to be happy 高興的；快樂的；令人愉快的 SYN **joyful**：*joyous laughter* 快樂的笑聲 ▸ **joy·ous·ly** *adv.*

joy·pad /ˈdʒɔɪpæd/ *noun* a device used with some computer games, with buttons that you use to move images on the screen（計算機）遊戲手柄，遊戲操縱器

joy·rid·ing /ˈdʒɔɪraɪdɪŋ/ *noun* [U] the crime of stealing a car and driving it for pleasure, usually in a fast and dangerous way 用偷來的車兜風（常指開快車或危險駕駛）；偷開車（罪）▸ **joy·ride** *noun* **joy·rider** *noun*

joy·stick /ˈdʒɔɪstɪk/ *noun* **1** a stick with a handle used with some computer games to move images on the screen（電腦遊戲的）遊戲桿，操縱桿，控制桿 **2** (*informal*) a stick with a handle in an aircraft that is used to control direction or height（飛機的）操縱桿

JP /ˌdʒeɪ ˈpiː/ *abbr.* JUSTICE OF THE PEACE：*Helen Alvey JP* 海倫•阿爾維治安法官

JPEG /ˈdʒeɪpeg/ *noun* (*computing* 計) **1** [U] the abbreviation for 'Joint Photographic Experts Group' (technology which reduces the size of files that contain images) * JPEG（靜止圖像壓縮）標準，聯合圖像專家組（全寫為 Joint Photographic Experts Group）：*JPEG files* * JPEG 文件 **2** [C] an image created using this technology * JPEG 圖像：*You can download the pictures as JPEGs.* 你可以用 JPEG 格式下載這些圖像。

Jr (also **Jnr**) (both *BrE*) (also **Jr.** *NAmE, BrE*) *abbr.* JUNIOR 年少者；年資較低者 ➲ compare SR

jua kali /ˌdʒʊə ˈkæli/ *noun* [U] (in Kenya) the informal jobs that people do to earn money, for example making useful things from old metal and wood（肯尼亞）家庭手工，小手工：*the* ***jua kali*** *sector* 小手工業

ju·bi·lant /ˈdʒuːbɪlənt/ *adj.* feeling or showing great happiness because of a success 喜氣洋洋的；歡欣鼓舞的；歡呼雀躍的 ▸ **ju·bi·lant·ly** *adv.*

jubi·la·tion /ˌdʒuːbɪˈleɪʃn/ *noun* [U] a feeling of great happiness because of a success 歡欣鼓舞；歡騰；歡慶

ju·bi·lee /ˈdʒuːbɪliː/ *noun* a special anniversary of an event, especially one that took place 25 or 50 years ago; the celebrations connected with it（尤指 25 週年或 50 週年的）週年紀念，週年大慶，週年慶祝 ➲ see also DIAMOND JUBILEE, GOLDEN JUBILEE, SILVER JUBILEE

Ju·da·ism /ˈdʒuːdeɪɪzəm; *NAmE* -dəɪzəm/ *noun* [U] the religion of the Jewish people, based mainly on the Bible (= the Christian Old Testament) and the Talmud 猶太教 ▸ **Ju·da·ic** /dʒuːˈdeɪɪk/ *adj.* [only before noun]：*Judaic tradition* 猶太教傳統

Judas /ˈdʒuːdəs/ *noun* a person who treats a friend badly by not being loyal 猶大；出賣朋友的人；叛徒 SYN **traitor**

jud·der /ˈdʒʌdə(r)/ *verb* [I] to shake violently（劇烈地）震動，震顫：*He slammed on the brakes and the car juddered to a halt.* 他猛踩剎車，汽車在劇烈震動中停下來。

judge 0━ /dʒʌdʒ/ *noun*, *verb*

■ *noun*

▸ IN COURT 法庭 **1** 0━ a person in a court who has the authority to decide how criminals should be punished or to make legal decisions 法官；審判員： *a High Court judge* 高等法院的法官 ◇ *a federal judge* 聯邦法院法官 ◇ *The case comes before Judge Cooper next week.* 本案下週交庫珀法官審理。◇ *The judge sentenced him to five years in prison.* 法官判他五年監禁。 ➲ compare JUSTICE OF THE PEACE, MAGISTRATE

▸ IN COMPETITION 競賽 **2** 0━ a person who decides who has won a competition 裁判員；評判員： *the panel of judges at the flower show* 花展評判小組 ◇ *The judges' decision is final.* 裁判的決定為最終決定。

▸ SB WHO GIVES OPINION 鑒定人 **3** 0━ [usually sing.] a person who has the necessary knowledge or skills to give their opinion about the value or quality of sb/sth 鑒定人；鑒賞家： *She's a **good judge** of character.* 她很善於鑒別人的性格。◇ *'I'm not sure that's a good way to do it.' '**Let me be the judge of that**.'* "我拿不準這樣做好不好。" "就讓我來判斷吧。"

■ *verb*

▸ FORM OPINION 判斷 **1** 0━ [I, T] to form an opinion about sb/sth, based on the information you have 判斷；斷定；認為： *As far as I can judge, all of them are to blame.* 依我看，他們都應承擔責任。◇ ***Judging by** her last letter, they are having a wonderful time.* 從她上封信看，他們過得非常愉快。◇ ***To judge from** what he said, he was very disappointed.* 從他的話判斷，他非常失望。◇ **~ sb/sth (on sth)** *Schools should not be judged only on exam results.* 學校的好壞不能僅憑考試結果來評判。◇ *Each painting must be judged on its own merits.* 任何一幅畫都必須根據其本身的價值來評判。◇ **~ sb/sth + noun** *The tour was judged a great success.* 這次巡迴演出被認為是大獲成功。◇ **~ sb/sth to be/do sth** *The concert was judged to have been a great success.* 這場音樂會被認為是大獲成功。◇ **~ sb/sth + adj.** *They judged it wise to say nothing.* 他們認為不說為妙。◇ **~ that ...** *He judged that the risk was too great.* 他認為風險太大。◇ **it is judged that ...** *It was judged that the risk was too great.* 據估計風險太大。◇ **~ how, what, etc. ...** *It was hard to judge how great the risk was.* 很難判斷風險有多大。

▸ ESTIMATE 估計 **2** 0━ [T] to guess the size, amount, etc. of sth 估計，猜測（大小、數量等）： **~ how, what, etc. ...** *It's difficult to judge how long the journey will take.* 很難估計這次旅行要花多長時間。◇ **~ sb/sth to be/do sth** *I judged him to be about 50.* 我估計他年紀在 50 左右。

▸ IN COMPETITION 競賽 **3** 0━ [T, I] **~ (sth)** to decide the result of a competition; to be the judge in a competition 裁判；評判；擔任裁判： *She was asked to judge the essay competition.* 她被邀請擔任作文比賽的評委。

▸ GIVE OPINION 評價 **4** 0━ [T, I] **~ (sb)** to give your opinion about sb, especially when you disapprove of them 評價；鑒定；（尤指）批評，指責： *What gives you the right to judge other people?* 你有什麼權利對別人評頭論足？

▸ IN COURT 法庭 **5** [T] to decide whether sb is guilty or innocent in a court 審判；審理；判決： **~ sth** *to judge a case* 審理案件 ◇ **~ sb + adj.** *to judge sb guilty/not guilty* 判某人有罪／無罪

IDM **don't judge a ˌbook by its ˈcover** (*saying*) used to say that you should not form an opinion about sb/sth from their appearance only 勿以貌取人；勿只憑外表判斷

judge·ment 0━ (also **judg·ment** especially in *NAmE*) /ˈdʒʌdʒmənt/ *noun*

1 0━ [U] the ability to make sensible decisions after carefully considering the best thing to do 判斷力；識別力： ***good/poor/sound judgement*** 判斷力強／弱；正確的判斷力 ◇ *She showed a lack of judgement when she gave Mark the job.* 她把這工作交給馬克表明她缺乏判斷力。◇ *It's not something I can give you rules for; you'll have to use your judgement.* 不是我把規則告訴你就行了，你得運用自己的判斷力。◇ *He achieved his aim **more by luck than judgement**.* 他達到目的主要是靠運氣而不是靠判斷力。◇ *The accident was caused by an **error of judgement** on the part of the pilot.* 此次事故是飛行員判斷失誤所致。 **2** 0━ [C, U] **~ (of/about/on sth)** an opinion that you form about sth after thinking about it carefully; the act of making this opinion known to others 看法；意見；評價： *He refused to **make a judgement** about the situation.* 他拒絕對形勢作出評價。◇ *Who am I to **pass judgement** on her behaviour?* (= to criticize it) 我有什麼資格對她的行為說三道四呢？◇ *I'd like to **reserve judgement** until I see the report.* 我還是想看到報告後再發表意見。◇ *It was, **in her judgement**, the wrong thing to do.* 在她看來，那樣做是錯誤的。◇ *I did it **against my better judgement*** (= although I thought it was perhaps the wrong thing to do). 我這樣做是違心的。 **3** (usually **judgment**) [C, U] the decision of a court or a judge 判決；裁決： *a judgment from the European Court of Justice* 歐洲法院的判決 ◇ *The judgment will be given tomorrow.* 此案將於明日宣判。◇ *The court has yet to **pass judgment*** (= say what its decision is) *in this case.* 此案還有待法庭判決。 **4** [C, usually sing.] **~ (on sth)** (*formal*) something bad that happens to sb that is thought to be a punishment from God 報應；天譴；（上帝對人的）審判 IDM see SIT

judge·men·tal (*BrE*) (also **judg·men·tal** *NAmE, BrE*) /dʒʌdʒˈmentl/ *adj.* **1** (*disapproving*) judging people and criticizing them too quickly 輕率評價的；動輒評頭論足的；動輒指責人的 **2** (*formal*) connected with the process of judging things 判斷的；裁決的；判決的： *the judgemental process* 判斷過程

ˈ**judgement call** *noun* (*informal*) a decision you have to make where there is no clear rule about what the right thing to do is, so that you have to use your own judgement 需憑判斷力作出的決定

ˈ**Judgement Day** (also **the ˌDay of ˈJudgement, the ˌLast ˈJudgement**) *noun* the day at the end of the world when, according to some religions, God will judge everyone who has ever lived（某些宗教指上帝對人類的）最後審判日，世界末日

ju·di·ca·ture /ˈdʒuːdɪkətʃə(r)/ *noun* (*law* 律) **1** [U] the system by which courts, trials, etc. are organized in a country 司法系統；審判制度 **2 the judicature** [sing.+sing./pl. v.] judges when they are considered as a group（統稱）審判人員

ju·di·cial /dʒuˈdɪʃl/ *adj.* [usually before noun] connected with a court, a judge or legal judgement 法庭的；法官的；審判的；司法的： *judicial powers* 司法權 ◇ *the judicial process/system* 司法程序／系統 ▸ **ju·di·cial·ly** /-ʃəli/ *adv.*

juˌdicial ˈactivism *noun* [U] (*law* 律) (in the US) the idea that it is not necessary to follow the exact words of the Constitution when new laws are made（美國）司法能動主義，司法積極主義（制訂新法律時不必嚴格遵循憲法）

juˌdicial reˈstraint *noun* [U] (*law* 律) (in the US) the idea that judges of the Supreme Court or other courts should not try to change a law that is allowed by the Constitution（美國）司法節制（最高法院或其他法院不應試圖更改符合憲法的法律）

juˌdicial reˈview *noun* (*law* 律) **1** [U] (in the US) the power of the Supreme Court to decide if sth is allowed by the Constitution（美國）司法審查（最高法院審查某事是否符合憲法的權力） **2** [C, U] (in Britain) a procedure in which a court examines an action or decision of a public body and decides whether it was right（英國）司法審查（法院審查公共機構的行動或決定是否正確的程序）： *There is to be a judicial review of the visa changes.* 對簽證程序變更將進行司法審查。

ju·di·ciary /dʒuˈdɪʃəri; *NAmE* -ʃieri/ *noun* (usually **the judiciary**) [C+sing./pl. v.] (*pl.* **-ies**) the judges of a country or a state, when they are considered as a group（統稱）審判人員；司法部；司法系統： *an independent judiciary* 獨立的司法系統 ➲ compare EXECUTIVE *n.* (3), LEGISLATURE

ju·di·cious /dʒuˈdɪʃəs/ *adj.* (*formal, approving*) careful and sensible; showing good judgement 審慎而明智的；明斷的；有見地的 OPP **injudicious** ▸ **ju·di·cious·ly** *adv.*： *a judiciously worded letter* 一封措辭審慎的信

judo /ˈdʒuːdəʊ; *NAmE* -doʊ/ *noun* [U] (from *Japanese*) a sport in which two people fight and try to throw each other to the ground 柔道：*He **does judo**.* 他是練柔道的。◇ *She's a **black belt in judo**.* 她是柔道黑帶高手。

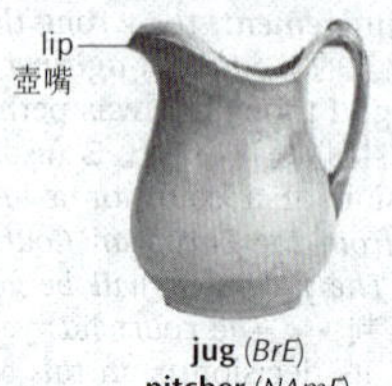

jug (*BrE*)
pitcher (*NAmE*)
帶柄大口壺

pitcher (*BrE*)
jug (*NAmE*)
帶柄大陶罐

jug /dʒʌg/ *noun* **1** (*BrE*) (*NAmE* **pitch·er**) a container with a handle and a LIP, for holding and pouring liquids（有柄有嘴的）壺，罐：*a milk/water jug* 奶杯；水罐 **2** (*NAmE*) a large round container with a small opening and a handle, for holding liquids（細口帶柄的）大罐：*a five-gallon jug of beer* 五加侖裝的啤酒罐 **3** the amount of liquid contained in a jug 一壺，一罐（的量）：*She spilled a jug of water.* 她把一罐子水弄灑了。**4 jugs** [pl.] (*taboo, slang*) an offensive word for a woman's breasts（女人的）奶子

jug·ful /ˈdʒʌgfʊl/ *noun* the amount of liquid contained in a jug 一罐的量；一壺的量

jugged hare /ˌdʒʌgd ˈheə(r); *NAmE* ˈher/ *noun* [U] a hot dish made from HARE that has been cooked slowly in liquid in a container with a lid 罐燉野兔肉；燜燉野兔肉

jug·ger·naut /ˈdʒʌgənɔːt; *NAmE* -gərn-/ *noun* **1** (*BrE*, often *disapproving*) a very large lorry/truck 重型卡車：*juggernauts roaring through country villages* 隆隆駛過村莊的重型卡車 **2** (*formal*) a large and powerful force or institution that cannot be controlled 不可抗拒的強大力量；無法控制的強大機構：*a bureaucratic juggernaut* 龐大的官僚機構

jug·gle /ˈdʒʌgl/ *verb* **1** [I, T] to throw a set of three or more objects such as balls into the air and catch and throw them again quickly, one at a time 玩雜耍（連續向空中拋接多個物體）：*My uncle taught me to juggle.* 我叔叔教我玩雜耍。◇ **~ with sth** *to juggle with balls* 拋接球 ◇ **~ sth** (*figurative*) *I was juggling books, shopping bags and the baby* (= I was trying to hold them all without dropping them). 我手裏又是書，又是購物袋，還抱着孩子，跟演雜技一樣。**2** [T, I] **~ (sth) (with sth)** to try to deal with two or more important jobs or activities at the same time so that you can fit all of them into your life 盡力同時應付（兩個或更多的重要工作或活動）：*Working mothers are used to juggling their jobs, their children's needs and their housework.* 為人母的職業女性已經習慣了既要工作，又要照顧孩子，還得做家務。**3** [T] **~ sth** to organize information, figures, the money you spend, etc. in the most useful or effective way 有效地組織，有效利用（信息、數字、開支等）

jug·gler /ˈdʒʌglə(r)/ *noun* a person who juggles, especially an entertainer 玩雜耍的人；要把戲的人；變戲法的人

jugu·lar /ˈdʒʌgjələ(r)/ (also **ˌjugular ˈvein**) *noun* any of the three large VEINS in the neck that carry blood from the head towards the heart 頸靜脈

IDM **go for the ˈjugular** (*informal*) to attack sb's weakest point during a discussion, in an aggressive way（討論中咄咄逼人地）抨擊對方的致命弱點，攻其要害

juice 🔑 /dʒuːs/ *noun, verb*

■ *noun* **1** 🔑 [U, C] the liquid that comes out of fruit or vegetables; a drink made from this 果汁；菜汁；果汁（或菜汁）飲料：*Add the juice of two lemons.* 加兩個檸檬的汁。◇ *a carton of apple juice* 一紙盒蘋果汁 ◇ *Two orange juices, please.* 請來兩份橙汁。**2** [C, usually pl., U] the liquid that comes out of a piece of meat when it is cooked 肉汁 **3** [C, usually pl.] the liquid in the stomach that helps you to DIGEST food 胃液；消化液：***digestive/gastric juices*** 消化／胃液 **4** [U] (*informal, especially BrE*) petrol/gas 汽油 **5** [U] (*NAmE, informal*) electricity 電

IDM see STEW *v.*

■ *verb* **~ sth** to get the juice out of fruit or vegetables 榨出（水果或蔬菜的）汁液；榨汁：*Juice two oranges.* 將兩個橙子榨汁。

PHR V **ˌjuice sth↔ˈup** (*informal, especially NAmE*) to make sth more exciting or interesting 使更活躍；給…增趣生色

ˈjuice bar *noun* a cafe serving drinks made from freshly squeezed fruit（鮮榨）果汁吧；水吧

juicer /ˈdʒuːsə(r)/ *noun* **1** a piece of electrical equipment for getting the juice out of fruit or vegetables 榨汁機 **2** (*NAmE*) (*BrE* **ˈlemon-squeezer**) a kitchen UTENSIL (= a tool) for squeezing juice out of a fruit 榨汁器 ➲ VISUAL VOCAB page V26

juicy /ˈdʒuːsi/ *adj.* (**juici·er**, **juici·est**) **1** (*approving*) containing a lot of juice and good to eat 多汁的；汁液豐富的：*soft juicy pears* 脆生多汁的梨 ◇ *The meat was tender and juicy.* 這肉又嫩汁又多。**2** (*informal*) interesting because you find it shocking or exciting 生動有趣的；妙趣橫生的；刺激的：*juicy gossip* 使人感興趣的流言 **3** (*informal*) attractive because it will bring you a lot of money or satisfaction 有吸引力的；報酬豐厚的；令人滿足的：*a juicy prize* 豐厚的獎品

ju-jitsu (also **jiu-jitsu**) /dʒuː ˈdʒɪtsuː/ *noun* [U] a Japanese system of fighting from which the sport of JUDO was developed 柔術（日本柔道由此發展而來）

juju /ˈdʒuːdʒuː/ *noun* **1** [C] an object used in W African magic（西非土著魔法中使用的）護符，物神 **2** [U] a type of magic in W Africa（西非土著的）魔法，法術 **3** [U] a type of Nigerian music that uses GUITARS and drums 祖祖音樂（尼日利亞音樂，用吉他和鼓演奏）

juke·box /ˈdʒuːkbɒks; *NAmE* -bɑːks/ *noun* a machine in a pub, bar, etc. that plays music when you put coins into it（酒吧等的投幣式）自動點唱機

julep /ˈdʒuːlep/ *noun* [U, C] **1** a sweet drink which may contain alcohol or medicine 甜藥酒；草藥飲料 **2** = MINT JULEP

Ju·lian cal·en·dar /ˌdʒuːliən ˈkælɪndə(r)/ *noun* [sing.] the system of arranging days and months in the year introduced by Julius Caesar, and used in Western countries until the GREGORIAN CALENDAR replaced it 儒略曆（凱撒大帝制訂的日曆，在西方國家一直使用至以陽曆取代為止）

July 🔑 /dʒuˈlaɪ/ *noun* [U, C] (*abbr.* **Jul.**) the 7th month of the year, between June and August 七月 **HELP** To see how **July** is used, look at the examples at **April**. * July 的用法見詞條 April 下的示例。

jum·ble /ˈdʒʌmbl/ *verb, noun*

■ *verb* [usually passive] **~ sth (together/up)** to mix things together in a confused or untidy way 使亂堆；使混亂；使雜亂：*Books, shoes and clothes were **jumbled together** on the floor.* 書、鞋子和衣服胡亂堆放在地上。▶ **jum·bled** *adj.*：*a jumbled collection of objects* 亂七八糟的一堆東西 ◇ *jumbled thoughts* 紛亂的思緒

■ *noun* **1** [sing.] **~ (of sth)** an untidy or confused mixture of things 雜亂的一堆；混亂的一團：*a jumble of books and paper* 一堆雜亂的書和紙 ◇ *The essay was a meaningless jumble of ideas.* 這篇文章思路混亂，使人不知所云。**2** [U] (*BrE*) a collection of old or used clothes, etc. that are no longer wanted and are going to be taken to a jumble sale 待義賣的一堆舊雜物

ˈjumble sale (*BrE*) (also **ˈrummage sale** *NAmE, BrE*) *noun* a sale of old or used clothes, etc. to make money for a church, school or other organization 舊雜物義賣（為教堂、學校或其他機構籌款）

jumbo /ˈdʒʌmbəʊ; *NAmE* -boʊ/ *noun, adj.*

■ *noun* (*pl.* **-os**) (also **ˌjumbo ˈjet**) a large plane that can carry several hundred passengers, especially a Boeing 747 大型客機（尤指波音 747）

■ *adj.* [only before noun] (*informal*) very large; larger than usual 巨型的；巨大的；特大的：*a jumbo pack of cornflakes* 一盒特大包裝的玉米片

jump 🔑 /dʒʌmp/ *verb, noun*

■ *verb*

▸ MOVE OFF/TO GROUND 跳 **1** 🔑 [I] to move quickly off the ground or away from a surface by pushing yourself with your legs and feet 跳；躍；跳躍：*'Quick, jump!' he shouted.* "趕快，跳！" 他大聲叫道。◇ **+ adv./prep.** *to jump into the air/over a wall/into the water* 跳到空中；躍過牆；跳進水裏 ◇ *The children were jumping up and down with excitement.* 孩子們興奮得跳來跳去。◇ *She jumped down from the chair.* 她從椅子上跳了下來。◇ *The pilot jumped from the burning plane* (= with a PARACHUTE). 飛行員從着火的飛機跳傘了。◇ **+ noun** *She has jumped 2.2 metres.* 她跳了 2.2 米。

▸ PASS OVER STH 跨躍 **2** 🔑 [T] to pass over sth by jumping 跳過；躍過；跨越：**~ sth** *Can you jump that gate?* 你能跳過那籬笆門嗎？◇ *His horse fell as it jumped the last hurdle.* 他的馬在跨躍最後一個欄時跌倒了。◇ **~ sth + adv./prep.** *I jumped my horse over all the fences.* 我縱馬躍過了所有的柵欄。**SYN** leap

▸ MOVE QUICKLY 快速移動 **3** 🔑 [I] **+ adv./prep.** to move quickly and suddenly 突然快速移動：*He* ***jumped to his feet*** *when they called his name.* 他們叫到他的名字時他一下子就站了起來。◇ *She jumped up and ran out of the room.* 她驀地跳起來跑出房間。◇ *Do you want a ride? Jump in.* 你想搭車嗎？快上來吧。**4** 🔑 [I] to make a sudden movement because of surprise, fear or excitement （因吃驚、害怕或激動而）猛地一動，突然一跳：*A loud bang made me jump.* 砰的一聲巨響嚇我一跳。◇ *Her heart jumped when she heard the news.* 聽到那消息她的心猛地一跳。

▸ INCREASE 增加 **5** 🔑 [I] to rise suddenly by a large amount 突升；猛漲；激增 **SYN** leap：**~ by ...** *Prices jumped by 60% last year.* 去年，物價暴漲 60%。◇ **~ (from ...) (to ...)** *Sales jumped from $2.7 billion to $3.5 billion.* 銷售額從 27 億元猛增到 35 億元。

▸ CHANGE SUDDENLY 突然改變 **6** 🔑 [I] **~ (about) (from sth to sth)** to change suddenly from one subject to another 突然改變，突然轉換（話題、題目）：*I couldn't follow the talk because he kept jumping about from one topic to another.* 我聽不明白他的講話，因為他老是轉換話題。◇ *The story then jumps from her childhood in New York to her first visit to London.* 故事接着從她在紐約的童年一下子轉到她第一次去倫敦。

▸ LEAVE OUT 略去 **7** [T] **~ sth** to leave out sth and pass to a further point or stage 略去；略過；跳過：*You seem to have jumped several steps in the argument.* 你在論證中似乎略去了好幾個步驟。

▸ OF MACHINE/DEVICE 機器；器具 **8** [I] (**+ adv./prep.**) to move suddenly and unexpectedly, especially out of the correct position 突然跳出正常位置；意外地離開正常位置：*The needle jumped across the dial.* 指針突然從刻度盤的一端跳到另一端。◇ *The film jumped during projection.* 電影放映時跳了片。

▸ ATTACK 襲擊 **9** [T, I] **~ (on) sb** (*informal*) to attack sb suddenly 突然襲擊（某人）；猛地撲向（某人）：*The thieves jumped him in a dark alleyway.* 一夥盜賊在一條漆黑的小巷裏突然撲向他。

▸ VEHICLE 車輛 **10** [T] **~ sth** (*NAmE*) to get on a vehicle very quickly 跳上（車輛等）：*to jump a bus* 跳上公共汽車 **11** (*NAmE*) = JUMP-START

▸ BE LIVELY 活潑 **12 be jumping** [I] (*informal*) to be very lively 歡躍；雀躍：*The bar's jumping tonight.* 今晚酒吧裏氣氛活躍。

IDM **be 'jumping up and down** (*informal*) to be very angry or excited about sth 暴跳如雷；歡欣雀躍 **jump down sb's 'throat** (*informal*) to react very angrily to sb 憤怒地反駁；猛烈回擊某人 **jump the 'gun** to do sth too soon, before the right time 搶跑；過早行動 **jump the 'lights** (*BrE*) (also **run a (red) 'light, run the 'lights** *NAmE, BrE*) (*informal*) to fail to stop at a red traffic light 闖紅燈 **jump out of your 'skin** (*informal*) to move violently because of a sudden shock 大吃一驚；嚇一大跳 **jump the 'queue** (*BrE*) (*US* **jump the 'line**) to go to the front of a line of people without waiting for your turn 插隊；加塞兒；不按次序排隊 **jump the 'rails** (of a train 火車) to leave the rails suddenly 出軌 **jump 'ship** **1** to leave the ship on which you are serving, without permission 擅自棄職離船 **2** to leave an organization that you belong to, suddenly and unexpectedly 擅自離隊；擅離職守 **jump through 'hoops** to do sth difficult or complicated in order to achieve sth（為達到目的而）經受磨難 **jump 'to it** (*NAmE* also **hop 'to it**) (*informal*) used to tell sb to hurry and do something quickly 趕快；加油；快點幹 ➲ more at BANDWAGON, CONCLUSION, DEEP *adj.*

PHR V **'jump at sb** (*NAmE*) = JUMP ON SB **'jump at sth** to accept an opportunity, offer, etc. with enthusiasm 迫不及待地接受，欣然接受（機會、建議等）**SYN** leap at **,jump 'in** **1** to interrupt a conversation 打斷談話：*Before she could reply Peter jumped in with an objection.* 她還沒來得及回答，彼得就迫不及待地表示反對。**2** to start to do sth very quickly without spending a long time thinking first 匆忙行動；急於從事 **'jump on sb** (*NAmE* also **'jump at sb**) (*informal*) to criticize sb 批評，責備（某人）**,jump 'out at sb** to be very obvious and easily noticed 極易引起某人的注意 **SYN** leap out at：*The mistake in the figures jumped out at me.* 我一眼就看出數字上有錯誤。

■ *noun*

▸ MOVEMENT 運動 **1** 🔑 an act of jumping 跳；躍；跳躍：*a jump of over six metres* 六米多的一跳 ◇ *The story takes a jump back in time.* 這故事一轉又回到以前發生的事情。◇ *Somehow he survived the jump from the third floor of the building.* 不知怎麼的，他從四樓跳下來竟然沒摔死。◇ *to do a parachute jump* 跳傘 ◇ *a ski jump champion* 跳台滑雪冠軍 ◇ *I sat up* ***with a jump*** (= quickly and suddenly). 我霍地坐起身來。◇ *The negotiations took a jump forward yesterday* (= they made progress). 談判昨天取得進展。➲ see also HIGH JUMP, LONG JUMP, SKI JUMP, TRIPLE JUMP

▸ BARRIER 障礙物 **2** 🔑 a barrier like a narrow fence that a horse or a runner has to jump over in a race or competition（比賽中需跳過的）障礙物：*The horse fell at the last jump.* 那匹馬在跨越最後一個障礙物時跌倒了。➲ VISUAL VOCAB page V46

▸ INCREASE 增加 **3** 🔑 **~ (in sth)** a sudden increase in amount, price or value 突升；猛漲；激增：*a 20 per cent jump in pre-tax profits* 稅前利潤 20% 的大幅增長 ◇ *unusually large price jumps* 非同尋常的大幅度漲價

IDM **to keep, etc. one jump ahead (of sb)** to keep your advantage over sb, especially your COMPETITORS, by taking action before they do or by making sure you know more than they do（尤指競爭中）保持優於（某人）的地位，（比某人）優先一步，（比某人）略勝一籌 ➲ more at HIGH JUMP, RUNNING *adj.*

'jump ball *noun* (in BASKETBALL 籃球) a ball that the REFEREE throws up between two opposing players to begin play 跳球；爭球

jump·cut /ˈdʒʌmpkʌt/ *noun* (*technical* 術語) (in films/movies 電影) a sudden change from one scene to another 跳格剪輯；跳切

'jumped-up *adj.* [only before noun] (*BrE, informal, disapproving*) thinking you are more important than you really are, particularly because you have risen in social status（尤因社會地位提高）妄自尊大的；自視甚高的

jump·er /ˈdʒʌmpə(r)/ *noun* **1** (*BrE*) a knitted piece of clothing made of wool or cotton for the upper part of the body, with long sleeves and no buttons（毛或棉的）針織套衫：*a woolly jumper* 套頭毛衣 ➲ VISUAL VOCAB page V63 **2** (*NAmE*) = PINAFORE (1) **3** a person, an animal or an insect that jumps 跳躍者；跳躍動物；跳蟲：*He's a good jumper.* 他的彈跳力特別好。

'jumper cable (*NAmE*) (*BrE* **jump lead**) *noun* [usually pl.] one of two cables that are used to start a car when it has no power in its battery. The jump cables connect the battery to the battery of another car. 跨接引線（用以將汽車上無電的電池連接到另一汽車的電池上以發動汽車）

,jumping-'off point (also **,jumping-'off place**) *noun* a place from which to start a journey or new activity 出發點；起點

'jump jet *noun* an aircraft that can take off and land by going straight up or down, without needing a RUNWAY 垂直起降噴氣機；垂直起降噴射機

jump lead /'dʒʌmp li:d/ (*BrE*) (*NAmE* **'jumper cable**) *noun* [usually pl.] one of two cables that are used to start a car when it has no power in its battery. The jump leads connect the battery to the battery of another car. 跨接引線（用以將汽車上無電的電池連接到另一汽車的電池上以發動汽車）

'jump-off (*NAmE* also **'ride-off**) *noun* (in the sport of SHOWJUMPING 超越障礙賽馬運動) an extra part of a competition in which horses that have the same score jump again to decide the winner 加賽決勝負

'jump rope *noun*, **,jump 'rope** *verb* (*NAmE*) ➲ SKIPPING ROPE, SKIP *v.* (2) ➲ VISUAL VOCAB page V37

'jump shot *noun* (in BASKETBALL 籃球) a shot made while jumping 跳投

'jump-start (*NAmE* also **jump**) *verb* **1** ~ **sth** to start the engine of a car by connecting the battery to the battery of another car with JUMP LEADS 用跨接引線啟動（汽車發動機） **2** ~ **sth** to put a lot of energy into starting a process or an activity or into making it start more quickly 全力啟動；加快開展

jump·suit /'dʒʌmpsu:t; *BrE* also -sju:t/ *noun* a piece of clothing that consists of trousers/pants and a jacket or shirt sewn together in one piece, worn especially by women（尤指女式）連衫褲

jumpy /'dʒʌmpi/ *adj.* (*informal*) nervous and anxious, especially because you think that sth bad is going to happen 膽戰心驚的；提心吊膽的；緊張不安的

junc·tion /'dʒʌŋkʃn/ *noun* **1** (*especially BrE*) (*NAmE* usually **inter·sec·tion**) the place where two or more roads or railway/railroad lines meet（公路或鐵路的）交叉路口，匯合處，樞紐站：*It was near the junction of City Road and Old Street.* 那是在城市路與老街的交叉路口附近。◇ *Come off the motorway at junction 6.* 在 6 號交叉路口駛離高速公路。 **2** a place where two or more cables, rivers or other things meet or are joined（電纜的）主接點；（河流的）匯合處；接合點：*a telephone junction box* 電話分線盒

junc·ture /'dʒʌŋktʃə(r)/ *noun* (*formal*) a particular point or stage in an activity or a series of events 特定時刻；關頭：*The battle had reached a crucial juncture.* 戰鬥已到了關鍵時刻。◇ ***At this juncture**, I would like to make an important announcement.* 此時此刻我要宣佈一項重要的事情。

June 0-π /dʒu:n/ *noun* [U, C] (*abbr.* **Jun.**) the 6th month of the year, between May and July 六月 **HELP** To see how **June** is used, look at the examples at **April**. * June 的用法見詞條 April 下的示例。

jun·gle /'dʒʌŋgl/ *noun* **1** [U, C] an area of tropical forest where trees and plants grow very thickly（熱帶）叢林，密林：*The area was covered in dense jungle.* 這個地區叢林密佈。◇ *the jungles of South-East Asia* 東南亞熱帶叢林 ◇ *jungle warfare* 叢林戰 ◇ *Our garden is a complete jungle.* 我們的花園雜草叢生。 **2** [sing.] an unfriendly or dangerous place or situation, especially one where it is very difficult to be successful or to trust anyone 爾虞我詐的環境；危險地帶：*It's a jungle out there—you've got to be strong to succeed.* 那是個弱肉強食的地方，要成功就得是強者。 ➲ see also CONCRETE JUNGLE **3** (also **'jungle music**) [U] a type of electronic dance music developed in Britain in the early 1990s, which has a fast drum beat and a strong slower BASS beat 叢林音樂（20 世紀 90 年代初發端於英國的一種伴以快速鼓點及強勁慢速低音節拍的電子舞曲） **IDM** see LAW

'jungle gym (*NAmE*) (*BrE* **'climbing frame**) *noun* a structure made of metal bars joined together for children to climb and play on（兒童遊樂設施）攀爬架 ➲ picture at FRAME ➲ VISUAL VOCAB page V37

jun·gli /'dʒʌŋgli/ *adj.* (*IndE*) wild; not educated 粗野的；沒教養的

jun·ior 0-π /'dʒu:niə(r)/ *adj., noun*

■ ***adj.***

▸ **OF LOW RANK** 低層 **1** 0-π [usually before noun] having a low rank in an organization or a profession 地位（或職位、級別）低下的：*junior employees* 低層雇員 ◇ **~ to sb** *She is junior to me.* 她職位比我低。

▸ **IN SPORT** 體育運動 **2** 0-π [only before noun] connected with young people below a particular age, rather than with adults, especially in sports 青少年的：*the world junior tennis championships* 世界青少年網球錦標賽

▸ **SON** 兒子 **3 Junior** (*abbr.* **Jnr**, **Jr**) (especially in US) used after the name of a man who has the same name as his father, to avoid confusion（尤用於美國，置於同名父子中兒子的姓名之後）小 ➲ compare THE YOUNGER at YOUNG *adj.* (6)

▸ **SCHOOL/COLLEGE** 學校；學院 **4** [only before noun] (*BrE*) (of a school or part of a school 學校或學校的一部份) for children under the age of 11 or 13 為 11 或 13 歲以下兒童設立的 **5** [only before noun] (*NAmE*) connected with the year before the last year in a HIGH SCHOOL or college（四年制中學或大學中）三年級生的，三年級的：*I spent my junior year in France.* 我三年級是在法國唸的。 ➲ compare SENIOR

■ ***noun***

▸ **LOW LEVEL JOB** 職位低的工作 **1** 0-π [C] (*especially BrE*) a person who has a job at a low level within an organization 職位較低者；低層次工作人員：*office juniors* 辦公室的低級職員

▸ **IN SPORT** 體育運動 **2** 0-π [C] a young person below a particular age, rather than an adult 青少年；青少年運動員：*She has coached many of our leading juniors.* 她訓練過我們許多名列前茅的青少年運動員。

▸ **IN SCHOOL/COLLEGE** 學校；學院 **3** [C] (*BrE*) a child who goes to JUNIOR SCHOOL 小學生 **4** [C] (*NAmE*) a student in the year before the last year at HIGH SCHOOL or college（中學或大學的）三年級學生 ➲ compare SOPHOMORE

▸ **SON** 兒子 **5** [sing.] (*NAmE, informal*) a person's young son 男孩子；年幼的兒子：*I leave junior with Mom when I'm at work.* 我工作時就把兒子留給母親照看。

IDM **be … years sb's 'junior | be sb's junior (by …)** to be younger than sb, by the number of years mentioned 小某人⋯歲；比某人小⋯歲：*She's four years his junior.* 她比他小四歲。◇ *She's his junior by four years.* 她比他小四歲。

,junior 'college *noun* (in the US) a college that offers programmes that are two years long. Some students go to a university or a college offering four-year programmes after they have finished studying at a junior college.（美國）兩年制專科學校，大專

,junior 'common room *noun* (*abbr.* **JCR**) (*BrE*) a room in a college, used for social purposes by students who have not yet taken their first degree（大學的）本科生交誼廳

'junior doctor *noun* (in Britain) a doctor who has finished medical school and who is working at a hospital to get further practical experience（英國）實習醫生 ➲ compare HOUSE OFFICER, INTERN *n.* (1)

,junior 'high school (also **,junior 'high**) *noun* [C, U] (in the US) a school for young people between the ages of 12 and 14（美國）初級中學 ➲ compare SENIOR HIGH SCHOOL

'junior school *noun* [C, U] (in Britain) a school for children between the ages of 7 and 11（英國）小學

ju·ni·per /'dʒu:nɪpə(r)/ *noun* [U, C] a bush with purple BERRIES that are used in medicine and to flavour GIN 刺柏，檜柏（有些種的果可供藥用和杜松子酒調味之用）

junk /dʒʌŋk/ *noun, verb*

■ ***noun*** **1** [U] things that are considered useless or of little value 無用的東西；無價值的東西 **SYN** **rubbish, garbage**：*I've cleared out all that old junk in the attic.* 我把閣樓裏所有的廢舊雜物都清除乾淨了。◇ *There's nothing but junk on the TV.* 電視上全是些無聊的東西。◇ (*informal, disapproving*) *Is this all your junk* (= are these all your things)? 這是你所有的家當嗎？ ➲ **SYNONYMS** at THING **2** [U] = JUNK FOOD **3** [C] a Chinese boat with a square sail and a flat bottom 中國式帆船

▪ *verb* **~ sth** (*informal*) to get rid of sth because it is no longer valuable or useful 把…當作廢物扔棄；丟棄；廢棄

ˈjunk bond *noun* (*business* 商) a type of BOND that pays a high rate of interest because there is a lot of risk involved, often used to raise money quickly in order to buy the shares of another company 風險債券，垃圾債券（利息高、風險大，常用於迅速集資進行收購）

jun·ket /ˈdʒʌŋkɪt/ *noun* (*informal, disapproving*) a trip that is made for pleasure by sb who works for the government, etc. and that is paid for using public money（政府官員的）公費旅遊

ˈjunk food (also **junk**) *noun* [U] (also **junk foods** [pl.]) (*informal, disapproving*) food that is quick and easy to prepare and eat but that is thought to be bad for your health（製作、食用方便卻有害健康的）垃圾食品

junkie /ˈdʒʌŋki/ *noun* (*informal*) a drug ADDICT (= a person who is unable to stop taking dangerous drugs) 有毒癮者；吸毒成癮者

ˈjunk mail *noun* [U] (*disapproving*) advertising material that is sent to people who have not asked for it（未經索要寄來的）郵寄廣告宣傳品，垃圾廣告郵件 ➲ compare SPAM (2)

ˌjunk ˈscience *noun* [U] (*disapproving*) used to refer to ideas and theories that seem to be well researched and scientific but in fact have little evidence to support them 垃圾科學（貌似嚴謹實則缺乏證據的思想和理論）

ˈjunk shop *noun* (*especially BrE*) a shop that buys and sells old furniture and other objects, at cheap prices 舊貨店；二手店

junky /ˈdʒʌŋki/ *adj.* (*informal, especially NAmE*) of poor quality or of little value 質量低劣的；無價值的

junk·yard /ˈdʒʌŋkjɑːd; *NAmE* -jɑːrd/ (*especially NAmE*) (*BrE* also **scrap·yard**) *noun* a place where old cars, machines, etc. are collected, so that parts of them, or the metal they are made of, can be sold to be used again（堆放舊汽車、舊機器等的）廢品場

junta /ˈdʒʌntə; *NAmE* ˈhʊntə/ *noun* a military government that has taken power by force（武力奪取政權的）軍人集團，軍政府

Ju·pi·ter /ˈdʒuːpɪtə(r)/ *noun* the largest planet of the SOLAR SYSTEM, fifth in order of distance from the sun 木星（太陽系中最大的行星）➲ VISUAL VOCAB page V73

Jur·as·sic /dʒʊˈræsɪk/ *adj.* (*geology* 地) of the PERIOD between around 208 to 146 million years ago, when the largest known dinosaurs lived; of the rocks formed during this time 侏羅紀的（距今約 2.08 億到 1.46 億年間，已知的最大的恐龍生活在這一時期）；侏羅紀岩系的 ▸ **the Jur·as·sic** *noun* [sing.]

jur·id·ic·al /dʒʊəˈrɪdɪkl; *NAmE* dʒʊˈr-/ *adj.* [usually before noun] (*formal*) connected with the law, judges or legal matters 法律的；司法的

jur·is·dic·tion /ˌdʒʊərɪsˈdɪkʃn; *NAmE* ˌdʒʊr-/ *noun* (*formal*) **1** [U, C] **~ (over sb/sth)** | **~ (of sb/sth) (to do sth)** the authority that an official organization has to make legal decisions about sb/sth 司法權；審判權；管轄權 **2** [C] an area or a country in which a particular system of laws has authority 管轄區域；管轄範圍 ▸ **jur·is·dic·tion·al** *adj.*

jur·is·pru·dence /ˌdʒʊərɪsˈpruːdns; *NAmE* ˌdʒʊr-/ *noun* [U] (*technical* 術語) the scientific study of law 法學；法律學：*a professor of jurisprudence* 法學教授

jur·ist /ˈdʒʊərɪst; *NAmE* ˈdʒʊr-/ *noun* (*formal*) a person who is an expert in law 法學家；法律學專家

juror /ˈdʒʊərə(r); *NAmE* ˈdʒʊr-/ *noun* a member of a jury 陪審團成員；陪審員

jury /ˈdʒʊəri; *NAmE* ˈdʒʊri/ *noun* [C+sing./pl. v.] (*pl.* **-ies**) **1** (also **panel**, **ˈjury panel** especially in *NAmE*) a group of members of the public who listen to the facts of a case in a court and decide whether or not sb is guilty of a crime 陪審團：***members of the jury*** 陪審團成員 ◇ *to **be/sit/serve on a jury*** 擔任陪審員 ◇ *The jury has/have returned a verdict of guilty.* 陪審團已作出有罪裁定。◇ *the right to trial **by jury*** 經由陪審團審判的權利 ➲ COLLOCATIONS at JUSTICE ➲ see also GRAND JURY **2** a group of people who decide who is the winner of a competition（比賽的）評判委員會，裁判委員會

IDM **the jury is (still) ˈout on sth** used when you are saying that sth is still not certain（某事）仍未定奪，懸而未決

ˈjury duty (*BrE* usually **ˈjury service**) *noun* [U] a period of time spent as a member of a jury in court 陪審義務；參與陪審期

jus /ʒuː; *NAmE* also dʒuːs/ *noun* [U] (from *French*) a thin sauce, especially one made from meat juices 調味（肉）汁

just 0⊸ /dʒʌst/ *adv.*, *adj.*

▪ *adv.* **1** 0⊸ exactly 正好；恰好：*This jacket is just my size.* 這件夾克正合我的尺碼。◇ *This gadget is **just the thing** for getting those nails out.* 這小玩意兒用來起那些釘子正合適。◇ ***Just my luck*** (= the sort of bad luck I usually have). *The phone's not working.* 我就是這麼倒霉。電話又壞了。◇ *You're **just in time**.* 你來得正是時候。◇ **~ like …** *She looks just like her mother.* 她看上去就像她母親。◇ **~ what …** *It's just what I wanted!* 這正是我想要的！◇ **~ as …** *It's just as I thought.* 我正是這樣想的。◇ (*BrE*) *It's **just on** six* (= exactly six o'clock). 現在六點整。 **2** 0⊸ **~ as …** at the same moment as 正當…時：*The clock struck six just as I arrived.* 我到達時，時鐘正敲六點。 **3** 0⊸ **~ as good, nice, easily, etc.** no less than; equally 不少於；同樣：*She's just as smart as her sister.* 她與她姐姐一樣聰明。◇ *You can get there just as cheaply by plane.* 你坐飛機到那兒同樣便宜。 **4** 0⊸ **(only) ~** | **~ after, before, under, etc. sth** by a small amount 剛好；差一點就不；勉強：*I got here just after nine.* 我到達這裏時剛過九點。◇ *I only just caught the train.* 我差一點沒趕上火車。◇ *Inflation fell to just over 4 per cent.* 通貨膨脹降至 4% 多一點。 **5** 0⊸ used to say that you/sb did sth very recently 剛才；方才：*I've just heard the news.* 我剛聽到這個消息。◇ *When you arrived he had only just left.* 你到時他剛走。◇ *She has just been telling us about her trip to Rome.* 她剛才一直在給我們講她的羅馬之行。◇ (*especially NAmE*) *I just saw him a moment ago.* 我剛才還見到過他。➲ note at ALREADY **6** 0⊸ at this/that moment; now 此時；那時；眼下；現在：*I'm just finishing my book.* 眼下我正在完成我的一本書。◇ *I was just beginning to enjoy myself when we had to leave.* 我剛開始玩得起勁我們就得離開了。◇ *I'm just off* (= I am leaving now). 我要走了。 **7** 0⊸ **~ about/going to do sth** going to do sth only a few moments from now or then 正要；正準備；馬上就要：*The water's just about to boil.* 水馬上就要開了。◇ *I was just going to tell you when you interrupted.* 我正準備告訴你，你突然把話打斷了。 **8** 0⊸ simply 只是；僅僅是：*It was just an ordinary day.* 那只是普普通通的一天。◇ *I **can't just** drop all my commitments.* 我答應要幹的事可不能都不幹了。◇ *This essay is **just not good enough**.* 這篇文章實在是不夠好。◇ *I didn't mean to upset you. **It's just that** I had to tell somebody.* 我本不想煩你，只是我非得找個人說說。◇ *This is not **just another** disaster movie—it's a masterpiece.* 不能說它只是又一部災難片，它是一部傑作。◇ ***Just because** you're older than me **doesn't mean** you know everything.* 你比我年長並不意味着你什麼都知道。 **9** 0⊸ only 僅僅；只不過：**~ (for sth)** *I decided to learn Japanese **just for fun**.* 我決定學日語只是為了好玩。◇ **~ (to do sth)** *I waited an hour just to see you.* 我等了一個小時只是為了看看你。◇ *There is just one method that might work.* 只有一個方法可能起作用。◇ *'Can I help you?' 'No thanks, **I'm just looking**.'* (= in a shop/store) "我能為你做點什麼嗎？" "不用，謝謝，我只是看看。" **10** (*informal*) really; completely 真正地；確實；完全：*The food was just wonderful!* 那吃的實在是好極了！◇ *I can just imagine his reaction.* 我完全可以想像出他的反應。 **11** used in orders to get sb's attention, give permission, etc.（引起注意、表示允許等）請，就：*Just listen to what I'm saying, will you!* 你就聽我說好嗎？◇ *Just help yourselves.* 請大家隨便吃。 **12** used to make a polite request, excuse, etc.（提出請求、表示歉意等）請：*Could you just help me with this box, please?* 請幫

J

我搬一搬這箱子好嗎？◇ *I've just got a few things to do first.* 對不起，我正好有點事要先做。 **13 could/might/may ~** used to show a slight possibility that sth is true or will happen（表示稍有可能）可能，也許：*Try his home number—he might just be there.* 試試他家的號碼，他也許在那兒。 **14** used to agree with sb（表示贊同）：*'He's very pompous.' 'Isn't he just?'* "他很自負。" "可不是嗎？"

IDM could/might just as well ... used to say that you/sb would have been in the same position if you had done sth else, because you got little benefit or enjoyment from what you did do 不如；還是…的好：*The weather was so bad we might just as well have stayed at home.* 天氣糟糕透了，還不如待在家裏好。 **it is just as 'well (that ...)** it is a good thing（…）還好，倒也不錯，還可以：*It is just as well that we didn't leave any later or we'd have missed him.* 還好，我們沒有晚些離開，要不然我們就見不到他了。 **just about** (*informal*) **1** almost; very nearly 幾乎；近乎；差不多：*I've met just about everyone.* 我幾乎每個人都見到了。◇ *'Did you reach your sales target?' 'Just about.'* "你的銷售目標達到了嗎？" "差不多了。" **2** approximately 大概；大約：*She should be arriving just about now.* 她現在該到了。 **just a 'minute/'moment/'second** (*informal*) used to ask sb to wait for a short time 稍等一會兒；請稍候：*'Is Mr Burns available?' 'Just a second, please, I'll check.'* "我可以見伯恩斯先生嗎？" "請稍等一會兒，我來查一下。" **just like 'that** suddenly, without warning or explanation（就是那樣）突如其來，冷不防，不加解釋 **just 'now 1** at this moment 此時；此刻；眼下：*Come and see me later—I'm busy just now.* 過些時候再來，我這會兒正忙着呢。 **2** during this present period 目前；現階段：*Business is good just now.* 目前生意很紅火。 **3** only a short time ago 剛才；剛剛；一會兒前：*I saw her just now.* 我剛剛見到過她。 **4** (*SAfrE, informal*) later; in a short period of time 以後；一會兒後 **just 'so** done or arranged very accurately or carefully（做或安排得）井井有條，有條不紊：*He liked polishing the furniture and making everything just so.* 他喜歡把傢具擦得亮亮的，一切都安排得井井有條。 **just 'then** at that moment 那時；就在那時：*Just then, someone knocked at the front door.* 就在那時，大門口有人敲門。 **not just 'yet** not now but probably quite soon 這會兒還不；可能很快：*I can't give you the money just yet.* 我這會兒還不能給你錢。 **I, etc. would just as soon do sth** used to say that you would equally well like to do sth as do sth else that has been suggested 樂意做某事（跟所建議的事一樣）：*I'd just as soon stay at home as go out tonight.* 今晚待在家裏或出去找都樂意。 ➲ more at CASE *n.*, JOB

■ *adj.* [usually before noun] **1** that most people consider to be morally fair and reasonable 公正的；正義的；正當的；合理的 **SYN fair**：*a just decision/law/society* 公正的判決／法律／社會 **2 the just** *noun* [pl.] people who are just 正直的人；公正的人 **3** appropriate in a particular situation 合適的；恰當的：*a **just reward/punishment*** 應有的報償／懲罰 ◇ *I think she got her **just deserts*** (= what she deserved). 我認為她罪有應得。 **OPP unjust** ▸ **just·ly** *adv.*：*to be treated justly* 受到公平待遇 ◇ *to be justly proud of sth* 有理由為某事而驕傲

just·ice /ˈdʒʌstɪs/ *noun*

1 [U] the fair treatment of people 公平；公正：*laws based on the principles of justice* 以公正為原則的法律 ◇ *They are demanding equal rights and justice.* 他們要求平等的權利和公正的待遇。 **OPP injustice** ➲ see also POETIC JUSTICE, ROUGH JUSTICE **2** [U] the quality of being fair or reasonable 公道；合理；公平合理：*Who can deny the justice of their cause?* 誰能否認他們的追求是合理的呢？ **OPP injustice 3** [U] the legal system used to punish people who have committed crimes 司法制度；法律制裁；審判：*the criminal justice system* 刑事審判制度 ◇ *The European Court of Justice* 歐洲法庭 ◇ (*BrE*) *They were accused of attempting to **pervert the course of justice**.* 他們因企圖妨礙司法公正而被控。◇ (*NAmE*) *They were accused of attempting to **obstruct justice**.* 他們被控企圖妨礙司法公正。 ➲ see also MISCARRIAGE OF JUSTICE **4** (also **Just·ice**) [C] (*NAmE*) a judge in a court (also used before the name of a judge) 法官（亦作稱謂） ➲ see also CHIEF JUSTICE **5 Just·ice** [C] (*BrE, CanE*) used before the name of a judge in a COURT OF APPEAL（稱謂）上訴庭法官：*Mr Justice Davies* 高等法院法官戴維斯先生

IDM bring sb to 'justice to arrest sb for a crime and put them on trial in court（將某人）繩之以法，緝拿歸案 **do justice to 'sb/'sth; do sb/sth 'justice 1** to treat or represent sb/sth fairly, especially in a way that shows how good, attractive, etc. they are 公平對待某人（或某事）；給以公正的評價：*That photo doesn't do you justice.* 那張照片把你給照走樣了。 **2** to deal with sb/sth correctly and completely 恰當處理某人（或某事）：*You cannot do justice to such a complex situation in just a few pages.* 你不可能僅僅幾頁就將這麼複雜的形勢恰如其分地描述出來。 **do yourself 'justice** to do sth as well as you can in order to show other people how good you are 充分發揮自己的能力：*She didn't do herself justice in the exam.* 她在考試中沒有充分發揮出自己的水平。 ➲ more at PERVERT *v.*

Justice of the 'Peace *noun* (*pl.* **Justices of the Peace**) (*abbr.* **JP**) (*formal*) an official who acts as a judge in the lowest courts of law 基層法院法官；治安法官；太平紳士 **SYN magistrate**

jus·ti·ciary /dʒʌˈstɪʃəri; *NAmE* dʒəˈstɪʃieri/ *noun* (*pl.* **-ies**) **1** (*ScotE*) [C] a judge or similar officer 司法官 **2** [U] the process by which justice is done 司法程序

jus·ti·fi·able AW /ˈdʒʌstɪfaɪəbl; ˌdʒʌstɪˈfaɪəbl/ *adj.* existing or done for a good reason, and therefore acceptable 有理由的；可證明是正當的；情有可原的 **SYN legitimate**：*justifiable pride* 無可非議的自豪感 ▸ **jus·ti·fi·ably** AW /-əbli/ *adv.*：*The university can be justifiably proud of its record.* 這所大學值得為自己的紀錄而自豪。

justifiable 'homicide *noun* [U] (*law* 律) in some countries, a killing which is not a criminal act, for example because you were trying to defend yourself 正當殺人（在一些國家中不構成犯罪，如因自衞） ➲ compare CULPABLE HOMICIDE

jus·ti·fi·ca·tion AW /ˌdʒʌstɪfɪˈkeɪʃn/ *noun* [U, C] **~ (for sth/doing sth)** a good reason why sth exists or is done 正當理由：*I can see no possible justification for any further tax increases.* 我看不出還能提出什麼理由來加稅了。◇ *He was getting angry—and **with some justification**.* 他生氣了，而這並不是沒有道理的。 ➲ SYNONYMS at REASON

IDM in justifi'cation (of sb/sth) as an explanation of why sth exists or why sb has done sth 作為（對…）的解釋（或辯護）：*All I can say in justification of her actions is that she was under a lot of pressure at work.* 我唯一能為她的行為辯解的理由是她工作壓力很大。

jus·ti·fied AW /ˈdʒʌstɪfaɪd/ *adj.*

1 ~ (in doing sth) having a good reason for doing sth（做某事）有正當理由的：*She felt fully justified in asking for her money back.* 她認為有充分的理由要求退款。 **2** existing or done for a good reason 事出有因的；合乎情理的：*His fears proved justified.* 他的恐懼後來證明是有原因的。 **OPP unjustified**

jus·tify AW /ˈdʒʌstɪfaɪ/ *verb* (**jus·ti·fies, jus·ti·fy·ing, jus·ti·fied, jus·ti·fied**)

1 to show that sb/sth is right or reasonable 證明…正確（或正當、有理）：**~ (sb/sth) doing sth** *How can they justify paying such huge salaries?* 他們怎能證明付這麼大筆薪金是正當的呢？◇ **~ sth** *Her success had justified the faith her teachers had put in her.* 她的成功證明了老師對她的信任是正確的。 **2 ~ sth/yourself (to sb)** | **~ (sb/sth) doing sth** to give an explanation or excuse for sth or for doing sth 對…作出解釋；為…辯解（或辯護） **SYN defend**：*The Prime Minister has been asked to justify the decision to Parliament.* 首相被要求就這一決定向議會解釋。◇ *You don't need to justify yourself to me.* 你不必向我解釋你的理由。 **3 ~ sth** (*technical* 術語) to arrange lines of printed text so that one or both edges are straight 調整使全行排滿；使每行排齊；使齊行

IDM see END *n.*

ˌjust-ˌin-ˈtime *adj.* (*abbr.* JIT) (*business* 商) used to describe a system in which parts or materials are only delivered to a factory just before they are needed 適時制（只有在需要時才將零部件或原材料送貨到廠）

jut /dʒʌt/ *verb* (-tt-) [I, T] to stick out further than the surrounding surface, objects, etc.; to make sth stick out （使）突出，伸出 SYN **protrude, project** : **~ (out) (from, into, over sth)** *A row of small windows jutted out from the roof.* 有一排小窗戶從房頂上突出來。◇ *A rocky headland jutted into the sea.* 嶙峋的岬角突入海中。◇ *a jutting chin* 突出的下巴 ◇ **~ sth (out)** *She jutted her chin out stubbornly.* 她倔強地把下巴翹得高高的。

jute /dʒuːt/ *noun* [U] FIBRES (= thin threads) from a plant, also called jute, used for making rope and rough cloth 黃麻纖維

ju·ven·ile /ˈdʒuːvənaɪl; *NAmE* -vənl/ *adj.*, *noun*

■ ***adj.*** **1** [only before noun] (*formal* or *law* 律) connected with young people who are not yet adults 少年的；未成年的：*juvenile crime/employment* 少年犯罪；童工的雇用 ◇ *juvenile offenders* 少年罪犯 **2** (*disapproving*) silly and more typical of a child than an adult 幼稚的；不成熟的；孩子氣的 SYN **childish** : *juvenile behaviour* 幼稚的行為 ◇ *Don't be so juvenile!* 別那麼孩子氣！

■ ***noun*** (*formal* or *law* 律) a young person who is not yet an adult 少年

ˌjuvenile ˈcourt *noun* a court that deals with young people who are not yet adults 少年法院；少年法庭

ˌjuvenile deˈlinquent *noun* a young person who is not yet an adult and who is guilty of committing a crime 少年犯 ▸ **ˌjuvenile deˈlinquency** *noun* [U]

ju·ven·ilia /ˌdʒuːvəˈnɪliə/ *noun* [pl.] (*formal*) writing, poetry, works of art, etc. produced by a writer or an artist when he/she was still young （統稱某作家或藝術家的）少年時代作品

juxta·pose /ˌdʒʌkstəˈpəʊz; *NAmE* -ˈpoʊz/ *verb* [usually passive] **~ A and/with B** (*formal*) to put people or things together, especially in order to show a contrast or a new relationship between them （尤指為對比或表明其關係而）把…並置，把…並列：*In the exhibition, abstract paintings are juxtaposed with shocking photographs.* 展覽會上抽象畫與令人震驚的照片並列展出。▸ **juxta·pos·ition** /ˌdʒʌkstəpəˈzɪʃn/ *noun* [U, C] : *the juxtaposition of realistic and surreal situations in the novel* 小說中現實主義與超現實主義情節的並置

J

Collocations 詞語搭配

Criminal justice 刑事審判

Breaking the law 犯法

- **break/violate/obey/uphold** the law 違反／違背／遵守／維護法律
- **be investigated/arrested/tried for** a crime/a robbery/fraud 因犯罪／搶劫／詐騙而被調查／逮捕／審判
- **be arrested**/(*especially NAmE*) **indicted/convicted** on charges of rape/fraud/(*especially US*) felony charges 因被控犯強姦罪／詐騙罪／重刑罪遭逮捕／起訴／定罪
- **be arrested** on suspicion of arson/robbery/shoplifting 因涉嫌縱火／搶劫／在商店行竊而被逮捕
- **be accused of/be charged with** murder/(*especially NAmE*) homicide/four counts of fraud 被指控犯有謀殺罪／殺人罪／四項詐騙罪
- **face** two charges of indecent assault 面臨兩項猥褻罪的指控
- **admit** your guilt/liability/responsibility (for sth) 承認（對某事的）罪責／責任
- **deny** the allegations/claims/charges 否認指控
- **confess to** a crime 坦白罪行
- **grant/be refused/be released on/skip/jump** bail 准許／不准保釋；交保釋金獲釋；棄保潛逃

The legal process 法律程序

- **stand/await/bring sb to/come to/be on** trial 受審；候審；把某人送交法院審判；開庭審理；受到審判
- **take sb to/come to/settle sth out of** court 把某人告上法庭；被法庭受理；庭外和解某事
- **face/avoid/escape** prosecution 面臨／免於／逃脫起訴
- **seek/retain/have the right to/be denied access to** legal counsel 尋求／聘請／有權聘用／無權聘用律師
- **hold/conduct/attend/adjourn** a hearing/trial 開庭；出庭；休庭
- **sit on/influence/persuade/convince** the jury 擔任／影響／說服陪審團
- **sit/stand/appear/be put/place sb** in the dock 坐在／站在／出現在／被送上／將某人送上被告席
- **plead** guilty/not guilty to a crime 認罪；不認罪
- **be called to/enter** (*BrE*) the witness box 被召喚進入／進入證人席
- **take/put sb on** the stand/(*NAmE*) the witness stand 出庭作證；讓某人出庭作證
- **call/subpoena/question/cross-examine** a witness 傳喚／以傳票傳喚／訊問／盤問證人
- **give/hear** the evidence against/on behalf of sb 提供／聽取對某人不利／有利的證據
- **raise/withdraw/overrule** an objection 提出／撤銷／否決異議
- **reach** a unanimous/majority verdict 作出一致的／多數人贊同的裁決
- **return/deliver/record** a verdict of not guilty/unlawful killing/accidental death 作出／宣佈無罪／非法殺人／意外死亡的裁決
- **convict/acquit** the defendant of the crime 宣判被告有罪／無罪
- **secure** a conviction/your acquittal 獲得有罪／無罪判決
- **lodge/file** an appeal 提出上訴
- **appeal (against)/challenge/uphold/overturn** a conviction/verdict 對判決／裁決提出上訴／質疑；維持／撤銷判決／裁決

Sentencing and punishment 判刑與懲罰

- **pass** sentence on sb 宣佈對某人的判決
- **carry/face/serve** a seven-year/life sentence 會被判處／面臨／服七年徒刑／無期徒刑
- **receive/be given** the death penalty 被判死刑
- **be sentenced to** ten years (in prison/jail) 被判十年（監禁）
- **carry/impose/pay** a fine (of $3 000)/a penalty (of 14 years imprisonment) 會被判處／處以／繳納（3 000 元的）罰金／（14 年的）監禁
- **be imprisoned/jailed for** drug possession/fraud/murder 因持有毒品罪／詐騙罪／謀殺罪被監禁
- **do/serve** time/ten years 服刑；服十年徒刑
- **be sent to/put sb in/be released from** jail/prison 被送進監獄；把某人送進監獄；被釋放出獄
- **be/put sb/spend X years** on death row 在／把某人關在死囚牢房；在死囚牢房度過 X 年
- **be granted/be denied/break** (your) parole 獲准假釋；假釋遭拒；違反假釋規定

➲ more collocations at CRIME

Kk

K /keɪ/ *noun, abbr.*

■ ***noun*** (also **k**) [C, U] (*pl.* **Ks, K's, k's** /keɪz/) the 11th letter of the English alphabet 英語字母表的第 11 個字母：*'King' begins with (a) K/'K'.* * king 一詞以字母 k 開頭。

■ ***abbr.*** (*pl.* **K**) **1** (*informal*) one thousand 一千：*She earns 40K (= £40 000) a year.* 她一年掙 4 萬英鎊。**2** kilometre(s) 千米；公里：*a 10K race* 萬米賽跑 **3** (*computing* 計) kilobyte(s) 千字節 **4** KELVIN(S) 開（溫度單位）

■ ***symbol*** the symbol for the chemical element potassium（化學元素）鉀

K-12 /ˌkeɪ ˈtwelv/ *adj.* (in the US) relating to education from KINDERGARTEN (= the class that prepares children for school) to 12th GRADE（美國）從幼兒園到 12 年級教育的，中小學及學前教育的

ka·baddi /ˈkʌbədi/ *noun* [U] a S Asian sport played by teams of seven players on a RECTANGULAR sand court. A player from one team tries to capture a player from the other team and must hold his/her breath while running. 卡巴迪（南亞運動比賽，每隊各有七人參加，在長方形沙地上舉行，運動員需屏氣追逐對手）

Kab·ba·lah (also **Ca·bala**, **Qa·ba·lah**) /kəˈbɑːlə; ˈkæbələ/ *noun* (in Judaism 猶太教) the ancient tradition of explaining holy texts through MYSTICAL means 喀巴拉（猶太教神秘主義體系）

ka·buki /kəˈbuːki/ *noun* [U] (from *Japanese*) traditional Japanese theatre, in which songs, dance and MIME are performed by men 歌舞伎（日本傳統劇種，由男子表演）

ka-ching /kəˈtʃɪŋ/ (*BrE* also **ker-ching**) (*NAmE* also **cha-ching**) *exclamation* (*informal*) used to say that sb is getting a lot of money 嘩啦（表示賺大錢）：*The money was rolling in, ka-ching, ka-ching!* 財富嘩啦啦地滾滾而來！◇ *Ka-ching! I just got my first cheque.* 嘩啦！我剛得到第一張支票。**ORIGIN** A way of representing the noise made by a CASH REGISTER. 源自對收銀機聲響的模仿。

kaffee·klatsch /ˈkæfeɪklætʃ/ *noun* (*NAmE*, from *German*) a social event at which people drink coffee 咖啡派對；咖啡敘談會

Kaf·fir /ˈkæfə(r)/ *noun* (*taboo, slang*) a very offensive word for a black African 卡菲爾人（對非洲黑人的一種蔑稱）

kaf·fi·yeh = KEFFIYEH

kafir /ˈkæfɪə(r); *NAmE* ˈkæfər/ *noun* a word used by Muslims to refer to a person who is not a Muslim, that can be considered offensive 卡菲爾（穆斯林對非伊斯蘭教教徒的稱呼，含侮慢意）

Kaf·ka·esque /ˌkæfkəˈesk/ *adj.* used to describe a situation that is confusing and frightening, especially one involving complicated official rules and systems that do not seem to make any sense 卡夫卡式的；恐怖而怪誕的：*My attempt to get a new passport turned into a Kafkaesque nightmare.* 我試圖申請新護照的過程變成了一場官樣文章的噩夢。**ORIGIN** From the name of the Czech writer Franz Kafka, whose novels often describe situations like this. 源自捷克作家弗朗茲 • 卡夫卡（Kafka）的名字，他的小說經常描寫此類情景。

kaf·tan (also **caf·tan**) /ˈkæftæn/ *noun* **1** a long loose piece of clothing, usually with a belt at the waist, worn by men in Arab countries（男式束腰帶）阿拉伯長袍 **2** a woman's long loose dress with long wide sleeves 寬大長袖女袍

ka·goul = CAGOULE

ka·huna /kəˈhuːnə/ *noun* (*NAmE, informal*) an important person; the person in charge 要人；負責人；大咖

kai /kaɪ/ *noun* (*NZE, informal*) food 食物

kai·ser /ˈkaɪzə(r)/ *noun* (from *German*) **1 Kaiser** (in the past) a ruler of Germany, of Austria, or of the Holy Roman Empire（舊時德國、奧地利或神聖羅馬帝國的）皇帝：*Kaiser Wilhelm* 威廉皇帝 **2** (also **ˈkaiser roll**) (*NAmE*) a crisp bread roll 王冠鬆脆小麪包

kai·zen /ˌkaɪˈzen/ *noun* [U] (*business* 商) (from *Japanese*) the practice of continuously improving the way in which a company operates（源自日本的公司經營模式的）持續改進

kajal /ˈkʌdʒəl/ *noun* [U] a type of black make-up used by S Asian women, that is put around the edge of the eyes to make them more noticeable and attractive（南亞女子用的）黑色眼影，燈黑

ka·kuro /ˌkɑːˈkʊərəʊ; *NAmE* -ˈkʊroʊ/ *noun* (*pl.* **-os**) [C, U] (from *Japanese*) a number puzzle in which you have to put numbers into white spaces in a diagram so that their total is the number given in a black space 數謎遊戲，數和（圖表中的白格所填數字之和等於黑格所給數字）：*She loves doing kakuros.* 她喜歡玩數謎。
➲ compare SUDOKU

Ka·lash·ni·kov /kəˈlæʃnɪkɒf; *NAmE* -kɔːf/ *noun* a type of RIFLE (= a long gun) that can fire bullets very quickly 卡拉什尼科夫步槍（或衝鋒槍）

kale /keɪl/ *noun* [U] (*NAmE* also **ˈcollard greens**) a dark green vegetable like a CABBAGE 羽衣甘藍

kal·eido·scope /kəˈlaɪdəskəʊp; *NAmE* -skoʊp/ *noun* **1** [C] a toy consisting of a tube that you look through with loose pieces of coloured glass and mirrors at the end. When the tube is turned, the pieces of glass move and form different patterns. 萬花筒 **2** [sing.] a situation, pattern, etc. containing a lot of different parts that are always changing（形勢、圖案等的）千變萬化，瞬息萬變
▸ **kal·eido·scop·ic** /kəˌlaɪdəˈskɒpɪk; *NAmE* -ˈskɑːpɪk/ *adj.*

ka·meez /kəˈmiːz/ *noun* (*pl.* **ka·meez** or **ka·meezes**) a piece of clothing like a long shirt worn by many people from S Asia 克米茲（許多南亞人穿的及膝長袍）

kami·kaze /ˌkæmɪˈkɑːzi/ *adj.* [only before noun] (from *Japanese*) used to describe the way soldiers attack the enemy, knowing that they too will be killed（向敵人進攻的方式）神風隊的，自殺性的 **SYN** **suicidal**：*a kamikaze pilot/attack* 神風隊飛行員；自殺性攻擊 ◇ (*figurative*) *He made a kamikaze run across three lanes of traffic.* 他不要命地衝過了三條車道。

kanga = KHANGA

kan·ga·roo /ˌkæŋɡəˈruː/ (also *informal* **roo**) *noun* (*pl.* **-oos**) a large Australian animal with a strong tail and back legs, that moves by jumping. The female carries its young in a pocket of skin (called a POUCH) on the front of its body. 袋鼠（產於澳大利亞）➲ VISUAL VOCAB page V12

ˌkangaroo ˈcourt *noun* (*disapproving*) an illegal court that punishes people unfairly 袋鼠法庭（不公正的非法法庭）；私設的公堂

kanji /ˈkændʒi; ˈkɑːn-/ *noun* [U, C] (*pl.* **kanji**) (from *Japanese*) a Japanese system of writing based on Chinese symbols, called CHARACTERS; a symbol in this system（日語中的）漢字體系；日本漢字

Kan·nada /ˈkænədə/ (also **Kan·ar·ese** /ˌkænəˈriːz/) *noun* [U] a language spoken in Karnataka in SW India 坎納達語，建那陀語，卡納拉語（印度西南部卡納塔克邦語言）

kanzu /ˈkænzuː/ *noun* (in E Africa) a long loose piece of outer clothing made from white cloth and worn by men 康祖長袍（東非男子穿的白色寬大長外套）

kao·lin /ˈkeɪəlɪn/ (also **ˌchina ˈclay**) *noun* [U] a type of fine white CLAY used in some medicines and in making PORCELAIN for cups, plates, etc. 高嶺土；瓷土

kapok /ˈkeɪpɒk; *NAmE* -pɑːk/ *noun* [U] a soft white material used for filling CUSHIONS, soft toys, etc. 木棉

kappa /ˈkæpə/ *noun* the 10th letter of the Greek alphabet (Κ, κ) 希臘字母表的第 10 個字母

kaput /kəˈpʊt/ *adj.* [not before noun] (*informal*) not working correctly; broken 運轉不正常；壞了：*The truck's kaput.* 卡車壞了。

kara·bin·er /ˌkærəˈbiːnə(r)/ *noun* a metal ring that can open to allow a rope to pass through, used by rock CLIMBERS to attach themselves safely to things（登山者使用的）穿索鐵鎖，岩釘鋼環

kar·aoke /ˌkæri'əʊki; *NAmE* -'oʊki/ *noun* [U] (from *Japanese*) a type of entertainment in which a machine plays only the music of popular songs so that people can sing the words themselves 卡拉 OK： *a karaoke machine/night/bar* 卡拉 OK 機 / 之夜 / 酒吧

karat (*NAmE*) = CARAT (2)

kar·ate /kə'rɑːti/ *noun* [U] a Japanese system of fighting in which you use your hands and feet as weapons 空手道： *a karate chop* (= a blow with the side of the hand) 空手道的掌側劈

karma /'kɑːmə; *NAmE* 'kɑːrmə/ *noun* [U] **1** (in Buddhism and Hinduism 佛教和印度教) the sum of sb's good and bad actions in one of their lives, believed to decide what will happen to them in the next life 羯磨，業（據信為可決定來生的個人善惡行為）**2 good/bad ~** (*informal*) the good/bad effect of doing a particular thing, being in a particular place, etc. 善報；惡報；因果報應： *Vegetarians believe that eating meat is bad karma.* 素食者認為吃肉食是造惡業。

kart /kɑːt; *NAmE* kɑːrt/ *noun* a small motor vehicle used for racing 小型賽車；卡丁賽車

kart·ing /'kɑːtɪŋ; *NAmE* 'kɑːrt-/ *noun* [U] the sport of racing in karts 卡丁車比賽

kas·bah (also **cas·bah**) /'kæzbɑː/ *noun* a castle on high ground in a N African city or the area around it （北非城市高地的）城堡，城堡周圍地區

ka·tab·ol·ism = CATABOLISM

kata·kana /ˌkætə'kɑːnə/ *noun* [U] (from *Japanese*) a set of symbols used in Japanese writing, used especially to write foreign words or to represent noises（日語中的）片假名 ➲ compare HIRAGANA

kayak /'kaɪæk/ *noun* a light CANOE in which the part where you sit is covered over（坐的部份遮蓋起來的）獨木舟，單人划子 ➲ **VISUAL VOCAB** page V55 ▶ **kayak·ing** *noun* [U]： *to go kayaking* 去划獨木舟

kayo /keɪ'əʊ; *NAmE* -'oʊ/ *noun* (*pl.* **-os**) = KO

kazoo /kə'zuː/ *noun* (*pl.* **-oos**) a small simple musical instrument consisting of a hollow pipe with a hole in it, that makes a BUZZING sound when you sing into it 卡佐膜管，卡祖笛（兩端點有薄膜的短管，通過對着一個側孔哼鳴或吟唱）

KB (also **K**) *abbr.* (in writing 書寫形式) KILOBYTE

Kb (also **Kbit**) *abbr.* (in writing 書寫形式) KILOBIT

Kbps *abbr.* (in writing 書寫形式) kilobits per second (a unit for measuring the speed of a MODEM) 千位每秒，每秒千比特（調制解調器傳輸速度單位）

KC /ˌkeɪ 'siː/ *noun* the highest level of BARRISTER, who can speak for the government in court in Britain. KC is the abbreviation for 'King's Counsel' and is used when there is a king in Britain. 英國王室法律顧問，英國御用大律師（全寫為 King's Counsel）➲ compare QC

kebab /kɪ'bæb/ (also **'shish kebab** especially in *NAmE*) *noun* small pieces of meat and vegetables cooked on a wooden or metal stick 烤肉串 ➲ see also DONER KEBAB

kedg·eree /'kedʒəriː/ *noun* [U] a hot dish of rice, fish and eggs cooked together 魚蛋燴飯

keel /kiːl/ *noun, verb*

■ ***noun*** the long piece of wood or steel along the bottom of a ship, on which the frame is built, and which sometimes sticks out below the bottom and helps to keep it in a vertical position in the water （船的）龍骨

IDM see EVEN *adj.*

■ ***verb*** [I, T] **~ (sth) (over)** (of a ship or boat 船隻) to fall over sideways; to make sth fall over sideways （使）傾覆，翻倒 SYN **capsize**

PHR V **ˌkeel 'over** to fall over unexpectedly, especially because you feel ill/sick （尤因病或感到不適）突然倒下，暈倒： *Several of them keeled over in the heat.* 他們中有好幾個人在酷暑中倒下。

keel·haul /'kiːlhɔːl/ *verb* **1 ~ sb** (*old use*) to punish a sailor by pulling him under a ship, from one side to the other or from one end to the other （把水手）拖曳過船底（作為懲罰）**2 ~ sb** (*humorous*) to punish sb very severely or speak very angrily to sb 重罰；怒斥

keen 0-w /kiːn/ *adj., verb*

■ ***adj.*** (**keen·er, keen·est**)

▸ **EAGER/ENTHUSIASTIC** 熱切；熱情 **1** 0-w (*especially BrE*) wanting to do sth or wanting sth to happen very much 渴望；熱切；熱衷於 SYN **eager** : **~ (to do sth)** *John was very keen to help.* 約翰很熱心，願意幫忙。◇ **~ (that …)** *We are keen that our school should get involved too.* 我們盼着自己學校也參與其中。◇ **~ (on doing sth)** *I wasn't too keen on going to the party.* 我不太想去參加這次聚會。**2** 0-w [usually before noun] (*especially BrE*) enthusiastic about an activity or idea, etc. 熱情的；熱心的： *a keen sportsman* 熱心運動的人 ◇ *one of the keenest supporters of the team* 這個隊最熱情的支持者之一

▸ **LIKING SB/STH** 喜愛 **3** 0-w (*BrE, informal*) liking sb/sth very much; very interested in sb/sth 喜愛；（對…）着迷，有興趣： **~ on sb/sth** *Tom's very keen on Anna.* 湯姆迷上了安娜。◇ **~ on doing sth** *She's not keen on being told what to do.* 她不喜歡別人向她發號施令。➲ **SYNONYMS** at LIKE

▸ **CLEVER** 聰明 **4** [only before noun] quick to understand 思維敏捷的；機靈的；機智的： *a **keen mind/intellect*** 敏捷的思考 / 頭腦 SYN **sharp, acute**

▸ **IDEAS/FEELINGS** 思想感情 **5** [usually before noun] strong or deep 強烈的；濃厚的；深厚的： *a keen sense of tradition* 強烈的傳統意識 ◇ *He took a **keen interest** in his grandson's education.* 他對孫子的教育很感興趣。

▸ **SENSES** 感官 **6** [only before noun] highly developed 靈敏的；敏銳的 SYN **sharp** : *Dogs have a keen sense of smell.* 狗的嗅覺很靈敏。◇ *My friend has **a keen eye** for* (= is good at noticing) *a bargain.* 我的朋友最會發現便宜貨。

▸ **COMPETITION** 競爭 **7** involving people competing very hard with each other for sth 激烈的；緊張的： *There is keen competition for places at the college.* 要在這所學院就讀競爭是非常激烈的。

▸ **PRICES** 價格 **8** (*especially BrE*) kept low in order to compete with other prices 低廉的；有競爭力的 SYN **competitive**

▸ **WIND** 風 **9** (*literary*) extremely cold 寒冷刺骨的

▸ **KNIFE** 刀 **10** [usually before noun] (*literary*) having a sharp edge or point 鋒利的；銳利的 SYN **sharp**

▶ **keen·ly** *adv.*： *a keenly fought contest* 爭奪激烈的比賽 ◇ *We were keenly aware of the danger.* 我們深知其危險。 **keen·ness** *noun* [U]

IDM **(as) ˌkeen as 'mustard** (*BrE, informal*) wanting very much to do well at sth; enthusiastic 極其渴望；極為熱心；非常熱情 ➲ more at MAD

■ ***verb*** [I] (usually used in the progressive tenses 通常用於進行時) (*old-fashioned*) to make a loud high sad sound, when sb has died （為死者）慟哭，哀號

keep 0-w /kiːp/ *verb, noun*

■ ***verb*** (**kept, kept** /kept/)

▸ **STAY** 保持 **1** 0-w [I, T] to stay in a particular condition or position; to make sb/sth do this （使）保持，處於： **+ adj.** *We huddled together to keep warm.* 我們擠在一起來保暖。◇ **+ adv./prep.** *The notice said 'Keep off* (= Do not walk on) *the grass'.* 牌子上寫着"勿踐踏草地"。◇ *Keep left along the wall.* 沿着牆靠左邊走。◇ **~ sb/sth + adj.** *She kept the children amused for hours.* 她陪孩子們玩了好幾個小時。◇ **~ sb/sth (+ adv./prep.)** *He kept his coat on.* 他一直穿着大衣。◇ *Don't **keep us in suspense**—what happened next?* 別跟我們賣關子了，接下來發生了什麼事？◇ *She had trouble **keeping her balance**.* 她保持平衡有困難。◇ **~ sb/sth doing sth** *I'm very sorry to **keep you waiting**.* 對不起，讓你久等了。

▸ **CONTINUE** 繼續 **2** 0-w [I] to continue doing sth; to do sth repeatedly 繼續，重複（做某事）： **~ doing sth** *Keep smiling!* 要保持笑容！◇ **~ on doing sth** *Don't keep on interrupting me!* 別老是跟我打岔！

▸ **DELAY** 耽擱 **3** [T] **~ sb** to delay sb 使耽擱；使延誤 SYN **hold sb up** : *You're an hour late—what kept you?* 你晚了一小時，什麼事把你給耽誤了？

▸ **NOT GIVE BACK** 不退還 **4** 0-w [T] **~ sth** to continue to have sth and not give it back or throw it away 保有；留着；不退還： *Here's a five dollar bill—please **keep the change**.* 給你一張五元的鈔票，零錢就不用找了。◇ *I keep all her letters.* 我把她所有的信都保留着。

K

▸ **SAVE FOR SB 為某人保留 5** [T] (*especially BrE*) to save sth for sb（為某人）保留，留下： **~ sth for sb** *Please keep a seat for me.* 請給我留個座位。◇ **~ sb sth** *Please keep me a seat.* 請給我留個座位。

▸ **PUT/STORE 放；存放 6** [T] **~ sth + adv./prep.** to put or store sth in a particular place 放，存放，貯存（在某處）： *Keep your passport in a safe place.* 把你的護照放在安全的地方。

▸ **SHOP/RESTAURANT 商店；餐館 7** [T] **~ sth** (*especially BrE*) to own and manage a shop/store or restaurant 開設，經營，管理（商店或餐館）： *Her father kept a grocer's shop.* 她父親開了個雜貨店。

▸ **ANIMALS 動物 8** [T] **~ sth** to own and care for animals 養；飼養：*to **keep bees/goats/hens*** 養蜜蜂／山羊／母雞

▸ **ABOUT HEALTH 健康 9** [I] **+ adv./prep.** (*informal*) used to ask or talk about sb's health（詢問或談論某人的健康）： ***How** is your mother **keeping**?* 你母親身體好嗎？◇ *We're all keeping well.* 我們都很健康。

▸ **OF FOOD 食物 10** [I] to remain in good condition 保持不壞： *Finish off the pie—it won't keep.* 把餡餅都吃了吧，這東西不耐放。◇ (*informal, figurative*) *'I'd love to hear about it, but I'm late already.' 'That's OK—**it'll keep*** (= I can tell you about it later).' "我很想聽聽，不過我已經遲到了。" "好吧，我以後再告訴你。"

▸ **SECRET 秘密 11** [T] **~ a secret | ~ sth secret (from sb)** to know sth and not tell it to anyone 保守（秘密）： *Can you keep a secret?* 你能保守秘密嗎？◇ *She kept her past secret from us all.* 她對我們所有人都避而不談她的過去。

▸ **PROMISE/APPOINTMENT 承諾；約會 12** [T] **~ your promise/word | ~ an appointment** to do what you have promised to do; to go where you have agreed to go 遵守；篤守；恪守： *She kept her promise to visit them.* 她遵守諾言去看望了他們。◇ *He failed to keep his appointment at the clinic.* 他未能按預約的時間去診所。

▸ **DIARY/RECORD 日記；記錄 13** [T] **~ a diary, an account, a record, etc.** to write down sth as a record 記下，記錄，記載（日記、賬目、記錄等）： *She kept a diary for over twenty years.* 她記了二十多年的日記。◇ *Keep a note of where each item can be found.* 把每樣物品的位置記錄下來。

▸ **SUPPORT SB 供養 14** [T] **~ sb/yourself** to provide what is necessary for sb to live; to support sb by paying for food, etc. 供養；養活： *He scarcely earns enough to keep himself and his family.* 他掙的錢幾乎不夠養活他自己和家人。

▸ **PROTECT 保護 15** [T] (*formal*) to protect sb from sth 保護；使免受： **~ sb** *May the Lord bless you and keep you* (= used in prayers in the Christian Church). 願上帝祝福你、保祐你（用於基督教的祈禱）。◇ **~ sb from sth** *His only thought was to keep the boy from harm.* 他一心想的就是不要讓這男孩受到傷害。

▸ **IN SPORT 體育運動 16** [T] **~ goal/wicket** (*BrE*) (in football (SOCCER), HOCKEY, CRICKET, etc. 足球、曲棍球、板球等) to guard or protect the goal or WICKET 守門；把守球門 ➲ see also GOALKEEPER, WICKETKEEPER

IDM Most idioms containing **keep** are at the entries for the nouns and adjectives in the idioms, for example **keep house** is at **house**. 大多數含 keep 的習語，都可在該等習語中的名詞及形容詞相關詞條找到，如 keep house 在詞條 house 下。 **ˌkeep ˈgoing 1** to make an effort to live normally when you are in a difficult situation or when you have experienced great suffering（在身處困境或遭難時）盡力維持下去，堅持活下去： *You just have to keep yourself busy and keep going.* 你只要讓自己忙起來，就能堅持下去。 **2** (*informal*) used to encourage sb to continue doing sth（用於鼓勵）繼續下去，堅持下去： *Keep going, Sarah, you're nearly there.* 堅持下去，薩拉，你已經快到了。 **ˌkeep sb ˈgoing** (*informal*) to be enough for sb until they get what they are waiting for 足以使某人維持（或支撐）： *Have an apple to keep you going till dinner time.* 吃個蘋果就能捱到吃晚飯了。

PHR V **ˌkeep sb ˈafter** (*NAmE*) (*BrE* **ˌkeep sb↔ˈback**) to make a student stay at school after normal hours as a punishment 罰（學生）課後留校

ˌkeep ˈat sth to continue working at sth 繼續做某事（或堅持幹）： *Come on, keep at it, you've nearly finished!* 快，要堅持，你馬上就要完成了！ **ˌkeep sb ˈat sth** to make sb continue working at sth 使某人繼續做（或堅持幹）某事： *He kept us at it all day.* 他讓我們不停地幹了一天。

ˌkeep aˈway (from sb/sth) to avoid going near sb/sth 避免接近；遠離；勿靠近： *Keep away from the edge of the cliff.* 切莫靠近懸崖邊。 **ˌkeep sb/sth aˈway (from sb/sth)** to prevent sb/sth from going somewhere 不讓接近某人（或某事物）；使離開： *Her illness kept her away from work for several weeks.* 她病得好幾週都上不了班。

ˌkeep ˈback (from sb/sth) to stay at a distance from sb/sth（與…）保持距離： *Keep well back from the road.* 離公路遠些。 **ˌkeep sb↔ˈback 1** (*BrE*) (*NAmE* **ˌkeep sb ˈafter**) to make a student stay at school after normal hours as a punishment 罰（學生）課後留校 **2** (*NAmE*) to make a student repeat a year at school because of poor marks/grades 使（學生）留級 **ˌkeep sb↔ˈback (from sb/sth)** to make sb stay at a distance from sb/sth 使某人（與…）保持距離： *Barricades were erected to keep back the crowds.* 設置了障礙，使人群無法靠近。 **ˌkeep sth↔ˈback 1** to prevent a feeling, etc. from being expressed 抑制（或阻止）感情等的流露 **SYN** **restrain**： *She was unable to keep back her tears.* 她無法忍住淚水。 **2** to continue to have a part of sth 保留（或扣留）某物的一部份：*He kept back half the money for himself.* 他把那筆錢留了一半給自己。 **ˌkeep sth↔ˈback (from sb)** to refuse to tell sb sth 拒絕告知某事；隱瞞： *I'm sure she's keeping something back from us.* 我肯定她有什麼事瞞着我們。

ˌkeep ˈdown to hide yourself by not standing up straight 隱蔽；隱伏；臥倒；蹲下： *Keep down! You mustn't let anyone see you.* 蹲下！千萬不要讓人看見你。 **ˌkeep sb↔ˈdown** to prevent a person, group, etc. from expressing themselves freely 壓制（或限制、控制）某人 **SYN** **oppress**： *The people have been kept down for years by a brutal regime.* 多年來人們一直受到殘暴統治的壓制。 **ˌkeep sth↔ˈdown 1** to make sth stay at a low level; to avoid increasing sth 使保持在低水平；抑制某事物的增長： *to keep down wages/prices/the cost of living* 保持低工資／物價／生活費用◇ *Keep your voice down—I don't want anyone else to hear.* 小聲點，別讓人聽見。◇ *Keep the noise down* (= be quiet). 小聲點兒。 **2** to not bring sth back through the mouth from the stomach; to not VOMIT 不使（胃中食物）吐出；不嘔吐： *She's had some water but she can't keep any food down.* 她喝了點兒水，但什麼食物都吃了就吐。

ˈkeep from sth | ˈkeep yourself from sth to prevent yourself from doing sth 忍住（或克制自己）不做某事： **~ doing sth** *She could hardly keep from laughing.* 她差一點兒笑了出來。◇ *I just managed to keep myself from falling.* 我差一點兒沒摔倒。 **ˈkeep sb from sth** to prevent sb from doing sth 阻止（或防止、阻礙）某人做某事： *I hope I'm not keeping you from your work.* 希望我沒有妨礙你工作。◇ **~ doing sth** *The church bells keep me from sleeping.* 教堂的鐘聲使我不能入睡。 **ˈkeep sth from sb** to avoid telling sb sth 不將某事告訴某人；瞞着某人： *I think we ought to keep the truth from him until he's better.* 我想我們應該等他身體好些再告訴他實情。 **ˈkeep sth from sth** to make sth stay out of sth 使置於某物之外；使與某物分開： *She could not keep the dismay from her voice.* 她無法使自己沉重的心情不流露在話音之中。

ˌkeep ˈin with sb (*BrE, informal*) to make sure that you stay friendly with sb, because you will get an advantage from doing so（為得到好處而）與某人友好相處，不得罪某人 **ˌkeep sth↔ˈin** to avoid expressing an emotion 控制（或抑制）感情 **SYN** **restrain**： *He could scarcely keep in his indignation.* 他幾乎控制不住自己的憤怒。 **ˌkeep sb ˈin** to make sb stay indoors or in a particular place 使某人留在室內（或某地）；使不外出 **ˈkeep sb/yourself in sth** to provide sb/yourself with a regular supply of sth 向某人持續供應某物

ˌkeep ˈoff if rain, snow, etc. **keeps off**, it does not fall（雨、雪等）未下 **ˌkeep ˈoff sth 1** to avoid eating, drinking or smoking sth 避免吃（或喝、吸）某物： *I'm trying to keep off fatty foods.* 我盡量不吃高脂肪食物。 **2** to avoid mentioning a particular subject 迴避某話題： *It's best to keep off politics when my father's around.* 我父親在場時最好不要談論政治。 **ˌkeep sb/sth↔ˈoff |**

K

ˌ**keep sb/sth ˈoff sb/sth** to prevent sb/sth from coming near, touching, etc. sb/sth 使…不接近（或不接觸、遠離）某人 / 事物： *They lit a fire to keep off wild animals.* 他們點燃篝火防止野獸靠近。◇ *Keep your hands off* (= do not touch) *me!* 別碰我！

ˌ**keep ˈon** to continue 繼續： *Keep on until you get to the church.* 一直往前走到教堂。 ˌ**keep sb↔ˈon** to continue to employ sb 繼續雇用某人 ˌ**keep sth ˈon** to continue to rent a house, flat/apartment, etc. 繼續租用房子（或套房等） ˌ**keep ˈon (at sb) (about sb/sth)** (*especially BrE*) to speak to sb often and in an annoying way about sb/sth （對…）糾纏不休；老是困擾；老是嘮叨 **SYN go on, nag**： *He does keep on so!* 他就是這樣糾纏不休！◇ *I'll do it—just don't keep on at me about it!* 我會做的，就別再對我嘮叨了！

ˌ**keep ˈout (of sth)** 🔑 to not enter a place; to stay outside 不進入；留在外面： *The sign said 'Private Property—Keep Out!'* 告示牌上寫着"私人產業，不得入內！" ˌ**keep sb/sth↔ˈout (of sth)** to prevent sb/sth from entering a place 使不進入；防止進入；把…關在外面： *Keep that dog out of my study!* 別讓那狗進我的書房！ ˌ**keep ˈout of sth** | ˌ**keep sb ˈout of sth** 🔑 to avoid sth; to prevent sb from being involved in sth or affected by sth 避免某事；使不捲入某事；使置身於…之外；使不受…的影響： *That child can't keep out of mischief.* 那孩子避不開別人的戲弄。◇ *Keep the baby out of the sun.* 別讓孩子曬着。

ˈ**keep to sth** **1** to avoid leaving a path, road, etc. 不偏離（或不離開）道路等 **SYN stick to sth**： *Keep to the track—the land is very boggy around here.* 順着道兒走，這一帶到處是沼澤地。 **2** to talk or write only about the subject that you are supposed to talk or write about 不偏離主題；不跑題： *Nothing is more irritating than people who do not* ***keep to the point***. 最煩人的就是那些談話不着邊際的人。 **3** to do what you have promised or agreed to do 遵守（或信守、履行）諾言： *to keep to an agreement/an undertaking/a plan* 遵守協議；信守承諾；執行計劃 **4** to stay in and not leave a particular place or position 堅守，不離開（某地或某個位置）： *She's nearly 90 and mostly keeps to her room.* 她快 90 歲了，大部份時間都待在房間裏。 ˌ**keep (yourself) to yourˈself** to avoid meeting people socially or becoming involved in their affairs 離群索居；不與人往來；不管別人的事： *Nobody knows much about him; he keeps himself very much to himself.* 誰對他都不太瞭解，因為他很少和人交往。 ˌ**keep sth to yourˈself** to not tell other people about sth 對…秘而不宣（或保守秘密）；不將…說出去： *I'd be grateful if you kept this information to yourself.* 你要是不把這消息傳出去，我會不勝感激的。

ˌ**keep sb ˈunder** to control or OPPRESS sb 控制，壓制（人）： *The local people are kept under by the army.* 當地居民受軍隊管制。

ˌ**keep ˈup** if particular weather **keeps up**, it continues without stopping （天氣）持續不變： *The rain kept up all afternoon.* 雨下了整整一個下午。 ˌ**keep ˈup (with sb/sth)** 🔑 to move, make progress or increase at the same rate as sb/sth （與…）齊步前進，並駕齊驅；跟上： *Slow down—I can't keep up!* 慢點，我跟不上了！◇ *I can't keep up with all the changes.* 我並非所有的變化都能跟得上。◇ *Wages are not keeping up with inflation.* 工資趕不上通貨膨脹。 ˌ**keep ˈup with sb** to continue to be in contact with sb 與（某人）保持聯繫： *How many of your old school friends do you keep up with?* 你與多少老同學保持着聯繫？ ˌ**keep ˈup with sth** **1** 🔑 to learn about or be aware of the news, current events, etc. 熟悉，瞭解（消息、形勢等）： *She likes to keep up with the latest fashions.* 她喜歡趕時髦。 **2** 🔑 to continue to pay or do sth regularly 繼續支付；繼續做： *If you do not keep up with the payments you could lose your home.* 如果你不繼續付款，你的住房就可能保不住了。 ˌ**keep sb ˈup** to prevent sb from going to bed 使某人熬夜（或開夜車、不睡覺）： *I hope we're not keeping you up.* 希望我們沒有耽誤你睡覺。 ˌ**keep sth↔ˈup** **1** 🔑 to make sth stay at a high level 使某事物保持在高水平： *The high cost of raw materials is keeping prices up.* 昂貴的原料費用使價格居高不下。 **2** 🔑 to continue sth at the same, usually high, level 使某事物保持（在同一水平，通常指高水平）： *The enemy kept up the bombardment day and night.* 敵人晝夜轟炸不停。◇ *We're having difficulty keeping up our mortgage payments.* 我們難以繼續償還按揭貸款。◇ *Well done!* ***Keep up the good work/Keep it up!*** 幹得好！繼續好好幹吧！ **3** to make sth remain at a high level 使處於高水平；使不低落： *They sang songs to keep their spirits up.* 他們唱歌以保持高昂的情緒。 **4** to continue to use or practise sth 沿用（或沿襲、保持）某事物： *to keep up old traditions* 保持老傳統◇ *Do you still keep up your Spanish?* 你還堅持說西班牙語嗎？ **5** to take care of a house, garden/yard, etc. so that it stays in good condition 保養，維護（房屋、花園等） **SYN maintain** ➲ related noun UPKEEP

■ *noun* **1** [U] food, clothes and all the other things that a person needs to live; the cost of these things 生活必需品；生活費用： *It's about time you got a job to* ***earn your keep***. 你該找個工作掙自己的生活費了。**2** [C] a large strong tower, built as part of an old castle 城堡主樓

IDM for ˈkeeps (*informal*) for ever 永遠；永久： *Is it yours for keeps or does he want it back?* 這東西是永遠屬於你了，還是要還給他？ ➲ more at EARN

keep·er /ˈkiːpə(r)/ *noun* **1** (especially in compounds 尤用於構成複合詞) a person whose job is to take care of a building, its contents or sth valuable 看守人；保管人： *the keeper of geology at the museum* 博物館地質資料的保管人 ➲ see also SHOPKEEPER **2** a person whose job is to take care of animals, especially in a zoo （尤指動物園的）飼養員 ➲ see also GAMEKEEPER, ZOOKEEPER **3** (*BrE, informal*) = GOALKEEPER, WICKETKEEPER **IDM** see FINDER

ˌ**keep-ˈfit** *noun* [U] (*BrE*) physical exercises that you do, usually in a class with other people, in order to improve your strength and to stay healthy（集體）健身鍛煉，健身操： *a keep-fit class* 健身班

keep·ing /ˈkiːpɪŋ/ *noun*

IDM in sb's ˈkeeping being taken care of by sb 由某人照料（或供養、飼養） ➲ see also SAFE KEEPING **in ˈkeeping (with sth)** appropriate or expected in a particular situation; in agreement with sth （與…）協調，一致： *The latest results are in keeping with our earlier findings.* 最新結果與我們先前的發現一致。 **out of ˈkeeping (with sth)** not appropriate or expected in a particular situation; not in agreement with sth（與…）不協調，不一致： *The painting is out of keeping with the rest of the room.* 這幅畫和這屋子不相稱。

keep·sake /ˈkiːpseɪk/ *noun* a small object that sb gives you so that you will remember them 紀念品 **SYN memento**

kef·fi·yeh (also **kaf·fi·yeh**) /kəˈfiːjə/ *noun* a square of cloth worn on the head by Arab men and fastened by a band （阿拉伯男子戴的）方頭巾

keg /keg/ *noun* **1** [C] a round wooden or metal container with a flat top and bottom, used especially for storing beer, like a BARREL but smaller （尤指盛啤酒的）小桶 **2** [U] (*BrE*) = KEG BEER

ˈ**keg beer** (*BrE* also **keg**) *noun* [U, C] (in Britain) beer served from metal containers, using gas pressure （英國，用氣壓出的）桶裝啤酒

keis·ter /ˈkiːstə(r)/ *noun* (*NAmE, informal*) the part of the body that you sit on 屁股 **SYN bottom**

Kejia /keɪˈdʒjɑː/ *noun* = HAKKA

kelim /kəˈliːm; ˈkelɪm; *NAmE* kiːˈliːm; ˈkeləm/ *noun* = KILIM

kelp /kelp/ *noun* [U] a type of brown SEAWEED, sometimes used as a FERTILIZER to help plants grow 巨藻；大型褐藻

kel·pie /ˈkelpi/ *noun* **1** (in Scottish stories 蘇格蘭傳說) a water spirit 水妖 **2** an Australian SHEEPDOG （澳大利亞）卡爾比犬

kel·vin /ˈkelvɪn/ *noun* (*abbr.* **K**) (*pl.* **kelvin** or **kelvins**) a unit for measuring temperature. One kelvin is equal to one degree Celsius, but the **Kelvin scale** starts at ABSOLUTE ZERO and water freezes at 273.15 kelvin. 開（開爾文溫標的計量單位，1 開相當於 1 攝氏度，但以絕對零度為計算起點，水的冰點為 273.15 開）

K

the ˌKelvin ˈscale *noun* [sing.] a scale of temperature in which water freezes at 273.15 degrees 絕對溫標；開爾文溫標；開氏溫標；克氏溫標

ken /ken/ *noun, verb*

■ ***noun***

IDM **beyond your ken** (*old-fashioned*) if sth is **beyond your ken**, you do not know enough about it to be able to understand it 為某人所不理解；在某人的知識範圍之外

■ ***verb*** (**-nn-**) [I, T] **~ (sth)** | **~ (that)** … | **~ what, where, etc.** … (*ScotE, NEngE*) to know 知道；懂得 **HELP** Kent is the usual form of the past tense used in Scotland. 在蘇格蘭過去時常用 kent。

kendo /ˈkendəʊ; *NAmE* -doʊ/ *noun* [U] (from *Japanese*) a Japanese form of the sport of FENCING, using light wooden weapons 劍道（日本劍術，用輕木質劍）

ken·nel /ˈkenl/ *noun* **1** (*NAmE* **dog·house**) a small shelter for a dog to sleep in 狗窩；犬舍 **2** (usually **kennels**) [C+sing./pl. v.] a place where people can leave their dogs to be taken care of when they go on holiday/vacation; a place where dogs are bred （寄養狗的）養狗場；狗繁殖場：*We put the dog* ***in kennels*** *when we go away.* 我們外出時把狗寄養在養狗場。➲ see also BOARDING KENNEL

kept *past tense, past part.* of KEEP

ˌkept ˈwoman *noun* (*old-fashioned*, usually *humorous*) a woman who is given money and a home by a man who visits her regularly to have sex （被包養的）姘婦，情婦

kera·tin /ˈkerətɪn/ *noun* [U] (*biology* 生) a PROTEIN that forms hair, feathers, horns, HOOFS, etc. （髮、羽、角、蹄等的）角蛋白

kerb (*BrE*) (*NAmE* **curb**) /kɜːb; *NAmE* kɜːrb/ *noun* the edge of the raised path at the side of a road, usually made of long pieces of stone （由條石砌成的）路緣；道牙；馬路牙子：*The bus mounted the kerb* (= went onto the PAVEMENT/SIDEWALK) *and hit a tree.* 那輛公共汽車開上路緣撞到了一棵樹。➲ VISUAL VOCAB page V3

ˈkerb-crawling *noun* [U] (*BrE*) the crime of driving slowly along a road in order to find a PROSTITUTE 路邊慢駛招妓（的罪行）▸ **ˈkerb-crawler** *noun*

kerb·side (*BrE*) (*NAmE* **curb·side**) /ˈkɜːbsaɪd; *NAmE* ˈkɜːrb-/ *noun* [U] the side of the street or path near the kerb 人行道靠近路緣的部份：*to stand at the kerbside* 站在馬路牙子上

kerb·stone (*BrE*) (*NAmE* **curb·stone**) /ˈkɜːbstəʊn; *NAmE* ˈkɜːrbstoʊn/ *noun* a block of stone or concrete in a kerb/curb 路緣石

ker·chief /ˈkɜːtʃɪf; *NAmE* ˈkɜːrtʃɪf/ *noun* (*old-fashioned*) a square piece of cloth worn on the head or around the neck 方頭巾；方圍巾

ker-ching /kəˈtʃɪŋ/ *exclamation* (*BrE, informal*) = KA-CHING

ker·fuf·fle /kəˈfʌfl; *NAmE* kərˈf-/ *noun* [sing.] (*BrE, informal*) unnecessary excitement or activity （不必要的）騷動，混亂，喧鬧 **SYN** **commotion, fuss**

ker·nel /ˈkɜːnl; *NAmE* ˈkɜːrnl/ *noun* **1** the inner part of a nut or seed （堅果或籽粒的）仁，核 **2** the central, most important part of an idea or a subject （思想或主題的）核心，中心，要點

kero·sene (also **kero·sine**) /ˈkerəsiːn/ *noun* [U] a type of fuel oil that is made from PETROLEUM and that is used in the engines of planes and for heat and light. In British English it is usually called PARAFFIN when it is used for heat and light. 煤油：*a kerosene lamp* 煤油燈

kes·trel /ˈkestrəl/ *noun* a small BIRD OF PREY (= a bird that kills other creatures for food) of the FALCON family 紅隼（小猛禽）

KET /ket/ *noun* [U] the abbreviation for 'Key English Test' (a British test, set by the University of Cambridge, that measures a person's ability to speak and write English as a foreign language at a basic level) 主流初級英語認證（全寫為 Key English Test，由英國劍橋大學命題）

keta·mine /ˈkiːtəmiːn/ (also *informal* **ket** /kiːt/) *noun* [U] a substance that is used as an ANAESTHETIC, and also as a drug that is taken illegally for pleasure 氯胺酮，K 粉（用作麻醉劑，也用作毒品）

ketch /ketʃ/ *noun* a sailing boat with two MASTS (= posts to support the sails) 雙桅帆船

ketchup /ˈketʃəp/ *noun* [U] a thick cold sauce made from tomatoes, usually sold in bottles 番茄醬

ket·tle /ˈketl/ *noun* a container with a lid, handle and a SPOUT, used for boiling water （燒水用的）壺，水壺：*an electric kettle* 電水壺 ◇ (*BrE*) *I'll* ***put the kettle on*** (= start boiling some water) *and make some tea.* 讓我來燒壺水沏茶。➲ VISUAL VOCAB page V25 **IDM** see DIFFERENT, POT *n.*

kettle·drum /ˈketldrʌm/ *noun* a large metal drum with a round bottom and a thin plastic top that can be made looser or tighter to produce different musical notes. A set of kettledrums is usually called TIMPANI. 定音鼓；鍋鼓 ➲ VISUAL VOCAB page V35

Kev·lar™ /ˈkevlɑː(r)/ *noun* [U] an artificial substance used to give strength to tyres and other rubber products 凱夫拉爾合成纖維，克維拉（用於強化輪胎等橡膠製品）

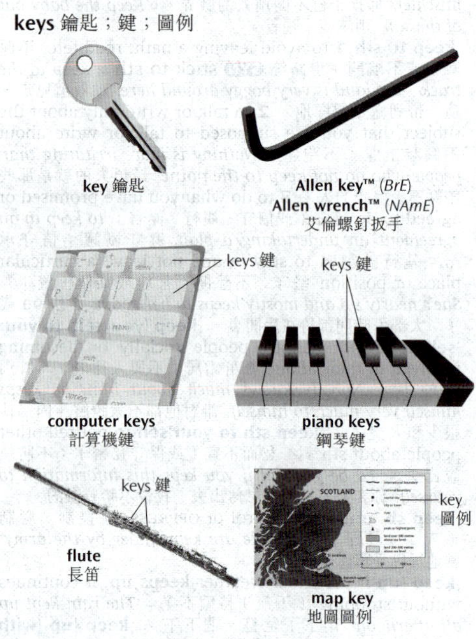

key 🗝 /kiː/ *noun, verb, adj.*

■ ***noun***

▸ **TOOL FOR LOCK** 開鎖工具 **1** 🗝 a specially shaped piece of metal used for locking a door, starting a car, etc. 鑰匙：*to* ***insert/turn the key*** *in the lock* 把鑰匙插入鎖孔；轉動鎖孔中的鑰匙 ◇ *the car keys* 汽車鑰匙 ◇ *a bunch of keys* 一串鑰匙 ◇ *the spare key to the front door* 前門備用鑰匙 ◇ *We'll have a duplicate key cut* (= made). 我們會配一把鑰匙。

▸ **MOST IMPORTANT THING** 最重要的事 **2** 🗝 [usually sing.] a thing that makes you able to understand or achieve sth 關鍵；要訣 **SYN** **secret**：**~ (to sth)** *The key to success is preparation.* 成功的關鍵是準備。◇ **~ (to doing sth)** *The driver of the car probably holds the key to solving the crime.* 這位汽車司機很可能掌握偵破這一罪案的關鍵證據。◇ (*especially NAmE*) ***The key is,*** *how long can the federal government control the inflation rate?* 關鍵在於聯邦政府對通貨膨脹率的控制能維持多久？

▸ **ON COMPUTER** 計算機 **3** 🗝 any of the buttons that you press to operate a computer or TYPEWRITER （計算機或打字機的）鍵：*Press the return key to enter the information.* 按回車鍵錄入信息。

▸ ON MUSICAL INSTRUMENT 樂器 **4** any of the wooden or metal parts that you press to play a piano and some other musical instruments（鋼琴或其他樂器的）鍵 ➲ VISUAL VOCAB page V34
▸ MUSIC 音樂 **5** a set of related notes, based on a particular note. Pieces of music are usually written mainly using a particular key 調：*a sonata in the key of E flat major* 一首降 E 大調奏鳴曲 ➲ compare SCALE *n.* (7)
▸ ANSWERS 答案 **6** a set of answers to exercises or problems 答案；題解：*Check your answers in the key at the back of the book.* 用書後的解答核對答案。
▸ ON MAP 地圖 **7** an explanation of the symbols used on a map or plan （地圖或平面圖的）符號說明，圖例 ➲ see also LOW-KEY IDM see LOCK *n.*
■ *verb* **1** ~ sth (in) | ~ sth (into sth) to put information into a computer using a keyboard 用鍵盤輸入；鍵入 SYN enter：*Key (in) your password.* 用鍵盤輸入密碼。 **2** to deliberately damage a car by scratching it with a key 用鑰匙劃壞（汽車）
PHR V **'key sb/sth to sth** [usually passive] (*especially NAmE*) to make sb/sth suitable or appropriate for a particular purpose 使某人（或某事）適合於某事 SYN gear：*The classes are keyed to the needs of advanced students.* 這些課是針對高年級學生的需要開設的。
■ *adj.* [usually before noun] most important; essential 最重要的；主要的；關鍵的 SYN critical, vital：*the key issue/factor/point* 關鍵問題 / 因素；要點 ◇ *He was a* **key figure** *in the campaign.* 他是這場運動的關鍵人物。◇ *She played a* **key role** *in the dispute.* 她在爭論中起着舉足輕重的作用。◇ *'Caution' is the* **key word** *in this situation.* 在此情形之下，caution 為關鍵詞。◇ *Good communication is key to our success.* 良好的溝通是我們成功的關鍵。◇ *His contribution could be key.* 他的貢獻可能是最重要的。 ➲ SYNONYMS at MAIN

key·board /'kiːbɔːd; *NAmE* -bɔːrd/ *noun, verb*
■ *noun* **1** the set of keys for operating a computer or TYPEWRITER（計算機或打字機的）鍵盤 ➲ VISUAL VOCAB page V66 **2** the set of black and white keys on a piano or other musical instrument（鋼琴或其他樂器的）琴鍵，鍵盤 ➲ VISUAL VOCAB page V36 **3** an electronic musical instrument that has keys like a piano and can be made to play in different styles or to sound like different instruments 鍵盤式電子樂器 ➲ compare SYNTHESIZER
■ *verb* [T, I] ~ (sth) to type information into a computer 用鍵盤輸入；將（信息）鍵入計算機 ▸ **key·board·ing** *noun* [U]

key·board·er /'kiːbɔːdə(r); *NAmE* -bɔːrd-/ *noun* a person whose job is to type data into a computer 操作鍵盤的人；鍵盤輸入員

key·board·ist /'kiːbɔːdɪst; *NAmE* -bɔːrd-/ *noun* a person who plays an electronic musical instrument with a keyboard 鍵盤（樂器）手

'key card *noun* (*especially NAmE*) = SWIPE CARD

ˌkeyed 'up *adj.* [not before noun] nervous and excited, especially before an important event（尤指重要事件前）緊張不安，激動萬分

key·hole /'kiːhəʊl; *NAmE* -hoʊl/ *noun* the hole in a lock that you put a key in 鎖眼；鑰匙孔

ˌkeyhole 'surgery *noun* [U] (*especially BrE*) medical operations which involve only a very small cut being made in the patient's body 微創手術

key·log·ger /'kiːlɒgə(r); *NAmE* -lɔːg-; -lɑːg-/ *noun* (*computing* 計) a computer program that records all the keys that a user hits so that it is possible to discover secret information such as code words 按鍵記錄程序；鍵盤監聽程式

key·note /'kiːnəʊt; *NAmE* -noʊt/ *noun* **1** [usually sing.] the central idea of a book, a speech, etc.（書、演說等的）要旨，主題，基調：*Choice is the keynote of the new education policy.* 新教育政策的主導原則是容許選擇。◇ *a* **keynote speech/speaker** (= a very important one, introducing a meeting or its subject) 主題發言；主要發言人 **2** (*music* 音) the note on which the KEY is based 主音 ▸ **key·noter** *noun*：*For the first time, a woman will be the keynoter at the convention this year.* 在今年的大會上將首次由一位女士當主要發言人。

key·pad /'kiːpæd/ *noun* a small set of buttons with numbers on used to operate a telephone, television, etc.; the buttons on the right of a computer keyboard （用於操作電話、電視等的）小鍵盤；（電話）按鍵；（計算機）輔助鍵盤

key·pal /'kiːpæl/ *noun* (*informal*) a person that you regularly send emails to, often sb you have never met 鍵友（經常用電子郵件聯繫，往往不曾謀面）

'key ring *noun* a small ring that you put keys on to keep them together 鑰匙圈；鑰匙環 ➲ picture at RING[1]

'key signature *noun* (*music* 音) the set of marks at the beginning of a printed piece of music to show what KEY the piece is in 調號 ➲ picture at MUSIC

key·stone /'kiːstəʊn; *NAmE* -stoʊn/ *noun* **1** (*architecture* 建) the central stone at the top of an ARCH that keeps all the other stones in position 拱頂石 ➲ VISUAL VOCAB page V14 **2** [usually sing.] the most important part of a plan or argument that the other parts depend on（計劃、論據的）主旨，基礎

key·stroke /'kiːstrəʊk; *NAmE* -stroʊk/ *noun* a single action of pressing a key on a computer or TYPEWRITER keyboard 擊鍵；按鍵

key·word /'kiːwɜːd; *NAmE* -wɜːrd/ *noun* **1** a word that tells you about the main idea or subject of sth 主題詞：*When you're studying a language, the keyword is patience.* 學習一門語言，最重要的是有耐心。 **2** a word or phrase that you type on a computer keyboard to give an instruction or to search for information about sth 關鍵詞，關鍵字（用於指令或檢索）：*Enter the keyword 'restaurants' and click on Search.* 鍵入關鍵詞 restaurants，點擊 Search 按鈕。

ˌkey 'worker *noun* (*BrE*) a worker in one of the essential services such as health, education or the police 關鍵工作人員（指醫療保健、教育或警察等重要服務行業的工作人員）：*The city council helps key workers find affordable housing.* 市政廳幫助關鍵工作人員尋找可負擔的住房。

kg *abbr.* (*pl.* **kg** or **kgs**) (in writing) kilogram(s) （書寫形式）千克，公斤：*10kg* * 10 公斤

the KGB /ˌkeɪ dʒiː 'biː/ *noun* [sing.] the state security police of the former USSR 克格勃，格別烏（前蘇聯國家安全委員會，為政治警察及安全機構）

khaki /'kɑːki/ *noun* **1** [U] a strong greenish or yellowish brown cloth, used especially for making military uniforms 卡其布（尤用以做軍裝） **2** [U] a dull greenish or yellowish brown colour 暗綠色；黃褐色 **3 khakis** [pl.] (*NAmE*) trousers/pants made from khaki cloth 卡其布長褲；卡其褲：*He wore a pair of baggy khakis.* 他穿了一條寬鬆的卡其褲。 ▸ **khaki** *adj.*：*khaki uniforms* 黃褐色卡其軍裝

khan /kɑːn/ *noun* a title given to rulers in some countries of central Asia 可汗，汗（一些中亞國家統治者或官員的稱號）

khan·ate /'kɑːneɪt/ *noun* **1** the area which is ruled by a khan 可汗的領土 **2** the position of a khan 可汗職位

khanga (also **kanga**) /'kæŋgə/ (also **lesso**) *noun* (*EAfrE*) a large piece of light cloth with designs printed on it and worn by women around the waist and legs or over the head and shoulders 肯加圍巾布（東非女子用作圍腰布或圍巾的印花薄布）

khat /kɑːt/ *noun* [U] the leaves of a plant that grows in Arabia and Africa, which people chew or drink in tea as a drug 阿拉伯茶葉（產於阿拉伯和非洲，有藥用）

khazi /'kɑːzi/ (also **kharzy** /'kɑːzi; *NAmE* 'kɑːrzi/) *noun* (*pl.* **-ies**) (*old-fashioned, BrE, slang*) a toilet 廁所；茅坑

kHz *abbr.* (in writing) KILOHERTZ（書寫形式）千赫（茲）

kia ora /ˌkiə 'ɔːrə/ *exclamation* (*NZE*) a GREETING wishing good health 你好；身體好

KiB *abbr.* (in writing 書寫形式) KIBIBYTE

Kib (also **Kibit**) *abbr.* (in writing 書寫形式) KIBIBIT

kib·bled /'kɪbld/ *adj.* [usually before noun] (of grain 穀粒) crushed into rough pieces 磨成粗粒的；粗磨的

K

kib·butz /kɪˈbʊts/ *noun* (*pl.* **kib·butz·im** /ˌkɪbʊtˈsiːm/) (in Israel) a type of farm or factory where a group of people live together and share all the work, decisions and income 基布兹，集體農場（以色列的共同生活、工作、決策和分配收入的合作農場或工廠）

kibi·bit /ˈkɪbibɪt/ *noun* (*abbr.* **Kib, Kibit**) (*computing* 計) = KILOBIT (2)

kibi·byte /ˈkɪbibaɪt/ *noun* (*abbr.* **KiB**) (*computing* 計) = KILOBYTE (2)

kib·itz /ˈkɪbɪts/ *verb* (*NAmE, informal*) **1** [I, T] (usually *disapproving*) to watch other people doing sth and make comments or give advice about it, often in an annoying way（旁觀者）指手畫腳，多嘴多舌：*It is rude to kibitz during a serious game.* 別人玩正經遊戲時在旁邊指指點點很不禮貌。◇ **~ sth** *I paused to kibitz a poker game.* 我停下來去指點別人玩紙牌。**2** [I] to talk in a friendly informal way 閒聊：*We sat around and kibitzed until about eleven.* 我們圍坐着，一直聊到大約 11 點。▶ **kib·itz·er** *noun*：*The kibitzers were second-guessing each move.* 多嘴的圍觀者對每一步棋都指手畫腳。

kibla = QIBLAH

ki·bosh /ˈkaɪbɒʃ; *NAmE* -bɑːʃ/ *noun* [sing.]
IDM **put the ˈkibosh on sth** (*informal*) to stop sth from happening; to spoil sb's plans 阻止某事發生；挫敗計劃

K

kick 🔑 /kɪk/ *verb, noun*
■ *verb* **1** 🔑 [T, I] to hit sb/sth with your foot 踢；踹：**~ (sb/sth)** *She was punched and kicked by her attackers.* 她遭到襲擊者的拳打腳踢。◇ *Stop kicking—it hurts!* 別踢了，好痛！◇ **~ sb/sth + adv./prep./adj.** *The boys were kicking a ball around in the yard.* 男孩們在院子裏踢球。◇ *Vandals had kicked the door down.* 破壞公物者把門踹倒了。**2** 🔑 [T, I] **~ (sth)** to move your legs as if you were kicking sth 踢蹬；踢（腿）：*The dancers kicked their legs in the air.* 舞蹈員做了空中踢腿的動作。◇ *The child was dragged away,* ***kicking and screaming***. 這孩子又踢又叫地被拖走了。**3** [T] **~ yourself** (*informal*) to be annoyed with yourself because you have done sth stupid, missed an opportunity, etc.（因幹了蠢事、失去良機等）對（自己）生氣：*He'll kick himself when he finds out he could have had the job.* 一旦發現他本可以得到這個工作，他會感到懊惱的。**4** [T] **~ sth** (in sports such as football (SOCCER) and RUGBY 體育運動，如足球和橄欖球) to score points by kicking the ball 踢球得分；射門得分：*to* ***kick a penalty/goal*** 罰球得分；射門得分

IDM **kick (some/sb's) ˈass** (*slang, especially NAmE*) to punish or defeat sb 懲罰，擊敗（某人） **kick the ˈbucket** (*informal or humorous*) to die 死；翹辮子；蹬腿兒 **kick the ˈhabit, ˈdrug, ˈbooze, etc.** to stop doing sth harmful that you have done for a long time 戒除惡習；戒毒；戒酒 **kick your ˈheels** (*BrE*) to have nothing to do while you are waiting for sb/sth 無聊地等待：*We were kicking our heels, waiting for some customers.* 我們百無聊賴地等待顧客光臨。**kick sb in the ˈteeth** to treat sb badly or fail to give them help when they need it 粗暴對待某人；使極度失望 **kick sth into the long ˈgrass/into ˈtouch** (*BrE*) to reject, remove or stop dealing with a problem 擱置；置之不理：*He tends to deal with disputes by kicking them into the long grass.* 他處理爭議的方法往往是置之不理。**kick over the ˈtraces** (*old-fashioned, BrE*) to start to behave badly and refuse to accept any discipline or control（開始）不聽話，不守規矩，不受管束 **kick up a ˈfuss, ˈstink, etc.** (*informal*) to complain loudly about sth 吵鬧；鬧事；起鬨 **kick up your ˈheels** (*informal, especially NAmE*) to be relaxed and enjoy yourself 輕輕鬆鬆；盡情享樂 **kick sb upˈstairs** (*informal*) to move sb to a job that seems to be more important but which actually has less power or influence 使某人明升暗降；以升遷為名排斥某人 **kick sb when they're ˈdown** to continue to hurt sb when they are already defeated, etc. 落井下石 ➲ more at ALIVE, HELL

PHR V **ˌkick aˈbout/aˈround** (*informal*) **1** (usually used in the progressive tenses 通常用於進行時) to be lying somewhere not being used 被閒置；閒置不用：*There's a pen kicking around on my desk somewhere.* 我書桌上什麼地方有支鋼筆老放着。**2** to go from one place to another with no particular purpose（無目的地）四處遊蕩，閒逛，到處走：*They spent the summer kicking around Europe.* 他們在歐洲各地晃悠了一夏天。**ˌkick sb aˈround** (*informal*) to treat sb in a rough or unfair way 粗暴地對待某人；虐待；凌辱 **ˌkick sth aˈbout/aˈround** (*informal*) to discuss an idea, a plan, etc. in an informal way 非正式談論（或討論）某事；隨便談談 **ˈkick against sth** to protest about or resist sth 反對，反抗，抵抗（某事）：*Young people often kick against the rules.* 年輕人常常違反規定。**ˌkick ˈback** (*especially NAmE*) to relax 放鬆：*Kick back and enjoy the summer.* 輕鬆愉快地享受這夏日的時光吧。**ˌkick ˈin** (*informal*) **1** to begin to take effect 開始生效（或見效）：*Reforms will kick in later this year.* 改革將於今年下半年開始見效。**2** (also **ˌkick ˈin sth**) (both *NAmE*) to give your share of money or help 捐獻；捐助；繳付 **ˌkick ˈoff 1** when a football (SOCCER) game or a team, etc. **kicks off**, the game starts（足球比賽等）開球，開始 ➲ related noun KICK-OFF (1) ➲ SYNONYMS at START **2** to suddenly become angry or violent 發怒；動怒 **ˌkick ˈoff (with sth)** (*informal*) to start 開始：*What time shall we kick off?* 我們什麼時候開始？◇ *Tom will kick off with a few comments.* 湯姆講話時要先發表幾點意見。➲ related noun KICK-OFF (2) **ˌkick sth↔ˈoff** to remove sth by kicking 踢開，踢掉（某物）：*to kick off your shoes* 把鞋踢掉 **ˌkick ˈoff sth** to start a discussion, a meeting, an event, etc. 開始進行討論（或會議、項目等）**SYN** open **ˌkick ˈout (at sb/sth) 1** to try to hit sb/sth with your legs because you are angry or upset（因氣憤或心煩意亂）用腳踢（人或物）**2** to react violently to sb/sth that makes you angry or upset（對令人氣憤或煩惱的人或事）作出強烈反應 **ˌkick sb ˈout (of sth)** (*informal*) to make sb leave or go away (from somewhere) 使某人離開；開除；逐出 **ˌkick ˈup** (*especially NAmE*) (of wind or a storm 風或風暴) to become stronger 越來越強；逐漸加強 **ˌkick sth↔ˈup** to make sth, especially dust, rise from the ground 揚起（尤指）塵埃

■ *noun* **1** 🔑 a movement with the foot or the leg, usually to hit sth with the foot 踢；踢腳；踢腿：*the first kick of the game* 比賽的開球 ◇ *She gave him a kick on the shin.* 她朝他的小腿踢了一腳。◇ *He aimed a kick at the dog.* 他對準狗踢了一腳。◇ *If the door won't open, give it a kick.* 門要是打不開就踹一下。◇ (*slang*) *She needs a* ***kick up the backside*** (= she needs to be strongly encouraged to do sth or to behave better). 她需要敲打敲打。➲ see also FREE KICK, PENALTY KICK, SPOT KICK **2** (*informal*) a strong feeling of excitement and pleasure 極度刺激；極度興奮；極大的樂趣 **SYN** thrill：*I* ***get a kick out of*** *driving fast cars.* 開快車給我帶來極大的樂趣。◇ *He* ***gets his kicks from*** *hurting other people.* 他以傷害他人為樂。◇ *What do you do* ***for kicks***? 你以什麼來尋求刺激呢？**3** [usually sing.] (*informal*) the strong effect that a drug or an alcoholic drink has（毒品或酒精的）效力，刺激性：*This drink has quite a kick.* 這酒的勁相當大。

IDM **a kick in the ˈteeth** (*informal*) a great disappointment; sth that hurts sb/sth emotionally 沉重打擊；嚴重挫折

ˈkick-ass (also **ˈass-kicking**) *adj.* (*slang, especially NAmE*) **1** powerful and aggressive 強橫的；粗暴的：*the film's kick-ass heroine* 這部影片潑辣的女主角 ◇ *his reputation as a kick-ass coach* 他那魔鬼教練的名聲 **2** extremely good and successful 極好的；非常成功的：*a kick-ass visual feast* 視覺大餐 ◇ *truly kick-ass quality* 超棒的質量

kick·back /ˈkɪkbæk/ *noun* (*informal, especially NAmE*) money paid illegally to sb in return for work or help（不合法的）回扣，酬金，佣金 **SYN** bribe

kick·ball /ˈkɪkbɔːl/ *noun* [U] a game that is based on BASEBALL in which players kick the ball instead of hitting it with a BAT 踢球戲（按棒球規則進行的足球戲）

ˈkick-boxing *noun* [U] a form of BOXING in which the people fighting each other can kick as well as punch (= hit with their hands) 散打；搏擊操

ˈkick drum *noun* (*informal*) a large drum played using a PEDAL 踏板鼓

kick·er /ˈkɪkə(r)/ *noun* **1** a person who kicks, especially the player in a sports team who kicks the ball to try to score points, for example in RUGBY 踢的人；（尤指）

踢球的運動員 **2** (*NAmE, informal*) a surprising end to a series of events（一連串事情的）意外結局

kick·ing /ˈkɪkɪŋ/ *adj., noun*

▪ **adj.** (*informal*) full of life and excitement 充滿活力的；充滿刺激的；令人興奮的：*The club was really kicking last night.* 昨晚俱樂部真是熱鬧非凡。

▪ **noun** [sing.] an act of kicking sb hard and repeatedly, especially when they are lying on the ground（尤指對躺在地上的人連續的）狠踢，猛踹：*They gave him a good kicking.* 他們狠狠地踢了他一頓。

ˈkick-off *noun* **1** [C, U] the start of a game of football (SOCCER)（足球賽的）開球，開賽：*The kick-off is at 3.* 足球比賽 3 時開球。 **2** [sing.] (*informal*) the start of an activity（活動的）開始，開幕

kick·stand /ˈkɪkstænd/ *noun* a long straight piece of metal fixed to a bicycle or a motorcycle, which is kept horizontal while the bicycle is being ridden but which can be moved to a vertical position when you need to stand the bicycle somewhere（自行車或摩托車的）撐腳架，支架 ➲ VISUAL VOCAB page V51

ˈkick-start *verb, noun*

▪ **verb** **1 ~ sth** to start a motorcycle by pushing down a LEVER with your foot 用腳踏啟動（摩托車） **2 ~ sth** to do sth to help a process or project start more quickly 促使…開始；使（項目）儘快啟動：*The government's attempt to kick-start the economy has failed.* 政府刺激經濟的努力失敗了。

▪ **noun** **1** (also **ˈkick-starter**) the part of a motorcycle that you push down with your foot in order to start it（摩托車的）腳踏啟動器 **2** a quick start that you give to sth by taking some action 迅速開始（採取行動）；快速啟動

ˈkick-turn *noun* **1** (in SKIING 滑雪) a turn made by lifting and turning each SKI separately so that you face the opposite direction 踢轉（分別將兩塊滑雪板翹起轉向所作的調頭） **2** a turn made with the front wheels of a SKATEBOARD off the ground 倒板（使滑板前輪抬起所作的調頭）

kid 🔑 /kɪd/ *noun, verb, adj.*

▪ **noun** **1** 🔑 [C] (*informal*) a child or young person 小孩；年輕人：*A bunch of kids were hanging around outside.* 一群年輕人在外面到處遊逛。◇ *a kid of 15* * 15 歲的年輕人 ◇ *She's a bright kid.* 她是個聰明孩子。◇ *How are the kids* (= your children)? 孩子們好嗎？◇ *Do you have any kids?* 你有孩子嗎？ HELP **Kid** is much more common than **child** in informal and spoken *NAmE*. 在非正式場合和美式英語口語中 kid 遠比 child 常見。 ➲ COLLOCATIONS at CHILD **2** [C] a young GOAT 小山羊 **3** [U] soft leather made from the skin of a young GOAT 小山羊皮革

IDM **handle/treat, etc. sb with kid ˈgloves** to deal with sb in a very careful way so that you do not offend or upset them 小心應付某人 **ˈkids' stuff** (*BrE*) (*NAmE* **ˈkid stuff**) something that is so easy to do or understand that it is thought to be not very serious or only suitable for children 極容易的事；"小兒科"；小孩子都懂得的道理 ➲ more at NEW

▪ **verb** (**-dd-**) (*informal*) **1** [I, T] (usually used in the progressive tenses 通常用於進行時) to tell sb sth that is not true, especially as a joke 戲弄；開玩笑 SYN **joke**：*I thought he was kidding when he said he was going out with a rock star.* 他說他在與一位搖滾樂歌星談戀愛，我還以為他在開玩笑呢。◇ *I didn't mean it. I was **only kidding**.* 我並沒有這個意思，我只是開開玩笑而已。◇ **~ sb** *I'm not kidding you. It does work.* 我不是戲弄你，那的確有效。 **2** [T] to allow sb/yourself to believe sth that is not true 欺騙；哄騙 SYN **deceive**：**~ sb/yourself** *They're kidding themselves if they think it's going to be easy.* 如果他們認為這會很容易，那是自己欺騙自己。◇ **~ sb/yourself (that)** ... *I tried to kid myself (that) everything was normal.* 我試圖讓自己相信一切都正常。

IDM **ˌno ˈkidding** (*informal*) **1** used to emphasize that sth is true or that you agree with sth that sb has just said（強調是真實的或同意別人剛說過的話）真的，可不是：*'It's cold!' 'No kidding!'* "天氣真冷！" "可不是！" **2** used to show that you mean what you are saying（表示認真）不是開玩笑，我說的是真的：*I want the money back tomorrow. No kidding.* 我希望明天錢就能退回來。這可不是開玩笑。 **you're ˈkidding** | **you must be ˈkidding** (*informal*) used to show that you are very surprised at sth that sb has just said（對對方剛說過的話感到非常驚奇）你是在開玩笑吧

PHR V **ˌkid aˈround** (*especially NAmE*) to behave in a silly way 做傻事；裝傻相

▪ **adj.** **~ sister/brother** (*informal, especially NAmE*) a person's younger sister/brother 妹妹；弟弟

kid·die (also **kiddy**) /ˈkɪdi/ (*pl.* **-ies**) *noun* (*informal*) a young child 小孩子；小傢伙：*a kiddies' party* 孩子們的聚會

kid·nap /ˈkɪdnæp/ *verb* (**-pp-**, *US* also **-p-**) **~ sb** to take sb away illegally and keep them as a prisoner, especially in order to get money or sth else for returning them 劫持；綁架 SYN **abduct, seize**：*Two businessmen have been kidnapped by terrorists.* 兩名商人遭恐怖分子綁架。 ▸ **kid·napper** *noun*：*The kidnappers are demanding a ransom of $1 million.* 劫持者索要 100 萬元贖金。 **kid·nap·ping** (also **kid·nap**) *noun* [U, C]：*He admitted the charge of kidnap.* 他對綁架的指控供認不諱。◇ *the kidnapping of 12 US citizens* 對 12 名美國公民的劫持

kid·ney /ˈkɪdni/ *noun* **1** [C] either of the two organs in the body that remove waste products from the blood and produce URINE 腎；腎臟：*a kidney infection* 腎感染 ➲ VISUAL VOCAB page V59 **2** [U, C] the kidneys of some animals that are cooked and eaten（食用的）動物腰子：*steak and kidney pie* 牛肉腰花餡餅

ˈkidney bean *noun* a type of reddish-brown BEAN shaped like a kidney that is usually dried before it is sold and then left in water before cooking 菜豆；芸豆；紅腰豆 ➲ VISUAL VOCAB page V31

ˈkidney machine *noun* a machine that does the work of a KIDNEY for sb whose kidneys are damaged or have been removed 人工腎；血液透析器；血液滲析器

kid·ol·ogy /kɪˈdɒlədʒi; *NAmE* -ˈdɑːl-/ *noun* [U] (*especially BrE, humorous*) the art or practice of making people believe sth which is not true 哄騙（術）；唬弄

kid·ult /ˈkɪdʌlt/ *noun* (*informal*) an adult who likes doing or buying things that are usually thought more suitable for children 童心未泯的成人，大小孩（喜歡做適合兒童做的事或購買適合兒童的物品）

kike /kaɪk/ *noun* (*taboo, slang, especially NAmE*) a very offensive word for a Jew 猶太佬；猶太鬼子

kikoi /kɪˈkɔɪ/ *noun* (*EAfrE*) a large piece of strong coloured cloth used mainly as an item of clothing around the waist and legs or over the shoulders 基科伊厚花布（主要用作圍腰布或披肩）

kilim /kɪˈliːm; ˈkiːlɪm; *NAmE* kiːˈliːm; ˈkɪləm/ (also **kelim**) *noun* a type of Turkish carpet or RUG（土耳其）基里姆地毯

kill 🔑 /kɪl/ *verb, noun*

▪ **verb** **1** 🔑 [T, I] **~ (sb/sth/yourself)** to make sb/sth die 殺死；弄死；導致死亡：*Cancer kills thousands of people every year.* 每年數以千計的人死於癌症。◇ *Three people were killed in the crash.* 三人在此次撞車事故中喪生。◇ *He tried to kill himself with sleeping pills.* 他試圖服安眠藥自殺。◇ *I bought a spray to kill the weeds.* 我買了一種噴劑來除草。◇ (*informal*) *My mother will kill me* (= be very angry with me) *when she finds out.* 我媽要是發現了會宰了我的。◇ *Don't kill yourself trying to get the work done by tomorrow. It can wait.* 別為了趕着明天把事情幹完而累壞身體。這事可以等一等嘛。◇ *Tiredness while driving can kill.* 疲勞駕駛會出人命的。 **2** [T] **~ sth** to destroy or spoil sth or make it stop 毀滅；破壞；扼殺；使停止：*to kill a rumour* 平息謠言 ◇ *Do you agree that television kills conversation?* 電視扼殺人與人之間的交談，你同意這種說法嗎？◇ *The defeat last night killed the team's chances of qualifying.* 昨晚的失敗使這個隊失去了獲得資格的機會。 **3** [T] **~ sb** | **it kills sb to do sth** (*informal*) (usually used in the progressive tenses and not used in the passive 通常用於進行時，不用於被動語態) to cause sb pain or suffering 使痛苦；使疼痛；使受折磨：*My feet are killing me.* 我的腳痛死了。 **4** [T] **~ sb** (*NAmE*) to make sb laugh a lot 使笑得前仰後合；使笑死了：*Stop it! You're killing me!* 別說了！你都把我笑死了！

K

IDM **kill the goose that lays the golden 'egg/'eggs** (*saying*) to destroy sth that would make you rich, successful, etc. 殺雞取卵；竭澤而漁；自絕財源 **,kill or 'cure** (*BrE*) used to say that what you are going to do will either be very successful or fail completely 要麼醫好要麼治死；不是成功便是失敗；成敗在此一舉 **kill 'time | kill an 'hour, a couple of 'hours, etc.** to spend time doing sth that is not important while you are waiting for sth else to happen（等待時）消磨時間，打發時光：*We killed time playing cards.* 我們打紙牌消磨時間。 **kill two birds with one 'stone** to achieve two things at the same time with one action 一石二鳥；一箭雙雕；一舉兩得 **,kill sb/sth with 'kindness** to be so kind to sb/sth that you in fact harm them 寵壞 **,kill yourself 'laughing** (*BrE*) to laugh a lot 樂死人；笑得前仰後合；笑破肚皮：*He was killing himself laughing.* 他笑得前仰後合。 ➲ more at CURIOSITY, DRESSED, LOOK *n.*, TIME *n.*

PHR V **,kill sb/sth↔'off** **1** to make a lot of plants, animals, etc. die 大量殺死，大量消滅（動植物等）：*Some drugs kill off useful bacteria in the user's body.* 某些藥物會殺死服用者體內的有益細菌。 **2** to stop or get rid of sth 使某事物停止；除掉；排除：*He has effectively killed off any political opposition.* 他實際上已消滅了一切對立的政見。

■ **noun** [usually sing.] **1** an act of killing, especially when an animal is hunted or killed 殺死，捕殺（尤指動物）：*A cat often plays with a mouse before the kill.* 貓在咬死老鼠之前常常要耍弄它一番。◇ *The plane prepared to* ***move in for the kill.*** 飛機已作好擊落敵機的準備。◇ *I was* ***in at the kill*** *when she finally lost her job* (= present at the end of an unpleasant process). 我親眼目睹了她最後失去工作的情景。 **2** an animal that has been hunted and killed 被捕殺的動物；獵物：*lions feeding on their kill* 正在吃獵物的獅子

kill·er /ˈkɪlə(r)/ *noun* **1** a person, an animal or a thing that kills 殺人者；殺手；導致死亡的人（或動物、事物）：*Police are hunting his killer.* 警方正在追捕殺害他的兇手。◇ *Heart disease is the biggest killer in Scotland.* 心臟病是蘇格蘭的頭號殺手。◇ *an electric insect killer* 電殺蟲器 ◇ *The players lacked* ***the killer instinct.*** 這些運動員缺乏拚殺本能。 ➲ see also LADYKILLER, SERIAL KILLER **2** (*informal*) something that is very difficult, very exciting or very skilful 棘手的事；令人激動的事物；精彩的事物：*The exam was a real killer.* 這考試可真費勁。◇ *The new movie is a killer.* 這部新影片精彩極了。

,killer appli'cation (also **,killer 'app**) *noun* (*computing* 計) a computer program that is so popular that it encourages people to buy or use the OPERATING SYSTEM, etc. that it runs on 殺手級應用程序（促使人們購買或使用其操作系統等的受歡迎計算機程序）

,killer 'bee *noun* a type of BEE that is very aggressive 非洲蜜蜂（攻擊性強）；非洲殺人蜂

'killer cell *noun* (*biology* 生) a white blood cell which destroys infected cells or cancer cells 殺傷細胞；殺手細胞

'killer whale (also **orca**) *noun* a black and white WHALE that eats meat 逆戟鯨；虎鯨；惡鯨；殺人鯨

kill·ing 0‑ /ˈkɪlɪŋ/ *noun, adj.*

■ **noun** 0‑ an act of killing sb deliberately 故意殺人；謀殺 SYN **murder**：*brutal killings* 殘殺 ➲ COLLOCATIONS at CRIME ➲ see also MERCY KILLING

IDM **,make a 'killing** (*informal*) to make a lot of money quickly 發大財；獲取暴利；財運亨通

■ **adj.** making you very tired 使人筋疲力盡的 SYN **exhausting**：*a killing schedule* 排得滿滿當當的時間表

'killing fields *noun* [pl.] a place where very many people were killed, for example during a war 大屠殺之地；殺戮戰場

kill·joy /ˈkɪldʒɔɪ/ *noun* (*disapproving*) a person who likes to spoil other people's enjoyment 使人掃興的人；大煞風景的人

kiln /kɪln/ *noun* a large oven for baking CLAY and bricks, drying wood and grain, etc. 窰

kilo /ˈkiːləʊ; *NAmE* ˈkiːloʊ/ *noun* (*pl.* **-os**) = KILOGRAM

kilo- /ˈkɪləʊ; *NAmE* ˈkɪloʊ/ *combining form* (in nouns; used in units of measurement 構成名詞，用於計量單位) **1** one thousand 千：*kilojoule* 千焦耳 **2** 2^{10}, or 1 024 千（二進制，等於 1 024）

kilo·bit /ˈkɪləbɪt/ *noun* (*abbr.* **Kb**, **Kbit**) (*computing* 計) **1** a unit for measuring computer memory or data, equal to 10^3, or 1 000 BITS 千比特（十進制計算機內存或數據的單位，等於 1 000 比特）➲ see also KBPS **2** (also **kibi·bit**) a unit for measuring computer memory or data, equal to 2^{10}, or 1 024 BITS 千比特（二進制計算機內存或數據的單位，等於 1 024 比特）

kilo·byte /ˈkɪləbaɪt/ *noun* (*abbr.* **K**, **KB**) (*computing* 計) **1** a unit for measuring computer memory or data, equal to 10^3, or 1 000 BYTES 千字節（十進制計算機內存或數據單位，等於 1 000 字節） **2** (also **kibi·byte**) a unit for measuring computer memory or data, equal to 2^{10}, or 1 024 BYTES 千字節（二進制計算機內存或數據單位，等於 1 024 字節）

kilo·gram 0‑ (*BrE* also **kilo·gramme**) /ˈkɪləɡræm/ (also **kilo**) *noun* (*abbr.* **kg**) a unit for measuring weight; 1 000 grams 千克；公斤：*2 kilograms of rice* * 2 公斤大米 ◇ *Flour is sold by the kilogram.* 麪粉按公斤出售。

kilo·hertz /ˈkɪləhɜːts; *NAmE* -hɜːrts/ *noun* (*abbr.* **kHz**) (*pl.* **kilo·hertz**) a unit for measuring radio waves 千赫（茲）

kilo·joule /ˈkɪlədʒuːl/ *noun* (*abbr.* **kJ**) a measurement of the energy that you get from food; 1 000 JOULES 千焦（耳）（食物能量單位）

kilo·metre 0‑ (*especially US* **kilo·meter**) /ˈkɪləmiːtə(r); *BrE* also kɪˈlɒmɪtə(r); *NAmE* also kɪˈlɑːm-/ *noun* (*abbr.* **k**, **km**) a unit for measuring distance; 1 000 metres 千米；公里

kilo·watt /ˈkɪləwɒt; *NAmE* -wɑːt/ *noun* (*abbr.* **kW**) a unit for measuring electrical power; 1 000 WATTS 千瓦（電的功率計量單位，等於 1 000 瓦特）

,kilowatt-'hour *noun* (*abbr.* **kWh**) a unit for measuring electrical energy equal to the power provided by one kilowatt in one hour 千瓦時；一度（電）

kilt /kɪlt/ *noun* a skirt made of TARTAN cloth that reaches to the knees and is traditionally worn by Scottish men; a similar skirt worn by women（蘇格蘭傳統男式）短褶裙；女式蘇格蘭格呢短褶裙

kilt·ed /ˈkɪltɪd/ *adj.* wearing a kilt 身着蘇格蘭格呢褶裙的

kil·ter /ˈkɪltə(r)/ *noun* [U]

IDM **out of 'kilter** **1** not agreeing with or the same as sth else（與…）不一致，不同：*His views are out of kilter with world opinion.* 他的觀點與世人的看法不一樣。 **2** no longer continuing or working in the normal way 不正常；失常：*Long flights throw my sleeping pattern out of kilter for days.* 長途飛行使我的睡眠習慣給打亂了好幾天。

ki·mono /kɪˈməʊnəʊ; *NAmE* kɪˈmoʊnoʊ/ *noun* (*pl.* **-os**) (from *Japanese*) a traditional Japanese piece of clothing like a long loose dress with wide sleeves, worn on formal occasions; a DRESSING GOWN or ROBE in this style（日本的）和服；和服式晨衣

kin /kɪn/ *noun* [pl.] (*old-fashioned* or *formal*) your family or your relatives（統稱）家屬，親屬，親戚 ➲ compare KINDRED ➲ see also NEXT OF KIN IDM see KITH

kind 0‑ /kaɪnd/ *noun, adj.*

■ **noun** 0‑ [C, U] a group of people or things that are the same in some way; a particular variety or type 同類的人（或事物）；種類：*three kinds of cakes/cake* 三種蛋糕 ◇ *music of* ***all/various/different kinds*** 各種類型的 / 不同種類的音樂 ◇ *Exercises of this kind are very popular.* 這種體育活動非常流行。◇ *What kind of house do you live in?* 你住的房子是哪一種？◇ *They sell all* ***kinds of things.*** 他們出售各種各樣的東西。◇ *The school is the first* ***of its kind*** *in Britain.* 這是英國同類學校中最早的一所。◇ *She isn't* ***that kind of*** *girl.* 她不是那種類型的女孩。◇ *The regions differ in size, but not* ***in kind.*** 這些地區大小各異，但類型相同。◇ *I need to buy paper and pencils, that* ***kind of thing.*** 我需要買紙和鉛筆之類的東西。◇ *I'll never have* ***that kind of*** *money* (= as much money as that). 我永遠不會有那麼多的錢。◇ (*formal*) *Would you like a drink of* ***some kind?*** 您想喝點什麼嗎？

IDM **in 'kind** **1** (of a payment 支付) consisting of goods or services, not money 以實物支付；以貨代款；以服務償付 **2** (*formal*) with the same thing 以同樣的方法（或手段）：*She insulted him and he responded in kind.* 她侮辱了他，他也以其人之道還治其人之身。 **a 'kind of** (*informal*) used to show that sth you are saying is not exact（表示不確切）某種，幾分，隱約：*I had a kind of feeling this might happen.* 我當時就隱約地感到會出這樣的事。 **'kind of** (*informal*) (also **'kinda** /'kaɪndə/) slightly; in some ways 稍微；有幾分；有點兒：*That made me feel kind of stupid.* 那使我感到有點兒愚蠢。◇ *I like him, kind of.* 我有點兒喜歡他。 **nothing of the 'kind/'sort** used to emphasize that the situation is very different from what has been said（強調情況與所說的大不相同）決不是那麼回事，一點也不，才不哩；沒有的事：*'I was terrible!' 'You were nothing of the kind.'* "我那時糟透了！" "你才不哩。" **of a 'kind** **1** (*disapproving*) not as good as it could be 不怎麼樣，徒有其名（指不如本應有的那麼好）：*You're making progress of a kind.* 你也算是有點進步的。 **2** very similar 同一類的；類似的：*They're two of a kind—both workaholics!* 他們倆一個樣，都是工作狂！ **one of a 'kind** the only one like this 獨一無二；獨特 **SYN** **unique**：*My father was one of a kind—I'll never be like him.* 我的父親很獨特，我決不會像他的。 **something of the/that 'kind** something like what has been said（與所言）類似的事物：*'He's resigning.' 'I'd suspected something of the kind.'* "他要辭職了。" "我料到會有這樣的事。"

■ ***adj.*** (**kind·er**, **kind·est**) **1** 🔑 caring about others; gentle, friendly and generous 體貼的；慈祥的；友好的；寬容的：*a very kind and helpful person* 肯幫忙的好人 ◇ *a kind heart/face* 仁慈的心；友好的面容 ◇ *a kind action/gesture/comment* 友好的行為／姿態／評論 ◇ *You've been very kind.* 你真是體貼入微。◇ **~ (to sb/sth)** *kind to animals* 愛護動物 ◇ (*figurative*) *Soft water is kinder to your hair.* 軟性水質不易損傷頭髮。◇ (*figurative*) *The weather was very kind to us.* 天氣非常宜人。◇ **~ (of sb) (to do sth)** *It was really kind of you to help me.* 你幫我的忙，我太感激了。◇ (*formal*) *Thank you for your kind invitation.* 感謝你的盛情邀請。◇ (*formal*) *'Do have another.' 'That's very kind of you* (= thank you).' "一定要再來一份。" "太謝謝你了。" **OPP** **unkind** **2** 🔑 (*formal*) used to make a polite request or give an order（客氣請求或命令）：*Would you be kind enough to close the window?* 請把窗子關上好嗎？➲ see also KINDLY, KINDNESS

kin·der /'kɪndə(r)/ *noun* (*AustralE*, *informal*) = KINDERGARTEN

kin·der·gar·ten /'kɪndəgɑːtn; *NAmE* -dərgɑːrtn/ *noun* (from *German*) **1** (*especially NAmE*) a school or class to prepare children aged five for school 學前班 **2** (*BrE*, *AustralE*, *NZE*) = NURSERY SCHOOL

ˌkind-'hearted *adj.* kind and generous 仁慈的；善良的；寬容的；好心的

kin·dle /'kɪndl/ *verb* **1** [I, T] to start burning; to make a fire start burning 開始燃燒；點燃：*We watched as the fire slowly kindled.* 我們看着火慢慢地燃燒起來。◇ **~ sth** *to* ***kindle a fire/flame*** 點火；點燃火焰 **2** [T, I] **~ (sth)** to make sth such as an interest, emotion, etc. start to grow in sb; to start to be felt by sb 激起（興趣、感情等）；發展起來；被感受到：*It was her teacher who kindled her interest in music.* 是她的老師激發了她對音樂的興趣。◇ *Suspicion kindled within her.* 她漸漸產生了懷疑。

kind·ling /'kɪndlɪŋ/ *noun* [U] small dry pieces of wood, etc. used to start a fire 引火柴；引火物

kind·ly 🔑 /'kaɪndli/ *adv.*, *adj.*

■ ***adv.*** **1** 🔑 in a kind way 體貼地；慈祥地；友好地；寬容地：*She spoke kindly to them.* 她與他們親切交談。◇ *He has kindly agreed to help.* 他友好地答應幫忙。 **2** 🔑 (*old-fashioned, formal*) used to ask or tell sb to do sth, especially when you are annoyed（尤用於煩惱時請人或讓人做某事）勞駕，請：*Kindly leave me alone!* 請不要打擾我！◇ *Visitors are kindly requested to sign the book.* 敬請參觀者在這本冊子上簽名。

IDM **look 'kindly on/upon sth/sb** (*formal*) to approve of sth/sb 贊同，接受，認可（某事或人）：*He hoped they would look kindly on his request.* 他希望他們接受他的請求。 **not take 'kindly to sth/sb** to not like sth/sb 不喜歡某事物／人：*She doesn't take kindly to sudden change.* 她不喜歡突然的改變。

■ ***adj.*** [only before noun] (*old-fashioned* or *literary*) kind and caring 和善的；親切的；關懷的；體貼的 ▸ **kind·li·ness** *noun* [U]

kind·ness 🔑 /'kaɪndnəs/ *noun* **1** 🔑 [U] the quality of being kind 仁慈；善良；體貼；寬容：*to treat sb with kindness and consideration* 待人體貼周到 **2** [C] a kind act 友好（或仁慈、體貼）的舉動：*I can never repay your many kindnesses to me.* 我無法報答你對我無微不至的關懷。 **IDM** see KILL *v.*, MILK *n.*

kin·dred /'kɪndrəd/ *noun*, *adj.*

■ ***noun*** (*old-fashioned* or *formal*) **1** [pl.] your family and relatives（統稱）家人，親屬 ➲ compare KIN **2** [U] the fact of being related to another person 親屬關係；血緣關係：*ties of kindred* 親屬關係

■ ***adj.*** [only before noun] (*formal*) very similar; related 類似的；相似的；相關的；有血緣關係的：*food and kindred products* 食物及類似產品 ◇ *I knew I'd found* ***a kindred spirit*** (= a person with similar ideas, opinions, etc.). 我知道我找到了志同道合的人。

kindy /'kɪndi/ *noun* (*pl.* **-ies**) (*AustralE*, *NZE*, *informal*) = KINDERGARTEN

kin·esis /kɪ'niːsɪs; kaɪ-/ *noun* [U] (*technical* 術語) movement 運動；動作

kin·et·ic /kɪ'netɪk; *BrE* also kaɪ-/ *adj.* [usually before noun] (*technical* 術語) of or produced by movement 運動的；運動引起的：*kinetic energy* 動能

kiˌnetic 'art *noun* [U] (*art* 美術) art, especially SCULPTURE, with parts that move 動態藝術（尤指雕刻）

Grammar Point 語法說明

kind / sort

- Use the singular (**kind/sort**) or plural (**kinds/sorts**) depending on the word you use before them. 用單數（kind/sort）還是複數（kinds/sorts）取決於之前的用詞：*each/one/every kind of animal* 每一種／一種／每一種動物 ◇ *all/many/other sorts of animals* 所有／許多／其他種類的動物
- **Kind/sort of** is followed by a singular or uncountable noun. * kind/sort of 後接單數名詞或不可數名詞：***This kind of question*** *often appears in the exam.* 這類問題在考試中經常出現。◇ ***That sort of behaviour*** *is not acceptable.* 那樣的行為是不允許的。
- **Kinds/sorts of** is followed by a plural or uncountable noun. * kinds/sorts of 後接複數名詞或不可數名詞：***These kinds of questions*** *often appear in the exam.* 這幾類問題在考試中經常出現。◇ ***These sorts of behaviour*** *are not acceptable.* 這種行為是不允許的。
- Other variations are possible but less common. 亦可能有其他結構，只是較少見：***These kinds of question*** *often appear in the exam.* 此類問題在考試中經常出現。◇ ***These sort of things*** *don't happen in real life.* 這類事情在現實生活中不會發生。(This example is very informal and is considered incorrect by some people. 此例很不正式，有些人認為不正確。)
- Note also that these examples are possible, especially in spoken English. 另注意下列例句，尤其在英語口語中可能出現：*The shelf was full of the* ***sort of books*** *I like to read.* 書架上擺滿了我喜歡讀的那種書。◇ *He faced* ***the same kind of problems*** *as his predecessor.* 他面臨着與他的前任同樣的問題。◇ *There are many* ***different sorts of animal*** *on the island.* 島上有許多不同種類的動物。◇ ***What kind of camera*** *is this?* 這是哪種型號的照相機？◇ ***What kind/kinds of cameras*** *do you sell?* 你們賣哪種／哪些型號的照相機？◇ *There were* ***three kinds of cakes/cake*** *on the plate.* 盤子上有三種蛋糕。

king 🔑 /kɪŋ/ *noun*
1 🔑 the male ruler of an independent state that has a royal family 君主；國王：*the kings and queens of England* 英國國王和王后 ◇ *to* ***be crowned king*** 接受加冕為國王 ◇ *King George V* 國王喬治五世 **2 ~ (of sth)** a person, an animal or a thing that is thought to be the best or most important of a particular type（人、動物、事物中的）首屈一指者，最重要者，大王：*the king of comedy* 喜劇之王 ◇ *The lion is the king of the jungle.* 獅子是叢林之王。 **3** used in compounds with the names of animals or plants to describe a very large type of the thing mentioned（與動植物名稱連用構成複合詞，表示巨型）…之最，…之王，巨型…：*a king penguin* 帝王企鵝 **4** the most important piece used in the game of CHESS, that can move one square in any direction（國際象棋中的）王 ➲ VISUAL VOCAB page V38 **5** a PLAYING CARD with the picture of a king on it（紙牌中的）老 K ➲ VISUAL VOCAB page V37
IDM **a ˌking's ˈransom** (*literary*) a very large amount of money 一筆巨款 **SYN** **fortune** **IDM** see EVIDENCE, UNCROWNED

king·dom /ˈkɪŋdəm/ *noun* **1** a country ruled by a king or queen 王國：*the United Kingdom* 聯合王國 ◇ *the kingdom of God* (= heaven) 天國 **2** an area controlled by a particular person or where a particular thing or idea is important 管轄範圍；領域 **3** one of the three traditional divisions of the natural world 自然三界之一：*the animal, vegetable and mineral kingdoms* 動物界、植物界及礦物界 **4** (*biology* 生) one of the five major groups into which all living things are organized 界（生物的五大類別之一）
IDM **blow sb/sth to kingdom ˈcome** (*informal*) to completely destroy sb/sth with an explosion 送…上西天；徹底炸毀 **till/until kingdom ˈcome** (*old-fashioned*) for ever 永遠；永久

king·fish /ˈkɪŋfɪʃ/ *noun* a long FRESHWATER fish with two parts that function as lungs and make it able to breathe air 王魚

king·fish·er /ˈkɪŋfɪʃə(r)/ *noun* a bird with a long beak, that catches fish in rivers. The European kingfisher is small and brightly coloured and the American kingfisher is larger and blue-grey in colour. 翠鳥

ˈking-hit *noun* (*AustralE, NZE, informal*) a hard KNOCKOUT blow 打倒對手的重擊；重拳 ▸ **ˈking-hit** *verb* **(-tt-) ~ sb**

king·ly /ˈkɪŋli/ *adj.* (*literary*) like a king; connected with or good enough for a king 國王似的；國王的；君主的；適合於君主身分的 **SYN** **regal**

king·maker /ˈkɪŋmeɪkə(r)/ *noun* a person who has a very strong political influence and is able to bring sb else to power as a leader 能扶植領導人的有影響人物；政界元老

king·pin /ˈkɪŋpɪn/ *noun* the most important person in an organization or activity（組織或活動中的）主要人物，領袖

ˌKing's ˈBench *noun* the word for QUEEN'S BENCH when the UK has a king 王座法庭，王座法院（英國高等法院的一部份，女王在位時稱 Queen's Bench）

ˌKing's ˈCounsel *noun* = KC

ˌKing's ˈEnglish *noun* [U] the word for QUEEN'S ENGLISH when the UK has a king 標準英語，規範英語（女王在位時稱 Queen's English）

ˌKing's ˈevidence *noun* [U] the word for QUEEN'S EVIDENCE when the UK has a king（刑事被告向法庭提供的）對同案犯不利的證據（女王在位時稱 Queen's evidence）

king·ship /ˈkɪŋʃɪp/ *noun* [U] the state of being a king; the official position of a king 國王身分；王位

ˈking-size (also **ˈking-sized**) *adj.* [usually before noun] very large; larger than normal when compared with a range of sizes 特大的；大於正常尺寸的：*a king-size bed* 特大號牀 ◇ *a king-sized headache* 特別厲害的頭痛

the ˌKing's ˈspeech *noun* the word for THE QUEEN'S SPEECH when the UK has a king 英王施政演說（議會期間開始時發表，女王在位時稱 the Queen's speech）

kink /kɪŋk/ *noun, verb*
■ ***noun*** **1** a bend or twist in sth that is usually straight（直線物體上的）彎，結：*a dog with a kink in its tail* 尾巴上有個結的狗 ◇ (*figurative*) *We need to iron out the kinks in the new system.* 我們需要理順新制度中的一些問題。 **2** (*informal, disapproving*) an unusual feature in a person's character or mind, especially one that does not seem normal 怪癖；怪念頭；奇想 **3** (*NAmE*) = CRICK
■ ***verb*** [I, T] **~ (sth)** to develop or make sth develop a bend or twist（使）彎曲，扭結，絞纏

kinky /ˈkɪŋki/ *adj.* (*informal*, usually *disapproving*) used to describe sexual behaviour that most people would consider strange or unusual 性行為變態的；性行為反常的

kins·folk /ˈkɪnzfəʊk; *NAmE* -foʊk/ *noun* [pl.] (*formal* or *old-fashioned*) a person's relatives（統稱個人的）親戚，親屬

kin·ship /ˈkɪnʃɪp/ *noun* (*formal*) **1** [U] the fact of being related in a family 親屬關係：*the ties of kinship* 親屬關係 **2** [U, sing.] a feeling of being close to sb because you have similar origins or attitudes（因出身或態度相似而產生的）親切感 **SYN** **affinity**

kins·man /ˈkɪnzmən/, **kins·woman** /ˈkɪnzwʊmən/ *nouns* (*pl.* **-men** /-mən/, **-women** /-wɪmɪn/) (*old-fashioned* or *literary*) a relative 親屬；親戚

kiondo /ˈkjɒndɒ; *NAmE* ˈkjɑːndɑː/ *noun* (*pl.* **-os**) (*EAfrE*) a bag with one or two long handles and made from SISAL (= dried grass twisted together) or other materials（用劍麻繩等編的）長帶挎包，長帶提包

kiosk /ˈkiːɒsk; *NAmE* -ɑːsk/ *noun* **1** a small shop/store, open at the front, where newspapers, drinks, etc. are sold. In some countries kiosks also sell food and things used in the home.（出售報紙、飲料等的）小亭；售貨亭；報刊亭 **SYN** **stand** **2** (*old-fashioned, BrE*) a public telephone box 公用電話亭 **SYN** **booth**

kip /kɪp/ *noun, verb*
■ ***noun*** [U, C, usually sing.] (*BrE, informal*) sleep 睡覺：*I must get some kip.* 我得睡會兒覺。◇ *Why don't you have a quick kip?* 你為什麼不小睡一會兒呢？
■ ***verb*** **(-pp-)** [I] (*BrE, informal*) to sleep 睡覺：*You can kip on the sofa, if you like.* 你想睡可以睡在沙發上。

kip·pa (also **kipa**, **kipah**, **kip·pah**) /kɪˈpɑː/ *noun* = YARMULKE

kip·per /ˈkɪpə(r)/ *noun* a HERRING (= a type of fish) that has been preserved using salt, then smoked（醃曬）煙熏鯡魚

ˌkipper ˈtie *noun* (*BrE*) a brightly coloured tie that is very wide 鮮豔寬大的領帶

Kir™ /kɪə(r); kɪr/ *noun* [U, C] a drink that is a mixture of white wine and a LIQUEUR (= a strong sweet alcoholic drink) made with BLACKCURRANTS 基爾酒（用白葡萄酒與黑加侖子酒調配而成）

kirby grip /ˈkɜːbi grɪp; *NAmE* ˈkɜːrbi/ *noun* (*BrE*) = HAIRGRIP

kirk /kɜːk; *NAmE* kɜːrk/ *noun* **1** [C] (*ScotE*) church 教堂：*the parish kirk* 堂區教堂 **2 the Kirk** [sing.] a name often used for the official Church of Scotland 蘇格蘭教會

kir·pan /kɪəˈpɑːn; *NAmE* kɪr-/ *noun* a pointed knife that is worn by SIKH men as a sign of their religion（錫克族男子佩帶的）聖刀

kirsch /kɪəʃ; *NAmE* kɪrʃ/ *noun* [U] a strong alcoholic drink made from CHERRIES 櫻桃白蘭地；櫻桃酒

kis·met /ˈkɪzmet/ *noun* [U] (*literary*) the idea that everything that happens to you in your life is already decided and that you cannot do anything to change or control it 命運；天命 **SYN** **destiny, fate**

kiss 🔑 /kɪs/ *verb, noun*
■ ***verb*** **1** 🔑 [I, T] to touch sb with your lips as a sign of love, affection, sexual desire, etc., or when saying hello or goodbye 親吻；接吻：*They stood in a doorway kissing* (= kissing each other). 他們站在門口親吻。◇ *Do people in Britain kiss when they meet?* 英國人見面時親吻嗎？

◇ **~ sb** *Go and kiss your mother goodnight.* 去親親你母親祝她晚安。◇ *She kissed him on both cheeks.* 她吻了吻他的雙頰。◇ *He lifted the trophy up and kissed it.* 他舉起獎杯吻了一下。➲ see also AIR KISS **2** [T] **~ sth** (*literary*) to gently move or touch sth 輕拂；輕觸：*The sunlight kissed the warm stones.* 陽光灑落在温暖的石塊上。

IDM **,kiss and 'tell** a way of referring to sb talking publicly, usually for money, about a past sexual relationship with sb famous（通常為了獲利）泄露與名人的私情 **kiss sb's 'arse** (*BrE*) (*NAmE* **kiss sb's 'ass**, **kiss 'ass**) (*taboo*, *slang*) to be very nice to sb in order to persuade them to help you or to give you sth 諂媚巴結某人；拍某人馬屁；奉承某人 **HELP** A more polite way to express this is **lick sb's boots.** 較禮貌的表達法是 lick sb's boots。**,kiss sth 'better** (*informal*) to take away the pain of an injury by kissing it 以吻消除疼痛；親一親就不痛了：*Come here and let me kiss it better.* 過來讓我親一親就不疼了。**kiss sth good'bye | kiss good'bye to sth** (*informal*) to accept that you will lose sth or be unable to do sth 任其失去；放棄某事物；承認對某事無能為力：*Well, you can kiss goodbye to your chances of promotion.* 嗳，你就甭想晉升了。

PHR V **,kiss sth↔a'way** to stop sb feeling sad or angry by kissing them 以吻消除（某人的悲傷或怒氣）：*He kissed away her tears.* 他吻了吻她，她就不哭了。

■ ***noun*** 🗝 the act of kissing sb/sth 吻：*Come here and **give me a kiss!*** 過來親親我吧！◇ *a kiss on the cheek* 在面頰上的一吻 ◇ *We were greeted with **hugs and kisses**.* 我們受到歡迎，又是擁抱，又是親吻。

IDM **the kiss of 'death** (*informal*, especially *humorous*) an event that seems good, but is certain to make sth else fail 貌似有利卻肯定會在別處導致失利的事物；表面有利實則有害的事物 **the kiss of 'life** (*BrE*) a method of helping sb who has stopped breathing to breathe again by placing your mouth on theirs and forcing air into their lungs 人工呼吸（口對口）**SYN** **mouth-to-mouth resuscitation** **IDM** see STEAL *v.*

kis·ser /'kɪsə(r)/ *noun* **1** **good, bad, etc. ~** a person who is very good, bad, etc. at kissing 善於（或不善於等）接吻的人 **2** (*informal*) a person's mouth 嘴巴

'kiss-off *noun* [usually sing.] (*NAmE*, *informal*) an occasion when sb is suddenly told they are no longer wanted, especially by a lover or by a company（關係等的）突然終止；解雇：*She gave her husband the kiss-off.* 她突然向丈夫提出了離婚。◇ *He got the kiss-off from his job.* 他突然被解雇了。

kisso·gram /'kɪsəgræm/ *noun* a humorous message on your birthday, etc., delivered by sb dressed in a special COSTUME who kisses you, arranged as a surprise by your friends 賀吻（為帶來驚喜，由穿着特別服裝者親吻致賀生日等）

the 'KISS principle *noun* [sing.] (*especially US*) the idea that products and advertising should be as simple as possible（產品與廣告的）最簡原則，單純原則 **ORIGIN** Formed from the first letters of the expression 'Keep it simple, stupid'. 以 Keep it simple, stupid 的首字母組合而成。

Ki·swa·hili /,kiːswə'hiːli; ,kɪswɑː'h-/ *noun* [U] = SWAHILI

kit /kɪt/ *noun, verb*

■ ***noun*** **1** [C] a set of parts ready to be made into sth 配套元件：*a kit for a model plane* 一套飛機模型元件 **2** [C, U] a set of tools or equipment that you use for a particular purpose 成套工具；成套設備：*a first-aid kit* 一套急救用品 ◇ *a drum kit* 一套擊鼓用具 ➲ SYNONYMS at EQUIPMENT ➲ see also TOOLKIT **3** [U] (*BrE*) a set of clothes and equipment that you use for a particular activity 全套衣服及裝備：*sports kit* 運動用品

IDM **get your 'kit off** (*BrE*, *slang*) to take your clothes off 把你的衣服都脱掉 ➲ more at CABOODLE

■ ***verb*** (-tt-)

PHR V **,kit sb 'out/'up (in/with sth)** [usually passive] (*BrE*) to give sb the correct clothes and/or equipment for a particular activity（為特定活動而）使某人裝備起來：*They were all kitted out in brand-new ski outfits.* 他們都一身全新的滑雪裝備。

kit·bag /'kɪtbæg/ *noun* (*especially BrE*) a long narrow bag, usually made of CANVAS in which soldiers, etc. carry their clothes and other possessions（士兵等的）行囊，背包

kit·chen 🗝 /'kɪtʃɪn/ *noun*

a room in which meals are cooked or prepared 廚房：*She's in the kitchen.* 她在廚房裏。◇ *We ate at the kitchen table.* 我們在廚房裏的桌子上吃飯。➲ VISUAL VOCAB page V25 ➲ see also SOUP KITCHEN

IDM **everything but the kitchen 'sink** (*informal*, *humorous*) a very large number of things, probably more than is necessary 過多的東西；大量的東西 ➲ more at HEAT *n.*

kit·chen·ette /,kɪtʃɪ'net/ *noun* a small room or part of a room used as a kitchen, for example in a flat/apartment 小廚房；套房裏用作廚房的一角

,kitchen 'garden *noun* (*BrE*) a part of a garden/yard where you grow vegetables and fruit for your own use 家庭菜園；花園中用作種蔬菜水果的部份

'kitchen paper (also **'kitchen roll**, **'kitchen towel**) (all *BrE*) (*NAmE* **,paper 'towel**) *noun* [U] thick paper on a roll, used for cleaning up liquid, food, etc. 廚房用捲紙 ➲ VISUAL VOCAB page V25

,kitchen 'porter *noun* (*BrE*) a person who works in the kitchen of a restaurant, hotel, etc., washing plates and doing other simple jobs（飯店、旅館等的）廚房雜務工

,kitchen-'sink *adj.* [only before noun] (of plays, films, novels, etc. 戲劇、電影、小説等) dealing with ordinary life and ordinary people, especially when this involves describing the boring or difficult side of their lives 生活化的；描寫普通人的生活的；揭示現實灰暗面的：*a kitchen-sink drama* 生活化戲劇

kit·chen·ware /'kɪtʃɪnweə(r); *NAmE* -wer/ *noun* [U] used in shops/stores to describe objects that you use in a kitchen, such as pans, bowls, etc.（商店用語）廚房用具

kite /kaɪt/ *noun, verb*

■ ***noun*** **1** a toy made of a light frame covered with paper, cloth, etc., that you fly in the air at the end of one or more long strings 風箏：*to fly a kite* 放風箏 ➲ VISUAL VOCAB page V37 **2** a BIRD OF PREY (= a bird that kills other creatures for food) of the HAWK family 鳶（猛禽）

IDM see FLY *v.*, HIGH *adj.*

■ ***verb*** **~ sth** (*NAmE*, *informal*) to use an illegal cheque to obtain money or to dishonestly change the amount written on a cheque 使用（非法支票）騙錢；塗改（支票）：*to kite checks* 用支票詐騙 ◇ *check kiting* 支票作弊

kite·surf·ing /'kaɪtsɜːfɪŋ; *NAmE* -sɜːrf-/ (also **kite·board·ing** /'kaɪtbɔːdɪŋ; *NAmE* -bɔːrd-/) *noun* [U] the sport of riding on water while standing on a short wide board and being pulled along by wind power, using a large kite 風箏衝浪（運動）➲ VISUAL VOCAB page V50

kith /kɪθ/ *noun*

IDM **kith and kin** (*old-fashioned*) friends and relatives 親戚朋友

kitsch /kɪtʃ/ *noun* [U] (*disapproving*) works of art or objects that are popular but that are considered to have no real artistic value and to be lacking in good taste, for example because they are SENTIMENTAL 庸俗的藝術作品；無真正藝術價值的作品；品位不高的傷感作品 ▸ **kitsch** (also **kitschy**) *adj.*

kit·ten /'kɪtn/ *noun* a young cat 小貓

IDM **have 'kittens** (*BrE*, *informal*) to be very anxious, angry or upset about sth 焦慮；煩躁；心慌意亂

'kitten heels *noun* [pl.] small thin curved heels on women's shoes（女鞋的）弧狀細矮跟 ➲ VISUAL VOCAB page V64

kit·ten·ish /'kɪtnɪʃ/ *adj.* (*old-fashioned*) (of a woman 女人) lively, and trying to attract men's attention 搔首弄姿的；賣弄風情的

kit·ti·wake /'kɪtɪweɪk/ *noun* a bird that lives in groups on sea CLIFFS 三趾鷗（海洋鷗類，營巢於懸崖）

kitty /'kɪti/ *noun* (*pl.* **-ies**) **1** (*informal*) if money is put in a **kitty**, a group of people all give an amount and the money is spent on sth they all agree on 共同湊集的一筆錢：*We each put £50 in the kitty to cover the bills.* 我們

K

每人湊 50 英鎊支付賬單。 **2** (in card games, etc. 紙牌遊戲等) the sum of money that all the players bet, which is given to the winner 全部賭注 **3** (*informal*) a way of referring to a cat 貓咪；小貓

ˌkitty-ˈcorner(ed) *adj., adv.* (*NAmE, informal*) = CATTY-CORNER(ED)

kiwi /ˈkiːwiː/ *noun* **1 Kiwi** (*informal*) a person from New Zealand 新西蘭人 **2** a New Zealand bird with a long beak, short wings and no tail, that cannot fly 幾維（新西蘭鳥，喙長、翼短、無尾、不能飛） **3** = KIWI FRUIT

ˈkiwi fruit *noun* (*pl.* **kiwi fruit**) (also **kiwi**) a small fruit with thin brown skin covered with small hairs, soft green flesh and black seeds 獼猴桃；奇異果 ➲ VISUAL VOCAB page V30

kJ *abbr.* KILOJOULE(S) 千焦（耳）

KKK /ˌkeɪ keɪ ˈkeɪ/ *abbr.* KU KLUX KLAN

klap /klʌp/ *verb* (**-pp-**) **~ sb/sth** (*SAfrE, informal*) to hit sb/sth 打，擊（某人或某物）：*I'll klap you!* 我要揍你！ ▸ **klap** *noun*：*to give sb a klap* 打某人

Klaxon™ /ˈklæksn/ *noun* (*BrE*) a horn, originally on a vehicle, that makes a loud sound as a warning 克萊克森高音喇叭（原為汽車喇叭）

Klee·nex™ /ˈkliːneks/ *noun* [U, C] (*pl.* **Klee·nex**) a paper HANDKERCHIEF; a TISSUE 舒潔紙巾；紙巾：*a box of Kleenex* 一盒紙巾 ◇ *Here, have a Kleenex to dry your eyes.* 喂，拿一張紙巾把眼睛擦乾。

K

klep·to·mania /ˌkleptəˈmeɪniə/ *noun* [U] a mental illness in which sb has a strong desire, which they cannot control, to steal things 偷竊狂；偷竊癖 ▸ **klep·to·maniac** /ˌkleptəˈmeɪniæk/ *noun*：*She's a kleptomaniac.* 她是個偷竊狂。

klick (also **click**) /klɪk/ *noun* (*NAmE, informal*) a kilometre 千米；公里：*We're twenty klicks south of your position.* 我們在你南面 20 公里處。

kludge /kluːdʒ/ *noun* (*computing* 計) a solution to a computer problem that has been quickly and badly put together 不成熟產品；蹩腳系統 ▸ **kludge** *verb* [I, T] **~ (sth)**

klutz /klʌts/ *noun* (*informal, especially NAmE*) a person who often drops things, is not good at sport(s), etc. 木頭人；不靈巧的人；笨手笨腳的人 ▸ **klutzy** /ˈklʌtsi/ *adj.*

km *abbr.* (*pl.* **km** or **kms**) (in writing) kilometre(s)（書寫形式）千米，公里

knack /næk/ *noun* [sing.] (*informal*) **1** a special skill or ability that you have naturally or can learn 技能；本領：*It's easy, once you've got the knack.* 你一旦掌握這個技能就容易了。◇ **~ of/for (doing) sth** *He's got a real knack for making money.* 他有賺錢的真本領。 **2 ~ of doing sth** (*BrE*) a habit of doing sth 習慣；癖好：*She has the unfortunate knack of always saying the wrong thing.* 不幸的是，她總是說錯話。

knacker /ˈnækə(r)/ *verb* (*BrE, slang*) **1 ~ sb** to make sb very tired 使筋疲力盡；使疲憊不堪 SYN **exhaust** **2 ~ sb/sth** to injure sb or damage sth 使受傷；破壞；損害 ▸ **knacker·ing** *adj.* [not usually before noun]：(*BrE, informal*) *I don't do aerobics any more—it's too knackering.* 我再不做有氧健身操了——太累人了。

knack·ered /ˈnækəd; *NAmE* -kərd/ *adj.* (*BrE, slang*) **1** [not usually before noun] extremely tired 筋疲力盡；疲憊不堪 SYN **exhausted, worn out** **2** too old or broken to use 舊（或破）得不能用了

ˈknacker's yard (also **the knackers**) *noun* [usually sing.] (*old-fashioned, BrE*) a place where old and injured horses are taken to be killed 老殘馬匹屠宰場

knap·sack /ˈnæpsæk/ *noun* (*old-fashioned* or *NAmE*) a small RUCKSACK 小背包

knave /neɪv/ *noun* **1** (*old-fashioned*) = JACK (3)：*the knave of clubs* 梅花傑克 **2** (*old use*) a dishonest man or boy 不誠實的男人（或男孩）；無賴；惡棍

knead /niːd/ *verb* **1 ~ sth** to press and stretch DOUGH, wet CLAY, etc. with your hands to make it ready to use 揉，捏（麵糰、濕黏土等） ➲ VISUAL VOCAB page V28 **2 ~ sth** to rub and squeeze muscles, etc. especially to relax them or to make them less painful 揉捏，按摩，推拿（肌肉等）

knee 0→ /niː/ *noun, verb*

■ *noun* **1** 0→ the joint between the top and bottom parts of the leg where it bends in the middle 膝；膝蓋；膝關節：*a knee injury* 膝關節受傷 ◇ *I grazed my knee when I fell.* 我摔了一跤，把膝蓋擦破了。◇ *He* ***went down on one knee*** *and asked her to marry him.* 他單膝跪下向她求婚。◇ *She was* ***on her knees*** *scrubbing the kitchen floor.* 她在廚房裏跪着刷洗地板。➲ VISUAL VOCAB page V59 **2** 0→ the part of a piece of clothing that covers the knee（褲子的）膝部：*These jeans are torn at the knee.* 這牛仔褲膝蓋那兒破了。◇ *a knee patch* 膝部的補丁 **3** 0→ the top surface of the upper part of the legs when you are sitting down（坐下時）大腿朝上的面 SYN **lap**：*Come and sit on Daddy's knee.* 來坐在爸爸腿上。

IDM **bring sb to their ˈknees** to defeat sb, especially in a war（尤指戰爭中）打敗某人，使某人屈膝投降 **bring sth to its ˈknees** to badly affect an organization, etc. so that it can no longer function 摧毀某物；使（組織等）癱瘓（或崩潰）：*The strikes brought the industry to its knees.* 罷工使得這個行業陷入癱瘓。 **put sb over your ˈknee** to punish sb by making them lie on top of your knee and hitting their bottom 把某人放在膝上打屁股 ➲ more at BEE, BEND *v.*, MOTHER *n.*, WEAK

■ *verb* (**kneed, kneed**) **~ sb/sth** to hit or push sb/sth with your knee 用膝蓋頂（或撞）：*He kneed his attacker in the groin.* 他用膝蓋猛撞攻擊者的下身。

knee·cap /ˈniːkæp/ *noun, verb*

■ *noun* the small bone that covers the front of the knee 膝蓋骨；髕骨 SYN **patella** ➲ VISUAL VOCAB page V59

■ *verb* (**-pp-**) **~ sb** to shoot or break sb's kneecaps as a form of punishment that is not official and is illegal 用槍擊穿膝蓋骨，擊碎膝蓋骨（非法刑罰） ▸ **knee·cap·ping** *noun* [C, U]

ˌknee-ˈdeep *adj.* up to your knees 沒膝的；齊膝深的：*The snow was knee-deep in places.* 有些地方的雪已齊膝深了。◇ (*figurative*) *I was knee-deep in work.* 我當時工作纏身。 ▸ **ˌknee-ˈdeep** *adv.*：*I waded in knee-deep.* 我在齊膝深的水中跋涉。

ˌknee-ˈhigh *adj.* high enough to reach your knees 齊膝高的

IDM **knee-high to a ˈgrasshopper** (*informal, humorous*) very small; very young 矮小；幼小

ˈknee-jerk *adj.* [only before noun] (*disapproving*) produced automatically, without any serious thought 本能地做出的；未經思考做出的：*It was* ***a knee-jerk reaction*** *on her part.* 這是她未加思索做出的反應。

kneel /niːl/ *verb* (**knelt, knelt** /nelt/) (*NAmE* also **kneeled, kneeled**) [I] to be in or move into a position where your body is supported on your knee or knees 跪；跪着；跪下：*a kneeling figure* 跪着的人影 ◇ **~ (down)** *We knelt (down) on the ground to examine the tracks.* 我們跪在地上察看蹤跡。

ˈknee-length *adj.* long enough to reach your knees 長及膝部的：*knee-length shorts/socks* 長及膝部的短褲／襪子

ˈknees-up *noun* [usually sing.] (*BrE, informal*) a noisy party, with dancing 喧鬧的社交集會；歡快的舞會

ˈknee trembler *noun* (*informal*) an act of sex that is done standing up 站立性交

knell /nel/ *noun* [sing.] = DEATH KNELL

knelt *past tense, past part.* of KNEEL

knew *past tense* of KNOW

knick·er·bockers /ˈnɪkəbɒkəz; *NAmE* ˈnɪkərbɑːkərz/ (*NAmE* also **knick·ers**) *noun* [pl.] short loose trousers/pants that fit tightly just below the knee, worn especially in the past（尤指舊時穿的膝下紮緊的）燈籠褲

knick·ers /ˈnɪkəz; *NAmE* -kərz/ *noun* [pl.] **1** (*BrE*) (also **pan·ties** *NAmE, BrE*) a piece of women's underwear that covers the body from the waist to the tops of the legs 女式短襯褲：*a pair of knickers* 一條女式短襯褲 **2** (*NAmE*) = KNICKERBOCKERS ▸ **knick·er** *adj.* [only before noun]：*knicker elastic*（女用）短襯褲鬆緊帶

IDM **get your 'knickers in a twist** (*BrE, slang*) to become angry, confused or upset 惱火；困惑；煩悶 ➲ more at WET *v.*

knick-knack /ˈnɪk næk/ *noun* [usually pl.] (*sometimes disapproving*) a small decorative object in a house（房子裏的）小裝飾物，小擺設 **SYN** **ornament**

knife 0‑ /naɪf/ *noun, verb*

■ ***noun*** 0‑ (*pl.* **knives** /naɪvz/) a sharp blade with a handle, used for cutting or as a weapon 刀： *knives and forks* 刀叉 ◇ *a sharp knife* 鋒利的刀 ◇ *a bread knife* (= one for cutting bread) 切麵包刀 ◇ *She was murdered in a frenzied knife attack.* 她被亂刀殘殺。 ➲ VISUAL VOCAB pages V22, V26 ➲ see also FLICK KNIFE, JACKKNIFE, PALETTE KNIFE, PAPERKNIFE, PENKNIFE, STANLEY KNIFE

IDM **the 'knives are out (for sb)** the situation has become so bad that people are preparing to make one person take the blame, for example by taking away their job（對某人）磨刀霍霍，興師問罪 **like a knife through 'butter** (*informal*) easily; without meeting any difficulty 輕而易舉；毫無困難 **put/stick the 'knife in | put/stick the 'knife into sb** (*informal*) to be very unfriendly to sb and try to harm them 對某人懷恨在心；加害於某人 **turn/twist the 'knife (in the wound)** to say or do sth unkind deliberately; to make sb who is unhappy feel even more unhappy 惡意地說（或做）；落井下石；往傷口上撒鹽 **under the 'knife** (*informal*) having a medical operation 接受手術；動手術

■ ***verb*** **~ sb** to injure or kill sb with a knife 用刀傷害（或殺害） **SYN** **stab**

'knife-edge *noun* [usually sing.] the sharp edge of a knife 刀刃

IDM **on a 'knife-edge** **1** (of a situation, etc. 形勢等) finely balanced between success and failure 勝負難料；成敗未定： *The economy is balanced on a knife-edge.* 經濟形勢尚不明朗。 **2** (of a person 人) very worried or anxious about the result of sth 十分焦慮；急於知道結果

knife·point /ˈnaɪfpɔɪnt/ *noun*

IDM **at 'knifepoint** while being threatened, or threatening sb, with a knife 在刀子威脅下： *She was raped at knifepoint.* 她遭持刀強姦。

knight /naɪt/ *noun, verb*

■ ***noun*** **1** (in the Middle Ages) a man of high social rank who had a duty to fight for his king. Knights are often shown in pictures riding horses and wearing ARMOUR.（中世紀的）騎士 ➲ see also WHITE KNIGHT **2** (in Britain) a man who has been given a special honour by the king or queen and has the title *Sir* before his name（英國）爵士（其名前冠以 Sir） ➲ compare BARONET **3** a piece used in the game of CHESS that is shaped like a horse's head（國際象棋中的）馬 ➲ VISUAL VOCAB page V38

IDM **a knight in shining 'armour** (usually *humorous*) a man who saves sb, especially a woman, from a dangerous situation 救人（尤指女子）於危難之中的男子；（拯救美人的）英雄

■ ***verb*** [usually passive] **~ sb** to give sb the rank and title of a knight 封（某人）為爵士： *He was knighted by the Queen for his services to industry.* 他因對工業界的貢獻獲女王封為爵士。

,knight 'errant *noun* (*pl.* **,knights 'errant**) (in the Middle Ages 中世紀) a KNIGHT who travelled around, looking for adventure 遊俠騎士

knight·hood /ˈnaɪthʊd/ *noun* (in Britain) the rank or title of a KNIGHT（英國）爵士頭銜，騎士頭銜，爵士稱號，騎士稱號： *He received a knighthood in the New Year's Honours list.* 他是新年受勳者之一，榮獲爵士稱號。

knight·ly /ˈnaɪtli/ *adj.* [usually before noun] (*literary*) consisting of knights; typical of a knight 由爵士（或騎士）組成的；爵士（或騎士）的；俠義的 **SYN** **chivalrous**

knit 0‑ /nɪt/ *verb, noun*

■ ***verb*** (**knit·ted, knit·ted**) **HELP** In senses 3 and 4 **knit** is usually used for the past tense and past participle. 作第 3 及第 4 義時，過去時和過去分詞常用 knit。 **1** 0‑ [T, I] to make clothes, etc. from wool or cotton thread using two long thin knitting needles or a machine 編織；針織；機織： **~ (sth)** *I knitted this cardigan myself.* 我自己織的這件開襟毛衣。 ◇ *Lucy was sitting on the sofa, knitting.* 露西坐在沙發上織毛線活兒。 ◇ **~ sb sth** *She's knitting the baby a shawl.* 她在給寶寶織一牀小被子。 **2** [T, I] **~ (sth)** to use a basic STITCH in knitting 織平針： *Knit one row, purl one row.* 織一趟平針，織一趟反針。 **3** [T, I] **~ (sb/sth) (together)** to join people or things closely together or to be joined closely together（使）緊密結合，嚴密，緊湊： *a* ***closely/tightly knit community*** (= one in which relationships are very close) 緊密團結的群體 ◇ *Society is knit together by certain commonly held beliefs.* 社會是靠某些共同的信念來維繫的。 **4** [I, T] **~ (sth)** (of broken bones 斷骨) to grow together again to form one piece; to make broken bones grow together again（使）癒合，接合 **SYN** **mend**： *The bone failed to knit correctly.* 骨頭癒合得不好。

IDM **knit your 'brow(s)** to move your EYEBROWS together, to show that you are thinking hard, feeling angry, etc. 皺眉（表示沉思、惱怒等） **SYN** **frown**

■ ***noun*** [usually pl.] a piece of clothing that has been knitted 編織的衣服；針織衫： *winter knits* 編織的冬衣

knit·ted 0‑ /ˈnɪtɪd/ (also **knit**) *adj.* made by knitting wool or thread 編織的；針織的： *knitted gloves* 編織手套 ◇ *a white knit dress* 白色針織連衣裙 ◇ *a hand-knitted sweater* 手工編織的毛衣 ◇ *a cotton-knit shirt* 針織棉襯衫

knit·ter /ˈnɪtə(r)/ *noun* a person who knits 編織者；針織工

knit·ting 0‑ /ˈnɪtɪŋ/ *noun* [U] **1** 0‑ an item that is being knitted 編織物；針織品： *Where's my knitting?* 我織的東西上哪兒去了？ **2** 0‑ the activity of knitting 編織；針織

'knitting needle *noun* a long thin stick with a round end that you use for knitting by hand 編織針；毛衣針 ➲ VISUAL VOCAB page V41

knit·wear /ˈnɪtweə(r); *NAmE* -wer/ *noun* [U] items of clothing that have been knitted 針織衫；針織衣物

knives *pl.* of KNIFE

knob /nɒb; *NAmE* nɑːb/ *noun* **1** a round switch on a machine such as a television that you use to turn it on and off, etc.（用以開關電視機等的）旋鈕： *the volume control knob* 音量控制旋鈕 **2** a round handle on a door or a drawer（門或抽屜的）球形把手 ➲ picture at HANDLE **3** a round lump on the surface or end of sth 疙瘩；節 **4** (*especially BrE*) a small lump of sth such as butter 小塊（黃油等） **5** (*BrE, taboo, slang*) a PENIS 陰莖

IDM **with 'knobs on** (*BrE, slang*) used to say that sth is a more complicated version of what you mention 有過之而無不及；更是如此；尤其突出： *It isn't art—it's just a horror movie with knobs on!* 那不是藝術，只是更加驚悚的恐怖片而已！

knob·bly /ˈnɒbli; *NAmE* ˈnɑːbli/ (*especially NAmE* **knobby** /ˈnɒbi; *NAmE* ˈnɑːbi/) *adj.* having small hard lumps 有節的；多疙瘩的： *knobbly knees* 骨節突出的膝蓋

knock 0‑ /nɒk; *NAmE* nɑːk/ *verb, noun*

■ ***verb***

▸ **AT DOOR/WINDOW 門窗** **1** 0‑ [I] to hit a door, etc. firmly in order to attract attention 敲；擊 **SYN** **rap**： *He knocked three times and waited.* 他敲了三下門就等着。 ◇ **~ at/on sth** *Somebody was knocking on the window.* 有人在敲窗戶。

▸ **HIT 擊** **2** 0‑ [T, I] to hit sth, often by accident, with a short, hard blow（常為無意地）碰，撞： **~ sth (against/on sth)** *Be careful you don't knock your head on this low beam.* 小心，別把頭撞在這矮梁上。 ◇ **~ against/on sth** *Her hand knocked against the glass.* 她的手碰了玻璃杯。 **3** [T] to put sb/sth into a particular state by hitting them/it 把…撞擊成（某種狀態）： **~ sb/sth + adj.** *The blow knocked me flat.* 那一拳把我打倒在地。 ◇ *He was knocked senseless by the blow.* 他被一拳打得不省人事。 ◇ **~ sb/sth doing sth** *She knocked my drink flying.* 她把我的飲料打翻了。 ◇ **~ sb/sth + adv./prep.** *The two rooms had been knocked into one* (= the wall between them had been knocked down). 那兩個房間打通了，成了一個房間。 ➲ SYNONYMS at HIT **4** 0‑ [T] to hit sth so that it moves or breaks 打掉；敲動；打破： **~ sth + adv./prep.**

He'd knocked over a glass of water. 他打翻了一杯水。◇ *I knocked the nail into the wall.* 我把釘子釘進牆裏。◇ *They had to knock the door down to get in.* 他們不得不破門而入。◇ *The boys were knocking (= kicking) a ball around in the back yard.* 男孩們在後院踢球玩兒。◇ **~ sth** (*figurative*) *The criticism had knocked (= damaged) her self-esteem.* 這一批評傷了她的自尊心。➲ SYNONYMS at HIT **5** [T] **~ sth + adv./prep.** to make a hole in sth by hitting it hard 打，鑿（洞）：*They managed to knock a hole in the wall.* 他們設法在牆上鑿了個洞。

▸ **OF HEART/KNEES** 心；膝蓋 **6** [I] if your heart **knocks**, it beats hard; if your knees **knock**, they shake, for example from fear （心）怦怦跳；（膝蓋）打哆嗦：*My heart was knocking wildly.* 我的心怦怦直跳。

▸ **OF ENGINE/PIPES** 發動機；管子 **7** [I] to make a regular sound of metal hitting metal, especially because there is sth wrong （尤指因故障）發碰撞聲，嘭嘭作響

▸ **CRITICIZE** 批評 **8** [T] **~ sb/sth** (*informal*) to criticize sb/sth, especially when it happens unfairly （不公平地）批評；貶責；挑剔；非難：*The newspapers are always knocking the England team.* 報紙總是攻擊英格蘭隊。◇ *'E-books?' 'Don't knock it—there's a great future in e-books.'* "電子書？" "別貶損它，電子書的前景大着呢。"

IDM **I'll knock your 'block/'head off!** (*BrE, informal*) used to threaten sb that you will hit them （威脅要打人）我非揍你不可，我要揍扁你 **knock sb 'dead** (*informal*) to impress sb very much 使某人傾倒：*You look fabulous—you'll knock 'em dead tonight.* 你看上去漂亮極了，今晚肯定把他們迷倒。 **knock sb/sth into a cocked 'hat** (*old-fashioned, BrE*) to be very much better than sb/sth 遠遠勝過某人（或事物）；大大超過；使相形見絀 **knock it 'off!** (*informal*) used to tell sb to stop making a noise, annoying you, etc. 別吵了；別煩人了 **knock sb off their 'pedestal/'perch** to make sb lose their position as sb/sth successful or admired 使某人喪失名位 **knock sth on the 'head** (*BrE, informal*) to stop sth from happening; to stop doing sth 阻止某事發生；停止做某事：*The recession knocked on the head any idea of expanding the company.* 經濟衰退使擴展公司的任何想法都化為泡影。 **knock on 'wood** (*NAmE, saying*) (*BrE* **touch 'wood**) used when you have just mentioned some way in which you have been lucky in the past, to avoid bringing bad luck 敲敲木頭，討個吉利（用於說了自己如何走運的話之後，表示希望繼續走好運） **knock sb 'sideways** (*informal*) to surprise or shock sb so much that they are unable to react immediately 使某人驚訝得不知所措（或目瞪口呆） **knock 'spots off sb/sth** (*BrE, informal*) to be very much better than sb/sth 遠遠勝過；大大超過；使相形見絀 **knock the 'stuffing out of sb** (*informal*) to make sb lose their confidence and enthusiasm 使某人喪失信心（或委靡不振） **you could have knocked me down with a 'feather** (*informal*) used to express surprise （表示驚奇）➲ more at DAYLIGHTS, HEAD *n.*, HELL, SENSE *n.*, SHAPE *n.*, SIX, SOCK *n.*

PHR V **,knock a'round ...** (*BrE* also **,knock a'bout ...**) (*informal*) **1** to travel and live in various places 漫遊：*He spent a few years knocking around Europe.* 他花了幾年時間漫遊歐洲。 **2** used to say that sth is in a place but you do not know exactly where （表示某物在一個地方但不知確切位置）：*It must be knocking around here somewhere.* 它肯定在這兒某個地方。 **,knock a'round with sb/together** (*BrE* also **,knock a'bout with sb/together**) (*informal*) to spend a lot of time with sb/together 常與某人交往（或做伴） **,knock sb/sth a'round** (*BrE* also **,knock sb/sth a'bout**) (*informal*) to hit sb/sth repeatedly; to treat sb/sth roughly 接連敲擊某人（或某物）；粗暴對待

,knock sb 'back **1** (*BrE*) to prevent sb from achieving sth or making progress, especially by rejecting them or sth that they suggest or ask 阻礙，妨礙（某人取得成果或進步，尤指以回絕方式）➲ related noun KNOCK-BACK **2** (*BrE*) to surprise or shock sb 使某人大吃一驚（或感到驚訝）：*Hearing the news really knocked me back.* 聽到這消息着實讓我大吃一驚。 **,knock sb 'back sth** (*BrE, informal*) to cost sb a lot of money 用掉某人一大筆錢：*That house must have knocked them back a bit.* 那房子一定花了他們不少錢。 **,knock sth↔'back** (*informal*) to drink sth quickly, especially an alcoholic drink 很快喝掉（酒等）

,knock sb 'down (from sth) (to sth) (*informal*) to persuade sb to reduce the price of sth 說服…降價；使降價；殺價：*I managed to knock him down to $400.* 我設法讓他把價格降到了 400 元。 **,knock sb↔'down/'over** 🔑 to hit sb and make them fall to the ground 打倒（或擊倒、撞倒）某人：*She was knocked down by a bus.* 她被一輛公共汽車撞倒在地。◇ *He knocked his opponent down three times in the first round.* 他第一局就將對手擊倒三次。 **,knock sth↔'down** 🔑 to destroy a building by breaking its walls 推倒（或拆掉、拆毀）建築物 SYN **demolish**：*These old houses are going to be knocked down.* 這些舊房子要拆了。 **,knock sth↔'down (from sth) (to sth)** (*informal*) to reduce the price of sth 減價；降價：*He knocked down the price from $80 to $50.* 他把價格從 80 元降到了 50 元。➲ see also KNOCK-DOWN

,knock 'off | ,knock 'off sth (*informal*) to stop doing sth, especially work 停止某事；中斷某事；（尤指）下班，收工：*Do you want to knock off early today?* 你今天想早點歇工嗎？◇ *What time do you knock off work?* 你什麼時候下班？◇ *Let's knock off for lunch.* 咱們收工吃午飯吧。 **,knock sb↔'off** (*slang*) to murder sb 殺死（或幹掉、除掉、結果）某人 **,knock sth↔'off** **1** (*informal*) to complete sth quickly and without much effort 迅速而輕鬆地完成：*He knocks off three novels a year.* 他一年趕出三部小說。 **2** (*BrE, slang*) to steal sth; to steal from a place 偷（東西）；搶劫（某處）：*to knock off a DVD player* 偷 DVD 影碟機 ◇ *to knock off a bank* 搶劫銀行 **,knock sth↔'off | ,knock sth↔'off sth** (*informal*) to reduce the price or value of sth 降價；減價；使貶值：*They knocked off $60 because of a scratch.* 因為有擦痕，他們將價格減了 60 元。◇ *The news knocked 13% off the company's shares.* 這消息使公司股價下跌 13%。

,knock sb↔'out **1** 🔑 to make sb fall asleep or become unconscious 使入睡；使昏睡；使不省人事：*The blow knocked her out.* 這一擊把她打昏了。 **2** (in boxing 拳擊運動) to hit an opponent so that they cannot get up within a limited time and therefore lose the fight 擊敗對手 ➲ related noun KNOCKOUT (1) **3** (*informal*) to surprise and impress sb very much 使大吃一驚；使傾倒；給某人留下深刻印象：*The movie just knocked me out.* 這電影着實令我讚歎不已。➲ related noun KNOCKOUT (2) **,knock sb/yourself 'out** to make sb/yourself very tired 使筋疲力盡；使疲憊不堪 SYN **wear out** **,knock sb↔'out (of sth)** to defeat sb so that they cannot continue competing 把…淘汰出（比賽） SYN **eliminate**：*England had been knocked out of the World Cup.* 英格蘭隊已被淘汰出世界杯足球賽。➲ see also KNOCKOUT *adj.* (1) **,knock sth↔'out** (*informal*) to produce sth, especially quickly and easily 完成；快速而輕易地做成：*He knocks out five books a year.* 他一年輕鬆寫出五本書。

,knock sb↔'over = KNOCK SB DOWN

,knock sth↔to'gether **1** (*informal*) to make or complete sth quickly and often not very well 草草做成；匆匆拼湊成：*I knocked some bookshelves together from old planks.* 我用舊木板拼拼湊湊做了些書架。 **2** (*BrE*) to make two rooms or buildings into one by removing the wall between them 把兩間屋（或兩座建築物）打通：*The house consists of two cottages knocked together.* 這房子是將兩棟小屋的隔牆打通合二為一的。

,knock 'up (in TENNIS, etc. 網球等) to practise for a short time before the start of a game 賽前練習 **,knock sb↔'up** **1** (*BrE, informal*) to wake sb by knocking on their door 敲門喚醒某人 **2** (*informal, especially NAmE*) to make a woman pregnant 使懷孕 **,knock sth↔'up** to prepare or make sth quickly and without much effort 迅速準備好；快速並輕易做成：*She knocked up a meal in ten minutes.* 她十分鐘就做好了一頓飯。

■ *noun*

▸ **AT DOOR/WINDOW** 門窗 **1** 🔑 the sound of sb hitting a door, window, etc. with their hand or with sth hard to attract attention 敲擊聲；敲門（或窗等）聲：*There was a* ***knock on/at*** *the door.* 有敲門聲。

▸ **HIT** 擊 **2** 🔑 a sharp blow from sth hard 捶擊；敲擊；撞擊 SYN **bang**：*He got a nasty knock on the head.* 他頭部遭到重重一擊。

IDM **take a (hard, nasty, etc.) 'knock** to have an experience that makes sb/sth less confident or successful; to be damaged 遭受（重大等）挫折；受到（沉重等）打擊；受到（嚴重等）破壞

knock·about /ˈnɒkəbaʊt; *NAmE* ˈnɑːk-/ *adj.* [usually before noun] (*BrE*) **knockabout** entertainment involves people acting in a deliberately silly way, for example falling over or hitting other people, in order to make the audience laugh 鬧劇的；喧鬧喜劇的 SYN **slapstick**

'knock-back *noun* (*informal*) a difficulty or problem that makes you feel less confident that you will be successful in sth that you are doing, especially when sb rejects you or sth you suggest or ask （尤指被人拒絕時受到的）挫折，挫傷，打擊

'knock-down *adj., noun*

■ *adj.* [only before noun] (*informal*) **1** (of prices, etc. 價格等) much lower than usual 低廉的 SYN **rock-bottom** **2** using a lot of force 強有力的；用力的： *a knock-down punch* 強有力的一拳

■ *noun* **1** (in boxing 拳擊運動) an act of falling to the ground after being hit 擊倒 **2** (in football (SOCCER) 足球) an act of hitting a high ball down to the ground or to another player 凌空抽射（將高球踢到地上或給另一球員）

,knock-down-'drag-out *adj.* [only before noun] (*NAmE, informal*) (of a fight or an argument) very aggressive and unpleasant（打架或爭吵）激烈的，猛烈的

knock·er /ˈnɒkə(r); *NAmE* ˈnɑːk-/ *noun* **1** (also **'door knocker**) [C] a metal object attached to the outside of the door of a house, etc. which you hit against the door to attract attention （固定在門上供敲門用的）門環 ➲ VISUAL VOCAB page V17 **2** [C] (*informal*) a person who is always criticizing sb/sth 吹毛求疵的人；一味批評的人 **3 knockers** [pl.] (*taboo, slang*) an offensive word for a woman's breasts （冒犯語）乳房，奶子

'knocking copy *noun* [U] (*BrE, informal*) advertising in which an opponent's product is criticized 詆譭性廣告（針對競爭對手）

'knocking shop *noun* (*BrE, informal*) a BROTHEL (= place where people can pay for sex) 妓院

,knock-'kneed *adj.* having legs that turn towards each other at the knees 膝外翻的

,knock 'knees *noun* [pl.] legs that turn towards each other at the knees 膝內翻；X 形腿

,knock-'on *adj.* (*especially BrE*) causing other events to happen one after another in a series 使產生連鎖反應的： *The increase in the price of oil had **a knock-on effect** on the cost of many other goods.* 石油價格上漲對其他許多商品的價格引起了連鎖反應。

knock·out /ˈnɒkaʊt; *NAmE* ˈnɑːk-/ *noun, adj.*

■ *noun* **1** (*abbr.* **KO**) (in boxing 拳擊運動) a blow that makes an opponent fall to the ground and be unable to get up, so that he or she loses the fight 擊敗對手的一擊；擊倒對手獲勝 **2** (*informal*) a person or thing that is very attractive or impressive 引人注目（或給人留下深刻印象的）的人（或物）

■ *adj.* [only before noun] **1** (*especially BrE*) a **knockout** competition is one in which the winning player/team at each stage competes in the next stage and the losing one no longer takes part in the competition 淘汰賽的；淘汰的： *the knockout stages of the tournament* 錦標賽的淘汰賽階段 **2** a **knockout** blow is one that hits sb so hard that they can no longer get up 擊敗對手的

'knock-up *noun* (*BrE*) a short practice before a game, especially of TENNIS （尤指網球的）賽前練習

knoll /nəʊl; *NAmE* noʊl/ *noun* a small round hill 圓丘；土墩 SYN **mound**

knot 0━ /nɒt; *NAmE* nɑːt/ *noun, verb*

■ *noun*

▸ IN STRING/ROPE 繩索 **1** 0━ a join made by tying together two pieces or ends of string, rope, etc. （用繩索等打的）結： *to **tie a knot*** 打結 ◇ *Tie the two ropes together with a knot.* 將這兩根繩子打結繫在一起。 ◇ (*figurative*) *hair full of knots and tangles* (= twisted in a way that is difficult to COMB) 纏結在一起亂糟糟的頭髮

▸ OF HAIR 頭髮 **2** a way of twisting hair into a small round shape at the back of the head 髮髻： *She had her hair in a knot.* 她把頭髮打了個髻。

▸ IN WOOD 木頭 **3** a hard round spot in a piece of wood where there was once a branch 節子；節疤

▸ GROUP OF PEOPLE 一群人 **4** a small group of people standing close together 一小群人

▸ OF MUSCLES 肌肉 **5** a tight, hard feeling in the stomach, throat, etc. caused by nerves, anger, etc. （由緊張、惱怒等引起的胃、喉等的）痙攣，鬱結，哽咽，哽塞： *My stomach was in knots.* 我的心揪得緊緊的。 ◇ *I could feel a knot of fear in my throat.* 我很害怕，感到喉嚨發緊。

▸ SPEED OF BOAT/PLANE 船／飛機的速度 **6** a unit for measuring the speed of boats and aircraft; one NAUTICAL MILE per hour 節（船和飛行器的速度計量單位，每小時一海里） IDM see RATE *n.*, TIE *v.*

■ *verb* (-tt-)

▸ TIE WITH KNOT 打結 **1** [T] **~ sth** to fasten sth with a knot or knots 把…打成結（或紮牢）： *He carefully knotted his tie.* 他仔細地打着領帶。

▸ TWIST 纏繞 **2** [I] to become twisted into a knot 纏結 SYN **tangle** **3** [T] **~ sth** to twist hair into a particular shape 打髮髻： *She wore her hair loosely knotted on top of her head.* 她在頭頂上打了個鬆鬆的髮髻。

▸ MUSCLES 肌肉 **4** [I, T] **~ (sth)** if muscles, etc. **knot** or sth **knots** them, they become hard and painful because of fear, excitement, etc. （因害怕、激動等而）痙攣，緊縮，使痙攣： *She felt her stomach knot with fear.* 她感到害怕，心都揪緊了。

IDM **get 'knotted** (*BrE, informal, slang*) a rude way of telling sb to go away or of telling them that you are annoyed with them 滾蛋；見鬼去；別煩人

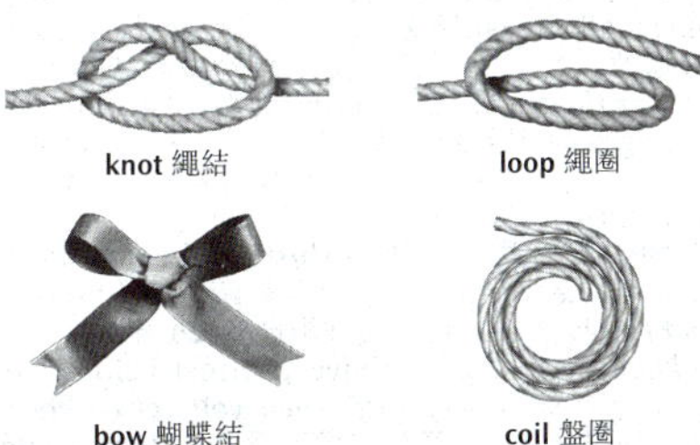

knot 繩結　loop 繩圈　bow 蝴蝶結　coil 盤圈

knotty /ˈnɒti; *NAmE* ˈnɑːti/ *adj.* (**knot·tier**, **knot·ti·est**) **1** complicated and difficult to solve 複雜的；難以解決的；棘手的 SYN **thorny**： *a knotty problem* 棘手的問題 **2** having parts that are hard and twisted together 有節的；纏繞在一起的： *the knotty roots of the old oak tree* 盤根錯節的老橡樹根

know 0━ /nəʊ; *NAmE* noʊ/ *verb, noun*

■ *verb* (**knew** /njuː; *NAmE* nuː/, **known** /nəʊn; *NAmE* noʊn/) (not used in the progressive tenses 不用於進行時)

▸ HAVE INFORMATION 知悉 **1** 0━ [T, I] to have information in your mind as a result of experience or because you have learned or been told it 知道；知悉；瞭解： **~ sth** *Do you know his address?* 你知道他的地址嗎？ ◇ *The cause of the fire is not yet known.* 火災的原因尚不清楚。 ◇ ***All I know** is that she used to work in a bank* (= I have no other information about her). 我只知道她曾在銀行工作過。 ◇ **~ (that)** ... *I know (that) people's handwriting changes as they get older.* 我知道人們的筆跡隨着年齡的增長而變化。 ◇ **it is known that** ... *It is widely known that CFCs can damage the ozone layer.* 眾所周知氯氟烴會破壞臭氧層。 ◇ **~ where, what, etc.** ... *I knew where he was hiding.* 我知道他藏在哪裏。 ◇ *I didn't know what he was talking about.* 我不知道他在談什麼。 ◇ **~ (of/about sth)** *'You've got a flat tyre.' 'I know.'* "你的車胎癟了。""我知道。" ◇ *'What's the answer?' 'I don't know.'* "答案是什麼？""我不知道。" ◇ *'There's no one in.' 'How do you know?'* "一個人都沒有。""你怎麼知道呢？" ◇

K

You know about Amanda's baby, don't you? 你知道阿曼達的小寶寶吧？◇ ***I don't know about you, but** I'm ready for something to eat.* 不管你怎麼樣，反正我要吃點東西。◇ ***I know of** at least two people who did the same thing.* 我知道至少有兩人幹過同樣的事。◇ *'Is anyone else coming?' **'Not that I know of.'*** "還有別的人要來嗎？" "據我所知沒有了。" ◇ *'Isn't that his car?' **'I wouldn't know./How should I know?'*** (= I don't know and I am not the person you should ask.) "那不是他的汽車嗎？" "我怎麼會知道呢？" ◇ (*informal*) *'What are you two whispering about?' **'You don't want to know.'*** (= because you would be shocked or wouldn't approve) "你們倆在說什麼悄悄話？" "你還是不知道的好。" ◇ **~ to do sth** *Does he know to come here* (= that he should come here) *first?* 他知道要先到這兒來嗎？◇ **~ sb/sth to be/do sth** *We know her to be honest.* 我們知道她很誠實。◇ *Two women are known to have died.* 據悉兩名婦女死了。
➲ see also NEED-TO-KNOW

▸ **REALIZE** 意識到 **2** 🗝 [T, I] to realize, understand or be aware of sth 認識到；懂得；意識到：**~ (that) …** *As soon as I walked in the room I knew (that) something was wrong.* 我剛走進屋就意識到出了事。◇ *She knew she was dying.* 她知道自己快死了。◇ **~ what, how, etc. …** *I knew perfectly well what she meant.* 我完全懂她的意思。◇ *I know exactly how you feel.* 我非常清楚你的感受。◇ **~ (sth)** *This case is hopeless **and he knows it*** (= although he will not admit it). 這個案子毫無希望，這一點他是清楚的。◇ *'Martin was lying all the time.' **'I should have known.'*** "馬丁一直在撒謊。" "我本該察覺到的。"

▸ **FEEL CERTAIN** 確信 **3** 🗝 [T, I] to feel certain about sth 確信；確知；肯定：**~ (that) …** *He knew (that) he could trust her.* 他確信她是可以信賴的。◇ *I know it's here somewhere!* 我肯定它在這兒某個地方！◇ *I don't know that I can finish it by next week.* 我沒有把握能在下週完成。◇ **~ (sth)** *'You were right—someone's been spreading rumours about you.' 'I knew it!'* "你說得對，有人一直在散佈你的謠言。" "我早就知道！" ◇ *'She's the worst player in the team.' 'Oh, **I don't know*** (= I am not sure that I agree)—*she played well yesterday.'* "她是最糟的隊員。" "哦，是嗎？她昨天表現可不錯。" ➲ see also DON'T-KNOW

▸ **BE FAMILIAR** 熟悉 **4** 🗝 [T] **~ sb/sth** to be familiar with a person, place, thing, etc. 熟悉；認識；瞭解：*I've known David for 20 years.* 我認識戴維已有 20 年了。◇ *Do you two know each other* (= have you met before)? 你們倆認識嗎？◇ *She's very nice when you **get to know** her.* 你瞭解她以後就會覺得她非常可愛。◇ ***Knowing Ben**, we could be waiting a long time* (= it is typical of him to be late). 本這個人我們瞭解，能叫我們等很長時間。◇ *This man **is known to the police*** (= as a criminal). 這男人是在警方掛了號的。◇ *I know Paris well.* 我很熟悉巴黎。◇ *Do you know the play* (= have you seen or read it before)? 你知道這齣戲嗎？◇ *The new rules could mean the end of football **as we know it*** (= in the form that we are familiar with). 這些新規則可能意味着我們熟悉的足球終結了。

▸ **REPUTATION** 名聲 **5** 🗝 [T, usually passive] to think that sb/sth is a particular type of person or thing or has particular characteristics 把…看作是；認為…是：**~ sb/sth as sth** *It's known as the most dangerous part of the city.* 人們都認為那是市內最危險的地段。◇ **~ sb/sth for sth** *She is best known for her work on the human brain.* 她在對人腦的研究方面最為知名。◇ **~ sb/sth to be/do sth** *He's known to be an outstanding physicist.* 他被公認為傑出的物理學家。

▸ **GIVE NAME** 命名 **6** 🗝 [T] **~ sb/sth as sth** [usually passive] to give sb/sth a particular name or title 將…稱為；把…叫做：*The drug is commonly known as Ecstasy.* 這種致幻藥通常稱作搖頭丸。◇ *Peter Wilson, also known as 'the Tiger'* 彼得・威爾遜，也稱"老虎"

▸ **RECOGNIZE** 認出 **7** 🗝 [T] **~ sb/sth** to be able to recognize sb/sth 能認出；能辨認出：*I couldn't see who was speaking, but I knew the voice.* 我看不到誰在講話，但我能辨認出聲音。◇ *She knows a bargain when she sees one.* 她一看就知道有沒有便宜可撿。➲ SYNONYMS at IDENTIFY

▸ **DISTINGUISH** 區分 **8** [T] **~ sb/sth from sb/sth** to be able to distinguish one person or thing from another 能區分；能分辨 SYN **differentiate**：*I hope we have taught our children to know right from wrong.* 我希望我們教給了孩子分辨是非的能力。

▸ **SKILL/LANGUAGE** 技能；語言 **9** 🗝 [T] to have learned a skill or language and be able to use it 學會；掌握：**~ sth** *Do you know any Japanese?* 你會日語嗎？◇ **~ how, what, etc. …** *Do you know how to use spreadsheets?* 你知道電子數據表的使用方法嗎？

▸ **EXPERIENCE** 經歷 **10** [T] (only used in the perfect tenses 僅用於完成時) to have seen, heard or experienced sth 看到過；聽到過；經歷過：**~ sb/sth (to) do sth** *I've never known it (to) snow in July before.* 我以前從未見到過七月份下雪。◇ **be known to do sth** *He has been known to spend all morning in the bathroom.* 聽說他整個上午都待在浴室裏。 **11** [T] **~ sth** to have personal experience of sth 親身體驗；親身經歷：*He has known both poverty and wealth.* 他貧富生活都親身經歷過。◇ *She may be successful now, but she has **known what it is like to be** poor.* 她現在算是成功了，但她嚐過貧窮的滋味。

IDM **before you know where you 'are** very quickly or suddenly 瞬息之間；轉眼間；一下子：*We were whisked off in a taxi before we knew where we were.* 還沒等我們弄清怎麼回事，出租車就一陣風似地把我們帶走了。 **be not to 'know** to have no way of realizing or being aware that you have done sth wrong 無從知道，並不知道（做錯了事）：*'I'm sorry, I called when you were in bed.' 'Don't worry—you weren't to know.'* "對不起，你睡覺時打電話打擾你了。" "別在意，你不是故意的嘛。" **for all you, I, they, etc. know** (*informal*) used to emphasize that you do not know sth and that it is not important to you（強調不知道對自己無關緊要的事）不知道，說不定，亦未可知：*She could be dead for all I know.* 她說不定已經死了。 **God/goodness/Heaven knows** (*informal*) **1** 🗝 used to emphasize that you do not know sth（強調不知道）誰知道，天曉得：*God knows what else they might find.* 誰知道他們還可能找到什麼。◇ *'Where are they?' 'Goodness knows.'* "他們在哪兒？" "天曉得。" **HELP** Some people may find the use of **God knows** offensive. 有人可能認為用 God knows 含冒犯意。 **2** used to emphasize the truth of what you are saying（強調所言屬實）老天作證，確實，的確：*She ought to pass the exam—goodness knows she's been working hard enough.* 她應該考合格，她可真夠努力了。 **I don't know how, why, etc. …** (*informal*) used to criticize sb's behaviour（批評某人的行為）真想不到，真不知道：*I don't know how you can say things like that.* 真想不到你怎麼會說出這種話來。 **I know** (*informal*) **1** 🗝 /aɪ ˈnəʊ; *NAmE* aɪ ˈnoʊ/ used to agree with sb or to show sympathy（表示同意或同情）我理解，我有同感，我知道：*'What a ridiculous situation!' 'I know.'* "這境況真荒唐！" "的確是。" **2** 🗝 /ˈaɪ nəʊ; *NAmE* ˈaɪ noʊ/ used to introduce a new idea or suggestion（引出新的想法或建議）我有個主意（或辦法、建議）：*I know, let's see what's on at the theatre.* 我有主意了，咱們看看劇院在上演什麼。 **know sth as well as 'I do** used to criticize sb by saying that they should realize or understand sth（用以批評）其實完全明白，哪會不知道，知道得很清楚：*You know as well as I do that you're being unreasonable.* 其實你完全明白你是在故意胡攪蠻纏。 **know sb/sth 'backwards** (*informal, especially BrE*) to know sb/sth extremely well 對…瞭如指掌（或倒背如流）；把…背得滾瓜爛熟：*She must know the play backwards by now.* 她現在對這個劇本肯定是倒背如流。 **know 'best** to know what should be done, etc. better than other people 最懂得，最知道，比誰都明白（該怎麼做等）：*The doctor told you to stay in bed, and she knows best.* 醫生叫你臥牀休息，她最清楚你該怎麼做。 **know better (than that/than to do sth)** to be sensible enough not to do sth 明白事理（而不至於）；不至於糊塗到：*He knows better than to judge by appearances.* 他明白得很，決不會憑表面現象來判斷。 **know sb by 'sight** to recognize sb without knowing them well 與某人面熟 **know 'different/'otherwise** (*informal*) to have information or evidence that the opposite is true 所知道的不是那麼回事；所掌握的情況大不一樣（或大相逕庭）：*He says he doesn't care about what the critics write, but I know different.* 他說他並不在乎批評家的評論，可我知道不是那麼回事。 **know full 'well** to be very aware of a fact and unable to deny or ignore it 非常清楚；不可否

認；不可忽視：*He knew full well what she thought of it.* 他非常清楚她對此事的看法。 **know sb/sth inside 'out | know sb/sth like the back of your 'hand** (*informal*) to be very familiar with sth 對…極為熟悉（或瞭如指掌）：*This is where I grew up. I know this area like the back of my hand.* 我在這兒長大的，我對這地方再熟悉不過了。 **know your own 'mind** to have very firm ideas about what you want to do 知道自己想做什麼；有主見 **know your 'stuff** (*informal*) to know a lot about a particular subject or job 精通業務；對工作很內行 **know your way a'round** to be familiar with a place, subject, etc. 熟悉周圍情況（或課題等） **know what you're 'talking about** (*informal*) to have knowledge about sth from your own experience 親身經歷過；作經驗之談 **know which side your 'bread is buttered** (*informal*) to know where you can get an advantage for yourself 知道自己的利益所在 **let it be known/make it known that ...** (*formal*) to make sure that people are informed about sth, especially by getting sb else to tell them （尤指通過他人傳達而）使人知曉，讓人知道：*The President has let it be known that he does not intend to run for election again.* 總統已經公開表示他不打算再次參加競選。 **let sb 'know** 🗝 to tell sb about sth 讓某人知道；告訴（或通知）某人：*Let me know how I can help.* 我能幫什麼忙，只管說。 **make yourself 'known to sb** to introduce yourself to sb 向某人作自我介紹：*I made myself known to the hotel manager.* 我向旅館老闆作了自我介紹。 **not know any 'better** to behave badly, usually because you have not been taught the correct way to behave （因缺乏教養而）表現不好；因無人指教而舉止不良 **not know your ˌarse from your 'elbow** (*BrE, taboo, slang*) to be very stupid or completely lacking in skill 愚蠢之至；屁都不懂 **not know 'beans about sth** (*NAmE, informal*) to know nothing about a subject 完全不懂行；對…一竅不通 **not know the first thing a'bout sb/sth** to know nothing at all about sb/sth 對…一無所知；對…一竅不通 **not know sb from 'Adam** (*informal*) to not know at all who sb is 根本不認識某人；與某人素不相識 **not know what 'hit you** (*informal*) to be so surprised by sth that you do not know how to react 因吃驚而不知所措；驚呆了 **not know where to 'look** (*informal*) to feel great embarrassment and not know how to react 尷尬得不知如何是好；狼狽不堪；感到很難堪 **not know whether you're 'coming or 'going** (*informal*) to be so excited or confused that you cannot behave or think in a sensible way （激動得）不知如何是好；糊裏糊塗；不知所措 **not know you are 'born** (*BrE, informal*) to have an easy life without realizing how easy it is 身在福中不知福：*You people without kids don't know you're born.* 你們沒孩子，真是身在福中不知福啊。 **there's no 'knowing** used to say that it is impossible to say what might happen 難以預料；無從知道；沒法說：*There's no knowing how he'll react.* 很難預料他會有什麼樣的反應。 **what does ... know?** used to say that sb knows nothing about the subject you are talking about （某人）知道什麼，懂什麼：*What does he know about football, anyway?* 不管怎麼說，他懂什麼足球？ **what do you 'know?** (*informal*) used to express surprise （表示驚奇）你看怪不怪，真沒想到：*Well, what do you know? Look who's here!* 唷，真想不到！你看誰來啦！ **ˌyou 'know** (*informal*) **1** 🗝 used when you are thinking of what to say next （說話人考慮接着說什麼時用）：*Well, you know, it's difficult to explain.* 唉，你知道，這很難解釋。 **2** 🗝 used to show that what you are referring to is known or understood by the person you are speaking to （表示對方知道或瞭解所言）你知道的：*Guess who I've just seen? Maggie! You know—Jim's wife.* 你猜我剛才看見誰了，瑪吉！你知道的，就是吉姆的妻子。◇ *You know that restaurant round the corner? It's closed down.* 拐角那家餐館，你知道吧？已經倒閉了。 **3** 🗝 used to emphasize sth that you are saying （加強語氣）你要知道：*I'm not stupid, you know.* 你要知道，我不是傻子。 **you 'know something/'what?** (*informal*) used to introduce an interesting or surprising opinion, piece of news, etc. （引出令人感興趣或吃驚的看法、消息等）要我告訴你嗎，你聽說了嗎：*You know something? I've never really enjoyed Christmas.* 要我告訴你嗎？聖誕節我從未真正快樂過。 **you know 'who/'what** (*informal*) used to refer to sb/sth without mentioning a name （不說出名稱）你知道是誰（或什麼） **you never know** 🗝 (*informal*) used to say that you can never be certain about what will happen in the future, especially when you are suggesting that sth good might happen （尤指可能會發生好事）很難說，很難預料 ➲ more at ANSWER *n.*, COST *n.*, DAY, DEVIL, FAR *adv.*, LORD *n.*, OLD, PAT *adv.*, ROPE *n.*, THING, TRUTH

■ ***noun***

IDM **in the 'know** (*informal*) having more information about sth than most people 知情；熟悉內幕；掌握內情：*Somebody in the know told me he's going to resign.* 有知情者告訴我他要辭職了。

'know-all (*BrE*) (also **'know-it-all** *NAmE, BrE*) *noun* (*informal, disapproving*) a person who behaves as if they know everything 自以為無所不知的人；百事通

Know·bot™ /ˈnəʊbɒt; *NAmE* ˈnoʊbɑːt/ *noun* (*computing* 計) a program that is designed to search for data in a large number of DATABASES when a user of a network has asked for information 知識機器人程序（用於網絡數據庫搜索）

'know-how *noun* [U] (*informal*) knowledge of how to do sth and experience in doing it 專門知識；技能；實際經驗：*We need skilled workers and technical know-how.* 我們需要熟練工人和專業技術知識。

know·ing /ˈnəʊɪŋ; *NAmE* ˈnoʊ-/ *adj.* [usually before noun] showing that you know or understand about sth that is supposed to be secret 會意的；心照不宣的；知情的：*a knowing smile* 會意的微笑 ➲ compare UNKNOWING

know·ing·ly /ˈnəʊɪŋli; *NAmE* ˈnoʊ-/ *adv.* **1** while knowing the truth or likely result of what you are doing 故意地；蓄意地 **SYN** **deliberately**：*She was accused of knowingly making a false statement to the police.* 她被指控故意向警方提供虛假供詞。 **2** in a way that shows that you know or understand about sth that is supposed to be secret 會意地；心照不宣地；知情地：*He glanced at her knowingly.* 他會意地看了她一眼。

'know-it-all (*especially NAmE*) (*BrE* also **'know-all**) *noun* (*informal, disapproving*) a person who behaves as if they know everything 自以為無所不知的人；百事通

know·ledge 🗝 /ˈnɒlɪdʒ; *NAmE* ˈnɑːl-/ *noun* **1** 🗝 [U, sing.] the information, understanding and skills that you gain through education or experience 知識；學問；學識：*practical/medical/scientific knowledge* 實際／醫學／科學知識 ◇ **~ of/about sth** *He has a wide knowledge of painting and music.* 他在繪畫和音樂方面知識淵博。◇ *There is a lack of knowledge about the tax system.* 大家對稅制缺乏瞭解。 **2** 🗝 [U] the state of knowing about a particular fact or situation 知曉；知悉；瞭解：*She sent the letter* ***without my knowledge***. 她背着我把信寄了出去。◇ *The film was made with the Prince's* ***full knowledge*** *and approval.* 這部影片是在王子充分瞭解和認可的情況下拍攝的。◇ *She was impatient* ***in the knowledge that*** *time was limited.* 她知道時間有限，所以很着急。◇ *I went to sleep* ***secure in the knowledge*** *that I was not alone in the house.* 我知道當時不是只有我一人在房子裏，就放心地睡覺了。◇ *They could relax* ***safe in the knowledge*** *that they had the funding for the project.* 他們得知工程撥款已有着落時就感到踏實輕鬆了。◇ *He* ***denied all knowledge of*** *the affair.* 他否認知道此事。 **3 ~ economy/industry/worker** working with information rather than producing goods 信息，知識（與產品製造相對）

IDM **be common/public 'knowledge** to be sth that everyone knows, especially in a particular community or group 常識；眾所周知 **come to sb's 'knowledge** (*formal*) to become known by sb 被某人知道；被某人獲悉：*It has come to our knowledge that you have been taking time off without permission.* 我們瞭解到你們時常未經允許就不上班。 **to your 'knowledge** from the information you have, although you may not know everything 據某人所知：*'Are they divorced?' 'Not to my knowledge.'* "他們離婚了嗎？" "據我所知沒有。" ➲ more at BEST *n.*

know·ledge·able /ˈnɒlɪdʒəbl; *NAmE* ˈnɑːl-/ *adj.* **~ (about sth)** knowing a lot 博學的；有見識的；知識淵

K

博的 SYN **well informed**： *She is very knowledgeable about plants.* 她對植物很在行。 ▸ **know·ledge·ably** /-əbli/ *adv.*

known /nəʊn; *NAmE* noʊn/ *adj.* [only before noun] known about, especially by a lot of people 知名的；出了名的；已知的： *He's a known thief.* 他是個出了名的小偷。◇ *The disease has no known cure.* 這種病目前還是不治之症。 ➲ see also KNOW *v.*

knuckle /ˈnʌkl/ *noun, verb*

■ *noun* **1** [C] any of the joints in the fingers, especially those connecting the fingers to the rest of the hand 指節；指關節 ➲ VISUAL VOCAB page V59 **2** (also **hock** especially in *NAmE*) [U, C] a piece of meat from the lower part of an animal's leg, especially a pig （豬等動物的）肘，蹄

IDM **near the ˈknuckle** (*BrE, informal*) (of a remark, joke, etc. 言語、玩笑等) concerned with sex in a way that is likely to offend people or make them feel embarrassed 近乎下流；近乎猥褻 ➲ more at RAP *n.*, RAP *v.*

■ *verb*

PHR V **ˌknuckle ˈdown (to sth)** (*informal*) to begin to work hard at sth 開始努力做 SYN **get down to**： *I'm going to have to knuckle down to some serious study.* 我得開始認認真真地學習了。 **ˌknuckle ˈunder (to sb/sth)** (*informal*) to accept sb else's authority 屈服；認輸

ˈknuckle-dragger *noun* (*informal*) a stupid man who thinks and behaves in simple, basic ways （缺心眼兒的）莽漢，笨蛋

knuckle·dust·er /ˈnʌkldʌstə(r)/ *noun* (*NAmE* also **ˌbrass ˈknuckles**) a metal cover that is put on the fingers and used as a weapon 指節金屬套（用作武器）

knuckle·head /ˈnʌklhed/ *noun* (*NAmE, informal*) a person who behaves in a stupid way 笨蛋；傻瓜

ˌknuckle ˈsandwich *noun* (*slang*) a punch in the mouth 對準嘴巴的一拳

KO (also **kayo**) /ˌkeɪ ˈəʊ; *NAmE* ˈoʊ/ *abbr.* KNOCKOUT 擊倒

koala /kəʊˈɑːlə; *NAmE* koʊ-/ (also **koˌala ˈbear**) *noun* an Australian animal with thick grey fur, large ears and no tail. Koalas live in trees and eat leaves. 樹袋熊；考拉；無尾熊 ➲ VISUAL VOCAB page V12

kofta /ˈkɒftə; *NAmE* ˈkɔːf-/ *noun* [U, C] a S Asian dish of meat, fish or cheese mixed with spices, crushed and shaped into balls; one of these balls 柯夫塔（用肉、魚或乾酪加香料壓碎調製成丸子的南亞菜肴）；柯夫塔丸子

kohl /kəʊl; *NAmE* koʊl/ *noun* [U] a black powder that is used especially in Eastern countries. It is put around the eyes to make them more attractive. 黑色眼影粉（尤指東方人用的）

kohl·rabi /ˌkəʊlˈrɑːbi; *NAmE* ˌkoʊl-/ *noun* [U] a vegetable of the CABBAGE family whose thick round white STEM is eaten 球莖甘藍；苤藍

koi /kɔɪ/ *noun* (*pl.* **koi**) a large fish originally from Japan, often kept in fish PONDS 錦鯉（觀賞魚，源自日本）

ˈkola nut *noun* = COLA NUT

kombi (also **combi**) /ˈkɒmbi; *NAmE* ˈkɑːm-/ *noun* (*SAfrE*) a vehicle that looks like a van, has windows at the sides and carries about ten people 康比小客車（可乘坐約十人）

Ko·modo dragon /kəˌməʊdəʊ ˈdræɡən; *NAmE* kəˌmoʊdoʊ/ *noun* a very large LIZARD from Indonesia 科莫多龍，科莫多巨蜥（產於印度尼西亞）

kook /kuːk/ *noun* (*informal, especially NAmE*) a person who acts in a strange or crazy way 怪人；狂人 ▸ **kooky** *adj.*

kooka·burra /ˈkʊkəbʌrə; *NAmE* -bɜːrə/ *noun* an Australian bird that makes a strange laughing cry 笑翠鳥（產於澳大利亞）

Koori /ˈkʊəri; *NAmE* ˈkʊri/ *noun* (*AustralE*) an Aboriginal person from the south-east of Australia （澳大利亞東南部的）土著

kop /kɒp; *NAmE* kɑːp/ *noun* **1** (*SAfrE, informal*) a head 頭；腦袋 **2** (*SAfrE*) (especially in place names 尤用於地名) a hill 小山 **3** (usually **the Kop**) (*BrE*) (especially in the past) an area of steps at a football (SOCCER) team's ground where that team's supporters stand to watch the game （尤指舊時足球隊主場的）主隊球迷看台

kop·pie /ˈkɒpi; *NAmE* ˈkɑːpi/ *noun* (*SAfrE*) a small hill 小山；小丘： *They went for a walk up the koppie.* 他們去小山上散步了。

kora /ˈkɔːrə/ *noun* a W African musical instrument with 21 strings that pass over a bowl-shaped body and are attached to a long wooden part 科拉琴（西非 21 弦樂器，狀似豎琴）

Koran (also **Qur'an**) /kəˈrɑːn/ *noun* **the Koran** [sing.] the holy book of the Islamic religion, written in Arabic, containing the word of Allah as REVEALED to the Prophet Muhammad《古蘭經》；《可蘭經》 ▸ **Kor·an·ic** /kəˈrænɪk/ *adj.*

korf·ball /ˈkɔːfbɔːl; *NAmE* ˈkɔːrf-/ *noun* [U] a game similar to BASKETBALL, played by two teams of eight players, four men and four women 合球，荷蘭式籃球運動，科爾夫球（比賽雙方各由四男四女組隊）

korma /ˈkɔːmə; *NAmE* ˈkɔːrmə/ *noun* [U, C] a S Asian dish or sauce made with cream or YOGURT, and often ALMONDS 奶油（或酸奶）浸肉（常加有杏仁的南亞菜肴或醬汁）： *chicken korma* 奶油浸雞肉

ko·sher /ˈkəʊʃə(r); *NAmE* ˈkoʊ-/ *adj.* **1** (of food 食物) prepared according to the rules of Jewish law 合猶太教教規及禮儀要求的） **2** (*informal*) honest or legal 誠實的；合法的： *Their business deals are not always completely kosher.* 他們的商業活動並不總是光明正大的。

kow·tow /ˌkaʊˈtaʊ/ *verb* [I] **~ (to sb/sth)** (*informal, disapproving*) to show sb in authority too much respect and be too willing to obey them 叩頭；磕頭；卑躬屈膝；唯命是從

KP /ˌkeɪ ˈpiː/ *noun* [U] (*NAmE*) work done by soldiers in the kitchen, usually as a punishment （常作為士兵懲罰的）伙房幫廚： *The sergeant assigned him to KP.* 中士派他下伙房去幫廚。 ORIGIN From 'kitchen police', a name for the soldiers. 源自 kitchen police （幫廚兵）一詞。

kph /ˌkeɪ piː ˈeɪtʃ/ *abbr.* kilometres per hour 每小時所行千米（或公里）數；千米每小時

kraal /krɑːl/ *noun* (*SAfrE*) **1** a traditional African village of HUTS surrounded by a fence 柵欄村莊（傳統的非洲茅屋村莊） **2** an area surrounded by a fence in which animals are kept 牲畜欄： *a cattle kraal* 牛欄

kra·ken /ˈkrɑːkən/ *noun* an extremely large imaginary creature which is said to appear in the sea near Norway （虛構的出沒於挪威附近的）北海巨妖

Kraut /kraʊt/ *noun* (*taboo, slang*) an offensive word for a person from Germany 德國佬；德國鬼子

krill /krɪl/ *noun* [pl.] very small SHELLFISH that live in the sea around the Antarctic and are eaten by WHALES 南極磷蝦；磷蝦

kris /kriːs/ *noun* a Malay or Indonesian knife with a blade with little curves on its edge （馬來或印度尼西亞的）波狀刃短劍，波形刃

Kriss Kringle /ˌkrɪs ˈkrɪŋɡl/ *noun* (*NAmE*) = SANTA CLAUS ORIGIN From *Christkindl*, the German for 'Christ child'. 源自表示"幼年基督"的德語詞 Christkindl。

krona /ˈkrəʊnə; *NAmE* ˈkroʊnə/ *noun* (*pl.* **kro·nor** /-nɔː(r); -nə(r)/) the unit of money in Sweden and Iceland 克朗（瑞典和冰島貨幣單位）

krone /ˈkrəʊnə; *NAmE* ˈkroʊnə/ *noun* (*pl.* **kro·ner** /-nə(r)/) the unit of money in Denmark and Norway 克朗（丹麥和挪威貨幣單位）

kryp·ton /ˈkrɪptɒn; *NAmE* -tɑːn/ *noun* [U] (*symb.* **Kr**) a chemical element. Krypton is a gas that does not react with anything, used in FLUORESCENT lights and LASERS. 氪；氪氣

kryp·ton·ite /ˈkrɪptənaɪt/ *noun* [U] a chemical element that exists only in stories, especially in stories about Superman, a character with special powers which he loses when he is near to kryptonite 氪（僅存在於超人等故事中的化學元素，超人若接近此元素即喪失超常能力）

kudos /ˈkjuːdɒs; *NAmE* ˈkuːdɑːs/ *noun* [U] the admiration and respect that goes with a particular achievement or position（隨某成就或地位而來的）榮譽，威信，光榮，名聲 SYN **prestige**：*the kudos of playing for such a famous team* 跟着這樣著名的隊參加比賽的榮譽

kudu /ˈkuːduː/ *noun* (*pl.* **kudu** or **kudus**) a large greyish or brownish African ANTELOPE with white stripes on its sides. The male kudu has long twisted horns. 撚角羚（見於非洲）

kudzu /ˈkʊdzuː/ *noun* [U] a climbing plant with purple flowers that grows very fast and is used as a food and in medicines 葛

Ku Klux Klan /ˌkuː klʌks ˈklæn/ *noun* [sing.+sing./pl. v.] (*abbr.* **KKK**) a secret organization of white men in the southern states of the US who use violence to oppose social change and equal rights for black people 三 K 黨（美國南部的白人秘密組織，通過暴力反對社會變革和為黑人爭取平等權利）

kulfi /ˈkʊlfi/ *noun* [C, U] a type of S Asian ice cream, usually served in the shape of a CONE （南亞）考非冰淇淋（通常為圓錐形）

kum·quat /ˈkʌmkwɒt; *NAmE* -kwɑːt/ *noun* a fruit like a very small orange with sweet skin that is eaten, and sour flesh 金柑；金橘

kung fu /ˌkʌŋ ˈfuː/ *noun* [U] (from *Chinese*) a Chinese system of fighting without weapons, similar to KARATE 功夫（中國拳術）

kurta /ˈkɜːtə; *NAmE* ˈkɜːrtə/ *noun* a loose shirt, worn by men or women in S Asia 庫爾塔衫，柯泰衫（南亞的寬鬆襯衫，男女皆宜）

kvetch /kvetʃ/ *verb* [I] (*NAmE, informal*) to complain about sth all the time 老是抱怨；總是發牢騷 SYN **moan, whine**

kW *abbr.* (*pl.* **kW**) (in writing) KILOWATT(S) （書寫形式）千瓦：*a 2kW electric fire* * 2 千瓦的電爐

kwaito /ˈkwaɪtəʊ; *NAmE* -toʊ/ *noun* [U] a type of South African dance music, often with words that are spoken or shouted rather than sung 庫威多舞曲（南非舞曲，常伴以說唱）

Kwan·zaa /ˈkwænzɑː/ *noun* [U] a cultural festival that is celebrated in the US by some African Americans from December 26 to January 1 匡扎節（一些非裔美國人於 12 月 26 日至次年 1 月 1 日舉行的節日）ORIGIN From a phrase in Swahili that means ‘first fruits’. 源自斯瓦希里語，意為“首批收穫的水果”。

kwashi·or·kor /ˌkwɒʃiˈɔːkɔː(r); ˌkwæʃ-; *NAmE* ˌkwɑːʃiˈɔːrkər/ *noun* [U] a dangerous form of MALNUTRITION that is caused by not eating enough PROTEIN 夸希奧科病；蛋白質營養不良

kwela /ˈkwelə/ *noun* [U] a type of South African JAZZ music in which the main part is usually played on a PENNY WHISTLE (= a type of long whistle with holes in it that you can cover with your fingers to produce different notes) 基維拉（南非爵士樂，主要部份由六孔小笛吹奏）

kWh *abbr.* (*pl.* **kWh**) (in writing) KILOWATT-HOUR(S)（書寫形式）千瓦時，一度（電）

kylie /ˈkaɪli/ *noun* (*AustralE*) a BOOMERANG 回力鏢；飛去來器

K

Ll

L /el/ *noun, abbr., symbol*

■ ***noun*** (also **l**) [C, U] (*pl.* **Ls, L's, l's** /elz/) the 12th letter of the English alphabet 英語字母表的第 12 個字母：*'Lion' begins with (an) L/'L'.* * lion 一詞以字母 l 開頭。➲ see also L-PLATE

■ ***abbr.*** **1 L.** (especially on maps) Lake（尤標於地圖上）湖：*L. Windermere* 温德米爾湖 **2** (especially for sizes of clothes) large（尤作衣服尺碼的標誌）大號：*S, M and L* (= small, medium and large) 小號、中號和大號

■ ***symbol*** (also **l**) the number 50 in ROMAN NUMERALS（羅馬數字）50

l *abbr.* **1** (*pl.* **l**) (in writing) litre(s)（書寫形式）升 **2** (also **l.**) (*pl.* **ll**) (in writing) line (on a page in a book)（書寫形式，指書頁上的）行

LA (also **L.A.**) /ˌel ˈeɪ/ *abbr.* the city of Los Angeles 洛杉磯市

la = LAH ➲ see also À LA

laa·ger /ˈlɑːɡə(r)/ *noun* (*SAfrE*) (in the past) a group of WAGONS that were put into a circle in order to protect people in the middle（舊時用馬車圍成的）臨時防禦陣地；車陣：*They drew their wagons into a laager and set up camp.* 他們把馬車圍成一圈紮起營地。◇ ***a laager mentality*** (= one that is not willing to accept new ideas) 守舊心態

Lab. *abbr.* (in British politics 英國政治) Labour 工黨

lab 🗝 /læb/ *noun* (*informal*) = LABORATORY：*science labs* 實驗室 ◇ *a lab technician* 實驗室技術員 ◇ *a lab coat* (= a white coat worn by scientists, etc. working in a laboratory) 實驗室白袍

label 標籤

price tag 價格標籤

ticket 票

label 🗝 AW /ˈleɪbl/ *noun, verb*

■ ***noun*** **1** 🗝 a piece of paper, etc. that is attached to sth and that gives information about it 標籤；籤條；標記 SYN **tag, ticket**：*The washing instructions are on the label.* 洗滌說明在標籤上。◇ *price/address labels* 價格標籤；地址籤條 ◇ *We tested various supermarkets' **own label** pasta sauces* (= those marked with the name of the shop/store where they are sold). 我們檢查了各大超市的自家商標意大利麪調味汁。◇ *He'll only wear clothes with a **designer label**.* 他只穿名牌服裝。➲ VISUAL VOCAB page V33 **2** (*disapproving*) a word or phrase that is used to describe sb/sth in a way that seems too general, unfair or not correct（不恰當的）稱謂，綽號，叫法：*I hated the label 'housewife'.* 我不喜歡"家庭主婦"這個稱謂。**3** a company that produces and sells music, CDs, etc. 唱片公司：*the Virgin record label* 維京唱片公司 ◇ *It's his first release for a major label.* 這是他在大唱片公司發行的第一張唱片。

■ ***verb*** (**-ll-**, *especially US* **-l-**) [often passive] **1** 🗝 **~ sth** to fix a label on sth or write information on sth 貼標籤於；用標籤標明：*We carefully labelled each item with the contents and the date.* 我們仔細地把每件物品用標籤標明成分和日期。◇ *The file was labelled 'Private'.* 那檔案上標明"私人"。**2** to describe sb/sth in a particular way, especially unfairly（尤指不公正地）把…稱為：**~ sb/sth (as) sth** | **~ sb/sth + noun** *He was labelled (as) a traitor by his former colleagues.* 他被以前的同事稱為叛徒。◇ **~ sb/sth + adj.** *It is unfair to label a small baby as naughty.* 硬說一個小小的嬰兒淘氣是不公平的。

Synonyms 同義詞辨析

label

tag • sticker

These are all words for a piece of paper, fabric or plastic that is attached to sth and gives information about it. 以上各詞均指標籤、標記。

label a small piece of paper, fabric or plastic that is attached to sth in order to show what it is or give information about it 指標籤、籤條、標記：*The washing instructions are on the label.* 洗滌說明在標籤上。◇ *address labels* 地址籤條 ◇ *He'll only wear clothes with a **designer label**.* 他只穿名牌服裝。

tag (often used in compounds) a small piece of paper, fabric or plastic that is attached to sth, or that sb wears, in order to give information about it/them（常構成複合詞）指標籤、標牌：*Everyone at the conference had to wear a name tag.* 所有與會者必須佩戴名牌。

LABEL OR TAG? 用 label 還是 tag？

Labels in clothes are usually made of fabric and sewn in. **Tags** on clothes are usually made of cardboard and cut off before you wear the clothes. A *name tag* can be stuck or tied onto sb to show who they are. 衣服上的 label 通常由織物做成並縫在衣服上，衣服上的 tag 通常指掛在衣服上的硬紙板標籤，穿衣服前要將其剪下。name tag 指可貼或繫在身上表明佩戴者身分的名牌：*All babies in the hospital have name tags tied round their ankles.* 醫院裏所有嬰兒的腳踝上都繫有姓名標籤。

Price tag is much more frequent than *price label* and is used for both literal and figurative meanings. * price tag 指價格標籤，遠較 price label 常用，既可用作字面意義也可用作比喻意義：*What does the price tag say?* 標價是多少？◇ *There is a £20 million price tag on the team's star player.* 這名球隊主將身價為 2 千萬英鎊。A **label** can also be a **sticker** that you put on an envelope. * label 亦可指貼在信封上的粘貼標籤。

sticker a sticky label with a picture or message on it, that you stick on to sth 指粘貼標籤、貼紙

PATTERNS

- a **price** label/tag/sticker
- to **have** a label/tag/sticker
- to **attach/put on/stick on** a label/tag/sticker
- The label/tag/sticker **says** …

labia /ˈleɪbiə/ *noun* [pl.] the four folds of skin at the entrance to a woman's VAGINA 陰唇

la·bial /ˈleɪbiəl/ *noun* (*phonetics* 語音) a speech sound made with the lips, for example /m/, /p/ and /v/ in *me*, *pea* and *very* 唇音 ▶ **la·bial** *adj.*

la·bio·den·tal /ˌleɪbiəʊˈdentl; *NAmE* -bioʊ-/ *noun* (*phonetics* 語音) a speech sound made by placing the top teeth against the bottom lip, for example /f/ and /v/ in *fan* and *van* 唇齒音 ▶ **la·bio·den·tal** *adj.*

la·bio·velar /ˌleɪbiəʊˈviːlə(r); *NAmE* -bioʊ-/ *noun* (*phonetics* 語音) a speech sound made using the lips and soft PALATE, for example /w/ in *we* 圓唇軟腭音；唇化軟腭音 ▶ **la·bio·velar** *adj.*

labor AW (*especially US*) = LABOUR

la·bora·tory 🗝 /ləˈbɒrətri; *NAmE* ˈlæbrətɔːri/ *noun* (*pl.* **-ies**) (also *informal* **lab**)
a room or building used for scientific research, experiments, testing, etc. 實驗室；實驗大樓：*a research laboratory* 研究實驗室 ◇ ***laboratory experiments/tests*** 實驗室的實驗／測試 ➲ see also LANGUAGE LABORATORY

ˈLabor Day *noun* a public holiday in the US and Canada on the first Monday of September, in honour of working people 勞工節（在美國和加拿大為九月的第一個星期一）➲ compare MAY DAY

la·bored, **la·bor·er**, **la·bor·ing** (*especially US*) = LABOURED, LABOURER, LABOURING

la·bori·ous /ləˈbɔːriəs/ *adj.* taking a lot of time and effort 耗時費力的；辛苦的 **SYN** **onerous, taxing**：*a **laborious task/process*** 艱巨的任務；艱難的過程 ◇ *Checking all the information will be slow and laborious.* 查看所有的信息既費時又費力。▶ **la·bori·ous·ly** *adv.*

ˈlabor union *noun* (*NAmE*) = UNION (1)

la·bour 🔑 **AW** (*especially US* **labor**) /ˈleɪbə(r)/ *noun, verb*

■ ***noun***

▸ WORK 勞動 **1** 🔑 [U] work, especially physical work 勞動；（尤指）體力勞動：***manual labour*** (= work using your hands) 體力勞動 ◇ *The price will include the labour and materials.* 此價格中包含人工費和材料費。◇ *The company wants to keep down **labour costs**.* 公司想保持低勞動成本。◇ *The workers voted to **withdraw their labour*** (= to stop work as a means of protest). 工人投票決定罷工以示抗議。◇ *He was sentenced to two years in a **labour camp*** (= a type of prison where people have to do hard physical work). 他被判處兩年勞改。**2** [C, usually pl.] (*formal*) a task or period of work 任務；（一段時間的）工作：*He was so exhausted from the day's labours that he went straight to bed.* 他工作了一天疲憊不堪，便直接上牀休息了。

▸ PEOPLE WHO WORK 勞動者 **3** 🔑 [U] the people who work or are available for work in a country or company（統稱）勞工，工人；勞動力：*a shortage of labour* 勞動力的短缺 ◇ *Employers are using immigrants as **cheap labour**.* 雇主正在把移民當作廉價勞動力使用。◇ *Repairs involve **skilled labour**, which can be expensive.* 修理需要熟練技工，人工費會很昂貴。◇ *good **labour relations*** (= the relationship between workers and employers) 良好的勞資關係

▸ HAVING BABY 分娩 **4** [U, C, usually sing.] the period of time or the process of giving birth to a baby 分娩期；分娩；生產：*Jane was **in labour** for ten hours.* 簡分娩花了十個小時。◇ *She **went into labour** early.* 她早產了。◇ *labour pains* 分娩時的陣痛

▸ POLITICS 政治 **5 Labour** [sing.+sing./pl. v.] (*abbr.* **Lab.**) the British Labour Party 英國工黨：*He always votes Labour.* 他老是投工黨的票。◇ *Labour was/were in power for many years.* 工黨曾執政多年。

IDM **a ˌlabour of ˈlove** a hard task that you do because you want to, not because it is necessary 為愛好而做的困難工作

■ ***verb***

▸ STRUGGLE 奮鬥 **1** [I] to try very hard to do sth difficult 努力做（困難的事）：**~ (away)** *He was in his study labouring away over some old papers.* 他在書房裏潛心研究一些舊材料。◇ **~ to do sth** *They laboured for years to clear their son's name.* 他們為洗刷兒子的罪名努力爭取了許多年。

▸ WORK HARD 努力工作 **2** [I] to do hard physical work 幹苦力活：*We laboured all day in the fields.* 我們在田地裏辛勤勞動了一整天。◇ (*old-fashioned*) *the labouring classes* (= the working class) 工人階級

▸ MOVE WITH DIFFICULTY 吃力地行進 **3** [I] (**+ adv./prep.**) to move with difficulty and effort 困難吃力地行進 **SYN** **struggle**：*The horses laboured up the steep slope.* 那些馬費力地爬上了陡坡。

IDM **labour the ˈpoint** to continue to repeat or explain sth that has already been said and understood 一再重複，反複解釋（已說明的事）

PHR V **ˈlabour under sth** (*formal*) to believe sth that is not true 為…所蒙蔽：*to **labour under a misapprehension/delusion, etc.*** 有誤解、錯覺等 ◇ *He's still labouring under the impression that he's written a great book.* 他仍然有這樣的錯覺，以為自己撰寫了一部巨著。

la·boured (*especially US* **la·bored**) /ˈleɪbəd; *NAmE* -bərd/ *adj.* **1** (of breathing 呼吸) slow and taking a lot of effort 緩慢而困難的 **2** (of writing, speaking, etc. 寫作、說話等) not natural and seeming to take a lot of effort 不自然的；費力的；矯揉造作的

la·bour·er (*especially US* **la·bor·er**) /ˈleɪbərə(r)/ *noun* a person whose job involves hard physical work that is not skilled, especially work that is done outdoors（尤指戶外的）體力勞動者，勞工，工人

ˈlabour force (*especially US* **ˈlabor force**) *noun* [C+sing./pl. v.] all the people who work for a company or in a country（全公司或全國的）勞動力 **SYN** **workforce**：*a skilled/an unskilled labour force* 熟練/非熟練工人

la·bour·ing (*especially US* **la·bor·ing**) /ˈleɪbərɪŋ/ *noun* [U] hard physical work that is not skilled 體力勞動：*a labouring job* 體力勞動工作

ˌlabour-inˈtensive (*especially US* **ˌlabor-inˈtensive**) *adj.* (of work 工作) needing a lot of people to do it 勞動密集型的：*labour-intensive methods* 勞動密集型方法 ➲ compare CAPITAL-INTENSIVE

ˈlabour market (*especially US* **ˈlabor market**) *noun* the number of people who are available for work in relation to the number of jobs available 勞動力市場：*young people about to enter the labour market* 即將進入勞動力市場的年輕人

the ˈLabour Party (also **Labour**) *noun* [sing.+sing./pl. v.] one of the main British political parties, on the political left, that has traditionally represented the interests of working people 工黨（英國主要政黨之一，傳統上代表勞動人民的利益）：*the Labour Party leader* 工黨領袖

ˈlabour-saving (*especially US* **ˈlabor-saving**) *adj.* [usually before noun] designed to reduce the amount of work or effort needed to do sth 省力的；節省勞力的；降低勞動強度的：*modern labour-saving devices such as washing machines and dishwashers* 諸如洗衣機和洗碗機之類的現代化省力設備

L

Lab·ra·dor /ˈlæbrədɔː(r)/ *noun* a large dog that can be yellow, black or brown in colour, often used by blind people as a guide 拉布拉多獵犬（常用於導盲）：*a **golden/black/chocolate Labrador*** 金黃色/黑色/深褐色拉布拉多犬

la·bur·num /ləˈbɜːnəm; *NAmE* -ˈbɜːrn-/ *noun* [C, U] a small tree with hanging bunches of yellow flowers 金鏈花（開懸垂黃花）

laby·rinth /ˈlæbərɪnθ/ *noun* (*formal*) a complicated series of paths, which it is difficult to find your way through 迷宮；曲徑：*We lost our way in the labyrinth of streets.* 我們在迷宮式的街道上迷了路。◇ (*figurative*) *a labyrinth of rules and regulations* 錯綜複雜的規章制度 ➲ compare MAZE (1) ▶ **laby·rin·thine** /ˌlæbəˈrɪnθaɪn; *NAmE* also -θɪn/ *adj.*：(*formal*) *labyrinthine corridors* 迷宮式的走廊 ◇ *labyrinthine legislation* 錯綜複雜的立法程序

lace /leɪs/ *noun, verb*

■ ***noun*** **1** [U] a delicate material made from threads of cotton, silk, etc. that are twisted into a pattern of holes 網眼織物；花邊；蕾絲：*a lace handkerchief* 蕾絲手帕 ◇ *a tablecloth edged with lace* 鑲有花邊的桌布 ◇ *lace curtains* 蕾絲窗簾 ➲ see also LACY **2** [C] = SHOELACE：*Your laces are undone.* 你的鞋帶鬆開了。➲ **VISUAL VOCAB** page V63

■ ***verb*** **1** [I, T] to be fastened with laces; to fasten sth with laces 由帶子繫緊；把…用帶子繫牢：**~ (up)** *She was wearing a dress that laced up at the side.* 她穿着一件在側面繫帶子的連衣裙。◇ **~ sth (up)** *He was sitting on the bed lacing up his shoes.* 他正坐在牀邊繫鞋帶。➲ see also LACE-UP **2** [T] **~ sth** to put a lace through the holes in a shoe, a boot, etc. 給（鞋、靴等）穿鞋帶 ➲ related noun LACE-UP **3** [T] **~ sth (with sth)** to add a small amount of alcohol, a drug, poison, etc. to a drink 給（飲料）摻（少量的酒、藥、毒藥等）**SYN** **spike**：*He had laced her milk with rum.* 他在她的牛奶裏加了少量朗姆酒。**4** [T] **~ sth (with sth)** to add a particular quality to a book, speech, etc. 給（書、講話等）潤色：*Her conversation was laced with witty asides.* 她談起話來帶着幾分俏皮。**5** [T] **~ sth** to twist sth together with another thing 使編織（或交織、纏繞）在一起：*They sat with their fingers laced.* 他們手指交叉着坐在那裏。

la·cer·ate /ˈlæsəreɪt/ *verb* (*formal*) **1 ~ sth** to cut skin or flesh with sth sharp 劃破，割裂（皮或肉）：*His hand had been badly lacerated.* 他的一隻手被嚴重劃傷了。**2 ~ sb** to criticize sb very severely 嚴厲抨擊；斥責

▸ **la·cer·ation** /ˌlæsəˈreɪʃn/ *noun* [C, U]： *She suffered multiple lacerations to the face.* 她的面部多處被劃傷。

ˈlace-up *noun* [usually pl.] (*especially BrE*) a shoe that is fastened with laces 繫帶鞋： *a pair of lace-ups* 一雙繫帶鞋 ◊ *lace-up boots* 繫帶靴子 ➲ compare OXFORD (1) ➲ VISUAL VOCAB page V64

lace·wing /ˈleɪswɪŋ/ *noun* an insect that has large transparent wings with lines on 草蛉（翅有網狀脈）

lach·ry·mose /ˈlækrɪməʊs; *NAmE* -moʊs/ *adj.* (*formal*) having a tendency to cry easily 愛哭的；愛流淚的 SYN **tearful**

lack 0‑π /læk/ *noun, verb*

■ **noun** 0‑π [U, sing.] **~ (of sth)** the state of not having sth or not having enough of sth 缺乏；匱乏；短缺 SYN **dearth, shortage**： *a lack of food/money/skills* 缺乏食物 / 金錢 / 技能 ◊ *The trip was cancelled* ***through lack of*** (= because there was not enough) *interest.* 因為缺乏興趣這次旅行被取消了。◊ *There was* ***no lack of*** *volunteers.* 志願者不乏其人。 IDM see TRY *v.*

■ **verb** 0‑π [no passive] **~ sth** to have none or not enough of sth 沒有；缺乏；不足；短缺： *Some houses still lack basic amenities such as bathrooms.* 有些住宅仍沒有像衞生間這樣的基本設施。◊ *He lacks confidence.* 他缺乏信心。◊ *She has the determination that her brother lacks.* 她有決心，而她弟弟卻沒有。➲ see also LACKING (1)

IDM **ˌlack (for) ˈnothing** (*formal*) to have everything that you need 沒有欠缺 ➲ more at COURAGE

lacka·dai·si·cal /ˌlækəˈdeɪzɪkl/ *adj.* not showing enough care or enthusiasm 無精打采的；委靡不振的；懶洋洋的；不熱心的

lackey /ˈlæki/ *noun* **1** (*old-fashioned*) a servant 僕人；用人；聽差；跟班 **2** (*disapproving*) a person who is treated like a servant or who behaves like one 被當作僕人看待者；卑躬屈膝的人；狗腿子；走狗

lack·ing 0‑π /ˈlækɪŋ/ *adj.* [not before noun]
1 0‑π **~ (in sth)** having none or not enough of sth 沒有；匱乏；缺乏；不足： *She's not usually lacking in confidence.* 她平時並不缺乏自信心。◊ *The book is completely lacking in originality.* 這部書完全沒有創意。◊ *He was taken on as a teacher but was* ***found lacking*** (= was thought not to be good enough). 他獲聘為教師，能力卻顯得一般。 **2** 0‑π not present or not available 不在場；得不到 SYN **missing**： *I feel there is something lacking in my life.* 我覺得我的生活中缺少點什麼。

lack·lustre (*especially US* **lack·lus·ter**) /ˈlæklʌstə(r)/ *adj.* not interesting or exciting; dull 無趣味的；單調的；枯燥乏味的： *a lacklustre performance* 枯燥乏味的表演 ◊ *lacklustre hair* 無光澤的頭髮

la·con·ic /ləˈkɒnɪk; *NAmE* -ˈkɑːn-/ *adj.* using only a few words to say sth 簡潔的；簡明扼要的；凝練的 ▸ **la·con·ic·al·ly** /-kli/ *adv.*

lac·quer /ˈlækə(r)/ *noun, verb*

■ **noun** [U] **1** a liquid that is used on wood or metal to give it a hard shiny surface 漆 **2** (*old-fashioned*) a liquid that is sprayed on the hair so that it stays in place 頭髮定型劑；噴髮膠 SYN **hairspray**

■ **verb 1 ~ sth** to cover sth such as wood or metal with lacquer 給（木製品或金屬）塗漆 **2 ~ sth** (*old-fashioned, BrE*) to put lacquer on your hair 給（頭髮）噴髮膠

la·crosse /ləˈkrɒs; *NAmE* -ˈkrɔːs; -ˈkrɑːs/ *noun* [U] a game played on a field by two teams of ten players who use sticks with curved nets on them to catch, carry, and throw the ball 長曲棍球（兩隊各十名隊員，用帶網兜的球棒接球、帶球和傳球）

lac·tate /lækˈteɪt/ *verb* [I] (*technical* 術語) (of a woman or female animal 婦女或雌性動物) to produce milk from the breasts to feed a baby or young animal 泌乳；哺乳
▸ **lac·ta·tion** /lækˈteɪʃn/ *noun* [U]： *the period of lactation* 哺乳期

lac·tic acid /ˌlæktɪk ˈæsɪd/ *noun* [U] an acid that forms in sour milk and is also produced in the muscles during hard exercise 乳酸

lacto·ba·cil·lus /ˌlæktəʊbəˈsɪləs; *NAmE* -toʊ-/ *noun* (*biology* 生) a type of bacteria that produces lactic acid 乳桿菌

lac·tose /ˈlæktəʊs; -təʊz; *NAmE* -toʊs; -toʊz/ *noun* [U] (*chemistry* 化) a type of sugar found in milk and used in some baby foods 乳糖

la·cuna /ləˈkjuːnə; *NAmE* also -ˈkuː-/ *noun* (*pl.* **-nae** /-niː/ or **la·cu·nas**) (*formal*) a place where sth is missing in a piece of writing or in an idea, a theory, etc.（文章、思想、理論等中的）缺漏，脱漏，空白，闕如 SYN **gap**

lacy /ˈleɪsi/ *adj.* made of or looking like LACE 網眼狀的；蕾絲的；似蕾絲的： *lacy underwear* 蕾絲內衣

lad /læd/ *noun* **1** [C] (*old-fashioned* or *informal, BrE*) a boy or young man 男孩兒；少年；男青年；小伙子： *Things have changed since I was a lad.* 從我幼時至今，一切都發生了變化。◊ *He's a nice lad.* 他是個好小伙子。➲ compare LASS **2 the lads** [pl.] (*BrE, informal*) a group of friends that a man works with or spends free time with 夥伴；哥們兒： *to go to the pub with the lads* 與夥伴一起去酒吧 **3** [C, usually sing.] (*BrE, informal*) a lively young man, especially one who is very interested in women and having sex, drinks a lot of alcohol and enjoys sport（精力旺盛的）放蕩小伙子： *Tony was* ***a bit of a lad*** *—always had an eye for the women.* 托尼這小子真是個花花公子，總是很會欣賞女人。➲ see also LADDISH **4** [C] (*BrE*) a person who works in a stable 馬夫；馬倌 ➲ see also STABLE BOY

lad·der /ˈlædə(r)/ *noun, verb*

■ **noun 1** a piece of equipment for climbing up and down a wall, the side of a building, etc., consisting of two lengths of wood or metal that are joined together by steps or RUNGS 梯子： *to* ***climb up/fall off a ladder*** 爬上 / 跌下梯子 ➲ VISUAL VOCAB page V20 ➲ see also STEPLADDER **2** [usually sing.] a series of stages by which you can make progress in your life or career（生活上進步或事業上晉升的）階梯，途徑： *to move up or down* ***the social ladder*** 爬上 / 跌下社會階梯 ◊ ***the career ladder*** 事業上的階梯 ◊ (*BrE*) *to get onto* ***the property ladder*** (= buy your first home) 首次進入有房階層 **3** (*BrE*) (*NAmE* **run**) a long thin hole in TIGHTS or STOCKINGS where some threads have broken（緊身褲襪或長筒襪的）滑絲，抽絲 **4** (also **ˈladder tournament**) a competition in a particular sport or game in which teams or players are arranged in a list and they can move up the list by defeating one of the teams or players above 階級比賽，階級遊戲（將參賽者排名，勝者名次前提）

■ **verb** [I, T] **~ (sth)** (*BrE*) if TIGHTS or STOCKINGS **ladder** or you **ladder** them, a long thin hole appears in them（緊身褲襪或長筒襪）出現滑絲，抽絲

lad·die /ˈlædi/ *noun* (*informal, especially ScotE*) a boy 男孩；小伙子 ➲ compare LASS

lad·dish /ˈlædɪʃ/ *adj.* (*informal*) behaving in a way that is supposed to be typical of a young man 小伙子的；有小伙子特徵的

laden /ˈleɪdn/ *adj.* **~ (with sth) 1** heavily loaded with sth 載滿的；裝滿的： *passengers laden with luggage* 攜帶大批行李的旅客 ◊ *The trees were laden with apples.* 樹上都掛滿了蘋果。◊ *a* ***heavily/fully laden*** *truck* 滿載的卡車 ➲ compare UNLADEN **2** (*literary*) full of sth, especially sth unpleasant 充滿的（尤指充滿令人不快的東西）： *His voice was soft, yet laden with threat.* 他說話的聲音很柔和，但充滿了恐嚇的語氣。 **3 -laden** used to form adjectives showing that sth is full of, or loaded with, the thing mentioned（用於構成形容詞）充滿…的，裝載…的： *calorie-laden cream cakes* 高熱量的奶油蛋糕

lad·ette /lædˈet/ *noun* (*BrE, informal*) a young woman who enjoys drinking alcohol, sport or other activities usually considered to be typical of young men 男性化的年輕女子，假小子（喜歡做年輕男子常做的事，如喝酒、參加體育運動等）

la-di-da (also **lah-di-da**) /ˌlɑː di ˈdɑː/ *adj., exclamation*

■ **adj.** (*informal, especially BrE*) used to describe a way of speaking or behaving that is typical of upper-class people but that is not natural or sincere（描述像上層人的說話或舉止）裝腔作勢的，裝模作樣的，做作的 SYN **affected**

▪ ***exclamation*** used when sb is irritating you, because they seem to think they are more important than they really are 真可笑（用於譏諷自視過高惹人討厭的人）

ˈladies' man (also **ˈlady's man**) *noun* a man who enjoys spending time with women and thinks he is attractive to them 喜歡厮混在女人中間的男人；自以為討女人喜歡的男子

ladle /ˈleɪdl/ *noun, verb*

▪ ***noun*** a large deep spoon with a long handle, used especially for serving soup 長柄勺；湯勺 ➲ VISUAL VOCAB page V26

▪ ***verb*** **~ sth** to place food on a plate with a large spoon or in large quantities（用大勺）舀，盛

PHR V **ˌladle sth↔ˈout** (sometimes *disapproving*) to give sb a lot of sth, especially money or advice 大量給予（尤指金錢或建議） **SYN** **dole sth out**

la dolce vita /lɑː ˌdɒltʃeɪ ˈviːtə; *NAmE* ˌdoʊl-/ *noun* [sing.] (from *Italian*) a life of pleasure and expensive things, without any worries 奢華無憂的生活

lady 0→ /ˈleɪdi/ (*pl.* **-ies**) *noun* **1** 0→ [C] a word used to mean 'woman' that some people, especially older people, consider is more polite 女士，女子（指成年女子，有些人尤其是長者認為這樣說比較禮貌）：*There's a lady waiting to see you.* 有位女士等着要見你。◇ *He was with an attractive young lady.* 他與一位漂亮的年輕女子在一起。◇ *the ladies' golf championship* 女子高爾夫球錦標賽 ◇ (*BrE*) *a tea lady* (= a woman who serves tea in an office)（辦公室的）上茶女侍 ◇ (*NAmE, approving*) *She's a tough lady.* 她是個能吃苦耐勞的女士。◇ *a lady doctor/golfer* 女醫生／高爾夫球手 **HELP** Some women object to the way **lady** is used in some of these examples and prefer it to be avoided if possible. 一些婦女反對上述某些例句中的用法，喜歡盡可能避免用 lady 一詞：*a doctor/a woman doctor* ◇ *There's someone waiting to see you.* ➲ see also BAG LADY, CLEANING LADY, DINNER LADY, FIRST LADY, LEADING LADY, LUNCH LADY, OLD LADY **2** 0→ [C] a woman who is polite and well educated, has excellent manners and always behaves well 舉止文雅且有教養的女子；淑女：*His wife was a real lady.* 他的妻子真是個嫻雅的淑女。➲ compare GENTLEMAN (1) **3** 0→ [C, usually pl.] (*formal*) used when speaking to or about a girl or woman, especially sb you do not know（尤用於稱呼或談及不認識的女子）女士，小姐：*Can I take your coats, ladies?* 女士們，我可以替你們拿大衣嗎？◇ *Could I have your attention, ladies and gentlemen?* 女士們，先生們，請注意！ **HELP** Some women do not like **ladies** used on its own, as in the first example, and prefer it to be left out. 在第一個例子的情況下，一些婦女不喜歡單獨使用 ladies，而更喜歡省去不用。 **4** [sing.] (*especially NAmE*) an informal way to talk to a woman, showing a lack of respect（不尊重的非正式稱呼）女人，女士：*Listen, lady, don't shout at me.* 聽着，女士，別對我大喊大叫的。 **5** [C] (*old-fashioned*) (in Britain) a woman belonging to a high social class（英國）貴婦人，夫人，小姐：*the lords and ladies of the court* 宮廷的貴族及夫人 ◇ *a lady's maid* 貴婦人的貼身女侍 **6** **Lady** [C] (in Britain) a title used by a woman who is a member of the NOBILITY, or by sb who has been given the title 'lady' as an honour. The wives and daughters of some members of the NOBILITY and the wives of KNIGHTS are also called 'Lady'.（在英國對女貴族、女爵士、貴族成員的妻女或爵士妻子的稱呼）夫人，女士，小姐：*Lady Howe* 豪夫人 ◇ *Lady Jane Grey* 簡•格雷小姐 ➲ compare LORD *n.* (1), (4), SIR (3) **7** **a/the ladies** [U] (*BrE*) (*NAmE* **ˈladies' room** [C]) a toilet/bathroom for women in a public building or place 女廁所；女衞生間；女洗手間；女盥洗室：*Could you tell me where the ladies is?* 請告訴我女衞生間在哪裏好嗎？ **8** **Our Lady** a title used to refer to Mary, the mother of Christ, especially in the Roman Catholic Church（羅馬天主教常用）聖母：*Our Lady of Lourdes* 露德聖母 **IDM** see FAT *adj.*, LEISURE

lady·bird /ˈleɪdibɜːd; *NAmE* -bɜːrd/ (*BrE*) (*NAmE* **lady·bug** /ˈleɪdibʌɡ/) *noun* a small flying insect, usually red with black spots 瓢蟲 ➲ VISUAL VOCAB page V13

lady·boy /ˈleɪdibɔɪ/ *noun* (*informal*) a TRANSVESTITE or TRANSSEXUAL 易裝癖者；易性癖者

lady·finger /ˈleɪdifɪŋɡə(r)/ *noun* (*NAmE*) a small long thin cake made with eggs, sugar and flour 手指鬆餅

ˌlady-in-ˈwaiting *noun* (*pl.* **ladies-in-waiting**) a woman who goes to places with, and helps, a queen or princess（女王或公主的）宮廷女侍，宮女，女侍臣

lady·kill·er /ˈleɪdikɪlə(r)/ *noun* (*old-fashioned* or *informal*) a man who is sexually attractive and successful with women, but who does not stay in a relationship with anyone for long 專門勾引女子的男人；使女子傾心的男人

lady·like /ˈleɪdilaɪk/ *adj.* (*old-fashioned*) polite and quiet; typical of what is supposed to be socially acceptable for a woman 文靜的；溫文爾雅的；淑女似的 **SYN** **refined**：*ladylike behaviour* 文靜嫻雅的舉止 ◇ *Her language was not very ladylike.* 她的用語不怎麼文雅。

ˌlady ˈmayor *noun* = MAYORESS (1)

lady·ship /ˈleɪdiʃɪp/ *noun* **1** **Her/Your Ladyship** a title used when talking to or about a woman who is a member of the NOBILITY（對女貴族的稱呼）夫人，小姐：*Does Your Ladyship require anything?* 夫人您需要點什麼？ **2** (*BrE, informal*) a way of talking to or about a girl or woman that you think is trying to be too important（對佯裝高貴的女子的用語）小姐，夫人：*Perhaps her ladyship would like to hang up her own clothes today!* 尊貴的夫人今天也許願意自己動手把衣服掛起來吧！ ➲ compare LORDSHIP (1)

ˈlady's man *noun* = LADIES' MAN

lag /læɡ/ *verb, noun*

▪ ***verb*** (**-gg-**) **1** [I] **~ (behind sb/sth)** | **~ (behind)** to move or develop slowly or more slowly than other people, organizations, etc. 緩慢移動；發展緩慢；滯後；落後於 **SYN** **trail**：*The little boy lagged behind his parents.* 那小男孩落在了父母的後面。◇ *We still lag far behind many of our competitors in using modern technology.* 我們在運用現代技術方面仍然遠遠落後於我們的許多競爭對手。 **2** [T] **~ sth (with sth)** (*BrE*) to cover pipes, etc. with a special material to stop the water in them from freezing, or to save heat 給（管道等）加防凍保暖層 **SYN** **insulate**

▪ ***noun*** = TIME LAG ➲ see also JET LAG, OLD LAG

lager /ˈlɑːɡə(r)/ *noun* (*BrE*) **1** [U, C] a type of light pale beer that usually has a lot of bubbles 拉格啤酒，貯陳啤酒，窖藏啤酒（味淡，通常多泡沫）：*a pint of lager* 一品脫拉格啤酒 ◇ *German lagers* 德國拉格啤酒 **2** [C] a glass, can or bottle of this 一杯（或一罐、一瓶）拉格啤酒（或貯藏啤酒）

ˈlager lout *noun* (*BrE*) a young man who drinks too much alcohol and then behaves in a noisy and unpleasant way 喝酒後行為不端的年輕人；耍酒瘋的青年

lag·gard /ˈlæɡəd; *NAmE* -ɡərd/ *noun* (*old-fashioned*) a slow and lazy person, organization, etc. 遲鈍懶散者；遲緩者；渙散的機構

la·goon /ləˈɡuːn/ *noun* **1** a lake of salt water that is separated from the sea by a REEF or an area of rock or sand 潟湖；環礁湖；瀕海湖 **2** (*NAmE*) a small area of fresh water near a lake or river（湖泊或江河附近的）小片淡水域，小淡水湖 **3** (*technical* 術語) an artificial area built to hold waste water before it is treated at a SEWAGE WORKS（人造）污水貯留池

lah (also **la**) /lɑː/ *noun* (*music* 音) the 6th note of a MAJOR SCALE 大調音階的第 6 音

lah-di-dah = LA-DI-DA

laid *past tense, past part.* of LAY

ˌlaid-ˈback *adj.* (*informal*) calm and relaxed; seeming not to worry about anything 安詳放鬆的；鬆弛的；彷彿無憂無慮的 **SYN** **easy-going**：*a laid-back attitude to life* 悠然自得的生活態度

lain *past part.* of LIE[1]

lair /leə(r); *NAmE* ler/ *noun* [usually sing.] **1** a place where a wild animal sleeps or hides 獸穴；獸窩 **2** a place where sb goes to hide or to be alone（人的）藏身處，躲藏處，獨居處 **SYN** **den, hideout**

laird /leəd; *NAmE* lerd/ *noun* (in Scotland) a person who owns a large area of land（蘇格蘭）地主

lairy /ˈleəri; *NAmE* ˈleri/ *adj.* (*BrE, informal*) behaving in a way that seems too loud and confident 張揚的；旁若無人的

laissez-faire /ˌleseɪ ˈfeə(r); *NAmE* ˈfer/ *noun* [U] (from *French*) the policy of allowing private businesses to develop without government control（政府對私有企業的）自由放任政策 ▸ **laissez-faire** *adj.*：*a laissez-faire economy* 自由放任的經濟 ◇ *They have a laissez-faire approach to bringing up their children* (= they give them a lot of freedom). 他們採用放任自由的方法來養育子女。

laity /ˈleɪəti/ *noun* **the laity** [sing.+sing./pl. v.] all the members of a Church who are not CLERGY（統稱）平信徒 ➲ see also LAYMAN (2)

lake 🔑 /leɪk/ *noun* (*abbr.* **L.**) a large area of water that is surrounded by land 湖；湖泊：*We swam in the lake.* 我們在湖裏游泳。◇ *Lake Ontario* 安大略湖 ◇ (*figurative*) *a wine lake* (= a large supply of wine that is not being used) 葡萄酒池 ➲ VISUAL VOCAB pages V4, V5

lake·side /ˈleɪksaɪd/ *noun* [sing.] the area around the edge of a lake 湖邊；湖岸；湖畔：*We went for a walk by the lakeside.* 我們沿湖邊散步。◇ *a lakeside hotel* 湖邊旅館

lakh /læk/ *number* (*plural verb*) (*pl.* **lakh** or **lakhs**) (*IndE*) a hundred thousand 十萬

la-la land /ˈlɑː lɑː lænd/ (also **cloud·land**) (both *NAmE*) (*BrE* ˌ**cloud ˈcuckoo land**) *noun* [U] (*informal, disapproving*) if you say that sb is living **in la-la land**, you mean that they do not understand what a situation is really like, but think it is much better than it is 幻想世界；脱離現實的幻境

lam /læm/ *noun, verb*

■ *noun*

IDM **on the ˈlam** (*NAmE, informal*) escaping from sb, especially from the police 在逃，逃匿（尤指逃避警方追緝）

■ *verb* (**-mm-**)

PHR V ˌ**lam ˈinto sb** (*BrE, informal*) to attack sb violently with blows or words 痛打某人；猛烈抨擊某人：*She really lammed into her opponent during the debate.* 在辯論中她着實給對手以猛烈的攻擊。

lama /ˈlɑːmə/ *noun* **1** a title given to a spiritual leader in Tibetan Buddhism 喇嘛（藏傳佛教高僧稱號）**2** a Buddhist MONK from Tibet or Mongolia 喇嘛（西藏和蒙古的佛教僧侶）

Lama·ism /ˈlɑːməɪzəm/ *noun* [U] Tibetan Buddhism 喇嘛教；藏傳佛教

lamb /læm/ *noun, verb*

■ *noun* **1** [C] a young sheep 羔羊；小羊 **2** [U] meat from a young sheep 羊羔肉：*a leg of lamb* 羔羊腿肉 ◇ *lamb chops* 羔羊排 ➲ compare MUTTON **3** [C] (*informal*) used to describe or address sb with affection or pity（慈愛或憐憫地描述或稱呼某人）寶貝，乖乖：*You poor lamb!* 可憐的寶貝！

IDM (**like**) **a lamb/lambs to the ˈslaughter** used to describe people who are going to do sth dangerous without realizing it（如同）羔羊被牽往屠宰場（指將遇危險而不自覺的人）➲ more at MUTTON, WELL *adv.*

■ *verb* [I] (of a sheep 羊) to give birth to a lamb 產羊羔

lam·bada /læmˈbɑːdə/ *noun* a fast Brazilian dance performed by couples who hold each other closely 蘭巴達（源自巴西的快步舞，二人緊擁對方舞蹈）

lam·baste (also **lam·bast**) /læmˈbeɪst/ *verb* **~ sb/sth** (*formal*) to attack or criticize sb/sth very severely, especially in public（尤指公開地）猛烈抨擊，狠狠批評 SYN **lay into**

lambda /ˈlæmdə/ *noun* the 11th letter of the Greek alphabet (Λ, λ) 希臘字母表的第 11 個字母

lambs·wool /ˈlæmzwʊl/ *noun* [U] soft fine wool from lambs, used for knitting clothes 羔羊毛（用以編織衣服）：*a lambswool sweater* 羔羊毛套衫

lame /leɪm/ *adj.* **1** (of people or animals 人或動物) unable to walk well because of an injury to the leg or foot 瘸的；跛的 **2** (of an excuse, explanation, etc. 藉口、解釋等) weak and difficult to believe 站不住腳的；無說服力的 SYN **feeble, unconvincing** ▸ **lame·ness** *noun* [U]：*The disease has left her with permanent lameness.* 那場病使她永遠不能直立走路了。

lamé /ˈlɑːmeɪ; *NAmE* lɑːˈmeɪ/ *noun* [U] a type of cloth into which gold or silver thread has been twisted 金銀錦緞

lame·brain /ˈleɪmbreɪn/ *noun* (*informal, especially NAmE*) a stupid person 呆子；笨蛋 ▸ **lame·brain** (also **lame·brained**) *adj.*：*They invented some lamebrain scheme to get rich quick.* 為發橫財，他們想出了個蠢辦法。

ˌ**lame ˈduck** *noun* **1** a person or an organization that is not very successful and that needs help 不太成功而需要幫助的人（或機構）；"跛腳鴨" **2** (*US, informal*) a politician or government whose period of office will soon end and who will not be elected again（不能繼續連任的）即將屆滿卸任的從政者（或政府）；"跛腳鴨"：***a lame-duck president/administration*** 跛腳鴨總統／政府

lame·ly /ˈleɪmli/ *adv.* in a way that does not sound very confident, or that does not persuade other people（聽起來）信心不足地，不具說服力地，站不住腳地 SYN **feebly**：*'I must have made a mistake,' she said lamely.* "我一定是弄錯了。"她膽怯地說。

lam·ent /ləˈment/ *verb, noun*

■ *verb* **~ sth** | **~ that …** | **+ speech** (*formal*) to feel or express great sadness or disappointment about sb/sth 對…感到悲痛；痛惜；對…表示失望 SYN **bemoan, bewail**：*In the poem he laments the destruction of the countryside.* 在那首詩裏他對鄉村遭到的破壞流露出悲哀。

■ *noun* (*formal*) a song, poem or other expression of great sadness for sb who has died or for sth that has ended 輓歌；哀詩；悼辭

lam·ent·able /ˈlæməntəbl; ləˈment-/ *adj.* (*formal*) very disappointing 十分令人失望的；令人遺憾的；使人惋惜的 SYN **deplorable, regrettable**：*She shows a lamentable lack of understanding.* 她顯得缺乏體諒，實在令人遺憾。▸ **lam·ent·ably** /-əbli/ *adv.*

lam·en·ta·tion /ˌlæmənˈteɪʃn/ *noun* [C, U] (*formal*) an expression of great sadness or disappointment 悲傷；悲痛；悲哀；十分失望

lam·ented /ləˈmentɪd/ *adj.* (*formal* or *humorous*) (of sb/sth that has died or disappeared 已死亡的人或已消失的事物) missed very much 令人悼念（或懷念）的；使人思念的：*her late lamented husband* 她那令人懷念的已故的丈夫 ◇ *the last edition of the much lamented newspaper* 那非常令人懷念的報紙的最後一期

lamin·ate /ˈlæmɪnət/ *noun* [U, C] a material that is laminated 薄片製成的材料；層壓（或粘合）材料

lamin·ated /ˈlæmɪneɪtɪd/ *adj.* **1** (of wood, plastic, etc. 木材、塑料等) made by sticking several thin layers together 由薄層粘製成的；層壓的；粘合的 **2** covered with thin transparent plastic for protection 用透明塑料薄膜覆蓋的；護貝的：*laminated membership cards* 壓膜會員卡

lam·ing·ton /ˈlæmɪŋtən/ *noun* (*AustralE, NZE*) a square piece of SPONGE cake that has been put in liquid chocolate and covered with small pieces of COCONUT 拉明頓蛋糕；椰絲巧克力方形海棉蛋糕

lamp 🔑 /læmp/ *noun, verb*

■ *noun* **1** 🔑 a device that uses electricity, oil or gas to produce light 燈：***a table/desk/bicycle, etc. lamp*** 枱燈、書桌燈、自行車燈等 ◇ ***to switch on/turn off a lamp*** 開／關燈 ◇ ***a street lamp*** 路燈 ➲ VISUAL VOCAB pages V21, V69 ➲ see also FOG LAMP, HURRICANE LAMP, LAVA LAMP, STANDARD LAMP **2** an electrical device that produces RAYS of heat and that is used for medical or scientific purposes（理療用的）發熱燈；（科學上用的）射線照射器：***an infra-red/ultraviolet lamp*** 紅外線／紫外線燈 ➲ see also BLOWLAMP, SUNLAMP

■ *verb* (*BrE, informal*) to hit sb very hard 重擊；狂毆：**~ sb** *The guy lamped me.* 那傢伙打得我不輕。◇ **~ sb sth** *I'd have lamped her one!* 我本想狠狠地揍她一頓！

lamp·light /ˈlæmplaɪt/ *noun* [U] light from a lamp 燈光

lamp·lit /ˈlæmplɪt/ *adj.* [usually before noun] given light by lamps; seen by the light from lamps 用燈光照明的；在燈光下可見的： *a lamplit room* 亮着燈的房間 ◇ *a lamplit figure in the chair* 燈光下坐在椅子上的人

lam·poon /læmˈpuːn/ *verb, noun*

■ ***verb* ~ sb/sth** to criticize sb/sth publicly in an amusing way that makes them or it look ridiculous 嘲諷；譏諷 **SYN** **satirize**： *His cartoons mercilessly lampooned the politicians of his time.* 他的漫畫毫不留情地嘲諷了他那個年代的政治人物。

■ ***noun*** a piece of writing that criticizes sb/sth and makes them or it look ridiculous 諷刺文章；幽默諷刺作品

ˈlamp post *noun* (*especially BrE*) a tall post in the street with a lamp at the top 路燈柱；燈杆： *The car skidded and hit a lamp post.* 那輛汽車打滑撞上了路燈杆。 ➲ compare STREET LIGHT ➲ **VISUAL VOCAB** page V2, V3

lam·prey /ˈlæmpri/ *noun* a FRESHWATER fish with a round mouth that attaches itself to other fish and sucks their blood 七鰓鰻，八目鰻（以口吸附於其他魚體，吸食宿主血液）

lamp·shade /ˈlæmpʃeɪd/ *noun* a decorative cover for a lamp that is used to make the light softer or to direct it 燈罩 ➲ **VISUAL VOCAB** page V21

LAN /læn/ *noun* (*computing* 計) the abbreviation for 'local area network' (a system for communicating by computer within a large building or group of buildings) 局部區域網，局域網，本地網（全寫為 local area network） ➲ compare WAN

lance /lɑːns; *NAmE* læns/ *noun, verb*

■ ***noun*** a weapon with a long wooden handle and a pointed metal end that was used by people fighting on horses in the past （舊時騎兵的）長矛

■ ***verb* 1** [T] **~ sth** to cut open an infected place on sb's body with a sharp knife in order to let out the PUS (= a yellow substance produced by infection) 用刀切開（感染處放膿）： *to lance an abscess* 切開膿腫 **2** [I] **+ adv./prep.** (of a pain 疼痛) to move suddenly and quickly and be very sharp 突然迅速傳導；突然劇烈起來： *Pain lanced through his body.* 疼痛傳到他的全身。

ˌlance ˈcorporal *noun* a member of one of the lower ranks in the British army （英國陸軍的）一等兵： *Lance Corporal Alan Smith* 一等兵艾倫 • 史密斯

lan·cer /ˈlɑːnsə(r); *NAmE* ˈlæn-/ *noun* in the past, a member of a REGIMENT that used LANCES （舊時的）長矛輕騎兵

lan·cet /ˈlɑːnsɪt; *NAmE* ˈlæn-/ *noun* a knife with a sharp point and two sharp edges, used by doctors for cutting skin and flesh （醫生用的）柳葉刀，小刀

land 🔑 /lænd/ *noun, verb*

■ ***noun***

▸ **SURFACE OF EARTH** 地球表面 **1** 🔑 [U] the surface of the earth that is not sea 陸地；大地： *It was good to be back* ***on land****.* 回到陸地上真好。◇ *We made the journey* ***by land****, though flying would have been cheaper.* 雖然乘飛機會便宜些，我們還是走了陸路。◇ *In the distance the crew sighted land.* 船員在遠處發現了陸地。◇ *The elephant is the largest living land animal.* 象是現今陸地上最大的動物。 ➲ **SYNONYMS** at FLOOR, SOIL ➲ see also DRY LAND

▸ **AREA OF GROUND** 土地 **2** 🔑 [U] (also **lands** [pl.]) an area of ground, especially of a particular type or used for a particular purpose（尤指某類型或作某種用途的）地帶，土地 **SYN** **terrain**： ***fertile/arid/stony, etc. land*** 肥沃、貧瘠、多石等的土地 ◇ ***flat/undulating/hilly, etc. land*** 平坦、波狀、丘陵等地帶 ◇ ***agricultural/arable/industrial, etc. land*** 農業用地、可耕地、工業用地等 ◇ *The land was very dry and hard after the long, hot summer.* 經過漫長的炎夏這塊土地又乾又硬。◇ *The land rose to the east.* 那地向東隆起。◇ *a piece of* ***waste/derelict land*** 一塊荒地／棄置的荒地 ◇ *Some of the country's richest grazing lands are in these valleys.* 全國最肥沃的一些牧場位於這些峽谷中。 **3** 🔑 [U] (also *formal* **lands** [pl.]) the area of ground that sb owns, especially when you think of it as property that can be bought or sold 地產；地皮： *The price of land is rising rapidly.* 地價正在迅速上漲。◇ *During the war their lands were occupied by the enemy.* 戰爭期間他們的土地被敵人佔據了。 ➲ see also NO-MAN'S-LAND

▸ **COUNTRYSIDE** 農村 **4 the land** [U] used to refer to the countryside and the way people live in the country as opposed to in cities （與城市相對的）農村，農村生活方式： *At the beginning of the 20th century almost a third of the population* ***lived off the land*** (= grew or produced their own food). * 20 世紀初幾乎有三分之一的人口依靠種地為生。◇ *Many people leave the land to find work in towns and cities.* 許多人離開農村到城鎮裏找工作。 ➲ **SYNONYMS** at COUNTRY

▸ **COUNTRY/REGION** 國家；地區 **5** [C] (*literary*) used to refer to a country or region in a way which appeals to the emotions or the imagination （涉及感情或想像）國家，地區： *She longed to return to her* ***native land****.* 她渴望回到她的祖國。◇ *They dreamed of travelling to* ***foreign lands****.* 他們夢想去外國旅遊。◇ *America is the land of freedom and opportunity.* 美國是一個擁有自由與機遇的國度。 ➲ see also CLOUD CUCKOO LAND, CLUBLAND, DOCKLAND, DREAMLAND, FAIRYLAND, NEVER-NEVER LAND, THE PROMISED LAND, WONDERLAND **HELP** There are many other compounds ending in **land**. You will find them at their place in the alphabet. 以 land 結尾的複合詞還有很多，可在各字母中的適當位置查到。

IDM **in the land of the ˈliving** (often *humorous*) awake or alive or no longer ill/sick 醒着；活着；在人世；康復 **the land of ˌmilk and ˈhoney** a place where life is pleasant and easy and people are very happy 富饒的樂土；豐裕之地 **in the ˌland of ˈNod** (*old-fashioned, humorous*) asleep 睡着；在夢鄉： *Pete and Jo were still in the land of Nod, so I went out for a walk in the morning sunshine.* 皮特和喬仍沉睡未醒，於是我就在晨光中出門散步去了。 **see, etc. how the ˈland lies** (*BrE*) to find out about a situation 弄清情況；摸清形勢： *Let's wait and see how the land lies before we do anything.* 咱們等弄清情況以後再行動吧。 ➲ more at LIE[1] *n.*, LIVE[1], SPY *v.*

■ ***verb***

▸ **OF BIRD/PLANE/INSECT** 鳥；飛機；昆蟲 **1** 🔑 [I] to come down through the air onto the ground or another surface 落；降落；着陸： *The plane landed safely.* 飛機安全着陸了。◇ *A fly landed on his nose.* 一隻蒼蠅落在他的鼻子上。 **OPP** **take off**

▸ **OF PILOT** 飛行員 **2** 🔑 [T] **~ sth** to bring a plane down to the ground in a controlled way 使（飛機）平穩着陸： *The pilot landed the plane safely.* 飛行員駕駛飛機安全着陸。

▸ **ARRIVE IN PLANE/BOAT** 乘飛機／船到達 **3** 🔑 [I] to arrive somewhere in a plane or a boat （乘飛機或船）着陸，登陸： *We shall be landing shortly. Please fasten your seatbelts.* 我們很快就要着陸，請您繫好安全帶。◇ *The troops landed at dawn.* 部隊已在黎明登陸。◇ *They were the first men to land on the moon.* 他們是首批登上月球的人。◇ *The ferry is due to land at 3 o'clock.* 渡輪預定 3 點鐘到岸。 **4** [T] **~ sb/sth** to put sb/sth on land from an aircraft, a boat, etc. （使）着陸，降落，靠岸，登陸： *The troops were landed by helicopter.* 部隊乘直升機降落。

▸ **FALL TO GROUND** 跌落地面 **5** 🔑 [I] to come down to the ground after jumping, falling or being thrown 跳落，跌落，被拋落（地面）： *I fell and landed heavily at the bottom of the stairs.* 我從樓梯上摔了下去，重重地摔在下面。◇ *A large stone landed right beside him.* 一大塊石頭正好落在他身旁。

▸ **DIFFICULTIES** 困難 **6** [I] **+ adv./prep.** to arrive somewhere and cause difficulties that have to be dealt with 降臨；使陷於（困境）；使不得不應付： *Why do complaints always* ***land on my desk*** (= why do I always have to deal with them)? 為什麼投訴總得要我來處理？

▸ **JOB** 工作 **7** [T] (*informal*) to succeed in getting a job, etc., especially one that a lot of other people want 成功得到，贏得，撈到（尤指許多人想得到的工作）： **~ sth** *He's just landed a starring role in Spielberg's next movie.* 他剛得到一個機會，在斯皮爾伯格執導的下一部電影裏擔任主角。◇ **~ sb/yourself sth** *She's just landed herself a company directorship.* 她剛在一家公司謀到一個主管的職位。

▸ **FISH** 魚 **8** [T] **~ sth** to catch a fish and bring it out of the water on to the land 捕到，釣到（魚）

L

IDM **land a 'blow, 'punch, etc.** to succeed in hitting sb/sth 打中；擊中：*She landed a punch on his chin.* 她對着他的下巴揍了一拳。➲ more at FOOT *n.*

PHR V **'land in sth | 'land sb/yourself in sth** (*informal*) to get sb/yourself into a difficult situation 使陷入（困境）：*She was arrested and landed in court.* 她被逮捕並送上了法庭。◇ *His hot temper has landed him in trouble before.* 他脾氣急躁，以前就遇到過麻煩。◇ *Now you've really* ***landed me in it!*** (= got me into trouble) 你這可把我坑苦了！ **,land 'up in, at ...** (*informal*) to reach a final position or situation, sometimes after other things have happened 終於到達（某位置）；最終落到（某種處境）**SYN** **end up**：*We travelled around for a while and landed up in Seattle.* 我們到處旅遊了一段時間，最後抵達西雅圖。◇ *He landed up in a ditch after he lost control of his car.* 他開車失控，栽進了溝裏。**'land sb/yourself with sth/sb** (*informal*) to give sb/yourself sth unpleasant to do, especially because nobody else wants to do it 把（苦差事）推給（某人）；主動承擔（苦差事）：*As usual, I got landed with all the boring jobs.* 所有枯燥乏味的工作都照例落在了我的頭上。

Synonyms 同義詞辨析

land

lot • ground • space • plot

These words all mean an area of land that is used for a particular purpose. 以上各詞均指作特定用途的土地。

land an area of ground, especially one that is used for a particular purpose 尤指作特定用途的土地、地帶：*agricultural land* 農業用地

lot (*NAmE*) a piece of land that is used or intended for a particular purpose 指作某種用途的一塊地、場地：*building lots* 建築用地◇ *a parking lot* 停車場

ground an area of land that is used for a particular purpose 指作特定用途的場地：*The kids were playing on waste ground near the school.* 孩子們在學校附近的荒地玩耍。◇ *the site of an ancient burial ground* 古代墓地舊址

LAND, LOT OR GROUND? 用 land、lot 還是 ground？

Land is used for large areas of open land in the country, especially when it is used for farming. A **lot** is often a smaller piece of land in a town or city, especially one intended for building or parking on. **Ground** is any area of open land; a **ground** is an area of land designed or used for a particular purpose or activity. * land 用以指鄉間廣闊的土地，尤指農業用地；lot 常指城鎮或城市中的一小塊地，尤指專用的建築或停車場地；ground 作不可數名詞指任何開闊地、空曠地，作可數名詞指特定用途或活動的場地。

space a large area of land that has no buildings on it 指無建築物的大片空地、開闊地：*The city has plenty of open space.* 這座城市有很多開闊的空地。◇ *the* ***wide open spaces*** *of the Canadian prairies* 加拿大一片片廣袤的草原

plot a small piece of land used or intended for a particular purpose 指專用的小塊土地：*She bought a small* ***plot of land*** *to build a house.* 她買了一小塊地蓋所房子。◇ *a vegetable plot* 一塊菜圃

LOT OR PLOT? 用 lot 還是 plot？

Either a **lot** or a **plot** can be used for building on. Only a **plot** can also be used for growing vegetables or burying people. * lot 和 plot 均可作建築用地。plot 亦可作菜地或墓地。

PATTERNS

- an **open** space
- **open/empty/vacant/waste/derelict** land/ground
- a/an **empty/vacant** lot/plot

'land agent *noun* (*especially BrE*) a person whose job is to manage land, farms, etc. for sb else 地產管理人

lan·dau /ˈlændɔː; -aʊ/ *noun* a CARRIAGE with four wheels and a roof that folds down in two sections, that is pulled by horses 雙排座活頂四輪馬車

'land-based *adj.* [usually before noun] located on or living on the land 位於陸地上的；棲息於陸地的：*land-based missiles* 陸基導彈◇ *land-based animals* 陸生動物

land·ed /ˈlændɪd/ *adj.* [only before noun] **1** owning a lot of land 擁有大量土地的：*the landed gentry* 擁有大量土地的鄉紳 **2** including a large amount of land 包括大量土地的：*landed estates* 地產

,landed 'immigrant *noun* (*CanE*) a person from another country who has permission to live permanently in Canada 落地移民（在加拿大獲准永久居留的外國移民）

land·fall /ˈlændfɔːl/ *noun* **1** [U, C] (*literary*) the land that you see or arrive at first after a journey by sea or by air（航海或飛行後）初見陸地，踏上陸地：*After three weeks they* ***made landfall*** *on the coast of Ireland.* 三個星期之後，他們登上了愛爾蘭的海岸。**2** [C] = LANDSLIDE (1)

land·fill /ˈlændfɪl/ *noun* **1** [C, U] an area of land where large amounts of waste material are buried under the earth 廢物填埋地（或場）：*The map shows the position of the new landfills.* 這張地圖上標有新的廢物填埋場的位置。◇ *a landfill site* 廢物填埋場地 ➲ **VISUAL VOCAB** page V6 **2** [U] the process of burying large amounts of waste material 廢物填埋：*the choice of landfill or incineration* 廢物填埋還是焚燒的選擇 **3** [U] waste material that will be buried 填埋的廢物

land·form /ˈlændfɔːm; *NAmE* -fɔːrm/ *noun* (*geology* 地) a natural feature of the earth's surface 地形；地貌

land·hold·ing /ˈlændhəʊldɪŋ; *NAmE* -hoʊld-/ *noun* [C, U] (*technical* 術語) a piece of land that sb owns or rents; the fact of owning or renting land 擁有（或租用）的一塊土地；擁有（或租用）土地 ▸ **land·hold·er** *noun*：*farmers and landholders* 農場主與土地所有者

land·ing /ˈlændɪŋ/ *noun* **1** [C] the area at the top of a set of stairs where you arrive before you go into an upstairs room or move onto another set of stairs 樓梯平台；（兩段樓梯間的）過渡平台 ➲ picture at STAIRCASE **2** [C, U] an act of bringing an aircraft or a SPACECRAFT down to the ground after a journey 降落；着陸：*a perfect/smooth/safe landing* 準確／順利／安全着陸◇ *the first Apollo* ***moon landing*** 阿波羅航天飛船首次登月着陸◇ *The pilot was forced to make* ***an emergency landing.*** 飛行員被迫緊急着陸。◇ *a landing site* 降落場 **OPP** **take-off** ➲ see also CRASH LANDING at CRASH-LAND **3** [C] an act of bringing soldiers to land in an area that is controlled by the enemy 登陸 **4** (*BrE* also **'landing stage**) [C] a flat wooden platform on the water where boats let people get on and off, and load and unload goods 碼頭；浮動碼頭；棧橋 **SYN** **jetty**

'landing craft *noun* (*pl.* **landing craft**) a boat with a flat bottom, carried on a ship. Landing craft open at one end so soldiers and equipment can be brought to land. 登陸艇

'landing gear *noun* [U] = UNDERCARRIAGE

'landing lights *noun* [pl.] **1** bright lamps on a plane that are switched on before it lands（飛機上的）着陸燈 **2** lights that are arranged along the sides of a RUNWAY to guide a pilot when he or she is landing a plane（飛機跑道兩邊的）着陸指示燈

'landing page *noun* (*computing* 計) the part of a website that you reach first when you click on a link on the Internet（網站）登陸頁：*Have a different landing page for each advertising campaign.* 為每個廣告宣傳活動設置不同的登陸頁。

'landing stage (*BrE*) (also **landing** *NAmE, BrE*) *noun* a flat wooden platform on the water where boats let people get on and off, and load and unload goods 碼頭；浮動碼頭；棧橋 **SYN** **jetty**

'landing strip *noun* = AIRSTRIP

land·lady /ˈlændleɪdi/ *noun* (*pl.* **-ies**) **1** a woman from whom you rent a room, a house, etc. 女房東；女地主 **2** (*BrE*) a woman who owns or manages a pub or a

GUEST HOUSE（酒吧或招待所的）女店主，女老闆 SYN proprietor ➲ compare LANDLORD

land·less /ˈlændləs/ *adj.* [usually before noun] not owning land for farming; not allowed to own land 無土地的；不准擁有土地的

land·line /ˈlændlaɪn/ *noun* a telephone connection that uses wires carried on poles or under the ground, in contrast to a mobile/cell phone（電話的）陸地線路，陸線，固網：*I'll call you later on the landline.* 晚些時候我會用固定線路給你打電話。➲ COLLOCATIONS at PHONE

land·locked /ˈlændlɒkt; *NAmE* -lɑːkt/ *adj.* almost or completely surrounded by land 幾乎（或完全）被陸地包圍的；陸圍的；內陸的：*Switzerland is completely landlocked.* 瑞士完全是個內陸國。

land·lord /ˈlændlɔːd; *NAmE* -lɔːrd/ *noun* **1** a person or company from whom you rent a room, a house, an office, etc. 業主；地主；房東 **2** (*BrE*) a man who owns or manages a pub or a GUEST HOUSE（酒吧或招待所的）店主，老闆 SYN proprietor ➲ compare LANDLADY

land·lub·ber /ˈlændlʌbə(r)/ *noun* (*informal*) a person with not much knowledge or experience of the sea or sailing 不諳航海的人

land·mark /ˈlændmɑːk; *NAmE* -mɑːrk/ *noun* **1** something, such as a large building, that you can see clearly from a distance and that will help you to know where you are 陸標，地標（有助於識別所處地點的大建築物等）：*The Empire State Building is a familiar landmark on the New York skyline.* 帝國大廈是紐約空中輪廓線中人們熟悉的地標。**2 ~ (in sth)** an event, a discovery, an invention, etc. that marks an important stage in sth（標誌重要階段的）里程碑 SYN **milestone**：*The cease-fire was seen as a major landmark in the fight against terrorism.* 停火協定被看作是與恐怖主義鬥爭的重要里程碑。◇ *a **landmark decision/ruling** in the courts* 具有里程碑意義的決策 / 法庭裁決 **3** (*especially NAmE*) a building or a place that is very important because of its history, and that should be preserved 有歷史意義的建築物（或遺址）SYN **monument**

ˈland mass *noun* (*technical* 術語) a large area of land, for example a continent 陸塊；地塊

land·mine /ˈlændmaɪn/ *noun* a bomb placed on or under the ground, which explodes when vehicles or people move over it 地雷

ˈland office (*NAmE*) (*BrE* **ˈland registry**) *noun* a government office that keeps a record of areas of land and who owns them 地政局；地籍局；土地登記處

land·owner /ˈlændəʊnə(r); *NAmE* -oʊn-/ *noun* a person who owns land, especially a large area of land 土地擁有者；地主 ▸ **land·owner·ship** (also **land·owning**) *noun* [U]：*private landownership* 土地私有制 **land·owning** *adj.* [only before noun]：*the great landowning families* 擁有大量土地的家族

ˈland reform *noun* [U, C] the principle of dividing land for farming into smaller pieces so that more people can own some 土地改革

ˈland registry (*BrE*) (*NAmE* **ˈland office**) *noun* a government office that keeps a record of areas of land and who owns them 地政局；地籍局；土地登記處

ˈLand Rover™ (also **ˈLand-Rover™**) *noun* a strong vehicle used for travelling over rough ground 路虎（越野車）

land·scape 🔑 /ˈlændskeɪp/ *noun, verb*

■ ***noun*** **1** 🔑 [C, usually sing.] everything you can see when you look across a large area of land, especially in the country（陸上，尤指鄉村的）風景，景色：*the **bleak/rugged/dramatic, etc. landscape** of the area* 那個地區荒蕪的景觀、崎嶇的地貌、引人入勝的風光等 ◇ *the woods and fields that are typical features of the English landscape* 具有典型英國風景特徵的森林與田野 ◇ *an **urban/industrial landscape*** 都市 / 工業景觀 ◇ (*figurative*) *We can expect changes in the **political landscape**.* 我們等着看政治舞台上的變化吧。➲ SYNONYMS at COUNTRY **2** 🔑 [C, U] a painting of a view of the countryside; this style of painting 鄉村風景畫；鄉村風景畫的風格：*an artist famous for his landscapes* 以風景畫聞名的畫家 ➲ COLLOCATIONS at ART ➲ compare TOWNSCAPE (2) **3** [U] (*technical* 術語) the way of printing a document in which the top of the page is one of the longer sides（文件的）橫向打印格式：*Select the landscape option when printing the file.* 打印文件時選擇橫向打印格式選項。➲ compare PORTRAIT *adj.* IDM see BLOT *n.*

■ ***verb* ~ sth** to improve the appearance of an area of land by changing the design and planting trees, flowers, etc. 對…做景觀美化；給…作園林美化；美化…的環境

ˌlandscape ˈarchitect *noun* a person whose job is planning and designing the environment, especially so that roads, buildings, etc. combine with the landscape in an attractive way 園林建築師；景觀設計師 ▸ **ˌlandscape ˈarchitecture** *noun* [U]

ˌlandscape ˈgardener *noun* a person whose job is designing and creating attractive parks and gardens 園林學家；造園師；園林設計師 ▸ **ˌlandscape ˈgardening** *noun* [U]

ˌLand's ˈEnd *noun* a place in Cornwall that is further west than any other place in England 蘭茲角（屬康沃爾郡，位於英格蘭最西邊）➲ compare JOHN O'GROATS

land·slide /ˈlændslaɪd/ *noun* **1** (also **land·fall**) a mass of earth, rock, etc. that falls down the slope of a mountain or a CLIFF（山坡或懸崖的）崩塌，塌方，滑坡，地滑 ➲ see also LANDSLIP **2** an election in which one person or party gets very many more votes than the other people or parties 一方選票佔壓倒多數的選舉；一方佔絕對優勢的選舉：*She was expected to win **by a landslide**.* 預計她會以壓倒多數的選票獲勝。◇ *a landslide victory* 壓倒性優勢的選舉勝利 ➲ COLLOCATIONS at VOTE

land·slip /ˈlændslɪp/ *noun* a mass of rock and earth that falls down a slope, usually smaller than a landslide（通常為小規模的）崩塌，塌方，滑坡，地滑

land·ward /ˈlændwəd; *NAmE* -wərd/ *adj.* [only before noun] facing the land; away from the sea 朝陸地的；向岸的 ▸ **land·ward** (also **land·wards**) *adv.*：*After an hour, the ship turned landward.* 一小時後，那艘船轉而駛向岸邊。

ˈland yacht *noun* **1** a small vehicle with a sail and no engine, that is used on land（帶風帆、無發動機的）快艇車，沙灘艇 **2** (*NAmE, informal*) a large car 大型汽車

lane 🔑 /leɪn/ *noun*

1 🔑 a narrow road in the country（鄉間）小路：*winding country lanes* 蜿蜒的鄉間小路 ◇ *We drove along a muddy lane to reach the farmhouse.* 我們駕車沿泥濘的小路到達農舍。➲ VISUAL VOCAB page V3 ➲ see also MEMORY LANE **2** 🔑 (especially in place names 尤用於地名) a street, often a narrow one with buildings on both sides 小巷；胡同；里弄：*The quickest way is through the back lanes behind the bus station.* 最近的路是穿過公共汽車站後面的小巷。◇ *Park Lane* 帕克里 **3** 🔑 a section of a wide road, that is marked by painted white lines, to keep lines of traffic separate 車道：*the **inside/middle lane*** 內 / 中車道 ◇ *the **northbound/southbound lane*** 北行 / 南行車道 ◇ *to change lanes* 變換車道 ◇ *She signalled and pulled over into the slow lane.* 她給信號後把車開進了慢車道。◇ *a four-lane highway* 四車道公路 ➲ see also BUS LANE, CYCLE LANE, FAST LANE, OUTSIDE LANE, PASSING LANE **4** a narrow marked section of a track or a swimming pool that is used by one person taking part in a race（比賽的）跑道，泳道：*The Australian in lane four is coming up fast from behind.* 第四道的澳大利亞選手正從後面快速追趕上來。➲ VISUAL VOCAB pages V40, V47 **5** a route used by ships or aircraft on regular journeys 航道；航線：*one of the world's busiest **shipping/sea lanes*** 世界上最繁忙的海運航線之一 IDM see FAST LANE

lan·gous·tine /ˈlɒŋɡʊstiːn; *NAmE* ˈlɑːŋ-/ (also **ˌNorway ˈlobster**, **ˌDublin Bay ˈprawn**) *noun* a type of SHELLFISH like a small LOBSTER 挪威海螯蝦；挪威龍蝦

lan·guage 🔑 /ˈlæŋɡwɪdʒ/ *noun*

▸ OF A COUNTRY 國家 **1** 🔑 [C] the system of communication in speech and writing that is used by people of a particular country or area 語言：*the Japanese language* 日語 ◇ *It takes a long time to learn to **speak a language***

L

well. 學會說好一種語言需要花很長的時間。◇ *Italian is my* ***first language***. 意大利語是我的母語。◇ *All the children must learn a* ***foreign language***. 所有的兒童必須學一門外語。◇ *She* ***has a good command of the Spanish language***. 她精通西班牙語。◇ *a qualification in* ***language teaching*** 語言教學的資格 ◇ *They fell in love in spite of* ***the language barrier*** (= the difficulty of communicating when people speak different languages). 儘管有語言障礙，他們還是相愛了。◇ *Why study Latin? It's a* ***dead language*** (= no longer spoken by anyone). 為什麼學拉丁語？它已經不再有人說了。◇ *Is English an* ***official language*** *in your country?* 英語在你們國家是官方語言嗎？ ➲ see also MODERN LANGUAGE

▸ COMMUNICATION 溝通 **2** [U] the use by humans of a system of sounds and words to communicate 言語；說話；語言： *theories about the origins of language* 有關語言起源的理論 ◇ *a study of* ***language acquisition*** *in two-year-olds* 對兩歲兒童語言習得的研究

▸ STYLE OF SPEAKING/WRITING 口語／書面語的風格 **3** [U] a particular style of speaking or writing 某種類型的言語（或語言）： ***bad/foul/strong language*** (= words that people may consider offensive) 髒罵；粗罵；罵人話 ◇ ***literary/poetic language*** 文學／詩歌語言 ◇ *the language of the legal profession* 法律專業用語 ◇ *Give your instructions in everyday language.* 用通俗的語言發佈指令。 ➲ see also BAD LANGUAGE

▸ MOVEMENTS/SYMBOLS/SOUND 動作；符號；聲音 **4** [C, U] a way of expressing ideas and feelings using movements, symbols and sound（用動作、符號和語音來表達思想感情的）表達方式，交際方式： *the language of mime* 啞劇的手勢語 ◇ *the* ***language of dolphins/bees*** 海豚／蜜蜂的交流方式 ➲ see also BODY LANGUAGE, SIGN LANGUAGE

▸ COMPUTING 計算機技術 **5** [C, U] a system of symbols and rules that is used to operate a computer 計算機語言： *a programming language* 程序設計語言

IDM **mind/watch your 'language** to be careful about what you say in order not to upset or offend sb 謹慎措辭；留神言辭： *Watch your language, young man!* 年輕人，注意你的言談！ **speak/talk the same 'language** to be able to communicate easily with another person because you share similar opinions and experience（因意見和經歷相似）能容易地溝通，說得來，有共同語言

,language engi'neering *noun* [U] (*computing* 計) the use of computers to process languages for industrial purposes 語言工程

'language laboratory *noun* a room in a school or college that contains special equipment to help students learn foreign languages by listening to tapes or CDs, watching videos or DVDs, recording themselves, etc. 語言實驗室；語音室

'language transfer *noun* [U] (*linguistics* 語言) the process of using your knowledge of your first language or another language that you know when speaking or writing a language that you are learning 語言遷移，語言介入（學習者在使用目標語時用第一語言或其他語言的知識）

langue /lɒ̃g; *NAmE* lɑːŋg/ *noun* (*linguistics* 語言) (from *French*) a language considered as a communication system of a particular community, rather than the way individual people speak（作為特定群體內交際系統的）語言 ➲ compare PAROLE *n.* (2)

lan·guid /'læŋgwɪd/ *adj.* moving slowly in an elegant manner, not needing energy or effort 慢悠悠的；慵懶的： *a languid wave of the hand* 懶洋洋一揮手 ◇ *a languid afternoon in the sun* 陽光下一個懶洋洋的下午 ▸ **lan·guid·ly** *adv.*： *He moved languidly across the room.* 他慢悠悠地穿過房間。

lan·guish /'læŋgwɪʃ/ *verb* (*formal*) **1** [I] ~ (**in sth**) to be forced to stay somewhere or suffer sth unpleasant for a long time 被迫滯留；長期受苦；受煎熬： *She continues to languish in a foreign prison.* 她繼續被囚禁在一所外國的監獄裏。 **2** [I] to become weaker or fail to make progress 變得衰弱；未能取得進展： *The share price languished at 102p.* 股票價格停滯在 102 便士上。

Synonyms 同義詞辨析

language

vocabulary • terms • wording • terminology

These are all terms for the words and expressions people use when they speak or write, or for a particular style of speaking or writing. 以上各詞均指措辭、用詞或某種類型的言語。

language a particular style of speaking or writing 指某種類型的言語或語言： *Give your instructions in everyday language.* 用通俗的語言發佈指令。◇ *the language of the legal profession* 法律專業用語

vocabulary all the words that a person knows or uses, or all the words in a particular language; the words that people use when they are talking about a particular subject 指一個人掌握或使用的詞彙、某種語言的詞彙、某一學科的詞彙： *to have a wide/limited vocabulary* 詞彙豐富／有限 ◇ *The word has become part of advertising vocabulary.* 這個詞已經成了廣告用語。

terms a way of expressing yourself or of saying sth 指表達方式、措辭、說法： *I'll try to explain in simple terms.* 我會盡量講得通俗易懂。

wording [usually sing.] the words that are used in a piece of writing or speech, especially when they have been carefully chosen 指措辭、用詞： *It was the standard form of wording for a consent letter.* 這是同意書的標準用詞。

terminology (*rather formal*) the set of technical words or expressions used in a particular subject; words used with particular meanings 指某學科的術語、有特別含義的用語、專門用語： *medical terminology* 醫學術語 ◇ *Scientists are constantly developing new terminologies.* 科學家不斷發展新的專門用語。 NOTE *Literary/poetic terminology* is used for talking about literature or poetry. *Literary/poetic language* is used for writing in a literary or poetic style. * literary/poetic terminology 用於談論文學或詩歌，literary/poetic language 用於文學或詩歌創作。

PATTERNS

- **formal/informal/everyday** language/vocabulary/terms
- **business/scientific/technical/specialized** language/vocabulary/terminology
- A word **enters** the language/the vocabulary.

lan·guor /'læŋgə(r)/ *noun* [U, sing.] (*literary*) the pleasant state of feeling lazy and without energy 倦怠；懶洋洋；慵懶： *A delicious languor was stealing over him.* 一種美滋滋懶洋洋的感覺悄悄傳遍他的全身。 ▸ **lan·guor·ous** /'læŋgərəs/ *adj.*： *a languorous pace of life* 慢悠悠的生活節奏 **lan·guor·ous·ly** *adv.*

La Niña /lɑː 'niːnjə/ *noun* [U] the cooling of the water in the central and eastern Pacific Ocean that happens every few years and that affects the weather in many parts of the world 拉尼娜現象，反聖嬰現象（指赤道附近太平洋中部和東部水溫每隔幾年異常降低並影響世界很多地區的氣候） ➲ compare EL NIÑO

lank /læŋk/ *adj.* **1** (of hair 毛髮) straight, dull and not attractive 平直而無光澤的 **2** (*SAfrE, informal*) large in number or amount 大量的；很多的： *I've got lank work to do.* 我有很多工作要做。

lanky /'læŋki/ *adj.* (**lank·ier**, **lank·iest**) (of a person 人) having long thin arms and legs and moving in an awkward way 瘦長（或胳膊、腿細長）而行動笨拙的： *a tall, lanky teenager* 身材瘦長的少年 SYN **gangling**

lano·lin /'lænəlɪn/ *noun* [U] an oil that comes from sheep's wool and is used to make skin creams 羊毛脂（用以製作護膚霜）

lan·tern /ˈlæntən; *NAmE* -tərn/ *noun* a lamp in a transparent case, often a metal case with glass sides, that has a handle, so that you can carry it outside 燈籠；提燈 ➲ see also CHINESE LANTERN

ˌlantern ˈjaw *noun* a long thin JAW with a large chin 瘦長突出的下巴；戽斗 ▸ **ˌlantern-ˈjawed** *adj.*

lanth·anum /ˈlænθənəm/ *noun* [U] (*symb.* **La**) a chemical element. Lanthanum is a silver-white metal. 鑭

lan·yard /ˈlænjɑːd; ˈlænjəd; *NAmE* -jərd/ *noun* **1** a string that you wear around your neck or wrist for holding sth 頸帶；腕帶：*A lanyard is useful for carrying your ID card.* 頸帶適合用來掛身分證。◇ *a whistle lanyard* 口哨帶 **2** a piece of equipment that you wear around your neck to hold the wire of an IPOD（蘋果播放器的）掛繩，頸繩：*lanyard headphones for use with your iPod* 配合蘋果播放器使用的掛繩耳機 **3** a rope used to fasten sth, for example the sail of a ship 牽索；（繫船帆的）收緊索，帆牽

lap /læp/ *noun, verb*

■ ***noun*** [C] **1** [usually sing.] the top part of your legs that forms a flat surface when you are sitting down（坐着時的）大腿部：*There's only one seat so you'll have to sit* ***on my lap****.* 只有一個座位，你只好坐在我腿上了。◇ *She sat with her hands* ***in her lap****.* 她雙手放在大腿上坐着。**2** one journey from the beginning to the end of a track used for running, etc.（跑道等的）一圈：*the fastest lap on record* 在紀錄上最快的一圈 ◇ *She has completed six laps.* 她跑完六圈了。◇ *He was overtaken on the final lap.* 他在最後一圈被超過。◇ *to do a* ***lap of honour*** (= go around the track again to celebrate winning) 繞場一週慶祝勝利 ◇ (*NAmE*) *to do a* ***victory lap*** 繞場一週慶祝勝利 **3** a section of a journey, or of a piece of work, etc.（行程或工作等中的）一段，環節：*They're off on the first lap of their round-the-world tour.* 他們踏上環遊世界的第一段行程。◇ *We've nearly finished. We're* ***on the last lap****.* 我們接近完工了，正在處理最後的一部份工作。

IDM **drop/dump sth in sb's ˈlap** (*informal*) to make sth the responsibility of another person 把（某事）推給他人負責：*They dropped the problem firmly back in my lap.* 他們把問題斷然給我推了回來。 **sth drops/falls into sb's lap** somebody has the opportunity to do sth pleasant without having made any effort（毫不費勁地）得到做稱心事的機會；賜良機：*My dream job just fell into my lap.* 我沒費勁就找到了夢寐以求的工作。 **in the lap of the ˈgods** if the result of sth is **in the lap of the gods**, you do not know what will happen because it depends on luck or things you cannot control 由神掌管；結果難以預料；非人力所能左右 **in the lap of ˈluxury** in easy, comfortable conditions, and enjoying the advantages of being rich 生活優裕；養尊處優

■ ***verb*** (**-pp-**) **1** [I] (of water 水) to touch sth gently and regularly, often making a soft sound（輕柔而有規律地）拍打：*The waves lapped around our feet.* 波浪輕輕地拍打着我們的腳。◇ *the sound of water lapping against the boat* 水輕輕拍打船幫的聲音 **2** [T] **~ sth** (of animals 動物) to drink sth with quick movements of the tongue 舔食；舔着喝 **3** [T] **~ sb** (in a race 賽跑) to pass another runner on a track who is one or more laps behind you 領先一圈（或數圈）

PHR V **ˌlap sth↔ˈup 1** (*informal*) to accept or receive sth with great enjoyment, without thinking about whether it is good, true or sincere（不加考慮地）樂於接受：*It's a terrible movie but audiences everywhere are lapping it up.* 這部電影很差勁，可各地的觀眾卻趨之若鶩。◇ *She simply lapped up all the compliments.* 什麼恭維話她都照單全收。 **2** to drink all of sth with great enjoyment 開懷暢飲：*The calf lapped up the bucket of milk.* 小牛把那桶牛奶津津有味地喝光了。

lapa /ˈlɑːpə/ *noun* (*SAfrE*) a shelter without walls on all sides, usually made of wooden poles and covered with THATCH (= dry grass), especially used as a place for relaxing and eating meals 草亭（尤用於休息和用餐）

lapar·os·copy /ˌlæpəˈrɒskəpi; *NAmE* -ˈrɑːs-/ *noun* (*pl.* **-ies**) (*medical* 醫) an examination of the inside of the body using a tube-shaped instrument that can be put through the wall of the ABDOMEN 腹腔鏡檢查

lapar·ot·omy /ˌlæpəˈrɒtəmi; *NAmE* -ˈrɑːt-/ *noun* (*pl.* **-ies**) (*medical* 醫) a cut in the ABDOMEN in order to perform an operation or an examination 剖腹手術；剖腹檢查

ˈlap belt *noun* a type of SEAT BELT that goes across your waist 安全腰帶

ˈlap dancing *noun* [U] sexually exciting dancing or STRIPTEASE which is performed close to, or sitting on, a customer in a bar or club（酒吧或夜總會中在顧客面前或坐在顧客腿上表演的）性感舞，脱衣舞

lap·dog /ˈlæpdɒg; *NAmE* -dɔːg; -dɑːg/ *noun* **1** a pet dog that is small enough to be carried（可攜帶的）寵物狗，叭兒狗 **2** (*disapproving*) a person who is under the control of another person or group 走狗 **SYN** **poodle**

lapel /ləˈpel/ *noun* one of the two front parts of the top of a coat or jacket that are joined to the COLLAR and are folded back（西服外衣或夾克上部胸前的）翻領 ➲ **VISUAL VOCAB** page V61

lapi·dary /ˈlæpɪdəri; *NAmE* -deri/ *adj.* **1** (*formal*) (especially of written language 尤指書面用語) elegant and exact 優雅精確的 **SYN** **concise**：*in lapidary style* 以優雅嚴謹的文體 **2** (*technical* 術語) connected with stones and the work of cutting and polishing them 鐫刻在石上的；（給石頭）切割磨光的

lapis laz·uli /ˌlæpɪs ˈlæzjʊli; *NAmE* ˈlæzəli/ *noun* [U] a bright blue stone, used in making jewellery 雜青金石（用於製作珠寶飾物）

lap·sang sou·chong /ˌlæpsæŋ ˈsuːʃɒŋ; *NAmE* -ʃɑːŋ/ *noun* [U] a type of tea that has a taste like smoke 正山小種紅茶（有煙熏味）

lapse /læps/ *noun, verb*

■ ***noun*** **1** a small mistake, especially one that is caused by forgetting sth or by being careless 小錯；（尤指）記錯，過失，疏忽：*a* ***lapse of concentration/memory*** 心不在焉；記錯 ◇ *A momentary lapse in the final set cost her the match.* 她最後一盤一走神兒，輸掉了整場比賽。 **SYN** **expire** **2** a period of time between two things that happen（兩件事發生的）間隔時間 **SYN** **interval**：*After a lapse of six months we met up again.* 相隔六個月之後我們又相遇了。 **3** an example or period of bad behaviour from sb who normally behaves well 行為失檢；（平時表現不錯的人一時的）失足

■ ***verb*** **1** [I] (of a contract, an agreement, etc. 合同、協議等) to be no longer valid because the period of time that it lasts has come to an end 失效；期滿終止：*She had allowed her membership to lapse.* 她的會員資格期滿終止，沒有再續。 **2** [I] to gradually become weaker or come to an end 衰退；衰弱；（逐漸）消失，結束：*His concentration lapsed after a few minutes.* 幾分鐘後他的注意力就下降了。 **3** [I] **~ (from sth)** to stop believing in or practising your religion 背棄，放棄（宗教信仰）：*He lapsed from Judaism when he was a student.* 他當學生時就放棄了猶太教。 ▸ **lapsed** *adj.* [only before noun]：*a lapsed subscription* 過期的訂購 ◇ *lapsed faith* 背棄的信仰 ◇ *a lapsed Catholic* 喪失信仰的天主教徒

PHR V **ˈlapse into sth 1** to gradually pass into a worse or less active state or condition（逐漸）陷入，進入：*to* ***lapse into unconsciousness/a coma*** 逐漸失去知覺／陷入昏迷狀態 ◇ *She* ***lapsed into silence*** *again.* 她又陷入了沉默。 **2** to start speaking or behaving in a different way, often one that is less acceptable 說話或舉止顯得異常（常令人難以接受）：*He soon lapsed back into his old ways.* 他很快又犯老毛病了。

lap·top /ˈlæptɒp; *NAmE* -tɑːp/ *noun* a small computer that can work with a battery and be easily carried 膝上型計算機；便攜式電腦；筆記本電腦 **SYN** **notebook** ➲ **VISUAL VOCAB** pages V66, V69 ➲ compare DESKTOP COMPUTER, NETBOOK, SUBNOTEBOOK

lap·wing /ˈlæpwɪŋ/ (also **pee·wit**) *noun* a black and white bird with a row of feathers (called a CREST) standing up on its head 鳳頭麥雞

lar·ceny /ˈlɑːsəni; *NAmE* ˈlɑːrs-/ *noun* [U, C] (*pl.* **-ies**) (*law* 律) (*NAmE* or *old-fashioned, BrE*) the crime of stealing sth from sb; an occasion when this takes place 盜竊罪；偷盜；盜竊 **SYN** **theft**：*The couple were charged with* ***grand/petty larceny*** (= stealing things that are valuable/not very valuable). 那對夫婦被指控犯有重大／輕微盜竊罪。

L

larch /lɑːtʃ; *NAmE* lɑːrtʃ/ *noun* [C, U] a tree with sharp pointed leaves that fall in winter and hard dry fruit called CONES 落葉松

lard /lɑːd; *NAmE* lɑːrd/ *noun, verb*

■ ***noun*** [U] a firm white substance made from the melted fat of pigs that is used in cooking（烹調用的）豬油

■ ***verb* ~ sth** to put small pieces of fat on or into sth before cooking it（烹飪前）塗豬油，放入豬油

PHR V **'lard sth with sth** [usually passive] (often *disapproving*) to include a lot of a particular kind of word or expressions in a speech or in a piece of writing（在講話或文章中）夾雜大量，大量穿插（某類詞語）：*His conversation was larded with Russian proverbs.* 他的談話夾雜了很多俄國諺語。

lard·ass /ˈlɑːdɑːs; *NAmE* ˈlɑːrdæs/ *noun* (*informal, especially NAmE, offensive*) a fat person, especially sb who is thought of as lazy（尤指被認為懶惰的）胖子

lar·der /ˈlɑːdə(r); *NAmE* ˈlɑːrd-/ *noun* (*especially BrE*) a cupboard/closet or small room in a house, used for storing food, especially in the past（尤指舊時的）食物櫥櫃，食物貯藏室 **SYN** **pantry**

large 0-ᵂ /lɑːdʒ; *NAmE* lɑːrdʒ/ *adj., verb*

■ ***adj.*** (**larger, larg·est**) **1** 0-ᵂ big in size or quantity 大的；大規模的；大量的：*a large area/family/house/car/appetite* 大面積／家庭／房子／汽車／胃口 ◇ *a large number of people* 很多人 ◇ *very large sums of money* 幾筆巨款 ◇ *He's a very large child for his age.* 就其年齡來說，這孩子個頭很大。◇ *A large proportion of old people live alone.* 一大部份老人都是獨居。◇ *Women usually do the larger share of the housework.* 婦女通常承擔大部份家務。◇ *Brazil is the world's largest producer of coffee.* 巴西是世界上最大的咖啡生產國。◇ *Who's the rather large (= fat) lady in the hat?* 那位戴帽子的豐滿女士是誰？**2** 0-ᵂ (*abbr.* L) used to describe one size in a range of sizes of clothes, food, products used in the house, etc.（服裝、食物、日用品等）大型號的：*small, medium, large* 小／中／大號 **3** 0-ᵂ wide in range and involving many things 廣泛的；眾多的：*a large and complex issue* 重大而複雜的問題 ◇ *Some drugs are being used on a much larger scale than previously.* 與以前相比，某些藥物的使用範圍更廣了。◇ *If we look at the larger picture of the situation, the differences seem slight.* 倘若我們對情況看得全面些，這些分歧就顯得微不足道了。➲ SYNONYMS at BIG ▸ **large·ness** *noun* [U]

IDM **at 'large 1** (used after a noun 用於名詞後) as a whole; in general 整個；全部；總地；一般地：*the opinion of the public at large* 普通大眾的意見 **2** (of a dangerous person or animal 危險的人或動物) not captured; free 未被捕獲的；自由的：*Her killer is still at large.* 殺害她的兇手仍然逍遙法外。 **by and 'large** used when you are saying something that is generally, but not completely, true 大體上；總體上；總的（或一般）說來：*By and large, I enjoyed my time at school.* 總的說來，我在學校的日子很開心。➲ LANGUAGE BANK at GENERALLY **give/have it 'large** (*BrE, slang*) to enjoy yourself, especially by dancing and drinking alcohol 玩個痛快；（尤指跳舞和飲酒）作樂 **in 'large part | in large 'measure** (*formal*) to a great extent 在很大程度上：*Their success is due in large part to their determination.* 他們的成功在很大程度上應歸功於他們的決心。 **(as) large as 'life** (*humorous*) used to show surprise at seeing sb/sth（表示驚訝地見到）本人，本身：*I hadn't seen her for fifteen years and then there she was, (as) large as life.* 我有十五年未見過她，卻在那裏遇見她了，沒錯，就是她。 **ˌlarger than 'life** looking or behaving in a way that is more interesting or exciting than other people, and so is likely to attract attention 外表行為惹人注目 **SYN** **flamboyant**：*He's a larger than life character.* 他這個人外表言行很招眼。➲ more at LOOM *v.*, WRIT *v.*

■ ***verb***

IDM **'large it | large it 'up** (*BrE, slang*) to enjoy yourself, especially by dancing and drinking alcohol 玩個痛快；（尤指跳舞和飲酒）作樂

large·ly 0-ᵂ /ˈlɑːdʒli; *NAmE* ˈlɑːrdʒli/ *adv.* to a great extent; mostly or mainly 在很大程度上；多半；主要地：*the manager who is largely responsible for the team's victory* 對該隊獲勝起主要作用的經理 ◇ *It was* **largely a matter of** *trial and error.* 這主要是個反複實驗的問題。◇ *He resigned largely because of the stories in the press.* 他的辭職多半是因為新聞界的一些報道。

ˌlarge-'scale *adj.* [usually before noun] **1** involving many people or things, especially over a wide area 大規模的；大批的；大範圍的：*large-scale development* 大規模的開發 ◇ *the large-scale employment of women* 對女性大批的雇用 **2** (of a map, model, etc. 地圖、模型等) drawn or made to a scale that shows a small area of land or a building in great detail 按大比例繪製（或製作）的；大比例尺的 **OPP** **small-scale**

lar·gesse (also **lar·gess**) /lɑːˈdʒes; *NAmE* lɑːrˈdʒes/ *noun* [U] (*formal* or *humorous*) the act or quality of being generous with money; money that you give to people who have less than you 慷慨解囊；施捨；（給窮人的）錢，贈款：*She is not noted for her largesse* (= she is not generous). 沒人聽說過她出手大方。◇ *to dispense largesse to the poor* 把錢施捨給窮人

lar·gish /ˈlɑːdʒɪʃ; *NAmE* ˈlɑːrdʒɪʃ/ *adj.* fairly large 相當大的

largo /ˈlɑːɡəʊ; *NAmE* ˈlɑːrɡoʊ/ *adv., adj., noun* (*music* 音) (from *Italian*)

■ ***adv., adj.*** (used as an instruction 指示語) in a slow, serious way 緩慢而莊嚴地（的）

■ ***noun*** (*pl.* **-os**) a piece of music to be performed in a slow, serious way 廣板（風格緩慢、莊嚴）

lark /lɑːk; *NAmE* lɑːrk/ *noun, verb*

■ ***noun* 1** a small brown bird with a pleasant song 百靈鳥；雲雀 ➲ see also SKYLARK **2** [usually sing.] (*informal*) a thing that you do for fun or as a joke 嬉戲；玩樂；玩笑：*The boys didn't mean any harm—they just did it for a lark.* 那些男孩並無惡意，他們只是鬧着玩罷了。**3** (*BrE, informal*) (used after another noun 用於另一名詞後) an activity that you think is a waste of time or that you do not take seriously（認為）浪費時間的活動；不受重視的活動：*Perhaps this riding lark would be more fun than she'd thought.* 也許這次騎馬的無聊活動比她所想像的要好玩一些。

IDM **be/get up with the 'lark** (*old-fashioned, BrE*) to get out of bed very early in the morning 清晨早起；雞鳴即起 **blow/sod that for a lark** (*BrE, slang*) used by sb who does not want to do sth because it involves too much effort（因太費力而不想幹時說）：*Sod that for a lark! I'm not doing any more tonight.* 拉倒吧！我今晚再也不做了。

■ ***verb***

PHR V **ˌlark a'bout/a'round** (*old-fashioned, informal, especially BrE*) to enjoy yourself by behaving in a silly way 傻玩；胡鬧；嬉戲 **SYN** **mess about/around**

lark·spur /ˈlɑːkspɜː(r); *NAmE* ˈlɑːrk-/ *noun* [C, U] a tall garden plant with blue, pink or white flowers growing up its STEM 飛燕草（高大花園植物，開藍色、粉紅或白色花）

lar·ney (also **lar·nie**) /ˈlɑːni; *NAmE* ˈlɑːr-/ *adj.* (*SAfrE*) very smart; expensive 很高檔的；昂貴的：*We were invited to a larney function.* 我們獲邀參加一個盛大的慶典。◇ *a larney hotel* 高檔酒店

lar·ri·kin /ˈlærɪkɪn/ *noun* (*AustralE, NZE*) a person who ignores the normal rules of society or of an organization 不守規矩的人；無視規章制度的人

larva /ˈlɑːvə; *NAmE* ˈlɑːrvə/ *noun* (*pl.* **lar·vae** /ˈlɑːviː; *NAmE* ˈlɑːrviː/) an insect at the stage when it has just come out of an egg and looks like a short fat WORM 幼蟲；幼體 ▸ **lar·val** /ˈlɑːvl; *NAmE* ˈlɑːrvl/ *adj.* [only before noun]：*an insect in its larval stage* 處於幼體階段的昆蟲 ➲ VISUAL VOCAB page V13

la·ryn·geal /ləˈrɪndʒiəl/ *adj.* (*biology* 生, *phonetics* 語音) related to or produced by the larynx 喉的；喉音的

laryn·gi·tis /ˌlærɪnˈdʒaɪtɪs/ *noun* [U] an infection of the larynx that makes speaking painful 喉炎

lar·ynx /ˈlærɪŋks/ *noun* (*pl.* **la·ryn·ges** /ləˈrɪndʒiːz/) (*anatomy* 解) the area at the top of the throat that contains the VOCAL CORDS 喉 SYN **voice box** ➲ VISUAL VOCAB page V59

la·sagne (also **la·sagna**) /lə'zænjə/ *noun* **1** [U] large flat pieces of PASTA 寬麵條 **2** [U, C] an Italian dish made from layers of lasagne, finely chopped meat and/or vegetables and white sauce 意大利千層麵（以多層寬麵條夾肉末、蔬菜和白汁製成）

la·scivi·ous /lə'sɪviəs/ *adj.* (*formal, disapproving*) feeling or showing strong sexual desire 好色的；淫蕩的；淫慾的；猥褻的：*a lascivious person* 淫蕩的人 ◇ *lascivious thoughts* 淫猥的念頭 ▸ **la·scivi·ous·ly** *adv.* **la·scivi·ous·ness** *noun* [U]

laser /'leɪzə(r)/ *noun* a device that gives out light in which all the waves OSCILLATE (= change direction and strength) together, typically producing a powerful beam of light that can be used for cutting metal, in medical operations, etc. 激光器；鐳射器：*a laser beam* 激光束 ◇ *a laser navigation device* 激光導航裝置 ◇ *The barcodes on the products are read by lasers.* 產品上的條碼是用激光讀取的。◇ *a **laser show*** (= lasers used as entertainment) 激光表演 ◇ *She's had **laser surgery** on her eye.* 她做了眼部激光手術。

laser·disc (also **laser·disk**) /'leɪzədɪsk; *NAmE* 'leɪzər-/ *noun* a plastic disc like a large CD on which large amounts of information, such as video or music, can be stored, and which can be read by a laser 激光光盤；激光影碟；鐳射光碟

'laser gun *noun* a piece of equipment which uses a laser to read a BARCODE or to find out how fast a vehicle or other object is moving 激光條碼掃描儀；激光測速儀；鐳射條碼掃描器；鐳射測速儀

'laser printer *noun* a printer that produces good quality printed material by means of a laser 激光打印機；鐳射打印機

lash /læʃ/ *verb, noun*

■ *verb* **1** [I, T] to hit sb/sth with great force 猛擊；狠打 SYN **pound**：**+ adv./prep.** *The rain lashed at the windows.* 雨點猛烈地打在窗戶上。◇ **~ sth** *Huge waves lashed the shore.* 巨浪拍打着海岸。➲ SYNONYMS at BEAT **2** [T] **~ sb/sth** to hit a person or an animal with a WHIP, rope, stick, etc. 鞭打；抽打 SYN **beat** **3** [T] **~ sb/sth** to criticize sb/sth in a very angry way 怒斥 SYN **attack** **4** [T] **~ sth + adv./prep.** to fasten sth tightly to sth else with ropes 捆綁；捆紮：*Several logs had been lashed together to make a raft.* 幾根原木捆紮在一起做成了木筏。◇ *During the storm everything on deck had to be lashed down.* 暴風雨中甲板上所有的東西都必須繫牢。**5** [I, T] **~ (sth)** to move or to move sth quickly and violently from side to side（使）迅猛擺動，甩動：*The crocodile's tail was lashing furiously from side to side.* 鱷魚的尾巴在急速地左右甩動。

PHR V **,lash 'out (at sb/sth)** **1** to suddenly try to hit sb（突然）狠打，痛打：*She suddenly lashed out at the boy.* 她突然狠狠地打那個男孩。**2** to criticize sb in an angry way 怒斥；嚴厲斥責：*In a bitter article he lashed out at his critics.* 他寫了一篇尖刻的文章，猛烈駁斥批評他的人。**,lash 'out on sth** (*BrE, informal*) to spend a lot of money on sth 在…上大量花費

■ *noun* **1** = EYELASH：*her long dark lashes* 她那長長的黑睫毛 **2** a hit with a WHIP, given as a form of punishment（作為懲罰的）鞭打，抽打：*They each received 20 lashes for stealing.* 他們因盜竊每人捱了 20 鞭。◇ (*figurative*) *to feel the lash of sb's tongue* (= to be spoken to in an angry and critical way) 領教某人利口如刀的厲害 **3** the thin leather part at the end of a WHIP 鞭端皮條；鞭梢

lash·ing /'læʃɪŋ/ *noun* **1** **lashings** [pl.] (*BrE, informal*) a large amount of sth, especially of food and drink 大量，許多（尤指食物和飲料）：*a bowl of strawberries with lashings of cream* 一碗澆了大量奶油的草莓 **2** [C] an act of hitting sb with a WHIP as a punishment（作為懲罰的）鞭打；笞刑：(*figurative*) *He was given a severe tongue-lashing* (= angry criticism). 他受到了嚴厲的斥責。**3** [C, usually pl.] a rope used to fasten sth tightly to sth else 捆綁用的繩索

lass /læs/ (also **las·sie** /'læsi/) *noun* (*ScotE, NEngE*) a girl; a young woman 女孩；少女；年輕女子 ➲ compare LAD (1), LADDIE

lassa fever /'læsə fiːvə(r)/ *noun* [U] a serious disease, usually caught from RATS and found especially in W Africa 拉沙熱（常由鼠類傳染，尤見於西非）

lassi /'læsi/ *noun* [U] a S Asian drink made from YOGURT（南亞）拉西酸奶奶昔

las·si·tude /'læsɪtjuːd; *NAmE* -tuːd/ *noun* [U] (*formal*) a state of feeling very tired in mind or body; lack of energy 倦怠；疲乏；無精打采

lasso /læ'suː; 'læsəʊ; *NAmE* 'læsoʊ/ *noun, verb*

■ *noun* (*pl.* **-os** or **-oes**) a long rope with one end tied into a LOOP that is used for catching horses, cows, etc.（捕馬、套牛等用的）套索

■ *verb* **~ sth** to catch an animal using a lasso 用套索套捕（動物）

Which Word? 詞語辨析

last / take

Last and **take** are both used to talk about the length of time that something continues. * last 和 take 均表示某事持續的時間。

- **Last** is used to talk about the length of time that an event continues. * last 表示某事持續的時間：*How long do you think this storm will last?* 你看這暴風雨會持續多久？◇ *The movie lasted over two hours.* 這部電影長兩個多小時。**Last** does not always need an expression of time. * last 並非總需要與表示時間的詞語連用：*His annoyance won't last.* 他的煩惱不會持續多久。**Last** is also used to say that you have enough of something. * last 亦可表示夠用、足夠維持：*We don't have enough money to last until next month.* 我們的錢不足以維持到下個月。
- **Take** is used to talk about the amount of time you need in order to go somewhere or do something. It must be used with an expression of time. * take 表示到某地或做某事需要的時間，必須與表示時間的詞語連用：*It takes (me) at least an hour to get home from work.*（我）下班回家至少得花一個小時。◇ *How long will the flight take?* 此次航班將飛行多長時間？◇ *The water took ages to boil.* 等上好半天水才開了。

last¹ 0→ /lɑːst; *NAmE* læst/ *det., adv., noun, verb* ➲ see also LAST²

■ *det.* **1** 0→ happening or coming after all other similar things or people 最後的；最末的；末尾的：*We caught the last bus home.* 我們趕上了回家的末班公共汽車。◇ *It's the last house on the left.* 是左邊盡頭那棟房子。◇ *She was last to arrive.* 她是最後到的。**2** 0→ [only before noun] most recent 最近的；上一個的：*last night/Tuesday/month/summer/year* 昨晚；上個星期二／月；剛過去的夏季；去年 ◇ *her last book* 她最近出版的書 ◇ *This last point is crucial.* 剛講的這一點是關鍵的。◇ *The **last time** I saw him was in May.* 我上次見到他是在五月份。**3** 0→ [only before noun] only remaining 僅剩下的；最終的 SYN **final**：*This is our last bottle of water.* 這是我們最後的一瓶水了。◇ *He knew this was his last hope of winning.* 他知道這是他取勝的最後希望。**4** used to emphasize that sb/sth is the least likely or suitable（強調）最不可能的，最不適當的：***The last thing she needed** was more work.* 她最不需要的就是更多的工作。◇ *He's the **last person** I'd trust with a secret.* 我要是有什麼秘密，告訴誰也不能告訴他。

IDM **be on your/its last 'legs** to be going to die or stop functioning very soon; to be very weak or in bad condition 瀕臨死亡；奄奄一息；行將就木；快不能用了 **the day, week, month, etc. before 'last** the day, week, etc. just before the most recent one; two days, weeks, etc. ago 前天；上上星期；上上月；兩天（或兩週等）以前：*I haven't seen him since the summer before*

L

last. 我已有兩個夏天沒見過他了。 **every last ...** every person or thing in a group （某群體中的）每一個，全部： *We spent every last penny we had on the house.* 我們把所有的錢都花在房子上了。 **have the last 'laugh** to be successful when you were not expected to be, making your opponents look stupid （在本未指望時）笑在最後，取得最後勝利 **in the last re'sort** when there are no other possible courses of action 作為最後的一招 SYN **at a pinch**： *In the last resort we can always walk home.* 頂多我們走回家就是了。 **your/the last 'gasp** the point at which you/sth can no longer continue living, fighting, existing, etc. 奄奄一息；苟延殘喘；臨終；垂死 ➲ see also LAST-GASP **the ˌlast 'minute/'moment** the latest possible time before an important event（重大事情前的）最後一刻，緊要關頭： *They changed the plans at the last minute.* 事到臨頭他們卻改變了計劃。◇ *Don't leave your decision to the last moment.* 別等到最後一刻才來做決定。 **a/your last re'sort** the person or thing you rely on when everything else has failed 最後可依賴的人（或事物）： *I've tried everyone else and now you're my last resort.* 其他人我都試過了，現在就靠你了。 **the ˌlast 'word (in sth)** the most recent, fashionable, advanced, etc. thing 最新（或時髦、先進等）的事物： *These apartments are the last word in luxury.* 這些寓所最為豪華。 ➲ more at ANALYSIS, BREATH, FAMOUS, LONG *adj.*, MAN *n.*, STRAW, THING, WEEK, WORD *n.*

■ ***adv.*** **1** 🔑 after anyone or anything else; at the end 最後；最終；終結： *He came last in the race.* 這次賽跑他得了最後一名。◇ *They arrived last of all.* 他們來得比誰都晚。 **2** 🔑 most recently 最新；最近；上一次： *When did you see him last?* 你最近什麼時候見過他？◇ *I saw him last/I last saw him in New York two years ago.* 我上一次是兩年前在紐約見到他的。◇ *They last won the cup in 2006.* 他們上一次獲得獎杯是在 2006 年。

L

IDM **ˌlast but not 'least** used when mentioning the last person or thing of a group, in order to say that they are not less important than the others（提及最後的人或事物時說）最後但同樣重要的： *Last but not least, I'd like to thank all the catering staff.* 最後但同樣重要的是，我要感謝所有的餐飲工作人員。 **ˌlast 'in, ˌfirst 'out** used, for example in a situation when people are losing their jobs, to say that the last people to be employed will be the first to go （形容裁員等情況）最後雇用的人最先被解雇，後來者先走 ➲ more at FIRST *adv.*, LAUGH *v.*

■ ***noun*** **the last** (*pl.* **the last**) **1** 🔑 the person or thing that comes or happens after all other similar people or things 最後來的人（或發生的事）： *Sorry I'm late—am I the last?* 對不起，我來晚了。我是最後到的人嗎？◇ *They were the last to arrive.* 他們是最後到達的人。 **2** 🔑 **~ of sth** the only remaining part or items of sth 僅剩下的部份（或事項）： *These are the last of our apples.* 這是我們最後剩下的幾個蘋果。

IDM **at (long) 'last** after much delay, effort, etc.; in the end （經過長時間的延誤或努力等之後）終於，最終 SYN **finally**： *At last we're home!* 我們終於到家了！◇ *At long last the cheque arrived.* 支票終於到了。 ➲ note at LASTLY **hear/see the 'last of sb/sth** to hear/see sb/sth for the last time 最後一次聽見（或看見）： *That was the last I ever saw of her.* 那是我最後一次見到她。◇ *Unfortunately, I don't think we've heard the last of this affair.* 遺憾的是，我認為這件事還沒有了結。 **the last I 'heard** used to give the most recent news you have about sb/sth （提供最新消息時說）我最近聽到的消息： *The last I heard he was still working at the garage.* 我最近聽到的消息是他還在汽車修理廠工作。 **next/second to 'last** (*BrE* also **ˌlast but 'one**) the one before the last one 倒數第二： *She finished second to last.* 她得了倒數第二。 **to/till the 'last** until the last possible moment, especially until death 直到最後一刻；（尤指）直至死亡： *He died protesting his innocence to the last.* 他至死都堅決辯稱自己無罪。 ➲ more at BREATHE, FIRST *n.*

■ ***verb*** **1** 🔑 [I] (not used in the progressive tenses 不用於進行時) to continue for a particular period of time 持續；繼續；延續： *The meeting only lasted (for) a few minutes.* 會議只開了幾分鐘。◇ *Each game lasts about an hour.* 每場比賽約一小時。◇ *How long does the play last?* 那齣戲要演多長時間？ **2** 🔑 [I, T] to continue to exist or to function well 繼續存在；持續起作用；持久： *This weather won't last.* 這種天氣持續不了多久。◇ *He's making a big effort now, and I hope it lasts.* 現在他正加緊努力，我希望他能堅持下去。◇ **~ sb** *These shoes should last you till next year.* 你這雙鞋應該能穿到明年。 **3** 🔑 [I, T] to survive sth or manage to stay in the same situation, despite difficulties （在困境等中）堅持下去；超逾（困境等）： *She won't last long in that job.* 她那份工作幹不了多久。◇ **~ (out)** *Can you last (out) until I can get help?* 你能支撐到有人來幫我嗎？◇ **~ (out) sth** *Doctors say that she probably won't last out the night* (= she will probably die before the morning). 醫生都說她很可能活不過今晚。◇ *He was injured early on and didn't last the match.* 他開賽後不久就受了傷，沒法堅持到底。 **4** 🔑 [I, T] to be enough for sb to use, especially for a particular period of time 夠用，足夠維持（尤指某段時間）： **~ (out)** *Will the coffee last out till next week?* 咖啡夠喝到下週嗎？◇ **~ sb (out)** *We've got enough food to last us (for) three days.* 我們的食物足夠維持三天。

last² /lɑːst; *NAmE* læst/ *noun* a block of wood or metal shaped like a foot, used in making and repairing shoes 鞋楦 ➲ see also LAST¹

ˌlast 'call *noun* **1** (*especially NAmE*) (*BrE* also **ˌlast 'orders**) the last opportunity for people to buy drinks in a pub or a bar before it closes （酒吧打烊前）買飲料的最後機會 **2** the final request at an airport for passengers to get on their plane （機場對旅客的）最後一次登機通知

ˌlast-'ditch *adj.* [only before noun] used to describe a final attempt to achieve sth, when there is not much hope of succeeding 作最後努力（或嘗試）的；孤注一擲的： *She underwent a heart transplant in a* ***last-ditch attempt*** *to save her.* 她動了心臟移植手術，這是為挽救她的生命而作的最後一次努力。

ˌlast-'gasp *adj.* [only before noun] done or achieved at the last possible moment 最後時刻做成（或取得）的；最後關頭的： *a last-gasp 2-1 victory* 最後一刻取得的 2:1 的勝利

last·ing /ˈlɑːstɪŋ; *NAmE* ˈlæstɪŋ/ *adj.* [usually before noun] continuing to exist or to have an effect for a long time 繼續存在的；持久的；耐久的 SYN **durable**： *Her words left a* ***lasting impression*** *on me.* 她的話給我留下了難忘的印象。◇ *I formed several lasting friendships at college.* 我在大學與幾個同學建立了牢固的友誼。◇ *The training was of no lasting value.* 這種訓練不會有長久的效果。 ➲ see also LONG-LASTING ▶ **last·ing·ly** *adv.*

the ˌLast 'Judgement *noun* [sing.] = JUDGEMENT DAY

last·ly /ˈlɑːstli; *NAmE* ˈlæstli/ *adv.* **1** used to introduce the final point that you want to make 最後一點；最後 SYN **finally**： *Lastly, I'd like to ask you about your plans.* 最後，我想問一下你們的計劃。 ➲ LANGUAGE BANK at FIRST **2** at the end; after all the other things that you have mentioned 最後；最後要說的是⋯： *Lastly, add the lemon juice.* 最後，加上檸檬汁。

Which Word? 詞語辨析

lastly / at last

- **Lastly** is used to introduce the last in a list of things or the final point you are making. * lastly 用以引出所列事情中的最後一項或最後一點： *Lastly, I would like to thank my parents for all their support.* 最後，我想感謝父母對我的全力支持。
- **At last** is used when something happens after a long time, especially when there has been some difficulty or delay. * at last 表示經過很長一段時間，尤其是經過困難或耽擱之後的事： *At last, after twenty hours on the boat, they arrived at their destination.* 乘船二十小時之後，他們終於到達了目的地。 You can also use **finally**, **eventually** or **in the end** with this meaning, but not *lastly*. 此義亦可用 finally、eventually 或 in the end，但不能用 lastly。

ˌlast-'minute *adj.* [usually before noun] done, decided or organized just before sth happens or before it is too late 最後一分鐘才完成（或決定、安排好）的；緊急關頭的： *a last-minute holiday* 最後一分鐘定下來的休假

ˈlast name *noun* your family name 姓 ➲ compare SURNAME

ˌlast ˈorders *noun* [pl.] (*BrE*) (also **ˌlast ˈcall** *NAmE, BrE*) the last opportunity for people to buy drinks in a pub or a bar before it closes （酒吧打烊前）買飲料的最後機會：*'Last orders, please!'* "要酒的，請抓住最後機會！"

the ˌlast ˈpost *noun* [sing.] (*BrE*) a tune played on a BUGLE at military funerals and at the end of the day in military camps 軍人葬禮號；軍營熄燈號

the ˌlast ˈrites *noun* [pl.] a Christian religious ceremony that a priest performs for, and in the presence of, a dying person （基督教的）臨終禮儀，臨終聖事：*to administer the last rites to sb* 給某人舉行臨終聖事 ◇ *to receive the last rites* 領受臨終聖事

lat. *abbr.* (in writing) LATITUDE （書寫形式）緯度

latch /lætʃ/ *noun, verb*

■ ***noun*** **1** a small metal bar that is used to fasten a door or a gate. You raise it to open the door, and drop it into a metal hook to fasten it. 門閂；插銷：*He lifted the latch and opened the door.* 他拉起門閂開了門。 **2** (*especially BrE*) a type of lock on a door that needs a key to open it from the outside 碰鎖；彈簧鎖：*She listened for his key in the latch.* 她留神聽着他把鑰匙插入門鎖。

IDM **on the ˈlatch** (*BrE*) closed but not locked 關着但未鎖上：*Can you leave the door on the latch so I can get in?* 你別鎖門好不好？我好進來。

■ ***verb*** **~ sth** to fasten sth with a latch 用插銷插上；用碰鎖鎖上

PHR V **ˌlatch ˈon (to sth)** | **ˌlatch ˈonto sth** (*informal*) to understand an idea or what sb is saying 理解，懂得，領會（想法或某人的話）：*It was a difficult concept to grasp, but I soon latched on.* 那是個難以弄明白的概念，但我很快就理解了。**ˌlatch ˈon (to sb/sth)** | **ˌlatch ˈonto sb/sth** (*informal*) **1** to become attached to sb/sth 變得依附於：*antibodies that latch onto germs* 依附於細菌的抗體 **2** to join sb and stay in their company, especially when they would prefer you not to be with them 糾纏，纏住（某人） **3** to develop a strong interest in sth 對…產生濃厚的興趣：*She always latches on to the latest craze.* 她總是對最新時尚有濃厚的興趣。

latch·key /ˈlætʃkiː/ *noun* a key for the front or the outer door of a house, etc. （房屋等前門或大門的）碰鎖鑰匙

ˈlatchkey child (also **ˈlatchkey kid**) *noun* (*usually disapproving*) a child who is at home alone after school because both parents are at work（因父母雙雙上班放學後獨自在家的）掛鑰匙兒童

late 🗝 /leɪt/ *adj., adv.*

■ ***adj.*** (**later, lat·est**) **1** 🗝 [only before noun] near the end of a period of time, a person's life, etc. 接近末期的；晚年的：*in the late afternoon* 傍晚 ◇ *in late summer* 夏末 ◇ *She married in her late twenties* (= when she was 28 or 29). 她快三十歲時才結婚。◇ *In later life he started playing golf.* 他晚年才開始打高爾夫球。◇ *The school was built in the late 1970s.* 這所學校建於 20 世紀 70 年代末。 **OPP** **early** **2** 🗝 [not usually before noun] arriving, happening or done after the expected, arranged or usual time 遲到；遲發生；遲做：*I'm sorry I'm late.* 對不起，我遲到了。◇ *She's late for work every day.* 她每天上班都遲到。◇ *My flight was an hour late.* 我那趟航班晚點了一小時。◇ *We apologize for the late arrival of this train.* 我們對本趟列車的晚點表示歉意。◇ *Because of the cold weather the crops are later this year.* 因天氣寒冷，農作物今年成熟得較晚。◇ *Interest will be charged for late payment.* 逾期付款必須支付利息。◇ *Here is a late news flash.* 現在插播剛剛收到的新聞。 **OPP** **early** **3** 🗝 near the end of the day 近日暮的；近深夜的：*Let's go home—it's getting late.* 咱們回家吧，時間不早了。◇ *Look at the time—it's much later than I thought.* 看看時間吧，比我想像的要晚多了。◇ *What are you doing up at this **late hour**?* 深更半夜的，你在做什麼？◇ *What is the latest time I can have an appointment?* 最晚的預約時間是幾點鐘？◇ *I've had too many **late nights** recently* (= when I've gone to bed very late). 我最近熬夜太多。 **OPP** **early** **4** [only before noun] (*formal*) (of a person 人) no longer alive 已故的：*her late husband* 她已故的丈夫 ◇ *the late Paul Newman* 已故的保羅 • 紐曼 ▸ **late·ness** /ˈleɪtnəs/ *noun* [U]：*They apologized for the lateness of the train.* 他們對火車晚點表示了歉意。◇ *Despite the lateness of the hour, the children were not in bed.* 儘管已是深夜，孩子們仍未就寢。 ➲ see also LATER, LATEST

IDM **be too ˈlate** 🗝 happening after the time when it is possible to do sth 為時已晚；已失時機：*It's too late to save her now.* 現在來拯救她的生命已為時太晚。◇ *Buy now before it's too late.* 欲購從速，勿失良機。

■ ***adv.*** (*comparative* **later**, *no superlative*) **1** 🗝 after the expected, arranged or usual time 遲；晚：*I got up late.* 我起晚了。◇ *Can I stay up late tonight?* 我今晚可以晚點兒睡嗎？◇ *She has to work late tomorrow.* 她明天得熬夜工作。◇ *The big stores are open later on Thursdays.* 每逢星期四大商店營業時間延長。◇ *She married late.* 她結婚晚。◇ *The birthday card arrived three days late.* 生日賀卡晚到了三天。 **2** 🗝 near the end of a period of time, a person's life, etc. 接近末期；在晚年：*late in March/the afternoon* 三月下旬；傍晚 ◇ *It happened late last year.* 那事發生在去年年底。◇ ***As late as*** (= as recently as) *the 1950s, tuberculosis was still a fatal illness.* 直到 20 世紀 50 年代，結核病仍然是一種致命的疾病。◇ *He became an author **late in life**.* 他到晚年才成為作家。 **3** 🗝 near the end of the day 臨近日暮；接近午夜：*There's a good film on late.* 深夜有一場好電影。◇ *Late that evening, there was a knock at the door.* 那天深夜，有人敲過門。◇ *Share prices fell early on but rose again late in the day.* 那天股票價格起先跌了，臨近收盤時又漲了。 **OPP** **early** ➲ see also LATER

IDM **ˌbetter ˌlate than ˈnever** (*saying*) used especially when you, or sb else, arrive/arrives late, or when sth such as success happens late, to say that this is better than not coming or happening at all 遲到總比不到好；遲發生總比不發生強 **ˌlate in the ˈday** (*disapproving*) after the time when an action could be successful 為時已晚；已失時機：*He started working hard much too late in the day—he couldn't possibly catch up.* 他太晚才開始努力工作，不可能趕上了。 **late of …** (*formal*) until recently working or living in the place mentioned 直至最近工作（或居住）的地方：*Professor Jones, late of Oxford University* 直到不久前還在牛津大學任教的瓊斯教授 **of ˈlate** (*formal*) recently 最近；新近；近來：*I haven't seen him of late.* 我最近沒見過他。 **too ˈlate** 🗝 after the time when it is possible to do sth successfully 過遲；太晚：*She's left it too late to apply for the job.* 她申請那份工作已為時太晚。◇ *I realized the truth too late.* 我太晚才知道真相了。 ➲ more at NIGHT, SOON

Grammar Point 語法說明

late / lately

- **Late** and **lately** are both adverbs, but **late** is used with similar meanings to the adjective **late**, whereas **lately** can only mean 'recently'. * late 和 lately 均為副詞，但 late 與作形容詞的 late 意義相似，而 lately 只含近來之意：*We arrived two hours late.* 我們遲到了兩小時。◇ *I haven't heard from him lately.* 我最近沒聽過他的消息。**Lately** is usually used with a perfect tense of the verb. * lately 常與動詞的完成時連用。
- Look also at the idioms **be too late** (at the adjective) and **too late** (at the adverb). 另見習語 be too late（形容詞部份）和 too late（副詞部份）。

late·comer /ˈleɪtkʌmə(r)/ *noun* a person who arrives late 遲到者；來遲者

late·ly /ˈleɪtli/ *adv.* recently; in the recent past 最近；新近；近來；不久前：*Have you seen her lately?* 你最近見過她嗎？◇ *It's only lately that she's been well enough to go out.* 她只是最近才康復，可出去走一走了。◇ (*BrE*) *I haven't been sleeping well just lately.* 我就是在最近才一直睡不好覺。◇ *She had lately returned from India.* 不久前她從印度回來了。

ˌlate-ˈnight *adj.* [only before noun] happening late at night; available after other things finish 深夜的；午夜

L

的；（其他事情完成後）可得到的： *a late-night movie* 午夜電影◇ *late-night shopping* 深夜購物

la·tent /ˈleɪtnt/ *adj.* [usually before noun] existing, but not yet very noticeable, active or well developed 潛在的；潛伏的；隱藏的： *latent disease* 潛伏性疾病◇ *These children have a huge reserve of latent talent.* 這些孩子蘊藏着極大的潛在天賦。 ▸ **la·tency** /ˈleɪtənsi/ *noun* [U]

later /ˈleɪtə(r)/ *adv., adj.*

▪ ***adv.*** **1** at a time in the future; after the time you are talking about 後來；以後；其後；隨後： *See you later.* 回頭見。◇ *I met her again three years later.* 三年後我又遇見她了。◇ *His father died later that year.* 那年晚些時候他的父親去世了。◇ *We're going to Rome later in the year.* 我們年內晚些時候要到羅馬去。◇ *She later became a doctor.* 她後來當了醫生。 OPP **earlier** **2 Later!** (*informal*) a way of saying goodbye, used by young people（年輕人告別時說）再見： *Later, guys!* 夥計們，再見！

IDM **later ˈon** (*informal*) at a time in the future; after the time you are talking about 後來；以後；其後；隨後： *I'm going out later on.* 我過一會兒要外出。◇ *Much later on, she realized what he had meant.* 過了好長時間，她才明白他的意思。 **not/no later than …** by a particular time and not after it 不晚於…；不遲於…： *Please arrive no later than 8 o'clock.* 請 8 點之前到達。

▪ ***adj.*** [only before noun] **1** coming after sth else or at a time in the future 後來的；以後的： *This is discussed in more detail in a later chapter.* 在後面的一章中對這一點有更詳細的討論。◇ *The match has been postponed to a later date.* 比賽已被推遲到以後的某個日期舉行。 **2** near the end of a period of time, life, etc. 接近末期的；晚年的： *the later part of the seventeenth century* ＊17 世紀末葉◇ *She found happiness in her later years.* 她在晚年才尋得幸福。 OPP **earlier** IDM see SOON

lat·eral /ˈlætərəl/ *adj., noun*

▪ ***adj.*** [usually before noun] (*technical* 術語) connected with the side of sth or with movement to the side 側面的；橫向的；向側面移動的： *the lateral branches of a tree* 樹的側枝◇ *lateral eye movements* 眼睛的兩側運動 ▸ **lat·eral·ly** /ˈlætərəli/ *adv.*

▪ ***noun*** (also ˌ**lateral** ˈ**consonant**) (*phonetics* 語音) a consonant sound which is produced by placing a part of the tongue against the PALATE so that air flows around it on both sides, for example /l/ in *lie* 邊音（如 lie 一詞中 /l/ 的發音）

ˌ**lateral** ˈ**thinking** *noun* [U] (*especially BrE*) a way of solving problems by using your imagination to find new ways of looking at the problem 水平思考，橫向思維（即用想像力尋求解決問題的新方法）

lat·est /ˈleɪtɪst/ *adj., noun*

▪ ***adj.*** [only before noun] the most recent or newest 最近的；最新的： *the latest unemployment figures* 最新失業數字◇ *the latest craze/fashion/trend* 最新時尚／款式／動向◇ *her latest novel* 她最近出版的小說◇ *Have you heard the latest news?* 你聽到最新消息了嗎？

▪ ***noun*** [U] **the latest** (*informal*) the most recent or the newest thing or piece of news 最新事物；最新消息： *This is the latest in robot technology.* 這是最新的機器人技術。◇ *Have you heard the latest?* 你聽到最新消息了嗎？

IDM **at the ˈlatest** no later than the time or the date mentioned 最遲；最晚；至遲： *Applications should be in by next Monday at the latest.* 最遲須於下星期一遞交申請書。

latex /ˈleɪteks/ *noun* [U] **1** a thick white liquid that is produced by some plants and trees, especially rubber trees. Latex becomes solid when exposed to air, and is used to make medical products.（天然）膠乳；（尤指橡膠樹的）橡漿： *latex gloves* 合成膠手套 **2** an artificial substance similar to this that is used to make paints, glues, etc. 人工合成膠乳（用於製作油漆、粘合劑等）

lath /lɑːθ; *NAmE* læθ/ *noun* (*pl.* **laths** /lɑːθs; *NAmE* læðz/) a thin narrow strip of wood that is used to support PLASTER (= material used for covering walls) on the inside walls and the ceilings of buildings 灰板條；板條；板筋

lathe /leɪð/ *noun* a machine that shapes pieces of wood or metal by holding and turning them against a fixed cutting tool 車牀

la·ther /ˈlɑːðə(r); *NAmE* ˈlæð-/ *noun, verb*

▪ ***noun*** [U, sing.] a white mass of small bubbles that is produced by mixing soap with water（皂液的）泡沫；皂沫

IDM **get into a ˈlather | work yourself into a ˈlather** (*BrE, informal*) to get anxious or angry about sth, especially when it is not necessary（尤指不必要地）焦躁不安，發怒 **in a ˈlather** (*BrE, informal*) in a nervous, angry or excited state 緊張；憤怒；激動 SYN **worked up**

▪ ***verb*** **1** [T] **~ sth** to cover sth with lather 給…塗上皂沫；用皂沫覆蓋： *I lathered my face and started to shave.* 我往臉上塗了皂沫，然後開始刮鬍子。 **2** [I] to produce lather 產生泡沫；起泡沫： *Soap does not lather well in hard water.* 肥皂在硬水中起不了多少泡沫。

lathi /ˈlɑːtiː/ *noun* (*IndE*) a long thick stick, especially one used as a weapon or by the police 長而粗的棍子；（尤指）警棍

Latin /ˈlætɪn; *NAmE* ˈlætn/ *noun, adj.*

▪ ***noun*** **1** [U] the language of ancient Rome and the official language of its empire 拉丁語 **2** [C] a person from countries where languages that have developed from Latin, such as Spanish, Portuguese, Italian or French, are spoken 拉丁人（來自拉丁語系國家如西班牙、葡萄牙、意大利或法國） **3** [U] music of a kind that came originally from Latin America, typically with strong dance rhythms 拉丁音樂（源自拉丁美洲，節奏感強，適於跳舞）

▪ ***adj.*** **1** of or in the Latin language 拉丁語的；用拉丁語寫成的： *Latin poetry* 拉丁語詩歌 **2** connected with or typical of the countries or peoples using languages developed from Latin, such as Spanish, Portuguese, Italian or French 拉丁語系國家（或民族）的（如西班牙、葡萄牙、意大利或法國）；拉丁人的： *a Latin temperament* 拉丁人的氣質

La·tina /læˈtiːnə/ *noun* a woman or girl, especially one who is living in the US, who comes from Latin America, or whose family came from there（尤指居住在美國的）拉丁美洲（裔）女子 ➲ compare LATINO ▸ **La·tina** *adj.* [usually before noun]

ˌ**Latin Aˈmerica** *noun* [U] the parts of the Americas in which Spanish or Portuguese is the main language 拉丁美洲（以西班牙語或葡萄牙語為主要語言的美洲地區） ➲ note at AMERICAN ➲ compare SOUTH AMERICA

Lat·in·ate /ˈlætɪneɪt/ *adj.* (of words or language 詞或語言) from Latin, or relating to Latin 從拉丁語派生（或演化）的；與拉丁語有關的： *formal Latinate terms* 正式拉丁術語

ˌ**Latin** ˈ**lover** *noun* (*informal*) a man from the Mediterranean region or from Latin America who is considered a good lover 拉丁情人（地中海地區或拉丁美洲男子，被視為有魅力的情人）

La·tino /læˈtiːnəʊ; *NAmE* -noʊ/ *noun* (*pl.* **-os**) a person, especially one who is living in the US, who comes from Latin America, or whose family came from there（尤指居住在美國的）拉丁美洲人，拉丁美洲人後裔 ➲ compare CHICANO ▸ **La·tino** *adj.* [usually before noun]

lati·tude /ˈlætɪtjuːd; *NAmE* -tuːd/ *noun* **1** (*abbr.* **lat.**) [U] the distance of a place north or south of the EQUATOR (= the line around the world dividing north and south), measured in degrees 緯度 ➲ compare LONGITUDE **2 latitudes** [pl.] a region of the world that is a particular distance from the EQUATOR 緯度地區： *the northern latitudes* 北緯地區 **3** [U] (*formal*) freedom to choose what you do or the way that you do it 選擇（做什麼事或做事方式）的自由 SYN **liberty** ➲ see also LEEWAY

la·trine /ləˈtriːn/ *noun* a toilet in a camp, etc., especially one made by digging a hole in the ground（營地等的）廁所；（尤指）茅坑，便坑

latte /ˈlɑːteɪ/ *noun* = CAFFÈ LATTE

lat·ter /ˈlætə(r)/ *adj., noun*

▪ ***adj.*** **1** being the second of two things, people or groups that have just been mentioned, or the last in a list（剛提及的兩者中）後者的；（系列中）最後的，末

尾的：*The latter point is the most important.* 後面提及的那一點是最重要的。 **2** nearer to the end of a period of time than the beginning 後半期的；後面的：*the latter half of the year* 下半年 ➲ compare FORMER

■ ***noun*** **the latter** (*pl.* **the latter**) the second of two things, people or groups that have just been mentioned, or the last in a list（剛提及的兩者中）後者；（系列中）最後一位，末位：*He presented two solutions. The latter seems much better.* 他提出了兩個解決方案，後一個看起來要好得多。◇ *The town has a concert hall and two theatres. The latter were both built in the 1950s.* 這座城鎮有一個音樂廳和兩個劇院。這兩個劇院都是在20 世紀 50 年代建成的。

'latter-day *adj.* [only before noun] being a modern version of a person or thing in the past（舊時的人或物的）現代翻版的：*a latter-day Robin Hood* 當代的羅賓漢

lat·ter·ly /ˈlætəli; *NAmE* -tərli/ *adv.* (*formal*) **1** most recently 最近；新近：*Latterly his painting has shown a new freedom of expression.* 最近，他的繪畫展示出一種新的自由表現形式。 **2** towards the end of a period of time 在最後一段時間：*Her health declined rapidly and latterly she never left the house.* 她的健康狀況急劇衰退，此後她再未離開過家。

lat·tice /ˈlætɪs/ *noun* [U, C] (also **ˈlat·tice·work** [U]) a structure that is made of strips of wood or metal that cross over each other with spaces shaped like a diamond between them, used, for example, as a fence; any structure or pattern like this 格子木架，格子金屬架，格柵（用作籬笆等）；斜條結構；斜格圖案：*a low wall of stone latticework* 石砌格構的矮牆 ◇ *a lattice of branches* 樹枝籬笆 ▸ **lat·ticed** /ˈlætɪst/ *adj.*

ˌlattice ˈwindow (also **ˌlat·ticed ˈwindow**) *noun* a window with small pieces of glass shaped like diamonds in a FRAMEWORK of metal strips 花格窗；斜條格構窗

laud /lɔːd/ *verb* **~ sb/sth** (*formal*) to praise sb/sth 讚揚；讚美；稱讚

laud·able /ˈlɔːdəbl/ *adj.* (*formal*) deserving to be praised or admired, even if not really successful 應受讚揚的；值得讚美的 SYN **commendable**：*a laudable aim/attempt* 值得稱讚的志向／嘗試 ▸ **laud·ably** /-əbli/ *adv.*

Vocabulary Building 詞彙擴充

Different ways of laughing 笑的不同方式

- **cackle** to laugh in a loud, unpleasant way, especially in a high voice * cackle 意為令人討厭地嘎嘎大笑，尤指高聲笑
- **chuckle** to laugh quietly, especially because you are thinking about something funny * chuckle 意為輕聲笑，尤指想到滑稽事時發笑
- **giggle** to laugh in a silly way because you are amused, embarrassed or nervous * giggle 意為因開心、難堪或緊張而傻笑
- **guffaw** to laugh noisily * guffaw 意為哄笑、狂笑、大笑
- **roar** to laugh very loudly * roar 意為放聲大笑
- **snigger/snicker** to laugh in a quiet unpleasant way, especially at something rude or at someone's problems or mistakes * snigger/snicker 意為竊笑、暗笑，尤指對無禮行為或因他人的問題或錯誤發笑
- **titter** to laugh quietly, especially in a nervous or embarrassed way * titter 意為竊笑，尤指緊張或尷尬地笑

You can also **be convulsed with laughter** or **dissolve into laughter** when you find something very funny. In *BrE* people also **shriek with laughter** or **howl with laughter**. 認為某事非常滑稽可笑亦可用 be convulsed with laughter（笑得前仰後合）或 dissolve into laughter（不禁大笑）。在英式英語中亦用 shriek with laughter（尖聲大笑）或 howl with laughter（狂笑）。

laud·anum /ˈlɔːdənəm/ *noun* [U] a drug made from OPIUM. In the past, people used to take laudanum to reduce pain and anxiety, and to help them sleep. 鴉片酊（舊時用以鎮痛、鎮靜及安眠）

laud·atory /ˈlɔːdətəri; *NAmE* -tɔːri/ *adj.* (*formal*) expressing praise or admiration 稱讚的；讚美的；頌揚的

laugh 🔑 /lɑːf; *NAmE* læf/ *verb, noun*

■ ***verb*** **1** 🔑 [I, T] to make the sounds and movements of your face that show you are happy or think sth is funny 笑；發笑：*to* ***laugh loudly/aloud/out loud*** 大聲／高聲／放聲地笑 ◇ **~ (at/about sth)** *You never laugh at my jokes!* 你聽了我的笑話從不發笑！◇ *The show was hilarious—I couldn't stop laughing.* 表演十分滑稽，弄得我笑個不停。◇ *She always* ***makes me laugh.*** 她老是引得我發笑。◇ *He* ***burst out laughing*** (= suddenly started laughing). 他突然大笑起來。◇ *She laughed to cover her nervousness.* 她笑了，想以此來掩飾自己緊張的心情。◇ *I told him I was worried but he laughed scornfully.* 我告訴他我很擔憂，可他卻輕蔑地一笑。◇ **+ speech** *'You're crazy!' she laughed.* "你瘋啦！"她哈哈大笑起來。 **2** [I] **be laughing** (*informal*) used to say that you are in a very good position, especially because you have done sth successfully（尤因成功而）處於有利地位：*If we win the next game we'll be laughing.* 要是贏了下一場比賽，我們就佔優勢了。

IDM **don't make me ˈlaugh** (*informal*) used to show that you think what sb has just said is impossible or stupid（認為不可能或愚蠢）別讓我笑掉大牙了，別開玩笑了：*'Will your dad lend you the money?' 'Don't make me laugh!'* "你父親會借給你錢嗎？""別開玩笑了！" **he who laughs ˌlast laughs ˈlongest** (*saying*) used to tell sb not to be too proud of their present success; in the end another person may be more successful 別高興得太早 **laugh all the way to the ˈbank** (*informal*) to make a lot of money easily and feel very pleased about it 發大財而喜笑顏開 **laugh in sb's ˈface** to show in a very obvious way that you have no respect for sb 當面嘲笑；公然蔑視 **laugh like a ˈdrain** (*BrE*) to laugh very loudly 哈哈大笑；放聲大笑 **laugh on the other side of your ˈface** (*BrE, informal*) to be forced to change from feeling pleased or satisfied to feeling disappointed or annoyed 轉喜為憂；得意變成失意；笑臉變為苦臉 **laugh sb/sth out of ˈcourt** (*BrE, informal*) to completely reject an idea, a story, etc. that you think is not worth taking seriously at all 對（某主意、說法等）一笑置之；置之不理；不屑一顧 **laugh till/until you ˈcry** to laugh so long and hard that there are tears in your eyes 笑得流淚；笑出眼淚 **laugh up your ˈsleeve (at sb/sth)** (*informal*) to be secretly amused about sth 暗自發笑；竊笑 **laugh your ˈhead off** to laugh very loudly and for a long time 大笑不止；狂笑不已 **not know whether to ˌlaugh or ˈcry** (*informal*) to be unable to decide how to react to a bad or unfortunate situation（面對惡劣或不幸情況）不知所措，哭笑不得 **you ˌhave/you've ˌgot to ˈlaugh** (*informal*) used to say that you think there is a funny side to a situation 還是值得一笑；還有可笑之處：*Well, I'm sorry you've lost your shoes, but you've got to laugh, haven't you?* 啊，真糟糕，你的鞋子丟了，可是這也挺逗的，是不是？➲ more at KILL *v.*, PISS *v.*

PHR V **ˈlaugh at sb/sth** 🔑 to make sb/sth seem stupid or not serious by making jokes about them/it 嘲笑；譏笑 SYN **ridicule**：*Everybody laughs at my accent.* 大家都拿我的口音取笑。◇ *She is not afraid to laugh at herself* (= is not too serious about herself). 她勇於自嘲。 **ˌlaugh sth↔ˈoff** (*informal*) to try to make people think that sth is not serious or important, especially by making a joke about it 一笑置之，付之一笑（尤指用笑話擺脫）：*He laughed off suggestions that he was going to resign.* 傳言他要辭職，他一笑置之。

■ ***noun*** **1** 🔑 [C] the sound you make when you are amused or happy 笑聲：*to* ***give a laugh*** 大笑一聲 ◇ *a short/nervous/hearty laugh* 短促的／緊張的／開心的笑聲 ◇ *His first joke* ***got the biggest laugh*** *of the night.* 他講的第一個笑話博得了當晚最開懷的笑聲。➲ see also BELLY LAUGH **2 a laugh** [sing.] (*informal*) an enjoyable and amusing occasion or thing that happens 令人開心的時

L

刻；引人發笑的事；笑料：*Come to the karaoke night—it should be a good laugh.* 來參加卡拉 OK 晚會吧，一定會很開心的。◇ *And he didn't realize it was you? What a laugh!* 他竟沒認出那是你？真有意思！ **3 a laugh** [sing.] a person who is amusing and fun to be with 引人發笑的人；逗笑好玩的人：*Paula's a good laugh, isn't she?* 葆拉是個活寶，是不是？

IDM **do sth for a 'laugh/for 'laughs** to do sth for fun or as a joke 逗趣；開玩笑：*I just did it for a laugh, but it got out of hand.* 我只是開開玩笑，然而卻一發不可收拾。 **have a (good) 'laugh (about sth)** to find sth amusing 覺得可笑（或有趣）：*I was angry at the time but we had a good laugh about it afterwards.* 我當時很生氣，可後來我們卻又覺得十分可笑。 ➲ more at BARREL *n.*, LAST[1] *det.*

laugh·able /ˈlɑːfəbl; *NAmE* ˈlæf-/ *adj.* silly or ridiculous, and not worth taking seriously 荒唐可笑的；荒謬的；不值得當真的 **SYN** **absurd** ▸ **laugh·ably** /-əbli/ *adv.*

laugh·ing /ˈlɑːfɪŋ; *NAmE* ˈlæfɪŋ/ *adj.* showing AMUSEMENT or happiness 笑的；帶笑意的：*his laughing blue eyes* 他帶着笑意的藍眼睛 ◇ *laughing faces* 笑臉

IDM **be no laughing 'matter** to be sth serious that you should not joke about 不是開玩笑的事；嚴肅的事 ➲ more at DIE *v.*, SPLIT *v.*

'laughing gas *noun* [U] (*informal*) = NITROUS OXIDE

laugh·ing·ly /ˈlɑːfɪŋli; *NAmE* ˈlæf-/ *adv.* **1** in an amused way 帶笑地；笑着：*He laughingly agreed.* 他笑着同意了。 **2** used to show that you think a particular word is not at all a suitable way of describing something and therefore seems ridiculous（表示用詞）荒唐可笑：*I finally reached what we laughingly call civilization.* 我終於到了我們戲稱為文明之地的地方。

'laughing stock *noun* [usually sing.] a person that everyone laughs at because they have done sth stupid 笑柄；笑料：*I can't wear that! I'd be a laughing stock.* 我可不能戴那個東西！否則會成為笑柄的。

,laugh-out-'loud *adj.* (*abbr.* **LOL**) [only before noun] (*informal*) extremely funny 非常滑稽的：*a laugh-out-loud moment* 十分逗樂的時刻 ◇ *The best scenes in the movie are laugh-out-loud funny.* 這部影片中最棒的幾個鏡頭簡直笑死人。 **HELP** The abbreviation **LOL** is also used in text messages, emails or Internet chat, to show that you think sth is funny or do not mean it seriously. 縮寫形式 LOL 也用於短信、電郵或互聯網聊天，表示認為某事滑稽，或隨便一說而已。

laugh·ter /ˈlɑːftə(r); *NAmE* ˈlæf-/ *noun* [U] the act or sound of laughing 笑；笑聲：*to* ***roar with laughter*** 放聲大笑 ◇ ***tears/gales/peals/shrieks of laughter*** 笑得流眼淚；陣陣笑聲；哈哈大笑；陣陣尖聲大笑 ◇ *to* ***burst/dissolve into laughter*** 突然／情不自禁大笑起來 ◇ *a house full of laughter* (= with a happy atmosphere) 充滿歡聲笑語的房子 **IDM** see SPLIT *v.*

launch 🔑 /lɔːntʃ/ *verb, noun*

■ *verb* **1** 🔑 **~ sth** to start an activity, especially an organized one 開始從事，發起，發動（尤指有組織的活動）：*to* ***launch an appeal/an inquiry/an investigation/a campaign*** 開始上訴／質詢／調查／一場運動 ◇ *to* ***launch an attack/invasion*** 發起攻擊；發動侵略 **2** 🔑 **~ sth** to make a product available to the public for the first time（首次）上市，發行：*a party to launch his latest novel* 他最新小說的首發式 ◇ *The new model will be launched in July.* 新型號產品將在七月推出。 **3** 🔑 **~ sth** to put a ship or boat into the water, especially one that has just been built 使（船，尤指新船）下水：*The Navy is to launch a new warship today.* 海軍今天有一艘新軍艦要下水。◇ *The lifeboat was launched immediately.* 那艘救生艇被立刻放下了水。 **4** 🔑 **~ sth** to send sth such as a SPACECRAFT, weapon, etc. into space, into the sky or through water 發射；把（航天器、武器等）發射上天；水中發射：*to launch a communications satellite* 發射通信衞星 ◇ *to* ***launch a missile/rocket/torpedo*** 發射導彈／火箭／魚雷 **5 ~ yourself at, from, etc. sth | ~ yourself forwards, etc.** to jump forwards with a lot of force 猛撲向前：*Without warning he launched himself at me.* 他突然向我猛撲過來。 **6 ~ sth** (*computing* 計) to start a computer program 啟動（計算機程序）：*You can launch programs and documents from your keyboard.* 你可以從鍵盤啟動程序和文件。

PHR V **'launch into sth | 'launch yourself into sth** to begin sth in an enthusiastic way, especially sth that will take a long time（熱情地）開始做，投入：*He launched into a lengthy account of his career.* 他開始囉囉嗦嗦地講述自己的工作經歷。 **,launch 'out** to do sth new in your career, especially sth more exciting 開始從事，投身於（新的、尤指更令人興奮的事業）：*It's time I launched out on my own.* 該是我自己創業的時候了。

■ *noun* **1** 🔑 [usually sing.] the action of launching sth; an event at which sth is launched（航天器的）發射；（船的）下水；（產品的）上市；（事件的）發起：*the successful launch of the Ariane rocket* 阿里亞娜火箭的成功發射 ◇ *a product launch* 產品的投放市場 ◇ *The official launch date is in May.* 正式的發行日期是在五月。 **2** a large boat with a motor 大型汽艇；機動大舢板；交通艇

launch·er /ˈlɔːntʃə(r)/ *noun* (often in compounds 常構成複合詞) a device that is used to send a ROCKET, a MISSILE, etc. into the sky（火箭、導彈等的）發射裝置，發射器：*a rocket launcher* 火箭發射裝置

'launch pad (also **'launching pad**) *noun* a platform from which a SPACECRAFT, etc. is sent into the sky（航天器等的）發射平台：(*figurative*) *She regards the job as a launch pad for her career in the media.* 她把這份工作當作她從事媒體職業的跳板。

laun·der /ˈlɔːndə(r)/ *verb* **1 ~ sth** (*formal*) to wash, dry and iron clothes, etc. 洗熨（衣物）：*freshly laundered sheets* 剛洗的被單 **2 ~ sth** to move money that has been obtained illegally into foreign bank accounts or legal businesses so that it is difficult for people to know where the money came from 洗錢

laun·der·ette (also **laun·drette**) /lɔːnˈdret/ (both *BrE*) (*NAmE* **Laun·dro·mat™** /ˈlɔːndrəmæt/) *noun* a place where you can wash and dry your clothes in machines that you operate by putting in coins 投幣式自助洗衣店

laun·dry /ˈlɔːndri/ *noun* (*pl.* **-ies**) **1** [U] clothes, sheets, etc. that need washing, that are being washed, or that have been washed recently 要（或正在）洗的衣物；剛洗好的衣物 **SYN** **washing**：*a pile of* ***clean/dirty laundry*** 一摞乾淨的／髒的衣物 ◇ *a* ***laundry basket/room*** 洗衣筐；洗衣間 **2** [U, sing.] the process or the job of washing clothes, sheets, etc. 洗衣物；洗衣物的活：*to do the laundry* 幹洗衣活 ◇ *The hotel has a laundry service.* 旅館提供洗衣服務。 **3** [C] a business or place where you send sheets, clothes, etc. to be washed 洗衣店；洗衣房

'laundry list *noun* a long list of people or things 一長串名單；清單：*a laundry list of problems* 一長串問題

Laur·asia /lɔːˈreɪʃə; -ʒə/ *noun* [sing.] (*geology* 地) a very large area of land that existed in the northern HEMISPHERE millions of years ago. It was made up of the present N America, Greenland, Europe and most of Asia. 勞亞古大陸（幾百萬年前存在於北半球的大片陸地，由如今的北美洲、格陵蘭、歐洲和亞洲大部份組成）

laure·ate /ˈlɒriət; *NAmE* ˈlɔːr-; ˈlɑːr-/ *noun* **1** a person who has been given an official honour or prize for sth important they have achieved 榮譽獲得者；獲獎者：*a Nobel laureate* 諾貝爾獎獲得者 **2** = POET LAUREATE

laurel /ˈlɒrəl; *NAmE* ˈlɔːr-; ˈlɑːr-/ *noun* **1** [U, C] a bush with dark smooth shiny leaves that remain on the bush and stay green through the year 月桂灌木；月桂樹 **2 laurels** [pl.] honour and praise given to sb because of sth that they have achieved 榮譽；讚譽；榮耀

IDM **look to your 'laurels** to be careful that you do not lose the success or advantage that you have over other people 小心翼翼地保持成就（或優勢） **rest/sit on your 'laurels** (usually *disapproving*) to feel so satisfied with what you have already achieved that you do not try to do any more 滿足於既得成就；不思進取

'laurel wreath *noun* a ring of laurel leaves that was worn on the head in the past as a sign of victory 桂冠（舊時作為勝利的象徵）

lav /læv/ *noun* (*BrE, informal*) a toilet 廁所

lava /ˈlɑːvə/ *noun* [U] **1** hot liquid rock that comes out of a VOLCANO（火山噴出的）熔岩，岩漿：*molten lava* 熔化的火山岩漿 **2** this type of rock when it has cooled and become hard 火山岩

lav·age /ˈlævɪdʒ; læˈvɑːʒ/ *noun* (*medical* 醫) the process of washing a space inside the body such as the stomach or COLON 灌洗（胃、腸等）

ˈlava lamp *noun* an electric lamp that contains a liquid in which a coloured substance like oil moves up and down in shapes that keep changing 熔岩燈（裝有可上下流動和變形的彩色油狀物）➲ VISUAL VOCAB page V21

lava·tor·ial /ˌlævəˈtɔːriəl/ *adj.* (*especially BrE*) **lavatorial** humour refers in a rude way to parts of the body, going to the toilet, etc. 粗俗的幽默（指粗俗地談論身體部位或上廁所等）

lav·atory /ˈlævətri; *NAmE* -tɔːri/ *noun* (*pl.* **-ies**) (*old-fashioned or formal*) **1** (*especially BrE*) a toilet, or a room with a toilet in it 抽水馬桶；廁所；衛生間；洗手間；盥洗室：*There's a bathroom and a lavatory upstairs.* 樓上有浴室和衛生間。 **2** (*BrE*) a public building or part of a building, with toilets in it 公共廁所（或衛生間、洗手間、盥洗室）：*The nearest public lavatory is at the station.* 最近的公共廁所在車站。

lav·en·der /ˈlævəndə(r)/ *noun* [U] **1** a garden plant or bush with bunches of purple flowers with a sweet smell 薰衣草（花園植物或灌木，開紫花，有香味） **2** the flowers of the lavender plant that have been dried, used for making sheets, clothes, etc. smell nice 乾薰衣草花（用以熏香牀單、衣物等）：*lavender oil* 薰衣草油 **3** a pale purple colour 淡紫色

lav·ish /ˈlævɪʃ/ *adj., verb*

■ ***adj.*** **1** large in amount, or impressive, and usually costing a lot of money 大量的；給人印象深刻的；耗資巨大的 SYN **extravagant, luxurious**：*lavish gifts/costumes/celebrations* 豐厚的禮品；昂貴的服裝；規模盛大的慶典 ◇ *They lived a very* ***lavish lifestyle.*** 他們過着揮霍無度的生活。◇ *They rebuilt the house on an even more* ***lavish scale*** *than before.* 他們重造了房子，規模甚至比以前更大。 **2** ~ (**with/in sth**) giving or doing sth generously 慷慨的；大方的：*He was lavish in his praise for her paintings.* 他大力讚揚她的繪畫。▸ **lav·ish·ly** *adv.*：*lavishly illustrated* 有大量插圖

■ ***verb***

PHR V **ˈlavish sth on/upon sb/sth** to give a lot of sth, often too much, to sb/sth 過分給予；濫施：*She lavishes most of her attention on her youngest son.* 她對她小兒子過於關愛。

law 🔑 /lɔː/ *noun*

▸ **SYSTEM OF RULES** 規則體系 **1** 🔑 (also **the law**) [U] the whole system of rules that everyone in a country or society must obey 法律（體系）：*If they entered the building they would be* ***breaking the law.*** 如果進入那棟大樓，他們就會觸犯法律。◇ *In Sweden it is* ***against the law*** *to hit a child.* 在瑞典打小孩是違法的。◇ *Defence attorneys can use any means* ***within the law*** *to get their client off.* 辯護律師可在法律許可的範圍內利用任何手段為當事人脫罪。◇ *British schools are now required* ***by law*** *to publish their exam results.* 現在英國的學校得按法律規定公佈考試結果。◇ *The reforms have recently* ***become law.*** 這些改革最近已成為法律。◇ *Do not think you are* ***above the law*** (= think that you cannot be punished by the law). 別以為你能凌駕於法律之上。◇ *the need for better* ***law enforcement*** 加強執法力度的必要 ◇ (*humorous*) *Kate's* ***word was law*** *in the Brown household.* 凱特的話在布朗家就是金科玉律。➲ COLLOCATIONS at JUSTICE

2 🔑 [U] a particular branch of the law 法規：***company/international/tax, etc. law*** 公司法、國際法、稅法等 ➲ see also CANON LAW, CASE LAW, CIVIL LAW, COMMON LAW, PRIVATE LAW, STATUTE LAW

▸ **ONE RULE** 一條法規 **3** 🔑 [C] a rule that deals with a particular crime, agreement, etc.（針對某項罪行、協議等的一條）法律，法規：~ (**against sth**) *the 1996 law against the hiring of illegal immigrants* 禁止雇用非法移民的 1996 法規 ◇ ~ (**on sth**) *The government has introduced some tough new laws on food hygiene.* 政府對食物衛生出台了一些強硬的新法規。◇ ***strict gun laws*** 嚴格的槍支法 ◇ ***a federal/state law*** 聯邦／州法律 ◇ ***to pass a law*** (= officially make it part of the system of laws) 通過一項法律 ◇ (*informal*) *There ought to be a law against it!* 應該立法加以禁止！➲ see also BY-LAW, LICENSING LAWS

▸ **SUBJECT/PROFESSION** 學科；職業 **4** 🔑 [U] the study of the law as a subject at university, etc.; the profession of being a lawyer 法學；法律學；律師業：*Jane is studying law.* 簡正在學習法律。◇ (*NAmE*) *He's in* ***law school.*** 他在讀法學院。◇ (*BrE*) *He's at law school.* 他在讀法學院。◇ *What made you go into law?* 是什麼促使你從事法律行業的呢？◇ *a law firm* 律師事務所

▸ **POLICE** 警察 **5** 🔑 **the law** [sing.] used to refer to the police and the legal system 警方；法律機構：*Jim is always getting into trouble with the law.* 吉姆總是因惹事落到警察手裏。

▸ **OF ORGANIZATION/ACTIVITY** 機構；活動 **6** [C] one of the rules which controls an organization or activity 規則；規章；條例：*the laws of the Church* 教會的戒律 ◇ *The first law of kung fu is to defend yourself.* 功夫的首要原則是自衞。◇ *the laws of cricket* 板球規則

▸ **OF GOOD BEHAVIOUR** 良好的品行 **7** [C] a rule for good behaviour or how you should behave in a particular place or situation 良好行為的準則；（某地或某場合下的）行為規範：*moral laws* 道德準則 ◇ *the unspoken laws of the street* 不言而喻的街頭行為規範

▸ **IN BUSINESS/NATURE/SCIENCE** 商業；自然；科學 **8** 🔑 [C] the fact that sth always happens in the same way in an activity or in nature 規律；法則；原理 SYN **principle**：*the laws of supply and demand* 供求律 ◇ *the law of gravity* 萬有引力之規律 **9** [C] a scientific rule that sb has stated to explain a natural process 定律：*the first law of thermodynamics* 熱力學第一定律 ➲ see also MURPHY'S LAW, PARKINSON'S LAW, SOD'S LAW, LEGAL, LEGALIZE, LEGISLATE

IDM **be a law unto yourˈself** to behave in an independent way and ignore rules or what other people want you to do 自行其是；我行我素 **go to ˈlaw** (*BrE*) to ask a court to settle a problem or disagreement 訴諸法律；提起訴訟；打官司 **ˌlaw and ˈorder** 🔑 a situation in which people obey the law and behave in a peaceful way 法治；治安；遵紀守法：*The government struggled to maintain law and order.* 政府努力維持治安。◇ *After the riots, the military was brought in to restore law and order.* 暴亂以後，軍隊出動來恢復治安。◇ *They claim to be the party of law and order.* 他們聲稱自己是重視治安問題的政黨。 **the ˌlaw of ˈaverages** the principle that one thing will happen as often as another if you try enough times 平均律：*Keep applying and by the law of averages you'll get a job sooner or later.* 繼續申請吧，根據平均律你遲早會找到工作的。 **the ˌlaw of the ˈjungle** a situation in which people are prepared to harm other people in order to succeed 叢林法則；弱肉強食 **lay down the ˈlaw** to tell sb with force what they should or should not do 發號施令；嚴格規定 **take the law into your own ˈhands** to do sth illegal in order to punish sb for doing sth wrong, instead of letting the police deal with them 不通過法律擅自處理 **there's no ˈlaw against sth** (*informal*) used to tell sb who is criticizing you that you are not doing anything wrong（對批評自己的人說）誰也管不着：*I'll sing if I want to—there's no law against it.* 我想唱就唱，誰也管不着。➲ more at LETTER *n.*, POSSESSION, RULE *n.*, WRONG *adj.*

ˈlaw-abiding *adj.* obeying and respecting the law 遵紀守法的；安分守己的：*law-abiding citizens* 遵紀守法的公民

law·break·er /ˈlɔːbreɪkə(r)/ *noun* a person who does not obey the law 不守法者；違法者；不法分子 ▸ **law-break·ing** *noun* [U]

ˈlaw court *noun* (*BrE*) = COURT OF LAW ➲ note at COURT

law·ful /ˈlɔːfl/ *adj.* (*formal*) allowed or recognized by law; legal 法定的；法律承認的；合法的：*his lawful heir* 他的合法繼承人 OPP **unlawful** ▸ **law·ful·ly** /-fəli/ *adv.*：*a lawfully elected government* 合法選舉產生的政府 **law·ful·ness** *noun* [U]

lawks /lɔːks/ *exclamation* (*old-fashioned, BrE*) used to show that you are surprised, angry or impatient（表示驚訝、生氣或不耐煩）天哪，啊呀

L

law·less /ˈlɔːləs/ *adj.* **1** (of a country or an area 國家或地區) where laws do not exist or are not obeyed 無法律的；不遵守法律的：*lawless streets* 沒有法紀的街區 ◇ *the lawless days of the revolution* 那場革命期間無法無天的日子 **2** (of people or their actions 人或其行為) without respect for the law 不遵守法律的；目無法紀的；不法的 **SYN** **anarchic, wild**：*lawless gangs* 目無法紀的團夥 ▸ **law·less·ness** *noun* [U]

ˈ**law lord** *noun* (*BrE*) a member of the British House of Lords who was qualified to perform its legal work. In 2009 the law lords' role was taken over by the judges of the new Supreme Court.（英國上議院的）司法議員（2009 年其職責由新的最高法院的法官接管）

law·maker /ˈlɔːmeɪkə(r)/ *noun* a person in government who makes the laws of a country 立法者 **SYN** **legislator**

law·man /ˈlɔːmæn/ *noun* (*pl.* **-men** /-men/) (*especially US*) an officer responsible for keeping law and order, especially a SHERIFF 執法官；（尤指）縣（或城鎮）治安官

lawn /lɔːn/ *noun* **1** [C] an area of ground covered in short grass in a garden/yard or park, or used for playing a game on 草坪；草地：*In summer we have to mow the lawn twice a week.* 夏天我們每週得修剪草坪兩次。◇ *a croquet lawn* 槌球場 ➲ **VISUAL VOCAB** page V19 **2** [U] a type of fine cotton or LINEN cloth used for making clothes 上等細棉布（或麻布）

ˈ**lawn bowling** *noun* [U] (*NAmE*) = BOWLS at BOWL *n.* (6)

ˈ**lawn chair** *noun* (*especially NAmE*) a chair that can be folded and that people use when sitting outside 草坪椅；戶外摺疊椅

lawn·mow·er /ˈlɔːnməʊə(r); *NAmE* -moʊ-/ (also **mower**) *noun* a machine for cutting the grass on LAWNS 割草機；剪草機 ➲ **VISUAL VOCAB** page V19

ˈ**lawn sign** *noun* (*NAmE*) a board that people put outside their house in order to advertise sth or to show that they support a particular politician or political party 草坪插牌，戶外告示牌（置於宅前，用於廣告或表明戶主支持某政治人物或政黨）

ˌ**lawn ˈtennis** *noun* [U] (*formal*) = TENNIS

More About 補充說明

lawyers

- **Lawyer** is a general term for a person who is qualified to advise people about the law, to prepare legal documents for them and/or to represent them in a court of law. * lawyer 為通用語，指律師，有資格提供法律咨詢、為當事人準備法律文件、在法庭上代表當事人。
- In England and Wales, a **lawyer** who is qualified to speak in the higher courts of law is called a **barrister**. In Scotland a **barrister** is called an **advocate**. 在英格蘭和威爾士，有資格在高等法院出庭辯護的律師叫 barrister；在蘇格蘭 barrister 稱作 advocate。
- In *NAmE* **attorney** is a more formal word used for a **lawyer** and is used especially in job titles. 在美式英語中，attorney 較 lawyer 正式，尤用於職務頭銜：*district attorney* 地方檢察官
- **Counsel** is the formal legal word used for a lawyer who is representing someone in court. * counsel 為正式的法律用語，指代表當事人出庭的律師：*counsel for the prosecution* 原告律師
- **Solicitor** is the *BrE* term for a lawyer who gives legal advice and prepares documents, for example when you are buying a house, and sometimes has the right to speak in a court of law. * solicitor 為英式英語，指提供法律咨詢、準備法律文件（如購買房屋時）、有時有權出庭辯護的律師。
- In *NAmE* **solicitor** is only used in the titles of some lawyers who work for the government. 在美式英語中，solicitor 只用於政府某些法務官員的頭銜：*Solicitor General* 司法部副部長

law·ren·cium /lɒˈrensiəm; *NAmE* lɔːˈr-/ *noun* [U] (*symb.* **Lr**) a chemical element. Lawrencium is a RADIOACTIVE metal. 鐒（放射性化學元素）

law·suit /ˈlɔːsuːt; *BrE* also -sjuːt/ (also **suit**) *noun* a claim or complaint against sb that a person or an organization can make in court 訴訟；起訴：*He **filed a lawsuit** against his record company.* 他對給他錄製唱片的公司提起了訴訟。

law·yer 0-m /ˈlɔːjə(r)/ *noun*
a person who is trained and qualified to advise people about the law and to represent them in court, and to write legal documents 律師

lax /læks/ *adj.* **1** (*disapproving*) not strict, severe or careful enough about work, rules or standards of behaviour 不嚴格的；不嚴厲的；馬虎的 **SYN** **slack, careless**：*lax security/discipline* 不嚴格的保安措施 / 紀律 ◇ *a lax attitude to health and safety regulations* 對衛生與安全條例的馬虎態度 **2** (*phonetics* 語音) (of a speech sound 語音) produced with the muscles of the speech organs relaxed 鬆的；鬆喉的 **OPP** **tense** ▸ **lax·ity** /ˈlæksəti/ *noun* [U]

laxa·tive /ˈlæksətɪv/ *noun* a medicine, food or drink that makes sb empty their BOWELS easily 輕瀉藥；通便劑；有通便作用的飲食 ▸ **laxa·tive** *adj.*

lay 0-m /leɪ/ *verb, adj., noun* ➲ see also LIE[1] *v.*

■ *verb* (**laid, laid** /leɪd/)

▸ **PUT DOWN/SPREAD** 放下；展開 **1** 0-m [T] to put sb/sth in a particular position, especially when it is done gently or carefully（尤指輕輕地或小心地）放置，安放，擱：**~ sb/sth + adv./prep.** *She laid the baby down gently on the bed.* 她把嬰兒輕輕地放在牀上。◇ *He laid a hand on my arm.* 他把手搭在我的胳膊上。◇ *The horse laid back its ears.* 那匹馬把耳朵往後豎着。◇ *Relatives laid wreaths on the grave.* 死者親屬在墓前獻了花圈。◇ **~ sb/sth + adj.** *The cloth should be laid flat.* 布應展開平放。**HELP** Some speakers confuse this sense of **lay** with **lie**, especially in the present and progressive tenses. However, **lay** has an object and **lie** does not. 有些人把 lay 的這一義項與 lie 混淆了，尤其是在現在時和進行時中。然而，lay 後可接賓語，lie 後則不接賓語：*She was lying on the beach.* ◇ ~~*She was laying on the beach.*~~ ◇ *Why don't you lie on the bed?* ◇ ~~*Why don't you lay on the bed?*~~ In the past tenses **laid** (from: *lay*) is often wrongly used for **lay** or **lain** (from: *lie*). 在過去時中，laid（詞根是 lay）常被誤作 lay 或 lain（詞根是 lie）：*She had lain there all night.* ◇ ~~*She had laid there all night.*~~ **2** 0-m [T] **~ sth (down)** to put sth down, especially on the floor, ready to be used 鋪，鋪放，鋪設（尤指在地板上）：*to **lay a carpet/cable/pipe*** 鋪地毯；鋪設電纜；鋪管道 ◇ *The foundations of the house are being laid today.* 今天正在給房子打地基。◇ (*figurative*) *They had laid the groundwork for future development.* 他們為此後的發展奠定了基礎。**3** 0-m [T] to spread sth on sth; to cover sth with a layer of sth（在某物上）攤開，塗，敷；用一層…覆蓋：**~ A (on/over B)** *Before they started they laid newspaper on the floor.* 他們開始前在地板上鋪了報紙。◇ *The grapes were laid to dry on racks.* 葡萄被攤放在架子上晾乾。◇ **~ B with A** *The floor was laid with newspaper.* 地板上鋪了報紙。

▸ **EGGS** 卵 **4** 0-m [T, I] **~ (sth)** if a bird, an insect, a fish, etc. **lays** eggs, it produces them from its body（鳥、昆蟲、魚等）下（蛋），產（卵）：*The cuckoo lays its eggs in other birds' nests.* 杜鵑在其他鳥的巢中下蛋。◇ *new-laid eggs* 鮮蛋 ◇ *The hens are not laying well* (= not producing many eggs). 母雞現在不愛下蛋。

▸ **TABLE** 桌子 **5** 0-m [T] **~ sth** (*BrE*) to arrange knives, forks, plates, etc. on a table ready for a meal 擺放餐具（準備就餐）**SYN** **set**：*to lay the table* 擺好餐具準備用餐

▸ **PRESENT PROPOSAL** 提出建議 **6** [T] **~ sth + adv./prep.** to present a proposal, some information, etc. to sb for them to think about and decide on 提出，提交（建議、信息等）：*The bill was laid before Parliament.* 議案已提交議會審議。

▸ **DIFFICULT SITUATION** 困境 **7** [T] **~ sth + adv./prep.** (*formal*) to put sb/sth in a particular position or state, especially a difficult or unpleasant one 使處於特定狀態（尤指困境）**SYN** **place**：*to lay a responsibility/burden on sb* 把責任 / 重擔加於某人身上 ◇ *to lay sb under an obligation to do sth* 使某人承擔做某事的義務

▸ WITH NOUNS 與名詞連用 **8** [T] **~ sth + adv./prep.** used with a noun to form a phrase that has the same meaning as the verb related to the noun（與名詞連用構成短語，其含義與該名詞的相關動詞相同）: *to lay the blame on sb* (= to blame sb) 歸咎於某人 ◇ *Our teacher lays great stress on good spelling* (= stresses it strongly). 我們老師着力強調要拼寫正確。

▸ PLAN/TRAP 計劃；圈套 **9** [T] **~ sth** to prepare sth in detail 周密準備；籌劃；設置：*to lay a trap for sb* 給某人設下圈套 ◇ *She began to **lay her plans** for her escape.* 她開始周密策劃準備逃走。◇ *Bad weather can upset even the **best-laid** plans.* 天氣不好，再好的計劃也會打亂。

▸ HAVE SEX 性交 **10** [T, often passive] **~ sb** (*slang*) to have sex with sb 與（某人）性交：*He went out hoping to **get laid** that night.* 他那天晚上外出希望找個女人睡一宿。

▸ FIRE 火 **11** [T] **~ sth** to prepare a fire by arranging wood, sticks or coal（擺好木、柴或煤）生火

▸ BET 打賭 **12** [T] to bet money on sth; to place a bet 對…下賭金；下賭注：**~ sth** *to lay a bet* 下賭注 ◇ **~ sth on sth** *She had laid $100 on the favourite.* 她在那匹特別喜愛的馬上下注 100 元。◇ **~ (sb) sth (that) …** *I'll lay you any money you like (that) he won't come.* 我看他不來了，你願意賭多少錢我都奉陪。**HELP** This pattern is not used in the passive. 此句型不用於被動語態。

IDM Idioms containing **lay** are at the entries for the nouns and adjectives in the idioms, for example **lay sth bare** is at **bare**. 含 lay 的習語，都可在該等習語中的名詞及形容詞相關詞條找到，如 lay sth bare 在詞條 bare 下。

PHR V **ˌlay aˈbout sb (with sth)** (*BrE*) to attack sb violently 襲擊（或猛打）某人：*The gang laid about him with sticks.* 那夥人用棍棒狠狠揍他。**ˌlay aˈbout you/yourself (with sth)** (*BrE*) to hit sb/sth without control or move your arms or legs violently in all directions 亂打；（向四面）拳打腳踢，猛打：*She laid about herself with her stick to keep the dogs off.* 她揮棒亂打以趕走那幾條狗。**ˌlay sth↔aˈside** (*formal*) **1** to put sth on one side and not use it or think about it 把…放在一邊（或擱置一旁）**SYN** **set aside**：*He laid aside his book and stood up.* 他把書放在一邊，站了起來。◇ (*figurative*) *Doctors have to lay their personal feelings aside.* 醫生不得不把個人的情感置之度外。**2** (also **ˌlay sth ˈby**) to keep sth to use, or deal with later 留存備用；留待以後處理 **SYN** **put aside**：*They had laid money aside for their old age.* 他們存錢防老。**ˌlay sth↔ˈdown 1** to put sth down or stop using it 放下；停止使用 **SYN** **put down**：*She laid the book down on the table.* 她把書放在桌上。◇ *Both sides were urged to lay down their arms* (= stop fighting). 雙方都被敦促放下武器。**2** (*formal*) to stop doing a job, etc. 中斷（工作）；辭（職）；放棄：*to lay down your duties* 停止履行職責 **3** if you **lay down** a rule or a principle, you state officially that people must obey it or use it 規定，制訂（條例或原則）：*You can't lay down hard and fast rules.* 規則不能定得太死。◇ **it is laid down that …** *It is laid down that all candidates must submit three copies of their dissertation.* 根據規定，所有學位答辯人均須提交論文一式三份。**4** [usually passive] to produce sth that is stored and gradually increases 積存某物：*If you eat too much, the surplus is laid down as fat.* 要是吃得太多，過剩的營養就會積聚成為脂肪。**ˌlay sth↔ˈin/ˈup** to collect and store sth to use in the future 貯備；貯存：*to lay in food supplies* 貯存食物 **ˌlay ˈinto sb/sth** (*informal*) to attack sb violently with blows or words 猛打；痛打；責罵；抨擊：*His parents really laid into him for wasting so much money.* 他因揮霍這麼多錢財被父母狠狠地責罵了一頓。**ˌlay ˈoff** | **ˌlay ˈoff sb/sth** (*informal*) used to tell sb to stop doing sth（讓人停止做某事）停止，別再打擾：*Lay off me will you—it's nothing to do with me.* 別找我好不好，這事與我無關。◇ **~ doing sth** *Lay off bullying Jack.* 別再欺負傑克。**ˌlay ˈoff sth** (*informal*) to stop using sth 停止使用：*I think you'd better lay off fatty foods for a while.* 我認為你最好暫時別吃油膩的食物。**ˌlay sb↔ˈoff** to stop employing sb because there is not enough work for them to do（因工作不多而）解雇 **SYN** **make sb redundant** ➲ related noun LAY-OFF **ˌlay sth↔ˈon** (*BrE, informal*) to provide sth for sb, especially food or entertainment 提供（尤指食物或娛樂）：*to lay on food and drink* 提供飲食 ◇ *A bus has been laid on to take guests to the airport.* 已安排公共汽車運送客人去機場。**ˌlay sth ˈon sb** (*informal*) to make sb have to deal with sth unpleasant or difficult 使不得不處理（討厭或困難的事）：*Stop laying a guilt trip on me* (= making me feel guilty). 別再讓我感到內疚了。**ˌlay sb↔ˈout 1** to knock sb unconscious 把…打昏 **2** to prepare a dead body to be buried（給死者）作殯葬準備 **ˌlay sth↔ˈout 1** to spread sth out so that it can be seen easily or is ready to use 鋪開；攤開；展開：*He laid the map out on the table.* 他把地圖在桌子上展開。◇ **+ adj.** *Lay the material out flat.* 把布料攤開放平。**2** [often passive] to plan how sth should look and arrange it in this way 佈置；策劃；安排；設計：*The gardens were laid out with lawns and flower beds.* 花園裏設置了草坪和花壇。◇ *a well-laid-out magazine* 設計精美的雜誌 ➲ related noun LAYOUT **3** to present a plan, an argument, etc. clearly and carefully 清晰謹慎地提出，策劃（計劃、論點等）**SYN** **set out**：*All the terms and conditions are laid out in the contract.* 所有的條款與條件在合同中均已清楚地列明。**4** (*informal*) to spend money 花錢 **SYN** **fork out**：*I had to lay out a fortune on a new car.* 我只好花一大筆錢買了輛新車。➲ related noun OUTLAY **ˌlay ˈover (at/in …)** (*NAmE*) to stay somewhere for a short time during a long journey（長途旅行期間）作短暫停留 ➲ related noun LAYOVER ➲ see also STOPOVER **ˌlay sb ˈup** [usually passive] if sb is **laid up**, they are unable to work, etc. because of an illness or injury（因病或受傷而）卧牀歇工：*She's laid up with a broken leg.* 她因腿部骨折卧牀養病。**ˌlay sth↔ˈup 1** = LAY STH IN **2** if you **lay up** problems or trouble for yourself, you do sth that will cause you problems later 自找（麻煩）；自討（苦吃）**3** to stop using a ship or other vehicle while it is being repaired（船或其他交通工具維修時）停止使用，擱置不用

■ ***adj.*** [only before noun] **1** not having expert knowledge or professional qualifications in a particular subject 外行的；非專業的；缺少專門知識的：*His book explains the theory for the lay public.* 他的書為大眾闡明了這個理論。**2** not in an official position in the Church 平信徒的；在俗的：*a lay preacher* 在俗傳道員 ➲ see also LAYMAN, LAYPERSON, LAYWOMAN

■ ***noun*** **1** (*taboo, informal*) a partner in sex, especially a woman 性夥伴；（尤指）性交的女人：***an easy lay*** (= a person who is ready and willing to have sex) 淫婦 ◇ *to be a great lay* 為荒淫無度的蕩婦 **2** (*old use*) a poem that was written to be sung, usually telling a story（供吟唱的）敍事詩

IDM **the ˌlay of the ˈland** (*NAmE*) (*BrE* **the ˌlie of the ˈland**) **1** the way the land in an area is formed and what physical characteristics it has 地貌；地勢；地形 **2** the way a situation is now and how it is likely to develop 目前的形勢及發展趨勢

lay·about /ˈleɪəbaʊt/ *noun* (*old-fashioned, BrE, informal*) a lazy person who does not do much work 遊手好閒的人；懶漢；二流子

lay·away /ˈleɪəweɪ/ *noun* [U] (*NAmE*) a system of buying goods in a store, where the customer pays a small amount of the price for an article and the store keeps the goods until the full price has been paid 預付訂金購貨法（餘額結清後取貨）

ˈlay-by *noun* **1** [C] (*BrE*) an area at the side of a road where vehicles may stop for a short time 路邊臨時停車處；路側停車帶 ➲ compare REST AREA **2** [U] (*AustralE, NZE, SAfrE*) a system of paying some money for an article so that it is kept for you and you can pay the rest of the money later 預付訂金購買：*You could secure it on lay-by.* 你可以預付訂金方式購買此貨。

layer 🔑 **AW** /ˈleɪə(r); ˈleə(r); *NAmE* ˈler/ *noun, verb*

■ ***noun*** **1** 🔑 a quantity or thickness of sth that lies over a surface or between surfaces 層；表層：*A thin layer of dust covered everything.* 所有的物品上都積了薄薄的一層灰塵。◇ *How many layers of clothing are you wearing?* 你穿了幾層衣服？**2** 🔑 a level or part within a system or set of ideas 層次；階層：*There were too many layers of management in the company.* 這家公司管理層太多。◇ *the layers of meaning in the poem* 這首詩不同層次的含義

L

■ *verb* [often passive] **~ sth** to arrange sth in layers 把…分層堆放：*Layer the potatoes and onions in a dish.* 把土豆和洋葱疊放在盤子裏。◇ *Her hair had been layered* (= cut to several different lengths). 她的頭髮已分層剪短。➲ VISUAL VOCAB page V60

lay·ette /leɪ'et/ *noun* a set of clothes and other things for a new baby 新生兒的全套用品

lay·man /'leɪmən/ *noun* (*pl.* **-men** /-mən/) (also **lay·per·son**) **1** a person who does not have expert knowledge of a particular subject 非專業人員；外行；門外漢：*a book written for professionals and laymen alike* 一本內行外行都可以讀的書 ◇ *to explain sth* ***in layman's terms*** (= in simple language) 用通俗易懂的語言解釋某事 **2** a person who is a member of a Church but is not a priest or member of the CLERGY 平信徒，在俗教徒（非神職人員）➲ see also LAYWOMAN ➲ note at GENDER

'lay-off *noun* **1** an act of making people unemployed because there is no more work left for them to do（因工作不多的）解雇，裁員 **2** a period of time when sb is not working or not doing sth that they normally do regularly 歇工期；停工期：*an eight-week lay-off with a broken leg* 因腿部骨折歇工休養八週

lay·out /'leɪaʊt/ *noun* [usually sing.] the way in which the parts of sth such as the page of a book, a garden or a building are arranged 佈局；佈置；設計；安排：*the layout of streets* 街道的佈局 ◇ *the magazine's attractive new page layout* 雜誌漂亮的新版面設計

lay·over /'leɪəʊvə(r); *NAmE* -oʊ-/ (*NAmE*) (*BrE* **stop·over**) *noun* a short stay somewhere between two parts of a journey 中途停留

lay·per·son /'leɪpɜːsn; *NAmE* -pɜːrsn/ *noun* (also **'lay person**) (*pl.* **lay people** or **lay·persons**) = LAYMAN：*The layperson cannot really understand mental illness.* 外行人無法完全瞭解精神疾病。

'lay-up *noun* **1** (in BASKETBALL 籃球) a shot made with one hand from under or beside the BASKET 單手上籃 **2** (in GOLF 高爾夫球) a shot made from a difficult position to a position that will allow an easier next shot 打點（將球送到較容易擊打的位置的一擊）

lay·woman /'leɪwʊmən/ *noun* (*pl.* **-women** /-wɪmɪn/) a woman who is a member of a Church but is not a priest or a member of the CLERGY 女平信徒，在俗女教徒（非神職人員）➲ see also LAYMAN (2), LAYPERSON ➲ note at GENDER

Laz·a·rus /'læzərəs/ *noun* used to refer to sb who improves or starts to be successful again after a period of failure 東山再起者（失敗後重新振作或再取得成功的人）**ORIGIN** From the story of **Lazarus** in the Bible. He was a man who died but was then brought back to life by Jesus Christ. 源自《聖經》中耶穌讓已死去的拉撒路（Lazarus）復活的故事。

laze /leɪz/ *verb* [I] to relax and do very little 懶散；懶惰；偷懶：*We lazed by the pool all day.* 我們整天都在池塘邊消磨。◇ **~ about/around** *I've spent the afternoon just lazing around.* 我一下午就那樣懶洋洋地打發了。

PHR V **'laze sth↔away** to spend time relaxing and doing very little 懶散地打發時間；混日子；消磨時光 **SYN** **lounge**：*They lazed away the long summer days.* 他們懶懶散散地混過了漫長的夏天。

lazy 🔑 /'leɪzi/ *adj.* (**lazi·er**, **lazi·est**)
1 🔑 (*disapproving*) unwilling to work or be active; doing as little as possible 不願工作的；懶散的；懶惰的 **SYN** **idle**：*He was not stupid, just lazy.* 他不笨，只是懶。◇ *I was feeling too lazy to go out.* 我當時懶得動，不願意外出。 **2** 🔑 not involving much energy or activity; slow and relaxed 無精打采的；懶洋洋的：*We spent a lazy day on the beach.* 我們在海灘上懶洋洋地度過了一天。 **3** (*disapproving*) showing a lack of effort or care 沒下工夫的；粗枝大葉的；馬虎的：*a lazy piece of work* 粗製濫造的作品 **4** (*literary*) moving slowly 行進緩慢的；慢吞吞的 **SYN** **torpid**：*the lazy river* 緩緩流淌的河水 ▸ **lazi·ly** *adv.*：*She woke up and stretched lazily.* 她醒來伸了個懶腰。 **lazi·ness** *noun* [U]

lazy·bones /'leɪzibəʊnz; *NAmE* -boʊnz/ *noun* [sing.] (*old-fashioned, informal*) used to refer to a lazy person 懶漢；懶蟲；懶骨頭：*Come on, lazybones, get up!* 趕快，你這懶骨頭，起牀了！

ˌlazy 'eye *noun* an eye that does not see well because it is not used enough（因少用而致的）弱視眼

ˌlazy 'Susan *noun* a round plate or TRAY on a base, which can be spun around so that the objects on it can be easily reached 餐桌轉盤（方便取食）

lb (*BrE*) (*NAmE* **lb.**) *abbr.* (*pl.* **lb** or **lbs**) a pound in weight, equal to about 454 grams (from Latin 'libra') 磅（源自拉丁語 libra，約等於 454 克）

lbw /ˌel biː 'dʌbljuː/ *abbr.* (in CRICKET 板球) leg before wicket (When the ball hits a player's leg instead of hitting his or her BAT, and would have hit the WICKET if the leg had not stopped it, then that player is **out lbw** and has to stop BATTING.) 腿碰球（擊球手用腿截球犯規出局）

l.c. /ˌel 'siː/ *abbr.* **1** in the piece of text that has been quoted (from Latin 'loco citato') 在引文中 **2** (in writing) LETTER OF CREDIT（書寫形式）信用證，信用狀 **3** (in writing) LOWER CASE（書寫形式）小寫字體

LCD /ˌel siː 'diː/ *abbr.* **1** liquid crystal display (a way of showing information in electronic equipment. An electric current is passed through a special liquid and numbers and letters can be seen on a small screen.) 液晶顯示；液晶顯示器：*a pocket calculator with LCD* 液晶顯示袖珍計算器 ◇ *an LCD screen* 液晶顯示屏 **2** LEAST/LOWEST COMMON DENOMINATOR

lea /liː/ *noun* (*literary*) an open area of land covered in grass 草原；草地

leach /liːtʃ/ *verb* (*technical* 術語) **1** [I] **~ (from sth) (into sth)** | **~ out/away** (of chemicals, minerals, etc. 化學物質、礦物質等) to be removed from soil, etc. by water passing through it 瀝濾；濾走：*Nitrates leach from the soil into rivers.* 硝酸鹽由土壤滲入江河。 **2** [T] **~ sth (from sth) (into sth)** | **~ sth out/away** (of a liquid 液體) to remove chemicals, minerals, etc. from soil 過濾；濾去：*The nutrient is quickly leached away.* 養分很快就被濾掉了。

lead¹ 🔑 /liːd/ *verb, noun* ➲ see also LEAD²
■ *verb* (**led**, **led** /led/)
▸ **SHOW THE WAY** 帶路 **1** 🔑 [I, T] to go with or in front of a person or an animal to show the way or to make them go in the right direction 帶路；領路；引領 **SYN** **guide**：*If you lead, I'll follow.* 你領頭，我跟着。◇ **~ sb/sth + adv./prep.** *He led us out into the grounds.* 他領我們進了庭園。◇ *The receptionist* ***led the way*** *to the boardroom.* 接待員領路到董事會會議室。◇ *She led the horse back into the stable.* 她把那匹馬牽回了馬廄。◇ (*figurative*) *I tried to lead the discussion back to the main issue.* 我試圖把討論引回到主要問題上。➲ SYNONYMS at TAKE
▸ **CONNECT TWO THINGS** 連接兩事物 **2** 🔑 [I] **~ from/to sth (to/from sth)** to connect one object or place to another（與…）相連，相通：*the pipe leading from the top of the water tank* 與水箱頂部相通的管道 ◇ *The wire led to a speaker.* 這電線連接着揚聲器。
▸ **OF ROAD/PATH/DOOR** 道路；小路；門 **3** 🔑 [I, T] to go in a particular direction or to a particular place 通向；通往：**+ adv./prep.** *A path led up the hill.* 有一條小路通往山上。◇ *Which door leads to the yard?* 哪扇門通向庭院？◇ **~ sb + adv./prep.** *The track led us through a wood.* 我們沿着那條小道穿過了樹林。
▸ **CAUSE** 原因 **4** 🔑 [I] **~ to sth** to have sth as a result 導致，造成（後果）**SYN** **result in**：*Eating too much sugar can lead to health problems.* 食用過多的糖會引起健康問題。➲ LANGUAGE BANK at CAUSE **5** 🔑 [T] to be the reason why sb does or thinks sth 使得出（觀點）；引導（某人）：**~ sb (to sth)** *What led you to this conclusion?* 你是如何得出這個結論的？◇ *He's too* ***easily led*** (= easily persuaded to do or think sth). 他太容易受人左右了。◇ **~ sb to do sth** *This has led scientists to speculate on the existence of other galaxies.* 這就使得科學家推測還有其他星系存在。◇ *The situation is far worse than we had been* ***led to believe.*** 情況比我們聽信的要糟糕得多。
▸ **LIFE** 生活 **6** 🔑 [T] **~ sth** to have a particular type of life 過（某種生活）：*to lead a quiet life/a life of luxury/*

a miserable existence 過寧靜／奢侈／悲慘的生活

▸ **BE BEST/FIRST** 屬最佳／第一 **7** [T, I] to be the best at sth; to be in first place 最擅長於；處於首位；處於領先地位：**~ (sb/sth) (in sth)** *The department led the world in cancer research.* 這個系在癌症研究方面走在了世界前列。◇ *We **lead the way** in space technology.* 我們在航天技術方面處於領先地位。◇ **~ (sb/sth) by sth** *The champion is leading (her nearest rival) by 18 seconds.* 冠軍領先了（緊隨其後的對手）18 秒鐘。

▸ **BE IN CONTROL** 控制 **8** [T, I] **~ (sth)** to be in control of sth; to be the leader of sth 控制；掌管；領導；率領：*to lead an expedition* 率領探險隊 ◇ *to lead a discussion* 主持討論 ◇ *Who will lead the party in the next election?* 下一屆選舉誰來領導這個黨？

▸ **IN CARD GAMES** 紙牌遊戲 **9** [I, T] to play first; to play sth as your first card 開牌；率先出牌：*It's your turn to lead.* 輪到你開牌了。◇ **~ sth** *to lead the ten of clubs* 先出梅花十

IDM **lead sb by the 'nose** to make sb do everything you want; to control sb completely 牽着某人的鼻子走；完全操縱（或控制）某人 **lead sb a (merry) 'dance** (*BrE*) to cause sb a lot of trouble or worry 給某人造成許多麻煩（或憂慮） **lead from the 'front** to take an active part in what you are telling or persuading others to do 帶頭；帶動；引導 **lead (sb) nowhere** to have no successful result for sb 毫無成果：*This discussion is leading us nowhere.* 我們這場討論將毫無結果。 **lead sb up/down the garden 'path** to make sb believe sth which is not true 給某人誤導的信息（或提示）；誤導某人 **SYN** **mislead** **IDM** see BLIND *adj.*, HORSE *n.*, LIFE, THING

PHR V **,lead 'off (from) sth** to start at a place and go away from it 起始於（某地）：*narrow streets leading off from the main square* 起始於大廣場的狹窄街道 **,lead 'off | ,lead sth↔'off** to start sth 開始（某事）：*Who would like to lead off the debate?* 誰願帶頭發言開始辯論？ **,lead sb 'on** (*informal*) to make sb believe sth which is not true, especially that you love them or find them attractive 使誤信，誤導某人（尤指謊稱自己喜愛對方或認為對方有魅力） **,lead 'up to sth** to be an introduction to or the cause of sth 是…的先導；是導致…的原因：*the weeks leading up to the exam* 臨近考試的幾個星期 ◇ *the events leading up to the strike* 導致罷工的事件 **'lead with sth** **1** (of a newspaper 報紙) to have sth as the main item of news 把…作為頭條新聞 **2** (in boxing 拳擊運動) to use a particular hand to begin an attack（用…手）率先出擊，開始進攻：*to **lead with your right/left*** 用右拳／左拳率先出擊

■ ***noun***

▸ **FIRST PLACE** 首位 **1** **the lead** [sing.] the position ahead of everyone else in a race or competition（競賽中的）領先地位：*She **took the lead** in the second lap.* 她在第二圈時領先。◇ *He has gone **into the lead**.* 他已處於領先地位。◇ *The Democrats now appear to be **in the lead**.* 現在看來好像民主黨人佔優勢。◇ *to **hold/lose the lead*** 保持／失去領先地位 ◇ *The lead car is now three minutes ahead of the rest of the field.* 現在跑在最前面的汽車較賽場上其餘的賽車領先三分鐘。 **2** [sing.] **~ (over sb/sth)** the amount or distance that sb/sth is in front of sb/sth else 超前量；領先的距離 **SYN** **advantage**：*He managed to **hold a lead** of two seconds over his closest rival.* 他比跟得最緊的對手勉強領先兩秒鐘。◇ *The polls have given Labour a five-point lead.* 投票選舉中工黨領先五個百分點。◇ *a **commanding/comfortable lead*** 遙遙／輕鬆領先 ◇ *to **increase/widen your lead*** 加大／擴大領先優勢 ◇ *Manchester lost their early two-goal lead.* 曼徹斯特隊失去了他們開場不久領先兩球的優勢。

▸ **EXAMPLE** 實例 **3** [sing.] an example or action for people to copy 實例；範例；榜樣：*If one bank raises interest rates, all the others will **follow their lead**.* 要是有一家銀行提高利率，所有其他銀行都會效法。◇ *If we **take the lead** in this (= start to act), others may follow.* 如果我們在這方面帶頭行動，其餘的人就會跟着來。◇ *You go first, I'll take my lead from you.* 你領頭，我來照樣做。

▸ **INFORMATION** 信息 **4** [C] a piece of information that may help to find out the truth or facts about a situation, especially a crime（尤指有關犯罪的）線索 **SYN** **clue**：*The police will **follow up** all possible **leads**.* 警方將追踪所有可能有用的線索。

▸ **ACTOR/MUSICIAN** 演員；音樂家 **5** [C] the main part in a play, film/movie, etc.; the person who plays this part（戲劇、電影等中的）主角；扮演主角的演員：*Who is **playing the lead**?* 誰是主演？◇ *the **male/female lead*** 男／女主角 ◇ *a lead role* 主角的角色 ◇ *the lead singer in a band* 樂隊的主唱歌手

▸ **FOR DOG** 狗 **6** (*BrE*) (also **leash** *NAmE*, *BrE*) [C] a long piece of leather, chain or rope used for holding and controlling a dog（牽狗用的）皮帶，鏈條，繩索：*Dogs must be kept on a lead in the park.* 狗在公園裏必須繫着牽狗帶。

▸ **FOR ELECTRICITY** 電 **7** [C] (*BrE*) a long piece of wire, usually covered in plastic, that is used to connect a piece of electrical equipment to a source of electricity 電線；導線 ➲ see also EXTENSION LEAD, JUMP LEAD

lead² /led/ *noun* ➲ see also LEAD¹ **1** [U] (*symb.* **Pb**) a chemical element. Lead is a heavy soft grey metal, used especially in the past for water pipes or to cover roofs. 鉛 **2** [C, U] the thin black part of a pencil that marks paper 鉛筆芯 ➲ **VISUAL VOCAB** page V69

IDM **go ,down like a lead bal'loon** (*informal*) to be very unsuccessful; to not be accepted by people 大失敗；終歸無效 ➲ more at SWING *v.*

lead·ed /'ledɪd/ *adj.* [usually before noun] **1** (of petrol, metal, etc. 汽油、金屬等) with lead added to it 加鉛的；含鉛的 **OPP** **unleaded** **2** with a cover or a frame of lead 鉛皮覆蓋的；鉛框的：*a leaded roof* 鉛屋頂

,leaded 'light (also **,leaded 'window**) *noun* [usually pl.] (*BrE*) a window made from small pieces of glass that are arranged in diamond shapes and are separated by strips of LEAD 菱形鉛條玻璃窗

lead·en /'ledn/ *adj.* (*literary*) **1** dull grey in colour, like LEAD 鉛灰色的：*leaden skies* 鉛灰色的天空 **2** dull, heavy or slow 沉悶的；陰鬱的；遲鈍的；呆滯的：*a leaden heart* (= because you are sad) 沉重的心情

lead·er /'liːdə(r)/ *noun*

1 a person who leads a group of people, especially the head of a country, an organization, etc. 領導者；領袖；首領：*a **political/spiritual, etc. leader*** 政治、精神等領袖 ◇ *the leader of the party* 該黨的領導人 ◇ *union leaders* 工會領導人 ◇ *He was not a **natural leader**.* 他並非天生的領袖。◇ *She's a **born leader**.* 她是個天生的領袖。 **2** a person or thing that is the best, or in first place in a race, business, etc. 最佳的人（或物）；（在賽跑、商業等活動中）處於領先地位的人（或物）：*She was among the leaders of the race from the start.* 比賽一開始她就與領先的幾位選手並駕齊驅。◇ *The company is a **world leader** in electrical goods.* 這家公司的電器產品在全世界首屈一指。 ➲ see also MARKET LEADER **3** (*BrE*) (also **con·cert·master** *NAmE*, *BrE*) the most important VIOLIN player in an ORCHESTRA（管弦樂隊的）首席小提琴手 **4** (*BrE*) = EDITORIAL *n.*

'leader board *noun* a sign showing the names and scores of the top players, especially in a GOLF competition（尤指高爾夫球比賽中的）領先選手積分牌

lead·er·less /'liːdələs; *NAmE* -dərl-/ *adj.* without a leader 無領導的：*Her sudden death left the party leaderless.* 她的猝然去世使該黨陷入群龍無首的境地。

the ,Leader of the 'House *noun* [sing.] (in Britain) a member of the government who is responsible for deciding what is discussed in Parliament（英國）國會領袖，上（或下）議院議長

lead·er·ship /'liːdəʃɪp; *NAmE* -dərʃ-/ *noun* **1** [U] the state or position of being a leader 領導；領導地位：*a leadership contest* 領導地位的角逐 ◇ *The party thrived **under his leadership**.* 該黨在他的領導下壯大起來。 **2** [U] the ability to be a leader or the qualities a good leader should have 領導才能；領導應有的品質：***leadership qualities/skills*** 領導的素質／技巧 ◇ *Strong leadership is needed to captain the team.* 擔任這個隊的隊長需要強有力的領導才能。 **3** [C+sing./pl. v.] a group of leaders of a particular organization, etc. 領導班子；領導層：*The party leadership is/are divided.* 這個黨的領導階層意見不合。

L

lead-free /ˌled ˈfriː/ *adj.* (of petrol, paint, etc. 汽油、塗料等) without any of the metal LEAD added to it 無鉛的

lead guitar /ˌliːd ɡɪˈtɑː(r)/ *noun* [U] a GUITAR style that consists mainly of SOLOS and tunes rather than only CHORDS 主音吉他，獨奏吉他，主奏吉他（主要為獨奏和奏出曲調而非只有和弦的吉他演奏風格）➲ compare RHYTHM GUITAR

lead-in /ˈliːd ɪn/ *noun* an introduction to a subject, story, show, etc.（主題、故事、表演等的）引子，介紹，開場白

lead·ing¹ 🔑 /ˈliːdɪŋ/ *adj.* [only before noun]
1 🔑 most important or most successful 最重要的；一流的：*leading experts* 最傑出的專家 ◇ *She was offered the* ***leading role*** *in the new TV series.* 她獲得主演那部新的電視連續劇的機會。◇ *He* ***played a leading part*** *in the negotiations.* 他在談判中起到了至關重要的作用。**2** 🔑 ahead of others in a race or contest（賽跑或比賽中）領先的，最前的：*She started the last lap just behind the leading group.* 她開始跑最後一圈時緊跟在領先的一組人後面。◇ *These are the leading first-round scores.* 這些是第一輪比賽的領先成績。

lead·ing² /ˈledɪŋ/ *noun* [U] (*technical* 術語) the amount of white space between lines of printed text 行距（相鄰兩個文本行之間的距離）

ˌleading ˈarticle (also **lead·er**) *noun* (both *BrE*) = EDITORIAL *n.*

ˌleading ˈedge *noun* **1** [sing.] the most important and advanced position in an area of activity, especially technology（某活動領域的）最重要位置，領先地位；（尤指技術上的）前沿，尖端：*at the leading edge of scientific research* 在科學研究的前沿 **2** [C] (*technical* 術語) the front or forward edge of sth moving, especially an aircraft wing 前緣；（尤指飛機的）機翼前緣 ➲ VISUAL VOCAB page V53 ▸ **ˌleading-ˈedge** *adj.* [only before noun] SYN **cutting edge**：*leading-edge technology* 尖端技術

ˌleading ˈlady, **ˌleading ˈman** *noun* the actor with the main female or male part in a play or film/movie 飾主角的女演員（或男演員）

ˌleading ˈlight *noun* an important, active or respected person in a particular area of activity（某活動範圍內）重要的活躍人物，受敬重的人物：*She's one of the leading lights in the opera world.* 她是歌劇界的一位大腕。

ˌleading ˈquestion *noun* a question that you ask in a particular way in order to get the answer you want 誘導性（或暗示性）問題

ˈlead-off *adj.* (*NAmE*) being the first of a series 開頭的；起始的：*the lead-off track on the album* 專輯的第一首歌

lead shot /ˌled ˈʃɒt; *NAmE* -ˈʃɑːt/ *noun* = SHOT *n.* (3)

lead story /ˈliːd stɔːri/ *noun* the main or first item of news in a newspaper, magazine or news broadcast 重要新聞；頭條新聞

lead time /ˈliːd taɪm/ *noun* the time between starting and completing a production process 從投產至完成生產間相隔的時間；訂貨交付時間

leaf 🔑 /liːf/ *noun, verb*
■ ***noun*** (*pl.* **leaves** /liːvz/) **1** 🔑 [C] a flat green part of a plant, growing from a STEM or branch or from the root 葉；葉片；葉子：*lettuce/cabbage/oak leaves* 萵苣／捲心菜／橡樹葉 ◇ *The trees are just* ***coming into leaf****.* 樹木正好在長葉子。◇ *the dead leaves of autumn/the fall* 秋天的枯葉 ➲ COLLOCATIONS at LIFE ➲ VISUAL VOCAB page V10 ➲ see also BAY LEAF, FIG LEAF **2 -leaf**, **-leafed**, **-leaved** (in adjectives 構成形容詞) having leaves of the type or number mentioned 有…狀葉的；有…片葉的：*a four-leaf clover* 四葉車軸草 ◇ *a broad-leaved plant* 闊葉植物 **3** [C] a sheet of paper, especially a page in a book（紙）頁，張；（尤指書的）頁 ➲ see also FLYLEAF, LOOSE-LEAF, OVERLEAF **4** [U] metal, especially gold or silver, in the form of very thin sheets 薄金屬片；（尤指金或銀）箔：*gold leaf* 金箔 **5** [C] a part of a table that can be lifted up or pulled into position in order to make the table bigger 活動桌板；摺疊桌板
IDM **take a leaf from/out of sb's ˈbook** to copy sb's behaviour and do things in the same way that they do, because they are successful 效仿，模仿（成功之人的舉止和行為）SYN **emulate** IDM see NEW
■ ***verb***
PHR V **ˈleaf through sth** to quickly turn over the pages of a book, etc. without reading them or looking at them carefully 匆匆翻閱；瀏覽

leaf·less /ˈliːfləs/ *adj.* having no leaves 無葉的 SYN **bare**

leaf·let /ˈliːflət/ *noun, verb*
■ ***noun*** a printed sheet of paper or a few printed pages that are given free to advertise or give information about sth 散頁印刷品；傳單；（宣傳或廣告）小冊子 SYN **booklet, pamphlet**：*a leaflet on local places of interest* 介紹當地名勝的小冊子
■ ***verb*** [I, T] **~ (sb/sth)** to give out leaflets to people 散發傳單（或小冊子）：*We did a lot of leafleting in the area.* 我們在此地散發了許多傳單。

ˈleaf mould (*BrE*) (*NAmE* **ˈleaf mold**) *noun* [U] soil consisting mostly of dead, decayed leaves 腐葉土

leafy /ˈliːfi/ *adj.* (**leaf·ier**, **leafi·est**) **1** having a lot of leaves 多葉的；葉茂的：*Eat plenty of leafy green vegetables.* 多吃綠葉蔬菜。**2** (*approving*) (of a place 地方) having a lot of trees and plants 多樹木的；多植物的：*leafy suburbs* 樹木茂密的郊區 **3** made by a lot of leaves or trees 葉製的；由樹木構成的：*We sat in the leafy shade of an oak tree.* 我們坐在一棵枝繁葉茂的櫟樹樹蔭下。

league 🔑 /liːɡ/ *noun*
1 🔑 a group of sports teams who all play each other to earn points and find which team is best（體育運動隊的）聯合會，聯賽：*major league baseball* 棒球大聯賽 ◇ *United were league champions last season.* 聯隊是上個賽季的聯賽冠軍。➲ see also MINOR-LEAGUE **2** (*informal*) a level of quality, ability, etc.（質量、能力等的）等級，級別，水平：*As a painter, he is* ***in a league of his own*** (= much better than others). 作為畫家，他獨領風騷。◇ *They're* ***in a different league*** *from us.* 他們與我們不屬同一個級別。◇ *When it comes to cooking, I'm* ***not in her league*** (= she is much better than me). 提到烹飪，我的水平遠比不上她。◇ *A house like that is* ***out of our league*** (= too expensive for us). 那樣的房子不是我們這號人買得起的。**3** a group of people or nations who have combined for a particular purpose 聯盟；同盟 SYN **alliance**：*the League of Nations* 國際聯盟 ◇ *a meeting of the Women's League for Peace* 婦女和平聯盟會議 ➲ see also IVY LEAGUE **4** (*old use*) a unit for measuring distance, equal to about 3 miles or 4 000 metres 里格（長度單位，約等於 3 英里或 4 000 米）
IDM **in ˈleague (with sb)** making secret plans with sb（與…）秘密串通，勾結

ˈleague table *noun* (*BrE*) **1** a table that shows the position of sports teams and how successfully they are performing in a competition（運動隊的）積分排名表 **2** a table that shows how well institutions such as schools or hospitals are performing in comparison with each other（學校、醫院等的）排名表

leak /liːk/ *verb, noun*
■ ***verb*** **1** [I, T] to allow liquid or gas to get in or out through a small hole or crack 漏；滲漏；泄漏：*a leaking pipe* 滲漏的管道 ◇ *The roof was leaking.* 屋頂在漏水。◇ **~ sth** *The tank had leaked a small amount of water.* 水箱滲漏出少量的水。**2** [I] (of a liquid or gas 液體或氣體) to get in or out through a small hole or crack in sth 滲入；漏出：*Water had started to leak into the cellar.* 水已開始滲入地下室。**3** [T] **~ sth (to sb)** to give secret information to the public, for example by telling a newspaper 泄露，透露（秘密信息）；走漏 SYN **disclose**：*The contents of the report were leaked to the press.* 報告的內容泄露到新聞界了。◇ *a leaked document* 已外泄的文件
PHR V **ˌleak ˈout** (of secret information 秘密信息) to become known to the public 泄露；走漏；透露：*Details of the plan soon leaked out.* 計劃的細節很快就泄露出去了。
■ ***noun*** **1** a small hole or crack that lets liquid or gas flow in or out of sth by accident 漏洞；裂縫；縫隙：*a leak in the roof* 屋頂的漏洞 ◇ *a leak in the gas pipe* 煤氣管道的裂縫 ➲ COLLOCATIONS at DECORATE **2** liquid or gas that escapes through a hole in sth 泄漏出的液體（或氣體）：*a gas leak* 煤氣泄漏 ◇ *oil leaks/leaks of oil* 漏油

3 a deliberate act of giving secret information to the newspapers, etc.（秘密信息的）透露：*a leak to the press about the government plans on tax* 有關政府稅收計劃的消息於新聞界的泄露 4 (*slang*) an act of passing URINE from the body 撒尿：*to* ***have/take a leak*** 撒尿 IDM see SPRING *v.*

leak·age /ˈliːkɪdʒ/ *noun* [C, U] an amount of liquid or gas escaping through a hole in sth; an occasion when there is a leak 泄漏量；漏損量；泄漏；滲漏：*a leakage of toxic waste into the sea* 有毒廢物的泄漏入海 ◇ *Check bottles for leakage before use.* 使用前應檢查瓶子是否滲漏。

leaky /ˈliːki/ *adj.* having holes or cracks that allow liquid or gas to escape 有漏洞的；有漏隙的；滲漏的：*a leaky roof* 漏水的屋頂

lean 0→ /liːn/ *verb, adj., noun*

■ ***verb*** (**leaned**, **leaned**) (*BrE* also **leant**, **leant** /lent/) **1** 0→ [I] (**+ adv./prep.**) to bend or move from a vertical position 前俯；後仰；傾斜：*I leaned back in my chair.* 我仰靠在椅背上。◇ *The tower is leaning dangerously.* 那座塔越來越斜，很危險。◇ *A man was leaning out of the window.* 一個人正探身窗外。 **2** 0→ [I] to rest on or against sth for support 倚靠；靠在；靠置：**~ against sth** *A shovel was leaning against the wall.* 一把鐵鏟靠牆放着。◇ **~ on sth** *She walked slowly, leaning on her son's arm.* 她倚靠着她兒子的手臂緩慢行走。 **3** 0→ [T] **~ sth against/on sth** to make sth rest against sth in a sloping position 使斜靠：*Can I lean my bike against the wall?* 我能把自行車靠在這牆上嗎？ IDM see BACKWARDS

PHR V **ˈlean on sb/sth** **1** to depend on sb/sth for help and support 依靠，依賴（…的幫助和支持） SYN **rely on**：*He leans heavily on his family.* 他在很大程度上依賴他的家庭。 **2** to try to influence sb by threatening them 對…施加壓力；威脅；恐嚇：*The government has been leaning on the TV company not to broadcast the show.* 政府一直給電視公司施加壓力，不准播放此節目。 **ˈlean to/towards/toward sth** to have a tendency to prefer sth, especially a particular opinion or interest 傾向，偏向（尤指某意見或利益）：*The UK leant towards the US proposal.* 英國傾向於美國的提案。

■ ***adj.*** (**lean·er**, **lean·est**) **1** (usually *approving*) (of people, especially men, or animals 人，尤指男人或動物) without much flesh; thin and fit 肉少的；瘦且健康的：*a lean, muscular body* 清瘦而肌肉發達的身體 ◇ *He was tall, lean and handsome.* 他長得瘦高而英俊。 **2** (of meat 肉) containing little or no fat 脂肪少的；無脂肪的 **3** [usually before noun] (of a period of time 一段時間) difficult and not producing much money, food, etc. 難以賺錢的；生產不出（食物等）的；貧乏的：*a* ***lean period/spell*** 不景氣時期 ◇ *The company recovered well after going through several* ***lean years***. 經歷了幾年的蕭條後，這家公司的業務才完全恢復了正常。 **4** (of organizations, etc. 機構等) strong and efficient because the number of employees has been reduced 精幹的；效率高的：*The changes made the company leaner and more competitive.* 改革使公司更精幹，更有競爭力。 ▸ **lean·ness** /ˈliːnnəs/ *noun* [U]

■ ***noun*** [U] the part of meat that has little or no fat 瘦肉

lean·ing /ˈliːnɪŋ/ *noun* [usually pl.] **~ (toward(s) sth)** a tendency to prefer sth or to believe in particular ideas, opinions, etc. 傾向；偏向；愛好 SYN **inclination, tendency**：*a leaning towards comedy rather than tragedy* 偏愛喜劇而不是悲劇 ◇ *a person with socialist leanings* 具有社會主義傾向的人

ˈlean-to *noun* (*pl.* **-tos** /-tuːz/) a small building with its roof leaning against the side of a large building, wall or fence（搭在高大建築物、牆壁或柵欄上建的）單坡屋頂小房，披屋，披棚：*a lean-to garage* 單坡屋頂車庫

leap /liːp/ *verb, noun*

■ ***verb*** (**leapt**, **leapt** /lept/ or **leaped**, **leaped**) **1** [I, T] to jump high or a long way 跳；跳躍；跳越：**+ adv./prep.** *A dolphin leapt out of the water.* 海豚躍出水面。◇ *We leapt over the stream.* 我們跳過了那條小溪。◇ **~ sth** *The horse leapt a five-foot wall.* 那匹馬躍過了一道五英尺高的牆。 **2** [I] **+ adv./prep.** to move or do sth suddenly and quickly 猛衝；突然做（某事）：*She leapt out of bed.* 她突然翻身下了牀。◇ *He leapt across the room to answer the door.* 他衝過房間去開門。◇ *I* ***leapt to my feet*** (= stood up quickly). 我趕緊站了起來。◇ *They* ***leapt into action*** *immediately.* 他們立即斷然採取了行動。◇ (*figurative*) *She was quick to* ***leap to my defence*** (= speak in support of me). 她馬上挺身而出為我辯護。◇ *The photo seemed to* ***leap off the page*** (= it got your attention immediately). 那張照片躍然紙上，引人注目。◇ *His name* ***leapt out at me*** (= I saw it immediately). 他的名字立刻映入了我的眼簾。 **3** [I] **~ (in sth) (from …) (to …)** to increase suddenly and by a large amount 驟增；劇增；猛漲 SYN **shoot up**：*The shares leapt in value from 476p to close at 536p.* 股價從 476 便士猛漲到收盤時的 536 便士。

IDM **ˌlook before you ˈleap** (*saying*) used to advise sb to think about the possible results or dangers of sth before doing it 三思而後行 ➲ more at CONCLUSION, HEART

PHR V **ˈleap at sth** to accept a chance or an opportunity quickly and with enthusiasm 趕緊抓住，急不可待地接受（機會） SYN **jump at**：*I leapt at the chance to go to France.* 我立刻抓住了去法國的機會。

■ ***noun*** **1** a long or high jump 跳越；跳躍；跳高：*a leap of six metres* 一跳跳了六米 ◇ *She took a* ***flying leap*** *and landed on the other side of the stream.* 她一個飛躍跳到小溪的對面。◇ (*figurative*) *His heart gave a sudden leap when he saw her.* 他看見她時，心猛地一跳。◇ (*figurative*) *Few people successfully make the leap from television to the movies.* 從電視業轉向電影業很少有人成功。 **2 ~ (in sth)** a sudden large change or increase in sth 驟變；劇增；激增：*a leap in profits* 利潤躍升 ➲ see also QUANTUM LEAP

IDM **by/in ˌleaps and ˈbounds** very quickly; in large amounts 非常迅速；飛躍地；突飛猛進；大量地：*Her health has improved in leaps and bounds.* 她的健康已迅速好轉。 **a leap in the ˈdark** an action or a risk that you take without knowing anything about the activity or what the result will be 冒險舉動

leap·frog /ˈliːpfrɒg; *NAmE* -frɔːg; -frɑːg/ *noun, verb*

■ ***noun*** [U] a children's game in which players take turns to jump over the backs of other players who are bending down 跳背遊戲（遊戲者輪流從其他彎背站立者身上跳過）

■ ***verb*** (**-gg-**) [T, I] **~ (sb/sth)** to get to a higher position or rank by going past sb else or by missing out some stages 越級提升：*The win allowed them to leapfrog three teams to gain second place.* 這場勝利使他們連超三個隊，躍居第二位。

ˈleap year *noun* one year in every four years when February has 29 days instead of 28 閏年

learn 0→ /lɜːn; *NAmE* lɜːrn/ *verb* (**learnt**, **learnt** /lɜːnt; *NAmE* lɜːrnt/ or **learned**, **learned**)

1 0→ [T, I] to gain knowledge or skill by studying, from experience, from being taught, etc. 學；學習；學到；學會：**~ sth** *to learn a language/a musical instrument/a skill* 學一種語言／樂器／技能 ◇ **~ sth from sb/sth** *I learned a lot from my father.* 我從父親那裏學到了許多東西。◇ **~ sth from doing sth** *You can learn a great deal just from watching other players.* 你只要注意看其他運動員怎麼做就能學到許多東西。◇ **~ (about sth)** *She's very keen to learn about Japanese culture.* 她熱衷於學習日本文化。◇ *The book is about how children learn.* 這本書是有關小孩怎樣學習的。◇ **~ to do sth** *He's learning to dance.* 他在學跳舞。◇ **~ how, what, etc. …** *Today we learnt how to use the new software.* 今天我們學習了怎樣使用這個新軟件。 **2** 0→ [I, T] to become aware of sth by hearing about it from sb else 聽到；得知；獲悉 SYN **discover**：**~ of/about sth** *I learnt of her arrival from a close friend.* 我從一位好友那裏聽說她到了。◇ **~ (that) …** *We were very surprised to learn (that) she had got married again.* 我們聽說她又結婚了，感到很驚訝。◇ **~ who, what, etc. …** *We only learned who the new teacher was a few days ago.* 我們幾天前才得知新教師是誰。◇ **~ sth** *How did they react when they learned the news?* 他們聽到這個消息有什麼反應？◇ **it is learned that …** *It has been learned that 500 jobs are to be lost at the factory.* 據悉工廠將要裁減 500 個工作崗位。 **3** 0→ [T] **~ sth** to study and repeat sth in order to be able to remember it 記住；背熟；熟記 SYN **memorize**：*We have to learn* *one of Hamlet's speeches for school tomorrow.* 我們明天上學得背誦一段哈姆雷特的台詞。 **4** [I, T] to gradually change your attitudes about sth so that you behave in a different way 認識到；意識到；（從…）吸取教訓： **~ (from sth)** *I'm sure she'll learn from her mistakes.* 我肯定她會從錯誤中吸取教訓。◇ **~ (that)** ... *He'll just have to learn (that) he can't always have his own way.* 他一定要明白不能老是隨心所欲。◇ **~ to do sth** *I soon learned not to ask too many questions.* 我很快就意識到不能問太多的問題。

IDM **,learn (sth) the 'hard way** to find out how to behave by learning from your mistakes or from unpleasant experiences, rather than from being told 歷經挫折才懂得 **learn your 'lesson** to learn what to do or not to do in the future because you have had a bad experience in the past 吸取教訓 ➲ more at COST *n.*, LIVE[1], ROPE *n.*

Vocabulary Building 詞彙擴充

Learning

- **learn** 學；學習： *He's learning Spanish/to swim.* 他在學西班牙語／游泳。
- **study** 學習；研究： *She studied chemistry for three years.* 她學了三年化學。
- **revise** (*BrE*) (*NAmE* **review**) 複習；溫習： *In this class we'll revise/review what we did last week.* 本節課我們將複習上週所學的內容。
- **practise** (*BrE*) (*NAmE* **practice**) 練習；實習： *If you practise speaking English, you'll soon improve.* 只要你練習說英語，很快就會進步。
- **rehearse** 排練： *We only had two weeks to rehearse the play.* 我們只有兩週時間排練此劇。

learn·ed /'lɜːnɪd; *NAmE* 'lɜːrnɪd/ *adj.* [usually before noun] **1** (*formal*) having a lot of knowledge because you have studied and read a lot 有學問的；知識淵博的；博學的： *a learned professor* 學識淵博的教授 ➲ see also FRIEND (5) **2** (*formal*) connected with or for learned people; showing and expressing deep knowledge （為）學者的；學術性的；學問精深的 **SYN** **scholarly**： *a learned journal* 學術性刊物 **3** /lɜːnd; *NAmE* lɜːrnd/ developed by training or experience; not existing at birth 通過訓練（或經歷）形成的；學到的；非天生的： *a learned skill* 學來的技能

learn·er /'lɜːnə(r); *NAmE* 'lɜːrn-/ *noun* **1** a person who is finding out about a subject or how to do sth 學習者： *a* ***slow/quick learner*** 遲鈍的／聰明的學生 ◇ *a dictionary for learners of English* 英語學習詞典 ◇ *learner-centred teaching methods* 以學生為中心的教學方法 **2** (also **,learner 'driver**) a person who is learning to drive a car 學習駕車者；學習駕駛員

'learner's permit (*NAmE*) (*BrE* **pro,visional 'licence**) *noun* an official document that you must have when you start to learn to drive 實習駕駛執照；學員駕照

learn·ing /'lɜːnɪŋ; *NAmE* 'lɜːrnɪŋ/ *noun* [U] **1** the process of learning sth 學習： *computer-assisted learning* 計算機輔助學習 ◇ *Last season was a learning experience for me.* 上個季度對我來說是一次學習。➲ see also DISTANCE LEARNING **2** knowledge that you get from reading and studying 知識；學問；學識： *a woman of great learning* 學識淵博的女子

'learning curve *noun* the rate at which you learn a new subject or a new skill; the process of learning from the mistakes you make 學習曲線；吸取教訓過程曲線

'learning difficulties *noun* [pl.] mental problems that people may have from birth, or that may be caused by illness or injury, that affect their ability to learn things 學習障礙（天生智力問題或由疾病、受傷引起）

'learning disability *noun* [usually pl.] a mental problem that people may have from birth, or that may be caused by illness or injury, that affects their ability to learn things 學習無能（先天性或由疾病、受傷引起）

lease /liːs/ *noun, verb*

■ ***noun*** a legal agreement that allows you to use a building, a piece of equipment or some land for a period of time, usually in return for rent（房屋、設備或土地的）租約，租契： *to* ***take out a lease*** *on a house* 辦理房屋租約 ◇ *The* ***lease expires/runs out*** *next year.* 這份租約明年到期。◇ *Under* ***the terms of the lease****, you have to pay maintenance charges.* 按租約的條款，你得支付維修費。➲ COLLOCATIONS at HOUSE

IDM **a (,new) lease of 'life** (*BrE*) (*NAmE* **a (,new) lease on 'life**) the chance to live or last longer, or with a better quality of life 延年益壽；生活質量更好： *Since her hip operation she's had a new lease of life.* 她自髖關節手術以後活得更有勁了。

■ ***verb*** to use or let sb use sth, especially property or equipment, in exchange for rent or a regular payment 租用，租借，出租（尤指房地產或設備） **SYN** **rent**： **~ sth** *We lease all our computer equipment.* 我們所有的計算機設備都是租來的。◇ **~ sth from sb** *They lease the land from a local farmer.* 他們從當地一位農場主手中租得這塊土地。◇ **~ sb sth** *A local farmer leased them the land.* 這塊地是當地的一個農場主租給他們的。◇ **~ sth (out) (to sb)** *Parts of the building are leased out to tenants.* 這棟大樓有一部份租出去了。▶ **leas·ing** *noun* [U]： *car leasing* 汽車租賃 ◇ *a leasing company* 租賃公司

lease·back /'liːsbæk/ (*US* also **re·ver·sion**) *noun* [U] (*law* 律) the process of allowing the former owner of a property to continue to use it if they pay rent to the new owner; a legal agreement where this happens 售後回租（將地產出售後再租回）；售後回租契約

lease·hold /'liːshəʊld; *NAmE* -hoʊld/ *adj., noun*

■ ***adj.*** (*especially BrE*) (of property or land 房產或土地) that can be used for a limited period of time, according to the arrangements in a LEASE 租賃的；租用的： *a leasehold property* 租賃的房地產 ▶ **lease·hold** *adv.*： *to purchase land leasehold* 購買有租約的土地 ➲ compare FREEHOLD

■ ***noun*** [U] (*especially BrE*) the right to use a building or a piece of land according to the arrangements in a LEASE（按租約使用房屋或土地的）租賃權： *to obtain/own the leasehold of a house* 獲得／擁有一所房子的租賃權 ➲ compare FREEHOLD

lease·hold·er /'liːshəʊldə(r); *NAmE* -hoʊld-/ *noun* (*especially BrE*) a person who is allowed to use a building or a piece of land according to the arrangements in a LEASE 租賃人；承租人；租借人 ➲ compare FREEHOLDER

leash /liːʃ/ *noun, verb*

■ ***noun*** (*especially NAmE*) (*BrE* also **lead**) a long piece of leather, chain or rope used for holding and controlling a dog（牽狗用的）皮帶，鏈條，繩索： *All dogs must be kept* ***on a leash*** *in public places.* 在公共場所所有的狗必須用皮帶牽住。 **IDM** see STRAIN *v.*

■ ***verb*** **~ sth** to control an animal, especially a dog, with a LEAD/LEASH 用皮帶繫住，拴住，縛住（尤指狗）

least /liːst/ *det., pron., adv.*

■ ***det., pron.*** (usually **the least**) smallest in size, amount, degree, etc. 最小的；最少的；程度最輕的： *He's the best teacher, even though he has the least experience.* 他雖然經驗最少，卻是最出色的老師。◇ *She never had the least idea what to do about it.* 這事怎麼辦，她一點主意都沒有。◇ *He gave (the) least of all towards the wedding present.* 買結婚禮物，他出的錢最少。◇ *How others see me is* ***the least of*** *my worries* (= I have more important things to worry about). 別人怎麼看我，我一點都不在乎。◇ *It's* ***the least I can do*** *to help* (= I feel I should do more). 這是我所能幫忙做的最起碼的事。

IDM **at the (very) 'least** used after amounts to show that the amount is the lowest possible（用於數量之後）至少，最少： *It'll take a year, at the very least.* 這至少需要一年時間。 **,not in the 'least** not at all 一點也不；絲毫不： *Really, I'm not in the least tired.* 說真的，我一點也不累。◇ *'Do you mind if I put the television on?' 'No, not in the least.'* "我開電視機你介意嗎？" "不，一點也不介意。" ➲ more at SAY *v.*

■ ***adv.*** to the smallest degree 最小；最少；微不足道： *He always turns up just when you least expect him.* 他總是在你最意料不到的時候出現。◇ *She chose the least expensive of the hotels.* 她挑了一家最便宜的旅館。◇

*I never hid the truth, **least of all** from you.* 我從不隱瞞事實，尤其是對你。

IDM at 'least 1 not less than 至少；不少於：*It'll cost at least 500 dollars.* 這東西至少要花 500 元。◇ *She must be at least 40.* 她至少應該有 40 歲了。◇ *Cut the grass at least once a week in summer.* 夏天至少每週割草一次。◇ *I've known her at least as long as you have.* 我認識她至少和你認識她的時間一樣久了。**2** used to add a positive comment about a negative situation（用於對否定情況補充肯定的評論）起碼：*She may be slow but at least she's reliable.* 她雖然遲鈍，但起碼還很可靠。**3** even if nothing else is true or you do nothing else 無論如何；反正：*You could at least listen to what he says.* 你至少可以聽一聽他說些什麼。◇ *Well, at least they weren't bored.* 唔，反正他們沒有厭煩。**4** used to limit or make what you have just said less definite（用以減輕前面所說的話的肯定性）至少 SYN **anyway**：*They seldom complained—officially at least.* 他們很少抱怨，至少不在正式場合這樣做。◇ *It works, at least I think it does.* 它行，反正我認為它行。**not 'least** especially 特別；尤其：*The documentary caused a lot of bad feeling, not least among the workers whose lives it described.* 那部紀錄片引起了許多人的反感，尤其是在片中描寫到其生活的工人。➲ more at LAST[1] *adv.*, LINE *n.*, SAY *v.*

,least ,common de'nominator *noun* (*NAmE*) = LOWEST COMMON DENOMINATOR

,least ,common 'multiple *noun* (*NAmE*) = LOWEST COMMON MULTIPLE

least·ways /'li:stweɪz/ *adv.* (*NAmE, informal*) at least 至少；起碼：*It isn't cheap to get there, leastways not at this time of year.* 去那裏費用可不低，至少在一年中的這個時節是這樣。

lea·ther /'leðə(r)/ *noun*

1 [U, C] material made by removing the hair or fur from animal skins and preserving the skins using special processes 皮革：*a leather jacket* 皮夾克 ◇ *The soles are made of leather.* 鞋底是皮革做的。◇ *a leather-bound book* 皮面裝幀的書 ➲ VISUAL VOCAB page V61 **2 leathers** [pl.] clothes made from leather, especially those worn by people riding motorcycles（尤指騎摩托車人穿的）皮衣，皮外套 ➲ see also CHAMOIS LEATHER at CHAMOIS (2), PATENT LEATHER IDM see HELL

lea·ther·back /'leðəbæk; *NAmE* -ðərb-/ (also **,leather-back 'turtle, ,leathery 'turtle**) *noun* a very large sea TURTLE with a shell that looks like leather 棱皮龜；革龜

lea·ther·ette /,leðə'ret/ *noun* [U] an artificial material that looks and feels like leather 人造革；人造皮

lea·thery /'leðəri/ *adj.* that looks or feels hard and tough like leather 堅韌粗糙的；似皮革的：*leathery skin* 粗糙的皮膚

leave /li:v/ *verb, noun*

■ *verb* (**left, left** /left/)

▸ **PLACE/PERSON** 地方；人 **1** [I, T] to go away from a person or a place 離開（某人或某處）：*Come on, it's time we left.* 快點，我們該走了。◇ **~ for …** *The plane leaves for Dallas at 12.35.* 飛機於 12:35 起飛前往達拉斯。◇ **~ sth** *I hate leaving home.* 我討厭離開家。◇ *The plane leaves Heathrow at 12.35.* 飛機於 12:35 在希思羅機場起飛。

▸ **HOME/JOB/SCHOOL** 家；工作；學校 **2** [I, T] to stop living at a place, belonging to a group, working for an employer, etc. 離開居住地點（或群體、工作單位等）：*My secretary has threatened to leave.* 我的秘書以辭職相要挾。◇ **~ sth** (*BrE*) *Some children leave school at 16.* 有些學生 16 歲就離校了。

▸ **WIFE/HUSBAND** 妻子；丈夫 **3** [T] **~ sb (for sb)** to leave your wife, husband or partner permanently 遺棄；丟棄：*She's leaving him for another man.* 她要拋棄他去跟另一個男人。

▸ **STH TO DO LATER** 以後要做的事 **4** [T] to not do sth or deal with sth immediately 不立刻做；不馬上處理：**~ sth** *Leave the dishes—I'll do them later.* 盤子先擱着吧，我等會兒再洗。◇ **~ sth until …** *Why do you always leave everything until the last moment?* 你怎麼什麼事都留到最後一刻才處理？

▸ **SB/STH IN CONDITION/PLACE** 處於某種狀態；在某地方 **5** [T] to make or allow sb/sth to remain in a particular condition, place, etc. 使保留，讓…處於（某種狀態、某地等）：**~ sb/sth (+ adj.)** *Leave the door open, please.* 請把門開着吧。◇ *The bomb blast left 25 people dead.* 那顆炸彈炸死了 25 個人。◇ **~ sb/sth doing sth** *Don't leave her waiting outside in the rain.* 別讓她在外邊雨下等着。◇ **~ sb/sth to do sth** *Leave the rice to cook for 20 minutes.* 把大米煮 20 分鐘。**6** [T] to make sth happen or remain as a result 使發生；造成，使留下為（某種結果）：**~ sth** *Red wine leaves a stain.* 紅葡萄酒會留下污漬。◇ **~ sb with sth** *She left me with the impression that she was unhappy with her job.* 她給我的印象是她不滿意自己的工作。◇ **~ sb sth** *I'm afraid you leave me no choice.* 恐怕你沒有給我選擇的餘地。**7 be left** [T] to remain to be used, sold, etc. 留下備用（或銷售等）：*Is there any coffee left?* 還有咖啡剩下嗎？◇ *How many tickets do you have left?* 你還剩下多少張票？◇ **~ of sth** (*figurative*) *They are fighting to save what is left of their business.* 他們在拚命搶救他們僅餘的業務。◇ **~ to sb** *The only course of action left to me was to notify her employer.* 我可以採取的唯一措施就是通知她的雇主。

8 [T] to go away from a place without taking sth/sb with you 忘了帶；丟下：**~ sth/sb (+ adv./prep.)** *I've left my bag on the bus.* 我把包忘在公共汽車上了。◇ **~ sth/sb behind** *Don't leave any of your belongings behind.* 別忘了帶上自己的隨身物品。◇ *He wasn't well, so we had to leave him behind.* 他身體不適，因此我們只好把他留下。

▸ **MATHEMATICS** 數學 **9** [T] **~ sth** to have a particular amount remaining 剩餘；餘下：*Seven from ten leaves three.* * 10 減 7 得 3。

▸ **AFTER DEATH** 死後 **10** [T] **~ sb** to have family remaining after your death 遺下（家人）：*He leaves a wife and two children.* 他遺下妻子和兩個孩子。**11** [T] to give sth to sb when you die（去世時）遺贈，遺留 SYN **bequeath**：**~ sth (to sb)** *She left £1 million to her daughter.* 她遺留給女兒 100 萬英鎊。◇ **~ sb sth** *She left her daughter £1 million.* 她遺留給女兒 100 萬英鎊。

▸ **RESPONSIBILITY TO SB** 留給某人的責任 **12** [T] to allow sb to take care of sth 把…留交；交託；委託：**~ sb/sth + adv./prep.** *You can leave the cooking to me.* 你可以把做飯的事交給我。◇ *She left her assistant in charge.* 她委託助手來負責。◇ ***Leave it with me**—I'm sure I can sort it out.* 把這事交給我吧，我相信自己可以解決的。◇ *'Where shall we eat?' 'I'll leave it entirely (up) to you* (= you can decide).' "我們上哪兒吃去？" "我全交給你來決定好了。" ◇ *They left me with all the clearing up.* 他們把什麼都留給我來收拾。◇ **~ sb/sth to do sth** *I was left to cope on my own.* 就剩下我一個人來單獨對付。

▸ **DELIVER** 遞送 **13** [T] to deliver sth and then go away 遞送；遞交；投遞：**~ sth (for sb)** *Someone left this note for you.* 有人給你送來了這張便條。◇ **~ sb sth** *Someone left you this note.* 有人給你送來了這張便條。

IDM Most idioms containing **leave** are at the entries for the nouns and adjectives in the idioms, for example **leave sb in the lurch** is at **lurch**. 大多數含 leave 的習語，都可在該等習語中的名詞及形容詞相關詞條找到，如 leave sb in the lurch 在詞條 lurch 下。**,leave 'go (of sth)** (*BrE, informal*) to stop holding on to sth 鬆手；撒手；放開 SYN **let go**：*Leave go of my arm—you're hurting me!* 放開我的手臂，你弄痛我了！**leave it at 'that** (*informal*) to say or do nothing more about sth 別再說了；到此為止；就這樣算了：*We'll never agree, so let's just leave it at that.* 咱們不可能意見一致，所以這事就這樣吧。**,leave it 'out** (*BrE, informal*) used to tell sb to stop doing sth（讓人停止做某事）行啦，就這樣吧 ➲ more at TAKE

PHR V ,leave sth↔a'side to not consider sth 不予考慮；擱置一邊：*Leaving the expense aside, do we actually need a second car?* 且不說費用多少，我們真的還需要一輛汽車嗎？**,leave sb/sth be'hind 1** [usually passive] to make much better progress than sb 比…取得好得多的進展；把…拋在後面；超過：*Britain is being left behind in the race for new markets.* 英國在開拓新市場方面正被甩在後面。**2** to leave a person, place or state permanently 永久離開（某人、某地或某國）：*She knew that she had left childhood behind.* 她知道童年已一去不復返了。➲ see also LEAVE *v.* (8) **,leave 'off** (*informal*) to stop doing sth 停止（做某事）；中斷：*Start reading from where you* *left off last time.* 從上次停下來的地方接着讀吧。◇ **~ doing sth** *He left off playing the piano to answer the door.* 他停止彈鋼琴，應門去了。**,leave sb/sth↔'off (sth)** to not include sb/sth on a list, etc. 不把⋯列入；不包括；不含：*You've left off a zero.* 你漏掉了一個零。◇ *We left him off the list.* 我們未把他列入名單。**,leave sb/sth 'out (of sth)** 🔑 to not include or mention sb/sth in sth 不包括；不提及：*Leave me out of this quarrel, please.* 請別把我牽扯進這場爭吵。◇ *He hadn't been asked to the party and was feeling very left out.* 他未被邀請參加聚會，感到頗受冷落。◇ *She left out an 'm' in 'accommodation'.* 她在 accommodation 一詞中漏掉了一個字母 m。**be ,left 'over (from sth)** 🔑 to remain when all that is needed has been used 剩下；殘留：*There was lots of food left over.* 飯菜剩下了不少。➲ related noun LEFTOVER

■ ***noun*** [U] **1** a period of time when you are allowed to be away from work for a holiday/vacation or for a special reason 假期；休假：*to take a month's* ***paid/unpaid leave*** 帶薪／不帶薪休假一個月 ◇ *soldiers home* ***on leave*** 回家休假的士兵 ◇ *to be on* ***maternity/study leave*** 休產假；脱產進修 ◇ *How much* ***annual leave*** *do you get?* 你們的年假有多少？➲ see also COMPASSIONATE LEAVE, SICK LEAVE **2** (*formal*) official permission to do sth 准許；許可：*to be absent* ***without leave*** 未經許可擅離職守 ◇ **~ to do sth** *The court granted him leave to appeal against the sentence.* 法庭准許他對判決提出上訴。◇ *She asked for* ***leave of absence*** (= permission to be away from work) *to attend a funeral.* 她請了假去參加葬禮。

IDM **,by/,with your 'leave** (*formal*) with your permission 如蒙您允許的話；承蒙俯允 **take ,leave of your 'senses** (*old-fashioned*) to start behaving as if you are crazy 喪失理智；發瘋 **take (your) 'leave (of sb)** (*formal*) to say goodbye 告辭；辭別：*With a nod and a smile, she took leave of her friends.* 她點頭微笑着向朋友告辭。**without a ,by your 'leave; without so much as a ,by your 'leave** (*old-fashioned*) without asking permission; rudely 擅自；未經許可；粗魯地；無禮地 ➲ more at BEG, FRENCH *adj.*

-leaved /-liːvd/ ➲ LEAF *n.* (2)

leaven /ˈlevn/ *noun, verb*

■ ***noun*** [U] a substance, especially YEAST, that is added to bread before it is cooked to make it rise 發酵劑；（尤指）酵母，麪肥：(*figurative*) *A few jokes add leaven to a boring speech.* 幾句笑話可給枯燥無味的演講增添活躍的氣氛。

■ ***verb*** [often passive] **~ sth (with sth)** (*formal*) to make sth more interesting or cheerful by adding sth to it （添加⋯）使較有趣，使更令人愉快：*Her speech was leavened with a touch of humour.* 幾分幽默使她的講話更為有趣。

leav·er /ˈliːvə(r)/ *noun* (often in compounds 常構成複合詞) a person who is leaving a place 離去者：*school-leavers* 中學畢業生

leaves *pl.* of LEAF

'leave-taking *noun* [U, C, usually sing.] (*formal*) the act of saying goodbye 告別；告辭 SYN **farewell**

leav·ings /ˈliːvɪŋz/ *noun* [pl.] something that you leave because you do not want it, especially food （不要的）剩餘物（尤指剩餘飯菜）

lech /letʃ/ *noun, verb* (*BrE, informal, disapproving*)

■ ***noun*** a man who shows an unpleasant sexual interest in sb 好色之徒；色鬼

■ ***verb***

PHR V **'lech after sb** (*BrE*) to show an unpleasant sexual interest in sb 對某人生邪念；對某人起色心

lech·er /ˈletʃə(r)/ *noun* (*disapproving*) a man who is always thinking about sex and looking for sexual pleasure 好色之徒；色鬼；淫棍 ▸ **lech·ery** *noun* [U]

lech·er·ous /ˈletʃərəs/ *adj.* (*disapproving*) having too much interest in sexual pleasure 好色的；淫蕩的 SYN **lustful, lascivious**

leci·thin /ˈlesɪθɪn/ *noun* [U] a natural substance found in animals, plants and in egg YOLKS. Lecithin is used as an ingredient in some foods. 卵磷脂，磷脂酰膽鹼（用作食物添加劑）

lec·tern /ˈlektən; *NAmE* -tərn/ (*NAmE* also **po·dium**) *noun* a stand for holding a book, notes, etc. when you are reading in church, giving a talk, etc. （教堂中的）誦經台；（演講的）講台

lec·tor /ˈlektɔː(r)/ *noun* a person who teaches in a university, especially sb who teaches their own language in a foreign country （尤指在國外教授本國語的）大學講師，大學教師 ➲ compare LECTRICE

lec·trice /lekˈtriːs; *NAmE* ˈlektrɪs/ *noun* a female LECTOR in a university （尤指在國外教授本國語的）大學女講師，大學女教師

lec·ture 🔑 AW /ˈlektʃə(r)/ *noun, verb*

■ ***noun*** **~ (to sb) (on/about sth)** **1** 🔑 a talk that is given to a group of people to teach them about a particular subject, often as part of a university or college course （通常指大學裏的）講座，講課，演講：*to* ***deliver/give a lecture*** *to first-year students* 給一年級學生講課 ◇ *to attend a* ***series of lectures*** *on Jane Austen* 聽關於簡•奧斯汀的系列講座 ◇ *a* ***lecture room/hall*** 演講室／廳 ➲ **SYNONYMS** at SPEECH ➲ **COLLOCATIONS** at EDUCATION **2** a long angry talk that sb gives to one person or a group of people because they have done sth wrong （冗長的）教訓，訓斥，譴責：*I know I should stop smoking—don't give me a lecture about it.* 我知道我該戒煙，別再教訓我了。

■ ***verb*** **1** [I] **~ (in/on sth)** to give a talk or a series of talks to a group of people on a subject, especially as a way of teaching in a university or college（尤指在大學裏）開講座，講授，講課：*She lectures in Russian literature.* 她講授俄羅斯文學。**2** [T] **~ sb (about/on sth)** | **~ sb (about doing sth)** to criticize sb or tell them how you think they should behave, especially when it is done in an annoying way （尤指惱人地）指責，訓斥，告誡：*He's always lecturing me about the way I dress.* 他對我的衣着總是指手畫腳的。

lec·tur·er AW /ˈlektʃərə(r)/ *noun* **1** a person who gives a lecture 講課者；講授者；講演者：*She's a superb lecturer.* 她是一個出色的演講者。**2** (especially in Britain) a person who teaches at a university or college （尤指英國大學的）講師：*He's a lecturer in French at Oxford.* 他是牛津大學的法語講師。

lec·ture·ship /ˈlektʃəʃɪp; *NAmE* -tʃərʃ-/ *noun* the position of lecturer at a British university or college （英國大學的）講師職位：*a lectureship in media studies* 大眾傳播學講師職位

'lecture theatre (*BrE*) (*NAmE* **'lecture theater**) *noun* a large room with rows of seats on a slope, where lectures are given 演講廳；階梯教室

LED /ˌel iː ˈdiː/ *abbr.* light emitting diode (a device that produces a light on electrical and electronic equipment) 發光二極管：*A single red LED shows that the power is switched on.* 單支紅色發光二極管表示電源已接通。

led /led/ **1** *past tense, past part.* of LEAD **2** **-led** (in adjectives 構成形容詞) influenced or organized by 起主導作用的：*a consumer-led society* 以消費者主導的社會 ◇ *student-led activities* 學生領導的活動

ledge /ledʒ/ *noun* **1** a narrow flat piece of rock that sticks out from a CLIFF 懸崖岩石突出部；岩架：*seabirds nesting on rocky ledges* 在岩架上築巢的海鳥 **2** a narrow flat shelf fixed to a wall, especially one below a window （平窄的）壁架，横檔；（尤指）窗台：*She put the vase of flowers on the window ledge.* 她把那瓶花放在窗台上。➲ see also SILL

ledger /ˈledʒə(r)/ *noun* a book in which a bank, a business, etc. records the money it has paid and received 收支總賬；分類賬簿；分戶賬簿：*to enter figures in the* ***purchase/sales ledger*** 把金額輸入購貨／銷售分類賬

lee /liː/ *noun* **1** [sing.] the side or part of sth that provides shelter from the wind 背風處；避風處 ➲ compare LEEWARD, WINDWARD **2** **lees** [pl.] the substance that is left at the bottom of a bottle of wine, a container of beer, etc. （酒瓶等容器中的）沉澱物，殘渣 SYN **dregs**

leech /liːtʃ/ *noun* **1** a small WORM that usually lives in water and that attaches itself to other creatures and sucks their blood. Leeches were used in the past by doctors to remove blood from sick people. 水蛭；螞蟥 **2** (*disapproving*) a person who depends on sb else for money, or takes the profit from sb else's work 依賴他人錢財者；攫取他人收益者；寄生蟲

leek /liːk/ *noun* a vegetable like a long onion with many layers of wide flat leaves that are white at the bottom and green at the top. Leeks are eaten cooked. The leek is a national symbol of Wales. 韭蔥（威爾士民族的象徵）➲ VISUAL VOCAB page V31

leer /lɪə(r); *NAmE* lɪr/ *verb, noun*

■ ***verb*** [I] **~ (at sb)** to look or smile at sb in an unpleasant way that shows an evil or sexual interest in them（邪惡地或色迷迷地）看；奸笑；淫笑

■ ***noun*** an unpleasant look or smile that shows sb is interested in a person in an evil or sexual way（邪惡的或色迷迷的）目光；奸笑；淫笑：*He looked at her with an evil leer.* 他用不懷好意的目光看着她。

leery /ˈlɪəri; *NAmE* ˈlɪri/ *adj.* (*informal*) **~ (of sth/sb)** | **~ (of doing sth)** suspicious or careful about sth/sb, and trying to avoid doing it or dealing with them 猜疑的；謹防的；極力躲避的 SYN **wary**：*The government is leery of changing the current law.* 政府對是否修改現行法律存有疑慮。

lee·ward /ˈliːwəd; *NAmE* -wərd; *or, in nautical use,* ˈluːəd; *NAmE* -ərd/ *adj., noun*

■ ***adj.*** on the side of sth that is sheltered from the wind 在背風面的；背風的；下風的：*a harbour on the leeward side of the island* 位於島的背風面的海港 ▸ **lee·ward** *adv.* ➲ compare WINDWARD

■ ***noun*** [U] the side or direction that is sheltered from the wind 背風面；下風 ➲ compare WINDWARD

lee·way /ˈliːweɪ/ *noun* [U] the amount of freedom that you have to change sth or to do sth in the way you want to 自由活動的空間 SYN **latitude**：*How much leeway should parents give their children?* 父母應該給孩子多少自由的空間？

IDM **make up ˈleeway** (*BrE*) to get out of a bad position that you are in, especially because you have lost a lot of time 擺脫逆境；（尤指）彌補損失的時間

left 🔑 /left/ *adj., adv., noun* ➲ see also LEAVE *v.*

■ ***adj.*** 🔑 [only before noun] on the side of your body which is towards the west when you are facing north 左邊的：*Fewer people write with their left hand than with their right.* 用左手寫字的人比用右手的人少。◇ *I broke my left leg.* 我的左腿骨折了。◇ *the left side of the field* 田地的左邊 ◇ *The university is on the left bank of the river.* 大學在河的左岸。◇ *Take a left turn at the intersection.* 在十字路口向左轉。◇ (*sport* 體) *a left back/wing* 左後衛；左邊鋒 ◇ *a left hook* 左鈎拳 OPP **right** ▸ **left** 🔑 *adv.*：*Turn left at the intersection.* 在十字路口向左拐。◇ *Look left and right before you cross the road.* 左右看一看，然後再過馬路。

IDM **have two left ˈfeet** (*informal*) to be very awkward in your movements, especially when you are dancing or playing a sport（尤指跳舞或體育運動時）非常笨拙，笨手笨腳 **ˌleft, right and ˈcentre** (also **ˌright, left and ˈcentre**) (*informal*) in all directions; everywhere 四面八方；到處；處處：*He's giving away money left, right and centre.* 他到處贈款。➲ more at RIGHT *adv.*

■ ***noun*** **1** 🔑 **the/sb's left** [sing.] the left side or direction 左邊；左方；左：*She was sitting **on my left**.* 她坐在我的左邊。◇ *Twist your body to the left, then to the right.* 先向左轉體，再向右轉體。◇ *Take the next road **on the left**.* 在下一個路口向左拐。◇ ***To the left of** the library is the bank.* 圖書館的左邊是銀行。 **2** 🔑 [sing.] **the first, second, etc. left** the first, second, etc. road on the left side 左邊的第一（或第二等）條路：*Take the first left.* 在下一個路口向左轉。 **3** **a left** [sing.] a turn to the left 左轉彎：(*BrE*) *to **take a left*** 往左拐 ◇ (*NAmE*) *to **hang/make a left*** 向左拐彎 **4** 🔑 **the left, the Left** [sing.+sing./pl. v.] political groups who support the ideas and beliefs of SOCIALISM（擁護社會主義思想和信念的）左派政治團體，左派：*The Left only has/have a small chance of winning power.* 左派取得政權的機會渺茫。◇ *a left-leaning newspaper* 思想左傾的報紙 **5** 🔑 **the left** [sing.+sing./pl. v.] the part of a political party whose members are most in favour of social change（政黨內的）激進派，激進分子：*She is on the far left of the party.* 她是這個黨的極左分子。 **6** [C] (in boxing 拳擊運動) a blow that is made with your left hand 左手拳：*He hit him with two sharp lefts.* 他給了他兩記猛烈的左手拳。OPP **right**

ˌleft ˈbrain *noun* [U, sing.] the left side of the human brain, that is thought to be used for analysing and for processing language 左腦 ➲ compare RIGHT BRAIN

ˌleft ˈfield *noun* [sing.] **1** (in BASEBALL 棒球) the left part of the field, or the position played by the person who is there 左外場；左場手位置 **2** (*informal, especially NAmE*) an opinion or a position that is strange or unusual and a long way from the normal position 離奇古怪的看法（或意見）；怪誕的態度（或立場）：*The governor is **way out/over in left field**.* 州長的看法怪得出了格。

ˈleft-field *adj.* (*informal, especially NAmE*) not following what is usually done; different, surprising and interesting 出乎意料的；怪誕有趣的：*a left-field comedy drama* 怪誕喜劇

ˈleft-hand *adj.* [only before noun] **1** on the left side of sth 左手的；左邊的；左面的：*the left-hand side of the street* 街的左側 ◇ *the top left-hand corner of the page* 頁面左上角 **2** connected with a person's left hand 左手的：*a tennis player with a left-hand grip* 左手握拍的網球運動員 ◇ *a left-hand glove* 左手用的手套 OPP **right-hand**

ˌleft-hand ˈdrive *adj.* (of a vehicle 車輛) with the STEERING WHEEL on the left side 左側駕駛的 OPP **right-hand drive**

ˌleft-ˈhanded *adj.* **1** (of a person 人) finding it easier to use the left hand to write, hit a ball, etc. than the right 慣用左手的；左撇子的：*a left-handed golfer* 左手握杆的高爾夫球手 ◇ *I'm left-handed.* 我是左撇子。 **2** (of tools, etc. 工具等) designed to be used by sb who finds it easier to use their left hand 供慣用左手者使用的：*left-handed scissors* 左手用的剪刀 **3** (of actions, etc. 動作等) done with your left hand 用左手做的：*a left-handed serve* 用左手發球 OPP **right-handed** ▸ **ˌleft-ˈhanded** *adv.*：*She writes left-handed.* 她用左手寫字。**ˌleft-ˈhanded·ness** *noun* [U]

IDM **ˌleft-handed ˈcompliment** (*NAmE*) = BACKHANDED COMPLIMENT at BACKHANDED

ˌleft-ˈhander *noun* a person who finds it easier to use their left hand to write, etc. with than their right 慣用左手的人；左撇子 OPP **right-hander**

leftie = LEFTY

left·ist /ˈleftɪst/ *noun* a person who supports LEFT-WING political parties and their ideas 左派人士；左翼分子 OPP **rightist** ▸ **left·ism** *noun* [U] **left·ist** *adj.*：*leftist groups* 左派團體

ˌleft-ˈluggage office (also **left ˈluggage**) *noun* (both *BrE*) a place where you can pay to leave bags or suitcases for a short time, for example at a station（車站等的）行李寄存處

left·most /ˈleftməʊst; *NAmE* -moʊst/ *adj.* [only before noun] furthest to the left 最左邊的；最左面的；最左的

ˌleft-of-ˈcentre *adj.* = CENTRE-LEFT

left·over /ˈleftəʊvə(r); *NAmE* -oʊv-/ *noun* **1** [usually pl.] food that has not been eaten at the end of a meal 吃剩的食物；殘羹剩飯 **2** an object, a custom or a way of behaving that remains from an earlier time 遺留物；殘存物；遺留下來的風俗習慣 SYN **relic**：*He's a leftover from the hippies in the 1960s.* 他是 20 世紀 60 年代嬉皮士的殘餘分子。 ▸ **left·over** *adj.* [only before noun] SYN **surplus**：*Use any leftover meat to make a curry.* 要是有剩肉就做咖哩菜。

left·ward /ˈleftwəd; *NAmE* -wərd/ (*BrE* also **left·wards**) *adj.* [only before noun] towards the left 向左的；向左側的：*a leftward swing in public opinion* 輿論向左轉變 ◇ *to move your eyes in a leftward direction* 目光向左移動 ▸ **left·ward** (*BrE* also **left·wards**) *adv.*

ˌleft ˈwing *noun* **1** [sing.+sing./pl. v.] the part of a political party whose members are most in favour of social change（政黨中的）左翼，左派：*on the left wing of the party* 屬於這個政黨的左翼 **2** [C, U] an attacking player or position on the left side of the field in a sports game（體育比賽的）左邊鋒，左翼

ˌleft-ˈwing *adj.* strongly supporting the ideas of SOCIALISM 左翼的；左派的：*left-wing groups* 左翼團體

ˌleft-ˈwinger *noun* **1** a person on the LEFT WING of a political party 左翼人士；左派成員：*a Labour left-winger* 工黨的左翼成員 **2** a person who plays on the left side of the field in a sports game（體育比賽的）左邊鋒，左翼 OPP **right-winger**

lefty (also **leftie**) /ˈlefti/ *noun* (*pl.* **-ies**) (*informal*) **1** (*disapproving, especially BrE*) a person who has SOCIALIST views 左派分子 **2** (*especially NAmE*) a person who uses their left hand to write, hit a ball, etc. 左撇子 ▸ **lefty** *adj.*：*a lefty feminist lecturer* 激進的女權主義講演者

leg /leg/ *noun, verb*

■ **noun**

▸ PART OF BODY 身體部位 **1** [C] one of the long parts that connect the feet to the rest of the body 腿：*I broke my leg playing football.* 我的腿踢足球時骨折了。◇ *How many legs does a centipede have?* 蜈蚣有多少條腿？◇ ***front/back legs*** 前腿；後腿 ◇ ***forelegs/hind legs*** 前腿；後腿 ◇ *a wooden leg* 木假腿 ➲ COLLOCATIONS at PHYSICAL ➲ VISUAL VOCAB page V59 ➲ see also BOW LEGS, DADDY-LONG-LEGS, INSIDE LEG, LEGGY, LEGROOM, PEG LEG, SEA LEGS

▸ MEAT 食用肉 **2** [C, U] the leg of an animal, especially the top part, cooked and eaten（尤指供食用的）動物的腿，腿肉：*frogs' legs* 青蛙腿 ◇ *chicken legs* 雞腿 ◇ **~ of sth** *roast leg of lamb* 烤羊腿

▸ OF TROUSERS/PANTS 褲子 **3** [C] the part of a pair of trousers/pants that covers the leg 褲腿：*a trouser/pant leg* 一隻褲腿 ◇ *These jeans are too long **in the leg**.* 這條牛仔褲的褲腿太長。

▸ OF TABLE/CHAIR 桌椅 **4** [C] one of the long thin parts on the bottom of a table, chair, etc. that support it（桌椅等的）腿：*a chair leg* 椅子腿

▸ -LEGGED 有…腿 **5** /ˈlegɪd; legd/ (in adjectives 構成形容詞) having the number or type of legs mentioned 有…腿的：*a three-legged stool* 三條腿的凳子 ◇ *a long-legged insect* 長腿昆蟲 HELP When **-legged** is used with numbers, it is nearly always pronounced /ˈlegɪd/; in other adjectives it can be pronounced /ˈlegɪd/ or /legd/. *-legged 與數字連用幾乎總是讀作 /ˈlegɪd/；構成其他形容詞時可讀作 /ˈlegɪd/ 或 /legd/。➲ see also CROSS-LEGGED

▸ OF JOURNEY/RACE 行程；賽跑 **6** [C] **~ (of sth)** one part of a journey or race 一段路程（或賽程）SYN **section, stage**

▸ SPORTS GAME 體育比賽 **7** [C] (*BrE*) one of a pair of matches played between the same opponents in a sports competition, which together form a single ROUND (= stage) of the competition（相同對手間兩回合比賽的）回合

IDM **break a ˈleg!** (*informal*) used to wish sb good luck（表示良好祝願）祝你好運！ **get your ˈleg over** (*BrE, informal*) to have sex 性交 **have ˈlegs** (*informal*) if you say that a news story, etc. **has legs**, you mean that people will continue to be interested in it for a long time（新聞報道等）會長期受到關注 **not have a ˌleg to ˈstand on** (*informal*) to be in a position where you are unable to prove sth or explain why sth is reasonable 無法證實；無法解釋（理由）；站不住腳：*Without written evidence, we don't have a leg to stand on.* 我們沒有書面證據就站不住腳。➲ more at ARM *n.*, FAST *adv.*, LAST[1] *det.*, PULL *v.*, SHAKE *v.*, STRETCH *v.*, TAIL *n.*, TALK *v.* ➲ see also LEG-UP

■ **verb** (**-gg-**)

IDM **ˈleg it** (*informal, especially BrE*) to run, especially in order to escape from sb 跑；（尤指）逃跑：*We saw the police coming and legged it down the road.* 我們看見警察來了就順着馬路逃跑了。

leg·acy /ˈlegəsi/ *noun, adj.*

■ **noun** (*pl.* **-ies**) **1** money or property that is given to you by sb when they die 遺產；遺贈財物 SYN **inheritance**：*They each received a legacy of $5 000.* 他們每人得到了 5 000 元的遺產。 **2** a situation that exists now because of events, actions, etc. that took place in the past 遺留問題；後遺症：*Future generations will be left with a legacy of pollution and destruction.* 留給子孫後代的將是環境的污染與破壞。

■ **adj.** [only before noun] used to describe a computer system or product that is no longer available to buy but is still used because it would be too difficult or expensive to replace it（計算機系統或產品）已停產的，老化的，老式的：*How can we integrate new technology with our legacy systems?* 我們該如何將新技術整合到我們老化的系統上？◇ *legacy hardware/software* 老式硬件／軟件

legal AW /ˈliːgl/ *adj.*

1 [only before noun] connected with the law 與法律有關的；法律的：*the **legal profession/system*** 法律專業／體系 ◇ *to take/seek **legal advice*** 聽取／尋求法律咨詢 ◇ *a legal adviser* 法律顧問 ◇ *legal costs* 律師費用 **2** allowed or required by law 法律允許的；合法的；法律要求的：*The driver was more than three times over the **legal limit*** (= the amount of alcohol you are allowed to have in your body when you are driving). 那名司機體內的酒精含量超過了法律允許限度的三倍。◇ *Should euthanasia be made legal?* 安樂死是否應定為合法？OPP **illegal** ▸ **le·gal·ly** AW /ˈliːgəli/ *adv.*：*a **legally binding** agreement* 具有法律約束力的協議 ◇ *to be legally responsible for sb/sth* 對某人／某事負有法律責任

ˌlegal ˈaction *noun* [U] (also **ˌlegal proˈceedings**) the act of using the legal system to settle a disagreement, etc. 法律訴訟：*to **take/begin legal action** against sb* 起訴某人 ◇ *They have threatened us with legal action.* 他們用起訴來要挾我們。

ˌlegal ˈaid *noun* [U] money that is given by the government or another organization to sb who needs help to pay for legal advice or a lawyer 法律援助（政府或某機構向需要幫助的人提供費用，使其能夠尋求法律咨詢或聘請律師）

ˌlegal ˈeagle (also **ˌlegal ˈbeagle**) *noun* (*humorous*) a lawyer, especially one who is very clever（尤指精明的）律師

le·gal·ese /ˌliːgəˈliːz/ *noun* [U] (*informal*) the sort of language used in legal documents that is difficult to understand（深奧難懂的）法律術語，法律用語

ˌlegal ˈholiday *noun* (in the US) a public holiday that is fixed by law（美國）法定假日 ➲ compare BANK HOLIDAY

le·gal·is·tic /ˌliːgəˈlɪstɪk/ *adj.* (*disapproving*) obeying the law too strictly 墨守法規的；條文主義的；死摳法律條文的：*a legalistic approach to family disputes* 死摳法律條文解決家庭糾紛的方法

le·gal·ity AW /liːˈgæləti/ *noun* (*pl.* **-ies**) **1** [U] the fact of being legal 合法（性）：*They intended to challenge the legality of his claim in the courts.* 他們打算在法庭上對他索賠的合法性提出質疑。◇ *The arrangement is of doubtful legality.* 這項約定是否合法值得懷疑。 **2** [C, usually pl.] the legal aspect of an action or a situation（某行為或情況的）法律方面：*You need a lawyer to explain all the legalities of the contracts.* 你需要律師來解釋這些合同在法律上的各項細節。➲ compare ILLEGALITY

le·gal·ize (*BrE* also **-ise**) /ˈliːgəlaɪz/ *verb* **~ sth** to make sth legal 使合法化；使得到法律認可 ▸ **le·gal·iza·tion, -isa·tion** *noun* [U]

ˈlegal pad *noun* (*NAmE*) a number of sheets of paper with lines on them, fastened together at one end 信箋簿；橫線簿

ˌlegal proˈceedings *noun* [pl.] = LEGAL ACTION

ˈlegal-size (also **legal**) *adj.* (*NAmE*) (of paper 紙張) 8½ inches (215.9 mm) wide and 14 inches (355.6 mm) long 法律文件尺寸的（寬 8½ 英寸或 215.9 毫米，長 14 英寸或 355.6 毫米）

ˌlegal ˈtender *noun* [U] money that can be legally used to pay for things in a particular country 法定貨幣

leg·ate /ˈlegət/ *noun* the official representative of the Pope in a foreign country 教宗使節：*a papal legate* 教宗使節

lega·tee /ˌlegəˈtiː/ *noun* (*law* 律) a person who receives money or property (= a LEGACY) when sb dies 遺產繼承人；受遺贈人

le·ga·tion /lɪ'geɪʃn/ *noun* **1** a group of DIPLOMATS representing their government in a foreign country in an office that is below the rank of an EMBASSY 公使館全體人員 **2** the building where these people work 公使館

le·gato /lɪ'gɑ:təʊ; *NAmE* -toʊ/ *adj.* (*music* 音) (from *Italian*) to be played or sung in a smooth, even manner 連音的 ▸ **le·gato** *adv.* **OPP** **staccato**

le·gend /'ledʒənd/ *noun* **1** [C, U] a story from ancient times about people and events, that may or may not be true; this type of story 傳說；傳奇故事 **SYN** **myth**：*the legend of Robin Hood* 羅賓漢的傳奇故事 ◇ *the heroes of Greek legend* 希臘傳說中的英雄 ◇ ***Legend has it*** *that the lake was formed by the tears of a god.* 據傳說這個湖是一位神仙的眼淚積聚而成的。 ➲ compare URBAN MYTH **2** [C] a very famous person, especially in a particular field, who is admired by other people （尤指某領域中的）傳奇人物：*a* ***jazz/tennis, etc. legend*** 爵士樂、網球等的傳奇人物 ◇ *She was* ***a legend in her own lifetime.*** 她在世的時候就是一個傳奇人物。◇ *Many of golf's* ***living legends*** *were playing.* 當時有許多當世高爾夫球傳奇選手在打球。 **3** [C] (*technical* 術語) the explanation of a map or a diagram in a book （地圖或書中圖表的）圖例，說明，解釋 **SYN** **key** **4** [C] (*formal*) a piece of writing on a sign, a label, a coin, etc. （標誌、徽記、硬幣等物品上的）刻印文字，銘文

le·gend·ary /'ledʒəndri; *NAmE* -deri/ *adj.* **1** very famous and talked about a lot by people, especially in a way that shows admiration 非常著名的；享有盛名的：*a legendary figure* 大名鼎鼎的人物 ◇ *the legendary Bob Dylan* 名揚四海的鮑勃 • 迪倫 ◇ *Her patience and tact are legendary.* 她的耐心與老練是出了名的。 **2** [only before noun] mentioned in stories from ancient times 傳奇的；傳說的：*legendary heroes* 傳奇故事中的英雄 ➲ compare FABLED

le·ger·de·main /'ledʒədəmeɪn; *NAmE* -dʒərd-/ *noun* [U] (from *French, formal*) = SLEIGHT OF HAND (1)

leg·gings /'legɪŋz/ *noun* [pl.] **1** trousers/pants for women that fit tightly over the legs, made of cloth that stretches easily 女式緊身褲：*a pair of leggings* 一條女式緊身褲 **2** outer coverings for the legs, worn as protection 護腿；綁腿；裹腿

leggy /'legi/ *adj.* (*informal*) (especially of girls and women 尤指女孩或婦女) having long legs 腿長的：*a tall leggy schoolgirl* 個高腿長的女學生

le·gible /'ledʒəbl/ *adj.* (of written or printed words 手寫或印刷文字) clear enough to read 清晰可讀的；清楚的：*legible handwriting* 清楚易讀的筆跡 ◇ *The signature was still legible.* 簽名仍清晰可辨。 **OPP** **illegible** ▸ **le·gi·bil·ity** /ˌledʒə'bɪləti/ *noun* [U] **le·gibly** /-əbli/ *adv.*

le·gion /'li:dʒən/ *noun, adj.*

■ ***noun*** **1** a large group of soldiers that forms part of an army, especially the one that existed in ancient Rome （尤指古羅馬的）軍團：*the French Foreign Legion* 法國軍隊中的外籍軍團 ◇ *Caesar's legions* 凱撒軍團 **2** (*formal*) a large number of people of one particular type 大量，大批（某類型的人）：*legions of photographers* 眾多的攝影師

■ ***adj.*** [not before noun] (*formal*) very many 很多；極多 **SYN** **numerous**：*The medical uses of herbs are legion.* 草本植物的醫藥效用數不勝數。

le·gion·ary /'li:dʒənəri; *NAmE* -neri/ *noun* (*pl.* **-ies**) a soldier who is part of a legion 軍團士兵 ▸ **le·gion·ary** *adj.* [only before noun]

le·gion·naire /ˌli:dʒə'neə(r); *NAmE* -'ner/ *noun* a member of a LEGION, especially the French Foreign Legion 軍團成員；（尤指法國軍隊中的）外籍軍團成員

ˌlegion'naires' disease *noun* [U] a serious lung disease caused by bacteria, especially spread by AIR CONDITIONING and similar systems 軍團病（由細菌引起的嚴重肺部疾病，尤通過空調及類似系統傳播）

le·gis·late **AW** /'ledʒɪsleɪt/ *verb* [I] **~ (for/against/on sth)** (*formal*) to make a law affecting sth 制訂法律；立法：*The government will legislate against discrimination in the workplace.* 政府將制訂法律，在工作場所禁止歧視。◇ (*figurative*) *You can't legislate against bad luck!* 你無法用立法手段來阻止惡運！◇ *They promised to legislate to protect people's right to privacy.* 他們承諾立法保護公民的隱私權。

le·gis·la·tion **AW** /ˌledʒɪs'leɪʃn/ *noun* [U] **1** a law or a set of laws passed by a parliament 法規；法律：*an important* ***piece of legislation*** 一條重要的法規 ◇ *New legislation on the sale of drugs will be introduced next year.* 有關藥物銷售的新法規將於明年出台。 ➲ COLLOCATIONS at POLITICS **2** the process of making and passing laws 立法；制訂法律：*Legislation will be difficult and will take time.* 立法既費力又耗時。

le·gis·la·tive **AW** /'ledʒɪslətɪv; *NAmE* -leɪtɪv/ *adj.* [only before noun] (*formal*) connected with the act of making and passing laws 立法的；制訂法律的：*a* ***legislative assembly/body/council*** 立法議會／機構／委員會 ◇ *legislative powers* 立法權

le·gis·la·tor **AW** /'ledʒɪsleɪtə(r)/ *noun* (*formal*) a member of a group of people that has the power to make laws 立法委員

le·gis·la·ture **AW** /'ledʒɪsleɪtʃə(r)/ *noun* (*formal*) a group of people who have the power to make and change laws 立法機關：*a democratically elected legislature* 民主選舉產生的立法機關 ◇ *the* ***national/state legislature*** 國家／州立法機構 ➲ compare EXECUTIVE *n.* (3), JUDICIARY

legit /lɪ'dʒɪt/ *adj.* (*informal*) legal, or acting according to the law or the rules 合法的；守法的；按法律（或法規）行事的：*The business seems legit.* 這筆生意看起來是合法的。

le·git·im·ate /lɪ'dʒɪtɪmət/ *adj.* **1** for which there is a fair and acceptable reason 正當合理的；合情合理的 **SYN** **valid, justifiable**：*a legitimate grievance* 合乎情理的抱怨 ◇ *It seemed a* ***perfectly legitimate*** *question.* 這似乎是完全合乎情理的問題。◇ *Politicians are legitimate targets for satire.* 政治人物理所當然成為諷刺的對象。 **2** allowed and acceptable according to the law 合法的；法律認可的；法定的 **SYN** **legal**：*the legitimate government of the country* 這個國家的合法政府 ◇ *Is his business strictly legitimate?* 他的生意是否絕對合法？ **OPP** **illegitimate** **3** (of a child 小孩) born when its parents are legally married to each other 合法婚姻所生的 **OPP** **illegitimate** ▸ **le·git·im·acy** /lɪ'dʒɪtɪməsi/ *noun* [U]：*the dubious legitimacy of her argument* 她的論點不一定站得住腳 ◇ *I intend to challenge the legitimacy of his claim.* 我打算對他的聲明是否正確提出質疑。 **le·git·im·ate·ly** *adv.*：*She can now legitimately claim to be the best in the world.* 現在她可以理所當然地聲稱自己是世界上最優秀的。

le·git·im·ize (*BrE* also **-ise**) /lɪ'dʒɪtəmaɪz/ *verb* (*formal*) **1 ~ sth** to make sth that is wrong or unfair seem acceptable 使（壞事或不正當的事）看起來可以接受：*The movie has been criticized for apparently legitimizing violence.* 這部電影因明顯地美化暴力而受到了指責。 **2 ~ sth** to make sth legal 使合法 **SYN** **legalize** **3 ~ sb** to give a child whose parents are not married to each other the same rights as those whose parents are 賦予（非婚生子）合法權利

leg·less /'legləs/ *adj.* **1** without legs 無腿的 **2** (*BrE, informal*) very drunk 醉醺醺的；爛醉如泥的

Lego™ /'legəʊ; *NAmE* -goʊ/ *noun* [U] a children's toy that consists of small coloured bricks that fit together 樂高（兒童積木玩具）

'leg-pull *noun* a joke played on sb, usually by making them believe sth that is not true 愚弄

leg·room /'legru:m; 'legrʊm/ *noun* [U] the amount of space available for your legs when you are sitting in a car, plane, theatre, etc. （汽車、飛機、劇院等座位前的）供伸腿的空間，放腿處

leg·ume /'legju:m; lɪ'gju:m/ *noun* (*technical* 術語) any plant that has seeds in long PODS. PEAS and BEANS are legumes. 豆科作物

leg·um·in·ous /lɪ'gju:mɪnəs/ *adj.* [usually before noun] (*technical* 術語) relating to plants of the legume family 豆科（植物）的

L

ˈleg-up *noun*
IDM **give sb a ˈleg-up** (*BrE, informal*) **1** to help sb to get on a horse, over a wall, etc. by allowing them to put their foot in your hands and lifting them up 用雙手托腳幫助（某人上馬、翻牆等）**2** to help sb to improve their situation 幫助，援助（改善處境）

ˈleg warmer *noun* [usually pl.] a kind of sock without a foot that covers the leg from the ankle to the knee, often worn when doing exercise 腿套；護腿

leg·work /ˈlegwɜːk; *NAmE* -wɜːrk/ *noun* [U] (*informal*) difficult or boring work that takes a lot of time and effort, but that is thought to be less important 跑腿活兒；吃力不討好的活兒

leis·ure /ˈleʒə(r); *NAmE* ˈliːʒər/ *noun* [U] time that is spent doing what you enjoy when you are not working or studying 閒暇；空閒；休閒：*These days we have more money and more leisure to enjoy it.* 如今我們錢多了，也有更多時間來花錢享受了。◇ ***leisure activities/interests/pursuits*** 業餘活動 / 愛好 / 嗜好
IDM **at ˈleisure** **1** with no particular activities; free 閒散；悠閒：*Spend the afternoon at leisure in the town centre.* 下午到城中心區玩兒去吧。**2** without hurrying 不慌不忙；從容：*Let's have lunch so we can talk at leisure.* 咱們吃午飯吧，邊吃邊談。**at your ˈleisure** (*formal*) when you have the time to do sth without hurrying 有空時；空閒時：*I suggest you take the forms away and read them at your leisure.* 我建議你把表格帶回去有空慢慢看。**a ˌgentleman/ˌlady of ˈleisure** (*humorous*) a man/woman who does not have to work 不必工作的男人（或女人）

ˈleisure centre *noun* (*BrE*) a public building where people can go to do sports and other activities in their free time 休閒（或業餘）活動中心

leis·ured /ˈleʒəd; *NAmE* ˈliːʒərd/ *adj.* **1** [only before noun] not having to work and therefore having a lot of time to do what you enjoy 有空的；悠閒自在的：*the leisured classes* 有閒階級 **2** = LEISURELY

leis·ure·ly /ˈleʒəli; *NAmE* ˈliːʒərli/ (also **leis·ured**) *adj.* [usually before noun] done without hurrying 不慌不忙的；慢悠悠的：*a leisurely meal* 悠閒的一餐 ◇ *They set off at a leisurely pace.* 他們步態悠閒地出發了。▸ **leis·ure·ly** *adv.*：*Couples strolled leisurely along the beach.* 成雙成對的情侶沿着海灘悠然漫步。

ˈleisure suit *noun* (*NAmE*) an informal suit consisting of a shirt and trousers/pants made of the same cloth, popular in the 1970s 休閒套裝（流行於 20 世紀 70 年代，包括相同布料的襯衣和褲子）

leis·ure·wear /ˈleʒəweə(r); *NAmE* ˈliːʒərwer/ *noun* [U] (used especially by shops/stores and clothes companies 尤用於商店和服裝公司) informal clothes worn for relaxing or playing sports in 休閒服；便裝；休閒運動服

leit·motif (also **leit·motiv**) /ˈlaɪtməʊtiːf; *NAmE* -moʊ-/ *noun* (from *German*) **1** (*music* 音) a short tune in a piece of music that is often repeated and is connected with a particular person, thing or idea（音樂的）主旋律，主導主題 **2** an idea or a phrase that is repeated often in a book or work of art, or is typical of a particular person or group（書、藝術品等的）中心思想，主題，主旨

lek·got·la /leˈxɒtlə; *NAmE* -ˈxɑːt-/ *noun* (*SAfrE*) an important meeting of politicians or government officials（政界人士或政府官員的）重要會議

lek·ker /ˈlekə(r)/ *adj., adv.* (*SAfrE, informal*)
▪ *adj.* good or nice; tasting good 好的；不錯的；味道好的：*It was lekker to see you again.* 很高興再次見到你。◇ *a lekker meal* 美味的一餐
▪ *adv.* very 很；非常：*I'm lekker full.* 我吃得很飽。

lemma /ˈlemə/ *noun* (*pl.* **lem·mas** or **lem·mata** /-mətə/) **1** (*technical* 術語) a statement that is assumed to be true in order to test the truth of another statement 引理；輔助定理 **2** (*linguistics* 語言) the basic form of a word, for example the singular form of a noun or the infinitive form of a verb, as it is shown at the beginning of a dictionary entry 詞根，詞元（詞的基本形式，如名詞單數或動詞的不定式形式）

lem·ming /ˈlemɪŋ/ *noun* a small animal like a mouse, that lives in cold northern countries. Sometimes large groups of lemmings MIGRATE (= move from one place to another) in search of food. Many of them die on these journeys and there is a popular belief that lemmings kill themselves by jumping off CLIFFS. 旅鼠（許多人認為旅鼠會集體從懸崖上跳下自殺）：*Lemming-like we rushed into certain disaster.* 我們像旅鼠一樣忙不迭地衝進災難。

lemon 🔑 /ˈlemən/ *noun, adj.*
▪ *noun* **1** 🔑 [C, U] a yellow CITRUS fruit with a lot of sour juice. Slices of lemon and lemon juice are used in cooking and drinks. 檸檬：*lemon tea* 檸檬茶 ◇ *a gin and tonic with ice and lemon* 一杯加冰和檸檬的杜松子酒奎寧水 ◇ *Squeeze the juice of half a lemon over the fish.* 把半個檸檬的汁擠在魚上。◇ *a lemon tree* 檸檬樹 ➲ **VISUAL VOCAB** page V30 **2** 🔑 [U] lemon juice or a drink made from lemon 檸檬汁；檸檬飲料 ➲ see also BITTER LEMON **3** 🔑 (also **ˌlemon ˈyellow**) [U] a pale yellow colour 淺黃色；檸檬色 **4** [C] (*informal, especially NAmE*) a thing that is useless because it does not work as it should 無用的東西；蹩腳貨；廢物 **SYN** **dud** **5** [C] (*BrE*) a stupid person 蠢人；無用的人 **SYN** **idiot**
▪ *adj.* (also **ˌlemon ˈyellow**) pale yellow in colour 淺黃色的；檸檬色的

lem·on·ade /ˌleməˈneɪd/ *noun* **1** [U] (*BrE*) a sweet FIZZY drink (= with bubbles) with a lemon flavour 檸檬味汽水 **2** [U] a drink made from lemon juice, sugar and water 檸檬飲料 **3** [C] a glass or bottle of lemonade 一杯（或一瓶）檸檬飲料 ➲ compare ORANGEADE

ˈlemon balm *noun* [U] a HERB with leaves that taste of lemon 檸檬薄荷（草本植物，葉子有檸檬香味）

ˌlemon ˈcurd *noun* [U] (*BrE*) a thick sweet yellow substance made from lemon, sugar, eggs and butter, spread on bread, etc. or used to fill cakes 檸檬酪（用檸檬、糖、雞蛋及黃油製作的果醬）

ˈlemon grass *noun* [U] a type of grass with a lemon flavour that grows in hot countries and is used especially in SE Asian cooking 檸檬草（生長在熱帶國家，尤用於東南亞烹飪）

ˌlemon ˈsole *noun* a common European FLATFISH, often eaten as food 檸檬鰨（常見的歐洲比目魚）

ˈlemon-squeezer (*BrE*) (*NAmE* **juicer**) *noun* a kitchen UTENSIL (= a tool) for squeezing juice out of a fruit 榨汁器 ➲ **VISUAL VOCAB** page V26

lem·ony /ˈleməni/ *adj.* tasting or smelling of lemon 檸檬味的；檸檬香的：*a lemony flavour* 檸檬味

lemur /ˈliːmə(r)/ *noun* an animal like a MONKEY, with thick fur and a long tail, that lives in trees in Madagascar 狐猴（棲居於馬達加斯加島）

lend 🔑 /lend/ *verb* (**lent**, **lent** /lent/)
1 🔑 [T] to give sth to sb or allow them to use sth that belongs to you, which they have to return to you later 借給；借出 **SYN** **loan**：**~ (out) sth (to sb)** *I've lent the car to a friend.* 我把車借給一位朋友了。◇ **~ sb sth** *Can you lend me your car this evening?* 你今晚能把汽車借給我用一下嗎？◇ *Has he returned that book you lent him?* 你借給他的那本書還你了嗎？➲ note at BORROW **2** 🔑 [T, I] (of a bank or financial institution 銀行或金融機構) to give money to sb on condition that they pay it back over a period of time and pay interest on it 貸（款）**SYN** **loan**：**~ (sth) (to sb)** *The bank refused to lend the money to us.* 銀行拒絕向我們貸款。◇ **~ sb sth** *They refused to lend us the money.* 他們拒絕向我們貸款。➲ compare BORROW (2) **3** [T] (*formal*) to give a particular quality to a person or a situation 給…增加，增添（特色）：**~ sth (to sb/sth)** *The setting sun lent an air of melancholy to the scene.* 落日給景色增添了傷感的氣氛。◇ **~ sb/sth sth** *Her presence lent the occasion a certain dignity.* 她的出席使那場面增添了幾分光彩。**4** [T] to give or provide help, support, etc. 給予，提供（幫助、支持等）：**~ sth (to sb/sth)** *I was more than happy to lend my support to such a good cause.* 我非常樂意給這樣崇高的事業提供援助。◇ **~ sb/sth sth** *He came along to lend me moral support.* 他來給予我精神上的支持。
IDM **lend an ˈear (to sb/sth)** to listen in a patient and sympathetic way to sb 聆聽；傾聽 **lend (sb) a (helping)**

'hand (with sth) (*informal*) to help sb with sth 幫助；援助；搭把手：*I went over to see if I could lend a hand.* 我走過去看我能不能幫上忙。**lend 'colour to sth** (*BrE*) to make sth seem true or probable 使顯得真實（或可能）：*Most of the available evidence lends colour to this view.* 現有的大部份證據支持這個觀點。**lend your name to sth** (*formal*) **1** to let it be known in public that you support or agree with sth 公開表示支持：*I am more than happy to lend my name to this campaign.* 我非常願意支持這個運動。**2** to have a place named after you 以…的名字命名（某地方）**lend sup'port, 'weight, 'credence, etc. to sth** to make sth seem more likely to be true or genuine 對…提供支持（如有重要或可靠的證據等而增加可信度）：*This latest evidence lends support to her theory.* 這一最新的證據印證了她的理論。➲ more at HELP *v.*

PHR V **'lend itself to sth** to be suitable for sth 適合於：*Her voice doesn't really lend itself well to blues singing.* 她的嗓子不是很適於唱布魯斯歌曲。

lend·er /ˈlendə(r)/ *noun* (*finance* 財) a person or an organization that lends money 放款人 ➲ compare BORROWER ➲ see also MONEYLENDER

lend·ing /ˈlendɪŋ/ *noun* [U] (*finance* 財) the act of lending money 放款；貸放：*Lending by banks rose to $10 billion last year.* 去年銀行發放的貸款增至 100 億元。

'lending library *noun* a public library from which you can borrow books and take them away to read at home（書籍可外借的）公共圖書館 ➲ compare REFERENCE LIBRARY

'lending rate *noun* (*finance* 財) the rate of interest that you must pay when you borrow money from a bank or another financial organization 貸款利率；放款利率

length 0┳ /leŋθ/ *noun*

▸ **SIZE/MEASUREMENT** 大小；度量 **1** 0┳ [U, C] the size or measurement of sth from one end to the other 長；長度：*This room is twice the length of the kitchen.* 這個房間的長度是廚房的兩倍。◇ *The river is 300 miles* ***in length.*** 這條河長 300 英里。◇ *The snake usually reaches a length of 100 cm.* 蛇一般長達 100 厘米。◇ *He ran the entire length of the beach* (= from one end to the other). 他從海灘一頭跑到另一頭。◇ *Did you see the length of his hair?* 你看見他頭髮有多長嗎？➲ compare BREADTH (1), WIDTH (1)

▸ **TIME** 時間 **2** 0┳ [U, C] the amount of time that sth lasts（持續）時間的長短：*We discussed shortening the length of the course.* 我們就縮短這門課程的時間進行了討論。◇ *He was disgusted at* ***the length of time*** *he had to wait.* 他非常討厭要等那麼長時間。◇ *She got a headache if she had to read* ***for any length of time*** (= for a long time). 她讀書時間長了就頭疼。◇ *Size of pension depends partly on length of service with the company.* 退休金的多少部份取決於為公司服務時間的長短。◇ *Each class is 45 minutes* ***in length.*** 每一節課為 45 分鐘。

▸ **OF BOOK/MOVIE** 書；電影 **3** 0┳ [U, C] the amount of writing in a book, or a document, etc.; the amount of time that a film/movie lasts（書或文件等的）篇幅；（電影的）片長：*Her novels vary in length.* 她的小說篇幅長短不一。

▸ **-LENGTH** …長度 **4** (in adjectives 構成形容詞) having the length mentioned 有…長度的：*shoulder-length hair* 長及肩的頭髮 ➲ see also FULL-LENGTH, KNEE-LENGTH

▸ **OF SWIMMING POOL** 游泳池 **5** [C] the distance from one end of a swimming pool to the other 游泳池長度（一端至另一端的距離）：*He swims 50 lengths a day.* 他每天游 50 個游泳池那麼長的距離。➲ compare WIDTH (3)

▸ **IN RACE** 賽跑 **6** [C] the size of a horse or boat from one end to the other, when it is used to measure the distance between two horses or boats taking part in a race（馬或船的）自身長度：*The horse won by two clear lengths.* 那匹馬以整整領先兩個馬身的優勢獲勝。

▸ **LONG THIN PIECE** 細長的段 **7** [C] a long thin piece of sth 細長的一段（或一節、一根等）：*a* ***length of rope/string/wire*** 一根繩子／細線／金屬線 ➲ see also LONG *adj.*

IDM **at 'length | at … length** **1** for a long time and in detail 長時間；詳盡地：*He quoted at length from the report.* 他大段大段地引用報告中的話。◇ *We have already discussed this matter at great length.* 我們已經十分詳盡地討論了這個問題。**2** (*literary*) after a long time 經過一段長時間以後；最後：*'I'm still not sure,' he said at length.* "我還是沒把握。" 他最後說道。**go to any, some, great, etc. 'lengths (to do sth)** to put a lot of effort into doing sth, especially when this seems extreme 竭盡全力；不遺餘力：*She goes to extraordinary lengths to keep her private life private.* 她竭盡全力讓自己的私生活不受干擾。**the length and 'breadth of …** in or to all parts of a place 到處；處處；各地：*They have travelled the length and breadth of Europe giving concerts.* 他們為舉行音樂會走遍了歐洲各地。➲ more at ARM *n.*

length·en /ˈleŋθən/ *verb* [I, T] to become longer; to make sth longer（使）變長：*The afternoon shadows lengthened.* 下午影子漸漸變長了。◇ **~ sth** *I need to lengthen this skirt.* 我需要把這條裙子放長。**OPP** **shorten**

length·ways /ˈleŋθweɪz/ (also **length·wise** /ˈleŋθwaɪz/) *adv.* in the same direction as the longest side of sth 縱向；縱長：*Cut the banana in half lengthways.* 把香蕉豎着切成兩半。➲ compare WIDTHWAYS

lengthy /ˈleŋθi/ *adj.* (**length·ier**, **lengthi·est**) very long, and often too long, in time or size 很長的；漫長的；冗長的：*lengthy delays* 多次長時間拖延 ◇ *the lengthy process of obtaining a visa* 取得簽證的漫長過程 ◇ *a lengthy explanation* 冗長的解釋

le·ni·ent /ˈliːniənt/ *adj.* not as strict as expected when punishing sb or when making sure that rules are obeyed（懲罰或執法時）寬大的，寬容的，仁慈的：***a lenient sentence/fine*** 從寬的判刑／罰款 ◇ *The judge was far too lenient with him.* 法官對他太寬容了。▶ **le·ni·ency** /-ənsi/ (also *less frequent* **le·ni·ence**) *noun* [U]：*She appealed to the judge for leniency.* 她向法官請求寬大處理。**le·ni·ent·ly** *adv.*：*to treat sb leniently* 寬待某人

Lenin·ism /ˈlenɪnɪzəm/ *noun* [U] the political and economic policies of Lenin, the first leader of the Soviet Union, which were based on Marxism 列寧主義（蘇聯第一任領導人列寧根據馬克思主義理論創立的政治和經濟政策）▶ **Lenin·ist** /ˈlenɪnɪst/ *noun, adj.*

lens /lenz/ *noun* **1** a curved piece of glass or plastic that makes things look larger, smaller or clearer when you look through it 透鏡；鏡片：*a pair of glasses with tinted lenses* 一副有色鏡片眼鏡 ◇ *a camera with an adjustable lens* 帶有可調鏡頭的照相機 ◇ *a* ***lens cap/cover*** 鏡頭帽／蓋 ➲ picture at BINOCULARS, FRAME ➲ see also FISHEYE LENS, TELEPHOTO LENS, WIDE-ANGLE LENS, ZOOM LENS **2** (*informal*) = CONTACT LENS：*Have you got your lenses in?* 你戴了隱形眼鏡嗎？**3** (*anatomy* 解) the transparent part of the eye, behind the PUPIL, that focuses light so that you can see clearly（眼球的）晶狀體 ➲ **VISUAL VOCAB** page V59

lens·man /ˈlenzmən/ *noun* (*pl.* **-men** /-mən/) a professional photographer or CAMERAMAN（專職）攝影師

Lent /lent/ *noun* [U] in the Christian Church, the period of 40 days from Ash Wednesday to the day before Easter, during which some Christians give up some type of food or activity that they enjoy in memory of Christ's suffering 大齋期，四旬期（從聖灰日至復活節前一日，共 40 天）

lent *past tense, past part.* of LEND

len·tigo /lenˈtaɪɡəʊ; *NAmE* -ɡoʊ/ *noun* [U] (*medical* 醫) a condition in which small brown areas appear on the skin, usually in old people 雀斑痣；（尤指）老人斑 ➲ see also LIVER SPOT

len·til /ˈlentl/ *noun* a small green, orange or brown seed that is usually dried and used in cooking, for example in soup or STEW 小扁豆；兵豆

Leo /ˈliːəʊ; *NAmE* ˈliːoʊ/ *noun* **1** [U] the fifth sign of the ZODIAC, the Lion 黃道第五宮；獅子宮；獅子（星）座 **2** [C] (*pl.* **-os**) a person born when the sun is in this sign, that is between 23 July and 22 August, approximately 屬獅子座的人（約出生於 7 月 23 日至 8 月 22 日）

leo·nine /ˈliːənaɪn/ *adj.* (*literary*) like a LION 像獅子一樣的；獅子般的

leop·ard /ˈlepəd; *NAmE* -ərd/ *noun* a large animal of the cat family, that has yellowish-brown fur with black spots. Leopards live in Africa and southern Asia. 豹 ➲ compare LEOPARDESS

IDM **a leopard cannot change its 'spots** (*saying*) people cannot change their character, especially if they have a bad character 本性難改；稟性難移

'leopard-crawl *verb* [I] + **adv./prep.** (*SAfrE*) (often used about soldiers 常用於士兵) to move with your body as close to the ground as possible, using your elbows and knees to push you forward 匍匐前進

leop·ard·ess /'lepədes; *NAmE* -ərd-/ *noun* a female leopard 母豹

leo·tard /'li:ətɑ:d; *NAmE* -tɑ:rd/ *noun* a piece of clothing that fits tightly over the body from the neck down to the tops of the legs, usually covering the arms, worn by dancers, women doing physical exercises, etc. （舞蹈演員、女性體育鍛煉者等穿的通常有袖的）緊身連衣褲

LEP /ˌel i: 'pi:/ *abbr.* [only before noun] (*NAmE, technical* 術語) Limited English Proficient (used to describe students who cannot speak English very well) 英語水平有限的（用於描述英語口語不夠流利的學生）：*schools with large numbers of LEP children* 有很多英語水平有限的學童的學校

leper /'lepə(r)/ *noun* **1** a person suffering from LEPROSY 麻風病患者 **2** a person that other people avoid because they have done sth that these people do not approve of （因其所為而）被大家躲避的人；別人唯恐躲之不及的人

lep·re·chaun /'leprəkɔ:n/ *noun* (in Irish stories) a creature like a little man, with magic powers （愛爾蘭傳說中像小矮人的）魔法精靈

lep·rosy /'leprəsi/ *noun* [U] an infectious disease that causes painful white areas on the skin and can destroy nerves and flesh 麻風 ➲ see also LEPER (1)

lep·rous /'leprəs/ *adj.* affected by LEPROSY 麻風病的

les·bian /'lezbiən/ (also *informal* **lezzy**, **lezzie**) *noun* a woman who is sexually attracted to other women 女同性戀者：*lesbians and gays* 女同性戀者與男同性戀者 ➲ compare GAY, HOMOSEXUAL ▶ **les·bian** *adj.*：*the lesbian and gay community* 男女同性戀群體 ◇ *a lesbian relationship* 女性同性戀關係 **les·bian·ism** *noun* [U]

lese-majesty /ˌli:z 'mædʒəsti; *NAmE* ˌleɪz/ *noun* [U] (from *French, formal*) the act or crime of insulting the king, queen or other ruler （對君主、元首等的）不敬罪，叛逆罪

le·sion /'li:ʒn/ *noun* (*medical* 醫) damage to the skin or part of the body caused by injury or by illness （因傷病導致皮膚或器官的）損傷，損害：*skin/brain lesions* 皮膚 / 大腦損傷

less 🔑 /les/ *det., pron., adv., prep.*

■ ***det., pron.*** 🔑 used with uncountable nouns to mean 'a smaller amount of'（與不可數名詞連用）較少的，更少的：*less butter/time/importance* 較少的黃油 / 時間；次要 ◇ *He was advised to smoke fewer cigarettes and drink less beer.* 有人勸他少抽煙、少喝啤酒。◇ *We have less to worry about now.* 現在我們要擔憂的事少一些了。◇ *It is* ***less of*** *a problem* ***than*** *I'd expected.* 問題不像我預料的那麼大。◇ *We'll be there in* ***less than no time*** (= very soon). 我們馬上就到。◇ *The victory was* ***nothing less than*** *a miracle.* 這場勝利是個不折不扣的奇跡。 **HELP** People often use **less** with countable nouns. * less 與可數名詞連用頗常見：*There were less cars on the road then.* This is not considered correct by some people, and **fewer** should be used instead. 有人認為這不正確，應用 fewer。

IDM **ˌless and 'less** 🔑 smaller and smaller amounts 越來越少：*As time passed, she saw less and less of all her old friends at home.* 隨着時間的消逝，她越來越見不到家鄉那些老朋友了。 **ˌless is 'more** (*saying*) include only what is essential in order to create an effective product or result 少即是多；以少見多；簡單就是美：*His simple, elegant paintings reflect his principle that less is more.* 他簡潔典雅的繪畫反映出他簡約就是美的原則。 **no 'less** (often *ironic*) used to suggest that sth is surprising or impressive （表示驚訝或欽佩）竟，居然：*She's having lunch with the Director, no less.* 她居然正在與主管一起進午餐。 **no less than ...** used to emphasize a large amount （強調大數量）不少於，多達：*The guide contains details of no less than 115 hiking routes.* 這本導遊指南包括多達 115 條徒步旅行路線的詳細介紹。

■ ***adv.*** 🔑 to a smaller degree; not so much 較少；較小；更少；更小；沒那麼多；少：*less expensive/likely/intelligent* 價錢較便宜；可能性較小；智力較差 ◇ *less often/enthusiastically* 不那麼經常 / 熱情 ◇ *I read much less now than I used to.* 我現在看的書比過去少得多。◇ *The receptionist was* ***less than*** (= not at all) *helpful.* 那接待員一點忙也幫不上。◇ *She wasn't* ***any the less*** *happy for* (= she was perfectly happy) *being on her own.* 她並不因獨自一人而有一丁點兒不快活。◇ *That this is a positive stereotype makes it* ***no less a*** *stereotype, and therefore unacceptable.* 這種成見即使是積極的也不失之為成見，因而是不可取的。

IDM **even/much/still 'less** and certainly not 更不用說；更何況：*No explanation was offered, still less an apology.* 連個解釋都不給，就更不用說道歉了。 **ˌless and 'less** 🔑 continuing to become smaller in amount 越來越少；越來越小：*She found the job less and less attractive.* 她發覺那工作越來越沒意思。 ➲ more at MORE *adv.*

■ ***prep.*** used before a particular amount that must be taken away from the amount just mentioned 減去；扣除 **SYN** **minus**：*a monthly salary of $2 000 less tax and insurance* 月薪 2 000 元，從中扣除稅款和保險費

-less /-ləs/ *suffix* (in adjectives 構成形容詞) **1** without 沒有；無：*treeless* 沒有樹木的 ◇ *meaningless* 無意義的 **2** not doing; not affected by 不做；不受影響：*tireless* 孜孜不倦的 ◇ *selfless* 無私的 ▶ **-less·ly** (in adverbs 構成副詞)：*hopelessly* 絕望地 **-less·ness** (in nouns 構成名詞)：*helplessness* 無助

les·see /le'si:/ *noun* (*law* 律) a person who has use of a building, an area of land, etc. on a LEASE 承租人；租戶 ➲ compare LESSOR

less·en /'lesn/ *verb* [I, T] to become or make sth become smaller, weaker, less important, etc. （使）變小，變少，減弱，減輕 **SYN** **diminish**：*The noise began to lessen.* 噪音開始減弱。◇ **~ sth** *to lessen the risk/impact/effect of sth* 減少某事物的風險 / 影響 / 效果 ▶ **less·en·ing** *noun* [sing., U]：*a lessening of tension* 緊張狀態的減緩

less·er /'lesə(r)/ *adj.* [only before noun] **1** not as great in size, amount or importance as sth/sb else 較小的；較少的；次要的：*people of lesser importance* 次要人物 ◇ *They were all involved* ***to a greater or lesser degree*** (= some were more involved than others). 他們或多或少都受到了牽連。◇ *The law was designed to protect wives, and, to a lesser extent, children.* 這條法律是為了保護妻子，其次是保護子女。◇ *He was encouraged to plead guilty to the lesser offence.* 有人慫恿他供認犯了那個較輕的罪行。 **2** used in the names of some types of animals, birds and plants which are smaller than similar kinds （用於比同類小的動植物名稱）小 **OPP** **greater** ▶ **less·er** *adv.*：*one of the lesser-known Caribbean islands* 加勒比海不甚知名的島嶼之一

IDM **the ˌlesser of two 'evils** | **the ˌlesser 'evil** the less unpleasant of two unpleasant choices 兩害相權之輕者

lesso /'lesəʊ; *NAmE* 'lesoʊ/ *noun* (*pl.* **-os**) = KHANGA

les·son 🔑 /'lesn/ *noun*

1 🔑 a period of time in which sb is taught sth 一節課；一課時：*She gives piano lessons.* 她教授鋼琴課。◇ *All new students are given* ***lessons in/on*** *how to use the library.* 所有新生都要上如何利用圖書館的課。◇ *I'm* ***having/taking*** *driving lessons.* 我在學開車。◇ (*especially BrE*) *Our first lesson on Tuesdays is French.* 我們星期二的第一節課是法語。◇ (*especially BrE*) *What did we do last lesson?* 我們上節課學了什麼內容？ ➲ COLLOCATIONS at EDUCATION ➲ compare CLASS *n.* (2) **2** 🔑 something that is intended to be learned 課；教學單元：*The course book is divided into 30 lessons.* 這本教科書分為 30 課。◇ *Other countries can* ***teach us a lesson*** *on industrial policy.* 其他國家的工業政策，我們可以借鑒一二。 **3** 🔑 an experience, especially an unpleasant one, that sb can learn from so that it does not happen again in the future 經驗；教訓：*a salutary lesson* 有益的經驗 ◇ *The accident* ***taught me a lesson*** *I'll never forget.* 那事故給我的教訓永遠也不會忘記。◇ **~ to sb** ***Let that be a lesson to you*** (= so that you do not make the same

L

mistake again). 你要以此為鑑。 ➲ see also OBJECT LESSON **4** a passage from the Bible that is read to people during a church service（教堂禮拜中的）《聖經》選讀 **IDM** see LEARN

les·sor /le'sɔː(r)/ *noun* (*law* 律) a person who gives sb the use of a building, an area of land, etc. on a LEASE 出租人 ➲ compare LESSEE

lest /lest/ *conj.* (*formal* or *literary*) **1** in order to prevent sth from happening 免得；以免：*He gripped his brother's arm lest he be trampled by the mob.* 他緊抓着他弟弟的胳膊，怕他讓暴民踩着。 **2** used to introduce the reason for the particular emotion mentioned（引出產生某種情感的原因）唯恐，擔心 **SYN** **in case**：*She was afraid lest she had revealed too much.* 她擔心她泄露得太多了。

let 🔑 /let/ *verb, noun*

■ *verb* (**let·ting, let, let**)

▸ ALLOW 允許 **1** 🔑 [no passive] to allow sb to do sth or sth to happen without trying to stop it 允許；讓：**~ sb/sth do sth** *Let them splash around in the pool for a while.* 讓他們在水池裏撲騰一會兒吧。◇ *Don't let her upset you.* 別讓她攪得你心煩。◇ *Let your body relax.* 讓你的身體放鬆。◇ **~ sb/sth** *He'd eat chocolate all day long if I let him.* 我要是不攔着，他會整天不停地吃巧克力。 **2** 🔑 to give sb permission to do sth 准許；許可；同意：**~ sb/sth do sth** *They won't let him leave the country.* 他們不許他離開這個國家。◇ **~ sb/sth** *She wanted to lend me some money but I wouldn't let her.* 她想借給我一些錢，可我不同意。 **3** 🔑 **~ sb/sth + adv./prep.** to allow sb/sth to go somewhere 允許（去某處）：*to let sb into the house* 允許某人進屋 ◇ *I'll give you a key so that you can let yourself in.* 我把鑰匙給你，你可以自己開門進去。◇ *Please let me past.* 請讓我過去。◇ *The cat wants to be let out.* 那隻貓想要出去。

▸ MAKING SUGGESTIONS 提出建議 **4** 🔑 **let's** [no passive] **~ (do sth)** used for making suggestions（提出建議時說）：*Let's go to the beach.* 咱們去海灘吧。◇ *Let's not tell her what we did.* 咱們幹的事可別告訴她。◇ (*BrE*) *Don't let's tell her what we did.* 咱們幹的事可別告訴她。◇ *I don't think we'll make it, but let's try anyway.* 我不認為我們會成功，但不管怎樣還是試一試吧。◇ *'Shall we check it again?' 'Yes, let's.'* "我們再檢查一下好嗎？" "好的。"

▸ OFFERING HELP 提供幫助 **5** 🔑 [no passive] **~ sb/sth do sth** used for offering help to sb（提出幫助時說）讓，由：*Here, let me do it.* 喂，讓我來吧。◇ *Let us get those boxes down for you.* 讓我們幫你把那些箱子搬下來吧。

▸ MAKING REQUESTS 提出要求 **6** [no passive] **~ sb/sth do sth** used for making requests or giving instructions（提出請求或給予指示時說）要：*Let me have your report by Friday.* 星期五以前要把你的報告交給我。

▸ CHALLENGING 挑戰 **7** [no passive] **~ sb/sth do sth** used to show that you are not afraid or worried about sb doing sth（表示不害怕或擔憂某人做某事）讓：*If he thinks he can cheat me, just let him try!* 要是他以為能夠騙過我，就讓他來試一下吧！

▸ WISHING 祝願 **8** [no passive] **~ sb/sth do sth** (*literary*) used to express a strong wish for sth to happen（表達強烈的願望）讓：*Let her come home safely!* 讓她平平安安回家吧！

▸ INTRODUCING STH 引出某事 **9** [no passive] **~ sb/sth do sth** used to introduce what you are going to say or do（引出要講或要做的事）讓：*Let me give you an example.* 讓我來舉一個例子吧。◇ *Let me just finish this and then I'll come.* 讓我把這個弄完，隨後就來。

▸ IN CALCULATING 計算 **10** [no passive] **~ sb/sth do sth** (*technical* 術語) used to say that you are supposing sth to be true when you calculate sth（計算時說）假設，設：*Let line AB be equal to line CD.* 設 AB 線與 CD 線等長。

▸ HOUSE/ROOM 房屋；房間 **11** 🔑 **~ sth (out) (to sb)** (*especially BrE*) to allow sb to use a house, room, etc. in return for regular payments 出租（房屋、房間等）：*I let the spare room.* 我把那間空房出租了。◇ *They decided to let out the smaller offices at low rents.* 他們決定以低租金把那些較小的辦公室租出去。 ➲ COLLOCATIONS at HOUSE ➲ note at RENT

IDM Most idioms containing **let** are at the entries for the nouns and adjectives in the idioms, for example **let alone** is at **alone**. 大多數含 let 的習語，都可在該等習語中的名詞及形容詞相關詞條找到，如 let alone 在詞條 alone 下。 **,let 'fall sth** to mention sth in a conversation, by accident or as if by accident 無意中提及；脫口說出 **SYN** **drop**：*She let fall a further heavy hint.* 她似乎無意中又說出了一個明顯的提示。 **,let sb 'go 1** 🔑 to allow sb to be free 放，釋放（某人） **SYN** **free**：*Will they let the hostages go?* 他們是否會釋放人質？ **2** to make sb have to leave their job 解雇；開除：*They're having to let 100 employees go because of falling profits.* 由於利潤下降，他們將不得不解雇 100 名員工。 **,let sb/sth 'go | ,let 'go (of sb/sth) 1** 🔑 to stop holding sb/sth 放開；鬆手：*Don't let the rope go.* 別鬆開繩子。◇ *Don't let go of the rope.* 別鬆開繩子。◇ *Let go! You're hurting me!* 放手！你把我弄疼了！ **2** to give up an idea or an attitude, or control of sth 放棄，摒棄（想法、態度或控制）：*It's time to let the past go.* 該忘掉過去了。◇ *It's time to let go of the past.* 該忘掉過去了。 **,let sth 'go** to stop taking care of a house, garden, etc. 不再照管，撒手不管（房屋、花園等）：*I'm afraid I've let the garden go this year.* 恐怕我今年沒有照看好園子。 **,let yourself 'go 1** to behave in a relaxed way without worrying about what people think of your behaviour 放鬆；隨心所欲：*Come on, enjoy yourself, let yourself go!* 來吧，盡情地玩，玩個痛快吧！ **2** to stop being careful about how you look and dress, etc. 不注重儀表；不修邊幅：*He has let himself go since he lost his job.* 他失業後就不修邊幅了。 **let sb 'have it** (*informal*) to attack sb physically or with words 打，揍，用言語攻擊（某人） **let it 'go (at 'that)** to say or do no more about sth 不再多說（或多做）；就到此為止：*I don't entirely agree, but I'll let it go at that.* 我不完全同意，但也就這樣吧。◇ *I thought she was hinting at something, but I let it go.* 我想她在暗示什麼，然而我也沒有再多問。 **,let me 'see/'think** 🔑 used when you are thinking or trying to remember sth 讓我想一想；讓我思考一下：*Now let me see—where did he say he lived?* 嗯，讓我想想，他說他住在哪裏呢？ **let us 'say** used when making a suggestion or giving an example（提議或舉例時）譬如說，比方說，例如：*I can let you have it for, well let's say £100.* 我可以把這東西賣給你，嗯，比如說給我 100 英鎊吧。

PHR V **,let sb↔down** 🔑 to fail to help or support sb as they had hoped or expected 不能幫助，不能支持（某人）；使失望：*I'm afraid she let us down badly.* 很遺憾，她讓我們大失所望。◇ *This machine won't let you down.* 你儘管放心，這台機器不會出毛病。◇ *He trudged home feeling lonely and let down.* 他步履艱難地往家走，感到孤獨而沮喪。 ➲ related noun LET-DOWN **,let sb/sth↔'down** to make sb/sth less successful than they/it should be（使）略遜一籌，美中不足：*She speaks French very fluently, but her pronunciation lets her down.* 她法語講得很流利，但美中不足的是發音不大好。 **,let sth↔'down 1** to let or make sth go down 放下；降低；降下：*We let the bucket down by a rope.* 我們用繩子把吊桶放下去。 **2** to make a dress, skirt, coat, etc. longer, by reducing the amount of material that is folded over at the bottom（把連衣裙、裙子、外套等）放長；放出（褶邊） **OPP** **take up 3** (*BrE*) to allow the air to escape from sth deliberately（故意地）放氣：*Some kids had let my tyres down.* 幾個小孩子故意把我的輪胎放了氣。 **,let sb/yourself 'in for sth** (*informal*) to involve sb/yourself in sth that is likely to be unpleasant or difficult 使陷入；使捲入；牽涉：*I volunteered to help, and then I thought 'Oh no, what have I let myself in for!'* 我自告奮勇要幫忙，然後又一想："啊，不好，我幹嗎把自己捲進去呢！" **,let sb 'in on sth | ,let sb 'into sth** (*informal*) to allow sb to share a secret 告知，透露（秘密）：*Are you going to let them in on your plans?* 你是不是打算讓他們知道你的計劃呀？ **,let sth 'into sth** to put sth into the surface of sth so that it does not stick out from it 把…置入，把…嵌進（某物的表層）：*a window let into a wall* 嵌進牆壁的窗戶 **,let sb 'off (with sth)** 🔑 to not punish sb for sth they have done wrong, or to give them only a light punishment 不懲罰；放過；寬恕；從輕處罰：*They let us off lightly.* 他們對我們從輕發落了。◇ *She was let off with a warning.* 她沒被處罰，只是受了個警告。 **,let sb 'off sth** (*BrE*) to allow sb not to do sth or not to go somewhere 允許（某人）不做；准許（某人）不去（某

L

處）：*He let us off homework today.* 他今天免了我們的家庭作業。**ˌlet sth ˈoff** to fire a gun or make a bomb, etc. explode 放（槍等）；使爆炸：*The boys were letting off fireworks.* 那些男孩在放花炮。**ˌlet ˈon (to sb)** (*informal*) to tell a secret（對某人）說出秘密，泄密：*I'm getting married next week, but please don't let on to anyone.* 我下週就要結婚了，但這事請對誰都不要說。◇ **~ that ...** *She let on that she was leaving.* 她透露說她要離開。**ˌlet ˈout** (*NAmE*) (of school classes, films/movies, meetings, etc. 課堂、電影、會議等) to come to an end, so that it is time for people to leave 結束；下課；散場；散會：*The movie has just let out.* 電影剛剛散場。**ˌlet sb ˈout** to make sb stop feeling that they are involved in sth or have to do sth 使某人解脫：*They think the attacker was very tall—so that lets you out.* 他們認為歹徒是個高個子，這樣就沒你什麼事兒了。➲ related noun LET-OUT **ˌlet sth ˈout 1** to give a cry, etc. 發出（叫聲等）：*to let out a scream of terror* 發出恐怖的尖叫 ◇ *to let out a gasp of delight* 滿意地鬆一口氣 OPP **hold in 2** to make a shirt, coat, etc. looser or larger（把襯衣、外套等）放大，放長，加寬 OPP **take in** **ˌlet ˈup** (*informal*) **1** to become less strong 減弱；減輕：*The pain finally let up.* 疼痛終於減輕了。**2** to make less effort 放鬆（努力）；鬆勁：*We mustn't let up now.* 我們現在決不能放鬆。➲ related noun LET-UP

■ **noun**

▸ IN TENNIS 網球 **1** a SERVE that lands in the correct part of the COURT but must be taken again because it has touched the top of the net（發球時的）擦網球

▸ HOUSE/ROOM 房屋；房間 **2** (*BrE*) an act of renting a home, etc. 出租；租借：*a* **long-term/short-term** *let* 長期 / 短期出租

IDM **without ˌlet or ˈhindrance** (*formal* or *law* 律) without being prevented from doing sth; freely 毫無阻礙；順暢地；自由地

-let *suffix* (in nouns 構成名詞) small; not very important 小的；不很重要的：*booklet* 小冊子 ◇ *piglet* 豬崽 ◇ *starlet* 渴望嶄露頭角的年輕女演員

ˈlet-down *noun* [C, usually sing., U] (*informal*) something that is disappointing because it is not as good as you expected it to be 令人失望的事；失望；沮喪 SYN **disappointment, anticlimax**

le·thal /ˈliːθl/ *adj.* **1** causing or able to cause death 致命的；可致死的 SYN **deadly, fatal**：*a lethal dose of poison* 毒藥的致死劑量 ◇ *a lethal weapon* 致命的武器 ◇ (*figurative*) *The closure of the factory dealt a lethal blow to the town.* 那家工廠的關閉對這座城鎮是致命的打擊。**2** (*informal*) causing or able to cause a lot of harm or damage 危害極大的；破壞性極大的：*You and that car—it's a lethal combination!* 你和那輛車真是致命的組合！▸ **le·thal·ly** /ˈliːθəli/ *adv.*

leth·argy /ˈleθədʒi; *NAmE* ˈleθərdʒi/ *noun* [U] the state of not having any energy or enthusiasm for doing things 無精打采；沒有熱情；冷漠 SYN **listlessness, inertia** ▸ **leth·ar·gic** /ləˈθɑːdʒɪk; *NAmE* -ˈθɑːrdʒ-/ *adj.*：*The weather made her lethargic.* 那天氣使得她無精打采。

Lethe /ˈliːθi/ *noun* [U] (in ancient Greek stories 古希臘故事) an imaginary river whose water, when drunk, was thought to make the dead forget their life on Earth 勒忒，忘川（假想的河流，死者飲此河的水即忘記塵世一生）

ˈlet-out *noun* [sing.] (*BrE*) an event or a statement that allows sb to avoid having to do sth 逃脫的機會；漏洞：*Good—we have a let-out now.* 好！我們現在有機可乘。◇ *a let-out clause* (= in a contract) 不適用條款

let's /lets/ *short form* let us 讓我們：*Let's break for lunch.* 咱們停下來吃午飯吧。

let·ter 0‑ /ˈletə(r)/ *noun, verb*

■ **noun 1** 0‑ a message that is written down or printed on paper and usually put in an envelope and sent to sb 信；函：*a* **business/thank-you, etc. letter** 商業信函、感謝信等 ◇ *a* **letter of** *complaint* 投訴信 ◇ (*BrE*) *to* **post a letter** 寄信 ◇ (*NAmE*) *to* **mail a letter** 寄信 ◇ *There's a letter for you from your mother.* 有你母親的一封來信。◇ *You will be notified* **by letter**. 將用信函通知你。HELP You will find compounds ending in **letter** at their place in the alphabet. 以 letter 結尾的複合詞可在各字母中適當的位置查到。➲ WRITING TUTOR page WT37 **2** 0‑ a written or printed sign representing a sound used in speech 字母：*'B' is the second letter of the alphabet.* * b 是字母表的第二個字母。◇ *Write your name* **in capital/block letters**. 用大寫字母書寫姓名。**3** (*NAmE*) a sign in the shape of a letter that is sewn onto clothes to show that a person plays in a school or college sports team（縫製在運動服上的）校運動隊字母標誌

IDM **the ˌletter of the ˈlaw** (often *disapproving*) the exact words of a law or rule rather than its general meaning 法律（或法規）的準確字面意義：*They insist on sticking to the letter of the law.* 他們堅持嚴守法律的字面意義。**to the ˈletter** doing/following exactly what sb/sth says, paying attention to every detail 絲毫不差；不折不扣；精確地：*I followed your instructions to the letter.* 我是嚴格遵照你的指示辦的。

■ **verb 1** [T, usually passive] **~ sth (+ noun)** to give a letter to sth as part of a series or list 用字母標明（於清單等上）：*the stars lettered Alpha and Beta* 以 α 和 β 命名的星 **2** [T, usually passive] **~ sth (in sth)** to print, paint, sew, etc. letters onto sth 把字母印刷（或縫製等）於：*a black banner lettered in white* 印有白色字母的黑色橫幅 **3** [I] (*NAmE*) to receive a letter made of cloth that you sew onto your clothes for playing in a school or college sports team 領取到學校運動隊布製字母標誌

ˈletter bomb *noun* a small bomb that is sent to sb hidden in a letter that explodes when the envelope is opened 書信炸彈（匿藏在書信中，開封即爆炸）➲ see also PARCEL BOMB

letter boxes 郵箱；信箱

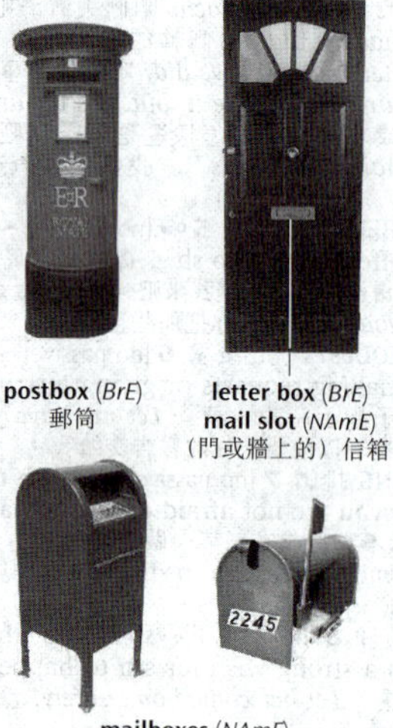

postbox (*BrE*) 郵筒

letter box (*BrE*) **mail slot** (*NAmE*)（門或牆上的）信箱

mailboxes (*NAmE*)（建築物大門口或路旁的）信箱

ˈletter box *noun* (*BrE*) **1** (*NAmE* **ˈmail slot**) a narrow opening in a door or wall through which mail is delivered（門或牆上的）信箱 ➲ VISUAL VOCAB page V17 **2** (*NAmE* **ˈmail·box**) a small box near the main door of a building or by the road, which mail is delivered to（建築物大門口或路旁的）信箱 **3** = POSTBOX ➲ compare PILLAR BOX

let·ter·box /ˈletəbɒks; *NAmE* ˈletərbɑːks/ *noun, verb*

■ **noun** [U] = WIDESCREEN

■ **verb ~ sth** to present a film/movie on television with the width a lot greater than the height, and with a black band at the top and bottom 寬銀幕模式播放：*a letterboxed edition* 寬銀幕模式的版本

ˈletter carrier *noun* (*NAmE*) = MAIL CARRIER

let·ter·head /ˈletəhed; *NAmE* -tərh-/ *noun* the name and address of a person, a company or an organization printed at the top of their writing paper 信頭（印於信箋上端的個人、公司或組織的名稱和地址）

let·ter·ing /ˈletərɪŋ/ *noun* [U] **1** letters or words that are written or printed in a particular style （用某種字體書寫或印刷的）字母，字： *Gothic lettering* 哥特體黑體字 **2** the process of writing, drawing or printing letters or words 寫字；描字；印字

ˌletter of ˈcredit *noun* (*pl.* **letters of credit**) (*finance* 財) a letter from a bank that allows you to get a particular amount of money from another bank 信用證；信用狀

ˈletter opener *noun* (*especially NAmE*) = PAPERKNIFE

ˌletter-ˈperfect *adj.* (*NAmE*) **1** correct in all details 準確無誤的；一字不差的；無訛的 **2** (*BrE* **ˌword-ˈperfect**) able to remember and repeat sth exactly without making any mistakes 能背得一字不差的；能背得滾瓜爛熟的

ˈletter-size (also **letter**) *adj.* (*NAmE*) (of paper 紙張) 8½ inches (215.9 mm) wide and 11 inches (279.4 mm) long 信紙尺寸的（寬 8½ 英寸或 215.9 毫米，長 11 英寸或 279.4 毫米）

let·ting /ˈletɪŋ/ *noun* (*BrE*) a period of time when you let a house or other property to sb else （房屋或其他財產的）出租期限： *holiday lettings* 假日出租

let·tuce /ˈletɪs/ *noun* [U, C] a plant with large green leaves that are eaten raw, especially in salad. There are many types of lettuce. 萵苣；生菜： *a bacon, lettuce and tomato sandwich* 鹹肉、生菜加番茄三明治 ◇ *Buy a lettuce and some tomatoes.* 買一個生菜和一些番茄。 ➲ VISUAL VOCAB page V31

ˈlet-up *noun* [U, sing.] **~ (in sth)** a period of time during which sth stops or becomes less strong, difficult, etc.; a reduction in the strength of sth（一段時間內的）停止，減弱，減少強度 SYN **lull**： *There is no sign of a let-up in the recession.* 經濟衰退沒有減弱的跡象。

leuco·cyte (also **leuko·cyte**) /ˈluːkəsaɪt; *BrE* also -kəʊs-/ *noun* (*biology* 生) = WHITE BLOOD CELL

leu·kae·mia (*BrE*) (*NAmE* **leu·ke·mia**) /luːˈkiːmiə/ *noun* [U] a serious disease in which too many white blood cells are produced, causing weakness and sometimes death 白血病

levee /ˈlevi/ *noun* (*NAmE*) **1** a low wall built at the side of a river to prevent it from flooding 防洪堤 **2** a place on a river where boats can let passengers on or off （河邊乘客上下船的）碼頭

level 🔑 /ˈlevl/ *noun, adj., verb*

■ ***noun***

▸ **AMOUNT** 數量 **1** 🔑 [C] the amount of sth that exists in a particular situation at a particular time （某時某情況下存在的）數量，程度，濃度： *a test that checks the level of alcohol in the blood* 對血液中酒精含量的測試 ◇ *a relatively **low/high level** of crime* 相對低的／高的罪案數字 ◇ ***low/high** pollution **levels*** 輕度／重度污染 ◇ *Profits were **at the same level** as the year before.* 利潤和前一年持平。

▸ **STANDARD** 標準 **2** 🔑 [C, U] a particular standard or quality 標準；水平；質量；品級： *a **high level** of achievement* 高水平的成就 ◇ *a computer game with 15 levels* * 15 級的電腦遊戲 ◇ *What is the level of this course?* 這門課程是什麼程度？ ◇ *He studied French to **degree level**.* 他的法語學到了拿學位的水平。 ◇ *Both players are **on a level*** (= of the same standard). 兩位選手的水平不相上下。 ◇ *I refuse to **sink to their level*** (= behave as badly as them). 我不願墮落到他們那種地步。 ➲ see also A LEVEL, ENTRY-LEVEL

▸ **RANK IN SCALE** 級別 **3** 🔑 [U, C] a position or rank in a scale of size or importance 層次；級別： *a decision taken at board level* 由董事會作出的決定 ◇ *Discussions are currently being held at national level.* 目前討論正在全國進行。

▸ **POINT OF VIEW** 觀察的角度 **4** 🔑 [C] a particular way of looking at, reacting to or understanding sth 看待（或應對、理解）事物的方式： *On a more personal level, I would like to thank Jean for all the help she has given me.* 從較為個人的角度我要感謝瓊所給予我的一切幫助。 ◇ *Fables can be understood on various levels.* 寓言可從不同的角度去理解。

▸ **HEIGHT** 高度 **5** 🔑 [C, U] the height of sth in relation to the ground or to what it used to be（與地面或過去位置相對的）高度： *the level of water in the bottle* 瓶中的水位 ◇ *The cables are buried one metre below **ground level**.* 電纜埋在地平面下一米深的地方。 ◇ *The floodwater nearly reached roof level.* 洪水幾乎漲到屋頂。 ◇ *The tables are not **on a level*** (= the same height). 這些桌子高矮不一。 ➲ see also EYE LEVEL, SEA LEVEL

▸ **FLOOR/LAYER** 樓層；層面 **6** 🔑 [C] a floor of a building; a layer of ground 樓層；地層： *The library is all on one level.* 圖書館全部在同一層樓上。 ◇ *Archaeologists found pottery in the lowest level of the site.* 考古學家在挖掘現場的最下層發現了陶器。 ◇ *a multi-level parking lot* 多層停車場 ➲ see also SPLIT-LEVEL

▸ **TOOL** 工具 **7** [C] = SPIRIT LEVEL

IDM **on the ˈlevel** (*NAmE* also **on the ˌup and ˈup**) (*informal*) honest; legal 誠實；誠懇；合法；正當 SYN **above board**： *I'm not convinced he's on the level.* 我不相信他是真誠的。 ◇ *Are you sure this deal is on the level?* 你確信這筆交易合法嗎？

■ ***adj.***

▸ **FLAT** 平坦 **1** 🔑 having a flat surface that does not slope 平的；平坦的： *Pitch the tent on level ground.* 把帳篷搭建在平地上。 ◇ *Add a **level tablespoon** of flour* (= enough to fill the spoon but not so much that it goes above the level of the edge of the spoon). 加一平匙麵粉。 ➲ compare HEAPED

▸ **EQUAL** 相等 **2** 🔑 having the same height, position, value, etc. as sth 等高的；地位相同的；價值相等的： *Are these pictures level?* 這些畫掛得一樣高嗎？ ◇ **~ with sth** *This latest rise is intended to keep wages level with inflation.* 最近這次加薪目的是使工資與通貨膨脹保持相同的水平。 ◇ *She **drew level with*** (= came beside) *the police car.* 她開車趕上來和警車並排行駛。 **3 ~ (with sb)** (*especially BrE, sport* 體) having the same score as sb 得分相同： *A good second round brought him level with the tournament leader.* 他第二輪發揮良好，與錦標賽領先選手得分持平。 ◇ *France took an early lead but Wales soon **drew level*** (= scored the same number of points). 法國隊開始領先，但很快就被威爾士隊把比分扳平。

▸ **VOICE/LOOK** 聲音；目光 **4** not showing any emotion; steady 平靜的；冷靜的；平穩的 SYN **even**： *a level gaze* 目光逼人的凝視 ➲ see also LEVELLY

IDM **be ˌlevel ˈpegging** (*BrE*) having the same score 勢均力敵；不分勝負： *The contestants were level pegging after round 3.* 參賽選手在第 3 輪以後成績不相上下。 **do/try your level ˈbest (to do sth)** to do as much as you can to try to achieve sth 盡自己最大的努力；竭盡全力；全力以赴 **a ˌlevel ˈplaying field** a situation in which everyone has the same opportunities 人人機會均等

■ ***verb*** (**-ll-**, *especially US* **-l-**)

▸ **MAKE FLAT** 使平坦 **1** [T] **~ sth (off/out)** to make sth flat or smooth 使平坦；使平整： *If you're laying tiles, the floor will need to be levelled first.* 你如果要鋪瓷磚，得先整平地面。

▸ **DESTROY** 摧毀 **2** [T] **~ sth** to destroy a building or a group of trees completely by knocking it down 摧毀，夷平（建築物或樹林） SYN **raze**： *The blast levelled several buildings in the area.* 那次爆炸把當地幾座建築物夷為平地。

▸ **MAKE EQUAL** 使相等 **3** [T, I] **~ (sth)** to make sth equal or similar 使相等；使平等；使相似： (*BrE*) *Davies levelled the score at 2 all.* 戴維斯把比分拉成 2:2 平。

▸ **POINT** 瞄準 **4** [T] **~ sth (at sb)** to point sth, especially a gun, at sb（尤指用槍）瞄準，對準： *I had a gun levelled at my head.* 有一支槍對準了我的頭。

IDM **ˌlevel the ˈplaying field** to create a situation where everyone has the same opportunities 創造人人機會均等的局面

PHR V **ˈlevel sth against/at sb** to say publicly that sb is to blame for sth, especially a crime or a mistake （尤指對犯罪或犯錯的人）公開指責，譴責： *The speech was intended to answer the charges levelled against him by his opponents.* 他演講的目的在於回應對手對他的公開指責。 **ˌlevel sth↔ˈdown** to make standards, amounts, etc. be of the same low or lower level 使（標準、數量等）降至同等水平；使降至更低水平： *Teachers are*

L

accused of levelling standards down to suit the needs of less able students. 有人指責教師降低標準以適應學習較差的學生的需要。**ˌlevel ˈoff/ˈout** **1** to stop rising or falling and remain horizontal（停止升降而）保持水平：*The plane levelled off at 1 500 feet.* 飛機在 1 500 英尺的高空保持水平飛行。◇ *After the long hill, the road levelled out.* 過了漫長的山路後，道路就變得平坦了。**2** to stay at a steady level of development or progress after a period of sharp rises or falls（經過急劇的漲落後）保持平穩發展：*Sales have levelled off after a period of rapid growth.* 銷售經過一段時間的快速增長後呈穩定狀態。**ˌlevel sth↔ˈup** to make standards, amounts, etc. be of the same high or higher level 把（標準、數量等）拉平；使達到更高水平 **ˈlevel with sb** (*informal*) to tell sb the truth and not hide any unpleasant facts from them 對某人說實話；直言相告

ˌlevel ˈcrossing (*BrE*) (*NAmE* **ˈrailroad crossing**) *noun* a place where a road crosses a railway/railroad line（公路與鐵路交匯的）道口，平面交叉

ˌlevel-ˈheaded *adj.* calm and sensible; able to make good decisions even in difficult situations 冷靜明智的；頭腦清醒的；（在困境中）能作出正確決策的

lev·el·ler (*especially US* **lev·el·er**) /ˈlevələ(r)/ *noun* [usually sing.] an event or a situation that makes everyone equal whatever their age, importance, etc. 使人人平等的事（或局面）：*death, the great leveller* 凡人皆要面對的死亡

lev·el·ly /ˈlevəli/ *adv.* in a calm and steady way 冷靜地；平靜地；穩定地：*She looked at him levelly.* 她平靜地看着他。

L

lever /ˈliːvə(r); *NAmE* ˈlevər/ *noun, verb*

■ ***noun*** **1** a handle used to operate a vehicle or piece of machinery（車輛或機器的）操縱桿，控制桿：*Pull the lever towards you to adjust the speed.* 把操縱桿往你身前拉動以調節速度。➲ see also GEAR LEVER **2** a long piece of wood, metal, etc. used for lifting or opening sth by sb placing one end of it under an object and pushing down on the other end 槓桿 **3 ~ (for/against sth)** an action that is used to put pressure on sb to do sth they do not want to do 施壓的行為：*The threat of sanctions is our most powerful lever for peace.* 實施制裁的威脅是我們爭取和平最有力的施壓手段。

■ ***verb*** to move sth with a lever（用槓桿）撬動 SYN **prise**：**~ sth + adv./prep.** *I levered the lid off the pot with a knife.* 我用刀撬掉了罐蓋。◇ **~ sth + adj.** *They managed to lever the door open.* 他們設法撬開了門。

le·ver·age /ˈliːvərɪdʒ; *NAmE* ˈlev-/ *noun, verb*

■ ***noun*** [U] **1** (*formal*) the ability to influence what people do 影響力：*diplomatic leverage* 外交影響力 **2** (*technical* 術語) the act of using a lever to open or lift sth; the force used to do this 槓桿作用；槓桿效力 **3** (*NAmE*) (*BrE* **gear·ing**) (*finance* 財) the relationship between the amount of money that a company owes and the value of its shares 資本與負債比率；聯動比率

■ ***verb*** **~ sth** (*business* 商) to get as much advantage or profit as possible from sth that you have 充分利用：*The company needs to leverage its resources.* 該公司需要充分利用其資源。

ˌleveraged ˈbuyout *noun* (*business* 商) (*especially NAmE*) the act of a small company buying a larger company using money that is borrowed based on the value of this larger company 槓桿式貸款收購，衡平收購（小公司以大公司的價值抵押貸款來收購這家大公司的方法）

lev·eret /ˈlevərət/ *noun* a young HARE 小野兔；野兔幼崽

le·via·than /ləˈvaɪəθən/ *noun* **1** (in the Bible) a very large sea MONSTER 里外雅堂，利章亞坦（《聖經》中的怪獸）**2** (*literary*) a very large and powerful thing 龐然大物：*the leviathan of government bureaucracy* 政府龐大的官僚機構

Levi's™ /ˈliːvaɪz/ *noun* [pl.] a US make of jeans (= trousers/pants made of DENIM)（美國）李維斯牛仔褲

levi·tate /ˈlevɪteɪt/ *verb* [I, T] **~ (sth)** to rise and float in the air with no physical support, especially by means of magic or by using special mental powers; to make sth rise in this way（尤指用魔力或特別的精神力量）升空，空中飄浮，使升空，使飄浮 ▸ **levi·ta·tion** /ˌlevɪˈteɪʃn/ *noun* [U]

lev·ity /ˈlevəti/ *noun* [U] (*formal*) behaviour that shows a lack of respect for sth serious and that treats it in an amusing way 輕率的舉止；輕浮；輕佻 SYN **frivolity**

levy AW /ˈlevi/ *noun, verb*

■ ***noun*** (*pl.* **-ies**) **~ (on sth)** an extra amount of money that has to be paid, especially as a tax to the government 徵收額；（尤指）稅款：*to* **put/impose a levy** *on oil imports* 對進口石油徵稅

■ ***verb*** (**lev·ies**, **levy·ing**, **lev·ied**, **lev·ied**) **~ sth (on sb/sth)** to use official authority to demand and collect a payment, tax, etc. 徵收；徵（稅）：*a tax levied by the government on excess company profits* 政府對公司超額利潤徵收的稅

lewd /luːd; *BrE* also ljuːd/ *adj.* referring to sex in a rude and offensive way 粗野下流的；淫蕩的；猥褻的 SYN **obscene**：*lewd behaviour/jokes/suggestions* 粗俗下流的行為／玩笑／暗示 ▸ **lewd·ly** *adv.* **lewd·ness** *noun* [U]

lex·eme /ˈleksiːm/ (also **ˌlexical ˈunit**) *noun* (*linguistics* 語言) a word or several words that have a meaning that is not expressed by any of its separate parts 詞位（最小的意義單位）

lex·ic·al /ˈleksɪkl/ *adj.* [usually before noun] (*linguistics* 語言) connected with the words of a language 詞彙的：***lexical items*** (= words and phrases) 詞項 ▸ **lex·ic·al·ly** /-kli/ *adv.*

ˈlexical meaning *noun* [U, C] the meaning of a word, without paying attention to the way that it is used or to the words that occur with it（不考慮用法或搭配的）詞彙意義，詞義

ˌlexical ˈunit *noun* = LEXEME

lexi·cog·raph·er /ˌleksɪˈkɒɡrəfə(r); *NAmE* -ˈkɑːɡ-/ *noun* a person who writes and EDITS dictionaries 詞典編纂者

lexi·cog·raphy /ˌleksɪˈkɒɡrəfi; *NAmE* -ˈkɑːɡ-/ *noun* [U] the theory and practice of writing dictionaries 詞典編纂學；詞典編纂

lexi·col·ogy /ˌleksɪˈkɒlədʒi; *NAmE* -ˈkɑːl-/ *noun* [U] the study of the form, meaning and behaviour of words 詞彙學

lexi·con /ˈleksɪkən; *NAmE* also -kɑːn/ *noun* **1** (also **the lexicon**) [sing.] (*linguistics* 語言) all the words and phrases used in a particular language or subject; all the words and phrases used and known by a particular person or group of people（某語言或學科、某人或群體使用的）全部詞彙：*the lexicon of finance and economics* 財經詞彙 **2** [C] a list of words on a particular subject or in a language in alphabetical order（某學科或語言的）詞彙表：*a lexicon of technical scientific terms* 科技術語詞彙表 **3** [C] a dictionary, especially one of an ancient language, such as Greek or Hebrew（尤指希臘語或希伯來語等古代語言的）詞典，字典

lexis /ˈleksɪs/ *noun* [U] (*linguistics* 語言) all the words and phrases of a particular language（某語言的）全部詞彙 SYN **vocabulary**

ley /leɪ/ *noun* **1** (also **ˈley line**) an imaginary line that is believed to follow the route of an ancient track and to have special powers（被認為是沿古代踪跡的路線並具有超常力量的）假想線 **2** (*technical* 術語) an area of land where grass is grown temporarily instead of crops 暫作草地的可耕地；輪作的草地

Ley·land cy·press /ˌleɪlənd ˈsaɪprəs/ (also **ley·landii** /leɪˈlændiaɪ/) *noun* a tree (a type of CONIFER) that grows very quickly, often used to divide gardens 萊蘭柏（生長迅速，常用以分隔花園）

lezzy (also **lezzie**) /ˈlezi/ *noun* (*pl.* **lez·zies**) *adj.* (*informal, especially BrE*) = LESBIAN

l.h. *abbr.* (in writing) LEFT HAND（書寫形式）左手

li·abil·ity /ˌlaɪəˈbɪləti/ *noun* (*pl.* **-ies**) **1** [U] **~ (for sth)** | **~ (to do sth)** the state of being legally responsible for sth（法律上對某事物的）責任，義務：*The company cannot accept liability for any damage caused by natural disasters.* 該公司對自然災害造成的任何損失概不承擔責任。**2** [C, usually sing.] (*informal*) a person or thing that causes you a lot of problems 惹麻煩的人（或事）：

Since his injury, Jones has become more of a liability than an asset to the team. 瓊斯負傷以來，與其說他是全隊的骨幹倒不如說他已成為隊裏的累贅。 **3** [C, usually pl.] the amount of money that a person or company owes 欠債；負債；債務： *The company is reported to have liabilities of nearly $90 000.* 據説公司負債近 9 萬元。 ➲ compare ASSET (2)

li·able /ˈlaɪəbl/ *adj.* [not before noun] **1 ~ (for sth)** legally responsible for paying the cost of sth （法律上）負有償付責任： *You will be liable for any damage caused.* 你必須對造成的任何損失負賠償責任。◇ *The court ruled he could not be held personally liable for his wife's debts.* 法庭裁定他個人不負有償付妻子債務的責任。 **2 ~ to do sth** likely to do sth 可能（做某事）： *We're all liable to make mistakes when we're tired.* 人在疲勞時都可能出差錯。◇ *The bridge is liable to collapse at any moment.* 那座橋可能隨時坍塌下來。 **3 ~ to sth** likely to be affected by sth 可能受…影響 **SYN** **prone**： *You are more liable to injury if you exercise infrequently.* 不經常運動就更容易受傷。 **4 ~ to sth** likely to be punished by law for sth 可能受法律懲處： *Offenders are liable to fines of up to $500.* 違者可能被處以最多 500 元的罰款。 **5 ~ for/to sth | ~ to do sth** having to do sth by law 必須按法律做（某事）；負有…責任： *People who earn under a certain amount are not liable to pay tax.* 收入低於一定數額者不必納税。

li·aise /liˈeɪz/ *verb* **1** [I] **~ (with sb)** (*especially BrE*) to work closely with sb and exchange information with them（與某人）聯絡，聯繫： *He had to liaise directly with the police while writing the report.* 寫報告的時候他不得不直接與警方取得聯繫。 **2** [I] **~ (between A and B)** to act as a link between two or more people or groups 做聯繫人；擔當聯絡員： *Her job is to liaise between students and teachers.* 她的工作是做師生間的聯繫人。

li·aison /liˈeɪzn; *NAmE* liˈeɪzɑːn; ˈliəzɑːn/ *noun* **1** [U, sing.] **~ (between A and B)** a relationship between two organizations or different departments in an organization, involving the exchange of information or ideas 聯絡；聯繫： *Our role is to ensure liaison between schools and parents.* 我們的職責是確保學校與家長間的聯繫。◇ *We work* ***in close liaison with*** *the police.* 我們與警方密切配合。 **2** [C] **~ (to/with sb/sth)** a person whose job is to make sure there is a good relationship between two groups or organizations 聯絡員；聯繫人： *the White House liaison to organized labor* 白宮與工會的聯絡人 **3** [C] **~ (with sb)** a secret sexual relationship, especially if one or both partners are married（尤指一方或雙方已婚的）私通，通姦 **SYN** **affair**

li'aison officer *noun* a person whose job is to make sure that there is a good relationship between two groups of people, organizations, etc. 聯絡人 ➲ see also LIAISON (2)

liar /ˈlaɪə(r)/ *noun* a person who tells lies 説謊者；撒謊者

lib /lɪb/ *noun* (*informal*) the abbreviation for 'liberation' (used in the names of organizations demanding greater freedom, equal rights, etc.) 解放（全寫為 liberation，用於組織名稱）： *women's lib* 婦女解放運動

li·ba·tion /laɪˈbeɪʃn/ *noun* (*formal*) (in the past) a gift of wine to a god（舊時供奉神的）奠酒，祭酒

Lib Dem /ˌlɪb ˈdem/ *abbr.* (in British Politics 英國政治) LIBERAL DEMOCRAT 自由民主黨（成員）： *I voted Lib Dem.* 我投了自由民主黨的票。

libel /ˈlaɪbl/ *noun, verb*

■ ***noun*** [U, C] the act of printing a statement about sb that is not true and that gives people a bad opinion of them（文字）誹謗，中傷： *He sued the newspaper for libel.* 他控告那家報社犯有誹謗罪。◇ *a libel action* (= a case in a court of law) 誹謗訴訟 ➲ compare SLANDER

■ ***verb*** (-ll-, *especially US* -l-) **~ sb** to publish a written statement about sb that is not true 發表文字誹謗（某人）： *He claimed he had been libelled in an article the magazine had published.* 他聲稱他遭到了那家雜誌發表的一篇文章的誹謗。 ➲ compare SLANDER

li·bel·lous (*especially US* **li·bel·ous**) /ˈlaɪbələs/ *adj.* containing a LIBEL about sb 含有誹謗性文字的： *a libellous statement* 誹謗性的聲明

lib·eral **AW** /ˈlɪbərəl/ *adj., noun*

■ ***adj.***

▸ **RESPECTING OTHER OPINIONS** 尊重他人意見 **1** willing to understand and respect other people's behaviour, opinions, etc., especially when they are different from your own; believing people should be able to choose how they behave 寬宏大度的；心胸寬闊的；開明的： *liberal attitudes/views/opinions* 開明的態度 / 觀點 / 意見

▸ **POLITICS** 政治 **2** wanting or allowing a lot of political and economic freedom and supporting gradual social, political or religious change（政治經濟上）自由的，開明的；支持（社會、政治或宗教）變革的： *Some politicians want more liberal trade relations with Europe.* 有些政治家想與歐洲大陸建立更加自由的貿易關係。◇ *liberal democracy* 自由民主◇ *liberal theories* 自由主義的理論◇ *a liberal politician* 支持改革的政治家 **3 Liberal** connected with the British Liberal Party in the past, or of a Liberal Party in another country（舊時）英國自由黨的；（英國以外國家）自由黨的

▸ **GENEROUS** 慷慨 **4 ~ (with sth)** generous; given in large amounts 慷慨的；大方的；大量給予的 **SYN** **lavish**： *She is very liberal with her money.* 她用錢很大方。◇ *I think Sam is too liberal with his criticism* (= he criticizes people too much). 我認為薩姆太愛批評人。

▸ **EDUCATION** 教育 **5** concerned with increasing sb's general knowledge and experience rather than particular skills 通識（教育）的： *a liberal education* 通識教育

▸ **NOT EXACT** 不精確 **6** not completely accurate or exact 不完全準確的；不精確的；不嚴格的 **SYN** **free**： *a liberal translation of the text* 不拘泥於原文的翻譯◇ *a* ***liberal interpretation*** *of the law* 對法律的靈活解釋

▸ **lib·er·al·ly** **AW** /-rəli/ *adv.*： *Apply the cream liberally.* 抹上大量的奶油。◇ *The word 'original' is liberally interpreted in copyright law.* * original 一詞在版權法中解釋很靈活。

■ ***noun***

▸ **SB WHO RESPECTS OTHERS** 尊重他人者 **1** a person who understands and respects other people's opinions and behaviour, especially when they are different from their own 理解且尊重他人意見的人；寬容的人；開明的人

▸ **POLITICS** 政治 **2** a person who supports political, social and religious change 支持（社會、政治或宗教）變革的人： *Reform is popular with middle-class liberals.* 改革受到了中產階級支持變革者的普遍歡迎。 **3 Liberal** (*politics* 政) a member of the British Liberal Party in the past, or of a Liberal Party in another country（舊時）英國自由黨成員；（英國以外國家的）自由黨成員

ˌliberal ˈarts *noun* [pl.] (*especially NAmE*) subjects of study that develop students' general knowledge and ability to think, rather than their technical skills 文科

ˌLiberal ˈDemocrat *noun* (*abbr.* **Lib Dem**) a member or supporter of the Liberal Democrats 自由民主黨成員（或支持者）

the ˌLiberal ˈDemocrats *noun* [pl.] (*abbr.* **Lib Dems**) one of the main British political parties, in favour of some political and social change, but not extreme（英國）自由民主黨 ➲ compare CONSERVATIVE PARTY, LABOUR PARTY

lib·er·al·ism **AW** /ˈlɪbərəlɪzəm/ *noun* [U] liberal opinions and beliefs, especially in politics 自由主義

lib·er·al·ity /ˌlɪbəˈræləti/ *noun* [U] (*formal*) **1** respect for political, religious or moral views, even if you do not agree with them（對政治、宗教或道德觀點的）尊重，寬容，寬宏大度 **2** the quality of being generous 慷慨；大方

lib·er·al·ize (*BrE* also **-ise**) **AW** /ˈlɪbrəlaɪz/ *verb* **~ sth** to make sth such as a law or a political or religious system less strict 使自由化；放寬對…的限制 ▸ **lib·er·al·iza·tion, -isa·tion** **AW** /ˌlɪbrəlaɪˈzeɪʃn; *NAmE* -ləˈz-/ *noun* [U]

lib·er·ate **AW** /ˈlɪbəreɪt/ *verb* **1 ~ sb/sth (from sb/sth)** to free a country or a person from the control of sb else 解放：*The city was liberated by the advancing army.* 軍隊向前挺進，解放了那座城市。 **2 ~ sb (from sth)** to free sb

L

from sth that restricts their enjoyment of life 使自由；使擺脱約束（或限制）：*Writing poetry liberated her from the routine of everyday life.* 寫詩使她從日常生活的例行公事中解脱出來。▸ **lib·er·ation** AW /ˌlɪbəˈreɪʃn/ *noun* [U, sing.]：*a war of liberation* 解放戰爭 ◇ *liberation from poverty* 擺脱貧困 ◇ *women's liberation* 婦女解放運動 **lib·er·ator** AW *noun*

lib·er·ated AW /ˈlɪbəreɪtɪd/ *adj.* free from the restrictions of traditional ideas about social and sexual behaviour（社會及性行為）不受傳統思想束縛的，解放的，開放的

libe,ration theˈology *noun* [U] a Christian movement, developed mainly by Latin American Catholics, which deals with social justice and the problems of people who are poor, as well as with spiritual matters 解放神學（拉丁美洲天主教徒倡導社會正義，針對窮人以及神學問題）

lib·er·tar·ian /ˌlɪbəˈteəriən; *NAmE* -bərˈter-/ *noun* a person who strongly believes that people should have the freedom to do and think as they like 自由論者

lib·er·tine /ˈlɪbətiːn; *NAmE* -bərt-/ *noun* (*formal, disapproving*) a person, usually a man, who leads an immoral life and is interested in pleasure, especially sexual pleasure 放蕩的男人；放蕩不羈的人；浪蕩公子

lib·erty /ˈlɪbəti; *NAmE* -bərti/ *noun* (*pl.* **-ies**) **1** [U] freedom to live as you choose without too many restrictions from government or authority 自由（自己選擇生活方式而不受政府或權威限制）：*the fight for justice and liberty* 爭取正義和自由的鬥爭 **2** [U] the state of not being a prisoner or a SLAVE 自由（不受關押或奴役的狀態）：*He had to endure six months' loss of liberty.* 他得忍受六個月失去自由之苦。 **3** [C] the legal right and freedom to do sth 自由（做某事的合法權利及行動自由）：*The right to vote should be a liberty enjoyed by all.* 投票權應當是人人享有的合法權利。◇ *People fear that security cameras could infringe personal liberties.* 人們擔心保安攝像機會侵犯人身自由。➲ see also CIVIL LIBERTY **4** [sing.] an act or a statement that may offend or annoy sb, especially because it is done without permission or does not show respect 冒犯行為（或言語）；放肆；失禮：*He* ***took the liberty of*** *reading my files while I was away.* 他趁我不在時擅自看我的文件。◇ *They've got a liberty, not even sending me a reply.* 他們真無禮，連個答覆也不給我回。

IDM **at liberty** (*formal*) (of a prisoner or an animal 囚犯或動物) no longer in prison or in a CAGE 不再受監禁；自由 SYN **free** **at liberty to do sth** (*formal*) having the right or freedom to do sth 有權做…；有…自由 SYN **free**：*You are at liberty to say what you like.* 你盡可暢所欲言。 **take ˈliberties with sb/sth 1** to make important and unreasonable changes to sth, especially a book（尤指對書）任意竄改：*The movie takes considerable liberties with the novel that it is based on.* 影片對小説原著作了相當大的改動。 **2** (*old-fashioned*) to be too friendly with sb, especially in a sexual way 過分親昵；放肆；狎昵；調戲

li·bid·in·ous /lɪˈbɪdɪnəs/ *adj.* (*formal*) having or expressing strong sexual feelings 性慾強的；好色的；淫蕩的

li·bido /lɪˈbiːdəʊ; ˈlɪbɪdəʊ; *NAmE* -doʊ/ *noun* (*pl.* **-os**) [U, C, usually sing.] (*technical* 術語) sexual desire 性慾；性衝動：*loss of libido* 性慾的喪失

Libra /ˈliːbrə/ *noun* **1** [U] the 7th sign of the ZODIAC, the SCALES 黃道第七宮；天秤宮；天秤（星）座 **2** [C] a person born when the sun is in this sign, that is between 23 September and 22 October, approximately 屬天秤座的人（約出生於 9 月 23 日至 10 月 22 日）▸ **Li·bran** *noun, adj.*

li·brar·ian /laɪˈbreəriən; *NAmE* -ˈbrer-/ *noun* a person who is in charge of or works in a library 圖書館館長；圖書管理員 ▸ **li·brar·ian·ship** *noun* [U]：*a degree in librarianship* 圖書管理學學位

li·brary O‑w /ˈlaɪbrəri; ˈlaɪbri; *NAmE* -breri/ *noun* (*pl.* **-ies**) **1** O‑w a building in which collections of books, CDs, newspapers, etc. are kept for people to read, study or borrow 圖書館；藏書樓：***a public/reference/university, etc. library*** 公共圖書館、參考書閱覽室、大學圖書館等 ◇ ***a library book*** 圖書館藏書 ◇ ***a toy library*** (= for borrowing toys from) 玩具圖書館 **2** a room in a large house where most of the books are kept 圖書室；資料室 **3** (*formal*) a personal collection of books, CDs, etc.（書、激光唱片等的）個人收藏：*a new edition to add to your library* 可收藏的新版本 **4** a series of books, recordings, etc. produced by the same company and similar in appearance 系列叢書（或錄製的音像等）；文庫：*a library of children's classics* 兒童文學名著系列叢書

the ˌLibrary of ˈCongress *noun* [sing.] the US national library（美國）國會圖書館

li·bret·tist /lɪˈbretɪst/ *noun* a person who writes the words for an OPERA or a musical play（歌劇或音樂劇的）劇本作者，歌詞作者

li·bretto /lɪˈbretəʊ; *NAmE* -toʊ/ *noun* (*pl.* **-os** or **li·bretti** /-tiː/) (*music* 音) the words that are sung or spoken in an OPERA or a musical play（歌劇或音樂劇的）唱詞，歌詞

lice *pl.* of LOUSE

li·cence O‑w AW (*especially US* **li·cense**) /ˈlaɪsns/ *noun* **1** O‑w [C] an official document that shows that permission has been given to do, own or use sth 許可證；執照：*a driving licence* 駕駛執照 ◇ **~ (for sth)** *a licence for the software* 軟件許可證 ◇ *Is there a licence fee?* 要交許可證費嗎？◇ *James lost his licence for six months* (= had his licence taken away by the police as a punishment). 詹姆斯的執照被警方扣了六個月。◇ **~ (to do sth)** *You need a licence to fish in this river.* 你在這條河裏釣魚要有許可證。◇ *a licence holder* (= a person who has been given a licence) 許可證持有人 **2** [U, sing.] **~ (to do sth)** (*formal*) freedom to do or say whatever you want, often sth bad or unacceptable 放肆；放縱：*Lack of punishment seems to give youngsters licence to break the law.* 由於缺少懲罰，年輕人似乎便恣意違法。 **3** [U] (*formal*) freedom to behave in a way that is considered sexually immoral 放蕩；縱慾；淫亂

IDM **artistic/poetic ˈlicence** the freedom of artists or writers to change facts in order to make a story, painting, etc. more interesting or beautiful 藝術上自由發揮的權利；詩的破格 **a licence to print ˈmoney** (*disapproving*) used to describe a business which makes a lot of money with little effort 不費勁掙大錢；一本萬利；搖錢樹 **under ˈlicence** (of a product 產品) made with the permission of a company or an organization 獲得生產許可

li·cense O‑w AW /ˈlaɪsns/ *verb, noun*

■ ***verb*** O‑w (*BrE* also *less frequent* **li·cence**) to give sb official permission to do, own, or use sth 批准；許可：**~ sth** *The new drug has not yet been licensed in the US.* 這種新藥尚未在美國獲得許可。◇ (*BrE*) *licensing hours* (= the times when alcohol can be sold at a pub, etc.) 限定的售酒時間 ◇ **~ sb/sth to do sth** *They had licensed the firm to produce the drug.* 他們批准了那家公司生產這種藥物。

■ ***noun*** O‑w (*NAmE*) = LICENCE：*a driver's license* 駕駛執照 ◇ *a license for the software* 軟件許可證 ◇ *a license holder* (= a person who has been given a license) 許可證持有人

li·censed AW /ˈlaɪsnst/ *adj.* **1** (*BrE*) having official permission to sell alcoholic drinks 有售酒許可的；獲准售酒的：*a licensed restaurant* 有售酒許可的餐館 **2** that you have official permission to own 獲准擁有的：*Is that gun licensed?* 那支槍有持槍執照嗎？ **3** having official permission to do sth 得到正式許可的：*She is licensed to fly solo.* 她已獲准單飛。

ˌlicensed ˈvictualler *noun* = VICTUALLER

li·cen·see /ˌlaɪsənˈsiː/ *noun* **1** (*BrE*) a person who has a licence to sell alcoholic drinks 售酒執照持有者 **2** a person or company that has a licence to make sth or to use sth 特許製作（或使用）…的人（或公司）

ˈlicense number (*NAmE*) (*BrE* **regiˈstration number**, **regis·tra·tion**) *noun* the series of letters and numbers that are shown on a LICENSE PLATE at the front and back of a vehicle to identify it（車輛的）登記號碼，牌照號碼

ˈlicense plate (*NAmE*) (*BrE* **ˈnumber plate**) *noun* a metal or plastic plate on the front and back of a vehicle that shows its LICENSE NUMBER（車輛的）牌照，號碼牌

ˈlicensing laws *noun* [pl.] British laws that state where and when alcoholic drinks can be sold（英國的）售酒法

li·cen·ti·ate /laɪˈsenʃiət/ *noun* (*technical* 術語) a person with official permission to work in a particular profession 持職業執照者

li·cen·tious /laɪˈsenʃəs/ *adj.* (*formal, disapproving*) behaving in a way that is considered sexually immoral 放蕩的；淫蕩的；淫亂的 ▶ **li·cen·tious·ness** *noun* [U]

li·chee = LYCHEE

li·chen /ˈlaɪkən; ˈlɪtʃən/ *noun* [U, C] a very small grey or yellow plant that spreads over the surface of rocks, walls and trees and does not have any flowers 地衣 ➲ **VISUAL VOCAB** page V11 ➲ compare MOSS

lich·gate ➲ LYCHGATE

licit /ˈlɪsɪt/ *adj.* (*formal*) allowed or legal 准許的；合法的 **OPP** illicit ▶ **licit·ly** *adv.*

lick /lɪk/ *verb, noun*

■ *verb* **1** [T] to move your tongue over the surface of sth in order to eat it, make it wet or clean it 舔：**~ sth** *He licked his fingers.* 他舔了一下自己的手指。◇ *I'm tired of licking envelopes.* 我舔信封都舔煩了。◇ *The cat sat licking its paws.* 那隻貓坐着舔爪子。◇ **~ sth + adj.** *She licked the spoon clean.* 她把調羹舔得乾乾淨淨。 **2** [T] **~ sth + adv./prep.** to eat or drink sth by licking it 舔吃；舔着喝：*The cat licked up the milk.* 貓把牛奶舔光了。◇ *She licked the honey off the spoon.* 她舔光了調羹上的蜂蜜。 **3** [T, I] (of flames 火焰) to touch sth lightly 輕輕觸及（某物）：**~ sth** *Flames were soon licking the curtains.* 火焰很快就燒着了窗簾。◇ **~ at sth** *The flames were now licking at their feet.* 火焰現正在他們腳下蔓延。 **4** [T] **~ sb/sth** (*informal*) to easily defeat sb or deal with sth 輕鬆戰勝；輕易對付：*We thought we* **had** *them* **licked**. 我們以為已經輕易地把他們對付過去了。◇ *It was a tricky problem but I think we've licked it.* 這是一個棘手的問題，但我認為我們輕而易舉地把它解決了。

IDM **lick sb's ˈboots** (also *taboo, slang* **lick sb's ˈarse**) (*disapproving*) to show too much respect for sb in authority because you want to please them 阿諛奉承；諂媚；拍馬屁 **SYN** **crawl** **lick your ˈwounds** to spend time trying to get your strength or confidence back after a defeat or disappointment（失敗或失望後）恢復元氣，重整旗鼓 ➲ more at LIP, SHAPE *n.*

■ *noun* **1** [C] an act of licking sth with the tongue 舔：*Can I have a lick of your ice cream?* 我能嚐一口你的冰淇淋嗎？ **2** [sing.] **a ~ of paint** (*informal*) a small amount of paint, used to make a place look better 一點兒（塗料）：*What this room needs is a lick of paint.* 這房間所需要的是刷點兒塗料。 **3** [C] (*informal*) a short piece of music which is part of a song and is played on a GUITAR（用吉他演奏的）小過門：*a* **guitar/blues lick** 用吉他演奏的／布魯斯樂的小過門

IDM **a lick and a ˈpromise** (*informal*) the act of performing a task quickly and carelessly, especially of washing or cleaning sth quickly 草草了事，敷衍塞責（尤指快速地洗刷東西） **at a (fair) ˈlick** (*informal*) fast; at a high speed 迅速；高速地

lickety-split /ˌlɪkəti ˈsplɪt/ *adv.* (*NAmE, old-fashioned, informal*) very quickly; immediately 急速地；立即

lick·ing /ˈlɪkɪŋ/ *noun* [sing.] (*informal*) a severe defeat in a battle, game, etc.（在戰爭、比賽等中的）慘敗，一敗塗地 **SYN** **thrashing**

lick·spit·tle /ˈlɪkspɪtl/ *noun* (*old-fashioned, disapproving*) a person who tries to gain the approval of an important person 諂媚者；阿諛奉承者

lic·orice *noun* [U] (*especially NAmE*) = LIQUORICE

lid 0-π /lɪd/ *noun*

1 0-π a cover over a container that can be removed or opened by turning it or lifting it（容器的）蓋，蓋子：*a dustbin lid* 垃圾箱蓋 ◇ *I can't get the lid off this jar.* 我打不開這廣口瓶的蓋子。 ➲ **VISUAL VOCAB** pages V22, V27, V33, V36 **2** = EYELID

IDM **keep a/the ˈlid on sth** **1** to keep sth secret or hidden 保守秘密；守口如瓶；遮掩；隱瞞 **2** to keep sth under control 把…控制住；抑制住：*The government is keeping the lid on inflation.* 政府正在控制通貨膨脹。 **lift the ˈlid on sth | take/blow the ˈlid off sth** to tell people unpleasant or shocking facts about sth 揭露…的真相：*Her article lifts the lid on child prostitution.* 她的文章揭露了兒童賣淫的醜聞。 **put the (tin) ˈlid on sth/things** (*BrE, informal*) to be the final act or event that spoils your plans or hopes 對…是最後的一擊；最後使計劃（或希望）落空 ➲ more at FLIP *v.*

Synonyms 同義詞辨析

lid

top • cork • cap • plug

These are all words for a cover for a container. 以上各詞均指容器的蓋、蓋子。

lid a cover over a container that can be removed or opened by turning or lifting it 指容器的蓋、蓋子：*a jar with a tight-fitting lid* 蓋子很緊的廣口瓶

top a thing that you put over the end of sth such as a pen or bottle in order to close it 指筆帽、瓶蓋、瓶塞

cork a small round object made of cork or plastic that is used for closing bottles, especially wine bottles 指尤用於酒瓶的軟木塞、塑料瓶塞

cap (often in compounds) a top for a pen or a protective cover for sth such as the lens of a camera（常構成複合詞）指鋼筆、照相機鏡頭等的蓋、帽

plug a round piece of material that you put into a hole in order to block it; a flat round rubber or plastic thing that you put into the hole of a sink in order to stop the water from flowing out 指栓塞、堵塞物、水池的塞子：*a bath plug* 浴缸塞子

PATTERNS

- a **tight-fitting** lid/top/cap
- a **screw** top/cap
- a **pen** lid/top
- to **put on/screw on/take off/unscrew** the lid/top/cap
- to **pull out** the cork/plug

lid·ded /ˈlɪdɪd/ *adj.* [usually before noun] **1** (of containers 容器) having a lid 有蓋的 **2** (*literary*) used to describe a person's expression when their EYELIDS appear large or their eyes are almost closed 眼瞼低垂的；瞇縫着眼的：*heavily-lidded eyes* 耷拉着眼皮的眼睛 ◇ *his lidded gaze* 他瞇縫着眼凝視

lido /ˈliːdəʊ; *NAmE* -doʊ/ *noun* (*pl.* **-os**) (*BrE*) a public outdoor swimming pool or part of a beach used by the public for swimming, water sports, etc. 公共露天游泳池；海濱浴場；海濱水上運動場

lido·caine /ˈlɪdəkeɪn; *BrE* also -dəʊk-/ (also **lig·no·caine**) *noun* [U] a substance used as a LOCAL ANAESTHETIC, for example to stop people feeling pain when teeth are removed 利多卡因（局部麻醉藥）

lie[1] 0-π /laɪ/ *verb, noun* ➲ see also LIE[2]

■ *verb* (**lies, lying, lay** /leɪ/, **lain** /leɪn/) **1** 0-π [I] (of a person or an animal 人或動物) to be or put yourself in a flat or horizontal position so that you are not standing or sitting 躺；平躺；平臥：**+ adv./prep.** *to* **lie on your back/side/front** 仰臥；側臥；俯臥 ◇ **+ adj.** *The cat was lying fast asleep by the fire.* 貓臥在爐火旁睡得很熟。 **2** 0-π [I] (of a thing 物品) to be or remain in a flat position on a surface 平放：**+ adv./prep.** *Clothes were lying all over the floor.* 地板上到處都堆放着衣服。◇ **+ adj.** *The book lay open on his desk.* 那本書攤開放在他的書桌上。 **3** 0-π [I] to be, remain or be kept in a particular state 處於，保留，保持（某種狀態）：**+ adj.** *Snow was lying thick on the ground.* 厚厚的積雪覆蓋着大地。◇ *These machines have lain idle since the factory closed.* 工廠關閉以來，這些機器就一直閒置着。◇ **+ adv./prep.** *a ship lying at anchor* 錨泊的船 ◇ *I'd rather use my money than leave it lying in the bank.* 我寧願把錢花掉也不願擱在銀行

L

裏不用。**4** [I] **+ adv./prep.** (of a town, natural feature, etc. 城鎮、自然特徵等) to be located in a particular place 位於；坐落在：*The town lies on the coast.* 這個小鎮位於海濱。 **5** [I] **+ adv./prep.** to be spread out in a particular place 伸展；鋪展；展開：*The valley lay below us.* 峽谷展現在我們的腳下。 **6** [I] **~ (in sth)** (of ideas, qualities, problems, etc. 思想、特徵、問題等) to exist or be found 存在；在於：*The problem lies in deciding when to intervene.* 問題在於決定何時介入。 **7** [I] (*BrE*) to be in a particular position during a competition（比賽時）名列，排名：**+ adv./prep.** *Thompson is lying in fourth place.* 湯姆森名列第四。◇ **+ adj.** *After five games the German team are lying second.* 經過五場比賽後，德國隊排名第二。 ➲ compare LAY

IDM **lie a'head/in 'store** to be going to happen to sb in the future 將來要發生：*You are young and your whole life lies ahead of you.* 你年紀輕，今後的日子還長着呢。 **lie in 'state** (of the dead body of an important person 重要人物的遺體) to be placed on view in a public place before being buried（安葬前停放在公共場所）供人瞻仰 **lie in 'wait (for sb)** to hide, waiting to surprise, attack or catch sb 隱蔽待機以出其不意；伏擊；埋伏以待：*He was surrounded by reporters who had been lying in wait for him.* 他被暗中守候他的記者團團圍住。 **lie 'low** (*informal*) to try not to attract attention to yourself 盡量不引起注意；不露面；不露聲色 **take sth lying 'down** to accept an insult or offensive act without protesting or reacting 甘受屈辱；逆來順受 ➲ more at BED *n.*, BOTTOM *n.*, HEAVY *adv.*, LAND *n.*, SLEEP *v.*

PHR V **lie a'round** (*BrE* also **lie a'bout**) **1** to be left somewhere in an untidy or careless way, not put away in the correct place 到處亂放；亂擱：*Don't leave toys lying around—someone might trip over them.* 別弄得到處是玩具，說不定會絆倒誰。 **2** (of a person 人) to spend time doing nothing and being lazy 無所事事地混日子；懶散度日；遊手好閒 ➲ related noun LAYABOUT **,lie 'back** to do nothing except relax 悠閒；休息；放鬆：*You don't have to do anything—just lie back and enjoy the ride.* 你什麼事也不必做，只管悠閒享受這次旅程的樂趣吧。 **,lie be'hind sth** to be the real reason for sth, often hidden 是…的真實原因（或理由）：*What lay behind this strange outburst?* 這反常的情緒激動的真正原因是什麼？ **,lie 'down** to be or get into a flat position, especially in bed, in order to sleep or rest 躺下，平卧（尤指在牀上睡覺或休息）：*Go and lie down for a while.* 去躺一會兒吧。◇ *He lay down on the sofa and soon fell asleep.* 他在沙發上躺下，很快就睡着了。 ➲ related noun LIE-DOWN **,lie 'in** (*BrE*) (also **,sleep 'in** *NAmE, BrE*) to stay in bed after the time you usually get up 睡懶覺；起得晚：*It's a holiday tomorrow, so you can lie in.* 明天放假，你可以睡懶覺了。 ➲ related noun LIE-IN **'lie with sb (to do sth)** (*formal*) to be sb's duty or responsibility 是…的職責（或責任）：*It lies with you to accept or reject the proposals.* 接受或是拒絕這些建議由你決定。

■ ***noun***

IDM **the ,lie of the 'land** (*BrE*) (*NAmE* **the ,lay of the 'land**) **1** the way the land in an area is formed and what physical characteristics it has 地貌；地勢；地形 **2** the way a situation is now and how it is likely to develop 目前的形勢及發展趨勢：*Check out the lie of the land before you make a decision.* 要摸清情況後再作決定。

lie² /laɪ/ *verb, noun* ➲ see also LIE¹

■ ***verb*** (**lies, lying, lied, lied**) [I] to say or write sth that you know is not true 說謊；撒謊；編造謊言：*You could see from his face that he was lying.* 從他的表情你可以看出他在說謊。◇ **~ (to sb) (about sth)** *Don't lie to me!* 別對我撒謊！◇ *She lies about her age.* 她謊報自己的年齡。◇ *The camera cannot lie* (= give a false impression). 照相機不會作假。 ➲ see also LIAR

IDM **lie through your 'teeth** (*informal*) to say sth that is not true at all 滿口謊言；撒彌天大謊；睜着眼說瞎話：*The witness was clearly lying through his teeth.* 那證人分明是在睜着眼睛說瞎話。 **lie your way into/out of sth** to get yourself into or out of a situation by lying 由於撒謊而處於某種境地（或擺脫某種處境）

■ ***noun*** a statement made by sb knowing that it is not true 謊言；謊話：*to **tell a lie*** 說謊 ◇ *The whole story is nothing but **a pack of lies**.* 整個敘述只不過是一派謊言。◇ *a **barefaced lie*** (= a lie that is deliberate and shocking) 厚顏無恥的謊話 ➲ see also WHITE LIE

IDM **give the lie to sth** (*formal*) to show that sth is not true 證實…是虛假的；證明不實；揭穿謊言 **I tell a 'lie** (*BrE, informal*) used to say that sth you have just said is not true or correct（表示剛說的話不真實或不正確）我說錯了，我說的不對：*We first met in 2006, no, I tell a lie, it was 2007.* 我們第一次見面是在 2006 年，不，我說錯了，是 2007 年。 ➲ more at LIVE¹, TISSUE

Lieb·frau·milch /ˈliːbfraʊmɪlʃ; -mɪlk; -mɪltʃ/ *noun* [U, C] (from *German*) a type of German white wine（德國）萊茵白葡萄酒

lied /liːd/ *noun* (*pl.* **lieder** /ˈliːdə(r)/) (from *German*) a German song for one singer and piano 利德（鋼琴伴奏的德國獨唱歌曲）

'lie detector (also *technical* 術語) (also *formal* **poly·graph**) *noun* a piece of equipment that is used, for example by the police, to find out if sb is telling the truth 測謊器

,lie-'down *noun* [sing.] (*BrE, informal*) a short rest, especially on a bed（尤指在牀上）小睡，小憩

lief /liːf/ *adv.* (*old use*) willingly; happily 樂意地；情願地；高興地：*I would as lief kill myself as betray my master.* 我寧願自殺也不會出賣我的主人。

liege /liːdʒ/ (also **,liege 'lord**) *noun* (*old use*) a king or lord 君主；領主

,lie-'in *noun* (*BrE*) a time when you stay in bed longer than normal in the morning 睡懶覺

lien /ˈliːən/ *noun* [U] **~ (in/over sth)** (*law* 律) the right to keep sb's property until a debt is paid 扣押權，留置權（扣押某人財產直至其償清債務）

lieu /luː; *BrE* also ljuː/ *noun* (*formal*)

IDM **in lieu (of sth)** instead of 替代：*They took cash in lieu of the prize they had won.* 他們沒有領獎品而是領了現金。◇ *We work on Saturdays and have a day off in lieu during the week.* 我們每週星期六上班，用其他的日子補休一天。

Lieut. (also **Lt**) (both *BrE*) (*NAmE* **Lt.**) *abbr.* (in writing) LIEUTENANT（書寫形式）（陸軍）中尉，（海軍或空軍）上尉

lieu·ten·ant /lefˈtenənt; *NAmE* luːˈt-/ *noun* (*abbr.* **Lieut.**, **Lt**) **1** an officer of middle rank in the army, navy, or AIR FORCE（陸軍）中尉；（海軍或空軍）上尉：*Lieutenant Paul Fisher* 保羅 • 費希爾陸軍中尉 ➲ see also FLIGHT LIEUTENANT, SECOND LIEUTENANT, SUB LIEUTENANT **2** (in compounds 構成複合詞) an officer just below the rank mentioned 僅低於…官階的官員：*a lieutenant colonel* 中校 **3** (in the US) a police officer of fairly high rank（美國警隊中）較高級別的警官 **4** a person who helps sb who is above them in rank or who performs their duties when that person is unable to 副職官員；助理官員；代理官員

lieu,tenant 'colonel *noun* an officer of middle rank in the US army, US AIR FORCE or British army（美國）陸軍中校，空軍中校；（英國）陸軍中校

lieu,tenant com'mander *noun* an officer of middle rank in the navy 海軍少校

lieu,tenant 'general *noun* an officer of very high rank in the army 陸軍中將

Lieu,tenant-'Govern·or *noun* (in Canada) the representative of the CROWN (2) in a PROVINCE（加拿大）省督

life /laɪf/ *noun* (*pl.* **lives** /laɪvz/)

▸ **STATE OF LIVING 生存狀態** **1** [U] the ability to breathe, grow, reproduce, etc. which people, animals and plants have before they die and which objects do not have 生命：*life and death* 生與死 ◇ *The body was cold and showed **no signs of life**.* 那軀體冰涼，顯現不出有生命的跡象。◇ *My father died last year—I wish I could bring him **back to life**.* 去年我父親逝世了，我要是能使他復活該多好啊。◇ *In spring the countryside bursts into life.* 鄉村在春天生機盎然。 **2** [U, C] the state of being alive as a human; an individual person's existence 人命；性

命；人的存活：*The floods caused a massive* ***loss of life*** (= many people were killed). 洪水造成許多人喪生。◇ *He* ***risked his life*** *to save his daughter from the fire.* 他冒着生命危險從火中救出他的女兒。◇ *Hundreds of lives were threatened when the building collapsed.* 數百條性命在大樓垮塌時受到了威脅。◇ *The operation* ***saved her life.*** 手術挽救了她的生命。◇ *My grandfather* ***lost his life*** (= was killed) *in the war.* 我的祖父在戰爭中喪生。◇ *Several attempts have been made on the President's life* (= several people have tried to kill him). 已有數人試圖謀殺總統。

▸ **LIVING THINGS 生物 3** 🔑 [U] living things 生物；活物：***plant/animal life*** 植物；動物 ◇ ***marine/pond life*** 海洋 / 池塘生物 ◇ *Is there intelligent life on other planets?* 在其他星球上存在具有智力的生命嗎？

▸ **PERIOD OF TIME 時期 4** 🔑 [C, U] the period between sb's birth and their death; a part of this period 一生；終身；壽命；一生中的部份時間：*He's lived here* ***all his life.*** 他在這裏住了一輩子了。◇ *I've lived in England for most of my life.* 我大半生都住在英格蘭。◇ *to have a* ***long/short life*** 壽命長；壽命短 ◇ *He became very weak towards the end of his life.* 他臨終時很虛弱。◇ *Brenda took up tennis* ***late in life.*** 布倫達在晚年打起網球來了。◇ *He will spend* ***the rest of his life*** (= until he dies) *in a wheelchair.* 他將在輪椅上度過他的餘生。◇ *There's no such thing as a job* ***for life*** *any longer.* 不會再有像終身職位這樣的事了。◇ *She is a* ***life member*** *of the club.* 她是這個俱樂部的終身會員。◇ *in* ***early/adult life*** 幼 / 成年 ➲ see also CHANGE OF LIFE **5** 🔑 [C] (used with an adjective 與形容詞連用) a period of sb's life when they are in a particular situation or job （某情景或工作的）一段生活經歷：*She has been an accountant all her* ***working life.*** 她在整個職業生涯中一直是會計師。◇ *He met a lot of interesting people during his life as a student.* 他在學生時代接觸過許多有趣的人。◇ *They were very happy throughout their* ***married life.*** 他們婚後生活一直很幸福。**6** 🔑 [C] the period of time when sth exists or functions 存在期；（某物的）壽命；有效期：*The International Stock Exchange* ***started life as*** *a London coffee shop.* 國際證券交易所起初就是倫敦的一家咖啡館。◇ *They could see that the company had a limited life* (= it was going to close). 他們意識到公司的壽命不長了。◇ *In Italy the average life of a government is eleven months.* 意大利每屆政府的平均壽命是十一個月。➲ see also SHELF LIFE

▸ **PUNISHMENT 懲罰 7** [U] the punishment of being sent to prison for life; life IMPRISONMENT 無期徒刑；終身監禁：*The judge* ***gave him life.*** 法官判他無期徒刑。

▸ **EXPERIENCE/ACTIVITIES 經歷；活動 8** 🔑 [U] the experience and activities that are typical of all people's existences 生活經歷：*the worries of everyday life* 日常生活中的操心事 ◇ *He is young and has little* ***experience of life.*** 他年輕，不諳世故。◇ *Commuting is a part of* ***daily life*** *for many people.* 乘車上下班是許多人日常生活的一部份。◇ *Jill wants to travel and see life for herself.* 吉爾想出去旅行，親身體驗一下生活。◇ *We bought a dishwasher* ***to make life easier.*** 為使生活輕鬆些我們買了一台洗碗機。◇ *In London life can be hard.* 在倫敦生活可以是很艱苦的。◇ *In* ***real life*** (= when she met him) *he wasn't how she had imagined him at all.* 一見面才發現他完全不是她所想像的那樣。◇ *Life isn't like in the movies, you know.* 你知道，生活不像在電影裏那樣。**9** 🔑 [U, C] the activities and experiences that are typical of a particular way of living （某種方式的）生活：***country/city life*** 鄉村 / 城市生活 ◇ *She enjoyed political life.* 她喜愛政治生活。◇ ***family/married life*** 家庭 / 婚後生活 ◇ *How do you find life in Japan?* 你覺得日本的生活如何？**10** 🔑 [C] a person's experiences during their life; the activities that form a particular part of a person's life 個人生活；個人經歷；個人生活某一方面的活動：*He has had* ***a good life.*** 他一直過着優裕的生活。◇ ***a hard/an easy life*** 艱難 / 安逸舒適的生活 ◇ *My* ***day-to-day life*** *is not very exciting.* 我的日常生活很平淡。◇ ***a life of*** *luxury* 奢侈的生活 ◇ *Her* ***daily life*** *involved meeting lots of people.* 她在日常生活中要接觸很多人。◇ *Many of these children have led very* ***sheltered lives*** (= they have not had many different experiences). 這些兒童中很多人都是溫室裏的花朵。◇ *They emigrated to* ***start a new life*** *in Canada.* 他們移居加拿大，開始了新的生活。◇ *He doesn't like to talk about his* ***private life.*** 他不願談及他的私生活。◇ *She has a full* ***social life.*** 她的社交活動非常頻繁。◇ *articles about the* ***love lives*** *of the stars* 有關明星愛情生活的文章 ➲ see also SEX LIFE

▸ **ENERGY/EXCITEMENT 活力；興奮 11** 🔑 [U] the quality of being active and exciting 活力；生命力；生氣 **SYN vitality**：*This is a great holiday resort that is* ***full of life.*** 這裏生氣勃勃，是一個絕妙的度假勝地。

▸ **IN ART 藝術 12** [U] a living model or a real object or scene that people draw or paint （繪畫的）模特兒，實物，實景：*She had lessons in drawing from life.* 她學了實物寫生課程。◇ *a* ***life class*** (= one in which art students draw a naked man or woman) 人體寫生課 ➲ see also STILL LIFE

▸ **STORY OF LIFE 傳記 13** [C] a story of sb's life 生平事跡；傳記 **SYN biography**：*She wrote a life of Mozart.* 她寫了一部莫扎特的傳記。

▸ **IN CHILDREN'S GAMES 兒童遊戲 14** [C] one of a set number of chances before a player is out of a game （玩遊戲者出局前幾次機會中的）一次機會：*He's lost two lives, so he's only got one left.* 他失去了兩次機會，所以只剩下一次了。

IDM be sb's 'life be the most important person or thing to sb 對某人至關重要的人（或事）：*My children are my life.* 我這幾個孩子就是我的命根子。◇ *Writing is his life.* 寫作是他的生命。 **bring sb/sth to 'life** to make sb/sth more interesting or exciting 使更有趣；使更生動：*The new teacher really brought French to life for us.* 新來的老師給我們把法語教得生動活潑。◇ *Flowers can bring a dull room back to life.* 鮮花可使沉悶的房間恢復生氣。 **come to 'life 1** to become more interesting, exciting or full of activity 變得更有趣（或使人興奮）；變得活躍：*The match finally came to life in the second half.* 比賽在下半場終於精彩起來。 **2** to start to act or move as if alive （彷彿活着）開始動起來：*In my dream all my toys came to life.* 在我的夢裏，玩具都活過來了。 **for dear 'life | for your 'life** as hard or as fast as possible 盡最大努力；拚命；儘快：*She was holding on to the rope for dear life.* 她死命抓着那根繩子。◇ *Run for your life!* 快跑啊！ **for the 'life of you** (*informal*) however hard you try 無論怎樣努力：*I cannot for the life of me imagine why they want to leave.* 我怎麼也想像不出他們為什麼要走。 **frighten/scare the 'life out of sb** to frighten sb very much 把某人嚇得魂不附體；使魂飛魄散 **full of 'beans/'life** having a lot of energy 充滿活力；精力充沛；生氣勃勃 **get a 'life** (*informal*) used to tell sb to stop being boring and to do sth more interesting （讓人別再令人厭煩，要做更有趣的事）來點兒有意思的 **lay down your 'life (for sb/sth)** (*literary*) to die in order to save sb/sth （為…）犧牲生命，獻身 **SYN sacrifice yourself** **lead/live the life of 'Riley** (*old-fashioned*, often *disapproving*) to live an enjoyable and comfortable life with no problems or responsibilities 無憂無慮地生活；安逸地生活；舒適愉快地生活 **life after 'death** the possibility or belief that people continue to exist in some form after they die 死後再生 **the life and 'soul of the party, etc.** (*BrE*) the most amusing and interesting person at a party, etc. （聚會等場合）最活躍風趣的人 **life is 'cheap** (*disapproving*) used to say that there is a situation in which it is not thought to be important if people somewhere die or are treated badly 把他人生死視同兒戲；視人性命如草芥；人命不值錢 **(have) a life of its 'own** (of an object 物體) seeming to move or function by itself without a person touching or working it （具有）自身生命力，原動力 **life's too 'short** (*informal*) used to say that it is not worth wasting time doing sth that you dislike or that is not important 人生苦短；不可枉費此生 **make life 'difficult (for sb)** to cause problems for sb （給某人）惹麻煩，造成困難，出難題 **the 'man/'woman in your life** (*informal*) the man or woman that you are having a sexual or romantic relationship with 闖進你生活中的男人（或女人） **not on your 'life** (*informal*) used to refuse very firmly to do sth （斷然拒絕）決不會 **take sb's 'life** to kill sb 殺死（某人）；取某人的性命 **take your (own) 'life** to kill yourself 自殺 **take your life in your 'hands** to risk being killed 冒生命危險；豁出性命；把腦袋掖在褲腰帶上：*You take your*

L

life in your hands just crossing the road here. 你在這裏過馬路簡直是冒險玩命。 **that's 'life** (*informal*) used when you are disappointed about sth but know that you must accept it （表示失望但無可奈何）這就是生活，生活就是這樣 **where there's 'life (, there's 'hope)** (*saying*) in a bad situation you must not give up hope because there is always a chance that it will improve 活着（就有希望）；留得青山在（，不怕沒柴燒） ➲ more at BET *v.*, BREATH, BREATHE, DEPART, DOG *n.*, END *v.*, FACT, FEAR *n.*, FIGHT *v.*, KISS *n.*, LARGE *adj.*, LEASE *n.*, LIGHT *n.*, MATTER *n.*, MISERY, NINE, RISK *v.*, SAVE *v.*, SLICE *n.*, SPRING *v.*, STAFF *n.*, STORY, TIME *n.*, TRUE *adj.*, VARIETY, WALK *n.*, WAY *n.*

ˌlife-and-ˈdeath (also **ˌlife-or-ˈdeath**) *adj.* [only before noun] extremely serious, especially when there is a situation in which people might die 生死攸關的；關係重大的： *a life-and-death decision/struggle* 生死攸關的決定；生死存亡的鬥爭

ˈlife assurance *noun* [U] (*BrE*) = LIFE INSURANCE

life·belt /ˈlaɪfbelt/ *noun* **1** (*BrE*) a large ring made of material that floats well, that is used to rescue sb who has fallen into water, to prevent them from DROWNING 救生圈 **2** (*NAmE*) a special belt worn to help sb float in water （使人不下沉的）救生帶 ➲ see also LIFE JACKET, LIFE PRESERVER

life·blood /ˈlaɪfblʌd/ *noun* [U] **1 ~ (of sth)** the thing that keeps sth strong and healthy and is necessary for successful development （事物的）命脈；生命線；命根子：*Tourism is the lifeblood of the city.* 旅遊業是這座城市的命脈。 **2** (*literary*) a person's blood, when it is thought of as the thing that is necessary for life （人的）命脈；生命必需的血液

life·boat /ˈlaɪfbəʊt; *NAmE* -boʊt/ *noun* **1** a special boat that is sent out to rescue people who are in danger at sea （派往海上救助的）救生艇，救生船： ***a lifeboat crew/station*** 救生船全體船員／停泊港 ➲ **VISUAL VOCAB** page V54 **2** a small boat carried on a ship in order to save the people on board if the ship sinks （船上備用的）救生艇

life·buoy /ˈlaɪfbɔɪ; *NAmE* also -buːi/ *noun* a piece of material that floats well, used to rescue sb who has fallen into water, by keeping them above water 救生帶；救生圈；救生衣

ˈlife coach (also **coach**) *noun* a person who is employed by sb to give them advice about how to achieve the things they want in their life and work 人生教練，生涯顧問（受雇幫助他人實現人生和工作目標） ▸ **ˈlife coaching** (also **coaching**) *noun* [U]

ˈlife cycle *noun* **1** (*biology* 生) the series of forms into which a living thing changes as it develops 生命週期，生活週期（生物發展過程的系列變形）： *the life cycle of the butterfly* 蝴蝶的生活週期 **2** the period of time during which sth, for example a product, is developed and used 生命週期，壽命（產品等從開發到使用完畢的一段時間）

ˈlife-enhancing *adj.* making you feel happier and making life more enjoyable 增加生活樂趣的

ˈlife expectancy (also **ˌexpectation of ˈlife**) *noun* [U, C] the number of years that a person is likely to live; the length of time that sth is likely to exist or continue for 預期壽命；預計存在（或持續）的期限

Collocations 詞語搭配

The living world 生物界

Animals 動物

- animals **mate/breed/reproduce/feed (on sth)** 動物交配／繁育／繁殖／以…為食
- fish/amphibians **swim/spawn** (= lay eggs) 魚／兩棲動物游動／產卵
- birds **fly/migrate/nest/sing** 鳥飛翔／遷徙／築巢／啼叫
- insects **crawl/fly/bite/sting** 昆蟲爬／飛／咬／叮
- insects/bees/locusts **swarm** 昆蟲／蜜蜂／蝗蟲成群地飛來飛去
- bees **collect/gather** nectar/pollen 蜜蜂採蜜／花粉
- spiders **spin/weave** a web 蜘蛛結網／織網
- snakes/lizards **shed their skins** 蛇／蜥蜴蛻皮
- bears/hedgehogs/frogs **hibernate** 熊／刺猬／青蛙冬眠
- insect larvae **grow/develop/pupate** 昆蟲的幼蟲生長／發育／化蛹
- an egg/a chick/a larva **hatches** 卵孵化；小雞出殼；幼蟲孵出
- **attract/find/choose** a mate 吸引／找到／選擇配偶
- **produce/release** eggs/sperm 產卵；排卵；產生／釋放精子
- **lay/fertilize/incubate/hatch** eggs 產卵；使卵受精；孵卵
- **inhabit** a forest/a reef/the coast 棲居於森林／礁石／海岸
- **mark/enter/defend** (a) territory 標出／進入／保衛領地
- **stalk/hunt/capture/catch/kill** prey 悄悄接近／獵殺／捕獲／殺死獵物

Plants and fungi 植物和真菌

- trees/plants **grow/bloom/blossom/flower** 樹木／植物生長／開花
- a seed **germinates/sprouts** 種子發芽
- leaves/buds/roots/shoots **appear/develop/form** 葉子／花蕾／根莖／幼苗長出來／長大／成形
- flower buds **swell/open** 花蕾含苞欲放／綻放
- a fungus **grows/spreads/colonizes sth** 菌類生長／擴散／長滿…
- **pollinate/fertilize** a flower/plant 給花／植物授粉
- **produce/release/spread/disperse** pollen/seeds/spores 長出／傳播花粉／種子／孢子
- **produce/bear** fruit 結果
- **develop/grow/form** roots/shoots/leaves 長出根莖／嫩芽／葉子
- **provide/supply/absorb/extract/release** nutrients 提供／吸收／提取／釋放營養物
- **perform/increase/reduce** photosynthesis 進行／增加／減少光合作用

Bacteria and viruses 細菌和病毒

- bacteria/microbes/viruses **grow/spread/multiply** 細菌／微生物／病毒生長／擴散／繁殖
- bacteria/microbes **live/thrive** in/on sth 細菌／微生物在…中存活／大量生長
- bacteria/microbes/viruses **evolve/colonize sth/cause disease** 細菌／微生物／病毒進化／長滿…／引發疾病
- bacteria **break sth down/convert sth (into sth)** 細菌（將某物）分解／轉化（成某物）
- a virus **enters/invades** sth/the body 病毒進入／侵入某物／身體
- a virus **mutates/evolves/replicates (itself)** 病毒變異／演化／（自我）複製
- **be infected with/contaminated with/exposed to** a new strain of a virus/drug-resistant bacteria 感染上／接觸到一種新病毒／抗藥性細菌
- **contain/carry/harbour** (*especially US*) **harbor** bacteria/a virus 帶有細菌／病毒
- **kill/destroy/eliminate** harmful/deadly bacteria 殺滅有害的／致命的細菌

ˈlife force *noun* [U] **1** the force that gives sb/sth their strength or energy 生命力；活力：*He looked very ill—his life force seemed to have drained away.* 他看上去病得很厲害，他的生命力似乎枯竭了。 **2** the force that keeps all life in existence 生命氣息；生命的能量：*In Hindi philosophy the life force is known as prana.* 在印度哲學中生命氣息稱為 prana（息）。

ˈlife form *noun* (*technical* 術語) a living thing such as a plant or an animal 生物；活物

ˈlife-giving *adj.* [usually before noun] (*literary*) that gives life or keeps sth alive 賦予生命的；維持生命的

life·guard /ˈlaɪfɡɑːd; *NAmE* -ɡɑːrd/ (*AustralE, NZE* **life-saver**, **ˈsurf lifesaver**) *noun* a person who is employed at a beach or a swimming pool to rescue people who are in danger in the water（海灘或游泳池的）救生員

ˌlife ˈhistory *noun* all the events that happen in the life of a person, animal or plant 生平；（生物的）生活史

ˈlife insurance (*BrE* also **ˈlife assurance**) *noun* [U] a type of insurance in which you make regular payments so that you receive a sum of money when you are a particular age, or so that your family will receive a sum of money when you die 人壽保險：*a life insurance policy* 人壽保險單

ˈlife jacket (*NAmE* also **ˈlife vest**) *noun* a jacket without sleeves, that can be filled with air, designed to help you float if you fall in water 救生衣 ➲ VISUAL VOCAB page V55

life·less /ˈlaɪfləs/ *adj.* **1** (*formal*) dead or appearing to be dead 死的；像是死的 SYN **inanimate** **2** not living; not having living things growing on or in it 無生命的；無生物生長的：*lifeless machines* 無生命的機器 ◇ *a lifeless planet* 沒有生命存在的行星 **3** dull; lacking the qualities that make sth/sb interesting and full of life 枯燥的；單調的；缺乏生氣的 SYN **lacklustre**：*his lifeless performance on stage* 他在舞台上死氣沉沉的表演

life·like /ˈlaɪflaɪk/ *adj.* exactly like a real person or thing 逼真的；生動的；栩栩如生的 SYN **realistic**：*a lifelike statue/drawing/toy* 栩栩如生的雕塑／繪畫；逼真的玩具

life·line /ˈlaɪflaɪn/ *noun* **1** a line or rope thrown to rescue sb who is in difficulty in the water（水上救援的）救生索 **2** a line attached to sb who goes deep under the sea（深海潛水員的）信號繩 **3** something that is very important for sb and that they depend on 命脈；生命線：*The extra payments are a lifeline for most single mothers.* 額外補助對大多數單身母親來說都是賴以生存的生命線。

life·long /ˈlaɪflɒŋ; *NAmE* -lɔːŋ; -lɑːŋ/ *adj.* [only before noun] lasting or existing all through your life 終身的；畢生的

ˌlife-or-ˈdeath *adj.* = LIFE-AND-DEATH

ˌlife ˈpeer *noun* (in Britain) a person who is given the title of PEER (= 'Lord' or 'Lady') but who cannot pass it on to their son or daughter（英國爵位不能世襲的）終身貴族

ˈlife preserver *noun* (*NAmE*) a piece of material that floats well, or a jacket made of such material, used to rescue a person who has fallen into water, by keeping them above water 救生用具

lifer /ˈlaɪfə(r)/ *noun* (*informal*) a person who has been sent to prison for their whole life 終身囚犯；無期徒刑犯

ˈlife raft *noun* an open rubber boat filled with air, used for rescuing people from sinking ships or planes 充氣救生船；橡皮救生筏

life·saver /ˈlaɪfseɪvə(r)/ *noun* **1** a thing that helps sb in a difficult situation; sth that saves sb's life 救助物；救命物：*The new drug is a potential lifesaver.* 這種新藥有可能成為一種救命藥。 **2** (also **ˈsurf lifesaver**) (*AustralE, NZE*) = LIFEGUARD

ˈlife-saving *adj., noun*

■ ***adj.*** [usually before noun] that is going to save sb's life 救命的；救生的：*a life-saving heart operation* 挽救生命的心臟手術

■ ***noun*** [U] the skills needed to save sb who is in water and is DROWNING（對溺水者的）救生術：*a life-saving qualification* 救生資格

ˈlife sciences *noun* [pl.] the sciences concerned with studying humans, animals or plants 生命科學 ➲ compare EARTH SCIENCE, NATURAL SCIENCE, PHYSICAL SCIENCE

ˈlife sentence *noun* the punishment by which sb spends the rest of their life in prison 無期徒刑；終身監禁

ˈlife-size (also **ˈlife-sized**) *adj.* the same size as a person or thing really is 與真人（或實物）一樣大小的：*a life-size statue* 與真人一樣大的雕像

life·span /ˈlaɪfspæn/ *noun* the length of time that sth is likely to live, continue or function 壽命；可持續年限；有效期：*Worms have a lifespan of a few months.* 蠕蟲的壽命為幾個月。

ˈlife story *noun* the story that sb tells you about their whole life 生平事跡

life·style /ˈlaɪfstaɪl/ *noun* [C, U] the way in which a person or a group of people lives and works 生活方式；工作方式：*a* ***comfortable/healthy/lavish, etc. lifestyle*** 舒適、健康、揮霍無度等的生活方式 ◇ *It was a big change in lifestyle when we moved to the country.* 我們遷居到鄉下，這在生活方式上是個巨大的變化。 ◇ *the lifestyle section of the newspaper* (= the part which deals with clothes, furniture, hobbies, etc.) 報紙的生活欄目

ˌlife supˈport *noun* [U] the fact of sb being on a life-support machine（用機器設備）維持生命：*Families want the right to refuse life support.* 病人親屬要求有權拒絕使用機器維持生命。◇ *She's critically ill,* ***on life support***. 她病情危急，靠機器來維持生命。

ˌlife-supˈport machine (also **ˌlife-supˈport system**) *noun* a piece of equipment that keeps sb alive when they are extremely ill/sick and cannot breathe without help 生命維持設備；用以維持生命的機器：*He was put on a life-support machine in intensive care.* 在特護期間給他使用了生命維持設備。

ˌlife's ˈwork (*BrE*) (*NAmE* **life·work** /ˌlaɪfˈwɜːk; *NAmE* -ˈwɜːrk/) *noun* [sing.] the main purpose or activity in a person's life, or their greatest achievement 畢生的主要目的（或活動）；終生最大的成就

ˈlife-threaten·ing *adj.* that is likely to kill sb 可能致命的；威脅着生命的：*His heart condition is not life-threatening.* 他的心臟病不會危及生命。

life·time /ˈlaɪftaɪm/ *noun* the length of time that sb lives or that sth lasts 一生；終身；有生之年；（某物的）存在期，壽命，使用期限：*His diary was not published during his lifetime.* 他的日記在他生前未曾發表過。◇ *a lifetime of experience* 畢生的經驗 ◇ *in the lifetime of the present government* 在本屆政府的任期內

IDM **the chance, etc. of a ˈlifetime** a wonderful opportunity, etc. that you are not likely to get again 終身難得的機遇；千載難逢的機會 **once in a ˈlifetime** used to describe sth special that is not likely to happen to you again（可能）一生只有一次：*An opportunity like this comes once in a lifetime.* 像這樣的機會一生也許只會遇到一次。◇ *a once-in-a-lifetime experience* 一生只會擁有一次的經歷

ˈlife vest *noun* (*NAmE*) = LIFE JACKET

lift 🔑 /lɪft/ *verb, noun*

■ ***verb***

▸ RAISE 提升 **1** 🔑 [T, I] to raise sb/sth or be raised to a higher position or level（被）提起，舉起，抬高，吊起：**~ sb/sth (up) (+ adv./prep.)** *He stood there with his arms lifted above his head.* 他站在那裏，胳臂舉過了頭頂。◇ *I lifted the lid of the box and peered in.* 我掀起箱蓋往裏看。◇ (*figurative*) *John lifted his eyes* (= looked up) *from his book.* 約翰從書本上抬起眼睛。◇ **~ (up)** *Her eyebrows lifted. 'Apologize? Why?'* 她的眉毛豎了起來：“道歉？為什麼？”

▸ MOVE SB/STH 挪動某人／某物 **2** 🔑 [T] **~ sb/sth (+ adv./prep.)** to take hold of sb/sth and move them/it to a different position 移開；移動：*I lifted the baby out of the chair.* 我把嬰兒從椅子上抱起來。◇ *He lifted the suitcase down from the rack.* 他把手提箱從行李架上搬下來。 **3** [T] **~ sb/sth (+ adv./prep.)** to transport people or things by air 空運：*The survivors were lifted to safety* by *helicopter.* 幸存者由直升機運往安全的地方。➲ see also AIRLIFT

▸ **REMOVE LAW/RULE** 撤銷法律／規則 **4** 🔑 [T] **~ sth** to remove or end restrictions 解除，撤銷，停止（限制）：*to **lift a ban/curfew/blockade*** 解除禁令／宵禁／封鎖 ◇ *Martial law has now been lifted.* 戒嚴令現已解除。

▸ **HEART/SPIRITS** 心情；情緒 **5** [I, T] to become or make sb more cheerful 高興起來；使更愉快：*His heart lifted at the sight of her.* 他一看見她心裏就高興起來了。◇ **~ sth** *The news lifted our spirits.* 這消息使我們群情振奮。

▸ **OF MIST/CLOUDS** 霧；雲 **6** [I] to rise and disappear 消散；消失 **SYN** **disperse**：*The fog began to lift.* 霧開始散了。◇ (*figurative*) *Gradually my depression started to lift.* 我的沮喪情緒開始逐漸消失。

▸ **STEAL** 偷盜 **7** [T] **~ sth (from sb/sth)** (*informal*) to steal sth 偷盜；盜竊：*He had been lifting electrical goods from the store where he worked.* 他一直從他工作的商店裏偷竊電器商品。➲ see also SHOPLIFT at SHOPLIFTING

▸ **COPY IDEAS/WORDS** 剽竊觀點／言語 **8** [T] **~ sth (from sth)** to use sb's ideas or words without asking permission or without saying where they come from 剽竊；盜用；抄襲 **SYN** **plagiarize**：*She lifted most of the ideas from a book she had been reading.* 大部份觀點都是她從一直在看的一本書裏抄來的。

▸ **VEGETABLES** 蔬菜 **9** [T] **~ sth** to dig up vegetables or plants from the ground 挖出，刨出，拔起（蔬菜或植物）：*to lift potatoes* 刨土豆

▸ **INCREASE** 增加 **10** [T, I] **~ (sth)** to make the amount or level of sth greater; to become greater in amount or level 提高；增加；（使）增長：*Interest rates were lifted yesterday.* 昨天利率提高了。

IDM **not lift/raise a finger/hand (to do sth)** (*informal*) to do nothing to help sb 一點忙也不幫；油瓶倒了都不扶：*The children never lift a finger to help around the house.* 孩子們從不幫着做家務。

PHR V **,lift 'off** (of a ROCKET or, less frequently, an aircraft 火箭，有時也指飛行器) to leave the ground and rise into the air 發射；起飛；升空 ➲ related noun LIFT-OFF

■ ***noun***

▸ **MACHINE** 機器 **1** 🔑 (*BrE*) (*NAmE* **ele·va·tor**) [C] a machine that carries people or goods up and down to different levels in a building or a mine 電梯；升降機：*It's on the sixth floor—let's **take the lift**.* 在七樓，咱們乘電梯吧。➲ see also CHAIRLIFT, SKI LIFT

▸ **FREE RIDE** 免費搭車 **2** 🔑 (*BrE*) (*NAmE* **ride**) [C] a free ride in a car, etc. to a place you want to get to 免費搭車；搭便車：*I'll **give you a lift** to the station.* 我用車順便送你去車站。◇ *She **hitched a lift** on a truck.* 她免費搭乘了一輛卡車。

▸ **HAPPIER FEELING** 更好的心情 **3** [sing.] a feeling of being happier or more confident than before 較好的心情；更大的信心 **SYN** **boost**：*Passing the exam gave him a real lift.* 他通過了考試，情緒好多了。

▸ **RISING MOVEMENT** 上升運動 **4** [sing.] a movement in which sth rises or is lifted up 提；抬；舉；上升；吊：*the puzzled lift of his eyebrows* 他迷惑不解地皺起眉頭

▸ **ON AIRCRAFT** 飛行器 **5** [U] the upward pressure of air on an aircraft when flying（飛行時的）提升力，升力 ➲ compare DRAG *n.* (5)

'lift-off *noun* [C, U] the act of a SPACECRAFT leaving the ground and rising into the air（航天器的）發射，起飛，升空 **SYN** **blast-off**：*Ten minutes to lift-off.* 離發射還有十分鐘。

liga·ment /ˈlɪɡəmənt/ *noun* a strong band of TISSUE in the body that connects bones and supports organs and keeps them in position 韌帶：*I've torn a ligament.* 我的韌帶撕裂了。➲ **COLLOCATIONS** at INJURY

li·gate /lɪˈɡeɪt; *NAmE* laɪˈɡ-/ *verb* **~ sth** (*medical* 醫) to tie up an ARTERY or other BLOOD VESSEL or tube in the body, with a LIGATURE 結紮，綁紮（動脈或血管等）▸ **li·ga·tion** *noun* [U]

liga·ture /ˈlɪɡətʃə(r)/ *noun* (*technical* 術語) something that is used for tying sth very tightly, for example to stop the loss of blood from a wound（用於緊縛的）帶子，繩索，繃帶；（用於止血等的）結紮絲，縛線

lig·ger /ˈlɪɡə(r)/ *noun* (*BrE, informal*) a person who always takes the opportunity to go to a free party or event that is arranged by a company to advertise its products 免費廣告活動常客

Which Word? 詞語辨析

light / lighting

■ The noun **light** has several different meanings and is used in many phrases. **Lighting** can only be used to talk about the type of light in a place or how lights are used to achieve a particular effect. 名詞 light 有幾個不同的含義，可用於許多短語中。lighting 只用以指照明或照明技術：*the lighting system* 照明系統◇ *the movie's interesting lighting effects* 這部電影精彩的燈光效果◇ *The lighting at the disco was fantastic.* 迪斯科舞廳裏燈光奇幻。

light 🔑 /laɪt/ *noun, adj., verb, adv.*

■ ***noun***

▸ **FROM SUN/LAMPS** 太陽；燈 **1** 🔑 [U] the energy from the sun, a lamp, etc. that makes it possible to see things 光；光線；光亮：***bright/dim light*** 明亮／暗淡的光線 ◇ *a room with good **natural light*** 採光好的房間◇ *in the fading light of a summer's evening* 在夏天漸漸暗淡的暮色中◇ *The light was beginning to fail* (= it was beginning to get dark). 天色漸暗。◇ *She could just see **by the light** of the candle.* 她藉着燭光勉強能看見。◇ *Bring it **into the light** so I can see it.* 把它拿到亮的地方，好讓我看見。◇ *a **beam/ray of light*** 一束／一縷光線◇ *The knife gleamed as it **caught the light*** (= as the light shone on it). 刀子被光線一照閃閃發亮。➲ see also FIRST LIGHT **2** 🔑 [C] a particular type of light with its own colour and qualities（具有某種顏色和特性的）光：*A cold grey light crept under the curtains.* 一絲幽暗陰冷的光從窗簾下面透過來。➲ see also THE NORTHERN LIGHTS

▸ **LAMP** 燈 **3** 🔑 [C] a thing that produces light, especially an electric light 發光體；光源；（尤指）電燈：*to **turn/switch the lights on/off*** 開／關燈◇ *to **turn out the light(s)*** 把燈關掉◇ *Suddenly all the **lights went out**.* 突然間所有的燈都滅了。◇ *It was an hour before the **lights came on** again.* 一個小時後燈才再亮了。◇ *to **turn down/dim the lights*** 把燈光調暗◇ *A light was still burning in the bedroom.* 卧室裏依然亮着燈。◇ ***ceiling/wall lights*** 頂燈；壁燈◇ *Keep going—the lights* (= traffic lights) *are green.* 不用停車，是綠燈。◇ *Check your car before you drive to make sure that your lights are working.* 開車前要檢查一下，燈一定都要運作正常。➲ **VISUAL VOCAB** page V41 ➲ see also BRAKE LIGHT, GREEN LIGHT, HEADLIGHT, LEADING LIGHT, RED LIGHT

▸ **FOR CIGARETTE** 香煙 **4** 🔑 [sing.] a match or device with which you can light a cigarette 火柴；打火機；點火器：(*BrE*) *Have you got a light?* 你有火兒嗎？◇ (*NAmE, BrE*) *Do you have a light?* 你有火兒嗎？

▸ **EXPRESSION IN EYES** 眼神 **5** [sing.] an expression in sb's eyes which shows what they are thinking or feeling 眼神：*There was a soft light in her eyes as she looked at him.* 她望着他，眼神很温柔。

▸ **IN PICTURE** 圖畫 **6** [U] light colours in a picture, which contrast with darker ones（圖畫中和暗色對比的）亮色，淺色：*the artist's use of light and shade* 畫家對明暗對比手法的運用

▸ **WINDOW** 窗戶 **7** [C] (*architecture* 建) a window or an opening to allow light in 窗；窗戶；光線進口；採光孔：*leaded lights* 花飾鉛條窗 ➲ see also SKYLIGHT

IDM **according to sb's/sth's 'lights** (*formal*) according to the standards which sb sets for himself or herself 根據…的標準；在…看來 **be/go out like a 'light** (*informal*) to go to sleep very quickly 很快入睡 **be in sb's 'light** to be between sb and a source of light 擋住某人的光線：*Could you move—you're in my light.* 挪動一下好嗎？你擋住我的光線了。 **bring sth to 'light** to make new information known to people 揭露；披露；暴露；揭發：*These facts have only just been brought to light.* 這些事實剛剛才被披露出來。 **cast/shed/throw 'light on sth** to make a problem, etc. easier to understand 使（問題等）較容易理解：*Recent research has* *thrown new light on the causes of the disease.* 最近的研究可以使人進一步瞭解導致這種疾病的原因。 **come to ˈlight** to become known to people 為人所知；變得眾所周知；暴露： *New evidence has recently come to light.* 新的證據最近已披露出來。 **in ˌa good, bad, favourable, etc. ˈlight** if you see sth or put sth **in a good, bad, etc. light**, it seems good, bad, etc. 從好（或壞、有利等）的角度： *You must not view what happened in a negative light.* 你切切不要從負面的角度來看待所發生的事。◇ *They want to present their policies in the best possible light.* 他們想盡可能從好的方面來介紹他們的政策。 **in the light of sth** (*BrE*) (*NAmE* **in light of sth**) after considering sth 考慮到；鑒於：*He rewrote the book in the light of further research.* 他根據進一步的研究重寫了那部書。 **the lights are ˈon but nobody's ˈhome** (*saying, humorous*) used to describe sb who is stupid, not thinking clearly or not paying attention 稀裏糊塗；沒頭腦；心不在焉 **light at the end of the ˈtunnel** something that shows you are nearly at the end of a long and difficult time or situation 快要熬出頭了；曙光在即 **(the) light ˈdawned (on sb)** somebody suddenly understood or began to understand sth 豁然開朗；恍然大悟： *I puzzled over the problem for ages before the light suddenly dawned.* 我對這個問題冥思苦想了很久才豁然開朗。 **the light of sb's ˈlife** the person sb loves more than any other 心愛的人；心肝寶貝 **run a (red) ˈlight | run the ˈlights** (both *especially NAmE*) (*BrE* also **jump the ˈlights**) (*informal*) to fail to stop at a red traffic light 闖紅燈 **see the ˈlight** **1** to finally understand or accept sth, especially sth obvious 終於領悟，最終明白，最後接受（尤指顯而易見的事） **2** to begin to believe in a religion 開始信教；皈依宗教 **see the ˈlight (of ˈday)** to begin to exist or to become publicly known about 開始存在；問世；開始為人所知：*He's written a lot of good material that has never seen the light of day.* 他寫了許多鮮為人知的好材料。 **set ˈlight to sth** (*especially BrE*) to make sth start burning 點燃；引火燒 **SYN** **ignite**： *A spark from the fire had set light to a rug.* 從火爐迸出的火星點燃了地毯。 ➲ more at BRIGHT *adj.*, COLD *adj.*, HIDE *v.*, JUMP *v.*, SWEETNESS

■ ***adj.*** (**light·er**, **light·est**)

▸ **WITH NATURAL LIGHT** 自然光 **1** 🔑 full of light; having the natural light of day 充滿亮光的；明亮的；有自然光的： *We'll leave in the morning as soon as **it's light**.* 明天早晨天一亮我們就出發。◇ *It **gets light** at about 5 o'clock.* 大約 5 點鐘天就亮了。◇ *It was a light spacious apartment at the top of the building.* 大樓頂層是一套寬敞明亮的房子。 **OPP** **dark**

▸ **COLOURS** 顏色 **2** 🔑 pale in colour 淺色的；淡色的： *light blue eyes* 淺藍色的眼睛 ◇ *Lighter shades suit you best.* 較淺色的衣服對你最合適。◇ *People with pale complexions should avoid wearing light colours.* 膚色白皙的人應當避免穿淺色衣服。 **OPP** **dark**

▸ **WEIGHT** 重量 **3** 🔑 easy to lift or move; not weighing very much 輕的；輕便的；不太重的： *Modern video cameras are light and easy to carry.* 新型的攝像機很輕，容易攜帶。◇ *Carry this bag—it's the lightest.* 你拿這個包，它最輕。◇ *He's lost a lot of weight—he's three kilos lighter than he was.* 他的體重減了許多，比以前輕了三公斤。◇ *The little girl was **as light as a feather**.* 那小女孩輕得很。◇ *The aluminium body is 12% lighter than if built with steel.* 用鋁製作比用鋼製作重量要輕 12%。 **OPP** **heavy** **4** 🔑 [usually before noun] of less than average or usual weight （比平均或平常重量）輕的： *light summer clothes* 輕薄的夏裝 ◇ *Only light vehicles are allowed over the old bridge.* 只有輕型車輛才准許通過那座舊橋。 **OPP** **heavy** **5** used with a unit of weight to say that sth weighs less than it should do （與重量單位連用）分量不足的： *The delivery of potatoes was several kilos light.* 送貨送來的土豆少了好幾公斤。

▸ **GENTLE** 輕柔 **6** 🔑 [usually before noun] gentle or delicate; not using much force 輕柔的；柔和的；不太用力的： *She felt a light tap on her shoulder.* 她感到有人在她肩上輕輕地拍了一下。◇ *the sound of quick light footsteps* 輕快的腳步聲 ◇ *You only need to apply light pressure.* 你只要輕輕地一壓就行了。◇ *As a boxer, he was always **light on his feet*** (= quick and elegant in the way he moved). 身為拳擊手，他的腳步總是十分輕盈。 **OPP** **heavy**

▸ **WORK/EXERCISE** 工作；鍛煉 **7** 🔑 [usually before noun] easy to do; not making you tired 容易做的；輕鬆的；不使人疲勞的： *After his accident he was moved to lighter work.* 他出事故以後就改做輕活兒了。◇ *some light housework* 一些輕鬆的家務活 ◇ *You are probably well enough to take a little light exercise.* 你恢復得不錯，大概可以做些輕微的運動了。

▸ **NOT GREAT** 不大 **8** 🔑 not great in amount, degree, etc. 少量的；程度低的： *light traffic* 來往車輛稀少 ◇ *The forecast is for light showers.* 天氣預報有小陣雨。◇ *light winds* 微風 ◇ *Trading on the stock exchange was light today.* 證券交易今日交易量很少。 **OPP** **heavy**

▸ **NOT SEVERE/SERIOUS** 不嚴厲；不嚴肅 **9** not severe 不嚴厲的；輕的： *He was convicted of assaulting a police officer but he got off with a **light sentence**.* 他被定了毆打警察罪，然而卻得到從輕判處。 **10** 🔑 entertaining rather than serious and not needing much mental effort 娛樂性的；消遣性的；輕鬆的： ***light reading** for the beach* 海灘消遣讀物 ◇ *a concert of light classical music* 古典輕音樂會 **11** 🔑 not serious 不嚴肅的： *She kept her tone light.* 她一直用溫和的語氣說話。◇ *This programme looks at the **lighter side** of politics.* 這個節目着眼於政治較輕鬆的方面。◇ *We all needed a little **light relief** at the end of a long day* (= something amusing or entertaining that comes after sth serious or boring). 在漫長的一天結束時我們都需要一點輕鬆的調劑。◇ ***On a lighter note**, we end the news today with a story about a duck called Quackers.* 為了輕鬆一下，我們最後講一個名叫"嘎嘎"的鴨子的故事來結束今天的新聞報道。

▸ **CHEERFUL** 愉快 **12** [usually before noun] free from worry; cheerful 無憂無慮的；愉快的；快活的： *I left the island with a light heart.* 我懷着愉快的心情離開了那個小島。

▸ **FOOD** 食物 **13** (of a meal 一餐飯) small in quantity 少量的： *a **light supper/snack**.* 簡單的晚餐；小吃 ◇ *I just want something light for lunch.* 我午飯稍微吃點就夠了。 **OPP** **heavy** **14** not containing much fat or not having a strong flavour and therefore easy for the stomach to DIGEST 不膩的；清淡的；易消化的： *Stick to a light diet.* 飲食要清淡。 ➲ see also LITE **15** containing a lot of air 含有許多空氣的；鬆軟的： *This pastry is so light.* 這種酥皮糕點可真鬆軟啊。

▸ **DRINK** 飲料 **16** low in alcohol 酒精含量低的；低度酒的： *a light beer* 低度啤酒 **17** (*IndE*) (of tea or coffee 茶或咖啡) containing a lot of water 淡味的 **SYN** **weak**： *I don't like my coffee too light.* 我不喜歡喝太淡的咖啡。 **OPP** **strong**

▸ **SLEEP** 睡眠 **18** [only before noun] a person in a **light** sleep is easy to wake 睡得不沉的；易醒的： *She drifted into a light sleep.* 她迷迷糊糊地睡得不沉。◇ *I've always been a light sleeper.* 我睡覺總是容易醒。 **OPP** **deep** ▸ **light·ness** *noun* [U] ➲ see also LIGHTLY

IDM **be light on sth** (*BrE*) to not have enough of sth 不足；缺乏： *We seem to be light on fuel.* 我們好像燃料不多了。 **a light touch** the ability to deal with sth in a delicate and relaxed way 靈巧的處事能力： *She handles this difficult subject with a light touch.* 她處理起這種難題來得心應手。 **make ˈlight of sth** to treat sth as not being important and not serious 輕視；對…等閒視之 **make light ˈwork of sth** to do sth quickly and with little effort 輕而易舉地做（某事） ➲ more at HAND *n.*

■ ***verb*** (**lit**, **lit** /lɪt/) **HELP** **Lighted** is also used for the past tense and past participle, especially in front of nouns. 過去時和過去分詞也用 lighted，尤置於名詞前。

▸ **START TO BURN** 開始燃燒 **1** 🔑 [T] **~ sth** to make sth start to burn 點燃；點火： *She lit a candle.* 她點着了蠟燭。◇ *The candles were lit.* 蠟燭都點着了。◇ *I put a lighted match to the letter and watched it burn.* 我劃了根火柴點着了那封信，然後看着它燃燒。 **2** 🔑 [I] to start to burn 開始燃燒；燃起來： *The fire wouldn't light.* 這火爐點不着。

▸ **GIVE LIGHT** 照亮 **3** 🔑 [T, usually passive] **~ sth** to give light to sth or to a place 照亮；使明亮： *The stage was lit by bright spotlights.* 舞台上有明亮的聚光燈照亮着。◇ ***well/badly lit** streets* 燈光明亮的／昏暗的街道 **4** [T] **~ sth** (*literary*) to guide sb with a light 用光指引： *Our way was lit by a full moon.* 一輪明月照亮了我們的路。

PHR V **ˈlight on/upon sth** (*literary*) to see or find sth by accident 偶然遇見；偶爾發現： *His eye lit upon a small boat on the horizon.* 他無意中看見地平線上有一條小船。

ˌlight ˈup | ˌlight sth↔ˈup **1** (*informal*) to begin to smoke a cigarette 開始抽煙： *They all lit up as soon as he left the room.* 他一離開房間他們就都抽起煙來。◇ *He sat back and lit up a cigarette.* 他往椅背上一靠，點上煙吸了起來。 **2** to become or to make sth become bright with light or colour（使）光亮，放光彩： *There was an explosion and the whole sky lit up.* 一聲爆炸照亮了整個天空。**3** if sb's eyes or face **light up**, or sth **lights them up**, they show happiness or excitement 喜形於色；喜氣洋洋： *His eyes lit up when she walked into the room.* 看見她走進房間，他兩眼一亮。◇ *A smile lit up her face.* 她微微一笑，臉上露出了喜色。

■ **adv.** IDM see TRAVEL *v.*

ˌlight ˈaircraft *noun* (*pl.* **light aircraft**) a small plane with seats for no more than about six passengers（最多六座的）輕型飛機 ➲ VISUAL VOCAB page V53

ˈlight bulb *noun* = BULB (1) ➲ VISUAL VOCAB page V8

ˌlight-ˈcoloured (*especially US* **ˌlight-ˈcolored**) *adj.* pale in colour; not dark 淺色的；淡色的

light·ed /ˈlaɪtɪd/ *adj.* **1** a **lighted** CANDLE, cigarette, match, etc. is burning 點燃的；燃燒的 **2** a **lighted** window is bright because there are lights on inside the room 燈火通明的；燈光照亮的 OPP **unlit**

light·en /ˈlaɪtn/ *verb* **1** [T] **~ sth** to reduce the amount of work, debt, worry, etc. that sb has 減輕，減少（工作量、債務、擔憂等）SYN **lessen**： *equipment to **lighten the load** of domestic work* 減輕家務工作的設備 ◇ *The measures will lighten the tax burden on small businesses.* 這些措施將減輕小型企業的納稅負擔。 **2** [I, T] to become or make sth become brighter or lighter in colour（使）變明亮，變成淡色： *The sky began to lighten in the east.* 東方開始透亮了。◇ **~ sth** *Use bleach to lighten the wood.* 用漂白劑把木材顏色漂淺。 **3** [I, T] to feel or make sb feel less sad, worried or serious（使）感到不那麼悲傷（或擔憂、嚴肅）；緩和 SYN **cheer**： **~ (up)** *My mood gradually lightened.* 我的心情漸漸好起來。◇ **~ sth (up)** *She told a joke to lighten the atmosphere.* 她講了個笑話以緩和氣氛。 **4** [T] **~ sth** to make sth lighter in weight 減輕重量

PHR V **ˌlighten ˈup** (*informal*) used to tell sb to become less serious or worried about sth 別那麼嚴肅；別擔憂： *Come on, John. Lighten up!* 約翰，加油，別緊張！

light·er /ˈlaɪtə(r)/ *noun* **1** (also **ciga'rette lighter**) a small device that produces a flame for lighting cigarettes, etc. 打火機 **2** a boat with a flat bottom used for carrying goods to and from ships in HARBOUR 駁船

ˌlight-ˈfingered *adj.* (*informal*) likely to steal things 慣扒竊的；慣偷的

ˌlight-ˈfooted *adj.* moving quickly and easily, in an elegant way 腳步輕鬆的；步履輕盈的

ˌlight-ˈheaded *adj.* not completely in control of your thoughts or movements; slightly faint 頭暈的；眩暈的： *After four glasses of wine he began to feel light-headed.* 他四杯酒下肚後開始感到頭暈目眩起來。

ˌlight-ˈhearted *adj.* **1** intended to be amusing or easily enjoyable rather than too serious 輕鬆的；愉快的： *a light-hearted speech* 輕鬆愉快的講話 **2** cheerful and without problems 無憂無慮的： *She felt light-hearted and optimistic.* 她感到無憂無慮，很樂觀。▸ **ˌlight-ˈhearted·ly** *adv.*

light·house /ˈlaɪthaʊs/ *noun* a tower or other building that contains a strong light to warn and guide ships near the coast 燈塔 ➲ VISUAL VOCAB pages V5, V15

ˌlight ˈindustry *noun* [U, C] industry that produces small or light objects such as things used in the house 輕工業 ➲ compare HEAVY INDUSTRY

light·ing /ˈlaɪtɪŋ/ *noun* [U] **1** the arrangement or type of light in a place 照明；燈光；佈光： ***electric/natural lighting*** 電力 / 自然照明 ◇ ***good/poor lighting*** 照明好 / 差 ◇ *The play had excellent sound and lighting effects.* 這齣戲劇的音響和燈光效果極佳。 **2** the use of electric lights in a place 照明： *the cost of heating and lighting* 供暖和照明費用 ◇ *street lighting* 街道照明 ➲ note at LIGHT

ˈlighting engineer *noun* a person who works in television, the theatre, etc. and whose job is to control and take care of the lights 照明工程師；燈光師

light·ly 🔑 /ˈlaɪtli/ *adv.*

1 🔑 gently; with very little force or effort 輕柔地；輕微地；輕輕地： *He kissed her lightly on the cheek.* 他輕輕吻了一下她的臉頰。 **2** 🔑 to a small degree; not much 少許；不多： *It began to snow lightly.* 開始下小雪了。◇ *She tended to sleep lightly nowadays* (= it was easy to disturb her). 她如今睡覺容易驚醒。◇ *I try to eat lightly* (= not to eat heavy or GREASY food). 我盡量不吃得太飽。 **3** in a way that sounds as though you are not particularly worried or interested 漫不經心地；滿不在乎地 SYN **nonchalantly**： *'I'll be all right,' he said lightly.* "我會好的。"他滿不在乎地說道。 **4** without being seriously considered 不慎重地；草率地；輕率地： *This is not a problem we should **take lightly**.* 這個問題我們可不能掉以輕心。

IDM **get off/be let off ˈlightly** (*informal*) to be punished or treated in a way that is less severe than you deserve or may have expected 只受輕罰；獲從輕發落

ˈlight meter *noun* a device used to measure how bright the light is before taking a photograph 曝光表

light·ning /ˈlaɪtnɪŋ/ *noun, adj.*

■ **noun** [U] a flash, or several flashes, of very bright light in the sky caused by electricity 閃電： ***a flash of lightning*** 一道閃電 ◇ *a violent storm with **thunder and lightning*** 夾着雷鳴電閃的暴風雨 ◇ *He was **struck by lightning** and killed.* 他被閃電擊中而死。◇ ***Lightning strikes** caused scores of fires across the state.* 雷擊給整個州造成了多起火災。➲ COLLOCATIONS at WEATHER

IDM **lightning never strikes (in the same place) twice** (*saying*) an unusual or unpleasant event is not likely to happen in the same place or to the same people twice 倒霉的事不可能在同一場所（或同一人身上）重複發生；一事不過二 **like (greased) ˈlightning** very fast 閃電般；飛快地；一溜煙地

■ **adj.** [only before noun] very fast or sudden 閃電般的；飛快的；突然的

ˈlightning bug *noun* (*NAmE*) = FIREFLY

ˈlightning conductor (*BrE*) (*NAmE* **ˈlightning rod**) *noun* a long straight piece of metal or wire leading from the highest part of a building to the ground, put there to prevent lightning damaging the building 避雷針

ˈlightning rod *noun* **1** (*NAmE*) = LIGHTNING CONDUCTOR **2** (*especially NAmE*) a person or thing that attracts criticism, especially if the criticism is then not directed at sb/sth else 引火燒身的人（或事）

ˌlightning ˈstrike *noun* **1** an incident in which LIGHTNING hits sb/sth 雷擊 **2** (*BrE*) a strike by a group of workers that is sudden and without warning 閃電式罷工

ˈlight pen *noun* **1** a piece of equipment, shaped like a pen, that is sensitive to light and that can be used to pass information to a computer when it touches the screen（用於向計算機輸入信息的）光筆 **2** a similar piece of equipment that is used for reading BARCODES 光筆；條形碼識讀器；光掃描器

ˈlight pollution *noun* [U] the existence of too much artificial light in the environment, for example from street lights, which makes it difficult to see the stars 光污染（人工照明造成）

light·ship /ˈlaɪtʃɪp/ *noun* a small ship that stays at a particular place at sea and that has a powerful light on it to warn and guide other ships（海上導航用的）燈船

ˈlight show *noun* a display of changing coloured lights, for example at a pop concert（流行音樂會等的）燈光變幻表演

ˈlight stick *noun* = GLOWSTICK

ˈlight water *noun* [U] **1** (*chemistry* 化) water that contains the normal amount of DEUTERIUM 輕水（水中氘含量正常）➲ compare HEAVY WATER **2** (*technical* 術語) a type of FOAM (= mass of bubbles) used to put out fires 滅火泡沫

light·weight /ˈlaɪtweɪt/ *adj., noun*

■ **adj.** **1** made of thinner material and less heavy than usual（布料）輕量的，薄型的： *a lightweight jacket* 輕便

的短上衣 **2** (*disapproving*) not very serious or impressive 不嚴肅的；給人印象不深的： *a lightweight book* 內容平庸的書 ◇ *He was considered too lightweight for the job.* 有人認為他資歷太淺，不適合做這工作。

■ ***noun*** **1** a BOXER weighing between 57 and 61 kilograms, heavier than a FEATHERWEIGHT 輕量級拳擊手（體重在 57 至 61 公斤之間）： *a lightweight champion* 輕量級拳擊冠軍 **2** a person or thing that weighs less than is usual 體重低於通常重量的人；比通常重量輕的東西 **3** (*informal, disapproving*) a person or thing of little importance or influence 無足輕重的人（或事）；沒有影響力的人（或事）： *a political lightweight* 政治上的無名之輩 ◇ *He's an intellectual lightweight* (= he does not think very deeply or seriously). 他是個智力平庸的人。

ˈlight year *noun* **1** (*astronomy* 天) the distance that light travels in one year, 9.4607×10^{12} kilometres 光年（指光在一年中走過的距離：9.4607×10^{12} 公里）： *The nearest star to earth is about 4 light years away.* 離地球最近的恒星距離地球約 4 光年。**2** **light years** [pl.] a very long time 很長時間；很久： *Full employment still seems light years away.* 充分就業好像依然是遙遙無期。

lig·nite /ˈlɪgnaɪt/ *noun* [U] a soft brown type of coal 褐煤

lig·no·caine /ˈlɪgnəkeɪn; *BrE* also -nəʊk-/ *noun* [U] = LIDOCAINE

lik·able (*especially NAmE*) = LIKEABLE

Synonyms 同義詞辨析

like

love • be fond of • be keen on sth • adore

These words all mean to find sth pleasant, attractive or satisfactory, or to enjoy sth. 以上各詞均含喜歡、喜愛某事物之意。

like to find sth pleasant, attractive or satisfactory; to enjoy sth 指喜歡、喜愛： *Do you like their new house?* 你喜歡他們的新房子嗎？◇ *I like to see them enjoying themselves.* 我就願意看着他們玩得高興。

love to like or enjoy sth very much 指非常喜歡、喜愛： *He loved the way she smiled.* 他喜歡她微笑的樣子。

be fond of sth to like or enjoy sth, especially sth you have liked or enjoyed for a long time 指喜愛（尤指已愛上很長時間的事物）： *We were fond of the house and didn't want to leave.* 我們喜歡上了這座房子，不想搬家。

be keen on sth (*BrE, informal*) (often used in negative statements) to like or enjoy sth （常用於否定句）指喜歡、喜愛： *I'm not keen on spicy food.* 我不喜歡加有香料的食物。◇ *She's not keen on being told what to do.* 她不喜歡別人向她發號施令。

adore (*informal*) to like or enjoy sth very much 指非常喜愛、熱愛： *She adores working with children.* 她熱愛為兒童工作。

LOVE OR ADORE? 用 love 還是 adore？

Adore is more informal than **love**, and is used to express a stronger feeling. * adore 較 love 非正式，用以表達更強烈的感情。

PATTERNS

- to like/love/be fond of/be keen on/adore **doing sth**
- to like/love **to do sth**
- to like/love sth **very much**
- **I** like/love/adore **it** here/there/when ...
- to like/love/adore **the way** sb does sth
- to **really** like/love/adore sb/sth
- to be **really** fond of/keen on sth

like 🔑 /laɪk/ *prep., verb, conj., noun, adj., adv.*

■ ***prep.*** **1** 🔑 similar to sb/sth 相似；類似；像： *She's wearing a dress like mine.* 她穿的連衣裙和我的相似。◇ *He's very like his father.* 他很像他的父親。◇ *She looks nothing like* (= not at all like) *her mother.* 她長得一點也不像她母親。◇ *That sounds like* (= I think I can hear) *him coming now.* 聽聲音像是他來了。**2** 🔑 used to ask sb's opinion of sb/sth （詢問意見）…怎麼樣： *What's it like studying in Spain?* 在西班牙唸書怎麼樣？◇ *This new girlfriend of his—what's she like?* 他這個新的女朋友是個什麼樣的人？ **3** 🔑 used to show what is usual or typical for sb （指某人常做的事）符合…的特點，像…才會： *It's just like her to tell everyone about it.* 她就是這麼個人兒，能把這事見誰就告訴誰。 **4** 🔑 in the same way as sb/sth 像…一樣： *Students were angry at being treated like children.* 學生對於把他們當小孩子對待感到氣憤。◇ *He ran like the wind* (= very fast). 他跑得飛快。◇ *You do it like this.* 你照這樣做。◇ *I, like everyone else, had read these stories in the press.* 我像大家一樣，也已經從報紙上看過這些報道。◇ *Don't look at me like that.* 別那樣看着我。◇ (*informal*) *The candles are arranged* **like so** (= in this way). 蠟燭都是像這樣排列的。 ➲ LANGUAGE BANK at SIMILARLY **5** 🔑 for example 例如；譬如；比方： *anti-utopian novels like 'Animal Farm' and '1984'* 諸如《動物莊園》和《1984》之類的反烏托邦小說 ➲ note at AS

IDM **more like ...** used to give a number or an amount that is more accurate than one previously mentioned （提供比以前更準確的數量）差不多，更接近： *He believes the figure should be more like $10 million.* 他認為數額若是 1 000 萬元就差不多了。 **more ˈlike (it)** (*informal*) **1** better; more acceptable 比較好；還差不多；才像話： *This is more like it! Real food—not that canned muck.* 這才像樣嘛！是新鮮的食物，而不是那種罐裝的垃圾食品。 **2** used to give what you think is a better description of sth （更恰當地描述）倒更像是，說…還差不多： *Just talking? Arguing more like it.* 僅僅是談論？說成是爭論還差不多。 **what is sb ˈlike?** (*BrE, informal*) used to say that sb has done sth annoying, silly, etc. （表示某人做了令人討厭、愚蠢之類的事）某人怎麼回事，某人怎麼會是這個樣子： *Oh, what am I like? I just completely forgot it.* 啊，我這是怎麼啦？我竟把這事忘得一乾二淨了。

■ ***verb*** (not usually used in the progressive tenses 通常不用於進行時) **1** 🔑 [T] to find sb/sth pleasant, attractive or of a good enough standard; to enjoy sth 喜歡；喜愛： **~ sb/sth** *She's nice. I like her.* 她人很好，我喜歡她。◇ *Do you like their new house?* 你喜歡他們的新房子嗎？◇ *Which tie do you like best?* 你最喜歡哪條領帶？◇ *How did you like Japan* (= did you find it pleasant)? 你覺得日本怎麼樣？◇ *I don't like the way he's looking at me.* 我討厭他看着我的樣子。◇ *You've got to go to school, whether you like it or not.* 不管你喜歡不喜歡，你得上學。◇ **~ doing sth** *She's never liked swimming.* 她從不喜歡游泳。◇ **~ sb/sth doing sth** *I didn't like him taking all the credit.* 我討厭他把所有的功勞歸於自己。◇ (*formal*) *I didn't like his taking all the credit.* 我討厭他把所有的功勞歸於自己。◇ **~ to do sth** *I like to see them enjoying themselves.* 我就願意看着他們玩得高興。◇ **~ it when ...** *I like it when you do that.* 我喜歡你那樣做。 ➲ SYNONYMS at LOVE **2** 🔑 [T, no passive] to prefer to do sth; to prefer sth to be made or to happen in a particular way 喜歡做；喜歡（以某種方式製作或產生的東西）： **~ to do sth** *At weekends I like to sleep late.* 週末我愛睡懶覺。◇ **~ sth + adj.** *I like my coffee strong.* 咖啡我愛喝濃的。 **3** 🔑 [T, no passive] **what/whatever sb ~** to want 想；要；希望： *Do what you like—I don't care.* 你想做什麼就做什麼，我不在乎。◇ *You can dye your hair whatever colour you like.* 你的頭髮你想怎麼染就怎麼染。 **4** 🔑 [T] used in negative sentences to mean 'to be unwilling to do sth' （用於否定句）願做： **~ to do sth** *I didn't like to disturb you.* 我本不願打攪你。◇ **~ doing sth** *He doesn't like asking his parents for help.* 他不願向父母求助。 **5** 🔑 [T, I] used with *would* or *should* as a polite way to say what you want or to ask what sb wants （與 would 或 should 連用表示客氣）想，想要，希望： **~ sth** *Would you like a drink?* 你想喝一杯嗎？◇ **~ to do sth** *I'd like to think it over.* 我想考慮一下這個問題。◇ *Would you like to come with us?* 你想不想和我們一塊兒去？◇ (*formal*) *We would like to apologize for the delay.* 我們對延遲表示歉意。◇ *How can they afford it? That's what I'd like to know.* 他們怎麼買得起這東西？這倒是我所想知道的。◇ **~ sb/sth to do sth** *We'd like you to come and visit us.*

我們想請你來我們這兒做客。◇ **~ for sb to do sth** (*NAmE*) *I'd like for us to work together.* 我希望我們在一起工作。 ➲ note at WANT

IDM **how would 'you like it?** used to emphasize that sth bad has happened to you and you want some sympathy（強調遭遇不佳並想得到同情）你會感覺怎麼樣呢：*How would you like it if someone called you a liar?* 如果有人說你撒謊，你會怎麼想呢？ **if you 'like** (*informal*) **1** 🗝 used to politely agree to sth or to suggest sth（禮貌地同意或建議）如果你要這樣做，你要是願意的話：*'Shall we stop now?' 'If you like.'* "我們現在停下來好嗎？" "聽你的。" ◇ *If you like, we could go out this evening.* 你如果願意的話，咱們今晚可以出去。 **2** used when you express sth in a new way or when you are not confident about sth（用新方式表達或不確定時說）換句話說，可以說：*It was, if you like, the dawn of a new era.* 換句話說，那就是新時代的黎明。 **I like 'that!** (*old-fashioned, informal*) used to protest that sth that has been said is not true or fair（抗議所言不實或不公）虧你說得出口：*'She called you a cheat.' 'Well, I like that!'* "她說你是騙子。" "哦，說得好哇！" **I/I'd like to think** used to say that you hope or believe that sth is true（表示希望或相信某事屬實）我倒想…：*I like to think I'm broad-minded.* 我倒想心胸開闊。 **ˌwhat's ˌnot to 'like?** (*informal, humorous*) used to say that sth is very good or enjoyable（用以表示非常好或令人愉快）：*You get paid to eat chocolate. So what's not to like?* 你吃巧克力還能得到報酬，這不很好嗎？

■ **conj.** (*informal*) **1** 🗝 in the same way as 像…一樣；如同：*No one sings the blues like she did.* 沒人像她那樣唱藍調歌曲。◇ *It didn't turn out like I intended.* 這結果與我的本意相悖。◇ ***Like I said*** (= as I said before), *you're always welcome to stay.* 正如我以前所說的一樣，我永遠都歡迎你留下來。 **2** 🗝 as if 好像；彷彿；似乎：*She acts like she owns the place.* 她的舉動就像那地方是她的一樣。 **HELP** You will find more information about this use of **like** at the entries for the verbs **act, behave, feel, look** and **sound** and in the note at **as**. 在動詞 act、behave、feel、look 和 sound 詞條下，以及在 as 用法說明中有 like 此種用法的更多說明。

■ **noun** **1 likes** [pl.] the things that you like 喜好；愛好：*We all have different **likes and dislikes**.* 我們各有不同的好惡。 **2** [sing.] a person or thing that is similar to another 類似的人（或物）：*jazz, rock **and the like*** (= similar types of music) 爵士樂、搖滾樂以及諸如此類的音樂 ◇ *a man whose like we shall not see again* 我們再也不願見到的那種男人 ◇ *You're not comparing **like with like**.* 你比較的不是同類的東西。 **3 the likes of sb/sth** (*informal*) used to refer to sb/sth that is considered as a type, especially one that is considered as good as sb/sth else（尤指被視為和某人或某事物一樣好的）種類，類型：*She didn't want to associate with the likes of me.* 她不想與我這種類型的人交往。

■ **adj.** [only before noun] (*formal*) having similar qualities to another person or thing 類似的；相似的：*a chance to meet people of like mind* (= with similar interests and opinions) 結識志趣相投的人的機會 ◇ *She responded in like manner.* 她以類似的方式作出了反應。

■ **adv.** **1** used in very informal speech, for example when you are thinking what to say next, explaining sth, or giving an example of sth（非正式口語，思考該說什麼、解釋或舉例時用）：*It was, like, weird.* 這事兒，就是說，有點怪。◇ *It was kind of scary, like.* 這還挺可怕的。◇ *It's really hard. Like I have no time for my own work.* 這事真費勁，弄得我沒時間做自己的工作了。 **2** used in very informal speech to show that what you are saying may not be exactly right but is nearly so（非正式口語）大概，可能：*I'm leaving in like twenty minutes.* 我大概 20 分鐘後離開。◇ *It's going to cost like a hundred dollars.* 這可能要花 100 元。 **3 I'm, he's, she's, etc. ~** used in very informal speech, to mean 'I say', 'he/she says', etc.（非正式口語）我說，他說，她說：*And then I'm like 'No Way!'* 接着我說 "沒門兒！" **4** used in informal speech instead of *as* to say that sth happens in the same way（非正式口語，代替 as）和…一樣，如，像：*There was silence, but not like before.* 沒有聲音，但與以前不一樣。 ➲ note at AS

IDM **(as) like as 'not | like e'nough | most/very 'like** (*old-fashioned*) quite probably 很可能；大概：*She would be in bed by now, as like as not.* 這時候她很可能睡了。

-like *combining form* (in adjectives 構成形容詞) similar to; typical of 類似…的；有…特徵的：*childlike* 孩子般的 ◇ *shell-like* 似殼的

like·able (*especially BrE*) (also **lik·able** *NAmE, BrE*) /ˈlaɪkəbl/ *adj.* pleasant and easy to like 可愛的；討人喜歡的：*a very likeable man* 十分討人喜愛的人

like·li·hood /ˈlaɪklihʊd/ *noun* [U, sing.] the chance of sth happening; how likely sth is to happen 可能；可能性 **SYN** **probability**：*There is very little likelihood of that happening.* 幾乎沒有發生那種事情的可能。◇ ***In all likelihood*** (= very probably) *the meeting will be cancelled.* 這次會議十有八九要被取消。◇ ***The likelihood is that*** (= it is likely that) *unemployment figures will continue to fall.* 很有可能失業人數會繼續下降。

like·ly 🗝 /ˈlaɪkli/ *adj., adv.*

■ **adj.** (**like·lier, like·li·est**) **HELP** **More likely** and **most likely** are the usual forms. 常用 more likely 和 most likely。 **1** 🗝 probable or expected 可能的；預料的；有希望的：*the most likely outcome* 最可能的結果 ◇ **~ (to do sth)** *Tickets are likely to be expensive.* 入場券可能很貴。◇ **~ (that ...)** *It's **more than likely that** the thieves don't know how much it is worth.* 盜賊很可能不知道此物的價值。◇ *They might refuse to let us do it, but it's **hardly likely**.* 他們也許不會讓我們做這工作，但這可能性太小。 ➲ LANGUAGE BANK at EXPECT **2** seeming suitable for a purpose 似乎合適的；彷彿恰當的 **SYN** **promising**：*She seems the most likely candidate for the job.* 這項工作，她似乎是最適宜的人選了。

IDM **a 'likely story** (*informal, ironic*) used to show that you do not believe what sb has said（表示不相信某人的話）說得好像真有這回事似的，像煞有介事

■ **adv.**

IDM **as ˌlikely as 'not | most/very 'likely** very probably 很可能：*As likely as not she's forgotten all about it.* 她很可能把這事忘得一乾二淨了。 **not 'likely!** (*informal, especially BrE*) used to disagree strongly with a statement or suggestion（表示堅決不同意）決不可能，絕對不會：*Me? Join the army? Not likely!* 我？參軍入伍？沒門兒！

Grammar Point 語法說明

likely

- In standard *BrE* the adverb **likely** must be used with a word such as *most, more* or *very*. 在標準的英式英語中，副詞 likely 必須與 most、more 或 very 等詞連用：*We will most likely see him later.* 我們很可能晚些時候會見到他。 In informal *NAmE* **likely** is often used on its own. 在非正式的美式英語中，likely 常單獨使用：*We will likely see him later.* 我們可能晚些時候會見到他。◇ *He said that he would likely run for President.* 他說他可能競選總統。

ˌlike-'minded *adj.* having similar ideas and interests 想法相同的；志趣相投的

liken /ˈlaɪkən/ *verb*

PHR V **'liken sth/sb to sth/sb** (*formal*) to compare one thing or person to another and say they are similar 把…比作…：*Life is often likened to a journey.* 人們常把人生比作旅程。

like·ness /ˈlaɪknəs/ *noun* **1** [C, U] the fact of being similar to another person or thing, especially in appearance; an example of this 相像；相似；相似之處 **SYN** **resemblance**：*Joanna bears a strong likeness to her father.* 喬安娜長得酷似她父親。◇ *Do you notice any family likeness between them?* 你看沒看出他們長得像是一家人？ **2** [C, usually sing.] a painting, drawing, etc. of a person, especially one that looks very like them（尤指畫得像的）肖像，畫像：*The drawing is said to be **a good likeness** of the girl's attacker.* 據說那幅嫌犯的畫像畫得很像襲擊女孩的歹徒真人。

likes *noun* ➲ LIKE *n.* (1)

like·wise AW /ˈlaɪkwaɪz/ *adv.* **1** (*formal*) the same; in a similar way 同樣地；類似地： *He voted for the change and he expected his colleagues to* ***do likewise.*** 他投票贊成變革並期望他的同事投同樣的票。 **2** (*formal*) also 也；還；亦；而且： *Her second marriage was likewise unhappy.* 她的第二次婚姻也不幸福。 **3** (*informal*) used to show that you feel the same towards sb or about sth（表示感覺相同）我也是，我有同感： *'Let me know if you ever need any help.' 'Likewise.'* "你要是需要幫助就告訴我。" "你也一樣。"

lik·ing /ˈlaɪkɪŋ/ *noun* [sing.] **~ (for sb/sth)** the feeling that you like sb/sth; the enjoyment of sth 喜歡；喜好；嗜好；樂趣 SYN **fondness**： *He* ***had a liking for*** *fast cars.* 他過去喜歡快車。◇ *She had* ***taken a liking to him*** *on their first meeting.* 她對他一見鍾情。
IDM **for your ˈliking** if you say, for example, that sth is too hot **for your liking**, you mean that you would prefer it to be less hot 適合…的口味（或願望）： *The town was too crowded for my liking.* 這座城鎮太擁擠了，我不喜歡。 **to sb's ˈliking** (*formal*) suitable, and how sb likes sth 適合某人的胃口；中某人的意： *The coffee was just to his liking.* 這咖啡正合他的口味。

lilac /ˈlaɪlək/ *noun* **1** [U, C] a bush or small tree with purple or white flowers with a sweet smell that grow closely together in the shape of a CONE 丁香 **2** [U] a pale purple colour 淡紫色；丁香紫 ▸ **lilac** *adj.*： *a lilac dress* 一件淡紫色的連衣裙

Lil·li·pu·tian /ˌlɪlɪˈpjuːʃn/ *adj.* (*formal*) extremely small 極小的；微小的 SYN **diminutive, tiny** ORIGIN From the land of **Lilliput**, in Jonathan Swift's *Gulliver's Travels*, where the people are only 15 cm high. 源自喬納森•斯威夫特的《格利佛遊記》中的小人國（Lilliput），那裏的居民僅有 15 厘米高。

lilo /ˈlaɪləʊ; *NAmE* -loʊ/ (also **Li-Lo™**) *noun* (*pl.* **-os**) (*BrE*) a plastic or rubber bed that is filled with air and used when camping or for floating on water 充氣墊（用於露營或水上漂浮）

lilt /lɪlt/ *noun* [sing.] **1** the pleasant way in which a person's voice rises and falls（說話聲的）抑揚頓挫： *Her voice had a soft Welsh lilt to it.* 她講話的聲音柔和而抑揚頓挫，有些威爾士口音。 **2** a regular rising and falling pattern in music, with a strong rhythm 節奏歡快的旋律；輕快活潑的曲調 ▸ **lilt·ing** *adj.*

lily /ˈlɪli/ *noun* (*pl.* **-ies**) a large white or brightly coloured flower with PETALS that curl back from the centre. There are many types of lily. 百合花 ➲ VISUAL VOCAB page V11 ➲ see also WATER LILY IDM see GILD

lily-livered /ˈlɪli lɪvəd; *NAmE* -vərd/ *adj.* (*old-fashioned*) lacking courage 膽怯的；懦弱的 SYN **cowardly**

ˌlily of the ˈvalley *noun* [C, U] (*pl.* **lilies of the valley**) a plant with small white flowers shaped like bells 鈴蘭

ˈlily pad *noun* a round floating leaf of a WATER LILY 睡蓮的漂浮葉

ˌlily-ˈwhite *adj.* **1** almost pure white in colour 近純白的： *lily-white skin* 白皙的皮膚 **2** morally perfect 純潔的；完美無瑕的： *They want me to conform, to be lily-white.* 他們要我循規蹈矩，要我清白無瑕。

lima bean /ˈliːmə biːn/ *noun* (*NAmE*) a type of round, pale green BEAN. Several lima beans grow together inside a flat POD. 利馬豆

limb /lɪm/ *noun* **1** an arm or a leg; a similar part of an animal, such as a wing 肢；臂；腿；翼；翅膀： *an artificial limb* 假肢 ◇ *For a while, she lost the use of her limbs.* 好一會兒她四肢都動彈不得。 **2 -limbed** (in adjectives 構成形容詞) having the type of limbs mentioned 有…肢（或翼、翅膀）的： *long-limbed* 四肢細長的 ◇ *loose-limbed* 四肢柔軟靈活的 **3** a large branch of a tree（樹的）大枝，主枝 ➲ VISUAL VOCAB page V10
IDM **out on a ˈlimb** (*informal*) not supported by other people 無人支持；孤立無援： *Are you prepared to* ***go out on a limb*** (= risk doing sth that other people are not prepared to do) *and make your suspicions public?* 你願意冒險把你懷疑的事公開嗎？ **tear/rip sb ˌlimb from ˈlimb** (often *humorous*) to attack sb very violently 猛烈攻擊某人 ➲ more at RISK *v.*

limba /ˈlɪmbə/ *noun* = AFARA

lim·ber /ˈlɪmbə(r)/ *verb*
PHR V **ˌlimber ˈup** to do physical exercises in order to stretch and prepare your muscles before taking part in a race, sporting activity, etc.（賽跑、體育運動等前）做準備活動，做熱身運動 SYN **warm up**

lim·bic sys·tem /ˈlɪmbɪk sɪstəm/ *noun* (*biology* 生) a system of nerves in the brain involving several different areas, concerned with basic emotions such as fear and anger and basic needs such as the need to eat and to have sex（大腦）邊緣系，邊緣系統

limbo /ˈlɪmbəʊ; *NAmE* -boʊ/ *noun* **1** [C] a West Indian dance in which you lean backwards and go under a bar which is made lower each time you go under it 林波舞（西印度群島舞蹈，舞者向後彎腰鑽過一次比一次降低的橫杆） **2** [U, sing.] a situation in which you are not certain what to do next, cannot take action, etc., especially because you are waiting for sb else to make a decision（尤指因等待他人作決定）處於不定狀態： *the limbo of the stateless person* 無國籍人的不安定狀態 ◇ *His life seemed stuck* ***in limbo****; he could not go forward and he could not go back.* 他的生活好像陷入了不知所措的境地，進退兩難。

lime /laɪm/ *noun, verb*
■ ***noun*** **1** (also **quick·lime**) [U] a white substance obtained by heating LIMESTONE, used in building materials and to help plants grow 石灰 **2** [C, U] a small green fruit, like a lemon, with a lot of sour juice, used in cooking and in drinks; the juice of this fruit 酸橙；萊姆；酸橙汁： *lime juice* 酸橙汁 ◇ *slices of lime* 酸橙片 ➲ VISUAL VOCAB page V30 **3** (also **ˈlime tree**) [C] a tree on which limes grow 酸橙樹 **4** (also **ˈlime tree**, **ˈlinden tree**, **linden**) [C] a large tree with light green heart-shaped leaves and yellow flowers 歐椴樹： *an avenue of limes* 兩邊栽有歐椴樹的林蔭道 **5** [U] = LIME GREEN
■ ***verb*** **~ sth** to add the substance lime to soil, especially in order to control the acid in it（尤指為控制酸度而給土壤）摻加石灰，撒石灰

lime·ade /laɪmˈeɪd/ *noun* [U, C] **1** a sweet FIZZY drink (= with bubbles) with a LIME flavour 酸橙汽水；萊姆汽水 **2** a drink made from LIME juice, sugar and water 酸橙汁飲料；萊姆汁飲料

ˌlime ˈgreen *adj.* (also **lime**) bright yellowish green in colour 酸橙綠的；淡綠色的 ▸ **ˌlime ˈgreen** (also **lime**) *noun* [U]

lime·light /ˈlaɪmlaɪt/ (usually **the limelight**) *noun* [U] the centre of public attention 公眾注意的中心： *to be* ***in the limelight*** 成為公眾注目的中心 ◇ *to stay* ***out of the limelight*** 避免引人注目 ◇ *to* ***steal/hog the limelight*** (= take attention away from other people) 把公眾的注意力吸引過來

lim·er·ick /ˈlɪmərɪk/ *noun* a humorous short poem, with two long lines that RHYME with each other, followed by two short lines that rhyme with each other and ending with a long line that rhymes with the first two 五行打油詩（幽默短詩，起始兩長句押韻，中間兩短句押韻，最後一長句與開頭兩句押韻）

lime·scale /ˈlaɪmskeɪl/ *noun* [U] (*BrE*) the hard white substance that is left by water on the inside of pipes, etc.（管道等內的）水垢

lime·stone /ˈlaɪmstəʊn; *NAmE* -stoʊn/ *noun* [U] a type of white stone that contains CALCIUM, used in building and in making CEMENT 石灰岩

ˈlime water *noun* [U] (*chemistry* 化) a liquid containing CALCIUM HYDROXIDE which shows the presence of CARBON DIOXIDE by turning white 石灰水

Limey /ˈlaɪmi/ *noun* (*old-fashioned*, *NAmE*) a slightly insulting word for a British person 英國佬

limit 0-w /ˈlɪmɪt/ *noun, verb*
■ ***noun*** **1** 0-w **~ (to sth)** a point at which sth stops being possible or existing 限度；限制： *There is a limit to the amount of pain we can bear.* 我們能忍受的疼痛是有限度的。◇ *The team performed* ***to the limit*** *of its capabilities.* 這個隊已竭盡全力。◇ *She knew the limits of her power.*

她知道自己的權限。◇ *to push/stretch/test sb/sth **to the limit*** 最大限度地推 / 拉 / 考查某人（或某物）◇ *His arrogance **knew** (= had) **no limits**.* 他極其傲慢。**2** ~ **(on sth)** the greatest or smallest amount of sth that is allowed 極限；限量；限額 SYN **restriction**：*a time/speed/age limit* 時間 / 速度 / 年齡限制 ◇ *The EU has set strict **limits** on levels of pollution.* 歐盟對污染程度訂下了嚴格的限制。◇ *They were travelling at a speed that was double the **legal limit**.* 他們正以兩倍於法定限速的速度行駛。◇ *You can't drive—you're **over the limit*** (= you have drunk more alcohol than is legal when driving). 你飲酒過量，不能駕車。**3** the furthest edge of an area or a place（地區或地方的）境界，界限，範圍：*We were reaching the limits of civilization.* 我們快到蠻荒地界了。◇ *the **city limits*** (= the imaginary line which officially divides the city from the area outside) 市區範圍 ➲ see also OFF-LIMITS

IDM **be the 'limit** (*old-fashioned, informal*) to be extremely annoying 極其令人討厭 **within 'limits** to some extent; with some restrictions 在某種程度上；有一定限制：*I'm willing to help, within limits.* 我願意幫忙，可有一定的限度。➲ more at SKY *n.*

■ *verb* **1** ~ **sth (to sth)** to stop sth from increasing beyond a particular amount or level 限制；限定 SYN **restrict**：*measures to limit carbon dioxide emissions from cars* 限制汽車二氧化碳排放的措施 ◇ *The amount of money you have to spend will limit your choice.* 你用作消費的金額會限制你的選擇。**2** ~ **yourself/sb (to sth)** to restrict or reduce the amount of sth that you or sb can have or use 限量；減量：*Families are limited to four free tickets each.* 每戶限發四張免費票。◇ *I've limited myself to 1 000 calories a day to try and lose weight.* 我為了減肥，限定自己每天攝入 1 000 卡的熱量。

PHR V **'limit sth to sb/sth** [usually passive] to make sth exist or happen only in a particular place or within a particular group 使（某事只在某地或某群體內）存在（或發生）：*Violent crime is not limited to big cities.* 暴力犯罪並不局限於大城市。◇ *The teaching of history should not be limited to dates and figures.* 教授歷史不應該局限於講年代和人物。

limi·ta·tion /ˌlɪmɪ'teɪʃn/ *noun* **1** [U] the act or process of limiting or controlling sb/sth 限制；控制 SYN **restriction**：*They would resist any limitation of their powers.* 他們會抵制對他們權力的任何限制。➲ SYNONYMS at LIMIT ➲ see also DAMAGE LIMITATION **2** [C] ~ **(on sth)** a rule, fact or condition that limits sth 起限制作用的規則（或事實、條件）SYN **curb, restraint**：*to impose limitations on imports* 對進口加以限制 ◇ *Disability is a physical limitation on your life.* 殘疾在身體方面限制了你的生活。➲ see also STATUTE OF LIMITATIONS **3** [C, usually pl.] a limit on what sb/sth can do or how good they or it can be 局限；限度：*This technique is useful but it **has its limitations**.* 這種技巧實用，但也有局限性。

limit·ed /'lɪmɪtɪd/ *adj.* **1** not very great in amount or extent 有限的：*We are doing our best with the limited resources available.* 我們利用可獲得的有限資源，盡最大的努力。**2** ~ **(to sth)** restricted to a particular limit of time, numbers, etc. 受（…的）限制：*This offer is for a limited period only.* 此次減價時間有限。➲ see also LTD

ˌlimited 'company (also **ˌlimited lia'bility company**) *noun* (in Britain) a company whose owners only have to pay a limited amount of its debts（英國的）有限責任公司，股份有限公司 ➲ see also LTD

ˌlimited e'dition *noun* a fixed, usually small, number of copies of a book, picture, etc. produced at one time（書、畫等的）限定版，限數本

ˌlimited lia'bility *noun* [U] (*law* 律) the legal position of having to pay only a limited amount of your or your company's debts 有限責任

limit·ing /'lɪmɪtɪŋ/ *adj.* putting limits on what is possible 限制性的：*Lack of cash is a limiting factor.* 現金短缺是一個制約因素。

limit·less /'lɪmɪtləs/ *adj.* without a limit; very great 無限制的；無界限的；無限度的；無止境的 SYN **infinite**：*the limitless variety of consumer products* 種類繁多的消

Synonyms 同義詞辨析

limit

restriction • control • constraint • restraint • limitation

These are all words for sth that limits what you can do or what can happen. 以上各詞均表示限制或限定。

limit the greatest or smallest amount of sth that is allowed 指極限、限量、限額：*The EU has set strict limits on pollution levels.* 歐盟對污染程度訂下了嚴格的限制。◇ *the speed limit* 速度限制

restriction (*rather formal*) a rule or law that limits what you can do 指限制規定、限制法規：*There are no restrictions on the amount of money you can withdraw.* 取款沒有限額。

control (often in compounds) the act of limiting or managing sth; a method of doing this（常構成複合詞）指限制、約束、管理、管制：*arms control* 軍備控制

constraint (*rather formal*) a fact or decision that limits what you can do 指限制、限定、約束：*We have to work within severe constraints of time and money.* 我們必須在時間緊迫、資金緊絀的限制下工作。

restraint (*rather formal*) a decision, a rule, an idea, etc. that limits what you can do; the act of limiting sth because it is necessary or sensible to do so 指約束力、管制措施、制約因素、控制、限制：*The government has imposed export restraints on some products.* 政府對一些產品實行了出口控制。◇ *The unions are unlikely to accept any sort of wage restraint.* 工會不大可能接受任何形式的工資限制。

limitation the act or process of limiting sth; a rule, fact or condition that limits sth 指限制、控制、起限制作用的規則、事實或條件：*They would resist any limitation of their powers.* 他們會抵制對他們權力的任何限制。

RESTRICTION, CONSTRAINT, RESTRAINT OR LIMITATION?
用 restriction、constraint、restraint 還是 limitation？

These are all things that limit what you can do. A **restriction** is rule or law that is made by sb in authority. A **constraint** is sth that exists rather than sth that is made, although it may exist as a result of sb's decision. A **restraint** is also sth that exists: it can exist outside yourself, as the result of sb else's decision; but it can also exist inside you, as a fear of what other people may think or as your own feeling about what is acceptable. 以上各詞均表示限制規定。restriction 指掌權者所作的限制規定或法規。constraint 指現存的、也可能是由於某人的決定而存在的限制或約束。restraint 亦指現存的限制或制約因素，可能是由於他人的決定而存在於自身之外的限制，也可能是由於擔心別人的想法或自己對接受事物的感受而自設的限制：*moral/social/cultural restraints* 道德 / 社會 / 文化制約因素 A **limitation** is more general and can be a rule that sb makes or a fact or condition that exists. * limitation 較通用，可指人為的規定，也可指客觀存在的構成限制的事實或條件。

PATTERNS

- limits/restrictions/controls/constraints/restraints/limitations **on** sth
- limits/limitations **to** sth
- **severe** limits/restrictions/controls/constraints/restraints/limitations
- **tight** limits/restrictions/controls/constraints
- to **impose/remove** limits/restrictions/controls/constraints/restraints/limitations
- to **lift** restrictions/controls/constraints/restraints

費產品 ◇ *The possibilities were almost limitless.* 可能性幾乎是無窮無盡的。

limo /ˈlɪməʊ; *NAmE* ˈlɪmoʊ/ *noun* (*pl.* **-os**) (*informal*) = LIMOUSINE

lim·ou·sine /ˈlɪməziːn; ˌlɪməˈziːn/ (also *informal* **limo**) *noun* **1** a large expensive comfortable car 大型高級轎車；豪華轎車： *a long black chauffeur-driven limousine* 由專職司機駕駛的黑色豪華長轎車 ➲ see also STRETCH LIMO **2** (*especially NAmE*) a van or small bus that takes people to and from an airport（往返機場接送旅客的）中型客車，小型公共汽車

limp /lɪmp/ *adj., verb, noun*

■ *adj.* **1** lacking strength or energy 無力的；無生氣的；無精神的： *His hand went limp and the knife clattered to the ground.* 他的手一軟，刀子嚓啷一聲掉到地上。◇ *She felt limp and exhausted.* 她感到渾身無力，累極了。 **2** not stiff or firm 柔軟的；不直挺的： *The hat had become limp and shapeless.* 這帽子軟得不成樣子了。 ▸ **limp·ly** *adv.*： *Her hair* **hung limply** *over her forehead.* 她的頭髮蓬鬆地垂在前額上。

■ *verb* **1** [I] to walk slowly or with difficulty because one leg is injured 瘸着走；跛行；蹣跚： *She had twisted her ankle and was limping.* 她把腳踝扭傷了，一瘸一拐地走着。◇ **+ adv./prep.** *Matt limped painfully off the field.* 馬特忍着痛歪歪斜斜地走出了運動場。 **2** [I] **+ adv./prep.** to move slowly or with difficulty after being damaged（受損後）緩慢行進，艱難地移動： *The plane limped back to the airport.* 飛機艱難地返回了機場。◇ (*figurative*) *The government was limping along in its usual way.* 政府按老一套掙扎着應付。

■ *noun* [usually sing.] a way of walking in which one leg is used less than normal because it is injured or stiff 跛行： *to walk with a* **slight/pronounced limp** 有點／明顯地一瘸一拐地走

lim·pet /ˈlɪmpɪt/ *noun* a small SHELLFISH that sticks very tightly to rocks 帽貝，鑰孔蝛（依附在岩石上）： *The Prime Minister clung to his job like a limpet, despite calls for him to resign.* 首相不顧眾人要求他辭職的呼聲，死賴在職位上不下台。

lim·pid /ˈlɪmpɪd/ *adj.* (*literary*) (of liquids, etc. 液體等) clear 清澈的；清晰的；透明的 **SYN** **transparent**： ***limpid eyes/water*** 明亮的眼睛；清澈的水

ˌlimp-ˈwristed *adj.* (*informal*) an offensive word for HOMOSEXUAL 娘娘腔的（含冒犯意，形容同性戀者）

LINC /lɪŋk/ *abbr.* Language Instruction for Newcomers to Canada (free language classes provided by the government to people from other countries who come to live in Canada) 加拿大新移民語言培訓（加拿大政府提供的免費課程）

linch·pin (also **lynch·pin**) /ˈlɪntʃpɪn/ *noun* a person or thing that is the most important part of an organization, a plan, etc., because everything else depends on them or it（組織、計劃等的）關鍵人物，關鍵事物

Lin·coln's Birth·day /ˌlɪŋkənz ˈbɜːθdeɪ; *NAmE* ˈbɜːrθ-/ *noun* [U] (in some US states) a legal holiday on 12 February in memory of the birthday of Abraham Lincoln 林肯誕辰紀念日（2 月 12 日，美國某些州的法定假日）

linc·tus /ˈlɪŋktəs/ *noun* [U] (*BrE*) thick liquid medicine that you take for a sore throat or a cough 潤喉止咳糖漿；藥糖劑： *cough linctus* 止咳糖漿

lin·den /ˈlɪndən/ (also **ˈlinden tree**) *noun* = LIME *n.* (4)

line 🔑 /laɪn/ *noun, verb*

■ *noun*

▸ **LONG THIN MARK** 線 **1** 🔑 [C] a long thin mark on a surface 線；線條： *a* ***straight/wavy/dotted/diagonal line*** 直／波狀／虛／對角線 ◇ *a* ***vertical/horizontal line*** 垂直／水平線 ◇ ***parallel lines*** 平行線 ◇ *Draw a thick black line across the page.* 在此頁上橫畫一條粗黑線。 **2** 🔑 [C] a long thin mark on the ground to show the limit or border of sth, especially of a playing area in some sports 界線；（尤指運動場地的）場地線，場界： *The ball* **went over the line**. 球越線出界了。◇ *Be careful not* **to cross the line** (= the broken line painted down the middle of the road). 小心別越過道路的中界線。◇ *Your feet must be behind the line when you serve* (= in TENNIS). 發球時你的腳必須站在底線的外面。◇ *They were all waiting on the* **starting line**. 他們全都在起跑線上等待着。 ➲ see also FINISHING LINE, GOAL LINE, SIDELINE, TOUCHLINE **3** 🔑 [C] a mark like a line on sb's skin that people usually get as they get older 皺紋；褶子 **SYN** **wrinkle**： *He has* **fine lines** *around his eyes.* 他的眼睛周圍有細細的皺紋。

▸ **DIVISION** 分界線 **4** 🔑 [C] an imaginary limit or border between one place or thing and another 分界線；邊界線： *He was convicted of illegally importing weapons across* **state lines**. 他被判犯有非法越州偷運武器罪。◇ *a* ***district/county line*** 行政區／郡界 ◇ ***lines of longitude and latitude*** 經線和緯線 ➲ see also COASTLINE, DATE LINE, DIVIDING LINE, PICKET LINE, TREELINE, WATERLINE **5** 🔑 [C] the division between one area of thought or behaviour and another（思想或行為的）界限，界線： *We want to cut across lines of race, sex and religion.* 我們要超越種族、性別和宗教的界限。◇ *There is* ***a fine line between*** *showing interest in what someone is doing and interfering in it.* 關心別人正在做的事情和進行干預之間存在着細微的差別。 ➲ see also RED LINE

▸ **SHAPE** 形狀 **6** 🔑 [C] the edge, outline or shape of sb/sth 邊線；輪廓線；形體；形狀： *He traced the line of her jaw with his finger.* 他用手指順着她的下巴外緣撫摸。◇ *a beautiful sports car with sleek lines* 線條流暢、美觀的跑車 ➲ see also BIKINI LINE

▸ **ROW OF PEOPLE/THINGS** 人或物的行列 **7** 🔑 [C] a row of people or things next to each other or behind each other 排；行；列： *a long line of trees* 一長排樹 ◇ *The children all stood* **in a line**. 孩子們全都站成一排。◇ *They were stuck in a line of traffic.* 他們塞在汽車長龍裏面了。 **8** 🔑 [C] (*NAmE*) a QUEUE of people（人）隊伍，行列： *to* ***stand/wait in line*** *for sth* 站隊／排隊等候某事物 ◇ *A line formed at each teller window.* 銀行每個出納員的窗口前都排起了隊。

▸ **IN FACTORY** 工廠 **9** [C] a system of making sth, in which the product moves from one worker to the next until it is finished 生產線；流水線 ➲ see also ASSEMBLY LINE, PRODUCTION LINE

▸ **SERIES** 系列 **10** 🔑 [C, usually sing.] a series of people, things or events that follow one another in time 按時間順序排列的人（或物、事件）；家系；家族： *She came from* ***a long line of*** *doctors.* 她來自一個醫生世家。◇ *to pass sth down through the* ***male/female line*** 通過父系／母系代代相傳某物 ◇ *This novel is the latest in a long line of thrillers that he has written.* 這部小說是他寫的系列驚險小說中最近出版的一部。 **11** [C, usually sing.] a series of people in order of importance 一系列按重要性排列的人： *Orders came down the line from the very top.* 命令從最高領導人逐級傳達下來。◇ *a line of command* 一系列按職務排序的指揮人員 ◇ *He is second* **in line** *to the chairman.* 他的地位僅次於主席。◇ *to be* **next in line** *to the throne* 為王位繼承人 ➲ see also LINE MANAGER at LINE MANAGEMENT

▸ **WORDS** 文字 **12** 🔑 [C] (*abbr.* **l**) a row of words on a page or the empty space where they can be written; the words of a song or poem 字行；便條；留言條；歌詞；詩行： *Look at line 5 of the text.* 看正文第 5 行。◇ *Write the title of your essay on the top line.* 把文章的標題寫在首行。◇ *I can only remember the first two lines of that song.* 我只記得那首歌的頭兩句歌詞。 ➲ see also BOTTOM LINE **13** 🔑 [C] the words spoken by an actor in a play or film/movie（戲劇或電影的）台詞，對白： *to learn your lines* 背台詞 ◇ *a line from the film 'Casablanca'* 電影《卡薩布蘭卡》裏的一句話 **14 lines** [pl.] (*BrE*) (in some schools) a punishment in which a child has to write out a particular sentence a number of times（某些學校）罰學生抄寫多次 **15** [C] (*informal*) a remark, especially when sb says it to achieve a particular purpose（尤指為達到某種目的說的）話，言語： *Don't give me that line about having to work late again.* 別再跟我說不得不工作到很晚這樣的話。◇ (*BrE*) *That's the worst* ***chat-up line*** *I've ever heard.* 我聽過的向人調情的話裏沒有比這更差勁的了。

▸ **ROPE/WIRE/PIPE** 繩索；金屬線；管子 **16** 🔑 [C] a long piece of rope, thread, etc., especially when it is used for a particular purpose 一段繩（或索、線等）： *a* *fishing line* 釣魚線 ◇ *He hung the towels out* **on the line** (= clothes line). 他把那些毛巾掛在曬衣繩上。◇ *They dropped the sails and threw a line to a man on the dock.* 他們放下風帆，把船纜拋給碼頭上的人。➲ see also LIFELINE **17** [C] a pipe or thick wire that carries water, gas or electricity from one place to another 管道；線路 ➲ see also POWER LINE

▸ **TELEPHONE 電話** **18** [C] a telephone connection; a particular telephone number 電話線路；電話號碼：*Your bill includes line rental.* 你的賬單包括電話線路的租用費。◇ *The company's lines have been jammed* (= busy) *all day with people making complaints.* 公司的電話整天都因人們打投訴電話而佔線。◇ *I was talking to John when the* **line** *suddenly* **went dead**. 我正和約翰談話，突然電話斷了。◇ *If you* **hold the line** (= stay on the telephone and wait), *I'll see if she is available.* 請你不要掛斷電話，我去看看她能不能接電話。➲ see also HELPLINE, HOTLINE, LANDLINE, OFFLINE, ONLINE

▸ **RAILWAY/RAILROAD 鐵道** **19** [C] a railway/railroad track; a section of a railway/railroad system 軌道；鐵道；(鐵路的)段，線路：*The train was delayed because a tree had fallen across the line.* 火車晚點是因為有一棵樹橫倒在鐵軌上。◇ *a branch line* 鐵路支線 ◇ *the East Coast line* 東海岸鐵路線 ➲ see also MAIN LINE

▸ **ROUTE/DIRECTION 路線；方向** **20** [C, usually sing.] the direction that sb/sth is moving or located in (行進的) 方向，路線；方位：*Just keep going* **in a straight line**; *you can't miss it.* 只管照直走，你不會找不到那地方的。◇ *The town is in a direct line between London and the coast.* 這個鎮在倫敦與海岸之間的直線上。◇ *Please move; you're right in my* **line of vision** (= the direction I am looking in). 請挪動一下，你正好擋住了我的視線。◇ *They followed the line of the river for three miles.* 他們沿着那條河走了三英里。◇ *Be careful to stay out of the* **line of fire** (= the direction sb is shooting in). 注意待在射擊路線以外。**21** [C] a route from one place to another especially when it is used for a particular purpose 路線；路徑；渠道：*Their aim was to block guerrilla* **supply lines**. 他們的目的是封鎖游擊隊的供給線。

▸ **ATTITUDE/ARGUMENT 態度；論點** **22** [C, usually sing.] an attitude or a belief, especially one that sb states publicly (尤指公開表明的) 態度，看法：*The government is* **taking a firm line on** *terrorism.* 政府現在對恐怖主義採取強硬的態度。◇ *He supported the* **official line** *on education.* 他支持官方的教育理念。➲ see also HARD LINE, PARTY LINE **23** [C] a method or way of doing or thinking about sth 方法；方式：*I don't follow your* **line of reasoning**. 我不理解你的推理方法。◇ *She decided to try a different* **line of argument** (= way of persuading sb of sth). 她決定換另一種說理方式。◇ *sb's first* **line of attack/defence** 某人進行抨擊／辯護的第一着 ◇ *The police are pursuing a new* **line of enquiry/inquiry** (= way of finding out information). 警方正在實施一種新的調查方法。

▸ **ACTIVITY 活動** **24** [sing.] a type or area of business, activity or interest 行業；活動的範圍：*My* **line of work** *pays pretty well.* 我的職業報酬頗豐厚。◇ *You can't do much in the art line without training.* 沒經過訓練，你在藝術行業是不會有多大作為的。➲ see also SIDELINE

▸ **PRODUCT 產品** **25** [C] a type of product 種類；類型：*We are starting a new line in casual clothes.* 我們將着手經營一組新的休閒服系列。◇ *Some lines sell better than others.* 有些品種的貨物銷售得好些，有些則較差。

▸ **TRANSPORT 運輸** **26** [C] (often used in names 常用於名稱) a company that provides transport for people or goods 運輸公司；航運公司：*a* **shipping/bus line** 航運／公共汽車公司 ➲ see also AIRLINE

▸ **SOLDIERS 士兵** **27** [C] a row or series of military defences where the soldiers are fighting during a war 防線；前線；戰線：*The regiment was sent to fight in* **the front line** (= the position nearest the enemy). 這個團被派到前線作戰。◇ *They were trapped* **behind enemy lines** (= in the area controlled by the enemy). 他們在敵人後方遭到圍困。

▸ **DRUGS 毒品** **28** [C] (*slang*) an amount of COCAINE that is spread out in a thin line, ready to take (準備吸用的) 散放成一條細線的可卡因

IDM **along/down the 'line** (*informal*) at some point during an activity or a process 在某一環節；在某一時刻：*Somewhere along the line a large amount of money went missing.* 有一筆巨款在某一環節上不翼而飛。◇ *We'll make a decision on that further down the line.* 我們將在以後的階段對此問題作出決策。 **along/on (the) ... 'lines** **1** (*informal*) in the way that is mentioned 按…方式：*The new system will operate* **along the same lines** *as the old one.* 新系統的運作方式將與舊系統一樣。◇ *They voted along class lines.* 他們按各社會等級進行投票。**2** (*informal*) similar to the way or thing that is mentioned 類似於(提及的方式或東西)：*Those aren't his exact words, but he said something along those lines.* 那些不是他的原話，但他說的大致就是這個意思。 **be, come, etc. on 'line** **1** to be working or functioning 正運轉；在運行：*The new working methods will come on line in June.* 新的操作方法將在六月實行。**2** using or connected to a computer or the Internet; communicating with other people by computer 聯機；在線：*All the new homes are on line.* 所有的新建住宅都已聯機。➲ see also ONLINE **bring sb/sth, come, get, fall, etc. into 'line (with sb/sth)** to behave or make sb/sth behave in the same way as other people or how they should behave 使一致；使規範；使符合；(和…) 一致：*Britain must be brought into line with the rest of Europe on taxes.* 英國必須在稅收上與其他歐洲國家保持一致。 **in (a) 'line (with sth)** in a position that forms a straight line with sth (與…) 成一排，成一直線：*An eclipse happens when the earth and moon are in line with the sun.* 地球和月亮與太陽處在一條直線上就會發生日蝕。 **in 'line for sth** likely to get sth 有可能獲得某物：*She is in line for promotion.* 她有可能得到提升。 **in the ˌline of 'duty** while doing a job 在執行任務時；在履行職責時：*A policeman was injured in the line of duty yesterday.* 昨天有一名警察在執行公務時受傷。 **in 'line with sth** similar to sth or so that one thing is closely connected with another 與…相似 (或緊密相連)：*Annual pay increases will be in line with inflation.* 每年加薪幅度將與通貨膨脹掛鈎。 **ˌlay it on the 'line** (*informal*) to tell sb clearly what you think, especially when they will not like what you say 坦率地說；實話實說：*The manager laid it on the line—some people would have to lose their jobs.* 經理開門見山地說，有些人將要失去工作。 **(choose, follow, take, etc.) the line of least re'sistance** (to choose, etc.) the easiest way of doing sth (採取) 最省事的方法 **(put sth) on the 'line** (*informal*) at risk 冒風險：*If we don't make a profit, my job is on the line.* 我們要是賺不了錢，我就有失業的危險。 **out of 'line (with sb/sth)** **1** not forming a straight line 不成直線 **2** different from sth 與…不同 (或不一致)；不符合：*London prices are way out of line with the rest of the country.* 倫敦的物價與英國其他地方的有很大的差異。**3** (*NAmE*) (*BrE* **ˌout of 'order**) (*informal*) behaving in a way that is not acceptable or right 行為不當；舉止讓人難以接受 **walk/tread a fine/thin line** to be in a difficult or dangerous situation where you could easily make a mistake 處於困境 (或險境)；如履薄冰；走鋼絲：*He was walking a fine line between being funny and being rude.* 他想滑稽而不粗魯，難以把握分寸。➲ more at BATTLE *n.*, DRAW *v.*, END *n.*, FIRING LINE, FIRM *adj.*, FRONT LINE, HARD *adj.*, HOOK *n.*, JUMP *v.*, OVERSTEP, PITCH *v.*, READ *v.*, SIGN *v.*, STEP *v.*, TOE *v.*

■ ***verb***

▸ **COVER INSIDE 做襯裏** **1** [often passive] **~ sth (with sth)** to cover the inside of sth with a layer of another material to keep it clean, make it stronger, etc. (用…) 做襯裏：*Line the pan with greaseproof paper.* 在烤盤裏墊一層防油紙。 **2 ~ sth** to form a layer on the inside of sth (在某物的內部) 形成一層：*the membranes that line the nose* 在鼻腔裏形成的一層內膜

▸ **FORM ROWS 形成行** **3** [often passive] to form lines or rows along sth 沿…形成行 (或列、排)：**~ sth** *Crowds of people lined the streets to watch the race.* 人群站在街道兩旁觀看比賽。◇ **~ sth with sth** *The walls were lined with books.* 靠牆是一排排的圖書。➲ see also LINED

IDM **line your (own)/sb's 'pockets** to get richer or make sb richer, especially by taking unfair advantage of a situation or by being dishonest (尤指通過佔便宜或欺詐而) 中飽私囊，(使) 發財

PHR V **ˌline ˈup** to stand in a line or row; to form a QUEUE/LINE 排成一行；站隊；排隊（等候）：*Line up, children!* 孩子們，站成一排！◇ *Cars lined up waiting to board the ship.* 汽車排隊等候上船。**ˌline sb/sth↔ˈup 1** to arrange people or things in a straight line or row 使站成一隊；使排列成一行：*The suspects were lined up against the wall.* 嫌疑犯靠牆站成了一排。◇ *He lined the bottles up along the shelf.* 他把瓶子排列在架子上。**2** to arrange for an event or activity to happen, or arrange for sb to be available to do sth 組織，安排（活動）；邀集（人做某事）：*Mark had a job lined up when he left college.* 馬克大學畢業時，工作已經安排好了。◇ *I've got a lot lined up this week* (= I'm very busy). 我這週有許多事要做。◇ *She's lined up a live band for the party.* 她為聚會安排了一個樂隊來現場演奏。**ˌline sth↔ˈup (with sth)** to move one thing into a correct position in relation to another thing 使…（與相關的另一物）排齊；使…對齊

lin·eage /ˈlɪniɪdʒ/ *noun* [U, C] (*formal*) the series of families that sb comes from originally 世系；宗系；家系；血統 **SYN** **ancestry**

lin·eal /ˈlɪniəl/ *adj.* [only before noun] (*formal*) coming in a direct line from an earlier or later generation of the same family as sb 直系的；嫡系的：*a lineal descendant of the company's founder* 公司創始人的直系後裔

lin·ea·ments /ˈlɪniəmənts/ *noun* [pl.] (*formal*) the typical features of sth（某物的）典型特徵

lin·ear /ˈlɪniə(r)/ *adj.* **1** of or in lines 線的；直線的；線狀的：*In his art he broke the laws of scientific linear perspective.* 他在自己的繪畫藝術中打破了科學的直線透視法規律。**2** going from one thing to another in a single series of stages（進展）直線式的：*Students do not always progress in a linear fashion.* 學生的進步不會總是直線式的。**OPP** **non-linear** **3** of length 長度的：*linear measurement* (= for example metres, feet, etc.) 長度測量 **4** (*mathematics* 數) able to be represented by a straight line on a GRAPH 線性的：*linear equations* 線性方程 ▶ **lin·ear·ity** /ˌlɪniˈærəti/ *noun* [U]：*She abandoned the linearity of the conventional novel.* 她摒棄了寫小說慣用的平鋪直敘的寫法。**lin·ear·ly** *adv.*

ˌLinear ˈB *noun* [U] the later of two early forms of writing found on stones in Crete（希臘克里特島上發現的）線形文字 B

line·back·er /ˈlaɪnbækə(r)/ *noun* (in AMERICAN FOOTBALL 美式足球) a DEFENSIVE player who tries to TACKLE members of the other team 中後衛

ˈline-caught *adj.* (of fish 魚) caught with a hook, not in a net 被釣到的：*We sell only line-caught wild fish.* 我們只賣釣來的野生魚。

lined /laɪnd/ *adj.* **1** (of skin, especially on the face 尤指面部皮膚) having folds or lines because of age, worry, etc. 有皺紋的 **SYN** **wrinkled**：*a deeply lined face* 佈滿深深皺紋的臉 **2** (of paper 紙) having lines printed or drawn across it 畫有橫線的；印有格的：*Lined paper helps keep handwriting neat.* 印有橫線的紙有助於書寫工整。**3** (of clothes 衣服) having a LINING inside them 有襯裏的；有內襯的：*a lined skirt* 帶襯裏的裙子 **4 -lined** having the object mentioned along an edge or edges, or as a LINING 沿邊緣有…的；有…作襯裏的：*a tree-lined road* 兩旁栽着樹的馬路

ˈline dancing *noun* [U] a type of dancing originally from the US, in which people dance in lines, all doing a complicated series of steps at the same time 隊列舞（源於美國）

ˈline drawing *noun* a drawing that consists only of lines 線條畫；白描

ˈline drive *noun* (in BASEBALL 棒球) a powerful hit in a straight line near to the ground 平直球，平飛球（貼近地面猛力擊打的直線球）

line·man /ˈlaɪnmən/ *noun* (*pl.* **-men** /-mən/) (*NAmE*) **1** a player in the front line of an AMERICAN FOOTBALL team（美式足球的）前鋒，線上的隊員 **2** = LINESMAN (2)

ˈline management *noun* [U] (*BrE*) the system of organizing a company, etc. in which information and instructions are passed from each employee and manager to the person one rank above or below them（公司等的）分級管理制 ▶ **ˈline manager** *noun*：*Review your training needs with your line manager.* 和你的部門經理探討一下你需要哪些方面的培訓。

linen /ˈlɪnɪn/ *noun* [U] **1** a type of cloth made from FLAX, used to make high-quality clothes, sheets, etc. 亞麻布：*a linen tablecloth* 亞麻桌布 **2** sheets, TABLECLOTHS, PILLOWCASES, etc. 亞麻織品；家用織品：(*BrE*) *a linen cupboard* 家庭日用織品壁櫥 ◇ (*NAmE*) *a linen closet* 家庭日用織品壁櫥 ➲ see also BEDLINEN **IDM** see WASH *v.*

ˌline of ˈsight (also **ˌline of ˈvision**, **ˈsight-line**) *noun* an imaginary line that goes from sb's eye to sth that they are looking at 視線：*There was a column directly in my line of sight, so I could only see half the stage.* 有一根柱子正擋着我的視線，所以我只能看見舞台的一半。

ˈline-out *noun* (in RUGBY 橄欖球) a situation that happens when the ball goes out of play, when players from opposing teams stand in lines and jump to try to catch the ball when it is thrown back in 界外球；球出界

ˈline printer *noun* a machine that prints very quickly, producing a complete line of print at a time 行式打印機

liner /ˈlaɪnə(r)/ *noun* **1** a large ship that carries passengers 郵輪：*an ocean liner* 遠洋客輪 ◇ *a luxury cruise liner* 豪華遊輪 ➲ VISUAL VOCAB page V54 **2** (especially in compounds 尤用於構成複合詞) a piece of material used to cover the inside surface of sth 襯裏；內襯：*bin/nappy liners* 襯在垃圾桶內的塑料袋；尿布襯墊 **3** = EYELINER

ˈliner note (*BrE* also **ˈsleeve note**) *noun* [usually pl.] information about the music or the performers that comes with a CD or is printed on the cover of a record（激光唱片或唱片的）封套內容簡介

lines·man /ˈlaɪnzmən/ *noun* (*pl.* **-men** /-mən/) **1** an official who helps the REFEREE in some games that are played on a field or court, especially in deciding whether or where a ball crosses one of the lines. Linesmen are now officially called **referee's assistants** in football (SOCCER).（足球等比賽中的）邊線裁判員，巡邊員，司線員 **2** (*BrE*) (*NAmE* **line·man**) a person whose job is to repair telephone or electricity power lines 架線工；線務員

ˈline-up *noun* [usually sing.] **1** the people who are going to take part in a particular event 陣容；陣式：*an impressive line-up of speakers* 給人印象深刻的演講者陣容 ◇ *the starting line-up* (= the players who will begin the game) 比賽首發隊員陣容 **2** a set of items, events etc. arranged to follow one another 節目安排；項目安排 **SYN** **programme**：*A horror movie completes this evening's TV line-up.* 今晚電視節目最後安排了一部恐怖影片。**3** (*especially NAmE*) (*BrE* also **iˌdentifiˈcation parade**, *informal* **iˈdentity parade**) a row of people, including one person who is suspected of a crime, who are shown to a witness to see if he or she can recognize the criminal 辨認行列，列隊認人（把嫌疑人同其他人排在一起，讓目擊者辨認）

ling /lɪŋ/ *noun* [U] a low plant that is a type of HEATHER and that grows on areas of wild open land (= MOORLAND) 帚石楠（低矮灌木，生長在荒野裏）

-ling /lɪŋ/ *suffix* (in nouns 構成名詞) (sometimes *disapproving*) small; not important 幼小；不重要：*duckling* 小鴨 ◇ *princeling* 小國的國君

lin·ger /ˈlɪŋɡə(r)/ *verb* **1** [I] to continue to exist for longer than expected 繼續存留；緩慢消失：*The faint smell of her perfume lingered in the room.* 房間裏仍飄溢着她那淡淡的香水味。◇ **~ on** *The civil war lingered on well into the 1930s.* 這次內戰到 20 世紀 30 年代還拖了好幾年。**2** [I] (**+ adv./prep.**) to stay somewhere for longer because you do not want to leave; to spend a long time doing sth 流連；逗留；徘徊；花很長時間做（某事）；磨蹭：*She lingered for a few minutes to talk to Nick.* 她多待了幾分鐘，想跟尼克談一談。◇ *We lingered over breakfast on the terrace.* 我們在平台上慢條斯理地吃着早餐。**3** [I] **~ (on sb/sth)** to continue to look at sb/sth or think about sth for longer than usual 持續看（或思考）：*His eyes lingered on the diamond ring on her finger.* 他一直

L

注視著她手指上的鑽戒。 **4** [I] **~ (on)** to stay alive but become weaker 苟延殘喘；奄奄一息：*He lingered on for several months after the heart attack.* 他心臟病發作後又拖了幾個月才去世。

lin·ge·rie /ˈlænʒəri; *NAmE* ˌlɑːndʒəˈreɪ/ *noun* [U] (used especially by shops/stores 尤用於商店) women's underwear 女內衣

lin·ger·ing /ˈlɪŋɡərɪŋ/ *adj.* slow to end or disappear 拖延的；纏綿的；緩慢消失的；遲遲不去的：*a painful and lingering death* 痛苦而拖延時日的死亡 ◇ *a last lingering look* 依依不捨的最後一瞥 ◇ *lingering doubts* 揮之不去的疑慮 ◇ *a lingering smell of machine oil* 飄浮不散的機油味 ▸ **lin·ger·ing·ly** *adv.*

lingo /ˈlɪŋɡəʊ; *NAmE* -ɡoʊ/ *noun* [sing.] (*informal*) **1** a language, especially a foreign language 語言；（尤指）外國語，外國話：*He doesn't speak the lingo.* 他不會講這種外國話。 **2** (*especially NAmE*) expressions used by a particular group of people 行話；術語 SYN **jargon**：*baseball lingo* 棒球術語

lin·gua franca /ˌlɪŋɡwə ˈfræŋkə/ *noun* [usually sing.] (*linguistics* 語言) a shared language of communication used between people whose main languages are different（母語不同的人共用的）通用語：*English has become a lingua franca in many parts of the world.* 英語在世界上許多地方都成了通用語。

lin·gual /ˈlɪŋɡwəl/ *adj.* **1** (*anatomy* 解) related to the tongue 舌的 **2** related to speech or language 話語的；語言的 **3** (*phonetics* 語音) (of a speech sound 語音) produced using the tongue 舌音的；用舌發出的 ▸ **lin·gual·ly** /ˈlɪŋɡwəli/ *adv.*

L

lin·guist /ˈlɪŋɡwɪst/ *noun* **1** a person who knows several foreign languages well 通曉數國語言的人：*She's an excellent linguist.* 她精通數國語言。 ◇ *I'm afraid I'm no linguist* (= I find foreign languages difficult). 對不起，我不懂外語。 **2** a person who studies languages or LINGUISTICS 語言學家

lin·guis·tic /lɪŋˈɡwɪstɪk/ *adj.* connected with language or the scientific study of language 語言的；語言學的：*linguistic and cultural barriers* 語言和文化上的障礙 ◇ *a child's innate linguistic ability* 兒童的先天語言能力 ◇ *new developments in linguistic theory* 語言學理論的新發展 ▸ **lin·guis·tic·al·ly** *adv.*

lin·guis·tics /lɪŋˈɡwɪstɪks/ *noun* [U] the scientific study of language or of particular languages 語言學：*a course in applied linguistics* 應用語言學課程

lini·ment /ˈlɪnəmənt/ *noun* [C, U] a liquid, especially one made with oil, that you rub on a painful part of your body to reduce the pain（尤指油質、鎮痛的）搽劑，擦劑；鎮痛油

lin·ing /ˈlaɪnɪŋ/ *noun* **1** [C] a layer of material used to cover the inside surface of sth 襯層；內襯；襯裏：*a pair of leather gloves with fur linings* 一雙毛皮襯裏的皮手套 ➲ VISUAL VOCAB page V61 **2** [U] the covering of the inner surface of a part of the body（身體器官內壁的）膜：*the stomach lining* 胃黏膜 IDM see CLOUD *n.*

link AW /lɪŋk/ *noun, verb*

■ *noun* **1** **~ (between A and B)** a connection between two or more people or things 聯繫；連接：*Police suspect there may be a link between the two murders.* 警方懷疑那兩樁兇殺案可能有關聯。 ◇ *evidence for a strong causal link between exposure to sun and skin cancer* 太陽曝曬與皮膚癌之間有緊密因果關係的證據 ➲ see also MISSING LINK **2** a relationship between two or more people, countries or organizations 關係；紐帶：**~ (with sth)** *to establish* **trade links** *with Asia* 與亞洲建立貿易關係 ◇ **~ (between A and B)** *Social customs provide a vital link between generations.* 社會風俗在不同世代之間起到了極其重要的紐帶作用。 **3** a means of travelling or communicating between two places 交通路線；通訊手段：*a high-speed* **rail link** 高速的鐵路交通 ◇ *a link road* 連接路 ◇ *a video link* 視頻線路 ◇ *The speech was broadcast via a* **satellite link**. 這次演講是通過衛星播放的。 **4** (*computing* 計) a place in an electronic document that is connected to another electronic document or to another part of the same document 鏈接：*To visit similar websites to this one, click on the links at the bottom of the page.* 要訪問與這個網站類似的網站，點擊網頁底部的鏈接。 ➲ VISUAL VOCAB page V68 ➲ see also HYPERLINK **5** each ring of a chain（鏈狀物的）環，節，圈 ➲ picture at ROPE ➲ see also CUFFLINK

IDM **a link in the ˈchain** one of the stages in a process or a line of argument 鏈條中的一個環節；整個過程中的一個階段 ➲ more at WEAK

■ *verb* [often passive] **1** to make a physical or electronic connection between one object, machine, place, etc. and another 把（物體、機器、地方等）連接起來 SYN **connect**：**~ A to B** *The video cameras are linked to a powerful computer.* 這些攝像機是與一台功能強大的計算機相連接的。 ◇ **~ A with B** *The Channel Tunnel links Britain with the rest of Europe.* 英吉利海峽隧道把英國和歐洲其他國家連接起來了。 ◇ **~ A and B (together)** *When computers are networked, they are linked together so that information can be transferred between them.* 計算機聯網連接，即彼此可供互傳信息。 **2** if sth **links** two things, facts or situations, or they **are linked**, they are connected in some way 聯繫；相關聯：**~ A to/with B** *Exposure to ultraviolet light is* **closely linked** *to skin cancer.* 受紫外線照射與皮膚癌緊密相關。 ◇ **~ A and B** *The two factors are* **directly linked**. 這兩個因素直接聯繫在一起。 ◇ *The personal and social development of the child are* **inextricably linked** (= they depend on each other). 兒童在自身和與人交往兩方面的成長是相輔相成的。 **3** **~ A to/with B** | **~ A and B** to state that there is a connection or relationship between two things or people 說明（兩件東西或兩人之間）有聯繫（或關係） SYN **associate**：*Detectives have linked the break-in to a similar crime in the area last year.* 偵探認為這起入室盜竊案與去年此地區一類似案件有關。 ◇ *Newspapers have linked his name with the singer.* 報章報道把他的名字與那名歌手連在一起。 **4** **~ A and B** to join two things by putting one through the other 挽住；鈎住；套在一起：*The two girls* **linked arms** *as they strolled down the street.* 兩個女孩挽着胳臂沿街漫步而行。

PHR V **ˌlink ˈup (with sb/sth)** to join or become joined with sb/sth（與…）連接，結合；使連接；使結合：*The two spacecraft will link up in orbit.* 兩艘宇宙飛船將在軌道上對接。 ◇ *The bands have linked up for a charity concert.* 這些樂隊已聯合起來，準備辦一場慈善音樂會。 ➲ related noun LINK-UP

link·age AW /ˈlɪŋkɪdʒ/ *noun* **1** [U, C] **~ (between A and B)** the act of linking things; a link or system of links 連接；聯繫；鏈環；連鎖 SYN **connection**：*This chapter explores the linkage between economic development and the environment.* 本章探討的是經濟發展與環境之間的關係。 **2** [C] a device that links two or more things 聯動裝置

ˈlinking verb (also **cop·ula**) *noun* (*grammar* 語法) a verb such as *be* or *become* that connects a subject with the adjective or noun (called the COMPLEMENT) that describes it 繫詞；連繫動詞：*In 'She became angry', the verb 'became' is a linking verb.* 在 She became angry 一句中，動詞 became 為連繫動詞。

link·man /ˈlɪŋkmæn/ *noun* (*pl.* **-men** /-men/) (*BrE*) **1** a person who helps two people or groups of people to communicate with each other 聯繫人；中間人；居間人 **2** a person who works on the radio or television introducing the programmes or telling people about future programmes（廣播或電視的）串聯主持人

links /lɪŋks/ *noun* = GOLF LINKS

ˈlink-up *noun* a connection formed between two things, for example two companies or two broadcasting systems 連接，聯繫（指兩事物如兩家公司或兩個廣播系統的結合）：*a live satellite link-up with the conference* 對會議的衛星實況轉播

Lin·naean (also **Lin·nean**) /lɪˈneɪən; -ˈniːən/ *adj.* (*biology* 生) relating to the system of naming and arranging living things into scientific groups which was invented by Carolus Linnaeus (Carl von Linné) 林奈式雙名法的，林奈式分類系統的（統一生物命名，定義生物屬種）

lin·net /ˈlɪnɪt/ *noun* a small brown and grey bird of the FINCH family 赤胸朱頂雀；麻籽雀

lino /ˈlaɪnəʊ; *NAmE* -noʊ/ *noun* [U] (*BrE, informal*) = LINOLEUM

lino·cut /ˈlaɪnəʊkʌt; *NAmE* -noʊ-/ *noun* a design or shape cut in a piece of LINO, used to make a print; a print made in this way 油氈浮雕圖案；油氈浮雕版印染品

li·no·leum /lɪˈnəʊliəm; *NAmE* -ˈnoʊ-/ (also *BrE, informal* **lino**) *noun* [U] a type of strong material with a hard shiny surface, used for covering floors 油地氈

Lino·type™ /ˈlaɪnəʊtaɪp; *NAmE* -noʊ-/ *noun* a machine used in the past for printing newspapers, that produces a line of words as one strip of metal 萊諾鑄排機（舊時用於報紙印刷）

lin·seed oil /ˌlɪnsiːd ˈɔɪl/ (also **flax·seed oil**) *noun* [U] an oil made from FLAX seeds, used in paint or to protect wood, etc. 亞麻籽油

lint /lɪnt/ *noun* [U] **1** (*especially BrE*) a type of soft cotton cloth used for covering and protecting wounds（敷傷口用的）紗布 **2** (*technical* 術語) short fine FIBRES that come off the surface of cloth when it is being made （織物在製作過程中從表面掉落的）纖維屑，飛花 **3** (*especially NAmE*) (*BrE* usually **fluff**) small soft pieces of wool, cotton, etc. that stick on the surface of cloth （毛料、棉布等的）絨毛

lin·tel /ˈlɪntl/ *noun* (*architecture* 建) a piece of wood or stone over a door or window, that forms part of the frame （門窗的）過梁；門楣

Linux™ /ˈlɪnəks/ *noun* [U] (*computing* 計) an OPERATING SYSTEM based on UNIX that is available free in the basic version * Linux 操作系統，Linux 作業系統 （基於 Unix 操作系統，基本版本可免費獲得）

lion /ˈlaɪən/ *noun* a large powerful animal of the cat family, that hunts in groups and lives in parts of Africa and southern Asia. Lions have yellowish-brown fur and the male has a MANE (= long thick hair round its neck). 獅；獅子 ➲ VISUAL VOCAB page V12 ➲ compare LIONESS ➲ see also MOUNTAIN LION

IDM **the ˈlion's den** a difficult situation in which you have to face a person or people who are unfriendly or aggressive towards you 龍潭虎穴 **the ˈlion's share (of sth)** (*BrE*) the largest or best part of sth when it is divided 最大（或最好）的一份 ➲ more at BEARD *v.* ➲ see also BRITISH LIONS

lion·ess /ˈlaɪənes/ *noun* a female lion 母獅

lion·ize (*BrE* also **-ise**) /ˈlaɪənaɪz/ *verb* **~ sb** (*formal*) to treat sb as a famous or important person 把（某人）視為名人；把（某人）當成要人對待

lip 0-w /lɪp/ *noun*

1 0-w [C] either of the two soft edges at the opening to the mouth 嘴唇： *The assistant pursed her lips.* 那女助手噘起了嘴。◇ *your **upper/lower/top/bottom lip*** 你的上／下嘴唇 ◇ *She kissed him **on the lips**.* 她吻了他的嘴唇。◇ *Not a drop of alcohol **passed my lips*** (= I didn't drink any). 我滴酒未沾。➲ COLLOCATIONS at PHYSICAL ➲ VISUAL VOCAB page V59 **2 -lipped** (in adjectives 構成形容詞) having the type of lips mentioned 嘴唇…的： *thin-lipped* 嘴唇薄的 ◇ *thick-lipped* 嘴唇厚的 ➲ see also TIGHT-LIPPED **3** [C] **~ (of sth)** the edge of a container or a hollow place in the ground （容器或凹陷地方的）邊，邊沿 SYN **rim**： *He ran his finger around the lip of the cup.* 他用手指沿杯口抹了一下。◇ *Lava bubbled a few feet below the lip of the crater.* 熔岩在火山口下幾英尺處沸騰。➲ picture at JUG **4** [U] (*informal*) words spoken to sb that are rude and show a lack of respect for that person 粗魯無禮的話 SYN **cheek**： *Don't let him **give you any lip!*** 不要讓他對你說粗魯無禮的話！

IDM **lick/smack your ˈlips** **1** to move your tongue over your lips, especially before eating sth good （尤指在吃好東西前）舔嘴唇 **2** (*informal*) to show that you are excited about sth and want it to happen soon 迫不及待；渴望： *They were licking their lips at the thought of clinching the deal.* 他們一想到馬上要做成這筆交易就顯得急不可待了。 **my lips are ˈsealed** used to say that you will not repeat sb's secret to other people （表示不會說出某人的秘密）我把嘴封住，我絕口不提 **on everyone's ˈlips** if sth is **on everyone's lips**, they are all talking about it 大家都在談論 ➲ more at BITE *v.*, PASS *v.*, READ *v.*, SLIP *n.*, STIFF *adj.*

lip·ase /ˈlaɪpeɪz/ *noun* [U] (*chemistry* 化) an ENZYME (= a chemical substance in the body) that makes fats change into acids and alcohol 脂（肪）酶

ˈlip gloss *noun* [U, C] a substance that is put on the lips to make them look shiny 唇彩 ➲ VISUAL VOCAB page V60

lipid /ˈlɪpɪd/ *noun* (*chemistry* 化) any of a group of natural substances which do not dissolve in water, including plant oils and STEROIDS 脂質；類脂

ˈlip liner *noun* [U] a substance that is put on the outline of the lips, to prevent LIPSTICK from spreading 唇線筆 ➲ VISUAL VOCAB page V60

lipo·pro·tein /ˈlɪpəprəʊtiːn; ˈlaɪ-; *NAmE* -proʊ-/ *noun* (*biology* 生) a PROTEIN that combines with a lipid and carries it to another part of the body in the blood 脂蛋白

lipo·some /ˈlɪpəsəʊm; ˈlaɪ-; *NAmE* -soʊm/ *noun* a very small bag formed of lipid MOLECULES, used to carry a drug to a particular part of the body 脂質體

lipo·suc·tion /ˈlɪpəʊsʌkʃn; ˈlaɪ-; *NAmE* ˈlaɪpoʊ-; ˈlɪ-/ *noun* [U] a way of removing fat from sb's body by using SUCTION 吸脂術；脂肪抽吸（術）

lippy /ˈlɪpi/ *adj.*, *noun*

■ ***adj.*** (*BrE, informal*) showing a lack of respect in the way that you speak to sb 出言不遜的；冒犯頂撞的 SYN **cheeky**

■ ***noun*** [U] (*BrE, informal*) = LIPSTICK

ˈlip-read *verb* [I, T] **~ (sb)** to understand what sb is saying by watching the way their lips move 觀唇辨意；唇讀 ▸ **ˈlip-reading** *noun* [U]

lip·salve /ˈlɪpsælv/ *noun* [U] (*BrE*) a substance in the form of a stick, like a LIPSTICK, that you put on your lips to stop them becoming sore 護唇膏；潤唇膏

ˈlip service *noun* [U] if sb pays **lip service** to sth, they say that they approve of it or support it, without proving their support by what they actually do 空口的應酬話；口惠： *All the parties pay lip service to environmental issues.* 對環境問題各方都是口惠而實不至。

lip·stick /ˈlɪpstɪk/ *noun* [U, C] a substance made into a small stick, used for colouring the lips; a small stick of this substance 口紅；唇膏： *She was wearing bright red lipstick.* 她搽着鮮紅色的口紅。➲ picture at STICK ➲ VISUAL VOCAB page V60

ˌlipstick ˈlesbian *noun* (*informal*) a LESBIAN who is a fashionable and attractive woman 口紅女同性戀者，口紅女同志（指時髦有魅力的女同性戀者）： *the lipstick lesbian stereotype* 口紅女同性戀者的模式化形象

lip-sync (also **lip-synch**) /ˈlɪp sɪŋk/ *verb* [I, T] to move your mouth, without speaking or singing, so that its movements match the sound on a recorded song, etc. （與錄製歌曲等）對口形，對嘴： **~ (to sth)** *She lip-synced to a Beatles song.* 她對口形假唱一首披頭士樂隊的歌曲。◇ **~ sth** *He lip-synced 'Return to Sender'.* 他對口形假唱了《退回寄信人》。

li·quefy /ˈlɪkwɪfaɪ/ *verb* (**li·que·fies**, **li·que·fy·ing**, **li·que·fied**, **li·que·fied**) [I, T] **~ (sth)** (*formal*) to become liquid; to make sth liquid （使）液化

li·queur /lɪˈkjʊə(r); *NAmE* -ˈkɜːr/ (*NAmE* also **cor·dial**) *noun* **1** [U, C] a strong sweet alcoholic drink, sometimes flavoured with fruit. It is usually drunk in very small glasses after a meal. （通常餐後少量飲用的）烈性甜酒 **2** [C] a glass of liqueur 一杯烈性甜酒

li·quid 0-w /ˈlɪkwɪd/ *noun*, *adj.*

■ ***noun*** 0-w [U, C] a substance that flows freely and is not a solid or a gas, for example water or oil 液體： *She poured the dark brown liquid down the sink.* 她把深棕色的液體倒進了洗碗槽。◇ *the transition from liquid to vapour* 從液體到蒸汽的轉化 ➲ see also WASHING-UP LIQUID

■ ***adj.*** **1** 0-w in the form of a liquid; not a solid or a gas 液體的；液態的： *liquid soap* 肥皂液 ◇ *liquid nitrogen* 液態氮 ◇ *The detergent comes in powder or **liquid form**.* 這種洗滌劑有粉狀或液態兩種選擇。◇ *a bar selling snacks and **liquid refreshment*** (= drinks) 售賣小吃和飲料的櫃

柗 **2** (*finance* 財) in cash, or that can easily be changed into cash 流動性好的；易變現的： *liquid assets* 流動資產 **3** (*literary*) clear, like water 清澈的；明亮的；晶瑩的 **SYN** **limpid**： *liquid blue eyes* 晶瑩的藍眼睛 **4** (*literary*) (of sounds 聲音) clear, pure and flowing 清脆的；清純的；流暢的： *the liquid song of a blackbird* 烏鶇清脆的鳴囀

li·quid·ate /ˈlɪkwɪdeɪt/ *verb* **1** [I, T] **~ (sth)** to close a business and sell everything it owns in order to pay debts 清算，清盤（停業後將資產出售，償還債務） **2** [T] **~ sth** (*finance* 財) to sell sth in order to get money 變賣；變現： *to liquidate assets* 變賣資產 **3** [T] **~ sth** (*finance* 財) to pay a debt 償還，清償（債務） **4** [T] **~ sb/sth** to destroy or remove sb/sth that causes problems 消滅；摧毀；清除 **SYN** **annihilate**： *The government tried to liquidate the rebel movement and failed.* 政府試圖肅清反叛運動，結果失敗了。

li·quid·ation /ˌlɪkwɪˈdeɪʃn/ *noun* [U] **1** (*BrE, AustralE, law* 律) the process of closing a company, selling what it owns and paying its debts（公司的）清盤，清算；（債務的）清償： *The company has* ***gone into liquidation.*** 這家公司已破產。➲ COLLOCATIONS at BUSINESS ➲ compare CHAPTER 11 **2** (*finance* 財) the action of selling sth to get money or to avoid losing money（資產的）變現，變賣： *Falling prices may lead to further liquidation of stocks.* 股價下跌可能導致股票的進一步變現。

li·quid·ator /ˈlɪkwɪdeɪtə(r)/ *noun* a person responsible for closing down a business and using any profits from the sale to pay its debts 清算人；清盤人

L

ˌliquid ˌcrystal disˈplay *noun* = LCD (1)

li·quid·ity /lɪˈkwɪdəti/ *noun* [U] (*finance* 財) the state of owning things of value that can easily be exchanged for cash 資產流動性；資產變現能力

li·quid·ize (*BrE* also **-ise**) /ˈlɪkwɪdaɪz/ *verb* **~ sth** (*especially BrE*) to crush fruit, vegetables, etc. into a thick liquid 把（水果、蔬菜等）榨成汁 **SYN** **purée**

li·quid·izer (*BrE* also **-iser**) /ˈlɪkwɪdaɪzə(r)/ *noun* (*BrE*) = BLENDER

ˌliquid ˈparaffin (*BrE*) (*NAmE* **ˈmineral oil**) *noun* [U] a liquid with no colour and no smell that comes from PETROLEUM and is used in medicines and COSMETICS 液狀石蠟，石蠟油（用於製造藥品和化妝品）

li·quor /ˈlɪkə(r)/ *noun* [U] **1** (*especially NAmE*) strong alcoholic drink 烈性酒 **SYN** **spirits**： *hard liquor* 烈性酒 ◊ *She drinks wine and beer but no liquor.* 她喝葡萄酒和啤酒，但不沾烈性酒。 **2** (*BrE, technical* 術語) any alcoholic drink 含酒精飲料： *intoxicating liquor* 烈酒

li·quor·ice (*especially BrE*) (*NAmE* usually **lic·orice**) /ˈlɪkərɪʃ; -rɪs/ *noun* [U, C] a firm black substance with a strong flavour, obtained from the root of a plant, used in medicine and to make sweets/candy; a sweet/candy made from this substance 甘草（用於製藥和糖果）；甘草糖

li·quor·ice all·sorts /ˌlɪkərɪʃ ˈɔːlsɔːts; -rɪs; *NAmE* -sɔːrts/ *noun* [pl.] (*BrE*) brightly coloured sweets/candy made with liquorice 什錦甘草糖果

ˈliquor store (also **ˈpackage store**) (both *US*) (*BrE* **ˈoff-licence**) *noun* a shop that sells alcoholic drinks in bottles and cans to take away 外賣酒店

lira /ˈlɪərə; *NAmE* ˈlɪrə/ *noun* (*pl.* **lire** /ˈlɪərə; *NAmE* ˈlɪreɪ/) (*abbr.* **l.**) the unit of money in Malta, Syria and Turkey, and formerly in Italy (replaced there in 2002 by the euro) 里拉（馬耳他、敍利亞、土耳其和意大利貨幣單位，在意大利於 2002 年為歐元所取代）

lisle /laɪl/ *noun* [U] a fine smooth cotton thread used especially for making TIGHTS and STOCKINGS 里爾線（尤用於織連褲襪和長襪）

lisp /lɪsp/ *noun, verb*

■ ***noun*** [usually sing.] a speech fault in which the sound 's' is pronounced 'th' 咬舌（語言缺陷，把 s 說成 th）： *She spoke with a slight lisp.* 她說話有點咬舌。

■ ***verb*** [I, T] (**+ speech**) to speak with a lisp 說話口齒不清；咬舌

lis·som (also **lis·some**) /ˈlɪsəm/ *adj.* (*literary*) (of sb's body 人體) thin and attractive 輕盈優美的；苗條的；裊娜的 **SYN** **lithe**

list /lɪst/ *noun, verb*

■ ***noun*** **1** [C] a series of names, items, figures, etc., especially when they are written or printed 一覽表；名單；目錄；清單： *a* ***shopping/wine/price list*** 購物單；酒類／價目表 ◊ *to* ***make a list*** *of things to do* 把要做的事列成清單 ◊ (*formal*) *to* ***draw up a list*** 造表 ◊ *Is your name* ***on the list****?* 表上有你的名字嗎？◊ *Having to wait hours came* ***high on the list*** *of complaints.* 在投訴當中，最多的是抱怨等候時間太長。➲ see also A-LIST, HIT LIST, LAUNDRY LIST, MAILING LIST, SHORTLIST, WAITING LIST, WAIT LIST **2** [sing.] the fact of a ship leaning to one side（船的）傾斜 **IDM** see DANGER

■ ***verb*** **1** [T] **~ sth** to write a list of things in a particular order（按某次序）把…列表，列清單，造表： *We were asked to list our ten favourite songs.* 我們應要求列出自己最喜愛的十首歌曲。◊ *Towns in the guide are listed alphabetically.* 旅遊指南裏的城鎮是按字母順序排列的。 **2** [T] **~ sb/sth** to mention or include sb/sth in a list 列舉；把…列入一覽表： *The koala is listed among Australia's endangered animals.* 樹袋熊已列為澳大利亞瀕臨絕種的動物之一。◊ *soldiers listed as missing* 列入失蹤名單的士兵 **3** [I, T] **~ (at sth)** | **~ sth** (*NAmE*) to be put or put sth in a list of things for sale（被）列入銷售清單，列入價目表： *This CD player lists at $200.* 這台激光唱片播放機在價目單上定為 200 元。 **4** [I] (of a ship 船) to lean to one side（向一側）傾斜

ˌlisted ˈbuilding *noun* (*BrE*) a building that is officially protected because it has artistic or historical value 正式列入文物保護範圍的建築物 ➲ see also LANDMARK

lis·ten /ˈlɪsn/ *verb, noun*

■ ***verb*** **1** [I] to pay attention to sb/sth that you can hear（注意地）聽；傾聽： *Listen! What's that noise? Can you hear it?* 聽！那是什麼響聲？你能聽見嗎？◊ *Sorry, I wasn't really listening.* 對不起，我沒注意聽。◊ **~ to sb/sth** *to listen to music* 聽音樂 ◊ *I listened carefully to her story.* 我認真聽了她說的情況。 **HELP** You cannot 'listen sth' (without 'to'). 不能說 listen sth（不帶介詞 to）： *I'm fond of listening to classical music.* ◊ ~~*I'm fond of listening classical music.*~~ **2** [I] **~ (to sb/sth)** to take notice of what sb says to you so that you follow their advice or believe them 聽信；聽從： *None of this would have happened if you'd listened to me.* 你要是聽了我的話，這一切就不會發生了。◊ *Why won't you* ***listen to reason****?* 你怎麼就不聽勸呢？ **3** [I] (*informal*) used to tell sb to take notice of what you are going to say（讓對方注意）聽着，注意聽： *Listen, there's something I have to tell you.* 聽着，我有事要告訴你。

PHR V **ˈlisten (ˈout) for sth** to be prepared to hear a particular sound 留心聽（某種聲音）： *Can you listen out for the doorbell?* 你能留心聽着門鈴嗎？ **ˌlisten ˈin (on/to sth)** **1** to listen to a conversation that you are not supposed to hear 竊聽；偷聽；監聽： *You shouldn't listen in on other people's conversations.* 你不應該偷聽別人的談話。 **2** to listen to a radio broadcast 收聽（無線電廣播） **ˌlisten ˈup** (*informal, especially NAmE*) used to tell people to listen carefully because you are going to say sth important 注意聽，留心聽（因有要事要講而要人注意聽）

■ ***noun*** [usually sing.] an act of listening 聽： *Have a listen to this.* 聽一聽這個。

lis·ten·able /ˈlɪsnəbl/ *adj.* (*informal*) pleasant to listen to 悅耳的；好聽的

lis·ten·er /ˈlɪsənə(r)/ *noun* **1** a person who listens 聽者： *a good listener* (= sb who you can rely on to listen with attention or sympathy) 認真傾聽的人 **2** a person listening to a radio programme 收聽廣播節目的人

ˈlistening post *noun* a place where people who are part of an army listen to enemy communications to try to get information that will give them an advantage（軍隊的）潛聽哨

lis·teria /lɪˈstɪəriə; *NAmE* -ˈstɪr-/ *noun* [U] a type of bacteria that makes people sick if they eat infected food 利斯特菌

list·ing /ˈlɪstɪŋ/ *noun* **1** [C] a list, especially an official or published list of people or things, often arranged in alphabetical order（常按字母順序排列的）表冊，目錄，列表：*a comprehensive listing of all airlines* 所有航線的總目錄 **2 listings** [pl.] information in a newspaper or magazine about what films/movies, plays, etc. are being shown in a particular town or city（報章或雜誌有關某城市電影、戲劇等的）上映信息，演出信息：*a listings magazine* 演出信息雜誌 **3** [C] a position or an item on a list（表冊上的）位置，項目：(*business* 商) *The company is seeking a stock exchange listing* (= for trading shares). 這家公司正在爭取上市。

list·less /ˈlɪstləs/ *adj.* having no energy or enthusiasm 沒有活力的；無精打采的；不熱情的 SYN **lethargic**：*The illness left her feeling listless and depressed.* 那場病使她感到虛弱無力，提不起精神。▶ **list·less·ly** *adv.* **list·less·ness** *noun* [U]

ˈ**list price** *noun* [usually sing.] (*business* 商) the price at which goods are advertised for sale, for example in a CATALOGUE（商品目錄等中的）價目表價格，定價

lit *past tense, past part.* of LIGHT

lit·any /ˈlɪtəni/ *noun* (*pl.* **-ies**) **1** a series of prayers to God for use in church services, spoken by a priest, etc., with set responses by the people 連禱文，總禱文（連禱啟應的禱文）**2 ~ (of sth)** (*formal*) a long boring account of a series of events, reasons, etc.（對一系列事件、原因等）枯燥冗長的陳述：*a litany of complaints* 喋喋不休的抱怨

lit·chi (*especially US*) = LYCHEE

lite /laɪt/ *adj.* (*informal*) **1** (*especially NAmE*) (of food or drink 食物或飲料) containing fewer CALORIES than other types of food, and therefore less likely to make you fat (a way of spelling 'light') 低熱量的，清淡的（light 的一種拼寫方法）：*lite ice cream* 低熱量冰淇淋 **2** (used after a noun 用於名詞後) (*disapproving*) used to say that a thing is similar to sth else but lacks many of its serious or important qualities 類似…的劣質品：*I would describe this movie as 'Hitchcock lite'.* 我把這部電影稱為"模仿希區柯克導演手法的平庸之作"。

liter (*NAmE*) = LITRE

lit·er·acy /ˈlɪtərəsi/ *noun* [U] the ability to read and write 讀寫能力：*a campaign to promote adult literacy* 提高成人文化水平的運動 ◇ *basic literacy skills* 基本的讀寫技巧 OPP **illiteracy** ➲ see also COMPUTER LITERACY at COMPUTER-LITERATE

lit·eral /ˈlɪtərəl/ *adj.* **1** [usually before noun] being the basic or usual meaning of a word or phrase 字面意義的：*I am not referring to 'small' people in the literal sense of the word.* 我指的不是字面意義上的"小"人。◇ *The literal meaning of 'petrify' is 'turn to stone'.* * petrify 的字面意思是 turn to stone（變成石頭）。➲ compare FIGURATIVE (1), METAPHORICAL **2** [usually before noun] that follows the original words exactly 完全按原文的：*a literal translation* 直譯 ➲ compare FREE *adj.* (13) **3** (*disapproving*) lacking imagination 缺乏想像力的：*Her interpretation of the music was too literal.* 她演奏的音樂太平淡乏味。▶ **lit·er·al·ness** *noun* [U]

lit·er·al·ly /ˈlɪtərəli/ *adv.* **1** in a literal way 按字面；字面上 SYN **exactly**：*The word 'planet' literally means 'wandering body'.* * planet 一詞字面上的意思是 wandering body。◇ *When I told you to 'get lost' I didn't expect to* ***be taken literally****.* 我叫你"滾開"，並沒讓你按字面意思來理解呀。**2** used to emphasize the truth of sth that may seem surprising（強調事實可能令人驚訝）真正地，確實地：*There are literally hundreds of prizes to win.* 可贏取的獎品真的有好幾百份。**3** (*informal*) used to emphasize a word or phrase, even if it is not actually true in a literal sense（用於加強語氣，雖然並非詞語的字面意義）簡直，真正地：*I literally jumped out of my skin.* 我簡直給嚇了一大跳。

lit·er·ary /ˈlɪtərəri; *NAmE* -reri/ *adj.* **1** connected with literature 文學的；文學上的：***literary criticism/theory*** 文學批評／理論 **2** (of a language or style of writing 語言或寫作文體) suitable for or typical of a work of literature 適於文學作品的；有典型文學作品特徵的：*It was Chaucer who really turned English into a literary language.* 是喬叟使英語真正變成了文學語言。**3** liking literature very much; studying or writing literature 愛好文學的；從事文學研究（或寫作）的：*a literary man* 文人

ˈ**literary agent** *noun* a person whose job is to represent authors and persuade companies to publish their work 作品經紀人，作家代理人（說服出版社出版作品）

lit·er·ate /ˈlɪtərət/ *adj.* able to read and write 有讀寫能力的；有文化的 OPP **illiterate** ➲ see also NUMERATE at NUMERACY, COMPUTER-LITERATE

lit·er·ati /ˌlɪtəˈrɑːti/ **the literati** *noun* [pl.] (*formal*) educated and intelligent people who enjoy literature 文人學士

lit·era·ture 0‑π /ˈlɪtrətʃə(r); *NAmE* also -tʃʊr/ *noun* [U] **1** 0‑π pieces of writing that are valued as works of art, especially novels, plays and poems (in contrast to technical books and newspapers, magazines, etc.) 文學；文學作品：*French literature* 法國文學 ◇ *great* ***works of literature*** 文學巨著 ➲ COLLOCATIONS at next page **2 ~ (on sth)** pieces of writing or printed information on a particular subject（某學科的）文獻，著作，資料：*I've read all the available literature on keeping rabbits.* 我閱讀了我能找到的關於養兔的全部資料。◇ *sales literature* 推銷商品的宣傳資料

lithe /laɪð/ *adj.* (of a person or their body 人或人體) moving or bending easily, in a way that is elegant 優美柔軟的；易彎曲的 ▶ **lithe·ly** *adv.*

lith·ium /ˈlɪθiəm/ *noun* [U] (*symb.* **Li**) a chemical element. Lithium is a soft, very light, silver-white metal used in batteries and ALLOYS. 鋰

litho·graph /ˈlɪθəɡrɑːf; *NAmE* -ɡræf/ *noun* a picture printed by lithography 平版印刷畫

lith·og·raphy /lɪˈθɒɡrəfi; *NAmE* -ˈθɑːɡ-/ *noun* (also *informal* **litho** /ˈlaɪθəʊ; *NAmE* -θoʊ/) [U] the process of printing from a smooth surface, for example a metal plate, that has been specially prepared so that ink only sticks to the design to be printed 平版印刷術 ▶ **litho·graph·ic** /ˌlɪθəˈɡræfɪk/ *adj.*

lith·ology /lɪˈθɒlədʒi; *NAmE* lɪˈθɑːl-/ *noun* [U] the study of the general physical characteristics of rocks 岩性學；岩石學

litho·sphere /ˈlɪθəsfɪə(r); *NAmE* -sfɪr/ *noun* [sing.] (*geology* 地) the layer of rock that forms the outer part of the earth 岩石圈；岩石層

liti·gant /ˈlɪtɪɡənt/ *noun* (*law* 律) a person who is making or defending a claim in court 訴訟當事人

liti·gate /ˈlɪtɪɡeɪt/ *verb* [I, T] **~ (sth)** (*law* 律) to take a claim or disagreement to court 提起訴訟；打官司 ▶ **liti·ga·tor** *noun*

liti·ga·tion /ˌlɪtɪˈɡeɪʃn/ *noun* [U] (*law* 律) the process of making or defending a claim in court 訴訟；打官司：*The company has been in litigation with its previous auditors for a full year.* 那家公司與前任審計員已打了整整一年的官司。

li·ti·gious /lɪˈtɪdʒəs/ *adj.* (*formal, disapproving*) too ready to take disagreements to court 好訴訟的；愛打官司的 ▶ **li·ti·gious·ness** *noun* [U]

lit·mus /ˈlɪtməs/ *noun* [U] a substance that turns red when it touches an acid and blue when it touches an ALKALI 石蕊（一種遇酸變紅而遇鹼則變藍的物質）：*litmus paper* 石蕊試紙

ˈ**litmus test** *noun* **1** (*especially NAmE*) = ACID TEST：*The outcome will be seen as a litmus test of government concern for conservation issues.* 這結果將被視為檢驗政府是否關注自然資源保護問題的試金石。**2** a test using litmus 石蕊試驗

li·to·tes /laɪˈtəʊtiːz; *NAmE* -ˈtoʊ-/ *noun* [U] (*technical* 術語) the use of a negative or weak statement to emphasize a positive meaning, for example *he wasn't slow to accept the offer* (= he was quick to accept the offer) 曲言（用否定或較弱的語氣加強表示肯定）➲ compare UNDERSTATEMENT (1)

litre ⚷ (*especially US* **liter**) /ˈliːtə(r)/ *noun* (*abbr.* **l**) a unit for measuring volume, equal to 1.76 British pints or 2.11 American pints 升（容量單位，等於英國的 1.76 品脫或美國的 2.11 品脫）：*3 litres of water* * 3 升水 ◇ *a litre bottle of wine* 一升容量的瓶裝酒 ◇ *a car with a 3.5 litre engine* 配有 3.5 升發動機的汽車

lit·ter /ˈlɪtə(r)/ *noun, verb*

■ ***noun*** **1** [U] small pieces of rubbish/garbage such as paper, cans and bottles, that people have left lying in a public place（在公共場所亂扔的）垃圾，廢棄物，雜物：*There will be fines for people who* ***drop litter***. 亂扔垃圾的人將被罰款。 **2** [sing.] **~ of sth** a number of things that are lying in an untidy way 亂七八糟的東西；亂放的雜物：*The floor was covered with a litter of newspapers, clothes and empty cups.* 地板上到處都是報紙、衣服和空杯子。 **3** [U] a dry substance that is put in a shallow open box for pets, especially cats, to use as a toilet when they are indoors（供寵物，尤指貓，在室內便溺的）貓砂：*cat litter* 貓砂 ◇ (*BrE*) *a litter tray* 貓砂盤 ◇ (*NAmE*) *a litter box* 鋪了便溺墊物的箱子 **4** [C] a number of baby animals that one mother gives birth to at the same time（動物一胎所生的）一窩幼崽：*a litter of puppies* 一窩小狗 ◇ *the runt* (= the smallest and weakest baby) *of the litter* 一窩中最弱小的幼畜 **5** [U] the substance, especially STRAW, that is used for farm animals to sleep on（供牲畜睡臥用的）墊草，褥草，鋪欄草 **6** [C] a kind of chair or bed that was used in the past for carrying important people（舊時抬要人的）轎，輿

■ ***verb*** **1** [T] **~ sth** to be spread around a place, making it look untidy 使亂七八糟；使凌亂：*Piles of books and newspapers littered the floor.* 地板上亂七八糟地堆了許多書和報紙。◇ *Broken glass littered the streets.* 街上到處是玻璃碎片。 **2** [T, usually passive, I] **~ (sth) (with sth)** to leave things in a place, making it look untidy 亂扔：*The floor was littered with papers.* 地板上亂七八糟扔了許多文件。◇ (*NAmE*) *He was arrested for littering.* 他因亂扔垃圾被拘捕。 **3** [T] **be littered with sth** to contain or involve a lot of a particular type of thing, usually sth bad 使飽含，使遍佈（一般指不好的東西）：*Your essay is littered with spelling mistakes.* 你的文章裏到處是拼寫錯誤。

ˈlitter bin (*BrE*) (*NAmE* **ˈtrash can**) *noun* a container for people to put rubbish/garbage in, in the street or in a public building（街道上或公共建築物裏的）垃圾箱，廢物箱 ➲ VISUAL VOCAB pages V2, V3

ˈlitter lout (*BrE*) (also **ˈlit·ter·bug** *NAmE, BrE*) *noun* (*informal, disapproving*) a person who leaves LITTER in public places（在公共場所）亂扔垃圾的人；垃圾蟲

lit·tle ⚷ /ˈlɪtl/ *adj., det., pron., adv.*

■ ***adj.*** [usually before noun] **HELP** The forms **littler** /ˈlɪtlə(r)/ and **littlest** /ˈlɪtlɪst/ are rare. It is more common to use **smaller** and **smallest**. * littler 和 littlest 都很少見，常用的是 smaller 和 smallest。**1** ⚷ not big; small; smaller than others 小的；比較小的：*a little house* 小房子 ◇ *a*

Collocations 詞語搭配

Literature 文學

Being a writer 當作家

- **write/publish** literature/poetry/fiction/a book/a story/a poem/a novel/a review/an autobiography 寫／發表文學作品／詩集／小說／書／故事／詩歌／長篇小說／評論／自傳
- **become** a writer/novelist/playwright 成為作家／小說家／劇作家
- **find/have** a publisher/an agent 找到／有出版商／代理人
- **have** a new book out 出版一部新書
- **edit/revise/proofread** a book/text/manuscript 編輯／修訂／校對書／文章／原稿
- **dedicate** a book/poem to … 把一本書／一首詩獻給…

Plot, character and atmosphere 情節、人物和氛圍

- **construct/create/weave/weave sth into** a complex narrative 構思／創作／編寫／把某事編成一部複雜的敘事小說
- **advance/drive** the plot 推進故事情節的發展
- **introduce/present** the protagonist/a character 介紹主人公／一個人物
- **describe/depict/portray** a character (as …)/(sb as) a hero/villain 描述人物／英雄／壞蛋；把一個人物描繪成…；把某人描繪成英雄／壞蛋
- **create** an exciting/a tense atmosphere 營造一種令人興奮／緊張的氣氛
- **build/heighten** the suspense/tension 製造／增加懸念／緊張氣氛
- **evoke/capture** the pathos of the situation 喚起對這種狀況的同情
- **convey** emotion/an idea/an impression/a sense of … 傳達…情感／思想；給人…印象／感覺
- **engage** the reader 吸引讀者
- **seize/capture/grip** the (reader's) imagination 抓住（讀者的）想像力
- **arouse/elicit** emotion/sympathy (in the reader) 喚起（讀者的）情感／同情
- **lack** imagination/emotion/structure/rhythm 缺乏想像力／情感／精心組織／節奏感

Language, style and imagery 語言、風格和形象語言

- **use/employ** language/imagery/humour/(*especially US*) humor/an image/a symbol/a metaphor/a device 使用語言／形象語言／幽默／意象／象徵／暗喻／手段
- **use/adopt/develop** a style/technique 使用／採用／形成一種風格／技巧
- **be rich in/be full of** symbolism 富含象徵意義
- **evoke** images of …/a sense of …/a feeling of … 喚起…的形象／感覺
- **create/achieve** an effect 創造／取得效果
- **maintain/lighten** the tone 維持／緩和基調
- **introduce/develop** an idea/a theme 引入／發展一種思想／一個主題
- **inspire** a novel/a poet/sb's work/sb's imagination 促成小說的創作；給詩人以靈感；促成某人作品的誕生；激發起某人的想像力

Reading and criticism 閱讀與評論

- **read** an author/sb's work/fiction/poetry/a text/a poem/a novel/a chapter/a passage 讀一個作家的作品／某人的著作／小說／詩集／一篇文章／一首詩／一部小說／一個章節／一段文章
- **review** a book/a novel/sb's work 評論一本書／一部小說／某人的作品
- **give sth/get/have/receive** a good/bad review 給某物／得到好評／惡評
- **be hailed** (as)/**be recognized as** a masterpiece 被譽為一部傑作
- **quote** a phrase/line/stanza/passage/author 引用一個短語／一行詩／一節詩／一段文章／作者的話
- **provoke/spark** discussion/criticism 引發討論／評論
- **study/interpret/understand** a text/passage 研讀／解讀／理解一篇文章／一段文章
- **translate** sb's work/a text/a passage/a novel/a poem 翻譯某人的作品／一篇文章／一段文章／一部小說／一首詩

little group of tourists 一小群遊客 ◇ *a little old lady* 個子小的老太太 ◇ *the classic little black dress* 典雅的黑色小連衣裙 ◇ *'Which do you want?' 'I'll take the little one.'* "你要哪一個？""我要那個小的。" ◇ *She gave a little laugh.* 她笑了一笑。 ◇ *(BrE) We should manage, with* ***a little bit*** *of luck.* 我們只要有一點點運氣就能應付過去。 ◇ *Here's* ***a little something*** (= a small present) *for your birthday.* 這是送給你的生日小禮物。 **2** 🗝 used after an adjective to show affection or dislike, especially in a PATRONIZING way (= one that suggests that you think you are better than sb)（用在形容詞的後面表示喜愛或厭惡，尤指屈尊俯就地）可愛的，可憐的，討厭的： *The* ***poor little thing!*** *It's lost its mother.* 這可憐的小傢伙！沒有了媽媽。 ◇ *What a nasty little man!* 多麼令人討厭的傢伙！ ◇ *She's a good little worker.* 她是個討人喜歡的工人。 ◇ *He'd become* ***quite the little*** *gentleman.* 他成了頗有風度的紳士了。 **3** 🗝 young 年幼的；幼小的： *a* ***little boy/girl*** 小男孩／女孩 ◇ *my* ***little brother/sister*** (= younger brother/sister) 我的弟弟／妹妹 ◇ *I lived in America when I was little.* 我小時候生活在美國。 **4** 🗝 (of distance or time 距離或時間) short 短的；近的；短暫的： *A* ***little while*** *later the phone rang.* 過了一小會兒電話響了起來。 ◇ *Shall we walk a little way?* 我們走一小段路好嗎？ **5** 🗝 not important; not serious 微不足道的；不嚴重的；不認真的：*I can't remember every little detail.* 我記不住每一個微小的細節。 ◇ *You soon get used to the little difficulties.* 你很快就會習慣這些小小的不便了。
▸ **lit·tle·ness** *noun* [U]

IDM **a little 'bird told me** (*informal*) used to say that sb told you sth but you do not want to say who it was（不想說出是誰告訴的）有人告訴我的，不告訴你我是怎麼知道的 ➲ more at OAK, WONDER *n.*

■ ***det., pron.*** **1** 🗝 used with uncountable nouns to mean 'not much'（與不可數名詞連用）不多的： *There was little doubt in my mind.* 我心裏幾乎沒有疑問。 ◇ *Students have* ***little or no*** *choice in the matter.* 學生在這個問題上很少有或沒有選擇餘地。 ◇ *I understood little of what he said.* 我幾乎聽不懂他所講的。 ◇ *She said* ***little or nothing*** (= hardly anything) *about her experience.* 她對自己的經歷幾乎隻字不提。 ◇ *Tell him* ***as little as possible.*** 盡量少告訴他。 **2** 🗝 **a little** used with uncountable nouns to mean 'a small amount', 'some'（與不可數名詞連用）少量的，一些： *a little milk/sugar/tea* 少許牛奶／糖／茶 ◇ *If you have any spare milk, could you give me a little?* 你要是有多餘的牛奶，給我一些好嗎？ ◇ *I've only read a little of the book so far.* 這本書我才讀了一小部份。 ◇ *(formal) It caused* ***not a little/no little*** (= a lot of) *confusion.* 這事引起了不小的混亂。 ◇ *After a little* (= a short time) *he got up and left.* 過了一會兒他站起來走了。

IDM **,little by 'little** 🗝 slowly; gradually 緩慢地；逐漸地；一點一點地： *Little by little the snow disappeared.* 雪漸漸融化了。 ◇ *His English is improving little by little.* 他的英語正在逐步提高。

■ ***adv.*** (**less**, **least**) **1** 🗝 not much; only slightly 不多；稍許；略微： *He is little known as an artist.* 幾乎沒人知道他是個藝術家。 ◇ *I slept very little last night.* 昨晚我幾乎沒怎麼睡。 ◇ ***Little did I know*** *that this spelled the end of my career.* 我一點也沒想到這會斷送了我的職業生涯。 **2** 🗝 **a little** (**bit**) to a small degree 少許；少量；一點： *She seemed a little afraid of going inside.* 她好像有點害怕進去。 ◇ *These shoes are a little (bit) too big for me.* 我穿這雙鞋太大了一點。 ◇ *(informal) Everything has become* ***just that little bit*** *harder.* 一切都變得更艱難了。 ◇ *(formal) She felt tired and* ***more than a little*** *worried.* 她感到既疲勞又非常擔憂。 ➲ note at BIT

the ,Little 'Bear *noun* = URSA MINOR

,Little 'Englander *noun* (*usually disapproving*) an English person who believes England (or, in practice, Britain) should not get involved in international affairs 英格蘭本土主義者（主張英國不參與國際事務）

,little 'finger *noun* the smallest finger of the hand 小指 **SYN** **pinky** ➲ VISUAL VOCAB page V59

IDM **twist/wrap/wind sb around your little 'finger** (*informal*) to persuade sb to do anything that you want 任意擺佈某人；左右某人

'Little League *noun* [sing., U] (in the US 美國) a BASEBALL league for children 少年棒球聯盟

'little people *noun* [pl.] **1** all the people in a country who have no power（統稱）平民，百姓，小老百姓 **2** extremely small people, who will never grow to a normal size because of a physical problem 異常矮小的人；侏儒；"袖珍"人 **3** **the little people** small imaginary people with magic powers 小精靈；小仙子 **SYN** **fairies**

lit·toral /ˈlɪtərəl/ *noun* (*technical* 術語) the part of a country that is near the coast 沿海地區 ▸ **lit·toral** *adj.* [only before noun]： *littoral states* 沿海各州

lit·urgy /ˈlɪtədʒi; *NAmE* ˈlɪtərdʒi/ *noun* (*pl.* **-ies**) a fixed form of public worship used in churches 禮拜儀式 ▸ **li·tur·gic·al** /lɪˈtɜːdʒɪkl; *NAmE* -ˈtɜːrdʒ-/ *adj.* **li·tur·gic·al·ly** /-kli/ *adv.*

liv·able *adj.* = LIVEABLE

live[1] 🗝 /lɪv/ *verb* ➲ see also LIVE[2]

▸ **IN A PLACE** 在某地 **1** 🗝 [I] **+ adv./prep.** to have your home in a particular place 住；居住： *to live in a house* 住在一座房子裏 ◇ *Where do you live?* 你住在什麼地方？ ◇ *She needs to find* ***somewhere to live.*** 她需要找個住的地方。 ◇ *We used to live in London.* 我們過去住在倫敦。 ◇ *Both her children still live at home.* 她的兩個孩子仍住在家裏。 ◇ *(BrE, informal) Where do these plates live* (= where are they usually kept)? 這些盤子通常放哪兒？

▸ **BE ALIVE** 活着 **2** 🗝 [I] to remain alive 生存；活着： *The doctors said he only had six months to live.* 醫生說他只能活六個月了。 ◇ *Spiders can live for several days without food.* 蜘蛛幾天不吃依然可存活。 ◇ **~ to do sth** *She lived to see her first grandchild.* 她一直活到抱上第一個孫子。 **3** 🗝 [I] to be alive, especially at a particular time（尤指在某時期）活着： *When did Handel live?* 亨德爾是什麼時期的人？ ◇ *He's the greatest player who ever lived.* 他是世上最出色的運動員。

▸ **TYPE OF LIFE** 生活方式 **4** 🗝 [I, T] to spend your life in a particular way（以某種方式）生活，過日子： *He lived in poverty most of his life.* 他大半輩子過的都是窮日子。 ◇ **~ sth** *She lived a very peaceful life.* 她過着十分寧靜的生活。 ◇ **+ noun** *She lived and died a single woman.* 她過了一輩子的獨身生活。

▸ **BE REMEMBERED** 被記住 **5** 🗝 [I] to continue to exist or be remembered 繼續存在；留存；被銘記 **SYN** **remain**： *This moment will live in our memory for many years to come.* 這一時刻將在我們的記憶中留存許多年。 ◇ *Her words have lived with me all my life.* 她的話我一輩子都銘記着。

▸ **HAVE EXCITEMENT** 興奮 **6** [I] to have a full and exciting life 享受充實而令人興奮的生活： *I don't want to be stuck in an office all my life—I want to live!* 我不想一輩子都憋在辦公室裏，我要享受人生樂趣！

IDM **,live and 'breathe sth** to be very enthusiastic about sth 熱衷於（某事）： *He just lives and breathes football.* 他非常熱衷於足球。 **live and 'let live** (*saying*) used to say that you should accept other people's opinions and behaviour even though they are different from your own 自己活也讓別人活；寬以待人；互相寬容 **live by your 'wits** to earn money by clever or sometimes dishonest means 靠耍小聰明賺錢；（有時）靠玩花招撈錢 **live** (**from**) **,hand to 'mouth** to spend all the money you earn on basic needs such as food without being able to save any money 僅夠餬口度日 **live in the 'past** to behave as though society, etc. has not changed, when in fact it has 彷彿生活在過去的社會中；落伍 **live in 'sin** (*old-fashioned* or *humorous*) to live together and have a sexual relationship without being married 未婚同居；姘居 **live it 'up** (*informal*) to enjoy yourself in an exciting way, usually spending a lot of money 盡情歡樂；狂歡；縱情揮霍享樂 **live a 'lie** to keep sth important about yourself a secret from other people, so that they do not know what you really think, what you are really like, etc. 過兩面人的生活；過騙人的生活；為人虛偽 **live off the fat of the 'land** to have enough money to be able to afford expensive things, food, drink, etc. 過奢侈的生活；錦衣玉食 **live off the 'land** to eat whatever food you can grow, kill or find yourself 靠耕

種（或狩獵）為生 **ˌlive to fight another ˈday** (*saying*) used to say that although you have failed or had a bad experience, you will continue（雖已失敗或經歷很糟但仍要）改日再戰，捲土重來 **you haven't ˈlived** used to tell sb that if they have not had a particular experience their life is not complete（表示若沒有某種經歷生活便不完整）你白活了：*You've never been to New York? You haven't lived!* 你從未去過紐約？你真是白活了！ **you live and ˈlearn** used to express surprise at sth new or unexpected you have been told（對得知的事物感到驚訝或意外）真是得活到老學到老，真想不到 ➲ more at BORROW, CLOVER, HALF *n.*, LIFE, LONG *adv.*, PEOPLE *n.*, POCKET *n.*, ROUGH *adv.*

PHR V **ˈlive by sth** to follow a particular belief or set of principles 按照（某信念或原則）生活：*That's a philosophy I could live by.* 那就是我所信奉的人生哲學。 **ˈlive by doing sth** to earn money or to get the things you need by doing a particular thing 靠做某事賺錢為生（或獲取所需）：*a community that lives by fishing* 靠捕魚為生的群體 **ˌlive sth↔ˈdown** to be able to make people forget about sth embarrassing you have done 能使人忘卻（你做過的令人尷尬的事）：*She felt so stupid. She'd never be able to live it down.* 她覺得自己做了傻事，恐怕永遠無法挽回自己的面子了。 **ˈlive for sb/sth** to think that sb/sth is the main purpose of or the most important thing in your life 以…為主要生活目的；為…而活着：*She lives for her work.* 她活着是為了工作。◇ *After his wife died, he had nothing to live for.* 妻子去世後，他便沒有了生活目標。 **ˌlive ˈin** to live at the place where you work or study 住在工作（或學習）的地方：*They have an au pair living in.* 他們有個換工姑娘住在家裏。 ➲ see also LIVE-IN **ˈlive off sb/sth** (often *disapproving*) to receive the money you need to live from sb/sth because you do not have any yourself 靠…過活；依賴…生活：*She's still living off her parents.* 她還在靠父母養活。◇ *to live off welfare* 靠救濟過活 **ˈlive off sth** to have one particular type of food as the main thing you eat in order to live 以食…為生：*He seems to live off junk food.* 他好像靠吃垃圾食品為生。 **ˌlive ˈon** to continue to live or exist 繼續活着；繼續存在：*She died ten years ago but her memory lives on.* 她十年前就去世了，但她還留在人們的記憶中。 **ˈlive on sth** **1** 🔑 to eat a particular type of food to live 以食…為生：*Small birds live mainly on insects.* 小鳥主要靠食昆蟲為生。 **2** (often *disapproving*) to eat only or a lot of a particular type of food 僅以（一種食物）為主要食物：*She lives on burgers.* 她只喜歡吃漢堡包。 **3** 🔑 to have enough money for the basic things you need to live 靠（…錢）生活：*You can't live on forty pounds a week.* 你靠每週四十英鎊沒法過活。 **ˌlive ˈout** to live away from the place where you work or study 不住在工作（或學習）的地方：*Some college students will have to live out.* 有些大學生將不得不住在校外。 **ˌlive ˈout sth** **1** to actually do what you have only thought about doing before 實踐（以前想要做的事）：*to live out your fantasies* 實現夢想 **2** to spend the rest of your life in a particular way（以某種方式）度過餘生：*He lived out his days alone.* 他獨自度過餘生。 **ˌlive ˈthrough sth** 🔑 to experience a disaster or other unpleasant situation and survive it 經歷（災難或其他困境）而幸存：*He has lived through two world wars.* 他經歷了兩次世界大戰。 **ˈlive together** (also **ˈlive with sb**) **1** 🔑 to live in the same house 在一起生活 **2** 🔑 to share a home and have a sexual relationship without being married 未婚同居；姘居 **SYN** **cohabit** **ˌlive ˈup to sth** to do as well as or be as good as other people expect you to 達到，符合，不辜負（他人的期望）：*He failed to live up to his parents' expectations.* 他辜負了父母的期望。◇ *The team called 'The No-Hopers' certainly lived up to its name.* 叫做"無望者"的球隊果真名副其實。 **ˈlive with sb** = LIVE TOGETHER **ˈlive with sth** to accept sth unpleasant 忍受，容忍（不快的事）：*I just had to learn to live with the pain.* 我不得不學會忍受痛苦。

live² 🔑 /laɪv/ *adj.*, *adv.* ➲ see also LIVE¹

■ *adj.* [usually before noun]

▸ **NOT DEAD** 活的 **1** 🔑 living; not dead 活的：*live animals* 活動物 ◇ *the number of live births* (= babies born alive) 活產嬰兒數 ◇ *We saw a **real live** rattlesnake!* 我們看見了一條活生生的響尾蛇！

▸ **NOT RECORDED** 非錄製 **2** 🔑 (of a broadcast 廣播) sent out while the event is actually happening, not recorded first and broadcast later 現場直播的；實況轉播的：*live coverage of the World Cup* 世界杯賽的實況轉播 **3** 🔑 (of a performance 表演) given or made when people are watching, not recorded 現場演出的：*The club has live music most nights.* 這俱樂部大多數晚上有現場演奏的音樂。◇ *a live recording made at Wembley Arena* 文布利運動場的現場錄音 ◇ *the band's new live album* 這個樂隊新出的演唱會專輯 ◇ *It was the first interview I'd done in front of a **live audience*** (= with people watching). 那是我首次在觀眾面前做現場採訪。

▸ **ELECTRICITY** 電 **4** (of a wire or device 電線或裝置) connected to a source of electrical power 連着電源的；通電的：*That terminal is live.* 那個端子有電。

▸ **BULLETS/MATCHES** 子彈；火柴 **5** still able to explode or light; ready for use 仍可爆炸的；仍可點燃的；隨時可用的：*live ammunition* 實彈

▸ **COALS** 煤塊 **6** **live** coals are burning or are still hot and red 燃燒着的；仍灼熱發紅的

▸ **YOGURT** 酸奶 **7** **live** YOGURT still contains the bacteria needed to turn milk into YOGURT 含乳酸菌的

▸ **QUESTION/SUBJECT** 問題；話題 **8** of interest or importance at the present time 當前所關心的；時下重大的：*Pollution is still very much a live issue.* 污染仍然是目前讓人非常關注的問題。

▸ **INTERNET** 互聯網 **9** (of an electronic link 電子鏈接) functioning correctly, so that it is connected to another document or page on the Internet 有效的；功能正常的；活的：*Here are some live links to other aviation-related web pages.* 這是另外一些與航空有關網頁的有效鏈接。

IDM **a live ˈwire** a person who is lively and full of energy 活躍而精力充沛的人；生龍活虎的人

■ *adv.* 🔑 broadcast at the time of an actual event; played or recorded at an actual performance 在現場直播；在現場表演（或錄製）：*The show is going out live.* 這場演出正在實況直播。

IDM **go ˈlive** (*computing* 計) (of a computer system 計算機系統) to become OPERATIONAL (= ready to be used) 隨時可用

live·able (also **liv·able**) /ˈlɪvəbl/ *adj.* **1** (*BrE* also **live-able in**) [not before noun]) (of a house, etc. 房屋等) fit to live in 適於居住的 **SYN** **habitable**：*safer and more liveable residential areas* 更安全和更適於居住的住宅區 ◇ *The place looks liveable in.* 這地方看起來適於居住。 **2** (of life 生活) worth living 值得一過的 **SYN** **endurable** **3** [not before noun] **~ with** that can be dealt with 能對付；可處理：*The problem is paying the mortgage—everything else is liveable with.* 問題在於償還按揭貸款 —— 別的一切事情都能對付。 **4** [only before noun] (of a wage, etc. 工資等) enough to live on 足夠維持生活的：*a liveable salary* 足以維持生活的薪水

live action /ˌlaɪv ˈækʃn/ *noun* [U] part of a film/movie that is made using real people or animals, rather than using drawings, models or computers（電影中的）真人實拍片段 ▸ **ˌlive-ˈaction** *adj.* [only before noun]：*a live-action movie* 一部真人實物影片

ˈlived-in *adj.* (of a place 地方) that has been used so continuously for so long that it does not look new 長期有人居住而不顯陌生的；長期使用過的：(*approving*) *The room had a comfortable, lived-in feel about it.* 這房間裏有一種一直有人居住的溫馨感覺。

live-in /ˈlɪv ɪn/ *adj.* **1** (of an employee 雇員) living in the house where they work 住在工作場所的：*a live-in nanny* 住在雇主家的保母 **2 ~ lover, boyfriend, girlfriend, etc.** a person who lives with their sexual partner but is not married to them 未婚同居者

live·li·hood /ˈlaɪvlihʊd/ *noun* [C, usually sing., U] a means of earning money in order to live 賺錢維生的手段；生計 **SYN** **living**：*Communities on the island depended on whaling for their livelihood.* 島上的居民靠捕鯨為生。◇ ***a means/source of livelihood*** 生計；生活來源

live·long /ˈlɪvlɒŋ; *NAmE* -lɔːŋ; -lɑːŋ/ *adj.*

IDM **the livelong ˈday** (*literary*) the whole length of the day 一整天

live·ly 🔑 /ˈlaɪvli/ *adj.* (**live·lier**, **live·li·est**)
1 🔑 full of life and energy; active and enthusiastic 精力充沛的；生氣勃勃的；活躍熱情的 SYN **animated**, **vivacious**：*an intelligent and lively young woman* 聰慧而充滿活力的年輕女士 ◇ *a lively and enquiring mind* 思維活躍、善於探索的頭腦 ◇ *He showed a lively interest in politics.* 他對政治表現出濃厚的興趣。 **2** 🔑 (of a place, an event, etc. 地方、事件等) full of interest or excitement 充滿趣味的；令人興奮的 SYN **bustling**：*a lively bar* 氣氛熱鬧的酒吧 ◇ *a lively debate* 熱烈的辯論 **3** (of colours 顏色) strong and definite 色濃的；鮮豔的：*a lively shade of pink* 鮮豔的粉紅色調 **4** (*especially BrE*) busy and active 繁忙活躍的；興旺的：*They do a lively trade in souvenirs and gifts.* 他們做紀念品和禮品生意，做得有聲有色。 ▸ **live·li·ness** *noun* [U]

liven /ˈlaɪvn/ *verb*
PHR V ˌ**liven ˈup** | ˌ**liven sb/sth ˈup** to become or to make sb/sth more interesting or exciting （使）更有趣，更令人興奮：*The game didn't liven up till the second half.* 那場比賽直到下半場才精彩起來。 ◇ *Let's put some music on to liven things up.* 咱們放些音樂活躍一下氣氛吧。

liver /ˈlɪvə(r)/ *noun* **1** [C] a large organ in the body that cleans the blood and produces BILE 肝臟 ➲ VISUAL VOCAB page V59 **2** [U, C] the liver of some animals that is cooked and eaten （動物供食用的）肝：*liver and onions* 洋蔥炒肝尖 ◇ *chicken livers* 雞肝

ˈ**liver fluke** *noun* a small WORM which, in an adult form, lives in the LIVER of people or animals, often causing disease 肝吸蟲（侵害宿主肝臟）

liv·er·ied /ˈlɪvərid/ *adj.* **1** (*BrE*) painted in a LIVERY 塗成專用顏色的：*liveried aircraft* 塗着航空公司專用顏色的飛機 **2** wearing LIVERY 穿制服的；穿號衣的：*liveried servants* 穿制服的僕人

Liv·er·pud·lian /ˌlɪvəˈpʌdliən; *NAmE* ˌlɪvərˈp-/ *noun* a person from Liverpool in NW England 利物浦人 ▸ **Liv·er·pud·lian** *adj.*

ˈ**liver sausage** (*BrE*) (*NAmE* **liv·er·wurst** /ˈlɪvəwɜːst; *NAmE* ˈlɪvərwɜːrst/) *noun* [U] a type of soft SAUSAGE made from finely chopped LIVER, usually spread cold on bread 肝泥香腸

ˈ**liver spot** *noun* a small brown spot on the skin, especially found in older people 雀斑；黃褐斑；（尤指）老人斑

liv·ery /ˈlɪvəri/ *noun* [U, C] (*pl.* **-ies**) **1** (*BrE*) the colours in which the vehicles, aircraft, etc. of a particular company are painted（車輛、飛機等塗的）公司專用色彩 **2** a special uniform worn by servants or officials, especially in the past （尤指舊時僕人或官員的）制服

ˈ**livery stable** *noun* a place where people can pay to keep their horses or can hire a horse （代客飼養馬或租馬的）馬房

lives *pl.* of LIFE

live·stock /ˈlaɪvstɒk; *NAmE* -stɑːk/ *noun* [U, pl.] the animals kept on a farm, for example cows or sheep 牲畜；家畜 ➲ VISUAL VOCAB pages V2, V3

live·ware /ˈlaɪvweə(r); *NAmE* -wer/ *noun* [U] (*informal*) people who work with computers, rather than the programs or computers with which they work 人件，活件（用計算機工作的人）

livid /ˈlɪvɪd/ *adj.* **1** extremely angry 暴怒的；狂怒的 SYN **furious** **2** dark bluish-grey in colour 烏青色的；青灰色的：*a livid bruise* 青瘀

liv·ing 🔑 /ˈlɪvɪŋ/ *adj., noun*
■ **adj.** **1** 🔑 alive now 活着的；活的：*all* ***living things*** 所有生物 ◇ *living organisms* 活的機體 ◇ *the finest living pianist* 健在的最傑出的鋼琴家 **2** 🔑 [only before noun] used or practised now 在使用的；在實施的：*living languages* (= those still spoken) 現用語言 ◇ *a living faith* 仍有人信奉的信仰
IDM **be living ˈproof of sth/that ...** to show by your actions or qualities that a particular fact is true （用行動或品格）證明…屬實：*He is living proof that not all engineers are boring.* 並非所有工程師都缺乏情趣，他就是活生生的例子。 **within/in ˌliving ˈmemory** at a time, or during the time, that is remembered by people still alive 在仍活着的人們的記憶中；記憶猶新：*the coldest winter in living memory* 人們記憶中最寒冷的冬天 ➲ more at DAYLIGHTS
■ **noun** **1** [C, usually sing.] money to buy the things that you need in life 生計；謀生；收入：*She* ***earns her living*** *as a freelance journalist.* 她靠做自由撰稿記者來維持生計。 ◇ *to* ***make a good/decent/meagre living*** 過優裕的／體面的／貧困的生活 ◇ *What do you* ***do for a living?*** 你靠什麼謀生？ ◇ *to* ***scrape/scratch a living*** *from part-time tutoring* 靠做兼職家庭教師勉強維持生活 **2** [U] a way or style of life 生活方式：*everyday living* 日常生活 ◇ *communal living* 集體生活 ◇ *plain living* 簡樸的生活 ◇ *Their* ***standard of living*** *is very low.* 他們的生活水平很低。 ◇ *The* ***cost of living*** *has risen sharply.* 生活費用已急劇上漲。 ◇ *poor* ***living conditions/standards*** 惡劣的生活條件；低下的生活水準 **3** **the living** [pl.] people who are alive now 活着的人：*the living and the dead* 生者與死者 IDM see LAND *n.* **4** [C] (*BrE*) (especially in the past) a position in the Church as a priest and the income and house that go with this （尤指舊時）有俸金住房的牧師職位 SYN **benefice**

ˌ**living ˈdeath** *noun* [sing.] a life that is worse than being dead 活受罪；生不如死

ˌ**living ˈhell** *noun* [sing.] a very unpleasant situation that causes a lot of suffering and lasts a long time 活受煎熬；活地獄；活受罪；人間地獄

ˈ**living roof** *noun* = GREEN ROOF

ˈ**living room** (*BrE* also ˈ**sitting room**) *noun* a room in a house where people sit together, watch television, etc. 客廳；起居室 SYN **lounge**

ˌ**living ˈwage** *noun* [sing.] a wage that is high enough for sb to buy the things that they need in order to live 基本生活工資；僅能維持生活的工資

ˌ**living ˈwill** *noun* a document stating your wishes concerning medical treatment in the case that you become so ill/sick that you can no longer make decisions about it, in particular asking doctors to stop treating you and let you die （尤指要求在病弱以致無法做決定時不再醫治的）生前意願

liz·ard /ˈlɪzəd; *NAmE* -ərd/ *noun* a small REPTILE with a rough skin, four short legs and a long tail 蜥蜴

ll *abbr.* (in writing) lines (the plural form of 'l') （書寫形式）行（l 的複數形式）

llama /ˈlɑːmə/ *noun* a S American animal kept for its soft wool or for carrying loads 美洲駝（產於南美）

LLB (*BrE*) (*NAmE* **LL.B**) /ˌel el ˈbiː/ *noun* the abbreviation for 'Bachelor of Laws' (a first university degree in law) 法學學士（全寫為 Bachelor of Laws，大學法學的初級學位）

LLD (*BrE*) (*NAmE* **LL.D**) /ˌel el ˈdiː/ *noun* the abbreviation for 'Doctor of Laws' (the highest university degree in law) 法學博士（全寫為 Doctor of Laws，大學法學的最高學位）

LLM (*BrE*) (*NAmE* **LL.M**) /ˌel el ˈem/ *noun* the abbreviation for 'Master of Laws' (a second university degree in law) 法學碩士（全寫為 Master of Laws，大學法學的中級學位）

lm *abbr.* LUMEN 流明（光通量單位）

LMS /ˌel em ˈes/ *noun* the abbreviation for 'learning management system' (a software system for managing training and education using the Internet) 學習管理系統（全寫為 learning management system，利用互聯網管理培訓與教育的軟件系統）

lo /ləʊ; *NAmE* loʊ/ *exclamation* (*old use* or *humorous*) used for calling attention to a surprising thing （引起對令人驚訝的事的注意）瞧，看哪
IDM ˌ**lo and beˈhold** (*humorous*) used for calling attention to a surprising or annoying thing （用於引起對令人驚訝或討厭之事的注意）哎喲，你瞧，嗨，真想不到

L

load 🗝 /ləʊd; *NAmE* loʊd/ *noun, verb*

■ ***noun***

▸ STH CARRIED 負載物 **1** 🗝 [C] something that is being carried (usually in large amounts) by a person, vehicle, etc. 負載；負荷 SYN **cargo**：*The trucks waited at the warehouse to pick up their loads.* 貨車在倉庫等着裝載貨物。◇ *The women came down the hill with their loads of firewood.* 婦女們背着柴火下了山。◇ *These backpacks are designed to* ***carry a heavy load.*** 這些背包是為攜帶重物設計的。◇ *A lorry* ***shed its load*** (= accidentally dropped its load) *on the motorway.* 一輛卡車意外地把運載的貨物掉落在高速公路上。 **2** 🗝 [C] (often in compounds 常構成複合詞) the total amount of sth that sth can carry or contain 裝載量；容納量：*a busload of tourists* 一公共汽車遊客◇ *They ordered three truckloads of sand.* 他們訂購了三卡車沙子。◇ *He put half a load of washing in the machine.* 他把要洗的衣物放進洗衣機，洗衣機裝了個半滿。◇ *The plane took off with a* ***full load.*** 飛機滿載起飛。

▸ WEIGHT 重量 **3** [C, usually sing.] the amount of weight that is pressing down on sth 承載量：*a load-bearing wall* 承重牆◇ *Modern backpacks spread the load over a wider area.* 新式背包把承重量分散在更大的面積上。

▸ LARGE AMOUNT 大量 **4** 🗝 [sing.] (*BrE* also **loads** [pl.]) **~ (of sth)** (*informal*) a large number or amount of sb/sth; plenty 大量；許多：*She's got loads of friends.* 她有很多朋友。◇ *There's loads to do today.* 今天有好多的事要做。◇ *He wrote loads and loads of letters to people.* 他給人們寫了很多很多的信。◇ *Uncle Jim brought a whole load of presents for the kids.* 吉姆大叔給孩子們帶來了一大堆禮物。

▸ RUBBISH/NONSENSE 胡說八道；廢話 **5** 🗝 [sing.] **~ of rubbish, garbage, nonsense, etc.** (*informal, especially BrE*) used to emphasize that sth is wrong, stupid, bad, etc.（強調錯誤、愚蠢、糟糕等）胡說八道，廢話：*You're talking a load of rubbish.* 你說的都是一派胡言。

▸ WORK 工作 **6** [C] an amount of work that a person or machine has to do 工作量；負荷：*Teaching loads have increased in all types of school.* 各種學校的教學工作量都增加了。 ➲ see also CASELOAD, WORKLOAD

▸ RESPONSIBILITY/WORRY 責任；憂慮 **7** [C, usually sing.] a feeling of responsibility or worry that is difficult to deal with（責任或憂慮的）沉重感 SYN **burden**：*She thought she would not be able to* ***bear the load*** *of bringing up her family alone.* 她認為她無法獨自一人擔負起養家活口的重任。◇ *Knowing that they had arrived safely* ***took a load off my mind.*** 得知他們平安到達後我如釋重負。

▸ ELECTRICAL POWER 電力 **8** [C] the amount of electrical power that is being supplied at a particular time 供電量

IDM **get a load of sb/sth** (*informal*) used to tell sb to look at or listen to sb/sth（用以讓人）看，聽：*Get a load of that dress!* 你瞧那件衣服！

■ ***verb***

▸ GIVE/RECEIVE LOAD 裝載；承載 **1** 🗝 [T, I] to put a large quantity of things or people onto or into sth（把大量…）裝上，裝入：**~ sth** *We loaded the car in ten minutes.* 我們十分鐘就裝好了車。◇ *Can you help me load the dishwasher?* 你幫我把碗碟放進洗碗機裏好嗎？◇ **~ sth (up) (with sth)** *Men were loading up a truck with timber.* 工人正在把木料裝上卡車。◇ **~ sth/sb (into/onto sth)** *Sacks were being loaded onto the truck.* 人們正在把麻袋裝上卡車。◇ **~ (up)** | **~ (up with sth)** *We finished loading and set off.* 我們裝完貨物就出發了。 OPP **unload** **2** [I] to receive a load 承載；裝載：*The ship was still loading.* 那條船還在裝貨。 OPP **unload** **3** 🗝 [T] **~ sb with sth** to give sb a lot of things, especially things they have to carry 大量給予（尤指得攜帶的東西）：*They loaded her with gifts.* 他們送了她很多禮物。

▸ GUN/CAMERA 槍；照相機 **4** 🗝 [T, I] to put sth into a weapon, camera or other piece of equipment so that it can be used 把…裝入（武器、照相機或其他設備）：**~ sth (into sth)** *She loaded film into the camera.* 她把膠捲裝到照相機裏。◇ **~ sth (with sth)** *She loaded the camera with film.* 她在照相機裏裝了膠捲。◇ **~ (sth)** *Is the gun loaded?* 那支槍子彈上膛了嗎？ OPP **unload**

▸ COMPUTING 計算機技術 **5** [T, I] **~ (sth)** to put data or a program into the memory of a computer 輸入，裝入，寫入，載入，存貯（數據或程序）：*Have you loaded the software?* 你裝上這種軟件了嗎？◇ *Wait for the game to load.* 等着遊戲軟件安裝完畢。 ➲ compare DOWNLOAD

IDM **load the 'dice (against sb)** [usually passive] to put sb at a disadvantage 使（某人）處於不利地位：*He has always felt that the dice were loaded against him in life.* 他總覺得自己一輩子都背運。

PHR V **,load sb/sth 'down (with sth)** [usually passive] to give sb/sth a lot of heavy things to carry 給…加以重負 SYN **weigh down**：*She was loaded down with bags of groceries.* 她提着很多裝着食品雜貨的袋子。

load·ed /'ləʊdɪd; *NAmE* 'loʊd-/ *adj.*

▸ FULL 滿 **1** carrying a load; full and heavy 裝載的；滿載而沉重的 SYN **laden**：*a fully loaded truck* 滿載貨物的卡車◇ **~ (with sth)** *a truck loaded with supplies* 裝滿供給品的卡車◇ *She came into the room carrying a loaded tray.* 她端着裝滿食物的托盤走進了房間。 **2 ~ with sth** (*informal*) full of a particular thing, quality or meaning 充滿…的：*cakes loaded with calories* 含高卡路里的糕點

▸ RICH 富有 **3** [not before noun] (*informal*) very rich 非常富有：*Let her pay—she's loaded.* 讓她付錢吧，她錢多得很。

▸ ADVANTAGE/DISADVANTAGE 有利；不利 **4 ~ in favour of sb/sth** | **~ against sb/sth** acting either as an advantage or a disadvantage to sb/sth in a way that is unfair（不公平地）對…有利，對…不利：*a system that is loaded in favour of the young* (= gives them an advantage) 對年輕人有利的體制

▸ WORD/STATEMENT 言語；陳述 **5** having more meaning than you realize at first and intended to make you think in a particular way 意味深長的；含蓄的：*It was a* ***loaded question*** *and I preferred not to comment.* 這是個帶有圈套的問題，我還是不作評論為好。

▸ GUN/CAMERA 槍支；照相機 **6** containing bullets, film, etc. 裝有（子彈、膠捲等）的：*a loaded shotgun* 裝有子彈的獵槍

▸ DRUNK 喝醉 **7** (*informal, especially NAmE*) very drunk 爛醉的；大醉的

load·ing /'ləʊdɪŋ; *NAmE* 'loʊd-/ *noun* [U, C] **1** (*AustralE, NZE*) extra money that sb is paid for their job because they have special skills or qualifications 附加工資（因有特別技能或資格） **2** an extra amount of money that you must pay in addition to the usual price 附加費用：*The 2% loading for using the card abroad has been removed.* 在國外使用此卡的 2% 附加費已經取消。

'load line *noun* = PLIMSOLL LINE

'load-shedding *noun* [U] the practice of stopping the supply of electricity for a period of time because the demand is greater than the supply 切負荷，減負荷，減（負）載（用電超過配電量時暫時切斷電力的做法）

load·star *noun* = LODESTAR

load·stone *noun* = LODESTONE

loaf /ləʊf; *NAmE* loʊf/ *noun, verb*

■ ***noun*** (*pl.* **loaves** /ləʊvz; *NAmE* loʊvz/) an amount of bread that has been shaped and baked in one piece 一條（麵包）：*a loaf of bread* 一條麵包◇ *Two white loaves, please.* 請拿兩條白麵包。◇ *a sliced loaf* 一條切片麵包 ➲ see also COTTAGE LOAF, FRENCH LOAF, MEAT LOAF IDM see HALF *det., pron.*, USE *v.*

■ ***verb*** [I] **~ (about/around)** (*informal*) to spend your time not doing anything, especially when you should be working 遊手好閒；無所事事；閒蕩 SYN **hang about/around**：*A group of kids were loafing around outside.* 一群小孩在外面四處遊蕩。

loaf·er /'ləʊfə(r); *NAmE* 'loʊf-/ *noun* **1** a person who wastes their time rather than working 虛度光陰者；遊手好閒者；浪子；二流子 **2** a flat leather shoe that you can put on your foot without fastening it 平底便鞋 ➲ VISUAL VOCAB page V64

loam /ləʊm; *NAmE* loʊm/ *noun* [U] (*technical* 術語) good quality soil containing sand, CLAY and decayed vegetable matter 壤土；肥土；沃土 ▸ **loamy** *adj.*

loan 🗝 /ləʊn; *NAmE* loʊn/ *noun, verb*

■ ***noun*** **1** 🗝 [C] money that an organization such as a bank lends and sb borrows 貸款；借款：*to* ***take out/***

repay a loan (= to borrow money/pay it back) 取得／償還貸款 ◇ ***bank loans*** *with low interest rates* 銀行低息貸款 ◇ *It took three years to repay my* ***student loan*** (= money lent to a student). 我花了三年的時間才還清我的學生貸款。◇ *a car loan* (= a loan to buy a car) 購車貸款 ➲ COLLOCATIONS at FINANCE **2** [sing.] **~ (of sth)** the act of lending sth; the state of being lent 借出；貸給；被借出：*I even* ***gave her the loan of*** *my car.* 我甚至把車也借給了她。◇ *an exhibition of paintings* ***on loan*** (= borrowed) *from private collections* 借用私人收藏品舉辦的畫展

■ ***verb*** **1** (*especially NAmE*) to lend sth to sb, especially money 借出，貸與（尤指錢）：**~ sth (to sb)** *The bank is happy to loan money to small businesses.* 銀行樂於貸款給小型企業。◇ **~ sb sth** *A friend loaned me $1 000.* 有一位朋友借給我 1 000 元。 **2** (*especially BrE*) to lend a valuable object to a museum, etc. 出借（貴重物品給博物館等）：**~ sth (out) (to sb/sth)** *This exhibit was kindly loaned by the artist's family.* 這件展品是藝術家的家人惠借而展出的。◇ **~ sb sth** *He loaned the museum his entire collection.* 他把自己的全部收藏品都借給了博物館。

'loan shark *noun* (*disapproving*) a person who lends money at very high rates of interest 放高利貸者；放印子錢者

'loan translation *noun* (*linguistics* 語言) = CALQUE

loan·word /'ləʊnwɜːd; *NAmE* 'loʊnwɜːrd/ *noun* (*linguistics* 語言) a word from another language used in its original form 借詞；外來詞：*'Latte' is a loanword from Italian.* * latte 是借自意大利語的外來詞。

loath (also *less frequent* **loth**) /ləʊθ; *NAmE* loʊθ/ *adj.* **~ to do sth** (*formal*) not willing to do sth 不情願；不樂意；勉強：*He was loath to admit his mistake.* 他不願承認自己的錯誤。

loathe /ləʊð; *NAmE* loʊð/ *verb* (not used in the progressive tenses 不用於進行時) **~ sb/sth | ~ doing sth** to dislike sb/sth very much 極不喜歡；厭惡 SYN **detest**：*I loathe modern art.* 我很不喜歡現代藝術。◇ *They loathe each other.* 他們相互討厭對方。 ➲ SYNONYMS at HATE

loath·ing /'ləʊðɪŋ; *NAmE* 'loʊð-/ *noun* [sing., U] **~ (for/of sb/sth)** (*formal*) a strong feeling of hatred 憎恨；憎惡；仇恨：*She looked at her attacker with* ***fear and loathing***. 她盯着襲擊她的歹徒，既害怕又憎恨。◇ *Many soldiers returned with a* ***deep loathing*** *of war.* 許多士兵回來時對戰爭都深惡痛絕。

loath·some /'ləʊðsəm; *NAmE* 'loʊð-/ *adj.* (*formal*) extremely unpleasant; disgusting 極不愉快的；令人厭惡的；討厭的 SYN **repulsive**

loaves *pl.* of LOAF

lob /lɒb; *NAmE* lɑːb/ *verb* (**-bb-**) **1 ~ sth + adv./prep.** (*informal*) to throw sth so that it goes quite high through the air（往空中）高扔，高拋，高擲：*Stones were lobbed over the wall.* 有人把石塊扔過了圍牆。 ➲ SYNONYMS at THROW **2 ~ sth (+ adv./prep.)** (*sport* 體) to hit or kick a ball in a high curve through the air, especially so that it lands behind the person you are playing against 吊高球，挑高球（尤指把球擊或踢到對方的身後）：*He lobbed the ball over the defender's head.* 他把球高挑過防守隊員的頭頂。 ▸ **lob** *noun*：*to play a lob* 放高球

lobby /'lɒbi; *NAmE* 'lɑːbi/ *noun, verb*

■ ***noun*** (*pl.* **-ies**) **1** [C] a large area inside the entrance of a public building where people can meet and wait（公共建築物進口處的）門廳，前廳，大廳 SYN **foyer**：*a hotel lobby* 旅館大廳 **2** [C] (in the British Parliament) a large hall that is open to the public and used for people to meet and talk to Members of Parliament（英國議會的）民眾接待廳 **3** [C+sing./pl. v.] a group of people who try to influence politicians on a particular issue（就某議題企圖影響從政者的）游說團體 SYN **pressure group**：*The gun lobby is/are against any change in the law.* 贊同擁有槍支的團體反對作任何法律上的修改。 **4** [C, sing.] (*BrE*) an organized attempt by a group of people to influence politicians on a particular issue（就某議題企圖影響從政者的）游說：*a recent lobby of Parliament by pensioners* 領養老金者近來在議會的游說

■ ***verb*** (**lob·bies, lobby·ing, lob·bied, lob·bied**) [T, I] **~ (sb) (for/against sth)** to try to influence a politician or the government and, for example, persuade them to support or oppose a change in the law 游説（從政者或政府）：*Farmers will lobby Congress for higher subsidies.* 農民將游説國會提高對農業的補貼。◇ *Women's groups are lobbying to get more public money for children.* 婦女組織在游説政府，要求增加對兒童的撥款。 ▸ **lobby·ist** /-ɪst/ *noun*：*political lobbyists* 政治說客

lobe /ləʊb; *NAmE* loʊb/ *noun* **1** = EAR LOBE **2** a part of an organ in the body, especially the lungs or brain（身體器官的）葉；（尤指）肺葉，腦葉

lo·belia /ləʊ'biːliə; *NAmE* loʊ-/ *noun* [C, U] a small garden plant with small blue, red or white flowers 半邊蓮（園圃植物，花小，呈藍、紅或白色）

lob·ola /lə'bəʊlə; lɒ'bɔːlə; *NAmE* loʊ'b-/ *noun* [U] (*SAfrE*) in traditional African culture, a sum of money or number of CATTLE that a man's family pays to a woman's family in order that he can marry her（非洲傳統文化中男方為娶親送給女方的）彩禮，彩牛禮：*to pay lobola* 出彩禮

lob·ot·om·ize (*BrE* also **-ise**) /lə'bɒtəmaɪz; *NAmE* -'bɑːt-/ *verb* **1 ~ sb** to perform a LOBOTOMY on sb 為…施行腦葉切斷術 **2 ~ sb** to make sb less intelligent or less mentally active 使遲鈍；使愚笨

lob·ot·omy /ləʊ'bɒtəmi; lə-; *NAmE* loʊ'bɑːt-/ *noun* (*pl.* **-ies**) a rare medical operation that cuts into part of a person's brain in order to treat mental illness 腦葉切斷術

lob·ster /'lɒbstə(r); *NAmE* 'lɑːb-/ *noun* **1** [C] a sea creature with a hard shell, a long body divided into sections, eight legs and two large CLAWS (= curved and pointed arms for catching and holding things). Its shell is black but turns bright red when it is boiled. 龍蝦 ➲ picture at SHELLFISH **2** [U] meat from a lobster, used for food（供食用的）龍蝦肉

'lobster pot *noun* a trap for lobsters that is shaped like a BASKET 誘捕龍蝦的籠

local /'ləʊkl; *NAmE* 'loʊkl/ *adj., noun*

■ ***adj.*** [usually before noun] **1** belonging to or connected with the particular place or area that you are talking about or with the place where you live 地方的；當地的；本地的：*a local farmer* 當地的農民 ◇ *A local man was accused of the murder.* 有一本地人被指控為這起謀殺案的兇手。◇ *Our children go to the local school.* 我們的小孩在本地學校就讀。◇ *a* ***local newspaper*** (= one that gives local news) 地方報紙 ◇ ***local radio*** (= a radio station that broadcasts to one area only) 地方廣播電台 ◇ *decisions made at local rather than national level* 地方性而非全國性的決策 ◇ *It was difficult to understand the local dialect.* 當地的方言很難懂。 **2** affecting only one part of the body （身體）局部的：*Her tooth was extracted under* ***local anaesthetic***. 她的牙齒是局部麻醉拔出的。 ▸ **lo·cal·ly** /-kəli/ *adv.*：*to work locally* 在本地工作 ◇ *Do you* ***live locally*** (= in this area)? 你住在這個地區嗎？◇ *locally grown fruit* 當地產的水果

■ ***noun*** **1** [usually pl.] a person who lives in a particular place or district 當地人；本地人：*The locals are very friendly.* 當地人很友好。 **2** (*BrE, informal*) a pub near where you live 住處附近的酒吧：*I called in at my local on the way home.* 我回家途中去了我住處附近的酒吧。 **3** (*NAmE*) a branch of a TRADE/LABOR UNION（工會的）地方分會 **4** (*NAmE*) a bus or train that stops at all places on the route （沿線每站都停的）公共汽車，火車

lo·cal /ˌləʊ 'kæl; *NAmE* ˌloʊ/ *adj.* (*informal*) = LOW-CAL

ˌlocal ˌarea 'network *noun* = LAN

ˌlocal au'thority *noun* (*BrE*) the organization which is responsible for the government of an area in Britain （英國的）地方當局，地方政府

'local call *noun* a telephone call to a place that is near 本地電話；市內電話

ˌlocal 'colour (*especially US* **ˌlocal 'color**) *noun* [U] the typical things, customs, etc. in a place that make it interesting, and that are used in a picture, story or film/movie to make it seem real （文藝作品的）地方特色，鄉土色彩

lo·cale /ləʊˈkɑːl; *NAmE* loʊˈkæl/ *noun* (*technical* 術語 or *formal*) a place where sth happens 發生地點；現場

ˌlocal ˈgovernment *noun* **1** [U] (*especially BrE*) the system of government of a town or an area by elected representatives of the people who live there 地方自治 **2** [C] (*NAmE*) the organization that is responsible for the government of a local area and for providing services, etc. 地方政府（機構）：*state and local governments* 國家和地方政府

lo·cal·ity /ləʊˈkæləti; *NAmE* loʊ-/ *noun* (*pl.* **-ies**) (*formal*) **1** the area that surrounds the place you are in or are talking about（圍繞所處或提及的）地區 SYN **vicinity**：*people living in the locality of the power station* 居住在發電站周圍地區的人 ◇ *There is no airport **in the locality**.* 這個地區沒有機場。 **2** the place where sb/sth exists（某人或某物存在的）地方，地點：*We talk of the brain as the locality of thought.* 我們把進行思維的地方叫做大腦。◇ *The birds are found in over 70 different localities.* 現已發現這種鳥棲息在 70 多個不同的地區。

lo·cal·ize (*BrE* also **-ise**) /ˈləʊkəlaɪz; *NAmE* ˈloʊ-/ *verb* **1 ~ sth** to limit sth or its effects to a particular area 使局限（於某地區）；使局部化 SYN **confine** **2 ~ sth** (*formal*) to find out where sth is 找出…的地點；發現…的位置：*animals' ability to localize sounds* 動物確定聲音發自某地點的能力 ▸ **lo·cal·iza·tion**, **-isa·tion** /ˌləʊkəlaɪˈzeɪʃn; *NAmE* ˌloʊkələˈz-/ *noun* [U]

lo·cal·ized (*BrE* also **-ised**) /ˈləʊkəlaɪzd; *NAmE* ˈloʊ-/ *adj.* (*formal*) happening within one small area 在小範圍內的；局部的：*a localized infection* (= in one part of the body) 局部感染 ◇ *localized fighting* 局部戰鬥

L

ˈlocal time *noun* [U] the time of day in the particular part of the world that you are talking about 地方時；當地時間：*We reach Delhi at 2 o'clock local time.* 我們在當地時間 2 時到達德里。

lo·cate 🔑 AW /ləʊˈkeɪt; *NAmE* ˈloʊkeɪt/ *verb* **1** 🔑 [T] **~ sb/sth** to find the exact position of sb/sth 找出…的準確位置；確定…的準確地點：*The mechanic located the fault immediately.* 機修工立即找到了出故障的地方。◇ *Rescue planes are trying to locate the missing sailors.* 救援飛機正在努力查明失踪水手的下落。 **2** 🔑 [T] **~ sth + adv./prep.** to put or build sth in a particular place 把…安置在（或建造於）SYN **site**：*They located their headquarters in Swindon.* 他們把總部設在了斯溫登。 ➲ compare RELOCATE **3** [I] **+ adv./prep.** (*especially NAmE*) to start a business in a particular place 創辦於（某地）：*There are tax breaks for businesses that locate in rural areas.* 在農村地區創辦企業享有稅收減免。

lo·cated 🔑 AW /ləʊˈkeɪtɪd; *NAmE* ˈloʊkeɪ-/ *adj.* [not before noun] if sth is **located** in a particular place, it exists there or has been put there 位於；坐落在 SYN **situated**：*a small town located 30 miles south of Chicago* 位於芝加哥以南 30 英里的一個小鎮 ◇ *The offices are conveniently located just a few minutes from the main station.* 辦事處所處的位置很方便，離總站僅有幾分鐘的路。

lo·ca·tion 🔑 AW /ləʊˈkeɪʃn; *NAmE* loʊ-/ *noun* **1** 🔑 [C] a place where sth happens or exists; the position of sth 地方；地點；位置：*a honeymoon in a secret location* 在一個祕密地點度的蜜月 ◇ *What is the exact location of the ship?* 那條船的確切位置在哪裏？ ➲ **SYNONYMS** at PLACE **2** [C, U] a place outside a film studio where scenes of a film/movie are made（電影的）外景拍攝地：*A mountain in the Rockies became the location for a film about Everest.* 落基山脈中的一座山成了一部有關珠穆朗瑪峰的電影的外景拍攝地。◇ *The movie was shot entirely **on location** in Italy.* 這部影片的外景全是在意大利拍攝的。 **3** [U] the act of finding the position of sb/sth 定位

loca·tive /ˈlɒkətɪv; *NAmE* ˈlɑːk-/ *adj.* (*grammar* 語法) (in some languages 用於某些語言) the form of a noun, pronoun or adjective when it expresses the idea of place（名詞、代詞或形容詞）表示位置的，方位格的 ➲ see also ACCUSATIVE, DATIVE, GENITIVE, NOMINATIVE, VOCATIVE

lo·ca·tor /ləʊˈkeɪtə(r); *NAmE* loʊˈkeɪtər; ˈloʊkeɪtər/ *noun* a device or system for finding sth 定位器；定位系統：*The company lists 5 000 stores on the store locator part of its website.* 這家公司在其網站的商店定位系統部份列出了 5 000 家商店。

loc. cit. /ˌlɒk ˈsɪt; *NAmE* ˌlɑːk/ *abbr.* in the piece of text quoted (from Latin 'loco citato') 在上述引文中（源自拉丁語 loco citato）

loch /lɒk; lɒx; *NAmE* lɑːk; lɑːx/ *noun* (in Scotland 蘇格蘭) a lake or a narrow strip of sea almost surrounded by land 湖；狹長的海灣 ➲ see also LOUGH

loci *pl.* of LOCUS

lock 🔑 /lɒk; *NAmE* lɑːk/ *verb, noun*

■ *verb* **1** 🔑 [T, I] **~ (sth)** to fasten sth with a lock; to be fastened with a lock（用鎖）鎖上；被鎖住：*Did you lock the door?* 你鎖門了嗎？◇ *This suitcase doesn't lock.* 這手提箱鎖不上。 **2** 🔑 [T] **~ sth + adv./prep.** to put sth in a safe place and lock it 把…鎖起來：*She locked her passport and money in the safe.* 她把自己的護照和錢鎖在了保險櫃裏。 **3** [I, T] **~ (sth) (in/into/around, etc. sth)** | **~ (sth) (together)** to become or make sth become fixed in one position and unable to move（使）固定，卡住，塞住：*The brakes locked and the car skidded.* 汽車刹車抱死，車在原地打滑。◇ *He locked his helmet into position with a click.* 他咔噠一聲把頭盔扣好。 **4** [T] **be locked in/into sth** to be involved in a difficult situation, an argument, a disagreement, etc. 陷入，捲入（困境、爭論、爭執等）：*The two sides are locked into a bitter dispute.* 雙方陷入了激烈的爭論。◇ *She felt locked in a loveless marriage.* 她覺得自己陷入了一樁沒有愛情的婚姻。 **5** [T] **be locked together/in sth** to be held very tightly by sb 被緊緊抓住（或抱住）：*They were locked in a passionate embrace.* 他們熱烈地擁抱在一起。 **6** [T] **~ sth** (*computing* 計) to prevent computer data from being changed or looked at by sb without permission 加鎖；鎖（定、緊）；封閉：*These files are locked to protect confidentiality.* 為了保密，這些文件都加了鎖。

IDM **ˌlock ˈhorns (with sb) (over sth)** to get involved in an argument or a disagreement with sb 涉及（與某人的）爭論（或爭端、糾紛）：*The company has locked horns with the unions over proposed pay cuts.* 公司與工會就減薪計劃爭論不休。

PHR V **ˌlock sb/sth aˈway** = LOCK SB/STH UP **ˌlock sb/yourself ˈin (...)** to prevent sb from leaving a place by locking the door 把…鎖在屋裏；把…關押起來：*At 9 p.m. the prisoners are locked in for the night.* 晚上 9 點犯人被鎖在牢房裏過夜。 **ˌlock ˈonto sth** (of a MISSILE, etc. 導彈等) to find the thing that is being attacked and follow it 尋找跟踪，鎖定（攻擊目標） **ˌlock sb/yourself ˈout (of sth)** to prevent sb from entering a place by locking the door 把…鎖在門外：*I'd locked myself out of the house and had to break a window to get in.* 我把自己鎖在了門外，不得不破窗而入。 **ˌlock sb ˈout** (of an employer 雇主) to refuse to allow workers into their place of work until they agree to particular conditions（在工人答應某些條件前）不准進入工作的地方 ➲ related noun LOCKOUT **ˌlock ˈup** | **ˌlock sth↔ˈup** 🔑 to make a building safe by locking the doors and windows 鎖好門窗：*Don't forget to lock up at night.* 晚上別忘了鎖好門窗。◇ *He locked up the shop and went home.* 他鎖好商店的門窗後回家了。 **ˌlock sb↔ˈup/aˈway** 🔑 (*informal*) to put sb in prison 把某人關進監獄 ➲ related noun LOCK-UP **ˌlock sth↔ˈup/aˈway** **1** 🔑 to put sth in a safe place that can be locked 把…收好並鎖起來 **2** to put money into an investment that you cannot easily turn into cash 把（錢）擱死（成為不易兌現的資本）：*Their capital is all locked up in property.* 他們把所有資金都擱死在地產上了。

■ *noun* **1** 🔑 [C] a device that keeps a door, window, lid, etc. shut, usually needing a key to open it 鎖：*She turned the key in the lock.* 她轉動鎖眼裏的鑰匙。 ➲ see also COMBINATION LOCK **2** 🔑 [C] a device with a key that prevents a vehicle or machine from being used 車鎖；制動器；鎖定器；制輪楔：*a bicycle lock* 自行車的車鎖 ◇ *a steering lock* 轉向鎖 **3** [U] a state in which the parts of a machine, etc. do not move（機器部件等的）鎖定 **4** [U, sing.] (*BrE*) (on a car, etc. 汽車等) the amount that the front wheels can be turned in one direction or the other in order to turn the vehicle 前輪轉向角度：*I had the steering wheel* ***on full lock*** (= I had turned it as far as it would turn). 我把方向盤轉到了底。 **5** [C] a section of CANAL or river with a gate at either end, in which the water level can be changed so that boats can move from one level of the canal or river to another（運河或河流的）閘，船閘 **6** [C] a few hairs that hang or lie together on your head 一綹（或一縷）頭髮：*John brushed a* ***lock of hair*** *from his eyes.* 約翰撩開眼前的一綹頭髮。 **7 locks** [pl.] (*literary*) a person's hair 頭髮：*She shook her long, flowing locks.* 她抖了抖她那飄逸的長髮。 **8** [C] (in RUGBY 橄欖球) a player in the second row of the SCRUM（並列爭球的）第二排前鋒 **9** [sing.] **a ~ (on sth)** (*NAmE*) total control of sth（對某物的）完全控制：*One company* ***had a*** *virtual* ***lock on*** *all orange juice sales in the state.* 有一家公司實際上壟斷了整個州所有的橙汁銷售。 ➲ see also ARMLOCK, HEADLOCK

IDM **ˌlock, stock and ˈbarrel** including everything 全部；所有：*He sold the business lock, stock and barrel.* 他把生意全盤賣掉了。 **(keep sth/put sth/be) under ˌlock and ˈkey** locked up safely somewhere; in prison 把…安全地鎖起來；在押；被囚禁：*We keep our valuables under lock and key.* 我們把貴重物品鎖起來收好了。◇ *I will not rest until the murderer is under lock and key.* 殺人兇手不關起來我是不會安心的。 ➲ more at PICK *v.*

lock·able /ˈlɒkəbl; *NAmE* ˈlɑːk-/ *adj.* that you can lock with a key 可鎖定的；能鎖的

lock·down /ˈlɒkdaʊn; *NAmE* ˈlɑːk-/ *noun* [C, U] (*especially NAmE*) an official order to control the movement of people or vehicles because of a dangerous situation（對人或交通工具的）活動限制，行動限制：*a three-day lockdown of American airspace* 美國為期三天的領空關閉 ◇ *Prisoners have been placed on lockdown to prevent further violence at the jail.* 已對囚犯實行活動限制，以免獄中再出現暴力行為。

lock·er /ˈlɒkə(r); *NAmE* ˈlɑːk-/ *noun* a small cupboard that can be locked, where you can leave your clothes, bags, etc. while you play a sport or go somewhere（體育館等的）有鎖存物櫃，寄物櫃 ➲ VISUAL VOCAB page V70

ˈlocker room *noun* (*especially NAmE*) a room with lockers in it, at a school, GYM, etc., where people can change their clothes（學校、體育館等設有鎖櫃的）更衣室，衣物間 ➲ compare CHANGING ROOM

locket /ˈlɒkɪt; *NAmE* ˈlɑːk-/ *noun* a piece of jewellery in the form of a small case that you wear on a chain around your neck and in which you can put a picture, piece of hair, etc. 盒式項鏈墜（可放照片、頭髮等） ➲ VISUAL VOCAB page V65

ˈlock-in *noun* (*BrE*) an occasion when customers are locked in a bar or club after it has closed so that they can continue drinking privately（酒吧或夜總會打烊後）留置顧客續飲

lock·jaw /ˈlɒkdʒɔː; *NAmE* ˈlɑːk-/ *noun* [U] (*old-fashioned, informal*) a form of the disease TETANUS in which the JAWS become stiff and closed 破傷風

ˈlock-keeper *noun* a person who is in charge of a LOCK on a CANAL or river, and opens and closes the gates（運河或河流上的）船閘管理員

lock·out /ˈlɒkaʊt; *NAmE* ˈlɑːk-/ *noun* a situation when an employer refuses to allow workers into their place of work until they agree to various conditions 閉廠，停工（雇主在工人答應各種條件前不准其進入工作場地）

lock·smith /ˈlɒksmɪθ; *NAmE* ˈlɑːk-/ *noun* a person whose job is making, fitting and repairing locks 鎖匠；修鎖工

lock·step /ˈlɒkstep; *NAmE* ˈlɑːk-/ *noun* [U] (*especially NAmE*) **1** a way of walking together where people move their feet at the same time 齊步走（步伐）：*The coffin was carried by six soldiers walking* ***in lockstep***. 靈柩由齊步行進的六名士兵抬着。◇ (*figurative*) *Politicians and the media are* ***marching in lockstep*** *on this issue* (= they agree). 政界和媒體在這一問題上保持一致。 **2** a situation where things happen at the same time or change at the same rate 同生同變：*a lockstep approach to teaching* 步伐一致的教學方法 ◇ *Cases of breathing difficulties increase* ***in lockstep with*** *air pollution.* 呼吸困難的病例隨空氣污染的加劇而增加。

ˈlock-up *noun* **1** a small prison where prisoners are kept for a short time 拘留所；（短期關押犯人的）監獄 **2** (*BrE*) a small shop that the owner does not live in; a garage that is usually separate from other buildings and that is rented to sb（店主不住在內的）小商店；（不和其他建築物相連供出租的）車庫 ▸ **ˈlock-up** *adj.* [only before noun]：*a lock-up garage* 出租的獨立車庫

loco /ˈləʊkəʊ; *NAmE* ˈloʊkoʊ/ *noun, adj.*

■ ***noun*** (*pl.* **-os**) (*informal*) = LOCOMOTIVE ➲ see also IN LOCO PARENTIS

■ ***adj.*** [not before noun] (*slang, especially NAmE*) crazy 發瘋；發狂

loco·mo·tion /ˌləʊkəˈməʊʃn; *NAmE* ˌloʊkəˈmoʊʃn/ *noun* [U] (*formal*) movement or the ability to move 移動（力）；運動（力）

loco·mo·tive /ˌləʊkəˈməʊtɪv; *NAmE* ˌloʊkəˈmoʊ-/ (also *informal* **loco**) *noun, adj.*

■ ***noun*** a railway engine that pulls a train 機車；火車頭：***steam/diesel/electric locomotives*** 蒸汽／內燃／電力機車 ➲ VISUAL VOCAB page V58

■ ***adj.*** (*formal*) connected with movement 移動的；運動的

locum /ˈləʊkəm; *NAmE* ˈloʊ-/ *noun* (*BrE*) a doctor or priest who does the work of another doctor or priest while they are sick, on holiday, etc. 代班醫生；代理牧師

locus /ˈləʊkəs; *NAmE* ˈloʊ-/ *noun* (*pl.* **loci** /ˈləʊsaɪ; *NAmE* ˈloʊ-/) (*technical* 術語 or *formal*) the exact place where sth happens or which is thought to be the centre of sth（某事發生的）確切地點；（被視為某物的）中心，核心

lo·cust /ˈləʊkəst; *NAmE* ˈloʊ-/ *noun* a large insect that lives in hot countries and flies in large groups, destroying all the plants and crops of an area 蝗蟲：*a swarm of locusts* 一大群蝗蟲

lo·cu·tion /ləˈkjuːʃn/ *noun* (*technical* 術語) **1** [U] a style of speaking 語言風格；語言表達方式 **2** [C] a particular phrase, especially one used by a particular group of people（尤指某類人的）慣用語，習語

lode /ləʊd; *NAmE* loʊd/ *noun* a line of ORE (= metal in the ground or in rocks) 礦脈

lode·star (also **load·star**) /ˈləʊdstɑː(r); *NAmE* ˈloʊd-/ *noun* **1** the POLE STAR (= a star that is used by sailors to guide a ship) 北極星（海員藉以導航） **2** (*formal*) a principle that guides sb's behaviour or actions（某人行為或行動的）指導原則

lode·stone (also **load·stone**) /ˈləʊdstəʊn; *NAmE* ˈloʊdstoʊn/ *noun* a piece of iron that acts as a MAGNET 天然磁石

lodge /lɒdʒ; *NAmE* lɑːdʒ/ *noun, verb*

■ ***noun*** **1** [C] a small house in the country where people stay when they want to take part in some types of outdoor sport（供參加戶外運動者暫住的）鄉間小屋，小舍：*a hunting lodge* 供打獵者居住的小屋 **2** [C] a small house at the gates of a park or in the land belonging to a large house（公園或宅第的）門口小屋，門房 **3** [C] a room at the main entrance to a building for the person whose job is to see who enters and leaves the building 管理員室；傳達室：*All visitors should report to the porter's lodge.* 所有來訪者都應先到傳達室通報。 **4** [C+sing./pl. v.] the members of a branch of a society such as the Freemasons; the building where they meet（共濟會等會社的）地方分會，集會處：*a masonic lodge* 共濟會的地方分會 **5** [C] the home of a BEAVER or an OTTER（河狸或水獺的）穴，窩 **6** [C] a Native American's tent or home built of LOGS（美洲土著人的）帳篷，原木住宅

■ ***verb*** **1** [T] **~ sth (with sb) (against sb/sth)** (*formal*) to make a formal statement about sth to a public organization or authority（向公共機構或當局）正式提出（聲明等） **SYN** **register, submit**：*They lodged a compensation claim against the factory.* 他們向工廠提出了賠償要求。◇ *Portugal has lodged a complaint with the International Court of Justice.* 葡萄牙向國際法院提出了申訴。 **2** [I] **+ adv./prep.** (*old-fashioned*) to pay to live in a room in sb's house（付款）寄住，借宿；租住 **SYN** **board**：*He lodged with Mrs Brown when he arrived in the city.* 他初

L

到這座城市時租房住在布朗太太的家裏。**3** [T] **~ sb (+ adv./prep.)** to provide sb with a place to sleep or live 為（某人）提供住宿 **SYN accommodate**：*The refugees are being lodged at an old army base.* 難民被安置在一座廢棄的軍事基地裏住宿。**4** [I, T] to become fixed or stuck somewhere; to make sth become fixed or stuck somewhere（被）固定，卡住：**~ in sth** *One of the bullets lodged in his chest.* 有一顆子彈嵌在了他的胸部。◇ **~ sth in sth** *She lodged the number firmly in her mind.* 她把號碼牢牢記在心中。**5** [T] **~ sth with sb/in sth** to leave money or sth valuable in a safe place 存放，寄存（錢或貴重物品）**SYN deposit**：*Your will should be lodged with your lawyer.* 你的遺囑應該交律師保管。

lodg·er /ˈlɒdʒə(r); *NAmE* ˈlɑːdʒ-/ *noun* (*especially BrE*) a person who pays rent to live in sb's house 租房人；房客

lodg·ing /ˈlɒdʒɪŋ; *NAmE* ˈlɑːdʒ-/ *noun* (*especially BrE*) **1** [U] temporary accommodation 暫住；寄宿；借宿：*full board and lodging* (= a room to stay in and all meals provided) 食宿全包 **2** [C, usually pl.] (*old-fashioned*) a room or rooms in sb else's house that you rent to live in 租住的房間：*It was cheaper to live in lodgings than in a hotel.* 住出租的房間比住旅館便宜。

ˈlodging house *noun* (*old-fashioned, BrE*) a house in which lodgings can be rented 有供出租用房間的公寓（或房屋）

loft /lɒft; *NAmE* lɔːft; lɑːft/ *noun, verb*

■ ***noun*** **1** (*especially BrE*) a space just below the roof of a house, often used for storing things and sometimes made into a room 閣樓，頂樓（常用以貯物，間或作房間）：*a **loft conversion*** (= one that has been made into a room or rooms for living in) 用閣樓改裝的居室 ➲ compare ATTIC, GARRET **2** an upper level in a church, or a farm or factory building（教堂的）樓廂；（農場的）廐樓；（工廠的）上層樓面：*the organ loft* 教堂內的管風琴台 **3** a flat/apartment in a former factory, etc., that has been made suitable for living in（由工廠等改建的）套房，公寓：*They lived in a SoHo loft.* 他們居住在索霍區改建的公寓裏。**4** (*NAmE*) a part of a room that is on a higher level than the rest（房間的）躍層：*The children slept in a loft in the upstairs bedroom.* 孩子們睡在樓上卧室裏的躍層上。

■ ***verb*** **~ sth** (*sport* 體) to hit, kick or throw a ball very high into the air 向高處擊（或踢、擲）

lofty /ˈlɒfti; *NAmE* ˈlɔːfti; ˈlɑːfti/ *adj.* (**loft·ier**, **lofti·est**) (*formal*) **1** (of buildings, mountains, etc. 建築物、山等) very high and impressive 巍峨的；高聳的：*lofty ceilings/rooms/towers* 高高的頂棚；屋頂高的房間；高聳的塔樓 **2** [usually before noun] (*approving*) (of a thought, an aim, etc. 思想、目標等) deserving praise because of its high moral quality 崇高的；高尚的：***lofty ambitions/ideals/principles*** 崇高的抱負／理想／原則 **3** (*disapproving*) showing a belief that you are worth more than other people 傲慢的；高傲的 **SYN haughty**：*her lofty disdain for other people* 她對別人不屑一顧的傲慢態度 ▸ **loft·ily** /-ɪli/ *adv.* **lofti·ness** *noun* [U]

log /lɒg; *NAmE* lɔːg; lɑːg/ *noun, verb*

■ ***noun*** **1** a thick piece of wood that is cut from or has fallen from a tree 原木：*logs for the fire* 燒火用的木材 ➲ VISUAL VOCAB page V10 **2** (also **log·book**) an official record of events during a particular period of time, especially a journey on a ship or plane（某時期事件的）正式記錄，日誌；（尤指）航海日誌，飛行日誌：*The captain keeps a log.* 船長記航海日誌。**3** (*informal*) = LOGARITHM **IDM** see EASY *adj.*, SLEEP *v.*

■ ***verb*** (**-gg-**) **1 ~ sth** to put information in an official record or write a record of events 把…載入正式記錄；記錄 **SYN record**：*The police log all phone calls.* 警方對所有電話都做了記錄。**2 ~ sth** to travel a particular distance or for a particular length of time 行駛，行進（若干距離或時間）**SYN clock up**：*The pilot has logged 1 000 hours in the air.* 這位飛行員有 1 000 小時的飛行記錄。**3 ~ sth** to cut down trees in a forest for their wood 採伐（森林的）樹木；伐木

PHR V **ˌlog ˈin/ˈon** (*computing* 計) to perform the actions that allow you to begin using a computer system 登錄，註冊，進入，登入（計算機系統）：*You need a password to log on.* 登錄需要密碼。**ˌlog sb ↔ˈin/ˈon** (*computing* 計) to allow sb to begin using a computer system 讓某人登錄，使註冊，使進入，使登入（計算機系統）：*The system is unable to log you on.* 這個系統無法讓你登錄。**ˌlog ˈoff/ˈout** (*computing* 計) to perform the actions that allow you to finish using a computer system 退出，註銷，登出（計算機系統）**ˌlog sb ↔ˈoff/ˈout** (*computing* 計) to cause sb to finish using a computer system 使註銷，使退出（計算機系統）

-log (*NAmE*) = -LOGUE

lo·gan·berry /ˈləʊgənbəri; *NAmE* ˈloʊgənberi/ *noun* (*pl.* **-ies**) a soft dark red fruit, like a large RASPBERRY, that grows on a bush 洛根莓

loga·rithm /ˈlɒgərɪðəm; *NAmE* ˈlɔːg-; ˈlɑːg-/ (also *informal* **log**) *noun* (*mathematics* 數) any of a series of numbers set out in lists which make it possible to work out problems by adding and SUBTRACTING instead of multiplying and dividing 對數 ▸ **loga·rith·mic** /ˌlɒgəˈrɪðmɪk; *NAmE* ˌlɔːg-; ˌlɑːg-/ *adj.*

log·book /ˈlɒgbʊk; *NAmE* ˈlɔːg-; ˈlɑːg-/ *noun* **1** (*BrE, becoming old-fashioned*) a document that records official details about a vehicle, especially a car, and its owner（交通工具，尤指小汽車的）行駛日誌 ➲ compare REGISTRATION (2) **2** = LOG *n.* (2)

ˌlog ˈcabin *noun* a small house built of logs 原木小屋 ➲ VISUAL VOCAB page V15

log·ger /ˈlɒgə(r); *NAmE* ˈlɔːg-; ˈlɑːg-/ *noun* = LUMBERJACK

log·ger·heads /ˈlɒgəhedz; *NAmE* ˈlɔːgər-; ˈlɑːg-/ *noun*

IDM **at loggerheads (with sb) (over sth)** in strong disagreement（與某人）不和；相爭；嚴重分歧：*The two governments are still at loggerheads over the island.* 兩國政府依然對這個島的歸屬問題爭執不下。

log·gia /ˈləʊdʒə; ˈlɒdʒiə; *NAmE* ˈloʊdʒə; ˈlɑːdʒiə/ *noun* (*BrE*) a room or GALLERY with one or more open sides, especially one that forms part of a house and has one side open to the garden 涼廊（敞向花園的房間或走廊）

log·ging /ˈlɒgɪŋ; *NAmE* ˈlɔːg-; ˈlɑːg-/ *noun* [U] the work of cutting down trees for their wood 伐木作業

logic 🔑 **AW** /ˈlɒdʒɪk; *NAmE* ˈlɑːdʒɪk/ *noun*

1 🔑 [U] a way of thinking or explaining sth 思維方式；解釋方法；邏輯：*I fail to see the logic behind his argument.* 我不明白支持他論據的是什麼邏輯。◇ *The two parts of the plan were governed by the same logic.* 計劃的兩個部份均受到了同一思維方式的制約。**2** 🔑 [U, sing.] sensible reasons for doing sth（做某事的）道理，合乎情理的原因：*Linking the proposals in a single package did have a certain logic.* 把這些提議聯繫起來成為一攬子提議確有一定的道理。◇ *a strategy based on sound commercial logic* 基於合理商業考慮的策略 ◇ *There is **no logic to/in** any of their claims.* 他們的說法全都不合理。**3** 🔑 [U] (*philosophy* 哲) the science of thinking about or explaining the reason for sth using formal methods 邏輯學：*the rules of logic* 邏輯學規則 **4** [U] (*computing* 計) a system or set of principles used in preparing a computer to perform a particular task 邏輯系統；操作規則

lo·gic·al 🔑 **AW** /ˈlɒdʒɪkl; *NAmE* ˈlɑːdʒ-/ *adj.*

1 🔑 (of an action, event, etc. 行動、事件等) seeming natural, reasonable or sensible 必然的；合乎情理的；合乎常理的：*a logical thing to do in the circumstances* 在那種環境下按理應做的事 ◇ *It was a logical conclusion from the child's point of view.* 從小孩的觀點來看這是個合乎情理的結論。**2** 🔑 following or able to follow the rules of logic in which ideas or facts are based on other true ideas or facts 符合邏輯的；按照邏輯的：*a logical argument* 合乎邏輯的論證 ◇ *Computer programming needs someone with a logical mind.* 編製計算機程序需要擅長邏輯思維的人。**OPP illogical** ▸ **lo·gic·al·ly** **AW** /-kli/ *adv.*：*to argue logically* 合乎邏輯地辯論

-logical, **-logic** ➲ -OLOGY

ˌlogical ˈpositivism *noun* [U] (*philosophy* 哲) the belief that the only problems which have meaning are those that can be solved using logical thinking 邏輯實證主義，邏輯經驗主義（認為只有能用邏輯思維解決的問題才有意義）

ˈlogic circuit *noun* (*computing* 計) a series of logic gates that performs operations on data that is put into a computer 邏輯電路（由一系列進行數據運算的邏輯門組成）

ˈlogic gate (also **gate**) *noun* (*computing* 計) an electronic switch that reacts in one of two ways to data that is put into it. A computer performs operations by passing data through a very large number of logic gates. 邏輯門，邏輯閘（以兩種方式之一對所輸入數據進行輸出的電子開關）

lo·gi·cian **AW** /ləˈdʒɪʃn/ *noun* a person who studies or is skilled in logic 邏輯學研究者；邏輯學家

login /ˈlɒɡɪn; *NAmE* ˈlɔːɡ-; ˈlɑːɡ-/ (also **logon**) *noun* **1** [U] the act of starting to use a computer system, usually by typing a name or word that you choose to use 註冊，登錄，登入（通過鍵入名稱或詞進入計算機系統的操作）：*If you've forgotten your login ID, click this link.* 如果忘記了自己的註冊賬號就點擊此鏈接。**2** [C] the name that you use to enter a computer system 登錄名；登入名稱：*Enter your login and password and press 'go'.* 鍵入登錄名和密碼，然後按下 go 按鈕。

-logist ➲ -OLOGY

lo·gis·tics /ləˈdʒɪstɪks/ *noun* **1** [U+sing./pl. v.] **~ (of sth)** the practical organization that is needed to make a complicated plan successful when a lot of people and equipment is involved 後勤；組織工作：*the logistics of moving the company to a new building* 把公司搬遷到一座新大樓的過程中需要進行的組織工作 **2** [U] (*business* 商) the business of transporting and delivering goods 物流 **3** [U] the activity of moving equipment, supplies and people for military operations 軍事後勤：*a revolution in military logistics* 軍隊後勤變革 ▸ **lo·gis·tic** (also **lo·gis·tic·al** /ləˈdʒɪstɪkl/) *adj.*：*logistic support* 後勤支持 ◇ *Organizing famine relief presents huge logistical problems.* 組織饑荒救濟工作涉及繁重的安排協調問題。 **lo·gis·tic·al·ly** /-kli/ *adv.*

log·jam /ˈlɒɡdʒæm; *NAmE* ˈlɔːɡ-; ˈlɑːɡ-/ *noun* **1** a difficult situation in which you cannot make progress easily because there are too many things to do（因事情太多造成的）困境，僵局 **SYN** **bottleneck** **2** a mass of LOGS floating on a river and blocking it（河面上）漂浮原木造成的阻塞

logo /ˈləʊɡəʊ; *NAmE* ˈloʊɡoʊ/ *noun* (*pl.* **-os**) a printed design or symbol that a company or an organization uses as its special sign（某公司或機構的）標識，標誌，徽標

log·off /ˈlɒɡɒf; *NAmE* ˈlɔːɡɔːf; ˈlɑːɡ-; -ɑːf/ (also **log·out**) *noun* [U] the act of finishing using a computer system（從計算機系統）退出，登出；註銷

logo·gram /ˈlɒɡəɡræm; *NAmE* ˈlɔːɡ-; ˈlɑːɡ-/ (also **logo·graph** /ˈlɒɡəɡrɑːf; *NAmE* ˈlɔːɡəɡræf; ˈlɑːɡəɡræf/) *noun* (*technical* 術語) a symbol that represents a word or phrase, for example those used in ancient writing systems 詞符；語符；速記符

logon /ˈlɒɡɒn; *NAmE* ˈlɔːɡɑːn; ˈlɑːɡ-; -ɔːn/ *noun* = LOGIN

log·out /ˈlɒɡaʊt; *NAmE* ˈlɔːɡ-; ˈlɑːɡ-/ *noun* = LOGOFF

log·roll·ing /ˈlɒɡrəʊlɪŋ; *NAmE* ˈlɔːɡroʊ-; ˈlɑːɡ-/ *noun* [U] (*NAmE*) **1** (in US politics 美國政治) the practice of agreeing with sb that you will vote to pass a law that they support so that they will later vote to pass a law that you support 互投贊成票（促使議案通過） **2** a sport in which two people stand on a LOG floating on water and try to knock each other off by moving the log with their feet 水上滾木比賽（兩人同時站在浮於水面的圓木上設法轉動滾木使對方落水）

-logue (*NAmE* also **-log**) *combining form* (in nouns 構成名詞) talk or speech 談話；講話：*a monologue* 獨白

-logy ➲ -OLOGY

loin /lɔɪn/ *noun* **1** [U, C] a piece of meat from the back or sides of an animal, near the tail（動物的）腰肉：*loin of pork* 豬後腰肉 **2** **loins** [pl.] (*old-fashioned*) the part of the body around the hips between the waist and the tops of the legs 腰部；後腰 **3** **loins** [pl.] (*literary*) a person's sex organs（人的）性器官，陰部，下身 **IDM** see GIRD

loin·cloth /ˈlɔɪnklɒθ; *NAmE* -klɔːθ; -klɑːθ/ *noun* a piece of cloth worn around the body at the hips by men in some hot countries, sometimes as the only piece of clothing worn（某些熱帶國家男子的）纏腰布，遮羞布

loi·ter /ˈlɔɪtə(r)/ *verb* [I] to stand or wait somewhere especially with no obvious reason 閒站着；閒蕩；徘徊 **SYN** **hang around**：*Teenagers were loitering in the street outside.* 青少年在外面街上閒蕩。

LOL /ˌel əʊ ˈel; *NAmE* oʊ/ *abbr.* LAUGH-OUT-LOUD

Lo·li·ta /ləʊˈliːtə; *NAmE* loʊ-/ *noun* a young girl who behaves in a more sexually developed way than is usual for her age, which makes her sexually attractive to older men（吸引年長男性的）早熟性感少女 **ORIGIN** From the name of the main character in Vladimir Nabokov's novel *Lolita.* 源自弗拉基米爾•納博科夫所著小說《洛麗塔》中主人公的名字。

loll /lɒl; *NAmE* lɑːl/ *verb* **1** [I] **+ adv./prep.** to lie, sit or stand in a lazy, relaxed way 懶洋洋地躺着（或坐着、站着）：*He lolled back in his chair by the fire.* 他懶洋洋地靠着椅背坐在爐火邊。**2** [I] **+ adv./prep.** (of your head, tongue, etc. 頭、舌等) to move or hang in a relaxed way 耷拉；下垂：*My head lolled against his shoulder.* 我把頭懶懶地靠在他的肩上。

lol·li·pop /ˈlɒlipɒp; *NAmE* ˈlɑːlipɑːp/ (also *BrE, informal* **lolly**) (also *NAmE, informal* **suck·er**) *noun* a hard round or flat sweet/candy made of boiled sugar on a small stick 棒棒糖

ˈlollipop man, ˈlollipop lady *noun* (*BrE, informal*) a person whose job is to help children cross a busy road on their way to and from school by holding up a sign on a stick telling traffic to stop（手持車輛暫停牌以幫助學童穿越馬路的）交通安全員

lol·lop /ˈlɒləp; *NAmE* ˈlɑːləp/ *verb* [I] (**+ adv./prep.**) (*informal, especially BrE*) to walk or run with long awkward steps 跌跌撞撞地走（或跑）：*The dog came lolloping towards them.* 那條狗蹣跚地向他們跑來。

lolly /ˈlɒli; *NAmE* ˈlɑːli/ *noun* (*pl.* **-ies**) (*informal*) **1** [C] (*BrE*) = LOLLIPOP **2** [C] (*BrE*) = ICE LOLLY **3** [U] (*old-fashioned, BrE*) money 錢 **4** [C] (*AustralE, NZE*) a sweet or a piece of candy 糖果；糖塊兒

Lon·don·er /ˈlʌndənə(r)/ *noun* a person from London in England 倫敦人

lone /ləʊn; *NAmE* loʊn/ *adj.* [only before noun] **1** without any other people or things 單獨的；獨自的；孤零零的 **SYN** **solitary**：*a lone sailor crossing the Atlantic* 獨自橫渡大西洋的人 **2** (*especially BrE*) without a husband, wife or partner to share the care of children 單親的 **SYN** **single**：*a **lone mother/parent/father*** 單親母親 / 父親 ➲ note at ALONE
IDM **a ˌlone ˈwolf** a person who prefers to be alone 好獨處的人；喜歡單幹的人

lone·ly 🔑 /ˈləʊnli; *NAmE* ˈloʊn-/ *adj.* (**lone·lier, lone·li·est**)
1 🔑 unhappy because you have no friends or people to talk to 孤獨的；寂寞的：*She lives alone and often feels lonely.* 她孑然一身，常感到寂寞。**2** 🔑 (of a situation or period of time 情況或一段時間) sad and spent alone 在孤單中度過的：*all those lonely nights at home watching TV* 所有那些在家看電視的孤寂夜晚 **3** 🔑 [only before noun] (of places 地方) where only a few people ever come or visit 偏僻的；人跡罕至的 **SYN** **isolated**：*a lonely beach* 人跡罕至的海灘 ➲ note at ALONE ▸ **lone·li·ness** *noun* [U]：*a period of loneliness in his life* 他一生中孤苦伶仃的一段時間

ˌlonely ˈhearts *adj.* [only before noun] a **lonely hearts column** in a newspaper, etc. is where people can advertise for a new lover or friend（在報紙等徵友專欄登廣告）徵求愛侶的，徵友的：*He placed a lonely hearts ad in a magazine.* 他在一份雜誌上刊登了徵友廣告。

ˌlone-parent ˈfamily *noun* = ONE-PARENT FAMILY

loner /ˈləʊnə(r); *NAmE* ˈloʊn-/ *noun* a person who is often alone or who prefers to be alone, rather than with other people 獨來獨往的人；喜歡獨處的人；不合群的人

lone·some /ˈləʊnsəm; *NAmE* ˈloʊn-/ *adj., noun*

■ *adj.* (*especially NAmE*) **1** unhappy because you are alone and do not want to be or because you have no friends 孤獨的；寂寞的：*I felt so lonesome after he left.* 他離開後我感到非常孤單。**2** (of a place 地方) where not many people go; a long way from where people live 人煙稀少的；荒涼的；偏僻的：*a lonesome road* 偏僻的路 ➲ note at ALONE

■ *noun*

IDM **(all) by/on your lonesome** (*informal*) alone 單獨；獨自：*Are you here all by your lonesome?* 只有你一個人在這兒嗎？

long 🔑 /lɒŋ; *NAmE* lɔːŋ; lɑːŋ/ *adj., adv., verb*

WORD FAMILY
long *adj., adv.*
length *noun*
lengthy *adj.*
lengthen *verb*

■ *adj.* (**long·er** /ˈlɒŋɡə(r); *NAmE* ˈlɔːŋ-; ˈlɑːŋ-/, **long·est** /ˈlɒŋɡɪst; *NAmE* ˈlɔːŋ-; ˈlɑːŋ-/)

▸ **DISTANCE** 距離 **1** 🔑 measuring or covering a great length or distance, or a greater length or distance than usual（長度或距離）長的：*She had long dark hair.* 她留着黑黑的長髮。◇ *He walked down the long corridor.* 他沿長廊走去。◇ *It was the world's longest bridge.* 那座橋當時是世界上最長的。◇ *a* ***long journey/walk/drive/flight*** 長途旅行／步行／駕駛／飛行 ◇ *We're* ***a long way*** *from anywhere here.* 我們這裏離任何一個地方都很遠。◇ *It's* ***a long way away.*** 那兒離這裏很遠。➲ VISUAL VOCAB page V60 **OPP** **short** **2** 🔑 used for asking or talking about particular lengths or distances（詢問或談論長度或距離）長：***How long*** *is the River Nile?* 尼羅河有多長？◇ *The table is six feet long.* 那張桌子長六英尺。◇ *The report is only three pages long.* 這份報告僅有三頁。

▸ **TIME** 時間 **3** 🔑 lasting or taking a great amount of time or more time than usual 長時間的；長久的；長期的：*He's been ill* (***for***) ***a long time.*** 他生病很久了。◇ *There was a long silence before she spoke.* 沉默了很長時間她才開口。◇ *I like it now the days are getting longer* (= it stays light for more time each day). 白天越來越長了，我很喜歡。◇ *a* ***long book/film/list*** (= taking a lot of time to read/watch/deal with) 篇幅長的書；放映時間長的電影；一份很長的清單 ◇ *Nurses have to work* ***long hours*** (= for more hours in the day than is usual). 護士都不得不長時間地工作。◇ (*NAmE*) *He stared at them* ***for the longest time*** (= for a very long time) *before answering.* 他盯着他們看了好長時間才回答。**OPP** **short** **4** 🔑 used for asking or talking about particular periods of time（詢問或談論某段時間）：***How long*** *is the course?* 這門課程要唸多久？◇ *I think it's only three weeks long.* 我想只有三個星期長。◇ *How long a stay did you have in mind?* 你原打算待多長時間？**5** 🔑 seeming to last or take more time than it really does because, for example, you are very busy or not happy（因忙或不愉快等）似乎比實際時間長的：*I'm tired. It's been a long day.* 我累了。這一天可真夠長的。◇ *We were married for ten long years.* 我們結婚有十年之久了。**OPP** **short**

▸ **CLOTHES** 衣物 **6** 🔑 covering all or most of your legs or arms 長的（完全或大部份覆蓋腿或臂的）：*She usually wears long skirts.* 她通常穿長裙。◇ *a long-sleeved shirt* 長袖襯衫 **OPP** **short**

▸ **VOWEL SOUNDS** 元音 **7** (*phonetics* 語音) taking more time to make than a short vowel sound in the same position 長音的 **OPP** **short**

IDM **as long as your ˈarm** (*informal*) very long 很長：*There's a list of repairs as long as your arm.* 有一份長得要命的修理單。**at long last** after a long time 最後；終於 **SYN** **finally** ：*At long last his prayers had been answered.* 他的祈望終於實現了。**at the ˈlongest** not longer than the particular time given 最長，至多（不超過某特定時間）：*It will take an hour at the longest.* 這事最多花一小時。**by a ˈlong way** by a great amount 大量地；大大地 **go back a long ˈway** (of two or more people 兩個或以上的人) to have known each other for a long time 相識很久：*We go back a long way, he and I.* 我跟他，我們倆相識很久了。**go a long ˈway** (of money, food, etc. 錢、食物等) to last a long time 經用；夠維持很長時間：*She seems to make her money go a long way.* 看起來她用錢細水長流。◇ *A small amount of this paint goes a long way* (= covers a large area). 這種塗料用一點就可塗一大片。◇ (*ironic*) *I find that* ***a little of*** *Jerry's company can* ***go a long way*** (= I quickly get tired of being with him). 我發覺跟傑里待上一會兒就受不了啦。**have come a long ˈway** to have made a lot of progress 取得大的進步；大有長進：*We've come a long way since the early days of the project.* 這項目開始以來我們已取得很大進展。**have a long way to ˈgo** to need to make a lot of progress before you can achieve sth 還有很長的路要走；還有很大差距：*She still has a long way to go before she's fully fit.* 她還需要很長時間才能完全恢復健康。**how long is a piece of ˈstring?** (*BrE, informal*) used to say that there is no definite answer to a question 一條線段有多長（意指沒有確切的答案）：*'How long will it take?' 'How long's a piece of string?'* "需要多長時間？" "沒準兒。" **in the ˈlong run** concerning a longer period in the future 從長遠來看：*This measure inevitably means higher taxes in the long run.* 從長遠來看這項措施的結果免不了要多納稅。**it's a ˌlong ˈstory** (*informal*) used to say that the reasons for sth are complicated and you would prefer not to give all the details 一言難盡；說來話長 **the long arm of sth** the power and/or authority of sth（某事物的）權力，權威：*There is no escape from the long arm of the law.* 法網恢恢，疏而不漏。**the long and (the) ˈshort of it** used when you are telling sb the essential facts about sth or what effect it will have, without explaining all the details 總而言之；總的情況 **(pull, wear, etc.) a long ˈface** (to have) an unhappy or disappointed expression 悶悶不樂；哭喪着臉；愁眉苦臉 **ˌlong in the ˈtooth** (*humorous, especially BrE*) old or too old 年齒漸長；老朽 **ORIGIN** This originally referred to the fact that a horse's teeth appear to be longer as it grows older, because its gums shrink. 源自馬越老因牙齦收縮而牙齒顯得越長。**ˈlong on sth** (*informal*) having a lot of a particular quality 擅長；頗具（某種特性）：*The government is long on ideas but short on performance.* 這個政府想法很多但做成的卻太少。**a ˈlong shot** an attempt or a guess that is not likely to be successful but is worth trying 成功希望不大的嘗試；把握不大的猜測；姑妄一猜：*It's a long shot, but it just might work.* 沒有什麼把握，但也許行得通。**long time no ˈsee** (*informal*) used to say hello to sb you have not seen for a long time 好久不見了 **not by a ˈlong chalk** (*BrE*) (also **not by a ˈlong shot** *NAmE, BrE*) not nearly; not at all 差得遠；絕不；一點也不：*It's not over yet—not by a long chalk.* 這事還沒有了結，還差得遠呢。**take a long (cool/hard) ˈlook at sth** to consider a problem or possibility very carefully and without hurrying 極其慎重地考慮（問題或可能性）：*We need to take a long hard look at all the options.* 我們需要十分謹慎地考慮所有的選擇。**take the ˈlong view (of sth)** to consider what is likely to happen or be important over a long period of time rather than only considering the present situation 從長遠考慮 **to cut a long story ˈshort** (*BrE*) (*NAmE* **to make a long story ˈshort**) (*informal*) used when you are saying that you will get to the point of what you are saying quickly, without including all the details 長話短說；扼要地說；簡而言之 ➲ more at BROAD *adj.*, KICK *v.*, TERM *n.*, WAY *n.*

■ *adv.* (**long·er** /ˈlɒŋɡə(r); *NAmE* ˈlɔːŋ-; ˈlɑːŋ-/, **long·est** /ˈlɒŋɡɪst; *NAmE* ˈlɔːŋ-; ˈlɑːŋ-/) **1** 🔑 for a long time 長期地；長久地：*Have you been here long?* 你來這裏時間長嗎？◇ *Stay as long as you like.* 你願待多久就待多久。◇ *The party went on long into the night.* 聚會持續到深夜。◇ *This may* ***take longer*** *than we thought.* 這事花的時間也許比我們預料的要多些。◇ *I won't* ***be long*** (= I'll return, be ready, etc. soon). 我一會兒就行。◇ ***How long*** *have you been waiting?* 你等了多久了？◇ *These reforms are long overdue.* 這些改革早就該進行了。**2** 🔑 a long time before or after a particular time or event（在某一時間或事件之前或以後）很久地：*He retired long before the war.* 他在戰爭之前早就退休了。◇ *It wasn't long before she had persuaded him* (= it only took a short time). 她沒用多久就把他說服了。◇ *We'll be home* ***before long*** (= soon). 我們很快就要到家了。◇ *The house was pulled down* ***long ago.*** 那棟房子很久以前就被拆掉了。◇ *They had* ***long since*** (= a long time before the present time) *moved away.* 他們早就搬走了。**3** used after a

L

noun to emphasize that sth happens for the whole of a particular period of time（用於名詞後強調某事發生在某整段時間）：*We had to wait* ***all day long.*** 我們不得不整天等候着。◇ *The baby was crying* ***all night long.*** 嬰兒整夜在哭。◇ *They stayed up* ***the whole night long.*** 他們徹夜未眠。

IDM **as/so 'long as** **1** only if 只要：*We'll go as long as the weather is good.* 只要天氣好我們就去。 **2** since; to the extent that 既然；由於；就…來說：*So long as there is a demand for these drugs, the financial incentive for drug dealers will be there.* 只要對這些毒品有需求，就會有對販毒者的經濟誘因。**for (so) 'long** for (such) a long time 長久地；（這麼）長時間地：*Will you be away for long?* 你要離開很久嗎？◇ *I'm sorry I haven't written to you for so long.* 真抱歉，我很長時間未給你寫信了。 **how long have you 'got?** (*BrE*) (*NAmE* **how long do you 'have?**) (*informal*) used to say that sth is going to take a long time to explain 你有多少時間（指需要很長時間來解釋）：*What do I think about it? How long have you got?* 這事我是怎麼想的？說來話長，你有時間聽嗎？ **long live sb/sth** used to say that you hope sb/sth will live or last for a long time …萬歲；…萬古常青 **no/any 'longer** used to say that sth which was possible or true before, is not now 不再；不復：*I can't wait any longer.* 我不能再等了。◇ *He no longer lives here.* 他不再住這兒了。 **so 'long** (*informal*) goodbye 再見 ➲ more at LAUGH *v.*

■ ***verb*** [I] to want sth very much especially if it does not seem likely to happen soon（尤指對看似不會很快發生的事）渴望 **SYN** **yearn**：**~ for sb/sth** *Lucy had always longed for a brother.* 露西一直渴望有個弟弟。◇ **~ for sb to do sth** *He longed for Pat to phone.* 他期盼着帕特來電話。◇ **~ to do sth** *I'm longing to see you again.* 我渴望再次見到你。 ➲ see also LONGED-FOR

Which Word? 詞語辨析

(for) long / (for) a long time

- Both **(for) long** and **(for) a long time** are used as expressions of time. In positive sentences **(for) a long time** is used. * (for) long 和 (for) a long time 均用以表示時間。肯定句用 (for) a long time：*We've been friends a long time.* 我們是老朋友了。 **(For) long** is not used in positive sentences unless it is used with *too, enough, as, so, seldom,* etc. * (for) long 只有與 too、enough、as、so、seldom 等詞連用時才用於肯定句中：*I stayed out in the sun for too long.* 我在太陽底下待的時間太長了。◇ *You've been waiting long enough.* 你等得夠久的了。 Both **(for) long** and **(for) a long time** can be used in questions, but **(for) long** is usually preferred. * (for) long 和 (for) a long time 均可用於疑問句，但 (for) long 較常用：*Have you been waiting long?* 你等了很長時間嗎？
- In negative sentences **(for) a long time** sometimes has a different meaning from **(for) long**. 在否定句中 (for) a long time 和 (for) long 有時含義不同。Compare 比較：*I haven't been here for a long time* (= It is a long time since the last time I was here). 我已很久沒來這裏了。 and 和 *I haven't been here long* (= I arrived here only a short time ago). 我到這裏沒多長時間。

long. *abbr.* (in writing) LONGITUDE（書寫形式）經度

,long-a'waited *adj.* that people have been waiting for for a long time 等待（或期待）已久的：*her long-awaited new novel* 她的令人期待已久的一部新小說

long·board /ˈlɒŋbɔːd; *NAmE* ˈlɔːŋbɔːrd/ *noun* a long board used in SURFING 衝浪板

long·boat /ˈlɒŋbəʊt; *NAmE* ˈlɔːŋboʊt; ˈlɑːŋboʊt/ *noun* a large ROWING BOAT, used especially for travelling on the sea（尤用於航海的）大划艇

long·bow /ˈlɒŋbəʊ; *NAmE* ˈlɔːŋboʊ; ˈlɑːŋboʊ/ *noun* a large BOW made of a long thin curved piece of wood that was used in the past for shooting arrows（舊時用於射箭的）長弓，大弓

,long-'distance *adj.* [only before noun] **1** travelling or involving travel between places that are far apart 長途的；長距離的：*a long-distance commuter* 長途通勤者 ◇ *long-distance flights* 長途航班 **2** operating between people and places that are far apart 長途運作的：*a long-distance phone call* 長途電話 ▶ **,long 'distance** *adv.*：*It's a relaxing car to drive long distance.* 這輛轎車跑長途，開起來很輕鬆。◇ *to call long distance* 打長途電話

,long-,distance 'footpath *noun* a route that people can walk along to see the countryside or the coast（鄉間或海岸的）觀光步道

,long di'vision *noun* [U] (*mathematics* 數) a method of dividing one number by another in which all the stages involved are written down 長除法（把每一步驟都寫下來）

,long-drawn-'out (also *less frequent* **'long-drawn, ,drawn-'out**) *adj.* lasting a very long time, often too long 持續很久的；拖長的 **SYN** **protracted**：*long-drawn-out negotiations* 曠日持久的談判

,long 'drink *noun* a cold drink that fills a tall glass, such as LEMONADE or beer 大杯冷飲料（如檸檬汽水或啤酒）

'longed-for *adj.* [only before noun] that sb has been wanting or hoping for very much 渴望的；期待已久的：*the birth of a longed-for baby* 一個盼望已久的嬰兒的出生

lon·gev·ity /lɒnˈdʒevəti; *NAmE* lɔːn-; lɑːn-/ *noun* [U] (*formal*) long life; the fact of lasting a long time 長壽；長命；持久：*We wish you both health and longevity.* 我們祝願您二位健康長壽。◇ *He prides himself on the longevity of the company.* 他為公司悠久的歷史而感到驕傲。

long·hair /ˈlɒŋheə(r); *NAmE* ˈlɔːŋher; ˈlɑːŋher/ *noun* a breed of cat with long hair 長毛貓 ➲ compare SHORT-HAIR

long·hand /ˈlɒŋhænd; *NAmE* ˈlɔːŋ-; ˈlɑːŋ-/ *noun* [U] ordinary writing, not typed or written in SHORTHAND 普通書寫（非打字或速記）

,long 'haul *noun* [usually sing.] a difficult task that takes a long time and a lot of effort to complete 費時費力的工作：*She knows that becoming world champion is going to be a long haul.* 她知道要成為世界冠軍需要長時間的艱苦努力。

IDM **be in sth for the long 'haul** (*especially NAmE*) to be willing to continue doing a task until it is finished 願意堅持到底：*I promise I am in this for the long haul.* 我保證我會堅持把這事做完。 **over the long 'haul** (*especially NAmE*) over a long period of time 長時間；長久

'long-haul *adj.* [only before noun] involving the transport of goods or passengers over long distances（運送貨物或旅客）長途的，遠距離的：***long-haul flights/routes*** 遠程航班；長途運輸路線 **OPP** **short-haul**

long·horn /ˈlɒŋhɔːn; *NAmE* -hɔːrn/ *noun* a type of cow with long horns 長角牛

long·house /ˈlɒŋhaʊs; *NAmE* ˈlɔːŋ-; ˈlɑːŋ-/ *noun* **1** (in Britain) an old type of house in which people and animals lived together（英國舊式人畜共居的）長屋 **2** (in the US) a traditional house used by some Native Americans（美國某些印第安人的傳統住宅）長屋

long·ing /ˈlɒŋɪŋ; *NAmE* ˈlɔːŋ-/ *noun, adj.*

■ ***noun*** [C, U] a strong feeling of wanting sth/sb（對…的）渴望，熱望：**~ (for sb/sth)** *a longing for home* 對故鄉的思念 ◇ **~ (to do sth)** *She was filled with longing to hear his voice again.* 她熱切希望再聽到他的聲音。◇ *romantic longings* 對愛情的渴望 ◇ *His voice was husky with longing* (= sexual desire). 他因慾火攻心而聲音嘶啞。

■ ***adj.*** [only before noun] feeling or showing that you want sth very much 渴望的；熱望的；表示渴望的：*He gave a longing look at the ice cream.* 他看了看那冰淇淋，顯出很想吃的樣子。 ▶ **long·ing·ly** *adv.*：*We looked longingly towards the hills.* 我們不勝嚮往地朝群山望去。

long·ish /ˈlɒŋɪʃ; *NAmE* ˈlɔːŋ-/ *adj.* [only before noun] fairly long 稍長的；較長的：*longish hair* 頗長的頭髮 ◇ *There was a longish pause.* 有一陣略長的停頓。

L

lon·gi·tude /ˈlɒŋɡɪtjuːd; ˈlɒndʒɪ-; *NAmE* ˈlɑːndʒətuːd; ˈlɔːndʒətuːd/ *noun* [U] (*abbr.* **long.**) the distance of a place east or west of the Greenwich MERIDIAN, measured in degrees 經度：*the longitude of the island* 那座島的經度 ➲ compare LATITUDE (1)

lon·gi·tu·din·al /ˌlɒŋɡɪˈtjuːdɪnl; ˌlɒndʒɪ-; *NAmE* ˌlɑːndʒəˈtuːdnl; ˌlɔːndʒəˈtuːdnl/ *adj.* (*technical* 術語) **1** going downwards rather than across 縱的；縱向的：*The plant's stem is marked with thin green longitudinal stripes.* 這種植物的莖上長有綠色的細長縱向條紋。**2** concerning the development of sth over a period of time 縱觀的：*a longitudinal study of ageing* 對衰老問題的縱向研究 **3** connected with longitude 經度的：*the town's longitudinal position* 這座城鎮的經度位置 ▸ **lon·gi·tu·din·al·ly** /-nəli/ *adv.*

longi,tudinal 'wave *noun* (*physics* 物) a wave that VIBRATES in the direction that it is moving 縱波 ➲ compare TRANSVERSE WAVE

'long johns *noun* [pl.] (*informal*) warm UNDERPANTS with long legs down to the ankles（至踝部的）長內褲，襯褲：*a pair of long johns* 一條長襯褲

the 'long jump (*NAmE* also **the 'broad jump**) *noun* [sing.] a sporting event in which people try to jump as far forward as possible after running up to a line 跳遠

,long-'lasting *adj.* that can or does last for a long time（可）持久的；長期的 **SYN** **durable**：*long-lasting effects* 長期的影響 ◇ *a long-lasting agreement* 長期的協議

,long-'life *adj.* **1** made to last longer than the ordinary type 長（壽）命的；經久耐用的；使用期限特別長的：*long-life batteries* 長效電池 **2** (*BrE*) made to remain fresh longer than the ordinary type 做過保鮮處理的；保鮮期特別長的：*long-life milk* 保鮮期長的牛奶

,long-'lived *adj.* having a long life; lasting for a long time 壽命長的；長壽的；經久耐用的；持久的 ➲ SYNONYMS at OLD

'long-lost *adj.* [only before noun] that you have not seen or received any news of for a long time 長時間沒見面的；杳無音信的：*a long-lost friend* 長久沒有音信的朋友

'long-range *adj.* [only before noun] **1** travelling a long distance 遠距離的；遠程的：*long-range missiles* 遠程導彈 **2** made for a period of time that will last a long way into the future 長遠的；長期的：*a long-range weather forecast* 遠期天氣預報 ◇ *long-range plans* 長遠的計劃 ➲ compare SHORT-RANGE

'long-running *adj.* [only before noun] that has been continuing for a long time 持續時間長的：*a long-running dispute* 長期的爭端 ◇ *a long-running TV series* 長期連播的電視系列片

'long-serving *adj.* [only before noun] having had the job or position mentioned for a long time 長期供職的：*long-serving employees* 高年資的雇員

long·ship /ˈlɒŋʃɪp; *NAmE* ˈlɔːŋ-; ˈlɑːŋ-/ *noun* a long narrow ship used by the Vikings 北歐海盜船；維金海盜船

long·shore drift /ˌlɒŋʃɔː ˈdrɪft; *NAmE* ˌlɔːŋʃɔːr; ˌlɑːŋ-/ *noun* [U] (*technical* 術語) the movement of sand, etc. along a beach caused by waves hitting the beach at an angle 沿岸泥沙流

long·shore·man /ˈlɒŋʃɔːmən; *NAmE* ˈlɔːŋʃɔːrmən; ˈlɑːŋʃɔːrmən/ *noun* (*pl.* **-men** /-mən/) (*NAmE*) a man whose job is moving goods on and off ships 碼頭工人；港口裝卸工

,long-'sighted (*especially BrE*) (also **,far-'sighted** especially in *NAmE*) *adj.* [not usually before noun] not able to see things that are close to you clearly 遠視 **OPP** **short-sighted** ▸ **,long-'sighted·ness** (also **,long 'sight**) *noun* [U]

,long-'standing *adj.* [usually before noun] that has existed or lasted for a long time 存在已久的；悠久的：*a long-standing relationship* 長期的關係

'long-stay *adj.* [usually before noun] **1** likely to need treatment or care for a long time 可能需要長期治療（或護理）的：*long-stay patients* 需要長期治療的病人 ◇ ***long-stay hospitals/institutions/wards*** (= for long-stay patients) 長期病人醫院／機構／病房 **2** for people who wish to park their cars for a long period 供長期停放汽車的：*long-stay parking* 長期停放車輛的停車場

,long-'suffer·ing *adj.* bearing problems or another person's unpleasant behaviour with patience 長期忍受的；忍耐的：*his long-suffering wife* 他那長期受罪的妻子

,long-'term *adj.* [usually before noun] **1** that will last or have an effect over a long period of time 長期的；長遠的；長期有效的：*a long-term strategy* 長期的策略 ◇ *the long-term effects of fertilizers* 肥料的長遠影響 ◇ *a long-term investment* 長線投資 **2** that is not likely to change or be solved quickly 近期不大可能改變的；不大可能很快解決的：*long-term unemployment* 長期失業 ➲ compare SHORT-TERM

'long-time *adj.* [only before noun] having been the particular thing mentioned for a long time 為時甚久的：*his long-time colleague* 他的老同事

lon·gueurs /lɒŋˈɡɜːz; *NAmE* lɔːŋˈɡɜːrz/ *noun* [pl.] (from *French, literary*) very boring parts or aspects of sth 冗長乏味的部份（或方面）

'long wave *noun* [U, C] (*abbr.* **LW**) a radio wave with a length of more than 1 000 metres 長波：*to broadcast **on long wave*** 用長波播送 ➲ compare SHORT WAVE

long·ways /ˈlɒŋweɪz; *NAmE* ˈlɔːŋ-; ˈlɑːŋ-/ (also **long·wise** /ˈlɒŋwaɪz; *NAmE* ˈlɔːŋ-/) *adv.* in the same direction as the longest side of sth 縱向地；長地 **SYN** **lengthways**

,long week'end *noun* a holiday/vacation of three or four days from Friday or Saturday to Sunday or Monday（三天或四天的）週末長假

,long-'winded *adj.* (*disapproving*) (especially of talking or writing 尤指說話或寫作) continuing for too long and therefore boring 冗長枯燥的；囉嗦的；嘮嘮叨叨的 **SYN** **tedious**

loo /luː/ *noun* (*pl.* **loos**) (*BrE, informal*) a toilet/bathroom 廁所；盥洗室；洗手間；浴室：*She's gone to the loo.* 她去盥洗室了。◇ *Can I use your loo, please?* 我可以用一下你的廁所嗎？

loo·fah /ˈluːfə/ *noun* a long rough bath SPONGE made from the dried fruit of a tropical plant（擦澡用的）絲瓜絡 ➲ VISUAL VOCAB page V24

look 0-ᵐ /lʊk/ *verb, noun, exclamation*

■ ***verb***

▸ **USE EYES 用眼睛** **1** 0-ᵐ [I] to turn your eyes in a particular direction 看；瞧：*If you look carefully you can just see our house from here.* 你要是仔細看，從這裏就可以看見我們的房子。◇ **~ (at sb/sth)** *She looked at me and smiled.* 她看了看我，笑了。◇ *'Has the mail come yet?' 'I'll **look and see**.'* "郵件來了嗎？" "我看看。" ◇ *Look! I'm sure that's Brad Pitt!* 看！那一定是布拉德•皮特！◇ *Don't look now, but there's someone staring at you!* 你現在別看，有人正盯着你呢！➲ see also FORWARD-LOOKING

▸ **SEARCH 搜尋** **2** 0-ᵐ [I] to try to find sb/sth 尋找；尋求：*I can't find my book—I've looked everywhere.* 我找不到我的書，我到處都找遍了。◇ **~ for sb/sth** *Where have you been? We've been looking for you.* 你上哪兒去了？我們一直在找你。◇ *Are you still looking for a job?* 你還在找工作嗎？

▸ **PAY ATTENTION 注意** **3** 0-ᵐ [I, T] to pay attention to sth 注意；留心；留神：**~ (at sth)** *Look at the time! We're going to be late.* 注意一下時間！我們要遲到了。◇ **~ where, what, etc. …** *Can't you look where you're going?* 你走路可不可以小心點？

▸ **APPEAR/SEEM 顯得；似乎** **4** 0-ᵐ *linking verb* to seem; to appear 看來好像；似乎；顯得：**+ adj.** *to look pale/happy/tired* 顯得蒼白／高興／疲倦 ◇ *That book looks interesting.* 那本書好像很有趣。◇ **~ (to sb) like sb/sth** *That looks like an interesting book.* 那好像是本有趣的書。◇ **+ noun** *That looks an interesting book.* 那好像是本有趣的書。◇ *You made me look a complete fool!* 你弄得我完全像個傻瓜！➲ see also GOOD-LOOKING **5** 0-ᵐ [I] (not usually used in the progressive tenses 通常不用於進行時) to have a similar appearance to sb/sth; to have an appearance that suggests that sth is true or will happen 與…外表相似；好像；彷彿：**~ (to sb) like sb/sth** *That photograph doesn't look like her at all.* 那張照片看

上去一點也不像她。◇ *It looks like rain* (= it looks as if it's going to rain). 像是要下雨的樣子。◇ **~ (to sb) as if .../ as though ...** *You look as though you slept badly.* 你好像沒睡好覺。 **HELP** In spoken English people often use **like** instead of **as if** or **as though** in this meaning, especially in *NAmE*. 英語口語中，尤其是美式英語，常用 like 代替 as if 或 as though 表示此義： *You look like you slept badly.* This is not considered correct in written *BrE*. 書面英式英語中，此用法被視為不正確。 **6** [I] to seem likely 看起來好像；似乎有可能： **~ (to sb) as if .../as though ...** *It doesn't look as if we'll be moving after all.* 看樣子我們還是不搬了。◇ **~ (to sb) like ...** (*informal*) ◇ *It doesn't look like we'll be moving after all.* 看樣子我們還是不搬了。 **HELP** This use of **like** instead of **as if** or **as though** is not considered correct in written *BrE*. 用 like 代替 as if 或 as though，此用法在書面英式英語中被視為不正確。

▸ **FACE 面向 7** [I] **+ adv./prep.** to face a particular direction 面向；正對；朝向： *The house looks east.* 這房子朝東。◇ *The hotel looks out over the harbour.* 從這家旅館朝外看可俯視港灣。

IDM Most idioms containing **look** are at the entries for the nouns and adjectives in the idioms, for example **look daggers at sb** is at **dagger**. 大多數含 look 的習語，都可在該等習語中的名詞及形容詞相關詞條找到，如 look daggers at sb 在詞條 dagger 下。 **be just 'looking** used in a shop/store to say that you are not ready to buy sth（在商店中表示無意購買某物）只是看一看： *'Can I help you?' 'I'm just looking, thank you.'* "請問您要買什麼？" "謝謝，我只是看看。" **be looking to do sth** to try to find ways of doing sth 試圖找到做某事的方法： *The government is looking to reduce inflation.* 政府正在力求降低通貨膨脹。 **look 'bad | not look 'good** to be considered bad behaviour or bad manners 被視為舉止不佳；失禮；不得體： *It looks bad not going to your own brother's wedding.* 連親兄弟的婚禮都不參加，這太不像話了。 **look 'bad (for sb)** to show that sth bad might happen 顯示不好的事可能發生；看來不利於： *He's had another heart attack; things are looking bad for him, I'm afraid.* 他又犯了一次心臟病，恐怕他情況不妙。 **look 'good** to show success or that sth good might happen 顯現成功（或好事可能發生）；看來充滿希望： *This year's sales figures are looking good.* 今年的銷售數字情況看好。 **look 'here** (*old-fashioned*) used to protest about sth（表示抗議）喂，聽着： *Now look here, it wasn't my fault.* 喂，那不是我的錯！ **look how/what/who ...** used to give an example that proves what you are saying or makes it clearer（用於舉例證實或說明）瞧： *Look how lazy we've become.* 瞧我們變得有多懶。◇ *Be careful climbing that ladder. Look what happened last time.* 爬那梯子時小心點兒。上次不就出事了麼。 **look sb ,up and 'down** to look at sb in a careful or critical way 上下仔細打量，苛求地審視（某人） **(not) look your'self** to not have your normal healthy appearance 氣色不像往常那樣好： *You're not looking yourself today* (= you look tired or ill/sick). 今天你看上去氣色不太好。 **never/not look 'back** (*informal*) to become more and more successful 一帆風順；蒸蒸日上： *Her first novel was published in 2007 and since then she hasn't looked back.* 她於 2007 年發表了第一部小說，自此她的寫作生涯一帆風順。 **not much to 'look at** (*informal*) not attractive 相貌平平；不起眼 **to 'look at sb/sth** judging by the appearance of sb/sth 由外表判斷： *To look at him you'd never think he was nearly fifty.* 看他的外表，誰也想不到他年近五十了。

PHR V **,look 'after yourself/sb/sth** (*especially BrE*) **1** to be responsible for or to take care of sb/sth 對…負責；照料；照顧： *Who's going to look after the children while you're away?* 你不在時誰來照料小孩？◇ *I'm looking after his affairs while he's in hospital.* 他住院時由我處理他的事務。◇ *Don't worry about me—I can look after myself* (= I don't need any help). 別擔心我，我能照顧好自己。 ➲ note at CARE **2** to make sure that things happen to sb's advantage 確保有利於： *He's good at looking after his own interests.* 他善於照顧自己的利益。

,look a'head (to sth) to think about what is going to happen in the future 展望未來；為將來設想

,look a'round/'round to turn your head so that you can see sth 環視；環顧；四下察看： *People came out of their houses and looked around.* 人們走出家門四處察看。

,look a'round/'round (sth) to visit a place or building, walking around it to see what is there 遊覽；參觀： *Let's look round the town this afternoon.* 咱們今天下午遊覽市區吧。 **,look a'round/'round for sth** to search for sth in a number of different places 到處尋找；搜尋： *We're looking around for a house in this area.* 我們正在這個地區四處找住房。

'look at sth 1 to examine sth closely（仔細）察看，檢查： *Your ankle's swollen—I think the doctor ought to look at it.* 你的腳踝腫了，我認為得找醫生檢查一下。◇ *I haven't had time to look at* (= read) *the papers yet.* 我還沒來得及看這些論文。 **2** to think about, consider or study sth 思考；考慮；研究： *The implications of the new law will need to be looked at.* 新法規可能造成的影響需要仔細研究一下。 **3** to view or consider sth in a particular way（用某種方式）看待，考慮： *Looked at from that point of view, his decision is easier to understand.* 從那個角度來看，他的決定比較容易理解。

,look 'back (on sth) to think about sth in your past 回首（往事）；回憶；回顧 **SYN reflect on**： *to look back on your childhood* 回顧自己的童年

,look 'down on sb/sth to think that you are better than sb/sth 蔑視；輕視；瞧不起： *She looks down on people who haven't been to college.* 她瞧不起沒上過大學的人。

'look for sth to hope for sth; to expect sth 期望；期待；盼望： *We shall be looking for an improvement in your work this term.* 我們期待你這學期功課有進步。

,look 'forward to sth to be thinking with pleasure about sth that is going to happen (because you expect to enjoy it)（高興地）盼望，期待： *I'm looking forward to the weekend.* 我盼着過週末呢。◇ **~ doing sth** *We're really looking forward to seeing you again.* 我們非常盼望能再見到你。

,look 'in (on sb) to make a short visit to a place, especially sb's house when they are ill/sick or need help（尤指當某人生病或需要幫助時到其住處）短暫探訪： *She looks in on her elderly neighbour every evening.* 她每天晚上都要看望一下年長的鄰居。◇ *Why don't you look in on me next time you're in town?* 你下次進城順便來看看我好嗎？

,look 'into sth to examine sth 調查；審查： *A working party has been set up to look into the problem.* 已成立一個工作小組來調查這個問題。

,look 'on to watch sth without becoming involved in it yourself 旁觀： *Passers-by simply looked on as he was attacked.* 他遭人襲擊，路人只在一邊袖手旁觀。 ➲ related noun ONLOOKER **'look on sb/sth as sb/sth** to consider sb/sth to be sb/sth 把…看作；把…視為： *She's looked on as the leading authority on the subject.* 她被視為這門學科的主要權威。 **'look on sb/sth with sth** to consider sb/sth in a particular way（以某種方式）看待 **SYN regard**： *They looked on his behaviour with contempt.* 他們對他的行為不屑一顧。

,look 'out used to warn sb to be careful, especially when there is danger（表示警告，尤指有危險）小心，當心，留神 **SYN watch out**： *Look out! There's a car coming.* 當心！有車來了。 **,look 'out for sb** to take care of sb and make sure nothing bad happens to them 關顧某人 **,look 'out for sb/sth 1** to try to avoid sth bad happening or doing sth bad 當心；提防；留心防備 **SYN watch out**： *You should look out for pickpockets.* 你應當提防扒手。◇ *Do look out for spelling mistakes in your work.* 一定要避免你作業中的拼寫錯誤。 **2** to keep trying to find sth or meet sb 留心尋覓： *I'll look out for you at the conference.* 我會在開會時來找你。 ➲ related noun LOOKOUT **,look 'out for sb/yourself** to think only of sb's/your own advantage, without worrying about other people 只考慮某人 / 自己的利益： *You should look out for yourself from now on.* 從現在起你應該多為自己着想。 **,look sth↔'out (for sb/sth)** (*BrE*) to search for sth from among your possessions 把…找出來： *I'll look out those old photographs you wanted to see.* 我會找出你想看的那些舊照片的。

,look sth↔'over to examine sth to see how good, big, etc. it is 查看；檢查： *We looked over the house again*

L

before we decided we would rent it. 那房子我們再看了一次才決定租下來。

ˌ**look ˈround** (*BrE*) to turn your head to see sb/sth behind you 轉過頭看；回頭看：*She looked round when she heard the noise.* 她聽到響聲，就回過頭去看。

ˌ**look ˈthrough sb** [no passive] to ignore sb by pretending not to see them 佯裝沒有看見而不理會某人：*She just looked straight through me.* 她竟然假裝沒看見我。 ˈ**look through sth** [no passive] to examine or read sth quickly 快速查看；瀏覽：*She looked through her notes before the exam.* 她考試前匆匆看了一下筆記。

ˈ**look to sb for sth** | ˈ**look to sb to do sth** (*formal*) to rely on or expect sb to provide sth or do sth 依賴，期待，指望（某人提供某物或做某事）：*We are looking to you for help.* 我們指望得到你的幫助。 ˈ**look to sth** (*formal*) to consider sth and think about how to make it better 注意，考慮（改進）：*We need to look to ways of improving our marketing.* 我們得考慮改進營銷方法。

ˌ**look ˈup** (*informal*) (of business, sb's situation, etc. 生意、某人的情況等) to become better 好轉；改善 **SYN** **improve**：*At last things were beginning to look up.* 情況終於開始好轉了。 ˌ**look ˈup (from sth)** to raise your eyes when you are looking down at sth（在低頭看某物時）抬頭往上看：*She looked up from her book as I entered the room.* 我進房間時，她從書本上抬起頭來看了看。 ˌ**look sb↔ˈup** [no passive] (*informal*) to visit or make contact with sb, especially when you have not seen them for a long time（尤指在久別之後）拜訪，看望，聯繫：*Do look me up the next time you're in London.* 你下次到倫敦，一定要來看我。 ˌ**look sth↔ˈup** to look for information in a dictionary or REFERENCE BOOK, or by using a computer（在詞典、參考書中或通過電腦）查閱，查檢：*Can you look up the opening times on the website?* 你可以在網站上查一下開放的時間嗎？◇ *I looked it up in the dictionary.* 我在詞典裏查過這個詞。 ˌ**look ˈup to sb** to admire or respect sb 欽佩；仰慕；尊敬

■ ***noun***

▸ **USING EYES 用眼睛 1** [C, usually sing.] **~ (at sb/sth)** an act of looking at sb/sth 看；瞧：*Here, **have a look** at this.* 來，看一看這個。◇ ***Take a look** at these figures!* 看一下這些數字吧！◇ *Make sure you get a **good look** at their faces.* 你一定要仔細看清他們的面孔。◇ ***One look** at his face and Jenny stopped laughing.* 珍妮一看見他那張臉，就止住不笑了。◇ *A look passed between them* (= they looked at each other). 他們互相看了一眼。◇ *It's an interesting place. Do you want to take **a look around**?* 這個地方很好玩，你要不要到處看看？◇ *We'll be taking a **close look** at these proposals* (= examining them carefully). 我們會仔細審查這些方案。

▸ **SEARCH 找尋 2** [C, usually sing.] **~ (for sth/sb)** an act of trying to find sth/sb 查找：*I've **had** a good **look** for it, but I can't find it.* 我仔細找過了，可是找不着。

▸ **EXPRESSION 表情 3** [C] an expression in your eyes or face 眼神；表情；神情；臉色：*a **look** of surprise* 驚訝的表情 ◇ *He didn't like the look in her eyes.* 他不喜歡她的眼神。◇ *She had a worried look on her face.* 她一臉擔憂的樣子。

▸ **APPEARANCE 外貌 4** [C, usually sing.] the way sb/sth looks; the appearance of sb/sth 樣子；外觀；相貌；外表：*It's going to rain today **by the look of it*** (= judging by appearances). 看樣子今天要下雨了。◇ *Looks can be deceptive.* 外表有時是靠不住的。◇ ***I don't like the look of** that guy* (= I don't trust him, judging by his appearance). 看他那副樣子，我不喜歡。 **5** **looks** [pl.] a person's appearance, especially when the person is attractive（尤指吸引人的）相貌，容貌：*She has her father's **good looks**.* 她有父親俊秀的容貌。◇ *He **lost his looks*** (= became less attractive) *in later life.* 他英俊的相貌在晚年已不復存在。 ➲ see also GOOD-LOOKING

▸ **FASHION 時尚 6** [sing.] a fashion; a style 時尚；式樣；風格：*The punk look is back in fashion.* 朋客式裝扮又時興起來了。◇ *They've given the place a completely new look.* 他們使得這地方的面貌煥然一新。 ➲ see also WET LOOK

IDM **if looks could ˈkill …** used to describe the very angry or unpleasant way sb is/was looking at you 眼神嚇死人；一臉怒氣；滿臉不高興：*I don't know what I've done to upset him, but if looks could kill …* 我不知道做了什麼惹他生氣了，但看他那嚇人的樣子… ➲ more at DIRTY *adj.*, LONG *adj.*

■ ***exclamation*** used to make sb pay attention to what you are going to say, often when you are annoyed（常為不悅時喚起他人注意）喂，聽我說：*Look, I think we should go now.* 喂，我想我們現在得走了。◇ *Look, that's not fair.* 嘿，那樣不公平。

look·alike /ˈlʊkəlaɪk/ *noun* (often used after a person's name 常用於人名後) a person who looks very similar to the person mentioned 長得極像（某人）的人：*an Elvis lookalike* 長得很像貓王的人

ˌ**look-and-ˈsay** *noun* [U] a method of teaching people to read based on the recognition of whole words, rather than on the association of letters with sounds 視讀法，直呼法（一種識字教學方法，根據整詞的辨認而不是字母與發音的聯繫） ➲ compare PHONICS

look·er /ˈlʊkə(r)/ *noun* (*informal*) a way of describing an attractive person, usually a woman 美人；靚女：*She's a real looker!* 她真是個美人！

ˈ**look-in** *noun*

IDM **(not) get/have a ˈlook-in** (*BrE, informal*) (not) to get a chance to take part or succeed in sth（沒）有參加的機會；（沒）有成功的機會；（沒）有份兒：*She talks so much that nobody else can get a look-in.* 她老是滔滔不絕，別人誰也插不上嘴。

ˈ**looking glass** *noun* (*old-fashioned*) a mirror 鏡子

Synonyms 同義詞辨析

look

watch • see • view • observe

These words all mean to turn your eyes in a particular direction. 以上各詞均含看、觀看之意。

look to turn your eyes in a particular direction 指看、瞧：*If you look carefully you can just see our house from here.* 你要是仔細看，從這裏就可以看見我們的房子。◇ *She **looked at** me and smiled.* 她看了看我，笑了。

watch to look at sb/sth for a time, paying attention to what happens 指看、注視、觀看、觀察：*to watch television* 看電視 ◇ *Watch what I do, then you try.* 你注意看我的動作，然後試着做。

see to watch a game, television programme, performance, etc. 指觀看（比賽、電視節目、演出等）：*In the evening we went to see a movie.* 晚上我們去看了一場電影。

view (*formal*) to look at sth, especially when you look carefully; to watch television, a film/movie, etc. 指看、觀看（尤指仔細觀察）；看（電視、電影等）：*People came from all over the world to view her work.* 觀眾從世界各地湧來欣賞她的作品。

WATCH, SEE OR VIEW? 用 watch、see 還是 view？

You can *see/view a film/movie/programme* 可以説 see/view a film/movie/programme，but you cannot 但不能說：~~*see/view television*~~ **View** is more formal than **see** and is used especially in business contexts. * view 較 see 正式，尤用於商務語境。

observe (*formal*) to watch sb/sth carefully, especially to learn more about them or it 指觀察、注視、監視：*The patients were observed over a period of several months.* 這些病人給觀察了數月之久。

PATTERNS

- to look/watch **for** sb/sth
- to watch/observe **what/who/how …**
- to look/watch/view/observe (sb/sth) **with** amazement/surprise/disapproval, etc.
- to watch/see/view a **film/movie/show/programme**
- to watch/see a **match/game/fight**
- to look (at sb/sth)/watch (sb/sth)/observe sb/sth **carefully/closely**

look·out /ˈlʊkaʊt/ *noun* **1** a place for watching from, especially for danger or an enemy coming towards you 監視處；觀察所；瞭望台： *a* ***lookout point/tower*** 瞭望哨；瞭望塔 **2** a person who has the responsibility of watching for sth, especially danger, etc. 監視員；觀察員；瞭望員： *One of the men stood at the door to act as a lookout.* 有一個人站在門口望風。

IDM **be ˈsb's lookout** (*BrE, informal*) used to say that you do not think sb's actions are sensible, but that it is their own problem or responsibility（認為某人的行為不明智）是某人自己的責任，是某人自己的事： *If he wants to waste his money, that's his lookout.* 他要亂花錢的話，那是他自己的事。 **be on the ˈlookout (for sb/sth)** | **keep a ˈlookout (for sb/sth)** (*informal*) to watch carefully for sb/sth in order to avoid danger, etc. or in order to find sth you want 注意；警戒；留心： *The public should be on the lookout for symptoms of the disease.* 公眾應當留心這種疾病的症狀。

ˌlook-ˈsee *noun* [sing.] (*informal, especially NAmE*) a quick look at sth 飛快一瞥： *Come and have a look-see.* 快來看一眼吧。

loom /luːm/ *verb, noun*

■ ***verb*** **1** [I] **(+ adv./prep.)** to appear as a large shape that is not clear, especially in a frightening or threatening way 赫然聳現；（尤指）令人驚恐地隱現： *A dark shape loomed up ahead of us.* 一個黑糊糊的影子隱隱出現在我們的前面。 **2** [I] to appear important or threatening and likely to happen soon 顯得突出；逼近： *There was a crisis looming.* 危機迫在眉睫。

IDM **ˌloom ˈlarge** to be worrying or frightening and seem hard to avoid 令人憂慮，令人驚恐（並似乎難以避免）： *The prospect of war loomed large.* 戰爭的陰影在逼近，令人憂慮。

■ ***noun*** a machine for making cloth by twisting threads between other threads which go in a different direction 織布機

loon /luːn/ *noun* **1** a large N American bird that eats fish and has a cry like a laugh 潛鳥（北美食魚大鳥，叫聲似笑聲） **2** = LOONY

Synonyms 同義詞辨析

look

glance • gaze • stare • glimpse • glare

These are all words for an act of looking, when you turn your eyes in a particular direction. 以上各詞均表示看的動作。

look an act of looking at sb/sth 指看、瞧： *Here, have a look at this.* 來，看一看這個。

glance a quick look 指匆匆一看、一瞥、掃視： *She stole a glance at her watch.* 她偷偷看了看錶。

gaze a long steady look at sb/sth 指凝視、注視： *She felt embarrassed under his steady gaze.* 她在他凝視的目光下感到很尷尬。

stare a long look at sb/sth, especially in a way that is unfriendly or that shows surprise 尤指不友善或吃驚的盯、凝視、注視： *She gave the officer a blank stare and shrugged her shoulders.* 她面無表情地看了那個軍官一眼，聳了聳肩。

glimpse a look at sb/sth for a very short time, when you do not see the person or thing completely 指一瞥、一看： *He caught a glimpse of her in the crowd.* 他在人群裏一眼瞥見了她。

glare a long angry look at sb/sth 指長久的怒視、瞪眼： *She fixed her questioner with a hostile glare.* 她帶着敵意地瞪着向她提問的人。

PATTERNS

- a look/glance **at** sb/sth
- a **penetrating/piercing** look/glance/gaze/stare
- a **long** look/glance/stare
- a **brief** look/glance/glimpse
- to **have/get/take** a look/glance/glimpse
- to **avoid** sb's glance/gaze/stare

loonie /ˈluːni/ *noun* (*CanE*) the Canadian dollar or a Canadian one-dollar coin 加拿大元；一加元硬幣

loony /ˈluːni/ *adj., noun*

■ ***adj.*** (*informal*) crazy or strange 發狂的；瘋狂的；怪異的；古怪的

■ ***noun*** (*pl.* **-ies**) (also **loon**) (*informal*) a person who has strange ideas or who behaves in a strange way 狂人；瘋子；怪人

ˈloony bin *noun* (*old-fashioned, slang*) a humorous and sometimes offensive way of referring to a hospital for people who are mentally ill 瘋人院（幽默用語，有時含冒犯意）

loop /luːp/ *noun, verb*

■ ***noun*** **1** a shape like a curve or circle made by a line curving right round and crossing itself 環形；環狀物；圓圈： *The road went in a huge loop around the lake.* 那條路環湖繞了一個大圈。 **2** a piece of rope, wire, etc. in the shape of a curve or circle（繩、電線等的）環，圈： *He tied a loop of rope around his arm.* 他在手臂上用繩子繫了一個圈。◇ *Make a loop in the string.* 在繩子上打個圈。◇ *a belt loop* (= on trousers/pants, etc. for holding a belt in place) 皮帶襻 ➲ picture at KNOT **3** a strip of film or tape on which the pictures and sound are repeated continuously 循環電影膠片；循環音像磁帶： *The film is on a loop.* 這部電影已製成循環音像磁帶。◇ (*figurative*) *His mind kept turning in an endless loop.* 他思緒萬千。 **4** (*computing* 計) a set of instructions that is repeated again and again until a particular condition is satisfied 循環；迴路；（程序中）一套重複的指令 **5** a complete CIRCUIT for electrical current 環路；迴線；迴路 **6** (*BrE*) a railway line or road that leaves the main track or road and then joins it again（鐵道或公路的）環線 **7** **the Loop** (*US, informal*) the business centre of the US city of Chicago 大環（指美國芝加哥市的商業中心）

IDM **in the ˈloop** | **out of the ˈloop** (*informal*) part of a group of people that is dealing with sth important; not part of this group 屬（處理要務的）圈內／圈外人士 **knock/throw sb for a ˈloop** (*NAmE, informal*) to shock or surprise sb 使震驚；使驚訝

■ ***verb*** **1** [T] **~ sth + adv./prep.** to form or bend sth into a loop 使成環；使繞成圈： *He looped the strap over his shoulder.* 他把帶子繞了一個圈挎在肩上。 **2** [I] **+ adv./prep.** to move in a way that makes the shape of a loop 成環形移動： *The river loops around the valley.* 那條河順着山谷繞了個大彎兒。◇ *The ball looped high up in the air.* 球高高飛起，在空中畫了一條弧線。

IDM **ˌloop the ˈloop** to fly or make a plane fly in a circle going up and down（使飛機）翻跟頭飛行

loop·hole /ˈluːphəʊl; *NAmE* -hoʊl/ *noun* **~ (in sth)** a mistake in the way a law, contract, etc. has been written which enables people to legally avoid doing sth that the law, contract, etc. had intended them to do（法律、合同等的）漏洞，空子： *a legal loophole* 法律的漏洞◇ *to close existing loopholes* 堵住現有的漏洞

loopy /ˈluːpi/ *adj.* (*informal*) **1** not sensible; strange 失去理智的；瘋狂的；奇怪的；怪異的 **SYN** **crazy** **2** (*BrE*) very angry 很生氣的；十分憤怒的 **SYN** **furious**： *He'll* ***go loopy*** *when he hears!* 他聽了會氣壞的！

loose ⚷ /luːs/ *adj., verb, noun*

■ ***adj.*** (**loos·er**, **loos·est**)

▸ **NOT FIXED/TIED** 不固定；未繫住 **1** ⚷ not firmly fixed where it should be; able to become separated from sth 未固定牢的；可分開的： *a loose button/tooth* 鬆動的鈕扣／牙齒◇ *Check that the plug has not* ***come loose***. 檢查一下別讓插頭鬆脫了。 **2** ⚷ not tied together; not held in position by anything or contained in anything 未繫（或捆）在一起的；未固定的；零散的： *She usually wears her hair loose.* 她通常披散着頭髮。◇ *The potatoes were sold loose, not in bags.* 土豆是散裝而不是袋裝出售。 **3** ⚷ [not usually before noun] free to move around without control; not tied up or shut in somewhere 不受約束；未束縛；自由： *The sheep had got out and were loose on the road.* 那些羊跑了出來在路上自由自在地走動。◇ *The horse had* ***broken loose*** (= escaped) *from*

L

its tether. 那匹馬掙脱繮繩跑了。◇ *During the night, somebody had cut the boat loose from its moorings.* 有人在夜間砍斷了泊船的纜繩。

▸ **CLOTHES** 衣服 **4** not fitting closely 寬鬆的：*a loose shirt* 寬大的襯衣 **OPP** **tight**

▸ **NOT SOLID/HARD** 不結實；不堅固 **5** not tightly packed together; not solid or hard 疏鬆的；不結實的；不堅固的：*loose soil* 疏鬆的土壤 ◇ *a fabric with a loose weave* 編織稀疏的織物

▸ **NOT STRICT/EXACT** 不嚴格；不精確 **6** not strictly organized or controlled 組織不嚴密的；未嚴加控制的：*a **loose alliance/coalition/federation*** 鬆散的聯盟／同盟／聯邦 **7** not exact; not very careful 不精確的；不嚴謹的；不周密的：*a loose translation* 不準確的譯文 ◇ *loose thinking* 不嚴密的思想

▸ **IMMORAL** 不道德 **8** [usually before noun] (*old-fashioned*) having or involving an attitude to sexual relationships that people consider to be immoral 放蕩的；淫蕩的：*a young man of loose morals* 生活放蕩的年輕人

▸ **BALL** 球 **9** (*sport* 體) not in any player's control 無球員控制的：*He pounced on a **loose ball**.* 他猛然撲向一個無人控制的球。

▸ **BODY WASTE** 人體糞便 **10** having too much liquid in it 稀的：*a baby with loose bowel movements* 患腹瀉的嬰兒

▸ **loose·ness** *noun* [U]

IDM **break/cut/tear (sb/sth) 'loose from sb/sth** to separate yourself or sb/sth from a group of people or their influence, etc. (使)擺脱，掙脱：*The organization broke loose from its sponsors.* 那家機構擺脱了贊助商。◇ *He cut himself loose from his family.* 他擺脱了家庭的束縛。 **hang/stay 'loose** (*informal, especially NAmE*) to remain calm; to not worry 保持鎮靜；不着急：*It's OK—hang loose and stay cool.* 沒事的，你要鎮定，冷靜。 **have a loose 'tongue** to talk too much, especially about things that are private (尤指對隱私)多嘴，饒舌 **let 'loose** (*BrE*) (*NAmE* **cut 'loose**) (*informal*) to do sth or to happen in a way that is not controlled 不受控制；自在發生：*Teenagers need a place to let loose.* 青少年需要一個可縱情嬉鬧的地方。 **let 'loose sth** to make a noise or remark, especially in a loud or sudden way (尤指大聲或突然)發出，喊出，發表：*She let loose a stream of abuse.* 她破口大罵起來。 **let sb/sth 'loose 1** to free sb/sth from whatever holds them/it in place 讓…自由；釋放；放開：*She let her hair loose and it fell around her shoulders.* 她的頭髮一解開，便順着肩膀垂了下來。◇ *Who's let the dog loose?* 誰把狗放出來了？ **2** to give sb complete freedom to do what they want in a place or situation 任(某人)自由行動；使隨心所欲；放任：*He was at last let loose in the kitchen.* 終於放手讓他幹廚房裏的活兒了。◇ *A team of professionals were **let loose on** the project.* 有一組專業人員可自主地做這個項目。 ➲ more at FAST *adv.*, HELL, SCREW *n.*

■ *verb* (*formal*)

▸ **RELEASE** 釋放 **1 ~ sth (on/upon sb/sth)** to release sth or let it happen or be expressed in an uncontrolled way 釋放；放任；不受約束地表達：*His speech loosed a tide of nationalist sentiment.* 他的講話表露出一種強烈的民族主義情緒。

▸ **MAKE STH LOOSE** 鬆開 **2 ~ sth** to make sth loose, especially sth that is tied or held tightly 鬆開，放開(尤指束緊或緊握的東西) **SYN** **loosen**：*He loosed the straps that bound her arms.* 他鬆開了綁在她手臂上的帶子。

▸ **FIRE BULLETS** 射子彈 **3 ~ sth (off) (at sb/sth)** to fire bullets, arrows, etc. 射出(子彈、箭等) **HELP** Do not confuse this verb with **to lose** = 'to be unable to find sth'. 不要將此動詞與 to lose（遺失）混淆。

■ *noun*

IDM **on the 'loose** (of a person or an animal 人或動物) having escaped from somewhere; free 已逃出；自由 **SYN** **at large**：*Three prisoners are still on the loose.* 有三名囚犯仍然在逃。

'loose box *noun* (*BrE*) a small area in a building or a vehicle where a horse can move freely 單廐間，散放圈(建築物或車輛中可供馬自由活動的一小塊地方)

ˌloose 'cannon *noun* a person, usually a public figure, who often behaves in a way that nobody can predict 大炮(指舉止無法預料的知名人士)

ˌloose 'change *noun* [U] coins that you have in a pocket or a bag (口袋或包裏隨身帶的)零錢

ˌloose 'cover (*BrE*) (*NAmE* **'slip cover**) *noun* [usually pl.] a cover for a chair, etc. that you can take off, for example to wash it (椅子等的)活套，活罩

ˌloose 'end *noun* [usually pl.] a part of sth such as a story that has not been completely finished or explained (故事等的)懸念，未了結的部份，未交代清楚的情節：*The play has too many loose ends.* 這部劇有太多地方未交代清楚。◇ *There are still **a few loose ends to tie up*** (= a few things to finish). 還有幾件小事需要了結。

IDM **at a loose 'end** (*BrE*) (*NAmE* **at loose 'ends**) having nothing to do and not knowing what you want to do 無所事事；無事可做：*Come and see us, if you're at a loose end.* 你要是閒着無事就來我們這兒坐坐吧。

ˌloose-'fitting *adj.* (of clothes 衣服) not fitting the body tightly 寬鬆的；肥大的

ˌloose 'forward *noun* (in RUGBY 橄欖球) a player who plays at the back of the SCRUM 爭球線後的前鋒

ˌloose 'head *noun* (in RUGBY 橄欖球) the player in the front row of a team in the SCRUM who is nearest to where the ball is put in 自由前鋒

ˌloose-'leaf *adj.* [usually before noun] (of a book, file, etc. 書、檔案等) having pages that can be taken out and put in separately 活頁的：*a loose-leaf binder* 活頁夾

ˌloose-'limbed *adj.* (*literary*) (of a person 人) moving in an easy, not stiff, way 四肢柔軟靈活的

loose·ly /'luːsli/ *adv.*

1 in a way that is not firm or tight 寬鬆地；鬆散地：*She fastened the belt loosely around her waist.* 她把皮帶鬆鬆地繫在腰上。 **2** in a way that is not exact 不精確地：*to use a term loosely* 寬泛地使用術語 ◇ *The play is loosely based on his childhood in Russia.* 那部劇大致上是根據他在俄羅斯的童年生活寫成的。

loos·en /'luːsn/ *verb* **1** [T, I] **~ (sth)** to make sth less tight or firmly fixed; to become less tight or firmly fixed (使)放鬆，變鬆 **SYN** **slacken**：*First loosen the nuts, then take off the wheel.* 先鬆開螺母，然後卸下車輪。◇ *The rope holding the boat loosened.* 繫船的繩子鬆了。 **2** [T] **~ sth** to make a piece of clothing, hair, etc. loose, when it has been tied or fastened 解開，鬆開(衣服、頭髮等) **3** [T] **~ your hands, hold, etc.** to hold sb/sth less tightly 鬆開，放開(手等)：*He loosened his grip and let her go.* 他鬆手放開了她。◇ (*figurative*) *The military regime has not loosened its hold on power.* 軍事政權尚未放鬆對權力的控制。 **4** [T] **~ sth** to make sth weaker or less controlled than before (使)變弱，鬆散，疏遠 **SYN** **relax**：*The party has loosened its links with big business.* 這個政黨與大企業的關係疏遠了。 **OPP** **tighten**

IDM **loosen sb's 'tongue** to make sb talk more freely than usual 使無拘束地說話；使自由自在地說：*A bottle of wine had loosened Harry's tongue.* 一瓶酒下肚，哈里的話匣子便打開了。

PHR V **ˌloosen 'up** to relax and stop worrying 放鬆不再擔憂：*Come on, Jo. Loosen up.* 得啦，喬，放鬆些，別再擔憂了。 **ˌloosen 'up | ˌloosen sb/sth↔'up** to relax your muscles or parts of the body or to make them relax, before taking exercise, etc. (在運動或其他活動前使肌肉或身體部位)放鬆

loot /luːt/ *verb, noun*

■ *verb* [T, I] **~ (sth)** to steal things from shops/stores or buildings after a RIOT, fire, etc. (暴亂、火災等後)打劫，搶劫，劫掠：*More than 20 shops were looted.* 有 20 多家商店遭到了搶劫。 ▸ **loot·er** /'luːtə(r)/ *noun* **loot·ing** *noun* [U]

■ *noun* [U] **1** money and valuable objects taken by soldiers from the enemy after winning a battle 戰利品；掠奪品 **SYN** **booty** **2** (*informal*) money and valuable objects that have been stolen by thieves 贓物；被盜物 **3** (*informal*) money 錢

lop /lɒp; *NAmE* lɑːp/ *verb* (**-pp-**) **~ sth** to cut down a tree, or cut some large branches off it 砍伐；剪(枝)

PHR V **ˌlop sth↔ˈoff (sth)** **1** to remove part of sth by cutting it, especially to remove branches from a tree 砍掉；剪掉；修剪（樹枝） **SYN** **chop** **2** to make sth smaller or less by a particular amount 削減；減少：*They lopped 20p off the price.* 他們把價格減了 20 便士。

lope /ləʊp; *NAmE* loʊp/ *verb* [I] **+ adv./prep.** to run taking long relaxed steps 輕鬆地大步跑：*The dog loped along beside her.* 那條狗在她身旁輕鬆地奔跑。◇ *He set off with a loping stride.* 他邁着輕快的步伐出發了。▶ **lope** *noun* [usually sing.]

ˈlop-ears *noun* [pl.] ears that hang down at the side of an animal's head 垂耳；耷拉耳 ▶ **ˈlop-eared** *adj.*：*a lop-eared rabbit* 垂耳兔

lop·sided /ˌlɒpˈsaɪdɪd; *NAmE* ˌlɑːp-/ *adj.* having one side lower, smaller, etc. than the other 一側比另一側低（或小等）的；向一側傾斜的；不平衡的：*a lopsided grin/mouth* 撇着嘴笑；撇嘴 ◇ *(figurative) The article presents a somewhat lopsided view of events.* 這篇文章對事情的看法顯得有些片面。▶ **lop·sided·ly** *adv.*

lo·qua·cious /ləˈkweɪʃəs/ *adj.* *(formal)* talking a lot 話多的；健談的；喋喋不休的 **SYN** **talkative** ▶ **lo·qua·city** /ləˈkwæsəti/ *noun* [U]

lo·quat /ˈləʊkwɒt; *NAmE* ˈloʊkwɑːt/ *noun* a round pale orange fruit that grows on bushes in China, Japan and the Middle East 枇杷

lord 🔑 /lɔːd; *NAmE* lɔːrd/ *noun, verb*

■ ***noun*** **1** 🔑 [C] (in Britain) a man of high rank in the NOBILITY (= people of high social class), or sb who has been given the title 'lord' as an honour （英國）貴族 ➲ compare LADY (6) **2** 🔑 **Lord** (in Britain) the title used by a lord 勳爵（英國貴族的稱號）：*Lord Beaverbrook* 比弗布魯克勳爵 **3** **Lord** a title used for some high official positions in Britain （英國用於某些高級官員的職位前）閣下，大人，大臣：*the Lord Chancellor* 大法官 ◇ *the Lord Mayor* 市長閣下 **4** **My Lord** (in Britain) a title of respect used when speaking to a judge, BISHOP or some male members of the NOBILITY (= people of high social class) （英國用以稱呼法官、主教或某些男性貴族成員，表示尊敬）大人，閣下 ➲ compare LADY (6) **5** a powerful man in MEDIEVAL Europe, who owned a lot of land and property （中世紀歐洲的）領主：*a feudal lord* 封建領主 ◇ *the lord of the manor* 莊園主 ➲ see also OVERLORD, WARLORD **6** (usually **the Lord**) [sing.] a title used to refer to God or Christ 主；上主；上帝：*Love the Lord with all your heart.* 要全心全意地愛主。 **7** **Our Lord** [sing.] a title used to refer to Christ 主耶穌；主基督 **8** **the Lords** [sing.+sing./pl. v.] = HOUSE OF LORDS：*The Lords has/have not yet reached a decision.* 上議院尚未作出決定。➲ compare COMMONS ➲ see also LAW LORD

IDM **(good) ˈLord! | oh ˈLord!** *exclamation* used to show that you are surprised, annoyed or worried about sth （表示驚訝、煩惱或憂慮）主啊，天哪：*Good Lord, what have you done to your hair!* 天啊，你把頭髮弄成什麼樣子啦！**ˈLord knows ...** used to emphasize what you are saying （強調所說的話）眾所周知，誰都知道：*Lord knows, I tried to teach her.* 誰都知道，我曾經努力想教她。**ˈLord (ˈonly) knows (what, where, why, etc.) ...** *(informal)* used to say that you do not know the answer to sth （表示不知道答案）天知道，天曉得：*'Why did she say that?' 'Lord knows!'* "她為何那樣說？" "只有天知道！" **HELP** Some people may find the use of **Lord** in these expressions offensive. 有人可能認為這些表達法用 Lord 含冒犯意。**IDM** see DRUNK *adj.*, YEAR

■ ***verb***

IDM **ˈlord it over sb** *(disapproving)* to act as if you are better or more important than sb 對某人舉止霸道（或逞威風）

ˌLord Lieuˈtenant *noun* in the UK, an officer in charge of local government and local judges （英國）郡治安長官

lord·ly /ˈlɔːdli; *NAmE* ˈlɔːrd-/ *adj.* **1** behaving in a way that suggests that you think you are better than other people 傲慢的；高傲的 **SYN** **haughty** **2** large and impressive; suitable for a lord 宏偉的；堂皇的；貴族氣派的 **SYN** **imposing**：*a lordly mansion* 富麗堂皇的宅第

ˌLord ˈMayor *noun* the title of the mayor of the City of London and some other large British cities 市長大人（倫敦市和其他一些英國大城市市長的稱號）

lord·ship /ˈlɔːdʃɪp; *NAmE* ˈlɔːrd-/ *noun* **1** **His/Your Lordship** a title of respect used when speaking to or about a judge, a BISHOP or a NOBLEMAN（對法官、主教或貴族的尊稱）閣下，大人，爵爺：*His Lordship is away on business.* 爵爺有事出去了。➲ compare LADYSHIP **2** *(BrE, informal)* a humorous way of talking to or about a boy or man that you think is trying to be too important （對自以為了不起的男孩或男子幽默的稱呼）閣下：*Can his lordship manage to switch off the TV?* 請閣下設法關掉電視機好不好？ **3** [U] the power or position of a LORD 貴族的權力（或身分、地位）

the ˌLord's ˈPrayer *noun* [sing.] the prayer that Jesus Christ taught the people who followed him, that begins 'Our Father ...' 主禱文；天主經

lore /lɔː(r)/ *noun* [U] knowledge and information related to a particular subject, especially when this is not written down; the stories and traditions of a particular group of people （尤指口頭流傳的）某一方面的學問；（某一群體的）傳說，傳統：*weather lore* 天氣的知識 ◇ *Celtic lore* 凱爾特人的傳說 ➲ see also FOLKLORE

lo-res /ˌləʊ ˈrez; *NAmE* ˌloʊ/ *adj.* = LOW-RESOLUTION

lor·gnette /lɔːˈnjet; *NAmE* lɔːrˈnjet/ *noun* an old-fashioned pair of glasses that you hold to your eyes on a long handle 長柄眼鏡

lori·keet /ˈlɒrɪkiːt; *NAmE* ˈlɔːrəkiːt; ˈlɑːr-/ *noun* a small bird found mainly in New Guinea 吸蜜鸚鵡（主要見於新幾內亞）

lorry 🔑 /ˈlɒri; *NAmE* ˈlɔːri; ˈlɑːri/ *(BrE) noun (pl. -ies)* (also **truck** *NAmE, BrE*)
a large vehicle for carrying heavy loads by road 卡車；貨運汽車：*a lorry driver* 卡車司機 ◇ *Emergency food supplies were brought in* ***by lorry***. 應急食物是用卡車運來的。◇ *a lorry load of frozen fish* 裝滿一卡車的冷凍魚 ➲ VISUAL VOCAB page V57 **IDM** see BACK *n.*

lose 🔑 /luːz/ *verb* (**lost**, **lost** /lɒst; *NAmE* lɔːst; lɑːst/)
▸ NOT FIND 找不到 **1** 🔑 [T] **~ sth/sb** to be unable to find sth/sb 遺失；丟失 **SYN** **mislay**：*I've lost my keys.* 我把鑰匙丟了。◇ *The tickets seem to have* ***got lost***. 那些票好像給弄丟了。◇ *She lost her husband in the crowd.* 她在人群中與丈夫走散了。
▸ HAVE STH/SB TAKEN AWAY 喪失 **2** 🔑 [T] **~ sth/sb** to have sth/sb taken away from you as a result of an accident, getting old, dying, etc. （因事故、年老、死亡等）損失，喪失，失去：*She lost a leg in a car crash.* 她在一次車禍中失去了一條腿。◇ *to* ***lose your hair/teeth*** (= as a result of getting old) 脫髮；掉牙 ◇ *He's* ***lost his job***. 他失業了。◇ *Some families* ***lost everything*** (= all they owned) *in the flood.* 有些家庭的財產在洪水中損失得精光。◇ *They lost both their sons* (= they were killed) *in the war.* 他們的兩個兒子都被戰爭奪去了生命。◇ *The ship was* ***lost at sea*** (= it sank). 那條船沉沒了。◇ *Many people* ***lost their lives*** (= were killed). 有許多人喪生。 **3** 🔑 [T] **~ sth (to sb/sth)** to have sth taken away by sb/sth 被…奪去：*The company has lost a lot of business to its competitors.* 公司的許多生意都被對手奪走了。 **4** 🔑 [T] **~ sth** to have to give up sth; to fail to keep sth 被迫放棄；失去：*You will lose your deposit if you cancel the order.* 如果撤銷訂單，訂金將不予退還。◇ *Sit down or you'll lose your seat.* 坐下吧，要不這個座位就沒啦。
▸ HAVE LESS 減少 **5** 🔑 [T] **~ sth** to have less and less of sth, especially until you no longer have any of it 降低；減少；漸漸喪失：*He* ***lost his nerve*** *at the last minute.* 他在最後一刻失去了勇氣。◇ *She seemed to have* ***lost interest*** *in food.* 她好像對食物不感興趣了。◇ *At that moment he* ***lost his balance*** *and fell.* 他在那一瞬間失去平衡摔倒了。◇ *I've lost ten pounds since I started this diet.* 這次節食開始以來我體重減了十磅。◇ *The train was* ***losing speed***. 火車當時正在減速。
▸ NOT WIN 未贏 **6** 🔑 [T, I] to be defeated; to fail to win a competition, a court case, an argument, etc. 被打敗；輸掉（比賽、訴訟案件、辯論等）：**~ sth (to sb)** *to lose*

L

a game/a race/an election/a battle/a war 輸掉比賽／賽跑／選舉／戰役／戰爭 ◇ **~ to sb** *We lost to a stronger team.* 我們輸給了一支實力更強的隊。◇ **~ (sth) (by sth)** *He lost by less than 100 votes.* 他以相差不到 100 張選票敗北。

▸ **NOT KEEP** 未保留 **7** [T, I] to fail to keep sth you want or need, especially money; to cause sb to fail to keep sth（使）失去（所需要的東西，尤指錢）：**~ sth** *The business is losing money.* 這家公司正在虧損。◇ *Poetry always loses something in translation.* 詩歌一經翻譯總會失去某些東西。◇ **~ sth (on sth/by doing sth)** *You have **nothing to lose** by telling the truth.* 你講真話是不會吃虧的。◇ **~ on sth/by doing sth** *We lost on that deal.* 我們那筆交易做虧了。◇ **~ sb sth** *His carelessness lost him the job.* 他粗枝大葉，丟了工作。

▸ **NOT UNDERSTAND/HEAR** 弄不懂；聽不見 **8** [T] **~ sth** to fail to get, hear or understand sth 不明白；聽不見；弄不懂：*His words were lost* (= could not be heard) *in the applause.* 他的講話讓掌聲淹沒了。**9** [T] **~ sb** (*informal*) to be no longer understood by sb 使弄不懂；使不理解：*I'm afraid **you've lost me** there.* 很抱歉，你把我弄糊塗了。

▸ **ESCAPE** 逃避 **10** [T] **~ sb/sth** to escape from sb/sth 逃避；逃脫 SYN **evade, shake off**：*We managed to lose our pursuers in the darkness.* 我們設法在黑暗中擺脫了追趕者。

▸ **TIME** 時間 **11** [T] **~ sth** to waste time or an opportunity 浪費（時間）；錯過（機會）：*We lost twenty minutes changing a tyre.* 我們換輪胎耽誤了二十分鐘。◇ *Hurry—**there's no time to lose!*** 快點，抓緊時間吧！◇ *He lost no **time in** setting out for London.* 他趕緊啟程去了倫敦。**12** [T, I] **~ (sth)** if a watch or clock **loses** or **loses time**, it goes too slowly or becomes a particular amount of time behind the correct time（鐘、錶）走慢，慢（若干時間）：*This clock loses two minutes a day.* 這時鐘每天慢兩分鐘。OPP **gain**

IDM Most idioms containing **lose** are at the entries for the nouns and adjectives in the idioms, for example **lose your bearings** is at **bearing**. 大多數含 lose 的習語，都可在該等習語中的名詞及形容詞相關詞條找到，如 lose your bearings 在詞條 bearing 下。**'lose it** (*informal*) to be unable to stop yourself from crying, laughing, etc.; to become crazy 禁不住（哭、笑等）；變得瘋狂：*Then she just lost it and started screaming.* 然後她再也控制不住，尖叫起來。

PHR V **'lose yourself in sth** to become so interested in sth that it takes all your attention 沉迷於；專心致志於 **,lose 'out (on sth)** (*informal*) to not get sth you wanted or feel you should have 得不到（想要或覺得應有的東西）：*While the stores make big profits, it's the customer who loses out.* 商店賺大錢，而吃虧的是顧客。**,lose 'out to sb/sth** (*informal*) to not get business, etc. that you expected or used to get because sb/sth else has taken it 被…取代：*Small businesses are losing out to the large chains.* 小商店被大型的連鎖店搶了生意。

loser /ˈluːzə(r)/ *noun* **1** a person who is defeated in a competition（比賽的）輸者，敗者：*winners and losers* 贏家與輸家 ◇ *He's **a good/bad loser*** (= he accepts defeat well/badly). 他是個輸得起／輸不起的人。**2** (*rather informal*) a person who is regularly unsuccessful, especially when you have a low opinion of them 屢屢失敗的人（尤指評價較低者）：*She's one of life's losers.* 她是個生活的失敗者。◇ *He's **a born loser**.* 他生來就走背運。**3** a person who suffers because of a particular action, decision, etc.（因某行為，決定等的）受損害者：*The real losers in all of this are the students.* 在這一切中真正受損害的是學生。

loss /lɒs; *NAmE* lɔːs; lɑːs/ *noun*
1 [U, C, usually sing.] the state of no longer having sth or as much of sth; the process that leads to this 喪失；損失；丟失：*I want to report the loss of a package.* 我要報告丟失了一個包裹。◇ ***loss of blood*** 失血 ◇ ***weight loss*** 體重減少 ◇ *The closure of the factory will lead to a number of **job losses**.* 工廠倒閉會使許多人失業。◇ *When she died I was filled with a **sense of loss**.* 她去世後我心裏充滿了失落感。◇ ***loss of earnings*** (= the money you do not earn because you are prevented from working) 收入損失 **2** [C] money that has been lost by a business or an organization 虧損；虧蝕：*The company has announced **net losses** of $1.5 million.* 公司宣告淨虧損 150 萬元。◇ *We **made a loss on*** (= lost money on) *the deal.* 我們做那筆交易虧了。◇ *We are now operating **at a loss**.* 我們現在是虧本經營。OPP **profit** **3** [C, U] the death of a person 去世；逝世：*The loss of his wife was a great blow to him.* 他妻子去世對他是個巨大的打擊。◇ *Enemy troops suffered **heavy losses**.* 敵軍傷亡慘重。◇ *The drought has led to widespread **loss of life**.* 旱災導致了許多人的死亡。**4** [sing.] the disadvantage that is caused when sb leaves or when a useful or valuable object is taken away; a person who causes a disadvantage by leaving（某人離開或珍貴物品被取走造成的）損失；因離去而造成損失者：*Her departure is a **big loss** to the school.* 她這一走對學校來說是一個巨大的損失。◇ *She will be a **great loss** to the school.* 她這一走對學校來說將是一個巨大的損失。◇ *If he isn't prepared to accept this money, then **that's his loss**.* 如果他不打算接受這筆錢，那他就虧了。⇨ see also DEAD LOSS **5** [C] a failure to win a contest 失敗；輸；失利：*Brazil's 2–1 loss to Argentina* 巴西對阿根廷 1:2 的落敗

IDM **at a 'loss** not knowing what to say or do 不知所措；困惑：*His comments left me **at a loss for words**.* 他的評論講我不知說什麼才好。◇ *I'm at a loss what to do next.* 我對下一步做什麼心裏沒譜。**cut your 'losses** to stop doing sth that is not successful before the situation becomes even worse 不成功就住手（免得情況更糟）；趁早罷手

'loss adjuster (*BrE*) (*NAmE* **in'surance adjuster**) *noun* a person who works for an insurance company and whose job is to calculate how much money sb should receive after they have lost sth or had sth damaged（保險公司的）險損估價師，損失理算人

'loss-leader *noun* an item that a shop/store sells at a very low price to attract customers 為招徠顧客而低價出售的商品

loss·less /ˈlɒsləs; *NAmE* ˈlɔːs-; ˈlɑːs-/ *adj.* (*technical* 術語) involving no loss of data or electrical energy（對數據或電能）無損的；無損耗的 OPP **lossy**

'loss-making *adj.* (of a company or business 公司或生意) not making a profit; losing money 虧損的

lossy /ˈlɒsi; *NAmE* ˈlɔːsi; ˈlɑːsi/ *adj.* (*technical* 術語) involving the loss of data or electrical energy（對數據或電能）有損的；有損耗的 OPP **lossless**

lost /lɒst; *NAmE* lɔːst; lɑːst/ *adj.*
1 unable to find your way; not knowing where you are 迷路的；迷失的：*We always **get lost** in London.* 我們在倫敦老是迷路。◇ *We're completely lost.* 我們完全迷路了。**2** that cannot be found or brought back 失去的；丟失的；喪失的；無法恢復的：*I'm still looking for that lost file.* 我還在找那份丟失的檔案。◇ *Your cheque must have **got lost** in the post.* 你的支票一定是郵寄中遺失的。**3** [usually before noun] that cannot be obtained; that cannot be found or created again 得不到的；無法再找到的；無法再造的：*The strike cost them thousands of pounds in **lost business**.* 罷工使他們失去了幾千英鎊的生意。◇ *She's trying to recapture her **lost youth**.* 她在努力追回逝去的青春。◇ *He regretted the **lost*** (= wasted) ***opportunity** to apologize to her.* 他後悔錯過了向她道歉的機會。**4** [not before noun] unable to deal successfully with a particular situation 不知所措；一籌莫展：*We would **be lost without** your help.* 我們沒有你的幫助就會一籌莫展。◇ *I felt so lost after my mother died.* 我母親去世後我覺得茫然無措。◇ *He's a **lost soul*** (= a person who does not seem to know what to do, and seems unhappy). 他是個迷惘的人。**5** [not before noun] unable to understand sth because it is too complicated 弄不懂；困惑：*They spoke so quickly I just got lost.* 他們說得太快，我簡直給弄糊塗了。◇ *Hang on a minute—I'm lost.* 等一下，我沒弄明白。⇨ see also LOSE *v.*

IDM **,all is not 'lost** there is still some hope of making a bad situation better 還有一線希望 **be lost for 'words** to be so surprised, confused, etc. that you do not know what to say（驚訝、困惑等而）不知說什麼才好 **be 'lost in sth** to be giving all your attention to sth so that you do not notice what is happening around you 全神貫注；沉浸於：*to be lost in thought* 陷入沉思 **be 'lost on sb** to be not understood or noticed by sb 未得某人理解（或注意）：*His jokes were completely lost on most of the students.* 他講的笑話大多數學生一點都沒能領會。 **be lost to the 'world** to be giving all your attention to sth so that you do not notice what is happening around you 全神貫注；沉浸於 **get 'lost** (*informal*) a rude way of telling sb to go away, or of refusing sth（讓人走開或拒絕某事的不禮貌說法）滾開，別來煩我 **give sb up for 'lost** (*formal*) to stop expecting to find sb alive 認為某人沒有生還的可能；認定某人已死 **make up for lost 'time** to do sth quickly or very often because you wish you had started doing it sooner（加快或加緊做某事以）彌補失去的時間 ➲ more at LOVE *n.*

,lost and 'found (*NAmE*) (*BrE* **,lost 'property**) *noun* [U] the place where items that have been found are kept until they are collected 失物招領處

,lost 'cause *noun* something that has failed or that cannot succeed 業已失敗的事情；沒有希望的事情

,lost 'property *noun* [U] (*BrE*) **1** items that have been found in public places and are waiting to be collected by the people who lost them（丟棄在公共場所的）失物：*a lost-property office* 失物招領處 **2** (*NAmE* **,lost and 'found**) the place where items that have been found are kept until they are collected 失物招領處

lot 🔑 /lɒt; *NAmE* lɑːt/ *pron., det., adv., noun*

■ ***pron.*** 🔑 **a lot** (also *informal* **lots**) **~ (to do)** a large number or amount 大量；許多：*'How many do you need?' 'A lot.'* "你需要多少？" "很多。" ◇ *Have some more cake. There's lots left.* 再吃點蛋糕吧。還剩下好多呢。◇ *She still has **an awful lot*** (= a very large amount) *to learn.* 她要學的還多着呢。◇ *He has invited nearly a hundred people but a lot aren't able to come.* 他邀請了差不多一百人，但很多人都來不了。➲ note at MANY, MUCH

■ ***det.*** 🔑 **a lot of** (also *informal* **lots of**) a large number or amount of sb/sth 大量；許多：*What a lot of presents!* 禮品真多啊！◇ *A lot of people are coming to the meeting.* 有很多人要來參加這次會議。◇ *black coffee with lots of sugar* 不加奶多放糖的咖啡 ◇ *I saw a lot of her* (= I saw her often) *last summer.* 去年夏天我經常見到她。➲ note at MANY, MUCH

■ ***adv.*** (*informal*) **1** 🔑 **a lot** (also *informal* **lots**) used with adjectives and adverbs to mean 'much'（與形容詞和副詞連用）很，非常：*I'm feeling a lot better today.* 我今天感覺好多了。◇ *I eat lots less than I used to.* 我比以前吃得少多了。 **2** 🔑 **a lot** used with verbs to mean 'a great amount'（與動詞連用）非常：*I care a lot about you.* 我非常在乎你。◇ *Thanks a lot for your help.* 非常感謝你的幫助。◇ *I play tennis quite a lot* (= often) *in the summer.* 我夏天常打網球。➲ note at MUCH

■ ***noun***

▸ **WHOLE AMOUNT/NUMBER** 全數 **1 the lot, the whole lot** [sing.+sing./pl. v.] (*informal*) the whole number or amount of people or things 全體；全部；整個：*He's bought a new PC, colour printer, scanner—the lot.* 他買了新的個人電腦、彩色打印機、掃描儀，樣樣齊備。◇ *Get out of my house, **the lot of you**!* 你們別待在我家裏，通通給我滾出去！◇ ***That's the lot!*** (= that includes everything) 全都在這兒了！◇ ***That's your lot!*** (= that's all you're getting) 你的那份兒全在那兒了！

▸ **GROUP/SET** 群；套 **2** [C+sing./pl. v.] (*especially BrE*) a group or set of people or things（一）組，群，批，套：*The first lot of visitors has/have arrived.* 首批遊客已經到達。◇ *I have several lots of essays to mark this weekend.* 這週末我有幾批文章要批改。◇ (*informal*) *What do **you lot** want?* 你們這幫人想要怎麼樣？

▸ **ITEMS TO BE SOLD** 待售物品 **3** [C] an item or a number of items to be sold, especially at an AUCTION 待售商品；（尤指）拍賣品：*Lot 46: six chairs* 拍賣品 46 號：六把椅子

▸ **AREA OF LAND** 一塊地 **4** [C] an area of land used for a particular purpose（作某種用途的）一塊地，場地：*a parking lot* 停車場 ◇ *a vacant lot* (= one available to be built on or used for sth) 一塊空地 ◇ (*especially NAmE*) *We're going to build a house on this lot.* 我們打算在這塊地上建造一座房子。➲ **SYNONYMS** at LAND

▸ **LUCK/SITUATION** 運氣；境況 **5** [sing.] a person's luck or situation in life 命運；生活狀況 **SYN destiny**：*She was feeling dissatisfied with her lot.* 她對自己的生活狀況感到不滿。

IDM **all 'over the lot** (*NAmE*) = ALL OVER THE PLACE at PLACE *n.* **a bad 'lot** (*old-fashioned, BrE*) a person who is dishonest 不誠實的人；騙子 **by 'lot** using a method of choosing sb to do sth in which each person takes a piece of paper, etc. from a container and the one whose paper has a special mark is chosen 抽籤；抓鬮 **draw/cast 'lots (for sth/to do sth)** to choose sb/sth by lot 抽籤（選定）；抓鬮（決定）：*They drew lots for the right to go first.* 他們拈鬮兒決定誰先走。 **fall to sb's 'lot (to do sth)** (*formal*) to become sb's task or responsibility 成為某人的任務（或責任）；落到某人肩上 **throw in your 'lot with sb** to decide to join sb and share their successes and problems 決心與某人共命運 ➲ more at BEST *n.*

,lo-'tech *adj.* = LOW-TECH

loth = LOATH

Loth·ario /ləˈθeəriəʊ; ləˈθɑːriəʊ; *NAmE* ləˈθerioʊ; ləˈθɑːrioʊ/ *noun* (*pl.* **-os**) a man who has sex with a lot of women 迷人浪子：*He has a reputation as the office Lothario.* 他在辦公室泡妞亂搞是出了名的。**ORIGIN** From the name of a character in an 18th century play by Nicholas Rowe. 源自 18 世紀尼古拉斯•羅所寫的戲劇人物洛薩里奧。

lo·tion /ˈləʊʃn; *NAmE* ˈloʊʃn/ *noun* [C, U] a liquid used for cleaning, protecting or treating the skin 潔膚液；護膚液；潤膚乳：*(a) **body/hand lotion*** 護膚 / 護手乳液 ◇ *suntan lotion* 防曬露

lotta /ˈlɒtə; *NAmE* ˈlɑːtə/ (also **lotsa** /ˈlɒtsə; *NAmE* ˈlɑːtsə/) (*informal, non-standard*) a written form of 'lot of' or 'lots of' that shows how it sounds in informal speech 許多：*We're gonna have a lotta fun.* 我們將玩得非常開心。 **HELP** You should not write this form unless you are copying somebody's speech. 只用於記錄講話。

lot·tery /ˈlɒtəri; *NAmE* ˈlɑːt-/ *noun* (*pl.* **-ies**) **1** [C] a way of raising money for a government, charity, etc. by selling tickets that have different numbers on them that people have chosen. Numbers are then chosen by chance and the people who have those numbers on their tickets win prizes.（用發行彩票為政府、慈善機構等集資的）抽彩給獎法：*the **national/state lottery*** 全國的 / 州的彩票抽獎 ◇ *a lottery ticket* 彩票 ➲ compare DRAW *n.* (3), RAFFLE *n.* **2** [sing.] (often *disapproving*) a situation whose success or result is based on luck rather than on effort or careful organization 碰運氣的事 **SYN gamble**：*Some people think that marriage is a lottery.* 有些人認為婚姻靠的是運氣。➲ see also POST-CODE LOTTERY

lotto /ˈlɒtəʊ; *NAmE* ˈlɑːtoʊ/ *noun* (*pl.* **lottos**) **1** [U] a game of chance similar to BINGO but with the numbers drawn from a container by the players instead of being called out 抽數碼賭博遊戲 **2** [C] a lottery 彩票

lotus /ˈləʊtəs; *NAmE* ˈloʊ-/ *noun* **1** a tropical plant with white or pink flowers that grows on the surface of lakes in Africa and Asia 蓮屬植物：*a lotus flower* 蓮花 ➲ **VISUAL VOCAB** page V11 **2** a picture in the shape of the lotus plant, used in art and ARCHITECTURE, especially in ancient Egypt 蓮花圖案，荷花飾（尤用於古埃及藝術和建築） **3** (in ancient Greek stories 古希臘故事) a fruit that is supposed to make you feel happy and relaxed when you have eaten it, as if in a dream 落拓棗，忘憂果（食後感到夢幻般的快樂輕鬆）

'lotus position *noun* [sing.] a way of sitting with your legs crossed, used especially when people MEDITATE or do YOGA（尤指冥想或做瑜伽時）跏趺坐，蓮花坐

louche /luːʃ/ *adj.* (*especially BrE, formal*) not socially acceptable, but often still attractive despite this 聲名不好卻有吸引力的

loud 🔑 /laʊd/ *adj., adv.*

■ ***adj.*** (**loud·er**, **loud·est**) **1** 🔑 making a lot of noise 喧鬧的；響亮的；大聲的：*loud laughter* 響亮的笑聲 ◇ *a*

L

deafeningly loud bang 震耳欲聾的巨響 ◇ *She spoke in a very loud voice.* 她聲音洪亮地講了話。◇ *That music's too loud—please turn it down.* 那音樂太吵了，請把音量調低一點。 **2** 🗝 (of a person or their behaviour 人或舉止) talking very loudly, too much and in a way that is annoying 說話太大聲的；吵鬧的 **3** (of colours, patterns, etc. 顏色、圖案等) too bright and lacking good taste 俗豔的；花哨的 SYN **gaudy, garish** ▸ **loud·ly** 🗝 *adv.*: *She screamed as loudly as she could.* 她聲嘶力竭地尖叫着。**loud·ness** *noun* [U]

■ ***adv.*** 🗝 (**loud·er**, **loud·est**) (*informal*) in a way that makes a lot of noise or can be easily heard 喧鬧地；大聲地；響亮地 SYN **loudly**: *Do you have to play that music so loud?* 你非得把音樂放那麼響嗎？◇ *You'll have to speak louder—I can't hear you.* 你得說大聲點，我聽不見你的話。

IDM **ˌloud and ˈclear** in a way that is very easy to understand 清楚明白：*The message is coming through loud and clear.* 消息傳達得清楚明白。**ˌout ˈloud** 🗝 in a voice that can be heard by other people 出聲；大聲地：*I laughed out loud.* 我放聲大笑了。◇ *Please read the letter out loud.* 請把信大聲唸出來。➲ compare ALOUD ➲ more at ACTION *n.*, CRY *v.*, THINK *v.*

Which Word? 詞語辨析

loud / loudly / aloud

- **Loudly** is the usual adverb from the adjective **loud**. * loudly 為形容詞 loud 的常用副詞：*The audience laughed loudly at the joke.* 觀眾聽到這笑話大笑起來。
- **Loud** is very common as an adverb in informal language. It is nearly always used in phrases such as **loud enough**, **as loud as** or with *too*, *very*, *so*, etc. * loud 作非正式用語常為副詞，幾乎總是用於 loud enough、as loud as 等短語中，或與 too、very、so 等詞連用：*Don't play your music too loud.* 你播放音樂聲音別太大。◇ *I shouted as loud as I could.* 我聲嘶力竭地喊着。
- **Louder** is also used in informal styles to mean 'more loudly'. * louder 亦作非正式用語指以更大的聲音：*Can you speak louder?* 你說話大聲些行嗎？
- **Out loud** is a common adverb meaning 'so that people can hear'. * out loud 為常用副詞，意為出聲地、大聲地：*Can you read the letter out loud?* 你把信大聲唸出來行嗎？◇ *He laughed out loud at his own joke.* 他對自己的笑話大笑起來。**Aloud** has the same meaning but is fairly formal. It can also mean 'in a loud voice'. * aloud 意義相同，但相當正式，亦含大聲之意。

loud·hail·er /ˌlaʊdˈheɪlə(r)/ (*BrE*) (*NAmE* **bull·horn**) *noun* an electronic device, shaped like a horn, with a MICROPHONE at one end, that you speak into in order to make your voice louder so that it can be heard at a distance 電子喇叭；擴音器 ➲ compare MEGAPHONE

loud·mouth /ˈlaʊdmaʊθ/ *noun* (*informal*) a person who is annoying because they talk too loudly or too much in an offensive or stupid way 說話大聲大氣的人；喋喋不休的人 ▸ **ˈloud-mouthed** *adj.*

loud·speak·er /ˌlaʊdˈspiːkə(r)/ *noun* **1** a piece of equipment that changes electrical signals into sound, used in public places for announcing things, playing music, etc. 揚聲器；擴音器；喇叭：*Their names were called **over the loudspeaker**.* 喇叭裏叫着他們的名字。➲ see also *PUBLIC ADDRESS SYSTEM*, TANNOY **2** (*old-fashioned*) the part of a radio or piece of musical equipment that the sound comes out of（收音機或音響設備的）揚聲器，喇叭 SYN **speaker**

lough /lɒk; lɒx; *NAmE* lɑːk; lɑːx/ *noun* (in Ireland 愛爾蘭) a lake or a long strip of sea that is almost surrounded by land 湖；狹長的海灣：*Lough Corrib* 科里布湖 ➲ see also LOCH

lounge /laʊndʒ/ *noun, verb*

■ ***noun*** **1** a room for waiting in at an airport, etc.（機場等的）等候室：*the departure lounge* 候機室 **2** a public room in a hotel, club, etc. for waiting or relaxing in（旅館、俱樂部等的）休息室：*the television lounge* 電視放映室 **3** (*BrE*) a room in a private house for sitting and relaxing in（私宅中的）起居室 SYN **living room, sitting room** ➲ see also SUN LOUNGE **4** (*BrE*) = LOUNGE BAR

■ ***verb*** [I] (+ **adv./prep.**) to stand, sit or lie in a lazy way 懶洋洋地站（或坐、躺）着 SYN **laze around**: *Several students were lounging around, reading newspapers.* 有幾個學生懶洋洋地坐着看報。

ˈlounge bar (also **sal·oon**) (both *BrE*) *noun* a bar in a pub, hotel, etc. which is more comfortable than the other bars and where the drinks are usually more expensive（酒館、旅館等的）高級酒吧，豪華酒吧 ➲ compare PUBLIC BAR

ˈlounge lizard *noun* (*old-fashioned, informal*) a person who does no work and who likes to be with rich, fashionable people（愛與時髦富人廝混的）二流子

loun·ger /ˈlaʊndʒə(r)/ *noun* (*especially BrE*) a long comfortable chair that supports your legs, used for sitting or lying on, especially outdoors 日光浴椅；日光浴牀 ➲ compare SUNLOUNGER

ˈlounge suit *noun* (*BrE*) a man's suit of matching jacket and trousers/pants, worn especially in offices and on fairly formal occasions（尤指在辦公室及較正式場合穿的）男式全套西服

lour *verb* = LOWER²

louse /laʊs/ *noun, verb*

■ ***noun*** **1** (*pl.* **lice** /laɪs/) a small insect that lives on the bodies of humans and animals 虱；虱子：*head lice* 頭虱 ➲ see also WOODLOUSE **2** (*pl.* **louses**) (*informal, disapproving*) a very unpleasant person 不受歡迎的人；討厭鬼

■ ***verb***

PHR V **ˌlouse sth↔ˈup** (*informal*) to spoil sth or do it very badly 搞壞；弄糟

lousy /ˈlaʊzi/ *adj.* (**lous·ier**, **lousi·est**) (*informal*) **1** very bad 非常糟的；極壞的；惡劣的 SYN **awful, terrible**: *What lousy weather!* 這天氣真糟糕！◇ *She felt lousy* (= ill). 她覺得很不舒服。 **2** [only before noun] used to show that you feel annoyed or insulted because you do not think that sth is worth very much（認為某物無太大價值而感到不滿或受辱）討厭的，倒霉的：*All she bought me was this lousy T-shirt.* 她給我買的就僅這件破 T 恤。 **3 ~ with sth/sb** (*NAmE*) having too much of sth or too many people（某事物或人）太多的：*This place is lousy with tourists in August.* 在八月份，這個地方擠滿遊人。

lout /laʊt/ *noun* (*BrE*) a man or boy who behaves in a rude and aggressive way 舉止粗野的男人（或男孩）SYN **yob** ➲ see also LAGER LOUT, LITTER LOUT ▸ **lout·ish** *adj.*: *loutish behaviour* 粗野無禮的行為

louvre (*especially US* **lou·ver**) /ˈluːvə(r)/ *noun* one of a set of narrow strips of wood, plastic, etc. in a door or a window that are designed to let air and some light in, but to keep out strong light or rain; a door or a window that has these strips across it 百葉窗板；百葉門；百葉窗 ▸ **louvred** (*especially US* **lou·vered**) *adj.*

lov·able (also **love·able**) /ˈlʌvəbl/ *adj.* having qualities that people find attractive and easy to love, often despite any faults 可愛的；惹人愛的；討人喜歡的 SYN **endearing**: *a lovable child* 討人喜歡的小孩 ◇ *a lovable rogue* 可愛的淘氣鬼

love 🗝 /lʌv/ *noun, verb*

■ ***noun***

▸ **AFFECTION** 喜愛 **1** 🗝 [U] a strong feeling of deep affection for sb/sth, especially a member of your family or a friend 愛；熱愛；慈愛：*a mother's love for her children* 母親對孩子的愛 ◇ *love of your country* 對祖國的熱愛 ◇ *He seems incapable of love.* 他好像不會疼愛人。

▸ **ROMANTIC** 浪漫 **2** 🗝 [U] a strong feeling of affection for sb that you are sexually attracted to 愛情；戀愛：*a **love song/story*** 愛情歌曲／故事 ◇ *We're **in love!*** 我們相愛了！◇ *She was **in love with him.*** 她與他相愛了。◇ *They **fell in love** with each other.* 他們彼此相愛了。◇

It was **love at first sight** (= they were attracted to each other the first time they met). 那是一見鍾情。◇ *They're* **madly in love.** 他們狂熱地相愛。◇ *Their love grew with the years.* 他們的愛逐年加深。 ➲ COLLOCATIONS at MARRIAGE

▸ **ENJOYMENT** 樂趣 **3** [U, sing.] the strong feeling of enjoyment that sth gives you 喜好；喜愛： *a* **love of** *learning* 對知識的愛好 ◇ *He's* **in love with** *his work.* 他熱愛自己的工作。◇ *I* **fell in love with** *the house.* 我喜歡上了這房子。

▸ **SB/STH YOU LIKE** 所愛的人／物 **4** [C] a person, a thing or an activity that you like very much 心愛的人；鍾愛之物；愛好：*Take care, my love.* 保重，我的愛人。◇ *He was* **the love of my life** (= the person I loved most). 他是我一生中最愛的人。◇ *I like most sports but tennis is my* **first love**. 大多數運動我都喜歡，而網球是我的第一愛好。

▸ **FRIENDLY NAME** 友好的稱呼 **5** [C] (*BrE, informal*) a word used as a friendly way of addressing sb（昵稱）親愛的： *Can I help you, love?* 親愛的，我能幫你忙嗎？ ➲ compare DUCK *n.* (4)

▸ **IN TENNIS** 網球 **6** [U] a score of zero (points or games) 零分： *40–love!* * 40 比 0！◇ *She won the first set* **six–love/six games to love.** 她以六比零贏了第一盤。

IDM **(just) for 'love | (just) for the 'love of sth** without receiving payment or any other reward 出於愛好；不收報酬；無償： *They're all volunteers, working for the love of it.* 他們都是義務工作的志願者。 **for the love of 'God** (*old-fashioned, informal*) used when you are expressing anger and the fact that you are impatient（表示憤怒和不耐煩）看在上帝的分上，哎呀，求求你： *For the love of God, tell me what he said!* 看在上帝的分上，告訴我他說了些什麼！ **give/send my love to sb** (*informal*) used to send good wishes to sb 向某人致意（或問候）： *Give my love to Mary when you see her.* 你見到瑪麗代我向她問好。◇ *Bob sends his love.* 鮑勃向你致意。 **'love from | lots of 'love (from)** (*informal*) used at the end of a letter to a friend or to sb you love, followed by your name（用於給朋友或所愛的人的信結尾具名前）愛你的： *Lots of love, Jenny* 非常愛你的珍妮 **love is 'blind** (*saying*) when you love sb, you cannot see their faults 愛情是盲目的，愛讓人蒙蔽雙眼（指戀愛中的人看不到對方缺點） **make 'love (to sb)** to have sex 有性行為；性交；做愛： *It was the first time they had made love.* 那是他們第一次發生性關係。 **not for love or/nor 'money** if you say you cannot do sth **for love nor money**, you mean it is completely impossible to do it 決不；無論怎樣也不： *We couldn't find a taxi for love nor money.* 我們無論如何也找不到一輛出租車。 **there's little/no 'love lost between A and B** they do not like each other（…之間）彼此厭惡，互無好感： *There's no love lost between her and her in-laws.* 她和她的姻親彼此嫌惡。 ➲ more at CUPBOARD, FAIR *adj.*, HEAD *n.*, LABOUR *n.*

■ *verb*

▸ **FEEL AFFECTION** 感到愛 **1** **~ sb/sth** (not used in the progressive tenses 不用於進行時) to have very strong feelings of affection for sb 愛；熱愛： *I love you.* 我愛你。◇ *If you love each other, why not get married?* 要是你們彼此相愛，幹嗎不結婚呢？◇ *Her much-loved brother lay dying of AIDS.* 她至愛的弟弟因艾滋病而瀕臨死亡。◇ *He had become a well-loved member of staff.* 他已成為受人喜愛的職員。◇ *Relatives need time to grieve over* **loved ones** *they have lost.* 親屬需要時間痛悼他們失去的至愛。◇ *to love your country* 熱愛你的祖國

▸ **LIKE/ENJOY** 喜歡；喜愛 **2** to like or enjoy sth very much 喜歡；喜愛 **SYN** **adore**： **~ sth** *I really love summer evenings.* 我非常喜歡夏天的夜晚。◇ ***I just love it when** you bring me presents!* 我就喜歡你送我禮物！◇ *He* **loved the way** *she smiled.* 他喜歡她微笑的樣子。◇ ***I love it*** *in Spain* (= I like the life there). 我喜歡西班牙的生活。◇ *It was one of his best-loved songs.* 這是他最受喜愛的歌曲之一。◇ (*ironic*) ***You're going to love this.*** *They've changed their minds again.* 你會感到高興的，他們又改變主意了。◇ **~ doing sth** (especially in *BrE*) *My dad loves going to football games.* 我父親愛去看足球賽。◇ **~ to do sth** (*especially NAmE*) *I love to go out dancing.* 我喜歡出去跳舞。◇ **~ sb/sth to do sth** *He loved her to sing to him.* 他喜歡讓她唱歌給他聽。 ➲ SYNONYMS at LIKE **3** **would love** used to say that you would very much like sth 很喜歡；很願意： **~ to do sth** *Come on Rory, the kids would love to hear you sing.* 來吧，羅里，孩子們都很喜歡聽你唱歌。◇ *I haven't been to Brazil, but I'd love to go.* 我沒去過巴西，但很想去。◇ **~ sb/sth to do sth** *I'd love her to come and live with us.* 我很願意讓她來和我們住在一起。◇ **~ sth** *'Cigarette?' 'I'd love one, but I've just given up.'* "要抽支煙嗎？" "我倒很樂意抽一支，可我剛把煙戒了。"

IDM **,love you and 'leave you** (*informal, humorous*) used to say that you must go, although you would like to stay longer（表示想留卻必須離開）不得不走： *Well, time to love you and leave you.* 唉，我該走了，不想走也得走哇。

Synonyms 同義詞辨析

love

like • be fond of sb • adore • be devoted to sb • care for sb • dote on sb

These words all mean to have feelings of love or affection for sb. 以上各詞均含喜愛、愛慕某人之意。

love to have strong feelings of affection for sb 指愛、熱愛： *I love you.* 我愛你。

like to find sb pleasant and enjoy being with them 指喜歡、喜愛： *She's nice. I like her.* 她人很好，我喜歡她。

be fond of sb to feel affection for sb, especially sb you have known for a long time 指喜愛（尤指認識已久的人）： *I've always been very fond of your mother.* 我一直非常喜歡你的母親。

adore to love sb very much 指熱愛、愛慕： *It's obvious that she adores him.* 她顯然深深地愛着他。

be devoted to sb to love sb very much and be loyal to them 指深愛、忠誠於某人： *They are devoted to their children.* 他們深愛着自己的孩子。

care for sb to love sb, especially in a way that is based on strong affection or a feeling of wanting to protect them, rather than sex 指深深地愛、非常喜歡，但不指性愛： *He cared for her more than she realized.* 她不知道他是多麼在乎她。 **NOTE** **Care for sb** is often used when sb has not told anyone about their feelings or is just starting to be aware of them. It is also used when sb wishes that sb loved them, or doubts that sb does. * care for sb 常用於未向任何人吐露感情或剛開始意識到這種感情時，亦用於希望別人愛自己或不知別人是否愛自己時： *If he really cared for you, he wouldn't behave like that.* 如果他真的在乎你，就不會幹出那樣的事。

dote on sb to feel and show great love for sb, ignoring their faults 指溺愛、寵愛、過分喜愛： *He dotes on his children.* 他溺愛自己的孩子。

PATTERNS

- to **really** love/like/adore/care for/dote on sb
- to be **really/genuinely** fond of/devoted to sb
- to love/like/care for sb **very much**

'love affair *noun* **1** a romantic and/or sexual relationship between two people who are in love and not married to each other 風流韻事；（非夫妻間的）性關係 **2** great enthusiasm for sth（對某事）極大的熱情，強烈的興趣 **SYN** **passion**： *the English love affair with gardening* 英國人對園藝的熱愛

love·bird /ˈlʌvbɜːd; *NAmE* -bɜːrd/ *noun* **1** [C] a small African PARROT (= a bird with brightly coloured feathers) 情侶鸚鵡，愛情鳥（產於非洲） **2** **lovebirds** [pl.] (*humorous*) two people who love each other very much and show this in their behaviour 恩愛情侶；熱戀的戀人

'love bite (*BrE*) (*NAmE* **hickey**) *noun* a red mark on the skin that is caused by sb biting or sucking their partner's skin when they are kissing 愛痕（接吻時在皮膚上咬或吮吸的紅色痕跡）

ˈlove child *noun* (used especially in newspapers, etc. 尤用於報刊等) a child born to parents who are not married to each other 私生子

ˌloved-ˈup *adj.* (*informal*) **1** happy and excited because of the effects of the illegal drug ECSTASY（因服用違禁迷幻藥而）興奮的，激情勃發的 **2** full of romantic love for sb（對某人）充滿愛戀的

ˈlove handles *noun* [pl.] (*informal, humorous*) extra fat on a person's waist 腰部贅肉

ˌlove-ˈhate relationship *noun* [usually sing.] a relationship in which your feelings for sb/sth are a mixture of love and hatred 愛恨交加的感情關係

ˈlove-in *noun* (*informal*) **1** (*old-fashioned*) a party at which people freely show their affection and sexual attraction for each other, associated with HIPPIES in the 1960s（20 世紀 60 年代嬉皮士的）愛情聚會 **2** (*disapproving*) an occasion when people are being especially pleasant to each other, in a way that you believe is not sincere 虛情假意的場合；假熱情

ˈlove interest *noun* [C, usually sing.] a character in a film/movie or story who has a romantic role, often as the main character's lover（電影或小說中的）戀愛角色（常為主角的情人）

love·less /ˈlʌvləs/ *adj.* without love 沒有愛的；無愛情的：*a loveless marriage* 沒有愛情的婚姻

ˈlove letter *noun* a letter that you write to sb telling them that you love them 情書

ˈlove life *noun* the part of your life that involves your romantic and sexual relationships 愛情生活

love·li·ness /ˈlʌvlinəs/ *noun* [U] (*formal*) the state of being very attractive 美麗動人；漂亮可愛；楚楚動人 SYN **beauty**

love·lorn /ˈlʌvlɔːn; *NAmE* -lɔːrn/ *adj.* (*literary*) unhappy because the person you love does not love you 單相思的；失戀的

love·ly 0-w /ˈlʌvli/ *adj., noun*

■ *adj.* (**love·lier**, **love·li·est**) HELP You can also use **more lovely** and **most lovely**. 亦可用 more lovely 和 most lovely。(*especially BrE*) **1** 0-w beautiful; attractive 美麗的；優美的；有吸引力的；迷人的：*lovely countryside/eyes/flowers* 美麗的鄉村／眼睛／花朵 ◇ *She* **looked** *particularly* **lovely** *that night.* 她那天晚上特別嫵媚動人。◇ *He has a lovely voice.* 他說話的聲音很好聽。➲ SYNONYMS at BEAUTIFUL **2** 0-w (*informal*) very enjoyable and pleasant; wonderful 令人愉快的；極好的：*'Can I get you anything?' 'A cup of tea would be lovely.'* "要我給你來點什麼嗎？" "一杯茶就很好了。" ◇ *What a lovely surprise!* 真讓人感到驚喜！◇ *How lovely to see you!* 見到你多麼讓人高興！◇ *Isn't it a lovely day?* 天氣真好呀！◇ *We've had a lovely time.* 我們玩得很痛快。◇ *It's a lovely old farm.* 那是個宜人的老農場。◇ *It's been lovely having you here.* 有你在這兒真是太好了。◇ (*ironic*) *You've got yourself into a lovely mess, haven't you?* 你惹的這麻煩可真夠瞧的，是吧？➲ SYNONYMS at WONDERFUL **3** 0-w (*informal*) (of a person 人) very kind, generous and friendly 親切友好的；慷慨大方的；可愛的：*Her mother was a lovely woman.* 她母親是個心地善良的女人。HELP **Very lovely** is not very common and is only used about the physical appearance of a person or thing. * very lovely 不很常見，僅用於形容人的外貌或事物的外觀。

IDM **lovely and ˈwarm, ˈcold, ˈquiet, etc.** (*BrE, informal*) used when you are emphasizing that sth is good because of the quality mentioned（用以強調某事物因具有所說的特質而很好）：*It's lovely and warm in here.* 這裏溫暖宜人。

■ *noun* (*pl.* **-ies**) (*old-fashioned*) a beautiful woman 美女；美人；佳人

love·mak·ing /ˈlʌvmeɪkɪŋ/ *noun* [U] sexual activity between two lovers, especially the act of having sex 性行為；做愛；性交

ˈlove match *noun* a marriage of two people who are in love with each other 戀愛結婚；愛情的結合

ˈlove nest *noun* [usually sing.] (*informal*) a house or an apartment where two people who are not married but are having a sexual relationship can meet 情侶幽會處；情人安樂窩

lover 0-w /ˈlʌvə(r)/ *noun*

1 0-w a partner in a sexual relationship outside marriage（婚外的）情人，情侶：*He denied that he was her lover.* 他否認是她的情夫。◇ *We were lovers for several years.* 我們相愛了好幾年。◇ *The park was full of young lovers holding hands.* 公園裏到處是手拉着手的年輕情侶。

2 0-w (often in compounds 常構成複合詞) a person who likes or enjoys a particular thing 愛好者；熱愛者：*a lover of music* 音樂愛好者 ◇ *an art-lover* 愛好藝術的人 ◇ *a nature-lover* 熱愛大自然的人

ˈlove seat *noun* (*NAmE*) a comfortable seat with a back and arms, for two people to sit on 雙人座椅；鴛鴦椅 ➲ VISUAL VOCAB page V21

love·sick /ˈlʌvsɪk/ *adj.* unable to think clearly or behave in a sensible way because you are in love with sb, especially sb who is not in love with you 害相思病的（尤指單相思的）

ˈlove triangle *noun* [usually sing.] a situation that involves three people, each of whom loves at least one of the others, for example a married woman, her husband, and another man that she loves 三角戀

lovey (also **luvvy**) /ˈlʌvi/ *noun* (*BrE, informal*) used as a friendly way of addressing sb（昵稱）親愛的，心肝，寶貝：*Ruth, lovey, are you there?* 魯思，寶貝，你在嗎？

lovey-dovey /ˌlʌvi ˈdʌvi/ *adj.* (*informal*) expressing romantic love in a way that is slightly silly 過於情意綿綿的

lov·ing /ˈlʌvɪŋ/ *adj.* **1** feeling or showing love and affection for sb/sth 愛的；充滿愛的 SYN **affectionate, tender**：*a warm and loving family* 溫馨而充滿愛的家庭 ◇ *She chose the present with loving care.* 她滿懷愛意精心挑選了這件禮物。**2 -loving** (in adjectives 構成形容詞) enjoying the object or activity mentioned 愛好…的；鍾愛…的：*fun-loving young people* 喜歡玩樂的年輕人 ▸ **lov·ing·ly** *adv.*：*He gazed lovingly at his children.* 他慈愛地注視着自己的孩子。◇ *The house has been lovingly restored.* 這所房子已經過精心修復。

ˈloving cup *noun* (*old use*) a large cup with two handles, which guests pass around and drink from 讚頌杯（雙耳大杯，供客人輪飲）

low 0-w /ləʊ; *NAmE* loʊ/ *adj., adv., noun, verb*

■ *adj.* (**lower**, **low·est**)

▸ NOT HIGH/TALL 低；矮 **1** 0-w not high or tall; not far above the ground 低的；矮的；離地面近的：*a low wall/building/table* 矮牆／建築物／桌子 ◇ *a low range of hills* 低矮的岡巒 ◇ *low clouds* 低雲 ◇ *flying at low altitude* 低空飛行 ◇ *The sun was low in the sky.* 太陽低掛在天空。OPP **high**

▸ NEAR BOTTOM 接近底部 **2** 0-w at or near the bottom of sth 在底部的；近底部的：*low back pain* 腰疼 ◇ *the lower slopes of the mountain* 山麓斜坡 ◇ *temperatures in the low 20s* (= no higher than 21–23°) 略高於 20 度的溫度 OPP **high**

▸ CLOTHING 衣服 **3** not high at the neck 領口開得低的：*a dress with a low neckline* 領口低的連衣裙 ➲ see also LOW-CUT

▸ LEVEL/VALUE 水平；價值 **4** 0-w (also **low-**) (often in compounds 常構成複合詞) below the usual or average amount, level or value 低於通常（或平均）數量（或水平、價值）的：*low prices* 低價 ◇ *low-income families* 低收入家庭 ◇ *a low-cost airline* 低成本運作的航空公司 ◇ *the lowest temperature ever recorded* 有記錄以來最低的溫度 ◇ *a low level of unemployment* 低失業率 ◇ *Yogurt is usually very low in fat.* 酸奶的脂肪含量通常很低。◇ *low-fat yogurt* 低脂酸奶 ◇ *low-tar cigarettes* 尼古丁含量低的捲煙 OPP **high** **5** 0-w having a reduced amount or not enough of sth（數量）減少的，縮減的；（某物）不足的：*The reservoir was low after the long drought.* 久旱之後水庫的水位下降了。◇ *Our supplies are* **running low** (= we only have a little left). 我們的供給品快用完了。◇ *They were* **low on** *fuel.* 他們的燃料快耗盡了。

‣ SOUND 聲音 **6** ⊶ not high; not loud 低聲的；小聲的；輕聲的： *The cello is lower than the violin.* 大提琴的聲音比小提琴低沉。◇ *They were speaking in low voices.* 他們在低聲說話。 OPP **high**
‣ STANDARD 標準 **7** ⊶ below the usual or expected standard 低於通常（或預期）標準的： *students with low marks/grades in their exams* 考試得分低的學生 ◇ *a low standard of living* 生活水平低 OPP **high**
‣ STATUS 地位 **8** ⊶ below other people or things in importance or status 低下的；次要的；低等的： *low forms of life* (= creatures with a very simple structure) 低等動物 ◇ *jobs with low status* 社會地位低下的職業 ◇ *Training was given a very low priority.* 培訓被擺在了非常次要的地位。◇ *the* **lower classes** *of society* 下層社會 OPP **high**
‣ OPINION 看法 **9** ⊶ [usually before noun] not very good 不好的；差的 SYN **poor**： *She has a very low opinion of her own abilities.* 她認為自己的能力很差。 OPP **high**
‣ DEPRESSED 沮喪 **10** weak or depressed; with very little energy 虛弱的；沮喪的；消沉的；無精打采的 SYN **down**： *I'm feeling really low.* 我現在很消沉。◇ *They were in low spirits.* 他們精神不振。
‣ NOT HONEST 不誠實 **11** (of a person 人) not honest 不誠實的；不正直的 SYN **disreputable**： *He mixes with some pretty low types.* 他和一些不三不四的人廝混在一起。
‣ LIGHT 光線 **12** not bright 暗淡的；微弱的 SYN **dim**： *The lights were low and romance was in the air.* 燈光暗淡，彌漫着浪漫情調。
‣ IN VEHICLE 交通工具 **13** if a vehicle is in **low gear**, it travels at a slower speed in relation to the speed of the engine 低速擋的
‣ PHONETICS 語音學 **14** (*phonetics* 語音) = OPEN *adj.* (19)

IDM **at a low 'ebb** in a poor state; worse than usual 處於低潮；狀況不佳： *Morale among teachers is at a low ebb.* 教師的精神面貌處於低潮。 **be brought 'low** (*old-fashioned*) to lose your wealth or your high position in society 失去財富；喪失社會地位 **lay sb 'low** if sb is **laid low** by/with an injury or illness, they feel very weak and are unable to do much （傷或病）使感到衰弱 **the ˌlowest of the 'low** people who are not respected at all because they are dishonest, immoral or not at all important 卑鄙小人；道德敗壞的人；無足輕重的人 ➲ more at PROFILE *n.*

■ ***adv.*** (**lower**, **low·est**)
‣ NOT HIGH 不高 **1** ⊶ in or into a low position, not far above the ground 低；向下；不高： *to crouch/bend low* 蹲下；俯身 ◇ *a plane flying low over the town* 在城鎮上方低空飛行的飛機 ◇ *low-flying aircraft* 低空飛行的飛機 ◇ *The sun sank lower towards the horizon.* 太陽漸漸西沉。
‣ NEAR BOTTOM 接近底部 **2** ⊶ in or into a position near the bottom of sth 在靠近…底部的位置；向…底部： *a window set low in the wall* 窗台低的窗戶 ◇ *The candles were burning low.* 蠟燭快燒完了。
‣ LEVEL 水平 **3** ⊶ (especially in compounds 尤用於構成複合詞) at a level below what is usual or expected 低於通常（或預期）的水平： *low-priced goods* 低價商品 ◇ *a low-powered PC* 低功率的個人電腦 ◇ *a very low-scoring game* 得分很低的比賽
‣ SOUND 聲音 **4** ⊶ not high; not loudly 低聲地；小聲地： *He's singing an octave lower than the rest of us.* 他唱的比我們其他人都低八度。◇ *Can you turn the music lower—you'll wake the baby.* 能不能把音樂放小點，別把孩子吵醒了。 IDM see HIGH *adv.*, LIE[1] *v.*, SINK *v.*, STOOP *v.*

■ ***noun***
‣ LEVEL/VALUE 水平；價值 **1** a low level or point; a low figure 低水平；低點；低數目： *The yen has fallen to* ***an all-time low*** *against the dollar.* 日元對美元的比價已跌至空前的低點。◇ *The temperature reached a record low in London last night.* 昨晚倫敦的氣溫降到了有記錄以來的最低點。◇ *The government's popularity has hit a new low.* 政府的聲望降到了一個新的低點。
‣ DIFFICULT TIME 艱難時期 **2** a very difficult time in sb's life or career （一生或事業中的）艱難時期，低谷： *The break-up of her marriage marked* ***an all-time low*** *in her life.* 婚姻破裂使她開始了人生中最艱難的日子。
‣ WEATHER 天氣 **3** an area of low pressure in the atmosphere 低氣壓區： *Another low is moving in from the Atlantic.* 另一個低氣壓區正從大西洋逼近。 OPP **high**

■ ***verb*** [I] (*literary*) when a cow **lows**, it makes a deep sound （牛）哞哞叫 SYN **moo**

low·ball /ˈləʊbɔːl; *NAmE* ˈloʊ-/ *verb* **~ sth** (*NAmE, informal*) to deliberately make an estimate of the cost, value, etc. of sth that is too low 有意壓低估價；虛報低價： *He lowballed the cost of the project in order to obtain federal funding.* 他為了得到聯邦資助而故意壓低項目的成本價格。 OPP **highball**

ˌlow-'born *adj.* (*old-fashioned* or *formal*) having parents who are members of a low social class 出身低微的 OPP **high-born**

low·brow /ˈləʊbraʊ; *NAmE* ˈloʊ-/ *adj.* (usually *disapproving*) having no connection with or interest in serious artistic or cultural ideas 無藝術文化修養的；對藝術文化無興趣的 OPP **highbrow** ➲ compare MIDDLEBROW

low-cal (also **lo-cal**) /ˌləʊ ˈkæl; *NAmE* ˌloʊ/ *adj.* (*informal*) (of food and drink 食物和飲料) containing very few CALORIES 低熱量的

ˌLow 'Church *adj.* connected with the part of the Anglican Church that considers priests and the traditional forms and ceremonies of the Anglican Church to be less important than personal faith and worship 低派教會的（聖公會的一派，認為牧師和傳統宗教儀式不如個人的信仰和崇拜重要）

ˌlow-'class *adj.* **1** of poor quality 低劣的；低級的 **2** connected with a low social class 社會地位低下的；下層社會的 OPP **high-class**

the 'Low Countries *noun* [pl.] the region of Europe which consists of the Netherlands, Belgium and Luxembourg (used especially in the past) 低地國家（包括荷蘭、比利時和盧森堡，尤用於舊時）

ˌlow-'cut *adj.* (of dresses, etc. 連衣裙等) with the top very low so that you can see the neck and the top of the chest 領口開得低的；袒胸露頸的

'low-down *adj., noun*
■ ***adj.*** [only before noun] (*informal*) not fair or honest 不公正的；不誠實的；欺詐的 SYN **mean**： *What a dirty, low-down trick!* 多麼骯髒、卑劣的伎倆！
■ ***noun*** **the low-down** [sing.] **~ on** (**sb/sth**) (*informal*) the true facts about sb/sth, especially those considered most important to know 真相；（尤指）重要事實： *Jane gave me the low-down on the other guests at the party.* 簡告訴了我聚會上其他來賓的真實情況。

'low-end *adj.* [usually before noun] at the cheaper end of a range of similar products （產品）低檔的

lower[1] /ˈləʊə(r); *NAmE* ˈloʊ-/ *adj., verb* ➲ see also LOWER[2]
■ ***adj.*** [only before noun] **1** located below sth else, especially sth of the same type, or the other of a pair（尤指位於同類物品或成對物品中另一個的）下面的，下方的： *the lower deck of a ship* 船的下甲板 ◇ *His lower lip trembled.* 他的下唇在顫抖。 **2** at or near the bottom of sth 在底部的；近底部的： *the mountain's lower slopes* 山麓斜坡 **3** (of a place 地方) located towards the coast, on low ground or towards the south of an area 朝海岸的；低窪的；向南的： *the lower reaches of the Nile* 尼羅河的下游 OPP **upper**
■ ***verb*** **1** [T] to let or make sth/sb go down 把…放低；使…降下： **~ sth** *He had to lower his head to get through the door.* 他得低頭才能過這道門。◇ *She lowered her newspaper and looked around.* 她放低報紙往四下看了看。◇ **~ sth/sb + adv./prep.** *They lowered him down the cliff on a rope.* 他們用繩索把他放下懸崖。 OPP **raise** **2** [T, I] **~ (sth)** to reduce sth or to become less in value, quality, etc. 減少；縮小；降低： *He lowered his voice to a whisper.* 他壓低了聲音悄悄地說。◇ *This drug is used to lower blood pressure.* 這種藥用於降血壓。◇ *Her voice lowered as she spoke.* 她一邊說一邊壓低了嗓音。 OPP **raise**

IDM **lower the 'bar** to set a new, lower standard of quality or performance 降低標準： *In the current economic climate we may need to lower the bar on quotas.* 在目前的經濟氣候下，我們可能需要降低配額標準。 OPP **raise the bar** ➲ compare SET THE BAR at BAR *n.* **'lower yourself (by doing sth)** (usually used in negative sentences 通常用於否定句) to behave in a way that makes other people respect you less 降低自己的身分；自貶人格 SYN **demean**：*I wouldn't lower myself by working for him.* 我不會貶低自己的身分去為他工作。➲ more at SIGHT *n.*, TEMPERATURE

lower² (also **lour**) /ˈlaʊə(r)/ *verb* [I] (*literary*) (of the sky or clouds 天空或雲) to be dark and threatening 變昏暗；變惡劣；變陰沉 ➲ see also LOWER¹

ˌlower ˈcase *noun* [U] (*technical* 術語) (in printing and writing 印刷和書寫) small letters 小寫字體：*The text is all in lower case.* 正文一律用小寫字體。◇ *lower-case letters* 小寫字母 ➲ compare CAPITAL *adj.* (2), UPPER CASE

ˌlowerˈchamber *noun* = LOWER HOUSE

the ˌlower ˈclasses *noun* [pl.] (also **the ˌlower ˈclass** [sing.]) the groups of people who are considered to have the lowest social status and who have less money and/or power than other people in society 下層社會；社會地位低下的階層 ▸ **ˌlower ˈclass** *adj.*：*The new bosses were condemned as 'too lower class'.* 這些新頭頭被指責為“層次太低”。◇ *a lower-class accent* 下層社會的口音 ➲ compare UPPER CLASS

ˌlower ˈhouse (also **ˌlower ˈchamber**) *noun* [sing.] the larger group of people who make laws in a country, usually consisting of elected representatives, such as the House of Commons in Britain or the House of Representatives in the US 下議院；（英國）平民院；（美國）眾議院 ➲ compare UPPER HOUSE

L

the ˌlower ˈorders *noun* [pl.] (*old-fashioned*) people who are considered to be less important because they belong to groups with a lower social status 下層社會

ˈlower school *noun* a school, or the classes in a school, for younger students, usually between the ages of 11 and 14 低年級學校，低年級班（學生年齡通常在 11 至 14 歲之間）➲ compare UPPER SCHOOL

ˌlowest ˌcommon deˈnominator *noun* **1** (*NAmE* usually **ˌleast ˌcommon deˈnominator**) (*mathematics* 數) the smallest number that the bottom numbers of a group of FRACTIONS can be divided into exactly 最小公分母 **2** (*NAmE* also **ˌleast ˌcommon deˈnominator**) (*disapproving*) something that is simple enough to seem interesting to, or to be understood by, the highest number of people in a particular group; the sort of people who are least intelligent or accept sth that is of low quality 大眾化的東西；最平庸的人：*The school syllabus seems aimed at the lowest common denominator.* 學校的教學大綱似乎是針對接受能力最差的學生制訂的。

ˌlowest ˌcommon ˈmultiple (*NAmE* usually **ˌleast ˌcommon ˈmultiple**) *noun* (*mathematics* 數) the smallest number that a group of numbers can be divided into exactly 最小公倍數

ˌlow-ˈfat *adj.* [usually before noun] containing only a very small amount of fat 低脂肪的

ˌlow-ˈgrade *adj.* [usually before noun] **1** of low quality 質量差的；劣質的 **2** (*medical* 醫) of a less serious type 不太嚴重的；輕度的：*a low-grade infection* 輕度感染

ˌlow-ˈimpact *adj.* [usually before noun] **1** involving movements that do not put a lot of stress on the body （動作）低力度的，低強度的：*low-impact aerobics* 低強度有氧運動 **2** not causing very many problems or changes, especially in the environment （尤指對環境）低衝擊的，負面影響小的：*low-impact tourism* 對環境負面影響甚小的旅遊業

ˌlow-ˈkey *adj.* not intended to attract a lot of attention 低調的；不招搖的：*Their wedding was a very low-key affair.* 他們的婚禮辦得很低調。

low·land /ˈləʊlənd; *NAmE* ˈloʊ-/ *adj.*, *noun*

■ ***adj.*** [only before noun] connected with an area of land that is fairly flat and not very high above sea level 低地的 ➲ compare HIGHLAND

■ ***noun*** [pl., U] an area of land that is fairly flat and not very high above sea level 低地：*the lowlands of Scotland* 蘇格蘭低地 ◇ *Much of the region is lowland.* 這地區大部份是低窪地。➲ compare HIGHLAND

low·land·er /ˈləʊləndə(r); *NAmE* ˈloʊ-/ *noun* a person who comes from an area which is flat and low 低地人 ➲ compare HIGHLANDER (1)

ˌlow-ˈlevel *adj.* [usually before noun] **1** close to the ground 離地面近的；低的：*low-level bombing attacks* 低空轟炸襲擊 **2** of low rank; involving people of junior rank 低級別的；初級的：*a low-level job* 低級職位 ◇ *low-level negotiations* 低級別的談判 **3** not containing much of a particular substance especially RADIOACTIVITY（尤指放射性）含量低的：*low-level radioactive waste* 放射性低的廢料 **4** (*computing* 計) (of a computer language 計算機語言) similar to MACHINE CODE in form 類似機器碼的；低級的 OPP **high-level**

ˈlow life *noun* [U] the life and behaviour of people who are outside normal society, especially criminals 下層社會的生活及行為；社會渣滓的生活及行為 ▸ **ˈlow-life** *adj.*：*a low-life bar* 社會渣滓聚集的酒吧

low·lights /ˈləʊlaɪts; *NAmE* ˈloʊl-/ *noun* [pl.] areas of hair that have been made darker than the rest, with the use of a chemical substance 顏色較暗的染髮部位 ➲ compare HIGHLIGHTS at HIGHLIGHT *n.* (2)

lowly /ˈləʊli; *NAmE* ˈloʊli/ *adj.* (**low·lier**, **low·li·est**) (often *humorous*) low in status or importance 地位低的；不重要的；無足輕重的 SYN **humble, obscure**

ˌlow-ˈlying *adj.* (of land 土地) not high, and usually fairly flat 低的；低窪的

ˌlow-ˈmaintenance *adj.* not needing much attention or effort 無須費神（或費力）的；易養護的：*a low-maintenance garden* 易於養護的花園 OPP **high-maintenance**

ˌlow-ˈpaid *adj.* earning or providing very little money 掙錢少的；報酬低的：*low-paid workers* 掙錢少的工人 ◇ *It is one of the lowest-paid jobs.* 那是薪水最低的一種職業。

ˌlow-ˈpitched *adj.* (of sounds 聲音) deep; low 低沉的；低聲的：*a low-pitched voice* 低沉的嗓音 OPP **high-pitched**

ˈlow point *noun* the least interesting, enjoyable or worst part of sth 最無趣的部份；最差的部份 OPP **high point**

ˌlow ˈpressure *noun* [U] **1** the condition of air, gas or liquid that is kept in a container with little force（氣體或液體的）低壓：*Water supplies to the house are **at low pressure**.* 這房子的供水水壓低。**2** a condition of the air which affects the weather when the pressure is lower than average（影響天氣的）低氣壓 ➲ compare HIGH PRESSURE

ˌlow-ˈprofile *adj.* [only before noun] receiving or involving very little attention 不引人注目的；不顯眼的；低調的；低姿態的：*a low-profile campaign* 不引人注目的運動 ➲ see also PROFILE *n.*

ˌlow-ˈranking *adj.* junior; not very important 初級的；位置不重要的：***a low-ranking officer/official*** 下級軍官／官員 OPP **high-ranking**

ˌlow-ˈrent *adj.* (*especially NAmE*) of poor quality or low social status 劣質的；社會地位低的：*her low-rent boyfriend* 她那卑微的男朋友

ˌlow-resoˈlution (also **lo-res**, **low-res** /ˌləʊ ˈrez; *NAmE* ˌloʊ/) *adj.* (of a photograph or an image on a computer or television screen 照片或計算機、電視屏幕影像) not showing a lot of clear detail 低分辨率的；低解析度的；低解像度的：*a low-resolution scan* 低清晰度掃描 OPP **high-resolution**

ˈlow-rise *adj.*, *noun*

■ ***adj.*** [only before noun] **1** (of a building 建築物) low, with only a few floors 樓層少的；低層的：*low-rise housing* 低層住宅 ➲ compare HIGH-RISE **2** (of a pair of jeans, etc. 牛仔褲等) cut so that the top is much lower than waist-level 低腰剪裁的

■ ***noun*** a low building with only a few floors 低層建築

ˌlow-ˈrisk *adj.* [usually before noun] involving only a small amount of danger and little risk of injury, death, damage, etc. 低風險的 SYN **safe**：*a low-risk investment* 低風險投資 ◇ *low-risk patients* (= who are very unlikely to get a particular illness) 患病幾率低的病人 **OPP** **high-risk**

ˈlow season (also **ˈoff season**) *noun* [U, sing.] (*especially BrE*) the time of year when a hotel or tourist area receives fewest visitors（旅館或旅遊地區的）淡季 **OPP** **high season**

ˌlow ˈslung *adj.* very low and close to the ground 低的；接近地面的

ˌlow-ˈtech (also **ˌlo-ˈtech**) *adj.* (*informal*) not involving the most modern technology or methods 低技術的；低科技的；不涉及最現代技術（或方法）的 **OPP** **high-tech**

ˌlow ˈtide (also **ˌlow ˈwater**) *noun* [U, C] the time when the sea is at its lowest level; the sea at this time（大海的）低潮時期，低潮：*The island can only be reached* ***at low tide.*** 這座島只能在退潮時上去。**OPP** **high tide**

ˌlow-ˈwater mark *noun* a line or mark showing the lowest point that the sea reaches at low tide 低潮線；低潮水位標記 **OPP** **high-water mark**

lox /lɒks; *NAmE* lɑːks/ *noun* [U] (*NAmE*) smoked SALMON (= a type of fish) 熏鮭魚；熏大麻哈魚

loyal 0‑ /ˈlɔɪəl/ *adj.*
~ (to sb/sth) remaining faithful to sb/sth and supporting them or it 忠誠的；忠實的 **SYN** **true**：*a* ***loyal friend/supporter*** 忠實的朋友／支持者 ◇ *She has always* ***remained loyal to*** *her political principles.* 她總是信守自己的政治原則。**OPP** **disloyal** ▸ **loy·al·ly** /ˈlɔɪəli/ *adv.*

loyal·ist /ˈlɔɪəlɪst/ *noun* **1** a person who is loyal to the ruler or government, or to a political party, especially during a time of change（尤指在變動時期對統治者、政府或政黨）忠誠的人 **2** **Loyalist** a person who supports the union between Great Britain and Northern Ireland 支持大不列顛和北愛爾蘭聯合的人 ➲ compare REPUBLICAN *n.* (3)

loy·alty /ˈlɔɪəlti/ *noun* (*pl.* **-ies**) **1** [U] **~ (to/towards sb/sth)** the quality of being faithful in your support of sb/sth 忠誠；忠實；忠心耿耿：*They swore their loyalty to the king.* 他們宣誓效忠國王。◇ *Can I count on your loyalty?* 我能指望你對我忠誠嗎？ **2** [C, usually pl.] a strong feeling that you want to be loyal to sb/sth 要忠於…的強烈感情：*a case of* ***divided loyalties*** (= with strong feelings of support for two different causes, people, etc.) 兩面效忠

ˈloyalty card *noun* (*BrE*) a card given to customers by a shop/store to encourage them to shop there regularly. Each time they buy sth they collect points which will allow them to have an amount of money taken off goods they buy in the future. 顧客忠誠卡，積分卡，集點卡（憑消費累積的集點可優惠購物）

loz·enge /ˈlɒzɪndʒ; *NAmE* ˈlɑːz-/ *noun* **1** (*geometry* 幾何) a figure with four sides in the shape of a diamond that has two opposite angles more than 90° and the other two less than 90° 菱形 **2** a small sweet/candy, often in a lozenge shape, especially one that contains medicine and that you dissolve in your mouth 菱形糖果；（尤指）菱形含片藥物：***throat/cough lozenges*** 潤喉／止咳糖片

LP /ˌel ˈpiː/ *noun* the abbreviation for 'long-playing record' (a record that plays for about 25 minutes each side and turns 33 times per minute) 密紋唱片（全寫為 long-playing record，每面約 25 分鐘、每分鐘 33 轉的唱片）

LPG /ˌel piː ˈdʒiː/ *noun* [U] the abbreviation for 'liquefied petroleum gas' (a fuel which is a mixture of gases kept in a liquid form by the pressure in a container) 液化石油氣（全寫為 liquefied petroleum gas）

ˈL-plate *noun* (in Britain and some other countries) a white sign with a large red letter L on it, that you put on a car when you are learning to drive 紅 L 字牌，學車牌（在英國等地學駕駛時置於車上的白色標誌）

LPN /ˌel piː ˈen/ *abbr.* (in the US) licensed practical nurse（美國）持執照臨牀護士

LSAT /ˌel es eɪ ˈtiː/ *abbr.* Law School Admission Test (a test taken by students who want to study law in the US)（美國）法學院入學考試

LSD /ˌel es ˈdiː/ (also *slang* **acid**) *noun* [U] a powerful illegal drug that affects people's minds and makes them see and hear things that are not really there 迷幻藥；致幻藥

Lt (*BrE*) (*NAmE* **Lt.**) *abbr.* (in writing) LIEUTENANT（書寫形式）（陸軍）中尉，（海軍或空軍）上尉：*Lt (Helen) Brown*（海倫）布朗陸軍中尉

Ltd *abbr.* Limited (used after the name of a British company or business) 有限責任公司，股份有限公司（用於英國公司或商行名稱之後）：*Pearce and Co. Ltd* 皮爾斯有限公司

lu·bri·cant /ˈluːbrɪkənt/ (also *informal* **lube** /luːb/) *noun* [U, C] a substance, for example oil, that you put on surfaces or parts of a machine so that they move easily and smoothly 潤滑劑；潤滑油

lu·bri·cate /ˈluːbrɪkeɪt/ *verb* **~ sth** to put a lubricant on sth such as the parts of a machine, to help them move smoothly 給…上潤滑油；上油 **SYN** **grease, oil** ▸ **lu·bri·ca·tion** /ˌluːbrɪˈkeɪʃn/ *noun* [U]

lu·bri·cious /luːˈbrɪʃəs/ *adj.* (*formal*) showing a great interest in sex in a way that is considered unpleasant or unacceptable 淫蕩的；淫穢的；猥褻的 **SYN** **lewd**

lucid /ˈluːsɪd/ *adj.* **1** clearly expressed; easy to understand 表達清楚的；易懂的 **SYN** **clear**：*a lucid style/explanation* 明白易懂的風格；清楚的解釋 **2** able to think clearly, especially during or after a period of illness or confusion（尤指生病期間或病癒後，糊塗狀態中或過後）頭腦清晰的，清醒的：*In a rare lucid moment, she looked at me and smiled.* 在難得清醒的時刻，她看看我，笑了笑。 ▸ **lu·cid·ity** /luːˈsɪdəti/ *noun* [U] **lu·cid·ly** *adv.*

Lu·ci·fer /ˈluːsɪfə(r)/ *noun* [sing.] the DEVIL 路濟弗爾（魔鬼）**SYN** **Satan**

luck 0‑ /lʌk/ *noun, verb*
■ ***noun*** [U] **1** 0‑ good things that happen to you by chance, not because of your own efforts or abilities 好運；幸運；僥幸：***With*** *(****any****)* ***luck****, we'll be home before dark.* 如果一切順利的話，我們可在天黑前回到家。◇ (*BrE*) ***With a bit of luck****, we'll finish on time.* 但願我們運氣好，能夠準時完成。◇ *So far I have had no luck with finding a job.* 我找工作一直不走運。◇ ***I could hardly believe my luck*** *when he said yes.* 聽他說行，我幾乎不敢相信自己會這麼走運。◇ *It was* ***a stroke of luck*** *that we found you.* 真巧我們找到了你。◇ ***By sheer luck*** *nobody was hurt in the explosion.* 萬幸的是，沒有人在爆炸中受傷。◇ *We* ***wish her luck*** *in her new career.* 我們祝願她在新的事業中一帆風順。◇ *You're* ***in luck*** (= lucky)—*there's one ticket left.* 你運氣不錯，還剩一張票。◇ *You're* ***out of luck****. She's not here.* 真不巧，她不在。◇ *What a piece of luck!* 運氣真好！ ➲ see also BEGINNER'S LUCK
2 0‑ chance; the force that causes good or bad things to happen to people 機遇；命運；運氣 **SYN** **fortune**：*to have* ***good/bad luck*** 運氣好；運氣壞 ➲ see also HARD-LUCK STORY

IDM **any ˈluck?** (*informal*) used to ask sb if they have been successful with sth（詢問是否成功）運氣怎麼樣：*'Any luck?' 'No, they're all too busy to help.'* "運氣怎麼樣？" "不怎麼樣，他們都沒空幫忙。" **as luck would ˈhave it** in the way that chance decides what will happen 碰巧；偶然；幸而；不巧：*As luck would have it, the train was late.* 不巧火車晚點了。 **bad, hard, etc. luck (on sb)** used to express sympathy for sb（表示同情）運氣不佳，不幸：*Bad luck, Helen, you played very well.* 海倫，你表現得非常好，只是運氣欠佳。◇ *It's hard luck on him that he wasn't chosen.* 他未被選中真是不幸。 **be down on your ˈluck** (*informal*) to have no money because of a period of bad luck 因一時不走運而沒有錢；窮困潦倒 **the best of ˈluck (with sth)** | **good ˈluck (with sth)** 0‑ (*informal*) used to wish sb success with sth 祝成功；祝好運：*The best of luck with your exams.* 祝你考試成功！◇ *Good luck! I hope it goes well.* 祝你交好運！我希望這事進展順利。 **ˌbetter luck ˈnext time** (*informal*) used to encourage sb who has not been successful at sth（鼓勵未成功的人）祝下次好運 **for ˈluck** **1** because you believe it will bring you good luck, or because this is a traditional belief 圖個吉利；為了帶來好運：*Take something blue. It's for luck.* 挑件藍色的東西吧，求個

吉利。 **2** (*informal*) for no particular reason 無緣無故：*I hit him once more for luck.* 我無故又打了他一下。 **good 'luck to sb** (*informal*) used to say that you do not mind what sb does as it does not affect you, but you hope they will be successful（與己無關而不介意某人的所為）祝某人成功，祝某人走運：*It's not something I would care to try myself but if she wants to, good luck to her.* 這件事我自己是不想做的，但如果她想試一試，祝願她成功。 **just my/sb's 'luck** (*informal*) used to show you are not surprised sth bad has happened to you, because you are not often lucky（對自己的遭遇並不驚訝）常不走運，就這運氣：*Just my luck to arrive after they had left.* 我總是這樣倒霉，他們離去後我才趕到。 **your/sb's 'luck is in** used to say that sb has been lucky or successful 交好運；走運 **the luck of the 'draw** the fact that chance decides sth, in a way that you cannot control 運氣的結果 **no such 'luck** used to show disappointment that sth you were hoping for did not happen（所希望的事情沒有發生而失望）沒那麼走運 ➲ more at HARD *adj.*, POT *n.*, PUSH *v.*, TOUGH *adj.*, TRY *v.*, WORSE *adj.*

■ *verb*

PHR V **,luck 'out** (*NAmE, informal*) to be lucky 走運；交好運：*I guess I really lucked out when I met her.* 我想，我遇到她真是交了好運。

luck·less /ˈlʌkləs/ *adj.* having bad luck 運氣不好的；不走運的；不幸的 SYN **unlucky**：*the luckless victim of the attack* 遭到襲擊的不幸受害者

lucky 0➡ /ˈlʌki/ *adj.* (**luck·ier, lucki·est**)
1 0➡ having good luck 有好運的；運氣好的；幸運的 SYN **fortunate**：**~ (to do sth)** *His friend was killed and he knows he is lucky to be alive.* 他的朋友喪了命，他知道自己還活着是僥幸。◇ *She was lucky enough to be chosen for the team.* 她很幸運被選中參加此隊。◇ **~ (that …)** *You were lucky (that) you spotted the danger in time.* 幸好你及時發現了險情。◇ *You can* ***think yourself lucky*** *you didn't get mugged.* 你未遭暴力搶劫，可算是萬幸了。◇ *She* ***counted herself lucky*** *that she still had a job.* 她認為自己很幸運，仍有一份工作。◇ *Mark is* ***one of the lucky ones*** *—he at least has somewhere to sleep.* 馬克是個幸運的人，他至少還有地方睡覺。◇ *the lucky winners* 幸運的獲勝者 **2** 0➡ **~ (for sb) (that …)** being the result of good luck 好運帶來的：***It was lucky for us that*** *we were able to go.* 我們能去是我們的運氣好。◇ *That was the luckiest escape of my life.* 那次逃脫是我一生中最大的幸運。◇ *a lucky guess* 僥幸猜中 **3** 0➡ bringing good luck 帶來好運的：*a lucky charm* 吉祥符 ▸ **luck·ily** /ˈlʌkɪli/ *adv.*：**~ (for sb)** *Luckily for us, the train was late.* 我們真湊巧，火車晚點了。◇ *Luckily, I am a good swimmer.* 幸好我是個游泳好手。

IDM **lucky 'you, 'me, etc.** (*informal*) used to show that you think sb is lucky to have sth, be able to do sth, etc. 你（或我等）真走運：*'I'm off to Paris.' 'Lucky you!'* "我要去巴黎了。" "你真幸運！" **,you'll be 'lucky** (*informal*) used to tell sb that sth that they are expecting probably will not happen（告訴某人所期盼的事很可能不會發生）但願你會走運：*'I was hoping to get a ticket for Saturday.' 'You'll be lucky.'* "我盼望弄到一張星期六的票。" "但願你會走運。" **,you, etc. should be so 'lucky** (*informal*) used to tell sb that they will probably not get what they are hoping for, and may not deserve it（告訴某人所希望之物可能得不到，且本不該其得到）你不見得這麼走運吧 ➲ more at STRIKE *v.*, THANK, THIRD *ordinal number*

,lucky 'dip (*BrE*) (*NAmE* **'grab bag**) *noun* [usually sing.] a game in which people choose a present from a container of presents without being able to see what it is going to be 摸彩遊戲

lu·cra·tive /ˈluːkrətɪv/ *adj.* producing a large amount of money; making a large profit 賺大錢的；獲利多的：*a* ***lucrative business/contract/market*** 利潤豐厚的生意 / 合同 / 市場 ➲ SYNONYMS at SUCCESSFUL ▸ **lu·cra·tive·ly** *adv.*

lucre /ˈluːkə(r)/ *noun* [U] (*disapproving*) money, especially when it has been obtained in a way that is dishonest or immoral（尤指來路不正的）錢財：*the lure of* ***filthy lucre*** 不義之財的誘惑

Lud·dite /ˈlʌdaɪt/ *noun* (*BrE, disapproving*) a person who is opposed to new technology or working methods 反對新技術（或新工作方法）的人 ORIGIN Named after Ned **Lud**, one of the workers who destroyed machinery in factories in the early 19th century, because they believed it would take away their jobs. 源自 19 世紀初的工人內德 • 盧德，他同其他一些工人認為機器會奪走其工作而將工廠機器搗毀。

ludic /ˈluːdɪk/ *adj.* (*formal*) showing a tendency to play and have fun, make jokes, etc., especially when there is no particular reason for doing this 頑皮的；愛開玩笑的

ludi·crous /ˈluːdɪkrəs/ *adj.* unreasonable; that you cannot take seriously 不合理的；不能當真的 SYN **absurd, ridiculous**：*a ludicrous suggestion* 荒謬的建議 ◇ *It was ludicrous to think that the plan could succeed.* 認為此計劃會取得成功是荒唐的。▸ **ludi·crous·ly** *adv.*：*ludicrously expensive* 貴得出奇 **ludi·crous·ness** *noun* [U]

ludo /ˈluːdəʊ; *NAmE* -doʊ/ *noun* [U] (*BrE*) a simple game played with DICE and COUNTERS on a special board, similar to the American game, PARCHEESI 盧多（一種用骰子和籌碼在棋盤上玩的遊戲，類似於美國的巴棋戲）

Synonyms 同義詞辨析

luck

chance • coincidence • accident • fate • destiny

These are all words for things that happen or the force that causes them to happen. 以上各詞均指機遇、命運、運氣。

luck the force that causes good or bad things to happen to people 指機遇、命運、運氣：*This ring has always brought me good luck.* 這戒指總是給我帶來好運。

chance the way that some things happen without any cause that you can see or understand 指偶然、碰巧、意外：*The results could simply be due to chance.* 這結果可能純屬意外。

coincidence the fact of two things happening at the same time by chance, in a surprising way 指出人意料的巧合、巧事：*They met through a series of strange coincidences.* 他們因一連串奇妙的巧合而相遇。

accident something that happens unexpectedly and is not planned in advance 指意外、偶然的事：*Their early arrival was just an accident.* 他們早到僅僅是偶然而已。

fate the power that is believed to control everything that happens and that cannot be stopped or changed 指命運、天數、定數、天意：*Fate decreed that she would never reach America.* 命中注定她永遠到不了美國。

destiny the power that is believed to control events 指主宰事物的力量、命運之神：*I believe there's some force guiding us—call it God, destiny or fate.* 我總認為有某種力量在指引着我們，稱之為上帝也罷，天意也罷，或是命運也罷。

FATE OR DESTINY? 用 fate 還是 destiny？

Fate can be kind, but this is an unexpected gift; just as often, **fate** is cruel and makes people feel helpless. **Destiny** is more likely to give people a sense of power: people who have *a strong sense of destiny* usually believe that they are meant to be great or do great things. * fate 有時是善意的，但那只是意外的恩賜；fate 往往是殘酷的，使人感到無能為力；destiny 更可能給人權力的感覺，have a strong sense of destiny 指人具有強烈使命感，通常認為自己必將不同凡響或成就偉業。

PATTERNS

- **by** … luck/chance/coincidence/accident
- **It's no** coincidence/accident **that** …
- **pure/sheer** luck/chance/coincidence/accident
- **to believe in** luck/coincidences/fate/destiny

lug /lʌg/ *verb, noun*

■ ***verb*** (-gg-) **~ sth + adv./prep.** (*informal*) to carry or drag sth heavy with a lot of effort 吃力地搬運；用力拖；使勁拉： *I had to lug my bags up to the fourth floor.* 我只得費勁地把我的幾個包拖上五樓。

■ ***noun*** **1** (*technical* 術語) a part of sth that sticks out, used as a handle or support 手柄；把柄；把手 **2** (also **lug·hole**) (both *BrE, humorous*) an ear 耳朵

luge /luːʒ; luːdʒ/ *noun* **1** [C] a type of SLEDGE (= a vehicle for sliding over ice) for racing, used by one person lying on their back with their feet pointing forwards 短雪橇，平底雪橇（比賽用的單人仰卧雪橇） **2 the luge** [sing.] the event or sport of racing down a track of ice on a luge 短雪橇運動；平底雪橇運動 ➲ VISUAL VOCAB page V48

Luger™ /ˈluːgə(r)/ *noun* a type of small gun which was made in Germany 魯格手槍（以前由德國製造）

lug·gage 0‑w /ˈlʌgɪdʒ/ (*especially BrE*) (also **bag·gage** especially in *NAmE*) *noun* [U] bags, cases, etc. that contain sb's clothes and things when they are travelling 行李： *There's room for one more piece of luggage.* 還有地方再放一件行李。◇ *You stay there with the luggage while I find a cab.* 你看着行李，我去找出租車。 ➲ COLLOCATIONS at TRAVEL ➲ note at BAGGAGE ➲ see also HAND LUGGAGE, LEFT-LUGGAGE OFFICE

ˈluggage rack *noun* **1** a shelf for luggage above the seats in a train, bus, etc. （火車、公共汽車等座位上方的）行李架 ➲ picture at RACK **2** (*especially NAmE*) = ROOF RACK

ˈluggage van (*BrE*) (*NAmE* **ˈbaggage car**) *noun* a coach/car on a train for carrying passengers' luggage （火車的）行李車廂

lug·hole /ˈlʌghəʊl; *NAmE* -hoʊl/ *noun* (*BrE, humorous*) = LUG *n.* (2)

lu·gu·bri·ous /ləˈguːbriəs/ *adj.* sad and serious 陰鬱的；悲傷的 SYN **doleful**： *a lugubrious expression* 悲傷的神情 ▸ **lu·gu·bri·ous·ly** *adv.*

lug·worm /ˈlʌgwɜːm; *NAmE* -wɜːrm/ *noun* a large WORM that lives in the sand by the sea. Lugworms are often used as BAIT on a hook to catch fish. 海蚯蚓，沙蠋（常用作釣餌）

luke·warm /ˌluːkˈwɔːm; *NAmE* -ˈwɔːrm/ *adj.* (often *disapproving*) **1** slightly warm 微温的；不冷不熱的；温和的 SYN **tepid**： *Our food was only lukewarm.* 我們的食物只是温乎的。 ➲ SYNONYMS at COLD **2** not interested or enthusiastic 無興趣的；不熱情的： *a lukewarm response* 冷淡的反應 ◇ **~ about sb/sth** *She was lukewarm about the plan.* 她對這個計劃不大感興趣。

lull /lʌl/ *noun, verb*

■ ***noun*** [usually sing.] **~ (in sth)** a quiet period between times of activity（活動間的）平靜時期，間歇： *a **lull in** the conversation/fighting* 談話 / 戰鬥中的沉寂 ◇ *Just before an attack everything would go quiet but we knew it was just **the lull before the storm*** (= before a time of noise or trouble). 就在攻擊開始前一切都變得沉寂，我們知道這只是風暴前的平靜。

■ ***verb*** **1** [T] **~ sb** to make sb relaxed and calm 使放鬆；使鎮靜 SYN **soothe**： *The vibration of the engine **lulled** the children **to sleep**.* 發動機的顫動使得孩子們睡着了。 **2** [T, I] **~ (sth)** to make sth, or to become, less strong （使）減弱；緩和： *His father's arrival lulled the boy's anxiety.* 男孩在他父親來了後便不那麼焦躁不安了。

PHR V **ˌlull sb ˈinto sth** to make sb feel confident and relaxed, especially so that they do not expect it when sb does sth bad or dishonest 麻痺；誘使： *His friendly manner **lulled her into a false sense of security*** (= made her feel safe with him when she should not have). 他友好的舉止使她產生了一種虛假的安全感。

lul·laby /ˈlʌləbaɪ/ *noun* (*pl.* **-ies**) a soft gentle song sung to make a child go to sleep 搖籃曲；催眠曲

lum·bago /lʌmˈbeɪgəʊ; *NAmE* -goʊ/ *noun* [U] pain in the muscles and joints of the lower back 腰痛

lum·bar /ˈlʌmbə(r)/ *adj.* [only before noun] (*medical* 醫) relating to the lower part of the back 腰（部）的

ˌlumbar ˈpuncture (*BrE*) (*NAmE* **ˈspinal tap**) *noun* the removal of liquid from the lower part of the SPINE with a hollow needle 腰椎穿刺

lum·ber /ˈlʌmbə(r)/ *noun, verb*

■ ***noun*** [U] **1** (*especially NAmE*) = TIMBER (2) **2** (*BrE*) pieces of furniture, and other large objects that you do not use any more 廢舊傢具；不用的大件物品： *a lumber room* (= for storing lumber in) 雜物貯藏室

■ ***verb*** **1** [I] **+ adv./prep.** to move in a slow, heavy and awkward way 緩慢吃力地移動；笨拙地行進： *A family of elephants lumbered by.* 一群大象邁着緩慢而沉重的步子從旁邊經過。 **2** [T, usually passive] **~ sb (with sb/sth)** (*informal*) to give sb a responsibility, etc., that they do not want and that they cannot get rid of 迫使擔負（職責等）： *When our parents went out, my sister got lumbered with me for the evening.* 父母外出時，晚上姐姐就得照管我。

lum·ber·ing /ˈlʌmbərɪŋ/ *adj.* moving in a slow, heavy and awkward way 緩慢吃力的；步態笨拙的： *a lumbering dinosaur* 邁着緩慢而沉重步子的恐龍

lum·ber·jack /ˈlʌmbədʒæk; *NAmE* -bərdʒ-/ (also **log·ger**) *noun* (especially in the US and Canada) a person whose job is cutting down trees or cutting or transporting wood （尤指美國和加拿大的）伐木工，木材採運工

lum·ber·yard /ˈlʌmbəjɑːd; *NAmE* ˈlʌmbərjɑːrd/ (*NAmE*) (*BrE* **ˈtim·ber yard**) *noun* a place where wood for building, etc. is stored and sold 木料場；貯木場

lu·men /ˈluːmen/ *noun* (*abbr.* **lm**) (*physics* 物) a unit for measuring the rate of flow of light 流明（光通量單位）

lu·mi·nance /ˈluːmɪnəns/ *noun* [U] (*physics* 物) the amount of light given out in a particular direction from a particular area 亮度

lu·mi·nary /ˈluːmɪnəri; *NAmE* -neri/ *noun* (*pl.* **-ies**) a person who is an expert or a great influence in a special area or activity 專家；權威；有影響的人物

lu·mi·nes·cence /ˌluːmɪˈnesns/ *noun* [U] (*technical* 術語 or *literary*) a quality in sth that produces light 發光；光輝 ▸ **lu·mi·nes·cent** *adj.*

lu·mi·nous /ˈluːmɪnəs/ *adj.* **1** shining in the dark; giving out light 夜光的；發光的；發亮的： *luminous paint* 發光漆 ◇ *luminous hands on a clock* 鐘的夜光指針 ◇ *staring with huge luminous eyes* 用亮晶晶的大眼睛盯着 ◇ (*figurative*) *the luminous quality of the music* 美妙動聽的音樂 **2** very bright in colour 鮮亮的；鮮豔的： *They painted the door a luminous green.* 他們把門漆成了翠綠色。 ▸ **lu·mi·nous·ly** *adv.* **lu·mi·nos·ity** /ˌluːmɪˈnɒsəti; *NAmE* -ˈnɑːs-/ *noun* [sing., U]

lumme /ˈlʌmi/ *exclamation* (*old-fashioned, BrE, informal*) used to show surprise or interest （表示驚訝或感興趣）哎呀，啊

lump 0‑w /lʌmp/ *noun, verb*

■ ***noun*** **1** 0‑w a piece of sth hard or solid, usually without a particular shape （通常為無定形的）塊： *a lump of coal/cheese/wood* 一塊煤 / 奶酪 / 木頭 ◇ *This sauce has lumps in it.* 這調味汁裏有結塊。 **2** (*BrE*) = SUGAR LUMP： *One lump or two?* 加一塊方糖還是兩塊？ **3** 0‑w a swelling under the skin, sometimes a sign of serious illness 腫塊；隆起： *He was unhurt apart from a lump on his head.* 除了頭上起了個包，他沒有別的傷。 ◇ *Check your breasts for lumps every month.* 每月要檢查一次乳房是否有腫塊。 **4** (*informal, especially BrE*) a heavy, lazy or stupid person 笨重的人；懶漢；傻大個

IDM **have, etc. a lump in your throat** to feel pressure in the throat because you are very angry or emotional （因憤怒或情緒激動而）喉嚨哽住，哽咽 **take your ˈlumps** (*NAmE, informal*) to accept bad things that happen to you without complaining 毫無怨言地忍受

■ ***verb*** **~ A and B together** | **~ A (in) with B** to put or consider different things together in the same group 把…歸併一起（或合起來考慮）： *You can't lump all Asian languages together.* 你不能把所有的亞洲語言混為一談。

IDM **ˈlump it** (*informal*) to accept sth unpleasant because there's no other choice （因別無選擇而）勉強接受，將

就，勉為其難：*I'm sorry you're not happy about it but you'll just have to lump it.* 你不滿意我很抱歉，可你只好將就一點了。◇ *That's the situation—like it or lump it!* 情況就是這樣，不管你高興還是不高興！

lump·ec·tomy /lʌmˈpektəmi/ *noun* (*pl.* **-ies**) an operation to remove a TUMOUR from sb's body, especially from a woman's breast（尤指女性乳房的）腫塊切除術

lump·en /ˈlʌmpən/ *adj.* (*BrE, literary*) looking heavy and awkward or stupid 看起來笨重的；樣子愚蠢的

lump·ish /ˈlʌmpɪʃ/ *adj.* heavy and awkward; stupid 笨重的；笨拙的；愚蠢的 SYN **clumsy**

ˌlump ˈsum (also **ˌlump ˌsum ˈpayment**) *noun* an amount of money that is paid at one time and not on separate occasions 一次總付的錢款

lumpy /ˈlʌmpi/ *adj.* full of lumps; covered in lumps 多塊狀物的；為塊狀物覆蓋的：*lumpy sauce* 有顆粒的調味汁 ◇ *a lumpy mattress* 凹凸不平的牀墊

lu·nacy /ˈluːnəsi/ *noun* [U] **1** behaviour that is stupid or crazy 愚蠢的行為；瘋狂 SYN **madness**：*It's sheer lunacy driving in such weather.* 天氣這樣糟糕還開車，真是瘋了。**2** (*old-fashioned*) mental illness 精神病；精神錯亂；精神失常 SYN **madness**

lunar /ˈluːnə(r)/ *adj.* [usually before noun] connected with the moon 月球的；月亮的：*a lunar eclipse/landscape* 月蝕；月球的地貌

ˌlunar ˈcycle *noun* (*astronomy* 天) a period of 19 years, after which the new moon and full moon return to the same day of the year 太陰週期，月運週期，默冬章（週期為 19 年，之後月相會在一年的同一天重現）

ˌlunar ˈmonth *noun* the average time between one new moon and the next (about 29½ days) 太陰月；會合月；朔望月 ➲ compare CALENDAR MONTH (1)

ˌlunar ˈyear *noun* a period of twelve lunar months (about 354 days) 太陰年（12 個太陰月，約 354 天）

lu·na·tic /ˈluːnətɪk/ *noun, adj.*

■ ***noun*** **1** a person who does crazy things that are often dangerous 精神錯亂者；狂人 SYN **maniac**：*This lunatic in a white van pulled out right in front of me!* 這個瘋子開着一輛白色貨車直接衝到了我前面！**2** (*old-fashioned*) a person who is severely mentally ill (the use of this word is now offensive) 嚴重精神病患者，瘋子（現為冒犯語）ORIGIN Originally from the Latin *lunaticus* (*luna* = moon), because people believed that the changes in the moon made people go mad temporarily. 源自拉丁文 lunaticus（luna 即月亮），因人們相信月的盈虧可引發暫時的神經錯亂。

■ ***adj.*** crazy, ridiculous or extremely stupid 瘋狂的；荒唐可笑的；極其愚蠢的：*lunatic ideas* 荒謬的想法 ◇ *a lunatic smile* 傻笑

IDM **the ˌlunatic ˈfringe** *noun* [sing.+sing./pl. v.] (*disapproving*) those members of a political or other group whose views are considered to be very extreme and crazy 極端分子；極端（或狂熱）分子集團

ˈlunatic asylum *noun* (*old-fashioned, especially BrE*) an institution where mentally ill people live 精神病院；瘋人院

lunch 🗝 /lʌntʃ/ *noun, verb*

■ ***noun*** 🗝 [U, C] a meal eaten in the middle of the day 午餐；午飯：*She's gone to lunch.* 她吃午飯去了。◇ *I'm ready for some lunch.* 我想吃點午飯了。◇ *What shall we have* ***for lunch***? 我們午餐吃什麼好呢？◇ *We serve hot and cold lunches.* 我們供應冷熱午餐。◇ *a one-hour* ***lunch break*** 一小時午餐時間 ◇ ***Let's do lunch*** (= have lunch together). 咱們共進午餐吧。➲ COLLOCATIONS at RESTAURANT ➲ note at MEAL ➲ see also BAG LUNCH, BOX LUNCH, PACKED LUNCH, PLOUGHMAN'S LUNCH

IDM **ˌout to ˈlunch** (*informal, especially NAmE*) behaving in a strange or confused way 行為怪異；心不在焉 ➲ more at FREE *adj.*

■ ***verb*** [I] (*formal*) to have lunch, especially at a restaurant（尤指在餐館）用午餐：*He lunched with a client at the Ritz.* 他與一位客戶在里茨餐館共進了午餐。

ˈlunch box *noun* **1** a container to hold a meal that you take away from home to eat（從家帶飯的）午餐盒，飯盒 **2** a small computer that you can carry around "飯盒"，手提電腦（便攜式小型電腦）

lunch·eon /ˈlʌntʃən/ *noun* [C, U] a formal lunch or a formal word for lunch 午餐，午宴（正式的午餐或正式用語）：*a charity luncheon* 慈善午餐會 ◇ *Luncheon will be served at one, Madam.* 夫人，午餐在一點鐘開始。

lunch·eon·ette /ˌlʌntʃəˈnet/ *noun* (*old-fashioned, NAmE*) a small restaurant serving simple meals 快餐館；小吃店

ˈluncheon meat *noun* [U] finely chopped cooked meat that has been pressed together in a container, usually sold in cans and served cold in slices（通常以罐裝出售的）午餐肉

ˈluncheon voucher *noun* a ticket given by some employers in Britain that sb can exchange for food at some restaurants and shops/stores（英國某些雇主提供的可在餐館用餐或在商店換取食物的）午餐券

ˈlunch home *noun* (*IndE*) a restaurant 餐館

ˈlunch hour *noun* the time around the middle of the day when you stop work or school to eat lunch 午餐時間；午休：*I usually go to the gym during my lunch hour.* 我通常在午休時間去健身房。

ˈlunch lady (*US*) (*BrE* **ˈdinner lady**) *noun* a woman whose job is to serve meals to children in schools（學校裏照顧孩子吃飯的）女膳食服務員

lunch·room /ˈlʌntʃruːm; -rʊm/ *noun* (*NAmE*) a large room in a school or office where people eat lunch（學校或辦公樓的）食堂，餐廳

lunch·time /ˈlʌntʃtaɪm/ *noun* [U, C] the time around the middle of the day when people usually eat lunch 午餐時間：*The package still hadn't arrived by lunchtime.* 包裹到午餐時間都還沒有送到。◇ *a lunchtime concert* 午間音樂會 ◇ *The sandwich bar is generally packed at lunchtimes.* 在午餐時間三明治櫃枱前通常都擠滿了人。

lung 🗝 /lʌŋ/ *noun*

either of the two organs in the chest that you use for breathing 肺：*lung cancer* 肺癌 ➲ VISUAL VOCAB page V59

lunge /lʌndʒ/ *verb, noun*

■ ***verb*** [I] ~ **(at/towards/for sb/sth)** | ~ **(forward)** to make a sudden powerful forward movement, especially in order to attack sb or take hold of sth 猛衝；猛撲

■ ***noun*** [usually sing.] **1** ~ **(at sb)** | ~ **(for sb/sth)** a sudden powerful forward movement of the body and arm that a person makes towards another person or thing, especially when attacking or trying to take hold of them 猛衝；猛撲：*He made a lunge for the phone.* 他向電話撲了過去。**2** (in the sport of FENCING 擊劍運動) a THRUST made by putting one foot forward and making the back leg straight 弓箭步刺；戳

lung·fish /ˈlʌŋfɪʃ/ *noun* (*pl.* **lung·fish**) a long fish that can breathe air and survive for a period of time out of water 肺魚

lung·ful /ˈlʌŋfʊl/ *noun* the amount of sth such as air or smoke that is breathed in at one time 一大口（一次吸入的空氣、煙等）

lungi /ˈlʊŋgiː/ *noun* a piece of clothing worn in S and SE Asia consisting of a piece of cloth, usually worn wrapped around the hips and reaching the ankles（南亞和東南亞人長及腳踝的）纏腰布，腰布

lunk·head /ˈlʌŋkhed/ *noun* (*NAmE, informal*) a stupid person 傻瓜；笨蛋

lupin (*BrE*) (*NAmE* **lu·pine**) /ˈluːpɪn/ *noun* a tall garden plant with many small flowers growing up its thick STEM 羽扇豆

lu·pine /ˈluːpaɪn/ *adj.* (*formal*) like a WOLF; connected with a wolf or wolves 狼似的；狼（群）的

lupus /ˈluːpəs/ *noun* [U] a disease that affects the skin or sometimes the joints 狼瘡

lurch /lɜːtʃ; *NAmE* lɜːrtʃ/ *verb, noun*

■ ***verb*** **1** [I] (+ **adv./prep.**) to make a sudden, unsteady movement forward or sideways 突然前傾（或向一側傾斜）SYN **stagger, sway**：*Suddenly the horse lurched to one side and the child fell off.* 馬突然歪向一邊，小孩

就摔了下來。◇ *The man lurched drunkenly out of the pub.* 那男人醉醺醺地踉蹌着走出了酒吧。◇ (*figurative*) *Their relationship seems to lurch from one crisis to the next.* 他們的關係好像坎坷不平，危機不斷。 **2** [I] if your heart or stomach **lurches**, you have a sudden feeling of fear or excitement （突然感到恐怖或激動時心或胃）猛地一跳（或動）

■ ***noun*** [usually sing.] a sudden strong movement that moves you forward or sideways and nearly makes you lose your balance 突然前傾（或向一側傾斜）：*The train gave a violent lurch.* 火車突然向前猛動了一下。◇ *His heart gave a lurch when he saw her.* 他見到她時心怦然一跳。

IDM **leave sb in the 'lurch** (*informal*) to fail to help sb when they are relying on you to do so （在某人需要幫助時）棄之不顧

lurch·er /ˈlɜːtʃə(r); *NAmE* ˈlɜːrtʃ-/ *noun* (*BrE*) a dog that is a mixture of two different breeds of dog, one of which is usually a GREYHOUND 混種狗；雜種獵狗

lure /lʊə(r); ljʊə(r); *NAmE* lʊr/ *verb, noun*

■ ***verb*** **~ sb** (**+ adv./prep.**) (*disapproving*) to persuade or trick sb to go somewhere or to do sth by promising them a reward 勸誘；引誘；誘惑 **SYN** **entice**：*The child was lured into a car but managed to escape.* 那小孩被誘騙上了車，但設法逃掉了。◇ *Young people are lured to the city by the prospect of a job and money.* 年輕人希望打工賺錢，從而被吸引到城市。

■ ***noun*** **1** [usually sing.] the attractive qualities of sth 吸引力；誘惑力；魅力：*Few can resist **the lure of** adventure.* 很少有人能抵擋歷險的誘惑力。 **2** a thing that is used to attract fish or animals, so that they can be caught 魚餌；誘餌

Lurex™ /ˈlʊəreks; ˈljʊə-; *NAmE* ˈlʊr-/ *noun* [U] a type of thin metal thread; a cloth containing this thread, used for making clothes 盧勒克斯金屬細線；盧勒克斯金屬絲織物

lurgy /ˈlɜːgi; *NAmE* ˈlɜːrgi/ *noun* (*pl.* **-ies**) [C, usually sing.] (*BrE, humorous*) a mild illness or disease 小恙；小病：*I've caught some kind of lurgy.* 我有點小病。◇ *It's the **dreaded lurgy**!* 就是那種嚇人的小病！

lurid /ˈlʊərɪd; ˈljʊər-; *NAmE* ˈlʊr-/ *adj.* (*disapproving*) **1** too bright in colour, in a way that is not attractive 俗豔的；花哨的 **2** (especially of a story or piece of writing 尤指故事或文章) shocking and violent in a way that is deliberate （故意地）駭人聽聞的，令人毛骨悚然的：*lurid headlines* 駭人的標題 ◇ *The paper gave all the lurid details of the murder.* 這份報紙對這起兇殺案聳人聽聞的細節描述得淋漓盡致。 ▸ **lur·id·ly** *adv.*

lurk /lɜːk; *NAmE* lɜːrk/ *verb, noun*

■ ***verb*** **1** [I] (**+ adv./prep.**) to wait somewhere secretly, especially because you are going to do sth bad or illegal （尤指為做不正當的事而）埋伏，潛伏 **SYN** **skulk**：*Why are you lurking around outside my house?* 你在我房子外面鬼鬼祟祟的，想幹什麼？◇ *A crocodile was lurking just below the surface.* 有條鱷魚就潛伏在水面下。 **2** [I] (**+ adv./prep.**) when sth unpleasant or dangerous **lurks**, it is present but not in an obvious way （不好或危險的事）潛在，隱藏着：*At night, danger lurks in these streets.* 夜晚這些街上隱藏着危險。 **3** [I] (*computing* 計) to read a discussion in a CHAT ROOM, etc. on the Internet, without taking part in it yourself "潛水"，隱身（在網上聊天室等閱讀別人的討論但不參與其中）

■ ***noun*** (*AustralE, NZE, informal*) a clever trick that is used in order to get sth 詭計；妙計；花招

lurve /lɜːv; *NAmE* lɜːrv/ *noun* [U] (*BrE, informal, humorous*) a non-standard spelling of 'love', used especially to refer to romantic love 愛（love 的非標準拼寫法，尤用於指愛情）：*It's Valentine's Day and lurve is in the air.* 今天是情人節，空氣中瀰漫着愛情的氣息。

lus·cious /ˈlʌʃəs/ *adj.* **1** having a strong pleasant taste 美味的；甘美的；可口的 **SYN** **delicious**：*luscious fruit* 香甜的水果 **2** (of cloth, colours or music 織物、顏色或音樂) soft and deep or heavy in a way that is pleasing to feel, look at or hear 柔軟的；柔和的；絢麗的；悅耳的 **SYN** **rich**：*luscious silks and velvets* 柔軟光滑的絲綢和天鵝絨 **3** (especially of a woman 尤指女人) sexually attractive 肉感的；性感的：*a luscious young girl* 性感的年輕女郎

lush /lʌʃ/ *adj., noun*

■ ***adj.*** **1** (of plants, gardens, etc. 植物、花園等) growing thickly and strongly in a way that is attractive; covered in healthy grass and plants 茂盛的；茂密的；草木繁茂的 **SYN** **luxuriant**：*lush vegetation* 茂盛的草木 ◇ *the lush green countryside* 鬱鬱葱葱的鄉村 **2** beautiful and making you feel pleasure; seeming expensive 華麗舒適的；豪華的：*a lush apartment* 豪華的公寓

■ ***noun*** (*NAmE, informal*) = ALCOHOLIC *n.*

luso·phone /ˈluːsəfəʊn; *NAmE* -foʊn/ *adj.* (*linguistics* 語言) speaking Portuguese as the main language 主要講葡萄牙語的；以葡萄牙語為主的

lust /lʌst/ *noun, verb*

■ ***noun*** (often *disapproving*) [U, C] **1 ~** (**for sb**) very strong sexual desire, especially when love is not involved 強烈的性慾；色慾；淫慾：*Their affair was driven by pure lust.* 他們私通純粹是受淫慾的驅使。 **2 ~** (**for sth**) very strong desire for sth or enjoyment of sth 強烈慾望；享受慾：*to satisfy his **lust for power*** 滿足他對權力的強烈慾望 ◇ *She has a real **lust for life*** (= she really enjoys life). 她真懂得享受生活。 ➲ see also BLOODLUST

■ ***verb***

PHR V **'lust after/for sb/sth** (often *disapproving*) to feel an extremely strong, especially sexual, desire for sb/sth 對…有極強的慾望（尤指性慾）

lust·ful /ˈlʌstfl/ *adj.* (often *disapproving*) feeling or showing strong sexual desire 有強烈性慾的；淫蕩的；好色的 **SYN** **lascivious**

lustre (*especially US* **lust·er**) /ˈlʌstə(r)/ *noun* [U] **1** the shining quality of a surface 光澤；光輝 **SYN** **sheen**：*Her hair had lost its lustre.* 她的頭髮失去了光澤。 **2** the quality of being special in a way that is exciting 榮光；光彩；榮耀：*The presence of the prince added lustre to the occasion.* 王子的出現給那場面增添了光彩。 ➲ compare LACKLUSTRE

lus·trous /ˈlʌstrəs/ *adj.* (*formal*) soft and shining 柔軟光亮的 **SYN** **glossy**：*thick lustrous hair* 濃密柔軟的亮髮

lusty /ˈlʌsti/ *adj.* healthy and strong 健壯的；強壯的 **SYN** **vigorous**：*a lusty young man* 健壯的年輕人 ◇ *lusty singing* 洪亮的歌聲 ▸ **lust·ily** /-ɪli/ *adv.*：*singing lustily* 起勁地唱歌

lute /luːt/ *noun* an early type of musical instrument with strings, played like a GUITAR 琉特琴，詩琴（撥弦樂器）

lu·ten·ist (also **lu·tan·ist**) /ˈluːtənɪst/ *noun* a person who plays the lute 琉特琴（或詩琴）彈奏者

lu·te·tium /luːˈtiːʃiəm; *BrE* also -siəm/ *noun* [U] (*symb.* **Lu**) a chemical element. Lutetium is a rare silver-white metal used in the nuclear industry. 鑥（用於核工業）

Lu·ther·an /ˈluːθərən/ *noun* a member of a Christian Protestant Church that follows the teaching of the 16th century German religious leader Martin Luther 信義宗信徒；路德宗信徒 ▸ **Lu·ther·an** *adj.*

luv /lʌv/ *noun* **1** (*BrE*) a way of spelling 'love', when used as an informal way of addressing sb （love 用於非正式稱呼的拼寫法）親愛的，寶貝：*Never mind, luv.* 沒關係，親愛的。 **2** an informal way of spelling 'love', for example when ending a letter （love 用於書信結尾等的非正式拼寫法）愛：*See you soon, lots of luv, Sue.* 盼早日見到你，非常愛你的，蘇。

luvvy (also **luv·vie**) /ˈlʌvi/ *noun* (*pl.* **-ies**) (*BrE, informal*) **1** (*disapproving*) an actor, especially when he or she behaves in a way that seems exaggerated and not sincere 演員；（尤指）表演造作的演員 **2** = LOVEY

lux·uri·ant /lʌgˈʒʊəriənt; *NAmE* -ˈʒʊr-/ *adj.* **1** (of plants or hair 植物或頭髮) growing thickly and strongly in a way that is attractive 茂盛的；濃密的：*luxuriant vegetation* 茂密的草木 ◇ *thick, luxuriant hair* 濃密的頭髮 **2** (especially of art or the atmosphere of a place 尤指藝術或氛圍) rich in sth that is pleasant or beautiful 豐富的；華麗的；富饒的：*the poet's luxuriant imagery* 詩人豐富的意象 ▸ **lux·uri·ance** /-əns/ *noun* [U]：*the luxuriance of the tropical forest* 茂密的熱帶森林

lux·uri·ant·ly /lʌɡˈʒʊəriəntli; *NAmE* -ˈʒʊr-/ *adv.* **1** in a way that is thick and attractive 茂盛地；濃密地：*a tall, luxuriantly bearded man* 留有濃密鬍鬚的高個子男人 **2** (especially of a way of moving your body 尤指身體動作) in a way that is comfortable and enjoyable 舒適愉快地：*She turned luxuriantly on her side, yawning.* 她打着哈欠，舒適地轉身側向一邊。

lux·uri·ate /lʌɡˈʒʊərieɪt; *NAmE* -ˈʒʊr-/ *verb*
PHR V **luˈxuriate in sth** to relax while enjoying sth very pleasant 盡情享受；縱情享樂：*She luxuriated in all the attention she received.* 她既備受關注，一路陶醉其中。

lux·uri·ous /lʌɡˈʒʊəriəs; *NAmE* -ˈʒʊr-/ *adj.* very comfortable; containing expensive and enjoyable things 十分舒適的；奢侈的 **SYN** **sumptuous**：*a luxurious hotel* 豪華旅館 ◇ *luxurious surroundings* 豪華舒適的環境 **OPP** **spartan** ▸ **lux·uri·ous·ly** *adv.*：*luxuriously comfortable* 豪華舒適 ◇ *a luxuriously furnished apartment* 佈置得富麗堂皇的公寓 ◇ *She stretched luxuriously on the bed.* 她愜意地在牀上舒展着身子。

lux·ury /ˈlʌkʃəri/ *noun* (*pl.* **-ies**) **1** [U] the enjoyment of special and expensive things, particularly food and drink, clothes and surroundings 奢侈的享受；奢華：*Now we'll be able to live **in luxury** for the rest of our lives.* 如今我們可在有生之年過豪華生活了。◇ *to lead a **life of luxury*** 過奢侈的生活 ◇ *a luxury hotel* 豪華酒店 ◇ *luxury goods* 奢侈品 **2** [C] a thing that is expensive and enjoyable but not essential 奢侈品 **SYN** **extravagance**：*small luxuries like chocolate and flowers* 像巧克力和鮮花之類的小奢侈品 ◇ *I love having a long, hot bath—it's one of **life's little luxuries**.* 我喜歡在熱水浴缸裏多泡一會兒，這是生活裏一種小小的享受。◇ *It was a luxury if you had a washing machine in those days.* 那時候有洗衣機就算是奢侈了。**3** [U, sing.] a pleasure or an advantage that you do not often have 不常有的樂趣（或享受、優勢）**SYN** **indulgence**：*We had the luxury of being able to choose from four good candidates for the job.* 我們的挑選餘地大，有四位出色的職位候選人可供選擇。**IDM** see LAP *n.*

LW *abbr.* (*especially BrE*) LONG WAVE 長波：*1 500m LW* 長波 1 500 米

-ly *suffix* **1** (in adverbs 構成副詞) in the way mentioned 以…方式：*happily* 幸福地 ◇ *stupidly* 愚蠢地 **2** (in adjectives 構成形容詞) having the qualities of 具有…性質：*cowardly* 怯懦的 ◇ *scholarly* 學者型的 **3** (in adjectives and adverbs 構成形容詞和副詞) at intervals of 每隔…時間：*hourly* 每小時 ◇ *daily* 每天

ly·chee (also **li·chee**) (also **lit·chi** especially in *US*) /ˌlaɪˈtʃiː; ˈlaɪtʃiː; *NAmE* ˈliːtʃi/ *noun* a small Chinese fruit with thick rough reddish skin, white flesh and a large seed inside 荔枝 ➲ VISUAL VOCAB page V30

lych·gate (also **lich·gate**) /ˈlɪtʃɡeɪt/ *noun* a gate with a roof at the entrance to a CHURCHYARD 停柩門（教堂墓地入口處有頂蓋的大門）

Lycra™ /ˈlaɪkrə/ (also **span·dex**) *noun* [U] an artificial material that stretches, used for making clothes that fit close to the body 萊卡（有彈性的人造材料，用於製作緊身衣）

lye /laɪ/ *noun* [U] a chemical used in various industrial processes, including washing 鹼液

lying *pres. part.* of LIE

ˌlying-ˈin *noun* [sing.] (*old-fashioned*) the period of time during which a woman in the past stayed in bed before and after giving birth to a child（舊時婦女產前產後的）臥牀期

ˌlying-in-ˈstate *noun* [U] the period when the dead body of a ruler is displayed to the public before being buried; the display of the body in this way（統治者死後的）遺體瞻仰（期）

Lyme disease /ˈlaɪm dɪziːz/ *noun* [U] a serious disease that causes fever and pain in the joints of the body, caused by bacteria carried by TICKS (= small insects) 萊姆病（由蜱傳播，症狀為發燒和關節疼痛）

lymph /lɪmf/ *noun* [U] a clear liquid containing white blood cells that helps to clean the TISSUES of the body and helps to prevent infections from spreading 淋巴 ▸ **lymph·at·ic** /lɪmˈfætɪk/ *adj.* [only before noun]：*the lymphatic system* 淋巴系統

ˈlymph node (also **ˈlymph gland**) *noun* one of the small round parts of the LYMPHATIC system that stores LYMPHOCYTES and helps fight infection 淋巴結

lympho·cyte /ˈlɪmfəsaɪt/ *noun* (*biology* 生) a type of small white blood cell with one round NUCLEUS, found especially in the LYMPHATIC system 淋巴細胞

lymph·oma /lɪmˈfəʊmə; *NAmE* -ˈfoʊ-/ *noun* [U] cancer of the LYMPH NODES 淋巴瘤

lynch /lɪntʃ/ *verb* **~ sb** if a crowd of people **lynch** sb whom they consider guilty of a crime, they capture them, do not allow them to have a trial in court, and kill them illegally, usually by hanging 用私刑處死（被認為有罪的人，通常為絞刑）▸ **lynch·ing** *noun* [C, U]

ˈlynch mob *noun* a crowd of people who gather to lynch sb 施用私刑的暴民

lynch·pin = LINCHPIN

lynx /lɪŋks/ *noun* (*pl.* **lynx** or **lynxes**) a wild animal of the cat family, with spots on its fur and a very short tail 猞猁

lyre /ˈlaɪə(r)/ *noun* an ancient musical instrument with strings fastened in a frame shaped like a U. It was played with the fingers. 里爾琴（古代 U 形撥弦樂器）

lyre·bird /ˈlaɪəbɜːd; *NAmE* ˈlaɪrbɜːrd/ *noun* a large Australian bird 琴鳥（棲於澳大利亞）

lyric /ˈlɪrɪk/ *adj.*, *noun*
■ *adj.* **1** (of poetry 詩歌) expressing a person's personal feelings and thoughts 抒情的 ➲ compare EPIC *adj.* (1) **2** connected with, or written for, singing 吟唱的；為吟唱譜寫的
■ *noun* **1** [C] a lyric poem 抒情詩 ➲ compare EPIC *n.* (1) **2** **lyrics** [pl.] the words of a song 歌詞：*music and lyrics by Rodgers and Hart* 由羅傑斯和哈特作詞作曲

lyr·ic·al /ˈlɪrɪkl/ *adj.* expressing strong emotion in a way that is beautiful and shows imagination 抒情的 **SYN** **expressive**：*a lyrical melody* 抒情的旋律 ◇ *He began to **wax lyrical*** (= talk in an enthusiastic way) *about his new car.* 他開始興高采烈地談論他的新車。

lyr·ic·al·ly /ˈlɪrɪkli/ *adv.* **1** in a way that expresses strong emotion 情感強烈地；抒情地 **2** connected with the words of a song 歌詞上：*Both musically and lyrically it is very effective.* 這首歌的音樂和歌詞都給人留下非常深刻的印象。

lyri·cism /ˈlɪrɪsɪzəm/ *noun* [U] the expression of strong emotion in poetry, art, music, etc.（詩歌、藝術、音樂等的）抒情

lyri·cist /ˈlɪrɪsɪst/ *noun* a person who writes the words of songs 歌詞作者

Mm

M /em/ *noun, abbr., symbol*

■ ***noun*** (also **m**) [C, U] (*pl.* **Ms**, **M's**, **m's** /emz/) the 13th letter of the English alphabet 英語字母表的第 13 個字母：*'Milk' begins with (an) M/'M'.* * milk 一詞以字母 m 開頭。

■ ***abbr.*** **1** (also **med.**) (especially for sizes of clothes) medium（尤指衣服尺碼）中號：*S, M and L* (= small, medium and large) 小號、中號、大號 **2** (used with a number to show the name of a British MOTORWAY) 高速公路（英國公路代號，後接數字）：*heavy traffic on the M25* * 25 號高速公路上繁忙的交通

■ ***symbol*** (also **m**) the number 1 000 in ROMAN NUMERALS（羅馬數字）1 000

m (*BrE*) (also **m.** *NAmE, BrE*) *abbr.* **1** male 男性 **2** married 已婚 **3** metre(s) 米：*800m medium wave* 中波 800 米 **4** million(s) 百萬：*population: 10m* 人口：1 000 萬

MA (*BrE*) (*NAmE* **M.A.**) /ˌem ˈeɪ/ *noun* the abbreviation for 'Master of Arts' (a second university degree in an ARTS subject, or, in Scotland, a first university degree in an arts subject) 文科碩士（全寫為 Master of Arts，大學文科中的中級學位，或蘇格蘭大學文科中的初級學位）：*to **be/have/do an MA*** 成為文科碩士；有 / 攻讀文科碩士學位 ◇ (*BrE*) *Julie Bell MA* 文科碩士朱莉 • 貝爾

ma /mɑː/ *noun* (*informal*) mother 母親；媽媽；媽：*I'm going now, ma.* 媽，我走啦。◇ *'I want my ma,' sobbed the little girl.* 小女孩抽泣着說："我要媽媽。"

ma'am *noun* [sing.] **1** /mæm/ (*NAmE*) used as a polite way of addressing a woman（尊稱）女士，夫人：*'Can I help you, ma'am?'* "要幫忙嗎，夫人？" ➲ compare SIR **2** /mɑːm/ (*BrE*) used when addressing the Queen or senior women officers in the police or army（對女王或高級女警官、女軍官的敬稱）= MADAM

maas /mɑːs/ *noun* (*SAfrE*) = AMASI

Mac /mæk/ *noun* [sing.] (*NAmE, informal*) used to address a man whose name you do not know（用於稱呼不知姓名的男子）老兄，老弟，夥計，哥們兒

mac (also **mack**) /mæk/ (also *old-fashioned* **mack·in·tosh**) *noun* (all *BrE*) a coat made of material that keeps you dry in the rain 雨衣；雨披

ma·cabre /məˈkɑːbrə/ *adj.* unpleasant and strange because connected with death and frightening things 可怕的，恐怖的（尤指與死亡等相聯繫的）**SYN** **ghoulish**, **grisly**：*a **macabre tale/joke/ritual*** 令人毛骨悚然的故事 / 笑話 / 儀式

mac·adam /məˈkædəm/ *noun* [U] a road surface made of layers of broken stones, mixed with TAR 柏油碎石路面

maca·da·mia /ˌmækəˈdeɪmiə/ (also **macaˈdamia nut**) *noun* the round nut of an Australian tree 澳洲堅果 ➲ **VISUAL VOCAB** page V32

ma·caque /məˈkæk; -ˈkɑːk/ *noun* a type of MONKEY that lives in Africa and Asia 獼猴

maca·roni /ˌmækəˈrəʊni; *NAmE* -ˈroʊni/ *noun* [U] PASTA in the shape of hollow tubes 通心粉；空心麪；通心麪

ˌmacaroni ˈcheese (*BrE*) (*NAmE* **ˌmacaroni and ˈcheese**) *noun* [U] a hot dish of macaroni in a cheese sauce 乾酪醬通心麪

maca·roon /ˌmækəˈruːn/ *noun* a soft round sweet biscuit/cookie made with ALMONDS or COCONUT 蛋白杏仁餅乾（或曲奇）；蛋白椰子餅乾（或曲奇）

macaw /məˈkɔː/ *noun* a large Central and S American tropical bird of the PARROT family, with bright feathers and a long tail 鸚鵡，金剛鸚鵡（熱帶美洲鸚鵡，尾長而毛色豔麗）

Mace™ /meɪs/ *noun* [U] a chemical that makes your eyes and skin sting, that some people, including police officers, carry in spray cans so that they can defend themselves against people attacking them 梅斯催淚氣體

mace /meɪs/ *noun* **1** [C] a decorative stick, carried as a sign of authority by an official such as a mayor 權杖 ➲ compare SCEPTRE **2** [C] a large heavy stick that has a head with metal points on it, used in the past as a weapon 狼牙棒（古代兵器）**3** [U] the dried outer covering of NUTMEGS (= the hard nuts of a tropical tree), used in cooking as a spice 肉豆蔻乾皮，肉豆蔻種衣（烹調香料）

ma·cer·ate /ˈmæsəreɪt/ *verb* [T, I] **~ (sth)** (*technical* 術語) to make sth (especially food) soft by leaving it in a liquid; to become soft in this way 把（食物等）浸軟；被浸軟

Mach /mɑːk; mæk/ *noun* [U] (often followed by a number 常後接數字) a measurement of speed, used especially for aircraft. Mach 1 is the speed of sound. 馬赫，馬赫數（速度單位，尤用於計算飛行速度，1 馬赫等於音速）：*a fighter plane with a top speed of Mach 3* (= 3 times the speed of sound) 最高速度為 3 馬赫的殲擊機

ma·chete /məˈʃeti/ *noun* a broad heavy knife used as a cutting tool and as a weapon 大刀；大砍刀

Ma·chia·vel·lian /ˌmækiəˈveliən/ *adj.* (*formal, disapproving*) using clever plans to achieve what you want, without people realizing what you are doing 馬基雅弗利主義的；不擇手段的；陰險狡詐的 **SYN** **cunning**, **unscrupulous** **ORIGIN** From the name of **Niccolò Machiavelli**, an Italian politician (1469-1527), who explained in his book *The Prince*, that it was often necessary for rulers to use immoral methods in order to achieve power and success. 源自意大利政治家尼科洛 • 馬基雅弗利（1469–1527），他在其《君主論》一書中聲稱，統治者為謀取權力和成功常需要採取一些不道德的手段。

ma·chin·ation /ˌmæʃɪˈneɪʃn/ *noun* [usually pl.] (*disapproving*) a secret and complicated plan 陰謀；詭計 **SYN** **plot**, **intrigue**

ma·chine 🔑 /məˈʃiːn/ *noun, verb*

■ ***noun*** **1** 🔑 (often in compounds 常構成複合詞) a piece of equipment with moving parts that is designed to do a particular job. The power used to work a machine may be electricity, steam, gas, etc. or human power. 機器；機械裝置：*Machines have replaced human labour in many industries.* 在許多行業中，機器已經替代了人力。◇ *to **operate/run a machine*** 操作機器 ◇ *How does this machine work?* 這部機器是如何運作的？◇ *a **washing/sewing machine*** 洗衣機；縫紉機 ◇ *a machine for making plastic toys* 生產塑料玩具的機器 ◇ *I left a message on her answering machine.* 我在她的電話答錄機上留了言。◇ *The potatoes are planted **by machine**.* 這些土豆是用機器種植的。➲ see also VOTING MACHINE **2** 🔑 (*informal*) a particular machine, for example in the home, when you do not refer to it by its full name（不提全稱時的簡略說法）機器：*Just put those clothes in the machine* (= the washing machine). 把那些衣服放到洗衣機裏就行了。◇ *The new machines* (= computers) *will be shipped next month.* 新計算機下個月推出市場。**3** a group of people that control an organization or part of an organization（組織的）核心機構：*the president's propaganda machine* 總統的宣傳團隊 **4** (often *disapproving*) a person who acts automatically, without allowing their feelings to show or to affect their work 機械化的人（做事呆板、感情不外露）➲ see also MECHANICAL, FRUIT MACHINE, SLOT MACHINE, TIME MACHINE **HELP** You will find other compounds ending in **machine** at their place in the alphabet. 其他以 machine 結尾的複合詞可在各字母中的適當位置查到。**IDM** see COG

■ ***verb*** [T, I] **~ (sth)** (*technical* 術語) to make or shape sth with a machine（用機器）製造，加工成型：*This material can be cut and machined easily.* 這種材料很容易用機器切割並加工成型。

maˈchine code (also **maˈchine language**) *noun* [C, U] (*computing* 計) a code in which instructions are written in the form of numbers so that a computer can understand and act on them 機器碼

maˈchine gun *noun* a gun that automatically fires many bullets one after the other very quickly 機關槍；機槍：*a **burst/hail of machine-gun fire*** 一陣猛烈的機關槍掃射

ma'chine-gun *verb* (-nn-) **~ sb/sth** to shoot at sb/sth with a machine gun 用機關槍射擊

ma,chine-'made *adj.* made by a machine 機器製造的；機製的 ➲ compare HANDMADE

ma,chine-'readable *adj.* (of data 數據或資料) in a form that a computer can understand 機器可讀的

ma·chin·ery /məˈʃiːnəri/ *noun*
1 [U] machines as a group, especially large ones（統稱）機器；（尤指）大型機器：***agricultural/industrial machinery*** 農業／工業機械 ◇ *a piece of machinery* 一部機器 **2** [U] the parts of a machine that make it work 機器的運轉部份；機械裝置 **3** [U, sing.] the organization or structure of sth; the system for doing sth 組織；機構；系統；體制：**~ (of sth)** *the machinery of government* 政府機構 ◇ **~ (for doing sth)** *There is no machinery for resolving disputes.* 根本沒有解決紛爭的機制。

ma'chine tool *noun* a tool for cutting or shaping metal, wood, etc., driven by a machine 機床；工具機

ma,chine trans'lation *noun* [U] the process of translating language by computer 機器翻譯；計算機翻譯

ma·chin·ist /məˈʃiːnɪst/ *noun* **1** a person whose job is operating a machine, especially machines used in industry for cutting and shaping things, or a sewing machine 機工；（尤指）車工，縫紉機工 **2** a person whose job is to make or repair machines 機械師；機械安裝修理工

mach·ismo /məˈtʃɪzməʊ; *NAmE* mɑːˈtʃiːzmoʊ/ *noun* [U] (from *Spanish*, usually *disapproving*) aggressive male behaviour that emphasizes the importance of being strong rather than being intelligent and sensitive 大男子氣概；大男子主義行為

M

macho /ˈmætʃəʊ; *NAmE* ˈmɑːtʃoʊ/ *adj.* (usually *disapproving*) male in an aggressive way 大男子氣的；男子漢的：*He's too macho to ever admit he was wrong.* 他太大男子主義了，從不認錯。◇ ***macho pride/posturing*** 大男子漢的高傲／姿態

mack = MAC

mack·erel /ˈmækrəl/ *noun* [C, U] (*pl.* **mack·erel**) a sea fish with greenish-blue bands on its body, that is used for food 鯖（魚）：*smoked mackerel* 熏鯖魚

mack·in·tosh /ˈmækɪntɒʃ; *NAmE* -tɑːʃ/ *noun* (*old-fashioned*) = MAC

mac·ramé /məˈkrɑːmi/ *noun* [U] the art of tying knots in string in a decorative way, to make things 裝飾編結藝術；編結藝術

macro /ˈmækrəʊ; *NAmE* ˈmækroʊ/ *noun* (*pl.* **-os**) (*computing* 計) a single instruction in a computer program that automatically causes a complete series of instructions to be put into effect, in order to perform a particular task 宏指令；巨集

macro- /ˈmækrəʊ; *NAmE* ˈmækroʊ/ *combining form* (in nouns, adjectives and adverbs 構成名詞、形容詞和副詞) large; on a large scale 大的；宏觀的；大規模的：*macroeconomics* 宏觀經濟學 OPP **micro-**

macro·bi·ot·ic /ˌmækrəʊbaɪˈɒtɪk; *NAmE* -kroʊbaɪˈɑːt-/ *adj.* consisting of whole grains and vegetables grown without chemical treatment 延年益壽的，養生飲食的（吃未經化學品助長的全穀和蔬菜）：*a macrobiotic diet* 長壽飲食

macro·cosm /ˈmækrəʊkɒzəm; *NAmE* -kroʊkɑːz-/ *noun* any large complete structure that contains smaller structures, for example the universe 大而完整的結構；宇宙；宏觀世界 ➲ compare MICROCOSM

macro·eco·nom·ics /ˌmækrəʊˌiːkəˈnɒmɪks; *NAmE* -kroʊˌekəˈnɑːm-/ *noun* [U] the study of large economic systems, such as those of whole countries or areas of the world 宏觀經濟學 ▶ **macro·eco·nom·ic** *adj.*：*macroeconomic policy* 宏觀經濟政策

mac·ron /ˈmækrɒn; *NAmE* ˈmeɪkrɑːn/ *noun* (*linguistics* 語言) the mark (¯) which is placed over a vowel in some languages and in the International Phonetic Alphabet to show that the vowel is stressed or long 長音符；平調符

macro·phage /ˈmækrəfeɪdʒ/ *noun* (*biology* 生) a large cell that is able to remove harmful substances from the body, and is found in blood and TISSUE 巨噬細胞

Synonyms 同義詞辨析

mad

crazy • nuts • batty • out of your mind • (not) in your right mind

These are all informal words that describe sb who has a mind that does not work normally. 以上各詞均為非正式用語，指人神經錯亂、精神失常。

mad (*informal, especially BrE*) having a mind that does not work normally 指瘋的、神經錯亂的、有精神病的：*I thought I'd go mad if I stayed any longer.* 我覺得再待久一點我就會發瘋。NOTE **Mad** is an informal word used to suggest that sb's behaviour is very strange, often because of extreme emotional pressure. It is offensive if used to describe sb suffering from a real mental illness; use **mentally ill** instead. **Mad** is not usually used in this meaning in North American English; use **crazy** instead. * mad 為非正式用語，暗指由於極度的精神壓力而行為怪異，用於真正的精神病患者意含冒犯，故用 mentally ill 代之。在美式英語中，通常不用 mad 表示此意，而用 crazy。

crazy (*informal, especially NAmE*) having a mind that does not work normally 指瘋的、神經錯亂的、有精神病的：*A crazy old woman rented the upstairs room.* 一個瘋老太婆租了樓上那個房間。NOTE Like **mad**, **crazy** is offensive if used to describe sb suffering from a real mental illness. 與 mad 一樣，crazy 用於真正的精神病患者具冒犯意。

nuts [not before noun] (*informal*) mad 指發瘋、神經錯亂：*That noise is driving me nuts!* 那噪音吵得我要瘋了！◇ *You guys are nuts!* 你們這些傢伙全瘋了！

batty (*informal, especially BrE*) slightly mad, in a harmless way 指瘋瘋癲癲的、古怪的：*Her mum's completely batty.* 她媽媽完全是瘋瘋癲癲的。

out of your mind (*informal*) unable to think or behave normally, especially because of extreme shock or anxiety 尤指因極度震驚或焦慮而心智失常、發瘋：*She was out of her mind with grief.* 她悲痛得精神失常了。

(not) in your right mind (*informal*) (not) mentally normal 指精神（不）正常：***No one in their right mind*** *would choose to work there.* 任何一個精神正常的人都不會選擇去那裏工作。

PATTERNS

- to be mad/crazy/nuts/out of your mind/not in your right mind **to do sth**
- to **go** mad/crazy/nuts/batty
- to **drive sb** mad/crazy/nuts/batty/out of their mind
- **completely** mad/crazy/nuts/batty/out of your mind

mad /mæd/ *adj.* (**mad·der**, **mad·dest**)
1 (*especially BrE*) having a mind that does not work normally; mentally ill 瘋的；神經錯亂的；有精神病的：*They realized that he had* ***gone mad***. 他們意識到他瘋了。◇ *Inventors are not mad scientists.* 發明家不是精神不正常的科學家。◇ ***I'll go mad*** *if I have to wait much longer.* 如果還要等更久的話，我會發瘋的。◇ *She seemed to have gone* ***stark raving mad***. 她好像是完全瘋了。➲ see also BARKING MAD **2** (*informal, especially BrE*) very stupid; not at all sensible 極愚蠢的；很不明智的：*You* ***must be mad*** *to risk it.* 你去冒這種風險，簡直是瘋了。◇ *It was a mad idea.* 那是個愚蠢透頂的想法。◇ *'I'm going to buy some new clothes.' 'Well, don't* ***go mad*** *(= spend more than is sensible).'* "我要去買幾件新衣服。" "去吧，可別亂花錢。" **3** [not before noun] **~ (at/with sb)** | **~ (about sth)** (*informal, especially NAmE*) very angry 很生氣；氣憤：*He* ***got mad*** *and walked out.*

他大動肝火，憤然離去。◇ *She's **mad at me** for being late.* 我遲到了，她非常氣憤。◇ *(BrE) That noise is **driving me mad**.* 那噪聲真讓我受不了。◇ *(BrE) He'll **go mad** when he sees the damage.* 他看到這樣的破壞準會氣瘋的。➲ SYNONYMS at ANGRY **4** [not usually before noun] **~ (about/on sth/sb)** (*BrE, informal*) liking sth/sb very much; very interested in sth 特別喜歡；痴迷；迷戀：*to be mad on tennis* 對網球着迷 ◇ *He's always been mad about kids.* 他一向特別喜歡孩子。◇ *football-mad boys* 迷戀足球的男孩兒 ◇ *She's completely power-mad.* 她權迷心竅。**5** done without thought or control; wild and excited 不理智的；瘋狂的；激動的：*The crowd made a **mad rush** for the exit.* 人群瘋狂地衝向出口處。◇ *Only a **mad dash** got them to the meeting on time.* 他們一陣狂奔，總算準時到達會場。◇ *(BrE) The team won and the fans **went mad**.* 球隊獲勝了，球迷欣喜若狂。◇ **~ with sth** (*BrE*) *to be **mad with anger/excitement/grief/love*** 因氣憤／興奮／悲傷／愛而喪失理智 ➲ compare CRAZY

IDM **be mad for sb/sth** (*BrE, informal*) to like or want sb/sth very much 非常喜歡；極為需要；對…想得發狂：*Scott's mad for peanuts.* 斯科特瘋狂地喜歡花生。 **like 'crazy/'mad** (*informal*) very fast, hard, much, etc. 非常快（或拚命、厲害等）：*I had to run like mad to catch the bus.* 為了趕上公共汽車，我不得不拚命跑。 **(as) mad as a 'hatter/a March 'hare** (*informal*) (of a person 人) mentally ill; very silly 發狂的；非常愚蠢的 **ORIGIN** From the Mad Hatter, a character in Lewis Carroll's *Alice's Adventures in Wonderland*. Because of the chemicals used in hat-making, workers often suffered from mercury poisoning, which can cause loss of memory and damage to the nervous system. A **March hare** was called mad because of the strange behaviour of hares during the mating season. 源於劉易斯 • 卡羅爾所著《艾麗斯漫遊奇境》一書中的瘋狂的帽商（Mad Hatter）這一形象。做帽子用的化學藥品經常使工人受汞毒毒害，破壞他們的記憶和神經系統。三月的兔子（March hare）在交配期行為怪異，因而被稱為瘋狂的兔子。 **mad 'keen (on sth/sb)** (*BrE, informal*) liking sth/sb very much; very interested in sth （對…）痴迷，迷戀；特別喜歡：*He's mad keen on planes.* 他對飛機十分着迷。 ➲ more at HOPPING *adv.*, RAVING *adv.*

madam /'mædəm/ *noun* **1** [sing.] (*formal*) used when speaking or writing to a woman in a formal or business situation 夫人；女士：*Can I help you, madam?* 要幫忙嗎，夫人？◇ *Dear Madam* (= used like *Dear Sir* in a letter) 尊敬的女士／夫人（用於書信開頭，同 Dear Sir） ➲ see also MA'AM (1) **2** [C] (*informal, disapproving, especially BrE*) a girl or young woman who expects other people to do what she wants 喜歡支使別人的年輕女子；任性妄為的年輕女子：*She's a proper little madam.* 她真是個說一不二的小姑奶奶。 **3** [C] a woman who is in charge of the PROSTITUTES in a BROTHEL 老鴇；鴇母；妓院女老闆

mad·cap /'mædkæp/ *adj.* [usually before noun] (*informal*) (of people, plans etc. 人、計劃等) crazy and not caring about danger; not sensible 魯莽的；狂妄的；不明智的 **SYN** reckless：***madcap schemes/escapades*** 冒險的計劃；魯莽的冒險行動

mad 'cow disease *noun* [U] (*informal*) = BSE

mad·den /'mædn/ *verb* [usually passive] **~ sb/sth** to make a person or an animal very angry or crazy 使非常生氣；使發瘋 **SYN** infuriate ▸ **mad·den·ing** /'mædnɪŋ/ *adj.*：*maddening delays* 令人非常氣惱的延誤 **mad·den·ing·ly** *adv.*：*Progress is maddeningly slow.* 進展慢得令人心煩。

mad·ding /'mædɪŋ/ *adj.* (*literary*) behaving in a crazy way; making you feel angry or crazy 瘋狂的；使人憤怒（或瘋狂）的

IDM **,far from the madding 'crowd** in a quiet and private place 遠離塵囂

made /meɪd/ **1** *past tense, past part.* of MAKE **2** **-made** (in adjectives 構成形容詞) made in the way, place, etc. mentioned …製造的；製作…的：*well-made* 製作精良的 ◇ *home-made* 家庭自製的 ➲ see also SELF-MADE

IDM **have (got) it 'made** (*informal*) to be sure of success; to have everything that you want 胸有成竹；具備所需的一切 **(be) 'made for sb/each other** to be completely suited to sb/each other 完全適合；非常般配：*Peter and Judy seem made for each other, don't they?* 彼得和朱迪像是天生的一對，不是嗎？ **what sb is 'made of** (*informal*) how sb reacts in a difficult situation 某人有多厲害（在困境中表現出來的應對能力）

Ma·deira /mə'dɪərə; *NAmE* mə'dɪrə/ (also **Ma,deira 'wine**) *noun* **1** [U, C] a strong wine, often sweet, from the island of Madeira 馬德拉白葡萄酒（產於大西洋馬德拉島，味甜，度數高） **2** [C] a glass of Madeira 一杯馬德拉白葡萄酒

Ma'deira cake (*BrE*) (*NAmE* **'pound cake**) *noun* [U, C] a plain yellow cake made with eggs, fat, flour and sugar 馬德拉蛋糕

mad·eleine /'mædleɪn; 'mædlen/ *noun* a type of small cake 瑪德琳小蛋糕

,made to 'measure *adj.* (of clothes, curtains, etc. 衣服、窗簾等) made specially to fit a particular person, window, etc. 量身訂製的；按尺寸製作的

,made to 'order *adj.* (*especially NAmE*) (of clothes, furniture, etc. 衣服、傢具等) made specially for a particular customer 訂製的；訂做的

'made-up *adj.* **1** wearing make-up 化妝的：*a heavily **made-up face/woman*** 濃妝的臉／女人 **2** not true or real; invented 不真實的；編造的：*a **made-up story/word/name*** 虛構的故事；謊話；假名

mad·house /'mædhaʊs/ *noun* **1** [usually sing.] (*informal*) a place where there is confusion and noise 混亂吵鬧的地方：*Don't work in that department; it's a madhouse.* 別在那個部門工作，那裏太亂。 **2** (*old use*) a hospital for people who are mentally ill 瘋人院；精神病院

Madi·son Av·enue /,mædɪsn 'ævənjuː/ *noun* [U] the US advertising industry 美國廣告業 **ORIGIN** From the name of the street in New York where many advertising companies have their offices. 源自紐約市美國廣告公司集中的麥迪遜大街街名。

madly /'mædli/ *adv.* **1** (only used *after* a verb 僅用於動詞後) in a way that shows a lack of control 發狂地；無法控制地：*She was rushing around madly trying to put out the fire.* 她瘋了似地跑來跑去，試圖把火撲滅。◇ *His heart thudded madly against his ribs.* 他的心都要跳出來了。 **2** (*informal*) very, extremely 極端地；非常地：***madly excited/jealous*** 非常激動／嫉妒 ◇ *She's **madly in love** with him.* 她瘋狂地愛着他。

mad·man /'mædmən/ *noun* (*pl.* **-men** /-mən/) a man who has a serious mental illness 瘋子；精神病患者：*The killing was the act of a madman.* 這起兇殺案是一個瘋子所為。◇ *He drove **like a madman**.* 他像瘋了似地開着車。◇ *Some madman* (= stupid person) *deleted all the files.* 不知哪個笨蛋把所有的文件都刪掉了。 ➲ see also MADWOMAN

mad·ness /'mædnəs/ *noun* [U] **1** (*old-fashioned*) the state of having a serious mental illness 精神失常；瘋狂 **SYN** insanity：*There may be a link between madness and creativity.* 在瘋狂和創造力之間也許有着某種聯繫。 **2** crazy or stupid behaviour that could be dangerous（會帶來危險的）瘋狂，瘋狂，愚蠢行為：*It would be sheer madness to trust a man like that.* 信任他這樣的人簡直是愚蠢至極。◇ *In a **moment of madness** she had agreed to go out with him.* 由於一時糊塗，她同意和他約會。 **IDM** see METHOD (2)

ma·donna /mə'dɒnə; *NAmE* mə'dɑːnə/ *noun* **1** **the Madonna** [sing.] the Virgin Mary, mother of Jesus Christ 聖母瑪利亞 **2** [C] a statue or picture of the Virgin Mary 聖母瑪利亞的雕像（或畫像等）

ma·dras /mə'dræs; -'drɑːs; *NAmE* also 'mædrəs/ *noun* [U, C] a spicy Indian dish, usually containing meat 馬德拉斯咖喱菜（通常含肉）：*chicken madras* 馬德拉斯咖喱雞

ma·dra·sa (also **ma·dra·sah** /mə'dræsə/) *noun* a college where the Islamic faith is taught 馬德拉沙（穆斯林高等教育機構）

mad·ri·gal /'mædrɪgl/ *noun* a song for several singers, usually without musical instruments, popular in the 16th century（流行於 16 世紀的）牧歌

M

mad·woman /ˈmædwʊmən/ *noun* (*pl.* **-women** /-wɪmɪn/) a woman who has a serious mental illness 瘋女人；女精神病患者 ➲ see also MADMAN

mael·strom /ˈmeɪlstrɒm; *NAmE* -strɑːm/ *noun* [usually sing.] **1** (*literary*) a situation full of strong emotions or confusing events, that is hard to control and makes you feel frightened（思想、感情、事態的）混亂，騷亂，動亂 **2** a very strong current of water that moves in circles 大漩渦 SYN **whirlpool**

maes·tro /ˈmaɪstrəʊ; *NAmE* -stroʊ/ *noun* (*pl.* **-os**) (often used as a way of addressing sb, showing respect 常作呼語，表尊敬) a great performer, especially a musician 大師；音樂大師：*Maestro Giulini* 音樂大師朱利尼 ◇ *The winning goal was scored by the maestro himself.* 致勝的一球是大師自己拿下的。

Mafia /ˈmæfiə; *NAmE* ˈmɑːf-/ *noun* **1** **the Mafia** [sing.+sing./pl. v.] a secret organization of criminals, that is active especially in Sicily, Italy and the US 黑手黨（尤活躍於意大利西西里和美國）**2** **mafia** [C+sing./pl. v.] a group of people within an organization or a community who use their power to get advantages for themselves 小集團；小幫派；團夥；社會黑幫：*a member of the local mafia* 當地黑社會中的一名成員 ◇ *Politics is still dominated by the middle-class mafia.* 政治仍然操縱在中產階級幫派手中。

Mafi·oso /ˌmæfiˈəʊsəʊ; *NAmE* ˌmɑːfiˈoʊsoʊ/ *noun* (*pl.* **Mafi·osi** /-siː/) a member of the Mafia 黑手黨成員

maga·zine 0━ /ˌmægəˈziːn; *NAmE* ˈmægəziːn/ *noun* **1** 0━ (also *informal* **mag** /mæg/) a type of large thin book with a paper cover that you can buy every week or month, containing articles, photographs, etc., often on a particular topic 雜誌；期刊：*a* ***weekly/monthly magazine*** 週刊；月刊 ◇ *a* ***magazine article/interview*** 雜誌文章／訪談 ◇ *an* ***online magazine*** 在線期刊 ◇ *Her designer clothes were from the pages of a glossy fashion magazine.* 她的名師設計的服裝取材於一份精美的時裝雜誌。**2** a radio or television programme that is about a particular topic（電視、廣播）專題節目：*a regional news magazine on TV* 以地區新聞為主題的電視節目 ◇ *a* ***magazine programme/program*** 專題節目 **3** the part of a gun that holds the bullets before they are fired 彈倉；彈盒；彈盤 **4** a room or building where weapons, EXPLOSIVES and bullets are stored 彈藥庫；軍火庫；軍械庫

ma·genta /məˈdʒentə/ *adj.* reddish-purple in colour 紫紅色的；洋紅色的 ▸ **ma·genta** *noun* [U]

mag·got /ˈmægət/ *noun* a creature like a small short WORM, that is the young form of a fly and is found in decaying meat and other food. Maggots are often used as BAIT on a hook to catch fish. 蛆

Magi /ˈmeɪdʒaɪ/ **the Magi** *noun* [pl.] (in the Bible《聖經》) the three wise men from the East who are said to have brought presents to the baby Jesus（帶禮物朝拜耶穌聖嬰的）東方三賢士

magic 0━ /ˈmædʒɪk/ *noun, adj., verb*

■ ***noun*** [U] **1** 0━ the secret power of appearing to make impossible things happen by saying special words or doing special things 魔法；法術；巫術：*Do you believe in magic?* 你相信巫術嗎？◇ *He suddenly appeared* ***as if by magic.*** 他突然神奇地出現了。◇ *A passage was cleared through the crowd* ***like magic.*** 好像有一股神奇的力量在人群中間開出了一條通道。➲ see also BLACK MAGIC **2** 0━ the art of doing tricks that seem impossible in order to entertain people 戲法；魔術 SYN **conjuring** **3** 0━ a special quality or ability that sb/sth has, that seems too wonderful to be real 魔力；魅力；神奇 SYN **enchantment**：*dance and music which capture the magic of India* 具有印度獨特魅力的舞蹈和音樂 ◇ *Like all truly charismatic people, he can* ***work his magic*** *on both men and women.* 像所有真正富有魅力的人一樣，他讓男人和女人都很着迷。◇ *Our year in Italy was* ***pure/sheer*** *magic.* 我們在意大利的那一年真是太有趣了。IDM see WEAVE *v.* (4)

■ ***adj.*** **1** 0━ having or using special powers to make impossible things happen or seem to happen 有魔力的；（施）巫術的；有神奇力量的：*a* ***magic spell/charm/potion/trick*** 魔咒；魔力；魔藥；魔法 ◇ *There is no magic formula for passing exams—only hard work.* 根本沒有通過考試的魔法，唯一的方法就是勤奮學習。**2** 0━ (*informal*) having a special quality that makes sth seem wonderful 神奇的；有魔力的；美好的：*It was a magic moment when the two sisters were reunited after 30 years.* * 30 年後姐妹倆重逢，就像做夢一樣。◇ *She has a* ***magic touch*** *with the children and they do everything she asks.* 她對孩子們很有兩下子，說什麼是什麼。◇ *Trust is the magic ingredient in our relationship.* 信任是維繫我們相互關係的神奇力量。**3** [not before noun] (*BrE, informal*) very good or enjoyable 好極了；棒極了：*'What was the trip like?' 'Magic!'* "旅行感覺如何？" "棒極了！"

■ ***verb*** (**-ck-**) **~ sb/sth + adv./prep.** to make sb/sth appear somewhere, disappear or turn into sth, by magic, or as if by magic（像）用魔法變出（或使消失、使變成…等）

magic·al /ˈmædʒɪkl/ *adj.* **1** containing magic; used in magic 有魔力的；用於巫術的：*magical powers* 魔力 ◇ *Her words had a magical effect on us.* 她的話對我們有一種魔力般的作用。**2** (*informal*) wonderful; very enjoyable 奇妙的；令人愉快的 SYN **enchanting**：*a truly magical feeling* 真正奇妙的感覺 ◇ *We spent a magical week in Paris.* 我們在巴黎度過了十分愉快的一週。▸ **ma·gic·al·ly** /-kli/ *adv.*

ˌmagical ˈrealism *noun* [U] = MAGIC REALISM

ˌmagic ˈbullet *noun* **1** (*medical* 醫) a medical treatment which works very quickly and effectively against a particular illness（針對某種疾病的）靈丹妙藥，神奇療法 **2** a fast and effective solution to a serious problem（解決某一問題的）靈丹妙藥

ˌmagic ˈcarpet *noun* (in stories 故事中) a carpet that can fly and carry people（可載人飛行的）魔毯

ma·gi·cian /məˈdʒɪʃn/ *noun* **1** a person who can do magic tricks 魔術師；變戲法的人 SYN **conjuror** **2** (in stories 故事中) a person who has magic powers 巫師；術士；施妖術的人 SYN **sorcerer**

ˌmagic ˈlantern *noun* a piece of equipment used in the past to make pictures appear on a white wall or screen 幻燈；幻燈機

ˌmagic ˈmushroom (*BrE* or becoming *old-fashioned*, *NAmE*) (*NAmE* usually *informal* **shroom**) *noun* a type of MUSHROOM that has an effect like some drugs and that may make people who eat it HALLUCINATE (= see things that are not there) 致幻蘑菇

ˌmagic ˈrealism (also **ˌmagical ˈrealism**) *noun* [U] a style of writing that mixes realistic events with FANTASY 魔幻現實主義

ˌmagic ˈwand *noun* = WAND：*I wish I could* ***wave a magic wand*** *and make everything all right again.* 真希望我能魔杖一揮使一切又都好起來。

magis·ter·ial /ˌmædʒɪˈstɪəriəl; *NAmE* -ˈstɪr-/ *adj.* (*formal*) **1** (especially of a person or their behaviour 尤指人或其行為) having or showing power or authority 權威的；威嚴的；傲慢的：*He talked with the magisterial authority of the head of the family.* 他說起話來儼然一副一家之主的口吻。**2** (of a book or piece of writing 書或文章) showing great knowledge or understanding 睿智的；有洞察力的；知識豐富的 SYN **authoritative**：*his magisterial work 'The Roman Wall in Scotland'* 他的睿智之作《蘇格蘭的羅馬牆》**3** [only before noun] connected with a magistrate 地方行政官的；地方法官的；治安官的 ▸ **magis·teri·al·ly** /-iəli/ *adv.*

the magis·tracy /ˈmædʒɪstrəsi/ *noun* [sing.+sing./pl. v.] magistrates as a group（統稱）地方行政官，地方執法官，治安官

magis·trate /ˈmædʒɪstreɪt/ *noun* an official who acts as a judge in the lowest courts of law 地方執法官 SYN **Justice of the Peace**：*a magistrates' court* 地方治安法庭 ◇ *to come up before the magistrates* 在地方法院出庭

magma /ˈmægmə/ *noun* [U] (*technical* 術語) very hot liquid rock found below the earth's surface 岩漿；熔岩

Magna Carta /ˌmæɡnə ˈkɑːtə; *NAmE* ˈkɑːrtə/ *noun* a document officially stating the political and legal rights of the English people, that King John was forced to sign in 1215 (often referred to as the basis for modern English law) 《大憲章》，《英格蘭大憲章》（1215 年英王約翰被迫簽署，保障英格蘭公民的政治和法律權利，常被視作現代英格蘭法律的基礎）

magna cum laude /ˌmæɡnə kʊm ˈlɔːdi; ˈlaʊdeɪ/ *adv., adj.* (from *Latin*) (in the US) at the second of the three highest levels of achievement that students can reach when they finish their studies at college（美國）以優異成績（三等優異成績的第二等）：*She graduated magna cum laude from UCLA.* 她以優異成績畢業於加州大學洛杉磯分校。➲ compare CUM LAUDE, SUMMA CUM LAUDE

mag·nani·mous /mæɡˈnænɪməs/ *adj.* (*formal*) kind, generous and forgiving, especially towards an enemy or a rival 寬宏的，大度的（尤指對敵人或對手）：*a magnanimous gesture* 大度的姿態 ◇ *He was magnanimous in defeat and praised his opponent's skill.* 他對失敗表現得很灑脫，並且讚揚了對手的才能。▸ **mag·na·nim·ity** /ˌmæɡnəˈnɪməti/ *noun* [U]：*She accepted the criticism with magnanimity.* 她很大度地接受了批評。**mag·nani·mous·ly** *adv.*

mag·nate /ˈmæɡneɪt/ *noun* a person who is rich, powerful and successful, especially in business 權貴；要人；富豪；（尤指）產業大亨：***a media/property/shipping magnate*** 媒體／房地產／航運業大亨

mag·ne·sia /mæɡˈniːʒə; *NAmE* -ʃə; *BrE* also -ziə/ *noun* [U] a white substance containing MAGNESIUM, used to help with INDIGESTION 氧化鎂（用於治療消化不良）

mag·ne·sium /mæɡˈniːziəm/ *noun* [U] (*symb.* **Mg**) a chemical element. Magnesium is a light, silver-white metal that burns with a bright white flame. 鎂

mag·net /ˈmæɡnət/ *noun* **1** a piece of iron that attracts objects made of iron towards it, either naturally or because of an electric current that is passed through it 磁鐵；磁石；吸鐵石 ➲ **VISUAL VOCAB** page V70 **2** [usually sing.] **~ (for sb/sth)** a person, place or thing that sb/sth is attracted to 有吸引力的人（或地方、事物）：*In the 1990s the area became a magnet for new investment.* 這個地區在 20 世紀 90 年代成了新的投資熱點。**3** an object with a magnetic surface that you can stick onto a metal surface 磁體；磁性物體：*fridge magnets of your favourite cartoon characters* 可吸附於冰箱表面的你最喜歡的動畫人物磁體

mag·net·ic /mæɡˈnetɪk/ *adj.* [usually before noun] **1** behaving like a magnet (1) 像磁鐵的；有磁性的：*magnetic materials* 磁性材料 ◇ *The block becomes magnetic when the current is switched on.* 一通上電流，這塊板就會有磁性。**2** connected with or produced by magnetism 磁的；磁性的：***magnetic properties/forces*** 磁性／力 ◇ ***a magnetic disk*** (= one containing magnetic tape that stores information to be used by a computer) 磁盤 **3** that people find very powerful and attractive 富有吸引力的；有魅力的：*a magnetic personality* 富有魅力的個性 ▸ **mag·net·ic·al·ly** /-kli/ *adv.*

magˌnetic ˈcompass *noun* = COMPASS (1)

magˌnetic ˈfield *noun* an area around a MAGNET or MAGNETIC object, where there is a force that will attract some metals towards it 磁場

magˌnetic ˈmedia *noun* [pl., U] the different methods, for example MAGNETIC TAPE, that are used to store information for computers 磁體媒介（計算機貯存信息的方法）

magˌnetic ˈnorth *noun* [U] the direction that is approximately north as it is shown on a magnetic compass 磁北 ➲ compare TRUE NORTH

magˌnetic ˈstorm *noun* a situation in which the magnetic field of the earth or of another planet, star, etc. is disturbed 磁暴（地球或其他星球等磁場的擾動）

magˌnetic ˈstrip *noun* a line of magnetic material on a plastic card, containing information（塑料卡上附有信息的）磁條

magˌnetic ˈtape *noun* [U] a type of plastic tape that is used for recording sound, pictures or computer information 磁帶

mag·net·ism /ˈmæɡnətɪzəm/ *noun* [U] **1** a physical property (= characteristic) of some metals such as iron, produced by electric currents, that causes forces between objects, either pulling them towards each other or pushing them apart 磁性；磁力 **2** the qualities of sth, especially a person's character, that people find powerful and attractive 吸引力；魅力：*She exudes sexual magnetism.* 她洋溢着女性的魅力。

mag·net·ize (*BrE* also **-ise**) /ˈmæɡnətaɪz/ *verb* **1** [usually passive] **~ sth** (*technical* 術語) to make sth metal behave like a MAGNET 磁化；使有磁性 **2 ~ sb** to strongly attract sb 吸引；迷住：*Cities have a powerful magnetizing effect on young people.* 城市對青年人有着強大的吸引力。

mag·neto /mæɡˈniːtəʊ; *NAmE* -ˈniːtoʊ/ *noun* (*pl.* **-os**) a small piece of equipment that uses MAGNETS (1) to produce the electricity that lights the fuel in the engine of a car, etc. 磁石發電機；永磁電機；永磁打火裝置

ˈmagnet school *noun* (*NAmE*) a school in a large city that offers extra courses in some subjects in order to attract students from other areas of the city（大城市中提供額外課程招收其他地區學生的）有吸引力的學校，磁力學校

mag·ni·fi·ca·tion /ˌmæɡnɪfɪˈkeɪʃn/ *noun* **1** [U] the act of making sth look larger 放大：*The insects were examined under magnification.* 這些昆蟲是放大後加以觀察的。**2** [C, U] the degree to which sth is made to look larger; the degree to which sth is able to make things look larger 放大率；放大倍數：*a magnification of 10 times the actual size* * 10 倍於實物的放大率 ◇ ***high/low magnification*** 高／低放大率 ◇ *The telescope has a magnification of 50.* 這個望遠鏡可以放大 50 倍。

mag·nifi·cent /mæɡˈnɪfɪsnt/ *adj.* extremely attractive and impressive; deserving praise 壯麗的；宏偉的；值得讚揚的 **SYN** **splendid**：*The Taj Mahal is a magnificent building.* 泰姬陵是一座宏偉的建築。◇ *She looked magnificent in her wedding dress.* 她穿着婚紗，看上去漂亮極了。◇ *You've all done a magnificent job.* 你們活兒幹得都很出色。▸ **mag·nifi·cence** /-sns/ *noun* [U]：*the magnificence of the scenery* 景色壯觀 **mag·nifi·cent·ly** *adv.*：*The public have responded magnificently to our appeal.* 對於我們的呼籲，公眾的反響極為熱烈。

mag·ni·fier /ˈmæɡnɪfaɪə(r)/ *noun* a piece of equipment that is used to make things look larger 放大器；放大鏡

mag·nify /ˈmæɡnɪfaɪ/ *verb* (**mag·ni·fies**, **mag·ni·fy·ing**, **mag·ni·fied**, **mag·ni·fied**) **1 ~ sth (to/by sth)** to make sth look bigger than it really is, for example by using a LENS or MICROSCOPE 放大 **SYN** **enlarge**：*bacteria magnified to 1 000 times their actual size* 放大了 1 000 倍的細菌 ◇ *an image magnified by a factor of 4* 放大了 4 倍的圖像 **2 ~ sth** to make sth bigger, louder or stronger 擴大；增強：*The sound was magnified by the high roof.* 高高的屋頂使聲音更響亮。◇ *The dry summer has magnified the problem of water shortages.* 乾燥的夏季加劇了缺水的問題。**3 ~ sth** to make sth seem more important or serious than it really is 誇大（重要性或嚴重性）；誇張 **SYN** **exaggerate**

ˈmagnifying glass *noun* a round piece of glass, usually with a handle, that you look through and that makes things look bigger than they really are 放大鏡 ➲ **VISUAL VOCAB** page V41

mag·ni·tude /ˈmæɡnɪtjuːd; *NAmE* -tuːd/ *noun* **~ (of sth)** **1** [U] (*formal*) the great size or importance of sth; the degree to which sth is large or important 巨大；重大；重要性：*We did not realize the magnitude of the problem.* 我們沒有意識到這個問題的重要性。◇ *a discovery **of the first magnitude*** 一項極重要的發現 **2** [C, U] (*astronomy* 天) the degree to which a star is bright 星等；星的亮度：*The star varies in brightness by about three magnitudes.* 星體的亮度大約分三個星等。**3** [C, U] (*geology* 地) the size of an EARTHQUAKE 震級

mag·no·lia /mæɡˈnəʊliə; *NAmE* -ˈnoʊ-/ *noun* **1** [C] a tree with large white, pink or purple flowers that smell sweet 木蘭；木蘭樹 **2** [U] (*BrE*) a very pale cream colour 淺乳白色

M

mag·num /ˈmæɡnəm/ *noun* a bottle containing 1.5 litres of wine, etc.（容量為 1.5 升的）大酒瓶，大瓶

ˌmagnum ˈopus *noun* [sing.] (from *Latin*) a large and important work of art, literature or music, especially one that people think is the best work ever produced by that artist, writer, etc. 代表作；傑作

mag·pie /ˈmæɡpaɪ/ *noun* a black and white bird with a long tail and a noisy cry. There is a popular belief that magpies like to steal small bright objects. 鵲；喜鵲

magus /ˈmeɪɡəs/ *noun* (*pl.* **magi** /ˈmeɪdʒaɪ/) **1** a member of the group to which priests in ancient Persia belonged 麻葛（古波斯祭司負責祭祀的氏族） **2** a man with magic powers 術士

maha·raja (also **maha·ra·jah**) /ˌmɑːhəˈrɑːdʒə/ *noun* an Indian prince, especially one who ruled over one of the states of India in the past（印度的）王公；（尤指過去的）土邦主

maha·rani (also **maha·ra·nee**) /ˌmɑːhəˈrɑːni/ *noun* the wife of a maharaja（印度的）王公妃；土邦主妃

Maha·rishi /ˌmɑːhəˈrɪʃi; -ˈriː-/ *noun* a Hindu spiritual leader or wise man（印度教）精神領袖；（印度教）哲人

ma·hatma /məˈhætmə; -ˈhɑːt-/ *noun* **1** a holy person in S Asia who is respected by many people（南亞的）聖人 **2** **the Ma·hatma** Mahatma Gandhi, the Indian spiritual leader who opposed British rule in India 聖雄甘地

Maha·yana /ˌmɑːhəˈjɑːnə/ (also **ˌMahaˌyana ˈBuddhism**) *noun* [U] one of the two major forms of Buddhism 大乘佛教（佛教兩個主要派別之一）➲ compare THERAVADA

mah·jong (also **mah·jongg** especially in *NAmE*) /mɑːˈdʒɒŋ; *NAmE* -ˈʒɑːŋ; -ˈʒɔːŋ/ *noun* [U] (from *Chinese*) a Chinese game played with small pieces of wood with symbols on them 麻將

ma·hog·any /məˈhɒɡəni; *NAmE* -ˈhɑːɡ-/ *noun* [U] **1** the hard reddish-brown wood of a tropical tree, used for making furniture 紅木；桃花心木：*a mahogany table* 紅木桌子 **2** a reddish-brown colour 紅褐色：*skin tanned to a deep mahogany* 曬成深紅褐色的皮膚

ma·hout /məˈhaʊt/ *noun* a person who works with, rides and cares for an ELEPHANT 象夫；騎象人；馴象人

maid /meɪd/ *noun* **1** (often in compounds 常構成複合詞) a female servant in a house or hotel 女僕；侍女；（旅館的）女服務員：*There is a maid to do the housework.* 有個女僕做家務事。➲ see also BARMAID, CHAMBERMAID, DAIRYMAID, HOUSEMAID, MILKMAID, NURSEMAID at NURSE *n.* (2) **2** (*old use*) a young woman who is not married 少女；年輕姑娘；未婚年輕女子 ➲ see also OLD MAID

mai·dan /maɪˈdɑːn/ *noun* an open space in or near a town in S Asia, usually covered with grass（南亞城鎮中或近郊的）草地，廣場，空地

maid·en /ˈmeɪdn/ *noun, adj.*

▪ ***noun*** **1** (*literary*) a young girl or woman who is not married 少女；處女；未婚女子：*stories of knights and fair maidens* 關於騎士和美女的故事 **2** (also **ˌmaiden ˈover**) (in CRICKET 板球) an OVER in which no points are scored 未得分的一輪投球

▪ ***adj.*** [only before noun] being the first of its kind 首次的；初次的：*a **maiden flight/voyage*** (= the first journey made by a plane/ship) 初次飛行；首航 ◇ *a **maiden speech*** (= the first speech made by an MP in the parliaments of some countries) 議員在議會的初次演講

ˌmaiden ˈaunt *noun* (*old-fashioned*) an aunt who has not married（未婚的）姑，姨

maid·en·hair /ˈmeɪdnheə(r); *NAmE* -her/ (also **ˌmaid·enhair ˈfern**) *noun* [U, C] a type of FERN with long thin STEMS and delicate pale green leaves that are shaped like fans 鐵線蕨

ˈmaidenhair tree *noun* = GINKGO

maid·en·head /ˈmeɪdnhed/ *noun* (*old use*) **1** the state of being a VIRGIN 處女身分；童貞 **2** = HYMEN

ˈmaiden name *noun* a woman's family name before marriage（女子的）娘家姓：*Kate kept her maiden name when she got married* (= did not change her surname to that of her husband). 凱特結婚後仍用她娘家的姓。

ˌmaid of ˈhonour (*especially US* **ˌmaid of ˈhonor**) *noun* (*pl.* **maids of honour/honor**) (especially in the US) a young woman or girl who is not married and who is the main BRIDESMAID at a wedding（尤用於美國，指未婚的）首席女儐相，伴娘 ➲ compare MATRON OF HONOUR

maid·ser·vant /ˈmeɪdsɜːvənt; *NAmE* -sɜːrv-/ *noun* (*old-fashioned*) a female servant in a house 女僕；女傭；侍女

mail 🔑 /meɪl/ *noun, verb*

▪ ***noun*** [U] **1** 🔑 (*BrE* also **post**) the official system used for sending and delivering letters, packages, etc. 郵政；郵遞系統：*a **mail service/train/van*** 郵政服務／列車／汽車 ◇ *the Royal Mail* 皇家郵政 ◇ *Your cheque is in the mail.* 你的支票在郵遞途中。◇ *We do our business **by mail**.* 我們通過郵遞做生意。➲ see also AIRMAIL, SNAIL MAIL, VOICEMAIL **2** 🔑 (*BrE* also **post**) letters, packages, etc. that are sent and delivered 郵件；信件；郵包：*There isn't much mail today.* 今天郵件不多。◇ *I sat down to open **the mail**.* 我坐下來打開信件。◇ *Is there a letter from them **in the mail**?* 郵件裏有他們來的信嗎？◇ ***hate mail*** (= letters containing insults and threats) 恐嚇侮辱信 ➲ see also JUNK MAIL, SURFACE MAIL ➲ note at POST **3** 🔑 messages that are sent or received on a computer 電子郵件；電郵：*Check regularly for new mail.* 定期查看新郵件。➲ see also ELECTRONIC MAIL, EMAIL **4** used in the title of some newspapers（用作報紙名稱）郵報：*the Mail on Sunday*《星期日郵報》 **5** = CHAIN MAIL：*a coat of mail* 一副鎖子甲

▪ ***verb*** **1** 🔑 (*especially NAmE*) to send sth to sb using the POSTAL system 郵寄：**~ sth (to sb/sth)** *Don't forget to mail that letter to your mother.* 別忘了把那封信給你媽寄去。◇ **~ sb sth** *Don't forget to mail your mother that letter.* 別忘了把那封信給你媽寄去。◇ **~ sb/sth** *The company intends to mail 50 000 households in the area.* 公司計劃給當地的 5 萬個家庭寄信。➲ note at POST **2** 🔑 (*BrE*) to send a message to sb by email 用電子郵件傳送；發電郵給：**~ sb** *Please mail us at the following email address.* 請按下面的電郵地址發電郵給我們。◇ **~ sth (to sb/sth)** *The virus mails itself forward to everyone in your address book.* 這種病毒通過電子郵件自動轉發給通訊錄中的所有人。◇ **~ sb sth** *Can you mail me that document you mentioned?* 你能把你提及的那份文件寄給我嗎？

PHR V **ˌmail sth↔ˈout** to send out a large number of letters, etc. at the same time 批量郵寄：*The brochures were mailed out last week.* 小冊子已於上週一批寄出去了。

mail·bag /ˈmeɪlbæɡ/ (*BrE* also **post·bag**) *noun* **1** a large strong bag that is used for carrying letters and packages 郵袋 **2** [usually sing.] all the letters, emails, etc. received by a newspaper, a TV station, a website, or an important person at a particular time or about a particular subject（寄給報紙、電視台、網站、要人等的）公眾來信

ˈmail bomb *noun, verb*

▪ ***noun*** **1** (*NAmE*) = LETTER BOMB **2** an extremely large number of email messages that are sent to sb 電郵轟炸（指發給某人的超大量電子郵件）

▪ ***verb*** **ˈmail-bomb** **~ sb/sth** to send sb an extremely large number of email messages 發動電郵轟炸（指向某人發送超大量電子郵件）：*The newspaper was mail-bombed by angry readers after the article was published.* 文章發表後，這家報紙受到了憤怒讀者的電郵轟炸。

mail·box /ˈmeɪlbɒks; *NAmE* -bɑːks/ *noun* **1** (*NAmE*) (*BrE* **ˈletter box**) a small box near the main door of a building or by the road, which mail is delivered to（建築物大門口或路旁的）信箱 **2** (*NAmE*) (*BrE* **post·box**, **ˈletter box**) a public box, for example in the street, that you put letters into when you send them 郵筒；郵箱 ➲ **VISUAL VOCAB** pages V2, V3 ➲ picture at LETTER BOX **3** the area of a computer's memory where email messages are stored 電子郵箱，信箱區（計算機的電存貯區）

'mail carrier (also **'letter carrier**) (both *NAmE*) *noun* ➲ MAILMAN

'mail drop *noun* **1** (*especially NAmE*) an address where sb's mail is delivered, which is not where they live or work 中轉通信地址；只作收郵件用的地址 **2** (*NAmE*) a box in a building where sb's mail is kept for them to collect （大樓內的）私人信箱 **3** (*BrE*) an occasion when mail is delivered 郵件的遞送

mail·er /'meɪlə(r)/ *noun* (*NAmE*) **1** = MAILING (2) **2** an envelope, box, etc. for sending small things by mail 郵件封套（或小箱、盒等）

mail·ing /'meɪlɪŋ/ *noun* **1** [U] the act of sending items by mail 郵遞；郵寄：*The strike has delayed the mailing of tax reminders.* 罷工耽擱了催稅單的投寄。◇ *a mailing address* 郵寄地址 **2** (*NAmE* also **mailer**) [C] a letter or package that is sent by mail, especially one that is sent to a large number of people 郵件（尤指成批寄發的）：*An order form is included in the mailing.* 隨信寄上訂購單一份。

'mailing list *noun* **1** a list of the names and addresses of people who are regularly sent information, advertising material, etc. by an organization 郵寄名單；郵寄名址錄：*I am already on your mailing list.* 我已經列在你的郵寄名單上了。 **2** a list of names and email addresses kept on a computer so that you can send a message to a number of people at the same time （計算機中存貯的）電郵發送清單

mail·man /'meɪlmæn/ *noun* (*pl.* **-men** /-men/) (also **'mail carrier**, **'letter carrier**) (all *NAmE*) a person whose job is to collect and deliver letters, etc. 郵遞員 ➲ see also POSTMAN ➲ note at GENDER

Mail·merge™ /'meɪlmɜːdʒ; *NAmE* -mɜːrdʒ/ *noun* [U] a computer program that allows names and addresses to be automatically added to letters and envelopes, so that letters with the same contents can be sent to many different people 郵件合併程序，郵件合併程式（可自動給內容相同的信件和信封添加姓名和地址以發給多人）

,mail 'order *noun* [U] a system of buying and selling goods through the mail 郵購（制度）：*All our products are available by mail order.* 我們的商品都可以郵購。◇ *a mail-order company* 郵購公司 ◇ *a mail-order catalogue* 郵購商品目錄

mail·shot /'meɪlʃɒt; *NAmE* -ʃɑːt/ *noun* advertising or information that is sent to a large number of people at the same time by mail 郵寄廣告材料；廣告郵件

'mail slot (*NAmE*) (*BrE* **'letter box**) *noun* a narrow opening in a door or wall through which mail is delivered （門或牆上的）信箱 ➲ picture at LETTER BOX

maim /meɪm/ *verb* **~ sb** to injure sb seriously, causing permanent damage to their body 使殘廢；使受重傷 **SYN** **incapacitate**：*Hundreds of people are killed or maimed in car accidents every week.* 每週都有數百人因車禍而喪命或致殘。

main 0-π /meɪn/ *adj.*, *noun*

■ ***adj.*** 0-π [only before noun] being the largest or most important of its kind 主要的；最重要的：*Be careful crossing the **main road**.* 過大馬路時小心點兒。◇ *the **main course*** (= of a meal) 主菜 ◇ *We have our main meal at lunchtime.* 我們的正餐是午飯。◇ *Reception is in the main building.* 接待處在主樓。◇ *Poor housing and unemployment are the main problems.* 住房條件差和失業是主要問題。◇ ***The main thing** is to stay calm.* 最重要的是要保持冷靜。 **IDM** see EYE *n.*

■ ***noun*** **1** [C] a large pipe that carries water or gas to a building; a large cable that carries electricity to a building （通往建築物的）主管道，總管，輸電幹線：*a leaking gas main* 漏氣的煤氣總管 ➲ see also WATER MAIN **2** a large pipe that carries waste/water and SEWAGE (= human waste, etc.) away from a building （建築物的）污水總管道 **3 the mains** [U, pl.] (*BrE*) the place where the supply of water, gas or electricity to a

M

Synonyms 同義詞辨析

main

major · key · central · principal · chief · prime

These words all describe sb/sth that is the largest or most important of its kind. 以上各詞均用以形容主要的、最重要的人或事物。

main [only before noun] largest or most important 指主要的、最重要的：*Be careful crossing the main road.* 過大馬路時小心點。◇ *The main thing is to remain calm.* 最重要的是要保持冷靜。

major [usually before noun] very large or important 指主要的、重要的、大的：*He played a major role in setting up the system.* 他對建立這個系統起了重要的作用。 **NOTE** **Major** is most often used after *a* with a singular noun, or no article with a plural noun. When it is used with *the* or *my/your/his/her/our/their* it means 'the largest or most important'. * major 最常用於不定冠詞 a 之後，與單數名詞連用；或不用冠詞，與複數名詞連用。major 與 the 或 my/your/his/her/our/their 連用時意為最主要的、最重要的：*Our major concern here is combatting poverty.* 在這裏我們最關心的是解決貧窮問題。 In this meaning it is only used to talk about ideas or worries that people have, not physical things, and it is also more formal than **main**. 在該含義中 major 只用以指人的想法或擔憂，而非物質的東西，且較 main 正式：~~*Be careful crossing the major road.*~~ ◇ ~~*The major thing is to remain calm.*~~

key [usually before noun] most important; essential 指最重要的、主要的、關鍵的：*He was a key figure in the campaign.* 他是這場運動的關鍵人物。 **NOTE** **Key** is used most frequently in business and political contexts. It can be used to talk about ideas, or the part that sb plays in a situation, but not physical things. It is slightly more informal than **major**, especially when used after a noun and linking verb. * key 最常用於商務和政治語境，可用以指想法或某人在某情勢下起的作用，而非物質的東西。key 較 major 稍非正式，用於名詞加連繫動詞後尤其如此：*Speed is key at this point.* 在這個時候速度是關鍵。

central (*rather formal*) most important. 指最重要的、首要的、主要的：*The central issue is that of widespread racism.* 最重要的問題是種族主義泛濫。 **NOTE** **Central** is used in a similar way to **key**, but is more formal. It is most frequently used in the phrase *sth is central to sth else.* * central 與 key 用法相似，但更正式，最常用於 be central to 短語中。

principal [only before noun] (*rather formal*) most important 指最重要的、主要的：*The principal reason for this omission is lack of time.* 略過這個的主要原因是時間不足。 **NOTE** **Principal** is mostly used for statements of fact about which there can be no argument. To state an opinion, or to try to persuade sb of the facts as you see them, it is more usual to use **key** or **central**. * principal 主要用於陳述無可爭辯的事實。表明意見或說服別人相信你所見到的事實，較常用 key 或 central：*The key/central issue here is ...* 這裏的關鍵問題是…

chief [only before noun] (*rather formal*) most important 指最重要的、首要的、主要的：*Unemployment was the chief cause of poverty.* 失業是貧窮的主要原因。

prime [only before noun] (*rather formal*) most important; to be considered first 指主要的、首要的：*My prime concern is to protect my property.* 我最關心的是保護自己的財產。

PATTERNS

- a/the main/major/key/central/principal/chief/prime **aim/concern**
- a/the main/major/principal **road/town/city**
- the main/key **thing** is to ...
- to be **of** major/key/central/prime **importance**

building or an area starts; the system of providing gas, water and electricity to a building or of carrying it away from a building 水源；煤氣源；電源；（水、煤氣、電等的）供應系統；下水道系統：*The house is not yet connected to the mains.* 這房子還沒有通水電。◇ *The electricity supply has been cut off* ***at the mains.*** 電的供應在電源處被切斷了。◇ *Plug the transformer into the mains* (= the place on a wall where electricity is brought into a room). 將變壓器插入電源。◇ ***mains gas/water/electricity*** 煤氣 / 水 / 電供應系統 ◇ *The shaver will run off batteries or mains.* 這個剃鬚刀可用電池或電源驅動。◇ *mains drainage* 排水系統

IDM **in the 'main** used to say that a statement is true in most cases 大體上；基本上：*The service here is, in the main, reliable.* 這裏的服務基本上是可靠的。

,main 'clause *noun* (*grammar* 語法) a group of words that includes a subject and a verb and can form a sentence 主句 ➲ compare SUBORDINATE CLAUSE

the ,main 'drag *noun* [sing.] (*NAmE, informal*) the most important or the busiest street in a town（城鎮的）大街，主要街道，最繁華的街道

main·frame /'meɪnfreɪm/ (also **,mainframe com'puter**) *noun* a large powerful computer, usually the centre of a network and shared by many users 主機；主計算機 ➲ compare MICROCOMPUTER, MINICOMPUTER, PERSONAL COMPUTER

the main·land /'meɪnlænd/ *noun* [sing.] the main area of land of a country, not including any islands near to it 大陸；（不包括附近島嶼的）國土的主體：*a boat* ***to/from the mainland*** 駛往大陸的 / 由大陸來的船 ◇ *The Hebrides are to the west of the Scottish mainland.* 赫布里底群島位於蘇格蘭本土的西面。▸ **main·land** *adj.* [only before noun]：*mainland Greece* 希臘大陸

,main 'line *noun* an important railway/railroad line between two cities（城際）鐵路主幹線 ▸ **,main-'line** *adj.*：*a main-line station* 幹線車站

main·line /'meɪnlaɪn/ *adj., verb*

■ ***adj.*** (*especially NAmE*) belonging to the system, or connected with the ideas that most people accept or believe in 傳統的；主流的 **SYN** **mainstream**：***mainline churches/faiths*** 主流教會 / 宗教

■ ***verb*** [T, I] **~ (sth)** (*slang*) to take an illegal drug by INJECTING it into a VEIN 靜脈注射（毒品）：*At 18 he was mainlining heroin.* 他 18 歲時就注射海洛因。

main·ly 🔑 /'meɪnli/ *adv.*

1 🔑 more than anything else; also used to talk about the most important reason for sth 主要地；首要地 **SYN** **chiefly, primarily**：*They eat mainly fruit and nuts.* 他們主要吃水果和堅果。◇ *'Where do you export to?' 'France, mainly.'* "你們出口到哪裏？" "主要是法國。" ◇ *The population almost doubles in summer,* ***mainly because of*** *the jazz festival.* 主要是爵士音樂節的緣故，在夏季這裏的人口幾乎比平時多一倍。**2** 🔑 in most cases; used to talk about the largest part of a group of people or things 大部份；大多：*Anorexia is an illness that occurs mainly in adolescents.* 厭食症是一種多發於青少年的疾病。◇ *The people in the hotel were mainly foreign tourists.* 酒店裏住的大多是外國遊客。➲ LANGUAGE BANK at GENERALLY

,main 'man *noun* [sing.] (*informal*) a man who is important to you because he is a trusted friend or employee 重要的人；密友；心腹雇員：*Of course I trust you—you're my main man!* 我當然信任你，你是我的左膀右臂！

main·sail /'meɪnseɪl; 'meɪnsl/ *noun* the largest and most important sail on a boat or ship 主帆 ➲ VISUAL VOCAB page V56

main·spring /'meɪnsprɪŋ/ *noun* **1** [usually sing.] **~ (of sth)** (*formal*) the most important part of sth; the most important influence on sth 主體部份；主要影響 **2** the most important spring in a watch, clock, etc.（鐘錶等的）主發條

main·stay /'meɪnsteɪ/ *noun* [usually sing.] **~ (of sth)** a person or thing that is the most important part of sth and enables it to exist or be successful 支柱；中流砥柱：*Cocoa is the country's economic mainstay.* 可可是這個國家的經濟支柱。

main·stream /'meɪnstriːm/ *noun, adj., verb*

■ ***noun*** **the mainstream** [sing.] the ideas and opinions that are thought to be normal because they are shared by most people; the people whose ideas and opinions are most accepted 主流思想；主流群體：*His radical views place him outside the mainstream of American politics.* 他的激進觀點使他脫離了美國政治的主流。▸ **main·stream** *adj.* [usually before noun]：*mainstream education* 主流教育

■ ***verb*** **1 ~ sth** to make a particular idea or opinion accepted by most people 使為大多數人所接受：*Vegetarianism has been mainstreamed.* 素食主義已為大多數人所接受。**2 ~ sb** (*especially NAmE*) to include children with mental or physical problems in ordinary school classes 讓（身心有缺陷的兒童）融入主流教育

'main street *noun* (*NAmE*) **1** (*BrE* **'high street**) [C] (especially in names 尤用於名稱) the main street of a town, where most shops/stores, banks, etc. are（市區的）大街 ➲ VISUAL VOCAB page V3 **2** **Main Street** [U] typical middle-class Americans 典型的美國中產階級：*Main Street won't be happy with this new program.* 中產階級不會對這個新計劃感到高興的。

main·tain 🔑 **AW** /meɪn'teɪn/ *verb*

1 🔑 **~ sth** to make sth continue at the same level, standard, etc. 維持；保持 **SYN** **preserve**：*to* ***maintain law and order/standards/a balance*** 維持治安；保持水平 / 平衡 ◇ *The two countries have always maintained close relations.* 這兩個國家一直保持着密切關係。◇ (*formal*) *She maintained a dignified silence.* 她一言不發，面容威嚴。◇ *to maintain prices* (= prevent them falling or rising) 維持價格的穩定 **2** 🔑 **~ sth** to keep a building, a machine, etc. in good condition by checking or repairing it regularly 維修；保養：*The house is large and difficult to maintain.* 房子很大，難以養護。**3** 🔑 to keep stating that sth is true, even though other people do not agree or do not believe it 堅持意見；固執己見 **SYN** **insist**：**~ (that)** ... *The men maintained (that) they were out of the country when the crime was committed.* 這幾個男人堅持說案發時他們在國外。◇ **~ sth** *She has always* ***maintained her innocence.*** 她一直堅持說她是無辜的。◇ **+ speech** *'But I'm innocent!' she maintained.* "但是我是無辜的！"她堅持道。➲ LANGUAGE BANK at ARGUE **4** 🔑 **~ sb/sth** to support sb/sth over a long period of time by giving money, paying for food, etc. 供養；扶養 **SYN** **keep**：*Her income was barely enough to maintain one child, let alone three.* 她的收入養活一個孩子都不夠，更不用說三個了。

main·ten·ance **AW** /'meɪntənəns/ *noun* [U] **1 ~ (of sth)** the act of keeping sth in good condition by checking or repairing it regularly 維護；保養：*The school pays for heating and the maintenance of the buildings.* 學校負擔這些大樓的供熱和維修費用。◇ *car maintenance* 汽車保養 **2 ~ (of sth)** the act of making a state or situation continue 維持；保持：*the maintenance of international peace* 維護世界和平 **3** (*law* 律) (*BrE*) money that sb must pay regularly to their former wife, husband or partner, especially when they have had children together（依法應負擔的）生活費；撫養費：*He has to pay maintenance to his ex-wife.* 他必須付給前妻生活費。◇ *child maintenance* 兒童撫養費 ◇ *a maintenance order* (= given by a court of law)（法院下達的）生活費支付令 ➲ see also ALIMONY

,main 'verb *noun* [usually sing.] (*grammar* 語法) the verb in a MAIN CLAUSE 主要動詞（主句中的動詞）

mai·son·ette /,meɪzə'net/ *noun* (*BrE*) a flat/apartment with rooms on two floors within a building, usually with a separate entrance 複式住宅；（跨）二層公寓

maître d' /,meɪtrə 'diː; *NAmE* also ,meɪtər/ *noun* (*pl.* **maître d's** /,meɪtrə 'diːz; *NAmE* also ,meɪtər/) (also *formal* **maître d'hôtel** /,meɪtrə dəʊ'tel; *NAmE* doʊ'tel; *NAmE* also ,meɪtər/ *pl.* **maîtres d'hôtel** /,meɪtrə dəʊ'tel; *NAmE* doʊ'tel; *NAmE* also ,meɪtər/) (from *French, informal*) **1** a head waiter 侍者總管；領班 **2** a man who manages a hotel 旅館經理；旅館老闆

maize /meɪz/ *noun* [U] **1** (*BrE*) (*NAmE* **corn**) a tall plant grown for its large yellow grains that are used for making flour or eaten as a vegetable; the grains of this plant 玉蜀黍；玉米 ➲ VISUAL VOCAB page V32 ➲ see also CORN ON THE COB, SWEETCORN **2** (*especially NAmE*) = INDIAN CORN

Maj. *abbr.* (in writing) MAJOR（書寫形式）少校：*Maj. (Tony) Davies*（托尼）戴維斯少校 ◇ *Maj. Gen.* (= Major General) 少將

ma·jes·tic /məˈdʒestɪk/ *adj.* impressive because of size or beauty 雄偉的；威嚴的；壯觀的 SYN **awe-inspiring, splendid**：*a majestic castle/river/view* 雄偉的城堡；壯麗的河流／景色 ▸ **ma·jes·tic·al·ly** /-kli/ *adv.*

maj·esty /ˈmædʒəsti/ *noun* (*pl.* **-ies**) **1** [U] the impressive and attractive quality that sth has 雄偉壯觀；莊嚴；威嚴：*the sheer majesty of St Peter's in Rome* 羅馬聖彼得大教堂的雄偉莊嚴 ◇ *the majesty of the music* 那音樂的莊嚴氣氛 **2** [C] **His/Her/Your Majesty** a title of respect used when speaking about or to a king or queen（對國王或女王的尊稱）陛下 **3** [U] royal power 王權

major 🔑 AW /ˈmeɪdʒə(r)/ *adj., noun, verb*

■ ***adj.*** **1** 🔑 [usually before noun] very large or important 主要的；重要的；大的：*a major road* 一條大馬路 ◇ *major international companies* 大跨國公司 ◇ *to play a major role in sth* 在某事中起重要作用 ◇ *We have encountered major problems.* 我們遇上了大問題。◇ *There were calls for major changes to the welfare system.* 有人要求對福利制度進行重大改革。OPP **minor** ➲ SYNONYMS at MAIN ➲ see also MINOR-LEAGUE (2) **2** [not before noun] (*NAmE*) serious 嚴重：*Never mind—it's not major.* 別擔心，這不嚴重。**3** (*music* 音) based on a SCALE (= a series of eight notes) in which the third note is two whole TONES/STEPS higher than the first note 大調的：*the key of D major* * D大調 ➲ compare MINOR *adj.* (2) **4** (*NAmE*) related to sb's main subject of study in college（課程）主修的

■ ***noun*** **1** [C] (*abbr.* **Maj.**) an officer of fairly high rank in the army or the US AIR FORCE 少校：*Major Smith* 史密斯少校 ◇ *He's a major in the US army.* 他是美國陸軍少校。➲ see also DRUM MAJOR, SERGEANT MAJOR **2** [C] (*NAmE*) the main subject or course of a student at college or university 主修課程；專業課：*Her major is French.* 她的專業課是法語。➲ compare MINOR *n.* (2) **3** [C] (*NAmE*) a student studying a particular subject as the main part of their course 主修學生；主修生：*She's a French major.* 她是法語專業的學生。**4 the majors** [pl.] (*sport* 體) (*NAmE*) the MAJOR LEAGUES 大聯盟

■ ***verb***

PHR V **ˈmajor in sth** (*NAmE*) to study sth as your main subject at a university or college 主修：*She majored in History at Stanford.* 她在斯坦福主修歷史。**ˈmajor on sth** (*BrE*) to pay particular attention to one subject, issue, etc. 專門研究（課題、問題等）

major-domo /ˌmeɪdʒə ˈdəʊməʊ; *NAmE* ˌmeɪdʒər ˈdoʊmoʊ/ *noun* (*pl.* **-os**) a senior servant who manages a large house（大宅的）總管家，大管家

ma·jor·ette /ˌmeɪdʒəˈret/ *noun* (*especially NAmE*) = DRUM MAJORETTE

ˌmajor ˈgeneral *noun* an officer of very high rank in the army or the US AIR FORCE 陸軍少將；（美）空軍少將：*Major General William Hunt* 陸軍少將威廉•亨特

ma·jor·ity 🔑 AW /məˈdʒɒrəti; *NAmE* -ˈdʒɔːr-; -ˈdʒɑːr-/ *noun* (*pl.* **-ies**)

1 🔑 [sing.+sing./pl. v.] **~ (of sb/sth)** the largest part of a group of people or things 大部份；大多數：*The majority of people interviewed prefer TV to radio.* 大多數接受採訪的人都喜歡看電視多於聽收音機。◇ *The majority was/were in favour of banning smoking*. 大多數人支持禁煙。◇ *This treatment is not available in the **vast majority** of hospitals.* 絕大部份醫院都不提供這種治療。◇ *a majority decision* (= one that is decided by what most people want) 根據大多數人的意見作出的決定 ◇ *In the nursing profession, women are **in a/the majority**.* 女性在護理行業中佔大多數。OPP **minority** ➲ see also MORAL MAJORITY, THE SILENT MAJORITY **2** 🔑 [C] (*BrE*) the number of votes by which one political party wins an election; the number of votes by which one side in a discussion, etc. wins（獲勝的）票數；多數票：*She was elected **by/with a majority** of 749.* 她以 749 票的多數票當選。◇ *a clear (= large) majority* 明顯多數票 ◇ **~ (over sb)** *They had a large majority over their nearest rivals.* 他們所得的票數遠遠超出名次僅次於他們的對手。◇ *The government does not have an **overall majority*** (= more members than all the other parties added together). 政府沒有獲得絕對多數票。◇ *The resolution was carried by a huge majority.* 這項決議以大多數票贊成而獲得通過。➲ COLLOCATIONS at VOTE ➲ see also ABSOLUTE MAJORITY **3** 🔑 [C] (*NAmE*) the difference between the number of votes given to the candidate who wins the election and the total number of votes of all the other candidates 超出其餘各方票數總和的票數 ➲ see also PLURALITY **4** [U] (*law* 律) the age at which you are legally considered to be an adult 成年的法定年齡

maˈjority leader *noun* the leader of the political party that has the majority in either the House of Representatives or the Senate in the US（美國眾議院或參議院的）多數派政黨領袖

maˌjority ˈrule *noun* [U] a system in which power is held by the group that has the largest number of members 多數裁定原則

maˌjority ˈverdict *noun* (*law* 律) a decision made by a JURY in a court case that most members, but not all, agree with 多數裁決（陪審團根據多數票作出）

ˈmajor league (also **ˈMajor league**) *noun* (*NAmE*) a league of professional sports teams, especially in BASEBALL, that play at the highest level（尤指棒球）第一流的職業隊伍聯盟；大聯盟

ˈmajor-league *adj.* [only before noun] (*NAmE*) **1** (*sport* 體) connected with teams that play in the major leagues, especially in BASEBALL（尤指棒球）職業體育總會的，大聯盟的：*a major-league team* 職業體育總會球隊 **2** very important and having a lot of influence 非常重要的；頗有影響力的：*a major-league business* 舉足輕重的企業

major·ly /ˈmeɪdʒəli; *NAmE* -dʒərli/ *adv.* (used before an adjective 用於形容詞前) (*informal, especially NAmE*) very; extremely 非常地；極端地：*majorly disappointed* 無比失望

make 🔑 /meɪk/ *verb, noun* ➲ see also MADE

■ ***verb*** (**made, made** /meɪd/)

▸ **CREATE** 製造 **1** 🔑 to create or prepare sth by combining materials or putting parts together 製造；做；組裝：**~ sth** *to make a table/dress/cake* 做桌子／連衣裙／蛋糕 ◇ *to make bread/cement/paper* 製作麵包；生產水泥／紙張 ◇ *She makes her own clothes.* 她自己做衣服。◇ *made in France* (= on a label) 法國製造 ◇ **~ sth (out) of sth** *What's your shirt made of?* 你的襯衣是用什麼做的？◇ **~ sth from sth** *Wine is made from grapes.* 葡萄酒是用葡萄做的。◇ **~ sth into sth** *The grapes are made into wine.* 這些葡萄用來做酒。◇ **~ sth for sb** *She made coffee for us all.* 她給我們大家沖了咖啡。◇ **~ sb sth** *She made us all coffee.* 她給我們大家沖了咖啡。➲ note at DO **2** 🔑 **~ sth** to write, create or prepare sth 寫；出產；制訂：*These regulations were made to protect children.* 這些規章制度是為了保護兒童而制訂的。◇ *My lawyer has been urging me to make a will.* 我的律師一直在催促我立遺囑。◇ *She has made* (= directed or acted in) *several movies.* 她已經出了好幾部電影。

▸ **A BED** 牀 **3** 🔑 **~ a bed** to arrange a bed so that it is neat and ready for use 鋪牀

▸ **CAUSE TO APPEAR/HAPPEN/BECOME/DO** 使出現／發生／成為／做 **4** 🔑 **~ sth (+ adv./prep.)** to cause sth to appear as a result of breaking, tearing, hitting or removing material 造成（破壞、破損等）：*The stone made a dent in the roof of the car.* 石頭把車頂砸了個坑。◇ *The holes in the cloth were made by moths.* 布上的窟窿是蟲子蛀的。**5** 🔑 **~ sth** to cause sth to exist, happen or be done 使出現；引發；使產生：*to **make a noise/mess/fuss*** 產生噪音；弄得一團糟；小題大做 ◇ *She tried to **make a good impression** on the interviewer.* 她努力給主持面試者留個好印象。◇ *I keep **making** the same **mistakes**.* 我總是犯同樣的錯誤。**6** 🔑 **~ sb/sth/yourself + adj.** to cause sb/sth

M

to be or become sth 使變得；使成為： *The news made him very happy.* 這則消息使他非常高興。◇ *She made her objections clear.* 她明確表示反對。◇ *He* ***made it clear that*** *he objected.* 他明確表示反對。◇ *The full story was never* ***made public****.* 全部情況從未公之於世。◇ *Can you* ***make yourself understood*** *in Russian?* 你能用俄語表達你的意思嗎？◇ *She couldn't* ***make herself heard*** *above the noise of the traffic.* 車輛噪音很大，她無法讓人聽到她的聲音。◇ *The terrorists* ***made it known that*** *tourists would be targeted.* 恐怖分子宣稱遊客將成為他們襲擊的目標。 **7** ⊶ **~ sb/sth do sth** to cause sb/sth to do sth 促使；使得： *She always makes me laugh.* 她總是讓我發笑。◇ *This dress makes me look fat.* 這衣服我穿着顯胖。◇ *What makes you say that* (= why do you think so)? 你為什麼這麼說？◇ *Nothing will make me change my mind.* 什麼也改變不了我的主意。 **8** ⊶ to cause sb/sth to be or become sth 使變得；使成為： **~ sth of sb/sth** *This isn't very important—I don't want to* ***make an issue of it****.* 這不太重要，我不想把它當回事兒。◇ *Don't* ***make a habit of it****.* 別養成習慣。◇ *You've* ***made a*** *terrible* ***mess of*** *this job.* 你把這件事兒搞得一團糟。◇ *It's important to try and* ***make something of*** (= achieve sth in) *your life.* 在一生中有所成就是很重要的。◇ *We'll make a tennis player of you yet.* 我們會讓你成為一名網球選手的。◇ **~ sth + noun** *I made painting the house my project for the summer.* 把房子粉刷了一遍，這就是我的夏季工程。◇ *She* ***made it her business*** *to find out who was responsible.* 她一定要查清楚到底該誰負責。

▸ **A DECISION/GUESS/COMMENT, ETC.** 決定、猜測、評論等 **9** ⊶ **~ a decision, guess, comment, etc.** to decide, guess, etc. sth 做，作出（決定、估計等）： *Come on! It's time we made a start.* 快點！我們該開始了。 **HELP** Make can be used in this way with a number of different nouns. These expressions are included at the entry for each noun. * make 可以和許多名詞這樣搭配使用，表達方式列在各有關名詞詞條下。

▸ **FORCE** 迫使 **10** ⊶ to force sb to do sth 迫使；強迫： **~ sb do sth** *They made me repeat the whole story.* 他們非讓我把整個事件再說一遍。◇ **be made to do sth** *She must be made to comply with the rules.* 必須讓她遵守規則。◇ **~ sb** *He never cleans his room and his mother never tries to make him.* 他從不收拾自己的房間，而他媽也從不要求他收拾。

▸ **REPRESENT** 表現 **11** ⊶ to represent sb/sth as being or doing sth 表現；表示；描繪： **~ sb/sth + adj.** *You've made my nose too big* (= for example in a drawing). 你把我的鼻子畫得太大了。◇ **~ sb/sth + noun** *He makes King Lear a truly tragic figure.* 他把李爾王刻畫成一個真正的悲劇人物。

▸ **APPOINT** 任命 **12** ⊶ **~ sb + noun** to elect or choose sb as sth 選舉；挑選；任命： *She made him her assistant.* 她挑選他做她的助手。

▸ **BE SUITABLE** 適合 **13** ⊶ *linking verb* **~ sb/sth + noun** to become or develop into sth; to be suitable for sth 成為；適合： *She would have made an excellent teacher.* 她本可以成為一位出色的教師。◇ *This room would make a nice office.* 這間屋子做辦公室挺不錯。

▸ **EQUAL** 等於 **14** ⊶ *linking verb* **+ noun** to add up to or equal sth 合計；等於： *5 and 7 make 12.* * 5 加 7 等於 12。◇ *A hundred cents make one euro.* 一百分等於一歐元。 **15** *linking verb* **+ noun** to be a total of sth 成為總數；是…的總和： *That makes the third time he's failed his driving test!* 他這已經是第三次駕駛考試不及格了！

▸ **MONEY** 錢 **16** ⊶ **~ sth** to earn or gain money 掙錢；賺錢： *She makes $100 000 a year.* 她一年賺 10 萬元。◇ *to* ***make a profit/loss*** 獲利；賠錢◇ *We need to think of ways to* ***make money****.* 我們需要想辦法掙錢。◇ *He* ***made a fortune*** *on the stock market.* 他在股票市場發了大財。◇ *He* ***makes a living*** *as a stand-up comic.* 他靠說單口相聲為生。

▸ **CALCULATE** 計算 **17** [no passive] **~ sth + noun** to think or calculate sth to be sth 估計；計算： *What time do you* ***make it****?* 你估計現在幾點了？◇ *I make that exactly $50.* 我算出正好是 50 元。

▸ **REACH** 達到 **18** [no passive] **~ sth** to manage to reach or go to a place or position （盡力）趕往，到達，達到： *Do you think we'll make Dover by 12?* 你覺得我們 12 點能到多佛嗎？◇ *I'm sorry I couldn't make your party last night.* 很抱歉，昨晚沒能參加你們的聚會。◇ *He'll never make* (= get a place in) *the team.* 他絕不可能成為該隊的隊員。◇ *The story made* (= appeared on) *the front pages of the national newspapers.* 這件事登在了全國性報紙的頭版。◇ *We just managed to* ***make the deadline*** (= to finish sth in time). 我們勉強按期完成。

▸ **STH SUCCESSFUL** 成功 **19** **~ sth** to cause sth to be a success 使成功；使圓滿： *Good wine can make a meal.* 酒美飯亦香。◇ *The news really* ***made my day****.* 這消息確實使我一天都很愉快。

IDM Most idioms containing **make** are at the entries for the nouns and adjectives in the idioms, for example **make merry** is at **merry**. 大多數含 make 的習語，都可在該等習語中的名詞及形容詞相關詞條找到，如 make merry 在詞條 merry 下。 **make as if to do sth** to make a movement that makes it seem as if you are just going to do sth 似乎；假裝： *He made as if to speak.* 他似乎要說點什麼。 **make 'do (with sth)** to manage with sth that is not really good enough 湊合；將就： *We were in a hurry so we had to make do with a quick snack.* 我們很匆忙，只好將就着來了點小吃。 **make 'good** to become rich and successful 變得富有；獲得成功 **make sth 'good** **1** to pay for, replace or repair sth that has been lost or damaged 賠償；替換；修理： *She promised to make good the damage.* 她答應賠償損失。 **2** to do sth that you have promised, threatened, etc. to do 履行，執行（曾承諾、威脅等的事） **SYN** fulfil **'make it** **1** ⊶ to be successful in your career 獲得成功： *He never really made it as an actor.* 他從來就不是一個成功的演員。 **2** ⊶ to succeed in reaching a place in time, especially when this is difficult （尤指在困難情況下）準時到達： *The flight leaves in twenty minutes—we'll never make it.* 再過二十分鐘飛機就起飛了，咱們無論如何也趕不上了。 **3** ⊶ to be able to be present at a place 能夠出席（或到場）： *I'm sorry I won't be able to make it* (= for example, to a party) *on Saturday.* 很抱歉，星期六我不能出席。 **4** ⊶ to survive after a serious illness or accident; to deal successfully with a difficult experience 幸免於難；渡過難關： *The doctors think he's going to make it.* 醫生認為他能挺過去。◇ *I don't know how I* ***made it through*** *the week.* 我不知道自己是怎麼熬過那個星期的。 **'make it with sb** (*NAmE, slang*) to have sex with sb （與某人）發生性關係 **make like ...** (*NAmE, informal*) to pretend to be, know or have sth in order to impress people （為給別人留下印象）假裝，裝出…樣子： *He makes like he's the greatest actor of all time.* 他裝模作樣，彷彿自己是有史以來最棒的演員。 **make the 'most of sth/sb/yourself** to gain as much advantage, enjoyment, etc. as you can from sb/sth 充分利用；盡情享受： *It's my first trip abroad so I'm going to make the most of it.* 這是我第一次出國，我要充分利用這個機會。◇ *She doesn't know how to make the most of herself* (= make herself appear in the best possible way). 她不知道如何充分表現自己。 **make 'much of sth/sb** to treat sth/sb as very important 重視；認為很重要： *He always makes much of his humble origins.* 他總是非常在意他卑微的出身。 **,make or 'break sb/sth** to be the thing that makes sb/sth either a success or a failure 為…成敗的關鍵： *This movie will make or break him as a director.* 這部電影將要決定他當導演是行還是不行。◇ *It's make-or-break time for the company.* 這是公司盛衰的關鍵時刻。 **'make something of yourself** to be successful in your life 獲得成功；事業有成

PHR V **'make for sth** **1** to move towards sth 向…移動 **SYN** head for **2** to help to make sth possible 促成： *Constant arguing doesn't make for a happy marriage.* 不斷爭吵不可能使婚姻幸福。 ➲ see also BE MADE FOR SB/EACH OTHER at MADE

'make sb/sth into sb/sth ⊶ to change sb/sth into sb/sth 把…變成 **SYN** turn into： *We're making our attic into an extra bedroom.* 我們要把閣樓改裝一下，增加一間臥室。

'make sth of sb/sth to understand the meaning or character of sb/sth 領會；理解；懂得： ***What do you make of*** *it all?* 你明白那都是什麼意思嗎？◇ *I can't make anything of this note.* 我根本不懂這封短信的意思。◇ *I don't know* ***what to make of*** (= think of) *the new manager.* 這位新經理，我不知道怎麼說他才好。

ˌmake ˈoff to hurry away, especially in order to escape 匆忙離開；（尤指）倉惶逃跑 **ˌmake ˈoff with sth** to steal sth and hurry away with it 偷走某物；順手牽羊
ˌmake ˈout 1 (*informal*) used to ask if sb managed well or was successful in a particular situation（詢問是否處理得當）應付，過：*How did he make out while his wife was away?* 他妻子不在家時他是怎麼過的？ **2 ~ (with sb)** (*NAmE, informal*) to kiss and touch sb in a sexual way; to have sex with sb 親吻撫摸（某人）；（與某人）性交
ˌmake sb ˈout to understand sb's character 看透，弄懂（某人）**ˌmake sb/sth↔ˈout 1** to manage to see sb/sth or read or hear sth 看清；聽清；分清；辨認清楚 **SYN distinguish**：*I could just make out a figure in the darkness.* 黑暗中我只看出了一個人的輪廓。◇ **~ what, who, etc. …** *I could hear voices but I couldn't make out what they were saying.* 我能聽到說話的聲音，卻聽不清他們在說什麼。➲ SYNONYMS at IDENTIFY **2** to say that sth is true when it may not be 聲稱；把…說成 **SYN claim**：*She's not as rich as people make out.* 她並不像人們說的那樣富有。◇ **~ that …** *He made out that he had been robbed.* 他說他被人搶劫了。◇ **~ to be/do sth** *She makes herself out to be smarter than she really is.* 她說自己多麼聰明，未免言過其實。 **ˌmake sth↔ˈout 1** to write out or complete a form or document 開具，填寫（表格或文件）：*He made out a cheque for €100.* 他開了一張 100 歐元的支票。◇ *The doctor made out a prescription for me.* 醫生給我開了一張處方。 **2** (used in negative sentences and questions 用於否定句和疑問句) to understand sth; to see the reasons for sth 理解；明白（事理）：*How do you make that out* (= what are your reasons for thinking that)? 你為什麼這麼想？◇ **~ what, why, etc. …** *I can't make out what she wants.* 我不明白她想要什麼。
ˌmake sth↔ˈover (to sb/sth) 1 to legally give sth to sb（合法地）給予，轉讓：*He made over the property to his eldest son.* 他把財產傳給了他的長子。 **2** to change sth in order to make it look different or use it for a different purpose; to give sb a different appearance by changing their clothes, hair, etc. 改造；修飾；徹底改變形象 **SYN transform** ➲ related noun MAKEOVER
ˈmake towards sth to start moving towards sth 向…移動；朝…走去：*He made towards the door.* 他向門口走去。
ˌmake ˈup | ˌmake yourself/sb↔ˈup to put powder, LIPSTICK, etc. on your/sb's face to make it more attractive or to prepare for an appearance in the theatre, on television, etc. 化妝；上妝 ➲ related noun MAKE-UP (1) **ˌmake sth↔ˈup 1** 🔑 to form sth 形成；構成 **SYN constitute**：*Women make up 56% of the student numbers.* 女生佔學生人數的 56%。➲ related noun MAKE-UP (3) ➲ SYNONYMS at CONSIST OF ➲ LANGUAGE BANK at PROPORTION **2** to put sth together from several different things 拼裝；組成 ➲ related noun MAKE-UP (3) **3** 🔑 to invent a story, etc., especially in order to trick or entertain sb 編造（故事、謊言等）：*He made up some excuse about his daughter being sick.* 他編造了一些託辭，說他的女兒病倒了。◇ *I told the kids a story, making it up as I went along.* 我給孩子們講了個故事，是現編的。◇ *You made that up!* 你瞎編！ **4** to complete a number or an amount required 湊數：*We need one more person to make up a team.* 我們還需要一個人才能組成一個隊。 **5** to replace sth that has been lost; to COMPENSATE for sth 補上（失去的東西）；作出補償：*Can I leave early this afternoon and make up the time tomorrow?* 我今天下午早點兒走，明天補上這段時間，可以嗎？ **6** to prepare a medicine by mixing different things together 配藥 **7** to prepare a bed for use; to create a temporary bed 鋪牀；臨時搭牀：*We made up the bed in the spare room.* 我們在空着沒用的房間裏搭了張牀。◇ *They made up a bed for me on the sofa.* 他們給我在沙發上鋪了個牀。 **8** (*especially NAmE*) to clean a hotel room and make the bed 打掃（酒店房間）：*The maid asked if she could make up the room.* 清潔女工問她是不是可以整理房間。 **ˌmake ˈup for sth** 🔑 to do sth that corrects a bad situation 彌補；補償 **SYN compensate**：*Nothing can make up for the loss of a child.* 失去一個孩子是任何東西都無法彌補的。◇ *After all the delays, we were anxious to* ***make up for lost time.*** 耽擱了這麼久，我們急着想彌補失去的時間。◇ *Her enthusiasm makes up for her lack of experience.* 她的熱情彌補了她經驗的不足。
ˌmake ˈup (to sb) for sth 🔑 to do sth for sb or give them sth because you have caused them trouble, suffering or disappointment and wish to show that you are sorry（對某人）表示歉意，給以補償 **SYN compensate**：*How can I make up for the way I've treated you?* 我這樣對你，該怎麼向你表示歉意呢？◇ (*informal*) *I'll* ***make it up to you,*** *I promise.* 我保證我一定會補償你的。
ˌmake ˈup to sb (*BrE, informal, disapproving*) to be pleasant to sb, praise them, etc. especially in order to get an advantage for yourself 獻媚；奉承；討好 **ˌmake ˈup (with sb)** (*BrE* also **ˌmake it ˈup**) to end a disagreement with sb and become friends again（與某人）言歸於好：*Why don't you two* ***kiss and make up****?* 你們兩個幹嗎不和好算了？◇ *Has he made it up with her yet?* 他跟她和好了嗎？◇ *Have they made it up yet?* 他們和解了嗎？➲ SYNONYMS at next page
■ ***noun*** 🔑 **~ (of sth)** the name or type of a machine, piece of equipment, etc. that is made by a particular company（機器、設備等的）品牌，型號：*What make of car does he drive?* 他開的是什麼品牌的車？◇ *There are so many different makes to choose from.* 有很多不同的型號可供選擇。◇ *a Swiss make of watch* 一塊瑞士錶
IDM on the ˈmake (*informal, disapproving*) trying to get money or an advantage for yourself 謀取利益

ˈmake-believe *noun* [U] **1** (*disapproving*) imagining or pretending things to be different or more exciting than they really are 虛構；想像；編造 **SYN fantasy**：*They live in a world of make-believe.* 他們生活在虛幻的世界裏。**2** imagining that sth is real, or that you are sb else, for example in a child's game 假扮；假裝：*'Let's play make-believe,' said Sam.* 薩姆說："咱們來玩假裝的遊戲吧。"

make·over /ˈmeɪkəʊvə(r); *NAmE* -oʊ-/ *noun* [C, U] the process of improving the appearance of a person or a place, or of changing the impression that sth gives（外觀的）改進，改善；修飾；翻新

maker /ˈmeɪkə(r)/ *noun* **1** [C] **~ (of sth)** (often in compounds 常構成複合詞) a person, company, or piece of equipment that makes or produces sth 生產者；製造者；制訂者：*a* ***decision/law/policy maker*** 作出決定／制訂法律／制訂政策的人◇ *programme makers* 方案擬訂者◇ *a new film/movie from the makers of 'Terminator'* 由《終結者》的製作班子製作的一部新電影◇ *If it doesn't work, send it back to the maker.* 如果不管用，就把它退還給製造廠家。◇ *an electric coffee-maker* 電咖啡壺◇ *one of the best winemakers in France* 法國最好的葡萄酒釀造廠之一 ➲ VISUAL VOCAB page V25 ➲ see also HOLIDAY-MAKER, PEACEMAKER, TROUBLEMAKER **2 the, his, your, etc. Maker** [sing.] God 上帝 **IDM** see MEET *v.*

make·shift /ˈmeɪkʃɪft/ *adj.* [usually before noun] used temporarily for a particular purpose because the real thing is not available 臨時替代的；權宜的 **SYN provisional, improvised**：*A few cushions formed a makeshift bed.* 臨時用幾個墊子拼了一張牀。

ˈmake-up 🔑 *noun*

1 🔑 [U] substances used especially by women to make their faces look more attractive, or used by actors to change their appearance 化妝品：*eye make-up* 眼妝◇ *to* ***put on your make-up*** 上妝◇ *She never* ***wears make-up.*** 她從來不化妝。◇ *a make-up artist* (= a person whose job is to put make-up on the faces of actors and models) 化妝師 ➲ COLLOCATIONS at FASHION ➲ VISUAL VOCAB page V60 **2** [sing.] the different qualities that combine to form sb's character or being 性格；氣質：*Jealousy is not part of his make-up.* 嫉妒不是他的本質。◇ *a person's genetic make-up* 一個人的遺傳性格 **3** [sing.] **~ (of sth)** the different things, people, etc. that combine to form sth; the way in which they combine 組成成分；構成方式：*the make-up of a TV audience* 電視觀眾的構成◇ (*technical* 術語) *the page make-up of a text* (= the way in which the words and pictures are arranged on a page) 文本的版面設計 **4** [C] (*NAmE*) a special exam taken by students who missed or failed an earlier one 補考

M

make·weight /ˈmeɪkweɪt/ *noun* an unimportant person or thing that is only added or included in sth in order to make it the correct number, quantity, size, etc. 充數的人（或物）

ˈmake-work *noun* [U] (*NAmE*) work that has little value but is given to people to keep them busy（佔用人手的）無價值的工作；幫閒工作： *In some departments there is too much make-work.* 有些部門的無聊瑣事太多。◇ *These are simply make-work schemes for accountants.* 這些方案只不過是讓會計師繼續忙碌而已。

Synonyms 同義詞辨析

make

do • create • develop • produce • generate • form

These words all mean to make sth from parts or materials, or to cause sth to exist or happen. 以上各詞均含製造、使產生之意。

make to create or prepare sth by combining materials or putting parts together; to cause sth to exist or happen 指製造、做、組裝、使產生： *She makes her own clothes.* 她自己做衣服。◇ *She* ***made a good impression*** *on the interviewer.* 她給主持面試者留下了很好的印象。

do (*rather informal*) to make or prepare sth, especially sth artistic or sth to eat 指製作、準備（尤指藝術品或食品）： *He did a beautiful drawing of a house.* 他畫了一棟漂亮的房子。◇ *Who's doing the food for the party?* 誰準備聚會的食物？

create to make sth exist or happen, especially sth new that did not exist before 指創造、創作、創建： *Scientists disagree about how the universe was created.* 科學家對宇宙是怎樣形成有分歧。

MAKE OR CREATE? 用 make 還是 create？

Make is a more general word and is more often used for physical things: you would usually *make a table/dress/cake* but *create jobs/wealth*. You can use **create** for sth physical in order to emphasize how original or unusual the object is. * make 較通用，較常用以指物質的東西，如製造桌子、做衣服、做蛋糕通常用 make，但創造就業機會／財富用 create。要強調某物品或實體事物是原創的或不同尋常，也可用 create： *Try this new dish, created by our head chef.* 品嚐一下這道新菜吧，是我們廚師長首創的。

develop (used especially in business contexts) to think of and produce a new product（尤用於商務語境）指開發、研製（產品）： *to develop new software* 開發新軟件

produce to make things to be sold; to create sth using skill 指生產、製造（商品），（運用技巧）製作、造出： *a factory that produces microchips* 微芯片製造廠

generate to produce or create sth, especially power, money or ideas 指創造、產生（電、財富或主意）： *to generate electricity* 發電 ◇ *Brainstorming is a good way of generating ideas.* 集思廣益是出主意的好辦法。

form [often passive] to make sth from sth else; to make sth into sth else 指製作、組成、製成： *Rearrange the letters to form a new word.* 重新排列字母，組成另一單詞。◇ *The chain is formed from 136 links.* 這根鏈條由 136 個鏈節組成。

PATTERNS

- to make/create/develop/produce/generate/form sth **from/out of** sth
- to make/form sth **into** sth
- to make/produce **wine**
- to create/develop a **new product**
- to create/produce/generate **income/profits/wealth**
- to produce/generate **electricity/heat/power**

M

mak·ing /ˈmeɪkɪŋ/ *noun* [U] **~ (of sth)** (often in compounds 常構成複合詞) the act or process of making or producing sth 生產；製造： *strategic decision making* 戰略決策 ◇ *film-making* 製片 ◇ *dressmaking* 製衣 ◇ *tea and coffee making facilities* 沏茶煮咖啡的用具 ◇ *the making of social policy* 社會政策的制訂 ➲ see also HAYMAKING, NON-PROFIT

IDM **be the ˈmaking of sb** to make sb become a better or more successful person 使成為更好（或更有作為）的人： *University was the making of Joe.* 大學造就了喬。 **have the ˈmakings of sth** to have the qualities that are necessary to become sth 具備了成為…的必要條件： *Her first novel has all the makings of a classic.* 她的第一部小說堪稱經典之作。 **in the ˈmaking** in the process of becoming sth or of being made 在生產（或形成）過程中： *This model was two years in the making.* 這種型號是用兩年時間製成的。◇ *These events are* ***history in the making****.* 這些事將載入史冊。 **of your own ˈmaking** (of a problem, difficulty, etc. 問題、困難等) created by you rather than by sb/sth else 自己造成的

ma·kuti /mæˈkuːti/ *noun* [pl.] the leaves of a PALM tree, used as a material to make fences, BASKETS, etc. and roofs , especially on the coast of E Africa 馬庫提（尤指東非海濱的一種棕櫚樹葉，用於籬笆、籃筐、屋頂等）： *a makuti roof* 馬庫提屋頂

mal- /mæl/ *combining form* (in nouns, verbs and adjectives 構成名詞、動詞和形容詞) bad or badly; not correct or correctly 糟糕；壞；錯誤： *malpractice* 玩忽職守 ◇ *malodorous* 有惡臭的 ◇ *malfunction* 故障

mal·ach·ite /ˈmæləkaɪt/ *noun* [U] a green mineral that can be polished, used to make decorative objects 孔雀石

mal·adjust·ed /ˌmæləˈdʒʌstɪd/ *adj.* (especially of children 尤指兒童) having mental and emotional problems that lead to unacceptable behaviour 適應不良的；心理失調的 ➲ compare WELL ADJUSTED ▸ **mal·adjust·ment** /ˌmæləˈdʒʌstmənt/ *noun* [U]

mal·admin·is·tration /ˌmælədˌmɪnɪˈstreɪʃn/ *noun* [U] (*formal*) the fact of managing a business or an organization in a bad or dishonest way 管理不善；腐敗

mal·adroit /ˌmæləˈdrɔɪt/ *adj.* (*formal*) done without skill, especially in a way that annoys or offends people 不靈巧的；笨拙的 SYN **clumsy**

mal·ady /ˈmælədi/ *noun* (*pl.* **-ies**) **1** (*formal*) a serious problem 嚴重問題；痼疾 SYN **ill**： *Violent crime is only one of the maladies afflicting modern society.* 暴力犯罪僅僅是困擾現代社會的嚴重問題之一。 **2** (*old use*) an illness 疾病

mal·aise /məˈleɪz/ *noun* [U, sing.] (*formal*) **1** the problems affecting a particular situation or group of people that are difficult to explain or identify（影響某個情況或某群人的）難以捉摸的問題，無法描述的問題： ***economic/financial/social malaise*** 揣摩不透的經濟／金融／社會問題 **2** a general feeling of being ill/sick, unhappy or not satisfied, without signs of any particular problem 莫名的不適（或不快、不滿等） SYN **unease**： *a serious malaise among the staff* 員工極為不滿的情緒

mala·prop·ism /ˈmæləprɒpɪzəm; *NAmE* -prɑːp-/ *noun* an amusing mistake sb makes when they use a word which sounds similar to the word they wanted to use, but means sth different 近音詞誤用所產生的滑稽效果 ORIGIN From Mrs Malaprop, a character in Richard Brinsley Sheridan's play *The Rivals*, who confuses words like this all the time. 源自理查德•布林斯利•謝里丹的戲劇《情敵》中的人物馬拉普洛普太太，她總是誤用詞語。

mal·aria /məˈleəriə; *NAmE* -ˈler-/ *noun* [U] a disease that causes fever and SHIVERING (= shaking of the body) caused by the bite of some types of MOSQUITO 瘧疾 ▸ **mal·ar·ial** /-iəl/ *adj.*： ***malarial insects/patients/regions*** 傳播瘧疾的昆蟲；瘧疾病人／流行區域

ma·lar·key /məˈlɑːki; *NAmE* məˈlɑːrki/ *noun* [U] (*informal, disapproving*) behaviour or an idea that you think is nonsense or has no meaning 無聊的話語（或行為）；廢話

Ma·lay·alam /ˌmʌləˈjɑːləm; ˌmɑːlə-/ *noun* [U] a language spoken in Kerala in SW India 馬拉雅拉姆語，馬拉亞蘭語（印度西南部喀拉拉邦的語言）

mal·con·tent /ˈmælkəntent; *NAmE* ˌmælkənˈtent/ *noun* [usually pl.] (*formal*, *disapproving*) a person who is not satisfied with a situation and who complains about it, or causes trouble in order to change it 不滿者；牢騷滿腹的人；反叛者

male /meɪl/ *adj.*, *noun*

■ *adj.* **1** (*abbr.* **m**) belonging to the sex that does not give birth to babies; connected with this sex 男性的；雄性的；男的：*a male bird* 雄鳥 ◇ *All the attackers were male, aged between 25 and 30.* 所有的襲擊者都是男性，年齡在 25 到 30 歲之間。◇ *a* ***male nurse/model/colleague*** 男護士／模特兒／同事 ◇ *male attitudes to women* 男人對女人的看法 ◇ ***male bonding*** (= the act of forming close friendships between men) 男性間的親密友誼 ◇ *the* ***male menopause*** (= emotional and physical problems that affect some men at about the age of 50) 男性更年期 ➲ compare MASCULINE *adj.* (1) ➲ see also ALPHA MALE **2** (*biology* 生) (of most plants 大多數植物) producing POLLEN 雄性的：*a male flower* 雄花 **3** (*technical* 術語) (of electrical PLUGS, parts of tools, etc. 電器插頭、工具部件等) having a part that sticks out which is designed to fit into a hole, SOCKET, etc. 陽的；凸形的 ➲ compare FEMALE ▸ **male·ness** *noun* [U]：*the chromosome that determines maleness* 決定男性性別的染色體

■ *noun* a male person, animal or plant 男性；雄性；雄株：*The male of the species has a white tail.* 這一物種的雄性有一條白色的尾巴。◇ *a male-dominated profession* 男性主宰的職業 ◇ (*formal*) *The body is that of a white male aged about 40.* 屍體是一名 40 歲上下的白人男子。➲ compare FEMALE

ˌmale ˈchauvinism (also **chauvinism**) *noun* [U] (*disapproving*) the belief held by some men that men are more important, intelligent, etc. than women 大男子主義

ˌmale ˈchauvinist (also **chauvinist**) *noun* (*disapproving*) a man who believes men are more important, intelligent, etc. than women 大男子主義者：*I hate working for that* ***male chauvinist pig*** *Steve.* 我討厭給史蒂夫這個可惡的大男子主義者幹活。

mal·efac·tor /ˈmælɪfæktə(r)/ *noun* (*rare*, *formal*) a person who does wrong, illegal or immoral things 犯罪分子；作惡的人；道德敗壞的人

ma·levo·lent /məˈlevələnt/ *adj.* [usually before noun] having or showing a desire to harm other people 有惡意的；有壞心腸的 SYN **malicious**, **wicked** OPP **benevolent** ▸ **ma·levo·lence** /-əns/ *noun* [U]：*an act of pure malevolence* 純粹惡意的舉動 **ma·levo·lent·ly** *adv.*

mal·for·ma·tion /ˌmælfɔːˈmeɪʃn; *NAmE* -fɔːrˈm-/ *noun* **1** [C] a part of the body that is not formed correctly（身體的）畸形部位：*Some foetal malformations cannot be diagnosed until late in pregnancy.* 有些胎兒的畸形部位得等到妊娠後期才能診斷出來。**2** [U] the state of not being correctly formed 畸形

mal·formed /ˌmælˈfɔːmd; *NAmE* -ˈfɔːrmd/ *adj.* (*technical* 術語) badly formed or shaped 畸形的

mal·func·tion /ˌmælˈfʌŋkʃn/ *verb* [I] (of a machine, etc. 機器等) to fail to work correctly 運轉失常；失靈；出現故障 ▸ **mal·func·tion** *noun* [C, U]

mal·ice /ˈmælɪs/ *noun* [U] a feeling of hatred for sb that causes a desire to harm them 惡意；怨恨：*He sent the letter* ***out of malice****.* 他出於惡意寄出了這封信。◇ *She is entirely without malice.* 她完全沒有惡意。◇ *He certainly* ***bears you no malice*** (= does not want to harm you). 他對你一定不會有什麼惡意。

IDM **with ˌmalice aˈforethought** (*law* 律) with the deliberate intention of committing a crime or harming sb（犯罪或傷人）有惡意預謀的

ma·li·cious /məˈlɪʃəs/ *adj.* having or showing hatred and a desire to harm sb or hurt their feelings 懷有惡意的；惡毒的 SYN **malevolent**, **spiteful**：***malicious gossip/lies/rumours*** 惡毒的流言蜚語／謊言／謠言 ◇ *He took malicious pleasure in telling me what she had said.* 他幸災樂禍地告訴我她說的那些話。▸ **ma·li·cious·ly** *adv.*

ma·lign /məˈlaɪn/ *verb*, *adj.*

■ *verb* ~ **sb/sth** (*formal*) to say bad things about sb/sth publicly（公開地）誹謗，譭謗，中傷 SYN **slander**：*She feels she has been* ***much maligned*** *by the press.* 她覺得她遭到了新聞界的恣意誹謗。

■ *adj.* [usually before noun] (*formal*) causing harm 有害的；引起傷害的：***a malign force/influence/effect*** 有害的勢力／影響／作用 ➲ compare BENIGN (2)

ma·lig·nancy /məˈlɪɡnənsi/ *noun* (*pl.* **-ies**) (*formal*) **1** [C] a malignant mass of TISSUE in the body 惡性腫瘤 SYN **tumour** **2** [U] the state of being malignant 惡性；惡毒

ma·lig·nant /məˈlɪɡnənt/ *adj.* **1** (of a TUMOUR or disease 腫瘤或疾病) that cannot be controlled and is likely to cause death 惡性的：*malignant cells* 惡性癌細胞 OPP **non-malignant** ➲ compare BENIGN (2) **2** (*formal*) having or showing a strong desire to harm sb 惡意的；惡毒的 SYN **malevolent**

ma·lin·ger /məˈlɪŋɡə(r)/ *verb* (usually **be malingering**) [I] (*disapproving*) to pretend to be ill/sick, especially in order to avoid work 裝病（尤指為逃避工作）▸ **ma·lin·ger·er** *noun*

mall /mɔːl; *BrE* also mæl/ *noun* (also **shopping mall**) (both *especially NAmE*) a large building or covered area that has many shops/stores, restaurants, etc. inside it 購物商場；購物廣場：*Let's go to the mall.* 我們去商場吧。◇ *Some teenagers were hanging out at the mall.* 有些青少年在大型購物中心裏閒逛。➲ COLLOCATIONS at SHOPPING ➲ compare ARCADE (3)

mal·lam /ˈmæləm/ (also **Mallam**) *noun* (*WAfrE*) a Muslim religious teacher; sometimes used as a title of respect for anybody who is seen as wise or highly educated, for example a university teacher 穆斯林宗教老師；馬拉姆（有時用作尊稱，指智者或學者，如大學教師）

mal·lard /ˈmælɑːd; *NAmE* ˈmælərd/ *noun* (*pl.* **mal·lards** or **mal·lard**) a common wild DUCK 綠頭鴨

mal·le·able /ˈmæliəbl/ *adj.* **1** (*technical* 術語) (of metal, etc. 金屬等) that can be hit or pressed into different shapes easily without breaking or cracking 可鍛造的；可軋壓的；易成型的 **2** (of people, ideas, etc. 人、思想等) easily influenced or changed 可塑的；易受影響（或改變）的 ▸ **mal·le·abil·ity** /ˌmæliəˈbɪləti/ *noun* [U]

mal·let /ˈmælɪt/ *noun* **1** a hammer with a large wooden head 木槌 ➲ VISUAL VOCAB page V20 **2** a hammer with a long handle and a wooden head, used for hitting the ball in the games of CROQUET and POLO（槌球和馬球運動的）球棍，球棒 ➲ VISUAL VOCAB page V46

mal·low /ˈmæləʊ; *NAmE* -loʊ/ *noun* [C, U] a plant with STEMS covered with small hairs and pink, purple or white flowers 錦葵

mall·rat /ˈmɔːlræt/ *noun* (*NAmE*, *informal*) a young person who spends a lot of time in SHOPPING MALLS, often in a large group of friends 愛（成群）逛商場的年輕人

malm·sey /ˈmɑːmzi/ *noun* [U, C] a type of strong sweet wine 瑪姆齊甜酒

mal·nour·ished /ˌmælˈnʌrɪʃt; *NAmE* -ˈnɜːr-/ *adj.* in bad health because of a lack of food or a lack of the right type of food 營養不良的

mal·nu·tri·tion /ˌmælnjuːˈtrɪʃn; *NAmE* -nuː-/ *noun* [U] a poor condition of health caused by a lack of food or a lack of the right type of food 營養不良 ➲ compare NUTRITION

mal·odor·ous /ˌmælˈəʊdərəs; *NAmE* -ˈoʊdərəs/ *adj.* (*formal* or *literary*) having an unpleasant smell 惡臭的

mal·prac·tice /ˌmælˈpræktɪs/ *noun* [U, C] (*law* 律) careless, wrong or illegal behaviour while in a professional job 瀆職；玩忽職守：*medical malpractice* 醫療失誤 ◇ *a malpractice suit* 瀆職訴訟 ◇ *He is currently standing trial for alleged malpractices.* 他被控營私舞弊，正在受審。

malt /mɔːlt; *BrE* also mɒlt; *NAmE* mɔːlt/ *noun* **1** [U] grain, usually BARLEY, that has been left in water for a period

M

of time and then dried, used for making beer, WHISKY, etc. 麥芽 **2** [U, C] = MALT WHISKY **3** [U, C] (*NAmE*) = MALTED MILK

malt·ed /ˈmɔːltɪd/ *adj.* [only before noun] **1** having been made into malt 成為麥芽的：*malted barley* 大麥芽 **2** having had malt added to it 加入麥芽的

ˌmalted ˈmilk (*NAmE* also **malt**) *noun* [U, C] a hot or cold drink made from MALT and dried milk mixed with water or milk and usually sugar, sometimes ice cream and/or chocolate added 麥乳精；麥芽奶

Mal·tese /ˌmɔːlˈtiːz/ *adj., noun* (*pl.* **Mal·tese**)

■ ***adj.*** from or connected with Malta 馬耳他的

■ ***noun*** **1** [C] a person from Malta 馬耳他人 **2** [U] the language of Malta 馬耳他語

ˌMaltese ˈcross *noun* a cross whose arms are equal in length and have wide ends with V-shapes cut out of them 馬耳他十字（四臂長度均等、末端呈寬大 V 字形）

malt·house /ˈmɔːlthaʊs/ (also **malt·ings** /ˈmɔːltɪŋz/ *BrE*) *noun* a building in which MALT is prepared and stored 麥芽作坊

Mal·thusian /mælˈθjuːziən/ *adj.* related to the theory of Thomas Malthus that, since populations naturally grow faster than the supply of food, failure to control their growth leads to disaster 馬爾薩斯人口論的（認為由於人口增長快於糧食供給，因此人口增長失控會導致災難）

mal·tose /ˈmɔːltəʊz; -təʊs; *NAmE* -toʊz; -toʊs/ *noun* [U] (*biology* 生) a sugar that substances in the body make from STARCH (= a food substance found in flour, rice, potatoes, etc.) 麥芽糖

M

mal·treat /ˌmælˈtriːt/ *verb* **~ sb/sth** to be very cruel to a person or an animal 虐待 SYN **ill-treat** ▸ **mal·treat·ment** *noun* [U]

ˌmalt ˈvinegar *noun* [U] VINEGAR which is made from grain rather than from wine 麥芽醋（用穀物而非果酒釀製）

ˌmalt ˈwhisky (also **malt**) *noun* [U, C] high quality WHISKY from Scotland; a glass of this（一杯）麥芽威士忌

mal·ware /ˈmælweə(r); *NAmE* -wer/ *noun* [U] software such as a virus on a computer or computer network that the user does not know about or want 惡意軟件；惡意軟體（指電腦病毒等）ORIGIN A combination of *malicious* and *software*. 該詞由 malicious 與 software 結合而成。

mam /mæm/ *noun* (*BrE, dialect, informal*) mother 媽媽

mama (also **mamma**) /ˈmæmə/ *noun* **1** /*BrE* also məˈmɑː/ (*NAmE* or *BrE, old-fashioned*) mother 媽媽 ➲ see also MUMMY (1) **2** in some places in Africa, a mother or older woman (often used as a title that shows respect) 媽媽，大媽（非洲某些地方對母親的稱呼或對年長婦女的尊稱）：*Leave this work to us, mama.* 這活兒留給我們幹吧，媽媽。◇ *Miriam Makeba became known as Mama Africa.* 米麗亞姆·馬凱巴被稱為非洲之母。◇ *Mama Ngina Kenyatta* 恩金納·肯雅塔夫人

ˈmama's boy (*NAmE*) (*BrE* **ˈmummy's boy**) *noun* (*disapproving*) a boy or man who depends too much on his mother 離不開媽媽的男孩（或男子）

mamba /ˈmæmbə/ *noun* a black or green poisonous African snake 樹眼鏡蛇（黑色或綠色，分佈於非洲，有劇毒）

mambo /ˈmæmbəʊ; *NAmE* -boʊ/ *noun* (*pl.* **-os**) **1** a lively Latin American dance 曼波舞（拉丁美洲輕快舞蹈）**2** a female VOODOO priest 伏都教女祭司；巫毒教女祭司

mam·mal /ˈmæml/ *noun* any animal that gives birth to live babies, not eggs, and feeds its young on milk. Cows, humans and WHALES are all mammals. 哺乳動物 ➲ VISUAL VOCAB page V12 ▸ **mam·ma·lian** /mæˈmeɪliən/ *adj.*

mam·mary /ˈmæməri/ *adj.* [only before noun] (*biology* 生) connected with the breasts 乳房的；乳腺的：*mammary glands* (= parts of the breast that produce milk) 乳腺

mam·mo·gram /ˈmæməɡræm/ *noun* an examination of a breast using X-RAYS to check for cancer 乳房 X 光檢查

mam·mog·raphy /mæˈmɒɡrəfi; *NAmE* -ˈmɑːɡ-/ *noun* [U] the use of X-RAYS to check for cancer in a breast 乳房 X 線照相術；乳房 X 光攝影術

Mam·mon /ˈmæmən/ *noun* [U] (*formal, disapproving*) a way of talking about money and wealth when it has become the most important thing in sb's life and as important as a god 瑪門（指財富、金錢）；財神

mam·moth /ˈmæməθ/ *noun, adj.*

■ ***noun*** an animal like a large ELEPHANT covered with hair, that lived thousands of years ago and is now EXTINCT 猛獁（象）；毛象

■ ***adj.*** [usually before noun] extremely large 極其巨大的；龐大的 SYN **huge**：*a mammoth task* 巨大的任務 ◇ *a financial crisis of mammoth proportions* 極其嚴重的金融危機

mammy /ˈmæmi/ *noun* (*pl.* **-ies**) **1** (*dialect, informal*) mother 媽；媽媽 **2** an offensive word used in the past in the southern states of the US for a black woman who cared for a white family's children 黑人保母（舊時美國南方各州對照看白人孩子的黑人女子的貶稱）

ˈmammy-wagon *noun* (*old-fashioned, WAfrE*) a lorry/truck with a roof and seats for people to travel in（帶頂棚的）小卡車，小客車

mam·para /mʌmˈpʌrə/ *noun* (*SAfrE*) = MOMPARA

man 🔑 /mæn/ *noun, verb, exclamation*

■ ***noun*** (*pl.* **men** /men/)

▸ **MALE PERSON** 男人 **1** 🔑 [C] an adult male human 成年男子；男人：*a good-looking young man* 英俊的年輕男子 ◇ *the relationships between men and women* 男女間的關係 ➲ see also DIRTY OLD MAN, LADIES' MAN, MEN'S ROOM

▸ **HUMANS** 人 **2** 🔑 [U] humans as a group or from a particular period of history 人類；（特定歷史時期的）人：*the damage caused by man to the environment* 人類給環境帶來的破壞 ◇ ***early/modern/Prehistoric man*** 早期人；現代人；史前人 ➲ note at GENDER **3** [C] (*literary* or *old-fashioned*) a person, either male or female（不論性別的）人：*All men must die.* 所有的人都會死。

▸ **PARTICULAR TYPE OF MAN** 某類人 **4** [C] (in compounds 構成複合詞) a man who comes from the place mentioned or whose job or interest is connected with the thing mentioned（來自某地、從事某種工作或有某種興趣等的）人：*a Frenchman* 法國人 ◇ *a businessman* 生意人 ◇ *a medical man* 醫務工作者 ◇ *a sportsman* 運動員 ➲ note at GENDER **5** [C] a man who likes or who does the thing mentioned（喜歡或做某事的）人：***a betting/drinking/fighting man*** 賭博／喝酒／打架的人 ➲ see also FAMILY MAN **6** [C] a man who works for or supports a particular organization, comes from a particular town, etc.（來自某處、支持某組織或為其工作的）人：*the BBC's man in Moscow* (= the man who reports on news from Moscow) 英國廣播公司駐莫斯科的新聞記者 ◇ *a loyal Republican Party man* 一名忠誠的共和黨人 ➲ see also RIGHT-HAND MAN, YES-MAN

▸ **SOLDIER/WORKER** 戰士；工人 **7** [C, usually pl.] a soldier or a male worker who obeys the instructions of a person of higher rank 士兵；（男性）工人：*The officer refused to let his men take part in the operation.* 這軍官拒絕讓他的士兵參加這項軍事行動。 **8** [C] a man who comes to your house to do a job 上門服務的人：*the gas man* 煤氣工人 ◇ *The man's coming to repair the TV today.* 修理工今天來修電視。

▸ **FORM OF ADDRESS** 稱呼 **9** [sing.] (*informal, especially NAmE*) used for addressing a male person 夥計；哥兒們：*Nice shirt, man!* 好漂亮的襯衣啊，哥兒們！◇ *Hey man. Back off!* 喂，夥計，退後！ **10** [sing.] (*old-fashioned*) used for addressing a male person in an angry or impatient way（不耐煩或生氣時對男人的稱呼）你這傢伙：*Don't just stand there, man—get a doctor!* 你這傢伙，別淨站着，趕緊去找醫生呀！

▸ **HUSBAND/BOYFRIEND** 丈夫；男友 **11** [C] (sometimes *disapproving*) a husband or sexual partner 丈夫；性伴侶：*What's her new man like?* 她的新男友怎麼樣？◇ *I now pronounce you man and wife* (= you are now officially married). 我現在正式宣佈你們結為夫婦。➲ see also OLD MAN

▸ **STRONG/BRAVE PERSON** 強壯的／勇敢的人 **12** [C] a person who is strong and brave or has other qualities that some people think are particularly male 勇敢強壯的人；男子漢：*Come on, now—be a man.* 加油，像個男子漢的樣子。◇ *She's more of a man than he is.* 她比他更像個男人。➲ see also HE-MAN, MUSCLEMAN, SUPERMAN

▸ **SERVANT** 僕人 **13** [sing.] (*old-fashioned, formal*) a male servant 男僕：*My man will drive you home.* 我的僕人會開車送你回家。

▸ **IN CHESS** 國際象棋 **14** [C] one of the figures or objects that you play with in a game such as CHESS 棋子 ➲ see also CHESSMAN

IDM **as one 'man** with everyone doing or thinking the same thing at the same time; in agreement 同心協力；協調一致 **be sb's 'man** to be the best or most suitable person to do a particular job, etc. 最合適的人；最佳人選：*For a superb haircut, David's your man.* 要想理個好髮型，你最好是去找戴維。 **be 'man enough (to do sth/for sth)** to be strong or brave enough 有足夠的勇氣或意志：*He was not man enough to face up to his responsibility.* 他沒有足夠的勇氣去承擔責任。 **every man for him'self** (*saying*) people must take care of themselves and not give or expect any help 人各為己；自己顧自己：*In business, it's every man for himself.* 生意場上都是人各為己。 **make a 'man (out) of sb** to make a young man develop and become more adult 使成為男子漢；使長大成人 **a/the ˌman about 'town** a man who frequently goes to fashionable parties, clubs, theatres, etc. 喜歡社交者；社交界名人 **ˌman and 'boy** from when sb was young to when they were old or older 從小到大；一輩子：*He's been doing the same job for 50 years—man and boy.* 他從小就幹着同一份工作，有 50 年了。 **the ˌman (and/or ˌwoman) in the 'street** an average or ordinary person, either male or female 平民；老百姓：*Politicians often don't understand the views of the man in the street.* 政治家通常不理解平民百姓的觀點。 **a ˌman of 'God/the 'cloth** (*old-fashioned, formal*) a religious man, especially a priest or a CLERGYMAN 神職人員；（尤指）牧師，司鐸 **the ˌman of the 'match** (*BrE, sport* 體) the member of a team who plays the best in a particular game（某場比賽的）最佳運動員 **a ˌman of the 'people** (especially of a politician 尤指政治家) a man who understands and is sympathetic to ordinary people 體恤民情者；體察民意者 **man's best 'friend** a way of describing a dog 人類的好朋友（指狗） **a ˌman's ˌhome is his 'castle** (*US*) (*BrE* **an ˌEnglishman's ˌhome is his 'castle**) (*saying*) a person's home is a place where they can be private and safe and do as they like 人之住宅即其城堡；人在家中，自成一統 **a 'man's man** a man who is more popular with men than with women 更受男人歡迎的男人 **be your own 'man/'woman** to act or think independently, not following others or being ordered 獨立自主 **ˌman to 'man** between two men who are treating each other honestly and equally（男人間）誠實相待，坦率：*I'm telling you all this man to man.* 我要把這一切都坦率地告訴你。◇ *a man-to-man talk* 坦率的談話 **one man's ˌmeat is another man's 'poison** (*saying*) used to say that different people like different things; what one person likes very much, another person does not like at all 興趣愛好因人而異；一人手中寶，他人腳下草 **separate/sort out the ˌmen from the 'boys** to show or prove who is brave, skilful, etc. and who is not 表明／證明誰有技能（或更勇敢等） **to a 'man | to the last 'man** used to emphasize that sth is true of all the people being described 一致；毫無例外：*They answered 'Yes,' to a man.* 他們異口同聲地回答："是。" ◇ *They were all destroyed, to the last man.* 他們無一例外全部被殲。 **you can't keep a good man 'down** (*saying*) a person who is determined or wants sth very much will succeed 有志者事竟成；決心大的人終有出頭之日 ➲ more at GRAND *adj.*, HEART, MARKED, NEXT *adj.*, ODD *adj.*, PART *n.*, POOR, POSSESSED, SUBSTANCE, THING, WORLD

■ ***verb*** (-nn-) **~ sth** to work at a place or be in charge of a place or a machine; to supply people to work somewhere 在…崗位上工作；操縱（機器等）；配備（人員） **SYN** **crew, staff**：*Soldiers manned barricades around the city.* 士兵把守着城市周圍的路障。◇ *The telephones are manned 24 hours a day by volunteers.* 每天 24 小時都有志願者接聽電話。

■ ***exclamation*** (*informal, especially NAmE*) used to express surprise, anger, etc.（表示驚奇、氣憤等）嘿，天哪：*Man, that was great!* 哇，太棒了！

man·acle /'mænəkl/ *noun, verb*

■ ***noun*** [usually pl.] one of two metal bands joined by a chain, used for fastening a prisoner's ankles or wrists together 手銬；腳鐐；鐐銬

■ ***verb*** [usually passive] **~ sb/sth** to put manacles on sb's wrists or ankles, to stop them from escaping 給…戴上鐐銬

man·age 0→ /'mænɪdʒ/ *verb*

▸ **DO STH DIFFICULT** 做難做的事 **1** 0→ [T, I] to succeed in doing sth, especially sth difficult 完成（困難的事）；勉力完成：**~ sth** *In spite of his disappointment, he managed a weak smile.* 儘管他很失望，他還是勉強露出一絲微笑。◇ *I don't know exactly how we'll **manage it**, but we will, somehow.* 我說不準我們如何去完成這件事，但不管怎樣我們一定會完成的。◇ *Can you manage another piece of cake?* (= eat one) 你還能再吃塊蛋糕嗎？◇ **~ (to do sth)** *We managed to get to the airport in time.* 我們設法及時趕到了機場。◇ *How did you manage to persuade him?* 你是怎麼說服他的？◇ (*humorous*) *He always manages to say the wrong thing.* 他總是哪壺不開提哪壺。◇ *We couldn't have managed without you.* 沒有你，我們就辦不成了。◇ *'Need any help?' 'No, thanks. I can manage.'* "要幫忙嗎？" "不了，謝謝。我應付得了。" ➲ note at CAN[1]

▸ **DEAL WITH PROBLEMS** 處理問題 **2** 0→ [I] to be able to solve your problems, deal with a difficult situation, etc. 能解決（問題）；應付（困難局面等） **SYN** **cope**：*She's 82 and can't manage on her own any more.* 她 82 歲了，照顧不了自己的生活了。◇ **~ with/without sb/sth** *How do you manage without a car?* 沒有車你怎麼應付的？

▸ **MONEY/TIME/INFORMATION** 金錢；時間；信息 **3** 0→ [I] **~ (on sth)** to be able to live without having much money 湊合着活下去；支撐：*He has to manage on less than £100 a week.* 他就靠每週不到 100 英鎊來維持生活。 **4** 0→ [T] **~ sth** to use money, time, information, etc. in a sensible way 明智地使用（金錢、時間、信息等）：*Don't tell me how to manage my affairs.* 用不着你來告訴我怎樣管我自己的事。◇ *a computer program that helps you manage data efficiently* 幫助你有效地處理數據的電腦程序 **5** 0→ [T] **~ sth** to be able to do sth at a particular time（在某一時間）能辦到，能做成：*Let's meet up again—can you manage next week sometime?* 我們再見一次面吧。下週找個時間，行嗎？

▸ **BUSINESS/TEAM** 公司；隊伍 **6** 0→ [T, I] **~ (sth)** to control or be in charge of a business, a team, an organization, etc. 管理，負責（公司、隊伍、組織等）：*to **manage a factory/bank/hotel/soccer team*** 管理工廠／銀行／酒店／足球隊 ◇ *to **manage a department/project*** 負責一個部門／項目 ◇ *We need people who are good at managing.* 我們需要擅長管理的人。

▸ **CONTROL** 控制 **7** 0→ [T] **~ sb/sth** to keep sb/sth under control; to be able to deal with sb/sth 控制住；操縱；能對付：*It's like trying to manage an unruly child.* 這就像試圖管住一個任性的孩子。◇ *Can you manage that suitcase?* 你弄得動那個箱子嗎？

man·age·able /'mænɪdʒəbl/ *adj.* possible to deal with or control 可操縱的；可處理的：*Use conditioner regularly to make your hair soft and manageable.* 經常使用護髮劑來使你的頭髮柔軟而且易於梳理。◇ *The debt has been reduced to a more manageable level.* 債務減到了比較能夠應付的程度。 **OPP** **unmanageable**

man·aged /'mænɪdʒd/ *adj.* [only before noun] carefully taken care of and controlled 妥善照看的；受監管的；受監督的：*The money will be invested in managed funds.* 這筆錢將投資於管理基金。◇ *Only wood from managed forests is used in our furniture.* 我們的傢具完全是用監管林中的木材做的。

man·age·ment 0→ /'mænɪdʒmənt/ *noun*

1 0→ [U] the act of running and controlling a business or similar organization 經營；管理：*a career in management* 管理方面的職業 ◇ ***hotel/project management*** 酒店／項目管理 ◇ *a management training course* 管理培訓課程

◇ *The report blames bad management.* 報告歸咎於管理不善。 **2** 🔑 [C+sing./pl. v., U] the people who run and control a business or similar organization 經營者；管理部門；資方： *The management is/are considering closing the factory.* 經營者在考慮關閉這家工廠。◇ *The shop is now **under new management**.* 這家商店現由新的經營者管理。◇ ***junior/middle/senior management*** 初級／中級／高級管理人員 ◇ *a **management decision/job*** 資方的決定／工作 ◇ *My role is to act as a mediator between employees and management.* 我的角色就是協調雇員與管理者之間的關係。◇ *Most managements are keen to avoid strikes.* 大多數經營者都很希望避免罷工的發生。 **3** 🔑 [U] the act or skill of dealing with people or situations in a successful way（成功的）處理手段；（有效的）處理能力： ***classroom management*** 課堂組織能力 ◇ ***time management*** (= the way in which you organize how you spend your time) 時間管理 ◇ *management of staff* 管理員工的能力 ◇ *Diet plays an important role in the management of heart disease.* 飲食對於心臟病的治療有重要作用。

man·ager 🔑 /ˈmænɪdʒə(r)/ *noun*
1 🔑 a person who is in charge of running a business, a shop/store or a similar organization or part of one（企業、店鋪等的）經理，經營者，老闆： ***a bank/hotel manager*** 銀行／酒店經理 ◇ *the **sales/marketing/personnel manager*** 銷售部／市場部／人事部經理 ◇ *a meeting of area managers* 地區經理會議 ➲ see also MIDDLE MANAGER **2** a person who deals with the business affairs of an actor, a musician, etc.（演員、音樂家等的）經理人，個人經理 **3** a person who trains and organizes a sports team（運動隊的）經理： *the new manager of Italy* 意大利隊的新經理

M

man·ager·ess /ˌmænɪdʒəˈres/ *noun* (*BrE*, becoming *old-fashioned*) a woman who is in charge of a small business, for example, a shop/store, restaurant or hotel 女經理；女老闆 ➲ note at GENDER

man·ager·ial /ˌmænəˈdʒɪəriəl; *NAmE* -ˈdʒɪr-/ *adj.* [usually before noun] connected with the work of a manager 經理的；管理的： *Does she have any managerial experience?* 她有沒有什麼管理經驗？

ˌmanaging diˈrector *noun* (*abbr.* **MD**) (*especially BrE*) the person who is in charge of a business 總裁；總經理；常務董事

ma·ñana /mænˈjɑːnə/ *adv.* (from *Spanish*) at some time in the future (used when a person cannot or will not say exactly when) 在將來某時；在以後的不確定時間

mana·tee /ˈmænətiː/ *noun* a large water animal with front legs and a strong tail but no back legs, that lives in America and Africa 熱帶海牛，海牛（水生哺乳動物，棲息於美洲和非洲）

ˈman bag *noun* a bag designed for men to carry money, keys, small pieces of equipment, etc. 男士包

ˈman boob *noun* [usually pl.] (*informal*) a man's breast that is large and fat 肥大的男性乳房；男波波

Man·cu·nian /mænˈkjuːniən/ *noun* a person from Manchester in NW England（英格蘭西北部的）曼徹斯特人 ▸ **Man·cu·nian** *adj.*

man·dala /ˈmændələ/ *noun* a round picture that represents the universe in some Eastern religions 曼荼羅（某些東方宗教用以代表宇宙的圓形圖）

man·da·rin /ˈmændərɪn/ *noun* **1** [C] a powerful official of high rank, especially in the CIVIL SERVICE 政界要員；（尤指）內務官員 SYN **bureaucrat** **2** [C] a government official of high rank in China in the past（舊時）中國政府高級官吏 **3 Mandarin** [U] the standard form of Chinese, which is the official language of China 普通話 **4** (also **ˌmandarin ˈorange**) [C] a type of small orange with loose skin that comes off easily 柑橘

ˌmandarin ˈcollar *noun* a small COLLAR that stands up and fits closely around the neck 中式領；緊口立領

man·date *noun, verb*
■ ***noun*** /ˈmændeɪt/ **1** the authority to do sth, given to a government or other organization by the people who vote for it in an election（政府或組織等經選舉而獲得的）授權： **~ (to do sth)** *The election victory gave the party a clear mandate to continue its programme of reform.* 選舉獲勝使得這個政黨擁有了明確的繼續推行改革的權力。◇ **~ (for sth)** *a mandate for an end to the civil war* 停止內戰的權力 **2** the period of time for which a government is given power（政府的）任期： *The presidential mandate is limited to two terms of four years each.* 總統的任期不得超過兩屆，每屆四年。 **3 ~ (to do sth)** (*formal*) an official order given to sb to perform a particular task 委託書；授權令： *The bank had no mandate to honour the cheque.* 銀行沒有得到指令來承兌這張支票。 **4** the power given to a country to govern another country or region, especially in the past（尤指舊時授予某國對別國或地區的）委任統治權
■ ***verb*** /ˈmændeɪt; ˌmænˈdeɪt/ [often passive] (*formal*) **1 ~ that ... | ~ sb (to do sth)** (*especially NAmE*) to order sb to behave, do sth or vote in a particular way 強制執行；委託辦理： *The law mandates that imported goods be identified as such.* 法律規定進口貨物必須如實標明。 **2 ~ sb/sth to do sth** to give sb, especially a government or a committee, the authority to do sth 授權： *The assembly was mandated to draft a constitution.* 大會獲授權起草一份章程。

man·dated /ˈmændeɪtɪd/ *adj.* [only before noun] (*formal*) **1** (of a country or state 國家) placed under the rule of another country 委託別國管轄的；託管的： *mandated territories* 託管地區 **2** required by law 依法的；按法律要求的： *a mandated curriculum* 法定課程 **3** having a mandate to do sth 獲得授權的： *a mandated government* 獲授權的政府

man·da·tory /ˈmændətəri; *NAmE* -tɔːri; *BrE* also mænˈdeɪtəri/ *adj.* (*formal*) required by law 強制的；法定的；義務的 SYN **compulsory**： *The offence carries a mandatory life sentence.* 這種罪行依照法律要判無期徒刑。◇ **~ (for sb) (to do sth)** *It is mandatory for blood banks to test all donated blood for the virus.* 血庫必須檢查所有捐獻的血是否含有這種病毒。

man·dazi /mænˈdɑːzi/ *noun* (*pl.* **man·dazi**) (*EAfrE*) a small cake made of fried DOUGH 油炸小麪餅

man·dible /ˈmændɪbl/ *noun* (*anatomy* 解) **1** the JAWBONE 下頜骨；頜 ➲ VISUAL VOCAB page V59 **2** the upper or lower part of a bird's beak 鳥喙的上部（或下部） **3** either of the two parts that are at the front and on either side of an insect's mouth, used especially for biting and crushing food（昆蟲的）上顎 ➲ VISUAL VOCAB page V13

man·dir /ˈmændɪə(r); *NAmE* -dɪr/ *noun* (*IndE*) a TEMPLE 印度教寺廟

man·do·lin /ˈmændəlɪn; ˌmændəˈlɪn/ *noun* a musical instrument with metal strings (usually eight) arranged in pairs, and a curved back, played with a PLECTRUM 曼陀林（撥弦樂器） ➲ VISUAL VOCAB page V36

man·drake /ˈmændreɪk/ *noun* [C, U] a poisonous plant used to make drugs, especially ones to make people sleep, thought in the past to have magic powers 茄參，毒參茄（可製藥，舊時認為具有魔力）

man·drill /ˈmændrɪl/ *noun* a large W African MONKEY with a red and blue face 山魈（面部有藍色和紅色的西非大猴）

mane /meɪn/ *noun* **1** the long hair on the neck of a horse or a LION（馬）鬃；（獅）鬣毛 ➲ VISUAL VOCAB page V12 **2** (*informal* or *literary*) a person's long or thick hair 長髮；濃密的頭髮

man·eater /ˈmæniːtə(r)/ *noun* **1** a wild animal that attacks and eats humans 食人獸 **2** (*humorous*) a woman who has many sexual partners 男士殺手（指有多個性伴侶的女子） ▸ **ˈman-eating** *adj.* [only before noun]: *a man-eating tiger* 噬人的老虎

man·eu·ver, man·eu·ver·able, man·eu·ver·ing (*especially US*) = MANOEUVRE, MANOEUVRABLE, MANOEUVRING

ˌman ˈFriday *noun* a male assistant who does many different kinds of work 得力的男助手；男僕 ➲ compare GIRL FRIDAY ORIGIN From a character in Daniel Defoe's novel *Robinson Crusoe* who is rescued by Crusoe and works for him. 源自丹尼爾・笛福所著的小說《魯賓遜

漂流記》中的人物。他為魯賓遜所救，後成為魯賓遜的僕人。

man·ful·ly /ˈmænfəli/ *adv.* using a lot of effort in a brave and determined way 有男子氣概地；勇敢堅定地 ▸ **man·ful** *adj.* [only before noun]

manga /ˈmæŋɡə/ *noun* [C, U] (from *Japanese*) a Japanese form of COMIC STRIP, often one with violent or sexual contents 日本連環漫畫（常有暴力或色情內容）

man·ga·nese /ˈmæŋɡəniːz/ *noun* [U] (*symb.* **Mn**) a chemical element. Manganese is a grey-white metal that breaks easily, used in making glass and steel. 錳

mange /meɪndʒ/ *noun* [U] a skin disease which affects MAMMALS, caused by a PARASITE 獸疥癬 ➲ see also MANGY (1)

man·ger /ˈmeɪndʒə(r)/ *noun* a long open box that horses and cows can eat from 馬槽；牛槽；飼料槽 **IDM** see DOG *n.*

mange·tout /ˌmɑːnʒˈtuː/ (*BrE*) (*NAmE* **ˈsnow pea**) *noun* [usually pl.] a type of very small PEA that grows in long, flat green PODS that are cooked and eaten whole 嫩豌豆；莢豆

man·gle /ˈmæŋɡl/ *verb, noun*

■ *verb* [usually passive] **1 ~ sth** to crush or twist sth so that it is badly damaged 壓碎；撕爛；嚴重損壞：*His hand was mangled in the machine.* 他的手捲到機器裏軋爛了。 **2 ~ sth** to spoil sth, for example a poem or a piece of music, by saying it wrongly or playing it badly 糟蹋（如蹩腳的詩朗誦或拙劣的演奏） **SYN** **ruin** ▸ **man·gled** *adj.*：***mangled bodies/remains*** 面目全非的屍體／遺跡

■ *noun* (also **wring·er**) a machine with two ROLLERS (1) used especially in the past for squeezing the water out of clothes that had been washed（尤指舊時的）軋布機，軋液機

mango /ˈmæŋɡəʊ; *NAmE* -ɡoʊ/ *noun* [C, U] (*pl.* **-oes** or **-os**) a tropical fruit with smooth yellow or red skin, soft orange flesh and a large seed inside 芒果 ➲ VISUAL VOCAB page V30

man·go·steen /ˈmæŋɡəstiːn/ *noun* a tropical fruit with a thick reddish-brown skin and sweet white flesh with a lot of juice 莽吉柿，倒捻子，山竹（熱帶水果，肉白，多汁） ➲ VISUAL VOCAB page V30

man·grove /ˈmæŋɡrəʊv; *NAmE* -ɡroʊv/ *noun* a tropical tree that grows in mud or at the edge of rivers and has roots that are above ground 紅樹林植物（生長在淤泥或河邊的熱帶樹木，有支柱根暴露在空氣中）：*mangrove swamps* 紅樹林沼澤地

mangy /ˈmeɪndʒi/ *adj.* [usually before noun] **1** (of an animal 動物) suffering from MANGE 患疥癬的：*a mangy dog* 患疥癬的狗 **2** (*informal*) dirty and in bad condition 污穢的；糟糕的 **SYN** **moth-eaten**：*a mangy old coat* 破爛不堪的舊外套

man·handle /ˈmænhændl/ *verb* **1 ~ sb** to push, pull or handle sb roughly（粗暴地）推搡，拉扯，對待：*Bystanders claim they were manhandled by security guards.* 旁觀者聲稱他們遭到了保安人員的粗暴推搡。 **2 ~ sth + adv./prep.** to move or lift a heavy object using a lot of effort 用力移動；用力舉起 **SYN** **haul**：*They were trying to manhandle an old sofa across the road.* 他們正努力要把一張舊沙發搬到馬路對面去。

man·hat·tan /ˌmænˈhætn/ *noun* an alcoholic drink made by mixing WHISKY or another strong alcoholic drink with VERMOUTH 曼哈頓雞尾酒（用威士忌或其他烈酒與苦艾酒調製而成）

man·hole /ˈmænhəʊl; *NAmE* -hoʊl/ *noun* a hole in the street that is covered with a lid, used when sb needs to go down to examine the pipes or SEWERS below the street（檢查地下管道用的）人孔，檢查井

man·hood /ˈmænhʊd/ *noun* **1** [U] the state or time of being an adult man rather than a boy 成年；成年時期 **2** [U] the qualities that a man is supposed to have, for example courage, strength and sexual power 男兒氣質：*Her new-found power was a threat to his manhood.* 她最近具有的能力對他的男子漢氣概是個威脅。 **3** [sing.] (*literary* or *humorous*) a man's PENIS. People use 'manhood' to avoid saying 'penis'.（與 penis 同義，即陰莖） **4** [U] (*literary*) all the men of a country 一國的男子：*The nation's manhood died on the battlefields of World War I.* 這個國家的男子都在第一次世界大戰的戰場上犧牲了。 ➲ compare WOMANHOOD

ˈman-hour *noun* [usually pl.] the amount of work done by one person in one hour 工時（每人每小時的工作量）

man·hunt /ˈmænhʌnt/ *noun* an organized search by a lot of people for a criminal or a prisoner who has escaped（對罪犯或逃犯的）搜捕，追捕

mania /ˈmeɪniə/ *noun* **1** [C, usually sing., U] **~ (for sth/for doing sth)** an extremely strong desire or enthusiasm for sth, often shared by a lot of people at the same time（通常指許多人共有的）強烈的慾望，狂熱，極大的熱情 **SYN** **craze**：*He had a mania for fast cars.* 他是個飛車狂。◇ *Football mania is sweeping the country.* 足球熱正風靡全國。 **2** [U] (*psychology* 心) a mental illness in which sb has an OBSESSION about sth that makes them extremely anxious, violent or confused 躁狂症

-mania *combining form* (in nouns 構成名詞) mental illness of a particular type …狂；…癖：*kleptomania* 偷竊癖 ▸ **-maniac** (in nouns 構成名詞)：*a pyromaniac* 縱火狂

ma·niac /ˈmeɪniæk/ *noun* **1** (*informal*) a person who behaves in an extremely dangerous, wild or stupid way 行為極其危險（或狂暴、愚蠢）的人；瘋子；狂人 **SYN** **madman**：*He was driving **like a maniac**.* 他發了瘋似地開車。 **2** a person who has an extremely strong desire or enthusiasm for sth, to an extent that other people think is not normal 狂熱分子；過激分子 **SYN** **fanatic** **3** (*psychology* 心) a person suffering from mania 躁狂症患者；瘋子：*a homicidal maniac* 殺人狂 ▸ **ma·niac** *adj.* [only before noun]：*a maniac driver/fan/killer* 發了瘋的司機；狂熱的愛好者；瘋狂殺手

ma·ni·acal /məˈnaɪəkl/ *adj.* wild or violent 狂野的；粗暴的：*maniacal laughter* 狂野的笑聲 ▸ **ma·ni·acal·ly** /-kli/ *adv.*

manic /ˈmænɪk/ *adj.* **1** (*informal*) full of activity, excitement and anxiety; behaving in a busy, excited, anxious way 狂熱的；興奮的；忙亂的 **SYN** **hectic**：*Things are manic in the office at the moment.* 這會兒辦公室裏一片忙亂。◇ *The performers had a manic energy and enthusiasm.* 表演者有一種瘋狂的勁頭和激情。 **2** (*psychology* 心) connected with MANIA (2) 躁狂的：*manic mood swings* 喜怒無常的情緒變化 ▸ **man·ic·al·ly** /-kli/ *adv.*：*I rushed around manically, trying to finish the housework.* 我手忙腳亂地跑來跑去，想把家務活幹完。

ˌmanic deˈpression *noun* [U] = BIPOLAR DISORDER

ˌmanic-deˈpres·sive *adj., noun* = BIPOLAR

Mani·chae·an (also **Mani·che·an**) /ˌmænɪˈkiːən/ *adj.* (*religion* 宗, *philosophy* 哲) based on the belief that there are two opposites in everything, for example good and evil or light and dark 二元對立論的

mani·cure /ˈmænɪkjʊə(r); *NAmE* -kjʊr/ *noun, verb*

■ *noun* [C, U] the care and treatment of a person's hands and nails 修剪指甲；指甲護理：*to have a manicure* 修指甲 ➲ compare PEDICURE

■ *verb* **~ sth** to care for and treat your hands and nails 修剪（指甲）；護理（手）

mani·cured /ˈmænɪkjʊəd; *NAmE* -kjʊrd/ *adj.* **1** (of hands or fingers 手或手指) with nails that are neatly cut and polished 精心護理的；修剪整齊的 **2** (of gardens, a LAWN, etc. 花園、草坪等) very neat and well cared for 整齊的；護理得很好的

mani·cur·ist /ˈmænɪkjʊərɪst; *NAmE* -kjʊr-/ *noun* a person whose job is the care and treatment of the hands and nails 指甲美容師；指甲修理師；護手師

mani·fest /ˈmænɪfest/ *verb, adj., noun*

■ *verb* (*formal*) **1 ~ sth (in sth)** to show sth clearly, especially a feeling, an attitude or a quality 表明，清楚顯示（尤指情感、態度或品質） **SYN** **demonstrate**：*Social tensions were manifested in the recent political crisis.* 最近的政治危機顯示了社會關係的緊張。 **2 ~ itself (in sth)** to appear or become noticeable 顯現；使人注意到 **SYN** **appear**：*The symptoms of the disease manifested*

M

themselves ten days later. 十天後，這種病的症狀顯現出來。

■ **adj. ~ (to sb) (in sth)** (*formal*) easy to see or understand 明顯的；顯而易見的 SYN **clear**: *His nervousness was manifest to all those present.* 所有在場的人都看出了他很緊張。◇ *The anger he felt is manifest in his paintings.* 他的憤怒明顯地表現在他的繪畫之中。▶ **mani·fest·ly** *adv.*: *manifestly unfair* 明顯不公平 ◇ *The party has manifestly failed to achieve its goal.* 這一政黨顯然沒有達到自己的目標。

■ **noun** (*technical* 術語) a list of goods or passengers on a ship or an aircraft（船或飛機的）貨單，旅客名單

mani·fest·ation /ˌmænɪfeˈsteɪʃn/ *noun* (*formal*) **1** [C, U] **~ (of sth)** an event, action or thing that is a sign that sth exists or is happening; the act of appearing as a sign that sth exists or is happening 顯示；表明；表示: *The riots are a clear manifestation of the people's discontent.* 騷亂清楚地表明了人們的不滿情緒。◇ *Some manifestation of your concern would have been appreciated.* 你當時要是表現出一些關心就好了。**2** [C] an appearance of a GHOST or spirit（幽靈的）顯現，顯靈: *The church is the site of a number of supernatural manifestations.* 這座教堂是個鬼魂屢次出沒的地方。

mani·festo /ˌmænɪˈfestəʊ; *NAmE* -ˈfestoʊ/ *noun* (*pl.* **-os**) a written statement in which a group of people, especially a political party, explain their beliefs and say what they will do if they win an election 宣言: *an election manifesto* 競選宣言 ◇ *the party manifesto* 政黨宣言

mani·fold /ˈmænɪfəʊld; *NAmE* -foʊld/ *adj., noun*

■ **adj.** (*formal*) many; of many different types 多的；多種多樣的；許多種類的: *The possibilities were manifold.* 有很多的可能性。

■ **noun** (*technical* 術語) a pipe or chamber with several openings for taking gases in and out of a car engine 歧管（汽車引擎用以進氣和排氣）: *the exhaust manifold* 排氣歧管

mani·kin (also **man·ni·kin**) /ˈmænɪkɪn/ *noun* **1** a model of the human body that is used for teaching art or medicine（醫療或藝術教學用的）人體模型 ➲ compare MANNEQUIN (1) **2** (*old-fashioned*) a very small man 侏儒；小矮人 SYN **dwarf**

Ma·nila (also **Ma·nilla**) /məˈnɪlə/ *noun* [U] strong brown paper, used especially for making envelopes 馬尼拉紙

man·ioc /ˈmæniɒk; *NAmE* -ɑːk/ *noun* [U] = CASSAVA

ma·nipu·late AW /məˈnɪpjuleɪt/ *verb* **1** (*disapproving*) to control or influence sb/sth, often in a dishonest way so that they do not realize it（暗中）控制，操縱，影響: **~ sb/sth** *She uses her charm to manipulate people.* 她利用自身的魅力來擺佈別人。◇ *As a politician, he knows how to manipulate public opinion.* 身為一位政客，他知道如何左右公眾輿論。◇ **~ sb into sth/into doing sth** *They managed to manipulate us into agreeing to help.* 他們總算促使我們答應提供幫助了。**2 ~ sth** (*formal*) to control or use sth in a skilful way（熟練地）操作，使用: *to manipulate the gears and levers of a machine* 熟練地操縱機器的排擋和變速桿 ◇ *Computers are very efficient at manipulating information.* 計算機在處理信息方面效率極高。**3 ~ sth** (*technical* 術語) to move a person's bones or joints into the correct position 正骨；治療脫臼 ▶ **ma·nipu·la·tion** AW /məˌnɪpjuˈleɪʃn/ *noun* [U, C]: *Advertising like this is a cynical manipulation of the elderly.* 作這樣的廣告宣傳就是要弄老年人。◇ *data manipulation* 數據操縱 ◇ *manipulation of the bones of the back* 對脊椎骨的推拿治療

ma·nipu·la·tive AW /məˈnɪpjələtɪv; *NAmE* -leɪtɪv/ *adj.* **1** (*disapproving*) skilful at influencing sb or forcing sb to do what you want, often in an unfair way 善於操縱的；會控制的；會擺佈人的 **2** (*formal*) connected with the ability to handle objects skilfully 熟練操作的；有操作能力的: *manipulative skills such as typing and knitting* 諸如打字、編織這樣的技能

ma·nipu·la·tor /məˈnɪpjuleɪtə(r)/ *noun* (often *disapproving*) a person who is skilful at influencing people or situations in order to get what they want 操縱者；控制者

man·kind /mænˈkaɪnd/ *noun* [U] all humans, thought about as one large group; the human race 人類: *the history of mankind* 人類的歷史 ◇ *an invention for the good of all mankind* 造福全人類的一項發明 ➲ note at GENDER ➲ compare WOMANKIND ➲ see also HUMANKIND

manky /ˈmæŋki/ *adj.* (*BrE, informal*) dirty and unpleasant 骯髒的；不潔的；令人生厭的

manly /ˈmænli/ *adj.* (often *approving*) (**man·lier**, **man·li·est**) having the qualities or physical features that are admired or expected in a man 有男子漢氣概的；強壯的 ▶ **man·li·ness** *noun* [U]

ˌman-ˈmade *adj.* made by people; not natural 人造的；非天然的 SYN **artificial**: *a man-made lake* 人工湖 ◇ *man-made fibres such as nylon and polyester* 尼龍和滌綸之類的人造纖維 ➲ SYNONYMS at ARTIFICIAL

manna /ˈmænə/ *noun* [U] (in the Bible《聖經》) the food that God provided for the people of Israel during their 40 years in the desert 嗎哪，瑪納（以色列人在荒野 40 年中神賜的食糧）: (*figurative*) *To the refugees, the food shipments were* ***manna from heaven*** (= an unexpected and very welcome gift). 對於難民來說，運來的食物有如天降嗎哪。

manned /mænd/ *adj.* if a machine, a vehicle, a place or an activity is **manned**, it has or needs a person to control or operate it（機器、車輛、地方或活動）有人控制的，需人操縱的: *manned space flight* 載人航天飛行 OPP **unmanned**

man·ne·quin /ˈmænɪkɪn/ *noun* **1** a model of a human body, used for displaying clothes in shops/stores（商店中用於陳列服裝的）人體模型 ➲ compare MANIKIN (1) **2** (*old-fashioned*) a person whose job is to wear and display new styles of clothes 時裝模特兒 SYN **model**

man·ner 🔑 /ˈmænə(r)/ *noun*

1 🔑 [sing.] (*formal*) the way that sth is done or happens 方式；方法: *She answered* ***in a*** *businesslike* ***manner***. 她回答時顯出一副公事公辦的樣子。◇ *The manner in which the decision was announced was extremely regrettable.* 宣佈決定的方式非常令人遺憾。**2** 🔑 [sing.] the way that sb behaves towards other people 舉止；行為方式: *to have an aggressive/a friendly/a relaxed manner* 帶着一副咄咄逼人的／友好的／悠閒的樣子 ◇ *His manner was polite but cool.* 他舉止有禮但很冷漠。➲ see also BEDSIDE MANNER **3** 🔑 **manners** [pl.] behaviour that is considered to be polite in a particular society or culture 禮貌；禮儀: *to have* ***good/bad manners*** 有／沒有禮貌 ◇ *It is bad manners to talk with your mouth full.* 嘴裏塞滿了東西跟人說話是不禮貌的。◇ *He* ***has no manners*** (= behaves very badly). 他毫無禮貌。➲ see also TABLE MANNERS **4 manners** [pl.] (*formal*) the habits and customs of a particular group of people 規矩；習俗: *the social morals and manners of the seventeenth century* 十七世紀的社會道德和習俗

IDM **all ˈmanner of sb/sth** many different types of people or things 各種各樣的人（或事）；形形色色的人（或事）: *The problem can be solved in all manner of ways.* 這個問題可以用各種方法加以解決。**in a manner of ˈspeaking** if you think about it in a particular way; true in some but not all ways 可以說；不妨說；從某種意義上說: *All these points of view are related, in a manner of speaking.* 所有這些觀點都在某方面相互關聯。**in the manner of sb/sth** (*formal*) in a style that is typical of sb/sth 以某人（或某物）的典型風格: *a painting in the manner of Raphael* 拉斐爾風格的繪畫 **(as/as if) to the manner ˈborn** (*formal*) as if sth is natural for you and you have done it many times in the past 彷彿天生的；生來就習慣的 **what manner of ...** (*formal* or *literary*) what kind of ... 什麼樣的…: *What manner of man could do such a terrible thing?* 究竟什麼人能做出這樣可怕的事呢？

man·nered /ˈmænəd; *NAmE* -nərd/ *adj.* **1** (*disapproving*) (of behaviour, art, writing, etc. 行為、藝術、寫作等) trying to impress people by being formal and not natural 矯揉造作的；不自然的 SYN **affected** **2 -mannered** (in compounds 構成複合詞) having the type of manners mentioned 態度…的；舉止…的：*a bad-mannered child* 沒有禮貌的孩子 ➲ see also ILL-MANNERED, MILD-MANNERED, WELL MANNERED

man·ner·ism /ˈmænərɪzəm/ *noun* **1** [C] a particular habit or way of speaking or behaving that sb has but is not aware of 習性；言談舉止：***nervous/odd/irritating mannerisms*** 緊張的／古怪的／令人不快的習慣 **2** [U] too much use of a particular style in painting or writing（繪畫、寫作中）過分的獨特風格 **3 Mannerism** [U] a style in 16th century Italian art that did not show things in a natural way but made them look strange or out of their usual shape 風格主義，矯飾主義（16 世紀意大利的一種藝術風格，以怪誕、變形的方式表現事物）

man·ner·ist /ˈmænərɪst/ (usually **Man·ner·ist**) *adj.* (of painting or writing 繪畫或寫作) in the style of Mannerism 風格主義的；矯飾主義的

man·ni·kin = MANIKIN

man·nish /ˈmænɪʃ/ *adj.* (usually *disapproving*) (of a woman or of sth belonging to a woman 婦女或其所有物) having qualities that are thought of as typical of or suitable for a man 像男人的；男子氣的；男性化的

mano-a-mano /ˌmɑːnəʊ æ ˈmɑːnəʊ; *NAmE* ˌmɑːnoʊ ɑː ˈmɑːnoʊ/ *adv., noun* (*informal, especially NAmE, from Spanish*)

■ ***adv.*** with two people facing each other directly in order to decide an argument or a competition（較量時）面對面：*It's time to settle this mano-a-mano.* 現在是當面解決這個問題的時候了。

■ ***noun*** (*pl.* **mano-a-manos**) a fight or contest, especially one between two people（尤指兩人間的）格鬥，較量，比試

man·oeuv·rable (*BrE*) (*NAmE* **man·euv·er·able**) /məˈnuːvərəbl/ *adj.* that can easily be moved into different positions 可調遣的；機動的；靈活的：*a highly manoeuvrable vehicle* 非常機動靈活的交通工具 ▸ **man·oeuv·ra·bil·ity** (*BrE*) (*NAmE* **man·eu·ver·abil·ity**) *noun* [U]

man·oeuvre (*especially US* **man·eu·ver**) /məˈnuːvə(r)/ *noun, verb*

■ ***noun*** **1** [C] a movement performed with care and skill 細緻巧妙的移動；機動動作：*a* ***complicated/skilful manoeuvre*** 複雜的／熟練的移動 ◇ *You will be asked to perform some standard manoeuvres during your driving test.* 駕駛考試中會要求你做幾個標準的機動動作。**2** [C, U] a clever plan, action or movement that is used to give sb an advantage 策略；手段；花招；伎倆 SYN **move**：*diplomatic manoeuvres* 外交策略 ◇ *a complex manoeuvre in a game of chess* 國際象棋中複雜的應對套路 **3 man·oeuvres** [pl.] military exercises involving a large number of soldiers, ships, etc. 軍事演習；作戰演習：*The army is* ***on manoeuvres*** *in the desert.* 軍隊在沙漠中進行軍事演習。

IDM **freedom of/room for maˈnoeuvre** the chance to change the way that sth happens and influence decisions that are made 改變事態的機會；迴旋餘地

■ ***verb*** **1** [I, T] to move or turn skilfully or carefully; to move or turn sth skilfully or carefully（使謹慎或熟練地）移動，運動，轉動：**~ (for sth)** *The yachts manoeuvred for position.* 那些遊艇靈活地尋找位置。◇ *There was very little room to manoeuvre.* 幾乎沒有什麼活動空間。◇ **~ sth (+ adv./prep.)** *She manoeuvred the car carefully into the garage.* 她小心翼翼地將車開進了車庫。**2** [I, T] to control or influence a situation in a skilful but sometimes dishonest way 操縱；控制；使花招：*The new laws have left us little* ***room to manoeuvre*** (= not much opportunity to change or influence a situation). 新法律沒給我們留下多少迴旋的餘地。◇ **~ sth + adv./prep.** *She manoeuvred her way to the top of the company.* 她施展手腕使自己進入了公司最高領導層。

man·oeuv·ring (*especially US* **man·eu·ver·ing**) /məˈnuːvərɪŋ/ *noun* [U, C] clever, skilful, and often dishonest ways of achieving your aims 手段；伎倆；花招

ˌman of ˈletters *noun* a man who is a writer, or who writes about literature 文人；作家

ˌman-of-ˈwar *noun* (*pl.* **ˌmen-of-ˈwar**) a sailing ship used in the past for fighting（舊時的）軍艦，戰艦

manor /ˈmænə(r)/ *noun* (*BrE*) **1** (also **ˈmanor house**) a large country house surrounded by land that belongs to it 莊園宅第 **2** an area of land with a manor house on it 莊園；莊園領地 **3** (*slang*) an area in which sb works or for which they are responsible, especially officers at a police station 工作區；（尤指警察的）管轄區

man·orial /məˈnɔːriəl/ *adj.* typical of or connected with a manor, especially in the past（尤指舊時）莊園的，采邑的

man·power /ˈmænpaʊə(r)/ *noun* [U] the number of workers needed or available to do a particular job 勞動力；人手；人力：*a need for* ***trained/skilled manpower*** 對受過培訓的／熟練的勞動力的需求 ◇ *a manpower shortage* 勞動力短缺

man·qué /ˈmɒŋkeɪ; *NAmE* mɑːŋˈkeɪ/ *adj.* (following nouns 用於名詞後) (from *French, formal* or *humorous*) used to describe a person who hoped to follow a particular career but who failed in it or never tried it 願望落空的；壯志未酬的；未成功的：*He's really an artist manqué.* 他很想當藝術家，但未能如願。

man·sard /ˈmænsɑːd; *NAmE* -sɑːrd/ (also **ˌmansard ˈroof**) *noun* (*technical* 術語) a roof with a double slope in which the upper part is less steep than the lower part 折線型屋頂，複折式屋頂（下部比上部陡）

manse /mæns/ *noun* the house of a Christian minister, especially in Scotland（尤指蘇格蘭的）牧師住宅

man·ser·vant /ˈmænsɜːvənt; *NAmE* -sɜːrv-/ *noun* (*pl.* **men·ser·vants**) (*old-fashioned*) a male servant, especially a man's personal servant 男僕；家丁；（尤指）隨身男侍從

man·sion /ˈmænʃn/ *noun* **1** [C] a large impressive house 公館；宅第：*an 18th century country mansion* * 18 世紀的鄉村宅第 **2 Mansions** [pl.] (*BrE*) used in the names of blocks of flats（用於公寓樓名）：*2 Moscow Mansions, Cromwell Road* 克倫威爾路莫斯科公寓 2 號

ˈman-sized *adj.* [only before noun] suitable or large enough for a man 宜於成年男人的；夠一個男人用的：*a man-sized breakfast* 夠一個大男人吃的早餐

man·slaugh·ter /ˈmænslɔːtə(r)/ *noun* [U] (*law* 律) the crime of killing sb illegally but not deliberately 過失殺人；誤殺 ➲ compare CULPABLE HOMICIDE, HOMICIDE, MURDER *n.* (1)

manta /ˈmæntə/ (also **ˌmanta ˈray**) *noun* a large fish that lives in tropical seas and swims by moving two parts like large flat wings 毯魟，雙吻前口蝠鱝（體寬大於長，見於暖水海域）

man·tel·piece /ˈmæntlpiːs/ (also **man·tel** especially in *NAmE* /ˈmæntl/) *noun* a shelf above a FIREPLACE 壁爐台 ➲ VISUAL VOCAB page V21

man·tis /ˈmæntɪs/ *noun* (*pl.* **man·tises** or **man·tids** /ˈmæntɪdz/) = PRAYING MANTIS

man·tle /ˈmæntl/ *noun, verb*

■ ***noun*** **1** [sing.] **the ~ of sb/sth** (*literary*) the role and responsibilities of an important person or job, especially when they are passed on from one person to another（可繼承的）責任，職責，衣鉢：*The vice-president must now* ***take on the mantle*** *of supreme power.* 副總統現在必須承擔起最高權力的重任。**2** [C] (*literary*) a layer of sth that covers a surface 覆蓋層：*hills with a mantle of snow* 白雪覆蓋的山巒 **3** [C] a loose piece of clothing without sleeves, worn over other clothes, especially in the past（尤指舊時的）披風，斗篷 SYN **cloak, covering 4** (also **ˈgas mantle**) [C] a cover around the flame of a gas lamp that becomes very bright when it is heated（煤氣燈的）白熾罩 **5** [sing.] (*geology* 地) the part of the earth below the CRUST and surrounding the core 地幔

■ ***verb*** **~ sth** (*literary*) to cover the surface of sth 覆蓋；遮蓋

man·tra /ˈmæntrə/ *noun* a word, phrase or sound that is repeated again and again, especially during prayer or MEDITATION 曼怛羅（某些宗教的唸咒）；唸咒聲：*a Buddhist mantra* 佛教的唸咒語

man·trap /ˈmæntræp/ *noun* **1** a trap used in the past for catching people, especially people who tried to steal things from sb's land（舊時私人地界防小偷等的）誘捕

M

陷阱 **2** any electronic device that is used to catch people who are doing sth dishonest 電子誘捕系統

man·ual AW /ˈmænjuəl/ *adj.*, *noun*
■ *adj.* **1** (of work, etc. 工作等) involving using the hands or physical strength 用手的；手工的；體力的：***manual labour/jobs/skills*** 體力勞動／活兒；手工技巧 ◇ *manual and non-manual workers* 體力勞動者和非體力勞動者 **2** operated or controlled by hand rather than automatically or using electricity, etc. 手動的；手控的；用手操作的：*a manual gearbox* 手動變速箱 ◇ *My camera has manual and automatic functions.* 我的照相機有手調和自動兩種功能。 **3** connected with using the hands 手工的；用手的：*manual dexterity* 手的靈巧 ▸ **manu·al·ly** AW /-juəli/ *adv.*：*manually operated* 手工操作的
■ *noun* a book that tells you how to do or operate sth, especially one that comes with a machine, etc. when you buy it 使用手冊；說明書；指南：*a **computer/car/instruction manual*** 電腦／汽車說明書；用法指南 ➲ compare HANDBOOK
IDM **on ˈmanual** not being operated automatically 處於非自動狀態；處於手動狀態：*Leave the controls on manual.* 讓操縱桿處於手動狀態。

manu·fac·ture 🔑 /ˌmænjuˈfæktʃə(r)/ *verb*, *noun*
■ *verb* **1** 🔑 **~ sth** to make goods in large quantities, using machinery（用機器）大量生產，成批製造 SYN **mass-produce**：*manufactured goods* 工業品 **2 ~ sth** to invent a story, an excuse, etc. 編造；捏造：*a news story manufactured by an unscrupulous journalist* 一個不道德的記者編造的一篇報道 **3 ~ sth** (*technical* 術語) to produce a substance 生成，產生（一種物質）：*Vitamins cannot be manufactured by our bodies.* 維生素不能由人體來生成。
■ *noun* **1** [U] the process of producing goods in large quantities 大量製造；批量生產 SYN **mass production**：*the manufacture of cars* 汽車製造 **2 manufactures** [pl.] (*technical* 術語) manufactured goods 工業品：*a major importer of cotton manufactures* 棉花產品的主要進口商

manu·fac·tur·er 🔑 /ˌmænjuˈfæktʃərə(r)/ *noun* a person or company that produces goods in large quantities 生產者；製造者；生產商 SYN **maker**：*a car/computer manufacturer* 汽車／計算機製造商 ◇ *Always follow the manufacturer's instructions.* 務必按廠家的用法說明使用。◇ *Faulty goods should be returned to the manufacturers.* 有問題的產品應退還生產廠家。

manu·fac·tur·ing 🔑 /ˌmænjuˈfæktʃərɪŋ/ *noun* [U] the business or industry of producing goods in large quantities in factories, etc. 製造業：*Many jobs in manufacturing were lost during the recession.* 在經濟衰退期，製造業有很多人失業了。

ma·nure /məˈnjʊə(r); *NAmE* məˈnʊr/ *noun*, *verb*
■ *noun* [U] the waste matter from animals that is spread over or mixed with the soil to help plants and crops grow 糞肥；肥料 SYN **dung**
■ *verb* **~ sth** to put manure on or in soil to help plants grow 給…施肥

manu·script /ˈmænjuskrɪpt/ *noun* (*abbr.* MS) **1** a copy of a book, piece of music, etc. before it has been printed 手稿；原稿：*an **unpublished/original manuscript*** 未經發表的／原始的手稿 ◇ *I read her poems **in manuscript**.* 我讀過她的詩作的手稿。 **2** a very old book or document that was written by hand before printing was invented（印刷術發明以前書籍或文獻的）手寫本，手抄本：*medieval illuminated manuscripts* 中世紀的裝飾過的手抄本

ˈmanuscript paper *noun* [U] paper printed with STAVES for writing music on 五線譜稿紙

Manx /mæŋks/ *adj.* of or connected with the Isle of Man, its people or the language once spoken there 馬恩島的；馬恩島人的；馬恩語的

ˌManx ˈcat *noun* a breed of cat with no tail 馬恩島貓（一種無尾家貓）

many 🔑 /ˈmeni/ *det.*, *pron.*
1 🔑 used with plural nouns and verbs, especially in negative sentences or in more formal English, to mean 'a large number of'. Also used in questions to ask about the size of a number, and with 'as', 'so' and 'too'. 許多（與複數名詞及動詞連用，尤用於否定句或正式用語，表示大量；也用於疑問句以詢問數字大小，並可與 as、so 和 too 連用）：*We don't have very many copies left.* 我們所剩的冊數不多。◇ *You can't have one each. We haven't got many.* 你們不能一人一個。我們沒有很多。◇ *Many people feel that the law should be changed.* 許多人都覺得這項法律應該修改。◇ *Many of those present disagreed.* 許多到場的人都不同意。◇ ***How many** children do you have?* 你有幾個孩子？◇ *There are **too many** mistakes in this essay.* 這篇文章錯誤太多。◇ *He made ten mistakes **in as many*** (= in ten) *lines.* 他在十行中就出了十個錯。◇ *New drivers have **twice as many** accidents as experienced drivers.* 新手司機所出的事故是熟練司機的兩倍。◇ *Don't take **so many**.* 別拿這麼多。◇ *I've known her for **a great many*** (= very many) *years.* 我認識她好多好多年了。◇ *Even if one person is hurt that is **one too many**.* 即使傷一個人，都嫌太多。◇ *It was one of my many mistakes.* 這是我犯的許多錯誤中的一個。◇ *a many-headed monster* 一隻多頭怪獸 **2 the many** used with a plural verb to mean 'most people'（與複數動詞連用）大多數人：*a government which improves conditions for the many* 為大多數人改善生活條件的政府 **3 many a** (*formal*) used with a singular noun and verb to mean 'a large number of'（與單數名詞及動詞連用）許多，大量：*Many a good man has been destroyed by drink.* 許多好人都毀在了飲酒上。
IDM **as many as ...** 🔑 used to show surprise that the number of people or things involved is so large（表示驚訝）多達，如此多：*There were as many as 200 people at the lecture.* 聽講的有 200 人之多。 **have had ˌone too ˈmany** (*informal*) to be slightly drunk 微醉；醉意朦朧 **many's the ...** (*formal*) used to show that sth happens often 許多次；常常：*Many's the time I heard her use those words.* 我不止一次聽她說過那樣的話。

Grammar Point 語法說明

many / a lot of / lots of

■ **Many** is used only with countable nouns. It is used mainly in questions and negative sentences. * many 只與可數名詞連用，主要用於疑問句和否定句中：*Do you go to many concerts?* 你常去聽音樂會嗎？◇ ***How many** people came to the meeting?* 多少人來參加了會議？◇ *I don't go to many concerts.* 我不常去聽音樂會。Although it is not common in statements, it is used after *so*, *as* and *too*. 該詞在陳述句中不很常用，但用於 so、as 和 too 之後：*You made too many mistakes.* 你犯的錯誤太多了。

■ In statements **a lot of** or **lots of** (*informal*) are much more common. 在陳述句中 a lot of 或 lots of（非正式）常用得多：*I go to a lot of concerts.* 我常去聽音樂會。◇ *'How many CDs have you got?' 'Lots!'* "你有幾張光盤？" "多着呢！" However, they are not used with measurements of time or distance. 不過，上述詞語不與表示時間和距離的量詞連用：*I stayed in England for many/quite a few/ten weeks.* 我在英格蘭逗留了許多週／好幾週／十週。◇ ~~*I stayed in England a lot of weeks.*~~ When **a lot of/lots of** means 'many', it takes a plural verb. * a lot of/lots of 意為 many 時，謂語動詞用複數：*Lots of people like Italian food.* 許多人喜歡意大利食物。You can also use **plenty of** (*informal*). 亦可用 plenty of（非正式）：*Plenty of stores stay open late.* 許多商店都營業到很晚。These phrases can also be used in questions and negative sentences. 以上短語亦可用於疑問句和否定句中。

■ **A lot of/lots of** is still felt to be informal, especially in *BrE*, so in formal writing it is better to use **many** or **a large number of** in statements. * a lot of/lots of 在英式英語中尤被視為非正式，因此在正式的書面陳述句中較宜用 many 或 a large number of。

➲ note at MUCH

Mao·ism /ˈmaʊɪzəm/ *noun* [U] the ideas of the 20th century Chinese COMMUNIST leader Mao Zedong 毛澤東主義；毛澤東思想 ▸ **Mao·ist** /ˈmaʊɪst/ *noun*, *adj.*

Maori /ˈmaʊri/ *noun* **1** [C] a member of a race of people who were the original people living in New Zealand（新西蘭）毛利人 **2** [U] the language of the Maori people 毛利語 ▶ **Maori** *adj.*

map /mæp/ *noun, verb*

■ ***noun*** a drawing or plan of the earth's surface or part of it, showing countries, towns, rivers, etc. 地圖：*a map of France* 法國地圖 ◇ *a street map of Miami* 邁阿密街區圖 ◇ *to* ***read a/the map*** (= understand the information on a map) 查看地圖 ◇ *large-scale maps* 大比例地圖 ◇ *Can you find Black Hill* ***on the map****?* 你能在地圖上找到布萊克山嗎？◇ *I'll draw you a map of how to get to my house.* 我給你畫一張到我家的路線圖。➲ VISUAL VOCAB page V40 ➲ see also ROAD MAP

IDM **put sb/sth on the ˈmap** to make sb/sth famous or important 使出名；使有重要性：*The exhibition has helped put the city on the map.* 展覽會使這個城市名揚四方。➲ more at WIPE *v.*

■ ***verb*** (**-pp-**) **1 ~ sth** to make a map of an area 繪製…的地圖 SYN **chart**：*an unexplored region that has not yet been mapped* 一個尚未繪製地圖的未經勘察的地區 **2 ~ sth** to discover or give information about sth, especially the way it is arranged or organized 瞭解信息，提供信息（尤指其編排或組織方式）：*It is now possible to map the different functions of the brain.* 現在已有可能瞭解大腦的各種功能。▶ **map·ping** *noun* [U]：*the mapping of the Indian subcontinent* 印度次大陸地圖的繪製 ◇ *gene mapping* 基因圖的繪製

PHR V **ˈmap sth on/onto sth** to link a group of qualities, items, etc. with their source, cause, position on a scale, etc. 把…與…相聯繫：*Grammar information enables students to map the structure of a foreign language onto their own.* 語法知識使學生能夠把外語結構和母語結構聯繫起來。**ˌmap sth↔ˈout** to plan or arrange sth in a careful or detailed way（精心細緻地）規劃，安排：*He has his career path clearly mapped out.* 他精心規劃了自己的事業前途。

maple /ˈmeɪpl/ *noun* **1** [C, U] (also **ˈmaple tree**) a tall tree with leaves that have five points and turn bright red or yellow in the autumn/fall. Maples grow in northern countries. 槭樹 **2** [U] the wood of the maple tree 槭木

ˈmaple leaf *noun* **1** [C] the leaf of the maple tree, used as a symbol of Canada 楓葉（加拿大的象徵）**2 the Maple Leaf** [sing.] the flag of Canada 楓葉旗（加拿大國旗）

ˌmaple ˈsyrup *noun* [U] a sweet sticky sauce made with liquid obtained from some types of maple tree, often eaten with PANCAKES 槭樹汁；槭糖漿

mar /mɑː(r)/ *verb* (**-rr-**) **~ sth** to damage or spoil sth good 破壞；毀壞；損毀；損害 SYN **blight, ruin**：*The game was marred by the behaviour of drunken fans.* 喝醉了的球迷行為不軌，把比賽給攪了。

ma·racas /məˈrækəz; *NAmE* -ˈrɑː-/ *noun* [pl.] a pair of simple musical instruments consisting of hollow balls containing BEADS or BEANS that are shaken to produce a sound 砂槌，響葫蘆（成對的打擊樂器，內裝珠子或豆粒，搖動以發聲）➲ VISUAL VOCAB page V35

mar·as·chino /ˌmærəˈʃiːnəʊ; -ˈskiːnəʊ; *NAmE* -noʊ/ *noun* (*pl.* **-os**) **1** [U, C] a strong sweet alcoholic drink made from black CHERRIES 馬拉斯加櫻桃酒；黑櫻桃酒 **2** (also **ˌmaraschino ˈcherry**) [C] a preserved CHERRY used to decorate alcoholic drinks 馬拉斯加酒漬櫻桃（用於裝點酒類飲料）

Ma·ra·thi (also **Mah·ratti**) /məˈrɑːti; -ˈræti/ *noun* [U] a language spoken in Maharashtra in western India 馬拉塔語（印度西部一種語言）

mara·thon /ˈmærəθən; *NAmE* -θɑːn/ *noun* **1** a long running race of about 42 kilometres or 26 miles 馬拉松賽跑（距離約 42 公里，合 26 英里）：*the London marathon* 倫敦馬拉松賽跑 ◇ *to run a marathon* 參加馬拉松賽跑 **2** an activity or a piece of work that lasts a long time and requires a lot of effort and patience 馬拉松式的活動（或工作）：*The interview was a real marathon.* 這次面試真是一場馬拉松。ORIGIN From the story that in ancient Greece a messenger ran from Marathon to Athens (22 miles) with the news of a victory over the Persians. 源自古希臘的傳說，一名通信兵從馬拉松奔跑 22 英里到雅典報捷。▶ **mara·thon** *adj.* [only before noun]：*a marathon journey lasting 56 hours* 持續了 56 小時的馬拉松式的旅程 ◇ *a marathon legal battle* 一場馬拉松式的法律鬥爭

ma·raud·ing /məˈrɔːdɪŋ/ *adj.* [only before noun] (of people or animals 人或動物) going around a place in search of things to steal or people to attack（到處）搶劫的，打劫的，劫掠的：*marauding wolves* 到處獵食的狼群 ▶ **ma·raud·er** /məˈrɔːdə(r)/ *noun*

mar·ble /ˈmɑːbl; *NAmE* ˈmɑːrbl/ *noun* **1** [U] a type of hard stone that is usually white and often has coloured lines in it. It can be polished and is used in building and for making statues, etc. 大理石：*a* ***slab/block of marble*** 一塊大理石板 ◇ *a* ***marble floor/sculpture*** 大理石地板／雕刻 **2** [C] a small ball of coloured glass that children roll along the ground in a game（玻璃）彈子 **3 marbles** [U] a game played with marbles 彈子遊戲：*Three boys were playing marbles.* 三個男孩兒在玩彈子遊戲。**4 marbles** [pl.] (*informal*) a way of referring to sb's intelligence or mental ability 理智；智力：*He's* ***losing his marbles*** (= he's not behaving in a sensible way). 他失去理智了。

mar·bled /ˈmɑːbld; *NAmE* ˈmɑːrbld/ *adj.* having the colours and/or patterns of marble 有大理石顏色（或花紋）的：*marbled wallpaper* 有大理石花紋的牆紙

marb·ling /ˈmɑːblɪŋ; *NAmE* ˈmɑːrb-/ *noun* [U] the method of decorating sth with a pattern that looks like MARBLE 大理石紋飾；仿大理石（裝飾）

marc /mɑːk; *NAmE* mɑːrk/ *noun* **1** [U, sing.] the substance left after GRAPES have been pressed to make wine（釀酒時將葡萄壓榨後的）殘渣；葡萄果渣 **2** [U, C] a strong alcoholic drink made from this substance 葡萄渣酒

March /mɑːtʃ; *NAmE* mɑːrtʃ/ *noun* [U, C] (*abbr.* **Mar.**) the 3rd month of the year, between February and April 三月 HELP To see how **March** is used, look at the examples at **April**. * March 的用法見詞條 April 下的示例。IDM see MAD

march /mɑːtʃ; *NAmE* mɑːrtʃ/ *verb, noun*

■ ***verb*** **1** [I] to walk with stiff regular steps like a soldier 齊步走；行進：(**+ adv./prep.**) *Soldiers were marching up and down outside the government buildings.* 士兵在政府大樓外面來回練習隊列行進。◇ *Quick march!* (= the order to start marching)（口令）齊步走！◇ **+ noun** *They marched 20 miles to reach the capital.* 他們行進了 20 英里才到達首都。**2** [I] **+ adv./prep.** to walk somewhere quickly in a determined way（堅定地向某地）前進，進發：*She marched over to me and demanded an apology.* 她毅然走過來，要我向她道歉。**3** [I] to walk through the streets in a large group in order to protest about sth 遊行示威；遊行抗議 SYN **demonstrate 4** [T] **~ sb + adv./prep.** to force sb to walk somewhere with you 使同行；強迫（某人）一起走：*The guards marched the prisoner away.* 衞兵押着囚犯離開了。

IDM **get your ˈmarching orders** (*BrE, informal*) to be ordered to leave a place, a job, etc. 奉命離開；被解職 **give sb their ˈmarching orders** (*informal*) to order sb to leave a place, their job, etc. 命令某人離開；解雇 **march to (the beat of) a different ˈdrummer/ˈdrum** to behave in a different way from other people; to have different attitudes or ideas 與眾不同：*She was a gifted and original artist who marched to a different drummer.* 她有天賦，具獨創性，是個與眾不同的藝術家。

PHR V **ˌmarch ˈon** to move on or pass quickly 繼續行進；快速經過：***Time marches on*** *and we still have not made a decision.* 時間過得飛快，而我們卻還沒有拿定主意。**ˈmarch on …** to march to a place to protest about sth or to attack it 向…行進（以示抗議或進行攻擊）：*Several thousand people marched on City Hall.* 數千人湧往市政廳進行抗議。

■ ***noun*** **1** [C] an organized walk by many people from one place to another, in order to protest about sth, or to express their opinions 示威遊行；抗議遊行：*protest marches* 抗議遊行 ◇ *to go on a march* 進行示威遊行 ➲ compare DEMONSTRATION (1) **2** [C] an act of

M

marching; a journey made by marching 行進；行軍：*The army began their long march to the coast.* 部隊開始了他們開往沿海地區的長途行軍。**3** [sing.] **the ~ of sth** the steady development or forward movement of sth 穩步發展；穩步前進：*the **march of progress/technology/time*** 平穩的進步；技術的穩步發展；時光的推移 **4** [C] a piece of music written for marching to 進行曲：*a funeral march* 葬禮進行曲

IDM **on the 'march** marching somewhere 在行軍中；在行進中；在進展中：*The enemy are on the march.* 敵人正在行軍途中。➲ more at STEAL *v.*

march·er /ˈmɑːtʃə(r); *NAmE* ˈmɑːrtʃ-/ *noun* a person who is taking part in a march as a protest 遊行示威者；抗議遊行者 SYN **demonstrator**

ˈmarching band *noun* [C+sing./pl. v.] a group of musicians who play while they are marching 行進樂隊；邊行走邊演奏的樂隊

ˈmarching season *noun* (in Northern Ireland) the time in July and August when PROTESTANT groups march through the streets in memory of victories over CATHOLICS in the 17th century 遊行季節（北愛爾蘭新教徒為紀念 17 世紀戰勝天主教而在七、八月份上街遊行）

mar·chion·ess /ˌmɑːʃəˈnes; *NAmE* ˌmɑːrʃ-/ *noun* **1** a woman who has the rank of a MARQUESS 女侯爵 **2** the wife of a MARQUESS 侯爵夫人 ➲ compare MARQUISE

ˈmarch past *noun* [sing.] a ceremony in which soldiers march past an important person, etc. 分列式（軍人列隊通過檢閱台）SYN **parade**

Mardi Gras /ˌmɑːdi ˈɡrɑː; *NAmE* ˈmɑːrdi ɡrɑː/ *noun* [U] (from *French*) the day before the beginning of Lent, celebrated as a holiday in some countries, with music and dancing in the streets 狂歡節（大齋期的前一天）➲ compare SHROVE TUESDAY

mare /meə(r); *NAmE* mer/ *noun* a female horse or DONKEY 母馬；母驢 ➲ compare BROOD MARE, FILLY, STALLION

IDM **a ˈmare's nest** **1** a discovery that seems interesting but is found to have no value（看似有趣但）毫無價值的發現 **2** a very complicated situation 複雜的形勢；變幻莫測的局勢

mar·gar·ine /ˌmɑːdʒəˈriːn; *NAmE* ˈmɑːrdʒərən/ (also *BrE informal* **marge** /mɑːdʒ; *NAmE* mɑːrdʒ/) *noun* [U] a yellow substance like butter made from animal or vegetable fats, used in cooking or spread on bread, etc. 人造黃油；人造奶油

mar·ga·rita /ˌmɑːɡəˈriːtə; *NAmE* ˌmɑːrɡ-/ *noun* an alcoholic drink made by mixing fruit juice with TEQUILA 瑪格麗特酒（用果汁與墨西哥龍舌蘭酒調製而成）

mar·gin AW /ˈmɑːdʒɪn; *NAmE* ˈmɑːrdʒən/ *noun* [C] **1** the empty space at the side of a written or printed page 頁邊空白；白邊：*the **left-hand/right-hand margin*** 左 / 右頁邊 ◇ *a **narrow/wide margin*** 窄 / 寬空白邊 ◇ *notes scribbled **in the margin*** 隨手寫在頁邊上的筆記 **2** [usually sing.] the amount of time, or number of votes, etc. by which sb wins sth（獲勝者在時間或票數上領先的）幅度，差額，差數：*He won by a **narrow margin**.* 他以微小的差額獲勝。◇ *She beat the other runners **by a margin of** ten seconds.* 她以領先十秒的優勢戰勝了其他賽跑者。**3** (*business* 商) = PROFIT MARGIN：*What are your average operating margins?* 你的平均營業利潤率是多少？◇ *a gross margin of 45%* * 45% 的毛利 **4** [usually sing.] an extra amount of sth such as time, space, money, etc. that you include in order to make sure that sth is successful 餘地；備用的時間（或空間、金錢等）：*a safety margin* 安全距離 ◇ *The narrow gateway left me little **margin for error** as I reversed the car.* 門口狹窄，弄得我倒車時幾乎不能出任何差錯。➲ see also MARGIN OF ERROR **5** (*formal*) the extreme edge or limit of a place 邊緣；極限；界限：*the eastern margin of the Indian Ocean* 印度洋的東岸 **6** [usually pl.] the part that is not included in the main part of a group or situation 邊緣部份；非主體部份 SYN **fringe**：*people living **on the margins** of society* 生活在社會邊緣的人 **7** (*AustralE, NZE*) an amount that is added to a basic wage, paid for special skill or responsibility（基本工資以外的）技術津貼，職務補貼

mar·gin·al AW /ˈmɑːdʒɪnl; *NAmE* ˈmɑːrdʒ-/ *adj., noun*

■ *adj.* **1** small and not important 小的；微不足道的；不重要的 SYN **slight**：*a marginal improvement in weather conditions* 天氣條件的略微好轉 ◇ *The story will only be of marginal interest to our readers.* 我們的讀者對這則故事不會很感興趣。**2** not part of a main or important group or situation 非主體的；邊緣的：*marginal groups in society* 社會中的非主流群體 **3** (*politics* 政) (*especially BrE*) won or lost by a very small number of votes and therefore very important or interesting as an indication of public opinion 以相差無幾的票數獲勝（或失敗）的；邊緣的：*a **marginal seat/constituency*** 邊緣席位 / 選區 **4** [only before noun] written in the margin of a page 寫在頁邊空白處的：***marginal notes/comments*** 頁邊的註解 / 評論 **5** (of land 土地) that cannot produce enough good crops to make a profit 貧瘠的（因而盈利有限）

■ *noun* (*BrE*) a seat in a parliament, on a local council, etc. that was won by a very small number of votes（議會或地方委員會的）邊緣席位：*a Labour marginal* 工黨的邊緣席位

mar·gi·na·lia /ˌmɑːdʒɪˈneɪliə; *NAmE* ˌmɑːrdʒ-/ *noun* [pl.] **1** notes written in the MARGINS of a book, etc.（書等的）旁註，邊註 **2** facts or details that are not very important 無足輕重的事情；細枝末節

mar·gin·al·ize (*BrE* also **-ise**) /ˈmɑːdʒɪnəlaɪz; *NAmE* ˈmɑːrdʒ-/ *verb* **~ sb** to make sb feel as if they are not important and cannot influence decisions or events; to put sb in a position in which they have no power 使顯得微不足道；使處於邊緣；使無實權 ▶ **mar·gin·al·iza·tion, -isa·tion** *noun* [U]：*the marginalization of the elderly* 對老年人的忽視

mar·gin·al·ly AW /ˈmɑːdʒɪnəli; *NAmE* ˈmɑːrdʒ-/ *adv.* very slightly; not very much 輕微地；很少地；微不足道地：*They now cost marginally more than they did last year.* 他們現在並不比去年貴多少。

ˌmargin of ˈerror *noun* [usually sing.] an amount that you allow when you calculate sth, for the possibility that a number is not completely accurate 誤差幅度：*The survey has a margin of error of 2.5%.* 測量的誤差幅度為 2.5%。

mar·guer·ite /ˌmɑːɡəˈriːt; *NAmE* ˌmɑːrɡ-/ *noun* a small white garden flower with a yellow centre 春白菊；濱菊；法蘭西菊

mari·achi /ˌmæriˈɑːtʃi/ *noun* [C, U] a musician who plays traditional Mexican music, usually as part of a small group that travels from place to place; the type of music played by these musicians 馬里亞奇音樂演奏者，墨西哥傳統音樂演奏者（常為街頭樂隊成員）；馬里亞奇音樂；墨西哥街頭音樂：*a mariachi band* 馬里亞奇樂隊

Mar·ian /ˈmeəriən; *NAmE* ˈmer-/ *adj.* (*religion* 宗) relating to the Virgin Mary in the Christian church（基督教）有關聖母瑪利亞的

mari·cul·ture /ˈmærɪkʌltʃə(r)/ *noun* [U] (*technical* 術語) a type of farming in which fish or other sea animals and plants are bred or grown for food 海產養殖業

Marie Celeste /ˌmæri sɪˈlest; ˌmɑːri/ *noun* [sing.] = MARY CELESTE

mari·gold /ˈmæriɡəʊld; *NAmE* -ɡoʊld/ *noun* an orange or yellow garden flower. There are several types of marigold. 萬壽菊；金盞花

ma·ri·juana (also **ma·ri·huana**) /ˌmærəˈwɑːnə/ (also *informal* **pot**) *noun* [U] a drug (illegal in many countries) made from the dried leaves and flowers of the HEMP plant, which gives the person smoking it a feeling of being relaxed 大麻；大麻毒品 SYN **cannabis**

ma·rimba /məˈrɪmbə/ *noun* a musical instrument like a XYLOPHONE 馬林巴琴；木琴

mar·ina /məˈriːnə/ *noun* a specially designed HARBOUR for small boats and YACHTS 小船塢；遊艇停靠區

mar·in·ade /ˌmærɪˈneɪd/ *noun* [C, U] a mixture of oil, wine, spices, etc., in which meat or fish is left before it is cooked in order to make it softer or to give it a particular flavour 醃泡汁

marin·ate /ˈmærɪneɪt/ (also **mar·in·ade**) *verb* [T, I] **~ (sth)** if you **marinate** food or it **marinates**, you leave it in a marinade before cooking it 醃，浸泡（食物）；（食物）醃，浸泡

mar·ine /məˈriːn/ *adj., noun*

■ ***adj.*** [only before noun] **1** connected with the sea and the creatures and plants that live there 海的；海產的；海生的：*marine life* 海洋生物 ◇ *a marine biologist* (= a scientist who studies life in the sea) 海洋生物學家 **2** connected with ships or trade at sea 海船的；貨船的；海上貿易的

■ ***noun*** a soldier who is trained to serve on land or at sea, especially one in the US Marine Corps or the British Royal Marines（尤指美國或英國皇家）海軍陸戰隊士兵

mari·ner /ˈmærɪnə(r)/ *noun* (*old-fashioned* or *literary*) a sailor 水手

mar·io·nette /ˌmæriəˈnet/ *noun* a PUPPET whose arms, legs and head are moved by strings 牽線木偶

mari·tal /ˈmærɪtl/ *adj.* [only before noun] connected with marriage or with the relationship between a husband and wife 婚姻的；夫妻關係的：***marital difficulties/breakdown*** 婚姻糾葛 / 破裂

ˌmarital ˈstatus *noun* [U] (*formal*) (used especially on official forms 尤用於正式表格) the fact of whether you are single, married, etc. 婚姻狀況：*questions about age, sex and marital status* 關於年齡、性別、婚姻狀況的問題

mari·time /ˈmærɪtaɪm/ *adj.* **1** connected with the sea or ships 海的；海事的；海運的；船舶的：*a maritime museum* 海洋博物館 **2** (*formal*) near the sea 靠近海的：*maritime Antarctica* 南極近海地區

mar·joram /ˈmɑːdʒərəm; *NAmE* ˈmɑːrdʒ-/ *noun* [U] a plant with leaves that smell sweet and are used in cooking as a HERB, often when dried 墨角蘭，牛至（葉子芳香，常在乾後用作烹調輔料）

mark 🔑 /mɑːk; *NAmE* mɑːrk/ *verb, noun*

■ ***verb***

▸ **WRITE/DRAW** 寫；畫 **1** 🔑 [T] to write or draw a symbol, line, etc. on sth in order to give information about it 作記號；作標記：**~ A (with B)** *Items marked with an asterisk can be omitted.* 打星號的項目可以刪去。◇ **~ B on A** *Prices are marked on the goods.* 價格標在商品上。◇ **~ sb/sth + adj.** *The teacher marked her absent* (= made a mark by her name to show that she was absent). 老師在她的名字旁做了個缺課的記號。◇ *Why have you marked this wrong?* 你為什麼批這道題為錯？◇ *Do not open any mail marked 'Confidential'.* 不要打開任何標有"機密"的郵件。

▸ **SPOIL/DAMAGE** 搞糟；損壞 **2** 🔑 [T, I] **~ (sth)** to make a mark on sth in a way that spoils or damages it; to become spoilt or damaged in this way 留下痕跡；弄污；使有污點：*A large purple scar marked his cheek.* 他的面頰上有一塊大紫疤。◇ *The surfaces are made from a material that doesn't mark.* 這些表層是由不會留下污漬的材料做的。

▸ **SHOW POSITION** 表示方位 **3** 🔑 [T] **~ sth** to show the position of sth 標明方位；標示 SYN **indicate**：*The cross marks the spot where the body was found.* 十字記號標明了發現死屍的地點。◇ *The route has been marked in red.* 路線用紅色標明了。

▸ **CELEBRATE** 慶賀 **4** 🔑 [T] **~ sth** to celebrate or officially remember an event that you consider to be important 紀念；慶賀：*a ceremony to mark the 50th anniversary of the end of the war* 紀念戰爭結束 50 週年的慶典

▸ **SHOW CHANGE** 標示變化 **5** [T] **~ sth** to be a sign that sth new is going to happen 是…的跡象；成為…的徵兆；表明：*This speech may* ***mark a change in*** *government policy.* 這篇演講表明政府的政策可能會有變化。◇ *The agreement marks a new phase in international relations.* 這一協議標誌着國際關係新時期的到來。

▸ **GIVE MARK/GRADE** 打分；給成績 **6** 🔑 [T, I] **~ (sth)** (*especially BrE*) to give marks to students' work 給（學生作業）打分，評分，評成績：*I hate marking exam papers.* 我討厭閱卷。◇ *I spend at least six hours a week marking.* 我每週至少要花六個小時批改作業。➲ compare GRADE *v.* (2)

▸ **GIVE PARTICULAR QUALITY** 賦予特徵 **7** [T, usually passive] (*formal*) to give sb/sth a particular quality or character 賦予特徵；給…確定性質 SYN **characterize**：**~ sb/sth** *a life marked by suffering* 痛苦的一生 ◇ **~ sb/sth as sth** *He was marked as an enemy of the poor.* 他被列為窮人的敵人。

▸ **PAY ATTENTION** 注意 **8** [T] (*old-fashioned*) used to tell sb to pay careful attention to sth 留心；留意；注意：**~ sth** *There'll be trouble over this,* ***mark my words.*** 記住我的話，這件事是會有麻煩的。◇ **~ what, how, etc. ...** *You mark what I say, John.* 約翰，注意聽着。

▸ **IN SPORT** 體育運動 **9** [T] **~ sb** (in a team game 成隊比賽) to stay close to an opponent in order to prevent them from getting the ball 釘人防守；釘住（對手）：*Hughes was marking Taylor.* 休斯在釘防泰勒。◇ *Our defence had him closely marked.* 我方後衛已經緊緊地釘住了他。➲ see also MARKING (4)

IDM **ˌmark ˈtime 1** to pass the time while you wait for sth more interesting 等待時機：*I'm just marking time in this job—I'm hoping to get into journalism.* 我幹這件工作只是在等待時機，我希望能從事新聞工作。 **2** (of soldiers 士兵) to make marching movements without moving forwards 原地踏步 **ˌmark ˈyou** (*old-fashioned, informal, especially BrE*) used to remind sb of sth they should consider in a particular case 無論如何；儘管如此；反正；然而：*She hasn't had much success yet. Mark you, she tries hard.* 她還沒取得什麼成功，可是她非常努力。

PHR V **ˌmark sb ˈdown** (*BrE*) to reduce the mark/grade given to sb in an exam, etc. 給低分；壓低成績：*She was marked down because of poor grammar.* 她因語法不好被扣了分。 **ˌmark sb ˈdown as sth** (*especially BrE*) to recognize sb as a particular type 將某人看作；認定某人為：*I hadn't got him marked down as a liberal.* 我當時還沒有把他看作自由主義者。 **ˌmark sth↔ˈdown 1** to reduce the price of sth 減價；打折：*All goods have been marked down by 15%.* 所有商品都打八五折。OPP **mark up** ➲ related noun MARKDOWN **2** to make a note of sth for future use or action 記下；將…記錄下：*The factory is already marked down for demolition.* 這家工廠已登記在案，準備拆除。 **ˌmark sb/sth ˈoff (from sb/sth)** to make sb/sth seem different from other people or things 使與眾不同；使有別於其他人（或物）：*Each of London's districts had a distinct character that marked it off from its neighbours.* 倫敦的每個區都有鮮明的特徵，與鄰近地區不同。 **ˌmark sth↔ˈoff** to separate sth by marking a line between it and sth else 畫線分隔；劃開：*The playing area was marked off with a white line.* 運動場地用白線劃了出來。 **ˌmark sb ˈout as/for sth** to make people recognize sb as special in some way 選定；挑選：*She was marked out for early promotion.* 她被選定要儘早得到擢升。 **ˌmark sth↔ˈout** to draw lines to show the edges of sth 畫出界限；畫出邊界；用線畫出範圍：*They marked out a tennis court on the lawn.* 他們在草坪上畫了個網球場。 **ˌmark sth↔ˈup 1** to increase the price of sth 提價；加價；漲價：*Share prices were marked up as soon as trading started.* 交易一開始，股票價格就漲上去了。OPP **mark down** ➲ related noun MARKUP (1) **2** (*technical* 術語) to mark or correct a text, etc., for example for printing 審校；標註排版說明：*to mark up a manuscript* 審校手稿

■ ***noun***

▸ **SPOT/DIRT** 污點 **1** 🔑 a small area of dirt, a spot or a cut on a surface that spoils its appearance 污點；污漬；斑點；疤痕：*The children left dirty marks all over the kitchen floor.* 孩子們把廚房的地板弄得污漬斑斑。◇ *a burn/scratch mark* 一塊灼傷的 / 抓傷的疤痕 ◇ *Detectives found no marks on the body.* 偵探沒有在屍體上發現任何斑痕。 **2** 🔑 a noticeable spot or area of colour on the body of a person or an animal which helps you to recognize them（人或動物身上有助於識別的）斑點，記號，色斑：*a horse with a white mark on its head* 頭上有塊白斑的馬 ◇ *He was about six feet tall, with no* ***distinguishing marks.*** 他身高約六英尺，沒什麼特別的記號。 ➲ **SYNONYMS** at PATCH ➲ see also BIRTHMARK, MARKING (1)

▸ **SYMBOL** 記號 **3** 🔑 a written or printed symbol that is used as a sign of sth, for example the quality of sth or who made or owns it 符號；記號；（顯示質量、製造者或所有者等的）標記：*punctuation marks* 標點符號 ◇ *Any piece of silver bearing his mark is extremely valuable.*

M

帶有他的印記的每一件銀器都極有價值。◇ *I put a mark in the margin to remind me to check the figure.* 我在頁邊做了個記號來提醒自己核對一下這個數字。➲ see also QUESTION MARK, EXCLAMATION MARK, TRADEMARK

▸ **SIGN 跡象** **4** a sign that a quality or feeling exists（品質或情感的）標誌，跡象，表示： *On the day of the funeral businesses remained closed as **a mark of respect**.* 葬禮那天，各行業都停業以示敬意。◇ *Such coolness under pressure is the mark of a champion.* 在壓力下仍能這樣保持冷靜，這就是冠軍相。

▸ **STANDARD/GRADE 標準；成績** **5** (*especially BrE*) a number or letter that is given to show the standard of sb's work or performance or is given to sb for answering sth correctly 成績；分數；等級： *to get a **good/poor mark** in English* 英語得分高／低 ◇ *to give sb a **high/low mark*** 給某人高分／低分 ◇ *What's the **pass mark** (= the mark you need in order to pass)?* 合格分數是多少？◇ *I got **full marks** (= the highest mark possible) in the spelling test.* 我在拼寫測驗中得了個滿分。◇ (*ironic*) *'You're wearing a tie!' '**Full marks for** observation.'* "你打領帶啦！""你真眼尖，我給你打滿分。" ➲ see also BLACK MARK, GRADE *n.* (3)

▸ **LEVEL 水平** **6** a level or point that sth reaches that is thought to be important（重要的）水平，標準點，指標： *Unemployment has passed the four million mark.* 失業人數已突破四百萬大關。◇ *She was leading at the half-way mark.* 賽程到一半時是她領先。

▸ **MACHINE/VEHICLE 機器；車輛** **7 Mark** (followed by a number 後接數詞) a particular type or model of a machine or vehicle 型號： *the Mark II engine* * II 型發動機

M

▸ **IN GAS OVEN 煤氣烤箱** **8 Mark** (*BrE*) (followed by a number 後接數詞) a particular level of temperature in a gas oven 燃氣擋；溫度刻度： *Preheat the oven to gas Mark 6.* 將烤箱預熱到 6 擋。

▸ **SIGNATURE 簽名** **9** a cross made on a document instead of a signature by sb who is not able to write their name（文盲在文件上代替簽名的）花押

▸ **TARGET 目標** **10** (*formal*) a target 目標；靶子： *Of the blows delivered, barely half found their mark.* 僅有不到半數的出拳擊中目標。◇ *to **hit/miss the mark*** 擊中／錯過目標

▸ **GERMAN MONEY 德國貨幣** **11** = DEUTSCHMARK

IDM **be close to/near the 'mark** to be fairly accurate in a guess, statement, etc.（猜測、陳述等）接近準確，幾乎無誤 **be off the 'mark** not to be accurate in a guess, statement, etc.（猜測、陳述等）不準確，相去甚遠，離題： *No, you're way off the mark.* 不行，你根本沒說到重點。 **be on the 'mark** to be accurate or correct 精確；準確無誤： *That estimate was right on the mark.* 那個估計分毫不差。 **get off the 'mark** to start scoring, especially in CRICKET（尤指板球運動）開始得分： *Stewart got off the mark with a four.* 斯圖爾特以一記四分球開始得分。 **ˌhit/ˌmiss the 'mark** to succeed/fail in achieving or guessing sth 達到／沒有達到目的；猜測正確／錯誤： *He blushed furiously and Robyn knew she had hit the mark.* 他滿臉通紅，羅賓一看便知道她擊中了要害。 **ˌleave your/its/a 'mark (on sth/sb)** to have an effect on sth/sb, especially a bad one, that lasts for a long time 留下久遠的影響（尤指壞影響）： *Such a traumatic experience was bound to leave its mark on the children.* 這樣的痛苦經歷一定會長期對孩子們有影響。 **ˌmake your/a 'mark (on sth)** to become famous and successful in a particular area（在某領域）取得成功，出名 **not be/feel ˌup to the 'mark** (*old-fashioned, BrE*) not to feel as well or lively as usual 感覺不舒服 **on your ˌmarks, get ˌset, 'go!** used to tell runners in a race to get ready and then to start（徑賽口令）各就各位，預備，跑！ **quick/slow off the 'mark** fast/slow in reacting to a situation（對形勢）反應敏捷／遲鈍 **ˌup to the 'mark** (*BrE*) (*NAmE* **ˌup to 'snuff**) as good as it/they should be 達到要求；符合標準 **SYN** **up to scratch**： *Your work isn't really up to the mark.* 你的工作沒有真正達到要求。➲ more at OVERSTEP, TOE *v.*, WIDE *adj.*

mark·down /ˈmɑːkdaʊn; *NAmE* ˈmɑːrk-/ *noun* [usually sing.] a reduction in price 減價；降價

Synonyms 同義詞辨析

mark

stain • fingerprint • streak • speck • blot • smear • spot

These are all words for a small area of dirt or another substance on a surface. 以上各詞均指污點、斑點、污跡。

mark a small area of dirt or other substance on the surface of sth, especially one that spoils its appearance 指污點、污跡、斑點： *The kids left dirty marks all over the kitchen floor.* 孩子們把廚房的地板弄得污跡斑斑。

stain a dirty mark on sth that is difficult to remove, especially one made by a liquid 指污點、污漬： *blood stains* 血跡

fingerprint a mark on a surface made by the pattern of lines on the end of a person's finger, often used by the police to identify criminals 指指紋、指印： *Her fingerprints were all over the gun.* 那支槍上佈滿了她的指紋。

streak a long thin mark or line that is a different colour from the surface it is on 指條紋、條痕： *She had streaks of grey in her hair.* 她頭上已是白髮縷縷。

speck a very small mark, spot or piece of a substance on sth 指小點、污點： *There isn't a speck of dust anywhere in the house.* 整間房子一塵不染。

blot a spot or dirty mark left on sth by a substance such as ink or paint being dropped on a surface 指污點、墨漬

smear a mark made by sth such as oil or paint being spread or rubbed on a surface 指污跡、油漬、污漬、污點

spot a small dirty mark on sth 指污跡、污漬、污點： *There were grease spots all over the walls.* 牆上滿是油漬。

PATTERNS

- a streak/speck/blot/smear/spot **of** sth
- a **greasy** mark/stain/smear
- an **ink** mark/stain/blot/spot
- a **grease** mark/stain/spot
- to **leave** a mark/stain/fingerprint/streak/speck/blot/smear

marked /mɑːkt; *NAmE* mɑːrkt/ *adj.* **1** easy to see 顯而易見的；明顯的；顯著的 **SYN** **noticeable, distinct**： *a **marked difference/improvement*** 明顯的差異／進步 ◇ *a marked increase in profits* 利潤的顯著提高 ◇ *She is quiet and studious, **in marked contrast to** her sister.* 她沉靜勤奮，與她妹妹形成了鮮明的對照。 **2** (*linguistics* 語言) (of a word or form of a word 單詞或詞形) showing a particular feature or style, such as being formal or informal 有標記成份的（如正式或非正式用語） **OPP** **unmarked** ▸ **mark·ed·ly** /ˈmɑːkɪdli; *NAmE* ˈmɑːrk-/ *adv.*： *Her background is markedly different from her husband's.* 她的背景和她丈夫的截然不同。◇ *This year's sales have risen markedly.* 今年的銷售額明顯提高了。

IDM **a ˌmarked 'man/'woman** a person who is in danger because their enemies want to harm them（遭計劃攻擊的）目標人物

mark·er /ˈmɑːkə(r); *NAmE* ˈmɑːrk-/ *noun* **1** [C] an object or a sign that shows the position of sth（表示方位的）標記，記號： *a boundary marker* 界標 ◇ *He placed a marker where the ball had landed.* 他在球落地的地方放了個標記。 **2** [sing.] **a ~ (of/for sth)** a sign that sth exists or that shows what it is like 標誌；標識；表示： *Price is not always an accurate marker of quality.* 價格並不總是質量的準確標誌。 **3** (*BrE* also **'marker pen**) a pen with a thick FELT tip 記號筆；氈頭筆 ➲ VISUAL VOCAB page V69 **4** (*BrE*) (*NAmE* **grader**) a person who marks/grades students' work or exam papers 閱卷人；判作業的人 **5** (*BrE*) (in team games, especially football (SOCCER) 團隊

比賽，尤指足球) a player who stays close to a player on the other team in order to stop them getting the ball 緊逼防守的隊員；釘人的防守隊員

mar·ket /ˈmɑːkɪt; *NAmE* ˈmɑːrk-/ *noun, verb*

■ ***noun*** **1** [C] an occasion when people buy and sell goods; the open area or building where they meet to do this 集市；市場；商場： ***a fruit/flower/antiques market*** 水果 / 鮮花 / 古玩市場 ◇ ***an indoor/a street market*** 室內 / 街頭市場 ◇ ***market stalls/traders*** 集市貨攤 / 商販 ◇ *We buy our fruit and vegetables* ***at the market***. 我們在市場上購買水果和蔬菜。◇ *Thursday is* ***market day***. 星期四是趕集日。◇ *a* ***market town*** (= a town in Britain where a regular market is or was held)（英國定期舉行集市貿易的）集鎮 ➲ VISUAL VOCAB pages V2, V3 ➲ see also FARMERS' MARKET **2** [sing.] business or trade, or the amount of trade in a particular type of goods 交易；買賣；交易量： *the world market in coffee* 世界咖啡交易 ◇ *They have increased their* ***share of the market*** *by 10%.* 他們將其所佔的市場份額增加了 10%。◇ *the* ***property/job market*** (= the number and type of houses, jobs, etc. that are available) 房地產 / 就業市場 ◇ *They have* ***cornered the market in*** *sportswear* (= sell the most). 他們壟斷了運動裝的銷售。➲ COLLOCATIONS at BUSINESS **3** [C] a particular area, country or section of the population that might buy goods 商品的銷售地；行銷地區；消費群體： *the Japanese market* 日本市場 ◇ *the* ***global/domestic market*** 全球 / 國內銷售市場 **4** [sing.] **~ (for sth)** the number of people who want to buy sth （顧客對貨物或服務的）需求 SYN **demand**： *a* ***growing/declining market*** *for second-hand cars* 不斷擴大的 / 萎縮的二手車市場 **5** (often **the market**) [sing.] people who buy and sell goods in competition with each other （處於競爭中的）市場經營者，市場： *The market will decide if the TV station has any future.* 電視台是否有前途將取決於市場。◇ *a* ***market-based/market-driven/market-led*** *economy* 以市場為基礎的 / 市場推動的 / 市場引導的經濟 ➲ see also BLACK MARKET, MARKET FORCES **6** [C] = STOCK MARKET： *the futures market* 期貨市場 ◇ *a market crash* 股市暴跌 HELP There are many other compounds ending in **market**. You will find them at their place in the alphabet. 以 market 結尾的複合詞還有很多，可在各字母中的適當位置查到。

IDM **in the ˈmarket for sth** interested in buying sth 有意購買： *I'm not in the market for a new car at the moment.* 我現在還不想買新車。 **on the ˈmarket** available for people to buy 出售；上市；有現貨供應： *to put your house on the market* 出售房屋 ◇ *The house came on the market last year.* 這棟房屋去年就上市了。◇ *There are hundreds of different brands on the market.* 有數百種不同的品牌供應。 **on the open ˈmarket** available to buy without any restrictions 敞開銷售；自由買賣 **play the ˈmarket** to buy and sell STOCKS and shares in order to make a profit 買賣證券和股票 ➲ more at BUYER, PRICE *v.*, SELLER

■ ***verb*** **~ sth (to sb) (as sth)** to advertise and offer a product for sale; to present sth in a particular way and make people want to buy it 推銷；促銷 SYN **promote**： *It is marketed as a low-alcohol wine.* 它作為一種低度酒投放市場。◇ *School meals need to be marketed to children in the same way as other food.* 校餐也要以其他食品的推銷方法推銷給孩子。➲ see also MARKETING

mar·ket·able /ˈmɑːkɪtəbl; *NAmE* ˈmɑːrk-/ *adj.* easy to sell; attractive to customers or employers 容易出售的；暢銷的；有銷路的： ***marketable products/skills/qualifications*** 受歡迎的產品 / 技能 / 條件 ▶ **mar·ket·abil·ity** /ˌmɑːkɪtəˈbɪləti; *NAmE* ˌmɑːrk-/ *noun* [U]

mar·ket·eer /ˌmɑːkɪˈtɪə(r); *NAmE* ˌmɑːrkəˈtɪr/ *noun* (usually in compounds 通常構成複合詞) a person who is in favour of a particular system of buying and selling 喜歡某種貿易體制的人： *a free marketeer* (= a person who believes in a FREE MARKET system of trade) 主張自由貿易者 ➲ see also BLACK MARKETEER

ˌmarket ˈforces *noun* [pl.] a free system of trade in which prices and wages rise and fall without being controlled by the government 市場調節作用；市場力量

ˌmarket ˈgarden (*BrE*) (*US* **ˈtruck farm**) *noun* a type of farm where vegetables are grown for sale 蔬菜農場 ▶ **ˌmarket ˈgardener** *noun* **ˌmarket ˈgardening** *noun* [U]

mar·ket·ing /ˈmɑːkɪtɪŋ; *NAmE* ˈmɑːrk-/ *noun* [U] the activity of presenting, advertising and selling a company's products in the best possible way 促銷；營銷；銷售活動： *a marketing campaign* 促銷活動 ◇ *She works in* ***sales and marketing***. 她在市場營銷部工作。➲ COLLOCATIONS at BUSINESS ➲ see also DIRECT MARKETING ▶ **mar·ket·er** *noun*： *a company that is a developer and marketer of software* 一家軟件開發和銷售公司

ˈmarketing mix *noun* (*business* 商) the combination of the features of a product, its price, the way it is advertised and where it is sold, each of which a company can adjust to persuade people to buy the product 營銷組合（即產品特徵、價格、廣告宣傳方式以及營銷地的組合，企業可調整這些項目來吸引消費者購買其產品）

ˌmarket ˈleader *noun* **1** the company that sells the largest quantity of a particular kind of product 同類商品的銷售大戶；市場份額的最大佔有者 **2** a product that is the most successful of its kind 最暢銷產品；同類商品中的佼佼者

mar·ket·place /ˈmɑːkɪtpleɪs; *NAmE* ˈmɑːrk-/ *noun* **1** **the marketplace** [sing.] the activity of competing with other companies to buy and sell goods, services, etc. 市場競爭： *Companies must be able to survive in the marketplace.* 公司必須有能力在市場競爭中生存下去。◇ *the education marketplace* 教育市場 **2** (also **ˌmarket ˈsquare**) [C] an open area in a town where a market is held 集市；市場

ˌmarket ˈprice *noun* the price that people are willing to pay for sth at a particular time 市場價；市價；時價

ˌmarket reˈsearch (also **ˌmarket ˈresearch**) *noun* [U] the work of collecting information about what people buy and why 市場調研；市場調查

ˌmarket ˈshare *noun* [U, sing.] (*business* 商) the amount that a company sells of its products or services compared with other companies selling the same things 市場佔有率；市場份額： *They claim to have a 40% worldwide market share.* 他們聲稱佔有全球 40% 的市場。➲ COLLOCATIONS at BUSINESS

ˌmarket ˈvalue *noun* [U, sing.] what sth would be worth if it were sold 市場價值；市值

mark·ing /ˈmɑːkɪŋ; *NAmE* ˈmɑːrk-/ *noun* **1** [C, usually pl.] a pattern of colours or marks on animals, birds or wood （獸類、鳥類或樹木的）斑紋，花紋，斑點 **2** [C, usually pl.] lines, colours or shapes painted on roads, vehicles, etc. （刷在道路、車輛等上的）線條，顏色，形狀： *Road markings indicate where you can stop.* 道路標誌告訴你哪裏可以停車。 **3** [U] (*especially BrE*) (*NAmE* usually **grading**) the activity of checking and correcting the written work or exam papers of students 批改；打分；閱卷： *She does her marking in the evenings.* 她晚上批改作業。 **4** [U] (in team games, especially football (SOCCER) 團隊比賽，尤指足球) the practice of staying close to a player on the other team in order to stop them getting the ball 釘人防守

marks·man /ˈmɑːksmən; *NAmE* ˈmɑːrk-/, **marks·woman** /ˈmɑːkswʊmən; *NAmE* ˈmɑːrk-/ *noun* (*pl.* **-men** /-mən/, **-women** /-wɪmɪn/) a person who is skilled in accurate shooting 神槍手；神射手

marks·man·ship /ˈmɑːksmənʃɪp; *NAmE* ˈmɑːrk-/ *noun* [U] skill in shooting 射擊術

mark·up /ˈmɑːkʌp; *NAmE* ˈmɑːrk-/ *noun* **1** [usually sing.] an increase in the price of sth based on the difference between the cost of producing it and the price it is sold at （基於成本價與銷售價之間差價的）加成： *an average markup of 10%* 平均 10% 的加成 **2** [U] (*computing* 計) the symbols used in computer documents which give information about the structure of the document and tell the computer how it is to appear on the computer screen, or how it is to appear when printed 標記，標記符號（標示計算機文檔結構和顯示、打印形式）： *a markup language* 標記語言

M

marl /mɑːl; *NAmE* mɑːrl/ *noun* **1** [U, C] soil consisting of CLAY and LIME (1) 泥灰岩；泥灰 **2** [U] a type of cloth with threads in it that are not of an even colour 夾花紗線織物： *blue marl leggings* 藍底兒夾花紗線綁腿

mar·lin /ˈmɑːlɪn; *NAmE* ˈmɑːrlɪn/ *noun* (*pl.* **mar·lin**) a large sea fish with a long sharp nose, that people catch for sport 穿索針魚，槍魚（吻呈長鏢槍狀）

mar·ma·lade /ˈmɑːməleɪd; *NAmE* ˈmɑːrm-/ *noun* [U] jam/jelly made from oranges, lemons, etc., eaten especially for breakfast 橘子醬；酸果醬 ➲ compare JAM (1)

Mar·mite™ /ˈmɑːmaɪt; *NAmE* ˈmɑːrm-/ *noun* [U] (*BrE*) a dark substance made from YEAST and spread on bread, etc. 馬麥醬（呈黑色，抹於麪包等食物上）**SYN** **yeast extract**： *Marmite sandwiches* 馬麥醬三明治

mar·mor·eal /mɑːˈmɔːriəl; *NAmE* mɑːrˈm-/ *adj.* (*literary*) made of or similar to MARBLE 大理石的；像大理石的

mar·mo·set /ˈmɑːməzet; *NAmE* ˈmɑːrm-/ *noun* a small MONKEY with a long thick tail, that lives in Central and S America 狨（棲於中南美洲的小長尾猴）

mar·mot /ˈmɑːmət; *NAmE* ˈmɑːrmət/ *noun* a small European or American animal that lives in holes in the ground 旱獺，土撥鼠（居於地穴，分佈於歐洲及美洲）

ma·roon /məˈruːn/ *adj.*, *noun*, *verb*

■ ***adj.*** dark brownish-red in colour 紫褐色的；褐紅色的

■ ***noun*** **1** [U] a dark brownish-red colour 褐紅色；紫褐色 **2** [C] a large FIREWORK that shoots into the air and makes a loud noise, used to attract attention, especially at sea（海上作為信號的）鞭炮

■ ***verb*** [usually passive] **~ sb** to leave sb in a place that they cannot escape from, for example an island 困住；使無法逃脱 **SYN** **strand**： *'Lord of the Flies' is a novel about English schoolboys marooned on a desert island.*《蠅王》是一本關於一群被困在荒島上的英國男學童的小説。

M

marque /mɑːk; *NAmE* mɑːrk/ *noun* (*formal*) a well-known make of a product, especially a car, that is expensive and fashionable 知名品牌（尤指汽車）： *the Porsche marque* 保時捷的品牌

mar·quee /mɑːˈkiː; *NAmE* mɑːrˈkiː/ *noun*, *adj.*

■ ***noun*** **1** a large tent used at social events（大型活動用的）大帳篷 **2** (*NAmE*) a covered entrance to a theatre, hotel, etc. often with a sign on or above it（戲院、酒店等入口處，通常帶有標記的）遮篷

■ ***adj.*** [only before noun] (*especially NAmE*) (especially in sport 尤用於體育運動) most important or most popular 最重要的；最受歡迎的；傑出的： *He is one of the marquee names in men's tennis.* 他是男子網球壇大名鼎鼎的人物之一。

mar·quess (also **mar·quis**) /ˈmɑːkwɪs; *NAmE* ˈmɑːrk-/ *noun* (in Britain) a NOBLEMAN of high rank between an EARL and a DUKE（英國）侯爵： *the Marquess of Bath* 巴斯侯爵 ➲ compare MARCHIONESS

mar·quet·ry /ˈmɑːkɪtri; *NAmE* ˈmɑːrk-/ *noun* [U] patterns or pictures made of pieces of wood on the surface of furniture, etc.; the art of making these patterns（傢具等的）鑲嵌細工，鑲嵌藝術

mar·quis /ˈmɑːkwɪs; *NAmE* ˈmɑːrk-/ *noun* **1** (in some European countries but not Britain) a NOBLEMAN of high rank between a COUNT and a DUKE（除英國外一些歐洲國家的）侯爵 **2** = MARQUESS

mar·quise /mɑːˈkiːz; *NAmE* mɑːrˈkiːz/ *noun* **1** the wife of a marquis 侯爵夫人 **2** a woman who has the rank of a marquis 女侯爵 ➲ compare MARCHIONESS

mar·ram grass /ˈmærəm grɑːs; *NAmE* græs/ (also **mar·ram**) *noun* [U] a type of grass that grows in sand, often planted to prevent sand DUNES from being destroyed by the wind, rain, etc. 濱草，沙茅草（用以固沙）

mar·riage 🔑 /ˈmærɪdʒ/ *noun*

1 🔑 [C] the legal relationship between a husband and wife 結婚；婚姻： *a* ***happy/unhappy marriage*** 幸福的／不幸福的婚姻 ◇ *All of her children's marriages ended in divorce.* 她的孩子們最終都離了婚。◇ *an* ***arranged marriage*** (= one in which the parents choose a husband or wife for their child) 一樁父母安排的婚姻 ◇ *She has two children by a previous marriage.* 她和前夫有兩個孩子。 ➲ see also MIXED **2** 🔑 [U] the state of being married 婚姻生活；已婚狀態： *They don't believe in marriage.* 他們不相信婚姻。◇ *My parents are celebrating 30 years of marriage.* 我的父母親即將慶祝結婚 30 週年。**3** 🔑 [C] the ceremony in which two people become husband and wife 婚禮： *Their marriage took place in a local church.* 他們的婚禮是在當地一所教堂裏舉行的。**HELP** **Wedding** is more common in this meaning. 表示 "婚禮"，wedding 更為常見。

IDM **by 'marriage** when sb is related to you **by marriage**, they are married to sb in your family, or you are married to sb in their family 通過姻親關係 ➲ more at HAND *n.*

mar·riage·able /ˈmærɪdʒəbl/ *adj.* (*old-fashioned*) suitable for marriage 適婚的： *She had reached marriageable age.* 當時她已經到了適婚年齡。

'marriage broker *noun* a person who is paid to arrange for two people to meet and marry（職業）婚姻介紹人，媒人

'marriage bureau *noun* (*old-fashioned*, *BrE*) an organization that introduces people who are looking for sb to marry 婚姻介紹所

'marriage certificate (*BrE*) (*US* **'marriage license**) *noun* a legal document that proves two people are married 結婚證書

,marriage 'guidance *noun* [U] (*BrE*) advice that is given by specially trained people to couples with problems in their marriage 婚姻指導；婚姻咨詢

'marriage licence (*BrE*) (*NAmE* **'marriage license**) *noun* **1** a document that allows two people to get married 結婚許可證 **2** (*US*) (*BrE* **'marriage certificate**) a legal document that proves two people are married 結婚證書

,marriage of con'venience *noun* a marriage that is made for practical, financial or political reasons and not because the two people love each other（出於實際需要、金錢或政治原因的）權宜婚姻

mar·ried 🔑 /ˈmærid/ *adj.*

1 🔑 having a husband or wife 已婚的： *a* ***married man/woman*** 已婚男子／女子 ◇ *Is he married?* 他結婚了嗎？◇ *a happily married couple* 一對幸福結合的伉儷 ◇ *She's* ***married to*** *John.* 她嫁給了約翰。◇ *Rachel and David are* ***getting married*** *on Saturday.* 雷切爾和戴維將在星期六結婚。◇ *How long have you been married?* 你結婚多長時間了？**OPP** **unmarried** ➲ COLLOCATIONS at MARRIAGE **2** 🔑 [only before noun] connected with marriage 婚姻的；結婚的： *Are you enjoying married life?* 你喜歡你的婚姻生活嗎？◇ *Her married name* (= the family name of her husband) *is Jones.* 她婚後隨夫姓瓊斯。 **3 ~ to sth** very involved in sth so that you have no time for other activities or interests 專心（於某事）；全神貫注（於某事）： *My brother is married to his job.* 我弟弟一心撲在工作上。

mar·row /ˈmærəʊ; *NAmE* -roʊ/ *noun* **1** [U] = BONE MARROW **2** (*BrE*) [U, C] a large vegetable that grows on the ground. Marrows are long and thick with dark green skin and white flesh. 西葫蘆 ➲ VISUAL VOCAB page V31

mar·row·bone /ˈmærəʊbəʊn; *NAmE* ˈmæroʊboʊn/ *noun* a bone which still contains the MARROW (= the substance inside) and is used in making food（烹飪用）髓骨

marry 🔑 /ˈmæri/ *verb* (**mar·ries**, **marry·ing**, **mar·ried**, **mar·ried**)

> **WORD FAMILY**
> **marry** *verb*
> **marriage** *noun*
> **married** *adj.* (≠ unmarried)

1 🔑 [T, I] to become the husband or wife of sb; to get married to sb（和某人）結婚；嫁；娶： **~ (sb)** *She married a German.* 她嫁給了一個德國人。◇ *He never married.* 他終身未娶。◇ *I guess I'm* ***not the marrying kind*** (= the kind of person who wants to get married). 我覺得我不是那種想結婚的人。◇ **+ adj.** *They married young.* 他們很年輕時就結了婚。**HELP** It is more common to say: *They're* ***getting married*** *next month* than: *They're* ***marrying*** *next month.* * They're getting married next month 比 They're marrying next month

更為常見。➲ COLLOCATIONS at MARRIAGE **2** [T] **~ sb** to perform a ceremony in which a man and woman become husband and wife 為…主持婚禮：*They were married by the local priest.* 當地牧師為他們主持了婚禮。 **3** [T] **~ sb (to sb)** to find a husband or wife for sb, especially your daughter or son 把…嫁給；為…娶親 **4** [T] **~ sth and/to/with sth** (*formal*) to combine two different things, ideas, etc. successfully（使不同的事物、觀點等）相結合，結合在一起 SYN **unite**：*The music business marries art and commerce.* 音樂行當將藝術和商業結合在一起。

IDM **marry in 'haste** (, **repent at 'leisure**) (*saying*) people who marry quickly, without really getting to know each other, may discover later that they have made a mistake 草草結婚後悔多 **marry 'money** to marry a rich person 和富人結婚

PHR V **,marry 'into sth** to become part of a family or group because you have married sb who belongs to it 因結婚而成為（家庭或團體的）成員：*She married into the aristocracy.* 她因為婚姻關係而躋身貴族。 **,marry sb↔'off (to sb)** (*disapproving*) to find a husband or wife for sb, especially your daughter or son 把…嫁給；為…娶親 **,marry sth↔'up (with sth)** to combine two things, people or parts of sth successfully（將兩個事物、人或部份）結合，匹配

Mars /mɑːz; *NAmE* mɑːrz/ *noun* the planet in the SOLAR SYSTEM that is fourth in order of distance from the sun, between the Earth and Jupiter 火星

Mar·sala /mɑːˈsɑːlə; *NAmE* mɑːrˈs-/ *noun* [U] a dark strong sweet wine from Sicily. It is usually drunk with the sweet course of a meal. 馬爾薩拉葡萄酒（產於西西里島的馬爾薩拉，通常吃甜食時飲用）

marsh /mɑːʃ; *NAmE* mɑːrʃ/ *noun* [C, U] an area of low land that is always soft and wet because there is nowhere for the water to flow away to 濕地；沼澤；草本沼澤：*Cows were grazing on the marshes.* 牛群在濕地上吃草。➲ VISUAL VOCAB page V3 ▶ **marshy** *adj.*：***marshy ground/land*** 沼澤地

mar·shal /ˈmɑːʃl; *NAmE* ˈmɑːrʃl/ *noun, verb*

■ ***noun*** **1** (usually in compounds 通常構成複合詞) an officer of the highest rank in the British army or AIR FORCE（英國）陸軍元帥，空軍元帥：*Field Marshal Lord Haig* 陸軍元帥黑格勳爵 ◇ *Marshal of the Royal Air Force* 皇家空軍元帥 ➲ see also AIR CHIEF MARSHAL, AIR MARSHAL, AIR VICE-MARSHAL, FIELD MARSHAL **2** a person responsible for making sure that public events, especially sports events, take place without any problems, and for controlling crowds 司儀；典禮官 SYN **steward** **3** (in the US) an officer whose job is to put court orders into effect（美國法院的）執行官：*a federal marshal* 聯邦法庭的執法官 **4** (in some US cities) an officer of high rank in a police or fire department（一些美國城市的）警察局長，消防局長

■ ***verb*** (-ll-, *US* -l-) (*formal*) **1 ~ sth** to gather together and organize the people, things, ideas, etc. that you need for a particular purpose 結集；收集；安排 SYN **muster**：*They have begun **marshalling forces** to send relief to the hurricane victims.* 他們已經開始結集隊伍將救濟物資送給遭受颶風侵害的災民。◇ ***to marshal your arguments/thoughts/facts*** 整理你的論點／想法／論據 **2 ~ sb** to control or organize a large group of people 控制人群；組織；維持秩序：*Police were brought in to marshal the crowd.* 警察奉命來維持秩序。

ˈmarshalling yard *noun* (*BrE*) a place where railway WAGONS are connected, prepared, etc. to form trains（鐵路的）調車場，編組站

M

Collocations 詞語搭配

Marriage and divorce 結婚和離婚

Romance 戀愛

- **fall/be** (madly/deeply/hopelessly) **in love** (with sb)（瘋狂地／深深地／無可救藥地）愛上／愛着（某人）
- **be/believe in/fall in** love at first sight 是／相信一見鍾情；一見鍾情
- **be/find** true love/the love of your life 是／找到真愛／一生的愛
- **suffer (from)** (the pains/pangs of) unrequited love 受單相思之苦
- **have/feel/show/express** great/deep/genuine affection for sb/sth 對某人／某事有着／表示出強烈的／深深的／真摯的愛慕之情
- **meet/marry** your husband/wife/partner/fiancé/fiancée/boyfriend/girlfriend 與丈夫／妻子／伴侶／未婚夫／未婚妻／男朋友／女朋友結識／結婚
- **have/go on** a (blind) **date** 有個／去約會／相親
- **be going out with**/(*especially NAmE*) **dating** a guy/girl/boy/man/woman 與一個小伙子／女生／男生／男人／女人在談戀愛
- **move in with/live with** your boyfriend/girlfriend/partner 與男朋友／女朋友／伴侶同居

Weddings 婚禮

- **get/be** engaged/married/divorced 訂婚；結婚；離婚
- **arrange/plan** a wedding 安排婚禮
- **have** a big wedding/a honeymoon/a happy marriage 舉行隆重的婚禮；度蜜月；婚姻幸福
- **have/enter into** an arranged marriage 有一個／走入包辦婚姻
- **call off/cancel/postpone** your wedding 取消／推遲婚禮
- **invite sb to/go to/attend** a wedding/a wedding ceremony/a wedding reception 邀請某人出席／參加婚禮／結婚典禮／結婚喜宴
- **conduct/perform** a wedding ceremony 舉行結婚典禮
- **exchange** rings/wedding vows/marriage vows 交換戒指；互致結婚誓言
- **congratulate/toast/raise a glass to** the happy couple 祝賀這對幸福的新人；為這對幸福的伉儷乾杯
- **be/go on** honeymoon (with your wife/husband)（與妻子／丈夫）在／去度蜜月
- **celebrate** your first (wedding) anniversary 慶祝第一個（結婚）紀念日

Separation and divorce 分居和離婚

- **be unfaithful to**/(*informal*) **cheat on** your husband/wife/partner/fiancé/fiancée/boyfriend/girlfriend 對丈夫／妻子／伴侶／未婚夫／未婚妻／男朋友／女朋友不忠
- **have an affair** (with sb)（和某人）有曖昧關係
- **break off/end** an engagement/a relationship 解除／終止婚約／戀愛關係
- **break up with/split up with**/(*informal*) **dump** your boyfriend/girlfriend 與男友／女友分手；甩掉男友／女友
- **separate from/be separated from/leave/divorce** your husband/wife 和丈夫／妻子分居；離棄丈夫／妻子；與丈夫／妻子離婚
- **annul/dissolve** a marriage 宣佈婚姻無效；解除婚姻關係
- **apply for/ask for/go through/get** a divorce 申請／要求／辦理離婚；離婚
- **get/gain/be awarded/have/lose** custody of the children 獲得／被判予／擁有／失去對孩子的監護權
- **pay** alimony/child support (to your ex-wife/husband)（向前妻／前夫）支付生活費／子女撫養費

ˌMarshal of the ˌRoyal ˈAir Force *noun* the highest rank of officer in the British AIR FORCE（英國）空軍元帥

ˈmarsh gas *noun* [U] a gas that is produced in a marsh when plants decay 沼氣

marsh·land /ˈmɑːʃlænd; *NAmE* ˈmɑːrʃ-/ *noun* [U, C] an area of soft wet land 沼澤地

marsh·mal·low /ˌmɑːʃˈmæləʊ; *NAmE* ˈmɑːrʃmeloʊ/ *noun* [C, U] a pink or white sweet/candy that feels soft and ELASTIC when you chew it 棉花軟糖

mar·su·pial /mɑːˈsuːpiəl; *NAmE* mɑːrˈs-/ *noun* any animal that carries its young in a pocket of skin (called a POUCH) on the mother's stomach. KANGAROOS and KOALAS are marsupials. 有袋動物（如袋鼠和樹袋熊）➲ VISUAL VOCAB page V12 ▸ **mar·su·pial** *adj.*

mart /mɑːt; *NAmE* mɑːrt/ *noun* (*especially NAmE*) a place where things are bought and sold 貿易場所；集市：*a used car mart* 舊車市場

mar·ten /ˈmɑːtɪn; *NAmE* ˈmɑːrtn/ *noun* a small wild animal with a long body, short legs and sharp teeth. Martens live in forests and eat smaller animals. 貂：*a pine marten* 松貂

mar·tial /ˈmɑːʃl; *NAmE* ˈmɑːrʃl/ *adj.* (*formal*) [only before noun] connected with fighting or war 戰爭的；軍事的

ˌmartial ˈart *noun* [usually pl.] any of the fighting sports that include JUDO and KARATE 武術

ˌmartial ˈlaw *noun* [U] a situation where the army of a country controls an area instead of the police during a time of trouble 軍事管制；戒嚴：*to* ***declare/impose/lift martial law*** 宣佈／實行／取消軍事管制 ◇ *The city remains firmly* ***under martial law****.* 這個城市仍實施嚴格的軍事管制。

M

Mar·tian /ˈmɑːʃn; *NAmE* ˈmɑːrʃn/ *adj., noun*

▪ **adj.** (*astronomy* 天) related to or coming from the planet Mars 火星的；來自火星的

▪ **noun** an imaginary creature from the planet Mars（假想的）火星人，火星生物

mar·tinet /ˌmɑːtɪˈnet; *NAmE* ˌmɑːrtnˈet/ *noun* (*formal*) a very strict person who demands that other people obey orders or rules completely 嚴格執行紀律的人

mar·tini /mɑːˈtiːni; *NAmE* mɑːrˈt-/ *noun* **1** **Martini™** [U] a type of VERMOUTH 馬提尼酒（一種品牌的味美思酒）**2** [U] an alcoholic drink made with GIN and VERMOUTH 馬提尼酒（由杜松子酒和味美思酒調配而成）**3** [C] a glass of martini 一杯馬提尼酒：*a dry martini* 一杯乾馬提尼酒

ˌMartin ˌLuther ˌKing ˈJr. Day *noun* a national holiday in the US on the third Monday in January to celebrate the birthday of Martin Luther King, Jr., who was active in the struggle to win more rights for Black Americans 馬丁•路德•金紀念日，金恩紀念日（美國假日，在一月份第三個星期一，紀念積極爭取美國黑人權利的馬丁•路德•金的生日）

mar·tyr /ˈmɑːtə(r); *NAmE* ˈmɑːrt-/ *noun, verb*

▪ **noun** **1** a person who suffers very much or is killed because of their religious or political beliefs 殉道者；烈士：*the early Christian martyrs* 早期基督教殉道者 ◇ ***a martyr to*** *the cause of freedom* 為了自由事業而獻身的烈士 **2** (usually *disapproving*) a person who tries to get sympathy from other people by telling them how much he or she is suffering 乞憐者（向人訴苦以博取同情）**3** **~ to sth** (*informal*) a person who suffers very much because of an illness, problem or situation（因疾病或困難局面）長期受苦者，長期受折磨者：*She's a martyr to her nerves.* 她長期忍受神經緊張之苦。

▪ **verb** [usually passive] **~ sb** to kill sb because of their religious or political beliefs（因宗教或政治信仰）使殉難，處死

mar·tyr·dom /ˈmɑːtədəm; *NAmE* ˈmɑːrtərdəm/ *noun* [U] the suffering or death of a martyr 殉難；殉道

mar·tyred /ˈmɑːtəd; *NAmE* ˈmɑːrtərd/ *adj.* [usually before noun] (*disapproving*) showing pain or suffering so that people will be kind and sympathetic towards you（為贏得同情）表現出痛苦的，滿臉苦相的：*She wore a perpetually martyred expression.* 她總是那麼一副可憐兮兮的樣子。

mar·vel /ˈmɑːvl; *NAmE* ˈmɑːrvl/ *noun, verb*

▪ **noun** **1** a wonderful and surprising person or thing 令人驚異的人（或事）；奇跡 SYN **wonder**：*the* ***marvels of nature/technology*** 大自然的／技術的奇跡 **2** **marvels** [pl.] wonderful results or things that have been achieved 不平凡的成果；成就；奇跡 SYN **wonders**：*The doctors have done marvels for her.* 醫生為她創造了奇跡。

▪ **verb** (-ll-, *US* -l-) [I, T] **~ (at sth)** | **~ that …** | **+ speech** to be very surprised or impressed by sth 感到驚奇；大為讚歎：*Everyone marvelled at his courage.* 人人都對他的勇氣驚歎不已。

mar·vel·lous (*US* **mar·vel·ous**) /ˈmɑːvələs; *NAmE* ˈmɑːrv-/ *adj.* extremely good; wonderful 極好的；非凡的 SYN **fantastic**, **splendid**：*This will be a marvellous opportunity for her.* 這對她可是千載難逢的機會。◇ *The weather was marvellous.* 天氣棒極了。◇ ***It's marvellous*** *what modern technology can do.* 現代技術所能做的真是太了不起了。▸ **mar·vel·lous·ly** (*US* **mar·vel·ous·ly**) *adv.*

Marx·ism /ˈmɑːksɪzəm; *NAmE* ˈmɑːrks-/ *noun* [U] the political and economic theories of Karl Marx (1818-83) which explain the changes and developments in society as the result of opposition between the social classes 馬克思主義 ▸ **Marx·ist** /ˈmɑːksɪst; *NAmE* ˈmɑːrks-/ *noun* **Marx·ist** *adj.*：***Marxist theory/doctrine/ideology*** 馬克思主義理論／信條／意識形態

Mary Celeste /ˌmeəri sɪˈlest; *NAmE* ˌmeri/ (also **Marie Celeste**) *noun* [sing.] used to talk about a place where all the people who should be there have disappeared in a mysterious way 神秘的失踪地：*Where is everyone? It's like the Mary Celeste here today.* 人都到哪兒去了？今天這裏的人都神秘失踪了。 ORIGIN From the name of the US ship *Mary Celeste*, which in 1872 was found at sea with nobody on board. 源自美國瑪麗•賽勒斯特號輪船船名，1872 年在海上被發現時船上空無一人。

mar·zi·pan /ˈmɑːzɪpæn; ˌmɑːzɪˈpæn; *NAmE* ˈmɑːrtsəpæn; ˈmɑːrz-/ *noun* [U] a sweet firm substance, sometimes with yellow colour added, made from ALMONDS, sugar and eggs and used to make sweets/candy and to cover cakes 杏仁蛋白糖（用於製作糖果或裝飾蛋糕）

ma·sala /məˈsɑːlə/ *noun* [U] **1** a mixture of spices used in S Asian cooking 馬薩拉（用於南亞烹飪的混合調味品）**2** a dish made with masala 馬薩拉菜肴：*chicken masala* 馬薩拉雞

mas·cara /mæˈskɑːrə; *NAmE* -ˈskærə/ *noun* [U] a substance that is put on EYELASHES to make them look dark and thick 睫毛膏；染睫毛油 ➲ VISUAL VOCAB page V60

mas·cot /ˈmæskət; *NAmE* -skɑːt/ *noun* an animal, a toy, etc. that people believe will bring them good luck, or that represents an organization, etc. 吉祥物：*The team's mascot is a giant swan.* 這個隊的吉祥物是隻大天鵝。◇ *Zakumi—the official mascot of the 2010 FIFA World Cup* * 2010 年世界杯足球賽的指定吉祥物 —— 紮庫米

mas·cu·line /ˈmæskjəlɪn/ *adj., noun*

▪ **adj.** **1** having the qualities or appearance considered to be typical of men; connected with or like men 男子漢的；男人的；像男人的：*He was handsome and strong, and very masculine.* 他英俊強壯，富有男子漢氣概。◇ *That suit makes her look very masculine.* 她穿那套衣服看起來很男性化。➲ compare FEMININE *adj.* (1), MALE *adj.* (1) **2** (*grammar* 語法) belonging to a class of words that refer to male people or animals and often have a special form 陽性的：*'He' and 'him' are masculine pronouns.* * he 和 him 都是陽性代詞。**3** (*grammar* 語法) (in some languages 用於某些語言) belonging to a class of nouns, pronouns or adjectives that have masculine GENDER, not FEMININE or NEUTER 陽性的：*The French word for 'sun' is masculine.* 法語單詞"太陽"是陽性的。

▪ **noun** **1** **the masculine** [sing.] the masculine GENDER (= form of nouns, adjectives and pronouns)（詞語的）陽性 **2** [C] a masculine word or word form 陽性詞；陽性詞形 ➲ compare FEMININE *n.*, NEUTER *adj.*

mas·cu·lin·ity /ˌmæskjuˈlɪnəti/ *noun* [U] the quality of being masculine 男子氣概；男性；陽性：*He felt it was a* *threat to his masculinity.* 他覺得這對他的男子氣概是一種威脅。

mas·cu·lin·ize (*BrE* also **-ise**) /ˈmæskjələmaɪz/ *verb* **~ sth/sb** (*formal*) to make sth or sb more like a man 使男性化；使雄性化

mash /mæʃ/ *noun, verb*

■ *noun* **1** (*especially BrE*) = MASHED POTATO **2** [U] grain cooked in water until soft, used to feed farm animals（煮軟的）穀物飼料 **3** [U] a mixture of MALT grains and hot water, used for making beer, etc. 麥芽漿（用於釀製啤酒） **4** [sing.] **a ~** (**of sth**) any food that has been crushed into a soft mass 糊狀食物：*The soup was a mash of grain and vegetables.* 那是用糧食和蔬菜做成的濃湯。➲ see also MISHMASH

■ *verb* **~ sth** (**up**) to crush food into a soft mass 搗爛，搗碎（食物）：*Mash the fruit up with a fork.* 用叉子將水果搗爛。➲ COLLOCATIONS at COOKING ➲ VISUAL VOCAB page V28 ▸ **mashed** *adj.*：*mashed banana* 香蕉泥

ˌmashed poˈtato (also **ˌmashed poˈtatoes**, **mash** especially in *BrE*) *noun* [U] potatoes that have been boiled and crushed into a soft mass, often with butter and milk 土豆泥，馬鈴薯泥（常調入黃油和牛奶）

mashup /ˈmæʃʌp/ *noun* a combination of elements from different sources used to create a new song, video, computer file, program, etc. 聚合應用，跨界，混搭（集成不同資源，創建新的歌曲、視頻、計算機文件、程序等）：*a video mashup* 視頻混搭

masks 面具；面罩

surgical mask 醫用口罩

Halloween mask 萬聖節面具

mask /mɑːsk; *NAmE* mæsk/ *noun, verb*

■ *noun* **1** a covering for part or all of the face, worn to hide or protect it 面具；面罩：*a **gas/surgical mask*** 防毒面具；醫用口罩 ◇ *The robbers wore stocking masks.* 強盜戴着長筒襪面罩。➲ VISUAL VOCAB pages V40, V44, V47 ➲ see also OXYGEN MASK **2** something that covers your face and has another face painted on it 假面具：*The kids were all wearing animal masks.* 孩子們都戴着動物面具。➲ see also DEATH MASK **3** a thick cream made of various substances that you put on your face and neck in order to improve the quality of your skin 護膚膜；面膜：*a face mask* 面膜 **4** [usually sing.] a manner or an expression that hides your true character or feelings 偽裝；掩飾：*He longed to throw off the mask of respectability.* 他渴望丟掉那副道貌岸然的偽裝。◇ *Her face was a cold blank mask.* 她裝出一副冷冰冰毫無表情的樣子。

■ *verb* **~ sth** to hide a feeling, smell, fact, etc. so that it cannot be easily seen or noticed 掩飾；掩藏 SYN **disguise, veil**：*She masked her anger with a smile.* 她用微笑來掩飾她的憤怒。➲ SYNONYMS at HIDE

masked /mɑːskt; *NAmE* mæskt/ *adj.* wearing a MASK 戴着面具（或面罩）的：*a masked gunman* 戴着面具的持槍歹徒

ˌmasked ˈball *noun* a formal party at which guests wear masks 假面舞會；化裝舞會

ˈmasking tape *noun* [U] sticky tape that you use to keep an area clean or protected when you are painting around or near it 膠紙帶，遮蓋膠帶（刷油漆時蓋住不需油漆的部份）

maso·chism /ˈmæsəkɪzəm/ *noun* [U] **1** the practice of getting sexual pleasure from being physically hurt 性受虐狂 ➲ compare SADISM (2) **2** (*informal*) the enjoyment of sth that most people would find unpleasant or painful 受虐狂：*You spent the whole weekend in a tent in the rain? That's masochism!* 下着雨，你就在帳篷裏度過了整個週末？真是自討苦吃！▸ **maso·chist** /-kɪst/ *noun* **maso·chis·tic** /ˌmæsəˈkɪstɪk/ *adj.*：***masochistic behaviour/tendencies*** 受虐狂行為／傾向

mason /ˈmeɪsn/ *noun* **1** a person who builds using stone, or works with stone 石匠；泥瓦匠 **2** **Mason** = FREEMASON

the Mason-Dixon Line /ˌmeɪsn ˈdɪksn laɪn/ *noun* [sing.] the border between the US states of Maryland and Pennsylvania that is thought of as the dividing line between the south of the US and the north. In the past it formed the northern border of the states where SLAVES were owned. 梅森—迪克森線（美國馬里蘭州與賓夕法尼亞州之間的分界線，為過去蓄奴州的最北邊界線）

Ma·son·ic /məˈsɒnɪk; *NAmE* -ˈsɑːn-/ *adj.* connected with FREEMASONS 共濟會會員的

Mason·ite™ /ˈmeɪsənaɪt/ *noun* [U] a US make of board that is used in building, made of small pieces of wood that are pressed together and stuck with glue（美國）美森耐複合板（建築材料）

ma·son·ry /ˈmeɪsənri/ *noun* [U] the parts of a building that are made of stone 磚石結構；磚石建築：*She was injured by falling masonry.* 她被倒塌的石牆砸傷了。◇ *He acquired a knowledge of carpentry and masonry* (= building with stone). 他掌握了木工和石工知識。

masque /mɑːsk; *NAmE* mæsk/ *noun* a play written in VERSE, often with music and dancing, popular in England in the 16th and 17th centuries 假面劇（16 至 17 世紀盛行於英國的一種詩劇，常伴以音樂和舞蹈）

mas·quer·ade /ˌmæskəˈreɪd; *BrE* also ˌmɑːsk-/ *noun, verb*

■ *noun* **1** (*formal*) a way of behaving that hides the truth or a person's true feelings 掩藏；掩飾 **2** (*especially NAmE*) a type of party where people wear special COSTUMES and MASKS over their faces, to hide their identities 化裝舞會；假面舞會

■ *verb* [I] **~ as sth** to pretend to be sth that you are not 假扮；喬裝；偽裝：*commercial advertisers masquerading as private individuals* 喬裝成普通百姓的商業廣告商

Mass /mæs/ *noun* **1** (sometimes **mass**) [U, C] (especially in the Roman Catholic Church) a ceremony held in memory of the last meal that Christ had with his DISCIPLES（尤指羅馬天主教的）彌撒：*to **go to Mass*** 參加彌撒 ◇ *a priest **celebrating/saying Mass*** 主持彌撒的神父 ➲ see also EUCHARIST, COMMUNION **2** [C] a piece of music that is written for the prayers, etc. of this ceremony 彌撒曲：*Bach's Mass in B minor* 巴赫的 B 小調彌撒曲

mass 0‑w /mæs/ *noun, adj., verb*

■ *noun* **1** 0‑w [C] **~** (**of sth**) a large amount of a substance that does not have a definite shape or form 團；塊；堆：*a mass of snow and rocks falling down the mountain* 從山上滾下來的一堆積雪和石塊 ◇ *The hill appeared as a black mass in the distance.* 遠遠地看去，那座山是黑魆魆一片。◇ *The sky was full of dark masses of clouds.* 天空中烏雲密佈。**2** 0‑w [C, usually sing.] **~ of sth** a large amount or quantity of sth 大量；許多：*a mass of blonde hair* 一頭金髮 ◇ *I began sifting through the mass of evidence.* 我開始認真篩選大量的證據。**3** 0‑w [sing.] **~ of sth** a large number of people or things grouped together, often in a confused way（常指混亂的）一群，一堆：*I struggled through the mass of people to the exit.* 我在人群裏擠來擠去，擠到了出口處。◇ *The page was covered with a mass of figures.* 紙上寫滿了密密麻麻的數字。**4** 0‑w **masses** [pl.] **~** (**of sth**) (*informal*) a large number or amount of sth 大量的東西 SYN **lots**：*There were masses of people in the shops yesterday.* 昨天商店裏人如潮湧。◇ *I've got masses of work to do.* 我有一大堆的工作要做。◇ *Don't give me any more. I've eaten masses!* 別再給我了，我已經吃了很多了！**5** **the masses** [pl.] the ordinary people in society who are not leaders or who are considered to be not very well educated 群眾；平民百姓：*government attempts to suppress dissatisfaction among the masses*

政府試圖壓制群眾不滿情緒的做法 ◇ *a TV programme that brings science to the masses* 普及科學知識的電視節目 **6 the mass of sth** [sing.] the most; the majority 大多數；多數：*The reforms are unpopular with the mass of teachers and parents.* 大多數教師和家長並不贊成這些改革。**7** [U] (*technical* 術語) the quantity of material that sth contains 質量：*calculating the mass of a planet* 計算一個行星的質量 **HELP** **Weight** is used in non-technical language for this meaning. 非技術性語言用 weight 表示此義。➲ see also BIOMASS, CRITICAL MASS, LAND MASS

IDM be a 'mass of to be full of or covered with sth 充滿；佈滿：*The rose bushes are a mass of flowers in June.* 六月的玫瑰園花團錦簇。◇ *Her arm was a mass of bruises.* 她的胳膊上傷痕纍纍。

■ ***adj.*** 🔑 [only before noun] affecting or involving a large number of people or things 大批的；數量極多的；廣泛的：***mass unemployment/production*** 大批失業；批量生產 ◇ *weapons of mass destruction* 大規模殺傷性武器 ◇ *Their latest product is aimed at the **mass market**.* 他們的最新產品瞄準了大眾市場。➲ see also MASS-MARKET

■ ***verb*** [I, T] to come together in large numbers; to gather people or things together in large numbers 集結；聚集：(**+ adv./prep.**) *Demonstrators had massed outside the embassy.* 示威者聚集在大使館的外面。◇ *Dark clouds massed on the horizon.* 天邊烏雲密佈。◇ **~ sb/sth** *The general massed his troops for a final attack.* 將軍把軍隊都集中起來準備發動最後的進攻。▶ **massed** *adj.*：*the **massed ranks** of his political opponents* 他的大批政敵

mas·sacre /ˈmæsəkə(r)/ *noun, verb*

■ ***noun*** [C, U] **1** the killing of a large number of people especially in a cruel way 屠殺；殘殺：*the bloody massacre of innocent civilians* 對無辜平民的血腥屠殺 ◇ *Nobody survived the massacre.* 這次大屠殺無人幸免。**2** (*informal*) a very big defeat in a game or competition（運動或比賽中的）慘敗：*The game was a 10–0 massacre for our team.* 這場比賽我們隊以 0:10 慘敗。

■ ***verb*** **1 ~ sb** to kill a large number of people, especially in a cruel way 屠殺；殺戮 **2 ~ sb** (*informal*) to defeat sb in a game or competition by a high score（在運動或比賽中）使慘敗

mas·sage /ˈmæsɑːʒ; *NAmE* məˈsɑːʒ/ *noun, verb*

■ ***noun*** [U, C] the action of rubbing and pressing a person's body with the hands to reduce pain in the muscles and joints 按摩：*Massage will help the pain.* 按摩能減輕疼痛。◇ *a back massage* 背部按摩 ◇ *to give sb a massage* 給某人按摩 ◇ *massage oils* 按摩油

■ ***verb*** **1 ~ sth** to rub and press a person's body with the hands to reduce pain in the muscles and joints 按摩；推拿：*He massaged the aching muscles in her feet.* 他給她按摩腳上疼痛的肌肉。◇ (*figurative*) *to massage sb's ego* (= to make sb feel better, more confident, attractive, etc.) 增強某人的自信心 **2 ~ sth into sth** to rub a substance into the skin, hair, etc. 用…揉擦（皮膚、頭髮等）：*Massage the cream into your skin.* 將護膚霜揉擦到皮膚上。**3 ~ sth** (*disapproving*) to change facts, figures, etc. in order to make them seem better than they really are 美化（事實）；虛報（數量）；粉飾：*The government was accused of massaging the unemployment figures.* 政府被指責謊報了失業數字。

'massage parlour (*especially US* **mas'sage parlor**) *noun* **1** a place where you can pay to have a massage 按摩院；按摩房 **2** a place that is supposed to offer the service of massage, but is also where men go to pay for sex with PROSTITUTES（打着按摩院幌子的）妓院

masse ➲ EN MASSE

mas·seur /mæˈsɜː(r)/ *noun* a person whose job is giving people massage 按摩師

mas·seuse /mæˈsɜːz; *NAmE* məˈsuːs/ *noun* a woman whose job is giving people massage 女按摩師

mas·sif /mæˈsiːf/ *noun* (*technical* 術語) a group of mountains that form a large mass 山巒；群山

mas·sive 🔑 /ˈmæsɪv/ *adj.*

1 🔑 very large, heavy and solid 巨大的；大而重的；結實的：*a massive rock* 一塊巨大的岩石 ◇ *the massive walls of the castle* 厚實堅固的城堡圍牆 **2** 🔑 extremely large or serious 巨大的；非常嚴重的：*The explosion made a massive hole in the ground.* 爆炸在地面留下了一個巨大的坑。◇ *a massive increase in spending* 開支的大幅度增加 ◇ *He suffered a massive heart attack.* 他的心臟病嚴重發作了。◇ (*BrE, informal*) *Their house is massive.* 他們的房子大極了。◇ *They have a massive great house.* 他們有一座非常大的房子。▶ **mas·sive·ly** *adv.*

ˌmass-'market *adj.* [only before noun] (of goods etc. 商品等) produced for very large numbers of people 面向大眾的；適銷對路的

the ˌmass 'media *noun* [pl.] sources of information and news such as newspapers, magazines, radio and television, that reach and influence large numbers of people 大眾傳媒

'mass noun *noun* (*grammar* 語法) **1** an uncountable noun 不可數名詞 **2** a noun that is usually uncountable but can be made plural or used with *a* or *an* when you are talking about different types of sth. For example, *bread* is used as a mass noun in *the shop sells several different breads*. 物質名詞（通常為不可數，但表示不同種類時可用複數或與 a 或 an 連用，例如 The shop sells several different breads 中的 bread）

'mass number *noun* (*chemistry* 化) the total number of PROTONS and NEUTRONS in an atom（原子）質量數

ˌmass-pro'duce *verb* **~ sth** to produce goods in large quantities, using machinery（用機器）批量生產，大量生產 ▶ **ˌmass-pro'duced** *adj.*：*mass-produced goods* 批量生產的貨品 **ˌmass pro'duction** *noun* [U]：*the mass production of consumer goods* 消費品的批量生產

mast /mɑːst; *NAmE* mæst/ *noun* **1** a tall pole on a boat or ship that supports the sails 桅杆；船桅 ➲ VISUAL VOCAB page V56 **2** a tall metal tower with an AERIAL that sends and receives radio or television signals 天線塔 **3** a tall pole that is used for holding a flag 旗杆

IDM see NAIL *v.* ➲ see also HALF MAST

mast·ec·tomy /mæˈstektəmi/ *noun* (*pl.* **-ies**) a medical operation to remove a person's breast 乳房切除術

mas·ter 🔑 /ˈmɑːstə(r); *NAmE* ˈmæs-/ *noun, verb, adj.*

■ ***noun***

▸ **OF SERVANTS** 僕人 **1** 🔑 (*old-fashioned*) a man who has people working for him, often as servants in his home（男）主人，雇主：*They lived in fear of their master.* 他們懼怕主人，提心吊膽地過日子。

▸ **PERSON IN CONTROL** 主宰 **2 ~ of sth** a person who is able to control sth 主宰；主人；有控制力的人：*She was no longer master of her own future.* 她已無法把握自己的未來。

▸ **SKILLED PERSON** 有技能的人 **3** 🔑 **~ (of sth)** a person who is skilled at sth 能手；擅長…者：*a master of disguise* 精於偽裝的人 ◇ *a master of the serve-and-volley game* 發球截擊的高手 ➲ see also PAST MASTER

▸ **DOG OWNER** 狗的主人 **4** the male owner of a dog 狗的男主人：*The dog saved its master's life.* 這條狗救了它的主人。➲ compare MISTRESS (4)

▸ **TEACHER** 教師 **5** (*BrE, old-fashioned*) a male teacher at a school, especially a private school（尤指私立學校的）男教師：*the physics master* 物理老師 ➲ compare SCHOOLMASTER, MISTRESS (2)

▸ **UNIVERSITY DEGREE** 大學學位 **6** 🔑 **master's** (also **'master's degree**) a second university degree, or, in Scotland, a first university degree, such as an MA 碩士學位（大學的中級學位；在蘇格蘭指初級學位）：*He has a Master's in Business Administration.* 他獲得了工商管理碩士學位。➲ see also MA, MB (1), MBA, MSc **7** (usually **Master**) a person who has a master's degree 碩士；有碩士學位的人：*a **Master of Arts/Science*** 文科／理科碩士

▸ **CAPTAIN OF SHIP** 船長 **8** the captain of a ship that transports goods（貨船的）船長

▸ **FAMOUS PAINTER** 著名畫家 **9** a famous painter who lived in the past（已故）著名畫家，繪畫大師：*an exhibition of work by the French master, Monet* 法國著名畫家莫奈的作品展 ➲ see also OLD MASTER (1)

▸ **ORIGINAL RECORD/TAPE/MOVIE** 原版錄音／磁帶／電影 **10** (often used as an adjective 常用作形容詞) a version of a record, tape, film/movie, etc. from which copies are made 母帶；母片；原始拷貝：*the master copy* 原始拷貝

▸ **TITLE 稱謂 11 Master** (*old-fashioned*) a title used when speaking to or about a boy who is too young to be called *Mr* (also used in front of the name on an envelope, etc.)（對年齡小而不便稱作“先生”的男孩的稱謂；也用在信封等處的人名前）少爺，君 **12 Master** (in Britain) the title of the head of some schools and university colleges（英國）校長，院長：*the Master of Wolfson College* 沃爾夫森學院院長 **13 Master** a title used for speaking to or about some religious teachers or leaders（對宗教導師或領袖的稱謂）大師，師傅 **HELP** There are many other compounds ending in **master**. You will find them at their place in the alphabet. 以 master 結尾的複合詞還有很多，可在各字母中的適當位置查到。

IDM **be your own 'master/'mistress** to be free to make your own decisions rather than being told what to do by sb else 獨立自主 ➲ more at SERVE *v.*

■ ***verb***

▸ **LEARN/UNDERSTAND 學會；理解 1 ~ sth** to learn or understand sth completely 精通；掌握：*to* ***master*** *new* ***skills/techniques*** 掌握新的技能 / 技術 ◇ *French was a language he had never mastered.* 法語他一直沒有學好。

▸ **CONTROL 控制 2 ~ sth** to manage to control an emotion 控制（情緒）：*She struggled hard to master her temper.* 她竭力按住性子，不發脾氣。 **3 ~ sth/sb** to gain control of an animal or a person 控制（動物或人）

■ ***adj.*** [only before noun]

▸ **SKILLED 熟練 1 ~ baker/chef/mason, etc.** used to describe a person who is very skilled at the job mentioned（描述精於某職業的人）熟練的，靈巧的，有技能的

▸ **MOST IMPORTANT 最重要 2** the largest and/or most important 最大的；最重要的：*the* ***master bedroom*** 主卧室 ◇ *a* ***master file/switch*** 主文件；總開關

mas·ter·class /'mɑːstəklɑːs; *NAmE* 'mæstərklæs/ *noun* a lesson, especially in music, given by a famous expert to very skilled students（大師授課的）高級音樂講習班；深造班

mas·ter·ful /'mɑːstəfl; *NAmE* 'mæstərfl/ *adj.* **1** (of a person, especially a man 人，尤指男人) able to control people or situations in a way that shows confidence as a leader 有控制能力的；有駕馭能力的 **2** = MASTERLY：*a masterful performance* 技藝高超的表演 ▸ **mas·ter·ful·ly** /-fəli/ *adv.*：*He took her arm masterfully and led her away.* 他很自然地挽着她的胳膊，帶引她走了。

'master key (also **'pass key**) *noun* a key that can be used to open many different locks in a building 萬能鑰匙

mas·ter·ly /'mɑːstəli; *NAmE* 'mæstərli/ (also **mas·ter·ful**) *adj.* showing great skill or understanding 技藝精湛的；理解透徹的：*a masterly performance* 精湛的表演 ◇ *Her handling of the situation was masterly.* 她對情勢的處理非常巧妙。

mas·ter·mind /'mɑːstəmaɪnd; *NAmE* 'mæstərm-/ *noun*, *verb*

■ ***noun*** [usually sing.] an intelligent person who plans and directs a complicated project or activity (often one that involves a crime)（極具才智的）決策者；主謀；出謀劃策者

■ ***verb*** **~ sth** to plan and direct a complicated project or activity 策劃，操縱，領導（複雜的事情）

,master of 'ceremonies *noun* (*abbr.* **MC**) a person who introduces guests or entertainers at a formal occasion 司儀；儀式主持人

mas·ter·piece /'mɑːstəpiːs; *NAmE* 'mæstərp-/ (also **mas·ter·work**) *noun* a work of art such as a painting, film/movie, book, etc. that is an excellent, or the best, example of the artist's work 代表作；傑作；名著：*The museum houses several of his Cubist masterpieces.* 博物館收藏了他的幾件立體派傑作。◇ *Her work is a masterpiece of* (= an excellent example of) *simplicity.* 她的作品是樸實的典範。

'master plan *noun* [sing.] a detailed plan that will make a complicated project successful 總體規劃；總計劃

'master's degree (also **master's**) *noun* a further university degree that you study for after a first degree 碩士學位

the Master's Tournament (also **the Master's**) *noun* a GOLF competition held in the US, in which skilled players are invited to compete（高爾夫球）美國大師賽；美國名人賽

mas·ter·stroke /'mɑːstəstrəʊk; *NAmE* 'mæstərstroʊk/ *noun* [usually sing.] something clever that you do that gives a successful result 絕招；高招；妙舉

mas·ter·work /'mɑːstəwɜːk; *NAmE* 'mæstərwɜːrk/ *noun* = MASTERPIECE

mas·tery /'mɑːstəri; *NAmE* 'mæst-/ *noun* **1** [U, sing.] **~ (of sth)** great knowledge about or understanding of a particular thing 精通；熟練掌握 **SYN** **command**：*She has mastery of several languages.* 她精通數門語言。 **2** [U] **~ (of/over sb/sth)** control or power 控制；駕馭；控制力量：*human mastery of the natural world* 人類對自然界的控制

mast·head /'mɑːsthed; *NAmE* 'mæst-/ *noun* **1** the top of a MAST on a ship 桅頂 **2** the name of a newspaper at the top of the front page（頭版頂部的）報紙名稱 **3** (*NAmE*) the part of a newspaper or a news website which gives details of the people who work on it and other information about it（報刊或新聞網站上載有其工作人員和其他相關信息的）刊頭

mas·tic /'mæstɪk/ *noun* [U] **1** a substance that comes from the BARK of a tree and is used in making VARNISH 乳香樹脂；乳香 **2** a substance that is used in building to fill holes and keep out water 膠泥；瑪琋脂

mas·ti·cate /'mæstɪkeɪt/ *verb* [I] (*technical* 術語) to chew food 咀嚼（食物） ▸ **mas·ti·ca·tion** /,mæstɪ'keɪʃn/ *noun* [U]

mas·tiff /'mæstɪf/ *noun* a large strong dog with short hair, often used to guard buildings 大馴犬（常用作守衛犬）

mas·titis /mæ'staɪtɪs/ *noun* [U] (*medical* 醫) painful swelling of the breast or UDDER usually because of infection 乳腺炎；乳房炎

mas·tur·bate /'mæstəbeɪt; *NAmE* -stərb-/ *verb* **1** [I, T] **~ (yourself)** to give yourself sexual pleasure by rubbing your sexual organs 手淫 **2** [T] **~ sb** to give sb sexual pleasure by rubbing their sexual organs 對（某人）行手淫 ▸ **mas·tur·ba·tion** /,mæstə'beɪʃn; *NAmE* -stər'b-/ *noun* [U] **mas·tur·ba·tory** /,mæstə'beɪtəri; *NAmE* 'mæstərbətɔːri/ *adj.*

mat /mæt/ *noun*, *adj.*

■ ***noun*** **1** a small piece of thick carpet or strong material that is used to cover part of a floor 小地毯；墊子：*Wipe your feet on the mat before you come in, please.* 請在墊子上擦擦腳再進來。➲ see also BATH MAT, DOORMAT (1), MOUSE MAT **2** a piece of thick material such as rubber or plastic used especially in some sports for people to lie on or fall onto（體育運動用的）厚墊子：***a judo/an exercise mat*** 柔道墊；健身墊 **3** a small piece of plastic, wood or cloth used on a table for decoration or to protect the surface from heat or damage（裝飾或保護桌面的）襯墊，小墊：*a beer mat* 啤酒杯墊 ➲ see also TABLE MAT **4** a thick mass of sth that is stuck together 團；簇；叢：*a mat of hair* 一團毛髮 ➲ see also MATTED

IDM **go to the 'mat (with sb) (for sb/sth)** (*NAmE*, *informal*) to support or defend sb/sth in an argument with sb（為支持或維護…）（與某人）爭辯 **take sb/sth to the 'mat** (*US*, *informal*) to get involved in an argument with sb/sth 與…進行辯論

■ ***adj.*** (*US*) = MATT

mata·dor /'mætədɔː(r)/ *noun* (from *Spanish*) a person who fights and kills the BULL in a BULLFIGHT 鬥牛士

Mata Hari /,mɑːtə 'hɑːri/ *noun* an attractive female SPY 美女間諜 **ORIGIN** From the name of a Dutch dancer who worked as a spy for the German government during the First World War. 源自第一次世界大戰期間為德國政府充當間諜的荷蘭舞蹈演員瑪塔・哈里的名字。

ma·tatu /mæ'tætuː/ *noun* (in Kenya) a small bus used as a taxi（肯尼亞）出租麪包車，小巴計程車

match 🔑 /mætʃ/ *noun, verb*

■ *noun*

▸ **FOR LIGHTING FIRES** 用於點火 **1** 🔑 [C] a small stick made of wood or cardboard that is used for lighting a fire, cigarette, etc. 火柴：*a box of matches* 一盒火柴 ◇ *to* ***strike a match*** (= to make it burn) 劃火柴 ◇ *to* ***put a match to sth*** (= set fire to sth) 用火柴點燃某物

▸ **IN SPORT** 體育運動 **2** 🔑 [C] (*especially BrE*) a sports event where people or teams compete against each other 比賽；競賽：(*BrE*) *a football match* 足球比賽 ◇ (*NAmE, BrE*) *a tennis match* 網球比賽 ◇ *They are playing an important match against Liverpool on Saturday.* 星期六他們和利物浦隊有一場重要比賽。◇ *to* ***win/lose a match*** 贏得／輸掉比賽 ➲ see also SHOOTING MATCH, SLANGING MATCH, TEST MATCH

▸ **AN EQUAL** 匹敵者 **3** [sing.] **a ~ for sb | sb's match** a person who is equal to sb else in strength, skill, intelligence, etc. 敵手；旗鼓相當的人：*I was* ***no match for*** *him at tennis.* 打網球我根本不是他的對手。◇ *I was his match at tennis.* 打網球我跟他難分伯仲。

▸ **SB/STH THAT COMBINES WELL** 相稱的人／物 **4** 🔑 [sing.] a person or thing that combines well with sb/sth else 相配的人（或物）；般配的人（或物）：*The curtains and carpet are a* ***good match****.* 窗簾和地毯非常相配。◇ *Jo and Ian are* ***a perfect match*** *for each other.* 喬和伊恩真是天設的一對，地配的一雙。

▸ **STH THE SAME** 相同的東西 **5** [C] a thing that looks exactly the same as or very similar to sth else 相同的東西；非常相似的東西：*I've found a vase that is an exact match of the one I broke.* 我找到了一隻花瓶，和我打碎的那個一模一樣。

M

▸ **MARRIAGE** 婚姻 **6** [C] (*old-fashioned*) a marriage or a marriage partner 婚姻；配偶 ➲ see also LOVE MATCH

IDM **find/meet your 'match (in sb)** to meet sb who is equal to, or even better than you in strength, skill or intelligence 遇到對手；棋逢對手 ➲ more at MAN *n.*

■ *verb*

▸ **COMBINE WELL** 匹配 **1** 🔑 [T, I] **~ (sth)** if two things **match**, or if one thing **matches** another, they have the same colour, pattern, or style and therefore look attractive together 般配；相配：*The doors were painted blue to match the walls.* 門漆成了藍色，使它與牆的顏色相配。◇ *a scarf with gloves* ***to match*** 一條圍巾還有和它相配的手套 ◇ *None of these glasses match* (= they are all different). 這些杯子沒有能配對兒的。➲ see also MATCHING

▸ **BE THE SAME** 相同 **2** 🔑 [T, I] **~ (sth)** if two things **match** or if one thing **matches** another, they are the same or very similar 相同；相似；相一致：*Her fingerprints match those found at the scene of the crime.* 她的指紋與犯罪現場的指紋相吻合。◇ *As a couple they are not very well matched* (= they are not very suitable for each other). 作為夫妻，他們並不十分般配。◇ *The two sets of figures don't match.* 這兩組數字不一致。

▸ **FIND STH SIMILAR/CONNECTED** 配對 **3** 🔑 [T] **~ sb/sth (to/with sb/sth)** to find sb/sth that goes together with or is connected with another person or thing 找相稱（或相關）的人（或物）；配對：*The aim of the competition is to match the quote to the person who said it.* 比賽的要求是把引文和它的作者配在一起。

▸ **BE EQUAL/BETTER** 一樣；更好 **4** [T] **~ sb/sth** to be as good, interesting, successful, etc. as sb/sth else 與…相匹敵；和…不相上下 SYN **equal**：*The profits made in the first year have never been matched.* 歷年獲得的利潤都比不上第一年的。◇ *The teams were* ***evenly matched****.* 各隊的水平旗鼓相當。 **5** [T] **~ sth** to make sth the same or better than sth else 使等同於；使優於：*The company was unable to match his current salary.* 當時公司付不起和他現在相同的工資。

▸ **PROVIDE STH SUITABLE** 提供合適的東西 **6** [T] **~ sth** to provide sth that is suitable for or enough for a particular situation 適應；滿足：*Investment in hospitals is needed now to match the future needs of the country.* 為了適應國家未來的需要，必須現在就投資醫院建設。

IDM see MIX *v.*

PHR V **'match sth against sth** to compare sth with sth else in order to find things that are the same or similar 拿…與…比較；對照：*New information is matched against existing data in the computer.* 新的資料和電腦中已有的數據作了比較。 **'match sb/sth against/with sb/sth** to arrange for sb to compete in a game or competition against sb else 讓…同…較量：*We are matched against last year's champions in the first round.* 我們第一輪即遭遇了去年的冠軍。 **,match 'up (to sb/sth)** (usually used in negative sentences 通常用於否定句) to be as good, interesting, successful as sb/sth 相稱；相當；配得上 SYN **measure up**：*The trip failed to match up to her expectations.* 這次旅行令她很失望。 **,match 'up (with sth)** 🔑 to be the same or similar（和某物）相同，相似 SYN **tally, agree**：*The suspects' stories just don't match up.* 各嫌疑犯交代的內容不一致。 **,match sth↔'up (with sth)** 🔑 to find things that belong together or that look attractive together 歸類；配套；搭配：*She spent the morning matching up orders with invoices.* 她花了一上午工夫把訂單和發票都給對好了。

match·book /ˈmætʃbʊk/ *noun* (*NAmE*) a piece of folded card containing matches and a surface to light them on 紙板火柴

match·box /ˈmætʃbɒks; *NAmE* -bɑːks/ *noun* a small box for holding matches 火柴盒 ➲ VISUAL VOCAB page V33

match·ing 🔑 /ˈmætʃɪŋ/ *adj.* [only before noun] (of clothing, material, objects, etc. 衣服、材料、物件等) having the same colour, pattern, style, etc. and therefore looking attractive together（顏色、形狀、款式等）相同的，相稱的，相配的：*a pine table with four matching chairs* 一張松木桌子和四把配套的椅子

match·less /ˈmætʃləs/ *adj.* (*formal*) so good that nothing can be compared with it 無可匹敵的；無比的；無雙的；無法媲美的 SYN **incomparable**：*matchless beauty/skill* 絕色；絕技

match·maker /ˈmætʃmeɪkə(r)/ *noun* a person who tries to arrange marriages or relationships between others 媒人；牽線搭橋的人；紅娘 ▸ **match·mak·ing** *noun* [U]

'match play *noun* [U] a way of playing GOLF in which your score depends on the number of holes that you win rather than the number of times you hit the ball in the whole game（高爾夫球）比洞賽（與計杆賽有別）➲ compare STROKE PLAY

,match 'point *noun* [U, C] (especially in TENNIS 指網球) a point that, if won by a player, will also win them the match 決勝分；賽點；賽末點

match·stick /ˈmætʃstɪk/ *noun* a single wooden match 火柴梗；火柴棍：*starving children with legs like matchsticks* 腿瘦得像火柴梗兒一樣的飢餓兒童

matchstick man 線條畫男子　matchstick woman 線條畫女子

'matchstick figure (*BrE*) (*NAmE* **'stick figure**) *noun* a picture of a person drawn only with thin lines for the arms and legs, a circle for the head, etc. 人物線條畫；簡筆人物畫

match·wood /ˈmætʃwʊd/ *noun* [U] very small pieces of wood 小木條；木料碎片

mate 🔑 /meɪt/ *noun, verb*

■ *noun*

▸ **FRIEND** 朋友 **1** 🔑 [C] (*BrE, AustralE, informal*) a friend 朋友；夥伴：*They've been best mates since school.* 他們從上學時期以來就是最要好的朋友。◇ *I was with a mate.* 我和一個朋友在一起。

▸ **FRIENDLY NAME** 友好的稱呼 **2** 🔑 [C] (*BrE, AustralE, informal*) used as a friendly way of addressing sb, especially between men（男人之間常用）哥兒們，夥計，老

兄：*Sorry mate, you'll have to wait.* 對不起，夥計，你得等着。◇ *All right, mate?* 行嗎，哥兒們？

▸ SB YOU SHARE WITH 夥伴 **3** [C] (in compounds 構成複合詞) a person you share an activity or accommodation with 同伴；同事；一同居住的人：***workmates/teammates/playmates/classmates*** 工友；隊友；遊戲夥伴；同學 ◇ *my **room-mate/flatmate*** 我的室友；和我同住一套公寓的人 ➲ see also RUNNING MATE, SOULMATE

▸ BIRD/ANIMAL 鳥；動物 **4** [C] either of a pair of birds or animals 偶；伴侶：*A male bird sings to attract a mate.* 雄鳥鳴唱以吸引雌鳥。

▸ SEXUAL PARTNER 性伴侶 **5** [C] (*informal*) a husband, wife or other sexual partner 配偶；性伴侶

▸ JOB 職業 **6** [C] (*BrE*) a person whose job is to help a skilled worker（熟練工人的）助手，下手：*a **builder's/plumber's mate*** 建築工的／管子工的助手

▸ ON SHIP 船舶 **7** [C] an officer in a commercial ship below the rank of captain or MASTER（商船的）大副 ➲ see also FIRST MATE

▸ IN CHESS 國際象棋 **8** [U] = CHECKMATE

■ *verb*

▸ ANIMALS/BIRDS 動物；鳥 **1** [I] **~ (with sth)** (of two animals or birds 一對動物或鳥) to have sex in order to produce young 交配；交尾：*Do foxes ever mate with dogs?* 狐狸會和狗交配嗎？ ➲ see also MATING **2** [T] **~ sth (to/with sth)** to put animals or birds together so that they will have sex and produce young 使交配

▸ IN CHESS 國際象棋 **3** [T] = CHECKMATE (1)

ma·ter·ial /məˈtɪəriəl; *NAmE* -ˈtɪr-/ *noun, adj.*

■ *noun* **1** [U, C] cloth used for making clothes, curtains, etc. 布料 SYN **fabric**：*a piece of material* 一塊布料 ◇ *'What material is this dress made of?' 'Cotton.'* "這件連衣裙是用什麼料子做的？" "棉布。" ➲ note at FABRIC **2** [C, U] a substance that things can be made from 材料；原料：***building materials*** (= bricks, sand, glass, etc.) 建築材料 ➲ see also RAW MATERIAL **3** [C, usually pl., U] things that are needed in order to do a particular activity（某一活動所需的）材料：*teaching materials* 教材 ◇ *The company produces its own training material.* 公司自行編寫培訓教材。◇ (*figurative*) *The teacher saw her as good university material* (= good enough to go to university). 老師認為她是塊上大學的料。➲ SYNONYMS at EQUIPMENT **4** [U] information or ideas used in books, etc. 素材；用以創作的材料（或構想）：*She's collecting material for her latest novel.* 她在為其最新的小說收集素材。**5** [U] items used in a performance 節目；曲目；劇目：*The band played all new material at the gig.* 在現場音樂會上，樂隊演奏的都是新曲目。

■ *adj.* **1** [only before noun] connected with money, possessions, etc. rather than with the needs of the mind or spirit 物質的，實際的（非精神需求的）：*material comforts* 物質享受 ◇ *changes in your material circumstances* 物質環境的改變 OPP **spiritual** **2** [only before noun] connected with the physical world rather than with the mind or spirit 物質的；客觀存在的：*the material world* 物質世界 OPP **immaterial** **3** (*formal* or *law* 律) important and needing to be considered 重要的；必要的：*material evidence* 重要的證據 ◇ **~ to sth** *She omitted information that was material to the case.* 她遺漏了此案的重要資料。➲ see also IMMATERIAL ▸ **ma·teri·ally** /-iəli/ *adv.*：*Materially they are no better off.* 他們的物質生活並沒有改善。◇ *Their comments have not materially affected our plans* (= in a noticeable or important way). 他們的評價並沒有對我們的計劃產生多麼重要的影響。

ma·teri·al·ism /məˈtɪəriəlɪzəm; *NAmE* -ˈtɪr-/ *noun* [U] **1** (usually *disapproving*) the belief that money, possessions and physical comforts are more important than spiritual values 實利主義；物質主義 **2** (*philosophy* 哲) the belief that only material things exist 唯物主義；唯物論 ➲ compare IDEALISM

ma·teri·al·ist /məˈtɪəriəlɪst; *NAmE* -ˈtɪr-/ *noun* **1** a person who believes that money, possessions and physical comforts are more important than spiritual values in life 物質享樂主義者；實利主義者 **2** a person who believes in the philosophy of materialism 唯物主義者；唯物論者

ma·teri·al·is·tic /məˌtɪəriəˈlɪstɪk; *NAmE* -ˌtɪr-/ *adj.* (*disapproving*) caring more about money and possessions than anything else 物質享樂主義的；貪圖享樂的

ma·teri·al·ize (*BrE* also **-ise**) /məˈtɪəriəlaɪz; *NAmE* -ˈtɪr-/ *verb* **1** [I] (usually used in negative sentences 通常用於否定句) to take place or start to exist as expected or planned 實現；發生；成為現實：*The promotion he had been promised failed to materialize.* 答應給他晉升的許諾未能實現。**2** [I] to appear suddenly and/or in a way that cannot be explained 突然顯現；奇怪地出現：*A tall figure suddenly materialized at her side.* 一個高高的身影突然出現在她的身邊。◇ (*informal*) *The train failed to materialize* (= it did not come). 列車始終沒有來。▸ **ma·teri·al·iza·tion**, **-isa·tion** /məˌtɪəriəlaɪˈzeɪʃn; *NAmE* -ˌtɪriələˈz-/ *noun* [U]

ma·ter·iel /məˌtɪəriˈel; *NAmE* -ˌtɪr-/ *noun* [U] (*technical* 術語) military weapons and equipment 軍用物資；武器裝備

ma·ter·nal /məˈtɜːnl; *NAmE* məˈtɜːrnl/ *adj.* **1** having feelings that are typical of a caring mother towards a child 母親的；母親般慈愛的：*maternal love* 母愛 ◇ *I'm not very maternal.* 我不太像個母親。◇ *She didn't have any maternal instincts.* 她沒有一點做母親的天性。**2** connected with being a mother 母親的；作為母親的：*Maternal age affects the baby's survival rate.* 母親的年齡影響嬰兒的成活率。**3** [only before noun] related through the mother's side of the family 母系的；母親方面的：*my maternal grandfather* (= my mother's father) 我的外祖父 ▸ **ma·ter·nal·ly** /-nəli/ *adv.*：*She behaved maternally towards her students.* 她以母親般的慈愛對待自己的學生。➲ compare PATERNAL

ma·ter·nity /məˈtɜːnəti; *NAmE* -ˈtɜːrn-/ *noun* [U] the state of being or becoming a mother 母親身分；懷孕：*maternity clothes* (= clothes for women who are pregnant) 孕婦裝 ◇ *a **maternity ward/hospital*** (= one where women go to give birth to their babies) 產科病房；婦產醫院

maˈternity leave *noun* [U] a period of time when a woman temporarily leaves her job to have a baby 產假 ➲ COLLOCATIONS at CHILD ➲ see also PARENTAL LEAVE, PATERNITY LEAVE

mate·ship /ˈmeɪtʃɪp/ *noun* [U] (*AustralE, NZE, informal*) friendship, especially between men（尤指男性之間的）友誼，友情，交情

matey /ˈmeɪti/ *adj., noun*

■ *adj.* **~ (with sb)** (*BrE, informal*) friendly, sometimes in a way that is not completely sincere 友好；親熱；套近乎：*She started off being quite matey with everyone.* 她一上來就和每個人套近乎。

■ *noun* (*BrE*) used by men as an informal way of addressing another man 哥兒們；兄弟

math /mæθ/ (*NAmE*) (*BrE* **maths**) *noun* [U] **1** mathematics, especially as a subject in school 數學（尤作為學校課程）：*a math teacher* 數學老師 **2** the process of calculating using numbers 運算；計算：*Is your math correct?* 你的計算正確嗎？

IDM **do the ˈmath** to think carefully about sth before doing it so that you know all the relevant facts or figures 周密估算；斟酌：*If only someone had done the math!* 要是有人事先合計過就好了！

math·em·at·ician /ˌmæθəməˈtɪʃn/ *noun* a person who is an expert in mathematics 數學家

math·emat·ics /ˌmæθəˈmætɪks/ (*formal*) (also *BrE* **maths** /mæθs/) (also *NAmE* **math** /mæθ/) *noun* **1** [U] the science of numbers and shapes. Branches of mathematics include ARITHMETIC, ALGEBRA, GEOMETRY and TRIGONOMETRY. 數學：*the school mathematics curriculum* 學校數學課程 **2** [U+sing./pl. v.] the process of calculating using numbers 運算；計算：*He worked out the very difficult mathematics in great detail.* 他詳細地解答了那些很難的運算。▸ **math·emat·ic·al** /ˌmæθəˈmætɪkl/ *adj.*：***mathematical calculations/problems/models*** 數學計算／問題／模型 ◇ *to assess children's mathematical ability* 評定孩子們的計算能力

M

math·emat·ic·al·ly /-kli/ *adv.*：*It's mathematically impossible.* 這在數學上是不可能的。◇ *Some people are very mathematically inclined* (= interested in and good at mathematics). 有些人特別喜歡並擅長數學。

maths /mæθs/ (*BrE*) (*NAmE* **math** /mæθ/) *noun* **1** [U] mathematics, especially as a subject in school 數學（尤作為學校課程）：*The core subjects are English, Maths and Science.* 主課是英語、數學和自然科學。◇ *a maths teacher* 數學老師 **2** [U+sing./pl. v.] the process of calculating using numbers 運算；計算：*If my maths is/are right, the answer is 142.* 如果我計算沒錯，答案是 142。
IDM **do the 'maths** to think carefully about sth before doing it so that you know all the relevant facts or figures 周密估算；斟酌：*Do the maths before you take on more debt.* 再借債之前要三思。

Ma·tilda /məˈtɪldə/ *noun* (*old use, AustralE, NZE*) a pack of things tied or wrapped together and carried by a BUSHMAN（布須曼人的）行囊，背囊

mat·inee (also **mat·inée**) /ˈmætɪneɪ; *NAmE* ˌmætnˈeɪ/ *noun* an afternoon performance of a play, etc.; an afternoon showing of a film/movie（戲劇、電影的）午後場，日場

'matinee idol (also **'matinée idol**) *noun* (*old-fashioned*) an actor who is popular with women 受女觀眾喜愛的男演員；偶像派男演員

mat·ing /ˈmeɪtɪŋ/ *noun* [U, C] sex between animals 交尾；交配：*the mating season* 交配季節

mat·ins (also **mat·tins**) /ˈmætɪnz; *NAmE* ˈmætnz/ *noun* [U] the service of morning prayer, especially in the Anglican Church（尤指聖公會的）晨禱 ➲ compare EVENSONG, VESPERS

ma·toke /mæˈtɒkə; *NAmE* mæˈtɑːkə/ *noun* [U] a type of green BANANA grown in Uganda and other places in E Africa and used for cooking; the cooked food made from this type of banana and eaten with STEW（烏干達等東非地帶用於烹調的）青香蕉；蒸香蕉（和燉菜一起食用）

ma·tri·arch /ˈmeɪtriɑːk; *NAmE* -ɑːrk/ *noun* a woman who is the head of a family or social group 女家長；女族長 ➲ compare PATRIARCH (1)

ma·tri·arch·al /ˌmeɪtriˈɑːkl; *NAmE* -ˈɑːrkl/ *adj.* (of a society or system 社會或體制) controlled by women rather than men; passing power, property, etc. from mother to daughter rather than from father to son 母系的；母權的：*The animals live in matriarchal groups.* 這些動物按母系群體生活。➲ compare PATRIARCHAL (1)

ma·tri·archy /ˈmeɪtriɑːki; *NAmE* -ɑːrki/ *noun* (*pl.* **-ies**) a social system that gives power and authority to women rather than men 母權制；母系社會 ➲ compare PATRIARCHY

ma·tric /məˈtrɪk/ *noun* [U] (*SAfrE*) **1** the final year of school（中學的）畢業學年：*We studied that book in matric.* 我們畢業那年學了那本書。 **2** the work and examinations in the final year of school 畢業學年的學業和考試：*He passed matric with four distinctions.* 他以四個優等成績通過畢業考試。◇ *She's preparing to write matric.* 她正準備參加畢業考試。

matri·ces *pl.* of MATRIX

maˌtric e'xemption *noun* [U] (*SAfrE*) the fact of successfully completing the final year of school and being able to study at university or college 中學畢業；具備大學入學資格：*A senior certificate with matric exemption is required for entry to university.* 上大學需要有中學畢業的資格證書。

matri·cide /ˈmætrɪsaɪd/ *noun* [U, C] (*formal*) the crime of killing your mother; a person who is guilty of this crime 弒母；弒母者 ➲ compare FRATRICIDE (1), PARRICIDE, PATRICIDE

ma·tric·ulate /məˈtrɪkjuleɪt/ *verb* **1** [I] (*formal*) to officially become a student at a university（正式）被大學錄取；註冊入大學：*She matriculated in 1995.* 她於 1995 年升入大學。 **2** [I] (*SAfrE*) to successfully complete the final year of school（從學校）畢業 ▸ **ma·tricu·la·tion** /məˌtrɪkjuˈleɪʃn/ *noun* [U]

matri·lin·eal /ˌmætrɪˈlɪniəl/ *adj.* (*technical* 術語) used to describe the relationship between mother and children that continues in a family with each generation, or sth that is based on this relationship 母系的；基於母系的：*She traced her family history by matrilineal descent* (= starting with her mother, her mother's mother, etc.). 她按母系血統追溯她的家族史。➲ compare PATRILINEAL

matri·mo·nial /ˌmætrɪˈməʊniəl; *NAmE* -ˈmoʊ-/ *adj.* [usually before noun] (*formal* or *technical* 術語) connected with marriage or with being married 婚姻的：*matrimonial problems* 婚姻問題◇ *the matrimonial home* 婚姻住所

matri·mony /ˈmætrɪməni; *NAmE* -moʊni/ *noun* [U] (*formal* or *technical* 術語) marriage; the state of being married 婚配：*holy matrimony* 婚配聖事

mat·rix /ˈmeɪtrɪks/ *noun* (*pl.* **matri·ces** /ˈmeɪtrɪsiːz/) **1** (*mathematics* 數) an arrangement of numbers, symbols, etc. in rows and columns, treated as a single quantity 矩陣 **2** (*formal*) the formal social, political, etc. situation from which a society or person grows and develops（人或社會成長發展的）社會環境，政治局勢：*the European cultural matrix* 歐洲文化的發源地 **3** (*formal* or *literary*) a system of lines, roads, etc. that cross each other, forming a series of squares or shapes in between 線路網；道路網 SYN **network**：*a matrix of paths* 縱橫交錯的小路 **4** (*technical* 術語) a MOULD in which sth is shaped 基體；鑄模 **5** (*computing* 計) a group of electronic CIRCUIT elements arranged in rows and columns like a GRID 矩陣轉接電路 ➲ see also DOT MATRIX PRINTER **6** (*geology* 地) a mass of rock in which minerals, PRECIOUS STONES, etc. are found in the ground 雜基

ma·tron /ˈmeɪtrən/ *noun* **1** (*BrE*) a woman who works as a nurse in a school（學校的）女舍監 **2** (*old-fashioned, BrE*) a senior female nurse in charge of the other nurses in a hospital (now usually called a **senior nursing officer**) 女護士長（現常稱為 senior nursing officer） **3** (*becoming old-fashioned*) an older married woman 上年紀的已婚婦女

ma·tron·ly /ˈmeɪtrənli/ *adj.* (*disapproving*) (of a woman 婦女) no longer young, and rather fat 韶華已逝而且肥胖的

'matron of honour (*especially US* **'matron of honor**) *noun* [sing.] a married woman who is the most important BRIDESMAID at a wedding（已婚的）首席女儐相，伴娘 ➲ compare MAID OF HONOUR

matro·nym·ic /ˌmætrəˈnɪmɪk/ *noun* (*technical* 術語) a name formed from the name of your mother or a female ANCESTOR especially by adding sth to the beginning or end of their name 從母名衍生出的姓或名字（尤指在母親或母系祖先之名前加前、後綴）➲ compare PATRONYMIC

matt (*BrE*) (*US* **mat**) (also **matte** *NAmE, BrE*) /mæt/ *adj.* (of a colour, surface, or photograph 色彩、表面或照片) not shiny 不光亮的；無光澤的；亞光的：*a matt finish* 亞光罩面漆◇ *matt white paint* 亞光白漆◇ *Prints are available on matt or glossy paper.* 相片可洗印在亞光相紙或亮光相紙上。

mat·ted /ˈmætɪd/ *adj.* (of hair, etc. 毛髮等) forming a thick mass, especially because it is wet and dirty 纏結的；濕髒蓬亂的

mat·ter 0━ /ˈmætə(r)/ *noun, verb*

■ ***noun***

▸ **SUBJECT/SITUATION** 課題；情況 **1** 0━ [C] a subject or situation that you must consider or deal with 課題；事情；問題 SYN **affair**：*It's a private matter.* 這是件私事兒。◇ *They had important matters to discuss.* 他們有些重要的問題要討論。◇ *She may need your help with some business matters.* 她也許需要你幫助處理一些生意方面的事情。◇ *I always consulted him on matters of policy.* 我總是向他咨詢一些政策問題。◇ *It's* ***a matter for*** *the police* (= for them to deal with). 這事須要由警方處理。◇ *That's a matter for you to take up with your boss.* 這個問題你得去和你的老闆進行交涉。◇ *Let's get on with the* ***matter in hand*** (= what we need to deal with now). 我們繼續解決手頭的問題吧。◇ *I wasn't prepared to* ***let*** *the matter drop* (= stop discussing it). 我沒打算把這件事擱下不提。◇ *It was **no easy matter** getting him to change his mind.* 讓他改變主意可不是件容易的事兒。◇ *It should have been a simple matter to check.* 檢查核對本來應該是件簡單的事情。◇ (*ironic*) *And then there's **the little matter** of the fifty pounds you owe me.* 還有件小事兒，你欠我五十英鎊呢。◇ (*formal*) *It was **a matter of** some concern to most of those present* (= something they were worried about). 這是當時在場的多數人關心的問題。◇ *I did not feel that we had got to **the heart of the matter*** (= the most important part). 我認為我們還沒有觸及問題的關鍵。◇ *And that is **the crux of the matter*** (= the most important thing about the situation). 這就是問題的癥結所在。 **2** **matters** [pl.] the present situation, or the situation that you are talking about 事態；當前的狀況 **SYN** **things**：*Unfortunately, there is nothing we can do to improve matters.* 很遺憾，我們無力改善目前的狀況。◇ *I'd forgotten the keys, which didn't **help matters**.* 我忘記帶鑰匙了，這讓我無能為力。◇ *Matters were made worse by a fire in the warehouse.* 倉庫失火使得事態更為嚴重。◇ *And then, **to make matters worse**, his parents turned up.* 接着，更糟糕的是，他的父母親來了。◇ *I decided to **take matters into my own hands*** (= deal with the situation myself). 我決定親自處理問題。◇ ***Matters came to a head*** (= the situation became very difficult) *with his resignation.* 隨着他的辭職，局面惡化得難以收拾。

▸ **PROBLEM 問題** **3** **the matter** [sing.] used (to ask) if sb is upset, unhappy, etc. or if there is a problem（用於詢問某人的情況）：***What's the matter?*** *Is there something wrong?* 怎麼了？出了什麼事兒嗎？◇ *Is **anything the matter**?* 有什麼問題嗎？◇ **~ with sb/sth** *Is **something the matter** with Bob? He seems very down.* 鮑勃有什麼事兒吧？他好像情緒很低落。◇ *There's something the matter with my eyes.* 我的眼睛出了點毛病。◇ *'We've bought a new TV.' 'What was the matter with the old one?'* "我們買了台新電視。" "那台舊的怎麼了？" ◇ ***What's the matter with you** today* (= why are you behaving like this)? 你今天是怎麼了？

▸ **A MATTER OF STH/OF DOING STH 關於…的問題** **4** [sing.] a situation that involves sth or depends on sth 關乎…的事情 **SYN** **question**：*Learning to drive is all a matter of coordination.* 學開車主要是靠協調。◇ *Planning a project is just a matter of working out the right order to do things in.* 規劃一個項目就是要設計出正確的工作順序。◇ *That's not a problem. It's **simply a matter of** letting people know in time.* 這沒問題，不就是及時通知大家麼。◇ *Some people prefer the older version to the new one. It's **a matter of taste**.* 有些人喜歡老版本而不喜歡新版本。這只是個愛好問題。◇ *She resigned over **a matter of principle**.* 她因為原則問題而辭職。◇ *The government must deal with this **as a matter of urgency**.* 政府必須將此事當作緊急的事情來處理。◇ *Just **as a matter of interest*** (= because it is interesting, not because it is important), *how much did you pay for it?* 我只是感興趣，你這是花多少錢買的？◇ *'I think this is the best so far.' 'Well, that's **a matter of opinion**'* (= other people may think differently). "我認為這是迄今為止最好的。" "唔，仁者見仁，智者見智嘛。"

▸ **SUBSTANCE 物質** **5** [U] (*physics* 物) physical substance in general that everything in the world consists of; not mind or spirit（統稱）物質：*to study the properties of matter* 研究物質的屬性 **6** [U] (*formal*) a substance or things of a particular sort（某種）東西，物品，材料：*Add plenty of organic matter to improve the soil.* 施用大量的有機肥料以改良土壤。◇ *elimination of **waste matter** from the body* 體內廢物的排除 ◇ *She didn't approve of their choice of **reading matter**.* 她不贊同他們選用的閱讀材料。 ➲ see also SUBJECT MATTER

IDM **as a matter of 'fact** **1** used to add a comment on sth that you have just said, usually adding sth that you think the other person will be interested in 事實上；其實；說真的：*It's a nice place. We've stayed there ourselves, as a matter of fact.* 那個地方不錯。事實上，我們在那兒待過。 **2** used to disagree with sth that sb has just said（表示不同意）事實上，其實 **SYN** **actually**：*'I suppose you'll be leaving soon, then?' 'No, as a matter of fact I'll be staying for another two years.'* "我想你快要離開了吧？" "不。事實上，我還要再待兩年呢。" **be another/a different 'matter** to be very different 另外一回事；又是一回事；另當別論：*I know which area they live in, but whether I can find their house is a different matter.* 我知道他們住在哪一地區，但能不能找到他們的房子則是另外一回事了。 **for 'that matter** used to add a comment on sth that you have just said 就此而論；在這方面：*I didn't like it much. Nor did the kids, for that matter.* 我不怎麼喜歡它。孩子們也同樣不喜歡。 **it's just/only a matter of 'time (before …)** used to say that sth will definitely happen, although you are not sure when 早晚的事；只是時間問題：*It's only a matter of time before they bring out their own version of the software.* 他們推出自己的軟件只是個時間問題。 **(as) a matter of 'course** (as) the usual and correct thing to do（作為）理所當然的事；（當作）常規：*We always check people's addresses as a matter of course.* 我們總是照例檢查一下人們的地址。 **a matter of 'hours, 'minutes, etc. | a matter of 'inches, 'metres, etc.** only a few hours, minutes, etc. 只有幾個小時、幾分鐘（或幾英寸、幾米等）之多；不多於…：*It was all over in a matter of minutes.* 幾分鐘就全部結束了。◇ *The bullet missed her by a matter of inches.* 子彈幾乎擦着她的身體飛過。 **a ˌmatter of ˌlife and 'death** used to describe a situation that is very important or serious 生死攸關的事；成敗的關鍵 **a ˌmatter of 'record** (*formal*) something that has been recorded as being true 有案可查的事 **no matter** used to say that sth is not important 沒關係；不要緊；不重要 **no matter who, what, where, etc.** used to say that sth is always true, whatever the situation is, or that sb should certainly do sth 不論…；無論…；不管…：*They don't last long no matter how careful you are.* 不管你如何小心，這些東西都維持不了很久。◇ *Call me when you get there, no matter what the time is.* 無論什麼時間，你到了那兒就給我打電話。 ➲ more at FACT, LAUGHING

■ ***verb*** [I, T] (not used in the progressive tenses 不用於進行時) to be important or have an important effect on sb/sth 事關緊要；要緊；有重大影響：**~ (to sb)** *The children matter more to her than anything else in the world.* 對於她來說，在這個世界上沒有比孩子更重要的了。◇ *'What did you say?' 'Oh, it doesn't matter* (= it is not important enough to repeat).' "你說什麼？" "噢，沒什麼。" ◇ *'I'm afraid I forgot that book again.' 'It doesn't matter* (= it is not important enough to worry about).' "很抱歉，我又忘了把那本書帶來了。" "沒事兒。" ◇ ***What does it matter** if I spent $100 on it—it's my money!* 我花 100 元錢買這東西有什麼關係，那是我的錢！◇ *As long as you're happy, that's **all that matters**.* 你幸福就行了，這才是最重要的。◇ *After his death, nothing seemed to matter any more.* 他死了以後，好像一切都無所謂了。◇ *He's been in prison, you know—**not that it matters*** (= that information does not affect my opinion of him). 你知道，他坐過牢，可那倒無關緊要。◇ **~ (to sb) who, what, etc. …** *Does it really matter who did it?* 是誰幹的真的很重要嗎？◇ ***It doesn't matter** to me what you do.* 你做什麼我無所謂。◇ **~ (to sb) that …** *It didn't matter that the weather was bad.* 天氣不好並沒什麼影響。

ˌmatter-of-'fact *adj.* said or done without showing any emotion, especially in a situation in which you would expect sb to express their feelings 不動感情的；據實的 **SYN** **unemotional**：*She told us the news of his death in a very matter-of-fact way.* 她很平靜地把他去世的消息告訴了我們。 ▸ **ˌmatter-of-'factly** *adv.*

mat·ting /'mætɪŋ/ *noun* rough WOVEN material for making MATS 編墊子的材料：*coconut matting* 製墊椰衣

mat·tins *noun* [U] = MATINS

mat·tock /'mætək/ *noun* a heavy garden tool with a long handle and a metal head, used for breaking up soil, cutting roots, etc. 鶴嘴鋤

mat·tress /'mætrəs/ *noun* the soft part of a bed, that you lie on 牀墊：*a **soft/hard mattress*** 軟 / 硬牀墊 ➲ VISUAL VOCAB page V23

mat·ur·ation **AW** /ˌmætʃu'reɪʃn/ *noun* [U] (*formal*) **1** the process of becoming or being made mature (= ready to

M

eat or drink after being left for a period of time) 成熟過程；成熟 **2** the process of becoming adult 成年過程；長大成人 ▸ **mat·ur·ation·al** AW *adj.*

ma·ture AW /mə'tʃʊə(r); -'tjʊə(r); *NAmE* -'tʃʊr; -'tʊr/ *adj.*, *verb*

■ *adj.* HELP Maturer is occasionally used instead of **more mature**. 有時不用 more mature，而用 maturer。

▸ SENSIBLE 明智 **1** (of a child or young person 兒童或年輕人) behaving in a sensible way, like an adult 明白事理的；成熟的；像成人似的： *Jane is very mature for her age.* 簡年齡不大，卻很成熟。◇ *a mature and sensible attitude* 一副深諳世事的態度 OPP **immature**

▸ FULLY GROWN 成熟 **2** (of a person, a tree, a bird or an animal 人、樹木、鳥或動物) fully grown and developed 成熟的；發育完全的： *sexually mature* 性成熟的 ◇ *a mature oak/eagle/elephant* 成熟的橡樹／鷹／象 OPP **immature** ➲ SYNONYMS at OLD

▸ WINE/CHEESE 葡萄酒；乾酪 **3** developed over a period of time to produce a strong, rich flavour 發酵成熟的；釀成的

▸ NO LONGER YOUNG 不再年輕 **4** used as a polite or humorous way of saying that sb is no longer young（禮貌或幽默的說法）成年的，不再年輕的： *clothes for the mature woman* 成年婦女的服裝 ◇ *a man of mature years* 中年人

▸ WORK OF ART 藝術作品 **5** created late in an artist's life and showing great understanding and skill 成熟的；技藝精湛的；創作於晚年的

▸ INSURANCE POLICY 保險單 **6** (*business* 商) ready to be paid 到期（應該支付）的 ▸ **ma·ture·ly** *adv.*

IDM **on mature re'flection/conside'ration** (*formal*) after thinking about sth carefully and for a long time 經過深思熟慮；經過審慎考慮

■ *verb*

▸ BECOME FULLY GROWN 成熟 **1** [I] to become fully grown or developed 成熟；長成： *This particular breed of cattle matures early.* 這一品種的牛發育成熟快。◇ *Technology in this field has matured considerably over the last decade.* 這一領域的技術經過過去十年的發展已經相當完善。

▸ BECOME SENSIBLE 變得明智 **2** [I] to develop emotionally and start to behave like a sensible adult（情感和認識）成熟；有判斷力： *He has matured a great deal over the past year.* 經過過去這一年，他成熟了許多。

▸ DEVELOP SKILL 提高技能 **3** [I] **~ (into sth)** to fully develop a particular skill or quality 使（技能或素質）成熟；充分發展： *She has matured into one of the country's finest actresses.* 她已經成長為這個國家一位最優秀的演員。

▸ WINE/CHEESE 葡萄酒；乾酪 **4** [I, T] **~ (sth)** if wine, cheese, etc. **matures** or **is matured**, it develops over a period of time to produce a strong, rich flavour 釀成；製成；發酵成熟

▸ INSURANCE POLICY 保險單 **5** [I] (*business* 商) to reach the date when it must be paid 到期（應付款）

ma,ture 'student *noun* (*BrE*) an adult student who goes to college or university some years after leaving school 成年學生（中學畢業幾年後再讀大學的學生）

ma·tur·ity AW /mə'tʃʊərəti; -'tjʊə-; *NAmE* -'tʃʊr-; -'tʊr-/ *noun* [U] **1** the quality of thinking and behaving in a sensible, adult manner（思想行為、作品等）成熟： *He has maturity beyond his years.* 他過於老成。◇ *Her poems show great maturity.* 她的詩歌顯得非常成熟。➲ compare IMMATURITY at IMMATURE **2** (of a person, an animal, or a plant 人或動植物) the state of being fully grown or developed 成熟；成年；完全長成： *The forest will take 100 years to* ***reach maturity***. 這片森林要花 100 年時間才能成材。➲ compare IMMATURITY at IMMATURE **3** (*business* 商) (of an insurance policy, etc. 保險單等) the time when money you have invested is ready to be paid 到期（應付款）

matzo /'mætsəʊ; *NAmE* 'mɑːtsoʊ/ *noun* [U, C] (*pl.* **-os**) a type of bread in the form of a large flat biscuit, traditionally eaten by Jews during Passover; one of these biscuits 無酵餅（猶太人在逾越節時吃）

maud·lin /'mɔːdlɪn/ *adj.* **1** talking in a silly, emotional way, often full of pity for yourself, especially when drunk（尤指醉酒時）言語傷感的，感情脆弱的，自憐的 SYN **sentimental** **2** (of a book, film/movie, or song 書籍、電影或歌曲) expressing or causing exaggerated emotions, especially in way that is not sincere 渲染感情的 SYN **sentimental**

maul /mɔːl/ *verb* **1 ~ sb** (of an animal 動物) to attack and injure sb by tearing their flesh 襲擊；撕咬 SYN **savage** **2 ~ sb/sth** to touch sb/sth in an unpleasant and/or violent way 粗手粗腳地擺弄；粗暴地對待 **3 ~ sth/sb** to criticize sth/sb severely and publicly 狠狠地批評；猛烈抨擊 SYN **savage** **4 ~ sb** (*informal*) to defeat sb easily 輕易擊敗 SYN **trash** ▸ **maul·ing** *noun* [sing.]： *The play received a mauling from the critics.* 這齣戲受到了劇評人無情的抨擊。◇ *They face a mauling by last year's winners.* 他們面臨去年的優勝者的嚴重威脅。

maun·der /'mɔːndə(r)/ *verb* [I] **~ (on) (about sth)** (*BrE*) to talk or complain about sth in a boring and/or annoying way 嘮叨；咕噥；抱怨

Maundy Thurs·day /,mɔːndi 'θɜːzdeɪ; -di; *NAmE* 'θɜːrz-/ *noun* [U, C] (in the Christian Church) the Thursday before Easter（基督教）聖星期四，濯足節

mau·so·leum /,mɔːsə'liːəm/ *noun* a special building made to hold the dead body of an important person or the dead bodies of a family 陵墓： *the royal mausoleum* 王室陵墓

mauve /məʊv; *NAmE* moʊv/ *adj.* pale purple in colour 淡紫色的 ▸ **mauve** *noun* [U]

maven /'meɪvn/ *noun* (*NAmE*) an expert on sth 專家；內行

mav·er·ick /'mævərɪk/ *noun* a person who does not behave or think like everyone else, but who has independent, unusual opinions 持不同意見者；獨行其是者；言行與眾不同者 ▸ **mav·er·ick** *adj.* [only before noun]： *a maverick film director* 獨行其是的電影導演

maw /mɔː/ *noun* **1** (*literary*) something that seems like a big mouth that swallows things up completely 無底洞；吞噬一切的深淵 **2** (*old-fashioned*) an animal's stomach or throat（動物的）胃，咽喉

mawk·ish /'mɔːkɪʃ/ *adj.* (*disapproving*) expressing or sharing emotion in a way that is exaggerated or embarrassing 無病呻吟的；自作多情的；多愁善感的 SYN **sentimental**： *a mawkish poem* 無病呻吟的詩歌 ▸ **mawk·ish·ness** *noun* [U]

max AW /mæks/ *abbr.*, *verb*

■ *abbr.* **1** (also **max.** especially in *NAmE*) maximum 最高的；最多的；最大極限的： *max temperature 18°C* 最高氣溫 18 攝氏度 **2** at the most 至多： (*informal*) *It'll cost $50 max.* 這東西至多花 50 元。OPP **min.**

IDM **to the 'max** to the highest level or greatest amount possible 最高程度地；最大數量地： *She believes in living life to the max.* 她認為人應當盡量活得充實。

■ *verb*

PHR V **,max (sth) 'out** (*NAmE, informal*) to reach, or make sth reach, the limit at which nothing more is possible（使）達到最高極限： *The car maxed out at 150 mph.* 汽車達到了每小時 150 英里的最快速度。

maxi /'mæksi/ *noun* a long coat, dress or skirt that reaches to the ankles（長至腳踝的）大衣，連衣裙，長裙

max·illa /mæk'sɪlə/ *noun* (*pl.* **max·il·lae** /-liː/) (*anatomy* 解) the JAW 上頜骨 ▸ **max·il·lary** /mæk'sɪləri/ *adj.*： *a maxillary fracture* 上頜骨骨裂

maxim /'mæksɪm/ *noun* a well-known phrase that expresses sth that is usually true or that people think is a rule for sensible behaviour 格言；箴言；座右銘

max·imal /'mæksɪml/ *adj.* [usually before noun] (*technical* 術語) as great or as large as possible 最大的；最高的 ➲ compare MINIMAL

maxi·mize (*BrE* also **-ise**) AW /'mæksɪmaɪz/ *verb* **1 ~ sth** to increase sth as much as possible 使增加到最大限度： *to* ***maximize efficiency/fitness/profits*** 最大限度地提高效率／增強體質／增加利潤 ◇ (*computing* 計) *Maximize the window to full screen.* 將窗口放至最大。 **2 ~ sth** to make the best use of sth 充分利用；最大限度地利用： *to* ***maximize opportunities/resources*** 充分利用機會／資源 OPP **minimize** ▸ **maxi·miza·tion**, **-isa·tion** AW /,mæksɪmaɪ'zeɪʃn; *NAmE* -mə'z-/ *noun* [U]

max·imum 🔑 AW /ˈmæksɪməm/ *adj., noun*

■ **adj.** 🔑 [only before noun] (*abbr.* **max**) as large, fast, etc. as is possible, or the most that is possible or allowed 最高的；最多的；最大極限的： *the **maximum speed/temperature/volume*** 最快速度；最高氣温；最大體積 ◇ ***For maximum effect** do the exercises every day.* 每天鍛煉以取得最佳效果。◇ *a maximum security prison* 最高戒備等級的監獄 ➲ compare MINIMUM

■ **noun** 🔑 [usually sing.] (*pl.* **max·ima** /ˈmæksɪmə/) (*abbr.* **max**) the greatest amount, size, speed, etc. that is possible, recorded or allowed 最大量；最大限度；最高限度： *a maximum of 30 children in a class* 每班至多 30 名學生 ◇ *The job will require you to use all your skills **to the maximum**.* 這項工作將要求你最大限度地發揮你的技能。◇ *The July maximum* (= the highest temperature recorded in July) *was 30°C.* 七月的最高氣温是 30 攝氏度。◇ *What is the absolute maximum you can afford to pay?* 你最多能出多少錢？ ➲ compare MINIMUM

May 🔑 /meɪ/ *noun* [U, C]
the fifth month of the year, between April and June 五月 HELP To see how **May** is used, look at the examples at **April**. * May 的用法見詞條 April 下的示例。

may 🔑 /meɪ/ *modal verb, noun*

■ **modal verb** (*negative* **may not**, *rare short form* **mayn't** /ˈmeɪənt/, *pt* **might** /maɪt/, *negative* **might not**, *rare short form* **mightn't** /ˈmaɪtnt/) **1** 🔑 used to say that sth is possible（有可能但不肯定）也許，可能： *That may or may not be true.* 這可能是真的，也可能不是。◇ *He may have* (= perhaps he has) *missed his train.* 他可能沒趕上火車。◇ *They **may well** win.* 他們完全可能贏。◇ *There is a range of programs on the market which may be described as design aids.* 市場上有各種程序，可以稱為設計輔助工具。 **2** 🔑 used when admitting that sth is true before introducing another point, argument, etc.（轉折前所述情況屬實）也許，可能： *He may be a good father but he's a terrible husband.* 他或許是一位好父親，但卻是個很糟糕的丈夫。 **3** 🔑 (*formal*) used to ask for or give permission（徵求同意或表示允許）可以： *May I come in?* 我可以進來嗎？◇ *You may come in if you wish.* 你想進來就進來吧。 ➲ note at CAN[1] **4** (*formal*) used as a polite way of making a comment, asking a question, etc.（禮貌地評價或提問等）可以： *You look lovely, if I may say so.* 我覺得你看上去很可愛。◇ *May I ask why you took that decision?* 我可否問一下你為什麼要作出那樣的決定？◇ *If I may just add one thing ...* 我想再補充一點… **5** (*formal*) used to express wishes and hopes（表示願望）但願： *May she rest in peace.* 願她安息。◇ *Business has been thriving in the past year. **Long may it continue** to do so.* 在過去的一年裏生意蒸蒸日上。但願這種情況能持續下去。 **6** (*formal*) used to say what the purpose of sth is（表明目的）可以，能夠： *There is a need for more resources so that all children may have a decent education.* 需要更多的財力支持，讓所有的孩子都受到良好的教育。 ➲ note at MODAL

IDM **be that as it ˈmay** (*formal*) despite that 儘管如此 SYN **nevertheless**： *I know that he has tried hard; be that as it may, his work is just not good enough.* 我知道他已經盡力了，儘管如此，他的工作仍不太理想。

■ **noun** [U] the white or pink flowers of the HAWTHORN 山楂花

maybe 🔑 /ˈmeɪbi/ *adv.*
1 🔑 used when you are not certain that sth will happen or that sth is true or is a correct number（不確定）大概，或許，可能 SYN **perhaps**： *Maybe he'll come, maybe he won't.* 他可能來，也可能不來。◇ *'Are you going to sell your house?' 'Maybe.'* "你要賣房子嗎？" "也許吧。" ◇ *It will cost two, maybe three hundred pounds.* 這個要花二百英鎊，或許三百英鎊。◇ *We go there maybe once or twice a month.* 我們每月大概去那裏一到兩次。 **2** 🔑 used when making a suggestion（提出建議）或許，也許 SYN **perhaps**： *I thought maybe we could go together.* 我覺得或許我們可以一起去。◇ *Maybe you should tell her.* 也許你應該告訴她。 **3** 🔑 used to agree with sb, and to add more information that should be thought about（贊同並補充信息）或許，也許，可能 SYN **perhaps**： *'You should stop work when you have the baby.' 'Maybe, but I can't afford to.'* "有了孩子你就不應該工作了。" "或許是吧，可我負擔不起呀。"

4 🔑 used when replying to a question or an idea, when you are not sure whether to agree or disagree（不置可否）也許，或許 SYN **perhaps**： *'I think he should resign.' 'Maybe.'* "我覺得他應該辭職。" "也許是吧。"

ˈMay bug *noun* = COCKCHAFER

ˈMay Day *noun* the first day of May, celebrated as a spring festival and, in some countries, as a holiday in honour of working people 五朔節；（某些國家的）五一勞動節 ➲ compare LABOR DAY

May·day /ˈmeɪdeɪ/ *noun* [U] an international radio signal used by ships and aircraft needing help when they are in danger（船隻或飛行器遇險時用的國際無線電求救信號） ORIGIN From the French *venez m'aider* 'come and help me'. 源自法語 venez m'aider，意為"速來救助"。

may·fly /ˈmeɪflaɪ/ *noun* (*pl.* **-ies**) a small insect that lives near water and only lives for a very short time 蜉蝣

may·hem /ˈmeɪhem/ *noun* [U] confusion and fear, usually caused by violent behaviour or by some sudden shocking event 騷亂；慌亂： *There was absolute mayhem when everyone tried to get out at once.* 眾人蜂擁而出，造成了極大的混亂。

may·on·naise /ˌmeɪəˈneɪz; *NAmE* ˈmeɪəneɪz/ (*also informal* **mayo** /ˈmeɪəʊ; *NAmE* ˈmeɪoʊ/) *noun* [U] a thick cold white sauce made from eggs, oil and VINEGAR, used to add flavour to SANDWICHES, salads, etc. 蛋黃醬（用作三明治、色拉等的調味品）： *egg mayonnaise* (= a dish made with hard-boiled eggs and mayonnaise) 雞蛋美奶滋（有煮老的雞蛋和蛋黃醬）

mayor 🔑 /meə(r); *NAmE* ˈmeɪər/ *noun*
1 🔑 (in England, Wales and Northern Ireland) the head of a town, BOROUGH or county council, chosen by other members of the council to represent them at official ceremonies, etc.（英格蘭、威爾士和北愛爾蘭由議員選舉產生的）鎮長，市長，郡長： *the Lord Mayor of London* 倫敦市長 ➲ compare PROVOST (3) **2** 🔑 the head of the government of a town or city, etc., elected by the public（民選的）市長，鎮長： *the Mayor of New York* 紐約市長 ◇ *Mayor Bob Anderson* 鮑勃•安德森市長 ► **may·oral** /ˈmeərəl; *NAmE* ˈmeɪə-/ *adj.* [only before noun]： ***mayoral robes/duties*** 市長的禮袍／職責

may·or·alty /ˈmeərəlti; *NAmE* ˈmeɪər-/ *noun* (*pl.* **-ies**) (*formal*) **1** the title or position of a mayor 市長頭銜；市長職位 **2** the period of time during which a person is a mayor 市長任期

may·or·ess /meəˈres; *NAmE* ˈmeɪərəs/ *noun* **1** (*also* **ˌlady ˈmayor**) a woman who has been elected mayor 女市長 ➲ note at GENDER **2** (in England, Wales and Northern Ireland) the wife of a mayor or a woman who helps a mayor at official ceremonies（英格蘭、威爾士和北愛爾蘭）市長（或鎮長、郡長）夫人，市長（或鎮長、郡長）女助理

may·pole /ˈmeɪpəʊl; *NAmE* -poʊl/ *noun* a decorated pole that people dance round in celebrations on MAY DAY 五朔節花柱；五月柱

maze /meɪz/ *noun* **1** a system of paths separated by walls or HEDGES built in a park or garden, that is designed so that it is difficult to find your way through 迷宮： *We got lost in the maze.* 我們在迷宮裏迷失了方向。◇ (*figurative*) *The building is a maze of corridors.* 這座建築長廊交錯，簡直就是一座迷宮。 ➲ compare LABYRINTH **2** [usually sing.] a large number of complicated rules or details that are difficult to understand 紛繁複雜的規則；複雜難懂的細節： *a maze of regulations* 一大堆紛繁複雜的規章制度 **3** (*NAmE*) a printed PUZZLE in which you have to draw a line that shows a way through a complicated pattern of lines 迷宮圖

ma·zurka /məˈzɜːkə; *NAmE* məˈzɜːrkə/ *noun* a fast Polish dance for four or eight couples, or a piece of music for this dance 馬祖卡舞（節奏輕快的波蘭舞，由四對或八對舞伴參加）；馬祖卡舞曲

MB *abbr.* **1** /ˌem ˈbiː/ (in Britain) Bachelor of Medicine (a university degree in medicine) 醫學學士（英國的大學醫學學位）： *Philip Watt MB* 醫學學士菲利普•瓦特

M

2 (in writing 書寫形式) MEGABYTE：*512MB of memory* * 512 兆內存

Mb (also **Mbit**) *abbr.* (in writing 書寫形式) MEGABIT

MBA /ˌem biː ˈeɪ/ *noun* the abbreviation for 'Master of Business Administration' (a second university degree in business) 工商管理碩士（全寫為 Master of Business Administration）：*to do an MBA* 攻讀工商管理學碩士學位

MBE /ˌem biː ˈiː/ *noun* the abbreviation for 'Member (of the Order) of the British Empire' (an award given to some people in Britain for a special achievement) 英帝國勳位獲得者，英帝國員佐勳銜獲得者（全寫為 Member (of the Order) of the British Empire，授予有特殊功勳者的獎章）：*She was made an MBE in 2007.* 她於 2007 年獲得英帝國勳位。◇ *Jim Cronin MBE* 英帝國勳位獲得者吉姆・克羅寧

MC /ˌem ˈsiː/ *noun* **1** the abbreviation for MASTER OF CEREMONIES 司儀，儀式主持人（全寫為 master of ceremonies）**2 M.C.** the abbreviation for 'Member of Congress' 議會議員，國會議員（全寫為 Member of Congress）**3** a person who speaks the words of a RAP song 說唱歌手

MCAT /ˈemkæt/ *abbr.* Medical College Admission Test (a test that students must pass in order to study medicine in the US)（美國）醫學院入學考試

Mc·Carthy·ism /məˈkɑːθiɪzəm; *NAmE* -ˈkɑːrθ-/ *noun* [U] an aggressive investigation during the 1950s against people in the US government and other institutions who were thought to be COMMUNISTS, in which many people lost their jobs 麥卡錫反共審查（20 世紀 50 年代在美國政府等機構中進行，很多人因此失業）

McCoy /məˈkɔɪ/ *noun*

IDM **the real Mc'Coy** (*informal*) something that is genuine and that has value, not a copy 真貨；真品：*It's an American flying jacket, the real McCoy.* 這是件真正的美國飛行員夾克。

ˈm-commerce *noun* [U] (*BrE, business* 商) the business of buying and selling products on the Internet by using mobile/cell phones and other similar technology 移動（電子）商務，行動商務（用手機等技術手段通過互聯網進行交易）：*m-tickets and other m-commerce products* 移動電子票務等移動業務產品

MD /ˌem ˈdiː/ *noun* **1** the abbreviation for 'Doctor of Medicine' 醫學博士（全寫為 Doctor of Medicine）：*Paul Clark MD* 醫學博士保羅・克拉克 **2** (*BrE*) the abbreviation for MANAGING DIRECTOR 總裁，總經理，常務董事（全寫為 managing director）：*Where's the MD's office?* 總經理辦公室在哪兒？

MDF /ˌem diː ˈef/ *noun* [U] the abbreviation for 'medium density fibreboard' (a building material made of wood or other plant FIBRES pressed together to form boards) 中密度纖維板（全寫為 medium density fibreboard，建築材料）

MDT /ˌem diː ˈtiː/ *abbr.* MOUNTAIN DAYLIGHT TIME 山區日光節約時間；山區夏令時間

ME /ˌem ˈiː/ *noun, abbr.*

■ **noun** (*BrE*) (also ˌ**chronic faˈtigue syndrome** *NAmE, BrE*) [U] the abbreviation for 'myalgic encephalomyelitis' (an illness that makes people feel extremely weak and tired and that can last a long time) 肌痛性腦脊髓炎（全寫為 myalgic encephalomyelitis）

■ **abbr.** (*NAmE*) MEDICAL EXAMINER

me 🔑 *pron., noun*

■ **pron.** 🔑 /mi; *strong form* miː/ the form of *I* that is used when the speaker or writer is the object of a verb or preposition, or after the verb *be*（I 的賓格）我：*Don't hit me.* 別打我。◇ *Excuse me!* 勞駕！◇ *Give it to me.* 給我。◇ *You're taller than me.* 你比我高。◇ *Hello, it's me.* 喂，是我。◇ *'Who's there?' 'Only me.'* "誰在那兒？" "只有我。" **HELP** The use of **me** in the last three examples is correct in modern standard English. **I** in these sentences would be considered much too formal for almost all contexts, especially in *BrE*. 後三例中 me 的用法符合現代英語的標準。若在這些句子中使用 I，幾乎在任何語境裏都會顯得過於正式，尤其是在英式英語中。

■ **noun** (also **mi**) /miː/ (*music* 音) the third note of a MAJOR SCALE 大調音階的第 3 音

mea culpa /ˌmeɪə ˈkʊlpə/ *exclamation* (from *Latin*, often *humorous*) used when you are admitting that sth is your fault 是我的錯；是我的責任

mead /miːd/ *noun* [U] a sweet alcoholic drink made from HONEY and water, drunk especially in the past（尤指舊時的）蜜糖酒，蜂蜜酒

meadow /ˈmedəʊ; *NAmE* -doʊ/ *noun* a field covered in grass, used especially for HAY 草地；牧場：*water meadows* (= near a river) 岸邊的草地 ➲ VISUAL VOCAB pages V2, V3

meadow·lark /ˈmedəʊlɑːk; *NAmE* -doʊlɑːrk/ *noun* a singing bird that lives on the ground 草地鷚（鳴禽，棲於地面）

meagre (*especially US* **mea·ger**) /ˈmiːɡə(r)/ *adj.* small in quantity and poor in quality 少量且劣質的 **SYN** **paltry**：*a meagre diet of bread and water* 只有麵包和水的簡樸飲食 ◇ *She supplements her meagre income by cleaning at night.* 她靠做夜間清潔工來補貼其微薄的收入。

More About 補充說明

meals

- People use the words **dinner**, **lunch**, **supper** and **tea** in different ways depending on which English-speaking country they come from. In Britain it may also depend on which part of the country or which social class a person comes from. 來自不同英語國家的人使用 dinner、lunch、supper 和 tea 的方式各不相同。在英國，這些詞的用法按某人來自的地區和社會階層而有所區別。
- A meal eaten in the middle of the day is usually called **lunch**. If it is the main meal of the day it may also be called **dinner** in *BrE*, especially in the north of the country. 午餐通常叫做 lunch，但在英式英語中，尤其在英國北部，如果是一天的主餐，亦可叫做 dinner。
- A main meal eaten in the evening is usually called **dinner**, especially if it is a formal meal. **Supper** is also an evening meal, but more informal than **dinner** and usually eaten at home. It can also be a late meal or something to eat and drink before going to bed. 晚上的主餐，尤其是正式用餐，通常叫做 dinner。supper 亦為晚餐，但不如 dinner 正式，而且一般在家裏吃，亦可指較晚的晚餐或睡前夜宵。
- In *BrE*, **tea** is a light meal in the afternoon with sandwiches, cakes, etc. and a cup of tea. 在英式英語中，tea 指下午的茶點，包括三明治、糕點等和一杯茶：*a cream tea* 奶油茶點 It can also be a main meal eaten early in the evening, especially by children. * tea 亦可指傍晚主餐，尤指孩子傍晚食用的：*What time do the kids have their tea?* 孩子們什麼時候用傍晚主餐？
- As a general rule, if **dinner** is the word someone uses for the meal in the middle of the day, they probably call the meal in the evening **tea** or **supper**. If they call the meal in the middle of the day **lunch**, they probably call the meal in the evening **dinner**. 一般說來，若午餐叫 dinner，晚餐則大多叫 tea 或 supper。如果午餐叫 lunch，晚餐則大多叫 dinner。
- **Brunch**, a combination of breakfast and lunch, is becoming more common, especially as a meal where your guests serve themselves. * brunch 是早餐和午餐合二為一的早午餐，如今日趨普遍，尤為自助餐形式。

meal 🔑 /miːl/ *noun*

1 🔑 [C] an occasion when people sit down to eat food, especially breakfast, lunch or dinner 早（或午、晚）餐；一頓飯：*Try not to eat between meals.* 兩餐之間盡量別吃東西。◇ *Lunch is his main meal of the day.* 午飯是他的正餐。◇ (*especially BrE*) *to* ***go out for a meal*** (= to

go to a restaurant to have a meal) 上館子用餐 ◇ *What time would you like your evening meal?* 你打算幾點鐘吃晚飯？ ➲ COLLOCATIONS at RESTAURANT **2** [C] the food that is eaten at a meal 一餐所吃的食物： *Enjoy your meal.* 請用餐。◇ *a three-course meal* 有三道菜的一頓飯 **3** [U] (often in compounds 常構成複合詞) grain that has been crushed to produce a powder, used as food for animals and for making flour 穀物粗粉（用作飼料或加工麵粉）➲ see also BONEMEAL, OATMEAL (1), WHOLEMEAL
IDM **make a 'meal of sth** (*informal*) to spend a lot of time, energy, etc. doing sth in a way that other people think is unnecessary and/or annoying 小題大做；做事過於認真 ➲ more at SQUARE *adj.*

meal·ie /'mi:li/ *noun* [C, usually pl., U] (*SAfrE*) **1** = MAIZE **2** = CORN ON THE COB

,meals on 'wheels *noun* [pl.] a service that takes meals to old or sick people in their homes （為老弱病殘者提供的）上門送餐服務

'meal ticket *noun* **1** (*informal*) a person or thing that you see only as a source of money and food 被視為金錢和食物來源的人（或物）： *He suspected that he was just a meal ticket for her.* 他感到對她來說自己不過是一張餐券。 **2** (*NAmE*) a card or ticket that gives you the right to have a cheap or free meal, for example at school 飯票；餐券

meal·time /'mi:ltaɪm/ *noun* a time in the day when you eat a meal 就餐時間；進餐時間

meal·worm /'mi:lwɜ:m; *NAmE* -wɜ:rm/ *noun* a LARVA which is used to feed pet birds 大黃粉蟲幼體（用作寵物鳥食）

mealy /'mi:li/ *adj.* (especially of vegetables or fruit 尤指蔬菜或水果) soft and dry when you eat them 乾軟的；麵的；吃起來鬆軟乾爽的

,mealy-'mouthed *adj.* (*disapproving*) not willing or honest enough to speak in a direct or open way about what you really think 不直爽的；說話拐彎抹角的： *mealy-mouthed politicians* 言不由衷的政客

mean 🔑 /mi:n/ *verb, adj., noun*

■ ***verb*** (**meant, meant** /ment/)

▸ **HAVE AS MEANING** 有含意 **1** 🔑 (not used in the progressive tenses 不用於進行時) to have sth as a meaning 表示…的意思： **~ sth** *What does this sentence mean?* 這個句子是什麼意思？◇ ***What is meant by** 'batch processing'?* * batch processing 是什麼意思？◇ **~ sth to sb** *Does the name 'Jos Vos' **mean anything to you*** (= do you know who he is)? 你知道喬斯 • 沃斯是誰嗎？◇ **~ (that) …** *The flashing light means (that) you must stop.* 閃爍的燈光表示你必須停下。

▸ **INTEND AS MEANING** 意思是 **2** 🔑 (not used in the progressive tenses 不用於進行時) to intend to say sth on a particular occasion 意思是；本意是： **~ sth** *What did he mean by that remark?* 他說那話是什麼意思？◇ *'Perhaps we should try another approach.' '**What do you mean?**'* (= I don't understand what you are suggesting.)' "也許我們應該試一試別的方法。" "你指的是什麼方法？" ◇ ***What do you mean**, you thought I wouldn't mind?* (= of course I mind and I am very angry) 你這是什麼意思？你以為我不會在意嗎？◇ ***What she means is** that there's no point in waiting here.* 她的意思是說在這兒等下去沒什麼意思。◇ *I always found him a little strange, **if you know what I mean*** (= if you understand what I mean by 'strange'). 我總覺得他有點兒怪，如果你明白我這話是什麼意思。◇ ***I know what you mean*** (= I understand and feel sympathy). *I hated learning to drive too.* 我明白你的意思。我也不願意學開車。◇ (*informal*) *It was like—weird. **Know what I mean?*** 它有點兒，怪異。你明白我的意思嗎？◇ ***I see what you mean*** (= I understand although I may not agree), *but I still think it's worth trying.* 我知道你是什麼意思，但我仍然認為值得一試。◇ ***See what I mean*** (= I was right and this proves it, doesn't it)? *She never agrees to anything I suggest.* 這下可證明我說的對了吧？我說什麼她都不聽。◇ *'But Pete doesn't know we're here!' '**That's what I mean!**'* (= that's what I have been trying to tell you.)' "可是皮特不知道我們在這兒呀！" "我就是這個意思嘛！" ◇ *Do you mean Ann Smith or Mary Smith?* 你是說安 • 史密斯，還是說瑪麗 • 史密斯？◇ **~ (that) …** *Did he mean (that) he was dissatisfied with our service?* 他是不是表示對我們的服務不滿意？◇ ***You mean*** (= are you telling me) *we have to start all over again?* 你是不是說我們必須從頭再來一遍？➲ LANGUAGE BANK at I.E.

▸ **HAVE AS PURPOSE** 有目的 **3** 🔑 to have sth as a purpose or intention 打算；意欲；有…的目的 **SYN** **intend**： **~ sth** *What did she mean by leaving so early* (= why did she do it)? 她為什麼這麼早就走了？◇ *Don't laugh! **I mean it*** (= I am serious). 別笑！我是認真的。◇ *He **means trouble*** (= to cause trouble). 他存心搗亂。◇ **~ sth as sth** *Don't be upset—I'm sure she meant it as a compliment.* 別不高興，我肯定她的原意是要稱讚你的。◇ **~ what …** *He **means what he says*** (= is not joking, exaggerating, etc.). 他說話是當真的。◇ **~ sth for sb/sth** *The chair was clearly meant for a child.* 這椅子顯然是專為兒童設計的。◇ *Don't be angry. I'm sure she **meant it for the best*** (= intended to be helpful). 別生氣了。我相信她是真心想要幫忙的。◇ **~ to do sth** *She means to succeed.* 她一意求成。◇ *I'm sorry I hurt you. **I didn't mean to.*** 對不起，弄疼你了。我不是故意的。◇ *I'm feeling very guilty—**I've been meaning** to call my parents for days, but still haven't got around to it.* 我感到非常內疚，幾天來我一直打算給父母打電話，但還是沒機會打。◇ **~ sb/sth to do sth** *I didn't mean you to read the letter.* 我沒打算讓你看那封信。◇ ***You're meant to*** (= you are supposed to) *pay before you go in.* 你要先交錢才能進去。◇ **~ (that) …** (*formal*) *I never meant (that) you should come alone.* 我從來沒打算讓你一個人來。

▸ **INTEND SB TO BE/DO STH** 讓某人成為 / 做 **4** 🔑 [often passive] to intend sb to be or do sth 想要某人成為；想要某人去做： **~ sb for sth/sb** *I **was never meant for** the army* (= did not have the qualities needed to become a soldier). 我根本就不是塊當兵的料。◇ *Duncan and Makiko **were meant for each other*** (= are very suitable as partners). 鄧肯和真紀子真是天生的一對。◇ **~ sb/sth to be sth** *His father meant him to be an engineer.* 他父親想讓他當工程師。◇ *She did everything to get the two of them together, but I guess it just wasn't **meant to be**.* 她極力撮合他們倆，但我覺得那根本不可能。

▸ **HAVE AS RESULT** 有結果 **5** 🔑 to have sth as a result or a likely result 產生…結果；意味着 **SYN** **entail**： **~ sth** *Spending too much now will mean a shortage of cash next year.* 現在花銷太多就意味着明年現金短缺。◇ **~ to be/do sth** *Do you have any idea **what it means to** be poor?* 你知不知道貧窮意味着什麼？◇ **~ (that) …** *We'll have to be careful with money but **that doesn't mean** (that) we can't enjoy ourselves.* 我們必須精打細算，可也並不是說我們就不能享受生活。◇ **~ doing sth** *This new order will mean working overtime.* 這新訂單一來，我們就得加班加點。◇ **~ sb/sth doing sth** *The injury could mean him missing next week's game.* 這次受傷可能使他無法參加下週的比賽。

▸ **BE IMPORTANT** 重要 **6** 🔑 [no passive] **~ sth to sb** to be of value or importance to sb 對某人重要（或有價值）： *Your friendship means a great deal to me.* 你的友誼對我來說是很珍貴的。◇ ***$20 means a lot*** (= represents a lot of money) *when you live on $100 a week.* 當你每週就靠 100 元維持生活時，20 元可是個大數目。◇ ***Money means nothing to him.*** 金錢對於他來說毫無價值。◇ *Her children **mean the world to her**.* 她的孩子就是她的一切。

IDM **be meant to be sth** 🔑 to be generally considered to be sth 被普遍認為是： *This restaurant is meant to be excellent.* 都說這家飯店很棒。 **I mean** 🔑 (*informal*) used to explain or correct what you have just said （解釋或更正剛說過的話）我是說，意思是說： *It was so boring—I mean, nothing happened for the first hour!* 真是無聊—我是說，一個小時都過去了，什麼事兒都沒發生！◇ *She's English—Scottish, I mean.* 她是英國人，更確切地說，她是蘇格蘭人。 **mean 'business** (*informal*) to be serious in your intentions 是認真的；說話算數： *He has the look of a man who means business.* 他看上去像是個說話算話的人。**mean (sb) no 'harm | not mean (sb) any 'harm** to not have any intention of hurting sb 沒有惡意；並非出於惡意 **mean to 'say** used to emphasize what you are saying or to ask sb if they really mean what they say（強調要說的話，或問對方是否真是這個意思）意思是說： *I mean to say, you should have known how he*

M

would react! 我的意思是説，你本應料到他會作何反應！◇ *Do you mean to say you've lost it?* 你是説你把那東西給弄丢了？ **'mean 'well** (usually *disapproving*) to have good intentions, although their effect may not be good 本意是好的；出於好心

■ *adj.* (**mean·er, mean·est**)

▸ **NOT GENEROUS** 吝嗇 **1** (*BrE*) (*NAmE* **cheap**) not willing to give or share things, especially money 吝嗇的；小氣的：*She's always been mean with money.* 她在花錢方面總是非常吝嗇。**OPP** **generous** ➲ see also STINGY

▸ **UNKIND** 不友善 **2** ~ (**to sb**) (of people or their behaviour 人或其行為) unkind, for example by not letting sb have or do sth 不善良；刻薄：*Don't be so mean to your little brother!* 別對你弟弟那麼刻薄！

▸ **ANGRY/VIOLENT** 憤怒；兇暴 **3** (*especially NAmE*) likely to become angry or violent 要發怒的；要發狂的：*That's a mean-looking dog.* 那狗看上去很兇。

▸ **SKILFUL** 熟練 **4** (*informal, especially NAmE*) very good and skilful 熟練的；出色的：*He's a mean tennis player.* 他是一名出色的網球選手。◇ *She plays a mean game of chess.* 她的國際象棋下得很棒。

▸ **AVERAGE** 平均 **5** [only before noun] (*technical* 術語) average; between the highest and the lowest, etc. 平均的；介於中間的：*the mean temperature* 平均氣溫

▸ **INTELLIGENCE** 智力 **6** (*formal*) (of a person's understanding or ability 人的理解力或能力) not very great 平庸的；一般的：*This should be clear even to the meanest intelligence.* 就是對智力最平庸的人來説，這也應當是非常明瞭的。

▸ **POOR** 低劣 **7** (*literary*) poor and dirty in appearance 低劣而骯髒的：***mean houses/streets*** 髒亂的房屋／街道 **8** (*old-fashioned*) born into or coming from a low social class 出身卑賤的；社會地位低下的

▸ **mean·ly** *adj.* **mean·ness** *noun* [U]

IDM **be no mean ...** (*approving*) used to say that sb is very good at doing sth 了不起；很出色：*His mother was a painter, and he's no mean artist himself.* 他的母親是畫家，他本人也是很出色的藝術家。

■ *noun* ➲ see also MEANS

▸ **MIDDLE WAY** 中間 **1** ~ (**between A and B**) a quality, condition, or way of doing sth that is in the middle of two extremes and better than either of them 中間；中庸；折衷：*He needed to find a mean between frankness and rudeness.* 他需要在坦誠與唐突之間找到折衷的方法。

▸ **AVERAGE** 平均 **2** (also **arith,metic 'mean**) (*mathematics* 數) the value found by adding together all the numbers in a group, and dividing the total by the number of numbers 平均數；平均值；算術中項 ➲ see also GEOMETRIC MEAN

IDM **the happy/golden 'mean** (*approving*) a course of action that is not extreme 中庸之道

me·ander /mi'ændə(r)/ *verb* **1** [I] (+ **adv./prep.**) (of a river, road, etc. 河流、道路等) to curve a lot rather than being in a straight line 蜿蜒而行；迂迴曲折：*The stream meanders slowly down to the sea.* 這條小河彎彎曲曲緩慢地流向大海。 **2** [I] (+ **adv./prep.**) to walk slowly and change direction often, especially without a particular aim 漫步；閒逛 **SYN** **wander 3** [I] (+ **adv./prep.**) (of a conversation, discussion, etc. 談話、討論等) to develop slowly and change subject often, in a way that makes it boring or difficult to understand（乏味地、令人費解地）漫談，閒聊 ▸ **me·ander** *noun*：*the meanders of a river* 河流的各處河曲 ➲ VISUAL VOCAB pages V4, V5

me·ander·ings /mi'ændrɪŋz/ *noun* [pl.] **1** a course that does not follow a straight line 蜿蜒曲折的路程：*the* ***meanderings of a river/path*** 曲折蜿蜒的一條河／小路 **2** walking or talking without any particular aim 漫步；閒逛；閒聊；漫話：*his philosophical meanderings* 他的哲學漫談

meanie (also **meany**) /'mi:ni/ *noun* (*pl.* **-ies**) (*informal*) used especially by children to describe an unkind person who will not give them what they want（兒童用語）小氣鬼，刻薄鬼

mean·ing 0-m /'mi:nɪŋ/ *noun, adj.*

■ *noun*

▸ **OF SOUND/WORD/SIGN** 聲音；文字；信號 **1** 0-m [U, C] ~ (**of sth**) the thing or idea that a sound, word, sign, etc. represents（聲音、文字、信號等傳遞的）意義，意思：*What's the meaning of this word?* 這個單詞的意思是什麼？◇ *Words often have several meanings.* 單詞往往有若干個意思。◇ *'Honesty'? He doesn't* ***know the meaning of the word!*** "誠實"？他不明白這個詞是什麼意思！

▸ **OF WHAT SB SAYS/DOES** 某人的言行 **2** 0-m [U, C] the things or ideas that sb wishes to communicate to you by what they say or do（想要表達的）意義，意思：*I don't quite* ***get your meaning*** (= understand what you mean to say). 我不太明白你要説的意思。◇ *What's the meaning of this? I explicitly told you not to leave the room.* 這是什麼意思？我明確地告訴過你不要離開這個房間。

▸ **OF FEELING/EXPERIENCE** 情感；經歷 **3** 0-m [U] the real importance of a feeling or experience 真正重要性；價值：*With Anna he learned the meaning of love.* 通過與安娜相處，他明白了愛意味着什麼。

▸ **OF BOOK/PAINTING** 書籍；繪畫 **4** 0-m [U, C] the ideas that a writer, artist, etc. wishes to communicate through a book, painting, etc.（作家或藝術家要表達的）意義，含義，思想：*several* ***layers of meaning*** 若干層意義◇ *There are, of course, deeper meanings in the poem.* 當然，這首詩裏還有更深層的含義。

▸ **SENSE OF PURPOSE** 追求的目標 **5** 0-m [U] the quality or sense of purpose that makes you feel that your life is valuable（人生的）意義，價值，目標：*Her life seemed to have lost all meaning.* 她的生活似乎已毫無價值。◇ *Having a child gave new meaning to their lives.* 有了孩子使他們的生活有了新的方向。

■ *adj.* [usually before noun] = MEANINGFUL (2)

mean·ing·ful /'mi:nɪŋfl/ *adj.* **1** serious and important 嚴肅的；重要的；重大的：*a* ***meaningful relationship/discussion/experience*** 重要的關係／討論／經歷 **2** (also *less frequent* **mean·ing**) intended to communicate or express sth to sb, without any words being spoken 意味深長的；意在言外的：*She gave me a* ***meaningful look.*** 她意味深長地看了我一眼。 **3** having a meaning that is easy to understand 意義明顯的；易於理解的：*These statistics are not very meaningful.* 這些統計數字説明不了什麼問題。 ▸ **mean·ing·ful·ly** /-fəli/ *adv.* **mean·ing·ful·ness** *noun* [U]

mean·ing·less /'mi:nɪŋləs/ *adj.* **1** without any purpose or reason and therefore not worth doing or having 毫無意義的；毫無目的的；無價值的 **SYN** **pointless**：*a meaningless existence* 毫無意義的存在◇ *We fill up our lives with meaningless tasks.* 我們終日忙忙碌碌，過得毫無意義。 **2** not considered important 不重要的；無所謂的 **SYN** **irrelevant**：*Fines are meaningless to a huge company like that.* 對於這樣一家大公司，罰金根本算不了什麼。 **3** not having a meaning that is easy to understand 意思不明確的；晦澀的：*To me that painting is completely meaningless.* 對我來説，這幅油畫晦澀難懂。 ▸ **mean·ing·less·ly** *adv.* **mean·ing·less·ness** *noun* [U]

means 0-m /mi:nz/ *noun* (*pl.* **means**)

1 0-m [C] ~ (**of sth/of doing sth**) an action, an object or a system by which a result is achieved; a way of achieving or doing sth 方式；方法；途徑：*Television is an effective means of communication.* 電視是一種有效的傳播途徑。◇ *Is there any means of contacting him?* 有沒有什麼辦法和他取得聯繫？◇ *Have you any* ***means of identification****?* 你有沒有任何身分證件？◇ *We needed to get to London but we had no* ***means of transport.*** 我們需要去倫敦，但卻沒有任何交通工具。 **2** [pl.] the money that a person has 財富；錢財：*People should pay* ***according to their means.*** 人們應該按照各自的負擔能力來消費。◇ *He doesn't have the means to support a wife and child.* 他無錢養活妻小。◇ *Private school fees are* ***beyond the means of most people*** (= more than they can afford). 私立學校的費用是大多數人無力支付的。◇ *Are the monthly repayments* ***within your means*** (= can you afford them)? 這樣按月還錢，你負擔得了嗎？◇ *Try to* ***live within your means*** (= not spend more money than you have). 要盡可能量入為出。◇ *a* ***man of means*** (= a rich man) 有錢人

IDM **by ˈall means** used to say that you are very willing for sb to have sth or do sth 可以；當然行；沒問題：*'Do you mind if I have a look?' 'By all means.'* "我看一眼行嗎？""當然可以。" **by means of sth** (*formal*) with the help of sth 借助…手段；依靠…方法：*The load was lifted by means of a crane.* 重物是用起重機吊起來的。 **by ˈno means | not by ˈany (manner of) means** not at all 決不；一點也不：*She is by no means an inexperienced teacher.* 她絕不是個毫無經驗的教師。◇ *We haven't won yet, not by any means.* 我們離成功還遠着呢。 **a ˌmeans to an ˈend** a thing or action that is not interesting or important in itself but is a way of achieving sth else（本身並不重要或有趣的）達到目的的手段：*He doesn't particularly like the work but he sees it as a means to an end.* 他不怎麼喜歡這項工作，只是把它看作達到目的的手段而已。➲ more at END *n.*, FAIR *adj.*, WAY *n.*

ˈmeans test *noun* an official check of sb's wealth or income in order to decide if they are poor enough to receive money from the government, etc. for a particular purpose 收入調查，經濟情況調查（以確定是否可領取政府補貼等）▶ **ˈmeans-test** *verb* **~ sb**

ˈmeans-tested *adj.* paid to sb according to the results of a means test 按收入調查結果支付的：*means-tested benefits* 按經濟情況調查結果支付的補助

meant *past tense, past part.* of MEAN

mean·time /ˈmiːntaɪm/ *noun, adv.*

■ ***noun***

IDM **for the ˈmeantime** (*BrE*) for a short period of time but not permanently 眼下；暫時：*I'm changing my email address but for the meantime you can use the old one.* 我要更換電郵地址，不過那個舊的暫時也還可以用。 **in the ˈmeantime** in the period of time between two times or two events 其間；同時 **SYN** **meanwhile**：*My first novel was rejected by six publishers. In the meantime I had written a play.* 我的第一部小說遭到六家出版商的拒絕。其間我又完成了一部戲劇。

■ ***adv.*** (*informal*) = MEANWHILE *adv.* (1), (2)：*I'll contact them soon. Meantime don't tell them I'm back.* 我會儘快和他們聯繫。在此期間，不要告訴他們我回來了。

mean·while /ˈmiːnwaɪl/ *adv., noun*

■ ***adv.*** **1** (also *informal* **mean·time**) while sth else is happening 同時；與此同時：*Bob spent fifteen months alone on his yacht. Ann, meanwhile, took care of the children on her own.* 鮑勃獨自在他的遊艇上待了十五個月。在這段時間，安一個人照顧孩子。 **2** (also *informal* **mean·time**) in the period of time between two times or two events 其間：*The doctor will see you again next week. Meanwhile, you must rest as much as possible.* 醫生下週還會給你看病。在此期間，你一定要盡可能多休息。 **3** used to compare two aspects of a situation（比較兩方面）對比之下：*Stress can be extremely damaging to your health. Exercise, meanwhile, can reduce its effects.* 壓力可能嚴重損害你的健康，鍛煉則可以減輕這些損害。

■ ***noun***

IDM **for the ˈmeanwhile** (*BrE*) for a short period of time but not permanently 一會兒；暫時：*We need some new curtains, but these will do for the meanwhile.* 我們需要一些新的窗簾，但這些暫時還可以用。 **in the ˈmeanwhile** in the period of time between two times or two events 在此期間；與此同時：*I hope to go to medical school eventually. In the meanwhile, I am going to study chemistry.* 我希望最終能上醫學院。這期間我打算學化學。

meany = MEANIE

mea·sles /ˈmiːzlz/ *noun* [U] an infectious disease, especially of children, that causes fever and small red spots that cover the whole body 麻疹 ➲ see also GERMAN MEASLES

measly /ˈmiːzli/ *adj.* (*informal, disapproving*) very small in size or quantity; not enough 很小的；很少的；不足的：*I get a measly £4 an hour.* 我每小時只拿少得可憐的 4 英鎊。

meas·ur·able /ˈmeʒərəbl/ *adj.* **1** that can be measured 可測量的；可度量的 **2** [usually before noun] large enough to be noticed or to have a clear and noticeable effect 顯著的；有明顯影響的：*measurable improvements* 顯著的改進 ▶ **meas·ur·ably** /-əbli/ *adv.*：*Working conditions have changed measurably in the last ten years.* 十年來，工作環境有了明顯的改變。

meas·ure /ˈmeʒə(r)/ *verb, noun*

■ ***verb***

▸ **SIZE/QUANTITY** 大小；數量 **1** to find the size, quantity, etc. of sth in standard units 測量；度量：**~ sth (in sth)** *A ship's speed is measured in knots.* 船速以節測量。◇ *a device that measures the level of radiation in the atmosphere* 測量大氣中輻射強度的儀器 ◇ ***measuring equipment/instruments*** 測量裝備／儀器 ◇ **~ sb/sth for sth** *He's gone to be measured for a new suit.* 他去量尺寸做新衣服去了。◇ **~ how much, how long, etc. ...** *A dipstick is used to measure how much oil is left in an engine.* 量油尺是用來探查引擎中的剩餘油量的。 **2** *linking verb* (not used in the progressive tenses 不用於進行時) **+ noun** to be a particular size, length, amount, etc.（指尺寸、長短、數量等）量度為：*The main bedroom measures 12ft by 15ft.* 主臥室寬 12 英尺，長 15 英尺。◇ *The pond measures about 2 metres across.* 這個池塘寬約 2 米。

▸ **JUDGE** 判斷 **3** **~ sth | ~ how, what, etc. ...** to judge the importance, value or effect of sth 估量，判定（重要性、價值或影響等）**SYN** **assess**：*It is difficult to measure the success of the campaign at this stage.* 在現階段還難以估量這場運動的成敗。

PHR V **ˈmeasure sb/sth against sb/sth** to compare sb/sth with sb/sth 使相比較：*The figures are not very good when measured against those of our competitors.* 和我們的競爭者相比，我們的數字並不樂觀。 **ˌmeasure sth↔ˈout** to take the amount of sth that you need from a larger amount 取出（或量出）所需量：*He measured out a cup of milk and added it to the mixture.* 他倒了一杯牛奶，摻了進去。 **ˌmeasure ˈup | ˌmeasure sb/sth↔ˈup** to measure sb/sth 測量；量度：*We spent the morning measuring up and deciding where the furniture would go.* 我們花了一上午量來量去，決定傢具怎麼擺。 **ˌmeasure ˈup (to sth/sb)** (usually used in negative sentences and questions 通常用於否定句和疑問句) to be as good, successful, etc. as expected or needed 達到預期的要求；符合標準 **SYN** **match up**：*Last year's intake just didn't measure up.* 去年納入的人數沒有達到預期的要求。◇ *The job failed to measure up to her expectations.* 這項工作沒有滿足她的期望。

■ ***noun***

▸ **OFFICIAL ACTION** 正式行動 **1** [C] an official action that is done in order to achieve a particular aim 措施；方法：***safety/security/austerity measures*** 安全／保安／緊縮措施 ◇ ***a temporary/an emergency measure*** 臨時／緊急措施 ◇ **~ (to do sth)** *We must take **preventive measures** to reduce crime in the area.* 我們必須採取預防措施來減少這個地區的犯罪。◇ *The government is introducing tougher measures to combat crime.* 政府正在引入更強硬的手段來打擊犯罪。◇ *measures against racism* 反種族主義措施 ◇ *Police in riot gear were in attendance as a **precautionary measure**.* 身着防暴服的警察到場戒備。➲ SYNONYMS at ACTION ➲ see also HALF MEASURES

▸ **UNIT OF SIZE/QUANTITY** 度量單位 **2** [C, U] a unit used for stating the size, quantity or degree of sth; a system or a scale of these units 度量單位；計量標準：*weights and measures* 度量衡 ◇ *The Richter Scale is a measure of ground motion.* 里氏震級是測量地動的單位。◇ ***liquid/dry measure*** 液量；乾量 ◇ *Which measure of weight do pharmacists use?* 藥劑師使用什麼劑量單位？ **3** [C] (especially of alcohol 尤指酒) a standard quantity 標準量：*a generous measure of whisky* 比標準量稍多一點的威士忌

▸ **AMOUNT** 程度 **4** [sing.] a particular amount of sth, especially a fairly large amount（一定的）量，程度 **SYN** **degree**：*A measure of technical knowledge is desirable in this job.* 做這項工作最好多懂一些技術知識。◇ *She achieved some measure of success with her first book.* 她出第一部書就得到了相當的成功。

▸ **INSTRUMENT FOR MEASURING** 測量儀器 **5** [C] an instrument such as a stick, a long tape or a container that is marked with standard units and is used for measuring 量器；計量工具 ➲ see also TAPE MEASURE

▸ **WAY OF SHOWING/JUDGING** 展示方式；判斷方法 **6** [sing.] a sign of the size or the strength of sth 尺度；標準；

M

程度： *Sending flowers is a measure of how much you care.* 送花能表明你有多關心。 **7** [C] a way of judging or measuring sth 判斷；衡量： *an accurate measure of ability* 能力的準確評判 ◇ *Is this test a good measure of reading comprehension?* 這種測試是判斷閱讀理解力的好方法嗎？

▸ **SUGGESTED NEW LAW** 法案 **8** [C] (*NAmE*) a written suggestion, especially one for a new law made by the lawmakers of a state（尤指州立法者的）提案，法案，議案：*a motion to refer the measure to another committee* 將提案提交給另一個委員會的動議 ◇ *a ballot measure* (= a change in the law that voters decide on) 投票表決的法案

▸ **IN MUSIC** 音樂 **9** (*NAmE*) (*BrE* **bar**) [C] one of the short sections of equal length that a piece of music is divided into, and the notes that are in it 小節（音樂節拍的單位）➲ picture at MUSIC

IDM **beyond 'measure** (*formal*) very much 非常；極其： *He irritated me beyond measure.* 他使我非常生氣。 **for good 'measure** as an extra amount of sth in addition to what has already been done or given 作為額外增添；外加的項目： *Use 50g of rice per person and an extra spoonful for good measure.* 按每人 50 克大米的分量，再額外加一勺。 **full/short 'measure** the whole of sth or less of sth than you expect or should have 足量；不足量： *We experienced the full measure of their hospitality.* 我們領受了他們十足的盛情。◇ *The concert only lasted an hour, so we felt we were getting short measure.* 音樂會僅僅持續了一個小時，讓我們有一種缺斤少兩的感覺。 **in full 'measure** (*formal*) to the greatest possible degree 最大程度地；最大限度地 **get/take/have the 'measure of sb | get/have/take sb's 'measure** (*formal*) to form an opinion about sb's character or abilities so that you can deal with them 摸清某人的底細： *After only one game, the chess champion had the measure of his young opponent.* 僅僅一局過後，這位國際象棋冠軍就摸清了年輕對手的實力。 **in no small 'measure | in some, equal, etc. 'measure** (*formal*) to a large extent or degree; to some, etc. extent or degree 在很大（或某種、同樣等）程度上： *The introduction of a new tax accounted in no small measure for the downfall of the government.* 這屆政府的垮台在很大程度上歸因於徵收一種新稅。◇ *Our thanks are due in equal measure to every member of the team.* 我們同樣感謝每一位隊員。 **,made to 'measure** (*BrE*) made especially for one person according to particular measurements 量身訂製的 **SYN** **bespoke**： *You'll need to get a suit made to measure.* 你得訂做一套西裝。◇ *a made-to-measure suit* 訂做的套裝 ➲ more at LARGE *adj.*

meas·ured /ˈmeʒəd; *NAmE* -ərd/ *adj.* [only before noun] slow and careful; controlled 緩慢謹慎的；慎重的；克制的： *She replied in a measured tone to his threat.* 她以很有分寸的語氣回應了他的威脅。◇ *He walked down the corridor with measured steps.* 他邁着緩慢而勻稱的腳步沿着走廊走去。

meas·ure·less /ˈmeʒələs; *NAmE* -ʒərl-/ *adj.* (*literary*) very great or without limits 極大的；無邊無際的： *the measureless oceans* 浩瀚的海洋

meas·ure·ment 0‑w /ˈmeʒəmənt; *NAmE* ˈmeʒərm-/ *noun*

1 0‑w [U] the act or the process of finding the size, quantity or degree of sth 測量；度量： *the metric system of measurement* 公制度量衡 ◇ *Accurate measurement is very important in science.* 在科學領域，精確的測量非常重要。 ➲ **COLLOCATIONS** at SCIENTIFIC **2** 0‑w [C, usually pl.] the size, length or amount of sth（某物的）尺寸，長度，數量：*to take sb's **chest/waist measurement*** 量某人的胸圍／腰圍 ◇ *Do you know your measurements* (= the size of parts of your body)? 你知道自己的尺寸嗎？◇ *The exact measurements of the room are 3 metres 20 by 2 metres 84.* 這間屋子的準確尺寸是長 3.20 米，寬 2.84 米。

'measuring cup *noun* a metal or plastic container used in the US for measuring quantities when cooking（美國烹飪用的）量杯 ➲ **VISUAL VOCAB** page V26

'measuring jug *noun* (*BrE*) a glass or plastic container for measuring liquids when cooking 量桶；量杯 ➲ **VISUAL VOCAB** page V26

'measuring spoon *noun* a metal or plastic spoon used in the US for measuring quantities when cooking（烹調用）量匙 ➲ **VISUAL VOCAB** page V26

'measuring tape *noun* = TAPE MEASURE

meat 0‑w /miːt/ *noun*

1 0‑w [U, C] the flesh of an animal or a bird eaten as food; a particular type of this 肉類；（某種）食用肉： *a **piece/slice of meat*** 一塊／一片肉 ◇ *horse meat* (= from a horse) 馬肉 ◇ *dog meat* (= for a dog) 餵狗的肉 ◇ *meat-eating animals* 食肉動物 ◇ *There's not much meat on this chop.* 這塊豬排沒什麼肉。◇ (*figurative, humorous*) *There's not much meat on her* (= she is very thin). 她太瘦了。 ➲ see also LUNCHEON MEAT, MINCEMEAT, RED MEAT, SAUSAGE MEAT, WHITE MEAT **2** [U] **~ (of sth)** the important or interesting part of sth 重要的部份；有趣的部份 **SYN** **substance**： *This chapter contains the real meat of the writer's argument.* 這一章包含了作者的主要論點。

IDM **,meat and 'drink to sb** something that sb enjoys very much 讓某人非常開心的事 ➲ more at DEAD *adj.*, MAN *n.*

,meat and po'tatoes *noun* [U] (*NAmE*) the most basic and important aspects or parts of sth 最基本的部份；最必要的部份： *Issues like this are the newspaper's meat and potatoes.* 像這樣的課題是報紙賴以生存的素材。

,meat-and-po'tatoes *adj.* [only before noun] (*NAmE*) **1** dealing with the most basic and important aspects of sth 根本的；基本的；主要的： *a meat-and-potatoes argument* 基本論據 **2** liking plain, simple things 喜歡簡樸的： *He's a real meat-and-potatoes guy.* 他是個十分崇尚簡樸的人。

,meat and two 'veg *noun* [U] (*BrE, informal*) a dish of meat with potatoes and another vegetable, considered as typical traditional British food 燉肉雙素（雙素之一為土豆，典型的傳統英國菜）

meat·ball /ˈmiːtbɔːl/ *noun* a small ball of finely chopped meat, usually eaten hot with a sauce 肉丸

'meat grinder *noun* (*NAmE*) = MINCER

,meat 'loaf *noun* [C, U] finely chopped meat, onions, etc. that are mixed together and shaped like a LOAF of bread and then baked 烤肉末條

'meat packing *noun* [U] (*NAmE*) the process of killing animals and preparing the meat for sale 肉類加工

meaty /ˈmiːti/ *adj.* (**meat·ier**, **meati·est**) **1** containing a lot of meat 含肉多的 **2** smelling, or tasting like meat 氣味（或味道）像肉的： *a meaty taste* 肉香的口味 **3** (*approving*) containing a lot of important or interesting ideas 富含重要（或有趣）的觀點的 **SYN** **substantial**： *a meaty discussion* 內容充實的討論 **4** (*informal*) large and fat; with a lot of flesh 肥碩的；多肉的 **SYN** **fleshy**： *a meaty hand* 肥胖的手 ◇ *big, meaty tomatoes* 又大又多肉的西紅柿

mebi·bit /ˈmebibɪt/ *noun* (*abbr.* **Mib**, **Mibit**) (*computing* 計) = MEGABIT (2)

mebi·byte /ˈmebibaɪt/ *noun* (*abbr.* **MiB**) (*computing* 計) = MEGABYTE (2)

Mecca /ˈmekə/ *noun* **1** a city in Saudi Arabia that is the holiest city of Islam, being the place where the Prophet Muhammad was born 麥加（沙特阿拉伯城市，伊斯蘭教聖地，先知穆罕默德出生地）**2** (usually **mecca**) a place that many people like to visit, especially for a particular reason 熱門地方： *The coast is a mecca for tourists.* 這個海岸是旅遊的熱門景點。

mech·an·ic /məˈkænɪk/ *noun* **1** [C] a person whose job is repairing machines, especially the engines of vehicles 機械師；機械修理工；技工： *a car mechanic* 汽車修理工 **2 mechanics** [U] the science of movement and force 力學 ➲ see also QUANTUM MECHANICS **3 mechanics** [U] the practical study of machinery 機械學： *the school's car maintenance department where students learn basic mechanics* 該校學生可以學習基礎機械學的汽車保養系 **4 the mechanics** [pl.] the way sth works or is done 方法；手段： *The exact mechanics of how payment will*

M

be made will be decided later. 確切的付款方法以後再作決定。

mech·an·ic·al /mə'kænɪkl/ *adj.* **1** operated by power from an engine 機動的；機械驅動的；機械的：*a* ***mechanical device/toy/clock*** 機械裝置 / 玩具 / 鐘錶◇ *mechanical parts* 機械部件 **2** connected with machines and engines 機器的；機械的；發動機的：***mechanical problems/defects*** 機械問題 / 缺陷◇ *The breakdown was due to a mechanical failure.* 拋錨是機械故障造成的。 **3** (*disapproving*) (of people's behaviour and actions 人的行為或行動) done without thinking, like a machine 機械般的；呆頭呆腦的；無思想的 SYN **routine**：*a* ***mechanical gesture/response*** 機械式的手勢 / 回答 **4** connected with the physical laws of movement and cause and effect (= with MECHANICS) 機械的；機械學的：*mechanical processes* 機械過程 **5** (of a person 人) good at understanding how machines work 擅長於機械原理的 ▶ **mech·an·ic·al·ly** /-kli/ *adv.*：*a mechanically powered vehicle* 機械驅動的交通工具◇ *She spoke mechanically, as if thinking of something else.* 她機械地說着話，彷彿在想着什麼別的事情。◇ *He's always been mechanically minded.* 他思想一向很僵化。

me,chanical engi'neering *noun* [U] the study of how machines are designed, built and repaired 機械工程學 ▶ **me,chanical engi'neer** *noun*

mech·an·ism AW /'mekənɪzəm/ *noun* **1** a set of moving parts in a machine that performs a task 機械裝置；機件：*a delicate watch mechanism* 精緻的手錶機件 **2** a method or a system for achieving sth 方法；機制：*mechanisms for dealing with complaints from the general public* 處理公眾投訴的機制 **3** a system of parts in a living thing that together perform a particular function （生物體內的）機制，構造：*the balance mechanism in the ears* 耳內的平衡機制◇ *Pain acts as a natural* ***defence mechanism.*** 疼痛起着自然防護機制的作用。

mech·an·is·tic /,mekə'nɪstɪk/ *adj.* (often *disapproving*) connected with the belief that all things in the universe can be explained as if they were machines 機械論的：*the mechanistic philosophy that compares the brain to a computer* 將人腦比作電腦的機械論哲學 ▶ **mech·an·is·ti·cal·ly** /-kli/ *adv.*

mech·an·ize (*BrE* also **-ise**) /'mekənaɪz/ *verb* [usually passive] **~ sth** to change a process, so that the work is done by machines rather than people 機械化；使機械化 SYN **automate**：*The production process is now highly mechanized.* 現在的生產過程高度機械化。 ▶ **mech·an·iza·tion, -isa·tion** /,mekənaɪ'zeɪʃn; *NAmE* -nə'z-/ *noun* [U]：*the increasing mechanization of farm work* 農活機械化的程度越來越高

Med /med/ **the Med** *noun* [sing.] (*informal*) the Mediterranean Sea 地中海

med /med/ *adj.* (*informal, especially NAmE*) = MEDICAL：*a med student* 醫學系的學生◇ *She's in med school.* 她在唸醫學。

medals 獎章 **shield** 盾形獎牌 **trophy** 獎座 **rosette** 玫瑰形飾物 **cup** 獎盃

medal /'medl/ *noun, verb*

■ ***noun*** a flat piece of metal, usually shaped like a coin, that is given to the winner of a competition or to sb who has been brave, for example in war 獎章；勳章：*to win a gold medal in the Olympics* 在奧林匹克運動會上贏得一枚金牌◇ *to award a medal for bravery* 獎賞一枚英勇勳章 IDM see DESERVE

■ ***verb*** (**-ll-**, *especially US* **-l-**) [I] to win a medal in a competition （在比賽中）獲得獎牌（或獎章）：*Evans has medalled at several international events.* 埃文斯已經多次在國際比賽中獲獎。

med·al·lion /mə'dæliən/ *noun* a piece of jewellery in the shape of a large flat coin worn on a chain around the neck （狀似大獎章的）項鏈垂飾 ⊃ VISUAL VOCAB page V65

med·al·list (*BrE*) (*US* **med·al·ist**) /'medəlɪst/ *noun* a person who has received a medal, usually for winning a competition in a sport （通常指體育比賽的）獎牌獲得者：*an Olympic medallist* 奧運會獎牌獲得者◇ *a* ***gold/silver/bronze medallist*** 金牌 / 銀牌 / 銅牌獲得者

,Medal of 'Freedom *noun* the highest award that the US gives to a CIVILIAN who has achieved sth very important 自由勳章（美國授予有傑出成就公民的最高獎賞）

,Medal of 'Honor *noun* the highest award that the US gives to a member of the armed forces who has shown very great courage in a war 榮譽勳章（美國授予英勇軍人的最高獎賞）

'medal play *noun* [U] = STROKE PLAY

med·dle /'medl/ *verb* (*disapproving*) **1** [I] **~ (in/with sth)** to become involved in sth that does not concern you 管閒事；干涉；干預 SYN **interfere**：*He had no right to meddle in her affairs.* 他無權干涉她的事情。 **2** [I] **~ (with sth)** to touch sth in a careless way, especially when it is not yours or when you do not know how to use it correctly 瞎搞，亂弄（尤指不應管或不懂的事物）：*Somebody had been meddling with her computer.* 有人擅自弄過她的電腦。 ▶ **med·dling** *noun* [U]

med·dler /'medlə(r)/ *noun* (*disapproving*) a person who tries to get involved in sth that does not concern them 管閒事的人 SYN **busybody**

meddle·some /'medlsəm/ *adj.* (*disapproving*) (of people 人) enjoying getting involved in situations that do not concern them 好管閒事的；愛干預的 SYN **interfering**

mede·vac /'medɪvæk/ *noun* [U] (*especially NAmE*) the movement of injured soldiers or other people to hospital in a HELICOPTER or other aircraft（傷員等的）空運救護，飛行送院 ⊃ compare AIR AMBULANCE

media 0➝ AW /'mi:diə/ *noun*

1 0➝ **the media** [U+sing./pl. v.] the main ways that large numbers of people receive information and entertainment, that is television, radio, newspapers and the Internet 大眾傳播媒介，大眾傳播工具（指電視、廣播、報紙、互聯網）：*the* ***news/broadcasting/national media*** 新聞 / 廣播 / 國家的大眾傳播媒介◇ *The trial was fully reported in the media.* 媒體對這次審判進行了全面報道。◇ *The media was/were accused of influencing the final decision.* 媒體受責左右了終審判決。◇ *Any event attended by the actor received widespread* ***media coverage.*** 這位演員參加任何一項活動，媒體都作了廣泛報道。 ⊃ see also MASS MEDIA, NEW MEDIA **2** *pl.* of MEDIUM

medi·aeval = MEDIEVAL

med·ial /'mi:diəl/ *adj.* (*technical* 術語) located in the middle, especially of the body or of an organ （身體或器官等）內側的，近中的

me·dian /'mi:diən/ *adj., noun*

■ ***adj.*** [only before noun] (*technical* 術語) **1** having a value in the middle of a series of values 中間值的；中間的：*the* ***median age/price*** 中年；中等價位 **2** located in or passing through the middle 在中間的；通過中點的：*a* ***median point/line*** 中點 / 線

■ ***noun*** **1** (*mathematics* 數) the middle value of a series of numbers arranged in order of size 中位數 **2** (*geometry*

幾何）a straight line passing from a point of a triangle to the centre of the opposite side（三角形的）中線 **3** (also **'median strip**) (both *NAmE*) (*BrE* **,central re'ser'vation**) a narrow strip of land that separates the two sides of a major road such as a MOTORWAY or INTERSTATE（高速公路、州際公路等的）中央隔離帶

'media studies *noun* [U+sing./pl. v.] the study of newspapers, television, radio, etc. as a subject at school, etc. 大眾傳播學；大眾傳媒學

me·di·ate AW /'miːdieɪt/ *verb* **1** [I, T] to try to end a disagreement between two or more people or groups by talking to them and trying to find things that everyone can agree on 調停；調解；斡旋：**~ (in sth)** *The Secretary-General was asked to mediate in the dispute.* 有人請秘書長來調解這次紛爭。◇ **~ between A and B** *An independent body was brought in to mediate between staff and management.* 由一個獨立機構介入，在勞資之間進行調解。◇ **~ sth** *to* ***mediate differences/disputes/problems*** 調解分歧／爭端／問題 **2** [T] **~ sth** to succeed in finding a solution to a disagreement between people or groups 找到（解決分歧的）方法；促成…的解決 SYN **negotiate**：*They mediated a settlement.* 他們找到了一個解決方案。 **3** [T, usually passive] **~ sth** (*formal* or *technical* 術語) to influence sth and/or make it possible for it to happen 影響…的發生；使…可能發生：*Educational success is mediated by economic factors.* 經濟因素影響着教育的成功。▸ **me·di·ation** AW /,miːdi'eɪʃn/ *noun* [U]

me·di·ator /'miːdieɪtə(r)/ *noun* a person or an organization that tries to get agreement between people or groups who disagree with each other 調停者；斡旋者；解決紛爭的人（或機構）

M

medic /'medɪk/ *noun* **1** (*informal, especially BrE*) a medical student or doctor 醫科學生；醫生；大夫 **2** (*NAmE*) a person who is trained to give medical treatment, especially sb in the armed forces（尤指軍隊中的）救護人員，護理人員

Me·dic·aid /'medɪkeɪd/ *noun* [U] (in the US) the insurance system that provides medical care for poor people 醫療援助制度（美國政府向貧困者提供醫療保險）

med·ic·al 🔑 AW /'medɪkl/ *adj., noun*

■ ***adj.*** [usually before noun] **1** 🔑 connected with illness and injury and their treatment 傷病的；疾病的；醫療的：***medical advances/care/research*** 醫學上的進展；醫療；醫學研究 ◇ *her* ***medical condition/history/records*** 她的病理狀況／病史／病歷 ◇ *the* ***medical profession*** 醫療職業 ◇ *a* ***medical student/school*** 醫科學生；醫學院 ◇ *a medical certificate* (= a statement by a doctor that gives details of your state of health) 健康證明 ➲ see also MED **2** connected with ways of treating illness that do not involve cutting the body 內科的：*medical or surgical treatment* 內科或外科療法 ▸ **med·ic·al·ly** AW /-kli/ *adv.*：***medically fit/unfit*** 體格健康／不佳

■ ***noun*** (also **,medical exami'nation**) a thorough examination of your body that a doctor does, for example, before you start a particular job 體格檢查 ➲ see also EXAM *n.* (2)

,medical e'xaminer *noun* (*abbr.* **ME**) (*NAmE*) a doctor whose job is to examine a dead body in order to find out the cause of death 法醫；驗屍官 ➲ compare PATHOLOGIST

'medical hall *noun* (*IndE, informal*) a chemist's shop/drugstore 藥店；藥房

'medical officer *noun* (*abbr.* **MO**) a person, usually a doctor, employed in an organization to deal with medical and health matters 衛生人員；衛生幹事；（某機構的）專職醫生

'medical school (*NAmE* also **'med school**, *informal*) *noun* a college where students study to obtain a degree in medicine 醫學院

Medi·care /'medɪkeə(r); *NAmE* -ker/ *noun* [U] **1** (in the US) the federal insurance system that provides medical care for people over 65 醫療保障制度，老年保健醫療制度（美國政府向 65 歲以上的人提供醫療保險） **2** (in Australia and Canada) the national medical care system for all people that is paid for by taxes (spelt 'medicare' in Canada) 醫療保健制度（澳大利亞和加拿大政府為所有國民而設，資源來自稅收；加拿大拼寫為 medicare）

medi·cate /'medɪkeɪt/ *verb* **~ sb** to give sb medicine, especially a drug that affects their behaviour 給…用藥（尤指影響行為的藥物）；用藥物治療

medi·cated /'medɪkeɪtɪd/ *adj.* containing a substance for preventing or curing infections of your skin or hair 藥物的，含藥的（用於防治皮膚或頭髮感染）：***medicated shampoo/soap*** 藥物洗髮液／肥皂

medi·ca·tion /,medɪ'keɪʃn/ *noun* [U, C] a drug or another form of medicine that you take to prevent or to treat an illness 藥；藥物：*to be* ***on medication*** 進行藥物治療 ◇ *Are you currently taking any medication?* 你在服用什麼藥嗎？◇ *Many flu medications are available without a prescription.* 許多流感藥不用處方就可以買到。➲ COLLOCATIONS at ILL

me·di·cin·al /mə'dɪsɪnl/ *adj.* helpful in the process of healing illness or infection 有療效的；藥用的；藥的：***medicinal herbs/plants*** 草藥；藥用植物 ◇ ***medicinal properties/use*** 藥性；藥用 ◇ (*humorous*) *He claims he keeps a bottle of brandy only* ***for medicinal purposes.*** 他說他存放着一瓶白蘭地只是為了藥用。

medi·cine 🔑 /'medsn; -dɪsn/ *noun*

1 🔑 [U] the study and treatment of diseases and injuries 醫學：*advances in modern medicine* 現代醫學的發展 ◇ *to* ***study/practise medicine*** 學醫；行醫 ◇ ***traditional/conventional/orthodox medicine*** 傳統／常規／正統醫學 ◇ ***alternative medicine*** 替代療法 ➲ see also AYURVEDIC MEDICINE, DEFENSIVE MEDICINE **2** 🔑 [U, C] a substance, especially a liquid that you drink or swallow in order to cure an illness 藥；（尤指）藥水：*Did you take your medicine?* 你吃過藥了嗎？◇ *cough medicine* 咳嗽藥 ◇ *Chinese herbal medicines* 中國草藥 ➲ COLLOCATIONS at ILL

IDM **the best 'medicine** the best way of improving a situation, especially of making you feel happier（改進狀況的）最佳方法；（尤指）除去心病的良方：*Laughter is the best medicine.* 歡笑是一副良藥。 **a taste/dose of your own 'medicine** the same bad treatment that you have given to others 自己曾給別人的苦頭：*Let the bully have a taste of his own medicine.* 讓那個惡棍得到報應吧。

'medicine ball *noun* a large heavy ball which is thrown and caught as a form of exercise 健身實心球

'medicine man *noun* a person who is believed to have special magic powers of healing, especially among Native Americans 巫醫（尤指美洲土著）➲ compare WITCH DOCTOR

med·ico /'medɪkəʊ; *NAmE* -koʊ/ *noun* (*pl.* **-os**) (*informal*) a doctor 醫生；大夫

medi·eval (also **medi·aeval**) /,medi'iːvl; *NAmE* also ,miːd-/ *adj.* [usually before noun] connected with the Middle Ages (about AD 1000 to AD 1450) 中世紀的（約公元 1000 到 1450 年）：*medieval architecture/castles/manuscripts* 中世紀的建築／城堡／手稿 ◇ *the literature of the late medieval period* 中世紀後期的文學

me·di·ocre /,miːdi'əʊkə(r); *NAmE* -'oʊkər/ *adj.* (*disapproving*) not very good; of only average standard 平庸的；普通的；平常的：*a mediocre musician/talent/performance* 平庸的音樂家／才能／表演 ◇ *I thought the play was only mediocre.* 我認為這部戲劇只是平庸之作。

me·di·oc·rity /,miːdi'ɒkrəti; *NAmE* -'ɑːk-/ *noun* (*pl.* **-ies**) (*disapproving*) **1** [U] the quality of being average or not very good 平庸；普通；平常：*His acting career started brilliantly, then sank into mediocrity.* 他的演藝生涯開場時轟轟烈烈，然後就變得庸庸碌碌。 **2** [C] a person who is not very good at sth 平庸之人；碌碌無為者：*a brilliant leader, surrounded by mediocrities* 周圍全是些庸才的傑出領導

medi·tate /'medɪteɪt/ *verb* **1** [I] **~ (on/upon sth)** to think deeply, usually in silence, especially for religious reasons or in order to make your mind calm 冥想；沉思 **2** [T] **~ sth** (*formal*) to plan sth in your mind; to consider doing sth 暗自策劃；考慮；謀劃 SYN **contemplate**：*They were meditating revenge.* 他們在謀劃進行報復。

medi·ta·tion /ˌmedɪˈteɪʃn/ *noun* **1** [U] the practice of thinking deeply in silence, especially for religious reasons or in order to make your mind calm 冥想；沉思；深思：*She found peace through yoga and meditation.* 她通過瑜伽和冥想找到了寧靜。◇ *He was deep **in meditation** and didn't see me come in.* 他正在沉思，沒有看見我進來。 **2** [C, usually pl.] **~ (on sth)** (*formal*) serious thoughts on a particular subject that sb writes down or speaks 沉思錄：*his meditations on life and art* 他對生活和藝術的沉思錄

medi·ta·tive /ˈmedɪtətɪv; *NAmE* -teɪt-/ *adj.* (*formal*) thinking very deeply; involving deep thought 深思的；陷入沉思的 SYN **thoughtful**：*She found him in a meditative mood.* 她發現他正在沉思。◇ *a meditative poem* 一首冥想詩

Medi·ter·ra·nean /ˌmedɪtəˈreɪniən/ *adj.* [only before noun] connected with the Mediterranean Sea or the countries and regions that surround it; typical of this area 地中海的：*a Mediterranean country* 地中海國家 ◇ *a Mediterranean climate* 地中海氣候

me·dium 0‑▬ AW /ˈmiːdiəm/ *adj., noun*

■ ***adj.*** 0‑▬ [usually before noun] (*abbr.* **M**) in the middle between two sizes, amounts, lengths, temperatures, etc. 中等的；中號的 SYN **average**：*a **medium-size** car/business/town* 中型汽車/企業；中等城鎮 ◇ *a man of **medium height/build*** 中等身材的人 ◇ *There are three sizes—small, medium and large.* 有三種尺寸——小號、中號和大號。◇ *Cook over a medium heat for 15 minutes.* 用中火煮 15 分鐘。◇ *a **medium dry** white wine* 中度乾白葡萄酒 ◇ *Choose **medium to large** tomatoes.* 挑選個頭中等到大個的西紅柿。 IDM see TERM *n.*

■ ***noun*** (*pl.* **media** /ˈmiːdiə/ or **me·diums**) **1** 0‑▬ a way of communicating information, etc. to people （傳播信息的）媒介，手段，方法：*the **medium of** radio/television* 廣播/電視媒介 ◇ ***electronic/audio-visual media*** 電子/視聽媒體 ◇ *Television is the modern **medium of communication**.* 電視是現代傳媒。◇ *A T-shirt can be an excellent medium for getting your message across.* * T 恤衫可以成為一種極好的表達信息的媒介。 HELP The plural in this meaning is usually **media**. 此義的複數形式通常為 media。 ➲ see also MEDIA, MASS MEDIA **2** 0‑▬ something that is used for a particular purpose 手段；工具；方法：*English is the **medium of instruction*** (= the language used to teach other subjects). 用英語進行教學。◇ *Video is a good medium for learning a foreign language.* 錄像是一種學習外語的好方法。 **3** the material or the form that an artist, a writer or a musician uses （文藝創作中使用的）材料，形式：*the **medium of** paint/poetry/drama* 繪畫/詩歌/戲劇的表現手法 ◇ *Watercolour is his favourite medium.* 水彩畫是他最喜歡的表現方式。 **4** (*biology* 生) a substance that sth exists or grows in or that it travels through 介質；培養基；環境：*The bacteria were growing in a sugar medium.* 細菌在糖基中生長。 **5** (*pl.* **me·diums**) a person who claims to be able to communicate with the spirits of dead people 通靈的人；靈媒；巫師 IDM see HAPPY

ˈmedium-sized *adj.* of average size 中等大小的；中型的；中號的：*a medium-sized saucepan* 中號的鍋

ˈmedium-term *adj.* used to describe a period of time that is a few weeks or months into the future 中期的：*the government's medium-term financial strategy* 政府的中期金融策略

ˈmedium wave (*abbr.* **MW**) *noun* [U] (also **the medium wave** [sing.]) a band of radio waves with a length of between 100 and 1 000 metres 中波（波長 100 到 1 000 米）：*648 m on (the) medium wave* 中波 648 米 ➲ compare SHORT WAVE

med·lar /ˈmedlə(r)/ *noun* a brownish fruit which is eaten when it has started to decay and become soft 歐楂果（開始凋萎時方能食用）

med·ley /ˈmedli/ *noun* **1** a piece of music consisting of several songs or tunes played or sung one after the other 混成曲（多首聲樂曲或器樂曲串聯在一起）：*a medley of Beatles hits* 披頭士樂隊歌曲大聯唱 **2** a mixture of people or things of different kinds 混雜物；混合物；混雜的人群：*a **medley of** flavours/smells* 各種味道/氣味混合在一起 **3** a swimming race in which each member of a team uses a different stroke 混合泳接力：*the 4×100 metres medley* * 4×100 米混合泳接力

ˈmed school *noun* (*NAmE, informal*) = MEDICAL SCHOOL

meek /miːk/ *adj.* (**meek·er**, **meek·est**) **1** quiet, gentle, and always ready to do what other people want without expressing your own opinion 溫順的；謙恭的；馴服的 SYN **compliant, self-effacing**：*They called her Miss Mouse because she was so **meek and mild**.* 他們稱她為"鼠小姐"，因為她總是那麼懦弱謙和。 **2 the meek** *noun* [pl.] people who are meek 溫順的人；謙恭的人 ▸ **meek·ly** *adv.*：*He meekly did as he was told.* 他溫順地聽從吩咐。 **meek·ness** *noun* [U]

meer·kat /ˈmɪəkæt; *NAmE* ˈmɪr-/ *noun* a small southern African animal with a long tail, which often stands up on its back legs. Meerkats are a type of MONGOOSE. 海貓

meet 0‑▬ /miːt/ *verb, noun*

■ ***verb*** (**met**, **met** /met/)

▸ BY CHANCE 偶然地 **1** 0‑▬ [I, T, no passive] to be in the same place as sb by chance and talk to them 相遇；相逢；遇見：*Maybe we'll meet again some time.* 說不定我們什麼時候還會再見面。◇ **~ sb** *Did you meet anyone in town?* 你在城裏碰見什麼人了嗎？

▸ BY ARRANGEMENT 通過安排 **2** 0‑▬ [I, T, no passive] to come together formally in order to discuss sth 開會；會晤：*The committee meets on Fridays.* 委員會每週五開會。◇ **~ sb** *The Prime Minister met other European leaders for talks.* 首相與其他歐洲首腦舉行會談。◇ **~ with sb** *The President met with senior White House aides.* 總統會見了白宮的高級幕僚。 **3** 0‑▬ [I, T, no passive] to come together socially after you have arranged it（與…）會面；集合：**~ (for sth)** *Let's meet for a drink after work.* 下班後我們一起去喝一杯吧。◇ **~ sb (for sth)** *We're meeting them outside the theatre at 7.* 我們 7 點鐘在劇院外面和他們會合。 **4** 0‑▬ [T] **~ sb/sth** to go to a place and wait there for a particular person to arrive 迎接：*Will you meet me at the airport?* 你到機場接我好嗎？◇ *The hotel bus meets all incoming flights.* 酒店有車在機場迎接各航班的旅客。◇ *I met him off the plane.* 他下飛機後我就接到了他。

▸ FOR THE FIRST TIME 初次 **5** 0‑▬ [T, no passive, I] **~ (sb)** to see and know sb for the first time; to be introduced to sb 相識；結識；被引見介紹（給某人）：*Where did you first meet your husband?* 你是在哪兒和你丈夫初次相識的？◇ (*especially BrE*) ***Pleased to meet you.*** 很高興認識你。◇ (*NAmE*) ***Nice meeting you.*** 很高興認識你。◇ *There's someone I want you to meet.* 我想介紹你認識一個人。◇ *I don't think we've met.* 我想我們沒見過面吧。

▸ IN CONTEST 比賽 **6** [I, T, no passive] to play, fight, etc. together as opponents in a competition 遭遇；交鋒：*Smith and Jones met in last year's final.* 史密斯和瓊斯在去年的決賽中相遇。◇ **~ sb** *Smith met Jones in last year's final.* 在去年的決賽中，史密斯與瓊斯交鋒。

▸ EXPERIENCE STH 經歷 **7** [T] **~ sth** to experience sth, often sth unpleasant 經歷（常指不愉快的事）：*Others have met similar problems.* 其他人遇到過同樣的問題。◇ *How she **met her death** will probably never be known.* 她的死因也許永遠無人知曉。 SYN **come across, encounter**

▸ TOUCH/JOIN 接觸；連接 **8** [I, T] to touch sth; to join 接觸（某物）；連接：*The curtains don't meet in the middle.* 這窗簾中間合不攏。◇ **~ sth** *That's where the river meets the sea.* 這條河就在這裏流入大海。◇ *His hand met hers.* 他的手碰到她的手。

▸ SATISFY 滿足 **9** [T] **~ sth** to do or satisfy what is needed or what sb asks for 滿足；使滿意 SYN **fulfil**：*How can we best **meet the needs** of all the different groups?* 我們怎樣才能最好地滿足各種人的需要呢？◇ *Until these **conditions are met** we cannot proceed with the sale.* 除非這些條件得到滿足，否則我們不能繼續這項交易。◇ *I can't possibly meet that deadline.* 我不可能如期完成。

▸ PAY 支付 **10** [T] **~ sth** to pay sth 支付；償付：*The cost **will be met** by the company.* 費用將由公司支付。

IDM **meet sb's ˈeye(s)** | **meet sb's ˈgaze, ˈlook, etc.** | **people's ˈeyes meet** **1** [T, I] if you **meet sb's eye(s)**, you look directly at them as they look at you; if two

M

people's **eyes meet**, they look directly at each other（和某人）對視，目光相遇：*She was afraid to meet my eye.* 她不敢正眼看我。◇ *Their eyes met across the crowded room.* 他們隔着擁擠的房間目光相遇了。◇ *She met his gaze without flinching.* 她毫不畏縮地與他對視。 **2** [T] **~ your eyes** if a sight **meets your eyes**, you see it 呈現；顯現：*A terrible sight met their eyes.* 一幅可怕的景象映入他們的眼簾。 **meet sb half'way** to reach an agreement with sb by giving them part of what they want 和某人妥協；對某人作出讓步 **meet your 'Maker** (especially *humorous*) to die 死；見上帝 **there is more to sb/sth than meets the 'eye** a person or thing is more complicated or interesting than you might think at first 某人（或物）比料想的更為複雜（或有趣）➲ more at END *n.*, MATCH *n.*, RUBBER, TWAIN

PHR V **,meet 'up (with sb)** 🔑 (rather *informal*) to meet sb, especially by arrangement（按照安排）見面，會面：*They met up again later for a drink.* 後來他們又在一起喝過酒。 **'meet with sb** 🔑 to meet sb, especially for discussions 和某人會晤（商討問題等）：*The President met with senior White House aides.* 總統會見了白宮的高級幕僚。 **'meet with sth** **1** to be received or treated by sb in a particular way 遭遇（某事）；受到某種對待：*Her proposal met with resistance from the Left.* 她的建議遭到了左翼的抵制。◇ *to meet with success/failure* 成功；失敗 **2** to experience sth unpleasant 經歷，體驗（不愉快的事）：*She was worried that he might have met with an accident.* 她怕他出了車禍。 **'meet sth with sth** to react to sth in a particular way（對某事）作出…反應；以…作為回應 **SYN** **receive**：*His suggestion was met with howls of protest.* 他的建議引起了一陣陣的抗議聲。

M

■ **noun** **1** (*especially NAmE*) a sports competition 體育比賽；運動會：*a track meet* 徑賽運動會 **2** (*BrE*) an event at which horse riders and dogs hunt FOXES. FOX-HUNTING with dogs is now illegal in the UK. 獵狐運動（現在於英國用狗獵狐屬違法行為）

,meet-and-'greet *adj.* [only before noun] (of an event 活動) arranged so that sb, especially a famous person, can meet and talk to people 為（名人與公眾等）見面閒聊幾句而安排的 ▶ **,meet and 'greet** *noun*

meet·ing 🔑 /'miːtɪŋ/ *noun*
1 🔑 [C] an occasion when people come together to discuss or decide sth 會議；集會：*to **have/hold/call/attend a meeting*** 召開／舉辦／召集／參加會議◇ *a **committee/staff meeting*** 委員會／員工會議◇ *What time is the meeting?* 什麼時候開會？◇ *Helen will **chair the meeting*** (= be in charge of it). 海倫將主持這次會議。◇ *I'll be **in a meeting** all morning—can you take my calls?* 我整個上午都要開會，你能不能幫我接一下電話？◇ *a meeting of the United Nations Security Council* 聯合國安理會會議 **2** **the meeting** [sing.] the people at a meeting（統稱）與會者：*The meeting voted to accept the pay offer.* 與會者投票接受這一工資提議。 **3** 🔑 [C] a situation in which two or more people meet together, because they have arranged it or by chance 會面；集會；集合 **SYN** **encounter**：*At our first meeting I was nervous.* 我們第一次見面時我很緊張。◇ *It was a **chance meeting** that would change my life.* 那次偶然的會面改變了我的一生。◇ *He remembered their childhood meetings with nostalgia.* 他懷念地回憶起他們孩提時代的聚會。 **4** [C] (*BrE*) a sports event or set of races, especially for horses 運動會；（尤指）賽馬：*an athletics meeting* 運動會◇ *a race meeting* 賽馬大會

IDM **a meeting of 'minds** a close understanding between people with similar ideas, especially when they meet to do sth or meet for the first time 彼此間的深刻理解（尤指初會時就意見一致）

'meeting house *noun* a place where Quakers meet for worship（貴格會的）禮拜堂

'meeting place *noun* a place where people often meet 聚集的地方；會場：*The cafe is a popular meeting place for students.* 咖啡館是學生喜歡的聚會場所。

meg /meg/ *noun* (*informal*) = MEGABYTE：*more than 512 megs of memory* 超過 512 兆的內存◇ *24-meg broadband* * 24 兆的寬帶

mega /'megə/ *adj.* [usually before noun] (*informal*) very large or impressive 巨大的；極佳的 **SYN** **huge, great**：*The song was a mega hit last year.* 這首歌是去年很熱門的歌曲。 ▶ **mega** *adv.*：*They're mega rich.* 他們極其富有。

mega- /'megə-/ *combining form* (in nouns 構成名詞) **1** very large or great 巨大的；了不起的：*a megastore* 大型專賣店 **2** (in units of measurement 用於計量單位) one million 百萬：*a megawatt* 百萬瓦特 **3** (in units of measurement 用於計量單位) 2^{20}, or 1 048 576 兆（二進制，等於 1 048 576）

mega·bit /'megəbɪt/ *noun* (*abbr.* **Mb**, **Mbit**) (*computing* 計) **1** a unit of computer memory or data, equal to 10^6, or 1 000^2, (= 1 000 000) BITS 百萬比特，兆比特（十進制計算機內存或數據單位，等於 1 000 000 比特） **2** (also **mebi·bit**) a unit of computer memory or data, equal to 2^{20}, or 1 024^2, (= 1 048 576) BITS 兆比特（二進制計算機內存或數據單位，等於 1 048 576 比特）

mega·bucks /'megəbʌks/ *noun* [pl.] (*informal*) a very large amount of money 一大筆錢：*He earns megabucks.* 他大筆大筆地賺錢。

mega·byte /'megəbaɪt/ (also *informal* **meg**) *noun* (*abbr.* **MB**) (*computing* 計) **1** a unit of computer memory or data, equal to 10^6, or 1 000^2, (= 1 000 000) BYTES 百萬字節，兆字節（十進制計算機內存或數據單位，等於 1 000 000 字節）：*a 512-megabyte flash drive* * 512 兆字節的閃存盤 **2** (also **mebi·byte**) a unit of computer memory or data, equal to 2^{20}, or 1 024^2, (= 1 048 576) BYTES 兆字節（二進制計算機內存或數據單位，等於 1 048 576 字節）

mega·hertz /'megəhɜːts; *NAmE* -hɜːrts/ *noun* (*pl.* **mega·hertz**) (*abbr.* **MHz**) a unit for measuring radio waves and the speed at which a computer operates; 1 000 000 HERTZ 兆赫；百萬赫茲

mega·lith /'megəlɪθ/ *noun* a very large stone, especially one put in a place that was used for ceremonies in ancient times（尤指古代用於祭祀的）巨石 ▶ **mega·lith·ic** /,megə'lɪθɪk/ *adj.*

meg·alo·mania /,megələ'meɪniə/ *noun* [U] **1** (*technical* 術語) a mental illness or condition in which sb has an exaggerated belief in their own importance or power 自大狂；誇大狂；妄自尊大 **2** a strong feeling that you want to have more and more power 渴望權力；權慾熏心

meg·alo·maniac /,megələ'meɪniæk/ *noun* a person suffering from or showing megalomania 誇大狂患者 ▶ **meg·alo·maniac** *adj.*

meg·alop·olis /,megə'lɒpəlɪs; *NAmE* -'lɑːp-/ *noun* (*formal*) a very large city or group of cities where a great number of people live 大都會（區）

megaphone 擴音器

mega·phone /'megəfəʊn; *NAmE* -foʊn/ *noun* a device for making your voice sound louder, that is wider at one end, like a CONE, and is often used at outside events 擴音器；喇叭筒；傳聲筒 ➲ compare LOUDHAILER

mega·pixel /'megəpɪksl/ *noun* a million PIXELS (= very small individual areas on a computer screen), used to measure the quality of a DIGITAL screen or image 百萬像素；百萬畫素：*a 12 megapixel digital camera* * 1 200 萬像素的數碼相機

mega·star /'megəstɑː(r)/ *noun* (*informal*) a very famous singer, actor or entertainer 演藝巨星；娛樂界的巨星

mega·store /'megəstɔː(r)/ *noun* a very large shop, especially one that sells one type of product, for example computers or furniture 大商店；（尤指）大型專賣店

mega·ton (also **mega·tonne**) /'megətʌn/ *noun* a unit for measuring the power of an EXPLOSIVE, equal to one million tons of TNT 百萬噸級（爆炸能量計量單位，相當於一百萬噸黃色炸藥的威力）：*a one megaton nuclear bomb* 一枚一百萬噸級的核炸彈

mega·watt /ˈmeɡəwɒt; *NAmE* -wɑːt/ *noun* (*abbr.* **MW**) a unit for measuring electrical power; one million WATTS 兆瓦，百萬瓦特（電能計量單位）

meh /me/ *exclamation, adj.* (*NAmE, informal*) used to show that you are not at all interested in or impressed by sth 哦（表示對某事根本不感興趣或全不在乎）：*'So how was the movie?' 'Meh. The action scenes aren't awful, but there's nothing great about it.'* "那麼電影怎麼樣呢？" "呃。動作鏡頭還不壞，不過沒什麼意思。" ◇ *She does an OK job on a meh song.* 那歌本來就不怎樣，她唱得還可以。

mei·osis /maɪˈəʊsɪs; *NAmE* -ˈoʊs-/ *noun* [U] (*biology* 生) the division of a cell in two stages that results in four cells, each with half the number of CHROMOSOMES of the original cell（細胞的）減數分裂，成熟分裂

-meister /ˈmaɪstə(r)/ *combining form* (in nouns 構成名詞) (*informal*) a person thought of as skilled at a particular activity or important in a particular field …方面的專家；…領域的高手：*a horror-meister* 恐怖大師

meit·ner·ium /maɪtˈnɪəriəm; *NAmE* -ˈnɪr-/ *noun* [U] (*symb.* **Mt**) a RADIOACTIVE chemical element. Meitnerium is produced when atoms COLLIDE (= crash into each other). 鿏（放射性化學元素）

mela·mine /ˈmeləmiːn/ *noun* [U] a strong hard plastic material, used especially for covering surfaces such as the tops of tables, and for making cups, etc. 蜜胺；三聚氰胺

mel·an·cho·lia /ˌmelənˈkəʊliə; *NAmE* -ˈkoʊ-/ *noun* (*old-fashioned*) a mental illness in which the patient is depressed and worried by unnecessary fears 憂鬱症

mel·an·chol·ic /ˌmelənˈkɒlɪk; *NAmE* -ˈkɑːl-/ *adj.* (*old-fashioned* or *literary*) feeling or expressing sadness, especially when the sadness is like an illness 憂鬱的；憂鬱症的

mel·an·choly /ˈmelənkəli; -kɒli; *NAmE* -kɑːli/ *noun, adj.*
■ ***noun*** [U] (*formal*) a deep feeling of sadness that lasts for a long time and often cannot be explained 憂鬱；傷悲：*A mood of melancholy descended on us.* 一種悲傷的情緒襲上我們的心頭。
■ ***adj.*** very sad or making you feel sadness（令人）悲哀的；（令人）沮喪的 SYN **mournful, sombre**：***melancholy thoughts/memories*** 悲哀的想法 / 記憶 ◇ *The melancholy song died away.* 哀婉的歌聲漸漸消失了。

me·lange /meɪˈlɑːnʒ/ *noun* (from *French, formal*) a mixture or variety of different things 混合物；大雜燴：*a melange of different cultures* 不同文化的融合

mel·anin /ˈmelənɪn/ *noun* [U] (*technical* 術語) a dark substance in the skin and hair that causes the skin to change colour in the sun's light 黑色素

mela·noma /ˌmeləˈnəʊmə; *NAmE* -ˈnoʊmə/ *noun* [C, U] (*medical* 醫) a type of cancer that appears as a dark spot or TUMOUR on the skin 黑素瘤；黑瘤

mela·to·nin /ˌmeləˈtəʊnɪn; *NAmE* -ˈtoʊ-/ *noun* [U] (*biology* 生) a HORMONE that affects skin colour and is thought to REGULATE the REPRODUCTIVE cycle 褪黑激素

meld /meld/ *verb* [I, T] **~ (A) with B | ~ (A and B) (together)** (*formal*) to combine with sth else; to make sth combine with sth else（使）融合，合併，結合 SYN **blend**

melee /ˈmeleɪ; *NAmE* ˈmeɪleɪ/ *noun* [sing.] (from *French*) a situation in which a crowd of people are rushing or pushing each other in a confused way 混亂；混亂的群眾

mel·lif·lu·ous /meˈlɪfluəs/ *adj.* (*formal*) (of music or of sb's voice 音樂或人的聲音) sounding sweet and smooth; very pleasant to listen to 甜美流暢的；悅耳動聽的

mel·low /ˈmeləʊ; *NAmE* -loʊ/ *adj., verb*
■ ***adj.*** (**mel·low·er, mel·low·est**) **1** (of colour or sound 色彩或聲音) soft, rich and pleasant 柔和豐富的：*mellow autumn colours* 宜人的秋色 ◇ *Mellow music and lighting helped to create the right atmosphere.* 柔和的音樂和燈光襯托出了適宜的氛圍。 **2** (of a taste or flavour 味道或香味) smooth and pleasant 醇香的；甘美的：*a mellow, fruity wine* 醇正濃香的葡萄酒 **3** (of people 人) calm, gentle and reasonable because of age or experience 老練的；成熟的：*Dad's certainly grown mellower with age.* 隨着年齡的增長，父親當然是更老練了。 **4** (*informal*) (of people 人) relaxed, calm and happy, especially after drinking alcohol 歡快的，安詳輕鬆的（尤指酒後）：*After two glasses of wine, I was feeling mellow.* 兩杯葡萄酒下肚，我就飄飄然了。
■ ***verb*** **1** [I, T] to become or make sb become less extreme in behaviour, etc., especially as a result of growing older（使）成熟，老成：*She had mellowed a great deal since their days at college.* 大學畢業以後，她成熟了許多。 ◇ **~ sb** *A period spent working abroad had done nothing to mellow him.* 他在海外工作了一段時間，卻沒有變得老練。 **2** [I, T] **~ (sth)** to become, or make a colour become less bright, especially over a period of time（使顏色）柔和 **3** [I, T] **~ (sth)** to develop or make wine develop a pleasant and less bitter taste over a period of time（使酒）更加醇香

PHR V **ˌmellow ˈout** (*informal, especially NAmE*) to enjoy yourself by relaxing and not doing much 悠然自得；怡然休閒

me·lod·ic /məˈlɒdɪk; *NAmE* -ˈlɑːd-/ *adj.* **1** [only before noun] connected with the main tune in a piece of music 主旋律的；旋律的：*The melodic line is carried by the two clarinets.* 主旋律由兩支單簧管奏出。 **2** = MELODIOUS

me·lod·ica /məˈlɒdɪkə; *NAmE* -ˈlɑːd-/ *noun* a musical instrument that has a keyboard and a part that you blow into 口風琴

me·lo·di·ous /məˈləʊdiəs; *NAmE* -ˈloʊ-/ (also **me·lod·ic**) *adj.* pleasant to listen to, like music 悅耳的；優美動聽的；像音樂的：*a rich melodious voice* 圓潤悅耳的嗓音 ▸ **me·lo·di·ous·ly** *adv.*

melo·dist /ˈmelədɪst/ *noun* a person who writes tunes; a person who is very good at writing tunes 作曲家；善於作曲的人

melo·drama /ˈmelədrɑːmə/ *noun* [U, C] **1** a story, play or novel that is full of exciting events and in which the characters and emotions seem too exaggerated to be real 情節劇；通俗劇；情節劇式故事（或小說）：*a gripping Victorian melodrama* 動人心弦的維多利亞時代情節劇 ◇ *Instead of tragedy, we got melodrama.* 我們看的是情節劇，不是悲劇。 **2** events, behaviour, etc. which are exaggerated or extreme 戲劇性的事件（或行為等）；過於誇大的事件（或行為等）：*Her love of melodrama meant that any small problem became a crisis.* 她喜歡誇大其詞，會把任何小問題說成危機。

melo·dra·mat·ic /ˌmelədrəˈmætɪk/ *adj.* (often *disapproving*) full of exciting and extreme emotions or events; behaving or reacting to sth in an exaggerated way 情節劇式的；誇大的；聳人聽聞的：*a melodramatic plot full of deceit and murder* 充滿欺騙和兇殺的聳人聽聞的情節 ▸ **melo·dra·mat·ic·al·ly** /-kli/ *adv.*

melo·dra·mat·ics /ˌmelədrəˈmætɪks/ *noun* [pl.] behaviour or events that are melodramatic 傳奇劇式行為（或事情）；誇張行為（或事情）：*Let's have no more melodramatics, if you don't mind.* 如果你不介意的話，咱們就別再誇張了。

mel·ody /ˈmelədi/ *noun* (*pl.* **-ies**) **1** [C] a tune, especially the main tune in a piece of music written for several instruments or voices 旋律；曲調；（尤指）主旋律：*a haunting melody* 縈繞心頭的旋律 ◇ *The melody is then taken up by the flutes.* 接着由長笛奏主旋律。 ➲ COLLOCATIONS at MUSIC **2** [C] a piece of music or a song with a clear or simple tune（旋律簡潔的）樂曲，歌曲：*old Irish melodies* 古老的愛爾蘭歌曲 **3** [U] the arrangement of musical notes in a tune 樂曲的音符編排：*A few bars of melody drifted towards us.* 幾小節樂曲從遠處傳來。

melon /ˈmelən/ *noun* [C, U] a large fruit with hard green, yellow or orange skin, sweet flesh and juice and a lot of seeds 甜瓜；瓜：*a slice of melon* 一片瓜 ➲ see also HONEYDEW MELON, WATERMELON

M

melt 🔑 /melt/ *verb*
1 🔑 [I, T] to become or make sth become liquid as a result of heating （使）熔化，融化：*The snow showed no sign of melting.* 雪没有一點融化的跡象。◇ *melting ice* 正在融化的冰 ◇ **~ sth** *The sun had melted the snow.* 陽光融化了積雪。◇ *First, melt two ounces of butter.* 先溶好兩盎司黃油。➲ COLLOCATIONS at COOKING ➲ compare DEFROST, DE-ICE **2** [I, T] to become or to make a feeling, an emotion, etc. become gentler and less strong （使）軟化，變得温柔：*The tension in the room began to melt.* 屋裏的緊張氣氛開始緩和。◇ **~ sth** *Her trusting smile melted his heart.* 她那信任的微笑使他的心變軟了。
IDM **,melt in your 'mouth** (of food 食物) to be soft and very good to eat 爽滑可口；柔嫩好吃 ➲ more at BUTTER *n.*
PHR V **,melt a'way** | **,melt sth↔a'way** to disappear or make sth disappear gradually （使）慢慢消失：*At the first sign of trouble, the crowd melted away.* 人群一看有麻煩，便作鳥獸散。 **,melt sth↔'down** to heat a metal or WAX object until it is liquid, especially so that the metal or wax can be used to make sth else 將（金屬或蠟）熔化 ➲ related noun MELTDOWN **'melt into sth** to gradually become part of sth and therefore become difficult to see 逐漸融入；漸漸與某物成為一體

melt·down /'meltdaʊn/ *noun* [U, C] **1** a serious accident in which the central part of a nuclear REACTOR melts, causing harmful RADIATION to escape 核反應堆核心熔毀（導致核輻射泄漏） **2** (*economics* 經) a situation where sth fails or becomes weaker in a sudden or dramatic way 崩潰；垮台：*The country is* **in** *economic* **meltdown**. 該國的經濟崩潰。◇ *a meltdown on the New York Stock Exchange* 紐約股票市場的崩盤

melt·ing /'meltɪŋ/ *adj.* [usually before noun] persuading you to feel love, pity or sympathy 感人的；柔情似水的；令人愛憐的；可同情的：*his melting eyes* 他那雙能打動人的眼睛 ▸ **melt·ing·ly** *adv.*

'melting point *noun* [U, C] the temperature at which a substance will melt 熔點

'melting pot *noun* [usually sing.] a place or situation in which large numbers of people, ideas, etc. are mixed together 熔爐（指多種民族、多種思想等融合混雜的地方或狀況）：*the vast melting pot of American society* 美國社會這個大熔爐
IDM **in the 'melting pot** (*especially BrE*) likely to change; in the process of changing 要起變化；處於變化之中

mem·ber 🔑 /'membə(r)/ *noun*
1 🔑 **~ (of sth)** a person, an animal or a plant that belongs to a particular group 成員；分子：*a* **member** ***of staff/society/the family*** 職工/社會/家庭中的一員 ◇ *characteristics common to all members of the species* 這一物種中所有個體的共同特點 **2** 🔑 a person, a country or an organization that has joined a particular group, club or team 成員；會員：***party/union members*** 黨員；工會會員 ◇ *a meeting of* ***member countries/states*** 成員國會議 ◇ *How much does it cost to become a member?* 要成為會員得花多少錢？◇ **~ of sth** *an active member of the local church* 當地教會的一名積極分子 **3** (*old use* or *literary*) a part of the body, especially an arm or a leg 身體部位（尤指胳膊或腿） **4** a PENIS. People say 'member' to avoid saying 'penis'. （委婉說法，與 penis 同義，即陰莖） **5 Member** (in Britain) a Member of Parliament （英國）下院議員：*the Hon. Member for Brent North* 布倫特北區議員閣下 ➲ see also PRIVATE MEMBER

,Member of 'Parliament *noun* = MP (1)

mem·ber·ship 🔑 /'membəʃɪp; *NAmE* -bərʃ-/ *noun*
1 🔑 [U] (*BrE*) **~ (of sth)** | (*NAmE*) **~ (in sth)** the state of being a member of a group, a club, an organization, etc. 會員資格；成員資格：*Who is eligible to apply for membership of the association?* 誰有資格申請加入這個協會？◇ *a* ***membership card/fee*** 會員卡；會費 **2** 🔑 [C+sing./pl. v.] the members, or the number of members, of a group, a club, an organization, etc. （統稱）會員，成員；會員人數；成員數：*The membership has/have not yet voted.* 會員還沒有進行投票。◇ *The club has a membership of more than 500.* 俱樂部的會員人數超過了500名。

mem·brane /'membreɪn/ *noun* [C, U] **1** a thin layer of skin or TISSUE that connects or covers parts inside the body （身體內的）膜 ➲ see also MUCOUS MEMBRANE **2** a very thin layer found in the structure of cells in plants （植物的）細胞膜 **3** a thin layer of material used to prevent air, liquid, etc. from entering a particular part of sth （可起防水、防風等作用的）膜狀物：*a waterproof membrane* 防水薄膜 ▸ **mem·bran·ous** /'membrənəs/ *adj.*

meme /miːm/ *noun* (*biology* 生) a type of behaviour that is passed from one member of a group to another, not in the GENES but by another means such as people copying it 模因，模仿傳遞行為（通過模仿等非遺傳方式傳遞的行為）

me·mento /mə'mentəʊ; *NAmE* -toʊ/ *noun* (*pl.* **-oes** or **-os**) a thing that you keep or give to sb to remind you or them of a person or place 紀念品 SYN **souvenir**：*a memento of our trip to Italy* 我們意大利之旅的紀念品

me·mento mori /mə,mentəʊ 'mɔːri; 'mɔːraɪ; *NAmE* -toʊ/ *noun* (*pl.* **me·mento mori**) an object or symbol that reminds or warns you of death 使人想到死亡的物品（或圖符）；死亡警告

memo /'meməʊ; *NAmE* -moʊ/ *noun* (*pl.* **-os**) (also *formal* **memo·ran·dum**) **~ (to sb)** an official note from one person to another in the same organization 備忘錄：*to* ***write/send/circulate a memo*** 寫/發送/傳閱備忘錄

mem·oir /'memwɑː(r)/ *noun* **1 memoirs** [pl.] an account written by sb, especially sb famous, about their life and experiences （尤指名人的）回憶錄；自傳 **2** [C] (*formal*) a written account of sb's life, a place, or an event, written by sb who knows it well 傳說；地方誌；大事記

mem·ora·bilia /,memərə'bɪliə/ *noun* [pl.] things that people collect because they once belonged to a famous person, or because they are connected with a particular interesting place, event or activity 收藏品；紀念品：*football/Beatles memorabilia* 足球/披頭士樂隊紀念品

mem·or·able /'memərəbl/ *adj.* **~ (for sth)** special, good or unusual and therefore worth remembering or easy to remember 值得紀念的；難忘的 SYN **unforgettable**：*a truly memorable occasion* 非常難忘的時刻 ▸ **mem·or·ably** /-əbli/ *adv.*

memo·ran·dum /,memə'rændəm/ *noun* (*pl.* **memo·randa** /,memə'rændə/) **1** (*formal*) = MEMO：*an internal memorandum* 內部備忘錄 **2** (*law* 律) a record of a legal agreement which has not yet been formally prepared and signed 協議備忘錄 **3** a proposal or report on a particular subject for a person, an organization, a committee, etc. 建議書；報告：*a detailed memorandum to the commission on employment policy* 呈交委員會的有關就業政策的詳細報告

me·mor·ial /mə'mɔːriəl/ *noun, adj.*
■ ***noun*** **1** [C] a statue, stone, etc. that is built in order to remind people of an important past event or of a famous person who has died 紀念碑（或像等）：*a* ***war memorial*** (= in memory of soldiers who died in a war) 陣亡將士紀念碑 ◇ **~ to sb/sth** *a memorial to victims of the Holocaust* 大屠殺遇難者的紀念碑 **2** [sing.] **~ to sb/sth** a thing that will continue to remind people of sb/sth 紀念物；紀念品：*The painting will be a lasting memorial to a remarkable woman.* 這幅油畫將成為對一位傑出女性的永久紀念。
■ ***adj.*** [only before noun] created or done in order to remember sb who has died 紀念的；悼念的：*a* ***memorial statue/plaque/prize*** 紀念像/牌/獎 ◇ *The* ***memorial service*** *will be held at a local church.* 悼念儀式將在當地的一所教堂舉行。◇ *the John F Kennedy Memorial Hospital* 肯尼迪紀念醫院

Me'morial Day *noun* a holiday in the US, usually the last Monday in May, in honour of members of the armed forces who have died in war 陣亡將士紀念日（美國假日，通常為五月的最後一個星期一）➲ see also REMEMBRANCE SUNDAY, VETERANS DAY

me·mor·ial·ize (*BrE* also **-ise**) /mə'mɔːriəlaɪz/ *verb* **~ sb/sth** (*formal*) to produce sth that will continue to exist and remind people of sb who has died or sth that has gone 紀念 SYN **commemorate**

me·mor·iam /mə'mɔːriəm/ ➲ IN MEMORIAM

mem·or·ize (*BrE* also **-ise**) /'meməraɪz/ *verb* **~ sth** to learn sth carefully so that you can remember it exactly 記憶；記住： *to memorize a poem* 記住一首詩

mem·ory /'meməri/ (*pl.* **-ies**) *noun*

▸ **ABILITY TO REMEMBER** 記憶力 **1** [C, U] **~ (for sth)** your ability to remember things 記憶力；記性： *I have a bad memory for names.* 我不善於記名字。◇ *People have* ***short memories*** (= they soon forget). 人是健忘的。◇ *He had* ***a long memory*** *for people who had disappointed him.* 誰讓他失望，他總是記恨在心。◇ *She can recite the whole poem* ***from memory***. 她能背誦全詩。◇ *He suffered loss of memory for weeks after the accident.* 事故之後他有幾個星期失去記憶。◇ *Are you sure? Memory can play tricks on you.* 你肯定嗎？記憶也會捉弄人的。 **2** [U] the period of time that sb is able to remember events 記憶所及的時期；回憶所及的範圍： *There hasn't been peace in the country* ***in/within my memory***. 在我的記憶裏，這個國家從沒太平過。◇ *It was the worst storm in recent memory.* 最近能記得的風暴中，這是最厲害的一次。◇ *This hasn't happened* ***in living memory*** (= nobody alive now can remember it happening). 在世的人都不記得發生過這樣的事。

▸ **STH YOU REMEMBER** 記住的事 **3** [C] a thought of sth that you remember from the past 回憶；記憶 SYN **recollection**： *childhood memories* 童年的回憶 ◇ *I have vivid memories of my grandparents.* 我依然清楚地記得我的祖父母。◇ *What is your earliest memory?* 你最早能記得的是什麼？◇ *The photos* ***bring back*** *lots of good* ***memories***. 這些照片喚起了許多美好的回憶。 **4** [U] (*formal*) what is remembered about sb after they have died 對死者的記憶： *Her memory lives on* (= we still remember her). 我們永遠懷念她。

▸ **COMPUTING** 計算機技術 **5** [C, U] the part of a computer where information is stored; the amount of space in a computer for storing information 存貯器；內存；記憶體 ➲ see also RAM

IDM **if (my) memory serves me well, correctly, etc.** if I remember correctly 如果我沒有記錯的話 **in memory of sb | to the memory of sb** intended to show respect and remind people of sb who has died 作為對某人的紀念： *He founded the charity in memory of his late wife.* 他創辦了這一慈善事業以紀念他已故的妻子。 ➲ more at ETCH, JOG *v.*, SIEVE *n.*

'memory bank *noun* the memory of a device such as a computer （計算機等的）存貯體，記憶庫

'memory card *noun* an electronic device that can be used to store data, used especially with DIGITAL cameras, mobile/cell phones, music players, etc. 存貯卡（尤用於數碼相機、手機、音樂播放器等）➲ compare SD CARD, SDHC CARD

memory 'lane *noun*

IDM **a trip/walk down ˌmemory 'lane** time that you spend thinking about and remembering the past or going to a place again in order to remind yourself of past experiences 回憶往事；重遊故地

'Memory Stick™ *noun* (*computing* 計) a CIRCUIT BOARD that can be put into a computer to give it more memory of the kind that does not lose data when the power supply is lost 記憶棒，存貯棒，內存擴展棒（斷電不會造成數據丟失）

'memory stick *noun* (*especially BrE*) a small memory device that can be used to store data from a computer and to move it from one computer to another 閃存盤；閃盤；U 盤 SYN **flash drive** ➲ VISUAL VOCAB page V66

mem·sahib /'memsɑːb/ *noun* used in India, especially in the past, to address a married woman with high social status, often a European woman （尤指舊時印度對來自歐洲等上層社會已婚婦女的稱呼）夫人，太太

men *pl.* of MAN

men·ace /'menəs/ *noun, verb*

■ *noun* **1** [C, usually sing.] **~ (to sb/sth)** a person or thing that causes, or may cause, serious damage, harm or danger 威脅；危險的人（或物）SYN **threat**： *a new initiative aimed at beating the menace of illegal drugs* 旨在打擊非法毒品威脅的新舉措 **2** [U] an atmosphere that makes you feel threatened or frightened 令人恐怖的氛圍；危險氣氛： ***a sense/an air/a hint of menace*** *in his voice* 他的話音裏的威脅語氣／腔調／意味 **3** [C, usually sing.] (*informal*) a person or thing that is annoying or causes trouble 煩人的人（或事物）；引起麻煩的人（或事物）SYN **nuisance** **4 menaces** [pl.] (*law* 律) (*BrE*) threats that sb will cause harm if they do not get what they are asking for 恐嚇；威脅： *to demand money* ***with menaces*** 勒索錢財

■ *verb* **~ sth/sb** (*formal*) to be a possible danger to sth/sb 對…構成危險；危及；威脅到 SYN **threaten**： *The forests are being menaced by major development projects.* 大型開發項目正在危及森林。

men·acing /'menəsɪŋ/ *adj.* seeming likely to cause you harm or danger 威脅的；恐嚇的；危險的 SYN **threatening**： *a* ***menacing face/tone*** 惡狠臉色／口吻 ◇ *At night, the dark streets become menacing.* 在夜晚，漆黑的街道變得陰森森的。 ▸ **men·acing·ly** *adv.*： *The thunder growled menacingly.* 雷聲轟鳴，叫人害怕。

mé·nage /meɪ'nɑːʒ/ *noun* [usually sing.] (from *French*, *formal* or *humorous*) all the people who live together in one house 家庭；全體家庭成員 SYN **household**

ménage à trois /ˌmenɑːʒ ɑː 'trwʌ/ *noun* (*pl.* **ménages à trois** /ˌmenɑːʒ ɑː 'trwʌ/) [usually sing.] (from *French*) a situation where three people, especially a husband, wife and lover, live together and have sexual relationships with each other 三人同居，三角家庭（尤指夫婦和情人同居）

men·agerie /mə'nædʒəri/ *noun* a collection of wild animals （一群）野生動物

mend /mend/ *verb, noun*

■ *verb* **1** [T] **~ sth** (*BrE*) to repair sth that has been damaged or broken so that it can be used again 修理；修補： *Could you mend my bike for me?* 你能幫我修一下自行車嗎？ ➲ see also FENCE-MENDING **2** [T] **~ sth** to repair a hole in a piece of clothing, etc. 縫補；織補： *He mended shoes for a living.* 他靠修鞋為生。 **3** [T] **~ sth** to find a solution to a problem or disagreement 彌合（分歧）；解決（爭端）： *They tried to mend their differences.* 他們試圖消除他們之間的分歧。 **4** [I] (*old-fashioned, BrE*) (of a person 人) to improve in health after being ill/sick 痊癒；恢復健康 SYN **recover**： *He's mending slowly after the operation.* 手術後，他正在緩慢好轉。 **5** [I] (of a broken bone 骨折) to heal 癒合；痊癒

IDM **mend (your) fences (with sb)** to find a solution to a disagreement with sb 解決紛爭；消除隔閡 **mend your 'ways** to stop behaving badly 改過自新；改邪歸正 ➲ more at SAY *v.*

■ *noun*

IDM **on the 'mend** (*informal*) getting better after an illness or injury; improving after a difficult situation 康復；好轉；改善；改進： *My leg is definitely on the mend now.* 我的腿正在明顯地好轉。◇ *Does he believe the economy's really on the mend?* 他相信經濟確實在復蘇嗎？

men·da·cious /men'deɪʃəs/ *adj.* (*formal*) not telling the truth 撒謊的；不真實的；捏造的 SYN **lying**

men·da·city /men'dæsəti/ *noun* [U] (*formal*) the act of not telling the truth 撒謊；捏造；說瞎話 SYN **lying**

men·del·evium /ˌmendə'liːviəm; -'leɪv-/ *noun* [U] (*symb.* **Md**) a chemical element. Mendelevium is a RADIOACTIVE element that does not exist naturally. 鍆（放射性化學元素）

mend·er /'mendə(r)/ *noun* (*BrE*) (usually in compounds 通常構成複合詞) a person who mends sth 修理工；修補者： *road menders* 修路工

men·di·cant /'mendɪkənt/ *adj.* (*formal*) (especially of members of religious groups 尤指宗教成員) living by asking people for money and food 化緣的；行乞的 ▸ **men·di·cant** *noun*

men·folk /'menfəʊk; *NAmE* -foʊk/ *noun* [pl.] (*old-fashioned*) men of a particular family or community （統稱家庭或社群中的）男人： *a society sending its menfolk off to war* 把男人送上戰場的社會 ➲ compare WOMENFOLK

M

me·nial /ˈmiːniəl/ *adj., noun*
■ ***adj.*** (usually *disapproving*) (of work 工作) not skilled or important, and often boring or badly paid 不需技巧的；枯燥的；報酬低的：***menial jobs/work*** 枯燥的工作 ◇ *menial tasks like cleaning the floor* 擦地板這種瑣碎的工作
■ ***noun*** (*old-fashioned*) a person with a menial job 僕人；用人

men·in·ges /məˈnɪndʒiːz/ *noun* [pl.] (*anatomy* 解) the three MEMBRANES (= thin layers of material) that surround the brain and SPINAL CORD 腦脊膜

men·in·gi·tis /ˌmenɪnˈdʒaɪtɪs/ *noun* [U] a serious disease in which the TISSUES surrounding the brain and SPINAL CORD become infected and swollen, causing severe headache, fever and sometimes death 腦膜炎；腦脊膜炎

me·nis·cus /məˈnɪskəs/ *noun* (*pl.* **me·nisci** /-saɪ/) **1** (*physics* 物) the curved surface of a liquid in a tube（液柱的）彎月面 **2** (*anatomy* 解) a thin layer of CARTILAGE between the surfaces of some joints, for example the knee（膝關節等的）半月板

Men·non·ite /ˈmenənaɪt/ *noun* a member of a PROTESTANT religious group that lives in the US and Canada. Mennonites live a simple life and do not work as public officials or soldiers. 門諾派教徒（美國和加拿大一個新教教派的成員，生活簡樸，不當公務員或服兵役）

meno·pause /ˈmenəpɔːz/ (also *informal* **the ˈchange (of life)**) *noun* [U] (often **the menopause**) [sing.] the time during which a woman gradually stops MENSTRUATING, usually at around the age of 50 絕經期；（婦女的）更年期：*to reach (the) menopause* 到更年期 ▸ **meno·pausal** /ˌmenəˈpɔːzl/ *adj.*：***menopausal women/symptoms*** 更年期的婦女／症狀

M

me·norah /mɪˈnɔːrə/ *noun* a traditional Jewish object to hold seven or nine CANDLES（傳統的猶太人所使用的可插七或九支蠟燭的）大燭台，多連燈燭台

mensch /menʃ/ *noun* (*NAmE, informal*) a good person, especially sb who does sth kind or helpful 好人；樂於助人的人

men·ses /ˈmensiːz/ *noun* (often **the menses**) [pl.] (*technical* 術語) the flow of blood each month from a woman's body 月經；行經

ˈmen's room *noun* (*NAmE*) a public toilet/bathroom for men 男廁所；男盥洗室

men·strual /ˈmenstruəl/ *adj.* connected with the time when a woman menstruates each month 月經的：*The average length of a woman's* ***menstrual cycle*** *is 28 days.* 婦女的平均月經週期是 28 天。◇ *menstrual blood* 經血 ◇ (*formal*) *a menstrual period* 月經期 ➲ compare PREMENSTRUAL

men·stru·ate /ˈmenstrueɪt/ *verb* [I] (*formal*) when a woman **menstruates**, there is a flow of blood from her womb, usually once a month 行經；來月經

men·stru·ation /ˌmenstruˈeɪʃn/ *noun* [U] (*formal*) the process or time of menstruating 行經；月經來潮 ➲ compare PERIOD

mens·wear /ˈmenzweə(r); *NAmE* -wer/ *noun* [U] used especially in shops/stores to describe clothes for men 男服（尤用於商店中）：*the menswear department* 男子服裝部

-ment *suffix* (in nouns 構成名詞) the action or result of …的行為（或結果）：*bombardment* 炮擊 ◇ *development* 發展 ▸ **-mental** (in adjectives 構成形容詞)：*governmental* 政府的 ◇ *judgemental* 審判的

men·tal 0┳ **AW** /ˈmentl/ *adj.*
1 0┳ [usually before noun] connected with or happening in the mind; involving the process of thinking 思想的；精神的；思考的；智力的：*the mental process of remembering* 記憶的心理過程 ◇ *Do you have a* ***mental picture*** *of what it will look like?* 在你想像中它會是什麼樣子？◇ *I* ***made a mental note*** *to talk to her about it.* 我記着要去和她談談這事兒。◇ *He has a complete* ***mental block*** (= difficulty in understanding or remembering) *when it comes to physics.* 他對物理一竅不通。 **2** 0┳ [usually before noun] connected with the state of health of the mind or with the treatment of illnesses of the mind 精神病治療的；精神健康的 **SYN** **psychological**：***mental health*** 精神健康 ◇ *a* ***mental disorder/illness/hospital*** 精神紊亂／病／病院 ◇ *She was suffering from physical and mental exhaustion.* 她當時已經是精疲力竭。➲ compare PSYCHIATRIC **3** [not usually before noun] (*BrE, slang*) crazy 瘋狂；發瘋：*Watch him. He's mental.* 小心，他瘋了。◇ *My dad* ***will go mental*** (= be very angry) *when he finds out.* 我父親要是發現了，他會氣瘋的。

Synonyms 同義詞辨析

mentally ill

insane • neurotic • psychotic • disturbed • unstable

These words all describe sb who is suffering from a mental illness. 以上各詞均用以形容患有精神疾病的人。

mentally ill suffering from an illness of the mind, especially in a way that affects the way you think and behave 指有精神病

insane [not usually before noun] (*rather formal*) suffering from a serious mental illness and unable to live in normal society 指精神失常、神經錯亂：*The question is, was the man insane when he committed the crime?* 問題在於這男人犯罪時是否處於精神失常狀態？ **NOTE** In informal English **insane** can describe sb who is not suffering from a mental illness, but whose mind does not work normally, especially because they are under pressure. This meaning is used especially in the phrases *go insane* and *drive sb insane*. 在非正式英語中，insane 可用於未患精神病但尤因壓力導致心智不正常的人。這一含義尤用於 go insane 和 drive sb insane 短語中。

neurotic (*medical*) suffering from or connected with neurosis (= a mental illness in which a person suffers strong feelings of fear and worry) 指神經機能病的、神經官能症的：*the treatment of anxiety in neurotic patients* 對神經官能症病人焦慮感的治療 **NOTE** In informal English **neurotic** is also used to describe sb who is not suffering from a mental illness, but is not behaving in a calm way because they are worried about sth 在非正式英語中，neurotic 亦用以指未患精神病、但因擔憂而變得神經質的人：*She became neurotic about keeping the house clean.* 她對保持房子清潔有點神經質。

psychotic (*medical*) suffering from or connected with psychosis (= a serious mental illness in which thought and emotions lose connection with external reality) 指精神錯亂的、有精神病的 **NOTE** In informal English **psychotic** is sometimes used to describe anyone suffering from a mental illness, but in correct medical usage it only describes people who have difficulty relating to external reality. It contrasts with **neurotic** which describes people who are less seriously mentally ill and are still able to distinguish what is real from what is not. 在非正式英語中，psychotic 有時用以泛指患有精神疾病，但在正確的醫學用語中，只用以描述難以與客觀現實建立聯繫的人，這與 neurotic 形成對比；neurotic 用以描述患有輕微精神錯亂，但仍能區分現實與虛幻的人。

disturbed mentally ill, especially because of very unhappy or shocking experiences 指有精神病的、心理不正常的、精神紊亂的，尤因不幸或受刺激所致：*He works with emotionally disturbed children.* 他從事跟精神異常兒童有關的工作。

unstable having emotions and behaviour that are likely to change suddenly and unexpectedly 指情緒、行為反覆無常的、不穩定的

PATTERNS

- neurotic/psychotic/disturbed/unstable **behaviour**
- neurotic/psychotic **illnesses/disorders/symptoms/patients**
- **seriously** mentally ill/neurotic/psychotic/disturbed
- **emotionally/mentally** disturbed/unstable

ˌmental ˈage *noun* [C, usually sing.] the level of sb's ability to think, understand, etc. that is judged by comparison with the average ability for children of a particular age 智力年齡；心理年齡： *She is sixteen but **has a mental age of** five.* 她十六歲，但智力年齡是五歲。 ➲ compare CHRONOLOGICAL (2)

ˌmental aˈrithmetic *noun* [U] adding, multiplying, etc. numbers in your mind without writing anything down or using a CALCULATOR 心算

men·tal·ity **AW** /menˈtæləti/ *noun* [usually sing.] (*pl.* **-ies**) the particular attitude or way of thinking of a person or group 心態；思想狀況；思想方法 **SYN** **mindset**： *I cannot understand the mentality of football hooligans.* 我無法理解足球流氓的心態。◇ *a **criminal/ghetto mentality*** 犯罪心態；種族聚居區的思想意識 ➲ see also SIEGE MENTALITY

men·tal·ly 🔑 **AW** /ˈmentəli/ *adv.* connected with or happening in the mind 精神上；智力上；思想上： *mentally ill* 有精神病 ◇ *The baby is very mentally alert.* 這孩子腦子很機靈。◇ *Mentally, I began making a list of things I had to do.* 我開始在腦子裏盤算我該做哪些事情。

ˌmentally ˈhandicapped *adj.* (*old-fashioned*) (of a person 人) slow to learn or to understand things because of a problem with the brain 弱智的；智力殘障的；精神殘疾的 **HELP** It is now more usual to say that people with this kind of problem **have learning difficulties**. 現在常把有此類問題的人說成 have learning difficulties（有學習障礙）。

men·tee /ˌmenˈtiː/ *noun* a person who is advised and helped by a more experienced person over a period of time 受指導者；門生： *the mentor/mentee relationship* 師徒關係 ➲ compare MENTOR

men·thol /ˈmenθɒl; *NAmE* -θɔːl; -θɑːl/ *noun* [U] a substance that tastes and smells of MINT, that is used in some medicines for colds and to give a strong cool flavour to cigarettes, TOOTHPASTE, etc. 薄荷醇

men·thol·ated /ˈmenθəleɪtɪd/ *adj.* containing menthol 含薄荷醇的： *mentholated sweets* 薄荷糖

men·tion 🔑 /ˈmenʃn/ *verb, noun*

■ ***verb*** 🔑 to write or speak about sth/sb, especially without giving much information 提到；寫到；說到： **~ sth/sb (to sb)** *Nobody mentioned anything to me about it.* 沒人跟我提過這事兒。◇ *Sorry, I won't mention it again.* 對不起，我再也不提它了。◇ ***Now that you mention it**, she did seem to be in a strange mood.* 既然你說到這事兒，她確實好像情緒不大對。◇ **~ sth/sb as sth/sb** *His name has been mentioned as a future MP.* 有人提到他，認為他將來可以當下院議員。◇ **~ where, why, etc. …** *Did she mention where she was going?* 她有沒有說起她要去哪兒？◇ **~ that …** *You mentioned in your letter that you might be moving abroad.* 你在信中談到你可能要移居國外。◇ **~ doing sth** *Did I mention going to see Vicky on Sunday?* 我說過週日要去看望維基了嗎？ ➲ see also ABOVE-MENTIONED, AFOREMENTIONED

IDM **don't ˈmention it** 🔑 (*informal*) used as a polite answer when sb has thanked you for sth（別人道謝時回答）不客氣 **SYN** **you're welcome**： *'Thanks for all your help.' 'Don't mention it.'* "多謝你幫忙。" "不用客氣。" **not to mention** used to introduce extra information and emphasize what you are saying 更不用說；且不說： *He has two big houses in this country, not to mention his villa in France.* 他在這個國家有兩座大房子，更別提他在法國的別墅了。

■ ***noun*** [U, C, usually sing.] an act of referring to sb/sth in speech or writing 提及；說起；寫上一筆： *He **made no mention of** her work.* 他根本沒提她的工作。◇ *The concert didn't even **get a mention** in the newspapers.* 報紙對這場音樂會隻字未提。◇ *Phil deserves (a) **special mention** for all the help he gave us.* 菲爾對我們的幫助很大，理應特別提一提。

men·tor /ˈmentɔː(r)/ *noun* an experienced person who advises and helps sb with less experience over a period of time 導師；顧問 ➲ compare MENTEE ▸ **men·tor·ing** *noun* [U]： *a mentoring programme* 指導計劃

menu 🔑 /ˈmenjuː/ *noun*

1 🔑 a list of the food that is available at a restaurant or to be served at a meal 菜單： *to **ask for/look at the menu*** 要 / 看菜單 ◇ *What's **on the menu*** (= for dinner) *tonight?* 今晚有什麼菜？ ➲ COLLOCATIONS at RESTAURANT **2** 🔑 (*computing* 計) a list of possible choices that are shown on a computer screen 功能選擇單；選單： *a pull-down menu* 下拉式選單 ➲ see also DROP-DOWN MENU

ˈmenu bar *noun* (*computing* 計) a horizontal bar at the top of a computer screen that contains PULL-DOWN menus such as 'File', 'Edit' and 'Help'（下拉）選單欄

meow (*especially NAmE*) (*BrE* usually **miaow**) /miˈaʊ/ *noun* the crying sound made by a cat 喵（貓叫聲） ➲ see also MEW ▸ **meow** (*especially NAmE*) (*BrE* usually **miaow**) *verb* [I]

MEP /ˌem iː ˈpiː/ *noun* the abbreviation for 'Member of the European Parliament' 歐洲議會議員（全寫為 Member of the European Parliament）： *the Labour MEP for South East Wales* 東南威爾士的工黨歐洲議會議員

Meph·is·toph·elian /ˌmefɪstəˈfiːliən; *NAmE* also ˌmefɪˌstɑːfəˈliən/ *adj.* (*formal*) very evil; like the DEVIL 十分邪惡的；魔鬼似的 **ORIGIN** From **Mephistopheles**, an evil spirit to whom, according to the German legend, Faust sold his soul. 源自魔鬼精靈墨菲斯托菲里斯（Mephistopheles）。根據德國民間傳說，浮士德把自己的靈魂出賣給了它。

Synonyms 同義詞辨析

mention

refer to sb/sth • speak • cite • quote

These words all mean to write or speak about sb/sth, often in order to give an example or prove sth. 以上各詞均含寫到、說到、談及或舉例說明之意。

mention to write or speak about sth/sb, especially without giving much information 指提到、寫到、說到，尤指未給出詳細信息： *Nobody mentioned anything to me about it.* 沒人跟我提過這事。

refer to sb/sth (*rather formal*) to mention or speak about sb/sth 指提到、談及、說起： *I promised not to refer to the matter again.* 我答應過再不提這事了。

speak to mention or describe sb/sth 指提起、講述： *Witnesses **spoke of** a great ball of flame.* 目擊者都談到有個大火球。

cite (*formal*) to mention sth as a reason or an example, or in order to support what you are saying 指提及（原因）、舉出（示例）證明： *He cited his heavy workload as the reason for his breakdown.* 他提到繁重的工作負荷是導致他累垮的原因。

quote to mention an example of sth to support what you are saying 指舉例說明： *Can you quote me an instance of when this happened?* 你能否給我舉例說明一下發生這事的情況？

CITE OR QUOTE? 用 cite 還是 quote？

You can **cite** reasons or examples, but you can only **quote** examples. * cite 可指提及原因或舉出示例，但 quote 只用於舉例： ~~*He quoted his heavy workload as the reason for his breakdown.*~~ **Cite** is a more formal word than **quote** and is often used in more formal situations, for example in descriptions of legal cases. * cite 較 quote 正式，常用於較正式的場合中，如說明法律案件。

PATTERNS

- to mention/refer to/speak of/cite/quote sb/sth **as** sb/sth
- to mention/refer to/cite/quote a(n) **example/instance/case** of sth
- **frequently/often** mentioned/referred to/spoken of/cited/quoted
- the example mentioned/referred to/cited/quoted **above/earlier/previously**

M

mer·can·tile /ˈmɜːkəntaɪl; *NAmE* ˈmɜːrk-; -tiːl/ *adj.* (*formal*) connected with trade and commercial affairs 商業的；貿易的

mer·can·til·ism /mɜːˈkæntɪlɪzəm; *NAmE* mɜːrˈk-/ *noun* [U] the economic theory that trade increases wealth 重商主義，商業本位（認為商業可增加財富）▸ **mer·can·til·ist** /-lɪst/ *adj.* **mer·can·til·ist** *noun*

Mer·ca·tor projection /mɜːˈkeɪtə prədʒekʃn; *NAmE* mɜːrˈkeɪtər/ *noun* [sing.] a traditional map of the world, on which the relative size of some countries is not accurate 墨卡托地圖投影（一種傳統的世界地圖投影，其中一些國家的面積失真）➲ compare PETERS PROJECTION

mer·cen·ary /ˈmɜːsənəri; *NAmE* ˈmɜːrsəneri/ *noun, adj.*
■ **noun** (*pl.* **-ies**) a soldier who will fight for any country or group that offers payment 雇傭兵：*foreign mercenaries* 外國雇傭兵 ◇ *mercenary soldiers* 雇傭兵
■ **adj.** (*disapproving*) only interested in making or getting money 只為金錢的：*a* ***mercenary society/attitude*** 唯利是圖的社會／態度 ◇ *She's interested in him for purely mercenary reasons.* 她對他感興趣完全是為了貪圖金錢。

mer·chan·dise *noun, verb*
■ **noun** /ˈmɜːtʃəndaɪs; -daɪz; *NAmE* ˈmɜːrtʃ-/ [U] **1** (*formal*) goods that are bought or sold; goods that are for sale in a shop/store 商品；貨品：*a wide selection of merchandise* 品種豐富的商品 ➲ **SYNONYMS** at PRODUCT **2** things you can buy that are connected with or that advertise a particular event or organization 相關商品；指定商品：*official Olympic merchandise* 奧林匹克運動會官方指定商品
■ **verb** /ˈmɜːtʃəndaɪz; *NAmE* ˈmɜːrtʃ-/ **~ sth** to sell sth using advertising, etc. 推銷；（運用廣告等進行）銷售

M

mer·chan·dis·ing /ˈmɜːtʃəndaɪzɪŋ; *NAmE* ˈmɜːrtʃ-/ *noun* [U] **1** (*especially NAmE*) the activity of selling goods, or of trying to sell them, by advertising or displaying them 推銷；展銷 **2** products connected with a popular film/movie, person or event; the process of selling these goods（根據受歡迎的電影、人物或事件而生產的）附帶產品；相關產品的銷售：*millions of pounds' worth of Batman merchandising* 價值數百萬英鎊的蝙蝠俠的附帶產品

mer·chant /ˈmɜːtʃənt; *NAmE* ˈmɜːrtʃ-/ *noun, adj.*
■ **noun** **1** a person who buys and sells goods in large quantities, especially one who imports and exports goods 商人；批發商；（尤指）進出口批發商：***builders' merchants*** (= who sell supplies to the building trade) 建材批發商 ◇ *a* ***coal/wine merchant*** 煤炭／葡萄酒批發商 ◇ *Venice was once a city of rich merchants.* 威尼斯曾是富商雲集的城市。➲ see also SQUEEGEE MERCHANT **2** (*BrE, informal, disapproving*) a person who likes a particular activity（某活動的）愛好者；熱衷於…的人：*a speed merchant* (= sb who likes to drive fast) 好開快車的人 ◇ *noise merchants* (= for example, a band who make a lot of noise) 噪音迷 **IDM** see DOOM *n.*
■ **adj.** [only before noun] connected with the transport of goods by sea 海上貨運的：*merchant seamen* 商船船員

mer·chant·able /ˈmɜːtʃəntəbl; *NAmE* ˈmɜːrtʃ-/ *adj.* (*law* 律) in a good enough condition to be sold 適於銷售的：*of merchantable quality* 質量符合銷售標準的

ˌmerchant ˈbank (*BrE*) (*NAmE* **inˈvestment bank**) *noun* a bank that deals with large businesses 商業銀行；投資銀行 ▸ **ˌmerchant ˈbanker** *noun* **ˌmerchant ˈbanking** *noun* [U]

mer·chant·man /ˈmɜːtʃəntmən; *NAmE* ˈmɜːrtʃ-/ (*pl.* **-men** /-mən/) (also **ˈmerchant ship**) *noun* a ship used for carrying goods for trade rather than a military ship 商船

ˌmerchant ˈnavy (*BrE*) (*NAmE* **ˌmerchant maˈrine**) *noun* [C+sing./pl. v.] a country's commercial ships and the people who work on them （國家的）商船隊；全體商船船員

mer·ci·ful /ˈmɜːsɪfl; *NAmE* ˈmɜːrs-/ *adj.* **1** ready to forgive people and show them kindness 寬大的；仁慈的；慈悲的 **SYN** **humane**：*a merciful God* 仁慈的上帝 ◇ *They asked her to be merciful to the prisoners.* 他們請求她對犯人仁慈。**2** (of an event 事件) seeming to be lucky, especially because it brings an end to sb's problems or suffering 還算幸運的，不幸而可取的（因能解決問題或能除痛苦）：*Death came as a merciful release.* 死神的到來算是一種幸運的解脫。➲ see also MERCY

mer·ci·ful·ly /ˈmɜːsɪfəli; *NAmE* ˈmɜːrs-/ *adv.* **1** used to show that you feel sb/sth is lucky because a situation could have been much worse （不幸中）幸運地 **SYN** **thankfully**：*Deaths from the disease are mercifully rare.* 這種疾病很少造成死亡，算是不幸中之幸。◇ *Mercifully, everyone arrived on time.* 幸而每個人都按時趕到。**2** in a kind way 仁慈地；寬大地：*He was treated mercifully.* 他受到了寬大對待。

mer·ci·less /ˈmɜːsɪləs; *NAmE* ˈmɜːrs-/ *adj.* showing no kindness or pity 毫不憐憫的；無情的；殘忍的 **SYN** **cruel**：*a* ***merciless killer/attack*** 無情的殺手／攻擊 ◇ *the merciless heat of the sun* 太陽的酷熱 ▸ **mer·ci·less·ly** *adv.* ➲ see also MERCY

mer·cur·ial /mɜːˈkjʊəriəl; *NAmE* mɜːrˈkjʊr-/ *adj.* **1** (*literary*) often changing or reacting in a way that is unexpected 多變的；變幻莫測的 **SYN** **volatile**：*Emily's mercurial temperament made her difficult to live with.* 埃米莉脾氣反覆無常，很難與她相處。**2** (*literary*) lively and quick 活潑的；機智的：*a brilliant, mercurial mind* 敏捷而富有才智的頭腦 **3** (*technical* 術語) containing MERCURY 含水銀的；水銀的

Mer·cury /ˈmɜːkjəri; *NAmE* ˈmɜːrk-/ *noun* the smallest planet in the SOLAR SYSTEM, nearest to the sun 水星

mer·cury /ˈmɜːkjəri; *NAmE* ˈmɜːrk-/ *noun* [U] (*symb.* **Hg**) a chemical element. Mercury is a poisonous silver liquid metal, used in THERMOMETERS. 汞；水銀

mercy /ˈmɜːsi; *NAmE* ˈmɜːrsi/ *noun* (*pl.* **-ies**) **1** [U] a kind or forgiving attitude towards sb that you have the power to harm or right to punish 仁慈；寬恕 **SYN** **humanity**：*to* ***ask/beg/plead for mercy*** 請求／乞求／祈求寬恕 ◇ *They* ***showed no mercy*** *to their hostages.* 他們對人質絲毫不講仁慈。◇ *God* ***have mercy on*** *us.* 上帝憐憫我們吧。◇ *The troops are on a* ***mercy mission*** (= a journey to help people) *in the war zone.* 部隊出發救助戰地民眾。**2** [C, usually sing.] (*informal*) an event or a situation to be grateful for, usually because it stops sth unpleasant 幸運；恩惠：***It's a mercy*** *she wasn't seriously hurt.* 幸運的是她傷勢不重。➲ see also MERCIFUL, MERCILESS
IDM **at the mercy of sb/sth** not able to stop sb/sth harming you because they have power or control over you 任…處置；對…無能為力；任由…擺佈：*I'm not going to put myself at the mercy of the bank.* 我不想任由銀行擺佈。◇ *We were at the mercy of the weather.* 我們受制於天氣。**leave sb/sth to the mercy/mercies of sb/sth** to leave sb/sth in a situation that may cause them to suffer or to be treated badly 聽任某人可能受苦或受到虐待（而無能為力）**throw yourself on sb's mercy** (*formal*) to put yourself in a situation where you must rely on sb to be kind to you and not harm or punish you 指望某人能夠善待（或寬恕）自己 ➲ more at SMALL *adj.*

ˈmercy killing *noun* [C, U] the act of killing sb out of pity, for example because they are in severe pain 安樂死；無疼痛致死術 **SYN** **euthanasia**

mere 🗝 /mɪə(r); *NAmE* mɪr/ *adj., noun*
■ **adj.** [only before noun] (*superlative* **mer·est**, no *comparative*) **1** 🗝 used when you want to emphasize how small, unimportant, etc. sb/sth is 僅僅的；只不過：*It took her a mere 20 minutes to win.* 她只花了 20 分鐘就贏了。◇ *A mere 2% of their budget has been spent on publicity.* 他們的預算開支只有 2% 用於宣傳。◇ *He seemed so young, a mere boy.* 他看來那麼年輕，只是個孩子。◇ *You've got the job. The interview will be a mere formality.* 你已經得到了這份工作。面試不過是個形式。**2** used when you are saying that the fact that a particular thing is present in a situation is enough to have an influence on that situation 只憑…就足以：*His mere presence* (= just the fact that he was there) *made her feel afraid.* 他當時在場，這就足以讓她害怕了。◇ *The* ***mere fact that*** *they were prepared to talk was encouraging.* 他們願意商談，這就很不錯了。◇ *The* ***mere thought of*** *eating made him feel sick.* 他一想到吃東西就覺得噁心。◇ *The merest*

(= the slightest) *hint of smoke is enough to make her feel ill.* 最細微的一絲煙就能使她感到不舒服。

■ ***noun*** (*BrE*, *literary*) (also used in names 也用於名稱) a small lake 小湖；池塘

mere·ly 0━ /ˈmɪəli; *NAmE* ˈmɪrli/ *adv.* used meaning 'only' or 'simply' to emphasize a fact or sth that you are saying 僅僅；只不過：*It is **not merely** a job, but a way of life.* 這不僅僅是一份工作，而且是一種生活方式。◇ *He said nothing, merely smiled and watched her.* 他什麼也沒說，只是微笑着看着她。◇ *They agreed to go merely because they were getting paid for it.* 他們同意去只是因為他們會得到酬勞。◇ *I'm merely stating what everybody knows anyway.* 我說的不過是些老生常談。

mere·tri·cious /ˌmerəˈtrɪʃəs/ *adj.* (*formal*) seeming attractive, but in fact having no real value 華而不實的；虛有其表的；金玉其外的

merge /mɜːdʒ; *NAmE* mɜːrdʒ/ *verb* **1** [I, T] to combine or make two or more things combine to form a single thing （使）合併，結合，併入：*The banks are set to merge next year.* 這幾家銀行準備明年合併。◇ *The two groups have merged to form a new party.* 兩大組織合併組成一個新黨。◇ **~ with sth** *His department will merge with mine.* 他的部門將和我的合併。◇ **~ into sth** *The villages expanded and merged into one large town.* 這些村莊擴大了並且結合成了一個大集鎮。◇ **~ (A and B) (together)** *Fact and fiction merge together in his latest thriller.* 在他最新的驚險小說中，真實和虛構交織在一起。◇ **~ A with B** *His department will be merged with mine.* 他的部門將和我的合併。◇ **~ sth** *The company was formed by merging three smaller firms.* 公司是由三家小公司合併組成的。 **2** [I] **~ (into sth)** if two things **merge**, or if one thing **merges into** another, the differences between them gradually disappear so that it is impossible to separate them 相融；融入；漸漸消失在某物中：*The hills merged into the dark sky behind them.* 山巒漸漸隱入背後漆黑的夜空之中。

IDM **merge into the ˈbackground** (of a person 人) to behave quietly when you are with a group of people so that they do not notice you 悄悄融入整體；不求聞達

mer·ger /ˈmɜːdʒə(r); *NAmE* ˈmɜːrdʒ-/ *noun* [C] the act of joining two or more organizations or businesses into one （機構或企業的）合併，歸併：**~ (between/of A and B)** *a merger between the two banks* 兩家銀行的合併 ◇ **~ (with sth)** *our proposed merger with the university* 我們與這所大學提議中的合併 ➲ COLLOCATIONS at BUSINESS

me·rid·ian /məˈrɪdiən/ *noun* one of the lines that is drawn from the North Pole to the South Pole on a map of the world 子午線；經線

mer·ingue /məˈræŋ/ *noun* [U, C] a sweet white mixture made from egg whites and sugar, usually baked until crisp and used to make cakes; a small cake made from this mixture 蛋白酥；蛋糖脆皮：*a lemon meringue pie* 檸檬蛋糖餡餅

me·rino /məˈriːnəʊ; *NAmE* -noʊ/ *noun* (*pl.* **-os**) **1** [C] a breed of sheep with long fine wool 美利奴羊（其絨細長） **2** [U] the wool of the merino sheep or a type of cloth made from this wool, used for making clothes 美利奴羊絨；美利奴羊毛織品

merit /ˈmerɪt/ *noun, verb*

■ ***noun*** **1** [U] (*formal*) the quality of being good and of deserving praise, reward or admiration 優點；美德；價值 **SYN** **worth**：*a work of outstanding artistic merit* 具有傑出藝術價值的作品 ◇ *The plan is entirely without merit.* 這個計劃毫無價值。◇ *I want to get the job **on merit**.* 我要憑才能得到這份工作。 **2** [C, usually pl.] a good feature that deserves praise, reward or admiration 值得讚揚（或獎勵、欽佩）的特點；功績；長處 **SYN** **strength**：*We will **consider each case on its** (**own**) **merits*** (= without considering any other issues, feelings, etc.). 我們將根據每件事情本身的情況來考慮。◇ *They weighed up the **relative merits** of the four candidates.* 他們對四名候選人各自的優點作了比較。 **3** [C] (*BrE*) a mark/grade in an exam or for a piece of work at school or university which is excellent （學校或大學考試或作業的）良好 **4** [C] (*BrE*) a mark/grade given as a reward for good behaviour at school （在校操行好而獲得的）良好

■ ***verb*** (not used in the progressive tenses 不用於進行時) **~ (doing) sth** (*formal*) to do sth to deserve praise, attention, etc. 應得；值得 **SYN** **deserve**：*He claims that their success was not merited.* 他聲稱他們不應該獲得成功。◇ *The case does not merit further investigation.* 這個案子不值得進一步調查。

mer·it·oc·racy /ˌmerɪˈtɒkrəsi; *NAmE* -ˈtɑːk-/ *noun* (*pl.* **-ies**) **1** [C, U] a country or social system where people get power or money on the basis of their ability 精英領導體制；英才管理制度 **2 the meritocracy** [sing.] the group of people with power in this kind of social system 精英管理班子 ► **mer·ito·crat·ic** /ˌmerɪtəˈkrætɪk/ *adj.*

meri·tori·ous /ˌmerɪˈtɔːriəs/ *adj.* (*formal*) deserving praise 值得讚揚的 **SYN** **praiseworthy**

mer·lin /ˈmɜːlɪn; *NAmE* ˈmɜːrlɪn/ *noun* a small BIRD OF PREY (= a bird that kills other creatures for food) of the FALCON family 灰背隼；鴿鷹

mer·maid /ˈmɜːmeɪd; *NAmE* ˈmɜːrm-/ *noun* (in stories) a creature with a woman's head and body, and a fish's tail instead of legs （傳說中的）美人魚

mer·man /ˈmɜːmæn; *NAmE* ˈmɜːr-/ *noun* (*pl.* **-men** /-men/) (in stories) a creature with a man's head and body and a fish's tail instead of legs, like a male MERMAID （傳說中的）人魚

mer·rily /ˈmerəli/ *adv.* **1** in a happy, cheerful way 高興地；愉快地：*They chatted merrily.* 他們愉快地聊着。 **2** without thinking about the problems that your actions might cause 自顧自地；毫無顧忌地 **SYN** **gaily**：*She carried on merrily, not realizing the offence she was causing.* 她毫無顧忌地胡鬧，沒意識到惹人生氣了。

mer·ri·ment /ˈmerimənt/ *noun* [U] (*formal*) happy talk, enjoyment and the sound of people laughing 歡樂；嬉戲；歡笑 **SYN** **jollity**, **mirth**

merry /ˈmeri/ *adj.* (**mer·rier**, **mer·ri·est**) **1** happy and cheerful 愉快的；高興的 **SYN** **cheery**：*a merry grin* 愉快的笑 **2 Merry Christmas** used at Christmas to say that you hope that sb has an enjoyable holiday（聖誕節祝賀語）聖誕快樂 **3** (*informal*, *especially BrE*) slightly drunk 微醺 **SYN** **tipsy**

IDM **make ˈmerry** (*old-fashioned*) to enjoy yourself by singing, laughing, drinking, etc. 行樂；宴樂 **the ˌmore the ˈmerrier** (*saying*) the more people or things there are, the better the situation will be or the more fun people will have 人越多越好玩；（東西）多多益善，越多越好：*'Can I bring a friend to your party?' 'Sure—the more the merrier!'* "我能帶個朋友來你的聚會嗎？" "當然，人越多越好玩嘛！" ➲ more at EAT, HELL, LEAD[1] *v.*

ˈmerry-go-round *noun* **1** (also **car·ou·sel** especially in *NAmE*) (*BrE* also **round·about**) a round platform with model horses, cars, etc. that turns around and around and that children ride on at a FAIRGROUND 旋轉木馬 ➲ picture at ROUNDABOUT **2** (*NAmE*) (*BrE* **round·about**) a round platform for children to play on in a park, etc. that is pushed round while the children are sitting on it （遊樂設施）旋轉平台 **3** continuous busy activity or a continuous series of changing events 一連串的繁忙活動；走馬燈似的更迭：*He was tired of the merry-go-round of romance and longed to settle down.* 他厭倦了沒完沒了的風流韻事，渴望安定下來。

merry·mak·ing /ˈmerimeɪkɪŋ/ *noun* [U] (*literary*) fun and enjoyment with singing, laughing, drinking, etc. 嬉笑玩樂；行樂 **SYN** **revelry**

mesa /ˈmeɪsə/ *noun* (*pl.* **mesas**) a hill with a flat top and steep sides that is common in the south-west of the US 桌子山，方山（常見於美國西南部）

mes·cal /ˈmeskæl; meˈskæl/ *noun* = PEYOTE (1)

mes·ca·line (also **mes·ca·lin**) /ˈmeskəlɪn/ *noun* [U] a drug obtained from a type of CACTUS, that affects people's minds and makes them see and hear things that are not really there 仙人球毒鹼，三甲氧苯乙胺（從某種仙人掌中提取的致幻劑）

mesh /meʃ/ *noun, verb*

■ ***noun*** **1** [U, C] material made of threads of plastic rope or wire that are twisted together like a net 網狀物；網狀織物：*wire mesh over the door of the cage* 罩在籠子門上的鐵絲網 **2** [C, usually sing.] a complicated situation or system that it is difficult to escape from 陷阱；困境；圈套 **SYN** **web**

■ ***verb*** (*formal*) **1** [I, T] to fit together or match closely, especially in a way that works well; to make things fit together successfully（使）吻合，相配，匹配，適合：**~ (sth) (with sth)** *This evidence meshes with earlier reports of an organized riot.* 這一證據和先前關於一次有組織暴亂的報告相吻合。◇ **~ (sth) (together)** *His theories mesh together various political and religious beliefs.* 他的理論把各種政治和宗教信仰完美地結合起來。**2** [I] (*technical* 術語) (of parts of a machine 機器零件) to fit together as they move 齧合：*If the cogs don't mesh correctly, the gears will keep slipping.* 如果嵌齒不能完好齧合，齒輪就會脱落。

mes·mer·ic /mezˈmerɪk/ *adj.* [usually before noun] (*formal*) having such a strong effect on people that they cannot give their attention to anything else 迷人的；不可抗拒的 **SYN** **hypnotic**

mes·mer·ize (*BrE* also **-ise**) /ˈmezməraɪz/ *verb* [usually passive] **~ sb** to have such a strong effect on you that you cannot give your attention to anything else 迷住；吸引 **SYN** **fascinate** ▸ **mes·mer·iz·ing, -is·ing** *adj.*：*Her performance was mesmerizing.* 她的表演讓人入迷。

meso·phyll /ˈmezəfɪl; ˈmiːz-; *BrE* also ˈmes-; miːs-/ *noun* [U] (*biology* 生) the material that the inside of a leaf is made of 葉肉

M

meso·sphere /ˈmezəsfɪə(r); ˈmiːz-; *NAmE* -sfɪr/ *noun* [usually sing.] the part of the earth's atmosphere which is between 50 and 80 kilometres from the ground, between the STRATOSPHERE and the THERMOSPHERE（大氣層的）中間層

mes·quite /meˈskiːt; ˈmeskiːt/ (also **meˈsquite tree**) *noun* a N American tree, often used for making CHARCOAL for GRILLING food 牧豆樹（產於北美，常用以製燒烤用的木炭）：*mesquite-grilled chicken* 牧豆樹炭烤雞

mess 0-w /mes/ *noun, verb*

■ ***noun***

▸ **UNTIDY STATE** 不整潔 **1** 0-w [C, usually sing.] a dirty or untidy state 骯髒；雜亂；不整潔：*The room was* ***in a mess.*** 這個房間雜亂不堪。◇ *The kids* ***made a mess*** *in the bathroom.* 孩子們把浴室搞得一塌糊塗。◇ ***'What a mess!'*** *she said, surveying the scene after the party.* 看着聚會後的場面，她説："真是一片狼藉！"◇ *My hair's a real mess!* 我的頭髮太亂了。

▸ **DIFFICULT SITUATION** 困境 **2** 0-w [C, usually sing.] a situation that is full of problems, usually because of a lack of organization or because of mistakes that sb has made（組織欠佳或人為導致的）麻煩，困境，混亂：*The economy is* ***in a mess.*** 經濟陷入了困境。◇ *I feel I've* ***made a mess of*** *things.* 我覺得我把事情搞糟了。◇ *The whole situation is a mess.* 整個情況都是一團糟。◇ *Let's try to sort out the mess.* 我們來收拾一下殘局吧。◇ *The biggest question is how they got into this mess in the first place.* 關鍵問題是他們是怎麼惹出這樣的麻煩的。

▸ **PERSON** 人 **3** [sing.] a person who is dirty or whose clothes and hair are not tidy 不整潔（或邋遢、不修邊幅）的人：*You're a mess!* 你真邋遢！**4** [sing.] (*informal*) a person who has serious problems and is in a bad mental condition 有嚴重問題且精神失常的人

▸ **ANIMAL WASTE** 動物糞便 **5** [U, C] (*informal*) the EXCREMENT (= solid waste matter) of an animal, usually a dog or cat（狗、貓等的）糞便

▸ **A LOT** 許多 **6** [sing.] **a ~ of sth** (*NAmE, informal*) a lot of sth 許多；大量：*There's a mess of fish down there, so get your lines in the water.* 那底下有很多魚，快下鉤吧。

▸ **ARMED FORCES** 武裝力量 **7** [C] (also **ˈmess hall** especially in *NAmE*) a building or room in which members of the armed forces have their meals（軍隊的）食堂，餐廳：*the officers' mess* 軍官食堂

■ ***verb***

▸ **MAKE UNTIDY** 使不整潔 **1** [T] **~ sth** (*informal, especially NAmE*) to make sth dirty or untidy 使不整潔；弄髒；弄亂：*Careful—you're messing my hair.* 小心，你弄亂我的頭髮了。

▸ **OF AN ANIMAL** 動物 **2** [I] to empty its BOWELS somewhere that it should not 隨地便溺

IDM **ˌno ˈmessing** (*informal*) used to say that sth has been done easily 毫不費力；不費吹灰之力；輕而易舉：*We finished in time, no messing.* 我們不費吹灰之力，就按時完成了。**not mess aˈround** (*BrE* also **not mess aˈbout**) (*informal*) to do sth quickly, efficiently or in the right way 不磨蹭；不拖沓；麻利地做；妥善處理：*When they decide to have a party they don't mess around.* 他們決定搞聚會，便會迅速操辦起來。

PHR V **ˌmess aˈround** (*BrE* also **ˌmess aˈbout**) **1** to behave in a silly and annoying way, especially instead of doing sth useful 胡鬧；瞎鬧 **SYN** **fool around**：*Will you stop messing around and get on with some work?* 別瞎鬧了，幹點正經事兒不行嗎？**2** to spend time doing sth for pleasure in a relaxed way 逍遙自在地做事：*We spent the day messing around on the river.* 我們在河邊閒逛了一整天。**ˌmess aˈround with sb** (*BrE* also **ˌmess aˈbout with sb**) to have a sexual relationship with sb, especially when you should not 勾搭；與某人調情；隨便與人發生性關係 **ˌmess aˈround with sth** (*BrE* also **ˌmess aˈbout with sth**) **1** to touch or use sth in a careless and/or annoying way 亂弄；玩弄：*Who's been messing around with my computer?* 誰瞎動過我的電腦？**2** to spend time playing with sth, repairing sth, etc. 花時間擺弄（或修理等）；瞎忙活 **ˌmess sb aˈbout/aˈround** (*BrE*) to treat sb in an unfair and annoying way, especially by changing your mind a lot or not doing what you said you would 粗魯地（或輕率地）對待 **ˌmess ˈup | ˌmess sth↔ˈup** to spoil sth or do it badly 把…弄糟；胡亂地做：*I've really messed up this time.* 這次我真的把事情給弄糟了。◇ *If you cancel now you'll mess up all my arrangements.* 如果你現在取消，就會破壞我所有的安排。**ˌmess sb↔ˈup** **1** (*informal*) to cause sb to have serious emotional or mental problems 使心情惡劣；使精神崩潰 **2** (*NAmE, informal*) to physically hurt sb, especially by hitting them 使身體受傷；毆打：*He was messed up pretty bad by the other guy.* 他被另一個傢伙打成了重傷。**ˌmess sth↔ˈup** to make sth dirty or untidy 使不整潔；弄髒；弄亂：*I don't want you messing up my nice clean kitchen.* 我不想讓你弄髒我這整潔的廚房。**ˈmess with sb/sth** (usually used in negative sentences 通常用於否定句) to get involved with sb/sth that may be harmful 捲入不好的事；與某人有牽連：*I wouldn't mess with him if I were you.* 我要是你就會離他遠點兒。

mes·sage 0-w /ˈmesɪdʒ/ *noun, verb*

■ ***noun*** **1** 0-w a written or spoken piece of information, etc. that you send to sb or leave for sb when you cannot speak to them yourself（書面或口頭的）信息，消息，音信：*There were no messages for me at the hotel.* 旅館裏沒有給我的留言。◇ *We've had an urgent message saying that your father's ill.* 我們得到個緊急消息説你父親病了。◇ *Jenny's not here at the moment.* ***Can I take a message?*** 珍妮這會兒不在。要我給你傳個話嗎？◇ ***I left a message*** *on her voicemail.* 我給她的語音信箱留言了。◇ *I've been trying to get you all day—don't you ever listen to your messages?* 我整天都在設法跟你聯繫，難道你就沒有聽一下電話留言？◇ **~ (from sb) (to sb)** *Messages of support have been arriving from all over the country.* 表示聲援的言論從全國各地紛至沓來。◇ *a televised message from the President to the American people* 電視播出的總統告美國人民書 ➲ see also ERROR MESSAGE **2** 0-w a piece of information sent in electronic form, for example by email or mobile/cell phone 電郵信息；（手機）短信息：*an email message* 電郵信息 ◇ *There were four messages in my inbox.* 我的收件箱裏有四封郵件。◇ *He sent me a message.* 他給我發了一條信息。**3** 0-w [usually sing.] an important moral, social or political idea that a book, speech, etc. is trying to communicate（書、演講等的）要旨，要點，教訓：*a film with a strong religious message* 有強烈的宗教啟示的電影 ◇ *The campaign is trying to* ***get the message across*** *to young people that drugs are dangerous.* 這次運動旨在讓年輕人認識毒品的危害。

4 a piece of information that is sent from the brain to a part of the body, or from a part of the body to the brain（從大腦發給身體某部位或身體某部位向大腦發送的）信息： *The message arrives in your brain in a fraction of a second.* 信息瞬間便可傳遞到大腦。 **5 messages** [pl.] (*ScotE*) shopping 購物；買東西： *to do the messages* 買東西 ◇ *to go for the messages* 去買東西 ◇ *You can leave your messages* (= the things that you have bought) *here.* 你可以把你買的東西放在這兒。

IDM **get the 'message** (*informal*) to understand what sb is trying to tell you indirectly 領悟，理解，明白（別人的暗示）： *When he started looking at his watch, I got the message and left.* 他開始看錶了，我明白他的意思，就走了。 **on/off 'message** (of a politician 從政者) stating/not stating the official view of their political party 説明（或不説明）所屬政黨的官方觀點

■ *verb* to send a TEXT MESSAGE to sb 向某人傳送（電子信息）： **~ sb** *Fiona just messaged me.* 菲奧納剛給我發來電郵。◇ **~ sb sth** *Brian messaged me the news.* 布賴恩用短信告訴我這個消息。 ▸ **mes·saging** *noun* [U] : *a multimedia messaging service* 多媒體信息服務 ◇ *picture messaging* 圖像傳送

'message board *noun* a place on a website where a user can write or read messages（網站）留言板： *I posted a question on the message board.* 我在留言板上貼出了一個問題。

mes·sen·ger /'mesɪndʒə(r)/ *noun* a person who gives a message to sb or who delivers messages to people as a job 送信人；通信員；郵遞員；信使： *He sent the order by messenger.* 他通過郵遞員發出訂單。◇ *a motorcycle messenger* 騎摩托車的郵遞員 **IDM** see SHOOT *v.*

Mes·siah /mə'saɪə/ *noun* **1 the Messiah** [sing.] (in Christianity 基督教) Jesus Christ who was sent by God into the world to save people from evil and SIN 彌賽亞；默西亞；救世主基督 **2 the Messiah** [sing.] (in Judaism 猶太教) a king who will be sent by God to save the Jewish people 彌賽亞（上帝要派去拯救猶太人民的國王） **3 messiah** a leader who people believe will solve the problems of a country or the world 人們信賴的領導者；救世主；救星 **SYN** **saviour** : *He's seen by many as a political messiah.* 許多人將他視為政治救星。

mes·si·an·ic /ˌmesi'ænɪk/ *adj.* (*formal*) **1** relating to a messiah 有關救世主的；救星的 **2** attempting to make big changes in society or to a political system in an extremely determined and enthusiastic way 有雄心壯志的；狂熱的： *The reforms were carried out with an almost messianic zeal.* 改革是以極大的熱情進行的。

Messrs (*BrE*) (*NAmE* **Messrs.**) /'mesəz; *NAmE* -sərz/ *abbr.* (used as the plural of 'Mr' before a list of names and before names of business companies)（Mr 的複數形式，用於一組人名或公司名稱前）： *Messrs Smith, Brown and Jones* 史密斯、布朗和瓊斯先生 ◇ *Messrs T Brown and Co* * T • 布朗公司諸位先生

messy /'mesi/ *adj.* (**mess·ier**, **messi·est**) **1** dirty and/or untidy 骯髒的；凌亂的；不整潔的 **SYN** **chaotic** : *The house was always messy.* 這房子總是亂糟糟的。◇ (*NAmE*) *Her long black hair was messy and dirty.* 她烏黑的長髮又髒又亂。 **2** making sb/sth dirty and/or untidy 使髒亂的；使不整潔的： *It was a messy job.* 這是項很髒的工作。 **3** (of a situation 狀況) unpleasant, confused or difficult to deal with 混亂的；難以處理的；令人厭煩的： *The divorce was painful and messy.* 那次離婚令人痛苦而又糾葛不清。

mes·tiza /me'sti:zə/ *noun* a female MESTIZO 梅斯蒂索女混血兒

mes·tizo /me'sti:zəʊ; *NAmE* -zoʊ/ *noun* (*pl.* **-os**) a Latin American who has both Spanish and Native American ANCESTORS 梅斯蒂索混血兒（有西班牙和美洲土著血統的拉丁美洲人）

Met /met/ *abbr.* (*informal*) **1** METEOROLOGICAL 氣象的；氣象學的： *the Met Office weather forecast service* 國家氣象局天氣預報處 **2 the Met** the Metropolitan Opera House (in New York)（紐約）大都會歌劇院 **3 the Met** the Metropolitan Police (the police force in London) 倫敦警隊

met *past tense, past part.* of MEET

meta- /'metə/ *combining form* (in nouns, adjectives and verbs 構成名詞、形容詞和動詞) **1** connected with a change of position or state（位置或狀態）變化的： *metamorphosis* 變形 ◇ *metabolism* 新陳代謝 **2** higher; beyond 高於；在上；在外： *metaphysics* 形而上學 ◇ *metalanguage* 元語言

me·tab·ol·ism /mə'tæbəlɪzəm/ *noun* [U, sing.] (*biology* 生) the chemical processes in living things that change food, etc. into energy and materials for growth 新陳代謝： *The body's metabolism is slowed down by extreme cold.* 嚴寒可以使身體新陳代謝的速度下降。 ▸ **meta·bol·ic** /ˌmetə'bɒlɪk; *NAmE* -'bɑ:l-/ *adj.* [usually before noun] : *a* ***metabolic process/disorder*** 新陳代謝過程／紊亂 ◇ *a* ***high/low metabolic rate*** 高／低新陳代謝速度

me·tab·ol·ize (*BrE* also **-ise**) /mə'tæbəlaɪz/ *verb* **~ sth** (*biology* 生) to turn food, minerals, etc. in the body into new cells, energy and waste products by means of chemical processes 新陳代謝（將食物、礦物質等通過化學過程轉換成新細胞、能量和廢料）

meta·car·pal /ˌmetə'kɑ:pl; *NAmE* -'kɑ:rpl/ *noun* (*anatomy* 解) any of the five bones in the hand between the wrist and the fingers 掌骨（人的腕骨與指骨之間的五根小型長骨）

meta·data /'metədeɪtə; -dɑ:tə; *NAmE* also -dætə/ *noun* [U] information that describes other information in order to help you understand or use it 元數據；元資料；後設資料： *In the metadata she found the author and location of the file.* 她從元數據中找到了文件的作者和位置。

meta·fic·tion /'metəfɪkʃn/ *noun* [U] a type of play, novel, etc. in which the author deliberately reminds the audience, reader, etc. that it is FICTION and not real life 元虛構作品，後設作品（敍事時有意識讓觀眾、讀者等意識到虛構性的戲劇或小說等）

metal 0‑ᴡ /'metl/ *noun* [C, U] a type of solid mineral substance that is usually hard and shiny and that heat and electricity can travel through, for example tin, iron and gold 金屬： *a piece of metal* 一塊金屬 ◇ *a* ***metal pipe/bar/box*** 金屬管／棍／盒子 ◇ *The frame is made of metal.* 框子是用金屬做的。 ➲ see also HEAVY METAL (2), PRECIOUS METAL

meta·lan·guage /'metəlæŋgwɪdʒ/ *noun* [C, U] (*linguistics* 語言) the words and phrases that people use to talk about or describe language or a particular language 元語言（用於講述或描述語言或某種語言的詞和短語）

'metal detector *noun* **1** an electronic device that you use to look for metal objects that are buried under the ground 金屬礦藏探測器 **2** an electronic machine that is used, for example at an airport, to see if people are hiding metal objects such as weapons（機場等處的）金屬物品檢測機

'metal fatigue *noun* [U] weakness in metal that is frequently put under pressure that makes it likely to break 金屬疲勞

meta·lin·guis·tic /ˌmetəlɪŋ'gwɪstɪk/ *adj.* (*linguistics* 語言) related to metalanguage 元語言的 ▸ **meta·lin·guis·tics** /ˌmetəlɪŋ'gwɪstɪks/ *noun* [U]

met·alled /'metld/ *adj.* (of a road or track 道路) made or repaired with small pieces of broken stone 碎石鋪面的

me·tal·lic /mə'tælɪk/ *adj.* [usually before noun] **1** that looks, tastes or sounds like metal 金屬般的；有金屬味（或聲音）的： ***metallic paint/colours/blue*** 有金屬光澤的顏料／顏色／藍色 ◇ *a metallic taste* 金屬味 ◇ *a* ***metallic sound/click*** 金屬聲；金屬碰撞的叮噹聲 ◇ *a metallic voice* (= that sounds unpleasant) 尖厲刺耳的聲音 **2** made of or containing metal 金屬製的；含金屬的： *a metallic object* 金屬物品 ◇ *metallic compounds* 金屬合成物

met·al·loid /'metlɔɪd/ (*BrE* also **semi·metal**) *noun* (*chemistry* 化) a chemical element which has properties both of metals and of other solid substances 準金屬

me·tal·lur·gist /mə'tælədʒɪst; *NAmE* 'metlɜ:rdʒɪst/ *noun* a scientist who studies metallurgy 冶金學家

M

me·tal·lurgy /mə'tælədʒi; *NAmE* 'metlɜ:rdʒi/ *noun* [U] the scientific study of metals and their uses 冶金學 ▸ **me·tal·lur·gical** /ˌmetə'lɜ:dʒɪkl; *NAmE* ˌmetl'ɜ:rdʒ-/ *adj.*

met·al·work /'metlwɜ:k; *NAmE* -wɜ:rk/ *noun* [U] **1** the activity of making objects out of metal; objects that are made out of metal 金屬製品的製造（或加工）；金屬製品 **2** the metal parts of sth 金屬配件：*cracks in the metalwork* 金屬件上的裂縫 ▸ **met·al·work·er** *noun*

meta·morph·ic /ˌmetə'mɔ:fɪk; *NAmE* -'mɔ:rf-/ *adj.* (*geology* 地) (of rocks 岩石) formed by the action of heat or pressure 變質的

meta·morph·ose /ˌmetə'mɔ:fəʊz; *NAmE* -'mɔ:rfoʊz/ *verb* [I, T] **~ (sth/sb) (from sth) (into sth)** (*formal*) to change or make sth/sb change into sth completely different, especially over a period of time（使）變形，變化，發生質變 **SYN** **transform**：*The caterpillar will eventually metamorphose into a butterfly.* 毛毛蟲最終將蛻變成一隻蝴蝶。

meta·mor·phosis /ˌmetə'mɔ:fəsɪs; *NAmE* -'mɔ:rf-/ *noun* (*pl.* **meta·mor·phoses** /-əsi:z/) [C, U] (*formal*) a process in which sb/sth changes completely into sth different 變形；質變 **SYN** **transformation**：*the metamorphosis of a caterpillar into a butterfly* 從毛毛蟲到蝴蝶的蛻變 ◇ *She had undergone an amazing metamorphosis from awkward schoolgirl to beautiful woman.* 她經歷了從笨女生到大美人這一令人驚訝的變化。

meta·phor /'metəfə(r); -fɔ:(r)/ *noun* [C, U] a word or phrase used to describe sb/sth else, in a way that is different from its normal use, in order to show that the two things have the same qualities and to make the description more powerful, for example *She has a heart of stone*; the use of such words and phrases 暗喻；隱喻：*a game of football used as a metaphor for the competitive struggle of life* 用來喻指生活中的激烈鬥爭的一場足球比賽 ◇ *the writer's striking use of metaphor* 這位作家對於隱喻的獨到運用 ➲ COLLOCATIONS at LITERATURE ➲ compare SIMILE

meta·phor·ical /ˌmetə'fɒrɪkl; *NAmE* -'fɔ:r-/ *adj.* connected with or containing metaphors 隱喻的；含比喻的；比喻性的：*metaphorical language* 比喻的語言 ➲ compare FIGURATIVE, LITERAL ▸ **meta·phor·ic·al·ly** /-kli/ *adv.*：*I'll leave you in Robin's capable hands—**metaphorically speaking**, of course!* 我要把你放到羅賓能幹的手中。當然，這只是打個比方。

meta,physical 'poets *noun* [pl.] a group of 17th century English POETS who explored the nature of the world and human life, and who used images that were surprising at that time（17世紀英國的）玄學派詩人

meta·phys·ics /ˌmetə'fɪzɪks/ *noun* [U] the branch of philosophy that deals with the nature of existence, truth and knowledge 形而上學；玄學 ▸ **meta·phys·ic·al** /ˌmetə'fɪzɪkl/ *adj.*：***metaphysical problems/speculation*** 形而上學的問題／思辨

me·tas·ta·sis /mə'tæstəsɪs/ *noun* [U] (*medical* 醫) the development of TUMOURS in different parts of the body resulting from cancer that has started in another part of the body（瘤）轉移 ▸ **me·tas·ta·tic** /ˌmetə'stætɪk/ *adj.*

meta·tar·sal /ˌmetə'tɑ:sl; *NAmE* -'tɑ:rsl/ *noun* (*anatomy* 解) any of the bones in the part of the foot between the ankle and the toes 蹠骨（組成人體足底的小型長骨）

mete /mi:t/ *verb*

PHR V **ˌmete sth↔'out (to sb)** (*formal*) to give sb a punishment; to make sb suffer bad treatment 給予懲罰；責罰；使受苦：*Severe penalties were meted out by the court.* 法庭判定予以嚴懲。◇ *the violence meted out to the prisoners* 施加在囚犯身上的暴力

me·teor /'mi:tiə(r); -iɔ:(r)/ *noun* a piece of rock from outer space that makes a bright line across the night sky as it burns up while falling through the earth's atmosphere 流星：*a meteor shower* 流星雨 ➲ see also SHOOTING STAR

me·teor·ic /ˌmi:ti'ɒrɪk; *NAmE* -'ɔ:r-/ *adj.* **1** achieving success very quickly 迅速成功的：*a meteoric rise to fame* 迅速成名 ◇ *a meteoric career* 迅速成功的事業 **2** connected with meteors 流星的：*meteoric craters* 流星撞擊形成的坑

me·teor·ite /'mi:tiəraɪt/ *noun* a piece of rock from outer space that hits the earth's surface 隕石

me·teor·olo·gist /ˌmi:tiə'rɒlədʒɪst; *NAmE* -'rɑ:l-/ *noun* a scientist who studies meteorology 氣象學家

me·teor·ology /ˌmi:tiə'rɒlədʒi; *NAmE* -'rɑ:l-/ *noun* [U] the scientific study of the earth's atmosphere and its changes, used especially in forecasting the weather (= saying what it will be like) 氣象學 ▸ **me·teoro·logic·al** /ˌmi:tiərə'lɒdʒɪkl; *NAmE* -'lɑ:dʒ-/ *adj.*

meter /'mi:tə(r)/ *noun, verb*

■ ***noun*** **1** (especially in compounds 尤用於構成複合詞) a device that measures and records the amount of electricity, gas, water, etc. that you have used or the time and distance you have travelled, etc.（用於測量電、煤氣、水等，以及時間和距離的）計量器，計量表：*A man came to read the gas meter.* 有個男子來查過煤氣表。◇ *The cab driver left the meter running while he waited for us.* 在等我們的時候，出租車司機讓計程表繼續走字。➲ see also LIGHT METER **2** = PARKING METER **3 -meter** (in compounds 構成複合詞) a device for measuring the thing mentioned 計；儀；表：*speedometer* 速度計 ◇ *altimeter* 高度表 ◇ *calorimeter* 熱量計 **4** (*NAmE*) = METRE：*Who holds the record in the 100 meters?* * 100 米紀錄是誰保持的？

■ ***verb*** **~ sth** to measure sth (for example how much gas, electricity, etc. has been used) using a meter 用儀表計量

meth /meθ/ (also **crystal meth**, **crystal**) *noun* [U] (*informal*) a powerful illegal drug, METHAMPHETAMINE, that looks like small pieces of glass 冰毒（即甲基苯丙胺）：*the growing meth problem in our rural communities* 我們鄉村社區越來越嚴重的冰毒問題

metha·done /'meθədəʊn; *NAmE* -doʊn/ *noun* [U] a drug that is used to treat people who are trying to stop taking the illegal drug HEROIN 美沙酮，美散痛（用於戒除海洛因毒癮）

meth·am·pheta·mine /ˌmeθæm'fetəmi:n/ (also *informal* **meth**, **'crystal meth**) *noun* [U] a powerful illegal drug 甲基苯丙胺；脫氧麻黃鹼；（俗稱）冰毒

me·thane /'mi:θeɪn; *NAmE* 'meθ-/ *noun* [U] (*symb.* CH_4) a gas without colour or smell, that burns easily and is used as fuel. Natural gas consists mainly of methane. 甲烷；沼氣

metha·nol /'meθənɒl; *NAmE* -nɔ:l; -noʊl/ *noun* [U] (*symb.* CH_3OH) a poisonous form of alcohol formed when METHANE reacts with OXYGEN 甲醇

methi·cil·lin /ˌmeθɪ'sɪlɪn/ *noun* [U] a drug that can be used against infections where PENICILLIN is not effective 甲氧苯青黴素；甲氧西林

me·thinks /mɪ'θɪŋks/ *verb* (*pt* **me·thought**) (not used in the perfect tenses 不用於完成時) [I, T] **~ (that) ...** (*old use* or *humorous*) I think 我想；我以為；據我看來

method 🔑 **AW** /'meθəd/ *noun*

1 🔑 [C] a particular way of doing sth 方法；辦法；措施：**~ (of sth)** *a **reliable/effective/scientific method** of data analysis* 可靠的／有效的／科學的數據分析方法 ◇ **~ (of doing sth)** *a new method of solving the problem* 解決問題的新方法 ◇ ***traditional/alternative methods*** 傳統的／另類的方式 ◇ **~ (for sth/for doing sth)** *the best method for arriving at an accurate prediction of the costs* 準確預測成本的最佳方法 ➲ see also DIRECT METHOD **2** [U] the quality of being well planned and organized 條理；有條不紊

IDM **there's (a) method in sb's madness** there is a reason for sb's behaviour and it is not as strange or as stupid as it seems 看來奇怪（或愚蠢）的行為有其道理

'method acting *noun* [U] a method of preparing for a role in which an actor tries to experience the life and feelings of the character he or she will play（深入角色生活和內心的）體驗派表演，方法演技 ▸ **'method actor** *noun*

meth·od·ic·al **AW** /mə'θɒdɪkl; *NAmE* -'θɑ:d-/ *adj.* **1** done in a careful and logical way 有條理的；有條不紊的：***a methodical approach/study*** 條理清晰的方法／研究 **2** (of a person 人) doing things in a careful and logical way 辦事有條不紊的 SYN **disciplined**, **precise**： *to have a methodical mind* 思想有條理 ▸ **meth·od·ic·al·ly** /-kli/ *adv.*： *They sorted slowly and methodically through the papers.* 他們慢慢地有條理地整理文件。

Meth·od·ist /ˈmeθədɪst/ *noun* a member of a Christian Protestant Church that broke away from the Church of England in the 18th century 循道宗信徒（18 世紀從英國國教分離出的基督教新教教徒） ▸ **Meth·od·ism** /ˈmeθədɪzəm/ *noun* [U] **Meth·od·ist** *adj.*： *a* ***Methodist church/preacher*** 循道宗教會 / 牧師

meth·od·ology AW /ˌmeθəˈdɒlədʒi; *NAmE* -ˈdɑːl-/ *noun* (*pl.* **-ies**) [C, U] (*formal*) a set of methods and principles used to perform a particular activity（從事某一活動的）方法，原則： *recent changes in the methodology of language teaching* 語言教學法最近的變化 ▸ **meth·odo·logic·al** AW /ˌmeθədəˈlɒdʒɪkl; *NAmE* -ˈlɑːdʒ-/ *adj.* [usually before noun]： *methodological problems* 方法問題 **meth·odo·logic·al·ly** /-kli/ *adv.*

meths /meθs/ *noun* [U] (*informal, especially BrE*) = METHYLATED SPIRIT

Me·thu·selah /məˈθjuːzələ/ *noun* used to describe a very old person（人）高壽： *I'm feeling older than Methuselah.* 我覺得自己老態龍鍾。 ORIGIN From Methuselah, a man in the Bible who is supposed to have lived for 969 years. 源自《聖經》人物瑪士撒拉，據傳享壽 969 歲。

meth·yl·ated spirit /ˌmeθəleɪtɪd ˈspɪrɪt/ (also **meth·yl·ated spirits**) (also *informal* **meths**) *noun* [U] a type of alcohol that is not fit for drinking, used as a fuel for lighting and heating and for cleaning off dirty marks 甲基化酒精（不適宜飲用，用作照明、加熱燃料或清洗劑）

me·ticu·lous /məˈtɪkjələs/ *adj.* paying careful attention to every detail 細心的；小心翼翼的 SYN **fastidious**, **thorough**： ***meticulous planning/records/research*** 周密的計劃；詳細的記錄；一絲不苟的研究 ◇ **~ in sth/doing sth** *He's always meticulous in keeping the records up to date.* 他總是十分細心地適時更新存檔資料。 ◇ **~ about sth** *My father was meticulous about his appearance.* 我父親對自己的外表很講究。 ▸ **me·ticu·lous·ly** *adv.*： *a meticulously planned schedule* 計劃周密的日程安排 ◇ *meticulously clean* 一塵不染 **me·ticu·lous·ness** *noun* [U]

mé·tier /ˈmetieɪ; *NAmE* ˈmeɪt-/ *noun* [usually sing.] (*from French, formal*) a person's work, especially when they have a natural skill or ability for it 職業；工作；行業；（尤指）專長

ˈme-time *noun* [U] (*informal*) time when a person who is normally very busy relaxes or does sth they enjoy 私人專屬時間；自我享受時間： *The spa is popular with women who want a bit of me-time.* 礦泉療養中心受到想找點時間自我放鬆一下的女士的青睞。

Metis /meɪˈtiː/ *noun* (*pl.* **Metis** /meɪˈtiː; meɪˈtiːz/) (*CanE*) (especially in Canada) a person with one Aboriginal parent and one European parent, or a person whose family comes from both Aboriginal and European backgrounds 梅蒂人；（加拿大土著和歐洲人或有土著和歐洲血統的）加歐混血兒

me·ton·ymy /məˈtɒnəmi; *NAmE* -ˈtɑːn-/ *noun* [U] (*technical* 術語) the act of referring to sth by the name of sth else that is closely connected with it, for example using *the White House* for *the US president* 轉喻（用一名稱來指代與之密切相關的事物，例如用 the White House 來指代 the US president）

ˌme-ˈtoo *adj.* [only before noun] (*BrE, informal*) done or produced because of sth successful that sb else has done 仿效別人（成功之事）的： *The magazine 'Hello!' gave rise to a number of me-too publications.*《你好！》雜誌帶動了許多效仿它的刊物問世。

metre 0➔ (*especially US* **meter**) /ˈmiːtə(r)/ *noun*
1 0➔ [C] (*abbr.* **m**) a unit for measuring length; a hundred centimetres 米；公尺 **2** [C, U] (*abbr.* **m**) used in the name of races 用於競賽名稱： *She came second in the 200 metres.* 在 200 米比賽中，她取得了第二名。◇ *the 4×100 metre(s) relay* * 4×100 米接力賽 **3** [U, C] the arrangement of strong and weak stresses in lines of poetry that produces the rhythm; a particular example of this（詩的）格律

met·ric /ˈmetrɪk/ *adj.* **1** based on the metric system 米制的；公制的： ***metric units/measurements/sizes*** 公制單位 / 尺寸 / 大小 ◇ *British currency went metric in 1971.* 英國的貨幣於 1971 年實行公制。 **2** made or measured using the metric system 按公制製作的；用公制測量的： *These screws are metric.* 這些螺絲釘是用公制尺碼製造的。 ➲ compare IMPERIAL **3** = METRICAL

met·ric·al /ˈmetrɪkl/ (also **met·ric**) *adj.* connected with the rhythm of a poem, produced by the arrangement of stress on the syllables in each line 格律的

met·ri·ca·tion /ˌmetrɪˈkeɪʃn/ *noun* [U] the process of changing to using the metric system 施行公制度量衡；公制化

the ˈmetric system *noun* [sing.] the system of measurement that uses the metre, the kilogram and the litre as basic units 公制；米制

ˌmetric ˈton *noun* = TONNE

metro /ˈmetrəʊ; *NAmE* ˈmetroʊ/ *noun, adj.*
■ ***noun*** (*pl.* **-os**) **1** (also **the Metro**) [sing.] an underground train system, especially the one in Paris 地下鐵路；（尤指）巴黎地鐵： *to travel* ***on the metro / by metro*** 乘地鐵旅行 ◇ *the Paris Metro* 巴黎地鐵 ◇ *a metro station* 地鐵車站 ➲ note at UNDERGROUND **2** (*IndE*) a large or capital city, especially Delhi, Kolkata, Mumbai or Chennai 大城市（尤指德里、加爾各答、孟買或欽奈）： *Here are the temperatures recorded at the four metros at 5 o'clock this morning.* 這是今天早晨 5 點鐘時四大城市的氣溫記錄。
■ ***adj.*** (*NAmE, informal*) = METROPOLITAN： *the New York metro areas* 紐約市區

me·trol·ogy /məˈtrɒlədʒi; *NAmE* -ˈtrɑːl-/ *noun* [U] the scientific study of measurement 計量學 ▸ **me·tro·logic·al** /ˌmetrəˈlɒdʒɪkl; *NAmE* -ˈlɑːdʒ-/ *adj.*

metronome 節拍器

met·ro·nome /ˈmetrənəʊm; *NAmE* -noʊm/ *noun* a device that makes a regular sound like a clock and is used by musicians to help them keep the correct rhythm when playing a piece of music 節拍器 ▸ **met·ro·nom·ic** /ˌmetrəˈnɒmɪk; *NAmE* -ˈnɑːm-/ *adj.*： *His financial problems hit the headlines with almost metronomic regularity.* 他的財政問題幾乎定期成為頭條新聞。

me·trop·olis /məˈtrɒpəlɪs; *NAmE* məˈtrɑːp-/ *noun* a large important city (often the capital city of a country or region) 大都會；大城市；首都；首府

met·ro·pol·itan /ˌmetrəˈpɒlɪtən; *NAmE* -ˈpɑːl-/ *adj.* [only before noun] **1** (also *NAmE informal* **metro**) connected with a large or capital city 大城市的；大都會的： *the New York metropolitan area* 紐約都市區 ◇ ***metropolitan districts/regions*** 都市區 **2** connected with a particular country rather than with the other regions of the world that the country controls 本土的： ***metropolitan France/Spain*** 法國 / 西班牙本土

met·ro·sex·ual /ˌmetrəˈsekʃuəl/ *noun* (*informal*) a HETEROSEXUAL man who lives in a city and is interested in things like fashion and shopping 都市麗男，都會美男（愛好時尚和購物等的異性戀男子） ▸ **met·ro·sex·ual** *adj.*

met·tle /ˈmetl/ *noun* [U] the ability and determination to do sth successfully despite difficult conditions 奮鬥精

神；毅力：*The next game will be a real test of their mettle.* 下一場比賽就要看他們的拚搏精神了。
IDM **on your 'mettle** prepared to use all your skills, knowledge, etc. because you are being tested 奮發起來；準備盡最大努力

mew /mjuː/ *noun* the soft high noise that a cat makes（貓叫聲）喵 ▸ **mew** *verb* [I] : *The kitten mewed pitifully.* 小貓喵喵地叫，挺可憐的。

mewl /mjuːl/ *verb* [I] to make a weak crying sound 嗚咽；啜泣 ▸ **mewl·ing** *noun* [U] **mewl·ing** *adj.* : *mewling babies* 嗚嗚哭的嬰兒

mews /mjuːz/ *noun* (*pl.* **mews**) (*BrE*) a short, narrow street with a row of stables (= buildings used to keep horses in) that have been made into small houses 馬廄街（周圍排列着馬廄改建的住房）

'mews house (*BrE*) (*US* **'carriage house**) *noun* a house in a mews 馬廄改建的房屋

Mex·ican /ˈmeksɪkən/ *adj.*, *noun*
■ ***adj.*** from or connected with Mexico 墨西哥的
■ ***noun*** a person from Mexico 墨西哥人

,Mexican 'wave (*BrE*) (*NAmE* **the 'wave**) *noun* a continuous movement that looks like a wave on the sea, made by a large group of people, especially people watching a sports game, when one person after another stands up, raises their arms, and then sits down again 墨西哥人浪（尤指體育比賽中看台上的觀眾依次站起坐下而形成的波浪狀場面）

mez·za·nine /ˈmezəniːn; ˈmetsə-/ *noun* **1** a floor that is built between two floors of a building and is smaller than the other floors（介於兩層樓之間、比其他樓層小的）夾樓層：*a bedroom on the mezzanine* 夾層樓面上的臥室 ◇ *a mezzanine floor* 夾樓層 **2** (*NAmE*) the first area of seats above the ground floor in a theatre; the first few rows of these seats（戲院的）最低層樓廳（前座）➲ see also DRESS CIRCLE

mezzo-soprano /ˌmetsəʊ səˈprɑːnəʊ; *NAmE* ˌmetsoʊ səˈprɑːnoʊ; -ˈpræn-/ (also **mezzo**) *noun* (*pl.* **mezzo-sopranos, mezzos**) (from *Italian*) a singing voice with a range between SOPRANO and ALTO; a woman with a mezzo-soprano voice 女中音；女中音歌手

mg *abbr.* (in writing) milligram(s)（書寫形式）毫克

Mgr (also **Mgr.** especially in *NAmE*) *abbr.* (in writing) MONSIGNOR（書寫形式）蒙席

MHA /ˌem eɪtʃ ˈeɪ/ *abbr.* (*CanE*) Member of the House of Assembly (the parliament in Newfoundland and Labrador)（紐芬蘭和拉布拉多的）議會議員

mhm /əmˈhm/ *exclamation* used to say 'yes', or to show sb that you are listening to them（表示同意或在聽對方說話）哦，嗯：*'Can I borrow your pen?' 'Mhm.'* "借你的鋼筆用一下好嗎？""可以。" ◇ *'I phoned Alan ...' 'Mhm.' '... and he said he's going to come.'* "我給艾倫打電話了…""噢。""…他說他要來。"

MHz *abbr.* (in writing) MEGAHERTZ（書寫形式）兆赫

mi = ME *n.*

MI5 /ˌem aɪ ˈfaɪv/ *noun* [U] the British government organization that deals with national security within Britain. Its official name is 'the Security Service'. 軍情五處（英國安全局，負責英國國內安全，正式名稱為 the Security Service）

MI6 /ˌem aɪ ˈsɪks/ *noun* [U] the British government organization that deals with national security from outside Britain. Its official name is 'the Secret Intelligence Service'. 軍情六處（負責與英國國家安全有關的海外情報，正式名稱為 the Secret Intelligence Service）

MIA /ˌem aɪ ˈeɪ/ *abbr.* (*especially NAmE*) (of a soldier 士兵) missing in action (missing after a battle) 在戰鬥中失踪

miaow (*BrE*) (also **meow** *NAmE, BrE*) /miˈaʊ/ *noun* the crying sound made by a cat（貓叫聲）喵 ➲ see also MEW ▸ **miaow** (*BrE*) (also **meow** *NAmE, BrE*) *verb* [I]

mi·asma /miˈæzmə; maɪˈæ-/ *noun* [C, usually sing., U] (*literary*) a mass of air that is dirty and smells unpleasant 污濁難聞的空氣：*A miasma of stale alcohol hung around him.* 他身上常帶着難聞的酒精味。◇ (*figurative*) *the miasma of depression* 壓抑的氣氛

MiB *abbr.* (in writing 書寫形式) MEBIBYTE

Mib (also **Mibit**) *abbr.* (in writing 書寫形式) MEBIBIT

mic /maɪk/ *noun* (*informal*) = MICROPHONE

mica /ˈmaɪkə/ *noun* [U] a clear mineral that splits easily into thin flat layers and is used to make electrical equipment 雲母

mice *pl.* of MOUSE

Mich·ael·mas /ˈmɪklməs/ *noun* [U] (in the Christian Church) the holy day in honour of St Michael, 29 September 米迦勒節（基督教節日，每年 9 月 29 日）

,Michaelmas 'daisy *noun* a plant that has blue, white, pink or purple flowers with dark centres, that appear in the autumn/fall 紫菀

Michelin man /ˈmɪtʃəlm mæn; ˈmɪʃ-/ *noun*
IDM **like the/a 'Michelin man** having a wide round body because of being very fat or wearing a lot of thick heavy clothes 身寬體圓；穿着臃腫 **ORIGIN** From the fat cartoon character made of tyres used as a symbol of the Michelin™ tyre company. 源自作為米其林輪胎公司標誌的肥胖卡通人物，全身用輪胎形象勾畫。

Mick /mɪk/ *noun* (*taboo, slang*) an offensive word for a person from Ireland（含侮慢意）愛爾蘭佬

mickey /ˈmɪki/ *noun*
IDM **take the 'mickey/'mick (out of sb)** (*BrE, informal*) to make sb look or feel silly by copying the way they talk, behave, etc. or by making them believe sth that is not true, often in a way that is not intended to be unkind（通過模仿某人或使其信以為真）取笑，戲弄 **SYN** **tease, mock**

Mickey Finn /ˌmɪki ˈfɪn/ *noun* a drink containing a drug or a lot of alcohol, given to sb who does not realize what is in it 蒙汗藥飲料（給不防備的人喝的，摻有藥或酒的飲料）

,Mickey 'Mouse *adj.* (*disapproving*) not of high quality; too easy 質量不高的；太容易的：*It's only a Mickey Mouse job.* 這活兒太容易了。

micro /ˈmaɪkrəʊ; *NAmE* -kroʊ/ *noun* (*pl.* **-os**) = MICROCOMPUTER

micro- /ˈmaɪkrəʊ; *NAmE* -kroʊ/ *combining form* **1** (in nouns, adjectives and adverbs 構成名詞、形容詞和副詞) small; on a small scale 微小的；規模小的：*microchip* 微芯片 ◇ *microorganism* 微生物 **OPP** **macro- 2** (in nouns; used in units of measurement 構成名詞，用於計量單位) one millionth 微；百萬分之一：*a microlitre* 百萬分之一升

mi·crobe /ˈmaɪkrəʊb; *NAmE* -kroʊb/ *noun* an extremely small living thing that you can only see under a MICROSCOPE and that may cause disease 微生物 ➲ COLLOCATIONS at LIFE

micro·biolo·gist /ˌmaɪkrəʊbaɪˈɒlədʒɪst; *NAmE* -kroʊbaɪˈɑːl-/ *noun* a scientist who studies microbiology 微生物學家

micro·biol·ogy /ˌmaɪkrəʊbaɪˈɒlədʒi; *NAmE* -kroʊbaɪˈɑːl-/ *noun* [U] the scientific study of very small living things, such as bacteria 微生物學 ▸ **micro·bio·logic·al** /ˌmaɪkrəʊˌbaɪəˈlɒdʒɪkl; *NAmE* -kroʊˌbaɪəˈlɑːdʒ-/ *adj.*

micro·blog·ging /ˈmaɪkrəʊblɒgɪŋ; *NAmE* -kroʊblɑːg-/ *noun* [U] the activity of sending regular short messages, photos or videos over the Internet, either to a selected group of people, or so that they can be viewed by anyone, as a means of keeping people informed about your activities and thoughts 微博客維護；微博客更新；微網誌 ▸ **micro·blog** /ˈmaɪkrəʊblɒg; *NAmE* -kroʊblɑːg/ *noun* **micro·blog** *verb* [I] ➲ compare TWITTER

micro·chip /ˈmaɪkrəʊtʃɪp; *NAmE* -kroʊ-/ *noun*, *verb*
■ ***noun*** (also **chip**) a very small piece of a material that is a SEMICONDUCTOR, used to carry a complicated electronic CIRCUIT 微芯片；微片
■ ***verb*** (**-pp-**) **~ sth** to put a microchip under the skin of an animal as a way of identifying it 植微（芯）片（在動物皮下，作識別用途）

micro·cli·mate /ˈmaɪkrəʊklaɪmət; *NAmE* -kroʊ-/ *noun* (*technical* 術語) the weather in a particular small area, especially when this is different from the weather in the surrounding area（尤指有別於周圍地區的）小氣候

micro·com·puter /ˈmaɪkrəʊkɒmpjuːtə(r); *NAmE* -kroʊ-/ (also **micro**) *noun* a small computer that contains a MICROPROCESSOR 微型計算機 ➲ compare MAINFRAME, MINICOMPUTER, PERSONAL COMPUTER

micro·cosm /ˈmaɪkrəʊkɒzəm; *NAmE* -kroʊkɑːz-/ *noun* a thing, a place or a group that has all the features and qualities of sth much larger 縮影；具體而微者：*The family is a microcosm of society.* 家庭是社會的縮影。➲ compare MACROCOSM

IDM **in microcosm** on a small scale 小規模地：*The developments in this town represent in microcosm what is happening in the country as a whole.* 這座城鎮的發展以小見大，體現了整個國家的發展。

micro·dot /ˈmaɪkrəʊdɒt; *NAmE* -kroʊdɑːt/ *noun* **1** a very small photograph about one millimetre in size, usually of a printed document 微點照片，縮微影印文件（約一毫米）**2** a very small round piece of a drug, especially the illegal drug LSD 超小型藥丸；（尤指）小粒迷幻藥

micro·elec·tron·ics /ˌmaɪkrəʊɪˌlekˈtrɒnɪks; *NAmE* -kroʊɪˌlekˈtrɑːn-/ *noun* [U] the design, production and use of very small electronic CIRCUITS 微電子學 ▸ **micro·elec·tron·ic** *adj.* [only before noun]

micro·fibre (*especially US* **micro·fiber**) /ˈmaɪkrəʊfaɪbə(r); *NAmE* -roʊf-/ *noun* [U] a very light and warm artificial material that is used especially for making coats and jackets 微纖維，超細纖維（輕柔溫暖的人造纖維，尤用以做外衣）

micro·fiche /ˈmaɪkrəʊfiːʃ; *NAmE* -kroʊ-/ *noun* [U, C] a piece of film with written information on it in print of very small size. Microfiches can only be read with a special machine. 縮微膠片；縮微平片：*The directory is available* ***on microfiche.*** 名錄有縮微膠片版。

micro·film /ˈmaɪkrəʊfɪlm; *NAmE* -kroʊ-/ *noun* [U, C] film used for storing written information on in print of very small size 縮微膠捲

micro·fi·nance /ˈmaɪkrəʊfamænsː; *NAmE* -kroʊ-/ *noun* [U] a system of providing services such as lending money and saving for people who are too poor to use banks 微金融（向無力使用銀行的窮人提供貸款和儲蓄服務的體系）

micro·gram /ˈmaɪkrəʊgræm; *NAmE* -kroʊ-/ *noun* (*symb.* **µg**) a unit for measuring weight; a millionth of a gram 微克（重量單位）；百萬分之一克

micro·light /ˈmaɪkrəʊlaɪt; *NAmE* -kroʊ-/ (*BrE*) (*NAmE* **ultra·light**) *noun* a very small light aircraft for one or two people 微型飛機 ➲ VISUAL VOCAB page V53

micro·manage /ˈmaɪkrəʊmænɪdʒ; *NAmE* -kroʊ-/ *verb* [T, I] ~ (**sth**) (*especially NAmE, disapproving*) to control every detail of a business, especially your employees' work 微觀管理，對…管頭管腳（尤指雇員的工作）：*The problem may be that you are micromanaging your team.* 問題可能是你對團隊的管理過於苛嚴而瑣細。◇ *bosses who micromanage* 管頭管腳的老闆 ▸ **micro·man·age·ment** *noun* [U] **micro·man·ager** *noun*

micro·meter /maɪˈkrɒmɪtə(r); *NAmE* -krɑːm-/ *noun* **1** (*especially US*) = MICROMETRE **2** a device used for measuring very small distances or spaces, using a screw with a very fine THREAD 螺旋測微器

micro·metre (*especially US* **micro·meter**) /ˈmaɪkrəʊmiːtə(r); *NAmE* -kroʊ-/ *noun* (*symb.* **µm**) a unit for measuring length, equal to one millionth of a metre 微米（= 百萬分之一米）

mi·cron /ˈmaɪkrɒn; *NAmE* -krɑːn/ *noun* (*old-fashioned*) = MICROMETRE

ˌmicro-ˈorganism *noun* (*technical* 術語) a very small living thing that you can only see under a MICROSCOPE 微生物

micro·phone /ˈmaɪkrəfəʊn; *NAmE* -foʊn/ (also *informal* **mic**, **mike**) *noun* a device that is used for recording sounds or for making your voice louder when you are speaking or singing to an audience 麥克風；話筒；傳聲器：*to speak into the microphone* 對着麥克風講話 ◇ *Their remarks were picked up by the hidden microphones.* 他們的話透過暗藏的麥克風傳了出去。

micro·por·tal /ˈmaɪkrəʊpɔːtl; *NAmE* ˈmaɪkroʊpɔːrtl/ *noun* (*computing* 計) a website that is used as a point of entry to the Internet where information has been collected that will be useful to a particular person or group 微門戶網站（針對特定個人或群體）

micro·pro·ces·sor /ˌmaɪkrəʊˈprəʊsesə(r); *NAmE* -kroʊˈproʊ-/ *noun* (*computing* 計) a small unit of a computer that contains all the functions of the CENTRAL PROCESSING UNIT 微處理器；微處理機

micro·scope /ˈmaɪkrəskəʊp; *NAmE* -skoʊp/ *noun* an instrument used in scientific study for making very small things look larger so that you can examine them carefully 顯微鏡：*a microscope slide* 顯微鏡載片 ◇ *The bacteria were then examined* ***under a/the microscope.*** 隨後把細菌放到顯微鏡下進行檢查。◇ (*figurative*) *In the play, love and marriage are* ***put under the microscope.*** 這部話劇對愛情和婚姻進行了細緻入微的探討。➲ VISUAL VOCAB page V70 ➲ see also ELECTRON MICROSCOPE

micro·scop·ic /ˌmaɪkrəˈskɒpɪk; *NAmE* -ˈskɑːpɪk/ *adj.* **1** [usually before noun] extremely small and difficult or impossible to see without a microscope 極小的；微小的；需用顯微鏡觀察的：*a* ***microscopic creature/particle*** 微生物；微粒 ◇ (*humorous*) *The sandwiches were microscopic!* 這些三明治小得都快看不見了！**2** [only before noun] using a microscope 使用顯微鏡的：*a* ***microscopic analysis/examination*** 顯微鏡分析／檢查 ▸ **micro·scop·ic·al·ly** /-kli/ *adv.*：*microscopically small creatures* 微生物 ◇ *All samples are examined microscopically.* 所有樣品都進行了精細的檢查。

micro·scopy /maɪˈkrɒskəpi; *NAmE* -ˈkrɑːs-/ *noun* [U] (*technical* 術語) the use of MICROSCOPES to look at very small creatures, objects, etc. 顯微術；顯微鏡觀察

micro·sec·ond /ˈmaɪkrəʊsekənd; *NAmE* -kroʊ-/ *noun* (*technical* 術語) (*symb.* **µs**) one millionth of a second 微秒；百萬分之一秒

micro·sur·gery /ˈmaɪkrəʊsɜːdʒəri; *NAmE* -kroʊsɜːr-/ *noun* [U] the use of extremely small instruments and MICROSCOPES in order to perform very detailed and complicated medical operations 顯微外科；顯微手術

micro·wave /ˈmaɪkrəweɪv/ *noun, verb*

■ *noun* **1** (also *formal* ˌ**microwave ˈoven**) a type of oven that cooks or heats food very quickly using ELECTROMAGNETIC waves rather than heat 微波爐：*Reheat the soup in the microwave.* 把湯放到微波爐裏再熱一熱。◇ ***microwave cookery/meals*** 微波爐烹飪／製作的食品 ➲ VISUAL VOCAB page V25 ➲ compare OVEN **2** (*technical* 術語) an ELECTROMAGNETIC wave that is shorter than a radio wave but longer than a light wave 微波

■ *verb* ~ **sth** to cook or heat sth in a microwave 用微波爐烹調（或加熱）➲ COLLOCATIONS at COOKING ▸ **micro·wave·able** (also **micro·wav·able**) *adj.*：*microwaveable meals* 可用微波爐製作的飯菜

mic·tur·ate /ˈmɪktjʊreɪt; *NAmE* ˈmɪktʃə-/ *verb* [I] (*formal*) to URINATE 排尿；小便 ▸ **mic·tur·ition** /ˌmɪktjuˈrɪʃn; *NAmE* -tʃəˈrɪʃn/ *noun* [U]

MID /ˌem aɪ ˈdiː/ *noun* the abbreviation for 'mobile Internet device' (a small computer that you can hold in your hand, larger than a SMARTPHONE but smaller than a TABLET PC. MIDs offer Internet-based services mainly for personal rather than business use.) 移動互聯網裝置，行動聯網裝置（全寫為 mobile Internet device，大小介於智能手機和平板電腦之間的掌上電腦，主要為個人提供互聯網服務）➲ compare MOBILE DEVICE

mid /mɪd/ *prep.* (*literary*) = AMID

mid- 0→ /mɪd/ *combining form* (in nouns and adjectives 構成名詞和形容詞) in the middle of 居中；在中間：*mid-morning coffee* 上午十點鐘左右的咖啡 ◇ *She's in her mid-thirties.* 她三十五六歲了。

ˌmid-ˈair *noun* [U] a place in the air or the sky, not on the ground 半空中；懸空：*The bird caught the insects* ***in mid-air.*** 鳥在半空中捕捉了昆蟲。▸ ˌ**mid-ˈair** *adj.*：*a mid-air collision* 在空中發生的碰撞

M

Midas touch /ˈmaɪdəs tʌtʃ/ *noun* (usually **the Midas touch**) [sing.] the ability to make a financial success of everything you do 事事都能賺大錢的本領 ORIGIN From the Greek myth in which King Midas was given the power to turn everything he touched into gold. 源自希臘神話，其中的邁達斯國王具有點石成金的能力。

ˌmid-Atˈlantic *adj.* [only before noun] **1** connected with the area on the east coast of the US, that is near New York and immediately to the south of it 美國東岸，紐約附近及其以南地區的：*the* ***mid-Atlantic states/coast*** 紐約附近各州；紐約附近的沿海地區 **2** in the middle of the Atlantic ocean 大西洋中部的；中大西洋的：*(figurative) a mid-Atlantic accent* (= a form of English that uses a mixture of British and American sounds) 大西洋中部地區口音（兼備英美發音特徵的英語）

mid·brain /ˈmɪdbreɪn/ *noun* (*anatomy* 解) a small central part of the brain 中腦

mid·day 0→ /ˌmɪdˈdeɪ/ *noun* [U] 12 o'clock in the middle of the day; the period around this time 中午；正午 SYN **noon**：*The train arrives at midday.* 列車正午到達。◇ *a midday meal* 午餐 ◇ *the heat of the midday sun* 正午驕陽的熱力

mid·den /ˈmɪdn/ *noun* a pile of waste near a house, in the past 貝丘（史前廢物堆）

mid·dle 0→ /ˈmɪdl/ *noun, adj.*

■ *noun* **1** 0→ **the middle** [sing.] the part of sth that is at an equal distance from all its edges or sides; a point or a period of time between the beginning and the end of sth 中間；中部；中央；中心：*a lake with an island* ***in the middle*** 中央有一個小島的湖 ◇ *He was standing in the middle of the room.* 他站在屋子的中間。◇ *The phone rang in the middle of the night.* 半夜裏響起了電話鈴聲。◇ *This chicken isn't cooked in the middle.* 這隻雞還沒有熟透。◇ *His picture was* ***right/bang*** (= exactly) ***in the middle*** *of the front page.* 他的照片就登在頭版的正中央。◇ *Take a sheet of paper and draw a line* ***down the middle.*** 拿出一張紙，在中間畫一條線。◇ *I should have finished* ***by the middle of*** *the week.* 我在這週過半的時候應該就能完成。➲ see also MONKEY IN THE MIDDLE, PIGGY IN THE MIDDLE **2** [C, usually sing.] (*informal*) a person's waist 腰部：*He grabbed her around the middle.* 他攔腰抱住她。

IDM **be in the middle of sth/of doing sth** to be busy doing sth 忙於做：*They were in the middle of dinner when I called.* 我打電話的時候，他們正在吃飯。◇ *I'm in the middle of writing a difficult letter.* 我正在寫一封很難寫的信。 **the middle of ˈnowhere** (*informal*) a place that is a long way from other buildings, towns, etc. 偏遠的地方：*She lives on a small farm in the middle of nowhere.* 她住在一個偏遠的小農場。 **ˌsplit/diˌvide sth down the ˈmiddle** to divide sth into two equal parts 平分；分為相等的兩半：*The country was split down the middle over the strike* (= half supported it, half did not). 國內支持和反對罷工的人勢均力敵。

■ *adj.* 0→ [only before noun] in a position in the middle of an object, group of objects, people, etc.; between the beginning and the end of sth 中間的；中央的；居中的；正中的：*Pens are kept in the middle drawer.* 鋼筆在中間那個抽屜裏。◇ *She's the middle child of three.* 三個孩子，她是老二。◇ *He was very successful in his middle forties.* 他在四十五六歲時很成功。◇ *a middle-sized room* 中等大小的房間 ◇ *the middle-income groups in society* 社會中等收入階層

IDM **(steer, take, etc.) a middle ˈcourse | (find, etc.) a/the middle ˈway** (to take/find) an acceptable course of action that avoids two extreme positions （走）中間道路；（取）中庸之道；（採取）折衷辦法

ˌmiddle ˈage *noun* [U] the period of your life when you are neither young nor old, between the ages of about 45 and 60 中年（45 歲到 60 歲左右）：*a pleasant woman in* ***early/late middle age*** 剛到中年的／接近老年的親切和藹的女人 ➲ COLLOCATIONS at AGE

ˌmiddle-ˈaged *adj.* **1** (of a person 人) neither young nor old 中年的 **2 the middle aged** *noun* [pl.] people who are middle-aged 中年人 **3** (*disapproving*) (of a person's attitudes or behaviour 人的態度或行為) rather boring and old-fashioned 煩人的；保守的；過時的

the ˌMiddle ˈAges *noun* [pl.] in European history, the period from about AD 1000 to AD 1450 中世紀（歐洲歷史上從公元 1000 年到 1450 年）

ˌmiddle-age ˈspread (also **ˌmiddle-aged ˈspread**) *noun* [U] (*humorous*) the fat around the stomach that some people develop in middle age 中年發福（某些人中年時腹部長出的脂肪）

ˌMiddle Aˈmerica *noun* [U] the middle class in the US, especially those people who represent traditional social and political values, and who come from small towns and SUBURBS rather than cities 美國中產階級（尤指那些來自小鎮或郊區、代表傳統社會和政治價值觀的人）

middle·brow /ˈmɪdlbraʊ/ *adj.* [usually before noun] (usually *disapproving*) (of books, music, art, etc. 書籍、音樂、藝術等) of good quality but not needing a lot of thought to understand 品位一般的；平庸的 ➲ compare HIGHBROW, LOWBROW

ˌmiddle ˈC *noun* [U] the musical note C near the middle of the piano keyboard 中央 C；中央 C 音

ˌmiddle ˈclass *noun* [C+sing./pl. v.] the social class whose members are neither very rich nor very poor and that includes professional and business people 中產階級；中等收入階層：*the* ***upper/lower middle class*** 中等偏上／偏下收入階層 ◇ *the growth of the middle classes* 中產階級的擴展 ➲ compare UPPER CLASS, WORKING CLASS

ˌmiddle-ˈclass *adj.* **1** connected with the middle social class 中產階級的；中等收入階層的：*a* ***middle-class background/family/suburb*** 中產階級背景／家庭／居住的郊區 **2** (*disapproving*) typical of people from the middle social class, for example having traditional views 典型中產階級特色的；帶有中產階級傳統觀念的；古板的：*a middle-class attitude* 中產階級的（保守）態度 ◇ *The magazine is very middle-class.* 這份雜誌太古板了。

the ˌmiddle ˈdistance *noun* [sing.] the part of a painting or a view that is neither very close nor very far away 中景：*His eyes were fixed on a small house in the middle distance.* 他凝視着不遠處的一座小房子。

ˌmiddle-ˈdistance *adj.* [only before noun] (*sport* 體) connected with running a race over a distance that is neither very short nor very long （賽跑）中距離的：*a middle-distance runner* (= for example, somebody who runs 800 or 1500 metre races) 中距離賽跑選手（如 800 米或 1 500 米跑選手）

ˌmiddle ˈear *noun* [sing.] the part of the ear behind the EARDRUM, containing the little bones that transfer sound VIBRATIONS 中耳

the ˌMiddle ˈEast (also *less frequent* **the ˌNear ˈEast**) *noun* [sing.] an area that covers SW Asia and NE Africa 中東（包括亞洲西南部和非洲東北部）➲ compare THE FAR EAST ▶ **ˌMiddle ˈEastern** (also *less frequent* **ˌNear ˈEastern**) *adj.*

ˌMiddle ˈEngland *noun* [U] the middle classes in England, especially people who have traditional social and political ideas and do not live in London（尤指持有傳統社會和政治觀念、不居住在倫敦的）英國中產階級

ˌMiddle ˈEnglish *noun* [U] an old form of English that was used between about AD 1150 and AD 1500 中古英語（約公元 1150 至 1500 年間的英語）➲ compare OLD ENGLISH

ˌMiddle-Euroˈpean *adj.* of or related to central Europe or its people 歐洲中部（人）的；中歐（人）的

ˌmiddle ˈfinger *noun* the longest finger in the middle of each hand 中指 ➲ VISUAL VOCAB page V59

ˈmiddle ground *noun* [U] a set of opinions, decisions, etc. that two or more groups who oppose each other can agree on; a position that is not extreme 中間立場；中間觀點：*Negotiations have failed to establish any middle ground.* 談判未能達成任何妥協。◇ *The ballet company now* ***occupies the middle ground between*** *classical ballet and modern dance.* 這個芭蕾舞團現在的風格介於古典芭蕾和現代舞之間。

middle·man /ˈmɪdlmæn/ *noun* (*pl.* **-men** /-men/) **1** a person or a company that buys goods from the

M

company that makes them and sells them to sb else 中間商；經銷商：*Buy direct from the manufacturer and **cut out the middleman**.* 直接從生產廠家購買，繞過中間商。 **2** a person who helps to arrange things between people who do not want to talk directly to each other **SYN** **intermediary**, **go-between** 經紀人；中間人；掮客

ˌmiddle ˈmanagement *noun* [U+sing./pl. v.] the people who are in charge of small groups of people and departments within a business organization but who are not involved in making important decisions that will affect the whole organization 中層管理人員；中間管理層 ▸ **ˌmiddle ˈmanager** *noun*

ˌmiddle ˈname *noun* a name that comes between your first name and your family name 中名（名和姓之間的名字）

IDM **be sb's middle ˈname** (*informal*) used to say that sb has a lot of a particular quality 是某人的突出個性：*'Patience' is my middle name!* 我的最大特點就是有耐心！

ˌmiddle-of-the-ˈroad *adj.* (of people, policies, etc. 人、政策等) not extreme; acceptable to most people 不極端的；多數人能接受的；取中間立場的 **SYN** **moderate**：*a middle-of-the-road newspaper* 觀點中立的報紙 ◇ *Their music is very middle-of-the-road.* 他們的音樂很大眾化。

ˌmiddle-ˈranking *adj.* [only before noun] having a responsible job or position, but not one of the most important 中層的；中級的

ˈmiddle school *noun* **1** (in Britain) a school for children between the ages of about 9 and 13 （英國為 9 到 13 歲兒童所設的）中間學校 **2** (in the US) a school for children between the ages of about 11 and 14 （美國為 11 到 14 歲兒童所設的）中學，初中 ➲ compare UPPER SCHOOL

middle·ware /ˈmɪdlweə(r); *NAmE* -wer/ *noun* [U] (*computing* 計) software that allows different programs to work with each other 中間件，中介軟件，中介軟體（允許不同程序協同工作）

middle·weight /ˈmɪdlweɪt/ *noun* a BOXER weighing between 67 and 72.5 kilograms, heavier than a WELTERWEIGHT 中量級拳擊手（體重在 67 到 72.5 公斤之間，略重於次中量級拳擊手）：*a middleweight champion* 中量級拳擊冠軍

the ˌMiddle ˈWest *noun* [sing.] = MIDWEST

mid·dling /ˈmɪdlɪŋ/ *adj.* [usually before noun] of average size, quality, status, etc. （大小、品質、地位等）中間的，普通的，中等的 **SYN** **moderate**, **unremarkable**：*a golfer of middling talent* 能力一般的高爾夫球手 **IDM** see FAIR *adv.*

mid·field /ˈmɪdfiːld; ˌmɪdˈfiːld/ *noun* [U, C, sing.] the central part of a sports field; the group of players in this position （運動場的）中場；中場隊員：*He plays (**in**) **midfield**.* 他是中場隊員。◇ *The team's midfield looks strong.* 這個球隊的中場顯得很強大。◇ *a midfield player* 中場球員 ▸ **mid·field·er** /ˌmɪdˈfiːldə(r)/ *noun*

midge /mɪdʒ/ *noun* a small flying insect that lives especially in damp places and that bites humans and animals 蠓；搖蚊

midget /ˈmɪdʒɪt/ *noun, adj.*

▪ ***noun*** **1** (*taboo, offensive*) an extremely small person, who will never grow to a normal size because of a physical problem; a person suffering from DWARFISM 侏儒；矮人 **2** (*informal*) a very small person or animal 小矮子；小東西（指人或動物）

▪ ***adj.*** [only before noun] very small 極小的

MIDI /ˈmɪdi/ *noun* [U] a connection or program that connects electronic musical instruments and computers （連接計算機的）電子樂器數字接口，樂器數位介面（或程序）

ˈmidi system *noun* (*BrE*) a SOUND SYSTEM with several parts that fit together into a small space 迷笛音響系統

Mid·lands /ˈmɪdləndz/ *noun* **the Midlands** [sing.+sing./pl. v.] the central part of a country, especially the central counties of England （一國的）中部，中部地區；（尤指）英格蘭中部地區 ▸ **Mid·land** *adj.* [only before noun]

mid·life /mɪdˈlaɪf/ *noun* [U] the middle part of your life when you are neither young nor old 中年；中年生活：*It is not difficult to take up a new career in midlife.* 人到中年開始新的事業並不難。◇ *midlife stresses* 中年生活的壓力

ˌmidlife ˈcrisis *noun* [usually sing.] the feelings of worry, disappointment or lack of confidence that a person may feel in the middle part of their life 中年危機（人在步入中年後可能產生的焦慮、失望和缺乏自信） ➲ COLLOCATIONS at AGE

mid·night 0→ /ˈmɪdnaɪt/ *noun* [U]

1 0→ 12 o'clock at night 半夜 12 點鐘；午夜；子夜：*They had to leave **at midnight**.* 他們不得不半夜離開。◇ *on the stroke of **midnight/shortly after midnight*** 半夜 12 點整；午夜時分 ◇ *She heard the clock strike midnight.* 她聽見鐘敲子夜 12 點。◇ *We have to catch the midnight train.* 我們得乘半夜 12 點的火車。 **2** (*especially NAmE*) = MIDNIGHT BLUE **IDM** see BURN *v.*, FLIT *n.*

ˌmidnight ˈblue (also **mid·night** especially in *NAmE*) *noun* [U] a very dark blue colour 深藍色 ▸ **ˌmidnight ˈblue** *adj.*

the ˌmidnight ˈsun *noun* [sing.] the sun that you can see in the middle of the summer near the North and South Poles 子夜太陽（在南北極的夏季能見到）

ˈmid-point *noun* [usually sing.] the point that is at an equal distance between the beginning and the end of sth; the point that is at an equal distance between two things 中點；正中央：*the mid-point of the decade* 十年過半的時候 ◇ *At its mid-point, the race had no clear winner.* 賽跑進行到一半時尚難分勝負。◇ *the mid-point between the first number and the last* 第一個數和最後一個數之間的中位數

ˌmid-ˈrange *adj.* [only before noun] (especially of a product for sale 尤指供銷售的產品) neither the best nor the worst that is available 中檔的；大眾型的：*a mid-range computer* 中檔電腦

mid·riff /ˈmɪdrɪf/ *noun* the middle part of the body between the chest and the waist 腹部；肚子：*a bare midriff* 裸露的腹部

mid·ship·man /ˈmɪdʃɪpmən/ *noun* (*pl.* **-men** /-mən/) a person training to be an officer in the navy 海軍軍官候補生；海軍學校學員：*Midshipman Paul Brooks* 海軍學校學員保羅 • 布魯克斯

ˌmid-ˈsized (also **ˌmid-ˈsize**) (both *especially NAmE*) *adj.* of average size, neither large nor small 中號的；中等尺寸的

midst /mɪdst/ *noun* (*formal*) (used after a preposition 用於介詞後) the middle part of sth 中部；中間 **SYN** **middle**：*Such beauty was unexpected **in the midst of** the city.* 市中心有這樣的美景真是出乎意料。

IDM **in the midst of sth/of doing sth** while sth is happening or being done; while you are doing sth 當某事發生時；在某人做某事時：*a country in the midst of a recession* 處於衰退中的國家 ◇ *She discovered it in the midst of sorting out her father's things.* 她在整理父親的東西時發現了它。 **in their/our/its/your midst** (*formal*) among or with them/us/it/you 在（他們、我們、你們等）中間；和…一起：*There is a traitor in our midst.* 我們中間有個叛徒。

mid·stream /ˌmɪdˈstriːm/ *noun* [U] the middle part of a river, stream, etc. 中流；河流中心：*We anchored in midstream.* 我們在河中心拋錨了。

IDM **(in) midstream** in the middle of doing sth; while sth is still happening 在進行中；在中途：*Their conversation was interrupted in midstream by the baby crying.* 他們的談話被嬰兒的啼哭打斷了。 ➲ more at CHANGE *v.*

mid·sum·mer /ˌmɪdˈsʌmə(r)/ *noun* [U] the middle of summer, especially the period in June in northern parts of the world, in December in southern parts 仲夏，中夏（尤指北半球六月間，南半球十二月間）：*a midsummer evening* 仲夏的夜晚

ˌMidsummer's ˈDay (*BrE*) (also **ˌMidsummer ˈDay** *NAmE, BrE*) *noun* 24 June, in northern parts of the world 施洗約翰節（世界北方地區的 6 月 24 日）

M

mid·term /ˌmɪdˈtɜːm; *NAmE* -ˈtɜːrm/ *adj.* [only before noun] **1** in the middle of the period that a government, a council, etc. is elected for（任期）中期的： *midterm elections* 中期選舉 **2** for or connected with a period of time that is neither long nor short; in the middle of a particular period 中期的： *a midterm solution* 中期解決方案 ◇ *midterm losses* 中期損失 ➲ see also LONG-TERM, SHORT-TERM **3** in the middle of one of the main periods of the academic year 學期中間的；期中的： *a* ***midterm examination/break*** 期中考試 / 休假 ➲ see also HALF-TERM

mid·town /ˈmɪdtaʊn/ *noun* [U] (*NAmE*) the part of a city that is between the central business area and the outer parts 市中心區： *a house in midtown* 市中心區的房子 ◇ *midtown Manhattan* 曼哈頓市中心區 ➲ compare DOWNTOWN, UPTOWN

mid·way /ˌmɪdˈweɪ/ *adv.* in the middle of a period of time; between two places 在（時間的）中途；在兩地之間 **SYN** **halfway**： *The goal was scored midway through the first half.* 上半場中段時攻進一球。 ▸ **mid·way** *adj.*： *to reach the midway point* 到達中間點

mid·week /ˌmɪdˈwiːk/ *noun* [U] the middle of the week 一週的中間： *to play a match* ***in midweek*** 在週中進行比賽 ◇ *By midweek he was too tired to go out.* 一週才剛過半，他就累得不想外出了。 ◇ *a midweek defeat for the team* 這個隊在週中比賽遭受的失敗 ▸ **mid·week** *adv.*： *It's cheaper to travel midweek.* 在星期中間旅行較便宜。

the Mid·west /ˌmɪdˈwest/ (also **the ˌMiddle ˈWest**) *noun* [sing.] the northern central part of the US（美國）中西部，中西部地區 ▸ **Mid·west·ern** /ˌmɪdˈwestən; *NAmE* -ərn/ *adj.*

M

mid·wife /ˈmɪdwaɪf/ *noun* (*pl.* **mid·wives** /-waɪvz/) a person, especially a woman, who is trained to help women give birth to babies 助產士；接生員；產婆 ➲ compare DOULA

mid·wif·ery /ˌmɪdˈwɪfəri; *NAmE* also -ˈwaɪf-/ *noun* [U] the profession and work of a midwife 助產；接生

mid·win·ter /ˌmɪdˈwɪntə(r)/ *noun* [U] the middle of winter, around December in northern parts of the world, June in southern parts 仲冬（北半球約在十二月，南半球約在六月）： *midwinter weather* 仲冬時節的天氣

mien /miːn/ *noun* [sing.] (*formal* or *literary*) a person's appearance or manner that shows how they are feeling 外表；樣子；風度

miffed /mɪft/ *adj.* [not before noun] (*informal*) slightly angry or upset 有點惱火；有點不高興 **SYN** **annoyed**

might 🔑 /maɪt/ *modal verb, noun*

■ ***modal verb*** (*negative* **might not**, *short form* **mightn't** /ˈmaɪtnt/) **1** 🔑 used as the past tense of *may* when reporting what sb has said（may 的過去時，用於間接引語）可能，可以： *He said he might come tomorrow.* 他說他明天可能來。 **2** 🔑 used when showing that sth is or was possible（表示可能性）可能： *He might get there in time, but I can't be sure.* 他有可能準時到達，但我不敢肯定。 ◇ *I know Vicky doesn't like the job, but I mightn't find it too bad.* 我知道維基不喜歡這工作，但我也許並不覺得它很差。 ◇ *The pills might have helped him, if only he'd taken them regularly.* 他當時要是按時服藥，也許可以對他有幫助的。 ◇ *He might say that now* (= it is true that he does), *but he can soon change his mind.* 他現在也許會那麼說，但他很快就會改變主意。 **3** 🔑 used to make a polite suggestion（用於有禮貌地提出建議）可以： *You might try calling the help desk.* 你可以試着給服務枱打個電話。 ◇ *I thought we might go to the zoo on Saturday.* 我覺得週六我們可以去動物園。 **4** 🔑 (*BrE*) used to ask permission politely（用於有禮貌地提出請求）可以： *Might I use your phone?* 我可以用一下你的電話嗎？ ◇ *If I might just say something …* 要是叫我說… **5** (*formal*) used to ask for information（用於詢問）： *How might the plans be improved upon?* 這些計劃還能怎麼改進呢？ ◇ *And who might she be?* 那麼她會是誰呢？ **6** used to show that you are annoyed about sth that sb could do or could have done（對某人未做某事表示不滿）應該： *I think you might at least offer to help!* 我認為你至少應該提出幫忙吧！ ◇ *Honestly, you might have told me!* 說實話，你事先應該告訴我呀！ **7** used to say that you are not surprised by sth（表示不感意外）： *I might have guessed it was you!* 我猜就是你！ **8** used to emphasize that an important point has been made（強調提出了重點）： *'And where is the money coming from?' 'You* ***might well ask****!'* "錢又從哪裏來呢？" "你這就問到點子上了！" ➲ note at MODAL **IDM** see WELL *adv.*

■ ***noun*** [U] (*formal* or *literary*) great strength, energy or power 強大力量；威力： *America's military might* 美國的軍事力量 ◇ *I pushed the rock* ***with all my might****.* 我用盡全力推這塊石頭。

IDM **ˌmight is ˈright** (*saying*) having the power to do sth gives you the right to do it 強權即公理： *Their foreign policy is based on the principle that 'might is right'.* 他們的外交政策遵循"強權即公理"的原則。

ˈmight-have-been *noun* [usually pl.] (*informal*) an event or situation that could have happened or that you wish had happened, but which did not 本來可能發生的事；未遂心願的事

might·ily /ˈmaɪtɪli/ *adv.* (*old-fashioned*) **1** very; very much 很；非常： ***mightily impressed/relieved*** 印象深刻的；如釋重負的 **2** (*formal*) with great strength or effort 全力以赴地；極其努力地： *We have struggled mightily to win back lost trade.* 我們已經盡了最大的努力以挽回損失的貿易額。

mighty /ˈmaɪti/ *adj., adv.*

■ ***adj.*** (**might·ier**, **mighti·est**) **1** (especially *literary*) very strong and powerful 強而有力的： *a mighty warrior* 威猛的鬥士 ◇ *He struck him with a mighty blow across his shoulder.* 他猛一下砸在他的肩膀上。 **2** large and impressive 巨大的；非凡的 **SYN** **great**： *the mighty Mississippi river* 浩蕩的密西西比河 **IDM** see HIGH *adj.*, PEN *n.*

■ ***adv.*** (*informal, especially NAmE*) (with adjectives and adverbs 與形容詞和副詞連用) very 非常；很；極其 **SYN** **really**： *mighty difficult* 極其困難 ◇ *driving mighty fast* 飛速駕駛

mi·graine /ˈmiːɡreɪn; ˈmaɪɡ-; *NAmE* ˈmaɪɡ-/ *noun* [U, C] a very severe type of headache which often makes a person feel sick and have difficulty in seeing 偏頭痛： *severe migraine* 嚴重的偏頭痛 ◇ *I'm getting a migraine.* 我得了偏頭痛。 ➲ **COLLOCATIONS** at ILL

mi·grant **AW** /ˈmaɪɡrənt/ *noun* **1** a person who moves from one place to another, especially in order to find work（為工作）移居者；移民： *migrant workers* 流動工人 ➲ **COLLOCATIONS** at RACE ➲ compare EMIGRANT, IMMIGRANT ➲ see also ECONOMIC MIGRANT **2** a bird or an animal that moves from one place to another according to the season 候鳥；遷徙動物

mi·grate **AW** /maɪˈɡreɪt; *NAmE* ˈmaɪɡreɪt/ *verb* **1** [I] (of birds, animals, etc. 鳥類、動物等) to move from one part of the world to another according to the season（隨季節變化）遷徙： *Swallows migrate south in winter.* 燕子在冬天遷徙到南方。 **2** [I] (of a lot of people 許多人) to move from one town, country, etc. to go and live and/or work in another 移居；遷移 **SYN** **emigrate**： *Thousands were forced to migrate from rural to urban areas in search of work.* 成千上萬的人為了尋找工作被迫從農村湧進城市。 **3** [I] (*technical* 術語) to move from one place to another 移動；轉移： *The infected cells then migrate to other areas of the body.* 受感染的細胞接着轉移到身體的其他部位。 **4** [I, T] **~ (sb)** (*computing* 計) to change, or cause sb to change, from one computer system to another（使）轉移到另一計算機系統 **5** [T] **~ sth** (*computing* 計) to move programs or HARDWARE from one computer system to another 將（程序或硬件）遷移，轉移（到另一系統）

mi·gra·tion **AW** /maɪˈɡreɪʃn/ *noun* [U, C] **1** the movement of large numbers of people, birds or animals from one place to another 遷移；移居；遷徙： *seasonal migration* 季節性遷徙 ◇ *mass migrations* 大規模的遷移 **2** the fact of changing from one computer system to another; the act of moving programs, etc. from one computer system to another（計算機系統的）改變；（程序或硬件的）遷移，轉移

mi·gra·tory **AW** /ˈmaɪɡrətri; maɪˈɡreɪtəri; *NAmE* ˈmaɪɡrətɔːri/ *adj.* (*technical* 術語) connected with, or having the habit of, regular migration 遷移的；遷徙的；移棲的： *migratory flights/birds* 遷徙飛行的鳥群；候鳥

mi·kado /mɪˈkɑːdəʊ; *NAmE* -doʊ/ *noun* (*pl.* **-os**) (from *Japanese*) a title given in the past to the EMPEROR of Japan（日本天皇的舊稱）

mike /maɪk/ *noun* (*informal*) = MICROPHONE ➲ see also OPEN MIKE

mi·lady /mɪˈleɪdi/ *noun* (*pl.* **-ies**) (*old use* or *humorous*) used when talking to or about a woman who is a member of the British NOBILITY or of high class（對英國貴族或上流社會婦女的稱呼）夫人，太太 ➲ compare MILORD

mil·age = MILEAGE

milch cow /ˈmɪltʃ kaʊ/ *noun* (*BrE*) a person, an organization or a product from which it is easy to make money 財源，搖錢樹（指人、機構或產品）

mild 0━ /maɪld/ *adj.*, *noun*

■ ***adj.*** (**mild·er**, **mild·est**) **1** 0━ not severe or strong 溫和的；和善的；不嚴厲的： *a **mild form** of the disease* 病勢不重 ◇ *a **mild punishment/criticism*** 輕微的責罰；和善的批評 ◇ *It's safe to take a mild sedative.* 服用藥性不強的鎮定劑沒有危險。◇ *Use a soap that is mild on the skin.* 使用對皮膚刺激性不強的肥皂。 **2** 0━ (of weather 天氣) not very cold, and therefore pleasant 溫和的；和煦的： *the mildest winter since records began* 自有記載以來最溫暖舒適的冬天 ◇ *a mild climate* 溫和的氣候 ➲ compare HARD **3** 0━ (of feelings 情感) not great or extreme 溫和的；不強烈的；輕微的 SYN **slight** ： ***mild irritation/amusement/disapproval*** 幾分惱怒／喜悅／不贊成 ◇ *She looked at him in mild surprise.* 她略帶吃驚地看着他。 **4** (of people or their behaviour 人或其行為) gentle and kind; not usually getting angry or violent 和善的；隨和的 SYN **equable** ： *a mild woman, who never shouted* 從不大聲叫喊的隨和的女人 **5** (of a flavour 味道) not strong, spicy or bitter 不濃的；淡味的： *a mild curry* 淡味咖喱 ◇ *mild cheese* 淡味奶酪 OPP **hot** ▸ **mild·ness** *noun* [U]： *the mildness of a sunny spring day* 春日陽光融融的溫暖 ◇ *her mildness of manner* 她溫柔隨和的舉止

■ ***noun*** [U] (*BrE*) a type of dark beer with a mild flavour 淡味啤酒： *Two pints of mild, please.* 請來兩品脫淡啤酒。➲ compare BITTER *n.* (1)

mil·dew /ˈmɪldjuː; *NAmE* -duː/ *noun* [U] a very small white FUNGUS that grows on walls, plants, food, etc. in warm wet conditions 黴；黴菌

mil·dewed /ˈmɪldjuːd; *NAmE* -duːd/ *adj.* with MILDEW growing on it 發霉的

mild·ly /ˈmaɪldli/ *adv.* **1** slightly; not very much 輕微地；稍微地： ***mildly surprised/irritated/interested*** 有點兒吃驚／生氣／感興趣 **2** in a gentle manner 和善地；溫和地： *'I didn't mean to upset you,' he said mildly.* 他和顏悅色地說："我並不是想讓你不高興。"

IDM **to put it ˈmildly** used to show that what you are talking about is much more extreme, etc. than your words suggest 說得委婉些；說得好聽一點： *The result was unfortunate, to put it mildly* (= it was extremely unfortunate). 說得好聽一點，結果是不幸的。

ˌmild-ˈmannered *adj.* (of a person 人) gentle and not usually getting angry or violent 溫和的；隨和的

ˌmild ˈsteel *noun* [U] a type of steel containing very little CARBON which is very strong but not easy to shape 軟鋼；低碳鋼

mile 0━ /maɪl/ *noun*

1 0━ [C] a unit for measuring distance equal to 1 609 metres or 1 760 yards 英里（＝1 609 米或 1 760 碼）： *a 20-mile drive to work* 開車 20 英里去上班 ◇ *an area of four square miles* 四平方英里的面積 ◇ *a mile-long procession* 一英里長的遊行隊伍 ◇ *The nearest bank is about half a mile down the road.* 最近的銀行沿着這條路要走半英里。◇ *We did about 30 miles a day on our cycling trip.* 我們騎車旅行，每天約騎 30 英里。◇ *The car must have been doing at least 100 miles an hour.* 這車速肯定每小時至少 100 英里。◇ (*BrE*) *My car does 35 miles to the gallon.* 我的車一加侖油能跑 35 英里。◇ (*NAmE*) *My car gets 35 miles to the gallon.* 我的車一加侖油能跑 35 英里。➲ see also AIR MILES, MPH, NAUTICAL MILE **2** 0━ **miles** [pl.] a large area or a long distance 大面積；長距離： *miles and miles of desert* 廣闊無垠的沙漠 ◇ *There isn't a house for miles around here.* 附近數英里以內沒有一座房子。◇ *I'm not walking—it's **miles away**.* 我不會走着去的，太遠了。 **3** [C, usually pl.] (*informal*) very much; far 很多；遠遠地： *I'm feeling miles better today, thanks.* 多謝，我今天感覺好多了。◇ *I'm miles behind with my work.* 我的工作遠遠地落在了後面。◇ *She's taller than you by a mile.* 她比你高多了。 **4 the mile** [sing.] a race over one mile 一英里賽跑： *He ran the mile in less than four minutes.* 他用了不到四分鐘就跑完一英里。◇ *a four-minute mile* 四分鐘一英里賽跑

IDM **be ˈmiles away** (*informal*) to be thinking deeply about sth and not aware of what is happening around you 想出了神 **go the ˌextra ˈmile (for sb/sth)** to make a special effort to achieve sth, help sb, etc. 孜孜以求；加倍努力；加把勁 **ˌmiles from ˈanywhere** (*informal*) in a place that is a long way from a town and surrounded only by a lot of open country, sea, etc. 在偏遠的地方： *We broke down miles from anywhere.* 在一個偏遠的地方，我們的車壞了。 **run a ˈmile (from sb/sth)** (*informal*) to show that you are very frightened of doing sth 盡量避開 **see, spot, tell, smell, etc. sth a ˈmile off** (*informal*) to see or realize sth very easily and quickly 輕而易舉地看出（或意識到）： *He's wearing a wig—you can see it a mile off.* 他戴着假髮，你一眼就能看出來。 **stand/stick out a ˈmile** to be very obvious or noticeable 顯而易見 ➲ more at INCH *n.*, MISS *n.*

mile·age (also **mil·age**) /ˈmaɪlɪdʒ/ *noun* **1** [U, C, usually sing.] the distance that a vehicle has travelled, measured in miles 英里里程： *My annual mileage is about 10 000.* 我一年的行駛里程大約為 1 萬英里。◇ *a used car with one owner and a low mileage* 只經過一人之手且行駛里程少的舊汽車 ◇ *The car rental included unlimited mileage, but not fuel.* 汽車租金不限里程，但不包括燃油費。◇ *I get a **mileage allowance** if I use my car for work* (= an amount of money paid for each mile I travel). 如果我因公開自己的車，就有一筆里程補貼。 **2** [U, C] the number of miles that a vehicle can travel using a particular amount of fuel（車輛使用某定量燃料可行駛的）英里數： *If you drive carefully you can get better mileage from your car.* 你只要小心開車，你的車就能多跑很多里程。 **3** [U] (*informal*) the amount of advantage or use that you can get from a particular event or situation 好處；利益： *I don't think the press can get any more mileage out of that story.* 我不認為報界可以再從那件事中撈到什麼好處。

mile·om·eter *noun* = MILOMETER

mile·post /ˈmaɪlpəʊst; *NAmE* -poʊst/ *noun* (*especially NAmE*) **1** a post by the side of the road that shows how far it is to the next town, and to other places 里程標 **2** = MILESTONE (1)

mile·stone /ˈmaɪlstəʊn; *NAmE* -stoʊn/ *noun* **1** (also **mile·post** especially in *NAmE*) a very important stage or event in the development of sth 重要事件；重要階段；轉折點；里程碑 SYN **landmark** **2** a stone by the side of a road that shows how far it is to the next town and to other places 里程碑

mi·lieu /miːˈljɜː/ *noun* [C, usually sing.] (*pl.* **mi·lieux** or **mi·lieus** /-ˈljɜːz/) (from *French*, *formal*) the social environment that you live or work in 社會環境；社會背景 SYN **background**

mili·tant /ˈmɪlɪtənt/ *adj.* using, or willing to use, force or strong pressure to achieve your aims, especially to achieve social or political change 動武的；好戰的；有戰鬥性的： ***militant groups/leaders*** 好戰團夥／頭目 ▸ **mili·tancy** /-ənsi/ *noun* [U]： *a growing militancy amongst the unemployed* 失業者中不斷增長的反抗傾向 **mili·tant** *noun*： *Student militants were fighting with the police.* 激進的學生在與警察對抗。 **mili·tant·ly** *adv.*

mili·tar·ism /ˈmɪlɪtərɪzəm/ *noun* [U] (usually *disapproving*) the belief that a country should have great military strength in order to be powerful 軍國主義 ▸ **mili·tar·ist** *noun*： *Militarists ran the country.* 軍國主義者把持這個國家。 **mili·tar·is·tic** /ˌmɪlɪtəˈrɪstɪk/ *adj.*： *militaristic government* 軍國主義政府

M

mili·tar·ize (*BrE* also **-ise**) /ˈmɪlɪtəraɪz/ *verb* [usually passive] **1 ~ sth** to send armed forces to an area 向（某地）派遣武裝力量： *a militarized zone* 軍事化地區 OPP **demilitarize 2 ~ sth** to make sth similar to an army 使具有軍事性質；武裝化： *a militarized police force* 武裝警察部隊 ▸ **mili·tar·iza·tion**, **-isa·tion** /ˌmɪlɪtəraɪˈzeɪʃn; *NAmE* -rəˈz-/ *noun* [U]

mili·tary AW /ˈmɪlətri; *NAmE* -teri/ *adj.*, *noun*

▪ *adj.* [usually before noun] connected with soldiers or the armed forces 軍事的；軍隊的；武裝的： ***military training/intelligence*** 軍訓；軍事情報 ◇ *a military coup* 軍事政變 ◇ *military uniform* 軍服 ◇ *We may have to take military action.* 我們可能不得不採取軍事行動。 ➲ COLLOCATIONS at WAR ➲ compare CIVILIAN ▸ **mili·tar·ily** *adv.*： *a militarily superior country* 軍事強國 ◇ *We may have to intervene militarily in the area.* 我們可能只好對這一地區進行軍事干涉。

▪ *noun* **the military** [sing.+sing./pl. v.] soldiers; the armed forces 軍人；軍隊；軍方： *The military was/were called in to deal with the riot.* 已調來軍隊平息暴亂。

ˌmilitary ˈband *noun* a large group of soldiers who play wind instruments and drums, sometimes while marching 軍樂隊 ➲ compare CONCERT BAND

ˌmilitary poˈlice *noun* (*abbr.* **MP**) (often **the military police**) [pl.] the police force which is responsible for the army, navy, etc. 憲兵

ˌmilitary ˈservice *noun* [U] **1** a period during which young people train in the armed forces 兵役： *to be* ***called up for military service*** 被徵召服兵役 ◇ *She has to* ***do her military service.*** 她必須服兵役。 **2** the time sb spends in the armed forces 服役期： *He's completed 30 years of active military service.* 他已經服完 30 年的現役。

M

mili·tate /ˈmɪlɪteɪt/ *verb*

PHR V **ˈmilitate against sth** (*formal*) to prevent sth; to make it difficult for sth to happen or exist 防止，阻礙（某事的發生或存在） SYN **hinder**： *The supervisor's presence militated against a relaxed atmosphere.* 主管人的出現驅散了鬆懈的氣氛。

mili·tia /məˈlɪʃə/ *noun* [sing.+sing./pl. v.] a group of people who are not professional soldiers but who have had military training and can act as an army 民兵組織；國民衛隊

mili·tia·man /məˈlɪʃəmən/ *noun* (*pl.* **-men** /-mən/) a member of a militia 民兵；國民衛隊隊員

milk /mɪlk/ *noun*, *verb*

▪ *noun* [U] **1** the white liquid produced by cows, GOATS and some other animals as food for their young and used as a drink by humans（牛或羊等的）奶： *a* ***pint/litre of milk*** 一品脫／一升奶 ◇ ***a bottle/carton of milk*** 一瓶／一紙盒奶 ◇ ***fresh/dried/powdered milk*** 鮮奶；奶粉 ◇ *Do you take milk in your tea?* 你茶裏加奶嗎？ ◇ *milk products* (= butter, cheese, etc.) 乳製品 ➲ see also BUTTERMILK, CONDENSED MILK, EVAPORATED MILK, MALTED MILK, SKIMMED MILK **2** the white liquid that is produced by women and female MAMMALS for feeding their babies（人或哺乳動物的）奶，乳汁： *breast milk* 母乳 **3** the white juice of some plants and trees, especially the COCONUT（椰子等植物的）白色汁液，乳液 ➲ VISUAL VOCAB page V30 ➲ see also SOYA MILK

IDM **the milk of human ˈkindness** (*literary*) kind behaviour, considered to be natural to humans 人的善良天性；惻隱之心 ➲ more at CRY *v.*, LAND *n.*

▪ *verb* **1 ~ sth** to take milk from a cow, GOAT, etc. 擠奶 **2** (*disapproving*) to obtain as much money, advantage, etc. for yourself as you can from a particular situation, especially in a dishonest way 趁機牟利；撈一把；撈好處： **~ A (from B)** *She's milked a small fortune from the company over the years.* 許多年來她揩公司的油，積攢了一筆小財。 ◇ **~ B (of A)** *She's milked the company of a small fortune.* 她揩公司的油，發了一筆小財。 ◇ *I know he's had a hard time lately, but he's certainly* ***milking it for all it's worth*** (= using it as an excuse to do things that people would normally object to). 我知道他最近的日子不好過，但他卻以此為藉口為所欲為。 IDM see DRY *adj.*

ˈmilk chocolate *noun* [U] light brown chocolate made with milk 牛奶巧克力 ➲ compare DARK CHOCOLATE

ˈmilk float *noun* (*BrE*) a small electric vehicle used for delivering milk to people's houses（電動）送奶車

milk·ing /ˈmɪlkɪŋ/ *noun* [U] the process of taking milk from a cow, etc. 擠奶： ***milking machines/sheds*** 擠奶機／棚

milk·maid /ˈmɪlkmeɪd/ *noun* (in the past) a woman whose job was to take milk from cows and make butter and cheese（舊時的）擠奶女工

milk·man /ˈmɪlkmən/ *noun* (*pl.* **-men** /-mən/) (especially in Britain) a person whose job is to deliver milk to customers each morning（尤指英國的）送奶人

ˈmilk powder (also **ˌpowdered ˈmilk**) (both *BrE*) (*US* **ˌdry ˈmilk**) *noun* [U] dried milk in the form of a powder 奶粉

ˌmilk ˈpudding *noun* [U, C] a PUDDING (= sweet dish) made with milk and rice, or with milk and another grain 牛奶布丁

ˈmilk round *noun* **1** (in Britain) the job of going from house to house regularly, delivering milk; the route taken by sb doing this job（英國）挨家送奶的工作；送奶路線 **2** (also **the milk round**) (in Britain) a series of visits that large companies make each year to colleges and universities, to talk to students who are interested in working for them（英國各大公司每年對高等院校進行的）巡迴招聘

ˈmilk run *noun* (*informal*) **1** [C] (*especially BrE*) a regular journey that is easy and in which nothing unusual happens, especially one by plane 輕鬆的例行旅程；（尤指）無風險的例行飛行 **2 the milk run** [sing.] (*NAmE*) a plane or train journey with stops in many places 沿途多處停靠的飛行（或火車旅程）： *We took the milk run back home.* 我們回家途中多次停留。

milk·shake /ˈmɪlkʃeɪk/ (also **shake**) *noun* a drink made of milk, and sometimes ice cream, with an added flavour of fruit or chocolate, which is mixed or shaken until it is full of bubbles 奶昔（將牛奶或冰淇淋，以及水果或巧克力味的香料混合或攪拌至起泡的飲料）： *a banana milkshake* 香蕉味奶昔

milk·sop /ˈmɪlksɒp; *NAmE* -sɑːp/ *noun* (*old-fashioned, disapproving*) a man or boy who is not brave or strong 懦弱的男子（或男孩）；弱不禁風的男子（或男孩）

ˈmilk tooth (*BrE*) (also **ˈbaby tooth** *NAmE, BrE*) *noun* any of the first set of teeth in young children that drop out and are replaced by others 乳齒；乳牙

milky /ˈmɪlki/ *adj.* **1** made of milk; containing a lot of milk 奶製的；含奶多的；奶的： *a hot milky drink* 熱奶飲料 ◇ ***milky tea/coffee*** 奶茶；牛奶咖啡 **2** like milk 像奶的；如奶般的： *milky* (= not clear) *blue eyes* 渾濁不清的藍眼睛 ◇ *milky* (= white) *skin* 乳白色的皮膚

the ˌMilky ˈWay *noun* [sing.] = GALAXY (2)

mill /mɪl/ *noun*, *verb*

▪ *noun* **1** a building fitted with machinery for GRINDING grain into flour 磨坊；麵粉廠 ➲ see also WATERMILL, WINDMILL (1) **2** (often in compounds 常構成複合詞) a factory that produces a particular type of material 工廠；製造廠： ***a cotton/cloth/steel/paper mill*** 紗／紡織／鋼／造紙廠 ◇ ***mill owners/workers*** 工廠主；工人 ➲ SYNONYMS at FACTORY ➲ see also ROLLING MILL, SAWMILL **3** (often in compounds 常構成複合詞) a small machine for crushing or GRINDING a solid substance into powder 磨粉機；磨麵機： *a pepper mill* 胡椒研磨機 ➲ VISUAL VOCAB page V26 ➲ see also RUN-OF-THE-MILL, TREADMILL

IDM **go through the ˈmill | put sb through the ˈmill** to have or make sb have a difficult time（使）陷於困境，經受磨難 ➲ more at GRIST

▪ *verb* [often passive] **~ sth** to crush or GRIND sth in a mill（用磨粉機）碾碎，磨成粉

PHR V **ˌmill aˈround** (*BrE* also **ˌmill aˈbout**) (especially of a large group of people 尤指一大群人) to move around an area without seeming to be going anywhere in particular 閒逛；轉悠： *Fans were milling around* *outside the hotel.* 追星族在酒店外徘徊。➲ see also MILLING

mil·len·ar·ian /ˌmɪlɪˈneəriən; *NAmE* -ˈner-/ *noun* a member of a religious group which believes in a future age of happiness and peace when Christ will return to Earth 千禧年信徒（篤信未來基督再臨地球時會出現太平盛世）▶ **mil·len·ar·ian** *adj.* **mil·len·ar·ian·ism** /-ˈneəriənɪzəm; *NAmE* -ˈner-/ *noun* [U]

mil·len·nium /mɪˈleniəm/ *noun* (*pl.* **mil·len·nia** /-niə/ or **mil·len·niums**) **1** a period of 1 000 years, especially as calculated before or after the birth of Christ 一千年，千年期（尤指公元紀年）：*the second millennium AD* 公元第二個千年 **2 the millennium** the time when one period of 1 000 years ends and another begins 千週年紀念日；千禧年：*How did you celebrate the millennium?* 你們是如何歡慶千禧年的？

mille·pede ➲ MILLIPEDE

mill·er /ˈmɪlə(r)/ *noun* a person who owns or works in a MILL for making flour 磨坊主；磨坊工人

mil·let /ˈmɪlɪt/ *noun* [U] a type of plant that grows in hot countries and produces very small seeds. The seeds are used as food, mainly to make flour, and also to feed to birds and animals. 黍類；穀子；粟 ➲ VISUAL VOCAB page V32

milli- /ˈmɪli/ *combining form* (in nouns; used in units of measurement 構成名詞，用於計量單位) one thousandth 千分之一：*milligram* 毫克

milli·bar /ˈmɪlibɑː(r)/ *noun* a unit for measuring the pressure of the atmosphere. One thousand millibars are equal to one BAR. 毫巴（大氣壓強單位）

milli·gram 0-π (*BrE* also **milli·gramme**) /ˈmɪligræm/ *noun* (*abbr.* **mg**)
a unit for measuring weight; a 1 000th of a gram 毫克；千分之一克

milli·litre (*especially US* **milli·liter**) /ˈmɪliliːtə(r)/ *noun* (*abbr.* **ml**) /mɪl/ a unit for measuring the volume of liquids and gases; a 1 000th of a litre 毫升；千分之一升

milli·metre 0-π (*especially US* **milli·meter**) /ˈmɪlimiːtə(r)/ *noun* (*abbr.* **mm**)
a unit for measuring length; a 1 000th of a metre 毫米；千分之一米

mil·liner /ˈmɪlɪnə(r)/ *noun* a person whose job is making and/or selling women's hats 女帽製造商；製造（或銷售）女帽的人

mill·in·ery /ˈmɪlɪnəri; *NAmE* ˈmɪlɪneri/ *noun* [U] **1** the work of a milliner 女帽業 **2** hats sold in shops/stores（商店的）帽類

mill·ing /ˈmɪlɪŋ/ *adj.* [only before noun] (of people 人) moving around in a large mass 成群亂轉的：*I had to fight my way through the **milling crowd**.* 我不得不在湧動的人潮中擠出一條路來。

mil·lion 0-π /ˈmɪljən/ *number* (*plural verb* 複數動詞)
1 0-π (*abbr.* **m**) 1 000 000 一百萬：*a population of half a million* 五十萬人口 ◇ *tens of millions of dollars* 數千萬元 ◇ *It must be worth a million* (= pounds, dollars, etc.). 它一定值一百萬。**HELP** You say **a, one, two, several, etc. million** without a final 's' on 'million'. **Millions (of ...)** can be used if there is no number or quantity before it. Always use a plural verb with **million** or **millions**, except when an amount of money is mentioned. * million 前有 a、one、two、several 等詞時，million 後面不加 s。若前面沒有數目或數量，可用 millions (of ...)。million 和 millions 均用複數動詞，指金額時除外：*Four million (people) were affected.* ◇ *Two million (pounds) was withdrawn from the account.*
2 0-π **a million** or **millions (of ...)** (*informal*) a very large amount 大量：*I still have a million things to do.* 我還有很多很多的事情要做。◇ *There were millions of people there.* 那裏人山人海。◇ *He **made his millions*** (= all his money) *on currency deals.* 他的萬貫家財都是通過外匯交易得到的。**HELP** There are more examples of how to use numbers at the entry for **hundred**. 更多數詞用法示例見 hundred 條。
IDM **look/feel like a million ˈdollars/ˈbucks** (*informal*) to look/feel extremely good 看上去／感覺好極了 **one, etc. in a ˈmillion** a person or thing that is very unusual or special 萬裏挑一的人（或物）；不同尋常的人（或物）：*He's a man in a million.* 他是個出類拔萃的人物。

mil·lion·aire /ˌmɪljəˈneə(r); *NAmE* -ˈner/ *noun* a person who has a million pounds, dollars, etc.; a very rich person 百萬富翁；大富豪：*an oil millionaire* 石油行業的百萬富翁 ◇ *She's a millionaire several times over.* 她是個億萬富婆。◇ *a millionaire businessman* 十分富有的商人

mil·lion·air·ess /ˌmɪljəˈneərəs; *NAmE* -ˈner-/ *noun* (*old-fashioned*) a woman who is a millionaire 女百萬富翁

mil·lionth 0-π /ˈmɪljənθ/ *ordinal number, noun*
■ ***ordinal number*** 0-π 1 000 000th 第一百萬
■ ***noun*** 0-π each of one million equal parts of sth 百萬分之一：*a/one millionth of a second* 百萬分之一秒

milli·pede (also **millepede**) /ˈmɪlɪpiːd/ *noun* a small creature like an insect, with a long thin body divided into many sections, each with two pairs of legs 馬陸；千足蟲

milli·sec·ond /ˈmɪlisekənd/ *noun* (*technical* 術語) a 1 000th of a second 毫秒；千分之一秒：(*figurative*) *I hesitated a millisecond too long.* 我稍稍猶豫了一下。

mil·li·volt /ˈmɪlivəʊlt; -vɒlt; *NAmE* -voʊlt/ *noun* (*physics* 物) a unit for measuring the force of an electric current; a 1 000th of a VOLT 毫伏（特）；千分之一伏特

mill·pond /ˈmɪlpɒnd; *NAmE* -pɑːnd/ *noun* a small area of water used especially in the past to make the wheel of a MILL turn（尤指舊時用於推動磨坊水車的）磨坊水池：*The sea was as calm as a millpond.* 海上風平浪靜。

ˌMills and ˈBoon™ *noun* a company that publishes popular romantic novels 米爾斯和布恩出版公司（出版通俗愛情小說）：*He was tall, dark and handsome, like a Mills and Boon hero.* 他個頭高大、皮膚黝黑、相貌堂堂，像通俗愛情小說的男主角。

mill·stone /ˈmɪlstəʊn; *NAmE* -stoʊn/ *noun* one of two flat round stones used, especially in the past, to crush grain to make flour 磨石；磨盤
IDM **a millstone around/round your ˈneck** a difficult problem or responsibility that it seems impossible to solve or get rid of 難以擺脫的沉重負擔：*My debts are a millstone around my neck.* 債務成了我難以擺脫的負擔。

mill·stream /ˈmɪlstriːm/ *noun* a stream whose water turns a wheel that provides power for machinery in a WATERMILL 水磨動力水流

ˈmill wheel *noun* a large wheel that is turned by water and that makes the machinery of a MILL work（帶動磨坊機器運轉的）水車輪

mil·om·eter (also **mile·ometer**) /maɪˈlɒmɪtə(r); *NAmE* -ˈlɑːm-/ (both *BrE*) (*NAmE* **odom·eter**) (also *informal* **the clock** *US, BrE*) *noun* an instrument in a vehicle that measures the number of miles it has travelled 里程表；計程器 ➲ VISUAL VOCAB page V52

mi·lord /mɪˈlɔːd; *NAmE* -ˈlɔːrd/ *noun* (*old use* or *humorous*) used when talking to or about a man who is a member of the British NOBILITY（對英國貴族的稱呼）老爺，大人 ➲ compare MILADY

mime /maɪm/ *noun, verb*
■ ***noun*** (also *less frequent* **dumb·show**) [U, C] (especially in the theatre) the use of movements of your hands or body and the expressions on your face to tell a story or to act sth without speaking; a performance using this method of acting 啞劇表演；啞劇；默劇：*The performance consisted of dance, music and mime.* 演出包括舞蹈、音樂和啞劇。◇ *a mime artist* 啞劇表演藝術家 ◇ *She performed a brief mime.* 她表演了一小段啞劇。
■ ***verb*** **1** [T, I] to act, tell a story, etc. by moving your body and face but without speaking 表演啞劇；用啞劇動作表現：**~ (sth)** *Each player has to mime the title of a movie, play or book.* 每一名參加者都得用啞劇動作表現出一部電影、戲劇或一本書的標題。◇ **~ doing sth** *He mimed climbing a mountain.* 他用啞劇形式表示爬山。**2** [I, T] **~ (to sth) | ~ (sth)** to pretend to sing a song that is actually being sung by sb else on a tape, etc.（按照播放錄音等）模擬歌唱；假唱：*The band was miming to*

M

a backing tape. 樂隊在用錄音帶播放歌曲的情況下模擬演唱。

mi·mesis /mɪˈmiːsɪs; maɪˈm-/ *noun* [U] **1** (*technical* 術語) the way in which the real world and human behaviour is represented in art or literature（文學藝術創作中的）模擬，模仿 **2** (*technical* 術語) the fact of a particular social group changing their behaviour by copying the behaviour of another social group（社會團體之間的）行為模仿 **3** (*biology* 生) the fact of a plant or animal developing a similar appearance to another plant or animal（生物的）擬態 **4** (*medical* 醫) the fact of a set of SYMPTOMS suggesting that sb has a particular disease, when in fact that person has a different disease or none 疾病模仿

mi·met·ic /mɪˈmetɪk/ *adj.* (*technical* 術語 or *formal*) copying the behaviour or appearance of sb/sth else 模仿的；擬態的

mimic /ˈmɪmɪk/ *verb, noun*

■ ***verb*** (**-ck-**) **1 ~ sb/sth** | **+ speech** to copy the way sb speaks, moves, behaves, etc., especially in order to make other people laugh 模仿（人的言行舉止）；（尤指）做滑稽模仿：*She's always mimicking the teachers.* 她總喜歡模仿老師的言談舉止。◇ *He mimicked her southern accent.* 他滑稽地模仿她的南方口音。 **2 ~ sth** (*technical* 術語 or *formal*) to look or behave like sth else（外表或行為舉止）像，似 SYN **imitate**：*The robot was programmed to mimic a series of human movements.* 機器人按程序設計可模仿人的一系列動作。

■ ***noun*** a person or an animal that can copy the voice, movements, etc. of others 會模仿的人（或動物）

mim·ic·ry /ˈmɪmɪkri/ *noun* [U] the action or skill of being able to copy the voice, movements, etc. of others 模仿；模仿的技巧：*a talent for mimicry* 模仿的天才

mi·mosa /mɪˈməʊzə; -ˈməʊsə; *NAmE* -ˈmoʊ-/ *noun* [C, U] **1** a tropical bush or tree with balls of yellow flowers and leaves that are sensitive to touch and light 含羞草屬植物 **2** (*NAmE*) (*BrE* ˌ**Buck's ˈFizz**) an alcoholic drink made by mixing SPARKLING white wine (= with bubbles) with orange juice 巴克泡騰酒（發泡白葡萄酒與橙汁調合而成）

Min /mɪn/ *noun* [U] a form of Chinese spoken mainly in SE China 閩方言；福建話

min. *abbr.* **1** (in writing) minute(s)（書寫形式）分鐘：*Cook for 8–10 min. until tender.* 煮 8 到 10 分鐘，至軟嫩為止。 **2** (in writing) minimum（書寫形式）最低的，最小的，最低限度的：*min. charge £4.50* 最低收費 4.5 英鎊 OPP **max**

min·aret /ˌmɪnəˈret/ *noun* a tall thin tower, usually forming part of a MOSQUE, from which Muslims are called to prayer 宣禮塔（常為清真寺的一部份）

min·atory /ˈmɪnətəri; *NAmE* -tɔːri/ *adj.* (*formal*) threatening 威脅的；恐嚇的：*minatory words* 威嚇的話

mince /mɪns/ *verb, noun*

■ ***verb*** **1** (*NAmE* also **grind**) [T] **~ sth** to cut food, especially meat, into very small pieces using a special machine (called a MINCER) 用絞肉機絞（食物，尤指肉）：*minced beef* 絞碎的牛肉 **2** [I] **+ adv./prep.** (*disapproving*) to walk with quick short steps, in a way that is not natural 裝模作樣地小步快走：*He minced over to serve us.* 他邁着碎步過來招待我們。

IDM **not mince (your) ˈwords** to say sth in a direct way even though it might offend other people 毫不隱諱；直言不諱

■ ***noun*** (*BrE*) [U] meat, especially beef, that has been finely chopped in a special machine 絞碎的肉，肉末（尤指牛肉）：*a pound of mince* 一磅碎肉 ➲ see also HAMBURGER (2)

mince·meat /ˈmɪnsmiːt/ *noun* [U] (*especially BrE*) a mixture of dried fruit, spices, etc. used especially for making PIES 百果餡（乾水果、香料等做成，尤用於做餡餅）

IDM **make ˈmincemeat of sb** (*informal*) to defeat sb completely in a fight, an argument or a competition 徹底擊敗；完全駁倒

ˌ**mince ˈpie** *noun* a small round PIE filled with mincemeat, traditionally eaten at Christmas, especially in Britain（尤指英國傳統上於聖誕節食用的）百果餡餅

min·cer /ˈmɪnsə(r)/ (*especially BrE*) (*NAmE* usually ˈ**meat grinder**) *noun* a machine for cutting food, especially meat, into very small pieces 食物絞碎機；（尤指）絞肉機

min·cing /ˈmɪnsɪŋ/ *adj.* (*disapproving*) (of a way of walking or speaking 言談步態) very delicate, and not natural 故作斯文的；裝模作樣的；忸怩作態的：*short mincing steps* 忸怩作態的小碎步

mind 🔑 /maɪnd/ *noun, verb*

■ ***noun***

▸ **ABILITY TO THINK** 思考能力 **1** 🔑 [C, U] the part of a person that makes them able to be aware of things, to think and to feel 頭腦；大腦：*the* ***conscious/subconscious mind*** 意識；潛意識 ◇ *There were all kinds of thoughts running through my mind.* 各種念頭在我腦海中閃過。◇ *There was no doubt in his mind that he'd get the job.* 他毫不懷疑自己能得到這份工作。◇ *'Drugs' are associated in most people's minds with drug abuse.* 大多數人把 drugs 與吸毒聯想在一起。◇ *She was in a disturbed* ***state of mind****.* 她的腦子裏一片混亂。◇ *I could not have complete* ***peace of mind*** *before they returned.* 他們不回來，我心裏就不踏實。➲ see also FRAME OF MIND, PRESENCE OF MIND **2** 🔑 [C] your ability to think and reason; your intelligence; the particular way that sb thinks 思考能力；智慧；思維方式 SYN **intellect**：*to have a* ***brilliant/good/keen mind*** 有非凡的智力／良好的思考能力／敏銳的頭腦 ◇ *a* ***creative/evil/suspicious mind*** 富創意的頭腦；邪惡的用心；懷疑的心態 ◇ *She had a lively and enquiring mind.* 她思想活躍，善於探索。◇ *His mind is as sharp as ever.* 他思維敏銳，一如既往。◇ *I've no idea how her mind works!* 我真不知道她是怎麼想的！◇ *He had the body of a man and the mind of a child.* 他四肢發達，頭腦簡單。◇ *insights into the criminal mind* 對罪犯內心世界的洞察 ➲ see also ONE-TRACK MIND

▸ **INTELLIGENT PERSON** 智者 **3** [C] a person who is very intelligent 聰明人；富有才智的人 SYN **brain** ➲ see also MASTERMIND：*She was one of the greatest minds of her generation.* 她是她那一代人中最聰慧的人之一。

▸ **THOUGHTS** 思想 **4** 🔑 [C] your thoughts, interest, etc. 心思：***Keep your mind on*** *your work!* 專心幹你的活吧！◇ *Her mind is completely occupied by the new baby.* 她一心撲在剛出世的寶寶身上。◇ *The lecture dragged on and my mind wandered.* 演講沒完沒了，我都心不在焉。◇ *He* ***gave his mind to*** *the arrangements for the next day.* 他認真考慮第二天的安排。◇ *As for avoiding you,* ***nothing could be further from my mind*** (= I was not thinking of it at all). 至於說躲避你，我根本就沒有這樣的想法。

▸ **MEMORY** 記憶 **5** 🔑 [C, usually sing.] your ability to remember things 記憶力：*When I saw the exam questions my* ***mind*** *just* ***went blank*** (= I couldn't remember anything). 我看到考題時，腦子裏一下子變得一片空白。◇ *Sorry—your name has gone right out of my mind.* 對不起，我想不起你的名字了。

IDM **be all in sb's/the ˈmind** to be sth that only exists in sb's imagination 只是憑空想像：*These problems are all in your mind, you know.* 你知道，這些問題都只是你的憑空想像而已。**bear/keep sb/sth in ˈmind | bear/keep in ˈmind that ...** 🔑 to remember sb/sth; to remember or consider that ... 將…記在心中；記住；考慮到 **be bored, frightened, pissed, stoned, etc. out of your ˈmind** (*informal*) to be extremely bored, etc. 感到非常無聊（或害怕等）；爛醉如泥；暈頭轉向 **be/go ˌout of your ˈmind** 🔑 to be unable to think or behave in a normal way; to become crazy 心智失常；發瘋：(*informal*) *You're lending them money? You must be out of your tiny mind!* 你要把錢借給他們？你真是瘋到家了。➲ SYNONYMS at MAD **be in two ˈminds about sth/about doing sth** (*BrE*) (*NAmE* **be of two ˈminds about sth/about doing sth**) to be unable to decide what you think about sb/sth, or whether to do sth or not 猶豫不決；拿不定主意：*I was in two minds about the book* (= I didn't know if I liked it or not). 我說不清我是否喜歡這本書。◇ *She's in two minds about accepting his invitation.* 是否接受他的邀請，她猶豫不決。**be of one/the same ˈmind (about sb/sth)** to have the same opinion about sb/sth

對…意見一致；對…看法相同 **be ˌout of your ˈmind with worry, etc.** to be extremely worried, etc. 極度焦慮（或愁苦等）；憂心忡忡 **bring/call sb/sth to ˈmind** (*formal*) **1** to remember sb/sth 想起；記起 SYN **recall**：*She couldn't call to mind where she had seen him before.* 她想不起來曾在哪裏見過他。 **2** to remind you of sb/sth 使想起；使記起 SYN **recall**：*The painting brings to mind some of Picasso's early works.* 這幅油畫使人想起了畢加索早期的作品。 **come/spring to ˈmind** 🔑 if sth **comes/springs to mind**, you suddenly remember or think of it 突然記起（或想到）：*When discussing influential modern artists, three names immediately come to mind.* 討論現代有影響力的藝術家時，一下子有三個名字出現在腦海中。 **have a good mind to do sth | have half a mind to do sth 1** used to say that you think you will do sth, although you are not sure 想去做某事，可能會做某事（但不確定）：*I've half a mind to come with you tomorrow.* 明天我可能會和你一起去。 **2** used to say that you disapprove of what sb has done and should do sth about it, although you probably will not （表明有心做某事，但未必採取行動）：*I've a good mind to write and tell your parents about it.* 我真想寫信給你父母，告訴他們這件事。 **have sb/sth in ˈmind (for sth)** 🔑 to be thinking of sb/sth, especially for a particular job, etc. 心中有適當人選（或想做的事等）：*Do you have anyone in mind for this job?* 你有沒有想到什麼人可以做這項工作？◇ *Watching TV all evening wasn't exactly what I had in mind!* 我才不願整個晚上看電視呢！ **have it in mind to do sth** (*formal*) to intend to do sth 打算做某事 **have a mind of your ˈown** to have your own opinion and make your own decisions without being influenced by other people 有主見；能自作決定：*She has a mind of her own and isn't afraid to say what she thinks.* 她有主見，並且敢於表達自己的觀點。◇ (*humorous*) *My computer seems to have a mind of its own!* 我的電腦好像也有它自己的想法！ **lose your ˈmind** 🔑 to become mentally ill 發瘋；神經錯亂 **make up your ˈmind | make your ˈmind up** 🔑 to decide sth 做出決定；下定決心：*They're both beautiful—I can't make up my mind.* 兩個都很漂亮，我難以決定。◇ *Have you made up your minds where to go for your honeymoon?* 你們決定好到哪裏去度蜜月了嗎？◇ *You'll never persuade him to stay—his* ***mind's made up*** (= he has definitely decided to go). 你根本無法勸他留下來，他已經拿定主意了。◇ *Come on—it's* ***make your mind up time!*** 嗨，你該作出決定了！ **ˌmind over ˈmatter** the use of the power of your mind to deal with physical problems 精神勝過物質（用精神力量處理物質問題） **your mind's ˈeye** your imagination 想像：*He pictured the scene in his mind's eye.* 他想像出了這一場面。 **on your ˈmind** if sb/sth is **on your mind**, you are thinking and worrying about them/it a lot 掛在心上；惦念：*You've been on my mind all day.* 我一整天都在為你擔心。◇ *Don't bother your father tonight—he's* ***got a lot on his mind.*** 今晚就別打擾你父親了，他的煩心事兒已經夠多了。 **put/get sth out of your ˈmind** to stop thinking about sb/sth; to deliberately forget sb/sth 不再想；有意忘記：*I just can't get her out of my mind.* 我就是忘不掉她。 **put sb in mind of sb/sth** (*old-fashioned*) to make sb think of sb/sth; to remind sb of sb/sth 使某人想起 **put/set sb's ˈmind at ease/rest** to do or say sth to make sb stop worrying about sth 安慰；寬解；使寬心 SYN **reassure put/set/turn your ˈmind to sth | set your ˈmind on sth** to decide you want to achieve sth and give this all your attention 集中精力做；下決心做：*She could have been a brilliant pianist if she'd put her mind to it.* 如果她專心致志，堅持到底，她本可以成為一名傑出的鋼琴家。 **take your mind off sth** to make you forget about sth unpleasant for a short time 轉移一下注意力；暫時將某事忘記 SYN **distract to ˈmy mind** in my opinion 依我看；以我之見：*It was a ridiculous thing to do, to my mind.* 依我看，這樣做是很荒唐的。 ➲ more at BACK *n.*, BEND *v.*, BLOW *v.*, BOGGLE, CAST *v.*, CHANGE *v.*, CHANGE *n.*, CLOSE[1] *v.*, CROSS *v.*, ETCH, GREAT *adj.*, KNOW *v.*, MEETING, OPEN *adj.*, OPEN *v.*, PIECE *n.*, PREY *v.*, PUSH *v.*, RIGHT *adj.*, SIEVE *n.*, SIGHT *n.*, SLIP *v.*, SPEAK, STICK *v.*, TURN *n.*, UNSOUND

■ ***verb***

▸ **BE UPSET/ANNOYED** 煩惱；苦惱 **1** 🔑 [T, I] (used especially in questions or with negatives; not used in the passive 尤用於疑問句或否定句，不用於被動句) to be upset, annoyed or worried by sth 對（某事）煩惱，苦惱，焦慮；介意：**~ (sth)** *I don't mind the cold—it's the rain I don't like.* 冷我不在乎，我是討厭下雨。◇ *I hope you don't mind the noise.* 希望你不介意這聲音。◇ *He wouldn't have minded so much if she'd told him the truth.* 如果她把真相告訴他，他就不會那麼着急了。◇ **~ about sth** *Did she mind about not getting the job?* 她沒得到這份工作是不是很介意？◇ **~ doing sth** *Did she mind not getting the job?* 她沒得到這份工作是不是很介意？◇ **~ sb/sth doing sth** *Do your parents mind you leaving home?* 你父母捨得你離開家嗎？◇ (*formal*) *Do your parents mind your leaving home?* 你父母捨得你離開家嗎？◇ **~ how, what, etc. …** *She never minded how hot it was.* 她從不在乎天氣有多熱。◇ **~ that …** *He minded that he hadn't been asked.* 沒被邀請，他很是耿耿於懷。

▸ **ASKING PERMISSION** 請求允許 **2** 🔑 [I, T] used to ask for permission to do sth, or to ask sb in a polite way to do sth （請求允許或客氣地請人做事）介意：*Do you mind if I open the window?* 我開開窗戶好嗎？◇ **~ sb doing sth** *Are you married, if you don't mind me asking?* 如果你不介意，請問你結婚了嗎？◇ (*formal*) *Are you married, if you don't mind my asking?* 如果你不介意，請問你結婚了嗎？◇ **~ doing sth** *Would you mind explaining that again, please?* 請你再解釋一遍行嗎？◇ *Do you mind driving? I'm feeling pretty tired.* 你來開車好嗎？我太累了。

▸ **NOT CARE/WORRY** 不關心；不擔心 **3** 🔑 **not mind** [I, T, no passive] to not care or not be concerned about sth 不關心；不在意；不考慮：*'Would you like tea or coffee?' 'I don't mind—either's fine.'* "你要茶還是要咖啡？""無所謂，什麼都行。" ◇ **~ sb** *Don't mind her—she didn't mean what she said.* 別理她，她只是隨便說說。◇ *Don't mind me* (= don't let me disturb you) *—I'll just sit here quietly.* 別管我，我就在這兒靜靜地坐坐。

▸ **BE WILLING** 願意 **4** 🔑 **not mind doing sth** [T] to be willing to do sth 願意做；樂意做：*I don't mind helping if you can't find anyone else.* 如果你找不到別人，我樂意幫忙。

▸ **WARNING** 警告 **5** 🔑 (*BrE*) (also **watch** *NAmE, BrE*) [T] used to tell sb to be careful about sth or warn them about a danger 當心；注意：**~ sth** *Mind* (= Don't fall on) *that step!* 注意台階！◇ *Mind your head!* (= for example, be careful you don't hit it on a low ceiling) 小心，別碰着頭！◇ *Mind your language!* (= don't speak in a rude or offensive way) 說話注意點！◇ **~ how, where, etc. …** *Mind how you go!* (= often used when you say goodbye to sb) 您走好！◇ *Mind where you're treading!* 當心腳下！◇ **~ (that) …** *Mind you don't cut yourself—that knife's very sharp.* 小心別傷着，這刀子快得很。◇ *You must be home for dinner, mind.* 記住，你一定得回來吃飯。 HELP 'That' is nearly always left out in this pattern. 這種句型一般都把 that 略去。

▸ **OBEY** 服從 **6** [T] **~ sb** (*NAmE, IrishE*) to pay attention to what sb says, and obey them 聽從：*And the moral of the story is: always mind your mother!* 這個故事的寓意是：一定要聽母親的話！

▸ **TAKE CARE OF** 關心 **7** (*especially BrE*) (*NAmE* usually **watch**) [T] **~ sb/sth** to take care of sb/sth 關心，照看（人或物） SYN **look after**：*Who's minding the children this evening?* 今天晚上誰看孩子？◇ *Could you mind my bags for a moment?* 你能不能照看一下我的袋子？

IDM **ˌdo you ˈmind?** (*ironic*) used to show that you are annoyed about sth that sb has just said or done 別這樣好不好：*Do you mind? I was here before you.* 你別這樣好不好？我比你先到。 **I don't mind adˈmitting, ˈtelling you … , etc.** used to emphasize what you are saying, especially when you are talking about sth that may be embarrassing for you 我不在乎承認（或告訴等）：*I was scared, I don't mind telling you!* 說真的，我嚇壞了。 **I don't mind if I ˈdo** (*informal*) used to say politely that you would like sth you have been offered （禮貌地表示願意接受）好的，可以：*'Cup of tea, Brian?' 'I don't mind if I do.'* "喝杯茶吧，布賴恩？""好的。" **if you ˌdon't ˈmind | if you ˌwouldn't ˈmind 1** 🔑 used to check that sb does not object to sth you want to do, or to ask sb politely to do sth （想要確保對方不反對，或客氣地請人做事）你不會在意吧，你若不介意的話：*I'd like to ask*

M

you a few questions, if you don't mind. 如果你不介意的話，我想問你幾個問題。◇ *Can you read that form carefully, if you wouldn't mind, and then sign it.* 請您仔細看一看那份表格，然後簽個字，行嗎？ **2** (often *ironic*) used to show that you object to sth that sb has said or done（表示反對某人所做的事或所說的話）如蒙你不在意：*I give the orders around here, if you don't mind.* 不好意思，在這裏我說了算。 **3** used to refuse an offer politely（表示委婉拒絕）：*'Will you come with us tonight?' 'I won't, if you don't mind—I've got a lot of work to do.'* "你今晚和我們一起去嗎？" "對不起，我不去了，我有好多事要做。" **if you ˌdon't mind me/my 'saying so ...** used when you are going to criticize sb or say sth that might upset them（批評等之前說）你不會在意我這麼說吧：*That colour doesn't really suit you, if you don't mind my saying so.* 這顏色並不十分適合你。我這麼說，你不會介意吧。 **I wouldn't mind sth/doing sth** 🗝 used to say politely that you would very much like sth/to do sth 我很想要；我很樂意做：*I wouldn't mind a cup of coffee, if it's no trouble.* 要是不麻煩的話，我很想來杯咖啡。◇ *I wouldn't mind having his money!* 我願意接受他的錢！ **ˌmind your ˌown 'business** (*informal*) to think about your own affairs and not ask questions about or try to get involved in other people's lives 想自己的事；別管閒事：*'What are you reading?' 'Mind your own business!'* "你在讀什麼呢？" "少管閒事！" ◇ *I was just sitting there, minding my own business, when a man started shouting at me.* 我就坐在那兒，也沒招誰惹誰，忽然有個男人對我大喊大叫。 **mind the 'shop** (*BrE*) (*NAmE* **mind the 'store**) to be in charge of sth for a short time while sb is away 臨時代管；幫忙關照：*Who's minding the shop while the boss is abroad?* 老闆出國期間由誰代管？ **ˌmind 'you** 🗝 (*informal*) used to add sth to what you have just said, especially sth that makes it less strong（對剛說過的話加以補充，尤使語氣減弱）請注意，說實話：*I've heard they're getting divorced. Mind you, I'm not surprised—they were always arguing.* 聽說他們要離婚了。告訴你吧，我並不感到意外，因為他們總是爭吵。 **ˌmind your Ps and 'Qs** (*informal*) to behave in the most polite way you can 要禮貌莊重 **ˌnever 'mind** **1** 🗝 (*especially BrE*) used to tell sb not to worry or be upset（用於安慰）沒關係：*Have you broken it? Never mind, we can buy another one.* 你把它打碎了？沒關係，我們可以再買一個。 **2** 🗝 used to suggest that sth is not important（表示並不重要）沒關係，無所謂：*This isn't where I intended to take you—but never mind, it's just as good.* 我沒想帶你到這裏來。不過沒什麼，這裏也不錯。 **3** used to emphasize that what is true about the first thing you have said is even more true about the second 更不用說 **SYN** **let alone**：*I never thought she'd win once, never mind twice!* 我還以為她一次都贏不了，更別說兩次了！ **never mind (about) (doing) sth** used to tell sb they shouldn't think about sth or do sth because it is not as important as sth else, or because you will do it（因為某事是次要的，或因為你要做某事）別想它，先別管：*Never mind your car—what about the damage to my fence?* 先別管你的車，我的圍欄撞壞了，怎麼辦？◇ *Never mind washing the dishes—I'll do them later.* 別管洗碟子的事了，等一下我會洗。 **ˌnever you 'mind** (*informal*) used to tell sb not to ask about sth because you are not going to tell them（表明不會告訴對方）不要問，別管：*'Who told you about it?' 'Never you mind!'* "誰告訴你這事兒的？" "別問了！" ◇ *Never you mind how I found out—it's true, isn't it?* 別問我是怎麼知道的。這是真的，對不對？ ➲ more at LANGUAGE, STEP *n.*

PHR V **ˌmind 'out** (*BrE, informal*) used to tell sb to move so that you can pass 請讓一下；借借光 **SYN** **watch out**：*Mind out—you're in the way there!* 請讓一讓，你擋着路啦！ **ˌmind 'out (for sb/sth)** (*BrE*) used to warn sb of danger 當心；注意：*Have some of my plum jam—but mind out for the stones.* 嚐嚐我的李子醬，但得當心有核兒。

'mind-bending *adj.* (*informal*) (especially of drugs 尤指麻醉品) having a strong effect on your mind 致幻的；使極度興奮的

'mind-blowing *adj.* (*informal*) very exciting, impressive or surprising 非常令人興奮的；給人印象極深的；非常令人吃驚的：*Watching your baby being born is a mind-blowing experience.* 看你的孩子出生是一次非常難忘的經歷。

'mind-boggling *adj.* (*informal*) very difficult to imagine or to understand; extremely surprising 難以想像的；難以理解的；令人驚愕的：*a problem of mind-boggling complexity* 複雜得難以想像的問題 ➲ compare BOGGLE

mind·ed /ˈmaɪndɪd/ *adj.* **1** (used with adjectives to form compound adjectives 與形容詞連用構成複合形容詞) having the way of thinking, the attitude or the type of character mentioned 思維（或態度、性格）…的：*a fair-minded employer* 公正的雇主 ◇ *high-minded principles* 高尚的原則 ◇ *I appeal to all like-minded people to support me.* 我呼籲所有志同道合的人來支持我。 ➲ see also ABSENT-MINDED, BLOODY-MINDED, SINGLE-MINDED **2** (used with adverbs to form compound adjectives 與副詞連用構成複合形容詞) having the type of mind that is interested in or able to understand the areas mentioned 對…有興趣（或能理解）；有…頭腦：*I'm not very politically minded.* 我對政治不怎麼感興趣。 **3** (used with nouns to form compound adjectives 與名詞連用構成複合形容詞) interested in or enthusiastic about the thing mentioned 對…感興趣的；對…有熱情的：*a reform-minded government* 熱衷於改革的政府 **4** [not before noun] **~ (to do sth)** (*formal*) wishing or intending to do sth 情願；有意 **SYN** **inclined**：*She was minded to accept their offer.* 她有意接受他們的提議。

mind·er /ˈmaɪndə(r)/ *noun* (*especially BrE*) a person whose job is to take care of and protect another person 看護人；照顧者：*a star surrounded by her minders* 被保鏢簇擁着的明星 ➲ see also CHILDMINDER

mind·ful /ˈmaɪndfl/ *adj.* **~ of sb/sth | ~ that ...** (*formal*) remembering sb/sth and considering them or it when you do sth 記着；想着；考慮到 **SYN** **conscious**：*mindful of our responsibilities* 意識到我們的責任 ◇ *Mindful of the danger of tropical storms, I decided not to go out.* 想到熱帶風暴的危險，我決定不出門。

'mind game *noun* something that you do or say in order to make sb feel less confident, especially to gain an advantage for yourself（尤指為了壓倒對方而展開的）心理遊戲，心理戰術

mind·less /ˈmaɪndləs/ *adj.* **1** done or acting without thought and for no particular reason or purpose 沒頭腦的；無謂的；盲目的 **SYN** **senseless**：*mindless violence* 無謂的暴力 ◇ *mindless vandals* 盲目破壞公物者 **2** not needing thought or intelligence 無需動腦筋的；機械的 **SYN** **dull**：*a mindless and repetitive task* 機械重複的工作 **3 ~ of sb/sth** (*formal*) not remembering sb/sth and not considering them or it when you do sth 不顧慮：*We explored the whole town, mindless of the cold and rain.* 我們不顧寒冷和下雨，在整個城市到處轉。 ▸ **mind·less·ly** *adv.*

'mind-numbing *adj.* very boring 非常乏味的；令人厭煩的：*mind-numbing conversation* 很無聊的談話 ▸ **mind-numbing·ly** *adv.*：*The lecture was mind-numbingly tedious.* 那堂課冗長乏味。

'mind-reader *noun* (often *humorous*) a person who knows what sb else is thinking without being told 洞悉他人心思的人

mind·set /ˈmaɪndset/ *noun* a set of attitudes or fixed ideas that sb has and that are often difficult to change 觀念模式；思維傾向 **SYN** **mentality**：*a conservative mindset* 保守的思維模式 ◇ *the mindset of the computer generation* 計算機時代的思維傾向

mind·share /ˈmaɪndʃeə(r); *NAmE* -ʃer/ *noun* [U] (*business* 商) the extent of knowledge of a company or product among consumers, compared with their knowledge of others of the same type 心理份額，心理佔有率（指公司或產品相對於同類為消費者所瞭解的程度）

mine 🗝 /maɪn/ *pron., noun, verb*

■ ***pron.*** 🗝 (the possessive form of *I* * I 的所有格形式) **1** of or belonging to the person writing or speaking 我的：*That's mine.* 這是我的。◇ *He's a friend **of mine*** (= one of my friends). 他是我的一個朋友。◇ *She wanted one like mine* (= like I have). 她想要一個和我的一樣的。 **2** (*BrE*, *informal*) my home 我的家： *Let's go back to mine after the show.* 看完表演後我們去我家吧。

■ ***noun*** **1** a deep hole or holes under the ground where minerals such as coal, gold, etc. are dug 礦井；礦： ***a copper/diamond mine*** 銅礦；鑽石礦 ➲ compare PIT *n.* (3), QUARRY *n.* (1) ➲ see also MINING, COAL MINE, GOLD MINE **2** a type of bomb that is hidden under the ground or in the sea and that explodes when sb/sth touches it 地雷；水雷 ➲ see also LANDMINE

IDM **a mine of inforˈmation** (**about/on sb/sth**) a person, book, etc. that can give you a lot of information on a particular subject 信息源泉；知識寶庫

■ ***verb*** **1** [T, I] to dig holes in the ground in order to find and obtain coal, diamonds, etc. （在某地）開礦，採礦： **~ sth** (**for sth**) *The area has been mined for slate for centuries.* 這個地區開採板岩有數百年了。◇ **~** (**for sth**) *They were mining for gold.* 他們在開採黃金。 **2** [T] **~ sth** to place MINES *n.* (2) below the surface of an area of land or water; to destroy a vehicle with mines 埋雷於；佈雷；用雷炸毀（車輛）： *The coastal route had been mined.* 沿海道路上佈了地雷。◇ *The UN convoy was mined on its way to the border.* 聯合國車隊在駛往邊界的途中觸雷被炸。

ˈmine dump *noun* (*SAfrE*) = DUMP (2)

mine·field /ˈmaɪnfiːld/ *noun* **1** an area of land or water where MINES (= bombs that explode when they are touched) have been hidden 雷區；佈雷區 **2** a situation that contains hidden dangers or difficulties 危機四伏的局面；充滿潛在危險的形勢： *a legal minefield* 法律上困難重重的局面 ◇ *Tax can be a minefield for the unwary.* 粗心大意的人在納稅方面很容易出錯。

mine·hunt·er /ˈmaɪnhʌntə(r)/ *noun* (*BrE*) a military ship for finding and destroying MINES (= bombs that explode when they are touched) 掃雷艇；獵雷艇

miner /ˈmaɪnə(r)/ *noun* a person who works in a mine taking out coal, gold, diamonds, etc. 礦工；採礦者 ➲ see also COAL MINER

min·eral /ˈmɪnərəl/ *noun*

1 [C, U] a substance that is naturally present in the earth and is not formed from animal or vegetable matter, for example gold and salt. Some minerals are also present in food and drink and in the human body and are essential for good health. 礦物；礦物質： ***mineral deposits/extraction*** 礦藏；礦物開採 ◇ *the recommended intake of vitamins and minerals* 維生素和礦物質的建議攝入量 ➲ COLLOCATIONS at DIET ➲ compare VEGETABLE (1) **2** [C, usually pl.] (*BrE, formal*) (*NAmE* **soda**) a sweet drink in various flavours that has bubbles of gas in it and does not contain alcohol 汽水： *Soft drinks and minerals sold here.* 此處銷售各種軟飲料和汽水。

min·er·al·ogist /ˌmɪnəˈrælədʒɪst/ *noun* a scientist who studies mineralogy 礦物學家

min·er·al·ogy /ˌmɪnəˈrælədʒi/ *noun* [U] the scientific study of minerals 礦物學 ▸ **min·er·al·ogic·al** /ˌmɪnərəˈlɒdʒɪkl; *NAmE* -ˈlɑːdʒ-/ *adj.*

ˈmineral oil *noun* [U] **1** (*BrE*) = PETROLEUM **2** (*NAmE*) (*BrE* **ˌliquid ˈparaffin**) a liquid with no colour and no smell that comes from PETROLEUM and is used in medicines and COSMETICS 液狀石蠟，石蠟油（用於製造藥品和化妝品）

ˈmineral water *noun* **1** [U, C] water from a SPRING in the ground that contains mineral salts or gases 礦泉水： *A glass of mineral water, please.* 請給我來杯礦泉水。 **2** [C] a glass or bottle of mineral water 一杯（或一瓶）礦泉水

mine·shaft /ˈmaɪnʃɑːft; *NAmE* -ʃæft/ *noun* a deep narrow hole that goes down to a mine 井筒；豎井

min·es·trone /ˌmɪnəˈstrəʊni; *NAmE* -ˈstroʊ-/ *noun* [U] an Italian soup containing small pieces of vegetables and PASTA（含蔬菜和意大利麵的）意大利濃菜湯

mine·sweeper /ˈmaɪnswiːpə(r)/ *noun* a ship used for finding and clearing away MINES (= bombs that explode when they are touched) 掃雷艇

mine·work·er /ˈmaɪnwɜːkə(r); *NAmE* -wɜːrk-/ *noun* a person who works in a mine 礦工

minge /mɪndʒ/ *noun* (*BrE, taboo, slang*) the female sex organs or PUBIC hair（女性）陰部，陰毛

ming·er /ˈmɪŋə(r)/ *noun* (*BrE, informal*) a person who is not attractive 毫無魅力的人

min·ging /ˈmɪŋɪŋ/ *adj.* (*BrE, informal*) very bad, unpleasant or ugly 非常糟糕的；令人不快的；醜陋的

min·gle /ˈmɪŋɡl/ *verb* **1** [I, T] to combine or make one thing combine with another（使）與…結合；使混合；使聯結： *The sounds of laughter and singing mingled in the evening air.* 笑聲和歌聲交織在夜空中。◇ **~** (**A**) (**with B**) *Her tears mingled with the blood on her face.* 她的淚水和臉上的血混在了一起。◇ *He felt a kind of happiness mingled with regret.* 他感到既高興又遺憾。◇ **~** (**A and B**) (**together**) *The flowers mingle together to form a blaze of colour.* 鮮花錦簇，色彩絢爛。 ➲ SYNONYMS at MIX **2** [I] to move among people and talk to them, especially at a social event（尤指在社交場所）相交往，混雜其中 **SYN** **circulate**： *The princess was not recognized and mingled freely with the crowds.* 公主沒有人認出，隨意混雜在人群之中。◇ *If you'll excuse me, I must go and mingle* (= talk to other guests). 對不起，我得去和其他客人聊聊。

mingy /ˈmɪndʒi/ *adj.* (*BrE, informal*) small, not generous 小的；吝嗇的 **SYN** **stingy**

mini /ˈmɪni/ *noun* = MINISKIRT

mini- /ˈmɪni/ *combining form* (in nouns 構成名詞) small 小的；短的： *mini-break* (= a short holiday/vacation) 短假 ◇ *minigolf* 小型高爾夫球

mini·ature /ˈmɪnətʃə(r); *NAmE* also -tʃʊr/ *adj., noun*

■ ***adj.*** [only before noun] very small; much smaller than usual 很小的；微型的；小型的： *miniature roses* 小玫瑰花 ◇ *a rare breed of miniature horses* 一種罕見的小矮馬 ◇ *It looks like a miniature version of James Bond's car.* 它看上去像一輛小型的詹姆斯•邦德的汽車。

■ ***noun*** **1** a very small detailed painting, often of a person 微型畫；小畫像 **2** a very small copy or model of sth; a very small version of sth 縮微模型；微型複製品： *brandy miniatures* (= very small bottles) 小瓶白蘭地

IDM **in miniature** on a very small scale 小規模的；小型的： *a doll's house with everything in miniature* 樣樣東西都很小的玩具小房子 ◇ *Through play, children act out in miniature the dramas of adult life.* 通過遊戲，孩子們演出了成年人生活的縮影。

ˈminiature golf *noun* [U] (*NAmE*) = MINIGOLF

mini·atur·ist /ˈmɪnɪtʃərɪst/ *noun* a painter who paints small works of art 細密畫畫家

mini·atur·ize (*BrE* also **-ise**) /ˈmɪnətʃəraɪz/ *verb* **~ sth** to make a much smaller version of sth 使微型化；使成為縮影 ▸ **mini·atur·iza·tion**, **-isa·tion** /ˌmɪnətʃəraɪˈzeɪʃn; *NAmE* -rəˈzeɪ-/ *noun* [U] **mini·atur·ized**, **-ised** *adj.* [only before noun]： *a miniaturized listening device* 微型監聽裝置

mini·bar /ˈmɪnibɑː(r)/ *noun* a small fridge/refrigerator in a hotel room, with drinks in it for guests to use 迷你吧（旅館房間裏放有飲料的小冰箱）

mini·beast /ˈmɪnibiːst/ *noun* (*BrE*) (used especially in schools 尤用於學校) any small animal that does not have a BACKBONE 小型無脊椎動物： *minibeasts such as worms, snails, centipedes and spiders* 蠕蟲、蝸牛、蜈蚣以及蜘蛛等小型無脊椎動物

mini·bus /ˈmɪnibʌs/ *noun* a small vehicle with seats for about twelve people 小型公共汽車；中巴 ➲ VISUAL VOCAB page V57

mini·cab /ˈmɪnikæb/ *noun* (*BrE*) a taxi that you have to order by telephone and cannot stop in the street（須電話預訂而不能自由攬客的）出租汽車

mini·cam /ˈmɪnikæm/ *noun* a video camera that is small enough to hold in one hand 迷你攝像機

mini·com·puter /ˈmɪnikəmpjuːtə(r)/ *noun* a computer that is smaller and slower than a MAINFRAME but larger and faster than a MICROCOMPUTER 小型計算機；小型電腦

mini·disc /ˈmɪnidɪsk/ *noun* a disc like a small CD that can record and play sound or data 小型磁盤；迷你光碟

mini·dress /ˈmɪnidres/ *noun* a very short dress 迷你連衣裙；超短連衣裙

mini·golf /ˈmɪnigɒlf; *NAmE* -gɑːlf; -gɔːlf/ (*NAmE* also **ˈminiature golf**) (*BrE* also **ˈcrazy golf**) *noun* [U] a type of GOLF in which people go around a small course hitting a ball through or over little tunnels, hills, bridges and other objects 迷你高爾夫球運動；微型高爾夫球運動

minim /ˈmɪnɪm/ (*BrE*) (*NAmE* **ˈhalf note**) *noun* (*music* 音) a note that lasts twice as long as a CROTCHET/QUARTER NOTE 二分音符；半音符 ➲ picture at MUSIC

min·imal AW /ˈmɪnɪməl/ *adj.* very small in size or amount; as small as possible 極小的；極少的；最小的：*The work was carried out at minimal cost.* 這項工作是以最少的開銷完成的。◇ *There's only a minimal amount of risk involved.* 所冒的風險極小。◇ *The damage to the car was minimal.* 汽車受到的損壞很小。➲ compare MAXIMAL ▸ **min·im·al·ly** AW *adv.*：*minimally invasive surgery* 微創手術 ◇ *The episode was reported minimally in the press.* 這段佚聞在報章雜誌中鮮有報道。

min·im·al·ist AW /ˈmɪnɪməlɪst/ *noun* an artist, a musician, etc. who uses very simple ideas or a very small number of simple things in their work 極簡抽象派藝術家；簡約主義者 ▸ **min·im·al·ism** *noun* [U] **min·im·al·ist** *adj.*

ˌminimal ˈpair *noun* (*phonetics* 語音) a pair of words, sounds, etc. which are distinguished from each other by only one feature, for example *pin* and *bin* 最小對立體（只在一個特徵上有區別的一對詞、發音等，如 pin 和 bin）

mini·mart /ˈmɪnimɑːt; *NAmE* -mɑːrt/ *noun* (*NAmE*) a small shop/store that sells food, newspapers, etc. and stays open very late（很晚才打烊的）雜貨鋪

min·im·ize (*BrE* also **-ise**) AW /ˈmɪnɪmaɪz/ *verb* **1** ~ sth to reduce sth, especially sth bad, to the lowest possible level 使減少到最低限度：*Good hygiene helps to minimize the risk of infection.* 保持清潔有助於最大限度地減少感染的危險。OPP **maximize** **2** ~ sth to try to make sth seem less important than it really is 降低；貶低；使顯得不重要 SYN **play down**：*He always tried to minimize his own faults, while exaggerating those of others.* 他總是試圖對自己的錯誤輕描淡寫，對別人的錯誤誇大其詞。**3** ~ sth to make sth small, especially on a computer screen（尤指在計算機屏幕上）使最小化：*Minimize any windows you have open.* 把你打開的所有窗口最小化。OPP **maximize** ▸ **mini·miza·tion**, **-isa·tion** /ˌmɪnɪmaɪˈzeɪʃn; *NAmE* -məˈz-/ *noun* [U]

mini·moto (also **mini-moto**) /ˈmɪniməʊtəʊ; *NAmE* -moʊtoʊ/ *noun* (*pl.* **-os**) a small motorcycle about 60cm high that people ride for fun and in races, but not on public roads 迷你摩托，迷你摩托車（用於遊戲和比賽，但不上路）

min·imum 0‑ AW /ˈmɪnɪməm/ *adj.*, *noun*

■ *adj.* 0‑ [usually before noun] (*abbr.* **min.**) the smallest that is possible or allowed; extremely small 最低的；最小的；最低限度的：*a* ***minimum charge/price*** 最低收費／價格 ◇ *the minimum age for retirement* 退休的最低年齡 ◇ *The work was done with the minimum amount of effort.* 做這項工作沒費什麼勁。OPP **maximum** ▸ **min·imum** *adv.*：*You'll need £200 minimum for your holiday expenses.* 你需要 200 英鎊作為你假日的最低開銷。

■ *noun* (*pl.* **min·ima** /-mə/) [C, usually sing.] **1** 0‑ (*abbr.* **min.**) the smallest or lowest amount that is possible, required or recorded 最小值；最少量；最低限度：*Costs should* ***be kept to a minimum.*** 成本應保持在最低限度。◇ *The class needs a minimum of six students to continue.* 這個班最少需要六名學生才可以繼續辦下去。◇ *As an* ***absolute minimum***, *you should spend two hours in the evening studying.* 你每天晚上應花兩個小時學習，這絕對是最低要求。◇ *Temperatures will fall to a minimum of 10 degrees.* 氣溫會降到最低點 10 度。**2** 0‑ [sing.] an extremely small amount 極小量：*He passed the exams with the minimum of effort.* 他沒費什麼勁就通過了考試。OPP **maximum**

ˌminimum seˈcurity prison (*NAmE*) (*BrE* **ˌopen ˈprison**) *noun* a prison in which prisoners have more freedom than in ordinary prisons 開放式監獄（對犯人的自由限制較少）

ˌminimum ˈwage *noun* [sing.] the lowest wage that an employer is allowed to pay by law 法定最低工資

min·ing /ˈmaɪnɪŋ/ *noun* [U] the process of getting coal and other minerals from under the ground; the industry involved in this 採礦；採礦業：***coal/diamond/gold/tin mining*** 煤礦／鑽石礦／金礦／錫礦開採 ◇ ***a mining company/community/engineer*** 採礦公司／界別／工程師 ➲ see also MINE *n.* (1)

ˈmini-note *noun* = SUBNOTEBOOK

min·ion /ˈmɪniən/ *noun* (*disapproving* or *humorous*) an unimportant person in an organization who has to obey orders; a servant 下屬；小卒；雜役

ˌmini-ˈroundabout *noun* (*BrE*) a white circle painted on a road at a place where two or more roads meet, that all traffic must go around in the same direction 迷你環島，微型環交，迷你圓環（道路交會處的環形白圈）

mini·ser·ies /ˈmɪnisɪəriːz; *NAmE* -sɪriːz/ *noun* (*pl.* **mini·ser·ies**) a television play that is divided into a number of parts and shown on different days 小型電視系列片；電視連續劇

mini·skirt /ˈmɪniskɜːt; *NAmE* -skɜːrt/ (also **mini**) *noun* a very short skirt 超短裙；迷你裙

min·is·ter 0‑ /ˈmɪnɪstə(r)/ *noun*, *verb*

■ *noun* **1** 0‑ (often **Minister**) (*BrE*) (in Britain and many other countries) a senior member of the government who is in charge of a government department or a branch of one（英國及其他許多國家的）部長，大臣：*the Minister of Education* 教育部長 ◇ *a meeting of EU Foreign Ministers* 歐盟外交部長會議 ◇ *senior ministers in the Cabinet* 內閣中的高級部長 ◇ *cabinet ministers* 內閣部長 ➲ see also FIRST MINISTER, PRIME MINISTER **2** 0‑ (in some Protestant Christian Churches 某些新教教會) a trained religious leader 牧師：*a Methodist minister* 循道宗牧師 ➲ compare PASTOR, PRIEST, VICAR **3** a person, lower in rank than an AMBASSADOR, whose job is to represent their government in a foreign country 公使；外交使節

■ *verb*

PHR V **ˈminister to sb/sth** (*formal*) to care for sb, especially sb who is sick or old, and make sure that they have everything they need 照料，服侍（年老或體弱者等）SYN **tend**

min·is·ter·ial AW /ˌmɪnɪˈstɪəriəl; *NAmE* -ˈstɪr-/ *adj.* connected with a government minister or ministers 部長的；大臣的：*decisions taken at ministerial level* 部長級的決定 ◇ *to* ***hold ministerial office*** (= to have the job of a government minister) 擔任部長職務

min·is·ter·ing /ˈmɪnɪstərɪŋ/ *adj.* [only before noun] (*formal*) caring for people 關心的；體貼的：*She could not see herself in the role of* ***ministering angel***. 她想像不出自己成為一名救死扶傷的天使會是什麼樣。

ˌMinister of ˈState *noun* a British government minister but not one who is in charge of a department（英國）國務大臣

min·is·tra·tions /ˌmɪnɪˈstreɪʃnz/ *noun* [pl.] (*formal* or *humorous*) the act of helping or caring for sb especially when they are ill/sick or in trouble 照料；服侍；看護

min·is·try 0‑ AW /ˈmɪnɪstri/ *noun* (*pl.* **-ies**)

1 0‑ [C] (*BrE*) a government department that has a particular area of responsibility（政府的）部：*the Ministry of Defence* 國防部 ◇ *a ministry spokesperson* 部發言人 **2** **the Ministry** [sing.+sing./pl. v.] ministers of religion, especially Protestant ministers, when they are mentioned as a group（尤指基督教新教的）全體牧師 **3** [C, usually sing.] the work and duties of a minister in the Church; the period of time spent working as a minister in the Church 神職；牧師職位；神職任期

mini·van (also **Mini Van™**) /ˈmɪnivæn/ (*especially NAmE*) (*BrE* **ˈpeople carrier**, **ˈpeople mover**) *noun* a large

M

car, like a van, designed to carry up to eight people 小型麪包車；（八人）小客車 ➲ VISUAL VOCAB page V52

mink /mɪŋk/ *noun* (*pl.* **mink** or **minks**) **1** [C] a small wild animal with thick shiny fur, a long body and short legs. Mink are often kept on farms for their fur. 水貂：*a mink farm* 水貂飼養場 **2** [U] the skin and shiny brown fur of the mink, used for making expensive coats, etc. 貂皮：*a mink jacket* 貂皮外套 **3** [C] a coat or jacket made of mink 貂皮大衣；貂皮外套

minke /ˈmɪŋki; -kə/ (also **ˈminke whale**) *noun* a small WHALE that is dark grey on top and white underneath 小鬚鯨

min·now /ˈmɪnəʊ; *NAmE* -noʊ/ *noun* **1** a very small FRESHWATER fish 米諾魚（多種小型魚類的總稱） **2** a company or sports team that is small or unimportant 無足輕重的（小）公司；不起眼的（小型）運動隊

minor **AW** /ˈmaɪnə(r)/ *adj., noun, verb*

■ ***adj.*** **1** [usually before noun] not very large, important or serious 較小的；次要的；輕微的：*a minor road* 小路 ◇ *minor injuries* 輕傷 ◇ *to undergo minor surgery* 做小手術 ◇ *youths imprisoned for minor offences* 因犯輕罪而被關押的年輕人 ◇ *There may be some minor changes to the schedule.* 時間安排上也許會有些微的變動。◇ *Women played a relatively minor role in the organization.* 在這個組織中，婦女發揮着相對次要的作用。**OPP** **major** **2** (*music* 音) based on a SCALE in which the third note is a SEMITONE/HALF TONE higher than the second note 小調的；小音階的：*the key of C minor* * C 小調 ➲ compare MAJOR *adj.* (3)

■ ***noun*** **1** (*law* 律) a person who is under the age at which you legally become an adult and are responsible for your actions 未成年人：*It is an offence to serve alcohol to minors.* 向未成年人提供含酒精的飲料是違法的。 **2** (*especially NAmE*) a subject that you study at university in addition to your MAJOR 輔修科目；輔修課程

■ ***verb***

PHR V **ˈminor in sth** (*NAmE*) to study sth at college, but not as your main subject 輔修 ➲ compare MAJOR

mi·nor·ity **AW** /maɪˈnɒrəti; *NAmE* -ˈnɔːr-/ *noun* (*pl.* **-ies**)

1 [sing.+sing./pl. v.] the smaller part of a group; less than half of the people or things in a large group 少數；少數派；少數人：*Only a small minority of students is/are interested in politics these days.* 目前，只有極少數學生對政治感興趣。◇ *minority shareholders in the bank* 銀行的小股東 **OPP** **majority** **2** [C] a small group within a community or country that is different because of race, religion, language, etc. 少數派；少數民族；少數群體：*the rights of* ***ethnic/racial minorities*** 少數民族/族裔的權利 ◇ *minority languages* 少數民族語言 ◇ *a large German-speaking minority in the east of the country* 在國家東部一個人口眾多的講德語的少數民族 ◇ (*NAmE*) *The school is 95 per cent minority* (= 95 per cent of children are not white Americans but from different groups). 這所學校裏 95% 的學生來自少數族裔。◇ (*NAmE*) *minority neighborhoods* (= where no or few white people live) 有色種族聚居區 ➲ COLLOCATIONS at RACE **3** [U] (*law* 律) the state of being under the age at which you are legally an adult 未成年

IDM **be in a/the miˈnority** to form much less than half of a large group 佔少數；成為少數派 **be in a minority of ˈone** (often *humorous*) to be the only person to have a particular opinion or to vote a particular way 是唯一持不同意見者；是唯一投此票者

miˌnority ˈgovernment *noun* [C, U] a government that has fewer seats in parliament than the total number held by all the other parties 少數黨政府（組成政府的政黨在議會中佔的席位少於其他政黨所佔席位的總和）

miˌnority ˈleader *noun* (in the US Senate or House of Representatives) a leader of a political party that does not have a majority（美國參議院和眾議院中的）少數黨領袖

ˈminor league (also **ˈMinor league**) *noun* (*NAmE*) a league of professional sports teams, especially in BASEBALL, that play at a lower level than the major leagues（尤指棒球）職業球隊小聯盟

ˈminor-league *adj.* [only before noun] (*NAmE*) **1** (*sport* 體) connected with teams in the minor leagues in BASEBALL 職業棒球小聯盟的：*a minor-league team* 職業棒球小聯盟球隊 **2** not very important and having little influence 次要的；無影響力的：*a minor-league business* 微不足道的一家企業

Mi·no·taur /ˈmaɪnətɔː(r); ˈmɪn-/ *noun* (in ancient Greek stories 古希臘神話) an imaginary creature who was half man and half BULL 彌諾陶洛斯（人身牛頭怪物）

min·ster /ˈmɪnstə(r)/ *noun* (*BrE*) a large or important church 大教堂：*York Minster* 約克大教堂

min·strel /ˈmɪnstrəl/ *noun* a musician or singer in the Middle Ages（中世紀的）遊方藝人

mint /mɪnt/ *noun, verb*

■ ***noun*** **1** [U] a plant with dark green leaves that have a fresh smell and taste and are added to food and drinks to give flavour, and used in cooking as a HERB and to decorate food 薄荷：*mint-flavoured toothpaste* 薄荷味的牙膏 ◇ *I decorated the fruit salad with a sprig of mint.* 我用小薄荷枝裝點水果色拉。◇ *roast lamb with mint sauce* 烤小羊肉蘸薄荷沙司 ➲ VISUAL VOCAB page V32 **2** [C] a sweet/candy flavoured with a type of mint called PEPPERMINT 薄荷糖：*after-dinner mints* 餐後薄荷糖 **3** [C] a place where money is made 鑄幣廠：*the Royal Mint* (= the one where British coins and notes are made) 皇家鑄幣廠 **4 a mint** [sing.] (*informal*) a large amount of money 大量的錢：*to* ***make/cost a mint*** 賺大錢；耗費大筆的錢

IDM **in mint conˈdition** new or as good as new; in perfect condition 嶄新；完美；完好無缺

■ ***verb*** **~ sth** to make a coin from metal 鑄（幣）；鑄造（硬幣）

mint·ed /ˈmɪntɪd/ *adj.* **1** **freshly/newly ~** recently produced, invented, etc. 新生產（或發明等）的：*a newly minted expression* 剛出現的詞語 **2** (of food 食物) flavoured with mint 薄荷味的 **3** (*BrE, informal*) very rich 富有的；富裕的

ˌmint ˈjulep (also **julep**) *noun* [U, C] an alcoholic drink made by mixing BOURBON with crushed ice, sugar and MINT 薄荷冰酒（用波旁威士忌、碎冰、糖和薄荷調製而成）

minty /ˈmɪnti/ *adj.* tasting or smelling of MINT 薄荷味的：*a* ***minty flavour/smell*** 薄荷口味/氣味

min·uet /ˌmɪnjuˈet/ *noun* a slow elegant dance that was popular in the 17th and 18th centuries; a piece of music for this dance 小步舞，小步舞曲（盛行於 17、18 世紀）

minus /ˈmaɪnəs/ *prep., noun, adj.*

■ ***prep.*** **1** used when you SUBTRACT (= take away) one number or thing from another one 減；減去：*Seven minus three is four* (7 - 3 = 4). 七減去三等於四。◇ *the former Soviet Union, minus the Baltic republics and Georgia* 前蘇聯，不包括波羅的海諸共和國及格魯吉亞 **2** used to express temperature below zero degrees 零下：*It was minus ten.* 氣溫為零下十度。◇ *The temperature dropped to minus 28 degrees centigrade* (-28°C). 氣温降到零下 28 攝氏度。 **3** (*informal*) without sth that was there before 無，欠缺（曾經有過的東西）：*We're going to be minus a car for a while.* 我們要過一段沒有車的日子。**OPP** **plus** **IDM** see PLUS *prep.*

■ ***noun*** **1** (also **ˈminus sign**) The symbol (-), used in mathematics 減號；負號 **2** (*informal*) a negative quality; a disadvantage 負值；缺點：*Let's consider the pluses and minuses of changing the system.* 我們來考慮一下改變系統的利弊吧。**OPP** **plus**

■ ***adj.*** **1** (*mathematics* 數) lower than zero 小於零的；負的：*a* ***minus figure/number*** 負數 **2** making sth seem negative and less attractive or good 負面的；使顯得有欠缺的：*What are the car's* ***minus points*** (= the disadvantages)? 這台車的缺點是什麼？◇ ***On the minus side,*** *rented property is expensive and difficult to find.* 不利因素是租房又貴又不好找。 **3** [not before noun] (used in a system of marks/grades 用於計分或計成績) slightly lower than the mark/grade A, B, etc. 略低於 A（或 B

M

等）：*I got (a) B minus (B-) in the test.* 這次考試我得了個 B-。**OPP** **plus**

min·us·cule /ˈmɪnəskjuːl/ *adj.* extremely small 極小的；微小的

min·ute¹ /ˈmɪnɪt/ *noun, verb* ➲ see also MINUTE²

■ *noun*

▸ **PART OF HOUR** 分鐘 **1** [C] (*abbr.* **min.**) each of the 60 parts of an hour, that are equal to 60 seconds 分鐘；分：*It's four minutes to six.* 差四分六點。◇ *I'll be back in a few minutes.* 我一會兒就回來。◇ *Boil the rice for 20 minutes.* 將米煮 20 分鐘。◇ *a ten-minute bus ride* 乘公共汽車十分鐘的路程 ◇ *I enjoyed every minute of the party.* 我在這次聚會上從頭到尾都非常開心。

▸ **VERY SHORT TIME** 短暫的時間 **2** [sing.] (*informal*) a very short time 一會兒；一會兒的工夫：*It only takes a minute to make a salad.* 只要一會兒就能做好色拉。◇ ***Hang on a minute***—*I'll just get my coat.* 等一下，我去拿外套。◇ *I just have to finish this—I won't be a minute.* 我得做完這活兒，一會兒就好。◇ *Could I see you for a minute?* 我能見你一下嗎？◇ *I'll be with you* ***in a minute***, *Jo.* 一會兒見，喬。◇ *Typical English weather—one minute it's raining and the next minute the sun is shining.* 典型的英國天氣，時雨時晴。

▸ **EXACT MOMENT** 時刻 **3** [sing.] an exact moment in time 時刻：*At that very minute, Tom walked in.* 就在這時候，湯姆走了進來。

▸ **ANGLES** 角 **4** [C] each of the 60 equal parts of a degree, used in measuring angles 分（角度單位，六十分之一度）：*37 degrees 30 minutes (37° 30′)* 37 度 30 分

▸ **RECORD OF MEETING** 會議記錄 **5 the minutes** [pl.] a summary or record of what is said or decided at a formal meeting 會議記錄；會議紀要：*We read through the minutes of the last meeting.* 我們認真通讀了上次會議的紀要。◇ *Who is going to* ***take the minutes*** (= write them)? 誰來做會議記錄？

▸ **SHORT NOTE** 簡短記錄 **6** [C] a short note on a subject, especially one that recommends a course of action 摘要；簡短記錄；備忘錄

IDM **(at) any ˈminute (ˈnow)** very soon 很快；馬上：*Hurry up! He'll be back any minute now.* 快點！他隨時都會回來。 **the minute (that) …** as soon as … 一…就：*I want to see him the minute he arrives.* 他一到我就要見他。 **ˌnot for a/one ˈminute** certainly not; not at all 當然不；絕不：*I don't think for a minute that she'll accept but you can ask her.* 我認為她絕不會接受，但你可以問問她。 **this minute** immediately; now 立刻；馬上；現在：*Come down this minute!* 馬上下來！◇ *I don't know what I'm going to do yet—I've* ***just this minute*** *found out.* 我還不知道我要怎麼做，我剛剛才弄清情況。 **to the ˈminute** exactly 準確地；確切地：*The train arrived at 9.05 to the minute.* 列車 9:05 準時到達。 **ˌup to the ˈminute** (*informal*) **1** fashionable and modern 時髦；緊跟時尚；入時：*Her styles are always up to the minute.* 她的裝束總是非常時髦。 **2** having the latest information 包含最新信息的；時時更新的：*The traffic reports are up to the minute.* 交通信息報道是最新的。➲ see also UP-TO-THE-MINUTE ➲ more at BORN *v.*, JUST *adv.*, LAST *det.*, WAIT *v.*

■ *verb* **~ sth | ~ that …** to write down sth that is said at a meeting in the official record (= the minutes) 將（某事）寫進會議記錄：*I'd like that last remark to be minuted.* 我希望把剛才那句話記錄在案。

mi·nute² /maɪˈnjuːt; *NAmE* also -ˈnuːt/ *adj.* ➲ see also MINUTE¹ (*superlative* **minut·est**, no *comparative*) **1** extremely small 極小的；微小的；細微的 **SYN** **tiny**：*minute amounts of chemicals in the water* 水中含量極小的化學成分 ◇ *The kitchen on the boat is minute.* 小船上的廚房小極了。**2** very detailed, careful and thorough 細緻入微的；詳細的：*a* ***minute examination/inspection*** 細緻的檢查／視察 ◇ *She remembered everything* ***in minute detail/in the minutest detail(s)***. 她記得每一件事的細節。▸ **mi·nute·ly** *adv.*：*The agreement has been examined minutely.* 協議經過了細緻入微的審查。

ˈminute hand *noun* [usually sing.] the hand on a watch or clock that points to the minutes（鐘錶的）分針 ➲ picture at CLOCK

Min·ute·man /ˈmɪnɪtmæn/ *noun* (*pl.* **-men** /-men/) (*US*) (during the American Revolution) a member of a group of men who were not soldiers but who were ready to fight immediately when they were needed（美國革命時期的）即召民兵

mi·nu·tiae /maɪˈnjuːʃiiː; *NAmE* mɪˈnuːʃiiː/ *noun* [pl.] very small details 微小的細節：*the minutiae of the contract* 合同細節

minx /mɪŋks/ *noun* [sing.] (*old-fashioned* or *humorous*) a girl or young woman who is clever at getting what she wants, and does not show respect 狡猾輕佻的女孩（或年輕女子）

MIPS /mɪps/ *abbr.* (*computing* 計) million instructions per second (a unit for measuring computer speed) 百萬條指令每秒（計算機速度單位）

miraa /ˈmɪrɑː/ *noun* [U] (*EAfrE*) a form of KHAT 米拉茶葉

mir·acle /ˈmɪrəkl/ *noun* **1** [C] an act or event that does not follow the laws of nature and is believed to be caused by God 聖跡；神跡 **SYN** **wonder** **2** [sing.] (*informal*) a lucky thing that happens that you did not expect or think was possible 奇跡；不平凡的事 **SYN** **wonder**：*an economic miracle* 經濟方面的奇跡 ◇ ***It's a miracle*** *(that) nobody was killed in the crash.* 撞車事故中竟然沒有一人喪生，這真是奇跡。◇ *It would take a miracle to make this business profitable.* 讓這個公司贏利簡直是天方夜譚。◇ *a* ***miracle cure/drug*** 有奇效的療法；靈丹妙藥 **3** [C] **~ of sth** a very good example or product of sth 極好的例子；精品 **SYN** **wonder**：*The car is a miracle of engineering.* 這輛車是汽車工業的精品。

IDM **work/perform ˈmiracles** to achieve very good results 創造奇跡；有奇效：*Her exercise programme has worked miracles for her.* 她的健身計劃對她很有效。

mi·racu·lous /mɪˈrækjələs/ *adj.* like a miracle; completely unexpected and very lucky 奇跡般的；不可思議的；不平凡的 **SYN** **extraordinary, phenomenal**：*miraculous powers of healing* 神奇的治病能力 ◇ *She's made a miraculous recovery.* 她奇跡般地康復了。▸ **mi·racu·lous·ly** *adv.*：*They miraculously survived the plane crash.* 在空難中，他們奇跡般地幸免於難。

mir·age /ˈmɪrɑːʒ; mɪˈrɑːʒ; *NAmE* məˈrɑːʒ/ *noun* **1** an effect caused by hot air in deserts or on roads, that makes you think you can see sth, such as water, which is not there 幻景；海市蜃樓 **2** a hope or wish that you cannot make happen because it is not realistic 幻想；妄想 **SYN** **illusion**：*His idea of love was a mirage.* 他的愛情觀不現實。

Mi·randa /mɪˈrændə/ *adj.* (in the US) relating to the fact that the police must tell sb who has been arrested about their rights, including the right not to answer questions, and warn them that anything they say may be used as evidence against them（美國）米蘭達原則的（即警察必須告訴被拘捕者其權利，包括有權保持緘默，以及他所說的話可能用作對他不利的證據）：*The police read him his Miranda rights.* 警察向他宣讀了他的米蘭達權利。**ORIGIN** From the decision of the Supreme Court on the case of Miranda v the State of Arizona in 1966. 源自 1966 年美國最高法院有關米蘭達訴亞利桑那州一案的裁決。

mire /ˈmaɪə(r)/ *noun* [U] an area of deep mud 泥潭；泥沼 **SYN** **bog**：*The wheels sank deeper into the mire.* 輪子在泥潭中陷得更深了。◇ (*figurative*) *My name had been dragged through the mire* (= my reputation was ruined). 我的名聲受到了玷污。◇ (*figurative*) *The government was sinking deeper and deeper* ***into the mire*** (= getting further into a difficult situation). 政府在泥潭中越陷越深。

mired /ˈmaɪəd; *NAmE* ˈmaɪərd/ *adj.* [not before noun] **~ in sth** (*literary*) **1** in a difficult or unpleasant situation that you cannot escape from 陷入困境；處境艱難：*The country was mired in recession.* 這個國家陷入了經濟衰退的困境。**2** stuck in deep mud 陷入泥沼；深陷泥潭

mir·ror /ˈmɪrə(r)/ *noun, verb*

■ *noun* **1** [C] a piece of special flat glass that reflects images, so that you can see yourself when you look in it 鏡子：*He looked at himself* ***in the mirror***. 他照了照鏡子。◇ *a rear-view mirror* (= in a car, so that the driver can see what is behind) (車內的)後視鏡 ◇ (*BrE*) *a wing mirror* (= on the side of a car) 裝在車外側面的後視鏡 ◇ (*NAmE*) *a side-view mirror* 側視鏡 ➲ VISUAL VOCAB pages V23, V51, V52, V60 **2** **a ~ of sth** [sing.] something that shows what sth else is like 寫照；反映某種情況的事物：*The face is the mirror of the soul.* 臉是反映靈魂的鏡子。

■ *verb* **1** **~ sth** to have features that are similar to sth else and which show what it is like 反映 SYN **reflect**：*The music of the time mirrored the feeling of optimism in the country.* 這個時期的音樂反映出這個國家的樂觀精神。**2** **~ sb/sth** to show the image of sb/sth on the surface of water, glass, etc. 映照；反射 SYN **reflect**：*She saw herself mirrored in the window.* 她看到自己在窗玻璃上照出的影像。

mir·ror·ball /ˈmɪrəbɔːl; *NAmE* ˈmɪrər-/ *noun* a decoration consisting of a large ball covered in small mirrors that hangs from the ceiling and turns to produce lighting effects (從天花板懸掛、產生燈光效果的)鏡面球，反光球

mir·rored /ˈmɪrəd; *NAmE* -rərd/ *adj.* [only before noun] having a mirror or mirrors or behaving like a mirror 有鏡子的；像鏡子的：***mirrored doors/sunglasses*** 有鏡子的門；反光太陽鏡

ˌmirror ˈimage *noun* an image of sth that is like a REFLECTION of it, either because it is exactly the same or because the right side of the original object appears on the left and the left side appears on the right 鏡像；映像；反像

ˈmirror site (also **mir·ror**) *noun* (*computing* 計) a website which is a copy of another website but has a different address on the Internet 鏡像站點；複製網絡站點

mirth /mɜːθ; *NAmE* mɜːrθ/ *noun* [U] happiness, fun and the sound of people laughing 歡樂；歡笑 SYN **merriment**：*The performance produced much mirth among the audience.* 這場演出使觀眾笑聲不斷。

mirth·less /ˈmɜːθləs; *NAmE* ˈmɜːrθ-/ *adj.* (*formal*) showing no real enjoyment or AMUSEMENT 不快樂的；憂鬱的：*a* ***mirthless laugh/smile*** 苦笑 ▸ **mirth·less·ly** *adv.*

MIS /ˌem aɪ ˈes/ *abbr.* (*computing* 計) management information system (a system that stores information for use by business managers) (商業)管理信息系統，管理資訊系統

mis- /mɪs/ *prefix* (in verbs and nouns 構成動詞和名詞) bad or wrong; badly or wrongly 壞(或錯)的；糟糕(或錯誤)地：*misbehaviour* 行為不端 ◇ *misinterpret* 誤解

mis·ad·ven·ture /ˌmɪsədˈventʃə(r)/ *noun* **1** [U] (*BrE, law* 律) death caused by accident, rather than as a result of a crime 意外致死：*a verdict of* ***death by misadventure*** 意外死亡的裁決 **2** [C, U] (*formal*) bad luck or a small accident 厄運；惡運；不幸遭遇 SYN **mishap**

mis·aligned /ˌmɪsəˈlaɪnd/ *adj.* not in the correct position in relation to sth else 方向偏離的；未對準的：*a misaligned vertebra* 錯位的脊椎骨 ▸ **mis·align·ment** /ˌmɪsəˈlaɪnmənt/ *noun* [U]：*The tests revealed a slight misalignment of the eyes.* 經檢測發現有輕度斜視。

mis·an·thrope /ˈmɪsənθrəʊp; *NAmE* -θroʊp/ *noun* (*formal*) a person who hates and avoids other people 厭惡人類的人；厭世者；不願與人交往者

mis·an·throp·ic /ˌmɪsənˈθrɒpɪk; *NAmE* -ˈθrɑːp-/ *adj.* (*formal*) hating and avoiding other people 厭世的；不願與別人交往的 ▸ **mis·an·thropy** /mɪˈsænθrəpi/ *noun* [U]

mis·ap·pli·ca·tion /ˌmɪsæplɪˈkeɪʃn/ *noun* [U, C] (*formal*) the use of sth for the wrong purpose or in the wrong way 誤用；不正當使用

mis·ap·ply /ˌmɪsəˈplaɪ/ *verb* (**mis·ap·plies**, **mis·ap·ply·ing**, **mis·ap·plied**, **mis·ap·plied**) [usually passive] **~ sth** (*formal*) to use sth for the wrong purpose or in the wrong way 誤用；濫用；挪用

mis·ap·pre·hen·sion /ˌmɪsæprɪˈhenʃn/ *noun* [U, C] (*formal*) a wrong idea about sth, or sth you believe to be true that is not true 誤解；誤會：*I was* ***under the misapprehension that*** *the course was for complete beginners.* 我誤以為這門課是給毫無基礎的初學者開的。

mis·ap·pro·pri·ate /ˌmɪsəˈprəʊprieɪt; *NAmE* -ˈproʊ-/ *verb* **~ sth** (*formal*) to take sb else's money or property for yourself, especially when they have trusted you to take care of it 私吞；挪用 SYN **embezzle** ➲ compare APPROPRIATE *v.* ▸ **mis·ap·pro·pri·ation** /ˌmɪsəˌprəʊpriˈeɪʃn; *NAmE* -ˌproʊ-/ *noun* [U]

mis·be·got·ten /ˌmɪsbɪˈɡɒtn; *NAmE* -ˈɡɑːtn/ *adj.* [usually before noun] (*formal*) badly designed or planned 設計(或規劃)拙劣的

mis·be·have /ˌmɪsbɪˈheɪv/ *verb* [I, T] to behave badly 行為不端：*Any child caught misbehaving was made to stand at the front of the class.* 搗蛋的孩子要是被當場抓住，都要在全班人前面罰站。◇ **~ yourself** *I see the dog has been misbehaving itself again.* 我發現這條狗又不乖了。OPP **behave** ▸ **mis·be·hav·iour** (*BrE*) (*NAmE* **mis·be·hav·ior**) /ˌmɪsbɪˈheɪvjə(r)/ *noun* [U]

mis·cal·cu·late /ˌmɪsˈkælkjuleɪt/ *verb* **1** [T, I] to estimate an amount, a figure, a measurement, etc. wrongly 錯誤地估計；誤算：**~ (sth)** *They had seriously miscalculated the effect of inflation.* 關於通貨膨脹的影響，他們的判斷嚴重失誤。◇ **~ how long, how much, etc. ...** *He had miscalculated how long the trip would take.* 這次旅行要花多少時間，他當時估計錯了。**2** [T, I] **~ (sth)** | **~ how, what, etc. ...** to judge a situation wrongly (對形勢)判斷錯誤 SYN **misjudge**：*She miscalculated the level of opposition to her proposals.* 她沒想到她的建議會受到這樣強烈的反對。▸ **mis·cal·cu·la·tion** /ˌmɪskælkjuˈleɪʃn/ *noun* [C, U]：*to make a miscalculation* 計算錯誤

mis·car·riage /ˈmɪskærɪdʒ; *BrE* also ˌmɪsˈk-/ *noun* [C, U] the process of giving birth to a baby before it is fully developed and able to survive; an occasion when this happens 流產：*to have a miscarriage* 流產 ◇ *The pregnancy ended in miscarriage at 11 weeks.* 懷孕到第 11 週便流產了。➲ COLLOCATIONS at CHILD ➲ compare ABORTION

misˌcarriage of ˈjustice *noun* [U, C] (*law* 律) a situation in which a court makes a wrong decision, especially when sb is punished when they are innocent 誤判；錯判；審判不公；司法不公

mis·carry /ˌmɪsˈkæri/ *verb* (**mis·car·ries**, **mis·carry·ing**, **mis·car·ried**, **mis·car·ried**) **1** [I, T] **~ (sth)** to give birth to a baby before it is fully developed and able to live 流產：*The shock caused her to miscarry.* 她因驚嚇而流產了。**2** [I] (*formal*) (of a plan 計劃) to fail 失敗 SYN **come to nothing**

mis·cast /ˌmɪsˈkɑːst; *NAmE* -ˈkæst/ *verb* (**mis·cast**, **mis·cast**) [usually passive] **~ sb (as sb/sth)** to choose an actor to play a role for which they are not suitable 角色選擇不當；給(演員)分配不適當的角色

mis·ce·gen·ation /ˌmɪsɪdʒəˈneɪʃn/ *noun* [U] (*formal*) the fact of children being produced by parents who are of different races, especially when one parent is white (尤指白人和非白人)混種生育子女，混種

mis·cel·lan·eous /ˌmɪsəˈleɪniəs/ *adj.* [usually before noun] consisting of many different kinds of things that are not connected and do not easily form a group 混雜的；各種各樣的 SYN **diverse**, **various**：*a sale of miscellaneous household items* 各種生活用品大減價 ◇ *She gave me some money to cover any miscellaneous expenses.* 她給了我一些零花錢。

mis·cel·lany /mɪˈseləni; *NAmE* ˈmɪsəleɪni/ *noun* [sing.] (*formal*) a group or collection of different kinds of things 雜集；混合體 SYN **assortment**

mis·chance /ˌmɪsˈtʃɑːns; *NAmE* -ˈtʃæns/ *noun* [U, C] (*formal*) bad luck 不幸；厄運

mis·chief /ˈmɪstʃɪf/ *noun* [U] **1** bad behaviour (especially of children) that is annoying but does not cause any serious damage or harm 淘氣；惡作劇；頑皮：*Those*

M

children are always ***getting into mischief.*** 那些孩子總是淘氣。◇ *I try to* ***keep out of mischief.*** 我盡量不胡鬧。◇ *It's very quiet upstairs; they must be* ***up to some mischief!*** 樓上很安靜，他們一定在搞什麼惡作劇！ **2** the wish or tendency to behave or play in a way that causes trouble 惡意；使壞的念頭： *Her eyes were full of mischief.* 她眼睛裏滿是使壞的神情。 **3** (*formal*) harm or injury that is done to sb or to their reputation 傷害；毀損： *The incident caused a great deal of political mischief.* 這一事件造成了嚴重的政治危害。

IDM **,do yourself a 'mischief** (*BrE, informal*) to hurt yourself physically 傷害自己的身體： *Watch how you use those scissors—you could do yourself a mischief!* 看你那是怎麼用剪刀啊，你會傷着自己的！ **make 'mischief** to do or say sth deliberately to upset other people, or cause trouble between them 搬弄是非；挑撥離間

'mischief-making *noun* [U] the act of deliberately causing trouble for people, such as harming their reputation 挑撥離間；搬弄是非

mis·chiev·ous /'mɪstʃɪvəs/ *adj.* **1** enjoying playing tricks and annoying people 頑皮的；搗蛋的 **SYN** **naughty**： *a mischievous boy* 淘氣的男孩 ◇ *a* ***mischievous grin/smile/look*** 頑皮地咧着嘴笑；頑皮地微微一笑；顯出淘氣的神情 **2** (*formal*) (of an action or a statement 行為或言論) causing trouble, such as damaging sb's reputation 招惹是非的；惡意的： ***mischievous lies/gossip*** 招惹是非的謊言／閒言碎語 ▸ **mis·chiev·ous·ly** *adv.*

mis·cible /'mɪsəbl/ *adj.* (*technical* 術語) (of liquids 液體) that can be mixed together 可混合的 **OPP** **immiscible**

M

mis·con·ceive /,mɪskən'si:v/ *verb* **~ sth** (*formal*) to understand sth in the wrong way 誤解；誤會 **SYN** **misunderstand**

mis·con·ceived /,mɪskən'si:vd/ *adj.* badly planned or judged; not carefully thought about 計劃不周的；判斷失誤的；欠考慮的： *a misconceived education policy* 考慮不周的教育政策 ◇ *their misconceived expectations of country life* 他們原先對鄉村生活的錯誤想法

mis·con·cep·tion /,mɪskən'sepʃn/ *noun* [C, U] **~ (about sth)** a belief or an idea that is not based on correct information, or that is not understood by people 錯誤認識；誤解： *frequently held misconceptions about the disease* 對這種疾病常見的誤解 ◇ *a* ***popular misconception*** (= one that a lot of people have) 很多人都有的錯誤觀念 ◇ *Let me deal with some* ***common misconceptions.*** 我來談談一些常見的錯誤認識。◇ *views based on misconception and prejudice* 由誤解和偏見而形成的觀點 ➲ compare PRECONCEPTION

mis·con·duct /,mɪs'kɒndʌkt; *NAmE* -'kɑ:n-/ *noun* [U] (*formal*) **1** unacceptable behaviour, especially by a professional person 失職；處理不當；行為不端： *a doctor accused of* ***gross misconduct*** (= very serious misconduct) 被控嚴重失職的醫生 ◇ *professional misconduct* 玩忽職守 **2** bad management of a company, etc. 管理不善： *misconduct of the company's financial affairs* 對公司財務的管理不善

mis·con·struc·tion /,mɪskən'strʌkʃn/ *noun* [U, C] (*formal*) a completely wrong understanding of sth 完全錯誤的理解；誤解

mis·con·strue /,mɪskən'stru:/ *verb* **~ sth (as sth)** (*formal*) to understand sb's words or actions wrongly 誤解（某人的言行） **SYN** **misinterpret**： *It is easy to misconstrue confidence as arrogance.* 很容易將信心誤解為傲慢。

mis·count /,mɪs'kaʊnt/ *verb* [T, I] **~ (sth)** to count sth wrongly 數錯： *The votes had been miscounted.* 票數計錯了。

mis·cre·ant /'mɪskriənt/ *noun* (*literary*) a person who has done sth wrong or illegal 缺德的人；不法之徒

mis·deed /,mɪs'di:d/ *noun* [usually pl.] (*formal*) a bad or evil act 惡行；不義之舉 **SYN** **wrongdoing**

mis·de·mean·our (*especially US* **mis·de·meanor**) /,mɪsdɪ'mi:nə(r)/ *noun* **1** (*formal*) an action that is bad or unacceptable, but not very serious 不正當的行為；不檢點的行為： *youthful misdemeanours* 年輕人的越軌行為 **2** (*law* 律) (*especially US*) a crime that is not considered to be very serious 輕罪 ➲ compare FELONY

mis·diag·nose /mɪs'daɪəgnəʊz; *NAmE* -noʊz/ *verb* **~ sth (as sth)** to give an explanation of the nature of an illness or a problem that is not correct 誤診；錯誤判斷： *Her depression was misdiagnosed as stress.* 她的抑鬱症被誤診為精神緊張。 ▸ **mis·diag·nosis** /,mɪsdaɪəg'nəʊsɪs; *NAmE* -'noʊ-/ *noun* (*pl.* **mis·diag·noses** /-si:z/)

mis·dial /,mɪs'daɪəl/ *verb* (**-ll-**, *NAmE* **-l-**) [I, T] **~ (sth)** to call the wrong telephone number by mistake 撥錯（電話號碼）

mis·dir·ect /,mɪsdə'rekt; -daɪ'rekt/ *verb* **1** [usually passive] **~ sth** to use sth in a way that is not appropriate to a particular situation 誤用；使用不當： *Their efforts over the past years have been largely misdirected.* 他們過去幾年的努力大都白費了。 **2 ~ sb/sth** to send sb/sth in the wrong direction or to the wrong place 指錯方向；引錯路；誤導 **3 ~ sb/sth** (*law* 律) (of a judge 法官) to give a JURY (= the group of people who decide if sb is guilty of a crime) wrong information about the law 誤導，錯誤指示（陪審團） ▸ **mis·dir·ec·tion** /,mɪsdə'rekʃn; -daɪ'rek-/ *noun* [U]

mise en scène /,mi:z ɒn 'sen; *NAmE* ɑ:n/ *noun* [sing.] (from *French*) **1** the arrangement of furniture, SCENERY, LIGHTING, etc. used on the stage for a play in the theatre, or in front of the camera in a film/movie 場景；舞台調度；場面調度 **2** (*formal*) the place or scene where an event takes place 事發地點；現場： *Venice provided the mise-en-scène for the conference.* 威尼斯是這次會議的地點。

miser /'maɪzə(r)/ *noun* (*disapproving*) a person who loves money and hates spending it 吝嗇鬼；守財奴

mis·er·able /'mɪzrəbl/ *adj.* **1** very unhappy or uncomfortable 痛苦的；非常難受的；可憐的： *We were cold, wet and thoroughly miserable.* 我們又冷又濕，難受極了。◇ *Don't look so miserable!* 別一副悶悶不樂的樣子！ ◇ *She knows how to* ***make life miserable*** *for her employees.* 她知道如何整治她的雇員。 **2** making you feel very unhappy or uncomfortable 使難受的；使不舒服的；令人不快的 **SYN** **depressing**： *miserable housing conditions* 惡劣的住房條件 ◇ *I spent a miserable weekend alone at home.* 我獨自一人在家度過了一個慘兮兮的週末。◇ *What a miserable day* (= cold and wet)*!* 多麼難受的天氣呀！◇ *The play was* ***a miserable failure.*** 這部話劇是個可悲的失敗。 **3** [only before noun] (*disapproving*) (of a person 人) always unhappy, bad-tempered and unfriendly 乖戾的；脾氣壞的 **SYN** **grumpy**： *He was a miserable old devil.* 他真是個令人厭煩的老傢伙。 **4** too small in quantity 太少的；少得可憐的 **SYN** **paltry**： *How can anyone live on such a miserable wage?* 這麼少的工資讓人怎麼活呀？ ▸ **mis·er·ably** /-əbli/ *adv.*： *They wandered around miserably.* 他們可憐兮兮地四處遊蕩。◇ *a miserably cold day* 令人難受的寒冷天氣 ◇ *He* ***failed miserably*** *as an actor.* 作為演員，他敗得很慘。 **IDM** see SIN *n.*

miser·ly /'maɪzəli; *NAmE* -ərli/ *adj.* (*disapproving*) **1** (of a person 人) hating to spend money 吝嗇的；小氣的 **SYN** **mean** **2** (of a quantity or amount 數量) too small 極少的；太小的 **SYN** **paltry**

mis·ery /'mɪzəri/ *noun* (*pl.* **-ies**) **1** [U] great suffering of the mind or body 痛苦；悲慘 **SYN** **distress**： *Fame brought her nothing but misery.* 名聲只給她帶來了痛苦。 **2** [U] very poor living conditions 窮困；悲慘的生活 **SYN** **poverty**： *The vast majority of the population lives in utter misery.* 這裏的人絕大多數生活在極度貧困之中。 **3** [C] something that causes great suffering of mind or body 不幸的事；痛苦的事： *the miseries of unemployment* 失業的痛苦 **4** [C] (*BrE, informal*) a person who is always unhappy and complaining 老發牢騷的人；不痛快的人： *Don't be such an old misery!* 別老這麼牢騷滿腹了！

IDM **make sb's life a 'misery** to behave in a way that makes sb else feel very unhappy 使別人遭殃；讓人痛苦 **put an animal, a bird, etc. out of its 'misery** to kill a creature because it has an illness or injury that cannot be treated 結束動物的生命以解除其痛苦 **put sb out of their 'misery** (*informal*) to stop sb worrying by telling them sth that they are anxious to know（告知情況以）

消除某人的憂慮：*Put me out of my misery—did I pass or didn't I?* 別再讓我着急了，我及不及格？

mis·file /ˌmɪsˈfaɪl/ *verb* **~ sth** to put away a document in the wrong place 歸錯（文檔）：*The missing letter had been misfiled.* 找不着的那封信放錯地方了。

mis·fire /ˌmɪsˈfaɪə(r)/ *verb* **1** [I] (of a plan or joke 計劃或笑話) to fail to have the effect that you had intended 不奏效；不起作用 SYN **go wrong 2** (also **miss**) [I] (of an engine 發動機) to not work correctly because the petrol/gas does not burn at the right time 不起動；不能正常運行 **3** [I] (of a gun, etc. 槍等) to fail to send out a bullet, etc. when fired 不發火；射不出子彈 ➲ compare BACKFIRE

mis·fit /ˈmɪsfɪt/ *noun* a person who is not accepted by a particular group of people, especially because their behaviour or their ideas are very different 與別人合不來的人；行為（或思想）怪異的人：*a social misfit* 與社會格格不入的人

mis·for·tune /ˌmɪsˈfɔːtʃuːn; *NAmE* -ˈfɔːrtʃ-/ *noun* **1** [U] bad luck 厄運；不幸：*He has known great misfortune in his life.* 他一生中經歷過巨大的不幸。◇ *We **had the misfortune to** run into a violent storm.* 我們不幸遭遇了猛烈的暴風雨。**2** [C] an unfortunate accident, condition or event 不幸的事故（或情況、事件）SYN **blow, disaster**：*She bore her misfortunes bravely.* 她勇敢地承受不幸的遭遇。

mis·giv·ing /ˌmɪsˈɡɪvɪŋ/ *noun* [C, usually pl., U] **~ about sth/about doing sth** feelings of doubt or anxiety about what might happen, or about whether or not sth is the right thing to do 疑慮；顧慮：*I had grave misgivings about making the trip.* 對於這次旅行我有過極大的顧慮。◇ *I read the letter with a sense of misgiving.* 我帶着疑慮看了那封信。

mis·govern /ˌmɪsˈɡʌvn; *NAmE* -ˈɡʌvərn/ *verb* **~ sth** to govern a country or state badly or unfairly 對（國家）治理不善（或失當）▸ **mis·gov·ern·ment** /ˌmɪsˈɡʌvənmənt; *NAmE* -ˈɡʌvərn-/ *noun* [U]

mis·guided /ˌmɪsˈɡaɪdɪd/ *adj.* wrong because you have understood or judged a situation badly（因理解或判斷失誤）搞錯的 SYN **inappropriate**：*She only did it in a misguided attempt to help.* 她是要幫忙，只是想法不對頭。▸ **mis·guided·ly** *adv.*

mis·handle /ˌmɪsˈhændl/ *verb* **1 ~ sth** to deal badly with a problem or situation 處理不當 SYN **mismanage**：*The entire campaign had been badly mishandled.* 整個活動搞得一塌糊塗。**2 ~ sb/sth** to touch or treat sb/sth in a rough and careless way 粗暴對待；胡亂操作：*The equipment could be dangerous if mishandled.* 這套設備如果使用不當會有危險。▸ **mis·hand·ling** *noun* [U]：*the government's mishandling of the economy* 政府對經濟問題處理不當

mis·hap /ˈmɪshæp/ *noun* [C, U] a small accident or piece of bad luck that does not have serious results 小事故；晦氣：*a slight mishap* 小小的不幸 ◇ *a series of mishaps* 一連串的倒霉事 ◇ *I managed to get home **without (further) mishap**.* 我總算平安回到了家。

mis·hear /ˌmɪsˈhɪə(r); *NAmE* -ˈhɪr/ *verb* (**mis·heard, mis·heard** /-ˈhɜːd; *NAmE* -ˈhɜːrd/) [T, I] **~ (sb)** | **~ what …** to fail to hear correctly what sb says, so that you think they said sth else 誤聽；聽錯：*You may have misheard her—I'm sure she didn't mean that.* 你可能聽錯她的話了，我肯定她不是這個意思。◇ *I thought he said he was coming today, but I must have misheard.* 我以為他說他今天來，不過我一定是聽錯了。

mis·hit /ˌmɪsˈhɪt/ *verb* (**mis·hit·ting, mis·hit, mis·hit**) **~ sth** (in a game 體育比賽) to hit the ball badly so that it does not go where you had intended 誤擊；把（球）打歪 ▸ **mis·hit** /ˈmɪshɪt/ *noun*

mish·mash /ˈmɪʃmæʃ/ *noun* [sing.] (*informal, usually disapproving*) a confused mixture of different kinds of things, styles, etc. 混雜物（或樣式等）；雜燴

mis·in·form /ˌmɪsɪnˈfɔːm; *NAmE* -ˈfɔːrm/ *verb* [often passive] **~ sb (about sth)** to give sb wrong information about sth 誤報；誤傳：*They were deliberately misinformed about their rights.* 有人故意向他們錯誤地說明了他們的權利。◇ *a misinformed belief* (= based on wrong information) 被誤導的信念 ▸ **mis·in·for·ma·tion** /ˌmɪsɪnfəˈmeɪʃn/ *noun* [U]：*a campaign of misinformation* 傳播假消息的活動

mis·in·ter·pret AW /ˌmɪsɪnˈtɜːprɪt; *NAmE* -ˈtɜːrp-/ *verb* **~ sth (as sth/doing sth)** to understand sth/sb wrongly 誤解；誤釋 SYN **misconstrue, misread**：*His comments were misinterpreted as a criticism of the project.* 他的評論被誤解為對這個項目的批評。➲ compare INTERPRET ▸ **mis·in·ter·pret·ation** AW /ˌmɪsɪntɜːprɪˈteɪʃn; *NAmE* -tɜːrp-/ *noun* [U, C]：*A number of these statements could be **open to misinterpretation*** (= could be understood wrongly). 這些話有許多可能被誤解。

mis·judge /ˌmɪsˈdʒʌdʒ/ *verb* [T, I] **1 ~ sb/sth** | **~ how, what, etc. …** to form a wrong opinion about a person or situation, especially in a way that makes you deal with them or it unfairly 形成錯誤認識；錯看：*She now realizes that she misjudged him.* 她現在意識到她錯看了他。**2 ~ sth** | **~ how long, how far, etc. …** to estimate sth such as time or distance wrongly 對（時間、距離等）判斷錯誤：*He misjudged the distance and his ball landed in the lake.* 他對距離判斷錯誤，使球落到了湖裏。▸ **mis·judge·ment** (also **mis·judg·ment**) *noun* [C, U]

mis·lay /ˌmɪsˈleɪ/ *verb* (**mis·laid, mis·laid** /-ˈleɪd/) **~ sth** (*formal, especially BrE*) to put sth somewhere and then be unable to find it again, especially for only a short time 隨意擱置，亂放（而一時找不到）SYN **lose**：*I seem to have mislaid my keys.* 我好像不知道把鑰匙放在哪兒了。

mis·lead /ˌmɪsˈliːd/ *verb* (**mis·led, mis·led** /-ˈled/) **~ sb (about sth)** | **~ sb (into doing sth)** to give sb the wrong idea or impression and make them believe sth that is not true 誤導；引入歧途；使誤信 SYN **deceive**：*He deliberately misled us about the nature of their relationship.* 關於他們究竟是什麼關係，他故意給我們留下錯誤印象。

mis·lead·ing /ˌmɪsˈliːdɪŋ/ *adj.* giving the wrong idea or impression and making you believe sth that is not true 誤導的；引入歧途的 SYN **deceptive**：***misleading information/advertisements*** 使人產生誤解的信息／廣告 ▸ **mis·lead·ing·ly** *adv.*：*These bats are sometimes misleadingly referred to as 'flying foxes'.* 這些蝙蝠有時被誤稱為"飛狐"。

mis·man·age /ˌmɪsˈmænɪdʒ/ *verb* **~ sth** to deal with or manage sth badly 對…處理失當；對…管理不當 SYN **mishandle** ▸ **mis·man·age·ment** *noun* [U]：*accusations of corruption and financial mismanagement* 對於腐敗和財務管理不當的指控

mis·match /ˈmɪsmætʃ/ *noun* **~ (between A and B)** a combination of things or people that do not go together well or are not suitable for each other 誤配；錯配；搭配不當：*a mismatch between people's real needs and the available facilities* 人民的切實需要和現有設施之間的錯配 ▸ **mis·match** /ˌmɪsˈmætʃ/ *verb* [often passive]：**~ sb/sth** *They made a mismatched couple.* 他們夫妻倆不般配。

mis·name /ˌmɪsˈneɪm/ *verb* [usually passive] **~ sb/sth** to give sb/sth a name that is wrong or not appropriate 錯誤命名；取名不當

mis·nomer /ˌmɪsˈnəʊmə(r); *NAmE* -ˈnoʊ-/ *noun* a name or a word that is not appropriate or accurate 使用不恰當（或不準確）的名稱；用詞不當：*'Villa' was **something of a misnomer**—the place was no more than an old farmhouse.* "別墅"一說有點不妥，那地方只不過是座舊農舍。

miso /ˈmiːsəʊ; *NAmE* -soʊ/ *noun* [U] a substance made from BEANS, used in Japanese cooking 味噌；日本豆醬

mis·ogyn·ist /mɪˈsɒdʒɪnɪst; *NAmE* -ˈsɑːdʒ-/ *noun* (*formal*) a man who hates women 厭惡女人的男人 ▸ **mis·ogyn·is·tic** /mɪˌsɒdʒɪˈnɪstɪk/ (also **mis·ogyn·ist**) *adj.*：*misogynistic attitudes* 厭惡女人的態度 **mis·ogyny** *noun* [U]

mis·place /ˌmɪsˈpleɪs/ *verb* **~ sth** to put sth somewhere and then be unable to find it again, especially for a short time 隨意擱置，亂放（而一時找不到）SYN **mislay**

M

mis·placed /ˌmɪsˈpleɪst/ *adj.* **1** not appropriate or correct in the situation 不合時宜的；不適宜的：*misplaced confidence/optimism/fear* 不應有的信心／樂觀精神／恐懼 **2** (of love, trust, etc. 愛情、信任等) given to a person who does not deserve or return those feelings 給錯對象的；不該給的：*misplaced loyalty* 無謂的忠誠

mis·print /ˈmɪsprɪnt/ *noun* a mistake such as a spelling mistake that is made when a book, etc. is printed 印刷錯誤 ➲ SYNONYMS at MISTAKE

mis·pro·nounce /ˌmɪsprəˈnaʊns/ *verb* **~ sth** to pronounce a word wrongly 發錯音；讀錯字音 ▸ **mis·pro·nun·ci·ation** /ˌmɪsprənʌnsiˈeɪʃn/ *noun* [C, U]

mis·quote /ˌmɪsˈkwəʊt; *NAmE* -ˈkwoʊt/ *verb* **~ sb/sth** to repeat what sb has said or written in a way that is not correct 錯誤地引用；誤引：*The senator claims to have been misquoted in the article.* 參議員聲稱文章錯誤地引用了他的話。▸ **mis·quo·ta·tion** /ˌmɪskwəʊˈteɪʃn; *NAmE* -kwoʊ-/ *noun* [C, U]

mis·read /ˌmɪsˈriːd/ *verb* (**mis·read, mis·read** /-ˈred/) **1** to understand sb/sth wrongly 誤解 SYN **misinterpret**: **~ sth** *I'm afraid I completely misread the situation.* 恐怕我完全看錯了形勢。◇ **~ sth as sth** *His confidence was misread as arrogance.* 他的信心被誤解為傲慢。**2 ~ sth (as sth)** to read sth wrongly 讀錯；誤讀：*I misread the 1 as a 7.* 我把 1 錯當成 7 了。

mis·re·port /ˌmɪsrɪˈpɔːt; *NAmE* -ˈpɔːrt/ *verb* **~ sth | ~ what, how, etc. … | it is misreported that …** to give a report of an event, etc. that is not correct 誤報；錯報；謊報：*The newspapers misreported the facts of the case.* 報紙沒有如實報道案情真相。

mis·rep·re·sent /ˌmɪsˌreprɪˈzent/ *verb* [often passive] (*formal*) to give information about sb/sth that is not true or complete so that other people have the wrong impression about them/it 誤傳；不實報道；歪曲：**~ sb/sth** *He felt that the book misrepresented his opinions.* 他覺得這本書歪曲了他的觀點。◇ **~ sb/sth as sth** *In the article she was misrepresented as an uncaring mother.* 這篇文章把她歪曲成一名缺少愛心的母親。◇ **~ what, how, etc. …** *The report misrepresented what the group believes.* 這個報告歪曲了小組成員的看法。▸ **mis·rep·re·sen·ta·tion** /ˌmɪsˌreprɪzenˈteɪʃn/ *noun* [C, U]：*a deliberate misrepresentation of the facts* 故意歪曲事實

mis·rule /ˌmɪsˈruːl/ *noun* [U] (*formal*) bad government 管治不善；暴政：*The regime finally collapsed after 25 years of misrule.* 在施行了 25 年的暴政後，這個政權最終垮台。

miss 🔑 /mɪs/ *verb, noun*

■ *verb*

▸ **NOT HIT, CATCH, ETC.** 未擊中；錯過 **1** 🔑 [T, I] to fail to hit, catch, reach, etc. sth 未擊中；未得到；未達到；錯過：**~ (sb/sth)** *How many goals has he missed this season?* 這個賽季他射丟了多少個球？◇ *The bullet missed her by about six inches.* 子彈從她身邊飛過，離她大約只有六吋。◇ *She threw a plate at him and only **narrowly missed**.* 她朝他甩出一個盤子，差一點打中他。◇ **~ doing sth** *She narrowly missed hitting him.* 她差一點沒打着他。

▸ **NOT HEAR/SEE** 不聞；不見 **2** 🔑 [T] **~ sth** to fail to hear, see or notice sth 未見到；未聽到；未覺察：*The hotel is the only white building on the road—**you can't miss it**.* 酒店是這條路上唯一的白色建築，你不會看不見的。◇ *Don't miss next week's issue!* 別錯過下週那一期！◇ *I missed her name.* 我沒聽清她的名字。◇ *Your mother will know who's moved in—she **doesn't miss much**.* 你媽會知道誰搬進來了，很少有她注意不到的。

▸ **NOT UNDERSTAND** 不懂 **3** 🔑 [T] **~ sth** to fail to understand sth 不理解；不懂：*He completely missed the joke.* 這個笑話他一點也沒聽懂。◇ *You're **missing the point*** (= failing to understand the main part) *of what I'm saying.* 你沒明白我的意思。

▸ **NOT BE/GO SOMEWHERE** 不在；不去 **4** 🔑 [T] **~ sth** to fail to be or go somewhere 不在；不去；錯過：*She hasn't missed a game all year.* 她一年中一場比賽都沒錯過。◇ *You missed a good party last night* (= because you did not go). 你昨晚錯過了一場愉快的聚會。◇ *'Are you coming to the school play?' '**I wouldn't miss it for the world.**'* "你來看學生演戲嗎？" "我說什麼也不能錯過呀。"

▸ **NOT DO STH** 不做 **5** 🔑 [T] **~ sth** to fail to do sth 不做；錯過：*You can't afford to miss meals* (= not eat meals) *when you're in training.* 你在接受訓練，可不能不吃飯呀。◇ *to miss a turn* (= to not play when it is your turn in a game) 錯過一輪比賽 **6** 🔑 [T] **~ (doing) sth** to not take the opportunity to do sth 錯過機會：*The sale prices were **too good to miss**.* 那次價格優惠真的不可錯過。◇ *It was an opportunity **not to be missed**.* 機不可失，時不再來。

▸ **BE LATE** 遲到 **7** 🔑 [T] **~ sth/sb | ~ doing sth** to be or arrive too late for sth 遲到；趕不上；錯過：*If I don't leave now I'll miss my plane.* 現在不走我就趕不上飛機了。◇ *Sorry I'm late—have I missed anything?* 對不起，我來晚了。我錯過什麼了嗎？◇ *'Is Ann there?' 'You've just missed her* (= she has just left).*'* "安在嗎？" "她剛走。"

▸ **FEEL SAD** 傷心 **8** 🔑 [T] to feel sad because you can no longer see sb or do sth that you like 懷念；思念：**~ sb/sth** *She will be greatly missed when she leaves.* 她走了以後，人們會非常思念她的。◇ *What did you miss most when you were in France?* 你在法國的時候最懷念的是什麼？◇ **~ (sb/sth) doing sth** *I don't miss getting up at six every morning!* 我才不想每天早上六點鐘起牀哩！

▸ **NOTICE STH NOT THERE** 發覺某物不在 **9** [T] **~ sb/sth** to notice that sb/sth is not where they/it should be 發覺丟失；發覺…不在原處：*When did you first miss the necklace?* 你最早發覺項鏈不見了是什麼時候？◇ *We seem to be missing some students this morning.* 今天早上我們好像有幾位同學沒到。

▸ **AVOID STH BAD** 避開壞事 **10** [T] to avoid sth unpleasant 避開（不愉快的事）SYN **escape**: **~ sth** *If you go now you should miss the crowds.* 你如果現在走就可以避開人群。◇ **~ doing sth** *He fell and just missed knocking the whole display over.* 他摔了一跤，差一點把全部展品碰翻。

▸ **OF ENGINE** 發動機 **11** = MISFIRE (2)

IDM **he, she, etc. doesn't miss a ˈtrick** (*informal*) used to say that sb notices every opportunity to gain an advantage 不失時機；很機敏 **ˌmiss the ˈboat** (*informal*) to be unable to take advantage of sth because you are too late 錯失良機：*If you don't buy now, you may find that you've missed the boat.* 你如果現在不買，你會錯失良機的。**ˌmiss your ˈguess** (*NAmE, informal*) to make a mistake 做錯；犯錯：***Unless I miss my guess**, your computer needs a new hard drive.* 我的判斷沒錯的話，你的電腦需要更換一個新的硬盤驅動器。➲ more at HEART, MARK *n.*

PHR V **ˌmiss sb/sth↔ˈout** 🔑 (*BrE*) to fail to include sb/sth in sth 不包括…在內；遺漏 SYN **omit**: *I'll just read through the form again to make sure I haven't missed anything out.* 我要再看一遍這份表格，免得漏掉什麼。**ˌmiss ˈout (on sth)** to fail to benefit from sth useful or enjoyable by not taking part in it 錯失獲利（或取樂等）的機會：*Of course I'm coming—I don't want to miss out on all the fun!* 我當然要來，我可不想錯失好玩的機會。

■ *noun*

▸ **TITLE/FORM OF ADDRESS** 稱謂 **1** 🔑 **Miss** used before the family name, or the first and family name, of a woman who is not married, in order to speak or write to her politely（用於未婚女子姓氏或姓名前，以示禮貌）小姐，女士：*That's all, thank you, Miss Lipman.* 就這些，謝謝，李普曼小姐。➲ compare MRS, MS **2 Miss** a title given to the winner of a beauty contest in a particular country, town, etc.（選美比賽優勝者的頭銜）小姐：*Miss Brighton* 布賴頓小姐 ◇ *the Miss World contest* 世界小姐選美比賽 **3 Miss** (*informal*) used especially by men to address a young woman when they do not know her name（稱呼不知姓名的年輕女子）小姐：*Will that be all, Miss?* 就這些嗎，小姐？**4 Miss** (*BrE, informal*) used as a form of address by children in some schools to a woman teacher, whether she is married or not（學生對女教師的稱呼）：*Good morning, Miss!* 老師早！➲ compare SIR **5** (*old-fashioned*) a girl or young woman 少女；年輕女子

M

▸ NOT HIT, CATCH, ETC. 未擊中；錯過 **6** a failure to hit, catch or reach sth 未擊中；未得到；未到達；錯過：*He scored two goals and had another two **near misses**.* 他攻進兩球，另有兩球也險些破門。

IDM **give sth a 'miss** (*informal, especially BrE*) to decide not to do sth, eat sth, etc. 不予理睬；不理會；決定不做：*I think I'll give badminton a miss tonight.* 我今晚不想打羽毛球了。 **a ˌmiss is as ˌgood as a 'mile** (*saying*) there is no real difference between only just failing in sth and failing in it badly because the result is still the same 錯誤再小也是錯；功敗垂成仍為敗

mis·sal /ˈmɪsl/ *noun* a book that contains the prayers etc. that are used at MASS in the Roman Catholic Church（天主教的）彌撒經書

mis·sel thrush = MISTLE THRUSH

mis·sha·pen /ˌmɪsˈʃeɪpən/ *adj.* with a shape that is not normal or natural 畸形的；扭曲變形的：*misshapen feet* 畸形腳

mis·sile /ˈmɪsaɪl; *NAmE* ˈmɪsl/ *noun* **1** a weapon that is sent through the air and that explodes when it hits the thing that it is aimed at 導彈：*nuclear missiles* 核導彈 ◇ *a **missile base/site*** 導彈基地／發射場 ➲ COLLOCATIONS at WAR ➲ see also BALLISTIC MISSILE, CRUISE MISSILE, GUIDED MISSILE **2** an object that is thrown at sb to hurt them 發射物；投擲物 SYN **projectile**

miss·ing 0-w /ˈmɪsɪŋ/ *adj.*
1 0-w that cannot be found or that is not in its usual place, or at home 找不到的；不在的；丟失的 SYN **lost**：*I never found the missing piece.* 我一直沒找到丟了的那件。◇ *My gloves have been missing for ages.* 我的手套已經丟了很久了。◇ *Two files have **gone missing**.* 兩個檔案不見了。◇ *They still hoped to find their missing son.* 他們仍然希望找到他們丟失的兒子。◇ (*especially BrE*) *Our cat's **gone missing** again.* 我們的貓又走丟了。 **2** 0-w that has been removed, lost or destroyed and has not been replaced 被去除的；丟失的；被損毀的；缺少的：*The book has two pages **missing/missing** pages.* 這本書缺了兩頁。◇ *He didn't notice there was anything missing from his room until later on.* 後來他才注意到他的屋裏丟了東西。 **3** 0-w (of a person 人) not present after an accident, battle, etc. but not known to have been killed 失踪的：*He was reported **missing, presumed dead**.* 有報道說他失踪了，據信已經喪生。◇ *Many soldiers were listed as **missing in action**.* 許多士兵都被列在戰鬥失踪人員名單上。 **4** 0-w not included, often when it should have been 缺少的；未被包括在內的：*Fill in the missing words in this text.* 填出文中空缺的單詞。◇ *There were several candidates missing from the list.* 有幾名候選人沒有出現在名單中。

ˌmissing ˈlink *noun* **1** [C] something, such as a piece of information, that is necessary for sb to be able to understand a problem or in order to make sth complete（理解問題或使事物完整的）必要的環節，缺少的一環 **2 the missing link** [sing.] an animal similar to humans that was once thought to exist at the time that APES were developing into humans 缺環（推想中從類人猿發展到人類之間的過渡動物）

ˌmissing ˈperson *noun* (*pl.* **missing persons**) a person who has disappeared from their home and whose family are trying to find them with the help of the police 失踪的人；下落不明者

mis·sion /ˈmɪʃn/ *noun, verb*

■ ***noun***

▸ OFFICIAL JOB/GROUP 官方使命；正式組織 **1** [C] an important official job that a person or group of people is given to do, especially when they are sent to another country 官方使命；使團的使命：*a trade mission to China* 赴華貿易代表團 ◇ *a fact-finding mission* 核查事實的工作 ◇ *a mercy mission to aid homeless refugees* 幫助無家可歸的難民的慈善工作 ➲ SYNONYMS TASK **2** [C] a group of people doing such a job; the place where they work 使團；代表團；執行任務的地點：*the head of the British mission in Berlin* 在柏林的英國使團團長

▸ TEACHING CHRISTIANITY 傳教 **3** [C, U] the work of teaching people about Christianity, especially in a foreign country; a group of people doing such work（尤指在海外的）傳教，佈道；佈道團：*a Catholic mission in Africa* 在非洲的天主教傳教士 ◇ *Gandhi's attitude to mission and conversion* 甘地對於佈道和改變信仰的態度 **4** [C] a building or group of buildings used by a Christian mission 佈道所；傳教區

▸ YOUR DUTY 職責 **5** [C] particular work that you feel it is your duty to do 使命；天職 SYN **vocation**：*Her **mission in life** was to work with the homeless.* 她以幫助無家可歸者為己任。

▸ OF ARMED FORCES 軍隊 **6** [C] an important job that is done by a soldier, group of soldiers, etc. 軍事行動：*The squadron flew on a reconnaissance mission.* 這支空軍中隊執行一項偵察任務。➲ COLLOCATIONS at WAR

▸ SPACE FLIGHT 太空飛行 **7** [C] a flight into space 太空飛行任務：*a US space mission* 美國的太空飛行 ◇ *mission control* (= the people on earth who control and communicate with the people on the mission) 太空飛行的地面指揮人員

▸ TASK 任務 **8** [C] (*BrE, informal*) a task or journey that is very difficult and takes a long time to complete（極其艱巨且需長時間才能完成的）任務，旅行：*It's a mission to get there.* 一路上要經歷艱辛才能到達那裏。

IDM **ˌmission acˈcomplished** used when you have successfully completed what you have had to do 任務已完成

■ ***verb*** [I] + **adv./prep.** (*informal*) to go on a long and difficult journey, especially one that involves going to many different places 作艱辛的長途旅行（尤指去許多地方）：*We had to mission round all the bars until we found him.* 我們跑遍了所有的酒吧才找到他。

mis·sion·ary /ˈmɪʃənri; *NAmE* -neri/ *noun* (*pl.* **-ies**) a person who is sent to a foreign country to teach people about Christianity 傳教士：*Baptist missionaries* 浸信會傳教士 ◇ *missionary work* 傳教士的工作 ◇ (*figurative*) *She spoke about her new project with **missionary zeal*** (= with great enthusiasm). 她以極大的熱忱談論自己的新項目。

the ˈmissionary position *noun* [sing.] a position for having sex in which a man and a woman face each other, with the man lying on top of the woman 正常體位，傳教士體位（男上女下的性交姿勢）

ˌmission-ˈcritical *adj.* essential for an organization to function successfully（對於機構的成功運作）關鍵的，至關重要的：*mission-critical employees* 不可或缺的雇員

ˈmission statement *noun* an official statement of the aims of a company or an organization（公司或組織的）宗旨說明，任務說明

mis·sis *noun* = MISSUS (1), (3)

mis·sive /ˈmɪsɪv/ *noun* (*formal* or *humorous*) a letter, especially a long or an official one 信函；（尤指）長信，公函

mis·spell /ˌmɪsˈspel/ *verb* (**mis·spelled, mis·spelled** or **mis·spelt, mis·spelt** /ˌmɪsˈspelt/) **~ sth** to spell a word wrongly 拼錯；寫錯 ▸ **mis·spell·ing** *noun* [C, U]

mis·spend /ˌmɪsˈspend/ *verb* (**mis·spent, mis·spent** /-ˈspent/) [usually passive] **~ sth** to spend time or money in a careless rather than a useful way 揮霍，浪費，濫用（時間或金錢）SYN **waste**：*He joked that being good at cards was the sign of **a misspent youth*** (= having wasted his time when he was young). 他開玩笑地說擅長打牌表明他虛度了青春年華。

mis·step /ˌmɪsˈstep/ *noun* (*NAmE*) a mistake; a wrong action 錯誤；失策

mis·sus /ˈmɪsɪz/ *noun* (*BrE*) **1** (also **mis·sis**) (*informal, becoming old-fashioned*) (used after 'the', 'my', 'your', 'his' 用於 the、my、your 和 his 之後) a man's wife 老婆；妻子：*How's the missus* (= your wife)? 你老婆怎麼樣？ **2** (*informal*) (used especially by young people 尤為年輕人使用) girlfriend 女友：*My missus doesn't like computer games.* 我女友不喜歡玩電腦遊戲。◇ *my current missus* 我的現任女友 **3** (also **mis·sis**) (*slang, becoming old-fashioned*) used by some people as a form of address to a woman whose name they do not know（稱呼不知姓名的婦女）大姐：*Is this your bag, missus?* 大姐，這是你的袋子嗎？

missy /ˈmɪsi/ *noun* used when talking to a young girl, especially to express anger or affection（表示生氣或喜愛）小姐，丫頭：*Don't you speak to me like that, missy!* 不許那樣對我講話，小姐！

mist /mɪst/ *noun, verb*

■ *noun* **1** [U, C] a cloud of very small drops of water in the air just above the ground, that make it difficult to see 薄霧；水汽：*The hills were **shrouded in mist**.* 這些小山籠罩在薄霧之中。◇ *Early morning mist patches will soon clear.* 清晨彌漫着的水汽很快會散盡。◇ *The origins of the story are **lost in the mists of time*** (= forgotten because it happened such a long time ago). 這個故事的起源由於年代久遠而變得模糊不清。◇ (*figurative*) *She gazed at the scene through a mist of tears.* 她淚眼模糊，凝視着面前的景象。➲ COLLOCATIONS at WEATHER ➲ compare FOG *n.* (1) ➲ see also MISTY **2** [sing.] a fine spray of liquid, for example, from an AEROSOL can 液體噴霧

■ *verb* **1** [T, I] **~ (sth) (up)** | **~ (over)** when sth such as glass **mists** or **is misted**, it becomes covered with very small drops of water, so that it is impossible to see through it 使結滿霧氣（模糊不清）：*The windows were misted up with condensation.* 窗戶上凝滿了水珠，一片模糊。◇ *As he came in from the cold, his glasses misted up.* 他從寒冷的戶外進來，眼鏡馬上蒙上了一層霧氣。**2** [I, T] if your eyes **mist** or sth **mists** them, they fill with tears（眼）含淚水；被淚水模糊：**~ (over/up)** *Her eyes misted over as she listened to the speech.* 她聽着演講，眼中噙滿了淚水。◇ **~ sth (up)** *Tears misted his eyes.* 淚水模糊了他的雙眼。**3** [T] **~ sth** to spray the leaves of a plant with very small drops of water 朝（植物）噴霧

M

mis·take 0-π /mɪˈsteɪk/ *noun, verb*

■ *noun* **1** 0-π an action or an opinion that is not correct, or that produces a result that you did not want（言語或行為上的）錯誤，失誤：*It's easy to **make a mistake**.* 犯錯誤很容易。◇ *This letter is addressed to someone else—there must be some mistake.* 這封信是給別人的，一定是搞錯了。◇ *It would be a mistake to ignore his opinion.* 忽略他的意見是不對的。◇ *Don't worry, we all **make mistakes**.* 沒關係，我們都會犯錯。◇ *You must try to **learn from your mistakes**.* 你得從所犯錯誤中吸取教訓。◇ *Leaving school so young was the biggest mistake of my life.* 我一生中最大的錯誤就是那麼年輕就離開了學校。◇ ***I made the mistake of** giving him my address.* 我真不該把我的地址給他。◇ *It was a big mistake on my part to have trusted her.* 我相信了她，這是我的一大錯誤。◇ *a **great/serious/terrible mistake*** 大錯；嚴重錯誤 ◇ *It's a **common mistake*** (= one that a lot of people make). 這是常犯的錯誤。**2** 0-π a word, figure, etc. that is not said or written down correctly（用詞或數字上的）錯誤，口誤，筆誤 SYN **error**：*It's a common mistake among learners of English.* 這是學英語的人常犯的錯誤。◇ *The waiter **made a mistake** (**in**) adding up the bill.* 服務員結賬時算錯了賬。◇ *Her essay is full of **spelling mistakes**.* 她的文章到處都是拼寫錯誤。

IDM **and ˈno mistake** (*old-fashioned, especially BrE*) used to show that you are sure about the truth of what you have just said 準確無誤；毫無疑問：*This is a strange business and no mistake.* 這確實是件怪事。**by miˈstake** 0-π by accident; without intending to 錯誤地；無意中：*I took your bag instead of mine by mistake.* 我不巧錯拿了你的包。**ˌmake no miˈstake (about sth)** used to emphasize what you are saying, especially when you want to warn sb about sth 別搞錯；注意：*Make no mistake (about it), this is one crisis that won't just go away.* 要知道，這是一場不會自行消失的危機。**in miˈstake for sth** thinking that sth is sth else 誤以為是；錯看成：*Children may eat pills in mistake for sweets.* 孩子可能會把藥片錯當成糖果吃。

■ *verb* 0-π (**mis·took** /mɪˈstʊk/, **mis·taken** /mɪˈsteɪkən/) to not understand or judge sb/sth correctly 誤會；誤解；看錯 SYN **misconstrue**：**~ sb/sth** *I admit that I mistook his intentions.* 我承認我誤解了他的意圖。◇ ***There was no mistaking*** (= it was impossible to mistake) *the bitterness in her voice.* 她的聲音裏流露出怨恨的情緒，這是很明顯的。◇ **~ sb/sth as sb/sth** *I mistook her offer as a threat.* 我把她的好心錯看成威脅了。◇ **~ what ...** *Sorry—I mistook what you said.* 不好意思，我誤解你的話了。

PHR V **miˈstake sb/sth for sb/sth** 0-π to think wrongly that sb/sth is sb/sth else 把…錯當成 SYN **confuse**：*I think you must be mistaking me for someone else.* 我看你準是認錯人了。

Synonyms 同義詞辨析

mistake

error • inaccuracy • slip • howler • misprint

These are all words for a word, figure or fact that is not said, written down or typed correctly. 以上各詞均指用詞、數字、事實等的錯誤、口誤、筆誤。

mistake a word or figure that is not said or written down correctly 指用詞或數字上的錯誤、口誤、筆誤：*It's a common mistake among learners of English.* 這是學英語的人常犯的錯誤。◇ *spelling mistakes* 拼寫錯誤

error (*rather formal*) a word, figure, etc. that is not said or written down correctly 指用詞、數字等的錯誤、口誤、筆誤：*There are too many errors in your work.* 你的工作失誤太多。NOTE **Error** is a more formal way of saying **mistake**. * error 為 mistake 的較正式用語。

inaccuracy (*rather formal*) a piece of information that is not exactly correct 指信息不準確、有誤：*The article is full of inaccuracies.* 這篇文章裏不準確的地方比比皆是。

slip a small mistake, usually made by being careless or not paying attention 指常因粗心或未予以重視造成的差錯、疏漏、紕漏

howler (*informal, especially BrE*) a stupid mistake, especially in what sb says or writes 尤指言談或行文中的愚蠢錯誤：*The report is full of howlers.* 這份報告錯漏百出。NOTE A **howler** is usually an embarrassing mistake which shows that the person who made it does not know sth that they really should know. * howler 通常指令人難堪的錯誤，表明犯錯誤者不知道應該知道的東西。

misprint a small mistake in a printed text 指印刷文本上的錯誤

PATTERNS

- a(n) mistake/error/inaccuracy/slip/howler/misprint **in** sth
- to **make** a(n) mistake/error/slip/howler
- to **contain/be full of** mistakes/errors/inaccuracies/howlers/misprints

mis·taken 0-π /mɪˈsteɪkən/ *adj.* **1** 0-π [not usually before noun] **~ (about sb/sth)** wrong in your opinion or judgement 錯誤；不正確：*You are completely mistaken about Jane.* 你對簡的看法完全錯了。◇ *Unless I'm very much mistaken, that's Paul's wife over there.* 要是我沒太弄錯的話，那邊那個就是保羅的妻子。**2** 0-π based on a wrong opinion or bad judgement 判斷錯誤的；被誤解的 SYN **misguided**：*mistaken **views/ideas*** 錯誤的觀點／想法 ◇ *I told her my secret **in the mistaken belief** that I could trust her.* 我誤以為可以相信她，就把我的秘密告訴了她。▸ **mis·taken·ly** *adv.*：*He mistakenly believed that his family would stand by him.* 他誤以為他的家人會支持他。

miˌstaken iˈdentity *noun* [U] a situation in which you think wrongly that you recognize sb or have found the person you are looking for 認錯人：*He was shot in what seems to have been **a case of mistaken identity**.* 他像是被人認錯了而遭到槍擊的。

mis·ter /ˈmɪstə(r)/ *noun* **1 Mister** the full form, not often used in writing, of the abbreviation *Mr* 先生（Mr 的全寫，書寫時不常用）**2** (*informal*) used, especially by children, to address a man whose name they do not know（兒童常用，稱呼不知姓名的男子）先生：*Please, mister, can we have our ball back?* 求求你，先生，能把球還給我們嗎？

mis·time /ˌmɪsˈtaɪm/ *verb* **~ sth** to do sth at the wrong time, especially when this makes sth bad or unpleasant happen 在不適當的時機做；選錯…的時機：*The horse completely mistimed the jump and threw its rider.* 這匹馬起跳完全不是時候，把騎手摔了下來。 ▸ **mis·tim·ing** *noun* [U]：*The failure of the talks was mainly due to insensitivity and mistiming.* 會談失敗主要是由於反應遲鈍和時機不對。

mis·tle thrush (also **mis·sel thrush**) /ˈmɪsl θrʌʃ/ *noun* a large THRUSH (= a type of bird) with spots on its front 槲鶇（前胸有斑點）

mistle·toe /ˈmɪsltəʊ; ˈmɪzl-; *NAmE* -toʊ/ *noun* [U] a plant with small shiny white BERRIES that grows on other trees and is often used as a decoration at Christmas 槲寄生（結白色小漿果，寄生於其他樹木，常用於聖誕節裝飾）：*the tradition of kissing under the mistletoe* 在槲寄生枝下親吻的習俗

mis·took *past tense* of MISTAKE

mis·tral /ˈmɪstrəl; mɪˈstrɑːl/ *noun* [sing.] a strong cold wind that blows through southern France, mainly in winter 密史脱拉風（法國南部主要出現於冬季的寒冷強風）

mis·treat /ˌmɪsˈtriːt/ *verb* **~ sb/sth** to treat a person or an animal in a cruel, unkind or unfair way 虐待 **SYN** **ill-treat, maltreat** ▸ **mis·treat·ment** *noun* [U]

mis·tress /ˈmɪstrəs/ *noun* **1** a man's (usually a married man's) **mistress** is a woman that he is having a regular sexual relationship with and who is not his wife 情婦 **2** (*BrE, old-fashioned*) a female teacher in a school, especially a private school （尤指私立學校的）女教師：*the Biology mistress* 生物科女教師 **3** (in the past) the female head of a house, especially one who employed servants （尤指舊時雇用僕人的）女主人，主婦：*the mistress of the house* 這房子的女主人 **4** the female owner of a dog or other animal （狗或其他動物的）女主人 **5** (*formal*) a woman who is in a position of authority or control, or who is highly skilled in sth 有權勢的女子；女能人；女強人；女主宰：*She wants to be mistress of her own affairs* (= to organize her own life). 她希望自己的事自己作主。 ➲ compare MASTER

mis·trial /ˌmɪsˈtraɪəl/ *noun* (*law* 律) **1** a trial that is not considered valid because of a mistake in the way it has been conducted （訴訟程序錯誤的）無效審判 **2** (*NAmE*) a trial in which the JURY cannot reach a decision （陪審團無法作出裁決的）未決審判

mis·trust /ˌmɪsˈtrʌst/ *verb, noun*

▪ *verb* **~ sb/sth** to have no confidence in sb/sth because you think they may be harmful; to not trust sb/sth 猜疑；不信任 **SYN** **distrust** ➲ note at DISTRUST

▪ *noun* [U, sing.] a feeling that you cannot trust sb/sth 猜疑；疑慮；不信任 **SYN** **suspicion**：*a climate of mistrust and fear* 充滿猜疑和恐懼的氛圍 ◇ *She has a deep mistrust of strangers.* 她對陌生人的猜疑極深。 ▸ **mis·trust·ful** /-fl/ *adj.*：**~ (of sb/sth)** *Some people are very mistrustful of computers.* 有些人對電腦很不放心。 **mis·trust·ful·ly** /-fəli/ *adv.*

misty /ˈmɪsti/ *adj.* **1** with a lot of MIST 多霧的；薄霧籠罩的：*a misty morning* 薄霧瀰漫的早晨 **2** not clear or bright 模糊的；不明晰的 **SYN** **blurred**：*misty memories* 朦朧的記憶 ◇ (*literary*) *His eyes grew misty* (= full of tears) *as he talked.* 他說話的時候雙眼模糊了。

ˌmisty-ˈeyed *adj.* feeling full of emotion, as if you are going to cry （十分激動）淚眼矇矓的

mis·un·der·stand /ˌmɪsʌndəˈstænd; *NAmE* -dərˈs-/ *verb* (**mis·un·der·stood, mis·un·der·stood** /-ˈstʊd/) [T, I] **~ (sb/sth)** | **~ what, how, etc. …** to fail to understand sb/sth correctly 誤解；誤會：*I completely misunderstood her intentions.* 我完全誤會了她的意圖。 ◇ *Don't misunderstand me—I am grateful for all you've done.* 別誤解我的意思，我對你所做的一切都很感激。 ◇ *I thought he was her husband—I must have misunderstood.* 我以為他是她丈夫，我一定是誤會了。

mis·un·der·stand·ing /ˌmɪsʌndəˈstændɪŋ; *NAmE* -dərˈs-/ *noun* **1** [U, C] a situation in which a comment, an instruction, etc. is not understood correctly 誤解；誤會：*There must be some misunderstanding—I thought I ordered the smaller model.* 一定是搞錯了，我以為我訂的是更小型號的。 ◇ **~ of/about sth** *There is still a fundamental misunderstanding about the real purpose of this work.* 對於這項工作的真正目的，仍然存在着嚴重的誤解。 ◇ **~ between A and B** *All contracts are translated to avoid any misunderstanding between the companies.* 所有的合同都經過翻譯，以避免公司間發生任何誤解。 **2** [C] a slight disagreement or argument 意見不一；不和；爭執：*We had a little misunderstanding over the bill.* 我們對這個提案的看法有點分歧。

mis·un·der·stood /ˌmɪsʌndəˈstʊd/ *adj.* having qualities that people do not see or fully understand 遭誤解的；不為人理解的：*a much misunderstood illness* 一種遭到許多人誤解的疾病 ◇ *She felt very alone and misunderstood.* 她覺得非常孤獨，得不到別人的理解。

mis·use *noun, verb*

▪ *noun* /ˌmɪsˈjuːs/ [U, C, usually sing.] (*formal*) the act of using sth in a dishonest way or for the wrong purpose 誤用；濫用；盜用 **SYN** **abuse**：***alcohol/drug misuse*** 酗酒；濫用藥物 ◇ ***the misuse of power/authority*** 濫用職權

▪ *verb* /ˌmɪsˈjuːz/ (*formal*) **1 ~ sth** to use sth in the wrong way or for the wrong purpose 誤用；濫用 **SYN** **abuse, ill-treat**：*individuals who misuse power for their own ends* 以權謀私的人 **2 ~ sb** to treat sb badly and/or unfairly 虐待

mite /maɪt/ *noun* **1** a very small creature like a spider that lives on plants, animals, carpets, etc. 螨（狀似蜘蛛的微小動物，在動植物、地毯等上生活）：*house dust mites* 房內的粉塵螨 ➲ see also DUST MITE **2** a small child or animal, especially one that you feel sorry for （可憐的）小孩子，小動物：*Poor little mite!* 可憐的小傢伙！ **3** (*old-fashioned*) a small amount of sth 少量：*The place looked* ***a mite*** (= a little) *expensive.* 這地方看上去稍微有點兒貴。

miter (*NAmE*) = MITRE

miti·gate /ˈmɪtɪgeɪt/ *verb* **~ sth** (*formal*) to make sth less harmful, serious, etc. 減輕；緩和 **SYN** **alleviate**：*action to mitigate poverty* 減輕貧窮的行動 ◇ *Soil erosion was mitigated by the planting of trees.* 水土流失的情況在經過植樹後緩和了。

miti·gat·ing /ˈmɪtɪgeɪtɪŋ/ *adj.* [only before noun] **~ circumstances/factors** (*law* 律 or *formal*) circumstances or factors that provide a reason that explains sb's actions or a crime, and make them easier to understand so that the punishment may be less severe 可考慮從輕處置的情節（或因素）

miti·ga·tion /ˌmɪtɪˈgeɪʃn/ *noun* [U] (*formal*) a reduction in how unpleasant, serious, etc. sth is 減輕；緩解 **IDM** **in mitiˈgation** (*law* 律) with the aim of making a crime seem less serious or easier to forgive 旨在減輕罪行；意在開脫罪責：*In mitigation, the defence lawyer said his client was seriously depressed at the time of the assault.* 為了減輕罪行，辯護律師說他的當事人在襲擊人的時候精神極度壓抑。

mi·to·chon·drion /ˌmaɪtəʊˈkɒndriən; *NAmE* ˌmaɪtoʊˈkɑːn-/ *noun* (*pl.* **mitochondria** /ˌmaɪtəʊˈkɒndriə; *NAmE* ˌmaɪtoʊˈkɑːn-/) (*biology* 生) a small part found in most cells, in which the energy in food is released （細胞內的）線粒體，粒線體 ▸ **mito·chon·drial** /-driəl/ *adj.*：*mitochondrial DNA* 線粒體 DNA

mi·tosis /maɪˈtəʊsɪs; *NAmE* -ˈtoʊs-/ *noun* [U] (*biology* 生) the process of cell division （細胞的）有絲分裂

mitre (*especially US* **miter**) /ˈmaɪtə(r)/ *noun, verb*

▪ *noun* **1** a tall pointed hat worn by BISHOPS at special ceremonies as a symbol of their position and authority 主教冠；牧冠 **2** (also **ˈmitre joint**) a corner joint, formed by two pieces of wood each cut at an angle, as in a picture frame 斜接頭；陽角接 ➲ picture at DOVETAIL

▪ *verb* **~ sth** (*technical* 術語) to join two pieces of wood together with a mitre joint 斜接

mitt /mɪt/ *noun* **1** = MITTEN **2** (in BASEBALL 棒球) a large thick leather glove worn for catching the ball 接球手

M

套；棒球手套 **3** [usually pl.] (*slang*) a hand 手：*I'd love to get my mitts on one of those.* 我很想得到一個那樣的東西。

mit·ten /ˈmɪtn/ (also **mitt**) *noun* a type of glove that covers the four fingers together and the thumb separately 連指手套 ➲ VISUAL VOCAB page V65

Mitty ➲ WALTER MITTY

mix 0➡ /mɪks/ *verb, noun*

■ *verb*

▸ COMBINE 結合 **1** 0➡ [I, T] if two or more substances **mix** or you **mix** them, they combine, usually in a way that means they cannot easily be separated（使）混合，摻和，融合：*Oil and water do not mix.* 油和水不相融。◇ **~ with sth** *Oil does not mix with water.* 油不融於水。◇ **~ A and B (together)** *Mix all the ingredients together in a bowl.* 把所有的配料放在碗裏，攪和一下。◇ *If you mix blue and yellow, you get green.* 藍色和黃色相混合就是綠色。◇ **~ A with B** *I don't like to **mix business with pleasure*** (= combine social events with doing business). 我不喜歡將社交活動和做生意混在一塊。**2** 0➡ [T] to prepare sth by combining two or more different substances 調配；配製：**~ sth** *With this range of paints, you can mix your own colours.* 用這一組油彩可以調配出你所需要的顏色。◇ **~ sth for sb** *Why don't you mix a cocktail for our guests?* 你何不給客人調製雞尾酒？◇ **~ sb sth** *Why don't you mix our guests a cocktail?* 你何不給客人調製雞尾酒？**3** 0➡ [I] if two or more things, people or activities **do not mix**, they are likely to cause problems or danger if they are combined 相容；平安相處：*Children and fireworks don't mix.* 孩子不宜玩煙火。

▸ MEET PEOPLE 與人交往 **4** 0➡ [I] **~ (with sb)** to meet and talk to different people, especially at social events 交往；相處；交際 SYN **socialize**：*They don't mix much with the neighbours.* 他們不怎麼與鄰居來往。

▸ MUSIC/SOUNDS 音樂；聲音 **5** [T] **~ sth** (*technical* 術語) to combine different recordings of voices and/or instruments to produce a single piece of music 混合錄音；混錄；混音

IDM **be/get mixed ˈup in sth** 0➡ to be/become involved in sth, especially sth illegal or dishonest 捲入（不正當的事）；與某事有牽連 **be/get mixed ˈup with sb** to be/become friendly with or involved with sb that other people do not approve of 與（不適合的人）交往；和某人廝混 **ˌmix and ˈmatch** to combine things in different ways for different purposes 混合重組；混合搭配：*You can mix and match courses to suit your requirements.* 你可以根據自己的要求將課程自由組合。**ˈmix it (with sb)** (*BrE*) (*NAmE* **ˌmix it ˈup (with sb)**) (*informal*) to argue with sb or cause trouble（與某人）吵架；找（某人的）茬

PHR V **ˌmix sth↔ˈin (with sth)** to add one substance to others, especially in cooking（烹調時）摻入，和入：*Mix the remaining cream in with the sauce.* 把剩下的奶油摻到調味醬裏。**ˈmix sth into sth** to combine one substance with others, especially in cooking（烹調時）摻和，將…和入；使與…混合：*Mix the fruit into the rest of the mixture.* 把水果和別的東西拌在一起。**ˈmix sth into/to sth** to produce sth by combining two or more substances, especially in cooking（烹調時）將…混合製成 SYN **blend**：*Add the milk and mix to a smooth dough.* 加入牛奶再揉成光滑的麪糰。**ˌmix sth↔ˈup** 0➡ to change the order or arrangement of a group of things, especially by mistake or in a way that you do not want 弄錯；弄亂 SYN **muddle**：*Someone has mixed up all the application forms.* 有人把申請表都弄亂了。➲ related noun MIX-UP **ˌmix sb/sth ˈup (with sb/sth)** 0➡ to think wrongly that sb/sth is sb/sth else 誤以為…是；弄錯；搞錯 SYN **confuse**：*I think you must be mixing me up with someone else.* 我覺得你一定是把我錯當成別人了。➲ see also MIXED UP

■ *noun*

▸ COMBINATION 結合 **1** 0➡ [C, usually sing.] a combination of different people or things 混合；混雜；結合 SYN **blend**：*a school with a good social mix of children* 有不同社會階層的孩子來上學的學校 ◇ *The town offers a fascinating mix of old and new.* 這個小鎮新舊結合，很有魅力。◇ *a pair of wool mix socks* (= made of wool and other materials) 一雙羊毛混紡襪子 **2** 0➡ [C, U] a combination of things that you need to make sth, often sold as a powder to which you add water, etc. 配料，混合料（常為粉狀）：*a cake mix* 蛋糕粉 ◇ *cement mix* 水泥配料

▸ IN POPULAR MUSIC 流行音樂 **3** [C] = REMIX **4** [sing.] the particular way that instruments and voices are arranged in a piece of music 混錄；混音 **5** [C] an arrangement of several songs or pieces of music into one continuous piece, especially for dancing 樂曲組合；連奏；連唱

Synonyms 同義詞辨析

mix

stir • mingle • blend

These words all refer to substances, qualities, ideas or feelings combining or being combined. 以上各詞均指物質、品質、想法或情感的混合、摻合、融合。

mix to combine two or more substances, qualities, ideas or feelings, usually in a way that means they cannot easily be separated; to be combined in this way 指（使）兩種或以上物質、品質、想法或情感等混合、摻合、融合：*Mix all the ingredients together in a bowl.* 把所有的配料放在碗裏攪和一下。◇ *Oil and water do not mix.* 油和水不相融。

stir to move a liquid or substance around, using a spoon or sth similar, in order to mix it thoroughly 指攪動、攪和、攪拌（液體或物質）：*She stirred her tea.* 她攪了攪茶。

mingle to combine or be combined 指（使）混合、摻合、融合 NOTE **Mingle** can be used to talk about sounds, colours, feelings, ideas, qualities or substances. It is used in written English to talk about how a scene or event appears to sb or how they experience it. * mingle 可用以指聲音、顏色、情感、想法、品質或物質等交織在一起，用於書面英語表示對某一場景或事件的感受或經歷：*The sounds of laughter and singing mingled in the evening air.* 笑聲和歌聲交織在夜空中。◇ *He felt a kind of happiness mingled with regret.* 他感到既高興又遺憾。

blend to mix two or more substances or flavours together; to be mixed together 指（使）兩種或以上物質或味道混合、摻合：*Blend the flour with the milk to make a smooth paste.* 把麪粉和牛奶調成均勻的麪糊。

MIX OR BLEND? 用 mix 還是 blend？

If you **blend** things when you are cooking you usually combine them more completely than if you just **mix** them. **Mix** can be used to talk about colours, feelings or qualities as well as food and substances. In this meaning **blend** is mostly used in the context of cooking. It is also used to talk about art, music, fashion, etc. with the meaning of 'combine in an attractive way'. 烹飪時用 blend 表示把各種材料完全摻和到一起，用 mix 只表示將這些東西混合在一起。mix 可指將食物、物質混合在一起，也可指顏色、情感、品質融合在一起。在這一含義中，blend 主要用於烹飪語境。blend 亦可表示藝術、音樂、時尚等元素和諧地融合在一起。

PATTERNS

- to mix/mingle/blend (sth) **with** sth
- to mix/stir/mingle/blend sth **into** sth
- to mix/stir/mingle/blend sth **together**
- to mix/stir/blend **ingredients**
- to mix/mingle/blend **flavours**
- to mix/blend **colours**
- mixed/mingled **feelings**
- to mix/stir/blend sth **thoroughly/well/gently**

mixed 0➡ /mɪkst/ *adj.*

1 0➡ having both good and bad qualities or feelings 混合的；混雜的：*The weather has been very mixed recently.* 最近天氣總是陰晴不定。◇ *I still **have mixed feelings** about going to Brazil* (= I am not sure what to think). 去不去巴西，我仍然拿不定主意。◇ *The play was given a **mixed reception** by the critics* (= some liked it, some did not). 劇評人對這齣戲的評價譭譽參半。◇ *British athletes had mixed fortunes in yesterday's competition.* 英國運動員在昨天的比賽中有輸有贏。 **2** [only before noun] consisting of different kinds of people, for example, people from different races and cultures 人員混雜的；由不同種族的人組成的：*a mixed community* 多文化的社區 ◇ *people of mixed race* 不同種族的人 ◇ *a mixed marriage* (= between two people of different races or religions) 異族或異教通婚 **3** [only before noun] consisting of different types of the same thing 混合的；摻雜在一起的：*a mixed salad* 什錦色拉 **4** [usually before noun] of or for both males and females 男女混雜的；男女混合的：*a mixed school* 男女同校的學校 ◇ *I'd rather not talk about it in mixed company.* 在男女混雜的場合，我不願意談論這件事。

ˌmixed-aˈbility *adj.* [usually before noun] with or for students who have different levels of ability 學生能力不一的；為各種水平的學生的：*a mixed-ability class* 學生能力水平不一的班級 ◇ *mixed-ability teaching* 針對能力不同的學生的教學

ˌmixed ˈbag *noun* [sing.] (*informal*) a collection of things or people of very different types 混合體；大雜燴

ˌmixed ˈblessing *noun* [usually sing.] something that has advantages and disadvantages 利弊並存之事；禍福參半之事

ˌmixed ˈdoubles *noun* [U+sing./pl. v.] (in TENNIS, etc. 網球等) a game in which a man and a woman play together against another man and woman 混合雙打

ˌmixed eˈconomy *noun* an economic system in a country in which some companies are owned by the state and some are private 混合經濟（國有與私營企業並存的經濟體系）

ˌmixed ˈfarming *noun* [U] a system of farming in which farmers both grow crops and keep animals（耕種和畜牧的）混合農業

ˌmixed ˈgrill *noun* (*BrE*) a hot dish of different types of meat and vegetables that have been GRILLED 烤雜排：*a mixed grill of bacon, sausages, tomatoes and mushrooms* 由鹹熏肉、香腸、番茄和蘑菇做成的烤雜排

ˌmixed ˈmetaphor *noun* a combination of two or more METAPHORS or idioms that produces a ridiculous effect, for example, 'He put his foot down with a firm hand.' 混合隱喻；多重隱喻

ˌmixed ˈnumber *noun* (*mathematics* 數) a number consisting of a whole number and a PROPER FRACTION, for example 3¼ 帶分數

ˌmixed ˈrace *adj.* (*especially BrE*) (*NAmE* usually **biracial**) concerning or containing members of two different races 混血的：*a mixed-race child* (= with parents of different races) 混血兒

ˌmixed ˈup *adj.* (*informal*) confused because of mental, emotional or social problems 迷茫的：*a **mixed-up** **kid/teenager*** 迷茫兒童／少年

mixer /ˈmɪksə(r)/ *noun* **1** a machine or device used for mixing things 攪拌器；混合器：*a food mixer* 食物攪拌器 ◇ (*BrE*) *a mixer tap* (= one in which hot and cold water can be mixed together before it comes out of the pipe) 冷熱水混合龍頭 ➲ see also CEMENT MIXER **2** a drink such as fruit juice that is not alcoholic and that can be mixed with alcohol 調酒用的飲料：*low-calorie mixers* 低熱量調酒配料 **3** (*technical* 術語) a device used for mixing together different sound or picture signals in order to produce a single sound or picture; a person whose job is to operate this device 聲音（或圖像）混合器；聲音（或圖像）混合操作員

IDM **a good/bad ˈmixer** a person who finds it easy/difficult to talk to people they do not know, for example at a party 擅長／不擅長交際的人

ˈmixing bowl *noun* a large bowl for mixing food in 拌菜碗；海碗

ˈmixing desk *noun* a piece of electronic equipment for mixing sounds, used especially when recording music or to improve its sound after recording it 混錄枱；調音枱

mix·ture /ˈmɪkstʃə(r)/ *noun*
1 [C, usually sing.] a combination of different things 混合；結合體：*The city is a mixture of old and new buildings.* 這座城市是新老建築兼而有之。◇ *We listened to the news with a mixture of surprise and horror.* 我們懷着驚恐交加的心情收聽了這則消息。 **2** [C, U] a substance made by mixing other substances together 混合物：*cake mixture* 蛋糕糊 ◇ *Add the eggs to the mixture and beat well.* 將雞蛋加進混合料中，攪拌均勻。 ➲ see also COUGH MIXTURE **3** [C] (*technical* 術語) a combination of two or more substances that mix together without any chemical reaction taking place 混合物；集合體 ➲ compare COMPOUND *n.* (2) **4** [U] the act of mixing different substances together 混合

ˈmix-up *noun* (*informal*) a situation that is full of confusion, especially because sb has made a mistake 混亂；雜亂 SYN **muddle**：*There has been a mix-up over the dates.* 日期完全攪亂了。

miz·zen (also **mizen**) /ˈmɪzn/ *noun* (*technical* 術語) **1** (also **miz·zen·mast** /ˈmɪznmɑːst; *NAmE* -mæst/) the MAST of a ship that is behind the main mast 後桅；次桅 **2** (also **miz·zen·sail** /ˈmɪznseɪl/) a sail on the mizzen of a ship 後桅縱帆；後帆

ml *abbr.* (*pl.* **ml** or **mls**) MILLILITRE(S) 毫升：*25ml water* * 25 毫升水

MLA /ˌem el ˈeɪ/ *abbr.* (in Canada and Northern Ireland 加拿大和北愛爾蘭) Member of the Legislative Assembly 立法會議員

M'lud /məˈlʌd/ *noun* (*BrE*) used when speaking to the judge in court（法庭用語）法官大人：*My client pleads guilty, M'lud.* 法官大人，我的當事人認罪。

mm *abbr., exclamation*
■ ***abbr.*** MILLIMETRE(S) 毫米：*rainfall 6mm* * 6 毫米的降雨量 ◇ *a 35mm camera* * 35 毫米照相機
■ ***exclamation*** (also **mmm**) the way of writing the sound /m/ that people make to show that they are listening to sb or that they agree, they are thinking, they like sth, they are not sure, etc. 唔，嗯（書寫中表示同意、思考中、喜歡、猶豫等發出的聲音）：*Mm, I know what you mean.* 唔，我知道你的意思。◇ *Mm, what lovely cake!* 唔，多好的蛋糕啊！◇ *Mmm, I'm not so sure that's a good idea.* 嗯，我不知道這想法行不行。

MMR /ˌem em ˈɑː(r)/ *abbr.* MEASLES, MUMPS, RUBELLA 麻疹—腮腺炎—風疹：*an MMR jab* (= a VACCINE given to small children to prevent these three diseases) 麻疹—腮腺炎—風疹疫苗

MMS /ˌem em ˈes/ *noun* [U, C] the abbreviation for 'Multimedia Messaging Service' (a system for sending colour pictures and sounds as well as short written messages from one mobile/cell phone to another)（手機）多媒體信息服務，彩信服務（全寫為 Multimedia Messaging Service）：*an MMS message* 多媒體短信 ◇ *He sent me an MMS.* 他給我發了條彩信。

MNA /ˌem en ˈeɪ/ *abbr.* (*CanE*) Member of the National Assembly 國會議員

mne·mon·ic /nɪˈmɒnɪk; *NAmE* -ˈmɑːn-/ *noun* a word, sentence, poem, etc. that helps you to remember sth 幫助記憶的詞句（或詩歌等）；助記符號 ▸ **mne·mon·ic** *adj.* [only before noun]：*a mnemonic device* 記憶手段

MO (*BrE*) (also **M.O.** *US, BrE*) /ˌem ˈəʊ; *NAmE* ˈoʊ/ *abbr.* **1** MEDICAL OFFICER（某機構的）專職醫生 **2** MODUS OPERANDI 工作方法

mo /məʊ; *NAmE* moʊ/ *noun* [sing.] (*BrE, informal*) a very short period of time 頃刻；瞬間 SYN **moment**：*See you in a mo!* 一會兒見！

moa /ˈməʊə; *NAmE* ˈmoʊə/ *noun* a large bird that could not fly, that was found in New Zealand but is now EXTINCT (= no longer exists) 恐鳥（曾發現於新西蘭，不能飛行，已滅絕）

moan /məʊn; *NAmE* moʊn/ *verb, noun*
■ ***verb*** **1** [I, T] (of a person 人) to make a long deep sound, usually expressing unhappiness, suffering or sexual pleasure 呻吟 SYN **groan**：*The injured man was lying on*

M

the ground, moaning. 受傷的人躺在地上呻吟着。◇ **~ in/with sth** *to moan in/with pain* 痛苦地呻吟 ◇ **+ speech** *'I might never see you again,' she moaned.* 她呻吟着說："我可能再也見不到你了。" **2** [I, T] **~ (at sb)** (*informal*) to complain about sth in a way that other people find annoying 抱怨 **SYN** **grumble, whine**：**~ (on) (about sth) (to sb)** *What are you moaning on about now?* 你在抱怨什麼呢？◇ **~ (at sb) (about sth)** *They're always **moaning and groaning** about how much they have to do.* 他們總是牢騷滿腹，抱怨有很多事要做。◇ **~ that ...** *Bella moaned that her feet were cold.* 貝拉抱怨說她的腳冷。➲ SYNONYMS at COMPLAIN **3** [I] (*literary*) (especially of the wind 尤指風) to make a long deep sound 呼嘯；發出蕭蕭聲 ▸ **moan·er** *noun*

■ **noun** **1** [C] a long deep sound, usually expressing unhappiness, suffering or sexual pleasure 呻吟聲 **SYN** **groan**：*a low **moan of despair/anguish*** 在絕望／痛苦中發出的低沉的呻吟聲 **2** [C] (*informal*) a complaint about sth 抱怨：*We had a good moan about work.* 我們對工作大大地抱怨了一番。◇ *His letters are full of the usual moans and groans.* 他的來信總是滿紙怨言。 **3** [sing.] (*literary*) a long deep sound, especially the sound that is made by the wind（尤指風的）呼嘯聲，蕭蕭聲

moat /məʊt; *NAmE* moʊt/ *noun* a deep wide channel that was dug around a castle, etc. and filled with water to make it more difficult for enemies to attack 護城河 ➲ VISUAL VOCAB page V15 ▸ **moat·ed** *adj.* [usually before noun]：*a moated manor house* 周圍有壕溝的莊園宅第

mob /mɒb; *NAmE* mɑːb/ *noun, verb*

■ **noun** **1** [C, sing.+sing./pl. v.] a large crowd of people, especially one that may become violent or cause trouble 人群；（尤指）暴民：*an **angry/unruly mob*** 憤怒的／失控的暴民 ◇ *The mob was/were preparing to storm the building.* 聚集的群眾準備猛攻大樓。◇ *an excited mob of fans* 一群激動的球迷 ◇ ***mob rule*** (= a situation in which a mob has control, rather than people in authority) 暴民統治 ➲ see also LYNCH MOB **2** [C, usually sing.] (*informal*) a group of people who are similar in some way 幫派；團夥 **SYN** **gang**：*All the usual mob were there.* 所有幫派成員都在那裏。 **3 the Mob** [sing.] (*informal*) the people involved in organized crime; the MAFIA 犯罪團夥；黑手黨 **4** [C] (*AustralE, NZE*) a group of animals（動物的）群 **SYN** **flock, herd**：*a mob of cattle* 一群牛 **IDM** see HEAVY *adj.*

■ **verb** (**-bb-**) [usually passive] **1 ~ sth** if a crowd of birds or animals **mob** another bird or animal, they gather round it and attack it（鳥群或獸群）圍攻，聚眾襲擊 **2 ~ sb** if a person is **mobbed** by a crowd of people, the crowd gathers round them in order to see them and try and get their attention（人群）圍聚，圍攏 **SYN** **besiege**

'mob cap *noun* a light cotton cap covering all the hair, worn by women in the 18th and 19th centuries（18、19世紀的）頭巾式女帽

mo·bile 🔑 /'məʊbaɪl; *NAmE* 'moʊbl/ *adj., noun*

■ **adj.** **1** 🔑 [usually before noun] that is not fixed in one place and can be moved easily and quickly 非固定的；可移動的：*mobile equipment* 可移動裝備 ◇ *a **mobile shop/library*** (= one inside a vehicle) 流動商店／圖書館 ➲ compare STATIONARY (1) **2** [not usually before noun] (of a person 人) able to move or travel around easily 行動方便；腿腳靈便：*a kitchen especially designed for the elderly or people who are less mobile* 專門為上了年紀或行動不便的人設計的廚房 ◇ *You really need to be mobile* (= have a car) *if you live in the country.* 如果你住在鄉村，你確實要有一輛汽車。 **OPP** **immobile** **3** (of people 人) able to change your social class, your job or the place where you live easily 易於變換社會階層（或工作、住處）的；流動的：*a highly mobile workforce* (= people who can move easily from place to place) 具有很強流動性的勞動力 ➲ see also UPWARDLY MOBILE **4** (of a face or its features 臉或面部特徵) changing shape or expression easily and often 多變的；易變的

■ **noun** **1** (*BrE*) = MOBILE PHONE：*Call me on my mobile.* 打手機給我。◇ *What's your mobile number?* 你的手機號碼是多少？◇ *the mobile networks* (= companies that provide mobile phone services) 移動電話網絡公司 **2** a decoration made from wire, etc. that is hung from the ceiling and that has small objects hanging from it which move when the air around them moves 風鈴；（可隨風擺動的）懸掛飾物

,mobile de'vice *noun* any small computing device that will fit into your pocket, such as a PDA or SMARTPHONE 移動電子裝置，行動裝置（如個人數字助理或智能手機）➲ compare MID

,mobile 'home *noun* **1** (*especially NAmE*) (also **trailer** *NAmE*) a small building for people to live in that is made in a factory and moved to a permanent place 活動住房 ➲ VISUAL VOCAB page V16 **2** (*BrE*) (*NAmE* **trailer**) a large CARAVAN that can be moved, sometimes with wheels, that is usually parked in one place and used for living in 旅遊房車；（拖車式）活動房屋 ➲ VISUAL VOCAB page V16

,mobile 'library (*BrE*) (*NAmE* **book·mobile**) *noun* a van/truck that contains a library and travels from place to place so that people in different places can borrow books 流動圖書館；圖書館車

,mobile 'phone 🔑 (also **mo·bile**) (both *BrE*) (also **cell phone**, **'cellular phone**, *informal* **cell** *NAmE, BrE*) *noun*
a telephone that does not have wires and works by radio, that you can carry with you and use anywhere 移動電話；手機：*Please make sure all mobile phones are switched off during the performance.* 請確保演出時關上所有手機。➲ COLLOCATIONS at PHONE

mo·bil·ity /məʊ'bɪləti; *NAmE* moʊ-/ *noun* [U] **1** the ability to move easily from one place, social class, or job to another（住處、社會階層、職業方面的）流動能力：***social/geographical/career mobility*** 社會地位／區域／職業流動性 ➲ see also UPWARD MOBILITY at UPWARD MOBILE **2** the ability to move or travel around easily 移動的能力；易於行走的能力：*An electric wheelchair has given her greater mobility.* 電動輪椅讓她行動起來方便多了。

mo·bil·ize (*BrE* also **-ise**) /'məʊbəlaɪz; *NAmE* 'moʊ-/ *verb* **1** [T, I] **~ (sb)** to work together in order to achieve a particular aim; to organize a group of people to do this 組織；鼓動；動員 **SYN** **rally**：*The unions mobilized thousands of workers in a protest against the cuts.* 各級工會組織了數千名工人抗議削減工資。 **2** [T] **~ sth** to find and start to use sth that is needed for a particular purpose 調動；調用 **SYN** **marshal**：*They were unable to mobilize the resources they needed.* 他們無法調用他們需要的資源。 **3** [T, I] **~ (sb/sth)** if a country **mobilizes** its army, or if a country or army **mobilizes**, it makes itself ready to fight in a war（戰時）動員：*The troops were ordered to mobilize.* 部隊接到了動員令。➲ compare DEMOBILIZE ▸ **mo·bil·iza·tion, -isa·tion** /,məʊbəlaɪ'zeɪʃn; *NAmE* ,moʊbələ'z-/ *noun* [U]

Möbius strip 麥比烏斯帶

Mö·bius strip (also **Moe·bius strip**) /'mɜːbiəs strɪp/ *noun* a surface with one continuous side, formed by joining the ends of a strip of material after twisting one end through 180 degrees 麥比烏斯帶（只有一面的連續曲面，把一條帶子的一端扭轉 180 度後將兩端連接起來構成）

mob·log /'mɒblɒg; 'məʊ-; *NAmE* 'mɑːblɑːg/ *noun* (*computing* 計) (*BrE*) a website that belongs to a particular person who puts pictures and other material from a mobile/cell phone on it 移動博客，手機博客，行動網誌（通過手機將圖片等上傳至網站）

mob·ster /ˈmɒbstə(r); *NAmE* ˈmɑːb-/ *noun* a member of a group of people who are involved in organized crime 暴徒；犯罪分子；匪徒

moc·ca·sin /ˈmɒkəsɪn; *NAmE* ˈmɑːk-/ *noun* a flat shoe that is made from soft leather and has large STITCHES around the front, of a type originally worn by Native Americans 莫卡辛軟皮鞋（原為美洲土著所穿）；軟幫皮鞋 ➲ VISUAL VOCAB page V64

mocha /ˈmɒkə; *NAmE* ˈmoʊkə/ *noun* **1** [U] a type of coffee of very good quality 摩卡咖啡；優等咖啡 **2** [C, U] a drink made or flavoured with this, often with chocolate added 加巧克力的摩卡咖啡飲料

mock /mɒk; *NAmE* mɑːk/ *verb, adj., noun*

■ ***verb*** **1** [T, I] **~ (sb/sth)** | **~ (sb) + speech** to laugh at sb/sth in an unkind way, especially by copying what they say or do 嘲笑；（模仿）嘲弄 SYN **make fun of**: *He's always mocking my French accent.* 他總是嘲笑我的法國口音。◇ *The other children mocked her, laughing behind their hands.* 其他孩子學她的樣子，用手捂着嘴笑。◇ *You can mock, but at least I'm willing to have a try!* 你可以嘲笑我，但我至少願意試一試。 **2** [T] **~ sth** (*formal*) to show no respect for sth 不尊重；蔑視：*The new exam mocked the needs of the majority of children.* 新的考試無視大多數孩子的需要。▸ **mock·er** *noun*

■ ***adj.*** [only before noun] **1** not sincere 虛假的；不誠實的 SYN **sham**：***mock horror/surprise*** 假裝恐懼；故作驚訝 **2** that is a copy of sth; not real 模仿的；模擬的：*a mock election* 模擬選舉 ◇ *a* ***mock interview/examination*** (= used to practise for the real one) 模擬面試／考試

■ ***noun*** (*informal*) (in Britain) a practice exam that you do before the official one （英國）模擬考試：*The mocks are in November.* 模擬考試在 11 月進行。◇ *What did you get in the mock?* 你的模擬考試得了多少分？

mock·ers /ˈmɒkəz; *NAmE* ˈmɑːkərz/ *noun* [pl.]

IDM **put the ˈmockers on sth/sb** (*BrE, informal*) to stop sth from happening; to bring bad luck to sth/sb 使（活動）告吹；使倒霉：*We were going to have a barbecue but the rain put the mockers on that idea.* 我們打算露天燒烤，但因為下雨，計劃泡湯了。

mock·ery /ˈmɒkəri; *NAmE* ˈmɑːk-/ *noun* **1** [U] comments or actions that are intended to make sb/sth seem ridiculous 嘲笑；愚弄 SYN **ridicule, scorn**：*She couldn't stand any more of their mockery.* 她再也無法忍受他們的愚弄了。 **2** [sing.] (*disapproving*) an action, a decision, etc. that is a failure and that is not as it is supposed to be 笑柄；被嘲笑的對象 SYN **travesty**：*It was a mockery of a trial.* 這次審判實在可笑。

IDM **make a ˈmockery of sth** to make sth seem ridiculous or useless 取笑；愚弄；嘲笑：*The trial made a mockery of justice.* 這次審判是對正義的嘲弄。

mock·ing /ˈmɒkɪŋ; *NAmE* ˈmɑːk-/ *adj.* (of behaviour, an expression, etc. 行為、臉色等) showing that you think sb/sth is ridiculous 嘲笑的；嘲弄的；愚弄的 SYN **contemptuous**：*a mocking smile* 嘲弄的微笑 ◇ *Her voice was faintly mocking.* 她的聲音略帶一絲嘲弄。 ▸ **mock·ing·ly** *adv.*

mock·ing·bird /ˈmɒkɪŋbɜːd; *NAmE* ˈmɑːkɪŋbɜːrd/ *noun* a grey and white American bird that can copy the songs of other birds 嘲鶇（美洲鳴禽，能模仿別種鳥的鳴叫）

mock·ney /ˈmɒkni; *NAmE* ˈmɑːkni/ *noun* [U] (*BrE, informal*, often *disapproving*) a way of speaking English by educated people from London which copies the words and sounds of COCKNEY speech (= a way of speaking typical of the East End of London)（英國受過教育的人中）仿倫敦東區口音：*She speaks in this ridiculous mockney accent.* 她模仿倫敦東區人的口音拿腔拿調地說話。

ˈmock-up *noun* a model or a copy of sth, often the same size as it, that is used for testing, or for showing people what the real thing will look like 實體模型；實尺寸模型

MOD /ˌem əʊ ˈdiː; *NAmE* oʊ/ *abbr.* Ministry of Defence (the government department in Britain that is responsible for defence)（英國）國防部

mod /mɒd; *NAmE* mɑːd/ *noun* a member of a group of young people, especially in Britain in the 1960s, who wore neat, fashionable clothes and rode MOTOR SCOOTERS 摩登派青年（尤指 20 世紀 60 年代英國的穿着時髦整潔、騎小型摩托車的青年）➲ compare ROCKER (3)

modal /ˈməʊdl; *NAmE* ˈmoʊdl/ (also **modal ˈverb, modal auˈxiliary, modal auˈxiliary verb**) *noun* (*grammar* 語法) a verb such as *can*, *may* or *will* that is used with another verb (not a modal) to express possibility, permission, intention, etc. 情態動詞（如 can、may 或 will 等，和實義動詞連用表示可能、許可、意圖等）▸ **modal** *adj.* ➲ compare AUXILIARY

Grammar Point 語法說明

modal verbs

- The **modal verbs** are **can, could, may, might, must, ought to, shall, should, will** and **would**. **Dare, need, have to** and **used to** also share some of the features of modal verbs. * can、could、may、might、must、ought to、shall、should、will 和 would 均為情態動詞。dare、need、have to 和 used to 亦具有情態動詞的某些特性。
- Modal verbs have only one form. They have no *-ing* or *-ed* forms and do not add *-s* to the 3rd person singular form. 情態動詞只有一種形式，沒有 -ing 或 -ed 形式，第三人稱單數也不加 -s：*He can speak three languages.* 他會說三種語言。◇ *She will try and visit tomorrow.* 她明天將設法去參觀。
- Modal verbs are followed by the infinitive of another verb without **to**. The exceptions are **ought to, have to** and **used to**. 情態動詞後跟不帶 to 的動詞不定式，但 ought to, have to 和 used to 例外：*You must find a job.* 你必須找到一份工作。◇ *You ought to stop smoking.* 你應當戒煙。◇ *I used to smoke but I gave up two years ago.* 我過去抽煙，但兩年前就戒了。
- Questions are formed without **do/does** in the present, or **did** in the past. 疑問句現在時不用 do/does，過去時不用 did：*Can I invite Mary?* 我可以邀請瑪麗嗎？◇ *Should I have invited Mary?* 我本該邀請瑪麗嗎？
- Negative sentences are formed with **not** or the short form **-n't** and do not use **do/does** or **did**. 否定句用 not 或簡約式 -n't，不用 do/does 或 did。

You will find more help with how to use modal verbs at the dictionary entries for each verb. 情態動詞的不同用法可參考本詞典裏各情態動詞詞條。

mo·dal·ity /məʊˈdæləti; *NAmE* moʊˈd-/ *noun* (*pl.* **-ies**) **1** [C] (*formal*) the particular way in which sth exists, is experienced or is done 形式；樣式；方式；形態：*They are researching a different modality of treatment for the disease.* 他們正在研究這種疾病的另一種療法。 **2** [U] (*linguistics* 語言) the idea expressed by modals 情態 **3** [C] (*biology* 生) the kind of senses that the body uses to experience things 感覺模式；感覺形式：*the visual and auditory modalities* 視覺和聽覺

mod cons /ˌmɒd ˈkɒnz; *NAmE* ˌmɑːd ˈkɑːnz/ *noun* [pl.] (*BrE, informal*) (especially in advertisements 尤用於廣告) the things in a house or flat/apartment that make living there easier and more comfortable 現代化的生活設備

mod·ding /ˈmɒdɪŋ; *NAmE* ˈmɑːdɪŋ/ *noun* [U] (*computing* 計) (*informal*) the activity of changing a piece of computer equipment or a computer program so that it works in a way that was not intended by the producer（電腦設備的）改裝；（電腦程序的）改編：*There are stiff penalties for illegal modding.* 非法改裝會受到重罰。 ▸ **mod** /mɒd; *NAmE* mɑːd/ *verb* (**-dd-**)：**~ sth** *a specially modded system* 經特別改編的系統

mode AW /məʊd; *NAmE* moʊd/ *noun* **1** [C] a particular way of doing sth; a particular type of sth 方式；風格；樣式：*a mode of communication* 交流方式 ◇ *a mode of behaviour* 行為模式 ◇ *environment-friendly modes of transport* 環保型的運輸模式 **2** [C, U] the way in which a

M

piece of equipment is set to perform a particular task（設備的）模式，工作狀態：*Switch the camera into the automatic mode.* 將照相機調到自動拍攝模式。 **3** [U] a particular way of feeling or behaving（情感或行為的）狀態，狀況：*to be in holiday mode* 處於假日的氣氛中 **4** [C, usually sing.] a particular style or fashion in clothes, art, etc.（衣着、藝術等的）形式，風格：*a pop video made by a director who really understands the mode* 由真正瞭解流行風格的製作人製作的流行音樂錄像帶 ➲ see also À LA MODE, MODISH **5** [sing.] (*technical* 術語) a set of notes in music which form a SCALE（音樂的）調式：***major/minor mode*** 大調／小調調式 **6** [sing.] (*mathematics* 數) the value that appears most frequently in a series of numbers 眾數（一組數字中出現次數最多的數）

model /ˈmɒdl; *NAmE* ˈmɑːdl/ *noun, verb*

■ ***noun***

▸ **SMALL COPY 模型** **1** a copy of sth, usually smaller than the original object（依照實物按比例製成的）模型：*a **working model** (= one in which the parts move) of a fire engine* 消防車的活動模型 ◇ *a model aeroplane* 飛機模型 ◇ *The architect had produced a **scale model** of the proposed shopping complex.* 建築師為計劃建設的購物中心做了一個比例模型。 ➲ VISUAL VOCAB page V41

▸ **DESIGN 設計** **2** a particular design or type of product 樣式；設計；型：*The latest models will be on display at the motor show.* 最新的車型將會在這次汽車展上展出。

▸ **DESCRIPTION OF SYSTEM 體系描述** **3** a simple description of a system, used for explaining how sth works or calculating what might happen, etc.（用於示範運作方法等的）模型：*a mathematical model for determining the safe level of pesticides in food* 測算食物中農藥的安全含量的數學模型 ➲ COLLOCATIONS at SCIENTIFIC

▸ **EXAMPLE TO COPY 可仿效的樣板** **4** something such as a system that can be copied by other people 樣本；範例：*The nation's constitution provided a model that other countries followed.* 這個國家的憲法成了別國仿效的範例。 **5** (*approving*) a person or thing that is considered an excellent example of sth 模範；典型：*It was a model of clarity.* 這是表達清晰的範例。◇ *a model student* 模範生 ◇ *a model farm (= one that has been specially designed to work well)* 示範農場 ➲ see also ROLE MODEL

▸ **FASHION 時裝** **6** a person whose job is to wear and show new styles of clothes and be photographed wearing them 模特兒：*a fashion model* 時裝模特兒 ◇ *a male model* 男模特兒

▸ **FOR ARTIST 藝術家的** **7** a person who is employed to be painted, drawn, photographed, etc. by an artist or photographer 模特兒

■ ***verb*** (**-ll-**, *especially US* **-l-**)

▸ **WORK AS MODEL 做模特兒** **1** [I] to work as a model for an artist or in the fashion industry 做模特兒

▸ **CLOTHES 衣服** **2** [T] **~ sth** to wear clothes in order to show them to people who might want to buy them（向顧客）穿戴展示：*The wedding gown is being modelled for us by the designer's daughter.* 結婚禮服正由設計者的女兒穿在身上給我們看。

▸ **CREATE COPY 複製** **3** [T] **~ sth** to create a copy of an activity, a situation, etc. so that you can study it before dealing with the real thing 將…做成模型；複製 SYN **simulate**：*The program can model a typical home page for you.* 這個程序可以使用模板幫你製作一個標準的主頁。

▸ **CLAY, ETC. 黏土等** **4** [T] **~ sth** to shape CLAY, etc. in order to make sth 將（黏土等）做成模型：*a statue modelled in bronze* 青銅像

PHR V **ˈmodel yourself on sb** to copy the behaviour, style, etc. of sb you like and respect in order to be like them 仿效；以某人為榜樣：*As a politician, he modelled himself on Churchill.* 作為一名從政者，他以丘吉爾為榜樣。 **ˈmodel sth on/after sth** to make sth so that it looks, works, etc. like sth else 模仿；仿照：*The country's parliament is modelled on the British system.* 這個國家的議會是模仿英國的體制建立的。

ˌmodel ˈhome (*NAmE*) (*BrE* **ˈshow house**, **ˈshow home**) *noun* a house in a group of new houses that has been painted and filled with furniture, so that people who might want to buy one of the houses can see what they will be like 樣品房，樣板房（供購買房子的顧客參觀）

mod·el·ler (*especially US* **mod·el·er**) /ˈmɒdələ(r); *NAmE* ˈmɑːd-/ *noun* **1** a person who makes models of objects（實物）模型製作者 **2** a person who makes a simple description of a system or a process that can be used to explain it, etc. 系統模型製作者；系統模型設計者

mod·el·ling (*especially US* **mod·el·ing**) /ˈmɒdəlɪŋ; *NAmE* ˈmɑːd-/ *noun* [U] **1** the work of a fashion model（時裝）模特兒工作，模特兒表演：*a career in modelling* 模特兒生涯 ◇ *a modelling agency* 模特兒經紀公司 **2** the activity of making models of objects（實物）模型製造：*clay modelling* 黏土模型製造 **3** the work of making a simple description of a system or a process that can be used to explain it, etc. 系統模型化，系統模型的建立：***mathematical/statistical/computer modelling*** 數學／統計學／電腦模型的建立

ˌmodel ˈvillage *noun* **1** a small model of a village, or a collection of small models of famous buildings arranged like a village（取材著名建築物製作的）模型村 **2** (*old use*) a village with good-quality houses, especially one built in the past by an employer for workers to live in 模範村（尤指舊時雇主為工人修建的優質房屋）

modem /ˈməʊdem; *NAmE* ˈmoʊ-/ *noun* a device that connects one computer system to another using a telephone line so that data can be sent 調制解調器

mod·er·ate *adj., verb, noun*

■ ***adj.*** /ˈmɒdərət; *NAmE* ˈmɑːd-/ **1** that is neither very good, large, hot, etc. nor very bad, small, cold, etc. 適度的；中等的：*students of moderate ability* 能力一般的學生 ◇ *Even moderate amounts of the drug can be fatal.* 這種藥的用量即使不很大也會致命。◇ *The team enjoyed only moderate success last season.* 上個賽季，這個隊伍只取得了中等成績。◇ *Cook over a moderate heat.* 用文火烹調。 **2** having or showing opinions, especially about politics, that are not extreme 溫和的；不激烈的；不偏激的：***moderate views/policies*** 溫和的見解／政策 ◇ *a moderate socialist* 溫和的社會主義者 **3** staying within limits that are considered to be reasonable by most people 適中的；合理的：*a moderate drinker* 不過多飲酒的人 ◇ *moderate wage demands* 合理的工資要求 OPP **immoderate**

■ ***verb*** /ˈmɒdəreɪt; *NAmE* ˈmɑːd-/ **1** [I, T] (*formal*) to become or make sth become less extreme, severe, etc. 緩和；使適中：*By evening the wind had moderated slightly.* 到黃昏時，風稍稍減弱了。◇ **~ sth** *We agreed to moderate our original demands.* 我們同意降低我們原先的要求。 **2** [T, I] **~ (sth)** (*BrE*) to check that an exam has been marked fairly and in the same way by different people 審核評分（查看不同閱卷人所打分數是否公平一致） **3** [T, I] **~ (sth)** to be in charge of a discussion or debate and make sure it is fair 主持（討論、辯論等）：*The television debate was moderated by a law professor.* 這場電視辯論由一位法學教授主持。◇ *a moderated newsgroup* 有主持人的網絡新聞組

■ ***noun*** /ˈmɒdərət; *NAmE* ˈmɑːd-/ a person who has opinions, especially about politics, that are not extreme 持溫和觀點者（尤指政見）

mod·er·ate·ly /ˈmɒdərətli; *NAmE* ˈmɑːd-/ *adv.* **1** to an average extent; fairly but not very 一般地；勉強地 SYN **reasonably**：*a moderately successful career* 還算成功的事業 ◇ *She only did moderately well in the exam.* 她這次考試成績還好。◇ *Cook in a moderately hot oven.* 用烤箱以中火烤製。 **2** within reasonable limits 適度；適量；適中：*He only drinks (alcohol) moderately.* 他喝酒不過量。

mod·er·ation /ˌmɒdəˈreɪʃn; *NAmE* ˌmɑːd-/ *noun* [U] **1** the quality of being reasonable and not being extreme 適度；適中；合理：*There was a call for moderation on the part of the trade unions.* 有人呼籲工會保持克制。◇ *Alcohol should only ever be taken **in moderation** (= in small quantities).* 酒只可少量飲用。 **2** (*BrE*) (in education 教育) the process of making sure that the same standards are used by different people in marking exams, etc. 評分審核制

mod·er·ator /ˈmɒdəreɪtə(r); *NAmE* ˈmɑːd-/ *noun* **1** a person whose job is to help the two sides in a disagreement to reach an agreement 調解人；調停人 ➲ see also

MEDIATOR **2** (*especially NAmE*) a person whose job is to make sure that a discussion or a debate is fair 會議主持；辯論會主席 **3** (*BrE*) a person whose job is to make sure that an exam is marked fairly 評分監督 **4** (*computing* 計) a person who is responsible for preventing offensive material from being published on a website（論壇等的）監管員，版主：*moderators of online discussion groups* 網上討論組的監管員 **5 Moderator** a religious leader in the Presbyterian Church who is in charge of the Church council 長老會會議主席

mod·ern 🔑 /ˈmɒdn; *NAmE* ˈmɑːdərn/ *adj.* **1** 🔑 [only before noun] of the present time or recent times 現代的；當代的；近代的 **SYN contemporary**：*the modern industrial world* 當今工業世界 ◇ *Modern European history* 歐洲近代史 ◇ *modern Greek* 現代希臘語 ◇ *Stress is a major problem of modern life.* 壓力是現代生活中的主要問題。 **2** 🔑 [only before noun] (of styles in art, music, fashion, etc. 藝術、音樂、時裝等的風格) new and intended to be different from traditional styles 新式的；有別於傳統的 **SYN contemporary**：***modern art/architecture/drama/jazz*** 現代藝術／建築／戲劇／爵士樂 **3** 🔑 (usually *approving*) using the latest technology, designs, materials, etc. 時新的；現代化的；最新的 **SYN up-to-date**：*a modern computer system* 時新的電腦系統 ◇ *modern methods of farming* 現代化的耕作方式 ◇ *the most modern, well-equipped hospital in London* 倫敦最先進的、設備最精良的醫院 **4** (of ways of behaving, thinking, etc. 行為、思想等的方式) new and not always accepted by most members of society 新式的，時髦的（大部份公眾不一定接受）：*She has very modern ideas about educating her children.* 在教育子女方面，她有非常新式的觀點。

ˌmodern ˈdance *noun* [U] a form of dance that was developed in the early 20th century by people who did not like the restrictions of traditional BALLET 現代舞（20 世紀初發展起來的一種擺脱芭蕾舞限制的舞蹈形式）

ˌmodern-ˈday *adj.* [only before noun] **1** of the present time 現代的；當代的 **SYN contemporary**：*modern-day America* 當代美國 **2** used to describe a modern form of sb/sth, usually sb/sth bad or unpleasant, that existed in the past 現代版的，翻新的（通常用於消極事物）：*It has been called modern-day slavery.* 人們稱之為現代版的奴隸制度。

ˌmodern ˈEnglish *noun* [U] the English language in the form it has been in since about 1500 現代英語（公元 1500 年前後至今的英語）

mod·ern·ism /ˈmɒdənɪzəm; *NAmE* ˈmɑːdərn-/ *noun* [U] **1** modern ideas or methods 現代主義；現代思想（或方法） **2** a style and movement in art, ARCHITECTURE and literature popular in the middle of the 20th century in which modern ideas, methods and materials were used rather than traditional ones 現代派，現代風格，現代主義（盛行於 20 世紀中期的藝術、建築和文學風格） ➲ compare POSTMODERNISM ▸ **mod·ern·ist** /ˈmɒdənɪst; *NAmE* ˈmɑːdərn-/ *adj.* [only before noun]：*modernist art* 現代派藝術 **mod·ern·ist** *noun*

mod·ern·is·tic /ˌmɒdəˈnɪstɪk; *NAmE* ˌmɑːdərˈn-/ *adj.* (of a painting, building, piece of furniture, etc. 繪畫、房屋、傢具等) painted, designed, etc. in a very modern style 現代派的；時髦的

mod·ern·ity /məˈdɜːnəti; *NAmE* -ˈdɜːrn-/ *noun* [U] the condition of being new and modern 現代性

mod·ern·ize (*BrE* also **-ise**) /ˈmɒdənaɪz; *NAmE* ˈmɑːdərn-/ *verb* **1** [T] **~ sth** to make a system, methods, etc. more modern and more suitable for use at the present time 使（制度、方法等）現代化 **SYN update**：*The company is investing $9 million to modernize its factories.* 這家公司要投資 900 萬元將其工廠現代化。 **2** [I] to start using modern equipment, ideas, etc. 使（設備、概念等）現代化：*Unfortunately we lack the resources to modernize.* 遺憾的是我們缺乏現代化所需的財力。 ▸ **mod·ern·iza·tion**, **-isa·tion** /ˌmɒdənaɪˈzeɪʃn; *NAmE* ˌmɑːdərnəˈz-/ *noun* [U]

ˌmodern ˈlanguage *noun* (*especially BrE*) a language that is spoken or written now, especially a European language, such as French or Spanish, that you study at school, university or college 現代語言（尤指在學校裏教授的歐洲語言）：*the department of modern languages* 現代語言系 ◇ *a degree in modern languages* 現代語言學的學位

mod·est /ˈmɒdɪst; *NAmE* ˈmɑːd-/ *adj.* **1** not very large, expensive, important, etc. 些許的；不太大（或貴、重要等）的：*modest improvements/reforms* 不太顯著的改進／改革 ◇ *He charged a relatively modest fee.* 他收取的費用不算高。 ◇ *a modest little house* 簡樸的小房子 ◇ *The research was carried out on a modest scale.* 這個研究項目開展的規模不算太大。 **2** (*approving*) not talking much about your own abilities or possessions 謙虛的；謙遜的：*She's very modest about her success.* 她對自己的成功非常謙虛。 ◇ *You're too modest!* 你太謙虛了！ **OPP immodest 3** (of people, especially women, or their clothes 人，尤指婦女或其衣着) shy about showing much of the body; not intended to attract attention, especially in a sexual way 莊重的；樸素的；不性感的 **SYN demure**：*a modest dress* 端莊的連衣裙 **OPP immodest** ▸ **mod·est·ly** *adv.*

mod·esty /ˈmɒdəsti; *NAmE* ˈmɑːd-/ *noun* [U] **1** the fact of not talking much about your abilities or possessions 謙虛；謙遜：*He accepted the award with characteristic modesty.* 他以他一貫的謙遜態度接受了獎項。 ◇ *I hate false* (= pretended) *modesty.* 我討厭虛偽的謙遜。 **2** the action of behaving or dressing so that you do not show your body or attract sexual attention 莊重；樸素；賢淑 **3** the state of being not very large, expensive, important, etc. 不突出；有限：*They tried to disguise the modesty of their achievements.* 他們成就不大，所以力圖掩蓋這一點。

modi·cum /ˈmɒdɪkəm; *NAmE* ˈmɑːd-; ˈmɔːd-/ *noun* [sing.] (*formal*) a fairly small amount, especially of sth good or pleasant 少量，一點點（好事或愉快的事）：*They should win, given a modicum of luck.* 只要有一點點運氣，他們就會贏。

modi·fi·ca·tion **AW** /ˌmɒdɪfɪˈkeɪʃn; *NAmE* ˌmɑːd-/ *noun* [U, C] **~ (of/to/in sth)** the act or process of changing sth in order to improve it or make it more acceptable; a change that is made 修改；改進；改變 **SYN adaptation**：*Considerable modification of the existing system is needed.* 需要對現有的系統進行相當大的改進。 ◇ *It might be necessary to make a few slight modifications to the design.* 也許有必要對這個設計稍作幾處修改。

modi·fier /ˈmɒdɪfaɪə(r); *NAmE* ˈmɑːd-/ *noun* (*grammar* 語法) a word or group of words that describes a noun phrase or restricts its meaning in some way 修飾語 ➲ compare POSTMODIFIER, PREMODIFIER

mod·ify **AW** /ˈmɒdɪfaɪ; *NAmE* ˈmɑːd-/ *verb* (**modi·fies**, **modi·fy·ing**, **modi·fied**, **modi·fied**) **1 ~ sth** to change sth slightly, especially in order to make it more suitable for a particular purpose 調整；稍作修改；使更適合 **SYN adapt**：*The software we use has been modified for us.* 我們使用的軟件已按我們的需要作過修改。 ◇ *Patients are taught how to modify their diet.* 病人獲得有關如何調節自己飲食的指導。 **2 ~ sth** to make sth less extreme 緩和；使溫和 **SYN adjust**：*to **modify** your **behaviour/language/views*** 使你的行為／語言／觀點更容易讓人接受 **3 ~ sth** (*grammar* 語法) a word, such as an adjective or adverb, that **modifies** another word or group of words describes it or restricts its meaning in some way 修飾：*In 'walk slowly', the adverb 'slowly' modifies the verb 'walk'.* 在 walk slowly 中，副詞 slowly 修飾動詞 walk。

mod·ish /ˈməʊdɪʃ; *NAmE* ˈmoʊ-/ *adj.* (sometimes *disapproving*) fashionable 時髦的；流行的

modu·lar /ˈmɒdjələ(r); *NAmE* ˈmɑːdʒə-/ *adj.* **1** (of a course of study, especially at a British university or college 尤指英國大學裏的課程) consisting of separate units from which students may choose several 分單元的（由獨立單元組成，學生可選修）：*a modular course* 單元課程 **2** (of machines, buildings, etc. 機器、建築等) consisting of separate parts or units that can be joined together 組合式的；模塊化的；標準組件的

modu·late /ˈmɒdjuleɪt; *NAmE* ˈmɑːdʒə-/ *verb* **1** [T] **~ sth** (*formal*) to change the quality of your voice in order to create a particular effect by making it louder, softer, lower, etc. 調節（嗓音的大小、強弱、高低等） **2** [I] **~ (from sth) (to/into sth)** (*music* 音) to change from one musical KEY (= set of notes) to another 變調；轉調 **3** [T] **~ sth** (*technical* 術語) to affect sth so that it becomes more regular, slower, etc. 調整；調節；控制：*drugs that effectively modulate the disease process* 可以有效控制疾病發展的藥品 **4** [T] **~ sth** (*technical* 術語) to change the rate at which a sound wave or radio signal VIBRATES (= the FREQUENCY) so that it is clearer 調制（聲波或無線電波頻率）；調諧 ▸ **modu·la·tion** /ˌmɒdjuˈleɪʃn; *NAmE* ˌmɑːdʒəˈl-/ *noun* [U, C]

mod·ule /ˈmɒdjuːl; *NAmE* ˈmɑːdʒuːl/ *noun* **1** a unit that can form part of a course of study, especially at a college or university in Britain 單元（尤指英國大學課程的一部份）：*The course consists of ten core modules and five optional modules.* 這門課程包括十個必修單元和五個選修單元。**2** (*computing* 計) a unit of a computer system or program that has a particular function 模塊；功能塊；程序塊 **3** one of a set of separate parts or units that can be joined together to make a machine, a piece of furniture, a building, etc. 組件；模塊；配件 **4** a unit of a SPACECRAFT that can function independently of the main part（航天器上獨立的）艙：*the lunar module* 登月艙

modus op·er·andi /ˌməʊdəs ˌɒpəˈrændiː; *NAmE* ˌmoʊdəs ˌɑːpə-/ *noun* [sing.] (from *Latin, formal*) (*abbr.* **MO**) a particular method of working 工作方法

modus vi·vendi /ˌməʊdəs vɪˈvendiː; *NAmE* ˌmoʊdəs/ *noun* [sing.] (from *Latin, formal*) an arrangement that is made between people, institutions or countries who have very different opinions or ideas, so that they can live or work together without arguing 妥協

M

Moe·bius strip *noun* = MÖBIUS STRIP

mog·gie (also **moggy**) /ˈmɒɡi; *NAmE* ˈmɑːɡi/ *noun* (*pl.* **-ies**) (*BrE, informal*) a cat 貓

mogul /ˈməʊɡl; *NAmE* ˈmoʊɡl/ *noun* **1** a very rich, important and powerful person 大亨；有權勢的人 **SYN** **magnate**：*a movie mogul* 電影大亨 **2 Mogul** (also **Mo·ghul**, **Mug·hal** /ˈmuːɡɑːl/) a member of the Muslim race that ruled much of India from the 16th to the 19th century 莫卧兒人（印度穆斯林，16 至 19 世紀統治印度大部份地區）**3** a raised area of hard snow that you jump over when you are SKIING 雪丘，雪墩，"貓跳"（滑雪坡道上需跳越的硬雪堆）

mo·hair /ˈməʊheə(r); *NAmE* ˈmoʊher/ *noun* [U] soft wool or cloth made from the fine hair of the ANGORA GOAT, used for making clothes 安哥拉山羊毛毛線（或織物）；馬海毛毛線（或織物）：*a mohair sweater* 馬海毛毛衣

Mo·ham·med *noun* = MUHAMMAD

Mo·hawk /ˈməʊhɔːk; *NAmE* ˈmoʊ-/ *noun* (*pl.* **Mohawk** or **Mohawks**) a member of a Native American people, many of whom live in New York State and Canada 莫霍克人（美洲土著，很多居於紐約州和加拿大）

Mo·hi·can /məʊˈhiːkən; *NAmE* moʊ-/ (*especially BrE*) (also **Mo·hawk** especially in *NAmE* /ˈməʊhɔːk; *NAmE* ˈmoʊ-/) *noun* a way of cutting the hair in which the head is shaved except for a strip of hair in the middle that is sometimes made to stick up 莫希干髮型，鶏坎髮型（只保留頭中間一道直立的頭髮）

moi /mwɑː/ *exclamation* (*humorous*, from *French*) me（賓格）我：*'Did you eat all the biscuits?' 'Who? Moi?'* "你把餅乾吃光了？" "誰？我？"

moire /mwɑː(r); *NAmE* also ˈmɔɪər/ (also **moiré** /ˈmwɑːreɪ/) *noun* [U] a type of silk cloth with a pattern on its surface like small waves 波紋絲綢

moist /mɔɪst/ *adj.* slightly wet 微濕的；濕潤的：*warm moist air* 温暖潮濕的空氣 ◇ *a rich moist cake* 鬆軟味濃的蛋糕 ◇ *Water the plants regularly to keep the soil moist.* 定時澆灌植物以保持土壤濕潤。◇ *Her eyes were moist* (= with tears). 她眼含淚水。➲ SYNONYMS at WET ▸ **moist·ness** *noun* [U]

mois·ten /ˈmɔɪsn/ *verb* [T, I] **~ (sth)** to become or make sth slightly wet（使）變得潮濕，變得濕潤：*He moistened his lips before he spoke.* 他潤了潤嘴唇，接着就開始講話。

mois·ture /ˈmɔɪstʃə(r)/ *noun* [U] very small drops of water that are present in the air, on a surface or in a substance 潮氣；水汽；水分：*the skin's natural moisture* 皮膚的天然水分 ◇ *a material that is designed to* ***absorb/retain moisture*** 用來吸收／保持水分的材料

mois·tur·ize (*BrE* also **-ise**) /ˈmɔɪstʃəraɪz/ *verb* [T, I] **~ (sth)** to put a special cream on your skin to make it less dry 使皮膚濕潤；（用脂膏）滋潤：*a* ***moisturizing cream/lotion*** 潤膚霜／液 ◇ *a product that soothes and moisturizes* 使皮膚柔軟濕潤的產品

mois·tur·izer (*BrE* also **-iser**) /ˈmɔɪstʃəraɪzə(r)/ *noun* [C, U] a cream that is used to make the skin less dry 潤膚霜；潤膚膏

mojo /ˈməʊdʒəʊ; *NAmE* ˈmoʊdʒoʊ/ *noun* (*pl.* **mojos**) (*especially NAmE*) **1** [U] magic power 魔力 **2** [C] a small object, or a collection of small objects in a bag, that is believed to have magic powers 符咒（袋）；護身符 **3** [U] the power of sb's attractive personality（人的）魅力

molar /ˈməʊlə(r); *NAmE* ˈmoʊ-/ *noun* any of the twelve large teeth at the back of the mouth used for crushing and chewing food 臼齒；磨牙 ➲ compare CANINE *n.* (1), INCISOR

mo·las·ses /məˈlæsɪz/ (*NAmE*) (*BrE* **trea·cle**) *noun* [U] a thick black sweet sticky liquid produced when sugar is REFINED (= made pure), used in cooking（製糖時產生的）糖漿，糖蜜

mold (*especially US*) (*BrE, CanE* **mould**) /məʊld; *NAmE* moʊld/ *noun, verb*

▪ ***noun*** **1** [C] a container that you pour a liquid or soft substance into, which then becomes solid in the same shape as the container, for example when it is cooled or cooked 模具；鑄模：*A clay mold is used for casting bronze statues.* 用黏土模具來澆鑄青銅塑像。◇ *Pour the chocolate into a heart-shaped mold.* 將巧克力倒入心形模子。◇ *They* ***broke the mold*** *when they made you* (= there is nobody like you). 塑人完畢，模子搗碎（意指世上沒有相同的人）。**2** [C, usually sing.] a particular style showing the characteristics, attitudes or behaviour that are typical of sb/sth（獨特）類型，個性，風格：*a hero in the 'Superman' mold* "超人"式的英雄 ◇ *He is cast in a different mold from his predecessor.* 他和他的前任作風不一樣。◇ *She doesn't fit (into) the traditional mold of an academic.* 她不像一個傳統的學者。**3** [U, C] a fine soft green, grey or black substance like fur that grows on old food or on objects that are left in warm wet air 黴；黴菌：*There's mold on the cheese.* 乾酪發霉了。◇ *molds and fungi* 黴菌和真菌 ◇ *mold growth* 黴的生長 ➲ see also LEAF MOULD

IDM **break the 'mold (of sth)** to change what people expect from a situation, especially by acting in a dramatic and original way 改變…模式；打破…模式而自成一格

▪ ***verb*** **1** [T] to shape a soft substance into a particular form or object by pressing it or by putting it into a mold（用模具）澆鑄，塑造：**~ A (into B)** *First, mold the clay into the desired shape.* 首先，將陶土揉捏成需要的形狀。◇ **~ B (from/out of/in A)** *The figure had been molded in clay.* 這座人像是用黏土塑造的。**2** [T] to strongly influence the way sb's character, opinions, etc. develop 對…影響重大；將…塑造成：**~ sb/sth** *The experience had molded and coloured her whole life.* 這次經歷影響了她的一生。◇ **~ sb/sth into sb/sth** *He molded them into a superb team.* 他將他們打造成一支非凡的團隊。**3** [I, T] **~ (sth) to sth** to fit or make sth fit tightly around the shape of sth（使）緊貼於，（使）與…吻合：*The fabric molds to the body.* 這種織物很貼身。

mol·der (*especially US*) (*BrE, CanE* **moulder**) /ˈməʊldə(r); *NAmE* ˈmoʊ-/ *verb* [I] to decay slowly and steadily 腐爛；腐朽：*The room smelt of disuse and moldering books.* 房間裏有一股荒置和書籍發霉的味道。

mold·ing (*especially US*) (*BrE, CanE* **mould·ing**) /ˈməʊldɪŋ; *NAmE* ˈmoʊ-/ *noun* a decorative strip of plastic, stone, wood, etc. around the top edge of a wall, on a door, etc. 線腳（用於簷口、門楣等的凹凸帶形裝飾）

moldy (*especially US*) (*BrE, CanE* **mouldy**) /ˈməʊldi; *NAmE* ˈmoʊ-/ *adj.* **1** covered with or containing MOLD 發霉的；帶霉斑的：*moldy bread/cheese* 發霉的麵包／乾酪 ◇ *Strawberries go moldy very quickly.* 草莓很容易發霉。**2** old and not in good condition 破舊的

mole /məʊl; *NAmE* moʊl/ *noun* **1** a small animal with dark grey fur, that is almost blind and digs tunnels under the ground to live in 鼴鼠（體小，視力極差，居住在挖掘的地道）➲ see also MOLEHILL **2** a small dark brown mark on the skin, sometimes slightly higher than the skin around it 色素痣 ➲ compare FRECKLE **3** a person who works within an organization and secretly passes important information to another organization or country 內奸 **4** (*chemistry* 化) a unit for measuring the amount of substance 摩爾（計量物質的數量單位）

mol·ecule /ˈmɒlɪkjuːl; *NAmE* ˈmɑːl-/ *noun* (*chemistry* 化) the smallest unit, consisting of a group of atoms, into which a substance can be divided without a change in its chemical nature 分子：*A molecule of water consists of two atoms of hydrogen and one atom of oxygen.* 水分子由兩個氫原子和一個氧原子構成。▸ **mo·lecu·lar** /məˈlekjələ(r)/ *adj.* [only before noun]：*molecular structure/biology* 分子結構／生物學

mole·hill /ˈməʊlhɪl; *NAmE* ˈmoʊl-/ *noun* a small pile of earth that a MOLE leaves on the surface of the ground when it digs underground 鼴丘（由鼴鼠挖洞扒出的泥土堆成）IDM see MOUNTAIN

mole·skin /ˈməʊlskɪn; *NAmE* ˈmoʊl-/ *noun* [U] a type of strong cotton cloth with a soft surface, used for making clothes 厚毛頭斜紋棉布

mo·lest /məˈlest/ *verb* **1 ~ sb** to attack sb, especially a child, sexually 對（兒童）性騷擾 SYN **abuse** **2 ~ sb** (*old-fashioned*) to attack sb physically 攻擊；傷害 ▸ **mo·lest·ation** /ˌmɒleˈsteɪʃn; *NAmE* ˌmoʊ-/ *noun* [U] **mo·lest·er** /məˈlestə(r)/ *noun*：*a child molester* 對兒童性騷擾者

moll /mɒl; *NAmE* mɑːl/ *noun* (*old-fashioned, slang*) the female friend of a criminal 惡棍的女友

mol·lify /ˈmɒlɪfaɪ; *NAmE* ˈmɑːl-/ *verb* (**mol·li·fies, mol·li·fy·ing, mol·li·fied, mol·li·fied**) **~ sb** (*formal*) to make sb feel less angry or upset 使平靜；撫慰 SYN **placate**

mol·lusc (*BrE*) (*US* **mol·lusk**) /ˈmɒləsk; *NAmE* ˈmɑːl-/ *noun* (*technical* 術語) any creature with a soft body that is not divided into different sections, and usually a hard outer shell. SNAILS and SLUGS are molluscs. 軟體動物 ➲ compare BIVALVE, SHELLFISH

molly·cod·dle /ˈmɒlikɒdl; *NAmE* ˈmɑːlikɑːdl/ *verb* (*disapproving*, becoming *old-fashioned*) **~ sb** to protect sb too much and make their life too comfortable and safe 溺愛；寵愛 ➲ compare CODDLE (1)

Molo·tov cock·tail /ˌmɒlətɒf ˈkɒkteɪl; *NAmE* ˌmɑːlətɔːf ˈkɑːk-; ˌmɔːl-/ (*BrE* also **ˈpetrol bomb**) *noun* a simple bomb that consists of a bottle filled with petrol/gas and a piece of cloth in the end that is made to burn just before the bomb is thrown 瓶裝汽油彈；莫洛托夫燃燒瓶

molt (*especially US*) (*BrE, CanE* **moult**) /məʊlt; *NAmE* moʊlt/ *verb* [I] (of a bird or an animal 鳥或動物) to lose feathers or hair before new feathers or hair grow 換羽；蛻毛

mol·ten /ˈməʊltən; *NAmE* ˈmoʊl-/ *adj.* (of metal, rock, or glass 金屬、岩石或玻璃) heated to a very high temperature so that it becomes liquid 熔化的；熔融的

mo·lyb·denum /məˈlɪbdənəm/ *noun* [U] (*symb.* **Mo**) a chemical element. Molybdenum is a silver-grey metal that breaks easily and is used in some ALLOY steels. 鉬

mom 0ᵚ /mɒm; *NAmE* mɑːm/ *noun* (*NAmE*) (*BrE* **mum**) (*informal*)
a mother 媽媽；媽：*Where's my mom?* 我媽在哪兒？◇ *Mom and Dad* 媽媽和爸爸 ◇ *Are you listening, Mom?* 媽，你在聽嗎？➲ see also SOCCER MOM

ˌmom-and-ˈpop *adj.* [only before noun] (*NAmE*) (of a shop/store or business 商店或企業) owned and run by a husband and wife, or by a family 夫妻（或家庭）經營的

mo·ment 0ᵚ /ˈməʊmənt; *NAmE* ˈmoʊ-/ *noun* **1** 0ᵚ a very short period of time 片刻；瞬間：*Could you wait a moment, please?* 請您稍等一下，好嗎？◇ ***One moment, please*** (= Please wait a short time). 請稍候。◇ *He thought **for a moment** before replying.* 他想了一下才回答。◇ *I'll be back **in a moment**.* 我一會兒就回來。◇ *We arrived **not a moment too soon*** (= almost too late). 我們到得一點也不早。◇ ***Moments later*** (= a very short time later), *I heard a terrible crash.* 過了一會兒，我聽到一聲可怕的撞擊聲。➲ see also SENIOR MOMENT **2** 0ᵚ [sing.] an exact point in time 某個時刻；當時：*We're busy **at the moment*** (= now). 我們這會兒很忙。◇ *I agreed **in a moment of** weakness.* 我一時心軟就答應了。◇ ***At that very moment**, the phone rang.* 就在那時，電話鈴響了。◇ ***From that moment on**, she never felt really well again.* 從那時候開始，她就再也沒真正好受過。**3** 0ᵚ [C] a particular occasion; a time for doing sth 時機；機遇；時光；做某事的時刻：*I'm waiting for **the right moment** to tell him the bad news.* 我得找個適當的時機告訴他這個壞消息。◇ *That was one of the happiest moments of my life.* 那是我一生中最快樂的一段時光。◇ *Have I caught you at a bad moment?* 我是不是來得不是時候？

IDM **(at) any ˈmoment (ˈnow)** 0ᵚ very soon 很快；隨時：*Hurry up! He'll be back any moment now.* 快點！他隨時都會回來。**at this moment in ˈtime** (*informal*) now, at the present time 現在；此時此刻：*At this moment in time, I don't know what my decision will be.* 此時此刻，我還未知道自己會作出什麼決定。**for the ˈmoment/ˈpresent** for now; for a short time 目前；暫時：*This house is big enough for the moment, but we'll have to move if we have children.* 這房子現在還夠大。要是有了孩子，我們還得搬。**have its/your ˈmoments** to have short times that are better, more interesting, etc. than others 有短暫的好時候：*The job isn't exciting all the time, but it has its moments.* 這工作並不總是很帶勁，但也有讓人興奮的時候。**the ˌmoment of ˈtruth** a time when sb/sth is tested, or when important decisions are made 考驗的時刻；（決策的）關鍵時刻 **the moment (that)** ... as soon as ... 一…就…：*I want to see him the moment he arrives.* 希望他一到我就見到他。**ˌnot for a/one ˈmoment** certainly not; not at all 當然不；一點也不：*I don't think for a moment that she'll accept but you can ask her.* 我覺得她一定不會接受的，不過你可以去問問她。**of ˈmoment** very important 非常重要：*matters of great moment* 極其重要的事 **of the ˈmoment** (of a person, a job, an issue, etc. 人、工作、議題等) famous, important and talked about a lot now 紅極一時；盛行一時；廣為談論：*She's the fashion designer of the moment.* 她是當前最紅的時裝設計師。➲ more at EVIL, JUST *adv.*, LAST *det.*, NOTICE *n.*, PSYCHOLOGICAL, SPUR *n.*, WAIT *v.*

mo·ment·ar·ily /ˈməʊməntrəli; *NAmE* ˌmoʊmənˈterəli/ *adv.* **1** for a very short time 短促地；片刻地 SYN **briefly**：*He paused momentarily.* 他稍作停頓。**2** (*NAmE*) very soon; in a moment 立即；馬上：*I'll be with you momentarily.* 我馬上就到你這兒來。

mo·ment·ary /ˈməʊməntri; *NAmE* ˈmoʊmənteri/ *adj.* lasting for a very short time 短促的；短暫的；片刻的 SYN **brief**：*a momentary lapse of concentration* 走神兒 ◇ *momentary confusion* 一時糊塗

mo·men·tous /məˈmentəs; *NAmE* moʊˈm-/ *adj.* very important or serious, especially because there may be important results 關鍵的；重要的；重大的 SYN **historic**：*a momentous decision/event/occasion* 重大決定／事件；重要時刻

mo·men·tum /məˈmentəm; *NAmE* moʊˈm-/ *noun* [U] **1** the ability to keep increasing or developing 推進力；動力；勢頭：*The fight for his release **gathers momentum** each day.* 爭取使他獲釋的鬥爭聲勢日益加強。◇ *They began to **lose momentum** in the second half of the game.* 在比賽的下半場，他們的勢頭就逐漸減弱。**2** a force that is gained by movement 衝力：*The vehicle **gained momentum** as the road dipped.* 那輛車順着坡越跑衝力越大。**3** (*technical* 術語) the quantity of movement of

M

a moving object, measured as its mass multiplied by its speed 動量

momma /ˈmɒmə; NAmE ˈmɑːmə/ *noun* (*NAmE, informal*) = MOMMY

mommy /ˈmɒmi; NAmE ˈmɑːmi/ *noun* (*pl.* **-ies**) (also **momma**) (both *NAmE*) (*BrE* **mummy**) (*informal*) a child's word for a mother（兒語）媽咪

mom·para /mɒmˈpʌrə; NAmE mɑːm-/ (also **mam·para**) *noun* (*SAfrE*) an insulting name for a person that you think is stupid（含侮慢意）傻瓜，蠢貨

mon- ➲ MONO-

monad /ˈmɒnæd; ˈməʊn-; NAmE ˈmɑːn-; ˈmoʊn-/ *noun* (*philosophy* 哲) a single simple thing that cannot be divided, for example an atom or a person 單子（不可分割的實體）

mon·arch /ˈmɒnək; NAmE ˈmɑːnərk; -ɑːrk/ *noun* a person who rules a country, for example a king or a queen 君主；帝王

mo·nar·chic·al /məˈnɑːkɪkl; NAmE -ˈnɑːrk-/ *adj.* [usually before noun] (*formal*) connected with a ruler such as a king or a queen or with the system of government by a king or queen 君主的；帝王的；君主制的

mon·arch·ist /ˈmɒnəkɪst; NAmE ˈmɑːnərk-/ *noun* a person who believes that a country should be ruled by a king or queen 擁護君主制度者；君主主義者 ▶ **mon·arch·ist** *adj.*

mon·archy /ˈmɒnəki; NAmE ˈmɑːnərki/ *noun* (*pl.* **-ies**) **1 the monarchy** [sing.] a system of government by a king or a queen 君主制；君主政體：*plans to abolish the monarchy* 廢除君主政體的計劃 ➲ COLLOCATIONS at POLITICS **2** [C] a country that is ruled by a king or a queen 君主國：*There are several constitutional monarchies in Europe.* 歐洲有若干個君主立憲國。➲ compare REPUBLIC **3 the monarchy** [sing.] the king or queen of a country and their family 君主及其家庭成員

M

mon·as·tery /ˈmɒnəstri; NAmE ˈmɑːnəsteri/ *noun* (*pl.* **-ies**) a building in which MONKS (= members of a male religious community) live together 隱修院；修道院；寺院 ➲ COLLOCATIONS at RELIGION

mo·nas·tic /məˈnæstɪk/ *adj.* **1** connected with MONKS or monasteries 僧侶的；隱修院的；修道院的 **2** (of a way of life 生活方式) simple and quiet and possibly CELIBATE 寧靜簡樸的；清修的；禁慾的 SYN **ascetic**

mo·nas·ti·cism /məˈnæstɪsɪzəm/ *noun* [U] the way of life of MONKS in MONASTERIES 僧侶生活；隱修院生活；修道院生活

Mon·day 0‑ /ˈmʌndeɪ; -di/ *noun* [C, U] (*abbr.* **Mon.**) the day of the week after Sunday and before Tuesday, the first day of the working week 星期一：*It's Monday today, isn't it?* 今天是星期一，對吧？◇ *She started work* ***last Monday***. 她上個星期一開始工作。◇ *Are you busy* ***next Monday***? 下週一你忙嗎？◇ ***Monday morning/afternoon/evening*** 星期一上午／下午／晚上 ◇ *We'll discuss this at Monday's meeting.* 我們將在星期一的會上討論這件事。◇ *Do we still have Monday's paper?* 我們還有週一的報紙嗎？◇ *I work Monday to Friday.* 我星期一到星期五上班。◇ *I work Mondays to Fridays.* 我每週星期一到星期五工作。◇ ***On Monday(s)*** (= Every Monday) *I do yoga.* 我每個星期一做瑜伽。◇ *I always do yoga* ***on a Monday***. 我總是在星期一做瑜伽。◇ *He was born on a Monday.* 他出生的那天是星期一。◇ *I went to Paris on Thursday, and came back the following Monday.* 我星期四去了巴黎，第二週的星期一就回來了。◇ *We'll meet* ***on Monday***. 我們星期一見。◇ (*BrE*) *'When did the accident happen?' 'It was the Monday* (= the Monday of the week we are talking about).' "事故是什麼時候發生的？" "就在那個星期一。" ◇ (*BrE*) *Come back Monday week* (= a week after next Monday). 下下星期一回來。◇ (*informal or NAmE*) *We'll meet Monday.* 咱們星期一見。 ORIGIN From the Old English for 'day of the moon', translated from Latin *lunae dies*. 源自古英語，原意為 day of the moon（月亮日），古英語則譯自拉丁文 lunae dies。

Monday morning ˈquarterback *noun* (*NAmE, informal, disapproving*) a person who criticizes or comments on an event after it has happened "星期一早上的四分衛"；事後指手畫腳的人 ORIGIN The quarterback directs the play in an American football match and matches are usually played at the weekend. 源自美式橄欖球，四分衛指揮比賽，而比賽往往在週末舉行。

mon·et·ar·ism /ˈmʌnɪtərɪzəm/ *noun* [U] the policy of controlling the amount of money available in a country as a way of keeping the economy strong 貨幣主義（控制貨幣量以調控經濟）

mon·et·ar·ist /ˈmʌnɪtərɪst/ *noun* a person who supports monetarism 貨幣主義者 ▶ **mon·et·ar·ist** *adj.*：*a monetarist economic policy* 貨幣主義經濟政策

mon·et·ary /ˈmʌnɪtri; NAmE -teri/ *adj.* [only before noun] connected with money, especially all the money in a country 貨幣的，錢的（尤指一國的金融）：***monetary policy/growth*** 貨幣政策／增長 ◇ *an item of little monetary value* 不怎麼值錢的東西 ◇ *closer European political, monetary and economic union* 更為密切的歐洲政治、貨幣及經濟聯盟 ➲ SYNONYMS at ECONOMIC

money 錢

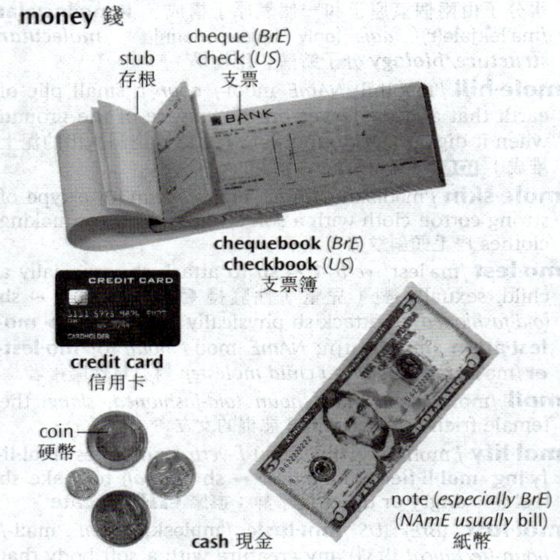

money 0‑ /ˈmʌni/ *noun*

1 0‑ [U] what you earn by working or selling things, and use to buy things 錢；薪水；收入：*to* ***borrow/save/spend/earn money*** 借錢；存錢；花錢；掙錢 ◇ *How much money is there in my account?* 我的賬上還有多少錢？◇ *The money is much better in my new job.* 我的新工作薪水高多了。◇ *If the item is not satisfactory, you will get your money back.* 東西不滿意，可以退款。◇ *We'll need to raise more money* (= collect or borrow it) *next year.* 明年我們需要籌集更多的錢。◇ *Can you lend me some money until tomorrow?* 能借我點兒錢嗎？明天就還。◇ *Be careful with that—it* ***cost a lot of money***. 小心別弄壞那東西，花了很多錢買的。➲ COLLOCATIONS at FINANCE **2** 0‑ [U] coins or paper notes 錢幣；鈔票：*I counted the money carefully.* 我仔細點了這筆錢。◇ *Where can I change my money into dollars?* 什麼地方能把我的錢兑換成美元？➲ see also FUNNY MONEY, PAPER MONEY, READY MONEY **3** 0‑ [U] a person's wealth including their property 財產；財富：*He lost all his money.* 他失去了全部財產。◇ *The family made their money in the 18th century.* 這個家族在 18 世紀創下了家業。**4 moneys** or **monies** [pl.] (*law* 律 or *old use*) sums of money 款項：*a statement of all monies paid into your account* 存入你的賬戶的所有金額的清單 HELP You will find other compounds ending in **money** at their place in the alphabet. 其他以 money 結尾的複合詞可在各字母中的適當位置查到。

IDM ▶ **be in the ˈmoney** (*informal*) to have a lot of money to spend 有錢 **for ˈmy money** (*informal*) in my opinion 依我看；我覺得：*For my money, he's one of the greatest* *comedians of all time.* 依我看，歷來的喜劇演員，他是數一數二的。 **get your 'money's worth** to get enough value or enjoyment out of sth, considering the amount of money, time, etc. that you are spending on it（錢或時間等）值得花 **good 'money** a lot of money; money that you earn with hard work 大筆的錢；辛苦掙來的錢： *Thousands of people paid good money to watch the band perform.* 成千上萬的人花很多錢去觀看這支樂隊的演出。◇ *Don't waste good money on that!* 別把辛苦掙來的錢浪費在那上頭！ **have money to 'burn** to have so much money that you do not have to be careful with it 錢多得花不完；有用不完的錢 **'made of money** (*informal*) very rich 極其富有 **make 'money** ⊶ to earn a lot of money; to make a profit 賺錢；獲利： *The movie should make money.* 這部電影應該賺大錢。◇ *There's money to be made from tourism.* 旅遊業非常有利可圖。 **make/lose money ˌhand over 'fist** to make/lose money very fast and in large quantities 賺大錢；破大財 **money for 'jam/old 'rope** (*BrE, informal*) money that is earned very easily, for sth that needs little effort 容易賺的錢財 **money is no 'object** money is not sth that needs to be considered, because there is plenty of it available 錢不成問題： *She travels around the world as if money is no object.* 她周遊世界，不把錢當一回事。 **money 'talks** (*saying*) people who have a lot of money have more power and influence than others 財大氣就粗；有錢就有勢 **on the 'money** correct; accurate 正確的；準確的： *His prediction was* ***right on the money.*** 他的預測準確無誤。 **put 'money into sth** to invest money in a business or a particular project 投資於： *We would welcome interest from anyone prepared to put money into the club.* 任何人有意向俱樂部投資，我們都歡迎。 **put your 'money on sb/sth** **1** to bet that a particular horse, dog, etc. will win a race 在（馬、狗等）上下賭注 **2** to feel very sure that sth is true or that sb will succeed 確信： *He'll be there tonight. I'd put money on it.* 我十分肯定他今晚會在那兒。 **put your money where your 'mouth is** (*informal*) to support what you say by doing sth practical; to show by your actions that you really mean sth 用行動證明自己的話 **throw your 'money about/around** (*informal*) to spend money in a careless and obvious way 肆意揮霍；大手大腳 **throw good money after 'bad** (*disapproving*) to spend more money on sth, when you have wasted a lot on it already 繼續花錢打水漂 **throw 'money at sth** (*disapproving*) to try to deal with a problem or improve a situation by spending money on it, when it would be better to deal with it in other ways 白（往某事上）扔錢： *It is inappropriate simply to throw money at these problems.* 只是用錢去處理這些問題是不適當的。 ➲ more at BEST *n.*, CAREFUL, COIN *v.*, COLOUR *n.*, EASY *adj.*, FOOL *n.*, GROW, LICENCE *n.*, LOVE *n.*, MARRY, OBJECT *n.*, PAY *v.*, POT *n.*, ROLL *v.*, RUN *n.*, TIME *n.*

ˌmoney-back guaran'tee *noun* an official promise by a shop/store, etc. to return the money you have paid for sth if it is not of an acceptable standard（商店對不合格商品的）退款保證

money·bags /'mʌnibæɡz/ *noun* (*pl.* **money·bags**) (*informal, humorous*) a very rich person 闊佬；大款

'money box *noun* (*especially BrE*) a small closed box with a narrow opening and sometimes with a lock and key, into which children put coins as a way of saving money 存錢罐；存錢盒 ➲ compare PIGGY BANK

mon·eyed (also **mon·ied**) /'mʌnid/ *adj.* [only before noun] (*formal*) having a lot of money 極有錢的；富有的 **SYN** **rich** : *the moneyed classes* 富有階層

'money-grubbing (also **'money-grabbing**) *adj.* [only before noun] (*informal, disapproving*) trying to get a lot of money 聚斂錢財的；試圖掙大錢的 ▸ **'money-grubber** (also **'money-grabber**) *noun*

money·lend·er /'mʌnilendə(r)/ *noun* (*old-fashioned*) a person whose business is lending money, usually at a very high rate of interest 放債者；放高利貸者

money·maker /'mʌnimeɪkə(r)/ *noun* a product, business, etc. that produces a large profit 賺大錢的產品（或企業等）▸ **money·mak·ing** *adj.*：*a moneymaking movie* 贏利頗豐的電影 **money·mak·ing** *noun* [U]

Synonyms 同義詞辨析

money

cash • change

These are all words for money in the form of coins or paper notes. 以上各詞均表示金錢，包括硬幣和鈔票。

money money in the form of coins or paper notes 指金錢，包括錢幣和鈔票： *I counted the money carefully.* 我仔細點了這筆錢。◇ *Where can I change my money into dollars?* 什麼地方能把我的錢兌換成美元？◇ ***paper money*** (= money that is made of paper, not coins) 紙幣

cash money in the form of coins or paper notes 指現金： *How much cash do you have on you?* 你身上帶着多少現金？◇ *Payments can be made by cheque or* ***in cash.*** 支票或現金付款均可。

MONEY OR CASH? 用 money 還是 cash？

If it is important to contrast money in the form of coins and notes and money in other forms, use **cash**. 強調現金而非其他形式的貨幣時用 cash： *How much money/cash do you have on you?* 你身上帶着多少現金？
◇ ~~*Payments can be made by cheque or in money.*~~
◇ ~~*Customers are offered a discount if they pay money.*~~

change the money that you get back when you have paid for sth giving more money than the amount it costs; coins rather than paper money 指找給的零錢、硬幣： *The ticket machine doesn't give change.* 自動售票機不找零。◇ *I don't have any* ***small change*** (= coins of low value). 我沒有零錢。

PATTERNS

- to **draw out/get out/take out/withdraw** money/cash
- **ready** money/cash (= money that you have available to spend immediately)

'money market *noun* the banks and other institutions that lend or borrow money, and buy and sell foreign money 貨幣市場；金融市場

'money order (*especially NAmE*) (*BrE* also **'postal order**) *noun* an official document that you can buy at a bank or a post office and send to sb so that they can exchange it for money（銀行或郵政）匯票

'money-saving *adj.* [only before noun] that helps you spend less money 省錢的；便宜的；廉價的： ***money-saving offers/tips*** 省錢的優惠價格／竅門

'money-spinner *noun* (*BrE, informal*) something that earns a lot of money 賺大錢的東西；搖錢樹

'money supply *noun* [sing., U] (*economics* 經) the total amount of money that exists in the economy of a country at a particular time 貨幣供應量

mon·gol /'mɒŋɡəl; *NAmE* 'mɑːŋ-/ (*NAmE* usually **mongoloid** /'mɒŋɡəlɔɪd; *NAmE* 'mɑːŋ-/) *noun* (*old-fashioned*) an offensive word for a person with Down's SYNDROME 患唐氏綜合症的人；蒙古症患者 ▸ **mon·gol·ism** *noun* [U]

mon·goose /'mɒŋɡuːs; *NAmE* 'mɑːŋ-/ *noun* (*pl.* **mon·gooses** /-sɪz/) a small tropical animal with fur, that kills snakes, RATS, etc. 獴，貓鼬（居於熱帶地區，捕食蛇、鼠等）

mon·grel /'mʌŋɡrəl/ (*especially BrE*) (also **mutt** especially in *NAmE*) *noun* a dog that is a mixture of different breeds 雜種狗

mon·ied = MONEYED

moni·ker /'mɒnɪkə(r); *NAmE* 'mɑːn-/ *noun* (*humorous*) a name 姓名；名

mon·ism /'mɒnɪzəm; 'məʊn-; *NAmE* 'mɑːn-; 'moʊn-/ *noun* (*religion* 宗) the belief that there is only one god 一神論

M

moni·tor 🔑 **AW** /ˈmɒnɪtə(r); *NAmE* ˈmɑːn-/ *noun, verb*

■ ***noun*** **1** 🔑 a television screen used to show particular kinds of information; a screen that shows information from a computer 顯示屏；監視器；（計算機）顯示器：*The details of today's flights are displayed on the monitor.* 今天航班的詳細資料都顯示在屏幕上。◇ *a PC with a 17-inch colour monitor* 帶 17 英寸彩色顯示器的個人電腦 ➲ VISUAL VOCAB page V66 ➲ see also VDU **2** a piece of equipment used to check or record sth 監控器；監測器：*a heart monitor* 心臟監測器 **3** a student in a school who performs special duties, such as helping the teacher 班長；級長；班代表 **4** a person whose job is to check that sth is done fairly and honestly, especially in a foreign country（尤指派往國外的）監督員，核查員：*UN monitors declared the referendum fair.* 聯合國核查員宣佈這次全民投票是公正的。 **5** a large tropical LIZARD (= a type of REPTILE) 巨蜥

■ ***verb*** **1** 🔑 **~ sth | ~ what, how, etc. …** to watch and check sth over a period of time in order to see how it develops, so that you can make any necessary changes 監視；檢查；跟蹤調查 **SYN** **track**：*Each student's progress is closely monitored.* 每一位同學的學習情況都受到密切的關注。 **2 ~ sth** to listen to telephone calls, foreign radio broadcasts, etc. in order to find out information that might be useful 監聽（電話、外國無線電廣播等）

monk /mʌŋk/ *noun* a member of a religious group of men who often live apart from other people in a MONASTERY and who do not marry or have personal possessions 僧侶；修道士：***Benedictine/Buddhist monks*** 本篤會修士；佛教僧侶 ➲ compare FRIAR, NUN ➲ see also MONKISH

mon·key /ˈmʌŋki/ *noun* **1** an animal with a long tail, that climbs trees and lives in hot countries. There are several types of monkey and they are related to APES and humans. 猴子 **2** (*informal*) a child who is active and likes playing tricks on people 頑皮的孩子；調皮鬼；搗蛋鬼：*Come here, you cheeky little monkey!* 過來，你這沒有教養的小搗蛋鬼！ **3** (*BrE, slang*) £500 * 500 英鎊

IDM **I don't/couldn't give a ˈmonkey's** (*BrE, slang*) used to say, in a way that is not very polite, that you do not care about sth, or are not at all interested in it 我根本無所謂；我壓根兒就不在乎 **make a ˈmonkey (out) of sb** to make sb seem stupid 捉弄；愚弄 ➲ more at BRASS

ˈmonkey business *noun* [U] (*informal*) dishonest or silly behaviour 欺騙；胡鬧；惡作劇

ˈmonkey chanting *noun* [U] (*BrE*) abuse of a black player by white people who are watching a contest, especially a football (SOCCER) game 猴舞般的哄罵（白人看比賽時對黑人運動員的咒罵，尤指足球比賽時）

ˌmonkey in the ˈmiddle (*NAmE*) (*BrE* **ˌpiggy in the ˈmiddle, ˌpig in the ˈmiddle**) *noun* **1** a children's game where two people throw a ball to each other over the head of another person who tries to catch it 過頂傳球（兒童遊戲，由兩人拋傳球，中間一人爭搶） **2** a person who is caught between two people or groups who are fighting or arguing （被夾在中間而）左右為難的人

ˈmonkey nut *noun* (*BrE*) a PEANUT with its shell still on 落花生

ˈmonkey puzzle (also **ˈmonkey puzzle tree**) *noun* a CONIFER tree with leaves like scales, that are thin, tough and very sharp 猴謎樹；智利南洋杉

ˌmonkey's ˈwedding *noun* (*SAfrE*) used to describe a period of time when it is raining while the sun is shining 晴雨天；太陽雨：*Look! It's a monkey's wedding!* 看！出着太陽還下雨！

ˈmonkey wrench (*BrE* also **ˌadjustable ˈspanner**) *noun* a tool that can be adjusted to hold and turn things of different widths 活動扳手 ➲ VISUAL VOCAB page V20 ➲ compare SPANNER, WRENCH

IDM **throw a ˈmonkey wrench in/into sth** (also **throw a ˈwrench in/into sth**) (*NAmE, informal*) to do sth to spoil sb's plans 破壞，阻撓（計劃）

monk·ish /ˈmʌŋkɪʃ/ *adj.* like a MONK; connected with MONKS 修士（般）的；僧侶（般）的

mono /ˈmɒnəʊ; *NAmE* ˈmɑːnoʊ/ *adj., noun*

■ ***adj.*** (also **mono·phon·ic**) (*music* 音) recording or producing sound which comes from only one direction 單聲道的：*a mono recording* 單聲道錄音 ➲ compare STEREO

■ ***noun*** [U] **1** a system of recording or producing sound which comes from only one direction 單聲道錄音（或放音）系統：*recorded in mono* 用單聲道錄音系統錄製的 ➲ compare STEREO **2** (*NAmE, informal*) = MONONUCLEOSIS

mono- /ˈmɒnəʊ; *NAmE* ˈmɑːnoʊ/ (also **mon-**) *combining form* (in nouns and adjectives 構成名詞和形容詞) one; single 單；單一：*monorail* 單軌鐵路 ◇ *monogamy* 一夫一妻制

mono·chrome /ˈmɒnəkrəʊm; *NAmE* ˈmɑːnəkroʊm/ *adj.* **1** (of photographs, etc. 照片等) using only black, white and shades of grey 黑白的：***monochrome illustrations/images*** 黑白插圖 / 肖像 ◇ (*figurative*) *a dull monochrome life* 枯燥單調的生活 **2** using different shades of one colour 單色的 ▸ **mono·chro·mat·ic** /ˌmɒnəkrəˈmætɪk; *NAmE* ˌmɑːnəkroʊˈm-/ *adj.*：*a monochromatic colour scheme* 單一色彩的調配 **mono·chrome** *noun* [U]：*an artist who works in monochrome* 從事單色繪畫的藝術家

mon·ocle /ˈmɒnəkl; *NAmE* ˈmɑːn-/ *noun* a single glass LENS for one eye, held in place by the muscles around the eye and used by people in the past to help them see clearly 單片眼鏡

mono·coty·ledon /ˌmɒnəʊˌkɒtɪˈliːdn; *NAmE* ˌmɑːnoʊˌkɑːt-/ (also **mono·cot** /ˈmɒnəkɒt; *NAmE* ˈmɑːnəkɑːt/) *noun* (*biology* 生) a plant whose seeds form EMBRYOS that produce a single leaf 單子葉植物 ➲ compare DICOTYLEDON

mono·cul·ture /ˈmɒnəkʌltʃə(r); *NAmE* ˈmɑːn-/ *noun* **1** [U] the practice of growing only one type of crop on a certain area of land 單作；單種栽培 **2** [C, U] a society consisting of people who are all the same race, all share the same beliefs, etc. 單一文化社會；單種族社會；一元化社會：*a global economic monoculture* 全球經濟一元化社會

mono·cycle /ˈmɒnəsaɪkl; *NAmE* ˈmɑːn-/ *noun* = UNICYCLE

mono·cyte /ˈmɒnəsaɪt; *NAmE* ˈmɑːn-/ *noun* (*biology* 生) a type of large white blood cell with a simple round NUCLEUS that can remove harmful substances from the body 單核細胞，單核白血球（能清除對肌體有害物質的大型白細胞）

mon·og·amy /məˈnɒɡəmi; *NAmE* məˈnɑːɡ-/ *noun* [U] **1** the fact or custom of being married to only one person at a particular time 一夫一妻（制）➲ compare BIGAMY, POLYGAMY **2** the practice or custom of having a sexual relationship with only one partner at a particular time 單配偶；單配性 ▸ **mon·og·am·ous** /məˈnɒɡəməs; *NAmE* məˈnɑːɡ-/ *adj.*：*a monogamous marriage* 一夫一妻制的婚姻 ◇ *Most birds are monogamous.* 大多數飛禽都是單配性的。

mono·glot /ˈmɒnəɡlɒt; *NAmE* ˈmɑːnəɡlɑːt/ *noun* (*technical* 術語) a person who speaks only one language 只說一種語言的人 ➲ compare POLYGLOT

mono·gram /ˈmɒnəɡræm; *NAmE* ˈmɑːn-/ *noun* two or more letters, usually the first letters of sb's names, that are combined in a design and marked on items of clothing, etc. that they own 字母組合圖案，交織字母，畫押字（常由姓名首字母組成，標在自己的衣服等物品上）▸ **mono·grammed** *adj.*：*a monogrammed handkerchief* 有字母組合圖案的手絹

mono·graph /ˈmɒnəɡrɑːf; *NAmE* ˈmɑːnəɡræf/ *noun* (*technical* 術語) a detailed written study of a single subject, usually in the form of a short book 專論；專題文章；專著

mono·lin·gual /ˌmɒnəˈlɪŋɡwəl; *NAmE* ˌmɑːnə-/ *adj.* speaking or using only one language 單語的；只用一種

M

語言的：*a monolingual dictionary* 單語詞典 ➲ compare BILINGUAL, MULTILINGUAL

mono·lith /ˈmɒnəlɪθ; *NAmE* ˈmɑːn-/ *noun* **1** a large single vertical block of stone, especially one that was shaped into a column by people living in ancient times, and that may have had some religious meaning（尤指古人鑿成、表示某種宗教意義的）單塊巨石，獨石柱 **2** (often *disapproving*) a single, very large organization, etc. that is very slow to change and not interested in individual people（少有變化，不關心個人的）單一龐大的組織 ▸ **mono·lith·ic** /ˌmɒnəˈlɪθɪk; *NAmE* ˌmɑːnə-/ *adj.*：*a monolithic block* 巨大的石塊 ◇ *the monolithic structure of the state* 統一龐大的國家結構

mono·logue (*NAmE* also **mono·log**) /ˈmɒnəlɒɡ; *NAmE* ˈmɑːnəlɔːɡ; -lɑːɡ/ *noun* **1** [C] a long speech by one person during a conversation that stops other people from speaking or expressing an opinion 滔滔不絕的講話；個人的長篇大論：*He went into a long monologue about life in America.* 他開始滔滔不絕地談起美國的生活。 **2** [U, C] a long speech in a play, film/movie, etc. spoken by one actor, especially when alone（戲劇、電影等的）獨白 **3** [C, U] a dramatic story, especially in VERSE, told or performed by one person 獨角戲：*a dramatic monologue* 戲劇獨白 ➲ compare DIALOGUE, SOLILOQUY

mono·mania /ˌmɒnəˈmeɪniə; *NAmE* ˈmɑːn-/ *noun* [U] (*psychology* 心) too much interest in or enthusiasm for just one thing so that it is not healthy 單狂（非理性的固執）

mono·nucle·osis /ˌmɒnəʊˌnjuːkliˈəʊsɪs; *NAmE* ˌmɑːnoʊˌnuːkliˈoʊsɪs/ (*NAmE* or *BrE, medical* 醫) (*NAmE, informal* **mono**) (*BrE* ˌ**glandular** ˈ**fever**) *noun* [U] an infectious disease that causes swelling of the LYMPH GLANDS and makes the person feel very weak for a long time 傳染性單核細胞增多症；腺熱

mono·phon·ic /ˌmɒnəˈfɒnɪk; *NAmE* ˌmɑːnəˈfɑːnɪk/ *adj.* (*music* 音) = MONO

mono·plane /ˈmɒnəpleɪn; *NAmE* ˈmɑː-/ *noun* an early type of plane with one set of wings 單翼飛機 ➲ compare BIPLANE

mon·op·ol·ist /məˈnɒpəlɪst; *NAmE* məˈnɑːp-/ *noun* (*technical* 術語) a person or company that has a MONOPOLY 壟斷者；專賣者；專營者

mon·op·ol·is·tic /məˌnɒpəˈlɪstɪk; *NAmE* məˌnɑːpə-/ *adj.* (*formal*) controlling or trying to get complete control over sth, especially an industry or a company 壟斷的；控制的；獨佔的

mon·op·ol·ize (*BrE* also **-ise**) /məˈnɒpəlaɪz; *NAmE* məˈnɑːp-/ *verb* **1 ~ sth** to have or take control of the largest part of sth so that other people are prevented from sharing it 獨佔；壟斷；包辦：*Men traditionally monopolized jobs in the printing industry.* 在傳統上，男人包攬了印刷行業中的所有工作。◇ *As usual, she completely monopolized the conversation.* 她和往常一樣，壟斷了這次談話。 **2 ~ sb** to have or take a large part of sb's attention or time so that they are unable to speak to or deal with other people 佔去（某人的大部份注意力或時間）；獨佔；霸佔；使無法擺脫 ▸ **mon·op·ol·iza·tion**, **-isa·tion** /məˌnɒpəlaɪˈzeɪʃn; *NAmE* məˌnɑːpələˈz-/ *noun* [U]

mon·op·oly /məˈnɒpəli; *NAmE* məˈnɑːp-/ *noun* (*pl.* **-ies**) **1 ~ (in/of/on sth)** (*business* 商) the complete control of trade in particular goods or the supply of a particular service; a type of goods or a service that is controlled in this way 壟斷；專營服務；被壟斷的商品（或服務）：*In the past central government had a monopoly on television broadcasting.* 過去，中央政府對電視節目播放實行壟斷。◇ *Electricity, gas and water were considered to be natural monopolies.* 電、煤氣和水壟斷經營過去被認為是理所當然的。 ➲ compare DUOPOLY **2** [usually sing.] **~ in/of/on sth** the complete control, possession or use of sth; a thing that belongs only to one person or group and that other people cannot share 獨佔；專利；專利品：*Managers do not have a monopoly on stress.* 並不只是經營管理者有壓力。◇ *A good education should not be the monopoly of the rich.* 良好的教育不應該成為富人的專利。 **3 Monopoly™** a BOARD GAME in which players have to pretend to buy and sell land and houses, using pieces of paper that look like money 大富翁（棋類遊戲，遊戲者以玩具鈔票買賣房地產）

Moˈnopoly money *noun* [U] money that does not really exist or has no real value 假鈔票；無實際價值的錢：*Inflation was so high that the notes were like Monopoly money.* 通貨膨脹嚴重，貨幣變得跟大富翁遊戲鈔票無異。 **ORIGIN** From the toy money used in the board game *Monopoly*™. 源自"大富翁"遊戲中使用的遊戲幣。

mono·rail /ˈmɒnəʊreɪl; *NAmE* ˈmɑːnoʊ-/ *noun* **1** [U] a railway/railroad system in which trains travel along a track consisting of a single rail, usually one placed high above the ground 單軌鐵路（通常為高架） **2** [C] a train used in a monorail system 單軌列車

mono·so·dium glu·ta·mate /ˌmɒnəˌsəʊdiəm ˈɡluːtəmeɪt; *NAmE* ˌmɑːnəˌsoʊ-/ *noun* [U] (*abbr.* **MSG**) a chemical that is sometimes added to food to improve its flavour 穀氨酸單鈉鹽；味精；味素

mono·syl·lab·ic /ˌmɒnəsɪˈlæbɪk; *NAmE* ˌmɑːn-/ *adj.* **1** having only one syllable 單音節的：*a monosyllabic word* 單音節詞 **2** (of a person or their way of speaking 人或說話方式) saying very little, in a way that appears rude to other people 寡言少語的；說話少而無禮的

mono·syl·lable /ˈmɒnəsɪləbl; *NAmE* ˈmɑːn-/ *noun* a word with only one syllable, for example, 'it' or 'no' 單音節詞

mono·the·ism /ˈmɒnəʊθiɪzəm; *NAmE* ˈmɑːnoʊ-/ *noun* [U] the belief that there is only one God 一神教；一神論 ➲ compare POLYTHEISM ▸ **mono·the·ist** /ˈmɒnəʊθiɪst; *NAmE* ˈmɑːnoʊ-/ *noun* **mono·the·is·tic** /ˌmɒnəʊθiˈɪstɪk; *NAmE* ˌmɑːnoʊ-/ *adj.*

mono·tone /ˈmɒnətəʊn; *NAmE* ˈmɑːnətoʊn/ *noun, adj.*

■ ***noun*** [sing.] a dull sound or way of speaking in which the tone and volume remain the same and therefore seem boring 單調；單調的聲音：*He spoke in a flat monotone.* 他說話單調低沉。

■ ***adj.*** [only before noun] without any changes or differences in sound or colour（聲音或色彩）單調的：*He spoke in a monotone drawl.* 他用慢吞吞又單調的語氣說話。◇ *monotone engravings* 單調的版畫

mon·ot·on·ous /məˈnɒtənəs; *NAmE* məˈnɑːt-/ *adj.* never changing and therefore boring 單調乏味的 **SYN** **dull, repetitious**：***a monotonous voice/diet/routine*** 單調乏味的聲音／飲食／日常事務 ◇ *monotonous work* 單調乏味的工作 ◇ *New secretaries came and went with **monotonous regularity**.* 秘書不停地更換，令人厭煩。 ▸ **mon·ot·on·ous·ly** *adv.*

mon·ot·ony /məˈnɒtəni; *NAmE* məˈnɑːt-/ *noun* [U] boring lack of variety 單調乏味；千篇一律：*She watches television to relieve the monotony of everyday life.* 她天天靠看電視來解悶兒。

mono·treme /ˈmɒnətriːm; *NAmE* ˈmɑːn-/ *noun* (*technical* 術語) a class of animal including the ECHIDNA and the PLATYPUS, which lays eggs, but also gives milk to its babies 單孔目動物（卵生哺乳動物）

mono·un·sat·ur·ated fat /ˌmɒnəʊʌnˌsætʃəreɪtɪd ˈfæt; *NAmE* ˌmɑːnoʊ-/ *noun* [C, U] a type of fat found, for example, in OLIVES and nuts, which does not encourage the harmful development of CHOLESTEROL 單元不飽和脂肪（橄欖和堅果等中所含脂肪，不會促進膽固醇的有害增長） ➲ see also POLYUNSATURATED FAT, SATURATED FAT, TRANS-FATTY ACID, UNSATURATED FAT

mono·zyg·ot·ic twin /ˌmɒnəʊzaɪˈɡɒtɪk twɪn; *NAmE* ˌmɑːnoʊzaɪˈɡɑːtɪk/ (also **mono·zyg·ous twin** /ˌmɒnəʊˈzaɪɡəs twɪn; *NAmE* ˌmɑːnoʊ-/) *adj.* (*technical* 術語) = IDENTICAL TWIN ➲ compare DIZYGOTIC TWIN

the Mon·roe Doc·trine /mənˌrəʊ ˈdɒktrɪn; *NAmE* mənˌroʊ ˈdɑːk-/ *noun* a part of US foreign policy that states that the US will act to protect its own interests in N and S America 門羅主義（美國外交政策，表明會採取行動維護其在南、北美洲的利益） **ORIGIN** From the name of US President James Monroe, who first stated the policy in 1823. 源自美國總統詹姆斯•門羅的名字，他於 1823 年首次宣佈這一政策。

Mon·si·gnor /mɒnˈsiːnjə(r); *NAmE* mɑːn-/ *noun* (*abbr.* **Mgr**) used as a title when speaking to or about a priest of high rank in the Roman Catholic Church 蒙席（羅馬天主教會授予某些聖職人員的榮銜）

mon·soon /ˌmɒnˈsuːn; *NAmE* ˌmɑːn-/ *noun* **1** a period of heavy rain in summer in S Asia; the rain that falls during this period （南亞地區的）雨季，雨季的降雨 **2** a wind in S Asia that blows from the south-west in summer, bringing rain, and the north-east in winter 季風，季節風（盛行於南亞地區，夏季颳西南風，帶來雨水，冬季颳東北風）

mons pubis /ˌmɒnz ˈpjuːbɪs; *NAmE* ˌmɑːnz/ (also **mons Ven·eris** /ˌmɒnz ˈvenərɪs; *NAmE* ˌmɑːnz/) *noun* (*formal*) the curved area of fat over the joint of the PUBIC bones, especially in women （尤指女性的）陰阜

mon·ster /ˈmɒnstə(r); *NAmE* ˈmɑːn-/ *noun, adj.*
■ *noun* **1** (in stories) an imaginary creature that is very large, ugly and frightening （傳說中的）怪物，怪獸：*a monster with three heads* 三頭怪獸 ◇ *prehistoric monsters* 史前怪物 **2** an animal or a thing that is very large or ugly 龐然大物；龐大的醜怪物；醜惡的東西：*Their dog's an absolute monster!* 他們那條狗好大喲！ **3** a person who is very cruel and evil 惡棍；惡魔 **4** (*humorous*) a child who behaves badly 小惡魔；小壞蛋
■ *adj.* [only before noun] (*informal*) unusually large 巨大的；龐大的 SYN **giant**：*monster mushrooms* 巨大的蘑菇

ˌmonster ˈtruck *noun* an extremely large PICKUP TRUCK with very large wheels, often used for racing 大腳車（輪子巨大的大卡車，常用於賽車）

mon·stros·ity /mɒnˈstrɒsəti; *NAmE* mɑːnˈstrɑːs-/ *noun* (*pl.* **-ies**) something that is very large and very ugly, especially a building 巨大而醜陋之物（尤指建築） SYN **eyesore**：*a concrete monstrosity* 混凝土建成的龐大怪物

mon·strous /ˈmɒnstrəs; *NAmE* ˈmɑːn-/ *adj.* **1** considered to be shocking and unacceptable because it is morally wrong or unfair 醜惡的；道德敗壞的；駭人的 SYN **outrageous**：*a* ***monstrous lie/injustice*** 彌天大謊；駭人聽聞的不公 **2** very large 巨大的 SYN **gigantic**：*a monstrous wave* 巨浪 **3** very large, ugly and frightening 巨大的；醜陋的；駭人的 SYN **horrifying**：*a* ***monstrous figure/creature*** 巨大的人影；駭人的動物 ▸ **mon·strous·ly** *adv.*：*monstrously unfair* 極不公正 ◇ *a monstrously fat man* 胖得嚇人的男子

mont·age /ˌmɒnˈtɑːʒ; ˈmɒn-; *NAmE* ˌmɑːnˈtɑːʒ/ *noun* **1** [C] a picture, film/movie or piece of music or writing that consists of many separate items put together, especially in an interesting or unusual combination 蒙太奇；剪輯組合物：*a photographic montage* 攝影的剪輯組合作品 **2** [U] the process of making a montage 剪輯；蒙太奇手法

mon·tane /ˈmɒnteɪn; *NAmE* ˈmɑːn-/ *adj.* [only before noun] (*technical* 術語) connected with mountains 山上的；山的

Mon·terey Jack /ˌmɒntəreɪ ˈdʒæk; *NAmE* ˌmɑːn-/ (*NAmE* also **ˈJack cheese**) *noun* [U] a type of white American cheese with a mild flavour 蒙特里傑克乾酪

month 0‑m /mʌnθ/ *noun*
1 0‑m [C] any of the twelve periods of time into which the year is divided, for example May or June 月；月份：*the month of August* 八月份 ◇ *We're moving house* ***next month***. 我們下個月搬家。◇ *She earns* ***$1 000 a month***. 她每月賺 1 000 元。◇ *The rent is* ***£300 per month***. 租金是每月 300 英鎊。◇ *Have you read this month's 'Physics World'?* 你看過這個月的《物理世界》嗎？◇ *Prices continue to rise* ***month after month*** (= over a period of several months). 近幾個月價格持續上升。◇ *Her anxiety mounted* ***month by month*** (= as each month passed). 她的焦慮之情逐月加重。➲ see also CALENDAR MONTH **2** 0‑m [C] a period of about 30 days, for example, 3 June to 3 July 約 30 天的時間；一個月的時間：*The baby is three months old.* 這嬰兒三個月大了。◇ *a three-month-old baby* 三個月大的嬰兒 ◇ *They lived in Toronto during their first few months of marriage.* 他們婚後的頭幾個月住在多倫多。◇ *several months later* 幾個月以後 ◇ *a six-month contract* 一份六個月的合約 ◇ *a month-long strike* 長達一個月的罷工 ◇ *He visits Paris once or twice a month.* 他一個月去一兩次巴黎。➲ see also LUNAR MONTH **3** 0‑m **months** [pl.] a long time, especially a period of several months 數月；很長時間：*He had to wait for months for the visas to come through.* 他不得不等好幾個月才領到簽證。◇ *It will be months before we get the results.* 我們要等很長時間才能得到結果。
IDM **in a ˌmonth of ˈSundays** (*informal*) used to emphasize that sth will never happen 遙遙無期；根本不會發生：*You won't find it, not in a month of Sundays.* 你找不到它的，根本不可能找到。➲ more at FLAVOUR *n.*

month·ly /ˈmʌnθli/ *adj., adv., noun*
■ *adj.* **1** happening once a month or every month 每月的；每月一次的：*a* ***monthly meeting/visit/magazine*** 每月一次的會議／拜訪；月刊 **2** paid, valid or calculated for one month 按月結算的；有效期為一個月的：*a monthly salary of £1 000* * 1 000 英鎊的月薪 ◇ *a monthly season ticket* 月票 ◇ *Summers are hot, with monthly averages above 22°C.* 夏天很熱，月平均溫度在 22 攝氏度以上。
■ *adv.* every month or once a month 每個月；每月一次：*She gets paid monthly.* 她按月領薪水。
■ *noun* (*pl.* **-ies**) a magazine published once a month 月刊：*the fashion monthlies* 時裝月刊

monty /ˈmɒnti; *NAmE* ˈmɑːnti/ *noun*
IDM **the ˌfull ˈmonty** the full amount that people expect or want 所期望的一切；全部：*They'll do the full monty* (= take off all their clothes) *if you pay them enough.* 如果你給足夠的錢，她們會把所有的衣服脫光。

monu·ment /ˈmɒnjumənt; *NAmE* ˈmɑːn-/ *noun* **1 ~ (to sb/sth)** a building, column, statue, etc. built to remind people of a famous person or event 紀念碑（或館、堂、像等）：*A monument to him was erected in St Paul's Cathedral.* 在聖保羅大教堂為他修了一座紀念碑。**2** a building that has special historical importance 歷史遺跡；有歷史價值的建築：*an ancient monument* 古跡 **3 ~ to sth** a thing that remains as a good example of sb's qualities or of what they did 典範；典型：*These recordings are a monument to his talent as a pianist.* 這些錄音是展現他鋼琴家才華的不朽之作。

monu·men·tal /ˌmɒnjuˈmentl; *NAmE* ˌmɑːn-/ *adj.* **1** [usually before noun] very important and having a great influence, especially as the result of years of work 重要的；意義深遠的；不朽的 SYN **historic**：*Gibbon's monumental work 'The Decline and Fall of the Roman Empire'* 吉本的不朽著作《羅馬帝國衰亡史》**2** [only before noun] very large, good, bad, stupid, etc. 非常大（或好、壞、蠢等）的 SYN **major**：*a book of monumental significance* 一本意義非凡的書 ◇ *We have a monumental task ahead of us.* 極其繁重的工作在等着我們。◇ *It seems like an act of monumental folly.* 這似乎是一種非常愚蠢的行為。**3** [only before noun] appearing in or serving as a monument 作為紀念碑的；紀念碑上的：*a* ***monumental inscription/tomb*** 碑文；陵墓 ◇ *a* ***monumental mason*** (= a person who makes monuments) 紀念碑石工

monu·men·tal·ly /ˌmɒnjuˈmentəli; *NAmE* ˌmɑːn-/ *adv.* (used to describe negative qualities) extremely （用於表述負面性質）極端地，極度地：***monumentally difficult/stupid*** 極其困難／愚蠢

moo /muː/ *noun* (*pl.* **moos**) the long deep sound made by a cow （牛叫聲）哞 ▸ **moo** *verb* [I]

mooch /muːtʃ/ *verb* (*informal*) **1** [I] **+ adv./prep.** (*BrE*) to walk slowly with no particular purpose; to be somewhere not doing very much 遛達；閒逛 SYN **potter**：*He's happy to mooch around the house all day.* 他就願意在家裏閒待着。**2** [I, T] **~ (sth) (off sb)** (*NAmE*) to get money, food, etc. from sb else instead of paying for it yourself 白吃（或用等）；要別人白給（金錢、食物等） SYN **cadge**：*He's always mooching off his friends.* 他總是向朋友討錢花。

mood 0‑m /muːd/ *noun*
1 0‑m [C] the way you are feeling at a particular time 情緒；心情：*She's* ***in a good mood*** *today* (= happy and friendly). 她今天心情很好。◇ *He's always* ***in a bad mood*** (= unhappy, or angry and impatient). 他總是情緒不好。◇ *to be in a* ***foul/filthy mood*** 情緒很差 ◇ *Some addicts*

suffer violent ***mood swings*** (= changes of mood) *if deprived of the drug.* 一些吸毒成瘾的人一旦沒有毒品就會出現情緒的極度波動。◇ *I'm just not* ***in the mood for*** *a party tonight.* 我今晚就是沒心情參加聚會。◇ *I'm not really* ***in the mood to*** *go out tonight.* 我今晚真的沒心情出門。◇ *He was* ***in no mood for*** *being polite to visitors.* 他當時沒心思以禮待客。 **2** [C] a period of being angry or impatient 壞心境；壞脾氣： *I wonder why he's* ***in such a mood*** *today.* 我不知道他為什麼今天脾氣這麼壞。◇ *She was* ***in one of her moods*** (= one of her regular periods of being angry or impatient). 她又鬧情緒了。 **3** [sing.] the way a group of people feel about sth; the atmosphere in a place or among a group of people 氣氛；氛圍： *The mood of the meeting was distinctly pessimistic.* 這次會議的氣氛顯然很悲觀。◇ *The movie captures the mood of the interwar years perfectly.* 這部電影恰如其分地捕捉到了兩次世界大戰中間這些年的氛圍。 **4** [C] (*grammar* 語法) any of the sets of verb forms that show whether what is said or written is certain, possible, necessary, etc. 表達語氣的動詞屈折變化 **5** [C] (*grammar* 語法) one of the categories of verb use that expresses facts, orders, questions, wishes or conditions（動詞的）語氣：*the* ***indicative/imperative/subjunctive mood*** 陳述 / 祈使 / 虛擬語氣

ˈmood-altering *adj.* (of drugs 藥物) having an effect on your mood 對情緒有影響的；改變情緒的：*mood-altering substances* 改變情緒的物質

ˈmood music *noun* [U] music intended to create a particular atmosphere, especially a relaxed or romantic one 情調音樂，氣氛音樂（營造輕鬆或浪漫的氣氛為主）

moody /ˈmuːdi/ *adj.* (**mood·ier**, **moodi·est**) **1** having moods that change quickly and often 情緒多變的；喜怒無常的： *Moody people are very difficult to deal with.* 喜怒無常的人很難打交道。 **2** bad-tempered or upset, often for no particular reason 脾氣壞的；鬱鬱寡歡的 SYN **grumpy** ： *Why are you so moody today?* 你今天怎麼這麼悶悶不樂啊？ **3** (of a film/movie, piece of music or place 電影、音樂或場所) suggesting particular emotions, especially sad ones 表現出…情調的；感傷的；抑鬱的；令人悲傷的 ▸ **mood·ily** /-ɪli/ *adv.* ： *He stared moodily into the fire.* 他憂鬱地盯着火光。 **moodi·ness** *noun* [U]

mooli /ˈmuːli/ (also **dai·kon**) *noun* [U, C] a long white root vegetable that you can eat 白蘿蔔（也稱“大根”） ➲ VISUAL VOCAB page V31

moon /muːn/ *noun, verb*

■ ***noun*** **1** (usually **the moon**), (also **the Moon**) [sing.] the round object that moves around the earth once every 27½ days and shines at night by light reflected from the sun 月球： *the surface of the moon* 月球表面 ◇ *a moon landing* 月球登陸 **2** [sing.] the moon as it appears in the sky at a particular time 月亮；月相： *a crescent moon* 新月 ◇ *There's no moon tonight* (= no moon can be seen). 今晚看不見月亮。◇ *By the light of the moon I could just make out shapes and outlines.* 月光下，我只能分辨出形狀和輪廓。 ➲ see also FULL MOON, HALF-MOON, NEW MOON **3** [C] a natural SATELLITE that moves around a planet other than the earth 衛星： *How many moons does Jupiter have?* 木星有多少顆衛星？

IDM **ask, cry, etc. for the ˈmoon** (*BrE, informal*) to ask for sth that is difficult or impossible to get or achieve 想做辦不到的事情；想要得不到的東西 **many ˈmoons ago** (*literary*) a very long time ago 很久以前 **over the ˈmoon** (*informal, especially BrE*) extremely happy and excited 欣喜若狂 ➲ more at ONCE *adv.*, PROMISE *v.*

■ ***verb*** [I] (*informal*) to show your bottom to people in a public place as a joke or an insult 以屁股示人（在公共場所進行的惡作劇或侮辱）

PHR V **ˌmoon aˈbout/aˈround** (*BrE, informal*) to spend time doing nothing or walking around with no particular purpose, especially because you are unhappy（尤指無精打采地）閒逛，消磨時光 **ˈmoon over sb** (*informal*) to spend time thinking about sb that you love, especially when other people think this is silly or annoying 痴痴地思念（所愛的人） SYN **pine for**

moon·beam /ˈmuːnbiːm/ *noun* a stream of light from the moon（一道）月光

ˈMoon Boot™ *noun* a thick warm boot made of cloth or plastic, worn in snow or cold weather 雪地靴

moong /muːŋ/ *noun* = MUNG

Moonie /ˈmuːni/ *noun* an offensive word for a member of the Unification Church 文鮮明信徒（含冒犯意，指文鮮明統一教教徒）

moonie /ˈmuːni/ *noun*

IDM **do a ˈmoonie** (*BrE, informal*) to show your naked bottom in public 當眾露臀部

moon·less /ˈmuːnləs/ *adj.* without a moon that can be seen 無月亮的： *a* ***moonless night/sky*** 沒有月亮的夜晚 / 天空

moon·light /ˈmuːnlaɪt/ *noun, verb*

■ ***noun*** [U] the light of the moon 月光： *to go for a walk by* ***moonlight/in the moonlight*** 在月光下散步 IDM see FLIT *n.*

■ ***verb*** (**moon·lighted**, **moon·lighted**) [I] (*informal*) to have a second job that you do secretly, usually without paying tax on the extra money that you earn（暗中）兼職，從事第二職業

moon·lit /ˈmuːnlɪt/ *adj.* lit by the moon 月光照耀的： *a* ***moonlit night/beach*** 月光照耀的夜晚 / 海濱

moon·scape /ˈmuːnskeɪp/ *noun* **1** a view of the surface of the moon 月球表面景色 **2** an area of land that is empty, with no trees, water, etc., and looks like the surface of the moon 像月球表面一樣荒涼的地區

moon·shine /ˈmuːnʃaɪn/ *noun* [U] **1** (*old-fashioned, NAmE*) WHISKY or other strong alcoholic drinks made and sold illegally 非法釀製並銷售的威士忌（或其他烈酒）；私釀酒 **2** (*informal*) silly talk 蠢話；胡言亂語 SYN **nonsense**

moon·stone /ˈmuːnstəʊn; *NAmE* -stoʊn/ *noun* [C, U] a smooth white shiny SEMI-PRECIOUS stone 月長石

moon·struck /ˈmuːnstrʌk/ *adj.* slightly crazy, especially because you are in love（尤指因愛）發痴的

moon·walk /ˈmuːnwɔːk/ *verb* **1** [I] to walk on the moon 在月球行走 **2** [I] to do a dance movement which consists of walking backwards, sliding the feet smoothly over the floor（舞蹈時）走太空步 ▸ **moon·walk** *noun*

Moor /mɔː(r); mʊə(r); *NAmE* mʊr/ *noun* a member of a race of Muslim people living in NW Africa who entered and took control of part of Spain in the 8th century 摩爾人（居住在非洲西北部的穆斯林，曾於 8 世紀侵佔西班牙部份地區） ▸ **Moor·ish** *adj.* ： *the Moorish architecture of Córdoba* 科爾多瓦市的摩爾式建築

moor /mɔː(r); mʊə(r); *NAmE* mʊr/ *noun, verb*

■ ***noun*** (*especially BrE*) **1** [C, usually pl.] a high open area of land that is not used for farming, especially an area covered with rough grass and HEATHER 曠野；荒野；高沼；漠澤： *the North York moors* 北約克郡的漠澤 ◇ *to go for a walk on the moors* 到曠野去散步 **2** [U] = MOORLAND ： *moor and rough grassland* 高沼地和蒼莽的草原

■ ***verb*** [I, T] to attach a boat, ship, etc. to a fixed object or to the land with a rope, or ANCHOR it 使停泊；繫泊 SYN **tie up** ： *We moored off the north coast of the island.* 我們停泊在島的北部岸邊。◇ **~ sth (to sth)** *A number of fishing boats were moored to the quay.* 很多漁船繫泊在碼頭。

moor·hen /ˈmɔːhen; ˈmʊə-; *NAmE* ˈmʊrhen/ *noun* a small black bird with a short reddish-yellow beak that lives on or near water 黑水雞；澤雞；雌蘇格蘭雷鳥；紅松雞

moor·ing /ˈmɔːrɪŋ; ˈmʊər-; *NAmE* ˈmʊr-/ *noun* **1** **moor·ings** [pl.] the ropes, chains, etc. by which a ship or boat is MOORED 繫泊用具： *The boat slipped its moorings and drifted out to sea.* 船的繫泊繩索滑落，船漂向大海。 **2** [C] the place where a ship or boat is MOORED 停泊處；繫泊區：*private moorings* 私人停泊區 ◇ *to find a mooring* 找一個停泊地 ◇ *mooring ropes* 停泊區的繩索

moor·land /ˈmɔːlənd; ˈmʊə-; *NAmE* ˈmʊrlənd/ (also **moor**) *noun* [U, C, usually pl.] (*especially BrE*) land that consists of MOORS 高沼地： *walking across open moorland* 穿越開闊的高沼地

M

moose /muːs/ *noun* (*pl.* **moose**) a large DEER that lives in N America. In Europe and Asia it is called an ELK. 駝鹿（產於北美；在歐洲和亞洲稱為麋鹿）➲ picture at ELK

ˈ**moose milk** *noun* (*CanE*) **1** [U, C] an alcoholic drink made by mixing RUM with milk 駝鹿奶酒（用朗姆酒和牛奶調製而成）**2** [U] any strong alcoholic drink which is made at home 家釀酒

moot /muːt/ *adj.*, *verb*

■ ***adj.*** (*NAmE*) unlikely to happen and therefore not worth considering（因不大可能發生而）無考慮意義的：*He argued that the issue had become moot since the board had changed its policy.* 他爭辯說這項議題已變得毫無實際意義，因為董事會已經改變了政策。

IDM **a moot ˈpoint/ˈquestion** (*BrE*, *NAmE*) a matter about which there may be disagreement or confusion 懸而未決的事；有爭議的問題

■ ***verb*** [usually passive] **~ sth** (*formal*) to suggest an idea for people to discuss 提出…供討論 **SYN** **propose, put forward**

ˈ**moot court** *noun* (*especially NAmE*) a MOCK court in which law students practise trials（法學專業學生實習的）模擬法庭

mop /mɒp; *NAmE* mɑːp/ *noun*, *verb*

■ ***noun*** **1** a tool for washing floors that has a long handle with a bunch of thick strings or soft material at the end 拖把；墩布：*a mop and bucket* 拖把和水桶 ➲ VISUAL VOCAB page V20 **2** a kitchen UTENSIL (= a tool) for washing dishes, that has a short handle with soft material at one end 洗碗刷 **3** a mass of thick, often untidy, hair 亂蓬蓬的頭髮：*a mop of curly red hair* 亂蓬蓬的紅色鬈髮

M

■ ***verb*** (**-pp-**) **1 ~ sth** to clean sth with a mop 用拖把擦乾淨：*She wiped all the surfaces and mopped the floor.* 她把所有的陳設都擦乾淨，還拖了地板。 **2 ~ sth (from sth)** to remove liquid from the surface of sth using a cloth 用布擦掉（表面的液體）：*He took out a handkerchief to **mop his brow*** (= to remove the sweat). 他拿出手絹來擦額頭上的汗水。 **IDM** see FLOOR *n.*

PHR V ˌ**mop sth/sb↔ˈup** to remove the liquid from sth using sth that absorbs it 吸乾淨；吸去…的水分：*Do you want some bread to mop up that sauce?* 要不要用塊麪包把這醬料蘸蘸吃了？◇ (*figurative*) *A number of smaller companies were mopped up* (= taken over) *by the American multinational.* 有若干較小的公司都被那家美國跨國集團兼併了。◇ (*figurative*) *New equipment mopped up* (= used up) *what was left of this year's budget.* 新設備用光了本年度的預算餘額。 ˌ**mop sb/sth↔ˈup** **1** to complete or end sth by dealing with the final parts 完成，結束（最後部份）；收尾：*There are a few things that need mopping up before I can leave.* 我還有幾件事兒，了結了才能走。 **2** to get rid of the last few people who continue to oppose you, especially by capturing or killing them 消滅（殘敵）：*Troops combed the area to mop up any remaining resistance.* 部隊對這一地區進行了清剿，以掃除一切殘餘的抵抗勢力。

mope /məʊp; *NAmE* moʊp/ *verb* [I] to spend your time doing nothing and feeling sorry for yourself 悶悶不樂；自怨自艾 **SYN** **brood**：*Moping won't do any good!* 自怨自艾一點用處都沒有！

PHR V ˌ**mope aˈbout/aˈround** (...) (*disapproving*) to spend time walking around a place with no particular purpose, especially because you feel sorry for yourself（尤指悶悶不樂地）閒蕩，閒逛：*Instead of moping around the house all day, you should be out there looking for a job.* 不要整天悶悶不樂地在家裏晃悠，你應該出去找份工作。

moped /ˈməʊped; *NAmE* ˈmoʊ-/ *noun* a motorcycle with a small engine and also PEDALS 機器腳踏車；摩托自行車

mop·pet /ˈmɒpɪt; *NAmE* ˈmɑːp-/ *noun* (*informal*) an attractive small child, especially a girl（可愛的）小孩，小娃娃，小女孩

mo·quette /mɒˈket; *NAmE* moʊ-/ *noun* [U] a type of thick cloth with a soft surface made of a mass of small threads, used for making carpets and covering furniture 絨頭織物，割絨織物（用於製作地毯和傢具罩單）

MOR /ˌem əʊ ˈɑː(r); *NAmE* oʊ/ *noun* [U] music that is pleasant to listen to, but is not exciting or original (the abbreviation for 'middle-of-the-road') 中庸音樂，大眾流行音樂（全寫為 middle-of-the-road，不刺激，無創新性）

mo·raine /məˈreɪn; *BrE* also mɒˈreɪn/ *noun* [U, C] (*technical* 術語) a mass of earth, stones, etc., carried along by a GLACIER and left when it melts 冰磧

moral 🗝 /ˈmɒrəl; *NAmE* ˈmɔːr-; ˈmɑːr-/ *adj.*, *noun*

■ ***adj.*** **1** 🗝 [only before noun] concerned with principles of right and wrong behaviour 道德的：*a **moral issue/dilemma/question*** 道德方面的議題／困境／問題 ◇ *traditional moral values* 傳統的道德觀念 ◇ *a decline in **moral standards*** 道德水準的下降 ◇ *moral philosophy* 道德哲學 ◇ *a deeply religious man with a highly developed **moral sense*** 道德意識極強的篤信宗教的人 ◇ *The newspapers were full of **moral outrage** at the weakness of other countries.* 報紙總是道貌岸然地說別的國家不好。 **2** 🗝 [only before noun] based on your own sense of what is right and fair, not on legal rights or duties 道義上的；道德上的 **SYN** **ethical**：***moral responsibility/duty*** 道義上的責任／義務 ◇ *Governments have at least a **moral obligation** to answer these questions.* 政府至少在道義上有責任回應這些問題。◇ (*BrE*) *The job was to call on all her diplomatic skills and **moral courage*** (= the courage to do what you think is right). 這項工作需要她發揮全部的外交才能和捍衛正義的勇氣。 **3** 🗝 following the standards of behaviour considered acceptable and right by most people 品行端正的；有道德的 **SYN** **good, honourable**：*He led a very moral life.* 他這個人一向很正派。◇ *a very moral person* 品行非常端正的人 ➲ compare AMORAL, IMMORAL **4** [only before noun] able to understand the difference between right and wrong 能辨別是非的：*Children are not naturally moral beings.* 兒童並非天生就能分辨是非。

IDM **take, claim, seize, etc. the moral ˈhigh ground** to claim that your side of an argument is morally better than your opponents' side; to argue in a way that makes your side seem morally better 聲稱自己的論點在道義上佔優勢

■ ***noun*** **1** **morals** [pl.] standards or principles of good behaviour, especially in matters of sexual relationships 品行，道德（尤指性關係方面）：*Young people these days have no morals.* 現在的年輕人根本不講道德。◇ *The play was considered an affront to **public morals**.* 人們認為這齣戲侮辱了公眾道德。◇ (*old-fashioned*) *a woman of **loose morals*** (= with a low standard of sexual behaviour) 放蕩的女人 **2** [C] a practical lesson that a story, an event or an experience teaches you 寓意；教益：*And the moral is that crime doesn't pay.* 寓意就是犯罪得不償失。

mor·ale /məˈrɑːl; *NAmE* -ˈræl/ *noun* [U] the amount of confidence and enthusiasm, etc. that a person or a group has at a particular time 士氣：*to **boost/raise/improve morale*** 提高士氣 ◇ *Morale amongst the players is very high at the moment.* 此刻各選手士氣高昂。◇ *Staff are suffering from low morale.* 員工士氣低落。

ˌ**moral ˈfibre** (*BrE*) (*NAmE* ˌ**moral ˈfiber**) *noun* [U] the inner strength to do what you believe to be right in difficult situations 道德力量；道義精神

mor·al·ist /ˈmɒrəlɪst; *NAmE* ˈmɔːr-/ *noun* **1** (*often disapproving*) a person who has strong ideas about moral principles, especially one who tries to tell other people how they should behave 道德說教者；衛道士 **2** a person who teaches or writes about moral principles 道德學家

mor·al·is·tic /ˌmɒrəˈlɪstɪk; *NAmE* ˌmɔːr-/ *adj.* (usually *disapproving*) having or showing very fixed ideas about what is right and wrong, especially when this causes you to judge other people's behaviour 是非觀念堅定的；道學的；說教的

mor·al·ity /məˈræləti/ *noun* (*pl.* **-ies**) **1** [U] principles concerning right and wrong or good and bad behaviour 道德；道德準則；道義：*matters of **public/private morality*** 公眾／個人道德問題 ◇ *Standards of morality seem to be dropping.* 道德標準似乎在下降。 **2** [U] the degree to which sth is right or wrong, good or bad, etc.

according to moral principles 合乎道德的程度：*a debate on the morality of abortion* 有關墮胎是否道德的辯論 **3** [U, C] a system of moral principles followed by a particular group of people 道德規範；道德體系 SYN **ethics** ➲ compare IMMORALITY

mo'rality play *noun* a type of play that was popular in the 15th and 16th centuries and was intended to teach a moral lesson, using characters to represent good and bad qualities 道德劇，寓意劇（流行於 15 和 16 世紀，劇中人物代表善與惡）

mor·al·ize (*BrE* also **-ise**) /'mɒrəlaɪz; *NAmE* 'mɔːr-; 'mɑːr-/ *verb* [I] (usually *disapproving*) to tell other people what is right and wrong especially in order to emphasize that your opinions are correct 進行道德說教 SYN **preach**

mor·al·ly 🔑 /'mɒrəli; *NAmE* 'mɔːr-/ *adv.* according to principles of good behaviour and what is considered to be right or wrong 道義上；道德上：*to act morally* 循規蹈矩 ◇ ***morally right/wrong/justified/unacceptable*** 從道義上講是正確的／錯誤的／正當的／不可接受的 ◇ *He felt morally responsible for the accident.* 他覺得在道義上應對這次事故負責。

the ˌmoral ma'jority *noun* [sing.+sing./pl. v.] the largest group of people in a society, considered as having very traditional ideas about moral matters, religion, sexual behaviour, etc.（對道德、宗教、性行為等）持傳統觀念的最大群體

ˌmoral sup'port *noun* [U] the act of giving encouragement by showing your approval and interest, rather than by giving financial or practical support 道義上的支持；精神支持：*My sister came along just to give me some moral support.* 我姐姐只是過來給我一些精神上的支持。

ˌmoral 'victory *noun* a situation in which your ideas or principles are proved to be right and fair, even though you may not have succeeded where practical results are concerned 道義上的勝利

mor·ass /mə'ræs/ *noun* [usually sing.] (*formal*) **1** an unpleasant and complicated situation that is difficult to escape from 困境；陷阱 SYN **web** **2** a dangerous area of low soft wet land 沼澤 SYN **bog, quagmire**

mora·tor·ium /ˌmɒrə'tɔːriəm; *NAmE* ˌmɔːr-/ *noun* (*pl.* **-riums** or **-toria** /-riə/) **~ (on sth)** a temporary stopping of an activity, especially by official agreement 暫停，中止（尤指經官方同意的）：*The convention called for a two-year moratorium on commercial whaling.* 會議呼籲兩年內暫停商業捕鯨活動。

moray /mɒ'reɪ; 'mɒreɪ; *NAmE* 'mɔːreɪ/ (also **ˌmoray 'eel**) *noun* a type of EEL that hides among rocks in tropical waters 海鱔（棲於熱帶水域岩礁間的鰻類）

mor·bid /'mɔːbɪd; *NAmE* 'mɔːrbɪd/ *adj.* **1** having or expressing a strong interest in sad or unpleasant things, especially disease or death 病態的；不正常的：*He had a morbid fascination with blood.* 他對血有着一種病態的喜好。◇ *'He might even die.' 'Don't be so morbid.'* "他甚至會死的。" "別胡思亂想。" **2** (*medical* 醫) connected with disease 病的；與疾病有關的 ▶ **mor·bid·ity** /mɔː'bɪdəti; *NAmE* mɔːr'b-/ *noun* [U] **mor·bid·ly** *adv.*

mor·dant /'mɔːdnt; *NAmE* 'mɔːrdnt/ *adj.* (*formal*) critical and unkind, but funny 尖刻而又風趣的；諷刺幽默的 SYN **caustic**：*His mordant wit appealed to students.* 他那尖刻的妙語受到學生的歡迎。▶ **mor·dant·ly** *adv.*

more 🔑 /mɔː(r)/ *det., pron., adv.*

■ ***det., pron.*** 🔑 (used as the comparative of 'much', 'a lot of', 'many' 用作 much、a lot of 和 many 的比較級) **~ (sth/of sth) (than …)** a larger number or amount of（數、量等）更多的，更大的：*more bread/cars* 更多的麪包／汽車 ◇ *Only two more days to go!* 僅僅剩下兩天了！◇ *people with more money than sense* 金錢多於智慧的人 ◇ *I can't stand much more of this.* 我可承受不了太多這樣的事。◇ *She earns a lot more than I do.* 她賺的錢比我多多了。◇ *There is room for* ***no more than*** *three cars.* 這地方只能停放三輛車。◇ *I hope we'll see more of you* (= see you again or more often). 希望我們能經常見面。

IDM **ˌmore and 'more** 🔑 continuing to become larger in number or amount（數量上）越來越多：*More and more people are using the Internet.* 越來越多人在使用互聯網。◇ *She spends more and more time alone in her room.* 她一個人待在屋裏的時間越來越多。

■ ***adv.*** **~ (than …)** **1** 🔑 used to form the comparative of adjectives and adverbs with two or more syllables（與兩個或更多音節的形容詞或副詞連用，構成比較級）更：*She was far more intelligent than her sister.* 她比她姐姐聰明多了。◇ *He read the letter more carefully the second time.* 他把信又更仔細地看了一遍。 **2** 🔑 to a greater degree than sth else; to a greater degree than usual（程度上）更強，更多：*I like her more than her husband.* 我喜歡她多於喜歡她丈夫。◇ *a course for more advanced students* 為更高程度的學生設置的課程 ◇ *It had more the appearance of a deliberate crime than of an accident.* 這件事看來是故意犯罪，而不是事故。◇ *Could you repeat that* ***once more*** (= one more time)? 你能再重複一遍嗎？◇ *I had no complaints and* ***no more*** (= neither) *did Tom.* 我沒什麼怨言，湯姆也沒有。◇ *Signing the forms is* ***little more than*** (= only) *a formality.* 在那些表格上簽名只是一種形式。◇ *I'm* ***more than*** *happy* (= extremely happy) *to take you there in my car.* 我非常樂意用我的車載你去那兒。◇ *She was* ***more than a little*** *shaken* (= extremely shaken) *by the experience.* 這次經歷使她非常震驚。◇ (*formal*) *I will torment you* ***no more*** (= no longer). 我再也不會讓你痛苦了。➲ see also ANY MORE

IDM **ˌmore and 'more** 🔑 continuing to become larger in number or amount（數量上）越來越多 SYN **increasingly**：*I was becoming more and more irritated by his behaviour.* 我對他的行為越來越感到惱火。**ˌmore or 'less** **1** 🔑 almost 幾乎；差不多：*I've more or less finished the book.* 我差不多已經讀完這本書了。 **2** 🔑 approximately 大概；大約：*She could earn $200 a night, more or less.* 她一晚上大約能掙 200 元。 **the more, less, etc. …, the more, less, etc. …** 🔑 used to show that two things change to the same degree 越…，越…；愈…，愈…：*The more she thought about it, the more depressed she became.* 這件事她越想越感到沮喪。◇ *The less said about the whole thing, the happier I'll be.* 對這整件事情談得越少，我越高興。 **what is 'more** used to add a point that is even more important 更有甚者；更為重要的是：*You're wrong, and what's more you know it!* 你錯了！而且你明明知道你錯了！➲ LANGUAGE BANK at ADDITION

more·ish /'mɔːrɪʃ/ *adj.* (*BrE, informal*) if food or drink is **moreish**, it tastes so good that you want to have more of it（食物、飲料滋味好）令人想再吃的

morel /mə'rel/ (also **moˌrel 'mushroom**) *noun* a type of MUSHROOM that you can eat, with a top that is full of holes 羊肚菌

more·over 🔑 /mɔːr'əʊvə(r); *NAmE* -'oʊvər/ *adv.* (*formal*) used to introduce some new information that adds to or supports what you have said previously 此外；而且 SYN **in addition**：*A talented artist, he was, moreover, a writer of some note.* 他是一位有才華的藝術家，同時也是頗有名氣的作家。➲ LANGUAGE BANK at ADDITION

mores /'mɔːreɪz/ *noun* [pl.] (*formal*) the customs and behaviour that are considered typical of a particular social group or community 風俗習慣；傳統 SYN **conventions**

morgue /mɔːg; *NAmE* mɔːrg/ *noun* **1** (*BrE*) a building in which dead bodies are kept before they are buried or CREMATED (= burned) 停屍房；太平間 ➲ compare MORTUARY **2** a place where dead bodies that have been found are kept until they can be identified（供辨認屍首的）陳屍所

MORI™ /'mɒri; *NAmE* 'mɔːri/ *noun* Market and Opinion Research International (an organization that finds out public opinion by asking a typical group of people questions) 摩利調查公司，市場與民意調查國際（全寫為 Market and Opinion Research International）：*A MORI poll showed that 68% of people opposed the ban.* 摩利公司的民意測驗顯示，有 68% 的人反對這一禁令。

mori·bund /'mɒrɪbʌnd; *NAmE* 'mɔːr-; 'mɑːr-/ *adj.* (*formal*) **1** (of an industry, an institution, a custom, etc. 企業、

M

機構、習俗等) no longer effective and about to come to an end completely 行將滅亡的；即將倒閉的；瀕於崩潰的 **2** in a very bad condition; dying 垂死的；瀕臨死亡的：*a moribund patient/tree* 瀕臨死亡的病人／樹

Mor·mon /ˈmɔːmən; *NAmE* ˈmɔːrmən/ *noun* a member of a religion formed by Joseph Smith in the US in 1830, officially called 'the Church of Jesus Christ of Latter-day Saints' 摩門教徒（摩門教正式名稱為"耶穌基督末世聖徒教會"，1830 年由約瑟夫 • 史密斯於美國創建）：*a Mormon church/chapel* 摩門教教會／教堂

morn /mɔːn; *NAmE* mɔːrn/ *noun* [usually sing.] (*literary*) morning 早晨；上午

morn·ing 0-w /ˈmɔːnɪŋ; *NAmE* ˈmɔːrnɪŋ/ *noun* **1** 0-w the early part of the day from the time when people wake up until midday or before lunch 早晨；上午：*They left for Spain early this morning.* 他們今天一早就出發去西班牙了。◇ *See you* **tomorrow morning**. 明天上午見。◇ *I prefer coffee* **in the morning**. 我早晨喜歡喝咖啡。◇ *She woke every morning at the same time.* 她每天早上都在同一時間醒來。◇ *Our group meets on Friday mornings.* 我們的組員每週五上午碰面。◇ *I walk to work most mornings.* 我大多數早晨步行去上班。◇ *We got the news* **on the morning of** *the wedding.* 我們在舉行婚禮的那天上午得到這個消息。◇ *He's been in a meeting all morning.* 他一上午都在開會。◇ *the morning papers* 晨報 ➲ see also GOOD MORNING **2** 0-w the part of the day from midnight to midday 午夜至正午的時間：*I didn't get home until two in the morning!* 我凌晨兩點才到家！◇ *He died in the early hours of Sunday morning.* 他於星期天凌晨去世。**3** **mornings** *adv.* in the morning of each day 在上午；在早晨；每天上午：*I only work mornings.* 我只在上午工作。

IDM **in the ˈmorning** **1** 0-w during the morning of the next day; tomorrow morning 次日上午；明天上午：*I'll give you a call in the morning.* 我明天上午給你打電話。**2** 0-w between midnight and midday 午夜至正午間：*It must have happened at about five o'clock in the morning.* 這件事一定發生在凌晨五點鐘左右。**morning, noon and ˈnight** at all times of the day and night (used to emphasize that sth happens very often or that it happens continuously) 從早到晚；一天到晚：*She talks about him morning, noon and night.* 她整天把他掛在嘴邊。◇ *The work continues morning, noon and night.* 這項工作從早到晚持續進行。➲ more at OTHER *adj.*

ˌmorning-ˈafter *adj.* [only before noun] **1** happening the next day, after an exciting or important event （令人興奮或重要之事後）次日發生的：*After his election victory, the president held a morning-after news conference.* 選舉獲勝後，總統於次日召開了新聞記者會。**2** used to describe how sb feels the next morning, after an occasion when they have drunk too much alcohol 宿醉的：*a morning-after headache* 宿醉頭痛

ˌmorning-ˈafter pill *noun* a drug that a woman can take some hours after having sex in order to avoid becoming pregnant （房事後服用的）女用口服避孕丸

ˈmorning coat (*BrE*) (*NAmE* **cut·away**) *noun* a black or grey jacket for men, short at the front and very long at the back, worn as part of morning dress （男子日間穿的黑色或灰色）晨燕尾服，常燕尾服 ➲ compare TAILS (6)

ˈmorning dress *noun* [U] clothes worn by a man on very formal occasions, for example a wedding, including a morning coat and dark trousers/pants 常禮服（男子在隆重場合穿的服裝，包括常燕尾服和黑褲子）

ˌmorning ˈglory *noun* [C, U] a climbing plant with flowers shaped like TRUMPETS that open in the morning and close in late afternoon 牽牛花

ˈmorning room *noun* (*old-fashioned, especially BrE*) (in some large houses, especially in the past 尤指過去的大房子) a room that you sit in in the morning 晨用起居室

ˈmorning sickness *noun* [U] the need to VOMIT that some women feel, often only in the morning, when they are pregnant, especially in the first months（孕婦）晨吐

the ˌmorning ˈstar *noun* [sing.] the planet Venus, when it shines in the east before the sun rises 晨星，啟明星（黎明前在東方閃爍的金星）

ˈmorning suit *noun* (*BrE*) a suit worn by a man on very formal occasions, for example a wedding, including a morning coat and dark trousers/pants 男式晨禮服，男式常禮服（在婚禮等很正式的場合穿，包括晨燕尾服和黑褲子）

mo·rocco /məˈrɒkəʊ; *NAmE* məˈrɑːkoʊ/ *noun* [U] fine soft leather made from the skin of a GOAT, used especially for making shoes and covering books 摩洛哥羊皮革（柔軟細膩，尤用於製鞋或書封皮）

moron /ˈmɔːrɒn; *NAmE* -rɑːn/ *noun* (*informal*) an offensive way of referring to sb that you think is very stupid 笨蛋；蠢貨：*They're a bunch of morons.* 他們是一群蠢貨。◇ *You moron—now look what you've done!* 你這個笨蛋，看你都幹了些什麼！▸ **mor·on·ic** /məˈrɒnɪk; *NAmE* -ˈrɑːn-/ *adj.*：*a moronic stare* 傻傻的凝視 ◇ *a moronic TV programme* 愚鈍的電視節目

mor·ose /məˈrəʊs; *NAmE* məˈroʊs/ *adj.* unhappy, bad-tempered and not talking very much 陰鬱的；脾氣不好的；悶悶不樂的 **SYN** **gloomy**：*She just sat there looking morose.* 她就那樣陰鬱地坐在那兒。▸ **mor·ose·ly** *adv.*

morph /mɔːf; *NAmE* mɔːrf/ *verb* **1** [I, T] **~ (sth) (into sth)** to change smoothly from one image to another using computer ANIMATION; to make an image change in this way（利用電腦動畫製作使圖像）平穩變換 **2** [I, T] **~ (sb/sth) (into sb/sth)** to change, or make sb/sth change into sth different （使）變化；（使）改變

mor·pheme /ˈmɔːfiːm; *NAmE* ˈmɔːrf-/ *noun* (*grammar* 語法) the smallest unit of meaning that a word can be divided into 詞素；語素：*The word 'like' contains one morpheme but 'un-like-ly' contains three.* * like 一詞含一個詞素，而 un-like-ly 則含三個。

mor·phine /ˈmɔːfiːn; *NAmE* ˈmɔːrf-/ (also *old-fashioned* **mor·phia** /ˈmɔːfiə; *NAmE* ˈmɔːrf-/) *noun* [U] a powerful drug that is made from OPIUM and used to reduce pain 嗎啡

morph·ology /mɔːˈfɒlədʒi; *NAmE* mɔːrˈfɑːl-/ *noun* [U] **1** (*biology* 生) the form and structure of animals and plants, studied as a science 形態學；形態論 **2** (*linguistics* 語言) the forms of words, studied as a branch of linguistics 詞法；形態學 ➲ compare GRAMMAR, SYNTAX (1) ▸ **mor·pho·logic·al** /ˌmɔːfəˈlɒdʒɪkl; *NAmE* ˌmɔːrfəˈlɑːdʒ-/ *adj.*

mor·ris dance /ˈmɒrɪs dɑːns; *NAmE* ˈmɔːrɪs dæns; ˈmɑːrɪs dæns/ *noun* a traditional English dance that is performed by people wearing special clothes decorated with bells and carrying sticks that they hit together 莫里斯舞（英格蘭的一種傳統民間化裝舞蹈）▸ **ˈmorris dancer** *noun* **ˈmorris dancing** *noun* [U]

mor·row /ˈmɒrəʊ; *NAmE* ˈmɔːr-; ˈmɑːroʊ/ *noun* **the morrow** [sing.] (*old-fashioned, literary*) the next day; tomorrow 次日；明天：*We had to leave* **on the morrow**. 我們明天就得離去。◇ *Who knows what the morrow (= the future) will bring?* 誰知道明天會是什麼樣？

Morse code /ˌmɔːs ˈkəʊd; *NAmE* ˌmɔːrs ˈkoʊd/ *noun* [U] a system for sending messages, using combinations of long and short sounds or flashes of light to represent letters of the alphabet and numbers 莫爾斯電碼

mor·sel /ˈmɔːsl; *NAmE* ˈmɔːrsl/ *noun* a small amount or a piece of sth, especially food 少量，一塊（食物）：*a tasty morsel of food* 一點可口的食物 ◇ *He ate it all, down to the last morsel.* 他全吃光了，一點不剩。

mor·tal /ˈmɔːtl; *NAmE* ˈmɔːrtl/ *adj., noun*

■ *adj.* **1** that cannot live for ever and must die 不能永生的；終將死亡的：*We are all mortal.* 我們都總有一死。**OPP** **immortal** **2** (*literary*) causing death or likely to cause death; very serious 導致死亡的；致命的；非常危急的：*a mortal blow/wound* 致命的一擊／傷口 ◇ *to be in mortal danger* 處於極度的危險之中 ◇ (*figurative*) *Her reputation suffered a mortal blow as a result of the scandal.* 這一醜聞毀了她的名聲。➲ compare FATAL (1) **3** [only before noun] (*formal*) lasting until death 至死方休的；不共戴天的 **SYN** **deadly**：*mortal enemies* 不共戴

天的敵人 ◊ *They were locked **in mortal combat*** (= a fight that will only end with the death of one of them). 他們陷入了一場你死我活的爭鬥中。**4** [only before noun] (*formal*) (of fear, etc. 恐懼等) extreme 極端的；非常大的：*We lived **in mortal dread** of him discovering our secret.* 因為害怕他發現我們的秘密，我們終日惶恐不安。

■ ***noun*** (often *humorous*) a human, especially an ordinary person with little power or influence 人；凡人；普通人 SYN **human being**：*old stories about gods and mortals* 關於天神和凡人的古老傳説 ◊ (*humorous*) *Such things are not for **mere mortals** like ourselves.* 這種事不會落在我們這樣的凡夫俗子身上。◊ (*humorous*) *She can deal with complicated numbers in her head, but we **lesser mortals** need calculators!* 她可以心算複雜的數字，而我們常人就需要計算器！

mor·tal·ity /mɔːˈtæləti; *NAmE* mɔːrˈt-/ *noun* (*pl.* **-ies**) **1** [U] the state of being human and not living for ever 生命的有限：*After her mother's death, she became acutely aware of her own mortality.* 她母親去世後，她開始強烈意識到自己的生命是有限的。**2** [U] the number of deaths in a particular situation or period of time 死亡數量；死亡率：*the infant mortality rate* (= the number of babies that die at or just after birth) 嬰兒死亡率 ◊ *Mortality from lung cancer is still increasing.* 死於肺癌的人數仍在上升。**3** [C] (*technical* 術語) a death 死亡：*hospital mortalities* (= deaths in hospital) 醫院裏的死亡數字

mor·tal·ly /ˈmɔːtəli; *NAmE* ˈmɔːrt-/ *adv.* (*literary*) **1** causing or resulting in death 致死；致命 SYN **fatally**：***mortally wounded/ill*** 受致命傷；得絕症 **2** extremely 極端；非常：***mortally afraid/offended*** 怕得要死；極為惱怒

ˌmortal ˈsin *noun* [C, U] (in the Roman Catholic Church 羅馬天主教) a very serious SIN for which you can be sent to HELL unless you CONFESS and are forgiven 死罪；大罪

mor·tar /ˈmɔːtə(r); *NAmE* ˈmɔːrt-/ *noun, verb*

■ ***noun*** **1** [U] a mixture of sand, water, LIME and CEMENT used in building for holding bricks and stones together 灰泥；砂漿 **2** [C] a heavy gun that fires bombs and SHELLS high into the air; the bombs that are fired by this gun 迫擊炮；迫擊炮彈：*to come under **mortar fire/attack*** 受到迫擊炮火的襲擊 **3** [C] a small hard bowl in which you can crush substances such as seeds and grains into powder with a special object (called a PESTLE) 研缽；臼 ➲ VISUAL VOCAB pages V26, V70 IDM see BRICK *n.*

■ ***verb*** [I, T] **~ (sb/sth)** to attack sb/sth using a mortar 用迫擊炮攻擊（或襲擊）

ˈmortar board *noun* a black hat with a stiff square top, worn by some university teachers and students at special ceremonies 學位帽，方頂帽（大學師生在一些隆重場合戴的黑色帽）➲ VISUAL VOCAB page V65 ➲ compare CAP (3)

mort·gage /ˈmɔːɡɪdʒ; *NAmE* ˈmɔːrɡ-/ *noun, verb*

■ ***noun*** (also *informal* **ˌhome ˈloan**) a legal agreement by which a bank or similar organization lends you money to buy a house, etc., and you pay the money back over a particular number of years; the sum of money that you borrow 按揭（由銀行等提供房產抵押借款）；按揭貸款：*to **apply for/take out/pay off a mortgage*** 申請／取得／還清抵押貸款 ◊ *mortgage rates* (= of interest) 按揭貸款利率 ◊ *a mortgage on the house* 一項房產按揭 ◊ *a mortgage of £60 000* * 6 萬英鎊的按揭貸款 ◊ *monthly mortgage payments* 房貸月供 ➲ COLLOCATIONS at HOUSE

■ ***verb*** **~ sth** to give a bank, etc. the legal right to own your house, land, etc. if you do not pay the money back that you have borrowed from the bank to buy the house or land（以房地產）做按揭貸款的抵押：*He had to mortgage his house to pay his legal costs.* 他不得不把房子抵押出去來付訴訟費。

ˈmortgage bond *noun* (*SAfrE*) = BOND (4)

mort·ga·gee /ˌmɔːɡɪˈdʒiː; *NAmE* ˌmɔːrɡ-/ *noun* (*technical* 術語) a person or an organization that lends money to people to buy houses, etc. 受抵押人；抵押權人

mort·ga·gor /ˈmɔːɡɪdʒɔː(r); *NAmE* ˈmɔːrɡ-/ *noun* (*technical* 術語) a person who borrows money from a bank or a similar organization to buy a house, etc. 抵押人；出押人

mor·ti·cian /mɔːˈtɪʃn; *NAmE* mɔːrˈt-/ *noun* (*NAmE*) = UNDERTAKER

mor·tify /ˈmɔːtɪfaɪ; *NAmE* ˈmɔːrt-/ *verb* (**mor·ti·fies**, **mor·ti·fy·ing**, **mor·ti·fied**, **mor·ti·fied**) [usually passive] **~ sb (to do sth)** | **it mortifies sb that …** to make sb feel very ashamed or embarrassed 使難堪；使羞愧 SYN **humiliate**：*She **was mortified to** realize he had heard every word she said.* 她意識到自己的每句話都被他聽到了，直羞得無地自容。▸ **mor·ti·fi·ca·tion** /ˌmɔːtɪfɪˈkeɪʃn; *NAmE* ˌmɔːrt-/ *noun* [U] **mor·ti·fy·ing** *adj.*：*How mortifying to have to apologize to him!* 要向他道歉，多難為情啊！

mor·tise (also **mor·tice**) /ˈmɔːtɪs; *NAmE* ˈmɔːrtɪs/ *noun* (*technical* 術語) a hole cut in a piece of wood, etc. to receive the end of another piece of wood, so that the two are held together 榫眼；卯眼 ➲ see also TENON

ˈmortise lock *noun* a lock that is fitted inside a hole cut into the edge of a door, not one that is screwed into the surface of one side 插鎖；暗鎖

mor·tu·ary /ˈmɔːtʃəri; *NAmE* ˈmɔːrtʃueri/ *noun* (*pl.* **-ies**) **1** a room or building, for example part of a hospital, in which dead bodies are kept before they are buried or CREMATED (= burned) 太平間；停屍房 **2** (*NAmE*) = FUNERAL PARLOUR ➲ compare MORGUE (1)

mo·saic /məʊˈzeɪɪk; *NAmE* moʊ-/ *noun* [C, U] a picture or pattern made by placing together small pieces of glass, stone, etc. of different colours 鑲嵌圖案；馬賽克：*a Roman mosaic* 羅馬鑲嵌畫 ◊ *a design in mosaic* 馬賽克圖案 ◊ *mosaic tiles* 馬賽克瓷磚 ◊ (*figurative*) *A mosaic of fields, rivers and woods lay below us.* 我們下方是由田野、河流和林木交織成的圖畫。

M

Mo·selle (*NAmE* usually **Mosel**) /məʊˈzel; *NAmE* moʊ-/ *noun* [U, C] a type of German white wine （德國）摩澤爾白葡萄酒

Moses basket /ˈməʊzɪz bɑːskɪt; *NAmE* ˈmoʊzɪz bæskɪt/ (*BrE*) (*NAmE* **bas·sinet**) *noun* a BASKET for a small baby to sleep in 摩西筐；嬰兒睡籃

mosey /ˈməʊzi; *NAmE* ˈmoʊzi/ *verb* [I] + **adv./prep.** (*informal*) to go in a particular direction slowly and with no definite purpose 漫步；遛達：*He moseyed on over to the bar.* 他遛達着朝酒吧走去。

mosh /mɒʃ; *NAmE* mɑːʃ/ *verb* [I] to dance and jump up and down violently or without control at a concert where rock music is played （在搖滾音樂會上）狂舞，勁舞

ˈmosh pit *noun* the place, just in front of the stage, where the audience at a concert of rock music moshes （搖滾音樂會的）舞台前觀眾狂舞區，搖滾區

Mos·lem /ˈmɒzləm; *NAmE* ˈmɑːz-/ *noun* = MUSLIM ▸ **Mos·lem** *adj.* = MUSLIM HELP The form **Moslem** is sometimes considered old-fashioned. Use **Muslim**. * Moslem 這一拼法有時被視為過時。用 Muslim。

mosque /mɒsk; *NAmE* mɑːsk/ *noun* a building in which Muslims worship 清真寺

mos·quito /məˈskiːtəʊ; *NAmE* -toʊ; *BrE* also mɒˈs-/ *noun* (*pl.* **-oes** or **-os**) a flying insect that bites humans and animals and sucks their blood. One type of mosquito can spread the disease MALARIA. 蚊子：*a mosquito bite* 蚊子叮傷 ➲ VISUAL VOCAB page V13

mosˈquito net *noun* a net that you hang over a bed, etc. to keep mosquitoes away from you 蚊帳

moss /mɒs; *NAmE* mɔːs/ *noun* [U, C] a very small green or yellow plant without flowers that spreads over damp surfaces, rocks, trees, etc. 苔蘚；地衣：*moss-covered walls* 青苔覆蓋的牆壁 ➲ VISUAL VOCAB page V11 ➲ compare LICHEN ➲ see also SPANISH MOSS IDM see ROLL *v.*

mossy /ˈmɒsi; *NAmE* ˈmɔːsi/ *adj.* covered with moss 苔蘚覆蓋的；長滿苔蘚的

most 0‑ /məʊst; NAmE moʊst/ det., pron., adv.
■ **det., pron.** (used as the superlative of 'much', 'a lot of', 'many' * much、a lot of 和 many 的最高級) **1** 0‑ the largest in number or amount（數量上）最多，最大：*Who do you think will get (the) most votes?* 你認為誰會得到最多的選票？◇ *She had the most money of all of them.* 在這些人當中，她最有錢。◇ *I spent most time on the first question.* 我在第一個問題上花的時間最多。◇ *Who ate the most?* 誰吃得最多？◇ *The director has **the most to lose**.* 主任的損失最大。HELP **The** can be left out in informal *BrE*. 在非正式英式英語中，the 可以省略。 **2** 0‑ more than half of sb/sth; almost all of sb/sth 大多數；幾乎所有：*I like most vegetables.* 幾乎什麼蔬菜我都喜歡。◇ *Most classical music sends me to sleep.* 大多數古典音樂都會讓我睡着。◇ *As most of you know, I've decided to resign.* 你們大多數人都知道，我已經決定辭職了。◇ *Most of the people I had invited turned up.* 我邀請的人多半都來了。◇ *There are thousands of verbs in English and most (of them) are regular.* 英語有數千個動詞，大多數是規則動詞。HELP **The** is not used with **most** in this meaning. 表達此義時，most 之前不加 the。
IDM **at (the) 'most** not more than 至多；不超過：*As a news item it merits a short paragraph at most.* 作為一則新聞，它至多只能佔一小段。◇ *There were 50 people there, at the very most.* 那兒最多只有 50 個人。
■ **adv.** **1** 0‑ used to form the superlative of adjectives and adverbs of two or more syllables（與兩個或更多音節的形容詞或副詞連用，構成最高級）最：*the most boring/beautiful part* 最煩人的／最美麗的部份 ◇ *It was the people with the least money who gave most generously.* 最沒錢的人最慷慨大方。HELP When **most** is followed only by an adverb, **the** is not used. * most 後只接副詞時不用 the：*This reason is mentioned most frequently*, but 但要說：*This is **the most** frequently mentioned reason.* **2** 0‑ to the greatest degree（程度上）最大，最多，最高：*What did you enjoy (the) most?* 你最欣賞的是什麼？◇ *It was what she wanted **most of all**.* 這就是她最想得到的。HELP **The** is often left out in informal English. 在非正式英語中，the 常常省略。 **3** (*formal*) very; extremely; completely 非常；極其；完全：*It was most kind of you to meet me.* 你來接我真是太好了。◇ *We shall most probably never meet again.* 我們極有可能再也見不到面了。◇ *This technique looks easy, but it most certainly is not.* 這項技術看上去簡單，但絕不是那麼回事。 **4** (*NAmE, informal*) almost 幾乎；差不多：*I go to the store most every day.* 我幾乎每天都去商店。

-most *suffix* (in adjectives 構成形容詞) the furthest 最遠的；最深遠的：*inmost* (= the furthest in) 最深處的 ◇ *southernmost* 最南方的 ◇ *topmost* (= the furthest up/nearest to the top) 最高處的

,most favoured 'nation *noun* a country to which another country allows the most advantages in trade, because they have a good relationship（貿易）最惠國

most·ly 0‑ /'məʊstli; NAmE 'moʊ-/ *adv.* mainly; generally 主要地；一般地；通常：*The sauce is mostly cream.* 這沙司主要是奶油。◇ *We're mostly out on Sundays.* 我們星期天一般不在家。

MOT /,em əʊ 'tiː; NAmE oʊ/ (also **MOT test**) *noun* the abbreviation for 'Ministry of Transport' (a test that any vehicle in Britain over three years old must take in order to make sure that it is safe and in good condition) 車輛性能檢測（英國對超過三年的機動車進行的強制性檢測，全寫為 Ministry of Transport）：*I've got to take the car in for its MOT.* 我得把車開去進行車檢。◇ *to **pass/fail the MOT*** 舊車性能檢測合格／不合格

mote /məʊt; NAmE moʊt/ *noun* (*old-fashioned*) a very small piece of dust 塵埃；微粒 SYN **speck**

motel /məʊ'tel; NAmE moʊ-/ (also **'motor lodge**) (*NAmE* also **'motor inn**) *noun* a hotel for people who are travelling by car, with space for parking cars near the rooms 汽車旅館（附有停車設施）

motet /məʊ'tet; NAmE moʊ-/ *noun* a short piece of church music, usually for voices only 經文歌（通常為清唱）➲ compare CANTATA

moth /mɒθ; NAmE mɔːθ/ *noun* a flying insect with a long thin body and four large wings, like a BUTTERFLY, but less brightly coloured. Moths fly mainly at night and are attracted to bright lights. 蛾；飛蛾 ➲ VISUAL VOCAB page V13

moth·ball /'mɒθbɔːl; NAmE 'mɔːθ-/ *noun, verb*
■ **noun** a small white ball made of a chemical with a strong smell, used for keeping moths away from clothes 衛生球；樟腦丸
IDM **in 'mothballs** stored and not in use, often for a long time（長期）封存；（長期）擱置
■ **verb** [usually passive] **~ sth** to decide not to use or develop sth, for a period of time, especially a piece of equipment or a plan 封存；擱置不用：*The original proposal had been mothballed years ago.* 最初的建議多年前就束之高閣了。SYN **shelve**

'moth-eaten *adj.* **1** (of clothes, etc. 衣服等) damaged or destroyed by moths 被蟲蛀的；蛀壞的 **2** (*informal, disapproving*) very old and in bad condition 破舊的；過時的 SYN **shabby**

mother 0‑ /'mʌðə(r)/ *noun, verb*
■ **noun** **1** 0‑ a female parent of a child or animal; a person who is acting as a mother to a child 母親；媽媽：*I want to buy a present for my mother and father.* 我想給爸爸媽媽買件禮物。◇ *the relationship between mother and baby* 母嬰關係 ◇ *She's the mother of twins.* 她有一對雙胞胎。◇ *a mother of three* (= with three children) 三個孩子的媽媽 ◇ *an expectant* (= pregnant) *mother* 孕婦 ◇ *She was a wonderful mother to both her natural and adopted children.* 她對親生的和領養的孩子一樣好。◇ *the mother chimpanzee caring for her young* 照料着幼崽的母猩猩 **2** the title of a woman who is head of a CONVENT (= a community of NUNS)（對女修道院院長的尊稱）➲ see also MOTHER SUPERIOR
IDM **at your ,mother's 'knee** when you were very young 小時候；孩提時：*I learnt these songs at my mother's knee.* 我小時候學過這些歌曲。 **the 'mother of (all) sth** (*informal*) used to emphasize that sth is very large, unpleasant, important, etc. 非常大（或討厭、重要等）的事情：*I got stuck in the mother of all traffic jams.* 我被困在一次超級嚴重的大塞車之中。➲ more at NECESSITY, OLD
■ **verb** **~ sb/sth** to care for sb/sth because you are their mother, or as if you were their mother 給以母親的關愛；像母親般地照顧：*He was a disturbed child who needed mothering.* 他是個心理失常的孩子，需要悉心照顧。◇ *Stop mothering me!* 我不要你的照顧！

mother·board /'mʌðəbɔːd; NAmE 'mʌðərbɔːrd/ *noun* (*computing* 計) the main board of a computer, containing all the CIRCUITS 主板；母板

'mother country *noun* [sing.] **1** the country where you or your family were born and which you feel a strong emotional connection with 祖國 **2** the country that controls or used to control the government of another country（控制別國的）母國

'mother figure *noun* an older woman that you go to for advice, support, help, etc., as you would to a mother（能向其討教、尋求支持或幫助等的）慈母般的人 ➲ see also FATHER FIGURE

mother·fuck·er /'mʌðəfʌkə(r); NAmE -ðərf-/ *noun* (*taboo, slang, especially NAmE*) an offensive word used to insult sb, especially a man, and to show anger or dislike（常用於男性）渾蛋，雜種

,mother 'hen *noun* (usually *disapproving*) a woman who likes to care for and protect people and who worries about them a lot 喜歡關心人的婦女；愛操心的女人

mother·hood /'mʌðəhʊd; NAmE -ðərh-/ *noun* [U] the state of being a mother 母親身分；母性：*Motherhood suits her.* 她很適合做母親。

mother·ing /'mʌðərɪŋ/ *noun* [U] the act of caring for and protecting children or other people 呵護；照料：*an example of **good/poor mothering*** 良好呵護的範例；照顧不周的例子

'Mother·ing Sun·day *noun* [U, C] (*BrE*, becoming *old-fashioned*) = MOTHER'S DAY

ˈ**mother-in-law** *noun* (*pl.* **mothers-in-law**) the mother of your husband or wife 婆婆；岳母 ➲ compare FATHER-IN-LAW

ˈ**mother-in-law apartment** *noun* (*NAmE*) = IN-LAW APARTMENT

mother·land /ˈmʌðəlænd; *NAmE* -ðərl-/ *noun* (*formal*) the country that you were born in and that you feel a strong emotional connection with 祖國 ➲ see also FATHERLAND

mother·less /ˈmʌðələs; *NAmE* -ðərl-/ *adj.* having no mother because she has died or does not live with you 無母親的；沒娘的

ˈ**mother lode** *noun* [usually sing.] (*especially NAmE*) a very rich source of gold, silver, etc. in a mine 主礦脈；母脈：(*figurative*) *Her own experiences have provided her with a mother lode of material for her songs.* 她自身的經歷為她的歌曲提供了取之不盡的素材。

mother·ly /ˈmʌðəli; *NAmE* -ərli/ *adj.* having the qualities of a good mother; typical of a mother 慈母般的；母親的 **SYN** **maternal**：*motherly love* 慈母般的愛 ◇ *She was a kind, motherly woman.* 她是一位善良的充滿母愛的女人。

ˌ**Mother ˈNature** *noun* [U] the natural world, when you consider it as a force that affects the world and humans 大自然；自然界

ˌ**mother-of-ˈpearl** (also **pearl**) *noun* [U] the hard smooth shiny substance in various colours that forms a layer inside the shells of some types of SHELLFISH and is used in making buttons, decorative objects, etc. 珠母層；珍珠母

ˈ**Mother's Day** *noun* a day on which mothers traditionally receive cards and gifts from their children, celebrated in Britain on the fourth Sunday in Lent and in the US on the 2nd Sunday in May 母親節

ˈ**mother ship** *noun* a large ship or SPACECRAFT that smaller ones go out from 母艦；航天運載飛船

ˌ**mother's ˈmilk** *noun* [U] a thing that a person really needs or enjoys 真正需要（或喜愛）的事物：*Jazz is mother's milk to me.* 爵士樂對於我來說是不可或缺的。

ˌ**mother's ˈruin** *noun* [U] (*old-fashioned, BrE, informal*) the alcoholic drink GIN 杜松子酒

ˌ**Mother Suˈperior** *noun* a woman who is the head of a female religious community, especially a CONVENT (= a community of NUNS) 女修道院院長

ˌ**mother-to-ˈbe** *noun* (*pl.* **mothers-to-be**) a woman who is pregnant 孕婦

ˌ**mother ˈtongue** *noun* the language that you first learn to speak when you are a child 母語；本國語 **SYN** **first language**

motif /məʊˈtiːf; *NAmE* moʊ-/ *noun* **1** a design or a pattern used as a decoration 裝飾圖案；裝飾圖形：*wallpaper with a flower motif* 有鮮花圖案的牆紙 **2** a subject, an idea or a phrase that is repeated and developed in a work of literature or a piece of music（文學作品或音樂的）主題，主旨，動機 ➲ see also LEITMOTIF **SYN** **theme**

mo·tion 🔑 /ˈməʊʃn; *NAmE* ˈmoʊʃn/ *noun, verb*

■ *noun* **1** 🔑 [U, sing.] the act or process of moving or the way sth moves 運動；移動；動：*Newton's laws of motion* 牛頓的運動定律 ◇ *The swaying motion of the ship was making me feel seasick.* 船身搖擺不定，讓我覺得噁心。◇ (*formal*) *Do not alight while the train is still* ***in motion*** (= moving). 列車未停穩時不要下車。◇ *Rub the cream in with a circular motion.* 一圈一圈地揉擦乳霜。➲ see also SLOW MOTION **2** [C] a particular movement made usually with your hand or your head, especially to communicate sth（為傳遞信息用手或頭做的）動作 **SYN** **gesture**：*At a single motion of his hand, the room fell silent.* 他手一揮，屋子裏便安靜了下來。**3** [C] a formal proposal that is discussed and voted on at a meeting 動議；提議：*to* ***table/put forward a motion*** 提出一項動議 ◇ *to propose a motion* (= to be the main speaker in favour of a motion) 提出動議 ◇ *The* ***motion*** *was* ***adopted/carried*** *by six votes to one.* 這項提議以六比一的票數通過。**4** [C] (*BrE, formal*) an act of emptying the BOWELS; the waste matter that is emptied from the bowels 通便；大便

IDM **go through the ˈmotions (of doing sth)** to do or say sth because you have to, not because you really want to 做姿態；走過場 **set/put sth in ˈmotion** to start sth moving 讓…動起來：*They set the machinery in motion.* 他們將機器開動起來。◇ (*figurative*) *The wheels of change have been set in motion.* 變革的車輪已經開始運轉。

■ *verb* [I, T] to make a movement, usually with your hand or head to show sb what you want them to do（以頭或手）做動作，示意：**~ to sb (to do sth)** *I motioned to the waiter.* 我向侍者打了個手勢。◇ **~ (for) sb to do sth** *He motioned for us to follow him.* 他示意我們跟他走。◇ **~ sb + adv./prep.** *She motioned him into her office.* 她示意他到她辦公室來。

mo·tion·less /ˈməʊʃnləs; *NAmE* ˈmoʊʃn-/ *adj.* not moving; still 靜止的；一動不動的：*She stood absolutely motionless.* 她紋絲不動地站在那裏。

ˌ**motion ˈpicture** *noun* (*especially NAmE*) a film/movie that is made for the cinema 電影

ˈ**motion sickness** *noun* [U] the unpleasant feeling that you are going to VOMIT, that some people have when they are moving, especially in a vehicle 暈動病（尤指暈車）

mo·tiv·ate **AW** /ˈməʊtɪveɪt; *NAmE* ˈmoʊ-/ *verb* **1** [often passive] **~ sb** to be the reason why sb does sth or behaves in a particular way 成為…的動機；是…的原因：*He is motivated entirely by self-interest.* 他做事完全出於私利。**2** to make sb want to do sth, especially sth that involves hard work and effort 推動…甘願苦幹；激勵；激發：**~ sb** *She's very good at motivating her students.* 她非常擅長激勵她的學生。◇ **~ sb to do sth** *The plan is designed to motivate employees to work more efficiently.* 這個計劃旨在促使員工更加卓有成效地工作。**3 ~ sth** (*SAfrE, formal*) to give reasons for sth that you have stated（就所說的話）給出理由；說明…的原因：*Please motivate your answer to question 5.* 請解釋你對第 5 題所作的回答。▸ **mo·tiv·ated** **AW** *adj.*：*a racially motivated attack* 種族問題引發的攻擊 ◇ *a highly motivated student* (= one who is very interested and works hard) 學習積極性很高的學生 **OPP** **unmotivated** **mo·tiv·ation** **AW** /ˌməʊtɪˈveɪʃn; *NAmE* ˌmoʊ-/ *noun* [C, U]：*What is the* ***motivation behind*** *this sudden change?* 這個突然轉變背後的動機是什麼？◇ *Most people said that pay was their main motivation for working.* 大多數人說賺取報酬是他們工作的主要動機。◇ *He's intelligent enough but he lacks motivation.* 他很聰明，但缺乏積極性。◇ (*SAfrE*) *All research proposals must be accompanied by a full motivation.* 所有研究計劃書均須詳述研究動機。 **mo·tiv·ation·al** /-ʃənl/ *adj.*：(*formal*) *an important motivational factor* 重要的促進因素 **mo·tiv·ator** /ˈməʊtɪveɪtə(r); *NAmE* ˈmoʊ-/ *noun*：*Desire for status can be a powerful motivator.* 追逐地位的慾望可以成為強大的動力。

mo·tive **AW** /ˈməʊtɪv; *NAmE* ˈmoʊ-/ *noun, adj.*

■ *noun* **~ (for sth)** a reason for doing sth 動機；原因；目的：*There seemed to be no motive for the murder.* 這起謀殺案看不出有什麼動機。◇ *I'm suspicious of his motives.* 我懷疑他的動機。◇ *the profit motive* (= the desire to make a profit) 謀利的動機 ◇ *I have an* ***ulterior motive*** *in offering to help you.* 我主動提出要幫助你是有私心的。➲ SYNONYMS at REASON ▸ **mo·tive·less** *adj.*：*an apparently* ***motiveless murder/attack*** 表面上沒有動機的謀殺／襲擊

■ *adj.* [only before noun] (*technical* 術語) causing movement or action 發動的；導致運動的：***motive power/force*** (= for example, electricity, to operate machinery) 原動力

mot juste /ˌməʊ ˈʒuːst; *NAmE* ˌmoʊ/ *noun* (*pl.* **mots justes** /ˌməʊ ˈʒuːst; *NAmE* ˌmoʊ/) (from *French*) the exact word that is appropriate for the situation 恰當的用詞；貼切的字眼

mot·ley /ˈmɒtli; *NAmE* ˈmɑːtli/ *adj.* (*disapproving*) consisting of many different types of people or things that do not seem to belong together 混雜的；雜七雜八的：*The room was filled with a motley collection of*

M

furniture and paintings. 屋子裏擺滿了五花八門的傢具和繪畫。◇ *The audience was a **motley crew** of students and tourists.* 觀眾是一群混雜在一起的學生和遊客。

moto·cross /ˈməʊtəʊkrɒs; NAmE ˈmoʊtoʊkrɔːs; ˈmoʊtoʊkrɑːs/ (*BrE* also **scram·bling**) *noun* [U] the sport of racing motorcycles over rough ground 摩托車越野賽

moto·neur·on /ˌməʊtəˈnjʊərɒn; NAmE ˌmoʊtəˈnjʊrɑːn; -ˈnuː-/ *noun* = MOTOR NEURON

motor /ˈməʊtə(r); NAmE ˈmoʊ-/ *noun, adj., verb*

■ ***noun*** **1** a device that uses electricity, petrol/gas, etc. to produce movement and makes a machine, a vehicle, a boat, etc. work 發動機；馬達：*an electric motor* 電動機 ◇ *He started the motor.* 他啟動了發動機。➲ see also OUTBOARD MOTOR **2** (*BrE, old-fashioned* or *humorous*) a car 汽車

■ ***adj.*** [only before noun] **1** having an engine; using the power of an engine 有引擎的；由發動機推動的：*motor vehicles* 機動車輛 **2** (*especially BrE*) connected with vehicles that have engines 機動車的；汽車的：*the **motor industry/trade*** 汽車工業／貿易 ◇ *a motor accident* 機動車事故 ◇ *motor insurance* 汽車保險 ◇ *motor fuel* 汽車燃料 **3** (*technical* 術語) connected with movement of the body that is produced by muscles; connected with the nerves that control movement 肌肉運動的；運動神經的：*uncoordinated motor activity* 不協調的肌肉運動 ◇ *Both motor and sensory functions are affected.* 運動功能和感覺功能都受到影響。

■ ***verb*** [I] + **adv./prep.** (*old-fashioned, BrE*) to travel by car, especially for pleasure 乘車旅行；駕車旅行 ▸ **motor·ing** *noun* [U]：*They're planning a motoring holiday to France this year.* 他們計劃今年駕車到法國去度假。

M

motor·bike /ˈməʊtəbaɪk; NAmE ˈmoʊtərb-/ *noun* **1** (*especially BrE*) = MOTORCYCLE：*Ben drove off on his motorbike.* 本騎着摩托車走了。 **2** (*NAmE*) a bicycle which has a small engine 機動自行車

motor·boat /ˈməʊtəbəʊt; NAmE ˈmoʊtərboʊt/ *noun* a small fast boat driven by an engine 摩托艇；汽艇；汽船

motor·cade /ˈməʊtəkeɪd; NAmE ˈmoʊtərk-/ *noun* a line of vehicles including one or more that famous or important people are travelling in（載着要人的）車隊，汽車行列：*The President's motorcade glided by.* 總統的車隊一溜風開了過去。

ˈ**motor car** *noun* (*BrE, formal*) a car 汽車

motor·cycle /ˈməʊtəsaɪkl; NAmE ˈmoʊtərs-/ (also **motor·bike** especially in *BrE*) *noun* a road vehicle with two wheels, driven by an engine, with one seat for the driver and often a seat for a passenger behind the driver 摩托車：*motorcycle racing* 摩托車賽 ◇ *a motorcycle accident* 摩托車事故 ➲ COLLOCATIONS at DRIVING ➲ VISUAL VOCAB page V51

motor·cyc·ling /ˈməʊtəsaɪklɪŋ; NAmE ˈmoʊtərs-/ *noun* [U] the sport of riding motorcycles 摩托車運動

motor·cyc·list /ˈməʊtəsaɪklɪst; NAmE ˈmoʊtərs-/ *noun* a person riding a motorcycle 騎摩托車的人：*a police motorcyclist* 駕駛摩托車的警察 ◇ *leather-clad motorcyclists* 穿着皮衣的摩托車手

motor·home /ˈməʊtəhəʊm; NAmE ˈmoʊtərhoʊm/ (*NAmE* also **RV**, **recreˌational ˈvehicle**) (*BrE* also **camp·er**, **ˈcamper van**) *noun* a large vehicle designed for people to live and sleep in when they are travelling 野營車（供旅行時居住）➲ VISUAL VOCAB page V58

motor·ing /ˈməʊtərɪŋ; NAmE ˈmoʊ-/ *adj.* [only before noun] connected with driving a car 開汽車的：*a motoring offence* 違章汽車駕駛

motor·ist /ˈməʊtərɪst; NAmE ˈmoʊ-/ *noun* a person driving a car 駕車者；開汽車的人 ➲ compare PEDESTRIAN

motor·ized (*BrE* also **-ised**) /ˈməʊtəraɪzd; NAmE ˈmoʊ-/ *adj.* [only before noun] **1** having an engine 有引擎的；機動的：*motorized vehicles* 機動車輛 ◇ *a motorized wheelchair* 機動輪椅 **2** (of groups of soldiers, etc. 部隊等) using vehicles with engines 使用機動車的；摩托化的；機動化的：***motorized forces/divisions*** 摩托化部隊／師

ˈ**motor lodge** (*NAmE* also ˈ**motor inn**) *noun* = MOTEL

motor·mouth /ˈməʊtəmaʊθ; NAmE ˈmoʊtərm-/ *noun* (*pl.* **motor·mouths** /-maʊðz/) (*informal*) a person who talks loudly and too much 說話大聲且健談者；喋喋不休的人

ˌ**motor ˈneuron** (also **moto·neur·on**) *noun* (*biology* 生) a nerve cell which sends signals to a muscle or GLAND 運動神經元

ˌ**motor ˈneuron disease** (also ˌ**motoˈneuron disease**) *noun* [U] a disease in which the nerves and muscles become gradually weaker until the person dies 運動神經元病（神經和肌肉逐漸萎縮，直到死亡）

ˈ**motor park** *noun* (*WAfrE*) a station for passengers to get on or off buses or taxis 公共汽車站；出租車停靠站：*Passengers are set down at Molete Motor Park.* 乘客在莫里特站下車。

ˈ**motor pool** (*especially US*) (*BrE* also ˈ**car pool**) *noun* a group of cars owned by a company or an organization, that its staff can use（公司或機構的）公用車隊

ˈ**motor racing** (*especially BrE*) (*NAmE* usually ˈ**auto racing**) *noun* [U] the sport of racing fast cars on a special track 賽道汽車賽

ˈ**motor scooter** (*especially NAmE*) (*BrE* also **scoot·er**) *noun* a light motorcycle, usually with small wheels and a curved metal cover at the front to protect the rider's legs 小型摩托車 ➲ VISUAL VOCAB page V51

motor·sport /ˈməʊtəspɔːt; NAmE ˈmoʊtərspɔːrt/ *noun* [U] (*especially BrE*) (*NAmE* usually **motorsports** [pl.]) the sport of racing fast cars or motorcycles on a special track 賽車運動

ˈ**motor vehicle** *noun* any road vehicle driven by an engine 機動車

motor·way /ˈməʊtəweɪ; NAmE ˈmoʊtərweɪ/ *noun* [C, U] (in Britain) a wide road, with at least two lanes in each direction, where traffic can travel fast for long distances between large towns. You can only enter and leave motorways at special JUNCTIONS.（英國）高速公路：***busy/congested motorways*** 繁忙的／擁擠的高速公路 ◇ *Join the motorway at Junction 19.* 在 19 號路口進入高速公路。◇ *Leave the motorway at the next exit.* 在下個出口駛出高速公路。◇ *A nine-mile stretch of motorway has been closed.* 一段九英里長的高速公路已關閉。◇ *a **motorway service area / service station*** 高速公路服務區／站 ➲ compare INTERSTATE

Mo·town™ /ˈməʊtaʊn; NAmE ˈmoʊ-/ *noun* [U] a style of music popular in the 1960s and 1970s, produced by a black music company based in Detroit 汽車城音樂（流行於 20 世紀 60 和 70 年代，由本部在底特律的一家黑人唱片公司發行）**ORIGIN** From the informal name for the city of Detroit. 源自底特律城的非正式名稱（汽車城）。

motte /mɒt; NAmE mɑːt/ *noun* the small hill on which the FORT is built in a motte-and-bailey castle 城堡丘陵（大型城堡中建有堡壘的高地或小山）

ˌ**motte-and-ˌbailey ˈcastle** *noun* an old type of castle that consists of a FORT on a small hill surrounded by an outer wall（舊時的）大型城堡（堡壘建在高地，帶圍牆）

mot·tled /ˈmɒtld; NAmE ˈmɑːtld/ *adj.* marked with shapes of different colours without a regular pattern 斑駁的；雜色的

motto /ˈmɒtəʊ; NAmE ˈmɑːtoʊ/ *noun* (*pl.* **-oes** or **-os**) a short sentence or phrase that expresses the aims and beliefs of a person, a group, an institution, etc. and is used as a rule of behaviour 座右銘；格言；箴言：*The school's motto is: 'Duty, Honour, Country'.* 這所學校的校訓是：盡責、知恥、愛國。◇ *'Live and let live.' That's my motto.* "待人寬如待己"，這是我的座右銘。

mould (*especially US* **mold**) /məʊld; NAmE moʊld/ *noun, verb*

■ ***noun*** **1** [C] a container that you pour a liquid or soft substance into, which then becomes solid in the same shape as the container, for example when it is cooled or cooked 模具；鑄模：*A clay mould is used for casting bronze statues.* 用黏土模具來澆鑄青銅塑像。◇ *Pour the chocolate into a heart-shaped mould.* 將巧克力倒入心形模子。◇ *They **broke the mould** when they made you* (= there is nobody like you). 你是世上獨一無二的。

2 [C, usually sing.] a particular style showing the characteristics, attitudes or behaviour that are typical of sb/sth（獨特）類型，個性，風格：*a hero in the 'Superman' mould* "超人"型的英雄 ◇ *He is cast in a different mould from his predecessor.* 他和他的前任性格不一樣。◇ *She doesn't fit (into) the traditional mould of an academic.* 她不像一個傳統的學者。 **3** [U, C] a fine soft green, grey or black substance like fur that grows on old food or on objects that are left in warm wet air 黴；黴菌：*There's mould on the cheese.* 乾酪發霉了。◇ *moulds and fungi* 黴菌和真菌 ◇ *mould growth* 黴的生長 ➲ see also LEAF MOULD

IDM **break the 'mould (of sth)** to change what people expect from a situation, especially by acting in a dramatic and original way 改變…模式；打破…模式

■ *verb* **1** [T] to shape a soft substance into a particular form or object by pressing it or by putting it into a mould（用模具）澆鑄，塑造：**~ A (into B)** *First, mould the clay into the desired shape.* 首先，將陶土做成需要的形狀。◇ **~ B (from/out of/in A)** *The figure had been moulded in clay.* 這座人像是用黏土塑造的。 **2** [T] to strongly influence the way sb's character, opinions, etc. develop 對…影響重大；將…塑造成：**~ sb/sth** *The experience had moulded and coloured her whole life.* 這次經歷影響了她的一生。◇ **~ sb/sth into sb/sth** *He moulded them into a superb team.* 他將他們塑造成一支非凡的隊伍。 **3** [I, T] **~ (sth) to sth** to fit or make sth fit tightly around the shape of sth（使）緊貼於，吻合：*The fabric moulds to the body.* 這種織物很貼身。

mould·er (*US* **mol·der**) /ˈməʊldə(r); *NAmE* ˈmoʊ-/ *verb* [I] to decay slowly and steadily 腐爛；腐朽：*The room smelt of disuse and mouldering books.* 房間裏有一股荒置和書籍發霉的味道。

mould·ing (*especially US* **mold·ing**) /ˈməʊldɪŋ; *NAmE* ˈmoʊ-/ *noun* a decorative strip of plastic, stone, wood, etc. around the top edge of a wall, on a door, etc. 線腳（用於簷口、門楣等的凹凸帶形裝飾）

mouldy (*especially US* **moldy**) /ˈməʊldi; *NAmE* ˈmoʊ-/ *adj.* **1** covered with or containing MOULD 發霉的：***mouldy bread/cheese*** 發霉的麪包／乾酪 ◇ *Strawberries **go mouldy** very quickly.* 草莓很容易發霉。 **2** old and not in good condition 破舊的

moult (*especially US* **molt**) /məʊlt; *NAmE* moʊlt/ *verb* [I] (of a bird or an animal 鳥或獸) to lose feathers or hair before new feathers or hair grow 換羽；蜕毛

mound /maʊnd/ *noun* **1** a large pile of earth or stones; a small hill 土墩；小丘；小山崗：*a Bronze Age burial mound* 青銅時代的墳塚 ◇ *The castle was built on top of a natural grassy mound.* 這座城堡建在一個天然的綠草如茵的小丘上。 **2** a pile 一堆 SYN **heap**：*a small **mound of rice/sand*** 一小堆米／沙子 **3 ~ of sth** (*informal*) a large amount of sth 許多；大量 SYN **heap**：*I've got a mound of paperwork to do.* 我有一堆文案工作要做。 **4** (in BASEBALL 棒球) the small hill where the player who throws the ball (called the PITCHER) stands 投手站立的土墩

mount 0-w /maʊnt/ *verb, noun*

■ *verb*

▸ ORGANIZE 組織 **1** 0-w [T] **~ sth** to organize and begin sth 準備；安排；組織開展 SYN **arrange**：*to **mount a protest/campaign/an exhibition*** 發起抗議／運動；舉辦展覽

▸ INCREASE 增加 **2** 0-w [I] to increase gradually 逐步增加：*Pressure is mounting on the government to change the law.* 迫使政府修改法律的壓力不斷增加。◇ *The death toll continues to mount.* 死亡人數持續增加。 ➲ see also MOUNTING *adj.*

▸ GO UP STH 攀登 **3** 0-w [T] **~ sth** (*formal*) to go up sth, or up on to sth that is raised 登上；爬上；攀登 SYN **ascend**：*She slowly mounted the steps.* 她慢慢地爬上台階。◇ *He mounted the platform and addressed the crowd.* 他登上講台對人群發表演說。

▸ BICYCLE/HORSE 自行車；馬 **4** 0-w [T, I] **~ (sth)** (rather *formal*) to get on a bicycle, horse, etc. in order to ride it 騎上；乘上；跨上：*He mounted his horse and rode away.* 他騎上馬走了。 OPP **dismount** ➲ see also MOUNTED (1)

▸ PICTURE/JEWEL, ETC. 圖畫、寶石等 **5** [T] **~ sth (on/onto/in sth)** to fix sth into position on sth, so that you can use it, look at it or study it 鑲嵌；安置：*The specimens were mounted on slides.* 標本安放在載片上。◇ *The diamond is mounted in gold.* 這顆鑽石鑲在金飾物上。

▸ OF MALE ANIMAL 雄性動物 **6** [T] **~ sth** to get onto the back of a female animal in order to have sex 爬上（雌性動物的背）交配 IDM see GUARD *n.*

PHR V **ˌmount ˈup** to increase gradually in size and quantity（尺寸和數量上）增加，上升 SYN **build up**：*Meanwhile, my debts were mounting up.* 同時，我的債務還在不斷增加。

■ *noun*

▸ MOUNTAIN 山 **1** 0-w **Mount** (*abbr.* **Mt**) (used in modern English only in place names 在現代英語裏僅用於地名) a mountain or a hill 山；山峰：*Mt Everest* 珠穆朗瑪峰 ◇ *St Michael's Mount* 聖邁克爾山

▸ HORSE 馬 **2** (*formal* or *literary*) a horse that you ride on 坐騎

▸ FOR DISPLAYING/SUPPORTING STH 用以展示／支持某物 **3** something such as a piece of card or glass that you put sth on or attach sth to, to display it 襯紙板；載片；裱褙 **4** (also **mount·ing**) something that an object stands on or is attached to for support 托架；支撐架：*an **engine/gun mount*** 發動機架；炮架

moun·tain 0-w /ˈmaʊntən; *NAmE* ˈmaʊntn/ *noun* **1** 0-w a very high hill, often with rocks near the top 高山；山嶽：*a **chain/range of mountains*** 山巒；山脈 ◇ *to climb a mountain* 爬山 ◇ *We spent a week walking **in the mountains**.* 我們在群山中走了一個星期。◇ *to enjoy the **mountain air/scenery*** 享受山上的空氣；欣賞山中景色 ◇ ***mountain roads/streams/villages*** 山路；山中的溪流；山村 ◇ *a **mountain rescue team*** 登山營救隊 ➲ VISUAL VOCAB pages V4, V5 **2 ~ of sth** (*informal*) a very large amount or number of sth 許多；大量：*a mountain of work* 大量的工作 ◇ *We made mountains of sandwiches.* 我們做了一大堆三明治。◇ *the problem of Europe's butter mountain* (= the large amount of butter that has to be stored because it is not needed) 歐洲的黃油過剩問題

IDM **make a ˌmountain out of a ˈmolehill** (*disapproving*) to make an unimportant matter seem important 小題大做；誇大其詞

ˌmountain ˈash *noun* = ROWAN

ˈmountain bike *noun* a bicycle with a strong frame, wide tyres and many gears, designed for riding on rough ground 山地自行車；越野單車 ▸ **ˈmountain biking** *noun* [U] ➲ VISUAL VOCAB page V51

moun·tain·board /ˈmaʊntənbɔːd; *NAmE* ˈmaʊntnbɔːrd/ (also **ˌall-terrain ˈboard**) *noun* a short narrow board with wheels like a SKATEBOARD that can be used for going down mountains 山地輪滑板；滑山板；越野雪板 ▸ **moun·tain·board·ing** *noun* [U]

ˌMountain ˈDaylight Time *noun* [U] (*abbr.* **MDT**) the time used in summer in parts of the US and Canada near the Rocky Mountains that is six hours earlier than GMT 山區夏令時間（美國和加拿大落基山脈地區的夏季時間，比格林尼治平時早六小時）

moun·tain·eer /ˌmaʊntəˈnɪə(r); *NAmE* -tnˈɪr/ *noun* a person who climbs mountains as a sport 登山者；登山運動員

moun·tain·eer·ing /ˌmaʊntəˈnɪərɪŋ; *NAmE* -tnˈɪrɪŋ/ *noun* [U] the sport or activity of climbing mountains 登山運動：*to go mountaineering* 去爬山 ◇ *a mountaineering expedition* 登山探險

ˈmountain lion *noun* (*NAmE*) = PUMA

ˈmountain man *noun* (*NAmE*) a man who lives alone in the mountains, especially one who catches and kills animals for their fur 山地人，山裏人（尤指獵取毛皮的）

moun·tain·ous /ˈmaʊntənəs/ *adj.* **1** having many mountains 多山的：*a **mountainous region/terrain*** 多山的地區／地形 **2** very large in size or amount; like a mountain 巨大的；山一般的 SYN **huge**：*mountainous waves* 如山的巨浪

moun·tain·side /ˈmaʊntənsaɪd/ *noun* the side or slope of a mountain 山坡：*Tracks led up the mountainside.* 小徑沿着山坡向上延伸。

M

ˌMountain ˈStandard Time *noun* [U] (*abbr.* **MST**) the time used in winter in parts of the US and Canada near the Rocky Mountains that is seven hours earlier than GMT 山區冬季時間（美國和加拿大落基山脈地區的冬季時間，比格林尼治平時早七小時）

ˈMountain time *noun* [U] the standard time in the parts of the US and Canada that are near the Rocky Mountains 山區標準時間（美國和加拿大落基山脈地區的時間）

moun·tain·top /ˈmaʊntəntɒp; *NAmE* ˈmaʊntntɑːp/ *noun* the top of a mountain 山頂 ▸ **moun·tain·top** *adj.* [only before noun]：*a mountaintop ranch* 山頂上的大牧場

moun·te·bank /ˈmaʊntɪbæŋk/ *noun* (*old-fashioned*) a person who tries to trick people, especially in order to get their money 江湖騙子

mount·ed /ˈmaʊntɪd/ *adj.* [only before noun] **1** (of a person, especially a soldier or a police officer 人，尤指士兵或警察) riding a horse 騎馬的：*mounted policemen* 騎警 **2** placed on sth or attached to sth for display or support 裝裱好的；安裝好的：*a mounted photograph* 裱好的照片 **3 -mounted** (in compounds 構成複合詞) attached to the thing mentioned for support 安裝在…上的：*a ceiling-mounted fan* 吊扇 ➲ see also WALL-MOUNTED

Moun·tie /ˈmaʊnti/ *noun* (*informal*) a member of the Royal Canadian Mounted Police 加拿大皇家騎警隊員

mount·ing /ˈmaʊntɪŋ/ *adj.*, *noun*

■ ***adj.*** [only before noun] increasing, often in a manner that causes or expresses anxiety 上升的；增長的 **SYN growing**：***mounting excitement/concern/tension*** 越來越興奮／關注／緊張 ◇ *There is mounting evidence of serious effects on people's health.* 有越來越多的證據表明對人的健康有嚴重影響。

■ ***noun*** = MOUNT：*The engine came loose from its mountings.* 發動機從托架上鬆開了。

mourn /mɔːn; *NAmE* mɔːrn/ *verb* [T, I] to feel and show sadness because sb has died; to feel sad because sth no longer exists or is no longer the same （因失去…而）哀悼，憂傷 **SYN grieve for**：**~ sth** *He was still mourning his brother's death.* 他仍然在為哥哥的去世而悲傷。◇ *They mourn the passing of a simpler way of life.* 他們對逝去的較為淳樸的生活感到惋惜。◇ **~ (for sb/sth)** *Today we mourn for all those who died in two world wars.* 今天，我們向所有在兩次世界大戰中死難的人表示哀悼。◇ *She mourned for her lost childhood.* 她為失去的童年而傷感。

mourn·er /ˈmɔːnə(r); *NAmE* ˈmɔːrn-/ *noun* a person who attends a funeral, especially a friend or a relative of the dead person 弔唁者；哀悼者

mourn·ful /ˈmɔːnfl; *NAmE* ˈmɔːrnfl/ *adj.* very sad 憂傷的；悲痛的 **SYN melancholy**：*mournful eyes* 憂傷的眼睛 ◇ *mournful music* 憂傷的音樂 ◇ *I couldn't bear the mournful look on her face.* 我受不了她臉上那憂傷的神情。▸ **mourn·ful·ly** /-fəli/ *adv.*：*The dog looked mournfully after its owner.* 狗悲傷地目送主人離去。

mourn·ing /ˈmɔːnɪŋ; *NAmE* ˈmɔːrn-/ *noun* [U] **1** sadness that you show and feel because sb has died 傷逝；哀悼 **SYN grief**：*The government announced a day of national mourning for the victims.* 政府宣佈全國為受害者哀悼一日。◇ *She was still* ***in mourning*** *for her husband.* 她仍在為丈夫服喪。 **2** clothes that people wear to show their sadness at sb's death 喪服

mouse 0→ /maʊs/ *noun*, *verb*

■ ***noun*** (*pl.* **mice** /maɪs/) **1** 0→ a small animal that is covered in fur and has a long thin tail. Mice live in fields, in people's houses or where food is stored. 老鼠；耗子：*a field mouse* 田鼠 ◇ *a house mouse* 家鼠 ◇ *The stores were overrun with rats and mice.* 倉庫裏到處都是大大小小的老鼠。◇ *She crept upstairs,* ***quiet as a mouse.*** 她像耗子一樣悄悄地爬上樓去。◇ *He was a weak little mouse of a man.* 他是個懦弱無能的人。➲ see also DORMOUSE **2** 0→ (*pl. also* **mouses**) (*computing* 計) a small device that is moved by hand across a surface to control the movement of the CURSOR on a computer screen 鼠標；滑鼠：*Click the left mouse button twice to highlight the program.* 雙擊鼠標左鍵來加亮突出這個程序。◇ *Use the mouse to drag the icon to a new position.* 用鼠標將圖標拖到一個新的位置。➲ VISUAL VOCAB page V66 **IDM** see CAT

■ ***verb***

PHR V ˈmouse over sth (*computing* 計) to use the mouse to move over sth on a computer screen 使鼠標懸停於：*Mouse over the link in the original message.* 使鼠標懸停在原始信息的鏈接上。▸ **mouse·over** /ˈmaʊsəʊvə(r); *NAmE* -oʊ-/ *noun*：*the use of mouseovers in web design* 網頁設計中鼠標懸停的使用

ˈmouse mat (*BrE*) (*especially NAmE* **ˈmouse pad**) *noun* a small square of plastic that is the best kind of surface on which to use a computer mouse 鼠標墊；滑鼠墊 ➲ VISUAL VOCAB page V69

ˈmouse potato *noun* (*informal, disapproving*) a person who spends too much time using a computer 電腦迷

mouser /ˈmaʊsə(r)/ *noun* a cat that catches mice 捕鼠的貓

mouse·trap /ˈmaʊstræp/ *noun* a trap with a powerful spring that is used, for example in a house, for catching mice 捕鼠器；老鼠夾

mousey = MOUSY

mous·saka /muːˈsɑːkə/ *noun* [U, C] a Greek dish made from layers of AUBERGINE and finely chopped meat with cheese on top （希臘菜肴）肉末茄子餅，茄合子

mousse /muːs/ *noun* [C, U] **1** a cold DESSERT (= a sweet dish) made with cream and egg whites and flavoured with fruit, chocolate, etc.; a similar dish flavoured with fish, vegetables, etc. 奶油凍，木斯，慕斯（用奶油和蛋清加水果、巧克力等做成甜食，或加魚肉、菜等做成涼菜）：***a chocolate/strawberry mousse*** 巧克力／草莓奶油凍 ◇ ***salmon/mushroom mousse*** 鮭魚／蘑菇奶油凍 **2** a substance that is sold in AEROSOLS, for example the light white substance that is used on hair to give it a particular style or to improve its condition 頭髮定型劑；摩絲

mous·tache (*especially US* **mus·tache**) /məˈstɑːʃ; *NAmE* ˈmʌstæʃ; məˈstæʃ/ *noun* **1** a line of hair that a man allows to grow on his upper lip 上唇的髭子；髭 ➲ COLLOCATIONS at PHYSICAL ➲ VISUAL VOCAB page V60 **2 moustaches** [pl.] a very long moustache 長髭 ➲ compare BEARD

mous·tached (*especially US* **mus·tached**) /məˈstɑːʃt; *NAmE* ˈmʌstæʃt; məˈstæʃt/ *adj.* [usually before noun] having a moustache 長髭子的；有髭子的 ➲ compare MUSTACHIOED

mous·tachi·oed = MUSTACHIOED

mousy (also **mousey**) /ˈmaʊsi/ *adj.* (*disapproving*) **1** (of hair 毛髮) of a dull brown colour 暗灰褐色的 **2** (usually *disapproving*) (of people 人) shy and quiet; without a strong personality 沉靜害羞的；個性不強的

mouth 0→ *noun*, *verb*

■ ***noun*** /maʊθ/ (*pl.* **mouths** /maʊðz/)

▸ PART OF FACE 臉的部位 **1** 0→ the opening in the face used for speaking, eating, etc.; the area inside the head behind this opening 嘴；口：*She* ***opened her mouth*** *to say something.* 她張開嘴要說什麼。◇ *His mouth twisted into a wry smile.* 他硬擠出一絲乾澀的微笑。◇ *Their* ***mouths fell open*** (= they were surprised). 他們張口結舌。◇ *Don't* ***talk with your mouth full*** (= when eating). 不要一邊吃一邊說話。◇ *The creature was foaming* ***at the mouth.*** 那隻動物在口吐白沫。➲ VISUAL VOCAB page V59 ➲ see also FOOT-AND-MOUTH DISEASE

▸ PERSON NEEDING FOOD 需要食物的人 **2** a person considered only as sb who needs to be provided with food 需要供養的人；食客：*Now there would be another* ***mouth to feed.*** 現在又多一個要吃飯的人。◇ *The world will not be able to support all these extra* ***hungry mouths.*** 這個世界養活不起這麼些額外的饑民。

▸ ENTRANCE/OPENING 入口；出口 **3** 0→ **~ (of sth)** the entrance or opening of sth 入口；開口：*the mouth of a cave/pit* 山洞／礦井口 ➲ see also GOALMOUTH

▸ OF RIVER 河流 **4** 0→ the place where a river joins the sea 入海口；河口

▸ **WAY OF SPEAKING 講話方式 5** a particular way of speaking 講話方式；言談：*He has a foul mouth on him!* 他滿嘴髒話！◇ *Watch your mouth!* (= stop saying things that are rude and/or offensive) 說話注意點兒！➲ see also LOUDMOUTH
▸ **-MOUTHED …口 6** (in adjectives 構成形容詞) having the type or shape of mouth mentioned 有…嘴的；…口的：*a wide-mouthed old woman* 大嘴的老太太 ◇ *a narrow-mouthed cave* 洞口狹窄的山洞 ➲ see also OPEN-MOUTHED **7** (in adjectives 構成形容詞) having a particular way of speaking 言談…的；口齒…的：*a rather crude-mouthed individual* 言談非常粗魯的人 ➲ see also FOUL-MOUTHED, MEALY-MOUTHED

IDM **be all 'mouth** (*informal*) if you say sb is **all mouth**, you mean that they talk a lot about doing sth, but are, in fact, not brave enough to do it 只說不做 **down in the 'mouth** unhappy and depressed 悶悶不樂；沮喪 **keep your 'mouth shut** (*informal*) to not talk about sth to sb because it is a secret or because it will upset or annoy them 守口如瓶；保持緘默：*I've warned them to keep their mouths shut about this.* 我警告他們對此事要守口如瓶。◇ *Now she's upset—why couldn't you keep your mouth shut?* 瞧她現在心煩意亂的樣子，你就不能閉上嘴？ **out of the ˌmouths of 'babes (and 'sucklings)** (*saying*) used when a small child has just said sth that seems very wise or clever 童言有道 **run off at the 'mouth** (*NAmE, informal*) to talk too much, in a way that is not sensible 夸夸其談；信口開河；喋喋不休 ➲ more at BIG *adj.*, BORN *v.*, BREAD, BUTTER *n.*, FOAM *v.*, FOOT *n.*, GIFT *n.*, HEART, HORSE *n.*, LIVE[1], MELT, MONEY, SHOOT *v.*, SHUT *v.*, TASTE *n.*, WATCH *v.*, WORD *n.*

■ *verb* /maʊð/ **1 ~ sth | + speech** to move your lips as if you were saying sth, but without making a sound（動嘴唇）不出聲地說：*He mouthed a few obscenities at us and then moved off.* 他不出聲地朝我們罵了幾句髒話然後離去。 **2 ~ sth | + speech** (*disapproving*) to say sth that you do not really feel, believe or understand 言不由衷地說：*They're just mouthing empty slogans.* 他們只是在空喊口號。

PHR V **ˌmouth 'off (at/about sth)** (*informal*) to talk or complain loudly about sth 大聲地講述；大聲地抱怨

mouth·ful /'maʊθfʊl/ *noun* **1** [C] an amount of food or drink that you put in your mouth at one time 一口，一滿口（的量）：*She took a mouthful of water.* 她喝了一大口水。 **2** [sing.] (*informal*) a word or a phrase that is long and complicated or difficult to pronounce 又長又拗口的詞（或短語）

IDM **give sb a 'mouthful** (*informal, especially BrE*) to speak angrily to sb, perhaps swearing at them 對某人惡言惡語；大罵某人 **say a 'mouthful** (*NAmE, informal*) to say sth important using only a few words 言簡意賅；說到點子上

mouth·guard /'maʊθgɑːd; *NAmE* -gɑːrd/ (*NAmE*) (*BrE* **gum·shield**) *noun* a cover that a sports player wears in his/her mouth to protect the teeth and GUMS（運動員所戴的）護齒

'mouth organ *noun* (*BrE*) = HARMONICA

mouth·piece /'maʊθpiːs/ *noun* **1** the part of the telephone that is next to your mouth when you speak（電話的）話筒 **2** the part of a musical instrument that you place between your lips（樂器的）吹口 ➲ VISUAL VOCAB page V34 **3 ~ (of/for sb)** a person, newspaper, etc. that speaks on behalf of another person or group of people 喉舌；代言人；發言人：*The newspaper has become the official mouthpiece of the opposition party.* 這份報紙已經成為反對黨的官方喉舌。◇ *The Press Secretary serves as the President's mouthpiece.* 新聞部長擔任總統的代言人。

ˌmouth-to-ˌmouth reˌsusci'tation (also **ˌmouth-to-'mouth**) *noun* [U] the act of breathing into the mouth of an unconscious person in order to fill their lungs with air 口對口人工呼吸 **SYN** **the kiss of life** ➲ compare ARTIFICIAL RESPIRATION

'mouth ulcer (*BrE*) (*NAmE* **'canker sore**) *noun* a small sore area in the mouth 口腔潰瘍

mouth·wash /'maʊθwɒʃ; *NAmE* -wɔːʃ; -wɑːʃ/ *noun* [C, U] a liquid used to make the mouth fresh and healthy 漱口劑

'mouth-watering *adj.* (*approving*) **mouth-watering** food looks or smells so good that you want to eat it immediately（食物）令人垂涎的，非常好吃的 **SYN** **tempting**：*a mouth-watering display of cakes* 令人垂涎的蛋糕展示 ◇ (*figurative*) *mouth-watering travel brochures* 誘人的旅遊手冊

mouthy /'maʊθi; -ði/ *adj.* (*informal, disapproving*) used to describe a person who talks a lot, sometimes expressing their opinions strongly and in a rude way 夸夸其談的

mov·able (also **move·able**) /'muːvəbl/ *adj., noun*
■ *adj.* **1** that can be moved from one place or position to another 可移動的；活動的：*movable partitions* 可移動的隔板 ◇ *a doll with a movable head* 頭可活動的洋娃娃 **2** (*law* 律) (of property 財產) able to be taken from one house, etc. to another 活動的；不固定的
■ *noun* [C, usually pl.] (*law* 律) a thing that can be moved from one house, etc. to another; a personal possession 動產；個人財物

ˌmovable 'feast *noun* a religious festival, such as Easter, whose date changes from year to year 因年而異的宗教節日（日期每年都可有變化）

move 🔑 /muːv/ *verb, noun*
■ *verb*
▸ **CHANGE POSITION 改變位置 1** 🔑 [I, T] to change position or make sb/sth change position in a way that can be seen, heard or felt（使）改變位置，移動：*Don't move—stay perfectly still.* 別動，一點都別動。◇ *The bus was already moving when I jumped onto it.* 我跳上車的時候，公共汽車已經開動了。◇ **+ adv./prep.** *He could hear someone moving around in the room above.* 他聽到樓上屋裏有人走動。◇ *Phil moved towards the window.* 菲爾朝窗戶走去。◇ ***You can hardly move** in this pub on Saturdays* (= because it is so crowded). 這家酒吧星期六總是擠得令人無法挪動。◇ ***You can't move for** books in her room.* 她的屋裏書多得挪不開步。◇ **~ sth** *I can't move my fingers.* 我的手指動不了了。◇ **~ sth + adv./prep.** *We moved our chairs a little nearer.* 我們把椅子挪近了一點。
▸ **CHANGE IDEAS/TIME 改變主意／時間 2** 🔑 [I, T] to change; to change sth 變化；改變；轉變 **SYN** **shift**：(**+ adv./prep.**) *The government has not moved on this issue.* 政府在這個問題上立場沒有轉變。◇ **~ sth (+ adv./prep.)** *Let's move the meeting to Wednesday.* 我們把開會時間改到星期三吧。
▸ **MAKE PROGRESS 取得進展 3** 🔑 [I] **~ (on/ahead)** to make progress in the way or direction mentioned 前進；進步；進展 **SYN** **progress**：*Time is moving on.* 時代在進步。◇ *Share prices moved ahead today.* 今天的股票價格上升了。◇ *Things are not moving as fast as we hoped.* 事情的進展不像我們希望的那麼快。
▸ **TAKE ACTION 採取行動 4** [I] to take action; to do sth 採取行動；做（事）**SYN** **act**：*The police moved quickly to dispel the rumours.* 警察迅速採取行動來消除謠言。 ➲ SYNONYMS at ACTION
▸ **CHANGE HOUSE/JOB 搬家；換工作 5** 🔑 [I, T] to change the place where you live, have your work, etc. 搬家；搬遷：*We don't like it here so we've decided to move.* 我們不喜歡這地方，所以決定搬走。◇ **~ (from …) (to …)** *The company's moving to Scotland.* 公司準備遷往蘇格蘭。◇ **~ away** *She's been all on her own since her daughter moved away.* 自從她女兒搬走以後，她一直獨自生活。◇ **~ house** (*BrE*) *We moved house last week.* 我們上星期搬家了。 **6** 🔑 [T] **~ sb (from …) (to …)** to make sb change from one job, class, etc. to another 使變換；調動 **SYN** **transfer**：*I'm being moved to the New York office.* 我要調到紐約辦事處去。
▸ **IN BOARD GAMES 棋類遊戲 7** 🔑 [I, T] (in CHESS and other board games 國際象棋和其他棋類遊戲) to change the position of a piece 走棋；移動棋子：*It's your turn to move.* 該你走棋了。◇ **~ sth** *She moved her queen.* 她挪動了棋盤上的王后。
▸ **CAUSE STRONG FEELINGS 使感動 8** 🔑 [T] to cause sb to have strong feelings, especially of sympathy or sadness 使感動（尤指因為同情或悲傷）；打動：**~ sb** *We were **deeply moved** by her plight.* 她的困境深深地打動了我們。◇ **~ sb to sth** *Grown men were **moved to tears** at*

M

the horrific scenes. 這樣悲慘的場面甚至讓錚錚漢子潸然淚下。➲ see also MOVING (1)

▸ MAKE SB DO STH 促使 **9** [T] (*formal*) to cause sb to do sth 促使，迫使（某人做某事）；使去做 SYN **prompt**: **~ sb to do sth** *She felt moved to address the crowd.* 她不由得想給大家講一番話。◇ **~ sb** *He works when the spirit moves him* (= when he wants to). 他只有在想幹活的時候才幹活。

▸ SUGGEST FORMALLY 正式提出 **10** [T] (*formal*) to suggest sth formally so that it can be discussed and decided（正式地）提出，提議 SYN **put forward**: **~ sth** *The Opposition moved an amendment to the Bill.* 反對派對法案提出修正案。◇ **~ that …** *I move that a vote be taken on this.* 我提議就此進行投票。

IDM **get 'moving** (*informal*) to begin, leave, etc. quickly 馬上行動；迅速開始（或離去等）: *It's late—we'd better get moving.* 天不早了，咱們走吧。 **get sth 'moving** (*informal*) to cause sth to make progress 使進步；推動: *The new director has really got things moving.* 新來的主任確實使事情有了進展。 **move heaven and 'earth** to do everything you possibly can in order to achieve sth 竭盡所能；竭盡全力 **move with the 'times** to change the way you think and behave according to changes in society 順應時代；順應潮流 ➲ more at ASS, FORWARD *adv.*

PHR V **,move a'long** to go to a new position, especially in order to make room for other people 移動一下，向前移動（以騰出空間）: *The bus driver asked them to move along.* 公共汽車司機讓他們往裏走走。 **,move 'in | ,move 'into sth** 🔑 to start to live in your new home 搬進新居: *Our new neighbours moved in yesterday.* 我們的新鄰居昨天搬來了。 OPP **move out** **,move 'in sth** to live, spend your time, etc. in a particular social group 涉足，出入，生活在（某群體）: *She only moves in the best circles.* 她只涉足那些精英圈子。 **,move 'in (on sb/sth)** to move towards sb/sth from all directions, especially in a threatening way 從四面八方逼近；進逼: *The police moved in on the terrorists.* 警察從四面八方向恐怖分子進逼。 **,move 'in with sb** to start living with sb in the house or flat/apartment where they already live 搬來和某人一起居住 **,move 'off** (especially of a vehicle 尤指交通工具) to start moving; to leave 啟動；離去 **,move 'on (to sth)** to start doing or discussing sth new 開始做（別的事）；換話題: *I've been in this job long enough—it's time I moved on.* 這工作我已經幹得夠久了，我該幹點別的了。◇ *Can we move on to the next item on the agenda?* 我們可以接着討論下一項議程嗎？ **,move sb 'on** (of police, etc. 警察等) to order sb to move away from the scene of an accident, etc. 讓（某人）離開（事故現場等） **,move 'out** 🔑 to leave your old home 搬出去；遷出 OPP **move in** **,move 'over** 🔑 (also **,move 'up**) to change your position in order to make room for sb 挪開；讓位: *There's room for another one if you move up a bit.* 如果你挪開一點，這裏還可以容納多一個人。

■ *noun*

▸ ACTION 行動 **1** 🔑 **~ (towards/to sth) | ~ (to do sth)** an action that you do or need to do to achieve sth 行動: *This latest move by the government has aroused fierce opposition.* 政府最近採取的行動引起了強烈的反對。◇ *The management have made no move to settle the strike.* 管理層沒有採取任何措施來解決罷工問題。◇ *Getting a job in marketing was a good* ***career move***. 找份市場營銷的工作是一個不錯的職業選擇。➲ see also FALSE MOVE

▸ CHANGE OF POSITION 位置變換 **2** 🔑 [usually sing.] a change of place or position 移動；活動: *Don't* ***make a move!*** 別動！◇ *Every move was painful.* 每動一下都很痛。◇ *She felt he was watching her* ***every move***. 她覺得他在注意她的一舉一動。➲ see also MOVEMENT (1), (2)

▸ CHANGE OF IDEAS/BEHAVIOUR 想法／行為的改變 **3** **~ to/away from sth** a change in ideas, attitudes or behaviour 改變；轉變；動搖 SYN **shift, trend**: *There has been a move away from nuclear energy.* 人們對於原子能的看法已經轉變。

▸ CHANGE OF HOUSE/JOB 搬家；調職 **4** 🔑 an act of changing the place where you live or work 搬家；搬遷；調動: *What's the date of your move?* 你什麼時候搬家？◇ *Their move from Italy to the US has not been a success.* 他們從意大利遷到美國並不成功。◇ *Her new job is just a sideways move.* 她的新工作只是平級調動。

▸ IN BOARD GAMES 棋類遊戲 **5** an act of changing the position of a piece in CHESS or other games that are played on a board 走棋；（棋子的）移動: *The game was over in only six moves.* 這盤棋只走了六步就結束了。◇ *It's your move.* 該你走了。

IDM **be on the 'move 1** to be travelling from place to place（經常）變換地點 **2** to be moving; to be going somewhere 在行進中；在移動中: *The car was already on the move.* 汽車已經開動了。◇ *The firm is on the move to larger offices.* 公司正在遷往更大的辦公樓。 **3** = BE ON THE GO **get a 'move on** (*informal*) you tell sb to **get a move on** when you want them to hurry 趕快 **make the first 'move** to do sth before sb else, for example in order to end an argument or to begin sth 搶先行動；搶佔先機: *If he wants to see me, he should make the first move.* 他要是想見我，就得採取主動。 **make a 'move** (*BrE, informal*) to begin a journey or a task 動身；開始行動: *It's getting late—we'd better make a move.* 時間不早了，我們得動身了。 **make a 'move on sb** (*informal*) **1** to try to start a sexual relationship with sb 意圖與某人發生性關係 **2** (*sport* 體) to try to pass sb who is in front of you in a race（速度競賽時）設法超越某人 **make a, your, etc. 'move** to do the action that you intend to do or need to do in order to achieve sth 採取行動；開始行動: *The rebels waited until nightfall before they made their move.* 叛亂者一直等到夜幕降臨才開始行動。

move·able *adj.* = MOVABLE

move·ment 🔑 /'muːvmənt/ *noun*

▸ CHANGING POSITION 改變位置 **1** 🔑 [C, U] an act of moving the body or part of the body（身體部位的）運動，轉動，活動: ***hand/eye movements*** 手／眼睛的活動 ◇ *She observed the gentle movement of his chest as he breathed.* 她觀察着他呼吸時胸部的微微起伏。◇ *Loose clothing gives you greater freedom of movement.* 衣服寬鬆，可以活動自如。◇ *There was a sudden movement in the undergrowth.* 矮樹叢裏突然有什麼東西動了一下。 **2** 🔑 [C, U] an act of moving from one place to another or of moving sth from one place to another 移動；遷移；轉移；活動: *enemy troop movements* 敵軍的調動 ◇ *laws to allow free movement of goods and services* 允許商品和服務自由流動的法律

▸ GROUP OF PEOPLE 群體 **3** 🔑 [C+sing./pl. v.] a group of people who share the same ideas or aims（具有共同思想或目標的）運動: *the* ***women's/peace movement*** 婦女／和平運動 ◇ *the Romantic movement* (= for example in literature) 浪漫主義運動 ◇ *a mass movement for change* 要求變革的群眾運動 ➲ COLLOCATIONS at POLITICS

▸ PERSON'S ACTIVITIES 人的活動 **4** **movements** [pl.] a person's activities over a period of time, especially as watched by sb else（尤指受監視者的）活動；行踪: *The police are keeping a close watch on the suspect's movements.* 警察正在密切監視嫌疑犯的活動。

▸ CHANGE OF IDEAS/BEHAVIOUR 想法／行為的改變 **5** [sing.] **~ (away from/towards sth)** a gradual change in what people in society do or think 逐步的轉變 SYN **trend**: *a movement towards greater sexual equality* 朝着更進一步的性別平等的轉變

▸ PROGRESS 進展 **6** [U] **~ (in sth)** progress, especially in a particular task（尤指某一工作的）進步，進展: *It needs cooperation from all the countries to get any movement in arms control.* 要在軍控方面取得進展需要所有國家的合作。

▸ CHANGE IN AMOUNT 量的改變 **7** [U, C] **~ (in sth)** a change in amount 量的變化；增減: *There has been no movement in oil prices.* 石油價格沒有變化。

▸ MUSIC 音樂 **8** [C] any of the main parts that a long piece of music is divided into 樂章: *the slow movement of the First Concerto* 第一協奏曲的和緩樂章

▸ OF BOWELS 腸 **9** [C] (*technical* 術語) = BOWEL MOVEMENT

mover /'muːvə(r)/ *noun* **1** a person or thing that moves in a particular way 以某方式移動的人（或物）: *a great mover on the dance floor* 舞場中舞姿優美的人 ➲ see also PRIME MOVER **2** a machine or a person that moves things from one place to another, especially sb who moves furniture from one house to another 運送物品的機器（或人）；搬運傢具的人：*an earth mover* 運土機 ◇ *professional furniture movers* 專業搬家工人 ➲ see also REMOVER (2)

IDM **ˌmovers and ˈshakers** people with power in important organizations（重要機構中）有權勢的人

movie 0➔ /ˈmuːvi/ *noun* (*especially NAmE*)
1 0➔ [C] a series of moving pictures recorded with sound that tells a story, shown at the cinema/movie theater 電影 **SYN** **film**：*to make a horror movie* 製作恐怖電影 ◇ *Have you seen the latest Miyazaki movie?* 你看過宮崎的新電影嗎？◇ *a famous* ***movie director/star*** 著名的電影導演／明星 ➲ COLLOCATIONS at CINEMA ➲ see also ROAD MOVIE **2** 0➔ **the movies** [pl.] = THE CINEMA (2)：*Let's go to the movies.* 我們去看電影吧。**3** 0➔ **the movies** [pl.] = CINEMA (3)：*I've always wanted to work in the movies.* 我一直想從事電影業。

movie·goer /ˈmuːvigəʊə(r); *NAmE* -goʊ-/ *noun* (*especially NAmE*) = FILM-GOER

ˈmovie star *noun* (*especially NAmE*) = FILM STAR

ˈmovie theater 0➔ (also **theater**) *noun* (*NAmE*) = CINEMA (1), THEATER (2)：*The documentary opens tomorrow in movie theaters nationwide.* 這部紀錄片明日起在全國各地的影院上映。

mov·ing 0➔ /ˈmuːvɪŋ/ *adj.*
1 0➔ causing you to have deep feelings of sadness or sympathy 動人的；令人感動的：*a deeply moving experience* 非常動人的經歷 **2** 0➔ [only before noun] (of things 事物) changing from one place or position to another 移動的；運動的：*the moving parts of a machine* 機器的活動部件 ◇ *fast-moving water* 快速流動的水 ◇ *a moving target* 活動靶 ▸ **mov·ing·ly** *adv.*：*She described her experiences in Africa very movingly.* 她十分動人地描述了她在非洲的經歷。

ˈmoving van (*NAmE*) (*BrE* **reˈmoval van**, **ˈfurniture van**) *noun* a large van used for moving furniture from one house to another 搬家卡車

mow /məʊ; *NAmE* moʊ/ *verb* (**mowed**, **mown** /məʊn; *NAmE* moʊn/ or **mowed**) [T, I] **~ (sth)** to cut grass, etc. using a machine or tool with a special blade or blades 刈；割；修剪：*I mow the lawn every week in summer.* 夏天我每週都要修剪草坪。◇ *the smell of new-mown hay* 新割的草料的氣味

PHR V **ˌmow sb↔ˈdown** to kill sb using a vehicle or a gun, especially when several people are all killed at the same time（用交通工具或槍）殺死，撂倒，掃倒

mower /ˈməʊə(r); *NAmE* ˈmoʊ-/ *noun* (especially in compounds 尤用於構成複合詞) a machine that cuts grass 割草機；剪草機：*a lawnmower* 剪草機 ◇ ***a motor/rotary mower*** 機動／滾筒割草機

moxie /ˈmɒksi; *NAmE* ˈmɑːksi/ *noun* [U] (*NAmE, informal*) courage, energy and determination 人格力量（指勇氣、精力和決心）

moz·za·rella /ˌmɒtsəˈrelə; *NAmE* ˌmɑːts-/ *noun* [U] a type of soft white Italian cheese with a mild flavour 莫澤雷勒乾酪（一種色白味淡的意大利乾酪）

moz·zie /ˈmɒzi; *NAmE* ˈmɑːzi; ˈmɔːzi/ *noun* (*pl.* **-ies**) (*informal*) a MOSQUITO 蚊子

MP /ˌem ˈpiː/ *noun* **1** the abbreviation for 'Member of Parliament' (a person who has been elected to represent the people of a particular area in a parliament) 議員（全寫為 Member of Parliament，經選舉在議會中代表某一選區者）：*Michael Phillips MP* 下院議員邁克爾•菲利普斯 ◇ *Write to your local MP to protest.* 給你們地區的議員寫信抗議。◇ *Conservative/Labour MPs* 議會中的保守黨／工黨議員 ◇ *the MP for Oxford East* 代表牛津東區的議員 ◇ *a Euro-MP* 歐洲議會議員 **2** a member of the MILITARY POLICE 憲兵

MP3 /ˌem piː ˈθriː/ *noun* [C, U] a method of reducing the size of a computer file containing sound, or a file that is reduced in size in this way * MP3 技術（指 MPEG 第三層聲音壓縮技術）；MP3 文件；MP3 檔案

MPˈ3 player *noun* a piece of computer equipment that can open and play MP3 files * MP3 播放機 ➲ VISUAL VOCAB page V66

MP4 /ˌem piː ˈfɔː(r)/ *noun* [C, U] a method of reducing the size of a computer file containing sound and images; a file that is reduced in size in this way * MP4 技術（一種影音壓縮技術）；MP4 文件

MPEG /ˈempeg/ *noun* (*computing* 計) **1** [U] technology which reduces the size of files that contain video images or sounds * MPEG（運動圖像壓縮）標準：*an MPEG file* * MPEG 文件；MPEG 檔 **2** [C] a file produced using this technology * MPEG 文件；MPEG 檔

mpg /ˌem piː ˈdʒiː/ *abbr.* miles per gallon (used for saying how much petrol/gas a vehicle uses) 每加侖燃料所行英里數；英里每加侖：*It does 40 mpg.* 這車每加侖跑 40 英里。◇ (*NAmE*) *It gets 40 mpg.* 這車每加侖跑 40 英里。

mph /ˌem piː ˈeɪtʃ/ *abbr.* miles per hour 每小時所行英里數；英里每小時：*a 60 mph speed limit* 每小時 60 英里的限速

MPV /ˌem piː ˈviː/ *noun* the abbreviation for 'multi-purpose vehicle' (a large car like a van) 多功能車，多用途車（全寫為 multi-purpose vehicle）**SYN** **people carrier**

Mr 0➔ (*BrE*) (also **Mr.** *NAmE, BrE*) /ˈmɪstə(r)/ *abbr.*
1 0➔ a title that comes before a man's family name, or before his first and family names together（用於男子的姓氏或姓名前）先生：*Mr Brown* 布朗先生 ◇ *Mr John Brown* 約翰•布朗先生 ◇ *Mr and Mrs Brown* 布朗先生和夫人 **2** a title used to address a man in some official positions（用於稱呼要員）先生：*Thank you, Mr Chairman.* 謝謝你，主席先生。◇ *Mr. President* 總統先生 ➲ see also MISTER (1)

IDM **ˌMr ˈNice Guy** (*informal*) a way of describing a man who is very honest and thinks about the wishes and feelings of other people 大好人；大善人：*I was tired of helping other people. From now on it was* ***no more Mr Nice Guy*** (= I would stop being pleasant and kind). 我已對幫助他人感到厭煩。從今以後我不做大善人了。 **Mr ˈRight** (*informal*) the man who would be the right husband for a particular woman 如意郎君；理想夫婿：*I'm not getting married in a hurry—I'm waiting for Mr Right to come along.* 我不想匆忙結婚，我在等着如意郎君出現。

ˌMr. ˈCharlie *noun* (*US, slang, offensive*) a name used by African Americans for a white man（非裔美國人對白人的稱呼）查理先生

ˌMr. ˈClean *noun* (*US, informal*) a man, especially a politician, who is considered to be very honest and good 清廉先生，正人君子（尤指從政者）：*The scandal destroyed his image as Mr. Clean.* 醜聞破壞了他的清廉形象。

Mr Fixit /ˌmɪstə ˈfɪksɪt/ *noun* (*BrE, informal*) a person who organizes things and solves problems 組織協調大王；解決問題能手

MRI /ˌem ɑːr ˈaɪ/ *abbr.* (*medical* 醫) magnetic resonance imaging (a method of using a strong MAGNETIC FIELD to produce an image of the inside of a person's body) 磁共振成像；磁力共振成像：*an MRI scan* 磁共振成像掃描

Mrs 0➔ (*BrE*) (also **Mrs.** *NAmE, BrE*) /ˈmɪsɪz/ *abbr.*
a title that comes before a married woman's family name or before her first and family names together（用於女子的姓氏或姓名前）太太，夫人：*Mrs Hill* 希爾太太 ◇ *Mrs Susan Hill* 蘇珊•希爾太太 ◇ *Mr and Mrs Hill* 希爾先生和夫人 ➲ compare MISS *n.* (1), (3), Ms

MRSA /ˌem ɑːr es ˈeɪ/ *noun* [U] the abbreviation for 'methicillin-resistant Staphylococcus aureus' (a type of bacteria that cannot be killed by standard ANTIBIOTICS) 抗甲氧西林金黃色葡萄球菌，抗甲氧苯青黴素金黃葡萄球菌（全寫為 methicilin-resistant Staphylococcus aureus，抗藥性細菌）：*rising rates of MRSA infections in hospitals* 醫院中感染抗甲氧西林金黃色葡萄球菌的病例增加得很快 ➲ see also SUPERBUG

MS (*NAmE* also **M.S.**) /ˌem ˈes/ *abbr.* **1** MULTIPLE SCLEROSIS 多發性硬化 **2** MANUSCRIPT (1) **3** = MSc

M

Ms 0┳ (*BrE*) (also **Ms.** *NAmE*, *BrE*) /mɪz; məz/ *abbr.* a title that comes before a woman's family name or before her first and family names together, and that can be used when you do not want to state whether she is married or not（用於女子的姓氏或姓名前，不指明婚否）女士：*Ms Murphy* 墨菲女士 ◇ *Ms Jean Murphy* 瓊・墨菲女士 ➲ compare MISS *n.* (1), (3), MRS

MSc /ˌem es ˈsiː/ (*BrE*) (*NAmE* **M.S.**, **MS**) *noun* the abbreviation for 'Master of Science' (a second university degree in science) 理科碩士（全寫為 Master of Science，大學理科中的中級學位）：(*BrE*) *to* **be/have/do an MSc** 是理科碩士；有理科碩士學位；攻讀理科碩士 ◇ (*BrE*) *J. Stevens MSc* 理科碩士 J・史蒂文斯

MSG /ˌem es ˈdʒiː/ *abbr.* MONOSODIUM GLUTAMATE 穀氨酸單鈉鹽；味精；味素

MSM /ˌem es ˈem/ *noun* [U+sing./pl. v.] (*computing* 計) the abbreviation for 'mainstream media' (traditional media such as newspapers and broadcasting) 主流媒體（全寫為 mainstream media，指報紙、廣播等傳統媒體）：*The line is beginning to blur between influential blogs and MSM.* 有影響的博客和主流媒體之間的界限開始變得模糊。

MSP /ˌem es ˈpiː/ *noun* the abbreviation for 'Member of the Scottish Parliament' 蘇格蘭議會議員（全寫為 Member of the Scottish Parliament）：*Alex Neil MSP* 蘇格蘭議會議員亞歷克斯・尼爾 ◇ *Write to your local MSP to protest.* 給你們地區的蘇格蘭議會議員寫信抗議。◇ *Labour MSPs* 蘇格蘭議會中的工黨議員

MST /ˌem es ˈtiː/ *abbr.* MOUNTAIN STANDARD TIME

Mt (also **Mt.** especially in *NAmE*) *abbr.* (especially on maps 尤用於地圖) MOUNT 山：*Mt Kenya* 肯尼亞山

MTV™ /ˌem tiː ˈviː/ *abbr.* music television (a television channel that shows music videos and other light entertainment programmes) 音樂電視頻道

mu /mjuː/ *noun* the 12th letter of the Greek alphabet (Μ, μ) 希臘字母表的第 12 個字母

much 0┳ /mʌtʃ/ *det., pron., adv.*

■ ***det., pron.*** 0┳ used with uncountable nouns, especially in negative sentences to mean 'a large amount of sth', or after 'how' to ask about the amount of sth. It is also used with 'as', 'so' and 'too'.（與不可數名詞連用，尤用於否定句；或與 how 連用以詢問數量；也可與 as、so 和 too 連用）許多，大量：*I don't have much money with me.* 我沒帶多少錢。◇ *'Got any money?' '***Not much.***'* "有錢嗎？" "不太多。" ◇ ***How much*** *water do you need?* 你要多少水？◇ ***How much is it*** (= What does it cost)? 這東西多少錢？◇ *Take* ***as much*** *time* ***as*** *you like.* 你想花多少時間就花多少時間。◇ *There was* ***so much*** *traffic* ***that*** *we were an hour late.* 路上交通很擁堵，我們因此遲到了一個小時。◇ *I've got far* ***too much to*** *do.* 我要做的事情太多了。◇ (*formal*) *I lay awake for much of the night.* 我大半夜都沒睡。◇ (*formal*) *There was much discussion about the reasons for the failure.* 就失敗的原因進行了大量的討論。

IDM **as ˈmuch** the same 一樣；同等：*Please help me get this job—you know I would do as much for you.* 請幫我弄到這份工作，你知道我也會為你的事同樣盡力。◇ *'Roger stole the money.' 'I* ***thought as much.***' "那錢是羅傑偷的。" "果然不出我所料。" **as much as sb can do** used to say that sth is difficult to do（表示難以做到）：*No dessert for me, thanks. It was as much as I could do to finish the main course.* 謝謝，別給我甜食了。我吃完這道主菜就不錯了。 **not much ˈin it** used to say that there is little difference between two things 沒什麼區別；差別不大：*I won, but there wasn't much in it* (= our scores were nearly the same). 我贏了，但比分相差不大。 **ˈnot much of a ...** not a good ... 不是很好；不怎麼樣：*He's not much of a tennis player.* 他算不上網球好手。 **ˈthis much** used to introduce sth positive or definite（引出正面的或肯定的話）：*I'll say this much for him—he never leaves a piece of work unfinished.* 我要為他說句公道話，他從不半途而廢。

■ ***adv.*** 0┳ (**more**, **most**) to a great degree 非常；十分；很：*Thank you* ***very much*** *for the flowers.* 非常感謝你的這些花。◇ *I would very much like to see you again.* 我很想再見到你。◇ *He isn't in the office much* (= often). 他不怎麼待在辦公室。◇ *You worry* ***too much.*** 你過於擔心了。◇ *My new job is* ***much the same as*** *the old one.* 我的新工作和原來的差不多。◇ ***Much to*** *her surprise he came back the next day.* 讓她非常吃驚的是他第二天就回來了。◇ *She's much better today.* 她今天好多了。◇ *The other one was* ***much too*** *expensive.* 另一個太貴了。◇ *Nikolai's English was* ***much the worst.*** 尼柯萊的英語糟糕透了。◇ *We are* ***very much aware*** *of the lack of food supplies.* 我們完全瞭解食物供應的缺乏。◇ *I'm* ***not much good at*** *tennis.* 我不太擅長打網球。◇ *He was much loved by all who knew him.* 認識他的人都很喜歡他。◇ *an appeal to raise much-needed cash* 籌集急需資金的呼籲

IDM **ˈmuch as** although 儘管；雖然：*Much as I would like to stay, I really must go home.* 儘管我想留下來，但我確實必須回家。➲ more at LESS *adv.*

Grammar Point 語法說明

much / a lot of / lots of

■ **Much** is used only with uncountable nouns. It is used mainly in questions and negative sentences. * much 只與不可數名詞連用，主要用於疑問句和否定句中：*Do you have much free time?* 你空閒時間多嗎？◇ ***How much*** *experience have you had?* 你經驗如何？◇ *I don't have much free time.* 我沒有多少空閒時間。

■ In statements **a lot of** or **lots of** (*informal*) is much more common. 在陳述句中 a lot of 或 lots of（非正式）常用得多：*'How much* (*money*) *does she earn?* "她掙多少（錢）？" ◇ *She earns a lot of money.* 她掙很多錢。You can also use **plenty** (**of**). These phrases can also be used in questions and negative sentences. 亦可用 plenty (of)。以上短語亦可用於疑問句和否定句中。

■ **A lot of/lots of** is still felt to be informal, especially in *BrE*, so in formal writing it is better to use **much**, **a great deal of** or **a large amount of**. * a lot of/lots of 仍被視為非正式，尤其在英式英語中，因此在正式的書面語中宜用 much、a great deal of 或 a large amount of。

■ **Very much** and **a lot** can be used as adverbs. * very much 和 a lot 可作副詞：*I miss my family very much.* 我很想念我的家人。◇ ~~*I miss very much my family.*~~ ◇ *I miss my family a lot.* 我很想念我的家人。◇ *Thanks a lot.* 多謝。In negative sentences you can use **much**. 在否定句中可用 much：*I didn't enjoy the film* (*very*) *much.* 我不大喜歡這部影片。

➲ note at MANY

much·ness /ˈmʌtʃnəs/ *noun*

IDM **ˌmuch of a ˈmuchness** very similar; almost the same 非常相似；幾乎相同；不分伯仲：*The two candidates are much of a muchness—it's hard to choose between them.* 兩位候選人不相上下，很難挑選。

muck /mʌk/ *noun, verb*

■ ***noun*** **1** waste matter from farm animals（牲畜的）糞便，糞肥 **SYN** **manure**：*to spread muck on the fields* 將糞肥撒到地裏 **2** (*informal, especially BrE*) dirt or mud 髒東西；泥漿；淤泥：*Can you wipe the muck off the windows?* 你把窗戶上的髒東西擦掉好嗎？ **3** (*informal, especially BrE*) something very unpleasant 令人厭惡的事物：*I can't eat this muck!* 我吃不下這些令人惡心的東西！

IDM **where there's ˌmuck there's ˈbrass** (*BrE, saying*) used to say that a business activity that is unpleasant or dirty can bring in a lot of money 哪兒髒活哪兒有錢賺；要掙大錢就別怕髒

■ ***verb***

PHR V **ˌmuck aˈbout/aˈround** (*BrE, informal*) to behave in a silly way, especially when you should be working or doing sth else 遊手好閒；遊蕩；胡混 **SYN** **mess about/around** **ˌmuck aˈbout/aˈround with sth** (*BrE, informal, disapproving*) to do sth, especially to a machine, so that it does not work correctly 瞎弄；亂搞 **SYN** **mess**

about/around: *Who's mucking around with my radio?* 誰在擺弄我的收音機呀？ **ˌmuck sb aˈbout/aˈround** (*BrE, informal*) to treat sb badly, especially by changing your mind a lot, or by not being honest 糊弄；耍弄 SYN **mess sb about/around**: *They've really mucked us about over our car insurance.* 在我們的汽車保險問題上他們確實糊弄了我們。 **ˌmuck ˈin** (*BrE, informal*) **1** to work with other people in order to complete a task 加入工作；合夥：*If we all muck in, we could have the job finished by the end of the week.* 如果我們大家一塊兒幹，到本週末就可以完成工作。 **2** to share food, accommodation, etc. with other people 分享；共享：*We didn't have much money, but everyone just mucked in together.* 我們沒有多少錢，只是大家都把錢拿出來一塊兒花。 **ˌmuck ˈout** | **ˌmuck sth↔ˈout** to clean out the place where an animal lives 打掃（畜欄） **ˌmuck sth↔ˈup** (*informal, especially BrE*) **1** to do sth badly so that you fail to achieve what you wanted or hoped to achieve 做得很糟 SYN **mess sth up**: *He completely mucked up his English exam.* 他英語考得一塌糊塗。 **2** to spoil a plan or an arrangement 破壞；弄糟；貽誤 SYN **mess sth up** **3** to make sth dirty 弄髒：*I don't want you mucking up my nice clean floor.* 我這地板又漂亮，又乾淨，不想讓你弄髒。

muck·er /ˈmʌkə(r)/ *noun* **1** (*BrE, informal*) used when talking to or about a friend to refer to them（用作稱呼）朋友，夥計：*It's my old mucker John!* 是我的老朋友約翰！ **2** (*old-fashioned, NAmE, informal*) a person who is rough and does not have good manners 粗魯的人；莽漢

muck·rak·ing /ˈmʌkreɪkɪŋ/ *noun* [U] (*informal, disapproving*) the activity of looking for information about people's private lives that they do not wish to make public 挖八卦；揭醜聞

mucky /ˈmʌki/ *adj.* (*informal, especially BrE*) **1** dirty 骯髒的；污穢的：*mucky hands* 骯髒的手 **2** sexually offensive 淫穢的；下流的 SYN **obscene**: ***mucky books/jokes*** 淫穢書籍；下流的笑話

ˌmucous ˈmembrane *noun* (*anatomy* 解) a thin layer of skin that covers the inside of the nose and mouth and the outside of other organs in the body, producing mucus to prevent these parts from becoming dry 黏膜

mucus /ˈmjuːkəs/ *noun* [U] a thick liquid that is produced in parts of the body, such as the nose, by a mucous membrane 黏液；鼻涕 ▸ **mu·cous** /ˈmjuːkəs/ *adj.*: *mucous glands* 分泌黏液的腺體

MUD /mʌd/ *noun* (*computing* 計) the abbreviation for 'multi-user dungeon/dimension' (a computer game played over the Internet by several players at the same time) "泥巴"遊戲，多用戶網絡遊戲（全寫為 multi-user dungeon/dimension）

mud 0-π /mʌd/ *noun* [U]
wet earth that is soft and sticky 泥；淤泥；泥漿：*The car wheels got stuck in the mud.* 汽車輪子陷到泥裏去了。◇ *Your boots are covered in mud.* 你的靴子上都是泥。◇ ***mud bricks/huts*** (= made of dried mud) 泥磚；土坯屋 ➲ SYNONYMS at SOIL
IDM **fling, sling, etc. ˈmud (at sb)** to criticize sb or accuse sb of bad or shocking things in order to damage their reputation, especially in politics（尤指政治上）故意抹黑，向…潑污水，污衊 ➲ see also MUD-SLINGING **ˌmud ˈsticks** (*saying*) people remember and believe the bad things they hear about other people, even if they are later shown to be false 惡事如泥巴，沾身洗不清；爛泥沾身洗不清 ➲ more at CLEAR *adj.*, NAME *n.*

mud·bath /ˈmʌdbɑːθ; *NAmE* -bæθ/ *noun* **1** a bath in hot mud that contains a lot of minerals, which is taken, for example, to help with RHEUMATISM 泥浴（用於減輕風濕症狀等） **2** a place where there is a lot of mud 泥沼；泥濘地：*Heavy rain turned the campsite into a mudbath.* 大雨把露營地變成了一片泥沼。

mud·dle /ˈmʌdl/ *verb, noun*
■ *verb* (*especially BrE*) **1** to put things in the wrong order or mix them up 弄亂；攪混：**~ sth** *Don't do that—you're muddling my papers.* 別動，你會弄亂我的文件的。◇ **~ sth up** *Their letters were all muddled up together in a drawer.* 他們的信都亂七八糟地放在一個抽屜裏。 **2 ~ sb (up)** to confuse sb 使困惑；使糊塗：*Slow down a little—you're muddling me.* 說慢點兒，你都把我搞糊塗了。 **3 ~ sb/sth (up)** | **~ A (up) with B** to confuse one person or thing with another 混淆；攪混；分不清 SYN **mix up**: *I muddled the dates and arrived a week early.* 我搞錯了日期，早到了一個星期。◇ *He **got all muddled up** about what went where.* 他對什麼東西放在哪裏全然記不清了。◇ *They look so alike, I always **get them muddled up**.* 他們看上去那麼像，我總是把他們給攪混了。
PHR V **ˌmuddle aˈlong** (*especially BrE*) to continue doing sth without any clear plan or purpose 混日子；得過且過：*We can't just keep muddling along like this.* 我們不能就這樣混日子。 **ˌmuddle ˈthrough** to achieve your aims even though you do not know exactly what you are doing and do not have the correct equipment, knowledge, etc. 胡亂應付過去：*We'll muddle through somehow.* 我們能想辦法應付過去。
■ *noun* (*especially BrE*) **1** [C, usually sing.] a state of mental confusion 糊塗；困惑；茫然：*Can you start from the beginning again—I'm **in a muddle**.* 請你從頭再來一遍吧，我還是搞不清楚。 **2** [C, usually sing., U] **~ (about/over sth)** a situation in which there is confusion about arrangements, etc. and things are done wrong（局面）一團糟，混亂：*There was a muddle over the theatre tickets.* 戲票問題搞得一團糟。◇ *There followed a long period of confusion and muddle.* 接下來是很長一段時間的困惑和混亂。 **3** [C, usually sing., U] a state of confusion in which things are untidy 混亂；亂七八糟 SYN **mess**: *My papers are all **in a muddle**.* 我的文件混亂不堪。

mud·dled /ˈmʌdld/ *adj.* (*especially BrE*) confused 糊塗的；困惑的；混亂的：*He gets muddled when the teacher starts shouting.* 老師一喊叫他就心煩意亂。◇ *muddled thinking* 混亂的思想

ˌmuddle-ˈheaded *adj.* confused or with confused ideas 頭腦混亂的；糊塗的：*muddle-headed thinkers* 思路混亂的人

mud·dling /ˈmʌdlɪŋ/ *adj.* (*especially BrE*) causing confusion; difficult to understand 引起困惑的；使人糊塗的；難以理解的

muddy /ˈmʌdi/ *adj., verb*
■ *adj.* (**mud·dier**, **mud·di·est**) **1** full of or covered in mud 多泥的；泥濘的：*a **muddy field/track*** 泥濘的田野／小徑 ◇ ***muddy boots/knees*** 沾滿泥漿的靴子／膝蓋 ➲ SYNONYMS at DIRTY **2** (of a liquid 液體) containing mud; not clear 含泥的；渾濁的：*muddy water* 泥水 ◇ *a muddy pond* 渾濁的池塘 **3** (of colours 色彩) not clear or bright 灰暗的；暗淡的：***muddy green/brown*** 暗綠色／褐色
■ *verb* (**mud·dies**, **muddy·ing**, **mud·died**, **mud·died**) **~ sth** to make sth muddy 使變得泥濘；使渾濁
IDM **muddy the ˈwaters, ˈissue, etc.** (*disapproving*) to make a simple situation confused and more complicated than it really is 攪渾水；添亂

mud·flap /ˈmʌdflæp/ *noun* one of a set of pieces of FLEXIBLE material that are fixed behind the wheels of a car, motorcycle, etc. to prevent them from throwing up mud, stones or water（車輪後的）擋泥簾，擋泥板

mud·flat /ˈmʌdflæt/ *noun* [usually pl.] an area of flat muddy land that is covered by the sea when it comes in at HIGH TIDE 潮泥灘

mud·guard /ˈmʌdgɑːd; *NAmE* -gɑːrd/ (*BrE*) (*NAmE* **fender**) *noun* a curved cover over a wheel of a bicycle（自行車）擋泥板

ˈmud pack *noun* a substance containing CLAY that you put on your face and take off after a short period of time, used to improve the condition of your skin（護膚用）泥面膜

ˌmud ˈpie *noun* wet earth that is made into the shape of a PIE as part of a game played by children（兒童遊戲時做的）泥餅

mud·slide /ˈmʌdslaɪd/ *noun* a large amount of mud sliding down a mountain, often destroying buildings and injuring or killing people below 泥流

M

ˌmud-slinging *noun* [U] (*disapproving*) the act of criticizing sb and accusing them of sth in order to damage their reputation 故意抹黑；惡意中傷

muesli /ˈmjuːzli/ *noun* [U] a mixture of grains, nuts, dried fruit, etc. served with milk and eaten for breakfast 牛奶什錦早餐（穀物、堅果、乾果加牛奶）

muez·zin /muːˈezm; mjuː-/ *noun* a man who calls Muslims to prayer, usually from the tower of a MOSQUE 宣禮員（通常在清真寺宣禮塔上召集穆斯林祈禱）

muff /mʌf/ *noun, verb*

■ ***noun*** a short tube of fur or other warm material that you put your hands into to keep them warm in cold weather 暖手筒；皮手筒 ➲ see also EARMUFFS

■ ***verb*** **~ sth** (*informal, disapproving*) to miss an opportunity to do sth well 錯過（機會）；做錯：*He muffed his lines* (= he forgot them or said them wrongly). 他忘了台詞。◇ *It was a really simple shot, and I muffed it.* 這確實是一記簡單的射門，而我竟然沒接住。

muf·fin /ˈmʌfɪn/ *noun* **1** (*BrE*) (*NAmE* **ˌEnglish ˈmuffin**) a type of round flat bread roll, usually TOASTED and eaten hot with butter 鬆餅（通常烤熱加黃油吃）**2** a small cake in the shape of a cup, often containing small pieces of fruit, etc. 杯狀小鬆糕（常含小塊水果等）：*a blueberry muffin* 藍莓鬆糕

muf·fle /ˈmʌfl/ *verb* **1 ~ sth** to make a sound quieter or less clear 壓抑（聲音）；使（聲音）降低；使聽不清：*He tried to muffle the alarm clock by putting it under his pillow.* 他把鬧鐘塞在枕頭底下，想減低聲音。 **2 ~ sb/sth (up) in sth** to wrap or cover sb/sth in order to keep them/it warm 裹住，覆蓋，蒙住（以保暖）：*She muffled the child up in a blanket.* 她用毯子將孩子裹得嚴嚴實實。

muf·fled /ˈmʌfld/ *adj.* (of sounds 聲音) not heard clearly because sth is in the way that stops the sound from travelling easily 沉悶的；壓抑的；模糊不清的：*muffled voices from the next room* 從隔壁房間裏傳來的沉悶聲音

muf·fler /ˈmʌflə(r)/ *noun* **1** (*old-fashioned*) a thick piece of cloth worn around the neck for warmth 圍巾 **SYN** **scarf** **2** (*NAmE*) (*BrE* **si·len·cer**) a device that is fixed to the EXHAUST of a vehicle in order to reduce the amount of noise that the engine makes（發動機的）消音器 ➲ **VISUAL VOCAB** page V51

mufti /ˈmʌfti/ *noun* **1** [C] (also **Mufti**) a Muslim who is an expert in legal matters connected with Islam 穆夫提（伊斯蘭教法典說明官）**2** [U] (*old-fashioned*) ordinary clothes worn by people such as soldiers who wear uniform in their job（穿制服上班的士兵等穿的）便裝，便服：*officers in mufti* 身着便裝的軍官

mug /mʌg/ *noun, verb*

■ ***noun*** **1** a tall cup for drinking from, usually with straight sides and a handle, used without a SAUCER（不用茶碟的有柄的）大杯，缸子，馬克杯：*a coffee mug* 咖啡缸子 ◇ *a beer mug* (= a large glass with a handle) 大啤酒杯 ➲ **VISUAL VOCAB** page V22 **2** a mug and what it contains 一缸子（的量）：*a mug of coffee* 一大杯咖啡 **3** (*slang*) a person's face（人的）臉：*I never want to see his ugly mug again.* 我再也不想看到他那張醜惡的面孔。 **4** (*informal*) a person who is stupid and easy to trick 傻瓜；笨蛋：*They made me look a complete mug.* 他們弄得我像個十足的傻瓜。◇ *He's no mug.* 他不傻。

IDM **a ˈmug's game** (*disapproving, especially BrE*) an activity that is unlikely to be successful or make a profit 徒勞無功的事；不易成功的事；不易獲利的事

■ ***verb*** (**-gg-**) **1** [T] **~ sb** to attack sb violently in order to steal their money, especially in a public place（公然）行兇搶劫，打劫：*She had been mugged in the street in broad daylight.* 光天化日之下，她在街上遭到搶劫。 **2** [I] **~ (for sb/sth)** (*informal, especially NAmE*) to make silly expressions with your face or behave in a silly, exaggerated way, especially on the stage or before a camera（尤指在舞台上或攝影機前）扮鬼臉，扮怪相：*to mug for the cameras* 在攝影機前扮怪相

PHR V **ˌmug sth↔ˈup** | **ˌmug ˈup on sth** (*BrE, informal*) to learn sth, especially in a short time for a particular purpose, for example an exam 突擊式學習

mug·ger /ˈmʌgə(r)/ *noun* a person who threatens or attacks sb in order to steal their money, especially in a public place 搶劫犯；攔路搶劫者

mug·ging /ˈmʌgɪŋ/ *noun* [U, C] the crime of attacking sb violently, or threatening to do so, in order to steal their money, especially in a public place 公然行兇搶劫案；攔路搶劫罪：*Mugging is on the increase.* 搶劫犯罪呈上升趨勢。◇ *There have been several muggings here recently.* 最近這裏發生了幾起行兇搶劫案。

mug·gins /ˈmʌgɪnz/ *noun* [sing.] (*BrE, informal, humorous*) used without 'a' or 'the' to refer to yourself when you feel stupid because you have let yourself be treated unfairly（不用 a 或 the，表示因受到不公正待遇而覺得自己很蠢）傻瓜，笨蛋：*And muggins here had to clean up all the mess.* 而我這個傻瓜現在不得不清理這個爛攤子。

muggy /ˈmʌgi/ *adj.* (of weather 天氣) warm and damp in an unpleasant way 悶熱潮濕的 **SYN** **close**：*a muggy August day* 八月裏悶熱的一天

Mug·hal /ˈmuːgɑːl/ *noun* = MOGUL

mug·shot /ˈmʌgʃɒt; *NAmE* -ʃɑːt/ *noun* (*informal*) a photograph of sb's face kept by the police in their records to identify criminals（警方存檔識別罪犯的）面部照片

mug·wump /ˈmʌgwʌmp/ *noun* (*NAmE*, often *disapproving*) a person who cannot decide how to vote or who refuses to support a political party 投票拿不定主意的人；（不支持任何政黨的）游離者

Mu·ham·mad (also **Mo·ham·med**) /məˈhæmɪd/ *noun* the Arab PROPHET through whom the Koran was REVEALED and the religion of Islam established and completed 穆罕默德（阿拉伯的先知、伊斯蘭教的創立人，揭示《古蘭經》的教義）

mu·ja·hi·deen (also **mu·ja·hi·din**) /ˌmuːdʒəhəˈdiːn/ *noun* [pl.] (in some Muslim countries 某些穆斯林國家) soldiers fighting in support of their strong Muslim beliefs 穆斯林聖戰者；穆斯林游擊隊員；聖戰者

muk·luk /ˈmʌklʌk/ *noun* (*CanE*) a high soft winter boot that is traditionally made with the skin of SEALS 高筒軟靴，高筒毛靴（傳統上以海豹皮製作）

mu·latto /mjuˈlætəʊ; məˈl-; *NAmE* -toʊ/ *noun* (*pl.* **-os** or **-oes**) (*offensive*) a person with one black parent and one white parent 黑白混血兒

mul·berry /ˈmʌlbəri; *NAmE* -beri/ *noun* (*pl.* **-ies**) **1** (also **ˈmulberry tree**) [C] a tree with broad dark green leaves and BERRIES that can be eaten. SILKWORMS (that make silk) eat the leaves of the white mulberry. 桑樹 **2** [C] the small purple or white BERRY of the mulberry tree 桑葚 **3** [U] a deep reddish-purple colour 深紫紅色

mulch /mʌltʃ/ *noun, verb*

■ ***noun*** [C, U] material, for example, decaying leaves, that you put around a plant to protect its base and its roots, to improve the quality of the soil or to stop WEEDS growing 覆蓋物，護根（用以保護植物根莖、改善土質或防止雜草生長）

■ ***verb*** **~ sth** to cover the soil or the roots of a plant with a mulch 用覆蓋物覆蓋（土壤或根部）

mule /mjuːl/ *noun* **1** an animal that has a horse and a DONKEY as parents, used especially for carrying loads 騾子：*He's as* ***stubborn as a mule.*** 他像騾子一樣倔。 **2** (*slang*) a person who is paid to take drugs illegally from one country to another 越境運毒者 **3** a SLIPPER (= a soft shoe for wearing indoors) that is open around the heel（室內使用的）拖鞋 ➲ **VISUAL VOCAB** page V64

mule·teer /ˌmjuːləˈtɪə(r); *NAmE* -ˈtɪr/ *noun* a person who controls MULES (= the animals) and makes them go in the right direction 趕騾人

mul·ish /ˈmjuːlɪʃ/ *adj.* unwilling to change your mind or attitude or to do what other people want you to do 執拗的；頑固的 **SYN** **stubborn**

mull /mʌl/ *verb*

PHR V **ˌmull sth↔ˈover** to spend time thinking carefully about a plan or proposal 認真琢磨，反複思考（計劃、建議等）**SYN** **consider**：*I need some time to mull it over before making a decision.* 在作出決定之前我需要一些時間來認真琢磨一下。

mul·lah /ˈmʌlə; ˈmʊlə/ *noun* a Muslim teacher of religion and holy law 毛拉（穆斯林宗教和聖法的教師）

mulled /mʌld/ *adj.* [only before noun] **mulled** wine has been mixed with sugar and spices and heated （指葡萄酒）放入糖和香料加熱的

mul·let /ˈmʌlɪt/ *noun* **1** (*pl.* **mul·let**) [C, U] a sea fish that is used for food. The two main types are **red mullet** and **grey mullet**. 鯔魚；鯡鯉 **2** [C] (*informal*) a HAIRSTYLE for men in which the hair is short at the front and sides and long at the back 胭脂魚髮型（男子髮型，前面和兩側的頭髮短，腦後的頭髮長）

mul·li·ga·tawny /ˌmʌlɪgəˈtɔːni/ *noun* [U] a hot spicy soup, originally from India （源自印度的）咖喱肉湯 **ORIGIN** From a Tamil word meaning 'pepper water'. 源自泰米爾語中表示"胡椒水"的詞。

mul·lion /ˈmʌliən/ *noun* (*architecture* 建) a solid vertical piece of stone, wood or metal between two parts of a window （窗扇間的）豎框，直欞 ▸ **mul·lioned** /ˈmʌliənd/ *adj.* [only before noun]： *mullioned windows* 有直欞的窗戶

multi- /ˈmʌlti/ *combining form* (in nouns and adjectives 構成名詞和形容詞) more than one; many 多個；許多： *multicoloured* 多色的 ◇ *a multimillionaire* 擁有幾百萬財產的富翁 ◇ *a multimillion-dollar business* 數百萬元資金的企業 ◇ *a multi-ethnic society* 多種族社會

ˌmulti-ˈaccess *adj.* (*computing* 計) allowing several people to use the same system at the same time （系統）多路接入的，多重存取的

multi·buy /ˈmʌltibaɪ/ *adj.* (*BrE*) used for describing items in a shop/store that are cheaper if you buy several of them （商品）多買可享優惠的： *Click here to see some of our multibuy offers.* 點擊此處查看我們的一些多買優惠商品。 ▸ **multi·buy** *noun*

multi·cast /ˈmʌltikɑːst; *NAmE* -kæst/ *verb* **~ sth** (*technical* 術語) to send data across a computer network to several users at the same time （在網絡上）多播（數據） ▸ **multi·cast** *noun* [U, C]

multi·chan·nel /ˈmʌltitʃænl/ *adj.* having or using many different television or communication channels 多頻道的；多通道的

multi·col·oured (*especially US* **multi·col·ored**) /ˌmʌltiˈkʌləd; *NAmE* -ˈkʌlərd/ (*BrE* also **multi·col·our**) (*US* also **multi·col·or**) *adj.* consisting of or decorated with many colours, especially bright ones 多色的；五彩斑斕的： *a multicoloured dress* 鮮豔的七彩連衣裙

multi·cul·tural /ˌmʌltiˈkʌltʃərəl/ *adj.* for or including people of several different races, religions, languages and traditions 多元文化的；多種文化融合的： *We live in a multicultural society.* 我們生活在一個多元文化的社會中。◇ *a multicultural approach to education* 多種文化融合的教育方法 ➲ COLLOCATIONS at RACE

multi·cul·tural·ism /ˌmʌltiˌkʌltʃərəlɪzəm/ *noun* [U] the practice of giving importance to all cultures in a society 多元文化主義（重視社會中各種文化） ➲ COLLOCATIONS at RACE

multi·di·men·sion·al **AW** /ˌmʌltidaɪˈmenʃənl; -dɪ-/ *adj.* having several DIMENSIONS (= measurements in space) 多維的： *multidimensional space* 多維空間

multi·dis·cip·lin·ary /ˌmʌltidɪsəˈplɪnəri; *NAmE* -ˈdɪsəpləneri/ *adj.* involving several different subjects of study （涉及）多門學科的： *a multidisciplinary course* 涉及多個學科的課程

multi·fa·cet·ed /ˌmʌltiˈfæsɪtɪd/ *adj.* (*formal*) having many different aspects to be considered 多方面的；要從多方面考慮的： *a complex and multifaceted problem* 一個複雜的需從多方面考慮的問題

multi·fari·ous /ˌmʌltɪˈfeəriəs; *NAmE* -ˈfer-/ *adj.* (*formal*) of many different kinds; having great variety 多種的；各種各樣的；多樣的： *the multifarious life forms in the coral reef* 珊瑚礁上的多種生命形式 ◇ *a vast and multifarious organization* 一個龐大而又形式多樣的機構

multi·func·tion·al /ˌmʌltiˈfʌŋkʃənl/ *adj.* having several different functions 多功能的；起多種作用的： *a multifunctional device* 多功能裝置

multi·grain /ˈmʌltigreɪn/ *adj.* containing several different types of grain 含多種穀物的；雜糧的： *multigrain bread* 雜糧麪包

multi·gym /ˈmʌltidʒɪm/ (*BrE*) *noun* a piece of equipment which can be used to exercise different parts of the body 多功能健身器

multi·lat·eral /ˌmʌltiˈlætərəl/ *adj.* **1** in which three or more groups, nations, etc. take part 多邊的；多國的： *multilateral negotiations* 多邊談判 **2** having many sides or parts 有多條邊的；有多個部份的 ➲ compare BILATERAL, TRILATERAL, UNILATERAL

multi·lat·eral·ism /ˌmʌltiˈlætərəlɪzəm/ *noun* [U] (*politics* 政) the policy of trying to make multilateral agreements in order to achieve nuclear DISARMAMENT 多邊主義，多邊政策（以促成核裁軍）

multi·lin·gual /ˌmʌltiˈlɪŋgwəl/ *adj.* **1** speaking or using several different languages 說（或用）多種語言的： ***multilingual translators/communities/societies*** 多語翻譯者／社群／社會 ◇ *a multilingual classroom* 多語課堂 **2** written or printed in several different languages 用多種語言書寫（或印刷）的： *a multilingual phrase book* 多種語言會話手冊 ➲ compare BILINGUAL, MONOLINGUAL

multi·media /ˌmʌltiˈmiːdiə/ *adj.* [only before noun] **1** (in computing 計算機技術) using sound, pictures and film in addition to text on a screen 多媒體的： ***multimedia systems/products*** 多媒體系統／產品 ◇ *the multimedia industry* (= producing CD-ROMs etc.) 多媒體工業 **2** (in teaching and art 教學和藝術) using several different ways of giving information or several different materials 使用多媒體的： *a multimedia approach to learning* 運用多媒體的學習方法 ▸ **multi·media** *noun* [U]： *the use of multimedia in museums* 多媒體在博物館中的運用

multi·mill·ion·aire /ˌmʌltimɪljəˈneə(r); *NAmE* -ˈner/ *noun* a person who has money and possessions worth several million pounds, dollars, etc. 擁有數百萬資產的富翁；千萬富翁

multi·nation·al /ˌmʌltiˈnæʃnəl/ *adj.*, *noun*

■ ***adj.*** existing in or involving many countries 跨國的；涉及多國的： ***multinational companies/corporations*** 跨國公司 ◇ *A multinational force is being sent to the trouble spot.* 一支多國部隊正趕往多事的地區。

■ ***noun*** a company that operates in several different countries, especially a large and powerful company 跨國公司

multi·party /ˌmʌltiˈpɑːti; *NAmE* -ˈpɑːrti/ *adj.* [only before noun] involving several different political parties 多黨派的；涉及多黨派的

mul·tiple /ˈmʌltɪpl/ *adj.*, *noun*

■ ***adj.*** [only before noun] many in number; involving many different people or things 數量多的；多種多樣的： *multiple copies of documents* 各種文件的大量的副本 ◇ *a multiple entry visa* 多次入境簽證 ◇ *to suffer multiple injuries* (= in many different places in the body) 多處受傷 ◇ *a multiple birth* (= several babies born to a mother at one time) 多胎分娩 ◇ *a multiple pile-up* (= a crash involving many vehicles) 連環車禍 ◇ *a house in* ***multiple ownership/occupancy*** (= owned/occupied by several different people or families) 多戶所有／使用的房屋

■ ***noun*** **1** (*mathematics* 數) a quantity that contains another quantity an exact number of times 倍數： *14, 21 and 28 are all multiples of 7.* * 14、21 和 28 都是 7 的倍數。◇ *18 is the lowest* ***common multiple*** *of 6 and 9.* * 18 是 6 和 9 的最小公倍數。◇ *Traveller's cheques are available in multiples of €10* (= to the value of €10, €20, €30, etc.). 購買旅行支票以 10 歐元的倍數計算面值。 **2** (also **ˌmultiple ˈstore**) (both *BrE*) = CHAIN STORE

ˌmultiple-ˈchoice *adj.* (of questions 問題) showing several possible answers from which you must choose the correct one 多項選擇的

ˌmultiple-persoˈnality disorder (also *less frequent* **ˌsplit-persoˈnality disorder**) *noun* (*psychology* 心) a rare condition in which a person seems to have one or more different personalities 多重人格障礙

ˌmultiple scleˈrosis *noun* [U] (*abbr.* **MS**) a disease of the nervous system that gets worse over a period of time with loss of feeling and loss of control of movement and speech 多發性硬化

multi·plex /ˈmʌltɪpleks/ (*BrE* also **ˌmultiplex ˈcinema**) *noun* a large cinema/movie theater with several separate rooms with screens 多廳影院；多銀幕電影院

multi·pli·ca·tion /ˌmʌltɪplɪˈkeɪʃn/ *noun* [U] the act or process of multiplying 乘；相乘；增加：*the multiplication sign* (×) 乘號（×）◇ *Multiplication of cells leads to rapid growth of the organism.* 細胞的繁殖導致有機體的迅速生長。➲ compare DIVISION (2)

ˌmultipliˈcation table (also **table**) *noun* a list showing the results when a number is multiplied by a set of other numbers, especially 1 to 12, in turn 乘法表

multi·pli·city /ˌmʌltɪˈplɪsəti/ *noun* [sing., U] (*formal*) a great number and variety of sth 多樣性；多種多樣：*This situation can be influenced by a multiplicity of different factors.* 當前的形勢可能受到各種不同因素的影響。

multi·plier /ˈmʌltɪplaɪə(r)/ *noun* (*mathematics* 數) a number by which another number is multiplied 乘數

multi·ply 🔑 /ˈmʌltɪplaɪ/ *verb* (**multi·plies**, **multi·ply·ing**, **multi·plied**, **multi·plied**)
1 🔑 [I, T] to add a number to itself a particular number of times 乘；乘以：*The children are already learning to multiply and divide.* 孩子們已經開始學習乘法和除法了。◇ **~ A by B** *2 multiplied by 4 is/equals/makes 8* (2×4 = 8) * 2 乘以 4 等於 8。◇ **~ A and B** (**together**) *Multiply 2 and 6 together and you get 12.* * 2 和 6 相乘得 12。
2 🔑 [I, T] to increase or make sth increase very much in number or amount 成倍增加；迅速增加：*Our problems have multiplied since last year.* 自去年以來，我們的問題成倍增加。◇ **~ sth** *Cigarette smoking multiplies the risk of cancer.* 抽煙會大大增加得癌症的風險。 **3** [I, T] (*biology* 生) to reproduce in large numbers; to make sth do this（使）繁殖，增殖：*Rabbits multiply rapidly.* 兔子繁殖迅速。◇ **~ sth** *It is possible to multiply these bacteria in the laboratory.* 在實驗室裏繁殖這些細菌是可以做到的。

multi·pro·ces·sor /ˌmʌltiˈprəʊsesə(r); *NAmE* -ˈprɑːs-; -ˈproʊ-/ *noun* a computer with more than one CENTRAL PROCESSING UNIT 多處理器

ˌmulti-ˈpurpose *adj.* able to be used for several different purposes 多用途的；多功能的：*a multi-purpose tool/machine* 多用途工具；多功能機 ➲ see also MPV

multi·racial /ˌmʌltiˈreɪʃl/ *adj.* including or involving several different races of people 多種族的：*a multi-racial society* 多種族的社會

ˌmulti-ˈskilling *noun* [U] (*business* 商) the fact of a person being trained in several different jobs which require different skills 多才多藝；（人才的）複合型技能

ˌmulti-storey ˈcar park (also **ˌmulti-ˈstorey**) (both *BrE*) (*NAmE* **ˈparking garage**) *noun* a large building with several floors for parking cars in 多層停車場；立體停車場

multi·task /ˌmʌltiˈtɑːsk; *NAmE* -ˈtæsk/ *verb* **1** [I] (of a computer 計算機) to operate several programs at the same time 多任務；多工 **2** [I] to do several things at the same time 同時做多件事情：*Women seem to be able to multitask better than men.* 女性似乎比男性更擅長同時做多件事情。

multi·tasking /ˌmʌltiˈtɑːskɪŋ; *NAmE* -ˈtæsk-/ *noun* [U] **1** (*computing* 計) the ability of a computer to operate several programs at the same time 多重任務處理 **2** the ability to do several things at the same time 能同時處理多項事情的

multi·track /ˈmʌltitræk/ *adj.* (*technical* 術語) relating to the mixing of several different pieces of music 多音軌混合的；多聲道的

multi·tude /ˈmʌltɪtjuːd; *NAmE* -tuːd/ *noun* (*formal*) **1** [C] **~ (of sth/sb)** an extremely large number of things or people 眾多；大量：*a multitude of possibilities* 眾多的可能性 ◇ *a multitude of birds* 一大群鳥 ◇ *These elements can be combined in a multitude of different ways.* 這些因素可以通過無數不同的方式進行組合。◇ *The region attracts tourists in their multitudes.* 這個地區吸引大批遊人。 **2 the multitude** [sing.+sing./pl. v.] (also **the multitudes** [pl.]) (sometimes *disapproving*) the mass of ordinary people 群眾；大批百姓；民眾：*It was an elite that believed its task was to enlighten the multitude.* 精英階層會認為自己的職責是啟迪群眾。◇ *to feed the starving multitudes* 使飢餓的群眾有飯吃 **3** [C] (*literary*) a large crowd of people 人群 SYN **throng**：*He preached to the assembled multitude.* 他向聚集在那裏的民眾佈道。
IDM **cover/hide a multitude of sins** (often *humorous*) to hide the real situation or facts when these are not good or pleasant 掩藏實情；掩蓋真相

multi·tu·di·nous /ˌmʌltɪˈtjuːdɪnəs; *NAmE* -ˈtuːdənəs/ *adj.* (*formal*) extremely large in number 大量的；眾多的

ˌmulti-ˈuser *adj.* (*computing* 計) able to be used by more than one person at the same time 多用戶（共享）的：*a multi-user software licence* 多用戶共享軟件許可

multi·vita·min /ˌmʌltiˈvɪtəmɪn; *NAmE* -ˈvaɪt-/ *noun* a pill or medicine containing several VITAMINS 多種維生素；綜合維他命

ˌmulti-ˈword *adj.* [only before noun] (*linguistics* 語言) consisting of more than one word 含多個單詞的；多詞組合的：*multi-word units such as 'fall in love'* 如 fall in love 的多詞組合單位

mum 🔑 /mʌm/ *noun, adj.*
■ ***noun*** 🔑 (*BrE*) (*NAmE* **mom**) (*informal*) a mother 媽媽；媽：*My mum says I can't go.* 我媽說我不能去。◇ *Happy Birthday, Mum.* 媽媽，生日快樂！◇ *A lot of* ***mums and dads*** *have the same worries.* 許多父母都有同樣的擔憂。
■ ***adj.***
IDM **keep mum** (*informal*) to say nothing about sth; to stay quiet 緘口不言；保持沉默：*He kept mum about what he'd seen.* 他對他所看到的隻字不說。 **ˌmum's the ˈword!** (*informal*) used to tell sb to say nothing about sth and keep it secret（提醒別人保守秘密）不要外傳

mum·ble /ˈmʌmbl/ *verb, noun*
■ ***verb*** [I, T] to speak or say sth in a quiet voice in a way that is not clear 嘟噥；口齒不清地說 SYN **mutter**：**~ (to sb/yourself)** *I could hear him mumbling to himself.* 我聽到他在喃喃自語。◇ **~ sth** (**to sb/yourself**) *She mumbled an apology and left.* 她嘟嘟囔囔地道了歉就走了。◇ **+ speech** *'Sorry,' she mumbled.* 她含含糊糊地說："對不起。" ◇ **~ that …** *She mumbled that she was sorry.* 她含含糊糊地說了聲對不起。
■ ***noun*** [usually sing.] (also **mum·bling** [C, usually pl., U]) speech or words that are spoken in a quiet voice in a way that is not clear 喃喃自語；嘟噥：*He spoke in a low mumble, as if to himself.* 他自言自語般地嘟噥着。◇ *They tried to make sense of her mumblings.* 他們試圖弄明白她在嘟噥些什麼。

mumbo jumbo /ˌmʌmbəʊ ˈdʒʌmbəʊ; *NAmE* ˌmʌmboʊ ˈdʒʌmboʊ/ *noun* [U] (*informal, disapproving*) language or a ceremony that seems complicated and important but is actually without real sense or meaning; nonsense 冠冕堂皇的空話；假大空言辭；繁文縟節；胡言亂語

mum·mer /ˈmʌmə(r)/ *noun* an actor in an old form of drama without words 啞劇演員

mum·mify /ˈmʌmɪfaɪ/ *verb* (**mum·mi·fies**, **mum·mi·fy·ing**, **mum·mi·fied**, **mum·mi·fied**) [usually passive] **~ sth** to preserve a dead body by treating it with special oils and wrapping it in cloth 把（屍體）製成木乃伊 SYN **embalm**

mummy /ˈmʌmi/ *noun* (*pl.* **-ies**) **1** (*BrE*) (*NAmE* **mommy**, **momma**) (*informal*) a child's word for a mother（兒語）媽咪：*'I want my mummy!' he wailed.* 他哭叫着："我要媽媽！" ◇ *It hurts, Mummy!* 媽媽，疼！◇ *Mummy and Daddy will be back soon.* 媽媽爸爸就要回來了。 **2** a body of a human or an animal that has been mummified 木乃伊；經處理保存的人體或動物乾屍：*an Egyptian mummy* 一具埃及木乃伊

ˈmummy's boy (*BrE*) (*NAmE* **ˈmama's boy**) *noun* (*disapproving*) a boy or man who depends too much on his mother 離不開媽媽的男孩（或男子）

mumps /mʌmps/ *noun* [U] a disease, especially of children, that causes painful swellings in the neck 腮腺炎

mumsy /ˈmʌmzi/ *adj.* (*BrE, informal*) having a comfortable, but dull and old-fashioned appearance 家常的；呆板的；不時髦的：*a mumsy dress* 式樣一般的連衣裙

munch /mʌntʃ/ *verb* [I, T] to eat sth steadily and often noisily, especially sth crisp 大聲咀嚼，用力咀嚼（脆的食物）SYN **chomp**：**~ on/at sth** *She munched on an apple.* 她在大口啃蘋果。◇ **~ sth** *He sat in a chair munching his toast.* 他坐在椅子上大嚼烤麪包片。◇ *I **munched my way through** a huge bowl of cereal.* 我狼吞虎嚥地吃了一大碗麥片粥。

Munch·ausen's syn·drome /ˈmʊntʃaʊzənz sɪndrəʊm; *NAmE* -droʊm/ *noun* [U] a mental condition in which sb keeps pretending that they are ill/sick in order to receive hospital treatment 閔希豪生綜合症，孟喬森氏症候群（表現為幻想生病以便求醫或住院的精神障礙）

munch·ies /ˈmʌntʃɪz/ *noun* [pl.] (*informal*) small pieces of food for eating with drinks at a party （聚會上提供的）小吃，點心

IDM **have the ˈmunchies** (*informal*) to feel hungry 感覺餓

mun·dane /mʌnˈdeɪn/ *adj.* (often *disapproving*) not interesting or exciting 單調的；平凡的 SYN **dull, ordinary**：*a **mundane task/job*** 平凡的任務／職業◇ *I lead a pretty mundane existence.* 我過着相當平淡的生活。◇ *On a more mundane level, can we talk about the timetable for next week?* 說點兒實際的吧，我們能談談下週的時間安排嗎？

mung /mʌŋ; muːŋ/ (also **moong**) *noun* **1** (also **ˈmung bean**) a small round green BEAN 綠豆 **2** the tropical plant that produces these beans 綠豆（指植物）

mu·ni·ci·pal /mjuːˈnɪsɪpl/ *adj.* [usually before noun] connected with or belonging to a town, city or district that has its own local government 市政的；地方政府的：***municipal elections/councils*** 地方政府選舉；市政委員會◇ *municipal workers* 市政工作者◇ *the Los Angeles Municipal Art Gallery* 洛杉磯市立美術館

mu·ni·ci·pal·ity /mjuːˌnɪsɪˈpæləti/ *noun* (*pl.* **-ies**) (*formal*) a town, city or district with its own local government; the group of officials who govern it 自治市；自治區；市（或區）政當局

mu·nifi·cent /mjuːˈnɪfɪsnt/ *adj.* (*formal*) extremely generous 極慷慨的：*a **munificent patron/gift/gesture*** 慷慨的贊助人／饋贈／表示 ▸ **mu·nifi·cence** /-sns/ *noun* [U]

mu·ni·tions /mjuːˈnɪʃnz/ *noun* [pl.] military weapons, AMMUNITION and equipment 軍需品；軍火：*a shortage of munitions* 軍需品缺乏◇ *a munitions factory* 兵工廠 ▸ **mu·ni·tion** *adj.* [only before noun]：*a munition store* 軍需庫

munt·jac (also **munt·jak**) /ˈmʌntdʒæk/ *noun* a type of small DEER, originally from SE Asia 麂（一種小鹿，產於東南亞）

mup·pet /ˈmʌpɪt/ *noun* (*BrE, informal*) a stupid person 笨蛋；蠢人

mural /ˈmjʊərəl; *NAmE* ˈmjʊrəl/ *noun* a painting, usually a large one, done on a wall, sometimes on an outside wall of a building 壁畫 ▸ **mural** *adj.*：*mural paintings* 壁畫

mur·der 0-w /ˈmɜːdə(r); *NAmE* ˈmɜːrd-/ *noun, verb*

■ *noun* **1** 0-w [U, C] the crime of killing sb deliberately 謀殺；兇殺 SYN **homicide**：*He was found guilty of murder.* 經裁決，他犯有謀殺罪。◇ *She has been charged with the **attempted murder** of her husband.* 她被指控意圖謀殺丈夫。◇ *to **commit (a) murder*** 犯謀殺罪◇ *a **murder case/investigation/trial*** 兇殺案件／調查；謀殺案的審判◇ *The rebels were responsible for the **mass murder** of 400 civilians.* 叛亂者對屠殺 400 名平民負有責任。◇ *What was the **murder weapon**?* 用的是什麼兇器？◇ *The play is a **murder mystery**.* 這齣戲說的是一樁神秘的兇殺案。➲ COLLOCATIONS at CRIME ➲ compare MANSLAUGHTER **2** [U] (*informal*) used to describe sth that is difficult or unpleasant 困難的事；討厭的事：*It's murder trying to get to the airport at this time of day.* 這個時候要趕到機場簡直要命。◇ *It was murder* (= very busy and unpleasant) *in the office today.* 今天辦公室裏忙亂得要命。

IDM **get away with ˈmurder** (*informal*, often *humorous*) to do whatever you want without being stopped or punished 逍遙法外；（做了錯事而）安然無事 ➲ more at SCREAM *v.*

■ *verb* **1** 0-w **~ sb** to kill sb deliberately and illegally 謀殺；兇殺：*He denies murdering his wife's lover.* 他否認謀殺了妻子的情人。◇ *The murdered woman was well known in the area.* 被殺害的女人在這個地區很有名氣。**2 ~ sth** to spoil sth because you do not do it very well 糟蹋；毀壞；弄壞 SYN **butcher**：*Critics accused him of murdering the English language* (= writing or speaking it very badly). 批評家指責他把英語給糟蹋了。**3 ~ sb** (*BrE, informal*) to defeat sb completely, especially in a team sport （尤指在團隊運動中）徹底打敗，打垮 SYN **thrash**

IDM **I could murder a ...** (*informal, especially BrE*) used to say that you very much want to eat or drink sth 我非常想吃（或喝）：*I could murder a beer.* 我很想來杯啤酒。**sb will ˈmurder you** (*informal*) used to warn sb that another person will be very angry with them 某人會要你的命

mur·der·er /ˈmɜːdərə(r); *NAmE* ˈmɜːrd-/ *noun* a person who has killed sb deliberately and illegally 殺人犯；殺人兇手 SYN **killer**：*a convicted murderer* 被判有罪的謀殺犯◇ *a mass murderer* (= who has killed a lot of people) 殺死很多人的兇手

mur·der·ess /ˈmɜːdəres; *NAmE* ˈmɜːrd-/ *noun* (*old-fashioned*) a woman who has killed sb deliberately and illegally; a female murderer 女殺人犯；女殺人兇手

mur·der·ous /ˈmɜːdərəs; *NAmE* ˈmɜːrd-/ *adj.* intending or likely to murder 蓄意謀殺的；兇殘的；兇惡的 SYN **savage**：*a **murderous villain/tyrant*** 兇殘的惡棍／暴君◇ *a murderous attack* 兇惡的進攻◇ *She gave him **a murderous look*** (= a very angry one). 她惡狠狠地瞪了他一眼。▸ **mur·der·ous·ly** *adv.*

murk /mɜːk; *NAmE* mɜːrk/ *noun* (usually **the murk**) [U] DARKNESS caused by smoke, FOG, etc. 陰暗；昏暗 SYN **gloom**

murky /ˈmɜːki; *NAmE* ˈmɜːrki/ *adj.* (**murk·ier, murki·est**) **1** (of a liquid 液體) not clear; dark or dirty with mud or another substance 渾濁的；污濁的 SYN **cloudy**：*She gazed into the murky depths of the water.* 她注視着那幽暗的水底。**2** (of air, light, etc. 空氣、光等) dark and unpleasant because of smoke, FOG, etc. 昏暗的；陰暗的；朦朧的：*a murky night* 昏暗的夜 **3** (*disapproving* or *humorous*) (of people's actions or character 人的行為或性格) not clearly known and suspected of not being honest 隱晦的；含糊的；曖昧可疑的：*He had a somewhat murky past.* 他有一段不清白的過去。◇ *the murky world of arms dealing* 黑暗的軍火生意

mur·mur /ˈmɜːmə(r); *NAmE* ˈmɜːrm-/ *verb, noun*

■ *verb* **1** [T, I] **~ (sth)** | **+ speech** | **~ that ...** to say sth in a soft quiet voice that is difficult to hear or understand 低語；喃喃細語：*She murmured her agreement.* 她低聲表示同意。◇ *He murmured something in his sleep.* 他在睡夢裏嘟囔了些什麼。◇ *She was murmuring in his ear.* 她在他耳邊悄聲說話。**2** [I] to make a quiet continuous sound 連續發出低沉的聲音：*The wind murmured in the trees.* 風在樹林中沙沙作響。**3** [I] **~ (against sb/sth)** (*literary*) to complain about sb/sth, but not openly （私下）發怨言，發牢騷

■ *noun* **1** [C] a quietly spoken word or words 低語；喃喃聲：*She answered in a faint murmur.* 她低聲應答。◇ *Murmurs of 'Praise God' went around the circle.* 周圍的人群發出了"讚美主"的低語聲。**2** [C] (also **mur·mur·ings** [pl.]) a quiet expression of feeling 嘟囔；咕噥：*a **murmur of agreement/approval/complaint*** 表示同意／贊同／抱怨的低語聲◇ *He paid the extra cost **without a murmur*** (= without complaining at all). 他一聲不吭地付了額外的費用。◇ *polite murmurings of gratitude* 有禮貌地連連低聲道謝 **3** (also **mur·mur·ing**) [sing.] a low continuous sound in the background 接連從遠處傳來的低沉的聲音：*the distant murmur of traffic* 遠處傳來的車輛的嘈雜聲 **4** [C] (*medical* 醫) a faint sound in the chest, usually a sign of damage or disease in the heart （胸部的）雜音：*a heart murmur* 心臟雜音

M

Murphy's Law /ˌmɜːfiz ˈlɔː; *NAmE* ˌmɜːrfiz/ *noun* (*humorous*) a statement of the fact that, if anything can possibly go wrong, it will go wrong 墨菲法則（認為任何可能出錯之事必將出錯）

mur·ram /ˈmʌrəm/ *noun* [U] a type of reddish soil that is often used to make roads in Africa（非洲築路的）紅土

Mus·ca·det /ˈmʌskədeɪ; ˈmʊsk-/ *noun* [U, C] a type of dry white French wine（法國）麝香白葡萄酒

mus·cat /ˈmʌskæt/ *noun* [U, C] **1** a type of wine, especially a strong sweet white wine 麝香葡萄酒（尤指一種白色烈性甜酒） **2** a type of GRAPE which can be eaten or used to make wine or RAISINS 麝香葡萄（用於釀酒或製葡萄乾）

mus·ca·tel /ˌmʌskəˈtel/ (also **mus·ca·delle**, **mus·ca·del** /-ˈdel/) *noun* [U, C] a type of GRAPE used in sweet white wines and for drying to make RAISINS 麝香葡萄

muscle 🔑 /ˈmʌsl/ *noun, verb*

■ *noun* **1** 🔑 [C, U] a piece of body TISSUE that you contract and relax in order to move a particular part of the body; the TISSUE that forms the muscles of the body 肌肉；肌：*a **calf/neck/thigh muscle*** 小腿／脖頸／大腿肌肉 ◇ *to **pull/tear/strain a muscle*** 拉傷／撕裂／扭傷肌肉 ◇ *This exercise will work the muscles of the lower back.* 這樣的運動可以鍛煉腰部的肌肉。◇ *He **didn't move a muscle*** (= stood completely still). 他一動不動地站着。➲ COLLOCATIONS at INJURY **2** [U] physical strength 體力：*He's an intelligent player but lacks the muscle of older competitors.* 他是個聰明的選手，但卻缺乏老對手的體力。 **3** [U] the power and influence to make others do what you want 權力；威信；影響力：*to exercise **political/industrial/financial muscle*** 運用在政治／產業／金融界的影響力 ▸ **muscled** *adj.*：*heavily muscled shoulders* 非常強壯的肩膀 IDM see FLEX *v.*

■ *verb*

PHR V **ˌmuscle ˈin (on sb/sth)** (*informal, disapproving*) to involve yourself in a situation when you have no right to do so, in order to get sth for yourself 強行干涉；粗暴干涉

ˈmuscle-bound *adj.* having large stiff muscles as a result of too much exercise（運動過度造成的）肌肉粗大僵硬的

muscle·man /ˈmʌslmæn/ *noun* (*pl.* **-men** /-men/) a big strong man, especially one employed to protect sb/sth 強壯的男子；保鏢；打手

mus·cu·lar /ˈmʌskjələ(r)/ *adj.* **1** connected with the muscles 肌肉的：***muscular tension/power/tissue*** 肌肉張力／力量／組織 **2** (also *informal* **muscly** /ˈmʌsli/) having large strong muscles 強壯的；肌肉發達的：*a **muscular body/build/chest*** 強壯的身體／體格；肌肉發達的胸部 ◇ *He was tall, lean and muscular.* 他高挑瘦削，強壯有力。

muscular dystrophy /ˌmʌskjələ ˈdɪstrəfi; *NAmE* -lər/ *noun* [U] a medical condition that some people are born with in which the muscles gradually become weaker 肌肉萎縮

mus·cu·lat·ure /ˈmʌskjələtʃə(r)/ *noun* [U, sing.] (*biology* 生) the system of muscles in the body or part of the body 肌肉系統

muse /mjuːz/ *noun, verb*

■ *noun* **1** a person or spirit that gives a writer, painter, etc. ideas and the desire to create things（作家、畫家等的）靈感；創作衝動的源泉 SYN **inspiration**：*He felt that his muse had deserted him* (= that he could no longer write, paint, etc.). 他覺得他已失去了創作靈感。 **2** **Muse** (in ancient Greek and Roman stories) one of the nine GODDESSES who encouraged poetry, music and other branches of art and literature 繆斯（古希臘和羅馬神話中執掌詩歌、音樂和其他文學藝術分支的九位女神之一）

■ *verb* (*formal*) **1** [I] ~ **(about/on/over/upon sth)** to think carefully about sth for a time, ignoring what is happening around you 沉思；冥想 SYN **ponder**：*I sat quietly, musing on the events of the day.* 我靜靜地坐着，沉思一天中所發生的事。➲ see also MUSING **2** [T] **+ speech** | **~ that …** to say sth to yourself in a way that shows you are thinking carefully about it 沉思地自言自語：*'I wonder why?' she mused.* "這是為什麼呢？" 她若有所思地問自己。

mu·seum 🔑 /mjuˈziːəm/ *noun* a building in which objects of artistic, cultural, historical or scientific interest are kept and shown to the public 博物館：*a museum of modern art* 現代藝術博物館 ◇ *a science museum* 科學博物館 ➲ VISUAL VOCAB pages V2, V3

muˈseum piece *noun* **1** an object that is of enough historical or artistic value to have in a museum 珍藏品；足以收入博物館的物品 **2** (*humorous*) a thing or person that is old-fashioned, or old and no longer useful 老古董；過時的物（或人）

mush /mʌʃ/ *noun* **1** [U, sing.] (usually *disapproving*) a soft thick mass or mixture 軟稠的一攤；糊狀物：*The vegetables had turned to mush.* 蔬菜都爛成了一堆。◇ *His insides suddenly felt like mush.* 他內心突然傷感起來。 **2** [U] (*NAmE*) a type of thick PORRIDGE made from CORN (MAIZE) 玉米粥

musher /ˈmʌʃə(r)/ *noun* (*NAmE*) a person who drives a dog SLED 趕狗拉雪橇的人

mush·room /ˈmʌʃrʊm; -ruːm/ *noun, verb*

■ *noun* a FUNGUS with a round flat head and short STEM. Many mushrooms can be eaten. 蘑菇；蕈；傘菌：*a field mushroom* (= the most common type that is eaten, often just called a 'mushroom', and often grown to be sold) 洋蘑菇 ◇ *fried mushrooms* 油炸蘑菇 ◇ *cream of mushroom soup* 奶油蘑菇湯 ➲ VISUAL VOCAB page V31 ➲ see also BUTTON MUSHROOM, TOADSTOOL

■ *verb* **1** [I] to rapidly grow or increase in number 快速生長；迅速增長：*We expect the market to mushroom in the next two years.* 我們期望未來兩年內市場會迅速發展。 **2** (usually **go mushrooming**) [I] to gather mushrooms in a field or wood 採蘑菇

ˈmushroom cloud *noun* a large cloud, shaped like a mushroom, that forms in the air after a nuclear explosion（核爆炸形成的）蘑菇雲

mushy /ˈmʌʃi/ *adj.* (**mush·ier**, **mushi·est**) **1** soft and thick, like mush 軟而稠的；糊狀的：*Cook until the fruit is soft but not mushy.* 將水果煮至柔軟，但不要煮成糊狀。 **2** (*informal, disapproving*) too emotional in a way that is embarrassing 多愁善感的；過於感傷多情的 SYN **sentimental**：*mushy romantic novels* 過於感傷的浪漫小說

ˌmushy ˈpeas *noun* [pl.] (*BrE*) cooked PEAS that are made into a soft mixture 豌豆粥；豌豆糊

music 🔑 /ˈmjuːzɪk/ *noun* [U]

1 🔑 sounds that are arranged in a way that is pleasant or exciting to listen to. People sing music or play it on instruments 音樂；樂曲：***pop/dance/classical/church music*** 流行音樂；舞曲；古典／教堂音樂 ◇ *to listen to music* 聽音樂 ◇ *She could hear music playing somewhere.* 她聽到某個地方在演奏音樂。◇ *It was a charming **piece of music**.* 那是一首動聽的樂曲。◇ *the popularity of Mozart's music* 對莫扎特樂曲的普遍歡迎 ◇ *He wrote the music but I don't know who wrote the words.* 他創作了樂曲，但我不知道誰填寫的歌詞。◇ *The poem has been **set to music**.* 這首詩被譜了曲。◇ *Every week they get together to **make music*** (= to play music or sing). 每個星期他們都聚在一起唱歌奏樂。➲ see also CHAMBER MUSIC, COUNTRY MUSIC, ROCK MUSIC, SOUL MUSIC **2** 🔑 the art of writing or playing music 音樂；樂曲創作（或演奏）藝術：*to study music* 學習音樂 ◇ *a career in music* 音樂生涯 ◇ *music lessons* 音樂課程 ◇ *the **music business/industry*** 音樂行業／產業 **3** 🔑 the written or printed signs that represent the sounds to be played or sung in a piece of music 樂譜：*Can you **read music*** (= understand the signs in order to play or sing a piece of music)? 你會讀樂譜嗎？◇ *I had to play it without the music.* 我只得不看樂譜演奏了。◇ *The music was still open on the piano* (= the paper or book with the musical notes on it). 樂譜仍攤開着放在鋼琴上。➲ see also SHEET MUSIC

IDM **music to your ˈears** news or information that you are very pleased to hear 好消息；令人滿意的信息 ➲ more at FACE *v.*

M

musical notation 樂譜

mu·sic·al 🗝 /ˈmjuːzɪkl/ *adj., noun*

■ ***adj.*** **1** 🗝 [only before noun] connected with music; containing music 音樂的；有音樂的：*the musical director of the show* 這場演出的音樂指導 ◇ ***musical talent/ability/skill*** 音樂天賦／才能／技巧 ◇ ***musical styles/tastes*** 音樂風格／品味 ◇ *a* ***musical production/entertainment*** 音樂作品／娛樂項目 **2** 🗝 (of a person 人) with a natural skill or interest in music 有音樂天賦的；喜愛音樂的：*She's very musical.* 她極具音樂天賦。**OPP** **unmusical** **3** (of a sound 聲音) pleasant to listen to, like music 悅耳的；音樂般的：*a musical voice* 悅耳的聲音 **OPP** **unmusical**

■ ***noun*** (also *old-fashioned* ˌ**musical ˈcomedy**) a play or a film/movie in which part or all of the story is told using songs and often dancing 音樂劇

ˈ**musical box** *noun* (*especially BrE*) = MUSIC BOX

ˌ**musical ˈchairs** *noun* [U] **1** a children's game in which players run round a row of chairs while music is playing. Each time the music stops, players try to sit down on one of the chairs, but there are always more players than chairs. 搶座位遊戲（參加者隨音樂繞一圈椅子走，音樂一停就搶椅子坐，但參加者總是比椅子多）**2** (often *disapproving*) a situation in which people frequently exchange jobs or positions 人員的經常更迭流動

ˌ**musical diˈrector** *noun* the person who is in charge of the music in a show in the theatre（舞台表演的）音樂總監

ˌ**musical ˈinstrument** (also **in·stru·ment**) *noun* an object used for producing musical sounds, for example a piano or a drum 樂器：*Most pupils learn (to play) a musical instrument.* 多數小學生都學習演奏樂器。◇ *the instruments of the orchestra* 管弦樂隊的樂器 ➲ **VISUAL VOCAB** pages V34, V35, V36

mu·sic·al·ity /ˌmjuːzɪˈkæləti/ *noun* [U] (*formal*) skill and understanding in performing music 樂感；音樂欣賞能力；音樂才能

music·al·ly /ˈmjuːzɪkli/ *adv.* **1** in a way that is connected with music 音樂上；在音樂方面：*musically gifted* 音樂方面有天賦的 ◇ *Musically speaking, their latest album is nothing special.* 在音樂方面，他們最新的專輯沒

M

Collocations 詞語搭配

Music 音樂

Listening 聽

- **listen to/enjoy/love/be into** music/classical music/jazz/pop/hip-hop, etc. 聽／欣賞／喜愛／迷上音樂／古典音樂／爵士樂／流行音樂／嘻哈音樂等
- **listen to** the radio/an MP3 player/a CD 聽收音機／MP3 播放器／CD
- **put on/play** a CD/a song/some music 播放 CD／歌曲／音樂
- **turn down/up** the music/radio/volume/bass 調小／調大音樂／收音機／音量／低音
- **go to** a concert/festival/gig/performance/recital 去聽音樂會；去看會演／流行音樂現場演唱會／演出／音樂演奏會
- **copy/burn/rip** music/a CD/a DVD 複製／燒錄／抄錄音樂／CD／DVD
- **download** music/an album/a song/a demo/a video 下載音樂／專輯／歌曲／錄音樣帶／視頻

Playing 演奏

- **play** a musical instrument/the piano/percussion/a note/a riff/the melody/a concerto/a duet/by ear 演奏樂器／鋼琴／打擊樂／音符／重複段／主旋律／協奏曲／二重奏；憑聽覺記憶演奏
- **sing** an anthem/a ballad/a solo/an aria/the blues/in a choir/soprano/alto/tenor/bass/out of tune 唱國歌／民歌；獨唱；唱詠歎調／藍調歌曲；在合唱團演唱；唱女高音／中音／男高音／男低音；唱歌走調
- **hum** a tune/a theme tune/a lullaby 哼曲子／主題曲／搖籃曲
- **accompany** a singer/choir 為歌手／合唱團伴奏
- **strum** a chord/guitar 彈奏和弦／吉他

Performing 表演

- **form/start/get together/join/quit/leave** a band 組建／創辦／組成／加入／退出／離開樂隊
- **give** a performance/concert/recital 表演節目；舉辦音樂會／音樂演奏會
- **do** a concert/recital/gig 開音樂會／音樂演奏會／流行音樂現場演唱會
- **play** a concert/gig/festival/venue 在音樂會／流行音樂現場演唱會／會演／音樂廳上演出
- **perform** (*BrE*) at/in a concert/(*especially NAmE*) a concert 在音樂會上演出
- **appear** at a festival/live 現身會演；現場表演
- **go on/embark on** a (world) tour 進行／開始（全球）巡演

Recording 錄製

- **write/compose** music/a ballad/a melody/a tune/a song/a theme song/an opera/a symphony 寫／創作音樂／民謠／旋律／曲子／歌曲／主題歌／歌劇／交響曲
- **land/get/sign** a record deal 獲得／簽署唱片合約
- **be signed to/be dropped by** a record company 與唱片公司簽約；被唱片公司解約
- **record/release/put out** an album/a single/a CD 錄製／發行／出版專輯／單曲／CD
- **be top of/top** the charts 高踞每週流行音樂排行榜之首
- **get to/go straight to/go straight in at/enter the charts at** number one 位列／一舉登上／進入排行榜首位

什麼特別的。 **2** with musical skill 有音樂技能： *He plays really musically.* 他的演奏嫻熟動聽。 **3** in a way that is pleasant to listen to, like music 和諧地；悅耳地；音樂般地： *to **laugh/speak musically*** 笑聲 / 講話悅耳

Grammar Point 語法說明

must / have (got) to / must not / don't have to

Necessity and Obligation 必要和義務

- **Must** and **have (got) to** are used in the present to say that something is necessary or should be done. **Have to** is more common in *NAmE*, especially in speech. * must 和 have (got) to 用於現在時，表示某事有必要或應該做。have to 較常用於美式英語，尤其是口語中： *You must be home by 11 o'clock.* 你必須在 11 點之前回家。◇ *I must wash the car tomorrow.* 我明天必須沖洗汽車。◇ *I have to collect the children from school at 3 o'clock.* 我得在 3 點鐘到學校接孩子。◇ *Nurses have to wear a uniform.* 護士必須穿制服。
- In *BrE* there is a difference between them. **Must** is used to talk about what the speaker or listener wants, and **have (got) to** about rules, laws and other people's wishes. 在英式英語中，兩詞之間有差異。must 是基於說話者或聽話者的主觀意願，have (got) to 關乎規定、法律和他人的願望： *I must finish this essay today. I'm going out tomorrow.* 我今天一定要完成這篇論文，因為我明天要出去。◇ *I have to finish this essay today. We have to hand them in tomorrow.* 我今天得完成這篇論文，因為我們明天必須交。
- There are no past or future forms of **must**. To talk about the past you use **had to** and **has had to**. * must 無過去或將來形式。表示過去用 had to 和 has had to： *I had to wait half an hour for a bus.* 我得等半小時的公共汽車。 **Will have to** is used to talk about the future, or **have to** if an arrangement has already been made. 說將來的事用 will have to，如果已作好安排亦可用 have to： *We'll have to borrow the money we need.* 我們需要的這筆錢只好去借了。◇ *I have to go to the dentist tomorrow.* 我明天得去看牙醫。
- Questions with **have to** are formed using **do**. 帶有 have to 的疑問句由 do 構成： *Do the children have to wear a uniform?* 孩子們必須穿制服嗎？ In negative sentences both **must not** and **don't have to** are used, but with different meanings. **Must not** is used to tell somebody not to do something. 在否定句中，用 must not 和 don't have to，但二者含義不同。must not 用於告訴某人不要做某事： *Passengers must not smoke until the signs have been switched off.* 指示燈未熄滅之前乘客不許抽煙。 The short form **mustn't** is used especially in *BrE*. 簡約式 mustn't 尤用於英式英語： *You mustn't leave the gate open.* 你一定不要讓大門敞開着。 **Don't have to** is used when it is not necessary to do something. 表示沒有必要做某事用 don't have to： *You don't have to pay for the tickets in advance.* 你不必預付票款。◇ *She doesn't have to work at weekends.* 她週末不用上班。

➲ note at NEED

Certainty 肯定

- Both **must** and **have to** are used to say that you are certain about something. **Have to** is the usual verb used in *NAmE* and this is becoming more frequent in *BrE* in this meaning. 表示肯定用 must 和 have to 均可。have to 通常用於美式英語中，在英式英語中也越來越常用於此義： *He has (got) to be the worst actor on TV!* 他無疑是最糟糕的電視演員！◇ *(BrE) This must be the most boring party I've ever been to.* 這無疑是我參加過的最無聊的聚會。 If you are talking about the past, use **must have**. 說過去的事用 must have： *Your trip must have been fun!* 你這次旅行一定很開心吧！

M

'music box (also **'musical box** especially in *BrE*) *noun* a box containing a device that plays a tune when the box is opened 音樂盒；八音盒

'music hall *noun* (*BrE*) **1** (also **vaude·ville** *NAmE, BrE*) [U] a type of entertainment popular in the late 19th and early 20th centuries, including singing, dancing and comedy（盛行於 19 世紀末 20 世紀初的）歌舞雜耍表演 **2** (*NAmE* **'vaudeville theater**) [C] a theatre used for popular entertainment in the late 19th and early 20th centuries 歌舞雜耍戲院

mu·si·cian 🗝 /mjuˈzɪʃn/ *noun* a person who plays a musical instrument or writes music, especially as a job 音樂家；作曲家；樂師： *a **jazz/rock musician*** 爵士樂 / 搖滾樂樂師

mu·si·cian·ship /mjuˈzɪʃnʃɪp/ *noun* [U] skill in performing or writing music 音樂才能；音樂技能

mu·sic·ology /ˌmjuːzɪˈkɒlədʒi; *NAmE* -ˈkɑːl-/ *noun* [U] the study of the history and theory of music 音樂學 ▸ **mu·sic·olo·gist** /ˌmjuːzɪˈkɒlədʒɪst; *NAmE* -ˈkɑːl-/ *noun*

'music stand *noun* a frame, especially one that you can fold, that is used for holding sheets of music while you play a musical instrument 樂譜架

'music video *noun* = VIDEO (4)

mus·ing /ˈmjuːzɪŋ/ *noun* [U, C, usually pl.] a period of thinking carefully about sth or telling people your thoughts about it 沉思；冥想；訴說想法： *We had to sit and listen to his musings on life.* 我們只好坐着聽他談論人生。

musk /mʌsk/ *noun* [U] a substance with a strong smell that is used in making some PERFUMES. It is produced naturally by a type of male DEER. 麝香 ▸ **musky** *adj.*： *a musky perfume* (= smelling of or like musk) 有麝香味的香水

mus·ket /ˈmʌskɪt/ *noun* an early type of long gun that was used by soldiers in the past（舊時的）火槍，滑膛槍，毛瑟槍

mus·ket·eer /ˌmʌskəˈtɪə(r); *NAmE* -ˈtɪr/ *noun* a soldier who uses a musket 火槍手；滑膛槍手

'musk ox *noun* a large animal of the cow family that is covered with hair and has curved horns 麝牛

musk·rat /ˈmʌskræt/ *noun* a N American water animal that has a strong smell and is hunted for its fur 麝鼠（北美洲半水棲鼠，有麝香味，毛皮可作商品）

Mus·lim /ˈmʊzlɪm; ˈmʌz-; -ləm/ *noun* a person whose religion is Islam 穆斯林；伊斯蘭教信徒 ▸ **Mus·lim** *adj.* ➲ see also MOSLEM

mus·lin /ˈmʌzlɪn/ *noun* [U] a type of fine cotton cloth that is almost transparent, used, especially in the past, for making clothes and curtains 平紋細布（舊時尤用於做衣物和窗簾）

muso /ˈmjuːzəʊ; *NAmE* -zoʊ/ *noun* (*pl.* **-os**) (*BrE, informal*) a person who plays, or is very interested in, music and knows a lot about it 樂師；樂迷；音樂通

mus·quash /ˈmʌskwɒʃ; *NAmE* -skwɑːʃ; -skwɔːʃ/ *noun* [U] the fur of the MUSKRAT 麝鼠皮

muss /mʌs/ *verb* **~ sth (up)** (*NAmE*) to make sb's clothes or hair untidy 弄亂（衣服或頭髮）；使邋遢： *Hey, don't muss up my hair!* 嗨，別弄亂了我的頭髮！

mus·sel /ˈmʌsl/ *noun* a small SHELLFISH that can be eaten, with a black shell in two parts 蚌；貽貝；淡菜 ➲ picture at SHELLFISH

must 🗝 *modal verb, noun*

■ ***modal verb***

■ /məst; *strong form* mʌst/ (*negative* **must not**, *short form* **mustn't** /ˈmʌsnt/) **1** 🗝 used to say that sth is necessary or very important (sometimes involving a rule or a law)（表示必要或很重要）必須： *All visitors must report to reception.* 所有來賓必須到接待處報到。◇ *Cars must not park in front of the entrance* (= it is not allowed). 車輛不得停在入口處。◇ *(formal) I must ask you not to do that again.* 我得勸你別再那樣做了。◇ *You mustn't say things like that.* 你千萬別說那樣的話。◇ *I must go to the bank and get some money.* 我得上銀行取點兒錢。◇ ***I must admit*** (= I feel that I should admit) *I was surprised it cost so little.* 我得承認，這麼便宜，真讓我驚訝。◇

(*especially BrE*) *Must you always question everything I say?* (= it is annoying) 我說什麼你都非要提出質疑嗎？◇ *'Do we have to finish this today?' 'Yes, you must.'* "我們今天一定得完成這工作嗎？" "對，必須完成。" **HELP** Note that the negative for the last example is *'No, you don't have to.'* 注意最後這個示例的否定式是 No, you don't have to。 **2** used to say that sth is likely or logical（表示很可能或符合邏輯）一定：*You must be hungry after all that walking.* 走了這麼遠的路，你一定餓了吧。◇ *He must have known* (= surely he knew) *what she wanted.* 他一定早已知道她想要什麼了。◇ *I'm sorry, she's not here. She must have left already* (= that must be the explanation). 抱歉，她不在這兒。準是走了。 **3** (*especially BrE*) used to recommend that sb does sth because you think it is a good idea（提出建議）應該，得：*You simply must read this book.* 這本書你可一定要看一看。◇ *We must get together soon for lunch.* 我們得馬上會合去吃午飯。 ➲ note at MODAL

IDM **if you 'must (do sth)** used to say that sb may do sth but you do not really want them to（表示雖不贊同但可允許）如果你一定要（那麼做）：*'Can I smoke?' 'If you must.'* "我可以抽煙嗎？" "好吧，如果你非要的話。" ◇ *It's from my boyfriend, **if you must know**.* 倘使你一定要知道的話，這是我男朋友給的。 **must-see/must-read/must-have, etc.** used to tell people that sth is so good or interesting that they should see, read, get it, etc. 必看（或必讀、必備等）：*Sydney is one of the world's must-see cities.* 悉尼是世界上的必遊城市之一。◇ *The magazine is a must-read in the show business world.* 這份雜誌是演藝界人士的必讀刊物。 ➲ more at NEED *n.*

■ ***noun*** /mʌst/ [usually sing.] (*informal*) something that you must do, see, buy, etc. 必須做（或看、買等）的事：*His new novel is a must for all lovers of crime fiction.* 他的新作是所有犯罪小說愛好者的必讀書。

mus·tache (*NAmE*) (*BrE* **mous·tache**) /məˈstɑːʃ; *NAmE* ˈmʌstæʃ; məˈstæʃ/ *noun* **1** a line of hair that a man allows to grow on his upper lip 上唇的鬍子；髭 ➲ VISUAL VOCAB page V60 **2 mustaches** [pl.] a very long mustache 長髭 ➲ compare BEARD

mus·tached (*NAmE*) (*BrE* **mous·tached**) /məˈstɑːʃt; *NAmE* ˈmʌstæʃt; məˈstæʃt/ *adj.* [usually before noun] having a mustache 長鬍子的；有鬍子的 ➲ compare MUSTACHIOED

mus·tachi·oed (also **mous·tachi·oed**) /məˈstæʃiəʊd; *NAmE* -ʃioʊd/ *adj.* (*literary*) having a large moustache with curls at the ends 有大髭曲八字鬍的

mus·tang /ˈmʌstæŋ/ *noun* a small American wild horse 北美野馬；卡尤塞馬

mus·tard /ˈmʌstəd; *NAmE* -tərd/ *noun* [U] **1** a thick cold yellow or brown sauce that tastes hot and spicy and is usually eaten with meat 芥末醬：*a jar of mustard* 一罐芥末醬 ◇ *mustard powder* 芥末粉 ◇ ***French/English mustard*** 法國／英國芥末 **2** a small plant with yellow flowers, grown for its seeds that are crushed to make mustard 芥；芥菜 **3** (*BrE*) the leaves of the mustard plant that are eaten raw in salads 芥菜葉：*mustard and cress* (= leaves of white mustard grown with CRESS) 芥菜葉和水芹 **4** a brownish-yellow colour 芥末黃；褐黃色 ▸ **mus·tard** *adj.*：*a mustard sweater* 芥末黃毛線衣

IDM **(not) cut the 'mustard** to (not) be as good as expected or required（不）如所期待的那麼好；（不）符合要求：*I didn't cut the mustard as a hockey player.* 我不是一個合格的曲棍球手。 ➲ more at KEEN *adj.*

'mustard gas *noun* [U] a poisonous gas that burns the skin, used in chemical weapons, for example during the First World War 芥子氣（損害皮膚，用於化學武器）

'mustard greens *noun* [pl.] the dark green leaves of a type of MUSTARD plant, that are cooked or eaten raw in salads, especially in the Southern US 芥菜葉（烹調或拌色拉用，尤見於美國南部）

mus·ter /ˈmʌstə(r)/ *verb, noun*

■ ***verb*** **1** [T] **~ sth (up)** to find as much support, courage, etc. as you can 找尋，聚集，激起（支持、勇氣等） **SYN** **summon**：*We mustered what support we could for the plan.* 我們極盡所能為這項計劃尋求支持。◇ *She left the room **with all the dignity she could muster**.* 她盡量莊重體面地走了出去。 **2** [I, T] to come together, or bring people, especially soldiers, together for example for military action 集合，召集，集結（尤指部隊） **SYN** **gather**：*The troops mustered.* 部隊集結起來。◇ **~ sb/sth** *to muster an army* 集合一支部隊 **3** [T] **~ sth** (*AustralE, NZE*) to gather together sheep or cows 趕攏（牛、羊）

■ ***noun*** a group of people, especially soldiers, that have been brought together 聚集的人群；（尤指）集結的兵力：***muster stations*** (= parts of a building, a ship, etc. that people must go to if there is an emergency) 集結站 **IDM** see PASS *v.*

musty /ˈmʌsti/ *adj.* (**must·ier**, **musti·est**) smelling damp and unpleasant because of a lack of fresh air 有霉味的；發霉的 **SYN** **dank**：*a musty room* 有霉味的房間

mut·able /ˈmjuːtəbl/ *adj.* (*formal*) that can change; likely to change 可變的；會變的 ▸ **mut·abil·ity** /ˌmjuːtəˈbɪləti/ *noun* [U]

mu·tant /ˈmjuːtənt/ *adj., noun*

■ ***adj.*** (*biology* 生) (of a living thing 生物) different in some way from others of the same kind because of a change in its GENETIC structure 因基因變異而不同的；變異的；突變的：*a mutant gene* 變異基因

■ ***noun*** **1** (*biology* 生) a living thing with qualities that are different from its parents' qualities because of a change in its GENETIC structure 突變型；突變體 **2** (*informal*) (in stories about space, the future, etc. 未來和太空等故事) a living thing with an unusual and frightening appearance because of a change in its GENETIC structure 突變異體怪物；異形

mu·tate /mjuːˈteɪt; *NAmE* ˈmjuːteɪt/ *verb* **1** [I, T] to develop or make sth develop a new form or structure, because of a GENETIC change（使）變異，突變：**~ (into sth)** *the ability of the virus to mutate into new forms* 病毒變種的能力 ◇ **~ sth** *mutated genes* 發生變異的基因 **2** [I] **~ (into sth)** to change into a new form 轉變；轉換：*Rhythm and blues mutated into rock and roll.* 節奏布魯斯演變成為搖滾樂。 ➲ see also MUTATION

mu·ta·tion /mjuːˈteɪʃn/ *noun* **1** [U, C] (*biology* 生) a process in which the GENETIC material of a person, a plant or an animal changes in structure when it is passed on to children, etc., causing different physical characteristics to develop; a change of this kind（生物物種的）變異，突變：*cells affected by mutation* 受到突變影響的細胞 ◇ *genetic mutations* 基因變異 **2** [U, C] a change in the form or structure of sth（形式或結構的）轉變，改變：(*linguistics* 語言) *vowel mutation* 元音變化

mu·ta·tis mu·tan·dis /mjuːˌtɑːtɪs mjuːˈtændɪs; muː-/ *adv.* (from *Latin*, *formal*) (used when you are comparing two or more things or situations) making the small changes that are necessary for each individual case, without changing the main points（用於比較兩種或以上的事物或狀況）針對具體情況作必要的小更改：*The same contract, mutatis mutandis, will be given to each employee* (= the contract is basically the same for everybody, but the names, etc. are changed). 把姓名等細節稍作修改之後，同一份合同將發給每個員工。

mute /mjuːt/ *adj., noun, verb*

■ ***adj.*** **1** not speaking 沉默的；不出聲的；無聲的 **SYN** **silent**：*a look of mute appeal* 默默請求的表情 ◇ *The child sat mute in the corner of the room.* 這孩子坐在屋子的角落裏，一聲不吭。 **2** (*old-fashioned*) (of a person 人) unable to speak 啞的 **SYN** **dumb**

■ ***noun*** **1** (*music* 音) a device made of metal, rubber or plastic that you use to make the sound of a musical instrument softer 弱音器 **2** (*old-fashioned*) a person who is not able to speak 啞巴

■ ***verb*** **1** **~ sth** to make the sound of sth, especially a musical instrument, quieter or softer, sometimes using a mute 消音；減音；減弱（尤指樂器）的聲音：*He muted the strings with his palm.* 他用手掌抹琴弦消音。 **2** **~ sth** to make sth weaker or less severe 減弱；緩解 **SYN** **tone down**：*She thought it better to mute her criticism.* 她覺得還是婉轉地提出批評比較好。

'mute button *noun* **1** a button on a telephone that you press in order to stop yourself from being heard by the person at the other end of the line (while you speak to sb else)（電話上的）靜音鍵 **2** a button that you press in order to switch off a television's sound（電視機的）靜音按鈕

muted /ˈmjuːtɪd/ *adj.* **1** (of sounds 聲音) quiet; not as loud as usual 靜靜的；減輕的：*They spoke in muted voices.* 他們輕聲說着話。**2** (of emotions, opinions, etc. 情感、意見等) not strongly expressed 含糊不清的；表達不明確的：*The proposals received only a muted response.* 這個倡議沒有得到明確的回應。**3** (of colours, light, etc. 色彩、光亮等) not bright 暗淡的；不明亮的：*a dress in muted shades of blue* 暗藍色調的連衣裙 **4** (of musical instruments 樂器) used with a mute 使用弱音器的：*muted trumpets* 裝有弱音器的小號

mute·ly /ˈmjuːtli/ *adv.* without speaking 無言地；一語不發地 SYN **silently**

muti /ˈmuːti/ *noun* [U] (*SAfrE*) **1** African medicines or magic CHARMS that are prepared from plants, animals, etc.（在非洲用植物、動物等製成的）草藥，土藥，符咒 **2** any kind of medicine 藥

mu·ti·late /ˈmjuːtɪleɪt/ *verb* **1 ~ sb/sth** to damage sb's body very severely, especially by cutting or tearing off part of it 使殘廢；使殘缺不全；毀傷：*The body had been badly mutilated.* 屍體被嚴重毀傷。**2 ~ sth** to damage sth very badly 嚴重損毀；毀壞 SYN **vandalize**：*Intruders slashed and mutilated several paintings.* 闖進來的人毀壞了好幾幅油畫。▶ **mu·ti·la·tion** /ˌmjuːtɪˈleɪʃn/ *noun* [U, C]：*Thousands suffered death or mutilation in the bomb blast.* 在炸彈爆炸事件中，數千人被炸死，或成為殘廢。

M

mu·tin·eer /ˌmjuːtəˈnɪə(r); *NAmE* -ˈnɪr/ *noun* a person who takes part in a MUTINY 叛變者；暴動者；反叛者

mu·tin·ous /ˈmjuːtənəs/ *adj.* **1** refusing to obey the orders of sb in authority; wanting to do this 不馴服的；桀驁不馴的；有意反抗的 SYN **rebellious**：*mutinous workers* 桀驁不馴的工人 ◇ *a mutinous expression* 反抗的神色 **2** taking part in a mutiny 參與叛亂的；參與暴動的 ▶ **mu·tin·ous·ly** *adv.*

mu·tiny /ˈmjuːtəni/ *noun, verb*

■ ***noun*** (*pl.* **-ies**) [U, C] the act of refusing to obey the orders of sb in authority, especially by soldiers or sailors（尤指士兵或船員的）譁變，暴動：*Discontent among the ship's crew finally led to the outbreak of mutiny.* 船員的不滿情緒最終釀成了暴亂。◇ *the famous movie 'Mutiny on the Bounty'* 著名電影《叛艦喋血記》◇ *We have a family mutiny on our hands!* 我們家出了叛逆之事，需要處理！

■ ***verb*** (**mu·tin·ies**, **mu·tiny·ing**, **mu·tin·ied**, **mu·tin·ied**) [I] (especially of soldiers or sailors 尤指士兵或船員) to refuse to obey the orders of sb in authority 不服從；反抗；反叛

mut·ism /ˈmjuːtɪzəm/ *noun* [U] (*medical* 醫) a medical condition in which a person is unable to speak 緘默症；啞症

mutt /mʌt/ *noun* (*informal, especially NAmE*) a dog, especially one that is not of a particular breed 狗；雜種狗 SYN **mongrel**

mut·ter /ˈmʌtə(r)/ *verb, noun*

■ ***verb*** **1** [T, I] to speak or say sth in a quiet voice that is difficult to hear, especially because you are annoyed about sth 嘀咕；嘟囔：**+ speech** *'How dare she,' he muttered under his breath.* 他輕聲嘀咕道："她怎麼敢。" ◇ **~ (sth) (to sb/yourself) (about sth)** *She just sat there muttering to herself.* 她坐在那兒獨自唧唧咕咕的。◇ *I muttered something about needing to get back to work.* 我嘀咕着說要接着幹活了。◇ **~ that** ... *He muttered that he was sorry.* 他輕聲嘀咕了一聲對不起。**2** [I, T] **~ (about sth)** | **~ that** ... to complain about sth, without saying publicly what you think（私下）抱怨，發牢騷 SYN **grumble**：*Workers continued to mutter about the management.* 工人私下對資方還是有怨言。

■ ***noun*** [usually sing.] a quiet sound or words that are difficult to hear 嘀咕；嘟噥；低語聲：*the soft mutter of voices* 柔和的低語聲

mut·ter·ing /ˈmʌtərɪŋ/ *noun* [U] **1** (also **mutterings** [pl.]) complaints that you express privately rather than openly（私下的）抱怨，牢騷：*There have been mutterings about his leadership.* 底下對他的領導一直怨聲不斷。**2** words that you speak very quietly to yourself 喃喃自語

mut·ton /ˈmʌtn/ *noun* [U] meat from a fully grown sheep 羊肉 ➲ compare LAMB *n.* (2)

IDM **mutton dressed as ˈlamb** (*BrE, informal, disapproving*) used to describe a woman who is trying to look younger than she really is, especially by wearing clothes that are designed for young people 扮俏的女人；老來俏

ˌmutton ˈchops (also **ˌmutton chop ˈwhiskers**) *noun* [pl.] hair at the sides of a man's face which is grown so that it is very wide and round in shape at the bottom 羊排絡腮鬍（長於臉頰兩邊，底部呈寬圓形）

mu·tual AW /ˈmjuːtʃuəl/ *adj.* **1** used to describe feelings that two or more people have for each other equally, or actions that affect two or more people equally 相互的；彼此的：***mutual respect/understanding*** 相互的尊敬／理解 ◇ ***mutual support/aid*** 相互的支持／幫助 ◇ *I don't like her, and I think **the feeling is mutual*** (= she doesn't like me either). 我不喜歡她，我覺得她也不喜歡我。**2** [only before noun] shared by two or more people 共有的；共同的：*We met at the home of a mutual friend.* 我們在彼此都認識的朋友家中會面。◇ *They soon discovered a mutual interest in music.* 他們很快發現對音樂有着共同的興趣。▶ **mu·tu·al·ity** /ˌmjuːtʃuˈæləti/ *noun* [U, C] (*formal*)

ˈmutual fund (*NAmE*) (*BrE* **ˌunit ˈtrust**) *noun* a company that offers a service to people by investing their money in various different businesses 共同基金，互惠基金（代客戶進行不同組合的投資）

mu·tu·al·ly AW /ˈmjuːtʃuəli/ *adv.* felt or done equally by two or more people 相互地；彼此；共同地：***a mutually beneficial/supportive*** *relationship* 互惠／互助的關係 ◇ *Can we find a mutually convenient time to meet?* 我們可以找個雙方都適當的時間會面嗎？◇ *The two views are not **mutually exclusive*** (= both can be true at the same time). 這兩種觀點並不互相排斥。

Muzak™ /ˈmjuːzæk/ *noun* [U] (often *disapproving*) continuous recorded music that is played in shops, restaurants, airports, etc. 米尤扎克背景音樂（常在商店、飯店、機場等地連續播放）➲ compare PIPE *v.* (3)

muz·zle /ˈmʌzl/ *noun, verb*

■ ***noun*** **1** the nose and mouth of an animal, especially a dog or a horse（狗、馬等動物的）口鼻 ➲ VISUAL VOCAB page V12 ➲ compare SNOUT (1) **2** a device made of leather or plastic that you put over the nose and mouth of an animal, especially a dog, to prevent it from biting people（防止動物咬人的）口套 **3** the open end of a gun, where the bullets come out 槍口；炮口

■ ***verb*** **1** [usually passive] **~ sth** to put a muzzle over a dog's head to prevent it from biting people（給狗）戴口套 **2 ~ sb/sth** to prevent sb from expressing their opinions in public as they want to 壓制，箝制（言論）；使緘默 SYN **gag**：*They accused the government of muzzling the press.* 他們指責政府壓制新聞自由。

muzzy /ˈmʌzi/ *adj.* (*BrE, informal*) **1** unable to think in a clear way 頭腦混亂的；迷糊的：*a muzzy head* 稀裏糊塗的頭腦 ◇ *Those drugs made me feel muzzy.* 那些藥使我昏昏欲睡。**2** not clear 模模糊糊的；不清楚的：*a muzzy voice* 模糊不清的聲音 ◇ *muzzy plans* 過於籠統的計劃

MV /ˌem ˈviː/ *abbr.* (*BrE*) (used before the name of a ship) motor vessel（用於船名前）內燃機船：*the MV Puma* 美洲獅號機動船

MVP /ˌem viː ˈpiː/ *abbr.* (*especially NAmE*) most valuable player (the best player in a team) 最優秀選手；最有價值球員：*He has just earned his fourth MVP award this season.* 這個賽季他剛獲得了他的第四個"最有價值球員獎"。

MW *abbr.* **1** MEDIUM WAVE 中波 **2** (*pl.* **MW**) MEGAWATT(S) 兆瓦（特）

MWA /ˌem dʌbljuː ˈeɪ/ *abbr.* Member of the Welsh Assembly 威爾士議會議員

mwah (also **mwa**) /mwɑː/ *exclamation* used to represent the sound that some people make when they kiss sb on the cheek（親吻臉頰的聲音）吧

mwa·limu /mwɑːˈliːmuː/ *noun* (*EAfrE*) **1** a teacher 教師；老師 **2 Mwalimu** a title or form of address for sb who is respected as a teacher（頭銜或尊稱）老師，導師：*Mwalimu Julius Nyerere* 朱利葉斯 • 尼雷爾導師

mwethya /mˈweθjə/ *noun* (*pl.* **mwethya**) (*EAfrE*) a group of people who are involved with projects in a community, for example building a school or repairing roads（建設學校、修路等的）社區項目工作組

my 🔑 /maɪ/ *det.*
(the possessive form of *I* * I 的所有格形式) **1** 🔑 of or belonging to the speaker or writer 我的：*Where's my passport?* 我的護照在哪兒？◇ *My feet are cold.* 我的腳冷。 **2** used in exclamations to express surprise, etc.（用於感歎句，表示吃驚等）：*My goodness! Look at the time!* 天哪！看看幾點了！ **3** used when addressing sb, to show affection（稱呼別人時使用，表示親切）：***my dear/darling/love*** 親愛的；我的寶貝兒／心肝兒 **4** used when addressing sb that you consider to have a lower status than you（對下級的稱呼）：*My dear girl, you're wrong.* 我親愛的姑娘，你錯了。

my·al·gia /maɪˈældʒə/ *noun* [U] (*medical* 醫) pain in a muscle 肌痛 ▸ **my·al·gic** /-dʒɪk/ *adj.* ➲ see also ME

my·al·gic en·ceph·alo·my·eli·tis /maɪˌældʒɪk enˌsefələʊmaɪəˈlaɪtɪs; *NAmE* -ˌsefələm-/ *noun* [U] = ME

my·col·ogy /maɪˈkɒlədʒi; *NAmE* -ˈkɑːl-/ *noun* [U] the scientific study of FUNGI 真菌學 ➲ see also FUNGUS

mye·lin /ˈmaɪəlɪn/ *noun* [U] (*biology* 生) a mixture of PROTEINS and fats that surrounds many nerve cells, increasing the speed at which they send signals 髓磷脂，髓鞘質（由脂質、蛋白質組成，包繞在神經纖維軸突上）

mye·loma /ˌmaɪəˈləʊmə; *NAmE* -ˈloʊmə/ (*pl.* **mye·lo·mas** or **mye·lo·mata** /-mətə/) *noun* (*medical* 醫) a type of cancer found as a TUMOUR inside the bone 骨髓瘤

mynah /ˈmaɪnə/ (also **ˈmynah bird**) *noun* a SE Asian bird with dark feathers, that can copy human speech 鷯哥，家八哥，八哥（東南亞一種能模仿人說話的黑羽鳥）

my·opia /maɪˈəʊpiə; *NAmE* -ˈoʊpiə/ *noun* [U] **1** (*technical* 術語) the inability to see things clearly when they are far away 近視 SYN **short sight**, **short-sightedness** **2** (*formal*, *disapproving*) the inability to see what the results of a particular action or decision will be; the inability to think about anything outside your own situation 目光短淺；缺乏遠見 SYN **short-sightedness** ▸ **my·opic** /maɪˈɒpɪk; *NAmE* -ˈɑːpɪk/ *adj.* (*technical* 術語) *a* ***myopic child/eye*** 近視的孩子／眼 ◇ (*disapproving*) *a myopic strategy* 缺乏遠見的策略 ◇ *myopic voters* 目光短淺的投票者 ➲ see also SHORT-SIGHTED **my·opic·al·ly** /maɪˈɒpɪkli; *NAmE* -ˈɑːpɪk-/ *adv.*

myr·iad /ˈmɪriəd/ *noun* (*literary*) an extremely large number of sth 無數；大量：*Designs are available in a myriad of colours.* 各種色彩的款式應有盡有。▸ **myr·iad** *adj.*：*the myriad problems of modern life* 現代生活中的大量問題

myrrh /mɜː(r)/ *noun* [U] a sticky substance with a sweet smell that comes from trees and is used to make PERFUME and INCENSE 沒藥（芳香液狀樹脂，用於製香水等）

myr·tle /ˈmɜːtl; *NAmE* ˈmɜːrtl/ *noun* [U, C] a bush with shiny leaves, pink or white flowers and bluish-black BERRIES 愛神木；香桃木；番櫻桃

my·self 🔑 /maɪˈself/ *pron.*
1 🔑 (the reflexive form of *I* * I 的反身形式) used when the speaker or writer is also the person affected by an action（用於動作影響說話人或作者時）我自己：*I cut myself on a knife.* 我用刀時割傷了自己。◇ *I wrote a message to myself.* 我給自己留了個便條。◇ *I found myself unable to speak.* 我發現自己說不出話了。◇ *I haven't been feeling myself recently* (= I have not felt well). 我最近感覺不太好。◇ *I needed space to be myself* (= not influenced by other people). 我需要給自己留點兒空間。 **2** 🔑 used to emphasize the fact that the speaker is doing sth（強調說話者在做某事）我本人，親自：*I'll speak to her myself.* 我要親自去跟她說。◇ *I myself do not agree.* 我本人不同意。

IDM **(all) by my'self** **1** alone; without anyone else（我）獨自，單獨：*I live by myself.* 我自己一個人生活。 **2** without help（我）獨立地：*I painted the room all by myself.* 我獨自一人粉刷了屋子。 **(all) to my'self** for the speaker or writer alone; not shared 獨自享用：*I had a whole pizza to myself.* 我獨自吃了一整個比薩餅。

My·Space™ /ˈmaɪspeɪs/ *noun* a SOCIAL NETWORKING website 聚友網

mys·teri·ous 🔑 /mɪˈstɪəriəs; *NAmE* -ˈstɪr-/ *adj.*
1 🔑 difficult to understand or explain; strange 神秘的；奇怪的；不易解釋的：*He died in mysterious circumstances.* 他的死因是個謎。◇ *A mysterious illness is affecting all the animals.* 一種奇怪的疾病正在侵襲所有的動物。 **2** 🔑 (especially of people 尤指人) strange and interesting because you do not know much about them 神秘的；陌生的 SYN **enigmatic**：*A mysterious young woman is living next door.* 一位神秘的年輕女子住在隔壁。 **3** (of people 人) not saying much about sth, especially when other people want to know more 詭秘的；故弄玄虛的：*He was being very mysterious about where he was going.* 他十分詭秘，閉口不談他要去的地方。 ▸ **mys·teri·ous·ly** *adv.*：*My watch had mysteriously disappeared.* 我的手錶不知怎麼就不見了。◇ *Mysteriously, the streets were deserted.* 不知怎的，街上空無一人。◇ *She was silent, smiling mysteriously.* 她沉默不語，神秘地笑着。 **mys·teri·ous·ness** *noun* [U]

mys·tery 🔑 /ˈmɪstri/ *noun* (*pl.* **-ies**)
1 🔑 [C] something that is difficult to understand or to explain 神秘的事物；不可理解之事；奧秘：*It is one of the great* ***unsolved mysteries*** *of this century.* 這是本世紀尚未解開的大奧秘之一。◇ *Their motives remain a mystery.* 他們的動機仍然是個謎。◇ ***It's a*** *complete* ***mystery to me why they chose him.*** 我真無法理解他們為什麼會選他。 **2** 🔑 [C] (often used as an adjective 常用作形容詞) a person or thing that is strange and interesting because you do not know much about them or it 神秘的人（或事物）；陌生而有趣的人（或事物）：*He's a bit of a mystery.* 他這個人有點兒神秘。◇ *There was a* ***mystery guest*** *on the programme.* 節目中有位神秘嘉賓。◇ *The band was financed by a mystery backer.* 這個樂隊是由一個不明身分的人資助的。◇ (*BrE*) *a* ***mystery tour*** (= when you do not know where you are going) 神秘之旅 **3** 🔑 [U] the quality of being difficult to understand or to explain, especially when this makes sb/sth seem interesting and exciting 神秘；不可思議；奧秘：*Mystery surrounds her disappearance.* 她的失踪引起了重重疑團。◇ *His past is* ***shrouded in mystery*** (= not much is known about it). 他來歷不明。◇ *The dark glasses give her an* ***air of mystery***. 這墨鏡使她顯得有些神秘。 **4** 🔑 [C] a story, a film/movie or a play in which crimes and strange events are only explained at the end 疑案小說（或電影、戲劇）：*I enjoy murder mysteries.* 我喜歡兇殺奇案作品。 **5 mysteries** [pl.] secret religious ceremonies; secret knowledge 秘密的宗教儀式；秘密知識：(*figurative*) *the teacher who initiated me into the mysteries of mathematics* 把我引進神秘的數學世界的老師 **6** [C] a religious belief that cannot be explained or proved in a scientific way（宗教信仰的）奧義，奧秘，奧跡：*the mystery of creation* 造物的奧秘

ˈmystery play (also **ˈmiracle play**) *noun* a type of play that was popular between the 11th and 14th centuries and was based on events in the Bible or the lives of the Christian SAINTS 奧跡劇，神秘劇（11 到 14 世紀間流行的一種宗教劇，以《聖經》故事或基督教聖徒的生活為素材）

ˌmystery ˈshopper *noun* a person whose job is to visit or telephone a shop/store or other business pretending to be a customer, in order to get information on the quality of the service, the facilities, etc. 神秘顧客（受雇假扮成顧客去瞭解服務質量等的人）▸ **ˌmystery ˈshopping** *noun* [U]

mys·tic /ˈmɪstɪk/ *noun* a person who tries to become united with God through prayer and MEDITATION and so understand important things that are beyond normal human understanding 潛修者；神秘主義者

mys·tic·al /ˈmɪstɪkl/ (also *less frequent* **mys·tic** /ˈmɪstɪk/) *adj.* **1** having spiritual powers or qualities that are difficult to understand or to explain 神秘的；不可思議的；難以解釋的：***mystical forces/powers*** 神秘的力量／能力 ◇ *mystic beauty* 不可思議的美麗 ◇ *Watching the sun rise over the mountain was an almost mystical experience.* 看着太陽爬上山岡，這幾乎是一種難以言傳的體驗。 **2** connected with mysticism 潛修的；神秘主義的：*the mystical life* 潛修生活 ▸ **mys·tic·al·ly** /-kli/ *adv.*

mys·ti·cism /ˈmɪstɪsɪzəm/ *noun* [U] the belief that knowledge of God and of real truth can be found through prayer and MEDITATION rather than through reason and the senses 神秘主義：*Eastern mysticism* 東方神秘主義

mys·tify /ˈmɪstɪfaɪ/ *verb* (**mys·ti·fies**, **mys·ti·fy·ing**, **mys·ti·fied**, **mys·ti·fied**) **~ sb** to make sb confused because they do not understand sth 迷惑；使迷惑不解；使糊塗 SYN **baffle**：*They were totally mystified by the girl's disappearance.* 那女孩失踪使他們大惑不解。 ▸ **mys·ti·fi·ca·tion** /ˌmɪstɪfɪˈkeɪʃn/ *noun* [U]：*He looked at her in mystification.* 他困惑地看着她。 **mys·ti·fy·ing** *adj.*

mys·tique /mɪˈstiːk/ *noun* [U, sing.] the quality of being mysterious or secret that makes sb/sth seem interesting or attractive 神秘性：*The mystique surrounding the monarchy has gone for ever.* 王室的神秘已經一去不復返了。

M

myth /mɪθ/ *noun* [C, U] **1** a story from ancient times, especially one that was told to explain natural events or to describe the early history of a people; this type of story 神話；神話故事 SYN **legend**：*ancient Greek myths* 古希臘神話 ◇ *a creation myth* (= that explains how the world began) 創世的神話 ◇ *the heroes of myth and legend* 神話和傳說中的英雄 **2** something that many people believe but that does not exist or is false 虛構的東西；荒誕的說法；不真實的事 SYN **fallacy**：*It is time to dispel the myth of a classless society* (= to show that it does not exist). 該消除那種無階級社會的神話了。◇ *Contrary to* ***popular myth****, women are not worse drivers than men.* 都說女人開車比男人差，其實不然。⊃ see also URBAN MYTH

myth·ic /ˈmɪθɪk/ *adj.* **1** = MYTHICAL (1), (2) **2** (also **myth·ic·al**) that has become very famous, like sb/sth in a myth 著名的；神話般的 SYN **legendary**：*Scott of the Antarctic was a national hero of mythic proportions.* 南極探險家斯科特是位赫赫有名的民族英雄。

myth·ic·al /ˈmɪθɪkl/ *adj.* [usually before noun] **1** (also *less frequent* **myth·ic**) existing only in ancient myths 神話的；神話裏的 SYN **legendary**：***mythical beasts/heroes*** 神話裏的野獸／英雄 **2** (also *less frequent* **myth·ic**) that does not exist or is not true 並不存在的；虛無的；不真實的 SYN **fictitious**：*the mythical 'rich uncle' that he boasts about* 他所吹噓而並不存在的"富伯" **3** = MYTHIC (2)

mytho·logic·al /ˌmɪθəˈlɒdʒɪkl; *NAmE* -ˈlɑːdʒ-/ *adj.* [usually before noun] connected with ancient MYTHS 神話的；神話學的：***mythological subjects/figures/stories*** 神話題材／人物／故事

myth·ology /mɪˈθɒlədʒi; *NAmE* -ˈθɑːl-/ *noun* (*pl.* **-ies**) [U, C] **1** ancient MYTHS in general; the ancient MYTHS of a particular culture, society, etc. (統稱)神話；某文化(或社會等)的神話：*Greek mythology* 希臘神話 ◇ *a study of the religions and mythologies of ancient Rome* 關於古羅馬的宗教和神話的研究 **2** ideas that many people think are true but that do not exist or are false 虛幻的想法；錯誤的觀點：*the popular mythology that life begins at forty* 生活四十方起步這種普遍的錯誤觀點

myxo·ma·tosis /ˌmɪksəməˈtəʊsɪs; *NAmE* -ˈtoʊ-/ *noun* [U] an infectious disease of RABBITS that usually causes death 兔黏液瘤病；多發黏液瘤病

mzee /mˈziː/ *noun* (*EAfrE*) **1** a person who is respected because of their age, experience or authority; an ELDER (因年長、閱歷豐富或有權力而)受尊敬的人；老人；長者；權威人士 **2** **Mzee** a title for a man that shows respect (對男子的尊稱)前輩，大人：*Mzee Kenyatta* 肯雅塔大人

Nn

N /en/ *noun, abbr., symbol*

■ ***noun*** (also **n**) (*pl.* **Ns**, **N's**, **n's** /enz/) **1** [C, U] the 14th letter of the English alphabet 英語字母表的第 14 個字母： *'Night' begins with (an) N/'N'.* * night 一詞以字母 n 開頭。**2** [U] (*mathematics* 數) used to represent a number whose value is not mentioned（表示不定數）： *The equation is impossible for any value of n greater than 2.* 這個等式對於任何大於 2 的數值都不成立。➲ see also NTH

■ ***abbr.*** **1** (*NAmE* also **No.**) north; northern 北方（的）；北部（的）： *N Ireland* 北愛爾蘭 **2** NEWTON(S) 牛頓（力的單位）

■ ***symbol*** the symbol for the chemical element nitrogen（化學元素）氮

n. *abbr.* noun 名詞

n/a *abbr.* **1** not applicable (used on a form as an answer to a question that does not apply to you)（用於回答表格問題）無關，不適用 **2** not available 沒有；無法得到

NAACP /ˌen dʌbəl ˌeɪ siː ˈpiː/ *abbr.* National Association for the Advancement of Colored People (an organization in the US that works for the rights of African Americans) 全國有色人種協進會（美國一黑人人權組織）

NAAFI /ˈnæfi/ *noun* [sing.] the abbreviation for 'Navy, Army and Air Force Institutes' (an organization which provides shops and places to eat for British soldiers) 海陸空軍小賣店經營機構（全寫為 Navy, Army and Air Force Institutes，負責英軍商店和食堂經營）

naan *noun* [U] = NAN²

naar·tjie /ˈnɑːtʃi; *NAmE* ˈnɑːrtʃi/ *noun* (*SAfrE*) a type of small orange with a loose skin that you can remove easily 南非柑橘

nab /næb/ *verb* (**-bb-**) (*informal*) **1 ~ sb** to catch or arrest sb who is doing sth wrong 捉住；當場逮捕 **SYN** **collar**： *He was nabbed by the police for speeding.* 他超速行駛被警察逮住了。 **2 ~ sth** to take or get sth 獲得；拿取： *Who's nabbed my drink?* 誰動了我的飲料？

nabob /ˈneɪbɒb; *NAmE* -bɑːb/ *noun* **1** a Muslim ruler or officer in the Mogul empire（印度莫卧兒帝國時代的）穆斯林官員，地方行政長官 **2** a rich or important person 富豪；要人

nachos /ˈnætʃəʊz; *NAmE* -tʃoʊz/ *noun* [pl.] (from *Spanish*) a Mexican dish of crisp pieces of TORTILLA served with BEANS, cheese, spices, etc. 墨西哥玉米片（可用豆、乾酪、辛香料等作配料食用）

nada /ˈnɑːdə/ *noun* [U] (from *Spanish, informal, especially NAmE*) nothing 無： *What is it worth? Zero, zilch, nada!* 它值多少？零，鴨蛋，啥也不值！

nadir /ˈneɪdɪə(r); *NAmE* -dɪr/ *noun* [sing.] (*formal*) the worst moment of a particular situation 最糟糕的時刻；最低點： *the nadir of his career* 他事業上的低谷 ◇ *Company losses reached their nadir in 2009.* * 2009 年公司的虧損額達到了最嚴重的程度。 **OPP** **zenith**

nae /neɪ/ *det.* (*ScotE*) no 無；沒有： *We have nae money.* 我們沒有錢。 ▸ **nae** *adv.*： *It's nae (= not) bad.* 還不壞。

naff /næf/ *adj.* (*BrE, informal*) lacking style, taste, quality, etc. 無特色的；沒有品位的；蹩腳的： *There was a naff band playing.* 有一支蹩腳的樂隊在演奏。

nag /næg/ *verb, noun*

■ ***verb*** (**-gg-**) **1** [I, T] to keep complaining to sb about their behaviour or keep asking them to do sth 嘮叨；不停地抱怨 **SYN** **pester**： **~ (at sb)** *Stop nagging—I'll do it as soon as I can.* 別嘮叨了，我會儘快做的。◇ **~ sb (to do sth)** *She had been nagging him to paint the fence.* 她一直嘮叨，要他把圍欄油漆一下。 **2** [I, T] to worry or irritate you continuously 不斷困擾；老使人煩惱： **~ at sb** *A feeling of unease nagged at her.* 一種不安的感覺一直困擾着她。◇ **~ sb** *Doubts nagged me all evening.* 我一晚上都沒有擺脫心中的疑慮。

■ ***noun*** (*old-fashioned, informal*) a horse 馬

na·gana /nəˈgɑːnə/ *noun* [U] (*EAfrE*) a serious illness that cows can get from a type of fly (= a TSETSE FLY) 非洲錐蟲病，那加那病（由舌蠅傳染，主要侵害牛）

nag·ging /ˈnægɪŋ/ *adj.* [only before noun] **1** continuing for a long time and difficult to cure or remove 糾纏不休的；難以擺脫的： *a **nagging pain/doubt*** 難以消除的疼痛 / 懷疑 **2** complaining 嘮叨的；抱怨的；訴苦的： *a nagging voice* 嘮嘮叨叨的聲音

nah /nɑː/ *exclamation* (*slang*) = NO

naiad /ˈnaɪæd/ *noun* (*pl.* **naiads** or **nai·ades** /-diːz/) (in ancient stories 神話故事) a water spirit 那伊阿得（水澤仙女）

nail 🔑 /neɪl/ *noun, verb*

■ ***noun*** **1** 🔑 thin hard layer covering the outer tip of the fingers or toes 指甲；趾甲： *Stop biting your nails!* 別咬指甲！◇ *nail clippers* 指甲鉗 ➲ VISUAL VOCAB page V59 ➲ see also FINGERNAIL, TOENAIL **2** 🔑 a small thin pointed piece of metal with a flat head, used for hanging things on a wall or for joining pieces of wood together 釘；釘子： *She hammered the nail in.* 她把釘子敲了進去。 ➲ COLLOCATIONS at DECORATE ➲ VISUAL VOCAB page V20 ➲ compare SCREW *n.* (1), TACK *n.* (3)

IDM **a nail in sb's/sth's 'coffin** something that makes the end or failure of an organization, sb's plans, etc. more likely to happen 導致失敗的事物；導致某事終結之物 **on the 'nail** (*BrE, informal*) (of payment 付款) without delay 立刻；馬上；毫不拖延： *They're good customers who always pay on the nail.* 他們是好主顧，付賬從不耽擱。 ➲ more at FIGHT *v.*, HARD *adj.*, HIT *v.*, TOUGH *adj.*

■ ***verb*** **1 ~ sth (+ adv./prep./adj.)** to fasten sth to sth with a nail or nails（用釘子）釘牢，固定： *I nailed the sign to a tree.* 我將標示牌釘到了一棵樹上。 **2 ~ sb** (*informal*) to catch sb and prove they are guilty of a crime or of doing sth bad 抓獲並證明有罪；抓住： *The police haven't been able to nail the killer.* 警方還沒有抓到殺人兇手。 **3 ~ sth** (*informal*) to prove that sth is not true 證明…不屬實；揭露；揭發： *We must nail this lie.* 我們一定要戳穿這個謊言。 **4 ~ sth** (*NAmE, informal*) to achieve sth or do sth right, especially in sport（尤指體育運動中）獲得，贏得，擊中： *He nailed a victory in the semi-finals.* 他在半決賽中獲勝。

IDM **nail your colours to the 'mast** (*especially BrE*) to say publicly and firmly what you believe or who you support 公開宣稱；公開表態

PHR V **ˌnail sth↔'down** **1** to fasten sth down with a nail or nails（用釘子）將…釘牢，將…固定 **2** to reach an agreement or a decision, usually after a lot of discussion 達成一致；作出決定： *All the parties seem anxious to nail down a ceasefire.* 各方面似乎都渴望將停火之事敲定。 **ˌnail sb↔'down (to sth)** to force sb to give you a definite promise or tell you exactly what they intend to do 迫使明確保證（或準確說出想做之事） **SYN** **pin down**： *She says she'll come, but I can't nail her down to a specific time.* 她說要來，但我無法讓她敲定具體什麼時候來。 **ˌnail sth↔'up** **1** to fasten sth to a wall, post, etc. with a nail or nails 用釘子將…固定到（牆上、柱子上等） **2** to put nails into a door or window so that it cannot be opened 用釘子封住，封死（門或窗）

'nail bar *noun* a place where you can pay to have your nails shaped, coloured and made more attractive 美甲店

'nail-biting *adj.* [usually before noun] making you feel very excited or anxious because you do not know what is going to happen 令人焦躁不安的；令人緊張的： *a nail-biting finish* 令人擔心的結局 ◇ *It's been a nail-biting couple of weeks waiting for my results.* 這兩個星期等結果，弄得我坐立不安。

'nail brush *noun* a small stiff brush for cleaning your nails 指甲刷 ➲ VISUAL VOCAB page V24

'nail clippers *noun* [pl.] a small tool for cutting the nails on your fingers and toes 指甲鉗；指甲刀 ➲ VISUAL VOCAB page V24

'nail file *noun* a small metal tool with a rough surface for shaping your nails 指甲銼 ➲ VISUAL VOCAB page V24 ➲ see also EMERY BOARD

'nail polish (*BrE* also **'nail varnish**) *noun* [U] clear or coloured liquid that you paint on your nails to make them look attractive 指甲油；趾甲油：*nail polish/varnish remover* 洗甲水

'nail scissors *noun* [pl.] small scissors that are usually curved, used for cutting the nails on your fingers and toes 指甲刀：*a pair of nail scissors* 一把指甲刀 ➲ VISUAL VOCAB page V24

naive (also **naïve**) /naɪ'iːv/ *adj.* **1** (*disapproving*) lacking experience of life, knowledge or good judgement and willing to believe that people always tell you the truth 缺乏經驗的；幼稚的；無知的；輕信的：*to be politically naive* 對政治一無所知 ◇ *I can't believe you were so naive as to trust him!* 真是難以相信你會幼稚到信任他！◇ *a naive question* 無知的問題 **2** (*approving*) (of people and their behaviour 人及其行為) innocent and simple 天真的；率直的 SYN **artless**：*Their approach to life is refreshingly naive.* 他們對待生活的態度天真率直，令人耳目一新。➲ compare SOPHISTICATED (1) **3** (*technical* 術語) (of art 藝術) in a style which is deliberately very simple, often uses bright colours and is similar to that produced by a child 稚拙派的（簡單質樸，色彩明快）▶ **naive·ly** (also **naïve·ly**) *adv.*：*I naively assumed that I would be paid for the work.* 我天真地以為這活兒是有報酬的。**naiv·ety** (also **naïv·ety**) /naɪ'iːvəti/ *noun* [U]：*They laughed at the naivety of his suggestion.* 他們嘲笑他提的建議太幼稚。◇ *She has lost none of her naivety.* 她絲毫沒有失去那份天真爛漫。

Synonyms 同義詞辨析

naked / bare

Both these words can be used to mean 'not covered with clothes' and are frequently used with the following nouns. 以上兩詞均含裸露、未穿衣服之意，常與下列名詞連用：

naked ~	**bare ~**
body	feet
man	arms
fear	walls
aggression	branches
flame	essentials

- **Naked** is more often used to describe a person or their body and **bare** usually describes a part of the body. * naked 較常用以表示赤身裸體，而 bare 通常指身體某部位裸露着。
- **Bare** can also describe other things with nothing on them. * bare 亦可用以描述其他沒有遮蓋或光秃的東西：*bare walls* 沒有裝飾的牆 ◇ *a bare hillside* 光秃秃的山腰 **Naked** can mean 'without a protective covering'. * naked 含無保護性遮蓋之義：*a naked sword* 出鞘的劍
- **Bare** can also mean 'just enough'. * bare 亦含僅夠之意：*the bare minimum* 最低限度 **Naked** can be used to talk about strong feelings that are not hidden. * naked 可用以表示赤裸裸、無掩飾的強烈感情：*naked fear* 不加掩飾的恐懼 Note also the idiom 另注意習語：*(visible) to/with the naked eye* 肉眼（可見）

N

naked 🔑 /'neɪkɪd/ *adj.* **1** 🔑 not wearing any clothes 裸體的；裸露的；不穿衣服的 SYN **bare**：*a naked body* 赤裸的身體 ◇ *naked shoulders* 裸露的肩膀 ◇ *They often wandered around the house **stark naked*** (= completely naked). 他們經常赤身裸體地在房子周圍漫步。◇ *They found him **half naked** and bleeding to death.* 他們發現他身體半裸，流着血，快不行了。◇ *The prisoners were **stripped naked**.* 囚犯被剝得赤條條的。➲ see also BUCK NAKED **2** [usually before noun] without the usual covering 無遮蓋的；裸露的 SYN **bare**：*a naked light* 無罩燈 ◇ *a naked sword* 出鞘之劍 ◇ *Mice are born naked* (= without fur). 老鼠出生時遍體無毛。◇ (*BrE*) *a naked flame* 明火 HELP In American English this is called an *open flame*. 美式英語稱作 open flame。**3** [only before noun] (of emotions, attitudes, etc. 情感、態度等) expressed strongly and not hidden 直白的；露骨的；毫不掩飾的：*naked aggression* 赤裸裸的攻擊 ◇ *the naked truth* 明擺着的事實 **4** [not usually before noun] unable to protect yourself from being harmed, criticized, etc. 缺乏保護；無力自衛 SYN **helpless**：*He still felt naked and drained after his ordeal.* 經歷了這場磨難之後，他仍然感到無法自衛，而且筋疲力盡。▶ **naked·ly** *adv.*：*nakedly aggressive* 赤裸裸地挑釁 **naked·ness** *noun* [U]

IDM **the naked 'eye** the normal power of your eyes without the help of an instrument 肉眼：*The planet should be visible **with/to the naked eye**.* 這顆行星肉眼就能看得見。

na·mas·kar /ˌnʌmʌs'kɑː(r)/ *noun* [U] (*IndE*) a way of GREETING sb in which the hands are placed together as in prayer and the head is bent forwards 合十禮（雙手合十並頷首的問候方式）

namby-pamby /ˌnæmbi 'pæmbi/ *adj.* (*informal, disapproving*) weak and too emotional 脆弱的；多愁善感的

name 🔑 /neɪm/ *noun, verb*

■ *noun* **1** 🔑 a word or words that a particular person, animal, place or thing is known by 名字；名稱：*What's your name?* 你叫什麼名字？◇ *What is/was the name, please?* (= a polite way of asking sb's name) 請問您叫什麼名字？◇ *Please write your full **name and address** below.* 請將您的姓名和地址寫在下面。◇ *Do you know the name of this flower?* 你知道這是什麼花嗎？◇ *Rubella is just another name for German measles.* 風疹只是德國麻疹的另一個名稱。◇ *Are you changing your name when you get married?* 結婚時你要改姓氏嗎？➲ see also ASSUMED NAME, BRAND NAME, CODE NAME, FAMILY NAME, FILENAME, FIRST NAME, FORENAME, HOUSEHOLD NAME, MAIDEN NAME, MIDDLE NAME, NICKNAME *n.*, PEN-NAME, PET NAME, PLACE NAME, SURNAME, TRADE NAME, USERNAME **2** [usually sing.] a reputation that sb/sth has; the opinion that people have about sb/sth 名譽；名聲；名氣：*She first **made her name** as a writer of children's books.* 她最初是以兒童讀物作家成名的。◇ *He's **made** quite **a name for himself*** (= become famous). 他闖出了名氣。◇ *The college has a **good name** for languages.* 這所大學的語言教學頗有名氣。◇ *This kind of behaviour **gives** students **a bad name**.* 這種行為使學生們背上罵名。**3** (in compound adjectives 構成複合形容詞) having a name or a reputation of the kind mentioned, especially one that is known by a lot of people 有…名稱的；以…著名的；有…名聲的：*a big-name company* 著名公司 ◇ *brand-name goods* 名牌產品 ➲ see also HOUSEHOLD NAME **4** a famous person 名人：*Some of the biggest names in the art world were at the party.* 一些藝術界的頭面人物參加了聚會。

IDM **by 'name** using the name of sb/sth 憑名字；用…的名字：*She asked for you by name.* 她點名要找你。◇ *The principal knows all the students by name.* 校長能叫出所有學生的姓名。◇ *I only know her by name* (= I have heard about her but I have not met her). 我只是聽說過她的名字。**by the name of …** (*formal*) who is called 名叫…的：*a young actor by the name of Tom Rees* 名叫湯姆•里斯的年輕演員 **enter sb's/your 'name (for sth)** | **put sb's/your 'name down (for sth)** to apply for a place at a school, in a competition, etc. for sb or yourself 申請參加；替…報名（入學、參賽等）：*Have you entered your name for the quiz yet?* 你申請參加這次問答比賽了嗎？**give your 'name to sth** to invent sth which then becomes known by your name 用自己的名字命名所發明之物 **go by the name of …** to use a name that may not be your real one 自稱為…；假稱是… **have your/sb's 'name on it** | **with your/sb's 'name on it** (*informal*) if sth **has your name on it**, or there is sth **with your name on it**, it is intended for you 是衝…來的；是為…準備的：*He took my place and got killed. It should have been me—that bullet had my name on it.* 他坐了我的位子而送了命。死的應該是我，那顆子彈是衝着我來的。◇ *Are you coming for dinner this evening? I've got a steak here with your name on it!* 今晚你來吃飯嗎？我為你準備了一塊牛排呢！**in ˌall but 'name** used to describe a situation which exists in reality but that is not officially recognized（表示實際存在但未得到正式認可）在只缺正式名分情況下：*He runs the company in all but name.* 他雖沒有名義，卻實際上在管理這家公司。 **in 'God's/'Heaven's name | in the name of 'God/'Heaven** used especially in questions to show that you are angry, surprised or shocked（尤用於疑問句，表示憤怒、驚奇和震驚）看在上帝的分兒上，到底，究竟：*What in God's name was that noise?* 那噪音究竟是怎麼回事？◇ *Where in the name of Heaven have you been?* 你到底上哪兒去了？ **in the name of 'sb/'sth | in sb's/sth's 'name** **1** 🔑 for sb; showing that sth officially belongs to sb 為（某人）；在…名下：*We reserved two tickets in the name of Brown.* 我們用布朗的名字預訂了兩張票。◇ *The car is registered in my name.* 這輛車是用我的名字登記的。 **2** using the authority of sb/sth; as a representative of sb/sth 憑…的權威；代表：*I arrest you in the name of the law.* 我依法逮捕你。 **3** used to give a reason or an excuse for doing sth, often when what you are doing is wrong 以…的名義；以…為藉口：*crimes committed in the name of religion* 以宗教名義進行的犯罪活動 **in 'name only** officially recognized but not existing in reality 名義上；有名無實：*He's party leader in name only.* 他只是名義上的政黨領袖。 **sb's name is 'mud** (*informal*, usually *humorous*) used to say that sb is not liked or popular because of sth they have done 某人臭名昭著 **the name of the 'game** (*informal*) the most important aspect of an activity; the most important quality needed for an activity 問題的實質；最為重要的方面：*Hard work is the name of the game if you want to succeed in business.* 要想生意興旺，勤奮工作是關鍵。 **a name to 'conjure with** (*BrE*) **1** (*NAmE* **a name to 'reckon with**) a person or thing that is well known and respected in a particular field 大名鼎鼎的人；重量級人物；影響巨大的事物：*Miyazaki is still a name to conjure with among anime fans.* 宮崎駿在日本動漫迷中仍是一個大名鼎鼎的名字。 **2** (*humorous*) used when you mention a name that you think is difficult to remember or pronounce 難記的名字；拗口的名字：*He comes from Tighnabruaich—now there's a name to conjure with!* 他來自 Tighnabruaich，這個名字真夠拗口的！ **put a 'name to sb/sth** to know or remember what sb/sth is called 知道…的名稱；記住…的稱呼：*I recognize the tune but I can't put a name to it.* 這曲子我聽過，但想不起叫什麼了。 **take sb's name in 'vain** to show a lack of respect when using sb's name 濫用…的名義；褻瀆…的名字：(*humorous*) *Have you been taking my name in vain again?* 你又在濫用我的名義吧？ **(have sth) to your 'name** to have or own sth 擁有；獲得；收歸某人的名下：*an Olympic athlete with five gold medals to his name* 奪得五枚金牌的一名奧林匹克運動員 ◇ *She doesn't have a penny/cent to her name* (= she is very poor). 她身無分文。 **under the name (of) ...** using a name that may not be your real name 用…名字；以…假名 ➲ more at ANSWER *v.*, BIG *adj.*, CALL *v.*, DOG *n.*, DROP *v.*, LEND, MIDDLE NAME, NAME *v.*, REJOICE, ROSE *n.*

■ *verb* **1** 🔑 to give a name to sb/sth 命名；給…取名 **SYN** **call**：**~ sb/sth (after sb)** | (*NAmE* also) **~ sb/sth (for sb)** *He was named after his father* (= given his father's first name). 他的名字跟他父親一樣。◇ **~ sb/sth + noun** *They named their son John.* 他們給兒子起了個名字叫約翰。 **2** 🔑 to say the name of sb/sth 說出…的名稱；叫出…的名字 **SYN** **identify**：**~ sb/sth** *The victim has not yet been named.* 受害人的姓名仍未得知。◇ *Can you name all the American states?* 你能說出美國所有的州名嗎？◇ **~ sb/sth as sb/sth** *The missing man has been named as James Kelly.* 失踪者已被確認為詹姆斯・凱利。 ➲ SYNONYMS at IDENTIFY **3** **~ sth** to state sth exactly 確定；說定；準確陳述 **SYN** **specify**：*Name your price.* 給個價吧。◇ *They're engaged, but they haven't yet **named the day*** (= chosen the date for their wedding). 他們訂婚了，但還未確定結婚日期。◇ *Activities available include squash, archery and swimming, **to name but a few**.* 所設活動項目包括壁球、射箭、游泳等等，不一而足。◇ *Chairs, tables, cabinets—**you name it**, she makes it* (= she makes anything you can imagine). 椅子、桌子、櫥櫃，凡是你說得出的她都能做。 **4** to choose sb for a job or position 任命；委任 **SYN** **nominate**：**~ sb (as) sth** | **~ sb + noun** *I had no hesitation in naming him (as) captain.* 我毫不猶豫地任命他為隊長。◇ **~ sb (to sth)** *When she resigned, he was named to the committee in her place.* 她辭職後，他被指定取代她進入委員會。

IDM **,name and 'shame** (*BrE*) to publish the names of people or organizations who have done sth wrong or illegal 公佈行為不當或違法者的名單；公佈黑名單 **name 'names** to give the names of the people involved in sth, especially sth wrong or illegal 供出，說出（犯事者等）的名字

More About 補充說明

names and titles 名字和稱謂

Names 名字

- Your **name** is either your whole name or one part of your name. * name 既指全名也指名字的一部份：*My name is Maria.* 我的名字叫瑪麗亞。◇ *His name is Tom Smith.* 他的名字叫湯姆・史密斯。
- Your **last name** or **family name** (also called **surname** in *BrE*) is the name that all members of your family share. * last name 或 family name 指姓氏（在英式英語中亦叫 surname）。
- Your **first name/names** (*formal* **forename**) is/are the name(s) your parents gave you when you were born. In *BrE* some people use the expression **Christian name**(s) to refer to a person's first name(s). * first name/names（正式用語為 forename）指出生時父母給取的名字。在英式英語中，有些人用 Christian name(s) 指 first name(s)（名字）。
- Your **middle name(s)** is/are any name your parents gave you other than the one that is placed first. The initial of this name is often used as part of your name, especially in America. * middle name(s) 指父母給取的第一名字外的名字。此名字的首字母常用作名字的一部份，尤其在美國：*John T. Harvey* 約翰・T・哈維
- Your **full name** is all your names, usually in the order: first + middle + last name. * full name 通常指以 first + middle + last name 為順序的全名。
- A woman's **maiden name** is the family name she had before she got married. Some women keep this name after they are married and do not use their husband's name. In North America, married women often use their maiden name followed by their husband's family name. * maiden name 指女子婚前娘家的姓。有的婦女婚後仍保留此姓，不用丈夫的姓。在北美，已婚婦女通常在自己娘家的姓後加上丈夫的姓：*Hillary Rodham Clinton* 希拉里・羅德漢姆・克林頓

Titles 稱謂

- **Mr** (for both married and unmarried men) 稱已婚和未婚男子
- **Mrs** (for married women) 稱已婚婦女
- **Miss** (for unmarried women) 稱未婚女子
- **Ms** (a title that some women prefer to use as it does not distinguish between married and unmarried women) 有些婦女喜歡用此稱謂，因為沒有指明已婚或未婚
- **Doctor**, **Professor**, **President**, **Vice-President**, **Reverend** (or **Rev**), etc. 醫生、教授、校長、副校長、牧師等

The correct way to talk to someone is 正確的稱呼為：

- first name, if you know them well 如果相熟可直呼其名：*Hello, Maria.* 你好，瑪麗亞。
- or title + surname 或稱謂 ＋ 姓：*Hello, Mr Brown.* 你好，布朗先生。
- or *Doctor* (medical), *Professor*, etc. on its own 或單獨用醫生、教授等：*Thank you, Doctor.* 謝謝你，醫生。This is only used for a very limited number of titles. 此說法只限於為數很少的幾個稱謂。

N

'name-calling *noun* [U] the act of using rude or insulting words about sb 辱罵

name·check /'neɪmtʃek/ *noun, verb*

■ ***noun*** an occasion when the name of a person or thing is mentioned or included in a list 提到名字；列出名字：*She started her speech by giving a namecheck to all the people who had helped her.* 她在講話開始時提到所有幫助過她的人的名字。

■ ***verb*** **~ sb/sth** to mention or include sb/sth in a list 提及，列出（某人或某事物的名字）：*The songs namecheck other artists and bands.* 這些歌提到了其他演員和樂隊的名字。◇ *The book was namechecked in today's paper.* 這本書在今天的報紙上提到了。

'name day *noun* a day which is special for a Christian with a particular name because it is the day which celebrates a SAINT with the same name 命名日（與基督徒同名的聖徒紀念日）

'name-dropping *noun* [U] (*disapproving*) the act of mentioning the names of famous people you know or have met in order to impress other people 提到所認識的名人以引起別人的注意 ▶ **'name-drop** *verb* [I] ➲ see also DROP NAMES at DROP *v.*

name·less /'neɪmləs/ *adj.* **1** [usually before noun] having no name; whose name you do not know 無名的；不知名的：*a nameless grave* 無名塚 ◇ *thousands of nameless and faceless workers* 成千上萬默默無聞的工人 **2** whose name is kept secret 匿名的；隱姓埋名的 **SYN** **anonymous**：*a nameless source in the government* 政府中的一位未透露姓名者 ◇ *a well-known public figure **who shall remain nameless*** 一位不便透露姓名的知名人士 **3** [usually before noun] (*literary*) difficult or too unpleasant to describe 不可名狀的；難以形容的：*nameless horrors* 不可名狀的恐懼 ◇ *a nameless longing* 難以形容的渴望

N

name·ly /'neɪmli/ *adv.* used to introduce more exact and detailed information about sth that you have just mentioned 即；也就是：*We need to concentrate on our target audience, namely women aged between 20 and 30.* 我們須針對我們的聽眾對象，即年齡在 20 到 30 歲之間的婦女。

name·plate /'neɪmpleɪt/ *noun* **1** a sign on the door or the wall of a building showing the name of a company or the name of a person who is living or working there（標明公司或居住、生活在該處的人的）名牌，標示牌，名匾 **2** a piece of metal or plastic on an object showing the name of the person who owns it, made it or presented it（標示所有者、製造者或捐獻者姓名的）名稱牌

name·sake /'neɪmseɪk/ *noun* a person or thing that has the same name as sb/sth else 同名的人（或物）：*Unlike his more famous namesake, this Gordon Brown has little interest in politics.* 這位戈登 • 布朗與那位同名的著名人物不同，對政治沒什麼興趣。

'name tag *noun* a small piece of plastic, paper or metal that you wear, with your name on it（佩帶於胸前的）名牌；胸佩

'name tape *noun* a small piece of cloth that is sewn or stuck onto a piece of clothing and that has the name of the owner on it（衣物上的）姓名標籤

nan¹ /næn/ *noun* (*BrE*) = NANNY (2)

nan² (also **naan**) /nɑːn/ (also **'nan bread**, **'naan bread**) *noun* [U] a type of soft flat S Asian bread 南亞式麪包（鬆軟扁平）

nana¹ (*BrE* also **nanna**) /'nænə/ *noun* (*informal*) = NANNY (2)

nana² /'nɑːnə/ *noun* (*old-fashioned, BrE, informal*) a stupid person 呆子；傻瓜 **SYN** **idiot**：*I felt a right nana.* 我覺得自己真傻。

nancy /'nænsi/ *noun* (*pl.* **-ies**) (also **'nancy boy**, **nance** /næns/) (*taboo, slang, especially BrE*) an offensive word for a HOMOSEXUAL man, or a man who behaves in a way that is thought to be typical of women 假娘兒們（含冒犯意，指同性戀男子或舉止像女性的男子）

nanny /'næni/ *noun* (*pl.* **-ies**) **1** a woman whose job is to take care of young children in the children's own home（兒童家中的）保母 **2** (also **nan**) (both *BrE*) (used by children, especially as a form of address 兒童用語，尤作稱呼) a grandmother 奶奶；姥姥：*When is Nanny coming to stay?* 奶奶什麼時候來住？◇ *my nan and grandad* 我的爺爺、奶奶 ➲ see also GRANNY

IDM **the 'nanny state** (*BrE*) a disapproving way of talking about the fact that government seems to get too much involved in people's lives and to protect them too much, in a way that limits their freedom 保母式國家

'nanny goat *noun* a female GOAT 母山羊；雌山羊 ➲ compare BILLY GOAT

nanny·ing /'næniɪŋ/ *noun* [U] **1** the job of being a child's NANNY 保母工作；照看小孩 **2** (*BrE, disapproving*) the fact of helping and protecting sb too much 幫忙過多；過於呵護；過分關心

nano- /'nænəʊ; *NAmE* 'nænoʊ/ *combining form* (*technical* 術語) (in nouns and adjectives; used especially in units of measurement 構成名詞和形容詞，尤用於計量單位) one billionth 納（諾）；毫微；十億分之一：*nanosecond* 毫微秒

nano·metre (*especially US* **nano·meter**) /'nænəʊmiːtə(r); *NAmE* 'nænoʊ-/ *noun* (*abbr.* **nm**) one thousand millionth of a metre 毫微米；十億分之一米；奈米

nano·par·ticle /'nænəʊpɑːtɪkl; *NAmE* 'nænoʊpɑːrt-/ *noun* a piece of matter less than 100 NANOMETRES long 納米粒子；奈米粒子

nano·scale /'nænəʊskeɪl; *NAmE* 'nænoʊ-/ *adj.* [usually before noun] of a size that can be measured in nanometres 納米（尺度）的；奈米的：*nanoscale particles/devices/electronics* 納米粒子 / 裝置 / 電子學

nano·sec·ond /'nænəʊsekənd; *NAmE* 'nænoʊ-/ *noun* (*abbr.* **ns**) one thousand millionth of a second 毫微秒；十億分之一秒；奈秒

nano·tech·nol·ogy /ˌnænəʊtek'nɒlədʒi; *NAmE* ˌnænoʊtek'nɑːlədʒi/ *noun* [U] the branch of technology that deals with structures that are less than 100 NANOMETRES long. Scientists often build these structures using individual MOLECULES of substances. 納米技術；奈米技術 ▶ **nano·tech·nolo·gist** *noun* **nano·tech·no·logic·al** /ˌnænəʊteknə'lɒdʒɪkl; *NAmE* ˌnænoʊteknə'lɑːdʒɪkl/ *adj.*：*nanotechnological research* 納米技術研究

nap /næp/ *noun, verb*

■ ***noun*** **1** [C] a short sleep, especially during the day（日間的）小睡，打盹 **SYN** **snooze**：*to **take/have a nap*** 打個盹 ➲ SYNONYMS at SLEEP ➲ compare SIESTA ➲ see also CATNAP, POWER NAP **2** [sing.] the short fine threads on the surface of some types of cloth, usually lying in the same direction（某些織物表面的）短絨毛 **3** [C] (*BrE*) advice given by an expert on which horse is most likely to win a race 賽馬情報；賽馬結果預測

■ ***verb*** (**-pp-**) [I] to sleep for a short time, especially during the day 打盹，小睡（尤指日間）**IDM** see CATCH *v.*

napa *noun* [U] = NAPPA

na·palm /'neɪpɑːm/ *noun* [U] a substance like jelly, made from petrol/gas, that burns and is used in making bombs 凝固汽油（用於製造炸彈）

nape /neɪp/ *noun* [sing.] **~ (of sb's neck)** the back of the neck 脖頸：*Her hair was cut short at the nape of her neck.* 她脖子後面的頭髮剪得很短。➲ VISUAL VOCAB page V59

naph·tha /'næfθə/ *noun* [U] a type of oil that starts burning very easily, used as fuel or in making chemicals 石腦油（作燃料或用於製造化學品）

naph·tha·lene /'næfθəliːn; *NAmE* also 'næpθə-/ *noun* [U] (*chemistry* 化) a substance used in products that keep MOTHS away from clothes, and in industrial processes 萘（用於製作衛生球等）

nap·kin /'næpkɪn/ *noun* **1** (also **'table napkin**) a piece of cloth or paper used at meals for protecting your clothes and cleaning your lips and fingers 餐巾；餐巾紙 **SYN** **serviette** ➲ VISUAL VOCAB page V22 **2** (*NAmE*) = SANITARY NAPKIN **3** (*BrE, old-fashioned* or *formal*) = NAPPY

nappa (also **napa**) /ˈnæpə/ *noun* [U] a type of soft leather made from the skin of sheep or GOATS 納帕軟羊皮革

nappe /næp/ *noun* [U] (*geology* 地) a thin layer of rock that lies on top of a different type of rock 推覆體（層狀岩體）

nappy /ˈnæpi/ *noun* (*pl.* **-ies**) (*BrE*) (*NAmE* **di·aper**) a piece of soft cloth or other thick material that is folded around a baby's bottom and between its legs to absorb and hold its body waste 尿布：*I'll change her nappy.* 我要給她換尿布。◇ *a disposable nappy* (= one that is made to be used once only) 一次性尿布 ◇ *nappy rash* 尿疹 ➲ COLLOCATIONS at CHILD

narc /nɑːk; *NAmE* nɑːrk/ (also **narco** /ˈnɑːkəʊ; *NAmE* ˈnɑːrkoʊ/) *noun* (*NAmE, informal*) a police officer whose job is to stop people selling or using drugs illegally 緝毒警察

nar·cis·sism /ˈnɑːsɪsɪzəm; *NAmE* ˈnɑːrs-/ *noun* [U] (*formal, disapproving*) the habit of admiring yourself too much, especially your appearance 自我陶醉，自賞，自戀（尤指對自己的容貌）▸ **nar·cis·sis·tic** /ˌnɑːsɪˈsɪstɪk; *NAmE* ˌnɑːrs-/ *adj.* ORIGIN From the Greek myth in which **Narcissus**, a beautiful young man, fell in love with his own reflection in a pool. He died and was changed into the flower which bears his name. 源自希臘神話，貌美青年那喀索斯（Narcissus）愛上了自己在水中的倒影。他死後化作水仙花，此花即因之命名。

nar·cis·sus /nɑːˈsɪsəs; *NAmE* nɑːrˈs-/ *noun* (*pl.* **nar·cissi** /nɑːˈsɪsaɪ; *NAmE* nɑːrˈs-/) a plant with white or yellow flowers that appear in spring. There are many types of narcissus, including the DAFFODIL. 水仙；水仙花

nar·co·lepsy /ˈnɑːkəʊlepsi; *NAmE* ˈnɑːrkoʊ-/ *noun* [U] (*medical* 醫) a condition in which sb falls into a deep sleep when they are in relaxing surroundings 發作性睡病；嗜睡症

nar·co·sis /nɑːˈkəʊsɪs; *NAmE* nɑːrˈkoʊsɪs/ *noun* [U] (*medical* 醫) a state caused by drugs in which sb is unconscious or keeps falling asleep 麻醉狀態

nar·cot·ic /nɑːˈkɒtɪk; *NAmE* nɑːrˈkɑː-/ *noun, adj.*

■ ***noun*** **1** (*formal*) a powerful illegal drug that affects the mind in a harmful way. HEROIN and COCAINE are narcotics. 致幻毒品；麻醉品：*a narcotics agent* (= a police officer investigating the illegal trade in drugs) 緝毒警察 **2** (*medical* 醫) a substance that relaxes you, reduces pain or makes you sleep 鎮靜劑；麻醉藥；催眠藥：*a mild narcotic* 藥性温和的鎮靜劑

■ ***adj.*** **1** (of a drug 藥物) that affects your mind in a harmful way 致幻的；麻醉的 **2** (of a substance 物質) making you sleep 催眠的：*a mild narcotic effect* 温和的催眠作用

nark /nɑːk; *NAmE* nɑːrk/ *noun* (*BrE, slang*) a person who is friendly with criminals and who gives the police information about them 警察的線人

narked /nɑːkt; *NAmE* nɑːrkt/ *adj.* [not usually before noun] (*old-fashioned, BrE, informal*) annoyed 厭煩；苦惱；惱火

narky /ˈnɑːki; *NAmE* ˈnɑːrki/ *adj.* (**nark·ier**, **narki·est**) (*BrE, informal*) easily becoming angry or annoyed 易怒的；脾氣壞的

nar·rate /nəˈreɪt; *NAmE* also ˈnæreɪt/ *verb* **1 ~ sth** (*formal*) to tell a story 講（故事）；敍述 SYN **relate**：*She entertained them by narrating her adventures in Africa.* 她講述她在非洲的歷險來逗他們開心。**2 ~ sth** to speak the words that form the text of a DOCUMENTARY film or programme 給（紀錄片或節目）作解說：*The film was narrated by Andrew Sachs.* 這部電影是由安德魯•薩克斯解說的。

nar·ra·tion /nəˈreɪʃn; næˈr-/ *noun* (*formal*) **1** [U, C] the act or process of telling a story, especially in a novel, a film/movie or a play （尤指小說、電影或戲劇中的）敍述，講述 **2** [C] a description of events that is spoken during a film/movie, a play, etc. or with music（電影、戲劇等中對情節的）解說；旁白：*He has recorded the narration for the production.* 他錄製了這部作品的解說詞。

nar·ra·tive /ˈnærətɪv/ *noun* (*formal*) **1** [C] a description of events, especially in a novel （尤指小說中的）描述，敍述 SYN **story**：*a gripping narrative of their journey up the Amazon* 他們沿亞馬孫河而上的扣人心弦的描述 ➲ COLLOCATIONS at LITERATURE **2** [U] the act, process or skill of telling a story 講故事；敍述；敍事技巧：*The novel contains too much dialogue and not enough narrative.* 這部小說對話過多，而敍述不足。▸ **nar·ra·tive** *adj.* [only before noun]：*narrative fiction* 敍事小說

nar·ra·tor /nəˈreɪtə(r)/ *noun* a person who tells a story, especially in a book, play or film/movie; the person who speaks the words in a television programme but who does not appear in it （書、戲劇或電影中的）敍述者，講述者；（電視節目中的）幕後解說員；旁白員：*a first-person narrator* 第一人稱敍述者

Synonyms 同義詞辨析

narrow / thin

These adjectives are frequently used with the following nouns. 以上形容詞常與下列名詞連用：

narrow ~	thin ~
road	man
entrance	legs
bed	ice
stairs	line
majority	layer
victory	material
range	cream

- **Narrow** describes something that is a short distance from side to side. **Thin** describes people, or something that has a short distance through it from one side to the other. * narrow 表示窄。thin 指人瘦或物細、薄。
- **Thin** is also used of things that are not as thick as you expect. **Narrow** can be used with the meanings 'only just achieved' and 'limited'. * thin 亦用以指薄。narrow 可表示勉強達到、僅僅。

nar·row 0ꟷ /ˈnærəʊ; *NAmE* -roʊ/ *adj., verb*

■ ***adj.*** (**nar·row·er**, **nar·row·est**) **1** 0ꟷ measuring a short distance from one side to the other, especially in relation to length 狹窄的；窄小的：*narrow streets* 狹窄的街道 ◇ *a narrow bed/doorway/shelf* 狹窄的牀／門口／架子 ◇ *narrow shoulders/hips* 窄小的肩頭／臀部 ◇ *There was only a narrow gap between the bed and the wall.* 牀和牆之間只有一條窄縫。◇ (*figurative*) *the narrow confines of prison life* 獄中生活的狹小範圍 OPP **broad**, **wide** **2** 0ꟷ [usually before noun] only just achieved or avoided 勉強的；剛剛好的：*a **narrow victory*** 險勝 ◇ *He lost the race by the **narrowest of margins**.* 他以極小的差距在賽跑中落敗。◇ *She was elected by a **narrow majority**.* 她以微弱多數當選。◇ *He had a **narrow escape** when his car skidded on the ice.* 車在冰上打滑，他險些出事。**3** 0ꟷ limited in a way that ignores important issues or the opinions of other people 狹隘的；目光短淺的：*narrow interests* 目光短淺的利益 ◇ *She has a very narrow view of the world.* 她對世界的認識是非常狹隘的。OPP **broad** **4** 0ꟷ limited in variety or numbers（種類或數目）有限的；範圍小的 SYN **restricted**：*The shop sells only a narrow range of goods.* 這家商店商品的種類有限。◇ *a narrow circle of friends* 有限的交友圈子 OPP **wide** **5** limited in meaning; exact 狹義的；嚴格的；準確的：*I am using the word 'education' in the narrower sense.* 我說的是較狹義的"教育"。OPP **broad** ▸ **nar·row·ness** *noun* [U]：*The narrowness of the streets caused many traffic problems.* 街道狹窄，造成很多交通問題。◇ *We were surprised by the narrowness of our victory.* 我們對自己勉強獲勝感到驚訝。◇ *His attitudes show a certain narrowness of mind.* 他的態度顯示他的思想有些狹隘。IDM see STRAIGHT *adj.*

■ ***verb*** [I, T] to become or make sth narrower 使窄小；變窄；縮小：*This is where the river narrows.* 這條河就是

N

在這裏變窄的。◇ *The gap between the two teams has narrowed to three points.* 兩隊之間的差距縮小到三分了。◇ *Her **eyes narrowed** (= almost closed) menacingly.* 她咄咄逼人地瞇起眼睛。◇ **~ sth** *He narrowed his eyes at her.* 他向她擠了擠眼睛。◇ *We need to try and narrow the health divide between rich and poor.* 我們需要設法縮小窮人和富人之間的健康差距。

PHR V **ˌnarrow sth↔'down (to sth)** to reduce the number of possibilities or choices 把（可能性或選擇）縮小（到）；縮小範圍：*We have narrowed down the list to four candidates.* 我們把範圍縮小到四位候選者。

nar·row·band /'nærəʊbænd; *NAmE* -roʊ-/ *noun* [U] (*technical* 術語) signals that use a narrow range of FREQUENCIES 窄帶；窄頻 ➲ compare BROADBAND (1)

nar·row·boat /'nærəʊbəʊt; *NAmE* 'næroʊboʊt/ *noun* (*BrE*) a long narrow boat, used on CANALS 運河船 ➲ **VISUAL VOCAB** page V54

nar·row·cast /'nærəʊkɑːst; *NAmE* 'næroʊkæst/ *verb* [I] (*technical* 術語) to send information by television or the Internet to a particular group of people（電視或互聯網為某一特定群體）小範圍播送，狹播，窄播 ➲ compare BROADCAST *v.* (1)

ˌnarrow 'gauge *noun* [U] a size of railway/railroad track that is not as wide as the standard track that is used in Britain and the US 窄軌：*a narrow-gauge railway* 窄軌鐵路

nar·row·ly /'nærəʊli; *NAmE* -roʊ-/ *adv.* **1** only by a small amount 勉強地；以毫厘之差：*The car narrowly missed a cyclist.* 汽車差點兒撞上一位騎自行車的人。◇ *She narrowly escaped injury.* 她險些兒受傷了。◇ *The team lost narrowly.* 這支隊伍以微弱差距敗北。 **2** (sometimes *disapproving*) in a way that is limited 狹隘地；嚴格地：*a narrowly defined task* 嚴格定明的任務◇ *a narrowly specialized education* 狹隘的專業教育 **3** closely; carefully 小心地；仔細地：*She looked at him narrowly.* 她仔細打量着他。

ˌnarrow-'minded *adj.* (*disapproving*) not willing to listen to new ideas or to the opinions of others 氣量小的；小心眼的；狹隘的 **SYN** **bigoted**, **intolerant**：*a narrow-minded attitude* 狹隘的態度◇ *a narrow-minded nationalist* 狹隘的民族主義者 **OPP** **broad-minded**, **open-minded** ▸ **ˌnarrow-'minded·ness** *noun* [U]

nar·rows /'nærəʊz; *NAmE* -roʊz/ *noun* [pl.] a narrow channel that connects two larger areas of water 海峽；（江河的）峽谷

nar·whal /'nɑːwəl; *NAmE* 'nɑːrwɑːl/ *noun* a small white WHALE from the Arctic region. The male narwhal has a long TUSK (= outer tooth). 獨角鯨（生活於北極地區，雄性有一長牙）

nary /'neəri; *NAmE* 'neri/ *adj.* (*old use* or *dialect*) not a; no 沒有一個的；沒有的

NASA /'næsə/ *abbr.* National Aeronautics and Space Administration (a US government organization that does research into space and organizes space travel)（美國）國家航空航天局，國家航空暨太空總署

nasal /'neɪzl/ *adj.* **1** connected with the nose 鼻的；與鼻子相關的：*the nasal passages* 鼻道◇ *a nasal spray* 鼻腔噴劑 **2** (of sb's voice 嗓音) sounding as if it is produced partly through the nose 帶鼻音的：*a nasal accent* 帶鼻音的口音 **3** (*phonetics* 語音) (of a speech sound 語音) produced by sending a stream of air through the nose. The nasal consonants in English are /m/, /n/ and /ŋ/, as in *sum*, *sun* and *sung*. 從鼻腔發出的；鼻音的

na·sal·ize (*BrE* also **-ise**) /'neɪzəlaɪz/ *verb* **~ sth** (*phonetics* 語音) to produce a speech sound, especially a vowel, with the air in the nose VIBRATING 使鼻音化（尤指元音）▸ **na·sal·iz·ation**, **-is·ation** /ˌneɪzəlaɪ'zeɪʃn/ *noun* [U]

nas·cent /'næsnt/ *adj.* (*formal*) beginning to exist; not yet fully developed 新生的；萌芽的；未成熟的

the NASDAQ /'næzdæk/ *noun* [sing.] National Association of Securities Dealers Automated Quotations (a computer system in the US that supplies the current price of shares to the people who sell them) 納斯達克；美國全國證券交易商協會自動報價系統

na·stur·tium /nə'stɜːʃəm; *NAmE* -'stɜːrʃ-/ *noun* a garden plant with round flat leaves and red, orange or yellow flowers that are sometimes eaten in salads 旱金蓮（有時用於色拉）

nasty /'nɑːsti; *NAmE* 'næsti/ *adj.* (**nas·tier**, **nas·ti·est**) **1** very bad or unpleasant 極差的；令人厭惡的；令人不悅的：*a nasty accident* 嚴重事故◇ *The news gave me a nasty shock.* 這消息可把我嚇死了。◇ *I had a nasty feeling that he would follow me.* 我覺得他會跟着我，這使我感到十分不快。◇ *He had a nasty moment when he thought he'd lost his passport.* 他以為護照丟了，苦惱極了。◇ *This coffee has a nasty taste.* 這咖啡真難喝。◇ *Don't buy that coat—it looks **cheap and nasty**.* 別買那件外套，一看就是差勁的便宜貨。 **2** unkind; unpleasant 不友好的；惡意的；令人不愉快的 **SYN** **mean**：*to make nasty remarks about sb* 說某人的壞話◇ *the nastier side of her character* 她個性較為惡毒的一面◇ *to have a nasty temper* 脾氣壞◇ *Don't be so nasty to your brother.* 別對你弟弟那麼兇。◇ *That was a nasty little trick.* 這是個可惡的小騙局。◇ *Life has a **nasty habit** of repeating itself.* 生活總是令人厭煩地重複着。 **3** dangerous or serious 危險的；嚴重的：*a nasty bend* (= dangerous for cars going fast) 危險的彎道◇ *a nasty injury* 重傷 **4** offensive; in bad taste 無禮的；污穢的；下流的：*to have a nasty mind* 思想齷齪◇ *nasty jokes* 下流的笑話 ➲ see also VIDEO NASTY ▸ **nas·tily** /-ɪli/ *adv.*：*'I hate you,' she said nastily.* 她咬牙切齒地說："我恨你。" **nas·ti·ness** *noun* [U]

IDM **get/turn 'nasty** **1** to become threatening and violent 翻臉；變兇：*You'd better do what he says or he'll turn nasty.* 你最好照他說的做，否則他就不客氣了。 **2** to become bad or unpleasant 變壞；變得令人討厭：*It looks as though the weather is going to turn nasty again.* 好像又要變天了。 **a nasty piece of 'work** (*BrE, informal*) a person who is unpleasant, unkind or dishonest 惡棍；令人討厭的人；靠不住的人 ➲ more at TASTE *n.*

natal /'neɪtl/ *adj.* [only before noun] (*formal*) relating to the place where or the time when sb was born 出生地的；出生時的：*her natal home* 她出生的家鄉

na·tal·ity /nə'tæləti/ *noun* [U] (*technical* 術語) the number of births every year for every 1 000 people in the population 出生率（每年每 1 000 人的出生人數）**SYN** **birth rate**

natch /nætʃ/ *adv.* (*slang*) used to say that sth is obvious or exactly as you would expect 當然；自然；毫無疑問 **SYN** **naturally**：*He was wearing the latest T-shirt, natch.* 當然啦，他穿着最新款式的 T 恤衫。

na·tion 0-w /'neɪʃn/ *noun*
1 0-w [C] a country considered as a group of people with the same language, culture and history, who live in a particular area under one government 國家；民族：*an independent nation* 獨立的國家◇ *the African nations* 非洲各國 **2** 0-w [sing.] all the people in a country 國民 **SYN** **population**：*The entire nation, it seemed, was watching TV.* 好像全國的人都在看電視。▸ **na·tion·hood** /'neɪʃnhʊd/ *noun* [U]：*Citizenship is about the sense of nationhood.* 公民身分涉及國家意識。

na·tion·al 0-w /'næʃnəl/ *adj., noun*
■ ***adj.*** [usually before noun] **1** 0-w connected with a particular nation; shared by a whole nation 國家的；民族的；全國的：*national and local newspapers* 全國性的和地方的報紙◇ *national and international news* 國內和國際新聞◇ *national and regional politics* 國家和地區政治◇ *a national election* 全國性選舉◇ *These buildings are part of our national heritage.* 這些建築是我們民族遺產的一部份。◇ *They are afraid of losing their national identity.* 他們擔心會失去他們的民族特色。 **2** 0-w owned, controlled or paid for by the government 國有的；國立的；國營的：*a national airline/museum/theatre* 國營航空公司；國立博物館；國家劇院
■ ***noun*** (*technical* 術語) a citizen of a particular country（某國的）公民：*Polish nationals living in Germany* 生活在德國的波蘭公民

ˌnational 'anthem *noun* the official song of a nation that is sung on special occasions 國歌

N

the ˌNational Asˌsembly for ˈWales *noun* = THE WELSH ASSEMBLY

ˌnational conˈvention *noun* a meeting held by a political party, especially in the US, to choose a candidate to take part in the election for President （尤指美國政黨推選總統候選人的）全國代表大會

ˌnational ˈcostume *noun* [C, U] (also **ˌnational ˈdress** [U]) the clothes traditionally worn by people from a particular country, especially on special occasions or for formal ceremonies （某一國家的）民族服裝

the ˌnational curˈriculum *noun* [sing.] (in Britain) a programme of study in all the main subjects that children aged 5 to 16 in state schools must follow （英國國立中小學）全國統一課程

ˌnational ˈdebt *noun* [usually sing.] the total amount of money that the government of a country owes 國債

the ˌNational ˈFront *noun* [sing.+sing./pl. v.] (in Britain) a small political party with extreme views, especially on issues connected with race （英國）民族陣線

ˌnational ˈgrid *noun* [sing.] (*BrE*) the system of power lines that joins the places where electricity is produced, and takes electricity to all parts of the country 全國高壓輸電線網

the ˌNational ˈGuard *noun* [sing.] **1** a small army, often used to protect a political leader（保護政界領導人的）警衛隊 **2** the army in each state of the US that can be used by the federal government if needed （美國）後備役軍人，國民警衛隊

the ˌNational ˈHealth Service *noun* [sing.] (*abbr.* **NHS**) the public health service in Britain that provides medical care and is paid for by taxes （英國）國民保健服務計劃： *I got my glasses on the National Health (Service).* 我配眼鏡是國民保健服務計劃資助的。

ˌNational Inˈsurance *noun* [U] (*abbr.* **NI**) (in Britain) a system of payments that have to be made by employers and employees to provide help for people who are sick, old or unemployed （英國）國民保險制度

na·tion·al·ism /ˈnæʃnəlɪzəm/ *noun* [U] **1** the desire by a group of people who share the same race, culture, language, etc. to form an independent country 國家主義： *Scottish nationalism* 蘇格蘭國家主義 **2** (sometimes *disapproving*) a feeling of love for and pride in your country; a feeling that your country is better than any other 民族主義；民族自豪感；民族優越感

na·tion·al·ist /ˈnæʃnəlɪst/ *noun* **1** a person who wants their country to become independent 國家主義者： *Scottish nationalists* 蘇格蘭國家主義者 **2** (sometimes *disapproving*) a person who has a great love for and pride in their country; a person who has a feeling that their country is better than any other 民族主義者；懷有本民族優越感者 ▸ **na·tion·al·ist** *adj.*： *nationalist sentiments* 民族主義感情

na·tion·al·is·tic /ˌnæʃnəˈlɪstɪk/ *adj.* (usually *disapproving*) having very strong feelings of love for and pride in your country, so that you think that it is better than any other 國家主義的；民族主義的

na·tion·al·ity /ˌnæʃəˈnæləti/ *noun* (*pl.* **-ies**) **1** [U, C] the legal right of belonging to a particular nation 國籍： *to* ***take/have/hold*** *French* ***nationality*** 獲得／持有／擁有法國國籍 ◇ *All applicants will be considered regardless of age, sex, religion or nationality.* 所有申請者，不論其年齡、性別、宗教信仰及國籍，都可考慮。◇ *The college attracts students of all nationalities.* 這所大學吸引着各國的學生。◇ *She has* ***dual nationality*** (= is a citizen of two countries). 她具有雙重國籍。**2** [C] a group of people with the same language, culture and history who form part of a political nation （構成國家一部份的）民族： *Kazakhstan alone contains more than a hundred nationalities.* 單是哈薩克斯坦就有一百多個民族。

na·tion·al·ize (*BrE* also **-ise**) /ˈnæʃnəlaɪz/ *verb* **~ sth** to put an industry or a company under the control of the government, which becomes its owner 將…國有化： *nationalized industries* 國有化企業 **OPP** **denationalize, privatize** ▸ **na·tion·al·iza·tion, -isa·tion** /ˌnæʃnəlaɪˈzeɪʃn; *NAmE* -ləˈz-/ *noun* [U, C]

the ˌNational ˈLeague *noun* (in the US) one of the two organizations for professional BASEBALL （美國）全國職業棒球聯盟，國家棒球聯盟 ➲ see also AMERICAN LEAGUE

na·tion·al·ly /ˈnæʃnəli/ *adv.* relating to a country as a whole; relating to a particular country 全國性地；與某國相關地： *The programme was broadcast nationally.* 這個節目曾在全國播放過。◇ *Meetings were held locally and nationally.* 舉行的會議有地方性的，也有全國性的。◇ *He's a talented athlete who competes nationally and internationally.* 他是一位有才華的運動員，既參加國內比賽，也參加國際比賽。

the ˌNational ˈMotto *noun* [sing.] the official US motto 'In God we trust' （美國）國家箴言（即"我們相信上帝"）

ˌnational ˈpark *noun* an area of land that is protected by the government for people to visit because of its natural beauty and historical or scientific interest 國家公園

ˌnational ˈservice *noun* [U] the system in some countries in which young people have to do military training for a period of time 兵役 **SYN** **military service**： *to do your national service* 服兵役

ˌNational ˈSocialism *noun* [U] (*politics* 政) the policies of the German Nazi party （德國納粹黨推行的）國家社會主義，納粹主義 ▸ **ˌNational ˈSocialist** *noun, adj.*

ˌnational ˈtrail *noun* a long route through beautiful country where people can walk or ride （修於美麗鄉間的）國家級步道，觀光道

the ˌNational ˈTrust *noun* an organization that owns and takes care of places of historical interest or natural beauty in England, Wales and Northern Ireland, so that people can go and visit them 全國託管協會（負責管理並保護英格蘭、威爾士及北愛爾蘭的歷史遺跡或自然景觀）

ˌnation ˈstate *noun* a group of people with the same culture, language, etc. who have formed an independent country 民族國家；單一民族的獨立國家

na·tion·wide /ˌneɪʃnˈwaɪd/ *adj.* happening or existing in all parts of a particular country 全國性的；遍及全國的；全國範圍的： *a nationwide campaign* 全國性運動 ▸ **na·tion·wide** *adv.*： *The company has over 500 stores nationwide.* 這家公司在全國各地有 500 多家商店。

na·tive /ˈneɪtɪv/ *adj., noun*

■ ***adj.*** **1** [only before noun] connected with the place where you were born and lived for the first years of your life 出生地的；兒時居住地的： *your* ***native land/country/city*** 你的故鄉／祖國／故里 ◇ *It is a long time since he has visited his native Chile.* 他很久沒有回故鄉智利了。◇ *Her native language is Korean.* 她的母語是朝鮮語。➲ see also NATIVE SPEAKER **2** [only before noun] connected with the place where you have always lived or have lived for a long time 本地的；當地的： *native Berliners* 土生土長的柏林人 **3** [only before noun] (sometimes *offensive*) connected with the people who originally lived in a country before other people, especially white people, came there 土著的；土著人的： *native peoples* 土著民族 ◇ *native art* 土著藝術 **4 ~ (to …)** (of animals and plants 動植物) existing naturally in a place 原產於某地的；土產的；當地的 **SYN** **indigenous**： *the native plants of America* 美國的土生植物 ◇ *The tiger is native to India.* 這種虎原產於印度。◇ *native species* 當地的物種 **5** [only before noun] that you have naturally without having to learn it 天賦的；與生俱來的 **SYN** **innate**： *native cunning* 與生俱來的狡猾

IDM **go ˈnative** (often *humorous*) (of a person staying in another country 移居異國的人) to try to live and behave like the local people 入鄉隨俗；同化

■ ***noun*** **1** a person who was born in a particular country or area 出生於某國（或某地）的人： *a native of New York* 紐約人 **2** a person who lives in a particular place, especially sb who has lived there a long time 本地人；當地人 **SYN** **local**： *You can always tell the difference between the tourists and the natives.* 遊客與當地人之間的區別一望即知。◇ *She speaks Italian like a native.* 她的

意大利語說得和意大利人一樣。 **3** (*old-fashioned, offensive*) a word used in the past by Europeans to describe a person who lived in a place originally, before white people arrived there（舊時歐洲人用以稱呼先於白人居住在某地的人）土著：*disputes between early settlers and natives* 早期移民和土著之間的紛爭 **4** an animal or a plant that lives or grows naturally in a particular area 本地的動物（或植物）：*The kangaroo is a native of Australia.* 袋鼠是產於澳大利亞的動物。

ˌNative Aˈmerican (also **Aˌmerican ˈIndian**) *noun* a member of any of the races of people who were the original people living in America 美洲土著居民 ▸ **ˌNative Aˈmerican** *adj.*：*Native American languages* 美洲土著語言

ˌNa·tive Caˈn·adian *noun* (*CanE*) an Aboriginal Canadian; a Canadian Indian, Inuit or Metis 加拿大土著居民；加拿大原住民；加拿大印第安人（或因努伊特人、梅蒂人）

ˌnative ˈspeaker *noun* a person who speaks a language as their first language and has not learned it as a foreign language 說本族語的人；母語使用者

na·tiv·ity /nəˈtɪvəti/ *noun* **1 the Nativity** [sing.] the birth of Jesus Christ, celebrated by Christians at Christmas 耶穌降生；聖誕 **2** a picture or a model of the baby Jesus Christ and the place where he was born 耶穌降生圖

naˈtivity play *noun* a play about the birth of Jesus Christ, usually performed by children at Christmas 聖誕劇（通常由兒童於聖誕節時演出）

NATO /ˈneɪtəʊ; *NAmE* -toʊ/ (also **Nato**) *abbr.* North Atlantic Treaty Organization. NATO is an organization to which many European countries and the US and Canada belong. They agree to give each other military help if necessary. 北約；北大西洋公約組織

N

nat·ter /ˈnætə(r)/ *verb* [I] **~ (away/on) (about sth)** (*BrE, informal*) to talk for a long time, especially about unimportant things 嘮叨；閒聊 SYN **chat** ▸ **nat·ter** *noun* [sing.]：(*BrE, informal*) *to have a good natter* 好好聊聊

natty /ˈnæti/ *adj.* (*old-fashioned, informal*) **1** neat and fashionable 整潔時髦的：*a natty suit* 筆挺時新的套裝 **2** well designed; clever 設計精妙的；聰明的：*a natty little briefcase* 設計精巧的小公文包 ▸ **nat·tily** *adv.*

nat·ural 0ᐧ /ˈnætʃrəl/ *adj., noun*

■ ***adj.***

▸ **IN NATURE** 自然 **1** 0ᐧ [only before noun] existing in nature; not made or caused by humans 自然的；天然的：*natural disasters* 自然災害 ◇ ***the natural world*** (= of trees, rivers, animals and birds) 自然界 ◇ *a country's* ***natural resources*** (= its coal, oil, forests, etc.) 一國的自然資源 ◇ *wildlife in its natural habitat* 自然棲息地裏的野生動植物 ◇ *natural yogurt* (= with no flavour added) 原味酸奶 ◇ *My hair soon grew back to its natural colour* (= after being DYED). 我的頭髮很快又恢復了本色。◇ *The clothes are available in warm natural colours.* 這些衣服有各種自然的暖色調可供挑選。 ➲ compare SUPERNATURAL (1)

▸ **EXPECTED** 期待 **2** 0ᐧ normal; as you would expect 正常的；自然的；意料之中的：*to die of* ***natural causes*** (= not by violence, but normally, of old age) 自然死亡 ◇ *He thought social inequality was all part of the natural order of things.* 他認為社會不平等完全合乎事物的自然規律。◇ *She was the natural choice for the job.* 做那份工作，她是當然人選。 ➲ compare UNNATURAL

▸ **BEHAVIOUR** 行為 **3** 0ᐧ used to describe behaviour that is part of the character that a person or an animal was born with 天生的；本能的；與生俱來的：*the natural agility of a cat* 貓天生的敏捷靈活 ◇ *the natural processes of language learning* 學習語言的自然過程 ◇ *It's only* ***natural*** *to worry about your children.* 為孩子操心是很自然的。

▸ **ABILITY** 能力 **4** 0ᐧ [only before noun] having an ability that you were born with 天賦的；天生具有某種能力的：*He's a natural leader.* 他天生是個領袖。

▸ **RELAXED** 放鬆 **5** relaxed and not pretending to be sb/sth different 不拘束的；不做作的；自然的：*It's difficult to look natural when you're feeling nervous.* 當你緊張的時候，很難顯得輕鬆自然。

▸ **PARENTS/CHILDREN** 父母；孩子 **6** [only before noun] (of parents or their children 父母或其子女) related by blood 有血緣關係的；親生的：*His natural mother was unable to care for him so he was raised by an aunt.* 他的生母不能照顧他，所以他是姑姑撫養大的。 **7** [only before noun] (*old use* or *formal*) (of a son or daughter 兒女) born to parents who are not married 非婚生的；私生的 SYN **illegitimate**：*She was a natural daughter of King James II.* 她是國王詹姆斯二世的私生女。

▸ **BASED ON HUMAN REASON** 符合理性 **8** [only before noun] based on human reason alone 符合人的理性的；正常的；自然的：***natural justice/law*** 自然公道／規律

▸ **IN MUSIC** 音樂 **9** used after the name of a note to show that the note is neither SHARP nor FLAT. The written symbol is (♮). 本位音的，標有還原號的（書寫符號為♮）：*B natural* * B 本位音 ➲ picture at MUSIC

■ ***noun***

▸ **PERSON** 人 **1 ~ (for sth)** a person who is very good at sth without having to learn how to do it, or who is perfectly suited for a particular job 有天賦的人；擅長做某事的人：*She took to flying like a natural.* 她迷上了飛行，彷彿天生就會似的。◇ *He's a natural for the role.* 他是這個角色的最佳人選。

▸ **IN MUSIC** 音樂 **2** a normal musical note, not its SHARP or FLAT form. The written symbol is (♮). 本位音，還原音，本位號（書寫符號為♮）

ˈnatural-born *adj.* [only before noun] having a natural ability or skill that you have not had to learn 天生的；天賦的；與生俱來的

ˌnatural ˈchildbirth *noun* [U] a method of giving birth to a baby in which a woman chooses not to take drugs and does special exercises to make her relaxed 自然分娩法

ˌnatural ˈgas *noun* [U] gas that is found under the ground or the sea and that is used as a fuel 天然氣

ˌnatural ˈhistory *noun* [U, C] the study of plants and animals; an account of the plant and animal life of a particular place 博物學；（某地區的）動植物研究：*the Natural History Museum* 自然歷史博物館 ◇ *He has written a natural history of Scotland.* 他寫了一本蘇格蘭博物誌。

nat·ur·al·ism /ˈnætʃrəlɪzəm/ *noun* [U] **1** a style of art or writing that shows people, things and experiences as they really are 自然主義（文學、藝術以反映現實為宗旨） **2** (*philosophy* 哲) the theory that everything in the world and life is based on natural causes and laws, and not on spiritual or SUPERNATURAL ones 自然主義（認為宇宙間存在的一切和生命都是受自然原因和自然規律支配，而非受精神或超自然力量支配）

nat·ur·al·ist /ˈnætʃrəlɪst/ *noun* a person who studies animals, plants, birds and other living things 博物學家

nat·ur·al·is·tic /ˌnætʃrəˈlɪstɪk/ *adj.* **1** (of artists, writers, etc. or their work 藝術家、作家等及其作品) showing things as they appear in the natural world 自然主義的；自然主義風格的 **2** copying the way things are in the natural world 寫實的；模仿自然的：*to study behaviour in laboratory and naturalistic settings* 研究實驗室裏的以及仿自然環境中的行為

nat·ur·al·ize (*BrE* also **-ise**) /ˈnætʃrəlaɪz/ *verb* [usually passive] **1** [T] **~ sb** to make sb who was not born in a particular country a citizen of that country 使加入…國籍；使成為某國公民；歸化 **2** [T] **~ sth** to introduce a plant or an animal to a country where it is not NATIVE 引進（動植物）；移植 **3** [I] (of a plant or an animal 動植物) to start growing or living naturally in a country where it is not NATIVE 適應異域生長環境 ▸ **nat·ur·al·iza·tion, -isa·tion** /ˌnætʃrəlaɪˈzeɪʃn; *NAmE* -ləˈz-/ *noun* [U]

ˌnatural ˈlanguage *noun* [C, U] a language that has developed in a natural way and is not designed by humans 自然語言（自然發展而成，並非人造）

ˌnatural ˈlanguage processing *noun* [U] (*abbr.* **NLP**) the use of computers to process natural languages, for example for translating（計算機）自然語言處理

ˌnatural ˈlaw *noun* [U] a set of moral principles on which human behaviour is based 自然法（人類行為所基於的道德原則）

nat·ur·al·ly /ˈnætʃrəli/ *adv.* **1** in a way that you would expect 順理成章地；自然地；當然地 SYN **of course**：*Naturally, I get upset when things go wrong.* 事情出了錯，我當然會很心煩。◇ *After a while, we naturally started talking about the children.* 過了一會兒，我們自然而然地談起了孩子。◇ *'Did you complain about the noise?' 'Naturally.'* "你是不是嫌吵了？" "那還用說。" **2** without special help, treatment or action by sb 天然地；自然而然地：*naturally occurring chemicals* 天然存在的化學物質 ◇ *plants that grow naturally in poor soils* 貧瘠土壤中自然生長的植物 **3** as a normal, logical result of sth 合理地；理所當然地；順理成章地：*This leads naturally to my next point.* 這必然引出我的下一個論點。 **4** in a way that shows or uses abilities or qualities that a person or an animal is born with 天生地；本能地：*to be naturally artistic* 有藝術天賦 ◇ *a naturally gifted athlete* 有天賦的運動員 **5** in a relaxed and normal way 自然地；大方地：*Just act naturally.* 放自然點兒就行了。
IDM **come ˈnaturally (to sb/sth)** if sth **comes naturally** to you, you are able to do it very easily and very well 輕而易舉：*Making money came naturally to him.* 賺錢對他來說輕而易舉。

nat·ur·al·ness /ˈnætʃrəlnəs/ *noun* [U] **1** the state or quality of being like real life 自然狀態；自然；逼真：*The naturalness of the dialogue made the book so true to life.* 自然逼真的對話使得這本書非常貼近生活。 **2** the quality of behaving in a normal, relaxed or innocent way 自然；大方；純真：*Teenagers lose their childhood simplicity and naturalness.* 十幾歲的青少年就不像兒時那麼淳樸天真了。 **3** the style or quality of happening in a normal way that you would expect 當然；必然性：*the naturalness of her reaction* 她的必然反應

ˌnatural ˈnumber *noun* (*mathematics* 數) a positive whole number such as 1, 2, or 3, and sometimes also zero 自然數

ˌnatural phiˈlosophy *noun* [U] (*old use*) the study of the physical world, which developed into the natural sciences 自然哲學（對物理世界的研究，後發展為自然科學）

ˌnatural ˈscience *noun* [C, U] a science concerned with studying the physical world. Chemistry, biology and physics are all natural sciences. 自然科學 ➲ compare EARTH SCIENCE, LIFE SCIENCES

ˌnatural seˈlection *noun* [U] the process by which plants, animals, etc. that can adapt to their environment survive and reproduce, while the others disappear 自然選擇；物競天擇

ˌnatural ˈwastage (*BrE*) (also **at·tri·tion** *NAmE, BrE*) *noun* [U] the process of reducing the number of people who are employed by an organization by, for example, not replacing people who leave their jobs 自然減員

na·ture /ˈneɪtʃə(r)/ *noun*

> **WORD FAMILY**
> **nature** *noun*
> **natural** *adj.* (≠ unnatural)
> **naturally** *adv.* (≠ unnaturally)

▸ **PLANTS, ANIMALS** 動植物 **1** (often **Nature**) [U] all the plants, animals and things that exist in the universe that are not made by people 宇宙中的萬物；自然界；大自然：*the beauties of nature* 自然界中美好的東西 ◇ *man-made substances not found in nature* 自然界裏找不到的人造物質 ◇ *nature conservation* 自然保護 HELP You cannot use 'the nature' in this meaning. 此義不可用 the nature：~~*the beauties of the nature*~~. It is often better to use another appropriate word, for example **the countryside**, **the scenery** or **wildlife**. 最好用其他恰當的詞，如 the countryside、the scenery 或 wildlife：*We stopped to admire the scenery.* 我們中途停下來欣賞一下風景。◇ ~~*We stopped to admire the nature.*~~ **2** (often **Nature**) [U] the way that things happen in the physical world when it is not controlled by people 自然；自然方式：*the* ***forces/laws of nature*** 自然力／規律 ◇ *Just let nature take its course.* 就順其自然吧。◇ *Her illness was Nature's way of telling her to do less.* 她的疾病是天意在告訴她不要太勞累。 ➲ see also MOTHER NATURE
▸ **CHARACTER** 性質 **3** [C, U] the usual way that a person or an animal behaves that is part of their character 天性；本性；性格：*It's* ***not in his nature*** *to be unkind.* 他天生不會刻薄。◇ *She is very sensitive* ***by nature***. 她生性很敏感。◇ *We appealed to his* ***better nature*** (= his kindness). 我們設法喚起他的善良本性。 ➲ see also GOOD NATURE, HUMAN NATURE, SECOND NATURE
▸ **BASIC QUALITIES** 基本特徵 **4** [sing.] the basic qualities of a thing 基本特徵；本質；基本性質：*the changing nature of society* 不斷變化的社會性質 ◇ *It's difficult to define the exact nature of the problem.* 很難給這個問題確切定性。◇ *My work is very specialized* ***in nature***. 我的工作性質非常專業化。
▸ **TYPE/KIND** 種類 **5** [sing.] a type or kind of sth 種類；類型：*books of a scientific nature* 科學書籍 ◇ *Don't worry about things of that nature.* 別擔心那類事情。
▸ **-NATURED** 本性 **6** (in adjectives 構成形容詞) having the type of character or quality mentioned 有…本性的；…性情的：*a good-natured man* 脾氣好的人
IDM **against ˈnature** not natural; not moral 違反自然的；有違天性的；不道德的：*Murder is a crime against nature.* 謀殺是一種有違天性的罪行。 **(get, go, etc.) back to ˈnature** to return to a simple kind of life in the country, away from cities 回歸自然；返璞歸真 **in the nature of ˈsth** similar to sth; a type of sth; in the style of sth 與…類似；…之類；以…風格：*His speech was in the nature of an apology.* 他的話也就是道歉。 **in the ˈnature of things** in the way that things usually happen 理所當然地；自然地：*In the nature of things, young people often rebel against their parents.* 年輕人常常會反抗他們的父母，這很自然。 ➲ more at CALL *n.*, FORCE *n.*

ˈnature reserve *noun* an area of land where the animals and plants are protected 自然保護區

ˈnature strip *noun* (*AustralE*) a piece of public land between the edge of a house, or other building, and the street, usually planted with grass （房屋或建築物前靠路邊的）公共綠化帶

ˈnature trail *noun* a path through countryside which you can follow in order to see the interesting plants and animals that are found there 自然景觀小徑

na·tur·ism /ˈneɪtʃərɪzəm/ *noun* [U] (*especially BrE*) = NUDISM

na·tur·ist /ˈneɪtʃərɪst/ *noun* (*especially BrE*) = NUDIST

na·tur·op·athy /ˌneɪtʃəˈrɒpəθi; *NAmE* -ˈrɑːp-/ *noun* [U] a system for treating diseases or conditions using natural foods and herbs and various other techniques, rather than artificial drugs 自然療法（指用天然食物、草藥等技術治療疾病，而不用人造藥物） ▸ **na·turo·path** /ˈneɪtʃərəpæθ/ *noun*：*A medical herbalist or naturopath will be able to advise on individual treatment plans.* 草藥醫士或自然療法醫士能夠對各別個體治療方案提供咨詢。 **na·turo·path·ic** /ˌneɪtʃərəˈpæθɪk/ *adj.* [only before noun]：*naturopathic medicine* 自然療法醫學 ◇ *a naturopathic physician* 自然療法醫師

naught *noun* = NOUGHT (2)

naughty /ˈnɔːti/ *adj.* (**naugh·tier**, **naugh·ti·est**) **1** (especially of children 尤指兒童) behaving badly; not willing to obey 頑皮的；淘氣的；不聽話的：*a naughty boy/girl* 淘氣的男孩／女孩 ◇ (*humorous*) *I'm being very naughty—I've ordered champagne!* 我今天放肆一回，我要了香檳了！ **2** (*informal*, often *humorous*) slightly rude; connected with sex 粗俗的；下流的 SYN **risqué**：*a naughty joke/word* 下流的笑話；粗俗的字眼 ▸ **naugh·tily** *adv.* **naugh·ti·ness** *noun* [U]

nau·sea /ˈnɔːziə; ˈnɔːsiə/ *noun* [U] the feeling that you have when you want to VOMIT, for example because you are ill/sick or are disgusted by sth 惡心；作嘔；反胃：*A wave of nausea swept over her.* 她覺得一陣惡心。◇ *Nausea and vomiting are common symptoms.* 惡心嘔吐是常見的症狀。 ➲ see also AD NAUSEAM

nau·se·ate /ˈnɔːzieɪt; ˈnɔːsieɪt/ *verb* **1 ~ sb** to make sb feel that they want to VOMIT 使惡心；使作嘔 **2 ~ sb** to make sb feel disgusted 使厭惡；使厭煩 SYN **revolt, sicken**：*I was nauseated by the violence in the movie.* 影片中的暴力場面讓我感到惡心。▸ **nau·se·at·ing** *adj.*：*a nauseating smell* 令人作嘔的氣味 ◇ *his nauseating behaviour* 他那令人厭惡的行為 **nau·se·at·ing·ly** *adv.*

nau·se·ous /ˈnɔːziəs; ˈnɔːsiəs; *NAmE* ˈnɔːʃəs/ *adj.* **1** feeling as if you want to VOMIT 惡心的；想嘔吐的：*She felt dizzy and nauseous.* 她覺得頭暈、惡心。**2** making you feel as if you want to VOMIT 令人作嘔的；令人厭惡的：*a nauseous smell* 令人作嘔的氣味

naut·ical /ˈnɔːtɪkl/ *adj.* connected with ships, sailors and sailing 航海的；海員的；船舶的：*nautical terms* 航海術語

ˌ**nautical ˈmile** (also ˈ**sea mile**) *noun* a unit for measuring distance at sea; 1 852 metres 海里（合 1 852 米）

naut·ilus /ˈnɔːtɪləs/ *noun* a creature with a shell that lives in the sea. It has TENTACLES around its mouth and its shell fills with gas to help it float. 鸚鵡螺

Nav·ajo (also **Nava·ho**) /ˈnævəhəʊ; *NAmE* -hoʊ/ *noun* (*pl.* **Nav·ajo** or **Nav·ajos**) a member of the largest group of Native American people, most of whom live in the US states of Arizona, New Mexico and Utah 納瓦霍人（美洲最大的土著民族成員，多數居於美國亞利桑那州、新墨西哥州和猶他州）

naval /ˈneɪvl/ *adj.* connected with the navy of a country 海軍的：*a naval base/officer/battle* 海軍基地／軍官；海戰

Nava·rat·ri /ˌnævəˈrætri/ (also **Nava·rat·ra** /-trə/) *noun* a Hindu festival lasting for nine nights, which takes place in the autumn/fall 那婆羅恆羅節，九夜節（印度教秋季的節日，歷時九個夜晚）

nave /neɪv/ *noun* the long central part of a church where most of the seats are 教堂正廳 ➲ compare TRANSEPT

navel /ˈneɪvl/ (also *informal* ˈ**belly button**) (*BrE* also ˈ**tummy button**) *noun* the small hollow part or lump in the middle of the stomach where the UMBILICAL CORD was cut at birth 肚臍；臍 ➲ VISUAL VOCAB page V59

ˈ**navel-gazing** *noun* [U] (*disapproving*) the fact of thinking too much about a single issue and how it could affect you, without thinking about other things that could also affect the situation 一根筋；鑽牛角尖

ˌ**navel ˈorange** *noun* a large orange without seeds that has a part at the top that looks like a navel 臍橙

nav·ig·able /ˈnævɪɡəbl/ *adj.* (of rivers, etc. 河流等) wide and deep enough for ships and boats to sail on 可航行的；適於通航的 ▸ **nav·ig·abil·ity** /ˌnævɪɡəˈbɪləti/ *noun* [U]

navi·gate /ˈnævɪɡeɪt/ *verb* **1** [I, T] to find your position or the position of your ship, plane, car etc. and the direction you need to go in, for example by using a map 導航；確定（船、飛機、汽車等）的位置和方向：*to navigate by the stars* 根據星辰確定航向 ◇ *I'll drive, and you can navigate.* 我開車，你引路。◇ **~ your way** ... *How do you navigate your way through a forest?* 你怎麼才能設法走出森林？ **2** [T] **~ sth** to sail along, over or through a sea, river etc. 航行；航海；橫渡：*The river became too narrow and shallow to navigate.* 河道變得又窄又淺，無法航行。**3** [T] **~ sth** to find the right way to deal with a difficult or complicated situation 找到正確方法（對付困難複雜的情況）：*We next had to navigate a complex network of committees.* 我們下一步必須設法使各級委員會予以通過。**4** [I, T] **~ (sth)** (*computing* 計) to find your way around on the Internet or on a particular website（在互聯網或網站上）導航

navi·ga·tion /ˌnævɪˈɡeɪʃn/ *noun* [U] **1** the skill or the process of planning a route for a ship or other vehicle and taking it there 導航；領航：*navigation systems* 導航系統 ◇ *an expert in navigation* 導航專家 **2** the movement of ships or aircraft 航行：*the right of navigation through international waters* 通過國際水域的航行權 ▸ **nav·iga·tion·al** /-ʃənl/ *adj.*：*navigational aids* 導航器材

navi·ga·tor /ˈnævɪɡeɪtə(r)/ *noun* a person who navigates, for example on a ship or an aircraft（飛機、船舶等上的）航行者，航海者，駕駛員，領航員

navvy /ˈnævi/ *noun* (*pl.* **-ies**) (*BrE*) a person employed to do hard physical work, especially building roads, etc. 壯工；苦力；（尤指）築路工

navy 🔑 /ˈneɪvi/ *noun* (*pl.* **-ies**)
1 🔑 [C+sing./pl. v.] the part of a country's armed forces that fights at sea, and the ships that it uses 海軍；海軍部隊：*the British and German navies* 英國和德國的海軍部隊 ◇ *He's joined **the navy/the Navy**.* 他參加了海軍。◇ *an officer in **the navy/the Navy*** 海軍軍官 ◇ *The navy is/are considering buying six new warships.* 海軍正在考慮購買六艘新戰艦。➲ COLLOCATIONS at WAR ➲ see also NAVAL **2** [U] = NAVY BLUE

ˈ**navy bean** (*NAmE*) (*BrE* **hari·cot**, ˌ**haricot ˈbean**) *noun* a type of small white BEAN that is usually dried before it is sold and then left in water before cooking 菜豆；扁豆；蕓豆

ˌ**navy ˈblue** (also **navy**) *adj.* very dark blue in colour 海軍藍的；深藍的：*a navy blue suit* 一套海軍藍的衣服 ▸ ˌ**navy ˈblue** (also **navy**) *noun* [U]：*She was dressed in navy blue.* 她穿着深藍色的衣服。

naw /nɔː/ *exclamation* (*informal*) no, used when answering a question（用於回答）不，不是，沒有：*'Want some toast?' 'Naw.'* "要吃烤麵包片嗎？" "不要。"

nawab /nəˈwɑːb/ *noun* **1** an Indian ruler during the Mogul empire 納瓦布（印度莫卧兒帝國時代的省級地方行政長官） **2** (*IndE*) a Muslim with high social status or rank 納瓦布；地位（或級別）較高的穆斯林

Naxa·lite /ˈnæksəlaɪt/ *noun* (in India) a member of a group which believes in political revolution in order to change the system of how land is owned. It took its name from Naxalbari in West Bengal, where it started. 納薩爾派分子（印度主張通過政治革命改變土地所有制的組織成員，因發起於西孟加拉邦的納薩爾巴里地區而得名）

nay /neɪ/ *adv.* **1** (*old-fashioned*) used to emphasize sth you have just said by introducing a stronger word or phrase（強調剛提及之事）不僅如此，而且：*Such a policy is difficult, nay impossible.* 這一政策很難實施，甚至是不可能的。**2** (*old use* or *dialect*) no 不 ➲ compare YEA

Nazi /ˈnɑːtsi/ *noun* **1** a member of the National Socialist party which controlled Germany from 1933 to 1945 納粹黨人，納粹分子（1933 至 1945 年間統治德國的國家社會主義工人黨成員） **2** (*disapproving*) a person who uses their power in a cruel way; a person with extreme and unreasonable views about race 兇殘的人；極端種族主義分子 ▸ **Nazi** *adj.* **Naz·ism** /ˈnɑːtsɪzəm/ *noun* [U]

NB (*BrE*) (also **N.B.** *US*, *BrE*) /ˌen ˈbiː/ *abbr.* used in writing to make sb take notice of a particular piece of information that is important (from Latin 'nota bene') 注意，留心（用於書面注意事項，譯自拉丁語 nota bene）：*NB The office will be closed from 1 July.* 注意：辦事處從 7 月 1 日起將關閉。

NBA /ˌen biː ˈeɪ/ *abbr.* National Basketball Association (the US organization responsible for professional BASKETBALL)（美國）全國職業籃球協會

NBC /ˌen biː ˈsiː/ *abbr.* National Broadcasting Company (a US company that produces television and radio programmes)（美國）全國廣播公司：*NBC News* 全國廣播公司新聞節目

NCO /ˌen siː ˈəʊ; *NAmE* ˈoʊ/ *abbr.* non-commissioned officer (a soldier who has a rank such as CORPORAL or SERGEANT) 軍士

NCT /ˌen siː ˈtiː/ *noun* (in Britain) the abbreviation for 'National Curriculum Test' (a test taken by children at the ages of 7 and 11, also called SAT)（英國）國家課程考試（全寫為 National Curriculum Test，學生在 7 歲和 11 歲時參加，又稱 SAT）

ndugu /n'dʊgʊ/ *noun* (*EAfrE*) (usually **Ndugu**) (in Tanzania) a title for a man or woman that shows respect（坦桑尼亞敬稱）大哥，大姐

NE *abbr.* north-east; north-eastern 東北方（的）；東北部（的）：*NE England* 英格蘭東北部

Ne·an·der·thal /ni'ændətɑːl; *NAmE* -dɔːrt-/ (also **nean·derthal**) *adj.* **1** used to describe a type of human being who used stone tools and lived in Europe during the early period of human history（石器時代生活於歐洲的）尼安德特人的 **2** (*disapproving*) very old-fashioned and not wanting any change 守舊的；僵化過時的：*neanderthal attitudes* 守舊的態度 **3** (*disapproving*) (of a man 男人) unpleasant, rude and not behaving in a socially acceptable way 令人厭煩的；粗魯無禮的 ▶ **Ne·an·der·thal** *noun*

neap tide /'niːp taɪd/ (also **neap**) *noun* a TIDE in the sea in which there is only a very small difference between the level of the water at HIGH TIDE and that at LOW TIDE 小潮

near /nɪə(r); *NAmE* nɪr/ *adj., adv., prep., verb*

■ ***adj.*** (**near·er**, **near·est**) HELP In senses 1 to 4 **near** and **nearer** do not usually go before a noun; **nearest** can go either before or after a noun. 第 1 至第 4 義中，near 和 nearer 通常不用於名詞前；nearest 可用於名詞之前或之後。 **1** a short distance away 距離近；不遠 SYN **close**：*His house is very near.* 他的房子就在附近。◇ *Where's the nearest bank?* 最近的銀行在哪兒？ ➲ note at NEXT **2** a short time away in the future 不久以後：*The conflict is unlikely to be resolved **in the near future*** (= very soon). 衝突短期內不可能解決。 **3** coming next after sb/sth 隨後；接近：*She has a 12-point lead over her nearest rival.* 她領先緊隨其後的對手 12 分。 **4** (usually **nearest**) similar; most similar 近似；相似；不分伯仲：*He was **the nearest thing to*** (= the person most like) *a father she had ever had.* 她接觸過的人中，他最像個父親。 ➲ see also O.N.O. **5** [only before noun] (no comparative or superlative 無比較級或最高級) close to being sb/sth 接近的；差不多的：*The election proved to be a near disaster for the party.* 這次選舉對該黨來說幾乎是一場災難。◇ *a near impossibility* 幾乎不可能的事 **6** **~ relative/relation** used to describe a close family connection（親屬關係）近親：*Only the nearest relatives were present at the funeral.* 只有幾位近親參加了葬禮。 ▶ **near·ness** *noun* [U]：*the nearness of death* 死亡的臨近

IDM **your ˌnearest and 'dearest** (*informal*) your close family and friends 至親；至愛；最親密的親友 **a ˌnear 'thing** a situation in which you are successful, but which could also have ended badly 僥幸做成的事：*Phew! That was a near thing! It could have been a disaster.* 哎呀！好險哪！差一點兒出事。◇ *We won in the end but it was a near thing.* 我們最後贏了，但比分很近。 **to the nearest ...** followed by a number when counting or measuring approximately 近似於；約等於：*We calculated the cost to the nearest 50 dollars.* 我們算計費用約為 50 元。

■ ***adv.*** (**near·er**, **near·est**) **1** at a short distance away 距離不遠；在附近：*A bomb exploded somewhere near.* 一顆炸彈在附近爆炸。◇ *She took a step nearer.* 她走近一步。◇ *Visitors came from **near and far**.* 遊客來自四面八方。 **2** a short time away in the future 不久以後：*The exams are **drawing near**.* 考試越來越近了。 **3** (especially in compounds 尤用於構成複合詞) almost 幾乎；差不多：*a near-perfect performance* 近乎完美的表演 ◇ *I'm as near certain as can be.* 我幾乎完全可以確定。

IDM **as near as** as accurately as 準確到…的程度；大約：*There were about 3 000 people there, as near as I could judge.* 據我判斷，大約有 3 000 人在那裏。 **as ˌnear as 'damn it/'dammit** (*BrE, informal*) used to say that an amount is so nearly correct that the difference does not matter（數量）相差無幾，沒什麼分別：*It will cost £350, or as near as dammit.* 這要花 350 英鎊上下。 **near 'enough** (*BrE, informal*) used to say that sth is so nearly true that the difference does not matter 確實；差不多：*We've been here twenty years, near enough.* 我們在這裏待了差不多二十年了。 **not anywhere near/nowhere near** far from; not at all 遠非；絕不是：*The job doesn't pay anywhere near enough for me.* 這份工作付給我的報酬遠遠不夠。 **so ˌnear and ˌyet so 'far** used to comment on sth that was almost successful but in fact failed 功敗垂成；功虧一簣 ➲ more at PRETTY *adv.*

■ ***prep.*** (also **near to**, **near·er (to)**, **near·est (to)**) HELP **Near to** is not usually used before the name of a place, person, festival, etc. * near to 通常不用於地點、人物、節日等名稱前。 **1** at a short distance away from sb/sth 在…附近；靠近：*Do you live near here?* 你住在這附近嗎？◇ *Go and sit nearer (to) the fire.* 坐得靠爐子近點兒。 ➲ note at NEXT **2** a short period of time from sth 接近；臨近：*My birthday is very near Christmas.* 我的生日離聖誕節很近。◇ *I'll think about it nearer **(to) the time*** (= when it is just going to happen). 到時候我會考慮的。 **3** used before a number to mean 'approximately', 'just below or above'（用於數詞前）大約，上下，接近：*Share prices are near their record high of last year.* 股票價格接近去年的最高紀錄。◇ *Profits fell from $11 million to nearer $8 million.* 利潤從 1 100 萬元下跌到大約 800 萬元。 **4** similar to sb/sth in quality, size, etc.（質量、大小等）相仿，接近：*Nobody else comes near her in intellect.* 誰也趕不上她聰明。◇ *He's nearer 70 than 60.* 他 60 多歲，快 70 歲了。◇ *This colour is nearest (to) the original.* 這種顏色最接近原色。 **5** **~ (doing) sth** close to a particular state 接近於（某種狀態）；瀕臨；快要：*a state near (to) death* 瀕臨死亡 ◇ *She was **near to tears*** (= almost crying). 她就要哭了。◇ *We **came near to** being killed.* 我們差點丟了性命。

IDM see HAND *n.*, HEART, MARK *n.*

■ ***verb*** [T, I] **~ (sth)** (rather *formal*) to come close to sth in time or space（時間或空間上）接近，靠近，臨近 SYN **approach**：*The project is **nearing completion**.* 這項工程就要竣工了。◇ *She was **nearing the end** of her life.* 她已經臨近生命的盡頭。◇ *We neared the top of the hill.* 我們快到山頂了。◇ *As Christmas neared, the children became more and more excited.* 快過聖誕節了，孩子們越來越興奮。

Which Word? 詞語辨析

near / close

■ The adjectives **near** and **close** are often the same in meaning, but in some phrases only one of them may be used. 形容詞 near 和 close 通常含義相同，但在某些短語中只能用其中一個：*the near future* 不久的將來 ◇ *a near neighbour* 近鄰 ◇ *a near miss* 差點兒命中 ◇ *a close contest* 勢均力敵的競賽 ◇ *a close encounter* 近距離接觸 ◇ *a close call* 僥幸脫險 **Close** is more often used to describe a relationship between people. * close 更常用於描述人與人之間的關係：*a close friend* 密友 ◇ *close family* 關係親密的家庭 ◇ *close links* 緊密的聯繫 You do not usually use **near** in this way. * near 通常不這樣用。

near·by /ˌnɪə'baɪ; *NAmE* ˌnɪr'baɪ/ *adj., adv.*

■ ***adj.*** [usually before noun] near in position; not far away 附近的；鄰近的：*Her mother lived in a nearby town.* 她母親住在附近一個小鎮上。◇ *There were complaints from nearby residents.* 附近的居民有些怨言。

■ ***adv.*** a short distance from sb/sth; not far away 在附近；不遠：*They live nearby.* 他們住在附近。◇ *The car is parked nearby.* 車就停在附近。

ˌnear-ˌdeath ex'perience *noun* an occasion when you almost die, which is often remembered as leaving your body or going down a tunnel 瀕死經歷（常留下靈魂出竅或墜入隧道的回憶）

the ˌNear 'East *noun* [sing.] = MIDDLE EAST

near·ly /'nɪəli; *NAmE* 'nɪrli/ *adv.* almost; not quite; not completely 幾乎；差不多；將近：*The bottle's nearly empty.* 這瓶子差不多空了。◇ *I've worked here for nearly two years.* 我已經在這裏工作了將近兩年。◇ *It's nearly time to leave.* 快該走了。◇ *The audience was nearly all men.* 觀眾幾乎全都是男的。◇ *He's nearly as tall as you are.* 他差不多和你一樣高了。◇

They're nearly always late. 他們幾乎總是遲到。◇ *She very nearly died.* 她差點兒死了。➲ SYNONYMS at ALMOST

IDM **not 'nearly** much less than; not at all 遠非；絕不是：*It's not nearly as hot as last year.* 天氣絕沒有去年那麼熱。◇ *There isn't nearly enough time to get there now.* 現在根本沒有足夠的時間趕到那兒。➲ more at PRETTY *adv.*

,near 'miss *noun* **1** a situation when a serious accident or a disaster very nearly happens 僥幸脫險 **2** a bomb or a shot that nearly hits what it is aimed at but misses it（炸彈或射擊）近距脫靶：(*figurative*) *He should have won the match—it was a near miss.* 這場比賽本該是他贏的，真是功虧一簣。➲ see also A NEAR THING at NEAR *adj.*

near·side /ˈnɪəsaɪd; *NAmE* ˈnɪrs-/ *adj.* [only before noun] (*BrE*) (for a driver) on the side that is nearest the edge of the road（對於駕駛員）靠近人行道的：*the car's nearside doors* 左邊的車門 ◇ *Keep to the nearside lane.* 不要偏離左邊的車道。▶ **the near·side** *noun* [sing.]：*The driver lost control and veered to the nearside.* 駕駛員失去控制，車猛地轉向左側。**OPP** **offside**

near·sight·ed /ˌnɪəˈsaɪtɪd; *NAmE* ˌnɪr-/ *adj.* (*especially NAmE*) = SHORT-SIGHTED (1) **OPP** **far-sighted** ▶ **near·sight·ed·ness** *noun* [U]

neat /niːt/ *adj.* (**neat·er**, **neat·est**)
1 tidy and in order; carefully done or arranged 整潔的；整齊的；有序的：*a neat desk* 整潔的課桌 ◇ *neat handwriting* 工整的筆跡 ◇ *neat rows of books* 一排排整齊的書 ◇ *She was wearing a neat black suit.* 她穿着整潔的黑色禮服。◇ *They sat in her **neat and tidy** kitchen.* 他們坐在她那乾淨整齊的廚房裏。**2** (of people 人) liking to keep things tidy and in order; looking tidy or doing things in a tidy way 有條理的；愛整潔的：*Try and be neater!* 乾淨利落點！**3** small, with a pleasing shape or appearance 小巧優雅的 **SYN** **trim**：*her neat figure* 她那嬌小玲瓏的身材 **4** simple but clever 簡潔的；睿智的；靈巧的：*a neat explanation* 簡明的解釋 ◇ *a neat solution to the problem* 解決這個問題的捷徑 **5** (*NAmE, informal*) good; excellent 好的；極好的：*It's a really neat movie.* 這真是一部極好的電影。◇ *We had a great time—it was pretty neat.* 我們玩得很痛快，棒極了。**6** (*BrE*) (*NAmE* **straight**) (especially of alcoholic drinks 尤指酒) not mixed with water or anything else 未摻水的；純的：*neat whisky* 純威士忌酒 ▶ **neat·ly** *adv.*：*neatly folded clothes* 摺疊整齊的衣服 ◇ *The box fitted neatly into the drawer.* 這盒子放在抽屜裏正合適。◇ *She summarized her plan very neatly.* 她非常簡明地總結了她的計劃。**neat·ness** *noun* [U]

neat·en /ˈniːtn/ *verb* ~ **sth** to make sth tidy 使整潔

neb·bish /ˈnebɪʃ/ *noun* (*NAmE, informal*) a man who behaves in an anxious and nervous way and without confidence 怯懦的男人；膽小鬼

neb·ula /ˈnebjələ/ *noun* (*pl.* **nebu·lae** /-liː/) (*astronomy* 天) a mass of dust or gas that can be seen in the night sky, often appearing very bright; a bright area in the night sky caused by a large cloud of stars that are far away 星雲狀積塵（或氣體）；星雲

nebu·lous /ˈnebjələs/ *adj.* (*formal*) not clear 模糊的；不清楚的 **SYN** **vague**：*a nebulous concept* 模糊的概念

ne·ces·sar·ies /ˈnesəsəriz; *NAmE* ˈnesəseriz/ *noun* [pl.] (*old-fashioned*) the things that you need, especially in order to live 必需品；（尤指）生活必需品

ne·ces·sar·ily /ˌnesəˈserəli; *BrE* also ˈnesəsərəli/ *adv.*
used to say that sth cannot be avoided 必然地；不可避免地：*The number of places available is necessarily limited.* 可用場所的數量不可避免地很有限。

IDM **,not neces'sarily** used to say that sth is possibly true but not definitely or always true 不一定；未必：*The more expensive articles are not necessarily better.* 較貴的東西不見得就較好。◇ *Biggest doesn't necessarily mean best.* 最大的不一定是最好的。◇ *'We're going to lose.' 'Not necessarily.'*"我們會輸的。""未必。"

ne·ces·sary /ˈnesəsəri; *NAmE* -seri/ *adj.*
1 ~ (**for sb/sth**) (**to do sth**) that is needed for a purpose or a reason 必需的；必要的 **SYN** **essential**：*It may be necessary to buy a new one.* 也許有必要買個新的了。◇ *It doesn't seem necessary for us to meet.* 我們似乎沒必要見面。◇ *Only use your car when absolutely necessary.* 非用不可的時候才用你的汽車。◇ ***If necessary**, you can contact me at home.* 必要的話，你可以打電話到我家找我。◇ *I'll make the necessary arrangements.* 我會做一些必要的安排。**2** [only before noun] that must exist or happen and cannot be avoided 必然的；無法避免的 **SYN** **inevitable**：*This is a necessary consequence of progress.* 這是發展的必然後果。

IDM **a ,necessary 'evil** a thing that is bad or that you do not like but which you must accept for a particular reason 無法避免的壞事；不得已的事

ne·ces·si·tate /nəˈsesɪteɪt/ *verb* (*formal*) to make sth necessary 使成為必要：~ **sth** *Recent financial scandals have necessitated changes in parliamentary procedures.* 最近的金融醜聞使得議會程序必須改革。◇ ~ **doing sth** *Increased traffic necessitated widening the road.* 交通量增大，這就需要拓寬道路。◇ ~ **sb/sth doing sth** *His new job necessitated him/his getting up at six.* 新工作使他不得不六點鐘起牀。

ne·ces·sity /nəˈsesəti/ *noun* **1** [U] the fact that sth must happen or be done; the need for sth 必然；必要；需要：~ (**for sth**) *We recognize the necessity for a written agreement.* 我們認為有必要簽訂一份書面協議。◇ ~ (**of sth/of doing sth**) *We were discussing the necessity of employing more staff.* 我們在討論是否需要雇用更多員工。◇ ~ (**for sb**) **to do sth** *There had never been any necessity for her to go out to work.* 她從來就沒有出去工作的必要。◇ *This is, **of necessity**, a brief and incomplete account.* 這必然是一個簡略的、不完全的描述。**2** [C] a thing that you must have and cannot manage without 必需的事物；必需品：*Many people cannot even afford **basic necessities** such as food and clothing.* 許多人甚至買不起食物和衣服之類的基本必需品。◇ *Air-conditioning is an absolute necessity in this climate.* 這樣的氣候絕對需要有空調。**3** [C, usually sing.] a situation that must happen and that cannot be avoided 必然性；不可避免的情況：*Living in London, he felt, was an unfortunate necessity.* 他覺得在倫敦生活是迫於無奈。

IDM **ne,cessity is the ,mother of in'vention** (*saying*) a difficult new problem forces people to think of a solution to it 需要是發明之母 ➲ more at VIRTUE

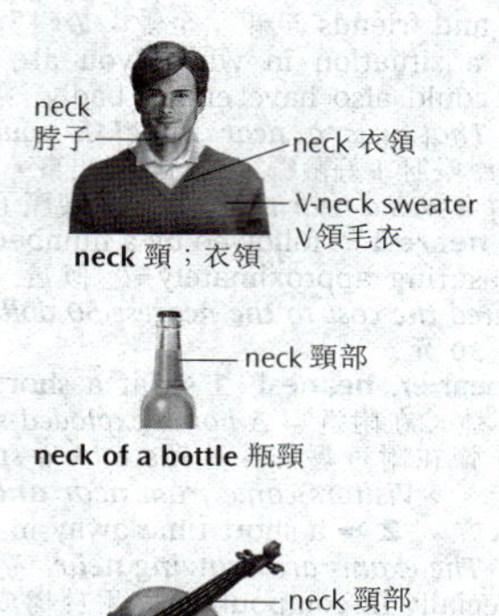

neck 頸；衣領

neck of a bottle 瓶頸

neck of a violin 小提琴琴頸

neck /nek/ *noun, verb*
■ *noun* **1** [C] the part of the body between the head and the shoulders 頸；脖子：*He tied a scarf around his neck.* 他脖子上圍着圍巾。◇ *Giraffes have very long necks.* 長頸鹿脖子很長。◇ *She **craned** (= stretched) **her neck** to get a better view.* 她伸長了脖子，想看得清楚一點。◇ *He broke his neck in the fall.* 他摔斷了脖子。◇ *Somebody's going to **break their neck** (= injure themselves) on these steps.* 會有人在這台階上摔傷的。➲ COLLOCATIONS at

PHYSICAL ➲ VISUAL VOCAB page V59 **2** [C] the part of a piece of clothing that fits around the neck 衣領；領子；領圈：*What neck size do you take?* 你穿多大的衣領？ ➲ see also CREW NECK, POLO NECK, TURTLENECK, V-NECK ➲ VISUAL VOCAB page V63 **3 -necked** (in adjectives 構成形容詞) having the type of neck mentioned 有…衣領的；有…脖子的：*a round-necked sweater* 一件圓領毛衣 ➲ see also OPEN-NECKED, STIFF-NECKED **4** [C] **~ (of sth)** a long narrow part of sth （物體的）細長部份，頸部：*the neck of a bottle* 瓶頸 ◇ *a neck of land* 地峽 **5** [U] **~ (of sth)** the neck of an animal, cooked and eaten （烹製食用的）動物頸肉：*neck of lamb* 小羊頸肉 ➲ see also BOTTLENECK, REDNECK, ROUGHNECK

IDM **be up to your neck in sth** to have a lot of sth to deal with 深陷於；忙於應付：*We're up to our neck in debt.* 我們債務累累。◇ *He's in it* (= trouble) *up to his neck.* 他遇上了麻煩，難以解脱。 **by a 'neck** if a person or an animal wins a race **by a neck**, they win it by a short distance 以微弱優勢（領先） **,get it in the 'neck** (*BrE, informal*) to be shouted at or punished because of sth that you have done 受到嚴厲責罵；受重罰 **,neck and 'neck (with sb/sth)** (also **,nip and 'tuck (with sb)** especially in *US*) level with sb in a race or competition （比賽中）勢均力敵，不分上下，平手 **,neck of the 'woods** (*informal*) a particular place or area 某地方；某地區：*He's from your neck of the woods* (= the area where you live). 他是你那一帶的人。 ➲ more at BLOCK *n.*, BRASS, BREATHE, MILLSTONE, PAIN *n.*, RISK *v.*, SAVE *v.*, SCRUFF, STICK *v.*, WRING

■ ***verb*** (usually **be necking**) [I] (*old-fashioned, informal*) when two people **are necking**, they are kissing each other in a sexual way 摟着脖子親吻；相擁互吻

neck·er·chief /ˈnekətʃiːf; *NAmE* -kər-/ *noun* a square of cloth that you wear around your neck 圍巾；領巾

neck·lace /ˈnekləs/ *noun, verb*

■ ***noun*** a piece of jewellery consisting of a chain, string of BEADS, etc. worn around the neck 項鏈：*a diamond necklace* 一條鑽石項鏈 ➲ VISUAL VOCAB page V65

■ ***verb*** **~ sb** to kill sb by putting a burning car tyre around their neck 給（某人）戴火項鏈（將燃燒的輪胎掛在脖子上將其燒死） ▸ **neck·lacing** *noun* [U]

neck·line /ˈneklaɪn/ *noun* the edge of a piece of clothing, especially a woman's, which fits around or below the neck （女裝的）領口，開領：*a dress with a **low/round/plunging neckline*** 低領／圓領／深 V 字領的連衣裙

neck·tie /ˈnektaɪ/ *noun* (*old-fashioned* or *NAmE*) = TIE *n.* (1)

necro·man·cer /ˈnekrəʊmænsə(r); *NAmE* ˈnekroʊ-/ *noun* a person who claims to communicate by magic with people who are dead 通靈者；巫師

necro·mancy /ˈnekrəʊmænsi; *NAmE* ˈnekroʊ-/ *noun* [U] **1** the practice of claiming to communicate by magic with the dead in order to learn about the future 通靈術；巫術 **2** the use of magic powers, especially evil ones 妖術；巫術

necro·philia /ˌnekrəˈfɪliə/ *noun* [U] sexual interest in dead bodies 戀屍癖 ▸ **necro·phil·iac** *noun*

ne·crop·olis /nəˈkrɒpəlɪs; *NAmE* -ˈkrɑːp-/ *noun* (*pl.* **ne·crop·olises** /-lɪsɪz/) a CEMETERY (= place where dead people are buried), especially a large one in an ancient city 墓場；（尤指古代城市的）大墓地

nec·ropsy /ˈnekrɒpsi; *NAmE* ˈnekrɑːpsi/ *noun* (*pl.* **-ies**) (*NAmE*) an official examination of a dead body (especially that of an animal) in order to discover the cause of death （尤指對動物的）屍體剖驗，屍檢 **SYN** **autopsy**

ne·cro·sis /neˈkrəʊsɪs; *NAmE* -ˈkroʊ-/ *noun* [U] (*medical* 醫) the death of most or all of the cells in an organ or TISSUE caused by injury, disease, or a loss of blood supply （器官或組織細胞的）壞死

nec·tar /ˈnektə(r)/ *noun* [U] **1** a sweet liquid that is produced by flowers and collected by BEES for making HONEY 花蜜：(*figurative*) *On such a hot day, even water was nectar* (= very good). 這麼熱的天，清水都是甘露。 **2** the thick juice of some fruits as a drink 果汁飲料：*peach nectar* 桃汁

nec·tar·ine /ˈnektəriːn/ *noun* a round red and yellow fruit, like a PEACH with smooth skin 油桃（桃的變種，果皮光滑）

née /neɪ/ *adj.* (from *French*) a word used after a married woman's name to introduce the family name that she had when she was born （用於已婚婦女姓名後，其娘家姓前）原姓的，娘家姓的：*Jane Smith, née Brown* 簡•史密斯，原姓布朗

need 🔑 /niːd/ *verb, modal verb, noun*

■ ***verb*** **1** 🔑 to require sth/sb because they are essential or very important, not just because you would like to have them 需要；必需：**~ sth/sb** *Do you need any help?* 你需要幫忙嗎？◇ *It's here if you need it.* 你要的話就拿去吧。◇ *Don't go—I might need you.* 別走，我可能要你幫忙。◇ *They **badly needed** a change.* 他們迫切需要變革。◇ *Food aid is urgently needed.* 迫切需要食物援助。◇ *What do you need your own computer for? You can use ours.* 你幹嗎還要自己買電腦？你可以用我們的。◇ *I don't need your comments, thank you.* 謝謝，我不需要你來評頭論足。◇ **~ to do sth** *I need to get some sleep.* 我需要睡會兒覺。◇ *He needs to win this game to stay in the match.* 他得贏下這場比賽以免被淘汰出局。◇ *You don't need to leave yet, do you?* 你不必現在就走吧？◇ *This shirt needs to be washed.* 這件襯衣該洗了。◇ **~ doing sth** *This shirt needs washing.* 這件襯衣該洗了。 **2** 🔑 **~ to do sth** used to show what you should or have to do （表示應該或不得不做）有必要：*All you need to do is complete this form.* 你要做的就是填好這個表格。◇ *I didn't need to go to the bank after all—Mary lent me the money.* 我最終不用去銀行，瑪麗借我錢了。 ➲ note at MODAL

IDM **need (to have) your 'head examined** (*informal*) to be crazy 發瘋

■ ***modal verb*** 🔑 (*negative* **need not**, *short form* **needn't** /ˈniːdnt/) used to state that sth is/was not necessary or that only very little is/was necessary; used to ask if sth is/was necessary （表示沒有必要或詢問是否有必要）需要：**~ (not) do sth** *You needn't bother asking Rick—I know he's too busy.* 你不必費神去問里克，我知道他太忙了。◇ *I **need hardly** tell you* (= you must already know) *that the work is dangerous.* 這工作很危險，這就不用我說了。◇ *If she wants anything, she **need only** ask.* 她想要什麼東西，只要開一下口就行了。◇ ***All you need** bring are sheets.* 你需要帶的就是牀單。◇ **~ (not) have done sth** *You needn't have worried* (= it was not necessary for you to worry, but you did)*—it all turned out fine.* 你本不必擔心，一切都很順利。◇ ***Need you** have paid so much?* 你用得着花那麼多錢嗎？

■ ***noun*** **1** 🔑 [sing., U] a situation when sth is necessary or must be done 需要；必須：*to **satisfy/meet/identify a need*** 滿足／迎合／看出某種需要◇ **~ (for sth)** *There is an urgent need for qualified teachers.* 迫切需要合資格教師。◇ *We will contact you again if the need arises.* 如果有必要，我們會再次和你聯繫。◇ *The house is **in need of** a thorough clean.* 這房子需要來個大掃除。◇ **~ (for sb/sth) to do sth** *There is **no need** for you to get up early tomorrow.* 你明天不必早起。◇ *I **had no need to** open the letter—I knew what it would say.* 我沒必要拆開那封信，我知道裏面會說些什麼。◇ *There's no need to cry* (= stop crying). 不要哭了。 **2** 🔑 [C, U] a strong feeling that you want sb/sth or must have sth 特別需要；迫切要求：*to fulfil an emotional need* 滿足感情的迫切需要◇ *She felt the need to talk to someone.* 她特別想和人聊聊。◇ *I'm **in need of** some fresh air.* 我很想呼吸一點新鮮空氣。◇ *She **had no more need of** me.* 她再也不需要我了。 **3** 🔑 [C, usually pl.] the things that sb requires in order to live in a comfortable way or achieve what they want 需要的事物；慾望：*financial needs* 經濟上的需要◇ *a programme to **suit** your individual **needs*** 滿足你個人需要的程序◇ *to **meet** children's special educational **needs*** 滿足兒童特殊教育的需要 **4** 🔑 [U] the state of not having enough food, money or support （食物、錢或生活來源的）短缺，缺乏 **SYN** **hardship**：*The charity aims to provide assistance to people **in need**.* 這個慈善機構的宗旨是向貧困者提供幫助。◇ *He helped me in my **hour of need**.* 在我生活困難的時候他幫助了我。 ➲ see also NEEDY

N

IDM **if need 'be** if necessary 如果需要的話；有必要的話： *There's always food in the freezer if need be.* 如果需要，冰箱裏總有食物。 ➲ more at CRYING *adj.*, FRIEND

Grammar Point 語法說明

need

- There are two separate verbs **need**. 有兩個各不相同的動詞 need。
- **Need** as a main verb has the question form **do you need?**, the negative **you don't need** and the past forms **needed**, **did you need?** and **didn't need**. It has two meanings. * need 作主要動詞時，疑問式為 do you need?，否定式為 you don't need，過去時為 needed、did you need? 和 didn't need。其含義有二： 1. to require something or to think that something is necessary 需要或認為有必要： *Do you need any help?* 你需要幫助嗎？ ◇ *I needed to get some sleep.* 我需要睡一會兒。 2. to have to or to be obliged to do sth 必須或一定要： *Will we need to show our passports?* 我們要出示護照嗎？
- **Need** as a modal verb has **need** for all forms of the present tense, **need you?** as the question form and **need not** (**needn't**) as the negative. The past is **need have**, **needn't have**. It is used to say that something is or is not necessary. * need 作情態動詞時，現在時均作 need，疑問式為 need you?，否定式為 need not (needn't)，過去時為 need have、needn't have，用以表示某事有必要或沒有必要： *Need I pay the whole amount now?* 我現在必須全部付清嗎？

N

'need-blind *adj.* (*US*) (of a university's or college's policy of choosing which people to offer places on a course of study 大學招生政策) depending only on sb's academic ability, without considering their ability to pay for it 不考慮經濟能力的（僅依據學生能力）： *a need-blind admissions policy* 不考慮經濟能力的錄取政策

need·ful /'ni:dfl/ *adj.* (*old-fashioned*) necessary 必要的；必需的；必然的

nee·dle 🔑 /'ni:dl/ *noun, verb*

■ *noun* [C]

▸ **FOR SEWING 縫紉** **1** 🔑 a small thin piece of steel that you use for sewing, with a point at one end and a hole for the thread at the other 針；縫衣針： *a* ***needle and thread*** 針和線 ◇ *the eye* (= hole) *of a needle* 針眼 ➲ **VISUAL VOCAB** page V41 ➲ see also PINS AND NEEDLES

▸ **FOR KNITTING 編織** **2** 🔑 a long thin piece of plastic or metal with a point at one end that you use for knitting. You usually use two together. 編織針： *knitting needles* 編織針 ➲ **VISUAL VOCAB** page V41

▸ **FOR DRUGS 藥品** **3** 🔑 a very thin, pointed piece of steel used on the end of a SYRINGE for putting a drug into sb's body, or for taking blood out of it 注射針；針頭： *a hypodermic needle* 皮下注射器針頭

▸ **ON INSTRUMENT 儀器** **4** 🔑 a thin piece of metal on a scientific instrument that moves to point to the correct measurement or direction 指針： *The compass needle was pointing north.* 羅盤指針指向北方。

▸ **ON PINE TREE 松樹** **5** [usually pl.] the thin, hard, pointed leaf of a PINE tree 松針；針葉 ➲ **VISUAL VOCAB** page V10

▸ **ON RECORD PLAYER 唱機** **6** the very small pointed piece of metal that touches a record that is being played in order to produce the sound 唱針；磁針 **SYN** **stylus**

IDM **a needle in a 'haystack** a thing that is almost impossible to find 草垛裏的針；幾乎不可能找到的東西： *Searching for one man in this city is like looking for a needle in a haystack.* 在這個城市裏找一個人無異於大海撈針。

■ *verb* **~ sb** (*informal*) to deliberately annoy sb, especially by criticizing them continuously 刺激；故意招惹；（尤指）不斷地數落 **SYN** **antagonize** : *Don't let her needle you.* 別讓她數落你。

needle·cord /'ni:dlkɔ:d; *NAmE* -kɔ:rd/ *noun* [U] (*BrE*) a type of fine CORDUROY 優質燈芯絨；細條紋光面呢

needle·point /'ni:dlpɔɪnt/ *noun* [U] a type of decorative sewing in which you use very small STITCHES to make a picture on strong cloth 針繡；帆布刺繡

need·less /'ni:dləs/ *adj.* **needless** death or suffering is not necessary because it could have been avoided 不必要的；可以避免的 **SYN** **unnecessary** : *needless suffering* 不必要的痛苦 ◇ *Banning smoking would save needless deaths.* 禁止吸煙會免除不必要的死亡。 ▸ **need·less·ly** *adv.* : *Many soldiers died needlessly.* 許多戰士白白地犧牲了。 ◇ *The process was needlessly slow.* 進程過於緩慢了。

IDM **,needless to 'say** used to emphasize that the information you are giving is obvious 不必說；不用說： *The problem, needless to say, is the cost involved.* 不用說，問題是所涉及的費用。

needle·woman /'ni:dlwʊmən/ *noun* (*pl.* **-women** /-wɪmɪn/) a woman who sews well 縫紉女工；女裁縫；擅做針線活的女子

needle·work /'ni:dlwɜ:k; *NAmE* -wɜ:rk/ *noun* [U] things that are sewn by hand, especially for decoration; the activity of making things by sewing 縫製品；刺繡品；女紅；針線活

needn't /'ni:dnt/ *short form* need not 不用；不必

needs /ni:dz/ *adv.* (*old use*) in a way that cannot be avoided 必定；必須： *We must needs depart.* 我們必須離開。

IDM **needs 'must (when the Devil drives)** (*saying*) in certain situations it is necessary for you to do sth that you do not like or enjoy（情勢所迫）只好如此；不得已而為之

need-to-'know *adj.*

IDM **on a ,need-to-'know basis** with people being told only the things they need to know when they need to know them, and no more than that 僅限於人們需要知道的範圍： *Information will be released strictly on a need-to-know basis.* 資訊發佈將嚴格限制在人們需要知道的範圍之內。

needy /'ni:di/ *adj.* (**need·ier**, **needi·est**) **1** (of people 人) not having enough money, food, clothes, etc. 缺乏生活必需品的；貧困的 ➲ **SYNONYMS** at POOR **2** **the needy** *noun* [pl.] people who do not have enough money, food, etc. 窮困的人 **3** (of people 人) not confident, and needing a lot of love and emotional support from other people 缺乏自信的；需要精神支持的

neep /ni:p/ *noun* (*ScotE, informal*) a SWEDE (= a large round yellow root vegetable) 蕪菁： *neeps and tatties* 蕪菁和土豆

ne'er /neə(r); *NAmE* ner/ *adv.* (*literary*) = NEVER

'ne'er-do-well *noun* (*old-fashioned*) a useless or lazy person 無用的人；懶漢

ne·fari·ous /nɪ'feəriəs; *NAmE* -'fer-/ *adj.* (*formal*) criminal; immoral 罪惡的；不道德的： *nefarious activities* 罪惡活動

neg. *abbr.* NEGATIVE

neg·ate **AW** /nɪ'geɪt/ *verb* (*formal*) **1 ~ sth** to stop sth from having any effect 取消；使無效 **SYN** **nullify** : *Alcohol negates the effects of the drug.* 酒精能使藥物失效。 **2 ~ sth** to state that sth does not exist 否定；否認

neg·ation /nɪ'geɪʃn/ *noun* (*formal*) **1** [C, usually sing., U] the exact opposite of sth; the act of causing sth not to exist or to become its opposite 反面；對立面；否定： *This political system was the negation of democracy.* 這種政治制度是對民主的否定。 **2** [U] disagreement or refusal 否定；拒絕： *She shook her head in negation.* 她搖頭表示拒絕。

nega·tive 🔑 **AW** /'negətɪv/ *adj., noun, verb*

■ *adj.*

▸ **BAD 壞** **1** 🔑 bad or harmful 壞的；有害的： *The crisis had a* ***negative effect on*** *trade.* 這次危機對貿易產生了很壞的影響。 ◇ *The whole experience was definitely more positive than negative.* 整個經歷當然是利多於弊。 **OPP** **positive**

▸ **NOT HOPEFUL 不樂觀 2** considering only the bad side of sth/sb; lacking enthusiasm or hope 消極的；負面的；缺乏熱情的：*Scientists have a fairly **negative attitude** to the theory.* 科學家對這個理論的態度是相當消極的。◇ *'He probably won't show up.' 'Don't be so negative.'* "他很可能不會露面。" "別那麼泄氣嘛。" **OPP positive**

▸ **NO 不 3** expressing the answer 'no' 否定的：*His response was negative.* 他的回答是否定的。◇ *They received a negative reply.* 他們得到一個否定的答覆。**OPP affirmative**

▸ **GRAMMAR 語法 4** containing a word such as 'no', 'not', 'never', etc. 含有否定詞的；否定的：*a **negative form/sentence*** 否定形式／句

▸ **SCIENTIFIC TEST 化驗 5** (*abbr.* **neg.**) not showing any evidence of a particular substance or medical condition 結果為陰性的（或否定的）：*Her pregnancy test was negative.* 她的孕檢呈陰性。**OPP positive**

▸ **ELECTRICITY 電 6** (*technical* 術語) containing or producing the type of electricity that is carried by an ELECTRON 負極的；陰極的：*a **negative charge/current*** 負電荷／電流 ◇ *the negative terminal of a battery* 電池的陰極 **OPP positive**

▸ **NUMBER/QUANTITY 數量 7** less than zero 負的；小於零的：*a negative trade balance* 貿易逆差 **OPP positive**
▸ **nega·tive·ly** AW *adv.*：*to react negatively to stress* 對壓力反應消極 ◇ *to respond negatively* 作出否定的回應 ◇ *negatively charged electrons* 帶負電荷的電子

■ **noun**

▸ **NO 不 1** a word or statement that means 'no'; a refusal or DENIAL 否定詞；否定；拒絕：(*formal*) *She answered **in the negative*** (= said 'no'). 她作了否定的回答。**OPP affirmative**

▸ **IN PHOTOGRAPHY 攝影 2** a developed film showing the dark areas of an actual scene as light and the light areas as dark 底片；負片 ➲ compare POSITIVE *n.* (2)

▸ **IN SCIENTIFIC TEST 化驗 3** the result of a test or an experiment that shows that a substance or condition is not present 屬陰性（或否定）的結果：*The percentage of **false negatives** generated by the cancer test is of great concern.* 癌症檢查的結果中，假陰性佔一定比例的現象受到極大關注。**OPP positive**

■ **verb** (*formal*) **1 ~ sth** to refuse to agree to a proposal or a request 拒絕；否定 **2 ~ sth** to prove that sth is not true 否定…的真實性；證偽

ˌnegative ˈequity *noun* [U] the situation in which the value of sb's house is less than the amount of money that is still owed to a MORTGAGE company, such as a bank 資產負值，負資產（資產值低於抵押款）

nega·tiv·ity /ˌnegəˈtɪvəti/ (also **nega·tiv·ism** /ˈnegətɪvɪzəm/) *noun* [U] (*formal*) a tendency to consider only the bad side of sth/sb; a lack of enthusiasm or hope 否定性；消極性

neg·lect /nɪˈglekt/ *verb, noun*

■ **verb 1 ~ sb/sth** to fail to take care of sb/sth 疏於照顧；未予看管：*She denies neglecting her baby.* 她否認沒有照看好她的孩子。◇ *The buildings had been neglected for years.* 這些大樓多年來一直無人看管。**2 ~ sth** to not give enough attention to sth 忽略；忽視；不予重視：*Dance has been neglected by television.* 電視節目一向不重視舞蹈。◇ *She has neglected her studies.* 她忽視了自己的學習。**3 ~ to do sth** (*formal*) to fail or forget to do sth that you ought to do 疏忽；疏漏 **SYN omit**：*You neglected to mention the name of your previous employer.* 你遺漏了你前雇主的名字。➲ see also NEGLIGENCE

■ **noun** [U] **~ (of sth/sb)** the fact of not giving enough care or attention to sth/sb; the state of not receiving enough care or attention 忽略；忽視；未被重視：*The law imposes penalties for the neglect of children.* 法律對疏於照管兒童有處罰措施。◇ *The buildings are crumbling from **years of neglect**.* 由於多年無人維修，這些建築物行將倒塌。◇ *The place smelled of decay and neglect.* 這地方有一股污濁腐朽的氣味。

neg·lect·ed /nɪˈglektɪd/ *adj.* not receiving enough care or attention 被忽略的；被忽視的；未被重視的：*neglected children* 無人照看的孩子 ◇ *a neglected area of research* 被人忽略了的研究領域

neg·lect·ful /nɪˈglektfl/ *adj.* (*formal*) not giving enough care or attention to sb/sth 馬虎的；不重視的；忽視的：*neglectful parents* 漫不經心的父母 ◇ **~ of sth/sb** *She became neglectful of her appearance.* 她變得不修邊幅起來。

neg·ligee (also **neg·ligée**) /ˈneglɪʒeɪ; *NAmE* ˌneglɪˈʒeɪ/ *noun* a woman's DRESSING GOWN made of very thin cloth（質地輕薄的）女式晨衣

neg·li·gence /ˈneglɪdʒəns/ *noun* [U] (*law* 律 or *formal*) the failure to give sb/sth enough care or attention 疏忽；失職；失誤；過失：*The accident was caused by negligence on the part of the driver.* 事故是由於司機的過失造成的。◇ *The doctor was sued for medical negligence.* 這名醫生因為引致醫療事故而被起訴。

neg·li·gent /ˈneglɪdʒənt/ *adj.* **1** (*law* 律 or *formal*) failing to give sb/sth enough care or attention, especially when this has serious results 疏忽的；造成過失的：*The school had been negligent in not informing the child's parents about the incident.* 校方疏忽了，沒有向這孩子的父母通報這件事。◇ *grossly negligent* 嚴重失職 **2** (*literary*) (of a person or their manner 人及其舉止) relaxed; not formal or awkward 放鬆的；隨便的；不拘謹的 **SYN nonchalant**：*He waved his hand in a negligent gesture.* 他漫不經心地揮了揮手。▸ **neg·li·gent·ly** *adv.*：*The defendant drove negligently and hit a lamp post.* 被告不小心駕駛，撞到一根路燈柱上了。◇ *She was leaning negligently against the wall.* 她很隨便地斜倚着牆。

neg·li·gible /ˈneglɪdʒəbl/ *adj.* of very little importance or size and not worth considering 微不足道的；不重要的；不值一提的 **SYN insignificant**：*The cost was negligible.* 費用不大，無關緊要。◇ *a negligible amount* 很小的量

ne·go·ti·able /nɪˈgəʊʃiəbl; *NAmE* -ˈgoʊ-/ *adj.* **1** that you can discuss or change before you make an agreement or a decision 可協商的；可討論的：*The terms of employment are negotiable.* 雇用的條件可以協商。◇ *The price was not negotiable.* 價格沒有商量的餘地。**2** (*business* 商) that you can exchange for money or give to another person in exchange for money 流通的；可兌現的；可轉讓的 **OPP non-negotiable**

ne·go·ti·ate /nɪˈgəʊʃieɪt; *NAmE* -ˈgoʊ-/ *verb* **1** [I] **~ (with sb) (for/about sth)** to try to reach an agreement by formal discussion 談判；磋商；協商：*The government will not negotiate with terrorists.* 政府不會和恐怖分子談判。◇ *We have been negotiating for more pay.* 我們一直在為增加工資進行協商。◇ *a strong negotiating position* 強硬的談判立場 ◇ *negotiating skills* 談判技巧 **2** [T] **~ sth** to arrange or agree sth by formal discussion 商定；達成協議：*to **negotiate a deal/contract/treaty/settlement*** 達成交易；確立合同；商定條約內容／解決措施 ◇ *We successfully negotiated the release of the hostages.* 我們成功地達成了釋放人質的協議。**3** [T] **~ sth** (*formal*) to successfully get over or past a difficult part on a path or route 通過，越過（險要路段）：*The climbers had to negotiate a steep rock face.* 攀登者必須攀越陡峭的岩壁。

the neˈgotiating table *noun* [sing.] (used mainly in newspapers 主要用於報章) a formal discussion to try and reach an agreement 談判桌（指正式的談判會議）：*We want to get all the parties back to the negotiating table.* 我們想把有關各方拉回到談判桌上來。

ne·go·ti·ation /nɪˌgəʊʃiˈeɪʃn; *NAmE* -ˌgoʊʃi-/ *noun* [C, usually pl., U] formal discussion between people who are trying to reach an agreement 談判；磋商；協商：***peace/trade/wage, etc. negotiations*** 和談、貿易洽談、工資談判等 ◇ *They begin another **round of negotiations** today.* 他們今天開始另一輪的談判。◇ *to **enter into/open/conduct negotiations** with sb* 和某人開始／展開／進行談判 ◇ *The rent is a **matter for negotiation** between the landlord and the tenant.* 租金可以由房東和租戶協商確定。◇ *A contract is prepared **in negotiation with** our clients.* 我們和客戶協商起草了一份合同。◇ *The issue is still **under negotiation**.* 這個問題還在商討之中。◇ *The price is generally **open to negotiation**.* 一般來講，價格可以商量。➲ COLLOCATIONS at INTERNATIONAL

ne·go·ti·ator /nɪˈgəʊʃieɪtə(r); *NAmE* -ˈgoʊʃi-/ *noun* a person who is involved in formal political or financial discussions, especially because it is their job 談判代表；協商者

Ne·gress /ˈniːɡres/ *noun* (*old-fashioned*, often *offensive*) a Negro woman or girl 黑人女子

neg·ri·tude /ˈneɡrɪtjuːd; *NAmE* -tuːd; *NAmE* also ˈniː-/ *noun* [U] (*formal*) the quality or fact of being of black African origin 非裔黑人特徵；非裔黑人血統

Negro /ˈniːɡrəʊ; *NAmE* -ɡroʊ/ *noun* (*pl.* **-oes**) (*old-fashioned*, often *offensive*) a member of a race of people with dark skin who originally came from Africa 黑人

ˌNegro ˈspiritual *noun* = SPIRITUAL

neigh /neɪ/ *verb* [I] when a horse **neighs** it makes a long high sound（馬）嘶鳴 ▶ **neigh** *noun*

neigh·bour (*especially US* **neigh·bor**) /ˈneɪbə(r)/ *noun*
1 a person who lives next to you or near you 鄰居；鄰人：*We've had a lot of support from all our* ***friends and neighbours***. 我們得到了朋友和鄰里的很多照顧。◇ *Our* ***next-door neighbours*** *are very noisy.* 我們隔壁的鄰居非常吵。**2** a country that is next to or near another country 鄰國：*What is Britain's nearest neighbour?* 英國最近的鄰國是哪個國家？**3** a person or thing that is standing or located next to another person or thing 身邊的人；靠近的東西；鄰近的人（或物）：*Stand quietly, children, and try not to talk to your neighbour.* 孩子們，站好，保持安靜，不要交頭接耳。◇ *The tree fell slowly, its branches caught in those of its neighbours.* 這棵樹慢慢地倒下，枝杈和旁邊的樹交錯在一起了。**4** (*literary*) any other human 他人；世人：*We should all love our neighbours.* 我們都要愛鄰人。

neigh·bour·hood (*especially US* **neigh·bor·hood**) /ˈneɪbəhʊd; *NAmE* ˈneɪbər-/ *noun*
1 a district or an area of a town; the people who live there 街區；城區；（統稱）某街區（或城區）的居民：*We grew up in the same neighbourhood.* 我們是在同一條街上長大的。◇ *a poor/quiet/residential neighbourhood* 貧困的街區；安靜的城區；住宅區 ◇ *Manhattan is divided into distinct neighborhoods.* 曼哈頓分為幾個區，風格各異。◇ *the neighbourhood police* 社區警察 ◇ *He shouted so loudly that the whole neighbourhood could hear him.* 他叫得那麼大聲，整條街的人都能聽到。**2** the area that you are in or the area near a particular place 所在地；鄰近的地方 SYN **vicinity**：*We searched the surrounding neighbourhood for the missing boy.* 我們在附近尋找失踪的男孩兒。◇ *Houses* ***in the neighbourhood*** *of Paris are extremely expensive.* 巴黎附近一帶的住房極其昂貴。
IDM **in the neighbourhood of** (of a number or an amount 數量) approximately; not exactly 大約；上下：*It cost in the neighbourhood of $500.* 這大約花費了500元。

ˌneighbourhood ˈwatch (*especially US* **ˌneighborhood ˈwatch**) *noun* [U] an arrangement by which a group of people in an area watch each other's houses regularly as a way of preventing crime 鄰里守護制（鄰居定期相互照看住宅，防止犯罪）

neigh·bour·ing (*especially US* **neigh·bor·ing**) /ˈneɪbərɪŋ/ *adj.* [only before noun] located or living near or next to a place or person 鄰近的；附近的；毗鄰的：*a neighbouring house* 附近的房子 ◇ *neighbouring towns* 毗鄰的城鎮 ◇ *a neighbouring farmer* 鄰近的農場主

neigh·bour·ly (*especially US* **neigh·bor·ly**) /ˈneɪbəli; *NAmE* -bərli/ *adj.* **1** involving people, countries, etc. that live or are located near each other 鄰近的；接壤的；住在附近的：*the importance of good neighbourly relations between the two states* 這兩國間睦鄰友好關係的重要性 ◇ *neighbourly help* 鄰里間的幫助 ◇ *a neighbourly dispute* 鄰居間的紛爭 **2** friendly and helpful 友好的；樂於助人的 SYN **kind**：*It was a neighbourly gesture of theirs.* 這是他們友好的表示。▶ **neigh·bour·li·ness** (*especially US* **neighbor·li·ness**) *noun* [U]：*good neighbourliness* 睦鄰關係 ◇ *a sense of community and neighbourliness* 社區互助意識

nei·ther /ˈnaɪðə(r); ˈniːðə(r)/ *det., pron., adv.*
■ *det., pron.* not one nor the other of two things or people 兩者都不：*Neither answer is correct.* 兩個答案都不對。◇ ***Neither of them*** *has/have a car.* 他們兩個都沒有汽車。◇ *They produced two reports,* ***neither of which*** *contained any useful suggestions.* 他們提交了兩個報告，都沒有任何有用的建議。◇ *'Which do you like?' 'Neither. I think they're both ugly.'* "你喜歡哪一個？" "兩個都不喜歡。我覺得兩個都很難看。"
■ *adv.* **1** used to show that a negative statement is also true of sb/sth else（否定的陳述同樣適用於其他人或物）也不：*He didn't remember and* ***neither did I***. 他沒記住，我也忘了。◇ *I hadn't been to New York before and* ***neither had Jane***. 我以前沒有去過紐約，簡也沒去過。◇ *'I can't understand a word of it.'* ***'Neither can I.'*** "我一個字都弄不懂。" "我也是。" ◇ (*informal*) *'I don't know.'* ***'Me neither.'*** "我不知道。" "我也不知道。" **2** **neither ... nor ...** used to show that a negative statement is true of two things（否定的陳述適用於兩方面）既不…也不…：*I neither knew nor cared what had happened to him.* 我既不知道也不關心他出了什麼事。◇ *Their house is neither big nor small.* 他們的房子不大也不小。◇ *Neither the TV nor the video actually work/works.* 電視機和錄像機都壞了。

Grammar Point 語法說明

neither / either

- After **neither** and **either** you use a singular verb. * neither 和 either 後用單數動詞：*Neither candidate was selected for the job.* 申請這個工作的兩個候選人都未獲選上。
- **Neither of** and **either of** are followed by a plural noun or pronoun and a singular or plural verb. A plural verb is more informal. * neither of 和 either of 後接複數名詞或代詞加單數或複數動詞，用複數動詞較非正式：*Neither of my parents speaks/speak a foreign language.* 我的父母都不會說外語。
- When **neither** … **nor** … or **either** … **or** … are used with two singular nouns, the verb can be singular or plural. A plural verb is more informal. * neither … nor … 或 either … or … 與兩個單數名詞連用時，謂語動詞可用單數或複數；用複數動詞較非正式。

nel·son /ˈnelsn/ *noun* a move in which a WRESTLER stands behind his/her opponent, puts one or both arms underneath the opponent's arm(s) and holds the back of the opponent's neck. When done with one arm it is called a **half nelson**, and with both arms a **full nelson**. 肩下握頸（從背後通過腋下鉤住對手後頸的摔跤動作，分單臂握頸和雙臂握頸）

nema·tode /ˈnemətəʊd; *NAmE* -toʊd/ (also **ˌnematode ˈworm**) *noun* a WORM with a thin, tube-shaped body that is not divided into sections 線蟲，圓蟲（身體不分節）

nem·esis /ˈneməsɪs/ *noun* [U, sing.] (*formal*) punishment or defeat that is deserved and cannot be avoided 報應；應得的懲罰；不可避免的失敗

neo- /ˈniːəʊ; *NAmE* ˈniːoʊ/ *combining form* (in adjectives and nouns 構成形容詞和名詞) new; in a later form 新的；新式的：*neo-Georgian* 新喬治王朝時代風格的 ◇ *neo-fascist* 新法西斯主義者

neo·clas·sic·al /ˌniːəʊˈklæsɪkl; *NAmE* ˌniːoʊ-/ *adj.* [usually before noun] used to describe art and ARCHITECTURE that is based on the style of ancient Greece or Rome, or music, literature, etc. that uses traditional ideas or styles 新古典主義的

neo·co·lo·nial·ism /ˌniːəʊkəˈləʊniəlɪzəm; *NAmE* ˌniːoʊkəˈloʊ-/ *noun* [U] (*disapproving*) the use of economic or political pressure by powerful countries to control or influence other countries 新殖民主義（強國通過施加經濟或政治壓力來控制或影響其他國家）

neo·con·ser·va·tive /ˌniːəʊkənˈsɜːvətɪv; *NAmE* ˌniːoʊkənˈsɜːrvətɪv/ *adj.* (*politics* 政) relating to political, economic, religious, etc. beliefs that return to traditional conservative views in a slightly changed form 新保守主義者的，新保守派的（在政治、經濟、宗教等信仰方面轉向傳統保守主義但形式稍有區別）▶ **neo·con·ser·va·tive** (also **neo·con**) *noun*

neo·cor·tex /ˌniːəʊˈkɔːteks; *NAmE* ˌniːoʊˈkɔːrteks/ *noun* (*anatomy* 解) part of the brain that controls sight and hearing（大腦）新皮質

neo·dym·ium /ˌniːəʊˈdɪmiəm; *NAmE* ˌniːoʊ-/ *noun* [U] (*symb.* **Nd**) a chemical element. Neodymium is a silver-white metal. 釹

neo·liberal /ˌniːəʊˈlɪbərəl; *NAmE* ˌniːoʊ-/ *adj.* [usually before noun] (*politics* 政) relating to a type of LIBERALISM that believes in a global free market, without government regulation, with businesses and industry controlled and run for profit by private owners 新自由主義的（主張不受政府調控的全球自由市場，工商企業由私有者經營以獲利）

Neo·lith·ic /ˌniːəˈlɪθɪk/ *adj.* of the later part of the STONE AGE 新石器時代的：*Neolithic stone axes* 新石器時代的石斧 ◇ *Neolithic settlements* 新石器時代的聚落

neolo·gism /niˈɒlədʒɪzəm; *NAmE* -ˈɑːl-/ *noun* (*formal*) a new word or expression or a new meaning of a word 新詞；新語彙；新義

neon /ˈniːɒn; *NAmE* ˈniːɑːn/ *noun* [U] (*symb.* **Ne**) a chemical element. Neon is a gas that does not react with anything and that shines with a bright light when electricity is passed through it. 氖；氖氣：***neon lights/signs*** 霓虹燈；霓虹燈廣告

neo·natal /ˌniːəʊˈneɪtl; *NAmE* ˌniːoʊ-/ *adj.* (*technical* 術語) connected with a child that has just been born 新生兒的：*the hospital's neonatal unit* 醫院的新生兒科 ◇ *neonatal care* 新生兒的護理

neo·nate /ˈniːəʊneɪt; *NAmE* ˈniːoʊ-/ *noun* (*medical* 醫) a baby that has recently been born, especially within the last four weeks（尤指出生不足四週的）新生兒

neo·phyte /ˈniːəfaɪt/ *noun* (*formal*) **1** a person who has recently started an activity 初學者；新手；生手：*The site gives neophytes the chance to learn from experts.* 這個網站給新手提供了向專家學習的機會。 **2** a person who has recently changed to a new religion 剛接受新宗教信仰的人；新皈依者 **3** a person who has recently become a priest or recently entered a religious order 新受聖職的司鐸；修會初學生

neo·prene /ˈniːəpriːn/ *noun* [U] an artificial material which looks like rubber, used for making WETSUITS 氯丁橡膠（用於製作潛水衣等的彈性合成橡膠）

NEPAD /ˈniːpæd/ *abbr.* (*SAfrE*) New Partnership for Africa's Development (= a plan decided by governments in Africa to help the continent's economy) 非洲發展新夥伴計劃（非洲各國政府制訂的促進非洲大陸經濟發展的計劃）

nephew 🔑 /ˈnefjuː; ˈnevjuː/ *noun* the son of your brother or sister; the son of your husband's or wife's brother or sister 姪子；外甥 ➲ compare NIECE

ne plus ultra /ˌneɪ plʊs ˈʊltrɑː; *NAmE* ˈʊltrə/ *noun* (from *Latin, formal*) the perfect example of sth 完美的範例；典範；典型

nepo·tism /ˈnepətɪzəm/ *noun* [U] (*disapproving*) giving unfair advantages to your own family if you are in a position of power, especially by giving them jobs 裙帶關係；任人唯親

Nep·tune /ˈneptjuːn; *NAmE* also -tuːn/ *noun* a planet in the SOLAR SYSTEM that is 8th in order of distance from the sun 海王星

nep·tun·ium /nepˈtjuːniəm; *NAmE* also -ˈtuːn-/ *noun* [U] (*symb.* **Np**) a chemical element. Neptunium is a RADIOACTIVE metal. 鎿（放射性化學元素）

nerd /nɜːd; *NAmE* nɜːrd/ *noun* (*informal, disapproving*) **1** a person who is boring, stupid and not fashionable 令人厭煩的人；愚蠢的人；落伍的人 **2** a person who is very interested in computers 電腦迷 SYN **geek** ▶ **nerdy** *adj.*

nerve 🔑 /nɜːv; *NAmE* nɜːrv/ *noun, verb*

■ *noun* **1** 🔑 [C] any of the long threads that carry messages between the brain and parts of the body, enabling you to move, feel pain, etc. 神經：*the optic nerve* 視神經 ◇ *nerve cells* 神經元 ◇ *nerve endings* 神經末梢 ◇ *Every nerve in her body was tense.* 她的每一根神經都繃得緊緊的。 ➲ VISUAL VOCAB page V59 **2** 🔑 **nerves** [pl.] feelings of worry or anxiety 神經質；神經緊張：*Even after years as a singer, he still suffers from nerves before a performance.* 儘管已做歌手多年，他在演出前仍然神經緊張。 ◇ *I need something to **calm/steady my nerves**.* 我需要點東西來穩定一下我的情緒。 ◇ *Everyone's **nerves were on edge*** (= everyone felt TENSE). 人人都覺得緊張。 ◇ *He **lives on his nerves*** (= is always worried). 他就愛神經緊張。 **3** [U] the courage to do sth difficult or dangerous 勇氣；氣魄 SYN **guts**：*It took a lot of nerve to take the company to court.* 將這個公司告上法庭需要極大的勇氣。 ◇ *I was going to have a go at parachuting but **lost my nerve** at the last minute.* 我想嘗試一下跳傘，可在最後關頭卻失去了勇氣。 ◇ *He **kept his nerve** to win the final set 6–4.* 他鼓足鬥志以 6 比 4 贏了最後一盤。 **4** [sing., U] (*informal*) a way of behaving that other people think is rude or not appropriate 魯莽；冒失；厚顏 SYN **cheek**：*I don't know how you **have the nerve** to show your face after what you said!* 真不知道你說了那些話以後怎麼還有臉露面！ ◇ *He's **got a nerve** asking us for money!* 他還腆着臉跟我們借錢！ ◇ *'Then she demanded to see the manager!' '**What a nerve!**'* "她還要求見經理！" "真不要臉！"

IDM **be a bag/bundle of ˈnerves** (*informal*) to be very nervous 非常緊張 **get on sb's ˈnerves** (*informal*) to annoy sb 煩擾；使心神不定 **have nerves of steel** to be able to remain calm in a difficult or dangerous situation 意志堅強；沉着冷靜 **hit/touch a (raw/sensitive) ˈnerve** to mention a subject that makes sb feel angry, upset, embarrassed, etc. 觸及要害；觸動痛處：*You touched a raw nerve when you mentioned his first wife.* 你談起他的第一任妻子，這就觸到了他的痛處。 ➲ more at BRASS, STRAIN *v.*, WAR

■ *verb* **~ yourself for sth/to do sth** to give yourself the courage or strength to do sth 鼓足勇氣；振作精神：*He nerved himself to ask her out.* 他鼓足勇氣去約她出來。

ˈnerve centre (*BrE*) (*NAmE* **ˈnerve center**) *noun* the place from which an activity or organization is controlled and instructions are sent out 神經中樞；控制中心

ˈnerve gas *noun* a poisonous gas used in war that attacks your CENTRAL NERVOUS SYSTEM 神經性毒氣，神經瓦斯（能損害神經系統正常功能）

nerve·less /ˈnɜːvləs; *NAmE* ˈnɜːrv-/ *adj.* **1** having no strength or feeling 無力的；麻木的：*The knife fell from her nerveless fingers.* 刀從她無力的手裏落下。 **2** having no fear 無畏的；鎮定從容的；勇敢的：*She is a nerveless rider.* 她是一位勇敢的騎手。 OPP **nervous**

ˈnerve-racking (also **ˈnerve-wracking**) *adj.* making you feel very nervous and worried 令人十分緊張的；令人焦慮不安的

ner·vous 🔑 /ˈnɜːvəs; *NAmE* ˈnɜːrvəs/ *adj.*

1 🔑 anxious about sth or afraid of sth 焦慮的；擔憂的；惶恐的：**~ (about/of sth)** *Consumers are very nervous about the future.* 消費者對未來非常憂慮。 ◇ *The horse may be nervous of cars.* 這匹馬可能害怕汽車。 ◇ **~ (about/of doing sth)** *He had been nervous about inviting us.* 他過去一直不敢邀請我們。 ◇ *I felt really nervous before the interview.* 面試前我感到惶恐不安。 ◇ ***a nervous glance/smile/voice*** (= one that shows that you feel anxious) 膽怯的一瞥／微笑／聲音 ◇ *By the time the police arrived, I was a **nervous wreck**.* 警察到達時，我已經緊張得不行了。 OPP **confident** ➲ SYNONYMS at WORRIED **2** 🔑 easily worried or frightened 神經質的；易緊張焦慮的；膽怯的：*She was a thin, nervous girl.* 她是個瘦削而又膽怯的女孩兒。 ◇ *He's not the nervous type.* 他不是那種好緊張的人。 ◇ *She was **of a nervous disposition**.* 她生性容易緊張。 **3** 🔑 connected with the body's nerves and often affecting you mentally or emotionally 神經系

統的： *a* ***nervous condition/disorder/disease*** 神經系統疾病；神經紊亂；神經症 ◇ *She was in a state of* ***nervous exhaustion.*** 她的神經處於極度疲勞狀態。 IDM see SHADOW *n.* ▶ **ner·vous·ly** *adv.*： *She smiled nervously.* 她露出不安的微笑。 **ner·vous·ness** *noun* [U]： *He tried to hide his nervousness.* 他試圖掩飾他的惶恐不安。

Synonyms 同義詞辨析

nervous

neurotic • on edge • jittery

These words all describe people who are easily frightened or are behaving in a frightened way. 以上各詞均形容人神經質、易緊張焦慮、膽怯。

nervous easily worried or frightened 指神經質的、易緊張焦慮的、膽怯的： *She was* ***of a nervous disposition.*** 她生性容易緊張。 NOTE See also the entry for **worried**. 另見 worried 詞條。

neurotic not behaving in a reasonable, calm way, because you are worried about sth 指神經質的、神經過敏的： *She became neurotic about keeping the house clean.* 她對保持房屋清潔有點神經質。

on edge nervous or bad-tempered 指緊張不安的、煩躁的、易怒的： *She was always on edge before an interview.* 她在面試前總是緊張不安。

jittery (*informal*) anxious and nervous 指緊張不安的、心神不寧的： *All this talk of job losses was making him jittery.* 所有這些關於失業的話題使他心神不寧。

PATTERNS

- a nervous/neurotic **man/woman/girl**
- to **feel** nervous/on edge/jittery
- **a bit** nervous/on edge/jittery

ˌnervous ˈbreakdown (also **break·down**) *noun* a period of mental illness in which sb becomes very depressed, anxious and tired, and cannot deal with normal life 神經衰弱： *to have a nervous breakdown* 患神經衰弱

ˈnervous system *noun* the system of all the nerves in the body 神經系統 ➲ see also CENTRAL NERVOUS SYSTEM

nervy /ˈnɜːvi; *NAmE* ˈnɜːrvi/ *adj.* (*informal*) **1** (*BrE*) anxious and nervous 焦慮的；緊張的 **2** (*NAmE*) brave and confident in a way that might offend other people, or show a lack of respect 大膽的；莽撞的

-ness *suffix* (in nouns 構成名詞) the quality, state or character of …的性質（或狀態、特點）： *dryness* 乾燥 ◇ *blindness* 失明 ◇ *silliness* 愚蠢

nest /nest/ *noun, verb*

■ *noun* **1** [C] a hollow place or structure that a bird makes or chooses for laying its eggs in and sheltering its young 鳥巢；鳥窩 ➲ VISUAL VOCAB page V12 **2** [C] a place where insects or other small creatures live and produce their young 巢穴；窩 **3** [sing.] a secret place which is full of bad people and their activities 藏匿處；秘密窩點： *a nest of thieves* 賊窩 **4** [sing.] the home, thought of as the safe place where parents bring up their children 家；安樂窩： ***to leave the nest*** (= leave your parents' home) 離開父母過獨立生活 ➲ see also EMPTY NEST **5** [C, usually sing.] a group or set of similar things that are made to fit inside each other（套疊在一起的）一套物件： *a nest of tables* 一套桌子 IDM see FEATHER *v.*, FLY *v.*, HORNET, MARE

■ *verb* **1** [I] to make and use a nest 築巢；巢居： *Thousands of seabirds are nesting on the cliffs.* 成千上萬的海鳥在懸崖上築巢。 **2** [T] **~ sth** (*technical* 術語) to put types of information together, or inside each other, so that they form a single unit 嵌套（信息）

ˈnest box (also **ˈnesting box**) *noun* a box provided for a bird to make its nest in 鳥巢箱；鳥舍箱

ˈnest egg *noun* (*informal*) a sum of money that you save to use in the future 備用的錢；儲備金

nes·tle /ˈnesl/ *verb* **1** [I] **+ adv./prep.** to sit or lie down in a warm or soft place 依偎；舒適地坐（或臥）： *He hugged her and she nestled against his chest.* 他擁抱着她，她則依偎在他的懷裏。 **2** [T] **~ sb/sth + adv./prep.** to put or hold sb/sth in a comfortable position in a warm or soft place 抱；安置： *He nestled the baby in his arms.* 他懷裏抱着孩子。 **3** [I] **+ adv./prep.** to be located in a position that is protected, sheltered or partly hidden 位處，坐落（於安全、隱蔽之處）： *The little town nestles snugly at the foot of the hill.* 這個小鎮偎依在小山腳下。

nest·ling /ˈnestlɪŋ/ *noun* a bird that is too young to leave the nest 雛鳥；未離巢的小鳥

net /net/ *noun, adj., verb*

■ *noun* **1** [U] a type of material that is made of string, thread or wire twisted or tied together, with small spaces in between 網；網狀物： *net curtains* 網眼簾子 ➲ see also FISHNET, NETTING **2** [C] (especially in compounds 尤用於構成複合詞) a piece of net used for a particular purpose, such as catching fish or covering sth 有專門用途的網： *fishing nets* 漁網 ◇ *a mosquito net* (= used to protect you from MOSQUITOES) 蚊帳 ➲ see also HAIRNET, SAFETY NET **3 the net** [sing.] (in sports 體育運動) the frame covered in net that forms the goal 球門網： *to kick the ball* ***into the back of the net*** 把球踢進網窩 **4 the net** [sing.] (in TENNIS, etc. 網球等) the piece of net between the two players that the ball goes over 球網 ➲ VISUAL VOCAB page V45 **5 the Net** (also **the net**) (*informal*) = THE INTERNET IDM see CAST *v.*, SLIP *v.*, SPREAD *v.*

■ *adj.* (*BrE* also **nett**) **1** [usually before noun] a **net** amount of money is the amount that remains when nothing more is to be taken away 淨得的；純的： *a* ***net profit*** *of £500* * 500 英鎊的純利潤 ◇ ***net income/earnings*** (= after tax has been paid) 純收入 ➲ compare GROSS *adj.* (1) **2** [only before noun] the **net** weight of sth is the weight without its container or the material it is wrapped in 淨的： *450 gms net weight* 淨重 450 克 ➲ compare GROSS *adj.* (1) **3** [only before noun] final, after all the important facts have been included 最後的；最終的： *The* ***net result*** *is that small shopkeepers are being forced out of business.* 最終結果是小店主被擠出了這個行業。 ◇ *Canada is now a substantial net importer of medicines* (= it imports more than it exports). 加拿大現在是一個藥物淨進口大國。 ◇ *a net gain* 最終收益 ▶ **net** *adv.*： *a salary of $50 000 net* * 5 萬元的稅後薪水 ◇ *Interest on the investment will be paid net* (= tax will already have been taken away). 投資的利息將按稅後的數額支付。 ➲ compare GROSS *adv.*

■ *verb* (**-tt-**) **1 ~ sth** to earn an amount of money as a profit after you have paid tax on it 淨賺；淨得： *The sale of paintings netted £17 000.* 賣畫淨得 17 000 英鎊。 **2 ~ sth** to catch sth, especially fish, in a net 用網捕捉（魚等） **3 ~ sb/sth** to catch sb or obtain sth in a skilful way（巧妙地）捕獲，得到： *A swoop by customs officers netted a large quantity of drugs.* 海關人員突擊搜查，緝獲大量毒品。 **4 ~ sth** (*especially BrE*) to kick or hit a ball into the goal（將球）踢入球門，射入球門 SYN **score**： *He has netted 21 goals so far this season.* 這個賽季至今他已射入 21 球。 **5 ~ sth** to cover sth with a net or nets 用網覆蓋

net·ball /ˈnetbɔːl/ *noun* [U] a game played by two teams of seven players, especially women or girls. Players score by throwing a ball through a high net hanging from a ring on a post.（尤指女子）無擋板籃球

net·book /ˈnetbʊk/ *noun* a small LAPTOP computer, designed especially for using the Internet and email 上網本；小筆電（尤用於上網和處理電子郵件的小型筆記本電腦） ➲ compare NOTEBOOK (3), SUBNOTEBOOK

ˌnet ˈcurtain (*BrE*) (*NAmE* **cur·tain**) *noun* a very thin curtain that you hang at a window, which allows light to enter but stops people outside from being able to see inside 網眼簾子

nether /ˈneðə(r)/ *adj.* [only before noun] (*literary* or *humorous*) lower 較低的；下方的：*a person's nether regions* (= their GENITALS) 人的下身

the neth·er·world /ˈneðəwɜːld; *NAmE* ˈneðərwɜːrld/ *noun* [sing.] (*literary*) the world of the dead 陰間；冥府；地獄 SYN **hell**

neti·quette /ˈnetɪket/ *noun* [U] (*informal, humorous*) the rules of correct or polite behaviour among people using the Internet 網絡禮儀

neti·zen /ˈnetɪzn/ *noun* (*informal, humorous*) a person who uses the Internet a lot 網民；網蟲；網迷；網路族

ˈNet surfer *noun* = SURFER (2)

nett *adj.* (*BrE*) = NET

net·ting /ˈnetɪŋ/ *noun* [U] material that is made of string, thread or wire twisted or tied together, with spaces in between 網；網狀材料：*wire netting* 金屬網

net·tle /ˈnetl/ *noun, verb*

■ *noun* (also **ˈstinging nettle**) a wild plant with leaves that have pointed edges, are covered in fine hairs and sting if you touch them 蕁麻 ➲ VISUAL VOCAB page V11 IDM see GRASP *v.*

■ *verb* [usually passive] **~ sb | it nettles sb that ...** (*informal, especially BrE*) to make sb slightly angry 使煩惱；使生氣 SYN **annoy**：*My remarks clearly nettled her.* 我的話顯然惹惱了她。

nettle·rash /ˈnetlræʃ/ *noun* [U] = URTICARIA

net·tle·some /ˈnetlsəm/ *adj.* (*especially NAmE*) causing trouble or difficulty 引起麻煩（或困難）的；棘手的；惱人的

net·work 🔑 AW /ˈnetwɜːk; *NAmE* -wɜːrk/ *noun, verb*

■ *noun* **1** 🔑 a complicated system of roads, lines, tubes, nerves, etc. that cross each other and are connected to each other 網絡；網狀系統：*a **rail/road/canal network*** 鐵路網；公路網；運河網 ◇ *a network of veins* 脈絡 **2** 🔑 a closely connected group of people, companies, etc. that exchange information, etc. 關係網；人際網；相互關係（或配合）的系統：*a **communications/distribution network*** 通信網；分銷網 ◇ *a network of friends* 朋友網 **3** 🔑 (*computing* 計) a number of computers and other devices that are connected together so that equipment and information can be shared（互聯）網絡，網路：*The office network allows users to share files and software, and to use a central printer.* 辦公室網絡讓用戶共享文件和軟件，並使用中央打印機。➲ see also LAN, WAN **4** 🔑 a group of radio or television stations in different places that are connected and that broadcast the same programmes at the same time 廣播網；電視網：*the four big US television networks* 美國四大電視網 IDM see OLD BOY

■ *verb* **1** [T] **~ sth** (*computing* 計) to connect a number of computers and other devices together so that equipment and information can be shared 將…連接成網絡 **2** [T] **~ sth** to broadcast a television or radio programme on stations in several different areas at the same time 聯播 **3** [I] to try to meet and talk to people who may be useful to you in your work 建立工作關係：*Conferences are a good place to network.* 各種會議是建立聯繫的好地方。

net·work·ing /ˈnetwɜːkɪŋ; *NAmE* -wɜːrk-/ *noun* [U] a system of trying to meet and talk to other people who may be useful to you in your work 人際關係網

neur·al /ˈnjʊərəl; *NAmE* ˈnʊrəl/ *adj.* (*technical* 術語) connected with a nerve or the NERVOUS SYSTEM 神經的；神經系統的：*neural processes* 神經系統的作用

neur·al·gia /njʊəˈrældʒə; *NAmE* nʊˈr-/ *noun* [U] (*medical* 醫) a sharp pain felt along a nerve, especially in the head or face（尤指頭部或面部）神經痛 ▶ **neur·al·gic** /njʊəˈrældʒɪk; *NAmE* nʊˈr-/ *adj.*

ˌneural ˈnetwork (also **ˌneural ˈnet**) *noun* (*computing* 計) a system with a structure which is similar to the human brain and nervous system 神經網絡

neur·as·the·nia /ˌnjʊərəsˈθiːniə; *NAmE* ˌnʊrəs-/ *noun* [U] (*old-fashioned*) a condition in which sb feels tired and depressed over a long period of time 神經衰弱

neuro- /ˈnjʊərəʊ; *NAmE* ˈnʊroʊ/ *combining form* (in nouns, adjectives and adverbs 構成名詞、形容詞和副詞) connected with the nerves 神經系統有關的：*neuroscience* 神經系統科學 ◇ *a neurosurgeon* 神經外科醫生

neuro·lin·guis·tic pro·gram·ming /ˌnjʊərəʊlɪŋˌɡwɪstɪk ˈprəʊɡræmɪŋ; *NAmE* ˌnʊroʊlɪŋˌɡwɪstɪk ˈproʊɡræmɪŋ/ (*abbr.* **NLP**) *noun* [U] (*psychology* 心) a technique that people use to help themselves or others think in a more positive way, and which uses neurolinguistics as its basis 神經語言程序技術；神經語言程式學

neuro·lin·guis·tics /ˌnjʊərəʊlɪŋˈɡwɪstɪks; *NAmE* ˌnʊroʊ-/ *noun* [U] (*psychology* 心) the study of the way the human brain processes language 神經語言學

neuro·logic·al /ˌnjʊərəˈlɒdʒɪkl; *NAmE* ˌnʊrəˈlɑːdʒ-/ *adj.* relating to nerves or to the science of NEUROLOGY 神經系統的；神經（病）學的：*neurological damage* 神經損傷

neurolo·gist /njʊəˈrɒlədʒɪst; *NAmE* nʊˈrɑːl-/ *noun* a doctor who studies and treats diseases of the nerves 神經病學家；神經科醫生

neurol·ogy /njʊəˈrɒlədʒi; *NAmE* nʊˈrɑːl-/ *noun* [U] the scientific study of nerves and their diseases 神經學；神經病學

neuron /ˈnjʊərɒn; *NAmE* ˈnʊrɑːn/ (also **neur·one** /ˈnjʊərəʊn; *NAmE* ˈnʊroʊn/ especially in *BrE*) *noun* (*biology* 生) a cell that carries information within the brain and between the brain and other parts of the body; a nerve cell 神經元 ➲ see also MOTOR NEURON DISEASE

neuro·physi·ology /ˌnjʊərəʊfɪziˈɒlədʒi; *NAmE* ˌnʊroʊfɪziˈɑːlədʒi/ *noun* [U] the scientific study of the normal functions of the NERVOUS SYSTEM 神經生理學

neuro·science /ˈnjʊərəʊsaɪəns; *NAmE* ˈnʊroʊ-/ *noun* [U] the science that deals with the structure and function of the brain and the NERVOUS SYSTEM 神經科學 ▶ **neuro·scientist** /-saɪəntɪst/ *noun*

neur·osis /njʊəˈrəʊsɪs; *NAmE* nʊˈroʊ-/ *noun* [C, U] (*pl.* **neur·oses** /-əʊsiːz; *NAmE* -oʊ-/) **1** (*medical* 醫) a mental illness in which a person suffers strong feelings of fear and worry 神經機能病；神經官能症；恐懼症 **2** any strong fear or worry 過分的恐懼（或焦慮）SYN **anxiety**

neuro·sur·gery /ˈnjʊərəʊsɜːdʒəri; *NAmE* ˈnʊroʊsɜːrdʒəri/ *noun* [U] medical operations performed on the nervous system, especially the brain 神經外科（學）

neur·ot·ic /njʊəˈrɒtɪk; *NAmE* nʊˈrɑː-/ *adj., noun*

■ *adj.* **1** caused by or suffering from neurosis 神經機能病的；神經官能症的：*neurotic obsessions* 神經症引起的強迫觀念 ➲ SYNONYMS at MENTALLY **2** not behaving in a reasonable, calm way, because you are worried about sth 神經質的；神經過敏的：*She became neurotic about keeping the house clean.* 她變得對保持房屋清潔有點神經質。◇ *a brilliant but neurotic actor* 傑出但有些神經質的男演員 ➲ SYNONYMS at NERVOUS ▶ **neur·ot·ic·al·ly** /-kli/ *adv.*

■ *noun* a neurotic person 神經官能症患者；神經質者

neuro·toxin /ˌnjʊərəʊˈtɒksɪn; *NAmE* ˌnʊroʊˈtɑːksɪn/ *noun* (*technical* 術語) a poison that affects the NERVOUS SYSTEM 神經毒素

neuro·trans·mit·ter /ˈnjʊərəʊtrænzmɪtə(r); *NAmE* ˈnʊroʊ-/ *noun* (*biology* 生) a chemical that carries messages from nerve cells to other nerve cells or muscles 神經遞質（在神經細胞間或向肌肉傳遞信息）

neu·ter /ˈnjuːtə(r); *NAmE* ˈnuːtər/ *adj., verb*

■ *adj.* (*grammar* 語法) (in some languages 用於某些語言) belonging to a class of nouns, pronouns, adjectives or verbs whose GENDER is not FEMININE or MASCULINE 中性的：*The Polish word for 'window' is neuter.* 波蘭語裏"窗戶"一詞是中性的。

■ *verb* **1 ~ sth** to remove part of the sex organs of an animal so that it cannot produce young 閹割（動物）：*Has your cat been neutered?* 你家的貓閹過了嗎？ **2 ~ sth** (*disapproving*) to prevent sth from having the effect that it ought to have 使失去作用

N

neu·tral AW /ˈnjuːtrəl; NAmE ˈnuː-/ *adj., noun*

■ ***adj.***

‣ **IN DISAGREEMENT/CONTEST 分歧；爭執** **1** not supporting or helping either side in a disagreement, competition, etc. 中立的；持平的；無傾向性的 SYN **impartial, unbiased**：*Journalists are supposed to be politically neutral.* 新聞工作者在政治上應持中立態度。◇ *I didn't take my father's or my mother's side; I tried to **remain neutral**.* 我既不支持父親也不袒護母親，盡力做到不偏不倚。

‣ **IN WAR 戰爭** **2** not belonging to any of the countries that are involved in a war; not supporting any of the countries involved in a war 中立國的；中立的：***neutral territory/waters*** 中立國的領土 / 水域 ◇ *Switzerland was neutral during the war.* 瑞士在戰爭期間保持了中立。

‣ **WITHOUT STRONG FEELING 不帶感情** **3** deliberately not expressing any strong feeling 中性的；不含褒貶義的：*'So you told her?' he said in a neutral tone of voice.* "那麼你告訴她了？" 他平靜地說。

‣ **COLOUR 色彩** **4** not very bright or strong, such as grey or light brown 素淨的；淡素的；不鮮豔的：*a neutral colour scheme* 中和色組合 ◇ *neutral tones* 淺色調

‣ **CHEMISTRY 化學** **5** neither acid nor ALKALINE 中性的；非酸性又非鹼性的

‣ **ELECTRICAL 與電有關** **6** (*abbr.* **N**) having neither a positive nor a negative electrical charge 中性的；不帶電的：*the neutral wire in a plug* 插頭上的不帶電的電線 ▸ **neu·tral·ly** /-rəli/ *adv.*

IDM **on neutral ground/territory** in a place that has no connection with either of the people or sides who are meeting and so does not give an advantage to either of them 在中立地區；在第三方地區：*We decided to meet on neutral ground.* 我們決定在第三方領土上會晤。

■ ***noun***

‣ **IN VEHICLE 車輛** **1** [U] the position of the gears of a vehicle in which no power is carried from the engine to the wheels（汽車排擋）空擋：*to leave the car **in neutral*** 將車的排擋置於空擋位

‣ **IN DISAGREEMENT/WAR 分歧；戰爭** **2** [C] a person or country that does not support either side in a disagreement, competition or war 中立者；中立國

‣ **COLOUR 色彩** **3** [C] a colour that is not bright or strong, such as grey or light brown 素淨色；中和色：*The room was decorated in neutrals.* 房間裝飾得素素淨淨。

neu·tral·ist /ˈnjuːtrəlɪst; NAmE ˈnuː-/ *noun* (*especially NAmE*) a person who does not support either side in a war 中立主義者 ▸ **neu·tral·ist** *adj.*：*a neutralist state* 中立國家

neu·tral·ity AW /njuːˈtræləti; NAmE nuː-/ *noun* [U] the state of not supporting either side in a disagreement, competition or war 中立；中立狀態

neu·tral·ize (*BrE* also **-ise**) AW /ˈnjuːtrəlaɪz; NAmE ˈnuː-/ *verb* **1 ~ sth** to stop sth from having any effect 使無效：*The latest figures should neutralize the fears of inflation.* 最新的數據應該可以消除對通貨膨脹的擔憂。**2 ~ sth** (*chemistry* 化) to make a substance NEUTRAL (5) 中和；使成為中性 **3 ~ sth** to make a country or an area NEUTRAL (2) 使中立 ▸ **neu·tral·iza·tion, -isa·tion** AW /ˌnjuːtrəlaɪˈzeɪʃn; NAmE ˌnuːtrələˈz-/ *noun* [U]

ˈ**neutral zone** *noun* **1** (in ICE HOCKEY 冰上曲棍球) an area that covers the central part of the RINK, between two blue lines 中立區 **2** (in AMERICAN FOOTBALL 美式足球) an imaginary area between the teams where no player except the CENTRE is allowed to step until play has started 中立區（比賽開始前對陣雙方之間球員不准進入的區域）

neu·trino /njuːˈtriːnəʊ; NAmE nuːˈtriːnoʊ/ *noun* (*pl.* **-os**) (*physics* 物) an extremely small PARTICLE that has no electrical charge, and which rarely reacts with other matter 中微子；微中子

neu·tron /ˈnjuːtrɒn; NAmE ˈnuːtrɑːn/ *noun* (*physics* 物) a very small piece of matter (= a substance) that carries no electric charge and that forms part of the NUCLEUS (= central part) of an atom 中子 ⊃ see also ELECTRON, PROTON

ˈ**neutron bomb** *noun* a bomb that can kill people by giving out neutrons, but does not cause a lot of damage to buildings 中子彈（可殺人，但對建築物損壞不大）

never 🔑 /ˈnevə(r)/ *adv., exclamation*

■ ***adv.*** **1** 🔑 not at any time; not on any occasion 從不；絕不；從未；未曾：*You never help me.* 你從不幫我。◇ *He has never been abroad.* 他從未出過國。◇ *'Would you vote for him?' 'Never.'* "你會投他一票嗎？" "決不。" ◇ *'I work for a company called Orion Technology.' 'Never heard of them.'* "我在一家名為奧里昂科技的公司工作。" "從來沒聽說過。" ◇ ***Never in all my life** have I seen such a horrible thing.* 我一輩子也沒見過這麼恐怖的事。◇ ***Never ever** tell anyone your password.* 不要把你的密碼告訴任何人。**2** 🔑 used to emphasize a negative statement instead of 'not'（與 not 同義，語氣較強）一點都不，從未：***I never knew** (= didn't know until now) you had a twin sister.* 我從來不知道你還有個雙胞胎姐姐。◇ (*especially BrE*) *Someone might find out, and that **would never do*** (= that is not acceptable). 也許有人會發現，那是絕對不行的。◇ *He **never so much as** smiled* (= did not smile even once). 他從未笑過。◇ (*especially BrE*) *'I told my boss exactly what I thought of her.' 'You never did!'* (= 'Surely you didn't!') "我對老闆說了我對她的真實看法。" "不可能！" ◇ (*BrE, slang*) *'You took my bike.' 'No, I never.'* "你把我的車騎走了吧。" "沒有，我沒騎。" ◇ (*old-fashioned* or *humorous*) ***Never fear*** (= Do not worry), *everything will be all right.* 別擔心，一切都會好的。

IDM **on the ˌnever-ˈnever** (*BrE, informal*) on HIRE PURCHASE (= by making payments over a long period) 以分期付款的方式：*to buy a new car on the never-never* 以分期付款的方式購買一輛新車 **Well, I never (did)!** (*old-fashioned*) used to express surprise or disapproval（表示驚奇或不贊同）不會吧，不行的

■ ***exclamation*** (*informal*) used to show that you are very surprised about sth because you do not believe it is possible（表示驚訝，因為覺得不可能）不會吧：*'I got the job.' 'Never!'* "我得到那份工作了。" "不可能吧！" IDM see MIND *v.*

ˌ**never-ˈending** *adj.* seeming to last for ever 永無止境的；沒完沒了的 SYN **endless, interminable**：*Housework is a never-ending task.* 家務活做起來真是沒完沒了。

never·more /ˌnevəˈmɔː(r); NAmE ˌnevərˈm-/ *adv.* (*old use*) never again 不再

ˌ**never-ˈnever land** *noun* [sing.] an imaginary place where everything is wonderful 虛妄的樂土；世外桃源

never·the·less 🔑 AW /ˌnevəðəˈles; NAmE -vərðə-/ *adv.* despite sth that you have just mentioned 儘管如此；不過；然而 SYN **nonetheless**：*There is little chance that we will succeed in changing the law. Nevertheless, it is important that we try.* 我們幾乎沒有可能改變法律。不過，重要的是我們要努力爭取。◇ *Our defeat was expected but it is disappointing nevertheless.* 我們的失敗是意料中的事，儘管如此，還是令人失望。

new 🔑 /njuː; NAmE nuː/ *adj.* (**newer, new·est**)

‣ **NOT EXISTING BEFORE 從前沒有** **1** 🔑 not existing before; recently made, invented, introduced, etc. 剛出現的；新的；新近推出的：*Have you read her new novel?* 你看過她新出的小說了嗎？◇ *new ways of doing things* 做事的新方法 ◇ *This idea isn't new.* 這主意不新鮮。◇ *The latest model has over 100 new features.* 最新的款式有 100 多種新特色。⊃ see also BRAND-NEW OPP **old 2 the new** *noun* [U] something that is new 新東西；新事物：*It was a good mix of the old and the new.* 這是新舊的完美結合。

‣ **RECENTLY BOUGHT 新買的** **3** 🔑 recently bought 新買的：*Let me show you my new dress.* 給你看看我新買的連衣裙。

‣ **NOT USED BEFORE 從未用過** **4** 🔑 not used or owned by anyone before 沒被用過的；未曾被人佔有過的；嶄新的：*A second-hand car costs a fraction of a new one.* 二手車的花費只是新車的零頭。

‣ **DIFFERENT 不同** **5** 🔑 different from the previous one 有別於從前的；新穎的：*I like your new hairstyle.* 我喜歡你的新髮型。◇ *When do you start your new job?* 你什麼時候開始你的新工作？◇ *He's made a lot of new friends.*

N

他交了許多新朋友。**OPP** old

▸ **NOT FAMILIAR** 不熟悉 **6** already existing but not seen, experienced, etc. before; not familiar 剛體驗到的；初見的；不熟悉的：*This is a new experience for me.* 對於我來說，這是一次從未有過的經歷。◇ *I'd like to learn a new language.* 我想學習一門新的語言。◇ *the discovery of a new star* 一顆新星的發現 ◇ **~ to sb** *Our system is probably new to you.* 你也許不熟悉我們的系統。

▸ **RECENTLY ARRIVED** 新到 **7** **~ (to sth)** not yet familiar with sth because you have only just started, arrived, etc. 初來乍到的；初學乍練的；新鮮的：*I should tell you, I'm completely new to this kind of work.* 我得告訴你，我幹這活完全是個新手。◇ *I am new to the town.* 我剛剛來到這座小鎮。◇ *a **new arrival/recruit*** 剛剛到達的人；新兵 ◇ *You're new here, aren't you?* 你是新來的，是嗎？

▸ **NEW-** 新… **8** used in compounds to describe sth that has recently happened （用於構成複合詞）新的，新近的：*He was enjoying his new-found freedom.* 他享受着剛剛獲得的自由。

▸ **MODERN** 現代 **9** (usually with *the* 通常與 the 連用) modern; of the latest type 現代的；最新型的：*the new morality* 現代的道德 ◇ *They called themselves the New Romantics.* 他們自稱新浪漫主義者。

▸ **JUST BEGINNING** 初始 **10** [usually before noun] just beginning or beginning again 剛開始的；初始的；重新開始的：*a new day* 新的一天 ◇ *It was a new era in the history of our country.* 這是我國歷史上的一個新紀元。◇ *She went to Australia to start a new life.* 她去澳大利亞開始新的生活。

▸ **WITH FRESH ENERGY** 有新鮮活力 **11** having fresh energy, courage or health 富有朝氣的；生氣勃勃的：*Since he changed jobs he's looked like a new man.* 他跳槽之後像換了一個人似的。

▸ **RECENTLY PRODUCED** 新近產生 **12** only recently produced or developed 新近產生的；新開發的；時鮮的：*The new buds are appearing on the trees now.* 樹上現在露出了新芽。◇ *new potatoes* (= ones dug from the soil early in the season) 早土豆 ▸ **new·ness** *noun* [U] ➲ see also NEWLY

IDM **ˌbreak new ˈground** to make a new discovery or do sth that has not been done before 有所發現；開拓創新 ➲ see also GROUNDBREAKING **(as) ˌgood as ˈnew | like ˈnew** in very good condition, as it was when it was new 完好如新：*I've had your coat cleaned—it's as good as new now.* 你的外套洗好了，像新的一樣。**… is the new …** (*BrE, informal*) used to say that sth has become very fashionable and can be thought of as replacing sth else（表示某事物已非常時髦，被視為可替代其他事物）：*Brown is the new black.* 棕色取代了黑色變得時髦起來。◇ *Comedy is the new rock and roll.* 現代搖滾滑稽有趣。◇ *Fifty is the new forty.* 四十已過時，五十正時興。**a new ˈbroom** (*BrE*, often *disapproving*) a person who has just started to work for an organization, department, etc., especially in a senior job, and who is likely to make a lot of changes 新就職者；（尤指）剛上任的新官：*Well, you know what they say—**a new broom sweeps clean**.* 俗語說，新官上任三把火。**a/the ˌnew kid on the ˈblock** (*informal*) a person who is new to a place, an organization, etc. （地方、機構等的）新來者，新手：*Despite his six years in politics, he was still regarded by many as the new kid on the block.* 儘管他已經從政六年，但很多人仍把他視為初出茅廬。**a new one on ˈme** (*informal*) used to say that you have not heard a particular idea, piece of information, joke, etc. before 未聽說過（或接觸過）的；很生疏的：*'Have you come across this before?' 'No, it's a new one on me.'* "你以前碰到過這樣的事嗎？" "沒有，從來沒聽說過。" **turn over a new ˈleaf** to change your way of life to become a better, more responsible person 改惡從善；重新做人 **what's ˈnew?** (*informal*) used as a friendly GREETING（友好的問候）你好嗎，怎麼樣：*Hi! What's new?* 嗨！你好嗎？➲ more at BLOOD *n.*, BRAVE *adj.*, BREATHE, COMPLEXION, TEACH

ˌNew ˈAge *adj.* connected with a way of life that rejects modern Western values and is based on spiritual ideas and beliefs, ASTROLOGY, etc. 新潮生活的，新時代生活方式的（摒棄西方現代價值觀，基於精神思想信仰、占星術等）：*a New Age festival* 新潮生活節 ◇ ***New Age travellers*** (= people in Britain who reject the values of modern society and travel from place to place, living in their vehicles) 新時代思潮的不時遷移者（摒棄現代社會價值的到處旅行者）▸ **ˌNew ˈAge** *noun* [U]

new·bie /ˈnjuːbi; *NAmE* ˈnuːbi/ *noun* (*informal*) a person who is new and has little experience in doing sth, especially in using computers（尤指使用電腦的）新手 **SYN** **novice**

new·born /ˈnjuːbɔːn; *NAmE* ˈnuːbɔːrn/ *adj.* [only before noun] recently born 新生的；初生的：*a newborn baby* 新生兒

ˌnew ˈbroom *noun* (*BrE*) a person who has just started to work for an organization, especially in a senior job, and who is likely to make a lot of changes 新就任者，新上任官員（可能進行很多變革）

ˈnew-build *noun* [C, U] (*BrE*) a building, ship or aircraft that has been built very recently or that is to be built soon; buildings, etc. of this type 新建物（指建築、船舶或飛機；亦指擬建中的）：*new-build properties/apartments* 新建樓房／公寓

New·cas·tle /ˈnjuːkɑːsl; *NAmE* ˈnuːkæsl/ *noun* [U] **IDM** see COAL

new·comer /ˈnjuːkʌmə(r); *NAmE* ˈnuː-/ *noun* **~ (to sth)** a person who has only recently arrived in a place or started an activity 新來者；新手

newel post /ˈnjuːəl pəʊst; *NAmE* ˈnuːəl poʊst/ (also **newel**) *noun* a post at the top or bottom of a set of stairs 樓梯端柱

Language Bank 用語庫

nevertheless

Conceding a point and making a counter-argument 承認一個觀點的正確性，並提出一個對立的觀點

- **While** the film is undoubtedly too long, it is **nevertheless** an intriguing piece of cinema. 雖然這部電影的確太長了，但它不失為一部有趣的影片。
- **It can be argued that** the movie is too long. It is **nonetheless** an intriguing piece of cinema. 可以認為這部電影太長了，但它不失為一部有趣的影片。
- The film is undoubtedly too long. **Still**, it is an intriguing piece of cinema. 這部電影的確太長了，但它仍不失為一部有趣的影片。
- **Of course**, huge chunks of the book have been sacrificed in order to make a two-hour movie, **but** it is **nevertheless** a successful piece of storytelling. 當然，為了製作一部兩小時的電影，該書中的大部份內容都被捨棄了，不過它仍不失為一部成功的故事片。
- Critics are wrong to argue that the film's plot is too complicated. **Certainly** there are a couple of major twists, **but** audiences will have no difficulty following them. 批評家認為這部電影的情節過於複雜，這種觀點是不恰當的。影片中確實有幾次大的情節變化，但觀眾還是不難看懂的。
- **It is true that** you cannot make a good movie without a good script, **but it is equally true** that a talented director can make a good script into an excellent film. 的確，沒有好的劇本不可能拍出好的電影，但有天賦的導演能將一般好的劇本製作成非常好的電影，這一點也是沒有疑問的。
- **It remains to be seen whether** these two movies herald a new era of westerns, **but there is no doubt that** they represent welcome additions to the genre. 這兩部電影是否預示着西部片新時代的來臨還有待觀察。但是毫無疑問，它們作為這一電影類型的新作而受到歡迎。

➲ Language Banks at ARGUE, HOWEVER, IMPERSONAL, OPINION

ˌNew ˈEngland *noun* an area in the north-eastern US that includes the states of Maine, New Hampshire, Vermont, Massachusetts, Rhode Island and Connecticut 新英格蘭（包括緬因、新罕布什爾、佛蒙特、馬薩諸塞、羅得島、康涅狄格諸州的美國東北部地區）

new·fan·gled /ˌnjuːˈfæŋɡld; *NAmE* ˌnuːˈf-/ *adj.* [usually before noun] (*disapproving*) used to describe sth that has recently been invented or introduced, but that you do not like because it is not what you are used to, or is too complicated 新奇怪異的；時髦複雜的

new·fie /ˈnjuːfi; *NAmE* ˈnuːfi/ *noun* (*CanE, informal*) a person from Newfoundland in Canada （加拿大）紐芬蘭人

ˌnew-ˈfound *adj.* [only before noun] recently discovered or achieved 新發現的；新取得的：*How is she handling her new-found fame?* 對於自己暴得大名，她是如何應付？◇ *his new-found freedom/confidence/enthusiasm* 他剛獲得的自由／找到的信心／產生的熱情

New·found·land Time /njuːˈfaʊndlənd taɪm; *NAmE* nuːˈf-/ *noun* [U] (*CanE*) the standard time system that is used in an area which includes the island of Newfoundland 紐芬蘭時間（紐芬蘭島地區標準時間）

ˌNew ˈLabour *noun* [sing.+sing./pl. v.] (in Britain) the modern Labour Party which moved away from the political left in the 1990s in order to appeal to more people （英國）新勞工黨，新工黨（對現今工黨的稱呼，因其於 20 世紀 90 年代脫離左派傳統以求獲得更多人的支持）

newly 🔑 /ˈnjuːli; *NAmE* ˈnuːli/ *adv.* (usually before a past participle 通常用於過去分詞前) recently 最近；新近：*a newly qualified doctor* 新近獲得行醫許可的醫生 ◇ *a newly created job* 新設置的崗位 ◇ *a newly independent republic* 剛獨立的共和國

ˈnewly-wed *noun* [usually pl.] a person who has recently got married 新婚者 ▸ **ˈnewly-wed** *adj.*

ˌnew ˈman *noun* (*BrE*) a man who shares the work in the home that is traditionally done by women, such as cleaning, cooking and taking care of children. New men are considered sensitive and not aggressive. 新派男子（分擔家務及照顧子女的工作）

ˌnew ˈmedia *noun* [pl.] new information and entertainment technologies, such as the Internet, CD-ROMs and DIGITAL TELEVISION 新媒體（像互聯網、光盤和數字電視等新的信息和娛樂技術）

ˌnew ˈmoon *noun* **1** the moon when it looks like a thin curved shape (= a CRESCENT) 新月 **2** the time of the month when the moon has this shape 新月期 ➲ compare FULL MOON, HALF-MOON (1)

the ˌNew ˈRight *noun* [sing.] (in the US) politicians and political groups who support conservative social and political policies and religious ideas based on Christian FUNDAMENTALISM （美國）新右派（支持保守的社會和政治政策和基於基督教基要主義的宗教思想）

news 🔑 /njuːz; *NAmE* nuːz/ *noun* [U]
1 🔑 new information about sth that has happened recently 消息；音信：*What's the latest news?* 有什麼最新消息嗎？◇ *Have you heard the news? Pat's leaving!* 你聽說了嗎？帕特要走了！◇ *That's great news.* 這真是好消息。◇ *Tell me all your news.* 把你最近的情況全都告訴我。◇ *Have you had any* **news of** *Patrick?* 你有沒有帕特里克的消息？◇ *Any news on the deal?* 這筆交易有消息嗎？◇ *Messengers brought* **news that** *the battle had been lost.* 通信員送來消息說這場戰鬥失敗了。◇ *Do you want the* **good news** *or the* **bad news** *first?* 你是想先聽好消息還是壞消息？◇ *a* **piece/bit of news** 一條／一則新聞 ◇ (*informal*) *It's* **news to me** (= I haven't heard it before). 這事我第一次聽說。 **2** 🔑 reports of recent events that appear in newspapers or on television or radio 媒體對重要事情的報道；新聞：*national/international news* 國內／國際新聞 ◇ *a news story/item/report* 一則新聞；新聞報道 ◇ *News of a serious road accident is just coming in.* 剛收到一則重大交通事故的消息。◇ *breaking news* (= news that is arriving about events that have just happened) 突發新聞 ◇ *She is always* **in the news**. 她老在媒體露面。◇ *The wedding was* **front-page news**. 這次婚禮成了頭版新聞。 **3** 🔑 **the news** a regular television or radio broadcast of the latest news （電視或廣播中的）新聞報道：*to* **listen to/watch the news** 收聽／收看新聞節目 ◇ *Can you put the news on?* 請你打開新聞好嗎？◇ *I saw it* **on the news**. 我是在新聞節目中看到的。◇ *the nine o'clock news* 九點的新聞報道 **4** a person, thing or event that is considered to be interesting enough to be reported as news 新聞人物；新聞事件：*Pop stars are always news.* 流行音樂明星總是新聞人物。➲ see also NEWSY

IDM **be bad ˈnews (for sb/sth)** to be likely to cause problems 對…不利：*Central heating is bad news for indoor plants.* 中央供暖系統不利於室內植物。 **break the ˈnews (to sb)** to be the first to tell sb some bad news 最先（向…）透露壞消息；說出實情 **be good news (for sb/sth)** to be likely to be helpful or give an advantage 對…有利（或有益處）：*The cut in interest rates is good news for homeowners.* 降低利率對於私房買主來說是個福音。 **ˌno news is ˈgood news** (*saying*) if there were bad news we would hear it, so as we have heard nothing, it is likely that nothing bad has happened 沒有消息就是好消息

ˈnews agency (also **ˈpress agency**) *noun* an organization that collects news and supplies it to newspapers and television and radio companies 通訊社

news·agent /ˈnjuːzeɪdʒənt; *NAmE* ˈnuːz-/ (*BrE*) (*US* **news·deal·er**) *noun* **1** a person who owns or works in a shop selling newspapers and magazines, and often sweets/candy and cigarettes 報刊經銷人；報刊經銷商 **2 news·agent's** (*pl.* **news·agents**) (*BrE* also **ˈpaper shop**) a shop/store that sells newspapers, magazines, sweets/candy, etc. 報刊經銷店；書報亭：*I'll go to the newsagent's on my way home.* 回家時我要去趟報刊店。

news·cast /ˈnjuːzkɑːst; *NAmE* ˈnuːzkæst/ *noun* (*especially NAmE*) a news programme on radio or television 新聞節目；新聞廣播

news·cast·er /ˈnjuːzkɑːstə(r); *NAmE* ˈnuːzkæstər/ (*BrE* also **news·read·er**) *noun* a person who reads the news on television or radio 新聞播音員

ˈnews conference *noun* (*especially NAmE*) = PRESS CONFERENCE

news·deal·er /ˈnjuːzdiːlə(r); *NAmE* ˈnuːz-/ (*US*) (*BrE* **news·agent**) *noun* **1** a person who owns or works in a shop selling newspapers and magazines, and often sweets/candy and cigarettes 報刊經銷人；報刊經銷商 **2** (*BrE* also **ˈpaper shop**) a shop/store that sells newspapers, magazines, sweets/candy, etc. 報刊經銷店；書報亭 ➲ see also NEWS-STAND

ˈnews desk *noun* the department of a newspaper office or a radio or television station where news is received and prepared for printing or broadcasting （報社、電台或電視台的）新聞編輯部，新聞採編部：*She works on the news desk.* 她在新聞採編部工作。

news·flash /ˈnjuːzflæʃ; *NAmE* ˈnuːz-/ (also **flash**) *noun* (*especially BrE*) a short item of important news that is broadcast on radio or television, often interrupting a programme （插播的）簡明新聞

news·gather·ing /ˈnjuːzɡæðərɪŋ; *NAmE* ˈnuːz-/ *noun* [U] the process of doing research on news items, especially ones that will be broadcast on television or printed in a newspaper （尤指電視或報紙的）新聞採集 ▸ **news·gather·er** /ˈnjuːzɡæðərə(r); *NAmE* ˈnuːz-/ *noun*

news·group /ˈnjuːzɡruːp; *NAmE* ˈnuːz-/ *noun* a place in a computer network, especially the Internet, where people can discuss a particular subject and exchange information about it （網絡）新聞組；（計算機系統）新聞組

news·let·ter /ˈnjuːzletə(r); *NAmE* ˈnuːz-/ *noun* a printed report containing news of the activities of a club or organization that is sent regularly to all its members （某組織的）內部通訊，簡訊

news·man /ˈnjuːzmæn; *NAmE* ˈnuːz-/, **news·woman** /ˈnjuːzwʊmən; *NAmE* ˈnuːz-/ *noun* (*pl.* **-men** /-men/, **-women** /-wɪmɪn/) a journalist who works for a newspaper or a television or radio station 新聞記者：*a* *crowd of reporters and TV newsmen* 一群記者和電視新聞採編人員

news·paper 0━ /ˈnjuːzpeɪpə(r); *NAmE* ˈnuːz-/ *noun* **1** 0━ [C] a set of large printed sheets of paper containing news, articles, advertisements, etc. and published every day or every week 報紙；報：*a* ***daily/weekly newspaper*** 日報；週報◇ *a* ***local/national newspaper*** 地方性／全國性報紙◇ *an* ***online newspaper*** 在線報紙◇ *a* ***newspaper article*** 報紙上發表的文章◇ *I read about it* ***in the newspaper***. 我在報上看到了這件事。◇ *a* ***newspaper cutting*** 剪報◇ *She works for the local newspaper* (= the company that produces it). 她在一家地方報社工作。◇ *newspaper proprietors* 報業老闆 ➲ see also PAPER *n.* (2) **2** [U] paper taken from old newspapers 舊報紙：*Wrap all your glasses in newspaper.* 把你的玻璃杯全用舊報紙包起來。

news·paper·man /ˈnjuːzpeɪpəmæn; *NAmE* ˈnuːzpeɪpərmæn/, **news·paper·woman** /ˈnjuːzpeɪpəwʊmən; *NAmE* ˈnuːzpeɪpər-/ *noun* (*pl.* **-men** /-men/, **-women** /-wɪmɪn/) a journalist who works for a newspaper 報社記者

new·speak /ˈnjuːspiːk; *NAmE* ˈnuː-/ *noun* [U] language that is not clear or honest, for example the language that is used in political PROPAGANDA 新話（模棱兩可的政治宣傳語言）

news·print /ˈnjuːzprɪnt; *NAmE* ˈnuːz-/ *noun* [U] the cheap paper that newspapers are printed on 新聞紙；白報紙

news·read·er /ˈnjuːzriːdə(r); *NAmE* ˈnuːz-/ *noun* (*BrE*) = NEWSCASTER

news·reel /ˈnjuːzriːl; *NAmE* ˈnuːz-/ *noun* a short film of news that was shown in the past in cinemas/movie theaters（舊時在電影院播放的）新聞短片

news·room /ˈnjuːzruːm; -rʊm; *NAmE* ˈnuːz-/ *noun* the room at a newspaper office or a radio or television station where news is received and prepared for printing or broadcasting（報社、電台或電視台的）新聞編輯室

ˈnews-sheet *noun* a small newspaper with only a few pages（只有幾頁的）小報

ˈnews-stand (*US* **ˈnewsstand**) *noun* a place on the street, at a station, etc. where you can buy newspapers and magazines 報攤；書報亭

ˈnews ticker (also **ticker**) *noun* a line of text containing news which passes across the screen of a computer or television（計算機或電視屏幕上的）滾動新聞條，新聞跑馬燈

news·wire /ˈnjuːzwaɪə(r); *NAmE* ˈnuːz-/ *noun* a service that provides the latest news, for example using the Internet 新聞專線（通過互聯網等提供最新新聞的服務）

news·worthy /ˈnjuːzwɜːði; *NAmE* ˈnuːzwɜːrði/ *adj.* interesting and important enough to be reported as news 有新聞價值的；值得報道的

newsy /ˈnjuːzi; *NAmE* ˈnuːzi/ *adj.* (*informal*) full of interesting and entertaining news 新聞多的；充滿有趣信息的：*a newsy letter* 一封有很多消息的信

newt /njuːt; *NAmE* nuːt/ *noun* a small animal with short legs, a long tail and cold blood, that lives both in water and on land (= is an AMPHIBIAN) 蠑螈（水陸兩棲）
IDM see PISSED

the ˌNew ˈTestament *noun* [sing.] the second part of the Bible, that describes the life and teachings of Jesus Christ《〈聖經〉新約》➲ compare THE OLD TESTAMENT

new·ton /ˈnjuːtən; *NAmE* ˈnuː-/ *noun* (*abbr.* **N**) (*physics* 物) a unit of force. One newton is equal to the force that would give a mass of one kilogram an ACCELERATION (= an increase in speed) of one metre per second per second. 牛頓（力的單位，1 牛頓等於使 1 千克質量的物體產生 1 米每平方秒的加速度所需要的力）

ˈnew town *noun* one of the complete towns that were planned and built in Britain after 1946（英國於 1946 年後規劃建設的）新市鎮

ˌnew ˌvariant CJˈD *noun* [U] a disease similar to CREUTZFELDT-JAKOB DISEASE (= a brain disease in humans that causes death) that is thought to be connected with BSE 新型克－雅氏病，新變異型庫賈氏症（據信與瘋牛病有關，類似克－雅氏病）

ˌnew ˈwave *noun* [U, sing.] **1** a group of people who together introduce new styles and ideas in art, music, cinema, etc. 新浪潮（統稱藝術、音樂、電影等領域的共同開拓創新者）：*one of the most exciting directors of the Australian new wave* 澳大利亞新浪潮派中最為振奮人心的導演之一◇ *new wave films* 新浪潮電影 **2** a style of rock music popular in the 1970s 新潮流音樂（流行於 20 世紀 70 年代的一種搖滾樂）

the ˌNew ˈWorld *noun* [sing.] a way of referring to N, Central and S America, used especially in the past 新大陸；美洲大陸 ➲ compare OLD WORLD

ˌnew ˈyear (also **ˌNew ˈYear**) *noun* [U, sing.] the beginning of the year 新年：*Happy New Year!* 新年快樂！◇ *We're going to Germany for Christmas and New Year.* 我們要去德國過聖誕和新年。◇ *I'll see you in the new year.* 新的一年裏再見。➲ see also RESOLUTION (4)

ˌNew Year's ˈDay (*NAmE* also **ˈNew Year's**) *noun* [U] 1 January 元旦；1 月 1 日

ˌNew Year's ˈEve (*NAmE* also **ˈNew Year's**) *noun* [U] 31 December, especially the evening of that day 除夕；12 月 31 日；（尤指）除夕夜

Which Word? 詞語辨析

next / nearest

- **(The) next** means 'after this/that one' in time or in a series of events, places or people. * (the) next 指下一個時間、事情、地點或人：*When is your next appointment?* 你下一次預約時間是什麼時候？◇ *Turn left at the next traffic lights.* 在下一個紅綠燈處向左拐。◇ *Who's next?* 下一個是誰？**(The) nearest** means 'closest' in space. * (the) nearest 指空間上最近：*Where's the nearest supermarket?* 最近的超市在哪兒？
- Notice the difference between the prepositions **nearest to** and **next to**. 注意介詞 nearest to 和 next to 的區別：*Janet's sitting nearest to the window* (= of all the people in the room). 珍妮特坐在（屋裏所有人中）離窗戶最近的地方。◇ *Sarah's sitting next to the window* (= right beside it). 薩拉坐在窗戶旁邊。In informal *BrE* **nearest** can be used instead of **nearest to**. 在非正式的英式英語中，nearest 可用以代替 nearest to：*Who's sitting nearest the door?* 誰坐在離門最近的地方？

next 0━ /nekst/ *adj., adv., noun*
■ ***adj.*** [only before noun] **1** 0━ (usually with *the* 通常與 the 連用) coming straight after sb/sth in time, order or space 下一個的；緊接着的；接下來的：*The next train to Baltimore is at ten.* 下一趟去巴爾的摩的列車十點鐘開。◇ *The next six months will be the hardest.* 接下來的六個月將是最難熬的。◇ *the next chapter* 下一章◇ *Who's next?* 下一位是誰？◇ *the woman in the next room* 隔壁房間裏的女子◇ *I fainted and* ***the next thing I knew*** *I was in the hospital.* 我昏迷了，醒來時只知道自己在醫院裏。◇ (*informal*) *Round here, you leave school at sixteen and* ***next thing you know***, *you're married with three kids.* 這一帶的人十六歲中學畢業，接着就結婚，生三個孩子。**2** 0━ (used without *the* 不與 the 連用) **~ Monday, week, summer, year, etc.** the Monday, week, etc. immediately following 緊隨其後的；下一個的：*Next Thursday is 12 April.* 下個星期四是 4 月 12 日。◇ ***Next time*** *I'll bring a book.* 下次我帶本書來。
IDM **the ˈnext man, woman, person, etc.** the average person 平常人；一般的人：*I can enjoy a joke* ***as well as the next man***, *but this is going too far.* 我和平常人一樣喜歡開玩笑，可這太過分了。➲ more at DAY, LUCK *n.*
■ ***adv.*** **1** 0━ after sth else; then; afterwards 緊接着；隨後：*What happened next?* 隨後發生了什麼？◇ *Next, I heard the sound of voices.* 接着，我聽到了說話的聲音。➲ LANGUAGE BANK at FIRST, PROCESS **2** 0━ **~ best, biggest, most important, etc. … (after/to sb/sth)**

N

following in the order mentioned 其次的；依次的；僅次於…的：*Jo was the next oldest after Martin.* 馬丁下面年齡最大的就是喬了。◇ ***The next best thing** to flying is gliding.* 好玩程度僅次於飛行的就是滑翔。 **3** used in questions to express surprise or confusion（用於詢問，表示吃驚或困惑）：*You're going bungee jumping? **Whatever next?*** 你要去蹦極？還想幹什麼？

■ **noun** (usually **the next**) [sing.] a person or thing that is next 下一位；下一個；下一件：*One moment he wasn't there, the next he was.* 他前一刻還不在那裏，一會兒又在了。◇ *the week **after next*** 下下週

ˌnext ˈdoor *adv., adj., noun*

■ **adv.** in the next room, house or building 在隔壁：*The cat is from the house next door.* 這隻貓是隔壁家的。◇ *The manager's office is just next door.* 經理辦公室就在隔壁。◇ *We live **next door to** the bank.* 我們住在銀行的隔壁。▸ **ˌnext-ˈdoor** *adj.* [only before noun]：*our next-door neighbours* 我們的隔壁鄰居 ◇ *the next-door house* 相鄰的房子

■ **noun** [U+sing./pl. v.] (*BrE, informal*) the people who live in the house or flat/apartment next to yours 隔壁鄰居；住在隔壁的人：*Is that next door's dog?* 那是鄰居家的狗嗎？

ˌnext of ˈkin *noun* [C, U] (*pl.* **next of kin**) your closest living relative or relatives 直系親屬；最近親：*I'm her next of kin.* 我是她的直系親屬。◇ *Her next of kin have been informed.* 她最近的親屬已得到通知了。◇ *The form must be signed by next of kin.* 這表格必須由直系親屬填寫。

ˈnext to *prep.*

1 in or into a position right beside sb/sth 緊鄰；在…近旁：*We sat next to each other.* 我們緊挨着坐在一起。➲ note at NEXT **2** following in order or importance after sb/sth 僅次於；緊接：*Next to skiing my favourite sport is skating.* 我最喜歡的運動除了滑雪就是溜冰。 **3** almost 幾乎：*Charles knew **next to nothing** about farming.* 查爾斯對耕作幾乎一無所知。◇ *The horse came **next to last** (= the one before the last one) in the race.* 這匹馬在比賽中跑了個倒數第二。 **4** in comparison with sb/sth 與…相比：*Next to her I felt like a fraud.* 和她相比，我覺得自己是濫竽充數。

N

nexus /ˈneksəs/ *noun* [sing.] (*formal*) a complicated series of connections between different things（錯綜複雜的）關係，連結，聯繫

Nez Percé /ˌnez ˈpɜːs; *NAmE* ˈpɜːrs/ *noun* (*pl.* **Nez Percé** or **Nez Percés**) a member of a Native American people, many of whom now live in the US state of Idaho 內茲佩爾塞人（美洲土著居民，其中許多居於美國愛達荷州）**ORIGIN** From the French for 'pierced nose'. 源自法語詞“穿鼻”。

NFC /ˌen ef ˈsiː/ *abbr.* **the NFC** (in the US) the National Football Conference (one of the two groups of teams in the National Football League)（美國）全國足球聯合會（全國足球聯盟的兩個聯合會之一）

NFL /ˌen ef ˈel/ *abbr.* (in the US) National Football League (the US organization for professional AMERICAN FOOTBALL with two groups of teams, the National Football Conference and the American Football Conference) 全國足球聯盟（美國職業足球組織，包括兩組球隊：全國足球聯合會和美國足球聯合會）

NGO /ˌen dʒiː ˈəʊ; *NAmE* ˈoʊ/ *abbr.* non-governmental organization (a charity, association, etc. that is independent of government and business) 非政府組織（獨立於政府或商界的慈善機構、協會等）

ngoma /əŋˈɡəʊmə; *NAmE* -ˈɡoʊ-/ *noun* **1** [C] a traditional drum from southern or eastern Africa 恩格瑪鼓（非洲南部或東部的一種傳統鼓） **2** [C, U] (*EAfrE*) a celebration or performance that involves dancing, singing and playing drums（伴有歌舞鼓樂的）狂歡慶典，盛大表演

NHS /ˌen eɪtʃ ˈes/ *noun* [sing.] the abbreviation for 'National Health Service' (the public health service in Britain that provides medical treatment and is paid for by taxes) 國民醫療服務體系（全寫為 National Health Service，英國靠賦稅維持的公眾醫療服務）：*an NHS hospital* 國民保健服務計劃所轄的醫院 ◇ *I had the operation done **on the NHS*** (= paid for by the NHS). 我做這次手術是國民保健服務計劃資助的。

NI *abbr.* (in Britain) NATIONAL INSURANCE（英國）國民保險制度

nia·cin /ˈnaɪəsɪn/ (also **ˌnico·tin·ic ˈacid**) *noun* [U] a VITAMIN of the B group that is found in foods such as milk and meat 煙酸，尼克酸，菸鹼酸（B 類維生素，存在於牛奶、肉類等食物中）

nib /nɪb/ *noun* the metal point of a pen 鋼筆尖 ➲ VISUAL VOCAB page V69

nib·ble /ˈnɪbl/ *verb, noun*

■ **verb** **1** [T, I] to take small bites of sth, especially food 小口咬，一點點地咬（食物）：**~ sth** *We sat drinking wine and nibbling olives.* 我們坐在那兒，喝着葡萄酒嚼着橄欖。◇ *He nibbled her ear playfully.* 他開玩笑地輕咬着她的耳朵。◇ **~ (at/on sth)** *She took some cake from the tray and nibbled at it.* 她從盤子裏拿了塊蛋糕小口地吃着。 **2** [I] **~ (at sth)** to show a slight interest in an offer, idea, etc.（對…）略微表現出興趣：*He nibbled at the idea, but would not make a definite decision.* 他對這個主意略感興趣，但還不願意作出明確決定。

PHR V **ˌnibble aˈway at sth** to take away small amounts of sth, so that the total amount is gradually reduced 慢慢地削弱；蠶食 **SYN** **erode**：*Inflation is nibbling away at spending power.* 通貨膨脹正在慢慢地減弱消費能力。

■ **noun** **1** [C] a small bite of sth 一小口 **2** **nibbles** [pl.] small things to eat with a drink before a meal or at a party（餐前或聚會中的）點心，小吃

nibs /nɪbz/ *noun*

IDM **his nibs** (*old-fashioned, BrE, informal*) used to refer to a man who is, or thinks he is, more important than other people（稱自命不凡的人）

nice /naɪs/ *adj.* (**nicer**, **nicest**)

▸ **PLEASANT/ATTRACTIVE** 令人愉快；吸引人 **1** pleasant, enjoyable or attractive 令人愉快的；宜人的；吸引人的：*a nice day/smile/place* 舒適的一天；舒心的微笑；宜人的地方 ◇ *nice weather* 好天氣 ◇ *Did you **have a nice time**?* 你玩得痛快嗎？◇ *You look very nice.* 你很好看。◇ *'Do you want to come, too?' 'Yes, **that would be nice**.'* "你也想來嗎？" "是啊，很高興來。" ◇ *The nicest thing about her is that she never criticizes us.* 她最大的好處就是從不批評我們。◇ **~ (to do sth)** ***Nice to meet you!*** (= a friendly GREETING when you meet sb for the first time) 很高興見到你！◇ **~ (doing sth)** ***It's been nice meeting you.*** 這次見到你真高興。◇ **~ (that …)** ***It's nice that** you can come with us.* 你能和我們一起去真是太好了。◇ ***It would be nice if** he moved to London.* 他要是搬到倫敦就好了。◇ *We all had the flu last week—it wasn't very nice.* 真不走運，上週我們都得了流感。◇ ***It's nice to know that** somebody appreciates what I do.* 知道有人欣賞我所做的事真讓人開心。 **2** used before adjectives or adverbs to emphasize how pleasant sth is（用於形容詞或副詞前以加強語氣）：*a nice hot bath* 舒舒服服的熱水浴 ◇ *a nice long walk* 長時間很愉快的散步 ◇ *It was nice and warm yesterday.* 昨天的天氣暖洋洋的。◇ *Everyone arrived nice and early.* 大家都早早地到了。 **HELP** **Nice and** with another adjective cannot be used before a noun. * nice and 加另一個形容詞不可用於名詞前：~~*a nice and quiet place*~~

▸ **KIND/FRIENDLY** 好心；友好 **3** kind; friendly 好心的；和藹的；友好的：*Our new neighbours are very nice.* 我們的新鄰居很和氣。◇ *He's a really nice guy.* 他真是個好人。◇ **~ to sb** *Be nice to me. I'm not feeling well.* 我有點不舒服，對我好點。◇ **~ of sb (to do sth)** *It was nice of them to invite us.* 他們真好，邀請了我們。◇ **~ about sth** *I complained to the manager and he was very nice about it.* 我向經理發牢騷，他很寬容。◇ *I asked him **in the nicest possible way** to put his cigarette out.* 我盡量客氣地請他把香煙掐了。**OPP** **nasty**

▸ **NOT NICE** 不好 **4** (*ironic*) bad or unpleasant 壞的；令人不愉快的：*That's a nice thing to say!* 這種話也說得出口！◇ *That's a nice way to speak to your mother!* 你竟然對你母親這麼說話！

▸ **SMALL DETAILS** 細節 **5** (*formal*) involving a very small detail or difference 細微的；精細的 **SYN** **subtle**：*a nice point of law* (= one that is difficult to decide) 法律上難以決斷之處

▸ **nice·ness** *noun* [U] : *In some professions, niceness does not get you very far.* 在某些行業，做老好人成不了大事。
IDM **as ˌnice as ˈpie** (*informal*) very kind and friendly, especially when you are not expecting it 非常友好的，很善良的（尤指出乎意料） **have a nice ˈday!** (*informal, especially NAmE*) a friendly way of saying goodbye, especially to customers （與顧客道別時常用）再見 **ˈnice one!** (*BrE, informal*) used to show you are pleased when sth good has happened or sb has said sth amusing 太好了；好極了： *You got the job? Nice one!* 你得到那份工作了？太好了！ **nice ˈwork!** (*informal, especially BrE*) used to show you are pleased when sb has done sth well 幹得好： *You did a good job today. Nice work, James!* 你今天幹得不錯。好樣的，詹姆斯！ **nice work if you can ˈget it** (*informal*) used when you wish that you had sb's success or good luck and think they have achieved it with little effort （認為對方耕耘少，收穫多）能有這樣的好事兒就好了 ➲ more at MR

Vocabulary Building 詞彙擴充

Nice and very nice

Instead of saying that something is **nice** or **very nice**, try to use more precise and interesting adjectives to describe things. 指某事物好或非常好，除了用 nice 或 very nice 外，盡量用更貼切更有意思的形容詞。

- **pleasant/perfect/beautiful** weather 宜人的／理想的／風和日麗的天氣
- a **cosy**/a **comfortable**/an **attractive** room 暖融融的／舒適的／招人喜愛的房間
- a **pleasant**/an **interesting**/an **enjoyable** experience 令人愉快的／有趣的／愉快的經歷
- **expensive/fashionable/smart** clothes 昂貴的／時尚的／漂亮的衣服
- a **kind**/a **charming**/an **interesting** man 和藹的／有魅力的／有趣的男子
- The party was **fun**. 這聚會真有意思。

In conversation you can also use **great**, **wonderful**, **lovely** and (in *BrE*) **brilliant**. 口語中亦可用 great、wonderful 和（英式英語） brilliant： *The party was great.* 這聚會真棒。◇ *We had a brilliant weekend.* 我們週末過得非常開心。

➲ note at GOOD

ˌnice-ˈlooking *adj.* attractive 好看的；有吸引力的： *What a nice-looking young man!* 多帥的小伙子啊！

nice·ly 🔑 /ˈnaɪsli/ *adv.*
1 🔑 in an attractive or acceptable way; well 有吸引力；令人滿意；令人愉快；很好地： *The room was nicely furnished.* 這房間佈置得很舒適。◇ *The plants are coming along nicely* (= growing well). 植物長勢良好。 **2** 🔑 in a kind, friendly or polite way 和善地；溫和地；友好地；有禮貌地： *If you ask her nicely she might say yes.* 好好地跟她說，她也許會同意的。 **3** (*formal*) carefully; exactly 細緻地；精確地： *His novels nicely describe life in Britain between the wars.* 他的小說細緻地描述了兩次大戰之間英國的生活狀況。
IDM **do ˈnicely** **1** to be making good progress 進展良好： *Her new business is doing very nicely.* 她的新事業一帆風順。 **2** to be acceptable 令人滿意： *Tomorrow at ten will do nicely* (= will be a good time). 明天上午十點挺合適。

ni·cety /ˈnaɪsəti/ *noun* (*pl.* **-ies**) (*formal*) **1** [C, usually pl.] the small details or points of difference, especially concerning the correct way of behaving or of doing things 細節；細微的差別 **2** [U] (*formal*) the quality of being very detailed or careful about sth 精確；準確；嚴密；仔細 SYN **precision** : *the nicety of his argument* 他那論點的精確嚴密

niche /niːʃ; nɪtʃ; *NAmE* nɪtʃ; niːʃ/ *noun* **1** a comfortable or suitable role, job, way of life, etc. 舒適或稱心的工作（或生活等）： *He eventually found his niche in sports journalism.* 最後他在體育新聞界找到了理想的工作。 **2** (*business* 商) an opportunity to sell a particular product to a particular group of people （產品的）商機；市場定位： *They spotted a niche in the market, with no serious competition.* 他們看到市場上一個競爭不激烈的商機。◇ *a niche market* 有利可圖的市場 ◇ *the development of **niche marketing*** (= aiming products at particular groups) 針對某群體的產品營銷開發 **3** a small hollow place, especially in a wall to contain a statue, etc., or in the side of a hill 壁龕；（山體）凹進的地方 SYN **nook** **4** (*biology* 生) a position or role taken by a kind of living thing within its community. Different living things may occupy the same niche in different places, for example ANTELOPES in Africa and KANGAROOS in Australia. 生態位（一種生物在生態環境中的地位或作用）

nick /nɪk/ *noun, verb*
■ ***noun*** **1** **the nick** [sing.] (*BrE, slang*) a prison or a police station 監獄；警察局： *He'll end up in the nick.* 他早晚得進局子。 **2** a small cut in the edge or surface of sth 裂口；刻痕
IDM **in good, etc. ˈnick** (*BrE, informal*) in good, etc. condition or health 身體健康（等）；狀況良好（等） **in the ˌnick of ˈtime** (*informal*) at the very last moment; just in time before sth bad happens 在最後一刻；緊要關頭；恰是時候
■ ***verb*** **1** [T] **~ sth/yourself** to make a small cut in sth 在…上劃刻痕；使有缺口；使有破損： *He nicked himself while shaving.* 他刮鬍子刮了個口子。 **2** [T] **~ sth (from sb/sth)** (*BrE, informal*) to steal sth 扒竊；偷竊 SYN **pinch** : *Who nicked my pen?* 誰偷走了我的鋼筆？ **3** [T] **~ sb (for sth)** (*BrE, informal*) to arrest sb for committing a crime 逮捕： *You're nicked!* 你被捕了！ **4** [I] **+ adv./prep.** (*AustralE, NZE, informal*) to go somewhere quickly 迅速去（某地）

nickel /ˈnɪkl/ *noun* **1** [U] (*symb.* **Ni**) a chemical element. Nickel is a hard silver-white metal used in making some types of steel and other ALLOYS. 鎳 **2** [C] a coin of the US and Canada worth 5 cents （美國和加拿大的）5 分鎳幣

ˌnickel-and-ˈdime *adj., verb*
■ ***adj.*** (*NAmE, informal*) involving only a small amount of money; not important 只涉小錢的；微不足道的
■ ***verb*** **~ sth/sb** (*NAmE*) to spend or save very small amounts of money; to charge small amounts of money for lots of extra items 一點一點地花錢；一分分地節省；只收一點小錢： *Set the money aside so you don't nickel-and-dime it away.* 把錢存起來，這樣你就不會一點一點地花掉了。◇ *She's careful not to nickel-and-dime clients for extra charges.* 她盡量不向客戶收取一點兒額外費用。

nicker /ˈnɪkə(r)/ *noun* (*pl.* **nicker**) (*BrE, slang*) a pound (in money) （一）英鎊

nick·name /ˈnɪkneɪm/ *noun, verb*
■ ***noun*** an informal, often humorous, name for a person that is connected with their real name, their personality or appearance, or with sth they have done 綽號；諢名；外號
■ ***verb*** [often passive] **~ sb/sth + noun** to give a nickname to sb/sth 給…起綽號： *She was nicknamed 'The Ice Queen'.* 她外號叫"冰上王后"。

nico·tine /ˈnɪkətiːn/ *noun* [U] a poisonous substance in TOBACCO that people become ADDICTED to, so that it is difficult to stop smoking 尼古丁；煙鹼

nico·tin·ic acid /ˌnɪkətɪnɪk ˈæsɪd/ *noun* [U] = NIACIN

niece 🔑 /niːs/ *noun*
the daughter of your brother or sister; the daughter of your husband's or wife's brother or sister 姪女；外甥女 ➲ compare NEPHEW

nifty /ˈnɪfti/ *adj.* (*informal*) **1** skilful and accurate 有技巧的；精確的： *There's some nifty guitar work on his latest CD.* 他最新的激光唱片裏有一些吉他曲彈得非常精彩。 **2** practical; working well 實用的；靈便的 SYN **handy** : *a nifty little gadget for slicing cucumbers* 片黃瓜的小巧工具

nig·gard·ly /ˈnɪɡədli; *NAmE* -ɡərd-/ *adj.* (*formal, disapproving*) **1** unwilling to be generous with money, time,

N

etc. 吝嗇的；小氣的；不大度的 SYN **mean 2** (of a gift or an amount of money 禮品或錢數) not worth much and given unwillingly 不值錢的；摳門兒的；小氣的 SYN **miserly**

nig·ger /ˈnɪɡə(r)/ *noun* (*taboo, slang*) a very offensive word for a black person（對黑人的冒犯稱呼）黑鬼

nig·gle /ˈnɪɡl/ *noun, verb*

■ ***noun* 1** (*BrE*) a small criticism or complaint 輕微的批評；小牢騷 **2** a slight feeling, such as worry, doubt, etc. that does not go away 一絲揮不去的煩惱（或疑慮等）: *a niggle of doubt* 一絲揮之不去的疑慮 **3** a slight pain 輕微疼痛: *He gets the occasional niggle in his right shoulder.* 他的右肩有時感到輕微的疼痛。

■ ***verb* 1** [I, T] to irritate or annoy sb slightly; to make sb slightly worried 使煩惱；使焦慮 SYN **bother**: **~ (at sb)** *A doubt niggled at her.* 一絲疑惑困擾着她。◇ **it niggles sb that …** (*BrE*) *It niggled him that she had not phoned back.* 她沒給他回電話，這使他很不安。◇ **~ sb** (*BrE*) *Something was niggling her.* 她有點煩心的事兒。 **2** [I] **~ (about/over sth)** | **~ (at sb) (for sth)** (*BrE*) to argue about sth unimportant; to criticize sb for sth that is not important 吹毛求疵；挑剔 SYN **quibble**

nig·gling /ˈnɪɡlɪŋ/ (also *less frequent* **nig·gly** /-li/) *adj.* **1** used to describe a slight feeling of worry or pain that does not go away（不嚴重卻不斷）煩人的，疼痛的: *She had niggling doubts about their relationship.* 她時常對他們的關係有一絲疑慮。◇ *a series of niggling injuries* 接連不斷的小傷痛 **2** not important 不重要的；微不足道的 SYN **petty**: *niggling details* 瑣碎的細節

nigh /naɪ/ *adv.* **1 ~ on** (*old-fashioned*) almost; nearly 幾乎；差不多: *They've lived in that house for nigh on 30 years.* 他們在那所房子裏住了差不多 30 年了。➲ see also WELL-NIGH **2** (*old use* or *literary*) near 靠近；近: *Winter was drawing nigh.* 冬天快到了。

night 🔑 /naɪt/ *noun* [U, C]

1 🔑 the time between one day and the next when it is dark, when people usually sleep 夜；夜晚: *These animals only come out **at night**.* 這些動物只在夜晚出來。◇ *They sleep by day and hunt **by night**.* 他們白天睡覺，夜晚捕獵。◇ *The accident happened on Friday night.* 事故發生在星期五夜裏。◇ ***on the night of** 10 January/January 10* 在 1 月 10 日晚上 ◇ *Did you hear the storm **last night**?* 昨天夜裏下大雨，你聽見了嗎？◇ *I lay awake **all night**.* 我一夜沒睡着。◇ *Where did you **spend the night**?* 你是在哪裏過夜的？◇ *You're welcome to **stay the night** here.* 歡迎你在這裏留宿。◇ *What is he doing calling **at this time of night**?* 他幹麼這麼晚了還打電話？◇ *You'll feel better after you've had **a good night's sleep**.* 你好好睡一夜就會覺得好些了。◇ *The trip was for ten nights.* 這次旅行要住十個晚上。◇ *The hotel costs €65 per person **per night**.* 住這家酒店，每人每天要 65 歐元。◇ *the **night train/boat/flight*** 夜間列車／輪船／飛機班次 ◇ ***Night fell*** (= it became dark). 夜幕降臨。 **2** 🔑 the evening until you go to bed 晚上，夜晚（夜裏就寢前的一段時間）: *Let's go out **on Saturday night**.* 我們星期六晚上出去吧。◇ *Bill's parents came for dinner **last night**.* 昨天晚上，比爾的父母來吃晚飯了。◇ *She doesn't like to walk home **late at night**.* 她不喜歡深夜步行回家。◇ *I saw her in town **the other night*** (= a few nights ago). 前兩天晚上我在城裏見過她。◇ *I'm working late **tomorrow night**.* 明晚我要工作到很晚。➲ see also GOODNIGHT **3** an evening when a special event happens（舉行盛事的）夜晚；…之夜: *the **first/opening night*** (= of a play, film/movie, etc.) 首映／首演之夜 ◇ *a karaoke night* 卡拉 OK 之夜 ◇ ***an Irish/a Scottish, etc. night*** (= with Irish/Scottish music, entertainment, etc.) 一場愛爾蘭、蘇格蘭等歌舞晚會 ➲ see also STAG NIGHT ▸ **nights** *adv.*: (*especially NAmE*) *He can't get used to working nights* (= at night). 他不能適應上夜班。

IDM **have an early/a late ˈnight** to go to bed earlier or later than usual 比平時睡得早／晚: *I've had a lot of late nights recently.* 最近我常常睡得很晚。 **have a good/bad ˈnight** to sleep well/badly during the night 夜裏睡得很好／很糟 **have a night on the ˈtiles** (*BrE, informal*) to stay out late enjoying yourself 深夜在外玩樂 **ˌnight and ˈday** | **ˌday and ˈnight** all the time; continuously 日日夜夜；夜以繼日；連續不斷: *The machines are kept running night and day.* 這些機器夜以繼日地運轉着。 **night ˈnight** used by children or to children, to mean 'Good night'（兒童用語或對兒童使用的語言）晚安: *'Night night, sleep tight!'* "寶寶睡覺覺，睡個好覺覺！" **a night ˈout** an evening that you spend enjoying yourself away from home 在外玩樂的夜晚: *They enjoy a night out occasionally.* 他們偶爾出去玩上一個晚上。 ➲ more at ALL RIGHT *adj.*, DANCE *v.*, DEAD *n.*, MORNING, SPEND *v.*, STILL *adj.*, THING

night·cap /ˈnaɪtkæp/ *noun* **1** a drink, usually containing alcohol, taken before going to bed 睡前飲料；（常指）夜酒 **2** (in the past) a soft cap worn in bed（舊時的）睡帽

night·clothes /ˈnaɪtkləʊðz; *NAmE* -kloʊðz/ *noun* [pl.] clothes that you wear in bed 睡衣

night·club /ˈnaɪtklʌb/ *noun* a place that is open late in the evening where people can go to dance, drink, etc. 夜總會

ˈnight depository (*US*) (*BrE* **ˈnight safe**) *noun* a SAFE in the outside wall of a bank where money, etc. can be left when the bank is closed 夜間保險箱，夜間保險櫃（裝於銀行外牆，銀行關門後供客戶存放現金等）

night·dress /ˈnaɪtdres/ (*BrE*) (*NAmE* or *old-fashioned* **night·gown**) (also *informal* **nightie** *BrE, NAmE*) *noun* a long loose piece of clothing like a thin dress, worn by a woman or girl in bed 女式睡衣；睡袍 ➲ VISUAL VOCAB page V63

ˈnight duty *noun* [U] work that people have to do at night, for example in a hospital 夜班；夜崗: *to be on night duty* 值夜班

night·fall /ˈnaɪtfɔːl/ *noun* [U] (*formal* or *literary*) the time in the evening when it becomes dark 黃昏；傍晚 SYN **dusk**

night·gown /ˈnaɪtɡaʊn/ *noun* (*NAmE* or *old-fashioned*) = NIGHTDRESS

nightie /ˈnaɪti/ *noun* (*informal*) = NIGHTDRESS

night·in·gale /ˈnaɪtɪŋɡeɪl/ *noun* a small brown bird, the male of which has a beautiful song 夜鶯

night·jar /ˈnaɪtdʒɑː(r)/ *noun* a brown bird with a long tail and a rough unpleasant cry, that is active mainly at night 夜鷹

night·life /ˈnaɪtlaɪf/ *noun* [U] entertainment that is available in the evening and at night 夜生活 ➲ COLLOCATIONS at TOWN

ˈnight light *noun* a light or CANDLE that is left on at night 夜間照明燈（或燭光）；夜燈

ˈnight-long *adj.* [only before noun] lasting all night 通宵的；徹夜的

night·ly /ˈnaɪtli/ *adj.* happening every night 每夜的；每晚的: *a nightly news bulletin* 每晚的新聞簡報 ▸ **night·ly** *adv.*

night·mare /ˈnaɪtmeə(r); *NAmE* -mer/ *noun* **1** a dream that is very frightening or unpleasant 噩夢；夢魘: *He still has nightmares about the accident.* 他仍然做噩夢夢見這場事故。 **2 ~ (for sb)** an experience that is very frightening and unpleasant, or very difficult to deal with 可怕的經歷；難以處理之事；噩夢: *The trip turned into a nightmare when they both got sick.* 這次旅行成了一場噩夢，他們倆都病了。◇ (*informal*) *Nobody knows what's going on—**it's a nightmare**!* 誰也不知道是怎麼回事，真是糟透了！◇ (*informal*) *Filling in all those forms was a nightmare.* 填寫了那麼多的表格，真是太可怕了。◇ *Losing a child is most people's **worst nightmare**.* 對於大多數人來說，喪子之痛是最可怕的夢魘。◇ *If it goes ahead, it will be the **nightmare scenario*** (= the worst thing that could happen). 這件事如果繼續下去就糟透了。◇ *a nightmare situation* 惡劣的形勢 ▸ **night·mar·ish** /ˈnaɪtmeərɪʃ; *NAmE* -mer-/ *adj.*: *nightmarish living conditions* 噩夢般的生活條件

ˈnight owl *noun* (*informal*) a person who enjoys staying up late at night 喜歡熬夜的人；夜貓子

ˈnight safe (*BrE*) (*US* **ˈnight depository**) *noun* a SAFE in the outside wall of a bank where money, etc. can be left when the bank is closed 夜間保險箱，夜間保險櫃（裝於銀行外牆，銀行關門後供客戶存放現金等）

ˈnight school *noun* [U, C] (*old-fashioned*) classes for adults, held in the evening （成人）夜校

night·shirt /ˈnaɪtʃɜːt; *NAmE* -ʃɜːrt/ *noun* a long loose shirt worn in bed 睡衣

night·spot /ˈnaɪtspɒt; *NAmE* -spɑːt/ *noun* (*informal*) a place people go to for entertainment at night 夜總會；夜間娛樂場所 SYN **nightclub**

night·stand /ˈnaɪtstænd/ (also **ˈnight table**) (both *NAmE*) *noun* = BEDSIDE TABLE

night·stick /ˈnaɪtstɪk/ *noun* (*NAmE*) = TRUNCHEON

ˈnight-time *noun* [U] the time when it is dark 夜間；黑夜；夜晚：*This area can be very noisy **at night-time**.* 這個地方夜間有時會非常吵。

night·watch·man /naɪtˈwɒtʃmən; *NAmE* -ˈwɑːtʃ-/ *noun* (*pl.* **-men** /-mən/) a man whose job is to guard a building such as a factory at night 守夜人

night·wear /ˈnaɪtweə(r); *NAmE* -wer/ *noun* [U] a word used by shops/stores for clothes that are worn in bed （商店用語）睡衣

ni·hil·ism /ˈnaɪɪlɪzəm/ *noun* [U] (*philosophy* 哲) the belief that nothing has any value, especially that religious and moral principles have no value 虛無主義 ▸ **ni·hil·is·tic** /ˌnaɪɪˈlɪstɪk/ *adj.*：*Her latest play is a nihilistic vision of the world of the future.* 她最近出的這個劇本對未來世界作了虛無主義的詮釋。

ni·hil·ist /ˈnaɪɪlɪst/ *noun* a person who believes in nihilism 虛無主義者

the Nikkei index /ˈnɪkeɪ ɪndeks/ (also **the ˈNikkei average**) *noun* [sing.] a figure that shows the relative price of shares on the Tokyo Stock Exchange 日經（平均）指數（日本東京證券交易所股票交易指數）

nil /nɪl/ *noun* [U] **1** (*especially BrE*) the number 0, especially as the score in some games （數碼）零；（體育比賽中的）0 分 SYN **zero**：*Newcastle beat Leeds four nil/by four goals to nil.* 紐卡斯爾隊以四比零戰勝利茲隊。**2** nothing 無；零：*The doctors rated her chances as nil* (= there were no chances). 醫生認為她沒有希望了。

nim·ble /ˈnɪmbl/ *adj.* (**nim·bler** /ˈnɪmblə(r)/, **nim·blest** /ˈnɪmblɪst/) **1** able to move quickly and easily 靈活的；敏捷的 SYN **agile**：*You need nimble fingers for that job.* 幹這活需要手指靈巧。◇ *She was extremely nimble on her feet.* 她的雙腳特別靈活。**2** (of the mind 頭腦) able to think and understand quickly 思路敏捷的；機敏的 ▸ **nim·bly** /ˈnɪmbli/ *adv.*

nim·bus /ˈnɪmbəs/ *noun* (*technical* 術語) **1** [C, usually sing., U] a large grey rain cloud （大片的）雨雲 **2** [C, usually sing.] a circle of light 光環

nimby /ˈnɪmbi/ *noun* (*pl.* **-ies**) (*disapproving, humorous*) a person who claims to be in favour of a new development or project, but objects if it is too near their home and will disturb them in some way 別在我家後院，有鄰避情結的人（聲稱支持某個建設項目卻反對在自家附近施工者）ORIGIN Formed from the first letters of 'not in my back yard'. 由 not in my back yard 的首字母構成。

nin·com·poop /ˈnɪŋkəmpuːp/ *noun* (*old-fashioned, informal*) a stupid person 頭腦簡單的人；幼稚的人；傻子

nine /naɪn/ *number*

9 九 HELP There are examples of how to use numbers at the entry for **five**. 數詞用法示例見 five 條。

IDM **have nine ˈlives** (especially of a cat 尤指貓) to be very lucky in dangerous situations 有九條命；命大 **a ˌnine days' ˈwonder** a person or thing that makes people excited for a short time but does not last very long 曇花一現；轟動一時的人（或事物） **ˌnine times out of ˈten** almost every time 十之八九；幾乎總是；差不多每次：*I'm always emailing her, but nine times out of ten she doesn't reply.* 我常常給她發電郵，但十之八九她都不回覆。 **ˌnine to ˈfive** the normal working hours in an office 九點至五點；正常辦公時間：*I work nine to five.* 我九點至五點上班。◇ *a nine-to-five job* 一份朝九晚五的工作 **the ˌwhole ˌnine ˈyards** (*informal, especially NAmE*) everything, or a situation which includes everything 一切；全部：*When Dan cooks dinner he always goes the whole nine yards, with three courses and a choice of dessert.* 丹做飯總是做全份的：三道菜，外加甜食供選擇。➲ more at DRESSED, POSSESSION

nine·pins /ˈnaɪnpɪnz/ *noun*

IDM **ˌgo down, ˌdrop, etc. like ˈninepins** (*BrE, informal*) to fall down or become ill/sick in great numbers 大量倒下；大批病倒

nine·teen /ˌnaɪnˈtiːn/ *number*

19 十九 ▸ **nine·teenth** /ˌnaɪnˈtiːnθ/ *ordinal number, noun* HELP There are examples of how to use ordinal numbers at the entry for **fifth**. 序數詞用法示例見 fifth 條。

IDM **talk, etc. nineteen to the ˈdozen** (*BrE, informal*) to talk, etc. without stopping 喋喋不休：*She was chatting away, nineteen to the dozen.* 她沒完沒了地聊着。

ninety /ˈnaɪnti/

1 *number* 90 九十 **2** *noun* **the nineties** [pl.] numbers, years or temperatures from 90 to 99 九十幾；九十年代：*The temperature must be in the nineties today.* 今天的氣溫肯定有九十多度。 ▸ **nine·ti·eth** /ˈnaɪntiəθ/ *ordinal number, noun* HELP There are examples of how to use ordinal numbers at the entry for **fifth**. 序數詞用法示例見 fifth 條。

IDM **in your nineties** between the ages of 90 and 99 ＊90 多歲 **ˌninety-nine ˌtimes out of a ˈhundred** almost always 幾乎沒有例外；幾乎總是

ning-nong /ˈnɪŋ nɒŋ; *NAmE* nɑːŋ/ (also **nong**) *noun* (*AustralE, NZE, informal*) a stupid person 呆子；傻瓜

ninja /ˈnɪndʒə/ *noun* (*pl.* **ninjas** or **ninja**) (from *Japanese*) a person trained in traditional Japanese skills of fighting and moving quietly 忍者（受過日本傳統打鬥和輕功訓練的人）

ninny /ˈnɪni/ *noun* (*pl.* **-ies**) (*old-fashioned, informal*) a stupid person 笨蛋；傻子

ninth /naɪnθ/ *ordinal number, noun*

■ ***ordinal number*** 9th 第九 HELP There are examples of how to use ordinal numbers at the entry for **fifth**. 序數詞用法示例見 fifth 條。

■ ***noun*** each of nine equal parts of sth 九分之一

nio·bium /naɪˈəʊbiəm; *NAmE* -ˈoʊ-/ *noun* [U] (*symb.* **Nb**) a chemical element. Niobium is a silver-grey metal used in steel ALLOYS. 鈮

nip /nɪp/ *verb, noun*

■ ***verb*** (**-pp-**) **1** [T, I] to give sb/sth a quick painful bite or PINCH 啃咬；掐；咬住；夾住：**~ sth** *He winced as the dog nipped his ankle.* 狗咬了他的腳腕子，疼得他齜牙咧嘴。◇ **~ (at sth)** *She nipped at my arm.* 她掐了一下我的胳膊。**2** [I, T] (of cold, wind, etc. 寒氣、風等) to harm or damage sth 傷害；損害：**~ (at sth)** *The icy wind nipped at our faces.* 寒風刺疼了我們的臉。◇ **~ sth** *growing shoots nipped by frost* 遭受霜凍的幼芽 **3** [I] **+ adv./prep.** (*BrE, informal*) to go somewhere quickly and/or for only a short time 快速去（某處）；急忙趕往 SYN **pop**：*He's just nipped out to the bank.* 他急匆匆去銀行了。◇ *A car nipped in* (= got in quickly) *ahead of me.* 一輛車突然插到我前面。

IDM **nip sth in the ˈbud** to stop sth when it has just begun because you can see that problems will come from it 將…扼殺在萌芽狀態；防患於未然

PHR V **ˌnip sth↔ˈoff** to remove a part of sth with your finger or with a tool 掐去；剪掉

■ ***noun*** **1** the act of giving sb a small bite or PINCH (= squeezing their skin between your finger and thumb) 啃咬；掐 **2** (*informal*) a feeling of cold 寒冷；寒意：*There was a real **nip in the air**.* 空中有一股刺骨的寒氣。➲ see also NIPPY (2) **3** (*informal*) a small drink of strong alcohol 少量的烈酒

ˌnip and ˈtuck *adj., adv., noun*

■ ***adj., adv.*** (*especially NAmE*) = NECK AND NECK at NECK *n.*：*The presidential contest is nip and tuck.* 總統競選勢均力敵。

■ ***noun*** (*informal*) a medical operation in which skin is removed or made tighter to make sb look younger or

N

more attractive, especially a FACELIFT 拉皮（或去皺）整形手術；（尤指）去皺整容手術，面部拉皮手術

nip·per /ˈnɪpə(r)/ *noun* (*informal*) a small child 小孩子

nip·ple /ˈnɪpl/ *noun* **1** either of the two small round dark parts on a person's chest. Babies can suck milk from their mother's breasts through the nipples. 乳頭 ➲ VISUAL VOCAB page V59 **2** (*NAmE*) (*BrE* **teat**) the rubber part at the end of a baby's bottle that the baby sucks in order to get milk, etc. from the bottle 奶嘴；橡膠乳頭 **3** a small metal, plastic or rubber object that is shaped like a nipple with a small hole in the end, especially one that is used as part of a machine to direct oil, etc. into a particular place 乳頭狀物品；（機器的）噴嘴：*a grease nipple* 油脂噴嘴

nippy /ˈnɪpi/ *adj.* **1** (*BrE*) able to move quickly and easily 靈巧的；敏捷的：*a nippy little sports car* 小巧靈便的跑車 **2** (*informal*) (of the weather 天氣) cold 冷的；寒冷的

niqab /nɪˈkɑːb/ *noun* a piece of cloth that covers the face but not usually the eyes, worn in public by some Muslim women 尼卡布（一些穆斯林婦女在公共場合戴的面紗，通常露出眼睛）

nir·vana /nɪəˈvɑːnə; *NAmE* nɪrˈv-/ *noun* [U] (in the religion of Buddhism 佛教) the state of peace and happiness that a person achieves after giving up all personal desires 涅槃（超脫一切煩惱的境界）

Nis·sen hut /ˈnɪsn hʌt/ (*BrE*) (*NAmE* **Quonset hut™**) *noun* a shelter made of metal with curved walls and roof 尼森式半筒形鐵皮屋

nit /nɪt/ *noun* **1** the egg or young form of a LOUSE (= a small insect that lives in human hair) 蝨子卵；小蝨子 **2** (*BrE, informal*) a stupid person 傻瓜；笨蛋

N

ˈnit-picking *noun* [U] (*informal, disapproving*) the habit of finding small mistakes in sb's work or paying too much attention to small details that are not important 吹毛求疵；挑刺兒 ▸ **ˈnit-picker** *noun* **ˈnit-picking** *adj.*

ni·trate /ˈnaɪtreɪt/ *noun* [U, C] (*chemistry* 化) a COMPOUND containing NITROGEN and OXYGEN. There are several different nitrates and they are used especially to make soil better for growing crops. 硝酸鹽；硝酸鹽類化肥：*We need to cut nitrate levels in water.* 我們需要降低水中的硝酸鹽含量。

ni·tric acid /ˌnaɪtrɪk ˈæsɪd/ *noun* [U] (*chemistry* 化) (*symb.* HNO_3) a powerful clear acid that can destroy most substances and is used to make EXPLOSIVES and other chemical products 硝酸

ni·trify /ˈnaɪtrɪfaɪ/ *verb* (**ni·tri·fies**, **ni·tri·fying**, **ni·tri·fied**, **ni·tri·fied**) **~ sth** (*chemistry* 化) to change a substance into a COMPOUND that contains NITROGEN 使與氮化合；用氮飽和；（使）硝化 ➲ see also NITRATE

ni·trite /ˈnaɪtraɪt/ *noun* [U, C] (*chemistry* 化) a COMPOUND containing NITROGEN and OXYGEN. There are several different nitrites. 亞硝酸鹽；亞硝酸酯

ni·tro·gen /ˈnaɪtrədʒən/ *noun* [U] (*symb.* **N**) a chemical element. Nitrogen is a gas that is found in large quantities in the earth's atmosphere. 氮；氮氣 ▸ **ni·tro·gen·ous** /naɪˈtrɒdʒənəs; *NAmE* -ˈtrɑːdʒ-/ *adj.*

ˈnitrogen cycle *noun* [C, U] the processes by which nitrogen is passed from one part of the environment to another, for example when plants decay 氮循環（各種形式的氮在自然界的循環）

ˌnitrogen diˈoxide *noun* [U] (*chemistry* 化) a brown poisonous gas. Nitrogen dioxide is formed when some metals are dissolved in NITRIC ACID. 二氧化氮

nitro·glyc·er·ine /ˌnaɪtrəʊˈɡlɪsəriːn; -rɪn; *NAmE* ˌnaɪtroʊˈɡlɪsərən/ (*especially BrE*) (*US* usually **nitro·gly·cerin** /-rɪn; *NAmE* -rən/) *noun* [U] a powerful liquid EXPLOSIVE 硝化甘油

ni·trous oxide /ˌnaɪtrəs ˈɒksaɪd; *NAmE* ˈɑːk-/ (also *informal* **ˈlaughing gas**) *noun* [U] a gas used especially in the past by dentists to prevent you from feeling pain 氧化亞氮，笑氣（舊時牙醫用作麻醉劑）

the nitty-gritty /ˌnɪti ˈɡrɪti/ *noun* [sing.] (*informal*) the basic or most important details of an issue or a situation 基本事實；重要細節：*Time ran out before we could **get down to the real nitty-gritty**.* 我們還沒來得及探討真正的細節，時間就過去了。

nit·wit /ˈnɪtwɪt/ *noun* (*informal*) a stupid person 笨蛋；傻瓜

nix /nɪks/ *verb, noun*

■ ***verb* ~ sth** (*NAmE, informal*) to prevent sth from happening by saying 'no' to it 阻止；拒絕

■ ***noun*** [U] (*NAmE, informal*) nothing 無；沒有什麼；沒有東西

NLP /ˌen el ˈpiː/ *abbr.* **1** NEUROLINGUISTIC PROGRAMMING **2** NATURAL LANGUAGE PROCESSING

No. *abbr.* **1** (also **no.**) (*pl.* **Nos**, **nos**) number 號碼：*Room No. 145* * 145 號房間 **2** (*NAmE*) north; northern 北方（的）；北部（的）

no 🔑 /nəʊ; *NAmE* noʊ/ *exclamation, det., adv., noun*

■ ***exclamation* 1** 🔑 used to give a negative reply or statement（用於否定的回答或陳述）不；沒有；不是：*Just say yes or no.* 只要說"是"或"不是"。◇ *'Are you ready?' 'No, I'm not.'* "準備好了嗎？""沒有，我沒準備好。" ◇ *Sorry, the answer's no.* 對不起，回答是不。◇ *'Another drink?' 'No, thanks.'* "再來一杯？""不要了，謝謝。" ◇ *It's about 70—no, I'm wrong—80 kilometres from Rome.* 距離羅馬大約是 70，不，不對，是 80 公里。◇ *No! Don't touch it! It's hot.* 別！別碰它！很燙。◇ *'It was Tony.' 'No, you're wrong. It was Ted.'* "是托尼。""不對，你錯了。是特德。" ◇ *'It's not very good, is it?' 'No, you're right, it isn't* (= I agree).*'* "這不太好，是吧？""你說得對，這不太好。" **2** 🔑 used to express shock or surprise at what sb has said（對某人所說的話感到驚訝）不，不要：*'She's had an accident.' 'Oh, no!'* "她發生了意外。""怎麼會呢！" ◇ *'I'm leaving!' 'No!'* "我要走了！""別走！"

IDM **not take no for an answer** to refuse to accept that sb does not want sth, will not do sth, etc. 非讓人接受（或聽從）：*You're coming and I won't take no for an answer!* 你一定要來，不來可不行！ ➲ more at YES *exclam.*

■ ***det.* 1** 🔑 not one; not any; not a 沒有；無：*No student is to leave the room.* 學生一律不許離開這房間。◇ *There were no letters this morning.* 今天早上一封信也沒有。◇ *There's no bread left.* 一片麪包都沒有了。◇ *No two days are the same.* 一天一個樣。➲ see also NO ONE **2** 🔑 used, for example on notices, to say that sth is not allowed 不准；禁止：*No smoking!* 禁止吸煙！ **3** 🔑 **there's ~ doing sth** used to say that it is impossible to do sth 沒有可能（做某事）：*There's no telling what will happen next.* 下一步還不定會發生什麼事。 **4** 🔑 used to express the opposite of what is mentioned（表示情況的反面）不是，並不：*She's no fool* (= she's intelligent). 她並不傻。◇ *It was no easy matter* (= it was difficult). 這件事不容易。

■ ***adv.*** used before adjectives and adverbs to mean 'not'（與 not 同義，用於形容詞和副詞前）不：*She's feeling no better this morning.* 她今天早晨還是不見好轉。◇ *Reply by no later than 21 July.* 請於 7 月 21 日前答覆。

■ ***noun*** (*pl.* **noes** /nəʊz; *NAmE* noʊz/) **1** an answer that shows you do not agree with an idea, a statement, etc.; a person who says 'no' 否定的回答；作否定回答的人：*Can't you give me a straight yes or no?* "是"還是"否"，你就不能給我個直截了當的回答嗎？◇ *When we took a vote there were nine yesses and 3 noes.* 我們投票表決，有九人贊同，三人反對。◇ *I'll put you down as a no.* 我就當你是反對了。 **2 the noes** [pl.] the total number of people voting 'no' in a formal debate, for example in a parliament（統稱）投反對票者：*The noes have it* (= more people have voted against sth than for it). 投反對票者佔多數。OPP **ayes**

Noah's ark /ˌnəʊəz ˈɑːk; *NAmE* ˌnoʊəz ˈɑːrk/ *noun* = ARK

nob /nɒb; *NAmE* nɑːb/ *noun* (*old-fashioned, BrE, informal*) a person who has a high social position; a member of the upper class 社會地位高的人；上層人士；大人物

ˌno-ˈball *noun* (in CRICKET 板球) a ball that is BOWLED (= thrown) in a way that is not allowed and which means that a RUN (= a point) is given to the other team 投球犯規

nob·ble /ˈnɒbl; NAmE ˈnɑːbl/ *verb* (*BrE, informal*) **1 ~ sth** to prevent a horse from winning a race, for example by giving it drugs 阻止（賽馬）取勝 **2 ~ sb** to persuade sb to do what you want, especially illegally, by offering them money 買通：*his attempts to nobble the jury* 他想收買陪審團的種種企圖 **3 ~ sb** to prevent sb from achieving what they want 阻撓；使遭受挫折 **SYN thwart** **4 ~ sb** to catch sb or get their attention, especially when they are unwilling（尤指有違其意願）抓住，引起注意：*He was nobbled by the press who wanted details of the affair.* 新聞界緊盯住他不放，要瞭解事件的詳情。▶ **nob·bling** *noun* [U]

no·bel·ium /nəʊˈbiːliəm; -ˈbel-; NAmE noʊ-/ *noun* [U] (*symb.* **No**) a chemical element. Nobelium is a RADIOACTIVE metal that does not exist naturally and is produced from CURIUM. 鍩（放射性化學元素）

Nobel Prize /nəʊˌbel ˈpraɪz; NAmE noʊ-/ *noun* one of six international prizes given each year for excellent work in physics, chemistry, medicine, literature, ECONOMICS and work towards world peace 諾貝爾獎

no·bil·ity /nəʊˈbɪləti; NAmE noʊ-/ *noun* **1 the nobility** [sing.+sing./pl. v.] people of high social position who have titles such as that of DUKE or DUCHESS 貴族 **SYN the aristocracy** **2** [U] (*formal*) the quality of being noble in character 高貴的品質

noble /ˈnəʊbl; NAmE ˈnoʊbl/ *adj., noun*

■ ***adj.*** (**no·bler** /ˈnəʊblə(r); NAmE ˈnoʊ-/, **nob·lest** /ˈnəʊblɪst; NAmE ˈnoʊ-/) **1** having fine personal qualities that people admire, such as courage, HONESTY and care for others 崇高的；品質高尚的：*a noble leader* 偉大的領袖 ◇ *noble ideals* 崇高的理想 ◇ *He died for a noble cause.* 他為了高尚的事業而犧牲。➲ compare IGNOBLE **2** very impressive in size or quality 宏偉的；壯麗的 **SYN splendid**：*a noble building* 雄偉的大樓 **3** belonging to a family of high social rank (= belonging to the nobility) 貴族的；高貴的 **SYN aristocratic**：*a man of noble birth* 出身高貴的人 ▶ **nobly** /ˈnəʊbli; NAmE ˈnoʊbli/ *adv.*：*She bore the disappointment nobly.* 她很失望，但表現得很大度。◇ *to be nobly born* 出身貴族

■ ***noun*** a person who comes from a family of high social rank; a member of the nobility 出身高貴的人；貴族成員 **SYN aristocrat**

ˌnoble ˈgas (also **iˌnert ˈgas**, **ˈrare gas**) *noun* (*chemistry* 化) any of a group of gases that do not react with other chemicals. ARGON, HELIUM, KRYPTON and NEON are noble gases. 惰性氣體；稀有氣體

noble·man /ˈnəʊblmən; NAmE ˈnoʊbl-/, **noble·woman** /ˈnəʊblwʊmən; NAmE ˈnoʊbl-/ *nouns* (*pl.* **-men** /-mən/, **-women** /-wɪmɪn/) a person from a family of high social rank; a member of the NOBILITY 出身高貴的人；貴族成員 **SYN aristocrat**

ˌnoble ˈsavage *noun* a word used in the past to refer in a positive way to a person or people who did not live in an advanced human society 高尚的野蠻人（指未開化原始人的善良、天真、不受文明罪惡玷污）：*The book contrasts modern civilization with the ideal of the noble savage who lived in harmony with nature.* 這本書將現代文明同與自然界和諧相處的高尚野蠻人的理想放在一起對比。

no·blesse ob·lige /nəʊˌbles əˈbliːʒ; NAmE noʊ-/ *noun* [U] (from *French*) the idea that people who have special advantages of wealth, etc. should help other people who do not have these advantages 位高則任重；顯貴者應有高尚品德；貴族義務

no·body 🔑 /ˈnəʊbədi; NAmE ˈnoʊ-/ *pron., noun*

■ ***pron.*** 🔑 = NO ONE：*Nobody knew what to say.* 誰也不知道該說什麼。**HELP** **Nobody** is more common than **no one** in spoken English. 在英語口語中，nobody 比 no one 更常用。**OPP somebody**

■ ***noun*** (*pl.* **-ies**) a person who has no importance or influence 小人物；無足輕重的人 **SYN nonentity**：*She rose from being a nobody to become a superstar.* 她從無名小輩一躍成為超級明星。➲ compare SOMEONE

ˌno-ˈbrain·er *noun* (*informal*) a decision or a problem that you do not need to think about much because it is obvious what you should do 無需用腦的事；容易的決定

ˌno-ˈclaims bonus (also **ˌno-ˈclaim bonus**, **ˌno-ˈclaim(s) discount**) *noun* (all *BrE*) a reduction in the cost of your insurance because you made no claims in the previous year 無索賠贈金（因前一年未申報保險賠償而獲得）

noc·tur·nal /nɒkˈtɜːnl; NAmE nɑːkˈtɜːrnl/ *adj.* **1** (of animals 動物) active at night 夜間活動的 **OPP diurnal** **2** (*formal*) happening during the night 夜間發生的：*a nocturnal visit* 夜訪

noc·turne /ˈnɒktɜːn; NAmE ˈnɑːktɜːrn/ *noun* a short piece of music in a romantic style, especially for the piano 夜曲（主要為鋼琴曲）

Nod /nɒd; NAmE nɑːd/ *noun* [U] **IDM** see LAND *n.*

nod /nɒd; NAmE nɑːd/ *verb, noun*

■ ***verb*** (**-dd-**) **1** [I, T] if you **nod**, **nod** your head or your head **nods**, you move your head up and down to show agreement, understanding, etc. 點頭：*I asked him if he would help me and he nodded.* 我問他能不能幫我一下，他點了點頭。◇ *Her head nodded in agreement.* 她點頭表示同意。◇ **~ sth** *He nodded his head sympathetically.* 他同情地點點頭。◇ *She nodded approval.* 她點頭表示贊同。**2** [I, T] to move your head down and up once to say hello to sb or to give them a sign to do sth 點頭致意；點頭示意：**~ (to/at sb)** *The president nodded to the crowd as he passed in the motorcade.* 當總統的車隊經過時，他向人群點頭致意。◇ **~ to/at sb to do sth** *She nodded at him to begin speaking.* 她點頭示意他開始講話。◇ **~ sth (to/at sb)** *to nod a greeting* 點頭問候 **3** [I] **+ adv./prep.** to move your head in the direction of sb/sth to show that you are talking about them/it（朝…方向）點頭（表示所談論的人或物）：*I asked where Steve was and she nodded in the direction of the kitchen.* 我問史蒂夫在哪兒，她朝廚房點了點頭。**4** [I] to let your head fall forward when you are sleeping in a chair 打盹；打瞌睡：*He sat nodding in front of the fire.* 他坐在火爐前打盹兒。

IDM **have a nodding acˈquaintance with sb/sth** to only know sb/sth slightly 與…有點頭之交；對…略知一二

PHR V **ˌnod ˈoff** (*informal*) to fall asleep for a short time while you are sitting in a chair 打盹；打瞌睡

■ ***noun*** a small quick movement of the head down and up again 點頭：*to give a **nod of approval/agreement/encouragement*** 點頭表示贊同／同意／鼓勵

IDM **get the ˈnod** (*informal*) to be chosen for sth; to be given permission or approval to do sth 獲選中；得到許可：*He got the nod from the team manager* (= he was chosen for the team). 他被球隊經理看中了。**give sb/sth the ˈnod** (*informal*) **1** to give permission for sth; to agree to sth 允許；對…表示同意：*We've been given the nod to expand the business.* 我們得到允許擴大企業規模。◇ *I hope he'll give the nod to the plan.* 我希望他會同意這個計劃。**2** to choose sb for sth 挑選 **a ˌnod and a ˈwink | a ˌnod is as good as a ˈwink** used to say that a suggestion or a HINT will be understood, without anything more being said 一點就懂；（心有靈犀）一點通：*Everything could be done by a nod and a wink.* 每件事只靠點撥一下就能辦妥了。**on the ˈnod** (*BrE, informal*) if a proposal is accepted **on the nod**, it is accepted without any discussion（未經討論）一致同意

nod·dle /ˈnɒdl; NAmE ˈnɑːdl/ (*NAmE* usually **noo·dle**) *noun* (*old-fashioned, slang*) your head; your brain 頭；腦袋

node /nəʊd; NAmE noʊd/ *noun* **1** (*biology* 生) a place on the STEM of a plant from which a branch or leaf grows 莖節 **2** (*biology* 生) a small swelling on a root or branch（根或枝上的）瘤，節，結 **3** (*technical* 術語, *computing* 計) a point at which two lines or systems meet or cross 結點；節點：*a network node* 網絡節點 **4** (*anatomy* 解) a small hard mass of TISSUE, especially near a joint in the human body（尤指人體關節附近的）硬結：*a lymph node* 淋巴結 ▶ **nodal** *adj.*

nod·ule /ˈnɒdjuːl; *NAmE* ˈnɑːdʒuːl/ *noun* a small round lump or swelling, especially on a plant（尤指植物上的）節結，小瘤

Noel /nəʊˈel; *NAmE* noʊ-/ *noun* [C, U] a word for 'Christmas' used especially in songs or on cards 聖誕節（尤用於歌曲和賀卡）: *Joyful Noel* 快樂的聖誕節

noes *pl.* of NO

ˌno-ˈfault *adj.* [only before noun] (*law* 律) (*especially NAmE*) not involving a decision as to who is to blame for sth 不追究責任的；無過失的：*no-fault insurance* (= in which the insurance company pays for damage, etc. without asking whose fault it was) 不追究責任的保險

ˌno-ˈfly zone *noun* an area above a country where planes from other countries are not allowed to fly 禁飛區（禁止別國飛機飛行的地區）

ˌno-ˈfrills *adj.* [only before noun] (especially of a service or product 尤指服務或產品) including only the basic features, without anything that is unnecessary, especially things added to make sth more attractive or comfortable 只包括基本元素的；無裝飾的：*a no-frills airline* 只提供基本服務的航空公司

ˌno-ˈgo area *noun* (*especially BrE*) an area, especially in a city, which is dangerous for people to enter, or that the police or army do not enter, often because it is controlled by a violent group 禁區（常因被暴力團夥控制）: (*figurative*) *Some clubs are no-go areas for people over 30.* 對於30歲以上的人來說，有些俱樂部是禁區。◇ (*figurative*) *This subject is definitely a no-go area* (= we must not discuss it). 這個話題絕對禁止談論。

ˈno-good *adj.* [only before noun] (*slang*) (of a person 人) bad or useless 壞的；無用的

Noh (also **No**) /nəʊ; *NAmE* noʊ/ *noun* [U] traditional Japanese theatre in which songs, dance, and MIME are performed by people wearing MASKS 能劇（日本傳統戲劇）

ˌno-ˈhoper *noun* (*informal*) a person or an animal that is considered useless or very unlikely to be successful 無望取勝的人（或動物）；無用之輩；無能之人

Which Word? 詞語辨析

noise / sound

- **Noise** is usually loud and unpleasant. It can be countable or uncountable. * noise 通常指噪音，既可作可數名詞，也可作不可數名詞：*Try not to make so much noise.* 別那麼吵吵鬧鬧的。◇ *What a terrible noise!* 多麼令人討厭的噪音啊！
- **Sound** is a countable noun and means something that you hear. * sound 為可數名詞，意為聽到的聲音或響聲：*All she could hear was the sound of the waves.* 她聽得到的只有海浪聲。You do not use words like *much* or *a lot of* with **sound**. * sound 不與 much 或 a lot of 等詞語連用。

noise 0 /nɔɪz/ *noun*

1 0 [C, U] a sound, especially when it is loud, unpleasant or disturbing 聲音；響聲；噪音；吵鬧聲：*a rattling noise* 咔噠咔噠的聲音 ◇ *What's that noise?* 哪來的響聲？◇ *Don't* **make a noise**. 別出聲。◇ *They were making too much noise.* 他們的噪聲太大了。◇ *I was woken by the noise of a car starting up.* 我被汽車的啟動聲吵醒了。◇ *We had to shout above the noise of the traffic.* 車輛噪聲太大，我們不得不扯着嗓子說話。◇ *to reduce* **noise levels** 減少噪音量 **2** [U] (*technical* 術語) extra electrical or electronic signals that are not part of the signal that is being broadcast or TRANSMITTED and which may damage it 干擾；電子干擾訊號 **3** [U] information that is not wanted and that can make it difficult for the important or useful information to be seen clearly 雜訊；垃圾信息：*There is some noise in the data which needs to be reduced.* 資料裏有一些需要刪除的不適用信息。

IDM **make a ˈnoise (about sth)** (*informal*) to complain loudly 大聲訴苦；大聲抱怨 **make ˈnoises (about sth)** (*informal*) **1** to talk in an indirect way about sth that you think you might do 放出…的風聲：*The company has been making noises about closing several factories.* 公司放出風聲說要關閉幾家工廠。**2** to complain about sth 抱怨；埋怨 **make soothing, encouraging, reassuring, etc. noises** to make remarks of the kind mentioned, even when that is not what you really think 說安慰（或鼓勵、使人放心等）的話（有時言不由衷地）：*He made all the right noises at the meeting yesterday* (= said what people wanted to hear). 在昨天的會上，他的話句句都合大家的胃口。➲ more at BIG *adj.*

noise·less /ˈnɔɪzləs/ *adj.* (*formal*) making little or no noise 沒有噪音的；寂靜的；不出聲的 SYN **silent**：*He moved with noiseless steps.* 他腳步輕輕地走動。▸ **noise·less·ly** *adv.*

ˌnoises ˈoff *noun* [pl.] **1** (in theatre 劇院) sounds made off the stage, intended to be heard by the audience 音響效果（為演出需要在後台發出的各種聲響）**2** (*humorous*) noise in the background which interrupts you 背景噪音

noi·some /ˈnɔɪsəm/ *adj.* (*formal*) extremely unpleasant or offensive 惡心的；極令人厭煩的；使人很不快的：*noisome smells* 令人厭惡的氣味

noisy 0 /ˈnɔɪzi/ *adj.* (**nois·ier**, **noisi·est**)

1 0 making a lot of noise 吵鬧的；聒噪的；嘈雜的：*noisy children/traffic/crowds* 吵鬧的孩子；喧鬧的交通；嘈雜的人群 ◇ *a noisy protest* (= when people shout) 吵吵嚷嚷的抗議聲 ◇ *The engine is very noisy at high speed.* 這個發動機轉速高時噪音非常大。**2** 0 full of noise 充滿噪音的；吵吵鬧鬧的：*a noisy classroom* 吵鬧的教室 ▸ **nois·ily** 0 /-ɪli/ *adv.*：*The children were playing noisily upstairs.* 孩子們在樓上吵鬧地玩耍。

nomad /ˈnəʊmæd; *NAmE* ˈnoʊ-/ *noun* a member of a community that moves with its animals from place to place 遊牧部落的人 ▸ **no·mad·ic** /nəʊˈmædɪk; *NAmE* noʊ-/ *adj.*：*nomadic tribes* 遊牧部落 ◇ *the nomadic life of a foreign correspondent* 駐國外記者的流浪生活

ˌno-man's-land *noun* [U, sing.] an area of land between the borders of two countries or between two armies, that is not controlled by either（邊境的）無人區域；（兩軍之間的）無人地帶

nom de guerre /ˌnɒm də ˈɡeə(r); *NAmE* ˌnɑːm də ˈɡer/ *noun* (*pl.* **noms de guerre** /ˌnɒm də ˈɡeə(r); *NAmE* ˌnɑːm də ˈɡer/) (from *French*, *formal*) a false name that is used, for example, by sb who belongs to a military organization that is not official 假名；化名

nom de plume /ˌnɒm də ˈpluːm; *NAmE* ˌnɑːm/ *noun* (*pl.* **noms de plume** /ˌnɒm də ˈpluːm; *NAmE* ˌnɑːm/) (from *French*) a name used by a writer instead of their real name 筆名 SYN **pen-name, pseudonym**

no·men·clat·ure /nəˈmenklətʃə(r); *NAmE* ˈnoʊmənkleɪtʃər/ *noun* [U, C] (*formal*) a system of naming things, especially in a branch of science（尤指某學科的）命名法

nom·in·al /ˈnɒmɪnl; *NAmE* ˈnɑːm-/ *adj.* **1** being sth in name only, and not in reality 名義上的；有名無實的；不真實的：*the nominal leader of the party* 這個政黨的名義領袖 ◇ *He remained in nominal control of the business for another ten years.* 他名義上又掌管了這家公司十年。**2** (of a sum of money 款額) very small and much less than the normal cost or change 很小的；象徵性的 SYN **token**：*We only pay a nominal rent.* 我們只象徵性地付一點租金。**3** (*grammar* 語法) connected with a noun or nouns 名詞性的；名詞的 ▸ **nom·in·al·ly** /-nəli/ *adv.*：*He was nominally in charge of the company.* 他名義上管理着這家公司。

nom·in·al·ize /ˈnɒmɪnəlaɪz; *NAmE* ˈnɑːm-/ *verb* **~ sth** (*grammar* 語法) to form a noun from a verb or adjective, for example 'truth' from 'true' 使（動詞或形容詞）轉變為名詞；使名詞化

nom·in·ate /ˈnɒmɪneɪt; *NAmE* ˈnɑːm-/ *verb* **1** to formally suggest that sb should be chosen for an important role, prize, position, etc. 提名；推薦 SYN **propose**：**~ sb (for sth)** *She has been nominated for the presidency.* 她已經獲得了董事長職位的提名。◇ **~ sb (as) sth** | **~ sb + noun** *He was nominated (as) best actor.* 他獲得了最佳男演員的提名。◇ **~ sb to do sth** *I nominated Paul* *to take on the role of treasurer.* 我推薦保羅擔任司庫。 **2** to choose sb to do a particular job 任命；指派 **SYN** **appoint**： **~ sb (to/as sth)** *I have been nominated to the committee.* 我被任命為委員會委員。◇ **~ sb to do sth** *She was nominated to speak on our behalf.* 她被指派代表我們發言。 **3 ~ sth (as sth)** to choose a time, date or title for sth 挑選，指定（時間、日期、名稱等） **SYN** **select**： *1 December has been nominated as the day of the election.* * 12 月 1 日被指定為選舉日。

nom·in·ation /ˌnɒmɪˈneɪʃn; *NAmE* ˌnɑːm-/ *noun* [U, C] the act of suggesting or choosing sb as a candidate in an election, or for a job or an award; the fact of being suggested for this 提名；推薦；任命；指派： *Membership of the club is by nomination only.* 俱樂部的會員資格僅可通過推薦獲得。◇ *He won the nomination as Democratic candidate for the presidency.* 他贏得了民主黨總統候選人的提名。◇ *They opposed her nomination to the post of Deputy Director.* 他們反對任命她為副主任。◇ *He has had nine Oscar nominations.* 他已經獲得九次奧斯卡提名。

nom·ina·tive /ˈnɒmɪnətɪv; *NAmE* ˈnɑːm-/ (also **sub·ject·ive**) *noun* (*grammar* 語法) (in some languages 用於某些語言) the form of a noun, a pronoun or an adjective when it is the subject of a verb 主格；主格詞 ➲ compare ABLATIVE, ACCUSATIVE, DATIVE, GENITIVE, VOCATIVE ▸ **nom·ina·tive** *adj.*： *nominative pronouns* 主格代詞

nom·inee /ˌnɒmɪˈniː; *NAmE* ˌnɑːm-/ *noun* **1** a person who has been formally suggested for a job, a prize, etc. 被提名人；被任命者： *a presidential nominee* 被提名為總統候選人的人◇ *an Oscar nominee* 獲得奧斯卡提名的人 **2** (*business* 商) a person in whose name money is invested in a company, etc. （投資等的）名義持有人

non- 🔑 /nɒn; *NAmE* nɑːn/ *prefix* (in nouns, adjectives and adverbs 構成名詞、形容詞和副詞) not 無；沒有： *nonsense* 廢話◇ *non-fiction* 紀實文學◇ *non-alcoholic* 不含酒精的◇ *non-profit-making* 非營利性的 ◇ *non-committally* 含糊其詞 **HELP** Most compounds with **non** are written with a hyphen in *BrE* but are written as one word with no hyphen in *NAmE*. 大多數含 non 的複合詞在英式英語裏要加連字符，而在美式英語裏則寫成一個詞。

nona·gen·ar·ian /ˌnɒnədʒəˈneəriən; ˌnəʊn-; *NAmE* ˌnɑːnədʒəˈner-; ˌnoʊn-/ *noun* a person who is between 90 and 99 years old * 90 多歲的人 ▸ **nona·gen·ar·ian** *adj.*

ˌnon-agˈgres·sion *noun* [U] (often used as an adjective 常用作形容詞) a relationship between two countries that have agreed not to attack each other （兩國間的）不侵犯，不侵略： *a policy of non-aggression* 互不侵犯政策◇ *a* ***non-aggression pact/treaty*** 互不侵犯協定 / 條約

ˌnon-alcoˈhol·ic *adj.* (of a drink 飲料) not containing any alcohol 不含酒精的： *a non-alcoholic drink* 軟飲料◇ *Can I have something non-alcoholic?* 給我來杯軟飲料好嗎？

ˌnon-aˈligned *adj.* not providing support for or receiving support from any of the powerful countries in the world 不結盟的 ▸ **ˌnon-aˈlignment** *noun* [U]： *a policy of non-alignment* 不結盟政策

ˌnon-alphaˈbet·ic (also **ˌnon-alphaˈbetical**) *adj.* not being one of the letters of the alphabet 不屬於字母表的；非字母的 ➲ compare ALPHABETIC

ˌnon-apˈpear·ance *noun* [U] (*formal*) failure to be in a place where people expect to see you 不露面；不到場

ˌnon-atˈtend·ance *noun* [U] failure to go to a place at a time or for an event where you are expected 缺席；不出席；不到場

ˌnon-biodeˈgrad·able *adj.* a substance or chemical that is **non-biodegradable** cannot be changed to a harmless natural state by the action of bacteria, and may therefore damage the environment （物質或化學品）不可生物降解的，非生物降解的 **OPP** **biodegradable**

nonce /nɒns; *NAmE* nɑːns/ *adj.* a **nonce** word or expression is one that is invented for one particular occasion （詞語）臨時造的，偶用的，只使用一次的

non·cha·lant /ˈnɒnʃələnt; *NAmE* ˌnɑːnʃəˈlɑːnt/ *adj.* behaving in a calm and relaxed way; giving the impression that you are not feeling any anxiety 若無其事的；冷靜的；漠不關心的 **SYN** **casual**： *to* ***appear/look/sound nonchalant*** 顯得 / 看上去 / 聽起來滿不在乎的樣子◇ *'It'll be fine,' she replied, with a nonchalant shrug.* 她若無其事地聳聳肩說："會沒事的。" ▸ **non·cha·lance** /-ləns; *NAmE* -ˈlɑːns/ *noun* [U]： *an air of nonchalance* 一副滿不在乎的樣子 **non·cha·lant·ly** *adv.*： *He was leaning nonchalantly against the wall.* 他漫不經心地斜倚着牆。

ˌnon-ˈcitizen *noun* (*NAmE*) = ALIEN (1)

ˌnon-ˈcombat·ant *noun* **1** a member of the armed forces who does not actually fight in a war, for example an army doctor （軍隊中的）非戰鬥人員 **2** in a war, a person who is not a member of the armed forces （戰爭時期的）平民，非軍事人員 **SYN** **civilian** ➲ compare COMBATANT

ˌnon-commisˈsioned ˈofficer *noun* (*abbr.* **NCO**) a soldier in the army, etc. who has a rank such as SERGEANT or CORPORAL, but not a high rank 軍士 ➲ compare COMMISSIONED OFFICER

ˌnon-coˈmmit·tal *adj.* not giving an opinion; not showing which side of an argument you agree with 態度不明朗的；不表態的；含糊的： *a* ***non-committal reply/tone*** 含糊其詞的回答 / 語調◇ *The doctor was non-committal about when I could drive again.* 關於我何時可以再開車的問題，醫生沒有表態。 ➲ see also COMMIT (4) ▸ **non·com·mit·tal·ly** *adv.*

ˌnon-comˈpli·ance *noun* [U] **~ (with sth)** the fact of failing or refusing to obey a rule 不服從；不順從；違反： *There are penalties for non-compliance with the fire regulations.* 不遵守消防規章的行為要受到處罰。 **OPP** **compliance**

ˌnon ˌcompos ˈmentis (also **ˌnon ˈcompos**) *adj.* (*formal*) not in a normal mental state 精神不健全的 **OPP** **compos mentis**

non·con·form·ist **AW** /ˌnɒnkənˈfɔːmɪst; *NAmE* ˌnɑːnkənˈfɔːrm-/ *noun* **1** **Nonconformist** (in England and Wales) a member of a Protestant Church that does not follow the beliefs and practices of the Church of England （英格蘭和威爾士）不從國教者，不遵奉聖公會的新教教徒 **2** a person who does not follow normal ways of thinking or behaving 不遵循傳統規範的人；不認同主流思想的人 ▸ **non·con·form·ist**, **Non·con·form·ist** *adj.*

non·con·form·ity **AW** /ˌnɒnkənˈfɔːmɪti; *NAmE* ˌnɑːnkənˈfɔːrm-/ (also **non·con·form·ism** /ˌnɒnkənˈfɔːmɪzəm; *NAmE* ˌnɑːnkənˈfɔːrm-/) *noun* [U] **1** the fact of not following normal ways of thinking and behaving 不遵從傳統規範；不認同主流思想 **2** **Nonconformity** the beliefs and practices of Nonconformist Churches 非國教教義；不信奉英國國教

ˌnon-ˈcontact sport *noun* a sport in which players do not have physical contact with each other 無身體接觸的體育運動；非接觸性體育運動 **OPP** **contact sport**

ˌnon-conˈtribu·tory *adj.* (of an insurance or pension plan 保險或養老金計劃) paid for by the employer and not the employee 全部由雇主承擔的；非分攤制的 **OPP** **contributory**

ˌnon-controˈver·sial *adj.* not causing, or not likely to cause, any disagreement 不會引起爭議的；一致的 **OPP** **controversial** **HELP** This is not as strong as **uncontroversial**, which is more common. 語氣沒有 uncontroversial 強，也較為少用。

ˌnon-coˌopeˈr·ation *noun* [U] refusal to help a person in authority by doing what they have asked you to do, especially as a form of protest 不合作（作為一種反抗的手段）： *A strike is unlikely, but some forms of non-cooperation are being considered.* 罷工不太可能，但是某種形式的不合作正在醞釀之中。

ˌnon-ˈcount *adj.* (*grammar* 語法) = UNCOUNTABLE

ˌnon-cuˈstod·ial *adj.* [only before noun] (*law* 律) **1** (of a punishment 懲罰) that does not involve a period of time

N

in prison 監外執行的： *a* ***non-custodial** sentence/penalty* 監外執行的判決／懲罰 **2** (of a parent 父或母) not having CUSTODY of a child 無監護權的 OPP **custodial**

ˌnon-ˈdairy *adj.* [only before noun] not made with milk or cream 非奶製的；非乳製的： *a non-dairy whipped topping* 打好的非奶製糕點配料

ˌnon-deˈfining *adj.* = NON-RESTRICTIVE

non·de·script /ˈnɒndɪskrɪpt; *NAmE* ˈnɑːn-/ *adj.* (*disapproving*) having no interesting or unusual features or qualities 無特徵的；平庸的；毫無個性的 SYN **dull**

none /nʌn/ *pron., adv.*

■ ***pron.*** **~** (**of sb/sth**) not one of a group of people or things; not any 沒有一個；毫無： *None of these pens works/work.* 這些鋼筆沒有一支能用。◇ *We have three sons but none of them lives/live nearby.* 我們有三個兒子，但他們都不住在附近。◇ *We saw several houses but none we really liked.* 我們看了幾所房子，但都不怎麼喜歡。◇ *Tickets for Friday? Sorry we've got none left.* 星期五的票？對不起，一張也沒有了。◇ *He told me all the news but none of it was very exciting.* 他告訴了我所有的新聞，但沒有一件激動人心的。◇ *'Is there any more milk?' 'No,* ***none at all.****'* "還有牛奶嗎？" "沒了，一點都沒了。" ◇ (*formal*) *Everybody liked him but none* (= nobody) *more than I.* 大家都喜歡他，但誰也比不過我。

IDM **ˈnone but** (*literary*) only 僅僅；只有： *None but he knew the truth.* 只有他知道真相。 **none ˈother than** used to emphasize who or what sb/sth is, when this is surprising（強調出人意料的人或事）竟然： *Her first customer was none other than Mrs Obama.* 她的第一位顧客竟然是奧巴馬夫人。 **have/want none of sth** to refuse to accept sth 拒絕接受；什麼也不要： *I offered to pay but he was having none of it.* 我提出付賬，但他堅決不讓我付。 **ˌnone the ˈless** = NONETHELESS

■ ***adv.*** **1** used with *the* and a comparative to mean 'not at all'（與 the 加比較級連用）一點都不，絕無： *She told me what it meant at great length but I'm afraid I'm* ***none the wiser.*** 她費盡口舌給我解釋它的意思，可我恐怕還是不明白。◇ *He seems* ***none the worse*** *for the experience.* 他的這次經歷似乎一點沒有給他造成傷害。 **2** used with *too* and an adjective or adverb to mean 'not at all' or 'not very'（與 too 加形容詞或副詞連用）絕不，不怎麼： *She was looking none too pleased.* 她看上去一點也不高興。

Grammar Point 語法說明

none of

■ When you use **none of** with an uncountable noun, the verb is in the singular. * none of 與不可數名詞連用時，動詞用單數： *None of the work was done.* 那些工作全都未幹。

■ When you use **none of** with a plural noun or pronoun, or a singular noun referring to a group of people or things, you can use either a singular or a plural verb. The singular form is used in a formal style in *BrE*. * none of 與複數名詞、代詞或單數集合名詞連用時，動詞用單數或複數均可。英式英語的正式文體用單數形式： *None of the trains is/are going to London.* 這些列車都不去倫敦。◇ *None of her family has/have been to college.* 她的一家誰都沒上過大學。

non·en·tity /nɒˈnentəti; *NAmE* nɑːˈn-/ *noun* (*pl.* **-ies**) (*disapproving*) a person without any special qualities, who has not achieved anything important 無專長的人；無成就的人 SYN **nobody**

ˌnon-esˈsential *adj.* [usually before noun] not completely necessary 非必需的；不重要的 ➲ compare ESSENTIAL *adj.* (1) HELP This is not as strong as **inessential** and is more common. **Inessential** can suggest disapproval. 不如 inessential 語氣強，但較常用。inessential 有不贊成的意思。 ▸ **ˌnon-esˈsential** *noun* [usually pl.]： *I have no money for non-essentials.* 我沒有錢應付那些非必要的花費。

nonet /nəʊˈnet; nɒˈnet; *NAmE* noʊˈnet/ *noun* **1** [C+sing./pl. v.] a group of nine people or things, especially nine musicians 九人組；九個一組；（尤指）九重奏樂團，九重唱組合 **2** [C] a piece of music for nine singers or musicians 九重奏（曲）；九重唱（曲）

none·the·less AW /ˌnʌnðəˈles/ (also **ˌnone the ˈless**) *adv.* (*formal*) despite this fact 儘管如此 SYN **nevertheless**： *The book is too long but, nonetheless, informative and entertaining.* 這本書太長，但是很有知識性和趣味性。◇ *The problems are not serious. Nonetheless, we shall need to tackle them soon.* 問題不嚴重。不過我們還是需要儘快處理。 ➲ LANGUAGE BANK at NEVERTHELESS

ˌnon-eˈvent *noun* (*informal*) an event that was expected to be interesting, exciting and popular but is in fact very disappointing 令人失望的事；掃興的事 SYN **anti-climax**

ˌnon-exˈecutive *adj.* [only before noun] (*BrE, business* 商) a **non-executive** director of a company can give advice at a high level but does not have the power to make decisions about the company 非執行的；非主管的；無決策權的

ˌnon-eˈxistent *adj.* not existing; not real 不存在的；不真實的： *a non-existent problem* 不存在的問題 ◇ *'How's your social life?' 'Non-existent, I'm afraid.'* "你的社交生活如何？" "我恐怕沒有社交生活。" ◇ *Hospital beds were scarce and medicines were* ***practically non-existent.*** 當時醫院病牀緊缺，藥物幾乎沒有。➲ compare EXISTENT ▸ **ˌnon-eˈxistence** *noun* [U]

ˌnon-ˈfiction *noun* [U] books, articles or texts about real facts, people and events 紀實文學： *I prefer reading non-fiction.* 我喜歡看紀實作品。◇ *the non-fiction section of the library* 圖書館的紀實文學類關區 OPP **fiction**

ˌnon-ˈfinite *adj.* (*grammar* 語法) a **non-finite** verb form or clause does not show a particular tense, PERSON or NUMBER 非限定的 OPP **finite**

ˌnon-ˈflammable *adj.* not likely to burn easily 不易燃的： *non-flammable nightwear* 不易燃的睡衣 OPP **flammable**

nong /nɒŋ; *NAmE* nɑːŋ; nɔːŋ/ *noun* (*AustralE, NZE, informal*) = NING-NONG

ˌnon-ˈgradable *adj.* (*grammar* 語法) (of an adjective 形容詞) that cannot be used in the comparative and superlative forms, or be used with words like 'very' and 'less' 不分級的；不與程度副詞連用的 OPP **gradable**

ˌnon-ˈhuman *adj.* not human 非人類的： *similarities between human and non-human animals* 人和其他動物之間的相似之處 ➲ compare HUMAN *adj.*, INHUMAN

ˌnon-iˌdentical ˈtwin *adj.* = FRATERNAL TWIN

ˌnon-interˈven·tion (also **ˌnon-interˈfer·ence**) *noun* [U] the policy or practice of not becoming involved in other people's disagreements, especially those of foreign countries（尤指對外國事務的）不干涉 ▸ **ˌnon-interˈven·tion·ism** *noun* [U] **ˌnon-interˈven·tion·ist** *adj.*

ˌnon-inˈvasive *adj.* (of medical treatment 治療) not involving cutting into the body 非侵害的；非創傷的；無創的

ˌnon-ˈissue *noun* a subject of little or no importance 無足輕重的事；不重要的事

ˌnon-ˈlinear *adj.* (*technical* 術語) that does not develop from one thing to another in a single smooth series of stages 非直線型的；非線性的 OPP **linear**

ˌnon-maˈlignant *adj.* (of a TUMOUR 腫瘤) not caused by cancer and not likely to be dangerous 非惡性的；良性的 SYN **benign** OPP **malignant**

ˌnon-ˈnative *adj.* **1** (of animals, plants, etc. 動物、植物等) not existing naturally in a place but coming from somewhere else 非本地的；引進的；移植的 **2** a **non-native** speaker of a language is one who has not spoken it from the time they first learnt to talk 非母語的 OPP **native**

ˌnon-neˈgoti·able *adj.* **1** that cannot be discussed or changed 不可談判解決的；無法改變的 **2** (of a cheque, etc. 支票等) that cannot be changed for money by anyone except the person whose name is on it 只限本人使用的；禁止轉讓的 OPP **negotiable**

ˌ**no-no** *noun* [sing.] (*informal*) a thing or a way of behaving that is not acceptable in a particular situation 不可幹的事；不可接受的行為

ˌ**non-obˈservance** *noun* [U] (*formal*) the failure to keep or to obey a rule, custom, etc. 違反，不遵從（規章、習俗等） OPP **observance**

ˌ**no-ˈnonsense** *adj.* [only before noun] simple and direct; only paying attention to important and necessary things 簡單直接的；言簡意賅的；不說廢話的

non·par·eil /ˌnɒnpəˈreɪl; *NAmE* ˌnɑːnpəˈrel/ *noun* [sing.] (*formal*) a person or thing that is better than others in a particular area 無與倫比的人（或事物）

ˌ**non-partiˈsan** *adj.* [usually before noun] not supporting the ideas of one particular political party or group of people strongly 無黨派之見的；中立的 OPP **partisan**

ˌ**non-ˈpayment** *noun* [U] (*formal*) failure to pay a debt, a tax, rent, etc. 未支付，不支付（欠債、稅款、租金等）

ˌ**non-ˈperson** *noun* (*pl.* ˌ**non-ˈpersons**) a person who is thought not to be important, or who is ignored 不受重視（或被忽視）的人；小人物

non·plussed (*US* also **non·plused**) /ˌnɒnˈplʌst; *NAmE* ˌnɑːn-/ *adj.* so surprised and confused that you do not know what to do or say 驚呆的；非常困惑的 SYN **dumbfounded**

ˌ**non-preˈscrip·tion** *adj.* (of drugs 藥品) that you can buy directly without a special form from a doctor 非處方類的；不用醫生處方可以買的

ˌ**non-proˈfes·sion·al** *adj.* **1** having a job that does not need a high level of education or special training; connected with a job of this kind 非專業的；未經專門訓練的；非專業性工作的： *training for non-professional staff* 對非專業員工的培訓 **2** doing sth as a hobby rather than as a paid job 非職業的；業餘的： *non-professional actors* 非職業演員 ➲ compare PROFESSIONAL *adj.*, UNPROFESSIONAL ➲ see also AMATEUR *adj.*

ˌ**non-ˈprofit** (*BrE* also ˌ**non-ˈprofit-making**) *adj.* (of an organization 機構) without the aim of making a profit 不以營利為目的的；非營利的：*an independent non-profit organization* 獨立的非營利機構 ◇ *The centre is run on a non-profit basis.* 這個中心的運作不以營利為目的。◇ *The charity is non-profit-making.* 這個慈善團體不以營利為目的。

ˌ**non-proˌlifeˈr·ation** *noun* [U] a limit to the increase in the number of nuclear and chemical weapons that are produced 限制核武器和化學武器的增加；防止核擴散

ˌ**non-proˈpri·etary** *adj.* not made by or belonging to a particular company 無產權的；非專屬的；非專利的： *non-proprietary medicines* 非專利藥物 OPP **proprietary**

ˌ**non-reˈfund·able** (also ˌ**non-reˈturnable**) *adj.* (of a sum of money 款額) that cannot be returned 不可償還的；不能退款的： *a non-refundable deposit* 不能退回的訂金 ◇ *a non-refundable ticket* (= you cannot return it and get your money back) 不可退的票

ˌ**non-reˈnewable** *adj.* **1** (of natural resources such as gas or oil 天然氣、石油等自然資源) that cannot be replaced after use 不能更新的；不可再生的 **2** that cannot be continued or repeated for a further period of time after it has ended 非延續性的；不可重複有效的： *a non-renewable contract* 不可延續的合同 OPP **renewable**

ˌ**non-ˈresident** *adj.*, *noun*

▪ ***adj.*** (*formal*) **1** (of a person or company 人或公司) not living or located permanently in a particular place or country 非當地居住（或營業的）；非常駐的 **2** not living in the place where you work or in a house that you own 不在（工作地點等）居住的；不寄宿的；非居民的 **3** not staying at a particular hotel 不在（某旅館）住宿的： *Non-resident guests are welcome to use the hotel swimming pool.* 歡迎非旅館住客使用本旅館的游泳池。

▪ ***noun*** **1** a person who does not live permanently in a particular country 非永久居民 **2** a person not staying at a particular hotel 不在某旅館住的人；非旅館住客

ˌ**non-resiˈdent·ial** *adj.* **1** that is not used for people to live in 不用於居住的；非住宅的 **2** that does not require you to live in the place where you work or study 通勤的；走讀的： *a non-residential course* 走讀課程

ˌ**non-reˈstric·tive** (also ˌ**non-deˈfining**) *adj.* (*grammar* 語法) (of RELATIVE CLAUSES 關係從句) giving extra information about a noun phrase, inside commas in writing or in a particular INTONATION in speech. In 'My brother, who lives in France, is coming to Rome with us', the part between the commas is a non-restrictive relative clause. 非限制性的；非限定的 ➲ compare RESTRICTIVE

ˌ**non-reˈturn·able** *adj.* **1** = NON-REFUNDABLE **2** that you cannot give back, for example to a shop/store, to be used again; that will not be given back to you 不可退回的；不回收的： *non-returnable bottles* 不回收的瓶子 ◇ *a non-returnable deposit* 不能退回的訂金 OPP **returnable**

ˌ**non-scienˈti·fic** *adj.* not involving or connected with science or scientific methods 不涉及科學的；與科學無關的 ➲ compare SCIENTIFIC, UNSCIENTIFIC

non·sense 🔑 /ˈnɒnsns; *NAmE* ˈnɑːnsens; -sns/ *noun* **1** 🔑 [U, C] ideas, statements or beliefs that you think are ridiculous or not true 謬論；胡扯；胡言亂語 SYN **rubbish**： *Reports that he has resigned are nonsense.* 有關他已經辭職的報道是無稽之談。◇ *You're **talking nonsense**!* 你在胡說八道！◇ *'I won't go.' 'Nonsense! You must go!'* "我不想去。" "胡扯！你一定得去！" ◇ ***It's nonsense to** say they don't care.* 說他們不在意那是瞎扯。◇ *The idea is an economic nonsense.* 這種觀點是經濟學上的謬論。 **2** 🔑 [U] silly or unacceptable behaviour 愚蠢的行為；冒失；不可接受的行為： *The new teacher won't stand for any nonsense.* 這位新教師不會容忍任何無禮行為。 ➲ see also NO-NONSENSE **3** 🔑 [U] spoken or written words that have no meaning or make no sense 毫無意義的話；沒有意義的文章： *a book of children's nonsense poems* 一本兒童打油詩集 ◇ *Most of the translation he did for me was complete nonsense.* 他給我做的大多數譯文完全不知所云。

IDM **make (a) ˈnonsense of sth** to reduce the value of sth by a lot; to make sth seem ridiculous 使…的價值大打折扣；使…顯得荒誕： *If people can bribe police officers, it makes a complete nonsense of the legal system.* 如果人們可以收買警察，法律體系就會變得一文不值。 ➲ more at STUFF *n.*

ˈ**nonsense word** *noun* a word with no meaning 無意義的詞

non·sens·ical /nɒnˈsensɪkl; *NAmE* nɑːn-/ *adj.* ridiculous; with no meaning 荒謬的；無意義的 SYN **absurd**

non sequi·tur /ˌnɒn ˈsekwɪtə(r); *NAmE* ˌnɑːn/ *noun* (from *Latin*, *formal*) a statement that does not seem to follow what has just been said in any natural or logical way 不合邏輯的推論；未根據前提的推理

ˌ**non-ˈslip** *adj.* that helps to prevent sb/sth from slipping; that does not slip 防滑的；不滑的： *a non-slip bath mat* 浴室防滑墊

ˌ**non-ˈsmoker** *noun* a person who does not smoke 不吸煙的人 OPP **smoker**

ˌ**non-ˈsmoking** (also ˌ**no-ˈsmoking**) *adj.* [usually before noun] **1** (of a place 地方) where people are not allowed to smoke 禁煙的；不允許吸煙的： *a non-smoking area in a restaurant* 餐廳裏的禁煙區 **2** (of a person 人) who does not smoke 不吸煙的： *She's a non-smoking, non-drinking fitness fanatic.* 她是一個不吸煙、不喝酒、熱愛健美的人。 ▸ ˌ**non-ˈsmoking** (also ˌ**no-ˈsmoking**) *noun* [U]： *Non-smoking is now the norm in most workplaces.* 大多數工作場所現在都已禁止吸煙。

ˌ**non-speˈcif·ic** *adj.* [usually before noun] **1** not definite or clearly defined; general 不明確的；非特定的；泛泛的： *The candidate's speech was non-specific.* 這位候選人的講話只是泛泛之談。 **2** (*medical* 醫) (of pain, a disease, etc. 疼痛、疾病等) with more than one possible cause 不止一種病因的；有多種致病可能的

ˌ**non-speˌcific ureˈthritis** *noun* [U] (*abbr.* NSU) (*medical* 醫) a condition in which the URETHRA becomes sore and swollen. It is often caused by an infection caught by having sex. 非特異性尿道炎（多因性交感染）

N

ˌnon-ˈstandard *adj.* **1** (of language 語言) not considered correct by most educated people 非標準的；不規範的： *non-standard dialects* 不規範的方言 ◇ *non-standard English* 非標準英語 ➲ compare STANDARD *adj.* (4) **2** not the usual size, type, etc. (尺寸、型號等) 不標準的，非常用的： *The paper was of non-standard size.* 這種紙的大小不標準。

ˌnon-ˈstarter *noun* (*informal*) a thing or a person that has no chance of success 無望取得成功的人（或事）： *As a business proposition, it's a non-starter.* 作為一個商業計劃，這不可能成功。

ˌnon-ˈstick *adj.* [usually before noun] (of a pan or a surface 鍋或物體表面) covered with a substance that prevents food from sticking to it 不粘食物的；不黏的

ˌnon-ˈstop *adj.* **1** (of a train, a journey, etc. 列車、旅程等) without any stops 直達的；不在途中停留的 SYN **direct**： *a non-stop flight to Tokyo* 到東京的直達航班 ◇ *a non-stop train/service* 直達列車／服務 **2** without any pauses or stops 不間斷的；不停的 SYN **continuous**： *non-stop entertainment/work* 連續不斷的娛樂／工作 ▸ **ˌnon-ˈstop** *adv.*： *We flew non-stop from Paris to Chicago.* 我們從巴黎直飛芝加哥。◇ *It rained non-stop all week.* 雨連續下了整整一個星期。

ˌnon-traˈditional AW *adj.* not following the usual methods, practices, etc. in a particular area of activity 非傳統的；不符合傳統的： *students from non-traditional backgrounds* 非傳統出身的學生 OPP **traditional**

ˌnon-ˈU *adj.* (*old-fashioned, informal*) (of language or social behaviour 語言或社交行為) not considered socially acceptable among the upper classes 不為上層階級所接受的 ORIGIN From the abbreviation **U** for 'upper class'. 源自 upper class 的縮寫字母 U。

ˌnon-ˈunion (also *less frequent* **ˌnon-ˈunionized, -ised**) *adj.* [usually before noun] **1** not belonging to a TRADE/LABOR UNION 不屬於工會的： *non-union labour/workers* 未加入工會的勞工／工人 **2** (of a business, company, etc. 企業、公司等) not accepting TRADE/LABOR UNION or employing TRADE/LABOR UNION members 不接受工會的；不雇用工會會員的

ˌnon-vegeˈtarian (also *informal* **ˌnon-ˈveg**) *noun* (*IndE*) a person who eats meat, fish, eggs, etc. 非素食者；葷食者： *They ordered a non-veg meal.* 他們要了一餐葷菜。

ˌnon-ˈverbal *adj.* [usually before noun] not involving words or speech 不涉及言語的；非言語的： *non-verbal communication* 非語言交際

ˌnon-ˈvintage *adj.* (of wine 葡萄酒) not made only from GRAPES grown in a particular place in a particular year 非特定地區特定年份釀造的 OPP **vintage**

ˌnon-ˈviolence *noun* [U] the policy of using peaceful methods, not force, to bring about political or social change 非暴力政策

ˌnon-ˈviolent *adj.* **1** using peaceful methods, not force, to bring about political or social change (政策) 非暴力的，不訴諸武力的： *non-violent resistance* 非暴力抵抗 ◇ *a non-violent protest* 非暴力抗議 **2** not involving force, or injury to sb (行為) 非暴力的： *non-violent crimes* 非暴力犯罪

ˌnon-ˈwhite *noun* a person who is not a member of a race of people who have white skin 非白種人 ▸ **ˌnon-ˈwhite** *adj.*

noo·dle /ˈnuːdl/ *noun* **1** [usually pl.] a long thin strip of PASTA, used especially in Chinese and Italian cooking 麪條： *chicken noodle soup* 雞湯麪 ◇ *Would you prefer rice or noodles?* 你喜歡吃米飯還是麪條？ **2** [C] (*old-fashioned, NAmE, slang*) = NODDLE

nook /nʊk/ *noun* a small quiet place or corner that is sheltered or hidden from other people 僻靜處；幽靜的角落： *a shady nook in the garden* 花園裏陰涼的一角 ◇ *dark woods full of secret **nooks and crannies*** 充滿了神秘色彩的幽暗的樹林

IDM **every ˌnook and ˈcranny** (*informal*) every part of a place; every aspect of a situation 到處；各個方面

nooky (also **nookie**) /ˈnʊki/ *noun* [U] (*slang*) sexual activity 性行為；性交

noon /nuːn/ *noun* [U] 12 o'clock in the middle of the day 正午；中午 SYN **midday**： *We should be there by noon.* 我們應該最晚中午到達。◇ *The conference opens at 12 noon on Saturday.* 這次會議在星期六中午 12 點開幕。◇ *the noon deadline for the end of hostilities* 中午結束敵對狀態這一最後期限 ◇ *I'm leaving on the noon train.* 我坐中午的火車走。◇ *the glaring light of **high noon*** 正午眩目的陽光 IDM see MORNING

noon·day /ˈnuːndeɪ/ *adj.* [only before noun] (*old-fashioned or literary*) happening or appearing at noon 正午發生的；中午出現的： *the noonday sun* 正午的太陽

ˈno one 🔑 (also **no·body**) *pron.* not anyone; no person 沒有人；沒有任何人： *No one was at home.* 沒有人在家。◇ *There was no one else around.* 周圍沒有其他人。◇ *We were told to speak to no one.* 要求我們不要和任何人說話。 HELP **No one** is much more common than **nobody** in written English. 在書面英語中，no one 比 nobody 更為常用。

noon·tide /ˈnuːntaɪd/ *noun* [U] (*literary*) around 12 o'clock in the middle of the day 正午；亭午

noose /nuːs/ *noun* a circle that is tied in one end of a rope with a knot that allows the circle to get smaller as the other end of the rope is pulled 繩套；套索；活扣： *a hangman's noose* 絞索 ◇ (*figurative*) *His debts were a noose around his neck.* 債務就像套在他脖子上的一條套索。

nope /nəʊp; *NAmE* noʊp/ *exclamation* (*informal*) used to say 'no' 不；不行；沒有： *'Have you seen my pen?' 'Nope.'* "你看見我的筆了嗎？""沒有。"

ˈno place *adv.* (*informal, especially NAmE*) = NOWHERE： *I have no place else to go.* 我沒有其他地方可去。

nor 🔑 /nɔː(r)/ *conj., adv.*

1 🔑 **neither … nor …** | **not … nor …** and not 也不： *She seemed neither surprised nor worried.* 她似乎既不驚訝也不擔心。◇ *He wasn't there on Monday. Nor on Tuesday, for that matter.* 他星期一沒在那兒。星期二也一樣，也不在。◇ (*formal*) *Not a building nor a tree was left standing.* 沒有一棟房屋一棵樹仍然立着沒倒。 **2** 🔑 used before a positive verb to agree with sth negative that has just been said (用於肯定動詞前，表示同意剛提及的否定命題) 也不： *She doesn't like them and nor does Jeff.* 她不喜歡他們，傑夫也不喜歡。◇ *'I'm not going.' 'Nor am I.'* "我不會去。" "我也不去。"

Nor·dic /ˈnɔːdɪk; *NAmE* ˈnɔːrdɪk/ *adj.* **1** of or connected with the countries of Scandinavia, Finland and Iceland 斯堪的納維亞的；北歐國家的 **2** typical of a member of a European race of people who are tall and have blue eyes and blonde hair 北歐人的；有北歐民族特徵的

ˌNordic ˈwalking *noun* [U] the sport of walking with special poles attached to your wrist 越野行走，北歐式健走 (使用特殊手杖快速行走的一種運動)

norm AW /nɔːm; *NAmE* nɔːrm/ *noun, verb*

■ *noun* **1** (often **the norm**) [sing.] a situation or a pattern of behaviour that is usual or expected 常態；正常行為 SYN **rule**： *a departure from the norm* 一反常態 ◇ *Older parents seem to be the norm rather than the exception nowadays.* 人們在年齡較大時才生育子女在今天似乎成了常事，而不是個例。 **2 norms** [pl.] standards of behaviour that are typical of or accepted within a particular group or society 規範；行為標準： ***social/cultural norms*** 社會／文化規範 ➲ COLLOCATIONS at RACE **3** [C] a required or agreed standard, amount, etc. 標準；定額；定量： *detailed education norms for children of particular ages* 針對具體年齡兒童的詳細教育標準

■ *verb* **~ sth** to adjust sth so that it is of the required standard; to establish a required or agreed standard for sth 規範；規定： *You can use the information to norm the test.* 你可以用這些資料去規範測試。◇ *to norm the practice of trading on the Internet* 規範網上交易行為

nor·mal 🔑 AW /ˈnɔːml; *NAmE* ˈnɔːrml/ *adj., noun*

■ *adj.* **1** 🔑 typical, usual or ordinary; what you would expect 典型的；正常的；一般的： ***quite/perfectly*** (= completely) ***normal*** 相當／完全正常 ◇ *Her temperature is normal.* 她的體溫正常。◇ ***It's normal to** feel tired*

N

after such a long trip. 這樣長途旅行之後感到疲勞是正常的。◇ *Divorce is complicated enough* ***in normal circumstances****, but this situation is even worse.* 在一般情況下，離婚已經夠複雜了，但這一次情況更糟。◇ ***Under normal circumstances****, I would say 'yes'.* 一般情況下，我會說"行"。◇ *He should be able to* ***lead a perfectly normal life****.* 他應該能夠過上完全正常的生活。◇ ***In the normal course of events*** *I wouldn't go to that part of town.* 通常我是不會到那個城區去的。◇ *We are open during normal office hours.* 我們在正常的辦公時間內開放。 **2** 🔑 not suffering from any mental DISORDER 精神正常的；意識健全的： *People who commit such crimes aren't normal.* 犯這種罪的人心理不正常。 OPP **abnormal** IDM see PER

■ ***noun*** 🔑 [U] the usual or average state, level or standard 常態；通常標準；一般水平： ***above/below normal*** 通常標準之上／之下 ◇ *Things soon returned* ***to normal****.* 情況很快恢復了正常。

ˌnormal distriˈbution *noun* (*statistics* 統計) the usual way in which a particular feature varies among a large number of things or people, represented on a GRAPH by a line that rises to a high SYMMETRICAL curve in the middle 正態分佈；常態分佈 ➲ compare BELL CURVE

nor·mal·ity AW /nɔːˈmæləti; *NAmE* nɔːrˈm-/ (also **nor·malcy** /ˈnɔːmlsi; *NAmE* ˈnɔːrm-/especially in *NAmE*) *noun* [U] a situation where everything is normal or as you would expect it to be 常態；正常的形勢： *They are hoping for a* ***return to normality*** *now that the war is over.* 既然戰爭結束了，他們希望一切都恢復常態。

nor·mal·ize (*BrE* also **-ise**) AW /ˈnɔːməlaɪz; *NAmE* ˈnɔːrm-/ *verb* [T, I] **~ (sth)** (*formal*) to fit or make sth fit a normal pattern or condition （使）正常化，標準化，常規化： *a lotion to normalize oily skin* 使油性皮膚恢復正常的護膚液 ◇ *The two countries agreed to* ***normalize relations*** (= return to a normal, friendly relationship, for example after a disagreement or war). 兩國同意恢復正常關係。◇ *It took time until the political situation had normalized.* 政治局勢過了很長時間才恢復正常。 ▸ **nor·mal·iza·tion, -isa·tion** AW /ˌnɔːməlaɪˈzeɪʃn; *NAmE* ˌnɔːrmələˈz-/ *noun* [U] ： *the normalization of relations* 關係的正常化

nor·mal·ly 🔑 AW /ˈnɔːməli; *NAmE* ˈnɔːrm-/ *adv.* **1** 🔑 usually; in normal circumstances 通常；正常情況下： *I'm not normally allowed to stay out late.* 通常情況下，我不能在外很晚不歸。◇ *It's normally much warmer than this in July.* 通常七月要比現在熱得多。◇ *It normally takes 20 minutes to get there.* 去那兒一般要花 20 分鐘。 **2** 🔑 in the usual or ordinary way 正常地；平常地： *Her heart is beating normally.* 她心跳正常。◇ *Just try to behave normally.* 盡量表現得若無其事。

Nor·man /ˈnɔːmən; *NAmE* ˈnɔːrm-/ *adj.* **1** used to describe the style of ARCHITECTURE in Britain in the 11th and 12th centuries that developed from the ROMANESQUE style 諾曼式的；諾曼式建築風格的： *a Norman church/castle* 諾曼式的教堂／城堡 **2** connected with the Normans (= the people from northern Europe who defeated the English in 1066 and then ruled the country) 諾曼人的： *the Norman Conquest* 諾曼征服

nor·ma·tive /ˈnɔːmətɪv; *NAmE* ˈnɔːrm-/ *adj.* (*formal*) describing or setting standards or rules of behaviour 規範的；標準的： *a normative approach* 規範的方法

Norse /nɔːs; *NAmE* nɔːrs/ *noun* [U] the Norwegian language, especially in an ancient form, or the Scandinavian language group 諾爾斯語；（古）挪威語；古斯堪的納維亞語

north 🔑 /nɔːθ; *NAmE* nɔːrθ/ *noun, adj., adv.*

■ ***noun*** [U, sing.] (*abbr.* **N**, **No.**) **1** 🔑 (usually **the north**) the direction that is on your left when you watch the sun rise; one of the four main points of the COMPASS 北；北方： *Which way is north?* 哪邊是北？◇ *cold winds coming from the north* 從北方襲來的寒風 ◇ *Mount Kenya is* ***to the north of*** (= further north than) *Nairobi.* 肯尼亞山在內羅畢以北。 ➲ picture at COMPASS ➲ compare EAST *n.* (1), SOUTH *n.* (1), WEST *n.* (1) ➲ see also MAGNETIC NORTH, TRUE NORTH **2** 🔑 **the north, the North** the northern part of a country, a region or the world 北部；北部地區： *birds migrating from the north* 從北方遷徙來的鳥 ◇ *Houses are less expensive in the North* (= of England) *than in the South.* 北方的房子比南方便宜。 **3 the North** the NE states of the US which fought against the South in the American Civil War（美國南北戰爭時與南方作戰的）北部各州，北方 **4 the North** the richer and more developed countries of the world, especially in Europe and N America 北方發達國家（尤指歐洲和北美各國）

■ ***adj.*** [only before noun] **1** 🔑 (*abbr.* **N**, **No.**) in or towards the north 北方的；向北的；北部的： *North London* 倫敦北區 ◇ *the north bank of the river* 這條河的北岸 **2** 🔑 a **north wind** blows from the north 北風的；北方吹來的 ➲ compare NORTHERLY *adj.*

■ ***adv.*** 🔑 **1** towards the north 向北；朝北： *The house faces north.* 這房子朝北。 **2 ~ of sth** nearer to the north than sth 某物以北： *They live ten miles north of Boston.* 他們居住在波士頓以北 10 英里處。 **3 ~ of sth** (*finance* 財 or *NAmE, informal*) more or higher than sth 超過： *The estimated value is north of $5.4 billion.* 估價高於 54 億元。 OPP **south**

IDM **up ˈnorth** (*informal*) to or in the north of a country, especially England 在北方，到北方（尤指英格蘭北部）： *They've gone to live up north.* 他們已經搬到北方去住了。

ˌNorth Aˈmerica *noun* [U] the continent consisting of Canada, the United States, Mexico, the countries of Central America and Greenland 北美洲，北美大陸（包括加拿大、美國、墨西哥、中美各國和格陵蘭）

the ˌNorth Atˌlantic ˈDrift *noun* [sing.] (*technical* 術語) a current of warm water in the Atlantic Ocean, that has the effect of making the climate of NW Europe warmer 北大西洋暖流（能使歐洲西北部氣候變暖）

north·bound /ˈnɔːθbaʊnd; *NAmE* ˈnɔːrθ-/ *adj.* travelling or leading towards the north 北行的；向北的： *northbound traffic* 北上的交通運輸 ◇ *the northbound carriageway of the motorway* 高速公路的北行車道

ˈnorth-country *adj.* [only before noun] connected with the northern part of a country or region 北國的；（國家或地區）北部的： *a north-country accent* 北部地區的口音

ˌnorth-ˈeast *noun* (usually **the north-east**) [sing.] (*abbr.* **NE**) the direction or region at an equal distance between north and east 東北；東北方；東北地區 ➲ picture at COMPASS ▸ **ˌnorth-ˈeast** *adv., adj.*

ˌnorth-ˈeast·er·ly *adj.* **1** [only before noun] in or towards the north-east 東北方的；向東北的；東北部的： *travelling in a north-easterly direction* 向東北行駛 **2** [usually before noun] (of winds 風) blowing from the north-east 從東北吹來的

ˌnorth-ˈeastern *adj.* [only before noun] (*abbr.* **NE**) connected with the north-east 東北的；東北方向的

ˌnorth-ˈeastwards (also **ˌnorth-ˈeastward**) *adv.* towards the north-east 向東北；朝東北 ▸ **ˌnorth-ˈeastward** *adj.*

north·er·ly /ˈnɔːðəli; *NAmE* ˈnɔːrðərli/ *adj., noun*

■ ***adj.*** **1** [only before noun] in or towards the north 北方的；向北的；北部的： *travelling in a northerly direction* 向北行駛 **2** [usually before noun] (of winds 風) blowing from the north 從北方吹來的： *a northerly breeze* 微微的北風 ➲ compare NORTH *adj.*

■ ***noun*** (*pl.* **-ies**) a wind that blows from the north 北風

north·ern 🔑 /ˈnɔːðən; *NAmE* ˈnɔːrðərn/ (also **Northern**) *adj.* [usually before noun] (*abbr.* **N**, **No.**) located in the north or facing north; connected with or typical of the north part of the world or a region 北方的；向北的；北部的： *the northern slopes of the mountains* 山脈的北坡 ◇ *northern Scotland* 蘇格蘭北部 ◇ *a northern accent* 北方口音

north·ern·er /ˈnɔːðənə(r); *NAmE* ˈnɔːrðən-/ *noun* a person who comes from or lives in the northern part of a country 北方人

the ˌNorthern ˌIreland Asˈsembly *noun* [sing.] **1** the regional government of Northern Ireland from 1973 to 1986（1973 至 1986 年間的）北愛爾蘭地方政府

N

2 the parliament of Northern Ireland that was first elected in 1998（1998 年首次通過選舉產生的）北愛爾蘭議會

the ˌNorthern ˈLights *noun* [pl.] (also **aurora borealis**) bands of coloured light, mainly green and red, that are sometimes seen in the sky at night in the most northern countries of the world 北極光

north·ern·most /ˈnɔːðənməʊst; *NAmE* ˈnɔːrðərnmoʊst/ *adj.* [usually before noun] furthest north 最北的；最北端的；最北部的：*the northernmost city in the world* 世界最靠北的城市

ˌnorth-north-ˈeast *noun* [sing.] (*abbr.* NNE) the direction at an equal distance between north and north-east 北東北；北東北方；北北東 ▸ **ˌnorth-north-ˈeast** *adv.*

ˌnorth-north-ˈwest *noun* [sing.] (*abbr.* NNW) the direction at an equal distance between north and north-west 北西北；北西北方；北北西 ▸ **ˌnorth-north-ˈwest** *adv.*

the ˌNorth ˈPole *noun* [sing.] the point on the surface of the earth that is furthest north 北極 ➲ VISUAL VOCAB page V72

the ˌNorth ˈSea *noun* [sing.] the part of the Atlantic Ocean that is next to the east coast of Britain 北海（英國東海岸附近的大西洋海域）

the ˌNorth-South Diˈvide *noun* [sing.] (*BrE*) the economic and social differences between the north of England and the richer south 南北鴻溝（指英格蘭北部和較富裕的南部之間的經濟與社會差別）

north·wards /ˈnɔːθwədz; *NAmE* ˈnɔːrθwərdz/ (also **north·ward**) *adv.* towards the north 向北；朝北：*to go/look/turn northwards* 向北走／看／掉轉 ▸ **north·ward** *adj.*：*in a northward direction* 向北方

ˌnorth-ˈwest *noun* (usually **the north-west**) [sing.] (*abbr.* NW) the direction or region at an equal distance between north and west 西北；西北方；西北地區 ➲ picture at COMPASS ▸ **ˌnorth-ˈwest** *adv.*, *adj.*

ˌnorth-ˈwester·ly *adj.* **1** [only before noun] in or towards the north-west 西北方的；向西北的；西北部的 **2** (of winds 風) blowing from the north-west 從西北吹來的

ˌnorth-ˈwestern *adj.* [only before noun] (*abbr.* NW) connected with the north-west 西北的；西北方向的

ˌnorth-ˈwestwards (also **ˌnorth-ˈwestward**) *adv.* towards the north-west 向西北；朝西北 ▸ **ˌnorth-ˈwestward** *adj.*

ˌNorway ˈlobster *noun* = LANGOUSTINE

ˌNorway ˈrat *noun* = BROWN RAT

nose 0‒ /nəʊz; *NAmE* noʊz/ *noun*, *verb*

■ *noun* **1** 0‒ [C] the part of the face that sticks out above the mouth, used for breathing and smelling things 鼻；鼻子：*He broke his nose in the fight.* 他打架時打斷了鼻梁。◇ *She wrinkled her nose in disgust.* 她厭惡地皺起鼻子。◇ *He **blew his nose*** (= cleared it by blowing strongly into a HANDKERCHIEF). 他擤了擤鼻子。◇ *a **blocked/runny nose*** 堵塞的／流鼻涕的鼻子 ◇ *Stop **picking your nose**!* (= removing dirt from it with your finger) 別摳鼻孔了！➲ COLLOCATIONS at PHYSICAL ➲ VISUAL VOCAB page V59 ➲ see also NASAL (1), PARSON'S NOSE, ROMAN NOSE **2 -nosed** (in adjectives 構成形容詞) having the type of nose mentioned 有…鼻子的：*red-nosed* 紅鼻子的 ◇ *large-nosed* 大鼻子的 ➲ see also HARD-NOSED, TOFFEE-NOSED **3** [C] the front part of a plane, SPACECRAFT, etc.（飛機、太空船等的）頭部，頭錐 ➲ VISUAL VOCAB page V53 **4** [sing.] **a ~ for sth** a special ability for finding or recognizing sth 發現（或辨別）事物的能力；嗅覺 SYN **instinct**：*As a journalist, she has always had a nose for a good story.* 作為一名記者，她總是能夠捕捉到好新聞。**5** [sing.] a sense of smell 嗅覺：*a dog with a good nose* 嗅覺靈敏的狗 **6** [sing.] (of wine 葡萄酒) a characteristic smell 特有的氣味 SYN **bouquet**

IDM **cut off your nose to spite your ˈface** (*informal*) to do sth when you are angry that is meant to harm sb else but which also harms you（惱怒之下）傷人害己，損人不利己 **get up sb's ˈnose** (*BrE, informal*) to annoy sb 煩擾 **have your nose in ˈsth** (*informal*) to be reading sth and giving it all your attention 專心致志地（閱讀）**have a nose ˈround** (*BrE, informal*) to look around a place; to look for sth in a place 環視（某地）；在（某地）尋找 **keep your ˈnose clean** (*informal*) to avoid doing anything wrong or illegal 循規蹈矩；不做違法的事：*Since leaving prison, he's managed to keep his nose clean.* 自從出獄以來，他已做到規規矩矩。**keep your nose out of sth** to try not to become involved in things that do not concern you 避免插手（他人的事）；盡力不捲入（或介入）**keep your nose to the ˈgrindstone** (*informal*) to work hard for a long period of time without stopping 連續辛勤地工作 **look down your ˈnose at sb/sth** (*informal, especially BrE*) to behave in a way that suggests that you think that you are better than sb or that sth is not good enough for you 對…不屑一顧；蔑視 SYN **look down on** **ˌnose to ˈtail** (*BrE*) if cars, etc. are **nose to tail**, they are moving slowly in a long line with little space between them（汽車等）首尾相連（緩緩行進）**on the ˈnose** (*informal, especially NAmE*) exactly 準確地；確切地：*The budget should hit the $136 billion target on the nose.* 預算應該正好達到 1 360 億元的目標。**poke/stick your nose into ˈsth** (*informal*) to try to become involved in sth that does not concern you 多管閒事；插手（與己無關的事）**put sb's ˈnose out of joint** (*informal*) to upset or annoy sb, especially by not giving them enough attention（冷落）使難堪；惹惱 **turn your ˈnose up at sth** (*informal*) to refuse sth, especially because you do not think that it is good enough for you 拒絕；看不上；看不起 **under sb's ˈnose** (*informal*) **1** if sth is **under sb's nose**, it is very close to them but they cannot see it 就在某人面前（卻看不見）：*I searched everywhere for the letter and it was under my nose all the time!* 我到處找這封信，可它一直就在我面前。**2** if sth happens **under sb's nose**, they do not notice it even though it is not being done secretly 當着某人的面，就在某人眼皮底下（卻沒有被察覺）：*The police didn't know the drugs ring was operating right under their noses.* 警方不知道販毒集團就在他們的眼皮底下運作。**with your nose in the air** (*informal*) in a way that is unfriendly and suggests that you think that you are better than other people 傲慢；看不起人；鼻孔朝天，自高自大 ➲ more at FOLLOW, LEAD[1] *v.*, PAY *v.*, PLAIN *adj.*, POWDER *v.*, RUB *v.*, SKIN *n.*, THUMB *v.*

■ *verb* **1** [I, T] to move forward slowly and carefully 小心翼翼地向前移動：**+ adv./prep.** *The plane nosed down through the thick clouds.* 飛機穿透厚厚的雲層慢慢向下降落。◇ **~ your way + adv./prep.** *The taxi nosed its way back into the traffic.* 出租車慢慢地匯入車流。**2** [I] **+ adv./prep.** (of an animal 動物) to search for sth or push sth with its nose（用鼻子）嗅，拱，頂：*Dogs nosed around in piles of refuse.* 一群狗在垃圾堆上嗅來嗅去。

PHR V **ˌnose aˈbout/aˈround (for sth)** to look for sth, especially information about sb 探查；打探；搜尋 SYN **poke about/around**：*We found a man nosing around in our backyard.* 我們發現有個人在我們後院裏找什麼東西。**ˌnose sth↔ˈout** (*informal*) to discover information about sb/sth by searching for it 偵察出；打探出；查出：*Reporters nosed out all the details of the affair.* 記者們打探出了這件事情的所有細節。

nose·bag /ˈnəʊzbæɡ; *NAmE* ˈnoʊz-/ (*BrE*) (*NAmE* **feedbag**) *noun* a bag containing food for a horse, that you hang from its head（掛在馬頭上的）飼料袋

nose·band /ˈnəʊzbænd; *NAmE* ˈnoʊz-/ *noun* a leather band that passes over a horse's nose and under its chin and is part of its BRIDLE（馬的）鼻羈

nose·bleed /ˈnəʊzbliːd; *NAmE* ˈnoʊz-/ *noun* a flow of blood that comes from the nose 鼻出血

ˈnose cone *noun* the pointed front end of a ROCKET, an aircraft, etc.（火箭、飛機等的）前錐體，鼻錐體，頭錐

nose·dive /ˈnəʊzdaɪv; *NAmE* ˈnoʊz-/ *noun*, *verb*

■ *noun* [sing.] **1** a sudden steep fall or drop; a situation where sth suddenly becomes worse or begins to fail 急劇下降；急轉直下；暴跌：*Oil prices **took a nosedive** in the crisis.* 危機期間，石油價格暴跌。◇ *These policies have sent the construction industry into an abrupt nosedive.* 這些政策使得建築業的形勢急轉直下。**2** the

N

sudden sharp fall of an aircraft towards the ground with its front part pointing down（飛行器的）俯衝

■ *verb* **1** [I] (of prices, costs, etc. 價格、費用等) to fall suddenly 驟降；急劇下跌；暴跌 SYN **plummet**：*Building costs have nosedived.* 建築費用猛跌下來。**2** [I] (of an aircraft 飛行器) to fall suddenly with the front part pointing towards the ground 俯衝

nose·gay /ˈnəʊzgeɪ; *NAmE* ˈnoʊz-/ *noun* (*old-fashioned*) a small bunch of flowers 小花束

ˈnose job *noun* (*informal*) a medical operation on the nose to improve its shape 鼻部整形手術

ˈnose ring *noun* **1** a ring that is put in an animal's nose for leading it（用於牽引動物的）鼻環，鼻圈 **2** a ring worn in the nose as a piece of jewellery 環形鼻飾；鼻環

nosey = NOSY

nosh /nɒʃ; *NAmE* nɑːʃ/ *noun, verb*

■ *noun* **1** [U, sing.] (*old-fashioned, BrE, slang*) food; a meal 食物；一餐：*She likes her nosh.* 她喜歡她的飯菜。◇ *Did you have a good nosh?* 你吃得好嗎？ **2** [C] (*especially NAmE*) a small meal that you eat quickly between main meals 小吃；點心

■ *verb* [I, T] **~ (sth)** (*informal*) to eat 吃

ˌno-ˈshow *noun* (*informal*) a person who is expected to be somewhere and does not come; a situation where this happens 沒有如期出現的人；失約；放棄預訂

ˈnosh-up *noun* (*slang, especially BrE*) a large meal 豐盛的一餐；大餐：*We went for a nosh-up at that new restaurant in town.* 我們到城裏那家新餐館大吃了一頓。

ˌno-ˈsmoking *adj.* = NON-SMOKING

nos·tal·gia /nɒˈstældʒə; *NAmE* nəˈs-; nɑːˈs-/ *noun* [U] a feeling of sadness mixed with pleasure and affection when you think of happy times in the past 懷舊；念舊：*a **sense/wave/pang of nostalgia*** 懷舊感；一陣強烈的懷舊之情 ◇ *She is filled with nostalgia for her own college days.* 她對自己的大學時代充滿了懷念之情。▸ **nos·tal·gic** /nɒˈstældʒɪk; *NAmE* nəˈs-; nɑːˈs-/ *adj.*：*nostalgic memories* 引起懷舊之情的回憶 ◇ *I feel quite nostalgic for the place where I grew up.* 我很懷念我成長的地方。 **nos·tal·gic·al·ly** /-kli/ *adv.*：*to look back nostalgically to your childhood* 懷緬童年時光

nos·tril /ˈnɒstrəl; *NAmE* ˈnɑːs-/ *noun* either of the two openings at the end of the nose that you breathe through 鼻孔 ➲ VISUAL VOCAB page V59

nos·trum /ˈnɒstrəm; *NAmE* ˈnɑːs-/ *noun* **1** (*formal, disapproving*) an idea that is intended to solve a problem but that will probably not succeed 並非靈驗的招數；不會奏效的計策 **2** (*old-fashioned*) a medicine that is not made in a scientific way, and that is not effective 江湖藥

nosy (also **nosey**) /ˈnəʊzi; *NAmE* ˈnoʊzi/ *adj.* (*informal, disapproving*) too interested in things that do not concern you, especially other people's affairs 好管閒事的；愛打聽的 SYN **inquisitive**：*nosy neighbours* 好管閒事的鄰居 ◇ *Don't be so nosy—it's none of your business.* 別管那麼多閒事，這與你無關。▸ **nosi·ly** *adv.* **nosi·ness** *noun* [U]

ˌnosy ˈparker *noun* (*BrE, informal*, becoming *old-fashioned*) a person who is too interested in other people's affairs 愛管閒事的人；好事者

not 0‑w /nɒt; *NAmE* nɑːt/ *adv.*

1 0‑w used to form the negative of the verbs *be, do* and *have* and modal verbs like *can* or *must* and often reduced to *n't*（構成動詞 be、do 和 have 及情態動詞 can 或 must 等的否定形式，常縮略為 n't）不，沒有：*She did not/didn't see him.* 她沒看見他。◇ *It's not/It isn't raining.* 沒下雨。◇ *I can't see from here.* 我從這兒看不見。◇ *He must not go.* 他決不能走。◇ *Don't you eat meat?* 你不吃肉嗎？◇ *It's cold, isn't it?* 很冷，是吧？ **2** 0‑w used to give the following word or phrase a negative meaning, or to reply in the negative（否定後面的詞或短語，或作否定的回答）不，沒有：*He warned me not to be late.* 他提醒我不要遲到。◇ *I was sorry not to have seen them.* 我很遺憾沒有見到他們。◇ *Not everybody agrees.* 不是每一個人都同意。◇ *'Who's next?' 'Not me.'* "下一位是誰？" "不是我。" ◇ *'What did you do at school?' '**Not a lot**.'* "你在學校幹什麼了？" "沒做多少事。" ◇ *It's not easy being a parent* (= it's difficult). 為人父母真不容易啊。 **3** 0‑w used after *hope, expect, believe,* etc. to give a negative reply（用於 hope、expect、believe 等動詞後，作為否定的回答）不，沒有：*'Will she be there?' 'I hope not.'* "她會在那兒嗎？" "但願不會。" ◇ *'Is it ready?' 'I'm afraid not.'* "準備好了嗎？" "恐怕還沒呢。" ◇ (*formal*) *'Does he know?' 'I believe not.'* "他知道嗎？" "我想他不知道。" **4** 0‑w **or ~** used to show a negative possibility（表示否定的可能性）否，不：*I don't know if he's telling the truth or not.* 我不知道他是否說了真話。 **5** 0‑w used to say that you do not want sth or will not allow sth（拒絕或不允許）不：*'Some more?' 'Not for me, thanks.'* "再來點兒嗎？" "我不要了，謝謝。" ◇ *'Can I throw this out?' 'Certainly not.'* "我把這個扔了，行嗎？" "當然不行。"

IDM **not a ... | not one ...** 0‑w used for emphasis to mean 'no thing or person'（用於強調）一個也不，一件也沒：*He didn't speak to me—not one word.* 他沒跟我說話，一個字也沒說。 **ˌnot at ˈall** 0‑w used to politely accept thanks or to agree to sth（禮貌地答謝或同意）別客氣，沒關係，沒什麼：*'Thanks a lot.' 'Not at all.'* "非常感謝。" "不客氣。" ◇ *'Will it bother you if I smoke?' 'Not at all.'* "我抽煙你介意嗎？" "沒關係。" **not only ... (but) also ...** 0‑w used to emphasize that sth else is also true 不僅…而且…：*She not only wrote the text but also selected the illustrations.* 她不僅寫了正文部份，而且還挑選了插圖。 **ˈnot that** used to state that you are not suggesting sth 倒不是；並不是說：*She hasn't written—not that she said she would.* 她還沒寫信來——倒不是她說過她要寫。

not·able /ˈnəʊtəbl; *NAmE* ˈnoʊ-/ *adj., noun*

■ *adj.* (rather *formal*) deserving to be noticed or to receive attention; important 值得注意的；顯著的；重要的 SYN **striking**：*a **notable success/achievement/example*** 顯著的成功／成就；明顯的事例 ◇ *His eyes are his most **notable feature**.* 他的雙眼是他最明顯的特徵。◇ **~ (for sth)** *The town is notable for its ancient harbour.* 這座小鎮因其古老的港口而出名。◇ ***With a few notable exceptions**, everyone gave something.* 人人都給了些東西，只有幾個人例外，很是顯眼。

■ *noun* [usually pl.] (*formal*) a famous or important person 名人；重要人物：*All the usual local notables were there.* 經常露面的地方名流都在那裏。

not·ably /ˈnəʊtəbli; *NAmE* ˈnoʊ-/ *adv.* **1** used for giving a good or the most important example of sth 尤其；特別 SYN **especially**：*The house had many drawbacks, most notably its price.* 這房子有很多缺陷，尤其是它的價格。 **2** to a great degree 極大程度上；非常 SYN **remarkably**：*This has not been a notably successful project.* 這個項目沒有取得很大的成功。

no·tar·ize (*BrE* also **-ise**) /ˈnəʊtəraɪz; *NAmE* ˈnoʊ-/ *verb* **~ sth** (*law* 律) if a document is **notarized**, it is given legal status by a NOTARY 公證；由公證人證實

no·tary /ˈnəʊtəri; *NAmE* ˈnoʊ-/ *noun* (*pl.* **-ies**) (also *technical* 術語 **ˌnotary ˈpublic** *pl.* **ˌnotaries ˈpublic**) a person, especially a lawyer, with official authority to be a witness when sb signs a document and to make this document valid in law 公證人

no·ta·tion /nəʊˈteɪʃn; *NAmE* noʊ-/ *noun* [U, C] a system of signs or symbols used to represent information, especially in mathematics, science and music（數學、科學和音樂中的）符號，記號，譜號 ➲ picture at MUSIC

notch /nɒtʃ; *NAmE* nɑːtʃ/ *noun, verb*

■ *noun* **1** a level on a scale, often marking quality or achievement 等級；檔次；位階：*The quality of the food here has dropped a notch recently.* 這裏的飯菜質量最近下降了一級。➲ see also TOP-NOTCH **2** a V-shape or a circle cut in an edge or a surface, sometimes used to keep a record of sth（表面或邊緣的）V 形刻痕，圓形切口：*For each day he spent on the island, he cut a new notch in his stick.* 他在島上每過一天，就在手杖上刻一個新的記號。◇ *She tightened her belt an extra notch.* 她將腰帶又束緊了一格。

■ *verb* **1 ~ sth (up)** (*informal*) to achieve sth such as a win or a high score 贏取；獲得：*The team has notched up*

N

20 goals already this season. 這支球隊本賽季已經攻進 20 個球。**2 ~ sth** to make a small V-shaped cut in an edge or a surface（在表面或邊緣）刻 V 形痕，刻下切口

note 0-ㅠ /nəʊt; *NAmE* noʊt/ *noun, verb*

■ ***noun***

▸ **TO REMIND YOU** 提醒自己 **1** 0-ㅠ [C] a short piece of writing to help you remember sth 筆記；記錄：*Please **make a note** of the dates.* 請記下日期。◇ *She **made a mental note** (= decided that she must remember) to ask Alan about it.* 她提醒自己要記住向艾倫問問這事。

▸ **SHORT LETTER** 短信 **2** 0-ㅠ [C] a short informal letter 短箋；便條：*Just a quick note to say thank you for a wonderful evening.* 僅以此短箋感謝您安排的美好的夜晚。◇ *She left a note for Ben on the kitchen table.* 她在廚房的餐桌上給本留了個便條。◇ *a suicide note* 絕命書

▸ **IN BOOK** 書籍 **3** 0-ㅠ [C] a short comment on a word or passage in a book 註釋；按語；批註：*a new edition of 'Hamlet', with explanatory notes* 附註釋的新版《哈姆雷特》◇ *See note 3, page 259.* 見 259 頁註釋 3。➲ see also FOOTNOTE (1)

▸ **INFORMATION** 資料 **4** 0-ㅠ **notes** [pl.] information that you write down when sb is speaking, or when you are reading a book, etc.（聽講或讀書等時的）記錄，筆記：*He sat **taking notes** of everything that was said.* 他坐在那兒記下了所說的每一件事。◇ *Can I borrow your **lecture notes**?* 我可以借你的課堂筆記看看嗎？◇ *Patients' **medical notes** have gone missing.* 患者的病歷丟失了。**5** 0-ㅠ [C, usually pl.] information about a performance, an actor's career, a piece of music, etc. printed in a special book or on a CD case, record cover, etc. 資料簡介（介紹某個演出、演員、音樂等，印製成小冊子或印在唱片盒或封套上）：*The sleeve notes include a short biography of the performers on this recording.* 封套上的介紹包括本唱片中的演奏者生平簡介。

N

▸ **MONEY** 錢幣 **6** 0-ㅠ (also **bank·note**) (both *especially BrE*) (*NAmE* usually **bill**) [C] a piece of paper money 紙幣：*a £5 note* 一張面值為 5 英鎊的紙幣◇ *We only exchange notes and traveller's cheques.* 我們只兌換紙幣和旅行支票。➲ picture at MONEY

▸ **IN MUSIC** 音樂 **7** 0-ㅠ [C] a single sound of a particular length and PITCH (= how high or low a sound is), made by the voice or a musical instrument; the written or printed sign for a musical note 單音；音調；音符：*He played the first few notes of the tune.* 他演奏了這支曲子開始的幾個音。◇ ***high/low notes*** 高音；低音 ➲ picture at MUSIC

▸ **QUALITY** 性質 **8** [sing.] **~ (of sth)** a particular quality in sth, for example in sb's voice or the atmosphere at an event 特徵；口氣；調子；氣氛 SYN **air**：*There was a note of amusement in his voice.* 聽他的口氣，是覺得很有意思。◇ ***On a more serious note*** (= speaking more seriously) ... 更嚴格地講⋯◇ ***On a slightly different note*** (= changing the subject slightly), *let's talk about ...* 咱們略微換一下話題，談談⋯

▸ **OFFICIAL DOCUMENT** 正式文件 **9** [C] an official document with a particular purpose 正式文件；票據；證明書：*a sick note from your doctor* 醫生開據的病假證明◇ *The buyer has to sign a delivery note as proof of receipt.* 購買者必須簽收送貨單表明貨已收到。➲ see also CREDIT NOTE, PROMISSORY NOTE **10** [C] (*technical* 術語) an official letter from the representative of one government to another（外交文書）照會；通牒：*an exchange of diplomatic notes* 外交照會的互換

IDM **of 'note** of importance or of great interest 重要的；引人注目的：*a scientist of note* 著名的科學家◇ *The museum contains nothing of great note.* 這家博物館沒有什麼很有價值的東西。**hit/strike the right/wrong 'note** (*especially BrE*) to do, say or write sth that is suitable/not suitable for a particular occasion 做（或說、寫）得得體／不得體 **sound/strike a 'note (of 'sth)** to express feelings or opinions of a particular kind 表達某種情感（或觀點）：*She sounded a note of warning in her speech.* 她在講話中提出了警告。**take 'note (of sth)** to pay attention to sth and be sure to remember it 注意到；將⋯銘記在心：*Take note of what he says.* 牢記他說的話。➲ more at COMPARE *v.*

■ ***verb*** (rather *formal*) **1** 0-ㅠ to notice or pay careful attention to sth 注意；留意：**~ sth** *Note the fine early Baroque altar inside the chapel.* 注意小教堂裏精緻的早期巴羅克風格的祭壇。◇ **~ (that)** ... *Please note (that) the office will be closed on Monday.* 請注意辦事處星期一將關閉。◇ **~ how, where, etc.** ... *Note how these animals sometimes walk with their tails up in the air.* 注意觀察這些動物如何有時翹起尾巴走路。◇ **it is noted that** ... *It **should be noted that** dissertations submitted late will not be accepted.* 應該注意的是遲交的論文將不予接受。➲ SYNONYMS at NOTICE ➲ LANGUAGE BANK at EMPHASIS **2 ~ sth | ~ that ... | ~ how, where, etc. ... | it is noted that ...** to mention sth because it is important or interesting 指出；特別提到：*It is worth noting that the most successful companies had the lowest prices.* 值得指出的是最成功的公司價格最低。➲ SYNONYMS at COMMENT ➲ LANGUAGE BANK at ARGUE

PHR V **,note sth↔'down** 0-ㅠ to write down sth important so that you will not forget it 記錄；記下 SYN **jot down**

note·book /ˈnəʊtbʊk; *NAmE* ˈnoʊt-/ *noun* **1** a small book of plain paper for writing notes in 筆記本 **2** (*NAmE*) (*BrE* **'exercise book**) a small book for students to write their work in 練習本 ➲ VISUAL VOCAB page V69 **3** (also **,notebook com'puter**) a small computer that can work with a battery and be easily carried 筆記本電腦；便攜式電腦 SYN **laptop** ➲ compare DESKTOP COMPUTER, NETBOOK, SUBNOTEBOOK

note·card /ˈnəʊtkɑːd; *NAmE* ˈnoʊtkɑːrd/ *noun* **1** a small folded card, sometimes with a picture on the front, that you use for writing a short letter on（正面有圖而摺疊的）便箋卡，萬用卡 ➲ see also NOTELET **2** (*especially NAmE*) a card on which notes are written, for example by sb to use when making a speech 摘記卡片；綱要卡片

noted /ˈnəʊtɪd; *NAmE* ˈnoʊt-/ *adj.* well known because of a special skill or feature（以⋯）見稱，聞名，著名 SYN **famous**：*a noted dancer* 著名的舞蹈演員◇ **~ for sth** *He is not noted for his sense of humour.* 他沒什麼幽默感。◇ **~ as sth** *The lake is noted as a home to many birds.* 這個湖作為許多鳥類的棲息地遐邇聞名。

note·let /ˈnəʊtlət; *NAmE* ˈnoʊt-/ *noun* (*BrE*) a small folded sheet of paper or card with a picture on the front that you use for writing a short letter on（正面有圖而摺疊的）便箋，便箋卡

No. 10 = NUMBER TEN

note·pad /ˈnəʊtpæd; *NAmE* ˈnoʊt-/ *noun* sheets of paper that are held together at the top and used for writing notes on 記事本；便條本：*a notepad by the phone for messages* 電話機旁用於記錄信息的記事本 ➲ VISUAL VOCAB page V69

note·paper /ˈnəʊtpeɪpə(r); *NAmE* ˈnoʊt-/ (also **'writing paper**) *noun* [U] paper for writing letters on 信紙；便箋

note·worthy /ˈnəʊtwɜːði; *NAmE* ˈnoʊtwɜːrði/ *adj.* deserving to be noticed or to receive attention because it is unusual, important or interesting 值得注意的；顯著的；重要的 SYN **significant**

'nother /ˈnʌðə(r)/ *adj.* (*non-standard*) = ANOTHER：*Now that's a whole 'nother question.* 但那完全是另一個問題。

noth·ing 0-ㅠ /ˈnʌθɪŋ/ *pron.*

1 0-ㅠ not anything; no single thing 沒有什麼；沒有一件東西：*There was nothing in her bag.* 她的包裏什麼都沒有。◇ *There's nothing you can do to help.* 你什麼忙也幫不上。◇ *The doctor said there was nothing wrong with me.* 醫生說我什麼毛病也沒有。◇ ***Nothing else** matters to him apart from his job.* 對他來說，除了工作以外，什麼事都無關緊要。◇ *It cost us nothing to go in.* 我們沒花錢就進去了。◇ (*BrE*) *He's five foot nothing* (= exactly five feet tall). 他正好五英尺高。**2** 0-ㅠ something that is not at all important or interesting 無關緊要的東西；毫無趣味的事：*'What's that in your pocket?' 'Oh, nothing.'* "你口袋裏裝的是什麼？" "哦，沒什麼重要的。" ◇ *We did nothing at the weekend.* 我們週末什麼也沒幹。

IDM **be 'nothing to sb** to be a person for whom sb has no feelings 對（某人）來說是無所謂的人：*I used to love her but she's nothing to me any more.* 我愛過她，但現在對她再也沒什麼感情了。**be/have nothing to do with sb/sth** 0-ㅠ to have no connection with sb/sth 與⋯毫不相干；與⋯無關：*Get out! It's nothing to do with you*

(= you have no right to know about it). 出去！這根本就不關你的事。◇ *That has nothing to do with what we're discussing.* 那與我們所討論的問題毫不相干。 **for 'nothing** **1** without payment 不花錢；免費 SYN free： *She's always trying to get **something for nothing**.* 她總想不勞而獲。 **2** with no reward or result 無酬勞；毫無結果；白白地： *All that preparation was for nothing because the visit was cancelled.* 訪問被取消，所有的準備工作都白費了。 **have nothing on sb** (*informal*) **1** to have much less of a particular quality than sb/sth 遠比不上某人；比某人差得多： *I'm quite a fast worker, but I've got nothing on her!* 我做事已經很麻利了，但比她還差得遠。 **2** (of the police, etc. 警察等) to have no information that could show sb to be guilty of sth 沒有某人的罪證 **not for 'nothing** for a very good reason 有充分理由；有正當理由： *Not for nothing was he called the king of rock and roll.* 他被稱作搖滾之王不是沒有道理的。 **'nothing but** only; no more/less than 只；只有；只是；僅僅： *Nothing but a miracle can save her now.* 現在只有出現奇跡才能救活她。◇ *I want nothing but the best for my children.* 我只想給我的孩子最好的一切。 **'nothing if not** extremely; very 極其；非常： *The trip was nothing if not varied.* 這次旅行極其豐富多彩。 **'nothing less than** used to emphasize how great or extreme sth is 簡直是；極其；不亞於： *It was nothing less than a disaster.* 這簡直就是一場災難。 **nothing 'like** (*informal*) **1** not at all like 完全不像；根本不像： *It looks nothing like a horse.* 它看上去根本不像一匹馬。 **2** not nearly; not at all 完全不；根本沒有： *I had nothing like enough time to answer all the questions.* 我根本來不及回答所有的問題。 **ˌnothing 'much** not a great amount of sth; nothing of great value or importance 不很多；不太重要；價值不太大： *There's nothing much in the fridge.* 冰箱裏沒什麼東西了。◇ *I got up late and did nothing much all day.* 我起來晚了，一天沒怎麼做事。 **(there's) ˌnothing 'to it** (it's) very easy（這事）輕而易舉，非常簡單： *You'll soon learn. There's nothing to it really.* 你很快就能學會。真的很簡單。 **there is/was nothing (else) 'for it (but to do sth)** there is no other action to take except the one mentioned（除了做某事）別無辦法： *There was nothing else for it but to resign.* 除了辭職，沒有別的辦法。 **there is/was nothing in sth** something is/was not true（某事）不可信，不真實： *There was a rumour she was going to resign, but there was nothing in it.* 有傳言說她要辭職，不過這靠不住。 **there's nothing like sth** used to say that you enjoy sth very much …非常好；…太棒了： *There's nothing like a brisk walk on a cold day!* 冷天出來快步走走，簡直太舒服了。 ➲ more at STOP *v.*, SWEET *adj.*

noth·ing·ness /ˈnʌθɪŋnəs/ *noun* [U] a situation where nothing exists; the state of not existing 不存在；虛無

no·tice /ˈnəʊtɪs; *NAmE* ˈnoʊ-/ *noun, verb*

■ ***noun***

▸ **PAYING ATTENTION** 注意 **1** [U] the fact of sb paying attention to sb/sth or knowing about sth 注意；理會；察覺： ***Don't take any notice of*** *what you read in the papers.* 別在意你在報上看到的東西。◇ ***Take no notice*** *of what he says.* 別理會他說的話。◇ *These protests have really made the government **sit up and take notice*** (= realize the importance of the situation). 這些抗議活動確實引起了政府的警覺和注意。◇ *It was Susan who **brought** the problem **to my notice*** (= told me about it). 是蘇珊使我注意到這個問題的。◇ *Normally, the letter would not have **come to my notice*** (= I would not have known about it). 通常情況下，我是不會看到這封信的。◇ (*formal*) *It will not have **escaped your notice** that there have been some major changes in the company.* 你肯定會注意到公司已經發生了一些重大的變化。

▸ **GIVING INFORMATION** 通報信息 **2** [C] a sheet of paper giving written or printed information, usually put in a public place 通告；佈告；通知： *There was a notice on the board saying the class had been cancelled.* 佈告牌上有一則通知說這堂課取消了。 **3** [C] a board or sign giving information, an instruction or a warning 公告牌；警示牌： *a notice saying 'Keep off the Grass'* 寫着“勿踏草地”的公告牌

▸ **ANNOUNCING STH** 宣佈 **4** [C] a small advertisement or ANNOUNCEMENT in a newspaper or magazine 啟事；聲

Synonyms 同義詞辨析

notice

note • detect • observe • witness

These words all mean to see sth, especially when you pay careful attention to it. 以上各詞均含看到、注意到之意。

notice to see, hear or become aware of sb/sth; to pay attention to sb/sth 指看（或聽）到、注意到、意識到、注意、留意： *The first thing I noticed about the room was the smell.* 我首先注意到的是這屋子裏的氣味。

note (*rather formal*) to notice or pay careful attention to sth 指注意、留意： *Please note (that) the office will be closed on Monday.* 請注意辦事處星期一將關閉。 NOTE This word is very common in business English. 該詞在商務英語中非常通用： *Note that the prices are inclusive of VAT.* 注意這些價格含增值税。

detect to discover or notice sth, especially sth that is not easy to see, hear, etc. 指發現、查明、偵察出： *The tests are designed to detect the disease early.* 這些檢查旨在及早查出疾病。

observe (*formal*) to see or notice sb/sth 指看到、注意到、觀察到： *Have you observed any changes lately?* 最近你注意到什麼變化沒有？◇ *The police observed a man enter the bank.* 警察注意到一個男人走進了銀行。

witness (*rather formal*) to see sth happen 指當場看到、目擊： *Police have appealed for anyone who witnessed the incident to contact them.* 警方呼籲目擊這一事故的人與他們聯繫。

PATTERNS

- to notice/note/detect/observe **that/how/what/where/who …**
- to notice/observe/witness **sth happen/sb do sth**

N

明： *notices of births, marriages and deaths* 出生喜報、結婚啟事和訃告 **5** [C] a short ANNOUNCEMENT made at the beginning or end of a meeting, a church service, etc. 通知： *There are just two notices this week.* 本週只有兩項通知。

▸ **WARNING** 警告 **6** [U] information or a warning given in advance of sth that is going to happen 預告；警告： *You must give **one month's notice**.* 你必須一個月前發出通知。◇ *Prices may be altered without notice.* 價格變動不另行通知。◇ *The bar is closed **until further notice*** (= until you are told that it is open again). 酒吧停止營業，直到另行通知。◇ *You are welcome to come and stay as long as you give us plenty of notice.* 只要你及時通知，我們都歡迎你來住宿。

▸ **WHEN LEAVING JOB/HOUSE** 辭職；搬遷 **7** [U] a formal letter or statement saying that you will or must leave your job or house at the end of a particular period of time 辭職信；搬遷通知： *He has **handed in his notice**.* 他遞交了辭呈。◇ *They **gave** her two weeks' **notice**.* 他們通知她兩週後搬走。

▸ **REVIEW OF BOOK/PLAY** 書評；劇評 **8** [C] a short article in a newspaper or magazine, giving an opinion about a book, play, etc.（報刊上對書籍、戲劇等的）評論，短評

IDM **at short 'notice | at a moment's 'notice** not long in advance; without warning or time for preparation 隨時；一經通知立即；沒有準備時間： *This was the best room we could get at such short notice.* 這是我們臨時能弄到的最好的房間了。◇ *You must be ready to leave at a moment's notice.* 你必須隨時準備出發。 **on short 'notice** (*NAmE*) = AT SHORT NOTICE

■ ***verb*** (not usually used in the progressive tenses 通常不用於進行時)

▸ **SEE/HEAR** 看到；聽到 **1** [I, T] to see or hear sb/sth; to become aware of sb/sth 看（或聽）到；注意到；意識到： *People were making fun of him but he didn't seem to notice.* 人們在拿他開玩笑，但他好像沒有意識到。◇

~ **sb/sth** *The first thing I noticed about the room was the smell.* 我首先注意到的是這屋子裏的氣味。◇ ~ **(that)** … *I couldn't help noticing (that) she was wearing a wig.* 我一眼就看出她戴着假髮。◇ ~ **how, what, etc.** … *Did you notice how Rachel kept looking at her watch?* 你有沒有注意到雷切爾在不停地看她的手錶？◇ ~ **sb/sth do sth** *I noticed them come in.* 我注意到他們進來了。◇ ~ **sb/sth doing sth** *I didn't notice him leaving.* 我沒有看到他離開。

▸ PAY ATTENTION 注意 **2** [T] ~ **sb/sth** to pay attention to sb/sth 注意；留意：*She wears those strange clothes just to get herself noticed.* 她穿那些奇裝異服不過是想引人注意而已。

no·tice·able /ˈnəʊtɪsəbl; *NAmE* ˈnoʊ-/ *adj.* easy to see or notice; clear or definite 顯著的；顯而易見的：*a noticeable improvement* 顯而易見的改進 ◇ ~ **in sb/sth** *This effect is particularly noticeable in younger patients.* 這種作用在年輕一些的病人身上尤為明顯。◇ ~ **that** … ***It was noticeable that*** *none of the family were present.* 很明顯這一家沒有人在場。▸ **no·tice·ably** /-əbli/ *adv.*：*Her hand was shaking noticeably.* 很明顯她的手在顫抖。◇ *Marks were noticeably higher for girls than for boys.* 女孩子的分數明顯地高於男孩子。

no·tice·board /ˈnəʊtɪsbɔːd; *NAmE* ˈnoʊtɪsbɔːrd/ (*BrE*) (*NAmE* ˈ**bulletin board**) (also **board** *BrE, NAmE*) *noun* a board for putting notices on 告示牌；佈告板 ⊃ VISUAL VOCAB page V69

no·ti·fi·able /ˈnəʊtɪfaɪəbl; *NAmE* ˈnoʊ-/ *adj.* [usually before noun] (*formal*) (of a disease or a crime 疾病或罪行) so dangerous or serious that it must by law be reported officially to the authorities 依法須報告當局的；依法須向官方彙報的

no·ti·fi·ca·tion /ˌnəʊtɪfɪˈkeɪʃn; *NAmE* ˌnoʊ-/ *noun* [U, C] (*formal*) the act of giving or receiving official information about sth 通知；通告；告示：***advance/prior notification*** (= telling sb in advance about sth) 預先通告 ◇ *written notification* 書面通知 ◇ *You should receive (a) notification of our decision in the next week.* 關於我們的決定，下週你會接到通知。

no·tify /ˈnəʊtɪfaɪ; *NAmE* ˈnoʊ-/ *verb* (**no·ti·fies, no·ti·fy·ing, no·ti·fied, no·ti·fied**) (*formal*) to formally or officially tell sb about sth （正式）通報，通知 SYN **inform**：~ **sb** *Competition winners will be notified by post.* 將發信通知競賽的優勝者。◇ ~ **sb of sth** *The police must be notified of the date of the demonstration.* 必須向警方報告遊行示威的日期。◇ ~ **sth to sb** *The date of the demonstration must be notified to the police.* 遊行示威的日期必須報告警方。◇ ~ **sb that** … *Members have been notified that there will be a small increase in the fee.* 會員已經得到通知，費用將有小幅上調。

no·tion AW /ˈnəʊʃn; *NAmE* ˈnoʊʃn/ *noun* an idea, a belief or an understanding of sth 觀念；信念；理解：~ **(of sth)** *a political system based on the notions of equality and liberty* 建立在自由平等觀念基礎上的政治體系 ◇ *She had only a vague notion of what might happen.* 對於可能發生的事她只有一個模糊的概念。◇ ~ **(that …)** *I have to reject the notion that greed can be a good thing.* 我不能接受那種認為貪慾也可以是件好事的想法。

no·tion·al /ˈnəʊʃənl; *NAmE* ˈnoʊ-/ *adj.* (*formal*) based on a guess, estimate or theory; not existing in reality 猜測的；估計的；理論上的；想像的 ▸ **no·tion·al·ly** /ˈnəʊʃənəli; *NAmE* ˈnoʊ-/ *adv.*

no·tori·ety /ˌnəʊtəˈraɪəti; *NAmE* ˌnoʊ-/ *noun* [U, sing.] fame for being bad in some way 惡名；壞名聲：~ **(for sth)** *She achieved notoriety for her affair with the senator.* 她因為和參議員的風流韻事而聲名狼藉。◇ ~ **(as sth)** *He gained a certain notoriety as a gambler.* 他落了個賭徒的惡名。

no·tori·ous /nəʊˈtɔːriəs; *NAmE* noʊ-/ *adj.* well known for being bad 聲名狼藉的；臭名昭著的：*a notorious criminal* 惡名昭彰的罪犯 ◇ ~ **for sth/for doing sth** *The country is notorious for its appalling prison conditions.* 這個國家因監獄狀況惡劣而臭名遠揚。◇ ~ **as sth** *The bar has become notorious as a meeting-place for drug dealers.* 這家酒吧作為毒品販子接頭的場所已變得聲名狼藉。▸ **no·tori·ous·ly** *adv.*：*Mountain weather is notoriously difficult to predict.* 山地氣候難以預料是人所共知的。

not·with·stand·ing AW /ˌnɒtwɪθˈstændɪŋ; -wɪð-; *NAmE* ˌnɑːt-/ *prep., adv.*

■ ***prep.*** (*formal*) (also used following the noun it refers to 亦用於其所指名詞之後) without being affected by sth; despite sth 雖然；儘管：*Notwithstanding some major financial problems, the school has had a successful year.* 雖然有些重大的經費問題，這所學校一年來還是很成功。◇ *The bad weather notwithstanding, the event was a great success.* 儘管天氣惡劣，活動還是取得了巨大的成功。

■ ***adv.*** (*formal*) despite this 儘管如此 SYN **however, nevertheless**：*Notwithstanding, the problem is a significant one.* 然而，這個問題仍很重要。

nou·gat /ˈnuːɡɑː; *NAmE* ˈnuːɡət/ *noun* [U] a hard sweet/candy that has to be chewed a lot, often containing nuts, CHERRIES, etc. and pink or white in colour 牛軋糖（含果仁、櫻桃等，呈粉紅色或白色）

nought /nɔːt/ *noun* **1** [C, U] (*BrE*) (also **zero** *NAmE, BrE*) the figure 0 （數碼）零：*A million is written with six noughts.* 一百萬寫出來有六個零。◇ *nought point one* (= written 0.1) 零點一 ◇ *I give the programme nought out of ten for humour.* 我給這個節目的幽默打零分。**2** (also **naught**) [U] (*literary*) used in particular phrases to mean 'nothing' （用於某些短語）無，零：*All our efforts have* ***come to nought*** (= have not been successful). 我們所付出的努力都已付諸東流。

the Nought·ies /ˈnɔːtiz/ *noun* [pl.] (*BrE*) the years from 2000 to 2009 * 21 世紀頭十年（即從 2000 年到 2009 年）

ˌ**noughts and** ˈ**crosses** (*BrE*) (*NAmE* ˌ**tic-tac-**ˈ**toe**) *noun* [U] a simple game in which two players take turns to write Os or Xs in a set of nine squares. The first player to complete a row of three Os or three Xs is the winner. 圈叉遊戲（二人輪流在井字形九格中畫 O 或 X，先將三個 O 或 X 連成一線者獲勝）⊃ VISUAL VOCAB page V38

noun /naʊn/ *noun* (*grammar* 語法) (*abbr.* **n.**) a word that refers to a person (such as *Ann* or *doctor*), a place (such as *Paris* or *city*) or a thing, a quality or an activity (such as *plant, sorrow* or *tennis*) 名詞 ⊃ see also ABSTRACT NOUN, COMMON NOUN, PROPER NOUN

ˈ**noun phrase** *noun* (*grammar* 語法) a word or group of words in a sentence that behaves in the same way as a noun, that is as a subject, an object, a COMPLEMENT, or as the object of a preposition 名詞短語；名詞詞組：*In the sentence 'I spoke to the driver of the car', 'the driver of the car' is a noun phrase.* 在句子 I spoke to the driver of the car 中，the driver of the car 是名詞短語。

nour·ish /ˈnʌrɪʃ; *NAmE* ˈnɜːrɪʃ/ *verb* **1** ~ **sb/sth** to keep a person, an animal or a plant alive and healthy with food, etc. 撫養；滋養；養育：*All the children were well nourished and in good physical condition.* 所有這些孩子都營養良好，身體健康。**2** ~ **sth** (*formal*) to allow a feeling, an idea, etc. to develop or grow stronger 培養，助長（情緒、觀點等）：*By investing in education, we nourish the talents of our children.* 我們通過教育投資，培養孩子們的才能。▸ **nour·ish·ing** *adj.*：*nourishing food* 滋補食品

nour·ish·ment /ˈnʌrɪʃmənt; *NAmE* ˈnɜːr-/ *noun* [U] (*formal* or *technical* 術語) food that is needed to stay alive, grow and stay healthy 營養；營養品：*Can plants obtain adequate nourishment from such poor soil?* 土壤這樣貧瘠，植物能獲得足夠的養分嗎？◇ (*figurative*) *As a child, she was starved of intellectual nourishment.* 她小時候缺乏吸取知識的機會。

nous /naʊs/ *noun* [U] (*BrE, informal*) intelligence and the ability to think and act in a practical way 智力；理性；常識 SYN **common sense**

nou·veau riche /ˌnuːvəʊ ˈriːʃ; *NAmE* ˌnuːvoʊ/ *noun* (*pl.* **nou·veaux riches** /ˌnuːvəʊ ˈriːʃ; *NAmE* ˌnuːvoʊ/ or **the nou·veau riche**) (from *French, disapproving*) a person who has recently become rich and likes to show how rich they are in a very obvious way 暴發戶 ▸ **nou·veau riche** *adj.*

N

nou·velle cui·sine /ˌnuːvel kwɪˈziːn/ *noun* [U] (from *French*) a modern style of cooking that avoids heavy foods and serves small amounts of different dishes arranged in an attractive way on the plate 新式烹飪（講求食物清淡，量少而精美）

nova /ˈnəʊvə; *NAmE* ˈnoʊvə/ *noun* (*pl.* **novae** /-viː/ or **novas**) (*astronomy* 天) a star that suddenly becomes much brighter for a short period 新星（短期內突然變得很亮）➲ compare SUPERNOVA

novel 🔑 /ˈnɒvl; *NAmE* ˈnɑːvl/ *noun, adj.*

■ ***noun*** 🔑 a story long enough to fill a complete book, in which the characters and events are usually imaginary （長篇）小說：*to write/publish/read a novel* 創作 / 發表 / 閱讀長篇小說 ◇ ***detective/historical/romantic novels*** 偵探 / 歷史 / 言情小說 ◇ *the novels of Jane Austen* 簡・奧斯汀的小說 ➲ **COLLOCATIONS** at LITERATURE

■ ***adj.*** (often *approving*) different from anything known before; new, interesting and often seeming slightly strange 新穎的；與眾不同的；珍奇的：*a novel feature* 新特徵

nov·el·ette /ˌnɒvəˈlet; *NAmE* ˌnɑːv-/ *noun* a short novel, especially a romantic novel that is considered to be badly written 中篇小說（尤指被認為很蹩腳的言情小說）

nov·el·ist /ˈnɒvəlɪst; *NAmE* ˈnɑːv-/ *noun* a person who writes novels 小說家：*a romantic/historical novelist* 言情 / 歷史小說家 ➲ **COLLOCATIONS** at LITERATURE

nov·el·is·tic /ˌnɒvəˈlɪstɪk; *NAmE* ˌnɑːv-/ *adj.* (*formal*) typical of or used in novels 小說的；小說中使用的

nov·ella /nəˈvelə/ *noun* a short novel 中篇小說

nov·elty /ˈnɒvlti; *NAmE* ˈnɑːv-/ *noun, adj.*

■ ***noun*** (*pl.* **-ies**) **1** [U] the quality of being new, different and interesting 新奇；新穎；新鮮：*It was fun working there at first but* ***the novelty soon wore off*** (= it became boring). 開始的時候在那裏工作很有趣，但這股新鮮勁很快就過去了。◇ *There's a certain* ***novelty value*** *in this approach.* 這種方法有一定的新意。**2** [C] a thing, person or situation that is interesting because it is new, unusual or has not been known before 新奇的事物（或人、環境）：*Electric cars are still something of a novelty.* 電動汽車仍然是一種新鮮玩意兒。**3** [C] a small cheap object sold as a toy or a decorative object 廉價小飾物；小玩意兒

■ ***adj.*** [only before noun] different and unusual; intended to be amusing and to catch people's attention 新奇的；風格獨特的：*a novelty teapot* 新穎獨特的茶壺

No·vem·ber 🔑 /nəʊˈvembə(r); *NAmE* noʊ-/ *noun* [U, C] (*abbr.* **Nov.**)

the 11th month of the year, between October and December 十一月 **HELP** To see how **November** is used, look at the examples at **April**. * November 的用法見詞條 April 下的示例。

nov·ice /ˈnɒvɪs; *NAmE* ˈnɑːv-/ *noun* **1** a person who is new and has little experience in a skill, job or situation 新手；初學者：*I'm a complete novice at skiing.* 滑雪我完全是個新手。◇ *computer software for novices/the novice user* 給初學者設計的電腦軟件 **2** a person who has joined a religious group and is preparing to become a MONK or a NUN 初學修士（或修女）；（修會等的）初學生 **3** a horse that has not yet won an important race 尚未贏過大賽的賽馬

novi·ti·ate (also **novi·ci·ate**) /nəʊˈvɪʃiət; *NAmE* noʊ-/ *noun* (*formal*) a period of being a novice (2) （修士或修女的）初學期

novo·caine /ˈnəʊvəkeɪn; *NAmE* ˈnoʊ-/ *noun* [U] (*medical* 醫) = PROCAINE

now 🔑 /naʊ/ *adv., conj.*

■ ***adv.*** **1** 🔑 (at) the present time 現在；目前；此刻：*Where are you living now?* 你現在住在哪裏？◇ *It's been two weeks now since she called.* 她上次來電距今已經有兩個星期了。◇ *It's too late now.* 現在太晚了。◇ ***From now on*** *I'll be more careful.* 從今以後，我會更加細心。◇ *He'll be home* ***by now.*** 他現在該到家了。◇ *I've lived at home* ***up till now.*** 我一直住在家裏。◇ *That's all* ***for now.*** 暫時就這些。**2** 🔑 at or from this moment, but not before 現在；從現在開始：*Start writing now.* 現在開始寫吧。◇ *I am now ready to answer your questions.* 我現在可以回答你們的問題了。**3** 🔑 (*informal*) used to show that you are annoyed about sth （表示厭煩）：*Now they want to tax food!* 他們竟然要對食品收稅！◇ *What do you want now?* 你又想要什麼？◇ *It's broken. Now I'll have to get a new one.* 舊的破了，我只好去買個新的了。**4** 🔑 used to get sb's attention before changing the subject or asking them to do sth （改變話題或要對方做某事前，引起對方注意）喂，哎，嗨：*Now, listen to what she's saying.* 嗨，聽聽她在講什麼。◇ *Now, the next point is quite complex.* 請注意，下一點非常複雜。◇ *Now come and sit down.* 喂，過來坐下。◇ *Now let me think ...* 嗯，讓我想想…

IDM **(every) now and aˈgain/ˈthen** 🔑 from time to time; occasionally 有時；偶爾；時常：*Every now and again she checked to see if he was still asleep.* 她隔一會兒就看看他是否還在睡覺。**now for ˈsb/ˈsth** used when turning to a fresh activity or subject （轉向新的活動或話題）：*And now for some travel news.* 下面播報幾條旅遊新聞。**ˌnow, ˈnow** (also **ˌnow ˈthen**) used to show in a mild way that you do not approve of sth （溫和地表示不贊同）可是，好啦：*Now then, that's enough noise.* 好啦，這夠吵了。**now ... now ...** at one time ... at another time ... 時而…時而…：*Her moods kept changing—now happy, now sad.* 她的情緒總是變幻不定，時而歡喜，時而憂傷。**(it's) ˌnow or ˈnever** this is the only opportunity sb will have to do sth 機不可失；勿失良機 **ˈnow then** **1** = NOW, NOW **2** used when making a suggestion or an offer （提出建議或提供幫助）喂，聽我說：*Now then, who wants to come for a walk?* 喂，誰想出來走走？**ˈnow what?** (*informal*) **1** (also **what is it ˈnow?**) used when you are annoyed because sb is always asking questions or interrupting you （對某人的不斷提問或打擾感到厭煩）又怎麼了：*'Yes, but Dad ...' 'Now what?'* "是的，可是爸爸…" "又怎麼了？" **2** used to say that you do not know what to do next in a particular situation （不知道下一步該做什麼）現在該怎麼辦

■ ***conj.*** 🔑 **~ (that)** ... because the thing mentioned is happening or has just happened 既然；由於：*Now that the kids have left home we've got a lot of extra space.* 孩子們都離開家了，我們住着就更寬綽了。

now·adays /ˈnaʊədeɪz/ *adv.* at the present time, in contrast with the past 現今；現在；目前：*Nowadays most kids prefer watching TV to reading.* 現在大多數孩子都喜歡看電視而不喜歡閱讀。

no·where 🔑 /ˈnəʊweə(r); *NAmE* ˈnoʊwer/ (also **ˈno place** especially in *NAmE*) *adv.*

not in or to any place 無處；哪裏都不：*This animal is found in Australia, and nowhere else.* 這種動物生長在澳大利亞，別處沒有。◇ *There was nowhere for me to sit.* 我無處可坐。◇ *'Where are you going this weekend?' 'Nowhere special.'* "這個週末你打算去哪兒？" "沒什麼地方可去。" ◇ *Nowhere is the effect of government policy more apparent than in agriculture.* 政府的政策對農業的影響最為顯著。

IDM **get/go ˈnowhere | get sb ˈnowhere** to make no progress or have no success; to not enable sb to make progress or have success （讓某人）毫無進展：*We discussed it all morning but got nowhere.* 我們就此事討論了一上午，可是毫無進展。◇ *Talking to him will get you nowhere.* 和他談話你會一無所獲。**nowhere to be ˈfound/ˈseen | nowhere in ˈsight** impossible for anyone to find or see 不可能找到（或看見）：*The children were nowhere to be seen.* 根本看不到孩子們在哪兒。◇ *A peace settlement is nowhere in sight* (= is not likely in the near future). 近期內看不到和平解決的跡象。➲ more at LEAD[1] *v.*, MIDDLE *n.*, NEAR *adv.*

ˌno-ˈwin *adj.* [only before noun] (of a situation, policy, etc. 情形、政策等) that will end badly whatever you decide to do 終將失敗的；無望取勝的：*We are considering the options available to us in this no-win situation.* 在這種取勝無望的情形下，我們在細想還有什麼選擇。

ˈnow-now *adv.* (*SAfrE, informal*) **1** within a short period of time 一會兒；立刻：*I'll be with you now-now.* 我馬

N

上就來。 **2** a short time ago 剛剛；剛才： *She left now-now.* 她剛走。

nowt /naʊt/ *pron.* (*BrE, dialect, informal*) nothing 無；沒有什麼： *There's nowt wrong with it.* 這沒什麼錯。

nox·ious /ˈnɒkʃəs; *NAmE* ˈnɑːk-/ *adj.* (*formal*) poisonous or harmful 有毒的；有害的： *noxious fumes* 有毒煙霧

noz·zle /ˈnɒzl; *NAmE* ˈnɑːzl/ *noun* a narrow piece that is attached to the end of a pipe or tube to direct the stream of liquid, air or gas passing through 管口；噴嘴

nr *abbr.* (*BrE*) near (used, for example, in the address of a small village) 靠近（用於小村莊等的地址中）： *Howden, nr Goole* 靠近古爾的豪頓村

NRA /ˌen ɑːr ˈeɪ/ *abbr.* National Rifle Association (a US organization that supports the right of citizens to own a gun)（美國）全國步槍協會（支持公民擁有槍支的權利）

NRI /ˌen ɑːr ˈaɪ/ *abbr.* (*IndE*) Non-Resident Indian (a person of Indian origin who is working somewhere else but who keeps links with India) 非常住印度人（不居住在印度但與印度保持聯繫的國外印度裔人）

ns *abbr.* NANOSECOND(S) 毫微秒；十億分之一秒；奈秒

NST /ˌen es ˈtiː/ *abbr.* (*CanE*) Newfoundland Standard Time 紐芬蘭標準時間

NSU /ˌen es ˈjuː/ *abbr.* NON-SPECIFIC URETHRITIS

nth /enθ/ *adj.* [only before noun] (*informal*) used when you are stating that sth is the last in a long series and emphasizing how often sth has happened（某事已發生多次，並強調其頻繁性）第 n 個的，第 n 次的： *It's the nth time I've explained it to you.* 這件事我已經向你解釋過無數遍了。

IDM **to the nth ˈdegree** extremely; to an extreme degree 極端地；非常地；極大程度上

N

NTSC /ˌen tiː es ˈsiː/ *noun* [U] (*technical* 術語) a television broadcasting system that is used in N America and Japan * NTSC 制式，全國電視系統委員會制式（北美和日本使用的電視廣播系統） ➲ compare PAL, SECAM

nu /njuː/ *noun* the 13th letter of the Greek alphabet (N, ν) 希臘字母表的第 13 個字母

nu·ance /ˈnjuːɑːns; *NAmE* ˈnuː-/ *noun* [C, U] a very slight difference in meaning, sound, colour or sb's feelings that is not usually very obvious（意義、聲音、顏色、感情等方面的）細微差別： *He watched her face intently to catch every nuance of expression.* 他認真地注視着她的臉，捕捉每一絲細微的表情變化。

nub /nʌb/ *noun* [sing.] **the ~ (of sth)** the central or essential point of a situation, problem, etc. 中心；要點；實質： ***The nub of the matter** is that business is declining.* 問題的核心是工商業在萎縮。

nu·bile /ˈnjuːbaɪl; *NAmE* ˈnuː-; ˈnuːbl/ *adj.* (of a girl or young woman 女孩或年輕女子) sexually attractive 性感的；迷人的

nu·buck /ˈnjuːbʌk; *NAmE* ˈnuː-/ *noun* [U] a type of leather that has been rubbed on one side to make it feel soft like SUEDE 正絨面革（單面打磨的軟皮革）

nu·clear 0-w **AW** /ˈnjuːkliə(r); *NAmE* ˈnuː-/ *adj.* [usually before noun]
1 0-w using, producing or resulting from nuclear energy 原子能的；核能的： *a nuclear power station* 核電站 ◇ *the nuclear industry* 原子能工業 ◇ *nuclear-powered submarines* 核動力潛艇 **2** 0-w connected with weapons that use nuclear energy 核武器的： ***a nuclear weapon/bomb/missile*** 核武器；核彈；核導彈 ◇ ***a nuclear explosion/attack/war*** 核爆炸 / 攻擊 / 戰爭 ◇ *the country's **nuclear capability*** (= the fact that it has nuclear weapons) 這個國家的核力量 ◇ ***nuclear capacity*** (= the number of nuclear weapons a country has) 核能力 **3** (*physics* 物) of the NUCLEUS (= central part) of an atom 核子的；原子核的： *nuclear particles* 核粒子 ◇ *a nuclear reaction* 核反應

ˌnuclear ˈenergy (also **ˌnuclear ˈpower**) *noun* [U] a powerful form of energy produced by converting matter into energy splitting the NUCLEI (= central parts) of atoms. It is used to produce electricity. 核能；原子能

ˌnuclear ˈfamily *noun* (*technical* 術語) a family that consists of father, mother and children, when it is thought of as a unit in society 核心家庭，小家庭（只包括父母和子女） ➲ compare EXTENDED FAMILY

ˌnuclear ˈfission *noun* [U] = FISSION

ˌnuclear-ˈfree *adj.* [usually before noun] (of a country or a region 國家或地區) not having or allowing nuclear energy, weapons or materials 無核的： *a nuclear-free zone* 無核區

ˌnuclear ˈfuel *noun* [U] a substance that can be used as a source of NUCLEAR ENERGY because it is capable of NUCLEAR FISSION 核燃料

ˌnuclear ˈfusion *noun* [U] = FUSION

nuclear option *noun* (*politics* 政) the most extreme possible response to a particular situation 核選擇（指可能做出的最極端反應）： *Currency controls would be the nuclear option.* 貨幣管制將是不得已而為之的選擇。

ˌnuclear ˈphysics *noun* [U] the area of physics which deals with the NUCLEUS of atoms and with nuclear energy（原子）核物理學 ▸ **ˌnuclear ˈphysicist** *noun*

ˌnuclear ˈpower *noun* [U] = NUCLEAR ENERGY

ˌnuclear reˈactor *noun* = REACTOR

ˌnuclear ˈwaste *noun* [U] waste material which is RADIOACTIVE, especially used fuel from nuclear power stations 核廢料

ˌnuclear ˈwinter *noun* a period without light, heat or growth which scientists believe would follow a nuclear war 核冬天，核子冬天（科學家認為核戰爭之後會出現的一段昏暗、寒冷、荒蕪的時期）

nu·cle·ic acid /njuːˌkliːɪk ˈæsɪd; -ˌkleɪk; *NAmE* nuː-/ *noun* [U] (*chemistry* 化) either of two acids, DNA and RNA, that are present in all living cells 核酸

nu·cleus /ˈnjuːkliəs; *NAmE* ˈnuː-/ *noun* (*pl.* **nu·clei** /-kliaɪ/) **1** (*physics* 物) the part of an atom that contains most of its mass and that carries a positive electric charge 核；原子核 ➲ see also NEUTRON, PROTON **2** (*biology* 生) the central part of some cells, containing the GENETIC material 細胞核 **3** the central part of sth around which other parts are located or collected 核心；中心： *These paintings will form the nucleus of a new collection.* 這些畫將構成新的收藏系列的基礎。

nude /njuːd; *NAmE* nuːd/ *adj., noun*

■ ***adj.*** **1** (especially of a human figure in art 尤指藝術人像) not wearing any clothes 裸體的 **SYN** **naked**： *a nude model* 裸體模特兒 ◇ *He asked me to pose nude for him.* 他請我給他擺裸體造型。 **2** involving people who are naked 裸體者的： *a nude photograph* 裸體照片 ◇ *Are there any nude scenes in the movie?* 電影裏有裸體鏡頭嗎？ **3** (*NAmE*) (of TIGHTS/PANTYHOSE, etc. 褲襪等) skin-coloured 肉色的

■ ***noun*** a work of art consisting of a naked human figure; a naked human figure in art 裸體畫；人物裸體作品；裸體人像： *a bronze nude by Rodin* 羅丹創作的青銅裸體像 ◇ *a reclining nude* 一個斜倚着的裸體人像

IDM **in the ˈnude** not wearing any clothes 裸體的 **SYN** **naked**： *She refuses to be photographed in the nude.* 她拒絕拍裸體照片。

nudge /nʌdʒ/ *verb, noun*

■ ***verb*** **1** [T] **~ sb/sth** to push sb gently, especially with your elbow, in order to get their attention（用肘）輕推，輕觸： *He nudged me and whispered, 'Look who's just come in.'* 他用胳膊肘碰了我一下，低聲說："瞧誰進來了。" **2** [T] **~ sb/sth + adv./prep.** to push sb/sth gently or gradually in a particular direction（朝某方向）輕推，漸漸推動： *He nudged the ball past the goalie and into the net.* 他輕鬆地將球推過守門員，送入網中。◇ *She nudged me out of the way.* 她將我慢慢地推開了。◇ (*figurative*) *He nudged the conversation towards the subject of money.* 他將談話逐步引到錢這個話題上。◇ (*figurative*) *She tried to nudge him into changing his mind* (= persuade him to do it). 她試圖慢慢說服他改變主意。 **3** [T, I] **~ (sth) + adv./prep.** to move forward by pushing with your elbow 用胳膊肘擠開往前走： *He **nudged his way** through the crowd.* 他用胳膊肘開路穿過人群。

4 [T] **~ sth (+ adv./prep.)** to reach or make sth reach a particular level（使）達到，接近：*Inflation is nudging 20%.* 通貨膨脹即將達到 20%。◇ *This afternoon's sunshine could nudge the temperature above freezing.* 今天下午的陽光可使溫度達到冰點以上。

■ ***noun*** a slight push, usually with the elbow（肘部的）輕推，碰：*She gave me a gentle nudge in the ribs to tell me to shut up.* 她用胳膊肘輕推了一下我的腰，讓我住口。◇ (*figurative*) *He can work hard but he needs a nudge now and then.* 他能夠努力工作，但偶爾需要督促一下。

IDM **ˌnudge ˈnudge, ˌwink ˈwink | a ˌnudge and a ˈwink** used to suggest sth to do with sex without actually saying it（暗指與性行為有關的事）眉來眼去：*They've been spending a lot of time together, nudge nudge, wink wink.* 他們長期廝混在一起，卿卿我我的。

nudie /ˈnjuːdi; *NAmE* ˈnuː-/ *adj.* (*informal*) showing or including people wearing no clothes 展示裸體的；有裸體的：*nudie photographs* 裸體照片

nud·ism /ˈnjuːdɪzəm; *NAmE* ˈnuː-/ (also **na·tur·ism** especially in *BrE*) *noun* [U] the practice of not wearing any clothes because you believe this is more natural and healthy 裸體主義（認為裸體更自然更有益健康）

nud·ist /ˈnjuːdɪst; *NAmE* ˈnuː-/ (also **na·tur·ist** especially in *BrE*) *noun* a person who does not wear any clothes because they believe this is more natural and healthy 裸體主義者：*a **nudist beach/camp*** 裸泳海灘；裸體營

nud·ity /ˈnjuːdəti; *NAmE* ˈnuː-/ *noun* [U] the state of being naked 裸體；赤裸：*The committee claimed that there was too much nudity on television.* 委員會指出電視裏的裸體鏡頭太多。

nuf·fin /ˈnʌfɪn/ (also **nuf·fink** /ˈnʌfɪŋk/) *pron.* (*BrE, informal*) nothing 沒有東西；沒有什麼

nu·ga·tory /ˈnjuːɡətəri; *NAmE* ˈnuːɡətɔːri/ *adj.* (*formal*) having no purpose or value 無目的的；無價值的 **SYN** **worthless**

nug·get /ˈnʌɡɪt/ *noun* **1** a small lump of a valuable metal or mineral, especially gold, that is found in the earth 天然貴重金屬塊；（尤指）天然金塊 **2** a small round piece of some types of food（某些食品的）小圓塊：*chicken nuggets* 雞肉塊 **3** a small thing such as an idea or a fact that people think of as valuable 有價值的小東西；有用的想法（或事實）**SYN** **snippet**：*a useful nugget of information* 一條有用的信息

nuis·ance /ˈnjuːsns; *NAmE* ˈnuː-/ *noun* **1** [C, usually sing.] a thing, person or situation that is annoying or causes trouble or problems 麻煩事；討厭的人（或東西）：*I don't want to **be a nuisance** so tell me if you want to be alone.* 我不想討人嫌，你要是想一個人待着就說一聲。◇ *I hope you're not **making a nuisance of yourself**.* 我希望你沒有討人嫌。◇ ***It's a nuisance** having to go back tomorrow.* 明天不得不回去，真煩人。◇ *What a nuisance!* 真麻煩！**2** [C, U] (*law* 律) behaviour by sb that annoys other people and that a court can order the person to stop 非法妨害；滋擾行為：*He was charged with causing a public nuisance.* 他被控妨害公共利益罪。

ˈnuisance value *noun* [U] (*BrE*) a quality that makes sth useful because it causes problems for your opponents 阻礙價值

nuke /njuːk; *NAmE* usually nuːk/ *verb, noun* (*informal*)

■ ***verb*** **~ sth** to attack a place with nuclear weapons 用核武器攻擊

■ ***noun*** a nuclear weapon 核武器

null /nʌl/ *adj.* (*technical* 術語) having the value zero 零值的；等於零的：*a null result* 毫無結果

IDM **ˌnull and ˈvoid** (*law* 律) (of an election, agreement, etc. 選舉、協議等) having no legal force; not valid 無法律效力的；無效的：*The contract was declared null and void.* 合同被宣佈無效。

ˈnull hypothesis *noun* (*statistics* 統計) the idea that an experiment that is done using two groups of people will show the same results for each group 零假設，原假設，虛無假設（即用兩組人分別實驗而結果相同）

nul·lify /ˈnʌlɪfaɪ/ *verb* (**nul·li·fies**, **nul·li·fy·ing**, **nul·li·fied**, **nul·li·fied**) (*formal*) **1 ~ sth** to make sth such as an agreement or order lose its legal force 使失去法律效力；廢止 **SYN** **invalidate**：*Judges were unwilling to nullify government decisions.* 法官們不願廢止政府決定。**2 ~ sth** to make sth lose its effect or power 使無效；抵消 **SYN** **negate**：*An unhealthy diet will nullify the effects of training.* 不健康的飲食會抵消鍛煉的效果。

null·ity /ˈnʌləti/ *noun* [sing.] (*formal* or *law* 律) the fact of sth, for example a marriage, having no legal force or no longer being valid; something which is no longer valid 無法律約束力；無效；無法律效力的事物

numb /nʌm/ *adj., verb*

■ ***adj.*** **1** if a part of your body is **numb**, you cannot feel anything in it, for example because of cold 麻木的；失去知覺的：*to **be/go numb*** 麻木；失去知覺 ◇ *numb with cold* 凍僵 ◇ *I've just been to the dentist and my face is still numb.* 我剛剛去看了牙醫，臉上現在還沒知覺呢。**2** unable to feel, think or react in the normal way 麻木的；遲鈍的；呆滯的：*He felt numb with shock.* 他驚呆了。➲ see also NUMBING ▶ **numb·ly** *adv.*：*Her life would never be the same again, she realized numbly.* 她模模糊糊地意識到她的生活不會和過去一樣了。**numb·ness** *noun* [U]：*pain and numbness in my fingers* 我的手指又疼又麻 ◇ *He was still in a state of numbness and shock from the accident.* 由於這事故，他還處於麻木與震驚狀態之中。

■ ***verb*** **1 ~ sth** to make a part of your body unable to feel anything, for example because of cold 使失去知覺；使麻木：*His fingers were numbed with the cold.* 他的手指凍僵了。**2 ~ sb** to make sb unable to feel, think or react in a normal way, for example because of an emotional shock 使麻木；使遲鈍 **SYN** **stun**：*We sat there in silence, numbed by the shock of her death.* 我們默默地坐在那裏發愣，因為她的死使我們感到震驚。

num·ber 🔑 /ˈnʌmbə(r)/ *noun, verb*

■ ***noun***

▸ **WORD/SYMBOL 單詞；符號** **1** 🔑 [C] a word or symbol that represents an amount or a quantity 數字；數；數量 **SYN** **figure**：*Think of a number and multiply it by two.* 想出一個數，然後乘以二。◇ *a **high/low number*** 高位 / 低位數 ◇ ***even numbers*** (= 2, 4, 6, etc.) 偶數 ◇ ***odd numbers*** (= 1, 3, 5, etc.) 奇數 ◇ *You owe me 27 dollars? Make it 30, that's a good **round number**.* 你欠我 27 元？湊到 30 吧，討個整數好記。➲ see also CARDINAL NUMBER at CARDINAL *n.* (2), ORDINAL, PRIME NUMBER, WHOLE NUMBER

▸ **POSITION IN SERIES 序列中的位置** **2** 🔑 [C] (*abbr.* **No.**) (*symb.* **#**) used before a figure to show the position of sth in a series 編號；序數：*They live at number 26.* 他們住在 26 號。◇ *The song reached number 5 in the charts.* 這首歌在排行榜中位列第 5。

▸ **TELEPHONE, ETC. 電話等** **3** 🔑 [C] (often in compounds 常構成複合詞) a number used to identify sth or communicate by telephone, FAX, etc.（電話、傳真等的）號碼：*My phone number is 266998.* 我的電話號碼是 266998。◇ *I'm sorry, I think you have the **wrong number*** (= wrong telephone number). 對不起，我想你打錯了。◇ *What is your account number, please?* 請問你的賬號是多少？➲ see also BOX NUMBER, E-NUMBER, PIN, REGISTRATION NUMBER, SERIAL NUMBER

▸ **QUANTITY 量** **4** 🔑 [C] **~ (of sb/sth)** a quantity of people or things 數量；數額：*A large number of people have applied for the job.* 許多人申請了這工作。◇ *The number of homeless people has increased dramatically.* 無家可歸者的人數急劇增加了。◇ *Huge numbers of* (= very many) *animals have died.* 有大量的動物死去。◇ ***A number of*** (= some) *problems have arisen.* 已經出現了一些問題。◇ *I could give you **any number of*** (= a lot of) *reasons for not going.* 我可以給你許多不去的理由。◇ *We were eight **in number*** (= there were eight of us). 我們有八個人。◇ *Nurses are leaving the profession in increasing numbers.* 越來越多的護士退出這一職業。◇ ***Sheer weight of numbers*** (= the large number of soldiers) *secured them the victory.* 他們只是靠重兵取勝。◇ *staff/student numbers* 員工 / 學生數量 **HELP** A plural verb is needed after **a/an (large, small, etc.) number of ...**. 在 a/an (large、small 等) number of ... 之後用複數動詞。

▸ **GROUP OF PEOPLE 人群** **5** [sing.] (*formal*) a group or quantity of people 一群人；許多人：*one of our number*

N

(= one of us) 我們中的一人 ◇ *The prime minister is elected by MPs from among their number.* 首相是下院議員從他們當中選出的。
▸ MAGAZINE 雜誌 **6** [C] (*BrE*) the version of a magazine, etc. published on a particular day, in a particular month, etc. 期；號 SYN **issue**：*the October number of 'Vogue'* 《時尚》十月號 ➲ see also BACK NUMBER
▸ SONG/DANCE 歌；舞蹈 **7** [C] a song or dance, especially one of several in a performance 一首歌，一段舞蹈（尤指演出的節目）：*They sang a slow romantic number.* 他們演唱了一首緩慢的浪漫歌曲。
▸ THING ADMIRED 令人羨慕的東西 **8** [sing.] (*informal*) (following one or more adjectives 接在一個或多個形容詞後) a thing, such as a dress or a car, that is admired 令人羨慕的東西：*She was wearing a black velvet number.* 她穿着一件時髦的黑天鵝絨禮服。
▸ GRAMMAR 語法 **9** [U] the form of a word, showing whether one or more than one person or thing is being talked about 數（表示所敍述的人或事物是一個或多個）：*The word 'men' is plural in number.* * men 一詞是複數形式。◇ *The subject of a sentence and its verb must agree in number.* 句子的主語和動詞的數必須一致。
IDM **by 'numbers** following a set of simple instructions identified by numbers 按數字指令：*painting by numbers* 按數字順序着色 **by the 'numbers** (*NAmE*) following closely the accepted rules for doing sth 循規蹈矩；一板一眼 **have (got) sb's 'number** (*informal*) to know what sb is really like and what they plan to do 瞭解某人的底細；對某人知根知底：*He thinks he can fool me but I've got his number.* 他以為他能糊弄我，但我清楚他的真面目。 **your 'number is up** (*informal*) the time has come when you will die or lose everything 劫數已到；死期已至 **'numbers game** a way of considering an activity, etc. that is concerned only with the number of people doing sth, things achieved, etc., not with who or what they are 數字遊戲（即只注重參與的人數、事情的達成數等，而不考慮參與者是誰、事情是什麼）：*MPs were playing the numbers game as the crucial vote drew closer.* 在至關重要的表決臨近時，下院議員們玩起了數字遊戲。 ➲ more at CUSHY, OPPOSITE *adj.*, SAFETY, WEIGHT *n.*
■ *verb*
▸ MAKE A SERIES 排序 **1** [T] to give a number to sth as part of a series or list 標號；給…編號：**~ sth** *All the seats in the stadium are numbered.* 運動場裏所有的座位都編了號。◇ *I couldn't work out the numbering system for the hotel rooms.* 我搞不清楚酒店房間的編號系統。◇ **~ sth from … to …** *Number the car's features from 1 to 10 according to importance.* 將車的特徵按重要性從 1 到 10 編號。◇ **~ sth + noun** *The doors were numbered 2, 4, 6 and 8.* 門上的編號為 2、4、6 和 8。
▸ MAKE STH AS TOTAL 總計 **2** [I] **+ noun** to make a particular number when added together 總計；共計；數以…計 SYN **add up to sth**：*The crowd numbered more than a thousand.* 聚集的人群共計一千多人。◇ *We numbered 20* (= there were 20 of us in the group). 我們總共 20 人。
▸ INCLUDE 包括 **3** [T, I] (*formal*) to include sb/sth in a particular group; to be included in a particular group 把…算作；（被）歸入：**~ sb/sth among sth** *I number her among my closest friends.* 我把她算作我最好的朋友之一。◇ **~ among sth** *He numbers among the best classical actors in Britain.* 他被看作是英國最好的古典劇目演員之一。 IDM see DAY

'number crunching *noun* [U] (*informal*) the process of calculating numbers, especially when a large amount of data is involved and the data is processed in a short space of time 數字密集運算

numbered *adj.* having a number to show that it is part of a series or list 編號的：*The players all wear numbered shirts.* 隊員都穿着有編號的運動衫。 IDM see DAY

num·ber·less /ˈnʌmbələs; *NAmE* -bərl-/ *adj.* (*literary*) too many to be counted 無數的；難以計數的 SYN **innumerable**

ˌnumber 'one *noun, adj.* (*informal*)
■ *noun* **1** [U] the most important or best person or thing 頭號人物（或事物）；最重要的人（或事物）；最好的人（或事物）：*We're number one in the used car business.* 在二手車交易中我們是老大。 **2** [U, C] the pop song or record that has sold the most copies in a particular week 週銷售量最高的流行歌曲（或唱片）：*The new album went straight to number one.* 這張新的歌曲專輯一舉登上了週銷售量榜首。◇ *She's had three number ones.* 她已有三張唱片曾經名列週銷售量排行榜榜首。 **3** [U] yourself 自己：***Looking after number one** is all she thinks about.* 她一心只顧着自己。 **4** [sing.] (*informal*) an expression used especially by children or when speaking to children to talk about passing liquid waste from the body （尤作為兒童用語）撒尿：*It's only a number one.* 只撒了尿。 ➲ compare NUMBER TWO
■ *adj.* most important or best 頭號的；最重要的；最好的：*the world's number one athlete* 世界頭號運動員 ◇ *the number one priority* 要最先處理的事

'number plate (*BrE*) (*NAmE* **'license plate**) *noun* a metal or plastic plate on the front and back of a vehicle that shows its REGISTRATION NUMBER（車輛的）牌照，號碼牌

ˌNumber 'Ten (also **No. 10**) *noun* [U+sing./pl. v.] 10 Downing Street, London, the official home of the British prime minister, often used to refer to the government 唐寧街十號（英國首相的倫敦官邸，常指英國政府）：*Number Ten had nothing to say on the matter.* 唐寧街十號對此不作評論。

ˌnumber 'two *noun* [sing.] (*informal*) an expression used especially by children or when speaking to children to talk about passing solid waste from the body （尤作為兒童用語）拉屉屉，拉屎：*Mum, I need a number two.* 媽媽，我要拉屉屉。 ➲ compare NUMBER ONE *n.* (4)

numb·ing /ˈnʌmɪŋ/ *adj.* (of an experience or a situation 經歷或情形) making you unable to feel anything 令人麻木的；使人失去知覺的：*numbing cold/fear* 令人麻木的嚴寒；使人發懵的恐懼 ◇ *Watching television had a numbing effect on his mind.* 看電視使他頭腦麻木。

numb·skull (also **num·skull**) /ˈnʌmskʌl/ *noun* (*informal*) a stupid person 蠢人；笨蛋

nu·mer·acy /ˈnjuːmərəsi; *NAmE* ˈnuː-/ *noun* [U] a good basic knowledge of mathematics; the ability to understand and work with numbers 數學基礎知識；識數；計算能力：*standards of literacy and numeracy* 讀寫和計算的水平 ▸ **nu·mer·ate** /ˈnjuːmərət; *NAmE* ˈnuː-/ *adj.*：*All students should be numerate and literate when they leave school.* 所有的學生畢業時都應具備計算和讀寫的能力。 OPP **innumerate**

nu·meral /ˈnjuːmərəl; *NAmE* ˈnuː-/ *noun* a sign or symbol that represents a number 數字；數碼 ➲ see also ARABIC NUMERAL, ROMAN NUMERAL

nu·mer·ator /ˈnjuːməreɪtə(r); *NAmE* ˈnuː-/ *noun* (*mathematics* 數) the number above the line in a FRACTION, for example 3 in the FRACTION ¾（分數中的）分子 ➲ compare DENOMINATOR

nu·mer·ic·al /njuːˈmerɪkl; *NAmE* nuː-/ (also *less frequent* **nu·mer·ic** /-ɪk/) *adj.* relating to numbers; expressed in numbers 數字的；用數字表示的：*numerical data* 數字數據 ◇ *The results are expressed in descending **numerical order**.* 結果按數字降序列出。 ▸ **nu·mer·ic·al·ly** /-kli/ *adv.*：*to express the results numerically* 按數字順序排列結果

nu·mer·ology /ˌnjuːməˈrɒlədʒi; *NAmE* ˌnuːməˈrɑːlədʒi/ *noun* [U] the use of numbers to try to tell sb what will happen in the future 數字命理學（用數字預測未來）；數字占卜術 ▸ **nu·mero·logic·al** /ˌnjuːmərəˈlɒdʒɪkl; *NAmE* ˌnuːmərəˈlɑːdʒɪkl/ *adj.*

nu·mer·ous /ˈnjuːmərəs; *NAmE* ˈnuː-/ *adj.* (*formal*) existing in large numbers 眾多的；許多的 SYN **many**：*He has been late on numerous occasions.* 他已經遲到過無數次了。◇ *The advantages of this system are too numerous to mention.* 這套系統的好處不勝枚舉。

nu·min·ous /ˈnjuːmɪnəs; *NAmE* ˈnuː-/ *adj.* (*formal*) having a strong religious and spiritual quality that makes you feel that God is present 超自然的；精神上的；神聖的

nu·mis·mat·ics /ˌnjuːmɪzˈmætɪks; *NAmE* ˌnuː-/ *noun* [U] the study of coins and MEDALS 錢幣學；獎章的研究 ▸ **nu·mis·mat·ic** *adj.*

nu·mis·ma·tist /njuːˈmɪzmətɪst; *NAmE* nuː-/ *noun* a person who collects or studies coins or MEDALS 錢幣（或獎章）收藏家；錢幣學家；獎章研究者

numpty /ˈnʌmpti/ (*pl.* **-ies**) *noun* (*ScotE, informal*) a stupid person 傻瓜；笨蛋

num·skull = NUMBSKULL

nun /nʌn/ *noun* a member of a religious community of women who promise to serve God all their lives and often live together in a CONVENT 修女；尼姑 ➲ compare MONK

nun·cio /ˈnʌnsiəʊ; *NAmE* -sioʊ/ *noun* (*pl.* **-os**) a representative of the POPE (= the leader of the Roman Catholic Church) in a foreign country 羅馬教廷大使：*a papal nuncio* 教廷大使

nun·nery /ˈnʌnəri/ *noun* (*pl.* **-ies**) (*old-fashioned* or *literary*) = CONVENT

nup·tial /ˈnʌpʃl/ *adj.* [only before noun] (*formal*) connected with marriage or a wedding 婚姻的；婚禮的：*nuptial bliss* 婚姻美滿 ◇ *a nuptial mass* 婚配彌撒

nup·tials /ˈnʌpʃlz/ *noun* [pl.] (*old-fashioned*) a wedding 婚禮

nurse 🔑 /nɜːs; *NAmE* nɜːrs/ *noun, verb*

▪ *noun* **1** 🔑 a person whose job is to take care of sick or injured people, usually in a hospital 護士：*a qualified/registered nurse* 合格的／註冊護士 ◇ *student nurses* 實習護士 ◇ *a male nurse* 男護士 ◇ *a dental nurse* (= one who helps a dentist) 牙科護士 ◇ *a psychiatric nurse* (= one who works in a hospital for people with mental illnesses) 精神病醫院的護士 ◇ *Nurse Bennett* 貝內特護士 ◇ *Nurse, come quickly!* 護士，快過來！ ➲ see also CHARGE NURSE, DISTRICT NURSE, PRACTICAL NURSE, REGISTERED NURSE, STAFF NURSE ➲ note at GENDER **2** (also **nurse·maid**) (*old-fashioned*) (in the past) a woman or girl whose job was to take care of babies or small children in their own homes（舊時雇主家中的）女保育員，保母，女僕 ➲ see also NURSERY NURSE, WET NURSE

▪ *verb* **1** [T] **~ sb** to care for sb who is ill/sick or injured 看護，照料（病人或傷者）：*He worked in a hospital for ten years nursing cancer patients.* 他在一所醫院裏工作了十年，護理癌症病人。◇ *She **nursed** her daughter **back to health**.* 她照料女兒恢復了健康。 **2** [T] **~ sth** to take care of an injury or illness 調治，調養（傷病）：*Several weeks after the match, he was still nursing a shoulder injury.* 比賽過去幾個星期了，他仍在療養肩傷。◇ *You'd better go to bed and nurse that cold.* 你最好上牀睡覺，把感冒治好。◇ (*figurative*) *She was nursing her hurt pride.* 她的自尊受挫，正在慢慢恢復。 ➲ COLLOCATIONS at ILL **3** [T] **~ sth** (*formal*) to have a strong feeling or idea in your mind for a long time 懷抱；懷有；心藏 **SYN** **harbour**：*to nurse an ambition/a grievance/a grudge* 心懷壯志／不滿／怨恨 ◇ *She had been nursing a secret desire to see him again.* 她一直暗暗渴望再次見到他。 **4** [T] **~ sth** to give special care or attention to sb/sth 培育；培養；悉心照料：*to nurse tender young plants* 悉心照料嫩苗 **5** [T] **~ sb/sth** to hold sb/sth carefully in your arms or close to your body 摟抱；小心抱着：*He sat nursing his cup of coffee.* 他坐在那裏小心翼翼地捧着他那杯咖啡。 **6** [I, T] (of a woman or female animal 婦女或雌性動物) to feed a baby with milk from the breast 餵奶；哺育 **SYN** **suckle**：*a **nursing mother*** 正在餵奶的母親 ◇ **~ sb/sth** *The lioness is still nursing her cubs.* 這隻母獅還在給它的幼崽餵奶。 ➲ compare BREASTFEED **7** [I] (of a baby 嬰兒) to suck milk from its mother's breast 吃奶；吸奶 **SYN** **suckle**

nurse·maid /ˈnɜːsmeɪd; *NAmE* ˈnɜːrs-/ *noun* (*old-fashioned*) = NURSE (2)

ˌnurse pracˈtitioner *noun* a nurse who is trained to do many of the tasks usually done by a doctor 從業護士

nur·sery /ˈnɜːsəri; *NAmE* ˈnɜːrs-/ *noun, adj.*

▪ *noun* (*pl.* **-ies**) **1** = DAY NURSERY **2** = NURSERY SCHOOL：*Her youngest child is **at nursery** now.* 她最小的孩子現在上幼兒園。 **3** (*NAmE* or *old-fashioned*) a room in a house where a baby sleeps 嬰兒室 **4** (*old-fashioned*) a room in a house where young children can play（供遊戲的）兒童室 **5** a place where young plants and trees are grown for sale or for planting somewhere else 苗圃

▪ *adj.* [only before noun] (*BrE*) connected with the education of children from 2 to 5 years old 幼兒教育的：*nursery education* 幼兒教育 ◇ *a nursery teacher* 幼兒教師

nur·sery·man /ˈnɜːsərimən; *NAmE* ˈnɜːrs-/ *noun* (*pl.* **-men** /-mən/) a person who owns or works in a nursery (5) 苗圃主；苗圃工人；園丁

ˈnursery nurse *noun* (*BrE*) a person whose job involves taking care of small children in a DAY NURSERY（日託）託兒所保育員

ˈnursery rhyme *noun* a simple traditional poem or song for children 童謠；兒歌

ˈnursery school *noun* a school for children between the ages of about two and five 幼兒園 **SYN** **preschool** ➲ compare KINDERGARTEN, PLAYGROUP

ˈnursery slope (*BrE*) (*NAmE* **ˈbunny slope**) *noun* [usually pl.] a slope that is not very steep and is used by people who are learning to SKI（初學滑雪者的）平緩坡地

nurs·ing /ˈnɜːsɪŋ; *NAmE* ˈnɜːrs-/ *noun* [U] the job or skill of caring for people who are sick or injured 護理；看護：*a career in nursing* 護理生涯 ◇ *nursing care* 看護 ◇ *the nursing profession* 護理職業

ˈnursing home *noun* a small private hospital, especially one where old people live and are cared for 小型私立療養院；（尤指）私立養老院

nur·ture /ˈnɜːtʃə(r); *NAmE* ˈnɜːrtʃ-/ *verb, noun*

▪ *verb* (*formal*) **1 ~ sb/sth** to care for and protect sb/sth while they are growing and developing 養育；養護；培養：*These delicate plants need careful nurturing.* 這些幼嫩的植物需要精心培育。◇ *children nurtured by loving parents* 受到慈愛的父母養育的孩子 **2 ~ sth** to help sb/sth to develop and be successful 扶持；幫助；支持 **SYN** **foster**：*It's important to nurture a good working relationship.* 維持良好的工作關係非常重要。 **3 ~ sth** to have a feeling, an idea, a plan, etc. for a long time and encourage it to develop 滋長；助長：*She secretly nurtured a hope of becoming famous.* 她暗暗滋生出成名的願望。

▪ *noun* [U] (*formal*) care, encouragement and support given to sb/sth while they are growing 養育；培養

nut 🔑 /nʌt/ *noun, verb*

▪ *noun* **1** 🔑 (often in compounds 常構成複合詞) a small hard fruit with a very hard shell that grows on some trees 堅果：*to **crack a nut*** (= open it) 破開堅果 ◇ *a Brazil nut* 巴西果 ◇ *a hazelnut* 榛子 ◇ *nuts and raisins* 果仁和葡萄乾 ➲ VISUAL VOCAB pages V10, V32 ➲ see also MONKEY NUT **2** a small piece of metal with a hole through the centre that is screwed onto a BOLT to hold pieces of wood, machinery, etc. together 螺母；螺帽：*to tighten a nut* 擰緊螺母 ◇ *a wheel nut* 車輪螺母 ➲ VISUAL VOCAB page V20 **3** (*BrE, slang*) a person's head or brain 人的頭（或大腦） **4** (*BrE* also **nut·ter**) (*informal*) a strange or crazy person 怪人；瘋子：*He's a complete nut, if you ask me.* 要我說，他是個十足的瘋子。 ➲ see also NUTS (1), NUTTY (2) **5** (*informal*) (in compounds 構成複合詞) a person who is extremely interested in a particular subject, activity, etc. 着迷的人；專注於某事的人；…迷：*a **fitness/tennis/computer, etc. nut*** 健美迷、網球迷、電腦迷等 **6 nuts** [pl.] (*slang*) a man's TESTICLES 睾丸

IDM **do your ˈnut** (*BrE, informal*) to become very angry 暴跳如雷；氣炸 **a hard/tough ˈnut** (*informal*) a person who is difficult to deal with or to influence 難對付的人；難說服的人 **a hard/tough ˈnut (to ˈcrack)** a difficult problem or situation to deal with 棘手的問題；不好對付的情形 **the ˌnuts and ˈbolts (of sth)** (*informal*) the basic practical details of a subject or an activity 基本

N

要點 ,**off your 'nut** (*BrE, informal*) crazy 瘋狂 ➲ more at SLEDGEHAMMER
■ *verb* (-tt-) **~ sb** (*BrE, informal*) to deliberately hit sb hard with your head （故意）以頭撞擊
PHR V ,**nut sth 'out** (*AustralE, NZE, informal*) to calculate sth or find the answer to sth 計算；找…的答案：*I'm going to have to nut it out on a piece of paper.* 我得在紙上計算一下。

,**nut-'brown** *adj.* dark brown in colour 栗色的；深棕色的：*nut-brown hair* 深棕色的頭髮

nut·case /'nʌtkeɪs/ *noun* (*informal*) a crazy person 瘋子

nut·crack·er /'nʌtkrækə(r)/ *noun* (*BrE* also **nut·crack·ers** [pl.]) a tool for cracking open the shells of nuts 堅果鉗 ➲ VISUAL VOCAB page V26

,**nut 'cutlet** *noun* nuts, bread and HERBS mixed together and cooked in a shape like a piece of meat 乾果蛋糕（用乾果、蔬菜和草本香料烤成）

nut·meg /'nʌtmeg/ *noun* [U, C] the hard seed of a tropical tree originally from SE Asia, used in cooking as a spice, especially to give flavour to cakes and sauces 肉豆蔻（尤用作調味料）：*freshly grated nutmeg* 新磨碎的肉豆蔻末 ➲ VISUAL VOCAB page V32

nutra·ceut·ical /,nju:trə'su:tɪkl/ *noun* = FUNCTIONAL FOOD

nu·tri·ent /'nju:triənt; *NAmE* 'nu:-/ *noun* (*technical* 術語) a substance that is needed to keep a living thing alive and to help it to grow 營養素；營養物：*a lack of **essential nutrients*** 基本營養的缺乏 ◇ *Plants draw minerals and other nutrients from the soil.* 植物從土壤中吸取礦物質和其他養分。◇ *children suffering from a serious **nutrient deficiency*** 嚴重缺乏營養的兒童 ➲ COLLOCATIONS at DIET, LIFE

nu·tri·tion /nju'trɪʃn; *NAmE* nu-/ *noun* [U] the process by which living things receive the food necessary for them to grow and be healthy 營養；滋養；營養的補給：*advice on diet and nutrition* 有關飲食和營養的建議 ◇ *to study food science and nutrition* 研究食物科學和營養 ➲ COLLOCATIONS at DIET ➲ compare MALNUTRITION ▶ **nu·tri·tion·al** /-ʃənl/ (also *less frequent* **nu·tri·tive**) *adj.*：*the nutritional value of milk* 牛奶的營養價值 **nu·tri·tion·al·ly** /-ʃənəli/ *adv.*：*a nutritionally balanced menu* 營養均衡的菜譜

nu·tri·tion·ist /nju'trɪʃənɪst; *NAmE* nu-/ *noun* a person who is an expert on the relationship between food and health 營養學家 ➲ see also DIETITIAN

nu·tri·tious /nju'trɪʃəs; *NAmE* nu-/ *adj.* (*approving*) (of food 食物) very good for you; containing many of the substances which help the body to grow 有營養的；營養豐富的 **SYN** **nourishing**：*tasty and nutritious meals* 既可口又有營養的飯菜

nuts /nʌts/ *adj.* [not before noun] (*informal*) **1** crazy 瘋狂：*My friends think I'm nuts for saying yes.* 朋友們認為我答應是瘋了。◇ *That phone ringing all the time is **driving me nuts!*** 那電話鈴一直響個不停，吵得我快要發瘋了。➲ SYNONYMS at MAD **2 ~ about sb/sth** very much in love with sb; very enthusiastic about sth 執著；迷戀；狂熱：*He's absolutely nuts about her.* 他絕對迷戀上她了。
IDM see SOUP *n.*

nut·shell /'nʌtʃel/ *noun*
IDM **(put sth) in a nutshell** (to say or express sth) in a very clear way, using few words 簡而言之；用簡明的話：*To put it in a nutshell, we're bankrupt.* 簡單地說，我們破產了。

nut·ter /'nʌtə(r)/ *noun* (*BrE, informal*) = NUT (4)

nutty /'nʌti/ *adj.* (**nut·tier**, **nut·ti·est**) **1** tasting of or containing nuts 堅果味的；含果仁的：*a nutty taste* 堅果口味 **2** (*informal*) slightly crazy 瘋瘋癲癲的：*She's got some nutty friends.* 她有幾個瘋瘋癲癲的朋友。◇ *He's **as nutty as a fruitcake*** (= completely crazy). 他瘋狂到了極點。

nuz·zle /'nʌzl/ *verb* [T, I] to touch or rub sb/sth with the nose or mouth, especially to show affection （用鼻子或嘴）摩擦，觸（尤指表達愛意）：**~ sb/sth** *She nuzzled his ear.* 她用嘴磨蹭他的耳朵。◇ **+ adv./prep.** *The child nuzzled up against his mother.* 這孩子依偎着他媽媽。

NVQ /,en vi: 'kju:/ *noun* the abbreviation for 'National Vocational Qualification' (a British qualification that shows that you have reached a particular standard in the work that you do) 國家職業資格證書，國家職業資格認證（全寫為 National Vocational Qualification，英國證明從業者專業水平的證書）：*NVQ Level 3 in Catering* 國家職業資格認證飲食業三級

NW *abbr.* north-west; north-western 西北方（的）；西北部（的）：*NW Australia* 澳大利亞西北部

NY *abbr.* New York 紐約

NYC *abbr.* New York City 紐約市

nylon /'naɪlɒn; *NAmE* -lɑ:n/ *noun* **1** [U] a very strong artificial material, used for making clothes, rope, brushes, etc. 尼龍：*a nylon fishing line* 尼龍釣線 ◇ *This material is 45% nylon.* 這種材料含 45% 的尼龍。**2 nylons** [pl.] (*old-fashioned*) women's STOCKINGS or TIGHTS/PANTYHOSE made of nylon （女用）尼龍長襪，尼龍連襪褲

nymph /nɪmf/ *noun* **1** (in ancient Greek and Roman stories) a spirit of nature in the form of a young woman, that lives in rivers, woods, etc. （古希臘、羅馬神話中居於山林水澤的）仙女 **2** (*biology* 生) a young insect that has a body form which compares with that of the adult 若蟲（與成蟲相似的昆蟲幼體）：*a dragonfly nymph* 蜻蜓幼蟲

nymph·et /'nɪmfet; nɪm'fet/ *noun* a young girl who is very sexually attractive 性感少女；美麗的少女

nym·pho·maniac /,nɪmfə'meɪniæk/ (also *informal* **nym·pho** /'nɪmfəʊ; *NAmE* -foʊ/ *pl.* **-os**) *noun* (*disapproving*) a woman who has, or wants to have, sex very often 女色情狂 ▶ **nym·pho·mania** *noun* [U]

NYSE /,en waɪ es 'i:/ *abbr.* New York Stock Exchange 紐約證券交易所

NZ (*BrE*) (also **N.Z.** *NAmE, BrE*) *abbr.* New Zealand 新西蘭

N

O /əʊ; *NAmE* oʊ/ *noun, exclamation, symbol*
■ ***noun*** (also **o**) (*pl.* **Os**, **O's**, **o's** /əʊz; *NAmE* oʊz/) **1** [C, U] the 15th letter of the English alphabet 英語字母表的第 15 個字母：*'Orange' begins with* (*an*) *O/'O'*. * orange 一詞以字母 o 開頭。 **2** used to mean 'zero' when saying telephone numbers, etc.（說電話號碼等時表示）零：*My number is six o double three* (= 6033). 我的號碼是六零三三。➲ see also O GRADE, O LEVEL
■ ***exclamation*** (especially *literary*) = OH
■ ***symbol*** the symbol for the chemical element Oxygen（化學元素）氧

o' /ə/ *prep.* used in written English to represent an informal way of saying *of*（在書面英語中，代替 of 的非正式說法）：*a couple o' times* 幾次

oaf /əʊf; *NAmE* oʊf/ *noun* a stupid, unpleasant or awkward person, especially a man 傻瓜，蠢材，笨蛋（尤指男人）：*Mind that cup, you clumsy oaf!* 當心那個杯子，你這笨手笨腳的傢伙！ ▸ **oaf·ish** *adj.*

oak /əʊk; *NAmE* oʊk/ *noun* **1** [C, U] (also **'oak tree** [C]) a large tree that produces small nuts called ACORNS. Oaks are common in northern countries and can live to be hundreds of years old. 櫟樹；橡樹：*a gnarled old oak tree* 多節瘤的老櫟樹 ◇ *forests of oak and pine* 長有松樹和櫟樹的森林 ➲ VISUAL VOCAB page V10 ➲ see also POISON OAK **2** [U] the hard wood of the oak tree 櫟木；橡木：*oak beams* 櫟木梁 ◇ *This table is made of solid oak.* 這張桌子是用實心櫟木製作的。
IDM **great/tall ˌoaks from little acorns ˈgrow** (*saying*) something large and successful often begins in a very small way 參天橡樹長自小小橡實；合抱之樹，生於毫末

oaken /ˈəʊkən; *NAmE* ˈoʊkən/ *adj.* [only before noun] (*literary*) made of oak 橡木的；橡木製作的

oakum /ˈəʊkəm; *NAmE* ˈoʊkəm/ *noun* [U] a material obtained by pulling old rope to pieces, a job done in the past by prisoners 麻刀，麻絮（舊時由囚犯製造）

OAP /ˌəʊ eɪ ˈpiː; *NAmE* ˌoʊ/ *noun* (*BrE*, becoming *old-fashioned*) the abbreviation for OLD-AGE PENSIONER 領養老金者（全寫為 old-age pensioner）

oar /ɔː(r)/ *noun* a long pole with a flat blade at one end that is used for ROWING a boat 船槳；槳：*He pulled as hard as he could on the oars.* 他拚命地划槳。➲ VISUAL VOCAB page V54 ➲ compare PADDLE *n.* (1)
IDM **put/stick your ˈoar in** (*BrE, informal*) to give your opinion, advice, etc. without being asked and when it is probably not wanted 多管閒事；橫插一槓子 SYN **interfere**

oar·lock /ˈɔːlɒk; *NAmE* ˈɔːrlɑːk/ (*NAmE*) (*BrE* **row·lock**) *noun* a device fixed to the side of a boat for holding an OAR（固定在小船邊緣的）槳架

oars·man /ˈɔːzmən; *NAmE* ˈɔːrz-/, **oars·woman** /ˈɔːzwʊmən; *NAmE* ˈɔːrz-/ *noun* (*pl.* **-men** /-mən/, **-women** /-wɪmɪn/) a person who ROWS a boat, especially as a member of a CREW (= team) 槳手；划槳人；（尤指）划艇隊員

OAS /ˌəʊ eɪ ˈes; *NAmE* ˌoʊ/ *abbr.* (*CanE*) OLD AGE SECURITY

oasis /əʊˈeɪsɪs; *NAmE* oʊ-/ *noun* (*pl.* **oases** /-siːz/) **1** an area in the desert where there is water and where plants grow（沙漠中的）綠洲 **2** a pleasant place or period of time in the middle of sth unpleasant or difficult（困苦中）令人快慰的地方（或時刻）；樂土；樂事 SYN **haven**：*an oasis of calm* 寧靜的一刻 ◇ *a green oasis in the heart of the city* 都市中心的綠茵

oast house /ˈəʊst haʊs; *NAmE* ˈoʊst/ *noun* (*especially BrE*) a building made of bricks with a round roof that was built to contain an oven used for drying HOPS（啤酒花）烘乾室

oat /əʊt; *NAmE* oʊt/ *adj.* [only before noun] made from or containing OATS 燕麥製的；含燕麥的：*oat cakes* 燕麥餅 ◇ *oat bran* 燕麥麩 ➲ see also OATMEAL

oat·cake /ˈəʊtkeɪk; *NAmE* ˈoʊt-/ *noun* a Scottish biscuit made with oats, which is not sweet（蘇格蘭不帶甜味的）燕麥餅

oater /ˈəʊtə(r); *NAmE* ˈoʊtər/ *noun* (*NAmE, informal*) a film/movie about life in the western US in the 19th century（以 19 世紀美國西部生活為題材的）西部影片

oath /əʊθ; *NAmE* oʊθ/ *noun* (*pl.* **oaths** /əʊðz; *NAmE* oʊðz/) **1** a formal promise to do sth or a formal statement that sth is true 宣誓；誓言：*to* ***take/swear an oath*** *of allegiance* 宣誓效忠 ◇ *Before giving evidence, witnesses in court have to* ***take the oath*** (= promise to tell the truth). 作證之前，證人必須當庭宣誓據實作證。➲ COLLOCATIONS at VOTE **2** (*old-fashioned*) an offensive word or phrase used to express anger, surprise, etc.; a swear word（表示憤怒、驚異等的）咒罵，詛咒的話：*She heard the sound of breaking glass, followed by a muttered oath.* 她聽到打碎玻璃的響聲，接着是低聲的咒罵。
IDM **on/under ˈoath** (*law* 律) having made a formal promise to tell the truth in court（在法庭上）宣誓說實話，經宣誓：*Is she prepared to give evidence on oath?* 她願意宣誓據實作證嗎？◇ *The judge reminded the witness that he was still under oath.* 法官提醒證人，他仍然受宣誓的約束。

oat·meal /ˈəʊtmiːl; *NAmE* ˈoʊt-/ *noun* [U] **1** flour made from crushed oats, used to make biscuits/cookies, PORRIDGE, etc. 燕麥粉；燕麥片 **2** (*NAmE*) = PORRIDGE (1) **3** a pale brown colour 淺棕色；淡棕色；燕麥黃 ▸ **oat·meal** *adj.*：*an oatmeal carpet* 一塊燕麥黃地毯

oats /əʊts; *NAmE* oʊts/ *noun* [pl.] grain grown in cool countries as food for animals and for making flour, PORRIDGE/OATMEAL, etc. 燕麥 ➲ VISUAL VOCAB page V32 ➲ see also OAT IDM see SOW[1] *v.*

ob·bli·gato (*NAmE* also **ob·li·gato**) /ˌɒblɪˈɡɑːtəʊ; *NAmE* ˌɑːblɪˈɡɑːtoʊ/ *noun* (*pl.* **-os**) (*music* 音) (from *Italian*) an important part for an instrument in a piece of music which cannot be left out 必需聲部；助奏

ob·dur·ate /ˈɒbdjərət; *NAmE* ˈɑːbdər-/ *adj.* (*formal*, usually *disapproving*) refusing to change your mind or your actions in any way 頑固的；固執的；執拗的 SYN **stubborn** ▸ **ob·dur·acy** /ˈɒbdjərəsi; *NAmE* ˈɑːbdər-/ *noun* [U] **ob·dur·ate·ly** *adv.*

OBE /ˌəʊ biː ˈiː; *NAmE* ˌoʊ/ *noun* the abbreviation for 'Officer of the Order of the British Empire' (an award given in Britain for a special achievement) 英帝國勳位軍官，英帝國官佐勳銜獲得者（全寫為 Officer of the Order of the British Empire，英國授予有特殊貢獻者的勳章）：*She was made an OBE.* 她榮獲英帝國官佐勳銜。◇ *Matthew Silk OBE* 英帝國官佐勳銜獲得者馬修 • 西爾克

obedi·ent /əˈbiːdiənt/ *adj.* doing what you are told to do; willing to obey 順從的；忠順的；唯命是從的：*an obedient child* 聽話的孩子 ◇ **~ to sb/sth** *He was always obedient to his father's wishes.* 他一向順從父親的意願。OPP **disobedient** ▸ **obedi·ence** /-əns/ *noun* [U]：***blind/complete/unquestioning/total obedience*** 盲目／絕對／無條件／完全的服從 ◇ **~ to sb/sth** *He has acted* ***in obedience*** *to the law.* 他是依法行事的。**obedi·ent·ly** *adv.*
IDM **your obedient servant** (*old use*) used to end a formal letter（用作正式信函的結束語）您恭順的僕人

obei·sance /əʊˈbeɪsns; *NAmE* oʊˈbiːsns/ *noun* (*formal*) **1** [U] respect for sb/sth or willingness to obey sb 景仰；尊敬；忠順；順從 **2** [C] the act of bending your head or the upper part of your body in order to show respect for sb/sth 鞠躬示敬；頷首行禮

ob·el·isk /ˈɒbəlɪsk; *NAmE* ˈɑːb-; ˈoʊb-/ *noun* a tall pointed stone column with four sides, put up in memory of a person or an event 方尖紀念碑 ➲ VISUAL VOCAB page V14

obese /əʊˈbiːs; *NAmE* oʊ-/ *adj.* (*formal* or *medical* 醫) (of people 人) very fat, in a way that is not healthy 臃腫的；虛胖的；病態肥胖的 ➲ COLLOCATIONS at DIET ▸ **obes·ity** /əʊˈbiːsəti; *NAmE* oʊ-/ *noun* [U]：*Obesity can increase the risk of heart disease.* 肥胖會增加患心臟病的危險。

obey /ə'beɪ/ *verb*
[T, I] ~ (**sb/sth**) to do what you are told or expected to do 服從；遵守；順從：*to obey a command/an order/rules/the law* 服從指揮 / 命令；遵守規章 / 法律 ◇ *He had always obeyed his parents without question.* 他對父母一向絕對服從。◇ *'Sit down!' Meekly, she obeyed.* "坐下！" 她乖乖地順從了。OPP **disobey**

ob·fus·cate /'ɒbfʌskeɪt; *NAmE* 'ɑːb-/ *verb* [I, T] ~ (**sth**) (*formal*) to make sth less clear and more difficult to understand, usually deliberately（故意地）混淆，使困惑，使模糊不清 SYN **obscure** ▸ **ob·fus·ca·tion** *noun* [U, C]

ob-gyn /ˌəʊ biː ˌdʒiː waɪ 'en; *NAmE* 'oʊ/ *noun* (*NAmE, informal*) **1** [U] the branches of medicine concerned with the birth of children (= OBSTETRICS) and the diseases of women (= GYNAECOLOGY) 婦產科 **2** [C] a doctor who is trained in this type of medicine 婦產科醫生

obi /'əʊbi; *NAmE* 'oʊ-/ *noun* (from *Japanese*) a wide piece of cloth worn around the waist of a Japanese KIMONO（日本和服的）寬腰帶

ob·itu·ary /ə'bɪtʃuəri; *NAmE* oʊ'bɪtʃueri/ *noun* (*pl.* **-ies**) an article about sb's life and achievements, that is printed in a newspaper soon after they have died 訃聞；訃告

Vocabulary Building 詞彙擴充

Objects you can use 可以使用的物體

It is useful to know some general words to help you describe objects, especially if you do not know the name of a particular object. 有些一般性詞彙可用於描述物品，尤其是名稱不詳的東西。

- A **device** is something that has been designed to do a particular job. * device 指為特定用途設計的裝置、器具、器械：*There is a new device for cars that warns drivers of traffic jams ahead.* 有一種新的汽車裝置可提醒司機前面有交通堵塞。
- A **gadget** is a small object that does something useful, but is not really necessary. * gadget 指有用、但不一定必需的小器具、小裝置：*His kitchen is full of gadgets he never uses.* 他廚房裏到處是他從不使用的小器具。
- An **instrument** is used especially for delicate or scientific work. * instrument 尤指用於精密或科學工作的儀器、器械、器具：*'What do you call the instrument that measures temperature?' 'A thermometer.'* "測量溫度的儀器叫什麼？" "溫度計。"
- A **tool** is something that you use for making and repairing things. * tool 指生產或修理用的工具、用具：*'Have you got one of those tools for turning screws?' 'Do you mean a screwdriver?'* "你有擰螺絲釘的工具嗎？" "你是指螺絲刀嗎？"
- A **machine** has moving parts and is used for a particular job. It usually stands on its own. * machine 指有特定用途的機器，通常為獨立設備：*'What's a blender?' 'It's an electric machine for mixing soft food or liquid.'* "攪拌器是什麼？" "是攪和軟食物或液汁的電動機器。"
- An **appliance** is a large machine that you use in the house, such as a washing machine. * appliance 指大型家用機器，如洗衣機。
- **Equipment** means all the things you need for a particular activity. * equipment 統稱某項活動所需的設備、裝備：*climbing equipment* 攀登用裝備
- **Apparatus** means all the tools, machines or equipment that you need for something. * apparatus 統稱做某事所用的設備、用具、器械、裝置：*firefighters wearing breathing apparatus* 戴着呼吸裝置的消防人員

ob·ject *noun, verb*
▪ *noun* /'ɒbdʒɪkt; *NAmE* 'ɑːbdʒekt; -dʒɪkt/ **1** a thing that can be seen and touched, but is not alive 物體；物品；東西：*everyday objects such as cups and saucers* 諸如杯碟之類的日用品 ◇ *Glass and plastic objects lined the shelves.* 架子上排列着玻璃和塑料製品。⊃ see also UFO **2** ~ **of desire, study, attention, etc.** a person or thing that sb DESIRES, studies, pays attention to, etc.（極欲得到、研究、注意等的）對象 ⊃ see also SEX OBJECT **3** an aim or a purpose 宗旨；目的；目標：*Her sole object in life is to become a travel writer.* 她人生的唯一目標就是當遊記作家。◇ *The object is to educate people about road safety.* 目的就是教育人們注意交通安全。◇ *If you're late, you'll defeat the whole* ***object of the exercise***. 如果你遲到了，便不能達到整個活動的目的。⊃ SYNONYMS at TARGET **4** (*grammar* 語法) a noun, noun phrase or pronoun that refers to a person or thing that is affected by the action of the verb (called the DIRECT OBJECT), or that the action is done to or for (called the INDIRECT OBJECT) 賓語（包括直接賓語、間接賓語）；受詞 ⊃ compare SUBJECT *n.* (5)
IDM **expense, money, etc. is no 'object** used to say that you are willing to spend a lot of money 費用不在話下；錢不成問題：*He always travels first class—expense is no object.* 他總是乘頭等艙旅行，從不計較花費多少。
▪ *verb* /əb'dʒekt/ **1** [I] to say that you disagree with, disapprove of or oppose sth 不同意；不贊成；反對：~ (**to sb/sth**) *Many local people object to the building of the new airport.* 許多當地的居民反對興建新機場。◇ *If nobody objects, we'll postpone the meeting till next week.* 如果沒有人反對，我們就把會議推遲到下週。◇ ~ **to doing sth/to sb doing sth** *I really object to being charged for parking.* 我非常反對收停車費。**2** [T] ~ **that ...** | + **speech** to give sth as a reason for opposing sth 提出…作為反對的理由；抗辯說 SYN **protest**：*He objected that the police had arrested him without sufficient evidence.* 他抗辯說警察沒有充分的證據就逮捕了他。⊃ SYNONYMS at COMPLAIN

'object code (also **'object language**) *noun* [U] (*computing* 計) the language into which a program is translated using a COMPILER or an ASSEMBLER（編譯或彙編程序的）目標碼，目標代碼，目的標

ob·ject·ifi·ca·tion /əbˌdʒektɪfɪ'keɪʃn/ *noun* [U] (*formal*) the act of treating people as if they are objects, without rights or feelings of their own（人格）物化（把人當成沒有權利或感情的物體）

ob·ject·ify /əb'dʒektɪfaɪ/ *verb* (**ob·ject·ifies, ob·ject·ify·ing, ob·ject·ified, ob·ject·ified**) ~ **sb/sth** (*formal*) to treat sb/sth as an object 將…物化；使…人格物化：*magazines that objectify women* 將婦女人格物化的雜誌

ob·jec·tion /əb'dʒekʃn/ *noun* ~ (**to sth/to doing sth**) | ~ (**that ...**) a reason why you do not like or are opposed to sth; a statement about this 反對的理由；反對；異議：*I have no* ***objection*** *to him coming to stay.* 我不反對他來小住。◇ *I'd like to come too, if you* ***have no objection***. 如果你不反對，我也想來。◇ *The main objection to the plan was that it would cost too much.* 反對這個計劃的主要理由是費用過高。◇ *to* ***raise an objection*** *to sth* 對某事提出異議 ◇ *No objections were raised at the time.* 當時沒人提出異議。◇ *The proposal will go ahead despite strong objections from the public.* 儘管公眾強烈反對，這項提案仍將付諸實施。

ob·jec·tion·able /əb'dʒekʃənəbl/ *adj.* (*formal*) unpleasant or offensive 令人不快的；令人反感的；討厭的：*objectionable people/odours* 討厭的人 / 氣味 ◇ *Why are you being so objectionable today?* 你今天怎麼這麼彆扭？

ob·ject·ive AW /əb'dʒektɪv/ *noun, adj.*
▪ *noun* **1** something that you are trying to achieve 目標；目的 SYN **goal**：*the* ***main/primary/principal objective*** 主要 / 首要 / 主要目標 ◇ *to* ***meet/achieve*** *your* ***objectives*** 達到 / 實現你的目標 ◇ *You must set realistic* ***aims and objectives*** *for yourself.* 你必須給自己確定切實可行的目的和目標。◇ *The main objective of this meeting is to give more information on our plans.* 這次會議的主要目的是進一步介紹我們的計劃。⊃ SYNONYMS at TARGET **2** (also **obˌjective 'lens**) (*technical* 術語) the LENS in a TELESCOPE or MICROSCOPE that is nearest to the object

being looked at （望遠鏡或顯微鏡的）物鏡 ➲ VISUAL VOCAB page V70

■ ***adj.*** **1** 🔑 not influenced by personal feelings or opinions; considering only facts 客觀的；就事論事的；不帶個人感情的 SYN **unbiased**： *an **objective analysis/assessment/report*** 客觀的分析／評價／報告 ◇ *objective criteria* 客觀標準 ◇ *I find it difficult to be objective where he's concerned.* 只要與他有關，我就難以客觀。 OPP **subjective** **2** (*philosophy* 哲) existing outside the mind; based on facts that can be proved 客觀存在的；基於事實的： *objective reality* 客觀現實 OPP **subjective** **3** [only before noun] (*grammar* 語法) the **objective** case is the one which is used for the object of a sentence 賓格的 ▶ **ob·ject·ive·ly** AW *adv.*： *Looked at objectively, the situation is not too bad.* 客觀地看，局面並不算太糟。◇ *Can these effects be objectively measured?* 這些結果能客觀地衡量嗎？ **ob·ject·iv·ity** AW /ˌɒbdʒekˈtɪvəti; *NAmE* ˌɑːb-/ *noun* [U]：*There was a lack of objectivity in the way the candidates were judged.* 對候選人的評定缺乏客觀性。◇ *scientific objectivity* 科學的客觀性 OPP **subjectivity**

ˈobject language *noun* **1** [C] (*linguistics* 語言) = TARGET LANGUAGE (1) **2** [U] (*computing* 計) = OBJECT CODE

ˈobject lesson *noun* [usually sing.] a practical example of what you should or should not do in a particular situation 借鑒；經驗教訓

ob·ject·or /əbˈdʒektə(r)/ *noun* ~ (**to sth**) a person who objects to sth 反對者： *There were no objectors to the plan.* 沒有人反對這個計劃。 ➲ see also CONSCIENTIOUS OBJECTOR

objet d'art /ˌɒbʒeɪ ˈdɑː; *NAmE* ˌɔːbdʒeɪ ˈdɑːr/ *noun* (*pl.* **ob·jets d'art** /ˌɒbʒeɪ ˈdɑː; *NAmE* ˌɔːbdʒeɪ ˈdɑːr/) (from *French*) a small artistic object, used for decoration（裝飾性的）小藝術品，小工藝品

ob·li·gated /ˈɒblɪgeɪtɪd; *NAmE* ˈɑːb-/ *adj.* ~ (**to do sth**) (*NAmE* or *BrE*, *formal*) having a moral or legal duty to do sth（道義或法律上）有義務的，有責任的，必須的 SYN **obliged**： *He felt obligated to help.* 他覺得有義務幫忙。

ob·li·ga·tion /ˌɒblɪˈgeɪʃn; *NAmE* ˌɑːb-/ *noun* **1** [U] ~ (**to do sth**) the state of being forced to do sth because it is your duty, or because of a law, etc. 義務；職責；責任： *You are **under no obligation** to buy anything.* 你不必非買什麼東西不可。◇ *She did not feel **under any obligation** to tell him the truth.* 她覺得沒有義務告訴他實情。◇ *I don't want people coming to see me out of a **sense of obligation**.* 我不想讓別人迫於無奈來看我。◇ *We will send you an estimate for the work **without obligation*** (= you do not have to accept it). 我們將寄上工程報價，以作參考。 **2** [C] something which you must do because you have promised, because of a law, etc.（已承諾的或法律等規定的）義務，責任 SYN **commitment**： *to fulfil your **legal/professional/financial obligations*** 履行法律／職業／財務責任 ◇ *They reminded him of his contractual obligations.* 他們提醒他注意合同規定的義務。◇ ~ **to do sth** *We have a **moral obligation** to protect the environment.* 我們有道義責任保護環境。

ob·li·gato = OBBLIGATO

ob·liga·tory /əˈblɪgətri; *NAmE* -tɔːri/ *adj.* **1** ~ (**for sb**) (**to do sth**) (*formal*) that you must do because of the law, rules, etc.（按法律、規定等）必須的，強制的 SYN **compulsory**： *It is obligatory for all employees to wear protective clothing.* 所有員工必須穿防護服裝。 OPP **optional** **2** (often *humorous*) that you do because you always do it, or other people in the same situation always do it 習慣性的；隨大溜的；趕時髦的： *In the mid 60s he took the almost obligatory trip to India.* * 60 年代中期，他也趕時髦到印度一遊。

ob·lige /əˈblaɪdʒ/ *verb* (*formal*) **1** [T, usually passive] ~ **sb to do sth** to force sb to do sth, by law, because it is a duty, etc.（以法律、義務等）強迫，迫使： *Parents are obliged by law to send their children to school.* 法律規定父母必須送子女入學。◇ *I **felt obliged** to ask them to dinner.* 我不得不請他們吃飯。◇ *He suffered a serious injury that obliged him to give up work.* 他受傷嚴重，不得已只好辭掉工作。 **2** [I, T] to help sb by doing what they ask or what you know they want（根據要求或需要）幫忙，效勞： *Call me if you need any help—I'd be **happy to oblige**.* 若有需要，儘管給我打電話。我很樂意幫忙。◇ ~ **sb** (**with sth**) *Would you oblige me with some information?* 拜託您給我透露些消息好嗎？◇ ~ **sb** (**by doing sth**) *Oblige me by keeping your suspicions to yourself.* 拜託你不要把你的懷疑聲張出去。

ob·liged /əˈblaɪdʒd/ *adj.* [not before noun] ~ (**to sb**) (**for sth/for doing sth**) (*formal*) used when you are expressing thanks or asking politely for sth, to show that you are grateful to sb 感激；感謝： *I'm **much obliged** to you for helping us.* 承蒙相助，本人不勝感激。◇ *I'd be obliged if you would keep this to yourself.* 如蒙保守這個秘密，我將感激不盡。

ob·li·ging /əˈblaɪdʒɪŋ/ *adj.* (*formal*) very willing to help 樂於助人的；熱情的 SYN **accommodating**, **helpful**： *They were very obliging and offered to wait for us.* 他們非常熱情，主動提出等候我們。 ▶ **ob·li·ging·ly** *adv.*

ob·lique /əˈbliːk/ *adj.*, *noun*

■ ***adj.*** **1** not expressed or done in a direct way 間接的；不直截了當的；拐彎抹角的 SYN **indirect**： *an **oblique reference/approach/comment*** 隱約提及；間接途徑；婉轉的評論 **2** (of a line 線) sloping at an angle 斜的；傾斜的 **3** ~ **angle** an angle that is not an angle of 90° 斜角 ▶ **ob·lique·ly** *adv.*： *He referred only obliquely to their recent problems.* 他只是隱約提到他們最近遇到的問題。◇ *Always cut stems obliquely to enable flowers to absorb more water.* 一定要斜剪花莖，讓花能多吸收些水分。

■ ***noun*** (*BrE*) = SLASH (3)

ob·lit·er·ate /əˈblɪtəreɪt/ *verb* [often passive] ~ **sth** to remove all signs of sth, either by destroying or covering it completely 毀掉；覆蓋；清除： *The building was completely obliterated by the bomb.* 炸彈把那座建築物徹底摧毀了。◇ *The snow had obliterated their footprints.* 白雪覆蓋了他們的足跡。◇ *Everything that happened that night was obliterated from his memory.* 那天夜裏發生的一切都從他的記憶中消失了。 ▶ **ob·lit·er·ation** /əˌblɪtəˈreɪʃn/ *noun* [U]

ob·liv·ion /əˈblɪviən/ *noun* [U] **1** a state in which you are not aware of what is happening around you, usually because you are unconscious or asleep 無意識狀態；沉睡；昏迷： *He often drinks himself into oblivion.* 他常常喝酒喝得不省人事。◇ *Sam longed for the oblivion of sleep.* 薩姆恨不得一睡不醒，了無心事。 **2** the state in which sb/sth has been forgotten and is no longer famous or important 被遺忘；被忘卻；湮沒 SYN **obscurity**： *An unexpected victory saved him from political oblivion.* 一次意外的勝利使得他在政治上不再默默無聞。◇ *Most of his inventions have been consigned to oblivion.* 他的大部份發明都湮沒無聞了。 **3** a state in which sth has been completely destroyed 被摧毀；被毀滅；被夷平： *Hundreds of homes were bombed into oblivion during the first weeks of the war.* 在戰爭的最初幾週內，數以百計的房屋被炸毀。

ob·livi·ous /əˈblɪviəs/ *adj.* [not usually before noun] not aware of sth 不知道；未注意；未察覺： ~ (**of sth**) *He drove off, oblivious of the damage he had caused.* 他車開走了，沒有注意到他所造成的損害。◇ ~ (**to sth**) *You eventually become oblivious to the noise.* 你終究會變得不在意吵鬧聲的。 ▶ **ob·livi·ous·ly** *adv.*

ob·long /ˈɒblɒŋ; *NAmE* ˈɑːblɔːŋ; ˈɑːblɑːŋ/ *adj.* **1** an **oblong** shape has four straight sides, two of which are longer than the other two, and four angles of 90° 矩形的；長方形的 **2** (*NAmE*) used to describe any shape that is longer than it is wide 橢圓形的；橢圓體的；長方形的：*an oblong melon* 橢圓形的瓜 ▶ **ob·long** *noun*：*a tiny oblong of glass in the roof* 嵌在屋頂上的一小塊矩形玻璃 ➲ see also RECTANGLE

ob·lo·quy /ˈɒbləkwi; *NAmE* ˈɑːb-/ *noun* [U] (*formal*) **1** strong public criticism 公開的抨擊；公開的譴責；辱罵 **2** loss of respect and honour 恥辱；不名譽

ob·nox·ious /əbˈnɒkʃəs; *NAmE* -ˈnɑːk-/ *adj.* extremely unpleasant, especially in a way that offends people 極討厭的；可憎的；令人作嘔的 SYN **offensive**： *obnoxious behaviour* 討厭的行為 ◇ *a thoroughly obnoxious little*

O

man 可惡至極的傢伙 ◇ *obnoxious odours* 難聞的氣味 ▸ **ob·nox·ious·ly** *adv.*

o.b.o. *abbr.* (*NAmE*) or best offer (used in small advertisements to show that sth may be sold at a lower price than the price that has been asked) 價格可商議：*$800 o.b.o.* * 800 元（可還價）➲ see also O.N.O.

oboe /ˈəʊbəʊ; *NAmE* ˈoʊboʊ/ *noun* a musical instrument of the WOODWIND group. It is shaped like a pipe and has a double REED at the top that you blow into. 雙簧管 ➲ VISUAL VOCAB page V34

obo·ist /ˈəʊbəʊɪst; *NAmE* ˈoʊboʊɪst/ *noun* a person who plays the oboe 雙簧管吹奏者

ob·scene /əbˈsiːn/ *adj.* **1** connected with sex in a way that most people find offensive 淫穢的；猥褻的；下流的：*obscene gestures/language/books* 淫穢的姿態／語言／書籍 ◇ *an obscene phone call* (= in which sb says obscene things) 色情騷擾電話 **2** extremely large in size or amount in a way that most people find unacceptable and offensive（數量等）大得驚人的，駭人聽聞的 SYN **outrageous**：*He earns an obscene amount of money.* 他撈了一大筆昧心錢。◇ *It's obscene to spend so much on food when millions are starving.* 當數以百萬的人忍飢挨餓時，飲食上揮霍無度是天理難容的。▸ **ob·scene·ly** *adv.*：*to behave obscenely* 舉止下流 ◇ *obscenely rich* 富得流油

ob·scen·ity /əbˈsenəti/ *noun* (*pl.* **-ies**) **1** [U] obscene language or behaviour 淫穢的語言；下流的行為：*The editors are being prosecuted for obscenity.* 編輯因刊載污穢文字而被起訴。◇ *the laws on obscenity* 禁止淫穢的言語及行為的法規 **2** [C, usually pl.] an obscene word or act 下流話（或動作）：*She screamed a string of obscenities at the judge.* 她衝着法官高聲罵了一連串的髒話。

ob·scur·ant·ism /ˌɒbskjuˈræntɪzəm; *NAmE* ɑːbˈskjʊr-/ *noun* [U] (*formal*) the practice of deliberately preventing sb from understanding or discovering sth 故弄玄虛；蒙蔽主義；矇騙政策 ▸ **ob·scur·ant·ist** *adj.*

O

ob·scure /əbˈskjʊə(r); *NAmE* əbˈskjʊr/ *adj.*, *verb*

■ *adj.* **1** not well known 無名的；鮮為人知的 SYN **unknown**：*an obscure German poet* 一個名不見經傳的德國詩人 ◇ *He was born around 1650 but his origins remain obscure.* 他生於 1650 年前後，但身世不詳。**2** difficult to understand 費解的；難以理解的：*I found her lecture very obscure.* 我覺得她的講座非常費解。◇ ***For some obscure reason**, he failed to turn up.* 他莫名其妙地沒有如期露面。▸ **ob·scure·ly** *adv.*：*They were making her feel obscurely worried* (= for reasons that were difficult to understand). 他們讓她無緣無故地擔憂起來。

■ *verb* **~ sth** to make it difficult to see, hear or understand sth 使模糊；使隱晦；使費解：*The view was obscured by fog.* 霧中景色朦朧。◇ *We mustn't let these minor details obscure the main issue.* 我們不能讓枝節問題掩蓋主要問題。

ob·scur·ity /əbˈskjʊərəti; *NAmE* -ˈskjʊr-/ *noun* (*pl.* **-ies**) **1** [U] the state in which sb/sth is not well known or has been forgotten 默默無聞；無名：*The actress was only 17 when she was plucked from obscurity and made a star.* 這個演員從無名少女一躍成為明星時年僅 17 歲。◇ *He spent most of his life working in obscurity.* 他在默默無聞的工作中度過了大半生。**2** [U, C, usually pl.] the quality of being difficult to understand; something that is difficult to understand 費解；晦澀；難懂的事：*The course teaches students to avoid ambiguity and obscurity of expression.* 這門課程教學生避免表達上的模稜兩可、含混不清。◇ *a speech full of obscurities* 一篇晦澀難懂的演說 **3** [U] (*literary*) the state of being dark 昏暗；黑暗 SYN **darkness**

ob·se·quies /ˈɒbsəkwiz; *NAmE* ˈɑːb-/ *noun* [pl.] (*formal*) funeral ceremonies 葬禮：*state obsequies* 國葬

ob·se·qui·ous /əbˈsiːkwiəs/ *adj.* (*formal, disapproving*) trying too hard to please sb, especially sb who is important 諂媚的；巴結奉迎的 SYN **servile**：*an obsequious manner* 諂媚的態度 ▸ **ob·se·qui·ous·ly** *adv.*：*smiling obsequiously* 諂媚地微笑着 **ob·se·qui·ous·ness** *noun* [U]

ob·serv·able /əbˈzɜːvəbl; *NAmE* -ˈzɜːrv-/ *adj.* that can be seen or noticed 能看得到的；能察覺到的：*observable differences* 可以察覺到的差異 ◇ *Similar trends are observable in mainland Europe.* 類似的趨勢在歐洲大陸也能見到。▸ **ob·serv·ably** /əbˈzɜːvəbli; *NAmE* -ˈzɜːrv-/ *adv.*

ob·ser·vance /əbˈzɜːvəns; *NAmE* -ˈzɜːrv-/ *noun* **1** [U, sing.] the practice of obeying a law, celebrating a festival or behaving according to a particular custom（對法律、習俗的）遵守，奉行；（節日的）慶祝：**~ (of sth)** *observance of the law* 守法 ◇ *a strict observance of the Sabbath* 對安息日的嚴格遵守 OPP **non-observance** **2** [C, usually pl.] an act performed as part of a religious or traditional ceremony 宗教（或傳統節日）的儀式：*religious observances* 宗教儀式

ob·ser·vant /əbˈzɜːvənt; *NAmE* -ˈzɜːrv-/ *adj.* **1** good at noticing things around you 善於觀察的；觀察力敏銳的 SYN **sharp-eyed**：*Observant walkers may see red deer along this stretch of the road.* 觀察敏銳的步行者能在這一路段看到赤鹿。◇ *How very observant of you!* 你真有眼力！**2** (*formal*) careful to obey religious laws and customs 謹慎遵守教規和習俗的

ob·ser·va·tion 0┳ /ˌɒbzəˈveɪʃn; *NAmE* ˌɑːbzərˈv-/ *noun*

1 0┳ [U, C] the act of watching sb/sth carefully for a period of time, especially to learn sth 觀察；觀測；監視：*Most information was collected by direct observation of the animals' behaviour.* 大部份信息都是通過直接觀察動物的行為收集到的。◇ *results based on scientific observations* 根據科學觀測得來的結果 ◇ *We managed to escape observation* (= we were not seen). 我們設法避開了人們的注意。◇ *The suspect is being kept **under observation*** (= watched closely by the police). 嫌疑人正受到監視。◇ *She has outstanding **powers of observation*** (= the ability to notice things around her). 她有超人的觀察力。◇ *an **observation post/tower*** (= a place from where sb, especially an enemy, can be watched) 瞭望哨／塔 ➲ COLLOCATIONS at SCIENTIFIC **2** 0┳ [C] **~ (about/on sth)** (*formal*) a comment, especially based on sth you have seen, heard or read（尤指據所見、所聞、所讀而作的）評論 SYN **remark**：*He began by making a few general observations about the report.* 開頭他先對這個報告作了幾點概括性的評論。◇ *She has some interesting observations on possible future developments.* 她對未來可能的發展有一些饒有興味的論述。➲ note at STATEMENT ▸ **ob·ser·va·tion·al** *adj.*

ˌobserˈvation car *noun* a coach/car on a train with large windows, designed to give passengers a good view of the passing landscape 觀光車廂，遊覽車廂（火車車廂，有大窗）

ob·ser·va·tory /əbˈzɜːvətri; *NAmE* əbˈzɜːrvətɔːri/ *noun* (*pl.* **-ies**) a special building from which scientists watch the stars, the weather, etc. 天文台；天文觀測站；氣象台

ob·serve 0┳ /əbˈzɜːv; *NAmE* əbˈzɜːrv/ *verb* [T]

1 0┳ (*formal*) to see or notice sb/sth 看到；注意到；觀察到：**~ sb/sth** *Have you observed any changes lately?* 最近你注意到什麼變化沒有？◇ *All the characters in the novel are closely observed* (= seem like people in real life). 小說中的人物個個栩栩如生。◇ **~ sb/sth do sth** *The police observed a man enter the bank.* 警察注意到一個男人走進了銀行。◇ **~ sb/sth doing sth** *They observed him entering the bank.* 他們看見他走進銀行。◇ **~ that ...** *She observed that all the chairs were already occupied.* 她發現所有的椅子都有人坐了。◇ **be observed to do sth** *He was observed to follow her closely.* 有人看到他緊跟着她。HELP This pattern is only used in the passive. 此句型僅用於被動語態。➲ SYNONYMS at COMMENT, NOTICE **2** 0┳ [T, I] (*formal*) to watch sb/sth carefully, especially to learn more about them 觀察；注視；監視 SYN **monitor**：**~ (sb/sth)** *I felt he was observing everything I did.* 我覺得他正在注視着我做的每一件事。◇ *The patients were observed over a period of several months.* 這些病人被觀察了數月之久。◇ *He observes keenly, but says little.* 他觀察敏銳，但言語寥寥。◇ **~ how, what, etc. ...** *They observed how the parts of the machine fitted together.* 他們觀看了機器零件的組裝過程。➲ SYNONYMS at LOOK **3** [T] **~ that ...** | **+ speech** (*formal*) to make a remark 說；評論 SYN **comment**：*She observed that it was getting late.* 她說天色晚了。**4** [T] **~ sth** to obey rules, laws, etc. 遵守（規則、法律等）：*Will the rebels observe the ceasefire?* 叛亂者會遵守停火協議嗎？◇ *The crowd* ***observed a minute's silence*** (= were silent for one minute) *in memory of those who had died.* 眾人為死者默哀一分鐘。 **5** [T] **~ sth** (*formal*) to celebrate festivals, birthdays, etc. 慶祝；慶賀；歡度：*Do they observe Christmas?* 他們過不過聖誕節？

ob·ser·ver /əbˈzɜːvə(r); *NAmE* -ˈzɜːrv-/ *noun* **1** a person who watches sb/sth 觀察者；觀測者；目擊者：*According to observers, the plane exploded shortly after take-off.* 據目擊者說，飛機起飛後不久就爆炸了。◇ *To the* ***casual observer*** (= somebody who does not pay much attention), *the system appears confusing.* 乍看起來，這個系統好像條理不清。➲ SYNONYMS at WITNESS **2** a person who attends a meeting, lesson, etc. to listen and watch but not to take part 觀察員；旁聽者：*A team of British officials were sent as observers to the conference.* 一組英國官員被派去做大會觀察員。 **3** a person who watches and studies particular events, situations, etc. and is therefore considered to be an expert on them 觀察家；觀察員；評論員：*a royal observer* 王室觀察家

ob·sess /əbˈses/ *verb* **1** [T, usually passive] **~ sb** to completely fill your mind so that you cannot think of anything else, in a way that is not normal 使痴迷；使迷戀；使着迷：*He's obsessed by computers.* 他迷上了電腦。◇ *She's completely obsessed with him.* 他讓她神魂顛倒。◇ *The need to produce the most exciting newspaper story obsesses most journalists.* 大多數記者夢寐以求的就是要寫出最撼動人心的新聞報道來。 **2** [I] **~ (about sth)** to be always talking or worrying about a particular thing, especially when this annoys other people 嘮叨；掛牽；念念不忘：*I think you should try to stop obsessing about food.* 我看你該歇歇了，別沒完沒了地嘮叨吃的東西。

ob·ses·sion /əbˈseʃn/ *noun* **1** [U] the state in which a person's mind is completely filled with thoughts of one particular thing or person in a way that is not normal 痴迷；着魔；困擾：*Her fear of flying is bordering on obsession.* 她怕乘飛機幾乎到了不可救藥的地步。◇ **~ with sb/sth** *The media's obsession with the young prince continues.* 新聞媒體繼續對年輕的王子作連篇累牘的報道。 **2** [C] **~ (with sb)** a person or thing that sb thinks about too much 使人痴迷的人（或物）：*Fitness has become an obsession with him.* 他迷上了健身。

ob·ses·sion·al /əbˈseʃənl/ *adj.* thinking too much about one particular person or thing, in a way that is not normal 痴迷的；迷戀的；耿耿於懷的：*She is obsessional about cleanliness.* 她有潔癖。◇ *obsessional behaviour* 痴迷的行為 ▶ **ob·ses·sion·al·ly** *adv.*

ob·ses·sive /əbˈsesɪv/ *adj., noun*

■ *adj.* thinking too much about one particular person or thing, in a way that is not normal 着迷的；迷戀的；難以釋懷的：*He's becoming more and more obsessive about punctuality.* 他對守時要求越來越過分了。◇ *an obsessive attention to detail* 過分注重細枝末節 ▶ **ob·ses·sive·ly** *adv.*：*obsessively jealous* 嫉妒得要命 ◇ *He worries obsessively about his appearance.* 他過度煩惱自己的外表。

■ *noun* (*psychology* 心) a person whose mind is filled with thoughts of one particular thing or person so that they cannot think of anything else 強迫症患者

ob,sessive com'pulsive disorder *noun* [U] (*abbr.* **OCD**) a mental DISORDER in which sb feels they have to repeat certain actions or activities to get rid of fears or unpleasant thoughts 強迫性神經（官能）症，強迫症（患者感到必須重複做某動作或活動以解除恐懼或不安）

ob·sid·ian /əbˈsɪdiən/ *noun* [U] a type of dark rock that looks like glass and comes from VOLCANOES 黑曜岩；黑曜石

ob·so·les·cence /ˌɒbsəˈlesns; *NAmE* ˌɑːb-/ *noun* [U] (*formal*) the state of becoming old-fashioned and no longer useful 過時；陳舊；淘汰：*products with* ***built-in/planned obsolescence*** (= designed not to last long so that people will have to buy new ones) 內在／計劃陳舊產品（故意設計成不耐使用而迫使人購買新的產品）▶ **ob·so·les·cent** /ˌɒbsəˈlesnt; *NAmE* ˌɑːb-/ *adj.*

ob·so·lete /ˈɒbsəliːt; *NAmE* ˌɑːbsəˈliːt/ *adj.* no longer used because sth new has been invented 淘汰的；廢棄的；過時的 **SYN** **out of date**：*obsolete technology* 過時技術 ◇ *With technological changes many traditional skills have become obsolete.* 隨着技術的革新，許多傳統技藝已被淘汰。

ob·stacle /ˈɒbstəkl; *NAmE* ˈɑːb-/ *noun* **1 ~ (to sth/to doing sth)** a situation, an event, etc. that makes it difficult for you to do or achieve sth 障礙；阻礙；絆腳石 **SYN** **hindrance**：*A lack of qualifications can be a major obstacle to finding a job.* 學力不足可能成為謀職的主要障礙。◇ *So far, we have managed to overcome all the obstacles that have been placed in our path.* 到目前為止，我們已設法克服了我們路上的一切障礙。 **2** an object that is in your way and that makes it difficult for you to move forward 障礙物；絆腳石：*The area was full of streams and bogs and other natural obstacles.* 此地遍佈小溪、泥潭和其他天然障礙。 **3** (in SHOWJUMPING 障礙賽馬) a fence, etc. for a horse to jump over 障礙柵欄；障礙

'obstacle course *noun* **1** a series of objects that people taking part in a race have to climb over, under, through, etc. 障礙賽跑場地 **2** a series of difficulties that people have to deal with in order to achieve a particular aim 艱險；重重困難 **3** (*NAmE*) (*BrE* **as'sault course**) an area of land with many objects that are difficult to climb, jump over or go through, which is used, especially by soldiers, for improving physical skills and strength 障礙訓練場

'obstacle race *noun* a race in which the people taking part have to climb over, under, through, etc. various objects 障礙賽跑

ob·stet·ri·cian /ˌɒbstəˈtrɪʃn; *NAmE* ˌɑːb-/ *noun* a doctor who is trained in obstetrics 產科醫生

ob·stet·rics /əbˈstetrɪks/ *noun* [U] the branch of medicine concerned with the birth of children 產科學 ▶ **ob·stet·ric** /əbˈstetrɪk/ *adj.*：*obstetric medicine* 產科學

ob·stin·ate /ˈɒbstɪnət; *NAmE* ˈɑːb-/ *adj.* **1** (*often disapproving*) refusing to change your opinions, way of behaving, etc. when other people try to persuade you to; behaviour that shows this 執拗的；固執的；頑固的 **SYN** **stubborn**：*He can be very obstinate when he wants to be!* 他的犟勁兒一上來，簡直執拗得要命！◇ *her obstinate refusal to comply with their request* 她對他們的請求堅持不從 **2** [usually before noun] difficult to get rid of or deal with 棘手的；難以去除的；難以對付的 **SYN** **stubborn**：*the obstinate problem of unemployment* 失業這個棘手的問題 ◇ *an obstinate stain* 除不掉的斑漬 ▶ **ob·stin·acy** /ˈɒbstɪnəsi; *NAmE* ˈɑːb-/ *noun* [U]：*an act of sheer obstinacy* 純屬固執的舉動 **ob·stin·ate·ly** *adv.*：*He obstinately refused to consider the future.* 他執意拒不考慮未來。

ob·strep·er·ous /əbˈstrepərəs/ *adj.* (*formal* or *humorous*) noisy and difficult to control 喧鬧的；桀驁不馴的；任性的

ob·struct /əbˈstrʌkt/ *verb* (*formal*) **1 ~ sth** to block a road, an entrance, a passage, etc. so that sb/sth cannot get through, see past, etc. 阻擋；阻塞；遮斷：*You can't park here, you're obstructing my driveway.* 你不能在這裏停車，你擋住了我家的車道。◇ *First check that the accident victim doesn't have an obstructed airway.* 首先要確保事故受傷者的氣道通暢。◇ *The pillar obstructed our view of the stage.* 柱子擋着，我們看不見舞台。 **2 ~ sb/sth** to prevent sb/sth from doing sth or making progress, especially when this is done deliberately（故意）妨礙，阻撓，阻礙 **SYN** **hinder**：*They were charged with obstructing the police in the course of their duty.* 他們被指控妨礙警察執行公務。◇ *terrorists attempting to obstruct the peace process* 企圖阻礙和平進程的恐怖分子

IDM **ob,struct 'justice** (*NAmE*) (*BrE* **per,vert the course of 'justice**) (*law* 律) to tell a lie or to do sth in order to prevent the police, etc. from finding out the truth about a crime 妨礙司法（如作偽證等）

ob·struc·tion /əbˈstrʌkʃn/ *noun* **1** [U, C] the fact of trying to prevent sth/sb from making progress 阻擋；阻礙；妨礙：*the obstruction of justice* 妨礙司法公正 ◇ *He was arrested for obstruction of a police officer in the*

O

execution of his duty. 他因妨礙警察執行公務而被逮捕。 **2** [U, C] the fact of blocking a road, an entrance, a passage, etc. 堵塞，阻擋（通道等）: *obstruction of the factory gates* 對工廠大門的堵塞 ◇ *The abandoned car was causing an obstruction.* 這輛被遺棄的汽車堵住了道路。 **3** [C] something that blocks a road, an entrance, etc. 路障；障礙；障礙物: *It is my job to make sure that all pathways are clear of obstructions.* 保證所有的道路通暢是我的職責。 **4** [C, U] (*medical* 醫) something that blocks a passage or tube in your body; a medical condition resulting from this 梗阻；阻塞；栓塞 **SYN** **blockage**: *He had an operation to remove an obstruction in his throat.* 他做了手術，取出喉頭的阻塞物。 ◇ ***bowel/intestinal obstruction*** 腸梗阻 **5** [U] (*sport* 體) the offence of unfairly preventing a player of the other team from moving to get the ball（球類運動）阻擋犯規

ob·struc·tion·ism /əbˈstrʌkʃənɪzəm/ *noun* [U] (*formal*) the practice of trying to prevent a parliament or committee from making progress, passing laws, etc.（對議會或委員會工作的）阻撓行為，妨礙 ▸ **ob·struc·tion·ist** /-ɪst/ *noun, adj.*

ob·struct·ive /əbˈstrʌktɪv/ *adj.* **1** trying to prevent sb/sth from making progress 阻撓；妨礙；阻止: *Of course she can do it. She's just being deliberately obstructive.* 這事她當然能做。她只是在刻意阻撓罷了。 ➲ compare CONSTRUCTIVE **2** [only before noun] (*medical* 醫) connected with a passage, tube, etc. in your body that has become blocked 梗阻的；阻塞的；栓塞的: *obstructive lung disease* 肺阻塞疾病

ob·tain 🔑 **AW** /əbˈteɪn/ *verb* (*formal*)
1 🔑 [T] **~ sth** to get sth, especially by making an effort（尤指經努力）獲得，贏得: *to obtain advice/information/permission* 得到忠告／信息／許可 ◇ *I finally managed to obtain a copy of the report.* 我終於設法弄到了這份報告的一個副本。 ◇ *To obtain the overall score, add up the totals in each column.* 要得出總計得分，就把各欄的小計加起來。 **2** [I] (not used in the progressive tenses 不用於進行時) (of rules, systems, customs, etc. 規則、制度、習俗等) to exist 存在；流行；沿襲 **SYN** **apply**: *These conditions no longer obtain.* 這些條件不再適用。

ob·tain·able **AW** /əbˈteɪnəbl/ *adj.* [not usually before noun] that can be obtained 可獲得；可得到 **SYN** **available**: *Full details are obtainable from any post office.* 詳情可至任何郵局索取。

ob·trude /əbˈtruːd/ *verb* [I, T] **~ (sth/yourself) (on/upon sb)** (*formal*) to become or make sth/yourself noticed, especially in a way that is not wanted 強行闖入；攪擾: *Music from the next room obtruded upon his thoughts.* 隔壁的音樂聲打攪了他的思緒。

ob·tru·sive /əbˈtruːsɪv/ *adj.* noticeable in an unpleasant way 扎眼的；過分炫耀的；顯眼的: *The sofa would be less obtrusive in a paler colour.* 沙發的顏色再淺一點就不那麼扎眼了。 ◇ *They tried to ensure that their presence was not too obtrusive.* 他們盡量做到在場時不引人注目。 ▸ **ob·tru·sive·ly** *adv.*

ob·tuse /əbˈtjuːs; *NAmE* -ˈtuːs/ *adj.* (*formal, disapproving*) slow or unwilling to understand sth 遲鈍的；愚蠢的；態度勉強的: *Are you being deliberately obtuse?* 你是不是故意裝傻？ ▸ **ob·tuse·ness** *noun* [U]

ob,tuse ˈangle *noun* an angle between 90° and 180° 鈍角 ➲ VISUAL VOCAB page V71 ➲ compare ACUTE ANGLE, REFLEX ANGLE, RIGHT ANGLE

ob·verse /ˈɒbvɜːs; *NAmE* ˈɑːbvɜːrs/ *noun* (usually **the obverse**) [sing.] **1** (*formal*) the opposite of sth 對立面；對應的事物: *The obverse of love is hate.* 愛的反面是恨。 **2** (*technical* 術語) the side of a coin or MEDAL that has the head or main design on it（硬幣或獎章的）正面

ob·vi·ate /ˈɒbvieɪt; *NAmE* ˈɑːb-/ *verb* **~ sth** (*formal*) to remove a problem or the need for sth 消除；排除；打消 **SYN** **preclude**: *This new evidence **obviates the need for** any further enquiries.* 這項新證據使事情沒必要再調查下去。

ob·vi·ous 🔑 **AW** /ˈɒbviəs; *NAmE* ˈɑːb-/ *adj.*
1 🔑 **~ (to sb) (that …)** easy to see or understand 明顯的；顯然的；易理解的 **SYN** **clear**: *It was obvious to everyone that the child had been badly treated.* 人人一看便知那個孩子受過虐待。 ◇ *It's obvious from what she said that something is wrong.* 根據她所說的，顯然是出問題了。 ◇ *I know you don't like her but try not to make it so obvious.* 我知道你不喜歡她，但盡量別表現得那麼明顯。 ◇ *He agreed with obvious pleasure.* 他同意了，顯然很高興。 ◇ ***For obvious reasons**, I'd prefer not to give my name.* 因為顯而易見的原因，我不願披露自己的姓名。 ◇ *The reasons for this decision were **not immediately obvious**.* 暫時還不清楚是基於什麼原因而有此決定。 ➲ SYNONYMS at CLEAR **2** 🔑 that most people would think of or agree to 公認的；當然的: *She was the obvious choice for the job.* 她是這一工作的當然人選。 ◇ *There's no obvious solution to the problem.* 這個問題尚無公認的解決辦法。 ◇ *This seemed the most obvious thing to do.* 這似乎是最順理成章的做法。 **3** 🔑 (*disapproving*) not interesting, new or showing imagination; unnecessary because it is clear to everyone 平淡無奇的；無創意的；因顯而易見而不必要的: *The ending was pretty obvious.* 結尾十分平淡。 ◇ *I may be **stating the obvious** but without more money the project cannot survive.* 我這話可能多餘，但是不投入更多資金，項目就難以為繼。 ▸ **ob·vi·ous·ness** *noun* [U]

ob·vi·ous·ly 🔑 **AW** /ˈɒbviəsli; *NAmE* ˈɑːb-/ *adv.*
1 🔑 used when giving information that you expect other people to know already or agree with（用於陳述認為別人已知道或希望別人同意的事）顯然，明顯地 **SYN** **clearly**: *Obviously, we don't want to spend too much money.* 很明顯，我們不想花太多的錢。 ◇ *Diet and exercise are obviously important.* 顯然，飲食和運動是重要的。 **2** 🔑 used to say that a particular situation or fact is easy to see or understand（用於說明某種情況或事實明顯）顯而易見，明顯，不言而喻: *He was obviously drunk.* 他顯然是喝醉了。 ◇ *They're obviously not coming.* 他們顯然不會來了。 ◇ *'I didn't realise it was a formal occasion.' 'Obviously!'* (= I can see by the way you are dressed) "我沒想到這是個正式場合。" "看得出來！"（看你的衣着就知道）

oca·rina /ˌɒkəˈriːnə; *NAmE* ˌɑːk-/ *noun* a small egg-shaped musical instrument that you blow into, with holes for the fingers 奧卡里納，小鵝笛，陶笛（管身橢圓形）

oc·ca·sion 🔑 /əˈkeɪʒn/ *noun, verb*
■ ***noun*** **1** 🔑 [C] a particular time when sth happens 某次；…的時候: *on this/that occasion* 這／那次 ◇ *I've met him on several occasions.* 我曾幾次見過他。 ◇ *I can remember very few **occasions when** he had to cancel because of ill health.* 我記得他因為健康不佳而被迫取消的情況絕無僅有。 ◇ *They have been seen together on two **separate occasions**.* 他們有兩次被人看見在一起。 ◇ *On one occasion, she called me in the middle of the night.* 有一次她深更半夜打電話給我。 ◇ *He used the occasion to announce further tax cuts.* 他利用這個機會宣佈再次減稅。 **2** 🔑 [C] a special event, ceremony or celebration 特別的事情（或儀式、慶典）: *a great/memorable/happy occasion* 盛大的／難忘的／歡樂的慶典 ◇ *Turn every meal into **a special occasion**.* 要把每一頓飯都弄得特別一些。 ◇ *They **marked the occasion** (= celebrated it) with an open-air concert.* 他們舉辦了露天音樂會來慶祝。 ◇ *Their wedding turned out to be quite an occasion.* 他們的婚禮辦得相當隆重。 ◇ *He was presented with the watch **on the occasion of** his retirement.* 他在退休儀式上獲贈這塊手錶。 **3** 🔑 [sing.] **~ (for sth/doing sth)** a suitable time for sth 適當的機會；時機: *It should have been an occasion for rejoicing, but she could not feel any real joy.* 原本應該是高興的時刻，她卻絲毫未感到快樂。 ◇ *I'll speak to him about it **if the occasion arises*** (= if I get a chance). 有機會的話，我要跟他談談這件事。 **4** [U, sing.] (*formal*) a reason or cause 理由；原因: **~ (to do sth)** *I've had no occasion to visit him recently.* 我最近無緣去拜訪他。 ◇ **~ (of/for sth)** *Her death was the occasion of mass riots.* 她的逝世引發了大規模的騷亂。 ◇ *I'm willing to go to court over this **if the occasion arises*** (= if it becomes necessary). 如果必要的話，我願意就此出庭。

IDM on oc'casion(s) sometimes but not often 偶爾；偶然；有時：*He has been known on occasion to lose his temper.* 大家都知道他有時會發脾氣。➲ more at SENSE *n.*

■ **verb** (*formal*) to cause sth 使發生；造成；導致：**~ sth** *The flight delay was occasioned by the need for a further security check.* 這次航班的延誤是由於必須做進一步的安全檢查。◇ **~ sb sth** *The decision occasioned us much anxiety.* 這個決定讓我們憂慮不堪。

oc·ca·sion·al /ə'keɪʒənl/ *adj.* [only before noun] happening or done sometimes but not often 偶爾的；偶然的；臨時的：*He works for us on an occasional basis.* 他在我們這裏做臨時工。◇ *I enjoy the occasional glass of wine.* 我喜歡偶爾喝一杯葡萄酒。◇ *He spent five years in Paris, with occasional visits to Italy.* 他在巴黎過了五年，偶爾去一去意大利。◇ *an occasional smoker* (= a person who smokes, but not often) 偶爾吸煙的人

oc·ca·sion·al·ly /ə'keɪʒnəli/ *adv.* sometimes but not often 偶然；偶爾；有時候：*We occasionally meet for a drink after work.* 我們下班後偶爾相聚小酌。◇ *This type of allergy can very occasionally be fatal.* 這類過敏症在極個別情況下有可能是致命的。

oc'casional table *noun* (*BrE*) a small light table that is easy to move, used for different things at different times 臨時茶几；小便桌 ➲ VISUAL VOCAB page V21

the Oc·ci·dent /'ɒksɪdənt; *NAmE* 'ɑːk-/ *noun* [sing.] (*formal*) the western part of the world, especially Europe and America 西方，西洋，西方世界（尤指歐洲和美洲）➲ compare ORIENT ▸ **oc·ci·den·tal** /ˌɒksɪ'dentl; *NAmE* ˌɑːk-/ *adj.*

Oc·ci·tan /'ɒksɪtən; *NAmE* 'ɑːksɪtæn/ *noun* [U] the traditional language of southern France 奧克西坦語（法國南部傳統語言）

oc·clude /ə'kluːd/ *verb* **~ sth** (*technical* 術語) to cover or block sth 使閉塞；堵塞：*an occluded artery* 閉塞的動脈 ▸ **oc·clu·sion** /ə'kluːʒn/ *noun* [U]

oc·cult /ə'kʌlt; *BrE* also 'ɒkʌlt/ *adj.* **1** [only before noun] connected with magic powers and things that cannot be explained by reason or science 神秘的；玄妙的；超自然的；不可思議的 SYN **supernatural**：*occult practices* 神秘的習俗 **2 the occult** *noun* [sing.] everything connected with occult practices, etc. 神秘的事物；玄機：*He's interested in witchcraft and the occult.* 他對巫術魔法情有獨鍾。

oc·cult·ist /ə'kʌltɪst; 'ɒkʌltɪst; *NAmE* 'ɑːk-/ *noun* a person who is involved in the occult 神秘學者；玄虛術士

oc·cu·pancy AW /'ɒkjəpənsi; *NAmE* 'ɑːk-/ *noun* [U] (*formal*) the act of living in or using a building, room, piece of land, etc.（房屋、土地等的）佔用，使用，居住：*Prices are based on full occupancy of an apartment.* 公寓租金按全套住用為基礎計算。◇ *to be in sole occupancy* 單獨佔用

oc·cu·pant AW /'ɒkjəpənt; *NAmE* 'ɑːk-/ *noun* **1** a person who lives or works in a particular house, room, building, etc.（房屋、建築等的）使用者，居住者：*All outstanding bills will be paid by the previous occupants.* 一切未支付的賬單將由前住戶償付。**2** a person who is in a vehicle, seat, etc. at a particular time（汽車等內的）乘坐者，佔用者：*The car was badly damaged but the occupants were unhurt.* 汽車嚴重損壞，但車內人員安然無恙。

oc·cu·pa·tion AW /ˌɒkju'peɪʃn; *NAmE* ˌɑːk-/ *noun* **1** [C] a job or profession 工作；職業：*Please state your name, age and occupation below.* 請在下面寫明姓名、年齡和職業。➲ SYNONYMS at WORK **2** [C] the way in which you spend your time, especially when you are not working 消遣；業餘活動：*Her main occupation seems to be shopping.* 逛商店購物似乎是她的主要消遣。**3** [U] the act of moving into a country, town, etc. and taking control of it using military force; the period of time during which a country, town, etc. is controlled in this way 侵佔；佔領；佔領期：*the Roman occupation of Britain* 羅馬人對不列顛的佔領 ◇ *The zones* ***under occupation*** *contained major industrial areas.* 被佔領地區涵蓋了主要的工業區。◇ *occupation forces* 佔領軍 **4** [U] (*formal*) the act of living in or using a building, room, piece of land, etc.（土地、房屋、建築等的）使用，居住，佔用：*The offices will be ready for occupation in June.* 辦公室將於六月交付使用。◇ *The following applies only to tenants in occupation after January 1 2010.* 以下規定僅適用於從 2010 年 1 月 1 日起入住的房客。◇ *The level of* ***owner occupation*** (= people owning their homes) *has increased rapidly in the last 30 years.* 擁有住房的人數在過去 30 年間急劇攀升。

oc·cu·pa·tion·al AW /ˌɒkju'peɪʃənl; *NAmE* ˌɑːk-/ *adj.* [only before noun] connected with a person's job or profession 職業的：*occupational health* 職業健康問題 ◇ *an* ***occupational risk/hazard*** 職業性危害 ◇ *an occupational pension scheme* 職業退休金計劃 ▸ **oc·cu·pa·tion·al·ly** *adv.*：*occupationally induced disease* 職業病

ˌoccuˌpational 'therapist *noun* a person whose job is to help people get better after illness or injury by giving them special activities to do 職業治療師（利用特定的技能訓練幫助病患者或受傷者恢復健康）

ˌoccuˌpational 'therapy *noun* [U] the work of an occupational therapist 職業療法

oc·cu·pied AW /'ɒkjupaɪd; *NAmE* 'ɑːk-/ *adj.* **1** [not before noun] being used by sb 使用中；有人使用（或居住）：*Only half of the rooms are occupied at the moment.* 目前只有半數的房間有人居住。➲ see also OWNER-OCCUPIED **2** [not before noun] busy 忙於：**~ (doing sth/in doing sth/in sth)** *He's fully occupied looking after three small children.* 照顧三個小孩把他忙得不可開交。◇ **~ (with sth/with doing sth)** *Only half her time is occupied with politics.* 她只用自己一半的時間從事政治活動。◇ *The most important thing is to* ***keep yourself occupied.*** 最重要的就是別讓自己閒着。**3** (of a country, etc. 國家等) controlled by people from another country, etc., using military force 被佔領的；被侵佔的：*He spent his childhood in occupied Europe.* 他在被佔領的歐洲度過了童年。OPP **unoccupied**

oc·cu·pier AW /'ɒkjupaɪə(r); *NAmE* 'ɑːk-/ *noun* **1 ~ (of sth)** (*formal*) a person who lives in or uses a building, room, piece of land, etc. 居住人；（土地、房屋等的）佔有者，佔用者 SYN **occupant**：*The letter was addressed to the occupier of the house.* 這封信是寫給這所房子的住戶的。➲ see also OWNER-OCCUPIER **2** [usually pl.] a member of an army that is occupying a foreign country, etc. 佔領者；佔領軍的一員

oc·cupy AW /'ɒkjupaɪ; *NAmE* 'ɑːk-/ *verb* (**oc·cu·pies, oc·cu·py·ing, oc·cu·pied, oc·cu·pied**)

1 ~ sth to fill or use a space, an area or an amount of time 使用，佔用（空間、面積、時間等）SYN **take up**：*The bed seemed to occupy most of the room.* 牀似乎佔去了大半個屋子。◇ *How much memory does the program occupy?* 這個程序佔用多少內存？◇ *Administrative work occupies half of my time.* 行政事務佔用了我一半的時間。**2 ~ sth** (*formal*) to live or work in a room, house or building 使用（房屋、建築）；居住：*He occupies an office on the 12th floor.* 他在 12 樓有一間辦公室。**3 ~ sth** to enter a place in a large group and take control of it, especially by military force 侵佔；佔領；佔據：*The capital has been occupied by the rebel army.* 叛軍已佔領了首都。◇ *Protesting students occupied the TV station.* 抗議的學生佔領了電視台。**4** to fill your time or keep you busy doing sth 使忙於（做某事）；忙着（做某事）：**~ sb/sth/yourself** *a game that will occupy the kids for hours* 能讓小孩一玩就是幾個小時的遊戲 ◇ *Problems at work continued* ***to occupy his mind*** *for some time.* 工作上的問題繼續在他的腦海中縈繞了一段時間。◇ **~ sb/sth/yourself with sb/sth** *She occupied herself with routine office tasks.* 她忙於辦公室的日常工作。◇ **~ sb/sth/yourself (in) doing sth** *She occupied herself doing routine office tasks.* 她忙於辦公室的日常工作。**5 ~ sth** to have an official job or position 任職；執政 SYN **hold**：*The president occupies the position for four years.* 總統任期四年。

occur AW /ə'kɜː(r)/ *verb* (**-rr-**)

1 [I] (*formal*) to happen 發生；出現：*When exactly did the incident occur?* 這一事件究竟是什麼時候發生的？◇ *Something unexpected occurred.* 發生了一件出乎意料的事。**2** [I] **+ adv./prep.** to exist or be found somewhere 存在於；出現在：*Sugar occurs naturally in fruit.* 水果天然含糖分。

O

PHR V **oc'cur to sb** (of an idea or a thought 觀念或想法) to come into your mind 被想到；出現在頭腦中：*The idea occurred to him in a dream.* 這個主意是他在夢中想到的。◇ **~ that** … *It didn't occur to him that his wife was having an affair.* 他沒有想到自己的妻子有婚外情。◇ **~ to do sth** *It didn't occur to her to ask for help.* 她沒想到請別人幫忙。

oc·cur·rence AW /əˈkʌrəns; NAmE əˈkɜːr-/ *noun (formal)* **1** [C] something that happens or exists 發生的事情；存在的事物：*a **common/everyday/frequent/regular occurrence*** 司空見慣的／每天發生的／經常發生的／定期發生的事情 ◇ *Vandalism used to be a **rare occurrence** here.* 過去這裏很少發生故意破壞公物的事。◇ *The program counts the number of occurrences of any word, within the text.* 這個程序可以統計任何單詞在文本中出現的次數。**2** [U] **~ (of sth)** the fact of sth happening or existing 發生；出現；存在：*a link between the occurrence of skin cancer and the use of computer monitors* 皮膚癌的發生與使用電腦顯示器之間的關聯

OCD /ˌəʊ siː ˈdiː; NAmE ˌoʊ/ *abbr.* OBSESSIVE COMPULSIVE DISORDER 強迫性神經（官能）症；強迫症

ocean /ˈəʊʃn; NAmE ˈoʊʃn/ *noun* **1** (usually **the ocean**) [sing.] (*especially NAmE*) the mass of salt water that covers most of the earth's surface 大海；海洋：*the depths of the ocean* 海洋的深處 ◇ *People were swimming in the ocean despite the hurricane warning.* 儘管有颶風警報，人們仍然在大海裏游泳。◇ *The plane hit the ocean several miles offshore.* 飛機在距離海岸數英里處墜入大海。◇ *Our beach house is just a couple of miles from the ocean.* 我家濱海的房子離大海只有幾英里。◇ *an ocean liner* 遠洋客輪 ◇ *Ocean levels are rising.* 海平面正在上升。**2** (usually **Ocean**) [C] one of the five large areas that the ocean is divided into（五大洋之一的）洋：*the **Antarctic/Arctic/Atlantic/Indian/Pacific Ocean*** 南極海；北冰洋；大西洋；印度洋；太平洋 ➲ note at SEA ➲ VISUAL VOCAB pages V4, V5

IDM **an ocean of sth** (*BrE* also **oceans of sth**) (*informal*) a large amount of sth 眾多；大量 ➲ more at DROP *n.*

ocean·arium /ˌəʊʃəˈneəriəm; NAmE ˌoʊʃəˈneriəm/ *noun* an extremely large container in which fish and other sea creatures are kept to be seen by the public or to be studied by scientists 大型海洋水族館 ➲ see also AQUARIUM

ocean·front /ˈəʊʃnfrʌnt; NAmE ˈoʊ-/ *adj.* (*NAmE*) located on land near the ocean 濱海的；臨海的；在海邊的：*an oceanfront hotel* 海濱旅館

'ocean-going *adj.* [only before noun] (of ships 船) made for crossing the sea or ocean, not for journeys along the coast or up rivers 遠洋航行的；遠洋的

Ocea·nia /ˌəʊsiˈɑːniə; -ʃi-; NAmE ˌoʊʃi-/ *noun* [U] a large region of the world consisting of the Pacific islands and the seas around them 大洋洲

ocean·ic /ˌəʊʃiˈænɪk; NAmE ˌoʊʃi-/ *adj.* [usually before noun] (*technical* 術語) connected with the ocean 海洋的；大海的；與海洋有關的：*oceanic fish* 海洋魚類

ocean·og·raphy /ˌəʊʃəˈnɒɡrəfi; NAmE ˌoʊʃəˈnɑːɡ-/ *noun* [U] the scientific study of the ocean 海洋學 ▸ **ocean·og·raph·er** *noun*

ˌocean 'trench *noun* = TRENCH (3)

oce·lot /ˈɒsəlɒt; NAmE ˈɑːsəlɑːt; ˈoʊs-/ *noun* a wild animal of the cat family, that has yellow fur with black lines and spots, found in Central and S America 豹貓（產於中南美洲的野生貓科動物，毛黃，有黑色斑紋和斑點）

och /ɒk; ɒx; NAmE ɑːk; ɑːx/ *exclamation* (*ScotE, IrishE*) used to express the fact that you are surprised, sorry, etc.（用於表示驚奇、遺憾等）啊，哦：*Och, aye* (= Oh, yes). 啊，對。

oche /ˈɒki; NAmE ˈɑːki/ *noun* [sing.] the line which players must stand behind in the game of DARTS（擲鏢遊戲的）投擲線

ochre (*US* also **ocher**) /ˈəʊkə(r); NAmE ˈoʊ-/ *noun* [U] **1** a type of red or yellow earth used in some paints and DYES 赭土；赭石 **2** the red or yellow colour of ochre 赭色；土黃色

ocker /ˈɒkə(r); NAmE ˈɑːk-/ *noun* (*AustralE, informal*) a rude or aggressive Australian man 粗魯（或無教養）的澳大利亞人 ▸ **ocker** *adj.*

o'clock /əˈklɒk; NAmE əˈklɑːk/ *adv.* used with the numbers 1 to 12 when telling the time, to mean an exact hour（表示整點）…點鐘：*He left between five and six o'clock.* 他是五六點鐘離開的。◇ *at/after/before eleven o'clock* 十一點整／後／前

OCR *abbr.* (*computing* 計) OPTICAL CHARACTER RECOGNITION

octa·gon /ˈɒktəɡən; NAmE ˈɑːktəɡɑːn/ *noun* (*geometry* 幾何) a flat shape with eight straight sides and eight angles 八邊形；八角形 ➲ VISUAL VOCAB page V71 ▸ **oc·tag·on·al** /ɒkˈtæɡənl; NAmE ɑːkˈt-/ *adj.*：*an octagonal coin* 八角形硬幣

oc·tane /ˈɒkteɪn; NAmE ˈɑːk-/ *noun* a chemical substance in petrol/gas, used as a way of measuring its quality 辛烷（汽油中的化學物質，用於檢測汽油的質量）：*high-octane fuel* 高辛烷值的燃料

oct·ave /ˈɒktɪv; NAmE ˈɑːk-/ *noun* (*music* 音) the difference (the INTERVAL) between the first and last notes in a series of eight notes on a SCALE 八度；八度音階：*to play an octave higher* 再奏高一個八度 ◇ *Orbison's vocal range spanned three octaves.* 奧畢森的音域跨越三個八度。

oc·tavo /ɒkˈteɪvəʊ; -ˈtɑːv-; NAmE ɑːk-; -voʊ/ *noun* (*pl.* **-os**) (*technical* 術語) a size of a book page that is made by folding each sheet of paper into eight LEAVES (= 16 pages) 八開本

octet /ɒkˈtet; NAmE ɑːk-/ *noun* **1** [C+sing./pl. v.] a group of eight singers or musicians 八重唱組合；八重奏樂團 **2** [C] a piece of music for eight singers or musicians 八重奏（曲）；八重唱（曲）

octo- /ˈɒktəʊ-; NAmE ˈɑːktoʊ-/ (also **oct-**) *combining form* (in nouns, adjectives and adverbs 構成名詞、形容詞和副詞) eight; having eight 八；八…的：*octagon* 八角形

Oc·to·ber /ɒkˈtəʊbə(r); NAmE ɑːkˈtoʊ-/ *noun* [U, C] (*abbr.* **Oct.**) the 10th month of the year, between September and November 十月 HELP To see how **October** is used, look at the examples at **April**. * October 的用法見詞條 April 下的示例。

oc·to·gen·ar·ian /ˌɒktədʒəˈneəriən; NAmE ˌɑːktədʒəˈner-/ *noun* a person between 80 and 89 years old 八旬老人；80 至 89 歲的人

octo·pus /ˈɒktəpəs; NAmE ˈɑːk-/ *noun* [C, U] (*pl.* **octo·puses**) a sea creature with a soft round body and eight long arms, that is sometimes used for food 章魚

'octopus trousers (*BrE*) (*NAmE* **'octopus pants**) *noun* [pl.] trousers/pants which have many strips of material hanging from them 章魚鬚長褲（綴有很多布條）

octo·syl·lable /ˈɒktəʊsɪləbl; NAmE ˈɑːktoʊ-/ *noun* (*technical* 術語) a line of poetry consisting of eight syllables 八音節詩行 ▸ **octo·syl·lab·ic** /ˌɒktəʊsɪˈlæbɪk; NAmE ˈɑːktoʊ-/ *adj.*

ocu·lar /ˈɒkjələ(r); NAmE ˈɑːk-/ *adj.* [only before noun] **1** (*technical* 術語) connected with the eyes 眼的；眼睛的：*ocular muscles* 眼部肌肉 **2** (*formal*) that can be seen 可以看見的；看得到的：*ocular proof* 目擊的證據

ocu·list /ˈɒkjəlɪst; NAmE ˈɑːk-/ *noun* (*old-fashioned*) a doctor who examines and treats people's eyes 眼科醫生

OD /ˌəʊ ˈdiː; NAmE ˌoʊ/ *verb* (**OD's**, **OD'ing**, **OD'd**, **OD'd**) [I] **~ (on sth)** (*informal*) = OVERDOSE

odd AW /ɒd; NAmE ɑːd/ *adj.* (**odder**, **oddest**)
▸ STRANGE 奇怪 **1** strange or unusual 奇怪的；怪異的；反常的：*They're very odd people.* 他們那些人都很古怪。◇ *There's something odd about that man.* 那個人有點兒怪。◇ *It's **most odd that*** (= very odd that) *she hasn't written.* 真怪了，她一直沒寫信。◇ ***The odd thing** was that he didn't recognize me.* 怪就怪在他沒認出我來。◇ *She had the oddest feeling that he was avoiding her.* 她有種異樣的感覺，覺得他在躲着她。➲ compare PECULIAR (1)
▸ ODD- （某方面）怪異 **2** (in compounds 構成複合詞) strange or unusual in the way mentioned（某方面）怪

異的，奇怪的：*an odd-looking house* 樣子怪異的房子 ◇ *an odd-sounding name* 聽起來奇怪的名字

▸ NOT REGULAR/OFTEN 不規則；不常 **3 the odd** [only before noun] (no comparative or superlative 無比較級或最高級) happening or appearing occasionally; not very regular or frequent 偶然出現的；偶爾發生的；不規律的 **SYN occasional**：*He makes the odd mistake—nothing too serious.* 他偶爾會犯錯誤，但不怎麼嚴重。

▸ VARIOUS 各種各樣 **4** [only before noun] (no comparative or superlative 無比較級或最高級) of no particular type or size; various 奇形怪狀的；各種各樣的：*decorations made of odd scraps of paper* 用各種各樣的紙片做的裝飾

▸ NOT MATCHING 不相配 **5** [usually before noun] (no comparative or superlative 無比較級或最高級) not with the pair or set that it belongs to; not matching 不成對的；不相配的：*You're wearing odd socks!* 你穿的襪子不成雙呀！

▸ NUMBERS 數字 **6** (no comparative or superlative 無比較級或最高級) (of numbers 數字) that cannot be divided exactly by the number two 奇數的：*1, 3, 5 and 7 are odd numbers.* * 1、3、5 和 7 是奇數。**OPP even**

▸ AVAILABLE 可得到的 **7** [only before noun] available; that sb can use 可得到的；可用的 **SYN spare**：*Could I see you when you've got an* ***odd moment****?* 你有空時，我能不能見見你？

▸ APPROXIMATELY 約略 **8** (no comparative or superlative; usually placed immediately after a number 無比較級或最高級；通常緊接在數字後面) approximately or a little more than the number mentioned 大約；略多：*How old is she—seventy odd?* 她多大年紀？七十出頭？◇ *He's worked there for twenty-odd years.* 他在那裏工作了二十多年。

▸ **odd·ness** *noun* [U]：*the oddness of her appearance* 她那怪樣子 ◇ *His oddness frightened her.* 他的反常把她嚇壞了。

IDM the odd man/one 'out a person or thing that is different from others or does not fit easily into a group or set 與其他不同（或合不來）的人（或物）；異類：*At school he was always the odd man out.* 在學校裏他總是與別人格格不入。◇ *Dog, cat, horse, shoe—which is the odd one out?* 狗、貓、馬、鞋，哪一個不屬同類？➲ more at FISH *n.*

odd·ball /ˈɒdbɔːl; *NAmE* ˈɑːd-/ *noun* (*informal*) a person who behaves in a strange or unusual way 行為古怪者；反常者；怪人 ▸ **odd·ball** *adj.*：*oddball characters* 古怪的人物

odd·ity /ˈɒdəti; *NAmE* ˈɑːd-/ *noun* (*pl.* **-ies**) **1** [C] a person or thing that is strange or unusual 古怪反常的人（或事物）；怪現象：*The book deals with some of the oddities of grammar and spelling.* 這本書專講語法和拼寫方面的某些不規則現象。 **2** [U] the quality of being strange or unusual 古怪；怪異；反常：*She suddenly realized the oddity of her remark and blushed.* 她突然意識到自己的話很可笑，臉一下子紅了。

ˌodd-ˈjob man *noun* (*especially BrE*) a person paid to do odd jobs 打零工的人；散工；短工

ˌodd ˈjobs *noun* [pl.] small jobs of various types 零散的工作；雜活；零活兒：*to do odd jobs around the house* 在家裏幹雜活

oddly /ˈɒdli; *NAmE* ˈɑːd-/ *adv.* **1** in a strange or unusual way 古怪地；怪異地；反常地 **SYN strangely**：*She's been behaving very oddly lately.* 她最近行為極其反常。◇ *oddly coloured clothes* 顏色古怪的衣裳 ◇ *He looked at her in a way she found oddly disturbing.* 他異樣地望着她，令她局促不安。 **2** used to show that sth is surprising 令人奇怪地；令人驚奇地 **SYN surprisingly**：*She felt, oddly, that they had been happier when they had no money.* 她感到奇怪的是，他們沒錢時生活得更幸福。◇ ***Oddly enough****, the most expensive tickets sold fastest.* 奇怪極了，最貴的票居然賣得最快。

odd·ments /ˈɒdmənts; *NAmE* ˈɑːd-/ *noun* [pl.] (*especially BrE*) **1** small pieces of cloth, wood, etc. that are left after a larger piece has been used to make sth 布頭；零木料；邊角料 **SYN remnants 2** small items that are not valuable or are not part of a larger set（無價值或派不上用場的）小物品，零碎 **SYN bits and pieces**

odds AW /ɒdz; *NAmE* ɑːdz/ *noun* [pl.] **1** (usually **the odds**) the degree to which sth is likely to happen（事物發生的）可能性，概率，幾率，機會：***The odds are*** *very much* ***in our favour*** (= we are likely to succeed). 我方勝算的幾率極大。◇ ***The odds*** *are heavily* ***against him*** (= he is not likely to succeed). 他成功的幾率很小。◇ ***The odds are that*** (= it is likely that) *she'll win.* 她有可能會贏。◇ ***What are the odds*** (= how likely is it) *he won't turn up?* 他不會露面的可能性有多大？ **2** something that makes it seem impossible to do or achieve sth 不利條件；掣肘的事情；逆境：*They secured a victory in the face of overwhelming odds.* 儘管情況非常不利，他們仍得到了勝利。◇ ***Against all*** (***the***) ***odds****, he made a full recovery.* 在凶多吉少的情形下，他終於完全康復了。**3** (in betting 打賭) the connection between two numbers that shows how much money sb will receive if they win a bet 投注賠率：*odds of ten to one* (= ten times the amount of money that has been bet by sb will be paid to them if they win) 十比一的賠率 ◇ *They are offering* ***long/short odds*** (= the prize money will be high/low because there is a high/low risk of losing) *on the defending champion.* 他們為衛冕者開出了高／低賠率。◇ (*figurative*) *I'll* ***lay odds*** *on him getting the job* (= I'm sure he will get it). 我敢說他能得到這份工作。

IDM be at 'odds (with sth) to be different from sth, when the two things should be the same（與…）有差異，相矛盾 **SYN conflict**：*These findings are at odds with what is going on in the rest of the country.* 這些研究結果與國內其他地區的實際情況並不相符。 **be at 'odds (with sb) (over/on sth)** to disagree with sb about sth（就某事）與…有分歧：*He's always at odds with his father over politics.* 他在政治上總是與他父親的意見相左。 **it makes no 'odds** (*informal, especially BrE*) used to say that sth is not important 沒關係；無所謂；無差別：*It makes no odds to me whether you go or stay.* 你的去留與我無關。 **over the 'odds** (*BrE, informal*) more money than you would normally expect（比期望的）價錢高：*Many collectors are willing to pay over the odds for early examples of his work.* 許多收藏家都肯出高價買他早期的作品。➲ more at STACKED

ˌodds and ˈends (*BrE* also **ˌodds and ˈsods**) *noun* [pl.] (*informal*) small items that are not valuable or are not part of a larger set 零碎；瑣碎的東西；小玩意：*She spent the day sorting through a box full of odds and ends.* 她花一天工夫整理裝滿小玩意兒的箱子。◇ *I've got a few odds and ends* (= small jobs) *to do before leaving.* 我臨行之前還有些雜事要處理。

ˌodds-ˈon *adj.* very likely to happen, win, etc. 很可能發生（或取勝等）的：*the* ***odds-on favourite*** (= the person, horse, etc. that is most likely to succeed, to win a race, etc.) 被看好會贏的人或馬等 ◇ ***It's odds-on that*** *he'll be late.* 他多半要遲到。◇ *Arazi is odds-on to win the Kentucky Derby.* 阿拉茲十有八九會在肯塔基賽馬會上獲勝。

ode /əʊd; *NAmE* oʊd/ *noun* a poem that speaks to a person or thing or celebrates a special event 頌詩；頌歌：*Keats's 'Ode to a Nightingale'* 濟慈的《夜鶯頌》

odi·ous /ˈəʊdiəs; *NAmE* ˈoʊ-/ *adj.* (*formal*) extremely unpleasant 令人作嘔的；令人討厭的；可憎的 **SYN horrible**：*What an odious man!* 真是個討厭透頂的傢伙！

odium /ˈəʊdiəm; *NAmE* ˈoʊ-/ *noun* [U] (*formal*) a feeling of hatred that a lot of people have towards sb, because of sth they have done 憎惡；厭惡；公憤

odom·eter /əʊˈdɒmɪtə(r); *NAmE* oʊˈdɑːm-/ (*NAmE*) (*BrE* **mil·om·eter, mile·ometer**) (also *informal* **the clock** *US, BrE*) *noun* an instrument in a vehicle that measures the number of miles it has travelled 里程表；計程器 ➲ VISUAL VOCAB page V52

odon·tol·ogy /ˌəʊdɒnˈtɒlədʒi; ˌɒd-; *NAmE* ˌoʊdɑːnˈtɑːlədʒi/ *noun* [U] the scientific study of the diseases and structure of teeth 牙科學 ▸ **odon·tolo·gist** /ˌəʊdɒnˈtɒlədʒɪst; ˌɒd-; *NAmE* ˌoʊdɑːnˈtɑːlədʒɪst/ *noun*

odor·ous /ˈəʊdərəs; NAmE ˈoʊ-/ *adj.* (*literary* or *technical* 術語) having a smell 有氣味的：*odorous gases* 有味兒的氣體

odour (*especially US* **odor**) /ˈəʊdə(r); NAmE ˈoʊ-/ *noun* [C, U] (*formal*) a smell, especially one that is unpleasant（尤指難聞的）氣味；臭味：*a* ***foul/musty/pungent, etc. odour*** 難聞的氣味、難聞的霉味、刺鼻的氣味等 ◇ *the stale odour of cigarette smoke* 香煙的臭味 ◇ (*figurative*) *the odour of suspicion* 事情很可疑 ➲ see also BODY ODOUR

IDM **be in good/bad ˈodour (with sb)** (*formal*) to have/not have sb's approval and support 得到／不得（某人的）青睞；受／不受（某人的）贊同

odour·less (*especially US* **odor·less**) /ˈəʊdələs; NAmE ˈoʊdərləs/ *adj.* without a smell 無氣味的：*an odourless liquid* 無臭的液體

odys·sey /ˈɒdəsi; NAmE ˈɑːd-/ *noun* [sing.] (*literary*) a long journey full of experiences 艱苦的跋涉；漫長而充滿風險的歷程 **ORIGIN** From the **Odyssey**, a Greek poem that is said to have been written by Homer, about the adventures of **Odysseus**. After a battle in Troy Odysseus had to spend ten years travelling before he could return home. 源自希臘史詩《奧德賽》，相傳為荷馬所作，描述了奧德修斯在特洛伊戰爭後，輾轉十年返回家園的種種經歷。

OECD /ˌəʊ iː siː ˈdiː; NAmE ˌoʊ/ *abbr.* Organization for Economic Cooperation and Development (an organization of industrial countries that encourages trade and economic growth) 經合組織，經濟合作與發展組織（工業化國家鼓勵貿易和經濟發展的組織）

the OED /ˌəʊ iː ˈdiː; NAmE ˌoʊ/ *abbr.* the Oxford English Dictionary (the largest dictionary of the English language, which was first published in Britain in 1928)《牛津英語大詞典》（最大的英語詞典，1928 年在英國發行初版）

O

oe·dema (*BrE*) (*NAmE* **edema**) /ɪˈdiːmə/ *noun* [U] (*medical* 醫) a condition in which liquid collects in the spaces inside the body and makes it swell 水腫

Oedi·pal /ˈiːdɪpl; *US* usually ˈed-/ *adj.* [usually before noun] connected with an Oedipus complex 戀母情結的

Oedi·pus com·plex /ˈiːdɪpəs kɒmpleks; NAmE ˈiːdɪpəs kɑːm-; *US* usually ˈedɪpəs kɑːm-/ *noun* [sing.] (*psychology* 心) feelings of sexual desire that a boy has for his mother and the jealous feelings towards his father that this causes 戀母情結 **ORIGIN** From the Greek story of **Oedipus**, whose father Laius had been told by the oracle that his son would kill him. Laius left Oedipus on a mountain to die, but a shepherd rescued him. Oedipus returned home many years later but did not recognize his parents. He killed his father and married his mother Jocasta. 源自希臘故事《俄狄浦斯》。拉伊俄斯由神諭得知，兒子俄狄浦斯將會殺害他，便將兒子置於山野，任其自滅。但俄狄浦斯為牧羊人所救，多年後返回家園，卻不認得父母。他殺死了父親，娶了母親伊俄卡斯塔。

o'er /ɔː(r)/ *adv., prep.* (*old use*) over 在…上面；越過

oe·sopha·gus (*BrE*) (*NAmE* **esopha·gus**) /iˈsɒfəgəs; NAmE iˈsɑː-/ *noun* (*pl.* **-pha·guses** or **-ph·agi** /-gaɪ/) (*anatomy* 解) the tube through which food passes from the mouth to the stomach 食道；食管 **SYN** **gullet** ➲ VISUAL VOCAB page V59

oes·tro·gen (*BrE*) (*NAmE* **es·tro·gen**) /ˈiːstrədʒən; NAmE ˈes-/ *noun* [U] a HORMONE produced in women's OVARIES that causes them to develop the physical and sexual features that are characteristic of females and that causes them to prepare their body to have babies 雌激素 ➲ compare PROGESTERONE, TESTOSTERONE

oes·trus (*BrE*) (*NAmE* **es·trus**) /ˈiːstrəs; NAmE ˈestrəs/ *noun* [U] (*technical* 術語) a period of time in which a female animal is ready to have sex（雌性動物的）動情期

oeuvre /ˈɜːvrə/ *noun* [sing.] (from *French, formal*) all the works of a writer, artist, etc.（作家、藝術家等的）全部作品：*Picasso's oeuvre* 畢加索的全部作品

of 0━ /əv; *strong form* ɒv; NAmE ʌv/ *prep.*
1 0━ belonging to sb; relating to sb 屬於（某人）；關於（某人）：*a friend of mine* 我的一個朋友 ◇ *the love of a mother for her child* 母親對孩子的愛 ◇ *the role of the teacher* 教師的角色 ◇ *Can't you throw out that old bike of Tommy's?* 難道你就不能把湯米那輛舊自行車給扔掉？◇ *the paintings of Monet* 莫奈的畫作 **HELP** When you are talking about everything someone has painted, written, etc., use **of**. When you are referring to one or more examples of somebody's work, use **by**. 指某人所畫或所著等的全部作品時，用 of；指其作品中的一部或多部時，則用 by：*a painting by Monet* **2** 0━ belonging to sth; being part of sth; relating to sth 屬於（某物）；（某事）部份的；關於（某物）：*the lid of the box* 盒子蓋 ◇ *the director of the company* 公司的董事 ◇ *a member of the team* 一名隊員 ◇ *the result of the debate* 辯論的結果 **3** 0━ coming from a particular background or living in a place 出身於（某背景）；住在（某地）：*a woman of Italian descent* 意大利裔女子 ◇ *the people of Wales* 威爾士人民 **4** 0━ concerning or showing sb/sth 關於，反映（某人或某事）：*a story of passion* 愛情故事 ◇ *a photo of my dog* 我那隻狗的照片 ◇ *a map of India* 印度地圖 **5** 0━ used to say what sb/sth is, consists of, or contains（用於表示性質、組成或涵蓋）即，由…組成：*the city of Dublin* 都柏林市 ◇ *the issue of housing* 住房問題 ◇ *a crowd of people* 一群人 ◇ *a glass of milk* 一杯牛奶 **6** 0━ used with measurements and expressions of time, age, etc.（用於表示計量、時間或年齡等）：*2 kilos of potatoes* 兩公斤馬鈴薯 ◇ *an increase of 2%* * 2% 的增長 ◇ *a girl of 12* * 12 歲的女孩 ◇ *the fourth of July* 七月四日 ◇ *the year of his birth* 他出生的那一年 ◇ (*old-fashioned*) *We would often have a walk of an evening.* 我們過去常在晚上散步。 **7** 0━ used to show sb/sth belongs to a group, often after *some, a few*, etc.（常用在 some、a few 等詞語之後，表示人或物的所屬）屬於…的：*some of his friends* 他的幾位朋友 ◇ *a few of the problems* 其中的幾個問題 ◇ *the most famous of all the stars* 最知名的一位明星 **8** 0━ used to show the position of sth/sb in space or time（表示人或事的時空位置）在，當：*just north of Detroit* 就在底特律以北 ◇ *at the time of the revolution* 在革命的年代 ◇ (*NAmE*) *at a quarter of eleven tonight* (= 10.45 p.m.) 在今晚十一點差一刻 **9** 0━ used after nouns formed from verbs. The noun after 'of' can be either the object or the subject of the action.（用於由動詞轉化的名詞之後，of 之後的名詞可以是受動者，也可以是施動者）：*the arrival of the police* (= they arrive) 警察的到來 ◇ *criticism of the police* (= they are criticized) 對警察的批評 ◇ *fear of the dark* 對黑暗的懼怕 ◇ *the howling of the wind* 狂風的呼嘯 **10** 0━ used after some verbs before mentioning sb/sth involved in the action（用於某些動詞後，後接動作所涉及的人或事）：*to deprive sb of sth* 剝奪某人的東西 ◇ *He was cleared of all blame.* 他所受的一切責難都澄清了。◇ *Think of a number, any number.* 想一個數字，隨便一個。 **11** 0━ used after some adjectives before mentioning sb/sth that a feeling relates to（用於某些形容詞後，後接與感情相關的人或事）因為，由於：*to be proud of sth* 為某事自豪 **12** 0━ used to give your opinion of sb's behaviour（用於對某人的行為發表看法）：*It was kind of you to offer.* 感謝你的好意。 **13** used when one noun describes a second one（用於一個名詞修飾另一個名詞時）：*Where's that idiot of a boy* (= the boy that you think is stupid)? 那個傻小子在哪兒？

IDM **of ˈall** used before a noun to say that sth is very surprising（用於名詞前，表示某事着實令人吃驚）竟然，偏偏：*I'm surprised that you of all people should say that.* 你竟然那麼說，真讓我吃驚！ **of all the ...** used to express anger（用以表示憤怒）：*Of all the nerve!* 竟然如此膽大包天！

off 0━ /ɒf; NAmE ɔːf; ɑːf/ *adv., prep., adj., noun, verb*
■ *adv.* **HELP** For the special uses of **off** in phrasal verbs, look at the entries for the verbs. For example **come off** is in the phrasal verb section at **come**. * off 在短語動詞中的特殊用法見有關動詞詞條。如 come off 在詞條 come 的短語動詞部份。 **1** 0━ away from a place; at a distance in space or time 離開（某處）；（在時間或空間上）距，離：*I called him but he ran off.* 我喊他，可他跑開了。◇ *Sarah's off in India somewhere.* 薩拉遠在印度某地。◇ *I must be off soon* (= leave). 我必須很快離開

這裏。◇ *Off you go!* 你走吧！◇ *Summer's not far off now.* 夏天已近在咫尺了。◇ *A solution is still some way off.* 解決辦法尚需時日。 **2** used to say that sth has been removed（用以表示除去了某物）: *He's had his beard shaved off.* 他把鬍子刮光了。◇ *Take your coat off.* 脱了外衣吧。◇ *Don't leave the toothpaste with the top off.* 用完了牙膏別讓蓋子開着。 **3** starting a race 起跑： *They're off* (= the race has begun). 他們起跑了。 **4** no longer going to happen; cancelled 不再會發生；被取消： *The wedding is off.* 婚禮被取消了。 **5** not connected or functioning 未連接；不工作： *The water is off.* 停水了。◇ *Make sure the TV is off.* 請注意關掉電視機。 **6** (*especially BrE*) (of an item on a menu 菜單中的項目) no longer available or being served 沒有；不再供應： *Sorry, the duck is off.* 對不起，鴨子賣光了。 **7** away from work or duty 休假；休息： *She's off today.* 她今天休假。◇ *I've got three days off next week.* 我下週有三天休假。◇ *How many days did you* ***take off****?* 你休了幾天假？◇ *I need some* ***time off****.* 我需要休息一段時間。 **8** taken from the price 減價的；削價的： *shoes with $20 off* 減價 20 元的鞋 ◇ *All shirts have/are 10% off.* 襯衣全部減價 10%。 **9** behind or at the sides of the stage in a theatre 在劇院舞台的後面（或旁邊） SYN **offstage**

IDM **be well/better/badly, etc. 'off** used to say how much money sb has（用於表示經濟情況）: *Families will be better off under the new law* (= will have more money). 這項新法律將使每個家庭的經濟較前寬裕。◇ *They are both comfortably off* (= have enough money to be able to buy what they want without worrying too much about the cost). 他們倆的生活都很寬裕。 **be better/worse off (doing sth)** to be in a better or worse situation（做某事）會較好／較糟： *She's better off without him.* 他不在身邊她反倒更快樂。◇ *The weather was so bad we'd have been better off staying at home.* 天氣太糟了，我們要是待在家裏就好了。◇ *We can't be any worse off than we are already.* 我們的狀況已經糟得不能再糟了。 **be ˌoff for 'sth** (*informal*) to have a particular amount of sth 有一定數量的東西： *How are we off for coffee* (= how much do we have)? 我們還有多少咖啡？ ➲ see also BADLY OFF **ˌoff and 'on/ˌon and 'off** from time to time; now and again 不時地；經常；斷斷續續地： *It rained on and off all day.* 雨斷斷續續地下了一整天。

■ ***prep.*** HELP For the special uses of **off** in phrasal verbs, look at the entries for the verbs. For example **take sth off sth** is in the phrasal verb section at **take**. * off 在短語動詞中的特殊用法見有關動詞詞條。如 take sth off sth 在詞條 take 的短語動詞部份。 **1** down or away from a place or at a distance in space or time 從（某處）落下；離開；（時空上）離，距： *I fell off the ladder.* 我從梯子上跌了下來。◇ *Keep off the grass!* 勿踐踏草坪！◇ *an island off the coast of Spain* 西班牙海岸附近的島 ◇ *They were still 100 metres off the summit.* 他們距山頂還有 100 米遠。◇ *Scientists are still a long way off finding a cure.* 科學家要找到一個治療方法，還遠着呢。◇ *We're getting right off the subject.* 我們完全離題了。 **2** leading away from sth, for example a road or room 離開；偏離： *We live off Main Street.* 我們住在大街附近。◇ *There's a bathroom off the main bedroom.* 主卧室旁邊有一個衞生間。 **3** used to say that sth has been removed 從…去掉；從…移開： *You need to take the top off the bottle first!* 你得先把瓶蓋子打開！◇ *I want about an inch off the back of my hair.* 我想把腦後的頭髮剪短約一英寸。 **4** away from work or duty 休假；休息： *He's had ten days off school.* 他有十天沒上學了。 **5** away from a price 偏離…價格；削價；殺價： *They knocked £500 off the car.* 他們對這輛汽車殺價 500 英鎊。 **6 off of** (*non-standard* or *NAmE, informal*) off; from 離開；來源於；從： *I got it off of my brother.* 這是我從我弟弟那裏弄到的。 **7** not wanting or liking sth that you usually eat or use 不想；戒除： *I'm off* (= not drinking) *alcohol for a week.* 我有一星期沒喝酒了。◇ *He's finally off drugs* (= he no longer takes them). 他終於把毒戒了。

■ ***adj.*** [not before noun] **1** (of food 食物) no longer fresh enough to eat or drink 不新鮮；變質： *This fish has gone off.* 這條魚已變質了。◇ *The milk smells off.* 這奶的味道不對勁。◇ *It's off.* 那東西壞了。 **2 ~ (with sb)** (*informal, especially BrE*) not polite or friendly 不禮貌；不熱情；冷淡： *He was a bit off with me this morning.* 他今天早晨對我有點冷淡。 **3** (*informal, especially BrE*) not acceptable 不能接受；難以容忍；不行： *It's a bit off expecting us to work on Sunday.* 讓我們星期天上班工作，那可不太行吧。

■ ***noun*** [sing.] **the off** the start of a race 起跑： *They're ready for the off.* 他們準備起跑了。

■ ***verb* ~ sb** (*informal, especially NAmE*) to kill sb 殺死（某人）

off- /ɒf; *NAmE* ɔːf; ɑːf/ *prefix* (in nouns, adjectives, verbs and adverbs 構成名詞、形容詞、動詞和副詞) not on; away from 不在…上；離開；去掉： *offstage* 不在舞台上 ◇ *offload* 卸掉

ˌoff-'air *adj.* (in radio and television 廣播及電視) not being broadcast 不在廣播中的： *off-air recording* 非廣播實況錄製 OPP **on-air** ▸ **ˌoff-'air** *adv.*： *to record off-air* 錄製廣播節目

offal /'ɒfl; *NAmE* 'ɔːfl; 'ɑːfl/ *noun* [U] (*US* also **va'riety meats** [pl.]) the inside parts of an animal, such as the heart and LIVER, cooked and eaten as food（食用的）動物內臟

off·beat /ˌɒf'biːt; *NAmE* ˌɔːf-; ˌɑːf-/ *adj.* [usually before noun] (*informal*) different from what most people expect 不尋常的；不落俗套的；標新立異的 SYN **unconventional**： *offbeat humour* 另類的幽默 ◇ *an offbeat approach to interviewing* 別開生面的採訪

ˌoff-'Broadway *adj.* (*NAmE*) **1** (of a theatre 劇院) not on Broadway, New York's main theatre district 不在百老匯的；外百老匯的 **2** (of a play 戲劇) unusual in some way and often by a new writer 不落俗的；有新意的；出自新人之手的 ➲ compare FRINGE THEATRE

ˌoff-'centre (*especially US* **ˌoff-'center**) *adv., adj.* not exactly in the centre of sth 不居中（的）

'off chance *noun*

IDM **do sth on the 'off chance** to do sth even though you think that there is only a small possibility of it being successful 僥幸一試；碰運氣： *She scanned the crowd on the off chance of seeing someone she knew.* 她掃視着人群，抱着一線希望看是否有熟人。◇ *I called in at the office on the off chance that you would still be there.* 我上了你的辦公室，想看看你是不是還在那裏。

ˌoff 'colour (*especially US* **ˌoff 'color**) *adj.* **1** [not before noun] (*BrE, informal*) not in good health; looking or feeling ill/sick 身體不舒服；氣色不佳 **2** [usually before noun] (*especially NAmE*) an **off-colour** joke is one that people think is rude, usually because it is about sex（笑話）粗俗的，下流的

off·cut /'ɒfkʌt; *NAmE* 'ɔːf-; 'ɑːf-/ *noun* (*especially BrE*) a piece of wood, paper, etc. that remains after the main piece has been cut 下腳料；邊角材料

'off day *noun* (*informal*) a day when you do not do things as well as usual 不順利的日子；倒霉的一天

ˌoff-'duty *adj.* not at work 非值勤的；歇班的： *an off-duty policeman* 休班警察

of·fence (*especially US* **of·fense**) /ə'fens/ *noun*
1 [C] **~ (against sb/sth)** an illegal act 違法行為；犯罪；罪行 SYN **crime**： ***a criminal/serious/minor/sexual, etc. offence*** 刑事罪、重罪、輕罪、性犯罪等 ◇ ***a first offence*** (= the first time that sb has been found guilty of a crime) 初犯 ◇ ***a capital offence*** (= one for which sb may be punished by death) 死罪 ◇ *He was not aware that he had* ***committed an offence****.* 他沒有意識到自己犯罪了。◇ *an* ***offence against society/humanity/the state*** 妨害社會／人類／國家的罪行 ◇ *New legislation makes it an offence to carry guns.* 新法律規定持槍為犯罪行為。 **2** [U] the act of upsetting or insulting sb 冒犯；攪擾；侮辱： *I'm sure he* ***meant no offence*** *when he said that.* 我相信他那麼説並無冒犯的意思。◇ *The photo may* ***cause offence*** *to some people.* 這張照片可能會引起一些人的反感。◇ *No one will* ***take offence*** (= feel upset or insulted) *if you leave early.* 你若早退誰也不會介意的。◇ *Don't be so quick to* ***take offence****.* 別動不動就生氣。

IDM **no of'fence** (*informal*) used to say that you do not mean to upset or insult sb by sth you say or do 無冒犯之意： *No offence, but I'd really like to be on my own.* 我無意冒犯，但我確實想自己一個人待着。

O

of·fend /ə'fend/ *verb*
1 [T, often passive, I] **~ (sb)** to make sb feel upset because of sth you say or do that is rude or embarrassing 得罪；冒犯：*They'll be offended if you don't go to their wedding.* 你若不參加他們的婚禮，他們會生氣的。◇ *Neil did not mean to offend anybody with his joke.* 尼爾開那個玩笑並非想冒犯誰。◇ *A TV interviewer must be careful not to offend.* 電視採訪者必須小心別得罪人。**2** [T] **~ sb/sth** to seem unpleasant to sb 令人不適：*The smell from the farm offended some people.* 農場散發的氣味讓一些人聞了不舒服。◇ *an ugly building that* ***offends the eye*** 一座醜陋礙眼的建築物 **3** [I] (*formal*) to commit a crime or crimes 犯罪；犯法：*He started offending at the age of 16.* 他 16 歲就開始犯法。**4** [I] **~ (against sb/sth)** (*formal*) to be against what people believe is morally right 違背（人情）；違反（常理）；有悖於：*comments that offend against people's religious beliefs* 有悖人們宗教信仰的評論 ▸ **of·fend·ed** *adj.*：*Alice looked rather offended.* 艾麗斯顯得憤憤不已。

of·fend·er /ə'fendə(r)/ *noun* **1** (rather *formal*) a person who commits a crime 犯罪者；違法者；罪犯：*a* ***persistent/serious/violent, etc. offender*** 慣犯、重犯、暴力犯等 ◇ *a young offender institution* 青少年罪犯管教所 ➲ see also FIRST OFFENDER, SEX OFFENDER **2** a person or thing that does sth wrong 妨害…的人（或事物）：*When it comes to pollution, the chemical industry is a major offender.* 談到環境污染問題，化工產業是一大禍害。

of·fend·ing /ə'fendɪŋ/ *adj.* [only before noun] **1** causing you to feel annoyed or upset; causing problems 煩人的；令人不安的；惹麻煩的：*The offending paragraph was deleted.* 令某些人不悅的那段話已經刪除。◇ *The traffic jam soon cleared once the offending vehicle had been removed.* 肇事車輛一經移走，交通擁堵很快就消除了。**2** guilty of a crime 有罪的；違法的：*The offending driver received a large fine.* 肇事司機被課以重額罰款。

O

of·fense 🔑 *noun* (*NAmE*)
1 🔑 /ə'fens/ [C] = OFFENCE：*to commit an offense* 犯罪 ◇ *The new law makes it a criminal offense to drink alcohol in public places.* 新法律將在公共場所飲酒定為刑事犯罪。◇ *a minor/serious offense* 輕罪；重罪 ◇ *She pleaded guilty to five traffic offenses.* 她承認曾五次違反交通法規。**2** 🔑 /'ɒfens; *NAmE* 'ɔːf-; 'ɑːf-/ [sing.+sing./pl. v., U] (*BrE* **at·tack** [sing.]) (*sport* 體) the members of a team whose main aim is to score points against the other team; a method of attack （球隊的）前鋒，鋒線隊員；進攻方法；攻勢：*The Redskins' offense is stronger than their defense.* 印第安人隊的進攻強於防守。◇ *He played offense for the Chicago Bulls.* 他在芝加哥公牛隊打前鋒。➲ compare DEFENCE (7)

of·fen·sive 🔑 /ə'fensɪv/ *adj., noun*
■ ***adj.*** **1** 🔑 rude in a way that causes you to feel upset, insulted or annoyed 冒犯的；得罪人的；無禮的：*offensive remarks* 冒犯的言論 ◇ *The programme contains language which some viewers may find offensive.* 節目裏使用了某些觀眾可能認為是犯忌的語言。◇ **~ to sb** *His comments were deeply offensive to a large number of single mothers.* 他的評論嚴重觸怒了眾多的單身母親。**OPP** **inoffensive** **2** (*formal*) extremely unpleasant 極其討厭的；令人不適的 **SYN** **obnoxious**：*an offensive smell* 刺鼻的氣味 ➲ SYNONYMS at DISGUSTING **3** [only before noun] connected with the act of attacking sb/sth 攻擊性的；進攻性的：*an offensive war* 侵略戰爭 ◇ *offensive action* 進攻行動 ◇ *He was charged with carrying an* ***offensive weapon***. 他被指控攜帶攻擊性武器。➲ compare DEFENSIVE *adj.* (1) **4** (*NAmE, sport* 體) connected with the team that has control of the ball; connected with the act of scoring points 攻方的；進攻型的；攻擊型的：*offensive play* 進攻動作 ➲ compare DEFENSIVE *adj.* (3) ▸ **of·fen·sive·ly** *adv.* **of·fen·sive·ness** *noun* [U]
■ ***noun*** **1** a military operation in which large numbers of soldiers, etc. attack another country 進攻；攻擊；侵犯 **SYN** **strike**：*an air offensive* 空中攻擊 ◇ *They* ***launched the offensive*** *on January 10.* 他們於 1 月 10 日發動了進攻。**2** a series of actions aimed at achieving sth in a way that attracts a lot of attention （引人注意的）系列行動；運動；攻勢 **SYN** **campaign**：*The government has launched a new offensive against crime.* 政府發動了新的打擊犯罪攻勢。◇ *a sales offensive* 銷售攻勢 ◇ *The public seems unconvinced by their latest* ***charm offensive*** (= their attempt to make people like them). 公眾似乎並不相信他們最近所表演的一連串笑臉攻勢。
IDM **be on the of'fensive** to be attacking sb/sth rather than waiting for them to attack you 發動攻勢；主動出擊 **go on (to) the of'fensive | take the of'fensive** to start attacking sb/sth before they start attacking you 先發制人

offer 🔑 /'ɒfə(r); *NAmE* 'ɔːf-; 'ɑːf-/ *verb, noun*
■ ***verb*** **1** 🔑 [T, I] to say that you are willing to do sth for sb or give sth to sb 主動提出；自願給予：**~ (sth)** *Josie had offered her services as a guide.* 喬西曾表示願意當嚮導。◇ *He offered some useful advice.* 他提出了一些有益的建議。◇ *I don't think they need help, but I think I should offer anyway.* 我想他們不需要幫助，但我認為我還是應該主動提出來。◇ **~ sth (to sb) (for sth)** *He offered $4 000 for the car.* 他出價 4 000 元買這輛汽車。◇ *They decided to offer the job to Jo.* 他們決定把這份工作給喬。◇ **~ sb sth** *They decided to offer Jo the job.* 他們決定讓喬做這件工作。◇ *I gratefully took the cup of coffee she offered me.* 我感激地接過她遞來的一杯咖啡。◇ *Taylor offered him 500 dollars to do the work.* 泰勒願出 500 元雇他做這件工作。◇ **~ to do sth** *The kids offered to do the dishes.* 孩子們主動要求洗盤子。◇ **+ speech** *'I'll do it,' she offered.* "這個我來做吧。" 她提議道。**2** 🔑 [T] **~ sth** to make sth available or to provide the opportunity for sth 提供（東西或機會）；供應：*The hotel offers excellent facilities for families.* 本旅館提供適合全家的優良設施。◇ *The job didn't offer any prospects for promotion.* 這份工作沒有任何升遷的希望。◇ *He did not offer any explanation for his behaviour.* 他沒有對自己的行為作出任何解釋。**3** [T] **~ sth/sb (up) (to sb)** (*formal*) to give sth to God 奉獻，祭獻（給上帝）：*We offered up our prayers for the men's safe return.* 我們祈求上蒼保佑他們平安歸來。
IDM **have sth to offer** to have sth available that sb wants 能提供；能適合要求：*Oxford has a lot to offer visitors in the way of entertainment.* 牛津向來訪者提供各式各樣的娛樂活動。◇ *a young man with a great deal to offer* (= who is intelligent, has many skills, etc.) 一個多才多藝的年輕人 **offer your 'hand** (*formal*) to hold out your hand for sb to shake 伸出手（以便同別人握手）
■ ***noun*** **1** 🔑 an act of saying that you are willing to do sth for sb or give sth to sb 主動提議；建議：**~ (of sth)** *Thank you for your kind offer of help.* 謝謝你的好心幫助。◇ *to* ***accept/refuse/decline an offer*** 接受 / 拒絕 / 謝絕好意 ◇ *I took him up on his offer of a loan.* 他主動借錢給我，我接受了。◇ *You can't just turn down offers of work like that.* 人家給你工作，你不能就那樣一一謝絕呀。◇ *an offer of marriage* 結婚的請求 ◇ **~ to do sth** *I accepted her offer to pay.* 她要付款，我同意了。**2** 🔑 **~ (for sth)** an amount of money that sb is willing to pay for sth 出價；報價：*I've had an offer of $2 500 for the car.* 有人向我出價 2 500 元買這輛汽車。◇ *They've decided to accept our original offer.* 他們已決定接受我們最初的報價。◇ *The offer has been withdrawn.* 那個報價已經撤銷了。◇ *They made me an offer I couldn't refuse.* 他們提出了一個使我不好拒絕的報價。◇ *The original price was £3 000, but I'm* ***open to offers*** (= willing to consider offers that are less than that). 原價為 3 000 英鎊，但價錢還可以商量。➲ see also O.N.O. **3** 🔑 a reduction in the normal price of sth, usually for a short period of time （通常為短期的）減價，削價；處理價；特價：*This* ***special offer*** *is valid until the end of the month.* 這個特價優惠月底前有效。◇ *See next week's issue for details of more* ***free offers***. 請見下週週刊有關更多免費贈品的詳情。◇ *They have an offer on beer at the moment.* 他們目下正在打折賣啤酒。
IDM **on 'offer** **1** that can be bought, used, etc. 提供的；可買到；可使用：*The following is a list of courses currently on offer.* 以下是目前所開設課程的清單。◇ *Prizes worth more than £20 000 are on offer.* 優勝者獎品總值逾 20 000 英鎊。**2** (*especially BrE*) on sale at a lower price than normal for a short period of time 短期內打折銷售；削價出售：*Italian wines are on (special)*

offer this week. 意大利葡萄酒本週特價銷售。**under 'offer** (*BrE*) if a house or other building is **under offer**, sb has agreed to buy it at a particular price（房屋或其他建築物）已有買主出價，在洽售中

of·fer·ing /ˈɒfərɪŋ; *NAmE* ˈɔːf-; ˈɑːf-/ *noun* **1** something that is produced for other people to use, watch, enjoy, etc. 用品；劇作；作品；供消遣的產品：*the latest offering from the Canadian-born writer* 在加拿大出生的那位作家的最新作品 **2** something that is given to a god as part of religious worship 祭品；供品 ➲ see also BURNT OFFERING, PEACE OFFERING

of·fer·tory /ˈɒfətri; *NAmE* ˈɔːfərtɔːri; ˈɑːf-/ *noun* (*pl.* **-ies**) **1** the offering of bread and wine to God at a church service 祭品（奉獻給上帝的餅和酒）**2** an offering or a collection of money during a church service 獻金（禮拜中收集的捐款）

ˌoff-ˈgrid *adj.* = OFF-THE-GRID

off·hand /ˌɒfˈhænd; *NAmE* ˌɔːf-; ˌɑːf-/ *adj.*, *adv.*

■ ***adj.*** (*disapproving*) not showing much interest in sb/sth 漫不經心的；不在乎的：*an offhand manner* 隨隨便便的態度 ◇ *He was very offhand with me.* 他完全是在敷衍我。

▸ **off·hand·ed·ly** /ˌɒfˈhændɪdli; *NAmE* ˌɔːf-; ˌɑːf-/ *adv.*：*He spoke offhandedly, making it clear I had no say in the matter.* 他漫不經心地説話，清楚表明這件事我無權發言。

■ ***adv.*** without being able to check sth or think about it 未經核實地；不假思索地；即席地：*I don't know offhand how much we made last year.* 我一時還真説不清我們去年賺了多少錢。

of·fice 🗝 /ˈɒfɪs; *NAmE* ˈɔːf-; ˈɑːf-/ *noun*

▸ **ROOM/BUILDING** 房屋；建築物 **1** 🗝 [C] a room, set of rooms or building where people work, usually sitting at desks 辦公室；辦公樓：*The company is moving to new offices on the other side of town.* 公司要遷往城另一邊的新辦公樓。◇ *Are you going to the office today?* 你今天去辦公室嗎？◇ *an **office job*** 辦公室工作 ◇ ***office workers*** 辦公室人員 ➲ COLLOCATIONS at JOB ➲ VISUAL VOCAB page V69 ➲ see also BACK OFFICE, HEAD OFFICE **2** 🗝 [C] a room in which a particular person works, usually at a desk（某人的）辦公室：*Some people have to share an office.* 有些人只好合用一間辦公室。◇ *Come into my office.* 到我的辦公室裏來。**3** [C] (*NAmE*) (*BrE* **sur·gery**) a place where a doctor, dentist or VET sees patients 診室；門診處：*a **doctor's/dentist's office*** 診室；牙醫診所 **4** 🗝 [C] (often in compounds 常構成複合詞) a room or building used for a particular purpose, especially to provide information or a service 辦事處；（尤指）問詢處，服務處：*the local tourist office* 當地旅遊辦事處 ◇ *a ticket office* 售票處 ➲ see also BOX OFFICE, REGISTRY OFFICE

▸ **GOVERNMENT DEPARTMENT** 政府部門 **5 Office** [C] used in the names of some British government departments（用於英國某些政府部門的名稱中）：*the Foreign Office* 外交部 ◇ *the Home Office* 內政部

▸ **IMPORTANT POSITION** 重要職位 **6** 🗝 [U, C] an important position of authority, especially in government; the work and duties connected with this 要職；重要官職；重要職務：*She **held office** as a cabinet minister for ten years.* 她擔任內閣部長長達十年。◇ *How long has he been **in office**?* 他任職多久了？◇ *The party has been **out of office** (= has not formed a government) for many years.* 那個黨已在野多年了。◇ *The present government **took office** in 2009.* 現政府於 2009 年上台執政。◇ *to **seek/run for office*** 謀求 / 競選公職 ◇ (*BrE*) *to **stand for office*** 競選要職 ◇ *the office of treasurer* 司庫的職務 ➲ COLLOCATIONS at VOTE

IDM **through sb's good 'offices** (*formal*) with sb's help 經某人斡旋；承某人協助

'office block (*BrE*) (also **'office building** *NAmE*, *BrE*) *noun* a large building that contains offices, usually belonging to more than one company 辦公大樓（通常為幾家公司合用的）➲ VISUAL VOCAB page V3

'office boy, **'office girl** *noun* (*old-fashioned*) a young person employed to do simple tasks in an office 辦公室勤雜員

'office-holder (also **'office-bearer**) *noun* a person who is in a position of authority, especially in the government or a government organization 官員；公務員；高級職員

'office hours *noun* [pl.] the time when people in offices are normally working 辦公時間：*Our telephone lines are open during normal office hours.* 我們的電話在正常辦公時間一直開通。

of·fi·cer 🗝 /ˈɒfɪsə(r); *NAmE* ˈɔːf-; ˈɑːf-/ *noun*

1 🗝 a person who is in a position of authority in the armed forces 軍官：***army/airforce/naval, etc. officers*** 陸軍、空軍、海軍等軍官 ◇ *a **commissioned/non-commissioned officer*** 軍官；軍士 ◇ *The matter was passed on to me, as your **commanding officer**.* 作為你的指揮官，這件事轉到了我這裏。➲ see also FLYING OFFICER, PETTY OFFICER, PILOT OFFICER, WARRANT OFFICER **2** 🗝 (often in compounds 常構成複合詞) a person who is in a position of authority in the government or a large organization（政府或大機構的）官員，高級職員：*an environmental health officer* 環境衞生官員 ◇ *a customs/prison/welfare officer* 海關 / 監獄 / 福利官員 ◇ *officers of state* (= ministers in the government)（政府各部）部長 ➲ see also CHIEF EXECUTIVE OFFICER, MEDICAL OFFICER, PRESS OFFICER, PROBATION OFFICER, RETURNING OFFICER **3** 🗝 (often used as a form of address 常用作稱謂) = POLICE OFFICER：*the officer in charge of the case* 負責本案的警察 ◇ *the investigating officer* 進行調查工作的警察 ◇ *Yes, officer, I saw what happened.* 是，警察先生，我看到了發生的事。**4** (*NAmE*) a title for a police officer 警察的頭銜：*Officer Dibble* 迪布爾警官

'office worker *noun* a person who works in the offices of a business or company（公司、企業的）辦事人員；公司職員；上班族

of·fi·cial 🗝 /əˈfɪʃl/ *adj.*, *noun*

■ ***adj.*** **1** 🗝 [only before noun] connected with the job of sb who is in a position of authority 公務的；公職的；公事的：*official responsibilities* 公務 ◇ *the Prime Minister's official residence* 首相官邸 ◇ *He attended in his official capacity as mayor.* 他以市長的官方身分蒞臨。◇ *This was her first official engagement.* 這是她的首樁公務。◇ *He made an official visit to Tokyo in March.* 他於三月到東京進行了一次公務訪問。**2** 🗝 [usually before noun] agreed to, said, done, etc. by sb who is in a position of authority 正式的；官方的；官方授權的：*an official announcement/decision/statement* 官方公告 / 決定 / 聲明 ◇ *according to official statistics/figures* 根據官方統計 / 數字 ◇ *An official inquiry has been launched into the cause of the accident.* 當局已對事故的原因展開調查。◇ *The country's official language is Spanish.* 這個國家的官方語言為西班牙語。◇ *I intend to lodge an official complaint* (= to complain to sb in authority). 我打算正式提出申訴。◇ *The news is not yet official.* 這消息尚未經官方證實。**3** 🗝 [only before noun] that is told to the public but may not be true 公開的；公佈的；據傳報的：*I only knew the official version of events.* 我對事情的瞭解僅限於官方的版本。◇ *The official story has always been that they are just good friends.* 官方一直説他們只不過是好朋友。**4** 🗝 [only before noun] formal and attended by people in authority 正式的；公務的；官方場合的：*an official function/reception* 官方活動 / 招待會 ◇ *The official opening is planned for October.* 正式開幕擬在十月。OPP **unofficial**

■ ***noun*** 🗝 (often in compounds 常構成複合詞) a person who is in a position of authority in a large organization 要員；官員；高級職員：*a bank/company/court/government official* 銀行 / 公司 / 法院 / 政府要員 ◇ *a senior official in the State Department* 國務院的高級官員

of·fi·cial·dom /əˈfɪʃldəm/ *noun* [U] (*disapproving*) people who are in positions of authority in large organizations when they seem to be more interested in following rules than in being helpful 官僚；當官的人

of·fi·cial·ese /əˌfɪʃəˈliːz/ *noun* [U] (*disapproving*) language used in official documents that is thought by many people to be too complicated and difficult to understand 官場用語（複雜而難以理解）

of·fi·cial·ly 0-π /əˈfɪʃəli/ *adv.*
1 0-π publicly and by sb who is in a position of authority 正式地；官方地；公開地：*The library will be officially opened by the local MP.* 圖書館將由當地下院議員正式揭幕。◇ *We haven't yet been told officially about the closure.* 我們尚未接到關閉的正式通知。◇ *The college is not an officially recognized English language school.* 那所學院不是官方認可的英語學校。 **2** 0-π according to a particular set of rules, laws, etc. 依據法規等：*Many of those living on the streets are not officially homeless.* 根據法律定義，許多流浪街頭的人並非無家可歸者。◇ *I'm not officially supposed to be here.* 按公事說，我是不該到這裏來的。 **3** 0-π according to information that has been told to the public but that may not be true 據傳；據公佈：*Officially, he resigned because of bad health.* 據官方說法，他是因健康狀況不佳而辭職的。 OPP **unofficially**

of,ficial re'ceiver *noun* (*law* 律) (*BrE*) = RECEIVER (3)

of,ficial 'secret *noun* (in Britain) a piece of information known only to the government and its employees, which it is illegal for them to tell anyone under the Official Secrets Act 國家機密，官方機密（英國根據"國家機密法案"政府工作人員不得泄露的信息）

the Of,ficial 'Secrets Act *noun* (in Britain) a law that prevents people giving information if the government wants it to remain secret 官方機密法（英國禁止泄露政府機密的法規）

of·fi·ci·ate /əˈfɪʃieɪt/ *verb* **1** [I, T] **~ (at sth)** | **~ sth** to act as an official in charge of sth, especially a sports event 履行職務；（尤指體育比賽）擔任裁判：*A referee from a neutral country will officiate (at) the game.* 一名來自中立國的裁判將擔任這場比賽的裁判。 **2** [I] **~ (at sth)** (*formal*) to do the official duties at a public or religious ceremony 主持（儀式）；履行職務

of·fi·cious /əˈfɪʃəs/ *adj.* (*disapproving*) too ready to tell people what to do or to use the power you have to give orders 愛指手畫腳的；愛發號施令的 SYN **self-important**：*a nasty officious little man* 討厭、好管閒事的傢伙 ▸ **of·fi·cious·ly** *adv.*：*'You can't park here,' he said officiously.* "此處不准停車。"他裝腔作勢地說。 **of·fi·cious·ness** *noun* [U]

off·ing /ˈɒfɪŋ; *NAmE* ˈɔːf-; ˈɑːf-/ *noun*
IDM **in the offing** (*informal*) likely to appear or happen soon 即將發生：*I hear there are more staff changes in the offing.* 我聽說有更多的人事變動在醞釀中。

,off-'key *adj.* **1** (of a voice or a musical instrument 聲音或樂器) not in tune 走調；不和諧 **2** not suitable or correct in a particular situation 不得體；不相宜；不恰當；不適當 SYN **inappropriate**：*Some of his remarks were very off-key.* 他有些話說得很不得體。 ▸ **,off-'key** *adv.*：*to sing off-key* 唱走了調

'off-licence (*BrE*) (*US* **'liquor store**, **'package store**) *noun* a shop that sells alcoholic drinks in bottles and cans to take away 外賣酒店

,off-'limits *adj.* **1 ~ (to sb)** (of a place 地方) where people are not allowed to go 不准進入的；禁止入內的：*The site is off-limits to the general public.* 這個場所不對公眾開放。 **2** not allowed to be discussed 不許談論的；禁止探討的：*The subject was ruled off-limits.* 規定禁止談論這個話題。

off·line /ˌɒfˈlaɪn; *NAmE* ˌɔːf-; ˌɑːf-/ *adj.* (*computing* 計) not directly controlled by or connected to a computer or to the Internet 未聯機的；未連線的；脱機的；離線的：*For offline orders, call this number.* 離線訂貨請撥打這個號碼。 ▸ **off·line** *adv.*：*How do I write an email offline?* 如何在離線時寫電子郵件？ ➲ see also ONLINE

off·load /ˌɒfˈləʊd; *NAmE* ˌɔːfˈloʊd; ˌɑːf-/ *verb* to get rid of sth/sb that you do not need or want by passing it/them to sb else 把（擔子等）轉移（給別人）；減輕（負擔）；卸（包袱）：**~ sth/sb** *They should stop offloading waste from oil tankers into the sea.* 他們應當停止從油輪上往海裏傾倒廢棄物。◇ **~ sth/sb on/onto sb** *It's nice to have someone you can offload your problems onto.* 有個能分憂的人真是不錯。

,off-'peak *adj.* [only before noun] happening or used at a time that is less popular or busy, and therefore cheaper 非高峰期的；淡季的；離峰的：*off-peak electricity/travel* 非高峰時間的電力；淡季旅遊 ▸ **,off-'peak** *adv.*：*Phone calls cost 20c per unit off-peak.* 非高峰時間電話費每單位兩角。 ➲ compare PEAK *adj.*

,off-'piste *adj.* away from the tracks of firm snow that have been prepared for SKIING on 在滑雪道外的；非滑雪場地的：*off-piste skiing* 道外滑雪 ▸ **,off-'piste** *adv.*：*We enjoy skiing off-piste.* 我們喜歡在滑道外滑雪。

off·print /ˈɒfprɪnt; *NAmE* ˈɔːf-; ˈɑːf-/ *noun* a separate printed copy of an article that first appeared as part of a newspaper, magazine, etc.（報紙、雜誌等文章的）單行本

'off-putting *adj.* (*informal, especially BrE*) not pleasant, in a way that prevents you from liking sb/sth 令人煩惱的；令人討厭的：*I find his manner very off-putting.* 我覺得他的舉止令人頗為厭惡。

'off-ramp *noun* (*NAmE, SAfrE*) a road used for driving off a major road such as an INTERSTATE（高速公路等的）出口匝道 ➲ compare ON-RAMP

'off-road *adj.* [usually before noun] not on the public road 非公路上的；越野的：*an **off-road vehicle*** (= one for driving on rough ground) 越野車

,off-'roader *noun* **1** a vehicle which is driven across rough ground as a sport 越野車 **2** a person who drives a vehicle across rough ground as a sport 越野賽車手 ▸ **,off-'roading** *noun* [U]

,off-'screen *adj.* [only before noun] in real life, not in a film/movie 真實的；生活中的；非屏幕上的：*They were off-screen lovers.* 他們是真實生活中的情侶。 ▸ **,off-'screen** *adv.*：*She looks totally different off-screen.* 她在現實生活中看上去判若兩人。 ➲ compare ON-SCREEN

'off season *noun* [sing.] **1** the time of the year that is less busy in business and travel（生意和旅遊的）淡季 SYN **low season** **2** (*NAmE*) (*BrE* **close season**) (*sport* 體) the time during the summer when teams do not play important games（夏季的）比賽淡季 ▸ **,off-'season** *adj.* [only before noun]：*off-season prices* 淡季價格 **,off-'season** *adv.*：*We prefer to travel off-season.* 我們喜歡在淡季旅遊。

off·set AW /ˈɒfset; *NAmE* ˈɔːf-; ˈɑːf-/ *verb, adj.*
■ ***verb*** (**off·set·ting**, **off·set**, **off·set**) to use one cost, payment or situation in order to cancel or reduce the effect of another 抵消；彌補；補償：**~ sth** *Prices have risen in order to offset the increased cost of materials.* 為補償原料成本的增加而提高了價格。◇ **~ sth against sth** (*BrE*) *What expenses can you **offset against tax**?* 什麼開支可以獲得稅項減免？
■ ***adj.*** [only before noun] used to describe a method of printing in which ink is put onto a metal plate, then onto a rubber surface and only then onto the paper 膠印的 ➲ see also CARBON OFFSET

off·shoot /ˈɒfʃuːt; *NAmE* ˈɔːf-; ˈɑːf-/ *noun* **1** a thing that develops from sth, especially a small organization that develops from a larger one 分支；（尤指）分支機構 **2** (*technical* 術語) a new STEM that grows on a plant 蘖枝；分枝

off·shore /ˌɒfˈʃɔː(r); *NAmE* ˌɔːf-; ˌɑːf-/ *adj.* [usually before noun] **1** happening or existing in the sea, not far from the land 海上的；近海的：*offshore drilling* 近海鑽探 ◇ *an offshore island* 近海的島 **2** (of winds 風) blowing from the land towards the sea 向海的；離岸的：*offshore breezes* 習習陸風 **3** (*business* 商) (of money, companies, etc. 資金、公司等) kept or located in a country that has more generous tax laws than other places 設在海外（尤指稅制較寬鬆的國家）的；投放國外的；離岸的：*offshore investments* 境外投資 ▸ **off·shore** *adv.*：*a ship anchored offshore* 一艘泊在海上的船 ◇ *profits earned offshore* 境外贏利 ➲ compare INSHORE, ONSHORE

off·shor·ing /ˌɒfˈʃɔːrɪŋ; *NAmE* ˌɔːf-; ˌɑːf-/ *noun* [U] the practice of a company in one country arranging for people in another country to do work for it（公司的）離岸外包業務，外包國外業務：*the offshoring of* *call-centre jobs to India* 對印度電話客戶服務中心業務的離岸外包 ▸ **off·shore** *verb* **~ sth**

off·side *adj., noun*

■ **adj.** /ˌɒfˈsaɪd; *NAmE* ˌɔːf-; ˌɑːf-/ **1** (*US* also **off·sides**) in some sports, for example football (SOCCER) and HOCKEY, a player is **offside** if he or she is in a position, usually ahead of the ball, that is not allowed（足球、曲棍球等體育運動中）越位的：*He was offside when he scored.* 他將球攻進門時已越位了。◇ *the offside rule* 越位規則 **OPP** **onside** **2** (*BrE*) on the side of a vehicle that is furthest from the edge of the road（車輛）外側的，右側的：*the offside mirror* 右側鏡 **OPP** **nearside**

■ **noun** [U] **1** /ˌɒfˈsaɪd; *NAmE* ˌɔːf-; ˌɑːf-/ (*US* also **off·sides**) the fact of being offside in a game such as football (SOCCER) or HOCKEY（足球、曲棍球等體育運動中的）越位：*The goal was disallowed for offside.* 因為越位，進球無效。**2** /ˈɒfsaɪd; *NAmE* ˈɔːf-; ˈɑːf-/ (*BrE*) the side of a vehicle that is furthest from the edge of the road（車輛的）外側，遠側，右側：*The offside was damaged.* 車輛外側受損。**OPP** **nearside**

off·sider /ɒfˈsaɪdə(r); *NAmE* ɔːf-; ɑːf-/ *noun* (*AustralE, NZE, informal*) a person who works with or helps sb else 同事；工友；幫手

off·spring /ˈɒfsprɪŋ; *NAmE* ˈɔːf-; ˈɑːf-/ *noun* (*pl.* **off·spring**) (*formal* or *humorous*) **1** a child of a particular person or couple 孩子；子女；後代：*the problems parents have with their teenage offspring* 父母與青少年子女之間的問題 ◇ *to **produce/raise offspring*** 生育 / 撫養後代 **2** the young of an animal or plant 崽獸；幼崽；幼苗

off·stage /ˌɒfˈsteɪdʒ; *NAmE* ˌɔːf-; ˌɑːf-/ *adj.* **1** not on the stage in a theatre; not where the audience can see 舞台外的；幕後的：*offstage sound effects* 幕後音響效果 **2** happening to an actor in real life, not on the stage（演員的）現實生活的，私生活的；舞台下的：*The stars were having an offstage relationship.* 這對明星在現實生活中發展出戀情。▸ **off·stage** *adv.*：*The hero dies offstage.* 劇中主角並非死在台上。**OPP** **onstage**

ˈoff-street *adj.* [usually before noun] not on the public road 不在大街上的；大街以外的；路外的；後街的：*an apartment with **off-street parking*** 有後街街邊可停車的公寓 **OPP** **on-street**

ˌoff-the-ˈcuff ➲ CUFF *n.* **HELP** You will also find other compounds beginning **off-the-** at the entry for the last word in the compound. 其他以 off-the- 開頭的複合詞可在最後一個詞的詞條下找到。

ˌoff-the-ˈgrid (also **ˌoff-ˈgrid**) *adj.* (*especially NAmE*) not using the public supplies of electricity, gas, water, etc. 不入網的（不使用公用輸電網、煤氣輸送網、自來水網等）：*an off-the-grid house, independent of traditional utility services* 一所不依賴傳統公用服務設施的網外房子 ➲ see also OFF THE GRID at GRID

ˌoff-the-ˈshelf *adj.* [only before noun] (of a product 產品) that can be bought immediately and does not have to be specially designed or ordered 從貨架直接取下買走的；現成的：*off-the-shelf software packages* 現買軟件包 ➲ see also SHELF

ˌoff-ˈwhite *adj.* very pale yellowish-white in colour 米色的；米黃色的 ▸ **ˌoff-ˈwhite** *noun* [U]

ˈoff year *noun* (*US*) a year in which there are no important elections, especially no election for president 無重要選舉的年份；（尤指）非大選年 ▸ **ˈoff-year** *adj.*

OFSTED /ˈɒfsted; *NAmE* ˈɔːf-/ *abbr.* the Office for Standards in Education (a British government department that is responsible for checking that standards in schools are acceptable) 教育標準局（英國負責評鑒學校標準的政府部門，全寫為 Office for Standards in Education）

oft /ɒft; *NAmE* ɔːft; ɑːft/ *adv.* (*old use*) often 時常

oft- /ɒft; *NAmE* ɔːft; ɑːft/ *prefix* (in adjectives 構成形容詞) often 時常：*an oft-repeated claim* 一再重複的說法

often **O-w** /ˈɒfn; ˈɒftən; *NAmE* ˈɔːfn; ˈɔːftən; ˈɑːf-/ *adv.*
1 **O-w** many times 時常；常常 **SYN** **frequently**：*We often go there.* 我們常去那裏。◇ *I've often wondered what happened to him.* 我時常納悶他出了什麼事。◇ ***How often** do you go to the theatre?* 你多長時間看一次戲？◇ *I see her quite often.* 我常常見到她。◇ *Try to exercise as often as possible.* 盡可能經常鍛煉。◇ *We should meet for lunch more often.* 我們應該更常相約一起吃午飯。◇ ***It is not often that** you get such an opportunity.* 你得到這樣的機會，可不是常有的事。**2** **O-w** in many cases 往往；大多 **SYN** **commonly**：*Old houses are often damp.* 老房子大多都潮濕。◇ *People are often afraid of things they don't understand.* 人往往對自己不懂的東西感到恐懼。◇ ***All too often** the animals die through neglect.* 動物因缺乏照料而死亡的事司空見慣。

IDM **as ˌoften as ˈnot | more ˌoften than ˈnot** usually; in a way that is typical of sb/sth 通常；往往；一貫：*As often as not, he's late for work.* 他上班往往遲到。**ˌevery so ˈoften** occasionally; sometimes 有時；偶爾 ➲ more at ONCE *adv.*

often·times /ˈɒfntaɪmz; ˈɒftən-; *NAmE* ˈɔːfn-; ˈɔːftən-; ˈɑːf-/ *adv.* (*old use* or *NAmE*) often 常常

ogham (also **ogam**) /ˈɒgəm; *NAmE* ˈɑːg-/ *noun* [U] an ancient British and Irish alphabet of twenty characters 歐甘字母表（古英國和愛爾蘭字母表，有 20 個字母）

ogle /ˈəʊgl; *NAmE* ˈoʊgl/ *verb* [T, I] **~ (sb)** to look hard at sb in an offensive way, usually showing sexual interest（色迷迷地）盯着看，痴痴地看：*He was not in the habit of ogling women.* 他沒有盯着女人看個沒完的習慣。

ˈO grade (also **ˈordinary grade**) *noun* [C, U] (in Scotland in the past) an exam in a particular subject, at a lower level than HIGHERS, usually taken at the age of 16. In 1988 it was replaced by the STANDARD GRADE. 普通等級考試（蘇格蘭舊時的單科考試，低於高級考試，通常在 16 歲時參加。1988 年由標準等級考試取代）

ogre /ˈəʊgə(r); *NAmE* ˈoʊ-/ *noun* **1** (in stories) a cruel and frightening giant who eats people（傳說中的）食人惡魔 **2** a very frightening person 兇惡的人；可怕的人：*My boss is a real ogre.* 我的上司是個十足的惡魔。

ogress /ˈəʊgres; *NAmE* ˈoʊ-/ *noun* a female ogre 吃人女妖

oh **O-w** (also especially *literary* **O**) /əʊ; *NAmE* oʊ/ *exclamation*
1 **O-w** used when you are reacting to sth that has been said, especially if you did not know it before（表示領悟）哦，唔：*'I saw Ben yesterday.' 'Oh yes, how is he?'* "我昨天看見本了。" "哦，他好嗎？" ◇ *'Emma has a new job.' 'Oh, has she?'* "埃瑪新找了一份工作。" "噢，是嗎？" **2** **O-w** used to express surprise, fear, joy, etc.（表示驚奇、恐懼、高興等）啊，哈，哎喲：*Oh, how wonderful!* 啊，真是妙極了！◇ *Oh no, I've broken it!* 哎喲，我把它給打碎了！**3** **O-w** used to attract sb's attention（用以引起注意）喂，嘿，嗨：*Oh, Sue! Could you help me a moment?* 嘿，蘇！你幫會兒忙行不行？**4** **O-w** used when you are thinking of what to say next（用於思索想說的話時）嗯：*I've been in this job for, oh, about six years.* 我做這項工作，嗯，有六年左右了吧。

ohm /əʊm; *NAmE* oʊm/ *noun* (*physics* 物) a unit for measuring electrical RESISTANCE 歐姆（電阻單位）

ohm·meter /ˈəʊmmiːtə(r); *NAmE* ˈoʊm-/ *noun* (*physics* 物) a device for measuring electrical RESISTANCE 歐姆計；電阻表

oho /əʊˈhəʊ; *NAmE* oʊˈhoʊ/ *exclamation* used for showing that you are surprised in a happy way, or that you recognize sb/sth（表示驚喜或辨認出）啊哈，哦嗬

ˈoh-oh *exclamation* = UH-OH

OHP /ˌəʊ eɪtʃ ˈpiː; *NAmE* ˌoʊ eɪtʃ ˈpiː/ *noun* the abbreviation for OVERHEAD PROJECTOR 投影儀（全寫為 overhead projector）：*Will you be using an OHP?* 你用不用投影儀？

ˈoh-so *adv.* (*informal*) extremely 極其；非常：*their oh-so ordinary lives* 他們極其平凡的生活

OHT /ˌəʊ eɪtʃ ˈtiː; *NAmE* ˌoʊ eɪtʃ ˈtiː/ *noun* the abbreviation for 'overhead transparency' (a transparent plastic sheet that you can write or print sth on and show on a screen using an OVERHEAD PROJECTOR) 投影膠片（全寫為 overhead transparency，用於投影儀）

oi (also **oy**) /ɔɪ/ *exclamation* (*BrE, informal*) used to attract sb's attention, especially in an angry way（用以引起注

意，尤指憤怒地）嘿，嗨：*Oi, you! What do you think you're doing?* 嗨，你！你以為你在幹什麼？

-oid *suffix* (in adjectives and nouns 構成形容詞和名詞) similar to 類似的；相像的：*humanoid* 類人的 ◇ *rhomboid* 長菱形

oik /ɔɪk/ *noun* (*BrE, slang*) an offensive way of referring to a person that you consider rude or stupid, especially a person of a lower social class 蠢貨；大老粗

oil /ɔɪl/ *noun, verb*

■ ***noun*** **1** [U] a thick liquid that is found in rock underground 石油；原油 SYN **petroleum**：*drilling for oil* 鑽探石油 **2** [U] a form of PETROLEUM that is used as fuel and to make parts of machines move smoothly 燃油；潤滑油：*engine oil* 機油 ◇ *an* ***oil lamp/heater*** 油燈；用燃油的暖氣機 ◇ *Put some oil in the car.* 給汽車加點潤滑油。 **3** [U, C] a smooth thick liquid that is made from plants or animals and is used in cooking 食用油：*olive oil* 橄欖油 ◇ *vegetable oils* 植物油 **4** [U, C] a smooth thick liquid that is made from plants, minerals, etc. and is used on the skin or hair 防護油；潤膚油；護髮油：*lavender bath oil* 薰衣草沐浴油 ◇ *suntan oil* 防曬油 ➲ see also ESSENTIAL OIL **5** [U] (also **oils** [pl.]) coloured paint containing oil used by artists（繪畫用）油彩：*a painting done* ***in oils*** 一幅油畫 ◇ *landscapes in oil* 風景油畫 ➲ COLLOCATIONS at ART ➲ see also OIL PAINT **6** [C] = OIL PAINTING (1)：*Among the more important Turner oils was 'Venus and Adonis'.*《維納斯和阿多尼斯》是透納比較重要的油畫作品之一。➲ see also OILY, CASTOR OIL, COD LIVER OIL, LINSEED OIL IDM see BURN *v.*, POUR

■ ***verb*** **~ sth** to put oil onto or into sth, for example a machine, in order to protect it or make it work smoothly 給…加潤滑油：*He oiled his bike and pumped up the tyres.* 他給自己的自行車上了油，給輪胎充了氣。

IDM **oil the 'wheels** (*BrE*) (*NAmE* **grease the 'wheels**) to help sth to happen easily and without problems, especially in business or politics（尤指在商業上或政治上）起促進作用

'oil-bearing *adj.* [only before noun] producing or containing oil 產油的；含油的

oil·can /'ɔɪlkæn/ *noun* a metal container for oil, especially one with a long thin SPOUT, used for putting oil onto machine parts 油壺；（尤指）長嘴油壺

oil·cloth /'ɔɪlklɒθ; *NAmE* -klɔːθ/ *noun* [U] a type of cotton cloth that is covered on one side with a layer of oil so that water cannot pass through it, used especially in the past for covering tables 油布（一面塗上油以防水防濕，舊時尤用作桌布）

'oil colour (*especially US* **'oil color**) *noun* [C, U] = OIL PAINT

oiled /ɔɪld/ *adj.* **well ~** (*BrE, informal*) drunk 喝醉酒的

oil·field /'ɔɪlfiːld/ *noun* an area where oil is found in the ground or under the sea 油田

,oil-'fired *adj.* (of a heating system, etc. 暖氣系統等) burning oil as fuel 燃油的

oil·man /'ɔɪlmæn/ *noun* (*pl.* **-men** /-men/) a man who owns an oil company or works in the oil industry 石油商；石油大亨；石油工人

'oil paint (also **'oil colour**) *noun* [C, U] a type of paint that contains oil 油漆；油畫顏料

'oil painting *noun* **1** (also **oil**) [C] a picture painted in OIL PAINT 油畫 **2** [U] the art of painting in OIL PAINT 油畫藝術

IDM **be no 'oil painting** (*BrE, humorous*) used when you are saying that a person is not attractive to look at 相貌平平；非美人兒

'oil pan *noun* (*NAmE*) = SUMP (2)

'oil rig (also **'oil platform**) *noun* a large structure with equipment for getting oil from under the ground or under the sea 石油鑽塔；鑽油平台；油井設備 ➲ VISUAL VOCAB page V15

,oilseed 'rape *noun* [U] = RAPE *n.* (3)

oil·skin /'ɔɪlskɪn/ *noun* **1** [U] a type of cotton cloth that has had oil put on it in a special process so that water cannot pass through it, used for making WATERPROOF clothing 防水油布，防雨布（用於製作防水衣） **2** [C] a coat or jacket made of oilskin 防水外衣 **3 oilskins** [pl.] a set of clothes made of oilskin, worn especially by sailors（尤指水手穿的）防水服裝

'oil slick *noun* = SLICK *n.* (1)

'oil tanker *noun* a large ship with containers for carrying oil 油輪

'oil well (also **well**) *noun* a hole made in the ground to obtain oil 油井

oily /'ɔɪli/ *adj.* (**oil·ier**, **oili·est**) **1** containing or covered with oil 含油的；油污的；塗油的：*oily fish* 含油多的魚 ◇ *an oily rag* 油污的抹布 **2** feeling, tasting, smelling or looking like oil（質地、味道、氣味、形態）像油的：*an oily substance* 油狀物質 **3** (*disapproving*) (of a person or their behaviour 人或舉止) trying to be too polite, in a way that is annoying 油滑的；油腔滑調的；奉迎的：*an oily smile* 諂媚的微笑 SYN **obsequious** ▸ **oili·ness** *noun* [U]

oink /ɔɪŋk/ *exclamation, noun* used to represent the sound a pig makes（豬叫聲）哼

oint·ment /'ɔɪntmənt/ *noun* [U, C] a smooth substance that you rub on the skin to heal a wound or sore place 藥膏；軟膏；油膏 SYN **cream**：*antiseptic ointment* 抗菌軟膏 IDM see FLY *n.*

OJ /'əʊ dʒeɪ; *NAmE* 'oʊ/ *noun* [U] (*NAmE, informal*) the abbreviation for 'orange juice' 橙汁（全寫為 orange juice）

Ojibwa /əʊ'dʒɪbwɑː; *NAmE* oʊ-/ (*pl.* **Ojibwa** or **Ojib·was**) *noun* a member of a Native American people, many of whom live in the US states of Michigan, Wisconsin and Minnesota and in Ontario in Canada 奥吉布瓦人（美洲土著，很多居於美國密歇根、威斯康星、明尼蘇達諸州以及加拿大安大略省）

OK (also **okay**) /əʊ'keɪ; *NAmE* oʊ-/ *exclamation, adj., adv., noun, verb*

■ ***exclamation*** (*informal*) **1** yes; all right 對；好；行：*'Shall we go for a walk?' 'OK.'* "咱們去散散步，好不好？" "好。" **2** used to attract sb's attention or to introduce a comment（用以引起注意或引入話題）好了，對了：*Okay, let's go.* 好了，咱們走吧。 **3** used to check that sb agrees with you or understands you（用於確保別人贊同或明白）好嗎，行不：*The meeting's at 2, OK?* 兩點開會，明白嗎？◇ *I'll do it my way, OK?* 我想怎麼做就怎麼做，行嗎？ **4** used to stop people arguing with you or criticizing you（用以制止對方爭辯或批評）得了，行了，好了：*OK, so I was wrong. I'm sorry.* 行了，是我不對。對不起。

■ ***adj., adv.*** (*informal*) **1** safe and well; in a calm or happy state 安然無恙；平安；快活：*Are you OK?* 你沒事吧？ ➲ SYNONYMS at WELL **2** **~ (for sb) (to do sth)** all right; acceptable; in an acceptable way 可以；可行；尚可；不錯：*Is it OK if I leave now?* 我現在離開，可以嗎？◇ *Is it OK for me to come too?* 我也去，行嗎？◇ *Does my hair look okay?* 我的頭髮還看得過去嗎？◇ *I think I did OK in the exam.* 我覺得我考得還不錯。◇ *Whatever you decide,* ***it's okay by me.*** 無論你怎麼決定對我來說都行。◇ *an okay movie* 一部不錯的電影

■ ***noun*** [sing.] (*informal*) permission 允許；准許；同意 SYN **go ahead**：*I'm still waiting for the boss to give me the OK.* 我還在等上司點頭呢。

■ ***verb*** (**OK's**, **OK'ing**, **OK'd**, **OK'd**) **~ sth** (*informal*) to officially agree to sth or allow it to happen 正式批准；同意：*She filled in an expenses claim and her manager OK'd it.* 她填寫了一張費用申請單，她的經理批准了。SYN **approve**

okapi /əʊ'kɑːpi; *NAmE* oʊ-/ *noun* an African animal that belongs to the same family as the GIRAFFE, but is smaller with a dark body and white lines across its legs 獾㹢狓（棲於非洲，長頸鹿科動物，黑色，腿部有白紋）

oke /əʊk; *NAmE* oʊk/ (also **ou**) *noun* (*SAfrE, informal*) a man or a boy 小伙子；男孩：*He's quite a big oke.* 他是個塊頭不小的男生。

okey-doke /ˌəʊki ˈdəʊk; *NAmE* ˌoʊki ˈdoʊk/ (also **okey-dokey** /ˌəʊki ˈdəʊki; *NAmE* ˌoʊki ˈdoʊki/) *exclamation* (*BrE, informal*) used to express agreement （用以表示同意）好吧，好了 **SYN** OK

okra /ˈəʊkrə; ˈɒkrə; *NAmE* ˈoʊkrə/ (also **bhindi**) *noun* [U] (also ˌ**ladies' ˈfingers**) the green seed cases of the okra plant, eaten as a vegetable 秋葵（可食用） ➲ VISUAL VOCAB page V31

Synonyms 同義詞辨析

old

elderly • aged • long-lived • mature

These words all describe sb/sth that has lived for a long time or that usually lives for a long time. 以上各詞均形容人年紀大、長壽或事物古老、經久耐用、持久。

old having lived for a long time; no longer young 指年老、年紀大： *She's getting old—she's 75 next year.* 她上年紀了，明年就 75 歲了。

elderly (*rather formal*) used as a polite word for 'old' * old 的委婉語，指年紀較大的、上了年紀的： *She is very busy caring for two elderly relatives.* 她在忙着照顧兩個年老的親戚。

aged (*formal*) very old 指年邁的、年老的： *Having aged relatives to stay in your house can be quite stressful.* 年邁的親戚住在家裏有時壓力相當大。

long-lived having a long life; lasting for a long time 指壽命長的、長壽的、經久耐用的、持久的： *Everyone in my family is exceptionally long-lived.* 我們家每個人都特別長壽。

mature used as a polite or humorous way of saying that sb is no longer young 禮貌或幽默的說法，指某人已成年或不再年輕： *clothes for the mature woman* 成年婦女的服裝

PATTERNS

- a(n) old/elderly/aged/long-lived/mature **man/woman**
- a(n) old/elderly/aged/mature **gentleman/lady/couple**

old 🔑 /əʊld; *NAmE* oʊld/ *adj.* (**old·er, old·est**)

▸ AGE 年齡 **1** 🔑 **be … years, months, etc. ~** of a particular age 具體年齡；（多少）歲；年紀： *The baby was only a few hours old.* 嬰兒才出生幾個小時。◇ *In those days most people left school when they were only fifteen years old.* 那時候，大多數人上學只上到十五歲。◇ *At thirty years old, he was already earning £40 000 a year.* 他三十歲時已拿到 4 萬英鎊的年薪了。◇ *two fourteen-year-old boys* 兩個十四歲的男孩 ◇ *a class for five-year-olds* (= children who are five) 為五歲兒童開的班 ◇ *I didn't think she was* ***old enough*** *for the responsibility.* 我認為她尚年輕，不足以擔當此任。◇ ***How old*** *is this building?* 這座建築已有多少年了？◇ *He's the oldest player in the team.* 他是隊裏年齡最大的隊員。◇ *She's much older than me.* 她的年齡比我大得多。

▸ NOT YOUNG 不年輕 **2** 🔑 having lived for a long time; no longer young 老的；年紀大的；不年輕的： *to* ***get/grow old*** 變老 ◇ *The old man lay propped up on cushions.* 老人靠在墊子上躺着。◇ *She was a woman grown* ***old before her time*** (= who looked older than she was). 她顯得未老先衰。 **OPP** **young** **3 the old** *noun* [pl.] old people 老年人： *The old feel the cold more than the young.* 老年人比年輕人怕冷。

▸ NOT NEW 舊 **4** 🔑 having existed or been used for a long time 存在（或使用）時間長的；陳舊的；古老的： *old habits* 舊習慣 ◇ *He always gives the* ***same old*** *excuses.* 他總是找那些老掉牙的藉口。◇ *This carpet's getting pretty old now.* 這塊地毯現在已經很舊了。 **OPP** **new** **5** 🔑 [only before noun] former; belonging to past times or a past time in your life 過去的；從前的： *Things were different in* ***the old days***. 從前的情況可不一樣。◇ *I went back to visit my old school.* 我回去拜訪了母校。◇ *Old and Middle English* 古英語和中古英語 **6** 🔑 [only before noun] used to refer to sth that has been replaced by sth else（用於指稱被替代的東西）原來的，原先的： *We had more room in our old house.* 我們原先的房子比較寬敞。 **OPP** **new** **7** 🔑 [only before noun] known for a long time 相識時間長的；結識久的： *She's an old friend of mine* (= I have known her for a long time). 她是我的一個老朋友。◇ *We're old rivals.* 我們是老對頭。 ➲ compare RECENT

▸ GOOD OLD/POOR OLD 可愛；可憐 **8** [only before noun] (*informal*) used to show affection or a lack of respect（表示親昵或不拘禮節）： ***Good old*** *Dad!* 可愛的老爸！◇ *You* ***poor old*** *thing!* 你這可憐的傢伙！◇ *I hate her, the silly old cow!* 我恨她，那個笨蛋老女人！

IDM ˈ**any old how** (*informal*) in a careless or untidy way 隨便地；淩亂地： *The books were piled up all over the floor any old how.* 地板上書堆得亂七八糟的，到處都是。 ˈ**any old …** (*informal*) any item of the type mentioned (used when it is not important which particular item is chosen) 任何一個；隨便哪個： *Any old room would have done.* 隨便哪間屋子都行。 **as old as the ˈhills** very old; ancient 古老的；悠久的 **for ˈold times' sake** if you do sth **for old times' sake**, you do it because it is connected with sth good that happened to you in the past 看在舊日的情分上；念及老交情 **the ˈgood/ˈbad old days** an earlier period of time in your life or in history that is seen as better/worse than the present 往昔的好 / 苦日子： *That was in the bad old days of rampant inflation.* 那是在物價飛漲、生活艱難的往昔。 **of ˈold** (*formal* or *literary*) in or since past times 在往昔；從以前： *in days of old* 從前 ◇ *We know him of old* (= we have known him for a long time). 我們認識他很久了。 **old ˈboy, ˈchap, ˈman, etc.** (*old-fashioned, BrE, informal*) used by older men of the middle and upper classes as a friendly way of addressing another man （中上階層男子對其他男子的友好稱呼）老兄，夥計，哥們兒 **old enough to be sb's ˈfather/ˈmother** (*disapproving*) very much older than sb (especially used to suggest that a romantic or sexual relationship between the two people is not appropriate) 論年齡足以當某人的爹 / 娘（尤指雙方在愛情或性關係方面不相配） **old enough to know ˈbetter** old enough to behave in a more sensible way than you actually did 已長大，該懂事了 (**have**) **an old head on young ˈshoulders** used to describe a young person who acts in a more sensible way than you would expect for a person of their age 年輕老練；少年老成 **the** (ˌ**same**) **old ˈstory** what usually happens 慣常的事情；（仍舊是）那麼回事： *It's the same old story of a badly managed project with inadequate funding.* 又是一樁資金短缺、經營不善的老故事。 **an old ˈwives' tale** (*disapproving*) an old idea or belief that has been proved not to be scientific 不經之談；不科學的陳腐思想 **one of the ˈold school** an old-fashioned person who likes to do things as they were done in the past 守舊的人；保守派人物 ➲ see also OLD SCHOOL ➲ more at CHIP *n.*, FOOL *n.*, GRAND *adj.*, HEAVE-HO, HIGH *adj.*, MONEY, RIPE, SETTLE *v.*, TEACH, TOUGH *adj.*, TRICK *n.*

Which Word? 詞語辨析

older / elder

- The usual comparative and superlative forms of **old** are **older** and **oldest**. * old 的比較級和最高級通常為 older 和 oldest： *My brother is older than me.* 我哥哥比我大。◇ *The palace is the oldest building in the city.* 這宮殿是城裏最古老的建築。 In *BrE* you can also use **elder** and **eldest** when comparing the ages of people, especially members of the same family, although these words are not common in speech now. As adjectives they are only used before a noun and you cannot say 'elder than'. 在英式英語中，比較人的年齡，尤其是家庭成員的年齡時亦可用 elder 和 eldest，不過這種說法在口語中已不常見；作形容詞時它們只能用於名詞前，而且不說 elder than： *my older/elder sister* 我的姐姐 ◇ *the elder/older of their two children* 他們的兩個孩子中大的一個 ◇ *I'm the eldest/oldest in the family.* 我是家中最年長的。

ˌold ˈage *noun* [U] the time of your life when you are old 老年；暮年： *Old age can bring many problems.* 人老麻煩多。◇ *He lived alone* ***in his old age****.* 他孑然一身度過晚年。➲ COLLOCATIONS at AGE

ˌold-age ˈpension *noun* (*BrE*) a regular income paid by the state to people above a particular age 養老金；老年撫恤金

ˌold-age ˈpensioner *noun* (*abbr.* **OAP**) (*BrE*, becoming *old-fashioned*) a person who receives an old-age pension 領養老金者 ➲ see also SENIOR CITIZEN

ˌold age seˈcurity *noun* [U] (*abbr.* **OAS**) (*CanE*) a regular income paid by the government to people above the age of 65（加拿大政府給 65 歲以上的人定期發放的）老年保障金，養老金

the Old Bai·ley /ˌəʊld ˈbeɪli; *NAmE* ˌoʊld/ *noun* [sing.] the main criminal court in London 老貝利（倫敦中央刑事法院）

ˌold ˈbat *noun* (*BrE, informal, disapproving*) a silly or annoying old person 愚蠢的老人；傻老帽兒

the ˌOld ˈBill *noun* [sing.] (*BrE, informal*) the police 警方

old boy *noun* **1 ˈold boy** (*BrE*) a man who used to be a student at a particular school, usually a private one（通常指私立學校的）校友 **2 ˌold ˈboy** (*informal, especially BrE*) an old man 老人；老頭： *The old boy next door has died.* 隔壁的老頭去世了。➲ see also OLD GIRL

IDM **the ˌold ˈboy network** (*BrE, informal*) the practice of men who went to the same school using their influence to help each other at work or socially 校友關係網；老同學間的互相關照

ˌold ˈbuffer *noun* (*BrE, old-fashioned*) = BUFFER *n.* (4)

the ˈold country *noun* [sing.] the country where you were born, especially when you have left it to live somewhere else 祖國；故國

ˌold ˈdear *noun* (*BrE, informal*) an old woman 老太太；老婆婆

olde /əʊld; ˈəʊldi; *NAmE* oʊld; ˈoʊldi/ *adj.* [only before noun] (*old use*) a way of spelling 'old' that was used in the past and is now sometimes used in names and advertisements to give the impression that sth is traditional（old 的舊式拼法，現有時用於名稱或廣告，以使人感到某物是傳統的）： *a pub that tries to recreate the flavour of olde England* 一家力圖重現古英國風情的酒館

olden /ˈəʊldən; *NAmE* ˈoʊldən/ *adj.* [only before noun] existing a long time ago in the past 古老的；悠久的： *What was life like* ***in the olden days****, Gran?* 從前的生活是什麼樣的，奶奶？

ˌOld ˈEnglish (also **ˌAnglo-ˈSaxon**) *noun* [U] the English language before about 1150, which is very different from modern English 古英語（約公元 1150 年前的英語，與現代英語差異很大）

ˌOld ˌEnglish ˈsheepdog *noun* a very large dog with very long grey and white hair 英國牧羊犬

ˌold-eˈstablished *adj.* [only before noun] that has existed for a long time 年代久遠的；古老的；悠久的；固有的

olde worlde /ˌəʊldi ˈwɜːldi; *NAmE* ˌoʊldi ˈwɜːrldi/ *adj.* [usually before noun] (*BrE, humorous*) (of a place or its atmosphere 地方或其氣氛) trying deliberately to seem old-fashioned（故意顯得）古色古香的，古樸的： *the olde worlde atmosphere of the tea room with its log fire* 壁爐中燃燒着木柴的茶室的古樸氣氛

ˌold-ˈfashioned 🔑 *adj.* (sometimes *disapproving*) **1** 🔑 not modern; no longer fashionable 陳舊的；過時的；不時髦的 **SYN** **dated**： *old-fashioned clothes/styles/methods/equipment* 過時的衣服／式樣／方法／設備 ➲ compare FASHIONABLE **2** 🔑 (of a person 人) believing in old or traditional ways; having traditional ideas 保守的；守舊的；迂腐的： *My parents are old-fashioned about relationships and marriage.* 我父母對男女關係和婚姻問題思想保守得很。

ˌold ˈflame *noun* a former lover 舊情人： *She met an old flame at the party.* 她在聚會上遇到了舊情郎。

old girl *noun* **1 ˈold girl** (*BrE*) a woman who used to be a student at a particular school, usually a private one（通常指私立學校的）女校友 **2 ˌold ˈgirl** (*informal, especially BrE*) an old woman 老婆婆；老太太： *The old girl next door has died.* 隔壁的老太太去世了。

ˌOld ˈGlory *noun* (*NAmE*) a name for the flag of the US 古老的榮耀（指美國國旗）；星條旗

the ˌold ˈguard *noun* [sing.+sing./pl. v.] the original members of a group or an organization, who are often against change（守舊的）元老派；保守派；衛道士

ˌold ˈhand *noun* ~ **(at sth/at doing sth)** a person with a lot of experience and skill in a particular activity 老手；經驗豐富的人；在行的人： *She's an old hand at dealing with the press.* 她是與新聞界打交道的老手。

ˌold ˈhat *noun* [U] something that is old-fashioned and no longer interesting 陳腐的事物；過時的東西： *Today's hits rapidly become old hat.* 今日紅極一時的東西，很快就會過時。

oldie /ˈəʊldi; *NAmE* ˈoʊldi/ *noun* (*informal*) an old person or thing 老人；舊事物 ➲ see also GOLDEN OLDIE

old·ish /ˈəʊldɪʃ; *NAmE* ˈoʊldɪʃ/ *adj.* fairly old 相當老的；相當舊的

ˌold ˈlady *noun* (*informal*) a person's wife or mother 老婆；老媽

ˌold ˈlag *noun* (*BrE, informal*) a person who has been in prison many times 多次坐牢的人；慣犯

ˌold ˈmaid *noun* (*old-fashioned, disapproving*) a woman who has never married and is now no longer young 老姑娘；老處女

ˌold ˈman *noun* (*informal*) a person's husband or father 老公；老爸

ˌold ˈmaster *noun* **1** a famous painter, especially of the 13th–17th centuries in Europe（尤指歐洲 13 至 17 世紀的）繪畫大師，名畫家 **2** a picture painted by an old master 繪畫大師的作品

ˌOld ˈNick *noun* (*old-fashioned, humorous*) the DEVIL 魔鬼；撒旦

ˌold ˈpeople's home (*BrE*) (also **reˈtirement home** *NAmE, BrE*) *noun* a place where old people live and are cared for 養老院；敬老院

ˈold school *adj.* old-fashioned or traditional 古老的；古舊的；傳統的

ˌold school ˈtie *noun* (*BrE*) **1** [C] a tie worn by former students of a particular school, especially a private one（尤指私立學校的）校友領帶 **2 the old school tie** [sing.] used to refer to the fact of men who went to the same private school using their influence to help each other at work or socially, and to the traditional attitudes they share（私立學校校友間的）相互關照，校友情誼，共同繼承的思想觀念

ˌold ˈstager *noun* (*informal*) a person who has great experience in a particular activity 老手；老資格

old·ster /ˈəʊldstə(r); *NAmE* ˈoʊld-/ *noun* (*informal*) an old person 老人；老者

ˈold-style *adj.* [only before noun] typical of past fashions or times 老派的；陳腐的；迂腐的： *an old-style dress shop* 老派服裝店 ◇ *old-style politics* 陳舊的政治觀點

the ˌOld ˈTestament *noun* [sing.] the first part of the Bible, that tells the history of the Jews, their beliefs and their relationship with God before the birth of Christ《〈聖經〉舊約》➲ compare THE NEW TESTAMENT

ˈold-time *adj.* [only before noun] typical of the past 昔日的；過去的；舊式的： *old-time dancing* 古典舞蹈

ˌold-ˈtimer *noun* **1** a person who has been connected with a club or an organization, or who has lived in a place, for a long time 老會員；老成員；老居民；老資格的人 **SYN** **veteran** **2** (*NAmE*) an old man 老人

ˌold ˈwoman *noun* **1** (*informal, especially BrE*) a person's wife or mother 老婆；老媽 **2** (*BrE, disapproving*) a man who worries too much about things that are not important 像管家婆似的男人

the ˌOld ˈWorld *noun* [sing.] Europe, Asia and Africa 舊世界（指歐洲、亞洲和非洲）➲ compare THE NEW WORLD

O

ˈ**old-world** *adj.* [only before noun] (*approving*) belonging to past times; not modern 古式的；非現代的： *an old-world hotel with character and charm* 一家風格典雅的古式飯店

ole /əʊl; *NAmE* oʊl/ *adj.* used in written English to represent how some people say the word 'old'（用於書面英語，代表有些人說 old 一詞的方式）老的： *My ole man used to work there.* 我老爸曾在那兒做事。

olé /əʊˈleɪ; *NAmE* oʊ-/ *exclamation* (from *Spanish, informal*) used for showing approval or happiness（表示贊成或高興）好哇，哇噻

ole·agin·ous /ˌəʊliˈædʒɪnəs; *NAmE* ˌoʊ-/ *adj.* (*formal*) covered in oil or GREASE or containing a lot of oil or grease 塗油脂的；油膩的；油質的

ole·an·der /ˌəʊliˈændə(r); *NAmE* ˌoʊli-/ *noun* [C, U] a Mediterranean bush or tree with white, pink or red flowers and long pointed thick leaves 夾竹桃

Ol·es·tra™ /ɒˈlestrə; *NAmE* oʊˈl-/ *noun* [U] a substance which is used instead of fat in some foods 奧利斯特拉油（食物油脂替代品）

ˈ**O level** (also ˈ**ordinary level**) *noun* [C, U] (in England and Wales in the past) an exam in a particular subject, at a lower level than A LEVEL, usually taken at the age of 16. In 1988 it was replaced by the GCSE. 普通證書考試（過去英格蘭、威爾士對某科目的考試，低於高級證書考試，通常在 16 歲時參加。1988 年被普通中等教育證書 (GCSE) 取代）： *O level French* 法語普通證書考試 ◇ *She took six subjects at O level.* 她參加了六門課程的普通證書考試。◇ *He's got an O level in Russian.* 他通過了俄語普通證書考試。 ➲ compare GCE

ol·fac·tory /ɒlˈfæktəri; *NAmE* ɑːl-; oʊl-/ *adj.* [only before noun] (*technical* 術語) connected with the sense of smell 嗅覺的： ***olfactory cells/nerves/organs*** 嗅覺細胞／神經／器官

oli·garch /ˈɒlɪɡɑːk; *NAmE* ˈɑːləɡɑːrk/ *noun* **1** a member of an oligarchy 寡頭政治家；寡頭統治集團成員 **2** an extremely rich and powerful person, especially a Russian who became rich in business after the end of the former Soviet Union 商業大亨（尤指前蘇聯解體後發跡的俄羅斯人）

oli·garchy /ˈɒlɪɡɑːki; *NAmE* ˈɑːləɡɑːrki/ *noun* (*pl.* **-ies**) **1** [U] a form of government in which only a small group of people hold all the power 寡頭政治 **2** [C+sing./pl. v.] the people who hold power in an oligarchy 寡頭統治集團 **3** [C] a country governed by an oligarchy 寡頭統治的國家

olive /ˈɒlɪv; *NAmE* ˈɑːlɪv/ *noun, adj.*

▪ ***noun*** **1** [C] a small green or black fruit with a strong taste, used in cooking and for its oil 油橄欖；齊墩果；橄欖 **2** (also ˈ**olive tree**) [C] a tree on which olives grow 橄欖樹： *olive groves* 橄欖樹叢 **3** (also ˌ**olive ˈgreen**) [U] a yellowish-green colour 橄欖綠

▪ ***adj.*** **1** (also ˌ**olive-ˈgreen**) yellowish-green in colour 橄欖綠的 **2** (of skin 皮膚) yellowish-brown in colour 黃褐色的；淡褐色的： *an olive complexion* 淺褐色的面容

ˈ**olive branch** *noun* [usually sing.] a symbol of peace; sth you say or do to show that you wish to make peace with sb 橄欖枝；和平的象徵： *Management is **holding out an olive branch** to the strikers.* 資方向罷工者擺出願意協商的姿態。

ˌ**olive ˈdrab** *noun* [U] a dull green colour, used in some military uniforms 草綠色，草黃色，灰橄欖色（用於軍服）

ˌ**olive ˈoil** *noun* [U] oil produced from OLIVES, used in cooking and on salad 橄欖油（用於烹飪和涼拌色拉） ➲ see also EXTRA VIRGIN

ollie /ˈɒli; *NAmE* ˈɑːli/ *noun* (in SKATEBOARDING 滑板運動) a jump that is done by pushing one foot down hard on the back of the board 豚跳（一腳猛踩滑板後部的帶板起跳）

ology /ˈɒlədʒi; *NAmE* ˈɑːl-/ *noun* (*pl.* **-ies**) (*informal, humorous*) a subject of study 學科： *They come here with their ologies knowing nothing about life.* 他們帶着自己的種種學問來到這裏，對人生卻一無所知。

-ology, -logy *combining form* (in nouns 構成名詞) **1** a subject of study 學科；科目： *sociology* 社會學 ◇ *genealogy* 宗譜學 **2** a characteristic of speech or writing 用語特徵；寫作特點： *phraseology* 措辭 ◇ *trilogy* 三部曲 ▸ **-ological, -logical** (also **-ologic, -logic**) (in adjectives 構成形容詞)： *pathological* 病理學的 **-ologist, -logist** (in nouns 構成名詞)： *biologist* 生物學家

Olym·piad /əˈlɪmpiæd/ *noun* **1** an occasion when the modern Olympic games are held 奧林匹克運動會；奧運會： *The 26th Olympiad took place in Atlanta, Georgia.* 第 26 屆奧運會是在佐治亞州的亞特蘭大舉辦的。 **2** an international competition in a particular subject, especially a science 奧林匹克大賽（常用於科學有關的國際比賽）： *the 14th International Physics Olympiad* 第 14 屆國際奧林匹克物理競賽

Olym·pian /əˈlɪmpiən/ *adj.* (*formal*) like a god; powerful and impressive 似神的；威嚴的；超凡的

Olym·pic /əˈlɪmpɪk/ *adj.* [only before noun] connected with the Olympic Games 奧林匹克運動會的： *an Olympic athlete/medallist* 奧林匹克運動員／獎牌獲得者

the Oˌlympic ˈGames (also **the Olym·pics**) *noun* [pl.] an international sports festival held every four years in a different country 奧林匹克運動會；奧運會： *the Beijing Olympics, held in 2008* * 2008 年在北京舉行的奧林匹克運動會

om·buds·man /ˈɒmbʊdzmən; -mæn; *NAmE* ˈɑːm-/ *noun* (*pl.* **-men** /-mən; -men/) an official whose job is to examine and report on complaints made by ordinary people about companies, the government or public authorities 政府巡查員，巡視官，申訴專員（政府處理民眾訴願的官員）

omega /ˈəʊmɪɡə; *NAmE* oʊˈmeɡə/ *noun* the last letter of the Greek alphabet (Ω, ω) 歐米加（希臘字母表的最後一個字母）

ˌ**Omega-ˈ3** /ˌəʊmɪɡə ˈθriː; *NAmE* oʊˌmeɪɡə/ (also ˌ**Omega-3 fatty ˈacid**) *noun* any of a group of acids, found mainly in fish oils, that many people think are important for human health * Ω-3 脂肪酸（魚油中多含，據信有利於人體健康）

om·elette (*NAmE* also **om·elet**) /ˈɒmlət; *NAmE* ˈɑːm-/ *noun* a hot dish of eggs mixed together and fried, often with cheese, meat, vegetables, etc. added 煎蛋捲，攤雞蛋（常加入奶酪、肉和蔬菜）： *a cheese and mushroom omelette* 奶酪、蘑菇蛋餅

IDM **you can't make an ˌomelette without breaking ˈeggs** (*saying*) you cannot achieve sth important without causing a few small problems 不打破雞蛋就炒不成蛋餅；不花代價就難成大事

omen /ˈəʊmən; *NAmE* ˈoʊ-/ *noun* a sign of what is going to happen in the future 預兆；前兆；徵兆 **SYN** **portent**： *a **good/bad omen*** 吉祥的／不祥的預兆 ◇ *an **omen of death/disaster*** 死亡／災難的徵兆 ◇ **~ for sth** *The omens for their future success are not good.* 他們未來成功的預兆不祥。

omi·cron /əʊˈmaɪkrɒn; *NAmE* ˈɑːməkrɑːn/ *noun* the 15th letter of the Greek alphabet (Ο, ο) 希臘字母表的第 15 個字母

om·in·ous /ˈɒmɪnəs; *NAmE* ˈɑːm-/ *adj.* suggesting that sth bad is going to happen in the future 不祥的；惡兆的；不吉利的 **SYN** **foreboding**： *There were ominous dark clouds gathering overhead.* 不祥的黑雲在頭頂上匯聚。◇ *She picked up the phone but there was an ominous silence at the other end.* 她拿起電話，但對方只有不祥的沉默。 ▸ **om·in·ous·ly** *adv.*

omis·sion /əˈmɪʃn/ *noun* (*formal*) **1** [U] **~ (from sth)** the act of not including sb/sth or not doing sth; the fact of not being included/done 省略；刪除；免除： *Everyone was surprised at her omission from the squad.* 她未列入該小組使大家感到驚訝。◇ *The play was shortened by the omission of two scenes.* 此劇刪減了兩場戲。◇ *sins of omission* (= not doing things that should be done) 瀆職罪 **2** [C] a thing that has not been included or done 遺漏；疏忽： *There were a number of errors and omissions in the article.* 這篇文章中有多處錯誤和疏漏。

omit /əˈmɪt/ *verb* (**-tt-**) (*formal*) **1** to not include sth/sb, either deliberately or because you have forgotten

O

it/them 刪除；忽略；漏掉；遺漏 SYN **leave out**：**~ sth/sb** *If you are a student, you can omit questions 16–18.* 學生可以免做 16–18 題。◇ **~ sth/sb from sth** *People were surprised that Smith was omitted from the team.* 人們感到驚訝，史密斯竟未列入該隊。 **2 ~ to do sth** to not do or fail to do sth 不做；未能做：*She omitted to mention that they were staying the night.* 她沒說他們當晚要留宿的事。

omni- /ˈɒmnɪ-; NAmE ˈɑːm-/ *combining form* (in nouns, adjectives and adverbs 構成名詞、形容詞和副詞) of all things; in all ways or places 總；全部；遍：*omnivore* 雜食動物 ◇ *omnipresent* 無所不在的

omni·bus /ˈɒmnɪbəs; NAmE ˈɑːm-/ *noun, adj.*

■ *noun* **1** (*BrE*) a television or radio programme that combines several recent programmes in a series（廣播、電視）綜合節目：*the 90-minute Sunday omnibus edition* 該節目長達 90 分鐘的週日綜合版 **2** a large book that contains a number of books, for example novels by the same author（若干種作品的）彙編，選集 **3** (*old-fashioned*) a bus 公共汽車

■ *adj.* (*NAmE*) including many things or different types of thing 綜合性的；選編的：*an omnibus law*（含多項法令的）綜合法令

omni·dir·ec·tion·al /ˌɒmnɪdəˈrekʃənl; -dɪˈr-; -daɪˈr-; NAmE ˌɑːmnɪ-/ *adj.* (*technical* 術語) receiving or sending signals in all directions（接收或發射信號）全向的：*an omnidirectional microphone* 全向話筒

om·nipo·tent /ɒmˈnɪpətənt; NAmE ɑːm-/ *adj.* (*formal*) having total power; able to do anything 萬能的；全能的；無所不能的：*an omnipotent God* 全能的上帝 ▶ **om·nipo·tence** /-təns/ *noun* [U]：*the omnipotence of God* 上帝的全能

omni·pres·ent /ˌɒmnɪˈpreznt; NAmE ˌɑːm-/ *adj.* (*formal*) present everywhere 無所不在的；遍及各處的：*These days the media are omnipresent.* 現在新聞媒體無處不在。▶ **omni·pres·ence** /ˌɒmnɪˈprezns; NAmE ˌɑːm-/ *noun* [U]

O

om·nis·ci·ent /ɒmˈnɪsiənt; NAmE ɑːm-/ *adj.* (*formal*) knowing everything 無所不知的；全知全能的；博聞廣識的：*The novel has an omniscient narrator.* 這部小說有一個全知全能的敘述者。▶ **om·nis·ci·ence** /-siəns/ *noun* [U]

omni·vore /ˈɒmnɪvɔː(r); NAmE ˈɑːm-/ *noun* an animal or a person that eats all types of food, especially both plants and meat 雜食動物；雜食的人 ➲ compare CARNIVORE, HERBIVORE, INSECTIVORE

om·niv·or·ous /ɒmˈnɪvərəs; NAmE ɑːm-/ *adj.* **1** (*technical* 術語) eating all types of food, especially both plants and meat 雜食的；（尤指）動、植物都吃的 ➲ compare CARNIVOROUS at CARNIVORE, HERBIVOROUS at HERBIVORE **2** (*formal*) having wide interests in a particular area or activity 興趣廣泛的：*She has always been an omnivorous reader.* 她一向閱讀興趣廣泛。

on 🔑 /ɒn; NAmE ɑːn; ɔːn/ *prep., adv.*

■ *prep.* HELP For the special uses of **on** in phrasal verbs, look at the entries for the verbs. For example **turn on sb** is in the phrasal verb section at **turn**. * on 在短語動詞中的特殊用法見有關動詞詞條。如 turn on sb 在詞條 turn 的短語動詞部份。 **1** 🔑 in or into a position covering, touching or forming part of a surface（覆蓋、附着）在…上（意指接觸物體表面或構成物體表面的一部份）：*a picture on a wall* 牆上的畫 ◇ *There's a mark on your skirt.* 你裙子上有一塊斑。◇ *the diagram on page 5* 第 5 頁上的圖解 ◇ *Put it down on the table.* 把它放在桌子上。◇ *He had been hit on the head.* 他被打中了腦袋。◇ *She climbed on to the bed.* 她爬上了牀。HELP This could also be written 此句亦可寫作：*onto the bed* **2** 🔑 supported by sb/sth 由…支撐着：*She was standing on one foot.* 她單腳站立着。◇ *Try lying on your back.* 試着仰卧。◇ *Hang your coat on that hook.* 把衣服掛在衣鈎上。 **3** 🔑 used to show a means of transport 在（運輸工具）上：*He was on the plane from New York.* 他在紐約來的飛機上。◇ *to travel on the bus/tube/coach* 乘公共汽車／地鐵／長途汽車 ◇ *I came on my bike.* 我騎自行車來的。◇ *a woman on horseback* 騎馬的女郎 **4** 🔑 used to show a day or date 在（某一天）：*He came on Sunday.* 他是星期天來的。◇ *We meet on Tuesdays.* 我們每星期二見面。◇ *on May the first/the first of May* 在五月一日 ◇ *on the evening of May the first* 在五月一日的晚上 ◇ *on one occasion* 曾經有一次 ◇ *on your birthday* 在你生日那天 **5** 🔑 immediately after sth 就在…之後；一…就：*On arriving home I discovered they had gone.* 我一到家就發現他們已經離開了。◇ *Please report to reception on arrival.* 到達後請立即到接待處報到。◇ *There was a letter waiting for him on his return.* 他一回來就有一封信在等着他看。 **6** 🔑 about sth/sb 關於（事或人）：*a book on South Africa* 一本關於南非的書 ◇ *She tested us on irregular verbs.* 她考了我們的不規則動詞。 **7** being carried by sb; in the possession of sb（身上）帶着；有：*Have you got any money on you?* 你帶錢了沒有？ **8** 🔑 used to show that sb belongs to a group or an organization 為（某團體或組織）的一員：*to be on the committee/staff/jury/panel* 為委員會／全體職員／陪審團／評判小組的成員 ◇ *Whose side are you on* (= which of two or more different views do you support)? 你支持哪一方的觀點？ **9** 🔑 eating or drinking sth; using a drug or a medicine regularly 吃；喝；按時服用（藥物）：*He lived on a diet of junk food.* 他把垃圾食品當飯吃。◇ *The doctor put me on antibiotics.* 醫生要我服用抗生素。 **10** 🔑 used to show direction（表示方向）在，向，對：*on the left/right* 在左邊／右邊 ◇ *He turned his back on us.* 他轉過身去背對着我們。 **11** 🔑 at or near a place 在，接近（某地）：*a town on the coast* 沿海的城鎮 ◇ *a house on the Thames* 泰晤士河畔的房子 ◇ *We lived on an estate.* 我們住在一處莊園上。 **12** 🔑 used to show the basis or reason for sth 根據；由於：*a story based on fact* 基於事實的小說 ◇ *On their advice I applied for the job.* 我聽從他們的建議申請了這份工作。 **13** 🔑 paid for by sth 以…支付；由…支付：*to live on a pension/a student grant* 靠養老金／助學金生活 ◇ *to be on a low wage* 掙低工資 ◇ *You can't feed a family on £50 a week.* 你無法靠每週 50 英鎊養活一家人。◇ *Drinks are* **on me** (= I am paying). 飲料錢由我付。 **14** 🔑 by means of sth; using sth 通過；使用；借助於：*She played a tune on her guitar.* 她用她的吉他彈了一支曲子。◇ *The information is available on the Internet.* 相關信息可從互聯網上找到。◇ *We spoke on the phone.* 我們通過電話談了談。◇ *What's on TV?* 電視上有什麼節目？◇ *The programme's on Channel 4.* 這個節目在 4 頻道。 **15** 🔑 used with some nouns or adjectives to say who or what is affected by sth（與某些名詞或形容詞連用，表示影響到）：*a ban on smoking* 對吸煙的禁令 ◇ *He's hard on his kids.* 他對自己的孩子很嚴厲。◇ *Go easy on the mayo!* (= do not take/give me too much) 少放一點蛋黃醬！ **16** compared with sb/sth 與…相比：*Sales are up on last year.* 銷售量比去年增長了。 **17** 🔑 used to describe an activity or a state（用於說明活動或狀態）：*to be on business/holiday/vacation* 在工作／度假中 ◇ *The book is currently on loan.* 該書已借出。 **18** 🔑 used when giving a telephone number（用於提供電話號碼）：*You can get me on 020 7946 0887.* 你找我可以撥打 020 7946 0887。◇ *She's on extension 2401.* 她的分機號是 2401。

■ *adv.* HELP For the special uses of **on** in phrasal verbs, look at the entries for the verbs. For example **get on** is in the phrasal verb section at **get**. * on 在短語動詞中的特殊用法見有關動詞詞條。如 get on 在詞條 get 的短語動詞部份。 **1** 🔑 used to show that sth continues（表示持續性）：*He worked on without a break.* 他毫不停歇地繼續工作。◇ *If you like a good story, read on.* 欲知故事的趣味所在，請往下讀。 **2** 🔑 used to show that sb/sth moves or is sent forward 向前（移動）：*She stopped for a moment, then walked on.* 她停了一會兒，然後又向前走。◇ *Keep straight on for the beach.* 一直向前走到海灘。◇ *From then on he never trusted her again.* 從那時起，他再也不信任她了。◇ *Please send the letter on to my new address.* 請把信件轉寄到我的新地址。 **3** 🔑 on sb's body; being worn 穿在身上；穿着；戴着：*Put your coat on.* 把外衣穿上。◇ *I didn't have my glasses on.* 我沒戴眼鏡。◇ *What did she have on* (= what was she wearing)? 她穿着什麼衣服？ **4** 🔑 covering, touching or forming part of sth（表示覆蓋、接觸某物或成為某物的一部份）：*Make sure the lid is on.* 要注意蓋上蓋子。 **5** 🔑 connected or operating; being used（表示已連接、處於工作狀態或使用中）：*The lights were all on.* 燈都亮着。◇ *The TV* *is always on in their house.* 他們家的電視總是開着。◇ *We were without electricity for three hours but it's on again now.* 我們停電三個小時了，不過現在又來電了。 **6** happening（表示發生）：*There was a war on at the time.* 當時正值戰爭。◇ *What's on at the movies?* 電影院在上演什麼片子？◇ *The band are on* (= performing) *in ten minutes.* 樂隊再過十分鐘開始演奏。 **7** planned to take place in the future（預先安排的事）將發生：*The game is still on* (= it has not been cancelled). 比賽仍將舉行。◇ *I don't think we've got anything on this weekend.* 我想這個週末我們沒安排活動。◇ *I'm sorry we can't come—we've* ***got a lot on***. 很抱歉我們去不了，我們安排得太滿了。 **8** on duty; working 值班；執行任務中：*I'm on now till 8 tomorrow morning.* 我正在值班，要值到明早 8 點鐘。 **9** in or into a vehicle 登上（車輛）：*The bus stopped and four people got on.* 公共汽車停下來，四個人上了車。◇ *They hurried on to the plane.* 他們匆忙登上了飛機。 ➲ see also ONTO

IDM **be 'on about sth** (*informal*) to talk about sth; to mean sth 談論（某事）；有…的意思：*I didn't know what he was on about. It didn't make sense.* 我不知道他說的是什麼，他說得不清不楚的。 **be/go/keep 'on about sth** (*informal, disapproving*) to talk in a boring or complaining way about sth 抱怨；嘮叨；發牢騷：*Stop keeping on about it!* 別再嘮叨那件事了！ **be/go/keep 'on at sb (to do sth)** (*informal, disapproving*) to keep asking or telling sb sth so that they become annoyed or tired（對某人）絮叨；說（或問）得令人生厭：*He was on at me again to lend him money.* 他又來纏着我借錢給他。 **be 'on for sth** (*informal*) to want to do sth 想要做某事：*Is anyone on for a drink after work?* 有人想下班後喝一杯嗎？ **it isn't 'on** (*informal*) used to say that sth is not acceptable 不行；沒門兒 **,on and 'on** without stopping; continuously 連續不停地；持續地：*She went on and on about her trip.* 她沒完沒了地談她的旅行。 **what are you, etc. 'on?** (*informal*) used when you are very surprised at sb's behaviour and are suggesting that they are acting in a similar way to sb using drugs 你鬼迷心竅了吧；你吃錯藥了吧 **you're 'on** (*informal*) used when you are accepting a bet（用於接受打賭）賭就賭吧 ➲ more at OFF *adv.*

,on-'air *adj.* (in radio and television 用於廣播及電視) being broadcast 正在播放：*She explains how she deals with on-air technical problems.* 她解釋了她是如何處理播放中的技術問題的。 OPP **off-air** IDM see AIR *n.*

onan·ism /'əʊnənɪzəm; *NAmE* 'oʊ-/ *noun* [U] (*formal*) **1** = MASTURBATION at MASTURBATE **2** = COITUS INTERRUPTUS

,on-'board *adj.* [only before noun] **1** on a ship, aircraft or vehicle 在船（或飛機、車）上的：*an on-board motor* 舷內發動機 **2** (*computing* 計) relating to, or controlled by, part of the main CIRCUIT BOARD 主板（控制）的；板上的：*a PC with on-board sound* 有板上聲卡的個人電腦

,on-'call [only before noun] (*especially NAmE*) (of a doctor, police officer, etc. 醫生、警察等) available for work if necessary, especially in an emergency（尤指緊急情況下）隨叫隨到的：*on-call doctors* 隨時應診的醫生 ➲ see also CALL *n.*

once /wʌns/ *adv., conj.*

■ ***adv.*** **1** on one occasion only; one time 僅一次；一次：*I've only been there once.* 我只去過那裏一次。◇ *He cleans his car* ***once a*** *week.* 他每週洗一次汽車。◇ *She only sees her parents* ***once every*** *six months.* 她每半年才探望一次父母。◇ (*informal*) *He only did it* ***the once***. 這種事兒他僅僅幹過一次。 **2** at some time in the past 曾；曾經：*I once met your mother.* 我曾經見過你母親。◇ *He once lived in Zambia.* 他曾在贊比亞生活過。◇ *This book was famous once, but nobody reads it today.* 這本書曾名噪一時，但現在卻無人問津。 **3** used in negative sentences and questions, and after *if* to mean 'ever' or 'at all'（用於否定句、疑問句和 if 後）曾，根本：*He never once offered to help.* 他從沒有主動提出過幫忙。◇ *If she once decides to do something, you won't change her mind.* 她一旦決定幹什麼，誰也改變不了她的主意。

IDM **,all at 'once** **1** suddenly 突然；驟然；忽然：*All at once she lost her temper.* 她突然大發脾氣。 **2** all together; at the same time 一起；同時 SYN **simultaneously**：*I can't do everything all at once—you'll have to be patient.* 我不能萬事一把抓呀。你可急不得。 **at 'once** **1** immediately; without delay 立即；馬上：*Come here at once!* 馬上到這裏來！ **2** at the same time 同時 SYN **simultaneously**：*Don't all speak at once!* 不要大家同時講！◇ *I can't do two things at once.* 我不能同時做兩件事。 **(just) for 'once | just this 'once** (*informal*) on this occasion (which is in contrast to what happens usually) 僅此一次（與通常情況對比而言）：*Just for once he arrived on time.* 只有這一次他按時到了。◇ *Can't you be nice to each other just this once?* 難道你們就不能彼此客氣哪怕一次？ **going 'once, going 'twice, 'sold** (*especially NAmE*) (*BrE* also **,going, ,going, 'gone**) said by an AUCTIONEER to show that an item has been sold（拍賣師用語）一次，二次，成交 **once a'gain | once 'more** one more time; another time 再一次；再次：*Once again the train was late.* 火車又一次晚點了。◇ *Let me hear it just once more.* 讓我再聽一遍。 **once a ..., always a ...** used to say that sb cannot change（表示一個人不能改變）一次為…便永遠是…：*Once an actor, always an actor.* 一朝從藝，永為藝人。 **once and for 'all** now and for the last time; finally or completely 最終地；最後地；徹底地；一次了結地：*We need to settle this once and for all.* 我們需要把這事一次解決。 **,once 'bitten, ,twice 'shy** (*saying*) after an unpleasant experience you are careful to avoid sth similar 一朝被蛇咬，十年怕井繩 **once in a blue 'moon** (*informal*) very rarely 極少地；難得地；破天荒地 **(every) ,once in a 'while** occasionally 偶爾地；間或 **,once or 'twice** a few times 一兩次；幾次：*I don't know her well, I've only met her once or twice.* 我跟她不很熟，我只見過她一兩次。 **,once too 'often** used to say that sb has done sth wrong or stupid again, and this time they will suffer because of it 僥幸難再：*You've tried that trick once too often.* 你故伎重施，可這次再逃不脫了。 **,once upon a 'time** used, especially at the beginning of stories, to mean 'a long time in the past'（用於故事的開頭）從前，很久以前：*Once upon a time there was a beautiful princess.* 從前，有一位美麗的公主。

■ ***conj.*** as soon as; when 一…就；一旦；當…時候：*We didn't know how we would cope once the money had gone.* 一旦錢花光了，我們就不知道該怎麼辦了。◇ *The water is fine once you're in!* 你一旦下了水，就會覺得水裏挺舒適。

'once-over *noun*

IDM **give sb/sth a/the 'once-over** (*informal*) **1** to look at sb/sth quickly to see what they or it are like 匆匆打量；隨便看一眼 **2** to clean sth quickly 匆匆打掃：*She gave the room a quick once-over before the guests arrived.* 趁客人還沒來，她匆匆把屋子打掃了一下。

on·col·ogy /ɒŋ'kɒlədʒi; *NAmE* ɑn'kɑːl-/ *noun* [U] the scientific study of and treatment of TUMOURS in the body 腫瘤學 ▸ **on·colo·gist** /ɒŋ'kɒlədʒɪst; *NAmE* ɑːn'kɑːl-/ *noun*

on·com·ing /'ɒnkʌmɪŋ; *NAmE* 'ɑːn-; 'ɔːn-/ *adj.* [only before noun] coming towards you 迎面而來的；即將來臨的 SYN **approaching**：*Always walk facing the oncoming traffic.* 走路一定要面向駛來的車輛。

'on-de'mand *adj.* [only before noun] done or happening whenever sb asks 按需的；隨選即行提供的：*The new network promises lightning-fast access to on-demand video.* 新的網絡會以閃電般的速度接入視頻點播。 ➲ see also DEMAND *n.*, PRINT ON DEMAND

one /wʌn/ *number, det., pron.*

■ ***number, det.*** **1** the number 1 一：*Do you want one or two?* 你要一個還是兩個？◇ *There's only room for one person.* 空間只能容一個人。◇ *One more, please!* 請再來一個！◇ *a one-bedroomed apartment* 一臥室的公寓房 ◇ *I'll see you at one* (= one o'clock). 我一點鐘見你。 **2** used in formal language or for emphasis before *hundred, thousand*, etc., or before a unit of measurement（正式用語或表示強調，用在 hundred、thousand 等或度量單位之前）一：*It cost one hundred and fifty pounds.* 那東西花了一百五十英鎊。◇ *He lost by less than one second.* 他以不到一秒鐘的差距輸了比賽。 **3** used for emphasis to mean 'a single' or 'just one'（表示強調）

O

單獨一個，僅僅一個：*There's only one thing we can do.* 我們能做的只有一件事。 **4** ⚷ a person or thing, especially when they are part of a group（尤指一組中的）一個人，一件事物：*One of my friends lives in Brighton.* 我有一個朋友住在布萊頓。◇ *One place I'd really like to visit is Bali.* 我真正想去看的一個地方就是巴厘島。 **5** ⚷ used for emphasis to mean 'the only one' or 'the most important one'（表示強調）唯一的一個，最重要的一個：*He's the one person I can trust.* 他是我唯一可以信賴的人。◇ *Her one concern was for the health of her baby.* 她唯一操心的就是孩子的健康。◇ *It's the one thing I can't stand about him.* 這是我最不能容忍他的一件事。 **6** ⚷ used when you are talking about a time in the past or the future, without actually saying which one（用於一般地談論過去或將來的某個時間）：*I saw her one afternoon last week.* 我在上週的一個下午見到了她。◇ ***One day*** (= at some time in the future) *you'll understand.* 總有一天你會明白的。 **7** ⚷ the same 同一個：*They all went off in one direction.* 他們都朝同一個方向走了。 **8** (*informal, especially NAmE*) used for emphasis instead of *a* or *an*（代替 a 或 an，表示強調）：*That was one hell of a game!* 那一場比賽簡直一塌糊塗！◇ *She's one snappy dresser.* 她的穿着很入時。 **9** used with a person's name to show that the speaker does not know the person（與人名連用，表示説話人不認識的人）某一個 SYN **a certain**：*He worked as an assistant to one Mr Ming.* 他給一位明先生當助手。

IDM **as 'one** (*formal*) in agreement; all together 一致；一齊：*We spoke as one on this matter.* 在這個問題上我們口徑一致。 **(be) at 'one (with sb/sth)** (*formal*) to feel that you completely agree with sb/sth, or that you are part of sth 完全一致；是…的一部份：*a place where you can feel at one with nature* 一個能讓你感到與大自然融為一體的地方 **for 'one** used to emphasize that a particular person does sth and that you believe other people do too 就是其中之一（表達意見時用以加強語氣）：*I, for one, would prefer to postpone the meeting.* 主張推遲會期的，我就是當中一人。 **get sth in 'one** to understand or guess sth immediately 立即明白（或猜到） **get one 'over (on) sb/sth** (*informal*) to get an advantage over sb/sth 佔上風；勝過；佔優勢：*I'm not going to let them get one over on me!* 我決不讓他們勝過我！ **go one 'better (than sb/sth)** to do sth better than sb else or than you have done before 勝人一籌；（比自己過去）做得更好 SYN **outdo**：*She did well this year and next year she hopes to go one better.* 今年她幹得不錯，她希望明年更上一層樓。 **in 'one** used to say that sb/sth has different roles, contains different things or is used for different purposes 集於一身（或一體）；多功能；多用途：*She's a mother and company director in one.* 她既是母親又是公司董事。◇ *It's a public relations office, a press office and a private office **all in one**.* 那兒既是公關辦公室，也是新聞辦公室，又是私人辦公室：三位一體。 ➲ see also ALL-IN-ONE **,one after a'nother/the 'other** first one person or thing, and then another, and then another, up to any number or amount 一個接一個地；陸續地；絡繹不絕地：*The bills kept coming in, one after another.* 賬單紛至沓來。 **,one and 'all** (*old-fashioned, informal*) everyone 各位；大家；每個人：*Happy New Year to one and all!* 祝各位新年快樂！ **,one and 'only** used to emphasize that sb is famous 絕無僅有的；唯一的；有名的：*Here he is, the one and only Van Morrison!* 他來了，這蓋世無雙的范•莫里森！ **,one and the 'same** used for emphasis to mean 'the same'（表示強調）同一個：*I never realized Ruth Rendell and Barbara Vine were one and the same* (= the same person using two different names). 我從未意識到魯思•蘭德爾和芭芭拉•瓦因原來是同一個人。 **,one by 'one** ⚷ separately and in order 逐個地；逐一地：*I went through the items on the list one by one.* 我逐條看了清單上的條目。 **,one or 'two** ⚷ a few 一些；一二：*We've had one or two problems—nothing serious.* 我們有一些問題，不過沒什麼大不了的。 **,one 'up (on sb)** having an advantage over sb 略勝一籌；強過別人 **when you've seen, heard, etc. 'one, you've seen, heard, etc. them 'all** (*saying*) used to say that all types of the things mentioned are very similar 所有的…都大同小異；知其一便知其全部：*I don't like science fiction novels much. When you've read one, you've read them all.* 我不太喜歡科幻小說。讀過一本，就知道其他的內容了。 ➲ more at ALL *pron.*, MINORITY, SQUARE *n.*

■ ***pron.*** **1** ⚷ used to avoid repeating a noun, when you are referring to sb/sth that has already been mentioned, or that the person you are speaking to knows about（用來避免重複已提過的或是聽者已知的事物的名稱）：*I'd like an ice cream. Are you having one, too?* 我想買份冰淇淋，你也要一份嗎？◇ *Our car's always breaking down. But we're getting a new one soon.* 我們的汽車老出毛病，但我們快要買新的了。◇ *She was wearing her new dress, the red one.* 她穿着她的新衣服，那件紅的。◇ *My favourite band? Oh, that's a hard one* (= a hard question). 我最喜愛的樂隊？哦，這可就難說了。◇ *What made you choose the one rather than the other?* 你怎麼選了這個而不是那個？◇ (*BrE*) *How about those ones over there?* 你看那邊那些怎麼樣？ **2** ⚷ used when you are identifying the person or thing you are talking about（用於辨別所談的人或事）：*Our house is the one next to the school.* 我家的房子就是學校旁邊的那座。◇ *The students who are most successful are usually the ones who come to all the classes.* 成績最好的學生往往是出全勤的那些。 **3** ⚷ **~ of** a person or thing belonging to a particular group 其中的一個人（或事物）：*It's a present for one of my children.* 這是送給我的一個孩子的禮物。◇ *We think of you as one of the family.* 我們把你看作家中的一員。 **4** ⚷ a person of the type mentioned（某類人中的）一個：*10 o'clock is too late for the **little ones**.* 十點鐘對那些小傢伙來說就太晚了。◇ *He ached to be home with his **loved ones**.* 他渴望着回家與親人團聚。◇ **~ to do sth** *She was never one to criticize.* 她是個從不愛批評人的人。 **5** ⚷ (*formal*) used to mean 'people in general' or 'I', when the speaker is referring to himself or herself 人們；本人：*One should never criticize if one is not sure of one's facts.* 一個人如果對自己掌握的事實沒有把握，就絕不該隨便批評。◇ *One gets the impression that they disapprove.* 據本人觀察，他們不贊成。 HELP This use of **one** is very formal and now sounds old-fashioned. It is much more usual to use **you** for 'people in general' and **I** when you are talking about yourself. * one 的這一用法頗為正式，現在聽起來過時了。現在更常用 you 指一般人，用 I 指自己。 **6 a 'one** (*old-fashioned, especially BrE*) a person whose behaviour is amusing or surprising（舉止）有趣的人，令人驚奇的人：*Oh, you are a one!* 哈！你這個活寶！ **7 the ~ about sth** the joke 玩笑；笑話：*Have you heard the one about the Englishman, the Irishman and the Scotsman?* 你聽沒聽過那個關於英格蘭人、愛爾蘭人和蘇格蘭人的笑話？

IDM **be (a) one for (doing) sth** to be a person who enjoys sth, or who does sth often or well 樂於（或長於）做某事的人：*I've never been a great one for fish and chips.* 我從來不是個好吃炸魚和薯條的人。

,one a'nother ⚷ *pron.*
one another is used when you are saying that each member of a group does sth to or for the other people in the group 互相：*We all try and help one another.* 我們都盡力互相幫助。◇ *I think we've learned a lot about one another in this session.* 我認為這一學期我們相互有了很多瞭解。

,one-armed 'bandit *noun* = SLOT MACHINE (2)

,one-horse 'town *noun* (*informal*) a small town with not many interesting things to do or places to go to 簡樸小鎮

,one-'liner *noun* (*informal*) a short joke or funny remark 小笑話；俏皮話；風趣的話：*He came out with some good one-liners.* 他講了幾個很有趣的小笑話。

,one-'man *adj.* [only before noun] done or controlled by one person only; suitable for one person 適於一個人的；由一個人操作的：*a **one-man show/business*** 獨角戲；一個人經營的生意◇ *a one-man tent* 單人帳篷 ➲ see also ONE-WOMAN

,one-man 'band *noun* a street musician who plays several instruments at the same time 一人樂隊（一個人同時演奏幾種樂器的街頭藝人）：(*figurative*) *He runs the business as a one-man band* (= one person does everything). 他是單槍匹馬辦企業。

Grammar Point 語法說明

one / ones

One/ones is used to avoid repeating a countable noun, but there are some times when you should not use it, especially in formal speech or writing.
* one/ones 用以避免重複可數名詞；但有時候，尤其在正式談話或書面語中，不應使用：

- After a possessive (*my, your, Mary's*, etc.), *some, any, both* or a number, unless it is used with an adjective. 在物主代詞（如 my、your、Mary's 等）、some、any、both 或數字之後不用 one/ones，除非與形容詞連用：*'Did you get any postcards?' 'Yes, I bought four nice ones.'*"你買明信片了嗎？""買了，我買了四張很精美的。"◇ ~~*I bought four ones.*~~
- It can be left out after superlatives, *this, that, these, those, either, neither, another, which*, etc. 在形容詞最高級、this、that、these、those、either、neither、another、which 等詞後可省略 one/ones：*'Here are the designs. Which (one) do you prefer?' 'I think that (one) looks the most original.'* "圖樣在這裏。你喜歡哪一張？""我認為那張看上去最有創意。"
- *These ones* and *those ones* are not used in *NAmE*, and are unusual in *BrE*. 美式英語中不用 these ones 和 those ones，英式英語也很少用：*Do you prefer these designs or those?* 你喜歡這些圖樣還是那些？
- It is never used to replace uncountable nouns and is unusual with abstract countable nouns. * one/ones 不用以取代不可數名詞，與抽象可數名詞連用也很少見：*The Scottish legal system is not the same as the English system, is better than … as the English one.* 用 The Scottish legal system is not the same as the English system（蘇格蘭法制與英格蘭法制不同）勝於用… as the English one。

one·ness /ˈwʌnnəs/ *noun* [U] (*formal*) the state of being completely united with sb/sth, or of being in complete agreement with sb 一體；一致；和諧：*a sense of oneness with the natural world* 與自然界的和諧感

ˌone-night ˈstand *noun* (*informal*) a sexual relationship that lasts for a single night; a person that sb has this relationship with 一夜情；露水姻緣；曾與之有一夜情的人：*I wanted it to be more than a one-night stand.* 我要的不只是一夜情緣。◇ *For her I was just a one-night stand.* 我不過是她玩一夜情的對象而已。

ˌone-ˈoff *adj., noun*
- **adj.** (*BrE*) (*NAmE* **ˈone-shot**) [only before noun] made or happening only once and not regularly 一次性的；非經常的：*a one-off payment* 一次性付款
- **noun** (*BrE*) a thing that is made or that happens only once and not regularly 絕無僅有的事物；僅出現一次的事物：*It was just a one-off; it won't happen again.* 這事絕無僅有，不會再發生了。

ˌone-on-ˈone *adj.* [usually before noun] (*NAmE*) = ONE-TO-ONE

ˌone-parent ˈfamily (also **ˌlone-parent ˈfamily**) *noun* a family in which the children live with one parent rather than two 單親家庭 ➲ see also SINGLE PARENT

ˈone-piece *adj.* [only before noun] (especially of clothes 尤指衣服) consisting of one piece, not separate parts 上下一件式的；連體式的：*a one-piece swimsuit* 一件式游泳衣

oner·ous /ˈəʊnərəs; *NAmE* ˈɑːn-; ˈoʊ-/ *adj.* (*formal*) needing great effort; causing trouble or worry 費力的；艱巨的；令人焦慮的 **SYN** **taxing**：*an **onerous duty/task/responsibility*** 繁重的義務／工作／職責

one's /wʌnz/ *det.* the possessive form of *one* （one 的所有格）個人的，自己的：*One tries one's best.* 一個人盡其所能。

one·self /wʌnˈself/ *pron.* (*formal*) **1** (the reflexive form of *one* * one 的反身形式) used as the object of a verb or preposition when 'one' is the subject of the verb or is understood as the subject （one 作動詞的主語時，oneself 作動詞或介詞的賓語）自己，自身：*One has to ask oneself what the purpose of the exercise is.* 大家必須問一問自己，這個鍛煉的目的是什麼。◇ *One cannot choose freedom for oneself without choosing it for others.* 人不能光為了自己的自由而不顧別人的自由。◇ *It is difficult to make oneself concentrate for long periods.* 讓自己長時間聚精會神是很困難的。**2** used to emphasize *one* （用以強調 one）親自，自己：*One likes to do it oneself.* 人都喜歡親自去做。**HELP** **One** and **oneself** are very formal words and now sound old-fashioned. It is much more usual to use **you** and **yourself** for referring to people in general and **I** and **myself** when the speaker is referring to himself or herself. * one 和 oneself 是非常正式的字眼，現在聽起來過時了。現在更常用 you 和 yourself 泛指一般人，用 I 和 myself 指說話人自己。
IDM **be oneˈself** to be in a normal state of body and mind, not influenced by other people 身心自在；怡然自得：*One needs space to be oneself.* 人要有空間才能怡然自得。**(all) by oneˈself** **1** alone; without anyone else （某人）獨自，單獨 **2** without help （某人）獨立地 **(all) to oneˈself** not shared with anyone 獨享的；獨自擁有的

ˈone-shot (*NAmE*) (*BrE* **ˌone-ˈoff**) *adj.* [only before noun] made or happening only once and not regularly 一次性的；非經常性的

ˌone-ˈsided *adj.* **1** (*disapproving*) (of an argument, opinion, etc. 論點、意見等) showing only one side of the situation; not balanced 片面的；偏頗的 **SYN** **biased**：*The press were accused of presenting a very one-sided picture of the issue.* 新聞界被指責對這件事的報道非常片面。**2** (of a competition or a relationship 競爭或關係) involving people who have different abilities; involving one person more than another 實力懸殊的；一邊倒的：*a totally one-sided match* 實力非常懸殊的比賽 ◇ *a one-sided conversation* (= in which one person talks most of the time) 一邊倒的交談

ˈOnesies™ /ˈwʌnzi/ *noun* (*NAmE*) a piece of clothing for babies that covers the top half of the body and sometimes also the legs. It fastens between the legs.（嬰兒）連體衣，連褲衣；寶寶衫 ➲ compare BABYGRO

ˌone-size-fits-ˈall *adj.* [only before noun] designed to be suitable for a wide range of situations or needs 通用的；一體適用的：*a one-size-fits-all monetary policy* 一體適用的貨幣政策

ˌone-ˈstar *adj.* [usually before noun] **1** having one star in a system that measures quality. The highest standard is usually represented by four or five stars.（服務質量）一星級的：*a one-star hotel* 一星級賓館 **2** (*NAmE*) having the fifth-highest military rank, and wearing uniform which has one star on it （軍階）一星級的：*a one-star general* 一星將軍

ˈone-stop *adj.* in which you can buy or do everything you want in one place 綜合性的；全方位服務的；一站式的；一切全包的：*Our agency is a one-stop shop for all your travel needs.* 我社是您旅遊方面的綜合服務站。

ˈone-time *adj.* [only before noun] **1** former 原先的；從前的；一度的：*her one-time best friend, Anna* 她以前的摯友——安娜 **2** not to be repeated 一次性的 **SYN** **one-off**：*a one-time fee of $500* * 500 元的一次性總費用

ˌone-to-ˈone (*especially BrE*) (*NAmE* usually **ˌone-on-ˈone**) *adj.* [usually before noun] **1** between two people only 一對一的；僅限兩人之間的：*a one-to-one meeting* 一對一的會見 **2** matching sth else in an exact way 一一對應的；完全對應的：*There is no one-to-one correspondence between sounds and letters.* 發音與字母之間沒有一對一的關係。▸ **ˌone-to-ˈone** *adv.*：*He teaches one-to-one.* 他一對一地個別教學。

ˌone-track ˈmind *noun* [usually sing.] if sb has a **one-track mind**, they can only think about one subject (often used to refer to sb thinking about sex) 單向褊狹的思路；一根筋；滿腦子只想着一件事（常指性愛）

ˌone-trick ˈpony *noun* (becoming *old-fashioned*, *disapproving*) a performer who is only famous for one song, etc.; a person or business that is only good at doing one thing "一招鮮"（指只有一首成名曲的歌手、單一

O

特長的人或單一經營的企業）：*This comedian is no one-trick pony.* 這位喜劇演員並不只有一招絕活。

one-upmanship /wʌnˈʌpmənʃɪp/ *noun* [U] (*disapproving*) the skill of getting an advantage over other people 取巧佔上風的伎倆

ˌone-ˈway *adj.* [usually before noun] **1** moving or allowing movement in only one direction 單行的；單向的：*one-way traffic* 單向交通 ◇ *a one-way street* 單行道 ◇ *a one-way valve* 單向閥門 **2** (*especially NAmE*) (*BrE* also **sin·gle**) a **one-way** ticket, etc. can be used for travelling to a place but not back again 單程的 ➲ compare RETURN *n.* (7) **3** operating in only one direction 單方面的；單向進行的：*Theirs was a one-way relationship* (= one person made all the effort). 他們的關係是一頭熱。◇ *They observed the prisoners through a* ***one-way mirror*** (= a mirror that allows a person standing behind it to see through it). 他們透過單向鏡子監視犯人。

ˌone-ˈwoman *adj.* [only before noun] done or controlled by one woman only 一個女人做的；由一個女人控制的：*a one-woman show* 女獨角戲

ˌon-ˈfield *adj.* at or on a sports field 運動場上的：*on-field medical treatment* 場上治療

on·going AW /ˈɒnɡəʊɪŋ; *NAmE* ˈɑːnɡoʊ-; ˈɔːn-/ *adj.* [usually before noun] continuing to exist or develop 持續存在的；仍在進行的；不斷發展的：*an ongoing debate/discussion/process* 持續的辯論／討論／過程 ◇ *The police investigation is ongoing.* 警方的調查在持續進行中。

onion 🔑 /ˈʌnjən/ *noun* [C, U] a round vegetable with many layers inside each other and a brown, red or white skin. Onions have a strong smell and flavour. 洋葱；葱頭：*Chop the onions finely.* 把洋葱切碎。◇ *French onion soup* 法式洋葱湯 ➲ VISUAL VOCAB page V31

ˌonion-skin ˈpaper *noun* [U] very thin smooth writing paper 葱皮紙；薄光澤紙

O

on·line /ˌɒnˈlaɪn; *NAmE* ˌɑːn-; ˌɔːn-/ *adj.* (*computing* 計) controlled by or connected to a computer or to the Internet 在線的；聯網的；聯機的：*Online shopping is both cheap and convenient.* 網上購物既便宜又方便。◇ *an online database* 在線數據庫 ▸ **on·line** *adv.*: *The majority of small businesses now do their banking online.* 大多數小企業現在都在網上辦理銀行業務。➲ COLLOCATIONS at EMAIL ➲ see also BE, COME, ETC. ON LINE at LINE *n.*

on·look·er /ˈɒnlʊkə(r); *NAmE* ˈɑːn-; ˈɔːn-/ *noun* a person who watches sth that is happening but is not involved in it 旁觀者 SYN **bystander**：*A crowd of onlookers gathered at the scene of the crash.* 在撞車現場聚集了一大群圍觀者。➲ SYNONYMS at WITNESS

only 🔑 /ˈəʊnli; *NAmE* ˈoʊnli/ *adj.*, *adv.*, *conj.*

■ ***adj.*** [only before noun] **1** 🔑 used to say that no other or others of the same group exist or are there 僅有的；唯一的：*She's their only daughter.* 她是他們的獨生女。◇ *We were the only people there.* 我們是唯一在場的人。◇ *His only answer was a grunt.* 他唯一的回答就只是哼了一聲。 **2** 🔑 used to say that sb/sth is the best and you would not choose any other 最好的；最適當的：*She's the only person for the job.* 她是這項工作最合適的人選。

IDM **the only thing ˈis ...** 🔑 (*informal*) used before mentioning a worry or problem you have with sth 問題是；麻煩的是；只是；不過：*I'd love to come—the only thing is I might be late.* 我很想去，只不過我可能會遲到。➲ more at NAME *n.*, ONE *number, det.*

■ ***adv.*** **1** 🔑 nobody or nothing except 只；只有；僅：*There are only a limited number of tickets available.* 剩下的票數量很有限。◇ *The bar is for* ***members only***. 這間酒吧只對會員開放。◇ ***You only have to*** *look at her to see she doesn't eat enough.* 你只消看一眼就知道她吃得不夠多。◇ *Only five people turned up.* 只來了五個人。 **2** 🔑 in no other situation, place, etc. 僅在…情況下（或地點等）：*I agreed, but only because I was frightened.* 我當時同意只是因為我受到了驚嚇。◇ *Children are admitted only if accompanied by an adult.* 兒童必須有成年人陪同方可入場。 HELP In formal written English **only**, or **only if** and its clause, can be placed first in the sentence. In the second part of the sentence, **be**, **do**, **have**, etc. come before the subject and the main part of the verb. 在正式書面英語中，only 或 only if 及其從句可置於句首。在句子的其餘部份，be、do、have 等置於主語及主要動詞前：***Only*** *in Paris* ***do*** *you find bars like this.* ◇ ***Only if*** *these conditions are fulfilled* ***can*** *the application proceed to the next stage.* **3** 🔑 no more important, interesting, serious, etc. than 只不過；僅…而已：*It was only a suggestion.* 這只是個提議罷了。◇ *Don't blame me, I'm only the messenger!* 別責怪我，我只不過是個傳話的！◇ *He was only teasing you.* 他只是逗你玩玩罷了。 **4** 🔑 no more than; no longer than 只有；僅；剛剛：*She's only 21 and she runs her own business.* 她只有 21 歲就經營起自己的企業了。◇ *It only took a few seconds.* 那只需要幾秒鐘。◇ *It took only a few seconds.* 那只需要幾秒鐘。 **5** 🔑 not until（直到）…才；（只是）…才：*We only got here yesterday.* 我們昨天才到這裏。◇ (*formal*) ***Only then did*** *she realize the stress he was under.* 直到那時她才意識到他所承受的壓力。 HELP When **only** begins a sentence **be**, **do**, **have**, etc. come before the subject and the main part of the verb. 當句子以 only 開始時，be、do、have 等詞要置於主語和主要動詞之前。 **6** 🔑 used to say that sb can do no more than what is mentioned, although this is probably not enough 僅此而已；只能：*We can only guess what happened.* 我們只能猜測發生了什麼事。◇ *He could only watch helplessly as the car plunged into the ravine.* 他只能眼睜睜地看着汽車衝落峽谷。◇ *I* ***only hope*** *that she never finds out.* 我唯有希望她永遠別發現真相。 **7** 🔑 used to say that sth will have a bad effect（用於說明事情的惡果）只會，愈加：*If you do that, it will only make matters worse.* 如果你那樣做，只會亂上加亂。◇ *Trying to reason with him only enrages him even more.* 跟他講理只會使他更加生氣。 **8 ~ to do sth** used to mention sth that happens immediately afterwards, especially sth that causes surprise, disappointment, etc. 不料；竟然：*She turned up the driveway, only to find her way blocked.* 她開上自家車道，不料發現路已被堵。

IDM **not only ... but (also) ...** 🔑 both ... and ... 不但…而且…：*He not only read the book, but also remembered what he had read.* 他不但讀了這本書，而且記得所讀的內容。➲ LANGUAGE BANK at ADDITION **only ˈjust** **1** not long ago/before 剛才；剛剛：*We've only just arrived.* 我們剛到。 **2** almost not 險些沒；差點沒；剛好：*He only just caught the train.* 他差點沒趕上火車。◇ *I can afford it, but only just.* 我的錢剛剛夠買這個。 **only too ...** very 很；非常：*I was only too pleased to help.* 我非常樂意幫忙。◇ *Children can be difficult as we know only too well.* 小孩子往往很難對付，對此我們都非常清楚。 **you're only young ˈonce** (*saying*) young people should enjoy themselves as much as possible, because they will have to work and worry later in their lives 行樂當及年少時；青春只有一次 ➲ more at EYE *n.*, IF *conj.*

■ ***conj.*** (*informal*) except that; but 不過；但是；可是：*I'd love to come, only I have to work.* 我很想去，但是我要上班。◇ *It tastes like chicken, only stronger.* 這東西嚐起來像雞肉，只是味道濃一點。

ˌonly ˈchild *noun* a child who has no brothers or sisters 獨生子（或女）：*I'm an only child.* 我是獨生子。

o.n.o. *abbr.* (*BrE*) or near/nearest offer (used in small advertisements to show that sth may be sold at a lower price than the price that has been asked) 或接近買方價格，可還價（用於小廣告中，表示某物可減價出售）：*Guitar £200 o.n.o.* 吉他 200 英鎊，可還價。➲ see also O.B.O.

ˌon-ˈoff *adj.* [only before noun] **1** (of a switch 開關) having the positions 'on' and 'off' 開 — 關的；雙位的；通斷的；離合的：*an on-off switch* 通斷開關 **2** (of a relationship 關係) interrupted by periods when the relationship is not continuing 斷斷續續的；間斷的

ono·mas·tics /ˌɒnəˈmæstɪks; *NAmE* ˌɑːnə-/ *noun* [U] the study of the history and origin of names, especially names of people（人名等）專有名稱詞源學；專名學

ono·mato·poeia /ˌɒnəˌmætəˈpiːə; *NAmE* ˌɑːn-/ *noun* [U] (*technical* 術語) the fact of words containing sounds similar to the noises they describe, for example *hiss*;

the use of words like this in a piece of writing 象聲；擬聲；擬聲法 ▶ **ono·mato·poe·ic** /-ˈpiːɪk/ *adj.*：*Bang and pop are onomatopoeic words.* * bang 和 pop 是擬聲詞。

ˈon-ramp *noun* (*NAmE, SAfrE*) a road used for driving onto a major road such as an INTERSTATE（高速公路等的）駛進匝道，駛進坡道 ➲ compare OFF-RAMP

on·rush /ˈɒnrʌʃ; *NAmE* ˈɑːn-; ˈɔːn-/ *noun* [sing.] a strong movement forward; the sudden development of sth 猛然向前；突如其來

ˌon-ˈscreen *adj.* [only before noun] **1** appearing or written on the screen of a computer, television or cinema/movie theater 屏幕上的；熒屏的；影視的：*on-screen courtroom dramas* 熒屏播映的法庭戲 ◇ *on-screen messages* 屏幕上的信息 **2** connected with the imaginary story of a film/movie and not with real life 扮演的；屏幕上的；非現實生活的：*His on-screen father is also his father in real life.* 他那熒幕上的父親也是他現實生活中的父親。➲ compare OFF-SCREEN ▶ **ˌon-ˈscreen** *adv.*

onset /ˈɒnset; *NAmE* ˈɑːn-; ˈɔːn-/ *noun* [sing.] the beginning of sth, especially sth unpleasant 開端，發生，肇始（尤指不快的事件）：*the onset of disease/old age/winter* 疾病的發作；老年的開始；冬天的來臨

on·shore /ˈɒnʃɔː(r); *NAmE* ˈɑːn-; ˈɔːn-/ *adj.* [usually before noun] **1** on the land rather than at sea 陸上的：*an onshore oil field* 陸上油田 **2** (of wind 風) blowing from the sea towards the land 吹向陸地的；向岸的 ▶ **on·shore** *adv.* ➲ compare OFFSHORE

on·side /ˌɒnˈsaɪd; *NAmE* ˌɑːn-; ˌɔːn-/ *adj.* (in football (SOCCER), HOCKEY, etc. 足球、曲棍球等) in a position on the field where you are allowed to play the ball 未越位；非越位 ▶ **on·side** *adv.* OPP **offside**

IDM **get/keep sb onˈside** (*BrE*) to get/keep sb's support 得到（或保持）某人的支持：*The party needs to keep the major national newspapers onside if it's going to win the next election.* 這個政黨要想在下次大選中獲勝，就需要全國各大報紙繼續給予支持。

on·slaught /ˈɒnslɔːt; *NAmE* ˈɑːn-; ˈɔːn-/ *noun* [C, usually sing.] a strong or violent attack 攻擊；猛攻：**~ (against/on sb/sth)** *the enemy onslaught on our military forces* 敵軍對我軍的進攻 ◇ **~ (of sth)** *The town survives the onslaught of tourists every summer.* 每年夏天，這座小城都要熬過一段旅遊者蜂擁而至的苦日子。◇ *an onslaught of abuse* 一陣謾罵

on·stage /ˌɒnˈsteɪdʒ; *NAmE* ˌɑːn-; ˌɔːn-/ *adj.* on the stage in a theatre; in front of an audience 舞台上的；表演的：*onstage fights* 舞台上的打鬥 ▶ **on·stage** *adv.* OPP **offstage**

ˌon-ˈstreet *adj.* [only before noun] (of parking facilities 停車設施) located at the side of a public road rather than in a garage, a drive, etc. 街邊的；路邊的 OPP **off-street**

onto 0-w /ˈɒntə; *before vowels* ˈɒntu; *NAmE* ˈɑːn-; ˈɔːn-/ (also **on to**) *prep.*

1 0-w used with verbs to express movement on or to a particular place or position（與動詞連用，表示朝某處或某位置運動）向，朝：*Move the books onto the second shelf.* 把書移到第二層架子上。◇ *She stepped down from the train onto the platform.* 她走下火車來到站台上。

2 0-w used to show that sth faces in a particular direction 朝向，面向（某個方向）：*The window looked out onto the terrace.* 窗戶外對着的是露天平台。

PHR V **be ˈonto sb 1** (*informal*) to know about what sb has done wrong 發現（某人做了壞事）：*She knew the police would be onto them.* 她知道警方將追查他們。 **2** to be talking to sb, usually in order to ask or tell them sth 與…談話；詢問：*They've been onto me for ages to get a job.* 很久以來，他們一直催促我找份工作。 **be ˈonto sth** to know about sth or be in a situation that could lead to a good result for you 瞭解；掌握；處於有利地位：*Scientists believe they are onto something big.* 科學家相信，他們將會有重大發現。◇ *She's onto a good thing with that new job.* 她在新工作中將大有作為。

ontol·ogy /ɒnˈtɒlədʒi; *NAmE* ɑːnˈtɑːl-/ *noun* **1** [U] a branch of philosophy that deals with the nature of existence 本體論；存在論 **2** [C] (*computing* 計) a list of concepts and categories in a subject area that shows the relationships between them 本體（一個主題下不同概念及類別）：*a guide to creating a marketing ontology* 市場本體構建指南 ▶ **onto·logic·al** /ˌɒntəˈlɒdʒɪkl; *NAmE* ˌɑːntəˈlɑːdʒ-/ *adj.*

onus /ˈəʊnəs; *NAmE* ˈoʊnəs/ *noun* (usually **the onus**) [sing.] (*formal*) the responsibility for sth 職責；責任：*The* **onus is on** *employers to follow health and safety laws.* 雇主有義務遵行健康安全法。

on·ward /ˈɒnwəd; *NAmE* ˈɑːnwərd; ˈɔːn-/ *adj.* [only before noun] (*formal*) continuing or moving forward 繼續的；向前的：*Ticket prices include your flight and onward rail journey.* 票價包括您的飛行航程和接續的鐵路旅費。

on·wards /ˈɒnwədz; *NAmE* ˈɑːnwərdz; ˈɔːn-/ (*especially BrE*) (*NAmE* usually **on·ward** /ˈɒnwəd; *NAmE* ˈɑːnwərd; ˈɔːn-/) *adv.* **1 from … onwards** continuing from a particular time 從（某時）起一直：*They lived there from the 1980s onwards.* 他們從 1980 年代起一直住在那裏。◇ *The pool is open from 7 a.m. onwards.* 游泳池從早上 7 點起開放。 **2** (*formal*) forward 向前；前往：*We drove onwards towards the coast.* 我們驅車前往海濱。

onyx /ˈɒnɪks; *NAmE* ˈɑːn-/ *noun* [U] a type of stone that has layers of different colours in it, usually used for decorative objects 縞瑪瑙

oo·dles /ˈuːdlz/ *noun* [pl.] **~ (of sth)** (*old-fashioned, informal*) a large amount of sth 大量；很多 SYN **loads**

oo-er /ˌuːˈɜː(r)/ *exclamation* (*humorous*) used for expressing surprise, especially about sth sexual（表示驚訝，尤指對性方面）啊喲，哎呀

ooh /uː/ *exclamation* used for expressing surprise, happiness or pain（表示驚訝、高興或疼痛）哎呀，啊哈，哎喲

oom·pah /ˈʊmpɑː; ˈuːm-/ (also **ˈoompah-pah**) *noun* (*informal*) used to refer to the sound produced by a group of BRASS instruments（銅管樂器組發出的）嗡姆吧聲：*an oompah band* 銅管樂隊

oomph /ʊmf/ *noun* [U] (*informal*) energy; a special good quality 精力；特質；氣質：*a styling product to give your hair more oomph* 使頭髮更靚麗的一種定型劑

oops /ʊps; uːps/ *exclamation* **1** used when sb has almost had an accident, broken sth, etc.（差點出事故、摔破物品等時說）哎喲：*Oops! I almost spilled the wine.* 哎喲！我差點把酒灑了。 **2** used when you have done sth embarrassing, said sth rude by accident, told a secret, etc.（做了令人尷尬的事、說了無理的話或泄露了秘密等時說）哎喲：*Oops, I shouldn't have said that.* 哎喲，我不應該那麼說。

oops-a-daisy /ˈʊpsə deɪzi; ˈʌpsə/ *exclamation* = UPSY-DAISY

ooze /uːz/ *verb, noun*

■ ***verb* 1** [I, T] if a thick liquid **oozes** from a place, or if sth **oozes** a thick liquid, the liquid flows from the place slowly（濃液體）滲出，慢慢流出：**~ from/out of/through sth** | **~ out** *Blood oozed out of the wound.* 血從傷口慢慢流出來。◇ **~ with sth** *an ugly swelling oozing with pus* 流着膿水的爛瘡 ◇ **~ sth** *The wound was oozing blood.* 傷口流着血。◇ *a plate of toast oozing butter* 一盤滲着黃油的烤麪包片 **2** [T, I] if sb/sth **oozes** a particular characteristic, quality, etc., they show it strongly 洋溢着，充滿（特質、氣質等）SYN **exude**：**~ sth** *She walked into the party oozing confidence.* 她信心十足地來到聚會上。◇ **~ with sth** *His voice oozed with sex appeal.* 他的聲音充溢着性感。

■ ***noun* 1** [U] very soft mud, especially at the bottom of a lake or river（河牀、湖底的）泥漿，稀泥 **2** [sing.] the very slow flow of a thick liquid（濃液的）緩慢滲出 ▶ **oozy** *adj.*

op /ɒp; *NAmE* ɑːp/ *noun* (*BrE, informal*) = OPERATION (1)：*I'm going in for my op on Monday.* 星期一我要住院動手術。

Op. (also **op.**) *abbr.* OPUS：*Webern's Five Pieces, Op. 10* 韋伯恩的第十號作品的五支樂曲

opa·city /əʊˈpæsəti; *NAmE* oʊ-/ *noun* [U] **1** (*technical* 術語) the fact of being difficult to see through; the fact of being OPAQUE 不透明性；模糊 **2** (*formal*) the fact of

O

being difficult to understand; the fact of being OPAQUE 費解；難懂；模糊 OPP **transparency**

opal /ˈəʊpl; *NAmE* ˈoʊpl/ *noun* [C, U] a white or almost clear SEMI-PRECIOUS STONE in which changes of colour are seen, used in jewellery 蛋白石；貓眼石：*an opal ring* 蛋白石戒指

opal·es·cent /ˌəʊpəˈlesnt; *NAmE* ˌoʊpə-/ *adj.* (*formal* or *literary*) changing colour like an opal 像貓眼石般變色的；色彩變幻的

opaque /əʊˈpeɪk; *NAmE* oʊ-/ *adj.* **1** (of glass, liquid, etc. 玻璃、液體等) not clear enough to see through or allow light through 不透明的；不透光的；渾濁的：*opaque glass* 不透明的玻璃 ◇ *opaque tights* 不透明的連褲襪 **2** (of speech or writing 說話或寫作) difficult to understand; not clear 難懂的；模糊的；隱晦的；不清楚的 SYN **impenetrable**：*The jargon in his talk was opaque to me.* 他談話中使用的行話對我是一團迷霧。OPP **transparent**

ˈ**op art** *noun* [U] a style of modern art that uses patterns and colours in a way that makes the images seem to move as you look at them 歐普藝術，光效應藝術（利用色彩圖形使畫面產生動感的現代藝術）

op. cit. *abbr.* used in formal writing to refer to a book or an article that has already been mentioned（用於正式文章中，指前文提到的書或文章）同上

op·code /ˈɒpkəʊd; *NAmE* ɑːpkoʊd/ *noun* = OPERATION CODE

OPEC /ˈəʊpek; *NAmE* ˈoʊ-/ *abbr.* Organization of Petroleum Exporting Countries (an organization of countries that produce and sell oil) 石油輸出國組織

ˈ**op-ed** (also **op-ˈed page**) *noun* (*NAmE*) the page in a newspaper opposite the EDITORIAL page that contains comment on the news and articles on particular subjects（報章上與社論版位置相對的）評論版，論壇版

O

open 0-w /ˈəʊpən; *NAmE* ˈoʊ-/ *adj., verb, noun*

■ *adj.*

▸ NOT CLOSED 開着 **1** 0-w allowing things or people to go through 開放的；敞開的：*A wasp flew in the open window.* 一隻黃蜂飛進了開着的窗子。◇ *She had left the door **wide open**.* 她把房門敞開着。OPP **closed** **2** 0-w (of sb's eyes, mouth, etc. 人的眼睛、嘴等) with EYELIDS or lips apart 張開的；張着的：*She had difficulty keeping her eyes open* (= because she was very tired). 她連睜開眼睛的力氣都沒有了。◇ *He was breathing through his open mouth.* 他張着嘴呼吸。OPP **closed** **3** 0-w spread out; with the edges apart 展開的；開放的：*The flowers are all open now.* 花現在都開了。◇ *The book lay open on the table.* 書攤開在桌子上。OPP **closed** **4** 0-w not blocked by anything 暢通的：*The pass is **kept open** all the year.* 通道一年到頭暢通無阻。OPP **closed**

▸ NOT FASTENED 未繫着 **5** 0-w not fastened or covered, so that things can easily come out or be put in 敞口的；未封的：*Leave the envelope open.* 別封上信封。◇ *The bag burst open and everything fell out.* 袋子爆開了，裏邊的東西都散落出來。**6** 0-w (of clothes 衣服) not fastened 沒扣上的；敞開的：*Her coat was open.* 她的外衣敞着。

▸ NOT ENCLOSED 未圍着 **7** 0-w not surrounded by anything; not confined 開闊的；未圍上的：***open country*** (= without forests, buildings, etc.) 空曠的田野 ◇ *a city with a lot of parks and **open spaces*** 有很多公園和空地的城市 ◇ *driving along the **open road*** (= part of a road in the country, where you can drive fast) 沿開闊的道路開車

▸ NOT COVERED 敞開 **8** 0-w with no cover or roof on 敞開的；露天的；裸露的：*an open drain* 一條明溝 ◇ *people working in **the open air*** (= not in a building) 在戶外作業的人 ◇ *The hall of the old house was open to the sky.* 舊房子的門廳是露天的。◇ *an open wound* (= with no skin covering it) 開放性傷口 ◇ (*NAmE*) *an open flame* 明火 HELP In British English this is called a *naked flame*. 英式英語稱作 naked flame。

▸ FOR CUSTOMERS/VISITORS 對賓客 **9** 0-w [not usually before noun] if a shop/store, bank, business, etc. is **open**, it is ready for business and will admit customers or visitors 開放；營業：*Is the museum open on Sundays?* 博物館每星期天都開放嗎？◇ *The new store will be open in the spring.* 新商店將在春天開業。◇ *The house had been **thrown open** to the public.* 這所宅院已向公眾開放。◇ *I declare this festival open.* 我宣佈慶祝活動開始。OPP **closed**

▸ OF COMPETITION/BUILDING 比賽；建築物 **10** if a competition, etc. is **open**, anyone can enter it 對大眾開放的；公開的；人人可以參加的 SYN **public**：*an open debate/championship/scholarship* 公開的辯論會；人人可以參加的錦標賽；人人均可申請的獎學金 ◇ *She was tried in **open court*** (= the public could go and listen to the trial). 她被公開審判。◇ *The debate was **thrown open** to the audience.* 辯論會對聽眾開放。**11** 0-w [not before noun] **~ to sb** if a competition, building, etc. is **open** to particular people, those people can enter it（比賽、建築物等）對特定群體開放：*The competition is open to young people under the age of 18.* 這項比賽讓 18 歲以下的青少年參加。◇ *The house is not open to the public.* 這所住宅不對外開放。OPP **closed**

▸ AVAILABLE 備有 **12** 0-w [not before noun] **~ (to sb)** to be available and ready to use 可得到；可使用：*What options are open to us?* 我們有什麼選擇？◇ *Is the offer still open?* 這個報價還有效嗎？◇ *I want to keep my Swiss bank account open.* 我想保留我的瑞士銀行賬戶。OPP **closed**

▸ NOT PROTECTED 無防範 **13** 0-w **~ (to sth)** likely to suffer sth such as criticism, injury, etc. 易受損害；脆弱 SYN **vulnerable**：*The system is open to abuse.* 這項制度容易被濫用。◇ *He has **laid himself wide open** to political attack.* 他在政治上已經處於極易受到攻擊的境地。

▸ NOT HIDDEN 不隱匿 **14** 0-w known to everyone; not kept hidden 人人皆知的；不保密的；公開的：*an open quarrel* 公開的爭吵 ◇ *open government* 透明的管理 ◇ *their open display of affection* 他們的公開示愛 ◇ *His eyes showed open admiration as he looked at her.* 他看她的時候，眼神裏明顯流露着敬佩之情。

▸ PERSON'S CHARACTER 性格 **15** 0-w honest; not keeping thoughts and feelings hidden 誠懇的；坦誠的；直率的 SYN **frank**：*She was always open with her parents.* 她總是與父母無話不談。◇ *He was quite open about his reasons for leaving.* 他對離開的原因完全未加隱瞞。➲ SYNONYMS at HONEST **16** 0-w **~ to sth** (of a person 人) willing to listen to and think about new ideas 思想開明的；不固執己見的：*I'm open to suggestions for what you would like to do in our classes.* 我很樂意聽聽你們對課堂活動的建議。

▸ NOT YET DECIDED 待定 **17** **~ (to sth)** not yet finally decided or settled 未決定的；待決定的：*The race is still **wide open*** (= anyone could win). 賽跑勝負未定。◇ *The price is not open to negotiation.* 價格不容商議。◇ *Some phrases in the contract are open to interpretation.* 合同中的某些條文容有不同詮釋。◇ *Which route is better remains **an open question*** (= it is not decided). 哪條路線較好尚待決定。◇ *In an interview try to ask **open questions*** (= to which the answer is not just 'yes' or 'no'). 主持面試時要盡量問一些討論性的問題。

▸ CLOTH 織物 **18** with wide spaces between the threads 稀疏的；不密的：*an open weave* 稀疏織法

▸ PHONETICS 語音學 **19** (also **low**) (of a vowel 元音) produced by opening the mouth wide 開的；開口的；低的 ➲ compare CLOSE² *adj.* (16)

IDM **be an ˌopen ˈsecret** if sth is **an open secret**, many people know about it, although it is supposed to be a secret 是公開的秘密 **have/keep an ˌopen ˈmind (about/on sth)** to be willing to listen to or accept new ideas or suggestions 願意聆聽（或接受）意見；（對…）不懷成見；思想開明 **keep your ˈears/ˈeyes open (for sth)** to be quick to notice or hear things（對…）保持警覺；注意；留心 **an ˌopen ˈbook** if you describe sb or their life as **an open book**, you mean that you can easily understand them and know everything about them 容易被瞭解的人；坦率的人 **an ˌopen inviˈtation (to sb)** **1** an invitation to sb to visit you at any time（給…）隨時可以來訪的邀請 **2** if sth is **an open invitation** to criminals, etc., it encourages them to commit a crime by making it easier 容易引誘人犯罪的行為：*Leaving your camera on the seat in the car is an* *open invitation to thieves.* 把照相機留在汽車座位上無異於開門揖盜。 **with ˌopen ˈarms** if you welcome sb **with open arms**, you are extremely happy and pleased to see them 熱烈地；熱情地；誠摯地 ➲ more at BURST *v.*, DOOR, EYE *n.*, MARKET *n.*, OPTION *n.*

■ ***verb***

▸ **DOOR/WINDOW/LID** 門窗；蓋子 **1** [T] **~ sth** to move a door, window, lid, etc. so that it is no longer closed 開；打開；開啟：*Mr Chen opened the car door for his wife.* 陳先生為妻子打開車門。 OPP **close 2** [I] to move or be moved so that it is no longer closed 打開；（使）開：*The door opened and Alan walked in.* 門開了，艾倫走了進去。 OPP **close**

▸ **CONTAINER/PACKAGE** 容器；包 **3** [T] **~ sth** to remove the lid, undo the FASTENING, etc. of a container, etc. in order to see or get what is inside 打開，開啟（瓶蓋、封口等）：*Shall I open another bottle?* 要不要我再開一瓶？◇ *He opened the letter and read it.* 他拆開信讀起來。

▸ **EYES** 眼睛 **4** [T, I] **~ (sth)** if you **open** your eyes or your eyes **open**, you move your EYELIDS upwards so that you can see 睜開 OPP **close**

▸ **MOUTH** 嘴 **5** [T, I] **~ (sth)** if you **open** your mouth or your mouth **opens**, you move your lips, for example in order to speak 張開：*He hardly ever opens his mouth* (= speaks). 他幾乎從不開口。

▸ **BOOK** 書籍 **6** [T] **~ sth** to turn the cover or the pages of a book so that it is no longer closed 打開；翻開：*Open your books at page 25.* 把書翻到第 25 頁。 OPP **close**

▸ **SPREAD OUT** 展開 **7** [I, T] to spread out or UNFOLD; to spread sth out or UNFOLD it 展開；打開：*What if the parachute doesn't open?* 降落傘打不開怎麼辦？◇ *The flowers are starting to open.* 花開始綻放了。◇ **~ sth** *Open the map on the table.* 把地圖攤在桌子上。◇ *He opened his arms wide to embrace her.* 他張開雙臂擁抱她。

▸ **BORDER/ROAD** 邊界；道路 **8** [T] **~ sth** to make it possible for people, cars, goods, etc. to pass through a place 讓（行人、車輛、貨物等）通行；開放：*When did the country open its borders?* 這個國家是何時開放邊界的？◇ *The road will be opened again in a few hours after police have cleared it.* 待警察清理完以後，道路在幾小時內就會重新開放。 OPP **close**

▸ **FOR CUSTOMERS/VISITORS** 對賓客 **9** [I, T] (of a shop/ store, business, etc. 商店、企業等) to start business for the day; to start business for the first time 開始營業；開業；開門：*What time does the bank open?* 這家銀行什麼時候開門？◇ **~ sth** *The company* ***opened its doors*** *for business a month ago.* 該公司一個月前開業。 OPP **close 10** [I] to be ready for people to go to 準備接待：*The new hospital opens on July 1st.* 這家新醫院七月一日開診。◇ *When does the play open?* 這個劇什麼時候上演？ OPP **close**

▸ **START STH** 開始某事 **11** [T] to start an activity or event 着手；開始：**~ sth** *You need just one pound to* ***open a bank account*** *with us.* 你只需一英鎊就可在我行開立一個賬戶。◇ *The police have opened an investigation into the death.* 警察已開始對這樁命案進行調查。◇ *Troops* ***opened fire on*** (= started shooting) *the crowds.* 軍隊向人群開火了。◇ **~ sth with sth** *They will open the new season with a performance of 'Carmen'.* 他們將以上演《卡門》來展開新的戲劇季。 ➲ SYNONYMS at START **12** [I] **~ (with sth)** (of a story, film/movie, etc. 故事、電影等) to start in a particular way 以…開篇；以…開頭：*The story opens with a murder.* 這個故事以謀殺案開始。

▸ **WITH CEREMONY** 以儀式 **13** [T] **~ sth** to perform a ceremony showing that a building can start being used 為（建築物）揭幕；宣佈啟用：*The bridge was opened by the Queen.* 女王為大橋開通揭幕。

▸ **COMPUTING** 計算機技術 **14** [T, I] **~ (sth)** to start a computer program or file so that you can use it on the screen 啟動，打開（計算機程序或文件）

IDM **open ˈdoors for sb** to provide opportunities for sb to do sth and be successful 為…敞開大門；提供良機 **open your/sb's ˈeyes (to sth)** to realize or make sb realize the truth about sth （使人）長見識（或開眼界、認清事實）：*Travelling really opens your eyes to other cultures.* 旅遊真正能使人開闊眼界，認識其他文化。 **open your/sb's mind to sth** to become or make sb aware of new ideas or experiences （使人）思想開闊，意識到某事 **open the way for sb/sth (to do sth)** to make it possible for sb to do sth or for sth to happen 開方便之門 ➲ more at HEART, HEAVEN

PHR V **ˈopen into/onto sth** to lead to another room, area or place 通向，通往（他處） **ˌopen ˈout** to become bigger or wider 變大；變寬：*The street opened out into a small square.* 街道豁然變寬，形成一個小廣場。 **ˌopen ˈout (to sb)** (*BrE*) = OPEN UP (TO SB) **ˌopen ˈup 1** to begin shooting 開火：*Anti-aircraft guns opened up.* 高射炮開始射擊。 **2** (often used in orders 常用於命令) to open a door, container, etc. 打開（門、容器等）：*Open up or we'll break the door down!* 開門！不然就砸門了！ **ˌopen ˈup (to sb)** (*BrE* also **ˌopen ˈout (to sb)**) to talk about what you feel and think; to become less shy and more willing to communicate 直抒胸臆；暢所欲言；不再拘謹：*It helps to discuss your problems but I find it hard to open up.* 與人談談自己面對的問題固然有益，但我覺得有些話很難說得出口。 **ˌopen sth↔ˈup | ˌopen ˈup 1** to become or make sth possible, available or able to be reached （使某事物）成為可能，可得到，可達到：*The railway opened up the east of the country.* 鐵路使這個國家的東部不再封閉。◇ *Exciting possibilities were opening up for her in the new job.* 新工作為她帶來了令人興奮的發展前途。 **2** to begin business for the day; to start a new business 開門；營業；開業：*I open up the store for the day at around 8.30.* 我的店每天早上大約 8:30 開門。 OPP **close up 3** to start a new business 開張；開業：*There's a new Thai restaurant opening up in town.* 城裏有一家新的泰國餐館開張了。 OPP **close down 4** to develop or start to happen or exist; to develop or start sth 發展；開始發生；出現：*A division has opened up between the two ministers over the issue.* 兩位部長在這個問題上出現了分歧。◇ *Scott opened up a 3-point lead in the first game.* 斯科特在第一局就以 3 分領先。 **5** to appear and become wider; to make sth wider when it is narrow or closed 張開；裂開；拓展；打開：*The wound opened up and started bleeding.* 傷口裂開，開始流血。◇ *The operation will open up the blocked passages around his heart.* 手術將把他心臟周圍被堵塞的通道打開。 OPP **close up ˌopen sth↔ˈup** to make sth open that is shut, locked, etc. 打開；翻開：*She laid the book flat and opened it up.* 她把書平攤開。

■ ***noun* the open** [sing.]

▸ **OUTDOORS** 戶外 **1** outdoors; the countryside 戶外；野外；曠野：*Children need to play out* ***in the open***. 孩子需要在戶外玩耍。

▸ **NOT HIDDEN** 不隱匿 **2** not hidden or secret 公開；非秘密：*Government officials do not want these comments* ***in the open***. 政府官員不想公開這些評論。◇ *They intend to* ***bring*** *their complaints* ***out into the open***. 他們想把心中的種種不滿公開講出來。

the ˌopen ˈair *noun* [sing.] a place outside rather than in a building 戶外；露天：*He likes to cook in the open air.* 他喜歡在戶外做飯。

ˌopen-ˈair *adj.* [only before noun] happening or existing outside rather than inside a building 戶外的；露天的：*an open-air swimming pool* 露天游泳池

ˌopen-and-shut ˈcase *noun* a legal case or other matter that is easy to decide or solve 容易解決的案件（或問題）：*The murder was an open-and-shut case.* 這樁謀殺案很容易偵破。

ˌopen ˈbar *noun* [U, C] an occasion when all the drinks at a party or other event have been paid for by sb else or are included in the ticket price（聚會等場合的）酒水免費，酒水已付

open·cast /ˈəʊpənkɑːst; *NAmE* ˈoʊpənkæst/ (*BrE*) (*NAmE* **ˌopen-ˈpit**) *adj.* [usually before noun] in **opencast** mines coal is taken out of the ground near the surface 露天開採的 ➲ see also STRIP MINING

ˈopen day (*BrE*) (*NAmE* **ˌopen ˈhouse**) *noun* a day when people can visit a school, an organization, etc. and see the work that is done there （學校、機構等的）開放參觀日，開放日

ˌopen ˈdoor *noun, adj.*
■ ***noun*** [sing.] a situation that allows sth to happen, or that allows people to go to a place or get information without restrictions 門戶開放；自由往來：*The government's policy is **an open door to** disaster.* 政府的政策為災難敞開了大門。◇ *An insecure computer system is an open door to criminals.* 不安全的電腦系統給罪犯提供了可乘之機。
■ ***adj.*** **ˌopen-ˈdoor** [only before noun] **1** (of a policy, system, principle, etc. 政策、制度、原則等) allowing people or goods freedom to come into a country; allowing people to go to a place or get information without restrictions 門戶開放的；自由往來的：*the country's **open-door policy** for refugees* 這個國家對難民的開放政策 **2** a policy within a company or other organization designed to allow people to freely communicate with the people in charge（公司或機構中下屬與主管）直接溝通的；政策開明的：*We operate an **open-door policy** here, and are always willing to listen to our students' suggestions.* 我們這裏實行"開門政策"，願意隨時聽取學生的建議。

ˌopen-ˈended *adj.* without any limits, aims or dates fixed in advance 無限制的；無確定目標的；無期限的：*an open-ended discussion* 無限制的自由討論 ◇ *The contract is open-ended.* 本合同並無限期。

open·er /ˈəʊpnə(r); *NAmE* ˈoʊ-/ *noun* **1** (usually in compounds 通常構成複合詞) a tool that is used to open things 開啟的工具：*a can opener* 罐頭起子 ◇ *a bottle-opener* 開瓶器 ➲ see also EYE-OPENER **2** the first in a series of things such as sports games; the first action in an event, a game, etc. 揭幕賽；開場戲：*They won the opener 4–2.* 他們以 4:2 贏了揭幕賽。◇ *Jones scored the opener.* 瓊斯首先得分。◇ *a good conversation opener* 一個很好的話題 **3** (in CRICKET 板球) either of the two BATSMEN who start play 開球員；首位擊球員
IDM **for ˈopeners** (*informal, especially NAmE*) as a beginning or first part of a process 首先；作為開始；開端 **SYN** **for starters**

ˌopen-faced ˈsandwich (also **ˌopen-face ˈsandwich**) *noun* (*NAmE*) a slice of bread with meat, cheese, etc. on top but without a second slice of bread to cover this 單片三明治，露餡三明治（頂層無麵包片覆蓋）

ˌopen-ˈhanded *adj.* **1** generous and giving willingly 慷慨的；大方的：*an open-handed host* 一位慷慨大方的東道主 **2** using the flat part of the hand 用手掌的：*an open-handed blow* 用巴掌打

ˌopen-ˈhearted *adj.* kind and friendly 善良誠懇的

ˌopen-heart ˈsurgery *noun* [U] a medical operation on the heart, during which the patient's blood is kept flowing by a machine 體外循環心臟手術；心臟直視手術；開心術

ˌopen ˈhouse *noun* **1** [U, sing.] a place or a time at which visitors are welcome（機關等的）開放，開放參觀日：*It's always open house at their place.* 他們的房舍隨時對外開放參觀。**2** (*NAmE*) (*BrE* **ˈopen day**) [C] a day when people can visit a school, an organization, etc. and see the work that is done there（學校、機關等的）開放日，開放參觀日 **3** [C] (*NAmE*) a time when people who are interested in buying a particular house or apartment can look around it（為欲購房者而設的）看房時間

open·ing 🔑 /ˈəʊpnɪŋ; *NAmE* ˈoʊ-/ *noun, adj.*
■ ***noun*** **1** 🔑 [C] a space or hole that sb/sth can pass through 孔；洞；缺口：*We could see the stars through an opening in the roof.* 我們從屋頂的小洞能看見星星。**2** 🔑 [C, usually sing.] the beginning or first part of sth 開始；開端：*The movie has an exciting opening.* 電影的開頭非常刺激。**OPP** **ending** **3** 🔑 [C, usually sing.] a ceremony to celebrate the start of a public event or the first time a new building, road, etc. is used 開幕式；落成典禮：*the opening of the Olympic Games* 奧林匹克運動會開幕式 ◇ *the official opening of the new hospital* 新建醫院的落成典禮 **4** 🔑 [C, U] the act or process of making sth open or of becoming open 開；開放；展開：*the opening of a flower* 花朵的綻放 ◇ *the opening of the new play* 新話劇的開演 ◇ *Late opening of supermarkets is common in Britain now.* 現在超市營業至很晚在英國司空見慣。**OPP** **closing** **5** [C] a job that is available 空缺的職位 **SYN** **vacancy**：*There are several openings in the sales department.* 銷售部有幾個空缺。**6** [C] a good opportunity for sb 良機：*Winning the competition was the opening she needed for her career.* 在這次比賽中獲勝是她未來事業發展的良好開端。**7** [C] part of a piece of clothing that is made to open and close so that it can be put on easily 開襟；開口：*The skirt has a side opening.* 這裙子是側面開口的。
■ ***adj.*** [only before noun] first; beginning 開始的；開篇的；開頭的：*his opening remarks* 他的開場白 ◇ *the opening chapter of the book* 該書的第一章 **OPP** **closing**

ˈopening hours *noun* [pl.] the time during which a shop/store, bank, etc. is open for business（商店、銀行等的）營業時間

ˌopening ˈnight *noun* [usually sing.] the first night that, for example, a play is performed or a film/movie is shown to the public（戲劇的）首夜演出；（電影的）首夜放映

ˈopening time *noun* [U] (*BrE*) the time when pubs can legally open and begin to serve drinks（酒館的法定）開始營業時間 **OPP** **closing time**

ˌopening ˈup *noun* [sing.] **1** the process of removing restrictions and making sth such as land or jobs available to more people 解禁；開放；供開發：*the opening up of new opportunities for women in business* 企業為婦女提供的新的工作機會 **2** the process of making sth ready for use 啟用；落成：*the opening up of a new stretch of highway* 一段新公路的開通啟用

ˌopen-ˈjaw *adj.* [only before noun] (of a plane ticket or FARE 機票或票價) allowing sb to fly to one place and fly back from another place 開口的，缺口的，不同點進出的（可選擇回程出發地）

ˌopen ˈletter *noun* a letter of complaint or protest to an important person or group that is printed in a newspaper so that the public can read it 公開信

ˌopen ˈline *noun, adj.*
■ ***noun*** a telephone communication in which conversations can be heard or recorded by others 可被監聽（或錄音）的電話；開放線路電話
■ ***adj.*** **ˌopen-ˈline** [only before noun] relating to a radio or television programme that the public can take part in by telephone（電台或電視節目）公眾可打電話參與的，開放式的，互動式的：*an open-line radio show* 互動式電台節目

open·ly 🔑 /ˈəʊpənli; *NAmE* ˈoʊ-/ *adv.* without hiding any feelings, opinions or information 公開地；毫不隱瞞地：*Can you talk openly about sex with your parents?* 你可以跟父母敞開談性的問題嗎？◇ *The men in prison would never cry openly* (= so that other people could see). 獄中犯人從不當眾哭泣。

ˌopen ˈmarket *noun* [sing.] a situation in which companies can trade without restrictions, and prices depend on the amount of goods and the number of people buying them 公開市場；自由市場：*to buy/sell/trade **on the open market*** 在自由市場上買／賣／交易

ˌopen ˈmike *noun* [U] an occasion in a club when anyone can sing, play music or tell jokes 即興表演式聚會（出席者都可上台唱歌、演奏或表演滑稽說笑）：*open-mike night* 即興表演晚會

ˌopen-ˈminded *adj.* willing to listen to, think about or accept different ideas 願意考慮不同意見的；思想開明的 **OPP** **narrow-minded** ▸ **ˌopen-ˈminded·ness** *noun* [U]

ˌopen-ˈmouthed *adj.* with your mouth open because you are surprised or shocked（因驚愕）張着口的，瞠目結舌的，目瞪口呆的

ˌopen-ˈnecked (also **ˌopen-ˈneck**) *adj.* (of a shirt 襯衣) worn without a tie and with the top button undone 未打領帶也未扣領扣的；敞領的

open·ness /ˈəʊpənnəs; *NAmE* ˈoʊ-/ *noun* [U] **1** the quality of being honest and not hiding information or feelings 誠實；率真；坦率 **2** the quality of being able to think about, accept or listen to different ideas or people 虛心

O

的品質；開明 **3** the quality of not being confined or covered 開闊；開放；未遮蓋

ˌopen-ˈpit (*NAmE*) (*BrE* **open·cast**) *adj.* [usually before noun] in **open-pit** mines coal is taken out of the ground near the surface 露天開採的 ➲ see also STRIP MINING

ˌopen-ˈplan *adj.* an **open-plan** building or area does not have inside walls dividing it up into rooms 開放式的；敞開式的；未隔間的：*an open-plan office* 敞開式的辦公室

ˌopen ˈprison (*BrE*) (*NAmE* **ˌminimum seˈcurity prison**) *noun* a prison in which prisoners have more freedom than in ordinary prisons 開放式監獄（對犯人的自由限制較少）

ˌopen ˈsandwich *noun* a SANDWICH which is served on a plate with no top piece of bread 單片三明治（頂層無麪包片覆蓋）

ˈopen season *noun* [sing.] **1 ~** (**for sth**) the time in the year when it is legal to hunt and kill particular animals or birds, or to catch fish, for sport （法定）漁獵開放季節 OPP **close season** **2 ~ for/on sb/sth** a time when there are no restrictions on criticizing particular groups of people or treating them unfairly （針對某些團體的）言論開放期，自由評論期：*It seems to be open season on teachers now.* 現在好像是自由批評教師的開放期。

ˌopen ˈsesame *noun* [sing.] an easy way to gain or achieve sth that is usually very difficult to get 開門咒語；通行手段；通行證：*Academic success is not always an open sesame to a well-paid job.* 在校成績好並非總是獲得高薪職位的敲門磚。ORIGIN From the fairy tale *Ali Baba and the Forty Thieves*, in which the magic words **open sesame** had to be said to open the cave where the thieves kept their treasure. 源自童話故事《阿里巴巴和四十大盜》。只有唸出咒語"芝麻，開門"，大盜藏寶洞的大門才能打開。

ˌopen ˈslather *noun* [U] (*AustralE, disapproving*) freedom to act without restrictions or limits 行動自由；無約束：*The changes will give developers open slather.* 這些變革將為開發商大開方便之門。

ˌopen-ˈsource *adj.* (*computing* 計) used to describe software for which the original SOURCE CODE is made available to anyone （軟件）開放源代碼的，提供源程序的，開放原始碼的

ˈopen syllable *noun* (*phonetics* 語音) a syllable which does not end with a consonant, for example *so* 開音節（以元音結束，如 so）

ˌopen-ˈtoed *adj.* (of shoes 鞋) not covering the toes 露趾的：*open-toed sandals* 露趾涼鞋

ˌopen-ˈtop (also **ˌopen-ˈtopped**) *adj.* (*BrE*) (of a vehicle 機動車) having no roof 敞篷的

ˌopen ˈverdict *noun* an official decision in a British court stating that the exact cause of a person's death is not known 死因未詳的裁決，存疑判決（英國法庭宣稱死因不明的判決）

opera /ˈɒprə; *NAmE* ˈɑːprə/ *noun* **1** [C, U] a dramatic work in which all or most of the words are sung to music; works of this type as an art form or entertainment 歌劇；歌劇劇本；歌劇藝術：*Puccini's operas* 普契尼的歌劇 ◇ *to go to the opera* 去看歌劇 ◇ *an opera singer* 歌劇演員 ◇ ***light/grand opera*** 輕 / 大歌劇 ➲ see also SOAP OPERA **2** [C] a company that performs opera; a building in which operas are performed 歌劇團；歌劇院：*the Vienna State Opera* 維也納國家歌劇院 ▶ **op·er·at·ic** /ˌɒpəˈrætɪk; *NAmE* ˌɑːp-/ *adj.*：*operatic arias/composers* 歌劇詠歎調 / 作曲家

op·er·able /ˈɒpərəbl; *NAmE* ˈɑːp-/ *adj.* **1** that functions; that can be used 運作的；可實行的；可使用的：*When will the single currency be operable?* 什麼時候實行單一貨幣？ **2** (of a medical condition 醫療狀況) that can be treated by an operation 可以動手術的 OPP **inoperable**

ˈopera glasses *noun* [pl.] small BINOCULARS that people use in a theatre to see the actors or singers on the stage 觀劇小望遠鏡

ˈopera house *noun* a theatre where operas are performed 歌劇院

op·er·and /ˈɒpərænd; *NAmE* ˈɑːp-/ *noun* (*mathematics* 數) the number on which an operation is to be done 操作數；運算數；運算元

op·er·ate 0-w /ˈɒpəreɪt; *NAmE* ˈɑːp-/ *verb*
▸ MACHINE 機器 **1** 0-w [I] **+ adv./prep.** to work in a particular way 運轉；工作 SYN **function**：*Most domestic freezers operate at below -18°C.* 多數家用冰櫃能製冷到零下 18 攝氏度以下。◇ *Solar panels can only operate in sunlight.* 太陽能電池板只能在日光下起作用。◇ (*figurative*) *Some people can only operate well under pressure.* 有些人只有在壓力下工作才會有好表現。 **2** 0-w [T] **~ sth** to use or control a machine or make it work 操作；控制；使運行：*What skills are needed to operate this machinery?* 操作這種機器需要什麼技能？
▸ SYSTEM/PROCESS/SERVICE 系統；過程；服務 **3** 0-w [I, T] to be used or working; to use sth or make it work （被）使用；（使）運轉：*A new late-night service is now operating.* 現在推出一項新的深夜服務。◇ *The regulation operates in favour of married couples.* 這一規定的實施有利於已婚夫婦。◇ **~ sth** *The airline operates flights to 25 countries.* 這家航空公司經營飛往 25 個國家的航班。◇ *France operates a system of subsidized loans to dairy farmers.* 法國對奶農實行補貼貸款制度。
▸ OF BUSINESS/ORGANIZATION 企業；機構 **4** [I] **+ adv./prep.** to work in a particular way or from a particular place （以某方式或從某地方）經營，營業：*They plan to operate from a new office in Edinburgh.* 他們計劃由愛丁堡的新辦事處經營。◇ *Illegal drinking clubs continue to operate in the city.* 非法飲酒俱樂部繼續在城內營業。
▸ MEDICAL 醫療 **5** 0-w [I] to cut open sb's body in order to remove a part that has a disease or to repair a part that is damaged 動手術：*The doctors operated last night.* 醫生昨夜做手術了。◇ **~** (**on sb**) (**for sth**) *We will have to operate on his eyes.* 我們得給他的眼睛動手術。
▸ OF SOLDIERS 士兵 **6** [I] (**+ adv./prep.**) to be involved in military activities in a place （在某地）採取軍事行動：*Troops are operating from bases in the north.* 部隊正從北部基地發動軍事行動。

ˈoperating system *noun* a set of programs that controls the way a computer works and runs other programs （計算機）操作系統

ˈoperating table *noun* a special table that you lie on to have a medical operation in a hospital 手術枱：*The patient died **on the operating table*** (= during an operation). 病人死在手術枱上。

ˈoperating theatre (also **theatre**) (both *BrE*) (*NAmE* **ˈoperating room**) *noun* a room in a hospital used for medical operations 手術室

op·er·ation 0-w /ˌɒpəˈreɪʃn; *NAmE* ˌɑːp-/ *noun*
▸ MEDICAL 醫療 **1** 0-w (also *BrE, informal* **op**) [C] the process of cutting open a part of a person's body in order to remove or repair a damaged part 手術：*Will I need to **have an operation**?* 我需要動手術嗎？◇ *He underwent a three-hour heart operation.* 他接受了三個小時的心臟手術。◇ **~** (**on sb/sth**) (**to do sth**) *an operation on her lung to remove a tumour* 為她做肺部腫瘤切除手術 ◇ **~** (**on sb/sth**) (**for sth**) *Doctors **performed an** emergency **operation** for appendicitis last night.* 醫生昨天夜裏做了緊急闌尾炎手術。 ➲ COLLOCATIONS at ILL
▸ ORGANIZED ACTIVITY 有組織的活動 **2** 0-w [C] an organized activity that involves several people doing different things （有組織的）活動，行動：*a security operation* 安全行動 ◇ *The police have launched a major operation against drug suppliers.* 警方展開了一次打擊毒販的大規模行動。◇ *the UN peacekeeping operations* 聯合國維持和平行動
▸ BUSINESS 商務 **3** 0-w [C, usually pl.] a business or company involving many parts （包括許多部份的）企業，公司：*a huge multinational operation* 龐大的跨國公司 **4** 0-w [C] the activity or work done in an area of business or industry （工商業）活動，業務：*the firm's banking operations overseas* 這家公司的國外銀行業務
▸ COMPUTER 計算機 **5** 0-w [C, U] an act performed by a machine, especially a computer 運算；運作：*The whole operation is performed in less than three seconds.* 全部運算在三秒內完成。
▸ MACHINE/SYSTEM 機器；系統 **6** 0-w [U] the way that parts of a machine or a system work; the process of making

O

sth work 運轉；運行；操作：*Regular servicing guarantees the smooth operation of the engine.* 定期維修可保持發動機的順暢運轉。◇ *Operation of the device is extremely simple.* 這個裝置的操作非常簡單。

▸ **MILITARY ACTIVITY** 軍事行動 **7** [C, usually pl.] military activity 軍事行動：*He was the officer in charge of operations.* 他是負責指揮作戰行動的軍官。

▸ **MATHEMATICS** 數學 **8** [C] a process in which a number or quantity is changed by adding, multiplying, etc. 運算

IDM **in ope'ration** working, being used or having an effect 工作中；使用中；有效：*The system has been in operation for six months.* 這個系統已經運行六個月了。◇ *Temporary traffic controls are in operation on New Road.* 新路正在實施臨時交通管制。**come into ope'ration** to start working; to start having an effect 開始工作；開始生效 SYN **come into force**：*The new rules come into operation from next week.* 新規定從下週起實施。**put sth into ope'ration** to make sth start working; to start using sth 實施；使…運轉；啟用：*It's time to put our plan into operation.* 現在應該執行我們的計劃了。

op·er·ation·al /ˌɒpəˈreɪʃənl; *NAmE* ˌɑːp-/ *adj.* **1** [usually before noun] connected with the way in which a business, machine, system, etc. works 操作的；運轉的；運營的；業務的：*operational activities/costs/difficulties* 營運上的活動／成本／困難 **2** [not usually before noun] ready to be used 可使用：*The new airport is now **fully operational**.* 新機場現在可全面投入運營。**3** [only before noun] connected with a military operation 軍事行動的：*operational headquarters* 作戰指揮部 ▸ **op·er·ation·al·ly** *adv.*

ˌoperational 'research (also **'operations research**) *noun* [U] (*technical* 術語) the study of how businesses are organized, in order to make them more efficient 運籌學

ˌope'ration code (also **op·code**) *noun* [U, C] (*computing* 計) an instruction written in MACHINE CODE which relates to a particular task 操作碼；運算碼

ope'rations room *noun* a room from which military or police activities are controlled（軍隊或警方的）作戰指揮室，行動指揮室

op·era·tive /ˈɒpərətɪv; *NAmE* ˈɑːpərətɪv; -reɪt-/ *noun, adj.*

■ ***noun*** **1** (*technical* 術語) a worker, especially one who works with their hands 工作人員；（尤指）體力勞動者，工人，操作員：*a factory operative* 工廠工人 ◇ ***skilled/unskilled operatives*** 技術／非技術工人 **2** (*especially NAmE*) a person who does secret work, especially for a government organization 密探；（尤指政府的）特工人員：*an intelligence operative* 情報人員

■ ***adj.*** **1** [not usually before noun] ready to be used; in use 可使用；在使用中 SYN **functional**：*This law becomes operative immediately.* 本法規即時生效。◇ *The station will be **fully operative** again in January.* 該站將於一月份全部恢復運營。**2** [only before noun] (*medical* 醫) connected with a medical operation 手術的：*operative treatment* 手術治療 ➲ see also POST-OPERATIVE

IDM **the operative word** used to emphasize that a particular word or phrase is the most important one in a sentence 關鍵詞；最重要的詞語：*I was in love with her—'was' being the operative word.* 在 I was in love with her 這句話中，was 是關鍵詞。

op·er·ator /ˈɒpəreɪtə(r); *NAmE* ˈɑːp-/ *noun* **1** (often in compounds 常構成複合詞) a person who operates equipment or a machine 操作人員；技工：*a computer/machine operator* 電腦／機器操作員 **2** (*BrE* also **tel·eph·on·ist**) a person who works on the telephone SWITCHBOARD of a large company or organization, especially at a TELEPHONE EXCHANGE 電話員；接線員 **3** (often in compounds 常構成複合詞) a person or company that runs a particular business（某企業的）經營者，專業公司：*a tour operator* 經營旅遊業者 ◇ *a bus operator* 公共汽車公司 **4** (*informal*, especially *disapproving*) a person who is skilful at getting what they want, especially when this involves behaving in a dishonest way 投機取巧者；善於鑽營的人；騙子：*a **smooth/slick/shrewd operator*** 一個八面玲瓏／油嘴滑舌／工於心計的取巧者 **5** (*mathematics* 數) a symbol or function which represents an operation in mathematics 算子

op·er·etta /ˌɒpəˈretə; *NAmE* ˌɑːpə-/ *noun* a short OPERA, usually with a humorous subject 輕歌劇

oph·thal·mic /ɒfˈθælmɪk; *NAmE* ɑːf-/ *adj.* (*medical* 醫) connected with the eye 眼科的；與眼睛有關的：*ophthalmic surgery* 眼科手術

ophˌthalmic op'tician *noun* (*BrE*) = OPTICIAN (1)

oph·thal·molo·gist /ˌɒfθælˈmɒlədʒɪst; *NAmE* ˌɑːfθælˈmɑːl-/ *noun* a doctor who studies and treats the diseases of the eye 眼科醫生

oph·thal·mol·ogy /ˌɒfθælˈmɒlədʒi; *NAmE* ˌɑːfθælˈmɑːl-/ *noun* [U] the scientific study of the eye and its diseases 眼科學

opi·ate /ˈəʊpiət; *NAmE* ˈoʊ-/ *noun* (*formal*) a drug derived from OPIUM. Opiates are used in medicine to reduce severe pain. 鴉片製劑；麻醉劑；鎮痛劑

opine /əʊˈpaɪn; *NAmE* oʊ-/ *verb* **~ that ...** (*formal*) to express a particular opinion 表達，發表（意見）：*He opined that Prague was the most beautiful city in Europe.* 他認為布拉格是歐洲最美麗的城市。

Language Bank 用語庫

opinion

Giving your personal opinion 表達個人意見

- **In my opinion**, everyone should have some understanding of science. 依我看，每個人都應該懂一點科學。
- Everyone should, **in my opinion**, have some understanding of science. 依我看，每個人都應該懂一點科學。
- **It seems to me that** many people in this country have a poor understanding of science. 在我看來，這個國家許多人都不太懂科學。
- This is, **in my view**, the result of a failure of the scientific community to get its message across. 依我看，這是科學界未能清楚傳達訊息所致。
- Another reason why so many people have such a poor understanding of science is, **I believe**, the lack of adequate funding for science in schools. 我認為，如此多的人對科學缺乏認識的另一個原因是學校對科學教育所投入的資金不足。
- Smith argues that science is separate from culture. **My own view is that** science belongs with literature, art, philosophy and religion as an integral part of our culture. 史密斯認為科學與文化是互不相干的。我的觀點是科學與文學、藝術、哲學以及宗教一起都是我們文化的不可或缺的一部份。
- **In this writer's opinion**, the more the public know about science, the less they will fear and distrust it. 在這個作家看來，公眾對科學瞭解得越多，他們就越不會懼怕科學並且會更加相信科學。

➲ Synonyms at THINK

➲ Language Banks at ACCORDING TO, ARGUE, IMPERSONAL, NEVERTHELESS, PERHAPS

opin·ion 🔑 /əˈpɪnjən/ *noun*

1 🔑 [C] your feelings or thoughts about sb/sth, rather than a fact 意見；想法；看法 SYN **view**：**~ (about/of/on sb/sth)** *We were invited to **give our opinions** about how the work should be done.* 我們應邀就如何開展工作提出意見。◇ *I've recently changed my opinion of her.* 我最近改變了對她的看法。◇ *Everyone **had an opinion** on the subject.* 大家對這個問題都有自己的看法。◇ **~ (that ...)** *The chairman **expressed the opinion** that job losses were inevitable.* 主席認為，失業在所難免。◇ *He has very strong political opinions.* 他的政見頗為堅定。◇ ***In my opinion**, it's a very sound investment.* 依我看，這是十分穩當的投資。◇ (*formal*) *It is our opinion that he should resign.* 我們認為他應該辭職。◇ *If you want my opinion, I think you'd be crazy not to accept.* 既然要我說嘛，我認為你不接受那才傻呢。➲ LANGUAGE BANK at ACCORDING TO **2** 🔑 [U] the beliefs or views of a group of people

（群體的）觀點，信仰：*legal/medical/political opinion* (= the beliefs of people working in the legal, etc. profession) 法學界／醫學界／政界的觀點 ◇ *There is **a difference of opinion*** (= people disagree) *as to the merits of the plan.* 關於這個計劃的優缺點，大家意見分歧。◇ ***Opinion is divided*** (= people disagree) *on the issue.* 大家對這件事意見有分歧。◇ *There is a wide body of opinion that supports this proposal.* 支持這項提議的大有人在。◇ *Which is the better is a **matter of opinion*** (= people have different opinions about it). 哪一個比較好只是看法問題。➲ see also PUBLIC OPINION **3** 🔑 [C] advice from a professional person 專家意見：*They called in a psychologist to give an independent opinion.* 他們徵詢一位心理學家的獨立意見。◇ *I'd like a **second opinion*** (= advice from another person) *before I make a decision.* 我在做決定之前，想聽聽別人的意見。

IDM **be of the opinion that ...** (*formal*) to believe or think that ... 相信；認為 **have a good, bad, high, low, etc. opinion of sb/sth** to think that sb/sth is good, bad, etc. 對…評價好／不好／高／低：*The boss has a very high opinion of her.* 老闆對她評價很高。➲ more at CONSIDER

opin·ion·ated /əˈpɪnjəneɪtɪd/ (also **ˌself-oˈpinion·ated**) *adj.* (*disapproving*) having very strong opinions that you are not willing to change 固執己見的；頑固的

oˈpinion poll *noun* = POLL *n.* (1)

opium /ˈəʊpiəm; *NAmE* ˈoʊ-/ *noun* [U] a powerful drug made from the juice of a type of POPPY (= a kind of flower), used in the past in medicines to reduce pain and help people sleep. Some people take opium illegally for pleasure and can become ADDICTED to it. 鴉片

opos·sum /əˈpɒsəm; *NAmE* əˈpɑːs-/ (*AustralE*, *NZE* or *NAmE*, *informal* **pos·sum**) *noun* a small American or Australian animal that lives in trees and carries its young in a POUCH (= a pocket of skin on the front of the mother's body) 負鼠（產於美洲或澳大利亞的小動物，在樹上生活，攜幼崽於母獸育兒袋中）

op·pon·ent 🔑 /əˈpəʊnənt; *NAmE* əˈpoʊ-/ *noun*
1 🔑 a person that you are playing or fighting against in a game, competition, argument, etc. 對手；競爭者 **SYN** **adversary**：*a political opponent* 政敵 ◇ *a **dangerous/worthy/formidable opponent*** 危險的／可敬的／強大的對手 ◇ *The team's opponents are unbeaten so far this season.* 該隊的競爭對手本賽季尚無敗績。**2** 🔑 **~ (of sth)** a person who is against sth and tries to change or stop it 反對者；阻止者：*opponents of abortion* 反對墮胎的人 ◇ *opponents of the regime* 反對政權的人

op·por·tune /ˈɒpətjuːn; *NAmE* ˌɑːpərˈtuːn/ *adj.* (*formal*)
1 (of a time 時間) suitable for doing a particular thing, so that it is likely to be successful 恰巧的；適當的；恰當的 **SYN** **favourable**：*The offer could not have come at a more opportune moment.* 那個建議提得正是時候。**2** (of an action or event 行動或事情) done or happening at the right time to be successful 及時的；適時的：*an opportune remark* 適時的言辭 **OPP** **inopportune**
▸ **op·por·tune·ly** *adv.*

op·por·tun·ism /ˌɒpəˈtjuːnɪzəm; *NAmE* ˌɑːpərˈtuː-/ *noun* [U] (*disapproving*) the practice of using situations unfairly to gain advantage for yourself without thinking about how your actions will affect other people 機會主義

op·por·tun·ist /ˌɒpəˈtjuːnɪst; *NAmE* ˌɑːpərˈtuː-/ (also **op·por·tun·is·tic**) *adj.* [usually before noun] (often *disapproving*) making use of an opportunity, especially to get an advantage for yourself; not done in a planned way 機會主義的；投機的；見風轉舵的：*an opportunist crime* 臨時起意的偶發犯罪 ▸ **op·por·tun·ist** *noun*：*80% of burglaries are committed by casual opportunists.* * 80% 的入室行竊都是臨時起意者所為。

op·por·tun·is·tic /ˌɒpətjuːˈnɪstɪk; *NAmE* ˌɑːpərtuːˈn-/ *adj.*
1 (*disapproving*) = OPPORTUNIST **2** [only before noun] (*medical* 醫) harmful to people whose IMMUNE SYSTEM has been made weak by disease or drugs 機會致病性的（對免疫系統差的人有害）：*an opportunistic infection* 機會性的感染

op·por·tun·ity 🔑 /ˌɒpəˈtjuːnəti; *NAmE* ˌɑːpərˈtuː-/ *noun* [C, U] (*pl.* **-ies**)
a time when a particular situation makes it possible to do or achieve sth 機會；時機 **SYN** **chance**：**~ (to do sth)** *You'll have the opportunity to ask any questions at the end.* 你們最後將有機會提問任何問題。◇ **~ (for sth/for doing sth)** *There was no opportunity for further discussion.* 沒有機會進行深入討論了。◇ **~ (of doing sth)** *At least give him the opportunity of explaining what happened.* 至少要給他機會解釋一下發生了什麼事。◇ *Our company promotes **equal opportunities** for women* (= women are given the same jobs, pay, etc. as men). 本公司提倡男女機會均等。◇ ***career/employment/job opportunities*** 職業發展／就業／工作機會 ◇ *I'd like to **take this opportunity** to thank my colleagues for their support.* 我謹藉此機會感謝同事的支持。◇ *He is rude to me **at every opportunity*** (= whenever possible). 他動不動就對我粗魯無禮。◇ *They intend to close the school **at the earliest opportunity*** (= as soon as possible). 他們打算儘早關閉學校。◇ *a **window of opportunity*** (= a period of time when the circumstances are right for doing sth) 行事的良機 ➲ see also PHOTO OPPORTUNITY

opporˈtunity shop (also **ˈop shop**) *noun* (*AustralE*, *NZE*) a shop/store that sells clothes and other goods given by people to raise money for a charity 義賣商店（為慈善事業募資）**SYN** **charity shop, thrift store**

op·pose 🔑 /əˈpəʊz; *NAmE* əˈpoʊz/ *verb*
1 🔑 to disagree strongly with sb's plan, policy, etc. and try to change it or prevent it from succeeding 反對（計劃、政策等）；抵制；阻撓：**~ sb/sth** *This party would bitterly oppose the re-introduction of the death penalty.* 這個黨會強烈反對恢復死刑。◇ *He threw all those that opposed him into prison.* 他把所有反對他的人都投進了監獄。◇ **~ (sb/sth) doing sth** *I would oppose changing the law.* 我將反對改變這個法規。➲ compare PROPOSE (4) **2 ~ sb** to compete with sb in a contest（在競賽中）與…對壘，與…角逐：*He intends to oppose the prime minister in the leadership election.* 在領導層選舉中，他欲與首相一決高下。

op·posed 🔑 /əˈpəʊzd; *NAmE* əˈpoʊzd/ *adj.*
[not usually before noun] **~ (to sth)** **1** 🔑 (of a person 人) disagreeing strongly with sth and trying to stop it 強烈反對：*She remained bitterly opposed to the idea of moving abroad.* 她仍然強烈反對移居國外。◇ *They are totally opposed to abortion.* 他們完全反對墮胎。**2** 🔑 (of ideas, opinions, etc. 意見、看法等) very different from sth 截然不同：*Our views are **diametrically opposed** on this issue.* 在這個問題上，我們的觀點大相逕庭。

IDM **as opposed to** 🔑 (*formal*) used to make a contrast between two things（表示對比）而，相對於：*200 attended, as opposed to 300 the previous year.* 出席的有 200 人，而前一年是 300 人。◇ *This exercise develops suppleness as opposed to* (= rather than) *strength.* 這項鍛煉不是增強力量，而是增強柔韌性的。

op·pos·ing 🔑 /əˈpəʊzɪŋ; *NAmE* əˈpoʊzɪŋ/ *adj.* [only before noun]
1 🔑 (of teams, armies, forces, etc. 隊組、軍隊、力量等) playing, fighting, working, etc. against each other 對立的；相競爭的；對抗的：*a player from the opposing side* 對方的運動員 ◇ *It is time for opposing factions to unite and work towards a common goal.* 現在是對立各派聯合起來、為共同目標而奮鬥的時候了。**2** 🔑 (of attitudes, views, etc. 態度、觀點等) very different from each other 相反的；極不相同的

op·pos·ite 🔑 /ˈɒpəzɪt; -sɪt; *NAmE* ˈɑːpəzət/ *adj.*, *adv.*, *noun*, *prep.*
■ ***adj.*** **1** 🔑 [only before noun] on the other side of a particular area from sb/sth and usually facing them 對面的；另一邊的：*Answers are given on the opposite page.* 答案在背面一頁上。◇ *We live further down on the opposite side of the road.* 我們住在馬路對面再遠一點的地方。◇ *It's not easy having a relationship when you live at opposite ends of the country.* 人雖同國卻各處東西；在這種情況下談戀愛，談何容易。**2** 🔑 (used after the noun 用於名詞後) facing the speaker or sb/sth that has been mentioned 對面的：*I could see smoke coming from the windows of the house directly opposite.* 我看到煙從正對

O

面房子的窗戶裏冒出來。◇ *He sat down in the chair opposite.* 他在對面的椅子上坐了下來。 **3** ⊶ [usually before noun] as different as possible from sth 相反的；迥然不同的：*I watched them leave and then drove off in the opposite direction.* 我目送他們離開，然後開車向相反的方向駛去。◇ *She tried calming him down but it seemed to be having the opposite effect.* 她試着讓他平靜下來，卻似乎火上澆油了。◇ *students at opposite ends of the ability range* 能力差距兩極的學生 ▸ **op·pos·ite** ⊶ *adv.*：*There's a newly married couple living opposite* (= on the other side of the road). 有一對新婚夫婦住在馬路對面。◇ *See opposite* (= on the opposite page) *for further details.* 詳情見對頁。

IDM **your ˌopposite ˈnumber** (*informal*) a person who does the same job as you in another organization（另一個單位內）與自己職位相等的人：*The Foreign Secretary is currently having talks with his opposite number in the White House.* 外交大臣現正和白宮的對等官員會談。 **the ˌopposite ˈsex** the other sex 異性：*He found it difficult to talk to members of the opposite sex.* 他覺得很難與異性交談。 ➲ more at PULL *v.*

▪ ***noun*** ⊶ a person or thing that is as different as possible from sb/sth else 對立的人（或物）；對立面；反面：*Hot and cold are opposites.* 熱和冷是對立面。◇ *What is the* ***opposite of*** *heavy?* 重的反義詞是什麼？◇ *I thought she would be small and blonde but she's* ***the complete opposite.*** 我原以為她是一位身材嬌小的金髮女郎，但她恰恰相反。◇ *Exactly the opposite is true.* 事實恰恰相反。◇ *'Is it better now?'* ***'Quite the opposite,*** *I'm afraid.'* "現在好點了嗎？" "恐怕正相反。"

IDM **ˌopposites atˈtract** used to say that people who are very different are often attracted to each other 相反相成；相異相吸

▪ ***prep.*** **1** ⊶ on the other side of a particular area from sb/sth, and usually facing them 與…相對；在…對面：*I sat opposite him during the meal* (= on the other side of the table). 席間我坐在他的對面。◇ *The bank is opposite the supermarket* (= on the other side of the road). 銀行在超市的正對面。◇ *Write your address opposite* (= next to) *your name.* 在姓名旁邊寫上你的地址。 **2** acting in a film/movie or play as the partner of sb 與…合演；與…聯袂演出：*She starred opposite Tom Hanks.* 她與湯姆•漢克斯聯袂主演。

O

op·pos·ition ⊶ /ˌɒpəˈzɪʃn; *NAmE* ˌɑːpə-/ *noun* **1** ⊶ [U] **~ (to sb/sth)** the act of strongly disagreeing with sb/sth, especially with the aim of preventing sth from happening（強烈的）反對，反抗，對抗：*Delegates expressed* ***strong opposition*** *to the plans.* 代表強烈反對這些計劃。◇ *The army* ***met with fierce opposition*** *in every town.* 軍隊在每一座城鎮都遭到了頑強的抵抗。◇ *He spent five years in prison for his opposition to the regime.* 他因為反對那個政權而過了五年的鐵窗生活。◇ ***opposition forces*** (= people who are arguing, fighting, etc. with another group) 反對勢力 **2** ⊶ **the opposition** [sing.+sing./pl. v.] the people you are competing against in business, a competition, a game, etc.（事業、競賽、遊戲等的）對手，敵手，競爭者：*He's gone to work for the opposition.* 他去為競爭對手工作了。◇ *The opposition is/are mounting a strong challenge to our business.* 對方正對我方企業逐漸形成強大的挑戰。◇ *Liverpool couldn't match the opposition in the final and lost 2–0.* 利物浦隊在決賽中不敵對手，以 0:2 輸掉比賽。 **3** ⊶ **the Opposition** (*NAmE* **the opposition**) [sing.+sing./pl. v.] the main political party that is opposed to the government; the political parties that are in a parliament but are not part of the government 反對黨；在野黨：*the* ***leader of the Opposition*** 反對黨領袖 ◇ ***Opposition MPs/parties*** 反對黨議員；反對黨派 ◇ *the Opposition spokesman on education* 反對黨教育事務發言人 **4** [U, C] (*formal*) the state of being as different as possible; two things that are as different as possible 對立；對立的事物：*the opposition between good and evil* 善與惡的對立 ◇ *His poetry is full of oppositions and contrasts.* 他的詩歌充滿了對立與對比。 ▸ **op·pos·ition·al** /-ʃənl/ *adj.* [usually before noun]：(*formal*) *oppositional groups/tactics* 反對團體／策略

IDM **in oppoˈsition** (of a political party 政黨) forming part of a parliament but not part of the government 反對黨的；在野的 **in oppoˈsition to sb/sth** **1** ⊶ disagreeing strongly with sb/sth, especially with the aim of preventing sth from happening 強烈反對（或抵制）某人／某事物：*Protest marches were held in opposition to the proposed law.* 為抗議新提出的法規舉行了示威遊行。 **2** contrasting two people or things that are very different 對比；對照：*Leisure is often defined in opposition to work.* 休閒常被定義為工作的反面。

op·press /əˈpres/ *verb* **1 ~ sb** to treat sb in a cruel and unfair way, especially by not giving them the same freedom, rights, etc. as other people 壓迫；欺壓；壓制：*The regime is accused of oppressing religious minorities.* 人們指控這個政權壓迫少數宗教群體。 **2 ~ sb** to make sb only able to think about sad or worrying things 壓抑；使窒息；使煩惱：*The gloomy atmosphere in the office oppressed her.* 辦公室的低沉氣氛使她感到鬱悶。 **SYN** **weigh down** ▸ **op·pres·sion** /əˈpreʃn/ *noun* [U]：*victims of oppression* 受壓迫者

op·pressed /əˈprest/ *adj.* **1** treated in a cruel and unfair way and not given the same freedom, rights, etc. as other people 被壓迫的；受迫害的：*oppressed minorities* 被壓迫的少數群體 **2** **the oppressed** *noun* [pl.] people who are oppressed 被壓迫者

op·pres·sive /əˈpresɪv/ *adj.* **1** treating people in a cruel and unfair way and not giving them the same freedom, rights, etc. as other people 壓迫的；壓制的；高壓的：*oppressive laws* 對部份人的壓制性法律 ◇ *an oppressive regime* 殘暴的政權 **2** (of the weather 天氣) extremely hot and unpleasant and lacking fresh air 悶熱的；令人窒息的 **SYN** **stifling**：*oppressive heat* 難熬的酷暑 **3** making you feel unhappy and anxious 令人苦惱的；令人焦慮的 **SYN** **stifling**：*an oppressive relationship* 令人苦惱的關係 ▸ **op·pres·sive·ly** *adv.*：*to behave oppressively* 表現得盛氣凌人 ◇ *oppressively hot* 熱得令人窒息 ◇ *He suffered from an oppressively dominant mother.* 他那武斷專橫的母親令他苦不堪言。

op·press·or /əˈpresə(r)/ *noun* a person or group of people that treats sb in a cruel and unfair way, especially by not giving them the same rights, etc. as other people 壓迫者；殘暴的統治者；暴君

op·pro·brium /əˈprəʊbriəm; *NAmE* əˈproʊ-/ *noun* [U] (*formal*) severe criticism of a person, country, etc. by a large group of people（眾人的）譴責，責難，抨擊 ▸ **op·pro·bri·ous** /əˈprəʊbriəs; *NAmE* əˈproʊ-/ *adj.*：*an opprobrious remark* 眾人的指摘

ˈop shop *noun* (*AustralE, NZE*) = OPPORTUNITY SHOP

opt /ɒpt; *NAmE* ɑːpt/ *verb* [I, T] to choose to take or not to take a particular course of action 選擇；挑選：**~ for/against sth** *After graduating she opted for a career in music.* 畢業後她選擇了從事音樂工作。◇ **~ to do sth** *Many workers opted to leave their jobs rather than take a pay cut.* 許多工人寧願離職也不接受減薪。 ➲ SYNONYMS at CHOOSE

PHR V **ˌopt ˈin (to sth)** to choose to be part of a system or an agreement 決定加入；選擇參與 **ˌopt ˈout (of sth)** **1** to choose not to take part in sth 決定退出；選擇不參與：*Employees may opt out of the company's pension plan.* 雇員可選擇不參加該公司的養老金計劃。 **2** (of a school or hospital in Britain 英國的學校或醫院) to choose not to be under the control of the local authority 選擇不受地方當局管理 ➲ related noun OPT-OUT

optic /ˈɒptɪk; *NAmE* ˈɑːp-/ *adj., noun*

▪ ***adj.*** [usually before noun] (*technical* 術語) connected with the eye or the sense of sight 眼的；視覺的：*the optic nerve* (= from the eye to the brain) 視神經

▪ ***noun*** a device for measuring amounts of strong alcoholic drinks in a bar 奧普蒂克量杯（酒吧用以量烈性酒）

op·tic·al /ˈɒptɪkl; *NAmE* ˈɑːp-/ *adj.* [usually before noun] **1** connected with the sense of sight or the relationship between light and sight 視力的；視覺的；光學的：*optical effects* 視覺效果 **2** used to help you see sth more clearly 有助於視力的；光學的：*optical aids* 助視器 ◇ *optical instruments such as microscopes and telescopes* 顯微鏡和望遠鏡等光學儀器 **3** (*computing* 計) using light for reading or storing information 光讀取的；光存

貯的： *optical storage* 光存貯器 ◇ *an optical disk* 光盤 ▸ **op·tic·al·ly** /-kli/ *adv.*

ˌoptical ˈcharacter recognition *noun* [U] (*abbr.* **OCR**) (*computing* 計) the process of using light to record printed information onto disks for use in a computer system 光符識別（用光學方法識別印刷字符，以便用於計算機系統）

ˌoptical ˈfibre (*BrE*) (*NAmE* **ˌoptical ˈfiber**) *noun* [C, U] a thin glass thread through which light can be TRANSMITTED (= sent) 光導纖維；光纖

optical illusions 視錯覺

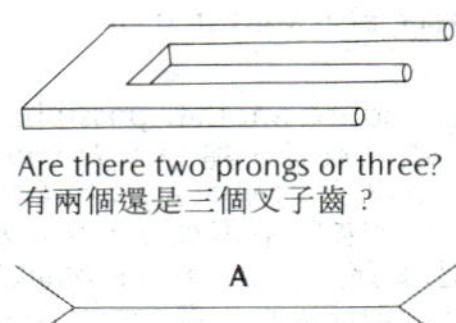

Are there two prongs or three?
有兩個還是三個叉子齒？

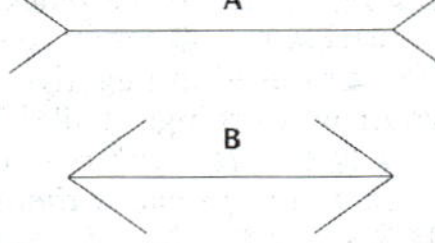

Horizontal line A and horizontal line B are of equal length, but horizontal line A appears to be longer.
水平線 A 和 B 長度相同，但 A 看起來要長些。

ˌoptical ilˈlusion *noun* something that tricks your eyes and makes you think that you can see sth that is not there, or makes you see sth as different from what it really is 視錯覺；錯視；視覺幻象

op·ti·cian /ɒpˈtɪʃn; *NAmE* ɑːp-/ *noun* **1** (also **ophˌthalmic opˈtician**) (both *BrE*) (also **op·tom·etrist** *NAmE, BrE*) a person whose job is to examine people's eyes and to recommend and sell glasses 眼鏡商；驗光師 **2 op·ti·cian's** (*pl.* **op·ti·cians**) the shop/store where an optician works 眼鏡商店： *to go to the optician's* 去眼鏡店 **3** a person who makes LENSES, glasses, etc. 光學儀器製造者

op·tics /ˈɒptɪks; *NAmE* ˈɑːp-/ *noun* [U] the scientific study of sight and light 光學 ➲ see also FIBRE OPTICS

op·ti·mal /ˈɒptɪməl; *NAmE* ˈɑːp-/ *adj.* = OPTIMUM (1) ▸ **op·ti·mal·ly** *adv.*

op·ti·mism /ˈɒptɪmɪzəm; *NAmE* ˈɑːp-/ *noun* [U] ~ (**about/for sth**) a feeling that good things will happen and that sth will be successful; the tendency to have this feeling 樂觀；樂觀主義： *optimism about/for the future* 對未來的樂觀 ◇ *We may now look forward* ***with optimism***. 我們現在可以樂觀地展望未來。◇ *a mood of* ***cautious optimism*** 謹慎樂觀的心情 ◇ *There are very real grounds for optimism.* 的確有理由可以樂觀。 OPP **pessimism**

op·ti·mist /ˈɒptɪmɪst; *NAmE* ˈɑːp-/ *noun* a person who always expects good things to happen or things to be successful 樂觀的人；樂天派 OPP **pessimist**

op·ti·mis·tic /ˌɒptɪˈmɪstɪk; *NAmE* ˌɑːp-/ *adj.* expecting good things to happen or sth to be successful; showing this feeling 樂觀的；抱樂觀看法的 SYN **positive**： ~ (**about sth**) *She's not very optimistic about the outcome of the talks.* 她對會談的結果不太樂觀。◇ ~ (**that** ...) *They are cautiously optimistic that the reforms will take place.* 他們對是否實行改革表示審慎的樂觀。◇ *We are now taking a more optimistic view.* 我們現在抱較樂觀的看法。◇ *in an optimistic mood* 以樂觀的情緒 ◇ *I think you're being a little* ***over-optimistic***. 我看你是有點過於樂觀了。 OPP **pessimistic** ▸ **op·ti·mis·tic·al·ly** /-kli/ *adv.*

op·ti·mize (*BrE* also **-ise**) /ˈɒptɪmaɪz; *NAmE* ˈɑːp-/ *verb* ~ **sth** to make sth as good as it can be; to use sth in the best possible way 使最優化；充分利用： *to optimize the use of resources* 充分利用資源

op·ti·mum /ˈɒptɪməm; *NAmE* ˈɑːp-/ *adj.* [only before noun] **1** (also **op·ti·mal**) the best possible; producing the best possible results 最佳的；最適宜的： *optimum growth* 最佳增長 ◇ *the optimum use of resources* 對資源的充分利用 ◇ *the optimum conditions for effective learning* 保證學習效果的最佳條件 **2 the optimum** *noun* [sing.] the best possible result, set of conditions, etc. 最佳結果；最好的條件 SYN **ideal**

op·tion 🔑 AW /ˈɒpʃn; *NAmE* ˈɑːp-/ *noun, verb*

■ ***noun*** **1** 🔑 [C, U] something that you can choose to have or do; the freedom to choose what you do 可選擇的事物；選擇；選擇權；選擇的自由： *As I see it, we have two options ...* 據我看，我們有兩種選擇… ◇ *There are various options open to you.* 你有多種選擇。◇ *Going to college was not an option for me.* 上大學不是我可以選擇的道路。◇ *I had* ***no option but to*** (= I had to) *ask him to leave.* 我別無選擇，只有請他離開。◇ ~ (**of doing sth**) *Students have the option of studying abroad in their second year.* 學生在二年級時可以選擇出國學習。◇ ~ (**to do sth**) *A savings plan that gives you the option to vary your monthly payments.* 一項允許你每月自由存款的儲蓄方案。◇ *This particular model comes with a wide range of options* (= things you can choose to have when buying sth but which you will have to pay extra for). 這一型號有各式各樣的配件可供選擇。➲ note at next page **2** 🔑 [C] a subject that a student can choose to study, but that they do not have to do 選修課： *The course offers options in design and computing.* 這一課程開了設計和計算機技術的選修科目。 **3** [C] the right to buy or sell sth at some time in the future（未來的）買賣選擇權： ~ (**on sth**) *We have an option on the house.* 我們有權購買這所房子。◇ *He has promised me first option on his car* (= the opportunity to buy it before anyone else). 他答應我可以優先買他的汽車。◇ ~ (**to do sth**) *The property is for rent with an option to buy at any time.* 這房子供出租，但可隨時買下。◇ *share options* (= the right to buy shares in a company) 認股選擇權 **4** [C] (*computing* 計) one of the choices you can make when using a computer program 選項；選擇： *Choose the 'Cut' option from the Edit menu.* 從編輯選單上選"剪切"項。

IDM **keep/leave your ˈoptions open** 🔑 to avoid making a decision now so that you still have a choice in the future 保留選擇餘地；暫不決定 **the ˌsoft/ˌeasy ˈoption** (often *disapproving*) a choice which is thought to be easier because it involves less effort, difficulty, etc. 輕鬆的選擇；捷徑： *They are anxious that the new course should not be seen as a soft option.* 他們盼望新辦法不會被視為捷徑。◇ *He decided to* ***take the easy option*** *and give them what they wanted.* 他決定順水推舟，他們要什麼就給什麼。

■ ***verb*** ~ **sth** to buy or sell the right to own or use sth, at some time in the future 購買（或出售）…的選擇權： *The novel has been optioned for the screen by his production company.* 這部小說改編成影視作品的權利已經被他的製作公司買下了。

op·tion·al AW /ˈɒpʃənl; *NAmE* ˈɑːp-/ *adj.* that you can choose to do or have if you want to 可選擇的；選修的： *Certain courses are compulsory; others are optional.* 有些課程是必修的，其他是選修的。◇ *This model comes with a number of* ***optional extras*** (= things you can choose to have but which you will have to pay extra for). 這一型號有一系列可供選擇的附件，價格另計。

op·tom·etrist /ɒpˈtɒmətrɪst; *NAmE* ɑːpˈtɑːm-/ (*BrE* also **op·ti·cian**, **ophˌthalmic opˈtician**) *noun* a person whose job is to examine people's eyes and to recommend and sell glasses 眼鏡商；驗光師

op·tom·etry /ɒpˈtɒmətri; *NAmE* ɑːpˈtɑːm-/ *noun* [U] the job of measuring how well people can see and checking their eyes for disease 驗光；視力測定

ˈopt-out *noun* (often used as an adjective 常用作形容詞) **1** (in Britain) the action of a school or hospital that decides to manage its own money and is therefore no longer controlled by a LOCAL AUTHORITY or similar organization（英國學校、醫院從地方當局財政管轄的）退出，脫離 **2** the act of choosing not to be involved in an agreement 不參與協議的決定： *an opt-out clause*

O

退出的條款 ◇ *MPs hoped to reverse Britain's opt-out from the treaty.* 國會議員希望推翻英國退出該條約的決定。

Synonyms 同義詞辨析

option

choice • alternative • possibility

These are all words for sth that you choose to do in a particular situation. 以上各詞均指某種情況下的選擇。

option something that you can choose to have or do; the freedom to choose what you do 指可選擇的事物、選擇、選擇權、選擇的自由： *As I see it, we have two options ...* 據我看，我們有兩種選擇⋯ ◇ *Students have the option of studying abroad in their second year.* 學生在二年級時可以選擇出國學習。

NOTE **Option** is also the word used in computing for one of the choices you can make when using a computer program. * option 亦指計算機程序裏的選項、選擇： *Choose the 'Cut' option from the Edit menu.* 從編輯選單上選擇"剪切"項。

choice the freedom to choose what you do; something that you can choose to have or do 指選擇權、選擇的自由、選擇、可選擇的事物： *If I had the choice, I would stop working tomorrow.* 如果讓我選擇，我明天就停止工作。◇ *There is a wide range of choices open to you.* 你有很多選擇。

alternative something that you can choose to have or do out of two or more possibilities 指可供選擇的事物、其中一種選擇： *You can be paid in cash weekly or by cheque monthly: those are the two alternatives.* 你的工資可以按週以現金支取，或按月以支票支取。二者可選其一。

OPTION, CHOICE OR ALTERNATIVE? 用 option、choice 還是 alternative？

Choice is slightly less formal than **option** and **alternative** is slightly more formal. **Choice** is most often used for 'the freedom to choose', although you can sometimes also use **option** (but not usually **alternative**). * choice 較 option 稍非正式，而 alternative 更正式些。表示選擇權或選擇的自由最常用 choice，不過有時也可用 option，但通常不用 alternative： *If I had the choice/option, I would ...* 如果讓我選擇，我會⋯ ◇ ~~*If I had the alternative, I would ...*~~ ◇ *parental choice in education* 父母在教育方面的選擇權 ◇ ~~*parental option/alternative in education*~~

Things that you can choose are **options, choices** or **alternatives**. However, **alternative** is more frequently used to talk about choosing between two things rather than several. 表示可選擇的事物用 option、choice 或 alternative 均可。不過，alternative 較常用以指兩個而非多個可選項。

possibility one of the different things that you can do in a particular situation 指某種情況下可選擇的事物： *We need to explore a wide range of possibilities.* 我們需要探究各種可能的情況。◇ *The possibilities are endless.* 可想的辦法是無窮的。

NOTE **Possibility** can be used in a similar way to **option, choice** and **alternative**, but the emphasis here is less on the need to make a choice, and more on what is available. * possibility 的用法與 option、choice 和 alternative 相似，不過其重點主要在於可選擇的事物而非需要作出選擇。

PATTERNS

- **with/without** the option/choice/possibility **of** sth
- a(n) **good/acceptable/reasonable/possible** option/choice/alternative
- the **only** option/choice/alternative/possibility **open to** sb
- to **have** a/an/the option/choice **of doing sth**
- to **have no** option/choice/alternative **but to** do sth
- a **number/range of** options/choices/alternatives/possibilities

O

opu·lent /ˈɒpjələnt; NAmE ˈɑːp-/ *adj.* (*formal*) **1** made or decorated using expensive materials 豪華的；富麗堂皇的；華麗的 SYN **luxurious** **2** (of people 人) extremely rich 極富有的；闊氣的 SYN **wealthy** ▶ **opu·lence** /-ləns/ *noun* [U] **opu·lent·ly** *adv.*

opus /ˈəʊpəs; NAmE ˈoʊ-/ *noun* (*pl.* **opera** /ˈɒpərə; NAmE ˈɑːp-/) [usually sing.] **1** (*abbr.* **op.**) a piece of music written by a famous COMPOSER and usually followed by a number that shows when it was written（按個別作曲家的創作排列的）編號樂曲，作品編號： *Beethoven's Opus 18* 貝多芬第十八號作品 **2** (*formal*) an important piece of literature, etc., especially one that is on a large scale 主要（文學等）作品；（尤指）大作，巨著 SYN **work** ➲ see also MAGNUM OPUS

or 🔑 /ɔː(r)/ *conj.*
1 🔑 used to introduce another possibility（用以引出另一種可能性）或，或者，還是： *Is your sister older or younger than you?* 你的姐妹比你大還是小？◇ *Are you coming or not?* 你來還是不來？◇ *Is it a boy or a girl?* 是個男孩還是女孩？◇ *It can be black, white or grey.* 它可能是黑的、白的或灰的。➲ compare EITHER ... OR ... at EITHER *adv.* (3) **2** 🔑 used in negative sentences when mentioning two or more things（用於否定句，提出兩種或多種事物時）也不： *He can't read or write.* 他不會讀，不會寫。◇ *There are people without homes, jobs or family.* 有人既無房屋，又無工作，又無家庭。➲ compare NEITHER ... NOR ... at NEITHER *adv.* (2) **3** 🔑 (also **or else**) used to warn or advise sb that sth bad could happen; otherwise（用於警告或忠告）否則，不然： *Turn the heat down or it'll burn.* 把爐火開小一些，不然就燒焦了。 **4** 🔑 used between two numbers to show approximately how many（用於兩個數字之間表示約略數目）大約： *There were six or seven of us there.* 我們約有六、七個人在場。 **5** 🔑 used to introduce a word or phrase that explains or means the same as another（用於引出解釋性詞語）或者說： *geology, or the science of the earth's crust* 地質學，或者說地殼的科學 ◇ *It weighs a kilo, or just over two pounds.* 這東西重一公斤，或者說兩磅多一點兒。 **6** 🔑 used to say why sth must be true（用於說明原因）不然，否則： *He must like her, or he wouldn't keep calling her.* 他一定喜歡她，不然他不會老給她打電話。 **7** 🔑 used to introduce a contrasting idea（用於引出對比的概念）： *He was lying—or was he?* 他在說謊，還是沒有說謊？

IDM **or so** 🔑 about 大約： *It'll cost €100 or so.* 這大約要花 100 歐元。 **or somebody/something/somewhere | somebody/something/somewhere or other** 🔑 (*informal*) used when you are not exactly sure about a person, thing or place（表示對人、事、地點不太有把握）： *He's a factory supervisor or something.* 他是工廠監督一類的人吧。◇ *'Who said so?' 'Oh, somebody or other. I can't remember who it was.'* "這是誰說的？" "啊，某一個人吧，我記不清是誰了。"

-or *suffix* (in nouns 構成名詞) a person or thing that ⋯的人（或物）： *actor* 演員 ➲ compare -EE (1), -ER (1)

or·acle /ˈɒrəkl; NAmE ˈɔːr-/ *noun* [C] **1** (in ancient Greece) a place where people could go to ask the gods for advice or information about the future; the priest or PRIESTESS through whom the gods were thought to give their message（古希臘的）神示所；（傳達神諭的）牧師，女祭司： *They consulted the oracle at Delphi.* 他們在德爾斐神示所向神請示。 **2** (in ancient Greece) the advice or information that the gods gave, which often had a hidden meaning（古希臘常有隱含意義的）神諭，神示 **3** [usually sing.] a person or book that gives valuable advice or information 能提供寶貴信息的人（或書）；權威；智囊： *My sister's the oracle on investment matters.* 我姐姐是個萬無一失的投資顧問。

or·acu·lar /əˈrækjələ(r)/ *adj.* (*formal* or *humorous*) of or like an oracle; with a hidden meaning 神諭般的；天書般的；晦澀難懂的

oral /ˈɔːrəl/ *adj., noun*
■ *adj.* **1** [usually before noun] spoken rather than written 口頭的： *a test of both oral and written French* 法語口試和筆試 ◇ *oral evidence* 口頭證據 ◇ *He was interested in **oral history*** (= history that is collected from interviews with people who have personal knowledge of past events). 他對口述歷史感興趣。 ➲ SYNONYMS at SPOKEN

➲ compare VERBAL (2) **2** [only before noun] connected with the mouth 用口的；口腔的；口服的：*oral hygiene* 口腔衞生 ◇ *oral sex* (= using the mouth to STIMULATE sb's sex organs) 口交 **3** (*phonetics* 語音) (of a speech sound 語音) produced without the air in the nose VIBRATING 口腔發聲的；口腔的 ➲ compare NASAL (3) ▸ **or·al·ly** /ˈɔːrəli/ *adv.*：*Answers can be written or presented orally on tape.* 答案可以寫下來或口述錄在磁帶上。◇ *Not to be taken orally* (= a warning on some medicines to show that they must not be swallowed). 不得口服。

▪ ***noun*** **1** (*especially BrE*) a spoken exam, especially in a foreign language（尤指外語考試中的）口試：*a French oral* 法語口試 ◇ *He failed the oral.* 他口試不及格。**2** (*NAmE*) a spoken exam in a university（大學裏的）口試

ˌoral ˈhistory *noun* [U] the collection and study of historical information using sound recordings of interviews with people who remember past events 口述歷史（用訪談錄音方法）；口述歷史學

oral·ism /ˈɔːrəlɪzəm/ *noun* [U] the system of teaching deaf people to communicate using speech and LIP-READING 口語教學法（教聾人通過講話和唇讀來交際）▸ **oral·ist** /-ɪst/ *adj.*

or·ange 🔑 /ˈɒrɪndʒ; *NAmE* ˈɔːr-; ˈɑːr-/ *noun, adj.*

▪ ***noun*** [C, U] **1** 🔑 a round CITRUS fruit with thick reddish-yellow skin and a lot of sweet juice 橙子；柑橘：*orange peel* 柑橘皮 ◇ *an orange tree* 橙樹 ◇ *freshly squeezed orange juice* 鮮榨橙汁 ◇ *orange groves* (= groups of orange trees) 橙樹叢 ◇ *orange blossom* 香橙花 ➲ VISUAL VOCAB page V30 ➲ see also BLOOD ORANGE **2** (*BrE*) orange juice, or a drink made from or tasting of oranges 橙汁；橘汁飲料：*Would you like some orange?* 您想喝點橙汁嗎？◇ *A vodka and orange, please.* 請來一份橙汁伏特加酒。**3** 🔑 a bright reddish-yellow colour 橙紅色；橘黃色 IDM see APPLE

▪ ***adj.*** **1** 🔑 bright reddish-yellow in colour 橙紅色的；橘黃色的：*yellow and orange flames* 黃色和橙紅色的火焰 **2 Orange** related to or belonging to a Protestant political group which believes that Northern Ireland should remain part of the UK 奧蘭治黨的，奧蘭治社團的（新教政治團體，主張北愛爾蘭繼續隸屬英國）：*an Orange march* 奧蘭治黨的遊行

or·ange·ade /ˌɒrɪndʒˈeɪd; *NAmE* ˌɔːr-; ˌɑːr-/ *noun* **1** [U] a sweet drink with an orange flavour. In Britain it always has bubbles in it; in the US it can be with or without bubbles. 橙汁飲料；橘子汁；橙汁汽水 **2** [C] a glass of orangeade 一杯橙汁汽水 ➲ compare LEMONADE

Or·ange·man /ˈɒrɪndʒmən; *NAmE* ˈɔːr-; ˈɑːr-/ *noun* (*pl.* **-men** /-mən/) a member of the Orange Order, a Protestant political organization that wants Northern Ireland to remain part of the United Kingdom 奧蘭治黨員，奧蘭治人（主張北愛爾蘭繼續隸屬英國的新教政治組織成員）

or·an·gery /ˈɒrɪndʒəri; *NAmE* ˈɔːr-; ˈɑːr-/ *noun* (*pl.* **-ies**) a glass building where orange trees are grown 柑橘暖房

ˌorange ˈsquash *noun* (*BrE*) **1** [U] a thick sweet liquid made with orange juice and sugar; a drink made from this with water added 加糖（或加水）橙汁飲料：*a bottle of orange squash* 一瓶橙子水飲料 **2** [C] a glass of orange squash 一杯橙汁飲料：*Two orange squashes, please.* 請來兩杯橙汁飲料。

orang-utan /ɔːˌræŋ uːˈtæn; əˈræŋ uːtæn; *NAmE* əˈræŋ ətæn/ *noun* a large APE (= an animal like a large MONKEY with no tail) with long arms and reddish hair, that lives in Borneo and Sumatra 猩猩，褐猿（產於婆羅洲和蘇門答臘）ORIGIN From Malay *orang utan/hutan*, meaning 'person of the forest'. 源自馬來語 orang utan/hutan，意為"森林人"。

ora·tion /ɔːˈreɪʃn/ *noun* (*formal*) a formal speech made on a public occasion, especially as part of a ceremony 演說，致辭（尤指作為儀式的一部份）

ora·tor /ˈɒrətə(r); *NAmE* ˈɔːr-; ˈɑːr-/ *noun* (*formal*) a person who makes formal speeches in public or is good at public speaking 講演者；雄辯家；善於演說的人：*a fine political orator* 優秀的政治演說家

ora·tor·ic·al /ˌɒrəˈtɒrɪkl; *NAmE* ˌɔːrəˈtɔːr-/ *adj.* (*formal, sometimes disapproving*) connected with the art of public speaking 演說的；講演術的：*oratorical skills* 演說技能

ora·torio /ˌɒrəˈtɔːriəʊ; *NAmE* ˌɔːrəˈtɔːrioʊ; ˌɑːrə-/ *noun* (*pl.* **-os**) a long piece of music for singers and an ORCHESTRA, usually based on a story from the Bible 清唱劇，神劇（通常以《聖經》故事為主題）➲ compare CANTATA

ora·tory /ˈɒrətri; *NAmE* ˈɔːrətɔːri; ˈɑːr-/ *noun* (*pl.* **-ies**) **1** [U] the skill of making powerful and effective speeches in public 講演術；雄辯術 SYN **rhetoric** **2** [C] a room or small building that is used for private prayer or worship（私人）祈禱室，小禮拜堂

orb /ɔːb; *NAmE* ɔːrb/ *noun* **1** (*literary*) an object shaped like a ball, especially the sun or moon 球體；（尤指）日，月 **2** a gold ball with a cross on top, carried by a king or queen at formal ceremonies as a symbol of power 王權寶球（國王或女王在正式儀式上攜帶的頂部飾十字架的金球，是權力的象徵）➲ compare SCEPTRE

orbit /ˈɔːbɪt; *NAmE* ˈɔːrbɪt/ *noun, verb*

▪ ***noun*** **1** [C, U] a curved path followed by a planet or an object as it moves around another planet, star, moon, etc.（天體等運行的）軌道：*the earth's orbit around the sun* 地球環繞太陽的軌道 ◇ *a space station **in orbit** round the moon* 繞月球運行的一個航天站 ◇ *A new satellite has been **put into orbit** around the earth.* 一顆新的人造衞星被送上了環繞地球的軌道。**2** [sing.] an area that a particular person, organization, etc. deals with or is able to influence（人、組織等的）影響範圍，勢力範圍：*to **come/fall/be within sb's orbit*** 進入／落入／屬於某人的勢力範圍

▪ ***verb*** [T, I] **~ (around) sth** to move in an orbit (= a curved path) around a much larger object, especially a planet, star, etc. 沿軌道運行；圍繞…運動：*The earth takes a year to orbit the sun.* 地球繞太陽一週要一年的時間。

or·bit·al /ˈɔːbɪtl; *NAmE* ˈɔːrb-/ *adj., noun*

▪ ***adj.*** [only before noun] **1** connected with the orbit of a planet or object in space（行星或空間物體）軌道的 **2** (*BrE*) (of a road 道路) built around the edge of a town or city to reduce the amount of traffic travelling through the centre（城市）外環路的

▪ ***noun*** (*BrE*) a very large RING ROAD, especially if it is a MOTORWAY 高速環行路：*the M25 London orbital* 倫敦 M25 高速環行路

or·bit·er /ˈɔːbɪtə(r); *NAmE* ˈɔːrb-/ *noun* a SPACECRAFT designed to move around a planet or moon rather than to land on it（繞天體作軌道運行的）宇宙飛船；軌道飛行器

orca /ˈɔːkə; *NAmE* ˈɔːrkə/ *noun* = KILLER WHALE

Or·ca·dian /ɔːˈkeɪdiən; ɔːrˈk-/ *noun* a person from the islands of Orkney in Scotland（蘇格蘭奧克尼群島的）奧克尼人 ▸ **Or·ca·dian** *adj.*

orch·ard /ˈɔːtʃəd; *NAmE* ˈɔːrtʃərd/ *noun* a piece of land, normally separated from the surrounding area, in which fruit trees are grown 果園 ➲ VISUAL VOCAB pages V2, V3

or·ches·tra /ˈɔːkɪstrə; *NAmE* ˈɔːrk-/ *noun* **1** [C+sing./pl. v.] a large group of people who play various musical instruments together, led by a CONDUCTOR 管弦樂隊：*She plays the flute in the school orchestra.* 她在校管弦樂隊裏吹長笛。◇ *the Scottish Symphony Orchestra* 蘇格蘭交響樂團 ➲ see also CHAMBER ORCHESTRA, SYMPHONY ORCHESTRA **2 the orchestra** [sing.] (*NAmE*) (*BrE* **the ˈorchestra stalls, the stalls**) the seats that are nearest to the stage in a theatre（劇場的）正廳前排座位

or·ches·tral /ɔːˈkestrəl; *NAmE* ɔːrˈk-/ *adj.* connected with an orchestra 管弦樂的；管弦樂隊的：*orchestral music* 管弦樂曲

ˈorchestra pit (also **pit**) *noun* the place in a theatre just in front of the stage where the orchestra sits and plays for an OPERA, a BALLET, etc. 樂池，樂隊席（舞台前樂隊演奏的地方）

O

or·ches·trate /ˈɔːkɪstreɪt; *NAmE* ˈɔːrk-/ *verb* **1 ~ sth** to arrange a piece of music in parts so that it can be played by an orchestra 編配（或創作）管弦樂曲 **2 ~ sth** to organize a complicated plan or event very carefully or secretly 精心安排；策劃；密謀 SYN **stage-manage**：*a carefully orchestrated publicity campaign* 精心策劃的一場宣傳運動 ▸ **or·ches·tra·tion** /ˌɔːkɪˈstreɪʃn; *NAmE* ˌɔːrk-/ *noun* [C, U]

or·chid /ˈɔːkɪd; *NAmE* ˈɔːrkɪd/ *noun* a plant with brightly coloured flowers of unusual shapes. There are many different types of orchid and some of them are very rare. 蘭科植物；蘭花 ➲ VISUAL VOCAB page V11

or·dain /ɔːˈdeɪn; *NAmE* ɔːrˈd-/ *verb* **1 ~ sb (as sth) | ~ sb + noun** to make sb a priest, minister or RABBI 授予聖秩（品）；授予聖職：*He was ordained (as) a priest last year.* 他去年接受任命為神父。➲ see also ORDINATION **2 ~ sth | ~ that …** *(formal)* (of God, the law or FATE 神、法律或命運) to order or command sth; to decide sth in advance 主宰；掌握；規定：*Fate had ordained that they would never meet again.* 他們命裏注定永遠不會再相見。

or·deal /ɔːˈdiːl; ˈɔːdiːl; *NAmE* ɔːrˈd-/ *noun* [usually sing.] **~ (of sth/of doing sth)** a difficult or unpleasant experience 磨難；折磨；煎熬；嚴酷的考驗：*They are to be spared the ordeal of giving evidence in court.* 他們將免受出庭作證的難堪。◇ *The hostages spoke openly about the terrible ordeal they had been through.* 人質公開陳述了他們所遭受的非人的折磨。◇ *The interview was less of an ordeal than she'd expected.* 面試並非如她想像的那樣可怕。

order 🗝 /ˈɔːdə(r); *NAmE* ˈɔːrd-/ *noun, verb*

■ *noun*

▸ **ARRANGEMENT** 安排 **1** 🗝 [U, C] the way in which people or things are placed or arranged in relation to each other 順序；次序：*The names are listed* ***in alphabetical order.*** 姓名是按字母順序排列的。◇ ***in chronological/numerical order*** 按時間／數字順序 ◇ ***arranged in order of*** *priority/importance/size* 按優先次序／重要性／大小排列 ◇ *The results, ranked* ***in descending/ascending order,*** *are as follows:* 結果按降序／升序排列如下：◇ *All the procedures must be done in the correct order.* 一切手續必須按正確順序辦理。◇ *Let's take the problems in a different order.* 咱們換一個順序來處理這些問題吧。 **2** 🗝 [U] the state of being carefully and neatly arranged 條理：*It was time she* ***put*** *her life* ***in order.*** 她到了該好好安排自己生活的時候了。◇ *The house had been kept in good order.* 房子保持得井井有條。◇ *Get your ideas into some sort of order before beginning to write.* 落筆之前，先要理清思路。◇ *It is one of the functions of art to bring order out of chaos.* 藝術的功能之一就是在混亂中整理出秩序。OPP **disorder**

▸ **CONTROLLED STATE** 有序狀態 **3** 🗝 [U] the state that exists when people obey laws, rules or authority 治安；秩序；規矩：*The army has been sent in to maintain order in the capital.* 軍隊被調進首都維持治安。◇ *Some teachers find it difficult to* ***keep*** *their classes* ***in order.*** 有些教師覺得難以維持課堂秩序。◇ *The police are trying to restore public order.* 警察正在努力恢復公共秩序。◇ *The argument continued until the chairman* ***called*** *them both* ***to order*** (= ordered them to obey the formal rules of the meeting). 爭論持續不休，直到主席要求雙方遵守議事規則。➲ compare DISORDER (2) ➲ see also POINT OF ORDER

▸ **INSTRUCTIONS** 指示 **4** 🗝 [C] something that sb is told to do by sb in authority 指示；命令：**~ (for sb/sth to do sth)** *He* ***gave orders*** *for the work to be started.* 他下令開始工作。◇ **~ (to do sth)** *The general* ***gave the order*** *to advance.* 將軍下令前進。◇ *I'm* ***under orders*** *not to let anyone in.* 我奉命不准任何人進入。◇ *She* ***takes orders*** *only from the president.* 她只聽從總裁的吩咐。◇ *Dogs can be trained to* ***obey orders.*** 狗可以訓練得聽從命令。◇ *(informal) No sugar for me—****doctor's orders.*** 我不要糖。這是醫生囑咐我的。◇ *Interest rates can be controlled* ***by order of*** *the central bank.* 利率可由中央銀行指示控制。

▸ **GOODS** 貨品 **5** 🗝 [C, U] **~ (for sth)** a request to make or supply goods 訂貨；訂購；訂單：*I would like to* ***place an order*** *for ten copies of this book.* 這本書我想訂購十冊。◇ *an order form* 訂貨單 ◇ *The machine parts are still* ***on order*** (= they have been ordered but have not yet been received). 機器零件尚在訂購之中。◇ *These items can be made* ***to order*** (= produced especially for a particular customer). 這幾項可以訂做。➲ see also MAIL ORDER **6** [C] goods supplied in response to a particular order that sb has placed 所訂的貨物；交付的訂貨：*The stationery order has arrived.* 訂購的文具到貨了。

▸ **FOOD/DRINKS** 食物；飲料 **7** 🗝 [C] a request for food or drinks in a restaurant, bar, etc.; the food or drinks that you ask for 點菜；所點的飲食菜肴：*May I* ***take your order?*** 您現在點菜嗎？◇ ***Last orders*** *at the bar now please!* (= because the bar is going to close) 本店（打烊前）最後一次點酒了！◇ *an order for steak and fries* 點一份牛排炸薯條 ◇ *a* ***side order*** (= for example, vegetables or salad that you eat with your main dish) 配菜（主菜以外的蔬菜、色拉等）➲ COLLOCATIONS at RESTAURANT

▸ **MONEY** 錢 **8** [C] a formal written instruction for sb to be paid money or to do sth 付款指令（或委託書）；書面指令；匯票 ➲ see also BANKER'S ORDER, COURT ORDER, MONEY ORDER, POSTAL ORDER, STANDING ORDER

▸ **SYSTEM** 制度 **9** [C, usually sing.] *(formal)* the way that a society, the world, etc. is arranged, with its system of rules and customs 秩序；結構：*a change in the political and social order* 政治和社會結構的改變 ◇ *the natural order of things* 天地萬物的自然秩序 ◇ *He was seen as a threat to* ***the established order.*** 他被視為現存制度的大敵。◇ *A* ***new order*** *seems to be emerging.* 新的秩序似乎正在顯現。

▸ **SOCIAL CLASS** 社會階級 **10** [C, usually pl.] *(disapproving or humorous)* a social class 階級；等級；階層：*the lower orders* 底層社會

▸ **BIOLOGY** 生物 **11** [C] a group into which animals, plants, etc. that have similar characteristics are divided, smaller than a CLASS and larger than a FAMILY（生物分類的）目：*the order of primates* 靈長目 ➲ compare GENUS

▸ **RELIGIOUS COMMUNITY** 宗教團體 **12** [C+sing./pl. v.] a group of people living in a religious community, especially MONKS or NUNS（按照一定的規範生活的）宗教團體；（尤指）修會：*religious orders* 修會 ◇ *the Benedictine order* 本篤會

▸ **SPECIAL HONOUR** 特殊榮譽 **13** [C+sing./pl. v.] a group of people who have been given a special honour by a queen, king, president, etc.（獲國王、女王、總統等）授勳的人；勳位；勳爵士團：*The Order of the Garter is an ancient order of chivalry.* 嘉德勳位是古代騎士勳位。 **14** [C] a BADGE or RIBBON worn by members of an order who have been given a special honour 勳章；綬帶

▸ **SECRET SOCIETY** 秘密社團 **15** [C+sing./pl. v.] a secret society whose members meet for special ceremonies（秘密）社團，集團，結社：*the Ancient Order of Druids* 古德魯伊特共濟會

IDM **be in/take (holy) 'orders** to be/become a priest 已領受／領受神品（或聖秩）；為／成為神職人員 **in 'order 1** 🗝 (of an official document 正式文件) that can be used because it is all correct and legal（依法）有效的 SYN **valid**：*Is your work permit in order?* 你的工作許可證有效嗎？ **2** 🗝 *(formal)* as it should be 正常；準備好；就緒：*Is everything in order, sir?* 一切都正常嗎，先生？ **3** if sth is **in order**, it is a suitable thing to do or say on a particular occasion 妥當；適宜：*I think a drink would be in order.* 我想應該喝杯飲料了吧。 **in 'order (to do sth)** *(formal)* allowed according to the rules of a meeting, etc. 符合議事規則：*Is it in order to speak now?* 依規定現在可以發言了嗎？ **in order that** 🗝 *(formal)* so that sth can happen 目的在於；為了；以便：*All those concerned must work together in order that agreement can be reached on this issue.* 一切有關人員必須通力合作，以便能在這個問題上達成協議。 **in order to do sth** 🗝 with the purpose or intention of doing or achieving sth 目的是；以便；為了：*She arrived early in order to get a good seat.* 她早早到場，好找個好位置。◇ *In order to get a complete picture, further information is needed.* 為掌握全面情況，還需要詳細資料。➲ LANGUAGE BANK at PROCESS **in running/working 'order** (especially of machines 尤指機器) working well 運轉正常；

運轉良好：*The engine is now in perfect working order.* 發動機現在運轉完全正常。**of a high order | of the highest/first order** of a high quality or degree; of the highest quality or greatest degree 高質量的；高品質的；一流的：*The job requires diplomatic skills of a high order.* 這項工作要求高超的外交技巧。◇ *She was a snob of the first order.* 她是天字第一號勢利鬼。**of/in the order of sth** (*BrE*) (*NAmE* **on the order of**) (*formal*) about sth; approximately sth 大約；差不多：*She earns something in the order of £80 000 a year.* 她的年收入為 8 萬英鎊左右。**the ˌorder of the ˈday** common, popular or suitable at a particular time or for a particular occasion 常見的；流行的；適宜的：*Pessimism seems to be the order of the day.* 悲觀失望似乎是當今司空見慣的情形。**Order! Order!** used to remind people to obey the rules of a formal meeting or debate（用於提醒人們遵守會議、辯論的規則）安靜！安靜！；別吵！別吵！**ˌout of ˈorder 1** (of a machine, etc. 機器等) not working correctly 有毛病；出故障：*The phone is out of order.* 電話壞了。**2** not arranged correctly or neatly 安排不當；不整潔：*I checked the files and some of the papers were out of order.* 我檢查過案卷，其中有些未按順序編排。**3** (*BrE*) (*NAmE* **ˌout of ˈline**) (*informal*) behaving in a way that is not acceptable or right 行為不當；舉止令人難以接受：*You were well out of order taking it without asking.* 你不問一聲就把它拿走，這是很不妥當的。**4** (*formal*) not allowed by the rules of a formal meeting or debate 違反規程的；不合乎（會議或辯論）規則的：*His objection was ruled out of order.* 他的反對被裁定為違反會議規則。➲ more at CALL *v.*, HOUSE *n.*, LAW, MARCH *v.*, PECK *v.*, SHORT *adj.*, STARTER, TALL

■ *verb*

▸ **GIVE INSTRUCTIONS** 下達指令 **1** [T] to use your position of authority to tell sb to do sth or say that sth must happen 命令；指揮；要求：**~ sb to do sth** *The company was ordered to pay compensation to its former employees.* 公司被勒令向以前的員工作出補償。◇ *The officer ordered them to fire.* 軍官命令他們開火。◇ **~ sb + adv./prep.** *They were ordered out of the class for fighting.* 他們因鬥毆被勒令退出課堂。◇ **~ sth** *The government has ordered an investigation into the accident.* 政府要求對事故進行調查。◇ **~ that ...** *They ordered that for every tree cut down two more be planted.* 他們要求每砍伐一棵樹就要補栽兩棵樹。◇ (*BrE* also) *They ordered that for every tree cut down two more should be planted.* 他們要求每砍伐一棵樹就要補栽兩棵樹。◇ **~ (sb) + speech** *'Sit down and be quiet,' she ordered.* "坐下，安靜點！"她命令道。

▸ **GOODS/SERVICE** 貨物；服務 **2** [T] to ask for goods to be made or supplied; to ask for a service to be provided 訂購；訂貨；要求提供服務：**~ sth (from sb)** *These boots can be ordered direct from the manufacturer.* 這些靴子可向廠方直接訂貨。◇ **~ sb sth** *Shall I order you a taxi?* 要我給你叫輛出租車嗎？◇ **~ sth for sb** *Shall I order a taxi for you?* 要我給你叫輛出租車嗎？

▸ **FOOD/DRINK** 食物；飲料 **3** [T, I] to ask for sth to eat or drink in a restaurant, bar, etc. 點（酒菜等）：**~ (sth)** *I ordered a beer and a sandwich.* 我要了一杯啤酒，一個三明治。◇ *Have you ordered yet?* 你點菜了沒有？◇ **~ sb/yourself sth** *He ordered himself a double whisky.* 他為自己點了一杯雙份威士忌。◇ **~ (sth) (for sb)** *Will you order for me while I make a phone call?* 我打個電話，幫我點下菜可以嗎？

▸ **ORGANIZE/ARRANGE** 組織；安排 **4** [T] **~ sth** (*formal*) to organize or arrange sth 組織；安排；整理：*I need time to order my thoughts.* 我需要時間梳理一下思路。➲ see also ORDERED, DISORDERED **IDM** see DOCTOR *n.*

PHR V **ˌorder sb aˈbout/aˈround** (*disapproving*) to keep telling sb what to do in a way that is annoying or unpleasant（不斷地）支使，命令，使喚

ˈorder book *noun* a record kept by a business of the products it has agreed to supply to its customers, often used to show how well the business is doing（公司業績的）訂貨簿：*We have a full order book for the coming year.* 我們來年的訂貨簿已經記滿了。

or·dered /ˈɔːdəd; *NAmE* ˈɔːrdərd/ *adj.* [usually before noun] carefully arranged or organized 精心安排的；組織有序的 **SYN** **orderly**：*an ordered existence* 井井有條的生活 ◇ *a well-ordered society* 井然有序的社會 **OPP** **disordered**

Synonyms 同義詞辨析

order

tell • instruct • direct • command

These words all mean to use your position of authority to say to sb that they must do sth. 以上各詞均含命令、指揮、要求之意。

order to use your position of authority to tell sb to do sth 指命令、指揮、要求：*The company was ordered to pay compensation to its former employee.* 公司被勒令向以前的員工作出補償。◇ *'Come here at once!' she ordered.* "馬上過來！"她命令道。

tell to say to sb that they must or should do sth 指命令、指示、吩咐：*He was told to sit down and wait.* 有人吩咐他坐下等着。◇ *Don't tell me what to do!* 別支使我做事！

instruct (*rather formal*) to tell sb to do sth, especially in a formal or official way 尤指以正式或官方的方式指示、命令、吩咐：*The letter instructed him to report to headquarters immediately.* 那封信指示他立即向總部彙報。

direct (*formal*) to give an official order 指正式發出指示、命令：*The judge directed the jury to return a verdict of not guilty.* 法官指示陪審團作出無罪裁決。

command to use your position of authority to tell sb to do sth 指利用權力命令：*He commanded his men to retreat.* 他命令手下撤退。

ORDER OR COMMAND? 用 order 還是 command？

Order is a more general word than **command** and can be used about anyone in a position of authority, such as a parent, teacher or government telling sb to do sth. **Command** is slightly stronger than **order** and is the normal word to use about an army officer giving orders, or in any context where it is normal to give orders without any discussion about them. It is less likely to be used about a parent or teacher. * order 含義較 command 寬泛，可指任何有權威的人，如父母、老師或政府下命令。command 的語氣稍強於 order，是指部隊長官發佈命令的常規用詞，或者用於指沒有商量餘地的命令。command 不大用於父母或老師下命令的情況。

PATTERNS

- to order/tell/instruct/direct/command sb **to do sth**
- to order/instruct/direct/command **that** ...
- to **do** sth **as** ordered/told/instructed/directed/commanded

ˈorder form *noun* a document filled in by customers when ordering goods 訂貨單

order·ing /ˈɔːdərɪŋ; *NAmE* ˈɔːrdər-/ *noun* [C, U] the way in which sth is ordered or arranged; the act of putting sth into an order 次序；組合；排列 **SYN** **arrangement**：*Many possible orderings may exist.* 組合方式可能有許多種。◇ *the successful ordering of complex data* 複雜數據的成功排列

or·der·ly /ˈɔːdəli; *NAmE* ˈɔːrdərli/ *adj.*, *noun*

■ *adj.* **1** arranged or organized in a neat, careful and logical way 整潔的；有秩序的；有條理的 **SYN** **tidy**：*a calm and orderly life* 平靜有序的生活 ◇ *vegetables planted in orderly rows* 一行行栽種整齊的蔬菜 **2** behaving well; peaceful 表現良好的；守秩序的：*an orderly demonstration* 秩序井然的示威 **OPP** **disorderly** ▸ **or·der·li·ness** /ˈɔːdəlinəs; *NAmE* ˈɔːrdər-/ *noun* [U]

■ *noun* (*pl.* **-ies**) **1** a person who works in a hospital, usually doing jobs that do not need any special training（醫院的）護理員 **2** a soldier who does jobs that do not need any special training 勤務兵

ˌorder of ˈmagnitude *noun* (*mathematics* 數) a level in a system of ordering things by size or amount, where each level is higher by a FACTOR of ten 數量級（量度物

理量大小的標準，用以 10 為底的指數表達）：*The actual measurement is two orders of magnitude* (= a hundred times) *greater than we expected.* 實際測量結果比我們預料的大兩個量級（即一百倍）。◇ (*figurative*) *The problem is of the same order of magnitude for all concerned.* 這個問題對有關各方的影響是一樣大的。

ˈOrder Paper *noun* (*BrE*) a list of the subjects to be discussed by Parliament on a particular day（議會的）議事日程表

or·din·al /ˈɔːdɪnl; *NAmE* ˈɔːrdənl/ (also **ˌordinal ˈnumber**) *noun* a number that refers to the position of sth in a series, for example 'first', 'second', etc. 序數詞（如第一、第二等）➲ compare CARDINAL *n.* (2) ▸ **or·din·al** *adj.*

or·din·ance /ˈɔːdɪnəns; *NAmE* ˈɔːrd-/ *noun* [C, U] (*formal*) an order or a rule made by a government or sb in a position of authority 法令；條例；指示；訓令

or·din·and /ˈɔːdɪnænd; *NAmE* ˈɔːrd-/ *noun* a person who is preparing to become a priest, minister or RABBI 待領聖職的人；領聖秩者

or·din·ar·ily /ˈɔːdnrəli; *NAmE* ˌɔːrdnˈerəli/ *adv.* **1** in a normal way 普通地；平常地；正常地 SYN **normally**：*To the untrained eye, the children were behaving ordinarily.* 在外行人眼裏，這些孩子表現正常。**2** used to say what normally happens in a particular situation, especially because sth different is happening this time 一般情況下；通常地 SYN **usually**：*Ordinarily, she wouldn't have bothered arguing with him.* 一般而言，她懶得跟他理論。◇ *We do not ordinarily carry out this type of work.* 我們通常不會實際去做這類工作。

or·din·ary 0-w /ˈɔːdnri; *NAmE* ˈɔːrdneri/ *adj.*
1 0-w [usually before noun] not unusual or different in any way 普通的；平常的；一般的；平凡的：*an ordinary sort of day* 平平常常的一天 ◇ *in the ordinary course of events* 在一般情況下 ◇ *ordinary people like you and me* 像你我這等普通人 ◇ *This was no ordinary meeting.* 這次會議非同尋常。**2** 0-w (*disapproving*) having no unusual or interesting features 平庸的；平淡無奇的：*The meal was very ordinary.* 這頓飯平常得很。➲ compare EXTRAORDINARY (2) ▸ **or·din·ari·ness** *noun* [U]

IDM **in the ordinary way** (*BrE*) used to say what normally happens in a particular situation 一般地；通常地：*In the ordinary way, she's not a nervous person.* 一般而言，她是個不愛緊張的人。**out of the ˈordinary** unusual or different 不尋常；特殊；超凡脫俗：*I'm looking for something a little more out of the ordinary.* 我正在找些稍不尋常的東西。

ˈordinary grade *noun* = O GRADE

ˈordinary level *noun* = O LEVEL

ˌordinary ˈseaman *noun* (*abbr.* OS) a sailor of the lowest rank in the British navy（英國的）二等水兵

ˌordinary ˈshare *noun* a fixed unit of a company's capital. People who own ordinary shares have voting rights in the company. 普通股（公司資本的固定單位，持有人在公司有投票權）

or·din·ate /ˈɔːdɪnət; *NAmE* ˈɔːrd-/ *noun* (*mathematics* 數) the COORDINATE that gives the distance along the vertical AXIS 縱坐標 ➲ compare ABSCISSA

or·din·ation /ˌɔːdɪˈneɪʃn; *NAmE* ˌɔːrdnˈeɪʃn/ *noun* [U, C] the act or ceremony of making sb a priest, minister or RABBI（聖職的）授予；派立禮；按立聖職；授神職禮 ➲ see also ORDAIN (1)

ord·nance /ˈɔːdnəns; *NAmE* ˈɔːrd-/ *noun* [U] **1** large guns on wheels（可移動）大炮 SYN **artillery** **2** military supplies and materials 軍備物資；軍需品；軍用器材：*an ordnance depot* 軍械庫

ˌOrdnance ˈSurvey map *noun* a very detailed map of an area of Britain or Ireland, prepared by an organization called the **Ordnance Survey**, which is supported by the government（由英國或愛爾蘭政府資助的全國地形測量局所繪製的）全國地形測繪詳圖

ord·ure /ˈɔːdjʊə(r); *NAmE* ˈɔːrdʒər/ *noun* [U] (*formal*) solid waste from the body of a person or an animal（人或動物的）糞；大便 SYN **faeces**

ore /ɔː(r)/ *noun* [U, C] rock, earth, etc. from which metal can be obtained 礦石；礦砂；礦：*iron ore* 鐵礦石

ore·gano /ˌɒrɪˈɡɑːnəʊ; *NAmE* əˈreɡənoʊ/ *noun* [U] a plant with leaves that have a sweet smell and are used in cooking as a HERB 牛至（葉可用於調味）➲ VISUAL VOCAB page V32

organ 0-w /ˈɔːɡən; *NAmE* ˈɔːrɡən/ *noun*
1 0-w a part of the body that has a particular purpose, such as the heart or the brain; part of a plant with a particular purpose（人體或動植物的）器官：*the **internal organs*** 內臟 ◇ *the **sense organs*** (= the eyes, ears, nose, etc.) 感覺器官 ◇ *the **sexual/reproductive organs*** 性／生殖器官 ◇ *an **organ transplant/donor*** 器官移植／捐贈者 ➲ VISUAL VOCAB page V59 **2** (especially *humorous*) a PENIS 陰莖；陽物：*the male organ* 雄性性器官 **3** 0-w (also **ˈpipe organ**) a large musical instrument with keys like a piano. Sounds are produced by air forced through pipes. 管風琴：*She plays the organ in church.* 她在教堂負責彈奏管風琴。◇ *organ music* 管風琴曲 ➲ compare HARMONIUM **4** a musical instrument similar to a pipe organ, but without pipes 風琴：*an electric organ* 電子琴 ➲ see also BARREL ORGAN, MOUTH ORGAN **5** (*formal*) an official organization that is part of a larger organization and has a special purpose（官方的）機構，機關：*the organs of government* 政府機關 **6** (*formal*) a newspaper or magazine that gives information about a particular group or organization; a means of communicating the views of a particular group 機關報刊；（某團體的）宣傳工具：*The People's Daily is the official organ of the Chinese Communist Party.*《人民日報》是中國共產黨的官方報紙。

or·gan·die (*NAmE* also **or·gandy**) /ˈɔːɡəndi; *NAmE* ˈɔːrɡ-/ *noun* [U] a type of thin cotton cloth that is slightly stiff, used especially for making formal dresses 蟬翼紗（細薄而稍硬的棉布，用於製作禮服）

ˈorgan-grinder *noun* a person who plays a BARREL ORGAN (= a large musical instrument played by turning a handle) 手搖風琴手；手搖風琴演奏者：(*humorous*) *He's only the **organ-grinder's monkey*** (= an unimportant person who does what he is told to do). 他不過是個聽喝的。

or·gan·ic /ɔːˈɡænɪk; *NAmE* ɔːrˈɡ-/ *adj.* [usually before noun] **1** (of food, farming methods, etc. 食品、耕作方式等) produced or practised without using artificial chemicals 有機的；不使用化肥的；綠色的：***organic cheese/vegetables/wine, etc.*** 有機奶酪、蔬菜、酒等 ◇ *an **organic farmer/gardener*** 實行有機栽培的農民／園藝師 ◇ ***organic farming/horticulture*** 有機耕作／園藝 ➲ VISUAL VOCAB page V8 **2** produced by or from living things 有機物的；生物的：*Improve the soil by adding **organic matter**.* 加入有機物以改良土壤。◇ ***organic compounds*** 有機化合物 OPP **inorganic** **3** (*technical* 術語) connected with the organs of the body 器官的；器質性的；官能的：*organic disease* 器官疾病 **4** (*formal*) consisting of different parts that are all connected to each other 有機的；統一的；關聯的：*the view of society as an organic whole* 視社會為一有機體的觀點 **5** (*formal*) happening in a slow and natural way, rather than suddenly 逐漸的；演進的；自然的：*the organic growth of foreign markets* 國外市場的逐步發展 ▸ **or·gan·ic·al·ly** /-kli/ *adv.*：*organically grown fruit* 用有機方式種植的水果 ◇ *The cardboard disintegrates organically.* 硬紙板是會自然分解的。◇ *Doctors could find nothing organically wrong with her.* 醫生找不出她的器官有什麼毛病。◇ *The organization should be allowed to develop organically.* 應該讓這個組織逐步發展。

orˌganic ˈchemistry *noun* [U] the branch of chemistry that deals with substances that contain CARBON 有機化學 ➲ compare INORGANIC CHEMISTRY

or·gan·ism /ˈɔːɡənɪzəm; *NAmE* ˈɔːrɡ-/ *noun* **1** (*biology* 生 or *formal*) a living thing, especially one that is extremely small 有機體；生物；（尤指）微生物 ➲ see also MICRO-ORGANISM **2** (*formal*) a system consisting of parts that depend on each other 有機組織；有機體系：*the social organism* (= society) 社會機體

or·gan·ist /ˈɔːɡənɪst; NAmE ˈɔːrɡ-/ *noun* a person who plays the organ 風琴演奏者；風琴手

or·gan·iza·tion 0‑w (BrE also **-isa·tion**) /ˌɔːɡənaɪˈzeɪʃn; NAmE ˌɔːrɡənəˈz-/ *noun* **1** 0‑w [C] a group of people who form a business, club, etc. together in order to achieve a particular aim 組織；團體；機構：*to work for a business/political/voluntary organization* 為一個商業 / 政治 / 志願機構工作 ◇ *the World Health Organization* 世界衛生組織 ◇ *He's the president of a large international organization.* 他是一個大型國際組織的主席。 **2** 0‑w [U] the act of making arrangements or preparations for sth 組織工作；籌備工作 SYN **planning**：*I leave most of the organization of these conferences to my assistant.* 我把這些會議的大部份籌備工作留給我的助手。 **3** 0‑w [U] the way in which the different parts of sth are arranged 安排；配置；分配 SYN **structure**：*The report studies the organization of labour within the company.* 這個報告研究了公司內部的人力分配問題。 **4** 0‑w [U] the quality of being arranged in a neat, careful and logical way 條理；系統性：*She is highly intelligent but her work lacks organization.* 她聰慧絕頂，工作卻缺乏條理。 ▶ **or·gan·iza·tion·al, -isa·tion·al** /-ʃənl/ *adj.*：*organizational skills* 組織技巧 ◇ *organizational change* 組織上的變化 **or·gan·iza·tion·al·ly, -isa·tion·al·ly** *adv.*

ˌorganiˈzation chart (also **or·gano·gram**) *noun* a diagram of the structure of an organization, especially a large business, showing the relationships between all the jobs in it（大企業等的）組織系統圖，組織架構圖

or·gan·ize (BrE also **-ise**) 0‑w /ˈɔːɡənaɪz; NAmE ˈɔːrɡ-/ *verb* **1** 0‑w [T] **~ sth** to arrange for sth to happen or to be provided 組織；籌備：*to organize a meeting/party/trip* 籌辦會議 / 聚會 / 旅行 ◇ *I'll invite people if you can organize food and drinks.* 如果你能備辦飲食，我就負責邀請人。 **2** 0‑w [T] **~ sth** to arrange sth or the parts of sth into a particular order or structure 安排；處理；分配：*Modern computers can organize large amounts of data very quickly.* 現代計算機能迅速處理大量的信息資料。◇ *You should try and organize your time better.* 你應該盡量更有效地分配你的時間。◇ *We do not fully understand how the brain is organized.* 我們不完全瞭解大腦是怎樣構成的。 **3** [T] **~ yourself/sb** to plan your/sb's work and activities in an efficient way 規劃；管理；照料：*I'm sure you don't need me to organize you.* 我相信你用不着我照顧你了吧。 **4** [T, I] **~ (sb/yourself) (into sth)** to form a group of people with a shared aim, especially a union or political party 成立，組建，建立（聯盟、黨派等）：*the right of workers to organize themselves into unions* 工人自行組織工會的權利 ➲ see also DISORGANIZED ▶ **or·gan·izer, -iser** *noun*：*the organizers of the festival* 節日活動的籌劃者 ➲ see also PERSONAL ORGANIZER

or·gan·ized (BrE also **-ised**) 0‑w /ˈɔːɡənaɪzd; NAmE ˈɔːrɡ-/ *adj.*
1 0‑w [only before noun] involving large numbers of people who work together to do sth in a way that has been carefully planned 有組織的；系統的：*an organized body of workers* 一個有組織的工人團體 ◇ ***organized religion*** (= traditional religion followed by large numbers of people who obey a fixed set of rules) 組織嚴密的傳統宗教信仰 ◇ ***organized crime*** (= committed by professional criminals working in large groups) 有組織的犯罪 ➲ compare UNORGANIZED **2** 0‑w arranged or planned in the way mentioned 有條理的；有安排的：*a carefully organized campaign* 精心策劃的運動 ◇ *a well-organized office* 井然有序的辦公室 ➲ compare DISORGANIZED **3** 0‑w (of a person 人) able to plan your work, life, etc. well and in an efficient way 有條理的；有效率的：*a very organized person* 很有條理的人 ◇ *Isn't it time you started to get organized?* 你該提高點效率了吧？ ➲ compare DISORGANIZED

ˈorgan loft *noun* a place where there is an organ high above the ground in a church or concert hall（教堂或音樂廳內的）風琴樓廂

or·gano·gram (also **or·gani·gram**) /ɔːˈɡænəɡræm; NAmE ɔːrˈɡ-/ *noun* (*business* 商) = ORGANIZATION CHART

or·gano·phos·phate /ˌɔːɡənəʊˈfɒsfeɪt; ɔːˌɡænəʊ-; NAmE ˌɔːrɡənoʊˈfɑːsfeɪt; ɔːrˌɡænoʊ-/ *noun* a chemical containing CARBON and PHOSPHORUS 有機磷酸酯

or·ganza /ɔːˈɡænzə; NAmE ɔːrˈɡ-/ *noun* [U] a type of thin stiff transparent cloth, used for making formal dresses 透明硬紗（用於製作禮服）

or·gasm /ˈɔːɡæzəm; NAmE ˈɔːrɡ-/ *noun* [U, C] the moment during sexual activity when feelings of sexual pleasure are at their strongest 性高潮：*to achieve/reach orgasm* 達到性高潮 ◇ *to have an orgasm* 出現性高潮

or·gas·mic /ɔːˈɡæzmɪk; NAmE ɔːrˈɡ-/ *adj.* [only before noun] connected with or like an orgasm 性高潮的；似性高潮的

or·gi·as·tic /ˌɔːdʒiˈæstɪk; NAmE ˌɔːrdʒ-/ *adj.* [usually before noun] (*formal*) typical of an orgy 縱慾的；放縱的；放蕩的

orgy /ˈɔːdʒi; NAmE ˈɔːrdʒi/ *noun* (*pl.* **-ies**) **1** a party at which there is a lot of eating, drinking and sexual activity 奢迷的聚會；狂歡會：*a drunken orgy* 縱酒狂歡會 **2 ~ (of sth)** (*disapproving*) an extreme amount of a particular activity 放縱；放蕩：*The rebels went on an orgy of killing.* 叛亂者肆意殺人。

oriel /ˈɔːriəl/ *noun* (*architecture* 建) a part of a building, like a small room with windows, that sticks out from a wall above the ground 突出主體牆外的建築；凸肚窗：*an oriel window* 凸肚窗

Ori·ent /ˈɔːriənt/ **the Orient** *noun* [sing.] (*literary*) the eastern part of the world, especially China and Japan 東方（尤指中國和日本）➲ compare OCCIDENT

ori·ent AW /ˈɔːrient/ (BrE also **orien·tate**) *verb* **1** [usually passive] **~ sb/sth (to/towards sb/sth)** to direct sb/sth towards sth; to make or adapt sb/sth for a particular purpose 朝向；面對；確定方向；使適應：*Our students are oriented towards science subjects.* 我們教的學生都適應學理科。◇ *policies oriented to the needs of working mothers* 針對在職母親的需要而制訂的政策 ◇ *We run a commercially oriented operation.* 我們經營一個商業性的企業。◇ *profit-orientated organizations* 以盈利為目的的機構 ◇ *Neither of them is politically oriented* (= interested in politics). 他們兩人都無意涉足政治。 **2 ~ yourself** to find your position in relation to your surroundings 確定方位；認識方向：*The mountaineers found it hard to orient themselves in the fog.* 登山者在大霧中很難辨認方向。 **3 ~ yourself** to make yourself familiar with a new situation 熟悉；適應：*It took him some time to orient himself in his new school.* 他經過了一段時間才熟悉新學校的環境。 ➲ compare DISORIENTATE

Orien·tal /ˌɔːriˈentl/ *noun* (*old-fashioned*, often *offensive*) a person from China, Japan or other countries in E Asia 東方人；東亞國家的人

orien·tal /ˌɔːriˈentl/ *adj.* connected with or typical of the eastern part of the world, especially China and Japan, and the people who live there 東方（尤指中國和日本）的；東方人的：*oriental languages* 東方語言

orien·tal·ist /ˌɔːriˈentəlɪst/ *noun* a person who studies the languages, arts, etc. of oriental countries 東方學專家；東方學者

orien·tate AW /ˈɔːriənteɪt/ *verb* (BrE) = ORIENT

orien·ta·tion AW /ˌɔːriənˈteɪʃn/ *noun* **1** [U, C] the type of aims or interests that a person or an organization has; the act of directing your aims towards a particular thing 方向；目標；定向：*The course is essentially theoretical in orientation.* 該課程的定位是以理論為主。◇ **~ to/towards sth** *Companies have been forced into a greater orientation to the market.* 各公司不得不轉變，更加面向市場。 **2** [U, C] a person's basic beliefs or feelings about a particular subject（個人的）基本信仰，態度，觀點：***religious/political orientation*** 宗教 / 政治取向 ◇ *a person's **sexual orientation*** (= whether they are attracted to men, women or both) 某人的性取向 **3** [U] training or information that you are given before starting a new job, course, etc.（任職等前的）培訓，訓練；迎新會：*an orientation course* 上崗培訓課 **4** [C] (*technical* 術語) the direction in which an object faces

O

方向：*The orientation of the planet's orbit is changing continuously.* 該行星軌道的方向不斷變化。

orien·teer·ing /ˌɔːriənˈtɪərɪŋ; *NAmE* -ˈtɪr-/ *noun* [U] the sport of following a route across country on foot, as quickly as possible, using a map and COMPASS 定向運動，定向越野，野外定向（利用指南針和地圖，徒步穿越曠野的運動）➲ **VISUAL VOCAB** page V40

ori·fice /ˈɒrɪfɪs; *NAmE* ˈɔːr-/ *noun* (*formal* or *humorous*) a hole or opening, especially one in the body（尤指身體上的）孔，穴，腔：*the nasal orifice* 鼻孔

ori·gami /ˌɒrɪˈɡɑːmi; *NAmE* ˌɔːr-/ *noun* [U] the Japanese art of folding paper into attractive shapes 日本摺紙藝術

ori·gin 0‑ᵚ /ˈɒrɪdʒɪn; *NAmE* ˈɔːr-/ *noun* [C, U] (also **origins** [pl.]) **1** 0‑ᵚ the point from which sth starts; the cause of sth 起源；源頭；起因：*the origins of life on earth* 地球上生命的起源 ◇ *Most coughs are viral* ***in origin*** (= caused by a virus). 咳嗽大多是由病毒引發的。◇ *The origin of the word remains obscure.* 該詞的來源尚不清楚。◇ *This particular custom* ***has its origins in*** *Wales.* 這一特殊風俗起源於威爾士。**2** 0‑ᵚ a person's social and family background 身世；出身：*She has risen from humble origins to immense wealth.* 她出身卑微，終成巨富。◇ *children of various ethnic origins* 各族裔的兒童 ◇ *people of German origin* 德裔民眾 ◇ *a person's country* ***of origin*** (= where they were born) 某人的出生國

ori·gin·al 0‑ᵚ /əˈrɪdʒənl/ *adj., noun*

▪ ***adj.*** **1** 0‑ᵚ [only before noun] existing at the beginning of a particular period, process or activity 原來的；起初的；最早的：*The room still has many of its original features.* 房間還保留着當初的許多特點。◇ *I think you should go back to your original plan.* 我認為你應該回頭執行你原來的計劃。**2** 0‑ᵚ new and interesting in a way that is different from anything that has existed before; able to produce new and interesting ideas 首創的；獨創的；有獨創性的：*an original idea* 獨到的見解 ◇ *That's not a very original suggestion.* 那個建議沒什麼新意。◇ *an original thinker* 有創意的人 **3** 0‑ᵚ [usually before noun] painted, written, etc. by the artist rather than copied 原作的；真跡的；非複製的：*an original painting by local artist Graham Tovey* 一幅本土藝術家格雷厄姆•托維的繪畫創作 ◇ *The original manuscript has been lost.* 原稿已經遺失。◇ *Only original documents* (= not photocopies) *will be accepted as proof of status.* 只有文件正本才能用作身分證明。

▪ ***noun*** **1** 0‑ᵚ a document, work of art, etc. produced for the first time, from which copies are later made 原件；正本；原稿；原作：*This painting is a copy; the original is in Madrid.* 這幅畫是複製品，原畫在馬德里。◇ *Send out the photocopies and keep the original.* 寄複印本，保留原件。**2** (*formal*) a person who thinks, behaves, dresses, etc. in an unusual way（思想、行為、衣着等）不同尋常的人，獨特的人，怪人

IDM **in the oˈriginal** in the language in which a book, etc. was first written, before being translated 用原著的語言；未經翻譯：*I studied Italian so that I would be able to read Dante in the original.* 我學習意大利語以便能讀但丁的原著。

ori·gin·al·ity /əˌrɪdʒəˈnæləti/ *noun* [U] the quality of being new and interesting in a way that is different from anything that has existed before 獨創性；創意；獨特構思：*This latest collection lacks style and originality.* 這本最新選集既無風格，又無創意。

ori·gin·al·ly 0‑ᵚ /əˈrɪdʒənəli/ *adv.* used to describe the situation that existed at the beginning of a particular period or activity, especially before sth was changed 原來；起初：*The school was originally very small.* 這所學校當初很小。◇ *She comes originally from York.* 她原本來自約克郡。◇ *Originally, we had intended to go to Italy, but then we won the trip to Greece.* 我們本來打算去意大利，但後來贏得機會去了希臘。

oˌriginal ˈsin *noun* [U] (in Christianity 基督教) the tendency to be evil that is believed to be present in everyone from birth 原罪（與生俱來的罪惡傾向）

ori·gin·ate /əˈrɪdʒɪneɪt/ *verb* (*formal*) **1** [I] (+ **adv./prep.**) to happen or appear for the first time in a particular place or situation 起源；發源；發端於：*The disease is thought to have originated in the tropics.* 這種疾病據說起源於熱帶地區。**2** [T] **~ sth** to create sth new 創立；創建；發明：*Locke originated this theory in the 17th century.* 洛克於 17 世紀創立了這個理論。▸ **ori·gin·ator** *noun*

ori·ole /ˈɔːriəʊl; *NAmE* -oʊl/ *noun* **1** a N American bird: the male is black and orange and the female is yellow-green 擬黃鸝（產於北美洲，雄鳥毛色黑與橘黃間隔，雌鳥黃綠色）**2** a European bird, the male of which is bright yellow with black wings 黃鸝（產於歐洲，雄鳥毛色鮮黃，雙翼黑色）

Oriya /ɒˈriːjə; *NAmE* ɔːˈr-/ *noun* [U] a language spoken in Orissa in eastern India 奧里雅語（印度東部奧里薩邦的語言）

or·molu /ˈɔːməluː; *NAmE* ˈɔːrm-/ *noun* [U] a gold metal made of a mixture of other metals, used to decorate furniture, make decorative objects, etc. 仿金銅；金色銅；銅鋅錫合金

or·na·ment *noun, verb*

▪ ***noun*** /ˈɔːnəmənt; *NAmE* ˈɔːrn-/ **1** [C] (*especially BrE*) an object that is used as decoration in a room, garden/yard, etc. rather than for a particular purpose 裝飾品：*a china/glass ornament* 瓷器 / 玻璃裝飾品 ◇ (*BrE, NAmE*) *Christmas tree ornaments* 聖誕樹裝飾品 ➲ **VISUAL VOCAB** page V21 **2** [C] (*formal*) an object that is worn as jewellery 首飾；飾物 **3** [U] (*formal*) the use of objects, designs, etc. as decoration 裝飾；擺設；點綴：*The clock is simply for ornament; it doesn't work any more.* 這架時鐘純屬擺設，它再也不走了。**4 ~ to sth** (*NAmE*) a person or thing whose good qualities improve sth 為…增添光彩的人（或事物）：*The building is an ornament to the city.* 這座建築物為整個城市增色不少。**5 ornaments** [pl.] (*music* 音) features that are added when playing individual notes to make them more beautiful or interesting 裝飾音

▪ ***verb*** /ˈɔːnəment; *NAmE* ˈɔːrn-/ [usually passive] **~ sth** (*formal*) to add decoration to sth 裝飾；點綴；美化 **SYN** **decorate**：*a room richly ornamented with carving* 雕飾得富麗堂皇的屋子

or·na·men·tal /ˌɔːnəˈmentl; *NAmE* ˌɔːrn-/ *adj.* used as decoration rather than for a practical purpose 裝飾性的；點綴的 **SYN** **decorative**：*an ornamental fountain* 裝飾性噴泉 ◇ *The chimney pots are purely ornamental.* 這些煙囪管帽純屬裝飾。

or·na·men·ta·tion /ˌɔːnəmenˈteɪʃn; *NAmE* ˌɔːrn-/ *noun* [U] the use of objects, designs, etc. to decorate sth 裝飾；點綴

or·nate /ɔːˈneɪt; *NAmE* ɔːrˈn-/ *adj.* covered with a lot of decoration, especially when this involves very small or complicated designs 華美的；富麗的；豪華的：*a mirror in an ornate gold frame* 鑲着豪華金框的鏡子 ▸ **or·nate·ly** *adv.*：*ornately carved chairs* 精雕細刻的椅子

or·nery /ˈɔːnəri; *NAmE* ˈɔːrn-/ *adj.* (*NAmE, informal*) bad-tempered and difficult to deal with 脾氣暴躁的；難對付的；彆扭的

or·ni·tholo·gist /ˌɔːnɪˈθɒlədʒɪst; *NAmE* ˌɔːrnɪˈθɑːl-/ *noun* a person who studies birds 鳥類學家 ➲ compare BIRD-WATCHER

or·ni·thol·ogy /ˌɔːnɪˈθɒlədʒi; *NAmE* ˌɔːrnɪˈθɑːl-/ *noun* [U] the scientific study of birds 鳥類學 ▸ **or·ni·tho·logic·al** /ˌɔːnɪθəˈlɒdʒɪkl; *NAmE* ˌɔːrnɪθəˈlɑːdʒ-/ *adj.*

or·ogeny /ɒˈrɒdʒəni; *NAmE* ɔːˈrɑːdʒ-/ *noun* [U] (*geology* 地) a process in which the outer layer of the earth is folded to form mountains 造山運動（地層褶皺形成山脈的過程）

oro·graph·ic /ˌɒrəˈɡræfɪk; *NAmE* ˌɔːrəˈɡræfɪk/ *adj.* (*geology* 地) connected with mountains, especially with their position and shape 山嶽（位置）的；山形的

oro·tund /ˈɒrətʌnd; *NAmE* ˈɔːrə-/ *adj.* (*formal*) (of the voice or the way something is said 嗓音或說話方式) using full and impressive sounds and language 洪亮的；令人難忘的 ▸ **oro·tund·ity** /ˌɒrəˈtʌndɪti; *NAmE* ˌɔːrə-/ *noun* [U]

orphan /ˈɔːfn; *NAmE* ˈɔːrfn/ *noun, verb*

■ **noun** a child whose parents are dead 孤兒： *He was an orphan and lived with his uncle.* 他是個孤兒，和他叔叔一起生活。◇ *orphan boys/girls* 父母雙亡的男孩／女孩

■ **verb** [usually passive] **~ sb** to make a child an orphan 使成為孤兒： *She was orphaned in the war.* 戰爭使她成為孤兒。

or·phan·age /ˈɔːfənɪdʒ; *NAmE* ˈɔːrf-/ *noun* a home for children whose parents are dead 孤兒院

ortho- /ˈɔːθəʊ; *NAmE* ˈɔːrθoʊ/ *combining form* (in nouns, adjectives and adverbs 構成名詞、形容詞和副詞) correct; standard 正確的；標準的： *orthodox* 正統的 ◇ *orthography* 拼寫法

ortho·don·tics /ˌɔːθəˈdɒntɪks; *NAmE* ˌɔːrθəˈdɑːn-/ *noun* [U] the treatment of problems concerning the position of the teeth and JAWS 正牙術 ▸ **ortho·don·tic** *adj.*： *orthodontic treatment* 矯牙治療

ortho·don·tist /ˌɔːθəˈdɒntɪst; *NAmE* ˌɔːrθəˈdɑːn-/ *noun* a dentist who treats problems concerning the position of the teeth and JAWS 正齒醫生；矯形牙醫

ortho·dox /ˈɔːθədɒks; *NAmE* ˈɔːrθədɑːks/ *adj.* **1** (especially of beliefs or behaviour 尤指信仰或行為) generally accepted or approved of; following generally accepted beliefs 普遍接受的；正統的；規範的 SYN **traditional**： *orthodox medicine* 傳統醫學 OPP **unorthodox** ➲ compare HETERODOX **2** following closely the traditional beliefs and practices of a religion 正統信仰的；正宗教義的： *an orthodox Jew* 正統的猶太教徒 **3 Orthodox** belonging to or connected with the Orthodox Church 正教的；東正教派的

the ˌOrthodox ˈChurch (also **the ˌEastern ˌOrthodox ˈChurch**) *noun* [sing.] a branch of the Christian Church in eastern Europe and Greece 東正教會；正教

ortho·doxy /ˈɔːθədɒksi; *NAmE* ˈɔːrθədɑːksi/ *noun* (*pl.* **-ies**) **1** [C, U] (*formal*) an idea or view that is generally accepted 正統觀念；普遍接受的觀點： *an economist arguing against the current financial orthodoxy* 一位批駁現行正統金融觀念的經濟學家 **2** [U, C, usually pl.] the traditional beliefs or practices of a religion, etc. 正統的信仰（或做法） **3 Orthodoxy** [U] the Orthodox Church, its beliefs and practices 正教會；正教信仰與做法

orth·og·raphy /ɔːˈθɒɡrəfi; *NAmE* ɔːrˈθɑːɡ-/ *noun* [U] (*formal*) the system of spelling in a language（文字的）拼寫體系，拼寫法 ▸ **or·tho·graph·ic** /ˌɔːθəˈɡræfɪk; *NAmE* ˌɔːrθ-/ *adj.*

ortho·paed·ics (*especially US* **ortho·ped·ics**) /ˌɔːθəˈpiːdɪks; *NAmE* ˌɔːrθə-/ *noun* [U] the branch of medicine concerned with injuries and diseases of the bones or muscles 矯形外科；整形外科學 ▸ **ortho·paed·ic** (*especially US* **ortho·ped·ic**) *adj.*： *an orthopaedic surgeon/hospital* 整形外科醫生／醫院

Or·well·ian /ɔːˈweliən; *NAmE* ɔːrˈw-/ *adj.* used to describe a political system in which a government tries to have complete control over people's behaviour and thoughts（政治制度）奧威爾式的，極權的 ORIGIN From the name of the English writer George Orwell, whose novel *Nineteen Eighty-Four* describes a government that has total control over the people. 源自英國作家喬治・奧威爾。他在小說《一九八四》中描寫對人民實行極權統治的政府。

-ory *suffix* **1** (in adjectives 構成形容詞) that does ...; involving the action concerned 起…作用的；包含相關動作的： *explanatory* 解釋性的 **2** (in nouns 構成名詞) a place for ...的地方： *observatory* 天文台

oryx /ˈɒrɪks; *NAmE* ˈɔːr-/ *noun* a large ANTELOPE with long straight horns 大羚羊（有長角）

OS /ˌəʊ ˈes; *NAmE* ˌoʊ/ *abbr.* **1** (*computing* 計) OPERATING SYSTEM **2** ORDINARY SEAMAN

Oscar™ /ˈɒskə(r); *NAmE* ˈɑːs-/ *noun* = ACADEMY AWARD： *The movie was nominated for an Oscar.* 這部電影獲奧斯卡金像獎提名。◇ *an* ***Oscar nomination/winner*** 奧斯卡金像獎提名／獲獎者

os·cil·late /ˈɒsɪleɪt; *NAmE* ˈɑːs-/ *verb* **1** [I] **~ (between A and B)** (*formal*) to keep changing from one extreme of feeling or behaviour to another, and back again（情感或行為）搖擺，波動，變化 SYN **swing**： *Her moods oscillated between depression and elation.* 她的情緒時而抑鬱，時而亢奮。 **2** [I] (*physics* 物) to keep moving from one position to another and back again 擺動；振動： *Watch how the needle on the dial oscillates.* 仔細看儀表盤上的指針如何擺動。 **3** [I] (*physics* 物) (of an electric current, radio waves, etc. 電流、無線電波等) to change in strength or direction at regular intervals 波動；振盪

os·cil·la·tion /ˌɒsɪˈleɪʃn; *NAmE* ˌɑːs-/ *noun* (*formal*) **1** [U, sing.] a regular movement between one position and another or between one amount and another 擺動；搖擺；振動： *the oscillation of the compass needle* 羅盤指針的擺動 ◇ **~ between A and B** *the economy's continual oscillation between growth and recession* 經濟增長與衰退之間的持續波動 **2** [C] **~ (between A and B)** | **~ (of sth) (against sth)** a single movement from one position to another of sth that is oscillating 一次波動；浮動；振幅： *the oscillations of the pound against foreign currency* 英鎊兌外幣匯價的波動 **3** [U, C] **~ (between A and B)** a repeated change between different feelings, types of behaviour or ideas（情感、行為、思想的）搖擺不定，變化無常，猶豫不定： *his oscillation, as a teenager, between science and art* 十幾歲的他對學文科還是學理科的猶豫不決

os·cil·la·tor /ˈɒsɪleɪtə(r); *NAmE* ˈɑːs-/ *noun* (*physics* 物) a piece of equipment for producing OSCILLATING electric currents 振盪器

os·cil·lo·scope /əˈsɪləskəʊp; *NAmE* -skoʊp/ *noun* (*physics* 物) a piece of equipment that shows changes in electrical current as waves in a line on a screen 示波器；示波管

osier /ˈəʊziə(r); *NAmE* ˈoʊʒər/ *noun* a type of WILLOW tree, with thin branches that bend easily and are used for making BASKETS 青剛柳；杞柳；柳樹

os·mium /ˈɒzmiəm; *NAmE* ˈɑːzmiəm/ *noun* [U] (*symb.* **Os**) a chemical element. Osmium is a hard silver-white metal. 鋨

os·mo·sis /ɒzˈməʊsɪs; *NAmE* ɑːzˈmoʊ-/ *noun* [U] **1** (*biology* 生 or *chemistry* 化) the gradual passing of a liquid through a MEMBRANE (= a thin layer of material) as a result of there being different amounts of dissolved substances on either side of the membrane 透析；滲透： *Water passes into the roots of a plant by osmosis.* 水經透析進入植物根部。 **2** the gradual process of learning or being influenced by sth, as a result of being in close contact with it 耳濡目染；潛移默化 ▸ **os·mot·ic** /ɒzˈmɒtɪk; *NAmE* ɑːzˈmɑːtɪk/ *adj.*： *osmotic pressure* 滲透壓力

os·prey /ˈɒspreɪ; *NAmE* ˈɑːs-/ *noun* a large BIRD OF PREY (= a bird that kills other creatures for food) that eats fish 鶚；魚鷹

os·se·ous /ˈɒsiəs; *NAmE* ˈɑːs-/ *adj.* (*technical* 術語) made of or turned into bone 骨的；骨質的；骨化的

os·sify /ˈɒsɪfaɪ; *NAmE* ˈɑːs-/ *verb* [usually passive] (**os·si·fies**, **os·si·fy·ing**, **os·si·fied**, **os·si·fied**) (*formal, disapproving*) **1** [I, T, usually passive] **~ (sth)** to become or make sth fixed and unable to change 僵化；使固定不變： *an ossified political system* 僵化的政治制度 **2** [I, T, usually passive] **~ (sth)** (*technical* 術語) to become or make sth hard like bone 使骨化；骨質化 ▸ **os·si·fi·ca·tion** *noun* [U] (*formal*)

os·ten·sible /ɒˈstensəbl; *NAmE* ɑːˈst-/ *adj.* [only before noun] (*formal*) seeming or stated to be real or true, when this is perhaps not the case 表面的；宣稱的；假託的 SYN **apparent**： *The ostensible reason for his absence was illness.* 他假託生病缺勤。 ▸ **os·ten·sibly** /-əbli/ *adv.*： *Troops were sent in, ostensibly to protect the civilian population.* 謊稱為保護平民而派駐了軍隊。

os·ten·ta·tion /ˌɒstenˈteɪʃn; *NAmE* ˌɑːs-/ *noun* [U] (*disapproving*) an exaggerated display of wealth, knowledge or skill that is made in order to impress people（對財富、知識、技能的）炫耀，賣弄，夸示

os·ten·ta·tious /ˌɒstenˈteɪʃəs; *NAmE* ˌɑːs-/ *adj.* **1** (*disapproving*) expensive or noticeable in a way that is intended to impress people 擺闊的；鋪張的；浮華的 SYN **showy** **2** (*disapproving*) behaving in a way that is

O

meant to impress people by showing how rich, important, etc. you are 炫耀的；賣弄的；夸示的 **3** (of an action 舉動) done in a very obvious way so that people will notice it 誇張的；招搖的：*He gave an ostentatious yawn.* 他張揚地打了個哈欠。▸ **os·ten·ta·tious·ly** *adv.*：*ostentatiously dressed* 招搖的打扮

osteo- /ˈɒstiəʊ; *NAmE* ˈɑːstioʊ/ *combining form* (in nouns and adjectives 構成名詞和形容詞) connected with bones 骨的：*osteopath* 骨療醫師

osteo·arth·ritis /ˌɒstiəʊɑːˈθraɪtɪs; *NAmE* ˌɑːstioʊɑːrˈθ-/ *noun* [U] (*medical* 醫) a disease that causes painful swelling and permanent damage in the joints of the body, especially the hips, knees and thumbs 骨關節炎

osteo·path /ˈɒstiəpæθ; *NAmE* ˈɑːs-/ *noun* a person whose job involves treating some diseases and physical problems by pressing and moving the bones and muscles 骨療醫師；整骨醫士 ➲ compare CHIROPRACTOR

oste·op·athy /ˌɒstiˈɒpəθi; *NAmE* ˌɑːstiˈɑːp-/ *noun* [U] the treatment of some diseases and physical problems by pressing and moving the bones and muscles 骨療學；整骨術 ▸ **osteo·path·ic** /ˌɒstiəˈpæθɪk; *NAmE* ˌɑːs-/ *adj.*

osteo·por·osis /ˌɒstiəʊpəˈrəʊsɪs; *NAmE* ˌɑːstioʊpəˈroʊ-/ (also ˌ**brittle** ˈ**bone disease**) *noun* [U] (*medical* 醫) a condition in which the bones become weak and are easily broken, usually when people get older or because they do not eat enough of certain substances 骨質疏鬆；骨質疏鬆症

ost·ler /ˈɒslə(r); *NAmE* ˈɑːs-/ (*NAmE* also **host·ler**) *noun* (in the past) a man who took care of guests' horses at an INN（昔日客棧的）馬夫

os·tra·cism /ˈɒstrəsɪzəm; *NAmE* ˈɑːs-/ *noun* [U] (*formal*) the act of deliberately not including sb in a group or activity; the state of not being included 排擠；排斥

os·tra·cize (*BrE* also **-ise**) /ˈɒstrəsaɪz; *NAmE* ˈɑːs-/ *verb* **~ sb** (*formal*) to refuse to let sb be a member of a social group; to refuse to meet or talk to sb 排擠；排斥 SYN **shun**：*He was ostracized by his colleagues for refusing to support the strike.* 他因拒絕支持罷工而受到同事的排斥。

os·trich /ˈɒstrɪtʃ; *NAmE* ˈɑːs-; ˈɔːs-/ *noun* **1** a very large African bird with a long neck and long legs, that cannot fly but can run very fast 鴕鳥 **2** (*informal*) a person who prefers to ignore problems rather than try and deal with them 逃避現實的人；不願正視現實者

OTC /ˌəʊ tiː ˈsiː; *NAmE* ˌoʊ/ *abbr.* = OVER-THE-COUNTER：*OTC medicines and food supplements* 非處方藥和膳食補充劑 ◇ *OTC trading of securities* 證券的場外交易

other 🔑 /ˈʌðə(r)/ *adj., pron.*
1 🔑 used to refer to people or things that are additional or different to people or things that have been mentioned or are known about 另外；其他：*Mr Harris and Mrs Bate and three other teachers were there.* 哈里斯老師、貝特老師和其他三位老師在場。◇ *Are there any other questions?* 還有其他問題沒有？◇ *I can't see you now—**some other time**, maybe.* 我現在不能見你，也許別的時候吧。◇ *Two buildings were destroyed and many others damaged in the blast.* 在這次爆炸中，兩座建築物被摧毀，還有許多建築物遭損壞。◇ *This option is preferable to any other.* 這個選擇比其他任何一個都好。◇ ***Some** designs **are better than others**.* 有一些設計比其他的好。➲ compare ANOTHER (1) **2** 🔑 **the, my, your, etc. ~** used to refer to the second of two people or things（指兩個人或事物中的第二個）那個，另一個：*My other sister is a doctor.* 我的另一個妹妹是醫生。◇ *One son went to live in Australia and **the other one** was killed in a car crash.* 一個兒子移居澳大利亞，另一個在撞車事故中身亡。◇ *He raised one arm and then the other.* 他先舉起一隻手，然後舉起另一隻。◇ *You must ask **one or other** of your parents.* 你必須問你的父親或母親。**3** 🔑 **the, my, your, etc. ~** used to refer to the remaining people or things in a group（指一組中其餘的人或事物）其餘的，另外的：*I'll wear my other shoes—these are dirty.* 這雙鞋髒了，我要穿別的鞋。◇ *'I like this one.' 'What about **the other ones**?'* "我喜歡這個。" "其他那些怎麼樣？" ◇ *I went swimming while the others played tennis.* 我去游泳，而其他人去打網球了。**4** 🔑 **the other ...** used to refer to a place, direction, etc. that is the opposite to where you are, are going, etc.（指與說話人所在位置等相反的方向或地點）另一邊，對面，相反的方向：*I work on the other side of town.* 我在城的另一邊工作。◇ *He crashed into a car coming the other way.* 他和迎面開來的汽車相撞了。◇ *He found me, not **the other way round/around**.* 他發現了我，而不是我發現了他。

IDM Most idioms containing **other** are at the entries for the nouns and verbs in the idioms, for example **in other words** is at **word**. 大多數含 other 的習語，都可在該等習語中的名詞及動詞相關詞條找到，如 in other words 在詞條 word 下。 **the** ˌ**other** ˈ**day/**ˈ**morning/**ˈ**evening/**ˈ**week** 🔑 recently 那天，那天早上，那天晚上，那個星期（用於指說話前不久的日子）：*I saw Jack the other day.* 我前幾天看到傑克了。**other than** (usually used in negative sentences 通常用於否定句) **1** 🔑 except 除…以外：*I don't know any French people other than you.* 除了你，我不認識別的法國人。◇ *We're going away in June but **other than that** I'll be here all summer.* 我們六月份外出；除此以外，我整個夏天都在這裏。**2** (*formal*) different or in a different way from; not 不同；不同於；不：*I have never known him to behave other than selfishly.* 我從沒見過他不自私。

ˌ**other** ˈ**half** (also ˌ**better** ˈ**half**) *noun* (*informal, humorous*) the person that you are married to, or your boyfriend or girlfriend 另一半（指配偶或男友、女友）

other·ness /ˈʌðənəs; *NAmE* ˈʌðərnəs/ *noun* [U] (*formal*) the quality of being different or strange 相異；奇特性；特別：*the otherness of an alien culture* 異域文化的不同情調

other·wise 🔑 /ˈʌðəwaɪz; *NAmE* ˈʌðərwaɪz/ *adv.*
1 🔑 used to state what the result would be if sth did not happen or if the situation were different 否則；不然：*My parents lent me the money. Otherwise, I couldn't have afforded the trip.* 我父母借錢給我了。否則，我可付不起這次旅費。◇ *Shut the window, otherwise it'll get too cold in here.* 把窗戶關好，不然屋子裏就太冷了。◇ *We're committed to the project. We wouldn't be here otherwise.* 我們是全心全意投入這項工作的，否則我們就不會到這裏來了。**2** apart from that 除此以外：*There was some music playing upstairs. Otherwise the house was silent.* 樓上有些音樂聲。除此以外，房子裏靜悄悄的。◇ *He was slightly bruised but otherwise unhurt.* 他除了一點青腫之外沒有受傷。**3** in a different way to the way mentioned; differently 以其他方式；另；亦：*Bismarck, **otherwise known as** 'the Iron Chancellor'* 俾斯麥，亦稱為“鐵血首相” ◇ *It is not permitted to sell or otherwise distribute copies of past examination papers.* 不准出售或以其他方式散發過去的試卷。◇ *You know what this is about. Why **pretend otherwise*** (= that you do not)? 你明明知道這是怎麼回事，為什麼裝作不知道？◇ *I wanted to see him but he was **otherwise engaged*** (= doing sth else). 我想見他，但他正忙着別的事情。

IDM **or otherwise** used to refer to sth that is different from or the opposite of what has just been mentioned 或其他情況；或相反：*It was necessary to discover the truth or otherwise of these statements.* 有必要查證這些說法是真是假。◇ *We insure against all damage, accidental or otherwise.* 我們的保險包括一切意外或其他損失。➲ more at KNOW *v.*

ˌ**other** ˈ**woman** *noun* [usually sing.] a woman with whom a man is having a sexual relationship, although he already has a wife or partner 情婦；女第三者

ˌ**other-**ˈ**worldly** *adj.* concerned with spiritual thoughts and ideas rather than with ordinary life 超脫世俗的；斷絕塵緣的；超凡入聖的；出世的 ▸ ˌ**other-**ˈ**worldli·ness** *noun* [U]

oti·ose /ˈəʊtiəʊs; *NAmE* ˈoʊʃioʊs/ *adj.* (*formal*) having no useful purpose 多餘的；無用的 SYN **unnecessary**：*an otiose round of meetings* 一輪無用的會議

ot·itis /əʊˈtaɪtɪs; *NAmE* oʊ-/ *noun* [U] (*medical* 醫) a painful swelling of the ear, caused by an infection 耳炎

OTT /ˌəʊ tiː ˈtiː; *NAmE* ˌoʊ/ *adj.* (*BrE, informal*) = OVER THE TOP at TOP *n.*：*Her make-up was a bit OTT.* 她化的妝有些過濃。

O

otter /ˈɒtə(r); *NAmE* ˈɑːtər/ *noun* a small animal that has four WEBBED feet (= with skin between the toes), a tail and thick brown fur. Otters live in rivers and eat fish. 水獺

otto /ˈɒtəʊ; *NAmE* ˈɑːtoʊ/ *noun* (*NAmE*) = ATTAR

ot·to·man /ˈɒtəmən; *NAmE* ˈɑːt-/ *noun* a piece of furniture like a large box with a soft top, used for storing things in and sitting on 褥榻，箱式凳（箱子式的坐凳，有軟墊）

OU /ˌəʊ ˈjuː; *NAmE* ˌoʊ/ *abbr.* (in Britain) Open University（英國的）開放大學，公開大學

ou /əʊ; *NAmE* oʊ/ *noun* (*pl.* **os** or **ouens** /ˈəʊənz; *NAmE* ˈoʊ-/) (*SAfrE*) = OKE

ouch /aʊtʃ/ *exclamation* used to express sudden pain（表示突然的疼痛）哎喲：*Ouch! That hurt!* 哎喲！疼死了！

oud /uːd/ *noun* a musical instrument similar to a LUTE played mainly in Arab countries 厄烏德琴（撥弦樂器，流行於阿拉伯國家）

ought to 0‑ /ˈɔːt tə; *before vowels and finally* ˈɔːt tu/ *modal verb* (*negative* **ought not to**, *short form* (*especially BrE*) **oughtn't to**)
1 0‑ used to say what is the right thing to do 應該；應當：*They ought to apologize.* 他們應該道歉。◇ *'Ought I to write to say thank you?' 'Yes, I think you ought (to).'* "我應該寫信致謝嗎？" "對，我覺得你應該。" ◇ *They ought to have apologized* (= but they didn't). 他們本該道歉的。◇ *Such things ought not to be allowed.* 這種事應該禁止。◇ *He oughtn't to have been driving so fast.* 他本不該把車開得那麼快。➲ note at SHOULD **2** 0‑ used to say what you expect or would like to happen（表示期望或可能發生的事）應該：*Children ought to be able to read by the age of 7.* 兒童 7 歲時應該識字了。◇ *Nurses ought to earn more.* 護士的薪資應該多一點。**3** 0‑ used to say what you advise or recommend（表示勸告或建議）應該：*We ought to be leaving now.* 我們現在該動身了。◇ *This is delicious. You ought to try some.* 這個菜很可口，你可得嚐嚐。◇ *You ought to have come to the meeting. It was interesting.* 會議可有意思了，你真該出席。**4** 0‑ used to say what has probably happened or is probably true（表示可能發生的或真實的事情）應該：*If he started out at nine, he ought to be here by now.* 他如果九點出發，現在應該到這裏了。◇ *That ought to be enough food for the four of us.* 這些食物應該夠咱們四個人吃了。◇ *Oughtn't the water to have boiled by now?* 水現在該開了吧？➲ note at MODAL

Ouija board™ /ˈwiːdʒə bɔːd; *NAmE* bɔːrd/ *noun* a board marked with letters of the alphabet and other signs, used in SEANCES to receive messages said to come from people who are dead 靈應牌，維佳博德牌（刻有字母和其他符號的板牌，用於降靈會中接收亡魂傳遞的信息）

ounce /aʊns/ *noun* **1** [C] (*abbr.* **oz**) a unit for measuring weight, 1/16 of a pound, equal to 28.35 grams 盎司（重量單位，1/16 磅，等於 28.35 克）➲ see also FLUID OUNCE **2** [sing.] **~ of sth** (*informal*) (used especially with negatives 尤與否定詞連用) a very small quantity of sth 少許；少量；一點點；絲毫：*There's not an ounce of truth in her story.* 她所說的一點都不真實。**IDM** see PREVENTION

our 0‑ /ɑː(r); ˈaʊə(r)/ *det.* (the possessive form of *we* * we 的所有格)
1 0‑ belonging to us; connected with us 我們的：*our daughter/dog/house* 我們的女兒 / 狗 / 房子 ◇ *We showed them some of our photos.* 我們給他們看了我們的一些照片。◇ *Our main export is rice.* 我們主要出口大米。◇ *And now, over to our Rome correspondent …* 現在是駐羅馬記者的報道… **2** **Our** used to refer to or address God or a holy person（用於稱上帝或聖人）：*Our Father* (= God) 上帝 ◇ *Our Lady* (= the Virgin Mary) 聖母瑪利亞

ours 0‑ /ɑːz; ˈaʊəz; *NAmE* ɑːrz; ˈaʊərz/ *pron.*
1 0‑ the one or ones that belong to us 我們的：*Their house is very similar to ours, but ours is bigger.* 他們的房子和我們的十分相像，但我們的要大些。◇ *No, those are Ellie's kids. Ours are upstairs.* 不，那些是埃利的孩子。我們的都在樓上。◇ *He's a friend of ours.* 他是我們的朋友。**2** (*BrE, informal*) our home 我們的住處：*Do you fancy coming to ours for Sunday dinner?* 週日來我們家吃晚飯怎麼樣？

our·selves 0‑ /ɑːˈselvz; ˌaʊəˈs-; *NAmE* ɑːrˈs-; ˌaʊərˈs-/ *pron.* **1** 0‑ the reflexive form of *we*; used when you and another person or other people together cause and are affected by an action（we 的反身形式）我們自己：*We shouldn't blame ourselves for what happened.* 我們不應該為發生的事責怪自己。◇ *Let's just relax and enjoy ourselves.* 咱們輕鬆一下，好好享受享受。◇ *We'd like to see it for ourselves.* 我們想親眼看看它。**2** 0‑ used to emphasize *we* or *us*; sometimes used instead of these words（用於強調或代替 we 或 us）我們自己，親自：*We've often thought of going there ourselves.* 我們常想親自到那裏去一趟。◇ *The only people there were ourselves.* 那裏僅有的人就是我們自己。
IDM **(all) by our'selves** **1** alone; without anyone else（我們）獨自，單獨 **2** without help（我們）獨立地 **(all) to our'selves** for us alone; not shared with anyone（完全）屬於我們自己：*We had the pool all to ourselves.* 這個游泳池完全供我們自己使用。

-ous *suffix* (in adjectives 構成形容詞) having the nature or quality of 有…性質的：*poisonous* 有毒的 ◇ *mountainous* 多山的 ▸ **-ously** (in adverbs 構成副詞)：*gloriously* 光榮地 **-ousness** (in nouns 構成名詞)：*spaciousness* 寬敞

oust /aʊst/ *verb* to force sb out of a job or position of power, especially in order to take their place 剝奪；罷免；革職：**~ sb (as sth)** *He was ousted as chairman.* 他的主席職務被革除了。◇ **~ sb (from sth)** *The rebels finally managed to oust the government from power.* 反叛者最後總算打倒了政府。

oust·er /ˈaʊstə(r)/ *noun* (*NAmE*) the act of removing sb from a position of authority in order to put sb else in their place; the fact of being removed in this way 罷免；廢黜；革職：*the president's ouster by the military* 軍方對總統的廢黜

out 0‑ /aʊt/ *adv., prep., noun, adj., verb*
■ *adv., prep.* **HELP** For the special uses of **out** in phrasal verbs, look at the entries for the verbs. For example **burst out** is in the phrasal verb section at **burst**. * out 在短語動詞中的特殊用法見有關動詞詞條。如 burst out 在詞條 burst 的短語動詞部份。**1** 0‑ **~ (of sth)** away from the inside of a place or thing（從…裏）出來：*She ran out into the corridor.* 她跑出來，衝進走廊。◇ *She shook the bag and some coins fell out.* 她抖了抖袋子，幾個硬幣掉了出來。◇ *I got out of bed.* 我起了牀。◇ *He opened the box and* **out jumped** *a frog.* 他打開盒子，從裏面跳出一隻青蛙來。◇ ***Out you go!*** (= used to order sb to leave a room) 滾出去！◇ (*informal*) *He ran out the door.* 他跑出門去。**2** 0‑ **~ (of sth)** (of people 人) away from or not at home or their place of work 不在家；不在工作地點；外出：*I called Liz but she was out.* 我打電話給利茲，但她不在家。◇ *Let's go out this evening* (= for example to a restaurant or club). 咱們今天晚上出去吧。◇ *We haven't had a* **night out** *for weeks.* 我們已經好幾個星期晚上沒出去過了。◇ *Mr Green is out of town this week.* 格林先生本週到外地去了。**3** 0‑ **~ (of sth)** away from the edge of a place 出去；離開（某地）邊緣：*The boy dashed out into the road.* 男孩子向路中間衝去。◇ *Don't lean out of the window.* 不要探出窗外。**4** 0‑ **~ (of sth)** a long or a particular distance away from a place or from land 遠離（某地或陸地）；離（某地或陸地）：*She's working out in Australia.* 她遠在澳大利亞工作。◇ *He lives right out in the country.* 他住在遠離此地的鄉間。◇ *The boats are all out at sea.* 船隻全都出海了。◇ *The ship sank ten miles out of Stockholm.* 那條船沉沒在距斯德哥爾摩十英里外海。**5** 0‑ **~ (of sth)** used to show that sth/sb is removed from a place, job, etc. 除掉；清除：*This detergent is good for getting stains out.* 這種洗滌劑能清除斑漬。◇ *We want this government out.* 我們想要這任政府下台。◇ *He got thrown out of the restaurant.* 他被逐出了餐館。**6** 0‑ **~ of sth/sb** used to show that sth comes from or is obtained from sth/sb（表示來源）從，用…製作：*He drank his beer out of the bottle.* 他從瓶口直接喝啤酒。◇ *a statue made out of bronze* 一尊青銅像 ◇ *a romance straight out of a fairy tale*

O

直接從童話改編的浪漫故事 ◇ *I paid for the damage out of my savings.* 我用自己的積蓄賠償了損失。◇ *We'll get the truth out of her.* 我們會從她那裏套出實情。**7** 🔑 **~ of sth** used to show that sb/sth does not have any of sth 沒有；缺少：*We're out of milk.* 我們沒有牛奶了。◇ *He's been* **out of work** *for six months.* 他已經失業六個月了。◇ *You're* **out of luck**—*she left ten minutes ago.* 你真不走運，她十分鐘前才離開。**8** 🔑 **~ of sth** used to show that sb/sth is not or no longer in a particular state or condition（表示不在原狀態）脫離，離開：*Try and stay out of trouble.* 盡量別惹麻煩。◇ *I watched the car until it was* **out of sight**. 我目送汽車，直到看不見為止。**9** 🔑 **~** (**of sth**) used to show that sb is no longer involved in sth（表示不再參與某事）脫離：*It was an awful job and I'm glad to be out of it.* 那件差事簡直是受罪，我很高興擺脫掉了。◇ *He gets out of the army in a few weeks.* 幾週之後他就要離開部隊。◇ *They'll be out* (= of prison) *on bail in no time.* 他們馬上就要獲得保釋出獄。◇ *Brown goes on to the semi-finals but Lee is out.* 布朗進入了半決賽，但李被淘汰了。**10 ~ of sth** used to show the reason why sth is done（表示原因）因為，出於：*I asked out of curiosity.* 我因為好奇問了問。◇ *She did it out of spite.* 她那麼做是出於惡意。**11** 🔑 **~ of sth** from a particular number or set 從（某個數目或集）中：*You scored six out of ten.* 總分十分你得了六分。◇ *Two out of three people think the President should resign.* 有三分之二的人認為總統應當辭職。**12** 🔑 (of a book, etc. 書籍等) not in the library; borrowed by sb else 不在圖書館；已借出：*The book you wanted is out on loan.* 你要的那本書借出去了。**13** 🔑 (of the TIDE 海潮) at or towards its lowest point on land 在退潮期；退潮：*I like walking on the wet sand when the tide is out.* 我喜歡退潮後走在濕潤的沙灘上。**14** 🔑 if the sun, moon or stars are or come **out**, they can be seen from the earth and are not hidden by clouds（日、月、星辰）出現，未被雲遮住 **15** (of flowers 花朵) fully open 開放：*There should be some snowdrops out by now.* 現在應該有雪花蓮開放了。**16** 🔑 available to everyone; known to everyone 公開；發行：*When does her new book come out?* 她的新書什麼時候出版？◇ **Word always gets out** (= people find out about things) *no matter how careful you are.* 無論你多麼小心，總會有消息走漏。◇ **Out with it!** (= say what you know) 你就說出來吧！**17** 🔑 clearly and loudly so that people can hear 大聲地：*to* **call/cry/shout out** 大聲叫／哭／喊 ◇ *Read it* **out loud**. 請大聲朗讀。◇ *Nobody* **spoke out** *in his defence.* 沒有人站出來替他辯護。**18** (*informal*) having told other people that you are HOMOSEXUAL 已公開同性戀身分：*I had been out since I was 17.* 我從 17 歲起就公開我是同性戀。**19** (in CRICKET, BASEBALL, etc. 板球、棒球等) if a team or team member is **out**, it is no longer their turn with the BAT 出局：*The West Indies were* **all out for** *364* (= after scoring 364 RUNS in CRICKET). 西印度群島隊以 364 分全隊出局。**20** (in TENNIS, etc. 網球等) if the ball is **out**, it landed outside the line 出界：*The umpire said the ball was out.* 裁判員判球出界。**21** 🔑 **~** (**in sth**) not correct or exact; wrong 錯誤；不準確：*I was slightly out in my calculations.* 我的計算出了點小錯。◇ *Your guess was a long way out* (= completely wrong). 你的猜測完全錯了。◇ *The estimate was* **out by** *more than $100.* 這個估計差了 100 多元。**22** not possible or not allowed 不可能；不允許：*Swimming is out until the weather gets warmer.* 天氣轉暖前，游泳是不可能的。**23** not fashionable 過時：*Black is out this year.* 今年黑色不時興了。**24** 🔑 (of fire, lights or burning materials 火、燈光、燃燒物等) not or no longer burning or lit 熄滅：*Suddenly all the lights went out.* 突然間所有的燈光都滅了。◇ *The fire had burnt itself out.* 爐火燒盡熄滅了。**25** at an end 結束：*It was summer and school was out.* 夏天，學校放假了。◇ *She was to regret her words* **before the day was out**. 她天黑前就會為自己說的話後悔。**26** unconscious 無知覺；昏迷：*He was out for more than an hour and came round in the hospital.* 他昏迷了一個多小時，在醫院才蘇醒過來。◇ *She was knocked* **out cold**. 她完全被打昏了。**27** (*BrE, informal*) on strike 罷工 **28** to the end; completely 到底；完全地：**Hear me out** *before you say anything.* 你聽我說完再講話。◇ *We left them to* **fight it out** (= settle a disagreement by fighting or arguing). 我們讓他們爭吵下去，爭出個輸贏。➲ see also ALL-OUT

IDM **be out for sth/to do sth** to be trying to get or do sth 試圖得到（或做）：*I'm not out for revenge.* 我不是來尋報復的。◇ *She's* **out for what she can get** (= trying to get something for herself). 她力圖得到自己能得的。◇ *The company is out to capture the Canadian market.* 這家公司竭盡全力搶佔加拿大市場。**ˌout and aˈbout** (*BrE*) **1** able to go outside again after an illness 病癒後能外出走動 **2** travelling around a place 遍遊某地：*We've been out and about talking to people all over the country.* 我們遊遍了全國，和各地的人交談。**ˈout of here** (*informal*) going or leaving 走；離去；離開：*As soon as I get my money I'm out of here!* 我一拿到錢就走！**ˈout of it** (*informal*) **1** sad because you are not included in sth（覺得自己是外人而）不是味兒：*We've only just moved here so we feel a little out of it.* 我們剛搬到這裏，所以心裏覺得有點不適應。**2** not aware of what is happening, usually because of drinking too much alcohol, or taking drugs（因酒或藥物作用而對周圍事情）茫然不覺，昏昏然

■ ***noun*** [sing.] a way of avoiding having to do sth 迴避的方法；託辭；出路：*She was desperately looking for an out.* 她在拚命找一條脫身之計。**IDM** see IN *n.*

■ ***adj.*** (*informal*) having told other people that you are HOMOSEXUAL 已公開同性戀身分的：*an out gay man* 已公開同性戀身分的男子

■ ***verb*** **~ sb** to say publicly that sb is HOMOSEXUAL, especially when they would prefer to keep the fact a secret 揭露，公佈（同性戀者）：*He is the latest politician to be outed by gay activists.* 他是被同性戀維權人士新近揭露的同性戀政治人物。

out- /aʊt/ *prefix* **1** (in verbs 構成動詞) greater, better, further, longer, etc. 超越；超過：*outnumber* 在數量上壓倒 ◇ *outwit* 在智慧上勝過 ◇ *outgrow* 長得比…快 ◇ *outlive* 活得比…長 **2** (in nouns and adjectives 構成名詞和形容詞) outside; OUTWARD; away from 在外面；向外；離開：*outbuildings* 附屬建築物 ◇ *outpatient* 門診病人 ◇ *outlying* 偏遠的 ◇ *outgoing* 向外的

out·age /ˈaʊtɪdʒ/ *noun* (*NAmE*) a period of time when the supply of electricity, etc. is not working（電等的）停供，斷供期：*a power outage* 停電

ˌout-and-ˈout *adj.* [only before noun] in every way 十足的；完全的；徹頭徹尾的 **SYN** **complete**：*What she said was an out-and-out lie.* 她說的是個漫天大謊。

out·back /ˈaʊtbæk/ *noun* **the outback** [sing.] the area of Australia that is a long way from the coast and the towns, where few people live（澳大利亞的）內地，內陸地區

out·bid /ˌaʊtˈbɪd/ *verb* (**out·bid·ding**, **out·bid**, **out·bid**) **~ sb** (**for sth**) to offer more money than sb else in order to buy sth, for example at an AUCTION（在拍賣等中）出價較高，出價高於（某人）

out·board /ˈaʊtbɔːd; *NAmE* -bɔːrd/ *adj.* (*technical* 術語) on, towards or near the outside of a ship or an aircraft（船或飛機）外側的，靠近外側的，舷外的

ˌoutboard ˈmotor (also **ˌoutboard ˈengine**, **out·board**) *noun* an engine that you can fix to the back of a small boat 船尾外裝發動機；舷外發動機

out·bound /ˈaʊtbaʊnd/ *adj.* (*formal*) travelling from a place rather than arriving in it 向外的；出港的；離開某地的：***outbound flights/passengers*** 出港航班／旅客 **OPP** **inbound**

ˈout box (*US*) (*BrE* **ˈout tray**) *noun* (in an office) a container on your desk for letters or documents that are waiting to be sent out or passed to sb else（辦公室的）待發信件盤 ➲ compare IN TRAY ➲ VISUAL VOCAB page V69

out·box /ˈaʊtbɒks; *NAmE* -bɑːks/ *noun* (*computing* 計) the place on a computer where new email messages that you write are stored before you send them（待）發件箱

out·break /ˈaʊtbreɪk/ *noun* the sudden start of sth unpleasant, especially violence or a disease（暴力、疾病等壞事的）爆發，突然發生：*the outbreak of war* 戰爭的爆發 ◇ *an outbreak of typhoid* 傷寒的爆發 ◇ *Outbreaks* *of rain are expected in the afternoon.* 下午將有暴雨。 ➲ COLLOCATIONS at ILL

out·build·ing /ˈaʊtbɪldɪŋ/ *noun* [usually pl.] a building such as a SHED or STABLE that is built near to, but separate from, a main building 附屬建築物

out·burst /ˈaʊtbɜːst; *NAmE* -bɜːrst/ *noun* **1** a sudden strong expression of an emotion（感情的）爆發，迸發：*an outburst of anger* 突然大怒 ◇ *She was alarmed by his violent outburst.* 他暴跳如雷，令她驚恐萬狀。**2** a sudden increase in a particular activity or attitude（活動的）激增；（態度的）激化：*an outburst of racism* 種族主義的突然高漲

out·cast /ˈaʊtkɑːst; *NAmE* -kæst/ *noun* a person who is not accepted by other people and who sometimes has to leave their home and friends 被拋棄者；被排斥者：*People with the disease were often treated as social outcasts.* 患有這種疾病的人常被社會擯棄。▸ **out·cast** *adj.*

out·class /ˌaʊtˈklɑːs; *NAmE* -ˈklæs/ *verb* [often passive] **~ sb/sth** to be much better than sb you are competing against 遠遠高出，遠遠超過（對手）：*Kennedy was outclassed 0–6 0–6 in the final.* 肯尼迪在決賽中以 0:6 和 0:6 連輸兩盤落敗。

out·come **AW** /ˈaʊtkʌm/ *noun* the result or effect of an action or event 結果；效果：*We are waiting to hear the final outcome of the negotiations.* 我們在等待談判的最終結果。◇ *These costs are payable whatever the outcome of the case.* 無論訟案結果如何，這些費用都應照付。◇ *We are confident of a successful outcome.* 我們相信會有圓滿的結果。◇ *Four possible outcomes have been identified.* 現已確定有四種可能的結果。 ➲ SYNONYMS at RESULT

out·crop /ˈaʊtkrɒp; *NAmE* -krɑːp/ *noun* a large mass of rock that stands above the surface of the ground（岩石）露出地面的部份；露頭

out·cry /ˈaʊtkraɪ/ *noun* [C, U] (*pl.* **-ies**) **~ (at/over/against sth)** a reaction of anger or strong protest shown by people in public 吶喊；怒吼；強烈的抗議：*an outcry over the proposed change* 對擬議的改革所發出的強烈抗議 ◇ *The new tax provoked a* ***public outcry***. 新稅項引起了公眾的強烈抗議。◇ *There was outcry at the judge's statement.* 法官的陳辭引起一片譁然。

out·dated /ˌaʊtˈdeɪtɪd/ *adj.* no longer useful because of being old-fashioned 過時的；陳舊的：*outdated equipment* 過時的設備 ◇ *These figures are now outdated.* 這些數字現在已經過時。 ➲ compare OUT OF DATE (1)

out·dis·tance /ˌaʊtˈdɪstəns/ *verb* **~ sb/sth** to leave sb/sth behind by going faster, further, etc.; to be better than sb/sth 遠遠超過；超越；優於 **SYN** **outstrip**

outdo /ˌaʊtˈduː/ *verb* (**out·does** /-ˈdʌz/, **out·did** /-ˈdɪd/, **outdone** /-ˈdʌn/) **~ sb/sth** to do more or better than sb else 勝過；優於 **SYN** **beat**：*Sometimes small firms can outdo big business when it comes to customer care.* 在顧客服務方面，有時小企業可能優於大企業。◇ ***Not to be outdone*** (= not wanting to let sb else do better), *she tried again.* 她不甘落後，又試了一次。

out·door 🔑 /ˈaʊtdɔː(r)/ *adj.* [only before noun] used, happening or located outside rather than in a building 戶外的；室外的：***outdoor clothing/activities*** 戶外穿的衣服／活動 ◇ *an outdoor swimming pool* 室外游泳池 ◇ *I'm not really the* ***outdoor type*** (= I prefer indoor activities). 我不太喜愛戶外活動。**OPP** **indoor**

out·doors 🔑 /ˌaʊtˈdɔːz; *NAmE* -ˈdɔːrz/ *adv., noun*
▪ ***adv.*** 🔑 outside, rather than in a building 在戶外；在野外：*The rain prevented them from eating outdoors.* 雨使他們無法戶外用餐。**OPP** **indoors**
▪ ***noun*** **the outdoors** [sing.] the countryside, away from buildings and busy places 野外；曠野；郊外：*They both have a love of the outdoors.* 他們倆都喜愛郊外的環境。◇ *Come to Canada and enjoy* ***the great outdoors***. 到加拿大來享受藍天碧野吧！ ➲ COLLOCATIONS at TOWN

outer 🔑 /ˈaʊtə(r)/ *adj.* [only before noun]
1 🔑 on the outside of sth 外表的；外邊的 **SYN** **external**：*the outer layers of the skin* 皮膚表層 **2** 🔑 furthest from the inside or centre of sth 遠離中心的；外圍的：*I walked along the outer edge of the track.* 我沿着跑道的外緣走。◇ *the outer suburbs of the city* 城市的遠郊 ◇ *Outer London/Mongolia* 倫敦的外圍地區；外蒙古 ◇ (*figurative*) *to explore the outer* (= most extreme) *limits of human experience* 探索人類經驗的極限 **OPP** **inner**

ˌ**outer ˈbelt** (*US*) (*BrE* ˈ**ring road**) *noun* a road that is built around a city or town to reduce traffic in the centre 環路；環城路

outer·most /ˈaʊtəməʊst; *NAmE* ˈaʊtərmoʊst/ *adj.* [only before noun] furthest from the inside or centre 最外邊的；最遠的：*the outermost planet* 最遠的行星 ◇ *He fired and hit the outermost ring of the target.* 他開槍射中了靶子的最外一環。**OPP** **innermost**

ˌ**outer ˈspace** *noun* [U] = SPACE (5)：*radio waves from outer space* 來自外層空間的無線電波

outer·wear /ˈaʊtəweə(r); *NAmE* ˈaʊtərwer/ *noun* [U] clothes such as coats, hats, etc. that you wear outside 外衣；戶外的穿着

out·face /ˌaʊtˈfeɪs/ *verb* **~ sb** (*formal*) to defeat an enemy or opponent by being brave and remaining confident 凜然面對；嚇退

out·fall /ˈaʊtfɔːl/ *noun* (*technical* 術語) the place where a river, pipe, etc. flows out into the sea（河流、管道等的）排放口，入海口；河口：*a sewage outfall* 污水排放口

out·field /ˈaʊtfiːld/ *noun, adv.*
▪ ***noun*** [sing.] the outer part of the field in BASEBALL, CRICKET and some other sports（棒球、板球等體育運動的）外場，外野 ➲ compare INFIELD
▪ ***adv.*** in or to the outfield 在外場；向外場

out·field·er /ˈaʊtfiːldə(r)/ *noun* (in CRICKET and BASEBALL 板球及棒球) a player in the outfield 外場手；外場員；外野手

out·fit /ˈaʊtfɪt/ *noun, verb*
▪ ***noun*** **1** [C] a set of clothes that you wear together, especially for a particular occasion or purpose 全套服裝，裝束（尤指為某場合或目的）：*She was wearing an expensive new outfit.* 她穿着一身昂貴的新衣裳。◇ *a wedding outfit* 一套結婚禮服 ◇ *a cowboy/Superman outfit* (= one that you wear for fun in order to look like the type of person mentioned) 一套牛仔／超人服裝 **2** [C+sing./pl. v.] (*informal*) a group of people working together as an organization, business, team, etc. 團隊；小組；分隊：*a market research outfit* 市場調查組 ◇ *This was the fourth album by the top rock outfit.* 這是這個頂級搖滾樂隊的第四張唱片專輯。**3** [C] a set of equipment that you need for a particular purpose 全套裝備；成套工具：*a bicycle repair outfit* 修自行車的整套工具
▪ ***verb*** (**-tt-**) [often passive] **~ sth/sb (with sth)** (*especially NAmE*) to provide sb/sth with equipment or clothes for a special purpose 裝備；配置設備；供給服裝 **SYN** **equip**：*The ship was outfitted with a 12-bed hospital.* 這艘船上配置了一個有 12 個牀位的醫療室。

out·fit·ter (also **out·fit·ters**) /ˈaʊtfɪtə(r)/ *noun* **1** (*old-fashioned, BrE*) a shop/store that sells men's clothes or school uniforms（出售男裝或校服的）服裝店 **2** (*NAmE*) a shop/store that sells equipment for camping and other outdoor activities 戶外活動用品店；露營裝備店

out·flank /ˌaʊtˈflæŋk/ *verb* **1 ~ sb/sth** to move around the side of an enemy or opponent, especially in order to attack them from behind 包抄；側翼包圍 **2 ~ sb/sth** to gain an advantage over sb, especially by doing sth unexpected（尤指出其不意地）勝過，佔先 **SYN** **outmanoeuvre**

out·flow /ˈaʊtfləʊ; *NAmE* -floʊ/ *noun* [usually sing.] **~ (of sth/sb) (from sth)** the movement of a large amount of money, liquid, people, etc. out of a place 外流；流出量：*There was a capital outflow of $22 billion in 2008.* * 2008 年的資金外流量為 220 億元。◇ *a steady outflow of oil from the tank* 石油從油罐裏不斷的流出 ◇ *the outflow of refugees* 難民湧出 **OPP** **inflow**

out·fox /ˌaʊtˈfɒks; *NAmE* -ˈfɑːks/ *verb* **~ sb** to gain an advantage over sb by being more clever than they are 以智力勝過（或超過）**SYN** **outwit**

out·going /ˈaʊtgəʊɪŋ; *NAmE* -goʊ-/ *adj.* **1** liking to meet other people, enjoying their company and being

O

friendly towards them 愛交際的；友好的；外向的 SYN **sociable** : *an outgoing personality* 外向的性格 **2** [only before noun] leaving the position of responsibility mentioned 將卸任的；離職的 : *the **outgoing president/government*** 即將下台的總統/政府 OPP **incoming** **3** [only before noun] going away from a particular place rather than arriving in it 向外的；離開的 : *This telephone should be used for outgoing calls.* 這部電話用來往外撥打電話。◇ ***outgoing flights/passengers*** 離境航班/旅客◇ *the outgoing tide* 退潮 OPP **incoming**

out·goings /ˈaʊtɡəʊɪŋz; NAmE -ɡoʊ-/ *noun* [pl.] (*BrE*) the amount of money that a person or a business has to spend regularly, for example every month 開支；經常性費用 SYN **expenditure** : ***low/high outgoings*** 開支低/高◇ *Write down your **incomings and outgoings**.* 把你的收入與支出記下來。

ˈ**out-group** *noun* the people who do not belong to a particular IN-GROUP in a society 外群體；外團體

out·grow /ˌaʊtˈɡrəʊ; NAmE -ˈɡroʊ/ *verb* (**out·grew** /-ˈɡruː/, **out·grown** /-ˈɡrəʊn; NAmE -ˈɡroʊn/) **1 ~ sth** to grow too big to be able to wear or fit into sth 長得穿不下（衣服）；增長得容不進（某地）SYN **grow out of** : *She's already outgrown her school uniform.* 她已經長得連校服都不能穿了。◇ *The company has outgrown its offices.* 公司發展得辦公室都不夠用了。 **2 ~ sb** to grow taller, larger or more quickly than another person 比…長得高（或大、快）: *He's already outgrown his older brother.* 他已長得比他哥哥還高。 **3 ~ sth** to stop doing sth or lose interest in sth as you become older 因長大而放棄；年增志移 SYN **grow out of** : *He's outgrown his passion for rock music.* 隨着年齡的增長，他已對搖滾樂失去了熱情。

out·growth /ˈaʊtɡrəʊθ; NAmE -ɡroʊθ/ *noun* **1** (*technical* 術語) a thing that grows out of sth else 長出物；分支 : *The eye first appears as a cup-shaped outgrowth from the brain.* 眼睛開始是從大腦長出，呈杯狀。 **2** (*formal*) a natural development or result of sth 自然發展（或結果）: *The law was an outgrowth of the 2008 presidential election.* 這項法律是 2008 年總統選舉的必然結果。

out·gun /ˌaʊtˈɡʌn/ *verb* (**-nn-**) [often passive] **~ sb/sth** to have greater military strength than sb（軍事上）勝過，超過 : (*figurative*) *The England team was completely outgunned.* 英格蘭隊毫無還手之力。

out·house /ˈaʊthaʊs/ *noun* **1** (*BrE*) a small building, such as a SHED, outside a main building（主建築的）外圍建築，附屬建築 **2** (*especially NAmE*) a toilet in a small building of its own 屋外廁所

out·ing /ˈaʊtɪŋ/ *noun* **1** [C] **~ (to …)** a trip that you go on for pleasure or education, usually with a group of people and lasting no more than one day（集體）出外遊玩（或學習等）；遠足 SYN **excursion** : *We went **on an outing** to London.* 我們遊覽了倫敦。◇ *a family outing* 全家遠足 ➲ SYNONYMS at TRIP **2** [C] (*sport* 體) (*informal*) an occasion when sb takes part in a competition 參賽；比賽 **3** [U, C] the practice of naming people as HOMOSEXUALS in public, when they do not want anyone to know（違背同性戀者本人意願）對（其）身分的公開挑明

out·land·ish /aʊtˈlændɪʃ/ *adj.* (usually *disapproving*) strange or extremely unusual 古怪的；極不尋常的；奇特的 SYN **bizarre** : *outlandish costumes/ideas* 奇裝異服；古怪的想法 ▸ **out·land·ish·ly** *adv.*

out·last /ˌaʊtˈlɑːst; NAmE -ˈlæst/ *verb* **~ sb/sth** to continue to exist or take part in an activity for a longer time than sb/sth 比…持續時間長 : *He can outlast anyone on the dance floor.* 在舞場上，他比誰都能跳。

out·law /ˈaʊtlɔː/ *verb, noun*

■ *verb* **1 ~ sth** to make sth illegal 宣佈…不合法；使…成為非法 SYN **ban** : *plans to outlaw the carrying of knives* 宣布攜帶刀具為非法的方案◇ *the outlawed nationalist party* 被宣佈為非法的民族主義黨 **2 ~ sb** (in the past) to make sb an outlaw（舊時）剝奪（某人的）法律權益

■ *noun* (used especially about people in the past) a person who has done sth illegal and is hiding to avoid being caught; a person who is not protected by the law（尤指過去的人）亡命徒，逃犯，草莽英雄，被剝奪法律權益者 : *Robin Hood, the world's most famous outlaw* 羅賓漢，蜚聲世界的綠林好漢

out·lay /ˈaʊtleɪ/ *noun* [C, U] **~ (on sth)** the money that you have to spend in order to start a new project（啟動新項目的）開支，費用 : *The business quickly repaid the initial outlay on advertising.* 這家公司很快償付了初期的廣告費。◇ *a massive **financial/capital outlay*** 大量的財政/資本開支 ➲ SYNONYMS at COST

out·let /ˈaʊtlet/ *noun* **1 ~ (for sth)** a way of expressing or making good use of strong feelings, ideas or energy（感情、思想、精力發泄的）出路；表現機會 : *She needed to find an outlet for her many talents and interests.* 她多才多藝、興趣廣泛，需要找個施展的機會。◇ *Sport became the perfect outlet for his aggression.* 運動成為他攻擊性心理的最佳出路。 **2** (*business* 商) a shop/store or an organization that sells goods made by a particular company or of a particular type 專營店；經銷店 : *The business has 34 retail outlets in this state alone.* 那家商號僅在本州就有 34 個零售店。 **3** (*especially NAmE*) a shop/store that sells goods of a particular make at reduced prices（某品牌的）折扣店 : *the Nike outlet in the outlet mall* 特價商品購物中心裏的耐克折扣店 **4** a pipe or hole through which liquid or gas can flow out 出口；排放管 : *a sewage outlet* 污水排放口◇ *an outlet pipe* 排水管道 OPP **inlet 5** (also **re·cep·tacle**) (both *NAmE*) (*BrE* **socket**, ˈ**power point**) a device in a wall that you put a plug into in order to connect electrical equipment to the power supply of a building（電源）插座 ➲ picture at PLUG

out·line 🔑 /ˈaʊtlaɪn/ *verb, noun*

■ *verb* **1** 🔑 **~ sth (to sb)** | **~ what, how, etc. …** to give a description of the main facts or points involved in sth 概述；略述 SYN **sketch** : *We outlined our proposals to the committee.* 我們向委員會提綱挈領地講了講我們的提案。 **2** 🔑 [usually passive] **~ sth (against sth)** to show or mark the outer edge of sth 顯示，勾勒，描畫（事物的輪廓）: *They saw the huge building outlined against the sky.* 他們看見了在天空的映襯下那座巨大建築的輪廓。

■ *noun* [C, U] **1** 🔑 a description of the main facts or points involved in sth 概述；梗概 : *This is a brief outline of the events.* 這就是事件的簡要情況。◇ *You should draw up a plan or outline for the essay.* 你應該為文章草擬個計劃或提綱。◇ *The book describes **in outline** the main findings of the research.* 本書扼要敘述了主要的研究結果。◇ *an **outline agreement/proposal*** 協議/建議綱要 **2** 🔑 the line that goes around the edge of sth, showing its main shape but not the details 輪廓線；略圖 : *At last we could see the dim outline of an island.* 我們終於能看到一小島朦朧的輪廓了。◇ *an **outline map/sketch*** 略圖；草圖◇ *She drew the figures **in outline**.* 她簡略地勾勒出人物的輪廓。

out·live /ˌaʊtˈlɪv/ *verb* **1 ~ sb** to live longer than sb 比…活得長 : *He outlived his wife by three years.* 他比妻子多活了三年。 **2 ~ sth** to continue to exist after sth else has ended or disappeared（在…結束或消失後）繼續存在 : *The machine had **outlived its usefulness*** (= was no longer useful). 這機器已無用了。

out·look /ˈaʊtlʊk/ *noun* [usually sing.] **1 ~ (on sth)** the attitude to life and the world of a particular person, group or culture 觀點；見解；世界觀；人生觀 : *He had a practical outlook on life.* 他的人生觀很實際。◇ *Most Western societies are liberal **in outlook**.* 西方社會大多思想觀念開放。 **2 ~ (for sth)** the probable future for sb/sth; what is likely to happen 前景；可能性 SYN **prospect** : *The outlook for jobs is bleak.* 就業市場前景暗淡。◇ *the country's economic outlook* 國家的經濟前景◇ *The outlook* (= the probable weather) *for the weekend is dry and sunny.* 週末天氣可望晴朗乾燥。 **3** (*formal*) a view from a particular place 景色；景致；景觀 : *The house has a pleasant outlook over the valley.* 房子俯瞰山谷，景色宜人。

out·ly·ing /ˈaʊtlaɪɪŋ/ *adj.* [only before noun] far away from the cities of a country or from the main part of a place 邊遠的；偏遠的；遠離市鎮的 : *outlying areas* 偏遠地區

out·man·oeuvre (*especially US* **out·ma·neu·ver**) /ˌaʊtməˈnuːvə(r)/ *verb* **~ sb/sth** to do better than an opponent by acting in a way that is cleverer or more skilful 比…高明；比…技高一籌：*The president has so far managed to outmanoeuvre his critics.* 到目前為止，總統面對批評者都能夠應付裕如。

out·moded /ˌaʊtˈməʊdɪd; *NAmE* -ˈmoʊd-/ *adj.* (*disapproving*) no longer fashionable or useful 過時的；已無用的：*an outmoded attitude* 陳腐的觀點

out·num·ber /ˌaʊtˈnʌmbə(r)/ *verb* **~ sb/sth** to be greater in number than sb/sth（在數量上）壓倒，比…多：*The demonstrators were heavily outnumbered by the police.* 示威者人數遠不及警察人數。◇ *In this profession, women outnumber men by two to one* (= there are twice as many women as men). 在這個行業，女性人數是男性的兩倍。

ˌout-of-ˌbody exˈperience *noun* a feeling of being outside your own body, especially when you feel that you are watching yourself from a distance 離體體驗，靈魂出竅體驗（尤指從遠處觀看自己的感覺）

ˌout of ˈdate *adj.* **1** old-fashioned or without the most recent information and therefore no longer useful 過時的；缺乏新信息的；陳腐的：*These figures are very out of date.* 這些數字早已過時。◇ *Suddenly she felt old and out of date.* 她猛然覺得自己老了，跟不上時代了。◇ *an out-of-date map* 已過時的地圖 ◇ *out-of-date technology* 落伍的技術 ➲ compare OUTDATED **2** no longer valid 失效的；過期的：*an out-of-date driving licence* 過期的駕駛執照 ➲ see also UP TO DATE

ˈout-of-pocket *adj.* **~ expenses/costs/expenditure/spending** small business expenses that you pay yourself, with your employer paying you back later（小額商務費用）墊付的：*On business trips she has some travel and other out-of-pocket expenses.* 她出差要墊付一些差旅費和其他費用。➲ compare POCKET *n.*

ˌout-of-ˈstate *adj.* [only before noun] (*US*) coming from or happening in a different state 外州的；州外的：*out-of-state license plates* 外州的汽車牌照

ˌout-of-the-ˈway *adj.* far from a town or city 偏僻的；偏遠的：*a little out-of-the-way place on the coast* 海邊一個偏遠的小地方

ˌout-of-ˈtown *adj.* [only before noun] **1** located away from the centre of a town or city 城外的；郊野的：*out-of-town superstores* 市郊超級商場 **2** coming from or happening in a different place 外地的；外來的：*an out-of-town guest* 外來客 ◇ *an out-of-town performance* 外地演出

ˌout-of-ˈwork *adj.* [only before noun] unemployed 失業的；下崗的：*an out-of-work actor* 待業演員

out·pace /ˌaʊtˈpeɪs/ *verb* **~ sb/sth** to go, rise, improve, etc. faster than sb/sth（在速度上）超過；比…快 **SYN** **outstrip**：*He easily outpaced the other runners.* 他輕而易舉地超過了其他賽跑選手。◇ *Demand is outpacing production.* 需求正在超過生產。

out·pa·tient /ˈaʊtpeɪʃnt/ *noun* a person who goes to a hospital for treatment but does not stay there 門診病人：*an outpatient clinic* 門診部 ➲ compare INPATIENT

out·per·form /ˌaʊtpəˈfɔːm; *NAmE* -pərˈfɔːrm/ *verb* **~ sb/sth** to achieve better results than sb/sth（效益上）超過，勝過 ▸ **out·per·form·ance** *noun* [U]

out·place·ment /ˈaʊtpleɪsmənt/ *noun* [U] (*business* 商) the process of helping people to find new jobs after they have been made unemployed 新工作安排；（對失業人員的）安置

out·play /ˌaʊtˈpleɪ/ *verb* **~ sb** to play much better than sb you are competing against（技勝一籌）戰勝，擊敗：*We were totally outplayed and lost 106–74.* 我們以 74:106 慘敗。

out·point /ˌaʊtˈpɔɪnt/ *verb* **~ sb** (especially in boxing 尤用於拳擊運動) to defeat sb by scoring more points 以點數取勝

out·post /ˈaʊtpəʊst; *NAmE* -poʊst/ *noun* **1** a small military camp away from the main army, used for watching an enemy's movements, etc. 前哨（基地） **2** a small town or group of buildings in a lonely part of a country 偏遠村鎮；孤零住區：*a remote outpost* 偏遠的村鎮 ◇ *the last outpost of civilization* 文明的邊緣地區

out·pour·ing /ˈaʊtpɔːrɪŋ/ *noun* **1** [usually pl.] a strong and sudden expression of feeling（感情的）迸發，傾瀉：*spontaneous outpourings of praise* 一片自然迸發的讚美聲 **2** a large amount of sth produced in a short time 湧現；噴湧：*a remarkable outpouring of new ideas* 新思想的大量湧現

out·put 0‑ **AW** /ˈaʊtpʊt/ *noun, verb*

▪ ***noun*** [U, sing.] **1** 0‑ the amount of sth that a person, a machine or an organization produces（人、機器、機構的）產量，輸出量：*Manufacturing output has increased by 8%.* 工業產量增長了 8%。**2** (*computing* 計) the information, results, etc. produced by a computer 輸出：*data output* 數據輸出 ◇ *an output device* 輸出裝置 ➲ compare INPUT **3** the power, energy, etc. produced by a piece of equipment 輸出功率；輸出量：*an output of 100 watts* 功率 100 瓦 **4** a place where energy, power, information, etc. leaves a system 輸出端：*Connect a cable to the output.* 把連線接到輸出端上。

▪ ***verb*** (**out·put·ting**, **out·put**, **out·put**) **~ sth** (*computing* 計) to supply or produce information, results, etc. 輸出：*Computers can now output data much more quickly.* 現在計算機能更快地輸出數據。➲ compare INPUT

out·rage /ˈaʊtreɪdʒ/ *noun, verb*

▪ ***noun*** **1** [U] a strong feeling of shock and anger 憤怒；義憤；憤慨：*The judge's remarks caused public outrage.* 裁判的話引起了公憤。◇ *Environmentalists have expressed outrage at the ruling.* 環境保護主義者對這一裁決表示憤慨。**2** [C] an act or event that is violent, cruel or very wrong and that shocks people or makes them very angry 暴行；駭人聽聞的事 **SYN** **atrocity**：*No one has yet claimed responsibility for this latest bomb outrage.* 迄今還沒有人宣稱對最近的爆炸暴行負責。

▪ ***verb*** [often passive] **~ sb** to make sb very shocked and angry 使震怒；激怒：*He was outraged at the way he had been treated.* 他對所遭受的待遇感到非常憤怒。

out·ra·geous /aʊtˈreɪdʒəs/ *adj.* **1** very shocking and unacceptable 駭人的；無法容忍的 **SYN** **scandalous**：*outrageous behaviour* 極端無禮的行為 ◇ *'That's outrageous!' he protested.* "簡直駭人聽聞！"他抗議說。**2** very unusual and slightly shocking 反常的；令人驚訝的：*She says the most outrageous things sometimes.* 她有時候儘說些聳人聽聞的事。◇ *outrageous clothes* 怪裏怪氣的服裝 ▸ **out·ra·geous·ly** *adv.*：*an outrageously expensive meal* 貴得嚇人的一頓飯 ◇ *They behaved outrageously.* 他們的行為表現讓人難以容忍。

out·ran *past tense* of OUTRUN

out·rank /ˌaʊtˈræŋk/ *verb* **~ sb** to be of higher rank, quality, etc. than sb（在職銜、質量等上）超過，在…之上

outré /ˈuːtreɪ; *NAmE* uːˈtreɪ/ *adj.* (from *French*, *formal*) very unusual and slightly shocking 反常的；驚人的；古怪的

out·reach /ˈaʊtriːtʃ/ *noun* [U] the activity of an organization that provides a service or advice to people in the community, especially those who cannot or are unlikely to come to an office, a hospital, etc. for help 外展服務（在服務機構以外的場所提供的社區服務等）：*an outreach and education programme* 外展服務及教育計劃 ◇ *outreach workers* 外展服務人員 ◇ *efforts to expand the outreach to black voters* 擴大對黑人選民外展服務的努力

out·rider /ˈaʊtraɪdə(r)/ *noun* a person who rides a motorcycle or a horse in front of or beside the vehicle of an important person in order to give protection（要人座車周圍的）騎士護衛，摩托護衛

out·rig·ger /ˈaʊtrɪɡə(r)/ *noun* a wooden structure that is fixed to the side of a boat or ship in order to keep it steady in the water; a boat fitted with such a structure 舷外托架；有舷外托架的小船

out·right /ˈaʊtraɪt/ *adj., adv.*

▪ ***adj.*** [only before noun] **1** complete and total 完全的；徹底的；絕對的：*an outright ban/rejection/victory* 完全禁止；斷然拒絕；徹底勝利 ◇ *She was the outright winner.* 她是絕對的優勝者。◇ *No one party is expected to gain an outright majority.* 沒有任何政黨可望獲得絕對多數。

O

2 open and direct 公開的；直率的；直截了當的：*There was outright opposition to the plan.* 該計劃遭到公開直接反對。

■ ***adv.*** **1** in a direct way and without trying to hide anything 公開地；直率地；毫無保留地：*Why don't you ask him outright if it's true?* 你為什麼不直截了當地問他那是否屬實？◇ *She couldn't help herself and she laughed outright.* 她忍不住大笑起來。**2** clearly and completely 完全徹底；乾淨利落：*Neither candidate won outright.* 兩個候選人誰也沒乾脆利落地獲勝。◇ *The group rejects outright any negotiations with the government.* 這個團體斷然拒絕與政府進行任何談判。**3** not gradually; immediately 一下子；驟然間；立即：*Most of the crash victims were **killed outright**.* 飛機墜毀的遇難者大都是立即慘死。◇ *We had saved enough money to buy the house outright.* 我們存了足夠的錢，能一次付清款項買下這所房子。

out·run /ˌaʊtˈrʌn/ *verb* (**out·run·ning**, **out·ran** /-ˈræn/, **out·run**) **1 ~ sb/sth** to run faster or further than sb/sth 跑得比…快（或遠）；超過：*He couldn't outrun his pursuers.* 他跑不過追他的人。**2 ~ sth** to develop faster than sth 發展更快；超過 SYN **outstrip**：*Demand for the new model is outrunning supply.* 新型號的產品供不應求。

out·sell /ˌaʊtˈsel/ *verb* (**out·sold**, **out·sold** /-ˈsəʊld; *NAmE* -ˈsoʊld/) **~ sb/sth** to sell more or to be sold in larger quantities than sb/sth 比…賣得多：*We are now outselling all our competitors.* 我們現在比所有競爭對手都賣得多。◇ *This year the newspaper has outsold its main rival.* 今年該報的發行量已超過了它的主要對手。

out·set /ˈaʊtset/ *noun*

IDM **at/from the ˈoutset (of sth)** at/from the beginning of sth 從開始：*I made it clear right from the outset that I disapproved.* 從一開始我就明確地說我不贊成。

out·shine /ˌaʊtˈʃaɪn/ *verb* (**out·shone**, **out·shone** /-ˈʃɒn; *NAmE* -ˈʃoʊn/) **~ sb/sth** to be more impressive than sb/sth; to be better than sb/sth 比…做得好；使遜色；高人一籌

O

out·side 0-w *noun, adj., prep., adv.*

■ ***noun*** /ˌaʊtˈsaɪd/ (usually **the outside**) **1** 0-w [C, usually sing.] the outer side or surface of sth 外部；外表 SYN **exterior**：*The outside of the house needs painting.* 房子的外表需要油漆一下。◇ *You can't open the door from the outside.* 你從外邊打不開這個門。**2** 0-w [sing.] the area that is near or around a building, etc. （建築物等的）周圍，外圍：*I walked around the outside of the building.* 我繞着這座房子四周散步。◇ *I didn't go into the temple—I only saw it from the outside.* 我沒有走進廟宇，只是從外面看了一下。**3** 0-w [sing.] the part of a road nearest to the middle （靠近路中央的）外側，外手：*Always overtake **on the outside**.* 超車務必走外側道。**4** [sing.] the part of a curving road or track furthest from the inner or shorter side of the curve （彎曲路面或軌道的）外道，外緣 OPP **the inside**

IDM **at the outside** at the most; as a maximum 至多：*There was room for 20 people at the outside.* 最多只能容納 20 個人。**on the outside 1** used to describe how sb appears or seems 從表面；從外表：*On the outside she seems calm, but I know she's worried.* 她貌似鎮定，但我知道她有心事。**2** not in prison 不在獄中：*Life on the outside took some getting used to again.* 出獄後的生活又需要慢慢適應了。

■ ***adj.*** /ˈaʊtsaɪd/ [only before noun] **1** 0-w of, on or facing the outer side 外部的；在外面的；向外的 SYN **external**：*The outside walls are damp.* 外牆潮濕。**2** 0-w not located in the main building; going out of the main building 主建築物以外的；向外面的 SYN **external**：*an outside toilet* 戶外廁所 ◇ *You have to pay to make outside calls.* 打外線電話必須付費。◇ *I can't get an outside line.* 我接不通外線。**3** 0-w not included in or connected with your group, organization, country, etc. 不屬於本團體（或機構、國家等）的；外部的；不相關的：*We plan to use an outside firm of consultants.* 我們計劃利用外面的咨詢公司。◇ *She has a lot of **outside interests*** (= not connected with her work). 她有許多業餘愛好。◇ *They felt cut off from the **outside world*** (= from other people and from other things that were happening). 他們覺得與外界隔絕了。**4** used to say that sth is very unlikely 不可能的；可能性極小的：*They have only an **outside chance** of winning.* 他們的勝算極小。◇ *150 is an outside estimate* (= it is very likely to be less). 估計最多不超過 150。

■ ***prep.*** /ˌaʊtˈsaɪd/ (also **out·side of** especially in *NAmE*) **1** 0-w on or to a place on the outside of sth 在…外面；向…外面：*You can park your car outside our house.* 你可以把汽車停在我們家屋外。OPP **inside** **2** 0-w away from or not in a particular place 離開；不在：*It's the biggest theme park outside the United States.* 這是美國以外最大的主題遊樂園。◇ *We live in a small village **just outside** Leeds.* 我們就住在利茲市外的一個小村子裏。**3** 0-w not part of sth 不在…範圍內；不屬於：*The matter is outside my area of responsibility.* 此事不屬於我的職責範圍。◇ *You may do as you wish outside working hours.* 上班時間以外，你愛幹什麼就幹什麼。OPP **within** **4 outside of** apart from 除了：*There was nothing they could do, outside of hoping things would get better.* 除了盼望情況好轉，他們無能為力。

■ ***adv.*** /ˌaʊtˈsaɪd/ **1** 0-w not in a room, building or container but on or to the outside of it 在外面；向外面：*I'm seeing a patient—please wait outside.* 我正在給病人看病，請在外面等候。◇ *The house is painted green outside.* 房子的外面漆成了綠色。**2** 0-w not inside a building 在戶外：*It's warm enough to eat outside.* 天氣暖和了，可以在露天吃飯了。◇ *Go outside and see if it's raining.* 去外邊看看是否下雨了。OPP **inside**

ˌoutside ˈbroadcast *noun* (*BrE*) a programme filmed or recorded away from the main studio 實地拍攝的節目；現場錄製的節目

ˌoutside ˈlane (*BrE*) (*NAmE* **ˌpassing ˈlane**) *noun* the part of a major road such as a MOTORWAY or INTERSTATE nearest the middle of the road, where vehicles drive fastest and can go past vehicles ahead （高速公路等靠近路中心的）外車道，超車道

out·sider /ˌaʊtˈsaɪdə(r)/ *noun* **1** a person who is not accepted as a member of a society, group, etc. 外人；局外人：*Here she felt she would always be an outsider.* 她在這裏總覺得是個外人。**2** a person who is not part of a particular organization or profession （組織、行業）外部的人；外來者：*They have decided to hire outsiders for some of the key positions.* 他們決定在某些關鍵職位上聘任外來人員。◇ *To an outsider it may appear to be a glamorous job.* 在外面的人看來，這似乎是一份令人嚮往的工作。**3** a person or an animal taking part in a race or competition that is not expected to win （比賽中）不被看好的人（或動物）：*The race was won by a 20–1 outsider.* 比賽獲勝者是個不被看好、20 賠 1 的賽馬。◇ *To everyone's surprise, the post went to **a rank outsider*** (= a complete outsider). 出人意料的是，那個職位竟然落到一個毫不起眼的人頭上。

out·size /ˈaʊtsaɪz/ (also **out·sized** /ˈaʊtsaɪzd/) *adj.* [usually before noun] **1** larger than the usual size 較大的；超過一般型號的：*an outsize desk* 一張特大號桌子 **2** designed for large people 特體的；特大號的：*outsize clothes* 特大號服裝

out·skirts /ˈaʊtskɜːts; *NAmE* -skɜːrts/ *noun* [pl.] the parts of a town or city that are furthest from the centre （市鎮的）邊緣地帶；市郊：*They live **on the outskirts** of Milan.* 他們住在米蘭市郊。

out·smart /ˌaʊtˈsmɑːt; *NAmE* -ˈsmɑːrt/ *verb* **~ sb** to gain an advantage over sb by acting in a clever way 比…精明；智勝 SYN **outwit**：*She always managed to outsmart her political rivals.* 她總有辦法表現得比她的政敵智高一籌。

out·source /ˈaʊtsɔːs; *NAmE* -sɔːrs/ *verb* [T, I] **~ (sth)** (*business* 商) to arrange for sb outside a company to do work or provide goods for that company 交外辦理；外購：*We outsource all our computing work.* 我們把全部計算機技術工作包給外邊去做。▶ **out·sourc·ing** *noun* [U]

out·spoken /aʊtˈspəʊkən; *NAmE* -ˈspoʊkən/ *adj.* saying exactly what you think, even if this shocks or offends people 直率的，直言不諱的（不怕得罪人）SYN **blunt**：*an outspoken opponent of the leader* 一個直言不諱反對領導的人 ◇ *outspoken comments* 直率的評論 ◇ **~ in sth**

She was outspoken in her criticism of the plan. 她直言不諱批評該計劃。➲ SYNONYMS at HONEST ▸ **out·spoken·ly** *adv.* **out·spoken·ness** *noun* [U]

out·spread /ˌaʊtˈspred/ *adj.* (*formal*) spread out completely 展開的；舒展的：*The bird soared high, with outspread wings.* 鳥兒展翅高飛。

out·stand·ing 🗝 /aʊtˈstændɪŋ/ *adj.*
1 🗝 extremely good; excellent 優秀的；傑出的；出色的：*an outstanding player/achievement/success* 傑出的運動員／成績／成就 ◇ *an area of* ***outstanding natural beauty*** 自然風景極美的地區 ➲ SYNONYMS at EXCELLENT **2** 🗝 [usually before noun] very obvious or important 突出的；明顯的；重要的 SYN **prominent**：*the outstanding features of the landscape* 這一風景的突出特徵 **3** (of payment, work, problems, etc. 款項、工作、困難等) not yet paid, done, solved, etc. 未支付的；未完成的；未解決的：*She has outstanding debts of over £500.* 她未清償的債務超過 500 英鎊。◇ *A lot of work is still outstanding.* 許多工作尚未完成。

out·stand·ing·ly /aʊtˈstændɪŋli/ *adv.* **1** used to emphasize the good quality of sth（用於正面強調）非常，極其 SYN **remarkably**：*outstandingly successful* 非常成功 **2** extremely well 優異；極好：*He performed well but not outstandingly.* 他表演得還不錯，但算不上非常出色。

out·stay /ˌaʊtˈsteɪ/ *verb* IDM see WELCOME *n.*

out·stretched /ˌaʊtˈstretʃt/ *adj.* (of parts of the body 身體部位) stretched or spread out as far as possible 伸展的；張開的：*He ran towards her* ***with arms outstretched/with outstretched arms.*** 他張開雙臂朝她飛奔而去。

out·strip /ˌaʊtˈstrɪp/ *verb* (**-pp-**) **1 ~ sth** to become larger, more important, etc. than sb/sth 比…大（或重要等）；超過；勝過：*Demand is outstripping supply.* 需求快超過供應了。 **2 ~ sth** to be faster, better or more successful than sb you are competing against 超過，超越（競爭對手）SYN **surpass**：*Their latest computer outstrips all its rivals.* 他們最新型的計算機超越了所有的對手。 **3 ~ sb** to run faster than sb in a race so that you pass them 比…跑得快；超越

outta (also **outa**) /ˈaʊtə/ *prep.* used for writing the way 'out of' is sometimes pronounced in informal speech（用於書寫，表示 out of 在非正式口語中的發音）：*I'm outta here!* (= I'm leaving now.) 我要走了！

ˈout-take *noun* a piece of a film that is removed before the film/movie is shown, for example because it contains a mistake（電影的）不選用鏡頭，不合格鏡頭

ˈout-there *adj.* (*NAmE, informal*) (of people) different, confident, having strong opinions, and attracting attention to yourself；(of ideas) different from what most people consider normal, but exciting（人）特立獨行的；（想法）吸引他人矚目的，讓人耳目一新的；自成一格的：*Wow, this is such an out-there character. This role is definitely going to be cool.* 哇，這是個如此個性鮮明的人物。這個角色一定很酷。◇ *It may be totally out-there but I think it could work.* 這可能離經叛道，但我認為行得通。

ˈout tray (*BrE*) (*US* **ˈout box**) *noun* (in an office) a container on your desk for letters or documents that are waiting to be sent out or passed to sb else（辦公室的）待發信件盤 ➲ compare IN TRAY ➲ VISUAL VOCAB page V69

out·vote /ˌaʊtˈvəʊt; *NAmE* -ˈvoʊt/ *verb* [usually passive] **~ sb/sth** to defeat sb/sth by winning a larger number of votes 得票超過 SYN **vote sb/sth down**：*His proposal was outvoted by 10 votes to 8.* 他的提案以 10 比 8 票被否決。

out·ward /ˈaʊtwəd; *NAmE* -wərd/ *adj.* [only before noun] **1** connected with the way people or things seem to be rather than with what is actually true 表面的；外表的：*Mark showed no outward signs of distress.* 馬克在外表上沒有現出沮喪的神色來。◇ *She simply observes the outward forms of religion.* 她只是表面上信教而已。◇ ***To all outward appearances*** (= as far as it was possible to judge from the outside) *they were perfectly happy.* 從外表上怎麼看他們都顯得無比幸福。OPP **inward** **2** going away from a particular place, especially one that you are going to return to 外出的；向外的：*the outward voyage/journey* 外出航程／旅程 **3** away from the centre or a particular point 朝外面的；向外的：*outward movement* 向外的運動 ◇ ***outward investment*** (= in other countries) 對外投資 ◇ *Managers need to become more* ***outward-looking*** (= more open to new ideas). 管理人員需要有更廣闊的視野。OPP **inward**

ˌoutward ˈbound *adj.* going away from home or a particular place 離家的；外出的

the ˌOutward ˌBound ˈTrust [sing.] (also **ˌOutward ˈBound™** [U]) *noun* an international organization that provides training in outdoor activities including sports for young people 野外拓展訓練信託，外展信託（為年輕人等提供野外活動培訓的國際組織）

out·ward·ly /ˈaʊtwədli; *NAmE* -wərd-/ *adv.* on the surface; in appearance 表面上；外表上：*Though badly frightened, she remained outwardly composed.* 她雖然非常害怕，但表面上依然很鎮靜。◇ *Outwardly, the couple seemed perfectly happy.* 表面上看，這對夫婦似乎幸福美滿。OPP **inwardly**

out·wards /ˈaʊtwədz; *NAmE* -wərdz/ (*BrE*) (also **out·ward** *NAmE, BrE*) *adv.* **~ (from sth)** towards the outside; away from the centre or from a particular point 向外；朝外：*The door opens outwards.* 這個門向外開。◇ *Factories were spreading outwards from the old heart of the town.* 工廠從舊城中心逐漸向外擴展。OPP **inwards**

out·weigh /ˌaʊtˈweɪ/ *verb* **~ sth** to be greater or more important than sth 重於；大於；超過：*The advantages* ***far outweigh*** *the disadvantages.* 利遠大於弊。

out·wit /ˌaʊtˈwɪt/ *verb* (**-tt-**) **~ sb/sth** to defeat sb/sth or gain an advantage over them by doing sth clever（智力上）超過，勝過 SYN **outsmart**：*Somehow he always manages to outwit his opponents.* 他反正總能設法智勝對手。

out·with /ˌaʊtˈwɪθ/ *prep.* (*ScotE*) outside of sth; not within sth 在…外面

out·work /ˈaʊtwɜːk; *NAmE* -wɜːrk/ *noun* [U] (*business* 商) (*BrE*) work that is done by people at home 外包活；家庭承攬的活 ▸ **out·work·er** *noun*

out·work·ing /ˈaʊtwɜːkɪŋ; *NAmE* -wɜːrk-/ *noun* [U] (*business* 商) (*BrE*) the activity of doing work away from the office or factory that provides the work 本單位外的工作

out·worn /ˈaʊtwɔːn; *NAmE* -wɔːrn/ *adj.* [usually before noun] old-fashioned and no longer useful 過時的；陳腐的；無用的 SYN **obsolete**：*outworn institutions* 陳腐的習俗 ➲ compare WORN OUT

ouzo /ˈuːzəʊ; *NAmE* ˈuːzoʊ/ *noun* [U] a strong alcoholic drink from Greece, made from ANISEED and usually drunk with water 茴香烈酒（希臘產，通常兌水飲用）

ova *pl.* of OVUM

oval /ˈəʊvl; *NAmE* ˈoʊvl/ *adj., noun*
▪ ***adj.*** shaped like an egg 橢圓形的；卵形的：*an oval face* 鵝蛋臉
▪ ***noun*** **1** an oval shape 橢圓形；卵形 **2** (*AustralE*) a ground for Australian Rules football 澳大利亞式橄欖球球場

the ˌOval ˈOffice *noun* [sing.] **1** the office of the US President in the White House（美國白宮的）橢圓形辦公室，總統辦公室 **2** a way of referring to the US President and the part of the government that is controlled by the President（美國）總統及政府行政部門：*Congress is waiting to see how the Oval Office will react.* 國會正觀望總統方面的反應。

ovary /ˈəʊvəri; *NAmE* ˈoʊ-/ *noun* (*pl.* **-ies**) **1** either of the two organs in a woman's body that produce eggs; a similar organ in female animals, birds and fish 卵巢 **2** the part of a plant that produces seeds（植物的）子房 ➲ VISUAL VOCAB page V11 ▸ **ovar·ian** /əʊˈveəriən; *NAmE* oʊˈver-/ *adj.* [only before noun]：*ovarian cancer* 卵巢癌

ova·tion /əʊˈveɪʃn; *NAmE* oʊ-/ *noun* enthusiastic clapping by an audience as a sign of their approval 熱烈鼓掌；熱烈歡迎：*to give sb a* ***huge/rapturous/rousing ovation*** 對某人萬分的／狂熱的／熱烈的歡迎 ◇ *The soloist*

O

got a ten-minute ***standing ovation*** (= in which people stand up from their seats). 獨奏演員受到了長達十分鐘的起立鼓掌歡呼。

oven 0━ /ˈʌvn/ *noun* the part of a cooker/stove shaped like a box with a door on the front, in which food is cooked or heated 烤箱；烤爐： *Take the cake out of the oven.* 把蛋糕從烤箱中取出來。◇ *a gas/an electric oven* 煤氣／電烤箱 ◇ *a* ***cool/hot/moderate oven*** 烤箱的低温／高温／中温擋 ◇ *Open a window, it's* ***like an oven*** *in here!* 打開窗戶。這兒熱得像火爐！➲ VISUAL VOCAB pages V25, V27 ➲ compare MICROWAVE *n.* (1) IDM see BUN

ˈoven glove (also **ˈoven mitt**) *noun* a glove made of thick material, used for holding hot dishes from an oven 烤箱手套；隔熱手套 ➲ VISUAL VOCAB page V25

oven·proof /ˈʌvnpruːf/ *adj.* suitable for use in a hot oven 適於烤箱內用的；耐熱的： *an ovenproof dish* 耐熱碟子

ˌoven-ˈready *adj.* [usually before noun] (of food 食物) bought already prepared and ready for cooking 已調製好的；加工過的；可直接入爐的

oven·ware /ˈʌvnweə(r); *NAmE* -wer/ *noun* [U] dishes that can be used for cooking food in an oven 烤箱器皿；烤盤

over 0━ /ˈəʊvə(r); *NAmE* ˈoʊ-/ *adv., prep., noun*

■ ***adv.*** HELP For the special uses of **over** in phrasal verbs, look at the entries for the verbs. For example **take sth over** is in the phrasal verb section at **take**. * over 在短語動詞中的特殊用法見有關動詞詞條。如 take sth over 在詞條 take 的短語動詞部份。 **1** 0━ downwards and away from a vertical position 從直立位置向下；落下；倒下： *Try not to knock that vase over.* 小心別把花瓶碰倒了。◇ *The wind must have blown it over.* 準是風把它吹倒了。 **2** 0━ from one side to another side 從一側到另一側；翻轉： *She turned over onto her front.* 她翻過身俯卧着。◇ *The car skidded off the road and rolled over and over.* 汽車滑出路面不斷翻滾。 **3** 0━ across a street, an open space, etc. 穿過（街道、開闊的空間等）： *I stopped and crossed over.* 我先停下來，然後走到對面。◇ *He rowed us over to the other side of the lake.* 他把我們擺渡到湖的對岸。◇ *They have gone over to France.* 他們渡海到法國去了。◇ *This is my aunt who's over from Canada.* 這是我姑姑，她是從加拿大過來的。◇ *I went over* (= across the room) *and asked her name.* 我走過去問她叫什麼名字。◇ *Put it down* ***over there.*** 把東西放到那邊去。 **4** 0━ so as to cover sb/sth completely 完全覆蓋（某人或某物）： *The lake was frozen over.* 湖面完全封凍了。◇ *Cover her over with a blanket.* 給她蓋條毯子。 **5** 0━ above; more 以上；大於；多於： *children of 14 and over* 14 歲或以上的兒童 ◇ *You get an A grade for scores of 75 and over.* * 75 分或以上的分數就是優等。 **6** 0━ remaining; not used or needed 剩餘；未用；不需要： *If there's any food left over, put it in the fridge.* 要是有剩下的飯菜，就放到冰箱裏。 **7** 0━ again 再；又： *He repeated it several times over until he could remember it.* 他重複了幾遍直到能記住為止。◇ (*NAmE*) *It's all wrong—you'll have to do it over.* 完全錯了。你得重做一遍。 **8** 0━ ended 結束： *By the time we arrived the meeting was over.* 我們到達時，會議已經結束了。◇ *Thank goodness that's over!* 謝天謝地，事情總算過去了！◇ *I was glad when it was* ***over and done with.*** 事情終告了結，我很高興。 **9** 0━ used to talk about sb/sth changing position（表示位置變換）改變，掉換： *He's gone over to the enemy* (= joined them). 他已變節投敵。◇ *Please change the wheels over* (= for example, put the front wheels at the back). 請把輪子調個個兒。◇ *Let's ask some friends over* (= to our home). 咱們邀請幾個朋友來家裏吧。◇ *Hand over the money!* 把錢交出來！ **10** used when communicating by radio（用於無線通話）完畢： *Message received. Over* (= it is your turn to speak). 消息收到了。完畢。◇ *Message understood.* ***Over and out.*** 消息聽懂了。通話完畢。

IDM **(all) over aˈgain** 0━ a second time from the beginning 再；重新： *He did the work so badly that I had to do it all over again myself.* 他活做得太糟糕了，我只好親自從頭再做一次。 **over against sth** in contrast with sth 與…對比（或相對） **ˌover and ˈover (aˈgain)** many times; repeatedly 多次；反複地；一再： *I've told you over and over again not to do that.* 我已一再跟你講不要再那麼做了。 **ˌover to ˈyou** used to say that it is sb's turn to do sth 輪到你了；該你了

■ ***prep.*** HELP For the special uses of **over** in phrasal verbs, look at the entries for the verbs. For example **get over sth** is in the phrasal verb section at **get**. * over 在短語動詞中的特殊用法見有關動詞詞條。如 get over sth 在詞條 get 的短語動詞部份。 **1** 0━ resting on the surface of sb/sth and partly or completely covering them/it（部份或全部覆蓋）在…上面： *She put a blanket over the sleeping child.* 她給熟睡的孩子蓋上毯子。◇ *He wore an overcoat over his suit.* 他在西服外面再加了一件大衣。◇ *She put her hand over her mouth to stop herself from screaming.* 她用手捂住嘴，以免叫出聲來。 **2** 0━ in or to a position higher than but not touching sb/sth; above sb/sth 懸在…上面；向…上方： *They held a large umbrella over her.* 他們給她撐起一把大傘。◇ *The balcony juts out over the street.* 陽台伸出在街道上方。◇ *There was a lamp hanging over the table.* 桌子上方吊着一盞燈。 **3** 0━ from one side of sth to the other; across sth 從一邊到另一邊；穿越： *a bridge over the river* 橫跨河面的橋 ◇ *They ran over the grass.* 他們跑過草地。◇ *They had a wonderful view over the park.* 他們放眼望去，把公園美麗的景色盡收眼底。 **4** 0━ on the far or opposite side of sth 在…的遠端（或對面）： *He lives over the road.* 他住在馬路對面。 **5** 0━ so as to cross sth and be on the other side 到另一邊；翻越： *She climbed over the wall.* 她翻過牆去。 **6** 0━ falling from or down from a place 從…落下： *The car had toppled over the cliff.* 汽車從山崖上跌落下去了。◇ *He didn't dare look over the edge.* 他不敢從邊緣向下看。 **7** 0━ **all ~** in or on all or most parts of sth 遍及： *Snow is falling all over the country.* 全國各地都在下雪。◇ *They've travelled all over the world.* 他們遊遍了全世界。◇ *There were papers lying around* ***all over the place.*** 文件散落一地。 **8** 0━ more than a particular time, amount, cost, etc. 多於（某時間、數量、花費等）： *over 3 million copies sold* 售出三百多萬冊 ◇ *She stayed in Lagos for over a month.* 她在拉各斯逗留了一個多月。◇ *He's over sixty.* 他六十多歲了。 **9** 0━ used to show that sb has control or authority（表示能控制、有權威）： *She has only the director over her.* 她的上司只有主任一個。◇ *He ruled over a great empire.* 他統治着一個大帝國。◇ *She has editorial control over what is included.* 她有權決定編輯的內容。 **10** 0━ during sth 在…期間： *We'll discuss it over lunch.* 我們吃午飯時商量此事吧。◇ *Over the next few days they got to know the town well.* 在以後幾天中，他們逐漸熟悉了這個小鎮。◇ *She has not changed much over the years.* 這些年來她沒有多大變化。◇ *He built up the business over a period of ten years.* 他用了十年時間把這個企業創建起來。◇ *We're away over* (= until after) *the New Year.* 新年期間我們會外出。 **11** 0━ past a particular difficult stage or situation 渡過（困難階段或局面）： *We're over the worst of the recession.* 我們已渡過了經濟衰退的最艱難時期。◇ *It took her ages to get over her illness.* 她花了很長時間才把病治好。 **12** 0━ because of or concerning sth; about sth 由於；關於： *an argument over money* 為了錢的爭吵 ◇ *a disagreement over the best way to proceed* 在如何推展工作才最好這一問題上出現的分歧 **13** 0━ using sth; by means of sth 利用；通過： *We heard it over the radio.* 我們從廣播中聽到的。◇ *She wouldn't tell me over the phone.* 她不肯在電話裏告訴我。 **14** louder than sth 聲音大於： *I couldn't hear what he said over the noise of the traffic.* 交通噪聲太大，我聽不清他說的話。➲ note at ABOVE

IDM **ˌover and aˈbove** in addition to sth 此外；另外： *There are other factors over and above those we have discussed.* 除了我們所討論的之外，還有其他因素。

■ ***noun*** (in CRICKET 板球) a series of six balls BOWLED by the same person 一輪投球（同一個投球手連續投出的六個球）

over- /ˈəʊvə(r); *NAmE* ˈoʊ-/ *prefix* (in nouns, verbs, adjectives and adverbs 構成名詞、動詞、形容詞和副詞) **1** more than usual; too much 太；過於： *overproduction* 生產過剩 ◇ *overload* 超載 ◇ *over-optimistic* 過分樂觀的 ◇ *overconfident* 過分自信的 ◇ *overanxious* 過於急切

2 completely 完全地： *overjoyed* 十分高興 **3** upper; outer; extra 上面；外面；額外： *overcoat* 長大衣 ◊ *overtime* 加班 **4** over; above 上方；上空： *overcast* 陰雲密佈的 ◊ *overhang* 懸掛

over·achieve /ˌəʊvərəˈtʃiːv; *NAmE* ˌoʊ-/ *verb* **1** [I] to do better than expected in your studies or work 學習（或工作）得比預期好；取得比預期好的成績 **2** [I] to try too hard to be successful in your work 過於努力；過於進取 ▸ **over·achiever** *noun*

over·act /ˌəʊvərˈækt; *NAmE* ˌoʊ-/ *verb* [I, T] **~ (sth)** (*disapproving*) to behave in a way that is exaggerated and not natural, especially when you are acting a part in a play 舉止過火；表現做作；（尤指）表演過火

over·active /ˌəʊvərˈæktɪv; *NAmE* ˌoʊvər-/ *adj.* [usually before noun] **1** (of an organ or part of the body 器官或身體部位) causing harm by doing sth too much 過度活動的： *an overactive thyroid* 亢進的甲狀腺 **2** (of sb's imagination 想像力) too active, especially so that they imagine things that are not true 過於活躍的；（尤指）想入非非的： *She suffers from an overactive imagination.* 她患上了狂想症。

over·age /ˌəʊvərˈeɪdʒ; *NAmE* ˌoʊ-/ *adj.* too old to be allowed to do a particular thing 超齡的；年齡過大的

overalls 工装服

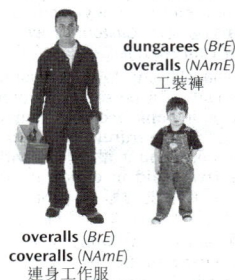

dungarees (*BrE*)
overalls (*NAmE*)
工裝褲

overalls (*BrE*)
coveralls (*NAmE*)
連身工作服

over·all 🔑 **AW** *adj., adv., noun*

■ *adj.* 🔑 /ˌəʊvərˈɔːl; *NAmE* ˌoʊ-/ [only before noun] including all the things or people that are involved in a particular situation; general 全面的；綜合的；總體的： *the person with* ***overall responsibility*** *for the project* 全面負責本項目的人 ◊ *There will be winners in each of three age groups, and one* ***overall winner***. 三個年齡組將各產生一位優勝者，另有一位總優勝者。◊ *an* ***overall improvement*** *in standards of living* (= affecting everyone) 生活水平的全面提高 ◊ *When she finished painting, she stepped back to admire the* ***overall effect***. 畫完以後，她退後一步，以審視總體效果。

■ *adv.* /ˌəʊvərˈɔːl; *NAmE* ˌoʊ-/ **1** 🔑 including everything or everyone; in total 全部；總計： *The company will invest $1.6m overall in new equipment.* 這個公司將總計投資 160 萬元購置新設備。 **2** 🔑 generally; when you consider everything 一般來說；大致上；總體上： *Overall, this is a very useful book.* 總的來說，這是一本很有用的書。 ➲ LANGUAGE BANK at CONCLUSION

■ *noun* /ˈəʊvərɔːl; *NAmE* ˈoʊ-/ **1** (*BrE*) [C] a loose coat worn over other clothes to protect them from dirt, etc. 外套；罩衣： *The lab assistant was wearing a white overall.* 實驗室助手穿着一件白罩衣。 **2 overalls** (*BrE*) (*NAmE* **cov·er·alls**) [pl.] a loose piece of clothing like a shirt and trousers/pants in one piece, made of heavy cloth and usually worn over other clothing by workers doing dirty work 工裝服；連身工作服： *The mechanic was wearing a pair of blue overalls.* 機修工穿着一件藍色工裝連衣褲。 ➲ compare BOILER SUIT **3 overalls** (also **ˈbib overalls**) (both *NAmE*) (*BrE* **dun·garees**) [pl.] a piece of clothing that consists of trousers/pants with an extra piece of cloth covering the chest, held up by strips of cloth over the shoulders 工裝褲

ˌoverall maˈjority *noun* [usually sing.] **1** more votes in an election or vote than all the other people or parties together 絕對多數，總體多數（票數超過其他人或政黨票數的總和） **2** the difference between the number of members that the government has in a parliament and the number that all the other political parties have together 絕對優勢（執政黨在議會中的議員人數與所有其他政黨議員總數的差額）： *a huge 101-seat overall majority* 多達 101 個席位的絕對優勢

over·am·bi·tious /ˌəʊvəræmˈbɪʃəs; *NAmE* ˌoʊ-/ *adj.* **1** (of a person 人) too determined to be successful, rich, powerful, etc. 進取心過強的；野心過大的 **2** (of a plan, task, etc. 計劃、任務等) unsuccessful or likely to be unsuccessful because of needing too much effort, money or time 所需投入過大的，目標過高的（因而成功機會甚微）： *Her plans were overambitious.* 她的計劃都過於宏大。

over·arch·ing /ˌəʊvərˈɑːtʃɪŋ; *NAmE* ˌoʊvərˈɑːrtʃɪŋ/ *adj.* [usually before noun] (*formal*) very important, because it includes or influences many things 非常重要的；首要的；概莫能外的

over·arm /ˈəʊvərɑːm; *NAmE* ˈoʊvərɑːrm/ (*especially BrE*) (also **over·hand** especially in *NAmE*) *adv.* if you throw a ball **overarm**, you throw it with your arm swung backwards and then lifted high above your shoulder 肩上投球（投球時舉手過肩） ▸ **over·arm** (*especially BrE*) (also **over·hand** especially in *NAmE*) *adj.*： *an overarm throw* 上手投球 ➲ compare UNDERARM

over·ate *past tense of* OVEREAT

over·awe /ˌəʊvərˈɔː; *NAmE* ˌoʊ-/ *verb* [usually passive] **~ sb** to impress sb so much that they feel nervous or frightened 使極為敬畏；使膽怯 ▸ **over·awed** *adj.*

over·bal·ance /ˌəʊvəˈbæləns; *NAmE* ˌoʊvərˈb-/ *verb* [I, T] **~ (sb/sth)** (*especially BrE*) to lose your balance and fall; to make sb/sth lose their balance and fall （使）失去平衡，摔倒： *He overbalanced and fell into the water.* 他失去了平衡，落入水中。

over·bear·ing /ˌəʊvəˈbeərɪŋ; *NAmE* ˌoʊvərˈber-/ *adj.* (*disapproving*) trying to control other people in an unpleasant way 專橫的；飛揚跋扈的 **SYN** **domineering**： *an overbearing manner* 專斷的作風

over·bite /ˈəʊvəbaɪt; *NAmE* ˈoʊvərb-/ *noun* [usually sing.] (*technical* 術語) a condition in which a person or animal's upper JAW is too far forward in relation to their lower JAW 覆咬合；上包齒

over·blown /ˌəʊvəˈbləʊn; *NAmE* ˌoʊvərˈbloʊn/ *adj.* **1** that is made to seem larger, more impressive or more important than it really is 過分的；誇張的；虛飾過度的 **SYN** **exaggerated** **2** (of flowers 花朵) past the best, most beautiful stage 殘敗的；盛期已過的

over·board /ˈəʊvəbɔːd; *NAmE* ˈoʊvərbɔːrd/ *adv.* over the side of a boat or a ship into the water 從船上落下： *to* ***fall/jump overboard*** 從船上落入／跳入水中 ◊ *Huge waves washed him overboard.* 巨浪把他沖下甲板捲入海中。

IDM **go ˈoverboard** (*informal*) to be too excited or enthusiastic about sth or about doing sth 過分熱情；過分熱衷： *Don't go overboard on fitness.* 熱衷健身運動別過頭。 **throw sb/sth ˈoverboard** to get rid of sb/sth that you think is useless 拋棄；扔掉

over·book /ˌəʊvəˈbʊk; *NAmE* ˌoʊvərˈbʊk/ *verb* [T, I] **~ (sth)** to sell more tickets on a plane or reserve more rooms in a hotel than there are places available 超額預訂（飛機座位或旅館客房）： *The flight was heavily overbooked.* 該班機售票大大超出機位數量。 ➲ compare DOUBLE-BOOK

over·bridge /ˈəʊvəbrɪdʒ; *NAmE* ˈoʊvərb-/ *noun* a bridge over a railway/railroad or road 天橋；上跨橋

over·bur·den /ˌəʊvəˈbɜːdn; *NAmE* ˌoʊvərˈbɜːrdn/ *verb* [usually passive] **~ sb/sth (with sth)** to give sb/sth more work, worry, etc. than they can deal with 使負擔過重

over·came *past tense of* OVERCOME

over·cap·acity /ˌəʊvəkəˈpæsəti; *NAmE* ˌoʊvərkə-/ *noun* [U, sing.] (*business* 商) the situation in which an industry

O

or a factory cannot sell as much as it is designed to produce 生產能力過剩

over·cast /ˌəʊvəˈkɑːst; *NAmE* ˌoʊvərˈkæst/ *adj.* covered with clouds; dull 陰天的；多雲的；陰暗的：*an overcast sky/day* 陰沉的天空／一天 ◇ *Today it will be dull and overcast.* 今天天氣將陰伴多雲。

over·cau·tious /ˌəʊvəˈkɔːʃəs; *NAmE* ˌoʊvərˈk-/ *adj.* too careful 過於謹慎的；過分小心的

over·charge /ˌəʊvəˈtʃɑːdʒ; *NAmE* ˌoʊvərˈtʃɑːrdʒ/ *verb* [T, I] **~ (sb) (for sth)** to make sb pay too much for sth 多收（某人的）錢：*Make sure they don't overcharge you for the drinks.* 注意別讓他們多收飲料費。◇ *We were overcharged by £5.* 我們讓人家多收了 5 英鎊。**OPP undercharge**

over·coat /ˈəʊvəkəʊt; *NAmE* ˈoʊvərkoʊt/ *noun* a long warm coat worn in cold weather 長大衣 ➲ VISUAL VOCAB page V61

over·come 🔑 /ˌəʊvəˈkʌm; *NAmE* ˌoʊvərˈkʌm/ *verb* (**over·came** /-ˈkeɪm/, **over·come**)
1 🔑 **~ sth** to succeed in dealing with or controlling a problem that has been preventing you from achieving sth 克服；解決：*She overcame injury to win the Olympic gold medal.* 她戰勝了傷痛，贏得了奧運會金牌。◇ *The two parties managed to overcome their differences on the issue.* 兩個政黨設法彌合了在這個問題上的分歧。
2 🔑 **~ sb/sth** to defeat sb 戰勝：*In the final game Sweden easily overcame France.* 在決賽中，瑞典隊輕鬆戰勝了法國隊。**3** 🔑 [usually passive] **~ sb** to be extremely strongly affected by sth 受到…的極大影響 **SYN overwhelm**：*Her parents were overcome with grief at the funeral.* 在葬禮上她的父母悲痛欲絕。◇ *The dead woman had been overcome by smoke.* 這個女人是被煙嗆死的。

over·com·pen·sate /ˌəʊvəˈkɒmpenseɪt; *NAmE* ˌoʊvərˈkɑːm-/ *verb* [I] **~ (for sth) (by doing sth)** to do too much when trying to correct a problem and so cause a different problem 過度補償（為糾正某事而做得過分）；矯枉過正：*She overcompensated for her shyness by talking too much and laughing too loud.* 她努力克服羞怯，卻矯枉過正，說話太多，笑聲太大。

O

over·con·fi·dent /ˌəʊvəˈkɒnfɪdənt; *NAmE* ˌoʊvərˈkɑːn-/ *adj.* too confident 過分自信的；自負的

over·cook /ˌəʊvəˈkʊk; *NAmE* ˌoʊvərˈkʊk/ *verb* **~ sth** to cook food for too long 煮得過熟；煮得過久

over·crit·ic·al /ˌəʊvəˈkrɪtɪkl; *NAmE* ˌoʊvərˈk-/ *adj.* too critical 過分挑剔的；吹毛求疵的

over·crowd·ed /ˌəʊvəˈkraʊdɪd; *NAmE* ˌoʊvərˈk-/ *adj.* (of a place 地方) with too many people or things in it 過於擁擠的：*overcrowded cities/prisons* 擁擠不堪的城市／監獄 ◇ *Too many poor people are living in* ***overcrowded conditions.*** 有太多貧民的居住環境十分擁擠。

over·crowd·ing /ˌəʊvəˈkraʊdɪŋ; *NAmE* ˌoʊvərˈk-/ *noun* [U] the situation when there are too many people or things in one place 過度擁擠；擁擠的狀況

over·de·veloped /ˌəʊvədɪˈveləpt; *NAmE* ˌoʊvərd-/ *adj.* that has grown too large 發育過度的；過於發達的：*overdeveloped muscles* 過於發達的肌肉 ◇ *an overdeveloped sense of humour* 過分的幽默感 ▶ **over·de·velop** *verb* **~ sth over·devel·op·ment** *noun* [U]

over·do /ˌəʊvəˈduː; *NAmE* ˌoʊvərˈduː/ *verb* (**over·does** /-ˈdʌz/, **over·did** /-ˈdɪd/, **over·done** /-ˈdʌn/) **1 ~ sth** to do sth too much; to exaggerate sth 做得過分；做得過火；誇張：*She really overdid the sympathy* (= and so did not seem sincere). 她真是同情得過火了。**2 ~ sth** to use too much of sth 過多使用；濫用：*Don't overdo the salt in the food.* 菜裏別放太多鹽。◇ *Use illustrations where appropriate but don't* ***overdo it.*** 要適當地使用插圖，但不宜過多。**3** [usually passive] **~ sth** to cook sth for too long 烹煮（飯菜）時間過長：*The fish was overdone and very dry.* 這魚燒的時間太長，都乾掉了。

IDM over'do it/things to work, study, etc. too hard or for too long（工作、學習等）過分努力：*He's been overdoing things recently.* 他最近過於努力了。◇ *I overdid it in the gym and hurt my back.* 我在健身房練得過火了，結果弄傷了背。

over·dog /ˈəʊvədɒg; *NAmE* ˈoʊvərdɔːg/ *noun* (*disapproving*) a person, organization or country that is successful or in a stronger position than others, especially when they seem to have an unfair advantage（尤指不公正地）佔上風者，佔優勢者：*political leaders who support the interests of the overdog* 支持特權階層利益的政治領導人 **OPP underdog**

over·dose /ˈəʊvədəʊs; *NAmE* ˈoʊvərdoʊs/ *noun, verb*
■ ***noun*** too much of a drug taken at one time（一次用藥）過量：*a* ***drug/drugs overdose*** 藥物劑量過大 ◇ *She took a massive overdose of sleeping pills.* 她服用了過量的安眠藥。
■ ***verb*** (also *informal* **OD**) [I] **~ (on sth)** to take too much of a drug at one time, so that it is dangerous 一次用藥過量：*He had overdosed on heroin.* 他過量服用了海洛因。◇ (*figurative*) *I had overdosed on sun.* 我曬太陽的時間過長了。

over·draft /ˈəʊvədrɑːft; *NAmE* ˈoʊvərdræft/ *noun* the amount of money that you owe to a bank when you have spent more money than is in your bank account; an arrangement that allows you to do this 透支額；透支安排：*to* ***run up/pay off an overdraft*** 透支；付清透支 ➲ COLLOCATIONS at FINANCE

over·draw /ˌəʊvəˈdrɔː; *NAmE* ˌoʊvərˈdrɔː/ *verb* (**over·drew** /-ˈdruː/, **over·drawn** /-ˈdrɔːn/) [T, I] **~ (sth)** (*especially BrE*) to take out more money from a bank account than it contains 透支：*Customers who overdraw their accounts will be charged a fee.* 透支的存戶須付手續費。

over·drawn /ˌəʊvəˈdrɔːn; *NAmE* ˌoʊvərˈd-/ *adj.* **1** [not usually before noun] (of a person 人) having taken more money out of your bank account than you have in it 已透支；有透支：*I'm overdrawn by £100.* 我透支了 100 英鎊。**2** (of a bank account 銀行賬戶) with more money taken out than was paid in or left in 被透支的：*an overdrawn account* 透支的賬戶 ◇ *Your account is £200 overdrawn.* 您的賬戶已透支 200 英鎊。

over·dressed /ˌəʊvəˈdrest; *NAmE* ˌoʊvərˈd-/ *adj.* (usually *disapproving*) wearing clothes that are too formal or too elegant for a particular occasion 穿着太正式的；打扮過分的

over·drive /ˈəʊvədraɪv; *NAmE* ˈoʊvərd-/ *noun* [U] an extra high gear in a vehicle, that you use when you are driving at high speeds（汽車的）超速擋：*to be in overdrive* 超速駕駛

IDM go into 'overdrive to start being very active and working very hard 加勁；加倍努力；拚命工作：*As the wedding approached, the whole family went into overdrive.* 隨着婚禮將近，全家人都忙得不亦樂乎。

over·dub /ˌəʊvəˈdʌb; *NAmE* ˌoʊvərˈd-/ *verb* (**-bb-**) **~ sb** to record new sounds over the sounds on an original recording so that both can be heard 把（錄音）配到原帶上；疊錄

over·due /ˌəʊvəˈdjuː; *NAmE* ˌoʊvərˈduː/ *adj.* **1** not paid, done, returned, etc. by the required or expected time（到期）未付的，未做的，未還的；過期的：*an overdue payment/library book* 逾期的付款；逾期未還的圖書 ◇ *The rent is now overdue.* 現在房租已屬拖欠。◇ *Her baby is two weeks overdue.* 她的胎兒已超過預產期兩週了。◇ *This car is overdue for a service.* 這輛汽車早就該維修了。**2** that should have happened or been done before now 早該發生的；早應完成的：*overdue reforms* 遲來的改革 ◇ *A book like this is* ***long overdue.*** 像這樣的書早就該有人出版了。

ˌover ˈeasy *adj.* (*NAmE*) (of fried eggs 煎蛋) turned over when almost cooked and fried for a short time on the other side 兩面煎的（一面快煎好時翻到另一面稍煎片刻）

over·eat /ˌəʊvərˈiːt; *NAmE* ˌoʊ-/ *verb* (**over·ate** /-ˈet; *NAmE* -ˈeɪt/, **over·eaten** /-ˈiːtn/) [I] to eat more than you need or more than is healthy 吃得過量；吃撐了 ▶ **over·eat·ing** *noun* [U]：*She went through periods of compulsive overeating.* 她經歷了強迫性暴食的幾個階段。

ˌover-ˈegg *verb*

IDM ˌover-egg the ˈpudding used to say that you think sb has done more than is necessary, or has added unnecessary details to make sth seem better or worse than it really is 做事過分；畫蛇添足：*If you're telling lies, keep it simple—never over-egg the pudding.* 如果撒謊，措辭要簡短；千萬別畫蛇添足。

over·empha·sis /ˌəʊvər'emfəsɪs; *NAmE* ˌoʊ-/ *noun* [U, sing.] **~ (on sth)** too much emphasis or importance 過分強調；過於重視：*an overemphasis on curing illness rather than preventing it* 過分強調治病而不事預防 ▸ **over·empha·size, -ise** /ˌəʊvər'emfəsaɪz; *NAmE* ˌoʊ-/ *verb* : **~ sth** *The importance of preparation* ***cannot be overemphasized***. 準備的重要性要一講再講。

over·esti·mate AW *verb, noun*

■ **verb** /ˌəʊvər'estɪmeɪt; *NAmE* ˌoʊ-/ **~ sth** to estimate sth to be larger, better, more important, etc. than it really is 高估：*They overestimated his ability when they promoted him.* 他們提拔他的時候高估了他的能力。◇ *The importance of these findings* ***cannot be overestimated*** (= is very great). 這些發現的重要性是無法充分估量的。OPP **underestimate** ▸ **over·esti·mation** *noun* [U, C]

■ **noun** /ˌəʊvər'estɪmət; *NAmE* ˌoʊ-/ [usually sing.] an estimate about the size, cost, etc. of sth that is too high 過高的評估 OPP **underestimate**

over·ex·cited /ˌəʊvərɪk'saɪtɪd; *NAmE* ˌoʊ-/ *adj.* too excited and not behaving in a calm or sensible way 過度興奮的；興奮得忘乎所以的：*Don't get the children overexcited just before bedtime.* 臨睡前不要讓孩子玩得過於興奮。

over·ex·pose /ˌəʊvərɪk'spəʊz; *NAmE* ˌoʊvərɪk'spoʊz/ *verb* [usually passive] **1 ~ sth** to affect the quality of a photograph or film by allowing too much light to enter the camera 使（膠片等）曝光過度 OPP **underexpose** **2 ~ sb/sth** to allow sb/sth to be seen too much on television, in the newspapers, etc. 對…報道過頻：*The club is careful not to let the younger players be overexposed, and rarely allows them to be interviewed.* 俱樂部不想讓年輕隊員過度曝光，因而很少允許他們接受採訪。▸ **over·ex·pos·ure** /ˌəʊvərɪk'spəʊʒə(r); *NAmE* ˌoʊvərɪk'spoʊ-/ *noun* [U]

over·ex·tend·ed /ˌəʊvərɪk'stendɪd; *NAmE* ˌoʊ-/ *adj.* [not usually before noun] involved in more work or activities, or spending more money, than you can manage without problems 承擔過多工作；開支過大 ▸ **over·ex·tend** *verb* : **~ yourself** *They should not overextend themselves on the mortgage.* 他們不應該用抵押借款過多。

over·feed /'əʊvəfiːd; *NAmE* 'oʊvərfiːd/ *verb* (**over·fed, over·fed** /'əʊvəfed; *NAmE* 'oʊvərfed/) **~ sb/sth** to give sb/sth too much food 給…餵食過度 ▸ **over·fed** *adj.* OPP **underfed**

over·fish·ing /ˌəʊvə'fɪʃɪŋ; *NAmE* ˌoʊvər'f-/ *noun* [U] the process of taking so many fish from the sea, a river, etc. that the number of fish in it becomes very low 捕撈過度

over·flow *verb, noun*

■ **verb** /ˌəʊvə'fləʊ; *NAmE* ˌoʊvər'floʊ/ **1** [I, T] to be so full that the contents go over the sides 漫出；溢出：*The bath is overflowing!* 浴盆溢水了！◇ **~ with sth** *Plates overflowed with party food.* 聚會上的食物碟滿盤盈。◇ (*figurative*) *Her heart overflowed with love.* 她的心裏充滿了愛。◇ **~ sth** *The river overflowed its banks.* 河水漲出了堤岸。**2** [I] **~ (with sth)** (of a place 地方) to have too many people in it 擠滿了人：*The streets were overflowing with the crowds.* 街上到處擠滿了人群。◇ *The hospitals are* ***filled to overflowing*** (= with patients). 醫院都人滿為患。**3** [I, T] **~ (into sth)** | **~ (sth)** to spread beyond the limits of a place or container that is too full 擴展出界；過度延伸：*The meeting overflowed into the street.* 集會的人群延伸到了大街上。

■ **noun** /'əʊvəfləʊ; *NAmE* 'oʊvərfloʊ/ **1** [U, sing.] a number of people or things that do not fit into the space available 容納不下的人（或物）：*A new office block was built to accommodate the overflow of staff.* 新建了一座辦公大樓以便容納多出的員工。◇ *an overflow car park* 備用停車場 **2** [U, sing.] the action of liquid flowing out of a container, etc. that is already full; the liquid that flows out 溢出；漫出；溢出的液體：*an overflow of water from the lake* 漫出的湖水 ◇ (*figurative*) *an overflow of powerful emotions* 橫流的激情 **3** (also **'overflow pipe**) [C] a pipe that allows extra liquid to escape 溢流管 **4** [C, usually sing.] (*computing* 計) a fault that happens because a number or data item (for example, the result of a calculation) is too large for the computer to represent it exactly 溢出，上溢（運算產生的數值位數或字的長度等超過存貯單元的長度）

over·fly /ˌəʊvə'flaɪ; *NAmE* ˌoʊvər'f-/ *verb* (**over·flies, over·fly·ing, over·flew** /-'fluː/, **over·flown** /-'fləʊn; *NAmE* -'floʊn/) [T, I] **~ (sth)** to fly over a place 飛越；飛過：*We overflew the war zone, taking photographs.* 我們飛越戰區攝影。◇ *the noise from overflying planes* 過往飛機發出的噪聲 ▸ **over·flight** *noun*

over·fond /ˌəʊvə'fɒnd; *NAmE* ˌoʊvər'fɑːnd/ *adj.* **~ of sb/sth** liking sb/sth too much（對…）過於喜歡，過分喜愛

over·gar·ment /'əʊvəgɑːmənt; *NAmE* 'oʊvərgɑːrm-/ *noun* (*formal*) an item of clothing that is worn over other clothes 罩袍；大衣

over·gen·er·al·ize (*BrE* also **-ise**) /ˌəʊvə'dʒenrəlaɪz; *NAmE* ˌoʊvər'dʒ-/ *verb* [I] to make a statement that is not accurate because it is too general 做過分概括的陳述；說話過於籠統 ▸ **over·gen·er·al·iza·tion, -isa·tion** /ˌəʊvədʒenrəlaɪ'zeɪʃn; *NAmE* ˌoʊvərdʒenrələ'zeɪʃn/ *noun* [C, U]

over·gen·er·ous /ˌəʊvə'dʒenərəs; *NAmE* ˌoʊvər'dʒ-/ *adj.* **~ (with sth)** giving too much of sth（施與某物時）過於慷慨，過分大方：*She is not overgenerous with praise.* 她不說過頭的恭維話。

over·graze /ˌəʊvə'greɪz; *NAmE* ˌoʊvər'g-/ *verb* **~ sth** if land is **overgrazed**, it is damaged by having too many animals feeding on it 在（土地）上過度放牧

over·ground /'əʊvəgraʊnd; *NAmE* 'oʊvərg-/ *adv.* (*BrE*) on or above the surface of the ground, rather than under it 在地面上；高出地面：*The new railway line will run overground.* 新鐵路線將鋪在地面上。▸ **over·ground** *adj.* : *overground trains* 地面火車 ➲ compare UNDERGROUND *adj.* (1)

over·grown /ˌəʊvə'grəʊn; *NAmE* ˌoʊvər'groʊn/ *adj.* **1** (of gardens, etc. 花園等) covered with plants that have been allowed to grow wild and have not been controlled 植物蔓生的；雜草叢生的：*an overgrown path* 長滿野草的小徑 ◇ **~ with sth** *The garden's completely overgrown with weeds.* 花園裏長滿了雜草。**2** (often *disapproving*) that has grown too large 發展過快的；長得過大的：*an overgrown village* 膨脹過大的村莊 ◇ *They act like a pair of overgrown children* (= they are adults but they behave like children). 他倆的舉動就像一對大孩子。

over·growth /'əʊvəgrəʊθ; *NAmE* 'oʊvərgroʊθ/ *noun* [U, sing.] (*technical* 術語) too much growth of sth, especially sth that grows on or over sth else 增生；瘋長

over·hand /'əʊvəhænd; *NAmE* 'oʊvərh-/ *adj., adv.* (*especially NAmE*) = OVERARM

over·hang *verb, noun*

■ **verb** /ˌəʊvə'hæŋ; *NAmE* ˌoʊvər'h-/ (**over·hung, over·hung** /-'hʌŋ/) [T, I] **~ (sth)** to stick out over and above sth else 懸垂；懸掛；突出於某物之上：*His big fat belly overhung his belt.* 他那碩大肥胖的肚子挺在腰帶上面。◇ *The path was cool and dark with overhanging trees.* 小路樹木掩映，涼爽幽暗。

■ **noun** /'əʊvəhæŋ; *NAmE* 'oʊvərh-/ **1** the part of sth that sticks out over and above sth else（…上的）伸出物，外伸物，懸垂物：*The roof has an overhang to protect the walls from the rain.* 屋頂有飛簷突出，保護牆壁不受雨淋。**2** the amount by which sth hangs over and above sth else 外伸量；突出量 **3** [usually sing.] (*business* 商) (*especially NAmE*) the state of being extra to what is required; the things that are extra 過剩（物）；積壓（物）：*attempts to reduce the overhang of unsold goods* 減少滯銷商品積壓的嘗試

over·hasty /ˌəʊvə'heɪsti; *NAmE* ˌoʊvər'h-/ *adj.* done too soon or doing sth too soon, especially without enough thought 過於匆忙的；過急的；過於草率的：*an overhasty decision* 過於草率的決定 ◇ *We were overhasty in making the choice.* 我們當初作選擇時太倉促了。

O

over·haul *noun, verb*

■ **noun** /ˈəʊvəhɔːl; *NAmE* ˈoʊvərh-/ an examination of a machine or system, including doing repairs on it or making changes to it 檢修；大修；改造：*a complete/major overhaul* 全面 / 大檢修◇*A radical overhaul of the tax system is necessary.* 有必要徹底改革稅制。

■ **verb** /ˌəʊvəˈhɔːl; *NAmE* ˌoʊvər-/ **1 ~ sth** to examine every part of a machine, system, etc. and make any necessary changes or repairs 徹底檢修：*The engine has been completely overhauled.* 發動機已徹底檢修過了。**2 ~ sb** to come from behind a person you are competing against in a race and go past them 趕上，超過（賽跑對手）**SYN** **overtake**：*He managed to overhaul the leader on the final lap.* 他在最後一圈發力超過了領先的選手。

over·head *adv., adj., noun*

■ **adv.** /ˌəʊvəˈhed; *NAmE* ˌoʊvərˈhed/ above your head; in the sky 在頭上方；在空中：*Planes flew overhead constantly.* 飛機不斷從頭頂上飛過。◇*Thunder boomed in the sky overhead.* 雷聲在天空中隆隆作響。

■ **adj.** /ˈəʊvəhed; *NAmE* ˈoʊvərhed/ **1** above your head; raised above the ground 頭上方的；地面以上的；高架的：*overhead power lines* 高架輸電線 **2** [only before noun] connected with the general costs of running a business or an organization, for example paying for rent or electricity 經費的；管理費用的：*overhead costs* 營運開支

■ **noun** [U] (*especially NAmE*) = OVERHEADS

ˌoverhead proˈjector *noun* (*abbr.* **OHP**) a piece of equipment that projects an image onto a wall or screen so that many people can see it 投影儀 ➲ compare DATA PROJECTOR, SLIDE PROJECTOR

over·heads /ˈəʊvəhedz; *NAmE* ˈoʊvərh-/ *noun* [pl.] (*especially BrE*) (also **over·head** [U], especially in *NAmE*) regular costs that you have when you are running a business or an organization, such as rent, electricity, wages, etc. 經費；營運費用；經常性開支 ➲ SYNONYMS at COST

over·hear /ˌəʊvəˈhɪə(r); *NAmE* ˌoʊvərˈhɪr/ *verb* (**over·heard, over·heard** /-ˈhɜːd; *NAmE* -ˈhɜːrd/) to hear, especially by accident, a conversation in which you are not involved 偶然聽到；無意中聽到：**~ sb/sth** *We talked quietly so as not to be overheard.* 我們低聲交談，以免別人聽到。◇*I overheard a conversation between two boys on the bus.* 我在公共汽車上無意中聽到兩個男孩的對話。◇**~ sb doing sth** *We overheard them arguing.* 我們碰巧聽到他們吵嘴。◇**~ sb do sth** *I overheard him say he was going to France.* 我偶然聽見他說他要去法國。➲ compare EAVESDROP

over·heat /ˌəʊvəˈhiːt; *NAmE* ˌoʊvərˈh-/ *verb* **1** [I, T] to become or to make sth become too hot 變得過熱；使過熱：*The engine is overheating.* 發動機過熱了。◇**~ sth** *It's vital not to overheat the liquid.* 最關鍵的是不要讓液體過熱。**2** [I] (of a country's economy 國家經濟) to be too active, with rising prices 發展過熱，過於活躍（以致物價高漲）▸ **over·heat·ing** *noun* [U]

over·heated /ˌəʊvəˈhiːtɪd; *NAmE* ˌoʊvərˈh-/ *adj.* **1** too hot 太熱的；過熱的：*Don't sleep in an overheated room.* 不要在太熱的屋子裏睡覺。**2** too interested or excited 過於熱心的；過於興奮的；痴迷的：*the figment of an overheated imagination* 想入非非而虛構的事物 **3** (of a country's economy 國家經濟) too active in a way that may cause problems 過熱的；增長過快的

over·hung *past tense* of OVERHANG

over·in·dulge /ˌəʊvərɪnˈdʌldʒ; *NAmE* ˌoʊ-/ *verb* **1** [I] **~ (in sth)** to have too much of sth nice, especially food or drink 過多地享用（尤指食物或飲料）**2** [T] **~ sb** to give sb more than is good for them 過分放任；過於縱容：*His mother overindulged him.* 他母親對他過於溺愛。

over·in·flated /ˌəʊvərɪnˈfleɪtɪd; *NAmE* ˌoʊ-/ *adj.* **1** (of a price or value 價格或價值) too high 過高的；過於高漲的：*overinflated house prices* 過高的房價 **2** made to seem better, worse, more important, etc. than it really is 誇張的；誇大的；言過其實的 **SYN** **exaggerated** **3** filled with too much air 過度充氣的：*Overinflated tyres burst more easily.* 充氣過量的輪胎更容易爆裂。

over·joyed /ˌəʊvəˈdʒɔɪd; *NAmE* ˌoʊvərˈdʒ-/ *adj.* [not before noun] extremely happy or pleased 非常高興；欣喜若狂 **SYN** **delighted**：**~ (at sth)** *He was overjoyed at my success.* 我的成功使他欣喜若狂。◇**~ (to do sth)** *We were overjoyed to hear their good news.* 聽到他們的好消息，我們都大喜過望。◇**~ (that …)** *She was overjoyed that her article had been published.* 她的文章發表了，這使她高興極了。

over·kill /ˈəʊvəkɪl; *NAmE* ˈoʊvərkɪl/ *noun* [U] (*disapproving*) too much of sth that reduces the effect it has 過猶不及；做得過火的事：*There is a danger of overkill if you plan everything too carefully.* 如果事事過分謹小慎微，那結果難免有適得其反的危險。

over·laid *past tense, past part.* of OVERLAY

over·land /ˈəʊvəlænd; *NAmE* ˈoʊvərl-/ *adj.* across the land; by land, not by sea or by air 橫跨陸地的；通過陸路的：*an overland route* 陸上路線 ▸ **over·land** *adv.*：*to travel overland* 作陸上旅行

over·lap **AW** *verb, noun*

■ **verb** /ˌəʊvəˈlæp; *NAmE* ˌoʊvərˈlæp/ (**-pp-**) **1** [T, I] **~ (sth)** if one thing **overlaps** another, or the two things **overlap**, part of one thing covers part of the other （物體）部份重疊，交疊：*A fish's scales overlap each other.* 魚鱗一片片上下交疊。◇*The floor was protected with overlapping sheets of newspaper.* 地板用一張搭着一張的報紙保護着。**2** [T] **~ sth** to make two or more things overlap 使部份重疊：*You will need to overlap the pieces of wood slightly.* 你得使這些木片像魚鱗片似的搭疊起來。**3** [I, T] **~ (sth)** if two events **overlap** or **overlap** each other, the second one starts before the first one has finished（時間上）部份重疊 **4** [I, T] to cover part of the same area of interest, knowledge, responsibility, etc. （範圍方面）部份重疊：*Our jobs overlap slightly, which sometimes causes difficulties.* 我們的工作略有重疊，所以有時引起一些困難。◇**~ (with) sth** *The language of science overlaps with that of everyday life.* 有些科學用語也用於日常生活。

■ **noun** /ˈəʊvəlæp; *NAmE* ˈoʊvərlæp/ **1** [C, U] **~ (between sth and sth)** a shared area of interest, knowledge, responsibility, etc. （範圍方面的）重疊部份：*There is (a) considerable overlap between the two subjects.* 兩門科目之間有相當多的共通之處。**2** [C, U] the amount by which one thing covers another thing （物體的）重疊部份，重疊量：*an overlap of 5 cm on each roof tile* 每片房瓦上 5 厘米的重疊度 **3** [U, sing.] a period of time in which two events or activities happen together （兩事發生的）重疊時間，交接時期：*There will be an overlap of a week while John teaches Ann the job.* 將有一週的交接期可以讓約翰教安如何接手工作。

over·lay *verb, noun*

■ **verb** /ˌəʊvəˈleɪ; *NAmE* ˌoʊvərˈleɪ/ (**over·laid, over·laid** /-ˈleɪd/) [usually passive] **1 ~ sth** (*technical* 術語) to put sth on top of a surface so as to cover it completely; to lie on top of a surface 覆蓋；包；鋪；鍍：*wood overlaid with gold* 包金木 **2 ~ sth (with sth)** (*literary*) to add sth, especially a feeling or quality, to sth else so that it seems to cover it （尤指以感情或品質）撒滿，遮掩：*The place was overlaid with memories of his childhood.* 這個地方處處都裝點着他童年的回憶。

■ **noun** /ˈəʊvəleɪ; *NAmE* ˈoʊvərleɪ/ **1** a transparent sheet with drawings, figures, etc. on it that can be placed on top of another sheet in order to change it 套圖透明膜；上襯：*An overlay showing population can be placed on top of the map.* 可以在地圖上加一層顯示人口的透明膜。**2** a thing that is laid on top of or covers sth else 覆蓋物；塗層：*an overlay of fibreglass insulation* 玻璃纖維絕緣層

over·leaf /ˌəʊvəˈliːf; *NAmE* ˌoʊvərˈliːf/ *adv.* on the other side of the page of a book, etc. 在（書頁等的）背面；在後面：*Complete the form overleaf.* 填妥背面的表格。◇*The changes are explained in detail overleaf.* 修改處在背面有詳細的說明。

over·lie /ˌəʊvəˈlaɪ; *NAmE* ˌoʊvərˈlaɪ/ *verb* (**over·ly·ing, over·lay** /-ˈleɪ/, **over·lain** /-ˈleɪn/) [I, T] **~ (sth)** (*technical* 術語) to lie over sth 疊加於；置於…上面：*overlying rock* 壓在上面的岩石

over·load *verb, noun*

■ ***verb*** /ˌəʊvəˈləʊd; *NAmE* ˌoʊvərˈloʊd/ [often passive] **1 ~ sth** to put too great a load on sth 使超載；使負荷過重：*an overloaded truck* 一輛超載的卡車 **2 ~ sb (with sth)** to give sb too much of sth 給…增加負擔：*He's overloaded with responsibilities.* 他擔負的責任過多。◇ *Don't overload the students with information.* 不要給學生灌輸過多的知識。 **3 ~ sth** to put too great a demand on a computer, an electrical system, etc. causing it to fail 使（計算機）超載運行；使（電路）超負荷

■ ***noun*** /ˈəʊvələʊd; *NAmE* ˈoʊvərloʊd/ [U, sing.] too much of sth 過多；過量；超負荷：*In these days of technological change we all suffer from* ***information overload****.* 在這科技日新月異的時代，過多的信息使人人都應接不暇。

over·long /ˌəʊvəˈlɒŋ; *NAmE* ˌoʊvərˈlɔːŋ; ˌoʊvərˈlɑːŋ/ (*BrE*) (*NAmE* **ˈoverly long**) *adj.* too long 過長的：*an overlong agenda* 過長的議程表

over·look /ˌəʊvəˈlʊk; *NAmE* ˌoʊvərˈlʊk/ *verb* **1 ~ sth** to fail to see or notice sth 忽略；未注意到 **SYN** **miss**：*He seems to have overlooked one important fact.* 他好像忽略了一個重要的事實。 **2 ~ sth** to see sth wrong or bad but decide to ignore it（對不良現象等）不予理會，視而不見 **SYN** **turn a blind eye to**：*We could not afford to overlook such a serious offence.* 對這樣嚴重的違法行為，我們決不能視若無睹。 **3 ~ sth** if a building, etc. **overlooks** a place, you can see that place from the building 俯視；眺望：*a restaurant overlooking the lake* 一家瀕湖餐廳 ◇ *Our back yard is overlooked by several houses.* 好幾棟房子都看得見我家的後院。 **4 ~ sb (for sth)** to not consider sb for a job or position, even though they might be suitable（提拔等時）對（某人）不予考慮 **SYN** **pass over**：*She's been overlooked for promotion several times.* 幾次提職時都沒有考慮她。

over·lord /ˈəʊvəlɔːd; *NAmE* ˈoʊvərlɔːrd/ *noun* (especially in the past) a person who has power over many other people（尤指舊時的）領主，莊主，大王：*feudal overlords* 封建領主

over·ly /ˈəʊvəli; *NAmE* ˈoʊvərli/ *adv.* (before an adjective 用於形容詞前) too; very 很；十分；過於 **SYN** **excessively**：*I'm not overly fond of pasta.* 我不怎麼喜歡吃意大利麪。◇ *We think you are being overly optimistic.* 我們認為你過於樂觀了。

over·manned /ˌəʊvəˈmænd; *NAmE* ˌoʊvərˈm-/ *adj.* (of a company, office, etc. 公司、辦公室等) having more workers than are needed 人浮於事的；人員過多的 **SYN** **overstaffed** **OPP** **undermanned** ▸ **over·man·ning** /ˌəʊvəˈmænɪŋ; *NAmE* ˌoʊvərˈm-/ *noun* [U]：*the problems of overmanning in industry* 產業界從業人員過多的問題

over·much /ˌəʊvəˈmʌtʃ; *NAmE* ˌoʊvərˈm-/ (*BrE*) (*NAmE* **ˈoverly much**) *adv.* (especially with a negative verb 尤與否定動詞連用) too much; very much 很多；過多；非常：*She didn't worry overmuch about it.* 她對此不太擔憂。 ▸ **over·much** *adj.*

over·night *adv., adj.*

■ ***adv.*** /ˌəʊvəˈnaɪt; *NAmE* ˌoʊvərˈn-/ **1** during or for the night 在夜間；在晚上：*We* ***stayed overnight*** *in London after the theatre.* 我們看完戲後在倫敦住了一晚。 **2** suddenly or quickly 突然；一夜之間；旋即：*Don't expect it to improve overnight.* 不要指望這事一下子就改善了。

■ ***adj.*** /ˈəʊvənaɪt; *NAmE* ˈoʊvərn-/ [only before noun] **1** happening during the night; for a night 夜間的；晚上的；只供一夜的：*an overnight flight* 夜間飛行 ◇ *overnight accommodation* 一夜住宿 ◇ *She took only* ***an overnight bag*** (= containing the things needed for a night spent away from home). 她只帶了一個外出住宿一晚的用品旅行袋。 **2** happening suddenly or quickly 突然的；很快的；一夜之間的：*The play was an overnight success.* 這部劇作一夜成名。

ˌover-optiˈmis·tic *adj.* **1** too confident that sth will be successful 過分樂觀的：*I'm not over-optimistic about my chances of getting the job.* 我對獲得這份工作不抱太大希望。 **2** showing more confidence that sth will be successful than is justified by later events 期望過高的；過於樂觀的：*The sales forecasts turned out to be over-optimistic.* 結果證明銷售預測過於樂觀。

over·pass /ˈəʊvəpɑːs; *NAmE* ˈoʊvərpæs/ (*NAmE*) (*BrE* **fly-over**) *noun* a bridge that carries one road over another one 高架橋；跨線橋；立交橋 ➲ compare UNDERPASS

over·pay /ˌəʊvəˈpeɪ; *NAmE* ˌoʊvərˈpeɪ/ *verb* (**over·paid**, **over·paid** /-ˈpeɪd/) [usually passive] **~ sb** to pay sb too much; to pay sb more than their work is worth 付款過多；多付報酬 **OPP** **underpay** ▸ **over·pay·ment** /-ˈpeɪmənt/ *noun* [C, U]

over·play /ˌəʊvəˈpleɪ; *NAmE* ˌoʊvərˈp-/ *verb* **~ sth** to give too much importance to sth 過分強調；過分重視 **OPP** **underplay**

IDM **overplay your ˈhand** to spoil your chance of success by judging your position to be stronger than it really is 因不自量力而毀掉勝機；高估自己的地位；錯估形勢

over·popu·lated /ˌəʊvəˈpɒpjuleɪtɪd; *NAmE* ˌoʊvərˈpɑːp-/ *adj.* (of a country or city 國家或城市) with too many people living in it 人口過多的 ▸ **over·popu·la·tion** /ˌəʊvəˌpɒpjuˈleɪʃn; *NAmE* ˌoʊvərˌpɑːp-/ *noun* [U]：*the problems of overpopulation* 人口過剩問題

over·power /ˌəʊvəˈpaʊə(r); *NAmE* ˌoʊvərˈp-/ *verb* **1 ~ sb** to defeat or gain control over sb completely by using greater strength（以較強力量）征服，制勝：*Police finally managed to overpower the gunman.* 警察最終制伏了持槍歹徒。 **2 ~ sb/sth** to be so strong or great that it affects or disturbs sb/sth seriously 壓倒；令人折服；使難以忍受 **SYN** **overwhelm**：*Her beauty overpowered him.* 她的美貌令他傾倒。◇ *The flavour of the garlic overpowered the meat.* 大蒜的味道蓋過了肉味。

over·power·ing /ˌəʊvəˈpaʊərɪŋ; *NAmE* ˌoʊvərˈp-/ *adj.* very strong or powerful 強烈的；極強大的；堅強的：*an overpowering smell of fish* 濃烈的魚腥味兒 ◇ *an overpowering personality* 極強的個性 ◇ *The heat was overpowering.* 酷熱難當。 ▸ **over·power·ing·ly** *adv.*

over·priced /ˌəʊvəˈpraɪst; *NAmE* ˌoʊvərˈp-/ *adj.* too expensive; costing more than it is worth 價格太高的；過於昂貴的 ➲ SYNONYMS at EXPENSIVE

over·print /ˌəʊvəˈprɪnt; *NAmE* ˌoʊvərˈp-/ *verb* **~ A (on B) | ~ B with A** to print sth on a document, etc. that already has printing on it（在印刷品上）套印，加印

over·pro·duce /ˌəʊvəprəˈdjuːs; *NAmE* ˌoʊvərprəˈduːs/ *verb* [T, I] **~ (sth)** to produce more of sth than is wanted or needed 過多地生產；過度生產 ▸ **over·pro·duc·tion** /ˌəʊvəprəˈdʌkʃn; *NAmE* ˌoʊvərp-/ *noun* [U]

over·pro·tect·ive /ˌəʊvəprəˈtektɪv; *NAmE* ˌoʊvərp-/ *adj.* too anxious to protect sb from being hurt, in a way that restricts their freedom 過分保護的；袒護的；溺愛有加的：*overprotective parents* 溺愛子女的父母

over·quali·fied /ˌəʊvəˈkwɒlɪfaɪd; *NAmE* ˌoʊvərˈkwɑːl-/ *adj.* having more experience or training than is necessary for a particular job, so that people do not want to employ you（對某職位而言）資歷過高的

over·ran *past tense of* OVERRUN

over·rate /ˌəʊvəˈreɪt; *NAmE* ˌoʊvərˈr-/ *verb* [usually passive] **~ sb/sth** to have too high an opinion of sb/sth; to put too high a value on sb/sth 對…評價過高；高估：*In my opinion, Hirst's work has been vastly overrated.* 依我看赫斯特的作品被大大地高估了。 **OPP** **underrate**

over·reach /ˌəʊvəˈriːtʃ; *NAmE* ˌoʊvərˈr-/ *verb* [T, I] **~ (yourself)** to fail by trying to achieve more than is possible 貪功致敗；不自量力：*In making these promises, the company had clearly overreached itself.* 這家公司作出這些承諾，顯然是不自量力。

over·react /ˌəʊvəriˈækt; *NAmE* ˌoʊ-/ *verb* [I] **~ (to sth)** to react too strongly, especially to sth unpleasant 反應過激，反應過火（尤指對不愉快的事情） ▸ **over·reac·tion** /-ˈækʃn/ *noun* [sing., U]

over·ride /ˌəʊvəˈraɪd; *NAmE* ˌoʊvərˈr-/ *verb* (**over·rode** /-ˈrəʊd; *NAmE* -ˈroʊd/, **over·rid·den** /-ˈrɪdn/) **1 ~ sth** to use your authority to reject sb's decision, order, etc.（以權力）否決，推翻，不理會 **SYN** **overrule**：*The chairman overrode the committee's objections and signed the agreement.* 主席不顧委員會的反對，逕行簽署了

O

協議。 **2 ~ sth** to be more important than sth 比⋯更重要；凌駕： *Considerations of safety override all other concerns.* 對安全的考慮高於一切。 **3 ~ sth** to stop a process that happens automatically and control it yourself 超馳控制，超控（使自動控制暫時失效，改用手工控制）： *A special code is needed to override the time lock.* 這定時鎖要用特定密碼才能打開。

over·rid·ing /ˌəʊvəˈraɪdɪŋ; NAmE ˌoʊvərˈr-/ *adj.* [only before noun] more important than anything else in a particular situation 最重要的；首要的；凌駕一切的： *the* ***overriding factor/consideration/concern*** 首要因素／考慮／關注的事 ◇ *Their overriding aim was to keep costs low.* 他們的首要目標是維持低成本。

over·ripe /ˌəʊvəˈraɪp; NAmE ˌoʊvərˈr-/ *adj.* too RIPE 過熟的： *overripe fruit* 熟過頭的水果

over·rule /ˌəʊvəˈruːl; NAmE ˌoʊvərˈr-/ *verb* [often passive] **~ sb/sth** to change a decision or reject an idea from a position of greater power （以權力）否定，拒絕，更改決定 SYN **override**： *to overrule a decision/an objection* （以權力）推翻決議／異議 ◇ *The verdict was overruled by the Supreme Court.* 最高法院駁回了那個裁決。

over·run /ˌəʊvəˈrʌn; NAmE ˌoʊ-/ *verb* (**over·ran** /-ˈræn/, **over·run**) **1** [T, often passive] **~ sth** (especially of sth bad or not wanted 尤指壞事或不欲之事) to fill or spread over an area quickly, especially in large numbers 泛濫；橫行；肆虐： *The house was completely overrun with mice.* 這房子簡直成了老鼠的天下。◇ *Enemy soldiers had overrun the island.* 敵軍士兵侵佔了該島。 **2** [I, T] to take more time or money than was intended 多用（時間、錢財等）；超時： *Her lectures never overrun.* 她講課從不拖堂。◇ **~ sth** *You've overrun your time by 10 minutes.* 你超時 10 分鐘了。 ▸ **over·run** /ˈəʊvərʌn; NAmE ˈoʊ-/ *noun*： *a cost overrun* 超出的成本

over·seas AW /ˌəʊvəˈsiːz; NAmE ˌoʊvərˈs-/ *adj., adv.*

■ ***adj.*** connected with foreign countries, especially those separated from your country by the sea or ocean 外國的；海外的： *overseas development/markets/trade* 海外發展／市場／貿易 ◇ *overseas students/visitors* 外國留學生／遊客 ➲ compare HOME *adj.* (3)

■ ***adv.*** to or in a foreign country, especially those separated from your country by the sea or ocean 在國外；向海外 SYN **abroad**： *to* ***live/work/go overseas*** 在國外生活／工作；出國 ◇ *The product is sold both at home and overseas.* 這個產品行銷國內外。

over·see /ˌəʊvəˈsiː; NAmE ˌoʊvərˈsiː/ *verb* (**over·saw** /-ˈsɔː/, **over·seen** /-ˈsiːn/) **~ sb/sth** to watch sb/sth and make sure that a job or an activity is done correctly 監督；監視 SYN **supervise**

over·seer /ˈəʊvəsɪə(r); NAmE ˈoʊvərsɪr/ *noun* **1** (*old-fashioned*) a person whose job is to make sure that other workers do their work 監工；工頭 **2** a person or an organization that is responsible for making sure that a system is working as it should （某體系的）監督者，監督機構，督察

over·sell /ˌəʊvəˈsel; NAmE ˌoʊvərˈsel/ *verb* (**over·sold**, **over·sold** /ˌəʊvəˈsəʊld; NAmE ˌoʊvərˈsoʊld/) [often passive] **1 ~ sb/sth/yourself** to say that sb/sth is better than they really are 吹噓；過分頌揚： *He has a tendency to oversell himself.* 他愛自我吹噓。 **2 ~ sth** (*business* 商) to sell too much or more of sth than is available 過多銷售；空頭銷售： *The seats on the plane were oversold.* 飛機上的座位超賣了。

over·sen·si·tive /ˌəʊvəˈsensɪtɪv; NAmE ˌoʊvərˈs-/ *adj.* too easily upset or offended 過於敏感的；愛生氣的；動不動就發脾氣的

over·sexed /ˌəʊvəˈsekst; NAmE ˌoʊvərˈs-/ *adj.* having stronger sexual desire than is usual 性慾過盛的

over·shadow /ˌəʊvəˈʃædəʊ; NAmE ˌoʊvərˈʃædoʊ/ *verb* [often passive] **1 ~ sb/sth** to make sb/sth seem less important, or successful 使顯得遜色；使黯然失色： *He had always been overshadowed by his elder sister.* 他與他姐姐相比總是相形見絀。 **2 ~ sth** to make an event less enjoyable than it should be 使掃興；使蒙上陰影 SYN **cloud**： *News of the accident overshadowed the day's events.* 出事的消息給這一天的活動蒙上了陰影。 **3 ~ sth** to throw a shadow over sth 掩蓋；遮蔽： *The garden is overshadowed by tall trees.* 花園中大樹濃蔭密佈。

over·shoe /ˈəʊvəʃuː; NAmE ˈoʊvərʃuː/ *noun* a shoe worn over another shoe, especially in wet weather or to protect a floor 套鞋，罩鞋（在雨天時或為保護地板而穿）

over·shoot /ˌəʊvəˈʃuːt; NAmE ˌoʊvərˈʃ-/ *verb* (**over·shot**, **over·shot** /-ˈʃɒt; NAmE -ˈʃɑːt/) **1** [T, I] to go further than the place you intended to stop or turn 超過，越過（預定地點）： **~ sth** *The aircraft overshot the runway.* 飛機衝出了跑道。◇ **~ (sth) (by sth)** *She had overshot by 20 metres.* 她超過了 20 米。 **2** [T] **~ sth (by sth)** to do more or to spend more money than you originally planned 超過（原計劃）；突破（預計費用）： *The department may overshoot its cash limit this year.* 這個部門今年的現金花費可能超過預算限額。

over·sight /ˈəʊvəsaɪt; NAmE ˈoʊvərs-/ *noun* **1** [C, U] the fact of making a mistake because you forget to do sth or you do not notice sth 疏忽；忽略；失察： *I didn't mean to leave her name off the list; it was an oversight.* 我不是有意在名單上漏掉她的名字的，這是個疏忽。 **2** [U] (*formal*) the state of being in charge of sb/sth 負責；照管： *The committee has oversight of finance and general policy.* 委員會負責處理財政和綜合政策。

over·sim·plify /ˌəʊvəˈsɪmplɪfaɪ; NAmE ˌoʊvərˈs-/ *verb* (**over·sim·pli·fies**, **over·sim·pli·fy·ing**, **over·sim·pli·fied**, **over·sim·pli·fied**) [T, I] **~ (sth)** to describe a situation, a problem, etc. in a way that is too simple and ignores some of the facts 陳述過於簡略；說明過於簡單化： *It's easy to oversimplify the issues involved.* 很容易把涉及的問題看得太簡單。◇ *an oversimplified view of human nature* 對人性過於簡單化的看法 ▸ **over·sim·pli·fi·ca·tion** /ˌəʊvəˌsɪmplɪfɪˈkeɪʃn; NAmE ˌoʊvərˌs-/ *noun* [C, usually sing., U]： *This is a gross oversimplification of the facts.* 這顯然把事實過分簡單化了。 ➲ compare SIMPLIFICATION

over·sized /ˈəʊvəsaɪzd; NAmE ˈoʊvərs-/ (also *less frequent* **over·size** /-saɪz/) *adj.* bigger than the normal size; too big 過大的；碩大的；大得超過正常的

over·sleep /ˌəʊvəˈsliːp; NAmE ˌoʊvərˈs-/ *verb* (**over·slept**, **over·slept** /-ˈslept/) [I] to sleep longer than you intended 睡過頭；睡得太久： *I overslept and missed the bus.* 我睡過了頭，因此誤了班車。

over·spend /ˌəʊvəˈspend; NAmE ˌoʊvərˈs-/ *verb* (**over·spent**, **over·spent** /-ˈspent/) [I, T] to spend too much money or more than you planned 花錢過多；比（預計的）花得多；超支： **~ (on sth)** *The company has overspent on marketing.* 這個公司在市場推廣方面開支過多。◇ **~ sth** *Many departments have overspent their budgets this year.* 許多部門今年開支都超過了預算。 ▸ **over·spend** /ˈəʊvəspend; NAmE ˈoʊvərs-/ *noun* [sing.]： (*BrE*) *a £1 million overspend* * 100 萬英鎊的超支額 **over·spent** /ˌəʊvəˈspent; NAmE ˌoʊvərs-/ *adj.*： *The organization is heavily overspent.* 這個機構嚴重超支。

over·spill /ˈəʊvəspɪl; NAmE ˈoʊvərs-/ *noun* [U, sing.] (*BrE*) people who move out of a city because it is too crowded to an area where there is more space 遷出城市的過剩人口： *New towns were designed to house London's overspill.* 新的城鎮是為容納倫敦的過剩人口而興建的。

over·staffed /ˌəʊvəˈstɑːft; NAmE ˌoʊvərˈstæft/ *adj.* (of a company, office, etc. 公司、辦公室等) having more workers than are needed 人手過多；人浮於事 SYN **overmanned** OPP **understaffed**

over·state /ˌəʊvəˈsteɪt; NAmE ˌoʊvərˈs-/ *verb* **~ sth** to say sth in a way that makes it seem more important than it really is 誇大；誇張；言過其實 SYN **exaggerate**： *He tends to* ***overstate his case*** *when talking politics.* 他一談政治便流於夸夸其談。◇ *The seriousness of the crime* ***cannot be overstated.*** 這一罪行的嚴重性怎麼說也不為過。 OPP **understate** ▸ **over·state·ment** /ˈəʊvəsteɪtmənt; NAmE ˈoʊvərs-/ *noun* [C, U]： *It is not an overstatement to say a crisis is imminent.* 說危機當頭絕非危言聳聽。

over·stay /ˌəʊvəˈsteɪ; NAmE ˌoʊvərˈs-/ *verb* **~ sth** to stay longer than the length of time you are expected or allowed to stay 停留過久： *They overstayed their visa.* 他們居留超過了簽證期限。 IDM see WELCOME *n.*

over·step /ˌəʊvəˈstep; *NAmE* ˌoʊvərˈs-/ *verb* (-pp-) **~ sth** to go beyond what is normal or allowed 超越（正常或允許的）範圍；越權；僭越： *to overstep your authority* 越權 ◇ *He tends to* ***overstep the boundaries of*** *good taste.* 他往往文雅過度而流於庸俗。

IDM **overstep the ˈmark/ˈline** to behave in a way that people think is not acceptable （行為）越軌

over·stock /ˌəʊvəˈstɒk; *NAmE* ˌoʊvərˈstɑːk/ *verb* **1** [T, I] **~ (sth)** to buy or make more of sth than you need or can sell 庫存過多（貨物）；進（貨）過多 **2** [T, I] **~ (sth)** to put too many animals in a place where there is not enough room or food for them （在空間、食物不足的地方）畜養過多的動物

over·stretch /ˌəʊvəˈstretʃ; *NAmE* ˌoʊvərˈs-/ *verb* **~ sb/sth/yourself** (*especially BrE*) to do more than you are capable of; to make sb/sth do more than they are capable of （使）勉強維持，硬撐着，超負荷運轉： *This will overstretch the prison service's resources.* 這將使監獄的資源不堪負荷。 ◇ *Credit cards can tempt you to overstretch yourself* (= spend more money than you can afford). 信用卡能誘使你超額消費。 ▸ **over·stretched** *adj.* ： *overstretched muscles* 過度疲勞的肌肉 ◇ *over-stretched services* 擴展過度的服務

over·sub·scribed /ˌəʊvəsəbˈskraɪbd; *NAmE* ˌoʊvərs-/ *adj.* if an activity, service, etc. is **oversubscribed**, there are fewer places, tickets, etc. than the number of people who are asking for them （活動、服務等）供不應求的，未能達到需求量的

overt /əʊˈvɜːt; ˈəʊvɜːt; *NAmE* oʊˈvɜːrt; ˈoʊvɜːrt/ *adj.* [usually before noun] (*formal*) done in an open way and not secretly 公開的；明顯的；不隱瞞的： *There was little overt support for the project.* 對這個項目公開表示支持的很少。 ➲ compare COVERT ▸ **overt·ly** *adv.* ： *overtly political activities* 公開的政治活動

over·take /ˌəʊvəˈteɪk; *NAmE* ˌoʊvərˈt-/ *verb* (**over·took** /-ˈtʊk/, **over·taken** /-ˈteɪkən/) **1** [T, I] **~ (sb/sth)** (*especially BrE*) to go past a moving vehicle or person ahead of you because you are going faster than they are 超過；趕上： *He pulled out to overtake a truck.* 他駛出車流，以超過一輛卡車。 ◇ *It's dangerous to overtake on a bend.* 在彎道強行超車是危險的。 **2** [T] **~ sb/sth** to become greater in number, amount or importance than sth else （在數量或重要性方面）大於，超過 SYN **outstrip**： *Nuclear energy may overtake oil as the main fuel.* 核能可能會超過石油成為主要燃料。 ◇ *We mustn't let ourselves be overtaken by our competitors.* 我們決不能讓競爭對手超過我們。 **3** [T, often passive] **~ sb/sth** if sth unpleasant **overtakes** a person, it unexpectedly starts to happen and to affect them （不愉快的事情）突然發生，突然降臨：*The climbers were overtaken by bad weather.* 登山者突然遭遇了惡劣天氣。 ◇ *Sudden panic overtook her.* 她突然感到一陣恐慌。 ◇ *Our original plan was* ***overtaken by events*** (= the situation changed very rapidly) *and we had to make a new one.* 我們原來的計劃沒趕上變化，只好再訂一個新的。

over·tax /ˌəʊvəˈtæks; *NAmE* ˌoʊvərˈt-/ *verb* **1 ~ sb/sth/yourself** to do more than you are able or want to do; to make sb/sth do more than they are able or want to do 使用過度；（使）超負荷工作： *to overtax your strength* 過度使用體力 ◇ *Take it easy. Don't overtax yourself.* 輕鬆一點，別讓自己勞累過度。 **2 ~ sb/sth** to make a person or an organization pay too much tax （對人或機構）課稅過重，多收稅款

ˌover-the-ˈcounter *adj.* [only before noun] **1** (of drugs and medicines 藥品) that can be obtained without a PRESCRIPTION (= a written order from a doctor) 無需處方可買到的；非處方的 **2** (*business* 商) (*NAmE*) (of stocks and shares 股票及證券) not appearing in an official STOCK EXCHANGE list 場外交易的

over·throw *verb, noun*

■ ***verb*** /ˌəʊvəˈθrəʊ; *NAmE* ˌoʊvərˈθroʊ/ (**over·threw** /-ˈθruː/, **over·thrown** /-ˈθrəʊn; *NAmE* -ˈθroʊn/) **~ sb/sth** to remove a leader or a government from a position of power by force 推翻；打倒；趕下台： *The president was over-thrown in a military coup.* 總統在軍事政變中被趕下台。

■ ***noun*** /ˈəʊvəθrəʊ; *NAmE* ˈoʊvərθroʊ/ [usually sing.] the act of taking power by force from a leader or government 推翻；打倒

over·time /ˈəʊvətaɪm; *NAmE* ˈoʊvərt-/ *noun* [U] **1** time that you spend working at your job after you have worked the normal hours 加班；加班的時間： *to* ***do/work overtime*** 加班 ◇ ***overtime pay/earnings/hours*** 加班費／收入／時間 ◇ *The union announced a ban on overtime.* 工會宣佈禁止加班。 ➲ COLLOCATIONS at JOB **2** the money sb earns for doing overtime 加班費： *They pay $150 a day plus overtime.* 他們支付每天 150 元的報酬，外加加班費。 **3** (*NAmE*) (*BrE* **ˌextra ˈtime**) (*sport* 體) a set period of time that is added to the end of a sports game, etc., if there is no winner at the end of the normal period （體育比賽等的）加時，加時賽

IDM **be working ˈovertime** (*informal*) to be very active or too active 非常活躍；過分活躍： *There was nothing to worry about. It was just her imagination working overtime.* 沒什麼可擔心的。那只是她的想像力太活躍了。

over·tired /ˌəʊvəˈtaɪəd; *NAmE* ˌoʊvərˈtaɪərd/ *adj.* extremely tired, so that you become irritated easily 勞累過度（而煩躁）的

over·tone /ˈəʊvətəʊn; *NAmE* ˈoʊvərtoʊn/ *noun* [usually pl.] an attitude or an emotion that is suggested and is not expressed in a direct way 弦外之音；言外之意；暗示： *There were political overtones to the point he was making.* 他的論點有政治寓意。 ➲ compare UNDERTONE

over·took *past tense* of OVERTAKE

over·train /ˌəʊvəˈtreɪn; *NAmE* ˌoʊvərˈt-/ *verb* [I] (of an ATHLETE 運動員) to train too hard or for too long 過度訓練

over·ture /ˈəʊvətʃʊə(r); -tjʊə(r); *NAmE* ˈoʊvərtʃər; -tʃʊr/ *noun* **1** a piece of music written as an introduction to an OPERA or a BALLET （歌劇或芭蕾舞的）序曲，前奏曲： *Prokofiev's overture to 'Romeo and Juliet'* 普羅科菲耶夫的《羅密歐與朱麗葉》的序曲 **2** [usually pl.] **~ (to sb)** a suggestion or an action by which sb tries to make friends, start a business relationship, have discussions, etc. with sb else 友好姿態；建議： *He began* ***making overtures to*** *a number of merchant banks.* 他開始主動同一些投資銀行接觸。

over·turn /ˌəʊvəˈtɜːn; *NAmE* ˌoʊvərˈtɜːrn/ *verb* **1** [I, T] if sth **overturns**, or if sb **overturns** it, it turns upside down or on its side 傾倒；傾覆；翻掉： *The car skidded and overturned.* 汽車打滑翻倒了。 ◇ **~ sth** *He stood up quickly, overturning his chair.* 他猛然站起來，弄翻了椅子。 **2** [T] **~ sth** to officially decide that a legal decision, etc. is not correct, and to make it no longer valid 推翻，撤銷（判決等）： *to* ***overturn a decision/conviction/verdict*** 撤銷決定／定罪／裁決 ◇ *His sentence was over-turned by the appeal court.* 上訴法庭撤銷了對他的判決。

over·use /ˌəʊvəˈjuːz; *NAmE* ˌoʊvərˈj-/ *verb* **~ sth** to use sth too much or too often 使用過度；濫用： *'Nice' is a very overused word.* * nice 一詞用得實在太濫了。 ▸ **over·use** /ˌəʊvəˈjuːs; *NAmE* ˌoʊvərˈj-/ *noun* [U, sing.]

over·value /ˌəʊvəˈvæljuː; *NAmE* ˌoʊvərˈv-/ *verb* [often passive] **~ sth** to put too high a value on sth 估計過高；過於重視： *Intelligence cannot be overvalued.* 智力是無比重要的。◇ (*business* 商) *overvalued currencies/stocks* 估價過高的貨幣／股票

over·view /ˈəʊvəvjuː; *NAmE* ˈoʊvərv-/ *noun* a general description or an outline of sth 概述；縱覽；概論；概況 SYN **survey, 10 000-foot view, helicopter view** ➲ LANGUAGE BANK at ABOUT

over·ween·ing /ˌəʊvəˈwiːnɪŋ; *NAmE* ˌoʊvərˈw-/ *adj.* [only before noun] (*formal, disapproving*) showing too much confidence or pride 傲慢的；自負的；過於自信的 SYN **arrogant**

over·weight /ˌəʊvəˈweɪt; *NAmE* ˌoʊvərˈw-/ *adj.* **1** (of people 人) too heavy and fat 太胖的；超重的： *She was only a few pounds overweight.* 她只是超重幾磅而已。 OPP **underweight** ➲ COLLOCATIONS at DIET **2** above an allowed weight 超過限制重量的；過重的： *overweight baggage* 超重的行李

O

over·whelm /ˌəʊvəˈwelm; *NAmE* ˌoʊvərˈw-/ *verb* [often passive] **1 ~ sb** to have such a strong emotional effect on sb that it is difficult for them to resist or know how to react（感情或感覺）充溢，難以禁受 SYN **overcome**：*She was overwhelmed by feelings of guilt.* 她感到愧疚難當。◇ *The beauty of the landscape overwhelmed me.* 秀麗的風光令我深深地陶醉。 **2 ~ sb** to defeat sb completely 壓倒；擊敗；征服 SYN **overpower**：*The army was overwhelmed by the rebels.* 軍隊被叛亂者完全擊敗了。 **3 ~ sb** to be so bad or so great that a person cannot deal with it; to give too much of a thing to a person 壓垮；使應接不暇：*We were overwhelmed by requests for information.* 各方的問訊使我們應接不暇。 **4 ~ sb/sth** (*literary*) (of water 水) to cover sb/sth completely 淹沒；漫過 SYN **flood**

over·whelm·ing /ˌəʊvəˈwelmɪŋ; *NAmE* ˌoʊvərˈw-/ *adj.* very great or very strong; so powerful that you cannot resist it or decide how to react 巨大的；壓倒性的；無法抗拒的：*The evidence against him was overwhelming.* 對他不利的證據確鑿，無法抵賴。◇ *The* ***overwhelming majority*** *of those present were in favour of the plan.* 絕大多數與會者都贊同這個計劃。◇ *an* ***overwhelming sense of*** *loss* 莫大的失落感◇ *She had the almost overwhelming desire to tell him the truth.* 她恨不得要告訴他實情。◇ *You may find it somewhat overwhelming at first.* 起初你可能覺得有些無法抗拒。▸ **over·whelm·ing·ly** *adv.*：*They voted overwhelmingly against the proposal.* 他們以壓倒多數票反對這項提案。

over·winter /ˌəʊvəˈwɪntə(r); *NAmE* ˌoʊvərˈw-/ *verb* [I, T] **~ (sth)** (of animals, birds and plants 鳥獸和植物) to spend the winter months in a place; to stay alive or to keep sth alive during the winter（使）越冬，度過冬天 ➲ compare WINTER *v.*

over·work /ˌəʊvəˈwɜːk; *NAmE* ˌoʊvərˈwɜːrk/ *verb, noun*

■ ***verb*** [I, T] to work too hard; to make a person or an animal work too hard（使）過度勞累，過分努力：*You look tired. Have you been overworking?* 你似乎很疲倦，是不是近來勞累過度了？◇ **~ sb/sth** *She overworks her staff.* 她讓員工過度勞累。

■ ***noun*** [U] the fact of working too hard 勞累過度；過分辛苦：*His illness was brought on by money worries and overwork.* 他的病是因操心錢和勞累過度而造成的。

over·worked /ˌəʊvəˈwɜːkt; *NAmE* ˌoʊvərˈwɜːrkt/ *adj.* **1** made to work too hard or too much 工作過多的；勞累過度的：*overworked nurses* 勞累過度的護士 **2** (of words or phrases 詞語) used too often so that the meaning or effect has become weaker 用得過濫的；濫而無效的

over·write /ˌəʊvəˈraɪt; *NAmE* ˌoʊvərˈr-/ *verb* (**over·wrote** /-ˈrəʊt; *NAmE* -ˈroʊt/, **over·writ·ten** /-ˈrɪtn/) **~ sth** (*computing* 計) to replace information on the screen or in a file by putting new information over it 蓋寫；重寫

over·wrought /ˌəʊvəˈrɔːt; *NAmE* ˌoʊvərˈr-/ *adj.* very worried and upset; excited in a nervous way 過度緊張的；過分憂煩的；緊張激動的 SYN **distraught**

over·zeal·ous /ˌəʊvəˈzeləs; *NAmE* ˌoʊvərˈz-/ *adj.* showing too much energy or enthusiasm 過於熱心的；激情過高的：*An overzealous fan ran onto the stage during the concert.* 音樂會上，一名狂熱的歌迷衝到了台上。

ovi·duct /ˈəʊvɪdʌkt; *NAmE* ˈoʊ-/ *noun* (*anatomy* 解) either of the tubes that carry eggs from the OVARIES in women and female animals 輸卵管

ovine /ˈəʊvaɪn; *NAmE* ˈoʊ-/ *adj.* (*technical* 術語) relating to sheep 羊的；與羊有關的

ovip·ar·ous /əʊˈvɪpərəs; *NAmE* oʊ-/ *adj.* (*biology* 生) (of an animal 動物) producing eggs rather than live babies 卵生的 ➲ compare OVOVIVIPAROUS, VIVIPAROUS

ovoid /ˈəʊvɔɪd; *NAmE* ˈoʊ-/ *adj.* (*formal*) shaped like an egg 蛋形的；卵形的 ▸ **ovoid** *noun*

ovo·vi·vip·ar·ous /ˌəʊvəʊvɪˈvɪpərəs; *NAmE* ˌoʊvoʊ-/ *adj.* (*biology* 生) (of an animal 動物) producing babies by means of eggs that are HATCHED inside the body of the parent, like some snakes 卵胎生的 ➲ compare OVIPAROUS, VIVIPAROUS

ovu·late /ˈɒvjuleɪt; *NAmE* ˈɑːv-/ *verb* [I] (of a woman or a female animal 女性或母獸) to produce an egg (called an OVUM), from the OVARY 產卵；排卵 ▸ **ovu·la·tion** /ˌɒvjuˈleɪʃn; *NAmE* ˌɑːv-/ *noun* [U]：*methods of predicting ovulation* 預測排卵的方法

ovule /ˈɒvjuːl; ˈəʊ-; *NAmE* ˈoʊ-/ *noun* (*biology* 生) the part of the OVARY of a plant containing the female cell, which becomes the seed when it is FERTILIZED 胚珠 ➲ **VISUAL VOCAB** page V11

ovum /ˈəʊvəm; *NAmE* ˈoʊ-/ *noun* (*pl.* **ova** /ˈəʊvə; *NAmE* ˈoʊvə/) (*biology* 生) a female cell of an animal or a plant that can develop into a young animal or plant when FERTILIZED 卵；卵子；卵細胞

ow /aʊ/ *exclamation* used to express sudden pain（表示疼痛）哎呦：*Ow! That hurt!* 哎呦！疼死我了！

owe 🗝 /əʊ; *NAmE* oʊ/ *verb* (not used in the progressive tenses 不用於進行時)
1 🗝 to have to pay sb for sth that you have already received or return money that you have borrowed 欠（債）；欠（賬）：**~ sb sth** *She still owes her father £3 000.* 她還欠她父親 3 000 英鎊。◇ (*figurative*) *I'm still owed three days' leave.* 還欠我三天假。◇ **~ sb sth for sth** *How much do I owe you for the groceries?* 買這些雜貨我得給你多少錢？◇ **~ sth (to sb) (for sth)** *She still owes £3 000 to her father.* 她還欠她父親 3 000 英鎊。◇ *The country owes billions of dollars to foreign creditors.* 這個國家欠外國債權人數十億元。 **2** 🗝 to feel that you ought to do sth for sb or give them sth, especially because they have done sth for you 欠（情）：**~ sth to sb** *I owe a debt of gratitude to all my family.* 我很感激我的全家人。◇ *You* ***owe it to*** *your staff to be honest with them.* 與下屬坦誠相待，這是你對他們應有的態度。◇ **~ sb sth** *You owe me a favour!* 你還欠我個人情哪！◇ *Thanks for sticking up for me—I* ***owe you one*** (= I owe you a favour). 謝謝你支持我，我欠你一個情。◇ *I think you owe us an explanation.* 我認為你應當給我們一個解釋。◇ *I think we're owed an apology.* 我認為得有人向我們道歉。 **HELP** The passive is not used in this meaning except with a person as the subject. 除了以人作主語外，這一義項不用被動語態：~~*An apology is owed to us.*~~ **3** to exist or be successful because of the help or influence of sb/sth 歸因於；歸功於；起源於：**~ sth to sb/sth** *He owes his success to hard work.* 他的成功是靠勤奮工作。◇ *The play owes much to French tragedy.* 這部戲頗受法國悲劇的影響。◇ *I owe everything to him.* 我的一切都歸功於他。◇ **~ sb sth** *I owe him everything.* 我的一切都歸功於他。◇ *I knew that I owed the surgeon my life.* 我明白外科醫生救了我的命。 **4 ~ allegiance/loyalty/obedience (to sb)** (*formal*) to have to obey or be loyal to sb who is in a position of authority or power（對位高權重者）忠誠，服從

owing /ˈəʊɪŋ; *NAmE* ˈoʊɪŋ/ *adj.* [not before noun] money that is **owing** has not been paid yet 拖欠；未付；未償還：*£100 is still owing on the loan.* 還有 100 英鎊貸款未還。

ˈowing to *prep.* because of 因為；由於：*The game was cancelled owing to torrential rain.* 比賽因大雨取消了。

owl /aʊl/ *noun* a BIRD OF PREY (= a bird that kills other creatures for food) with large round eyes, that hunts at night. Owls are traditionally thought to be wise. 貓頭鷹，鴞（傳統上認為是智慧的象徵）：*An owl hooted nearby.* 一隻貓頭鷹在附近啼叫。➲ see also BARN OWL, NIGHT OWL, TAWNY OWL

owlet /ˈaʊlət/ *noun* a young OWL 鴞類幼體；小型貓頭鷹

owl·ish /ˈaʊlɪʃ/ *adj.* looking like an owl, especially because you are wearing round glasses, and therefore seeming serious and intelligent 似貓頭鷹的；儒雅的 ▸ **owl·ish·ly** *adv.*：*She blinked at them owlishly.* 她斯文地向他們眨了眨眼。

own 🗝 /əʊn; *NAmE* oʊn/ *adj., pron., verb*

■ ***adj., pron.*** **1** 🗝 used to emphasize that sth belongs to or is connected with sb（用於強調）自己的，本人的：*It was her own idea.* 那是她自己的主意。◇ *I saw it with my own eyes* (= I didn't hear about it from somebody else). 我親眼看見的。◇ *Is the car your own?* 這輛汽車是你自己的嗎？◇ *Your day off is your own* (= you can spend it as you wish). 你的假日歸你自己支配。◇ *Our children* *are grown up and have children* ***of their own.*** 我們的子女都已長大成人，有了自己的孩子。◇ ***For reasons of his own*** (= particular reasons that perhaps only he knew about), *he refused to join the club.* 由於他個人的原因，他謝絕加入俱樂部。◇ *The accident happened* ***through no fault of her own.*** 這一事故的發生不是她本人的過錯。◇ *He wants to come into the business* ***on his own terms.*** 他想依自己開出的條件加入該公司。◇ *I need a room* ***of my own.*** 我需要有一間自己的房間。◇ *I have my* ***very own*** *room at last.* 我終於有了我自己的房間了！ **HELP** Own cannot be used after an article. * own 不能用在冠詞之後： *I need my own room.* ◇ *~~I need an own room.~~* ◇ *It's good to have your own room.* ◇ *~~It's good to have the own room.~~* **2** done or produced by and for yourself 自己做的；為自己的： *She makes all her own clothes.* 她的衣服都是自己做。◇ *He has to cook his own meals.* 他必須自己做飯。

IDM **come into your/its 'own** to have the opportunity to show how good or useful you are or sth is 得到充分的發揮： *When the traffic's this bad, a bicycle really comes into its own.* 在交通如此擁堵的時候，自行車就顯出了它的價值。 **get your 'own back (on sb)** (*informal*) to do sth to sb in return for harm they have done to you; to get REVENGE 報復： *I'll get my own back on him one day, I swear!* 我發誓，我總有一天要報復他的！ **hold your 'own (against sb/sth) (in sth)** to remain in a strong position when sb is attacking you, competing with you, etc. 堅守立場；（使自己）立於不敗之地： *Business isn't good but we're managing to hold our own.* 生意不景氣，但我們正設法堅持下去。◇ *She can hold her own against anybody in an argument.* 她在辯論中不會讓任何人佔上風。◇ *The patient is holding her own although she is still very sick.* 病人的病情仍然很重，但她還在支持着。 **(all) on your 'own** **1** alone; without anyone else 獨自；單獨： *I'm all on my own today.* 今天就我一個人。◇ *She lives on her own.* 她一個人生活。 **2** without help 獨立地： *He did it on his own.* 這件事他獨立完成了。 ➲ more at DEVIL, MIND *n.*, SOUND *n.*

■ ***verb*** (not used in the progressive tenses 不用於進行時) **1** [T] **~ sth** to have sth that belongs to you, especially because you have bought it 擁有，有（尤指買來的東西）： *Do you own your house or do you rent it?* 你的房子是自己的，還是租的？◇ *I don't own anything of any value.* 我沒有任何值錢的東西。◇ *Most of the apartments are privately owned.* 多數公寓房都是私人的。◇ *an American-owned company* 一家美資公司 **2** [I, T] (*old-fashioned*) to admit that sth is true 承認： **~ to sth/to doing sth** *He owned to a feeling of guilt.* 他承認有歉疚感。◇ **~ (that)** ... *She owned (that) she had been present.* 她承認她當時在場。

IDM **,behave/,act as if you 'own the place | think you 'own the place** (*disapproving*) to behave in a very confident way that annoys other people, for example by telling them what to do（言行）喧賓奪主

PHR V **,own 'up (to sth/to doing sth)** to admit that you are responsible for sth bad or wrong 承擔責任；認錯；坦白 **SYN** **confess**： *I'm still waiting for someone to own up to the breakages.* 我還在等着有人承認把東西打碎了。

,own-'brand (also **,own-'label**) (both *BrE*) (*US* **'store-brand**) *adj.* used to describe goods that are marked with the name of the shop/store in which they are sold rather than with the name of the company that produced them 自有品牌的（指產品以商店自定的品牌出售）

owner /'əʊnə(r); *NAmE* 'oʊ-/ *noun* a person who owns sth 物主；所有權人；主人： *a dog/factory owner* 狗的主人；廠主◇ *The painting has been returned to its* ***rightful owner.*** 這幅畫已歸還給合法所有權人。◇ *He's now the* ***proud owner*** *of a cottage in Wales.* 現在他很得意自己在威爾士有一座小別墅。 ➲ see also HOMEOWNER, LANDOWNER

,owner-'occupied *adj.* (of a house, etc. 房子等) lived in by the owner rather than rented to sb else 房主自用的

,owner-'occupier *noun* a person who owns the house, flat/apartment, etc. that they live in 住自家房屋者；房屋自用者

own·er·ship /'əʊnəʃɪp; *NAmE* 'oʊnərʃɪp/ *noun* [U] the fact of owning sth 所有權；產權；物主身分： *a growth in home ownership* 房屋所有權的增長◇ *Ownership of the land is currently being disputed.* 這塊土地的所有權現在還有爭議。◇ *to be in* ***joint/private/public ownership*** 為共有／私有／公有產權◇ *The restaurant is under new ownership.* 這家餐廳已換了新的經營者。

,own 'goal *noun* [usually sing.] (*BrE*) **1** (in football (SOCCER) 足球) a goal that is scored by mistake by a player against his or her own team 烏龍球；射進自家球門的球 **2** something that you do that achieves the opposite of what you wanted and that brings you a disadvantage 幫倒忙的事；無意中讓自己吃虧的事

,own-'label *adj.* (*BrE*) = OWN-BRAND

owt /aʊt/ *pron.* (*BrE, dialect, informal*) anything 任何事物；任何東西： *I didn't say owt.* 我什麼也沒說。

ox /ɒks; *NAmE* ɑːks/ *noun* (*pl.* **oxen** /'ɒksn; *NAmE* 'ɑːksn/) **1** a BULL (= a male cow) that has been CASTRATED (= had part of its sex organs removed), used, especially in the past, for pulling farm equipment, etc. （閹割的）公牛；去勢公牛 ➲ compare BULLOCK, STEER *n.* (2) **2** (*old-fashioned*) any cow or BULL on a farm 飼養的牛 ➲ see also CATTLE

oxbow 曲流灣

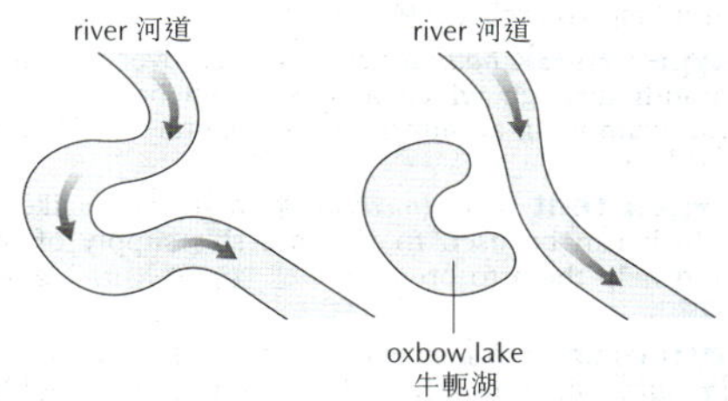

oxbow /'ɒksbəʊ; *NAmE* 'ɑːksboʊ/ *noun* (*technical* 術語) a bend in a river that almost forms a full circle; a lake that forms when this bend is separated from the river 河道曲流灣；牛軛湖

Ox·bridge /'ɒksbrɪdʒ; *NAmE* 'ɑːks-/ *noun* [U] the universities of Oxford and Cambridge, when they are thought of together 牛津劍橋大學： *an Oxbridge education* 牛津劍橋的教育 ➲ compare IVY LEAGUE, RED-BRICK (2)

ox·ford /'ɒksfəd; *NAmE* 'ɑːksfərd/ *noun* **1** **oxfords** [pl.] (*especially NAmE*) leather shoes that fasten with LACES 牛津鞋（一種繫鞋帶的皮鞋） ➲ compare LACE-UP ➲ **VISUAL VOCAB** page V64 **2** [U] = OXFORD CLOTH： *an oxford shirt* 一件牛津布襯衣

,oxford 'cloth (also **ox·ford**) *noun* [U] (*NAmE*) a type of heavy cotton cloth used mainly for making shirts 牛津布（厚棉布，做襯衫用）

oxi·dant /'ɒksɪdənt; *NAmE* 'ɑːks-/ *noun* (*chemistry* 化) a substance that makes another substance combine with oxygen 氧化劑

oxide /'ɒksaɪd; *NAmE* 'ɑːk-/ *noun* [U, C] (*chemistry* 化) a COMPOUND of OXYGEN and another chemical element 氧化物： *iron oxide* 氧化鐵◇ *an oxide of tin* 氧化錫

oxi·dize (*BrE* also **-ise**) /'ɒksɪdaɪz; *NAmE* 'ɑːk-/ *verb* [T, I] **~ (sth)** (*chemistry* 化) to remove one or more ELECTRONS from a substance, or to combine or to make sth combine with OXYGEN, especially when this causes metal to become covered with RUST （使）氧化；（尤指使）生銹 ▸ **oxi·da·tion** /,ɒksɪ'deɪʃn; *NAmE* ,ɑːk-/ *noun* [U] ➲ compare REDUCE (4), REDUCTION (4)

Oxon /'ɒksɒn; *NAmE* 'ɑːksɑːn/ *abbr.* (used after degree titles) of Oxford University（用於學位名稱後）牛津大學的： *Alice Tolley MA (Oxon)* 文科碩士艾麗斯 • 托利（牛津大學）

Oxon·ian /ɒk'səʊniən; *NAmE* ɑːk'soʊ-/ *adj.* (*formal* or *humorous*) relating to Oxford in England, or to Oxford University（英格蘭）牛津的，牛津大學的

ox·tail /'ɒksteɪl; *NAmE* 'ɑːks-/ *noun* [U, C] meat from the tail of a cow, used especially for making soup 牛尾肉（通常用於做湯）：*oxtail soup* 牛尾湯

oxter /'ɒkstə(r); *NAmE* 'ɑːks-/ *noun* (*BrE, dialect, informal*) a person's ARMPIT 胳肢窩；腋窩

oxy·acet·yl·ene /ˌɒksiə'setəliːn; *NAmE* ˌɑːk-/ *adj.* connected with a mixture of oxygen and ACETYLENE gas which produces a very hot flame, used especially for cutting or joining metal 氧乙炔的（尤用於切割或焊接金屬）：*an oxyacetylene torch* 氧乙炔炬

oxy·gen /'ɒksɪdʒən; *NAmE* 'ɑːk-/ *noun* [U] (*symb.* **O**) a chemical element. Oxygen is a gas that is present in air and water and is necessary for people, animals and plants to live. 氧；氧氣

oxy·gen·ate /'ɒksɪdʒəneɪt; *NAmE* 'ɑːk-/ *verb* ~ **sth** (*technical* 術語) to supply sth with oxygen 供氧；輸氧 ▸ **oxy·gen·ation** *noun* [U]

oxy·gen·ator /'ɒksɪdʒəneɪtə(r); *NAmE* 'ɑːks-/ *noun* **1** (*medical* 醫) a device for putting oxygen into the blood 氧合器；人工肺 **2** a water plant that puts oxygen into the water around it 富氧水草；富氧水生植物

'oxygen bar *noun* a place where you can pay to breathe pure oxygen in order to improve your health and help you relax 氧吧

'oxygen mask *noun* a device placed over the nose and mouth through which a person can breathe OXYGEN, for example in an aircraft or a hospital 氧氣面具；氧氣面罩

'oxygen tent *noun* (*medical* 醫) a structure like a tent which can be used to increase sb's supply of oxygen and help them to breathe（急救輸氧用的）氧幕；氧氣帳

O

oxy·moron /ˌɒksɪ'mɔːrɒn; *NAmE* ˌɑːksɪ'mɔːrɑːn/ *noun* (*technical* 術語) a phrase that combines two words that seem to be the opposite of each other, for example *a deafening silence* 矛盾修辭法

oy *exclamation* = OI

oyez (also **oyes**) /əʊ'jeɪ; *NAmE* oʊ-/ *exclamation* used by a TOWN CRIER or an officer in court to tell people to be quiet and pay attention（街頭公告員或法庭官員用語）肅靜

oys·ter /'ɔɪstə(r)/ *noun* a large flat SHELLFISH. Some types of oyster can be eaten and others produce shiny white JEWELS called PEARLS. 牡蠣；蠔：*Oyster beds, on the mudflats, are a form of fish farming.* 灘塗牡蠣養殖場是一種水產養殖方式。➲ picture at SHELLFISH **IDM** see WORLD

oys·ter·catch·er /'ɔɪstəkætʃə(r); *NAmE* 'ɔɪstərk-/ *noun* a black bird with long legs and a long red beak that lives near the coast and feeds on SHELLFISH 蠣鷸（捕食貝類的濱鳥）

'oyster mushroom *noun* a type of wide, flat FUNGUS that grows on trees and that you can eat 平菇；蠔菇

oy vey /ˌɔɪ 'veɪ/ *exclamation* used for showing disappointment or sadness (mainly by Yiddish speakers or Jewish people)（主要為講依地語者或猶太人使用，表示失望或悲傷）哎呀，天哪

Oz /ɒz; *NAmE* ɑːz/ *noun* [U] (*BrE, AustralE, NZE, informal*) Australia 澳大利亞；澳洲

oz *abbr.* OUNCE(S)：*4oz sugar* * 4 盎司的糖

ozone /'əʊzəʊn; *NAmE* 'oʊzoʊn/ *noun* [U] **1** (*chemistry* 化) a poisonous gas with a strong smell that is a form of OXYGEN 臭氧 **2** (*BrE, informal*) air near the sea that smells fresh and pure 海邊的清新空氣

ˌozone-'friend·ly *adj.* not containing substances that will damage the OZONE LAYER 無害臭氧層的；不含損害臭氧層物質的

'ozone hole *noun* an area in the ozone layer where the amount of OZONE has been very much reduced so that harmful RADIATION from the sun can pass through it 臭氧洞

'ozone layer *noun* [sing.] a layer of OZONE high above the earth's surface that helps to protect the earth from harmful RADIATION from the sun 臭氧層 ➲ COLLOCATIONS at ENVIRONMENT

Oz·zie = AUSSIE

Pp

P (also **p**) /piː/ *noun* [C, U] (*pl.* **Ps**, **P's**, **p's** /piːz/) the 16th letter of the English alphabet 英語字母表的第 16 個字母：*'Pizza' begins with (a) P/'P'.* * pizza 一詞以字母 p 開頭。**IDM** see MIND *v.*

p (also **p.**) *abbr.* **1** (*pl.* **pp.**) page 頁：*See p.34 and pp.63-72.* 見第 34 頁及第 63–72 頁。**2** PENNY, PENCE 便士：*a 30p stamp* 一枚 30 便士的郵票 **3** (*music* 音) quietly (from Italian 'piano') 輕柔地；安靜地；弱 ➲ see also P. AND P., P. AND H.

PA /ˌpiː ˈeɪ/ *abbr.* **1** PUBLIC ADDRESS (SYSTEM)：*Announcements were made over the PA.* 通告是從廣播系統播出的。**2** (*especially BrE*) PERSONAL ASSISTANT：*She's the Managing Director's PA.* 她是總經理的私人助理。

Pa *abbr.* PASCAL 帕（斯卡）（標準壓強單位）

pa /pɑː/ *noun* (*old-fashioned, informal*) father 爹；爸爸：*I used to know your pa.* 我過去跟你爸爸很熟。

p.a. *abbr.* per year (from Latin 'per annum') 每年（源自拉丁語 per annum）：*an increase of 3% p.a.* 每年 3% 的增長

paan (also **pan**) /pɑːn/ *noun* [U, C] (*IndE*) a BETEL leaf, usually folded into a shape with three sides and filled with spices for eating 蔞葉，蒟醬葉包檳榔，包葉檳榔（通常摺成粽子狀食用）

PAC /ˌpiː ei ˈsiː/ *abbr.* POLITICAL ACTION COMMITTEE

pace¹ 🔑 /peɪs/ *noun, verb* ➲ see also PACE²

■ ***noun*** **1** 🔑 [sing., U] the speed at which sb/sth walks, runs or moves（移動的）速度；步速：*to set off **at a steady/gentle/leisurely pace*** 以穩定的／徐緩的／悠閒的步子出發 ◇ *Congestion frequently reduces traffic to **walking pace**.* 交通阻塞經常把車流的速度降低得如步行一般緩慢。◇ *The ball **gathered pace** as it rolled down the hill.* 球向山下滾動，速度越來越快。◇ *The runners have noticeably quickened their pace.* 賽跑者明顯加快了腳步。**2** 🔑 [sing., U] **~ (of sth)** the speed at which sth happens 發生的速度；步伐；節奏：*It is difficult to keep up with the rapid pace of change.* 跟上快速的變化步伐是很困難的。◇ *We encourage all students to work **at their own pace*** (= as fast or as slow as they can). 我們鼓勵學生都按自己的節奏學習。◇ *I prefer the relaxed **pace of life** in the country.* 我喜愛鄉間那悠閒的生活節奏。◇ *Rumours of corruption and scandal **gathered pace*** (= increased in number). 腐化墮落的傳聞日益增多。**3** 🔑 [C] an act of stepping once when walking or running; the distance travelled when doing this（走或跑時）邁出的一步，一步的距離；步幅 **SYN** **step**：*She took two paces forward.* 她向前走了兩步。**4** [U] the fact of sth happening, changing, etc. quickly 迅速出現（或變化等）；快節奏：*He gave up his job in advertising because he couldn't **stand the pace**.* 他辭去了廣告業的工作，因為他承受不了那種快節奏。◇ *The novel lacks pace* (= it develops too slowly). 這部小說缺乏節奏感。➲ see also PACY

IDM **go through your 'paces | show your 'paces** to perform a particular activity in order to show other people what you are capable of doing 展示自己的能力 **keep 'pace (with sb/sth)** to move, increase, change, etc. at the same speed as sb/sth（與…）並駕齊驅；（與…）步調一致：*She found it hard to keep pace with him as he strode off.* 他大步走開了，她感到很難跟上他。◇ *Until now, wage increases have always kept pace with inflation.* 到目前為止，工資的增長與通貨膨脹始終保持同步。**off the 'pace** (in sport 體育運動) behind the leader or the leading group in a race or a competition（賽跑或比賽中）在領頭人之後，在領頭隊之後：*Tiger Woods is still three shots off the pace* (= in GOLF). 泰格 • 伍茲仍落後領先選手三杆。**put sb/sth through their/its 'paces** to give sb/sth a number of tasks to perform in order to see what they are capable of doing 考察，考驗（某人的能力）**set the 'pace 1** to do sth at a particular speed or to a particular standard so that other people are then forced to copy it if they want to be successful 確定速度；確立標準；領先：*The company is no longer setting the pace in the home computer market.* 這家公司再也不能在國內計算機市場上獨領風騷了。**2** (in a race 跑步比賽) to run faster than the other people taking part, at a speed that they then try to copy 領跑 ➲ more at FORCE *v.*, SNAIL

■ ***verb*** **1** [I, T] to walk up and down in a small area many times, especially because you are feeling nervous or angry 來回踱步；走來走去：**+ adv./prep.** *She **paced up and down** outside the room.* 她在屋子外面來回走着。◇ **~ sth** *Ted paced the floor restlessly.* 特德焦躁地在屋裏走來走去。**2** [T] **~ sth** to set the speed at which sth happens or develops 確定速度；調整節奏：*He paced his game skilfully.* 他巧妙地控制着自己的比賽節奏。**3** [T] **~ yourself** to find the right speed or rhythm for your work or an activity so that you have enough energy to do what you have to do 調整自己的工作（或活動）節奏：*He'll have to learn to pace himself in this job.* 他必須學會使自己適應這項工作的節奏。

PHR V **ˌpace sth↔'off/'out** to measure the size of sth by walking across it with regular steps 以步丈量

pace² /ˈpɑːkeɪ; ˈpɑːtʃeɪ; ˈpeɪsi/ *prep.* (from *Latin, formal*) used before a person's name to express polite disagreement with what they have said（用於人名前，委婉提出不同意見）請…原諒：*The evidence suggests, pace Professor Jones, that ...* (= Professor Jones has a different opinion). 請瓊斯教授原諒，證據表明… ➲ see also PACE¹

ˌpace 'bowler *noun* = FAST BOWLER

pace·maker /ˈpeɪsmeɪkə(r)/ *noun* **1** an electronic device that is put inside a person's body to help their heart beat regularly 心臟起搏器；心律調整器 **2** (also **pace·setter** especially in *NAmE*) a person or an animal that begins a race quickly so that the other people taking part will try to copy the speed and run a fast race 領跑人；領跑動物：(*figurative*) *The big banks have been the pacesetters in developing the system.* 大銀行歷來是發展這一體系的先驅。**3** (also **pace·setter** especially in *NAmE*) a person or team that is winning in a sports competition（競賽中的）領先者，領先隊伍：*The local club are now only one point off the pacemakers.* 當地俱樂部與領先者只差一分。

pace·man /ˈpeɪsmæn/ *noun* (*pl.* **-men** /-men/) = FAST BOWLER

pace·setter /ˈpeɪssetə(r)/ *noun* (*especially NAmE*) = PACEMAKER

pacey = PACY

pa·chinko /pəˈtʃɪŋkəʊ; *NAmE* -koʊ/ *noun* [U] (from *Japanese*) a Japanese form of PINBALL, in which you can win prizes 彈球盤，柏青哥（一種日本賭博遊戲）

pachy·derm /ˈpækidɜːm; *NAmE* -dɜːrm/ *noun* (*technical* 術語) a type of animal with a very thick skin, for example, an ELEPHANT 厚皮動物（如大象）

pa·cif·ic /pəˈsɪfɪk/ *adj.* [usually before noun] (*literary*) peaceful or loving peace 平靜的；和平的；愛和平的

Paˌcific 'Daylight Time *noun* [U] (*abbr.* **PDT**) the time used in summer in the western parts of Canada and the US that is seven hours earlier than GMT 太平洋日光節約時間，太平洋夏令時間（加拿大和美國西部地區的夏季時間，比格林尼治平時早七個小時）

the Paˌcific 'Rim *noun* [sing.] the countries around the Pacific Ocean, especially the countries of eastern Asia, considered as an economic group 太平洋周邊地區，環太平洋圈（尤指被視為經濟集團的東亞諸國）

Paˌcific 'Standard Time *noun* [U] (*abbr.* **PST**) the time used in winter in the western parts of Canada and the US that is eight hours earlier than GMT 太平洋標準時間（加拿大和美國西部地區的冬季時間，比格林尼治平時早八個小時）

Pa'cific time *noun* [U] the standard time on the west coast of the US and Canada 太平洋時間（加拿大和美國西海岸的標準時間）

paci·fier /ˈpæsɪfaɪə(r)/ (*NAmE*) (*BrE* **dummy**) *noun* a specially shaped rubber or plastic object for a baby to suck 橡皮奶嘴；橡皮奶頭

paci·fism /ˈpæsɪfɪzəm/ *noun* [U] the belief that war and violence are always wrong 和平主義；綏靖主義；反戰主義

paci·fist /ˈpæsɪfɪst/ *noun* a person who believes in pacifism and who refuses to fight in a war 和平主義者；綏靖主義者；反戰主義者 ➲ compare CONSCIENTIOUS OBJECTOR ▸ **paci·fist** *adj.* [usually before noun]: *pacifist beliefs* 和平主義者的信仰

pacify /ˈpæsɪfaɪ/ *verb* (**paci·fies**, **paci·fy·ing**, **paci·fied**, **paci·fied**) **1 ~ sb** to make sb who is angry or upset become calm and quiet 使平靜；平息；撫慰 SYN **placate**: *The baby could not be pacified.* 嬰兒怎麼也不能平靜下來。◇ *The speech was designed to pacify the irate crowd.* 演講的目的是安撫憤怒的群眾。 **2 ~ sth** to bring peace to an area where there is fighting or a war 平息戰爭；使實現和平 ▸ **paci·fi·ca·tion** /ˌpæsɪfɪˈkeɪʃn/ *noun* [U]

pack 0‑ /pæk/ *verb, noun*

■ *verb*

▸ PUT INTO CONTAINER 裝入容器 **1** 0‑ [I, T] to put clothes, etc. into a bag in preparation for a trip away from home 收拾（行李）；裝（箱）: *I haven't packed yet.* 我還沒收拾行李呢。◇ **~ sth** *I haven't packed my suitcase yet.* 我的行李箱還沒收拾好呢。◇ *He packed a bag with a few things and was off.* 他裝了幾件衣物就走了。◇ *He packed a few things into a bag.* 他裝了幾件衣物。◇ *Did you pack the camera?* 你裝進照相機了嗎？◇ **~ sb sth** *I've packed you some food for the journey.* 我給你打點了些路上吃的食物。 **2** 0‑ [T] **~ sth (up) (in/into sth)** to put sth into a container so that it can be stored, transported or sold 打包；包裝: *The pottery was packed in boxes and shipped to the US.* 陶器已裝箱運往美國。◇ *I carefully packed up the gifts.* 我小心翼翼地把禮品包好。 OPP **unpack**

▸ PROTECT 保護 **3** 0‑ [T] **~ sth (in/with sth)** to protect sth that breaks easily by surrounding it with soft material（在四周填入軟料以）包裝（易損物品）: *The paintings were carefully packed in newspaper.* 這些畫被仔細地用報紙裹了起來。

▸ PRESERVE FOOD 保存食品 **4** 0‑ [T] **~ sth (in sth)** to preserve food in a particular substance（用某物）保存，保藏: *fish packed in ice* 用冰塊保存的鮮魚

▸ FILL 填入 **5** 0‑ [I, T] to fill sth with a lot of people or things 塞進；擠進: **+ adv./prep.** *We all packed together into one car.* 我們大家擠進一輛汽車裏。◇ **~ sth (with sth)** *Fans packed the hall to see the band.* 樂迷為了一睹樂隊丰采，把大廳擠得水泄不通。 ➲ see also PACKED, PACKED OUT

▸ SNOW/SOIL 雪；土壤 **6** [T] **~ sth (down)** to press sth such as snow or soil to form a thick hard mass 堆積；壓實: *Pack the earth down around the plant.* 把植物周圍的泥土壓實。◇ *a patch of packed snow* 一片壓實的雪地

▸ CARRY GUN 攜槍 **7** [T, I] **~ (sth)** (*NAmE, informal*) to carry a gun 佩帶，攜帶（槍支）: *to pack a gun* 佩帶槍支 ◇ *Is he packing?* 他有帶槍嗎？

▸ STORM 暴風雨 **8** [T] **~ sth** to have sth 夾帶着: *A storm packing 75 mph winds swept across the area last night.* 昨晚暴雨夾帶着每小時 75 英里的狂風橫掃該地區。

IDM **pack a (powerful, real, etc.) ˈpunch** (*informal*) **1** (of a BOXER 拳擊手) to be capable of hitting sb very hard 能重拳出擊；能重擊 **2** to have a powerful effect on sb 產生巨大影響；十分有效力: *The advertising campaign packs quite a punch.* 這次廣告造勢產生了相當大的影響。 **pack your ˈbags** (*informal*) to leave a person or place permanently, especially after a disagreement（尤指產生分歧後）永遠離開 ➲ more at SEND

PHR V **ˌpack aˈway** to be capable of being folded up small when it is not being used 能摺疊（以縮小體積）: *The tent packs away in a small bag.* 帳篷可以摺疊裝進小袋子裏。 **ˌpack sth↔aˈway** to put sth in a box, etc. when you have finished using it（用後）收拾好: *We packed away the summer clothes.* 我們把夏裝收藏起來了。 **ˌpack sb↔ˈin** [no passive] (of plays, performers, etc. 戲劇、演員等) to attract a lot of people to see it/them 吸引（大批觀眾）: *The show is still* ***packing them in.*** 演出仍然吸引着大批觀眾。 **ˌpack sth↔ˈin** (*informal*) to stop doing sth 停止做某事 SYN **give up**: *She decided to pack in her job.* 她決定辭職不幹了。◇ (*especially BrE*) ***Pack it in*** (= stop behaving badly or annoying me), *you two!* 別鬧了，你們倆！ **ˌpack sb/sth ˈin/ˈinto sth** **1** to do a lot of things in a limited period of time 在（有限時間裏）做（大量工作）: *You seem to have packed a lot into your life!* 你生活中好像有做不完的事情！ **2** to put a lot of things or people into a limited space 在（有限空間裏）塞進（大量的人或物）；塞滿 SYN **cram in**: *They've managed to pack a lot of information into a very small book.* 他們設法把大量的信息編進了一本很小的書中。 **ˌpack ˈinto sth** to go somewhere in large numbers so that all available space is filled 使爆滿 SYN **cram**: *Over 80 000 fans packed into the stadium to watch the final.* * 8 萬多名球迷湧入了體育場觀看決賽。 ➲ see also PACK (5) **ˌpack sb↔ˈoff (to …)** (*informal*) to send sb somewhere, especially because you do not want them with you 把…打發走: *My parents always packed me off to bed early.* 我父母總是早早就打發我上牀。 **ˌpack sth↔ˈout** (of shows, performers, etc. 表演、演員等) to attract enough people to completely fill a theatre, etc. 吸引（足夠的觀眾）；使…滿座: *The band can still pack out concert halls.* 這支樂隊仍能使音樂廳爆滿。 ➲ see also PACKED OUT **ˌpack ˈup** (*informal, especially BrE*) (of a machine 機器) to stop working 停止工作；壞了: *The TV's packed up again.* 電視機又壞了。 **ˌpack ˈup** | **ˌpack sth↔ˈup** **1** 0‑ to put your possessions into a bag, etc. before leaving a place 打行李；收拾行裝: *Are you packing up already? It's only 4 o'clock.* 你已經開始打點行李了？現在才剛剛 4 點鐘。◇ *We arrived just as the musicians were packing up their instruments.* 我們到場時樂隊已開始收拾樂器了。 **2** (*BrE, informal*) to stop doing sth, especially a job 停止；放棄；辭掉 SYN **give up**: *What made you pack up a good job like that?* 什麼原因使你辭去了那麼好的工作？ ➲ see also PACK *v.* (2)

■ *noun*

▸ CONTAINER 容器 **1** 0‑ [C] (*especially NAmE*) a container, usually made of paper, that holds a number of the same thing or an amount of sth, ready to be sold（商品的）紙包，紙袋，紙盒: *a pack of cigarettes/gum* 一盒香煙／口香糖 ◇ *You can buy the envelopes in packs of ten.* 你可以整沓地買信封，每沓十個。 ➲ VISUAL VOCAB page V33 ➲ compare PACKAGE *n.* (1), (2), PACKET (1) ➲ see also FLAT-PACK, SIX-PACK

▸ SET 套 **2** 0‑ [C] a set of different things that are supplied together for a particular purpose（一起供應的）全套東西: *Send for your free information pack today.* 今天就來信索取免費資訊包。

▸ THINGS TIED FOR CARRYING 成捆攜帶的東西 **3** [C] a number of things that are wrapped or tied together, especially for carrying 一捆，一包（尤指適於攜帶的東西）: *donkeys carrying packs of wool* 馱着成捆羊毛的驢 ◇ (*figurative*) *Everything she told us is a* ***pack of lies*** (= a story that is completely false). 她對我們說的全是一派謊言。

▸ LARGE BAG 大包 **4** [C] a large bag that you carry on your back 大背包: *We passed a group of walkers, carrying huge packs.* 我們與一批背着超大行囊的步行者擦肩而過。 ➲ see also BACKPACK, FANNY PACK

▸ OF ANIMALS 動物 **5** [C+sing./pl. v.] a group of animals that hunt together or are kept for hunting 一群（動物或獵狗）: *packs of savage dogs* 成群的野狗 ◇ *wolves hunting in packs* 成群獵食的狼 ◇ *a pack of hounds* 一群獵犬

▸ OF PEOPLE 人 **6** [C+sing./pl. v.] a group of similar people or things, especially one that you do not like or approve of 群；幫；團夥: *We avoided a pack of journalists waiting outside.* 我們避開了等在門外的一群記者。◇ *He's the leader of the pack.* 他是那個團夥的頭目。 **7** [C+sing./pl. v.] all the people who are behind the leaders in a race, competition, etc.（統稱）競賽中的落後者: *measures aimed at keeping the company ahead of the pack* 旨在使公司領先所有競爭對手的措施

▸ OF CARDS 紙牌 **8** (*BrE*) (also **deck** *NAmE, BrE*) [C] a complete set of 52 PLAYING CARDS 一副（為 52 張）: *a pack of cards* 一副紙牌 ➲ VISUAL VOCAB page V37

▸ OF CUBS/BROWNIES 男／女幼童軍 **9** [C+sing./pl. v.] an organized group of CUBS/CUB SCOUTS or BROWNIES 一隊（男或女幼童軍）: *to join a Brownie pack* 加入一隊幼女童軍

P

▸ **FOR WOUND** 用於傷口 **10** [C] a hot or cold piece of soft material that absorbs liquid, used for treating a wound（治創傷用的）裹布，填塞物，敷料 ➲ see also FACE PACK, ICE PACK, MUD PACK **IDM** see JOKER

pack·age 🗝 /ˈpækɪdʒ/ *noun, verb*

■ ***noun*** **1** 🗝 (*especially NAmE*) = PARCEL *n.* (1)：*A large package has arrived for you.* 你有一個大包裹來了。**2** 🗝 (*NAmE*) a box, bag, etc. in which things are wrapped or packed; the contents of a box etc. 包；盒；袋；包裝好的東西：*Check the list of ingredients on the side of the package.* 檢查一下包裝盒側面的成分清單。◇ *a package of hamburger buns* 一袋做漢堡包用的圓麵包 ➲ **VISUAL VOCAB** page V33 ➲ compare PACK *n.* (1), PACKET (1) **3** (also ˈ**package deal**) a set of items or ideas that must be bought or accepted together（必須整體接收的）一套東西，一套建議；一攬子交易：*a benefits package* 一套福利措施 ◇ *an aid package* 綜合援助計劃 ◇ *a package of measures to help small businesses* 扶助小企業的整套措施 **4** (also ˈ**software package**) (*computing* 計) a set of related programs for a particular type of task, sold and used as a single unit 軟件包：*The system came with a database software package.* 本系統配有數據庫軟件包。

■ ***verb*** [often passive] **1** 🗝 to put sth into a box, bag, etc. to be sold or transported 將…包裝好：**~ sth** *packaged food/goods* 包裝好的食品／商品 ◇ *We package our products in recyclable materials.* 我們用可回收的材料包裝我們的產品。◇ **~ sth up** *The orders were already packaged up, ready to be sent.* 訂貨已包裝好待運。**2 ~ sb/sth (as sth)** to present sb/sth in a particular way 包裝成；使改頭換面；把…裝扮為：*an attempt to package news as entertainment* 把新聞包裝成娛樂形式的嘗試

ˈ**package store** *noun* (*US*) = LIQUOR STORE

ˈ**package tour** (*BrE* also ˈ**package holiday**) *noun* a holiday/vacation that is organized by a company at a fixed price and that includes the cost of travel, hotels, etc. 包價旅遊（費用固定、一切由旅行社代辦的度假旅遊）

pack·aging 🗝 /ˈpækɪdʒɪŋ/ *noun* [U]

1 🗝 materials used to wrap or protect goods that are sold in shops/stores 包裝材料；外包裝：*Attractive packaging can help to sell products.* 精美的包裝有助於產品的銷售。➲ **VISUAL VOCAB** page V33 **2** the process of wrapping goods 包裝工作；包裝：*His company offers a flexible packaging service for the food industry.* 他的公司為食品工業提供靈活的包裝業務。

ˈ**pack animal** *noun* an animal used for carrying loads, for example a horse 馱畜；役畜

packed /pækt/ *adj.* **1** extremely full of people 異常擁擠的；擠滿人的 **SYN** **crowded**：*The restaurant was packed.* 餐館裏坐滿了客人。◇ *The show played to* ***packed houses*** (= large audiences). 演出場場爆滿。**2** containing a lot of a particular thing 有大量…的；…極多的：**~ with sth** *The book is packed with information.* 這本書資料豐富。◇ **~ -packed** *an information-packed book* 一本資料豐富的書 **3 tightly ~** pressed closely together 緊密壓在一起的：*The birds' nests are lined with tightly packed leaves.* 鳥巢有一層壓得密密實實的樹葉。**4** [not before noun] (*informal*) having put everything you need into cases, boxes, etc. before you go somewhere 收拾好行李：*I'm all packed and ready to go.* 我已打點好行裝，準備出發了。

ˌ**packed ˈlunch** *noun* (*BrE*) a meal of SANDWICHES, fruit, etc. that is prepared at home and eaten at school, work, etc. 自備的午餐 ➲ compare BAG LUNCH, BOX LUNCH

ˌ**packed ˈout** *adj.* [not before noun] (*informal, especially BrE*) completely full of people or things 爆滿；擠滿人（或物）：*Opera houses are packed out wherever she sings.* 每逢她演唱，任何歌劇院都場場爆滿。

pack·er /ˈpækə(r)/ *noun* a person, machine or company that puts food, goods, etc. into containers to be sold or sent to sb 包裝工；包裝機；包裝公司

packet 🗝 /ˈpækɪt/ *noun*

1 🗝 (*BrE*) a small paper or cardboard container in which goods are packed for selling（商品的）小包裝紙袋，小硬紙板盒：*a packet of biscuits/cigarettes/crisps* 一包餅乾／香煙／油炸土豆片 ➲ **VISUAL VOCAB** page V33 ➲ compare PACK *n.* (1), PACKAGE *n.* (2) ➲ see also PAY PACKET **2** 🗝 a small object wrapped in paper or put into a thick envelope so that it can be sent by mail, carried easily or given as a present（郵政）小件包裹：*A packet of photographs arrived with the mail.* 一包照片郵寄來了。**3** (*NAmE*) (*BrE* **sa·chet**) a closed plastic or paper package that contains a very small amount of liquid or a powder（塑料或紙質）密封小袋：*a packet of instant cocoa mix* 一袋混合速溶可可粉 ➲ **VISUAL VOCAB** page V33 **4** [sing.] (*BrE, informal*) a large amount of money 一筆巨款：*That car must have cost a packet.* 買那輛汽車一定花了一大筆錢。**5** (*computing* 計) a piece of information that forms part of a message sent through a computer network 信息包；數據包；資訊包 **6** (*NAmE*) a set of documents that are supplied together for a particular purpose（為某種用途的）一套文件；一套資料：*a training packet* 一套培訓材料

ˈ**packet switching** *noun* [U] (*computing* 計) a process in which data is separated into parts before being sent, and then joined together after it arrives 分組交換，包交換，封包交換（將數據分組發送後再連接）

pack·horse /ˈpækhɔːs; *NAmE* -hɔːrs/ *noun* a horse that is used to carry heavy loads 馱馬

ˈ**pack ice** *noun* [U] a large mass of ice floating in the sea, formed from smaller pieces that have frozen together 聚集的浮冰；大塊的浮冰

pack·ing /ˈpækɪŋ/ *noun* [U] **1** the act of putting your possessions, clothes, etc. into bags or boxes in order to take or send them somewhere 打行李；收拾行囊：*Have you finished your packing?* 你收拾好行李了嗎？**2** material used for wrapping around delicate objects in order to protect them, especially before sending them somewhere 包裝材料：(*BrE*) *The price includes* ***postage and packing.*** 本價格包括郵資和包裝費。

ˈ**packing case** *noun* (*BrE*) a large strong box for packing or transporting goods in 包裝箱；裝貨箱

ˈ**pack rat** *noun* **1** (*NAmE*) a person who collects and stores things that they do not really need 馱鼠（指愛收藏雜物的人）**2** a small N American animal like a mouse that collects small sticks, etc. in its hole 馱鼠；林鼠

pact /pækt/ *noun* **~ (between A and B)** | **~ (with sb) (to do sth)** a formal agreement between two or more people, groups or countries, especially one in which they agree to help each other 條約；協議；公約：*a non-aggression pact* 互不侵犯條約 ◇ *They have* ***made a pact*** *with each other not to speak about their differences in public.* 他們彼此達成協議，不公開談論他們的歧見。◇ *a* ***suicide pact*** (= an agreement by two or more people to kill themselves at the same time) 自殺協議（兩人或多人約定同時自殺）

pacy (also **pacey**) /ˈpeɪsi/ *adj.* (*BrE, informal*) **1** (of a book, film/movie, etc. 書、電影等) having a story that develops quickly 快節奏的；劇情發展快的 **2** able to run quickly（奔跑）速度快的；能跑快的 **SYN** **fast**：*a pacy winger who can also score goals* 能射門得分的快速邊鋒

pad /pæd/ *noun, verb*

■ ***noun***

▸ **OF SOFT MATERIAL** 軟材料 **1** a thick piece of soft material that is used, for example, for absorbing liquid, cleaning or protecting sth（吸收液體、保潔或保護用的）軟墊，護墊，墊狀物：*medicated cleansing pads for sensitive skin* 敏感皮膚藥物清洗棉 ◇ *sanitary pads* (= that a woman uses during her PERIOD) 衛生棉墊 ➲ see also SHOULDER PAD

▸ **OF PAPER** 紙張 **2** a number of pieces of paper for writing or drawing on, that are fastened together at one edge 便箋本；拍紙簿：*a* ***sketch/writing pad*** 速寫／拍紙簿 ➲ see also NOTEPAD, SCRATCH PAD

▸ **OF ANIMAL'S FOOT** 動物的足 **3** the soft part under the foot of a cat, dog, etc. 爪墊；肉掌

▸ **FOR CLEANING** 用於清洗 **4** a small piece of rough material used for cleaning pans, surfaces, etc. 百潔布，菜瓜布（刷鍋等的小塊粗糙材料）：*a scouring pad* 刷洗用的金屬絲球

P

▸ **FOR SPACECRAFT/HELICOPTER 航天器；直升機** **5** a flat surface where a SPACECRAFT or a HELICOPTER takes off and lands 發射台；停機坪 ➲ see also HELIPAD, LAUNCH PAD

▸ **FOR PROTECTION 用於防護** **6** [usually pl.] a piece of thick material that you wear in some sports, for example football and CRICKET, to protect your legs, elbows, etc. （運動用）防護墊（如護腿、護肘等） ➲ **VISUAL VOCAB** page V44

▸ **OF WATER PLANTS 水生植物** **7** the large flat leaf of some water plants, especially the WATER LILY 浮葉（尤見於睡蓮）: *floating lily pads* 睡蓮的浮葉

▸ **FLAT/APARTMENT 公寓** **8** [usually sing.] (*old-fashioned, informal*) the place where sb lives, especially a flat/apartment 住所；（尤指）公寓 ➲ see also INK-PAD, KEYPAD

■ ***verb*** (-dd-)

▸ **ADD SOFT MATERIAL 添加軟材料** **1** [T, often passive] **~ sth (with sth)** to put a layer of soft material in or on sth in order to protect it, make it thicker or change its shape （用軟材料）填充，覆蓋，保護: *All the sharp corners were padded with foam.* 所有的棱角都墊上了泡沫塑料。◇ *a padded jacket* 有夾層的外套 ◇ *a* ***padded envelope*** (= for sending delicate objects) 有墊料層的封套

▸ **WALK QUIETLY 輕步行走** **2** [I] **+ adv./prep.** to walk with quiet steps 躡手躡腳地走: *She padded across the room to the window.* 她躡手躡腳地穿過屋子走到窗前。

▸ **BILLS 賬單** **3** [T] **~ sth** (*NAmE*) to dishonestly add items to bills to obtain more money 虛報（賬目）；做黑賬: *to* ***pad bills/expense accounts*** 在賬單上／開支賬上做手腳

PHR V ˌ**pad sth↔ˈout** **1** to put soft material into a piece of clothing in order to change its shape 給（衣服）加襯墊 **2** to make sth such as an article, seem longer or more impressive by adding things that are unnecessary （用多餘的話）延長（文章等）；充篇幅: *The report was padded out with extracts from previous documents.* 該報告摘抄過去的文件而加長了篇幅。

ˌpadded ˈcell *noun* a room in a hospital for mentally ill people, with soft walls to prevent violent patients from injuring themselves （精神病院的）軟壁病房

P

pad·ding /ˈpædɪŋ/ *noun* [U] **1** soft material that is placed inside sth to make it more comfortable or to change its shape 襯料；襯墊 **2** words that are used to make a speech, piece of writing, etc. longer, but that do not contain any interesting information 贅語；廢話；湊篇幅的文字

pad·dle /ˈpædl/ *noun, verb*

■ ***noun*** **1** [C] a short pole with a flat wide part at one or both ends, that you hold in both hands and use for moving a small boat, especially a CANOE, through water 槳；船槳 ➲ **VISUAL VOCAB** page V55 ➲ compare OAR **2** [C] a tool or part of a machine shaped like a paddle, especially one used for mixing food （機具的）槳狀部份；（尤指）食物攪拌器的槳葉 **3** **a paddle** [sing.] (*BrE*) an act or period of walking in shallow water with no shoes or socks 蹚水；赤腳涉水: *Let's go for a paddle.* 咱們去玩水吧。 ➲ see also DOG-PADDLE **4** [C] (*NAmE*) a BAT used for playing TABLE TENNIS 乒乓球拍 **5** [C] (*NAmE*) a piece of wood with a handle, used for hitting children as a punishment 戒尺（體罰兒童的工具） **IDM** see CREEK

■ ***verb*** **1** [I, T] to move a small boat through water using a paddle 用槳划船: (**+ adv./prep.**) *We paddled downstream for about a mile.* 我們划船順流而下約一英里。◇ **~ sth** (**+ adv./prep.**) *We paddled the canoe along the coast.* 我們划着獨木舟沿海岸而行。 **2** (*BrE*) (*NAmE* **wade**) [I] to walk or stand with no shoes or socks in shallow water in the sea, a lake, etc. 蹚水；赤足涉水: *The children have* ***gone paddling***. 孩子們蹚水去了。 **3** [I] to swim with short movements of your hands or feet up and down 狗趴式游泳 **4** [T] **~ sb/sth** (*NAmE*) to hit a child with a flat piece of wood as a punishment 用戒尺打（孩子）

ˈpaddle steamer (*BrE*) (also **paddle·boat** *NAmE, BrE*) *noun* an old-fashioned type of boat driven by steam and moved forward by a large wheel or wheels at the side 槳輪蒸汽船；明輪船 ➲ **VISUAL VOCAB** page V54

ˈpaddling pool (*BrE*) (*NAmE* **ˈwading pool**) *noun* a shallow swimming pool for children to play in, especially a small plastic one that you fill with water （尤指小型的塑料）淺水池，嬉水池

pad·dock /ˈpædək/ *noun* **1** a small field in which horses are kept （牧馬的）小圍場 **2** (in horse racing or motor racing 賽馬或賽車) an area where horses or cars are taken before a race and shown to the public 檢閱場 **3** (*AustralE, NZE*) any field or area of land that has fences around it 設有圍欄的一片土地

Paddy /ˈpædi/ *noun* (*pl.* **-ies**) (*informal*) an offensive word for a person from Ireland 帕迪（對愛爾蘭人的蔑稱）

paddy /ˈpædi/ *noun* (*pl.* **-ies**) **1** (also **ˈpaddy field**) a field in which rice is grown 稻田；水田: *a rice paddy* 水稻田 **2** [usually sing.] (*BrE, informal*) a state of being angry or in a bad mood 發火；發怒 **SYN** **temper**: *The news put him in a bit of a paddy.* 這消息讓他肝火上升。

ˈpaddy wagon *noun* (*informal, NAmE*) = PATROL WAGON

pad·kos /ˈpʌtkɒs; *NAmE* -kɑːs/ *noun* [U] (*SAfrE*) food that you take with you to eat while on a journey 旅行食物；乾糧

padlock 掛鎖

pad·lock /ˈpædlɒk; *NAmE* -lɑːk/ *noun, verb*

■ ***noun*** a type of lock that is used to fasten two things together or to fasten one thing to another. Padlocks are used with chains on gates, etc. 掛鎖

■ ***verb*** to lock sth with a padlock 用掛鎖鎖住: **~ sth to sth** *She always padlocked her bike to the railings.* 她總是用掛鎖把自行車鎖在欄杆上。◇ **~ sth** *The doors were padlocked.* 門都用掛鎖鎖着。

padre /ˈpɑːdreɪ/ *noun* (often used as a form of address 常用於稱謂) a priest, or other Christian minister, especially in the armed forces 牧師；神父；（尤指）隨軍牧師 ➲ compare CHAPLAIN

paean /ˈpiːən/ *noun* (*literary*) a song of praise or victory 讚歌；凱歌

paed- (*BrE*) (*NAmE* **ped-**) /piːd-/ *combining form* (in nouns and adjectives 構成名詞和形容詞) connected with children 與兒童有關的；兒童的: *paediatrician* 兒科醫生

paed·er·ast, paed·er·asty *nouns* (*BrE*) = PEDERAST, PEDERASTY

paedi·at·ri·cian (*BrE*) (*NAmE* **pedi·at·ri·cian**) /ˌpiːdiəˈtrɪʃn/ *noun* a doctor who studies and treats the diseases of children 兒科醫生；兒科學家

paedi·at·rics (*BrE*) (*NAmE* **pedi·at·rics**) /ˌpiːdiˈætrɪks/ *noun* [U] the branch of medicine concerned with children and their diseases 兒科學 ▸ **paedi·at·ric** (*BrE*) (*NAmE* **pedi-**) *adj.*: *paediatric surgery* 小兒外科

paedo·phile (*BrE*) (*NAmE* **pedo-**) /ˈpiːdəʊfaɪl; *NAmE* -doʊ-/ *noun* a person who is sexually attracted to children 戀童癖者

paedo·philia (*BrE*) (*NAmE* **pedo-**) /ˌpiːdəˈfɪliə/ *noun* [U] the condition of being sexually attracted to children; sexual activity with children 戀童癖；與兒童的性行為

pa·ella /paɪˈelə/ *noun* [U, C] a Spanish dish of rice, chicken, fish and vegetables, cooked and served in a large shallow pan 西班牙雜燴菜飯（由大米、雞肉、魚肉和蔬菜用平底鍋烹製而成）

pagan /ˈpeɪɡən/ *noun* (often *disapproving*) **1** a person who holds religious beliefs that are not part of any of the world's main religions 異教徒（信奉非主流宗教者） **2** used in the past by Christians to describe a person who did not believe in Christianity 教外人（舊時的基督徒用以指非基督徒）▶ **pagan** *adj.*：*a pagan festival* 異教節日 **pa·gan·ism** /ˈpeɪɡənɪzəm/ *noun* [U]

page /peɪdʒ/ *noun, verb*

■ ***noun*** **1** (*abbr.* **p**) one side or both sides of a sheet of paper in a book, magazine, etc.（書刊或紙張的）頁，面，張，版：*Turn to page 64.* 翻到第 64 頁。◇ *Someone has torn a page out of this book.* 有人從這本書裏撕掉了一張。◇ *a **blank/new page*** 空白頁；新的一頁 ◇ *the **sports/financial pages** of the newspaper* 報紙的體育 / 金融版 ◇ *on the **opposite/facing page*** 在對面的一頁上 ◇ ***over the page*** (= on the next page) 在下一頁 ➲ see also FRONT PAGE, FULL-PAGE, YELLOW PAGES **2** a section of data or information that can be shown on a computer screen at any one time（計算機的）頁面，版面 ➲ see also HOME PAGE **3** (*literary*) an important event or period of history 歷史篇章，歷史篇頁（指歷史大事或時期）：*a glorious page of Arab history* 阿拉伯歷史上光輝的篇章 **4** (*especially NAmE*) = PAGEBOY (1) **5** (*NAmE*) a student who works as an assistant to a member of the US Congress（美國議員的）青年助理（本身為學生）**6** (in the Middle Ages 中世紀) a boy or young man who worked for a KNIGHT while training to be a knight himself 學習騎士（接受訓練期間做侍從，可晉升騎士）

IDM **on the same ˈpage** (*especially NAmE*) if two or more people or groups are **on the same page**, they agree about what they are trying to achieve 目標一致；就目標達成共識 **turn the ˈpage** to begin doing things in a different way and thinking in a more positive way after a period of difficulties（經過困難後）翻開新的一頁，開始新的生活 ➲ more at PRINT *v.*

■ ***verb*** **1 ~ sb** to call sb's name over a PUBLIC ADDRESS SYSTEM in order to find them and give them a message（在公共傳呼系統上）呼叫：*Why don't you have him paged at the airport?* 你為何不在機場擴音喇叭上呼叫他呢？**2 ~ sb** to contact sb by sending a message to their PAGER 用傳呼機傳呼（某人）：*Page Dr Green immediately.* 立即傳呼格林醫生。

PHR V **ˌpage ˈthrough sth** (*NAmE*) to quickly turn the pages of a book, magazine, etc. and look at them without reading them carefully or in detail 隨意翻閱；瀏覽 **SYN** **flick through sth, leaf through sth**

pa·geant /ˈpædʒənt/ *noun* **1** a public entertainment in which people dress in historical COSTUMES and give performances of scenes from history 穿古代服裝的遊行；再現歷史場景的娛樂活動 **2** (*NAmE*) a competition for young women in which their beauty, personal qualities and skills are judged 選美比賽：*a beauty pageant* 選美比賽 ➲ compare BEAUTY CONTEST (1) **3 ~ (of sth)** (*literary*) something that is considered as a series of interesting and different events 內容繁雜有趣的場面；盛大華麗的情景：*life's rich pageant* 豐富的人生畫卷

pa·geant·ry /ˈpædʒəntri/ *noun* [U] impressive and exciting events and ceremonies involving a lot of people wearing special clothes 壯觀的場面；隆重的儀式；盛典：*the pageantry of royal occasions* 王室慶典的盛況

page·boy /ˈpeɪdʒbɔɪ/ *noun* **1** (also **page** especially in *NAmE*) a small boy who helps or follows a BRIDE during a marriage ceremony 新娘的伴童；小男儐相 ➲ compare BRIDESMAID **2** (also **page**) (*old-fashioned*) a boy or young man, usually in uniform, employed in a hotel to open doors, deliver messages for people, etc.（旅館的）行李員，門童 **3** a HAIRSTYLE for women in which the hair is shoulder-length and turned under at the ends 女子齊肩內鬈髮；扣邊女式髮型

pager /ˈpeɪdʒə(r)/ *noun* a small electronic device that you carry around with you and that shows a message or lets you know when sb is trying to contact you, for example by making a sound 尋呼機；傳呼機；BP 機 ➲ see also BEEPER, BLEEPER

ˌpage-ˈthree girl *noun* (*BrE*) a naked or partly naked young woman whose picture is printed in a newspaper 三版女郎（報紙上裸體或半裸體年輕女子）**ORIGIN** From page three of the *Sun* newspaper, where one of these pictures is or was printed every day. 源自《太陽報》第三版，每日印有裸女或半裸女照片。

ˈpage-turner *noun* (*informal*) a book that is very exciting 令人欲罷不能的書；扣人心弦的讀物

ˈpage view *noun* [C, sing.] (*business* 商) one visit to a single page on a website（一次）網頁瀏覽：*a surge in page views* 網頁瀏覽量的激增

pa·gin·ate /ˈpædʒɪneɪt/ *verb* **~ sth** (*technical* 術語) to give a number to each page of a book, piece of writing, etc. 給（書等）標頁碼，編頁碼

pa·gin·ation /ˌpædʒɪˈneɪʃn/ *noun* [U] (*technical* 術語) the process of giving a page number to each page of a book; the page numbers given 標頁碼；編頁碼；頁碼

pa·goda /pəˈɡəʊdə; *NAmE* -ˈɡoʊ-/ *noun* a TEMPLE (= religious building) in S or E Asia in the form of a tall tower with several levels, each of which has its own roof that extends beyond the walls（南亞或東亞的）佛塔 ➲ **VISUAL VOCAB** page V15

pah /pɑː/ *exclamation* used to represent the sound that people make when they disagree with sth or disapprove of sth strongly（表示強烈不滿或不同意）哼！

paid /peɪd/ *adj.* [usually before noun] **1** (of work, etc. 工作等) for which people receive money 有償的；付費的：*Neither of them is currently in paid employment.* 他們倆目前都沒有掙錢的差事。◇ *a well-paid job* 報酬不菲的工作 **2** (of a person 人) receiving money for doing work 有報酬的；有薪金的：*Men still outnumber women in the paid workforce.* 在上班掙錢的人口中，男性仍然多於女性。◇ *a poorly paid teacher* 收入微薄的教師 **OPP** **unpaid**

IDM **put ˈpaid to sth** (*informal*) to stop or destroy sth, especially what sb plans or wants to do 使終止；使（希望等）破滅

ˈpaid-up *adj.* [only before noun] **1** having paid all the money necessary to be a member of a club or an organization 已付清會費的；已繳款的：*a fully paid-up member* 會費完全付清的會員 **2** (*BrE, informal*) strongly supporting sb/sth 堅決支持的；付出全部心力的：*a fully paid-up environmental campaigner* 全力投入的環保運動者

pail/peɪl/, **pail·ful** /ˈpeɪlfʊl/ *noun* (*NAmE* or *old-fashioned*) = BUCKET *n.* (1), (3)

P

pain /peɪn/ *noun, verb*

■ ***noun*** ➲ see also PAINS **1** [U, C] the feelings that you have in your body when you have been hurt or when you are ill/sick（身體上的）疼痛：*a cry of pain* 痛苦的喊叫 ◇ *She was clearly **in** a lot of **pain**.* 她顯然疼痛萬分。◇ *He felt a sharp pain in his knee.* 他感到膝蓋一陣劇痛。◇ *patients suffering from acute back pain* 患劇烈背痛的病人 ◇ ***stomach/chest pains*** 胃 / 胸痛 ◇ *You get more **aches and pains** as you get older.* 年紀越大，疼痛就越多。◇ *The booklet contains information on **pain relief** during labour.* 這本小冊子介紹了減輕分娩疼痛的知識。◇ *This cream should help to **relieve the pain**.* 這種藥膏應有助於止痛。➲ see also GROWING PAINS (1) **2** [U, C] mental or emotional suffering 痛苦；苦惱；煩惱：*the pain of separation* 離別的痛苦 ◇ *I never meant to cause her pain.* 我從沒有讓她痛苦之意。◇ *the **pleasures and pains** of growing old* 老年的苦與樂 **3** [C] (*informal*) a person or thing that is very annoying 討厭的人（或事）；令人頭痛的人（或事）：*She can be a real pain when she's in a bad mood.* 她脾氣不好時，真是令人頭痛。◇ ***It's a pain** having to go all that way for just one meeting.* 只為開一次會，要跑那麼遠的路，真煩死人了。

IDM **no ˌpain, no ˈgain** (*saying*) used to say that you need to suffer if you want to achieve sth 不勞則無獲 **on/under pain of sth** (*formal*) with the threat of having sth done to you as a punishment if you do not obey 違則受到某種懲罰；違則以…論處：*They were required to cut pollution levels, on pain of a £10 000 fine if they disobeyed.* 他們被要求降低污染水平，違則罰款 1 萬英鎊。 **a pain in the ˈneck** (*BrE* also **a pain in the ˈarse/ˈbackside**) (*NAmE* also **a pain in the ˈass/ˈbutt**) (*informal*) a person or thing that is very annoying 極討厭的人（或事物）

■ ***verb*** (not used in the progressive tenses 不用於進行時) (*formal*) to cause sb pain or make them unhappy 使痛

苦；使苦惱 SYN **hurt**： **~ sb** *She was deeply pained by the accusation.* 這一指控使她極為痛苦。◇ (*old use*) *The wound still pained him occasionally.* 他還是感到傷口不時疼痛。◇ **it pains sb to do sth** *It pains me to see you like this.* 看到你這副模樣真令我難過。◇ **it pains sb that ...** *It pained him that she would not acknowledge him.* 讓他難過的是，她不願意理睬他。

'pain barrier *noun* [usually sing.] the moment at which sb doing hard physical activity feels the greatest pain, after which the pain becomes less 痛苦極限，痛障（艱苦體力活動的最痛苦時刻，此後疼痛會減輕）： *He broke through the pain barrier at 25 kilometres and went on to win his first marathon.* 他克服了 25 公里時的痛苦極限，進而贏得了他的第一個馬拉松冠軍。

pained /peɪnd/ *adj.* showing that sb is feeling annoyed or upset 顯出痛苦（或難過、苦惱）的： *a **pained expression/voice*** 痛苦的表情 / 聲音

Synonyms 同義詞辨析

painful

sore • raw • inflamed • excruciating • burning • itchy

These words all describe sth that causes you physical pain. 以上各詞均指使人肉體上疼痛的。

painful causing you physical pain 指使人肉體上疼痛的 NOTE **Painful** can describe a part of the body, illness, injury, treatment or death. * painful 可用於描述身體部位、疾病、傷害、治療或死亡等： *Is your knee still painful?* 你的膝蓋還疼嗎？◇ *a series of painful injections* 一次又一次令人痛苦的注射◇ *a slow and painful death* 緩慢而痛苦的死亡

sore (of a part of the body) painful and often red, especially because of infection or because a muscle has been used too much 指（身體部位）發炎疼痛的、肌肉痠痛的： *a sore throat* 咽喉疼◇ *Their feet were sore after hours of walking.* 他們走了幾小時的路，把腳都走疼了。

raw (of a part of the body) red and painful, for example because of an infection or because the skin has been damaged 指（身體部位）紅腫疼痛的、破損的、擦傷的： *The skin on her feet had been rubbed raw.* 她腳上的皮磨破了。

inflamed (of a part of the body) painful, red and hot because of an infection or injury 指（身體部位）發炎的、紅腫的： *The wound had become inflamed.* 傷口發炎了。

excruciating extremely painful 指極痛苦的、極苦惱的 NOTE **Excruciating** can describe feelings, treatments or death but not parts of the body. * excruciating 可用於描述情感、治療或死亡，而非身體部位： ~~*an excruciating throat/back/knee*~~

burning painful and giving a feeling of being very hot 指火辣辣地痛的： *She felt a burning sensation in her throat.* 她感到咽喉火辣辣的疼。

itchy giving an uncomfortable feeling on your skin that makes you want to scratch; having this feeling 指發癢的： *an itchy rash* 發癢的皮疹◇ *I feel itchy all over.* 我覺得渾身發癢。

PATTERNS
- sore/inflamed/itchy **eyes**
- raw/inflamed/itchy **skin**
- a painful/an excruciating **death**
- a painful/burning **sensation**
- excruciating/burning **pain**

pain·ful 0-w /'peɪnfl/ *adj.* **1** 0-w causing you pain 令人疼痛的： *Is your back still painful?* 你的背還疼嗎？◇ *a painful death* 痛苦的死亡◇ *My ankle is still too painful to walk on.* 我的腳腕子還是疼得不能走路。 **2** 0-w **~ (for sb) (to do sth)** | **~ (doing sth)** causing you to feel upset or embarrassed 令人痛苦（或難過、難堪）的： *a **painful experience/memory*** 痛苦的經歷 / 回憶◇ *Their efforts were painful to watch.* 看着他們辛勞真是令人心痛。 **3** 0-w unpleasant or difficult to do 不愉快的；困難的；艱難的 SYN **trying**： *Applying for jobs can be a long and painful process.* 求職可以是漫長而又艱難的過程。

pain·ful·ly /'peɪnfəli/ *adv.* **1** extremely, and in a way that makes you feel annoyed, upset, etc. 非常地；令人痛苦地；令人煩惱地： *Their son was **painfully shy**.* 他們的兒子非常害羞。◇ *The dog was **painfully thin**.* 那條狗瘦得可憐。◇ *He was **painfully aware** of his lack of experience.* 他痛苦地意識到自己缺乏經驗。◇ *Progress has been **painfully slow**.* 進度慢得令人焦急。 **2** in a way that causes you physical or emotional pain 使人疼痛地；令人苦惱地： *He banged his knee painfully against the desk.* 他的膝蓋撞到桌子上，疼得很。 **3** with a lot of effort and difficulty 吃力地；艱難地： *painfully acquired experience* 艱難獲得的經驗

pain·kill·er /'peɪnkɪlə(r)/ *noun* a drug that reduces pain 止痛藥： *She's on (= taking) painkillers.* 她在服止痛藥。 ▶ **pain·kill·ing** *adj.* [only before noun]： ***painkilling drugs/injections*** 止痛藥物 / 注射劑

pain·less /'peɪnləs/ *adj.* **1** causing you no pain 無痛的： *a painless death* 無痛死亡◇ *The treatment is painless.* 這種治療無疼痛。 **2** not unpleasant or difficult to do 愉快的；輕鬆的；不難的；不討厭的： *The interview was relatively painless.* 此次面試相對輕鬆。 ▶ **pain·less·ly** *adv.*

pains /peɪnz/ *noun* [pl.]
IDM **be at pains to do sth** to put a lot of effort into doing sth correctly 下苦功；花大力氣： *She was at great pains to stress the advantages of the new system.* 她極力強調新制度的優點。 **for your 'pains** (*especially BrE*, often *ironic*) as payment, reward or thanks for sth you have done 作為回報；作為答謝： *I told her what I thought and got a mouthful of abuse for my pains!* 我跟她講了我的感受，而得到的回報竟是破口大罵！ **take (great) pains (to do sth)** | **go to great pains (to do sth)** to put a lot of effort into doing sth 兢兢業業地做某事；費力地做某事： *The couple went to great pains to keep their plans secret.* 這對夫婦煞費苦心，對計劃守口如瓶。 **take (great) pains with/over sth** to do sth very carefully 小心翼翼地做某事： *He always takes great pains with his lectures.* 他總是仔細用心地準備講稿。

pains·tak·ing /'peɪnzteɪkɪŋ/ *adj.* [usually before noun] needing a lot of care, effort and attention to detail 需細心的；辛苦的；需專注的 SYN **thorough**： *painstaking research* 細心的研究◇ *The event had been planned with painstaking attention to detail.* 這次活動的細節是經過精心計劃的。 ▶ **pains·tak·ing·ly** *adv.*

paint 0-w /peɪnt/ *noun, verb*
■ ***noun*** **1** 0-w [U] a liquid that is put on surfaces to give them a particular colour; a layer of this liquid when it has dried on a surface 油漆；油漆塗層： *white paint* 白漆◇ ***gloss/matt/acrylic paint*** 亮光 / 亞光 / 樹脂漆◇ *The woodwork has recently been given a fresh **coat of paint**.* 木建部份最近新刷了一層漆。◇ ***Wet paint!*** (= used as a sign) 油漆未乾！◇ *The paint is starting to peel off.* 油漆開始起皮剝落了。 ➲ see also GREASEPAINT, OIL PAINT, WARPAINT **2** 0-w **paints** [pl.] tubes or blocks of paint used for painting pictures 繪畫顏料： *oil paints* 油畫顏料
■ ***verb*** **1** 0-w [T, I] **~ sth (with sth)** to cover a surface or object with paint 在…上刷油漆： **~ (sth)** *We've had the house painted.* 我們已經把房子油漆過了。◇ *Paint the shed with weather-resistant paint.* 用抗風雨的油漆把棚子漆一漆。◇ *a brightly painted barge* 塗得很鮮豔的畫舫◇ **~ sth + adj./noun** *The walls were painted yellow.* 牆壁漆成了黃色。 ➲ COLLOCATIONS at DECORATE **2** 0-w [T, I] to make a picture or design using paints 用顏料畫： **~ sth/sb** *to paint portraits* 畫肖像◇ *A friend painted the children for me (= painted a picture of the children).* 一位朋友給我畫了這張孩子們的畫像。◇ **~ sth on sth** *Slogans had been painted on the walls.* 標語塗在牆上。◇ **~ (in sth)** *She paints in oils.* 她畫油畫。◇ *My mother paints well.* 我母親很會畫畫。 ➲ COLLOCATIONS at ART **3** [T] to give a particular impression of sb/sth 把…描

P

繪成 SYN **portray**：**~ sb/sth as sth** *The article paints them as a bunch of petty criminals.* 文章把他們描繪成一夥小犯罪分子。◇ **~ sb/sth in ...** *The documentary painted her in a bad light.* 紀錄片的描繪對她很不利。 **4** [T] **~ sth** to put coloured make-up on your nails, lips, etc. 往（指甲、嘴唇等上）施化妝品；染（指甲）；塗（唇膏）

IDM **paint a (grim, gloomy, rosy, etc.) 'picture of sb/sth** to describe sb/sth in a particular way; to give a particular impression of sb/sth 給人以…印象；把…描繪成：*The report paints a vivid picture of life in the city.* 報告生動地描繪了都市生活。◇ *Journalists paint a grim picture of conditions in the camps.* 記者描繪了營裏的惡劣狀況。 **paint the town 'red** (*informal*) to go to a lot of different bars, clubs, etc. and enjoy yourself 花天酒地地玩樂；出沒於各娛樂場所 **paint sth with a ,broad 'brush** to describe sth in a general way, ignoring the details 大致地描述 ➲ more at BLACK *adj.*

PHR V **,paint sth↔'out** to cover part of a picture, sign, etc. with another layer of paint 用油漆等塗掉 **,paint 'over sth** to cover sth with a layer of paint 刷油漆覆蓋：*We painted over the dirty marks on the wall.* 我們把牆上的髒印子用油漆蓋上了。

paint·ball /ˈpeɪntbɔːl/ *noun* [U] a game in which people shoot balls of paint at each other 彩彈遊戲

paint·box /ˈpeɪntbɒks; *NAmE* -bɑːks/ *noun* a box containing a set of paints 顏料盒

paint·brush /ˈpeɪntbrʌʃ/ *noun* a brush that is used for painting 畫筆；漆刷 ➲ VISUAL VOCAB page V20

,paint-by-'numbers *adj.* [only before noun] **1** (of pictures 圖畫) having sections with different numbers showing which colours should be used to fill them in 用數字標明填色區域的 **2** (*disapproving*) used to describe sth that is produced without using the imagination 缺乏想像力的；呆板的；刻板的：*He accused the government of relying on paint-by-numbers policies.* 他指責政府依賴一成不變的政策。

'paint chip *noun* **1** a small piece of paint that has broken off sth or the small area where the paint has come off 剝落的油漆；油漆剝落處 **2** (*NAmE*) a strip of card with samples of paint in different colours, provided in shops/stores to help customers decide what paint to buy（供選購者用的）油漆色樣條，油漆色卡

paint·er 0‑w /ˈpeɪntə(r)/ *noun*
1 0‑w a person whose job is painting buildings, walls, etc. 油漆匠：*He works as a painter and decorator.* 他的職業是油漆匠和裝潢師傅。 **2** 0‑w an artist who paints pictures 畫家：*a famous painter* 著名畫家 ◇ *a **portrait/landscape painter*** 肖像／風景畫家 **3** a rope fastened to the front of a boat, used for tying it to a post, ship, etc.（繫船的）纜繩

paint·er·ly /ˈpeɪntəli; *NAmE* -ərli/ *adj.* typical of artists or painting 有畫家（或繪畫）特徵的 SYN **artistic**

paint·ing 0‑w /ˈpeɪntɪŋ/ *noun*
1 0‑w [C] a picture that has been painted 繪畫；油畫：*a collection of paintings by American artists* 美國藝術家繪畫作品集 ◇ *cave paintings* 洞窟裏的壁畫 ➲ SYNONYMS at PICTURE ➲ COLLOCATIONS at ART ➲ see also OIL PAINTING **2** 0‑w [U] the act or art of using paint to produce pictures 作畫；繪畫：*Her hobbies include music and painting.* 她的愛好包括音樂和繪畫。 ➲ VISUAL VOCAB page V41 **3** 0‑w [U] the act of putting paint onto the surface of objects, walls, etc. 塗漆；刷油漆：*painting and decorating* 油漆和裝潢

'paint stripper *noun* [U] a liquid used to remove old paint from surfaces 脫漆劑；除漆劑

paint·work /ˈpeɪntwɜːk; *NAmE* -wɜːrk/ *noun* [U] (*especially BrE*) the layer of paint on the surface of a door, wall, car, etc. 漆面；油漆層：*The paintwork is beginning to peel.* 漆面已經開始剝落了。

pair 0‑w /peə(r); *NAmE* per/ *noun, verb*
■ *noun*
▸ TWO THINGS THE SAME 相同的兩樣東西 **1** 0‑w [C] two things of the same type, especially when they are used or worn together 一雙；一對：*a **pair of gloves/shoes/earrings, etc.*** 一副手套、一雙鞋、一對耳環等 ◇ *a huge pair of eyes* 一雙大眼睛 ◇ *The vase is one of a **matching pair**.* 這隻花瓶是一對中的一隻。

▸ TWO PARTS JOINED 連接的兩部份 **2** 0‑w [C] an object consisting of two parts that are joined together 分兩個相連接部份的物體：*a **pair of trousers/pants/jeans, etc.*** 一條長褲、褲子、牛仔褲等 ◇ *a **pair of glasses/binoculars/scissors, etc.*** 一副眼鏡、一架雙筒望遠鏡、一把剪刀等 HELP A plural verb is sometimes used with **pair** in the singular in senses 1 and 2. In informal *NAmE* some people use **pair** as a plural form. 在第 1 及第 2 義中，pair 有時以單數形式與複數動詞搭配。在非正式的美式英語中，有些人把 pair 作為複數：*three pair of shoes* 三雙鞋子 This is not considered correct in written English. 在書面英語中，這種用法被認為不正確。

▸ TWO PEOPLE 兩個人 **3** 0‑w [C+sing./pl. v.] two people who are doing sth together or who have a particular relationship 兩個共事（或有特殊關係）的人；倆；對：*Get pairs of students to act out the dialogue in front of the class.* 叫學生兩人一組在課堂上演出這個對話。◇ *Get the students to do the exercise as **pair work*** (= two students work together). 讓學生兩人一組做練習。◇ (*informal*) *I've had enough of the pair of you!* 你們倆讓我煩透了！ HELP In *BrE* a plural verb is usually used. 在英式英語中常用複數動詞：*A pair of children were kicking a ball about.* ◇ *The pair are planning a trip to India together.*

▸ TWO ANIMALS/BIRDS 兩個動物；兩隻鳥 **4** [C+sing./pl. v.] two animals or birds of the same type that are breeding together（同時馴養的）兩個同類的鳥（或獸）；一對：*a breeding pair* 用於繁殖的一對 ◇ *a pair of swans* 一對天鵝

▸ TWO HORSES 兩匹馬 **5** [C] two horses working together to pull a CARRIAGE 一起拉車的兩匹馬：*a carriage and pair* 雙駕馬車 ➲ see also AU PAIR

IDM **a pair of 'hands** (*informal*) a person who can do, or is doing, a job 一個能做事的人；人手；正在工作的人：*We need an extra pair of hands if we're going to finish on time.* 要想按時完成，我們就要再增加一個人。◇ *Colleagues regard him as a **safe pair of hands*** (= sb who can be relied on to do a job well). 同事認為他辦事可靠。 **in 'pairs** 0‑w in groups of two objects or people 成對的；成雙的：*Students worked in pairs on the project.* 學生兩人一組做這個項目。 **I've only got one pair of 'hands** (*informal*) used to say that you are too busy to do anything else 我只有一雙手 ➲ more at SAFE *adj.*

■ *verb*
▸ MAKE GROUPS OF TWO 配對 **1** [T, usually passive] to put people or things into groups of two 使成對；配對：**~ A with B** *Each blind student was paired with a sighted student.* 每個盲人學員都與一個視力正常的同學配對。◇ **~ A (and B) (together)** *All the shoes on the floor were neatly paired.* 地板上的鞋子都整齊成雙地擺着。

▸ OF ANIMALS/BIRDS 獸；鳥 **2** [I] (*technical* 術語) to come together in order to breed 配對（以繁殖）；交配：*Many of the species pair for life.* 許多物種都終生配對。

PHR V **,pair 'off (with sb)** | **,pair sb↔'off (with sb)** to come together, especially in order to have a romantic relationship; to bring two people together for this purpose（使）結對，配對：*It seemed that all her friends were pairing off.* 好像她的朋友全都成雙結對了。◇ *He's always trying to pair me off with his cousin.* 他總想把我和他表弟配成一對。 **,pair 'up (with sb)** | **,pair sb↔'up (with sb)** to come together or to bring two people together to work, play a game, etc.（使兩人）結組工作（或遊戲等）

pair·ing /ˈpeərɪŋ; *NAmE* ˈper-/ *noun* **1** [C] two people or things that work together or are placed together; the act of placing them together 結對的兩個人（或物）；配對；搭配：*Tonight they take on a Chinese pairing in their bid to reach the final tomorrow.* 今晚他們將挑戰一對中國選手，爭取進入明天的決賽。 **2** [U] (in the British Parliament) the practice of an MP agreeing with an MP of a different party that neither of them will vote in a debate so that they do not need to attend the debate 配對，結對（英國議會中來自不同政黨的兩名議員約定放棄投票從而不必參加辯論進行表決）

paisa /ˈpaɪsɑː; -sə/ *noun* (*pl.* **paise** /-seɪ; -sə/) a coin of India, Pakistan and Nepal. There are one hundred paise in a RUPEE. 派士（印度、巴基斯坦和尼泊爾的硬幣，100 派士等於 1 盧比）

pais·ley /ˈpeɪzli/ *noun* [U] a detailed pattern of curved shapes that look like feathers, used especially on cloth 佩斯利（羽狀）圖案：*a paisley tie* 一條佩斯利花紋領帶

Pai·ute /ˈpaɪuːt/ *noun* (*pl.* **Pai·ute** or **Pai·utes**) a member of a Native American people many of whom live in the south-western US 派尤特人（美洲土著，很多居於美國西南部）

pa·ja·mas (*NAmE*) (*BrE, CanE* **py·ja·mas**) /pəˈdʒɑːməz; *NAmE* -ˈdʒæm-/ *noun* [pl.] a loose jacket and pants/trousers worn in bed （一套）睡衣褲 ➲ VISUAL VOCAB page V63

pak choi /ˌpæk ˈtʃɔɪ/ (*BrE*) (*NAmE* **ˌbok ˈchoy**) *noun* [U] a type of CHINESE CABBAGE with long dark green leaves and thick white STEMS 小白菜

Pak·eha /ˈpɑːkihɑː/ *noun* (*NZE*) a white person from New Zealand (that is, not a Maori) 新西蘭白種人

Paki /ˈpæki/ *noun* (*BrE, informal, taboo*) a very offensive word for a person from Pakistan, especially one living in Britain. The word is often also used for people from India or Bangladesh. （對巴基斯坦人，尤指在英國居住者的蔑稱，也常用於印度人和孟加拉人）

pa·kora /pəˈkɔːrə/ *noun* a flat piece of spicy S Asian food consisting of meat or vegetables fried in BATTER （南亞）油炸辣肉菜片

PAL /pæl/ *noun* [U] a television broadcasting system that is used in most of Europe * PAL 制式（歐洲大部份地區使用的電視廣播系統）➲ compare NTSC, SECAM

pal /pæl/ *noun, verb*

■ *noun* **1** (*informal, becoming old-fashioned*) a friend 朋友；夥伴；哥們兒：*We've been pals for years.* 我們是多年的哥們兒了。➲ see also PEN PAL **2** (*informal*) used to address a man in an unfriendly way（對男子的不友好的稱呼）傢伙，小子：*If I were you, pal, I'd stay away from her!* 我要是你呀，小子，我就離她遠遠的！▸ **pally** *adj.*：*I got very pally (= friendly) with him.* 我跟他的關係鐵着呢。

■ *verb* (**-ll-**)

PHR V **ˌpal aˈround (with sb)** (*informal, especially NAmE*) to do things with sb as a friend （和某人）一起共事，結夥出沒：*I palled around with him and his sister at school.* 我上學時常常與他和他姐姐在一起。**ˌpal ˈup (with sb)** (*BrE*) (*NAmE* **ˌbuddy ˈup (to/with sb)**) (*informal*) to become friendly with sb （和某人）成為：*They palled up while they were at college.* 他們上大學時成了朋友。

pal·ace 0┳ /ˈpæləs/ *noun*

1 0┳ [C] the official home of a king, queen, president, etc. 王宮；宮殿；總統府：*Buckingham Palace* 白金漢宮 ◇ *the royal/presidential palace* 王宮；總統府 ➲ VISUAL VOCAB page V15 **2** (often **the Palace**) [sing.] the people who live in a palace, especially the British royal family 住在王宮裏的人；（尤指英國的）王室：*The Palace last night refused to comment on the reports.* 昨晚王室拒絕對報道作出評論。◇ *a Palace spokesman* 王室發言人 **3** [C] any large impressive house 豪華住宅；宮殿：*The Old Town has a whole collection of churches, palaces and mosques.* 舊城區集了許多教堂、大宅院和清真寺。**4** [C] (*old-fashioned*) (sometimes used in the names of buildings 有時用於建築物名稱) a large public building, such as a hotel or cinema/movie theater 大的公共建築（如旅館、影劇院）：*the Strand Palace Hotel* 濱河王宮飯店

ˌpalace ˈcoup (also **ˌpalace revoˈlution**) *noun* a situation in which a ruler or leader has their power taken away from them by sb within the same party, etc. 宮廷政變；宮廷革命

palaeo- (*especially BrE*) (*NAmE* usually **paleo-**) /ˈpæliəʊ; ˈpeɪl-; *NAmE* -ioʊ/ *combining form* (in nouns, adjectives and adverbs 構成名詞、形容詞和副詞) connected with ancient times 古代的

palae·og·raphy (*BrE*) (*NAmE* **pale·og·raphy**) /ˌpæliˈɒɡrəfi; ˌpeɪl-; *NAmE* -ˈɑːɡ-/ *noun* [U] the study of ancient writing systems 古文字學 ▸ **palae·og·rapher** (also **pale·og·rapher**) /ˌpæliˈɒɡrəfə(r); ˌpeɪl-; *NAmE* -ˈɑːɡ-/ *noun*

Palaeo·lith·ic (*especially BrE*) (*NAmE* usually **Paleo-**) /ˌpæliəˈlɪθɪk; ˌpeɪl-/ *adj.* from or connected with the early part of the Stone Age 舊石器時代的

palae·on·tolo·gist (*especially BrE*) (*NAmE* usually **paleo-**) /ˌpæliɒnˈtɒlədʒɪst; ˌpeɪl-; *NAmE* ˌpeɪliɑːnˈtɑːl-/ *noun* a person who studies FOSSILS 古生物學家；化石學家

palae·on·tology (*especially BrE*) (*NAmE* usually **paleo-**) /ˌpæliɒnˈtɒlədʒi; ˌpeɪl-; *NAmE* ˌpeɪliɑːnˈtɑːl-/ *noun* [U] the study of FOSSILS (= the remains of animals or plants in rocks) as a guide to the history of life on earth 古生物學；化石學

pal·ais /ˈpæleɪ/ (also **ˌpalais de ˈdanse** /ˌpæleɪ də ˈdɑːns/) *noun* (*BrE*) (in the past) a large public building used for dancing; a dance hall （舊時的）舞場，舞廳

pal·at·able /ˈpælətəbl/ *adj.* **1** (of food or drink 食物或飲料) having a pleasant or acceptable taste 可口的；味美的 **2 ~ (to sb)** pleasant or acceptable to sb 宜人的；可意的；可接受的：*Some of the dialogue has been changed to make it more palatable to an American audience.* 有些對白有所修改以適應美國觀眾的口味。OPP **unpalatable**

pal·atal /ˈpælətl/ *noun* (*phonetics* 語音) a speech sound made by placing the tongue against or near the hard PALATE of the mouth, for example /j/ at the beginning of *yes* 腭音 ▸ **pal·atal** *adj.*

pal·at·al·ize (*BrE* also **-ise**) /ˈpælətəlaɪz/ *verb* **~ sth** (*phonetics* 語音) to make a speech sound by putting your tongue against or near your hard PALATE 使（語音）腭化 ▸ **pal·at·al·iz·ation, -is·ation** /ˌpælətəlaɪˈzeɪʃn/ *noun* [U]

pal·ate /ˈpælət/ *noun* **1** the top part of the inside of the mouth 腭；上腭：*the **hard/soft palate*** (= the hard/soft part at the front/back of the palate) 硬腭；軟腭 ➲ see also CLEFT PALATE **2** [usually sing.] the ability to recognize and/or enjoy good food and drink 味覺；品嚐力：*a menu to tempt even the most **jaded palate*** 能引起最沒胃口的人食慾的食譜

pa·la·tial /pəˈleɪʃl/ *adj.* [usually before noun] (of a room or building 房間或建築物) very large and impressive, like a palace 宮殿般的；富麗堂皇的 SYN **splendid**

pa·lat·in·ate /pəˈlætɪnət/ *noun* **1** [C] the area ruled by a Count Palatine (= a ruler with the power of a king or queen) 巴拉丁領地（行使王權的巴拉丁伯爵的轄地）**2 the Palatinate** [sing.] the land of the German Empire that was ruled over by the Count Palatine of the Rhine 巴拉丁領地（萊恩的巴拉丁伯爵統轄的德意志帝國領地）

pal·at·ine /ˈpælətaɪn/ *adj.* [only before noun] **1** (of an official, etc. in the past 舊時官員等) having the power in a particular area that a king or queen usually has （在領地內）行使王權的 **2** (of an area of land 地域) ruled over by sb who has the power of a king or queen 歸行使王權者統轄的；屬於巴拉丁領地的

pa·la·ver /pəˈlɑːvə(r); *NAmE* also -ˈlæv-/ *noun* (*informal*) **1** [U, sing.] (*BrE*) a lot of unnecessary activity, excitement or trouble, especially caused by sth that is unimportant 麻煩；瑣事；忙亂 SYN **fuss**：*What's all the palaver about?* 這些雞毛蒜皮的事到底是為什麼？◇ *What a palaver it is, trying to get a new visa!* 申請新簽證真煩死人了！**2** [U] (*NAmE*) talk that does not have any meaning; nonsense 空話；廢話：*He's talking palaver.* 他在信口開河。

pa·lazzo pants /pəˈlætsəʊ pænts; *NAmE* pəˈlɑːtsoʊ/ *noun* [pl.] women's trousers/pants with wide loose legs 帕拉柔寬腿女褲

pale 0┳ /peɪl/ *adj., verb, noun*

■ *adj.* (**paler, pal·est**) **1** 0┳ (of a person, their face, etc. 人、面孔等) having skin that is almost white; having skin that is whiter than usual because of illness, a strong emotion, etc. 灰白的；蒼白的；白皙的：*a pale complexion* 慘白的面容 ◇ *pale with fear* 害怕得臉色蒼白 ◇ *to **go/turn pale*** 變得蒼白 ◇ *You look pale. Are you OK?*

你氣色不好，沒事吧？◇ *The ordeal left her looking* ***pale and drawn***. 這場磨難使她看來蒼白而又憔悴。 **2** light in colour; containing a lot of white 淺色的；淡色的： *pale blue eyes* 淡藍色的眼睛 ◇ *a paler shade of green* 淡綠的色調 ◇ *a pale sky* 天色昏暗 **OPP dark, deep 3** (of light 光線) not strong or bright 暗淡的；微弱的： *the cold pale light of dawn* 破曉時分的魚白寒光 ⮌ see also PALLID, PALLOR ▸ **pale·ly** /ˈpeɪlli/ *adv.* : *Mark stared palely (= with a pale face) at his plate.* 馬克面色蒼白，呆呆地望着盤子。 **pale·ness** *noun* [U]

■ ***verb*** [I] **~ (at sth)** to become paler than usual 變得比平常白；變蒼白： *She (= her face) paled visibly at the sight of the police car.* 她一看見警車，臉色就刷地變白了。◇ *The blue of the sky paled to a light grey.* 天空的藍色漸變成了淺灰色。

IDM **ˈpale beside/next to sth** | **ˈpale in/by comparison (with/to sth)** | **ˈpale into insignificance** to seem less important when compared with sth else 相形見絀；顯得遜色： *Last year's riots pale in comparison with this latest outburst of violence.* 去年的騷亂與最近這次暴亂相比，可說是小巫見大巫。

■ ***noun***

IDM **beˌyond the ˈpale** considered by most people to be unacceptable or unreasonable 出格；出圈；越軌；令人不能容忍： *His remarks were clearly beyond the pale.* 他的話顯然過分了。

pale·face /ˈpeɪlfeɪs/ *noun* (used in film/movies, etc. 用於電影等) a name for a white person, said to have been used by Native Americans 白臉人（據説美洲土著稱呼白人曾使用的名稱）

paleo- (*NAmE*) = PALAEO-

pal·ette /ˈpælət/ *noun* **1** a thin board with a hole in it for the thumb to go through, used by an artist for mixing colours on when painting 調色板 ⮌ **VISUAL VOCAB** page V41 **2** [usually sing.] (*technical* 術語) the colours used by a particular artist（畫家使用的）主要色彩，主色調： *Greens and browns are typical of Ribera's palette.* 綠色和棕色是里貝拉的主色調。

ˈpalette knife *noun* a knife with a blade that bends easily and has a round end, used by artists and in cooking 調色刀；畫刀；（炊具中的）鏟刀 ⮌ **VISUAL VOCAB** page V26

pali·mony /ˈpælɪməni/ *noun* [U] (*informal, especially NAmE*) money that a court orders sb to pay regularly to a former partner when they have lived together without being married（法院判定定期付給前未婚同居對象的）生活費，贍養費 ⮌ compare ALIMONY

pal·imp·sest /ˈpælɪmpsest/ *noun* **1** an ancient document from which some or all of the original text has been removed and replaced by a new text 再生羊皮紙卷，重寫羊皮書卷（全部或部份原有文字被刮去，在上面另行書寫） **2** (*formal*) something that has many different layers of meaning or detail 具有多重意義的事物；多層次的東西

pal·in·drome /ˈpælɪndrəʊm; *NAmE* -droʊm/ *noun* a word or phrase that reads the same backwards as forwards, for example *madam* or *nurses run* 迴文（正反讀都一樣的詞語或短語）

pal·ing /ˈpeɪlɪŋ/ *noun* [C, usually pl., U] a metal or wooden post that is pointed at the top; a fence made of these posts 尖木樁；尖鐵條；圍欄

pal·is·ade /ˌpælɪˈseɪd/ *noun* **1** a fence made of strong wooden or metal posts that are pointed at the top, especially used to protect a building in the past 木柵欄；金屬柵欄 **2 palisades** [pl.] (*US*) a line of high steep CLIFFS, especially along a river or by the sea or ocean（尤指河邊、海邊的）絕壁，峭壁

pall /pɔːl/ *noun, verb*

■ ***noun*** **1** [usually sing.] **~ of sth** a thick dark cloud of sth 濃密的雲煙；塵煙： *a* ***pall of smoke/dust*** 一團煙霧 / 沙塵 ◇ (*figurative*) *News of her death* ***cast a pall*** *over the event.* 她的死亡消息給這件事蒙上了陰影。 **2** a cloth spread over a COFFIN (= a box used for burying a dead person in) 柩衣；棺材罩布

■ ***verb*** [I] (not used in the progressive tenses 不用於進行時) **~ (on sb)** to become less interesting to sb over a period of time because they have done or seen it too much（因見或做得過多而）失去魅力，使人厭倦： *Even the impressive scenery began to pall on me after a few hundred miles.* 行經了數百英里以後，即使秀麗風光也使我感到索然無味了。

pal·la·dium /pəˈleɪdiəm/ *noun* [U] (*symb.* **Pd**) a chemical element. Palladium is a rare silver-white metal that looks like PLATINUM. 鈀（銀白色稀有化學元素）

ˈpall-bearer *noun* a person who walks beside or helps to carry the COFFIN at a funeral 扶靈者；抬棺者

pal·let /ˈpælət/ *noun* **1** a heavy wooden or metal base that can be used for moving or storing goods 托盤；平台；運貨板 **2** a cloth bag filled with STRAW, used for sleeping on（睡覺用的）草墊子

pal·li·asse /ˈpæliæs; *NAmE* ˌpælˈjæs/ *noun* a cloth bag filled with STRAW, used for sleeping on 草薦；草褥 **SYN pallet**

pal·li·ate /ˈpælieɪt/ *verb* **~ sth** (*formal*) to make a disease or an illness less painful or unpleasant without curing it 減輕，緩和（疾病或不適）

pal·lia·tive /ˈpæliətɪv/ *noun* **1** (*medical* 醫) a medicine or medical treatment that reduces pain without curing its cause 治標藥物；緩解劑；治標措施；保守療法 **2** (*formal*, usually *disapproving*) an action, a decision, etc. that is designed to make a difficult situation seem better without actually solving the cause of the problems 權宜之計；消極措施；緩衝劑 ▸ **pal·lia·tive** *adj.* [usually before noun] : *palliative treatment* 保守療法 ◇ *short-term palliative measures* 短期的權宜之計

pal·lid /ˈpælɪd/ *adj.* **1** (of a person, their face, etc. 人、面色等) pale, especially because of illness（尤指因病）蒼白的： *a pallid complexion* 蒼白的臉色 **2** (of colours or light 顏色或光線) not strong or bright, and therefore not attractive 暗淡的；微弱的；乏味的： *a pallid sky* 暗淡的天空

pal·lor /ˈpælə(r)/ *noun* [U] pale colouring of the face, especially because of illness or fear 蒼白的臉色（尤指因病或恐懼）：*Her cheeks had an unhealthy pallor.* 她面色蒼白，顯得虛弱。

pally /ˈpæli/ *adj.* ⮌ PAL

palm /pɑːm/ *noun, verb*

■ ***noun*** **1** the inner surface of the hand between the wrist and the fingers 手掌；手心： *He held the bird gently in* ***the palm of his hand***. 他把小鳥輕輕地托在掌心。◇ *sweaty palms* 汗涔涔的手掌 ◇ ***to read sb's palm*** (= to say what you think will happen to sb by looking at the lines on their palm) 看手相 ⮌ **VISUAL VOCAB** page V59 **2** (also **ˈpalm tree**) a straight tree with a mass of long leaves at the top, growing in tropical countries. There are several types of palm tree, some of which produce fruit. 棕櫚樹： *a date palm* 棗椰樹 ◇ *a coconut palm* 椰子樹 ◇ ***palm leaves/fronds/groves*** 棕櫚葉 / 樹叢 ⮌ **VISUAL VOCAB** page V10

IDM **have sb in the ˌpalm of your ˈhand** to have complete control or influence over sb 完全控制某人；把某人攥在手心裏 ⮌ more at CROSS *v.*, GREASE *v.*

■ ***verb*** **~ sth** to hide a coin, card, etc. in your hand, especially when performing a trick 把…藏在手中（尤指玩戲法）

PHR V **ˌpalm sb↔ˈoff (with sth)** (*informal*) to persuade sb to believe an excuse or an explanation that is not true, in order to stop them asking questions or complaining（藉口某事）欺騙搪塞某人，騙過某人 **ˌpalm sth↔ˈoff (on/onto sb)** | **ˌpalm sb↔ˈoff (with sth)** (*informal*) to persuade sb to accept sth that has no value or that you do not want, especially by tricking them. 哄騙他人接受（無價值或自己不要的東西）；用假貨行騙： *She's always palming the worst jobs off on her assistant.* 她總是哄騙她的助手做最苦的差事。◇ *Make sure he doesn't try to palm you off with faulty goods.* 當心別上當讓他把殘次品賣給你。 **ˌpalm sth ˈoff as sth** (*informal*) to tell sb that sth is better than it is, especially in order to sell it 推銷假貨；以假亂真： *They were trying to palm the table off as a genuine antique.* 他們在設法把那張普通桌子當真正的古董推銷出去。

P

Palm·cord·er™ /ˈpɑːmkɔːdə(r); *NAmE* -kɔːrd-/ *noun* a small CAMCORDER (= video camera that records pictures and sound) that can be held in the PALM of one hand 掌中寶攝像機；掌上型數位攝影機

pal·metto /pælˈmetəʊ; *NAmE* -toʊ/ *noun* (*pl.* **-os**) a small PALM tree that grows in the south-eastern US 矮棕櫚（生長於美國東南部）

palm·ist /ˈpɑːmɪst/ *noun* a person who claims to be able to tell what a person is like and what will happen to them in the future, by looking at the lines on the PALM of their hand 手相術士；看手相的人

palm·is·try /ˈpɑːmɪstri/ *noun* [U] the art of telling what a person is like and what will happen to them by looking at the lines on the PALM of their hand 手相術

ˈpalm oil *noun* [U] oil obtained from the fruit of some types of PALM tree, used in cooking and in making soap, CANDLES, etc. 棕櫚油

ˌPalm ˈSunday *noun* [U, C] (in the Christian Church) the Sunday before Easter 棕枝主日，聖枝主日（復活節前的星期日）

palm·top /ˈpɑːmtɒp; *NAmE* -tɑːp/ *noun* a small computer that can be held in the PALM of one hand 掌上電腦；掌上機

palmy /ˈpɑːmi/ *adj.* (**palm·ier**, **palmi·est**) used to describe a time in the past when life was good（指昔日）繁榮昌盛的，美好年華的：*That's a picture of me in my palmier days.* 那是我風華正茂時的照片。

palo·mino /ˌpæləˈmiːnəʊ; *NAmE* -noʊ/ *noun* (*pl.* **-os**) a horse that is a cream or gold colour with a white MANE and tail 帕洛米諾馬（體毛奶白色或金黃色、鬃毛和尾毛為白色）

palp·able /ˈpælpəbl/ *adj.* that is easily noticed by the mind or the senses 易於察覺的；可意識到的；明顯的：*a* **palpable sense** *of relief* 如釋重負 ◇ *The tension in the room was almost palpable.* 屋子裏的緊張氣氛幾乎能感覺到。▸ **palp·ably** /-əbli/ *adv.*：*It was palpably clear what she really meant.* 她的本意是什麼，那是一清二楚的。

P

pal·pate /pælˈpeɪt/ *verb* **~ sth** (*medical* 醫) to examine part of the body by touching it 觸診；捫診；觸摸檢查 ▸ **pal·pa·tion** *noun* [U]

pal·pi·tate /ˈpælpɪteɪt/ *verb* [I] (of the heart 心臟) to beat rapidly and/or in an IRREGULAR way especially because of fear or excitement 急速跳動，悸動（尤指因恐懼或興奮）

pal·pi·ta·tions /ˌpælpɪˈteɪʃnz/ *noun* [pl.] a physical condition in which your heart beats very quickly and in an IRREGULAR way 心悸：*Just the thought of flying gives me palpitations* (= makes me very nervous). 一想到飛行我的心就嘣嘣地跳。

palsy /ˈpɔːlzi/ *noun* [U] (*old-fashioned*) PARALYSIS (= loss of control or feeling in part or most of the body), especially when the arms and legs shake without control 癱瘓，麻痹（尤指四肢顫動類）➲ see also CEREBRAL PALSY ▸ **pal·sied** /ˈpɔːlzid/ *adj.*

pal·try /ˈpɔːltri/ *adj.* [usually before noun] **1** (of an amount 數量) too small to be considered as important or useful 可忽略不計的；微小的；微不足道的 SYN **meagre**：*This account offers a paltry 1% return on your investment.* 這個賬戶給你投資的回報僅是微不足道的 1%。◇ *a paltry sum* 小得可憐的數額 **2** having no value or useful qualities 無價值的；無用的：*a paltry gesture* 沒有意義的姿態

pam·pas /ˈpæmpəs; *NAmE* also -pəz/ *noun* (usually **the pampas**) [sing.+sing./pl. v.] the large area of land in S America that has few trees and is covered in grass（南美洲的）大草原，草甸

ˈpampas grass *noun* [U] a type of tall grass from S America that is often grown in gardens/yards for its long silver-white flowers that look like feathers 潘帕斯草，蒲葦（產於南美洲，開銀白色長羽毛狀花，常見於園子）

pam·per /ˈpæmpə(r)/ *verb* **~ sb** (sometimes *disapproving*) to take care of sb very well and make them feel as comfortable as possible 細心照顧；精心護理；嬌慣；縱容 SYN **cosset**：*Pamper yourself with our new range of beauty treatments.* 盡情享受一下我們的新系列美容服務吧。◇ *a spoilt and pampered child* 一個嬌生慣養的孩子

pamph·let /ˈpæmflət/ *noun* a very thin book with a paper cover, containing information about a particular subject 小冊子；手冊 SYN **leaflet**

pamph·let·eer /ˌpæmfləˈtɪə(r); *NAmE* -ˈtɪr/ *noun* a person who writes pamphlets on particular subjects 撰寫小冊子的人；小冊子作者

pan¹ O-w /pæn/ *noun, verb*

■ ***noun*** **1** O-w a container, usually made of metal, with a handle or handles, used for cooking food in 平鍋；平底鍋：*pots and pans* 鍋壺瓢盆 ◇ *a large stainless steel pan* 一隻不銹鋼大平鍋 ➲ see also FRYING PAN, SAUCEPAN **2** O-w the amount contained in a pan 一鍋的量：*a pan of boiling water* 一鍋開水 **3** (*NAmE*) (*BrE* **tin**) a metal container used for cooking food in（烘煮食物用的）烤盤，烤模：*a cake pan* 蛋糕烤盤 ➲ **VISUAL VOCAB** page V27 **4** either of the dishes on a pair of SCALES that you put things into in order to weigh them（天平的）稱盤 **5** (*BrE*) the bowl of a toilet 馬桶 ➲ see also BEDPAN, DUSTPAN, SKIDPAN, WARMING PAN

IDM **go down the ˈpan** (*BrE, informal*) to be wasted or spoiled 被浪費；被糟蹋：*That's another brilliant idea down the pan.* 又一個好主意被糟蹋了！➲ more at FLASH *n.*

■ ***verb*** (**-nn-**) **1** [T, usually passive] **~ sth** (*informal*) to severely criticize sth such as a play or a film/movie 嚴厲批評，抨擊（戲劇、電影等）SYN **slate** **2** [I, T] if a television or video camera **pans** somewhere, or a person **pans** or **pans a camera**, the camera moves in a particular direction, to follow an object or to film a wide area（移動攝像機）追拍，搖攝：**+ adv./prep.** *The camera panned back to the audience.* 攝像機搖回拍攝觀眾。◇ **~ sth + adv./prep.** *He panned the camera along the row of faces.* 他移動攝像機順着這一排面孔拍攝。**3** [I, T] **~ (for) sth** to wash soil or small stones in a pan to find gold or other valuable minerals（用淘選盤）淘洗；淘（金）：*panning for gold* 淘金

PHR V **ˌpan ˈout** (*informal*) (of events or a situation 事情或局面) to develop in a particular way 以一定方式發展：*I'm happy with the way things have panned out.* 我對事情的結果感到很滿意。

pan² = PAAN

pan- /pæn/ *combining form* (in adjectives and nouns 構成形容詞和名詞) including all of sth; connected with the whole of sth 包含一切的；全部的；泛：*pan-African* 泛非洲的 ◇ *pandemic* 大流行病

pana·cea /ˌpænəˈsiːə/ *noun* **~ (for sth)** something that will solve all the problems of a particular situation 萬靈藥；萬能之計

pan·ache /pəˈnæʃ; pæˈn-; *NAmE* also -ˈnɑːʃ/ *noun* [U] the quality of being able to do things in a confident and elegant way that other people find attractive 神氣十足；瀟灑氣質 SYN **flair, style**

pan·ama /ˈpænəmɑː/ (also **ˌpanama ˈhat**) *noun* a man's hat made from fine STRAW 巴拿馬草帽 ➲ **VISUAL VOCAB** page V65

pana·tella (*BrE*) (*NAmE* **pana·tela**) /ˌpænəˈtelə/ *noun* a long thin CIGAR 細長雪茄

pan·cake /ˈpænkeɪk/ *noun* **1** [C] a thin flat round cake made from a mixture of flour, eggs and milk that is fried on both sides, usually eaten hot for breakfast in the US, and in Britain either as a DESSERT with sugar, jam, etc. or as a main course with meat, cheese, etc. 烙餅；薄餅 **2** [U] thick make-up for the face, used especially in the theatre（尤指舞台化妝用的）粉餅 IDM see FLAT *adj.*

ˈPancake Day *noun* (*informal*) the day before the beginning of Lent, when people traditionally eat PANCAKES 薄餅日（封齋期的前一天，按傳統習慣吃薄餅）➲ compare SHROVE TUESDAY

ˈpancake race *noun* a traditional race in Britain on Pancake Day, in which each runner keeps throwing a PANCAKE into the air from a pan 薄餅賽跑（薄餅日舉行

的英國傳統賽跑，參加者不斷將平底鍋中的薄烤餅拋向空中）

pan·chay·at /pʌnˈtʃaɪət/ *noun* (in some S Asian countries 某些南亞國家) **1** a village council 潘查耶特；村務委員會 **2** the official organization that governs local areas in the country, outside large towns （大城市以外的）地方當局；村（或縣、地區）評議會

pan·creas /ˈpæŋkriəs/ *noun* an organ near the stomach that produces INSULIN and a liquid that helps the body to DIGEST food 胰；胰腺 ➲ **VISUAL VOCAB** page V59 ▸ **pan·cre·at·ic** /ˌpæŋkriˈætɪk/ *adj.* [only before noun]

panda /ˈpændə/ *noun* **1** (also ˌ**giant** ˈ**panda**) a large black and white animal like a BEAR, that lives in China and is very rare 大貓熊；大熊貓 **2** (also ˌ**red** ˈ**panda**) an Asian animal like a RACCOON, with reddish-brown fur and a long thick tail 小貓熊，小熊貓（產於亞洲，毛棕紅色，尾巴粗長）

ˈ**panda car** *noun* (*old-fashioned, BrE, informal*) a small police car 巡邏警車

pan·dem·ic /pænˈdemɪk/ *noun* a disease that spreads over a whole country or the whole world （全國或全球性）流行病；大流行病 ▸ **pan·dem·ic** *adj.*：*a pandemic disease* 大範圍流行的疾病 ➲ compare ENDEMIC, EPIDEMIC

pan·de·mon·ium /ˌpændəˈməʊniəm; *NAmE* -ˈmoʊ-/ *noun* [U] a situation in which there is a lot of noise, activity and confusion, especially because people are feeling angry or frightened 騷動；群情沸騰 **SYN** **chaos**：*Pandemonium broke out when the news was announced.* 這消息一宣佈，立即亂成一片。

pan·der /ˈpændə(r)/ *verb*
PHR V ˈ**pander to sth/sb** (*disapproving*) to do what sb wants, or try to please them, especially when this is not acceptable or reasonable 迎合；奉迎；投其所好：*to pander to sb's wishes* 迎合某人的願望 ◇ *The speech was pandering to racial prejudice.* 這篇講話是在縱容種族偏見。

p. and h. (also **p. & h.**) /ˌpiː ənd ˈeɪtʃ/ *abbr.* (*NAmE*) postage and handling 郵資和手續費 ➲ compare P. AND P.

pan·dit /ˈpændɪt/ (also **pun·dit**) *noun* **1** a Hindu priest or wise man （印度的）祭司，哲人 **2** (*IndE*) a teacher 教師 **3** (*IndE*) a skilled musician 樂師

Pandora's box /pænˌdɔːrəz ˈbɒks; *NAmE* ˈbɑːks/ *noun* [sing., U] a process that, if started, will cause many problems that cannot be solved 潘多拉魔盒（指邪惡之源）：*This court case could* ***open a Pandora's box*** *of similar claims.* 這宗訴訟案會為類似的申訴開啟潘多拉魔盒。
ORIGIN From the Greek myth in which **Pandora** was created by the god Zeus and sent to the earth with a box containing many evils. When she opened the box, the evils came out and infected the earth. 源自希臘神話。主神宙斯創造了潘多拉並派其帶着裝滿邪惡的盒子下凡。當她打開盒子時，各種邪惡奔湧而出，泛濫人間。

pan·dowdy /pænˈdaʊdi/ *noun* (*pl.* **-ies**) [C, U] (*US*) a sweet dish of apples and spices covered with a mixture of butter, milk and eggs, that is baked 蘋果布丁（用黃油、牛奶和雞蛋覆蓋蘋果和香料烤製而成）

p. and p. (also **p. & p.**) /ˌpiː ən ˈpiː/ *abbr.* (*BrE*) postage and packing (= the cost of packing sth and sending it by post) 郵資與包裝費：*Add £2 for p. and p.* 另加郵資及包裝費 2 英鎊。➲ compare P. AND H., S AND H

pane /peɪn/ *noun* a single sheet of glass in a window （一片）窗玻璃：*a pane of glass* 一片窗玻璃 ◇ *a windowpane* 一塊窗玻璃

pan·eer (also **panir**) /pæˈnɪə(r); *NAmE* -ˈnɪr/ *noun* [U] a type of soft cheese used in Asian cooking 奶豆腐（亞洲烹飪用軟乾酪）

pan·egyr·ic /ˌpænəˈdʒɪrɪk/ *noun* (*formal*) a speech or piece of writing praising sb/sth 頌辭；頌文

panel 🔑 **AW** /ˈpænl/ *noun, verb*
■ *noun* **1** 🔑 [C] a square or RECTANGULAR piece of wood, glass or metal that forms part of a larger surface such as a door or wall （門、牆等上面的）嵌板，鑲板，方格板塊：*One of the glass panels in the front door was cracked.* 前門的一塊方玻璃破裂了。➲ **VISUAL VOCAB** page V24 ➲ see also SOLAR PANEL **2** [C] a piece of metal that forms part of the outer frame of a vehicle （車身的）金屬板，板金 **3** [C] a piece of cloth that forms part of a piece of clothing （衣服上的）鑲條，嵌條，飾片：*The trousers have double thickness knee panels for extra protection.* 這條褲子上有雙倍厚的護膝片以加強保護。**4** 🔑 [C+sing./pl. v.] a group of specialists who give their advice or opinion about sth; a group of people who discuss topics of interest on television or radio 專家咨詢組；（廣播、電視上的）討論小組：*an advisory panel* 顧問組 ◇ *a panel of experts* 專家組 ◇ *We have two politicians on tonight's panel.* 今天晚上出席座談會的有兩位政界人士。◇ *a panel discussion* 專家小組討論 **5** (also ˈ**jury panel**) [C] (both *especially NAmE*) = JURY (1) **6** [C] a flat board in a vehicle or on a piece of machinery where the controls and instruments are fixed （汽車或其他機械的）控制板，儀表盤：*an* ***instrument panel*** 儀表盤 ◇ *a* ***control/display panel*** 控制／顯示面板
■ *verb* (**-ll-**, *especially US* **-l-**) [usually passive] **~ sth** to cover or decorate a surface with flat strips of wood, glass, etc. 鑲板（用木或玻璃板等鑲嵌或裝飾）：*The walls were panelled in oak.* 牆壁鑲了橡木飾片。◇ *a* ***glass-/wood-panelled*** *door* 鑲玻璃／木板的門

ˈ**panel beater** *noun* (*BrE*) a person whose job is to remove the DENTS from the outer frame of a vehicle that has been in an accident （汽車）板金工

ˈ**panel game** *noun* (*BrE*) a game in which a team of people try to answer questions correctly, especially on television or radio （尤指電視或電台等的）分組答題競賽，分組智力競賽

pan·el·ling **AW** (*especially US* **pan·el·ing**) /ˈpænəlɪŋ/ *noun* [U] square or RECTANGULAR pieces of wood used to cover and decorate walls, ceilings, etc. （裝飾牆壁、天花板等的）嵌板，飾塊

pan·el·list (*especially US* **pan·el·ist**) /ˈpænəlɪst/ *noun* a person who is a member of a panel answering questions during a discussion, for example on radio or television （廣播、電視節目中的）討論會成員

ˈ**panel van** (*AustralE, NZE, SAfrE*) (*NAmE* ˈ**panel truck**) *noun* a small van/truck, especially one without windows at the sides or seats for passengers （密封式）小貨車，箱式貨車

ˈ**pan-fry** *verb* (**pan-fries, pan-frying, pan-fried, pan-fried**) **~ sth** to fry food in a pan in shallow fat 用平鍋煎：*pan-fried chicken* 用平鍋攤煎的雞肉

pang /pæŋ/ *noun* a sudden strong feeling of physical or emotional pain 突然的疼痛（或痛苦）；一陣劇痛：***hunger pangs/pangs of hunger*** 飢餓之苦 ◇ *a sudden* ***pang of jealousy*** 突然湧來的嫉妒

panga /ˈpæŋɡə/ *noun* (*EAfrE, SAfrE*) a large heavy knife that is used for cutting grass or small sticks or for removing WEEDS 大砍刀

Pan·gaea /pænˈdʒiːə/ *noun* [sing.] (*geology* 地) an extremely large area of land which existed millions of years ago, made up of all the present continents 泛大陸，泛古陸（原始大陸，由現在的所有大陸組成）

pan·go·lin /ˈpæŋɡəlɪn; *BrE also* pæŋˈɡəʊlɪn/ (also ˌ**scaly** ˈ**anteater**) *noun* a small animal from Africa or Asia that eats insects, and has a long nose, tongue and tail, and hard SCALES on its body 穿山甲，有鱗食蟻獸（見於非洲和亞洲）

pan·han·dler /ˈpænhændlə(r)/ *noun* (*NAmE, informal*) a person who asks other people for money in the street 叫化子；乞丐 ▸ **pan·han·dle** *verb* [I]

panic /ˈpænɪk/ *noun, verb*
■ *noun* [U, C, usually sing.] **1** a sudden feeling of great fear that cannot be controlled and prevents you from thinking clearly 驚恐；恐慌：*a moment of panic* 一時驚慌 ◇ *They were in a state of panic.* 他們驚恐萬狀。◇ *Office workers fled* ***in panic*** *as the fire took hold.* 起火時，辦公室人員驚慌逃出。◇ *There's no point* ***getting into a panic*** *about the exams.* 對考試驚惶失措是沒有用的。◇ *a* ***panic attack*** (= a condition in which you suddenly feel very anxious, causing your heart to beat faster, etc.) 一陣心慌意亂 ◇ *a panic decision* (= one that is made when you

P

are in a state of panic) 慌亂中作出的決定 ➲ SYNONYMS at FEAR **2** a situation in which people are made to feel very anxious, causing them to act quickly and without thinking carefully 人心惶惶的局面；惶恐不安：*News of the losses caused (a) panic among investors.* 虧損的消息令投資者人心惶惶。◇ *Careful planning at this stage will help to avoid a last-minute panic.* 現在仔細規劃就可以避免事到臨頭手忙腳亂。◇ ***There's no panic*** (= we do not need to rush), *we've got plenty of time.* 不用着急，我們有的是時間。◇ ***panic buying/selling*** (= the act of buying/selling things quickly and without thinking carefully because you are afraid that a particular situation will become worse) 恐慌性搶購 / 拋售

IDM **'panic stations** (*BrE, informal*) a situation in which people feel anxious and there is a lot of confused activity, especially because there is a lot to do in a short period of time 慌亂的狀態；（尤指）忙亂的狀況

■ ***verb*** (**-ck-**) [I, T] to suddenly feel frightened so that you cannot think clearly and you say or do sth stupid, dangerous, etc.; to make sb do this （使）驚慌，驚慌失措：*I panicked when I saw smoke coming out of the engine.* 我看見發動機冒煙時，嚇得手足無措。◇ **~ sb/sth** *The gunfire panicked the horses.* 槍聲驚嚇到馬匹。

PHR V **'panic sb into doing sth** [usually passive] to make sb act too quickly because they are afraid of sth 使倉惶行事；使倉促行動

'panic button *noun* a button that sb working in a bank, etc. can press to call for help if they are in danger （銀行等的）緊急呼救按鈕

IDM **press/push the 'panic button** (*BrE*) to react in a sudden or extreme way to sth unexpected that has frightened you 驚慌失措；倉促行事；採取緊急行動

pan·icky /'pænɪki/ *adj.* (*informal*) anxious about sth; feeling or showing panic 焦慮不安的；驚慌的 SYN **hysterical**

'panic room (also **'safe room**) *noun* a room in a home or an office building where people can go to avoid a dangerous situation（家中或辦公樓中的）緊急避險室，避難室

'panic-stricken *adj.* extremely anxious about sth, in a way that prevents you from thinking clearly 驚慌失措的 SYN **hysterical**

pa·nini /pə'niːni/ (also **pa·nino** /pə'niːnəʊ; *NAmE* -noʊ/) *noun* (*pl.* **pa·nini** or **pa·ninis**) a sandwich made with Italian bread, usually toasted 意式帕尼尼三明治（通常經烘烤）

panir = PANEER

pan·nier /'pæniə(r)/ *noun* each of a pair of bags or boxes carried on either side of the back wheel of a bicycle or motorcycle; each of a pair of BASKETS carried on either side of its back by a horse or DONKEY （自行車、摩托車後架兩側的）掛籃，貨筐；（牲畜背上馱的）馱籠，馱籃

pan·oply /'pænəpli/ *noun* [sing., U] (*formal*) a large and impressive number or collection of sth 巨大的數量（或收藏品）SYN **array**

pan·or·ama /ˌpænə'rɑːmə; *NAmE* -'ræmə/ *noun* **1** a view of a wide area of land 全景 SYN **vista**：*There is a superb panorama of the mountains from the hotel.* 從旅館可飽覽峰巒疊嶂的雄偉景觀。➲ SYNONYMS at VIEW **2** a description, study or set of pictures that presents all the different aspects or stages of a particular subject, event, etc.（某專題或事件的）全面敘述，綜合研究；全景畫卷 ▸ **pan·or·am·ic** /ˌpænə'ræmɪk/ *adj.* [usually before noun]：*a panoramic view over the valley* 山谷的全景

'pan pipes *noun* [pl.] (*BrE*) (*NAmE* **'pan·pipe** [C]) a musical instrument made of a row of pipes of different lengths that you play by blowing across the open ends 排簫；牧神簫

pansy /'pænzi/ *noun* (*pl.* **-ies**) **1** a small garden plant with brightly coloured flowers 三色堇；蝴蝶花 **2** (*taboo, slang*) an offensive word for a HOMOSEXUAL man 娘娘腔的男人（對同性戀男人的蔑稱）

pant /pænt/ *verb* [I, T] (**+ speech**) to breathe quickly with short breaths, usually with your mouth open, because you have been doing some physical exercise, or because it is very hot 氣喘；喘息：*She finished the race panting heavily.* 她跑完比賽氣喘吁吁的。◇ *She could hear him panting up the stairs* (= running up and breathing quickly). 她聽見他氣喘吁吁地跑上樓。◇ *He found her* ***panting for breath*** *at the top of the hill.* 上到山頂他發現她上氣不接下氣。▸ **pant** *noun* [usually pl.]：*His breath came in short pants.* 他氣息急促。➲ see also PANTS

IDM see PUFF *v.*

PHR V **'pant for/after sb/sth** to want sth/sb very much 渴望：*The end of the novel leaves you panting for more.* 小說的結尾讓人感到意猶未盡。

pan·ta·loons /ˌpæntə'luːnz/ *noun* [pl.] **1** women's loose trousers/pants with wide legs that fit tightly at the ankles 女式燈籠褲 **2** (in the past) men's tight trousers/pants fastened at the foot （舊時的）男式緊身褲，馬褲

pan·tech·nicon /pæn'teknɪkən/ *noun* (*old-fashioned, BrE*) = REMOVAL VAN

pan·the·ism /'pænθiɪzəm/ *noun* [U] **1** the belief that God is present in all natural things 泛神論（認為神存在於萬事萬物）**2** belief in many or all gods 泛神崇拜；泛神信仰 ▸ **pan·the·ist** /-θiɪst/ *noun* **pan·the·ist·ic** /ˌpænθi'ɪstɪk/ *adj.*

pan·theon /'pænθiən; *NAmE* -θiɑːn/ *noun* **1** (*technical* 術語) all the gods of a nation or people （一國或一個民族信仰的）眾神，諸神：*the ancient Egyptian pantheon* 古埃及眾神 **2** (*formal*) a group of people who are famous within a particular area of activity （統稱某一領域的）名人，名流 **3** a TEMPLE (= religious building) built in honour of all the gods of a nation; a building in which famous dead people of a nation are buried or HONOURED 萬神廟；先賢祠；偉人祠

pan·ther /'pænθə(r)/ *noun* **1** a black LEOPARD (= a large wild animal of the cat family) 黑豹 **2** (*NAmE*) = PUMA

pantie girdle *noun* = PANTY GIRDLE

pan·ties /'pæntiz/ (*especially NAmE*) (*BrE* also **knick·ers**) *noun* [pl.] a piece of women's underwear that covers the body from the waist to the tops of the legs 女式短襯褲

pan·tile /'pæntaɪl/ *noun* a curved TILE used for roofs 波形瓦；筒瓦

panto /'pæntəʊ; *NAmE* -toʊ/ *noun* (*pl.* **-os** /-təʊz; *NAmE* -toʊz/) (*BrE, informal*) = PANTOMIME (1)

panto·graph /'pæntəgrɑːf; *NAmE* -græf/ *noun* a device used for copying a drawing in a bigger or smaller size 縮放儀；比例繪圖儀

panto·mime /'pæntəmaɪm/ *noun* **1** (also *BrE informal* **panto**) [C, U] (in Britain) a type of play with music, dancing and jokes, that is based on a FAIRY TALE and is usually performed at Christmas （英國多在聖誕節期間上演的）童話劇 **2** [U, C, usually sing.] the use of movement and the expression of your face to communicate sth or to tell a story 啞劇；默劇 SYN **mime 3** [C, usually sing.] (*BrE*) a ridiculous situation, usually with a lot of confusion 滑稽可笑的局面 SYN **farce**

ˌ**pantomime 'dame** (also **dame**) *noun* (*BrE*) a female character in a PANTOMIME (1), that is usually played by a man 童話劇中的女性（通常由男人扮演）

ˌ**pantomime 'horse** *noun* (*BrE*) a character in a PANTOMIME (1) that is supposed to be a horse, played by two people in a special COSTUME 童話劇中的馬（由兩人共穿一件戲裝扮演）

pan·try /'pæntri/ *noun* (*pl.* **-ies**) a cupboard/closet or small room in a house, used for storing food 食品貯藏室；食品貯藏櫃 SYN **larder**

pants 0-w /pænts/ *noun* [pl.]

1 0-w (*BrE*) UNDERPANTS or KNICKERS 內褲；短襯褲：*a pair of pants* 一件內褲 **2** 0-w (*especially NAmE*) trousers 褲子：*a new pair of pants* 一條新褲子 ◇ *ski pants* 滑雪褲 ➲ VISUAL VOCAB page V61 ➲ see also CARGO PANTS **3** (*BrE, slang*) (also used as an adjective 也用作形容詞) something you think is of poor quality 次品；劣質品 SYN **rubbish**：*Their new CD is absolute pants!* 他們的新光盤絕對是次貨！◇ *Do we have to watch this pants programme?* 我們非要看這種爛節目嗎？

P

IDM **bore, scare, etc. the ˈpants off sb** (*informal*) to make sb extremely bored, frightened, etc. 把…煩死（或嚇死等）➲ more at ANT, CATCH *v.*, SEAT *n.*, WEAR *v.*, WET *v.*

pant·suit /ˈpæntsuːt; *BrE* also -sjuːt/ (*NAmE*) (*BrE* **ˈtrouser suit**) *noun* a woman's suit of jacket and trousers/pants（女子的）衣褲套裝

pant·sula /ˌpæntˈsuːlə/ *noun* [U] a style of South African dancing in which each person takes a turn to perform dance movements in front of a group of other dancers who are in a circle 潘祖拉圈舞（南非舞，參加者依次在圍成一圈的其他舞者前跳舞）

panty girdle (also **pantie girdle**) /ˈpænti ɡɜːdl; *NAmE* ɡɜːrdl/ *noun* a tight piece of women's underwear that combines KNICKERS/PANTIES and a GIRDLE（女式）緊身褡短褲

panty·hose /ˈpæntihəʊz; *NAmE* -hoʊz/ (*NAmE*) (*BrE* **tights**) *noun* [pl.] a piece of clothing made of very thin cloth that fits closely over a woman's hips, legs and feet（女用）連褲襪，緊身褲 ➲ compare STOCKING

pap /pæp/ *noun* [U] **1** (*disapproving*) books, magazines, television programmes, etc. that have no real value 無價值的讀物（或電視節目等）**2** soft or almost liquid food eaten by babies or people who are ill/sick（嬰兒或病人吃的）軟食，流食 **3** (*SAfrE*) PORRIDGE made with flour from MAIZE/CORN 玉米粥

papa /pəˈpɑː; *NAmE* ˈpɑːpə/ *noun* (*BrE, old-fashioned* or *NAmE*) used to talk about or to address your father 爸爸

pap·acy /ˈpeɪpəsi/ *noun* **1 the papacy** [sing.] the position or the authority of the POPE 教宗的職位（或權力）**2** [C, usually sing.] the period of time when a particular POPE is in power（某教宗）任職的時期

papal /ˈpeɪpl/ *adj.* [only before noun] connected with the POPE 教宗的；教皇的：*papal authority* 教宗的權力 ◇ *a papal visit to Mexico* 教宗對墨西哥的訪問

pap·ar·azzo /ˌpæpəˈrætsəʊ; *NAmE* -ˈrætsoʊ/ *noun* (*pl.* **pap·ar·azzi** /-tsi/) [usually pl.] a photographer who follows famous people around in order to get interesting photographs of them to sell to a newspaper 獵奇名流的攝影記者；狗仔隊

pa·paya /pəˈpaɪə/ (*BrE* also **paw·paw**) *noun* a tropical fruit with yellow and green skin, sweet orange or red flesh and round black seeds 番木瓜；（俗稱）木瓜 ➲ VISUAL VOCAB page V30

paper 🔑 /ˈpeɪpə(r)/ *noun, verb*

■ *noun*

▸ **FOR WRITING/WRAPPING** 供書寫／包裝 **1** 🔑 [U] (often in compounds 常構成複合詞) the thin material that you write and draw on and that is also used for wrapping and packing things 紙；紙張：***a piece/sheet of paper*** 一片／一張紙 ◇ *a package wrapped in brown paper* 一個用牛皮紙包紮的包裹 ◇ *recycled paper* 再造紙 ◇ *She wrote her name and address on **a slip*** (= a small piece) ***of paper***. 她把姓名和地址寫在一張紙條上。◇ *Experience is more important for this job than **paper qualifications*** (= that exist on paper, but may not have any real value). 就這項工作而言，經驗比紙面上的資格重要。◇ ***paper losses/profits*** (= that are shown in accounts but which may not exist in reality) 賬面虧損／利潤 ◇ *This journal is available in paper and electronic form.* 這份刊物有印刷版本和電子版本。➲ see also NOTEPAPER, WRAPPING PAPER, WRITING PAPER

▸ **NEWSPAPER** 報紙 **2** 🔑 [C] a newspaper 報紙：*a **local/national paper*** 地方性／全國性報紙 ◇ *a(n) **daily/evening/Sunday paper*** 日報；晚報；星期日報 ◇ *I read about it **in the paper**.* 我從報上得知這件事。◇ *Have you seen today's paper?* 你看了今天的報紙沒有？◇ ***The papers*** (= newspapers in general) *soon got hold of the story.* 報紙很快就獲悉了這件事的來龍去脈。

▸ **DOCUMENTS** 文件 **3** 🔑 **papers** [pl.] pieces of paper with writing on them, such as letters, pieces of work or private documents 文件；文獻：*His desk was covered with books and papers.* 他的辦公桌上全是書籍和文件。**4** 🔑 **papers** [pl.] official documents that prove your identity, give you permission to do sth, etc. 證明；證件：***divorce/identification papers*** 離婚／身分證件 ➲ see also WALKING PAPERS, WORKING PAPER

▸ **EXAM** 考試 **5** [C] (*BrE*) a set of exam questions on a particular subject; the answers that people write to the questions 試卷；試題；答卷：*The Geography paper was hard.* 地理試題難極了。◇ *She spent the evening marking exam papers.* 她用一個晚上批閱試卷。

▸ **ARTICLE** 文章 **6** [C] an academic article about a particular subject that is written by and for specialists 論文：*a recent paper in the Journal of Medicine* 最近刊在《醫學學報》上的一篇論文 ◇ *She was invited to **give a paper*** (= a talk) *on the results of her research.* 她應邀發表一篇論文，報告她的研究結果。➲ COLLOCATIONS at SCIENTIFIC ➲ see also GREEN PAPER, ORDER PAPER, POSITION PAPER, WHITE PAPER, WORKING PAPER (1) **7** [C] (*NAmE*) a piece of written work done by a student（學生的）研究報告，論文：*Your grade will be based on four papers and a final exam.* 你的成績將根據四篇研究報告和期末考試決定。➲ see also TERM PAPER

▸ **ON WALLS** 牆壁上 **8** [C, U] paper that you use to cover and decorate the walls of a room 壁紙：*The room was damp and the paper was peeling off.* 屋子很潮濕，壁紙都一片片剝落了。**HELP** There are many other compounds ending in **paper**. You will find them at their place in the alphabet. 以 paper 結尾的複合詞還有很多，可在各字母中的適當位置查到。

IDM **on paper 1** 🔑 when you put sth **on paper**, you write it down 寫下來；筆錄 **2** judged from written information only, but not proved in practice 僅照字面看；理論上：*The idea **looks good on paper**.* 僅就字面看，這個主意不錯。➲ more at PEN *n.*, WORTH *adj.*

■ ***verb*** **~ sth** to decorate the walls of a room by covering them with WALLPAPER 貼壁紙

PHR V **ˌpaper ˈover sth 1** to cover a wall with WALLPAPER in order to hide sth 糊壁紙遮蓋 **SYN** **wallpaper**：*The previous owners had obviously papered over any damp patches.* 原先的房主顯然是用壁紙把潮斑都蓋起來了。**2** to try to hide a problem or disagreement in a way that is temporary and not likely to be successful 暫時掩蓋，權且掩飾（問題或分歧）：*The government is trying to **paper over the cracks** in the cabinet.* 政府正竭力掩飾內閣出現的裂痕。◇ *We can't just paper over the problem.* 我們不能就這麼掩飾這個問題。

paper·back /ˈpeɪpəbæk; *NAmE* -pərb-/ *noun* [C, U] a book that has a thick paper cover 平裝書；簡裝書：*a cheap paperback* 一本廉價的簡裝書 ◇ *When is it coming out **in paperback**?* 這本書的平裝本什麼時候出版？◇ *a **paperback book/edition*** 平裝書／版本 ➲ compare HARDBACK

ˈpaper boy, ˈpaper girl *noun* a boy or girl who delivers newspapers to people's houses 男（或女）報童

pa·per·chase /ˈpeɪpətʃeɪs; *NAmE* -pərtʃ-/ *noun* **1** (*BrE*) a game in which one runner drops pieces of paper for the other runners to follow 撒紙追逐遊戲（領頭者沿途撒下紙屑，供追趕者尋蹤追逐）**2** (*NAmE, informal*) the fact of producing too much work on paper 過多的書面工作；文牘追求

ˈpaper clip *noun* a piece of bent wire or plastic that is designed to hold loose sheets of paper together 迴形針；曲別針；紙夾 ➲ VISUAL VOCAB page V69

ˈpaper cutter (*US*) (*BrE* **guil·lo·tine**) *noun* [C] a device with a long blade for cutting paper 裁切機；切紙機

paper·knife /ˈpeɪpənaɪf; *NAmE* ˈpeɪpər-/ *noun* (*pl.* **-knives**) (*especially BrE*) (*NAmE* usually **ˈletter opener**) a knife used for opening envelopes 拆信刀；開信刀

paper·less /ˈpeɪpələs; *NAmE* -pərləs/ *adj.* using computers, telephones, etc. rather than paper to exchange information 無紙的；不用紙交換信息的：*the paperless office* 無紙辦公室 ◇ *a system of paperless business transactions* 無紙商業交易系統

ˌpaper ˈmoney *noun* [U] money that is made of paper, not coins 紙幣；鈔票 **SYN** **notes**

ˌpaper ˈplate *noun* a cardboard plate that can be thrown away after it is used（一次性）紙盤子

P

ˈpaper-pusher *noun* (*disapproving*) a person who does unimportant office work as their job 辦公室小職員；小文書

ˈpaper round (*BrE*) (*NAmE* **ˈpaper route**) *noun* the job of delivering newspapers to houses; the route taken when doing this 送報；送報路線

ˈpaper shop *noun* (*BrE*) = NEWSAGENT (2)

ˌpaper-ˈthin *adj.* (of objects 物品) very thin and delicate 薄如紙的；極薄的：*paper-thin slices of meat* 像紙一樣薄的肉片 ➲ compare WAFER-THIN

ˌpaper ˈtiger *noun* a person, a country or a situation that seems or claims to be powerful or dangerous but is not really（指人、國家或局勢）紙老虎，外強中乾者

ˌpaper ˈtowel *noun* **1** [C] a thick sheet of paper that you use to dry your hands or to absorb water 厚紙巾 **2** [U] (*NAmE*) (*BrE* **ˈkitchen paper**, **ˈkitchen roll**, **ˈkitchen towel**) thick paper on a roll, used for cleaning up liquid, food, etc. 廚房用捲紙 ➲ VISUAL VOCAB page V25

ˈpaper trail *noun* (*informal, especially NAmE*) a series of documents that provide evidence of what you have done or what has happened（揭示來龍去脈的）系列文件：*He was a shrewd lawyer with a talent for uncovering paper trails of fraud.* 他是個精明強幹的律師，能從一連串文件中找出詐騙的蛛絲馬跡。

paper·weight /ˈpeɪpəweɪt; *NAmE* -pərw-/ *noun* a small heavy object that you put on top of loose papers to keep them in place 鎮紙

paper·work /ˈpeɪpəwɜːk; *NAmE* ˈpeɪpərwɜːrk/ *noun* [U] **1** the written work that is part of a job, such as filling in forms or writing letters and reports 文書工作：*We're trying to cut down on the amount of paperwork involved.* 我們正在努力降低有關此事的文書工作量。 **2** all the documents that you need for sth, such as a court case or buying a house（訴訟案件、購置房產等所需的）全部文件，全部資料：*How quickly can you prepare the paperwork?* 你要多久才能把全部文件備好？

P

pa·pery /ˈpeɪpəri/ *adj.* like paper; thin and dry 紙一樣的；薄而乾的

pa·pier mâché /ˌpæpieɪ ˈmæʃeɪ; *NAmE* ˌpeɪpər məˈʃeɪ; ˌpæpjeɪ/ *noun* [U] (from *French*) paper mixed with glue or flour and water, that is used to make decorative objects 混凝紙，製型紙（加進膠水等經漿狀處理的紙，用以做裝飾品）

pap·il·loma /ˌpæpɪˈləʊmə; *NAmE* -ˈloʊ-/ *noun* (*medical* 醫) a small lump like a WART that grows on the skin and is usually harmless 乳頭狀瘤（通常為良性）

pap·ist /ˈpeɪpɪst/ *noun* (*taboo*) an offensive word for a Roman Catholic, used by some Protestants 教皇黨人（某些新教教徒對天主教徒的蔑稱）▸ **pap·ist** *adj.*

pa·poose /pəˈpuːs/ *noun* a type of bag that can be used for carrying a baby in, on your back or in front of you 嬰兒袋，嬰兒兜（可背負或放在胸前）

pap·rika /pəˈpriːkə; *BrE* also ˈpæprɪkə/ *noun* [U] a red powder made from a type of PEPPER, used in cooking as a spice 紅辣椒粉 ➲ VISUAL VOCAB page V32

ˈPap smear (*NAmE*) (*BrE* **ˈsmear test**, **smear**, **ˌcervical ˈsmear**) *noun* a medical test in which a very small amount of TISSUE from a woman's CERVIX is removed and examined for cancer cells 塗片試驗（從婦女子宮頸取少許組織，以檢查是否有癌細胞）

pa·pyrus /pəˈpaɪrəs/ *noun* (*pl.* **pa·pyri** /pəˈpaɪriː/) **1** [U] a tall plant with thick STEMS that grows in water 紙莎草 **2** [U] paper made from the STEMS of the papyrus plant, used in ancient Egypt for writing and drawing on（古埃及用的）紙莎草紙 **3** [C] a document or piece of paper made of papyrus（寫在紙莎草紙上的）文獻，文稿

par /pɑː(r)/ *noun* [U] **1** (in GOLF 高爾夫球) the number of strokes a good player should need to complete a course or to hit the ball into a particular hole 標準杆數：*a par five hole* 五標準杆的洞 ◇ *Par for the course is 72.* 一場球的標準杆數是 72 杆。 **2** (also **ˈpar value**) (*business* 商) the value that a share in a company had originally（股票的）面值，票面價值：*to be redeemed **at par*** 以面值兑換

IDM **below/under ˈpar** less well, good, etc. than is usual or expected 不太好；不佳；不及平常好；不如預期：*Teaching in some subjects has been well below par.* 一些科目的教學一直遠達不到標準。 **be ˌpar for the ˈcourse** (*disapproving*) to be just what you would expect to happen or expect sb to do in a particular situation 不出所料；果不其然 SYN **the norm**：*Starting early and working long hours is par for the course in this job.* 開工早以及工時長是這份工作的常態。 **on a par with sb/sth** as good, bad, important, etc. as sb/sth else 與…同樣好（或壞、重要等）；不相上下；不相伯仲 **up to ˈpar** as good as usual or as good as it should be 達到通常（或應有）的水準 SYN **up to scratch**

par. (also **para.**) *abbr.* (in writing) paragraph（書寫形式）段：*See par. 3.* 參見第 3 段。

para /ˈpærə/ *noun* (*informal*) = PARATROOPER

para- /ˈpærə/ *prefix* (in nouns and adjectives 構成名詞和形容詞) **1** beyond 超越：*paranormal* 超常的 **2** similar to but not official or not fully qualified 準；近似：*paramilitary* 準軍事的 ◇ *a paramedic* 醫務輔助人員

par·able /ˈpærəbl/ *noun* a short story that teaches a moral or spiritual lesson, especially one of those told by Jesus as recorded in the Bible（尤指《聖經》中的）寓言故事

para·bola /pəˈræbələ/ *noun* (*geometry* 幾何) a curve like the path of an object thrown into the air and falling back to earth 拋物線 ➲ VISUAL VOCAB page V71 ▸ **para·bol·ic** /ˌpærəˈbɒlɪk; *NAmE* -ˈbɑːlɪk/ *adj.*：*parabolic curves* 拋物曲線

para·ceta·mol /ˌpærəˈsiːtəmɒl; -ˈset-; *NAmE* -mɔːl/ (*BrE*) (*NAmE* **acet·amino·phen**) *noun* [U, C] (*pl.* **para·ceta·mol** or **para·ceta·mols**) a drug used to reduce pain and fever 醋氨酚；撲熱息痛：*Do you have any paracetamol?* 你有撲熱息痛嗎？◇ *Take two paracetamol(s) and try to sleep.* 服兩片撲熱息痛，好好睡一覺。

para·chute /ˈpærəʃuːt/ *noun, verb*

▪ *noun* (also *informal* **chute**) a device that is attached to people or objects to make them fall slowly and safely when they are dropped from an aircraft. It consists of a large piece of thin cloth that opens out in the air to form an umbrella shape. 降落傘：*Planes dropped supplies by parachute.* 飛機用降落傘空投補給。◇ *a **parachute drop/jump*** 空投；跳傘 ◇ *a parachute regiment* 空降兵團

▪ *verb* **1** [I] (+ **adv./prep.**) to jump from an aircraft using a parachute 跳傘：*The pilot was able to parachute to safety.* 飛行員得以安全跳傘。◇ *She regularly **goes parachuting**.* 她經常去玩跳傘。 **2** [T] **~ sb/sth + adv./prep.** to drop sb/sth from an aircraft by parachute 傘降；空投

para·chut·ist /ˈpærəʃuːtɪst/ *noun* a person who jumps from a plane using a parachute 跳傘者

para·clin·ical /ˌpærəˈklɪnɪkl/ *adj.* (*technical* 術語) related to the parts of medicine, especially laboratory sciences, that are not directly involved in the care of patients 臨牀旁學的，輔助臨牀的（關於實驗室科學等）

par·ade /pəˈreɪd/ *noun, verb*

▪ *noun*

▸ PUBLIC CELEBRATION 公共慶典 **1** [C] a public celebration of a special day or event, usually with bands in the streets and decorated vehicles 慶祝遊行 SYN **procession**：*the Lord Mayor's parade* 倫敦市長就職遊行 ◇ *St Patrick's Day parade in New York* 紐約市聖帕特里克節慶祝遊行

▸ OF SOLDIERS 士兵 **2** [C, U] a formal occasion when soldiers march or stand in lines so that they can be examined by their officers or other important people 檢閱；閱兵：*a military parade* 軍事檢閱 ◇ *They stood as straight as soldiers **on parade**.* 他們像接受檢閱的士兵一樣站得筆直。◇ (*figurative*) *The latest software will be on parade at the exhibition.* 最新電腦軟件將在展覽會上展出。 ➲ see also IDENTIFICATION PARADE

▸ SERIES 系列 **3** [C] a series of things or people 一系列（人或事）：*Each generation passes through a similar parade of events.* 每一代人都要經歷一系列類似的事。

▸ **WEALTH/KNOWLEDGE** 財富；知識 **4** [C, usually sing.] **~ of wealth, knowledge, etc.** (often *disapproving*) an obvious display of sth, particularly in order to impress other people 夸示；炫耀

▸ **ROW OF SHOPS** 一排商店 **5** [C] (*especially BrE*) (often in names 常用於名稱) a street with a row of small shops 有一排小商店的街道：*a shopping parade* 購物街 **IDM** see RAIN *v.*

■ ***verb***

▸ **WALK TO CELEBRATE/PROTEST** 遊行慶祝／抗議 **1** [I] **(+ adv./prep.)** to walk somewhere in a formal group of people, in order to celebrate or protest about sth 遊行；遊行慶祝；遊行示威：*The victorious team will parade through the city tomorrow morning.* 明天上午獲勝隊將在城內舉行慶祝遊行。

▸ **SHOW IN PUBLIC** 公開展示 **2** [I] **+ adv./prep.** to walk around in a way that makes other people notice you 招搖過市；大搖大擺：*People were parading up and down showing off their finest clothes.* 人們走來走去，炫耀着他們最漂亮的服裝。 **3** [T] **~ sb/sth + adv./prep.** to show sb/sth in public so that people can see them/it 展覽；展示：*The trophy was paraded around the stadium.* 獎杯被環繞着體育場高舉展示。◇ *The prisoners were paraded in front of the crowd.* 囚犯被押解遊街示眾。◇ (*figurative*) *He is not one to parade his achievements.* 他不是一個愛炫耀自己成就的人。

▸ **OF SOLDIERS** 士兵 **4** [I, T] to come together, or to bring soldiers together, in order to march in front of other people（使）列隊行進，接受檢閱：**+ adv./prep.** *The crowds applauded as the guards paraded past.* 衛隊列隊走過時，人群鼓掌歡迎。◇ **~ sb + adv./prep.** *The colonel paraded his men before the Queen.* 上校指揮士兵列隊行進，接受女王的檢閱。

▸ **PRETEND** 佯裝 **5** [I, T] to pretend to be, or to make sb/sth seem to be, good or important when they are not（使）冒充，偽裝，打扮成：**~ as sth** *myth parading as fact* 外表看似真實的神話 ◇ **~ sb/sth/yourself as sth** *He paraded himself as a loyal supporter of the party.* 他把自己偽裝成該黨的忠實支持者。

pa'rade ground *noun* a place where soldiers gather to march or to be INSPECTED by an officer or an important visitor 閱兵場

para·digm **AW** /ˈpærədaɪm/ *noun* **1** (*technical* 術語 or *formal*) a typical example or pattern of sth 典範；範例；樣式：*a paradigm for students to copy* 供學生效法的榜樣 ◇ *The war was a paradigm of the destructive side of human nature.* 那場戰爭盡顯人性中具有破壞性的一面。 **2** (*grammar* 語法) a set of all the different forms of a word 詞形變化表：*verb paradigms* 動詞詞形變化表 ▸ **para·dig·mat·ic** /ˌpærədɪɡˈmætɪk/ *adj.*

ˈparadigm shift *noun* a great and important change in the way sth is done or thought about 範式轉移（指行事或思維方式的重大變化）

para·dise /ˈpærədaɪs/ *noun* **1** (often **Paradise**) [U] (in some religions) a perfect place where people are said to go when they die（某些宗教所指的）天堂，天國 **SYN** **heaven**：*The ancient Egyptians saw paradise as an idealized version of their own lives.* 古埃及人把天堂視為人生活的理想形式。 **2** [C] a place that is extremely beautiful and that seems perfect, like heaven 天堂，樂土，樂園（指美好的環境）：*a tropical paradise* 一處熱帶的人間樂土 **3** [C] a perfect place for a particular activity or kind of person（某類活動或某類人的）樂園，完美去處：*The area is a birdwatcher's paradise.* 這一地區是鳥類觀察者的樂園。 **4** [U] a state of perfect happiness 至福；極樂 **SYN** **bliss**：*Being alone is his idea of paradise.* 他視獨處為至樂之事。 **5** **Paradise** [U] (in the Bible《聖經》) the garden of Eden, where Adam and Eve lived 伊甸園

para·dox /ˈpærədɒks; *NAmE* -dɑːks/ *noun* **1** [C] a person, thing or situation that has two opposite features and therefore seems strange 矛盾的人（或事物、情況）：*He was a paradox—a loner who loved to chat to strangers.* 他真是個矛盾人物，生性孤僻卻又喜歡和陌生人閒聊。◇ *It is a curious paradox that professional comedians often have unhappy personal lives.* 這真是個奇怪的矛盾現象：職業喜劇演員的私人生活往往並不快樂。 **2** [C, U] a statement containing two opposite ideas that make it seem impossible or unlikely, although it is probably true; the use of this in writing 似非而是的雋語；悖論；悖論修辭：*'More haste, less speed' is a well-known paradox.* "欲速則不達"是人們熟知的似非而是的雋語。◇ *It's a work full of paradox and ambiguity.* 這部作品充滿了似非而是及模稜兩可之處。 ▸ **para·dox·ical** /ˌpærəˈdɒksɪkl; *NAmE* -ˈdɑːks-/ *adj.*：*It is paradoxical that some of the poorest people live in some of the richest areas of the country.* 某些最貧窮的人卻住在這個國家一些最富有的地區，這似乎很矛盾。 **para·dox·ic·al·ly** /-kli/ *adv.*：*Paradoxically, the less she ate, the fatter she got.* 很矛盾的是，她吃得越少，卻變得越胖。

par·af·fin /ˈpærəfɪn/ (also **ˌparaffin ˈoil**) (both *BrE*) (*NAmE* **kero·sene**) *noun* [U] a type of oil obtained from PETROLEUM and used as a fuel for heat and light 煤油：*a **paraffin heater/lamp/stove*** 煤油取暖器／燈／爐

ˈparaffin wax *noun* [U] a soft white substance that is made from PETROLEUM or coal, and is used especially for making CANDLES 石蠟（尤用以製造蠟燭）

para·glider /ˈpærəɡlaɪdə(r)/ *noun* **1** a structure consisting of a big thin piece of cloth like a PARACHUTE, and a HARNESS which is attached to a person when they jump from a plane or a high place in the sport of PARAGLIDING 滑翔傘；飛行傘 **2** a person who does paragliding 滑翔傘運動員；飛行傘運動員

para·glid·ing /ˈpærəɡlaɪdɪŋ/ *noun* [U] a sport in which you wear a special structure like a PARACHUTE, jump from a plane or a high place and are carried along by the wind before coming down to earth 滑翔傘運動；飛行傘運動：*to go paragliding* 去傘翼滑翔 ➲ **VISUAL VOCAB** page V49

para·gon /ˈpærəɡən; *NAmE* -ɡɑːn/ *noun* a person who is perfect or who is a perfect example of a particular good quality 完人；典範：*I make no claim to be a paragon.* 我沒有說過自己是完人。◇ *He wasn't the **paragon of virtue** she had expected.* 他不是她想像中的那種美德典範。

para·graph **AW** /ˈpærəɡrɑːf; *NAmE* -ɡræf/ *noun* (*abbr.* **par.**, **para.**) a section of a piece of writing, usually consisting of several sentences dealing with a single subject. The first sentence of a paragraph starts on a new line. 段；段落：*an **opening/introductory paragraph*** 開頭的／導引的一段 ◇ *Write a paragraph on each of the topics given below.* 就下面所列主題各寫一個段落。◇ *See paragraph 15 of the handbook.* 參見手冊第 15 段。

para·graph·ing **AW** /ˈpærəɡrɑːfɪŋ; *NAmE* -ɡræf-/ *noun* [U] the way that a piece of writing is divided into paragraphs 段落劃分；分段（方式）

para·keet (also **parra·keet**) /ˈpærəkiːt/ *noun* a small bird of the PARROT family, usually with a long tail 長尾小鸚鵡

para·legal /ˌpærəˈliːɡl/ *noun* (*especially NAmE*) a person who is trained to help a lawyer 律師助理 ▸ **para·legal** *adj.*

para·lin·guis·tic /ˌpærəlɪŋˈɡwɪstɪk/ *adj.* (*linguistics* 語言) relating to communication through ways other than words, for example tone of voice, expressions on your face and actions 副語言的，輔助語言的，伴隨語言的（通過聲調、表情、行動等交流）

par·all·ax /ˈpærəlæks/ *noun* [U] (*technical* 術語) the effect by which the position or direction of an object appears to change when the object is seen from different positions 視差（從不同位置觀察物體所產生的位置或方向上的差別）

par·al·lel 🔑 **AW** /ˈpærəlel/ *adj., noun, verb*

■ ***adj.*** **1** 🔑 two or more lines that are **parallel** to each other are the same distance apart at every point 平行的：*parallel lines* 平行線 ◇ **~ to/with sth** *The road and the canal are parallel to each other.* 道路與運河平行。 **2** very similar or taking place at the same time 極相似的；同時發生的；相應的；對應的：*a parallel case* 同類型事例 ◇ *parallel trends* 並行發展的趨勢 **3** (*computing* 計) involving several computer operations at the same time 並行的：*parallel processing* 並行處理 ▸ **par·al·lel** *adv.*：*The road and the canal **run parallel** to each other.* 道路

P

與運河平行。◇ *The plane flew parallel to the coast.* 飛機沿海岸線飛行。

■ ***noun*** **1** [C, U] a person, a situation, an event, etc. that is very similar to another, especially one in a different place or time（尤指不同地點或時間的）極其相似的人（或情況、事件等）SYN **equivalent**：*These ideas have parallels in Freud's thought too.* 這些觀念與弗洛伊德思想中的某些觀點非常相似。◇ *This is an achievement **without parallel** in modern times.* 這一成就在當代無人可及。◇ *This tradition **has no parallel** in our culture.* 這種傳統在我們的文化中是沒有的。**2** [C, usually pl.] similar features 相似特徵；相似特點：*There are interesting parallels between the 1960s and the late 1990s.* * 20 世紀 60 年代和 90 年代後期有些頗有意思的相似之處。◇ *It is possible to **draw a parallel between*** (= find similar features in) *their experience and ours.* 在他們的經歷和我們的經歷之間找到相似點是可能的。**3** (also **ˌparallel of ˈlatitude**) [C] an imaginary line around the earth that is always the same distance from the EQUATOR; this line on a map（地球或地圖的）緯線，緯圈：*the 49th parallel* 第 49 緯度線

IDM **in ˈparallel (with sth/sb)** with and at the same time as sth/sb else（與…）同時：*The new degree and the existing certificate courses would run in parallel.* 新的學位課程和現有的證書課程將同時開設。

■ ***verb*** **1 ~ sth** to be similar to sth; to happen at the same time as sth 與…相似；與…同時發生：*Their legal system parallels our own.* 他們的法律制度與我們的相似。◇ *The rise in unemployment is paralleled by an increase in petty crime.* 在失業率上升的同時，輕度犯罪也跟着增長。**2 ~ sth** to be as good as sth 與…媲美；比得上 SYN **equal**：*a level of achievement that has never been paralleled* 絕無僅有的最高成就 ➲ compare UNPARALLELED

ˌparallel ˈbars *noun* [pl.] two bars on posts that are used for doing GYMNASTIC exercises 雙槓

ˌparallel ˈimports *noun* [pl.] (*economics* 經) goods that are imported into a country without the permission of the company that produced them, and sold at a lower price than the company sells them at 平行進口貨物，水貨（未經廠家許可進口並低價銷售的產品）

P

par·al·lel·ism /ˈpærəlelɪzəm/ *noun* [U, C] (*formal*) the state of being similar; a similar feature 相似；相似的特點：*I think he exaggerates the parallelism between the two cases.* 我認為他誇大了兩件事的相似之處。

par·al·lelo·gram /ˌpærəˈleləɡræm/ *noun* (*geometry* 幾何) a flat shape with four straight sides, the opposite sides being parallel and equal to each other 平行四邊形

ˈparallel port *noun* (*computing* 計) a point on a computer where you connect a device such as a printer that sends or receives more than one piece of data at a time 並行端口；平行埠

ˌparallel ˈprocessing *noun* [U] (*computing* 計) the division of a process into different parts, which are performed at the same time by different PROCESSORS in a computer 並行處理；平行處理

ˌparallel ˈruler *noun* a device for drawing lines that are always the same distance apart, consisting of two connected rulers 平行線尺（由兩把相連接的尺子組成）

the Para·lym·pics /ˌpærəˈlɪmpɪks/ *noun* [pl.] an international ATHLETICS competition for people who are disabled 殘疾人奧運會；殘奧會

para·lyse (*BrE*) (*NAmE* **para·lyze**) /ˈpærəlaɪz/ *verb* [often passive] **1 ~ sb** to make sb unable to feel or move all or part of their body 使癱瘓；使麻痹：*The accident left him **paralysed from the waist down**.* 那場事故使他腰部以下都癱瘓了。◇ (*figurative*) *paralysing heat* 令人頭昏腦脹的炎熱 ◇ (*figurative*) *She stood there, paralysed with fear.* 她站在那裏，嚇得呆若木雞。**2 ~ sth** to prevent sth from functioning normally 使不能正常工作：*The airport is still paralysed by the strike.* 機場仍因為罷工而陷於癱瘓。

par·aly·sis /pəˈræləsɪs/ *noun* (*pl.* **par·aly·ses** /-siːz/) **1** [U, C] a loss of control of, and sometimes feeling in, part or most of the body, caused by disease or an injury to the nerves 麻痹；癱瘓：*paralysis of both legs* 雙腿癱瘓 **2** [U] a total inability to move, act, function, etc.（活動、工作等）能力的完全喪失，癱瘓：*The strike caused total paralysis in the city.* 罷工使這座城市完全癱瘓。

para·lyt·ic /ˌpærəˈlɪtɪk/ *adj.* **1** [not before noun] (*BrE, informal*) very drunk 爛醉；酩酊大醉 **2** [usually before noun] (*formal*) suffering from PARALYSIS; making sb unable to move 癱瘓的；麻痹的；使動彈不得的：*a paralytic illness* 一種麻痹症 ◇ *paralytic fear* 令人不知所措的恐懼

para·med·ic /ˌpærəˈmedɪk/ *noun* a person whose job is to help people who are sick or injured, but who is not a doctor or a nurse 護理人員；醫務輔助人員：*Paramedics treated the injured at the roadside.* 護理人員在路旁為傷者治療。▸ **para·med·ic·al** /-ɪkl/ *adj.*：*paramedical staff* 醫務輔助人員

par·am·eter AW /pəˈræmɪtə(r)/ *noun* [usually pl.] (*formal*) something that decides or limits the way in which sth can be done 決定因素；規範；範圍：*to **set/define the parameters*** 制訂／設定規範 ◇ *We had to work within the parameters that had already been established.* 我們必須在已設定的範圍內工作。

para·mili·tary /ˌpærəˈmɪlətri; *NAmE* -teri/ *adj., noun*

■ ***adj.*** [usually before noun] **1** a **paramilitary** organization is an illegal group that is organized like an army 非法軍事組織的：*a right-wing paramilitary group* 一個右翼非法軍事集團 **2** helping the official army of a country 輔助軍事的；準軍事的：*paramilitary police, such as the CRS in France* 法國的共和國保安部隊之類的軍事輔助警察

■ ***noun*** [usually pl.] (*pl.* **-ies**) **1** a member of an illegal paramilitary group or organization 非法軍事集團（或組織）的成員 **2** a member of an organization that helps the official army of a country 輔助軍事組織的成員；準軍事組織的成員

para·mount /ˈpærəmaʊnt/ *adj.* **1** more important than anything else 至為重要的；首要的：*This matter is **of paramount importance**.* 此事至關重要。◇ *Safety is paramount.* 安全至上。➲ LANGUAGE BANK at VITAL **2** (*formal*) having the highest position or the greatest power 至高無上的；至尊的；權力最大的：*China's paramount leader* 中國的最高領導人 ▸ **para·mount·cy** /-maʊntsi/ *noun* [U]

par·amour /ˈpærəmʊə(r); *NAmE* -mʊr/ *noun* (*old-fashioned* or *literary*) a person that sb is having a romantic or sexual relationship with 情人；情婦；情夫 SYN **lover**

para·noia /ˌpærəˈnɔɪə/ *noun* [U] **1** (*medical* 醫) a mental illness in which a person may wrongly believe that other people are trying to harm them, that they are sb very important, etc. 妄想症；偏執狂 **2** (*informal*) fear or suspicion of other people when there is no evidence or reason for this（對別人的）無端恐懼，多疑

para·noid /ˈpærənɔɪd/ *adj., noun*

■ ***adj.*** (also *less frequent* **para·noiac** /ˌpærəˈnɔɪɪk; -ˈnɔɪæk/) **1** afraid or suspicious of other people and believing that they are trying to harm you, in a way that is not reasonable 多疑的；恐懼的：*She's getting really paranoid about what other people say about her.* 她開始對別人怎麼議論她變得十分猜疑。➲ SYNONYMS at AFRAID **2** suffering from a mental illness in which you wrongly believe that other people are trying to harm you or that you are very important 患偏執症的；有妄想狂的：*paranoid delusions* 偏執妄想 ◇ *paranoid schizophrenia* 妄想型精神分裂症 ◇ *a paranoid killer* 偏執型殺人兇手

■ ***noun*** (also **para·noiac** /ˌpærəˈnɔɪɪk; -ˈnɔɪæk/) a person who suffers from paranoia 偏執狂；妄想症患者

para·nor·mal /ˌpærəˈnɔːml; *NAmE* -ˈnɔːrml/ *adj.*

■ ***adj.*** **1** that cannot be explained by science or reason and that seems to involve mysterious forces 超自然的；無法用科學解釋的；超常的 SYN **supernatural** **2** **the paranormal** *noun* [sing.] events or subjects that are paranormal 超常事件（或話題）SYN **the supernatural**

para·pet /ˈpærəpɪt; -pet/ *noun* a low wall along the edge of a bridge, a roof, etc. to stop people from falling 防護矮牆：(*figurative*) *He was not prepared to **put his***

***head above the parapet** and say what he really thought* (= he did not want to risk doing it). 他不想冒然出頭說出自己的真實想法。

para·pher·na·lia /ˌpærəfəˈneɪliə; *NAmE* also -fərˈn-/ *noun* [U] a large number of objects or personal possessions, especially the equipment that you need for a particular activity（尤指某活動所需的）裝備，大量用品，私人物品：*skiing paraphernalia* 滑雪裝備 ◇ *an electric kettle and all the paraphernalia for making tea and coffee* 電水壺及沏茶沖咖啡的全套用具

para·phrase /ˈpærəfreɪz/ *verb, noun*

■ ***verb*** [T, I] **~ (sth)** to express what sb has said or written using different words, especially in order to make it easier to understand（用更容易理解的文字）解釋，釋義，意譯：*Try to paraphrase the question before you answer it.* 先試解釋一下問題再作回答。

■ ***noun*** a statement that expresses sth that sb has written or said using different words, especially in order to make it easier to understand 解釋；釋義；意譯

para·ple·gia /ˌpærəˈpliːdʒə/ *noun* [U] PARALYSIS (= loss of control or feeling) in the legs and lower body 截癱；下身麻痺

para·ple·gic /ˌpærəˈpliːdʒɪk/ *noun* a person who suffers from paraplegia 截癱病人；下身麻痺患者 ▸ **para·ple·gic** *adj.*

para·psych·ology /ˌpærəsaɪˈkɒlədʒi; *NAmE* -ˈkɑːl-/ *noun* [U] the study of mental powers that seem to exist but that cannot be explained by scientific knowledge 心靈學；超心理學

para·quat /ˈpærəkwɒt; *NAmE* -kwɑːt/ *noun* [U] an extremely poisonous liquid used to kill plants that are growing where they are not wanted（巨毒）滅草劑；百草枯

para·sail·ing /ˈpærəseɪlɪŋ/ *noun* [U] the sport of being pulled up into the air behind a boat while wearing a special PARACHUTE 帆傘運動；水上拖傘運動

par·as·cend·ing /ˈpærəsendɪŋ/ *noun* [U] (*BrE*) a sport in which you wear a PARACHUTE and are pulled along behind a boat, car, etc. so that you rise up into the air（汽船、汽車等牽引的）傘翼滑翔運動：*to go parascending* 進行傘翔運動

para·site /ˈpærəsaɪt/ *noun* **1** a small animal or plant that lives on or inside another animal or plant and gets its food from it 寄生生物；寄生蟲；寄生植物 **2** (*disapproving*) a person who always relies on or benefits from other people and gives nothing back 寄生蟲；依賴他人過活者

para·sit·ic /ˌpærəˈsɪtɪk/ (also *less frequent* **para·sit·ical** /ˌpærəˈsɪtɪkl/) *adj.* **1** caused by a parasite 寄生生物引起的：*a **parasitic disease/infection*** 寄生物誘發的疾病 / 感染 **2** living on another animal or plant and getting its food from it 寄生的；依附性的：*a parasitic mite* 寄生蟎 **3** (*disapproving*) (of a person 人) always relying on or benefiting from other people and giving nothing back 寄生蟲似的；依賴他人的 ▸ **para·sit·ic·al·ly** /-kli/ *adv.*

para·sol /ˈpærəsɒl; *NAmE* -sɔːl; -sɑːl/ *noun* **1** a type of light umbrella that women in the past carried to protect themselves from the sun（舊時的）女用陽傘 **2** a large umbrella that is used for example on beaches or outside restaurants to protect people from hot sun（海灘上、餐館外等處的）大遮陽傘 ➲ VISUAL VOCAB page V19 ➲ compare SUNSHADE (1)

para·statal /ˌpærəˈsteɪtl/ *adj.* (*technical* 術語) (of an organization 機構) having some political power and serving the state 國有的；部份國有的

para·taxis /ˌpærəˈtæksɪs/ *noun* [U] (*grammar* 語法) the placing of clauses and phrases one after the other, without words to link them or show their relationship 無連詞並列；意合連接 ➲ compare HYPOTAXIS

par·atha /pəˈrɑːtə/ *noun* a type of S Asian bread made without YEAST, usually fried on a GRIDDLE 抛餅（南亞食品，不發酵，通常用鏊子煎成）

para·troop·er /ˈpærətruːpə(r)/ (also *informal* **para**) *noun* a member of the paratroops 傘兵；空降兵

para·troops /ˈpærətruːps/ *noun* [pl.] soldiers who are trained to jump from planes using a PARACHUTE 空降兵部隊；傘兵部隊 ▸ **para·troop** *adj.* [only before noun]：*a paratroop regiment* 傘兵團

par·boil /ˈpɑːbɔɪl; *NAmE* ˈpɑːrb-/ *verb* **~ sth** to boil food, especially vegetables, until it is partly cooked（尤指將蔬菜）煮成半熟

par·cel /ˈpɑːsl; *NAmE* ˈpɑːrsl/ *noun, verb*

■ ***noun*** **1** (*especially BrE*) (*NAmE* usually **pack·age**) something that is wrapped in paper or put into a thick envelope so that it can be sent by mail, carried easily, or given as a present 包裹；小包：*There's a parcel and some letters for you.* 有你的一個包裹和幾封信。◇ *She was carrying a parcel of books under her arm.* 她腋下夾着一包書。◇ *The prisoners were allowed food parcels.* 囚犯可以收食物包裹。 **2** a piece of land 一塊地；一片地：*50 five-acre parcels have already been sold.* 五英畝一塊的土地已經售出 50 塊。**3** (*especially BrE*) a small amount of food that is wrapped in sth, usually pastry, before it is cooked 油酥包（通常以油酥皮包裹少許食物烹製）：*filo pastry parcels* 千層油酥包 **IDM** see PART *n.*

■ ***verb*** (*especially BrE*) (**-ll-**, *especially US* **-l-**) **~ sth (up)** to wrap sth up and make it into a parcel 包；裹好；打包：*She parcelled up the books to send.* 她把要寄走的書包了起來。

PHR V **ˌparcel sth↔ˈout** to divide sth into parts or between several people 把某物分開；把某物（在幾個人之間）分：*The land was parcelled out into small lots.* 這塊地被分成了若干小塊。

ˈparcel bomb *noun* (*BrE*) a bomb that is sent to sb in a package and that explodes when the package is opened 郵包炸彈；包裹炸彈

parch /pɑːtʃ; *NAmE* pɑːrtʃ/ *verb* **~ sth** (especially of hot weather 尤指炎熱天氣) to make an area of land very dry 使（土地）極乾燥

parched /pɑːtʃt; *NAmE* pɑːrtʃt/ *adj.* **1** very dry, especially because the weather is hot 焦乾的；曬焦的：*dry parched land* 焦乾的土地 ◇ *soil parched by drought* 旱災造成的焦乾的土壤 ◇ *She licked her parched lips.* 她舔了舔乾裂的雙唇。 **2** (*informal*) very thirsty 乾渴的；極渴的：*Let's get a drink—I'm parched.* 咱們喝點飲料吧，我嗓子都乾得冒煙兒了。

ˌparched ˈrice *noun* [U] rice that has been pressed flat and dried, used in Asian cooking 大米片（扁平乾燥）

Par·cheesi™ /pɑːˈtʃiːzi; *NAmE* pɑːrˈtʃ-/ *noun* [U] (*NAmE*) a simple game played with DICE and COUNTERS on a special board, similar to the British game, LUDO 巴棋戲（一種用骰子和籌碼在棋盤上玩的遊戲，類似英國的“盧多”）

parch·ment /ˈpɑːtʃmənt; *NAmE* ˈpɑːrtʃ-/ *noun* **1** [U] material made from the skin of a sheep or GOAT, used in the past for writing on 羊皮紙：*parchment scrolls* 羊皮紙卷 **2** [U] a thick yellowish type of paper 仿羊皮紙 **3** [C] a document written on a piece of parchment 羊皮紙文獻

pard·ner /ˈpɑːdnə(r); *NAmE* ˈpɑːrd-/ *noun* (*NAmE, informal, non-standard*) a way of saying or writing 'partner' in informal speech 搭檔，夥伴（partner 的非正式表達方式）

par·don /ˈpɑːdn; *NAmE* ˈpɑːrdn/ *exclamation, noun, verb*

■ ***exclamation*** **1** (also **ˌpardon ˈme** especially in *NAmE*) used to ask sb to repeat sth because you did not hear it or did not understand it（用於請求別人重複某事）什麼，請再說一遍：*'You're very quiet today.' 'Pardon?' 'I said you're very quiet today.'* "你今天話很少啊。" "什麼？" "我說你今天話很少。" **2** (also **ˌpardon ˈme**) used by some people to say 'sorry' when they have accidentally made a rude noise, or said or done sth wrong 抱歉；對不起

■ ***noun*** **1** (also *law* 律) (also *BrE* **ˌfree ˈpardon**) [C] an official decision not to punish sb for a crime, or to say that sb is not guilty of a crime 赦免；特赦：***to ask/grant/receive a pardon*** 請求 / 准予 / 獲得赦免 ◇ ***a royal/presidential pardon*** 皇家 / 總統特赦 **2** [U] (*formal*)

P

~ (for sth) the action of forgiving sb for sth 原諒；寬恕 **SYN** **forgiveness**：*He asked her pardon for having deceived her.* 他欺騙了她，向她請求原諒。 **IDM** see BEG

■ ***verb*** (not usually used in the progressive tenses 通常不用於進行時) **1 ~ sb** to officially allow sb who has been found guilty of a crime to leave prison and/or avoid punishment 赦免；特赦：*She was pardoned after serving ten years of a life sentence.* 她被判終身監禁，服刑十年後被赦免了。 **2** to forgive sb for sth they have said or done (used in many expressions when you want to be polite) 原諒（表示禮貌時常用的詞語） **SYN** **excuse**：**~ sth** *Pardon my ignorance, but what is a 'duplex'?* 請原諒我無知，duplex 是什麼呢？◇ *The place was,* ***if you'll pardon the expression****, a dump.* 那個地方，請恕我直言，簡直是個垃圾場。◇ **~ sb (for sth/for doing sth)** (*BrE*) *You could be pardoned for thinking* (= it is easy to understand why people think) *that education is not the government's priority.* 人們認為政府沒有優先考慮教育，這是不難理解的。◇ *Pardon me for interrupting you.* 對不起，打擾您了。◇ **~ sb doing sth** *Pardon my asking, but is that your husband?* 請原諒我多問，那位是您的先生嗎？

IDM ˌ**pardon** ˈ**me** (*informal*) **1** (*especially NAmE*) used to ask sb to repeat sth because you did not hear it or do not understand it（用於請別人重複某事）什麼，請再說一次 **2** used by some people to say 'sorry' when they have accidentally made a rude noise or done sth wrong（為偶爾的冒失響聲或過失表示歉意）對不起 ➲ see also I BEG YOUR PARDON at BEG ˌ**pardon me for** ˈ**doing sth** used to show that you are upset or offended by the way that sb has spoken to you（對別人的說話方式表示煩惱或生氣）原諒我不得不做某事：*'Oh, just shut up!' 'Well, pardon me for breathing!'* "你給我閉嘴！""哦，真抱歉，我呼吸也打擾到你了！" ➲ more at FRENCH *n.*

par·don·able /ˈpɑːdnəbl; *NAmE* ˈpɑːrdn-/ *adj.* that can be forgiven or excused 可原諒的；可以寬恕的 **SYN** **excusable** **OPP** **unpardonable**

pare /peə(r); *NAmE* per/ *verb* **1** to remove the thin outer layer of sth, especially of fruit 削皮，去皮（尤指果皮）：**~ sth** *She pared the apple.* 她削了蘋果。◇ **~ sth from sth** *First, pare the rind from the lemon.* 首先把檸檬皮剝掉。◇ **~ sth off/away** *He pared away the excess glue with a razor blade.* 他用剃鬚刀片將溢膠刮去。➲ see also PARING KNIFE **2 ~ sth (back/down)** to gradually reduce the size or amount 逐步減小（數量或體積）；使縮小：*The training budget has been pared back to a minimum.* 培訓預算已被削減到最低限度。◇ *The workforce has been* ***pared to the bone*** (= reduced to the lowest possible level). 公司員工已被裁減到極限。 **3 ~ sth** (*especially BrE*) to cut away the edges of sth, especially your nails, in order to make them smooth and neat 修剪（指甲等） ➲ see also PARINGS

par·ent 0‑ /ˈpeərənt; *NAmE* ˈper-/ *noun*
1 0‑ [usually pl.] a person's father or mother 父親；母親：*He's still living with his parents.* 他還和父母住在一起。◇ *her adoptive parents* 她的養父母 ◇ *Sue and Ben have recently become parents.* 蘇和本最近當了爸爸媽媽了。➲ see also ONE-PARENT FAMILY, SINGLE PARENT, STEP-PARENT **2** an animal or a plant which produces other animals or plants（動、植物的）親本，親代，父本，母本：*the parent bird/tree* 親代鳥／樹 **3** (often used as an adjective 常用作形容詞) an organization that produces and owns or controls smaller organizations of the same type 創始機構；母公司；總部：*a parent bank and its subsidiaries* 總行及其附屬銀行 ◇ *the parent company* 母公司

par·ent·age /ˈpeərəntɪdʒ; *NAmE* ˈper-/ *noun* [U] the origin of a person's parents and who they are 出身；世系；家世：*a young American of German parentage* 一個年輕的德裔美國人 ◇ *Nothing is known about her parentage and background.* 她的家世和來歷不明。

par·en·tal /pəˈrentl/ *adj.* [usually before noun] connected with a parent or parents 父親的；母親的；父母的；雙親的：*parental responsibility/rights* 父母的職責／權利 ◇ *parental choice in education* 父母在教育上的選擇 ◇ *the parental home* 父母的家

paˌrental conˈtrols *noun* [pl.] (also **paˌrental ˈlock** [C]) a feature that is offered in some computer, mobile/cell phone and DIGITAL television services, that enables parents or other adults to control children's access to material that is not suitable for them 家長監護（一些計算機、手機、數字電視所提供的功能，保護孩子不接觸"兒童不宜"的內容） ▸ **parental control** *adj.* [only before noun]：*parental control software* 家長監護軟件

paˌrental ˈleave *noun* [U] time when a parent is allowed to be away from work to care for a child（照顧孩子的）父母假，家長假，育兒假：*paid/unpaid parental leave* 帶薪／不帶薪家長假 ◇ *fathers who take parental leave* 休育兒假的父親們 ➲ see also MATERNITY LEAVE, PATERNITY LEAVE

par·en·thesis /pəˈrenθəsɪs/ *noun* (*pl.* **par·en·theses** /-əsiːz/) **1** a word, sentence, etc. that is added to a speech or piece of writing, especially in order to give extra information. In writing, it is separated from the rest of the text using brackets, commas or DASHES. 插入語 **2** (*formal* or *NAmE*) (*BrE* **bracket**, ˈ**round bracket**) [usually pl.] either of a pair of marks, ( ) placed around extra information in a piece of writing or part of a problem in mathematics 括號：*Irregular forms are given* ***in parentheses****.* 不規則形式標註在括號內。

par·en·thet·ical /ˌpærənˈθetɪkl/ (also **par·en·thet·ic** /-ɪk/) *adj.* [usually before noun] (*formal*) given as extra information in a speech or piece of writing 插入的；插入成分的：*parenthetical remarks* 補充的話 ▸ **par·en·thet·ic·al·ly** /-kli/ *adv.*

par·ent·hood /ˈpeərənthʊd; *NAmE* ˈper-/ *noun* [U] the state of being a parent 做父母的身分：*the* ***responsibilities/joys of parenthood*** 做父母的責任／歡樂

par·ent·ing /ˈpeərəntɪŋ; *NAmE* ˈper-/ *noun* [U] the process of caring for your child or children 養育；撫養；教養：***good/poor parenting*** 教養有方／無方 ◇ ***parenting skills*** 教養子女的技巧 ➲ COLLOCATIONS at CHILD

par·en·tis ➲ IN LOCO PARENTIS

ˈ**parents-in-law** *noun* [pl.] the parents of your husband or wife 配偶的雙親；公婆；岳父母 ➲ see also IN-LAWS

ˌ**parent-ˈteacher association** *noun* = PTA

par excellence /ˌpɑːr ˈeksəlɑːns; *NAmE* ˌeksəˈlɑːns/ *adj.* (from *French*) (only used after the noun it describes 僅用於所修飾的名詞之後) better than all the others of the same kind; a very good example of sth 最好的；最優秀的；典型的；卓越的：*She turned out to be an organizer par excellence.* 結果表明她是一個非常出色的組織者。 ▸ **par excellence** *adv.*：*Chemistry was par excellence the laboratory science of the early nineteenth century.* 化學是 19 世紀初期最傑出的實驗室科學。

par·iah /pəˈraɪə/ *noun* a person who is not acceptable to society and is avoided by everyone 被社會遺棄者；賤民 **SYN** **outcast**

ˈ**paring knife** *noun* a small sharp knife, used especially for cutting and PEELING fruit 水果刀；削皮小尖刀 ➲ see also PARE ➲ VISUAL VOCAB page V26

par·ings /ˈpeərɪŋz; *NAmE* ˈper-/ *noun* [pl.] thin pieces that have been cut off sth 削下之物；切下的碎屑：*cheese parings* 奶酪碎屑 ➲ see also PARE

par·ish /ˈpærɪʃ/ *noun* **1** [C] an area that has its own church and that a priest is responsible for 堂區；教區：*a* ***parish church/priest*** 堂區的教堂／神父 ◇ *He is vicar of a large rural parish.* 他是鄉下一個大教區的代牧。 **2** [C] (in England) a small country area that has its own elected local government（英國）鄉村的行政小區：*the parish council* 行政區議會 **3** [C+sing./pl. v.] the people living in a particular area, especially those who go to church 教區的居民；（尤指）教區教徒

par·ish·ad /ˈpʌrɪʃʌd/ *noun* (*IndE*) a council 委員會；議會

ˌ**parish** ˈ**clerk** *noun* an official who organizes the affairs of a church in a particular area 教區秘書

pa·rish·ion·er /pəˈrɪʃənə(r)/ *noun* a person living in a parish, especially one who goes to church regularly 教區居民；（尤指）教區的教徒

ˌ**parish-ˈpump** *adj.* [only before noun] (*BrE*, *disapproving*) connected with local affairs only (and therefore not thought of as being very important) 地方主義的；區域性的；地方性的 SYN **parochial**：*parish-pump politics* 地方主義政治

ˌparish ˈregister *noun* a book that has a list of all the BAPTISMS, marriages and funerals that have taken place at a particular PARISH church 教區記事冊（記錄洗禮、婚喪等事）

par·ity /ˈpærəti/ *noun* (*pl.* **-ies**) **1** [U] **~ (with sb/sth)** | **~ (between A and B)** (*formal*) the state of being equal, especially the state of having equal pay or status（尤指薪金或地位）平等，相同，對等：*Prison officers are demanding pay parity with the police force.* 獄警正要求與警察部隊同工同酬。 **2** [U, C] (*finance* 財) the fact of the units of money of two different countries being equal（兩國貨幣的）平價：*to achieve parity with the dollar* 取得與美元的平價

park /pɑːk; *NAmE* pɑːrk/ *noun, verb*

■ ***noun*** **1** [C] an area of public land in a town or a city where people go to walk, play and relax 公園：*Hyde Park* 海德公園 ◇ *We went for a walk in the park.* 我們去公園散了散步。◇ *a park bench* 公園的長凳 **2** [C] (in compounds 構成複合詞) an area of land used for a particular purpose 專用區；園區：*a business/science park* 商業／科學園區 ◇ *a wildlife park* 野生動物園 ➲ see also AMUSEMENT PARK, CAR PARK, NATIONAL PARK, RETAIL PARK, SAFARI PARK, THEME PARK **3** [C] (in Britain) an area of land, usually with fields and trees, attached to a large country house（英國）莊園，庭院 **4** [C] (*NAmE*) a piece of land for playing sports, especially BASEBALL 運動場；（尤指）棒球場 ➲ see also BALLPARK **5 the park** [sing.] (*BrE*) a football (SOCCER) or RUGBY field 足球場；橄欖球場：*the fastest man on the park* 足球場上速度最快的人 IDM see WALK *n.*

■ ***verb*** **1** [I, T] **~ (sth)** to leave a vehicle that you are driving in a particular place for a period of time 停車；泊車：*You can't park here.* 此處不准停車。◇ *You can't park the car here.* 此處禁止停車。◇ *He's parked very badly.* 他的車停放得很不好。◇ *a badly parked truck* 一輛沒有停放好的卡車 ◇ *A red van was parked in front of the house.* 一輛紅色麪包車停在房前。◇ *a parked car* 一輛停放的轎車 ◇ (*informal, figurative*) *Just park your bags in the hall until your room is ready.* 你的房間收拾好之前，請先把行李放在大廳。➲ see also DOUBLE-PARK **2** [T] **~ yourself + adv./prep.** (*informal*) to sit or stand in a particular place for a period of time（在某處）坐下，站着：*She parked herself on the edge of the bed.* 她坐在牀沿上。 **3** [T] **~ sth** (*business* 商) (*informal*) to decide to leave an idea or issue to be dealt with or considered at a later meeting 把…擱置，推遲（在以後的會議上討論或處理）：*Let's park that until our next meeting.* 咱們把這留到下次開會時再處理吧。

PHR V **ˌpark ˈup** | **ˌpark sth↔ˈup** (*especially BrE* or *AustralE*) to find a place where you can park your vehicle 泊車；停放（車輛）：*There was a police car parked up outside the warehouse.* 有一輛警車停在倉庫外面。◇ *I couldn't* ***get parked up*** *anywhere near the restaurant.* 在這家餐館附近我找不到地方停車。

parka /ˈpɑːkə; *NAmE* ˈpɑːrkə/ *noun* a very warm jacket or coat with a HOOD that often has fur inside 派克大衣；風雪外套

park·ade /pɑːˈkeɪd; *NAmE* pɑːrˈk-/ *noun* (*CanE*) a parking garage for many cars 停車場

ˌpark and ˈride *noun* a system designed to reduce traffic in towns in which people park their cars on the edge of a town and then take a special bus or train to the town centre; the area where people park their cars before taking the bus 停車轉乘體系（把汽車停在城外，然後乘公交車輛到市中心，以減少市區的車輛）；轉乘停車場：*Use the park and ride.* 請使用停車轉乘系統。◇ *I've left my car in the park and ride.* 我把汽車停在轉乘停車場了。◇ *a park-and-ride service* 停車轉乘服務

par·kin /ˈpɑːkɪn; *NAmE* ˈpɑːrkɪn/ *noun* [U] (*BrE*) a dark brown sticky cake made with OATMEAL and TREACLE, flavoured with GINGER 燕麥薑餅

park·ing /ˈpɑːkɪŋ; *NAmE* ˈpɑːrk-/ *noun* [U] **1** the act of stopping a vehicle at a place and leaving it there for a period of time 停車；泊車：*There is no parking here between 9 a.m. and 6 p.m.* 上午 9 時至下午 6 時此處禁止停車。◇ *I managed to find a* ***parking space.*** 我終於找到了一個停車位。◇ *a parking fine* (= for parking illegally) 違章停車罰款 **2** a space or an area for leaving vehicles 停車場；停車位：*The hotel is centrally situated with ample free parking.* 旅館坐落在市中心，有充裕的免費停車位。

ˈparking brake *noun* (*NAmE*) = HANDBRAKE

ˈparking garage (*NAmE*) (*BrE* **ˌmulti-storey ˈcar park, ˌmulti-ˈstorey**) *noun* a large building with several floors for parking cars in 多層停車場；立體停車場

ˈparking lot *noun* (*NAmE*) an area where people can leave their cars 停車場 ➲ compare CAR PARK

ˈparking meter (also **meter**) *noun* a machine beside the road that you put money into when you park your car next to it 停車收費器 ➲ VISUAL VOCAB pages V2, V3

ˈparking ticket (also **ticket**) *noun* an official notice that is put on your car when you have parked illegally, ordering you to pay money 違章停車傳票

Par·kin·son's dis·ease /ˈpɑːkɪnsnz dɪziːz; *NAmE* ˈpɑːrk-/ (also **par·kin·son·ism** /ˈpɑːkɪnsənɪzəm; *NAmE* ˈpɑːrk-/) *noun* [U] a disease of the nervous system that gets worse over a period of time and causes the muscles to become weak and the arms and legs to shake 帕金森病（神經系統疾病，能致肌肉無力和四肢顫抖）

ˈParkinson's law *noun* [U] (*humorous*) the idea that work will always take as long as the time available for it 帕金森定律（工作總是到時限最後一刻才會完成）

park·land /ˈpɑːklænd; *NAmE* ˈpɑːrk-/ *noun* [U] open land with grass and trees, for example around a large house in the country（如鄉村大宅院周圍的）有草木的開闊地

par·kour /pɑːˈkʊə(r); *NAmE* pɑːrˈkʊr/ *noun* [U] the sport of moving through a city by running, jumping and climbing under, around and through things 跑酷，城市疾走（在城市中奔跑、跳躍、攀爬、蛇行、穿越的運動）➲ compare FREE RUNNING ORIGIN From French *parcours du combatant*, a type of military training. 源自法語 parcours du combatant，一種軍事訓練課程。➲ VISUAL VOCAB page V50

park·way /ˈpɑːkweɪ; *NAmE* ˈpɑːrk-/ *noun* (*NAmE*) a wide road with trees and grass along the sides or middle（有草木的）大路；綠化道路；林蔭大道

parky /ˈpɑːki; *NAmE* ˈpɑːrki/ *adj.* (*BrE, informal, old-fashioned* or *humorous*) (of the weather 天氣) cold 寒冷的

par·lance /ˈpɑːləns; *NAmE* ˈpɑːrl-/ *noun* [U] (*formal*) a particular way of using words or expressing yourself, for example one used by a particular group 說法；術語；用語：*in* ***common/legal/modern parlance*** 用普通／法律／現代用語 ◇ *A Munro, in climbing parlance, is a Scottish mountain exceeding 3 000 feet.* "芒羅"在登山術語裏是指高度超過 3 000 英尺的蘇格蘭山峰。

par·lay /ˈpɑːleɪ; *NAmE* ˈpɑːrleɪ/ *verb*

PHR V **ˈparlay sth into sth** (*NAmE*) to use or develop sth such as money or a skill to make it more successful or worth more 成功地利用；有效發展；使增值：*She hopes to parlay her success as a model into an acting career.* 她希望利用自己當模特兒的成功經歷進而發展演藝事業。

par·ley /ˈpɑːli; *NAmE* ˈpɑːrli/ *noun, verb*

■ ***noun*** (*old-fashioned*) a discussion between enemies or people who disagree, in order to try and find a way of solving a problem（敵對或有異議的雙方間的）和談，會談，對話

■ ***verb*** [I] **~ (with sb)** (*old-fashioned*) to discuss sth with sb in order to solve a disagreement（和某人）和談，談判，會談

par·lia·ment /ˈpɑːləmənt; *NAmE* ˈpɑːrl-/ *noun* **1** [C, sing.+sing./pl. v.] the group of people who are elected to make and change the laws of a country 議會；國會：*The German parliament is called the 'Bundestag'.* 德國的議會稱為 Bundestag。➲ COLLOCATIONS at POLITICS **2** **Parliament** [U+sing./pl. v.] the parliament of the United Kingdom, consisting of the House of Commons and the House of Lords 英國議會

P

（包括下議院和上議院）：*a Member of Parliament* 議會議員 ◇ *The issue was debated **in Parliament**.* 議會就這個問題進行了辯論。◇ *an Act of Parliament* 議會法案 ◇ *to **win a seat in Parliament*** 贏得議會中的一個席位 ◇ *to **be elected to Parliament*** 當選為議會議員 **3** (also **Parliament**) [C, U] a particular period during which a parliament is working; Parliament as it exists between one GENERAL ELECTION and the next 一屆議會的會期；（兩次大選之間的）一屆議會：*We are now into the second half of the parliament.* 我們現已進入了本屆議會的後半任期。◇ *to dissolve Parliament* (= formally end its activities) *and call an election* 解散議會並舉行大選 ➲ see also HOUSES OF PARLIAMENT, HUNG (1)

par·lia·men·tar·ian /ˌpɑːləmenˈteəriən; *NAmE* ˌpɑːrləmənˈter-/ *noun* a member of a parliament, especially one with a lot of skill and experience 議會議員；（尤指）資深議員，老道的議員

par·lia·men·tary /ˌpɑːləˈmentri; *NAmE* ˌpɑːrl-/ *adj.* [usually before noun] connected with a parliament; having a parliament 議會的；國會的；設有議會的：*parliamentary elections* 議會選舉 ◇ *a parliamentary democracy* 議會民主政體 ➲ compare UNPARLIAMENTARY

ˌparliamentary private ˈsecretary *noun* = PPS

ˌparliamentary ˈprivilege *noun* [U] the special right of Members of Parliament to speak freely in Parliament, especially about another person, without risking legal action 議員特權，言論免責權（在議會中針對他人等自由發言而不會被起訴）：*He made the allegation under the protection of parliamentary privilege.* 他是在議員特權的保護下說出那種毫無根據的話的。

ˌparliamentary ˈsecretary *noun* a Member of Parliament who works in a government department below the minister 政務次官（大臣掌管的政府部門的議員）➲ compare PARLIAMENTARY PRIVATE SECRETARY, PARLIAMENTARY UNDERSECRETARY

parliaˌmentary ˌunderˈsecretary *noun* (in the UK) a Member of Parliament in a government department, below a minister in rank 政務次官（英國政府部門任職的議員，級別低於大臣）

P

par·lour (*especially US* **par·lor**) /ˈpɑːlə(r); *NAmE* ˈpɑːrl-/ *noun* **1** (*old-fashioned*) a room in a private house for sitting in, entertaining visitors, etc.（私人住房的）起居室，客廳 **2** (in compounds 構成複合詞) (*especially NAmE*) a shop/store that provides particular goods or services（專營某種商品或業務的）店鋪：*a beauty/an ice-cream parlour* 美容院；冰淇淋店 ➲ see also FUNERAL PARLOUR, MASSAGE PARLOUR

ˈparlour game (*especially US* **ˈparlor game**) *noun* a game played in the home, especially a word game or guessing game 室內遊戲；（尤指）填字遊戲，猜謎遊戲

par·lour·maid (*especially US* **par·lor·maid**) /ˈpɑːləmeɪd; *NAmE* ˈpɑːrlərmeɪd/ *noun* (*old use*) a female servant who was employed in the past to serve food at the dinner table（舊時侍候用餐的）客廳侍女

par·lous /ˈpɑːləs; *NAmE* ˈpɑːrləs/ *adj.* (*formal*) (of a situation 形勢) very bad and very uncertain; dangerous 惡劣的；動盪的；危險的 **SYN** **perilous**

Parma vio·let /ˌpɑːmə ˈvaɪələt; *NAmE* ˌpɑːrmə/ *noun* a strong-smelling plant with light purple flowers 帕爾馬紫羅蘭

Par·mesan /ˈpɑːmɪzæn; ˌpɑːmɪˈzæn; *NAmE* ˈpɑːrməzɑːn; -zæn/ (also **ˌParmesan ˈcheese**) *noun* [U] a type of very hard Italian cheese that is usually GRATED and eaten on Italian food 帕爾馬乾酪（一種意大利硬奶酪，常磨碎放在食品上）

pa·ro·chial /pəˈrəʊkiəl; *NAmE* -ˈroʊ-/ *adj.* **1** [usually before noun] (*formal*) connected with a church PARISH 教區的；堂區的：*parochial schools* 教區學校 ◇ *a member of the parochial church council* 教區教堂理事會成員 **2** (*disapproving*) only concerned with small issues that happen in your local area and not interested in more important things 只關心本地區的；地方觀念的 ▸ **pa·ro·chial·ism** /-ɪzəm/ *noun* [U]：*the parochialism of a small community* 小圈子的狹隘觀念

paˌrochial ˈschool *noun* (*NAmE*) a private school supported by a particular Christian church（由特定基督教派辦的）教區學校 ➲ compare FAITH SCHOOL

par·od·ist /ˈpærədɪst/ *noun* a person who writes parodies 滑稽模仿作品作者

par·ody /ˈpærədi/ *noun, verb*

■ ***noun*** (*pl.* **-ies**) **~ (of sth)** **1** [C, U] a piece of writing, music, acting, etc. that deliberately copies the style of sb/sth in order to be amusing 滑稽模仿作品（文章、音樂作品或表演等的滑稽模仿）：*a parody of a horror film* 一部恐怖電影的仿作 **2** [C] (*disapproving*) something that is such a bad or unfair example of sth that it seems ridiculous 拙劣的模仿；荒誕不經的事 **SYN** **travesty**：*The trial was a parody of justice.* 那次審判是對正義的嘲弄。

■ ***verb*** (**par·odies**, **par·ody·ing**, **par·odied**, **par·odied**) **~ sb/sth** to copy the style of sb/sth in an exaggerated way, especially in order to make people laugh 滑稽地模仿；誇張地演繹 **SYN** **lampoon**

par·ole /pəˈrəʊl; *NAmE* pəˈroʊl/ *noun, verb*

■ ***noun*** [U] **1** permission that is given to a prisoner to leave prison before the end of their SENTENCE on condition that they behave well 假釋；有條件的釋放：*to be eligible for parole* 符合假釋條件 ◇ *She was released **on parole**.* 她獲得假釋。➲ COLLOCATIONS at JUSTICE **2** (*linguistics* 語言) language considered as the words individual people use, rather than as the communication system of a particular community 言語 ➲ compare LANGUE

■ ***verb*** [usually passive] **~ sb** to give a prisoner permission to leave prison before the end of their SENTENCE on condition that they behave well 假釋；有條件地釋放：*She was paroled after two years.* 她兩年後獲假釋。

par·ox·ysm /ˈpærəksɪzəm/ *noun* **~ (of sth)** **1** a sudden strong feeling or expression of an emotion that cannot be controlled 突然發作：*paroxysms of hate* 突然滿腔仇恨 ◇ *a paroxysm of laughter* 一陣狂笑 **2** (*medical* 醫) a sudden short attack of pain, causing physical shaking that cannot be controlled（病痛的）突然發作，陣發

par·quet /ˈpɑːkeɪ; *NAmE* pɑːrˈkeɪ/ *noun* [U] a floor covering made of flat pieces of wood fixed together in a pattern 拼花地板；鑲木地板：*parquet flooring* 拼花地板 ➲ compare WOODBLOCK (1)

parra·keet ➲ PARAKEET

parri·cide /ˈpærɪsaɪd/ *noun* [U, C] (*formal*) the crime of killing your father, mother or a close relative; a person who is guilty of this crime 殺父（或母、近親）罪；殺父（或母、近親）者 ➲ compare FRATRICIDE (1), MATRICIDE, PATRICIDE

par·rot /ˈpærət/ *noun, verb*

■ ***noun*** a tropical bird with a curved beak. There are several types of parrot, most of which have bright feathers. Some are kept as pets and can be trained to copy human speech. 鸚鵡 **IDM** see SICK *adj.*

■ ***verb*** **~ sb/sth** (*disapproving*) to repeat what sb else has said without thinking about what it means 鸚鵡學舌

ˈparrot-fashion *adv.* (*BrE, disapproving*) if sb learns or repeats sth **parrot-fashion**, they do it without thinking about it or understanding what it means 鸚鵡學舌般地；盲從地；亦步亦趨地

parry /ˈpæri/ *verb* (**par·ries**, **parry·ing**, **par·ried**, **par·ried**) **1** [T, I] **~ (sth)** to defend yourself against sb who is attacking you by pushing their arm, weapon, etc. to one side 擋開，擱擋（攻擊等）**SYN** **deflect**：*He parried a blow to his head.* 他擋開了砸向頭部的一擊。◇ *The shot was parried by the goalie.* 射門的球被守門員擋出去了。**2** [T] **~ sth | + speech** to avoid having to answer a difficult question, criticism, etc., especially by replying in the same way 逃避，躲避，迴避（難題、批評等）**SYN** **fend off**：*She parried all questions about their relationship.* 她迴避了關於他們之間關係的所有問題。▸ **parry** *noun* (*pl.* **-ies**)

parse /pɑːz; *NAmE* pɑːrs/ *verb* **~ sth** (*grammar* 語法) to divide a sentence into parts and describe the grammar of each word or part（對句子）作語法分析；作句法分析

Par·see (also **Parsi**) /ˌpɑːˈsiː; ˈpɑːsiː; *NAmE* ˌpɑːrˈsiː; ˈpɑːrsiː/ *noun* a member of a religious group whose ANCESTORS originally came from Persia and whose religion is Zoroastrianism 帕西人（拜火教徒後裔，祖先為波斯人）

par·si·mo·ni·ous /ˌpɑːsɪˈməʊniəs; *NAmE* ˌpɑːrsəˈmoʊ-/ *adj.* (*formal*) extremely unwilling to spend money 慳吝的；吝嗇的；小氣的 SYN **mean** ▸ **par·si·mo·ni·ous·ly** *adv.*

par·si·mony /ˈpɑːsɪməni; *NAmE* ˈpɑːrsəmoʊni/ *noun* [U] (*formal*) the fact of being extremely unwilling to spend money 慳吝；吝嗇；小氣 SYN **meanness**

pars·ley /ˈpɑːsli; *NAmE* ˈpɑːrsli/ *noun* [U] a plant with curly green leaves that are used in cooking as a HERB and to decorate food 歐芹；荷蘭芹： *fish with parsley sauce* 歐芹沙司煮魚 ➲ VISUAL VOCAB page V32 ➲ see also COW PARSLEY

pars·nip /ˈpɑːsnɪp; *NAmE* ˈpɑːrs-/ *noun* [C, U] a long pale yellow root vegetable 歐洲防風；歐洲蘿蔔 ➲ VISUAL VOCAB page V31

par·son /ˈpɑːsn; *NAmE* ˈpɑːrsn/ *noun* **1** (*old-fashioned*) an Anglican VICAR or PARISH priest 聖公會教區牧師；教區牧師 **2** (*informal*) a Protestant CLERGYMAN 新教牧師

par·son·age /ˈpɑːsənɪdʒ; *NAmE* ˈpɑːrs-/ *noun* a parson's house 教區牧師的住所

ˌparson's ˈnose (*NAmE* also **ˌpope's ˈnose**) *noun* the piece of flesh at the tail end of a cooked bird, usually a chicken（烹調過的禽類、尤指雞的）尾部的肉

part 0━ /pɑːt; *NAmE* pɑːrt/ *noun, verb, adv.*

■ ***noun***

▸ **SOME** 一些 **1** 0━ [U] **~ of sth** some but not all of a thing 部份： *We spent part of the time in the museum.* 我們花了一部份時間在博物館。◇ *Part of the building was destroyed in the fire.* 大樓的一部份毀於火災。◇ *Voters are given* ***only part of the story*** (= only some of the information). 只對選民透露了部份情況。◇ ***Part of me*** *feels sorry for him* (= I feel partly, but not entirely, sorry for him). 我有點同情他。

▸ **PIECE** 片段 **2** 0━ [C] a section, piece or feature of sth 片段；部份；一點： *The early part of her life was spent in Paris.* 她年輕時生活在巴黎。◇ *The novel is good* ***in parts***. 小說的一些章節不錯。◇ *We've done the difficult part of the job.* 我們已完成了工作的困難部份。◇ *The procedure can be divided into two parts.* 這一程序可以分為兩部份。◇ *The worst part was having to wait three hours in the rain.* 最糟糕的是必須在雨中等待三個小時。

▸ **MEMBER** 成員 **3** 0━ [U] a member of sth; a person or thing that, together with others, makes up a single unit 成員；成分： *You need to be able to work as part of a team.* 你必須能作為團隊的一員去工作。

▸ **OF MACHINE** 機器 **4** 0━ [C] a piece of a machine or structure 部件；零件： *aircraft parts* 飛行器零件◇ *the working parts of the machinery* 機器的運作部件◇ ***spare parts*** 備用零件

▸ **OF BODY/PLANT** 身體；植物 **5** 0━ [C] a separate piece or area of a human or animal body or of a plant 器官；部位；組成部份： *the parts of the body* 身體各部位 ➲ see also PRIVATE PARTS

▸ **REGION/AREA** 地區；區域 **6** 0━ [C] an area or a region of the world, a country, a town, etc.（世界、國家或城鎮等的）區域，地區： *the northern part of the country* 這個國家的北部地區◇ *a plant that grows in many parts of the world* 生長在世界許多地區的一種植物◇ *Which part of Japan do you come from?* 你是日本哪個地區的人？◇ *Come and visit us if you're ever in our part of the world.* 什麼時候到我們這個地方來，請來看看我們。 **7 parts** [pl.] (*old-fashioned, informal*) a region or an area 區域；地區： *She's not from these parts.* 她不是這一帶的人。◇ *He's just arrived back from foreign parts.* 他剛從外地回來。

▸ **OF BOOK/SERIES** 書；系列片 **8** 0━ [C] (*abbr.* **pt**) a section of a book, television series, etc., especially one that is published or broadcast separately（書、電視系列片等的、尤指單獨發行或播出的）部，集，部份： *an encyclopedia published in 25 weekly parts* 每週出版一部，共 25 部的百科全書。◇ *Henry IV, Part II* 《亨利四世》第二篇◇ *The final part will be shown next Sunday evening.* 最後一集將於下星期天晚上播出。

▸ **FOR ACTOR** 演員 **9** 0━ [C] a role played by an actor in a play, film/movie, etc.; the words spoken by an actor in a particular role 角色；台詞： *She was very good in the part.* 她這個角色演得很好。◇ *Have you learned your part yet?* 你記住你的台詞了嗎？◇ (*figurative*) *He's always* ***playing a part*** (= pretending to be sth that he is not). 他總是裝模作樣的。

▸ **INVOLVEMENT** 參與 **10** [C, usually sing., U] the way in which sb/sth is involved in an action or situation 參加；參與： *He* ***had no part in*** *the decision.* 他沒有參與這項決定。

▸ **IN MUSIC** 音樂 **11** [C] music for a particular voice or instrument in a group singing or playing together 部；聲部；音部；段落： *the clarinet part* 單簧管部◇ *four-part harmony* 四部和聲

▸ **EQUAL PORTION** 等份 **12** [C] a unit of measurement that allows you to compare the different amounts of substances in sth（度量單位的）等份，份： *Add three parts wine to one part water.* 一份水兌上三份葡萄酒。

▸ **IN HAIR** 髮式 **13** (*NAmE*) (*BrE* **part·ing**) [C] a line on a person's head where the hair is divided with a COMB（頭髮的）分縫，髮縫，分線 ➲ VISUAL VOCAB page V60

IDM **the best/better part of sth** most of sth, especially a period of time; more than half of sth（事物、時間的）絕大部份，多半： *The journey took her the better part of an hour.* 旅程花去了她半個多小時。 **for the ˈmost part** 0━ mostly; usually 多半；通常： *The contributors are, for the most part, professional scientists.* 投稿者大多是專業科學家。➲ LANGUAGE BANK at GENERALLY **for ˈmy, ˈhis, ˈtheir, etc. part** speaking for myself, etc. 就我（或他、他們等）而言 SYN **personally** **have a part to ˈplay (in sth)** to be able to help sth 能幫助，能在…中發揮作用： *We all have a part to play in the fight against crime.* 打擊犯罪，我們大家都有一份責任。 **have/play a ˈpart (in sth)** to be involved in sth 參與某事： *She plays an active part in local politics.* 她積極參與地方政治活動。 **have/play/take/want no ˈpart in/of sth** to not be involved in or refuse to be involved in sth, especially because you disapprove of it 不參與，不捲入，拒絕加入（尤指不贊成的事情）： *I want no part of this sordid business.* 我決不想捲入這一卑鄙勾當。 **in ˈpart** 0━ partly; to some extent 部份地；在某種程度上： *Her success was due in part to luck.* 她的成功在某種程度上是由於運氣好。 **look/dress the ˈpart** to have an appearance or wear clothes suitable for a particular job, role or position 外貌／穿着與工作（或身分、職務）相宜 **a man/woman of (many) ˈparts** a person with many skills 多才多藝的人；多面手 **on the part of sb/on sb's part** made or done by sb 由某人所為： *It was an error on my part.* 那是我的過失。 **part and parcel of sth** an essential part of sth 重要部份；基本部份： *Keeping the accounts is part and parcel of my job.* 記賬是我的主要工作。 **part of the ˈfurniture** a person or thing that you are so used to seeing that you no longer notice them 見慣了的人（或東西）；存在已久故不為人注意的人（或事物）： *I worked there so long that I became part of the furniture.* 我在那裏工作得太久，都不為人注意了。 **take sth in good ˈpart** (*BrE*) to accept sth slightly unpleasant without complaining or being offended 從容面對，不介意地接受（不太愉快的事） **take ˈpart (in sth)** 0━ to be involved in sth 參與某事 SYN **participate**： *to take part in a discussion/demonstration/fight/celebration* 參加討論／示威／戰鬥／慶祝◇ *How many countries took part in the last Olympic Games?* 有多少國家參加了上屆奧運會？ **take sb's ˈpart** (*BrE*) to support sb, for example in an argument（在辯論等中）支持某人，站在某人一邊 SYN **side with**： *His mother always takes his part.* 他母親總是護着他。➲ more at DISCRETION, LARGE *adj.*, SUM *n.*

■ ***verb***

▸ **LEAVE SB** 離開某人 **1** [I] (*formal*) if a person **parts** from another person, or two people **part**, they leave each other 離開；分別： *We parted at the airport.* 我們在機場分手了。◇ *I hate to part on such bad terms.* 我討厭以那麼惡劣的方式分手。◇ **~ from sb** *He has recently parted*

P

from his wife (= they have started to live apart). 他最近與妻子分居了。➲ see also PARTING *adj.*

▸ **KEEP APART** 隔離 **2** [T, often passive] **~ sb (from sb)** (*formal*) to prevent sb from being with sb else 分離；分開；隔離：*I hate being parted from the children.* 我不願與孩子們分開。◇ *The puppies were parted from their mother at birth.* 小狗崽兒一出生就和它們的媽媽分開了。

▸ **MOVE AWAY** 移開 **3** [I, T] if two things or parts of things **part** or you **part** them, they move away from each other 分散；分開；解散：*The crowd parted in front of them.* 人群在他們面前分開了。◇ *The elevator doors parted and out stepped the President.* 電梯門打開了，總統從裏面步出。◇ **~ sth** *Her lips were slightly parted.* 她的嘴唇微微張開。◇ *She parted the curtains a little and looked out.* 她略扒開窗簾，向外張望。

▸ **HAIR** 頭髮 **4** [T] **~ sth** to divide your hair into two sections with a COMB, creating a line that goes from the back of your head to the front 分開；梳成分頭：*He parts his hair in the middle.* 他梳着中分頭。➲ see also PARTING *n.* (2)

IDM **part 'company (with/from sb)** **1** to leave sb; to end a relationship with sb 離開；分手；斷絕關係：*This is where we part company* (= go in different directions). 這就是我們分手的地方。◇ *The band have parted company with their manager.* 樂隊與其經理人已散夥了。◇ *The band and their manager have parted company.* 樂隊與其經理人已散夥了。 **2** to disagree with sb about sth（與某人）有意見分歧：*Weber parted company with Marx on a number of important issues.* 韋伯與馬克思在若干重大問題上意見有分歧。➲ more at FOOL *n.*

PHR V **'part with sth** to give sth to sb else, especially sth that you would prefer to keep 放棄，交出（尤指不捨得的東西）：*Make sure you read the contract before parting with any money.* 一定要注意先看清合約再交錢。

■ ***adv.*** (often in compounds 常構成複合詞) consisting of two things; to some extent but not completely 由兩部份構成；在一定程度上；部份地：*She's part French, part English.* 她是英法血統各半。◇ *His feelings were part anger, part relief.* 他感到既憤怒，又解脫。◇ *The course is part funded by the European Commission.* 這個課程由歐洲委員會部份出資贊助。◇ *He is part owner of a farm in France.* 他擁有法國某農場的一部份。

par·take /pɑː'teɪk; *NAmE* pɑːr't-/ *verb* (**par·took** /-'tʊk/, **par·taken** /-'teɪkən/) (*formal*) **1** [I] **~ (of sth)** (*old-fashioned* or *humorous*) to eat or drink sth especially sth that is offered to you 吃，喝，享用（尤指給予的食物）：*Would you care to partake of some refreshment?* 你想吃些東西嗎？ **2** [I] **~ (in sth)** (*old-fashioned*) to take part in an activity 參加；參與：*They preferred not to partake in the social life of the town.* 他們不想參加這個鎮的社交活動。

PHR V **par'take of sth** (*formal*) to have some of a particular quality 具有（部份特性）；有點：*His work partakes of the aesthetic fashions of his time.* 他的作品具有當時的某些審美時尚。

par·terre /pɑː'teə(r); *NAmE* pɑːr'ter/ *noun* (from *French*) **1** a flat area in a garden, with plants arranged in a formal design 花壇；花圃 **2** (*especially NAmE*) the lower level in a theatre where the audience sits, especially the area underneath the BALCONY（尤指戲院樓廳底下的）正廳觀眾席

,part ex'change *noun* [U] (*BrE*) a way of buying sth, such as a car, in which you give the old one as part of the payment for a more expensive one 部份抵價交易；以舊換新交易：*We'll take your car **in part exchange**.* 我們收下你的舊車，以抵付購買新車的部份款額。▸ **,part-ex'change** *verb* **~ sth**

par·theno·gen·esis /ˌpɑːθənəʊ'dʒenɪsɪs; *NAmE* ˌpɑːrθənoʊ-/ *noun* [U] (*biology* 生) the process of producing new plants or animals from an OVUM that has not been FERTILIZED 孤雌生殖；單性生殖 ▸ **par·theno·gen·et·ic** /ˌpɑːθənəʊdʒə'netɪk; *NAmE* ˌpɑːrθənoʊ-/ *adj.*：*parthenogenetic species* 單性生殖物種 **par·theno·gen·et·ic·ally** /-kli/ *adj.*：*These organisms reproduce parthenogenetically.* 這些生物體通過單性生殖進行繁殖。

par·tial /'pɑːʃl; *NAmE* 'pɑːrʃl/ *adj.* **1** not complete or whole 部份的；不完全的：*It was only a partial solution to the problem.* 那只是部份地解決了這個問題。◇ *a partial eclipse of the sun* 日偏蝕 **2** [not before noun] **~ to sb/sth** (*old-fashioned*) liking sb/sth very much 熱愛；鍾愛：*I'm not partial to mushrooms.* 我不太愛吃蘑菇。 **3** [not usually before noun] **~ (towards sb/sth)** (*disapproving*) showing or feeling too much support for one person, team, idea, etc., in a way that is unfair 偏頗；偏袒 **SYN** **biased** **OPP** **impartial**

par·ti·al·ity /ˌpɑːʃi'æləti; *NAmE* ˌpɑːrʃ-/ *noun* (*formal*) **1** [U] (*disapproving*) the unfair support of one person, team, idea, etc. 偏袒 **SYN** **bias** **OPP** **impartiality** **2** [sing.] **~ for sth/sb** a feeling of liking sth/sb very much 特別喜愛；酷愛 **SYN** **fondness**：*She has a partiality for exotic flowers.* 她特別喜愛異國花卉。

par·tial·ly /'pɑːʃəli; *NAmE* 'pɑːrʃ-/ *adv.* partly; not completely 部份地；不完全地：*The road was partially blocked by a fallen tree.* 倒下的一棵樹擋住了部份道路。◇ *a society for the blind and **partially sighted*** (= people who can see very little). 一個盲人及弱視者協會 ➲ note at PARTLY

par·tici·pant **AW** /pɑː'tɪsɪpənt; *NAmE* pɑːr't-/ *noun* **~ (in sth)** a person who is taking part in an activity or event 參與者；參加者：*He has been an active participant in the discussion.* 他一直積極參與這次討論。

par·tici·pate **AW** /pɑː'tɪsɪpeɪt; *NAmE* pɑːr't-/ *verb* [I] **~ (in sth)** (rather *formal*) to take part in or become involved in an activity 參加；參與：*She didn't participate in the discussion.* 她沒有參加討論。◇ *We encourage students to participate fully in the running of the college.* 我們鼓勵學生全面參與學院的運作。◇ *Details of the competition are available at all participating stores.* 比賽的詳情可在各參與商店取閱。

par·tici·pa·tion **AW** /pɑːˌtɪsɪ'peɪʃn; *NAmE* pɑːrˌt-/ *noun* [U] the act of taking part in an activity or event 參加；參與：*a show with lots of **audience participation*** 觀眾熱烈參與的演出 ◇ **~ in sth** *A back injury prevented active participation in any sports for a while.* 背傷曾一度妨礙積極參加任何體育運動。

par·tici·pa·tory **AW** /pɑːˌtɪsɪ'peɪtəri; *NAmE* pɑːr'tɪsəpətɔːri/ *adj.* [usually before noun] allowing everyone in a society, business, etc. to give their opinions and to help make decisions 參與式的（允許所有成員參與）：*Participatory democracy is a fundamental principle of cooperative businesses.* 參與式民主制是合作企業的基本原則。

par·ti·ciple /pɑː'tɪsɪpl; *NAmE* 'pɑːrtɪsɪpl/ *noun* (*grammar* 語法) (in English) a word formed from a verb, ending in *-ing* (= the PRESENT PARTICIPLE) or *-ed*, *-en*, etc. (= the PAST PARTICIPLE) 分詞（現在分詞或過去分詞）▸ **par·ti·ci·pial** /ˌpɑːtɪ'sɪpiəl; *NAmE* ˌpɑːrt-/ *adj.*

par·ticle /'pɑːtɪkl; *NAmE* 'pɑːrt-/ *noun* **1** a very small piece of sth 顆粒；微粒：*particles of dust* 灰塵 ◇ *dust particles* 塵埃 ◇ *There was **not a particle of** evidence* (= no evidence at all) *to support the case.* 沒有絲毫證據支持這個論點。 **2** (*physics* 物) a very small piece of matter, such as an ELECTRON or PROTON, that is part of an atom 粒子 ➲ see also ALPHA PARTICLE, ELEMENTARY PARTICLE **3** (*grammar* 語法) an adverb or a preposition that can combine with a verb to make a phrasal verb 小品詞（與動詞構成短語動詞的副詞或介詞）：*In 'She tore up the letter', the word 'up' is a particle.* 在 She tore up the letter 句中，up 是小品詞。➲ see also ADVERBIAL PARTICLE

'particle physics *noun* [U] the scientific study of very small pieces of matter that are parts of an atom 粒子物理學

par·ticu·lar 🔑 /pə'tɪkjələ(r); *NAmE* pər't-/ *adj.*, *noun*

■ ***adj.*** **1** 🔑 [only before noun] used to emphasize that you are referring to one individual person, thing or type of thing and not others 專指的，特指的（與泛指相對） **SYN** **specific**：*There is one particular patient I'd like you to see.* 我想讓你見一個病人。◇ *Is there a particular type of book he enjoys?* 他特別喜愛哪一類的書籍嗎？ **2** 🔑 [only before noun] greater than usual; special 不尋常的；格外的；特別的：*We must pay particular attention* *to this point.* 我們必須特別注意這一點。◇ *These documents are of particular interest.* 這些文件讓人很感興趣。**3 ~** (**about/over sth**) very definite about what you like and careful about what you choose 講究；挑剔 **SYN fussy**：*She's very particular about her clothes.* 她對衣着特別挑剔。

IDM in par'ticular 1 especially or particularly 尤其；特別；格外：*He loves science fiction in particular.* 他特別喜愛科幻小說。➲ LANGUAGE BANK at EMPHASIS **2** special or specific 特殊的；專門的；具體的：*Peter was lying on the sofa doing **nothing in particular**.* 彼得躺在沙發上，無所事事。◇ *Is there **anything in particular** you'd like for dinner?* 晚飯你想吃點什麼特別的嗎？◇ *She directed the question at **no one in particular**.* 她的問題並沒有針對任何個人。

■ ***noun*** (*formal*) **1** [usually pl.] a fact or detail, especially one that is officially written down（正式記下的）細節，詳情：*The police officer took down all the particulars of the burglary.* 這名警察記下了竊案發生的詳細情況。◇ *The nurse asked me for my particulars* (= personal details such as your name, address, etc.). 護士向我詢問了我的個人資料。◇ *The new contract will be the same in every particular as the old one.* 新合同與舊合同的各項細節將完全相同。**2 particulars** [pl.] written information and details about a property, business, job, etc. 詳細資料；詳細介紹材料：*Application forms and further particulars are available from the Personnel Office.* 申請表格及其他詳細資料可向人事部索取。

par·ticu·lar·ity /pəˌtɪkju'lærəti; *NAmE* pər't-/ *noun* (*pl.* **-ies**) (*formal*) **1** [U] the quality of being individual or unique 個性；獨特性：*the particularity of each human being* 每個人的獨特個性 **2** [U] attention to detail; being exact 考究；準確；精確 **3 particularities** [pl.] the special features or details of sth 特徵；特性；細節；詳情

par·ticu·lar·ize (*BrE* also **-ise**) /pə'tɪkjələraɪz; *NAmE* pər't-/ *verb* [I, T] **~ (sth)** (*formal*) to give details of sth, especially one by one; to give particular examples of sth 詳細說明；逐一列舉；以具體的例子說明

par·ticu·lar·ly /pə'tɪkjələli; *NAmE* pər'tɪkjələrli/ *adv.*
especially; more than usual or more than others 特別；尤其：*particularly good/important/useful* 特別好／重要／有用 ◇ *Traffic is bad, particularly in the city centre.* 交通狀況很差，尤其是在市中心。◇ *I enjoyed the play, particularly the second half.* 我很欣賞那部劇，特別是後半段。◇ *The lecture was **not particularly*** (= not very) *interesting.* 講座並不特別精彩。◇ *'Did you enjoy it?' 'No, **not particularly*** (= not very much).' "你玩得開心嗎？" "不很開心。"

par·ticu·late /pɑː'tɪkjələt; -leɪt; *NAmE* pɑːr't-/ *adj.*, *noun* (*chemistry* 化)
■ ***adj.*** relating to, or in the form of, PARTICLES 微粒（形式）的；顆粒（狀）的：*particulate pollution* 微塵污染
■ ***noun* particulates** [pl.] matter in the form of PARTICLES 微粒；顆粒；粒子

part·ing /'pɑːtɪŋ; *NAmE* 'pɑːrt-/ *noun*, *adj.*
■ ***noun* 1** [U, C] the act or occasion of leaving a person or place 離別；分手；分別：*the moment of parting* 離別的時刻 ◇ *We had a tearful parting at the airport.* 我們在機場灑淚而別。**2** (*BrE*) (*NAmE* **part**) [C] a line on a person's head where the hair is divided with a COMB（頭髮的）分縫，髮縫，分線：*a **side/centre parting*** 偏分；中分 ➲ VISUAL VOCAB page V60 **3** [U, C] the act or result of dividing sth into parts 分開；分離；散開：*the parting of the clouds* 雲破天開

IDM a/the ˌparting of the 'ways a point at which two people or groups of people decide to separate 岔路口；分道揚鑣處；分手處

■ ***adj.*** [only before noun] said or done by sb as they leave 離別時說的（或做的）：*a parting kiss* 臨別之吻 ◇ *His parting words were 'I love you.'* 他臨別的話是"我愛你"。

IDM ˌparting 'shot a final remark, especially an unkind one, that sb makes as they leave 臨別的放話（尤指不友善的）

par·ti·san /ˌpɑːtɪ'zæn; 'pɑːtɪzæn; *NAmE* 'pɑːrtəzn/ *adj.*, *noun*
■ ***adj.*** (often *disapproving*) showing too much support for one person, group or idea, especially without considering it carefully（對個別人、團體或思想）過分支持的，偏護的，盲目擁護的 **SYN one-sided**：*Most newspapers are politically partisan.* 大多數報紙都有政治傾向。
■ ***noun* 1** a person who strongly supports a particular leader, group or idea 堅定的支持者；鐵桿擁護者 **SYN follower 2** a member of an armed group that is fighting secretly against enemy soldiers who have taken control of its country 游擊隊員 ▸ **par·ti·san·ship** /-ʃɪp/ *noun* [U]

par·ti·tion /pɑː'tɪʃn; *NAmE* pɑːr't-/ *noun*, *verb*
■ ***noun* 1** [C] a wall or screen that separates one part of a room from another 隔斷；隔扇；隔板牆：*a glass partition* 玻璃隔板 ◇ *partition walls* 隔斷牆 ➲ VISUAL VOCAB page V69 **2** [U] the division of one country into two or more countries 分割；分治；瓜分：*the partition of Germany after the war* 戰後對德國的分割
■ ***verb*** [often passive] to divide sth into parts 分割；使分裂：**~ sth** *to partition a country* 分割一個國家 ◇ **~ sth into sth** *The room is partitioned into three sections.* 這間屋子被隔為三小間。

PHR V parˌtition sth↔'off to separate one area, one part of a room, etc. from another with a wall or screen（把地方、房間等）分隔，隔開

par·ti·tive /'pɑːtətɪv; *NAmE* 'pɑːrt-/ *noun* (*grammar* 語法) a word or phrase that shows a part or quantity of sth 表示部份的詞（或詞組）；表量詞語：*In 'a spoonful of sugar', the word 'spoonful' is a partitive.* 在 a spoonful of sugar 中，spoonful 一詞是表量詞。▸ **par·ti·tive** *adj.*

part·ly /'pɑːtli; *NAmE* 'pɑːrt-/ *adv.*
to some extent; not completely 一定程度上；部份地：*Some people are unwilling to attend the classes **partly because** of the cost involved.* 有些人不願來上課，部份原因是所需的費用問題。◇ *He was only partly responsible for the accident.* 他對這次事故只負有部份責任。

Which Word? 詞語辨析

partly / partially

- **Partly** and **partially** both mean 'not completely'.
  * partly 和 partially 均指部份：*The road is partly/partially finished.* 道路完工了一部份。**Partly** is especially used to talk about the reason for something, often followed by *because* or *due to*.
  * partly 尤用以說明原因，其後常跟 because 或 due to：*I didn't enjoy the trip very much, partly because of the weather.* 我旅行過得不太愉快，部份是因為天氣的緣故。**Partially** should be used when you are talking about physical conditions. 指身體狀況時應用 partially：*His mother is partially blind.* 他的母親失去了部份視力。

part·ner AW /'pɑːtnə(r); *NAmE* 'pɑːrt-/ *noun*, *verb*
■ ***noun* 1** the person that you are married to or having a sexual relationship with 配偶；性伴侶：*Come to the New Year disco and bring your partner!* 攜伴來參加新年迪斯科舞會吧！◇ *a marriage partner* 配偶 ➲ COLLOCATIONS at MARRIAGE **2** one of the people who owns a business and shares the profits, etc. 合夥人：*a partner in a law firm* 法律事務所的合夥人 ◇ *a **junior/senior partner*** 次要／主要合夥人 **3** a person that you are doing an activity with, such as dancing or playing a game 搭檔；同伴；舞伴：*a **dancing/tennis, etc. partner*** 舞伴、網球搭檔等 ➲ see also SPARRING PARTNER **4** a country or an organization that has an agreement with another country 夥伴（與另一國家有協議關係的國家或組織）：*a trading partner* 貿易夥伴 ➲ see also SLEEPING PARTNER
■ ***verb* ~ sb** to be sb's partner in a dance, game, etc.（在跳舞、遊戲等中）結成夥伴，做搭檔，配對：*Gerry offered to partner me at tennis.* 格里提出和我搭檔打網球。

P

part·ner·ship 0‑w AW /ˈpɑːtnəʃɪp; NAmE ˈpɑːrtnərʃɪp/ *noun* **1** 0‑w [U] the state of being a partner in business 夥伴關係；合夥人身分： *to be in/to go into partnership* 結成合作關係 ◇ **~ with sb/sth** *He developed his own program in partnership with an American expert.* 他與一位美國專家合作開發自己的程序。 **2** 0‑w [C, U] a relationship between two people, organizations, etc.; the state of having this relationship 合作關係；合作： *Marriage should be an equal partnership.* 婚姻應當是平等的伴侶關係。 ◇ **~ with sb/sth** *the school's partnership with parents* 學校與家長的合作 ◇ **~ between A and B** *a partnership between the United States and Europe* 美國與歐洲的合作 **3** 0‑w [C] a business owned by two or more people who share the profits 合夥企業： *a junior member of the partnership* 企業的次要合夥人

ˌpart of ˈspeech *noun* (*grammar* 語法) one of the classes into which words are divided according to their grammar, such as noun, verb, adjective, etc. 詞類；詞性 SYN **word class**

par·took *past tense of* PARTAKE

par·tridge /ˈpɑːtrɪdʒ; NAmE ˈpɑːrt-/ *noun* [C, U] (*pl.* **par·tridges** or **par·tridge**) a brown bird with a round body and a short tail, that people hunt for sport or food; the meat of this bird 山鶉；山鶉肉

ˌpart-ˈtime *adj.* (*abbr.* **PT**) for part of the day or week in which people work 部份時間的；兼職的： *She's looking for a part-time job.* 她在尋找兼職工作。 ◇ *to study on a part-time basis* 兼讀式學習 ◇ *part-time workers* 兼職工作者 ◇ *I'm only part-time at the moment.* 我現在只是兼職。 ▸ **ˌpart-ˈtime** *adv.*： *Liz works part-time from 10 till 2.* 利茲的兼職時間是 10 點到 2 點。 ➲ compare FULL-TIME

ˌpart-ˈtimer *noun* a person who works part-time 兼職者；部份時間工作的人

par·tur·ition /ˌpɑːtjʊˈrɪʃn; NAmE ˌpɑːrt-/ *noun* [U] (*technical* 術語) the act of giving birth 分娩

ˈpart-way *adv.* some of the way 半途；部份地： *They were part-way through the speeches when he arrived.* 他到達的時候講演已經進行一段時間了。

ˈpart-work *noun* (*BrE*) a book that is published in several parts that people can collect over a period of time 分期發表的作品；分冊出版的書

party 0‑w /ˈpɑːti; NAmE ˈpɑːrti/ *noun*, *verb*

■ ***noun*** (*pl.* **-ies**) **1** 0‑w (also **Party**) [C+sing./pl. v.] a political organization that you can vote for in elections and whose members have the same aims and ideas 政黨；黨派： *the Democratic and Republican Parties in the United States* 美國的民主黨和共和黨 ◇ *She belongs to the Labour Party.* 她是工黨黨員。 ◇ *the* ***ruling/opposition party*** 執政 / 反對黨 ◇ *the* ***party leader/manifesto/policy*** 黨的領袖 / 宣言 / 政策 ➲ COLLOCATIONS at POLITICS **2** 0‑w [C] (especially in compounds 尤用於構成複合詞) a social occasion, often in a person's home, at which people eat, drink, talk, dance and enjoy themselves 聚會；宴會；聯歡會；派對： *a* ***birthday/dinner/garden, etc. party*** 生日聚會、晚宴、遊園會等 ◇ *to* ***give/have/throw a party*** 搞聚會 ◇ *Did you* ***go to the party?*** 你去參加聚會了嗎？ ◇ *party games* 聯歡會遊戲 ➲ see also HEN PARTY, HOUSE PARTY, STAG PARTY at STAG NIGHT **3** 0‑w [C+sing./pl. v.] a group of people who are doing sth together such as travelling or visiting somewhere（一起旅行或參觀等的）群，隊，組： *The school is taking a party of 40 children to France.* 學校將帶領一個 40 人的兒童團隊前往法國。 ◇ *The theatre gives a 10% discount to parties of more than ten.* 劇場給十人以上的團體打九折。 ➲ see also SEARCH PARTY, WORKING PARTY **4** [C] (*formal*) one of the people or groups of people involved in a legal agreement or argument（契約或爭論的）當事人，一方： *the* ***guilty/innocent party*** 有罪的 / 無罪的一方 ◇ *The contract can be terminated by either party with three months' notice.* 合同的任何一方如提前三個月通知，均可終止本合同。 ➲ see also INJURED PARTY, THIRD PARTY

IDM **be (a) party to sth** (*formal*) to be involved in an agreement or action 參與，參加（協議或行動）： *to be party to a decision* 參與作出決議 ◇ *He refused to be a party to any violence.* 他拒絕參與任何暴力活動。 **ˌbring sth to the ˈparty/ˈtable** to contribute sth useful to a discussion, project, etc. 為（討論、項目等）作出貢獻： *What Hislop brought to the party was real commitment and energy.* 希斯洛普對黨的貢獻是他全身心的投入和十足的幹勁。

■ ***verb*** (**par·ties**, **party·ing**, **par·tied**, **par·tied**) [I] (*informal*) to enjoy yourself, especially by eating, drinking alcohol and dancing 尋歡作樂；吃喝玩樂： *They were out partying every night.* 他們每晚都外出尋歡作樂。

ˌparty ˈfavors (also **favors**) (both *NAmE*) *noun* [pl.] small gifts that are often given to children at a party（聚會上贈給兒童的）小禮品

ˈparty-goer *noun* a person who enjoys going to parties or who is a guest at a particular party 愛參加聚會的人；聚會的客人

ˌparty ˈline *noun* [usually sing.] the official opinions and policies of a political party, which members are expected to support 政黨的路線 IDM see TOE *v.*

ˈparty piece *noun* (*BrE*, *informal*) a thing that sb does to entertain people, especially at parties, for example singing a song（聚會上的某項）娛樂活動

ˌparty poˈlitical *adj.* [only before noun] (*especially BrE*) made by or relating to a political party 政黨的；黨派政治的： *a party political broadcast* 黨派政治廣播

ˌparty ˈpolitics *noun* [U+sing./pl. v.] political activity that involves political parties 政黨政治： *The President should stand above party politics.* 總統應當置身於政黨政治之上。 ◇ *Many people think that party politics should not enter into local government.* 許多人都認為，黨派政治不應關涉到地方政府。

party-pooper /ˈpɑːti puːpə(r); NAmE ˈpɑːrti puːpər/ *noun* (*informal*) a person who does not want to take part in an enjoyable activity and spoils the fun for other people（在聚會等上）令眾人掃興者

ˌparty ˈspirit *noun* [U] the sort of mood in which you can enjoy a party and have fun 社交情結；愛社交的心情

ˌparty ˈwall *noun* a wall that divides two buildings or rooms and belongs to both owners 界牆；隔斷牆；共用牆

par·venu /ˈpɑːvənjuː; NAmE ˈpɑːrvənuː/ *noun* (*pl.* **-us**) (*formal*, *disapproving*) a person from a low social or economic position who has suddenly become rich or powerful 暴發戶；新貴

pas·cal /ˈpæskl/ *noun* **1** (*abbr.* **Pa**) the standard unit for measuring pressure 帕（斯卡）（標準壓強單位） **2 Pascal, PASCAL** a language used for writing programs for computer systems 帕斯卡語言；Pascal（計算機系統編程）語言

pas·chal /ˈpɑːskl; NAmE ˈpæskl/ *adj.* (*formal*) **1** relating to Easter 復活節的 **2** relating to the Jewish Passover 逾越節的

pas de deux /ˌpɑː də ˈdɜː/ *noun* (*pl.* **pas de deux** /ˌpɑː də ˈdɜː/) (from *French*) a dance, often part of a BALLET, that is performed by two people（芭蕾舞等中的）雙人舞

pash·mi·na /pæʃˈmiːnə/ *noun* a long piece of cloth made of fine soft wool from a type of GOAT and worn by a woman around the shoulders 羊絨披肩

Pashto /ˈpæʃtəʊ; NAmE -toʊ/ *noun* [U] the official language of Afghanistan, also spoken in northern Pakistan 普什圖語（阿富汗官方語言，也用於巴基斯坦北部地區）

pass 0‑w /pɑːs; NAmE pæs/ *verb*, *noun*

■ ***verb***

▸ MOVE 移動 **1** 0‑w [I, T] to move past or to the other side of sb/sth 通過；走過： *Several people were passing but nobody offered to help.* 有幾個人擦肩而過，卻沒有人主動伸出援手。 ◇ *I hailed a passing taxi.* 我招了一輛路過的出租車。 ◇ *The road was so narrow that cars were unable to pass.* 道路太窄，汽車無法通過。 ◇ **~ sb/sth** *to pass a barrier/sentry/checkpoint* 通過障礙 / 崗哨 / 檢查站 ◇ *You'll pass a bank on the way to the train station.* 你在去火車站的路上會經過一家銀行。 ◇ *She passed me in the street without even saying hello.* 她在街上與我擦肩而

過，卻連一聲招呼也沒打。◇ (*especially NAmE*) *There was a truck behind that was trying to pass me.* 後面有一輛卡車想要超過我。 **HELP** The usual word in British English in the last example is **overtake**. 在上一例句中，英式英語通常用 overtake。 **2** [I] **+ adv./prep.** to go or move in the direction mentioned 沿某方向前進；向某方向移動：*The procession passed slowly along the street.* 隊伍沿街緩緩行進。◇ *A plane passed low overhead.* 一架飛機從頭上低空飛過。 **3** [T] **~ sth + adv./prep.** to make sth move in the direction or into the position mentioned 使沿某方向移動；使達到某位置：*He passed the rope around the post three times to secure it.* 他把繩索在柱子上繞了三匝纏緊。

▸ **GIVE** 給予 **4** [T] to give sth to sb by putting it into their hands or in a place where they can easily reach it 給；遞；傳遞：**~ sth (to sb)** *Pass the salt, please.* 請把鹽遞過來。◇ *Pass that book over.* 把那本書遞過來。◇ **~ sb sth** *Pass me over that book.* 遞給我那本書。

▸ **BALL** 球 **5** [T, I] (in ball games 球類運動) to kick, hit or throw the ball to a player of your own side 傳球：**~ sth (to sb)** *He passed the ball to Rooney.* 他把球傳給了魯尼。◇ **~ (to sb)** *Why do they keep passing back to the goalie?* 他們為什麼老是把球回傳給守門員？

▸ **AFTER DEATH** 死後 **6** [I] **~ to sb** to be given to another person after first belonging to sb else, especially after the first person has died 轉移給，遺留給（繼承人等）：*On his death, the title passed to his eldest son.* 他死後，封號傳給長子。

▸ **BECOME GREATER** 變大 **7** [T] **~ sth** (of an amount 數量) to become greater than a particular total 大於；超過 **SYN** **exceed**：*Unemployment has now **passed the** three **million mark**.* 失業人口現已突破三百萬大關。

▸ **CHANGE** 變化 **8** [I] **~ from sth to/into sth** to change from one state or condition to another 轉變；變化；過渡：*She had passed from childhood to early womanhood.* 她已由童年進入了少女期。

▸ **TIME** 時間 **9** [I] when time **passes**, it goes by 推移；逝去：*Six months passed and we still had no news of them.* 半年過去了，我們仍然沒有他們的音訊。◇ *We grew more anxious **with every passing day**.* 一天天過去，我們的焦慮與日俱增。 **10** [T] **~ sth** to spend time, especially when you are bored or waiting for sth 消磨；度過；打發：*We sang songs to **pass the time**.* 我們藉唱歌消磨時間。◇ *How did you pass the evening?* 你是怎麼打發那個晚上的？

▸ **END** 結束 **11** [I] to come to an end; to be over 結束；完結：*They waited for the storm to pass.* 他們等待暴風雨過去。

▸ **TEST/EXAM** 測驗；考試 **12** [I, T] to achieve the required standard in an exam, a test, etc. 及格；合格：*I'm not really expecting to pass first time.* 我真不指望第一次就能合格。◇ **~ sth** *She hasn't passed her driving test yet.* 她還沒有通過駕駛執照考試。 **OPP** **fail** **13** [T] **~ sb** to test sb and decide that they are good enough, according to an agreed standard 准予通過；承認合格：*The examiners passed all the candidates.* 主考人評定考生全部及格。 **OPP** **fail**

▸ **LAW/PROPOSAL** 法律；建議 **14** [T] **~ sth** to accept a proposal, law, etc. by voting 經表決通過（動議、法律等）：*The bill was passed by 360 votes to 280.* 這個法案以 360 票對 280 票獲得通過。

▸ **HAPPEN** 發生 **15** [I] to be allowed 得到允許：*I don't like it, but I'll **let it pass*** (= will not object). 我不喜歡，但我也不會反對。◇ *Her remarks passed without comment* (= people ignored them). 人們對她的言論未予理睬。 **16** [I] to happen; to be said or done 發生；說出（或做出）：**~ (between A and B)** *They'll never be friends again after all that has passed between them.* 經過了這麼多事情，他們已經友誼難再了。◇ **+ adj.** *His departure **passed unnoticed**.* 他神不知、鬼不覺地離開了。

▸ **NOT KNOW** 不知 **17** [I] **~ (on sth)** to say that you do not know the answer to a question, especially during a QUIZ 不知道，過（尤在回答競賽問題時所用）：*'What's the capital of Peru?' 'I'll have to pass on that one.'* "秘魯的首都是哪裏？" "不知道。" ◇ *'Who wrote 'Catch-22'?' 'Pass* (= I don't know).' "誰寫了《第二十二條軍規》？" "不知道。"

▸ **NOT WANT** 不要 **18** [I] **~ (on sth)** to say that you do not want sth that is offered to you 不要；免掉：*Thanks. I'm going to pass on dessert, if you don't mind.* 謝謝，您若不介意，我就免了飯後甜點吧。

▸ **SAY/STATE STH** 陳述 **19** [T] **~ sth (on sb/sth)** to say or state sth, especially officially 宣佈；聲明：*The court waited in silence for the judge to **pass sentence**.* 全體出庭人員默默等待法官宣判。◇ *It's not for me to **pass judgement** on your behaviour.* 我無權評判你的行為作風。◇ *The man smiled at the girl and passed a friendly remark.* 男子對姑娘微微一笑，又說了句親切的話。

▸ **BELIEF/UNDERSTANDING** 相信；理解 **20** [T] **~ belief, understanding, etc.** (*formal*) to go beyond the limits of what you can believe, understand, etc. 超出…的限度：*It passes belief* (= is impossible to believe) *that she could do such a thing.* 很難相信她會做出這等事來。

▸ **IN CARD GAMES** 紙牌遊戲 **21** [I] to refuse to play a card or make a BID when it is your turn 不出牌；不叫牌；過

▸ **FROM THE BODY** 排出體外 **22** [T] **~ sth** to send sth out from the body as or with waste matter 排泄；排出：*If you're passing blood you ought to see a doctor.* 如果便中帶血，你就應該找大夫看看。

IDM **ˌcome to ˈpass** (*old use*) to happen 發生；出現 **not pass your ˈlips** **1** if words do **not pass your lips**, you say nothing 未說話；未開口 **2** if food or drink does **not pass your lips**, you eat or drink nothing 未吃；未喝；（水米）未沾 **pass the ˈhat round/around** (*informal*) to collect money from a number of people, for example to buy a present for sb 湊份子（送禮）；湊集金錢 **pass ˈmuster** to be accepted as of a good enough standard 達到要求；獲得接受 **pass the time of ˈday (with sb)** to say hello to sb and have a short conversation with them（與某人）寒暄，打招呼，閒談一會兒 **pass ˈwater** (*formal*) to URINATE 小便；小解；解小手

PHR V **ˌpass sth↔aˈround/ˈround** (*BrE*) to give sth to another person, who gives it to sb else, etc. until everyone has seen it 挨個傳遞某物；傳閱：*Can you pass these pictures around for everyone to look at, please?* 請你把這些畫傳給每個人看一看好嗎？ **ˈpass as sb/sth** = PASS FOR/AS SB/STH **ˌpass aˈway** **1** (also **ˌpass ˈon**) to die. People say 'pass away' to avoid saying 'die'.（婉辭，指去世）亡故：*His mother passed away last year.* 他母親去年去世了。 **2** to stop existing 消失；消逝：*civilizations that have passed away* 不復存在的文明 **ˌpass ˈby (sb/sth)** to go past 通過；經過（…旁邊）：*The procession passed right by my front door.* 隊伍正好從我家門前經過。 **ˌpass sb/sth ˈby** to happen without affecting sb/sth 未影響（某人或某事）：*She feels that life is passing her by* (= that she is not enjoying the opportunities and pleasures of life). 她覺得人生所有的機遇和歡樂都與她無緣。 **ˌpass sth↔ˈdown** [often passive] to give or teach sth to your children or people younger than you, who will then give or teach it to those who live after them, and so on 使世代相傳；流傳 **SYN** **hand down** **ˈpass for/as sb/sth** to be accepted as sb/sth 被認為是；被當作：*He speaks the language so well he could easily pass for a German.* 他德語講得好極了，很容易被當成德國人。◇ *We had some wine—or what passes for wine in that area.* 我們有一些酒，或是在那個地區當作酒的東西。 **ˈpass into sth** to become a part of sth 變為其中一部份；融入；納入：*Many foreign words have passed into the English language.* 許多外來詞語已變成英語的一部份。 **ˌpass ˈoff** (*BrE*) (of an event 事情) to take place and be completed in a particular way（以某方式）發生並完成：*The demonstration passed off peacefully.* 示威遊行始終和平地進行。 **ˌpass sb/yourself/sth ˈoff as sb/sth** to pretend that sb/sth is sth they are not 裝作；佯裝；假裝：*He escaped by passing himself off as a guard.* 他偽裝成看守人而得以脫逃。 **ˌpass ˈon** = PASS AWAY **ˌpass sth↔ˈon (to sb)** to give sth to sb else, especially after receiving it or using it yourself 轉交；（用後）遞給，傳給：*Pass the book on to me when you've finished with it.* 你看完那本書後請傳給我。◇ *I passed your message on to my mother.* 我把你的留言轉給我媽了。◇ *Much of the discount is pocketed by retailers instead of being passed on to customers.* 折扣的大部份進了零售商的腰包，而顧客沒有得到實惠。 **ˌpass ˈout** to become unconscious 昏迷；失去知覺 **SYN** **faint** **ˌpass ˈout (of sth)** (*BrE*) to leave a military college after finishing a

P

course of training 從軍校畢業：*a passing-out ceremony* 軍校畢業典禮 **,pass sb↔'over** to not consider sb for promotion in a job, especially when they deserve it or think that they deserve it（考慮提職等時）跳過某人：*He was passed over in favour of a younger man.* 他未被擢升，卻提拔了一個比他年輕的人。**,pass 'over sth** to ignore or avoid sth 避免提及；不考慮 SYN **overlook**：*They chose to pass over her rude remarks.* 他們決定不計較她的粗魯言辭。**,pass 'through …** 🔑 to go through a town, etc., stopping there for a short time but not staying 經過；路過：*We were passing through, so we thought we'd come and say hello.* 我們路過此地，所以想來問候一聲。**,pass sth↔'up** (*informal*) to choose not to make use of a chance, an opportunity, etc. 放棄，不要（機會等）：*Imagine passing up an offer like that!* 真想不到居然放棄人家提供的大好機會！

■ ***noun***

▸ **IN EXAM** 考試 **1** (*especially BrE*) a successful result in an exam 及格；合格；通過：*She got a pass in French.* 她法語考試及格了。◇ *12 passes and 3 fails* * 12 門及格，3 門不及格 ◇ *Two A-level passes are needed for this course.* 本課程要求有兩個高級證書考試的及格成績。◇ *The **pass mark** is 50%.* * 50% 為及格成績。◇ *The school has a 90% **pass rate*** (= 90% of students pass their exams). 該校學生的及格率為 90%。

▸ **OFFICIAL DOCUMENT** 正式文件 **2** an official document or ticket that shows that you have the right to enter or leave a place, to travel on a bus or train, etc. 通行證；車票；乘車證：*a boarding pass* (= for a plane) 登機卡 ◇ *There is no admittance without a security pass.* 無保安通行證不得入內。➲ see also BUS PASS

▸ **OF BALL** 球類運動 **3** (in some sports) an act of hitting or throwing the ball to another player in your team（某些運動中）傳球：*a long pass to Rooney* 給魯尼的一個長傳 ◇ *a back pass to the goalkeeper* 回傳給守門員

▸ **THROUGH MOUNTAINS** 穿越山脈 **4** a road or way over or through mountains 關口；關隘；山路：*a mountain pass* 山口 ➲ VISUAL VOCAB page V5

▸ **MOVING PAST/OVER** 經過；越過 **5** an act of going or moving past or over sth 越過；飛躍：*The helicopter made several passes over the village before landing.* 直升機在村落上空盤旋數次才降落。

▸ **STAGE IN PROCESS** 階段 **6** a stage in a process, especially one that involves separating things from a larger group 階段；步驟：*In the first pass all the addresses are loaded into the database.* 第一步，所有地址均輸入數據庫。

IDM **come to such a 'pass | come to a pretty 'pass** (*old-fashioned* or *humorous*) to reach a sad or difficult state 陷於不妙的（或困難的）境地；落到這步田地 **make a pass at sb** (*informal*) to try to start a sexual relationship with sb 勾引；與某人調情

pass·able /'pɑːsəbl; *NAmE* 'pæs-/ *adj.* **1** fairly good but not excellent 過得去的；尚可的 SYN **satisfactory** **2** [not usually before noun] if a road or a river is **passable**, it is not blocked and you can travel along or across it 通行無阻 OPP **impassable**

pass·ably /'pɑːsəbli; *NAmE* 'pæs-/ *adv.* in a way that is acceptable or good enough 過得去；尚可；還可以 SYN **reasonably**：*He speaks passably good French.* 他法語講得還可以。

pas·sage 🔑 /'pæsɪdʒ/ *noun*

▸ **LONG NARROW WAY** 狹長通路 **1** 🔑 (also **pas·sage·way** /'pæsɪdʒweɪ/) [C] a long narrow area with walls on either side that connects one room or place with another 通道；走廊 SYN **corridor**：*a secret underground passage* 地下秘密通道 ◇ *A dark narrow passage led to the main hall.* 一條陰暗狹窄的走廊通向大廳。

▸ **IN THE BODY** 體內 **2** [C] a tube in the body through which air, liquid, etc. passes（體內通氣、輸液等的）管路，通道：*blocked nasal passages* 鼻腔堵塞 ➲ see also BACK PASSAGE

▸ **SECTION FROM BOOK** 章節 **3** 🔑 [C] a short section from a book, piece of music, etc. 章節；段落；樂段 SYN **excerpt, extract**：*Read the following passage and answer the questions below.* 閱讀下面這段文章並回答後面的問題。➲ COLLOCATIONS at LITERATURE

▸ **OF TIME** 時間 **4** [sing.] **the ~ of time** (*literary*) the process of time passing（時間的）流逝，推移：*Her confidence grew with the passage of time.* 她的信心與日俱增。

▸ **OF BILL IN PARLIAMENT** 議會的議案 **5** [sing.] the process of discussing a BILL in a parliament so that it can become law 通過：*The bill is now guaranteed an easy passage through the House of Representatives.* 現在該法案保證能在眾議院順利通過。

▸ **JOURNEY BY SHIP** 海程 **6** [sing.] a journey from one place to another by ship（乘船的）航程，旅程：*Her grandfather had **worked his passage*** (= worked on a ship to pay for the journey) *to America.* 她的祖父一路在船上打工支付船費來到美國。

▸ **GOING THROUGH** 通過 **7** [sing.] **a ~ (through sth)** a way through sth 通路；通道：*The officers forced a passage through the crowd.* 警察在人群中闢開一條通路。**8** [U] (*formal*) the action of going across, through or past sth 穿過；穿越：*Large trees may obstruct the passage of light.* 大樹可能阻止光線穿過。**9** [U, C, usually sing.] the permission to travel across a particular area of land 通行許可：*We were promised (a) safe passage through the occupied territory.* 我們得到保證，可以安全通過佔領區。➲ see also BIRD OF PASSAGE, RITE OF PASSAGE

pas·sant ➲ EN PASSANT

pass·book /'pɑːsbʊk; *NAmE* 'pæs-/ *noun* a small book containing a record of the money you put into and take out of an account at a BUILDING SOCIETY or a bank 銀行存摺；房屋互助協會儲蓄簿

passé /'pæseɪ; 'pɑːs-; *NAmE* pæ'seɪ/ *adj.* [not usually before noun] (from *French, disapproving*) no longer fashionable 過時；陳舊；不再流行 SYN **outmoded**

pas·sen·ger 🔑 /'pæsɪndʒə(r)/ *noun*
1 🔑 a person who is travelling in a car, bus, train, plane or ship and who is not driving it or working on it 乘客；旅客：*a passenger train* (= carrying passengers, not goods) 客運列車 **2** (*informal, disapproving, especially BrE*) a member of a group or team who does not do as much work as the others 白吃飯的人；閒散人員：*The firm cannot afford to carry passengers.* 公司養不起白吃飯的人。

'passenger seat *noun* the seat in a car which is next to the driver's seat（汽車駕駛員旁邊的）乘客座位；副駕駛座 ➲ VISUAL VOCAB page V52

,passer-'by *noun* (*pl.* **passers-by**) a person who is going past sb/sth by chance, especially when sth unexpected happens 路人；過路的人：*Police asked passers-by if they had seen the accident.* 警察詢問過路的人是否目擊了這次事故。➲ SYNONYMS at WITNESS

,pass-'fail *adj.* (*US*) connected with a grading system for school classes, etc. in which a student passes or fails rather than receiving a grade as a letter (for example, A or B) 及格—不及格評分制的（不細分為 A、B 之類的等級）▸ **,pass-'fail** *adv.*：*to take a class pass-fail* 選修一門只給及格—不及格兩種評分的課程

pas·sim /'pæsɪm/ *adv.* (from *Latin*) used in the notes to a book or an article to show that a particular name or subject appears in several places in it（用於書、文章註釋，表示某個名稱或題目出現於該書、該文的）各處，多處

pass·ing 🔑 /'pɑːsɪŋ; *NAmE* 'pæs-/ *noun, adj.*

■ ***noun*** [U] **1** 🔑 **the ~ of time/the years** the process of time going by（時間、歲月的）流逝，推移 **2** (*formal*) the fact of sth ending or of sb dying（事物的）結束，消亡；（人的）亡故，逝世：*When the government is finally brought down, no one will mourn its passing.* 當政府最終垮台，將不會有人為它的消亡而悲哀。◇ *the passing of the old year* (= on New Year's Eve) 辭舊歲 ◇ *Many will mourn her passing* (= her death, when you do not want to say this directly). 很多人將會為她的過世而悲傷。**3** 🔑 **the ~ of sth** the act of making sth become a law（法律等的）通過：*the passing of a resolution/law* 決議 / 法律的通過

IDM **in passing** done or said while you are giving your attention to sth else 順便；隨便 SYN **casually**：*He only mentioned it in passing and didn't give any details.* 他只是隨口提及而已，並沒有談任何細節。

■ *adj.* [only before noun] **1** lasting only for a short period of time and then disappearing 暫時的；瞬間的 SYN **brief**：*a* ***passing phase/thought/interest*** 過渡階段；一閃念；一時之興 ◇ *He makes only a* ***passing reference*** *to the theory in his book* (= it is not the main subject of his book). 他在書中對這個理論只是一筆帶過。◇ *She* ***bears*** *more than* ***a passing resemblance to*** (= looks very like) *your sister.* 她酷似你姐姐。**2** going past 經過的；過往的：*I love him more with each passing day.* 隨着時間的流逝，我越發愛他了。◇ *the noise of passing cars* 過往車輛的嘈雜 **3 ~ grade/mark** (*NAmE*) a grade/mark that achieves the required standard in an exam, a test, etc.（考試、測驗等）及格的

'passing lane (*NAmE*) (*BrE* **,outside 'lane**) *noun* the part of a major road such as a MOTORWAY or INTERSTATE nearest the middle of the road, where vehicles drive fastest and can go past vehicles ahead （高速公路等靠近路中央的）快車道，超車道

'passing shot *noun* (in TENNIS 網球) a shot which goes past your opponent, and which he or she cannot reach 超身球，穿越球（越過對手使其無法接住）

pas·sion /'pæʃn/ *noun* **1** [C, U] a very strong feeling of love, hatred, anger, enthusiasm, etc. 強烈情感；激情：*He's a man of violent passions.* 他是個性情暴烈的人。◇ *a* ***crime of passion*** 因情慾妒忌而造成的犯罪 ◇ *She argued her case with considerable passion.* 她相當激動地為自己的主張提出論據。◇ ***Passions were running high*** (= people were angry and emotional) *at the meeting.* 會上群情沸騰。**2** [sing.] (*formal*) a state of being very angry 盛怒；激憤 SYN **rage**：*She* ***flies into a passion*** *if anyone even mentions his name.* 哪怕是有人提到他的名字，她也會勃然大怒。**3** [U] **~ (for sb)** a very strong feeling of sexual love 強烈的愛（尤指兩性間的）：*His passion for her made him blind to everything else.* 他鍾情於她，達到了不顧一切的地步。**4** [C] **~ (for sth)** a very strong feeling of liking sth; a hobby, an activity, etc. that you like very much 酷愛；熱衷的愛好（或活動等）：*The English have a passion for gardens.* 英國人酷愛花園。◇ *Music is a passion with him.* 他對音樂情有獨鍾。**5 the Passion** [sing.] (in Christianity 基督教) the suffering and death of Jesus Christ 耶穌的受難

pas·sion·ate /'pæʃənət/ *adj.* **1** having or showing strong feelings of sexual love or of anger, etc. 擁有（或表現出）強烈性愛的；情意綿綿的；怒不可遏的：*to have a passionate nature* 天性易激動 **2** having or showing strong feelings of enthusiasm for sth or belief in sth 熱誠的；狂熱的：*a passionate interest in music* 對音樂的濃厚興趣 ◇ *a passionate defender of civil liberties* 公民自由權利的積極捍衛者 ▸ **pas·sion·ate·ly** *adv.*：*He took her in his arms and kissed her passionately.* 他把她摟在懷裏狂熱地親吻。◇ *They are all passionately interested in environmental issues.* 他們都熱衷於環境問題。

'passion flower *noun* a tropical climbing plant with large brightly coloured flowers 西番蓮

'passion fruit *noun* [C, U] (*pl.* **passion fruit**) a small tropical fruit with a thick purple skin and many seeds inside, produced by some types of passion flower 百香果，西番蓮果（一種熱帶水果）➲ VISUAL VOCAB page V30

pas·sion·less /'pæʃnləs/ *adj.* without emotion or enthusiasm 冷淡的；冷漠的；無情的

'Passion play *noun* a play about the suffering and death of Jesus Christ 耶穌受難劇

pas·sive AW /'pæsɪv/ *adj., noun*

■ *adj.* **1** accepting what happens or what people do without trying to change anything or oppose them 消極的；被動的：*He played a passive role in the relationship.* 他在他們的關係中處於被動地位。◇ *a passive observer of events* 列席觀察員 **2** (*grammar* 語法) connected with the form of a verb used when the subject is affected by the action of the verb, for example *He was bitten by a dog.* is a passive sentence（動詞形式）被動語態的 ➲ compare ACTIVE *adj.* (6) ▸ **pas·sive·ly** AW *adv.*

■ *noun* (also **,passive 'voice**) [sing.] (*grammar* 語法) the form of a verb used when the subject is affected by the action of the verb 動詞被動形式；被動語態 ➲ compare ACTIVE *n.*

,passive-ag'gressive *adj.* being angry without expressing your anger openly, but resisting people in authority by refusing to do what they want or to accept responsibility for your actions 消極對抗的：*He exhibited passive-aggressive tendencies.* 他表現出了消極抵抗傾向。

,passive re'sistance *noun* [U] a way of opposing a government or an enemy by peaceful means, often by refusing to obey laws or orders 消極反抗；和平抵抗

,passive 'smoking *noun* [U] the act of breathing in smoke from other people's cigarettes 被動吸煙；吸二手煙

pas·siv·ity AW /pæ'sɪvəti/ *noun* [U] the state of accepting what happens without reacting or trying to fight against it 被動；消極狀態

pas·siv·ize (*BrE* also **-ise**) /'pæsɪvaɪz/ *verb* **~ sth** (*grammar* 語法) to put a verb into the passive form 將（動詞）變成被動語態形式；使被動化

'pass key *noun* = MASTER KEY

Pass·over /'pɑːsəʊvə(r); *NAmE* 'pæsoʊ-/ *noun* [U, C] the Jewish religious festival and holiday in memory of the escape of the Jews from Egypt 逾越節（猶太人的宗教節日）

pass·port /'pɑːspɔːt; *NAmE* 'pæspɔːrt/ *noun*
1 an official document that identifies you as a citizen of a particular country, and that you may have to show when you enter or leave a country 護照：*a valid passport* 有效護照 ◇ *a South African passport* 南非護照 ◇ *I was stopped as I went through* ***passport control*** (= where passports are checked). 在經過護照查驗卡時，我被叫住了。◇ *a passport photo* 護照相片 **2 ~ to sth** a thing that makes sth possible or enables you to achieve sth 途徑；路子；手段 SYN **key**：*The only passport to success is hard work.* 獲得成功的唯一途徑就是艱苦奮鬥。

pass·word /'pɑːswɜːd; *NAmE* 'pæswɜːrd/ *noun* **1** a secret word or phrase that you need to know in order to be allowed into a place 暗語；暗號；口令 **2** (*computing* 計) a series of letters or numbers that you must type into a computer or computer system in order to be able to use it 口令；密碼：*Enter a username and password to get into the system.* 進入系統請鍵入用戶名稱和密碼。

past /pɑːst; *NAmE* pæst/ *adj., noun, prep., adv.*

■ *adj.* **1** gone by in time 過去的；昔日的：*in past years/centuries/ages* 在過去的歲月／世紀／時代 ◇ *in times past* 在過去 ◇ *The time for discussion is past.* 討論的時間已過。**2** [only before noun] gone by recently; just ended 剛過去的；剛結束的：*I haven't seen much of her in the past few weeks.* 近幾週來我很少見到她。◇ *The past month has been really busy at work.* 上個月工作實在是忙。**3** [only before noun] belonging to an earlier time 從前的；以往的：*past events* 以往的事件 ◇ *From past experience I'd say he'd probably forgotten the time.* 根據過去的經驗，我想他可能把時間忘了。◇ ***past and present students*** *of the college* 學院的老校友和現在的在校生 ◇ *Let's forget about who was more to blame—it's all* ***past history***. 咱們且忘掉更該責怪誰吧，那都是陳年舊賬了。**4** [only before noun] (*grammar* 語法) connected with the form of a verb used to express actions in the past（動詞）過去式的

■ *noun* **1 the past** [sing.] the time that has gone by; things that happened in an earlier time 過去；昔日；過去的事情：*I used to go there often in the past.* 過去我常去那裏。◇ *the* ***recent/distant past*** 最近的／遙遠的過去 ◇ *She looked back on the past without regret.* 她回首往事毫無遺憾。◇ *Writing letters seems to be* ***a thing of the past***. 寫信好像已是昔日的事情了。**2** [C] a person's past life or career（某人）過去的經歷（或事業）：*We don't know anything about his past.* 我們對他的過去一無所知。◇ *They say she has a 'past'* (= bad things in her past life that she wishes to keep secret). 據說她有一段"過去"（不名譽的秘史）。**3 the past** [sing.] (*grammar* 語法) = PAST TENSE IDM see BLAST *n.*, DISTANT, LIVE[1]

P

■ ***prep.*** **1** (*NAmE* also **after**) later than sth 晚於；在…之後： *half past two* 兩點半 ◇ *ten (minutes) past six* 六點過十分 ◇ *There's a bus at twenty minutes past the hour* (= at 1.20, 2.20, etc.). 每小時逢二十分發一班公共汽車。 ◇ *We arrived at two o'clock and left at ten past* (= ten minutes past two). 我們兩點鐘到達，十分鐘後離開。◇ *It was past midnight when we got home.* 我們到家已是午夜之後了。 **2** on or to the other side of sb/sth 在另一邊；到另一側： *We live in the house just past the church.* 我們就住在挨着教堂那邊的房子裏。◇ *He hurried past them without stopping.* 他匆匆走過他們身邊，連停都沒停。◇ *He just walked **straight past** us!* 他逕直與我們擦肩而過！ **3** above or further than a particular point or stage 多於；超過： *Unemployment is now past the 3 million mark.* 失業人口現在已超過了 300 萬大關。◇ *The flowers are past their best.* 這些花已過了盛開的季節。◇ *He's past his prime.* 他已不再年富力強了。◇ *She's long past retirement age.* 她早已超過了退休年齡。◇ *Honestly, I'm **past caring** what happens* (= I can no longer be bothered to care). 老實說，我已什麼事都不關心了。

IDM **'past it** (*BrE, informal*) too old to do what you used to be able to do; too old to be used for its normal function （人）過老而無用；（物）舊得不宜使用： *In some sports you're past it by the age of 25.* 在某些運動中，人過 25 歲就難有作為了。◇ *That coat is looking decidedly past it.* 那件外衣看來絕對穿不出去了。

■ ***adv.*** **1** from one side of sth to the other 從一側到另一側；經過： *I called out to him as he ran past.* 他跑過時，我大聲喊他。 **2** used to describe time passing （時間）過去，逝去 **SYN** **by**： *A week went past and nothing had changed.* 一個星期過去了，情況毫無變化。

pasta /ˈpæstə; *NAmE* ˈpɑːstə/ *noun* [U] an Italian food made from flour, water and sometimes eggs, formed into different shapes and usually served with a sauce. It is hard when dry and soft when cooked. 意大利麪食

paste /peɪst/ *noun, verb*

■ ***noun*** **1** [sing.] a soft wet mixture, usually made of a powder and a liquid 麪糊： *She mixed the flour and water to a smooth paste.* 她把麪和水和成細滑的麪糊。 **2** [C] (especially in compounds 尤用於構成複合詞) a smooth mixture of crushed meat, fish, etc. that is spread on bread or used in cooking 肉（或魚等）醬（作塗抹料或烹飪用） **3** [U] a type of glue that is used for sticking paper to things 糨糊： *wallpaper paste* 貼壁紙的糨糊 **4** [U] a substance like glass, that is used for making artificial JEWELS, for example diamonds （製作人造寶石的）鉛質玻璃

■ ***verb*** **1** [T] **~ sth + adv./prep.** to stick sth to sth else using glue or paste 粘貼；粘合： *He pasted the pictures into his scrapbook.* 他把畫片貼到他的剪貼本裏。◇ *Paste the two pieces together.* 把這兩片粘在一起。◇ *Paste down the edges.* 把邊緣貼合起來。 **2** [T] **~ sth** to make sth by sticking pieces of paper together 拼貼： *The children were busy cutting and pasting paper hats.* 孩子們忙着剪裁和粘貼紙帽子。 **3** [T, I] **~ (sth)** (*computing* 計) to copy or move text into a document from another place or another document 粘貼；貼入；插入： *This function allows you to **cut and paste** text.* 本功能可使你剪切並粘貼文本。◇ *It's quicker to cut and paste than to retype.* 剪切和粘貼比重新打字要快。

paste·board /ˈpeɪstbɔːd; *NAmE* -bɔːrd/ *noun* [U] a type of thin board made by sticking sheets of paper together （用多層紙粘貼的）硬紙板

pas·tel /ˈpæstl; *NAmE* pæˈstel/ *noun* **1** [U] soft coloured CHALK, used for drawing pictures 彩色粉筆；蠟筆： *drawings in pastel* 蠟筆畫 **2 pastels** [pl.] small sticks of CHALK 粉筆： *a box of pastels* 一盒粉筆 **3** [C] a picture drawn with pastels 彩色粉筆畫；蠟筆畫 ➲ COLLOCATIONS at ART **4** [C] a pale delicate colour 淡雅的色彩： *The whole house was painted in soft pastels.* 整座房屋都漆成柔和淡雅的色彩。

pas·tern /ˈpæstən; *NAmE* -tərn/ *noun* (*anatomy* 解) the part of a horse's foot between the FETLOCK and the HOOF （馬足部的）骹

pas·teur·ize (*BrE* also **-ise**) /ˈpɑːstʃəraɪz; *NAmE* ˈpæs-/ *verb* **~ sth** to heat a liquid, especially milk, to a particular temperature and then cool it, in order to kill harmful bacteria 用巴氏殺菌法消毒 ▸ **pas·teur·iza·tion**, **-isa·tion** /ˌpɑːstʃəraɪˈzeɪʃn; *NAmE* ˌpæstʃərəˈzeɪʃn/ *noun* [U]

pas·tiche /pæˈstiːʃ/ *noun* **1** [C] a work of art, piece of writing, etc. that is created by deliberately copying the style of sb/sth else 刻意模仿的文藝作品；模仿作品： *a pastiche of the classic detective story* 經典偵探故事的仿作 **2** [C] a work of art, etc. that consists of a variety of different styles （集多種風格於一身的）混成作品，集錦 **3** [U] the art of creating a pastiche 模仿藝術；模仿技藝

pas·tille /ˈpæstəl; *NAmE* pæˈstiːl/ *noun* (*especially BrE*) a small sweet/candy that you suck, especially one that is flavoured with fruit or that contains medicine for a sore throat 含片；含片狀藥物： *fruit pastilles* 果味含片 ◇ *throat pastilles* 喉片

pas·time /ˈpɑːstaɪm; *NAmE* ˈpæs-/ *noun* something that you enjoy doing when you are not working 消遣；休閒活動 **SYN** **hobby** ➲ SYNONYMS at INTEREST

past·ing /ˈpeɪstɪŋ/ *noun* [sing.] (*especially BrE*) **1** a heavy defeat in a game or competition（比賽中的）慘敗，大敗 **2** an instance of being hit very hard as a punishment 痛打，鞭打，棒打（作為體罰） **SYN** **thrashing**

pas·tis /pæˈstiːs/ *noun* [U, C] (*pl.* **pas·tis**) (from *French*) a strong alcoholic drink usually drunk before a meal, that has the flavour of ANISEED 法國茴香酒（常作開胃酒）

ˌpast ˈmaster *noun* **~ (at sth/at doing sth)** a person who is very good at sth because they have a lot of experience in it 老手；內行；專家 **SYN** **expert**： *She's a past master at getting what she wants.* 她可是個精明幹練的人，想要什麼就能得到什麼。

pas·tor /ˈpɑːstə(r); *NAmE* ˈpæs-/ *noun* a minister in charge of a Christian church or group, especially in some NONCONFORMIST churches （尤指非英國國教的）牧師

pas·tor·al /ˈpɑːstərəl; *NAmE* ˈpæs-/ *adj.* **1** relating to the work of a priest or teacher in giving help and advice on personal matters, not just those connected with religion or education 牧靈的，牧師的，教牧的（有關聖職人員及教師對個人幸福的關顧）： *pastoral care* 牧師對教友的關懷 **2** showing country life or the countryside, especially in a romantic way 田園的；鄉村生活的；村野風情的： *a pastoral scene/poem/symphony* 田園風光／詩／交響樂 **3** relating to the farming of animals 畜牧的： *agricultural and pastoral practices* 農牧業活動

pas·tor·al·ism /ˈpɑːstərəlɪzəm; *NAmE* ˈpæs-/ *noun* [U] a way of keeping animals such as CATTLE, sheep, etc. that involves moving them from place to place to find water and food 遊牧（牧者帶着牲口逐水草而居） ▸ **pas·tor·al·ist** *noun, adj.*

ˌpast ˈparticiple *noun* (*grammar* 語法) the form of a verb that in English ends in *-ed*, *-en*, etc. and is used with the verb *have* to form PERFECT tenses such as *I have eaten*, with the verb *be* to form passive sentences such as *It was destroyed*, or sometimes as an adjective as in *an upset stomach* 過去分詞 ➲ compare PRESENT PARTICIPLE

the ˌpast ˈperfect (also **the ˌpast ˌperfect ˈtense**, **the plu·per·fect**) *noun* [sing.] (*grammar* 語法) the form of a verb that expresses an action completed before a particular point in the past, formed in English with *had* and the past participle 過去完成時；過去完成式

pas·trami /pæˈstrɑːmi/ *noun* [U] cold spicy smoked beef 五香熏牛肉

pas·try /ˈpeɪstri/ *noun* (*pl.* **-ies**) **1** [U] a mixture of flour, fat and water or milk that is rolled out flat and baked as a base or covering for PIES, etc. 油酥麪糰；油酥麪皮 ➲ see also CHOUX PASTRY, FILO PASTRY, PUFF PASTRY, SHORTCRUST PASTRY **2** [C] a small cake made using pastry 油酥糕點 ➲ see also DANISH PASTRY

ˈpastry cook *noun* a professional cook whose main job is to make pastry, cakes, etc. 糕點師傅；糕點廚師

the ˌpast ˈtense (also **the past**) *noun* [sing.] (*grammar* 語法) the form of a verb used to describe actions in the past 過去時；過去式：*The past tense of 'take' is 'took'.* take 的過去時是 took。

pas·tur·age /ˈpɑːstʃərɪdʒ; *NAmE* ˈpæs-/ *noun* [U] (*technical* 術語) land covered with grass for animals to eat 牧場

pas·ture /ˈpɑːstʃə(r); *NAmE* ˈpæs-/ *noun, verb*

■ ***noun*** **1** [U, C] land covered with grass that is suitable for feeding animals on 牧場；牧草地：*an area of permanent/rough/rich pasture* 一片永久的 / 高低不平的 / 富饒的牧場 ◇ *high mountain pastures* 高山牧場 ◇ *The cattle were put* ***out to pasture.*** 牛群放牧在牧場草地上。➲ VISUAL VOCAB pages V2, V3 **2 pastures** [pl.] the circumstances of your life, work, etc. 生活狀況；工作條件；個人發展的機遇：*I felt we were off to* ***greener pastures*** (= a better way of life). 我覺得我們在邁向更好的生活。◇ (*BrE*) *She decided it was time to move on to* ***pastures new*** (= a new job, place to live, etc.). 她認定換個新工作的時候到了。

■ ***verb*** **~ sth** to put animals in a field to feed on grass 放牧

pas·ture·land /ˈpɑːstʃəlænd; *NAmE* ˈpæstʃərl-/ *noun* [U, pl.] (also **pas·tur·age** [U]) land where animals can feed on grass 牧場；牧草地

pasty¹ /ˈpæsti/ *noun* (*pl.* **-ies**) (*BrE*) a small PIE containing meat and vegetables 餡餅 ➲ see also CORNISH PASTY

pasty² /ˈpeɪsti/ *adj.* pale and not looking healthy 面色蒼白的 SYN **pallid**：*a* ***pasty face/complexion*** 蒼白的面孔 / 容顏

pat /pæt/ *verb, noun, adj., adv.*

■ ***verb*** (**-tt-**) to touch sb/sth gently several times with your hand flat, especially as a sign of affection（喜愛地）輕拍：**~ sth** *She patted the dog on the head.* 她輕輕地拍着狗的頭。◇ *He patted his sister's hand consolingly.* 他輕拍着妹妹的手安慰她。◇ **~ sth + adj.** *Pat your face dry with a soft towel.* 用軟毛巾把臉揩乾。

IDM **pat sb/yourself on the ˈback** (*informal*) to praise sb or yourself for doing sth well 表揚，稱讚（某人或自己）

■ ***noun*** **1** [usually sing.] a gentle friendly touch with your open hand or with a flat object（友善的）輕拍，拍打：*a pat on the head* 輕輕拍一下頭 ◇ *He gave her knee an affectionate pat.* 他溫情地拍了拍她的膝蓋。**2 ~ of butter** a small, soft, flat lump of butter 一小塊黃油 ➲ see also COWPAT

IDM **a ˌpat on the ˈback (for sth/for doing sth)** (*informal*) praise or approval for sth that you have done well 表揚；讚許：*He deserves a pat on the back for all his hard work.* 他工作兢兢業業，值得嘉許。

■ ***adj.*** (usually *disapproving*) (of an answer, a comment, etc. 答案、評論等) too quick, easy or simple; not seeming natural or realistic 過於簡易的；不自然的；油滑的 SYN **glib**：*The ending of the novel is a little too pat to be convincing.* 小說的結尾有點過於簡單，不能令人信服。◇ *There are no pat answers to these questions.* 這些問題沒有簡單的答案。

■ ***adv.***

IDM **have/know sth off ˈpat** (*BrE*) (*NAmE* **have/know sth down ˈpat**) to know sth perfectly so that you can repeat it at any time without having to think about it 瞭如指掌；滾瓜爛熟：*He had all the answers off pat.* 所有的答案他都胸有成竹。**stand ˈpat** (*especially NAmE*) to refuse to change your mind about a decision you have made or an opinion you have 固執己見；拒不改變決定

patch /pætʃ/ *noun, verb*

■ ***noun***

▸ SMALL AREA 小塊 **1** a small area of sth, especially one which is different from the area around it 色斑；斑點；（與周圍不同的）小塊，小片：*a black dog with a white patch on its back* 背上有一塊白斑的黑狗 ◇ *a bald patch on the top of his head* 他頭頂的禿塊 ◇ *damp patches on the wall* 牆上的片片濕漬 ◇ *patches of dense fog* 團團濃霧

▸ PIECE OF MATERIAL 小片材料 **2** a small piece of material that is used to cover a hole in sth or to make a weak area stronger, or as decoration 補丁；補塊：*I sewed patches on the knees of my jeans.* 我在我的牛仔褲膝部打了個補丁。**3** a piece of material that you wear over an eye, usually because the eye is damaged 眼罩：*He had a black patch over one eye.* 他一隻眼戴着黑眼罩。➲ see also EYEPATCH **4** (*NAmE*) (*BrE* **badge**) a piece of material that you sew onto clothes as part of a uniform（制服上的）標記，標識 **5** a piece of material that people can wear on their skin to help them to stop smoking 戒煙貼片：*nicotine patches* 尼古丁戒煙貼片

▸ PIECE/AREA OF LAND 地塊 **6** a small piece of land, especially one used for growing vegetables or fruit 小塊土地；（尤指）菜地，果園：*a vegetable patch* 菜地 ➲ VISUAL VOCAB page V19 **7** (*BrE, informal*) an area that sb works in, knows well or comes from 工作地；熟悉的地區；家鄉：*He knows every house in his patch.* 他熟悉他那地區的每一座房子。◇ *She has had a lot of success in her* ***home patch.*** 她在自己的家鄉地區真是一帆風順。

▸ DIFFICULT TIME 艱難時刻 **8** (*informal, especially BrE*) a period of time of the type mentioned, usually a difficult or unhappy one 一段（艱難）歲月；一段（痛苦）日子：*to go through a* ***bad/difficult/sticky patch*** 經歷艱難 / 困難 / 不幸的時期 ➲ see also PURPLE PATCH

▸ IN COMPUTING 計算機技術 **9** a small piece of code (= instructions that a computer can understand) which can be added to a computer program to improve it or to correct a fault 修補程序；補丁：*Follow the instructions below to download and install the patch.* 按照下面的說明下載並安裝修補程序。

IDM **be not a ˈpatch on sb/sth** (*informal, especially BrE*) to be much less good, attractive, etc. than sb/sth else 遠不如；遠比…遜色

Synonyms 同義詞辨析

patch

dot • mark • spot

These are all words for a small part on a surface that is a different colour from the rest. 以上各詞均指斑點、色斑。

patch an area of sth, especially one which is different from the area around it 指色斑、斑點、（與周圍不同的）小塊、小片：*a white dog with a black patch on its head* 頭上有一塊黑斑的白狗 ◇ *patches of dense fog* 團團濃霧

dot a small round mark on sth, especially one that is printed 指點、小點、小圓點，尤指印出來的點：*The letters 'i' and 'j' have dots over them.* 字母 i 和 j 上面都有一點。◇ *The island is a small green dot on the map.* 這個島在地圖上是一個小綠點。

mark a noticeable area of colour on the body of a person or animal 指人或動物身上的斑、記號、色斑：*The horse had a white mark on its head.* 這匹馬頭上有塊白斑。

spot a small round area that is a different colour or feels different from the surface it is on 指斑點：*Which has spots, a leopard or a tiger?* 有斑點的是豹還是虎？

PATTERNS

- a patch/dot/mark/spot **on** sth
- **with** patches/dots/marks/spots
- **a blue/black/red, etc.** patch/dot/mark/spot

■ ***verb*** **~ sth (with sth)** to cover a hole or a worn place, especially in clothes, with a piece of cloth or other material 打補丁；縫補；修補 SYN **mend**：*patched jeans* 帶補丁的牛仔褲 ◇ *to patch a hole in the roof* 修補屋頂的漏洞

PHR V **ˌpatch sb/sth ˈthrough (to sb/sth)** to connect telephone or electronic equipment temporarily（臨時把電話、電子設備）接通，連通：*She was patched through to London on the satellite link.* 她經衛星線路與倫敦接通了。**ˌpatch sth↔toˈgether** to make sth from several different parts, especially in a quick careless way 拼湊；草草拼合：*They hope to be able to patch together a temporary settlement.* 他們希望能快速搭好一個臨時安置區。**ˌpatch sth/sb↔ˈup** (rather *informal*) **1** to repair

P

sth, especially in a temporary way by adding a new piece of material or a patch 修理；（尤指）臨時修補：*Just to patch the boat up will cost £10 000.* 小船簡單地修一下就得花 1 萬英鎊。**2** to treat sb's injuries, especially quickly or temporarily 臨時包紮（傷口）；倉促處理（損傷）：*The doctor will soon patch you up.* 大夫很快就會給你處理包紮好的。**3** to try to stop arguing with sb and be friends again 言歸於好：*They've managed to patch up their differences.* 他們終於彌合了分歧。◇ *Have you tried* ***patching things up*** *with her?* 你有沒有試試跟她恢復和好？**4** to agree on sth, especially after long discussions and even though the agreement is not exactly what everyone wants 勉強同意：*They managed to patch up a deal.* 他們勉強達成交易。

patch·ouli /ˈpætʃʊli; pəˈtʃuːli/ *noun* [U] a PERFUME made with oil from the leaves of a SE Asian bush 廣藿香水

patch·work /ˈpætʃwɜːk; *NAmE* -wɜːrk/ *noun* **1** [U] a type of NEEDLEWORK in which small pieces of cloth of different colours or designs are sewn together （不同圖案雜色布塊的）拼縫物；拼布工藝：*a patchwork quilt* 拼布絎縫蓋被 ➲ compare CRAZY QUILT ➲ **VISUAL VOCAB** page V23 **2** [sing.] a thing that is made up of many different pieces or parts 拼湊之物：*a patchwork of different styles and cultures* 不同風格和文化的拼合 ◇ *From the plane, the landscape was just a patchwork of fields.* 從飛機上俯瞰，滿目是田園交錯的景色。

patchy /ˈpætʃi/ *adj.* **1** existing or happening in some places and not others 零散的；散落的；分佈不勻的 **SYN** **uneven**：*patchy fog* 團團的霧 ◇ *The grass was dry and patchy.* 草都乾了，東一片西一片的。**2** (*NAmE* also **spotty**) not complete; good in some parts, but not in others 不完整的；參差不齊的：*a patchy knowledge of Spanish* 對西班牙語一知半解 ◇ *It was a patchy performance.* 那是一場水準參差的演出。▸ **patch·ily** *adv.* **patchi·ness** *noun* [U]

pate /peɪt/ *noun* (*old use* or *humorous*) the top part of the head, especially when there is no hair on it 頭頂；（尤指）禿頂，光頂：*The sun beat down on his bald pate.* 灼熱的陽光直射到他那光光的禿頂上。

P

pâté /ˈpæteɪ; *NAmE* pɑːˈteɪ/ *noun* [U] a soft mixture of very finely chopped meat or fish, served cold and used for spreading on bread, etc. 魚醬，肉醬（用作冷盤、塗於麪包等上）

pâté de foie gras /ˌpæteɪ də fwʌ ˈɡrɑː; *NAmE* pɑːˌteɪ/ (also **ˌfoie ˈgras**) *noun* [U] (from *French*) an expensive type of pâté made from the LIVER of a GOOSE 鵝肝醬

pa·tel·la /pəˈtelə/ *noun* (*pl.* **pa·tel·lae** /-liː/) (*anatomy* 解) the KNEECAP 膝蓋骨；髕骨 ➲ **VISUAL VOCAB** page V59

pa·tent *noun, adj., verb*

■ **noun** /ˈpætnt; *BrE* also ˈpeɪtnt/ [C, U] an official right to be the only person to make, use or sell a product or an invention; a document that proves this 專利權；專利證書：*to* ***apply for/obtain a patent*** *on an invention* 申請／獲得發明專利權 ◇ *The device was protected* ***by patent***. 這一裝置受專利保護。

■ **adj.** /ˈpeɪtnt; *NAmE* also ˈpætnt/ [only before noun] **1** connected with a patent 有專利的；受專利保護的：*patent applications/laws* 專利申請；專利法 ◇ *the US Patent Office* 美國專利局 **2** (of a product 產品) made or sold by a particular company 專利生產的；專利經銷的：*patent medicines* 專利藥品 **3** (*formal*) used to emphasize that sth bad is very clear and obvious 明顯的；赤裸裸的 **SYN** **blatant**：*It was a patent lie.* 那是赤裸裸的謊言。

■ **verb** /ˈpætnt; *BrE* also ˈpeɪtnt/ **~ sth** to obtain a patent for an invention or a process 獲得專利權

pa·tent·ee /ˌpætənˈtiː; *BrE* also ˌpeɪt-/ *noun* a person or an organization that holds the patent for sth 專利權（所有）人；專利獲得者

patent leather /ˌpeɪtnt ˈleðə(r); *NAmE* usually ˈpætnt/ *noun* [U] a type of leather with a hard shiny surface, used especially for making shoes and bags 漆革；漆皮

pa·tent·ly /ˈpeɪtəntli; ˈpætəntli; *NAmE* ˈpæt-/ *adv.* (*formal*) without doubt 毫無疑問；顯然 **SYN** **clearly**：*Her explanation was patently ridiculous.* 她的解釋顯然是荒唐可笑的。◇ *It was* ***patently obvious*** *that she was lying.* 她顯然是在撒謊。

pater /ˈpeɪtə(r)/ *noun* (*old-fashioned, BrE*) father 父親

pater·famil·ias /ˌpeɪtəfəˈmɪliæs; *NAmE* ˌpætərf-/ *noun* [sing.] (*formal* or *humorous*) the man who is the head of a family（男性）家長

pa·ter·nal /pəˈtɜːnl; *NAmE* -ˈtɜːrnl/ *adj.* **1** connected with being a father; typical of a kind father 父親的；慈父般的：*paternal love* 父愛 ◇ *He gave me a piece of paternal advice.* 他給了我慈父般的忠告。**2** related through the father's side of the family 父系的：*my paternal grandmother* (= my father's mother) 我的祖母 ▸ **pa·ter·nal·ly** *adv.*：*He smiled paternally at them.* 他像慈父一樣對他們微笑着。➲ compare MATERNAL

pa·ter·nal·ism /pəˈtɜːnəlɪzəm; *NAmE* -ˈtɜːrn-/ *noun* [U] (*sometimes disapproving*) the system in which a government or an employer protects the people who are governed or employed by providing them with what they need, but does not give them any responsibility or freedom of choice 家長作風；家長式管理；專制 ▸ **pa·ter·nal·is·tic** /pəˌtɜːnəˈlɪstɪk; *NAmE* -ˌtɜːrn-/ (also **pa·ter·nal·ist**) *adj.*：*a paternalistic employer* 家長式雇主

pa·ter·nity /pəˈtɜːnəti; *NAmE* -ˈtɜːrn-/ *noun* [U] the fact of being the father of a child 父親的身分（或地位）：*He refused to admit paternity of the child.* 他拒不承認是那孩子的父親。➲ compare MATERNITY

paˈternity leave *noun* [U] time that the father of a new baby is allowed to have away from work 男人侍產假（父親照顧新生兒的休假）➲ **COLLOCATIONS** at CHILD ➲ see also MATERNITY LEAVE, PARENTAL LEAVE

paˈternity suit (also **paˈternity case**) *noun* a court case that is intended to prove who a child's father is, especially so that he can be ordered to give the child financial support 確認生父的訴訟（請求法院確認生父並使其承擔撫養義務）

path 🔑 /pɑːθ; *NAmE* pæθ/ (*pl.* **paths** /pɑːðz; *NAmE* pæðz/) (also **path·way**) *noun*

1 🔑 a way or track that is built or is made by the action of people walking 小路；小徑：*a concrete path* 混凝土小路 ◇ *the* ***garden path*** 花園小徑 ◇ ***Follow the path*** *through the woods.* 沿着這條小路穿過樹林。◇ *to walk along a path* 沿小徑前行 ◇ *The* ***path led*** *up a steep hill.* 小路通向一座陡峭的山丘。◇ *a* ***coastal path*** 海邊的小路 ➲ see also FOOTPATH **2** 🔑 [usually sing.] a line along which sb/sth moves; the space in front of sb/sth as they move 路線；道路 **SYN** **way**：*He threw himself* ***into the path of*** *an oncoming vehicle.* 他衝入迎面有汽車駛來的路中。◇ *The avalanche forced its way down the mountain, crushing everything* ***in its path***. 雪崩衝下山來，摧毀了沿途的一切。◇ *Three men blocked her path.* 三個男人擋住了她的去路。➲ see also FLIGHT PATH **3** 🔑 a plan of action or a way of achieving sth 行動計劃；成功的途徑：*a career path* 職業道路 ◇ *the path to success* 成功之道 **IDM** see BEAT *v.*, CROSS *v.*, LEAD[1] *v.*, PRIMROSE, SMOOTH *v.*

path·et·ic /pəˈθetɪk/ *adj.* **1** making you feel pity or sadness 可憐的；可悲的；令人憐惜的 **SYN** **pitiful**：*a pathetic and lonely old man* 可憐又孤獨的老翁 ◇ *The starving children were a pathetic sight.* 飢餓的兒童看起來是一幅悽慘的景象。**2** (*informal, disapproving*) weak and not successful 無力的；不成功的 **SYN** **feeble**：*a pathetic excuse* 牽強的藉口 ◇ *She made a pathetic attempt to smile.* 她勉強地微微一笑。◇ *You're pathetic!* 你真是廢物！▸ **path·et·ic·al·ly** /-kli/ *adv.*：*He cried pathetically.* 他哭得很悲傷。◇ *a pathetically shy woman* 令人憐憫的靦腆女人

paˌthetic ˈfallacy *noun* [U, sing.] (in art and literature 用於藝術和文學) the act of describing animals and things as having human feelings 擬人謬化（對動物或物體賦予人類感情）

path·find·er /ˈpɑːθfaɪndə(r); *NAmE* ˈpæθ-/ *noun* **1** a person, group or thing that goes before others and shows the way over unknown land 探路者；開路人 **2** a person, group or thing that finds a new way of doing sth 先鋒；開拓者 **SYN** **trailblazer**：*The company* *is a pathfinder in computer technology.* 這家公司是計算機技術的開拓者。

patho- /ˈpæθəʊ; *NAmE* -θoʊ/ *combining form* (in nouns, adjectives and adverbs 構成名詞、形容詞和副詞) connected with disease 與疾病相關： *pathogenesis* (= the development of a disease) 發病機制 ◇ *pathophysiology* 病理生理學

patho·gen /ˈpæθədʒən/ *noun* (*technical* 術語) a thing that causes disease 病原體 ▸ **patho·gen·ic** /-ˈdʒenɪk/ *adj.*

patho·gen·esis /ˌpæθəˈdʒenɪsɪs/ *noun* (*medical* 醫) the way in which a disease develops 發病機制；病原

patho·logic·al /ˌpæθəˈlɒdʒɪkl; *NAmE* -ˈlɑːdʒ-/ *adj.* **1** not reasonable or sensible; impossible to control 不理智的；無道理的；無法控制的： *pathological fear/hatred/violence* 無理由的恐懼／憎恨／暴行 ◇ *a* ***pathological liar*** (= a person who cannot stop telling lies) 說謊成性者 **2** caused by, or connected with, disease or illness 病態的；與疾病有關的： *pathological depression* 病態的抑鬱 **3** (*technical* 術語) connected with PATHOLOGY 病理學的；與病理學相關的 ▸ **patho·logic·al·ly** /-kli/ *adv.*： *pathologically jealous* 有嫉妒狂的

path·olo·gist /pəˈθɒlədʒɪst; *NAmE* -ˈθɑːl-/ *noun* a doctor who studies pathology and examines dead bodies to find out the cause of death 病理學醫生；病理學家 ➲ compare MEDICAL EXAMINER

path·ology /pəˈθɒlədʒi; *NAmE* -ˈθɑːl-/ *noun* **1** [U] (*medical* 醫) the scientific study of diseases 病理學 **2** [C] an aspect of sb's behaviour that is extreme and unreasonable and that they cannot control 變態；反常

pathos /ˈpeɪθɒs; *NAmE* -θɑːs; -θɔːs/ *noun* [U] (in writing, speech and plays 文章、講話和戲劇) the power of a performance, description, etc. to produce feelings of sadness and sympathy 感染力；令人產生悲憫共鳴的力量

path·way /ˈpɑːθweɪ; *NAmE* ˈpæθ-/ *noun* = PATH

pa·tience 🔑 /ˈpeɪʃns/ *noun* [U]
1 🔑 **~ (with sb/sth)** the ability to stay calm and accept a delay or sth annoying without complaining 耐心；忍耐力： *She* ***has little patience with*** (= will not accept or consider) *such views.* 她很難接受這類觀點。◇ *People have* ***lost patience with*** (= have become annoyed about) *the slow pace of reform.* 人們對改革的緩慢速度已經失去耐性。◇ *I have run out of patience with her.* 我對她已失去耐性了。◇ *My patience is wearing thin.* 我要忍耐不住了。◇ *Teaching children with special needs requires patience and understanding.* 教導有特殊需要的兒童需要耐心和體諒。 **2** 🔑 the ability to spend a lot of time doing sth difficult that needs a lot of attention and effort 毅力；堅忍；恒心： *It takes time and patience to photograph wildlife.* 拍攝野生動物要肯花時間，還要有毅力。◇ *I don't* ***have the patience to*** *do jigsaw puzzles.* 我沒有耐性玩拼圖遊戲。 **3** (*BrE*) (*NAmE* **soli·taire**) a card game for only one player 單人紙牌遊戲 **IDM** see JOB, TRY *v.*

pa·tient 🔑 /ˈpeɪʃnt/ *noun, adj.*
■ ***noun*** **1** 🔑 a person who is receiving medical treatment, especially in a hospital 接受治療者，病人（尤指醫院裏的）： *cancer patients* 癌症病人 **2** 🔑 a person who receives treatment from a particular doctor, dentist, etc.（某個醫生或牙醫等的）病人： *He's one of Dr Shaw's patients.* 他是肖醫生的病人之一。 **3** (*grammar* 語法) the person or thing that is affected by the action of the verb. In the sentence 'I started the car', the patient is *car*. 受動者 ➲ compare AGENT (6)
■ ***adj.*** 🔑 **~ (with sb/sth)** able to wait for a long time or accept annoying behaviour or difficulties without becoming angry 有耐心的；能忍耐的： *She's very patient with young children.* 她對幼兒特別有耐心。◇ *You'll just have to be patient and wait till I'm finished.* 你只能耐心點，等我把事情做完。 ▸ **pa·tient·ly** *adv.*： *She sat patiently waiting for her turn.* 她耐心地坐着等候輪到自己。

pat·ina /ˈpætɪnə; *NAmE* pəˈtiːnə/ *noun* [usually sing.] **1** a green, black or brown layer that forms on the surface of some metals（金屬表面的）綠銹，銅銹，氧化層 **2** a thin layer that forms on other materials; the shiny surface that develops on wood or leather when it is polished 薄層；（木器或皮革的）光澤： (*figurative*) *He looked relaxed and elegant and had the patina of success.* 他神態輕鬆瀟灑，給人成功的印象。

pat·in·ation /ˌpætɪˈneɪʃn/ *noun* [U, C] (*technical* 術語) a shiny layer on the surface of metal, wood, etc.; the process of covering sth with a shiny layer 綠銹；生綠銹

patio /ˈpætiəʊ; *NAmE* -oʊ/ *noun* (*pl.* **-os**) a flat hard area outside, and usually behind, a house where people can sit（房屋外面或後面的）露台，平台： *Let's have lunch out* ***on the patio****.* 咱們在外面平台上吃午飯吧。 ➲ VISUAL VOCAB page V19

ˌpatio ˈdoor *noun* [usually pl.] (*especially BrE*) a large glass sliding door that leads to a garden or BALCONY（通往花園或陽台的）滑動玻璃門

pa·tis·serie /pəˈtiːsəri/ *noun* (from *French*) **1** [C] a shop/store that sells cakes, etc. 糕點店 **2** [U] (also **pa·tis·series** [pl.]) (*formal*) cakes 糕點

Pat Malone /ˌpæt məˈləʊn; *NAmE* -loʊn/ *noun*
IDM **on your Pat Maˈlone** (*AustralE, NZE, informal*) alone; without anybody else 單獨；獨自

pat·ois /ˈpætwɑː/ *noun* (*pl.* **pat·ois** /-twɑːz/) a form of a language, spoken by people in a particular area, that is different from the standard language of the country 方言；土語；土話

patri·arch /ˈpeɪtriɑːk; *NAmE* -ɑːrk/ *noun* **1** the male head of a family or community（男性）家長，族長，酋長 ➲ compare MATRIARCH **2** an old man that people have a lot of respect for 德高望重的男長者 **3 Patriarch** the title of a most senior BISHOP (= a senior priest) in the Orthodox or Roman Catholic Church（東正教和天主教的）牧首，宗主教

patri·arch·al /ˌpeɪtriˈɑːkl; *NAmE* -ˈɑːrkl/ *adj.* **1** ruled or controlled by men; giving power and importance only to men 男人統治的；男性主宰的： *a patriarchal society* 父權社會 **2** connected with a patriarch 族長的；家長的 ➲ compare MATRIARCHAL

patri·arch·ate /ˈpeɪtriɑːkət; *NAmE* -ɑːrk-/ *noun* (*formal*) **1** the title, position or period of office of a patriarch (3) 宗主教（或牧首）的職務（或在任期等） **2** the area governed by a patriarch (3) 宗主教（或牧者）區

patri·archy /ˈpeɪtriɑːki; *NAmE* -ɑːrki/ *noun* [C, U] (*pl.* **-ies**) a society, system or country that is ruled or controlled by men 男性統治的社會（或制度、國家）；男權政治；父權制 ➲ compare MATRIARCHY

pa·tri·cian /pəˈtrɪʃn/ *adj.* (*formal*) connected with or typical of the highest social class 貴族的；上流社會的 **SYN** **aristocratic** ▸ **pa·tri·cian** *noun* ➲ compare PLEBEIAN

patri·cide /ˈpætrɪsaɪd/ *noun* [U, C] (*formal*) the crime of killing your father; a person who is guilty of this crime 弒父罪；弒父者 ➲ compare FRATRICIDE (1), MATRICIDE, PARRICIDE

patri·lin·eal /ˌpætrɪˈlɪniəl/ *adj.* (*formal*) used to describe the relationship between father and child that continues in a family with each generation, or sth that is based on this relationship 父子相傳的；父系的： *In that society, inheritance of land is patrilineal* (= the children get the land that their father owned). 在那個社會，土地世襲是父傳子的。 ➲ compare MATRILINEAL

patri·mony /ˈpætrɪməni; *NAmE* -moʊni/ *noun* [sing.] (*formal*) **1** property that is given to sb when their father dies 遺產；祖傳財產 **SYN** **inheritance** **2** the works of art and TREASURES of a nation, church, etc. 文化遺產；文物；國家（或教堂等）的財產 **SYN** **heritage**

pat·riot /ˈpeɪtriət; *BrE* also ˈpæt-/ *noun* a person who loves their country and who is ready to defend it against an enemy 愛國者

pat·ri·ot·ic /ˌpeɪtriˈɒtɪk; ˌpæt-; *NAmE* ˌpeɪtriˈɑːtɪk/ *adj.* having or expressing a great love of your country 愛國的： *a patriotic man who served his country well* 為國盡忠的愛國者 ◇ *patriotic songs* 愛國歌曲 ▸ **pat·ri·ot·ic·al·ly** *adv.* /-kli/

P

pat·ri·ot·ism /ˈpeɪtriətɪzəm; *BrE* also ˈpæt-/ *noun* [U] love of your country and willingness to defend it 愛國主義；愛國精神

pa·trol /pəˈtrəʊl; *NAmE* pəˈtroʊl/ *verb, noun*

■ *verb* (-ll-) **1** [T, I] ~ (sth) to go around an area or a building at regular times to check that it is safe and that there is no trouble 巡邏；巡查：*Troops patrolled the border day and night.* 軍隊日夜在邊境地區巡邏。◇ *Guards can be seen patrolling everywhere.* 到處都能見到衛兵在巡邏。 **2** [T] ~ sth to drive or walk around a particular area, especially in a threatening way（尤指威脅性地）逛蕩，閒逛：*Gangs of youths patrol the streets at night.* 夜裏成幫結夥的年輕人在街上閒逛。

■ *noun* **1** [C, U] the act of going to different parts of a building, an area, etc. to make sure that there is no trouble or crime 巡邏；巡查：*Security guards make regular patrols at night.* 夜間保安人員定時巡邏。◇ *a police car* ***on patrol*** 巡邏的警車 **2** [C] a group of soldiers, vehicles, etc. that patrol an area 巡邏隊；巡邏車隊：*a naval/police patrol* 海軍／警察巡邏隊 ◇ *a patrol car/boat* 巡邏車／船 **3** [C] a group of about six BOY SCOUTS or GIRL GUIDES/SCOUTS that forms part of a larger group 童子軍小隊

pa·trol·man /pəˈtrəʊlmən; *NAmE* -ˈtroʊ-/, **pa·trol·woman** /pəˈtrəʊlwʊmən; *NAmE* -ˈtroʊ-/ *noun* (*pl.* **-men** /-mən/, **-women** /-wɪmɪn/) **1** (in the US) a police officer who walks or drives around an area to make sure that there is no trouble or crime（美國的）巡警：*Patrolman Don Lilly* 巡警唐•利利 **2** (in Britain) an official of an association for car owners who goes to give help to drivers who have a problem with their cars（英國汽車協會幫助車主解決困難的）公路巡查員，巡視員

paˈtrol wagon (also *informal* **ˈpaddy wagon**) (both *NAmE*) *noun* a police van for transporting prisoners in 囚車

pat·ron /ˈpeɪtrən/ *noun* **1** a person who gives money and support to artists and writers（藝術家的）贊助人，資助者：*Frederick the Great was the patron of many artists.* 腓特烈大帝是許多藝術家的贊助人。 **2** a famous person who supports an organization such as a charity and whose name is used in the advertisements, etc. for the organization 名義贊助人（支持慈善組織等的名人，名字常用於有關的廣告宣傳中） **3** (*formal*) a person who uses a particular shop/store, restaurant, etc. 老主顧；顧客；常客：*Patrons are requested not to smoke.* 請顧客不要吸煙。

pat·ron·age /ˈpætrənɪdʒ; ˈpeɪt-/ *noun* [U] **1** the support, especially financial, that is given to a person or an organization by a patron 資助；贊助：*Patronage of the arts comes from businesses and private individuals.* 對藝術的資助來自企業和個人。 **2** the system by which an important person gives help or a job to sb in return for their support（掌權者給予提挈以換取支持的）互惠互利 **3** (*especially NAmE*) the support that a person gives a shop/store, restaurant, etc. by spending money there 惠顧；光顧

pat·ron·ess /ˌpeɪtrənˈes/ *noun* a female PATRON (1) 女贊助人；女資助人 ➲ note at GENDER

pat·ron·ize (*BrE* also **-ise**) /ˈpætrənaɪz; *NAmE* ˈpeɪt-/ *verb* **1** [T, I] ~ (sb) (*disapproving*) to treat sb in a way that seems friendly, but which shows that you think that they are not very intelligent, experienced, etc. 屈尊俯就地對待；擺出高人一等的派頭：*Some television programmes tend to patronize children.* 有些電視節目往往以大人的觀點對待兒童。 **2** [T] ~ sth (*formal*) to be a regular customer of a shop/store, restaurant, etc. 經常光顧：*The club is patronized by students and locals alike.* 學生和當地居民都經常去那個俱樂部。 **3** [T] ~ sb/sth to help a particular person, organization or activity by giving them money 贊助；資助：*She patronizes many contemporary British artists.* 她贊助許多英國當代藝術家。

pat·ron·iz·ing (*BrE* also **-is·ing**) /ˈpætrənaɪzɪŋ; *NAmE* ˈpeɪtrənaɪzɪŋ/ *adj.* (*disapproving*) showing that you feel better, or more intelligent than sb else 自認為高人一等的；擺派頭的 SYN **superior**：*a patronizing smile* 屈尊俯就的一笑 ◇ *I was only trying to explain; I didn't want to sound patronizing.* 我只是想解釋一下而已，絕無自詡清高之意。 ▸ **pat·ron·iz·ing·ly**, **-is·ing·ly** *adv.*：*He patted her hand patronizingly.* 他以上級姿態拍了拍她的手。

ˌpatron ˈsaint *noun* a Christian SAINT who is believed to protect a particular place or group of people 主保；主保聖人；守護聖人：*St Patrick, Ireland's patron saint* 聖帕特里克，愛爾蘭的主保聖人 ◇ *St Christopher, patron saint of travellers* 聖克利斯托弗，旅行主保

patro·nym·ic /ˌpætrəˈnɪmɪk/ *noun* (*technical* 術語) a name formed from the name of your father or a male ANCESTOR, especially by adding sth to the beginning or end of their name 從父名衍生出的姓或名字（尤指在父親或父系祖先之名加前、後綴）➲ compare MATRONYMIC

patsy /ˈpætsi/ *noun* (*pl.* **-ies**) (*informal, especially NAmE*) a weak person who is easily cheated or tricked, or who is forced to take the blame for sth that sb else has done wrong 容易吃虧上當者；容易成為替罪羊者

pat·ter /ˈpætə(r)/ *noun, verb*

■ *noun* **1** [sing.] the sound that is made by sth repeatedly hitting a surface quickly and lightly 吧嗒吧嗒的響聲；急速的輕拍聲：*the* ***patter of feet/footsteps*** 噠噠的腳步聲 ◇ *the patter of rain on the roof* 雨打屋頂的啪噠聲 **2** [U, sing.] fast continuous talk by sb who is trying to sell you sth or entertain you（為推銷或娛樂的）不間斷說話：*sales patter* 推銷員的一口氣說話

IDM **the patter of tiny feet** (*informal* or *humorous*) a way of referring to children when sb wants, or is going to have, a baby（用於想要或即將有孩子時）小寶寶的腳步聲：*We can't wait to hear the patter of tiny feet.* 我們恨不得早點有個小寶寶。

■ *verb* **1** [I] + adv./prep. to make quick, light sounds as a surface is being hit several times 發出輕快的拍打聲：*Rain pattered against the window.* 雨點啪噠啪噠地敲擊着窗子。 **2** [I] + adv./prep. to walk with light steps in a particular direction 輕盈地走：*I heard her feet pattering along the corridor.* 我聽到她步履輕盈地在走廊上走過。

pat·tern 🔑 /ˈpætn; *NAmE* -tərn/ *noun, verb*

■ *noun* **1** 🔑 the regular way in which sth happens or is done 模式；方式：***changing patterns*** *of behaviour* 行為變化模式 ◇ *an irregular sleeping pattern* 不規律的睡眠模式 ◇ *The murders all seem to* ***follow a (similar) pattern*** (= happen in the same way). 這些兇殺案似乎同出一轍。 **2** 🔑 [usually sing.] an excellent example to copy 範例；典範；榜樣；樣板：*This system* ***sets the pattern*** *for others to follow.* 這個系統堪為他人仿效的典範。 **3** 🔑 a regular arrangement of lines, shapes, colours, etc. as a design on material, carpets, etc. 圖案；花樣；式樣：*a pattern of diamonds and squares* 菱形和正方形構成的圖案 ◇ *a shirt with a floral pattern* 一件花襯衣 **4** 🔑 a design, set of instructions or shape to cut around that you use in order to make sth 模型；底樣；紙樣：*a knitting pattern* 編織圖樣 ◇ *She bought a dress pattern and some material.* 她買了一幅衣服紙樣和一些衣料。 **5** a small piece of material, paper, etc. that helps you choose the design of sth 樣品；樣本 SYN **sample**：*wallpaper patterns* 壁紙樣品

■ *verb* **1** ~ sth to form a regular arrangement of lines or shapes on sth 構成圖案（或花樣）：*Frost patterned the window.* 霜在窗子上形成了圖案。◇ *a landscape patterned by vineyards* 由一片片葡萄園構成的風景圖 **2** ~ sth (*technical* 術語) to cause a particular type of behaviour to develop 使形成，促成（某行為模式）：*Adult behaviour is often patterned by childhood experiences.* 成年人的行為模式往往是童年經歷造成的。

PHR V **ˈpattern sth on sth** (*BrE*) (*NAmE* **ˈpattern sth after sth**) [usually passive] to use sth as a model for sth; to copy sth 模仿；仿效：*a new approach patterned on Japanese ideas* 模仿日本概念而設計的新方法

pat·terned /ˈpætənd; *NAmE* -tərnd/ *adj.* decorated with a pattern 有圖案的；帶花樣的：*patterned wallpaper* 印有圖案的壁紙 ◇ **~ with sth** *cups patterned with yellow flowers* 有黃花圖案的杯子 ➲ VISUAL VOCAB page V61

pat·tern·ing /ˈpætənɪŋ; *NAmE* -tərn-/ *noun* [U] **1** (*technical* 術語) the forming of fixed ways of behaving by copying or repeating sth 固有行為方式的形成：*cultural* *patterning* 文化形態的形成 ◇ *the patterning of husband-wife roles* 夫妻角色的形成 **2** the arrangement of shapes or colours to make patterns（形狀、色彩的）排列，造型：*a red fish with black patterning* 有黑色花紋的紅魚

patty /ˈpæti/ *noun* (*pl.* **-ies**) (*especially NAmE*) finely chopped meat, fish, etc. formed into a small round flat shape 碎肉餅；魚肉餅：*a hamburger patty* 漢堡包肉餅

pau·city /ˈpɔːsəti/ *noun* [sing.] **~ (of sth)** (*formal*) a small amount of sth; less than enough of sth 少量；少許；貧乏：*a paucity of information* 信息的短缺

paunch /pɔːntʃ/ *noun* a fat stomach on a man（男人的）大肚子，啤酒肚 ▸ **paunchy** *adj.*

pau·per /ˈpɔːpə(r)/ *noun* (*old use*) a very poor person 窮人；貧民；乞丐

pause 0┳ /pɔːz/ *verb, noun*

■ *verb* **1** 0┳ [I] to stop talking or doing sth for a short time before continuing 暫停；停頓：*Anita paused for a moment, then said: 'All right'.* 安尼塔略停了一會兒，然後說："好吧"。◇ *The woman spoke almost without* ***pausing for breath*** (= very quickly). 那女人說話像放連珠炮似的。◇ *I paused at the door and looked back.* 我停在門口，回頭看了看。◇ ***Pausing only to*** *pull on a sweater, he ran out of the house.* 他只停下來穿了件毛衣就衝出了屋外。 **2** 0┳ [T] **~ sth** to stop a tape, CD, etc. for a short time using the pause button（按暫停鍵）暫停放音，暫停放像：*She paused the DVD and went to answer the phone.* 她暫停了 DVD 去接電話。

■ *noun* **1** 0┳ [C] **~ (in sth)** a period of time during which sb stops talking or stops what they are doing 停頓；停頓的時間：*There was a long pause before she answered.* 她停了好一會兒才回答。◇ *David waited for a pause in the conversation so he could ask his question.* 戴維等着談話停下來，好問個問題。◇ *After a brief pause, they continued climbing.* 他們略停了一下就繼續爬山。◇ *The rain fell* ***without pause***. 雨不停地下着。 **2** [C] (*especially BrE*) (also **fer·mata** especially in *NAmE*) (*music* 音) a sign (𝄐) over a note or a REST to show that it should be longer than usual 延長記號 **3** [U] (also **ˈpause button**) a control that allows you to stop a TAPE RECORDER, CD player, etc. for a short time 暫停鍵：*Press pause to stop the tape.* 按暫停鍵停下磁帶。

IDM **give (sb) ˈpause** (*BrE* also **give (sb) pause for ˈthought**) (*formal*) to make sb think seriously about sth or hesitate before doing sth 使認真考慮；使猶豫 ➲ more at PREGNANT

pav·ane /pəˈvæn; -ˈvɑːn/ (also **pavan** /ˈpævən/) *noun* a slow dance popular in the 16th and 17th centuries; a piece of music for this dance 帕凡舞（流行於 16 和 17 世紀的慢步舞）；帕凡舞曲

pave /peɪv/ *verb* [often passive] **~ sth (with sth)** to cover a surface with flat stones or bricks（用磚石）鋪（地）：*a paved area near the back door* 後門旁一塊石板地

IDM **ˌpave the ˈway (for sb/sth)** to create a situation in which sb will be able to do sth or sth can happen（為…）鋪平道路，創造條件：*This decision paved the way for changes in employment rights for women.* 這項決議為修改婦女就業權利創造了條件。➲ more at ROAD, STREET *n.*

pave·ment /ˈpeɪvmənt/ *noun* **1** [C] (*BrE*) (*NAmE* **side·walk**) a flat part at the side of a road for people to walk on（馬路邊的）人行道：*a pavement cafe* 路邊咖啡館 ➲ VISUAL VOCAB page V3 **2** [C, U] (*BrE*) any area of flat stones on the ground 石板鋪的地面：*a mosaic pavement* 馬賽克地面 **3** [U] (*NAmE*) the surface of a road 路面：*Two cars skidded on the icy pavement.* 兩輛汽車在結冰的路面上打滑。

ˈpavement artist (*BrE*) (*NAmE* **ˈsidewalk artist**) *noun* an artist who draws pictures in CHALK on the PAVEMENT/SIDEWALK, hoping to get money from people who pass 街頭畫家，馬路畫家（在人行道上用粉筆作畫討錢）

pa·vil·ion /pəˈvɪliən/ *noun* **1** a temporary building used at public events and exhibitions（公共活動或展覽用的）臨時建築物：*the US pavilion at the Trade Fair* 交易會上的美國展覽館 **2** (*BrE*) a building next to a sports ground, used by players and people watching the game（運動場旁設立的）運動員席，看台：*a cricket pavilion* 板球場看台 **3** (*NAmE*) a large building used for sports or entertainment 大型文體館：*the Pauley Pavilion, home of the university's basketball team* 普萊文體中心，這所大學的籃球隊之家 **4** a building that is meant to be more beautiful than useful, built as a shelter in a park or used for concerts and dances（公園中的）亭，閣；（音樂會、舞會的）華美建築：*his first show at the Winter Gardens Pavilion, Blackpool* 他在布萊克浦冬園閣的首次演出

pav·ing /ˈpeɪvɪŋ/ *noun* [U] **1** a surface of flat stones or material like stone on the ground 石板等鋪的地面：*Weeds grew through the cracks in the paving.* 雜草從鋪石路面的縫隙中長出來。➲ see also CRAZY PAVING **2** the stones or material that are used to make a flat surface on the ground 鋪料；鋪地的材料：*We'll use concrete paving.* 我們將使用混凝土鋪地面。

ˈpaving stone *noun* a flat, usually square, piece of stone that is used to make a hard surface for walking on 鋪地石板；方石板 SYN **flagstone**

pav·lova /pævˈləʊvə; *NAmE* -ˈloʊ-/ *noun* a cold DESSERT (= sweet dish) made of MERINGUE, cream and fruit 巴甫洛娃蛋糕（用蛋白酥、奶油和水果製成）

Pav·lov·ian /pævˈləʊviən; *NAmE* -ˈloʊ-/ *adj.* (of an animal's or human's reaction 動物或人的反應) happening in response to a particular STIMULUS 巴甫洛夫氏條件作用的；經典條件反射的：*Her yawn was a Pavlovian response to my yawn.* 她打哈欠是對我打哈欠的條件反射。 ORIGIN From the name of the Russian scientist, I P Pavlov, who carried out experiments on dogs, showing how they could be conditioned to react to certain stimuli. 源自俄羅斯科學家巴甫洛夫的名字，他對狗隻的實驗表明它們經過訓練能夠對某些刺激作出反應。

paw /pɔː/ *noun, verb*

■ *noun* **1** the foot of an animal that has CLAWS or nails（動物的）爪 ➲ VISUAL VOCAB page V12 **2** (*informal*) a person's hand（人的）手：*Take your filthy paws off me!* 把你的髒手從我身上拿開！

■ *verb* **1** [I, T] (of an animal 動物) to scratch or touch sth repeatedly with a paw（不斷地）撓，抓：**~ at sth** *The dog pawed at my sleeve.* 狗一直撓我的衣袖。◇ **~ sth** *The stallion pawed the ground impatiently.* 種馬焦躁地用蹄刨着地面。 **2** [T] **~ sb** (sometimes *humorous*) to touch sb in a rough sexual way that they find offensive 猥褻地亂摸；動手動腳；動手挑逗

pawn /pɔːn/ *noun, verb*

■ *noun* **1** a CHESS piece of the smallest size and least value. Each player has eight pawns at the start of a game.（國際象棋的）兵，卒 ➲ VISUAL VOCAB page V38 **2** a person or group whose actions are controlled by more powerful people 被利用的人；走卒：*The hostages are being used as political pawns.* 人質正被用作政治卒子。

IDM **in pawn** if sth is **in pawn**, it has been pawned 被抵押；被典當：*All her jewellery was in pawn.* 她把首飾全典當了。

■ *verb* **~ sth** to leave an object with a pawnbroker in exchange for money. The object is returned to the owner if he or she pays back the money within an agreed period of time. If not, it can be sold. 質押；典當

pawn·broker /ˈpɔːnbrəʊkə(r); *NAmE* -broʊ-/ *noun* a person who lends money in exchange for articles left with them. If the money is not paid back by a particular time, the pawnbroker can sell the article. 典當商人；當鋪老闆

Paw·nee /ˈpɔːniː/ *noun* (*pl.* **Paw·nee** or **Paw·nees**) a member of a Native American people, many of whom live in the US state of Oklahoma 波尼人（美洲土著，很多居於美國俄克拉何馬州）

pawn·shop /ˈpɔːnʃɒp; *NAmE* -ʃɑːp/ *noun* a pawnbroker's shop/store 當鋪

paw·paw /ˈpɔːpɔː/ *noun* (*BrE*) = PAPAYA

pay 0┳ /peɪ/ *verb, noun*

■ *verb* (**paid, paid** /peɪd/) **1** 0┳ [I, T] to give sb money for work, goods, services, etc. 付費；付酬：**~ (for sth)**

P

I'll pay for the tickets. 我來買票。◇ *Are you* **paying** *in* **cash** *or* **by credit card**? 您付現金還是用信用卡？◇ *My company* **pays well** (= pays high salaries). 我公司給的工資很高。◇ **~ for sb to do sth** *Her parents paid for her to go to Canada.* 她父母出錢送她去加拿大。◇ **~ sth** *to* **pay cash** 付現金 ◇ **~ sth for sth** *She pays £200 a week for this apartment.* 這套房子她每週要付租金 200 英鎊。◇ **~ sb (for sth)** *Would you mind paying the taxi driver?* 您付出租車費好嗎？◇ **~ sb sth** *He still hasn't* **paid** *me* **the money** *he owes me.* 他還沒歸還欠我的錢呢。◇ *I'm paid $100 a day.* 我每天工資 100 元。◇ **~ sb/sth to do sth** *I don't pay you to sit around all day doing nothing!* 我不是花錢雇你整天閒坐着的！➲ see also LOW-PAID, PRE-PAY, WELL PAID **2** 🗝 [T] to give sb money that you owe them 交納；償還：**~ sth** *to* **pay a bill/debt/fine/ransom, etc.** 繳付賬單、債款、罰金、贖金等 ◇ **~ sth to sb** *Membership fees should be paid to the secretary.* 會員費應交給秘書。◇ **~ sb sth** *Have you paid him the rent yet?* 你向他付房租了沒有？ **3** 🗝 [I] (of a business, etc. 企業等) to produce a profit 贏利；創收：*It's hard to make farming pay.* 種莊稼獲利很不容易。 **4** 🗝 [I, T] to result in some advantage or profit for sb 受益；划算：*Crime doesn't pay.* 犯罪是划不來的。◇ **it pays to do sth** *It pays to keep up to date with your work.* 工作能跟上時代是有利的。◇ **it pays sb to do sth** *It would probably pay you to hire an accountant.* 聘一名會計師或許對你有好處。 **5** 🗝 [I] to suffer or be punished for your beliefs or actions 付代價；遭受懲罰：**~ (for sth)** *You'll pay for that remark!* 你會為你的話付出代價的！◇ **~ (with sth)** *Many people paid with their lives* (= they died). 許多人付出了生命。 **6** 🗝 [T] used with some nouns to show that you are giving or doing the thing mentioned（與某些名詞結合使用，表示做某事或付出某事物）：**~ sth** *I didn't* **pay attention** *to what she was saying.* 我沒有注意她在說什麼。◇ *The director* **paid tribute** *to all she had done for the charity.* 董事讚揚她為慈善事業所做的一切。◇ *I'll* **pay a call on** (= visit) *my friends.* 我將去看朋友。◇ **~ sb sth** *I'll pay you a call when I'm in town.* 我在城裏的時候將去拜訪你。◇ *He's always* **paying me compliments**. 他總是誇獎我。

P

IDM **the ˈdevil/ˈhell to pay** (*informal*) a lot of trouble 大麻煩；大亂子：*There'll be hell to pay when he finds out.* 一旦他發現了真相，那麻煩就大了。 **he who pays the piper calls the ˈtune** (*saying*) the person who provides the money for sth can also control how it is spent 花錢的人說了算；財大者氣粗 **pay ˈcourt to sb** (*old-fashioned*) to treat sb with great respect in order to gain favour with them 獻殷勤；奉迎；討好 **pay ˈdividends** to produce great advantages or profits 有所收穫；產生效益：*Exercising regularly will pay dividends in the end.* 經常運動最終會對身體大有好處的。 **ˌpay for itˈself** (of a new system, sth you have bought, etc. 新系統、所買的東西等) to save as much money as it cost 使損益相當；夠本：*The rail pass will pay for itself after about two trips.* 火車周遊券大約只需乘兩次車就夠本了。 **pay good ˈmoney for sth** used to emphasize that sth cost(s) a lot of money, especially if the money is wasted 為…花費很多錢（尤指錢白花了）：*I paid good money for this jacket, and now look at it—it's ruined!* 這件夾克是我花大價錢買的。瞧瞧，全給毀了！ **pay its ˈway** (of a business, etc. 企業等) to make enough money to pay what it costs to keep it going 贏利運作；不負債；收支平衡：*The bridge is still not paying its way.* 這座橋現在還入不敷出。 **pay the ˈpenalty (for sth/for doing sth)** | **pay a/the ˈprice (for sth/for doing sth)** to suffer because of bad luck, a mistake or sth you have done 因…受害／付代價：*He looked terrible this morning. I think he's paying the penalty for all those late nights.* 他今天上午臉色很不好，我想這是他一直熬夜造成的。◇ *They're now paying the price for past mistakes.* 他們現在正為過去的錯誤付出代價。 **pay your reˈspects (to sb)** (*formal*) to visit sb or to send a message of good wishes as a sign of respect for them（拜訪或問候某人）表示敬意：*Many came to* **pay their last respects** (= by attending sb's funeral). 許多人前來參加葬禮向逝者告別。 **pay through the ˈnose (for sth)** (*informal*) to pay too much money for sth（為…）付過高的價 **pay your ˈway** to pay for everything yourself without having to rely on anyone else's money 自力償付一切；自食其力 **you pays your ˌmoney and you takes your ˈchoice** (*informal, especially BrE*) used for saying that there is very little difference between two or more things that you can choose 如何選擇由你做主（表示各種選擇的分別不大）➲ more at ARM *n.*, HEED *n.*, ROB

PHR V **ˌpay sb ˈback (sth)** | **ˌpay sth↔ˈback (to sb)** 🗝 to return money that you borrowed from sb（向某人）還錢 **SYN** **repay**：*I'll pay you back next week.* 我下週把錢還給你。◇ *You can pay back the loan over a period of three years.* 你可以在三年內分期歸還貸款。◇ *Did he ever pay you back that $100 he owes you?* 他把欠你的 100 塊錢還給你沒有？ **ˌpay sb ˈback (for sth)** 🗝 to punish sb for making you or sb else suffer 報復；懲罰：*I'll pay him back for making me look like a fool in front of everyone.* 他讓我當眾出醜，我非治治他不可。➲ related noun PAYBACK **ˌpay sth↔ˈdown** (*NAmE*) to reduce an amount of money that you owe by paying some of it（分期或部份）支付，償還：*She used the money to pay down her mortgage.* 她把這筆錢用於償還她的部份抵押貸款。 **ˌpay sth↔ˈin** | **ˌpay sth ˈinto sth** to put money into a bank account 存款；存入賬戶：*I paid in a cheque this morning.* 我今天上午存入一張支票。◇ *I'd like to pay some money into my account.* 我想在我的賬戶裏存一些錢。 **ˌpay ˈoff** (*informal*) (of a plan or an action, especially one that involves risk 尤指冒險的計劃或行動) to be successful and bring good results 成功；奏效；達到目的：*The gamble paid off.* 賭博贏了。 **ˌpay sb↔ˈoff** **1** to pay sb what they have earned and tell them to leave their job 付清工資後解雇；遣散：*The crew were paid off as soon as the ship docked.* 船一泊港，船員就被付酬解雇了。 **2** (*informal*) to give sb money to prevent them from doing sth or talking about sth illegal or dishonest that you have done 用錢封某人的口；買通某人：*All the witnesses had been paid off.* 所有的證人都被買通了。➲ related noun PAY-OFF (1) **ˌpay sth↔ˈoff** to finish paying money owed for sth 付清；償清：*We paid off our mortgage after fifteen years.* 我們歷經十五年的時間還清了抵押借款。 **ˌpay sth↔ˈout** **1** 🗝 to pay a large sum of money for sth 付巨款：*I had to pay out £500 to get my car repaired.* 我只好花 500 英鎊的高價修理我的汽車。➲ related noun PAYOUT **2** to pass a length of rope through your hands（從手中）徐徐放出繩索 **ˌpay ˈup** 🗝 to pay all the money that you owe to sb, especially when you do not want to or when the payment is late 總算付清全部欠款：*I had a hard time getting him to pay up.* 我好不容易讓他還清了全部欠款。

■ *noun* 🗝 [U] the money that sb gets for doing regular work 工資；薪水：*Her job is hard work, but the pay is good.* 她工作雖辛苦，但薪水不低。◇ *a* **pay increase** 加薪 ◇ (*BrE*) *a* **pay rise** 加薪 ◇ (*NAmE*) *a* **pay raise** 加薪 ◇ *a 3%* **pay offer** * 3% 的加薪 ◇ *holiday pay* 假日薪金 ◇ *to make a* **pay claim** (= to officially ask for an increase in pay) 正式要求加薪 ➲ **SYNONYMS** at INCOME ➲ see also SICK PAY

IDM **in the pay of sb/sth** (usually *disapproving*) working for sb or for an organization, often secretly 秘密（為某人或某組織）工作；由…豢養；被…收買

pay·able /ˈpeɪəbl/ *adj.* [not before noun] **1** that must be paid or can be paid 應付；可償付：*A 10% deposit is payable in advance.* 須預付 10% 的押金。◇ *The price is payable in monthly instalments.* 本價格可按月分期付款。 **2** when a cheque, etc. is made **payable to** sb, their name is written on it and they can then pay it into their bank account 應付予（抬頭人、收款人等）

ˌpay and disˈplay *noun* [U] (*BrE*) a system of car parking in which you buy a ticket from a machine for a period of time and put it in the window of the car 泊車付費系統（從售票機購得泊車證置於車窗）

ˌpay as you ˈearn *noun* [U] = PAYE ➲ compare WITHHOLDING TAX

ˌpay-as-you-ˈgo *adj.* connected with a system of paying for a service just before you use it rather than paying for it later 付費後使用的；預付費的：*pay-as-you-go phones* 預先付費電話

pay·back /ˈpeɪbæk/ *noun* [C, U] **1** the money that you receive back on money that you have invested (especially when this is equal to the amount that you invested to start with); the time that it takes to get your money back 本金返還；還本；投資的回收期：*a 10-year payback* * 10 年的投資回收期 **2** the advantage or reward that sb receives for sth they have done; the act of paying sth back 報償；回報：*His victory was seen as payback for all the hard work he'd put in during training.* 他的勝利被視為訓練期間所有辛苦努力的回報。◇ (*informal*) *It's **payback time**!* (= a person will have to suffer for what they have done) 現在該遭到報應了！

'pay bed *noun* (in the UK) a bed for private patients that they pay to use in a free public hospital （英國免費公立醫院的）自費病牀，私人病牀

'pay channel *noun* a television channel that you must pay for separately in order to watch it 付費電視頻道

'pay cheque (*BrE*) (*US* **pay·check** /ˈpeɪtʃek/) *noun* **1** the cheque that you are given when your wages are paid to you 工資支票 **2** (*especially NAmE*) a way of referring to the amount of money that you earn 收入；進項；進賬：*a huge paycheck* 巨額收入

pay·day /ˈpeɪdeɪ/ *noun* [U, C] the day on which you get your wages or salary 發薪日；發工資日：*Friday is payday.* 星期五是發薪日。

'pay dirt *noun* [U] (*especially NAmE*) earth that contains valuable minerals or metal such as gold （含貴重礦物或金屬的）礦石，礦砂

IDM **hit/strike 'pay dirt** (*informal*) to suddenly be in a successful situation, especially one that makes you rich 驟然成功；暴富

PAYE /ˌpiː eɪ waɪ ˈiː/ *abbr.* pay as you earn (a British system of paying income tax in which money is taken from your wages by your employer and paid to the government) 預扣所得税（英國制度，雇主從職工工資中扣除應繳税款，直接上繳政府）

payee /ˌpeɪˈiː/ *noun* (*technical* 術語) a person that money or a cheque is paid to 受款人；收款人

'pay envelope (*NAmE*) (*BrE* **'pay packet**, **'wage packet**) *noun* an envelope containing your wages; the amount a person earns 工資袋；所得工資

payer /ˈpeɪə(r)/ *noun* a person who pays or who has to pay for sth 付款人；交款人：*mortgage payers* 按揭付款人 ◇ *The company are not very good payers* (= they are slow to pay their bills, or they do not pay their employees well). 這家公司財務支付信譽不佳。

ˌpay-for-perˈformance *adj.* [only before noun] (*NAmE*) paying more or less money depending on how well a person does their job 按工作表現付酬的；按績效付酬的：*There has been an increase in pay-for-performance plans all over the US.* 績效付酬計劃在全美各地已經日益普及。➲ compare PERFORMANCE (3), PERFORMANCE-RELATED

ˌpaying 'guest *noun* a person who pays to live in sb's house with them, usually for a short time （付費並同在一處居住的）臨時住宿者

pay·load /ˈpeɪləʊd; *NAmE* -loʊd/ *noun* (*technical* 術語) **1** the passengers and goods on a ship or an aircraft for which payment is received （飛機、船隻的）有效載荷，有酬負載 **2** the goods that a vehicle, for example a lorry/truck, is carrying; the amount it is carrying （車輛等的）裝載貨物，裝載量 **3** the EXPLOSIVE power of a bomb or a MISSILE（炸彈、導彈的）爆炸力，炸藥量 **4** the equipment carried by a SPACECRAFT or SATELLITE （航天器、衞星的）裝備

pay·mas·ter /ˈpeɪmɑːstə(r); *NAmE* -mæs-/ *noun* **1** (usually *disapproving*) a person or group of people that pays another person or organization and therefore can control their actions 操縱者；後台老闆 **2** an official who pays the wages in the army, a factory, etc. （軍隊、工廠等的）工薪出納員

pay·ment 0→ /ˈpeɪmənt/ *noun*
1 0→ [U] **~ (for sth)** the act of paying sb/sth or of being paid 付款；支付；收款：***payment in instalments/in advance/by cheque/in cash*** 分期／預先／支票／現金付款 ◇ *There will be a penalty for late payment of bills.* 賬單拖延付款要收滯納金。 **2** 0→ [C] **~ (for sth)** a sum of money paid or expected to be paid （將付或應付的）款額，款項：*a **cash payment*** 現金付款 ◇ *They are finding it difficult to **meet the payments** on their car.* 他們感到很難償付汽車款。◇ *He agreed to make ten **monthly payments** of £50.* 他同意每月付款 50 英鎊，十次付清。➲ COLLOCATIONS at FINANCE ➲ see also BALANCE OF PAYMENTS, DOWN PAYMENT **3** 0→ [U, sing.] **~ (for sth)** a reward or an act of thanks for sth you have done 報答；報償 SYN **recompense**：*We'd like you to accept this gift **in payment for** your kindness.* 謹以薄禮答謝厚愛，敬請笑納。◇ *Is this all the payment I get for my efforts?* 這就是對我辛勞的全部報償嗎？

IDM **on payment of sth** when sth has been paid 付款後：*Entry is only allowed on payment of the full registration fee.* 繳付全數登記費用方可進入。

Synonyms 同義詞辨析

payment

premium • contribution • subscription • repayment • deposit • instalment

These are all words for an amount of money that you pay or are expected to pay, or for the act of paying. 以上各詞均指款額、款項、付款。

payment an amount of money that you pay or are expected to pay; the act of paying 指款額、款項、付款：*ten monthly payments of $50* 每月付款 50 元，十次付清 ◇ *payment in advance* 預先付款

premium an amount of money that you pay once or regularly for an insurance policy; an extra payment added to the basic rate; a higher amount of money than usual 指保險費、額外費用、附加費、溢價：*an insurance premium* 保險費 ◇ *a premium for express delivery* 快遞附加費

contribution a sum of money that you pay regularly to your employer or the government in order to pay for benefits such as health insurance, a pension, etc. 指（給雇主或政府用作醫療保險、養老金等福利的）定期繳款：*You can increase your monthly contributions to the pension plan.* 你可以增加你的養老金計劃每月供款。

subscription an amount of money you pay in advance to receive regular copies of a newspaper or magazine or to receive a service 指（報刊的）訂閱費、訂購款，（服務的）用戶費：*a subscription to 'Newsweek'*《新聞週刊》的訂閱費

repayment (*BrE*) an amount of money that you pay regularly to a bank, etc. until you have returned all the money that you owe; the act of paying this money 指按期償還的款項、分期償還、償還債務、歸還借款：*the repayments on the loan* 貸款的分期償還額

deposit an amount of money that you pay as the first part of a larger payment 指訂金：*We've put down a 5% deposit on the house.* 我們已支付了房款的 5% 作為訂金。

instalment one of a number of payments that you make regularly over a period of time until you have paid for sth 指分期付款的一期付款：*We paid for the car by/in instalments.* 我們以分期付款買了這輛車。

PATTERNS

- (a/an) **annual/monthly/regular** payment/premium/contributions/subscription/repayment/deposit/instalment
- payment/repayment **in full**
- to **pay** a(n) premium/contribution/subscription/deposit/instalment
- to **make** (a) payment/repayment/deposit
- to **meet/keep up** (**with**) (the) payment(s)/the premiums/(the) repayment(s)/the instalments

'pay-off *noun* (*informal*) **1** a payment of money to sb so that they will not cause you any trouble or to make them keep a secret （用以買通別人的）黑錢；行賄錢

P

SYN **bribe** **2** a payment of money to sb to persuade them to leave their job 辭退金；遣散費 **3** an advantage or a reward from sth you have done 回報；報償

pay·ola /peɪˈəʊlə; *NAmE* -ˈoʊlə/ *noun* [U] (*NAmE, informal*) the practice of giving or taking payments for doing sth illegal, especially for illegally influencing the sales of a particular product 買通，賄賂（尤指為非法影響銷售）**SYN** **bribery**

pay·out /ˈpeɪaʊt/ *noun* a large amount of money that is given to sb 付出的巨款： *an insurance payout* 巨額保險償付 ◇ *a lottery payout* 彩票大額獎金

ˈ**pay packet** (also ˈ**wage packet**) (both *BrE*) (*NAmE* ˈ**pay envelope**) *noun* an envelope containing your wages; the amount a person earns 工資袋；所得工資

ˌ**pay-per-ˈview** *noun* [U] a system of television broadcasting in which you pay an extra sum of money to watch a particular programme, such as a film/movie or a sports event （電視節目的）付費點播系統

pay·phone /ˈpeɪfəʊn; *NAmE* -foʊn/ *noun* a telephone, usually in a public place, that is operated using coins or a card 公用（付費）電話

pay·roll /ˈpeɪrəʊl; *NAmE* -roʊl/ *noun* **1** a list of people employed by a company showing the amount of money to be paid to each of them （公司員工的）工資名單： *We have 500 people **on the payroll**.* 我們在編員工有 500 人。 **2** [usually sing.] the total amount paid in wages by a company （公司的）工資總支出

pay·slip /ˈpeɪslɪp/ *noun* (*BrE*) a piece of paper given to an employee that shows how much money they have been paid and how much has been taken away for tax, etc. （給員工的）工資明細表，工資計算單

ˌ**pay TˈV** (also ˈ**pay television**) *noun* [U] a system of television broadcasting in which you pay extra money to watch particular television programmes or channels 收費電視

PBS /ˌpiː biː ˈes/ *abbr.* the Public Broadcasting Service (an organization in the US that broadcasts television programmes to local stations that do not show advertisements) （美國）公共電視網（給不播廣告的地方台播放電視節目）

P

PC /ˌpiː ˈsiː/ *abbr.* **1** personal computer (a small computer that is designed for one person to use at work or at home) 個人電腦；個人計算機 ➲ VISUAL VOCAB pages V66, V69 **2** (*BrE*) Police Constable (a police officer of the lowest rank) 警察；警員： *PC Tom March* 警員湯姆 • 馬什 ➲ see also WPC **3** POLITICALLY CORRECT

PCB /ˌpiː siː ˈbiː/ *abbr.* printed circuit board 印刷電路板

ˌ**PˈC card** *noun* (*computing* 計) a plastic card with a PRINTED CIRCUIT on it that can be put into a computer to allow it to work with other devices 印刷電路卡；PC 卡

PCP /ˌpiː siː ˈpiː/ *abbr.* **1** PRIMARY CARE PHYSICIAN **2** PRIMARY CARE PROVIDER

PC Plod /ˌpiː siː ˈplɒd; *NAmE* ˈplɑːd/ *noun* (*BrE, informal, humorous*) a junior police officer 初級警員

PCSO /ˌpiː siː es ˈəʊ; *NAmE* ˈoʊ/ *abbr.* (in England and Wales) police community support officer (a person who is not a police officer but works in an area to help the work of the police) （英格蘭和威爾士的）警察社區支援員

PDA /ˌpiː diː ˈeɪ/ *noun* the abbreviation for 'personal digital assistant' (a very small computer that is used for storing personal information and creating documents, and that may include other functions such as telephone, FAX, connection to the Internet, etc.) 個人數字助理，個人數位助理，掌上型電腦（全寫為 personal digital assistant） ➲ VISUAL VOCAB page V66

PDF /ˌpiː diː ˈef/ (also ˌ**PDˈF file**) *noun* (*computing* 計) the abbreviation for 'Portable Document Format' (a type of computer file that can contain words or pictures. It can be read using any system, can be sent from one computer to another, and will look the same on any computer.) 可移植文檔格式，可攜式文件格式（全寫為 Portable Document Format）： *I'll send it to you as a PDF.* 我會用 PDF 格式把它發給你。

p.d.q. /ˌpiː diː ˈkjuː/ *abbr.* pretty damn/damned quick (= very fast) 火速；馬上；立即： *Make sure you get here p.d.q.* 你馬上給我趕到這兒來。

PDT /ˌpiː diː ˈtiː/ *abbr.* PACIFIC DAYLIGHT TIME

PE (*BrE*) (*US* **P.E.**) /ˌpiː ˈiː/ *noun* [U] the abbreviation for 'physical education' (sport and exercise that is taught in schools) 體育（課）（全寫為 physical education）： *a PE class* 一堂體育課

pea /piː/ *noun* a small round green seed, eaten as a vegetable. Several peas grow together inside a long thin POD on a climbing plant also called a pea. 豌豆；豌豆粒： *frozen peas* 冷凍豌豆 ◇ *pea soup* 豌豆湯 ➲ VISUAL VOCAB page V31 ➲ see also CHICKPEA, MUSHY PEAS, SPLIT PEA, SWEET PEA

peace 0‑ᵤ /piːs/ *noun*

1 0‑ᵤ [U, sing.] a situation or a period of time in which there is no war or violence in a country or an area 和平；太平： *war and peace* 戰爭與和平 ◇ ***peace talks/negotiations*** 和平談判／協商 ◇ *The negotiators are trying to **make peace** between the warring factions.* 談判者正努力使交戰各派議和。 ◇ *A UN force has been sent to **keep the peace*** (= to prevent people from fighting). 一支聯合國部隊已受遣前去維護和平。 ◇ *After years of war, the people long for a lasting peace.* 歷經多年戰亂之後，人民渴望永久和平。 ◇ *the Peace of Utrecht, 1713* (= the agreement ending the war) * 1713 年的烏得勒支和平協議 ◇ *The two communities live together **in peace**.* 這兩個社區和平相處。 ◇ *The countries have been **at peace** for more than a century.* 這些國家和平共處已有一個多世紀。 ◇ *the **peace movement*** (= that tries to prevent war by protesting, persuading politicians, etc.) 爭取和平運動 ➲ COLLOCATIONS at WAR **2** 0‑ᵤ [U] the state of being calm or quiet 平靜；安靜；寧靜： *She lay back and enjoyed the peace of the summer evening.* 她輕鬆地躺着享受夏日傍晚的寧靜。 ◇ *I would work better if I had some **peace and quiet**.* 四周若再安靜一些，我會幹得更好。 ◇ *He just wants to be **left in peace*** (= not to be disturbed). 他只希望不受打擾。 ◇ *I need to check that she is all right, just for my own **peace of mind*** (= so that I do not have to worry). 我必須看到她安然無恙，心裏才踏實。 ◇ *He never felt really **at peace** with himself.* 他從未真正感到心裏平靜過。 **3** 0‑ᵤ [U] the state of living in friendship with sb without arguing 和睦；融洽；和諧： *They simply can't seem to live in peace with each other.* 他們好像就是不能和睦相處。 ◇ *She felt **at peace with** the world.* 她感覺與世無爭。 ➲ see also BREACH, JUSTICE OF THE PEACE

IDM ˌ**hold your ˈpeace/ˈtongue** (*old-fashioned*) to say nothing although you would like to give your opinion （想說卻）保持沉默，緘口不語 **make (your) peace with sb** to end an argument with sb, usually by saying you are sorry （經道歉）與人和解，言歸於好 ➲ more at WICKED *n.*

Which Word? 詞語辨析

peace / peacefulness

- The noun **peace** can be used to talk about a peaceful state or situation. 名詞 peace 指和平、平靜、安寧的狀態或形勢： *world peace* 世界和平 ◇ *I just need some peace and quiet.* 我需要的只是平靜與安寧。 **Peacefulness** is not a common word. It means 'the quality of being peaceful'.
* peacefulness 不常用，指和平、平靜、安寧的性質。

peace·able /ˈpiːsəbl/ *adj.* **1** not involving or causing argument or violence 不惹事的；和平的；安寧的 **SYN** **peaceful**： *A peaceable settlement has been reached.* 已經達成和解。 **2** not liking to argue; wishing to live in peace with others 不愛爭吵的；愛好和平的；溫和的 **SYN** **peaceful, calm**： *a peaceable character* 性格溫和的人 ▸ **peace·ably** /-əbli/ *adv.*

the ˈPeace Corps *noun* [sing.] a US organization that sends young Americans to work in other countries without pay in order to create international friendship 和平隊，和平工作團（美國機構，送美國青年去其他國家義務工作以建立國際友誼）

ˈpeace dividend *noun* [usually sing.] money previously spent on weapons and the defence of a country and now available to be used for other things because of a reduction in a country's military forces 和平紅利，和平增益（指國家因裁軍而得以用於其他方面的原軍備和國防費用）

peace·ful 0-w /ˈpiːsfl/ *adj.*
1 0-w not involving a war, violence or argument 不訴諸戰爭（或暴力、爭論）的；和平的：*a **peaceful protest/demonstration/solution*** 和平抗議／示威／解決辦法 ◊ *They hope for a **peaceful settlement** of the dispute.* 他們希望和平解決爭端。 **2** 0-w quiet and calm; not worried or disturbed in any way 安靜的；平靜的 SYN **tranquil**：*a peaceful atmosphere* 寧靜的氣氛 ◊ *peaceful sleep* 安靜的睡眠 ◊ *It's so peaceful out here in the country.* 這裏的郊外一切都是那麼寧靜。◊ *He had a peaceful life.* 他過着平靜的生活。 **3** 0-w trying to create peace or to live in peace; not liking violence or disagreement 愛好和平的；和睦的；尋求和平的 SYN **peaceable**：*a peaceful society* 和諧的社會 ◊ *The aims of the organization are wholly peaceful.* 這個組織的宗旨完全是追求和平。 ▶ **peace·ful·ly** /-fəli/ *adv.*：*The siege has ended peacefully.* 圍城已經和平地結束了。◊ *The baby slept peacefully.* 嬰兒睡得很安穩。 **peace·ful·ness** *noun* [U] ➲ note at PEACE

peace·keep·er /ˈpiːskiːpə(r)/ *noun* **1** a member of a military force who has been sent to help stop people fighting in a place where war or violence is likely 維和部隊士兵 **2** a person who tries to stop people arguing or fighting 調解人；勸架者：*She's the peacekeeper in that family.* 那個家庭的糾紛都由她來調解。

peace·keep·ing /ˈpiːskiːpɪŋ/ *adj.* [only before noun] intended to help stop people fighting and prevent war or violence in a place where this is likely 維護和平的：*peacekeeping operations* 維和行動 ◊ *a United Nations peacekeeping force* 聯合國維持和平部隊 ➲ COLLOCATIONS at WAR

ˈpeace-loving *adj.* preferring to live in peace and to avoid arguments and fighting 愛好和平的 SYN **peaceable**

peace·maker /ˈpiːsmeɪkə(r)/ *noun* a person who tries to persuade people or countries to stop arguing or fighting and to make peace 調解人；調停人

peace·nik /ˈpiːsnɪk/ *noun* (*informal*, sometimes *disapproving*) a PACIFIST (= sb who believes war and violence are always wrong and refuses to fight) 反戰分子；和平主義分子

ˈpeace offering *noun* a present given to sb to show that you are sorry for sth or want to make peace after an argument 表示和解的禮物；致歉的禮物

ˈpeace pipe *noun* a TOBACCO pipe offered and smoked as a symbol of peace by Native Americans 和平煙斗（美洲土著作為和平象徵請人抽的）

ˈpeace process *noun* [usually sing.] a series of talks and agreements designed to end war or violence between two groups 和平進程

peace·time /ˈpiːstaɪm/ *noun* [U] a period of time when a country is not at war 和平時期 ➲ compare WARTIME

peach /piːtʃ/ *noun, adj.*
■ *noun* **1** [C] a round fruit with soft red and yellow skin, yellow flesh and a large rough seed inside 桃；桃子：*a peach tree* 桃樹 ➲ VISUAL VOCAB page V30 ➲ compare NECTARINE **2** [sing.] **~ (of a ...)** (*old-fashioned, informal*) a particularly good or attractive person or thing 極好的人（或物）；特別漂亮的東西（或人） **3** [U] a pinkish-orange colour 桃紅色；粉紅色
■ *adj.* pinkish-orange in colour 粉紅色的；桃紅色的

peach Melba /ˌpiːtʃ ˈmelbə/ *noun* [U, C] a cold DESSERT (= a sweet dish) made from half a PEACH, ice cream and RASPBERRY sauce 山莓醬桃子冰淇淋（用半個桃子、冰淇淋和山莓醬製成）

peachy /ˈpiːtʃi/ *adj.* **1** like a peach in colour or appearance（顏色或外形）像桃的：*pale peachy skin* 白裏透紅的皮膚 **2** (*NAmE, informal*) fine; very nice 順利；很好：*Everything is just peachy.* 一切順利。

ˈpea coat (also **ˈpea jacket**) *noun* (*NAmE*) a type of thick short coat 水手短外套（一種厚呢短大衣）

pea·cock /ˈpiːkɒk; *NAmE* -kɑːk/ *noun* a large male bird with long blue and green tail feathers that it can spread out like a fan 雄孔雀：*as proud as a peacock* 孔雀般地驕傲 ➲ see also PEAHEN

ˌpeacock ˈblue *adj.* deep greenish-blue in colour 孔雀藍的；暗綠光藍的 ▶ **ˌpeacock ˈblue** *noun* [U]

pea·fowl /ˈpiːfaʊl/ *noun* (*pl.* **pea·fowl**) a large PHEASANT found mainly in Asia. The male is called a PEACOCK and the female is called a PEAHEN. 孔雀（主要見於亞洲，peacock 指雄孔雀，peahen 指雌孔雀）

ˌpea-ˈgreen *adj.* bright green in colour, like PEAS 淺綠色的；豆綠的

pea·hen /ˈpiːhen/ *noun* a large brown bird, the female of the peacock 雌孔雀

peak 0-w /piːk/ *noun, verb, adj.*
■ *noun* **1** 0-w [usually sing.] the point when sb/sth is best, most successful, strongest, etc. 頂峰；高峰 SYN **height**：*Traffic **reaches its peak** between 8 and 9 in the morning.* 上午 8、9 點鐘之間是交通高峰期。◊ *She's **at the peak of** her career.* 她正處在事業的巔峰。◊ *the **peaks and troughs** of married life* 婚後生活的起起伏伏 ➲ compare OFF-PEAK **2** 0-w the pointed top of a mountain; a mountain with a pointed top 山峰；峰巒：*a **mountain peak*** 山峰 ◊ ***snow-capped/jagged peaks*** 積雪覆蓋的／嶙峋怪異的群峰 ◊ *The climbers made camp halfway up the peak.* 登山者在半山腰設置營地。➲ VISUAL VOCAB page V5 **3** any narrow and pointed shape, edge, etc. 尖形；尖端；尖頭：*Whisk the egg whites into stiff peaks.* 把蛋清攪成硬尖狀。 **4** (*BrE*) (*NAmE* **bill**, **visor**) the stiff front part of a cap that sticks out above your eyes 帽舌；帽簷 ➲ VISUAL VOCAB page V65
■ *verb* [I] to reach the highest point or value 達到高峰；達到最高值：*Oil production peaked in the early 1980s.* * 20 世紀 80 年代初期，石油產量達到了最高峰。◊ *Unemployment peaked at 17%.* 失業率達到 17% 的最高點。◊ *an athlete who peaks* (= produces his or her best performance) *at just the right time* 一位恰在最佳時刻締造出最佳成績的運動員
■ *adj.* [only before noun] used to describe the highest level of sth, or a time when the greatest number of people are doing sth or using sth 最高度的；高峰時期的；巔峰狀態的：*It was a time of **peak demand** for the product.* 那是對該產品需求最旺的時期。◊ *March is one of the **peak periods** for our business.* 三月是我們公司業務最繁忙的時期之一。◊ *The athletes are all in **peak condition**.* 所有運動員都處在巔峰狀態。◊ *We need extra help during the **peak season**.* 我們在最繁忙的季節需要額外人手。➲ compare OFF-PEAK

peaked /piːkt/ *adj.* **1** having a PEAK *n.* (4) 有帽簷的；有帽舌的 **2** (*NAmE*) (*BrE* **peaky**) ill/sick or pale 有病的；憔悴的；蒼白的

ˌpeak ˈoil *noun* [U] the point in time when world oil production reaches its highest rate, after which it goes into permanent decline 石油峰值（指世界石油生產達到峰值的時間點）

ˌpeak ˈrate *noun* the busiest time, which is therefore charged at the highest rate 高峰期，高峰時段（收費最高）：*peak-rate phone calls* 高峰時段通話

ˈpeak time (also **ˌpeak ˈviewing time**) *noun* (*BrE*) = PRIME TIME

peaky /ˈpiːki/ (*BrE, informal*) (*NAmE* **peaked**) *adj.* ill/sick or pale 有病的；憔悴的；蒼白的：*You're looking a little peaky. Are you OK?* 你看來有點憔悴。你沒事吧？

peal /piːl/ *noun, verb*
■ *noun* **1 ~ (of sth)** a loud sound or series of sounds 響亮的聲音；轟轟的響聲：*She burst into peals of laughter.* 她忽然哈哈大笑起來。 **2** the loud ringing sound of a bell 洪亮的鐘聲：*a peal of bells rang out* 洪亮的鐘聲響了起來 **3** a set of bells that all have different notes;

P

a musical pattern that can be rung on a set of bells 編鐘；編鐘音樂
■ **verb 1** [I] **~ (out)** (of bells 鐘或鈴) to ring loudly 大聲作響：*The bells of the city began to peal out.* 都市的鐘聲齊鳴。**2** [I] **~ (with sth)** to suddenly laugh loudly 轟然大笑：*Ellen pealed with laughter.* 埃倫忽然大笑起來。

pea·nut /ˈpiːnʌt/ *noun* **1** (*BrE* also **ground·nut**) [C] a nut that grows underground in a thin shell 花生：*a packet of salted peanuts* 一包鹹花生 ◇ *peanut oil* 花生油 ➲ VISUAL VOCAB page V32 **2 peanuts** [pl.] (*informal*) a very small amount of money 很少的錢：*He gets paid peanuts for doing that job.* 他幹那件工作報酬很低。

ˌpeanut ˈbutter *noun* [U] a thick soft substance made from very finely chopped PEANUTS, usually eaten spread on bread 花生醬：(*NAmE*) *a peanut butter and jelly sandwich* 一份花生醬加果醬三明治

pear /peə(r); *NAmE* per/ *noun* a yellow or green fruit that is narrow at the top and wide at the bottom 梨：*a pear tree* 梨樹 ➲ see also PRICKLY PEAR

pearl /pɜːl; *NAmE* pɜːrl/ *noun* **1** [C] a small hard shiny white ball that forms inside the shell of an OYSTER and is of great value as a JEWEL 珍珠：*a string of pearls* 一掛珍珠 ◇ *a pearl necklace* 珍珠項鏈 ◇ *She was wearing her pearls* (= a NECKLACE of pearls). 她戴着她的珍珠項鏈。➲ VISUAL VOCAB page V65 ➲ see also SEED PEARL **2** [C] a copy of a pearl that is made artificially 人造珍珠 **3** [U] = MOTHER-OF-PEARL：*pearl buttons* 珍珠母鈕扣 **4** [C, usually sing.] a thing that looks like a pearl in shape or colour（形狀或顏色）像珍珠之物：*pearls of dew on the grass* 草上的露珠 **5** [C] a thing that is very highly valued 極有價值的東西：*She is a pearl among women.* 她是女中人傑。
IDM **cast, throw, etc. pearls before ˈswine** to give or offer valuable things to people who do not understand their value 明珠暗投；對牛彈琴 **a ˌpearl of ˈwisdom** (usually *ironic*) a wise remark 睿智的語言；雋語；妙語如珠：*Thank you for those pearls of wisdom.* 謝謝你的金玉良言。

P

ˌpearl ˈbarley *noun* [U] smooth grains of BARLEY, which are added to soups and other dishes 珍珠大麥，大麥粉粒（添加於湯和菜中）

pearly /ˈpɜːli; *NAmE* ˈpɜːrli/ *adj.* of or like a pearl 珍珠的；似珍珠的：*pearly white teeth* 珍珠般的皓齒

the ˌPearly ˈGates *noun* [pl.] (*humorous*) the gates of heaven 天堂之門

ˈpear-shaped *adj.* **1** shaped like a pear 梨形的；像梨一樣的 **2** a **pear-shaped** person is wider around their waist and hips than around the top part of their body（指人）罐子狀的，腹大腰圓的
IDM **go ˈpear-shaped** (*BrE, informal*) if things **go pear-shaped**, they go wrong 出毛病；出問題

peas·ant /ˈpeznt/ *noun* **1** (especially in the past, or in poorer countries) a farmer who owns or rents a small piece of land（尤指舊時或貧窮國家的）農民，小農，佃農：*peasant farmers* 自耕農 **2** (*informal, disapproving*) a person who is rude, behaves badly, or has little education 老粗；土包子；沒教養的人 SYN **lout**

peas·ant·ry /ˈpezntri/ *noun* [sing.+sing./pl. v.] all the peasants in a region or country（統稱）一個地區或國家的農民：*the local peasantry* 當地的農民

pease pudding /ˌpiːz ˈpʊdɪŋ/ *noun* [U] (*BrE*) a hot dish made from dried PEAS that are left in water and then boiled until they form a soft mass, usually served with HAM or PORK 豌豆布丁（用煮爛的乾豌豆製成，通常和火腿或豬肉一起吃）

ˈpea-shooter *noun* (*BrE*) a small tube that children use to blow small objects such as dried PEAS at sb/sth, in order to hit them or it 射豆吹管；射豆槍

pea-souper /ˌpiː ˈsuːpə(r)/ *noun* (*old-fashioned, BrE, informal*) a very thick yellowish FOG 黃色濃霧

peat /piːt/ *noun* [U] a soft black or brown substance formed from decaying plants just under the surface of the ground, especially in cool wet areas. It is burned as a fuel or used to improve garden soil. 泥煤；泥炭：*peat bogs* 泥炭沼 ▸ **peaty** *adj.*：*peaty soils* 泥炭土

peb·ble /ˈpebl/ *noun* a smooth, round stone that is found in or near water 鵝卵石；礫石

ˈpebble-dash *noun* [U] (*BrE*) CEMENT mixed with small stones used for covering the outside walls of houses（抹房屋外牆的）小礫石灰漿

pebbly /ˈpebli/ *adj.* covered with pebbles 礫石覆蓋的：*a pebbly beach* 遍佈卵石的海灘

pecan /ˈpiːkən; pɪˈkæn; *NAmE* pɪˈkɑːn/ *noun* the nut of the American **pecan tree** with a smooth pinkish-brown shell 美洲山核桃 ➲ VISUAL VOCAB page V32

pecca·dillo /ˌpekəˈdɪləʊ; *NAmE* -ˈdɪloʊ/ *noun* (*pl.* **-oes** or **-os**) a small unimportant thing that sb does wrong 過失；岔子；輕罪

pec·cary /ˈpekəri/ (*pl.* **-ies**) *noun* an animal like a pig, which lives in the southern US, Mexico and Central and S America 西貒，矛牙野豬，貒豬（見於美國南部、墨西哥和中、南美洲）

peck /pek/ *verb, noun*
■ **verb 1** [I, T] (of birds 鳥) to move the beak forward quickly and hit or bite sth 啄；鶴：**~ (at sth)** *A robin was pecking at crumbs on the ground.* 一隻知更鳥在地上啄食麵包渣。◇ **~ sth** *A bird had pecked a hole in the sack.* 一隻鳥把袋子啄了個洞。◇ **~ sth out** *Vultures had pecked out the dead goat's eyes.* 禿鷲啄出了死羊的眼睛。**2** [T] (*informal*) to kiss sb lightly and quickly 匆匆地輕吻：**~ sb on sth** *He pecked her on the cheek as he went out.* 他出門時匆匆輕吻了一下她的面頰。◇ **~ sth** *She pecked his cheek.* 她輕吻了一下他的臉。
IDM **a/the ˈpecking order** (*informal*, often *humorous*) the order of importance in relation to one another among the members of a group 等級排序 SYN **hierarchy**：*New Zealand is at the top of the pecking order of rugby nations.* 新西蘭在橄欖球國家中首屈一指。
PHR V **ˈpeck at sth** to eat only a very small amount of a meal because you are not hungry（因不餓而）淺嚐幾口 SYN **pick at**
■ **noun 1** (*informal*) a quick kiss 匆匆的吻：*He gave her a friendly peck on the cheek.* 他友好地在她臉上輕輕一吻。**2** an act of pecking sb/sth 啄：*The budgerigar gave a quick peck at the seed.* 虎皮鸚鵡匆匆地啄了一下種子。

peck·er /ˈpekə(r)/ *noun* (*slang, especially NAmE*) a PENIS 陰莖；雞巴
IDM **ˌkeep your ˈpecker up** (*BrE, informal*) to remain cheerful despite difficulties（在困難中）振作精神，打起精神

peck·ish /ˈpekɪʃ/ *adj.* (*BrE, informal*) slightly hungry 有點餓的

pecs /peks/ *noun* [pl.] (*informal*) = PECTORALS

pec·tin /ˈpektɪn/ *noun* [U] (*chemistry* 化) a substance similar to sugar that forms in fruit that is ready to eat, and is used to make jam/jelly firm as it is cooked 果膠

pec·toral /ˈpektərəl/ *adj., noun*
■ **adj.** (*anatomy* 解) relating to or connected with the chest or breast 胸部的；胸的：*pectoral muscles* 胸肌
■ **noun pectorals** (also *informal* **pecs**) [pl.] the muscles of the chest 胸肌

pe·cu·liar /pɪˈkjuːliə(r)/ *adj.* **1** (*BrE* or rather *formal, NAmE*) strange or unusual, especially in a way that is unpleasant or worrying 怪異的；奇怪的；不尋常的 SYN **odd**：*a peculiar smell/taste* 奇怪的氣味／味道 ◇ *There was something peculiar in the way he smiled.* 他笑起來有點怪。◇ *I had a peculiar feeling we'd met before.* 我有一種奇怪的感覺，覺得我們以前見過面。◇ ***For some peculiar reason,*** *she refused to come inside.* 出於某種奇怪的原因，她拒絕到裏面來。➲ compare ODD (1) **2 ~ (to sb/sth)** belonging or relating to one particular place, situation, person, etc., and not to others（某人、某地、某種情況等）特有的，特殊的：*a humour that is peculiar to American sitcoms* 美國情景喜劇特有的幽默 ◇ *a species of bird peculiar to Asia* 亞洲獨有的鳥類 ◇ *He has his own peculiar style which you'll soon get used to.* 他有自己獨特的風格，你會很快習慣的。◇ *the peculiar properties of mercury* 水銀的特殊性質 **3** (*BrE, informal*) slightly ill/sick 不適；不舒服 IDM see FUNNY

pe·cu·li·ar·ity /pɪˌkjuːliˈærəti/ *noun* (*pl.* **-ies**) **1** [C] a strange or unusual feature or habit 怪異的性質（或習慣）；怪癖：*a physical peculiarity* 身體上的特徵 **2** [C] a feature that only belongs to one particular person, thing, place, etc.（人、物、地等的）個性，特色，特點 **SYN** **characteristic**：*the cultural peculiarities of the English* 英國人的文化特點 **3** [U] the quality of being strange or unusual 奇怪；怪異

pe·cu·li·ar·ly /prˈkjuːliəli; *NAmE* -ərli/ *adv.* **1** very; more than usually 很；不尋常地；特別 **SYN** **particularly, especially**：*These plants are peculiarly prone to disease.* 這些植物特別容易發生病變。 **2** in a way that relates to or is especially typical of one particular person, thing, place, etc. 獨特地；特有地 **SYN** **uniquely**：*He seemed to believe that it was a peculiarly British problem.* 他似乎認為那是英國獨有的問題。 **3** in a strange or unusual way 奇怪地；異常地

pe·cu·ni·ary /pɪˈkjuːniəri; *NAmE* -ieri/ *adj.* (*formal*) relating to or connected with money 金錢的；與錢相關的：*pecuniary advantage* 金錢方面的好處

ped- (*NAmE*) (*BrE* **paed-**) /piːd-/ *combining form* (in nouns and adjectives 構成名詞和形容詞) connected with children 與兒童有關的；兒童的

peda·gogic /ˌpedəˈɡɒdʒɪk; *NAmE* -ˈɡɑːdʒ-/ (also **peda·gogic·al** /-ɪkl/) *adj.* (*formal*) concerning teaching methods 教學法的：*pedagogic principles* 教學原則 ▸ **peda·gogic·al·ly** /ˌpedəˈɡɒdʒɪkli; *NAmE* -ˈɡɑːdʒ-/ *adv.*

peda·gogue /ˈpedəɡɒɡ; *NAmE* -ɡɑːɡ/ *noun* (*old use* or *formal*) a teacher; a person who likes to teach people things, especially because they think they know more than other people 教師；好為人師的人

peda·gogy /ˈpedəɡɒdʒi; *NAmE* -ɡɑːdʒ-/ *noun* [U] (*technical* 術語) the study of teaching methods 教育學；教學法

pedal /ˈpedl/ *noun, verb*

■ ***noun*** **1** a flat bar on a machine such as a bicycle, car, etc. that you push down with your foot in order to make parts of the machine move or work（自行車、汽車等的）腳蹬子，踏板：*I couldn't reach the pedals on her bike.* 我騎她的車夠不到腳蹬子。◇ *She pressed her foot down sharply on the brake pedal.* 她猛踩剎車踏板。➲ VISUAL VOCAB page V51 **2** a bar on a musical instrument such as a piano or an organ that you push with your foot in order to control the sound（鋼琴、風琴等的）踏板，踏瓣，腳踏鍵 ➲ VISUAL VOCAB page V36

■ ***verb*** (**-ll-**, *US* also **-l-**) **1** [I, T] to ride a bicycle somewhere 騎自行車：**+ adv./prep.** *I saw her pedalling along the towpath.* 我看見她在縴道上騎自行車。◇ *He jumped on his bike and pedalled off.* 他跳上自行車就騎走了。◇ **~ sth + adv./prep.** *She pedalled her bicycle up the track.* 她騎車上了小路。 **2** [I, T] to turn or press the pedals on a bicycle or other machine 踩踏板：(**+ adv./prep.**) *You'll have to pedal hard up this hill.* 走上坡時你必須用力蹬車。◇ **~ sth** *She had been pedalling her exercise bike all morning.* 她整個上午都在蹬健身車。➲ see also BACK-PEDAL, SOFT-PEDAL

ˈpedal bin *noun* (*BrE*) a container for rubbish, usually in a kitchen, with a lid that opens when a pedal is pressed 腳踏式垃圾桶

ped·alo /ˈpedələʊ; *NAmE* -loʊ/ *noun* (*pl.* **-oes** or **-os**) (*BrE*) a small pleasure boat that you move through the water by pushing PEDALS with your feet 腳踏遊船；腳踏輪槳船

ˈpedal pushers *noun* [pl.] (*BrE*) women's trousers/pants that reach just below the knee 長及小腿的女褲；女式六分褲

ped·ant /ˈpednt/ *noun* (*disapproving*) a person who is too concerned with small details or rules especially when learning or teaching 迂夫子；書呆子；學究

pe·dan·tic /pɪˈdæntɪk/ *adj.* (*disapproving*) too worried about small details or rules 迂腐的；學究氣的 ▸ **pe·dan·tic·al·ly** /-kli/ *adv.*

ped·ant·ry /ˈpedntri/ *noun* [U] (*disapproving*) too much attention to small details or rules 迂腐；謹小慎微

ped·dle /ˈpedl/ *verb* **1 ~ sth** to try to sell goods by going from house to house or from place to place 挨戶銷售；巡迴銷售：*He worked as a door-to-door salesman peddling cloths and brushes.* 他的工作是上門推銷抹布和刷子。◇ *to peddle illegal drugs* 販賣毒品 **2 ~ sth** to spread an idea or story in order to get people to accept it 兜售，宣傳，傳播（思想、消息）：*to peddle malicious gossip* 散佈惡意的流言蜚語 ◇ *This line* (= publicly stated opinion) *is being peddled by all the government spokesmen.* 所有的政府發言人都在宣揚這個官方路線。

ped·dler /ˈpedlə(r)/ *noun* **1** (also **ˈdrug peddler**) (both *BrE*) a person who sells illegal drugs 毒品販子 **2** (*NAmE*) (*BrE* **ped·lar**) a person who in the past travelled from place to place trying to sell small objects（舊時的）流動小販

ped·er·ast (*BrE* also **paed·er·ast**) /ˈpedəræst/ *noun* (*formal*) a man who has sex with a boy（與男童發生性關係的）戀童癖男子 ▸ **ped·er·asty** (*BrE* also **paed·er·asty**) /ˈpedəræsti/ *noun* [U]

ped·es·tal /ˈpedɪstl/ *noun* the base that a column, statue, etc. rests on（柱子或雕塑等的）底座，基座：*a pedestal basin* (= a WASHBASIN supported by a column) 有底座的洗臉盆 ◇ *I replaced the vase carefully on its pedestal.* 我小心地把花瓶放回基座上。➲ VISUAL VOCAB page V14

IDM **to put/place sb on a ˈpedestal** to admire sb so much that you do not see their faults 把某人奉為完人；盲目崇拜某人 ➲ more at KNOCK *v.*

pe·des·trian /pəˈdestriən/ *noun, adj.*

■ ***noun*** a person walking in the street and not travelling in a vehicle 行人；步行者 ➲ compare MOTORIST

■ ***adj.*** **1** [only before noun] used by or for the use of pedestrians; connected with pedestrians 行人使用的；行人的：*pedestrian areas* 步行區 ◇ *Pedestrian accidents are down by 5%.* 行人受傷事故下降了 5%。 **2** without any imagination or excitement; dull 缺乏想像的；乏味的；無趣的 **SYN** **unimaginative**

peˌdestrian ˈcrossing (*BrE*) (*NAmE* **cross·walk**) *noun* a part of a road where vehicles must stop to allow people to cross 人行橫道；行人穿越道 ➲ VISUAL VOCAB pages V2, V3 ➲ see also ZEBRA CROSSING

pe·des·tri·an·ize (*BrE* also **-ise**) /pəˈdestriənaɪz/ *verb* **~ sth** to make a street or part of a town into an area that is only for people who are walking, not for vehicles 使為行人專用；行人專用化 ▸ **pe·des·tri·an·iza·tion, -isa·tion** /pəˌdestriənaɪˈzeɪʃn/ *noun* [U]

peˌdestrian ˈprecinct (*BrE*) (*NAmE* **peˌdestrian ˈmall**) *noun* a part of a town, especially a shopping area, that vehicles are not allowed to enter 步行區；行人專用區 ➲ VISUAL VOCAB pages V2, V3

pedi·at·ri·cian (*NAmE*) (*BrE* **paedi·at·ri·cian**) /ˌpiːdiəˈtrɪʃn/ *noun* a doctor who studies and treats the diseases of children 兒科醫生；兒科專家

pedi·at·rics (*NAmE*) (*BrE* **paedi·at·rics**) /ˌpiːdiˈætrɪks/ *noun* [U] the branch of medicine concerned with children and their diseases 兒科學 ▸ **pedi·at·ric** (*NAmE*) (*BrE* **paedi-**) *adj.*

pedi·cure /ˈpedɪkjʊə(r); *NAmE* -kjʊr/ *noun* [C, U] care and treatment of the feet and TOENAILS 足部保養；足部護理 ➲ compare MANICURE

pedi·gree /ˈpedɪɡriː/ *noun, adj.*

■ ***noun*** **1** [C] knowledge of or an official record of the animals from which an animal has been bred 動物血統記錄；動物純種系譜：*dogs with good pedigrees* (= their ANCESTORS are known and of the same breed) 純種的狗 **2** [C, U] a person's family history or the background of sth, especially when this is impressive 家譜；門第；世系；起源：*She was proud of her long pedigree.* 她為自己源遠流長的家世而自豪。◇ *The product has a pedigree going back to the last century.* 這項產品的淵源可追溯到上個世紀。

■ ***adj.*** (*BrE*) (*NAmE* **pedi·greed**) [only before noun] (of an animal 動物) coming from a family of the same breed that has been officially recorded for a long time and is thought to be of a good quality 優良品種的；純種的：*pedigree sheep* 純種綿羊

pedi·ment /ˈpedɪmənt/ *noun* (*architecture* 建) the part in the shape of a triangle above the entrance of a building

P

in the ancient Greek style （古典希臘式建築入口處上方的）三角形楣飾

ped·lar (*BrE*) (*NAmE* **ped·dler**) /ˈpedlə(r)/ *noun* a person who in the past travelled from place to place trying to sell small objects （舊時的）流動小販

ped·ometer /peˈdɒmɪtə(r); *NAmE* -ˈdɑːm-/ *noun* an instrument for measuring how far you have walked 計步器；步程計

pedo·phile (*NAmE*) (*BrE* **paedo-**) /ˈpiːdəʊfaɪl; *NAmE* -doʊ-/ *noun* a person who is sexually attracted to children 戀童癖者

pedo·philia (*NAmE*) (*BrE* **paedo-**) *noun* [U] the condition of being sexually attracted to children; sexual activity with children 戀童癖；與兒童的性行為

pee /piː/ *verb, noun*

■ *verb* (**peed**, **peed**) [I] (*informal*) to pass waste liquid from your body 撒尿 SYN **urinate**：*I need to pee.* 我要撒尿。

■ *noun* (*informal*) **1** [sing.] an act of passing liquid waste from your body 撒尿：(*BrE*) *to go for a pee* 去撒尿 ◇ *to have a pee* 去小便 ◇ (*NAmE*) *to take a pee* 尿尿 **2** [U] liquid waste passed from your body; URINE 尿；小便

peek /piːk/ *verb* **1** [I] to look at sth quickly and secretly because you should not be looking at it 窺視；偷看 SYN **peep**：*No peeking!* 禁止窺探！◇ **+ adv./prep.** *She peeked at the audience from behind the curtain.* 她從帷幕後面窺視了一下觀眾。◇ *I couldn't resist peeking in the drawer.* 我不由得偷看了一下抽屜裏面。 **2** [I] **~ out/over/through, etc.** to be just visible 微露出；探出：*Her feet peeked out from the end of the blanket.* 她的腳從毯子末端露了出來。 ▶ **peek** *noun* [sing.]：*I took a quick peek inside.* 我匆匆向裏面偷看了一眼。

peek·aboo /ˌpiːkəˈbuː/ (*BrE* also **ˈpeep-bo**) *noun* [U] a simple game played to amuse young children, in which you keep hiding your face and then showing it again, saying 'Peekaboo!' or 'Peep-bo!' 藏貓貓（把臉隱藏而後閃現以逗幼兒的遊戲）；（做這種遊戲時發的聲音）貓兒

peel /piːl/ *verb, noun*

■ *verb* **1** [T] **~ sth** to take the skin off fruit, vegetables, etc. 剝（水果、蔬菜等的）皮；去皮：*to peel an orange/a banana* 剝橙子／香蕉 ◇ *Have you peeled the potatoes?* 你給土豆刮皮了嗎？ ➲ COLLOCATIONS at COOKING **2** [T, I] **~ (sth) away/off/back** to remove a layer, covering, etc. from the surface of sth; to come off the surface of sth 剝掉；揭掉；剝落：*Carefully peel away the lining paper.* 小心剝掉襯着的那層紙。◇ *The label will peel off if you soak it in water.* 標籤浸到水中就會脱落。 **3** [I] **~ (off)** (of a covering 覆蓋層) to come off in strips or small pieces 脱落；剝落：*The wallpaper was beginning to peel.* 壁紙開始剝落了。 **4** [I] (of a surface 表面) to lose strips or small pieces of its covering 起皮；剝落：*Put on some cream to stop your nose from peeling.* 抹點乳霜，以免你的鼻子再脱皮。◇ *The walls have begun to peel.* 牆壁開始破皮了。 IDM see EYE *n.*

PHR V **ˌpeel ˈoff** to leave a group of vehicles, aircraft, etc. and turn to one side （車輛、飛機等）離隊，轉向一側：*The leading car in the motorcade peeled off to the right.* 汽車隊的先導車轉向右側。 **ˌpeel ˈoff | ˌpeel (sth)↔ˈoff** (*informal*) to remove some or all of your clothes 脱衣服：*You look hot—why don't you peel off?* 你看來很熱，為何不脱掉衣服？◇ *He peeled off his shirt.* 他脱下了襯衣。 **ˌpeel ˈout** (*NAmE, informal*) to leave quickly and in a noisy way, especially in a car, on a motorcycle, etc. （尤指乘汽車、摩托車等）喧囂地迅速離去

■ *noun* **1** [U, C] the thick skin of some fruits and vegetables （某些水果、蔬菜的）外皮；果皮：*orange/lemon peel* 橙子／檸檬皮 ◇ (*NAmE* also) *an orange/a lemon peel* 一片橙子／檸檬皮 ➲ VISUAL VOCAB page V30 ➲ compare RIND (1), SKIN *n.* (4), ZEST (3) **2** **peels** [pl.] (*NAmE*) = PEELINGS

peel·er /ˈpiːlə(r)/ *noun* (usually in compounds 通常構成複合詞) a special type of knife for taking the skin off fruit and vegetables 去皮器；削皮器：*a potato peeler* 土豆去皮器 ➲ VISUAL VOCAB page V26

peel·ings /ˈpiːlɪŋz/ (*NAmE* also **peels**) *noun* [pl.] the skin of fruit or vegetables that has been removed 刮掉的果皮（或菜皮）

peep /piːp/ *verb, noun*

■ *verb* **1** [I] (**+ adv./prep.**) to look quickly and secretly at sth, especially through a small opening. （尤指通過小孔）窺視，偷看：*We caught her peeping through the keyhole.* 她從鎖孔偷看時被我們撞着了。◇ *Could I just peep inside?* 我能不能看一眼裏邊？◇ *He was peeping at her through his fingers.* 他從指縫偷看她。 **2** [I] **+ adv./prep.** to be just visible 微露出；部份現出：*The tower peeped above the trees.* 塔尖從樹梢上露出來。◇ *The sun peeped out from behind the clouds.* 太陽從雲層裏露了一下臉。 **3** [I, T] **~ (sth)** to make a short high sound; to make sth make this sound. （使）發出尖細的聲音，發出吱吱聲

■ *noun* **1** [C, usually sing.] a quick or secret look at sth 偷偷一瞥：*Dave* **took a quick peep** *at the last page.* 戴夫迅速地瞟了一下最後一頁。 **2** [sing.] (*informal*) something that sb says or a sound that sb makes 說話；出聲音：*We did* **not hear a peep out of** *the baby all night.* 我們整夜都沒聽到嬰兒出聲。 **3** [C] a short high sound like the one made by a young bird or by a whistle 啾啾聲；嘟嘟聲 **4** (also **peep ˈpeep**) [C] (*BrE*) a word for the sound of a car's horn, used especially by children 嘟嘟（兒語，指汽車喇叭聲）

peep-bo /ˈpiːpbəʊ; ˈpiːpəʊ; *NAmE* -boʊ; -poʊ/ *noun* [U] (*BrE*) = PEEKABOO

peep·hole /ˈpiːphəʊl; *NAmE* -hoʊl/ *noun* a small opening in a wall, door, etc. that you can look through （牆或門上等的）窺視孔，瞭望孔

ˌPeeping ˈTom *noun* (*disapproving*) a person who likes to watch people secretly when they are taking off their clothes 窺視者湯姆；有窺裸癖者 SYN **voyeur**

ˈpeep show *noun* **1** a series of moving pictures in a box that you look at through a small opening 拉洋片；西洋鏡 **2** a type of show in which sb pays to watch a woman take off her clothes in a small room 女子脱衣表演；偷窺秀

peer /pɪə(r); *NAmE* pɪr/ *noun, verb*

■ *noun* **1** [usually pl.] a person who is the same age or who has the same social status as you 身分（或地位）相同的人；同齡人；同輩：*She enjoys the respect of her peers.* 她受到同儕的尊敬。◇ *Children are worried about failing in front of their peers.* 兒童都怕在同伴面前失敗。◇ **Peer pressure** *is strong among young people* (= they want to be like other people of the same age). 年輕人受到強大的同輩壓力。 **2** (in Britain) a member of the NOBILITY （英國）貴族成員 ➲ see also LIFE PEER, PEERESS

■ *verb* [I] (**+ adv./prep.**) to look closely or carefully at sth, especially when you cannot see it clearly 仔細看；端詳：*We peered into the shadows.* 我們往陰暗處仔細瞧。◇ *He went to the window and peered out.* 他走到窗前仔細往外瞧。◇ *She kept peering over her shoulder.* 她不停地回頭看。◇ *He peered closely at the photograph.* 他聚精會神地端詳着相片。 ➲ SYNONYMS at STARE

peer·age /ˈpɪərɪdʒ; *NAmE* ˈpɪr-/ *noun* **1** [sing.] all the peers (2) as a group （統稱）貴族：*a member of the peerage* 一位貴族成員 **2** [C] the rank of a peer (2) or peeress 貴族的爵位

peer·ess /ˈpɪəres; *NAmE* ˈpɪrəs/ *noun* a female PEER (2) 女貴族

ˈpeer group *noun* a group of people of the same age or social status 同齡群體；社會地位相同的群體：*She gets on well with her peer group.* 她和同齡人相處融洽。◇ *peer-group pressure* 同儕壓力

peer·less /ˈpɪələs; *NAmE* ˈpɪrləs/ *adj.* better than all others of its kind 無雙的；傑出的；出眾的 SYN **unsurpassed**：*a peerless performance* 出色的表演

ˌpeer reˈview *noun* [U, C] a judgement on a piece of scientific or other professional work by others working in the same area （對科研、專業成果等作出的）同行評議，同行評估，同儕審查：*All research proposals are subject to peer review before selection.* 所有研究建議均須經過同行評議後再行篩選。 ▶ **ˌpeer-reˈviewed** *adj.*：*peer-reviewed journals* 實行同行評審制的期刊

ˌpeer-to-ˈpeer *adj.* [only before noun] (*computing* 計) (of a computer system 計算機系統) in which each computer can act as a SERVER for the others, allowing data to be shared without the need for a central server 對等的，點對點的（系統中的任何一台計算機均可用作服務器，允許文件共享）➲ compare CLIENT-SERVER

peeve /piːv/ *noun*
IDM **sb's pet ˈpeeve** (*NAmE*) (*BrE* **sb's pet ˈhate**) something that you particularly dislike 特別厭惡的東西

peeved /piːvd/ *adj.* **~ (about sth)** (*informal*) annoyed 惱怒的；生氣的：*He sounded peeved about not being told.* 沒人通知他，為此他氣哼哼的。

peev·ish /ˈpiːvɪʃ/ *adj.* easily annoyed by unimportant things; bad-tempered 愛生氣的；易怒的；脾氣壞的 **SYN** **irritable** ▸ **peev·ish·ly** *adv.*

pee·wit /ˈpiːwɪt/ *noun* = LAPWING

pegs 鈎；楔；栓；椿

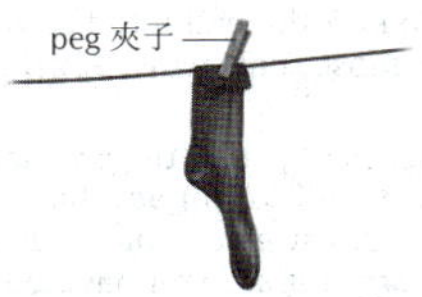

coat pegs
衣服掛鈎

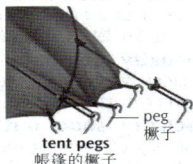

peg
橛子
tent pegs
帳篷的橛子

peg 夾子
clothes peg (*NAmE* **clothespin**)
晾衣夾子

peg
琴栓
tuning pegs
琴栓

peg /peg/ *noun, verb*
■ ***noun*** **1** a short piece of wood, metal or plastic used for holding things together, hanging things on, marking a position, etc.（木、金屬或塑料）釘子，楔子，橛子，短樁：*There's a peg near the door to hang your coat on.* 門邊有個鈎子可以掛衣服。 **2** (also **ˈtent peg**) a small pointed piece of wood or metal that you attach to the ropes of a tent and push into the ground in order to hold the tent in place（木製或金屬）帳篷短樁，橛子 **3** (also **ˈclothes peg**) (both *BrE*) (*NAmE* **clothes·pin**) a piece of wood or plastic used for attaching wet clothes to a clothes line 晾衣夾子 **4** (also **ˈtuning peg**) a wooden, metal or plastic screw used for making the strings of a musical instrument tighter or looser 弦鈕；琴栓 ➲ VISUAL VOCAB page V34
IDM **ˌoff the ˈpeg** (*BrE*) (*NAmE* **ˌoff the ˈrack**) (of clothes 衣服) made to a standard average size and not made especially to fit you 成品的；現成的：*He buys his clothes off the peg.* 他買的是成衣。◇ *off-the-peg fashions* 成衣的流行式樣 **ˌbring/ˌtake sb ˈdown a peg (or two)** to make sb realize that they are not as good, important, etc. as they think they are 煞某人的威風；挫某人的鋭氣：*He needed to be taken down a peg or two.* 需要煞煞他的威風。 **a peg to ˈhang sth on** something that gives you an excuse or opportunity to discuss or explain sth 藉口；理由；話頭 ➲ more at SQUARE *adj.*
■ ***verb*** (**-gg-**) **1** to fasten sth with pegs 用夾子夾住；用楔子釘住：**~ sth (out) + adv./prep.** *All their wet clothes were pegged out on the line.* 他們的濕衣服都夾在繩子上晾着。◇ **~ sth to sth** *She was busy pegging her tent to the ground.* 她忙着用橛子把帳篷釘牢在地上。 **2** [usually passive] to fix or keep prices, wages, etc. at a particular level 使工資、價格等固定於某水平（或與…掛鈎）：**~ sth (at sth)** *Pay increases will be pegged at 5%.* 工資調升率將限定在 5%。◇ **~ sth (to sth)** *Loan repayments are pegged to your income.* 分期付還貸款按你的收入計算。 **3 ~ sb as sth** (*NAmE, informal*) to think of sb in a particular way 視為；看作：*She pegged him as a big spender.* 她覺得他是個花錢大手大腳的人。 **IDM** see LEVEL *adj.*
PHR V **ˌpeg aˈway (at sth)** (*informal, especially BrE*) to continue working hard at sth or trying to achieve sth difficult 堅持不懈地工作（或努力） **ˌpeg sb/sth↔ˈback** (especially in sport 尤用於體育運動) to stop sb/sth from winning or increasing the amount by which they are ahead 扼止；止住；拖住：*Each time we scored we were pegged back minutes later.* 每次我們得分，幾分鐘後便被追上。 **ˌpeg ˈout** (*BrE, informal*) to die 死；斷氣

ˈpeg leg *noun* (*informal*) an artificial leg, especially one made of wood 假腿（尤指木製的）

pe·jora·tive /pɪˈdʒɒrətɪv; *NAmE* -ˈdʒɔːr-; -ˈdʒɑːr-/ *adj.* (*formal*) a word or remark that is **pejorative** expresses disapproval or criticism 貶損的；輕蔑的 **SYN** **derogatory**：*I'm using the word 'academic' here in a pejorative sense.* 我這裏使用的"學術"一詞是貶義的。 ▸ **pe·jora·tive·ly** *adv.*

Pe·kin·ese (also **Pe·king·ese**) /ˌpiːkɪˈniːz/ *noun* (*pl.* **Pe·kin·ese** or **Pe·kin·eses**) a very small dog with long soft hair, short legs and a flat nose 北京狗；獅子狗

pe·la·gic /pəˈlædʒɪk/ *adj.* (*technical* 術語) connected with, or living in, the parts of the sea that are far from land 公海的；遠洋的

peli·can /ˈpelɪkən/ *noun* a large bird that lives near water, with a bag of skin under its long beak for storing food 鵜鶘

ˌpelican ˈcrossing *noun* (in Britain) a place on a road where you can stop the traffic and cross by operating a set of TRAFFIC LIGHTS（英國由行人控制紅綠燈的）人行橫道，行人穿越道

pel·lagra /pəˈlægrə/ *noun* [U] a disease caused by a lack of good food, that causes the skin to crack and may lead to mental illness 糙皮病，玉米紅斑病（因缺乏營養而引起的皮膚皸裂，可導致精神障礙）

pel·let /ˈpelɪt/ *noun* **1** a small hard ball of any substance, often of soft material that has become hard 小球；團粒；丸：*food pellets for chickens* 團粒雞食 **2** a very small metal ball that is fired from a gun 小彈丸

pell-mell /ˌpelˈmel/ *adv.* (*old-fashioned*) very quickly and in a way that is not controlled 匆忙地；倉促；混亂地

pel·lu·cid /pəˈluːsɪd/ *adj.* (*literary*) extremely clear 清澈的；清晰的 **SYN** **transparent**

Pel·man·ism /ˈpelmənɪzəm/ *noun* [U] a game in which players must remember cards or other objects that they have seen 佩爾曼記憶訓練紙牌戲（參加者必須記住所見到的紙牌或其他物品）

pel·met /ˈpelmɪt/ (also **val·ance** especially in *NAmE*) *noun* a strip of wood or cloth above a window that hides the curtain rail 窗簾盒；窗簾短帷幔

pe·lota /pəˈlɒtə; -ˈləʊ-; *NAmE* -ˈloʊ-/ *noun* **1** [U] a game from Spain in which players hit a ball against a wall using a kind of BASKET attached to their hand 西班牙回力球運動（運動員戴籃狀手套對牆擊球） **2** [C] the ball used in the game of pelota 回力球

the pelo·ton /ˈpelətɒn; *NAmE* -tɑːn/ *noun* [sing.] (from *French*) the main group of riders in a bicycle race（自行車賽中的）主車群

pelt /pelt/ *verb, noun*
■ ***verb*** **1** [T] **~ sb (with sth)** to attack sb by throwing things at them 投物攻擊；向…投擲：*The children pelted him with snowballs.* 孩子們向他投擲雪球。 **2** [I] **~ (down)** (of rain 雨) to fall very heavily 傾瀉；下得很大 **3** [I] **+ adv./prep.** (*informal*) to run somewhere very fast 飛跑 **SYN** **dash**：*We pelted down the hill after the car.* 我們飛奔下山追趕那輛汽車。
■ ***noun*** the skin of an animal, especially with the fur or hair still on it（動物的）皮，毛皮
IDM **(at) full ˈpelt/ˈtilt** as fast as possible 急速；疾速；儘快

ˌpelvic ˈfloor *noun* (*anatomy* 解) the muscles at the base of the ABDOMEN, attached to the pelvis（骨）盆底肌

P

pel·vis /ˈpelvɪs/ *noun* the wide curved set of bones at the bottom of the body that the legs and SPINE are connected to 骨盆 ➲ VISUAL VOCAB page V59 ▸ **pel·vic** /ˈpelvɪk/ *adj.* [only before noun]：*the pelvic bones* 骨盆骨

pem·mican /ˈpemɪkən/ *noun* [U] a food made from crushed dried meat, originally made by Native Americans 乾肉餅，肉糜餅（最初為美洲土著的食品）

pen 0━ /pen/ *noun, verb*

▪ ***noun*** **1** 0━ (often in compounds 常構成複合詞) an instrument made of plastic or metal used for writing with ink 筆；鋼筆：*pen and ink* 鋼筆和墨水 ◇ *a new book from the pen of Martin Amis* 馬丁•埃米斯寫的新書 ➲ see also BALLPOINT PEN, FELT-TIP PEN, FOUNTAIN PEN **2** a small piece of land surrounded by a fence in which farm animals are kept 圈；圍欄；畜欄：*a sheep pen* 羊圈 **3** (*NAmE, slang*) = PENITENTIARY

IDM **the ˌpen is ˌmightier than the ˈsword** (*saying*) people who write books, poems, etc. have a greater effect on history and human affairs than soldiers and wars 筆誅勝於劍伐 **put pen to ˈpaper** to write or start to write sth 寫；動筆 ➲ more at SLIP *n.*

▪ ***verb*** (**-nn-**) **1 ~ sth** (*formal*) to write sth 寫：*He penned a letter to the local paper.* 他給當地報紙寫了一封信。**2 ~ sb/sth (in/up)** to shut an animal or a person in a small space（把…）關起來，圈起來：*At clipping time sheep need to be penned.* 在剪羊毛時，需要把羊圈起來。◇ *The whole family were penned up in one room for a month.* 全家人被關在一間屋子裏達一個月之久。

penal /ˈpiːnl/ *adj.* [usually before noun] **1** connected with or used for punishment, especially by law 懲罰的；刑罰的：*penal reforms* 刑罰改革 ◇ *the* ***penal system*** 刑罰制度 ◇ *Criminals could at one time be sentenced to* ***penal servitude*** (= prison with hard physical work). 曾經有個時期，罪犯可以被判服勞役刑。◇ *a* ***penal colony*** (= a place where criminals were sent as a punishment in the past) 罪犯流放地 **2** that can be punished by law 應受刑罰的：*a penal offence* 刑事犯罪 **3** very severe 嚴重的；嚴厲的：*penal rates of interest* 很重的利率

P

ˈpenal code *noun* a system of laws connected with crime and punishment 刑法典

pen·al·ize (*BrE* also **-ise**) /ˈpiːnəlaɪz/ *verb* **1 ~ sb (for sth)** to punish sb for breaking a rule or law by making them suffer a disadvantage 處罰；懲罰；處以刑罰：*You will be penalized for poor spelling.* 你拼寫不好將會受到處罰。**2** to punish sb for breaking a rule in a sport or game by giving an advantage to their opponent（體育運動中）判罰：**~ sb (for sth)** *He was penalized for time-wasting.* 他因拖延時間而受罰。◇ **~ sth** *Foul play will be severely penalized.* 比賽犯規將受到嚴厲處罰。**3 ~ sb** to put sb at a disadvantage by treating them unfairly 置於不利地位；不公正地對待：*The new law appears to penalize the poorest members of society.* 新法規似乎不利於社會中的最貧困者。

pen·alty /ˈpenəlti/ *noun* (*pl.* **-ies**) **1** a punishment for breaking a law, rule or contract 懲罰；處罰；刑罰：*to impose a penalty* 予以懲罰 ◇ *Assault* ***carries a*** *maximum* ***penalty*** *of seven years' imprisonment.* 侵犯人身罪可判處最高七年的監禁。◇ **~ (for sth)** *The penalty for travelling without a ticket is £200.* 無票乘車的罰款為 200 英鎊。◇ *Contractors who fall behind schedule incur heavy financial penalties.* 承包商如延誤工期將被處以巨額罰款。◇ *a penalty clause in a contract* 合同中的懲罰條款 ◇ *You can withdraw money from the account at any time* ***without penalty***. 您可以隨時從賬戶中提款，不收罰金。➲ see also DEATH PENALTY **2 ~ (of sth)** a disadvantage suffered as a result of sth 害處；不利：*One of the penalties of fame is loss of privacy.* 成名的弊端之一是失掉了隱私。**3** (in sports and games 體育運動) a disadvantage given to a player or a team when they break a rule（對犯規者的）判罰，處罰：*He incurred a ten-second penalty in the first round.* 他在第一輪受到停賽十秒鐘的處罰。**4** (in football (SOCCER) and some other similar sports 足球和其他類似體育運動) a chance to score a goal or point without any defending players, except the GOALKEEPER, trying to stop it; the goal or point that is given if it is successful. This chance is given because the other team has broken the rules. 點球；罰點球得分：*Two minutes later Ford equalized with a penalty.* 兩分鐘後，福特以一記點球將比分扳平。◇ *We were* ***awarded a penalty*** *after a late tackle.* 對方鏟球犯規後，我們得到了一個點球。◇ *I volunteered to* ***take the penalty*** (= be the person who tries to score the goal/point) 我自願主罰點球。◇ *He* ***missed a penalty*** *in the last minute of the game.* 在比賽的最後一刻，他罰失了點球。

IDM see PAY *v.*

ˈpenalty area (*BrE* also **ˈpenalty box**, **area**) *noun* (in football (SOCCER) 足球) the area in front of the goal. If the defending team breaks the rules within this area, the other team is given a penalty. 罰球區；禁區

ˈpenalty box *noun* **1** (*BrE*) = PENALTY AREA **2** (in ICE HOCKEY 冰上曲棍球) an area next to the ice where a player who has broken the rules must wait for a short time 犯規隊員臨時座席；受罰席

ˈpenalty kick (*BrE* also **ˈspot kick**) *noun* a kick that is taken as a PENALTY in the game of football (SOCCER)（足球比賽的）罰點球，罰球

ˈpenalty point *noun* (*BrE*) a note on sb's DRIVING LICENCE showing they have committed an offence while driving（司機的）違章駕駛記錄

ˌpenalty ˈshoot-out *noun* (in football (SOCCER) 足球) a way of deciding the winner when both teams have the same score at the end of a game. Each team is given a number of chances to kick the ball into the goal and the team that scores the most goals wins. 罰點球決定勝負

pen·ance /ˈpenəns/ *noun* **1** [C, usually sing., U] (especially in particular religions 尤見於某些宗教) an act that you give yourself to do, or that a priest gives you to do in order to show that you are sorry for sth you have done wrong 補贖；悔罪；修和聖事：*an act of penance* 贖罪善功 ◇ **~ for sth** *to do penance for your sins* 為自己的罪過做補贖 ➲ COLLOCATIONS at RELIGION **2** [sing.] something that you have to do even though you do not like doing it 苦差事；被迫做的事：*She regards living in New York as a penance; she hates big cities.* 她把住在紐約視為苦事，她討厭大都市。

ˌpen-and-ˈink *adj.* [usually before noun] drawn with a pen 用鋼筆畫的：*pen-and-ink drawings* 鋼筆畫

pence /pens/ (*BrE*) (*abbr.* **p**) *pl.* of PENNY

pen·chant /ˈpɒ̃ʃɒ̃; *NAmE* ˈpentʃənt/ *noun* **~ for sth** a special liking for sth 愛好；嗜愛 SYN **fondness**：*She* ***has a penchant for*** *champagne.* 她酷愛香檳酒。

pen·cil 0━ /ˈpensl/ *noun, verb*

▪ ***noun*** 0━ [C, U] a narrow piece of wood, or a metal or plastic case, containing a black or coloured substance, used for drawing or writing 鉛筆：*a pencil drawing* 鉛筆畫 ◇ *I'll get a pencil and paper.* 我去拿鉛筆和紙。◇ *She scribbled a note* ***in pencil***. 她用鉛筆草草寫了張便條。◇ *coloured pencils* 彩色鉛筆 ➲ VISUAL VOCAB page V69 ➲ see also EYEBROW PENCIL, PROPELLING PENCIL

▪ ***verb*** (**-ll-**, *especially US* **-l-**) **~ sth** to write, draw or mark sth with a pencil 用鉛筆寫（或畫、作記號）：*a pencilled portrait* 鉛筆畫像 ◇ *A previous owner had pencilled 'First Edition' inside the book's cover.* 這本書過去的主人在書的封面內頁上用鉛筆寫了"第一版"。

PHR V **ˌpencil sth/sb↔ˈin** to write down sb's name or details of an arrangement with them that you know might have to be changed later 臨時記下（約會的人名或安排細節）：*We've pencilled in a meeting for Tuesday afternoon.* 我們暫定星期二下午開會。◇ *Shall I pencil you in for Friday?* (= for a meeting) 我要不要先記下你星期五開會？

ˈpencil case *noun* a small bag, etc. for holding pencils and pens 鉛筆盒；鉛筆袋 ➲ VISUAL VOCAB page V70

ˈpencil-pusher *noun* (*NAmE*) = PEN-PUSHER

ˈpencil sharpener *noun* a small device with a blade inside, used for making pencils sharp 削鉛筆器；轉筆刀 ➲ VISUAL VOCAB page V69

ˈpencil skirt *noun* (*BrE*) a narrow straight skirt 窄身直筒裙；鉛筆裙

pen·dant /ˈpendənt/ *noun* a piece of jewellery that you wear around your neck on a chain（項鏈上的）垂飾，飾墜 ➲ VISUAL VOCAB page V65

pend·ing /ˈpendɪŋ/ *prep., adj.*

■ ***prep.*** (*formal*) while waiting for sth to happen; until sth happens 在等待…時期；直到…為止：*He was released on bail pending further inquiries.* 他獲得保釋，等候進一步調查。

■ ***adj.*** (*formal*) **1** waiting to be decided or settled 待定的；待決的：*Nine cases are still pending.* 尚有九宗案件待決。◇ *a* ***pending file/tray*** (= where you put letters, etc. you are going to deal with soon) 待辦卷宗 / 文件盤 **2** going to happen soon 即將發生的 SYN **imminent**：*An election is pending in Italy.* 意大利即將舉行選舉。◇ *his pending departure* 他即將離開

ˈpen drive *noun* = FLASH DRIVE

pen·du·lous /ˈpendjələs; *NAmE* -dʒələs/ *adj.* (*formal*) hanging down loosely and swinging from side to side 懸垂擺動的

pen·du·lum /ˈpendjələm; *NAmE* -dʒələm/ *noun* a long straight part with a weight at the end that moves regularly from side to side to control the movement of a clock 鐘擺：(*figurative*) *In education, the pendulum has swung back to traditional teaching methods.* 教育界又恢復了傳統教學法。◇ *the pendulum of public opinion* 輿論的轉變 ➲ picture at CLOCK

pene·trable /ˈpenətrəbl/ *adj.* (*formal*) that allows sth to be pushed into or through it; that can have a way made through it 可被穿透的；能穿透的：*soil that is easily penetrable with a fork* 能輕易下耙的土壤 OPP **impenetrable**

pene·trate /ˈpenətreɪt/ *verb* **1** [T, I] to go into or through sth 穿過；進入：**~ sth** *The knife had penetrated his chest.* 刀子刺入了他的胸膛。◇ *The sun's radiation penetrates the skin.* 太陽的輻射能透進皮膚。◇ (*figurative*) *The war penetrates every area of the nation's life.* 戰爭波及到全國國民生活的各個領域。◇ **~ into/through/to sth** *These fine particles penetrate deep into the lungs.* 這些微小的塵埃可深深地吸入肺部。 **2** [T, I] to succeed in entering or joining an organization, a group, etc. especially when this is difficult to do 滲透，打入（組織、團體等）：**~ sth** *They had penetrated airport security.* 他們已滲透機場保安組織。◇ *The party has been penetrated by extremists.* 極端分子已經打入了這個黨。◇ *This year the company has been trying to penetrate new markets* (= to start selling their products there). 今年這家公司一直試圖打入新市場。◇ **~ into sth** *The troops had penetrated deep into enemy lines.* 部隊已經深入敵軍防線。 **3** [T] **~ sth** to see or show a way into or through sth 看透；透過…看見：*Our eyes could not penetrate the darkness.* 我們的眼睛在黑暗中什麼也看不見。◇ *The flashlights barely penetrated the gloom.* 手電筒勉強照見那幽暗處。 **4** [T] **~ sth** to understand or discover sth that is difficult to understand or is hidden 洞察；發現；揭示：*Science can penetrate many of nature's mysteries.* 科學能揭示自然界的許多奧秘。 **5** [I, T] to be understood or realized by sb 被領悟；被理解：*I was at the door before his words penetrated.* 我走到門口才聽懂了他說的話。◇ **~ sth** *None of my advice seems to have penetrated his thick skull* (= he has not listened to any of it). 他那木腦袋似乎一點也聽不進我的忠告。 **6** [T] **~ sb/sth** (of a man 男人) to put the PENIS into the VAGINA or ANUS of a sexual partner（以陰莖）插入

pene·trat·ing /ˈpenətreɪtɪŋ/ *adj.* **1** (of sb's eyes or the way they look at you 眼睛或眼神) making you feel uncomfortable because the person seems to know what you are thinking 銳利的；犀利的；尖利的：*penetrating blue eyes* 銳利的藍眼睛◇ *a* ***penetrating gaze/look/stare*** 洞察一切的凝視 / 目光 / 注視 **2** (of a sound or voice 聲音或嗓音) loud and hard 響亮的；尖厲的 SYN **piercing**：*Her voice was shrill and penetrating.* 她的聲音尖厲刺耳。 **3** showing that you have understood sth quickly and completely 深刻的；精闢的：*a* ***penetrating comment/criticism/question*** 精闢的評論；入木三分的批評；尖銳的問題 **4** spreading deeply or widely 瀰漫的；滲透的：*a penetrating smell* 刺鼻的氣味◇ *the* ***penetrating cold/damp*** 刺骨的寒氣；很重的濕氣

pene·tra·tion /ˌpenəˈtreɪʃn/ *noun* [U] **1** the act or process of making a way into or through sth 穿透；滲透；進入：*The floor is sealed to prevent water penetration.* 地板加了密封塗料防止滲水。◇ *the company's successful penetration of overseas markets* 公司對海外市場的順利開拓 **2** the act of a man putting his PENIS into his partner's VAGINA or ANUS（男人陰莖的）插入

pene·tra·tive /ˈpenətrətɪv; *NAmE* -treɪtɪv/ *adj.* **1** (of sexual activity 性行為) involving putting the PENIS into sb's VAGINA or ANUS 行房的；交媾的：*penetrative sex* 行房事 **2** able to make a way into or through sth 能穿透的；能進入的：*penetrative weapons* 穿透性武器 **3** deep and thorough 深入的；徹底的：*a penetrative survey* 全面深入的調查

pen·friend /ˈpenfrend/ (*BrE*) (also **ˈpen pal** *NAmE, BrE*) *noun* a person that you make friends with by writing letters, often sb you have never met 筆友

pen·guin /ˈpeŋgwɪn/ *noun* a black and white bird that lives in the Antarctic. Penguins cannot fly but use their wings for swimming. There are several types of penguin, some of them very large but some of them quite small. 企鵝

peni·cil·lin /ˌpenɪˈsɪlɪn/ *noun* [U] a substance obtained from MOULD, used as a drug to treat or prevent infections caused by bacteria; a type of ANTIBIOTIC 青黴素；盤尼西林

pen·ile /ˈpiːnaɪl/ *adj.* [only before noun] (*technical* 術語) relating to the PENIS 陰莖的

pen·in·sula /pəˈnɪnsjələ; *NAmE* -sələ/ *noun* an area of land that is almost surrounded by water but is joined to a larger piece of land 半島：*the Iberian peninsula* (= Spain and Portugal) 伊比利亞半島

pen·in·su·lar /pəˈnɪnsjələ(r); *NAmE* -sələr/ *adj.* on or connected with a peninsula 半島上的；與半島有關的：*peninsular Spanish* (= that is spoken in Spain, not in Latin America) 半島本土西班牙語

penis /ˈpiːnɪs/ *noun* the organ on the body of a man or male animal that is used for URINATING and sex 陰莖

peni·tence /ˈpenɪtəns/ *noun* [U] a feeling of being sorry because you have done sth wrong 懺悔；悔罪；愧疚

peni·tent /ˈpenɪtənt/ *adj., noun*

■ ***adj.*** feeling or showing that you are sorry for having done sth wrong 懺悔的；後悔的；愧疚的 SYN **remorseful**

■ ***noun*** a person who shows that they are sorry for doing sth wrong, especially a religious person who wants God to forgive them 懺悔者；（尤指宗教）悔罪者

peni·ten·tial /ˌpenɪˈtenʃl/ *adj.* (*formal*) showing that you are sorry for having done sth wrong 悔悟的；悔罪的；懺悔的

peni·ten·tiary /ˌpenɪˈtenʃəri/ *noun* (*pl.* **-ies**) (also *slang* **pen**) (both *NAmE*) a prison 監獄

penknife 小摺刀

pen·knife /ˈpennaɪf/ *noun* (*pl.* **-knives** /-naɪvz/) (also **pock·et·knife** especially in *NAmE*) a small knife with one or more blades that fold down into the handle 小摺刀 ➲ VISUAL VOCAB page V20

pen·man·ship /ˈpenmənʃɪp/ *noun* [U] (*formal*) the art of writing by hand; skill in doing this 書寫藝術；書法；書寫技巧

ˈpen-name *noun* a name used by a writer instead of their real name 筆名 SYN **nom de plume** ➲ compare PSEUDONYM

P

pen·nant /ˈpenənt/ *noun* **1** a long narrow pointed flag, for example one used on a ship to give signals（船上用作信號等的）三角旗 **2** (in the US 美國) a flag given to the winning team in a sports league, especially in BASEBALL（獎給棒球等聯賽優勝隊的）錦旗

pen·ni·less /ˈpeniləs/ *adj.* having no money; very poor 一文不名的；窮困的 **SYN** **destitute** ➲ SYNONYMS at POOR

penn'orth /ˈpenəθ; *NAmE* -nərθ/ *noun* [usually sing.] (*old-fashioned, BrE*) = PENNYWORTH

Penn·syl·va·nia Dutch /ˌpensɪlveɪniə ˈdʌtʃ/ *noun* **1 the Pennsylvania Dutch** [pl.] a group of people originally from Germany and Switzerland who settled in Pennsylvania in the 17th and 18th centuries 德裔賓州人（17 至 18 世紀定居在賓夕法尼亞州的德國人和瑞士人後裔）**2** [U] a type of German mixed with English spoken by the Pennsylvania Dutch 賓州德語（德裔賓州人講的德語與英語的混合語）

penny 0‑ᴡ /ˈpeni/ *noun* (*pl.* **pen·nies** or **pence**)
HELP In senses 1 and 2, **pennies** is used to refer to the coins, and **pence** to refer to an amount of money. In sense 3, the plural is **pennies**. 在第 1 及第 2 義中，pennies 指硬幣，pence 指款額。在第 3 義中，複數形式為 pennies。
1 0‑ᴡ (*abbr.* **p**) a small British coin and unit of money. There are 100 pence in one pound (£1). 便士（英國的小硬幣和貨幣單位，1 英鎊為 100 便士）：*He had a few pennies in his pocket.* 他口袋裏有幾個便士的硬幣。◇ *That will be 45 pence, please.* 一共是 45 便士。◇ *They cost 20p each.* 這些東西每個要 20 便士。**2** (*abbr.* **d**) a British coin in use until 1971. There were twelve pennies in one SHILLING. 便士（英國 1971 年前使用的硬幣，十二便士為一先令）**3** 0‑ᴡ (*NAmE*) a cent 分
IDM ˌ**every** ˈ**penny** all of the money 所有的錢；每一分錢：*We collected £700 and every penny went to charity.* 我們募集了 700 英鎊，悉數捐給了慈善機構。ˌ**in for a** ˈ**penny,** ˌ**in for a** ˈ**pound** (*BrE, saying*) used to say that since you have started to do sth, it is worth spending as much time or money as you need to in order to complete it 一不做，二不休；有始有終 **not a** ˈ**penny** no money at all 分文沒有；根本不用錢：*It didn't cost a penny.* 那東西沒花一分錢。**the** ˈ**penny drops** (*informal, especially BrE*) used to say that sb has finally understood or realized sth that they had not understood or realized before 恍然大悟；終於明白；茅塞頓開 **a** ˌ**penny for your** ˈ**thoughts** | **a penny for them** (*saying*) used to ask sb what they are thinking about（用於詢問別人想什麼）你在呆呆地尋思什麼呢 **turn up like a bad** ˈ**penny** (*informal*) (of a person 人) to appear when they are not welcome or not wanted, especially when this happens regularly（不願碰上的）卻總出現；冤家路窄 ˌ**two**/ˌ**ten a** ˈ**penny** (*BrE*) (*NAmE* **a** ˌ**dime a** ˈ**dozen**) very common and therefore not valuable 普通得不值錢；（因常見而）價值低 ➲ more at PINCH *v.*, PRETTY *adj.*, SPEND *v.*

ˌ**penny** ˈ**black** *noun* an old British stamp worth one penny, first used in 1840. It was the first stamp in the world that could be stuck to an envelope. 黑便士（英國 1840 年首次發行的 1 便士郵票，是世界上第一枚可粘貼在信封上的郵票）

ˌ**penny-**ˈ**farthing** *noun* (*BrE*) an early type of bicycle with a very large front wheel and a very small back wheel 早期的自行車（前輪大，後輪小）

ˈ**penny-pinching** *adj.* (*disapproving*) unwilling to spend money 吝嗇的；慳吝的；小氣的 **SYN** **mean** ▸ ˈ**penny-pinching** *noun* [U]

ˌ**penny** ˈ**whistle** *noun* = TIN WHISTLE

penny·worth /ˈpeniwɜːθ; *NAmE* -wɜːrθ/ *noun* [sing.] (*old-fashioned, BrE*) as much as you can buy with a penny; a small amount of sth 值一便士的量；少量；些許
IDM **put in your two** ˈ**pennyworth** (also **put in your two** ˈ**penn'orth**) (both *BrE*) (*NAmE* **put in your two** ˈ**cents' worth**) (*informal*) to give your opinion about sth, even if other people do not want to hear it 發表意見（即使別人不想聽）

pen·ology /piːˈnɒlədʒi; pɪ-; *NAmE* -ˈnɑːl-/ *noun* [U] the scientific study of the punishment of criminals and the operation of prisons 刑罰學；監獄管理學 ▸ **pen·olo·gist** /piːˈnɒlədʒɪst; pɪ-; *NAmE* -ˈnɑːl-/ *noun*

ˈ**pen pal** (*especially NAmE*) (*BrE* also **pen·friend**) *noun* a person that you make friends with by writing letters, often sb you have never met 筆友

ˈ**pen-pusher** (*especially BrE*) (*NAmE* usually ˈ**pencil-pusher**) *noun* (*informal, disapproving*) a person with a boring job, especially in an office, that involves a lot of writing 抄寫匠；文書

pen·sion[1] 0‑ᴡ /ˈpenʃn/ *noun, verb* ➲ see also PENSION[2]
■ *noun* 0‑ᴡ an amount of money paid regularly by a government or company to sb who is considered to be too old or too ill/sick to work 養老金；退休金；撫恤金：*to receive an* ***old-age/a retirement pension*** 領養老金 / 退休金 ◇ *a* ***disability/widow's pension*** 殘疾 / 遺孀撫恤金 ◇ *a* ***state pension*** 國家撫恤金 ◇ *to live* ***on a pension*** 靠退休金生活 ◇ *to take out a* ***personal/private pension*** 獲得個人 / 私人撫恤金 ◇ *a* ***pension fund*** 退休金基金 ➲ COLLOCATIONS at AGE, FINANCE
■ *verb*
PHR V ˌ**pension sb** ˈ**off** (*especially BrE*) [usually passive] to allow or force sb to retire and to pay them a pension 准許某人退休，強迫某人退休（並發給養老金）：*He was pensioned off and his job given to a younger man.* 他被迫退休，工作交給了一個比他年輕的人。◇ (*informal, figurative*) *That car of yours should have been pensioned off years ago.* 你那輛汽車早就該報廢了。

pen·sion[2] /ˈpɒ̃sjɒ̃; *NAmE* pɑːnsiˈoʊn/ *noun* (from *French*) a small, usually cheap, hotel in some European countries, especially France（歐洲，尤指法國的）廉價小旅店 ➲ see also PENSION[1]

pen·sion·able /ˈpenʃənəbl/ *adj.* giving sb the right to receive a pension 有權享受養老金（或撫恤金、退休金）的：*people of pensionable age* 達到領養老金年齡的人 ◇ *pensionable pay* 可供計算退休金的薪酬

pen·sion·er /ˈpenʃənə(r)/ *noun* (*especially BrE*) a person who is receiving a pension, especially from the government 領養老金（或退休金、撫恤金）者：*an old-age pensioner* 領養老金的人 ➲ see also OAP, SENIOR CITIZEN

ˈ**pension plan** (*BrE* usually ˈ**pension scheme**) (*NAmE* also **re**ˈ**tirement plan**) *noun* a system in which you, and usually your employer, pay money regularly into a fund while you are employed. You are then paid a PENSION when you retire. 退休金計劃，養老金計劃（通常雇主定期交納基金，雇員退休後便可領取退休金）

pen·sive /ˈpensɪv/ *adj.* thinking deeply about sth, especially because you are sad or worried 沉思的；憂傷的；憂戚的：*a pensive mood* 沉重的心情 ◇ *to look pensive* 神情憂傷 ▸ **pen·sive·ly** *adv.*

penta- /ˈpentə/ *combining form* (in nouns, adjectives and adverbs 構成名詞、形容詞和副詞) five; having five 五；五…的：*pentagon* 五邊形 ◇ *pentathlon* 現代五項運動

penta·gon /ˈpentəgən; *NAmE* -gɑːn/ *noun* **1** [C] (*geometry* 幾何) a flat shape with five straight sides and five angles 五邊形；五角形 ➲ VISUAL VOCAB page V71 **2 the Pentagon** [sing.] the building near Washington DC that is the HEADQUARTERS of the US Department of Defense and the military leaders 五角大樓（美國國防部所在地）：*a spokesman for the Pentagon* 美國國防部發言人

pen·tagon·al /penˈtægənl/ *adj.* (*geometry* 幾何) having five sides 五邊形的；五角形的

penta·gram /ˈpentəgræm/ *noun* a flat shape of a star with five points, formed by five straight lines. Pentagrams are often used as magic symbols. 五角星形（常用於象徵魔力）

pen·tam·eter /penˈtæmɪtə(r)/ *noun* [C, U] (*technical* 術語) a line of poetry with five stressed syllables; the rhythm of poetry with five stressed syllables to a line 五音步詩行；五音步詩律

pent·ath·lon /penˈtæθlən/ *noun* a sporting event in which people compete in five different sports (running, riding, swimming, shooting and FENCING) 現代五項運動，五項全能運動（賽跑、騎馬、游泳、射擊、擊劍）

P

➲ compare BIATHLON, DECATHLON, HEPTATHLON, TRIATHLON

penta·tonic /ˌpentəˈtɒnɪk; NAmE -ˈtɑːn-/ *adj.* (*music* 音) related to or based on a SCALE of five notes 五聲音階的；五音的

Pente·cost /ˈpentɪkɒst; NAmE -kɔːst; -kɑːst/ *noun* [U, C] **1** (*BrE* also ˌ**Whit** ˈ**Sunday**) (in the Christian Church) the 7th Sunday after Easter when Christians celebrate the Holy Spirit coming to the APOSTLES 聖靈降臨節，五旬節（基督教節日，為復活節後的第 7 個星期日）**2** = SHAVUOTH

Pente·cos·tal /ˌpentɪˈkɒstl; NAmE -ˈkɔːs-; -ˈkɑːs-/ *adj.* connected with a group of Christian Churches that emphasize the gifts of the Holy Spirit, such as the power to heal the sick 五旬節派的（強調神恩作用，如治病的能力）▸ **Pente·costal·ist** *noun*

pent·house /ˈpenthaʊs/ *noun* an expensive and comfortable flat/apartment or set of rooms at the top of a tall building 頂層豪華公寓；閣樓套房

pent-up /ˌpent ˈʌp/ *adj.* **1** (of feelings, energy, etc. 感情、精力等) that cannot be expressed or released 壓抑的；積壓的：*pent-up frustration/energy* 壓抑的挫折感／精力 **2** having feelings that you cannot express 感情抑鬱的；難以抒懷的：*She was too pent-up to speak.* 她悶悶不樂，不想說話。

pen·ul·ti·mate /penˈʌltɪmət/ *adj.* [only before noun] immediately before the last one 倒數第二的 SYN **last but one**：*the penultimate chapter/day/stage* 倒數第二章／天／階段

pen·um·bra /pəˈnʌmbrə/ *noun* (*technical* 術語) **1** an area of shadow which is between fully dark and fully light（黑暗與光明之間的）半影 **2** (*astronomy* 天) the shadow made by the earth or the moon during a PARTIAL ECLIPSE（偏蝕期間的）半影 ➲ compare UMBRA

pen·uri·ous /pəˈnjʊəriəs; NAmE -ˈnʊr-/ *adj.* (*formal*) very poor 貧窮的；窮困的；赤貧的 SYN **destitute, penniless**

pen·ury /ˈpenjəri/ *noun* [U] (*formal*) the state of being very poor 貧困；貧窮 SYN **poverty**

peon /ˈpiːən/ *noun* **1** a worker on a farm in Latin America（拉丁美洲的）農場工人 **2** (*NAmE, humorous*) a person with a hard or boring job that is not well paid and not considered important 苦力；苦工

peony /ˈpiːəni/ *noun* (*pl.* **-ies**) a garden plant with large round white, pink or red flowers 牡丹；芍藥

people 🔑 /ˈpiːpl/ *noun, verb*

■ *noun* **1** 🔑 [pl.] persons; men, women and children 人：*At least ten people were killed in the crash.* 至少有十人在撞車事故中喪生。◇ *There were a lot of people at the party.* 有許多人參加聚會。◇ *Many young people are out of work.* 很多年輕人失業。**2** 🔑 [pl.] persons in general or everyone 人們；大家：*He doesn't care what people think of him.* 他不在乎人們怎樣看他。◇ *She tends to annoy people.* 她的舉止往往惹人煩。HELP Use **everyone** or **everybody** instead of 'all people'. 用 everyone 或 everybody，不用 all people。**3** 🔑 [C] all the persons who live in a particular place or belong to a particular country, race, etc.（統稱）人民，國民；民族，種族：*the French people* 法國人 ◇ *the native peoples of Siberia* 西伯利亞原住民族 ➲ see also TOWNSPEOPLE **4** 🔑 **the people** [pl.] the ordinary men and women of a country rather than those who govern or have a special position in society 平民；百姓；大眾：*the life of the common people* 普通人的生活 ◇ *It was felt that the government was no longer in touch with the people.* 人們覺得政府已脫離了民眾。➲ see also LITTLE PEOPLE **5** 🔑 [pl.] men and women who work in a particular type of job or are involved in a particular area of activity（統稱某行業或領域的）人：*a meeting with business people and bankers* 與商界和銀行界人士的會晤 ◇ *These garments are intended for professional sports people.* 這些服裝是為專業運動員製作的。**6** [pl.] (*literary*) the men, women and children that a person leads（某人轄下的）國民，人民，臣民，群眾：*The king urged his people to prepare for war.* 國王呼籲臣民百姓準備作戰。**7** [pl.] the men and women who work for you or support you 雇員；支持者；下屬人員：*I've had my people watching the house for a few days.* 我讓傭人照看了幾天房子。**8** [pl.] (*BrE, informal*) guests or friends 客人；朋友：*I'm having people to dinner this evening.* 今晚我在家裏宴請客人。**9** [pl.] (*old-fashioned*) the men, women and children that you are closely related to, especially your parents, grandparents, etc. 家人；親人；家屬；（尤指）父母，祖父母：*She's spending the holidays with her people.* 她正與家人一起度假。➲ see also BOAT PEOPLE, STREET PEOPLE, TRADESPEOPLE

IDM **of ˈall people** when you say **of all people**, you are emphasizing that sb is the person you would most or least expect to do sth（在所有的人中）偏偏，唯有：*She of all people should know the answer to that.* 在所有的人中，她是最應知道那個問題的答案的。**people (who live) in glass houses shouldn't throw ˈstones** (*saying*) you should not criticize other people, because they will easily find ways of criticizing you 身居玻璃房，投石招禍殃；自身毛病多，勿挑他人錯 ➲ more at MAN *n.*, THING

■ *verb* [usually passive] **~ sth (with sth)** to live in a place or fill it with people 居住在；把…擠滿人；住滿居民：*The town was peopled largely by workers from the car factory and their families.* 這個鎮上的居民大部份都是汽車廠的工人及其家屬。◇ *The ballroom was peopled with guests.* 舞廳裏滿堂賓客。

ˈ**people carrier** (also ˈ**people mover**) (both *BrE*) (*NAmE, BrE* **mini·van, Mini Van**™) *noun* a large car, like a van, designed to carry up to eight people 小型麪包車；（八人）小客車 ➲ VISUAL VOCAB page V52

ˈ**people person** *noun* (*informal*) a person who enjoys, and is good at, being with and talking to other people 喜歡（或擅長）交際的人

Pe·oria /piˈɔːriə/ *noun* a small city in the US state of Illinois. The opinions of the people who live there are considered to be typical of opinions in the whole of the US. 皮奧里亞（美國伊利諾伊州小城，據信此地居民的觀點在美國很有代表性）：*Ask yourself what the folks in Peoria will think of it.* 想一想皮奧里亞的人會如何看待這件事。

pep /pep/ *verb, noun*

■ *verb* (-pp-)

PHR V ˌ**pep sb/sth**↔ˈ**up** (*informal*) to make sb/sth more interesting or full of energy 增加…的趣味；使興致勃勃；激勵；使活躍 SYN **liven up**：*Pep up meals by adding more unusual spices.* 加些特別的調料使飯菜味道更佳。◇ *A walk in the fresh air will pep you up.* 在清新空氣中散散步會使你精神振奮。

■ *noun* [U] energy and enthusiasm 精力；活力；熱情

pep·per 🔑 /ˈpepə(r)/ *noun, verb*

■ *noun* **1** 🔑 [U] a powder made from dried BERRIES (called PEPPERCORNS), used to give a hot flavour to food 胡椒粉：*Season with **salt and pepper*** 用鹽和胡椒粉調味 ◇ *freshly **ground pepper*** 新研磨的胡椒粉 ➲ see also BLACK PEPPER, CAYENNE, WHITE PEPPER **2** (*BrE*) (also ˌ**sweet** ˈ**pepper** *BrE, NAmE*) (*NAmE* ˈ**bell pepper**) [C, U] a hollow fruit, usually red, green or yellow, eaten as a vegetable either raw or cooked 甜椒；柿子椒；燈籠椒 ➲ VISUAL VOCAB page V31

■ *verb* **~ sth** to put pepper on food（在食物上）撒胡椒粉：*peppered steak* 撒了胡椒粉的牛排 ◇ *Salt and pepper the potatoes.* 給土豆放上鹽和胡椒粉。

PHR V ˈ**pepper sb/sth with sth** [usually passive] to hit sb/sth with a series of small objects, especially bullets（以小物體）頻繁擊打；（尤指）向…不斷射擊 SYN **spray** ˈ**pepper sth with sth** [often passive] to include large numbers of sth in sth 大量加入：*He peppered his speech with jokes.* 他在講演中插入了許多笑話。

ˌ**pepper-and-ˈsalt** (also ˌ**salt-and-ˈpepper**) *adj.* (especially of hair 尤指頭髮) having two colours that are mixed together, especially a dark colour and a light one 兩色相間的；（尤指）深淺色相間的，花白的

pep·per·corn /ˈpepəkɔːn; NAmE -pərkɔːrn/ *noun* a dried BERRY from a tropical plant, that is crushed to make pepper 胡椒粒；乾胡椒籽 ➲ VISUAL VOCAB page V32

P

ˌpeppercorn ˈrent *noun* (*BrE*) a very low rent 極低的租金；象徵性租金

pep·per·mint /ˈpepəmɪnt; *NAmE* -pərm-/ *noun* **1** [U] a type of MINT (= a plant used to give flavour to food that produces an oil with a strong flavour) 胡椒薄荷；薄荷 ➲ compare SPEARMINT **2** [C] a sweet/candy flavoured with peppermint oil 薄荷糖

pep·per·oni /ˌpepəˈrəʊni; *NAmE* -ˈroʊ-/ *noun* [U] a type of spicy SAUSAGE 意大利辣肉腸：*a pepperoni pizza* 辣香腸比薩餅

ˈpepper pot (*especially BrE*) (*NAmE* usually **ˈpepper shaker**) *noun* a small container with holes in the top, used for putting pepper on food 胡椒瓶 ➲ VISUAL VOCAB page V22

pep·pery /ˈpepəri/ *adj.* **1** tasting of pepper 胡椒味的；辣的 **2** bad-tempered 脾氣不好的；愛發火的：*a peppery old man* 脾氣暴躁的老頭

ˈpep pill *noun* (*informal*) a pill containing a drug that gives you more energy or makes you happy for a short time 興奮藥丸

peppy /ˈpepi/ *adj.* (**pep·pier**, **pep·pi·est**) (*informal, especially NAmE*) lively and full of energy or enthusiasm 生機勃勃的；精力充沛的；滿腔熱情的：*a peppy advertising jingle* 熱情洋溢的廣告歌

ˈpep rally *noun* (*NAmE, informal*) a meeting of school students before a sports event to encourage support for the team （競賽前的）動員會，誓師集會：(*figurative*) *The Democrats held a pep rally on Capitol Hill yesterday.* 民主黨昨天在國會山召開了競選誓師大會。

pep·sin /ˈpepsɪn/ *noun* [U] (*biology* 生) a substance in the stomach that breaks down PROTEINS in the process of DIGESTION 胃蛋白酶

ˈpep talk *noun* (*informal*) a short speech intended to encourage sb to work harder, try to win, have more confidence, etc. 激勵的話；鼓舞士氣的話

P

pep·tic ulcer /ˌpeptɪk ˈʌlsə(r)/ *noun* an ULCER in the DIGESTIVE SYSTEM, especially in the stomach 消化系統潰瘍；（尤指）胃潰瘍

pep·tide /ˈpeptaɪd/ *noun* (*chemistry* 化) a chemical consisting of two or more AMINO ACIDS joined together 肽

per 0┳ /pə(r); *strong form* pɜː(r)/ *prep.* used to express the cost or amount of sth for each person, number used, distance travelled, etc. 每；每一：*Rooms cost £50 per person, per night.* 房價每人每晚 50 英鎊。◇ *60 miles per hour* 每小時 60 英里

IDM **as per sth** following sth that has been decided 按照；依據：*The work was carried out as per instructions.* 工作是按指示進行的。 **as per ˈnormal/ˈusual** (*informal*) in the way that is normal or usual; as often happens 照常；按慣例；一如既往：*Everyone blamed me as per usual.* 大家照例是責怪我。

per·am·bu·la·tion /pəˌræmbjuˈleɪʃn/ *noun* [C] (*formal* or *humorous*) a slow walk or journey around a place, especially one made for pleasure 漫步；散步；溜彎；兜風 ▸ **per·am·bu·late** /pəˈræmbjuleɪt/ *verb* [I, T] ~ (sth)

per·am·bul·ator /pəˈræmbjuleɪtə(r)/ *noun* **1** (*technical* 術語) a device consisting of a wheel on a long handle, which is pushed along the ground to measure distances 測距儀 **2** (*old-fashioned, BrE*) = PRAM

per annum /pər ˈænəm/ *adv.* (*abbr.* **p.a.**) (from *Latin*) for each year 每年：*earning £30 000 per annum* 每年賺 3 萬英鎊

per·cale /pəˈkeɪl; *NAmE* pərˈkeɪl/ *noun* [U] a type of cotton or POLYESTER cloth used for making sheets 高級密織棉布（用以製作被單）

per cap·ita /pə ˈkæpɪtə; *NAmE* pər/ *adj.* (from *Latin*) for each person 每人的；人均的：*Per capita income rose sharply last year.* 去年人均收入猛增。 ▸ **per cap·ita** *adv.*：*average earnings per capita* 人均收益

per·ceive **AW** /pəˈsiːv; *NAmE* pərˈs-/ *verb* (*formal*) **1** to notice or become aware of sth 注意到；意識到；察覺到：**~ sth** *I perceived a change in his behaviour.* 我注意到他舉止有些改變。◇ **~ that …** *She perceived that all was not well.* 她意識到一切都不順利。◇ **~ sb/sth to be/have sth** *The patient was perceived to have difficulty in breathing.* 發現病人呼吸困難。 **HELP** This pattern is usually used in the passive. 此句型通常用於被動語態。 **2** to understand or think of sb/sth in a particular way 將…理解為；將…視為；認為 **SYN** see：**~ sb/sth/yourself (as sth)** *This discovery was perceived as a major breakthrough.* 這一發現被視為一項重大突破。◇ *She did not perceive herself as disabled.* 她沒有把自己看成殘疾人。◇ **~ sb/sth to be/have sth** *They were widely perceived to have been unlucky.* 人們普遍認為他們的運氣不佳。 **HELP** This pattern is usually used in the passive. 此句型通常用於被動語態。

> **WORD FAMILY**
> perceive *verb*
> perception *noun*
> perceptive *adj.*
> perceptible *adj.*
> (≠ imperceptible)

per cent 0┳ (*especially BrE*) (*NAmE* usually **per·cent**) /pə ˈsent; *NAmE* pər ˈsent/ (*symb.* **%**) *noun, adj., adv.*

■ **noun** 0┳ (*pl.* **per cent**, **per·cent**) one part in every hundred 百分之…：*Poor families spend about 80 to 90 per cent of their income on food.* 貧困家庭大約花費收入的 80% 到 90% 購買食物。◇ *It is often stated that we use only 10 per cent of our brain.* 常有報告指人只運用了大腦的 10%。◇ *What per cent of the population is/are overweight?* 體重超重的人佔人口多大的百分比？

■ **adj., adv.** 0┳ by, in or for every hundred 每一百中：*a 15 per cent rise in price* 價格上揚 15% ◇ *House prices rose five per cent last year.* 去年房價上漲了百分之五。

per·cent·age **AW** /pəˈsentɪdʒ; *NAmE* pərˈs-/ *noun* **1** [C+sing./pl. v.] the number, amount, rate of sth, expressed as if it is part of a total which is 100; a part or share of a whole 百分率；百分比：*What percentage of the population is/are overweight?* 身體超重的人佔人口多大的百分比？◇ *A high percentage of the female staff are part-time workers.* 女職員中，兼職工作的人佔很高的比例。◇ *Interest rates are expected to rise by one* ***percentage point*** (= one per cent). 利率預計將提高一個百分點。◇ *The figure is* ***expressed as a percentage***. 數字是用百分率表示的。◇ *The results were analysed* ***in percentage terms***. 結果是按百分比分析的。 **2** [C, usually sing.] a share of the profits of sth 利潤的分成；提成：*He gets a percentage for every car sold.* 他每售出一輛車便可得到一份提成。

> **Grammar Point 語法說明**
>
> **expressing percentages 百分比的表示法**
>
> - Percentages (= numbers of per cent) are written in words as *twenty-five per cent* and in figures as *25%*. 百分比用文字表示有如 twenty-five per cent，用數字表示有如 25%。
> - If a percentage is used with an uncountable or a singular noun the verb is generally singular. 百分比與不可數名詞或單數名詞連用時，動詞一般為單數：*90% of the land is cultivated.* * 90% 的土地已耕種。
> - If the noun is singular but represents a group of people, the verb is singular in *NAmE* but in *BrE* it may be singular or plural. 如果是單數集合名詞，美式英語動詞用單數，英式英語用單、複數均可：*Eighty per cent of the work force* ***is/are*** *against the strike.* 百分之八十的勞動者都反對這次罷工。
> - If the noun is plural, the verb is plural. 如果名詞為複數，動詞用複數：*65% of children* ***play*** *computer games.* * 65% 的孩子玩電腦遊戲。

per·cent·ile /pəˈsentaɪl; *NAmE* pərˈs-/ *noun* (*technical* 術語) one of the 100 equal groups that a larger group of people can be divided into, according to their place on a scale measuring a particular value 百分位數：*Overall these students rank in the 21st percentile on the tests—that is, they did worse than 79 per cent of all children* *taking the test.* 這些考生的總體百分位排名佔第 21 位。就是說，79% 的應試兒童比他們考得好。

per·cep·tible /pəˈseptəbl; *NAmE* pərˈs-/ *adj.* **1** (*formal*) great enough for you to notice it 可察覺到的；看得出的 SYN **noticeable**：*a perceptible change/increase/decline/impact* 可以察覺的變化／增長／下降／影響 ◇ *The price increase has had no perceptible effect on sales.* 這次提價沒有對銷售產生明顯的影響。◇ *Her foreign accent was* ***barely perceptible***. 她的外國口音幾乎聽不出來。 **2** (*technical* 術語) that you can notice or feel with your senses 可感知的；可感覺的：*the perceptible world* 可感知的世界 OPP **imperceptible** ▸ **per·cep·tibly** /-əbli/ *adv.*：*Income per head rose perceptibly.* 人均收入明顯提高了。◇ *It was perceptibly colder.* 天氣明顯地冷了。

per·cep·tion AW /pəˈsepʃn; *NAmE* pərˈs-/ *noun* **1** [U] (*technical* 術語 or *formal*) the way you notice things, especially with the senses 知覺；感知：*our perception of reality* 我們對現實的認識 ◇ *visual perception* 視覺 ➲ see also EXTRASENSORY PERCEPTION **2** [U] (*formal*) the ability to understand the true nature of sth 洞察力；悟性 SYN **insight**：*She showed great perception in her assessment of the family situation.* 她對家庭狀況的分析顯示出敏銳的洞察力。 **3** [U, C] (*formal*) an idea, a belief or an image you have as a result of how you see or understand sth 看法；見解：*a campaign to change public perception of the police* 改變警察公眾形象的運動 ◇ **~ that …** *There is a general public perception that standards in schools are falling.* 公眾普遍認為，學校的水平都在下降。

per·cep·tive /pəˈseptɪv; *NAmE* pərˈs-/ *adj.* **1** (*approving*) having or showing the ability to see or understand things quickly, especially things that are not obvious 理解力強的；有洞察力的；思維敏捷的：*a* ***highly perceptive*** *comment* 見地高明的評論 ◇ *It was very perceptive of you to notice that.* 你能注意到此事，真夠敏銳的。 **2** (*technical* 術語 or *formal*) connected with seeing, hearing and understanding 視覺的；聽覺的；感覺的；知覺的：*our innate perceptive abilities* 我們天生的五官感覺能力 ▸ **per·cep·tive·ly** *adv.* **per·cep·tive·ness** *noun* [U]

per·cep·tual /pəˈseptʃuəl; *NAmE* pərˈs-/ *adj.* [only before noun] (*technical* 術語) relating to the ability to PERCEIVE things or the process of PERCEIVING 知覺的；感知的：*perceptual skills* 知覺技能

perch /pɜːtʃ; *NAmE* pɜːrtʃ/ *verb, noun*

■ ***verb*** **1** [I] **~ (on sth)** (of a bird 鳥) to land and stay on a branch, etc. 棲息；停留：*A robin was perching on the fence.* 一隻知更鳥落在籬笆上。 **2** [I, T] (*informal*) to sit or to make sb sit on sth, especially on the edge of it （使）坐，坐在…邊沿：**~ (on sth)** *We perched on a couple of high stools at the bar.* 我們坐在酒吧的幾張高腳凳上。◇ **~ sb/yourself (on sth)** *She perched herself on the edge of the bed.* 她坐在牀沿上。➲ SYNONYMS at SIT **3** [I] **~ (on sth)** to be placed on the top or the edge of sth 置於（頂上或邊上）：*The hotel perched precariously on a steep hillside.* 旅店立在陡峭的山坡上狀似搖搖欲墜。

■ ***noun*** **1** a place where a bird rests, especially a branch or bar for this purpose, for example in a bird's CAGE （鳥的）棲息處，棲木 **2** a high seat or position 高座；高處：*He watched the game from his precarious perch on top of the wall.* 他無視安全，高坐在牆頭上觀看比賽。 **3** (*pl.* **perch**) a FRESHWATER fish that is sometimes used for food 鱸魚；河鱸 IDM see KNOCK *v.*

per·chance /pəˈtʃɑːns; *NAmE* pərˈtʃæns/ *adv.* (*old use*) perhaps 也許；可能

perched /pɜːtʃt; *NAmE* pɜːrtʃt/ *adj.* **~ on, etc. sth** **1** (especially of a bird 尤指鳥) sitting or resting on sth 棲息；停留：*There was a bird perched on the roof.* 有一隻鳥落在屋頂上。 **2** placed in a high and/or dangerous position 被置於高處（或危險處）：*a hotel perched high on the cliffs* 高高矗立在懸崖上的旅館

per·cipi·ent /pəˈsɪpiənt; *NAmE* pərˈs-/ *adj.* (*formal*) having or showing the ability to understand things, especially things that are not obvious 敏銳的；理解透徹的；明察秋毫的 SYN **perceptive**

per·co·late /ˈpɜːkəleɪt; *NAmE* ˈpɜːrk-/ *verb* **1** [I] (**+ adv./prep.**) (of a liquid, gas, etc. 液體、氣體等) to move gradually through a surface that has very small holes or spaces in it 滲入；滲透；滲漏：*Water had percolated down through the rocks.* 水從岩縫間滲漏下去。 **2** [I] to gradually become known or spread through a group or society 逐漸流傳；傳開：*It had percolated through to us that something interesting was about to happen.* 我們聽到傳言說，將要發生一件有趣的事。 **3** [T, I] **~ (sth)** to make coffee in a percolator; to be made in this way （用滲濾式咖啡壺）濾煮；濾煮咖啡 ▸ **per·co·la·tion** /ˌpɜːkəˈleɪʃn; *NAmE* ˌpɜːrk-/ *noun* [U]

per·co·la·tor /ˈpɜːkəleɪtə(r); *NAmE* ˈpɜːrk-/ *noun* a pot for making coffee, in which boiling water is forced up a central tube and then comes down again through the coffee 滲濾式咖啡壺

per·cus·sion /pəˈkʌʃn; *NAmE* pərˈk-/ *noun* **1** [U] musical instruments that you play by hitting them with your hand or with a stick, for example drums 打擊樂器；敲擊樂器：*percussion instruments* 打擊樂器 ◇ *The track features Joey Langton* ***on percussion***. 唱片的這段樂曲是喬伊•蘭頓演奏的打擊樂。➲ VISUAL VOCAB page V35 **2 the percussion** [sing.] (also **perˈcussion section** [C]) the players of percussion instruments in an ORCHESTRA （管弦樂團的）打擊樂器組 ➲ compare BRASS (2), STRINGS *n.* (6), WOODWIND

per·cus·sion·ist /pəˈkʌʃənɪst; *NAmE* pərˈk-/ *noun* a person who plays percussion instruments 打擊樂器演奏員

per·cus·sive /pəˈkʌsɪv; *NAmE* pərˈk-/ *adj.* (*technical* 術語) connected with sounds made by hitting things, especially PERCUSSION instruments 打擊聲的；打擊樂器聲的

per·cu·tan·eous /ˌpɜːkjuːˈteɪniəs; *NAmE* ˌpɜːrk-/ *adj.* (*medical* 醫) made or done through the skin 經皮的；通過皮膚的：*a percutaneous injection* 皮下注射

per diem /ˌpɜː ˈdiːem; *NAmE* ˌpɜːr/ *adj., noun* (from *Latin*, *especially NAmE*)

■ ***adj.*** [only before noun] (of money 錢) for each day 每日的；按日計的：*a per diem allowance* 每日津貼 ▸ **per diem** *adv.*：*He agreed to pay at specified rates per diem.* 他同意每天按規定的數額付款。

■ ***noun*** [U, C] money paid, for example to employees, for things they need to buy every day 日補貼；日津貼：*He will get $14 000 a year in per diem to help with the higher costs of living in Washington.* 他每年將得到 14 000 元的日補貼，以彌補華盛頓較高的生活費。

per·di·tion /pɜːˈdɪʃn; *NAmE* pɜːrˈd-/ *noun* [U] (*formal*) punishment that lasts for ever after death 永劫不復；墮地獄

pere·grin·ation /ˌperəgrɪˈneɪʃn/ *noun* [usually pl.] (*literary* or *humorous*) a journey, especially a long slow one （尤指漫長而緩慢的）旅程

pere·grine /ˈperɪgrɪn/ (also **ˌperegrine ˈfalcon**) *noun* a grey and white BIRD OF PREY (= a bird that kills other creatures for food) that can be trained to hunt for sport 游隼

per·emp·tor·ily /pəˈremptrəli/ *adv.* (*formal, disapproving*) in a way that allows no discussion or refusal 專橫地；霸道地；不容商量地：*She peremptorily rejected the request.* 她斷然拒絕了請求。

per·emp·tory /pəˈremptəri/ *adj.* (*formal, disapproving*) (especially of sb's manner or behaviour 尤指態度、舉止) expecting to be obeyed immediately and without question or refusal 強硬的；強制的；不容分辯的：*a peremptory summons* 強制性傳票 ◇ *The letter was peremptory in tone.* 信中的語氣強硬。

per·en·nial /pəˈreniəl/ *adj., noun*

■ ***adj.*** **1** continuing for a very long time; happening again and again 長久的；持續的；反複出現的：*the perennial problem of water shortage* 缺水這個老問題 ◇ *that perennial favourite, hamburgers* 漢堡包，永遠受人喜愛的食品 **2** (of plants 植物) living for two years or more 多年生的 ▸ **per·en·ni·al·ly** /-niəli/ *adv.*：*a perennially popular subject* 長年的熱門話題

■ ***noun*** any plant that lives for more than two years 多年生植物 ➲ compare ANNUAL *n.* (2), BIENNIAL

P

per·fect 0🔑 *adj., verb, noun*

■ **adj.** /ˈpɜːfɪkt; *NAmE* ˈpɜːrf-/ **1** 0🔑 having everything that is necessary; complete and without faults or weaknesses 完備的；完美的；完全的： *in perfect condition* 狀況極佳 ◇ *a perfect set of teeth* 一副完美的牙齒 ◇ *Well I'm sorry—but **nobody's perfect*** (= used when sb has criticized you). 呃，對不起。不過，人無完人嘛。 **2** 0🔑 completely correct; exact and accurate 完全正確的；準確的；地道的： *She speaks perfect English.* 她講一口地道的英語。◇ *a **perfect copy/fit/match*** 精確的副本；絕對合身；天作之合 ◇ *What **perfect timing**!* 時機掌握得恰到好處！ ➲ see also WORD-PERFECT **3** 0🔑 the best of its kind 優秀的；最佳的： *a **perfect example** of the painter's early style* 這位畫家早期風格的典範 ◇ *the **perfect crime*** (= one in which the criminal is never discovered) 一樁無頭案 **4** 0🔑 excellent; very good 極好的；很好的： *The weather was perfect.* 天氣好極了。 ➲ SYNONYMS at EXCELLENT **5** 0🔑 **~ for sb/sth** exactly right for sb/sth 對…正合適的 SYN **ideal** : *It was a perfect day for a picnic.* 那天是野餐最理想的天氣。◇ *She's the perfect candidate for the job.* 她是這項工作的最佳人選。◇ *'Will 2.30 be OK for you?' 'Perfect, thanks.'* "2:30 對你合適嗎？" "正合適，謝謝。" **6** [only before noun] total; complete 全部的；完全的；純然的： *I don't know him—he's a perfect stranger.* 我不認識他，他是百分之百的陌生人。 **7** (*grammar* 語法) connected with the form of a verb that consists of part of the verb *have* with the past participle of the main verb, used to express actions completed by the present or a particular point in the past or future （動詞）完成時的，完成式的： *'I have eaten' is the present perfect tense of the verb 'to eat', 'I had eaten' is the past perfect and 'I will have eaten' is the future perfect.* * I have eaten 是動詞 eat 的現在完成時；I had eaten 是過去完成時；I will have eaten 是將來完成時。 ➲ see also FUTURE PERFECT, PAST PERFECT, PRESENT PERFECT IDM see PRACTICE *n.*, WORLD

■ **verb** /pəˈfekt; *NAmE* pərˈf-/ **~ sth** to make sth perfect or as good as you can 使完善；使完美；使完備： *As a musician, she has spent years perfecting her technique.* 身為音樂家，她多年來不斷在技藝上精益求精。

P

■ **noun** /ˈpɜːfɪkt; *NAmE* ˈpɜːrf-/ **the perfect** (also **the ˌperfect ˈtense**) [sing.] (*grammar* 語法) the form of a verb that expresses actions completed by the present or a particular point in the past or future, formed in English with part of the verb *have* and the past participle of the main verb （動詞的）完成時（態），完成式 ➲ see also FUTURE PERFECT, PAST PERFECT, PRESENT PERFECT

per·fec·tion /pəˈfekʃn; *NAmE* pərˈf-/ *noun* [U, sing.] **1** the state of being perfect 完善；完美： *physical perfection* 體格健全 ◇ *The fish was cooked **to perfection**.* 這魚烹得恰到好處。◇ *The novel achieves a perfection of form that is quite new.* 小說的形式新穎完美。◇ *His performance was perfection* (= sth perfect). 他的演技真是爐火純青。 **2** the act of making sth perfect by doing the final improvements 最後加工；完美；圓滿： *They have been working on the perfection of the new model.* 他們一直在努力完善新型號。 IDM see COUNSEL *n.*

per·fec·tion·ist /pəˈfekʃənɪst; *NAmE* pərˈf-/ *noun* (sometimes *disapproving*) a person who likes to do things perfectly and is not satisfied with anything less 完美主義者；至善論者 ► **per·fec·tion·ism** /pəˈfekʃənɪzəm; *NAmE* pərˈf-/ *noun* [U]

per·fect·ly 0🔑 /ˈpɜːfɪktli; *NAmE* ˈpɜːrf-/ *adv.*

1 0🔑 completely 完全地；非常；十分： *It's perfectly normal to feel like this.* 有這樣的感覺是完全正常的。◇ *It's perfectly good as it is* (= it doesn't need changing). 現在這樣已經非常好了。◇ *You **know perfectly well** what I mean.* 我的意思你是一清二楚的。◇ *To be **perfectly honest**, I didn't want to go anyway.* 說真心話，無論如何我是真的不想去。◇ *He stood perfectly still until the danger had passed.* 他一動不動地站在那裏，直到危險解除。◇ *'Do you understand?' 'Perfectly.'* "你明白嗎？" "完全明白。" ◇ (*old-fashioned*) *How perfectly awful!* 簡直是一塌糊塗！ **2** 0🔑 in a perfect way 完美地；完好地；圓滿地： *The TV works perfectly now.* 這台電視機現在運作得很好。◇ *It fits perfectly.* 那正合適。

ˌperfect ˈpitch *noun* [U] (*music* 音) the ability to identify or sing a musical note correctly without the help of an instrument 絕對音高，絕對音感（指不需借助樂器準確識別或唱出音符的能力）

ˌperfect ˈstorm *noun* [sing.] (*especially NAmE*) an occasion when several bad things happen at the same time, creating a situation that could not be worse 禍不單行；屋漏偏逢連夜雨

per·fidi·ous /pəˈfɪdiəs; *NAmE* pərˈf-/ *adj.* (*literary*) that cannot be trusted 不可信任的；背叛的；不忠的 SYN **treacherous**

per·fidy /ˈpɜːfədi; *NAmE* ˈpɜːrf-/ *noun* [U] (*literary*) unfair treatment of sb who trusts you 背叛；背信棄義 SYN **treachery**

per·for·ate /ˈpɜːfəreɪt; *NAmE* ˈpɜːrf-/ *verb* **~ sth** to make a hole or holes through sth 打孔；穿孔；打眼： *The explosion perforated his eardrum.* 爆炸震破了他的耳膜。◇ *a perforated line* (= a row of small holes in paper, made so that a part can be torn off easily) 齒孔線

per·for·ation /ˌpɜːfəˈreɪʃn; *NAmE* ˌpɜːrf-/ *noun* **1** [C, usually pl.] a small hole in a surface, often one of a series of small holes 齒孔： *Tear the sheet of stamps along the perforations.* 沿齒孔把郵票撕開。 **2** [U] (*medical* 醫) the process of splitting or tearing in such a way that a hole is left 穿孔；穿通： *Excessive pressure can lead to perforation of the stomach wall.* 過大的壓力會導致胃壁穿孔。

per·force /pəˈfɔːs; *NAmE* pərˈfɔːrs/ *adv.* (*old use* or *formal*) because it is necessary or cannot be avoided 必須；必定；勢必 SYN **necessarily**

per·form 0🔑 /pəˈfɔːm; *NAmE* pərˈfɔːrm/ *verb*

1 0🔑 [T] **~ sth** to do sth, such as a piece of work, task or duty 做；履行；執行 SYN **carry out** : *to perform an experiment/a miracle/a ceremony* 做實驗；創奇跡；舉行儀式 ◇ *She performs an important role in our organization.* 她在我們的組織中發揮着重要的作用。◇ *This operation has never been performed in this country.* 這個國家從未做過這種手術。◇ *A computer can perform many tasks at once.* 電腦能同時做多項工作。 **2** 0🔑 [T, I] **~ (sth)** to entertain an audience by playing a piece of music, acting in a play, etc. 演出；表演： *to perform somersaults/magic tricks* 表演空翻／魔術 ◇ *The play was first performed in 2007.* 這部劇於 2007 年首次上演。◇ *I'd like to hear it performed live.* 我希望聽現場演出。◇ *to perform on the flute* 吹奏長笛 ◇ *I'm looking forward to seeing you perform.* 我期待着看你演出。 **3** 0🔑 [I] **~ (well/badly/poorly)** to work or function well or badly 工作，運轉（好／不好）： *The engine seems to be performing well.* 發動機看起來運轉良好。◇ *The company has been performing poorly over the past year.* 這家公司過去一年業績欠佳。 IDM see MIRACLE

per·form·ance 0🔑 /pəˈfɔːməns; *NAmE* pərˈfɔːrm-/ *noun*

1 0🔑 [C] the act of performing a play, concert or some other form of entertainment 表演；演出： *The performance starts at seven.* 演出七點開始。◇ *an evening performance* 晚場演出 ◇ *a performance of Ravel's String Quartet* 拉威爾弦樂四重奏的演出 ◇ *a series of performances by the Kirov Ballet* 基洛夫芭蕾舞團的系列演出 ◇ *one of the band's rare **live performances*** 那個樂隊少見的一次現場演出 ➲ COLLOCATIONS at MUSIC **2** 0🔑 [C] the way a person performs in a play, concert, etc. 藝術上的表現；演技： *She **gave the** greatest **performance** of her career.* 她做了演藝生涯中最精彩的表演。◇ *an Oscar-winning performance from Kate Winslet* 凱特•溫斯萊特榮獲奧斯卡獎的演出 ➲ COLLOCATIONS at CINEMA **3** 0🔑 [U, C] how well or badly you do sth; how well or badly sth works 表現；性能；業績；工作情況： *the country's economic performance* 國家的經濟狀況 ◇ *It was an impressive performance by the French team.* 那是法國隊一次令人歎服的表現。◇ *The new management techniques aim to improve performance.* 新的管理技術旨在提高效率。◇ *He criticized the recent poor performance of the company.* 他批評公司近期業績不佳。◇ ***high-performance*** (= very powerful) *cars* 高性能汽車 ◇ ***performance indicators*** (= things that show how well or badly sth is working) 性能指標 ➲ compare

PAY-FOR-PERFORMANCE, PERFORMANCE-RELATED **4** [U, sing.] (*formal*) the act or process of performing a task, an action, etc. 做；執行；履行：*She has shown enthusiasm in the performance of her duties.* 她在工作中表現出對工作的熱忱。◇ *He did not want **a repeat performance** of the humiliating defeat he had suffered.* 他不想讓失敗的恥辱重演。 **5** [sing.] (*informal, especially BrE*) an act that involves a lot of effort or trouble, sometimes when it is not necessary（不必要的）麻煩，忙亂 SYN **carry-on**：*It's such a performance getting the children off to school in the morning.* 早上打發孩子上學可要忙亂一陣子呢。

per'formance art *noun* [U] an art form in which an artist gives a performance, rather than producing a physical work of art 行為藝術（通過行為表現而非實物創作所展示的藝術形式）

per'formance-enhancing *adj.* [only before noun] (of a substance, especially a drug) that people take so that they will be more successful in a sports competition（尤指藥物）興奮性的（以提高在體育競賽的表現）：*steroids and other performance-enhancing drugs* 類固醇等興奮劑

per,formance-re'lated *adj.* [only before noun] depending on how well a person does their job 基於工作表現的；按績效的：*Is there any evidence that **performance-related pay** actually improves performance?* 是否有證據表明績效工資確實會提高業績？ ➲ compare PAY-FOR-PERFORMANCE, PERFORMANCE (3)

per·forma·tive /pə'fɔːmətɪv; *NAmE* pər'fɔːrm-/ *adj.* (*grammar* 語法) when sb uses a performative word or expression, for example 'I promise' or 'I apologize', they are also doing sth (promising or apologizing) 表述行為的（如說 I promise 或 I apologize，同時表示許諾或道歉）➲ see also CONSTATIVE

per·form·er 🔑 /pə'fɔːmə(r); *NAmE* pər'fɔːrm-/ *noun* **1** 🔑 a person who performs for an audience in a show, concert, etc. 表演者；演出者；演員：*a brilliant/polished/seasoned performer* 卓越的／優雅的／嫻熟的表演者 **2** a person or thing that behaves or works in the way mentioned 表現得…者；表現了…者：*He was a poor performer at school and left with no qualifications.* 他在校學習成績不好，沒有畢業就離開學校。◇ *VW is the **star performer** of the motor industry this year.* 大眾汽車在本年度汽車行業中出類拔萃。

the per,forming 'arts *noun* [pl.] arts such as music, dance and drama which are performed for an audience 表演藝術

per·fume /'pɜːfjuːm; *NAmE* pər'fjuːm/ *noun, verb*
■ ***noun*** [C, U] **1** a liquid, often made from flowers, that you put on your skin to make yourself smell nice 香水：*a bottle of expensive perfume* 一瓶昂貴的香水 ◇ *We stock a wide range of perfumes.* 我們備有各種各樣的香水。◇ *the perfume counter of the store* 商店的香水櫃枱 ◇ *She was wearing too much perfume.* 她噴了太多的香水。 **2** a pleasant, often sweet, smell 芳香；香味；馨香 SYN **scent**：*the heady perfume of the roses* 玫瑰撲鼻的香味
■ ***verb*** [often passive] **1 ~ sth (with sth)** (*literary*) (especially of flowers 尤指花) to make the air in a place smell pleasant 使香氣瀰漫 SYN **scent**：*The garden was perfumed with the smell of roses.* 花園裏瀰漫着玫瑰的芳香。 **2 ~ sth (with sth)** to put perfume in or on sth 在…上撒香水；抹香水：*She perfumed her bath with fragrant oils.* 她沐浴時在浴缸內灑了些芳香油。 ▸ **per·fumed** *adj.*：*perfumed soap* 香皂

per·fumery /pə'fjuːməri; *NAmE* pər'f-/ *noun* (*pl.* **-ies**) **1** [C] a place where perfumes are made and/or sold 香水製造廠；香水商店 **2** [U] the process of making perfume 香水製造

per·func·tory /pə'fʌŋktəri; *NAmE* pər'f-/ *adj.* (*formal*) (of an action 行為) done as a duty or habit, without real interest, attention or feeling 敷衍的；例行公事般的；潦草的：*a perfunctory nod/smile* 敷衍的點頭／微笑 ◇ *They only made a perfunctory effort.* 他們只是敷衍了事。 ▸ **per·func·tor·ily** /-trəli/ *adv.*：*to nod/smile perfunctorily* 漫不經心地點頭／微笑

per·gola /'pɜːɡələ; *NAmE* 'pɜːrɡ-/ *noun* an ARCH in a garden/yard with a frame for plants to grow over and through 花架；蔓藤架 ➲ VISUAL VOCAB page V19

per·haps 🔑 /pə'hæps; præps; *NAmE* pər'h-/ *adv.* **1** 🔑 possibly 可能；大概；也許 SYN **maybe**：*'Are you going to come?' 'Perhaps. I'll see how I feel.'* "你來不來？" "也許來。要看我身體情況了。" ◇ *Perhaps he's forgotten.* 也許是他忘掉了。 **2** 🔑 used when you want to make a statement or opinion less definite（用以減弱肯定語氣）也許，可能：*This is perhaps his best novel to date.* 這也許是他迄今最好的小說。 **3** 🔑 used when making a rough estimate（用於粗略的估計）或許，可能：*a change which could affect perhaps 20% of the population* 一項可能影響 20% 人口的改革 **4** 🔑 used when you agree or accept sth unwillingly, or do not want to say strongly that you disapprove（表示勉強同意或其實不贊成）也許，大概：*'You could do it yourself.' 'Yeah, perhaps.'* "你可以自己做。" "嗯，也許吧。" **5** 🔑 used when making a polite request, offer or suggestion（用於委婉的請求、主動承諾或提出建議）也許，如果：*Perhaps it would be better if you came back tomorrow.* 如果你明天回來，也許更好。◇ *I think perhaps you've had enough to drink tonight.* 我想今晚你已經喝得夠多了。

Language Bank 用語庫

perhaps

Making an opinion sound less definite
以不確定的語氣表達意見

- Most cybercrime involves traditional crimes, such as theft and fraud, being committed in new ways. Phishing is **perhaps/possibly/probably** the best-known example of this. 大多數網絡犯罪都包含盜竊、詐騙等傳統犯罪，只是犯罪的方式有了新的變化。網絡誘騙大概是這類犯罪中最著名的例子。
- It **seems/appears** that the more personal data which organizations collect, the more opportunity there is for this data to be lost or stolen. 看來各種機構收集的個人資料越多，這些資料丟失或被盜的可能性就越大。
- **It seems clear that** introducing national ID cards would do little to prevent identity theft. 看來很明顯的是，採用全國通用身分證對防止身分盜用起不了什麼作用。
- **It could be argued that** the introduction of national ID cards might actually make identity theft easier. 可以說採用全國通用身分證實際上可能使身分盜用更容易。
- **It is possible that / It may be that** the only way to protect ourselves against DNA identity theft is to avoid the creation of national DNA databases. 或許保護自己免遭 DNA 身分盜用的唯一途徑就是不要建立全國 DNA 數據庫。

➲ Language Banks at IMPERSONAL, OPINION

per·igee /'perɪdʒiː/ *noun* (*astronomy* 天) the point in the ORBIT of the moon, a planet or other object in space when it is nearest the planet, for example the earth, around which it turns 近地點（繞地運動的天體軌道上離地心最近點）➲ compare APOGEE

peril /'perəl/ *noun* (*formal* or *literary*) **1** [U] serious danger 嚴重危險：*The country's economy is now in grave peril.* 現在，這個國家的經濟陷入了嚴重危機。 **2** [C, usually pl.] **~ (of sth)** the fact of sth being dangerous or harmful 禍害；險情：*a warning about the perils of drug abuse* 對吸毒之害的警告
IDM **do sth at your (own) 'peril** used to warn sb that if they do sth, it may be dangerous or cause them problems（警告對方）自冒風險

P

per·il·ous /ˈperələs/ *adj.* (*formal* or *literary*) very dangerous 危險的；艱險的 SYN **hazardous** ▸ **per·il·ous·ly** *adv.*：*We came* ***perilously close*** *to disaster.* 我們險些出了大亂子。

per·im·eter /pəˈrɪmɪtə(r)/ *noun* **1** the outside edge of an area of land （土地的）外緣，邊緣：*Guards patrol the perimeter of the estate.* 保安人員在莊園四周巡邏。◇ *a* ***perimeter fence/track/wall*** 圍繞四周的柵欄／小徑／牆 **2** (*mathematics* 數) the total length of the outside edge of an area or a shape 周長 ➲ compare CIRCUMFERENCE

peri·natal /ˌperɪˈneɪtl/ *adj.* (*technical* 術語) at or around the time of birth 臨產的；圍產期的：*perinatal care* 圍產期護理 ◇ *perinatal mortality* 圍產期死亡率

peri·neum /ˌperɪˈniːəm/ *noun* (*pl.* **peri·nea** /-ˈniːə/) (*anatomy* 解) the area between the ANUS and the SCROTUM or VULVA 會陰

period 0‒ AW /ˈpɪəriəd; NAmE ˈpɪr-/ *noun, adv., adj.*

■ ***noun***

▸ **LENGTH OF TIME** 時間長度 **1** 0‒ a particular length of time 一段時間；時期：*a period of consultation/mourning/uncertainty* 磋商／哀悼／形勢不明朗的期間 ◇ *The factory will be closed down over a 2-year period/a period of two years.* 這家工廠將在兩年內關閉。◇ *This compares with a 4% increase for the same period last year.* 這個數字與去年同期的 4% 升幅相若。◇ *This offer is available for a* ***limited period*** *only.* 這項優惠僅在限期內有效。◇ *All these changes happened over* ***a period of time.*** 所有這些變化都是在一段時間內發生的。◇ *The aim is to reduce traffic at* ***peak periods.*** 目的是降低高峰時段的交通流量。◇ *You can have it for a* ***trial period*** (= in order to test it). 這東西你可以試用一段時間。➲ see also COOLING-OFF PERIOD **2** 0‒ a length of time in the life of a particular person or in the history of a particular country（人生或國家歷史的）階段，時期，時代：*Which period of history would you most like to have lived in?* 你最喜歡生活在哪一個歷史時期？◇ *the post-war period* 戰後時期 ◇ *Like Picasso, she too had a blue period.* 和畢加索一樣，她也有過一段消沉時期。◇ *Most teenagers go through a period of rebelling.* 大多數青少年都要經歷一段叛逆期。**3** (*geology* 地) a length of time which is a division of an ERA. A period is divided into EPOCHS. 紀（地質年代，代下分紀）：*the Jurassic period* 侏羅紀

▸ **LESSON** 課時 **4** any of the parts that a day is divided into at a school, college, etc. for study 節；學時；課：*'What do you have next period?' 'French.'* "你下一節是什麼課？" "法語。" ◇ *a* ***free/study period*** (= for private study) 自習課

▸ **WOMAN** 婦女 **5** the flow of blood each month from the body of a woman who is not pregnant 月經；經期；例假：*period pains* 痛經 ◇ *monthly periods* 月經 ◇ *When did you last* ***have a period?*** 你上一次月經是什麼時候？➲ compare MENSTRUATION

▸ **PUNCTUATION** 標點 **6** (*NAmE*) (*BrE* **ˌfull ˈstop**) the mark (.) used at the end of a sentence and in some abbreviations, for example *e.g.* 句點；句號

■ ***adv.*** (*especially NAmE*) (*BrE* also **ˌfull ˈstop**) (*informal*) used at the end of a sentence to emphasize that there is nothing more to say about a subject（用於句末，強調不再多說）到此為止，就是這話：*The answer is no, period!* 答覆是不，不再說了！

■ ***adj.*** [only before noun] having a style typical of a particular time in history 具有某個時代特徵的：*period costumes/furniture* 代表某一時期的服裝／傢具

peri·od·ic AW /ˌpɪəriˈɒdɪk; NAmE ˌpɪriˈɑːdɪk/ (also *less frequent* **peri·od·ical** /-kl/) *adj.* [usually before noun] happening fairly often and regularly 間發性的；定期的；週期的：*Periodic checks are carried out on the equipment.* 設備定期進行檢查。▸ **peri·od·ic·al·ly** AW /-kli/ *adv.*：*Mailing lists are updated periodically.* 郵寄名單定期更新。

peri·od·ical AW /ˌpɪəriˈɒdɪkl; NAmE ˌpɪriˈɑːd-/ *noun* a magazine that is published every week, month, etc., especially one that is concerned with an academic subject（學術）期刊

the ˌperiodic ˈtable *noun* [sing.] (*chemistry* 化) a list of all the chemical elements, arranged according to their ATOMIC NUMBER 元素週期表

peri·odon·tal /ˌperiəˈdɒntl; NAmE -ˈdɑːn-/ *adj.* (*medical* 醫) related to or affecting the parts of the mouth that surround and support the teeth 牙周的

peri·odon·titis /ˌperiədɒnˈtaɪtɪs; NAmE -dɑːn-/ (*BrE* also **pyor·rhoea**) (*NAmE* also **pyor·rhea**) *noun* [U] (*medical* 醫) a condition in which the area around the teeth becomes sore and swollen, which may make the teeth fall out 牙周炎；牙周病

ˈperiod piece *noun* **1** a play, film/movie, etc. that is set in a particular period of history 古裝戲劇（或電影等） **2** a decorative object, piece of furniture, etc. that was made during a particular period of history and is typical of that period 具有某個時代特徵的裝飾品（或傢具等）

peri·pat·et·ic /ˌperipəˈtetɪk/ *adj.* (*formal*) going from place to place, for example in order to work 巡迴工作的；流動的：*a peripatetic music teacher* 一名流動的音樂教師

per·iph·eral /pəˈrɪfərəl/ *adj., noun*

■ ***adj.*** **1** (*formal*) not as important as the main aim, part, etc. of sth 次要的；附帶的：*peripheral information* 輔助信息 ◇ **~ to sth** *Fund-raising is peripheral to their main activities.* 相對於他們的主要活動，籌集資金是次要的。**2** (*technical* 術語) connected with the outer edge of a particular area 外圍的；周邊的：*the peripheral nervous system* 周圍神經系統 ◇ *peripheral vision* 周邊視覺 **3** (*computing* 計) (of equipment 設備) connected to a computer 與計算機相連的：*a peripheral device* 外圍設備 ▸ **per·iph·er·al·ly** /pəˈrɪfərəli/ *adv.*

■ ***noun*** (*computing* 計) a piece of equipment that is connected to a computer 外圍設備；周邊設備：*monitors, printers and other peripherals* 顯示器、打印機及其他外圍設備

per·iph·ery /pəˈrɪfəri/ *noun* [usually sing.] (*pl.* **-ies**) (*formal*) **1** the outer edge of a particular area 邊緣；周圍；外圍：*industrial development* ***on the periphery of*** *the town* 城鎮周邊地區工業的發展 ◇ *The condition makes it difficult for patients to see objects at the periphery of their vision.* 這種病症使患者難於看見視覺邊緣的物體。**2** the less important part of sth, for example of a particular activity or of a social or political group 次要部份；次要活動；邊緣：*minor parties* ***on the periphery*** *of American politics* 處於美國政治邊緣的小黨派

peri·phrasis /pəˈrɪfrəsɪs/ *noun* [U] **1** (*technical* 術語) the use of an indirect way of speaking or writing 迂迴表達；迂說 **2** (*grammar* 語法) the use of separate words to express a GRAMMATICAL relationship, instead of verb endings, etc. 加詞表達法，迂說法（非通過詞綴等表示語法關係） ▸ **peri·phras·tic** /ˌperɪˈfræstɪk/ *adj.*

peri·scope /ˈperɪskəʊp; NAmE -skoʊp/ *noun* a device like a long tube, containing mirrors which enable the user to see over the top of sth, used especially in a SUBMARINE (= a ship that can operate underwater) to see above the surface of the sea 潛望鏡

per·ish /ˈperɪʃ/ *verb* **1** [I] (*formal* or *literary*) (of people or animals 人或動物) to die, especially in a sudden violent way 死亡；暴死：*A family of four perished in the fire.* 一家四口死於此次火災之中。**2** [I] (*formal*) to be lost or destroyed 喪失；湮滅；毀滅：*Early buildings were made of wood and have perished.* 早期建築物為木質結構，已經消失殆盡。**3** [I, T] **~ (sth)** (*BrE*) if a material such as rubber **perishes** or **is perished**, it becomes damaged, weaker or full of holes（使橡膠等）老化，脆裂

IDM **ˌperish the ˈthought** (*informal* or *humorous*) used to say that you find a suggestion unacceptable or that you hope that sth will never happen（用於拒絕一項建議或希望某事永不發生）沒門兒，甭想了，下輩子吧：*Me get married? Perish the thought!* 我結婚？下輩子再說吧！

per·ish·able /ˈperɪʃəbl/ *adj.* (especially of food 尤指食物) likely to decay or go bad quickly 易腐爛的；易變質的：***perishable goods/foods*** 易腐爛變質的商品／食物

per·ish·ables /ˈperɪʃəblz/ *noun* [pl.] (*technical* 術語) types of food that decay or go bad quickly 易腐食物

per·ished /ˈperɪʃt/ *adj.* [not before noun] (*BrE, informal*) (of a person 人) very cold 極冷： *We were perished.* 我們冷極了。

per·isher /ˈperɪʃə(r)/ *noun* (*old-fashioned, BrE, informal*) a child, especially one who behaves badly 小孩；（尤指）淘氣包，討厭鬼

per·ish·ing /ˈperɪʃɪŋ/ *adj.* (*BrE, informal*) **1** extremely cold 冰冷的；酷寒的 SYN **freezing**： *It's perishing outside!* 外邊冷極了。◇ *I'm perishing!* 我都快凍死了！ **2** [only before noun] (*old-fashioned*) used to show that you are annoyed about sth 討厭的；可惡的： *I've had enough of this perishing job!* 這討厭的差事，我真受夠了！

peri·stal·sis /ˌperɪˈstælsɪs/ *noun* [U] (*biology* 生) the wave-like movements of the INTESTINE, etc. caused when the muscles contract and relax（腸壁等的）蠕動

peri·ton·eum /ˌperɪtəˈniəm/ *noun* (*pl.* **peri·ton·eums** or **peri·ton·ea** /-ˈniə/) (*anatomy* 解) the MEMBRANE (= very thin layer of TISSUE) on the inside of the ABDOMEN that covers the stomach and other organs 腹膜

peri·ton·itis /ˌperɪtəˈnaɪtɪs/ *noun* [U] (*medical* 醫) a serious condition in which the inside wall of the body becomes swollen and infected 腹膜炎

peri·win·kle /ˈperiwɪŋkl/ *noun* **1** [C, U] a small plant that grows along the ground 蔓長春花 **2** (*BrE* also **win·kle**) [C] a small SHELLFISH, like a SNAIL, that can be eaten 濱螺，玉黍螺（可食用）

per·jure /ˈpɜːdʒə(r); *NAmE* ˈpɜːrdʒ-/ *verb* **~ yourself** (*law* 律) to tell a lie in court after you have sworn to tell the truth 作偽證；發假誓 ▸ **per·jurer** /ˈpɜːdʒərə(r); *NAmE* ˈpɜːrdʒ-/ *noun*

per·jury /ˈpɜːdʒəri; *NAmE* ˈpɜːrdʒ-/ *noun* [U] (*law* 律) the crime of telling a lie in court 偽證；偽誓；偽證罪

perk /pɜːk; *NAmE* pɜːrk/ *noun, verb*

■ ***noun*** (also *formal* **per·quis·ite**) [usually pl.] something you receive as well as your wages for doing a particular job（工資之外的）補貼，津貼，額外待遇： *Perks offered by the firm include a car and free health insurance.* 公司給予的額外待遇包括一輛汽車和免費健康保險。◇ (*figurative*) *Not having to get up early is just one of the perks of being retired.* 不必早起只是退休生活的好處之一。

■ ***verb***

PHR V **ˌperk ˈup** | **ˌperk sb↔ˈup** (*informal*) to become or to make sb become more cheerful or lively, especially after they have been ill/sick or sad（使）振奮，活躍，快活 SYN **brighten**： *He soon perked up when his friends arrived.* 朋友一來他就精神起來了。**ˌperk ˈup** | **ˌperk sth↔ˈup** (*informal*) to increase, or to make sth increase in value, etc. 上揚；增加；使增值： *Share prices had perked up slightly by close of trading.* 收盤時股價略有上揚。 **ˌperk sth↔ˈup** (*informal*) to make sth more interesting, more attractive, etc. 使更有趣；使更誘人 SYN **liven up**： *ideas for perking up bland food* 給無味的食品增添味道的主意

perky /ˈpɜːki; *NAmE* ˈpɜːrki/ *adj.* (**perk·ier**, **perki·est**) (*informal*) cheerful and full of energy 高興的；快活的；精力充沛的 ▸ **perki·ness** *noun* [U]

perm /pɜːm; *NAmE* pɜːrm/ *noun, verb*

■ ***noun*** a way of changing the style of your hair by using chemicals to create curls that last for several months 捲髮；燙髮： *to have a perm* 燙鬈髮

■ ***verb*** **~ sth** to give sb's hair a perm 燙（髮）： *to have your hair permed* 燙鬈髮 ◇ *a shampoo for permed hair* 適用於燙過的頭髮的洗髮液 ➲ VISUAL VOCAB page V60

perma·frost /ˈpɜːməfrɒst; *NAmE* ˈpɜːrməfrɔːst; ˈpɜːrmə-frɑːst/ *noun* [U] (*technical* 術語) a layer of soil that is permanently frozen, in very cold regions of the world（寒帶）永凍土層；永凍層

per·man·ence /ˈpɜːmənəns; *NAmE* ˈpɜːrm-/ (also *less frequent* **per·man·ency** /-nənsi/) *noun* [U] the state of lasting for a long time or for all time in the future 永久；持久性： *The spoken word is immediate but lacks permanence.* 口頭之言便捷，但不持久。◇ *We no longer talk of the permanence of marriage.* 如今，再沒有人說婚姻要天長地久了。

per·man·ent 0‑w /ˈpɜːmənənt; *NAmE* ˈpɜːrm-/ *adj., noun*

■ ***adj.*** 0‑w lasting for a long time or for all time in the future; existing all the time 永久的；永恒的；長久的： *a permanent job* 固定工作 ◇ *permanent staff* 固定職工 ◇ *They are now living together on a permanent basis.* 他們現在是長期同住。◇ *The accident has not done any permanent damage.* 那場事故沒有造成什麼永久性損傷。◇ *a permanent fixture* (= a person or an object that is always in a particular place) 固定於某處的人或物品 OPP **impermanent**, **temporary** ▸ **per·man·ent·ly** 0‑w *adv.*： *The stroke left his right side permanently damaged.* 中風使他的右半身永久受損。◇ *She had decided to settle permanently in France.* 她已經決定永久定居法國。

■ ***noun*** (*old-fashioned, NAmE*) = PERM

ˌPermanent ˈResident Card *noun* an official card that shows that sb from another country is allowed to live and work in Canada（加拿大）永久居民卡

ˌPermanent ˈUndersecretary (also **ˌPermanent ˈSecretary**) *noun* (in Britain) a person of high rank in the CIVIL SERVICE, who advises a SECRETARY OF STATE（英國）常務次官 ➲ compare UNDERSECRETARY (1)

ˌpermanent ˈwave *noun* (*old-fashioned*) = PERM

perma·tan /ˈpɜːmətæn; *NAmE* ˈpɜːrmə-/ *noun* (*BrE, informal, humorous*) the brown skin colour that a person with pale skin gets from being in the sun, when they have this skin colour all year 持久古銅色（指曬黑後終年不退的膚色）

per·me·able /ˈpɜːmiəbl; *NAmE* ˈpɜːrm-/ *adj.* **~ (to sth)** (*technical* 術語) allowing a liquid or gas to pass through 可滲透的；可滲入的： *The skin of amphibians is permeable to water.* 兩棲動物的皮膚是透水的。◇ *permeable rocks* 滲透性岩石 OPP **impermeable** ▸ **per·mea·bil·ity** /ˌpɜːmiəˈbɪləti; *NAmE* ˌpɜːrm-/ *noun* [U]

per·me·ate /ˈpɜːmieɪt; *NAmE* ˈpɜːrm-/ *verb* (*formal*) **1** [T, I] (of a liquid, gas, etc. 液體、氣體等) to spread to every part of an object or a place 滲透；瀰漫；擴散： **~ sth** *The smell of leather permeated the room.* 屋子裏瀰漫着皮革的氣味。◇ **+ adv./prep.** *rainwater permeating through the ground* 滲入地下的雨水 **2** [T, I] (of an idea, an influence, a feeling, etc. 思想、影響、感情等) to affect every part of sth 感染；傳播；擴散： **~ sth** *a belief that permeates all levels of society* 深入社會各階層的看法 ◇ **+ adv./prep.** *Dissatisfaction among the managers soon permeated down to members of the workforce.* 管理人員的不滿情緒很快傳染給了全體職工。 ▸ **per·me·ation** /ˌpɜːmiˈeɪʃn; *NAmE* ˌpɜːrm-/ *noun* [U] (*formal*)

per·mis·sible /pəˈmɪsəbl; *NAmE* pərˈm-/ *adj.* (*formal*) acceptable according to the law or a particular set of rules 容許的；許可的： *permissible levels of nitrates in water* 水中硝酸鹽含量的容許度 ◇ **~ (for sb) (to do sth)** *It is not permissible for employers to discriminate on grounds of age.* 資方不得以年齡為由歧視職工。

per·mis·sion 0‑w /pəˈmɪʃn; *NAmE* pərˈm-/ *noun*
1 0‑w [U] the act of allowing sb to do sth, especially when this is done by sb in a position of authority 准許；許可；批准： **~ (for sth)** *You must **ask permission** for all major expenditure.* 一切重大開支均須報請批准。◇ **~ (for sb/sth) (to do sth)** *The school has been refused permission to expand.* 學校擴充未得到許可。◇ *No official **permission** has been **given** for the event to take place.* 這項活動未得到正式批准，不能舉行。◇ *She took the car **without permission**.* 她未經許可擅自使用了汽車。◇ *poems reprinted **by kind permission of** the author* 經作者慨然許可後重印的詩歌 ◇ (*formal*) *With your permission, I'd like to say a few words.* 如蒙允許，我想講幾句話。**2** [C, usually pl.] an official written statement allowing sb to do sth 許可證；書面許可： *The publisher is responsible for obtaining the necessary permissions to reproduce illustrations.* 出版者負責申辦准予使用他人插圖的必要許可文件。 ➲ see also PLANNING PERMISSION

per·mis·sive /pəˈmɪsɪv; *NAmE* pərˈm-/ *adj.* allowing or showing a freedom of behaviour that many people do not approve of, especially in sexual matters 放任的；縱

P

容的；姑息的；（尤指两性關係）放縱的：*permissive attitudes* 縱容的態度 ◇ *permissive parents* (= who allow their children a lot of freedom) 放任的父母 ▶ **per·mis·sive·ness** *noun* [U]

the per,missive so'ciety *noun* [sing.] (*often disapproving*) the changes towards greater freedom in attitudes and behaviour that happened in many countries in the 1960s and 1970s, especially the greater freedom in sexual matters 寬容社會，（尤指）性開放社會（20 世紀 60 和 70 年代出現在很多國家）

per·mit 🔑 *verb, noun*

■ ***verb*** /pə'mɪt; *NAmE* pər'm-/ (**-tt-**) (*formal*) **1** 🔑 [T] to allow sb to do sth or to allow sth to happen 允許；准許：**~ sth** *Radios are not permitted in the library.* 圖書館內不許使用收音機。◇ *There are fines for exceeding permitted levels of noise pollution.* 噪音超標會處以罰款。◇ **~ sb/yourself sth** *We were not permitted any contact with each other.* 我們不許彼此有任何接觸。◇ *Jim permitted himself a wry smile.* 吉姆勉強苦笑了一下。◇ **~ sb/yourself to do sth** *Visitors are not permitted to take photographs.* 參觀者請勿拍照。◇ *She would not permit herself to look at them.* 她避免看他們。◇ (*formal*) *Permit me to offer you some advice.* 請允許我向你提些建議。**2** 🔑 [I, T] to make sth possible 允許；使有可能：*We hope to visit the cathedral, if time permits.* 如果時間允許，我們希望能參觀一下主教座堂。◇ *I'll come tomorrow, **weather permitting*** (= if the weather is fine). 天氣許可的話，我明天過來。◇ **~ sth** *The password permits access to all files on the hard disk.* 這個密碼可調出硬盤上的所有文檔。◇ **~ sb/sth to do sth** *Cash machines permit you to withdraw money at any time.* 取款機可讓你隨時取款。

■ ***noun*** /'pɜːmɪt; *NAmE* 'pɜːrmɪt/ an official document that gives sb the right to do sth, especially for a limited period of time 許可證，特許證（尤指限期的）：*a **fishing/residence/parking, etc. permit*** 釣魚、居住、停車等許可證 ◇ *to **apply for a permit*** 申請許可證 ◇ *to **issue a permit*** 簽發許可證 ➲ see also WORK PERMIT

per·mu·ta·tion /,pɜːmju'teɪʃn; *NAmE* ,pɜːrm-/ *noun* [usually pl.] any of the different ways in which a set of things can be ordered 排列（方式）；組合（方式）；置換：*The possible permutations of x, y and z are xyz, xzy, yxz, yzx, zxy and zyx.* * x、y 和 z 的可能的組合方式為 xyz、xzy、yxz、yzx、zxy 和 zyx。

per·ni·cious /pə'nɪʃəs; *NAmE* pər'n-/ *adj.* (*formal*) having a very harmful effect on sb/sth, especially in a way that is gradual and not easily noticed 有害的，惡性的（尤指潛移默化地）

per·nick·ety /pə'nɪkəti; *NAmE* pər'n-/ (*especially BrE*) (*NAmE* usually **per·snick·ety**) *adj.* (*informal, disapproving*) worrying too much about unimportant details; showing this 愛挑剔的；吹毛求疵的 **SYN** **fussy**

per·or·ation /,perə'reɪʃn/ *noun* (*formal*) **1** the final part of a speech in which the speaker gives a summary of the main points（講話的）結尾，結論，總結 **2** (*disapproving*) a long speech that is not very interesting 冗長乏味的演說

per·ox·ide /pə'rɒksaɪd; *NAmE* -'rɑːk-/ (also **,hydrogen pe'roxide**) *noun* [U] a clear liquid used to kill bacteria and to BLEACH hair (= make it lighter) 過氧化物；過氧化氫：*a woman with peroxide blonde hair* 漂染金髮的女子

per·pen·dicu·lar /,pɜːpən'dɪkjələ(r); *NAmE* ,pɜːrp-/ *adj., noun*

■ ***adj.*** **1 ~ (to sth)** (*technical* 術語) forming an angle of 90° with another line or surface; vertical and going straight up 垂直的；成直角的：*Are the lines perpendicular to each other?* 這些直線相互垂直嗎？◇ *The staircase was almost perpendicular* (= very steep). 樓梯幾乎成垂直的了。**2** **Perpendicular** (*architecture* 建) connected with a style of ARCHITECTURE common in England in the 14th and 15th centuries, that makes use of vertical lines and wide ARCHES 垂直式的（英國 14、15 世紀盛行的建築風格）

■ ***noun*** **the perpendicular** [sing.] a line, position or direction that is exactly perpendicular 垂直線（或位置、方向）：*The wall is a little out of the perpendicular.* 牆壁有點傾斜。

per·pet·rate /'pɜːpətreɪt; *NAmE* 'pɜːrp-/ *verb* (*formal*) to commit a crime or do sth wrong or evil 犯（罪）；做（錯事）；幹（壞事）：**~ sth** *to **perpetrate a crime/fraud/massacre*** 犯罪；行騙；進行屠殺 ◇ **~ sth against/upon/on sb** *violence perpetrated against women and children* 針對婦女和兒童的暴力行為 ▶ **per·pet·ra·tion** /,pɜːpə'treɪʃn; *NAmE* ,pɜːrp-/ *noun* [U]

per·pet·ra·tor /'pɜːpətreɪtə(r); *NAmE* 'pɜːrp-/ *noun* a person who commits a crime or does sth that is wrong or evil 作惡者；行兇者；犯罪者：*the perpetrators of the crime* 該項罪行的犯案者

per·pet·ual /pə'petʃuəl; *NAmE* pər'p-/ *adj.* **1** [usually before noun] continuing for a long period of time without interruption 不間斷的；持續的；長久的 **SYN** **continuous**：*the perpetual noise of traffic* 持續不斷的交通噪聲 ◇ *We lived for years in a perpetual state of fear.* 多年來我們一直生活在恐懼中。**2** [usually before noun] frequently repeated, in a way that is annoying 一再反複的；無盡無休的；沒完沒了的 **SYN** **continual**：*How can I work with these perpetual interruptions?* 打擾不斷，讓我怎麼工作？**3** [only before noun] (of a job or position 工作或職位) lasting for the whole of sb's life 終身的；永久的：*He was elected perpetual president.* 他被選為終身會長。◇ (*humorous*) *She's a perpetual student.* 她是個終身學習者。▶ **per·petu·al·ly** /-tʃuəli/ *adv.*

per,petual 'motion *noun* [U] a state in which sth moves continuously without stopping, or appears to do so 永動：*We're all in a state of **perpetual motion** in this office* (= we're always moving around or changing things). 我們這個辦公室裏大家總在忙得團團轉。

per·petu·ate /pə'petʃueɪt; *NAmE* pər'p-/ *verb* **~ sth** (*formal*) to make sth such as a bad situation, a belief, etc. continue for a long time 使永久化；使持久化；使持續：*to perpetuate injustice* 持續造成不公正 ◇ *This system perpetuated itself for several centuries.* 這一制度維持了幾個世紀。◇ *Comics tend to perpetuate the myth that 'boys don't cry'.* 連環畫往往在延續着"男兒有淚不輕彈"的迷思。▶ **per·petu·ation** /pə,petʃu'eɪʃn; *NAmE* pər,p-/ *noun* [U]

per·petu·ity /,pɜːpə'tjuːəti; *NAmE* ,pɜːrpə'tuː-/ *noun* [U]
IDM **in perpetuity** (*formal*) for all time in the future 永遠；永久 **SYN** **forever**：*They do not own the land in perpetuity.* 他們並不永久擁有這片土地。

per·plex /pə'pleks; *NAmE* pər'p-/ *verb* [usually passive] **~ sb | it perplexes sb that …** if sth **perplexes** you, it makes you confused or worried because you do not understand it 迷惑；使困惑 **SYN** **puzzle**：*They were perplexed by her response.* 她的答覆令他們困惑不解。▶ **per·plex·ing** *adj.*：*a perplexing problem* 令人不解的問題

per·plexed /pə'plekst; *NAmE* pər'p-/ *adj.* confused and anxious because you are unable to understand sth; showing this 困惑的；迷惑不解的：*a perplexed expression* 困惑的表情 ◇ *She looked perplexed.* 她看來茫然若失。▶ **per·plex·ed·ly** /-ɪdli/ *adv.*

per·plex·ity /pə'pleksəti; *NAmE* pər'p-/ *noun* (*pl.* **-ies**) (*formal*) **1** [U] the state of feeling confused and anxious because you do not understand sth 困惑；迷惘 **SYN** **confusion**：*Most of them just stared at her in perplexity.* 他們多數人茫然地凝視着她。**2** [C, usually pl.] something that is difficult to understand 難以理解的事物；疑團：*the perplexities of life* 人生的困惑

per·quis·ite /'pɜːkwɪzɪt; *NAmE* 'pɜːrk-/ *noun* (*formal*) **1** [usually pl.] = PERK **2 ~ (of sb)** something to which sb has a special right because of their social position 特權；利益：*Politics used to be the perquisite of the property-owning classes.* 政治曾經是有產階級的特權。

perry /'peri/ *noun* [U] a slightly sweet alcoholic drink made from the juice of PEARS 梨酒 ➲ compare CIDER

per se /,pɜː 'seɪ; *NAmE* ,pɜːr/ *adv.* (from *Latin*) used meaning 'by itself' to show that you are referring to sth on its own, rather than in connection with other things 本身；本質上：*The drug is not harmful per se, but is dangerous when taken with alcohol.* 這種藥本身無害，但與酒同服就危險了。

per·se·cute /ˈpɜːsɪkjuːt; *NAmE* ˈpɜːrs-/ *verb* [often passive] **1 ~ sb (for sth)** to treat sb in a cruel and unfair way, especially because of their race, religion or political beliefs（因種族、宗教或政治信仰）迫害，殘害，壓迫：*Throughout history, people have been persecuted for their religious beliefs.* 人們因宗教信仰而受迫害的情況貫穿了整個歷史。◇ *persecuted minorities* 被迫害的少數群體 **2 ~ sb** to deliberately annoy sb all the time and make their life unpleasant 騷擾；打擾；為…找麻煩 SYN **harass**：*Why are the media persecuting him like this?* 新聞媒體為什麼總這樣揪住他不放？▶ **per·se·cu·tion** /ˌpɜːsɪˈkjuːʃn; *NAmE* ˌpɜːrs-/ *noun* [U, C]：*the victims of religious persecution* 宗教迫害的受難者 ➲ COLLOCATIONS at RACE

perseˈcution complex *noun* a type of mental illness in which sb believes that other people are trying to harm them 受迫害妄想症

per·se·cu·tor /ˈpɜːsɪkjuːtə(r); *NAmE* ˈpɜːrs-/ *noun* a person who treats another person or group of people in a cruel and unfair way 迫害者；殘害者

per·se·ver·ance /ˌpɜːsɪˈvɪərəns; *NAmE* ˌpɜːrsəˈvɪr-/ *noun* [U] (*approving*) the quality of continuing to try to achieve a particular aim despite difficulties 毅力；韌性；不屈不撓的精神：*They showed great perseverance in the face of difficulty.* 他們面對困難表現了堅強的毅力。◇ *The only way to improve is through hard work and dogged perseverance.* 要更上一層樓，唯一的途徑就是艱苦奮鬥，不屈不撓。

per·se·vere /ˌpɜːsɪˈvɪə(r); *NAmE* ˌpɜːrsəˈvɪr/ *verb* [I] (*approving*) to continue trying to do or achieve sth despite difficulties 堅持；孜孜以求：**~ (in sth/in doing sth)** *Despite a number of setbacks, they persevered in their attempts to fly around the world in a balloon.* 雖屢遭挫折，他們仍不斷嘗試乘氣球環遊世界。◇ **~ (with sth/sb)** *She persevered with her violin lessons.* 她孜孜不倦地學習小提琴。◇ *You have to persevere with difficult students.* 對難教的學生你必須堅持誨人不倦的精神。

per·se·ver·ing /ˌpɜːsɪˈvɪərɪŋ; *NAmE* ˌpɜːrsəˈvɪrɪŋ/ *adj.* [usually before noun] (*approving*) showing determination to achieve a particular aim despite difficulties 堅韌不拔的；不屈不撓的

Per·sian /ˈpɜːʃn; -ʒn; *NAmE* ˈpɜːrʒn/ *noun* **1** [C] a person from ancient Persia, or modern Persia, now called Iran 波斯人 **2** (also **Farsi**) [U] the official language of Iran 波斯語 **3** [C] = PERSIAN CAT ▶ **Per·sian** *adj.*

ˌPersian ˈcarpet (also **ˌPersian ˈrug**) *noun* a carpet of traditional design from the Near East, made by hand from silk or wool 波斯地毯

ˌPersian ˈcat (also **Per·sian**) *noun* a breed of cat with long hair, short legs and a round flat face 波斯貓

per·si·flage /ˈpɜːsɪflɑːʒ; *NAmE* ˈpɜːrs-/ *noun* [U] (*formal*) comments and jokes in which people laugh at each other in a fairly unkind but not serious way 取笑；插科打諢

per·sim·mon /pəˈsɪmən; *NAmE* pərˈs-/ *noun* a sweet fruit that looks like a large orange tomato 柿子 ➲ VISUAL VOCAB page V30

per·sist AW /pəˈsɪst; *NAmE* pərˈs-/ *verb* **1** [I, T] to continue to do sth despite difficulties or opposition, in a way that can seem unreasonable 頑強地堅持；執著地做：**~ (in doing sth)** *Why do you persist in blaming yourself for what happened?* 你何必為已發生的事沒完沒了地自責？◇ **~ (in sth)** *She persisted in her search for the truth.* 她執著地追求真理。◇ **~ (with sth)** *He persisted with his questioning.* 他問個不停。◇ **+ speech** *'So, did you agree or not?' he persisted.* "那麼你同意了沒有？"他叮問道。 **2** [I] to continue to exist 維持；保持；持續存在：*If the symptoms persist, consult your doctor.* 如果症狀持續不退，就得去看醫生。

per·sist·ence AW /pəˈsɪstəns; *NAmE* pərˈs-/ *noun* [U] **1** the fact of continuing to try to do sth despite difficulties, especially when other people are against you and think that you are being annoying or unreasonable 堅持；鍥而不捨：*His persistence was finally rewarded when the insurance company agreed to pay for the damage.* 保險公司同意賠償損失，他的堅持不懈終於得到了回報。◇ *It was her sheer persistence that wore them down in the end.* 最終把他們拖垮的純粹是她的不屈不撓。 **2** the state of continuing to exist for a long period of time 持續存在；維持：*the persistence of unemployment in the 1970s and 1980s* * 20 世紀 70 年代和 80 年代的持續失業狀況

per·sist·ent AW /pəˈsɪstənt; *NAmE* pərˈs-/ *adj.* **1** determined to do sth despite difficulties, especially when other people are against you and think that you are being annoying or unreasonable 執著的；不屈不撓的；堅持不懈的：*How do you deal with persistent salesmen who won't take no for an answer?* 你怎麼對付那些不輕言放棄、一直糾纏下去的推銷員？◇ *a **persistent offender*** (= a person who continues to commit crimes after they have been caught and punished) 慣犯 **2** continuing for a long period of time without interruption, or repeated frequently, especially in a way that is annoying and cannot be stopped 連綿的；持續的；反複出現的 SYN **unrelenting**：*persistent rain* 陰雨連綿 ◇ *a persistent cough* 持續不斷的咳嗽 ▶ **per·sist·ent·ly** AW *adv.*：*They have persistently denied claims of illegal dealing.* 他們一再否認進行非法交易的說法。◇ *persistently high interest rates* 居高不下的利率

perˌsistent ˌvegetative ˈstate *noun* (*medical* 醫) a condition in which a person's body is kept working by medical means but the person shows no sign of brain activity 持續植物狀態；植物人狀態

per·snick·ety /pəˈsnɪkəti; *NAmE* pərˈs-/ *adj.* (*NAmE*) = PERNICKETY

per·son 0-w /ˈpɜːsn; *NAmE* ˈpɜːrsn/ *noun* (*pl.* **people** /ˈpiːpl/ or, especially in formal use, 正式用語常作 **persons**)

1 0-w a human as an individual 人；個人：*What sort of person would do a thing like that?* 什麼人會幹那樣的事呢？◇ *He's a fascinating person.* 他是個魅力十足的人。◇ *What is she like as a person?* 她的人品怎麼樣？◇ *He's just the person we need for the job.* 他正是我們需要的適合這項工作的人。◇ *I had a letter from the people who used to live next door.* 我接到了過去的鄰居寫來的一封信。◇ *I'm not really a city person* (= I don't really like cities). 我不是一個很喜歡城市生活的人。➲ see also PEOPLE PERSON HELP Use **everyone** or **everybody** instead of 'all people'. 可用 everyone 或 everybody，不用 all people。 **2** 0-w (*formal* or *disapproving*) a human, especially one who is not identified 人；某人：*A certain person* (= somebody that I do not wish to name) *told me about it.* 有人告訴了我這件事。◇ *The price is $40 per person.* 價格為每人 40 元。◇ *This vehicle is licensed to carry 4 persons.* (= in a notice) 此車准乘 4 人。◇ (*law* 律) *The verdict was murder by a person or persons unknown.* 裁斷是一人或多人謀殺，兇手身分未明。➲ see also VIP **3** 0-w **-person** (in compounds 構成複合詞) a person working in the area of business mentioned; a person concerned with the thing mentioned 從事…工作（或擔任…職務）的人；人員：*a salesperson* 推銷員 ◇ *a spokesperson* 發言人 **4** (*grammar* 語法) any of the three classes of personal pronouns. The **first person** (*I/we*) refers to the person(s) speaking; the **second person** (*you*) refers to the person(s) spoken to; the **third person** (*he/she/it/they*) refers to the person(s) or thing(s) spoken about. 人稱（第一人稱 I/we 指說話人，第二人稱 you 指聽話的人，第三人稱 he/she/it/they 指談到的人或事物）

IDM **about/on your ˈperson** if you have or carry sth **about/on your person**, you carry it about with you, for example in your pocket 身上帶着；身上有 **in ˈperson** 0-w if you do sth **in person**, you go somewhere and do it yourself, instead of doing it by letter, asking sb else to do it, etc. 親自；親身 **in the person of sb** (*formal*) in the form or shape of sb 以某人的形骸；通過某人體現：*Help arrived in the person of his mother.* 來幫忙的是他的母親。➲ more at RESPECTER

per·sona /pəˈsəʊnə; *NAmE* pərˈsoʊnə/ *noun* (*pl.* **per·sonae** /-niː; -naɪ/ or **per·so·nas**) (*formal*) the aspects of a person's character that they show to other people, especially when their real character is different 偽裝；假象；人格面具：*His public persona is quite different from the family man described in the book.* 他的公開形象

P

與書中描寫的戀家男人相去甚遠。➲ see also DRAMATIS PERSONAE

per·son·able /ˈpɜːsənəbl; NAmE ˈpɜːrs-/ *adj.* (of a person 人) attractive to other people because of having a pleasant appearance and character 品貌兼優的；英俊瀟灑的

per·son·age /ˈpɜːsənɪdʒ; NAmE ˈpɜːrs-/ *noun* (*formal*) an important or famous person 要人；名人：*a royal personage* 王室要人

per·son·al /ˈpɜːsənl; NAmE ˈpɜːrs-/ *adj.*

▸ **YOUR OWN** 自己 **1** [only before noun] your own; not belonging to or connected with anyone else 個人的；私人的：*personal effects/belongings/possessions* 私人物品／財產／財物 ◇ *personal details* (= your name, age, etc.) 個人基本資料 ◇ *Of course, this is just a personal opinion.* 當然了，這只是個人意見。◇ *Coogan has run a* ***personal best*** *of just under four minutes.* 庫根跑出了剛好低於四分鐘的個人最好成績。◇ *The novel is written from* ***personal experience****.* 這部小說是根據個人親身經歷寫成的。◇ *Use stencils to add a few* ***personal touches*** *to walls and furniture.* 用型板給牆壁和傢具增添些個人風格。◇ *All hire cars are for* ***personal use*** *only.* 所有租賃車輛僅供個人使用。

▸ **FEELINGS/CHARACTER/RELATIONSHIPS** 感情；性格；關係 **2** [only before noun] connected with individual people, especially their feelings, characters and relationships 人際的；個性的：*Having good* ***personal relationships*** *is the most important thing for me.* 具有良好的人際關係對我最為重要。◇ *He was popular as much for his personal qualities as for his management skills.* 他的人品和他的管理技巧同樣受到人們的喜愛。

▸ **NOT OFFICIAL** 非公事 **3** not connected with a person's job or official position 私人的；私事的：*The letter was marked 'Personal'.* 信上標註着"私人"字樣。◇ *I'd like to talk to you about a personal matter.* 我想和你談點私事。◇ *I try not to let work interfere with my* ***personal life****.* 我盡量不讓工作干擾我的私生活。◇ *She's a personal friend of mine* (= not just somebody I know because of my job). 她是我的私人朋友。

▸ **DONE BY PERSON** 本人做 **4** [only before noun] done by a particular person rather than by sb who is acting for them 親自做的：*The President made a personal appearance at the event.* 總統親臨現場。◇ *I shall give the matter my personal attention.* 我將親自處理此事。

▸ **DONE FOR PERSON** 為個人 **5** [only before noun] made or done for a particular person rather than for a large group of people or people in general 為某人做的；個別的：*We offer a* ***personal service*** *to all our customers.* 我們為所有顧客提供個別服務。◇ *a* ***personal pension plan*** (= a pension organized by a private company for one particular person)（私營公司的）個人養老金計劃

▸ **OFFENSIVE** 冒犯 **6** referring to a particular person's character, appearance, opinions, etc. in a way that is offensive 針對個人的；人身攻擊的：*Try to avoid making personal remarks.* 要盡量避免針對個人的言論。◇ *There's no need to* ***get personal****!* 沒有必要搞人身攻擊嘛！◇ ***Nothing personal*** (= I do not wish to offend you), *but I do have to go now.* 我沒有得罪之意，不過我現在不得不告辭了。

▸ **CONNECTED WITH BODY** 身體 **7** [only before noun] connected with a person's body 人身的；身體的：*personal cleanliness/hygiene* 人體清潔；個人衛生

ˈpersonal ad *noun* a private advertisement in a newspaper, etc., especially from sb who is looking for a romantic or sexual partner（尤指交友或尋性伴侶的）私人廣告

ˌpersonal alˈlowance (*BrE*) (*NAmE* **ˌpersonal exˈemption**) *noun* the amount of money you are allowed to earn each year before you have to pay INCOME TAX 個人免稅額

ˌpersonal asˈsistant *noun* (*abbr.* **PA**) a person who works as a secretary or an assistant for one person 私人助理；私人秘書

ˈpersonal column *noun* a part of a newspaper or magazine for private messages or small advertisements（報刊的）人事廣告欄

ˌpersonal comˈputer *noun* (*abbr.* **PC**) a small computer that is designed for one person to use at work or at home 個人電腦；個人計算機 ➲ compare MAINFRAME, MICROCOMPUTER, MINICOMPUTER

ˈpersonal day *noun* (*NAmE*) a day that you take off work for personal reasons, but not because you are ill/sick or on holiday/vacation（非病假或節假日的）事假日 ➲ compare DUVET DAY

ˌpersonal ˌdigital asˈsistant *noun* = PDA

ˌpersonal exˈemption (*NAmE*) (*BrE* **ˌpersonal alˈlowance**) *noun* the amount of money you are allowed to earn each year before you have to pay INCOME TAX 個人免稅額

ˌpersonal inforˈmation manager *noun* (*abbr.* **PIM**) a computer program in which you write names, addresses, things that you have to do, etc. 個人信息管理員（程序）

ˌpersonal ˈinjury *noun* [U] (*law* 律) physical injury, rather than damage to property or to sb's reputation 人身傷害；人身損害

per·son·al·ity /ˌpɜːsəˈnæləti; NAmE ˌpɜːrs-/ *noun* (*pl.* **-ies**)
1 [C, U] the various aspects of a person's character that combine to make them different from other people 性格；個性；人格：*His wife has a strong personality.* 他妻子的個性很強。◇ *The children all have very different personalities.* 孩子們的性格各不相同。◇ *He maintained order by sheer force of personality.* 他純憑人格力量維護秩序。◇ *There are likely to be tensions and* ***personality clashes*** *in any social group.* 任何社會團體都容易出現關係緊張和性格衝突。 **2** [U] the qualities of a person's character that make them interesting and attractive 魅力；氣質；氣度：*We need someone with lots of personality to head the project.* 我們需要一位富有魅力的人來主持這個項目。 **3** [C] a famous person, especially one who works in entertainment or sport 名人，風雲人物（尤指娛樂界或體育界的）SYN **celebrity**：*personalities from the world of music* 音樂界名流 ◇ *a* ***TV/sports personality*** 電視圈／體育界名人 **4** [C] a person whose strong character makes them noticeable 性格鮮明的人；有突出個性的人：*Their son is a real personality.* 他們的兒子真是有個性。 **5** [U] the qualities of a place or thing that make it interesting and different 特色；特徵 SYN **character**：*The problem with many modern buildings is that they lack personality.* 許多現代建築物的問題在於缺乏特色。

persoˈnality cult *noun* (*disapproving*) a situation in which people are encouraged to show extreme love and admiration for a famous person, especially a political leader 個人迷信；個人崇拜

persoˈnality disorder *noun* (*technical* 術語) a serious mental condition in which sb's behaviour makes it difficult for them to have normal relationships with other people or a normal role in society 人格障礙，性格障礙（有嚴重異常人格特質，以至難以與人正常交往或影響社會功能）

per·son·al·ize (*BrE* also **-ise**) /ˈpɜːsənəlaɪz; NAmE ˈpɜːrs-/ *verb* **1** [usually passive] **~ sth** to mark sth in some way to show that it belongs to a particular person 在…上標明主人姓名：*All the towels were personalized with their initials.* 所有毛巾上都標有物主姓名的首字母。 **2 ~ sth** to design or change sth so that it is suitable for the needs of a particular person 為個人特製（或專設）：*All our courses are personalized to the needs of the individual.* 我們的全部課程都是針對個人需要設計的。 **3 ~ sth** to refer to particular people when discussing a general subject 針對個人；個人化：*The mass media tends to personalize politics.* 大眾傳媒往往把政治個人化。▸ **per·son·al·ized, -ised** *adj.*：*a highly personalized service* 高度個性化的服務 ◇ (*BrE*) *a personalized number plate* (= on a car) 標有姓名（首字母）的車牌

P

per·son·al·ly /ˈpɜːsənəli; *NAmE* ˈpɜːrs-/ *adv.* **1** used to show that you are giving your own opinion about sth 就本人而言；就個人意見：*Personally, I prefer the second option.* 就我個人而言，我傾向第二種選擇。◇ *'Is it worth the effort?' 'Speaking personally, yes.'* "值得為它費工夫嗎？" "就本人而言，值得。" **2** by a particular person rather than by sb acting for them 本人；親自：*All letters will be answered personally.* 一切信函都將由本人親自答覆。◇ *Do you know him personally* (= have you met him, rather than just knowing about him from other people)? 你本人認識他嗎？ **3** in a way that is connected with one particular person rather than a group of people 個別地；單個地 SYN **individually**：*He was personally criticized by inspectors for his incompetence.* 他因不稱職而受到督查專員的個別批評。◇ *You will be held personally responsible for any loss or breakage.* 如有丟失或損壞，將由你個人負責。 **4** in a way that is intended to be offensive 無禮地；冒犯地：*I'm sure she didn't mean it personally.* 我相信她絕無冒犯之意。 **5** in a way that is connected with sb's personal life rather than with their job or official position 私人地（與工作相對）：*Have you had any dealings with any of the suspects, either personally or professionally?* 你是否與任何嫌疑人有過私人或業務來往？

IDM **take sth ˈpersonally** to be offended by sth 認為某事針對自己而不悅：*I'm afraid he took your remarks personally.* 恐怕你的話激怒了他。

ˌpersonal ˈorganizer (*BrE* also **-iser**) *noun* a small file with loose sheets of paper in which you write down information, addresses, what you have arranged to do, etc.; a very small computer for the same purpose 私人記事本；電子記事簿 ➲ see also FILOFAX

ˌpersonal ˈpronoun *noun* (*grammar* 語法) any of the pronouns *I, you, he, she, it, we, they, me, him, her, us, them* 人稱代詞；人稱代名詞

ˌpersonal ˈshopper *noun* a person whose job is to help sb else buy things, either by going with them around a shop/store or by doing their shopping for them （私人）購物助理，購物代理人

ˌpersonal ˈspace *noun* [U] the space directly around where you are standing or sitting 個人空間（站立或坐着時與他人保持的距離範圍）：*He leaned towards her and she stiffened at this invasion of her personal space.* 他向她俯過身去，這種侵犯她個人空間的舉動讓她繃緊了身子。

ˌpersonal ˈstereo *noun* a small CD or CASSETTE player with HEADPHONES that you carry with you and use while you are moving around 個人音響（可隨身攜帶的備有耳機的激光唱片或磁帶小型放音機）

ˌpersonal ˈtrainer *noun* a person who is paid by sb to help them exercise, especially by deciding what types of exercise are best for them 私人健身教練

persona non grata /pɜːˌsəʊnə nɒn ˈɡrɑːtə; nəʊn; *NAmE* pɜːrˌsoʊnə nɑːn/ *noun* [U] (from *Latin*) a person who is not welcome in a particular place because of sth they have said or done, especially one who is told to leave a country by the government 不受歡迎的人（尤指政府令其離開某國者）

per·soni·fi·ca·tion /pəˌsɒnɪfɪˈkeɪʃn; *NAmE* pərˌsɑːn-/ *noun* **1** [C, usually sing.] **~ of sth** a person who has a lot of a particular quality or characteristic 體現某品質或特點的人；化身；典型 SYN **epitome**：*She was the personification of elegance.* 她是典雅的化身。 **2** [U, C] the practice of representing objects, qualities, etc. as humans, in art and literature; an object, quality, etc. that is represented in this way 擬人；人格化；擬人化的東西（或品質等）：*the personification of autumn in Keats's poem* 濟慈詩歌中對秋天的擬人化

per·son·ify /pəˈsɒnɪfaɪ; *NAmE* pərˈsɑːn-/ *verb* (**per·soni·fies**, **per·soni·fy·ing**, **per·soni·fied**, **per·soni·fied**) **1 ~ sth** to be an example of a quality or characteristic, or to have a lot of it 是…的典型；集中表現 SYN **typify**：*These children personify all that is wrong with the education system.* 這些兒童充分體現了教育制度的缺陷。◇ *He is kindness personified.* 他是仁慈的化身。 **2** [usually passive] **~ sth (as sb)** to show or think of an object, quality, etc. as a person 擬人化；把…人格化：*The river was personified as a goddess.* 這條河被人格化，成為一位女神。

per·son·nel /ˌpɜːsəˈnel; *NAmE* ˌpɜːrs-/ *noun* **1** [pl.] the people who work for an organization or one of the armed forces （組織或軍隊中的）全體人員，職員：*skilled personnel* 熟練人員 ◇ ***sales/technical/medical/security/military, etc. personnel*** 推銷、技術、醫務、保安、軍事等人員 **2** [U+sing./pl. v.] the department in a company that deals with employing and training people 人事部門 SYN **human resources**：*the **personnel department/manager*** 人事部門／經理 ◇ *She works in personnel.* 她在人事部工作。◇ *Personnel is/are currently reviewing pay scales.* 人事部現在正審核工資級別。

ˌpersonˈnel carrier *noun* a military vehicle for carrying soldiers 運兵車；士兵運輸車

ˌperson-to-ˈperson *adj.* [usually before noun] **1** happening between two or more people who deal directly with each other rather than through another person 通過個人接觸的；個人之間的：*Technical support is offered on a person-to-person basis.* 技術支持是向個人直接提供的。 **2** (*especially NAmE*) (of a telephone call 電話) made by calling the OPERATOR (= a person who works at a telephone exchange) and asking to speak to a particular person. If that person is not available, the call does not have to be paid for. 指定受話人的，叫人的（請接線員接通；如果指定受話人不在，可免交電話費）：*a person-to-person call* 叫人的電話

per·spec·tive AW /pəˈspektɪv; *NAmE* pərˈs-/ *noun* **1** [C] a particular attitude towards sth; a way of thinking about sth 態度；觀點；思考方法 SYN **viewpoint**：*a global perspective* 全面的看法 ◇ *Try to see the issue **from a different perspective**.* 試以不同的角度看待這件事。◇ *a report that looks at the education system **from the perspective of** deaf people* 從聾人的角度看待教育制度的報告 ◇ **~ on sth** *His experience abroad provides a wider perspective on the problem.* 他在國外的經歷使他以更廣闊的視角看待這個問題。 **2** [U] the ability to think about problems and decisions in a reasonable way without exaggerating their importance 客觀判斷力；權衡輕重的能力：*She was aware that she was losing all sense of perspective.* 她意識到自己正在失掉一切正確判斷的能力。◇ *Try to **keep** these issues **in perspective**.* 要盡量恰當地處理這些問題。◇ *Talking to others can often help to **put** your own problems **into perspective**.* 跟別人談談往往有助於正確處理自己的問題。◇ *It is important not to let things **get out of perspective**.* 重要的是不要把事情輕重倒置。 **3** [U] the art of creating an effect of depth and distance in a picture by representing people and things that are far away as being smaller than those that are nearer the front 透視法：*We learnt how to draw buildings **in perspective**.* 我們學習如何用透視法畫建築物。◇ *The tree on the left is **out of perspective**.* 左側的樹不成比例。 **4** [C] (*formal*) a view, especially one in which you can see far into the distance 景觀；遠景：*a perspective of the whole valley* 山谷全景

Per·spex™ /ˈpɜːspeks; *NAmE* ˈpɜːrs-/ (*BrE*) (*NAmE* **Plexi·glas™**) *noun* [U] a strong transparent plastic material that is often used instead of glass 珀斯佩有機玻璃

per·spi·ca·cious /ˌpɜːspɪˈkeɪʃəs; *NAmE* ˌpɜːrs-/ *adj.* (*formal*) able to understand sb/sth quickly and accurately; showing this 敏銳的；有洞察力的；精闢的：*a perspicacious remark* 入木三分的評論 ▸ **per·spi·ca·city** /ˌpɜːspɪˈkæsəti; *NAmE* ˌpɜːrs-/ *noun* [U]

per·spir·ation /ˌpɜːspəˈreɪʃn; *NAmE* ˌpɜːrs-/ *noun* [U] **1** drops of liquid that form on your skin when you are hot 汗；汗珠 SYN **sweat**：*Beads of perspiration stood out on his forehead.* 他的前額上掛着汗珠。◇ *Her skin was damp with perspiration.* 她的皮膚上汗津津的。 **2** the act of perspiring 排汗；出汗：*Perspiration cools the skin in hot weather.* 熱天出汗可使皮膚降温。

per·spire /pəˈspaɪə(r); *NAmE* pərˈs-/ *verb* [I] (*formal*) to produce sweat on your body 出汗；排汗；發汗 SYN **sweat**

per·suade /pəˈsweɪd; *NAmE* pərˈs-/ *verb* **1** to make sb do sth by giving them good reasons for doing it 勸說；說服：**~ sb to do sth** *Try to persuade*

P

him to come. 盡量勸他來。◇ **~ sb** *Please try and persuade her.* 請盡力說服她。◇ *She's always easily persuaded.* 她向來禁不住勸。◇ *I'm sure he'll come with a bit of persuading.* 我相信，勸一勸他就會來的。◇ **~ sb into sth/into doing sth** *I allowed myself to be persuaded into entering the competition.* 我擱不住人家的勸說，就參加了比賽。 **2** to make sb believe that sth is true 使信服；使相信 SYN **convince**：**~ sb/yourself that …** *It will be difficult to persuade them that there's no other choice.* 很難讓他們相信別無選擇。◇ *She had persuaded herself that life was not worth living.* 她自認為人生沒有價值。◇ **~ sb** *No one was persuaded by his arguments.* 沒人相信他的論點。◇ **~ sb of sth** (*formal*) *I am still not fully persuaded of the plan's merits.* 我還不能完全信服這個計劃的優點。

Which Word? 詞語辨析

persuade / convince

- The main meaning of **persuade** is to make someone agree to do something by giving them good reasons for doing it. * persuade 的主要意思為說服、勸說：*I tried to persuade her to see a doctor.* 我極力勸她去看醫生。 The main meaning of **convince** is to make someone believe that something is true. * convince 的主要意思為使確信、信服：*He convinced me he was right.* 他使我相信他是正確的。
- It is quite common, however, for each of these words to be used with both meanings, especially for **convince** to be used as a synonym for **persuade**. 不過，上述兩詞兩種含義都用的情況相當普遍，尤其是 convince 常作同義詞替代 persuade：*I persuaded/convinced her to see a doctor.* 我勸她去看醫生。 Some speakers of *BrE* think that this is not correct. 有些說英式英語的人認為此用法不正確。

P

per·sua·sion /pəˈsweɪʒn; *NAmE* pərˈs-/ *noun* **1** [U] the act of persuading sb to do sth or to believe sth 說服；勸說：*It didn't take much persuasion to get her to tell us where he was.* 我們沒費什麼口舌就讓她說出了他的下落。◇ *After a little gentle persuasion, he agreed to come.* 耐心勸說一下，他就同意來了。◇ *She has great powers of persuasion.* 她的游說能力極強。 **2** [C, U] a particular set of beliefs, especially about religion or politics （宗教或政治）信仰：*politicians of all persuasions* 信仰各異的政治人物 ◇ *every shade of religious persuasion* 形形色色的宗教信仰

per·sua·sive /pəˈsweɪsɪv; *NAmE* pərˈs-/ *adj.* able to persuade sb to do or believe sth 有說服力的；令人信服的：*persuasive arguments* 令人信服的論點 ◇ *He can be very persuasive.* 他有時很會說服人。 ▸ **per·sua·sive·ly** *adv.*：*They argue persuasively in favour of a total ban on handguns.* 他們以雄辯的論據支持全面禁用手槍。 **per·sua·sive·ness** *noun* [U]

pert /pɜːt; *NAmE* pɜːrt/ *adj.* **1** (especially of a girl or young woman 尤指青少年女子) showing a lack of respect, especially in a cheerful and amusing way 無禮的；冒失的；輕佻的 SYN **impudent**：*a pert reply* 無禮的答覆 **2** (of a part of the body 身體部位) small, firm and attractive 小巧玲瓏的；誘人的；硬實的：*a pert nose* 小巧筆挺的鼻子 ◇ *pert features* 俊俏的面龐 ▸ **pert·ly** *adv.*

per·tain /pəˈteɪn; *NAmE* pərˈt-/ *verb* [I] (*formal*) to exist or to apply in a particular situation or at a particular time 存在；適用：*Living conditions are vastly different from those pertaining in their country of origin.* 生活條件與他們的出生國大不相同。◇ *Those laws no longer pertain.* 那些法律已不適用了。

PHR V **perˈtain to sth/sb** (*formal*) to be connected with sth/sb 與…相關；關於：*the laws pertaining to adoption* 有關收養的法律

per·tin·acious /ˌpɜːtɪˈneɪʃəs; *NAmE* ˌpɜːrtnˈeɪ-/ *adj.* (*formal*) determined to achieve a particular aim despite difficulties or opposition 堅定不移的；堅決的；義無反顧的 ▸ **per·tin·acity** /ˌpɜːtɪˈnæsəti; *NAmE* ˌpɜːrtnˈæ-/ *noun* [U]

per·tin·ent /ˈpɜːtɪnənt; *NAmE* ˈpɜːrtnənt/ *adj.* (*formal*) appropriate to a particular situation 有關的；恰當的；相宜的 SYN **relevant**：*a* ***pertinent question/fact*** 有關的問題／事實 ◇ **~ to sth** *Please keep your comments pertinent to the topic under discussion.* 請勿發表與討論主題無關的言論。 ▸ **per·tin·ent·ly** *adv.* **per·tin·ence** /-əns/ *noun* [U]

per·turb /pəˈtɜːb; *NAmE* pərˈtɜːrb/ *verb* **~ sb** (*formal*) to make sb worried or anxious 使焦慮；使不安 SYN **alarm**：*Her sudden appearance did not seem to perturb him in the least.* 她的突然出現似乎一點也沒有令他不安。 ▸ **per·turbed** /-ˈtɜːbd; *NAmE* -ˈtɜːrbd/ *adj.*：*a perturbed young man* 煩惱的年輕人 ◇ **~ at/about sth** *She didn't seem perturbed at the change of plan.* 她對改變計劃似乎毫不在意。 OPP **unperturbed**

per·turb·ation /ˌpɜːtəˈbeɪʃn; *NAmE* ˌpɜːrtərˈb-/ *noun* **1** [U] (*formal*) the state of feeling anxious about sth that has happened 憂慮；不安；煩惱 SYN **alarm 2** [C, U] (*technical* 術語) a small change in the quality, behaviour or movement of sth 攝動；微擾；小變異：*temperature perturbations* 溫度的些微變化

per·use /pəˈruːz/ *verb* **~ sth** (*formal* or *humorous*) to read sth, especially in a careful way 細讀；研讀：*A copy of the report is available for you to peruse at your leisure.* 現有一份報告，供你閒暇時細讀。 ▸ **per·usal** /pəˈruːzl/ *noun* [U, sing.]：*The agreement was signed after careful perusal.* 合同是仔細閱讀以後才簽署的。

perv (also **perve**) /pɜːv; *NAmE* pɜːrv/ *noun* (*informal*) **1** = PERVERT **2** (*AustralE, NZE*) a look at sb/sth that shows sexual interest in them or it, in an unpleasant way 色迷迷地看；用好色的眼神看

per·vade /pəˈveɪd; *NAmE* pərˈv-/ *verb* **~ sth** (*formal*) to spread through and be noticeable in every part of sth 滲透；瀰漫；遍及 SYN **permeate**：*a pervading mood of fear* 普遍的恐懼情緒 ◇ *the sadness that pervades most of her novels* 充斥她大部份小說的悲愴情緒 ◇ *The entire house was pervaded by a sour smell.* 整所房子都充滿了酸味。

per·va·sive /pəˈveɪsɪv; *NAmE* pərˈv-/ *adj.* existing in all parts of a place or thing; spreading gradually to affect all parts of a place or thing 遍佈的；充斥各處的；瀰漫的：*a pervasive smell of damp* 四處瀰漫的潮濕味兒 ◇ *A sense of social change is pervasive in her novels.* 她的小說裏充斥着社會變化的意識。 ▸ **per·va·sive·ly** *adv.* **per·va·sive·ness** *noun* [U]

per·verse /pəˈvɜːs; *NAmE* pərˈvɜːrs/ *adj.* showing deliberate determination to behave in a way that most people think is wrong, unacceptable or unreasonable 執拗的；任性的；不通情理的：*a perverse decision* (= one that most people do not expect and think is wrong) 悖謬的決定 ◇ *She finds a perverse pleasure in upsetting her parents.* 她讓父母擔驚受怕，從中取得任性的快樂。◇ *Do you really mean that or are you just being* ***deliberately perverse****?* 你是真要那樣，還是故意作對？ ▸ **per·verse·ly** *adv.*：*She seemed perversely proud of her criminal record.* 她似乎不通人事，拿自己的前科當榮耀。 **per·vers·ity** *noun* [U]：*He refused to attend out of sheer perversity.* 他拒不出席，純屬任性固執。

per·ver·sion /pəˈvɜːʃn; *NAmE* pərˈvɜːrʒn/ *noun* [U, C] **1** behaviour that most people think is not normal or acceptable, especially when it is connected with sex; an example of this type of behaviour 反常行為；（性）變態：*sexual perversion* 性變態 ◇ *sadomasochistic perversions* 施虐受虐的變態行為 **2** the act of changing sth that is good or right into sth that is bad or wrong; the result of this 顛倒；歪曲；顛倒是非：*the perversion of justice* 對正義的歪曲 ◇ *Her account was a perversion of the truth.* 她的報告顛倒了是非。

per·vert *verb*, *noun*

■ *verb* /pəˈvɜːt; *NAmE* pərˈvɜːrt/ **1 ~ sth** to change a system, process, etc. in a bad way so that it is not what it used to be or what it should be 敗壞；使走樣；誤導；誤用：*Some scientific discoveries have been perverted to create weapons of destruction.* 某些科學發明被濫用來生產毀滅性武器。 **2 ~ sb/sth** to affect sb in a way that makes them act or think in an immoral or unacceptable way 腐蝕；侵害；使墮落 SYN **corrupt**：*Some people* *believe that television can pervert the minds of children.* 有些人認為，電視能腐蝕兒童的心靈。

IDM **per,vert the course of 'justice** (*BrE*) (*NAmE* **ob'struct justice**) (*law* 律) to tell a lie or to do sth in order to prevent the police, etc. from finding out the truth about a crime 作偽證；妨礙司法

■ ***noun*** /ˈpɜːvɜːt; *NAmE* ˈpɜːrvɜːrt/ (also *informal* **perv**) a person whose sexual behaviour is not thought to be normal or acceptable by most people 性變態者 SYN **deviant**： *a sexual pervert* 性變態者

per·verted /pəˈvɜːtɪd; *NAmE* pərˈvɜːr-/ *adj.* not thought to be normal or acceptable by most people 反常的；變態的： *sexual acts, normal and perverted* 正常的和變態的性行為 ◇ *She was having difficulty following his perverted logic.* 她很難理解他那反常的邏輯。◇ *They clearly take a perverted delight in watching others suffer.* 他們看別人受罪時顯然得到一種病態的快感。

pe·seta /pəˈseɪtə/ *noun* the former unit of money in Spain (replaced in 2002 by the euro) 比塞塔（西班牙以前的貨幣單位，於 2002 年為歐元所取代）

pesky /ˈpeski/ *adj.* [only before noun] (*informal, especially NAmE*) annoying 惱人的；討厭的： *pesky insects* 討厭的昆蟲

peso /ˈpeɪsəʊ; *NAmE* -soʊ/ *noun* (*pl.* **-os**) the unit of money in many Latin American countries and the Philippines 比索（多個拉美國家和菲律賓貨幣單位）

pes·sary /ˈpesəri/ *noun* (*pl.* **-ies**) **1** a small piece of solid medicine that is placed inside a woman's VAGINA and left to dissolve, used to cure an infection or to prevent her from becoming pregnant （治療炎症或避孕用的）陰道栓劑 ➲ see also SUPPOSITORY **2** a device that is placed inside a woman's VAGINA to support the WOMB 子宮托

pes·sim·ism /ˈpesɪmɪzəm/ *noun* [U] ~ (**about/over sth**) a feeling that bad things will happen and that sth will not be successful; the tendency to have this feeling 悲觀；悲觀情緒；悲觀主義： *There is a mood of pessimism in the company about future job prospects.* 公司中有一種對未來職場前景悲觀的情緒。OPP **optimism**

pes·sim·ist /ˈpesɪmɪst/ *noun* a person who always expects bad things to happen 悲觀主義者；悲觀論者： *You don't have to be a pessimist to realize that we're in trouble.* 不是悲觀論者也能意識到我們有了麻煩。OPP **optimist**

pes·sim·is·tic /ˌpesɪˈmɪstɪk/ *adj.* ~ (**about sth**) expecting bad things to happen or sth not to be successful; showing this 悲觀的；悲觀主義的： *They appeared surprisingly pessimistic about their chances of winning.* 他們對勝利的可能性顯得出奇地悲觀。◇ *a pessimistic view of life* 對人生悲觀的看法 ◇ *I think you're being far too pessimistic.* 我覺得你過於悲觀了。OPP **optimistic**

▸ **pes·sim·is·tic·al·ly** /-kli/ *adv.*

pest /pest/ *noun* **1** an insect or animal that destroys plants, food, etc. 害蟲；害獸；害鳥： *pest control* 害蟲防治 ◇ ***insect/plant/garden pests*** 害蟲；作物 / 花園害蟲 **2** (*informal*) an annoying person or thing 討厭的人（或物）： *That child is being a real pest.* 那個孩子真討厭。

pes·ter /ˈpestə(r)/ *verb* [T, I] to annoy sb, especially by asking them sth many times 打擾；糾纏；煩擾 SYN **badger**： **~ sb for sth** *Journalists pestered neighbours for information.* 記者纏着鄰居打聽消息。◇ **~ sb with sth** *He has been pestering her with phone calls for over a week.* 他打電話騷擾她有一個多星期了。◇ **~ sb/sth** *The horses were continually pestered by flies.* 馬不斷地被蒼蠅叮咬。◇ **~ (sb to do sth)** *The kids kept pestering me to read to them.* 孩子們老纏着我給他們讀故事書。

'pester power *noun* [U] (*informal*) the ability that children have to make their parents buy things, by repeatedly asking them until they agree（孩子要求父母買東西的）纏磨力，纏功

pesti·cide /ˈpestɪsaɪd/ *noun* [C, U] a chemical used for killing pests, especially insects 殺蟲劑；除害藥物： *vegetables grown without the use of pesticides* 未用殺蟲劑種植的蔬菜 ◇ *crops sprayed with pesticide* 噴灑過殺蟲劑的莊稼 ➲ see also HERBICIDE, INSECTICIDE

pesti·lence /ˈpestɪləns/ *noun* [U, sing.] (*old use* or *literary*) any infectious disease that spreads quickly and kills a lot of people 瘟疫

pesti·len·tial /ˌpestɪˈlenʃl/ *adj.* **1** [only before noun] (*literary*) extremely annoying 極討厭的；極煩人的 **2** (*old use*) connected with or causing a pestilence 瘟疫的；引起瘟疫的

pes·tle /ˈpesl/ *noun* a small heavy tool with a round end used for crushing things in a special bowl called a MORTAR 杵，碾槌（研磨食品工具）➲ **VISUAL VOCAB** pages V26, V70

pesto /ˈpestəʊ; *NAmE* ˈpestoʊ/ *noun* [U] an Italian sauce made of BASIL leaves, PINE NUTS, cheese and oil 意大利松子青醬（用羅勒葉、松子、乾酪和油調製而成）

PET *noun* [U] **1** /ˌpiː iː ˈtiː/ the abbreviation for 'polyethylene terephthalate' (an artificial substance used to make materials for packaging food, including plastic drinks bottles) 聚對苯二甲酸乙二醇酯（全寫為 polyethylene terephthalate，可做食品飲料包裝材料）**2** /pet/ (*medical* 醫) the abbreviation for 'positron emission tomography' (a process that produces an image of your brain or of another part inside your body) 正電子發射掃描（全寫為 positron emission tomography，大腦或其他體內部位的成像）： *a PET scan* 正電子發射掃描 **3** /pet/ the abbreviation for 'Preliminary English Test' (a British test, set by the University of Cambridge, that measures a person's ability to speak and write English as a foreign language at an INTERMEDIATE level) 中級英語證書考試（全寫為 Preliminary English Test，由英國劍橋大學命題，測試英語作為外語的口語和寫作能力是否達到中級水平）

pet 0‑ᴡ /pet/ *noun, verb, adj.*

■ ***noun*** **1** 0‑ᴡ an animal, a bird, etc. that you have at home for pleasure, rather than one that is kept for work or food 寵物： *Do you have any pets?* 你有沒有養寵物？◇ *a **pet dog/hamster, etc.*** 養作寵物的狗、倉鼠等 ◇ *a **family/domestic pet*** 家庭 / 家養寵物 ◇ ***pet food*** 寵物食品 ◇ *a **pet shop*** (= where animals are sold as pets) 寵物店 **2** (usually *disapproving*) a person who is given special attention by sb, especially in a way that seems unfair to other people 寵兒；寶貝；紅人 SYN **favourite**： *She's **the teacher's pet**.* 她是老師的寶貝疙瘩。 **3** (*BrE, informal*) used when speaking to sb to show affection or to be friendly（昵稱）寶貝兒，乖乖： *What's wrong, pet?* 怎麼啦，寶貝兒？◇ *Be a pet* (= be kind) *and post this letter for me.* 乖啊，替我把這封信寄了。

■ ***verb*** (**-tt-**) **1** [T] **~ sb/sth** (*especially NAmE*) to touch or move your hand gently over an animal or a child in a kind and loving way 撫摸；（愛撫地）摩挲 **2** [I] (*informal*) (of two people 兩人) to kiss and touch each other in a sexual way 親吻；調情；愛撫 ➲ see also PETTING

■ ***adj.*** [only before noun] that you are very interested in 很喜歡的；鍾愛的；很感興趣的： *his **pet subject/theory/project, etc.*** 他所喜愛的學科、理論、項目等 ➲ see also PET NAME

IDM **sb's pet 'hate** (*BrE*) (*NAmE* **sb's pet 'peeve**) something that you particularly dislike 特別厭惡的東西

petal /ˈpetl/ *noun* a delicate coloured part of a flower. The head of a flower is usually made up of several petals around a central part. 花瓣 ➲ **VISUAL VOCAB** page V11

pe·tard /pəˈtɑːd; *NAmE* pəˈtɑːrd/ *noun* IDM see HOIST *v.*

Peter /ˈpiːtə(r)/ *noun* IDM see ROB

peter /ˈpiːtə(r)/ *verb*

PHR V **ˌpeter 'out** to gradually become smaller, quieter, etc. and then end 逐漸減少；逐漸減弱；慢慢消失： *The campaign petered out for lack of support.* 那場運動因缺乏支持者而最終煙消雲散。◇ *The road petered out into a dirt track.* 大道延伸到一條泥路小徑。

ˌPeter 'Pan *noun* a person who looks unusually young for their age, or who behaves in a way that would be more appropriate for sb younger 外表異常年輕的人；行為像孩子的成人 ORIGIN From a story by J M Barrie about a boy with magic powers who never grew up.

源自詹姆斯・巴里的小説《彼得・潘》，主人公是個永遠長不大的有魔力的男孩。

ˈPeters projection *noun* [sing.] a map of the world on which the relative size, but not the shape of countries is more accurate than on more traditional maps 彼得斯投影世界地圖（其中各國的相對面積而不是形狀比傳統地圖更準確）➲ compare MERCATOR PROJECTION

peth·id·ine /ˈpeθədiːn/ *noun* [U] a drug used to reduce severe pain, especially for women giving birth 哌替啶，度冷丁（一種鎮痛藥）

petit bourgeois /ˌpeti ˈbʊəʒwɑː; *NAmE* ˈbʊrʒ-/ (also **ˌpetty ˈbourgeois**) *noun* (*pl.* **petits/petty bourgeois**) (*disapproving*) a member of the lower middle class in society, especially one who thinks that money, work and social position are very important 小資產階級分子 ▸ **ˌpetit ˈbourgeois** (also **ˌpetty ˈbourgeois**) *adj.* [usually before noun]

pe·tite /pəˈtiːt/ *adj.* (*approving*) (of a girl, woman or her figure 女孩、婦女或其身材) small and thin 纖弱的；嬌小的： *a petite blonde* 嬌小的金髮女郎

the peˌtite ˌbourgeoiˈsie (also **ˌpetty ˌbourgeoiˈsie**) *noun* [sing.] the lower middle class in society 小資產階級

petit four /ˌpeti ˈfɔː(r)/ *noun* [usually pl.] (*pl.* **petits fours** /ˌpeti ˈfɔː(r)/) (from *French*) a very small decorated cake or biscuit/cookie that is served with coffee or tea 花式小點心；小茶點

pe·ti·tion /pəˈtɪʃn/ *noun, verb*

■ *noun* **1 ~ (against/for sth)** a written document signed by a large number of people that asks sb in a position of authority to do or change sth 請願書： *a petition against experiments on animals* 反對用動物做實驗的請願書 ◇ *The workers are getting up* (= starting) *a petition for tighter safety standards.* 工人正發起請願，要求提高安全標準。 **2** (*law* 律) an official document asking a court to take a particular course of action 申訴書；申請書 **3** (*formal*) a formal prayer to God or request to sb in authority 祈禱；祈求

■ *verb* **1** [I, T] to make a formal request to sb in authority, especially by sending them a petition 祈求；請求；請願： **~ for/against sth** *Local residents have successfully petitioned against the siting of a prison in their area.* 當地居民反對在區內興建監獄的請願成功了。◇ **~ sb/sth (for sth)** *The group intends to petition Parliament for reform of the law.* 這個團體準備請求議會修改法律。◇ **~ sb/sth to do sth** *Parents petitioned the school to review its admission policy.* 家長請願懇求學校修訂招生政策。 **2** [I, T] **~ (sb) (for sth)** | **~ sb/sth to do sth** to formally ask for sth in court （向法庭）請求，申請： *to petition for divorce* 申請離婚

pe·ti·tion·er /pəˈtɪʃənə(r)/ *noun* **1** a person who organizes or signs a petition 請願者 **2** (*law* 律) a person who asks a court to take a particular course of action 訴願人；上訴人 **3** (*formal*) a person who makes a formal request to sb in authority 懇求者；請求者

petit mal /ˌpeti ˈmæl/ *noun* [U] a form of EPILEPSY that is not very serious, in which sb becomes unconscious only for very short periods 癲癇小發作

ˈpet name *noun* a name you use for sb instead of their real name, as a sign of affection 昵稱；愛稱

pet·rel /ˈpetrəl/ *noun* a black and white bird that can fly over the sea a long way from land 圓尾鸌；海燕

Petri dish /ˈpetri dɪʃ; ˈpiːtri/ *noun* a shallow covered dish used for growing bacteria, etc. in 皮氏培養皿（作細菌等培養用的有蓋玻璃碟）➲ VISUAL VOCAB page V70

petri·fied /ˈpetrɪfaɪd/ *adj.* **1** extremely frightened 非常害怕；恐慌的 SYN **terrified**： *a petrified expression* 惶恐的表情 ◇ **~ (of sth)** *I'm petrified of snakes.* 我特別怕蛇。 ◇ *They were petrified with fear* (= so frightened that they were unable to move or think). 他們都嚇呆了。◇ **~ (that ...)** *She was petrified that the police would burst in at any moment.* 她感到懼怕的是警察隨時都可能破門而入。 **2** [only before noun] **petrified** trees, insects, etc. have died and been changed into stone over a very long period of time 石化的： *a petrified forest* 石化林

pet·rify /ˈpetrɪfaɪ/ *verb* (**petri·fies**, **petri·fy·ing**, **petri·fied**, **petri·fied**) **1** [T] **~ sb** to make sb feel extremely frightened 使嚇呆；使驚呆 SYN **terrify** **2** [I, T] **~ (sth)** to change or to make sth change into a substance like stone（使）石化

petro- /ˈpetrəʊ; *NAmE* ˈpetroʊ/ *combining form* (in nouns, adjectives and adverbs 構成名詞、形容詞和副詞) **1** connected with rocks 岩石的： *petrology* 岩石學 **2** connected with petrol/gas 石油的；汽油的： *petrochemical* 石油化學產品

petro·chem·ical /ˌpetrəʊˈkemɪkl; *NAmE* ˌpetroʊ-/ *noun* any chemical substance obtained from PETROLEUM oil or natural gas 石油化學產品： *the petrochemical industry* 石油化學工業

petro·dol·lar /ˈpetrəʊdɒlə(r); *NAmE* ˈpetroʊdɑːlər/ *noun* a unit of money that is used for calculating the money earned by countries that produce and sell oil 石油美元（計算石油生產及銷售國收入的單位）

pet·rol 0➡ /ˈpetrəl/ (*BrE*) (*NAmE* **gas**, **gas·oline**) *noun* [U] a liquid obtained from PETROLEUM, used as fuel in car engines, etc. 汽油： *to fill a car up with petrol* 給汽車油箱裝滿汽油 ◇ *to run out of petrol* 用光汽油 ◇ *the petrol tank of a car* 汽車的油箱 ◇ *an increase in petrol prices* 汽油價格的上漲 ◇ *leaded/unleaded petrol* 含鉛／無鉛汽油 ➲ compare DIESEL (1)

ˌpetrol ˈblue *adj.* a deep greenish blue in colour 深藍綠色的： *petrol-blue eyes* 藏藍色的雙眸 ▸ **ˌpetrol ˈblue** *noun* [U]

ˈpetrol bomb *noun* (*BrE*) = MOLOTOV COCKTAIL

ˈpetrol bunk *noun* (*IndE*) a petrol station 汽車加油站

pet·rol·eum /pəˈtrəʊliəm; *NAmE* -ˈtroʊ-/ *noun* [U] mineral oil that is found under the ground or the sea and is used to produce petrol/gas, PARAFFIN, DIESEL oil, etc. 石油；原油

peˌtroleum ˈjelly (*NAmE* also **pet·rol·atum** /ˌpetrəˈleɪtəm/) *noun* [U] a soft clear substance obtained from petroleum, used to heal injuries on the skin or to make machine parts move together more smoothly 凡士林；礦脂 SYN **Vaseline**

pet·rology /pəˈtrɒlədʒi; *NAmE* -ˈtrɑːl-/ *noun* [U] the scientific study of how rocks are made and what they are made of 岩石學

ˈpetrol station (*BrE*) (*NAmE* **ˈgas station**) (also **ˈfilling station**, **ˈservice station** *NAmE*, *BrE*) *noun* a place at the side of a road where you take your car to buy petrol/gas, oil, etc. 汽車加油站

petti·coat /ˈpetɪkəʊt; *NAmE* -koʊt/ *noun* (*old-fashioned*) a piece of women's underwear like a thin dress or skirt, worn under a dress or skirt 襯裙 SYN **slip**

petti·fog·ging /ˈpetɪfɒgɪŋ; *NAmE* -fɔːg-; -fɑːg-/ *adj.* [only before noun] (*old-fashioned*) paying too much attention to unimportant details; concerned with unimportant things 吹毛求疵；挑剔的；瑣碎的 SYN **petty**

pet·ting /ˈpetɪŋ/ *noun* [U] the activity of kissing and touching sb, especially in a sexual way 親吻撫摸；調情： *heavy petting* (= sexual activity which avoids PENETRATION) 熱烈的愛撫

ˈpetting zoo *noun* (*NAmE*) a zoo with animals that children can touch（允許兒童觸摸動物的）愛畜動物園

pet·tish /ˈpetɪʃ/ *adj.* behaving in a bad-tempered or unreasonable way, especially because you cannot have or do what you want 發脾氣的（尤因未能遂願）；使性子的 ▸ **pet·tish·ly** *adv.*

petty /ˈpeti/ *adj.* (usually *disapproving*) **1** [usually before noun] small and unimportant 小的；瑣碎的；次要的 SYN **minor**： *petty squabbles* 小口角 ◇ *petty crime/theft* (= that is not very serious) 輕微罪行／偷竊 ◇ *a petty criminal/thief* 輕罪犯；小竊賊 ◇ *a petty bureaucrat/official* (= who does not have much power or authority, although they might pretend to) 小官僚；小官員 **2** caring too much about small and unimportant matters, especially when this is unkind to other people 小氣的；狹隘的 SYN **small-minded**： *How could you be so petty?* 你怎麼那麼小氣呢？ ▸ **petti·ness** *noun* [U]

P

ˌpetty ˈbourgeois *noun, adj.* = PETIT BOURGEOIS

the ˌpetty ˌbourgeoiˈsie *noun* [sing.] = PETITE BOURGEOISIE

ˌpetty ˈcash *noun* [U] a small amount of money kept in an office for small payments（辦公室的）小額備用現金

ˌpetty ˈofficer *noun* (*abbr.* **PO**) a sailor of middle rank in the navy 海軍軍士

petu·lant /ˈpetjulənt; *NAmE* ˈpetʃə-/ *adj.* bad-tempered and unreasonable, especially because you cannot do or have what you want 鬧脾氣的；愛耍性子的；賭氣的；任性的 ▸ **petu·lant·ly** *adv.* **petu·lance** /-əns/ *noun* [U]

pe·tu·nia /pəˈtju:niə; *NAmE* -ˈtu:-/ *noun* a garden plant with white, pink, purple or red flowers 矮牽牛

pew /pju:/ *noun* a long wooden seat in a church 教堂長椅 **IDM** **ˌtake a ˈpew!** (*BrE, informal, humorous*) used to tell sb to sit down 坐下！

pew·ter /ˈpju:tə(r)/ *noun* [U] a grey metal made by mixing tin with LEAD, used especially in the past for making cups, dishes, etc.; objects made from pewter 白鑞；錫鑞；白鑞製品

pey·ote /peɪˈəʊti; *NAmE* -ˈoʊ-/ *noun* **1** (also **mes·cal**) [C, U] a small, blue-green CACTUS that contains a powerful drug that affects people's minds 佩奧特掌（藍綠色小仙人掌，具致幻作用）**2** [U] the drug that comes from this plant 佩奧特鹼（從佩奧特掌中提取的致幻劑）

PG /ˌpi: ˈdʒi:/ *abbr.* (*BrE*) parental guidance. A film that has the label 'PG' is not suitable for children to watch without an adult. * PG 類影片，家長指引（建議家長對兒童加以引導）

PGCE /ˌpi: dʒi: si: ˈi:/ *noun* the abbreviation for 'Postgraduate Certificate in Education' (a British teaching qualification taken by people who have a university degree) 研究生教育證書（全寫為 Postgraduate Certificate in Education，有大學學位者取得的英國教師資格證書）

pH /ˌpi: ˈeɪtʃ/ *noun* [sing.] (*chemistry* 化) a measurement of the level of acid or ALKALI in a SOLUTION or substance. In the pH range of 0 to 14 a reading of below 7 shows an acid and of above 7 shows an alkali. * pH 值（溶液或物質的酸鹼度。pH 值介於 0 至 14，7 以下為酸，7 以上為鹼）：*a pH of 7.5* * pH 值 7.5 ◇ *to test the pH level of the soil* 測試土壤的酸鹼度

phago·cyte /ˈfægəsaɪt/ *noun* (*biology* 生) a type of cell present in the body that is able to absorb bacteria and other small cells 吞噬細胞

phal·anx /ˈfælæŋks/ *noun* (*formal*) a group of people or things standing very close together 密集的人（或東西）

phal·lic /ˈfælɪk/ *adj.* of or like a phallus 似陰莖的；陰莖的：*phallic symbols* 陰莖的象徵物

phal·locen·tric /ˌfæləʊˈsentrɪk; *NAmE* -loʊˈs-/ *adj.* (*formal*) related to men, male power, or the phallus as a symbol of male power 男性中心的；陽具中心的 ▸ **phal·locen·trism** /ˌfæləʊˈsentrɪzəm; *NAmE* -loʊˈs-/ *noun* [U]

phal·lus /ˈfæləs/ *noun* **1** (*technical* 術語) the male sexual organ, especially when it is ERECT (= stiff)（尤指勃起的）陰莖 **2** a model or an image of the male sexual organ that represents power and FERTILITY 陰莖模型，陰莖圖像（力量與生殖力的象徵）

phan·tasm /ˈfæntæzəm/ *noun* (*formal*) a thing seen in the imagination 幻覺；幻影；幻想 **SYN** **illusion**

phan·tas·ma·goria /ˌfæntæzməˈgɒriə; *NAmE* -ˈgɔ:r-/ *noun* [sing.] (*formal*) a changing scene of real or imagined figures, for example as seen in a dream or created as an effect in a film/movie（真實或幻覺形象的）變換情景，幻覺效應 ▸ **phan·tas·ma·gor·ical** /-ˈgɒrɪkl; *NAmE* -ˈgɔ:r-/ *adj.*

phan·tasy *noun* [C, U] (*old use*) = FANTASY

phantom /ˈfæntəm/ *noun, adj.*

■ ***noun*** **1** a GHOST 鬼；鬼魂；幽靈：*the phantom of his dead father* 他已故父親的幽靈 **2** a thing that exists only in your imagination 幻覺；幻象

■ ***adj.*** [only before noun] **1** like a GHOST 像鬼的；幽靈似的：*a phantom horseman* 幽靈似的騎士 **2** existing only in your imagination 幻覺的；幻象的；虛幻的：*phantom profits* 虛幻的利潤 ◇ *phantom illnesses* 幻覺疾病 ◇ *a phantom pregnancy* (= a condition in which a woman seems to be pregnant but in fact is not) 精神性假妊娠

phar·aoh /ˈfeərəʊ; *NAmE* ˈferoʊ/ *noun* a ruler of ancient Egypt 法老（古埃及國王）

Phari·see /ˈfærɪsi:/ *noun* **1** a member of an ancient Jewish group who followed religious laws and teaching very strictly 法利賽人（嚴守律法的古猶太教派成員）**2** (*disapproving*) a person who is very proud of the fact that they have high religious and moral standards, but who does not care enough about other people 自詡聖潔者；自恃清高者；偽善者 **SYN** **hypocrite**

pharma·ceut·ical /ˌfɑ:məˈsu:tɪkl; -ˈsju:-; *NAmE* ˌfɑ:rməˈsu:-/ *adj., noun*

■ ***adj.*** [only before noun] connected with making and selling drugs and medicines 製藥的；配藥的；賣藥的：*pharmaceutical products* 藥物 ◇ *the pharmaceutical industry* 製藥業

■ ***noun*** [usually pl.] (*technical* 術語) a drug or medicine 藥物：*the development of new pharmaceuticals* 新藥的開發 ◇ *the pharmaceuticals industry* 藥物業

pharma·cist /ˈfɑ:məsɪst; *NAmE* ˈfɑ:rm-/ *noun* **1** (*NAmE* also **drug·gist**) a person whose job is to prepare medicines and sell or give them to the public in a shop/store or in a hospital 藥劑師：*We had to wait for the pharmacist to make up her prescription.* 我們只得等藥劑師給她配好藥。➲ compare CHEMIST (1) **2** **pharma·cist's** (*pl.* **pharma·cists**) (*BrE*) a shop that sells medicines 藥店；藥房：*They sell vitamin supplements at the pharmacist's.* 那藥店賣維生素補劑。➲ compare CHEMIST (2) ➲ see also PHARMACY

pharma·colo·gist /ˌfɑ:məˈkɒlədʒɪst; *NAmE* ˌfɑ:rməˈkɑ:l-/ *noun* a scientist who studies pharmacology 藥物學家；藥理學家

pharma·col·ogy /ˌfɑ:məˈkɒlədʒi; *NAmE* ˌfɑ:rməˈkɑ:l-/ *noun* [U] the scientific study of drugs and their use in medicine 藥物學；藥理學 ▸ **pharma·co·logic·al** /ˌfɑ:məkəˈlɒdʒɪkl; *NAmE* ˌfɑ:rməkəˈlɑ:dʒ-/ *adj.*：*pharmacological research* 藥物學研究

pharma·co·poeia (*NAmE* also **pharma·co·peia**) /ˌfɑ:məkəˈpi:ə; *NAmE* ˌfɑ:rmə-/ *noun* (*technical* 術語) an official book containing a list of medicines and drugs and instructions for their use 藥典

phar·macy /ˈfɑ:məsi; *NAmE* ˈfɑ:rm-/ *noun* (*pl.* **-ies**) **1** [C] a shop/store, or part of one, that sells medicines and drugs 藥房；藥店；醫藥櫃枱 ➲ compare CHEMIST (2), DRUGSTORE **2** [C] a place in a hospital where medicines are prepared（醫院的）藥房，配藥室 ➲ see also DISPENSARY (1) **3** [U] the study of how to prepare medicines and drugs 藥劑學；製藥學

pharm·ing /ˈfɑ:mɪŋ; *NAmE* ˈfɑ:rmɪŋ/ *noun* [U] **1** **pharming™** the process of changing the GENES of an animal or a plant so that it produces large quantities of a substance, especially for use in medicine 藥耕（指通過改變動植物基因大量生產某種物質，尤為醫用）**ORIGIN** From 'farming' and 'pharmaceutical'. 源自 farming 和 pharmaceutical 的縮合。**2** the practice of secretly changing computer files or software so that visitors to a popular website are sent to a different website instead, without their knowledge, where their personal details are stolen and used to steal money from them 域欺騙，網址嫁接（指暗中修改計算機文件或軟件將網站訪客騙到其他網站，從而盜取其個人資料並進而盜取錢財）➲ compare PHISHING

pha·ryn·geal /fəˈrɪndʒiəl; ˌfærɪnˈdʒiəl/ *adj., noun*

■ ***adj.*** (*medical* 醫) relating to the pharynx 咽的

■ ***noun*** (also **phaˌryngeal ˈconsonant**) (*phonetics* 語音) a speech sound produced by the root of the tongue using the PHARYNX 咽音

pha·ryn·gitis /ˌfærɪnˈdʒaɪtɪs/ *noun* [U] (*medical* 醫) a condition in which the throat is red and sore 咽炎

phar·ynx /ˈfærɪŋks/ *noun* (*pl.* **pha·ryn·ges** /fəˈrɪndʒi:z/) (*anatomy* 解) the soft area at the top of the throat where the passages to the nose and mouth connect with the throat 咽 ➲ VISUAL VOCAB page V59

phase 0-π AW /feɪz/ *noun, verb*
■ *noun* **1** 0-π a stage in a process of change or development 階段；時期：*during the first/next/last phase* 在第一／下一／最後階段 ◇ *the **initial/final phase** of the project* 工程的初始／最後階段 ◇ ***a critical/decisive phase*** 關鍵性／決定性階段 ◇ *the **design phase*** 設計階段 ◇ *His anxiety about the work was just **a passing phase**.* 他對工作的擔心只是暫時的。◇ *She's going through a **difficult phase**.* 她正處於困難時期。◇ *The wedding marked the beginning of a **new phase** in Emma's life.* 婚禮標誌着埃瑪生活新階段的開始。**2** each of the shapes of the moon as we see it from the earth at different times of the month 月相；（月亮的）盈虧
IDM **in phase/out of phase (with sth)** (*BrE*) working/not working together in the right way 協調；不協調：*The traffic lights were out of phase.* 紅綠燈信號不協調。
■ *verb* [usually passive] **~ sth** to arrange to do sth gradually in stages over a period of time 分階段進行；逐步做：*the phased withdrawal of troops from the area* 從該地區分期逐步的撤軍 ◇ *Closure of the hospitals was phased over a three-year period.* 這些醫院的關閉是在三年期間逐步進行的。
PHR V **ˌphase sth↔ˈin** to introduce or start using sth gradually in stages over a period of time 逐步引入；分階段開始：*The new tax will be phased in over two years.* 新稅種將在兩年內逐步實行。**ˌphase sth↔ˈout** to stop using sth gradually in stages over a period of time 逐步廢除：*Subsidies to farmers will be phased out by next year.* 對農民的補貼將在明年之前逐步廢除。

phat /fæt/ *adj.* (*slang, especially NAmE*) very good 精彩的；極棒的

phat·ic /ˈfætɪk/ *adj.* (*linguistics* 語言) relating to language used for social purposes rather than to give information or ask questions 純交際性的；用於寒暄交際的：*phatic communication* 客套話

PhD (also **Ph.D.** especially in *NAmE*) /ˌpiː eɪtʃ ˈdiː/ *noun* the abbreviation for 'Doctor of Philosophy' (a university degree of a very high level that is given to sb who has done research in a particular subject) 哲學博士學位，博士學位（全寫為 Doctor of Philosophy，授予完成某學科研究者的高級學位）：*to **be/have/do a PhD*** 是一位博士；有博士學位；攻讀博士學位 ◇ *Anne Thomas, PhD* 安妮・托馬斯博士 ➲ COLLOCATIONS at EDUCATION

P

pheas·ant /ˈfeznt/ *noun* [C, U] (*pl.* **pheas·ants** or **pheas·ant**) a large bird with a long tail, the male of which is brightly coloured. People sometimes shoot pheasants for sport or food. Meat from this bird is also called pheasant. 野雞；雉；野雞肉：(*BrE*) *to shoot pheasant* 射獵野雞 ◇ (*NAmE*) *to hunt pheasant* 打野雞 ◇ *roast pheasant* 烤野雞 ➲ VISUAL VOCAB page V12

phe·nol /ˈfiːnɒl; *NAmE* -nɔːl; -nɑːl/ *noun* [U] (*chemistry* 化) a poisonous white chemical. When dissolved in water it is used as an ANTISEPTIC and DISINFECTANT, usually called CARBOLIC ACID. 酚；石碳酸

phen·ology /fəˈnɒlədʒi; *NAmE* -ˈnɑːl-/ *noun* [U] the study of patterns of events in nature, especially in the weather and in the behaviour of plants and animals 物候學

phe·nom /fəˈnɒm; ˈfiːnɒm; *NAmE* -nɑːm/ *noun* (*NAmE, informal*) a person or thing that is very successful or impressive 非凡的人（或事物）；了不起的人（或事物）SYN **phenomenon**

phe·nom·enal AW /fəˈnɒmɪnl; *NAmE* -ˈnɑːm-/ *adj.* very great or impressive 了不起的；非凡的 SYN **extraordinary**：*The product has been a phenomenal success.* 這一產品獲得了極大的成功。

phe·nom·en·al·ly /fəˈnɒmɪnəli; *NAmE* -ˈnɑːm-/ *adv.* **1** in a very great or impressive way 了不起地；非凡地；難以置信地 SYN **extraordinarily**：*This product has been phenomenally successful.* 這種產品獲得了極大的成功。**2** extremely; very 極其；十分：*phenomenally bad weather* 非常糟糕的天氣

phe·nom·en·ology /fɪˌnɒmɪˈnɒlədʒi; *NAmE* -ˌnɑːməˈnɑːl-/ *noun* [U] the branch of philosophy that deals with what you see, hear, feel, etc. in contrast to what may actually be real or true about the world 現象學 ▸ **phe·nom·eno·logic·al** /fɪˌnɒmɪnəˈlɒdʒɪkl; *NAmE* -ˌnɑːmənəˈlɑːdʒ-/ *adj.*

phe·nom·enon AW /fəˈnɒmɪnən; *NAmE* fəˈnɑːm-/ *noun* (*pl.* **phe·nom·ena** /-mə/) **1** a fact or an event in nature or society, especially one that is not fully understood 現象：***cultural/natural/social phenomena*** 文化／自然／社會現象 ◇ *Globalization is a phenomenon of the 21st century.* 全球化是 21 世紀的現象。**2** (*pl.* **phe·nom·enons** in *NAmE*) a person or thing that is very successful or impressive 傑出的人；非凡的人（或事物）

phe·no·type /ˈfiːnətaɪp/ *adj., noun* (*biology* 生) the set of characteristics of a living thing, resulting from its combination of GENES and the effect of its environment 表型（的），表現型（的）（基因和環境作用的結合而形成的一組生物特徵）➲ compare GENOTYPE

phero·mone /ˈferəməʊn; *NAmE* -moʊn/ *noun* (*biology* 生) a substance produced by an animal as a chemical signal, often to attract another animal of the same SPECIES 外激素；信息素

phew /fjuː/ *exclamation* a sound that people make to show that they are hot, tired, or happy that sth bad has finished or did not happen 哦（表示熱、累或寬慰）：*Phew, it's hot in here!* 哦，這裏真熱呀！◇ *Phew, I'm glad that's all over.* 哦，這檔事總算結束了！➲ compare WHEW

phi /faɪ/ *noun* the 21st letter of the Greek alphabet (Φ, ø) 希臘字母表的第 21 個字母

phial /ˈfaɪəl/ (also **vial** especially in *NAmE*) *noun* (*formal*) a small glass container, for medicine or PERFUME 管形瓶；小藥瓶

ˌPhi ˌBeta ˈKappa *noun* (in the US) a society for college and university students who are very successful in their studies * ΦβK 聯誼會（美國大學高材生組織）

phil·an·der·er /fɪˈlændərə(r)/ *noun* (*old-fashioned, disapproving*) a man who has sexual relationships with many different women 色鬼；玩弄女性者

phil·an·dering /fɪˈlændərɪŋ/ *noun* [U] (*old-fashioned, disapproving*) (of a man 男人) the fact of having sexual relationships with many different women 淫亂；玩弄女性；調戲婦女 SYN **womanizing** ▸ **phil·an·dering** *adj.* [only before noun]

phil·an·throp·ist /fɪˈlænθrəpɪst/ *noun* a rich person who helps the poor and those in need, especially by giving money 慈善家；樂善好施的人

phil·an·thropy /fɪˈlænθrəpi/ *noun* [U] the practice of helping the poor and those in need, especially by giving money 博愛；慈善；樂善好施 ▸ **phil·an·throp·ic** /ˌfɪlənˈθrɒpɪk; *NAmE* -ˈθrɑːp-/ *adj.*：*philanthropic work* 慈善工作 **phil·an·throp·ic·al·ly** /ˌfɪlənˈθrɒpɪkli; *NAmE* -ˈθrɑːp-/ *adv.*

phila·tel·ist /fɪˈlætəlɪst/ *noun* (*technical* 術語) a person who collects or studies stamps 集郵愛好者；郵票專家

phil·ately /fɪˈlætəli/ *noun* [U] (*technical* 術語) the collection and study of stamps 集郵；郵票研究 ▸ **phila·tel·ic** /ˌfɪləˈtelɪk/ *adj.*

-phile *combining form* (in nouns and adjectives 構成名詞和形容詞) liking a particular thing; a person who likes a particular thing 愛好…的；…愛好者：*Anglophile* 親英者 ◇ *bibliophile* 藏書家 ➲ compare -PHOBE

phil·har·mon·ic /ˌfɪlɑːˈmɒnɪk; *NAmE* ˌfɪlərˈmɑːnɪk/ *adj.* used in the names of ORCHESTRAS, music societies, etc.（用於樂隊、音樂團體等名稱中）愛好音樂的：*the Berlin Philharmonic (Orchestra)* 柏林愛樂（管弦）樂團

-philia *combining form* (in nouns 構成名詞) love of sth, especially connected with a sexual attraction that is not considered normal（尤指不正常的）性嗜好；癖好；怪癖：*paedophilia* 戀童癖 ➲ compare -PHOBIA

phil·is·tine /ˈfɪlɪstaɪn; *NAmE* -stiːn/ *noun* (*disapproving*) a person who does not like or understand art, literature, music, etc. 對文化藝術無知的人；文化修養低的人 ▸ **phil·is·tine** *adj.*：*philistine attitudes* 厭惡藝術的態度 **phil·is·tin·ism** /-tɪnɪzəm/ *noun* [U]：*the philistinism of the tabloid press* 小報新聞界之庸俗

Phil·lips /ˈfɪlɪps/ *adj.* (of a screw or SCREWDRIVER 螺絲釘或螺絲刀) with a cross-shaped part for turning 十字形的 ➲ compare FLATHEAD, SLOTTED (2)

philo- /ˈfɪləʊ; *NAmE* ˈfɪloʊ/ (also **phil-**) *combining form* (in nouns, adjectives, verbs and adverbs 構成名詞、形容詞、動詞和副詞) liking 愛好；喜愛：*philanthropy* 博愛

phil·olo·gist /fɪˈlɒlədʒɪst; *NAmE* -ˈlɑːl-/ *noun* a person who studies philology 語文學家；語文研究者

phil·ology /fɪˈlɒlədʒi; *NAmE* -ˈlɑːl-/ *noun* [U] the scientific study of the development of language or of a particular language 語文學；語文研究 ▸ **phil·olo·gic·al** /ˌfɪləˈlɒdʒɪkl; *NAmE* -ˈlɑːdʒ-/ *adj.*

phil·oso·pher **AW** /fəˈlɒsəfə(r); *NAmE* -ˈlɑːs-/ *noun* **1** a person who studies or writes about philosophy 哲學家：*the Greek philosopher Aristotle* 希臘哲學家亞里士多德 **2** a person who thinks deeply about things 深思的人；善於思考的人：*He seems to be a bit of a philosopher.* 他像個思想家似的。

the phiˌlosopher's ˈstone *noun* [sing.] an imaginary substance that, in the past, people believed could change any metal into gold or silver, or could make people live for ever 魔法石（舊時被認為能使其他金屬變為金銀或能使人長生不老的仙石）

philo·soph·ical **AW** /ˌfɪləˈsɒfɪkl; *NAmE* -ˈsɑːf-/ (also **philo·soph·ic** /-ˈsɒfɪk; *NAmE* -ˈsɑːfɪk/) *adj.* **1** connected with philosophy 哲學的：*the philosophical writings of Kant* 康德的哲學論著 ◇ *philosophic debate* 哲學辯論 **2 ~ (about sth)** (*approving*) having a calm attitude towards a difficult or disappointing situation 達觀的；處亂不驚的 **SYN** **stoical**：*He was philosophical about losing and said that he'd be back next year to try again.* 他對失敗處之泰然，聲稱來年將再來一試身手。▸ **philo·soph·ic·al·ly** **AW** /-kli/ *adv.*：*This kind of evidence is philosophically unconvincing.* 這類證據在哲學上是不足為信的。◇ *She took the bad news philosophically.* 她鎮定地面對這個壞消息。

philo·so·phize (*BrE* also **-ise**) **AW** /fəˈlɒsəfaɪz; *NAmE* -ˈlɑːs-/ *verb* [I] **~ (about/on sth)** to talk about sth in a serious way, especially when other people think this is boring 鄭重論述；高談闊論：*He spent the evening philosophizing on the meaning of life.* 他整個晚上大談人生的意義。▸ **phil·oso·phiz·ing, -is·ing** **AW** *noun* [U]

phil·oso·phy 🔑 **AW** /fəˈlɒsəfi; *NAmE* -ˈlɑːs-/ *noun* **1** 🔑 [U] the study of the nature and meaning of the universe and of human life 哲學：*moral philosophy* 倫理學 ◇ *the philosophy of science* 科學原理 ◇ *a professor of philosophy* 哲學教授 ◇ *a degree in philosophy* 哲學學位 **2** 🔑 [C] a particular set or system of beliefs resulting from the search for knowledge about life and the universe 哲學體系；思想體系：*the philosophy of Jung* 榮格的哲學體系 **3** 🔑 [C] a set of beliefs or an attitude to life that guides sb's behaviour 人生哲學；生活的信條（或態度）：*Her philosophy of life is to take every opportunity that presents itself.* 她的處世態度是不放過任何呈現眼前的機會。

phil·tre (*especially US* **phil·ter**) /ˈfɪltə(r)/ *noun* (*literary*) a magic drink that is supposed to make people fall in love 春藥

phish·ing /ˈfɪʃɪŋ/ *noun* [U] the activity of tricking people by getting them to give their identity, bank account numbers, etc. over the Internet or by email, and then using these to steal money from them 網絡誘騙（通過互聯網或電郵騙取他人身分、銀行賬號等以盜取金錢）➲ compare PHARMING (2)

phle·bitis /fləˈbaɪtɪs/ *noun* [U] (*medical* 醫) a condition in which the walls of a VEIN become sore and swollen 靜脈炎

phle·bot·omy /fləˈbɒtəmi; *NAmE* -ˈbɑːt-/ *noun* [C, U] (*pl.* **-ies**) (*medical* 醫) the opening of a VEIN in order to remove blood or put another liquid in 靜脈切開術

phlegm /flem/ *noun* [U] **1** the thick substance that forms in the nose and throat, especially when you have a cold 痰 **2** the ability to remain calm in a situation that is difficult or upsetting 冷靜；鎮定；自制力

phleg·mat·ic /flegˈmætɪk/ *adj.* not easily made angry or upset 冷靜的；鎮定的；不易衝動的 **SYN** **calm**：*a phlegmatic temperament* 平和的性情 ▸ **phleg·mat·ic·al·ly** /-kli/ *adv.*

phloem /ˈfləʊem; *NAmE* ˈfloʊ-/ *noun* [U] (*biology* 生) the material in a plant containing very small tubes that carry sugars produced in the leaves around the plant 韌皮部（由篩管等將葉製造的糖分輸送到各部位的植物組織）➲ compare XYLEM

phlox /flɒks; *NAmE* flɑːks/ *noun* **1** a tall garden plant with groups of white, blue or red flowers with a sweet smell 福祿考（高大開花植物，可種植在花園）**2** a low, spreading plant with small white, blue or pink flowers 叢生福祿考（低矮蔓生開花植物）

-phobe *combining form* (in nouns 構成名詞) a person who dislikes a particular thing or particular people 厭惡…的人：*Anglophobe* 仇英者 ◇ *xenophobe* 仇外者 ➲ compare -PHILE

pho·bia /ˈfəʊbiə; *NAmE* ˈfoʊ-/ *noun* **1** a strong unreasonable fear of sth 恐怖症，恐懼症（無名的極度恐懼）：*He **has a phobia about** flying.* 他有飛行恐懼症。**2 -phobia** (in nouns 構成名詞) a strong unreasonable fear or hatred of a particular thing 對…的恐懼症：*claustrophobia* 幽閉恐怖症 ◇ *xenophobia* 恐外症 ➲ compare -PHILIA

pho·bic /ˈfəʊbɪk; *NAmE* ˈfoʊ-/ *noun* **1** a person who has a strong unreasonable fear or hatred of sth 恐懼症患者；極端仇視者：*cat phobics* 特別怕貓的人 **2 -phobic** (in adjectives 構成形容詞) having a strong unreasonable fear or hatred of a particular thing 恐懼…的；仇恨…的：*claustrophobic* 幽閉恐怖的 ◇ *xenophobic* 仇外的 ▸ **pho·bic** *adj.*：*phobic anxiety* 由恐懼而生的焦慮

phoe·nix /ˈfiːnɪks/ *noun* (in stories) a magic bird that lives for several hundred years before burning itself and then being born again from its ASHES（傳說中的）鳳凰，長生鳥：*to rise like a phoenix from the ashes* (= to be powerful or successful again) 雄起如再生的鳳凰

British/American 英式/美式英語

phone / call / ring

Verbs 動詞

- In *BrE*, **to phone, to ring** and **to call** are the usual ways of saying **to telephone**. In *NAmE* the most common word is **call**, but **phone** is also used. Speakers of *NAmE* do not say **ring**. **Telephone** is very formal and is used mainly in *BrE*. 在英式英語中，phone、ring 和 call 為表示打電話的慣常用語。在美式英語中，call 最常用，但也用 phone。說美式英語的人不用 ring。telephone 非常正式，主要用於英式英語。

Nouns 名詞

- You can use **call** or **phone call** (more formal) in both *BrE* and *NAmE*. 在英式英語和美式英語中，用 call 或 phone call（較正式）均可：*Were there any phone calls for me?* 有我的電話嗎？◇ *How do I make a local call?* 本地電話怎麼打？The idiom **give sb a call** is also common. 習語 give sb a call 亦常用：*I'll give you a call tonight.* 我今晚會給你打電話。In informal *BrE* you could also say 非正式英式英語中亦可說：*I'll give you a ring tonight.* 我今晚會給你打電話。

phone 🔑 /fəʊn; *NAmE* foʊn/ *noun, verb*
■ *noun* **1** 🔑 [U, C] a system for talking to sb else over long distances using wires or radio; a machine used for this; a telephone 電話；電話系統；電話機：*I have to **make a phone call**.* 我得打個電話。◇ *The **phone rang** and Pat answered it.* 電話響起，帕特接了。◇ *They like to do business **by phone/over the phone**.* 他們喜歡用電話／在電話上談生意。◇ *His phone must be switched off.* 他的電話一定是關機了。◇ *I hadn't got my phone with me.* 我沒有帶手機。◇ *a phone bill* 電話費單 ➲ see also CAR PHONE, CELL PHONE, ENTRYPHONE, MOBILE PHONE, PAYPHONE,

P

TELEPHONE *n.* (1) **2** 🔑 [C] the part of a phone that you hold in your hand and speak into; a telephone 電話聽筒；電話： *to* ***pick up the phone*** 拿起電話 ◇ *to* ***put the phone down*** 放下電話 ◇ *He left the phone off the hook as he didn't want to be disturbed.* 他不想被電話打擾，就把電話聽筒摘下來了。➲ see also ANSWERPHONE, TELEPHONE *n.* (2) **3 -phone** (in nouns 構成名詞) an instrument that uses or makes sound（發聲或使用聲音的）工具，儀器： *dictaphone* 口述錄音機 ◇ *xylophone* 木琴 **4 -phone** (in adjectives and nouns 構成形容詞和名詞) speaking a particular language; a person who does this 說某種語言的；講某種語言的人： *anglophone* 講英語的（人）◇ *francophone* 講法語的（人） **5** (*phonetics* 語音) a sound made in speech, especially when not considered as part of the sound system of a particular language 音子；音素 ➲ compare PHONEME

IDM **be on the 'phone** **1** to be using the telephone 在打電話中： *He's been on the phone to Kate for more than an hour.* 他給凱特打電話講了一個多小時了。 **2** (*BrE*) to have a telephone in your home or place of work（在家中或工作單位）有電話，安了電話： *They're not on the phone at the holiday cottage.* 他們的度假別墅沒裝電話。

■ ***verb*** 🔑 (*especially BrE*) (*BrE* also **ˌphone 'up**) [I, T] to make a telephone call to sb 打電話 SYN **call**： *I was just phoning up for a chat.* 我只是打電話聊聊天。◇ *He phoned to invite me out for dinner.* 他打電話請我外出吃飯。◇ *Someone phone for an ambulance!* 找人打電話叫救護車！◇ *Could you* ***phone back*** *later?* 您過一會兒再打電話來好嗎？◇ *He* ***phoned home****, but there was no reply.* 他往家裏打電話，但沒有人接。◇ **~ sb/sth** *Don't forget to phone New York.* 別忘了往紐約打電話。◇ *For reservations, phone 020 281 3964.* 預訂請撥打 020 281 3964。◇ *Phone them up and find out when they are coming.* 給他們打個電話，問問他們什麼時候來。

PHR V **ˌphone 'in** (*especially BrE*) **1** to make a telephone call to the place where you work 往工作單位打電話： **+ adj.** *Three people have* ***phoned in sick*** *already this morning.* 今天上午已有三個人打電話來請病假。**2** to make a telephone call to a radio or television station 往（電台或電視台）打電話；打熱線電話： *Listeners are invited to phone in with their comments.* 歡迎聽眾撥打熱線電話發表意見。➲ related noun PHONE-IN **ˌphone sth↔'in** (*especially BrE*) to make a telephone call to the place where you work in order to give sb some information 往工作單位打電話通報某事： *I need you to phone the story in before five.* 我要你在五點鐘前打電話來報告整件事。

'phone book *noun* = TELEPHONE DIRECTORY

'phone booth (also **'telephone booth**) *noun* a place that is partly separated from the surrounding area, containing a public telephone, in a hotel, restaurant, in the street, etc.（半封閉的）公用電話間，電話亭

'phone box (also **'telephone box**, **'telephone kiosk**, **'call box**) (all *BrE*) *noun* a small unit with walls and a roof, containing a public telephone, in the street, etc.（全封閉的）公用電話亭，電話間

'phone call *noun* = CALL *n.* (1)

phone·card /ˈfəʊnkɑːd; *NAmE* ˈfoʊnkɑːrd/ *noun* (*NAmE* also **'calling card**) **1** a plastic card that you can use in some public telephones instead of money（公共電話用）電話卡 **2** (*NAmE*) a card with a number on it that you use in order to pay to make a call from any phone. The cost of the call is charged to your account and you pay it later.（轉賬付費）電話卡

'phone-in (*BrE*) (*NAmE* **'call-in**) *noun* a radio or television programme in which people can telephone and make comments or ask questions about a particular subject（廣播、電視的）熱線直播節目，聽眾來電直播節目

phon·eme /ˈfəʊniːm; *NAmE* ˈfoʊ-/ *noun* (*phonetics* 語音) any one of the set of smallest units of speech in a language that distinguish one word from another. In English, the /s/ in *sip* and the /z/ in *zip* represent two different phonemes. 音位（區分單詞的最小語音單位，英語 sip 中的 /s/ 和 zip 中的 /z/ 是兩個不同的音素）▸ **phon·em·ic** /fəˈniːmɪk/ *adj.*

Collocations 詞語搭配

Phones 電話

Making and receiving phone calls 打 / 接電話

- the phone/telephone **rings** 電話鈴響了
- **answer/pick up/hang up** the phone/telephone 接 / 掛電話
- **lift/pick up/hold/replace** the receiver 拿起 / 拿着 / 放回聽筒
- **dial** a (phone/extension/wrong) number/an area code 撥打（電話 / 分機）號碼；撥錯號碼；撥打區號
- **call sb/talk (to sb)/speak (to sb)** on the phone/telephone; from home/work/the office 給某人打電話；從家裏 / 工作地點 / 辦公室給某人打電話
- **make/get/receive** a phone call 打 / 接電話
- **take** the phone **off the hook** (= remove the receiver so that the phone does not ring) 摘下電話聽筒
- the line is (*BrE*) **engaged**/(*especially NAmE*) **busy** 佔線
- the phones have been (*NAmE*) **ringing off the hook** (= ringing frequently) 電話鈴聲不斷
- **put sb through/get through** to the person you want to speak to 給某人接通另一人的電話；打通電話
- **put sb** on hold (= so that they must wait for the person they want to speak to) 讓某人不要掛上電話（以便等想找的人接電話）
- **call from/use** a landline 用固定線路打電話

Mobile/cell phones 手機

- **be/talk** on a (*both BrE*) mobile phone/mobile/(*especially NAmE*) cell phone/(*informal, especially NAmE*) cell 用手機講電話
- **use/answer/call (sb on)/get a message on** your mobile phone/mobile/cell phone/cell 使用 / 接聽 / 撥打某人的手機；用手機接收信息
- **switch/turn on/off** your mobile phone/mobile/cell phone/cell 開啟 / 關閉手機
- **charge/recharge** your mobile phone/mobile/cell phone/cell 給手機充電
- a mobile/cell phone **is on/is off/rings/goes off** 手機開着 / 關機 / 響鈴 / 沒電關機
- (*BrE*) **top up** your mobile (phone) 給手機充值
- **send/receive** a text (message)/an SMS (message)/a fax 發送 / 接收信息 / 短信 / 傳真
- **insert/remove/change** a SIM card 插入 / 取出 / 更換 SIM 卡

'phone number *noun* = TELEPHONE NUMBER

'phone tapping *noun* = TELEPHONE TAPPING

phon·et·ic /fəˈnetɪk/ *adj.* **1** using special symbols to represent each different speech sound 表示語音的；音標的： *the International Phonetic Alphabet* 國際音標 ◇ *a phonetic symbol/transcription* 音標；注音 **2** (of a spelling or spelling system 拼寫或拼寫系統) that closely matches the sounds represented 拼音的；與發音近似的： *Spanish spelling is phonetic, unlike English spelling.* 與英語不同，西班牙語的拼寫與發音相近。 **3** connected with the sounds of human speech 語音的 ▸ **phon·et·ic·al·ly** /-kli/ *adv.*

phon·et·ics /fəˈnetɪks/ *noun* [U] the study of speech sounds and how they are produced 語音學 ▸ **phon·et·ician** /ˌfəʊnəˈtɪʃn; ˌfɒn-; *NAmE* ˌfoʊn-; ˌfɑːn-/ *noun*

pho·ney (also **phony** especially in *NAmE*) /ˈfəʊni; *NAmE* ˈfoʊni/ *adj., noun*

■ ***adj.*** (**pho·nier**, **pho·ni·est**) (*informal, disapproving*) not real or true; false, and trying to trick people 假的；冒充的；欺騙的 SYN **fake**： *She spoke with a phoney Russian accent.* 她用一種偽裝的俄國腔調說話。

P

■ ***noun*** (*pl.* **-neys** or **-nies**) (*informal*) a person who is not honest or sincere; a thing that is not real or true 不誠實的人；冒充的人（或東西）；冒牌貨

,phoney 'war *noun* [sing.] (*BrE*) a period of time when two groups are officially at war but not actually fighting（戰爭時期並未真正交戰的）假戰爭

phon·ic /ˈfɒnɪk; *NAmE* ˈfɑːnɪk/ *adj.* **1** (*technical* 術語) relating to sound; relating to sounds made in speech 聲音的；語音的 **2 -phonic** (in adjectives 構成形容詞) connected with an instrument that uses or makes sound 用…傳聲的；用…發聲的： *telephonic* 電話的

phon·ics /ˈfɒnɪks; *NAmE* ˈfɑːn-/ *noun* [U] a method of teaching people to read based on the sounds that letters represent 語音教學法；拼讀法

phono- /ˈfəʊnəʊ; *NAmE* ˈfoʊnoʊ-/ (also **phon-**) *combining form* (in nouns, adjectives and adverbs 構成名詞、形容詞和副詞) connected with sound or sounds 聲的；聲音的；語音的： *phonetic* 語音的

phono·graph /ˈfəʊnəɡrɑːf; *NAmE* ˈfoʊnəɡræf/ *noun* (*old-fashioned*) = RECORD PLAYER

phon·ology /fəˈnɒlədʒi; *NAmE* -ˈnɑːl-/ *noun* [U] (*linguistics* 語言) the speech sounds of a particular language; the study of these sounds 音系；音系學 ▸ **phono·logic·al** /ˌfəʊnəˈlɒdʒɪkl; ˌfɒn-; *NAmE* ˌfoʊnəˈlɑːdʒ-; ˌfɑːn-/ *adj.*： *phonological analysis* 音系分析 **phon·olo·gist** /fəˈnɒlədʒɪst; *NAmE* fəˈnɑːl-/ *noun*

phony (*especially NAmE*) = PHONEY

phooey /ˈfuːi/ *exclamation* used when you think sb/sth is wrong or silly（表示不信、輕蔑等）錯了，真傻，呸，啐 ▸ **phooey** *noun* [U]： *It's all phooey!* 全錯了！

phos·gene /ˈfɒzdʒiːn; *NAmE* ˈfɑːz-/ *noun* [U] a poisonous gas that was used as a CHEMICAL WEAPON during the First World War 光氣，碳醯氯（第一次世界大戰中用作化學武器）

phos·phate /ˈfɒsfeɪt; *NAmE* ˈfɑːs-/ *noun* [C, U] (*chemistry* 化) any COMPOUND containing phosphorus, used in industry or for helping plants to grow 磷酸鹽；含磷化合物；磷肥： *phosphate-free washing powder* 無磷洗衣粉

phos·phor·es·cent /ˌfɒsfəˈresnt; *NAmE* ˌfɑːs-/ *adj.* (*technical* 術語) **1** producing a faint light in the dark（在黑暗中）發微光的，發熒光的 ➲ compare FLUORESCENT **2** producing light without heat or with so little heat that it cannot be felt 發磷光的 ▸ **phos·phor·es·cence** /-sns/ *noun* [U]

phosphoric acid /fɒsˌfɒrɪk ˈæsɪd; *NAmE* fɑːsˌfɔːrɪk/ *noun* [U] an acid used in FERTILIZERS and in the production of DETERGENTS and food 磷酸（用於化肥，以及生產洗滌劑和食品）

phos·phorus /ˈfɒsfərəs; *NAmE* ˈfɑːs-/ *noun* [U] (*symb.* **P**) a chemical element. Phosphorus is found in several different forms, including as a poisonous, pale yellow substance that shines in the dark and starts to burn as soon as it is placed in air. 磷

phot·ic /ˈfəʊtɪk; *NAmE* ˈfoʊ-/ *adj.* (*technical* 術語) **1** relating to, or caused by, light 光的；光引起的 **2** relating to the part of the ocean which receives enough light for plants to grow（海洋）光照充足的，透光的： *the photic zone* 透光帶

photo 0-ᴛ /ˈfəʊtəʊ; *NAmE* ˈfoʊtoʊ/ *noun* (*pl.* **-os**) = PHOTOGRAPH： *a* ***colour/black-and-white photo*** 彩色／黑白照片 ◇ *a* ***passport photo*** 護照照片 ◇ ***a photo album*** (= a book for keeping your photos in) 相冊 ◇ *I'll* ***take a photo*** *of you.* 我來給你拍個照。 **HELP** The usual phrase in *NAmE* is **take a picture**. 美式英語常用 take a picture。 ➲ SYNONYMS at PHOTOGRAPH

photo- /ˈfəʊtəʊ; *NAmE* ˈfoʊtoʊ/ *combining form* (in nouns, adjectives, verbs and adverbs 構成名詞、形容詞、動詞和副詞) **1** connected with light 光的；關於光的： *photosynthesis* 光合作用 **2** connected with photography 攝影的；照相的： *photogenic* 上相的

ˈphoto booth *noun* a small structure with walls and a roof where you can put money in a machine and get a photograph of yourself in a few minutes 自助快照亭

photo·call /ˈfəʊtəʊkɔːl; *NAmE* ˈfoʊtoʊ-/ *noun* a time that is arranged in advance when newspaper photographers are invited to take photographs of sb（攝影記者預約的）拍照時間；媒體拍照時間： *The president joined the team for a photocall.* 總統加入到團隊中接受媒體拍照。

photo·cell /ˈfəʊtəʊsel; *NAmE* ˈfoʊtoʊ-/ *noun* = PHOTOELECTRIC CELL

photo·chem·ical /ˌfəʊtəʊˈkemɪkl; *NAmE* ˌfoʊtoʊ-/ *adj.* (*chemistry* 化) caused by or relating to the chemical action of light 光化作用的；光化學的： *photochemical smog* 光化煙霧

photo·copier /ˈfəʊtəʊkɒpiə(r); *NAmE* ˈfoʊtoʊkɑːp-/ (also **copier** especially in *NAmE*) *noun* a machine that makes copies of documents, etc. by photographing them 複印機；影印機 ➲ VISUAL VOCAB page V69

photo·copy 0-ᴛ /ˈfəʊtəʊkɒpi; *NAmE* ˈfoʊtoʊkɑːpi/ *noun, verb*

■ ***noun*** 0-ᴛ (also **copy**) (*pl.* **-ies**) a copy of a document, etc. made by the action of light on a specially treated surface 影印本；複印件： *Make as many photocopies as you need.* 你需要多少複印件就複印多少吧。

■ ***verb*** (**photo·cop·ies**, **photo·copy·ing**, **photo·cop·ied**, **photo·cop·ied**) (also **copy** especially in *BrE*) **1** 0-ᴛ [T, I] **~ (sth)** to make a photocopy of sth 影印；複製；複印： *a photocopied letter* 複印的信 ◇ *Can you get these photocopied for me by 5 o'clock?* 你能不能在 5 點鐘前把這些給我複印好？ ◇ *I seem to have spent most of the day photocopying.* 我這一天的大部份時間似乎都花在複印上了。 **2** [I] **~ well/badly** (of printed material 印刷品) to produce a good/bad photocopy 影印得好／不好： *The comments in pencil haven't photocopied very well.* 用鉛筆寫的評語沒有複印清楚。

photo·elec·tric /ˌfəʊtəʊɪˈlektrɪk; *NAmE* ˌfoʊtoʊ-/ *adj.* using an electric current that is controlled by light 光電的

ˌphotoelectric ˈcell (also **photo·cell**) *noun* an electric device that uses a stream of light. When the stream is broken it shows that sb/sth is present, and can be used to control alarms, machinery, etc. 光電池；光電感應器；光電管

ˌphoto ˈfinish *noun* [usually sing.] the end of a race in which the leading runners or horses are so close together that only a photograph of them passing the finishing line can show which is the winner 攝影定名次（競賽成績十分接近，以終點線攝影決定結果）

photo·fit /ˈfəʊtəʊfɪt; *NAmE* ˈfoʊtoʊfɪt/ *noun* (*BrE*) a picture of a person who is wanted by the police, made by putting together photographs of different features of faces from information that is given by sb who has seen the person 通緝犯拼像（根據目擊者提供的信息拼湊而成） ➲ compare E-FIT, IDENTIKIT

photo·gen·ic /ˌfəʊtəʊˈdʒenɪk; *NAmE* ˌfoʊtoʊ-/ *adj.* looking attractive in photographs 上鏡的；上相的： *I'm not very photogenic.* 我不大上相。

photo·graph 0-ᴛ /ˈfəʊtəɡrɑːf; *NAmE* ˈfoʊtəɡræf/ *noun, verb*

■ ***noun*** 0-ᴛ (also **photo**) a picture that is made by using a camera that has a film sensitive to light inside it 照片；相片： ***aerial/satellite photographs*** 飛機航拍／衛星照片 ◇ *colour photographs* 彩色照片 ◇ *Please enclose a recent passport-sized photograph of yourself.* 請附寄一張近照，大小同護照用相片。 ◇ *I spent the day* ***taking photographs*** *of the city.* 我花了一天時間拍攝這座城市的照片。 **HELP** The usual phrase in *NAmE* is **take pictures**. 美式英語常用 take pictures。 ➲ SYNONYMS at next page

■ ***verb*** **1** 0-ᴛ [T] to take a photograph of sb/sth 拍照；照相： **~ sb/sth** *He has photographed some of the world's most beautiful women.* 他為幾位傾世佳麗拍過照片。 ◇ *a beautifully photographed book* (= with good photographs in it) 一本有精美照片的書 ◇ **~ sb/sth + adj.** *She refused to be photographed nude.* 她拒拍裸體照片。 ◇ **~ sb/sth doing sth** *They were photographed playing with their children.* 他們跟孩子一起嬉戲的情景被拍成了照片。 **2** [I] **~ well, badly, etc.** to look or not look attractive in photographs（很、不等）上相，上鏡： *Some people just don't photograph well.* 有些人就是不上相。

Synonyms 同義詞辨析

photograph

picture • photo • shot • snapshot/snap • print

These are all words for a picture that has been made using a camera. 以上各詞均指照片、相片。

photograph a picture that has been made using a camera 指照片、相片： *a photograph of the house* 這座房子的照片 ◇ *Can I take a photograph?* 我可以拍個照嗎？

picture a photograph 指照片、相片： *We had our picture taken in front of the hotel.* 我們在旅館前照了相。

photo a photograph 指照片、相片： *a passport photo* 護照照片

PHOTOGRAPH, PICTURE OR PHOTO? 用 photograph、picture 還是 photo？

Photograph is slightly more formal and **photo** is slightly less formal. **Picture** is used especially in the context of photographs in newspapers, magazines and books. * photograph 較正式而 photo 較非正式。picture 尤指報紙、雜誌和書籍中的照片。

shot a photograph 指照片、相片： *I tried to get a shot of him in the water.* 我試着給他拍一張在水中的照片。 **NOTE** **Shot** often places more emphasis on the process of taking the photograph, rather than the finished picture. * shot 通常更強調拍攝照片的過程，而非已拍出的照片。

snapshot/snap an informal photograph that is taken quickly, and not by a professional photographer 指非攝影專業的人隨手抓拍的照片： *holiday snaps* 度假時拍的照片

print a copy of a photograph that is produced from film or from a digital camera 指（由膠片或數碼相機洗印的）照片： *a set of prints* 一套照片

PATTERNS

- a **colour** photograph/picture/photo/snap/print
- to **take** a photograph/picture/photo/shot/snapshot

pho·tog·raph·er /fəˈtɒɡrəfə(r); *NAmE* fəˈtɑːɡ-/ *noun* a person who takes photographs, especially as a job 拍照者；攝影師： *a **wildlife/fashion/portrait photographer*** 野生動物 / 時裝 / 人像攝影師

photo·graph·ic /ˌfəʊtəˈɡræfɪk; *NAmE* ˌfoʊ-/ *adj.* connected with photographs or photography 攝影的；攝製的；照片的： *photographic equipment/film/images* 攝影設備 / 膠片 / 圖像 ◇ *They produced a photographic record of the event.* 他們為這一事件製作了一套照片實錄。◇ *His paintings are almost photographic in detail.* 他的繪畫細緻得簡直和照片一樣逼真。 ▸ **photo·graph·ic·al·ly** /-kli/ *adv.*

ˌphotographic ˈmemory *noun* [usually sing.] the ability to remember things accurately and in great detail after seeing them 精確的記憶力

pho·tog·raphy /fəˈtɒɡrəfi; *NAmE* fəˈtɑːɡ-/ *noun* [U] the art, process or job of taking photographs or filming sth 照相術；攝影： ***colour/flash/aerial, etc. photography*** 彩色、閃光、空中等攝影 ◇ ***fashion photography** by David Burn* 戴維 • 伯恩的時裝攝影 ◇ *Her hobbies include hiking and photography.* 她的業餘愛好包括徒步旅行和攝影。◇ *the **director of photography*** (= the person who is in charge of the actual filming of a film/movie, programme, etc.) 攝影導演 ◇ *Did you see the film about Antarctica? The photography was superb!* 你看了關於南極的那部電影沒有？攝影棒極了！ ➲ VISUAL VOCAB page V41

photo·jour·nal·ism /ˌfəʊtəʊˈdʒɜːnəlɪzəm; *NAmE* ˌfoʊtoʊˈdʒɜːrn-/ *noun* [U] the work of giving news using mainly photographs, especially in a magazine 圖片新聞報道；攝影新聞報道；攝影新聞工作

photo·mon·tage /ˌfəʊtəʊmɒnˈtɑːʒ; *NAmE* ˌfoʊtoʊmɑːnˈtɑːʒ/ *noun* [C, U] a picture which is made up of different photographs put together; the technique of producing these pictures 合成照片（術）；照相剪接

pho·ton /ˈfəʊtɒn; *NAmE* ˈfoʊtɑːn/ *noun* (*physics* 物) a unit of ELECTROMAGNETIC energy 光子；光量子

ˈphoto opportunity *noun* an occasion when a famous person arranges to be photographed doing sth that will impress the public 為名人拍照的時機；（為宣傳）拍照名人的時間

photo·real·ism /ˌfəʊtəʊˈriːəlɪzəm; -ˈrɪəl-; *NAmE* ˌfoʊtoʊˈriːəlɪzəm/ *noun* [U] an artistic style that represents a subject in an accurate and detailed way, like a photograph 照相寫實主義（如照片一般精確細緻地表現主題）

photo·recep·tor /ˈfəʊtəʊrɪseptə(r); *NAmE* ˈfoʊtoʊ-/ *noun* (*biology* 生) a cell or an organ that is sensitive to light 光感受器

photo·sensi·tive /ˌfəʊtəʊˈsensətɪv; *NAmE* ˌfoʊtoʊ-/ *adj.* (*technical* 術語) reacting to light, for example by changing colour or producing an electrical signal 光敏的；感光的

ˈphoto shoot *noun* an occasion when a photographer takes pictures of sb, for example a famous person, fashion model, etc. for use in a magazine, etc.（為名人、時裝模特等所作的）專業攝影： *I **went on a photo shoot** to Rio with him.* 我和他一起去里約拍照了。

photo·shop /ˈfəʊtəʊʃɒp; *NAmE* ˈfoʊtoʊʃɑːp/ (also **Photoshop**) *verb* (**-pp-**) **~ sth** to change a picture or photograph using a computer 用計算機修改（圖片或照片）： *I'm sure this picture has been photoshopped.* 我敢說這張圖片準用電腦修改過。

photo·stat /ˈfəʊtəstæt; *NAmE* ˈfoʊ-/ *noun* a photocopy or a machine that produces them 直接影印本；直接複印機

photo·syn·thesis /ˌfəʊtəʊˈsɪnθəsɪs; *NAmE* ˌfoʊtoʊ-/ *noun* [U] (*biology* 生) the process by which green plants turn CARBON DIOXIDE and water into food using energy obtained from light from the sun 光合作用 ➲ COLLOCATIONS at LIFE

photo·syn·the·size (*BrE* also **-ise**) /ˌfəʊtəʊˈsɪnθəsaɪz; *NAmE* ˌfoʊtoʊ-/ *verb* [I, T] **~ (sth)** (*biology* 生) (of plants 植物) to make food by means of PHOTOSYNTHESIS 通過光合作用產生（養料）；進行光合作用

photo·trop·ism /ˌfəʊtəʊˈtrəʊpɪzəm; *NAmE* ˌfoʊtoʊˈtroʊ-/ *noun* [U] (*biology* 生) the action of a plant turning towards or away from light （植物的正或負）向光性 ▸ **photo·trop·ic** /-ˈtrɒpɪk; *NAmE* -ˈtrɑːpɪk/ *adj.*

phrasal /ˈfreɪzl/ *adj.* of or connected with a phrase 短語的；詞組的

ˌphrasal ˈverb *noun* (*grammar* 語法) a verb combined with an adverb or a preposition, or sometimes both, to give a new meaning, for example *go in for*, *win over* and *see to* 短語動詞；動詞詞組；片語動詞

phrase /freɪz/ *noun, verb*

■ *noun* **1** (*grammar* 語法) a small group of words without a FINITE verb that together have a particular meaning and that typically form part of a sentence. 'the green car' and 'on Friday morning' are phrases. 短語；詞組；片語 ➲ SYNONYMS at WORD ➲ see also NOUN PHRASE **2** a group of words which have a particular meaning when used together 成語；習語；慣用法；警句： *a memorable phrase* 易記的警句 ◇ *She was, in her own favourite phrase, 'a woman without a past'.* 用她自己最喜歡的字眼說，她是個"沒有不清白過去的女人"。 ➲ see also CATCHPHRASE **3** (*music* 音) a short series of notes that form a unit within a longer passage in a piece of music 樂句；樂節 **IDM** see COIN *v.*, TURN *n.*

■ *verb* **1** [T] to say or write sth in a particular way （以某種方式）表達，措辭，推敲： **~ sth** (+ **adv./prep.**) *a carefully phrased remark* 措辭謹慎的話語 ◇ *I agree with what he says, but I'd have phrased it differently.* 我贊同他說的，但我會以不同的方式表述。◇ **~ sth as sth** *Her order was phrased as a suggestion.* 她的命令表述得像是一項建議。 **2** [I, T] **~ (sth)** to divide a piece of music into small groups of notes; to play or sing these in a particular way, especially in an effective way 劃分樂句，分樂節（尤指為奏樂或歌唱）

ˌ**phrase book** *noun* a book containing lists of common expressions translated into another language, especially for people visiting a foreign country 常用語手冊，會話手冊（出國旅遊者常用）

phrase·ology /ˌfreɪziˈɒlədʒi; *NAmE* -ˈɑːlə-/ *noun* [U] (*formal*) the particular way in which words and phrases are arranged when saying or writing sth 措辭；遣詞造句

phras·ing /ˈfreɪzɪŋ/ *noun* [U] **1** the words used to express sth 措辭；用語：*The phrasing of the report is ambiguous.* 這份報告的措辭模稜兩可。 **2** (*music* 音) the way in which a musician or singer divides a piece of music into phrases by pausing in suitable places 樂句劃分法；分句法

phreak·ing /ˈfriːkɪŋ/ *noun* [U] (*informal, especially NAmE*) the act of getting into a communications system illegally, usually in order to make telephone calls without paying 非法竊入通訊系統；（通常指）竊用電話 ▸ **phreak·er** *noun*

phren·ology /frəˈnɒlədʒi; *NAmE* -ˈnɑːl-/ *noun* [U] the study of the shape of the human head, which some people think is a guide to a person's character 顱相學 ▸ **phren·olo·gist** /frəˈnɒlədʒɪst; *NAmE* -ˈnɑːl-/ *noun*

phwoah (also **phwoor**, **phwoar**) /ˈfwɔːə/ *exclamation* (*BrE, informal*) used when you find sth or sb very impressive and attractive, especially in a sexual way（對某事物或某人的性感魅力等表示讚歎）哇噻

phylum /ˈfaɪləm/ *noun* (*pl.* **phyla** /-lə/) (*biology* 生) a group into which animals, plants, etc. are divided, smaller than a KINGDOM and larger than a CLASS（生物分類學的）門 ➲ compare GENUS

phys·ic·al 0▬ AW /ˈfɪzɪkl/ *adj., noun*

■ ***adj.***

▸ **THE BODY 身體 1** 0▬ [usually before noun] connected with a person's body rather than their mind 身體的；肉體的；軀體的：*physical fitness* 健康體魄 ◇ *physical appearance* 外貌 ◇ *The ordeal has affected both her mental and physical health.* 痛苦的經歷損害了她的身心健康。◇ *He tends to avoid all physical contact.* 他傾向於避免一切身體接觸。

▸ **REAL THINGS 實物 2** 0▬ [only before noun] connected with things that actually exist or are present and can be seen, felt, etc. rather than things that only exist in a person's mind 客觀存在的；現實的；物質的；有形的：*the* ***physical world/universe/environment*** 客觀世界／宇宙／環境 ◇ *the* ***physical properties*** (= the colour, weight, shape, etc.) *of copper* 銅的物理性質

▸ **NATURE/SCIENCE 自然；科學 3** 0▬ [only before noun] according to the laws of nature 根據自然規律的；符合自然法則的：*It is a physical impossibility to be in two places at once.* 同時身處兩地在自然法則上是不可能的。 **4** 0▬ [only before noun] connected with the scientific study of forces such as heat, light, sound, etc. and how they affect objects 物理學的：*physical laws* 物理定律

▸ **SEX 性 5** 0▬ involving sex 性慾的；肉慾的：*physical love* 性愛 ◇ *They are having a physical relationship.* 他們一直有性關係。

▸ **PERSON 人 6** (*informal*) (of a person 人) liking to touch other people a lot 愛觸摸他人的；愛動手動腳的：*She's not very physical.* 她不愛摩摩挲挲的。

▸ **VIOLENT 暴力 7** (*informal*) violent (used to avoid saying this in a direct way) 使用武力的；粗暴的：*Are you going to cooperate or do we have to get physical?* 你是合作呢，還是要我們動手？

■ ***noun*** (also ˌ**physical exami'nation**) a medical examination of a person's body, for example, to check that they are fit enough to do a particular job 體檢；體格檢查 ➲ SYNONYMS at next page

ˌ**physical edu'cation** *noun* = PE

ˌ**physical ge'ography** *noun* [U] **1** the scientific study of the natural features on the surface of the earth, for example mountains and rivers 自然地理學 **2** the way in which the natural features of a place are arranged 地貌特徵；地形；地勢：*the physical geography of Scotland* 蘇格蘭的地形

phys·ic·al·ity /ˌfɪzɪˈkæləti/ *noun* [U] (*formal*) the quality of being physical rather than emotional or spiritual 肉體性

phys·ic·al·ly 0▬ AW /ˈfɪzɪkli/ *adv.*

1 0▬ in a way that is connected with a person's body rather than their mind 身體上；肉體上：*mentally and physically handicapped* 身心俱殘 ◇ *physically and emotionally exhausted* 身心交瘁 ◇ *I felt physically sick before the exam.* 大考前我感到身體不適。◇ *I don't find him physically attractive.* 我不覺得他外表吸引人。◇ *They were physically prevented from entering the building.* 他們被擋在大樓門外。 **2** 0▬ according to the laws of nature or what is probable 依據自然規律；按自然法則；根本上：*It's physically impossible to finish by the end of the week.* 根本不可能在本週末之前完成。

ˌ**physical 'science** *noun* [U] (also **the physical sciences** [pl.]) the areas of science concerned with studying natural forces and things that are not alive, for example physics and chemistry 自然科學；物理科學 ➲ compare LIFE SCIENCES

ˌ**physical 'therapist** (*US*) (*BrE* **physio·ther·ap·ist**, *informal* **physio**) *noun* a person whose job is to give patients physical therapy 物理治療師；理療師

ˌ**physical 'therapy** (*US*) (*BrE* **physio·ther·apy**, *informal* **physio**) *noun* [U] the treatment of disease, injury or weakness in the joints or muscles by exercises, MASSAGE and the use of light and heat 物理治療；理療

ˌ**physical 'training** *noun* = PT (1)

phys·ician /fɪˈzɪʃn/ *noun* (*especially NAmE*) a doctor, especially one who is a specialist in general medicine and not SURGERY 醫師；（尤指）內科醫生 ➲ compare SURGEON **HELP** This word is now old-fashioned in *BrE*. **Doctor** or **GP** is used instead. 在英式英語中，本詞現已過時，而代之以 doctor 或 GP。

physi·cist /ˈfɪzɪsɪst/ *noun* a scientist who studies physics 物理學家；物理學研究者：*a nuclear physicist* 核物理學家

phys·ics 0▬ /ˈfɪzɪks/ *noun* [U]

the scientific study of matter and energy and the relationships between them, including the study of forces, heat, light, sound, electricity and the structure of atoms 物理學：*a degree in physics* 物理學學位 ◇ ***particle/nuclear/theoretical physics*** 粒子／核／理論物理學 ◇ *the laws of physics* 物理定律 ◇ *a school physics department* 學校的物理系 ◇ *to study the physics of the electron* 研究電子物理 ➲ see also ASTROPHYSICS, GEOPHYSICS

physio /ˈfɪziəʊ; *NAmE* ˈfɪzioʊ/ *noun* (*pl.* **-os**) (*BrE, informal*) **1** [U] = PHYSIOTHERAPY **2** [C] = PHYSIOTHERAPIST

physio- /ˈfɪziəʊ; *NAmE* ˈfɪzioʊ/ *combining form* (in nouns, adjectives and adverbs 構成名詞、形容詞和副詞) **1** connected with nature 自然的 **2** connected with PHYSIOLOGY 生理學的

physi·ognomy /ˌfɪziˈɒnəmi; *NAmE* -ˈɑːnə-/ *noun* (*pl.* **-ies**) (*formal*) the shape and features of a person's face 容貌；相貌；面相

physi·olo·gist /ˌfɪziˈɒlədʒɪst; *NAmE* -ˈɑːlə-/ *noun* a scientist who studies physiology 生理學家；生理學研究者

physi·ology /ˌfɪziˈɒlədʒi; *NAmE* -ˈɑːlə-/ *noun* **1** [U] the scientific study of the normal functions of living things 生理學：*the department of anatomy and physiology* 解剖生理學系 **2** [U, sing.] the way in which a particular living thing functions 生理機能：*plant physiology* 植物的生理機能 ◇ *the physiology of the horse* 馬的生理機能 ▸ **physio·logic·al** /ˌfɪziəˈlɒdʒɪkl; *NAmE* -ˈlɑːdʒ-/ *adj.*：*the physiological effect of space travel* 宇宙航行的生理影響 **physio·lo·gic·al·ly** /-ɪkli/ *adv.*

physio·ther·ap·ist /ˌfɪziəʊˈθerəpɪst; *NAmE* ˌfɪzioʊ-/ (also *informal* **physio**) (both *BrE*) (*US* ˌ**physical 'therapist**) *noun* a person whose job is to give patients physiotherapy 物理治療師；理療師

physio·ther·apy /ˌfɪziəʊˈθerəpi; *NAmE* ˌfɪzioʊ-/ (also *informal* **physio**) (both *BrE*) (*US* ˌ**physical 'therapy**) *noun* [U] the treatment of disease, injury or weakness in the joints or muscles by exercises, MASSAGE and the use

P

of light and heat 物理治療；理療 ➲ COLLOCATIONS at INJURY

phys·ique /fɪ'ziːk/ *noun* [C, U] the size and shape of a person's body 體格；體形 SYN **build**: *He has the physique of a rugby player.* 他有橄欖球運動員的體形。◇ *a powerful physique* 健壯的體格

pi /paɪ/ *noun* **1** (*geometry* 幾何) the symbol π used to show the RATIO of the CIRCUMFERENCE of (= distance around) a circle to its DIAMETER (= distance across), that is 3.14159 ... 圓周率 **2** the 16th letter of the Greek alphabet (Π, π) 希臘字母表的第 16 個字母

pi·an·is·simo /ˌpiə'nɪsɪməʊ; *NAmE* -moʊ/ *adv.* (*abbr.* **pp**) (*music* 音) played or sung very quietly 極輕柔地；很弱 OPP **fortissimo** ▸ **pi·an·is·simo** *adj.*

pi·an·ist /'pɪənɪst/ *noun* a person who plays the piano 鋼琴彈奏者；鋼琴家：*a concert pianist* 音樂會的鋼琴演奏者 ◇ *a jazz pianist* 爵士樂的鋼琴演奏者

piano *noun, adv.*

■ **noun** /pi'ænəʊ; *NAmE* -noʊ/ (*pl.* **-os**) (also *old-fashioned, formal* **pi·ano·forte** /piˌænəʊ'fɔːti; *NAmE* piˌænoʊ'fɔːr-/) a large musical instrument played by pressing the black and white keys on the keyboard. The sound is produced by small HAMMERS hitting the metal strings inside the piano. 鋼琴：*to play the piano* 彈鋼琴 ◇ *playing jazz*

Collocations 詞語搭配

Physical appearance 外貌

- A person may be described as **having** 描述一個人的長相可用 have 一詞：

Eyes 眼睛

- (bright) blue/green/(dark/light) brown/hazel **eyes** （明亮的）藍／綠／（深／淺）棕色／淺綠褐色眼睛
- deep-set/sunken/bulging/protruding **eyes** 凹陷的／凸出的眼睛
- small/beady/sparkling/twinkling/(*informal*) shifty **eyes** 小的／小珠般圓亮的／亮晶晶的／閃閃發亮的／賊溜溜的眼睛
- piercing/penetrating/steely **eyes** 敏銳的／銳利的眼睛；冷冰冰的眼神
- bloodshot/watery/puffy **eyes** 佈滿血絲的／水汪汪的／腫脹的眼睛
- bushy/thick/dark/raised/arched **eyebrows** 濃密的／揚起的／弓形的眉毛
- long/dark/thick/curly/false **eyelashes/lashes** 長長的／濃密的／彎曲的／假的眼睫毛

Face 臉

- a flat/bulbous/pointed/sharp/snub **nose** 塌／蒜頭／尖頭／尖／短平而上翹的鼻子
- a straight/a hooked/a Roman/(*formal*) an aquiline **nose** 挺直的鼻子；鷹鉤鼻；高鼻梁；鷹鉤鼻
- full/thick/thin/pouty **lips** 豐滿的／厚／薄／翹嘴唇
- dry/chapped/cracked **lips** 乾的／皸裂的／乾裂的嘴唇
- flushed/rosy/red/ruddy/pale **cheeks** 發紅的／紅潤的／蒼白的面頰
- soft/chubby/sunken **cheeks** 柔嫩的／胖乎乎的／凹陷的面頰
- white/perfect/crooked/protruding **teeth** 潔白的／完好無缺的／參差不齊的／凸出來的牙齒
- a large/high/broad/wide/sloping **forehead** 大大的／高高的／寬大的／後傾的前額
- a strong/weak/pointed/double **chin** 硬朗的／瘦削的／尖／雙下巴
- a long/full/bushy/wispy/goatee **beard** 長／大／濃密的／一小撮／山羊鬍子
- a long/thin/bushy/droopy/handlebar/pencil **moustache**/(*especially US*) **mustache** 長長的／稀疏的／濃密的／耷拉着的／翹／細直的八字鬍

Hair and skin 頭髮和皮膚

- pale/fair/olive/dark/tanned **skin** 蒼白的／白皙的／橄欖色的／黝黑的／曬黑的皮膚
- dry/oily/smooth/rough/leathery/wrinkled **skin** 乾性的／油性的／光滑的／粗糙的／有皺紋的皮膚
- a dark/pale/light/sallow/ruddy/olive/swarthy/clear **complexion** 黝黑的／蒼白的／淺淡的／蠟黃的／紅潤的／橄欖色的／黝黑的／清秀的面容
- deep/fine/little/facial **wrinkles** 深深的／細小的／小的／面部的皺紋
- blonde/blond/fair/(light/dark) brown/(jet-)black/auburn/red/(*BrE*) ginger/grey **hair** 金黃色的／淺色的／（淺／深）棕色的／烏黑的／紅褐色的／紅色的／薑黃色的／灰白色的頭髮
- straight/curly/wavy/frizzy/spiky **hair** 直髮；鬈髮；波浪形的／鬈曲的／刺猬式的頭髮
- thick/thin/fine/bushy/thinning **hair** 厚密的／稀疏的／纖細的／濃密的／逐漸稀少的頭髮
- dyed/bleached/soft/silky/dry/greasy/shiny **hair** 染了色的／漂白了的／柔順的／絲滑的／乾性的／油性的／有光澤的頭髮
- long/short/shoulder-length/cropped **hair** 長／短／齊肩／剪短了的頭髮
- a bald/balding/shaved **head** 禿頭；開始禿頂的頭；剃光了的頭
- a receding **hairline** 後移的髮際線
- a bald **patch/spot** 禿了的一塊
- a side/centre/(*US*) center (*BrE*) **parting**/(*NAmE*) **part** 偏分；中分

Body 身體

- a long/short/thick/slender/(*disapproving*) scrawny **neck** 長／短／粗／細／乾瘦的脖子
- broad/narrow/sloping/rounded/hunched **shoulders** 寬／窄／斜／圓／聳肩膀
- a bare/broad/muscular/small/large **chest** 赤裸的／寬闊的／肌肉發達的胸膛；小胸；大胸
- a flat/swollen/bulging **stomach** 扁平的／鼓脹的／鼓起的肚子
- a small/tiny/narrow/slim/slender/28-inch **waist** 纖細的／28 英寸的腰
- big/wide/narrow/slim **hips** 大的／寬的／窄小的／苗條的臀部
- a straight/bent/arched/broad/hairy **back** 直的／彎曲的／弓著的／寬大的／多毛的背部
- thin/slender/muscular **arms** 瘦削的／細長的／肌肉發達的臂膀
- big/large/small/manicured/calloused/gloved **hands** 大的／小的／修剪整齊的／有老繭的／戴著手套的手
- long/short/fat/slender/delicate/bony **fingers** 長的／短的／粗的／細長的／纖細的／瘦削的手指
- long/muscular/hairy/shapely/(*both informal, often disapproving*) skinny/spindly **legs** 長的／肌肉發達的／多毛的／有曲線美的／皮包骨的／乾瘦的腿
- muscular/chubby/(*informal, disapproving*) flabby **thighs** 肌肉發達的／胖乎乎的／肥胖的大腿
- big/little/small/dainty/wide/narrow/bare **feet** 大的／小的／嬌小可愛的／寬的／窄的／光著的腳
- a good/a slim/a slender/an hourglass **figure** 好的／修長的／苗條的／沙漏形身材
- **be of** slim/medium/average/large/athletic/stocky **build** 有著苗條的／中等的／普通的／大塊頭的／健壯的／矮壯的身材

P

on the piano 用鋼琴彈奏爵士樂 ◇ *piano music* 鋼琴曲 ◇ *a **piano teacher/lesson*** 鋼琴教師／課 ◇ *Ravel's piano concerto in G* 拉威爾的 G 大調鋼琴協奏曲 ➲ see also GRAND PIANO, THUMB PIANO, UPRIGHT PIANO
▪ ***adv.*** /ˈpjɑːnəʊ; *NAmE* -noʊ/ (*abbr.* **p**) (*music* 音) played or sung quietly 輕柔地；安靜地；弱 **OPP** **forte** ▸ **piano** *adj.*

piˌano acˈcordion *noun* a type of ACCORDION that you press buttons and keys on to produce the different notes（鍵盤式）手風琴

Pi·an·ola™ /ˌpiəˈnəʊlə; *NAmE* -ˈnoʊ-/ *noun* a piano that plays automatically by means of a PIANO ROLL 皮阿諾拉自動鋼琴（用穿孔氣動紙捲控制琴鍵）**SYN** **player piano**

piˈano roll *noun* a roll of paper full of very small holes that controls the movement of the keys in a PLAYER PIANO 自動鋼琴打孔紙捲（用於自動鋼琴琴鍵彈奏）

pi·azza /piˈætsə; *NAmE* piˈɑːzə/ *noun* a public square, especially in an Italian town（尤指意大利城鎮中的）廣場

pi·broch /ˈpiːbrɒk; -brɒx; *NAmE* -brɑːk; -brɑːx/ *noun* [C, U] a piece of music played on the BAGPIPES, especially at military occasions or funerals; music of this type 風笛變奏曲（常在軍事場合或葬禮上吹奏）

pic /pɪk/ *noun* (*informal*) a picture 圖片；畫片

pica /ˈpaɪkə/ *noun* (*technical* 術語) a unit for measuring the size of printed letters and the length of a line of printed text 派卡（印刷字母規格和字行長度單位）

pi·can·te /pɪˈkɑːnteɪ/ *adj.* (from *Spanish*, *NAmE*) (of food 食物) hot and spicy 香辣的：*tortilla chips dipped in a picante sauce* 蘸香辣調味汁的玉米薄片

pic·ar·esque /ˌpɪkəˈresk/ *adj.* (*formal*) connected with literature that describes the adventures of a person who is sometimes dishonest but easy to like 流浪漢小說題材的：*a picaresque novel* 一部流浪漢小說

Pic·ca·dilly Cir·cus /ˌpɪkədɪli ˈsɜːkəs; *NAmE* ˈsɜːrkəs/ *noun* (*BrE*) used to describe a place that is very busy or crowded 熱鬧忙碌的地方；擁擠的地方：*It's been like Piccadilly Circus in this house all morning.* 這房子裏整個上午都忙亂得像皮卡迪利廣場。**ORIGIN** From the name of a busy area in the centre of London where several large roads meet and where there is always a lot of traffic. 源自倫敦市中心繁忙地帶皮卡迪利廣場，幾條大街在此交匯，車輛川流不息。➲ compare GRAND CENTRAL STATION

pic·ca·ninny (also **picka·ninny**) /ˌpɪkəˈnɪni/ *noun* (*pl.* **-ies**) (*old-fashioned*) an offensive word for a small black child（含冒犯意）小黑人，小黑崽

pic·colo /ˈpɪkələʊ; *NAmE* -loʊ/ *noun* (*pl.* **-os**) a musical instrument of the WOODWIND group, like a small FLUTE that plays high notes 短笛 ➲ **VISUAL VOCAB** page V34

pick 🗝 /pɪk/ *verb, noun*
▪ ***verb*** **1** 🗝 [T] (rather *informal*) to choose sb/sth from a group of people or things 選擇；挑選：**~ sb/sth** *Pick a number from one to twenty.* 從一至二十中挑選一個數。◇ *She picked the best cake for herself.* 她為自己挑了一塊最好的蛋糕。◇ *He **picked his words** carefully.* 他用詞細心謹慎。◇ *Have I picked a bad time to talk to you?* 我是不是挑了個不恰當的時間跟你談話？◇ **~ sb/sth to do sth** *He has been picked to play in this week's game.* 他已入選參加本週的比賽。➲ **SYNONYMS** at CHOOSE ➲ see also HAND-PICKED **2** 🗝 [T] **~ sth** to take flowers, fruit, etc. from the plant or the tree where they are growing 採；摘：*to pick grapes* 摘葡萄 ◇ *flowers freshly picked from the garden* 剛從花園採的鮮花 ◇ *to go blackberry picking* 去採黑莓 **3** 🗝 [T] to pull or remove sth or small pieces of sth from sth else, especially with your fingers（用手指）摘掉，剔除，掐去：**~ sth + adv./prep.** *She picked bits of fluff from his sweater.* 她摘掉他毛衣上的絨毛。◇ *He picked the nuts off the top of the cake.* 他把蛋糕上面的果仁拿掉。◇ **~ sth** *to **pick your nose*** (= put your finger inside your nose to remove dried MUCUS) 摳鼻子 ◇ *to **pick your teeth*** (= use a small sharp piece of wood to remove pieces of food from your teeth) 剔牙 ◇ **~ sth + adj.** *The dogs picked the bones clean* (= ate all the meat from the bones). 狗把骨頭啃得乾乾淨淨。**4** [I, T] **~ (sth)** (*NAmE*) = PLUCK (3)

IDM **ˌpick and ˈchoose** to choose only those things that you like or want very much 挑揀；精挑細選：*You have to take any job you can get—you can't pick and choose.* 你只能有什麼工作就幹什麼，沒得挑三揀四了。**pick sb's ˈbrains** (*informal*) to ask sb a lot of questions about sth because they know more about the subject than you do 討教；請教；不斷地問（以向別人學習）**pick a ˈfight/ˈquarrel (with sb)** to deliberately start a fight or an argument with sb 找碴兒；找麻煩；挑釁 **pick ˈholes in sth** to find the weak points in sth such as a plan, suggestion, etc. 挑刺兒；挑毛病；找漏洞：*It was easy to pick holes in his arguments.* 找他論據中的漏洞很容易。**pick a ˈlock** to open a lock without a key, using sth such as a piece of wire（用鐵絲等）捅開鎖 **pick sb's ˈpocket** to steal sth from sb's pocket without them noticing 扒竊；掏包兒 ➲ related noun PICKPOCKET **pick up the ˈbill, ˈtab, etc. (for sth)** (*informal*) to pay for sth 付賬：*The company picked up the tab for his hotel room.* 公司為他付旅館費。◇ *The government will continue to pick up college fees for some students.* 政府將繼續替一些學生繳納學費。**pick up the ˈpieces** to return or to help sb return to a normal situation, particularly after a shock or a disaster（使）恢復；補救；收拾殘局：*You cannot live your children's lives for them; you can only be there to pick up the pieces when things go wrong.* 你不能替孩子過活，只能在出現問題時幫忙解決。**pick up ˈspeed** to go faster 加速 **pick up the ˈthreads** to return to an earlier situation or way of life after an interruption 恢復原狀 **pick your ˈway (across, along, among, over, through sth)** to walk carefully, choosing the safest, driest, etc. place to put your feet 擇路而行；小心看着路行走：*She picked her way delicately over the rough ground.* 她小心翼翼地在高低不平的地面上行走。**pick a ˈwinner** **1** to choose a horse, etc. that you think is most likely to win a race 認定勝利者（如賽馬中）**2** (*informal*) to make a very good choice 挑選得當；選得很準 ➲ more at BONE *n.*, PIECE *n.*, SHRED *n.*

PHR V **ˈpick at sth** **1** to eat food slowly, taking small amounts or bites because you are not hungry 磨蹭着吃；（因為不餓而）小口吃 **2** to pull or touch sth several times（反複地）揪，扯：*He tried to undo the knot by picking at it with his fingers.* 他用手指不停地扯，想把繩結解開。

ˌpick sb↔ˈoff (*informal*) to aim carefully at a person, an animal or an aircraft, especially one of a group, and then shoot them 選擇（目標）射擊：*Snipers were picking off innocent civilians.* 狙擊手專揀無辜的平民射擊。**ˌpick sth↔ˈoff** to remove sth from sth such as a tree, a plant, etc. 去除；剪除：*Pick off all the dead leaves.* 把枯葉全部摘掉。

ˈpick on sb/sth **1** to treat sb unfairly, by blaming, criticizing or punishing them（跟某人）鬧彆扭；故意刁難挑剔：*She was picked on by the other girls because of her size.* 她因為個頭關係被其他女孩欺負。**2** to choose sb/sth 挑選；選中：*He picked on two of her statements which he said were untrue.* 他從她的話中挑出了兩處他認為不真實的地方。

ˌpick sb/sth↔ˈout **1** to choose sb/sth carefully from a group of people or things 精心挑選 **SYN** **select**：*She was picked out from dozens of applicants for the job.* 她從大批的求職者中被選中承擔這項工作。◇ *He picked out the ripest peach for me.* 他給我挑了個熟透了的桃子。**2** to recognize sb/sth from among other people or things 認出來；辨別出：*See if you can pick me out in this photo.* 看你能不能把我從這張照片上認出來。**ˌpick sth↔ˈout** **1** to play a tune on a musical instrument slowly without using written music（不用樂譜）慢慢地彈奏（樂曲）：*He picked out the tune on the piano with one finger.* 他憑記憶用一個手指在鋼琴上慢慢彈出了那支曲子。**2** to discover or recognize sth after careful study（經仔細研究）找出，認識到：*Read the play again and pick out the major themes.* 重讀劇本，把主題找出來。**3** to make sth easy to see or hear 使顯著；使容易看見（或聽見）：*a sign painted cream, with the lettering picked out in black* 印着醒目黑字的乳白色標牌

ˌpick sth↔ˈover | **ˌpick ˈthrough sth** to examine a group of things carefully, especially to choose the ones you want 用心挑選；篩選：*Pick over the lentils and remove any little stones.* 仔細挑揀豆子，把小石子揀出去。◇ *I picked through the facts of the case.* 我仔細審查本案的事實。

ˌpick ˈup 1 to get better, stronger, etc.; to improve 改善；好轉；增強：*Trade usually picks up in the spring.* 貿易一般在春天回升。◇ *The wind is picking up now.* 現在風愈颳愈大了。◇ *Sales have picked up 14% this year.* 今年銷售額增長了 14%。➲ related noun PICKUP (3) **2** (*informal*) to start again; to continue 重新開始；繼續：*Let's* **pick up where we left off** *yesterday.* 咱們從昨天停下的地方繼續吧。**3** (*informal, especially NAmE*) to put things away and make things neat, especially for sb else（為某人）收拾，整理：*All I seem to do is cook, wash and pick up after the kids.* 燒飯、洗衣、跟在孩子屁股後頭收拾東西，好像這就是我全部的活兒。**ˌpick ˈup | ˌpick sth ˈup** to answer a phone 接電話：*The phone rang and rang and nobody picked up.* 電話鈴響了又響，但沒人接。**ˌpick sb↔ˈup 1** 🔑 to go somewhere in your car and collect sb who is waiting for you（開車）接人 SYN **collect**：*I'll pick you up at five.* 我五點鐘來接你。**2** to allow sb to get into your vehicle and take them somewhere 讓人乘車；搭載：*The bus picks up passengers outside the airport.* 公共汽車在機場外接送乘客。**3** to rescue sb from the sea or from a dangerous place, especially one that is difficult to reach（從海裏或危險處）營救，搭救：*A lifeboat picked up survivors.* 救生艇把幸存者救起來。**4** (*informal, often disapproving*) to start talking to sb you do not know because you want to have a sexual relationship with them（猥褻地與生人）搭訕，勾搭：*He goes to clubs to pick up girls.* 他到俱樂部去泡妞。➲ related noun PICKUP (2) **5** (*informal*) (of the police 警察) to arrest sb 逮捕；抓捕：*He was picked up by police and taken to the station for questioning.* 警察把他抓到局子問話去了。**6** to make sb feel better 使人覺得舒服；提神：*Try this—it will pick you up.* 嚐嚐這個，能讓你提提神的。➲ related noun PICK-ME-UP **ˌpick sb/sth↔ˈup** 🔑 to take hold of sb/sth and lift them/it up 拿起；舉起；提起：*She went over to the crying child and picked her up.* 她走到啼哭的孩子身邊，把她抱了起來。**ˌpick sth↔ˈup 1** 🔑 to get information or a skill by chance rather than by making a deliberate effort（偶然）得到，聽到，學會：*to pick up bad habits* 染上壞習慣 ◇ *Here's a tip I picked up from my mother.* 告訴你一個竅門，是我從媽媽那裏學來的。◇ *She picked up Spanish when she was living in Mexico.* 她旅居墨西哥時順便學會了西班牙語。**2** to identify or recognize sth 辨認；識別出：*Scientists can now pick up early signs of the disease.* 現在科學家能夠辨認這種疾病的早期症狀。**3** 🔑 to collect sth from a place 取回；收集：*I picked up my coat from the cleaners.* 我從乾洗店取回了外衣。➲ related noun PICKUP (4) **4** 🔑 to receive an electronic signal, sound or picture 接收（信號、聲音、圖像等）：*We were able to pick up the BBC World Service.* 我們能收到英國廣播公司國際廣播節目。**5** (*informal*) to buy sth, especially cheaply or by chance（碰巧）買到（便宜的東西）：*We managed to pick up a few bargains at the auction.* 我們從拍賣場買到了幾件便宜貨。**6** (*informal*) to get or obtain sth 得到；感染；得到：*I seem to have picked up a terrible cold from somewhere.* 我似乎從什麼地方染上了重感冒。◇ *I picked up £30 in tips today.* 我今天得到 30 英鎊的小費。**7** to find and follow a route 找到；跟蹤；追尋：*to pick up the scent of an animal* 追蹤動物的臭跡 ◇ *We can pick up the motorway in a few miles.* 經過幾英里以後我們就能上高速公路。**8** to return to an earlier subject or situation in order to continue it 回到（本題）；恢復原狀 SYN **take up**：*He picks up this theme again in later chapters of the book.* 在該書的後幾章，他又重回到這個主題上。**9** to notice sth that is not very obvious; to see sth that you are looking for 察覺；發現；注意到：*I picked up the faint sound of a car in the distance.* 我聽到遠處傳來微弱的汽車聲。**10** (*especially NAmE*) to put things away neatly 收拾；整理：*Will you pick up all your toys?* 把你的玩具都收起來好不好？**11** (*NAmE*) to put things away and make a room neat 收拾房間：*to pick up a room* 整理房間 **ˌpick ˈup on sth 1** to notice sth and perhaps react to it 領略；意會；意識到：*She failed to pick up on the humour in his remark.* 她沒有領悟他話中的幽默。**2** to return to a point that has already been mentioned or discussed 回到（某課題等）；重提（要點等）：*If I could just pick up on a question you raised earlier.* 請允許我重提一下您早先提出的問題。**ˌpick sb ˈup on sth** to mention sth that sb has said or done that you think is wrong 提到某人的錯誤；挑毛病；算舊賬：*I knew he would pick me up on that slip sooner or later.* 我知道他遲早會提起我那個小過失的。**ˌpick yourself ˈup** to stand up again after you have fallen（跌倒後）站起來：*He just picked himself up and went on running.* 他爬起來繼續跑。◇ (*figurative*) *She didn't waste time feeling sorry for herself—she just picked herself up and carried on.* 她沒有浪費時間自憐，而是振作起來繼續幹。

■ **noun 1** [sing.] (rather *informal*) an act of choosing sth 挑選；選擇：***Take your pick*** (= choose). 自己選吧。◇ *The winner gets first pick of the prizes.* 獲勝者可先挑獎品。**2** [C] (*informal*) a person or thing that is chosen 選中的人（或物）：*She was his pick for best actress.* 她是他選中的最佳女演員。➲ SYNONYMS at CHOICE **3** [sing.] **the ~ of sth** (rather *informal*) the best thing or things in a group 精品；精華；最好的東西：*We're reviewing the pick of this month's new books.* 我們正在做本月的精品新書評介。◇ *I think we got* ***the pick of the bunch*** (= the best in the group). 我認為我們得到了其中的極品。**4** [C] = PICKAXE：*picks and shovels* 鎬與平鍬 **5** [C] (*informal*) = PLECTRUM ➲ see also ICE PICK, TOOTHPICK IDM see BUNCH *n.*

ˈpick-and-mix *adj.* (*BrE*) used to describe a way of putting sth together by choosing things from among a large variety of different items 組合的；綜合的；拼合的：*a pick-and-mix programme of study* 綜合課程

picka·ninny = PICCANINNY

pick·axe (*NAmE* also **pick·ax**) /ˈpɪkæks/ (also **pick**) *noun* a large heavy tool that has a curved metal bar with sharp ends fixed at the centre to a wooden handle. It is used for breaking rocks or hard ground. 鎬；尖嘴鎬；鶴嘴鋤 ➲ picture at AXE

pick·er /ˈpɪkə(r)/ *noun* a person or machine that picks flowers, vegetables, etc. 採摘者；採摘機；採摘工具：*cotton pickers* 採棉人

picket /ˈpɪkɪt/ *noun, verb*

■ **noun 1** a person or group of people who stand outside the entrance to a building in order to protest about sth, especially in order to stop people from entering a factory, etc. during a strike; an occasion at which this happens（罷工期間糾察妥協分子的）糾察員，糾察隊；罷工警戒：*Five pickets were arrested by police.* 五名糾察隊員被警方逮捕。◇ *I was on picket duty at the time.* 當時我正執行罷工的糾察工作。◇ *a mass picket of the factory* 工廠的大規模罷工糾察隊 ➲ see also FLYING PICKET, PICKETER **2** a soldier or group of soldiers guarding a military base（軍營的）警戒哨，警戒隊，哨兵 **3** a pointed piece of wood that is fixed in the ground, especially as part of a fence（尤指柵欄的）尖木樁，尖板條：*a picket fence* 尖板條柵欄

■ **verb** [T, I] **~ (sth)** to stand outside somewhere such as your place of work to protest about sth or to try and persuade people to join a strike 在…外抗議；做罷工糾察：*200 workers were picketing the factory.* * 200 名工人在工廠外罷工抗議。◇ *Striking workers picketed outside the gates.* 罷工工人圍在大門外擔任糾察（禁止出入）。

pick·et·er /ˈpɪkɪtə(r)/ *noun* (*NAmE*) a person who takes part in a picket（罷工行動的）糾察隊員

picket·ing /ˈpɪkɪtɪŋ/ *noun* [U] the activity of standing outside the entrance to a building in order to protest about sth and stop people from entering the building 進行糾察封鎖；擔任警戒；圍廠抗議：*mass picketing of the factory* 罷工工人集體對工廠的封鎖

ˈpicket line *noun* a line or group of PICKETS (1) 糾察線；糾察隊人牆：*Fire crews refused to cross the picket line.* 消防人員拒不衝破圍廠隊伍人牆。

pick·ings /ˈpɪkɪŋz/ *noun* [pl.] something, especially money, that can be obtained from a particular situation in an easy or a dishonest way 油水；（不正當的）外

快；不義之財：*There were only* ***slim pickings*** *to be made at the fair.* 在交易會上只能撈些小油水。◇ *There are* ***rich pickings*** *to be had by investing in this sort of company.* 向這類公司投資大有油水可撈。◇ *The strike affecting the country's largest airline is producing* ***easy pickings*** *for smaller companies.* 罷工給全國最大航空公司帶來的影響使得較小的航空公司輕易撿到便宜。

pickle /ˈpɪkl/ *noun, verb*

■ ***noun*** **1** [C, usually pl.] (*BrE*) a vegetable that has been preserved in VINEGAR or salt water and has a strong flavour, served cold with meat, salads, etc. 泡菜；醃菜 **2** [U] (*BrE*) a cold thick spicy sauce made from fruit and vegetables that have been boiled, often sold in JARS and served with meat, cheese, etc. 菜醬 **3** (*NAmE*) (*BrE* **gher·kin**) [U, C] a small CUCUMBER that has been preserved in VINEGAR before being eaten 醋泡小黃瓜

IDM **in a ˈpickle** (*informal*) in a difficult or unpleasant situation 處於困境；處境窘迫

■ ***verb*** **~ sth** to preserve food in VINEGAR or salt water 醃漬

pickled /ˈpɪkld/ *adj.* **1** (of food 食物) preserved in VINEGAR 醃漬的：*pickled cabbage/herring/onions* 醃漬洋白菜／鯡魚／洋葱 **2** (*old-fashioned, informal*) drunk 醉醺醺的

ˌpick-me-up *noun* (*informal*) something that makes you feel better, happier, healthier, etc., especially medicine or an alcoholic drink 提神物品，興奮劑（尤指藥物或酒精飲料）：(*figurative*) *This deal would offer the best possible pick-me-up to the town's ailing economy.* 這筆交易對該鎮每況愈下的經濟是一服最好的強心劑。

pick·off /ˈpɪkɒf; *NAmE* -ɔːf; -ɑːf/ *noun* (*NAmE*) (in BASEBALL 棒球) a situation in which a player running to a BASE is out because a FIELDER or the PITCHER suddenly throws the ball to that base 牽制出局（指守場員或投球手對跑壘員突然傳殺致使其出局）

pick·pocket /ˈpɪkpɒkɪt; *NAmE* -pɑːkɪt/ *noun* a person who steals money, etc. from other people's pockets, especially in crowded places 扒手；小偷

pick·up /ˈpɪkʌp/ *noun, adj.*

■ ***noun*** **1** (also **ˈpickup truck**) [C] a vehicle with low sides and no roof at the back used, for example, by farmers 輕型貨車；敞篷小貨車；皮卡貨車 ➲ VISUAL VOCAB page V46 **2** [C] a person sb meets for the first time, for example in a bar, with whom they start a sexual relationship 偶然結識的調情者：*casual pickups* 遊戲鴛鴦 **3** [C] **~ (in sth)** an improvement 改進；好轉；改善：*a pickup in the housing market* 房市景氣的好轉 **4** [U, C] an occasion when sb/sth is collected 接人；收取物品；提貨：*Goods are delivered not later than noon on the day after pickup.* 貨物遞送不遲於收件後的第二天中午。**5** [C] the part of a record player or musical instrument that changes electrical signals into sound, or sound into electrical signals （唱機的）唱頭，磁頭 **6** [U] (*NAmE*) a vehicle's ability to ACCELERATE (= increase in speed) （車輛的）加速能力

■ ***adj.*** [only before noun] (*NAmE*) (of a sports game 體育比賽) often not planned in advance and that anyone who wants to can join in 臨時拼湊的；臨時組織的：*A group of kids started a pickup game of basketball on the street outside.* 一群孩子在外面開始了即興街頭籃球賽。

picky /ˈpɪki/ *adj.* (*informal*) (of a person 人) liking only particular things and difficult to please 挑剔的；難伺候的 **SYN** **fussy**

ˌpick-your-ˈown *adj.* [only before noun] (of fruit or vegetables 水果或蔬菜) picked by the customer on the farm where they are grown（顧客到農田）自己採摘的：*pick-your-own strawberries* 供人親手採摘的草莓

pic·nic /ˈpɪknɪk/ *noun, verb*

■ ***noun*** **1** an occasion when people pack a meal and take it to eat outdoors, especially in the countryside 野餐：*It's a nice day. Let's* ***go for a picnic.*** 天氣不錯；咱們去野餐吧。◇ *We* ***had a picnic*** *beside the river.* 我們在河邊野餐。**2** the meal, usually consisting of SANDWICHES, salad and fruit, etc. that you take with you when you go on a picnic 野餐食物：*Let's eat our picnic by the lake.* 咱們到湖邊去吃野餐吧。◇ *a picnic lunch* 午間野餐 ◇ *a picnic basket* 野餐提籃

IDM **be no ˈpicnic** (*informal*) to be difficult and cause a lot of problems 可不容易；不是好玩的：*Bringing up a family when you're unemployed is no picnic.* 失了業還要養家可不是容易的事。

■ ***verb*** **(-ck-)** [I] to have a picnic 野餐：*No picnicking allowed* (= on a sign) 禁止野餐

pic·nick·er /ˈpɪknɪkə(r)/ *noun* a person who is having a picnic 野餐者

pico- /ˈpiːkəʊ-; ˈpaɪkəʊ-; *NAmE* -koʊ-/ *combining form* (in nouns; used in units of measurement 構成名詞，用於計量單位) 10^{-12}; one million millionth 皮（可）；微微；萬億分之一

picto·gram /ˈpɪktəgræm/ *noun* **1** a picture representing a word or phrase 圖畫文字 **2** a diagram that uses pictures to represent amounts or numbers of a particular thing 統計圖表

pic·tor·ial /pɪkˈtɔːriəl/ *adj.* [usually before noun] **1** using or containing pictures 用圖片的；有插圖的：*a* ***pictorial account/record*** *of the expedition* 對遠征的圖片記述／記錄 **2** connected with pictures 畫片的；圖畫的：*pictorial traditions* 繪圖傳統 ▸ **pic·tori·al·ly** /-əli/ *adv.*

pic·ture 🔑 /ˈpɪktʃə(r)/ *noun, verb*

■ ***noun***

▸ **PAINTING/DRAWING 繪畫** **1** 🔑 [C] a painting or drawing, etc. that shows a scene, a person or thing 圖畫；繪畫：*A picture of flowers hung on the wall.* 牆上掛着一張花卉的圖畫。◇ *The children were* ***drawing pictures*** *of their pets.* 孩子們在畫他們的寵物。◇ *She wanted a famous artist to* ***paint her picture*** (= a picture of herself). 她想請一位名畫家為自己畫像。◇ *a book with lots of pictures in it* 一本有大量插圖的書

▸ **PHOTOGRAPH 照片** **2** 🔑 [C] a photograph 相片；照片：*We had our* ***picture taken*** *in front of the hotel.* 我們在旅館前照了像。◇ *The picture shows the couple together on their yacht.* 照片顯示這對情侶一同在他們的遊艇上。◇ *Have you got any pictures of your trip?* 你有這次旅行的照片嗎？ ➲ SYNONYMS at PHOTOGRAPH

▸ **ON TV 電視** **3** 🔑 [C] an image on a television screen 電視圖像：*harrowing television pictures of the famine* 電視上悲慘的饑荒畫面 ◇ *satellite pictures* 衛星圖像 ◇ *The picture isn't very clear tonight.* 今晚電視畫面不怎麼清楚。

▸ **DESCRIPTION 描述** **4** 🔑 [C, usually sing.] a description that gives you an idea in your mind of what sth is like 描繪；描述：*The writer paints a gloomy picture of the economy.* 作者把經濟狀況描繪得一片慘淡。◇ *The police are trying* ***to build up a picture*** *of what happened.* 警方正試圖掌握事情發生的經過。

▸ **MENTAL IMAGE 印象** **5** 🔑 [C, usually sing.] a mental image or memory of sth 頭腦中的情景；記憶；印象：*I have a vivid picture of my grandfather smiling down at me when I was very small.* 我清楚地記得很小的時候祖父低頭向我微笑的情景。

▸ **GENERAL SITUATION 局面** **6** **the picture** [sing.] the general situation concerning sb/sth 狀況；情形；形勢：*Just a few years ago the picture was very different.* 幾年前的情況就大不相同。◇ *The overall picture for farming is encouraging.* 農業的總體形勢是令人鼓舞的。

▸ **MOVIES 電影** **7** [C] a film/movie 電影：*The movie won nine Academy Awards, including Best Picture.* 這部電影榮獲九項奧斯卡金像獎，包括最佳影片獎。◇ (*especially NAmE*) *I believe her husband's* ***in pictures*** (= he acts in movies or works in the movie industry). 我想她丈夫是在電影圈工作。➲ see also MOTION PICTURE **8** **the pictures** [pl.] (*old-fashioned, informal*) the cinema/the movies 電影院；影劇院：*Shall we go to the pictures tonight?* 今晚我們去看電影好嗎？

IDM **be/look a ˈpicture** to look very beautiful or special 好看；悅目 **be the picture of ˈhealth, ˈguilt, ˈmisery, etc.** (*informal*) to look extremely healthy, guilty, unhappy, etc. 顯得非常健康（或內疚、不愉快等） **get the ˈpicture** (*informal*) to understand a situation, especially one that sb is describing to you 明白，瞭解（別人描述的情形）：*'I pretended that I hadn't heard.' 'I get the picture.'* "我裝作沒聽見。" "我明白了。" **in/out of the ˈpicture** (*informal*) involved/not involved in a

P

situation 在局內／局外： *Morris is likely to win, with Jones out of the picture now.* 瓊斯現已出局，莫里斯極有可能勝出。 **put/keep sb in the ˈpicture** (*informal*) to give sb the information they need in order to understand a situation 介紹情況；使瞭解情況： *Just to put you in the picture—there have been a number of changes here recently.* 只是讓你瞭解一下情況吧，最近這裏出現了許多變化。 ➲ more at BIG *adj.*, PAINT *v.*, PRETTY *adj.*

■ *verb*

▸ **IMAGINE 想像 1** to imagine sb/sth; to create an image of sb/sth in your mind 想像；設想；憶起： **~ sb/sth** *I can still picture the house I grew up in.* 我還能回憶起我童年時住的那座房子。◇ **~ sb/sth as sth** *We found it hard to picture him as the father of teenage sons.* 我們很難想像他居然是有幾個十幾歲兒子的父親了。◇ **~ sb/sth doing sth** *When he did not come home she pictured him lying dead on the roadside somewhere.* 當他沒有回家，她想像着他已橫屍路邊了。◇ **~ what, how, etc. …** *I tried to picture what it would be like to live alone.* 我努力想一個人單獨生活是什麼情景。

▸ **DESCRIBE 描繪 2** [often passive] **~ sb/sth as sth** to describe or present sb/sth in a particular way 描述；描寫 **SYN portray**： *Before the trial Liz had been pictured as a frail woman dominated by her husband.* 審訊之前，利茲被描繪成受丈夫操縱的孱弱女子。

▸ **SHOW IN PHOTOGRAPH 照片顯示 3** [usually passive] to show sb/sth in a photograph or picture 顯示在照片上；用圖片顯示： **~ sb/sth (+ adv./prep/adj.)** *She is pictured here with her parents.* 這張照片顯示她和父母在一起。◇ **~ sb/sth doing sth** *The team is pictured setting off on their European tour.* 圖片顯示，這個隊正開始歐洲之行。

Synonyms 同義詞辨析

picture

painting • drawing • portrait • print • sketch

These are all words for a scene, person or thing that has been represented on paper by drawing, painting, etc. 以上各詞均表示圖畫、繪畫。

picture a scene, person or thing that has been represented on paper using a pencil, a pen or paint 指用鉛筆、鋼筆或顏料畫出的圖畫、繪畫： *The children were drawing pictures of their pets.* 孩子在畫他們的寵物。

painting a picture that has been made using paint 指用顏料畫出的圖畫、繪畫： *a collection of paintings by American artists* 美國藝術家的繪畫作品集

drawing a picture that has been made using a pencil or pen, not paint 指用鉛筆或鋼筆而非顏料畫出的圖畫、素描畫： *a pencil/charcoal drawing* 鉛筆／炭筆畫

portrait a painting, drawing or photograph of a person, especially of the head and shoulders 指肖像、半身畫像、半身照： *Vermeer's 'Portrait of the artist in his studio'* 弗美爾的"藝術家在畫室的肖像" ◇ *a self-portrait* (= a painting that you do of yourself) 自畫像

print a picture that has been copied from a painting using photography 指（用照相製版法製作的）繪畫複製品： *a Renoir print* 一張雷諾阿畫作的影印件

sketch a simple picture that is drawn quickly and does not have many details 指素描、速寫、草圖： *I usually do a few very rough sketches before I start on a painting.* 我開始作畫之前通常會畫幾幅草圖。

PATTERNS

- to **draw** a picture/portrait/sketch
- to **paint** a picture/portrait
- to **make** a painting/drawing/portrait/print/sketch
- to **do** a painting/drawing/portrait/sketch

P

ˈpicture book *noun* a book with a lot of pictures, especially one for children 畫冊；圖畫書

ˈpicture messaging *noun* [U] a system of sending images from one mobile/cell phone to another （手機的）圖像傳輸系統 **SYN EMS**

ˌpicture-ˈperfect *adj.* (*NAmE*) exactly right in appearance or in the way things are done 完美的；圓滿的

ˌpicture ˈpostcard *noun* (*old-fashioned*) a POSTCARD with a picture on one side 美術明信片；風景明信片

ˌpicture-ˈpostcard *adj.* [only before noun] (*especially BrE*) (of places 地方) very pretty 優美的；漂亮的： *a picture-postcard village* 風景如畫的村莊

ˈpicture rail *noun* a narrow strip of wood attached to the walls of a room below the ceiling and used for hanging pictures from 掛畫的板條；掛畫線

pic·tur·esque /ˌpɪktʃəˈresk/ *adj.* **1** (of a place, building, scene, etc. 地方、建築物、景色等) pretty, especially in a way that looks old-fashioned 優美的；古色古香的 **SYN quaint**： *a picturesque cottage/setting/village* 畫兒一般的小屋／環境／村落 **2** (of language 語言) producing strong mental images by using unusual words 生動的；栩栩如生的： *a picturesque description of life at sea* 對海上生活生動的描述 ▸ **pic·tur·esque·ly** *adv.*： *The inn is picturesquely situated on the banks of the river.* 小客棧坐落在河畔，構成一幅美麗的圖畫。

ˈpicture window *noun* a very large window made of a single piece of glass （整塊玻璃做的）大觀景窗；落地窗

pic·tur·ize (*BrE* also **-ise**) /ˈpɪktʃəraɪz/ *verb* **~ sth** (*IndE*) to adapt a story or play as a film/movie; to create a film SEQUENCE to accompany a song 將…改編成電影；為（歌曲）配電影鏡頭： *The novel has been picturized twice.* 這部小說已兩度改編為電影。 ▸ **pic·tur·iza·tion, -isa·tion** /ˌpɪktʃəraɪˈzeɪʃn/ *noun* [C, U]： *It was one of the few song picturizations that created magic with both music and visuals.* 那是創造音樂和視覺神奇效果的少數音樂電影之一。

pid·dle /ˈpɪdl/ *verb* [I] (*old-fashioned, informal*) to URINATE 撒尿

pid·dling /ˈpɪdlɪŋ/ *adj.* [only before noun] (*informal, disapproving*) small and unimportant 瑣碎的；雞毛蒜皮的 **SYN trivial**

pidgin /ˈpɪdʒɪn/ *noun* [U] **1** a simple form of a language, especially English, Portuguese or Dutch, with a limited number of words, that are used together with words from a local language. It is used when people who do not speak the same language need to talk to each other. 洋涇浜語；皮欽語 **2 Pidgin** = TOK PISIN **3 ~ English, French, Japanese, etc.** a way of speaking a language that uses simple words and forms, used when a person does not speak the language well, or when he or she is talking to sb who does not speak the language well 洋涇浜英語（或法語、日語等）；洋涇浜式；混雜語式： *I tried to get my message across in my pidgin Italian.* 我嘗試用我的洋涇浜意大利語表達出我的意思。

pi-dog = PYE-DOG

pie /paɪ/ *noun* [C, U] **1** fruit baked in a dish with PASTRY on the bottom, sides and top 果餡餅；果餡派： *a slice of apple pie* 一塊蘋果派 ◇ *Help yourself to some more pie.* 請隨意再吃些果餡餅吧。◇ *a pie dish* 一份果餡餅 ➲ see also CUSTARD PIE **2** (*especially BrE*) meat, vegetables, etc. baked in a dish with PASTRY on the bottom, sides and top 肉餡餅；蔬菜餡餅： *a steak and kidney pie* 牛肉腰子餡餅 ➲ see also MINCE PIE, PORK PIE, SHEPHERD'S PIE

IDM a ˌpiece/ˌslice/ˌshare of the ˈpie a share of sth such as money, profits, etc. （金錢、利潤等的）一份；一杯羹 **ˌpie in the ˈsky** (*informal*) an event that sb talks about that seems very unlikely to happen 難以實現的事；幻想的事；空中樓閣： *This talk of moving to Australia is all just pie in the sky.* 移居澳大利亞之說純屬異想天開。 ➲ more at AMERICAN *adj.*, EASY *adj.*, EAT, FINGER *n.*, NICE

pie·bald /ˈpaɪbɔːld/ *adj.* (of a horse 馬) with areas on it of two colours, usually black and white 花斑的；有黑白兩色的 ➲ compare SKEWBALD

Vocabulary Building 詞彙擴充

Pieces

If you want to talk about a small amount or one example of something that is normally an uncountable noun, there is a range of words you can use. You must choose the right one to go with the substance you are talking about. 許多表示少量、一個等的詞可用以修飾不可數名詞，但必須選擇能與該物質名詞搭配得當的詞。

- **Piece** and (*BrE, informal*) **bit** are very general words and can be used with most uncountable nouns. * piece 和 bit（非正式英式英語）是十分通用的詞，可與大多數不可數名詞連用： *a piece of paper/wood/string/cake/fruit/meat/work/research/advice* 一張紙；一塊木頭；一根繩子；一塊蛋糕；一個水果；一塊肉；一件工作；一項研究；一個忠告 ◇ *a bit of paper/work/chocolate/luck.* 一小片紙；一點工作；一小塊巧克力；一點運氣
- A **slice** is a thin flat piece. * slice 指薄片： *a slice of bread/cake/salami/cheese/pie/apple* 一片麪包／蛋糕／薩拉米香腸／乾酪／餡餅／蘋果 ◇ (*figurative*) *a slice of life*（電影、戲劇或書中的）現實生活片斷
- A **chunk** is a thick, solid piece. * chunk 指厚厚的一塊： *a chunk of cheese/bread/rock* 一塊厚乾酪／麪包／岩石 ◇ *a chunk of land* (= a fairly large piece) 一大塊土地
- A **lump** is a piece of something solid without any particular shape. * lump 指無一定形狀的一塊、一團： *a lump of coal/rock/mud* 一塊煤／岩石；一團泥
- A **fragment** is a very small piece of something that is broken or damaged. * fragment 指碎片、破片： *fragments of glass* 玻璃碎片 ◇ (*figurative*) *fragments of conversation* 談話片斷 It can also be used with countable nouns to mean a small part of something. 該詞亦可與可數名詞連用表示小部份： *a fragment of the story* 故事的一個片段
- A **speck** is a tiny piece of powder. * speck 指小顆粒、微粒： *a speck of dust/dirt* 一點灰塵／污垢 You can also say 也可以說： *a speck of light* 一點光
- **Drop** is used with liquids. * drop 用於液體： *a drop of water/rain/blood/milk/whisky* 一滴水／雨／血／牛奶／威士忌酒
- A **pinch** is as much as you can hold between your finger and thumb. * pinch 指一撮、一捏、一掐： *a pinch of salt/cinnamon* 一撮鹽／肉桂粉
- A **portion** is enough for one person. * portion 指夠一人用的一份、一客： *a portion of chicken* 一份雞肉

piece 🔑 /piːs/ *noun, verb*

■ ***noun***

▸ **SEPARATE AMOUNT 分離的量** **1** 🔑 [C] **~ (of sth)** (used especially with *of* and uncountable nouns 尤與 of 和不可數名詞連用) an amount of sth that has been cut or separated from the rest of it; a standard amount of sth 片；塊；段；截；標準的量： *a piece of string/wood* 一截繩子；一塊木頭 ◇ *She wrote something on a small piece of paper.* 她在一小片紙上寫了點什麼。◇ *a large piece of land* 一大片土地 ◇ *a piece of cake/cheese/meat* 一塊蛋糕／奶酪／肉 ◇ *He cut the pizza into bite-sized pieces.* 他把比薩餅切成一口一塊的小塊。◇ *I've got a piece of grit in my eye.* 我眼裏進了一粒沙子。

▸ **PART 部份** **2** 🔑 [C, usually pl.] one of the bits or parts that sth breaks into 碎片；碎塊： *There were tiny pieces of glass all over the road.* 道路上佈滿了碎玻璃。◇ *The boat had been smashed* ***to pieces*** *on the rocks.* 小船在岩石上撞得粉碎。◇ *The vase lay* ***in pieces*** *on the floor.* 花瓶碎片散落在地上。 **3** 🔑 [C] one of the parts that sth is made of 零件；部件： *He* ***took*** *the clock* ***to pieces.*** 他把鐘拆散了。◇ *a missing piece of the puzzle* 拼圖玩具丟失的一片 ◇ *The bridge was taken down* ***piece by piece.*** 橋梁被一部份一部份地拆毀。◇ *a 500-piece jigsaw* 一副 500 片的拼圖玩具 ➲ see also ONE-PIECE, TWO-PIECE, THREE-PIECE

▸ **SINGLE ITEM 單件** **4** 🔑 [C] (used especially with *of* and uncountable nouns 尤與 of 和不可數名詞連用) a single item of a particular type, especially one that forms part of a set（尤指一套中的）一件，一台： *a piece of clothing/furniture/luggage* 一件衣服／傢具／行李 ◇ *a piece of equipment/machinery* 一台設備／機器 ◇ *a 28-piece dinner service* 一套 28 件的餐具 **5** 🔑 [C] **~ of sth** used with many uncountable nouns to describe a single example or an amount of sth 條；項；點： *a* ***piece of advice/information/news*** 一條建議／信息／消息 ◇ *an interesting piece of research* 一項有趣的研究 ◇ *Isn't that a* ***piece of luck?*** 那難道不是有點運氣？ **6** 🔑 [C] **~ (of sth)** a single item of writing, art, music, etc. that sb has produced or created（文章、藝術品、音樂作品等的）一件，一篇，一首，一支： *a* ***piece of art/music/poetry, etc.*** 一件藝術品、一支樂曲、一首詩歌等 ◇ *They performed pieces by Bach and Handel.* 他們演奏了巴赫和亨德爾的幾支曲子。◇ (*formal*) *They have some beautiful pieces* (= works of art, etc.) *in their home.* 他們家中珍藏了一些精美的藝術品。➲ see also MASTERPIECE, MUSEUM PIECE, PARTY PIECE, PERIOD PIECE, SHOWPIECE

▸ **NEWS ARTICLE 新聞報道** **7** [C] an article in a newspaper or magazine or a broadcast on television or radio（新聞傳媒的）文章，報道： *Did you see her piece about the Internet in the paper today?* 你看了今天報紙上她寫的關於互聯網的文章沒有？ ➲ see also SET PIECE (1)

▸ **COIN 硬幣** **8** [C] a coin of the value mentioned（某價值的）硬幣： *a 50p piece* 一枚 50 便士的硬幣 ◇ *a five-cent piece* 一枚五分的硬幣

▸ **IN CHESS, ETC. 國際象棋等** **9** [C] one of the small figures or objects that you move around in games such as CHESS 棋子

▸ **SHARE OF STH 份額** **10** [sing.] **~ of sth** (*especially NAmE*) a part or share of sth 部份；份額： *companies seeking a piece of the market* 爭取市場份額的公司

▸ **GUN 槍** **11** [C] (*NAmE, slang*) a gun 槍支；槍

▸ **DISTANCE 距離** **12 a piece** [sing.] (*old-fashioned, NAmE, informal*) a short distance 短距離；一小段距離： *She lives down the road a piece from here.* 她住在路那頭離這裏不遠的地方。 **HELP** You will find other compounds ending in **piece** at their place in the alphabet. 其他以 piece 結尾的複合詞可在各字母中的適當位置查到。

IDM **a/some ˌpiece of ˈwork** (*NAmE, informal*) used to express the fact that you admire sb or find them amusing, often when they have done sth that surprises you 了不起的人；與眾不同的人： *You're some piece of work, Jack, do you know that?* 你知道嗎，傑克？你真了不起。 **fall to ˈpieces** 🔑 **1** 🔑 (usually used in the progressive tenses 通常用於進行時) (of things 東西) to become very old and in bad condition because of long use 用太久而變得破舊不堪 **SYN** **fall apart**： *Our car is falling to pieces, we've had it so long.* 我們的汽車已破舊不堪，我們已用了它很久了。 **2** 🔑 (of a person, an organization, a plan, etc. 人、機構、計劃等) to stop working; to be destroyed 停止運作；崩潰；瓦解： *He's worried the business will fall to pieces without him.* 他擔心沒有了他企業將會倒閉。 **give sb a piece of your ˈmind** (*informal*) to tell sb that you disapprove of their behaviour or are angry with them 表明對某人的行為不滿；向某人表示惱火 **go to ˈpieces** (*informal*) (of a person 人) to be so upset or afraid that you cannot manage to live or work normally 身心崩潰；沮喪至極 **(all) in one ˈpiece** (*informal*) safe; not damaged or hurt, especially after a journey or dangerous experience 安然無恙（尤指旅行或經歷危險之後）： *They were lucky to get home in one piece.* 他們能平安返家真是幸運。 **(all) of a ˈpiece** (*formal*) **1** all the same or similar 一模一樣；相仿： *The houses are all of a piece.* 這些房子千篇一律。 **2** all at the same time 同時；一起： *The house was built all of a piece in 1754.* 整所房子是在 1754 年建造完成的。 **pick/pull/tear sb/sth to ˈpieces/ˈshreds** (*informal*) to criticize sb, or their work or ideas, very severely 嚴厲斥責；痛斥；批評得體無完膚 **a ˌpiece of ˈcake** (*informal*) a thing that is very easy to do 輕而易舉的事；舉手之勞 **a ˌpiece of ˈpiss** (*BrE, taboo, slang*) a thing that is very easy to do 小菜一碟；輕而易舉的事 ➲ more at ACTION, BIT, LONG *adj.*, NASTY, PICK *v.*, PIE, SAY *v.*, VILLAIN

■ *verb*

PHR V ˌpiece sth↔toˈgether **1** to understand a story, situation, etc. by taking all the facts and details about it and putting them together 組合資料（以便瞭解情況）：*Police are trying to piece together the last hours of her life.* 警方正努力理清她在死亡之前數小時的情況。**2** to put all the separate parts of sth together to make a complete whole 拼湊；拼合 SYN **assemble** : *to piece together a jigsaw* 拼合拼圖

pièce de ré·sist·ance /ˌpjes də reˈzɪstɒ̃s; *NAmE* -stɑːns/ *noun* [usually sing.] (*pl.* **pièces de ré·sist·ance** /ˌpjes də reˈzɪstɒ̃s; *NAmE* ˌreziːˈstɑːns/) (from *French*) the most important or impressive part of a group or series of things 成功之作；最重要的項目

piece·meal /ˈpiːsmiːl/ *adj.* [usually before noun] (often *disapproving*) done or happening gradually at different times and often in different ways, rather than carefully planned at the beginning 逐漸做成（或發生）的；零敲碎打的；零散的：*a piecemeal approach to dealing with the problem* 全無章法的解決問題的方式 ◇ *piecemeal changes* 零星的變化 ▶ **piece·meal** *adv.* : *The reforms were implemented piecemeal.* 改革在零零星星地進行。

ˌpiece of ˈeight *noun* (*pl.* **ˌpieces of ˈeight**) an old Spanish coin 八里亞爾幣比索（西班牙舊幣名）

ˈpiece rate *noun* an amount of money paid for each thing or amount of sth that a worker produces 計件酬金；計件工資

piece·work /ˈpiːswɜːk; *NAmE* -wɜːrk/ *noun* [U] work that is paid for by the amount done and not by the hours worked 計件工作 ▶ **piece·work·er** *noun*

ˈpie chart *noun* a diagram consisting of a circle that is divided into sections to show the size of particular amounts in relation to the whole 圓形統計圖；餅分圖 ⊃ LANGUAGE BANK at ILLUSTRATE ⊃ WRITING TUTOR page WT16

pied /paɪd/ *adj.* (especially of birds 尤指鳥) of two or more different colours, especially black and white 黑白雙色的；多色的；雜色的

pied-à-terre /ˌpjeɪd ɑː ˈteə(r); *NAmE* ˈter/ *noun* (*pl.* **pieds-à-terre** /ˌpjeɪd ɑː/) (from *French*) a small flat/apartment, usually in a town, that you do not live in as your main home but keep for use when necessary 備用小公寓；備用房

pie-dog = PYE-DOG

ˌPied ˈPiper *noun* a person who persuades a lot of other people to follow them or do sth with them 有感召力的人；有號召力的人 ORIGIN From the old German story of the Pied Piper of Hamelin, who made first rats and later children follow him by playing beautiful music on his pipe. 源自古老的德國傳說，哈默爾恩的花衣魔笛手吹奏美妙的樂曲，先後誘走老鼠和孩子。

ˌpie-ˈeyed *adj.* (*informal*) very drunk 爛醉的

pier /pɪə(r); *NAmE* pɪr/ *noun* **1** a long structure built in the sea and joined to the land at one end, often with places of entertainment on it（常設有娛樂場所的）突堤 **2** a long low structure built in a lake, river or the sea and joined to the land at one end, used by boats to allow passengers to get on and off（突入湖、河、海中的）碼頭；突碼頭 SYN **landing stage** **3** (*technical* 術語) a large strong piece of wood, metal or stone that is used to support a roof, wall, bridge, etc. 柱子；牆墩；橋墩

pierce /pɪəs; *NAmE* pɪrs/ *verb* **1** [T, I] to make a small hole in sth, or to go through sth, with a sharp object 扎；刺破；穿透：**~ sth** *The arrow pierced his shoulder.* 箭頭射入他的肩膀。◇ *He pierced another hole in his belt with his knife.* 他用刀子在皮腰帶上又扎了一個洞。◇ *to **have your ears/nose, etc. pierced*** (= to have a small hole made in your ears/nose, etc. so that you can wear jewellery there) 在耳朵、鼻子等上扎洞 ◇ **~ sb** (*figurative*) *She was pierced to the heart with guilt.* 她萬般愧疚，心如刀割。◇ **~ through sth** *The knife pierced through his coat.* 刀子刺穿了他的外衣。**2** [T, I] **~ (through) sth** (*literary*) (of light, sound, etc. 光、聲等) to be suddenly seen or heard 刺破；穿過；透入：*Sirens pierced the silence of the night.* 警笛聲劃破了夜晚的寧靜。◇ *Shafts of sunlight pierced the heavy mist.* 縷縷陽光穿透了濃霧。**3** [T, I] **~ (through) sth** to force a way through a barrier 衝破；突破 SYN **penetrate** : *They failed to pierce the Liverpool defence.* 他們未能突破利物浦隊的防線。

pier·cing /ˈpɪəsɪŋ; *NAmE* ˈpɪrsɪŋ/ *adj., noun*

■ *adj.* **1** [usually before noun] (of eyes or the way they look at sb 眼睛或眼神) seeming to notice things about another person that would not normally be noticed, especially in a way that makes that person feel anxious or embarrassed 銳利的；逼人的；尖利的：*She looked at me with piercing blue eyes.* 她用一雙敏銳的藍眼睛盯着我。◇ *a piercing look* 洞悉一切的目光 **2** [usually before noun] (of sounds 聲音) very high, loud and unpleasant 尖利的；刺耳的 SYN **shrill** : *a piercing shriek* 尖厲的叫聲 ◇ *She has such a **piercing voice**.* 她的聲音是那麼刺耳。**3** [only before noun] (of feelings 感情) affecting you very strongly, especially in a way that causes you pain 深切的；刻骨的：*piercing sadness* 深深的悲哀 **4** (of the wind or cold 風或寒氣) very strong and feeling as if it can pass through your clothes and skin 刺骨的；凜冽的 **5** [only before noun] sharp and able to make a hole in sth 鋒利的；銳利的：*The animal is covered in long piercing spines.* 這種動物渾身長滿了鋒利的長刺。▶ **pier·cing·ly** *adv.* : *His eyes were piercingly blue.* 他有一雙敏銳的藍眼睛。◇ *The weather remained piercingly cold.* 天氣依舊徹骨地寒冷。

■ *noun* **1** [U] = BODY PIERCING **2** [C] the hole that is made in your ear, nose or some other part of your body so that you can wear jewellery there（耳朵、鼻子或其他身體部位為戴首飾打的）穿孔，洞眼：*She has a tongue piercing.* 她為佩戴首飾穿了個舌洞。

Pier·rot /ˈpɪərəʊ; ˈpjerəʊ; *NAmE* ˈpɪəroʊ/ *noun* a male character in traditional French plays, with a sad white face and a pointed hat（法國傳統劇中表情哀傷、臉上用粉塗成白色，頭戴尖頂帽的）白面男丑角

pietà /pjerˈtɑː/ *noun* (*art* 美術) a picture or SCULPTURE of the Virgin Mary holding the dead body of Christ 聖母憐子圖，聖母慟子圖（或雕像）（顯示聖母抱着耶穌的遺體）

piety /ˈpaɪəti/ *noun* [U] the state of having or showing a deep respect for sb/sth, especially for God and religion; the state of being PIOUS 虔誠 OPP **impiety**

pif·fle /ˈpɪfl/ *noun* [U] (*old-fashioned, informal*) nonsense 胡言亂語；廢話；蠢話 SYN **rubbish**

pif·fling /ˈpɪflɪŋ/ *adj.* (*informal, disapproving*) small and unimportant 渺小的；微不足道的：*piffling amounts* 微不足道的數量

pig 🔑 /pɪɡ/ *noun, verb*

■ *noun* **1** 🔑 (also **hog** especially in *NAmE*) an animal with pink, black or brown skin, short legs, a broad nose and a short tail which curls round itself. Pigs are kept on farms for their meat (called PORK) or live in the wild. 豬：*a pig farmer* 養豬的農民 ◇ *Pigs were grunting and squealing in the yard.* 豬在院子裏哼哼地叫個不停。⊃ see also BOAR, PIGLET, SOW², SWINE (3), GUINEA PIG **2** (*informal, disapproving*) an unpleasant or offensive person; a person who is dirty or GREEDY 令人不快（或討厭）的人；貪婪（或骯髒）的人：*Arrogant pig!* 傲慢的傢伙！◇ *Don't be such a pig!* 別那麼討厭嘛！◇ *The greedy pig's eaten all the biscuits!* 那個饞貓把餅乾都吃光了！◇ *She **made a pig of herself** with the ice cream* (= ate too much). 她大吃了一通冰淇淋。◇ *He's a real **male chauvinist pig*** (= a man who does not think women are equal to men). 他是個徹頭徹尾的大男子主義者。**3** (*slang*) an offensive word for a police officer（對警察的蔑稱）

IDM **make a ˈpig's ear (out) of sth** (*BrE, informal*) to do sth badly; to make a mess of sth 把事情辦砸；弄得一團糟 **(buy) a pig in a ˈpoke** if you **buy a pig in a poke**, you buy sth without seeing it or knowing if it is good enough（買）未看過的東西；（買）不知優劣的東西 **a pig of a sth** (*BrE, informal*) a difficult or unpleasant thing or task 撓頭的事；煩人的事；苦差：*I've had a pig of a day.* 我這一天倒霉透了。**pigs might ˈfly** (*BrE*) (*NAmE* **when pigs ˈfly**) (*ironic, saying*) used to show that you do not believe sth will ever happen（表示不相信某事會發生）太陽從西出：*'With a bit of luck, we'll be finished*

P

by the end of the year.' 'Yes, and pigs might fly!' "運氣不錯的話，我們年底就能完成。" "是啊，太陽能打西邊出嘛！"

■ *verb* (-gg-) (*BrE, informal*) to eat too much of sth 吃得過量；大吃特吃：**~ sth** *I had a whole box of chocolates and pigged the lot!* 我把一整盒巧克力吃了個精光！◇ **~ yourself (on sth)** *Don't give me cakes—I'll just pig myself.* 可別給我拿糕點，那我會吃個沒夠的。

PHR V ˌ**pig** ˈ**out (on sth)** (*informal*) to eat too much food 大吃；猛吃：*They pigged out on pizza.* 他們猛搶着吃比薩餅。

pi·geon /ˈpɪdʒɪn/ *noun* a fat grey and white bird with short legs. Pigeons are common in cities and also live in woods and fields where people shoot them for sport or food. 鴿子：*the sound of pigeons cooing* 鴿子咕咕的叫聲 ➲ compare DOVE[1] (1) ➲ see also CARRIER PIGEON, CLAY PIGEON SHOOTING, HOMING PIGEON, WOOD PIGEON

IDM **be sb's pigeon** (*old-fashioned, BrE*) to be sb's responsibility or business 是某人的職責（或事情）➲ more at CAT

pi·geon·hole /ˈpɪdʒɪnhəʊl; *NAmE* -hoʊl/ *noun, verb*

■ *noun* one of a set of small boxes that are fixed on a wall and open at the front, used for putting letters, messages, etc. in; one of a similar set of boxes that are part of a desk, used for keeping papers, documents, etc. in 信件格；開口文件格：*If you can't come, leave a note in my pigeonhole.* 你若不能來就在我的信件格裏留張便條。

■ *verb* **1 ~ sb (as sth)** to decide that sb belongs to a particular group or type without thinking deeply enough about it and considering what other qualities they might have 將某人輕率分類；主觀劃分（某人）為 **SYN** **categorize, label**：*He has been pigeonholed as a children's writer.* 他硬被歸入兒童文學作家之列。**2 ~ sth** to decide to deal with sth later or to forget it 擱置；將…束之高閣；不予處理 **SYN** **shelve**：*Plans for a new school have been pigeonholed.* 建新學校的計劃擱在一邊了。

ˌ**pigeon-ˈtoed** *adj.* having feet that point towards each other and not straight forward 足內翻的；內八字腳的

pig·gery /ˈpɪɡəri/ *noun* (*pl.* **-ies**) a place where pigs are kept or bred 豬圈；豬欄；養豬場

piggy /ˈpɪɡi/ *noun, adj.*

■ *noun* (*pl.* **-ies**) a child's word for a pig（兒童用語）豬豬，小豬

■ *adj.* [only before noun] (*informal, disapproving*) (of a person's eyes 人的眼睛) like those of a pig 像豬一樣的

pig·gy·back /ˈpɪɡibæk/ *noun, verb*

■ *noun* a ride on sb's back, while he or she is walking 背着；肩馱：*Give me a piggyback, Daddy!* 背背我，爸爸！◇ *a piggyback ride* 肩馱 ▶ **pig·gy·back** *adv.*：*to ride piggyback* 騎在肩上

■ *verb*

PHR V ˈ**piggyback on sb/sth** to use sth that already exists as a support for your own work; to use a larger organization, etc. for your own advantage 利用；借助；攀附利用

ˈ**piggy bank** *noun* a container in the shape of a pig, with a narrow opening in the top for putting coins in, used by children to save money 豬形儲錢罐；撲滿 ➲ compare MONEY BOX

ˌ**piggy in the ˈmiddle** (also ˌ**pig in the ˈmiddle**) (both *BrE*) (*NAmE* ˌ**monkey in the ˈmiddle**) *noun* **1** a children's game where two people throw a ball to each other over the head of another person who tries to catch it 過頂傳球（兒童遊戲，由兩人拋傳球，中間一人爭搶）**2** a person who is caught between two people or groups who are fighting or arguing 左右為難的人

ˌ**pig-ˈheaded** *adj.* unwilling to change your opinion about sth, in a way that other people think is annoying and unreasonable 頑固的；固執的 **SYN** **obstinate, stubborn** ▶ ˌ**pig-ˈheaded·ness** *noun* [U]

ˌ**pig-ˈignorant** *adj.* (*informal*) very stupid or badly educated 蠢笨的；粗鄙的

ˈ**pig iron** *noun* [U] a form of iron that is not pure 生鐵；鑄鐵

pig·let /ˈpɪɡlət/ *noun* a young pig 豬仔；小豬

pig·ment /ˈpɪɡmənt/ *noun* [U, C] **1** a substance that exists naturally in people, animals and plants and gives their skin, leaves, etc. a particular colour 色素 **2** a coloured powder that is mixed with a liquid to produce paint, etc. 顏料

pig·men·ta·tion /ˌpɪɡmenˈteɪʃn/ *noun* [U] the presence of pigments in skin, hair, leaves, etc. that causes them to be a particular colour 色素沉着；天然顏色

pig·ment·ed /pɪɡˈmentɪd/ *adj.* (especially of skin 尤指皮膚) having a natural colour 天然色的；本色的

pigmy *noun, adj.* = PYGMY

pig·skin /ˈpɪɡskɪn/ *noun* **1** [U] leather made from the skin of a pig 豬皮革 **2** [sing.] (*NAmE, informal*) the ball used in AMERICAN FOOTBALL（美式足球使用的）球

pig·sty /ˈpɪɡstaɪ/ (also **sty**) *noun* (*pl.* **-ies**) (*NAmE* also ˈ**pig·pen** /ˈpɪɡpen/) **1** [C] a small building or a confined area where pigs are kept 豬圈；豬場 **2** [sing.] (*informal*) a very dirty or untidy place 骯髒的地方；豬窩般邋遢的地方

pig·swill /ˈpɪɡswɪl/ *noun* [U] = SWILL *n.* (1)

pig·tail /ˈpɪɡteɪl/ (*BrE*) (also **braid** *NAmE, BrE*) *noun* hair that is tied together into one or two bunches and twisted into a PLAIT or PLAITS, worn either at the back of the head or one on each side of the head 辮子：*She wore her hair* ***in pigtails***. 她梳着兩條辮子。➲ VISUAL VOCAB page V60 ➲ compare PONYTAIL

pike /paɪk/ *noun, verb*

■ *noun* **1** (*pl.* **pike**) a large FRESHWATER fish with very sharp teeth 狗魚；梭子魚 **2** a weapon with a sharp blade on a long wooden handle, used in the past by soldiers on foot 長矛 **3** (*NAmE*) = TURNPIKE **4** (*dialect*) a pointed top of a hill in the north of England（英格蘭北部的）山峰，陡峰

IDM **come down the ˈpike** (*NAmE, informal*) to happen; to become noticeable 發生；顯現：*We're hearing a lot about new inventions coming down the pike.* 我們經常聽說新發明不斷問世。

■ *verb* (*AustralE, NZE, informal*)

PHR V ˌ**pike ˈout** to decide not to do sth that you had agreed to do 背約；退出；出爾反爾 ˈ**pike on sb** to fail to help or support sb as they had hoped or expected 未能如某人所願提供幫助（或支持）；辜負別人的期望

pike·staff /ˈpaɪkstɑːf; *NAmE* -stæf/ *noun* **IDM** see PLAIN *adj.*

pikey /ˈpaɪki/ *noun* (*BrE, informal, offensive*) **1** a name for a GYPSY 吉普賽鬼 **2** a person who is poor and not educated 沒教養的窮鬼：*He referred to them as dirty pikey scum.* 他稱他們是骯髒又無知的叫花子。

pilaf (also **pilaff**) /ˈpiːlæf; *NAmE* pɪˈlɑːf/ (also **pilau** /ˈpiːlaʊ/) *noun* [U, C] a hot spicy Eastern dish of rice and vegetables and often pieces of meat or fish 辣味菜肉飯

pi·las·ter /pɪˈlæstə(r)/ *noun* (*technical* 術語) a flat column that sticks out from the wall of a building, used as decoration 壁柱；半露柱

Pi·la·tes /pɪˈlɑːtiːz/ *noun* [U] a system of stretching and pushing exercises using special equipment, which help make your muscles stronger and make you able to bend parts of your body more easily 普拉提，皮拉提斯（利用特殊設備做伸展推拉等動作以達到鍛煉肌肉和提高身體柔韌性的一種健身運動）

pil·chard /ˈpɪltʃəd; *NAmE* -tʃərd/ *noun* a small sea fish that is used for food 歐洲沙丁魚；沙丁魚

pile 0‑w /paɪl/ *noun, verb*

■ *noun* ➲ see also PILES **1** 0‑w [C] a number of things that have been placed on top of each other 摞；垛；沓：*a pile of books/clothes/bricks* 一摞書籍／衣物／磚塊 ◇ *He arranged the documents in neat piles.* 他把文件一摞摞地碼得整整齊齊。◇ *She looked in horror at the mounting pile of letters on her desk.* 她惶恐地望着桌子上堆積如山的信函。**2** 0‑w [C] a mass of sth that is high in the middle and wider at the bottom than at the top 堆；成堆的東西 **SYN** **heap**：*a pile of sand* 一堆沙 ◇ *piles of*

P

dirty washing 成堆待洗的髒衣物 **3** 🔑 [C, usually pl.] **~ of sth** (*informal*) a lot of sth 大量；許多：*I have got piles of work to do.* 我有大量工作要做。◇ *He walked out leaving a pile of debts behind him.* 他出走了，留下累累債務。**4** [U, sing.] the short threads, pieces of wool, etc. that form the soft surface of carpets and some types of cloth such as VELVET 絨頭；絨毛：*a deep-pile carpet* 一塊厚絨地毯 **5** [C] a large wooden, metal or stone post that is fixed into the ground and used to support a building, bridge, etc. 樁；樁柱 **6** [C] (*formal* or *humorous*) a large impressive building 宏偉建築物

IDM **(at the) bottom/top of the 'pile** in the least/most important position in a group of people or things 處於無足輕重的／舉足輕重的地位 **make a/your 'pile** (*informal*) to make a lot of money 賺很多錢

■ ***verb*** **1** 🔑 [T] to put things one on top of another; to form a pile 堆放；摞起；叠放：**~ sth** *She* ***piled*** *the boxes* ***one on top of the other.*** 她把盒子一個個地摞起來。◇ *The clothes were* ***piled high*** *on the chair.* 衣服在椅子上堆得高高的。◇ **~ sth up** *Snow was piled up against the door.* 積雪封門。**2** 🔑 [T] to put sth on/into sth; to load sth with sth 放置；裝入：**~ A with B** *The sofa was* ***piled high*** *with cushions.* 沙發上高高地堆着一些墊子。◇ *He piled his plate with as much food as he could.* 他把食物猛往自己盤子裏堆。◇ **~ B on(to) A** *He piled as much food as he could onto his plate.* 他把食物猛往自己盤子裏堆。◇ **~ B in(to) A** *She piled everything into her suitcase.* 她把一應物品裝進衣箱。➲ see also STOCKPILE **3** [I] **+ adv./prep.** (*informal*) (of a number of people 許多人) to go somewhere quickly without order or control 蜂擁；擁擠：*The coach finally arrived and we all piled on.* 長途汽車終於開來了，我們一擁而上。

IDM **pile on the 'agony/'gloom** (*informal, especially BrE*) to make an unpleasant situation worse 使雪上加霜；傷口上撒鹽：*Bosses piled on the agony with threats of more job losses.* 老闆威脅要削減更多的職位，令情況更加惡化。

PHR V **,pile 'on** (especially of a person's weight 尤指體重) to increase quickly 劇增；猛增：*The weight just piled on while I was abroad.* 我出國期間體重一個勁地增加。**,pile sth↔'on** **1** to make sth increase rapidly 使迅速增加；猛增：*The team piled on the points in the first half of the game.* 球隊在上半場連連得分。◇ *I've been piling on the pounds* (= I have put on weight) *recently.* 我最近體重猛增。**2** to express a feeling in a much stronger way than is necessary 誇張；誇大其詞：*Don't pile on the drama!* 別再添油加醋了！◇ *Things aren't really that bad—she does tend to* ***pile it on.*** 事情並沒有那麼糟糕，她的確有意誇張。**3** to give sb more or too much of sth 過度施加；猛增某物：*The German team* ***piled on the pressure*** *in the last 15 minutes.* 在最後 15 分鐘，德國隊施加了強大的壓力。**,pile sth 'on(to) sb** to give sb a lot of sth to do, carry, etc. 給…增加工作；使負擔加重：*He felt his boss was piling too much work on him.* 他覺得上司派給他的工作太多。**,pile 'up** 🔑 to become larger in quantity or amount 堆積；積壓 **SYN** **accumulate**：*Work always piles up at the end of the year.* 年底總是積壓一大堆工作。

pile·driver /'paɪldraɪvə(r)/ *noun* **1** (*BrE, informal*) a very heavy kick or blow 狠踢；重擊 **2** a machine for forcing heavy posts into the ground 打樁機

piles /paɪlz/ *noun* [pl.] painful swollen VEINS at or near the ANUS 痔；痔瘡 **SYN** **haemorrhoids**

'pile-up *noun* a road accident involving several vehicles crashing into each other 連環車禍；連續撞車：*Three people died in a multiple pile-up in freezing fog.* 有三人死於凍霧引起的連環車禍中。

pil·fer /'pɪlfə(r)/ *verb* [I, T] to steal things of little value or in small quantities, especially from the place where you work 偷竊（小東西）；小偷小摸；（尤指員工）偷竊：**~ (from sb/sth)** *He was caught pilfering.* 他行竊時被抓個正着。◇ **~ sth (from sb/sth)** *She regularly pilfered stamps from work.* 她常從工作單位順手牽羊拿走郵票。▶ **pil·fer·age** /'pɪlfərɪdʒ/ *noun* [U]：(*formal*) *pilferage of goods* 貨物盜竊 **pil·fer·er** *noun*：*Certain types of goods are preferred by pilferers.* 某些類型的商品較為小偷所喜歡。**pil·fering** *noun* [U]：*We know that pilfering goes on.* 我們知道常有小偷小摸的事情。

pil·grim /'pɪlɡrɪm/ *noun* **1** a person who travels to a holy place for religious reasons 朝覲者；朝聖的人；香客：*Muslim pilgrims on their way to Mecca* 前往麥加的穆斯林朝聖者 ◇ *Christian pilgrims visiting Lourdes* 赴盧爾德朝聖的基督徒 **2 Pilgrim** a member of the group of English people (**the Pilgrim Fathers**) who sailed to America on the ship *The Mayflower* in 1620 and started a COLONY in Massachusetts 清教徒前輩移民（1620 年乘五月花號赴美洲，在馬薩諸塞建立英國殖民地）

pil·grim·age /'pɪlɡrɪmɪdʒ/ *noun* [C, U] **1** a journey to a holy place for religious reasons 朝聖之旅：*to* ***go on/make a pilgrimage*** 前往朝聖 ➲ COLLOCATIONS at RELIGION **2** a journey to a place that is connected with sb/sth that you admire or respect 參拜之行；瞻仰之旅：*His grave has become a* ***place of pilgrimage.*** 他的陵墓成了參拜之地。

pill 🔑 /pɪl/ *noun, verb*

■ ***noun*** **1** 🔑 [C] a small flat round piece of medicine that you swallow without chewing it 藥丸；藥片：*a vitamin pill* 維生素片 ➲ see also PEP PILL, SLEEPING PILL **2 the pill** or **the Pill** [sing.] a pill that some women take to prevent them becoming pregnant 口服避孕藥：*the contraceptive pill* 避孕藥丸 ◇ *to be/go* ***on the pill*** 在服用避孕藥 ➲ see also MORNING-AFTER PILL **3** [C] (*NAmE*) an annoying person 討厭的人；討厭鬼

IDM **sugar/sweeten the pill** to do sth that makes an unpleasant situation seem less unpleasant 藥裏加糖；緩和情況；緩解苦感 **SYN** **sugar-coat** ➲ more at BITTER *adj.*

■ ***verb*** [I] (of a piece of clothing, especially one made of wool 尤指毛織衣物) to become covered in very small balls of FIBRE 起球；結絨

pil·lage /'pɪlɪdʒ/ *verb* [I, T] to steal things from a place or region, especially in a war, using violence 搶劫；劫掠；掠奪 **SYN** **plunder**：*The rebels went looting and pillaging.* 叛亂者趁火打劫，掠奪財物。◇ **~ sth** *The town had been pillaged and burned.* 這座城鎮被洗劫焚燬。◇ **~ sth from sth** *Works of art were pillaged from churches and museums.* 教堂和博物館的藝術品被劫掠一空。▶ **pil·lage** *noun* [U]：*They brought back horrific accounts of murder and pillage.* 他們帶回了殘殺擄掠的可怕消息。**pil·la·ger** *noun* ➲ compare LOOT, PLUNDER

pil·lar /'pɪlə(r)/ *noun* **1** a large round stone, metal or wooden post that is used to support a bridge, the roof of a building, etc., especially when it is also decorative （尤指兼作裝飾的）柱子，橋墩 **2** a large round stone, metal or wooden post that is built to remind people of a famous person or event 紀念柱 **SYN** **column** **3 ~ of sth** a mass of sth that is shaped like a pillar 柱狀物：*a* ***pillar of smoke/rock*** 煙柱；石柱 **4 ~ of sth** a strong supporter of sth; an important member of sth 台柱子；主心骨；中流砥柱：*a pillar of the Church* 教會的骨幹分子 ◇ *a pillar of society* 社會中堅 **5 ~ of sth** a person who has a lot of a particular quality 富有某種素質的人；某種素質的化身：*She is a* ***pillar of strength*** *in a crisis.* 她在危難中表現非常堅強。**6** a basic part or feature of a system, organization, belief, etc.（組織、制度、信仰等的）核心，基礎，支柱：*the central pillar of this theory* 這一理論的核心支柱

IDM **be driven, pushed, etc. from ,pillar to 'post** to be forced to go from one person or situation to another without achieving anything 被迫四處碰壁（或到處奔波）

'pillar box *noun* (*old-fashioned, BrE*) a tall red metal box in the street, used for putting letters in which are being sent by post 郵筒；信筒 ➲ compare LETTER BOX, POSTBOX

,pillar-box 'red *adj.* (*BrE*) very bright red in colour 鮮紅的 ▶ **,pillar-box 'red** *noun* [U]

pil·lared /'pɪləd; *NAmE* -ərd/ *adj.* [only before noun] (of a building or part of a building 建築物) having PILLARS 有立柱的；柱式的

pill·box /'pɪlbɒks; *NAmE* -bɑːks/ *noun* a small shelter for soldiers, often partly underground, from which a gun can be fired（士兵的）掩體，隱蔽所，碉堡

pil·lion /ˈpɪliən/ *noun* a seat for a passenger behind the driver of a motorcycle 摩托車後座：*a **pillion passenger/seat*** 摩托車後座乘客；摩托車後座 ▸ **pil·lion** *adv.*：*to ride pillion* 坐在摩托車的後座上

pil·lock /ˈpɪlək/ *noun* (*BrE, slang*) a stupid person 蠢材；笨蛋

pil·lory /ˈpɪləri/ *verb, noun*

■ ***verb*** (**pil·lor·ies, pil·lory·ing, pil·lor·ied, pil·lor·ied**) [often passive] **~ sb** to criticize sb strongly in public 公開批評；抨擊：*He was regularly pilloried by the press for his radical ideas.* 他因觀點極端而經常受到新聞界的抨擊。

■ ***noun*** (*pl.* **-ies**) a wooden frame, with holes for the head and hands, which people were locked into in the past as a punishment （古刑具）木枷，頸手枷 ➲ compare STOCK *n.* (9)

pil·low /ˈpɪləʊ; *NAmE* -loʊ/ *noun, verb*

■ ***noun*** **1** a square or RECTANGULAR piece of cloth filled with soft material, used to rest your head on in bed 枕頭：*She lay back against the pillows.* 她半躺半坐靠在枕頭上。◇ ***pillow talk*** (= conversations in bed between lovers) 枕邊細語 ◇ *He lay back on the grass using his backpack as a pillow.* 他用背包當枕頭仰卧在草地上。➲ **VISUAL VOCAB** page V23 **2** (*NAmE*) = CUSHION *n.* (1)

■ ***verb*** **~ sth (+ adv./prep.)** (*literary*) to rest sth, especially your head, on an object 枕着（某物）：*She lay on the grass, her head pillowed on her arms.* 她頭枕着胳膊躺在草地上。

pil·low·case /ˈpɪləʊkeɪs; *NAmE* -loʊ-/ (also **ˈpil·low·slip** /ˈpɪləʊslɪp; *NAmE* -loʊ-/) *noun* a cloth cover for a PILLOW, that can be removed 枕頭套 ➲ **VISUAL VOCAB** page V23

pilot 🔑 /ˈpaɪlət/ *noun, verb, adj.*

■ ***noun*** **1** 🔑 a person who operates the controls of an aircraft, especially as a job 飛行員；（飛行器）駕駛員：*an airline pilot* 民航飛機飛行員 ◇ *a fighter pilot* 戰鬥機飛行員 ◇ *The accident was caused by pilot error.* 這場事故是飛行員的失誤造成的。➲ see also AUTOMATIC PILOT, AUTOPILOT, CO-PILOT, TEST PILOT **2** a person with special knowledge of a difficult area of water, for example, the entrance to a HARBOUR, whose job is to guide ships through it 領航員；引水員；領港員 **3** a single television programme that is made in order to find out whether people will like it and want to watch further programmes （電視的）試播節目 **4** = PILOT LIGHT

■ ***verb*** **1 ~ sth** to fly an aircraft or guide a ship; to act as a pilot 駕駛（飛行器）；領航（船隻）：*The plane was piloted by the instructor.* 飛機由教練員駕駛。◇ *The captain piloted the boat into a mooring.* 船長把船駛向泊位。**2 ~ sth (through sth)** to guide sb/sth somewhere, especially through a complicated place or system 引導；使通過（尤指複雜的地方或系統）：*She piloted a bill on the rights of part-time workers through parliament.* 她幾經周折終於使兼職勞工權利法案在議會中得以通過。**3 ~ sth** to test a new product, idea, etc. with a few people or in a small area before it is introduced everywhere 試點；試行

■ ***adj.*** [only before noun] done on a small scale in order to see if sth is successful enough to do on a large scale 試驗性的；試點的：*a **pilot project/study/survey*** 試驗性項目／研究／調查 ◇ *a **pilot episode*** (= of a radio or television series) 系列節目試播的一集

ˈpilot light (also **pilot**) *noun* a small flame that burns all the time, for example on a gas BOILER, and lights a larger flame when the gas is turned on 引火火種；長明火

ˈpilot officer *noun* (*abbr.* **PO**) an officer of the lowest rank in the British AIR FORCE 英國空軍少尉

ˈpilot whale *noun* a small WHALE that lives in warm seas 巨頭鯨；領航鯨

Pils /pɪlz; pɪls/ (also **Pilsner** /ˈpɪlznə(r); ˈpɪls-/) *noun* [U] a type of strong light-coloured beer originally made in what is now the Czech Republic 比而森啤酒（原產地在現在的捷克共和國境內）

PIM /ˌpiː aɪ ˈem; pɪm/ *abbr.* PERSONAL INFORMATION MANAGER

Pima /ˈpiːmə/ *noun* (*pl.* **Pima** or **Pimas**) *noun* a member of a Native American people, many of whom live in the US state of Arizona 皮馬人（美洲土著，很多居於美國亞利桑那州）

pi·mento /pɪˈmentəʊ; *NAmE* -toʊ/ *noun* (*pl.* **-os**) a small red PEPPER with a mild taste 西班牙甜椒

pimp /pɪmp/ *noun, verb*

■ ***noun*** a man who controls PROSTITUTES and lives on the money that they earn 拉皮條的男人

■ ***verb*** **1** [I] **~ (for sb)** to get customers for a PROSTITUTE 拉嫖客；做淫媒；拉皮條 **2** [T] (*informal*) to add things to sth to make it look or sound better, especially by making it more individual 修飾，改裝，加工（尤指使事物更具個人特色）：**~ sth** *Pimp your car with stylish custom wheels!* 給你的車裝上時尚的訂製車輪！◇ **~ sth up** *I would love to pimp the songs up.* 我很想讓這些歌曲更具獨有的特色。

pim·per·nel /ˈpɪmpənel; *NAmE* -pərnel/ *noun* a small wild plant with red, white or blue flowers 海綠（開紅、白或藍花的矮小野生植物）

pim·ple /ˈpɪmpl/ *noun* a small raised red spot on the skin 丘疹；粉刺；小膿包 ➲ compare SPOT *n.* (3) ➲ see also GOOSE PIMPLES ▸ **pim·ply** /ˈpɪmpli/ *adj.*：*pimply skin* 長丘疹的皮膚 ◇ *a pimply youth* 長粉刺的青年人

PIN /pɪn/ (also **ˈPIN number**) *noun* the abbreviation for 'personal identification number' (a number given to you, for example by a bank, so that you can use a plastic card to take out money from a cash machine) 個人身分識別號碼，個人密碼（全寫為 personal identification number，銀行等向顧客提供的可與提款卡配合使用的號碼）➲ see also CHIP AND PIN

pin 🔑 /pɪn/ *noun, verb*

■ ***noun***

▸ **FOR FASTENING/JOINING** 用於固定／連接 **1** 🔑 a short thin piece of stiff wire with a sharp point at one end and a round head at the other, used especially for fastening together pieces of cloth when sewing 大頭針 ➲ see also BOBBY PIN, DRAWING PIN, HAIRPIN, LINCHPIN, PINS AND NEEDLES, SAFETY PIN

▸ **JEWELLERY** 首飾 **2** a short thin piece of stiff wire with a sharp point at one end and an item of decoration at the other, worn as jewellery 胸針；飾針：*a diamond pin* 一枚鑽石胸針 ➲ see also TIEPIN **3** (*especially NAmE*) = BROOCH

▸ **BADGE** 徽章 **4** (*especially NAmE*) a type of BADGE that is fastened with a pin at the back （有別針的）徽章：*He supports the group and wears its pin on his lapel.* 他支持這個團體，為此在翻領上佩戴該團體的徽章。

▸ **MEDICAL** 醫療 **5** a piece of steel used to support a bone in your body when it has been broken （接骨用的）鋼釘

▸ **ELECTRICAL** 電器 **6** one of the metal parts that stick out of an electric plug and fit into a SOCKET （插頭的）管腳：*a 2-pin plug* 雙芯插頭 ➲ picture at PLUG

▸ **IN GAMES** 遊戲 **7** a wooden or plastic object that is shaped like a bottle and that players try to knock down in games such as BOWLING （保齡球等的）木瓶，瓶柱 ➲ **VISUAL VOCAB** page V40 ➲ see also NINEPINS, TENPIN

▸ **IN GOLF** 高爾夫球 **8** a stick with a flag on top of it, placed in a hole so that players can see where they are aiming for 旗杆

▸ **LEGS** 腿 **9 pins** [pl.] (*informal*) a person's legs（人的）雙腿

▸ **ON SMALL BOMB** 小炸彈上 **10** a small piece of metal on a HAND GRENADE that stops it from exploding and is pulled out just before the HAND GRENADE is thrown （手榴彈上的）保險栓，保險針 ➲ see also LINCHPIN

IDM **for two ˈpins** (*old-fashioned, BrE*) used to say that you would like to do sth, even though you know that it would not be sensible 恨不得；恨不能：*I'd kill him for two pins.* 我恨不得殺了他。➲ more at HEAR

■ ***verb*** (**-nn-**)

▸ **FASTEN/JOIN** 固定；連接 **1** 🔑 **~ sth + adv./prep.** to attach sth onto another thing or fasten things together with a pin, etc. （用大頭釘等）固定，別上，釘住：*She pinned the badge onto her jacket.* 她把徽章別到外衣上。◇ *A message had been pinned to the noticeboard.* 佈告牌上釘着一條消息。◇ *Pin all the pieces of material together.*

P

把這些材料都釘到一起。◇ *She always wears her hair pinned back.* 她總是把頭髮往後別。

▸ **PREVENT MOVEMENT** 阻礙 **2 ~ sb/sth + adv./prep.** to make sb unable to move by holding them or pressing them against sth 使不能動彈；按住；箝住：*They pinned him against a wall and stole his wallet.* 他們把他擠在牆邊，偷走了他的錢包。◇ *He grabbed her arms and pinned them to her sides.* 他抓住她的雙臂，按在她的腰間。◇ *They found him pinned under the wreckage of the car.* 人們發現他被卡在汽車殘骸下。

IDM **,pin (all) your 'hopes on sb/sth | ,pin your 'faith on sb/sth** to rely on sb/sth completely for success or help 完全依賴；寄希望於；指望：*The company is pinning its hopes on the new project.* 這家公司對此新項目寄予厚望。

PHR V **,pin sb↔'down 1** to make sb unable to move by holding them firmly 按住；使動彈不得：*Two men pinned him down until the police arrived.* 兩個人按住他直到警察趕來。**2** to find sb and make them answer a question or tell you sth you need to know 找某人查問；使說清楚：*I need the up-to-date sales figures but I can never pin him down at the office.* 我需要最新的銷售數字，可就是不能在辦公室找到他問清楚。**,pin sb↔'down (to sth/doing sth)** to make sb make a decision or say clearly what they think or what they intend to do 使決定；使說明意向：*It's difficult to pin her down to fixing a date for a meeting.* 讓她確定個開會日期實在是難。**,pin sth↔'down** to explain or understand sth exactly 確切說明（或理解）：*The cause of the disease is difficult to pin down precisely.* 病因目前還難以解釋清楚。**'pin sth on sb** to make sb be blamed for sth, especially for sth they did not do 讓（無辜的人）受過：*No one would admit responsibility. They all tried to* ***pin the blame on*** *someone else.* 誰也不肯負責，大家都竭力把過失推給別人。◇ *You can't pin this one on me—I wasn't even there!* 這事你不能怪罪我。我當時根本不在場！

pina co·lada /ˌpiːnə kəˈlɑːdə/ *noun* [C, U] an alcoholic drink made by mixing RUM with PINEAPPLE juice and COCONUT 菠蘿汁朗姆酒（用朗姆酒和菠蘿汁、椰汁調製而成）

P

pina·fore /ˈpɪnəfɔː(r)/ *noun* **1** (also **'pinafore dress**) (both *especially BrE*) (*NAmE* usually **jumper**) a loose dress with no sleeves, usually worn over a BLOUSE or sweater 無袖女裝（通常套在襯衣或針織套衫外面）；圍裙裝 **2** (*old-fashioned*) (also *informal* **pinny**) (both *BrE*) a long loose piece of clothing without sleeves, worn by women over the front of their clothes to keep them clean, for example when cooking （女用）圍裙 ➲ compare APRON (1) **3** a loose piece of clothing like a dress without sleeves, worn by children over their clothes to keep them clean, or by young girls over a dress （小孩）圍裙，圍嘴；（女孩的）連胸圍裙

pi·ña·ta (also **pi·na·ta**) /pɪnˈjɑːtə/ *noun* (from *Spanish*) (in Spanish-speaking communities in the US) a brightly decorated figure, filled with toys and sweets/candy, which children try to hit with a stick with their eyes covered in order to break it open, as a party game 彩色禮品包（內裝玩具和糖果，美國西班牙語社區兒童聚會玩遊戲時蒙眼用小棍戳破）

pin·ball /ˈpɪnbɔːl/ *noun* [U] a game played on a **pinball machine**, in which the player sends a small metal ball up a sloping board and scores points as it BOUNCES off objects. The player tries to prevent the ball from reaching the bottom of the machine by pressing two buttons at the side. 彈球遊戲

pin·board /ˈpɪnbɔːd; *NAmE* -bɔːrd/ *noun* (*BrE*) a board made of CORK that is fixed to an indoor wall, on which you can display messages, notices, etc. 軟木告示牌（用於留言、發佈通知等）

pince-nez /ˌpæs ˈneɪ/ *noun* (*pl.* **pince-nez**) (from *French*) a pair of glasses, worn in the past, with a spring that fits on the nose, instead of parts at the sides that fit over the ears （舊時的）夾鼻眼鏡

pin·cer /ˈpɪnsə(r)/ *noun* **1** **pincers** [pl.] a tool made of two crossed pieces of metal, used for holding things firmly and pulling things, for example nails out of wood 鉗子：*a pair of pincers* 一把鉗子 **2** [C] one of a pair of curved CLAWS of some types of animal, for example CRABS and LOBSTERS （蟹、蝦等的）螯 ➲ VISUAL VOCAB page V13

'pincer movement *noun* [usually sing.] a military attack in which an army attacks the enemy from two sides at the same time 鉗形運動；鉗形攻勢

pinch /pɪntʃ/ *verb, noun*

■ *verb*

▸ **WITH THUMB AND FINGER** 用拇指和手指 **1** [T] **~ sb/sth/yourself** to take a piece of sb's skin between your thumb and first finger and squeeze hard, especially to hurt the person 擰；捏；掐：*My sister's always pinching me and it really hurts.* 我姐姐老擰我，真的很痛。◇ *He pinched the baby's cheek playfully.* 他捏着寶寶的臉頰逗着玩。◇ (*figurative*) *She had to pinch herself to make sure she was not dreaming.* 她不得不掐一下自己，弄清楚自己不是在做夢。**2** [T] **~ sth (+ adv./prep.)** to hold sth tightly between the thumb and finger or between two things that are pressed together 捏住；夾緊：*Pinch the nostrils together between your thumb and finger to stop the bleeding.* 用手指捏住鼻孔止血。◇ *a pinched nerve in the neck* 脖子上一條被擠壓的神經

▸ **OF A SHOE** 鞋 **3** [I, T] **~ (sb/sth)** if sth such as a shoe **pinches** part of your body, it hurts you because it is too tight 夾（腳）；夾痛：*These new shoes pinch.* 這雙新鞋夾腳。

▸ **STEAL** 偷竊 **4** [T] **~ sth (from sb/sth)** (*BrE, informal*) to steal sth, especially sth small and not very valuable 偷摸；行竊 **SYN** **nick**：*Who's pinched my pen?* 誰拿了我的筆？

▸ **COST TOO MUCH** 昂貴 **5** [T] **~ sb/sth** to cost a person or an organization a lot of money or more than they can spend 使花費過多；使入不敷出：*Higher interest rates are already pinching the housing industry.* 提高利率已使住房產業不堪負荷。

▸ **ARREST** 拘捕 **6** [T] **~ sb** (*old-fashioned, BrE, informal*) to arrest sb 逮捕：*I was pinched for dangerous driving.* 我因危險駕駛而被抓住。

IDM **pinch 'pennies** (*informal*) to try to spend as little money as possible 一毛不拔；吝嗇

PHR V **,pinch sth↔'off/'out** to remove sth by pressing your fingers together and pulling 掐掉；摘掉

■ *noun*

▸ **WITH THUMB AND FINGER** 用拇指和手指 **1** an act of squeezing a part of sb's skin tightly between your thumb and finger, especially in order to hurt them 捏；掐；擰：*She gave him a pinch on the arm to wake him up.* 她擰一下他的胳膊把他喚醒。

▸ **SMALL AMOUNT** 少量 **2** the amount of sth that you can hold between your finger and thumb 一撮：*a pinch of salt* 一撮鹽

IDM **at a 'pinch** (*BrE*) (*NAmE* **in a 'pinch**) used to say that sth could be done or used in a particular situation if it is really necessary 必要時；不得已時：*We can get six people round this table at a pinch.* 必要時，這張桌子可以坐六個人。**take sth with a pinch of 'salt** to be careful about believing that sth is completely true 不完全相信；半信半疑 ➲ more at FEEL *v.*

pinched /pɪntʃt/ *adj.* (of a person's face 人的臉) pale and thin, especially because of illness, cold or worry （因疾病、寒冷、愁苦等）蒼白清瘦的，清癯的

'pinch-hit *verb* (*NAmE*) **1** [I] (in BASEBALL 棒球) to hit the ball for another player 代擊球；替補擊球 **2** [I] **~ (for sb)** (*informal*) to do sth for sb else who is suddenly unable to do it 臨時頂替；緊急替代

'pinch run *verb* [I] (in BASEBALL 棒球) to take the place of a player who is on a BASE 替補（跑壘員）：*Gordon pinch ran for Gomez.* 戈登上場替補跑壘員戈麥斯。

pin·cush·ion /ˈpɪnkʊʃn/ *noun* a small thick PAD made of cloth, used for sticking pins in when they are not being used 針墊；針插

pine /paɪn/ *noun, verb*

■ *noun* **1** [C, U] (also **'pine tree** [C]) an EVERGREEN forest tree with leaves like needles 松樹：*pine forests* 松樹林 ◇ *pine needles* 松針 ◇ *a Scots pine* 歐洲赤松 **2** (also

pine·wood) [U] the pale soft wood of the pine tree, used in making furniture, etc. 松木：*a pine table* 松木桌子

■ ***verb*** [I] to become very sad because sb has died or gone away（因死亡、離別）難過，悲傷：*She pined for months after he'd gone.* 他死了以後，她難過了好幾個月。

PHR V **ˌpine aˈway** to become very sick and weak because you miss sb/sth very much（因思念等）病重虛弱，憔悴：*After his wife died, he just pined away.* 妻子死後，他日漸憔悴。 **ˈpine for sb/sth** to want or miss sb/sth very much 懷念；思念；渴望：*She was pining for the mountains of her native country.* 她對祖國的青山思念不已。

pin·eal /paɪˈniːəl/ (also **piˈneal gland**) *noun* (*anatomy* 解) a small organ in the brain that releases a HORMONE 松果腺；松果體

pine·apple /ˈpaɪnæpl/ *noun* [C, U] a large tropical fruit with thick rough skin, sweet yellow flesh with a lot of juice and stiff leaves on top 菠蘿；鳳梨：*fresh pineapple* 新鮮菠蘿 ◇ *a tin of pineapple chunks* 一罐菠蘿塊 ◇ *pineapple juice* 菠蘿汁 ➲ **VISUAL VOCAB** page V30 **IDM** see ROUGH *adj.*

ˈpine cone *noun* the hard dry fruit of the PINE tree 松球；松果

ˈpine marten *noun* a small wild animal with a long body, short legs and sharp teeth. Pine martens live in forests and eat smaller animals. 松貂

ˈpine nut (*BrE* also **ˈpine kernel**) *noun* the white seed of some PINE trees, used in cooking 松子；松仁

pine·wood /ˈpaɪnwʊd/ *noun* = PINE (2)

ping /pɪŋ/ *noun, verb*

■ ***noun*** a short high sound made when a hard object hits sth that is made of metal or glass（硬物碰擊金屬或玻璃發出的響聲）乒，砰

■ ***verb*** **1** [I, T] **~ (sth)** to make a short, high ringing sound; to make sth produce this sound（使）乒乓作響，發乒乓聲 **2** (*NAmE*) (*BrE* **pink**) [I] (of a car engine 汽車發動機) to make knocking sounds because the fuel is not burning correctly 發爆聲；敲缸 **3** [T] **~ sth** to test whether an Internet connection is working by sending a signal to a computer and waiting for a reply 乒網（向計算機發送信號等待回覆測試是否連通互聯網） **4** [T] **~ sth (to sb)** (*informal*) to send an email or TEXT MESSAGE to sb 發送（電子郵件、手機短信）：*I'll ping it to you later.* 我隨後把它發送給你。

ping·er /ˈpɪŋə(r)/ *noun* a device that makes a series of short high sounds, for example on a cooker/stove to tell you that the cooking time has ended（廚灶等的）響鈴定時器

ˈping-pong (*BrE, informal*) (*NAmE* **ˈPing-Pong™**) *noun* [U] a game played like TENNIS with BATS and a small plastic ball on a table with a net across it 乒乓球運動 ➲ **VISUAL VOCAB** page V45

pin·head /ˈpɪnhed/ *noun* the very small flat surface at one end of a pin 大頭針的平頭

pin·hole /ˈpɪnhəʊl; *NAmE* -hoʊl/ *noun* a very small hole, especially one made by a pin 針刺的孔；針孔

pin·ion /ˈpɪnjən/ *verb* **~ sb/sth + adv./prep.** to hold or tie sb, especially by their arms, so that they cannot move 捆住，縛住（雙臂）；固定住：*His arms were pinioned to his sides.* 他的雙臂被綁在身體兩側。◇ *They were pinioned against the wall.* 他們被牢牢地靠牆綁着。

pink 🔑 /pɪŋk/ *adj., noun, verb*

■ ***adj.*** **1** 🔑 pale red in colour 粉紅色的：*pale pink roses* 淡粉色的玫瑰 ◇ *She went bright pink with embarrassment.* 她尷尬得滿臉緋紅。 **2** [only before noun] (*BrE*) connected with HOMOSEXUAL people 與同性戀者有關的：*the pink pound* (= money spent by HOMOSEXUALS as an influence in the economy) 同性戀族群消費力 **3** (*politics* 政) (*informal, disapproving*) having or showing slightly LEFT-WING political views 政治觀點偏左的；略呈左傾的 ➲ compare RED *adj.* (5) ▸ **pink·ness** *noun* [U] **IDM** see TICKLE *v.*

■ ***noun*** **1** 🔑 [U, C] the colour that is produced when you mix red and white together 粉紅色：*She was dressed in pink.* 她穿着粉紅色的衣服。◇ *The bedroom was decorated in pale pinks.* 卧室塗成了淡粉紅色。 **2** [C] a garden plant with pink, red or white flowers that have a sweet smell 香石竹；石竹

IDM **in the ˈpink** (*old-fashioned, informal*) in good health 滿面紅光；容光煥發

■ ***verb*** (*BrE*) (*NAmE* **ping**) [I] (of a car engine 汽車發動機) to make knocking sounds because the fuel is not burning correctly 發爆聲；敲缸

ˌpink-ˈcollar *adj.* [only before noun] (*especially NAmE*) connected with low-paid jobs done mainly by women, for example in offices and restaurants（辦公室、餐館等）以女性為主低薪職業的；粉領的：*pink-collar workers* 粉領職工 ➲ compare BLUE-COLLAR, WHITE-COLLAR

ˌpink ˈgin *noun* **1** [U] an alcoholic drink made from GIN mixed with ANGOSTURA that gives it a bitter flavour 苦味杜松子酒；紅杜松子酒 **2** [C] a glass of pink gin 一杯苦味杜松子酒

ˈpink·ing shears *noun* [pl.] special scissors used for cutting cloth so that it will not FRAY at the edges 鋸齒形布邊剪刀；花齒剪

pink·ish /ˈpɪŋkɪʃ/ *adj.* fairly pink in colour 淺粉色的；略帶桃紅色的

pinko /ˈpɪŋkəʊ; *NAmE* -koʊ/ *noun* (*pl.* **-os** or **-oes**) **1** (*NAmE, informal, disapproving*) a COMMUNIST or a SOCIALIST 共產主義者；社會主義者 **2** (*BrE, informal*) a person who is slightly LEFT-WING in their ideas, but not very 觀點偏左的人；左傾分子 ➲ compare RED *n.* (3) ▸ **pinko** *adj.*

ˌpink ˈslip *noun* (*NAmE, informal*) a letter given to sb to say that they must leave their job 解雇通知書

pinky (also **pinkie**) /ˈpɪŋki/ *noun* (*pl.* **-ies**) (*NAmE, ScotE*) the smallest finger of the hand（手的）小指：*a pinky ring* (= worn on the smallest finger) 戴在小指上的戒指 **SYN** **little finger**

ˈpin money *noun* [U] a small amount of money that you earn, especially when this is used to buy things that you want rather than things that you need 小額閒錢

pin·na·cle /ˈpɪnəkl/ *noun* **1** [usually sing.] **~ of sth** the most important or successful part of sth 頂點；頂峰；鼎盛時期：*the pinnacle of her career* 她事業的頂峰 **2** a small pointed stone decoration built on the roof of a building（建築物）小尖頂 **3** a high pointed piece of rock, especially at the top of a mountain（尤指山頂的）尖岩，兀立岩石

pinny /ˈpɪni/ *noun* (*pl.* **-ies**) (*BrE, informal*) = PINAFORE

Pinoc·chio /pɪˈnəʊkiəʊ; *NAmE* -ˈnoʊkioʊ/ *noun* a character in a children's story who changes from a wooden figure into a boy. Whenever he tells a lie, his nose grows longer. 皮諾曹（從木偶變成男孩的童話人物，說謊時鼻子就變長）：*Cartoons showed the Minister as a long-nosed Pinocchio.* 漫畫把部長描畫成長鼻子皮諾曹。

pin·point /ˈpɪnpɔɪnt/ *verb, adj., noun*

■ ***verb*** **1 ~ sth** to find and show the exact position of sb/sth or the exact time that sth happened 明確指出，確定（位置或時間）：*He was able to pinpoint on the map the site of the medieval village.* 他能在地圖上準確找出那個中世紀村莊的位置。 **2 ~ sth** to be able to give the exact reason for sth or to describe sth exactly 準確解釋（或說明）：*The report pinpointed the areas most in need of help.* 報告精確說明了亟待援助的地區。

■ ***adj.*** if sth is done with **pinpoint accuracy**, it is done exactly and in exactly the right position 準確的；精確的：*The pilots bombed strategic targets with pinpoint accuracy.* 飛行員準確地轟炸了戰略目標。

■ ***noun*** a very small area of sth, especially light 極小的範圍；光點

pin·prick /ˈpɪnprɪk/ *noun* **1** a very small area of sth, especially light（光等的）點：*His eyes narrowed to two small pinpricks.* 他把眼睛瞇成了兩條細縫。 **2** a very small hole in sth, especially one that has been made by a pin 小孔；針孔 **3** something that annoys you even though it is small and unimportant 煩心的小事；令人不快的瑣事

ˌpins and ˈneedles *noun* [U] an uncomfortable feeling in a part of your body, caused when a normal flow

P

of blood returns after it has been partly blocked, especially because you have been sitting or lying in an awkward position 發麻；麻木：*to have pins and needles* 感覺麻木

IDM **be on ˌpins and ˈneedles** (*NAmE*) = BE ON TENTERHOOKS

pin·stripe /ˈpɪnstraɪp/ *noun* **1** [C] one of the white vertical lines printed on dark cloth that is used especially for making business suits（深色西裝衣料上）白色細條紋 **2** [U, C] dark cloth with white vertical lines printed on it; a suit made from this cloth 帶有白色細條紋的深色衣料；細條紋西服：*a pinstripe suit* 一套細條紋西裝 ▸ **pin·striped** *adj.* [only before noun]：*a pinstriped suit* 一套細條紋西裝 ◇ *a pinstriped official* (= who is wearing a pinstriped suit) 一個穿細條紋套裝的官員

pint 0┳ /paɪnt/ *noun*
1 0┳ (*abbr.* **pt**) a unit for measuring liquids and some dry goods. There are 8 pints in a gallon, equal to 0.568 of a litre in the UK and some other countries, and 0.473 of a litre in the US 品脫（容量單位，為 ⅛ 加侖，在英國等國家約合 0.568 升，在美國約合 0.473 升）：*a* **pint of beer/milk** 一品脫啤酒 / 牛奶 ◇ *We'd better get a couple of extra pints (= of milk) tomorrow.* 明天我們最好再多買幾品脫牛奶。◇ *Add half a pint of cream.* 加上半品脫奶油。 **2** 0┳ (*BrE*) a pint of beer (especially in a pub) 一品脫啤酒（尤用於酒吧）：*Do you want to* **go for a pint** *later?* 待會兒你想去喝杯啤酒嗎？

pinta /ˈpaɪntə/ *noun* (*old-fashioned, BrE, informal*) a pint of milk 一品脫牛奶

pinto /ˈpɪntəʊ; *NAmE* -toʊ/ *adj.* (*NAmE*) (of a horse 馬) with areas on it of two colours, usually black and white 有兩色花斑的；（通常指）黑白斑紋的 **SYN** **piebald** ▸ **pinto** *noun* (*pl.* **-os**)

ˈpinto bean *noun* a type of curved BEAN with coloured marks on the skin 斑豆；花腰豆

ˌpint ˈpot *noun* a beer glass, often with a handle, that holds one pint 一品脫啤酒杯（常帶柄） **IDM** see QUART

P

ˈpint-sized *adj.* (*informal*) (of people 人) very small 矮小的

ˈpin-up *noun* **1** a picture of an attractive person, especially one who is not wearing many clothes, that is put on a wall for people to look at 名人（或美人）海報；掛在牆上的半裸美人像 **2** a person who appears in a pin-up 半裸海報畫中的模特兒；海報中的名人（或美女）

pin·wheel /ˈpɪnwiːl/ *noun* (*NAmE*) **1** (*BrE* **wind·mill**) a toy with curved plastic parts that form the shape of a flower which turns round on the end of a stick when you blow on it 玩具風車 **2** = CATHERINE WHEEL

Pin·yin /ˌpɪnˈjɪn/ *noun* [U] the standard system of ROMAN spelling in Chinese 漢語拼音（採用羅馬拼寫體系）

pi·on·eer /ˌpaɪəˈnɪə(r); *NAmE* -ˈnɪr/ *noun, verb*
▪ ***noun*** **1** ~ (**in/of sth**) a person who is the first to study and develop a particular area of knowledge, culture, etc. that other people then continue to develop 先鋒；先驅；帶頭人 **SYN** **trailblazer**：*a pioneer in the field of microsurgery* 顯微外科領域的創始人 ◇ *a computer pioneer* 計算機方面的先驅 ◇ *a pioneer aviator* 航空探索者 ◇ *a pioneer design* (= one that introduces new ideas, methods, etc.) 開創性設計 **2** one of the first people to go to a particular area in order to live and work there 開發者；拓荒者：*the pioneer spirit* 拓荒者的精神
▪ ***verb*** **~ sth** when sb **pioneers** sth, they are one of the first people to do, discover or use sth new 當開拓者；做先鋒；倡導：*a new technique pioneered by surgeons in a London hospital* 由倫敦一家醫院的外科醫生率先採用的新技術

pi·on·eer·ing /ˌpaɪəˈnɪərɪŋ; *NAmE* -ˈnɪr-/ *adj.* [usually before noun] introducing ideas and methods that have never been used before 開拓性的；先驅性的；探索性的：*pioneering work on infant mortality* 嬰兒死亡率方面的探索性研究工作 ◇ *the pioneering days of radio* 無線電的初創時期

pious /ˈpaɪəs/ *adj.* **1** having or showing a deep respect for God and religion 虔誠的；虔敬的 **SYN** **devout**：*pious acts* 虔誠之舉 **OPP** **impious** ➲ see also PIETY **2** (*disapproving*) pretending to be religious, moral or good in order to impress other people 道貌岸然的；偽善的；假正經的 **SYN** **sanctimonious**：*pious sentiments* 虛情假意 **3** **~ hope** something that you want to happen but is unlikely to be achieved 可望而不可及的；難以實現的：*Such reforms seem likely to remain little more than pious hopes.* 這類改革可能只是畫餅充饑而已。▸ **pi·ous·ly** *adv.*

pip /pɪp/ *noun, verb*
▪ ***noun*** **1** (*especially BrE*) (*NAmE* usually **seed**) the small hard seed that is found in some types of fruit（某些水果的）種子，籽：*an* **apple/orange pip** 蘋果籽；橙子籽 ➲ VISUAL VOCAB page V26 **2** **the pips** [pl.] (*old-fashioned, BrE*) a series of short high sounds, especially those used when giving the exact time on the radio 嘟嘟聲；（尤指電台的）報時信號 **3** (*NAmE*) one of the dots showing the value on DICE and DOMINOES; one of the marks showing the value and SUIT of a PLAYING CARD（色子、骨牌、紙牌上的）點
▪ ***verb*** (**-pp-**) **~ sb** (*BrE, informal*) to beat sb in a race, competition, etc. by only a small amount or at the last moment 以微弱優勢擊敗；險勝；終於戰勝：*She pipped her rival for the gold medal.* 她險勝對手，奪得金牌。◇ *He was* **pipped at/to the post** *for the top award.* 他到終點時以些微之差被超越，失去了冠軍。

pipes 管；煙斗

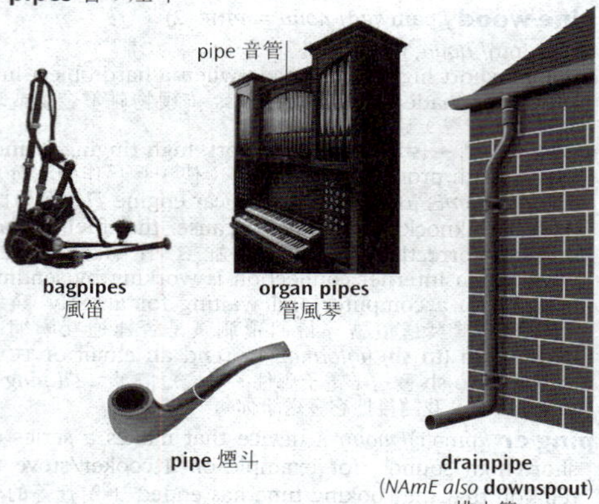

pipe 音管

bagpipes 風笛

organ pipes 管風琴

pipe 煙斗

drainpipe (*NAmE also* **downspout**) 排水管

pipe 0┳ /paɪp/ *noun, verb*
▪ ***noun*** **1** 0┳ [C, U] a tube through which liquids and gases can flow 管子；管道：*hot and cold water pipes* 冷、熱水管 ◇ *lead/plastic pipes* 鉛 / 塑料管子 ◇ *a leaking gas pipe* 漏氣的煤氣管 ◇ *Copper pipe is sold in lengths.* 銅管按長度出售。◇ *a* **burst pipe** 有破洞的管子 ➲ COLLOCATIONS at DECORATE ➲ see also DRAINPIPE, EXHAUST *n.* (2), WINDPIPE **2** 0┳ [C] a narrow tube with a bowl at one end, used for smoking TOBACCO 煙斗；煙袋：*to smoke a pipe* 抽煙斗 ◇ *He puffed on his pipe.* 他吸着煙斗。◇ *pipe tobacco* 煙斗絲 **3** [C] a musical instrument in the shape of a tube, played by blowing 管樂器 ➲ see also PAN PIPES **4** [C] any of the tubes from which sound is produced in an organ（管風琴的）音管 **5** **pipes** [pl.] = BAGPIPES
▪ ***verb*** **1** [T] **~ sth** (**+ adv./prep.**) to send water, gas, oil, etc. through a pipe from one place to another 用管道輸送：*to pipe oil across the desert* 用管子把石油輸送過沙漠 ◇ *Water is piped from the reservoir to the city.* 水從水庫經管子輸送到城裏。 **2** [T] **~ sth** (**+ adv./prep.**) [usually passive] to send sounds or signals through a wire or cable from one place to another 用線路系統傳輸（或傳送）：*The speech was piped over a public address system.* 講話經廣播系統傳送出去。 **3** [T, I] **~** (**sb**) to play music on a pipe or the BAGPIPES, especially to welcome sb who has arrived 用管樂器演奏（尤指迎賓曲）：*Passengers were piped aboard ship at the start of the cruise.* 遊客在管樂迎賓曲中登船開始水上遊。◇ *a prize for piping*

and drumming 笛鼓演奏獎 **4** [I, T] (+ **speech**) to speak or sing in a high voice or with a high sound 尖聲地說（或唱）；尖聲啼鳴：*Outside a robin piped.* 外面有一隻知更鳥在啼鳴。 **5** [T] **~ sth** (**on sth**) to decorate food, especially a cake, with thin lines of ICING, etc. by squeezing it out of a special bag or tube 裱花（用裱花袋把糖霜等裱在糕點上）：*The cake had 'Happy Birthday' piped on it.* 蛋糕上裱了"生日快樂"的字樣。

PHR V **,pipe 'down** (*informal*) used especially in orders, to tell sb to stop talking or to be less noisy 安靜些；別說話；別嚷嚷 **,pipe 'up (with sth)** (*informal*) to begin to speak 開始說；說起來：*The person next to me piped up with a silly comment.* 我旁邊那位愚蠢地評論起來。◇ **+ speech** *'I know the answer,' piped up a voice at the back of the room.* "我知道答案。" 房間後邊有個聲音叫起來。

'pipe band *noun* a marching band consisting of BAGPIPES and drums（行進）風笛鼓樂隊

'pipe cleaner *noun* a short piece of wire, covered with soft material, used for cleaning inside a TOBACCO pipe 煙斗通條

,piped 'music *noun* [U] (*BrE*) recorded music that is played continuously in shops, restaurants, etc.（商店、餐館等處不斷播放的）背景音樂

'pipe dream *noun* a hope or plan that is impossible to achieve or not practical 脱離實際的願望；行不通的計劃；妄想

pipe·line /'paɪplaɪn/ *noun* a series of pipes that are usually underground and are used for carrying oil, gas, etc. over long distances 輸油管道，輸氣管道，輸送管線（通常指地下的）

IDM **in the 'pipeline** something that is **in the pipeline** is being discussed, planned or prepared and will happen or exist soon 在討論（或規劃、準備）中；在醞釀中

'pipe organ *noun* = ORGAN (3)

piper /'paɪpə(r)/ *noun* a person who plays music on a pipe or the BAGPIPES 吹笛者；風笛吹奏者 IDM see PAY *v.*

pip·ette /pɪ'pet; *NAmE* paɪ'p-/ *noun* (*technical* 術語) a narrow tube used in a laboratory for measuring or transferring small amounts of liquids（實驗室用的）吸管，移液管 ➲ VISUAL VOCAB page V70

pipe·work /'paɪpwɜːk; *NAmE* -wɜːrk/ *noun* [U] the pipes used for carrying oil, gas or water around a machine, building, etc.（統稱機器、建築物等的）管道；管路系統

pip·ing /'paɪpɪŋ/ *noun, adj.*

■ ***noun*** [U] **1** a pipe or pipes of the type or length mentioned（某種或某長度的）管道，管子：*ten metres of lead piping* 十米長的鉛管 **2** a folded strip of cloth, often with a length of string inside, used to decorate a piece of clothing, a CUSHION, etc.（衣服、靠墊等的）緄邊：*a uniform with gold piping* 帶金色緄邊的制服 **3** lines of cream or ICING/FROSTING as decoration on a cake（用糖霜等裱成的）糕點條紋花飾 **4** the sound of a pipe or pipes being played 笛聲；管樂器聲

■ ***adj.*** (of a person's voice 人的聲音) high 尖的；高的

,piping 'hot *adj.* (of liquids or food 液體或食物) very hot 滾燙的；燙手的；炙熱的

pipit /'pɪpɪt/ *noun* (often in compounds 常構成複合詞) a small brown bird with a pleasant song 鷚；小百靈：*a meadow/rock/tree pipit* 草地 / 岩石 / 樹鷚

pip·squeak /'pɪpskwiːk/ *noun* (*old-fashioned, informal*) a person that you think is unimportant or does not deserve respect because they are small or young 無足輕重的人；小人物；小子

pi·quancy /'piːkənsi/ *noun* [U] the quality of being piquant 趣味；興奮；辛辣：*The tart flavour of the cranberries adds piquancy.* 越橘的酸味很可口。◇ *The situation has an added piquancy since the two men are also rivals in love.* 事情更加有趣的是，這兩個人也是情敵。

pi·quant /'piːkənt/ *adj.* **1** having a pleasantly strong or spicy taste 辛辣的；開胃的 **2** exciting and interesting 刺激的；令人興奮的；有趣的

pique /piːk/ *noun, verb*

■ ***noun*** [U] (*formal*) annoyed or bitter feelings that you have, usually because your pride has been hurt 怨恨；憤恨；惱怒：*When he realized nobody was listening to him, he left in a **fit of pique**.* 他發覺他說話無人理睬，就憤然離去。

■ ***verb*** **~ sb/sth** (*formal*) to make sb annoyed or upset 使憤恨；使惱怒 SYN **wound** ▸ **piqued** *adj.* [not before noun]：*She couldn't help feeling a little piqued by his lack of interest.* 她不禁對他的淡漠感到有些不樂。

IDM **,pique sb's 'interest, curi'osity, etc.** (*especially NAmE*) to make sb very interested in sth 使…興趣盎然；引起…的好奇

piqué /'piːkeɪ/ *noun* [U] a type of stiff cloth with a raised pattern 凸紋堅挺布料；珠地布；凹凸織物

pir·acy /'paɪrəsi/ *noun* [U] **1** the crime of attacking ships at sea in order to steal from them 海上搶劫 **2** the act of making illegal copies of DVDs, computer programs, books, etc., in order to sell them 盜版行為；非法複製：*software piracy* 軟件盜版行為 ➲ see also PIRATE

pi·ranha /pɪ'rɑːnə/ *noun* a small S American FRESHWATER fish that attacks and eats live animals 水虎魚，鋸脂鯉（南美的一種捕食動物的小淡水魚）

pir·ate /'paɪrət/ *noun, verb*

■ ***noun*** **1** (especially in the past) a person on a ship who attacks other ships at sea in order to steal from them（尤指舊時的）海盜：*a pirate ship* 海盜船 **2** (often used as an adjective 常用作形容詞) a person who makes illegal copies of DVDs, computer programs, books, etc., in order to sell them 盜版者；盜印者：*a pirate edition* 盜版 ◇ *software pirates* 軟件盜版者 **3** (often used as an adjective 常用作形容詞) a person or an organization that broadcasts illegally 非法播音的人（或組織）：*a pirate radio station* 非法電台 ➲ see also PIRACY ▸ **pir·at·ical** /,paɪ'rætɪkl/ *adj.*

■ ***verb*** **~ sth** to copy and use or sell sb's work or a product without permission and without having the right to do so 盜印；竊用：*pirated computer games* 盜版電腦遊戲

piri-piri /,pɪri 'pɪri/ *noun* [U] a type of spicy sauce made from CHILLIES 辣椒醬

pirou·ette /,pɪru'et/ *noun* a fast turn or spin that a person, especially a BALLET dancer, makes on one foot（尤指芭蕾舞中的）單腳尖旋轉 ▸ **pirou·ette** *verb* [I]：*She pirouetted across the stage.* 她用單腳尖旋轉着從舞台的一邊轉到另一邊。

pisca·tor·ial /,pɪskə'tɔːriəl/ (also **pisca·tory** /'pɪskətəri; *NAmE* -tɔːri/) *adj.* (*formal*) relating to fishing or to FISHERMEN 捕魚的；漁業的；漁民的

Pis·ces /'paɪsiːz/ *noun* **1** [U] the 12th sign of the ZODIAC, the Fishes 黃道第十二宮；雙魚宮；雙魚（星）座 **2** [sing.] a person born when the sun is in this sign, that is between 20 February and 20 March 屬雙魚座的人（約出生於 2 月 20 日至 3 月 20 日）▸ **Pis·cean** /'paɪsiən/ *noun, adj.*

pis·cine /'pɪsaɪn; 'paɪsiːn/ *adj.* (*formal* or *technical* 術語) of or related to fish 魚的；魚類的

piss /pɪs/ *verb, noun* (*taboo, slang*)

■ ***verb*** [I] to URINATE 撒尿 HELP A more polite way of expressing this is **go to the toilet/loo** (*BrE*), **go to the bathroom** (*NAmE*) or simply **go** (*NAmE, BrE*). 較委婉的表達方式為 go to the toilet/loo（英式英語）、go to the bathroom（美式英語）或直接用 go（美式英語、英式英語均可）。

IDM **'piss yourself (laughing)** to laugh very hard 大笑不止；笑破肚皮

PHR V **,piss a'bout/a'round** (*BrE*) to waste time by behaving in a silly way 浪費時間；混日子 HELP A more polite, informal way of saying this is **mess about** (*BrE*) or **mess around** (*NAmE, BrE*). 較禮貌和非正式的說法是 mess about（英式英語）或 mess around（美式、英式英語）。**,piss sb a'bout/a'round** (*BrE*) to treat sb in a way that is deliberately not helpful to them or wastes their time 存心折騰（某人）；故意搗亂 HELP A more polite, informal way of saying this is **mess sb about/around**.

P

較禮貌和非正式的說法是 mess sb about/around。**ˈpiss down** (*BrE*) to rain heavily 下大雨 **ˌpiss ˈoff** (*especially BrE*) (usually used in orders 通常用於命令) to go away 走開：*Why don't you just piss off and leave me alone?* 你就不能滾開，讓我清靜清靜？**ˌpiss sb↔ˈoff** to make sb annoyed or bored 使生氣；使厭煩：*Her attitude really pisses me off.* 她的態度讓我厭煩極了。

■ ***noun*** **1** [U] = URINE **2** [sing.] an act of URINATING 撒尿：*to go for a piss* 去撒尿

IDM **be on the ˈpiss** (*BrE*) to be out at a pub, club, etc. and drinking a large amount of alcohol （在酒館等）暴飲 **take the ˈpiss (out of sb/sth)** (*BrE*) to make fun of sb, especially by copying them or laughing at them for reasons they do not understand 拿…開心；嘲弄模仿 ➲ more at PIECE *n.*

ˈpiss artist *noun* (*BrE, taboo, slang*) **1** a person who drinks too much alcohol 酒鬼 **SYN** **alcoholic** **2** a person who behaves in a stupid way 傻瓜；蠢豬；笨蛋

pissed /pɪst/ *adj.* **1** (*BrE, taboo, slang*) drunk 爛醉的；醉醺醺的 **2** (*NAmE, slang*) (also **ˌpissed ˈoff** *BrE, NAmE*) very angry or annoyed 氣瘋了；怒沖沖的：*I'm pissed off with the way they've treated me.* 他們那樣對待我使我很生氣。

IDM **(as) pissed as a ˈnewt** (*BrE*) very drunk 爛醉如泥

ˌpiss-ˈpoor *adj.* (*taboo, slang*) **1** of a very low standard 差勁的；水平極低的：*That band really was piss-poor.* 那支樂隊糟糕透頂。 **2** not having enough money for basic needs 拮据的；貧窮的

piss·pot /ˈpɪspɒt; *NAmE* -pɑːt/ *noun* (*slang, offensive*) = CHAMBER POT

ˈpiss-take *noun* (*BrE, taboo, slang*) a joke that is intended to make sb/sth seem ridiculous 挖苦的笑話；戲謔的玩笑

ˈpiss-up *noun* (*BrE, taboo, slang*) an occasion when a large amount of alcohol is drunk 暴飲；狂飲 **HELP** A more polite, informal word for this is **booze-up**. 較禮貌和非正式的說法是 booze-up。

pis·ta·chio /pɪˈstæʃiəʊ; -ˈstɑːʃiəʊ; *NAmE* -ʃioʊ/ *noun* (*pl.* **-os**) **1** (also **piˈstachio nut**) [C] the small green nut of an Asian tree 開心果；阿月渾子 ➲ VISUAL VOCAB page V32 **2** [U] a pale green colour 淡綠色

piste /piːst/ *noun* a track of firm snow prepared for SKIING on 滑雪道 ➲ see also OFF-PISTE

pis·til /ˈpɪstɪl/ *noun* (*biology* 生) the female organs of a flower, which receive the POLLEN and produce seeds 雌蕊

pis·tol /ˈpɪstl/ *noun* a small gun that you can hold and fire with one hand 手槍：*an automatic pistol* 自動手槍 ◇ *a starting pistol* (= used to signal the start of a race) 發令槍 ➲ see also WATER PISTOL

ˈpistol-whip *verb* **~ sb** to hit sb with the BUTT of a pistol many times 用手槍柄連續擊打

piston 活塞

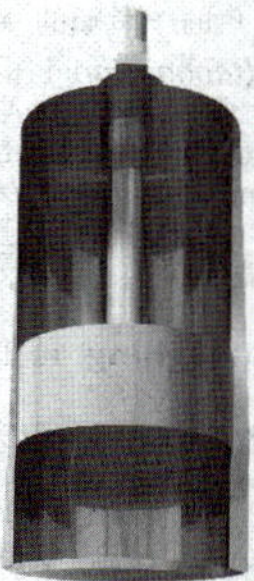

pis·ton /ˈpɪstən/ *noun* a part of an engine that consists of a short CYLINDER that fits inside a tube and moves up and down or backwards and forwards to make other parts of the engine move 活塞

pit /pɪt/ *noun, verb*

■ ***noun***

▸ **DEEP HOLE** 深洞 **1** [C] a large deep hole in the ground 深洞；深坑：*We dug a deep pit in the yard.* 我們在院子中挖了個深洞。◇ *The body had been dumped in a pit.* 屍體被扔進了深坑。 **2** [C] (especially in compounds 尤用於構成複合詞) a deep hole in the ground from which minerals are dug out 礦井：*a* ***chalk/gravel pit*** 白堊 / 沙礫礦坑

▸ **MINE** 礦 **3** [C] = COAL MINE：*pit closures* 煤礦關閉◇ (*BrE*) *He went down the pit* (= started work as a MINER) *when he left school.* 他中學一畢業就當礦工了。

▸ **IN SKIN** 皮膚 **4** [C] a small shallow hole in the surface of sth, especially a mark left on the surface of the skin by some disease, such as CHICKENPOX 麻子；痘瘢 ➲ see also PITTED (1)

▸ **IN FRUIT** 水果 **5** [C] (*especially NAmE*) = STONE (5)：*a peach pit* 桃核

▸ **IN MOTOR RACING** 汽車賽 **6 the pits** [pl.] (*BrE*) (*NAmE* **the pit** [C]) a place near the track where cars can stop for fuel, new tyres, etc. during a race （賽車道旁的）修理加油站 ➲ see also PIT STOP

▸ **IN THEATRE** 劇場 **7** [C] = ORCHESTRA PIT

▸ **PART OF BODY** 身體部位 **8** [C] (*NAmE, informal*) = ARMPIT

▸ **IN BUSINESS** 商業 **9** [C] (*NAmE*) the area of a STOCK EXCHANGE where a particular product is traded （交易所中某一商品的）交易場所：*the corn pit* 玉米交易廳 ➲ compare FLOOR (6) ➲ see also SANDPIT

IDM **be the ˈpits** (*informal*) to be very bad or the worst example of sth 是壞典型；是拙劣典型；最糟糕 **the pit of your/the ˈstomach** the bottom of the stomach where people say they feel strong feelings, especially fear 心窩；心底：*He had a sudden sinking feeling in the pit of his stomach.* 他內心深處突然有一種不祥之感。 ➲ more at BOTTOMLESS

■ ***verb*** (**-tt-**) [usually passive]

▸ **MAKE HOLES** 打洞 **1 ~ sth** to make marks or holes on the surface of sth 使…表面有斑點；在…上打洞：*The surface of the moon is pitted with craters.* 月亮的表面佈滿隕石坑。◇ *Smallpox scars had pitted his face.* 他滿臉是麻子。

▸ **FRUIT** 水果 **2** (*BrE* also **stone**) **~ sth** to remove the stone from the inside of a fruit 去掉…的果核：*pitted olives* 去核橄欖

PHR V **ˈpit sb/sth against sth** to test sb or their strength, intelligence, etc. in a struggle or contest against sb/sth else 使競爭；使較量；使經受考驗：*Lawyers and accountants felt that they were being pitted against each other.* 律師和會計師都覺得他們要一爭高下。◇ *a chance to* ***pit your wits against*** *the world champions* (= in a test of your intelligence) 一次與世界冠軍級高手鬥智的機會

pita, **ˈpita bread** *noun* [U] (*NAmE*) = PITTA

pit-a-pat /ˌpɪtəˈpæt/ (also **ˈpitter-patter**) *adv.* with quick light steps or beats 撲撲的響聲；劈啪聲；噠噠聲：*Her heart went pit-a-pat.* 她心裏撲撲直跳。 ▸ **pit-a-pat** (also **pitter-patter**) *noun* [sing.]：*I could hear the pit-a-pat of feet in the corridor.* 我能聽見走廊上啪噠啪噠的腳步聲。

ˌpit ˌbull ˈterrier (also **ˈpit bull**) *noun* a small strong aggressive dog, sometimes used in dog fights where people bet on which dog will win 鬥獸場鬥牛㹴狗（有時用於鬥狗）

pitch 0→ /pɪtʃ/ *noun, verb*

■ ***noun***

▸ **FOR SPORT** 體育運動 **1** 0→ (*BrE*) (also **field** *NAmE, BrE*) [C] an area of ground specially prepared and marked for playing a sports game （體育比賽的）場地；球場：*a* ***football/cricket/rugby pitch*** 足球 / 板球 / 橄欖球場◇ *The rugby tour was a disaster both on and off the pitch.* 這次橄欖球巡迴賽在場上、場下都徹底失敗。 ➲ VISUAL VOCAB page V44

▸ **OF SOUND** 聲音 **2** 0→ [sing., U] how high or low a sound is, especially a musical note （尤指樂音的）音高：*A basic sense of rhythm and pitch is essential in a music teacher.* 基本的韻律感和音高感是音樂教師的必備素質。 ➲ see also PERFECT PITCH

▸ **DEGREE/STRENGTH 程度；強度 3** [sing., U] the degree or strength of a feeling or activity; the highest point of sth（感情、活動等的）程度，力度；（事物的）最高點：*a frenetic pitch of activity* 活動的狂熱極點 ◇ *Speculation has reached such a pitch that a decision will have to be made immediately.* 種種猜測甚囂塵上，以至必須立即作出決定。➲ see also FEVER PITCH

▸ **TO SELL STH 銷售 4** [C, usually sing.] talk or arguments used by a person trying to sell things or persuade people to do sth 推銷的話；說教；宣傳論點：*an aggressive **sales pitch*** 強有力的推銷行話 ◇ *the candidate's campaign pitch* 候選人的競選宣傳 ◇ *Each company was given ten minutes to **make its pitch**.* 每個公司有十分鐘時間做推銷宣傳。

▸ **IN BASEBALL 棒球 5** [C] an act of throwing the ball; the way in which it is thrown 投球；投球方法 ➲ **SYNONYMS** at THROW

▸ **BLACK SUBSTANCE 黑色物質 6** [U] a black sticky substance made from oil or coal, used on roofs or the wooden boards of a ship to stop water from coming through 瀝青；柏油

▸ **IN STREET/MARKET 街道；市場 7** [C] (*BrE*) a place in a street or market where sb sells things, or where a street entertainer usually performs 街頭售貨攤點；街頭藝人表演地點

▸ **OF SHIP/AIRCRAFT 船；飛機 8** [U] (*technical* 術語) the movement of a ship up and down in the water or of an aircraft in the air（船在水上的）上下顛簸，縱搖；（飛機在空中的）俯仰 ➲ compare ROLL *n.* (6)

▸ **OF ROOF 屋頂 9** [sing., U] (*technical* 術語) the degree to which a roof slopes 傾斜度

IDM **make a 'pitch for sb/sth | make a 'pitch to sb** to make a determined effort to get sth or to persuade sb of sth 決心獲得；決心勸服 ➲ more at QUEER *v.*

■ ***verb***

▸ **THROW 拋 1** [T] **~ sb/sth + adv./prep.** to throw sb/sth with force 用力扔；投；拋：*The explosion pitched her violently into the air.* 爆炸把她猛烈地拋向空中。◇ (*figurative*) *The new government has already been pitched into a crisis.* 新政府已被拋入危機之中。

▸ **IN SPORTS 體育運動 2** [I, T] **~ (sth)** (in BASEBALL 棒球) to throw the ball to the person who is BATTING 將（球）投給擊球員；投球；當投手 **3** [I, T] **~ (sth) + adv./prep.** (of the ball in the games of CRICKET or GOLF 板球或高爾夫球) to hit the ground; to make the ball hit the ground 觸地；（使球）定點落地：*The ball pitched a yard short.* 球差一碼落了地。**4** [T, I] **~ (sth)** (in GOLF 高爾夫球) to hit the ball in a high curve 擊出大曲線球；擊高球

▸ **FALL 倒下 5** [I] **+ adv./prep.** to fall heavily in a particular direction 重跌；踉蹌倒下：*With a cry she pitched forward.* 她大叫一聲向前跌倒了。

▸ **OF SHIP/AIRCRAFT 船；飛機 6** [I] to move up and down on the water or in the air 顛簸；上下飄盪：*The sea was rough and the ship pitched and rolled all night.* 大海波濤洶湧，船整夜顛簸搖晃。

▸ **SET LEVEL 定標準 7** [T] to set sth at a particular level 確定標準：**~ sth (+ adv./prep./adj.)** *They have pitched their prices too high.* 他們把價格定得太高了。◇ **~ sth (at sth)** *The test was pitched at too low a level for the students.* 這次考試太低估學生的程度了。

▸ **TRY TO SELL 推銷 8** [T] to aim or direct a product or service at a particular group of people（使產品或服務）針對，面向；確定銷售對象（或目標市場）：**~ sth (at sb)** *The new software is being pitched at banks.* 這種新軟件以銀行為目標市場。◇ **~ sth (as sth)** *Orange juice is to be pitched as an athlete's drink.* 橙汁將作為運動員飲料進行推銷。 **9** [T, I] to try to persuade sb to buy sth, to give you sth or to make a business deal with you 推銷；爭取支持（或生意等）：**~ sth** *Representatives went to Japan to pitch the company's newest products.* 銷售代表前往日本推銷公司的最新產品。◇ **~ (for sth)** *We were pitching against a much larger company for the contract.* 我們在與一家比我們大得多的公司競爭這項合同。

▸ **SOUND/MUSIC 聲音；音樂 10** [T] **~ sth + adj.** to produce a sound or piece of music at a particular level 定音高：*You pitched that note a little flat.* 你把那個音符定得有點低了。◇ *The song was pitched too low for my voice.* 這首歌起調太低，不適合我的嗓音。➲ see also HIGH-PITCHED, LOW-PITCHED

▸ **TENT 帳篷 11** [T] **~ sth** to set up a tent or a camp for a short time 搭（帳篷）；紮（營）：*We could **pitch our tent** in that field.* 我們可以臨時把帳篷搭在那塊地上。◇ *They **pitched camp** for the night near the river.* 他們靠河邊紮營過夜。➲ see also PITCHED

IDM **,pitch a 'story/'line/'yarn (to sb)** (*informal*) to tell sb a story or make an excuse that is not true（對某人）編謊話

PHR V **,pitch 'in (with sb/sth)** (*informal*) to join in and help with an activity, by doing some of the work or by giving money, advice, etc. 投入；參與；支援：*Everyone pitched in with the work.* 每個人都投入了這項工作。◇ *Local companies pitched in with building materials and labour.* 當地的公司支援了建築材料和勞動力。 **,pitch sth ↔'in** to give a particular amount of money in order to help with sth 參與；出力；出份子：*We all pitched in $10 to buy her a gift.* 我們每人出 10 元錢給她買禮物。 **,pitch 'into sb** (*informal*) to attack or criticize sb 攻擊；批判；批評：*She started pitching into me as soon as I arrived.* 我剛一到她就劈頭蓋臉地批評起我來。 **,pitch 'into sth** (*informal*) to start an activity with enthusiasm 蓬勃開展；大幹：**~ doing sth** *I rolled up my sleeves and pitched into cleaning the kitchen.* 我捲起袖子，給廚房做大掃除。 **,pitch 'up** (*BrE, informal*) to arrive somewhere, especially late or without planning 到達（尤指遲到或不約而至）**SYN** **turn up**：*You can't just pitch up and expect to get in without a ticket.* 你可不能說來就來，還想無票入場。

,pitch and 'putt *noun* [U] (*BrE*) GOLF played on a very small course 小場地高爾夫球

,pitch-'black *adj.* completely black or dark 漆黑的；烏黑的

,pitch-'dark *adj.* completely dark 漆黑的

pitched /pɪtʃt/ *adj.* (of a roof 屋頂) sloping; not flat 傾斜的

,pitched 'battle *noun* **1** a fight that involves a large number of people 群毆；聚眾打鬥：*The demonstration escalated into a pitched battle with the police.* 示威逐步升級，演變成了一場同警察的混戰。 **2** a military battle fought with soldiers arranged in prepared positions（軍事上的）對陣戰

pitch·er /ˈpɪtʃə(r)/ *noun* **1** (*NAmE*) (*BrE* **jug**) a container with a handle and a LIP, for holding and pouring liquids（有柄有嘴的）壺，罐：*a pitcher of water* 一罐水 **2** (*BrE*) a large CLAY container with a small opening and one or two handles, used, especially in the past, for holding liquids（尤指舊時的）帶柄的陶罐 ➲ picture at JUG **3** (in BASEBALL 棒球) the player who throws the ball to the BATTER 投球手 ➲ **VISUAL VOCAB** page V44

pitch·fork /ˈpɪtʃfɔːk; *NAmE* -fɔːrk/ *noun* a farm tool in the shape of a large fork with a long handle and two or three sharp metal points, used especially for lifting and moving HAY (= dried grass), etc. 杈子；乾草叉

'pitch invasion *noun* (*BrE*) an occasion when a crowd of people who are watching a sports game run onto the field, for example to celebrate sth or protest about sth（觀眾為慶祝或抗議等的）闖入比賽場地，侵入運動場

pitch·out /ˈpɪtʃaʊt/ *noun* **1** (in BASEBALL 棒球) a BALL deliberately thrown so that it is too far away to hit so that the CATCHER can throw it to get a player out who is running between BASES 戰術壞球；故意壞球 **2** (in AMERICAN FOOTBALL 美式足球) a ball thrown sideways 橫傳球

pit·eous /ˈpɪtiəs/ *adj.* [usually before noun] (*literary*) deserving pity or causing you to feel pity 可憐的；令人憐憫的；令人同情的 **SYN** **pathetic**：*a piteous cry/sight* 可憐的哭聲／景象 ▸ **pit·eous·ly** *adv.*

pit·fall /ˈpɪtfɔːl/ *noun* a danger or difficulty, especially one that is hidden or not obvious at first 危險；困難；（尤指）陷阱，隱患：*the potential pitfalls of buying a house* 購買房屋可能遇到的圈套

pith /pɪθ/ *noun* [U] **1** a soft dry white substance inside the skin of oranges and some other fruits（橙子等水果皮中的）木髓 ➲ **VISUAL VOCAB** page V30 **2** the essential

P

or most important part of sth 精髓；核心；要點：*the pith of her argument* 她論據的核心

pit·head /ˈpɪthed/ *noun* the entrance to a coal mine and the offices, machinery, etc. in the area around it 礦井井口；坑口周圍設施

ˈpith helmet *noun* a light hard hat worn to give protection from the sun in very hot countries（熱帶國家用的）木髓遮陽帽

pithy /ˈpɪθi/ *adj.* (*approving*) (**pith·ier**, **pithi·est**) (of a comment, piece of writing, etc. 說話或文章等) short but expressed well and full of meaning 言簡意賅的；精練的 ▸ **pith·ily** /-ɪli/ *adv.*：*pithily expressed* 簡潔地表達的

piti·able /ˈpɪtiəbl/ *adj.* (*formal*) **1** deserving pity or causing you to feel pity 值得同情的；可憐的：*The refugees were in a pitiable state.* 難民處境可憐。 **2** not deserving respect 卑鄙的；卑劣的：*a pitiable lack of talent* 令人遺憾的無能表現 ▸ **piti·ably** /-əbli/ *adv.*

piti·ful /ˈpɪtɪfl/ *adj.* **1** deserving pity or causing you to feel pity 可憐的；令人憐憫的；令人同情的 SYN **pathetic**：*The horse was a* ***pitiful sight*** (= because it was very thin or sick). 這匹馬看上去可憐兮兮的。 **2** not deserving respect 卑微的；卑鄙的 SYN **poor**：*a pitiful effort/excuse/performance* 不值一提的努力／藉口／表現 ▸ **piti·fully** /-fəli/ *adv.*：*The dog was whining pitifully.* 那條狗可憐巴巴地哀叫着。◇ *She was pitifully thin.* 她瘦骨嶙峋，令人憐憫。◇ *The fee is pitifully low.* 酬金低得可憐。

piti·less /ˈpɪtiləs/ *adj.* **1** showing no pity; cruel 冷酷的；無情的 SYN **callous**：*a pitiless killer/tyrant* 殘忍的兇手／暴君 **2** very cruel or severe, and never ending 嚴酷而無盡的 SYN **relentless**：*a scorching, pitiless sun* 灼熱的驕陽 ▸ **piti·less·ly** *adv.*

piton /ˈpiːtɒn; *NAmE* -tɑːn/ *noun* a short pointed piece of metal used in rock-climbing. The piton is fixed into the rock and has a rope attached to it through a ring at the other end.（登山用的）鋼錐，岩釘

ˈpit pony *noun* a small horse that was used in the past for moving coal in a mine（舊時煤礦的）馱煤小馬

P

ˈpit prop *noun* a large piece of wood used to support the roof of part of a coal mine from which coal has been removed（煤礦的）坑木，坑柱

ˈpit stop *noun* **1** (in motor racing 賽車運動) an occasion when a car stops during a race for more fuel, etc. 停車加油（或修理等） **2** (*NAmE, informal*) a short stop during a long trip for a rest, a meal, etc.（長途旅行中的）短暫休息，歇腳

pitta (*BrE*) (*NAmE* **pita**) /ˈpiːtə; *BrE* also ˈpɪtə/ (also **ˈpitta bread**, **ˈpita bread**) *noun* [U, C] a type of flat bread in the shape of an OVAL that can be split open and filled 皮塔餅，填餡麪包，口袋麪包（一種扁平的橢圓麪包，可加入餡料）

pit·tance /ˈpɪtns/ *noun* [usually sing.] a very small amount of money that sb receives, for example as a wage, and that is hardly enough to live on 微薄的工資；極少的報酬：*to pay sb a pittance* 付給某人菲薄的工資 ◇ *to work for a pittance* 為一點小錢而工作

pit·ted /ˈpɪtɪd/ *adj.* **1** having small marks or holes in the surface 表面有小點（或小洞）的；坑坑窪窪的 **2** (of fruit 水果) having had the large hard seed (= the PIT) removed 去核的：*pitted olives* 去核橄欖

pitter-patter /ˈpɪtə pætə(r)/ *adv., noun* = PIT-A-PAT

pi·tu·it·ary /pɪˈtjuːɪtəri; *NAmE* -ˈtuːəteri/ (also **piˈtuitary gland**) *noun* a small organ at the base of the brain that produces HORMONES that influence growth and sexual development 腦下垂體；垂體

pity 0‑ᴛ /ˈpɪti/ *noun, verb*

WORD FAMILY
pity *noun, verb*
pitiful *adj.*
pitiless *adj.*
pitiable *adj.*
piteous *adj.*

■ ***noun*** **1** 0‑ᴛ [U] **~ (for sb/sth)** a feeling of sympathy and sadness caused by the suffering and troubles of others 同情；憐憫：*I could only feel pity for what they were enduring.* 對他們所受的苦難我唯有同情而已。◇ *a* ***look/feeling/surge of pity*** 憐憫的表情／感覺／湧動 ◇ ***I took pity on*** *her and lent her the money.* 我同情她，就把錢借給了她。◇ (*formal*) *I beg you to* ***have pity on*** *him.* 請你可憐可憐他吧。◇ *I don't want your pity.* 我用不着你可憐。 **2** 0‑ᴛ [sing.] used to show that you are disappointed about sth（用於表示失望）遺憾，可惜 SYN **shame**：**a ~ (that ...)** ***It's a pity*** *that you can't stay longer.* 你不能再多停留些時間，真是可惜。◇ *'I've lost it!' 'Oh,* ***what a pity****.'* "我把東西弄丟了！" "哎呀，真可惜。" ◇ *What a pity that she didn't tell me earlier.* 真遺憾，她沒有早點告訴我。◇ **a ~ (to do sth)** *It* ***seems a pity*** *to waste this food.* 浪費這些食物真可惜。◇ *This dress is really nice. Pity it's so expensive.* 這件連衣裙真不錯，只可惜太貴了。◇ *Oh,* ***that's a pity****.* 唉，那可真遺憾。◇ *It would be* ***a great pity*** *if you gave up now.* 你要是現在放棄，那就太可惜了。

IDM **more's the ˈpity** (*BrE, informal*) unfortunately 不幸地：*'Was the bicycle insured?' 'No, more's the pity!'* "自行車上保險沒有？" "沒有。真倒霉！"

■ ***verb*** (**pit·ies**, **pity·ing**, **pit·ied**, **pit·ied**) (not used in the progressive tenses 不用於進行時) to feel sorry for sb because of their situation; to feel pity for sb 同情；憐憫；可憐：**~ sb** *He pitied people who were stuck in dead-end jobs.* 他很同情那些工作上毫無前途的人。◇ *Compulsive gamblers are more* ***to be pitied*** *than condemned.* 對嗜賭成癮者要多些同情，少些譴責。◇ **~ sb doing sth** *I pity her having to work such long hours.* 她不得不加班加點工作，真讓我同情。

pity·ing /ˈpɪtiɪŋ/ *adj.* [usually before noun] showing pity for sb, often in a way that shows that you think you are better than them 憐憫的，同情的（常帶優越感）：*a pitying look/smile* 垂憐的眼神／微笑 ▸ **pity·ing·ly** *adv.*

pivot /ˈpɪvət/ *noun, verb*

■ ***noun*** **1** the central point, pin or column on which sth turns or balances 支點；樞軸；中心點 **2** the central or most important person or thing 最重要的人（或事物）；中心；核心：*West Africa was the pivot of the cocoa trade.* 西非曾是可可豆貿易的中心。◇ *The pivot on which the old system turned had disappeared.* 維繫舊制度的支柱已經消失了。

■ ***verb*** [I, T] **~ (sth) (+ adv./prep.)** to turn or balance on a central point (= a pivot); to make sth do this（使）在樞軸上旋轉（或轉動）：*Windows that pivot from a central point are easy to clean.* 沿中軸轉動的窗子容易擦洗。◇ *She pivoted around and walked out.* 她一轉身走了出去。

PHR V **ˈpivot on/around sth** (of an argument, a theory, etc. 論點、理論等) to depend completely on sth 圍繞（主旨）；以…為核心 SYN **hinge on**

piv·otal /ˈpɪvətl/ *adj.* of great importance because other things depend on it 關鍵性的；核心的：*a pivotal role in European affairs* 在歐洲事務中的關鍵作用

pixel /ˈpɪksl/ *noun* (*computing* 計) any of the small individual areas on a computer screen, which together form the whole display 像素（組成屏幕圖像的最小獨立元素）

pix·el·ate (also **pix·el·late**) /ˈpɪksəleɪt/ *verb* **1 ~ sth** to divide an image into PIXELS 使像素化；將（圖像）分解成像素 **2 ~ sth** to show an image on television as a small number of large PIXELS, especially in order to hide sb's identity（尤指為了不透露當事人身分而）使電視圖像模糊，打上馬賽克

pixie /ˈpɪksi/ *noun* (in stories) a creature like a small person with pointed ears, who has magic powers（傳說中的）小精靈，小仙子，小妖怪

pizza /ˈpiːtsə/ *noun* [C, U] an Italian dish consisting of a flat round bread base with cheese, tomatoes, vegetables, meat, etc. on top 比薩餅；意大利餅：*a ham and mushroom pizza* 火腿蘑菇比薩餅 ◇ *Is there any pizza left?* 還有比薩餅嗎？

piz·azz /pɪˈzæz/ *noun* [U] (*informal*) a lively and exciting quality or style 激情；活潑；風度 SYN **flair**：*We need someone with youth, glamour and pizzazz.* 我們需要一位年富力強、魅力十足、風度翩翩的人。

piz·zeria /ˌpiːtsəˈriːə/ (*NAmE* also **ˈpizza parlor**) *noun* a restaurant that serves mainly pizzas 比薩餅店；比薩餅餐廳

pizzi·cato /ˌpɪtsɪˈkɑːtəʊ; *NAmE* -toʊ/ *adj., adv.* (*music* 音) played using the fingers instead of a BOW to pull at the strings of a musical instrument such as a VIOLIN 彈撥（的）；撥奏（的）

Pl. *abbr.* (used in written addresses) PLACE（用於書寫地址）街道，廣場：*Grosvenor Pl.* 格羅夫諾街

pl. *abbr.* (in writing) plural（書寫形式）複數

plac·ard /ˈplækɑːd; *NAmE* -kɑːrd/ *noun* a large written or printed notice that is put in a public place or carried on a stick in a march 標語牌；廣告牌；招貼；海報：*They were carrying placards and banners demanding that he resign.* 人們手持標語牌和橫額，要求他下台。

pla·cate /pləˈkeɪt; *NAmE* ˈpleɪkeɪt/ *verb* **~ sb** to make sb feel less angry about sth 安撫；平息（怒氣）SYN **pacify**：*a placating smile* 按撫的微笑 ◇ *The concessions did little to placate the students.* 讓步根本沒能平息學生的憤怒。

pla·ca·tory /pləˈkeɪtəri; *NAmE* ˈpleɪkətɔːri/ *adj.* (*formal*) designed to make sb feel less angry by showing that you are willing to satisfy or please them 和解的；安撫性的；安慰的：*a* ***placatory remark/smile/gesture*** 撫慰的話／微笑／姿態

place 0➡ /pleɪs/ *noun, verb*

■ ***noun***

▸ **POSITION/POINT/AREA 位置；地點；區域** **1** 0➡ [C] a particular position, point or area 位置；地點；場所；地方：*Is this the place where it happened?* 這就是事發現場嗎？◇ *This would be a good place for a picnic.* 這可是個野餐的好地方。◇ *I can't be in two places at once.* 我不能同時身處兩地。

▸ **CITY/TOWN/BUILDING 城；鎮；建築物** **2** 0➡ [C] a particular city, town, building, etc. 某處地方（如城鎮或建築物等）：*I can't remember all the places we visited in Thailand.* 我記不清在泰國參觀過的所有地方。◇ *I used to live in York and I'm still fond of the place.* 我以前住在約克，現在仍然喜歡那裏。◇ *The police searched the place.* 警察搜查了那個地方。◇ *We were looking for a* ***place to eat***. 我們想找個吃飯的地方。◇ *Let's get out of this place!* 咱們離開這兒吧！ **3** 0➡ [C] (especially in compounds or phrases 尤用於構成複合詞或詞組) a building or an area of land used for a particular purpose 有某用途的建築（或土地）：*a* ***meeting place*** 聚會地點 ◇ *The town has many excellent* ***eating places***. 本鎮有許多上好的餐館。◇ (*formal*) *churches and other* ***places of worship*** 教堂和其他禮拜場所 ◇ *He can usually be contacted at his* ***place of work***. 一般都能在他的工作單位找到他。➲ see also RESTING PLACE

▸ **AREA ON SURFACE 表面區域** **4** 0➡ [C] a particular area on a surface, especially on a person's body 表面的某處；（尤指）身體某處：*He broke his arm in three places.* 他胳膊上有三處骨折。◇ *The paint was peeling off the wall* ***in places***. 牆上有幾處油漆剝落了。

▸ **IN BOOK/SPEECH, ETC. 書、講話等** **5** 0➡ [C] a point in a book, speech, piece of music, etc., especially one that sb has reached at a particular time 段；點；節；（尤指）讀到的（或說到的）某點：*She had marked her place with a bookmark.* 她把書籤夾在讀到的地方。◇ *Excuse me, I seem to have* ***lost my place***. 對不起，我好像忘了在哪裏接下去了。

▸ **SEAT 座位** **6** 0➡ [C] a position, seat, etc., especially one that is available for or being used by a person or vehicle（尤指佔用或空着的）座位，位置，泊位：*Come and sit here—I've* ***saved you a place***. 到這兒來坐吧。我給你留了個座位。◇ *I don't want to* ***lose my place*** *in the line.* 我可不想失去排隊的位置。◇ *Would you like to* ***change places*** *with me so you can see better?* 你想跟我換個位子看得更清楚點嗎？◇ *I've* ***set a place*** *for you at the table.* 我在餐桌上給你安排好了座位。

▸ **ROLE/IMPORTANCE 角色；重要性** **7** [sing.] **~ (in sth)** the role or importance of sb/sth in a particular situation, usually in relation to others 身分；地位；資格：*He is assured of his place in history.* 他確信自己會在歷史上留名。◇ *Accurate reporting* ***takes second place*** *to lurid detail.* 準確的報道在其次，聳人聽聞的細節最重要。◇ *My father believed that people should* ***know their place*** (= behave according to their social position). 我父親認為人應該安分守己。◇ *It's* ***not your place*** (= your role) *to give advice.* 還輪不到你來做指導。◇ *Anecdotes* ***have no place in*** (= are not acceptable in) *an academic essay.* 學術文章容不得奇聞佚事。

▸ **AT UNIVERSITY/SCHOOL 學校** **8** 0➡ [C] an opportunity to take part in sth, especially to study at a school or university or on a course 求學機會；進修機會；入學名額：*She's been offered a place at Bath to study Business.* 她已被錄取到巴斯大學讀商科。◇ *There are very few places left on the course.* 這門課程沒剩幾個學生名額了。

▸ **IN SPORTS TEAM 運動隊** **9** [C] the position of being a member of a sports team 隊員身分；隊員資格：*She has* ***won a place*** *in the Olympic team.* 她已獲得奧運代表隊的隊員資格。◇ *He* ***lost his place*** *in the first team.* 他失去了甲級隊員的資格。

▸ **CORRECT POSITION 正確位置** **10** 0➡ [C] the natural or correct position for sth 恰當位置；適當的地方：*Is there a place on the form to put your address?* 表格上有填寫地址的空白嗎？◇ *Put it back in its place when you've finished with it.* 用畢放回原處。

▸ **SAFE AREA 安全地區** **11** [C] (usually with a negative 通常與否定詞連用) a suitable or safe area for sb to be 適當的（或安全的）處所：*These streets are* ***no place for*** *a child to be out alone at night.* 這些街道可不是小孩子夜間單獨去的地方。

▸ **HOME 家** **12** 0➡ [sing.] (*informal*) a house or flat/apartment; a person's home 家；住處：*What about dinner at* ***my place***? 到我家吃晚飯好不好？◇ *I'm fed up with living with my parents, so I'm looking for* ***a place of my own***. 我膩煩跟父母同住了，所以正在找一個屬於自己的住處。

▸ **IN RACE/COMPETITION 競賽** **13** 0➡ [C, usually sing.] a position among the winners of a race or competition（速度比賽或競賽獲勝者的）名次：*He finished in third place.* 他得了第三名。

▸ **MATHEMATICS 數學** **14** [C] the position of a figure after a DECIMAL POINT（小數點後的）位：*The number is correct to three decimal places.* 這個數目精確到小數點後三位數。

▸ **STREET/SQUARE 街道；廣場** **15 Place** [sing.] (*abbr.* **Pl.**) used as part of a name for a short street or square（作短街道或廣場名稱的一部份）：*66 Portland Place* 波特蘭街 66 號

IDM **all ˈover the place** (*BrE* also **all ˈover the shop**) (*US* also **all ˈover the lot**) (*informal*) **1** everywhere 到處；各處：*New restaurants are appearing all over the place.* 新餐館如雨後春筍般紛紛出現了。 **2** not neat or tidy; not well organized 凌亂；狼藉；雜亂無章：*Your calculations are all over the place* (= completely wrong). 你的計算錯得一塌糊塗。 **change/swap ˈplaces (with sb)** (usually used in negative sentences 通常用於否定句) to be in sb else's situation（與某人）交換位置，交換處境：*I'm perfectly happy—I wouldn't change places with anyone.* 我幸福極了，誰也甭想跟我交換位置。 **fall/slot into ˈplace** if sth complicated or difficult to understand **falls** or **slots into place**, it becomes organized or clear in your mind 明朗化；清晰；理出頭緒 **give ˈplace to sb/sth** (*formal*) to be replaced by sb/sth 讓位於；被…代替 SYN **give way to**：*Houses and factories gave place to open fields as the train gathered speed.* 火車逐漸加速駛過了房屋和工廠進入曠野。 **be ˈgoing places** (*informal*) to be getting more and more successful in your life or career 事業順利；春風得意：*a young architect who's really going places* 一個春風得意的青年建築師 **if ˌI was/were in ˈyour place** used to introduce a piece of advice you are giving to sb 若是換了我呀；我若在你的位置：*If I were in your place, I'd resign immediately.* 我要是你呀，我就立即辭職。 **in the ˈfirst place** used at the end of a sentence to talk about why sth was done or whether it should have been done or not（用於句尾，談論某事為何或是否應該做）究竟，到底，當初：*I still don't understand why you chose that name in the first place.* 我仍不明白你究竟為什麼取了這麼個名字。◇ *I should never have taken that job in the first place.* 我當初就不該接受那份工作。 **in the ˈfirst, ˈsecond, etc. place** used at the beginning of a sentence to introduce the different points you are making in an argument（用於句首）第一、第二等等：*Well, in the first place he has all the right qualifications.* 嗯，首先，他符合一切條件。 **in ˈmy, ˈyour, etc. place** in my, your, etc. situation

P

處於我（或你等）的境況：*I wouldn't like to be in your place.* 我可不想處於你的境地。**in 'place** **1** (also **into 'place**) in the correct position; ready for sth 在正確位置；準備妥當：*Carefully lay each slab in place.* 要仔細鋪好每一塊石板。◇ *The receiver had already clicked into place.* 聽筒咔地一聲放回原位了。**2** working or ready to work 在工作；準備就緒：*All the arrangements are now in place for their visit.* 他們來訪的一切事宜都安排好了。**3** (*NAmE*) = ON THE SPOT (3) at SPOT *n.* **in place of sb/sth | in sb's/sth's 'place** instead of sb/sth 代替；頂替：*You can use milk in place of cream in this recipe.* 這道食譜可以用牛奶代替奶油。◇ *He was unable to come to the ceremony, but he sent his son to accept the award in his place.* 他不能親自來參加儀式，但派了他兒子前來代他領獎。**out of 'place** **1** not in the correct place 位置不當：*Some of these files seem to be out of place.* 有些檔案似乎沒放對地方。**2** not suitable for a particular situation 不得體；不適當：*Her remarks were out of place.* 她出言不當。◇ *I felt completely out of place among all these successful people.* 夾在這些事業有成的人中間我覺得自己格格不入。**a place in the 'sun** a position in which you are comfortable or have an advantage over other people 舒適的狀態；有利地位；優越境況 **put yourself in sb else's/sb's 'place** to imagine that you are in sb else's situation 設身處地替別人着想；設想自己處於別人的境地：*Of course I was upset—just put yourself in my place.* 我當然不高興，你設身處地為我想想。**put sb in their 'place** to make sb feel stupid or embarrassed for showing too much confidence 挫某人的銳氣；煞某人的威風；使明白自己的身分：*At first she tried to take charge of the meeting but I soon put her in her place.* 起初她試圖主導會議，但我很快就把她轟下去了。**take 'place** to happen, especially after previously being arranged or planned（尤指根據安排或計劃）發生，進行：*The film festival takes place in October.* 電影節將於十月舉行。◇ *We may never discover what took place that night.* 我們可能永遠不會知道那一夜發生了什麼事。**take sb's/sth's 'place | take the place of sb/sth** to replace sb/sth 代替；替換：*She couldn't attend the meeting so her assistant took her place.* 她不能參加會議，所以她的助手代她出席。◇ *Computers have taken the place of typewriters in most offices.* 在大多數辦公室，電腦已經取代了打字機。**take your 'place** **1** to go to the physical position that is necessary for an activity 就位；入座：*Take your places for dinner.* 請各位入席。**2** to take or accept the status in society that is correct or that you deserve 得到應有的社會地位；名副其實 ➲ more at HAIR, HEART, LIGHTNING *n.*, OWN *v.*, PRIDE *n.*, ROCK *n.*

P

■ *verb*

▸ **IN POSITION** 位置 **1** [T] **~ sth + adv./prep.** to put sth in a particular place, especially when you do it carefully or deliberately（小心或有意）放置，安放：*He placed his hand on her shoulder.* 他把手搭在她的肩上。◇ *A bomb had been placed under the seat.* 座位下面放了一枚炸彈。◇ *The parking areas in the town are few, but strategically placed.* 城內停車場雖少，但都設在關鍵地方。

▸ **IN SITUATION** 境況 **2** [T] **~ sb/yourself + adv./prep.** (more formal than *put* 比 put 正式) to put sb/yourself in a particular situation 使（人）處於某位置；安置；安頓：*to place sb in command* 讓某人指揮 ◇ *She was placed in the care of an uncle.* 她由一位叔父照顧。◇ *His resignation placed us in a difficult position.* 他的辭職使我們不知所措。◇ *The job places great demands on me.* 這項工作對我的要求很高。

▸ **ATTITUDE** 態度 **3** [T] **~ sth on sth/doing sth** used to express the attitude sb has towards sb/sth 以某種態度對待（或看待）：*Great emphasis is placed on education.* 教育受到高度重視。◇ *They place a high value on punctuality.* 他們對守時極為重視。

▸ **RECOGNIZE** 辨認 **4** [T] **~ sb/sth** (usually used in negative sentences 通常用於否定句) to recognize sb/sth and be able to identify them/it 認出；辨認；識別：*I've seen her before but I just can't place her.* 我從前見過她，不過現在認不出她來。◇ *His accent was impossible to place.* 他的口音無法辨認。

Synonyms 同義詞辨析

place

site • area • position • point • location • scene • spot • venue

These are all words for a particular area or part of an area, especially one used for a particular purpose or where sb/sth is situated or happens. 以上各詞均表示地點、場所、位置。

place a particular point, area, city, town, building, etc, especially one used for a particular purpose or where a particular thing happens 指有特定用途或事情發生的地點、場所、城鎮、建築物、地方：*This would be a good place for a picnic.* 這可是個野餐的好地方。

site the place where sth, especially a building, is or will be situated; a place where sth happened or that is used for a particular purpose 尤指建築物的地點、位置，事情發生或有特定用途的地點、場所：*They've chosen a site for the new school.* 他們為新學校選了校址。

area a part of a room, building or particular space that is used for a special purpose; a particular place on an object 指（房間、建築物、處所劃為某用途的）地方、場地，（物體上的）區、部位：*the hotel reception area* 旅館接待處 ◇ *Move the cursor to a blank area on the screen.* 把光標移至電腦屏幕的空白區。

position the place where a person or thing is situated; the place where sb/sth is meant to be 指位置、方位、恰當的位置：*From his position at the top of the hill, he could see the harbour.* 他在山頭那個位置可以俯瞰海港。**NOTE** The **position** of sb/sth is often temporary: the place where sb/sth is at a particular time. * position 指人／物所處的位置常常是暫時性的，即在某段時間所在的位置。

point a particular place within an area, where sth happens or is supposed to happen 指（某事發生或將要發生的）地點、某個地方：*the point at which the river divides* 河流分叉點

location a place where sth happens or exists, especially a place that is not named or not known 指事情發生或存在的地方、地點、位置，尤指無名或鮮為人知的地方：*The company is moving to a new location.* 公司準備遷移新址。

scene a place where sth happens, especially sth unpleasant 尤指不愉快事件發生的地點、現場：*the scene of the accident* 事故現場

spot a particular point or area, especially one that has a particular character or where sth particular happens 尤指具有某種特點或某一事件發生的地點、場所：*The lake is one of the local **beauty spots**.* 這個湖是當地的一個風景點。

venue the place where people meet for an organized event such as a performance or sports event 指演出、體育比賽等的聚會地點、場館、會場

PATTERNS

- **at** a place/site/position/point/location/scene/spot/venue
- **in** a(n) place/area/position/location/venue
- the place/site/point/location/spot/venue **where …**
- the **right** place/site/position/location/spot/venue
- a **central** site/position/location/venue
- the/sb's/sth's **exact/precise** place/site/position/point/location/spot

▸ **BET/ORDER/ADVERTISEMENT** 打賭；訂單；廣告 **5** [T] **~ sth** to give instructions about sth or make a request for sth to happen 下指示；請求：*to place a bet/an order* 下注；下訂單 ◇ *We placed an advertisement for a cleaner in the local paper.* 我們在本地報紙上登了廣告，招一名清潔工。

▸ **FIND HOME/JOB** 找家／工作 **6** [T] to find a suitable home, job, etc. for sb 安置家庭（或工作等）：**~ sb (with sb/sth)**

The children were placed with foster parents. 這些小孩已安頓好，交給寄養父母了。◇ **~ sb (in sth)** *The agency placed about 2 000 secretaries last year.* 去年，這家中介所為大約 2 000 名秘書找到了工作。

▸ **GIVE RANK** 排檔次 **7** [T] **~ sb/sth + adv./prep.** to decide that sb/sth has a particular position or rank compared with other people or things（經比較）歸類，劃分，排名次：*I would place her among the top five tennis players in the world.* 我會把她排在世界五名頂尖網球選手之列。◇ *Nursing attracts people who place relationships high on their list of priorities.* 護理工作對重視人際關係的人具有吸引力。

▸ **IN RACE** 體育競賽 **8** [T, I] used to describe a person, a team, a horse, etc. finishing in a particular position in a race 排名；獲名次：**~ sb/sth + adj.** *He was placed fifth in last Saturday's race.* 在上週六的徑賽中，他名列第五。◇ **~ (sth)** (*BrE*) *My horse has been placed several times* (= it was among the first three or four to finish the race). 我的馬在競賽中屢獲名次。◇ (*NAmE*) *His horse placed in the last race* (= it was among the first three to finish the race, usually in second place). 他的馬在上次比賽中得了名次（常指亞軍）。

IDM **be well, ideally, uniquely, better, etc. placed for sth/to do sth** **1** to be in a good, very good, etc. position or have a good, etc. opportunity to do sth 有良好的（或理想的、獨特的等）機遇；處於有利等的位置：*Engineering graduates are well placed for a wide range of jobs.* 工程科畢業生在很多職業中處於優勢。◇ *The company is ideally placed to take advantage of the new legislation.* 這家公司條件理想得很，恰好可以充分利用新法規。 **2** to be located in a pleasant or convenient place 坐落在方便宜人的地方；位於合宜的地點：*The hotel is well placed for restaurants, bars and clubs.* 這家賓館位置很好，附近有很多餐廳、酒吧和俱樂部。➲ more at PEDESTAL, PREMIUM *n.*, RECORD *n.*

pla·cebo /plə'siːbəʊ; *NAmE* -boʊ/ *noun* (*pl.* **-os**) a substance that has no physical effects, given to patients who do not need medicine but think that they do, or used when testing new drugs（給無實際治療需要者的）安慰劑；（試驗藥物用的）無效對照劑：*the* ***placebo effect*** (= the effect of taking a placebo and feeling better) 安慰劑效應

'place card *noun* a small card with a person's name on it, placed on a table to show where they are to sit（標有姓名的）座位卡

place·hold·er /'pleɪshəʊldə(r); *NAmE* -hoʊld-/ *noun* **1** (*technical* 術語) a symbol or piece of text which replaces sth that is missing（替代缺失部份的）佔位符，佔位文字 **2** (*linguistics* 語言) an item which is necessary in a sentence, but does not have real meaning, for example the word 'it' in 'It's a pity she left.' 位標（句子中必要但無實際意義的詞項，如 It's a pity she left 中的 it）

'place kick *noun* (in RUGBY and AMERICAN FOOTBALL 橄欖球和美式足球) a kick made by putting the ball on the ground first 定位球

place·man /'pleɪsmən/ *noun* (*pl.* **-men** /-mən/) (*BrE, disapproving*) a person who is given an official position as a reward for supporting a politician or government 獲贈官祿者（因支持某從政者或政府而得官職）

'place mat *noun* a MAT on a table on which a person's plate is put 餐具墊 ➲ VISUAL VOCAB page V22

place·ment /'pleɪsmənt/ *noun* **1** [U] the act of finding sb a suitable job or place to live（對人的）安置，安排：*a job placement service* 職業介紹所 ◇ *placement with a foster family* 安置到寄養家庭 **2** (also **'work placement**) [U, C] (*BrE*) a job, often as part of a course of study, where you get some experience of a particular kind of work 實習工作；實習課：*The third year is spent* ***on placement*** *in selected companies.* 第三年是在選定的公司裏實習。◇ *The course includes a placement in Year 3.* 本課程第 3 年有實習課。➲ compare INTERNSHIP (1), WORK EXPERIENCE (2) **3** [U] the act of placing sth somewhere（對物件的）安置，放置：*This procedure ensures correct placement of the catheter.* 這個程序可保證導液管的正確置入。➲ see also ADVANCED PLACEMENT, PRODUCT PLACEMENT

'placement test *noun* a test which is designed to find the appropriate level for students in a course or programme of study（課程等的）分班考試，分級考試

'place name *noun* a name of a town or other place 地名

pla·centa /plə'sentə/ (usually **the placenta**) *noun* (*anatomy* 解) the material that comes out of a woman or female animal's body after a baby has been born, and which was necessary to feed and protect the baby 胎盤 **SYN** **afterbirth**

pla·cen·tal /plə'sentl/ *adj.* [usually before noun] **1** (*medical* 醫) of or related to the PLACENTA 胎盤的 **2** (*biology* 生) having a PLACENTA 有胎盤的；有胎座的：*placental mammals* 胎盤哺乳動物

'place setting *noun* a set or an arrangement of knives, forks and spoons, and/or plates and dishes for one person（供一人用的）一套餐具

pla·cid /'plæsɪd/ *adj.* **1** (of a person or an animal 人或動物) not easily excited or irritated 温和的；平和的；文靜的：*a placid baby/horse* 安靜的嬰兒；馴良的馬 **OPP** **high-spirited** **2** calm and peaceful, with very little movement 平靜的；寧靜的；安靜的 **SYN** **tranquil**：*the placid waters of the lake* 平靜的湖水 ▸ **pla·cid·ity** /plə'sɪdəti/ *noun* [U] **pla·cid·ly** *adv.*

pla·cing /'pleɪsɪŋ/ *noun* the position of sb/sth in a race or a competition or in a list arranged in order of success 名次；排名：*He needs a high placing in today's qualifier to reach the final.* 在今天的資格賽中，他必須排名靠前才能進入決賽。

pla·giar·ism /'pleɪdʒərɪzəm/ *noun* [U, C] (*disapproving*) an act of plagiarizing sth; sth that has been plagiarized 抄襲；剽竊；剽竊作品：*There were accusations of plagiarism.* 曾有過剽竊的指控。◇ *a text full of plagiarisms* 滿篇剽竊他人著作的文章 ➲ WRITING TUTOR page WT11 ▸ **pla·giar·ist** /'pleɪdʒərɪst/ *noun*

pla·giar·ize (*BrE* also **-ise**) /'pleɪdʒəraɪz/ *verb* [T, I] **~ (sth)** (*disapproving*) to copy another person's ideas, words or work and pretend that they are your own 剽竊；抄襲：*He was accused of plagiarizing his colleague's results.* 他被指控剽竊同事的成果。

plague /pleɪg/ *noun, verb*

■ *noun* **1** (also **the plague**) [U] = BUBONIC PLAGUE：*an outbreak of plague* 鼠疫的爆發 **2** [C] any infectious disease that kills a lot of people 死亡率高的傳染病 **SYN** **epidemic**：*the plague of AIDS* 艾滋病這種嚴重的傳染病 **3** [C] **~ of sth** large numbers of an animal or insect that come into an area and cause great damage（大批動物或昆蟲肆虐造成的）災害，禍患：***a plague of locusts/rats, etc.*** 蝗災、鼠害等 **IDM** see AVOID

■ *verb* **1 ~ sb/sth (with sth)** to cause pain or trouble to sb/sth over a period of time 給…造成長時間的痛苦（或麻煩）；困擾；折磨；使受煎熬 **SYN** **trouble**：***to be plagued by*** *doubt* 為疑慮所困擾 ◇ *Financial problems are plaguing the company.* 財政問題使這家公司焦頭爛額。◇ *The team has been plagued by injury this season.* 本賽季這支隊一直為隊員受傷所困擾。 **2 ~ sb (with sth)** to annoy sb or create problems, especially by asking for sth, demanding attention, etc. 糾纏；纏磨；纏擾 **SYN** **hound**：*Rock stars have to get used to being plagued by autograph hunters.* 搖滾歌星必須習慣歌迷要求簽名的糾纏。

plaice /pleɪs/ *noun* [C, U] (*pl.* **plaice**) a flat sea fish that is used for food 鰈（一種可食用的比目海魚）

plaid /plæd/ *noun* **1** [U] a type of thick cloth with a pattern of lines and squares of different colours and widths, especially a TARTAN pattern 格子呢；毛呢 ➲ VISUAL VOCAB page V61 **2** [C] a long piece of plaid made of wool, worn over the shoulders as part of the Scottish national dress 方格花呢長披肩（蘇格蘭民族服飾的一部份）

Plaid Cymru /ˌplaɪd 'kʌmriː/ *noun* [U+sing./pl. v.] (*WelshE*) a Welsh political party that wants Wales to be an independent state 威爾士黨，威爾士民族主義黨（主張威爾士獨立）

Synonyms 同義詞辨析

plain

simple • stark • bare • unequivocal

These words all describe statements, often about sth unpleasant, that are very clear, not trying to hide anything, and not using more words than necessary. 以上各詞常形容令人不快的陳述清楚明白、直截了當、簡單明瞭。

plain used for talking about a fact that other people may not like to hear; honest and direct in way that other people may not like 用於他人可能不樂意聽的事實或指直率、直接得讓人不喜歡：*The plain fact is that nobody really knows.* 事實很明顯，沒有人真正瞭解。

simple [only before noun] used for talking about a fact that other people may not like to hear; very obvious and not complicated by anything else 用於他人可能不樂意聽的事實或指事物簡單明瞭：*The simple truth is that we just can't afford it.* 事實很簡單，我們就是付不起。

PLAIN OR SIMPLE? 用 plain 還是 simple？

When it is being used to emphasize facts that other people may not like to hear, **plain** is usually used in the expression *the plain fact/truth is that …* . **Simple** can be used in this way too, but it can also be used in a wider variety of structures and collocations (such as *reason* and *matter*). 用以強調他人可能不樂意聽的事實時，plain 通常用於 the plain fact/truth is that … 短語中。simple 也可用這種表達方式，但是還可用於更多種類的結構，與更多的詞語（如 reason 和 matter）搭配：*The problem was due to the simple fact that …* 問題源於這一簡單的事實… ◇ ~~*The problem was due to the plain fact that …*~~ ◇ ~~*for the plain reason that …*~~ ◇ ~~*It's a plain matter of …*~~ Expressions with **simple** often suggest impatience with other people's behaviour. 與 simple 構成的表達法通常暗指對別人的行為不耐煩。

stark (*rather formal*) used for describing an unpleasant fact or difference that is very obvious 用於描述令人不快的事實或區別十分明顯、鮮明：*The stark truth is that there is not enough money left.* 明擺着的事實是剩下的錢已經不夠了。**NOTE** The *simple/plain truth* may be sth that some people do not want to hear, but it may be good for them to hear it anyway. The *stark truth* is sth particularly unpleasant and has no good side to it at all. * simple/plain truth 指所談的事儘管不中聽，但聽了可能會有好處。stark truth 指所談之事特別令人不快，而且沒有任何好處。

bare [only before noun] the most basic or simple, with nothing extra 指最基本的、最簡單的：*She gave me only the bare facts of the case.* 她只給我介紹了這個案件的一些基本情況。

unequivocal (*formal*) expressing your opinion or intention very clearly and firmly 指表達明確的、毫不含糊的、斬釘截鐵的：*The reply was an unequivocal 'no'.* 回答是個乾脆利落的"不"字。

PATTERNS

- the plain/simple/stark/bare/unequivocal **truth**
- a(n) plain/simple/stark/bare/unequivocal **fact/statement**
- a(n) plain/simple/unequivocal **answer**

plain /pleɪn/ *adj., noun, adv.*

■ **adj.** (**plain·er**, **plain·est**) **1** easy to see or understand 清楚的；明顯的；淺白的 **SYN** **clear**：*He made it plain that we should leave.* 他明確表示要我們離開。◇ *She made her annoyance plain.* 她滿臉不耐煩。◇ *The facts were* **plain to see**. 事實顯而易見。◇ *It was a rip-off,* **plain and simple**. 這是一個不折不扣的冒牌貨。➲ SYNONYMS at CLEAR **2** not trying to trick anyone; honest and direct 坦誠的；直率的；直接的：*The plain fact is that nobody really knows.* 事實很明顯，沒有人真正瞭解。◇ *a politician with a reputation for* **plain speaking** 說話直率出了名的一個政治人物 **3** not decorated or complicated; simple 不尚修飾的；樸素的；簡單的：*a plain but elegant dress* 樸素淡雅的連衣裙 ◇ *plain food* 清淡的食物 ◇ *The interior of the church was plain and simple.* 教堂內部樸素無華。◇ *plain yogurt* (= without sugar or fruit) 純酸奶 ➲ compare FANCY *adj.* (2) **4** without marks or a pattern on it 素的；無花紋的；單色的：*covers in plain or printed cotton* 單色或印花的罩布 ◇ *Write on plain paper* (= without lines). 用無格白紙書寫。**5** [only before noun] used to emphasize that sth is very ordinary, not special in any way 極普通的；平庸的；平凡的 **SYN** **everyday**：*You don't need any special skills for this job, just plain common sense.* 這項工作不需要任何特殊技能，只要有普通常識就夠了。**6** (especially of a woman 尤指女人) not beautiful or attractive 相貌平平的；無姿色的 **7** describing a simple STITCH used in knitting（編織）平針的，平紋的 ▶ **plain·ness** *noun* [U]

IDM **be plain 'sailing** (*US* also **be clear 'sailing**) to be simple and free from trouble 順利；一帆風順 **in plain 'English** simply and clearly expressed, without using technical language 用簡易的言語（或文字） **(as) plain as a 'pikestaff | (as) plain as 'day | (as) plain as the nose on your 'face** very obvious 一清二楚；一目瞭然；顯而易見

■ **noun** (also **plains** [pl.]) a large area of flat land 平原：*the flat coastal plain of Thassos* 薩索斯島平坦的濱海平原 ◇ *the Great Plains* 北美洲大平原 ➲ see also FLOODPLAIN

■ **adv.** (*informal*) used to emphasize how bad, stupid, etc. sth is（用於強調）簡直，絕對地：*plain stupid/wrong* 簡直愚蠢至極；絕對錯誤

plain·chant /ˈpleɪntʃɑːnt; *NAmE* -tʃænt/ *noun* [U] = PLAINSONG

ˌplain ˈchocolate *noun* [U] (*BrE*) = DARK CHOCOLATE

ˌplain ˈclothes *noun* [pl.] ordinary clothes, not uniform, when worn by police officers on duty（警察執行任務時穿的）便衣，便服：*officers* **in plain clothes** 便衣警察 ▶ **ˌplain-ˈclothes** *adj.* [only before noun]：*plain-clothes police officers* 便衣警察

ˌplain ˈflour (*BrE*) (*NAmE* **ˌall-purpose ˈflour**) *noun* [U] flour that does not contain BAKING POWDER（不含發酵粉的）普通麪粉 ➲ compare SELF-RAISING FLOUR

plain·ly /ˈpleɪnli/ *adv.* **1** in a way that is easy to see, hear, understand or believe 清晰地；明顯地；清楚地 **SYN** **clearly**：*The sea was plainly visible in the distance.* 大海在遠處清晰可見。◇ *The lease plainly states that all damage must be paid for.* 租約明確規定，一切損壞必須賠償。◇ *She had no right to interfere in what was plainly a family matter.* 這事明擺着是別人的家事，她無權干涉。◇ *Plainly* (= obviously) *something was wrong.* 很顯然什麼地方出了問題。**2** using simple words to say sth in a direct and honest way 簡單明瞭地；直截了當地：*To put it plainly, he's a crook.* 實話實說吧，他是個騙子。**3** in a simple way, without decoration 簡樸地；樸素地：*She was plainly dressed and wore no make-up.* 她衣着樸素，粉黛不施。

plain·song /ˈpleɪnsɒŋ; *NAmE* -sɔːŋ; -sɑːŋ/ (also **plain·chant**) *noun* [U] a type of church music for voices alone, used since the Middle Ages 素歌（中世紀以來的教堂音樂）

plaint /pleɪnt/ *noun* **1** (*BrE, law* 律) a complaint made against sb in court 起訴；訴狀 **2** (*literary*) a sad cry or sound 淒涼的哭泣（或聲音）

ˈplain text *noun* [U] (*technical* 術語) data that is stored in the form of ASCII (= a standard code used so that data can be moved between computers that use different programs). Plain text cannot be FORMATTED (= displayed in a particular way on the screen). 純文本數據，明文（以 ASCII 形式貯存的數據）

plain·tiff /ˈpleɪntɪf/ (*BrE, less frequent* **com·plain·ant**) *noun* (*law* 律) a person who makes a formal complaint against sb in court 原告；起訴人 ➲ compare DEFENDANT

plaint·ive /ˈpleɪntɪv/ *adj.* sounding sad, especially in a weak complaining way（聲音）悲傷的，哀怨的

SYN mournful : *a plaintive cry/voice* 悽楚的哭泣／聲音 ▸ **plaint·ive·ly** *adv.*

plait /plæt/ (*BrE*) (also **braid** *NAmE, BrE*) *noun, verb*
■ ***noun*** a long piece of sth, especially hair, that is divided into three parts and twisted together 辮狀物；髮辮；辮子： *She wore her hair* ***in plaits****.* 她梳着辮子。 ➲ VISUAL VOCAB page V60
■ ***verb*** **~ sth** to twist three or more long pieces of hair, rope, etc. together to make one long piece 將（頭髮、繩子等）編成辮

plan 🔑 /plæn/ *noun, verb*
■ ***noun***
▸ **INTENTION** 意圖 **1** 🔑 something that you intend to do or achieve 計劃；打算： **~** (**for sth**) *Do you have any plans for the summer?* 這個夏天你有什麼打算？◇ **~** (**to do sth**) *There are no plans to build new offices.* 現在沒有建新辦公樓的計劃。◇ *Your* ***best plan*** (= the best thing to do) *would be to go by car.* 你開車去是上策。◇ *There's been* ***a change of plan****.* 計劃作了變動。◇ *We can't change our plans now.* 我們現在不能改變計劃了。 ➲ SYNONYMS at PURPOSE
▸ **ARRANGEMENT** 安排 **2** 🔑 a set of things to do in order to achieve sth, especially one that has been considered in detail in advance（詳細）規劃，方案；精心安排： **~** (**for sth**) *Both sides agreed to a detailed plan for keeping the peace.* 雙方都同意維護和平的詳細方案。◇ **~** (**to do sth**) *The government has announced plans to create one million new training places.* 政府已經宣佈開設一百萬個新培訓名額的計劃。◇ *a* ***development/business/peace, etc. plan*** 發展計劃、營業規劃、和平規劃等◇ *a five-point plan* 五點規劃◇ *a three-year plan* 三年計劃◇ *We need to* ***make plans*** *for the future.* 我們必須規劃未來。◇ *a* ***plan of action/campaign*** 行動／運動方案◇ *Let's hope everything will* ***go according to plan****.* 但願一切都會按計劃進行。 ➲ see also MASTER PLAN
▸ **MAP** 地圖 **3** 🔑 a detailed map of a building, town, etc.（建築、城鎮等的）詳圖： *a plan of the museum* 博物館詳圖◇ *a street plan of the city* 城市街道詳圖
▸ **DRAWING** 繪圖 **4** 🔑 [usually pl.] **~** (**for/of sth**) (*technical* 術語) a detailed drawing of a machine, building, etc. that shows its size, shape and measurements（機器、建築等的）設計圖，平面圖；圖解： *The architect is* ***drawing up plans*** *for the new offices.* 建築師正在繪製新辦公樓的設計圖。 ➲ compare ELEVATION (4), GROUND PLAN (1) **5** 🔑 a diagram that shows how sth will be arranged 分佈圖；示意圖： *a* ***seating plan*** (= showing where each person will sit, for example at a dinner) 座位安排示意圖◇ *a* ***floor plan*** (= showing how furniture is arranged) 樓層平面圖
▸ **MONEY** 錢 **6** 🔑 (especially in compounds 尤用於構成複合詞) a way of investing money for the future 投資方式： *a savings plan* 儲蓄計劃
IDM **,make a 'plan** (*SAfrE*) to think of sth you can do to solve a problem or make sth happen 想辦法；設法解決： *It's going to be difficult to find the time but I'll make a plan.* 要抽出時間很難，不過我會想辦法的。 ➲ more at SOUND *v.*
■ ***verb*** (**-nn-**)
▸ **MAKE ARRANGEMENTS** 安排 **1** 🔑 [T, I] to make detailed arrangements for sth you want to do in the future 精心安排；計劃；謀劃： **~ sth** *to plan a trip* 計劃一次旅行◇ *Everything* ***went*** *exactly* ***as planned****.* 一切都嚴格地按計劃進行。◇ *We planned the day down to the last detail.* 我們極為詳細地安排了這一天的日程。◇ **~ sth for sth** *A meeting has been planned for early next year.* 會議計劃明年年初召開。◇ **~** (**for sth**) *to plan for the future* 規劃未來◇ **~ how, what, etc. …** *I've been planning how I'm going to spend the day.* 我一直在籌劃怎樣度過這一天。◇ **~ that …** *They planned that the two routes would connect.* 他們計劃讓兩條路接上。
▸ **INTEND/EXPECT** 意欲；期待 **2** 🔑 [I, T] to intend or expect to do sth 打算；期待： **~ on sth/on doing sth** *We hadn't planned on going anywhere this evening.* 我們今晚沒打算外出。◇ **~ to do sth** *They plan to arrive some time after three.* 他們預計在三點鐘以後到達。◇ **~ sth** *We're planning a trip to France in the spring—are you interested?* 我們打算春天去法國旅遊。你有意去嗎？
▸ **DESIGN** 設計 **3** 🔑 [T] **~ sth** to make a design or an outline for sth 設計；安排；組織；策劃： *to plan an essay/a garden* 構思一篇文章；設計一個花園◇ *a well-planned campaign* 一場精心策劃的活動
PHR V **,plan sth↔'out** to plan carefully and in detail sth that you are going to do in the future 精心安排；籌劃： *Plan out your route before you go.* 出發前要仔細設計好你的路線。◇ *She has her career all planned out.* 她對自己的前途事業已作了精心規劃。

Plan 'A *noun* [sing.] the thing or things sb intends to do if everything happens as they expect（一切如所預料的情況下使用的）第一行動方案，甲案

pla·nar /'pleɪnə(r)/ *adj.* (*technical* 術語) of or related to a flat surface 平面的

Plan 'B *noun* [sing.] the thing or things sb intends to do if their first plan is not successful（第一方案不可行的情況下使用的）第二行動方案，次選方案，乙案： *If Plan A fails, go to Plan B.* 假如第一方案失敗了，就執行第二方案。

plane 🔑 /pleɪn/ *noun, adj., verb*
■ ***noun*** **1** 🔑 (*BrE* also **aero·plane**) (also **air·plane** especially in *NAmE*) a flying vehicle with wings and one or more engines 飛機： *She left* ***by plane*** *for Berlin.* 她乘飛機去柏林了。◇ *a* ***plane crash*** 飛機墜毀◇ *I* ***caught the*** *next* ***plane*** *to Dublin.* 我趕上了下一班飛機去都柏林。◇ *The* ***plane took off*** *an hour late.* 飛機延遲了一小時起飛。◇ *The* ***plane landed*** *at Geneva.* 飛機在日內瓦降落。 ➲ COLLOCATIONS at TRAVEL ➲ VISUAL VOCAB page V53 **2** (*geometry* 幾何) any flat or level surface, or an imaginary flat surface through or joining material objects 平面： *the* ***horizontal/vertical plane*** 水平／垂直平面 **3** a level of thought, existence or development（思想、存在或發展的）水平，程度，階段，境界： *to reach a higher plane of achievement* 取得更高的成就 **4** a tool with a blade set in a flat surface, used for making the surface of wood smooth by shaving very thin layers off it 木工刨；刨子 ➲ VISUAL VOCAB page V20
■ ***adj.*** [only before noun] (*technical* 術語) completely flat; level 平的；平坦的： *a plane surface* 平面
■ ***verb*** **1** [T] to make a piece of wood smoother or flatter with a PLANE *n.* (4) 用刨子刨平： **~ sth** *Plane the surface down first.* 首先要把表面刨平。◇ **~ sth + adj.** *Then plane the wood smooth.* 然後把木頭刨光。 **2** [I] (of a bird 鳥) to fly without moving the wings, especially high up in the air 滑翔 **3** [I] (of a boat, etc. 船等) to move quickly across water, only just touching the surface 擦着水面疾駛

plane·load /'pleɪnləʊd; *NAmE* -loʊd/ *noun* the number of people or the amount of goods that can be carried in a plane 飛機載客量（或裝載量）： *two planeloads of refugees* 兩飛機的難民

planer /'pleɪnə(r)/ *noun* an electric tool for making wooden surfaces smooth（電動）刨牀

planet 🔑 /'plænɪt/ *noun*
1 🔑 [C] a large round object in space that moves around a star (such as the sun) and receives light from it 行星： *the planets of our solar system* 太陽系的行星◇ *the planet Earth/Venus/Mars* 地球；金星；火星 **2** 🔑 **the planet** [sing.] used to mean 'the world', especially when talking about the environment 地球（尤指環境）： *the battle to save the planet* 拯救地球的戰鬥
IDM **to be on another 'planet | what 'planet is sb on?** (*informal, humorous*) used to suggest that sb's ideas are not realistic or practical（指某人的想法完全不切實際）： *He thinks being a father is easy. What planet is he on?* 他認為做父親很容易，他真是在做白日夢！

plan·et·arium /,plænɪ'teəriəm; *NAmE* -'ter-/ *noun* (*pl.* **-iums**) a building with a curved ceiling to represent the sky at night, with moving images of the planets and stars, used to educate and entertain people 天文館；天象館

plan·et·ary /'plænətri; *NAmE* -teri/ *adj.* [only before noun] (*technical* 術語) relating to a planet or planets 行星的： *a planetary system* 行星系

P

ˈplane tree *noun* a tree with spreading branches and broad leaves, that is often found in towns in northern countries 懸鈴木

plan·gent /ˈplændʒənt/ *adj.* **1** (*formal*) (of sounds 聲音) loud, with a strong beat 洪亮的；轟鳴的 **2** (*literary*) (of sounds or images 聲音或圖像) expressing sadness 哀婉的；淒涼的 SYN **plaintive**：*the plangent sound of the harpsichord* 撥弦鍵琴如泣如訴的聲音

plank /plæŋk/ *noun* **1** a long narrow flat piece of wood that is used for making floors, etc. 木板；板條：*a plank of wood* 一塊木板條 ◇ *a wooden plank* 一條木板 **2** a main point in the policy of an organization, especially a political party（政黨等的）政策準則，政綱的核心：*The* ***central plank*** *of the bill was rural development.* 這一法案的核心是農村發展。IDM see THICK *adj.*, WALK *v.*

plank·ing /ˈplæŋkɪŋ/ *noun* [U] planks used to make a floor, etc. 板材；地板木料

plank·ton /ˈplæŋktən/ *noun* [U+sing./pl. v.] the very small forms of plant and animal life that live in water 浮游生物

ˌplanned eˈconomy (also **comˌmand eˈconomy**) *noun* an economy in which production, prices and incomes are decided and fixed by the central government 計劃經濟

plan·ner /ˈplænə(r)/ *noun* **1** (also **ˌtown ˈplanner**) a person whose job is to plan the growth and development of a town 城市規劃者 **2** a person who makes plans for a particular area of activity 設計者；規劃者：*curriculum planners* 課程規劃人員 **3** a book, chart, computer program, etc. that contains dates and is used for recording information, arranging meetings, etc. 記事簿；規劃簿：*a journey planner* 旅程安排表 ◇ *a wall planner* 壁掛記事簿 ➲ VISUAL VOCAB page V69

plan·ning 🔑 /ˈplænɪŋ/ *noun* [U]
1 🔑 the act or process of making plans for sth 計劃制訂；規劃過程：*financial planning* 財政計劃 ➲ see also FAMILY PLANNING **2** = TOWN PLANNING

P

ˈplanning permission *noun* [U] (*BrE*) official permission to build a new building or change one that already exists 規劃許可；建築（或改建）許可

plant 🔑 /plɑːnt; *NAmE* plænt/ *noun, verb*

■ ***noun***

▸ **LIVING THING 生物** **1** 🔑 [C] a living thing that grows in the earth and usually has a STEM, leaves and roots, especially one that is smaller than a tree or bush 植物：*All plants need light and water.* 一切植物都需要陽光和水。◇ ***flowering/garden/indoor plants*** 開花 / 花園 / 室內植物 ◇ *a tomato/potato plant* 番茄秧；馬鈴薯秧 ◇ *the animal and plant life of the area* 本地區的動植物 ➲ COLLOCATIONS at LIFE ➲ VISUAL VOCAB page V11 ➲ see also BEDDING PLANT, HOUSE PLANT, POT PLANT, RUBBER PLANT

▸ **FACTORY 工廠** **2** 🔑 [C] a factory or place where power is produced or an industrial process takes place 發電廠；工廠：*a nuclear reprocessing plant* 核物質再處理廠 ◇ *Japanese car plants* 日本汽車製造廠 ◇ *a chemical plant* 化工廠 ➲ see also SEWAGE PLANT ➲ SYNONYMS at FACTORY

▸ **MACHINERY 機械** **3** [U] the large machinery that is used in industrial processes（工業用的）大型機器，設備：*The company has been investing in new plant and equipment.* 這家公司一直在投資購置新機器和設備。

▸ **STH ILLEGAL 不合法的東西** **4** [C, usually sing.] (*informal*) something that sb has deliberately placed among another person's clothes or possessions in order to make them appear guilty of a crime 栽贓物品

▸ **PERSON 人** **5** [C] a person who joins a group of criminals or enemies in order to get and secretly report information about their activities 坐探；內線；卧底

■ ***verb***

▸ **SEEDS/PLANTS 種子；植物** **1** 🔑 **~ sth** to put plants, seeds, etc. in the ground to grow 栽種；種植；播種：*to plant and harvest rice* 栽種並收割水稻 ◇ *Plant these shrubs in full sun.* 把這些灌木栽在陽光充足的地方。**2** 🔑 to cover or supply a garden/yard, area of land, etc. with plants 在（某處）栽種：**~ sth** *a densely planted orange grove* 栽植稠密的橘樹叢 ◇ **~ sth with sth** *The field had been ploughed and planted with corn.* 這塊地已犁過並種上了玉米。

▸ **PUT IN POSITION 安放** **3 ~ sth/yourself + adv./prep.** to place sth or yourself firmly in a particular place or position 立穩；豎立；安放：*They planted a flag on the summit.* 他們在山頂上插了一面旗子。◇ *He planted himself squarely in front of us.* 他穩穩地站在我們面前。

▸ **BOMB 炸彈** **4 ~ sth (+ adv./prep.)** to hide sth such as a bomb in a place where it will not be found（秘密）放置，安置

▸ **STH ILLEGAL 不合法的東西** **5 ~ sth (on sb)** to hide sth, especially sth illegal, in sb's clothing, possessions, etc. so that when it is found it will look as though they committed a crime（給某人）栽（贓）：*He claims that the drugs were planted on him.* 他聲稱這些毒品是別人給他栽的贓。

▸ **PERSON 人** **6 ~ sb (in sth)** to send sb to join a group, etc., especially in order to make secret reports on its members 使卧底；安插（密探）

▸ **THOUGHT/IDEA 思想；意見** **7 ~ sth (in sth)** to make sb think or believe sth, especially without them realizing that you gave them the idea（使思想、信念等）植根於：*He planted the first seeds of doubt in my mind.* 是他最初啟發我起疑心的。

PHR V **ˌplant sth↔ˈout** to put plants in the ground so that they have enough room to grow 均勻栽植（彼此保持適當距離以利生長）

plan·tain /ˈplæntɪn/ *noun* **1** [C, U] a fruit like a large BANANA, but less sweet, that is cooked and eaten as a vegetable 大蕉 **2** [C] a wild plant with small green flowers and broad flat leaves that spread out close to the ground 車前草

plan·tar /ˈplæntə(r)/ *adj.* [only before noun] (*anatomy* 解) of or related to the bottom of the foot 蹠的；腳底的

ˌplantar ˈwart (*NAmE*) (*BrE* **ver·ruca**) *noun* a small hard lump like a WART on the bottom of the foot, which can be easily spread from person to person 足底疣；跖疣

plan·ta·tion /plɑːnˈteɪʃn; *NAmE* plæn-/ *noun* **1** a large area of land, especially in a hot country, where crops such as coffee, sugar, rubber, etc. are grown 種植園，種植場（尤指熱帶國家種植咖啡、甘蔗、橡膠等的大莊園）：*a banana plantation* 香蕉種植園 **2** a large area of land that is planted with trees to produce wood 木材林地；人造林：*conifer/forestry plantations* 針葉樹林地；種植林

plant·er /ˈplɑːntə(r); *NAmE* ˈplæn-/ *noun* **1** an attractive container to grow a plant in 花盆 ➲ VISUAL VOCAB page V19 **2** a person who owns or manages a PLANTATION in a tropical country 種植園主；種植園經營者：*a tea planter* 茶園園主 **3** a machine that plants seeds, etc. 播種機；插秧機

plant·ing /ˈplɑːntɪŋ; *NAmE* ˈplæn-/ *noun* [U, C] an act of planting sth; sth that has just been planted 種植；栽種；栽種物：*The Tree Council promotes tree planting.* 林木委員會倡導植樹造林。◇ *These bushes are fairly recent plantings.* 這些灌木叢是最近栽植的。

ˈplant pot *noun* a container for growing plants in 花盆 ➲ VISUAL VOCAB page V21

plants·man /ˈplɑːntsmən; *NAmE* ˈplænts-/, **plants·woman** /ˈplɑːntswʊmən; *NAmE* ˈplænts-/ *noun* (*pl.* **-men** /-mən/, **-women** /-wɪmɪn/) an expert in garden plants and GARDENING 花卉栽培技術員；園藝師

plaque /plæk; *BrE* also plɑːk/ *noun* **1** [C] a flat piece of stone, metal, etc., usually with a name and dates on, attached to a wall in memory of a person or an event（紀念性的）牌匾，匾額；紀念匾 **2** [U] a soft substance that forms on teeth and encourages the growth of harmful bacteria 牙斑；牙菌斑 ➲ compare SCALE *n.* (10)

plasma /ˈplæzmə/ (also **plasm** /ˈplæzəm/) *noun* [U] **1** (*biology* 生 or *medical* 醫) the clear liquid part of blood, in which the blood cells, etc. float 血漿 **2** (*physics* 物) a gas that contains approximately equal numbers of positive and negative electric charges and is present in the sun and most stars 等離子體；等離子體

ˈplasma screen *noun* a type of television or computer screen that is larger and thinner than most screens and produces a very clear image（電視機或電腦的）等離子屏幕，電漿顯示器

ˌplasma TˈV *noun* a television set with a plasma screen 等離子電視；電漿電視

plas·ter /ˈplɑːstə(r); *NAmE* ˈplæs-/ *noun, verb*

■ *noun* **1** [U] a substance made of LIME, water and sand, that is put on walls and ceilings to give them a smooth hard surface 灰泥：*an old house with crumbling plaster and a leaking roof* 一所灰泥剝落、屋頂漏水的老房子 **2** (also *less frequent* **ˌplaster of ˈParis**) [U] a white powder that is mixed with water and becomes very hard when it dries, used especially for making copies of statues or holding broken bones in place 熟石膏：*a plaster bust of Julius Caesar* 一尊尤利烏斯 • 凱撒的半身石膏塑像 ◇ (*BrE*) *She broke her leg a month ago and it's still* ***in plaster***. 她一個月前腿骨骨折，至今仍打着石膏。 **3** (also **ˈsticking plaster**) (both *BrE*) (also **ˈBand-Aid™** *NAmE, BrE*) [C, U] material that can be stuck to the skin to protect a small wound or cut; a piece of this 膏藥；創可貼；護創膠布 ➲ COLLOCATIONS at INJURY

■ *verb* **1** **~ sth** to cover a wall, etc. with plaster 抹灰；用灰泥抹（牆等）➲ COLLOCATIONS at DECORATE **2** **~ sb/sth/yourself in/with sth** to cover sb/sth with a wet or sticky substance 用…塗抹：*She plastered herself in suntan lotion.* 她往身上抹防曬液。◇ *We were plastered from head to foot with mud.* 我們渾身上下都沾滿了泥。 **3** **~ sth + adv./prep.** to make your hair flat and stick to your head 把（頭髮）梳平；使頭髮粘在（頭上）：*His wet hair was plastered to his head.* 他那濕透的頭髮緊貼在頭皮上。**4** **~ sth + adv./prep.** to completely cover a surface with pictures or POSTERS 貼滿，遍貼（畫片或招貼畫）：*Her bedroom wall was plastered with photos of him.* 她臥室的牆上貼滿了他的照片。◇ *She had photos of him plastered all over her bedroom wall.* 她把他的照片貼滿了臥室的牆。◇ *The next day their picture was plastered all over the newspapers.* 第二天，他們的照片被刊登在各家報紙上。

PHR V **ˌplaster ˈover sth** to cover sth such as a crack or an old wall with plaster 用灰泥抹（裂縫或舊牆）

plas·ter·board /ˈplɑːstəbɔːd; *NAmE* ˈplæstərbɔːrd/ (*NAmE* also **ˈdry wall**) *noun* [U] a building material made of sheets of cardboard with plaster between them, used for inside walls and ceilings 灰泥板；紙面石膏板

ˈplaster cast *noun* **1** (also **cast**) a case made of PLASTER OF PARIS that covers a broken bone and protects it（固定骨折部位的）石膏繃帶，石膏夾 **2** a copy of sth, made from PLASTER OF PARIS 石膏模型：*They took a plaster cast of the teeth for identification purposes.* 他們做了這副牙的石膏模型作鑒別之用。

plas·tered /ˈplɑːstəd; *NAmE* ˈplæstərd/ *adj.* [not before noun] (*informal*) drunk 醉：*to be/get plastered* 喝醉酒

plas·terer /ˈplɑːstərə(r); *NAmE* ˈplæs-/ *noun* a person whose job is to put plaster on walls and ceilings 抹灰工；泥水匠；粉刷工

plaster of Paris /ˌplɑːstər əv ˈpærɪs; *NAmE* ˌplæs-/ *noun* [U] = PLASTER (2)

ˌplaster ˈsaint *noun* a person who tries to appear to have no moral faults or weaknesses, especially when this appearance is false 道貌岸然者；（尤指）偽聖人，偽君子

plas·ter·work /ˈplɑːstəwɜːk; *NAmE* ˈplæstərwɜːrk/ *noun* [U] the dry PLASTER on ceilings when it has been formed into shapes and patterns for decoration（天花板的）灰泥裝飾圖案

plas·tic 0‑ˉ /ˈplæstɪk/ *noun, adj.*

■ *noun* **1** 0‑ˉ [U, C, usually pl.] a light strong material that is produced by chemical processes and can be formed into shapes when heated. There are many different types of plastic, used to make different objects and FABRICS. 塑料；塑膠：*The pipes should be* ***made of plastic***. 這些管子應該是用塑料製作的。◇ *a sheet of clear plastic* 一張透明的塑料 ◇ *the plastic industry* 塑料工業 **2** **plastics** [U] the science of making plastics 塑料學；塑膠學 **3** [U] (*informal*) a way of talking about CREDIT CARDS 信用卡：*Do they take plastic?* 他們收信用卡嗎？

■ *adj.* **1** 0‑ˉ made of plastic 塑料製的；塑料的；塑膠的：*a plastic bag/cup/toy* 塑料袋／杯／玩具 **2** (of a material or substance 材料或物質) easily formed into different shapes 可塑的；有塑性的 SYN **malleable**：*Clay is a plastic substance.* 黏土是可塑物質。 **3** (*disapproving*) that seems artificial; false; not real or sincere 做作的；虛偽的；矯飾的 SYN **false**：*TV game show hosts with their banal remarks and plastic smiles* 語言陳腐、笑容刻板的電視競賽節目主持人

ˌplastic ˈarts *noun* [pl.] (*technical* 術語) art forms that involve making models or representing things so that they seem solid 造型藝術：*The plastic arts include sculpture, pottery and painting.* 造型藝術包括雕塑、陶藝和繪畫。

ˌplastic ˈbullet *noun* a bullet made of plastic, that is intended to injure but not to kill people 塑料子彈；橡皮子彈；塑膠子彈

ˌplastic exˈplosive *noun* [U, C] an EXPLOSIVE that is used to make bombs 塑性炸藥

Plas·ti·cine™ /ˈplæstəsiːn/ *noun* [U] (*BrE*) a soft substance like CLAY that is made in different colours, used especially by children for making models 普萊斯蒂辛橡皮泥

plas·ti·city /plæˈstɪsəti/ *noun* [U] (*technical* 術語) the quality of being easily made into different shapes 可塑性；塑性

plas·ti·cize (*BrE* also **-ise**) /ˈplæstɪsaɪz/ *verb* **~ sth** (*technical* 術語) to add sth to a substance so that it becomes easy to bend and form into different shapes 使增塑；使塑化；使可塑

ˌplastic ˈsurgeon *noun* a doctor who is qualified to perform plastic surgery 整形外科醫生

ˌplastic ˈsurgery *noun* [U] medical operations to repair injury to a person's skin, or to improve a person's appearance 整形手術；整形外科

ˈplastic wrap (also **Saran Wrap™**) (both *NAmE*) (*BrE* **ˈcling film**) *noun* [U] a thin transparent plastic material that sticks to a surface and to itself, used especially for wrapping food（尤指包裝食物的）透明薄膜，保鮮塑料膜

plate 0‑ˉ /pleɪt/ *noun, verb*

■ *noun*

▸ FOOD 食物 **1** 0‑ˉ [C] a flat, usually round, dish that you put food on 盤子；碟子：*sandwiches on a plate* 盤子上的三明治 ◇ *a pile of dirty plates* 一摞髒盤子 ◇ *dinner plates* 餐盤 ➲ VISUAL VOCAB page V22 **2** 0‑ˉ [C] the amount of food that you can put on a plate 一盤所盛之量；一盤：*a plate of sandwiches* 一盤三明治 ◇ *two large plates of pasta* 兩大盤意大利麵 ➲ compare PLATEFUL **3** [C] (*especially NAmE*) a whole main course of a meal, served on one plate 一道主菜：*Try the seafood plate.* 嚐嚐這道海鮮吧。

▸ FOR STRENGTH 強化用 **4** 0‑ˉ [C] a thin flat piece of metal, used especially to join or make sth stronger（金屬）板條，板材：*The tanks were mainly constructed of steel plates.* 這些坦克車主要是用鋼板製造的。◇ *She had a metal plate inserted in her arm.* 她的胳膊裏嵌着一塊接骨板。

▸ FOR INFORMATION 提供信息 **5** [C] a flat piece of metal with some information on it, for example sb's name（刻有名字等的）金屬牌子：*A brass plate beside the door said 'Dr Alan Tate'.* 門旁的銅牌上寫着"艾倫 • 泰特醫生"。➲ see also NAMEPLATE

▸ ON VEHICLE 車輛上 **6** [usually pl.] the pieces of metal or plastic at the front and back of a vehicle with numbers and letters on it（車輛的）號碼牌 ➲ see also L-PLATE, LICENSE PLATE, NUMBER PLATE

▸ SILVER/GOLD 銀；金 **7** [U] ordinary metal that is covered with a thin layer of silver or gold 鍍金（或鍍銀）的金屬：*The cutlery is plate, not solid silver.* 這套餐具是鍍銀的，不是純銀的。➲ see also GOLD PLATE, SILVER PLATE, TINPLATE **8** [U] dishes, bowls, etc. that are made of silver or gold 金的（或銀的）餐具

P

▸ **ON ANIMAL 動物 9** [C] (*biology* 生) one of the thin flat pieces of horn or bone that cover and protect an animal 盾片；鱗甲；護甲：*the armadillo's protective shell of bony plates* 犰狳的一層防護性鱗甲

▸ **GEOLOGY 地質學 10** [C] one of the very large pieces of rock that form the earth's surface and move slowly 板塊：*the Pacific plate* 太平洋板塊 ◇ *Earthquakes are caused by two **tectonic plates** bumping into each other.* 地震是由兩塊地殼構造板塊互相碰撞造成的。➲ see also PLATE TECTONICS

▸ **PRINTING/PHOTOGRAPHY 印刷；攝影 11** [C] a photograph that is used as a picture in a book, especially one that is printed on a separate page on high quality paper 書籍插圖照片；（尤指優質紙上的）整頁插圖：*The book includes 55 colour plates.* 本書有 55 幅彩色插圖。◇ *See plate 4.* 見彩圖 4。 **12** [C] a sheet of metal, plastic, etc. that has been treated so that words or pictures can be printed from it （印刷用的）印版，圖版：*a printing plate* 印版 **13** [C] a thin sheet of glass, metal, etc. that is covered with chemicals so that it reacts to light and can form an image, used in larger or older cameras （玻璃、金屬等）底片，感光板

▸ **IN MOUTH 口內 14** [C] a thin piece of plastic with wire or artificial teeth attached to it which fits inside your mouth in order to make your teeth straight 假牙托；托牙板；假牙牀 ➲ compare BRACE *n.* (2), DENTURES

▸ **IN BASEBALL 棒球 15** [sing.] (*NAmE*) = HOME PLATE

▸ **IN CHURCH 教堂 16** (usually **the plate**) [sing.] a flat dish that is used to collect money from people in a church 奉獻盤；捐款盤 ➲ see also BOOKPLATE, BREASTPLATE, FOOTPLATE, HOTPLATE

IDM **have enough/a lot/too much on your 'plate** (*informal*) to have a lot of work or problems, etc. to deal with 問題（或工作等）成堆 ➲ more at HAND *v.*, STEP *v.*

■ ***verb*** [usually passive] **1 ~ sth (with sth)** to cover a metal with a thin layer of another metal, especially gold or silver 電鍍（尤指鍍金、鍍銀）：*a silver ring plated with gold* 一枚鍍金的銀戒指 ➲ see also GOLD-PLATED, SILVER PLATE **2 ~ sth (with sth)** to cover sth with sheets of metal or another hard substance 為…加設護板；（用金屬板等）覆蓋：*The walls of the vault were plated with steel.* 保險庫的牆壁都裝了鋼板。➲ see also ARMOUR-PLATED

P

plat·eau /ˈplætəʊ; *NAmE* plæˈtoʊ/ *noun, verb*

■ ***noun*** (*pl.* **plat·eaux** or **plat·eaus** /-təʊz; *NAmE* -ˈtoʊz/) **1** an area of flat land that is higher than the land around it 高原 ➲ VISUAL VOCAB pages V4, V5 **2** a time of little or no change after a period of growth or progress （發展、增長後的）穩定期，停滯期：*Inflation has reached a plateau.* 通貨膨脹停了下來。

■ ***verb*** [I] **~ (out)** to stay at a steady level after a period of growth or progress （在一段時期的發展後）保持穩定水平，處於停滯狀態：*Unemployment has at last plateaued out.* 失業情況終於穩定了下來。

plate·ful /ˈpleɪtfʊl/ *noun* the amount that a plate holds 一盤之量；盤：*She ate three platefuls of spaghetti.* 她吃了三盤意大利麪。➲ compare PLATE

ˌplate ˈglass *noun* [U] very clear glass of good quality, made in thick sheets, used for doors, windows of shops/stores, etc. 平板玻璃；厚玻璃板

plate·lay·er /ˈpleɪtleɪə(r)/ *noun* (*BrE*) a person whose job is to lay and repair railway tracks （鐵路）鋪軌工，養路工

plate·let /ˈpleɪtlət/ *noun* a very small part of a cell in the blood, shaped like a disc. Platelets help to CLOT the blood from a cut or wound. 血小板

ˌplate tecˈtonics *noun* [U] (*geology* 地) the movements of the large sheets of rock (called PLATES) that form the earth's surface; the scientific study of these movements 板塊運動；板塊構造學；大地構造學

plat·form 0▬ /ˈplætfɔːm; *NAmE* -fɔːrm/ *noun*

▸ **AT TRAIN STATION 火車站 1** 0▬ the raised flat area beside the track at a train station where you get on or off the train 站台；月台：(*BrE*) *What platform does it go from?* 火車從哪個站台發車？◇ (*BrE*) *The train now standing at platform 1 is for Leeds.* 停靠在 1 號站台的火車是開往利茲的。➲ compare TRACK *n.* (4) ➲ VISUAL VOCAB page V58

▸ **FOR PERFORMERS 表演用 2** 0▬ a flat surface raised above the level of the ground or floor, used by public speakers or performers so that the audience can see them 講台；舞台 **SYN** **rostrum**：*Coming onto the platform now is tonight's conductor, Jane Glover.* 現在出場的是今晚的指揮簡•格洛弗。◇ *Representatives of both parties shared a platform* (= they spoke at the same meeting). 兩黨的代表同台發言。

▸ **RAISED SURFACE 凸起的平面 3** 0▬ a raised level surface, for example one that equipment stands on or is operated from 平台：*an **oil/gas platform*** 石油／天然氣鑽井平台 ◇ *a **launch platform*** (= for SPACECRAFT) 發射平台 ◇ *a **viewing platform** giving stunning views over the valley* 縱覽山谷美景的觀景台

▸ **POLITICS/OPINIONS 政治；觀點 4** [usually sing.] the aims of a political party and the things that they say they will do if they are elected to power （政黨的）綱領，政綱，宣言：*They are campaigning on an anti-immigration platform.* 他們正在宣傳反對外來移民的政綱。 **5** an opportunity or a place for sb to express their opinions publicly or make progress in a particular area （公開表達意見或在某方面發展的）機會，陣地，講壇：*She used the newspaper column as a platform for her feminist views.* 她以這個報紙專欄為講壇，宣傳她的女權主義觀點。

▸ **COMPUTING 計算機技術 6** the type of computer system or the software that is used 計算機平台：*an IBM platform* 國際商用機器公司平台 ◇ *a multimedia platform* 多媒體平台

▸ **SHOES 鞋子 7** a type of shoe with a high, thick SOLE; the sole on such a shoe 厚底鞋；厚鞋底：*platform shoes* 厚底鞋 ➲ VISUAL VOCAB page V64

▸ **ON BUS 公共汽車 8** (*BrE*) the open part at the back of a DOUBLE-DECKER bus where you get on or off （雙層汽車的）上下車出入口，入口平台

British/American 英式／美式英語

platform / track

- In British stations the platforms, where passengers get on and off trains, have numbers. 在英國火車站，旅客上下火車的站台（platform）有編號：*The Edinburgh train is waiting at platform 4.* 去愛丁堡的火車在 4 號站台等候。
- In stations in the USA, it is the track that the train travels along that has a number. 在美國火車站，按火車的軌道（track）編號：*The train for Chicago is on track 9.* 往芝加哥的火車在第 9 道。

ˈplatform game (also **plat·form·er** /ˈplætfɔːmə(r); *NAmE* -fɔːrm-/) *noun* a computer game in which the player controls a character who jumps and climbs between platforms at different positions on the screen （電腦）平台遊戲，跳爬遊戲

plat·ing /ˈpleɪtɪŋ/ *noun* [U] **1** a thin covering of a metal, especially silver or gold, on another metal 鍍層（鍍在金屬上的其他金屬薄層） **2** a layer of coverings, especially of metal plates 外層；（尤指）金屬板護層：*armour plating* 裝甲敷板

plat·inum /ˈplætɪnəm/ *noun* [U] (*symb.* **Pt**) a chemical element. Platinum is a silver-grey PRECIOUS METAL, used in making expensive jewellery and in industry. 鉑；白金

ˌplatinum ˈblonde *noun* (*informal*) a woman whose hair is a very pale silver colour, especially because it has been coloured with chemicals; this colour of hair 銀髮女郎（尤指染髮的）；（頭髮的）銀色 ▸ **ˌplatinum ˈblonde** *adj.*

ˌplatinum ˈdisc *noun* a platinum record in a frame, given to a singer, etc. who has sold a very high number of records （給唱片銷售量極高的歌手等頒發的）白金唱片

plati·tude /ˈplætɪtjuːd; *NAmE* -tuːd/ *noun* (*disapproving*) a comment or statement that has been made very often before and is therefore not interesting 陳詞濫調；老生

常談 ▸ **plati·tud·in·ous** /ˌplætɪˈtjuːdɪnəs; *NAmE* -ˈtuːdənəs/ *adj.* (*formal*)

pla·ton·ic /pləˈtɒnɪk; *NAmE* -ˈtɑːn-/ *adj.* (of a relationship 關係) friendly but not involving sex 柏拉圖式的（指不含性愛）：*platonic love* 柏拉圖式的愛 ◇ *Their relationship is strictly platonic.* 他們的關係完全是純友誼。

Pla·ton·ism /ˈpleɪtənɪzəm/ *noun* [U] (*philosophy* 哲) the ideas of the ancient Greek PHILOSOPHER Plato and those who followed him 柏拉圖主義；柏拉圖學說 ▸ **Pla·ton·ist** /ˈpleɪtənɪst/ *adj., noun*

pla·toon /pləˈtuːn/ *noun* a small group of soldiers that is part of a COMPANY and commanded by a LIEUTENANT（軍隊的）排

plat·ter /ˈplætə(r)/ *noun* a large plate that is used for serving food 大平盤：*a silver platter* 大銀盤子 ◇ *I'll have the fish platter* (= several types of fish and other food served on a large plate). 我來一盤魚套餐吧。 **IDM** see SILVER *n.*

platy·pus /ˈplætɪpəs/ (also ˌ**duck-billed** ˈ**platypus**) *noun* an Australian animal that is covered in fur and has a beak like a DUCK, WEBBED feet (= with skin between the toes) and a flat tail. Platypuses lay eggs but give milk to their young. 鴨嘴獸，鴨獺（棲於澳大利亞）

plau·dits /ˈplɔːdɪts/ *noun* [usually pl.] (*formal*) praise and approval 讚譽；稱讚；褒揚：*His work* ***won him plaudits*** *from the critics.* 他的作品贏得了評論家的讚賞。

plaus·ible /ˈplɔːzəbl/ *adj.* **1** (of an excuse or explanation 藉口或解釋) reasonable and likely to be true 有道理的；可信的：*Her story sounded perfectly plausible.* 她的說辭聽起來言之有理。◇ *The only plausible explanation is that he forgot.* 唯一合理的解釋就是他忘掉了。 **OPP** **implausible** **2** (*disapproving*) (of a person 人) good at sounding honest and sincere, especially when trying to trick people 巧言令色的；花言巧語的：*She was a plausible liar.* 她是個巧言令色的說謊高手。 ▸ **plausi·bil·ity** /ˌplɔːzəˈbɪləti/ *noun* [U] **plaus·ibly** /-əbli/ *adv.*：*He argued very plausibly that the claims were true.* 他花言巧語地辯解說那些說法屬實。

play 🔑 /pleɪ/ *verb, noun*

■ ***verb***

▸ **OF CHILDREN** 兒童 **1** 🔑 [I, T] to do things for pleasure, as children do; to enjoy yourself, rather than work 玩耍；遊戲；玩樂：*You'll have to play inside today.* 你今天只能在屋裏玩耍。◇ *There's a time to work and a time to play.* 工作、玩耍皆有時。◇ **~ with sb/sth** *A group of kids were playing with a ball in the street.* 一群孩子在街上玩球。◇ *I haven't got anybody to play with!* 沒有人跟我玩兒！◇ **~ sth** *Let's play a different game.* 咱們玩點別的遊戲吧。 ➲ **SYNONYMS** at ENTERTAINMENT **2** 🔑 [T, no passive, I] to pretend to be or do sth for fun（為玩耍）假裝，假扮：**~ sth** *Let's play pirates.* 咱們假扮海盜玩吧。◇ **~ at doing sth** *They were playing at being cowboys.* 他們裝扮成牛仔玩。

▸ **TRICK** 把戲 **3** 🔑 [T] **~ a trick/tricks** (**on sb**) to trick sb for fun 捉弄；戲弄

▸ **SPORTS/GAMES** 運動；比賽 **4** 🔑 [T, I] **~ (sth) (with/against sb)** to be involved in a game; to compete against sb in a game 參加比賽；（同某人）比賽：**~ sth** *to* ***play football/chess/cards, etc.*** 踢足球、下棋、玩紙牌等 ◇ **~ sb** *France are playing Wales tomorrow.* 明天法國隊和威爾士隊比賽。◇ **~ sb at sth** *Have you played her at squash yet?* 你跟她打過壁球沒有？◇ **~ for sb** *He plays for Cleveland.* 他代表克利夫蘭參賽。◇ **~ against sb** *France are playing against Wales on Saturday.* 星期六法國隊迎戰威爾士隊。◇ **+ adv./prep.** *Evans played very well.* 埃文斯比賽很出色。 **5** [I] to take a particular position in a sports team（在運動隊中）擔當，充任：**+ adv./prep.** *Who's playing on the wing?* 誰擔任邊鋒？◇ **+ noun** *I've never played right back before.* 我過去從來未當過右後衛。 **6** [T] **~ sb** (**+ adv./prep.**) to include sb in a sports team 派…出場；讓…加入運動隊：*I think we should play Matt on the wing.* 我認為我們應該讓麥特打邊鋒。 **7** [T] **~ sth** to make contact with the ball and hit or kick it in the way mentioned 觸，帶，踢，擊（球）：*She played the ball and ran forward.* 她帶球向前衝。◇ *He played a backhand volley.* 他用反手截擊球。 **8** [T] **~ sth** (in CHESS 國際象棋) to move a piece in CHESS, etc. 走（子）；行（棋）：*She played her bishop.* 她走象。 **9** [T, I] **~ (sth)** (in card games 紙牌遊戲) to put a card face upwards on the table, showing its value 出牌：*to play your ace/a trump* 出 A / 王牌 ◇ *He played out of turn!* 他搶出牌！

▸ **MUSIC** 音樂 **10** 🔑 [T, I] **~ (sth) (on sth)** to perform on a musical instrument; to perform music 彈撥，吹奏（樂器）；演奏：**~ (sth)** *to* ***play the piano/violin/flute, etc.*** 彈鋼琴、拉小提琴、吹長笛等 ◇ *In the distance a band was playing.* 遠處有個樂隊在演奏。◇ **~ sth (on sth)** *He played a tune on his harmonica.* 他用口琴吹奏了一支曲子。◇ **~ sth to sb** *Play that new piece to us.* 給我們演奏那支新曲子吧。◇ **~ sb sth** *Play us that new piece.* 給我們演奏那支新曲子吧。 **11** 🔑 [T, I] to make a tape, CD, etc. produce sound 播放：**~ sth (for sb)** *Play their new CD for me, please.* 請把他們的新唱片放給我聽一下吧。◇ **~ (sb sth)** *Play me their new CD, please.* 請給我放一下他們的新唱片吧。◇ *My favourite song was playing on the radio.* 收音機裏播放着我最喜愛的歌曲。◇ *For some reason this CD won't play.* 不知什麼原因，這張唱片不能播放。

▸ **DVD/VIDEO** * DVD 光盤；視頻 **12** [I, T] (of a DVD or video * DVD 光盤或視頻) to start working; to make a DVD or video start working 開始播放；播放（光盤或視頻）：*This DVD won't play on my computer.* 這張 DVD 光盤在我的電腦上不能播放。◇ **~ sth** *Click below to play videos.* 點擊下方播放視頻。

▸ **ACT/PERFORM** 扮演；演出 **13** 🔑 [T] **~ sth** to act in a play, film/movie, etc.; to act the role of sb（在電影、話劇中）扮角色，扮演，表演：*The part of Elizabeth was played by Cate Blanchett.* 伊麗莎白這一角色由凱特 • 布蘭切特扮演。◇ *He had always wanted to play Othello.* 他一直想扮演奧賽羅。 **14** 🔑 [I] to pretend to be sth that you are not 佯裝；假裝：**+ adj.** *I decided it was safer to* ***play dead.*** 我拿定主意裝死會更安全些。◇ **+ noun** *She enjoys playing the wronged wife.* 她很喜歡扮演受委屈的妻子。 **15** [I] **~ (to sb)** to be performed 上演；演出：*A production of 'Carmen' was playing to packed houses.*《卡門》一劇上演場場爆滿。

▸ **HAVE EFFECT** 起作用 **16** [T] **~ a part/role (in sth)** to have an effect on sth 發揮作用：*The media played an important part in the last election.* 大眾傳媒在上一次選舉中發揮了重要作用。

▸ **SITUATION** 局面 **17** [T] **~ sth + adv./prep.** to deal with a situation in the way mentioned（以某種方式）應付，處理：*He played the situation carefully for maximum advantage.* 他謹慎應付局面以獲得最大利益。

▸ **OF LIGHT/A SMILE** 光；微笑 **18** [I] **+ adv./prep.** to move or appear quickly and lightly, often changing direction or shape 閃爍；浮現；掠過：*Sunlight played on the surface of the lake.* 陽光在湖面上閃爍。

▸ **OF FOUNTAIN** 噴泉 **19** [I] when a FOUNTAIN **plays**, it produces a steady stream of water 噴湧；湧流

IDM Most idioms containing **play** are at the entries for the nouns and adjectives in the idioms, for example **play the game** is at **game**. 大多數含 play 的習語，都可在該等習語中的名詞及形容詞相關詞條找到，如 play the game 在詞條 game 下。 **have money, time, etc. to** ˈ**play with** (*informal*) to have plenty of money, time, etc. for doing sth 有的是金錢（或時間等） **what is sb** ˈ**playing at?** used to ask in an angry way about what sb is doing（氣憤時的質問語）某人在搞什麼名堂？：*What do you think you are playing at?* 你以為你在搞什麼名堂？ ˈ**play with yourself** (*informal*) to MASTURBATE 手淫

PHR V ˌ**play aˈbout/aˈround (with sb/sth)** **1** 🔑 to behave or treat sth in a careless way 玩弄；亂弄；胡弄：*Don't play around with my tools!* 別瞎擺弄我的工具！ **2** (*informal*) to have a sexual relationship with sb, usually with sb who is not your usual partner 鬼混；廝混：*Her husband is always playing around.* 她的丈夫總是在外拈花惹草。 ˌ**play aˈlong (with sb/sth)** to pretend to agree with sb/sth 假意順從：*I decided to play along with her idea.* 我決定假意聽從她的意見。 ˈ**play at sth/at doing sth** (often *disapproving*) to do sth without being serious about it or putting much effort into it 敷衍應付；虛與委蛇 **play aˈway (from home)** (*BrE*) **1** (of a sports team 體育運動隊) to play a match at the opponent's ground or STADIUM 在客場打比賽 **2** (of a person who is married or who has a regular sexual partner 已婚或有固定性伴侶者) to have a secret sexual relationship with sb else 有外遇；搞婚外戀 **,play sth↔'back (to sb)** to play music, film, etc. that has been recorded on a tape, video, etc. 播放錄音（或錄像等）：*Play that last section back to me again.* 把最後一節再給我放一次。➲ related noun PLAYBACK **,play sth↔'down** to try to make sth seem less important than it is 減低…的重要性；貶低；淡化 SYN **downplay** OPP **play up** **,play A 'off against B** (*BrE*) (*NAmE* **'play A off B**) to put two people or groups in competition with each other, especially in order to get an advantage for yourself 挑撥離間（以便漁利）：*She played her two rivals off against each other and got the job herself.* 她挑撥兩個對手相爭，使自己弄到了那份工作。➲ related noun PLAY-OFF **,play 'on** (*sport* 體) to continue to play; to start playing again 繼續比賽；恢復比賽：*The home team claimed a penalty but the referee told them to play on.* 主隊要求判罰，但裁判卻要他們繼續比賽。**'play on/upon sth** to take advantage of sb's feelings, etc. 利用（感情等）SYN **exploit**：*Advertisements often play on people's fears.* 廣告常利用人們的恐懼心理。**,play sth↔'out** when an event **is played out**, it happens 發生；出現 SYN **enact**：*Their love affair was played out against the backdrop of war.* 他們在戰爭的背景下發生戀情。**,play yourself/itself 'out** to become weak and no longer useful or important 消耗淨盡；使精疲力竭 **,play 'up | ,play sb 'up** (*informal, especially BrE*) to cause sb problems or pain（給某人）添麻煩；使痛苦：*The kids have been playing up all day.* 孩子們整天慣惹麻煩。◇ *My shoulder is playing me up today.* 我的肩膀今天疼起來了。**,play sth↔'up** to try to make sth seem more important than it is 誇大…的重要性；渲染；吹噓 SYN **overplay** OPP **play down** **'play with sb/sth** to treat sb who is emotionally attached to you in a way that is not serious and which can hurt their feelings 玩弄人；玩弄感情：*She tends to play with men's emotions.* 她總是玩弄男人的感情。◇ *She realized that Patrick was merely playing with her.* 她意識到帕特里克只是和她逢場作戲而已。**'play with sth** **1** 🔑 to keep touching or moving sth 擺弄；玩弄：*She was playing with her hair.* 她在撫弄自己的頭髮。◇ *Stop playing with your food!* 別老是擺弄食物！**2** to use things in different ways to produce an interesting or humorous effect, or to see what effect they have 巧妙地利用；新奇（或幽默等地）運用：*In this poem Fitch plays with words which sound alike.* 在這首詩中，菲奇巧妙地運用了些近音詞。◇ *The composer plays with the exotic sounds of Japanese instruments.* 作曲者運用了日本樂器的異國音調。

■ ***noun***

▸ **CHILDREN** 兒童 **1** 🔑 [U] things that people, especially children, do for pleasure rather than as work 遊戲；玩耍；娛樂：*the happy sounds of children* ***at play*** 兒童嬉戲的歡鬧聲 ◇ *the importance of learning through play* 寓教於樂的重要性 ◇ *a play area* 遊戲的場地

▸ **IN THEATRE** 劇院 **2** 🔑 [C] a piece of writing performed by actors in a theatre or on television or radio 戲劇；劇本：*to* ***put on*** (= perform) *a play* 演出戲劇 ◇ *a play by Shakespeare* 一齣莎士比亞的戲劇 ◇ *a radio play* 廣播劇 ➲ see also MYSTERY PLAY, PASSION PLAY

▸ **IN SPORT** 體育運動 **3** [U] the playing of a game 比賽；賽風；比賽中的表現：*Rain stopped play.* 因雨停賽。◇ *There was some excellent play in yesterday's match.* 昨天的比賽有精彩的場面。➲ see also FAIR PLAY, FOUL PLAY (2) **4** [C] (*NAmE*) an action or move in a game 比賽中的動作：*a defensive play* 防守動作

▸ **IN ROPE** 繩索 **5** [U] the possibility of free and easy movement 間隙；活動空間：*We need more play in the rope.* 我們需要再鬆一鬆繩子。

▸ **ACTIVITY/INFLUENCE** 活動；影響 **6** [U] the activity or operation of sth; the influence of sth on sth else 活動；作用；影響：*the free play of market forces* 市場力量的自由調節作用 ◇ *The financial crisis has* ***brought*** *new factors* ***into play***. 財政危機已引發了新的變數。◇ *Personal feelings should not* ***come into play*** *when you are making business decisions.* 為公事作決策不應摻入個人感情。

▸ **OF LIGHT/A SMILE** 光；笑容 **7** [U] (*literary*) a light, quick movement that keeps changing 輕快變幻的動作；閃爍；閃現：*the play of sunlight on water* 陽光在水面上的閃爍

IDM **have a 'play (with sth)** to spend time playing with a toy, game, etc. 玩（玩具、遊戲等）：*I had a play with the new computer game.* 我玩了一下這個新的電腦遊戲。**in/out of 'play** (*sport* 體) (of a ball 球) inside/outside the area allowed by the rules of the game 在非死球／死球區域；在可繼續／不能繼續比賽區域：*She just managed to keep the ball in play.* 她把球勉強保持在界內。**make a 'play for sb/sth** to try to obtain sth; to do things that are intended to produce a particular result 企圖得到；處心積慮做事：*She was making a play for the sales manager's job.* 她千方百計要取得銷售部經理的位置。**make great/much 'play of sth** to emphasize the importance of a particular fact 強調；着重說明：*He made great play of the fact that his uncle was a duke.* 他特別強調自己的叔父是位公爵。**a play on 'words** the humorous use of a word or phrase that can have two different meanings 雙關語；語帶雙關 SYN **pun** ➲ more at CALL *v.*, CHILD, STATE *n.*, WORK *n.*

play·able /ˈpleɪəbl/ *adj.* **1** (of a piece of music or a computer game 樂曲或計算機遊戲) easy to play 容易演奏的；容易掌握的 **2** (of a sports field 運動場) in a good condition and suitable for playing on 適於使用的；可用以比賽的 OPP **unplayable**

'play-acting *noun* [U] behaviour that seems to be honest and sincere when in fact the person is pretending 假裝；偽善；演戲 ▸ **'play-act** *verb* [I]：*He thought she was play-acting but in fact she had really hurt herself.* 他以為她是裝出來的，但實際上她真的受了傷。

play·back /ˈpleɪbæk/ *noun* [U, C, usually sing.] the act of playing music, showing a film/movie or listening to a telephone message that has been recorded before; a recording that you listen to or watch again 錄音（或錄像、電話留言等的）播放；（回放的）錄音，錄像

play·bill /ˈpleɪbɪl/ *noun* **1** a printed notice advertising a play 戲劇海報 **2** (*NAmE*) a theatre programme 戲單；戲劇演出節目單

play·boy /ˈpleɪbɔɪ/ *noun* a rich man who spends his time enjoying himself 尋歡作樂的有錢男子；花花公子；紈絝子弟

,play-by-'play *noun* [usually sing.] (*NAmE*) a report on what is happening in a sports game, given as the game is being played 體育比賽現場解說

,played 'out *adj.* [not before noun] (*informal*) no longer having any influence or effect 失去影響（或作用）

play·er 🔑 /ˈpleɪə(r)/ *noun*

1 🔑 a person who takes part in a game or sport 遊戲者；運動員；參賽選手：***a tennis/rugby/chess, etc. player*** 網球、橄欖球、國際象棋等選手 ◇ *a game for four players* 四人玩的遊戲 ◇ *a midfield player* 中場球員 **2** a company or person involved in a particular area of business or politics（商業或政治方面的）參與者，競爭者，玩家：*The company has emerged as a* ***major player*** *in the London property market.* 那家公司已嶄露頭角，成為倫敦物業市場的主要競爭者。➲ see also TEAM PLAYER **3** 🔑 (in compounds 構成複合詞) a machine for reproducing sound or pictures that have been recorded on CDs, etc. 播放機：***a CD/DVD/cassette/record player*** 激光唱片／數字光碟／盒式磁帶／唱片播放機 **4** 🔑 (usually in compounds 通常構成複合詞) a person who plays a musical instrument 演奏者：*a trumpet player* 小號手 **5** (*old-fashioned*) (especially in names 尤用於名稱) an actor 演員：*Phoenix Players present 'Romeo and Juliet'.* 鳳凰劇社獻演《羅密歐與朱麗葉》。

'player piano *noun* a piano that plays automatically by means of a PIANO ROLL 自動鋼琴（用打孔紙捲控制琴鍵）SYN **Pianola**

play·ful /ˈpleɪfl/ *adj.* **1** full of fun; wanting to play 有趣的；愛嬉戲的；愛玩的：*a playful puppy* 頑皮的小狗 **2** (of a remark, an action, etc. 話語、動作等) made or done in fun; not serious 打趣的；鬧着玩的；嬉戲的 SYN **light-hearted**：*He gave her a playful punch on the arm.* 他開玩笑地捶了一下她的胳膊。▸ **play·ful·ly** /-fəli/ *adv.* **play·ful·ness** *noun* [U]

play·goer /ˈpleɪɡəʊə(r); *NAmE* -ɡoʊər/ *noun* = THEATRE-GOER

play·ground /ˈpleɪɡraʊnd/ *noun* **1** an outdoor area where children can play, especially at a school or in a park （尤指學校或公園中的）遊戲場，遊樂場；操場 ➲ VISUAL VOCAB page V57 ➲ compare SCHOOLYARD ➲ see also ADVENTURE PLAYGROUND **2** a place where a particular type of people go to enjoy themselves（某些集體聚會遊樂的）園地，天地，活動場所：*The resort is a playground of the rich and famous.* 這個度假勝地是富翁名流的娛樂場所。

play·group /ˈpleɪɡruːp/ (also **play·school**) (both *BrE*) *noun* [C, U] a place where children who are below school age go regularly to play together and to learn through playing（學齡前兒童的）幼兒遊戲班 ➲ compare NURSERY SCHOOL

play·house /ˈpleɪhaʊs/ *noun* **1** used in names of theatres（用於劇場名稱）劇院：*the Liverpool Playhouse* 利物浦劇院 **2** (*BrE* also **ˈWendy house**) a model of a house large enough for children to play in 遊戲房（供兒童進入玩耍的大模型房子）

play·ing /ˈpleɪɪŋ/ *noun* **1** [U] the way in which sb plays sth, especially a musical instrument（演奏等的）表現，風格：*The orchestral playing is superb.* 這個管弦樂團的演奏棒極了。 **2** [C] the act of playing a piece of music（樂曲）演奏：*repeated playings of the National Anthem* 國歌反複的演奏

ˈplaying card (also **card**) *noun* any one of a set of 52 cards with numbers and pictures printed on one side, which are used to play various card games 紙牌；撲克牌：(*BrE*) *a pack of (playing) cards* 一副紙牌 ◇ (*NAmE*) *a deck of (playing) cards* 一副紙牌 ➲ VISUAL VOCAB page V37

ˈplaying field *noun* a large area of grass, usually with lines marked on it, where people play sports and games 運動場；操場：*the school playing fields* 學校的運動場 IDM see LEVEL *adj.*

play·let /ˈpleɪlət/ *noun* a short play 短劇

play·list /ˈpleɪlɪst/ *noun* a list of all the songs and pieces of music that are played by a radio station or on a radio programme（電台節目的）音樂播放清單

play·maker /ˈpleɪmeɪkə(r)/ *noun* a player in a team game who starts attacks or brings other players on the same side into a position in which they could score 組織進攻的隊員

play·mate /ˈpleɪmeɪt/ *noun* a friend with whom a child plays（兒童）玩耍的夥伴

ˈplay-off *noun* a match/game, or a series of them, between two players or teams with equal points or scores to decide who the winner is（平分後決出勝負的）附加賽：*They lost to Chicago in the play-offs.* 在附加賽中他們負於芝加哥隊。

play·pen /ˈpleɪpen/ *noun* a frame with wooden bars or NETTING that surrounds a small area in which a baby or small child can play safely（幼兒）玩耍護欄

play·room /ˈpleɪruːm; -rʊm/ *noun* a room in a house for children to play in 遊戲室

play·scheme /ˈpleɪskiːm/ *noun* (*BrE*) a project that provides organized activities for children, especially during school holidays（尤指學校放假期間的）組織活動計劃

play·school /ˈpleɪskuːl/ *noun* (*BrE*) = PLAYGROUP

play·suit /ˈpleɪsuːt; *BrE* also -sjuːt/ *noun* **1** a piece of clothing for babies or small children that covers the body, arms and legs 寶寶連身衣；幼兒連褲裝 **2** (*BrE*) a set of clothes that children wear for fun so that they look like a particular person（兒童）模仿套裝：*a Spiderman playsuit* 蜘蛛俠裝扮套裝 **3** a piece of women's underwear that covers the upper body to the tops of the legs（長及大腿根部的）女式連體內衣

play·thing /ˈpleɪθɪŋ/ *noun* **1** a person or thing that you treat like a toy, without really caring about them or it 玩物；玩樂對象：*She was an intelligent woman who refused to be a rich man's plaything.* 她是個有頭腦的女性，拒不肯做富人的玩物。 **2** (*old-fashioned*) a toy 玩具：*The teddy bear was his favourite plaything.* 軟毛玩具熊是他最心愛的玩具。

play·time /ˈpleɪtaɪm/ *noun* [U, C] **1** (*especially BrE*) a time at school when teaching stops for a short time and children can play（學校的）遊戲時間，課間休息時間 **2** a time for playing and having fun 娛樂時間：*With so much homework to do, her playtime is now very limited.* 因為作業太多，她現在的娛樂時間很少。

play·wright /ˈpleɪraɪt/ *noun* a person who writes plays for the theatre, television or radio 劇作家 SYN **drama·tist** ➲ compare SCREENWRITER, SCRIPTWRITER

plaza /ˈplɑːzə; *NAmE* ˈplæzə/ *noun* (*especially NAmE*) **1** a public outdoor square especially in a town where Spanish is spoken（尤指西班牙語城鎮的）露天廣場 **2** a small shopping centre, sometimes also with offices 購物中心：*a downtown shopping plaza* 市中心的購物區

plc /ˌpiː el ˈsiː/ (also **PLC**) *abbr.* (*BrE*) public limited company (used after the name of a company or business) 公開股份有限公司（用於公司、企業名稱之後）：*Lloyd's Bank plc* 勞埃德銀行

plea /pliː/ *noun* **1** (*formal*) an urgent emotional request 請求；懇求：**~ (for sth)** *She made an impassioned plea for help.* 她懇切地求助。◇ **~ (to sb) (to do sth)** *a plea to industries to stop pollution* 請求各個行業停止污染 ◇ *He refused to listen to her tearful pleas.* 他對她聲淚俱下的懇求置之不理。 **2** (*law* 律) a statement made by sb or for sb who is accused of a crime（被告或被告律師的）抗辯，答辯，辯護：*a* ***plea of guilty/not guilty*** 承認／不承認有罪 ◇ *to* ***enter a*** *guilty* ***plea*** 正式表示認罪 **3 ~ of sth** (*law* 律) a reason given to a court for doing or not doing sth（向法庭提供的）理由，藉口，辯解：*He was charged with murder, but got off on a plea of insanity.* 他被指控犯了謀殺罪，但以精神錯亂為由逃過懲罰。

ˈplea-bargain·ing *noun* [U] (*law* 律) an arrangement in court by which a person admits to being guilty of a smaller crime in the hope of receiving less severe punishment for a more serious crime 認罪協商，認罪求情協議，辯訴交易（在法庭上由被告承認輕罪以期減輕刑罰的安排）➲ compare COP A PLEA at COP *v.*, TURN KING'S/QUEEN'S EVIDENCE at EVIDENCE ▸ **ˈplea bargain** *noun*：*He reached a plea bargain with the authorities.* 他和當局達成了辯訴交易。

plead /pliːd/ *verb* (**pleaded**, **pleaded**, *NAmE* also **pled**, **pled** /pled/) **1** [I, T] to ask sb for sth in a very strong and serious way 乞求；懇求 SYN **beg**：**~ (with sb) (to do sth)** *She pleaded with him not to go.* 她懇求他不要離開。◇ **~ (with sb) (for sth)** *I was forced to plead for my child's life.* 我被迫苦苦哀求給我的孩子一條生路。◇ *pleading eyes* 乞求的眼神 ◇ **~ to do sth** *He pleaded to be allowed to see his mother one more time.* 他懇求准許他再看媽媽一眼。◇ **+ speech** *'Do something!' she pleaded.* "幫幫忙吧！"她央求道。 **2** [I, T, no passive] to state in court that you are guilty or not guilty of a crime（在法庭）申辯，認罪，辯護：**(+ adj.)** *to* ***plead guilty/not guilty*** 認罪；不認罪 ◇ *How do you plead?* (= said by the judge at the start of the trial) 你有何辯護？◇ **~ sth** *He advised his client to plead insanity* (= say that he/she was mentally ill and therefore not responsible for his/her actions). 他建議他的當事人以精神不正常作為辯護理由。 **3** [T] **~ sth** to present a case to a court（向法庭）陳述案情：*They hired a top lawyer to plead their case.* 他們聘請了一位頂級律師幫他們陳述案情。**4** [T, no passive] **~ sth (for sth)** | **~ that ...** to give sth as an explanation or excuse for sth 解釋；推說；找藉口：*He pleaded family problems for his lack of concentration.* 他解釋說他不能集中精神是因為有家庭問題。 **5** [T, I] to argue in support of sb/sth 為…辯護；聲援；支持：**~ sth** *She appeared on television to plead the cause of political prisoners everywhere.* 她出現在電視上為所有政治犯聲援請命。◇ **~ for sb/sth** *The United Nations has pleaded for a halt to the bombing.* 聯合國已呼籲停止轟炸。

plead·ing /ˈpliːdɪŋ/ *noun* **1** [C, U] an act of asking for sth that you want very much, in an emotional way 懇求；央求：*He refused to give in to her pleadings.* 他拒不接受她的請求。 **2** [C, usually pl.] (*law* 律) a formal statement

P

of sb's case in court 訴狀；答辯狀 ➲ see also SPECIAL PLEADING

plead·ing·ly /ˈpliːdɪŋli/ *adv.* in an emotional way that shows that you want sth very much but are not certain that sb will give it to you 懇求地；乞求地：*He looked pleadingly at her.* 他以乞求的目光望着她。

pleas·ant 0‑ /ˈpleznt/ *adj.* (**pleas·ant·er**, **pleas·ant·est**) HELP **More pleasant** and **most pleasant** are more common. * more pleasant 和 most pleasant 較常見。**1** 0‑ enjoyable, pleasing or attractive 令人愉快的；可喜的；宜人的；吸引人的：*a pleasant climate/evening/place* 令人愉快的氣候／夜晚／地方◇*What a pleasant surprise!* 這真是一樁令人又驚又喜的事！◇*to live in pleasant surroundings* 生活在宜人的環境中◇*music that is pleasant to the ear* 悅耳的音樂◇*a pleasant environment to work in* 舒適的工作環境◇***It was pleasant** to be alone again.* 又只剩下一個人了，真自在。**2** 0‑ friendly and polite 友好的；和善的；文雅的：*a pleasant young man* 彬彬有禮的年輕人◇*a pleasant smile/voice/manner* 和藹可親的笑容／聲音／態度◇**~ to sb** *Please try to be pleasant to our guests.* 請對我們的客人盡量客氣點。OPP **unpleasant** ▸ **pleas·ant·ly** 0‑ *adv.*：*a pleasantly cool room* 涼爽宜人的房間◇*I was pleasantly surprised by my exam results.* 我的考試成績真讓我喜出望外。◇*'Can I help you?' he asked pleasantly.* "需要幫忙嗎？"他和悅地問道。**pleas·ant·ness** *noun* [U]：*She remembered the pleasantness of the evening.* 她對那個愉快的夜晚記憶猶新。

pleas·ant·ry /ˈplezntri/ *noun* [C, usually pl., U] (*pl.* **-ies**) (*formal*) a friendly remark made in order to be polite 客氣話；客套：*After exchanging the usual pleasantries, they got down to serious discussion.* 互致寒暄之後，他們便開始嚴肅的討論了。

please 0‑ /pliːz/ *exclamation, verb*

■ ***exclamation*** **1** 0‑ used as a polite way of asking for sth or telling sb to do sth（用於客氣地請求或吩咐）請，請問：*Please sit down.* 請坐。◇*Two coffees, please.* 請來兩杯咖啡。◇*Quiet please!* 請安靜！◇*Please could I leave early today?* 請問我今天早走一會兒行嗎？**2** 0‑ used to add force to a request or statement（用於加強請求或陳述的語氣）請千萬，請務必，的確：*Please don't leave me here alone.* 請千萬別把我一個人留在這兒。◇*Please, please don't forget.* 請務必務必不要忘記呀。◇*Please, I don't understand what I have to do.* 我的確不明白我該做什麼。**3** 0‑ used as a polite way of accepting sth（表示接受的客氣話）太感謝了，太好了：*'Would you like some help?' 'Yes, please.'* "您需要幫忙嗎？""是的。太感謝了。"◇*'Coffee?' 'Please.'* "要咖啡嗎？""那太好了。"**4** **Please!** (*informal*, often *humorous*) used to ask sb to stop behaving badly（用於讓別人停止不規矩行為）別鬧了，收斂點兒：*Children, please! I'm trying to work.* 孩子們，別鬧了！我在幹活哪。◇*John! Please!* 約翰！老實點兒吧！**5** **Please/P-lease** /pəˈliːz/ used when you are replying to sb who has said sth that you think is stupid（認為對方說話荒唐時用）得了吧，算了吧：*Oh, please! You cannot be serious.* 喔，得了吧！你準是在打哈哈。

■ ***verb*** **1** 0‑ [T, I] **~ (sb)** | **it pleases sb to do sth** to make sb happy 使滿意；使愉快：*You can't please everybody.* 你無法讓每個人都滿意。◇*He's a difficult man to please.* 他是個難以取悅的人。◇***There's just no pleasing some people*** (= some people are impossible to please). 有些人你是沒法讓他們滿意的。◇*I did it to please my parents.* 我這麼做是要讓父母高興。◇*She's always very eager to please.* 她總是急欲取悅別人。OPP **displease** **2** [I] often used after *as* or *what*, *where*, etc. to mean 'to want', 'to choose' or 'to like' to do sth（常用在 as 或 what、where 等詞後）想，選擇，喜歡：*You may stay as long as you please.* 你想待多久就待多久。◇*She always does exactly as she pleases.* 她總是我行我素。◇*I'm free now to live wherever I please.* 我現在想住哪裏就住哪裏。

IDM **if you ˈplease** **1** (*old-fashioned, formal*) used when politely asking sb to do sth（用於特別表示客氣）請：*Take a seat, if you please.* 請坐吧。**2** (*old-fashioned, especially BrE*) used to say that you are annoyed or surprised at sb's actions（用於對某人的行為表示氣憤或驚異）你們聽聽，豈有此理：*And now, if you please, he wants me to rewrite the whole thing!* 哼！你們聽聽，他竟要我全部重寫！**ˌplease the ˈeye** to be very attractive to look at 十分悅目 **ˌplease ˈGod** used to say that you very much hope or wish that sth will happen（表示殷切期望）但願老天幫忙，上帝保佑：*Please God, don't let him be dead.* 老天爺呀！千萬別讓他死啊。**ˌplease yourˈself** (*informal*) used to tell sb that you are annoyed with them and do not care what they do（表示惱怒和不關心）隨你的便，悉聽尊便：*'I don't think I'll bother finishing this.' 'Please yourself.'* "我想我不會費力做完這件事。""隨你的便。"**ˌplease yourˈself** | **ˌdo as you ˈplease** to be able to do whatever you like 能夠隨心所欲：*There were no children to cook for, so we could just please ourselves.* 因為不用給孩子做飯，我們就可以自便了。

pleased 0‑ /pliːzd/ *adj.*

1 0‑ feeling happy about sth 高興；滿意；愉快：**~ (with sb/sth)** *She was very pleased with her exam results.* 她對考試成績非常滿意。◇*The boss should be pleased with you.* 上司應該對你滿意了。◇**~ (that …)** *I'm really pleased that you're feeling better.* 你覺得好些了，我真高興。◇**~ (to hear, know, etc. sth)** *I'm pleased to hear about your news.* 聽到你的消息我很高興。◇*You're coming? I'm so pleased.* 你要來呀？我太高興了。◇*He did not look too pleased when I told him.* 我告訴他時，他似乎不是很高興。➲ SYNONYMS at GLAD **2** 0‑ **~ to do sth** happy or willing to do sth 高興，樂於（做某事）：*We are always pleased to be able to help.* 我們一向樂意能幫忙。◇*I was **pleased to hear** you've been promoted.* 聽說你高升了，我很高興。◇*Aren't you pleased to see me?* 見到我你不高興嗎？◇(*especially BrE*) ***Pleased to meet you*** (= said when you are introduced to sb). 很高興認識您。◇*Thank you for your invitation, which I am very pleased to accept.* 承蒙邀請，我欣然接受。◇*I am pleased to inform you that the book you ordered has arrived.* 謹此欣然奉告，您所訂的書已到。

IDM **(as) ˌpleased as ˈPunch** (*BrE*) very pleased 稱心滿意；自滿自足 **far from ˈpleased** | **none too ˈpleased** not pleased; angry 不悅；氣憤：*She was none too pleased at having to do it all again.* 工作必須重做，這使她氣憤不已。**only too ˈpleased (to do sth)** very happy or willing to do sth 十分情願，巴不得（做某事）：*We're only too pleased to help.* 我們非常願意幫忙。**ˈpleased with yourself** (often *disapproving*) too proud of sth you have done 自鳴得意；飄飄然：*He was looking very pleased with himself.* 他顯得沾沾自喜。

pleas·ing 0‑ /ˈpliːzɪŋ/ *adj.*

that gives you pleasure or satisfaction 令人高興的；令人滿意的：*a pleasing design* 令人滿意的設計◇**~ to sb/sth** *The new building was **pleasing to the eye**.* 這座新樓真漂亮。➲ SYNONYMS at SATISFYING ▸ **pleas·ing·ly** *adv.*：*She had a pleasingly direct manner.* 她為人直爽，令人愉快。

pleas·ur·able /ˈpleʒərəbl/ *adj.* (*formal*) giving pleasure 愉快的；快活的；適意的 SYN **enjoyable**：*a pleasurable experience* 愉快的經歷◇*We do everything we can to make your trip pleasurable.* 我們會盡力使你的旅途愉快。

pleas·ur·ably /ˈpleʒərəbli/ *adv.* with pleasure 愉快地；怡然：*He sipped his coffee pleasurably.* 他怡然地品味着咖啡。

pleas·ure 0‑ /ˈpleʒə(r)/ *noun*

1 0‑ [U] a state of feeling or being happy or satisfied 高興；快樂；愉快；欣慰；滿意 SYN **enjoyment**：*to read **for pleasure*** 讀書以自娛◇**~ (in sth/in doing sth)** *He **takes** no **pleasure** in his work.* 他從他的工作中得不到絲毫樂趣。◇**~ (of sth/of doing sth)** *She **had the pleasure** of seeing him look surprised.* 看他好像吃了一驚，她感到開心。◇(*formal*) *We request the pleasure of your company at the marriage of our daughter Lisa.* 敬請光臨小女莉薩的婚禮。◇***It gives me great pleasure*** *to introduce our guest speaker.* 我很榮幸來介紹我們的特約演講人。➲ SYNONYMS at FUN **2** 0‑ [U] the activity of enjoying yourself, especially in contrast to working 玩樂；休閒：*Are you in Paris on business or pleasure?* 你來巴黎是公幹還是遊玩？➲ SYNONYMS at ENTERTAINMENT **3** 0‑ [C] a thing that makes you happy or satisfied 樂事；快事：*the pleasure and pains of everyday life* 日常生活的苦與樂

P

◇ *the simple pleasures of the countryside* 鄉村淳樸的樂趣 ◇ ***It's a pleasure** to meet you.* 很高興認識你。◇ *'Thanks for doing that.' **'It's a pleasure.'*** "這事真勞您大駕了。" "不客氣。" ➲ compare DISPLEASURE

IDM **at your/sb's 'pleasure** (*formal*) as you want; as sb else wants 根據你的（或某人的）意願；隨意：*The land can be sold at the owner's pleasure.* 這塊地可隨主人的意願出售。 **my 'pleasure** used as a polite way of replying when sb thanks you for doing sth, to show that you were happy to do it（對別人表示感謝的一種禮貌回答）不客氣，很樂意效勞 **with 'pleasure** 🔑 used as a polite way of accepting or agreeing to sth（客氣地接受或同意）當然了，很願意：*'May I sit here?' 'Yes, with pleasure.'* "我可以坐在這兒嗎？" "當然可以。"

Synonyms 同義詞辨析

pleasure

delight • joy • privilege • treat • honour

These are all words for things that make you happy or bring you enjoyment. 以上各詞均指令人愉快、高興的事。

pleasure a thing that brings you enjoyment or satisfaction 指樂事、快事：*the pleasures and pains of everyday life* 日常生活的苦與樂◇ ***It's been a pleasure** meeting you.* 很高興認識您。

delight a thing or person that brings you great enjoyment or satisfaction 指令人高興的事或人、樂事、樂趣：*the delights of living in the country* 生活在鄉村的樂趣

joy a thing or person that brings you great enjoyment or happiness 指令人高興的事或人、樂事、樂趣：*the joys and sorrows of childhood* 童年的歡樂與悲傷

PLEASURE, DELIGHT OR JOY? 用 pleasure、delight 還是 joy？

A **delight** or **joy** is greater than a **pleasure**; a person, especially a child, can be a **delight** or **joy**, but not a **pleasure**; **joys** are often contrasted with **sorrows**, but **delights** are not. * delight 或 joy 語氣較 pleasure 強。令人高興的人，尤其是孩子，可以是一種 delight 或 joy，但不能是一種 pleasure。joys 常與 sorrows 形成對比，但 delights 無這種對比。

privilege (*rather formal*) something that you are proud and lucky to have the opportunity to do 指榮幸、榮耀、光榮：*It was a great privilege to hear her sing.* 聽她唱歌是莫大的榮幸。

treat (*informal*) a thing that sb enjoyed or is likely to enjoy very much 指樂事、樂趣：*You've never been to this area before? Then you're **in for a real treat**.* 你以前從來沒有到過這一地區？那麼你一定會喜之不盡。

honour/honor (*formal*) something that you are very pleased or proud to do because people are showing you great respect 指榮幸、光榮：*It was a great honour to be invited here today.* 今天承蒙邀請到此，深感榮幸。

PATTERNS

- the pleasures/delights/joys **of** sth
- **It's a** great pleasure/joy **to me that** ...
- **It's a** pleasure/delight/joy/privilege/treat/honour **to do sth**
- **It's a** pleasure/delight/joy **to see/find** ...
- a pleasure/delight/joy **to behold/watch**
- a **real** pleasure/delight/joy/privilege/treat
- a **great** pleasure/joy/privilege/honour
- a **rare** joy/privilege/treat/honour

'pleasure boat (also **'pleasure craft**) *noun* a boat used for short pleasure trips 遊艇；遊船

pleat /pliːt/ *noun* a permanent fold in a piece of cloth, made by sewing the top or side of the fold（布料上縫的）褶

pleat·ed /ˈpliːtɪd/ *adj.* having pleats 打褶的；有褶的：*a pleated skirt* 有褶的裙子

plea·ther /ˈpleðə(r)/ *noun* [U] a plastic material that looks like leather 塑料皮革；人造皮：*a pleather jacket* 塑料皮革上衣 **ORIGIN** From 'plastic' and 'leather'. 源自 plastic 和 leather 的縮合。

pleb /pleb/ *noun* (*disapproving*) an ordinary person, especially one who is poor or not well educated 普通人；（尤指）社會地位低下的人

plebe /pliːb/ *noun* (*US, informal*) a first-year student at a military or NAVAL college in the US（美國軍校）一年級學生，新生

ple·beian /pləˈbiːən/ *adj., noun*

■ ***adj.*** **1** connected with ordinary people or people of the lower social classes 平民的；百姓的；下層社會的 **2** (*disapproving*) lacking in culture or education 粗俗的；俗鄙的：*plebeian tastes* 庸俗的趣味

■ ***noun*** (usually *disapproving*) a person from a lower social class (used originally in ancient Rome) 下層人；平民；庶民 ➲ compare PATRICIAN

pleb·is·cite /ˈplebɪsɪt; -saɪt/ *noun* **~ (on sth)** (*politics* 政) a vote by the people of a country or a region on an issue that is very important 公民投票；全民公決 **SYN** **referendum**：*to **hold a plebiscite** on the country's future system of government* 就國家未來的政府體制舉行公民投票

plebs /plebz/ *noun* (usually **the plebs**) [pl.] (*informal*) an offensive way of referring to ordinary people, especially those of the lower social classes 平頭百姓；市井小民；賤民

plec·trum /ˈplektrəm/ *noun* (*pl.* **plec·trums** or **plec·tra** /-trə/) (also *informal* **pick**) a small piece of metal, plastic, etc. used for PLUCKING the strings of a GUITAR or similar instrument（彈撥琴弦用的）琴撥，撥子

pled (*US*) *past tense, past part.* of PLEAD

pledge /pledʒ/ *noun, verb*

■ ***noun*** **1** a serious promise 保證；諾言；誓約 **SYN** **commitment**：**~ (of sth)** *a pledge of support* 支援的許諾◇ **~ (to do sth)** *Will the government **honour its** election **pledge** not to raise taxes?* 政府會履行其競選諾言，不增加稅收嗎？◇ **~ (that ...)** *Management has **given a pledge** that there will be no job losses this year.* 資方保證今年不會削減工作職位。 **2** a sum of money or sth valuable that you leave with sb to prove that you will do sth or pay back money that you owe 抵押；質錢；抵押品

IDM **sign/take the 'pledge** (*old-fashioned*) to make a promise never to drink alcohol 發誓戒酒

■ ***verb*** **1** [T] to formally promise to give or do sth 保證給予（或做）；正式承諾：**~ sth** *Japan has pledged $100 million in humanitarian aid.* 日本已承諾提供一億元人道主義援助。◇ *The government **pledged their support** for the plan.* 政府保證支持這項計劃。◇ **~ sth to sb/sth** *We all had to **pledge allegiance** to the flag* (= state that we are loyal to our country). 我們都必須對國旗宣誓效忠。◇ **~ to do sth** *The group has pledged to continue campaigning.* 這個組織發誓繼續投入運動。◇ **~ (that)** ... *The group has pledged that they will continue campaigning.* 這個組織發誓他們將繼續投入運動。 **2** [T] to make sb or yourself formally promise to do sth 使保證；使發誓 **SYN** **swear**：**~ sb/yourself (to sth)** *They were all pledged to secrecy.* 他們都宣誓保密。◇ **~ sb/yourself to do sth** *The government has pledged itself to root out corruption.* 政府已承諾剷除腐敗。 **3** [T] **~ sth** to leave sth with sb as a pledge (2) 抵押；典當 **4** [I, T] (*NAmE*) to promise to become a junior member of a FRATERNITY or SORORITY 宣誓參加美國大學生聯誼會：*Do you think you'll pledge this semester?* 這學期你會加入大學生聯誼會嗎？◇ **~ sth** *My brother pledged Sigma Nu.* 我哥哥宣誓加入 Σ NU 聯誼會。

the ˌPledge of Alˈlegiance *noun* [sing.] a formal promise to be loyal to the US, which Americans make standing in front of the flag with their right hand on their heart 宣誓效忠（美國人站在國旗前右手貼左胸宣誓）

plen·ary /ˈpliːnəri/ *adj., noun*

■ ***adj.*** [only before noun] (*formal*) **1** (of meetings, etc. 會議等) to be attended by everyone who has the right to attend 全體參加的：*The new committee holds its first **plenary session** this week.* 新委員會本週舉行第一次全會。 **2** without any limit; complete 無限的；完全的；絕對的：*The Council has plenary powers to administer the agreement.* 理事會擁有全權執行這項協議。

■ ***noun*** (*pl.* **-ies**) a plenary meeting 全體會議；全會

pleni·po·ten·tiary /ˌplenɪpəˈtenʃəri; *NAmE* also -ʃieri/ *noun* (*pl.* **-ies**) (*technical* 術語) a person who has full powers to take action, make decisions, etc. on behalf of their government, especially in a foreign country (尤指在國外代表政府的) 全權代表；全權大使 ▸ **pleni·po·ten·tiary** *adj.*：*plenipotentiary powers* 全權

pleni·tude /ˈplenɪtjuːd; *NAmE* -tuːd/ *noun* [sing., U] (*formal*) a large amount of sth 大量；充裕；眾多 SYN **abundance**

plent·eous /ˈplentiəs/ *adj.* (*literary*) = PLENTIFUL

plen·ti·ful /ˈplentɪfl/ (also **plent·eous**) *adj.* available or existing in large amounts or numbers 大量的；眾多的；充足的；豐富的 SYN **abundant**：*a **plentiful supply** of food* 充足的食物供應 ◇ *In those days jobs were plentiful.* 那時期工作崗位多得很。 ▸ **plen·ti·ful·ly** /-fəli/ *adv.*：*Evidence is plentifully available.* 證據俯拾即是。 ◇ *She kept them plentifully supplied with gossip.* 她不斷向他們散播大量的流言蜚語。

plenty 🔑 /ˈplenti/ *pron., adv., noun, det.*

■ ***pron.*** 🔑 **~ (of sth)** a large amount; as much or as many as you need 大量；眾多；充足：*plenty of eggs/money/time* 充裕的雞蛋／錢／時間 ◇ *'Do we need more milk?' 'No, there's plenty in the fridge.'* "我們要不要再買些牛奶？" "不必了。冰箱裏還多着呢。" ◇ *They always gave us plenty to eat.* 他們總是給我們好多東西吃。 ◇ *We had plenty to talk about.* 我們有說不完的話。 ➲ note at MANY, MUCH

■ ***adv.*** **1** 🔑 **~ more (of) (sth)** a lot 大量；很多：*We have plenty more of them in the warehouse.* 我們倉庫裏這類東西還多得很。 ◇ *There's plenty more paper if you need it.* 你要是需要紙，還有很多。 **2 ~ big, long, etc. enough (to do sth)** (*informal*) more than big, long, etc. enough 足夠有餘：*The rope was plenty long enough to reach the ground.* 這根繩子長及地面依然有餘。 **3** (*NAmE*) a lot; very 非常；十分；很：*We talked plenty about our kids.* 我們談了很多關於孩子的事。 ◇ *You can be married and still be plenty lonely.* 結了婚也可能非常孤寂。 IDM see FISH *n.*

■ ***noun*** [U] (*formal*) a situation in which there is a large supply of food, money, etc. 富裕；充裕：*Everyone is happier **in times of plenty**.* 在富足的歲月裏，每個人都比較快樂。 ◇ *We had food and drink **in plenty**.* 我們的食物和飲料十分充足。

■ ***det.*** (*NAmE* or *informal*) a lot of 很多；大量：*There's plenty room for all of you!* 這裏有足夠的地方容納你們所有人！

ple·num /ˈpliːnəm/ *noun* a meeting attended by all the members of a committee, etc.; a PLENARY meeting (委員會等的) 全體會議，全會

ple·on·asm /ˈpliːənæzəm/ *noun* [U, C] (*technical* 術語) the use of more words than are necessary to express a meaning. For example, 'see with your eyes' is a pleonasm because the same meaning can be expressed using 'see'. 冗筆；冗述；贅述 ▸ **ple·on·as·tic** /ˌpliːəˈnæstɪk/ *adj.*

pleth·ora /ˈpleθərə/ *noun* [sing.] (*formal*) an amount that is greater than is needed or can be used 過多；過量；過剩 SYN **excess**

pleura /ˈplʊərə; *NAmE* ˈplʊrə/ *noun* (*pl.* **pleurae** /-riː/) (*anatomy* 解) one of the two MEMBRANES that surround the lungs 胸膜

pleur·isy /ˈplʊərəsi; *NAmE* ˈplʊr-/ *noun* [U] a serious illness that affects the inner covering of the chest and lungs, causing severe pain in the chest or sides 胸膜炎；肋膜炎

Plexi·glas™ /ˈpleksiglɑːs; *NAmE* -glæs/ (*NAmE*) (*BrE* **Perspex™**) *noun* [U] a strong transparent plastic material that is often used instead of glass 普列克斯玻璃

plexus ➲ SOLAR PLEXUS

pli·able /ˈplaɪəbl/ *adj.* **1** easy to bend without breaking 易彎曲的；柔韌的 SYN **flexible** **2** (of people 人) easy to influence or control 易受影響的；可塑的；容易擺佈的 SYN **impressionable**

pli·ant /ˈplaɪənt/ *adj.* **1** (of a person or their body 人或人體) soft and giving way to sb, especially in a sexual way 綿軟順從的；柔順的：*her pliant body* 她那柔軟的肢體 ◇ *She lay pliant in his arms.* 她順從地偎依在他的懷中。 **2** (sometimes *disapproving*) willing to accept change; easy to influence or control 溫順的；容易擺佈的：*He was deposed and replaced by a more pliant successor.* 他被趕下台，由一個比較容易擺佈的繼任者取代。 ▸ **pli·ancy** /ˈplaɪənsi/ *noun* [U] **pli·ant·ly** *adv.*

pli·ers /ˈplaɪəz; *NAmE* -ərz/ *noun* [pl.] a metal tool with handles, used for holding things firmly and twisting and cutting wire 鉗子；夾鉗：*a pair of pliers* 一把鉗子 ➲ VISUAL VOCAB page V20

plight /plaɪt/ *noun, verb*

■ ***noun*** [sing.] a difficult and sad situation 苦難；困境；苦境：*the plight of the homeless* 無家可歸者的艱難困苦 ◇ *The African elephant is in a desperate plight.* 非洲象正面臨絕境。

■ ***verb***

IDM **plight your 'troth** (*old use* or *humorous*) to make a promise to a person saying that you will marry them; to marry sb 許婚；以身相許

plim·soll /ˈplɪmsəl/ (also **pump**) (both *BrE*) (also **'gym shoe** *BrE, NAmE*) *noun* a light simple sports shoe made of CANVAS (= strong cotton cloth) with a rubber SOLE 橡膠底帆布鞋；體操鞋：*a pair of plimsolls* 一雙體操鞋

'Plimsoll line (also **'load line**) *noun* a line on the side of a ship showing the highest point that the water can safely reach when the ship is loaded (船的) 載重線標誌，國際載重線標誌，吃水線

plinth /plɪnθ/ *noun* a block of stone on which a column or statue stands (雕像或柱子的) 底座，柱基 ➲ VISUAL VOCAB page V14

plod /plɒd; *NAmE* plɑːd/ *verb* (**-dd-**) [I, T] to walk slowly with heavy steps, especially because you are tired 艱難地行走；吃力地行進 SYN **trudge**：**+ adv./prep.** *Our horses plodded down the muddy track.* 我們的馬沿着泥濘小路蹣跚而行。 ◇ *We plodded on through the rain.* 我們冒雨艱難地跋涉。 ◇ **~ your way + adv./prep.** *I watched her plodding her way across the field.* 我注視着她步履艱難地穿過田野。 ▸ **plod** *noun* [sing.]

PHR V **ˌplod aˈlong/ˈon** to make very slow progress, especially with difficult or boring work 進展緩慢 (尤指艱難枯燥的工作) SYN **slog**

plod·der /ˈplɒdə(r); *NAmE* ˈplɑːd-/ *noun* a person who works slowly and steadily but without imagination 幹活慢條斯理而缺乏想像力的人；沉悶苦幹者

plod·ding /ˈplɒdɪŋ; *NAmE* ˈplɑːd-/ *adj.* working or doing sth slowly and steadily, especially in a way that other people think is boring 老牛拖破車似的；做事慎重而呆板的

plonk /plɒŋk; *NAmE* plɑːŋk/ *verb, noun*

■ ***verb*** (*especially BrE*) (*NAmE* usually **plunk**) (*informal*) **1 ~ sth + adv./prep.** to put sth down on sth, especially noisily or carelessly 隨意放下；砰然扔下：*He plonked the books down on the table.* 他嘭地一聲把書籍扔到了桌子上。 ◇ *Just plonk your bag anywhere.* 把你的袋子隨便擱在哪兒吧。 **2 ~ yourself (down)** to sit down heavily or carelessly 重重地坐下；不經意地坐下：*He just plonked himself down and turned on the TV.* 他一屁股坐下來，打開了電視。

■ ***noun*** (*informal, especially BrE*) **1** [U] cheap wine that is not of good quality 廉價劣質酒；便宜酒 **2** [C, usually sing.] a low sound like that of sth heavy falling and hitting a surface (重物落下碰到物體表面發出的) 嘭的聲響，撲通聲：*She sat down with a plonk.* 她撲通一聲坐下來。

plonk·er /ˈplɒŋkə(r); *NAmE* ˈplɑːŋk-/ *noun* (*BrE, slang*) a stupid person 傻子；呆子；笨蛋

plop /plɒp; *NAmE* plɑːp/ *noun, verb*
▪ *noun* [usually sing.] a short sound like that of a small object dropping into water（物體落入水的）撲通聲，咚
▪ *verb* (-pp-) **1** [I] + **adv./prep.** to fall, making a plop 咚地落下：*The frog plopped back into the water.* 青蛙撲通一聲跳回水中。◇ *A tear plopped down onto the page she was reading.* 一滴眼淚啪噠一聲落在她正在讀的書頁上。 **2** [T] **~ sth + adv./prep.** to drop sth into sth, especially a liquid, so that it makes a plop 撲通一聲把…放入（尤指液體）：*Can you just plop some ice in my drink?* 能在我的飲料中放點冰塊嗎？ **3** [T, I] **~ (yourself) (down)** to sit or lie down heavily or in a relaxed way（重重地或懶洋洋地）坐下，躺下

plo·sive /ˈpləʊsɪv; *NAmE* ˈploʊ-/ *noun* (*phonetics* 語音) a speech sound made by stopping the flow of air coming out of the mouth and then suddenly releasing it, for example /t/ and /p/ in *top* 破裂音（如 top 中的 /t/ 和 /p/）▶ **plo·sive** *adj.*

plot 0-w /plɒt; *NAmE* plɑːt/ *noun, verb*
▪ *noun* **1** 0-w [C, U] the series of events that form the story of a novel, play, film/movie, etc. 故事情節；佈局：*a conventional plot about love and marriage* 傳統的婚戀故事情節 ◇ *The book is well organized in terms of plot.* 這本書的故事佈局十分嚴謹。➲ COLLOCATIONS at LITERATURE **2** 0-w [C] **~ (to do sth)** a secret plan made by a group of people to do sth wrong or illegal 陰謀；密謀 SYN **conspiracy** **3** 0-w [C] a small piece of land that is used or intended for a special purpose（專用的）小塊土地：*She bought a small plot of land to build a house on.* 她買了一小塊地蓋所房子。◇ *a vegetable plot* 一塊菜圃 ➲ SYNONYMS at LAND

IDM **ˌlose the ˈplot** (*BrE, informal*) to lose your ability to understand or deal with what is happening 迷惘；不知所措 **the plot ˈthickens** used to say that a situation is becoming more complicated and difficult to understand 情況變得複雜起來
▪ *verb* (-tt-) **1** 0-w [I, T] to make a secret plan to harm sb, especially a government or its leader 密謀；暗中策劃 SYN **conspire**：**~ (with sb) (against sb)** *They were accused of plotting against the state.* 他們被指控密謀叛亂。◇ **~ sth** *Military officers were suspected of plotting a coup.* 人們懷疑軍方在策劃政變。◇ **~ to do sth** *They were plotting to overthrow the government.* 他們在密謀顛覆政府。 **2** [T] **~ sth (on sth)** to mark sth on a map, for example the position or course of sth（在地圖上）畫出，標出：*The earthquake centres had been plotted on a world map.* 地震震中均被標示在一張世界地圖上。 **3** [T] **~ sth (on sth)** to make a diagram or chart from some information 繪製（圖表）：*We carefully plotted each patient's response to the drug on a chart.* 我們仔細繪出了每個病人對這種藥物反應的圖表。 **4** [T] **~ sth (on sth)** to mark points on a GRAPH and draw a line or curve connecting them 繪製（圖表的曲線）：*First, plot the temperature curve on the graph.* 首先，在圖表上繪出溫度曲線來。 **5** [T] **~ sth** to write the plot of a novel, play, etc.（為小說、戲劇等）設計情節，佈局：*a tightly-plotted thriller* 情節絲絲入扣的驚險刺激小說

plot·ter /ˈplɒtə(r); *NAmE* ˈplɑːtər/ *noun* **1** a person who makes a secret plan to harm sb 陰謀家；秘密策劃者 SYN **conspirator** **2** a device that turns data from a computer into a GRAPH, usually on paper（計算機）繪圖儀，描繪器

plough (*NAmE* **plow**) /plaʊ/ *noun, verb*
▪ *noun* **1** [C] a large piece of farming equipment with one or several curved blades, pulled by a TRACTOR or by animals. It is used for digging and turning over soil, especially before seeds are planted. 犁 ➲ see also SNOWPLOUGH *n.* **2 the Plough** (*BrE*) (*NAmE* **the ˌBig ˈDipper**) [sing.] a group of seven bright stars that can only be seen from the northern half of the world 北斗七星；大熊星座

IDM **under the ˈplough** (*BrE, formal*) (of land 土地) used for growing crops, not for keeping animals on 用於耕作的；作農田的 SYN **arable**
▪ *verb* [T, I] **~ (sth)** to dig and turn over a field or other area of land with a plough 犁（田）；耕（地）；翻（土）：*ploughed fields* 犁過的田地 ➲ COLLOCATIONS at FARMING

IDM **ˌplough a lonely, your own, etc., ˈfurrow** (*literary*) to do things that other people do not do, or be interested in things that other people are not interested in 自耕孤疇（指自行其是或自得其樂）

PHR V **ˌplough sth↔ˈback (in/into sth)** | **ˌplough sth ↔back ˈin** **1** to turn over growing crops, grass, etc. with a plough and mix them into the soil to improve its quality 犁埋；使秸稈還田 **2** to put money made as profit back into a business in order to improve it 把（利潤）再投資：*The money was all ploughed back into the company.* 所有的錢都再投資到這個公司。 **ˈplough into sb/sth** (especially of a vehicle or its driver 尤指汽車或司機) to crash violently into sth, especially because you are driving too fast or not paying enough attention 猛撞（尤因開車太快或不小心所致）：*A truck ploughed into the back of the bus.* 一輛卡車猛撞到公共汽車的尾部。 **ˌplough sth ˈinto sth** to invest a large amount of money in a company or project 把（大批資金）投入；大量投資於：*The government has ploughed more than $20 billion into building new schools.* 政府已投放 200 多億元興建新學校。 **ˌplough ˈon (with sth)** to continue doing sth that is difficult or boring 堅持做，繼續進行（艱難或乏味的事）；苦撐：*No one was listening to her, but she **ploughed on regardless**.* 沒有人在聽她講話，但她仍不加理會，喋喋不休。 **ˌplough (your way) ˈthrough sth** **1** to force a way through sth 費勁地穿越（或通過）：*She ploughed her way through the waiting crowds.* 她從等候的人群中擠過去。 **2** (of a vehicle or an aircraft 車輛或飛機) to go violently through sth, out of control 猛衝過；失控地穿過：*The plane ploughed through the trees.* 飛機猛衝過樹林。 **3** to make slow progress through sth difficult or boring, especially a book, a report, etc. 艱難地進行，緩慢地推進（尤指讀書、做報告等）；埋頭苦幹：*I had to plough through dozens of legal documents*. 我得慢慢地埋頭閱讀幾十份法律文件。 **ˌplough sth↔ˈup** **1** to turn over a field or other area of land with a plough to change it from grass, for example, to land for growing crops（用犁）開墾；犁地 **2** to break up the surface of the ground by walking or driving across it again and again 軋翻，碾壞（地面）：*The paths get all ploughed up by motorbikes.* 鄉間小路全讓摩托車給軋壞了。

plough·man (*NAmE* **plow·man**) /ˈplaʊmən/ *noun* (*pl.* **-men** /-mən/) a man whose job is guiding a plough, especially one pulled by animals 扶犁者（尤指畜力拉的犁）

ˌploughman's ˈlunch (also **ˈploughman's**) *noun* (*BrE*) a cold meal of bread, cheese, PICKLE and salad, often served in pubs 農夫午餐（包括麪包、奶酪、泡菜和色拉，常在酒館供應）

plough·share (*NAmE* **plow·share**) /ˈplaʊʃeə(r); *NAmE* -ʃer/ (*NAmE* also **share**) *noun* the broad curved blade of a PLOUGH 犁鏵；鏵 IDM see SWORD

plover /ˈplʌvə(r)/ *noun* a bird with long legs and a short tail that lives on wet ground 千鳥；鴴

plow, **plow·man**, **plow·share** (*NAmE*) = PLOUGH, PLOUGHMAN, PLOUGHSHARE

ploy /plɔɪ/ *noun* words or actions that are carefully planned to get an advantage over sb else 計謀；策略；手法；花招 SYN **manoeuvre**：*a clever marketing ploy* 巧妙的銷售策略 ◇ **~ to do sth** *It was all a ploy to distract attention from his real aims.* 那全是障眼法，藉以轉移對他真實目的的注意。

pluck /plʌk/ *verb, noun*
▪ *verb*
▸ HAIR 毛髮 **1** [T] **~ sth (out)** to pull out hairs with your fingers or with TWEEZERS 摘；拔：*She plucked out a grey hair.* 她拔掉了一根灰白頭髮。◇ *expertly plucked eyebrows* 拔得精巧的眉毛
▸ CHICKEN, ETC. 雞等 **2** [T] **~ sth** to pull the feathers off a dead bird, for example a chicken, in order to prepare it for cooking 拔掉，退去（死禽的毛）
▸ MUSICAL INSTRUMENT 樂器 **3** (*NAmE* also **pick**) [T, I] **~ (at) sth** to play a musical instrument, especially a GUITAR, by pulling the strings with your fingers 彈，彈

P

撥（樂器的弦）： *to pluck the strings of a violin* 彈撥小提琴的弦 ◇ *He took the guitar and plucked at the strings.* 他拿起吉他撥動起琴弦來。

▸ **REMOVE SB/STH 移開人／物 4** [T] **~ sb (from sth) (to sth)** to remove sb from a place or situation, especially one that is unpleasant or dangerous 解救；搭救： *Police plucked a drowning girl from the river yesterday.* 昨天警方從河裏救起了一名溺水少女。◇ *Survivors of the wreck were **plucked to safety** by a helicopter.* 沉船的幸存者被直升機營救脱險。◇ *She was plucked from obscurity to instant stardom.* 她從默默無聞中得到提攜，轉瞬成為明星。 **5** [T] **~ sth (from sth)** to take hold of sth and remove it by pulling it 搶奪： *He plucked the wallet from the man's grasp.* 他搶走了那個男人緊抓着的錢包。

▸ **FRUIT/FLOWER 果；花 6** [T] **~ sth (from sth)** (*old-fashioned* or *literary*) to pick a fruit, flower, etc. from where it is growing 摘；掐；採摘： *I plucked an orange from the tree.* 我從樹上摘了一個橙子。

IDM **pluck sth out of the 'air** to say a name, number, etc. without thinking about it, especially in answer to a question 脱口而出；隨意回答： *I just plucked a figure out of the air and said: 'Would £1 000 seem reasonable to you?'* 我隨口說出一個數字問道："你看 1 000 英鎊合適嗎？" **pluck up (the) 'courage (to do sth)** to make yourself do sth even though you are afraid to do it 鼓起勇氣（做某事）： *I finally plucked up the courage to ask her for a date.* 我終於鼓起勇氣約她出去。

PHR V **'pluck at sth** to hold sth with the fingers and pull it gently, especially more than once 揪；拽；拉；扯 **SYN** **tug** : *The child kept plucking at his mother's sleeve.* 小孩不停地拉扯着他媽媽的衣袖。◇ (*figurative*) *The wind plucked at my jacket.* 風不時地吹動着我的上衣。

■ **noun** [U] (*informal*) courage and determination 膽識；膽量；意志： *It takes a lot of pluck to do what she did.* 她這麼做需要很大的膽量。

plucky /'plʌki/ *adj.* (*informal*) (**pluck·ier**, **plucki·est**) having a lot of courage and determination 勇敢的；有膽量的；剛毅的 **SYN** **brave** ▸ **pluck·ily** *adv.*

plugs 插頭；塞子

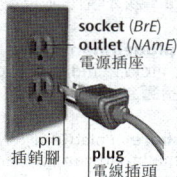

tap (*especially BrE*) (*NAmE usually* faucet) 水龍頭
socket (*BrE*) outlet (*NAmE*) 電源插座
plug 塞子
sink 洗滌池
pin 插銷腳
plug 電線插頭

plug /plʌg/ *noun, verb*

■ **noun**

▸ **ELECTRICAL EQUIPMENT 電氣設備 1** a small plastic object with two or three metal pins, that connects a piece of electrical equipment to the main supply of electricity 插頭： *a three-pin plug* 三相插頭 ◇ *I'll have to **change the plug** on my hairdryer.* 我必須更換吹風機的插頭。 **2** (*informal, especially BrE*) a small opening in a wall, by which you connect a piece of electrical equipment to the main supply of electricity（電源）插座 **SYN** **socket** : *Can I use this plug for my iron?* 我能用這個插座插熨斗嗎？ **3** a small object that connects a wire from one piece of electrical equipment to an opening in another 連接插頭： *the plug from the computer to the printer* 連接電腦和打印機的插頭

▸ **IN ENGINE 發動機 4** = SPARK PLUG

▸ **IN BATH/SINK 浴缸；水池 5** a thick round piece of plastic, rubber or metal that you put in the hole in a bath/BATHTUB or a SINK to stop the water flowing out 塞子： *She **pulled out the plug** and let the water drain away.* 她拔起塞子放掉了水。 ➲ SYNONYMS at LID ➲ VISUAL VOCAB page V24

▸ **IN HOLE 洞 6** a round piece of material that fits into a hole and blocks it 堵塞物；塞子： *She took the plug of cotton wool from her ear.* 她從耳朵中取出棉毛耳塞來。 ➲ see also EARPLUG **7** (*NAmE*) = STOPPER ➲ SYNONYMS at LID

▸ **FOR SCREW 螺絲 8** a small plastic tube that you put into a hole in a wall so that it will hold a screw 螺釘楔子；螺釘塞栓（塞入洞中用來固定螺絲的小塑料管）

▸ **FOR BOOK/MOVIE 書籍；電影 9** (*informal*) praise or attention that sb gives to a new book, film/movie, etc. in order to encourage people to buy or see it 推銷；宣傳： *He managed to get in a plug for his new book.* 他設法為自己的新書插入了一條宣傳信息。 **IDM** see PULL *v.*

■ **verb** (-gg-)

▸ **FILL HOLE 堵洞 1 ~ sth (up)** to fill a hole with a substance or piece of material that fits tightly into it 堵塞；封堵： *He plugged the hole in the pipe with an old rag.* 他用一塊破布把管子上的那個洞塞住了。

▸ **PROVIDE STH MISSING 彌補不足 2 ~ sth** to provide sth that has been missing from a particular situation and is needed in order to improve it 補足；補充；供給： *A cheaper range of products was introduced to **plug the gap** at the lower end of the market.* 推出相對廉價的一系列產品是為了填補較低端市場的缺口。

▸ **BOOK/MOVIE 書籍；電影 3 ~ sth** (*informal*) to give praise or attention to a new book, film/movie, etc. in order to encourage people to buy or see it 推廣；宣傳 **SYN** **promote** : *She came on the show to plug her latest album.* 她上電視節目宣傳新唱片專輯。

▸ **SHOOT 射擊 4 ~ sb** (*old-fashioned, NAmE, informal*) to shoot sb 射擊；射殺

PHR V **,plug a'way (at sth)** to continue working hard at sth, especially sth that you find difficult 堅持不懈地做（尤指困難的工作） **,plug sth↔'in | ,plug sth 'into sth** 🔑 to connect a piece of electrical equipment to the main supply of electricity or to another piece of electrical equipment 接通（電源）；把（插頭）插進（插座）： *Is the printer plugged in?* 打印機接上電源沒有？ **OPP** **unplug** **,plug sth 'into sth 1** = TO PLUG STH IN **2** to connect a computer to a computer system 把（計算機）聯網： *All our computers are plugged into the main network.* 我們所有的電腦都和主網絡聯網了。 **,plug 'into sth 1** (of a piece of electrical equipment 電器) to be able to be connected to the main supply of electricity or to another piece of electrical equipment 能與（電源或其他電器）連接： *The DVD player plugs into the back of the television.* * DVD 播放機在電視機的後部連接。 **2** to become involved with a particular activity or group of people 參與；加入： *The company has doubled its profits since plugging into lucrative overseas markets.* 自從這家公司進入賺錢的海外市場以後，利潤翻了一番。

,Plug and 'Play *noun* [U] (*computing* 計) a system that makes it possible for a piece of equipment, such as a printer, to be connected to a computer and to work immediately, without the user needing to do anything 即插即用系統 ▸ **,plug-and-'play** *adj.* : *plug-and-play peripherals* 即插即用式外圍設備

plug·hole /'plʌghəʊl; *NAmE* -hoʊl/ (*BrE*) (*US* **drain**) *noun* a hole in a bath/BATHTUB, SINK, etc. where the water flows away and into which a plug fits（水池、浴缸等的）排水孔，漏眼，滲水孔 ➲ VISUAL VOCAB page V24

IDM **(go) down the 'plughole** (*BrE*) = (GO) DOWN THE DRAIN at DRAIN *n.*

'plug-in *adj., noun*

■ **adj.** [only before noun] **1** able to be connected using a plug 可插入插頭的；插入式的： *a plug-in kettle* 電源插入式水壺 **2** (*computing* 計) able to be added to a computer system so that it can do more things 插入（以擴展功能）的；外掛的： *a plug-in graphics card* 插入式圖形卡

■ **noun 1** (*computing* 計) a piece of computer software that can be added to a system so that it can do more things 插件；外掛程式 **2** (*CanE*) a connection to an electricity supply in a garage, etc. so that you can use an electric HEATER to warm the engine of a car, so that it starts more easily（連接車庫等電源的）發動機預熱器接線

ˌplug-ˈugly *adj.* (*informal*) very ugly 極醜陋的；很難看的

plum /plʌm/ *noun, adj.*

▪ ***noun*** **1** [C] a soft round fruit with smooth red or purple skin, sweet flesh and a large flat seed inside 李子；梅子：*a plum tree* 李樹 **2** [U, C] a dark reddish-purple colour 紫紅色

▪ ***adj.*** [only before noun] (of a job, etc. 工作等) considered very good and worth having 稱心的；值得擁有的：*She's landed a plum job at the BBC.* 她在英國廣播公司謀得稱心如意的工作。

plum·age /ˈpluːmɪdʒ/ *noun* [U] the feathers covering a bird's body（鳥的）全身羽毛

plumb /plʌm/ *verb, adv.*

▪ ***verb*** **~ sth** (*literary*) to try to understand or succeed in understanding sth mysterious 探索；鑽研；探究 **SYN** **fathom**：*She spent her life plumbing the mysteries of the human psyche.* 她畢生探索人類心靈的奧秘。

IDM **plumb the depths of sth** to be or to experience an extreme example of sth unpleasant 陷入（痛苦等的）深淵；深入…深處：*His latest novel plumbs the depths of horror and violence.* 他的最新小說簡直是充斥着極端恐怖和暴力的代表作。◇ *The team's poor performances* ***plumbed new depths*** *last night when they lost 10-2.* 昨晚這個隊的糟糕表現達到了新低紀錄，以 2:10 輸掉了。

PHR V **ˌplumb sth↔ˈin** (*especially BrE*) to connect a WASHING MACHINE, toilet, etc. to the water supply in a building 把（洗衣機、馬桶等）與水管連接

▪ ***adv.*** **1** (used before prepositions 用於介詞前) exactly 恰恰；正好：*He was standing plumb in the middle of the road.* 他站在路正中間。 **2** (*old-fashioned, NAmE, informal*) completely 完全；徹底：*He's plumb crazy.* 他徹底瘋了。

plumb·er /ˈplʌmə(r)/ *noun* a person whose job is to fit and repair things such as water pipes, toilets, etc. 水暖工；管子工；鉛管工

plumb·ing /ˈplʌmɪŋ/ *noun* [U] **1** the system of pipes, etc. that supply water to a building（建築物的）管路系統，自來水管道 ➲ COLLOCATIONS at DECORATE **2** the work of a plumber 水暖工的工作

ˈplumb line *noun* a piece of thick string with a weight attached to one end, used to find the depth of water or to test whether a wall, etc. is straight（測水深或垂直面用的）重錘線，鉛垂線

plume /pluːm/ *noun* **1** a cloud of sth that rises and curves upwards in the air 飄升之物：*a plume of smoke* 一縷青煙 **2** a large feather 翎；羽毛：*a black hat with an ostrich plume* 飾有一根鴕鳥羽毛的黑帽子 **3** a group of feathers or long thin pieces of material tied together and often used as a decoration（常用作飾物的）連在一起的羽毛，羽狀物；羽飾 ➲ see also NOM DE PLUME

plumed /pluːmd/ *adj.* having or decorated with a plume or plumes 有羽毛的；用羽毛裝飾的：*a plumed helmet* 一副羽飾頭盔

plum·met /ˈplʌmɪt/ *verb* [I] to fall suddenly and quickly from a high level or position 暴跌；速降 **SYN** **plunge**：*Share prices plummeted to an all-time low.* 股票價格暴跌到歷史最低點。◇ *Her spirits plummeted at the thought of meeting him again.* 一想到又要見到他，她的心情便直往下沉。◇ *The jet plummeted into a row of houses.* 那架噴氣式飛機一頭栽進一排房子裏。

plummy /ˈplʌmi/ *adj.* **1** (*BrE, informal, usually disapproving*) (of a voice 嗓音) having a sound that is typical of upper-class English people 拿腔拿調的；做作的：*a plummy accent* 一副矯揉造作的腔調 **2** like a PLUM in colour, taste, etc.（顏色、味道等）像梅子的

plump /plʌmp/ *adj., verb*

▪ ***adj.*** (**plump·er, plump·est**) **1** having a soft, round body; slightly fat 豐腴的；微胖的：*a short, plump woman* 一個矮胖的女人 ◇ *a plump face* 飽滿的面龐 **2** looking soft, full and attractive to use or eat 鬆軟的；豐滿的；飽滿的：*plump cushions* 鬆軟的墊子 ◇ *plump tomatoes* 滾圓的番茄 ▶ **plump·ness** *noun* [U]

▪ ***verb*** **~ sth (up)** to make sth larger, softer and rounder 使變大變鬆軟；使蓬鬆：*He leaned forward while the nurse plumped up his pillows.* 他往前夠了夠身子，讓護士把枕頭拍鬆了。

PHR V **ˈplump for sb/sth** (*informal*) to choose sb/sth from a number of people or things, especially after thinking carefully 慎重挑選；篩選

ˌplum ˈpudding *noun* [U, C] (*old-fashioned, BrE*) = CHRISTMAS PUDDING

ˌplum toˈmato *noun* an Italian tomato that is long and thin, rather than round（意大利）李形番茄

plun·der /ˈplʌndə(r)/ *verb, noun*

▪ ***verb*** [I, T] to steal things from a place, especially using force during a time of war（尤指戰亂時用武力）搶劫，掠奪 **SYN** **loot**：*The troops crossed the country, plundering and looting as they went.* 部隊經過鄉村，一路搶劫擄掠。◇ **~ sth (of sth)** *The abbey had been plundered of its valuables.* 寺院的珍寶被洗劫一空。◇ **~ sth (from sth)** *Only a small amount of the money that he plundered from his companies has been recovered.* 他從公司搜刮的錢只有一小部份被追回。➲ compare PILLAGE ▶ **plun·der·er** *noun*

▪ ***noun*** [U] **1** the act of plundering 搶掠；掠奪 **2** things that have been stolen, especially during a war, etc.（尤指戰爭中）掠奪的財物 ➲ compare PILLAGE

plunge /plʌndʒ/ *verb, noun*

▪ ***verb*** **1** [I, T] to move or make sb/sth move suddenly forwards and/or downwards 使突然前衝（或下落）：**+ adv./prep.** *She lost her balance and plunged 100 feet to her death.* 她沒有站穩，從 100 英尺的高處跌下摔死了。◇ **~ sb/sth + adv./prep.** *The earthquake plunged entire towns over the edge of the cliffs.* 地震將整座整座的城鎮掀到懸崖之下。 **2** [I] (of prices, temperatures, etc. 價格、溫度等) to decrease suddenly and quickly 暴跌；驟降；突降 **SYN** **plummet**：*Stock markets plunged at the news of the coup.* 政變的消息一傳來，股票市場便暴跌。 **3** [I] **+ adv./prep.** (of a road, surface, etc. 道路、表面等) to slope down steeply 陡峭地向下傾斜：*The track plunged down into the valley.* 小路陡然而下，直插山谷。 **4** [I] to move up and down suddenly and violently（劇烈）顛簸，震盪：*The horse plunged and reared.* 馬猛然躍起，用後腿直立。◇ (*figurative*) *His heart plunged* (= because of a strong emotion). 他的心怦怦亂跳。

PHR V **ˌplunge ˈin | ˌplunge ˈinto sth** **1** to jump into sth, especially with force（尤指用力地）投入，跳進：*The pool was declared open and eager swimmers plunged in.* 游泳池剛剛宣佈開門，游泳的人就急切地跳入池中。 **2** to start doing sth in an enthusiastic way, especially without thinking carefully about what you are doing 熱情投入；貿然行動：*She was about to plunge into her story when the phone rang.* 她剛要開始大談她的經歷，電話響了。◇ *He's always plunging in at the deep end* (= becoming involved in difficult situations without being well enough prepared). 他總是貿然行動，屢屢捲入困境。 **ˌplunge sth ˈin | ˌplunge sth ˈinto sth** to push sth quickly and with force into sth else 猛力插入；扎進：*She plunged the knife deep into his chest.* 她把刀子深深地刺進他的胸膛。 **ˌplunge ˈinto sth** **1** = PLUNGE IN **2** to experience sth unpleasant 經歷，陷入（不快的事）：*The country plunged deeper into recession.* 那個國家進一步陷入經濟蕭條之中。 **ˌplunge sb/sth ˈinto sth** to make sb/sth experience sth unpleasant 使經歷，使陷入（不快的事情）：*The news plunged them into deep depression.* 這條消息立即使他們深感沮喪。◇ *There was a flash of lightning and the house was* ***plunged into darkness.*** 雷電閃過，房子陷入一片黑暗之中。

▪ ***noun*** [usually sing.] **1** a sudden movement downwards or away from sth 突然跌落；突然分離 **SYN** **drop**：*The calm water ends there and the river begins a headlong plunge.* 平靜的河水突然中斷，開始奔騰直瀉而下。 **2** **~ (in sth)** a sudden decrease in an amount or the value of sth（價格、數量的）暴跌，猛降，驟減 **SYN** **drop**：*a dramatic plunge in profits* 利潤銳減 **3** **~ into sth** the act of becoming involved in a situation or activity 捲入；參與：*The company is planning a deeper plunge into the commercial market.* 這家公司正計劃進一步投入商業市場。 **4** an act of jumping or DIVING into water; a quick swim 跳水；快速游泳：*He took the plunge into the deep end.* 他跳入深水區。◇ *She went for a plunge.* 她去游泳了。

P

IDM **take the 'plunge** (*informal*) to decide to do sth important or difficult, especially after thinking about it for a long time（尤指深思熟慮後）果斷行事，毅然決定

'plunge pool *noun* a small deep artificial pool filled with cold water, especially one that you jump into in order to get cooler after a SAUNA（尤指沐完桑拿浴後跳入的）冷水池

plun·ger /ˈplʌndʒə(r)/ *noun* **1** a part of a piece of equipment that can be pushed down 柱塞；活塞 ➲ VISUAL VOCAB page V25 **2** a piece of equipment used for clearing kitchen and bathroom pipes, that consists of a rubber cup fixed to a handle（疏通管道用的）搋子

plun·ging /ˈplʌndʒɪŋ/ *adj.* [only before noun] (of a dress, BLOUSE, etc. 連衣裙、女襯衫等) cut in a deep V shape at the front 低領的；凹領的；深開領的：*a plunging neckline* 深開式領口

plunk /plʌŋk/ *verb* (*informal*) **1** **~ sth + adv./prep.** (*NAmE*) = PLONK：*He plunked the package down on the desk.* 他把包裹砰地撂到桌子上。 **2** **~ sth** to play a GUITAR, a keyboard, etc. with your fingers and produce a rough unpleasant sound 彈撥，刮奏（吉他、琴鍵等） ▸ **plunk** *noun*：*the plunk, plunk of the banjo* 班卓琴咚咚的弦聲

PHR V **'plunk down sth** to pay money for sth, especially a large amount 重金買下；付錢買

plu·per·fect /ˌpluːˈpɜːfɪkt; *NAmE* -ˈpɜːrf-/ *noun* (*grammar* 語法) = PAST PERFECT

plural /ˈplʊərəl; *NAmE* ˈplʊrəl/ *noun, adj.*

■ ***noun*** (*grammar* 語法) (*abbr.* **pl.**) a form of a noun or verb that refers to more than one person or thing（名詞或動詞的）複數，複數形式：*The plural of 'child' is 'children'.* * child 一詞的複數形式是 children。◇ *The verb should be **in the plural**.* 這個動詞應該用複數形式。➲ compare SINGULAR *n.*

■ ***adj.*** **1** (*grammar* 語法) (*abbr.* **pl.**) connected with or having the plural form 複數的；複數形式的：*Most plural nouns in English end in 's'.* 英語中多數複數名詞以 s 結尾。 **2** relating to more than one 多樣的；多元的：*a plural society* (= one with more than one RACIAL, religious, etc. group) 多元社會

P

plur·al·ism /ˈplʊərəlɪzəm; *NAmE* ˈplʊr-/ *noun* [U] (*formal*) **1** the existence of many different groups of people in one society, for example people of different races or of different political or religious beliefs 多元化，多元性（不同種族、不同政治或宗教信仰的多種群體共存）：*cultural pluralism* 文化的多元性 **2** the belief that it is possible and good for different groups of people to live together in peace in one society 多元主義（不同群體可以有益地在同一社會中和平共處的主張） **3** (*usually disapproving*) the fact of having more than one job or position at the same time, especially in the Church 兼職，兼任神職（指同時擔任兩個或以上的職務）

plur·al·ist /ˈplʊərəlɪst; *NAmE* ˈplʊr-/ *adj., noun*

■ ***adj.*** (also **plur·al·is·tic** /ˌplʊərəˈlɪstɪk; *NAmE* ˌplʊr-/) **1** (of a society 社會) having many different groups of people and different political parties in it 多元性的；多元化的：*a pluralist democracy* 多元化的民主 **2** (*philosophy* 哲) not based on a single set of principles or beliefs 多元主義的；多元論的：*a pluralist approach to politics* 多元主義的政治手段

■ ***noun*** **1** a person who believes that it is possible and good for different groups of people to live together in peace in our society 多元主義者（認為社會中不同群體可以有益地和平共處的人） **2** a person who has more than one job or position at the same time, especially in the Church 兼職者；（尤指）兼任神職者（同時擔任兩個或以上的職務）

plur·al·ity /plʊəˈræləti; *NAmE* plʊˈr-/ *noun* (*pl.* **-ies**) **1** [C, usually sing.] (*formal*) a large number 眾多；大量：*a plurality of influences* 眾多的影響 **2** [C, usually sing.] (*politics* 政) (*US*) the number of votes given to one person, political party, etc. when this number is less than 50% but more than any other single person, etc. receives（未超過半數的）最多數票：*In order to be elected, a candidate needs only a plurality of the votes cast.* 候選人只需要得票最多就能當選。➲ compare MAJORITY (3) **3** [U] (*grammar* 語法) the state of being plural 複數

plur·al·ize (*BrE* also **-ise**) /ˈplʊərəlaɪz; *NAmE* ˈplʊrə-/ *verb* **~ sth** to make a word plural 使（單詞）成複數；使構成複數 ▸ **plur·al·iza·tion** /ˌplʊərəlaɪˈzeɪʃn; *NAmE* ˌplʊrələˈzeɪʃn/ *noun* [U]

plus[1] **AW** /plʌs/ *prep., noun, adj., conj.*

■ ***prep.*** **1** used when the two numbers or amounts mentioned are being added together 加：*Two plus five is seven.* 二加五等於七。◇ *The cost is £22, plus £1 for postage.* 費用為 22 英鎊，另加 1 英鎊的郵費。 **2** as well as sth/sb; and also 和；也；外加：*We have to fit five of us plus all our gear in the car.* 我們五人和全部用具都得塞進車裏。**OPP** **minus**

IDM **plus or 'minus** used when the number mentioned may actually be more or less by a particular amount 或多或少；左右；大約 **SYN** **give or take**：*The margin of error was plus or minus three percentage points.* 誤差幅度在三個百分點左右。

■ ***noun*** **1** (*informal*) an advantage; a good thing 優勢；好處；長處：*Knowledge of French is a plus in her job.* 通曉法文使她在工作中佔優勢。◇ *There were a lot of pluses in the performance.* 這次演出有多處值得嘉許。**2** (also **'plus sign**) the symbol (+), used in mathematics 加號：*He put a plus instead of a minus.* 他填了個加號而不是減號。**OPP** **minus**

■ ***adj.*** **1** used after a number to show that the real number or amount is more than the one mentioned（在數字後）多，餘：*The work will cost £10 000 plus.* 這項工作將耗資萬餘英鎊。 **2** above zero 零度以上；零上：*The temperature is plus four degrees.* 溫度為零上四度。**OPP** **minus** **3** [only before noun] used to describe an aspect of sth that you consider to be a good thing 優點的；好的：*One of the hotel's **plus points** is that it is very central.* 那個旅館的優勢之一是它處於市中心。◇ ***On the plus side**, all the staff are enthusiastic.* 好的方面是職員的工作熱忱都很高。**OPP** **minus** **4** [not before noun] (used in a system of marks/grades 用於評分或評等級) slightly higher than the mark/grade A, B, etc. 略高於（A、B 等）：*I got B plus (B+) in the test.* 我考試得了個 B+。**OPP** **minus**

■ ***conj.*** (*informal*) used to add more information 而且；此外；況且 **SYN** **furthermore**：*I've got too much on at work. Plus my father is not well.* 我工作負擔太重了，而且我父親身體也不好。

plus[2] /pluː/

IDM **plus ça change** /ˌpluː sæ ˈʃɒ̃ʒ; *NAmE* -sɑː ˈʃɑːnʒ/ (*saying, from French*) used as a way of saying that people and situations never really change over time, although they may appear to 變來變去還是老樣子；表面雖變本質猶存

ˌplus 'fours *noun* [pl.] (*BrE*) wide loose trousers/pants that end just below the knees, where they fit closely, and that used to be worn, for example, by men playing GOLF（過膝下四英寸的）燈籠褲；寬大運動褲：*a pair of plus fours* 一條燈籠褲

plush /plʌʃ/ *noun, adj.*

■ ***noun*** [U] a type of silk or cotton cloth with a thick soft surface made of a mass of threads（絲或棉的）長毛絨：*red plush armchairs* 紅色長毛絨扶手椅

■ ***adj.*** (*informal*) very comfortable; expensive and of good quality 舒適的；豪華的 **SYN** **luxurious**：*a plush hotel* 豪華的旅館

ˌplus-'minus *adv.* (*SAfrE*) (used when you are giving a figure that is not exact) approximately（表示數字不十分準確）大約，差不多：*'How many people were there?' 'Plus-minus thirty.'* "當時有多少人？" "三十人上下。"

Pluto /ˈpluːtəʊ; *NAmE* -toʊ/ *noun* one of a number of round objects in space that are not as large as planets but which go around the sun. In August 2006, the International Astronomical Union declared that Pluto should be called a DWARF PLANET because it is smaller and has different characteristics from the other planets in our SOLAR SYSTEM; in 2008 it declared that DWARF PLANETS further from the sun than Neptune could also be called plutoids. 冥王星（比行星小但圍繞太陽旋轉的星體之一。2006 年 8 月，國際天文學聯合會宣佈應將其

稱為矮行星，因為它比我們太陽系的其他行星小，而且有着不同的特點。2008 年，國際天文學聯合會宣佈較海王星離太陽更遠的矮行星也可稱為類冥矮行星。）

plu·toc·racy /pluːˈtɒkrəsi; *NAmE* -ˈtɑːk-/ *noun* (*pl.* **-ies**) **1** [U] government by the richest people of a country 富豪統治；財閥當政 **2** [C] a country governed by the richest people in it 富豪統治的國家

plu·to·crat /ˈpluːtəkræt/ *noun* (often *disapproving*) a person who is powerful because of their wealth 有錢有勢的人；財閥

plu·toid /ˈpluːtɔɪd/ *noun* any DWARF PLANET that is further from the sun than the planet Neptune 類冥矮行星（指比海王星更遠離太陽的矮行星）

plu·to·nium /pluːˈtəʊniəm; *NAmE* -ˈtoʊ-/ *noun* [U] (*symb.* **Pu**) a chemical element. Plutonium is RADIOACTIVE and is used in nuclear weapons and in producing nuclear energy. 鈈（放射性化學元素）

ply /plaɪ/ *verb, noun*

■ ***verb*** (**plies**, **ply·ing**, **plied**, **plied**) **1** [I, T] (*literary* or *IndE*) (of ships, buses, etc. 船、公共汽車等) to travel regularly along a particular route or between two particular places 定時往來；定期行駛：**+ adv./prep.** *Ferries ply across a narrow strait to the island.* 渡船定時穿越狹窄的海峽駛向海島。◇ *Buses ply regularly to and from these places.* 公交車定時往返於這些地方。◇ **~ sth** *canals plied by gondolas and steam boats* 有小划船和蒸汽船往來的運河 **2** [T] **~ sth** (*formal*) to use a tool, especially in a skilful way （嫻熟地）使用：*The tailor delicately plied his needle.* 裁縫精巧地飛針走線。

IDM **ply your ˈtrade** to do your work or business 從事工作；做事 **ply for ˈhire/ˈtrade/ˈbusiness** (*BrE*) to look for customers, passengers, etc. in order to do business 招徠顧客；等生意：*taxis plying for hire outside the theatre* 在劇院外招攬乘客的出租車

PHR V **ˈply sb with sth** **1** to keep giving sb large amounts of sth, especially food and/or drink 持續大量提供（食物、飲料等） **2** to keep asking sb questions 不停地提問：*He plied me with questions from the moment he arrived.* 他一到就不斷地向我提問題。

■ ***noun*** [U] (especially in compounds 尤用於構成複合詞) a measurement of wool, rope, wood, etc. that tells you how thick it is （毛線、繩子、木板等的計量單位）股，層，厚：*four-ply knitting yarn* 四股毛線

Ply·mouth Breth·ren /ˌplɪməθ ˈbreðrən/ *noun* [pl.] a strict Protestant group started in England around 1830 普利茅斯兄弟會（約 1830 年成立於英格蘭的嚴格的基督教新教派別）

ply·wood /ˈplaɪwʊd/ *noun* [U] board made by sticking thin layers of wood on top of each other 膠合板；壓合板；夾板：*plywood furniture* 膠合板傢具

PM /ˌpiː ˈem/ *noun* (*informal, especially BrE*) the abbreviation for 'prime minister' 首相，總理（全寫為 prime minister）：*an interview with the PM* 對首相的訪問

p.m. 🔑 (*NAmE* also **P.M.**) /ˌpiː ˈem/ *abbr.* after 12 o'clock NOON (from Latin 'post meridiem') 下午，午後（源自拉丁文 post meridiem）：*The appointment is at 3 p.m.* 約會定於下午 3 點。➲ compare A.M.

PMP /ˌpiː em ˈpiː/ *noun* the abbreviation for 'portable media player' (a piece of equipment that stores and plays sound and pictures) 便攜式媒體播放器，PMP 播放器（全寫為 portable media player，用於貯存與播放聲音和圖像）

PMS /ˌpiː em ˈes/ (*BrE*) (also **PMT** /ˌpiː em ˈtiː/ *NAmE, BrE*) *noun* [U] physical and emotional problems such as pain and feeling depressed that many women experience before their PERIOD (= flow of blood) each month. PMS/PMT are abbreviations for 'premenstrual syndrome/tension'. 月經前綜合症，月經前緊張（全寫為 premenstrual syndrome 及 premenstrual tension）➲ see also PREMENSTRUAL

pneu·mat·ic /njuːˈmætɪk; *NAmE* nuː-/ *adj.* [usually before noun] **1** filled with air 充氣的：*a pneumatic tyre* 充氣輪胎 **2** worked by air under pressure 由壓縮空氣操作的；氣動的；風動的：*pneumatic tools* 風動工具

pneuˌmatic ˈdrill (*BrE*) (*NAmE* **jack·ham·mer**) *noun* a large powerful tool, worked by air pressure, used especially for breaking up road surfaces 風鑽

pneu·mo·nia /njuːˈməʊniə; *NAmE* nuːˈmoʊ-/ *noun* [U] a serious illness affecting one or both lungs that makes breathing difficult 肺炎

PO /ˌpiː ˈəʊ; *NAmE* ˈoʊ/ *abbr.* **1** POST OFFICE 郵局 ➲ see also PO BOX **2** POSTAL ORDER

poach /pəʊtʃ; *NAmE* poʊtʃ/ *verb* **1** [T] **~ sth** to cook food, especially fish, gently in a small amount of liquid 水煮，燉，煨（尤指魚）：*poached salmon* 清燉鮭魚 **2** [T] **~ sth** to cook an egg gently in nearly boiling water after removing its shell 水煮（去殼的蛋） **3** [T, I] **~ (sth)** to illegally hunt birds, animals or fish on sb else's property or without permission （在他人地界）偷獵，偷捕：*The elephants are poached for their tusks.* 為獲取象牙而偷獵大象。 **4** [T, I] **~ (sb/sth)** (**from sb/sth**) to take and use sb/sth that belongs to sb/sth else, especially in a secret, dishonest or unfair way 盜用；挖走（人員等）：*The company poached the contract from their main rivals.* 這家公司竊取了其主要競爭對手的合同。◇ *Several of our employees have been poached by a rival firm.* 我們公司有好幾名職員被對手公司給挖走了。◇ *I hope I'm not* ***poaching on your territory*** (= doing sth that is actually your responsibility). 但願我沒有侵犯你的職權。

poach·er /ˈpəʊtʃə(r); *NAmE* ˈpoʊtʃ-/ *noun* **1** a person who illegally hunts birds, animals or fish on sb's else's property 偷獵者；非法捕獵的人 **2** a special pan for POACHING eggs 水煮荷包蛋鍋 **3** (also **ˈgoal poacher**) (especially in football (SOCCER) 尤指足球) a player who waits near the opposite team's goal in order to try to score if they get the ball （在對方球門附近伺機進球的）偷襲球員

IDM **poacher turned ˈgamekeeper** (*especially BrE*) a person who has changed from one situation or attitude to the opposite one, especially sb who used to oppose people in authority but is now in a position of authority 經過角色轉換的人；當年造反今天掌權的人

ˌP'O box (also **ˈpost office box**) *noun* used as a kind of address, so that mail can be sent to a post office where it is kept until it is collected 郵政信箱：*Radio Netherlands, PO Box 222, Hilversum* 希爾弗瑟姆郵政信箱 222 號，荷蘭廣播電台

P

pocked /pɒkt; *NAmE* pɑːkt/ *adj.* having holes or hollow marks on the surface （表面）有洞的，有坑的 **SYN** pitted

pocket 🔑 /ˈpɒkɪt; *NAmE* ˈpɑːk-/ *noun, verb*

■ ***noun***

▸ **IN CLOTHING 衣服** **1** 🔑 a small piece of material like a small bag sewn into or onto a piece of clothing so that you can carry things in it 衣袋；口袋；兜：*a coat pocket* 上衣口袋 ◇ *I put the note in my pocket.* 我把紙幣裝進了衣袋。◇ ***Turn out your pockets*** (= empty your pockets). 把口袋裏的東西通通拿出來。◇ *Take your hands out of your pockets!* 不要把手插在口袋裏！◇ *a pocket dictionary* (= one that is small enough to fit in your pocket) 袖珍詞典 ➲ VISUAL VOCAB page V63

▸ **SMALL CONTAINER 小容器** **2** 🔑 a small bag or container fastened to sth so that you can put things in it, for example, in a car door or in a bag （附在車門上、提包內等的）小口袋，小容器：*Information about safety procedures is in the pocket in front of you* (= on a plane). 安全求生的資料放在您前方的小袋子裏。

▸ **MONEY 錢** **3** [usually sing.] used to talk about the amount of money that you have to spend 錢財；財力；資金：*We have holidays to* ***suit every pocket****.* 我們有適合各種程度消費的度假方式。◇ *He had no intention of paying for the meal* ***out of his own pocket****.* 他不想自己掏腰包付飯錢。◇ *The Foundation is reputed to have very* ***deep pockets*** (= to have a lot of money). 據說這個基金會資金雄厚。

▸ **SMALL GROUP/AREA 小團體／範圍** **4** a small group or area that is different from its surroundings （與周圍不同的）小組織，小區域：*There are still a few isolated pockets of resistance to the new regime.* 現在仍有零星個

別的勢力反對新政權。◇ *a pocket of air* 氣阱 ➲ see also AIR POCKET

▸ **IN BILLIARDS, ETC.** 枱球等 **5** any of the holes or nets around the edges of the table used in the games of BILLIARDS, POOL or SNOOKER, which you have to hit the ball into 球袋；網袋 ➲ **VISUAL VOCAB** page V40

IDM **be in sb's 'pocket** to be controlled or strongly influenced by sb 受某人的控制（或極大影響）；在某人掌握之中 **be/live in each other's 'pockets** (*BrE*) if two people are **in each other's pockets**, they are too close to each other or spend too much time with each other 過從甚密；形影不離 **have sb in your 'pocket** to have influence or power over sb, for example, a police officer or a politician, especially by threatening them or by offering them money 駕馭，讓…聽使喚（尤指通過恐嚇或賄賂） **have sth in your 'pocket** to be certain to win sth 勝利在握；穩操勝券 **ˌin/ˌout of 'pocket** (*especially BrE*) having gained/lost money as a result of sth 得到 / 損失錢財：*That one mistake left him thousands of pounds out of pocket.* 那一次失誤讓他損失了數千英鎊。➲ compare OUT-OF-POCKET ➲ more at BURN *v.*, DIP *v.*, HAND *n.*, LINE *v.*, PICK *v.*

■ ***verb***

▸ **PUT INTO POCKET** 放入衣袋 **1 ~ sth** to put sth into your pocket 把…放進衣袋：*She paid for the drink and pocketed the change without counting it.* 她付了飲料費，把找回的零錢數都沒數就裝進了口袋。

▸ **MONEY** 錢 **2 ~ sth** to take or keep sth, especially an amount of money, that does not belong to you 攫取；揩油；中飽私囊：*He regularly charges passengers more than the normal fare and pockets the difference.* 他經常多收乘客票錢，把差額塞進自己的腰包。 **3 ~ sth** to earn or win an amount of money 掙；賺下：*Last year, she pocketed over $1 million in advertising contracts.* 去年，她從廣告合同中賺了 100 多萬元。

▸ **IN BILLIARDS, ETC.** 枱球等 **4 ~ sth** (in the games of BILLIARDS, POOL and SNOOKER 枱球、普爾和斯諾克) to hit a ball into a POCKET *n.* (5) 擊（球）入球袋 **SYN** **pot**

pock·et·book /ˈpɒkɪtbʊk; *NAmE* ˈpɑːk-/ *noun* **1** (*NAmE*) used to refer to the financial situation of a person or country. (In the past it was a small flat case for carrying papers or money.)（個人或國家的）財政狀況，財力，錢袋子：*Many foreign goods are too expensive for American pocketbooks.* 許多外國貨都太貴，與一般美國人的財力不符。◇ *The increase is likely to hit the pocketbooks of consumers.* 提價可能會砸到消費者的錢袋子。 **2** (*especially BrE*) a small book for writing in 記事本；小筆記本 **SYN** **notebook 3** (*old-fashioned, NAmE*) = HANDBAG

pock·et·ful /ˈpɒkɪtfʊl; *NAmE* ˈpɑːk-/ *noun* the amount a pocket holds 一衣袋（的量）：*a pocketful of coins* 一衣袋硬幣

pock·et·knife /ˈpɒkɪtnaɪf; *NAmE* ˈpɑːk-/ *noun* (*especially NAmE*) = PENKNIFE

ˈpocket money *noun* [U] **1** (*especially BrE*) (also **al·low·ance** especially in *NAmE*) a small amount of money that parents give their children, usually every week or every month（父母給孩子的）零花錢 **2** a small amount of money that you can spend on things you need or want 零用錢；小額私用款 ➲ compare SPENDING MONEY

ˈpocket-sized (also **ˈpocket-size**) *adj.* small enough to fit into your pocket or to be carried easily 袖珍的；便攜的

ˌpocket ˈveto *noun* (in the US) a method by which the President can stop a new law from being introduced by not signing it and keeping it until a session of Congress has finished 擱置否決（美國總統阻止新法律實施的一種方法，即不予簽字並將其保留至國會休會後）

pock·mark /ˈpɒkmɑːk; *NAmE* ˈpɑːkmɑːrk/ *noun* a hollow mark on the skin, often caused by disease or infection（皮膚上的）麻點，麻坑

ˈpock-marked *adj.* covered with hollow marks or holes 有麻子的；佈滿坑洞的：*a pock-marked face* 一張麻子臉 ◇ *The district is pock-marked with caves.* 這個地區佈滿了坑洞。

pod /pɒd; *NAmE* pɑːd/ *noun* **1** a long thin case filled with seeds that develops from the flowers of some plants, especially PEAS and BEANS 莢；莢果：*a pea pod* 豌豆莢 ◇ *a vanilla pod* 香子蘭蒴果 ➲ **VISUAL VOCAB** pages V31, V32 **2** a long narrow container that is hung under an aircraft and used to carry fuel, equipment, weapons, etc.（飛機的）吊艙，發射架 **3** part of a SPACECRAFT or a boat that can be separated from the main part 分離艙 **4** [C] a small group of sea animals, such as DOLPHINS or WHALES, swimming together（海豚或鯨等海洋動物的）一群：*a pod of adult dolphins* 一群成年海豚

pod·cast /ˈpɒdkɑːst; *NAmE* ˈpɑːdkæst/ *noun* a recording of a radio broadcast or a video that can be taken from the Internet 播客：*To listen to the podcast, click on the link below.* 點擊下面的鏈接收聽播客。➲ **COLLOCATIONS** at EMAIL ▸ **pod·caster** *noun*：*The US has an estimated 60 million podcasters.* 美國約有 6 000 萬播客發佈者。 **pod·cast·ing** *noun* [U]：*Podcasting could turn into an audio form of blogging.* 播客製作可變成博客的有聲形式。

podgy /ˈpɒdʒi; *NAmE* ˈpɑːdʒi/ (*BrE*) (also **pudgy** *NAmE, BrE*) *adj.* (*informal*, usually *disapproving*) slightly fat 微胖的：*podgy arms* 胖乎乎的胳膊

po·dia·trist /pəˈdaɪətrɪst/ *noun* (*especially NAmE*) = CHIROPODIST

po·dia·try /pəˈdaɪətri/ *noun* [U] (*especially NAmE*) = CHIROPODY

po·dium /ˈpəʊdiəm; *NAmE* ˈpoʊ-/ *noun* **1** a small platform that a person stands on when giving a speech or CONDUCTING an ORCHESTRA, etc. 講台；講壇；（樂隊的）指揮台 **SYN** **rostrum 2** (*NAmE*) = LECTERN

Po·dunk /ˈpəʊdʌŋk; *NAmE* ˈpoʊ-/ *adj.* (*US, informal*) (of a town 小鎮) small, dull and not important 無生氣的；無足輕重的 **ORIGIN** From a place name of southern New England. 源自新英格蘭南部地名波敦克。

poem 0‑ᵂ /ˈpəʊɪm; *NAmE* ˈpoʊəm/ *noun* a piece of writing in which the words are chosen for their sound and the images they suggest, not just for their obvious meanings. The words are arranged in separate lines, usually with a repeated rhythm, and often the lines RHYME at the end. 詩；韻文 ➲ **COLLOCATIONS** at LITERATURE

poesy /ˈpəʊəzi; -si; *NAmE* ˈpoʊ-/ *noun* [U] (*literary*) poetry 詩；詩篇

poet /ˈpəʊɪt; *NAmE* ˈpoʊət/ *noun* a person who writes poems 詩人

poet·ess /ˌpəʊɪˈtes; *NAmE* ˌpoʊəˈtes/ *noun* (*old-fashioned*) a woman who writes poems 女詩人

poet·ic /pəʊˈetɪk; *NAmE* poʊ-/ (also *less frequent* **poet·ical** /-ɪkl/) *adj.* **1** [only before noun] connected with poetry; being poetry 詩歌的；詩的：*poetic language* 詩歌語言 ◇ *Byron's Poetical Works* 拜倫詩作 **2** (*approving*) like or suggesting poetry, especially because it shows imagination and deep feeling 像詩一般的；富有詩意的 **SYN** **lyrical**：*There is a poetic quality to her playing.* 她的演奏富有詩意。 **IDM** see LICENCE ▸ **poet·ic·al·ly** /-kli/ *adv.*

poˌetic ˈjustice *noun* [U] a situation in which sth bad happens to sb, and you think that this is what they deserve 報應；應得的懲罰

poˌetic ˈlicence (*NAmE* **poˌetic ˈlicense**) *noun* [U] the freedom to change facts, the normal rules of language, etc. in a special piece of writing or speech in order to achieve a particular effect（寫作或演講中的）破格修辭法，破格用語

poet·ics /pəʊˈetɪks; *NAmE* poʊ-/ *noun* [U] **1** the art of writing poetry 詩歌寫作；詩藝 **2** the study of poetry, literature, etc. 詩學

ˌPoet ˈLaureate *noun* **1** (especially in Britain) a person who has been officially chosen to write poetry for the country's important occasions 桂冠詩人（尤指英國正式選定為國家重要場合賦詩者） **2** (*especially NAmE*) a person whose poetry is considered to be the best, or most typical of their country or region（某國或地區的）最傑出詩人，代表詩人

poet·ry 🔑 /ˈpəʊətri; *NAmE* ˈpoʊ-/ *noun*
1 🔑 [U] a collection of poems; poems in general 詩集；詩歌；詩作 SYN **verse**：*epic/lyric/pastoral, etc. poetry* 史詩、抒情詩、田園詩等 ◇ *Maya Angelou's poetry* 瑪雅•安吉羅的詩作 ◇ *a poetry reading* 詩歌朗誦 ➲ COLLOCATIONS at LITERATURE ➲ compare PROSE **2** [U, sing.] (*approving*) a beautiful and elegant quality 美好的品質；優雅的氣質；詩意：*There was poetry in all her gestures.* 她一舉一動都很優美。

po-faced /ˈpəʊ feɪst; *NAmE* ˈpoʊ/ *adj.* (*BrE, informal, disapproving*) looking very serious and as though you do not approve of sb/sth 一本正經的；不以為然的；孤傲的；板着臉的

pogo stick /ˈpəʊgəʊ stɪk; *NAmE* ˈpoʊgoʊ/ *noun* a pole with a bar to stand on and a spring at the bottom, that you jump around on for fun 蹦蹦蹺；彈簧單高蹺

pog·rom /ˈpɒgrəm; *NAmE* ˈpoʊg-/ *noun* the organized killing of large numbers of people, because of their race or religion (originally the killing of Jews in Russia) 大屠殺，集體迫害（因種族或宗教原因，原指俄國對猶太人的殺戮）

poign·ant /ˈpɔɪnjənt/ *adj.* having a strong effect on your feelings, especially in a way that makes you feel sad 令人沉痛的；悲慘的；酸楚的 SYN **moving**：*a poignant image/moment/memory, etc.* 悲慘的形象、時刻、回憶等 ◇ *Her face was a **poignant reminder** of the passing of time.* 她的容顏顯示青春已逝，教人感傷。 ▶ **poign·ancy** /-jənsi/ *noun* [U]：*the poignancy of parting and separation* 別離的痛苦 ◇ *Of particular poignancy was the photograph of their son with his sisters, taken the day before he died.* 特別令人感傷的是他們的兒子去世前一天和姐妹們的合影。 **poign·ant·ly** /-jəntli/ *adv.*

poin·set·tia /ˌpɔɪnˈsetiə/ *noun* a tropical plant with large red or pink leaves that grow to look like flowers, often grown indoors in pots 一品紅；猩猩木

point 🔑 /pɔɪnt/ *noun, verb*

■ **noun**

▸ **OPINION/FACT** 看法；事實 **1** 🔑 [C] a thing that sb says or writes giving their opinion or stating a fact 論點；觀點；見解：*She **made** several interesting **points** in the article.* 她在文章中提出了幾個有趣的觀點。◇ ***I take your point*** (= understand and accept what you are saying). 我贊同你的看法。◇ *He's just saying that to **prove a point*** (= to show his idea is right). 他那樣説只是為了證明他的看法。◇ *OK, you've **made your point**!* 好了，你已經把話説清楚了！ ➲ see also TALKING POINT

▸ **MAIN IDEA** 要點 **2** 🔑 [C] (usually **the point**) the main or most important idea in sth that is said or done 重點；要點；核心問題：***The point is** you shouldn't have to wait so long to see a doctor.* 關鍵是看病不該等那麼長時間。◇ *I wish he would **get to the point*** (= say it quickly). 但願他快點説正題。◇ *I'll **come straight to the point**: we need more money.* 我就直説吧：我們還需要錢。◇ *Do you **see my point*** (= understand)? 你明白我的意思嗎？◇ *I think **I missed the point*** (= did not understand). 我想我沒聽懂。◇ *You **have a point*** (= your idea is right)—*it would be better to wait till this evening.* 你説的有道理，還是等到今天晚上比較好。◇ *'There won't be anywhere to park.' 'Oh, **that's a** (**good**) **point*** (= I had not thought of that).' "會找不到地方停車。" "嗯，還真是。" ◇ *It just isn't true. That's **the whole point*** (= the only important fact). 最重要的是，那根本不是事實。◇ *'He's been married before.' '**That's beside the point*** (= not important).' "他結過婚。" "那不重要。" ◇ *I know it won't cost very much but **that's not the point*** (= not the important thing). 我知道那花不了多少錢，但這不是重點。

▸ **PURPOSE** 目的 **3** 🔑 [U, sing.] the purpose or aim of sth 意圖；目的；理由：*What's the point of all this violence?* 這些暴行的意圖何在？◇ *There's **no point** in getting angry.* 發火是沒有用的。◇ ***I don't see the point of** doing it all again.* 我就不明白，再做一次有什麼意義。◇ *The point of the lesson is to compare the two countries.* 本課的目的是比較這兩個國家。 ➲ SYNONYMS at PURPOSE

▸ **DETAIL** 細節 **4** 🔑 [C] a particular detail or fact 具體細節（或事實）：*Here are the **main points** of the news.* 以下是新聞摘要。◇ *Can you explain that point again?* 你能再解釋一下那一點嗎？

▸ **QUALITY** 素質 **5** 🔑 [C] a particular quality or feature that sb/sth has 特點；特性；特徵：*Tact is not one of her **strong points**.* 她不善於圓通處事。◇ *Read the manual to learn the program's **finer points*** (= small details). 讀一下指南，以瞭解這一程序的細節。◇ *Living in Scotland **has its good points** but the weather is not one of them.* 在蘇格蘭生活有其優點，但天氣不好。◇ *One of the hotel's **plus points*** (= good features) *is that it is very central.* 這個旅館的一大優點是它處於市中心。 ➲ see also SELLING POINT

▸ **TIME** 時間 **6** 🔑 [C] a particular time or stage of development 時刻；關頭；瞬間；階段：*The climber was **at/on the point of** death when they found him.* 當他們發現那個登山者的時候，他已奄奄一息。◇ *We were **on the point of** giving up.* 我們當時幾乎要放棄了。◇ *Many people suffer from mental illness **at some point** in their lives.* 許多人在人生的某個階段都會得精神病。◇ *We had **reached the point** when there was no money left.* 我們曾落到身無分文的地步。◇ ***At this point in time** we just have to wait.* 到這種時刻，我們只好等待了。◇ ***At this point** I don't care what you decide to do.* 到這個時候，我不在乎你決定要怎麼做了。 ➲ see also HIGH POINT, LOW POINT, SATURATION POINT, STARTING POINT, STICKING POINT, TURNING POINT

▸ **PLACE** 地方 **7** 🔑 [C] a particular place or area 某地方；地點：*I'll wait for you at the meeting point in the arrivals hall.* 我將在入境大廳的迎接處等你。◇ *the point at which the river divides* 河流分叉點 ◇ *Draw a line from point A to point B.* 從 A 點到 B 點畫一條線。◇ *No parking beyond this point.* 請勿越界停車。 ➲ SYNONYMS at PLACE ➲ see also FOCAL POINT, JUMPING-OFF POINT, THREE-POINT TURN, VANISHING POINT, VANTAGE POINT

▸ **DIRECTION** 方向 **8** [C] one of the marks of direction around a COMPASS（羅盤上的）羅經點，方位點：*the points of the compass* (= N, S, E, W, etc.) 羅盤上的羅經點

▸ **IN COMPETITION** 競賽 **9** 🔑 [C] (*abbr.* **pt**) an individual unit that adds to a score in a game or sports competition 得分；點：*to **win/lose a point*** 贏／輸一分 ◇ *Australia finished 20 points ahead.* 澳大利亞隊終局領先 20 分。◇ *They won **on points*** (= by scoring more points rather than by completely defeating their opponents). 他們以點數取勝。 ➲ see also BROWNIE POINT, MATCH POINT

▸ **MEASUREMENT** 計量 **10** [C] a mark or unit on a scale of measurement（單位）點；標度：*The party's share of the vote fell by ten percentage points.* 該黨的得票率下跌了十個百分點。 ➲ see also BOILING POINT, FREEZING POINT, MELTING POINT

▸ **SHARP END** 尖兒 **11** 🔑 [C] the sharp thin end of sth 尖端；尖頭：*the point of a pencil/knife/pin* 鉛筆／刀／大頭針尖 ➲ VISUAL VOCAB page V26 ➲ see also BALL-POINT, GUNPOINT, KNIFEPOINT

▸ **LAND** 土地 **12** [C] (also **Point**) a narrow piece of land that stretches into the sea 岬角；尖地；海角：*The ship sailed around the point.* 那條船繞過了岬角。◇ *Pagoda Point* 寶塔角

▸ **PUNCTUATION** 標點 **13** [C] a small dot used in writing, especially the dot that separates a whole number from the part that comes after it 小數點；點：*two point six* (2.6) 二點六 ◇ *a decimal point* 小數點 ◇ *We broadcast on ninety-five point nine* (95.9) *FM.* 我們以調頻 95.9 播音。 ➲ see also BULLET POINT, FULL STOP *n.*

▸ **OF LIGHT/COLOUR** 光；色 **14** [C] a very small dot of light or colour 光點；色點：*The stars were points of light in the sky.* 天空中的點點光亮就是星星。

▸ **FOR ELECTRICITY** 電 **15** [C] (*BrE*) a place in a wall, etc. where a piece of equipment can be connected to electricity（電源）插座：*a **power/shaver/telephone point*** 電源／剃鬚刀／電話插座

▸ **IN BALLET** 芭蕾舞 **16 points** [pl.] = POINTE

▸ **ON RAILWAY TRACK** 鐵軌 **17 points** [pl.] (*BrE*) (*NAmE* **switch** [C]) a piece of track at a place where a railway/railroad line divides that can be moved to allow a train to change tracks 道岔；尖軌；轉轍器

▸ **SIZE OF LETTERS** 字符大小 **18** [U] a unit of measurement for the size of letters in printing or on a computer screen, etc.（印刷物或計算機屏幕上字體大小的單位）點，磅值：*Change the text to 10 point.* 把文本字體大小變為 10 點。

P

IDM **if/when it comes to the ˈpoint** used when you have to decide sth or say what you really think 必須做決定（或亮明觀點）時： *When it comes to the point, he always changes his mind.* 他總是臨時變卦。 **in point of ˈfact** used to say what is true in a situation 實際上；其實： *In point of fact, she is their adopted daughter.* 實際上，她是他們的養女。 **make a ˈpoint of doing sth** to be or make sure you do sth because it is important or necessary（因重要或必要）保證做，必定做： *I made a point of closing all the windows before leaving the house.* 我離家前必定要把所有的窗子都關好。 **ˌmore to the ˈpoint** used to say that sth is more important than sth else 更為重要的是： *I couldn't do the job—I've never been to Spain and, more to the point, I don't speak Spanish.* 這個工作我做不了——我從未去過西班牙；而更重要的是，我不會說西班牙語。 **on point** (*NAmE*) appropriate or relevant to the situation 適合的；相關的；相符的： *The quotation was directly on point.* 這段話引用得恰到好處。◇ *Let's stay on point.* 咱們不要偏離主題。 **ˌpoint of ˈcontact** a place where you go or a person that you speak to when you are dealing with an organization 聯繫地點；聯繫人： *The receptionist is the first point of contact most people have with the clinic.* 多數人與診所接觸的第一個人是接待員。 **a ˌpoint of deˈparture** **1** a place where a journey starts 出發點 **2** (*formal*) an idea, a theory or an event that is used to start a discussion, an activity, etc. 拋磚引玉的事物；起點 **a ˌpoint of ˈhonour** a thing that sb considers to be very important for their honour or reputation 事關名譽的大事 **the ˌpoint of ˌno reˈturn** the time when you must continue with what you have decided to do, because it is not possible to get back to an earlier situation 欲罷不能的時刻；已無退路；不可能回頭 **ˌpoint ˈtaken** used to say that you accept that sb else is right when they have disagreed with you or criticized you（接受相反的意見）同意，好吧，算你有理： *Point taken. Let's drop the subject.* 好吧。咱們就拋開這個話題吧。 **to the ˈpoint** expressed in a simple, clear way without any extra information or feelings 簡明恰當；簡潔中肯 **SYN** **pertinent**： *The letter was short and to the point.* 這封信簡短扼要。 **to the ˈpoint of (doing) sth** to a degree that can be described as sth 達到某種程度；近乎： *He was rude to the point of being aggressive.* 他粗魯到蠻不講理的地步。 **up to a (certain) ˈpoint** to some extent; to some degree but not completely 在某種程度上： *I agree with you up to a point.* 我在某種程度上同意你的看法。 ➲ more at BELABOUR, CASE *n.*, FINE *adj.*, LABOUR *v.*, MOOT *adj.*, SCORE *v.*, SORE *adj.*, STRETCH *v.*

■ *verb*

▸ **SHOW WITH FINGER** 用手指示意 **1** 🔑 [I, T, no passive] to stretch out your finger or sth held in your hand towards sb/sth in order to show sb where a person or thing is（用手指頭或物體）指，指向： **~ (at/to/towards sb/sth)** *'What's your name?' he asked, pointing at the child with his pen.* 他用筆指着小孩問："你叫什麼名字？"◇ *He pointed to the spot where the house used to stand.* 他指出那所房子原來所在的地方。◇ *She pointed in my direction.* 她指向我這邊。◇ *It's rude to point!* 用手指人很不禮貌啊！◇ **~ sth** *She pointed her finger in my direction.* 她指着我這個方向。

▸ **AIM** 瞄準 **2** 🔑 [T] **~ sth (at sb/sth)** to aim sth at sb/sth 瞄準： *He pointed the gun at her head.* 他舉槍對準了她的頭。

▸ **FACE DIRECTION** 朝向 **3** 🔑 [I] **+ adv./prep.** to face in or be directed towards a particular direction 對着；朝向： *The telescope was pointing in the wrong direction.* 望遠鏡對錯了方向。◇ *The signpost pointed straight ahead.* 路標直指前方。◇ *A compass needle points north.* 羅盤指針指向北方。

▸ **LEAD TO** 指引 **4** [I, T] to lead to or suggest a particular development or logical argument（意思上）指向；引導；指引： **+ adv./prep.** *The evidence seems to point in that direction.* 證據似乎指向那個方向。◇ **~ the way + adv./prep.** *The fans are looking to the new players to point the way to victory.* 球迷都在指望新球員打出勝利之路。

▸ **SHOW THE WAY** 指路 **5** [T] to show sb which way to go 指路；指點： **~ sb + adv./prep.** *I wonder if you could point me in the right direction for the bus station.* 請問您能指點我到公共汽車站往哪個方向走嗎？◇ **~ the way + adv./prep.** *A series of yellow arrows pointed the way to reception.* 連續的黃色箭頭標出往接待站的路。

▸ **WALL** 牆壁 **6** [T] **~ sth** to put MORTAR between the bricks of a wall（用灰泥）抹磚縫，勾縫

IDM **point a/the ˈfinger (at sb)** to accuse sb of doing sth 指責： *The article points an accusing finger at the authorities.* 那篇文章譴責了當局。

PHR V **ˌpoint sb/sth↔ˈout (to sb)** 🔑 to stretch your finger out towards sb/sth in order to show sb which person or thing you are referring to 指（給某人）看： *I'll point him out to you next time he comes in.* 他下次來的時候，我指給你看。 **ˌpoint ˈout (to sb) | ˌpoint sth↔ˈout (to sb)** 🔑 to mention sth in order to give sb information about it or make them notice it（向某人）指出： *She tried in vain to point out to him the unfairness of his actions.* 她試圖向他指出他的做法不公正，但無濟於事。◇ *He pointed out the dangers of driving alone.* 他指出單獨駕車的危險性。◇ **~ that …** *I should point out that not one of these paintings is original.* 我應當指出，這些畫中沒有一幅是真跡。◇ **+ speech** *'It's not very far,' she pointed out.* "那裏不太遠。"她說道。 ➲ LANGUAGE BANK at ARGUE **ˈpoint to sth** **1** to mention sth that you think is important and/or the reason why a particular situation exists 提出，指出（重要的事或理由）： *The board of directors pointed to falling productivity to justify their decision.* 董事會指出生產率下降一事為其決策辯護。 **2** to suggest that sth is true or likely 暗示；預示： *All the signs point to a successful year ahead.* 一切跡象都預示着來年將一帆風順。 **ˌpoint sth↔ˈup** (*formal*) to emphasize sth so that it becomes more noticeable 強調；明確顯示 **SYN** **highlight**： *The conference merely pointed up divisions in the party.* 這次會議只是顯現了該黨內部的分歧。

ˌpoint-and-ˈclick *adj.* [usually before noun] (*computing* 計) able to be used with a mouse 可用鼠標的；可點擊的

ˌpoint-and-ˈshoot *adj.* (of a camera 照相機) easy to use, without a person needing to adjust controls on it "傻瓜"型的；全自動的

ˌpoint-ˈblank *adj.* [only before noun] **1** (of a shot 射擊) fired with the gun touching or very close to the person or thing it is aimed at 挨着的；近身的；近距離的： *The officer was shot dead* **at point-blank range**. 這位軍官被近距離開槍打死。 **2** (of sth that is said 說的話) very definite and direct and not very polite 直截了當（缺乏禮貌）的 **SYN** **blunt**： *a point-blank refusal* 斷然拒絕 ▸ **ˌpoint-ˈblank** *adv.*： *She fired point-blank at his chest.* 她抵住他的胸口開了槍。◇ *He refused point-blank to be photographed.* 他斷然拒絕被拍照。

ˈpoint duty *noun* [U] (*BrE*) the job of controlling traffic that is done by a police officer standing in the middle of the road（交通警察）值勤，指揮交通： *to be on point duty* 指揮交通

pointe /pwæt/ *noun* [U] (also **pointes** /pwæt/, **points** [pl.]) the hard tops of the toes of a kind of shoe that a BALLET dancer balances on（芭蕾舞鞋的）硬鞋尖

point·ed 🔑 /ˈpɔɪntɪd/ *adj.*
1 🔑 having a sharp end 尖的；有尖頭的： *a pointed chin* 尖下巴◇ *pointed teeth* 尖尖的牙齒◇ *a pointed instrument* 銳器 ➲ see also POINTY **2** aimed in a clear and often critical way against a particular person or their behaviour 尖銳的；尖刻的；明確的： *a pointed* **comment/remark** 一針見血的評論／說話◇ *His words were a pointed reminder of her position.* 他刻意提醒了她的身分。

point·ed·ly /ˈpɔɪntɪdli/ *adv.* in a way that is clearly intended to show what you mean or to express criticism 明確地；尖銳地；直言不諱地： *She yawned and looked pointedly at her watch.* 她打了個哈欠，又刻意地看了看手錶。

point·er /ˈpɔɪntə(r)/ *noun* **1** (*informal*) a piece of advice 提示；建議： *Here are some pointers on how to go about the writing task.* 關於這項寫作任務，以下有幾點建議。 **2 ~ (to sth)** a sign that sth exists; a sign that shows how sth may develop in the future 標誌；跡象；兆頭；動向：*The surge in car sales was regarded as an encouraging pointer to an improvement in the economy.* 汽車銷售量的激增被視為經濟回升的指標。 **3** a thin strip of metal that points to the numbers on a DIAL on a piece of equipment for measuring sth（刻度盤的）指針 **4** a stick used to point to things on a map or picture on a wall 指示杆 **5** (*computing* 計) a small symbol, for example an arrow, that marks a point on a computer screen 指針（光標）**6** a large dog used in hunting, trained to stand still with its nose pointing towards the birds that are being hunted 指示犬（經訓練用以指示獵物等）

'pointer finger *noun* (*NAmE*) a child's word for the INDEX FINGER（兒語）食指

'point guard *noun* (in BASKETBALL 籃球) the player who directs the team's attacking players（球隊進攻的）控球後衛，組織後衛

poin·til·lism /'pɔɪntɪlɪzəm; 'pwænt-/ *noun* [U] a style of painting that was developed in France in the late 19th century in which very small dots of colour are used to build up the picture 點彩畫法，點描技法（19 世紀末葉興起於法國的繪畫風格）▸ **poin·til·list** /-lɪst/ *adj.* **poin·til·list** *noun*：*Seurat, the French pointillist* 修拉，法國點彩派畫家

point·ing /'pɔɪntɪŋ/ *noun* [U] (*BrE*) the MORTAR that is put in the spaces between the bricks or stones in a wall; the method of filling in the spaces with MORTAR（勾牆磚、石縫用的）灰泥，灰漿；勾縫

'pointing device *noun* (*computing* 計) a mouse or other device which allows you to move the CURSOR on a computer screen 點擊設備；指標裝置

point·less /'pɔɪntləs/ *adj.* having no purpose; not worth doing 無意義的；無目標的；不值得做的：*We searched until we knew it would be pointless to continue.* 我們搜索又搜索，直到覺得繼續下去也枉然時才罷手。 ▸ **point·less·ly** *adv.*：*He argued pointlessly with his parents.* 他無謂地和父母爭論。 **point·less·ness** *noun* [U]：*the pointlessness of war* 戰爭的無意義

'point man *noun* a soldier who goes in front of the others to look for danger 尖兵；先遣兵：(*figurative, NAmE*) *the President's point man on education* (= the person who is responsible for it) 總統在教育方面的特派員

,point of 'order *noun* (*pl.* **points of order**) (*formal*) a question about whether the rules of behaviour in a formal discussion or meeting are being followed correctly 議事規劃問題；議事程序問題

,point of 'reference *noun* (*pl.* **points of reference**) something that you already know that helps you understand a situation or explain sth to sb 參照物；參考依據

,point of 'sale *noun* [usually sing.] the place where a product is sold 銷售點；售貨點：*More information on healthy foods should be provided* ***at the point of sale.*** 銷售點應提供更多有關健康食品的資料。

,point of 'use *noun* [usually sing.] the place where a product or a service is actually used（產品的）使用地點；（服務的）提供地點：*Medical care is still free* ***at the point of use.*** 醫療保健在實際提供點仍然是免費的。

,point of 'view *noun* (*pl.* **points of view**) **1** the particular attitude or opinion that sb has about sth 觀點；態度；意見；看法：*Why can't you ever see my point of view?* 你怎麼老不明白我的觀點呢？◇ *There are a number of different points of view on this issue.* 在這個問題上意見紛紜。◇ ***From my point of view*** (= as far as I was concerned), *the party was a complete success.* 依我看這次聚會非常圓滿。 **2** a particular way of considering or judging a situation 考慮角度；判斷方法 SYN **angle** *These statistics are important from an ecological point of view.* 就生態學而言，這些統計數字很重要。◇ *The book is written from the father's point of view.* 這本書是從父親的角度寫的。

,point-to-'point *noun* (*BrE*) a race on horses that goes over a marked course across fields and has fences or walls for the horses to jump over 定點越野賽馬

pointy /'pɔɪnti/ *adj.* (*informal*) with a point at one end 尖的；有尖頭的 SYN **pointed**：*pointy ears* 尖耳朵 ◇ (*humorous*) *Don't try to argue when you find yourself at the* ***pointy end*** *of a knife* (= when sb is threatening you with a knife). 有人用刀尖頂着你時，不要試圖去爭辯。

poise /pɔɪz/ *noun, verb*

■ ***noun*** [U] **1** a calm and confident manner with control of your feelings or behaviour 沉着自信；穩重；自若 **2** the ability to move or stand in an elegant way with good control of your body 優雅的舉止；儀態

■ ***verb*** [I, T] to be or hold sth steady in a particular position, especially above sth else 保持（某種姿勢）；抓緊；使穩定：**+ adv./prep.** *The hawk poised in mid-air ready to swoop.* 老鷹在半空中盤旋，準備俯衝。◇ **~ sth/yourself to do sth** *He was poising himself to launch a final attack.* 他穩定住自己，以發動最後攻擊。◇ **~ sth/yourself + adv./prep.** *She poised the javelin in her hand before the throw.* 她把標槍握穩，然後投了出去。

poised /pɔɪzd/ *adj.* **1** [not before noun] in a position that is completely still but is ready to move at any moment 處於準備狀態；蓄勢待發：**~ (on, above, over, etc. sth)** *Tina was tense, her hand poised over the telephone.* 蒂娜心情緊張，手懸在電話機上。◇ *He stopped writing and looked at me, pen poised.* 他手握鋼筆，停下來望着我。◇ **~ to do sth** *The cat crouched in the grass, poised to jump.* 貓兒蹲踞在草叢中，準備跳躍。 **2** [not before noun] **~ (in, on, above, etc. sth)** in a position that is balanced but likely to change in one direction or another（暫時）平衡，穩固：*The cup was poised on the edge of the chair.* 杯子放在椅子邊上（隨時可能掉下來）。◇ (*figurative*) *The world stood poised between peace and war.* 世界處於戰爭與和平之間。 **3** [not before noun] completely ready for sth or to do sth 有充分準備；準備好；蓄勢待發 SYN **set**：**~ for sth** *The economy is poised for recovery.* 經濟呈復蘇之勢。◇ **~ to do sth** *Kate is poised to become the highest-paid supermodel in the fashion world.* 凱特決心成為時裝界最高薪的超級模特兒。 **4** having a calm and confident manner and in control of your feelings and behaviour 泰然自若的；沉着自信的；穩健的 SYN **assured**：*He is a remarkably poised young man.* 他是個特別穩健的年輕人。

P

poi·son 0▬ /'pɔɪzn/ *noun, verb*

■ ***noun*** [C, U] **1** 0▬ a substance that causes death or harm if it is swallowed or absorbed into the body 毒藥；毒物；毒素：*Some mushrooms contain a deadly poison.* 有些蘑菇含有致命毒素。◇ *How did he die? Was it poison?* 他是怎麼死的？是中毒嗎？◇ *The dog was killed by rat poison* (= poison intended to kill RATS). 狗被耗子藥毒死了。◇ *to hunt with poison arrows* 用毒箭狩獵 ◇ *bombs containing poison gas* 毒氣彈 **2** an idea, a feeling, etc. that is extremely harmful 極有害的思想（或心情等）；精神毒藥：*the poison of racial hatred* 種族仇恨這種害人的思想

IDM **what's your 'poison?** (*informal, humorous*) used to ask sb what alcoholic drink they would like（用於問別人想喝什麼酒）➲ more at MAN *n.*

■ ***verb*** **1** 0▬ **~ sb/yourself (with sth)** to harm or kill a person or an animal by giving them poison 毒死；毒害 **2** 0▬ **~ sth** to put poison in or on sth 下毒；在…中放毒：*a poisoned arrow* 毒箭 ◇ *Someone had been poisoning his food.* 有人一直在他的食物裏下毒。◇ *Large sections of the river have been poisoned by toxic waste from factories.* 工廠的有毒廢棄物污染了大段大段的河流。 **3 ~ sth** to have a bad effect on sth 毒化；敗壞；使惡化：*His comment served only to poison the atmosphere still further.* 他的評論只是令氣氛更加惡化了。◇ *She succeeded in* ***poisoning their minds*** *against me.* 是她令他們仇視我的。

IDM **a poisoned 'chalice** (*especially BrE*) a thing that seems attractive when it is given to sb but which soon becomes unpleasant 金杯毒酒

poi·son·er /'pɔɪzənə(r)/ *noun* a person who murders sb by using poison 投毒殺人者；毒死別人的人

poi·son·ing /'pɔɪzənɪŋ/ *noun* [U, C] **1** the fact or state of having swallowed or absorbed poison 中毒；服毒：*a series of deaths caused by carbon monoxide poisoning* 一氧化碳中毒引起的一連串死亡 ◇ *At least 10 000 children are involved in accidental poisonings every year.* 每年

至少有 1 萬名兒童意外中毒。 **2** the act of killing or harming sb/sth by giving them poison 毒害；毒殺；投毒： *The police suspected poisoning.* 警方懷疑有人下毒。◇ *The rats were controlled by poisoning.* 用毒殺法使老鼠受到控制。 ➲ see also BLOOD POISONING, FOOD POISONING

ˌpoison ˈivy *noun* [U] a N American climbing plant that causes painful spots on the skin when you touch it 毒常春藤，氣根毒藤（原產於北美，接觸後會引起皮炎）

ˌpoison ˈoak *noun* [U] a N American bush that causes painful spots on the skin when you touch it 櫟葉漆，毒櫟（原產於北美，接觸後會引起皮炎）

poi·son·ous /ˈpɔɪzənəs/ *adj.*
1 causing death or illness if swallowed or absorbed into the body 引起中毒的；有毒的 **SYN toxic**： *poisonous chemicals/plants* 有毒化學物質 / 植物 ◇ *This gas is highly poisonous.* 這種氣體有劇毒。◇ *The leaves of certain trees are poisonous to cattle.* 某些樹的葉子會毒害牛。 **2** (of animals and insects 動物和昆蟲) producing a poison that can cause death or illness if the animal or insect bites you 分泌毒素的；能毒傷人的 **SYN venomous**： *poisonous snakes* 毒蛇 **3** extremely unpleasant or unfriendly 極端討厭（或不友善）的；惡毒的；邪惡的： *the poisonous atmosphere in the office* 辦公室裏的惡劣氣氛

ˌpoison ˈpen letter *noun* an unpleasant letter that is not signed and is intended to upset the person who receives it 惡意的匿名信；匿名誹謗信

ˌpoison ˈpill *noun* (*informal*, *business* 商) a form of defence used by a company to prevent, or to reduce the effect of, a TAKEOVER bid that they do not want, for example by selling some of their important possessions（公司為防止被兼併而採取的）自戕式防禦；（出售某些重要財產以求最終自保的）掏空政策

poke /pəʊk; *NAmE* poʊk/ *verb*, *noun*
■ *verb* **1** [T] to quickly push your fingers or another object into sb/sth（用手指或其他東西）捅，戳，杵 **SYN prod**： **~ sb/sth with sth** *She poked him in the ribs with her elbow.* 她用胳膊肘頂他的肋部。◇ **~ sth into sth** *She poked her elbow into his ribs.* 她用胳膊肘頂他的肋部。◇ **~ sb/sth** *I'm sick of being poked and prodded by doctors.* 我討厭讓醫生在我身上戳戳點點的。◇ *She got up and poked the fire* (= to make it burn more strongly). 她起來撥了撥火。 **2** [T] **~ sth + adv./prep.** to push sth somewhere or move it in a particular direction with a small quick movement 推；捅；戳；探： *He poked his head around the corner to check that nobody was coming.* 他從轉角處探出頭來，查看有沒有人過來。◇ *Someone had poked a message under the door.* 有人從門底下塞進了一張紙條。◇ *Don't poke her eye out with that stick!* 別讓那根棍子戳着她的眼！ **3** [I] **+ adv./prep.** if an object is **poking out of, through, etc.** sth, you can see a part of it that is no longer covered by sth else 露出；伸出；探出： *The end of the cable was left poking out of the wall.* 電纜頭從牆裏露出來了。◇ *Clumps of grass poked up through the snow.* 一簇簇的草破雪而出。 **4** [T] **~ a hole in sth (with sth)** to make a hole in sth by pushing your finger or another object into it 捅窟窿；扎洞： *The kids poked holes in the ice with sticks.* 孩子們用棍子在冰上戳洞。 **5** [T] **~ sb** (*taboo*, *slang*) (of a man 男人) to have sex with sb 與（某人）性交

IDM **poke ˈfun at sb/sth** to say unkind things about sb/sth in order to make other people laugh at them 拿…開心；奚落；嘲弄 **SYN ridicule**： *Her novels poke fun at the upper class.* 她的小說嘲弄上流社會。 ➲ more at NOSE *n.*

PHR V **ˌpoke aˈbout/aˈround** (*informal*) to look for sth, especially sth that is hidden among other things that you have to move 搜查；翻找： *The police spent the day poking around in his office but found nothing.* 警察花了一天時間搜查他的辦公室，但一無所獲。◇ (*figurative*) *We've had journalists poking around and asking a lot of questions.* 我們給記者不斷追問。 **ˈpoke at sth** to push a pointed object, your finger, etc. at sth repeatedly with small quick movements（用手指、物件等反複地）捅，戳，扎： *He poked at the spaghetti with a fork.* 他用叉子撥弄着意大利麵。

■ *noun* **1** [C, usually sing.] the action of quickly pushing your fingers or another object into sb/sth 捅；戳；撥；挑： *to give the fire a poke* 撥一撥火 ◇ *He gave me a poke in the ribs to wake me up.* 他捅了一下我的肋部把我叫醒。 **2** [U] (*BrE*) power in a car（汽車的）馬力，推進力： *I prefer something with a bit more poke.* 我想要馬力再大些的。

IDM **have a ˌpoke aˈround** (*informal*) to look carefully around a place to see what you can find; to try to find out information about sb/sth 仔細尋覓；探究；打探 **take a ˈpoke at sb/sth** (*old-fashioned*, *NAmE*, *informal*) to make an unkind remark about sb/sth; to laugh at sb/sth 嘲弄；奚落；嘲笑 ➲ more at PIG *n.*

poker /ˈpəʊkə(r); *NAmE* ˈpoʊ-/ *noun* **1** [U] a card game for two or more people, in which the players bet on the values of the cards they hold 撲克牌遊戲 **2** [C] a metal stick for moving or breaking up coal in a fire 通條；撥火棍 ➲ VISUAL VOCAB page V21

ˈpoker-faced *adj.* (*informal*) with an expression on your face that does not show what you are thinking or feeling 不露聲色的；毫無表情的 ▶ **ˈpoker face** *noun*： *He maintained a poker face.* 他一直面無表情。

poky /ˈpəʊki; *NAmE* ˈpoʊki/ *adj.* (*informal*) (**poki·er**, **poki·est**) **1** (of a room or a building 屋子或建築物) too small; without much space 狹窄的；窄小的 **SYN cramped**： *a poky little room* 窄小的屋子 **2** (also **pokey**) (both *NAmE*) extremely slow and annoying 極慢的；遲鈍的；拖沓的；慢騰騰的

pol /pɒl; *NAmE* pɑːl/ *noun* (*NAmE*, *informal*) = POLITICIAN (1)

Po·lack /ˈpəʊlæk; *NAmE* ˈpoʊ-/ *noun* (*taboo*, *slang*, *especially NAmE*) an offensive word for a person from Poland, or a person of Polish origin 波蘭佬（含冒犯意，指波蘭人或波蘭後裔）

polar /ˈpəʊlə(r); *NAmE* ˈpoʊ-/ *adj.* [only before noun]
1 connected with, or near the North or South Pole 極地的；近地極的；南極（或北極）的： *the polar regions* 極區 ◇ *polar explorers* 極地探險家 **2** (*technical* 術語) connected with the POLES (= the positive and negative ends) of a MAGNET 磁極的： *polar attraction* 極向引力 **3** (*formal*) used to describe sth that is the complete opposite of sth else 完全相反的；截然對立的： *The parents' position is often the polar opposite of the child's.* 父母的觀點常與孩子的完全相反。

ˈpolar bear *noun* a white BEAR that lives near the North Pole 北極熊；白熊

po·lar·ity /pəˈlærəti/ *noun* [U] **1 ~ (between A and B)** (*formal*) the situation when two tendencies, opinions, etc. oppose each other（兩種傾向、意見等的）截然對立，兩極化： *the growing polarity between the left and right wings of the party* 黨內左右兩派間日益明顯的對立 **2** [U, C] (*physics* 物) the condition of having two POLES with opposite qualities 兩極並存的狀態；極性

po·lar·ize (*BrE* also **-ise**) /ˈpəʊləraɪz; *NAmE* ˈpoʊ-/ *verb* **1** [I, T] to separate or make people separate into two groups with completely opposite opinions（使）兩極化，截然對立：*Public opinion has polarized on this issue.* 在這個問題上公眾意見已呈兩極化。◇ **~ sth** *The issue has polarized public opinion.* 這個問題已使公眾意見兩極化。 **2** [T] **~ sth** (*physics* 物) to make waves of light, etc. VIBRATE in a single direction 使（光波等）偏振 **3** [T] **~ sth** (*physics* 物) to give polarity to sth 使（物體）極化： *to polarize a magnet* 使磁體極化 ▶ **po·lar·iza·tion**, **-isa·tion** /ˌpəʊləraɪˈzeɪʃn; *NAmE* ˌpoʊlərəˈz-/ *noun* [U, C]

Po·lar·oid™ /ˈpəʊlərɔɪd; *NAmE* ˈpoʊ-/ *noun* **1** [C] (also **ˌPolaroid ˈcamera**) a camera that can produce a photograph within a few seconds 寶麗來照相機；拍立得照相機 **2** [C] a photograph that has been taken with a Polaroid camera 寶麗來一次成像照片；拍立得相片 **3** [U] a transparent substance that is put on SUNGLASSES and car windows to make the sun seem less bright（太陽鏡或汽車玻璃上的）偏光薄膜： *Polaroid sunglasses* 偏光膜太陽鏡 **4 Polaroids** [pl.] (also **ˌPolaroid ˈsunglasses**) SUNGLASSES that have a layer of Polaroid on them 偏光膜太陽鏡；貼膜太陽鏡

pole 0→ /pəʊl; *NAmE* poʊl/ *noun, verb*
■ *noun* **1** 0→ a long thin straight piece of wood or metal, especially one with the end placed in the ground, used as a support 柱子；杆子；棍；杖：*a tent pole* 帳篷支柱◇ *a ski pole* 滑雪杖◇ *a curtain pole* 窗簾杆 ➲ VISUAL VOCAB pages V21, V55 ➲ see also BARGEPOLE, FLAGPOLE, TELEGRAPH POLE, TOTEM POLE **2** 0→ either of the two points at the opposite ends of the line on which the earth or any other planet turns （行星的）極；地極：*the* ***North/South Pole*** 北極；南極 **3** (*physics* 物) either of the two ends of a MAGNET, or the positive or negative points of an electric battery 磁極；電極 **4** either of two opposite or contrasting extremes （對立或相反的）任何一方；極端：*Their opinions were at opposite poles of the debate.* 他們的意見在辯論中截然相反。
IDM **be 'poles apart** to be widely separated; to have no interests that you share 天南地北；南轅北轍；截然相反 **up the 'pole** (*old-fashioned, BrE, informal*) crazy 發狂的；瘋狂的 ➲ more at GREASY, TOUCH *v.*
■ *verb* [T, I] **~ (sth) + adv./prep.** to move a boat by pushing on the bottom of a river, etc. with a pole 用篙撐船；擺船

pole·axe (*BrE*) (*US* **pole·ax**) /'pəʊlæks; *NAmE* 'poʊl-/ *verb* **1 ~ sb** to hit sb very hard so that they fall down and cannot stand up again 打垮；擊倒 **2** [usually passive] **~ sb** to surprise or shock you so much that you do not know what to say or do 使驚慌失措；使手足無措 SYN **dumbfound**

pole·cat /'pəʊlkæt; *NAmE* 'poʊl-/ *noun* **1** a small European wild animal with a long thin body, dark brown fur and a strong unpleasant smell 艾鼬，臭貂（體長，有臭味） **2** (*NAmE*) = SKUNK

'pole dancing *noun* [U] sexually exciting dancing that is performed in a bar or club, with the dancer moving his or her body around a long pole 鋼管舞（在酒吧或夜總會跳的豔舞，舞者繞長杆扭動身體） ▶ **'pole dancer** *noun*

po·lem·ic /pə'lemɪk/ *noun* (*formal*) **1** [C] a speech or a piece of writing that argues very strongly for or against sth/sb 激烈爭論；辯論文章；論戰 **2** [U] (also **polemics** [pl.]) the practice or skill of arguing strongly for or against sth/sb 辯論術；辯論法：*Her speech was memorable for its polemic rather than its substance.* 她的演說之所以令人難忘，不是因其內容而是因其辯論方法。

po·lem·ic·al /pə'lemɪkl/ (also *less frequent* **po·lem·ic**) *adj.* (*formal*) involving strong arguments for or against sth, often in opposition to the opinion of others 爭論的；挑起辯論的

po·lemi·cist /pə'lemɪsɪst/ *noun* (*formal*) a person who makes skilful use of POLEMIC 善於辯論的人；善辯者；有辯才的人

po·lenta /pə'lentə/ *noun* [U] **1** a yellow food made with MAIZE (CORN) flour, used in Italian cooking（意大利烹飪中的）玉米糊 **2** the flour used to make polenta 玉米粉

'pole position *noun* [U, C] the leading position at the start of a race involving cars or bicycles （汽車、自行車比賽的）首發位置

the 'Pole Star *noun* [sing.] the star that is above the North Pole in the sky 北極星

the 'pole vault *noun* [sing.] a sporting event in which people try to jump over a high bar, using a long pole to push themselves off the ground 撐杆跳高 ➲ VISUAL VOCAB page V46 ▶ **'pole-vaulter** *noun* **'pole-vaulting** *noun* [U]

po·lice 0→ /pə'li:s/ *noun, verb*
■ *noun* 0→ (often **the police**) [pl.] an official organization whose job is to make people obey the law and to prevent and solve crime; the people who work for this organization 警察部門；警方：*A man was arrested by the police and held for questioning.* 一名男子被警方逮捕並拘押訊問。◇ *Get out of the house or* ***I'll call the police.*** 滾出這所房子，不然我就叫警察了。◇ *Police suspect a local gang.* 警方懷疑當地的一個不良幫派。◇ *a* ***police car*** 警車◇ *Hundreds of police in riot gear struggled to control the violence.* 數以百計的警察身披防暴裝備，奮力鎮壓暴亂。 ➲ see also SECRET POLICE
■ *verb* **1 ~ sth** (of the police, army, etc. 警察、軍隊等) to go around a particular area to make sure that nobody is breaking the law there 巡查；維護治安：*The border will be policed by UN officials.* 邊境將由聯合國官員巡查。 **2 ~ sth** (of a committee, etc. 委員會等) to make sure that a particular set of rules is obeyed 監督；管制 SYN **monitor**：*The profession is policed by its own regulatory body.* 這個行業由其自律機構監督。

po'lice commissioner *noun* (*especially NAmE*) = COMMISSIONER (2)

po,lice 'constable (also **constable**) *noun* (*abbr.* **PC**) (in Britain and some other countries) a police officer of the lowest rank （英國和其他一些國家的）警察，警員：*Police Constable Jordan* 警員喬丹

po'lice department *noun* (in the US) the police organization of a particular city（美國城市中的）警察局

po'lice dog *noun* a dog that is trained to find or attack suspected criminals 警犬

po'lice force *noun* the police organization of a country, district or town （國家、地區或城鎮的）警力，警察部隊

po·lice·man /pə'li:smən/ *noun* (*pl.* **-men** /-mən/) a male police officer （男）警察 ➲ note at GENDER

po'lice officer (also **officer**) *noun* a member of the police 警察

po'lice state *noun* (*disapproving*) a country where people's freedom, especially to travel and to express political opinions, is controlled by the government, with the help of the police 警察國家（通過警察部門控制人民旅行及言論等自由）

po'lice station (*NAmE* also **'station house**) *noun* the office of a local police force 警察局；警察分局；派出所：*The suspect was taken to the nearest police station for questioning.* 嫌疑犯被帶到最近的警察局訊問。

po·lice·wo·man /pə'li:swʊmən/ *noun* (*pl.* **-women** /-wɪmɪn/) a female police officer 女警察 ➲ note at GENDER

po·licing /pə'li:sɪŋ/ *noun* [U] **1** the activity of keeping order in a place with police （用警察）維護治安；治安保衛：*community policing* 社區治安的維護 **2** the activity of controlling an industry, an activity, etc. to make sure that people obey the rules （對行業、活動等的）監督，管理，檢查

pol·icy 0→ AW /'pɒləsi; *NAmE* 'pɑ:l-/ *noun* (*pl.* **-ies**) **1** 0→ [C, U] **~ (on sth)** a plan of action agreed or chosen by a political party, a business, etc. 政策；方針：*the present government's policy on education* 現政府的教育政策◇ *The company has* ***adopted a*** *firm* ***policy*** *on shoplifting.* 那家公司對店內行竊採取了嚴厲的措施。◇ *We have tried to* ***pursue a policy*** *of neutrality.* 我們設法奉行中立的政策。◇ *US* ***foreign/domestic policy*** 美國的外交／國內政策◇ *They have had a significant* ***change in policy*** *on paternity leave.* 他們對男人侍產假制度作了重大改變。◇ *a policy document* 政策文件 ➲ COLLOCATIONS at POLITICS **2** [C, U] (*formal*) a principle that you believe in that influences how you behave; a way in which you usually behave 原則；為人之道：*She is following her usual policy of ignoring all offers of help.* 她遵循着自己的一貫原則，對於他人的主動幫助一概不予理睬。◇ (*saying*) *Honesty is the best policy.* 誠實為上。 **3** 0→ [C] a written statement of a contract of insurance 保險單：*Check the terms of the policy before you sign.* 仔細閱讀保險單的條款後再簽字。

pol·icy·hold·er /'pɒləsihəʊldə(r); *NAmE* 'pɑ:ləsihoʊl-/ *noun* (*formal*) a person or group that holds an insurance policy 保險單持有人（或機構）

polio /'pəʊliəʊ; *NAmE* 'poʊlioʊ/ (also *formal* **polio·my·el·itis** /ˌpəʊliəʊˌmaɪə'laɪtɪs; *NAmE* ˌpoʊlioʊ-/) *noun* [U] an infectious disease that affects the central nervous system and can cause temporary or permanent PARALYSIS (= loss of control or feeling in part or most of the body) 脊髓灰質炎；小兒麻痺症

P

pol·ish /ˈpɒlɪʃ; NAmE ˈpɑːl-/ *noun, verb*
■ *noun* **1** [U, C] a substance used when rubbing a surface to make it smooth and shiny 擦光劑；上光劑；亮光劑：*furniture/floor/shoe/silver polish* 傢具上光漆；地板蠟；鞋油；銀光劑 ◇ *wax polish* 亮光蠟 ➲ see also FRENCH POLISH, NAIL POLISH ➲ VISUAL VOCAB page V60 **2** [sing.] an act of polishing sth 拋光；上光；擦亮：*I give it a polish now and again.* 我不時把它擦亮。 **3** [sing.] the shiny appearance of sth after it has been polished 擦光的面；打磨光亮的面 SYN **lustre, sheen** **4** [U] a high quality of performance achieved with great skill（表演的）完美，嫻熟，精湛 SYN **brilliance**：*She played the cello with the polish of a much older musician.* 她演奏大提琴頗有資深演奏家的風範。 **5** [U] high standards of behaviour; being polite 文雅；優雅；品味；禮貌 SYN **refinement** IDM see SPIT *n.*
■ *verb* **1** [T, I] to make sth smooth and shiny by rubbing it 擦光；磨光；拋光：**~ (sth)** *Polish shoes regularly to protect the leather.* 要經常擦鞋，以保護皮革。◇ **~ sth (up) (with sth)** *He polished his glasses with a handkerchief.* 他用手絹揩拭眼鏡。➲ see also FRENCH POLISH **2** [T] to make changes to sth in order to improve it 修改；潤飾；潤色：**~ sth** *The statement was carefully polished and checked before release.* 這項聲明是經仔細潤色檢查後才發表的。◇ **~ sth up** *The hotel has polished up its act* (= improved its service) *since last year.* 這家酒店自去年以來已經改善了服務水平。
PHR V **,polish sb↔ˈoff** (*informal, especially NAmE*) to kill sb 幹掉；殺死 **,polish sth↔ˈoff** (*informal*) to finish sth, especially food, quickly 很快做完；（尤指）迅速吃光：*He polished off the remains of the apple pie.* 他把剩下的蘋果派趕快吃完。

pol·ished /ˈpɒlɪʃt; NAmE ˈpɑːl-/ *adj.* **1** shiny as a result of polishing 拋光的；磨光的；擦亮的 SYN **gleaming** **2** elegant, confident and/or highly skilled 優雅的；嫻熟的 SYN **fine**

pol·ish·er /ˈpɒlɪʃə(r); NAmE ˈpɑːl-/ *noun* a machine for polishing sth 上光機；磨光機；打蠟機：*a floor polisher* 地板上光機

P

pol·it·buro /ˈpɒlɪtbjʊərəʊ; NAmE ˈpɑːlɪtbjʊroʊ/ *noun* (*pl.* **-os**) the most important committee of a Communist party, with the power to decide on policy（共產黨的）政治局

po·lite /pəˈlaɪt/ *adj.* (**po·liter, po·litest**) HELP **More polite** and **most polite** are also common. * more polite 和 most polite 也常用。
1 having or showing good manners and respect for the feelings of others 有禮貌的；客氣的；儒雅的 SYN **courteous**：*Please be polite to our guests.* 請禮貌待客。◇ *We were all too polite to object.* 我們都太客氣了，沒有反對。 OPP **impolite** **2** socially correct but not always sincere 應酬的；禮節性的；客套的：*I don't know how to make **polite conversation**.* 我不曉得怎麼說應酬話。◇ *The performance was greeted with polite applause.* 這場演出得到了禮貌性的掌聲。 **3** [only before noun] from a class of society that believes it is better than others 上流社會的：*'Bum' is not a word we use in polite company.* "屁股"可不是我們當着文雅人的面說的字眼。▶ **po·lite·ly** *adv.* **po·lite·ness** *noun* [U]

poli·tesse /ˌpɒlɪˈtes; NAmE ˌpɑːl-/ *noun* [U] (from *French, literary*) formal POLITENESS 正規禮節

pol·it·ic /ˈpɒlətɪk; NAmE ˈpɑːl-/ *adj.* (*formal*) (of actions 行為) based on good judgement 謹慎的；得當的；明智的 SYN **prudent, wise**：*It seemed politic to say nothing.* 沉默似乎是上策。➲ see also BODY POLITIC

pol·it·ical /pəˈlɪtɪkl/ *adj.*
1 connected with the state, government or public affairs 政治的；政府的；政權的：*a monarch without political power* 沒有政治權力的君主 ◇ *He was a **political prisoner*** (= one who was put in prison because he was thought to be harmful to the state). 他曾是個政治犯。 **2** connected with the different groups working in politics, especially their policies and the competition between them 政黨的；黨派的：*a political debate/party/leader* 政治辯論 / 黨派 / 領袖 ◇ *What are your political sympathies?* 你認同哪個政黨？ **3** (of people 人) interested in or active in politics 關心政治的；政治上活躍的：*She became very political at university.* 她上大學時開始十分熱衷於政治。◇ *I'm not a **political animal*** (= person who is interested in politics). 我不是搞政治的那種人。 **4** concerned with power, status, etc. within an organization, rather than with matters of principle 爭權奪利的；人事糾紛的：*I suspect that he was dismissed for political reasons.* 我懷疑他被解職是人事上的原因。 ➲ see also POLITICALLY

po,litical ˈaction committee *noun* (*abbr.* **PAC**) (in the US) a group of people who collect money to support the candidates and policies that will help them achieve their political and social aims 政治行動委員會（美國組織，為所支持的公職候選人籌集資金）

po,litical aˈsylum *noun* [U] (*formal*) = ASYLUM (1)

po,litical corˈrectness *noun* [U] (sometimes *disapproving*) the principle of avoiding language and behaviour that may offend particular groups of people 政治上正確（言行避免有歧視之嫌）

po,litical eˈconomy *noun* [U] the study of how nations organize the production and use of wealth 政治經濟學

po,litical geˈography *noun* [U] the way in which the world is divided into different countries, especially as a subject of study 政治地理學

pol·it·ic·al·ly /pəˈlɪtɪkli/ *adv.*
in a way that is connected with politics 政治上：*a politically sensitive issue* 一個政治上敏感的議題 ◇ *politically motivated crimes* 政治犯罪 ◇ *It makes sense politically as well as economically.* 這在經濟上和政治上都有道理。

po,litically corˈrect *adj.* (*abbr.* **PC**) used to describe language or behaviour that deliberately tries to avoid offending particular groups of people 政治上正確的（言行避免有歧視之嫌）

po,litically incorˈrect *adj.* failing to avoid language or behaviour that may offend particular groups of people 政治上不正確的（言行有歧視之嫌）

po,litical ˈscience (also **pol·it·ics**) *noun* [U] the study of government and politics 政治學

po,litical ˈscientist *noun* an expert in political science 政治學家

pol·it·ician /ˌpɒləˈtɪʃn; NAmE ˌpɑːl-/ *noun*
1 (also *NAmE informal* **pol**) a person whose job is concerned with politics, especially as an elected member of parliament, etc. 從政者；政治家 **2** (*disapproving*) a person who is good at using different situations in an organization to try to get power or advantage for himself or herself 政客；見風駛舵者；投機鑽營者

pol·iti·cize (*BrE* also **-ise**) /pəˈlɪtɪsaɪz/ *verb* [often passive] **1 ~ sth** to make sth a political issue 使政治化；使帶有政治色彩：*the highly politicized issue of unemployment* 高度政治化的失業問題 **2 ~ sb/sth** to make sb/sth become more involved in politics 使參與（或捲入）政治；使對政治敏感：*The rural population has become increasingly politicized in recent years.* 近年來，農村人口對政治愈來愈感興趣。▶ **pol·iti·ciza·tion, -isa·tion** /pəˌlɪtɪsaɪˈzeɪʃn/ *noun* [U]：*the politicization of education* 教育的政治化

pol·it·ick·ing /ˈpɒlətɪkɪŋ; NAmE ˈpɑːl-/ *noun* [U] (often *disapproving*) political activity, especially to win support for yourself 政治活動；（尤指）拉攏活動

pol·it·ico /pəˈlɪtɪkəʊ; NAmE -koʊ/ *noun* (*pl.* **-os**) (*informal, disapproving*) a politician; a person who is active in politics 政客；熱衷政治的人

pol·it·ics /ˈpɒlətɪks; NAmE ˈpɑːl-/ *noun*
1 [U+sing./pl. v.] the activities involved in getting and using power in public life, and being able to influence decisions that affect a country or a society 政治；政治事務（或活動）：*party politics* 黨派政治 ◇ *local politics* 地方政治活動 ◇ *He's thinking of **going into politics*** (= trying to become a Member of Parliament, Congress, etc.). 他打算步入政壇。◇ *a major figure in British politics* 英國政壇的風雲人物 **2** [U+sing./pl. v.] (*disapproving*)

matters concerned with getting or using power within a particular group or organization 權術；鈎心鬥角：*I don't want to get involved in office politics.* 我不想捲入辦公室的政治。◇ *the internal politics of the legal profession* 法律界內部的鈎心鬥角 ◇ *sexual politics* (= concerning relationships of power between the sexes) 兩性間的權勢之爭 **3** [pl.] a person's political views or beliefs（個人的）政治觀點，政見，政治信仰：*His politics are extreme.* 他的政治觀點偏激。**4** [U] = POLITICAL SCIENCE：*a degree in Politics* 政治學學位 **5** [sing.] a system of political beliefs; a state of political affairs 政治思想體系；政治局勢：*A politics of the future has to engage with new ideas.* 未來的政治制度必須同新思想結合。

pol·ity /ˈpɒləti; *NAmE* ˈpɑːl-/ *noun* (*pl.* -ies) (*technical* 術語) **1** [C] a society as a political unit 政體；國家組織 **2** [U] the form or process of government 政體；政權形態；政治制度

polka /ˈpɒlkə; *NAmE* ˈpoʊlkə/ *noun* a fast dance for two people together that was popular in the 19th century; a piece of music for this dance 波爾卡舞（盛行於 19 世紀的一種輕快的雙人舞）；波爾卡舞曲

ˈ**polka dot** *noun* one of many dots that together form a pattern, especially on cloth（織物等圓點圖案中的）大圓點：*a polka-dot tie* 圓點領帶 ➲ **VISUAL VOCAB** page V61 ➲ compare SPOT *n.* (1)

poll /pəʊl; *NAmE* poʊl/ *noun, verb*

■ ***noun*** **1** (also **oˈpinion poll**) [C] the process of questioning people who are representative of a larger group in order to get information about the general opinion 民意測驗；民意調查 **SYN** **survey**：*to **carry out/conduct** a poll* 進行／做民意測驗 ◇ *A recent poll suggests some surprising changes in public opinion.* 最近的調查反映民意有了出人意表的變化。 **2** [C] (also **the polls** [pl.]) the process of voting at an election; the process of counting the votes 選舉投票；計票：*The final result of the poll will be known tomorrow.* 投票結果將於明天公佈。◇ *Thursday is traditionally the day when Britain **goes to the polls*** (= when elections are held). 英國傳統的投票選舉日是星期四。◇ *Polls close* (= voting ends) *at 9 p.m.* 投票於晚上 9 點結束。 ➲ **SYNONYMS** at ELECTION

Collocations 詞語搭配

Politics 政治

Power 權力

- **create/form/be the leader of** a political party 創建／組建／領導政黨
- **gain/take/win/lose/regain** control of Congress 獲得／失去／奪回對國會的控制權
- **start/spark/lead/be on the brink of** a revolution 發起／引發／領導一場革命；革命一觸即發
- **be engaged/locked in** an internal power struggle 參與／陷入內部權力鬥爭
- **lead/form** a rival/breakaway faction 領導／組建反對派／分裂派
- **seize/take** control of the government/power 奪取／接手對政府／政權的控制權
- **bring down/overthrow/topple** the government/president/regime 推翻政府／總統／政權
- **abolish/overthrow/restore** the monarchy 廢除／推翻／恢復君主制
- **establish/install** a military dictatorship/a stable government 建立軍事獨裁／穩定的政府
- **be forced/removed/driven from** office/power 被迫離職／下台；被免職／趕下台
- **resign/step down as** party leader/an MP/president/prime minister 辭去政黨領袖／議員／總統／總理的職位
- **enter/retire from/return to** political life 開始／退出／重回政治生涯

Political debate 政治辯論

- **spark/provoke** a heated/hot/intense/lively debate 引發激烈的辯論
- **engage in/participate in/contribute to** (the) political/public debate (on/over sth) 參與（關於某事的）政治／公開辯論
- **get involved in/feel excluded from** the political process 參與／感覺被排擠出政治進程
- **launch/start/lead/spearhead** a campaign/movement 發起／領導一場運動
- **join/be linked with** the peace/anti-war/feminist/civil rights movement 參與和平／反戰／女權／民權運動；與和平／反戰／女權／民權運動有聯繫
- **criticize/speak out against/challenge/support** the government 批評／公開反對／質疑／支持政府
- **lobby/put pressure on** the government (to do sth) 游說／施壓於政府（去做某事）
- **come under fire/pressure from** opposition parties 受到來自反對黨的抨擊／壓力

Policy 政策

- **call for/demand/propose/push for/advocate** democratic/political/land reform(s) 呼籲／強烈要求／提議／敦促／倡導民主／政治／土地改革
- **formulate/implement** domestic economic policy 制訂／執行國內經濟政策
- **change/influence/shape/have an impact on** government/economic/public policy 改變／影響政府／經濟／公共政策
- **be consistent with/be in line with/go against/be opposed to** government policy 符合／違背政府政策
- **reform/restructure/modernize** the tax system 改革／重組／革新稅收制度
- **privatize/improve/deliver/make cuts in** public services 私有化／改善／提供／削減公共服務
- **invest** (**heavily**) **in/spend sth on** schools/education/public services/(the) infrastructure 在學校／教育／公共服務／基礎設施上投入（大量）資金
- **nationalize** the banks/the oil industry 使銀行／石油產業國有化
- **promise/propose/deliver/give** ($80 billion in/significant/substantial/massive) tax cuts 承諾／提議／兌現／實行（800 億元／大幅度的）減稅
- a/the budget is **approved**/(*especially NAmE*) **passed** by parliament/congress 預算經議會／國會通過

Making laws 制定法律

- **have a majority in/have seats in** Parliament/Congress/the Senate 在議會／國會／參議院中佔多數席位／佔有席位
- **propose/sponsor** a bill/legislation/a resolution 提交法案／法規／決議
- **introduce/bring in/draw up/draft/adopt/pass** a bill/a law/legislation/measures 推出／提出／擬定／起草／採用／通過法案／法律／法規／措施
- **amend/repeal** an act/a law/legislation 修正／廢除法案／法律／法規
- **veto/vote against/oppose** a bill/legislation/a measure/a proposal/a resolution 否決／投票反對／反對法案／法規／措施／提議／決議
- **get/require/be decided by** a majority vote 獲得／需要多數票；由多數票決定

➲ more collocations at ECONOMY, VOTE

P

3 [sing.] the number of votes given in an election 投票數 SYN **ballot**：*Labour is ahead in the poll.* 工黨的得票數領先。◇ *They gained 20% of the poll.* 他們得到了 20% 的選票。➲ see also DEED POLL, EXIT POLL, STRAW POLL

■ *verb* **1** [T, I] to receive a particular number of votes in an election 獲得（票數）：**~ sth** *They polled 39% of the vote in the last election.* 在上屆選舉中，他們獲得了 39% 的選票。◇ **+ adv./prep.** *The Republicans have polled well* (= received many votes) *in recent elections.* 共和黨在最近的選舉中得票數都很高。 **2** [T, usually passive] **~ sb** to ask a large number of members of the public what they think about sth 做民意調查 SYN **survey**：*Over 50% of those polled were against the proposed military action.* 民調中有超過 50% 的人反對擬議的軍事行動。

pol·lard /ˈpɒləd; -lɑːd; *NAmE* ˈpɑːlərd/ *verb* [usually passive] **~ sth** (*technical* 術語) to cut off the branches at the top of a tree so that the lower branches will grow more thickly 修剪樹冠；給（樹木）去頂

pol·len /ˈpɒlən; *NAmE* ˈpɑːlən/ *noun* [U] fine powder, usually yellow, that is formed in flowers and carried to other flowers of the same kind by the wind or by insects, to make those flowers produce seeds 花粉 ➲ COLLOCATIONS at LIFE

ˈpollen count *noun* [usually sing.] a number that shows the amount of pollen in the air, used to warn people whose health is affected by it 花粉計數（用於警示花粉過敏者空氣中花粉的含量）

ˈpollen tube *noun* (*biology* 生) a tube that grows when pollen lands on the STIGMA (= a part of the female organ) of a flower to carry the male cell to the OVULE (= the part that contains the female cell) 花粉管

pol·lin·ate /ˈpɒləneɪt; *NAmE* ˈpɑːl-/ *verb* **~ sth** to put POLLEN into a flower or plant so that it produces seeds 授粉；傳粉：*flowers pollinated by bees/the wind* 由蜜蜂 / 風傳粉的花卉 ▸ **pol·lin·ation** /ˌpɒləˈneɪʃn; *NAmE* ˌpɑːl-/ *noun* [U]

poll·ing /ˈpəʊlɪŋ; *NAmE* ˈpoʊ-/ *noun* [U] **1** the activity of voting 投票：*Polling has been heavy since 8 a.m.* 從早上 8 點以來投票很踴躍。 **2** the act of asking questions as part of an opinion POLL 民意測驗

ˈpolling booth (*especially BrE*) (*NAmE* usually **ˈvoting booth**) *noun* a small place in a POLLING STATION, separated from the surrounding area, where people vote by marking a card, etc. 投票亭，寫票間（設在投票站）

ˈpolling day *noun* [U, C] (*BrE*) a day on which people vote in an election 投票日；選舉日：*a week before polling day* 投票日前一週（的那天）

ˈpolling station (*especially BrE*) (*NAmE* usually **ˈpolling place**) *noun* a building where people go to vote in an election 投票站；投票點 ➲ COLLOCATIONS at VOTE

polli·wog (also **polly·wog**) /ˈpɒliwɒg; *NAmE* ˈpɑːliwɑːg/ *noun* (*NAmE*) = TADPOLE

poll·ster /ˈpəʊlstə(r); *NAmE* ˈpoʊl-/ *noun* a person who makes or asks the questions in an OPINION POLL 民意測驗主辦人；民意調查員

ˈpoll tax *noun* a tax that must be paid at the same rate by every person or every adult in a particular area 人頭稅

pol·lu·tant /pəˈluːtənt/ *noun* (*formal*) a substance that pollutes sth, especially air and water 污染物；污染物質

pol·lute /pəˈluːt/ *verb* to add dirty or harmful substances to land, air, water, etc. so that it is no longer pleasant or safe to use 污染；弄髒：**~ sth** *the exhaust fumes that are polluting our cities* 污染我們城市的廢氣 ◇ **~ sth by/with sth** *The river has been polluted with toxic waste from local factories.* 當地工廠排放的有毒廢棄物污染了這條河。◇ (*figurative*) *a society polluted by racism* 受種族主義污染的社會 ➲ COLLOCATIONS at ENVIRONMENT

pol·luter /pəˈluːtə(r)/ *noun* a person, company, country, etc. that causes pollution 污染源；污染者

pol·lu·tion 0┳ /pəˈluːʃn/ *noun* [U] **1** 0┳ the process of making air, water, soil, etc. dirty; the state of being dirty 污染；玷污；弄髒：***air/water pollution*** 空氣 / 水污染 ◇ *to reduce levels of environmental pollution* 降低環境污染的程度 ➲ COLLOCATIONS at ENVIRONMENT **2** 0┳ substances that make air, water, soil, etc. dirty 污染物；穢物；垃圾：*beaches covered with pollution* 穢物狼藉的海灘 **3 noise/light ~** harmful or annoying levels of noise, or of artificial light at night 噪音污染；（夜間擾人的）強烈燈光

Polly·anna /ˌpɒliˈænə; *NAmE* ˈpɑːl-/ *noun* [usually sing.] a person who is always cheerful and expects only good things to happen 盲目樂觀的人；無憂無慮的人 ORIGIN From the name of a character created by the US writer of children's stories, Eleanor Hodgman Porter. 源自美國兒童文學作家埃莉諾•霍奇曼•波特所創作的人物波莉亞娜。

polly·wog = POLLIWOG

polo /ˈpəʊləʊ; *NAmE* ˈpoʊloʊ/ *noun* [U] a game in which two teams of players riding on horses try to hit a ball into a goal using long wooden hammers (called MALLETS) 馬球（運動）➲ VISUAL VOCAB page V46 ➲ see also WATER POLO

pol·on·aise /ˌpɒləˈneɪz; *NAmE* ˌpɑːl-/ *noun* a slow Polish dance that was popular in the 19th century; a piece of music for this dance 波洛奈茲舞（盛行於 19 世紀的波蘭慢步舞）；波洛奈茲舞曲

ˈpolo neck (*BrE*) (*NAmE* **turtle·neck**) *noun* a high round COLLAR made when the neck of a piece of clothing is folded over; a piece of clothing with a polo neck 高圓翻領；高圓翻領衣服：*a polo-neck sweater* 高翻領套衫 ◇ *You can wear a polo neck with that jacket.* 你可以穿件高圓翻領衫配那件外衣。➲ VISUAL VOCAB page V63

po·lo·nium /pəˈləʊniəm; *NAmE* -ˈloʊ-/ *noun* [U] (*symb.* **Po**) a chemical element. Polonium is a RADIOACTIVE metal that is present in nature when URANIUM decays. 釙（放射性化學元素）

ˈpolo shirt *noun* an informal shirt with short sleeves, a COLLAR and a few buttons at the neck 馬球衫（開領短袖）➲ VISUAL VOCAB page V63

pol·ter·geist /ˈpəʊltəgaɪst; ˈpɒl-; *NAmE* ˈpoʊltərg-/ *noun* a GHOST that makes loud noises and throws objects 促狹鬼（有時發怪聲、亂扔東西）

pol·troon /pɒlˈtruːn; *NAmE* pɑːlˈt-/ *noun* (*old use, disapproving*) a COWARD (= a person who lacks courage) 膽小鬼；懦夫

poly /ˈpɒli; *NAmE* ˈpɑːli/ *noun* (*pl.* **polys**) (*BrE, informal*) = POLYTECHNIC

poly- /ˈpɒli; *NAmE* ˈpɑːli/ *combining form* (in nouns, adjectives and adverbs 構成名詞、形容詞和副詞) many 多；複：*polygamy* 一夫多妻 ◇ *polyphonic* 複調的

poly·an·dry /ˌpɒliˈændri; *NAmE* ˌpɑːl-/ *noun* [U] (*technical* 術語) the custom of having more than one husband at the same time 一妻多夫（制）➲ compare POLYGAMY ▸ **poly·an·drous** /ˌpɒliˈændrəs; *NAmE* ˌpɑːl-/ *adj.*

poly·an·thus /ˌpɒliˈænθəs; *NAmE* ˌpɑːl-/ *noun* [C, U] a small garden plant with round brightly coloured flowers, several of which grow at the end of each STEM 西洋櫻草（矮小花園植物，開鮮豔圓形花）

poly·car·bon·ate /ˌpɒliˈkɑːbənət; *NAmE* ˌpɑːliˈkɑːrb-/ *noun* [U, C] (*technical* 術語) a very strong transparent plastic used, for example, in windows and LENSES 聚碳酸酯（堅硬透明塑料，用於窗子和鏡頭等）

poly·clinic /ˈpɒliklɪnɪk; *NAmE* ˈpɑːl-/ *noun* (*BrE*) a medical centre that is not part of a hospital, where both general doctors and specialists work 綜合診所；綜合診療中心

poly·es·ter /ˌpɒliˈestə(r); *NAmE* ˌpɑːli-; ˈpɑːliestər/ *noun* [U] a strong material made of FIBRES (called polyesters) which are produced by chemical processes, often mixed with other materials and used especially for making clothes 聚酯纖維；滌綸：*a cotton and polyester shirt* 滌棉混紡襯衫

poly·ethyl·ene /ˌpɒliˈeθəliːn; *NAmE* ˌpɑːl-/ (*NAmE*) (*BrE* **poly·thene**) *noun* [U] a strong thin plastic material, used especially for making bags or for wrapping things in 聚乙烯

pol·yg·amy /pəˈlɪɡəmi/ *noun* [U] (*technical* 術語) the custom of having more than one wife at the same time 一夫多妻（制）➲ compare POLYANDRY ▸ **pol·yg·am·ist** /pəˈlɪɡəmɪst/ *noun* **pol·yg·am·ous** /pəˈlɪɡəməs/ *adj.*：*a polygamous marriage/society* 一夫多妻制婚姻／社會

poly·glot /ˈpɒliɡlɒt; *NAmE* ˈpɑːliɡlɑːt/ *adj.* (*formal*) knowing, using or written in more than one language 通曉（或使用）多種語言的；用多種語言寫成的 **SYN** **multilingual**：*a polyglot nation* 多語種民族 ▸ **poly·glot** *noun*

poly·gon /ˈpɒlɪɡən; *NAmE* ˈpɑːliɡɑːn/ *noun* (*geometry* 幾何) a flat shape with at least three straight sides and angles, and usually five or more 多邊形；多角形 ➲ **VISUAL VOCAB** page V71 ▸ **pol·yg·on·al** /pəˈlɪɡənl/ *adj.*

poly·graph /ˈpɒliɡræf; *NAmE* ˈpɑːli-; *BrE* also -ɡrɑːf/ *noun* (*technical* 術語) (*formal*) = LIE DETECTOR

poly·he·dron /ˌpɒliˈhiːdrən; -ˈhed-; *NAmE* ˌpɑːli-/ *noun* (*pl.* **poly·he·dra** /-ˈhiːdrə; -ˈhed-/ or **poly·he·drons**) (*geometry* 幾何) a solid shape with many flat sides, usually more than six 多面體（通常指多於六面）▸ **poly·he·dral** *adj.*

poly·math /ˈpɒlimæθ; *NAmE* ˈpɑːl-/ *noun* (*formal, approving*) a person who knows a lot about many different subjects 博學家；博學大師

poly·mer /ˈpɒlɪmə(r); *NAmE* ˈpɑːl-/ *noun* (*chemistry* 化) a natural or artificial substance consisting of large MOLECULES (= groups of atoms) that are made from combinations of small simple MOLECULES 聚合物；聚合體

poly·mer·ize (*BrE* also **-ise**) /ˈpɒlɪməraɪz; *NAmE* ˈpɑːli-/ *verb* [I, T] **~ (sth)** (*chemistry* 化) to combine, or to make units of a chemical combine, to make a POLYMER（使）聚合：*The substance polymerizes to form a hard plastic.* 這種物質聚合形成堅硬的塑料。▸ **poly·mer·iza·tion** /ˌpɒlimәraɪˈzeɪʃn; *NAmE* ˌpɑːli-/ *noun* [U]

poly·morph·ous /ˌpɒliˈmɔːfəs; *NAmE* ˌpɑːliˈmɔːrfəs/ (also **poly·morph·ic** /-fɪk/) *adj.* (*formal* or *technical* 術語) having or passing through many stages of development（發展）呈多種形式的，多態的

polyp /ˈpɒlɪp; *NAmE* ˈpɑːlɪp/ *noun* **1** (*medical* 醫) a small lump that grows inside the body, especially in the nose, that is caused by disease but is usually harmless 息肉；（尤指）鼻息肉 **2** a small and very simple sea creature with a body shaped like a tube（水螅型）珊瑚蟲；水螅蟲

pol·yph·ony /pəˈlɪfəni/ *noun* [U] (*music* 音) the combination of several different patterns of musical notes sung together to form a single piece of music 複調音樂；複調樂曲 **SYN** **counterpoint** ▸ **poly·phon·ic** /ˌpɒliˈfɒnɪk; *NAmE* ˌpɑːliˈfɑːnɪk/ *adj.*

poly·pro·pyl·ene /ˌpɒliˈprəʊpəliːn; *NAmE* ˌpɑːliˈproʊ-/ *noun* [U] a strong plastic often used for objects such as toys or chairs that are made in a MOULD 聚丙烯

poly·sem·ous /ˌpɒliˈsiːməs; *NAmE* ˌpɑːl-/ *adj.* (*linguistics* 語言) (of a word 詞) having more than one meaning（一詞）多義的

poly·semy /pəˈlɪsɪmi/ *noun* [U] (*linguistics* 語言) the fact of having more than one meaning（一詞）多義；多義性；多義現象

poly·styr·ene /ˌpɒliˈstaɪriːn; *NAmE* ˌpɑːl-/ (also **Styro·foam™** especially in *NAmE*) *noun* [U] a very light soft plastic that is usually white, used especially for making containers that prevent heat loss. 聚苯乙烯：*polystyrene cups* 聚苯乙烯杯子

poly·syl·lable /ˈpɒlisɪləbl; *NAmE* ˈpɑːl-/ *noun* (*technical* 術語) a word of several (usually more than three) syllables 多音節詞 ▸ **poly·syl·lab·ic** /ˌpɒlisɪˈlæbɪk; *NAmE* ˌpɑːl-/ *adj.*

poly·tech·nic /ˌpɒliˈteknɪk; *NAmE* ˌpɑːl-/ (also *BrE informal* **poly**) *noun* (in Britain in the past) a college for higher education, especially in scientific and technical subjects. Most polytechnics are now called, and have the same status as, universities.（舊時英國的）理工學院（現在多已改為大學）

poly·the·ism /ˈpɒliθiɪzəm; *NAmE* ˈpɑːl-/ *noun* [U] the belief that there is more than one god 多神論；多神信仰 ➲ compare MONOTHEISM ▸ **poly·the·is·tic** /ˌpɒliθiˈɪstɪk; *NAmE* ˌpɑːl-/ *adj.*

poly·thene /ˈpɒlɪθiːn; *NAmE* ˈpɑːl-/ (*BrE*) (*NAmE* **poly·ethyl·ene**) *noun* [U] a strong thin plastic material, used especially for making bags or for wrapping things in 聚乙烯：*a polythene bag* 聚乙烯袋

poly·tun·nel /ˈpɒlitʌnl; *NAmE* ˈpɑːl-/ *noun* a long low structure covered with plastic, used for growing seeds or young plants outdoors 塑料大棚；塑料暖房 ➲ **VISUAL VOCAB** pages V2, V3

poly·un·sat·ur·ated fat /ˌpɒliʌnˌsætʃəreɪtɪd ˈfæt; *NAmE* ˌpɑːl-/ *noun* [C, U] a type of fat found, for example, in seeds and vegetable oils, which does not encourage the harmful development of CHOLESTEROL 多不飽和脂肪（存在於種子和植物油等中，不促進膽固醇的有害增長）：*foods that are high in polyunsaturated fats* 富含多不飽和脂肪的食物 ➲ see also MONOUNSATURATED FAT, SATURATED FAT, TRANS-FATTY ACID, UNSATURATED FAT ▸ **poly·un·sat·ur·ates** /ˌpɒliʌnˈsætʃərəts; *NAmE* ˌpɑːl-/ *noun* [pl.]：*foods that are high in polyunsaturates* (= polyunsaturated fats) 富含多不飽和脂肪的食物

poly·ur·eth·ane /ˌpɒliˈjʊərəθeɪn; *NAmE* ˌpɑːliˈjʊr-/ *noun* [U] (*technical* 術語) a type of plastic material used in making paints, glues, etc. 聚氨酯；聚氨基甲酸酯

poly·va·lent /ˌpɒliˈveɪlənt; *NAmE* ˌpɑːl-/ *adj.* **1** (*chemistry* 化) having a VALENCY of 3 or more 多價的 **2** (*formal*) having many different functions or forms 多功能的；多形式的：*polyvalent managerial skills* 多方面的管理技能 ▸ **poly·va·lence** /ˌpɒliˈveɪləns; *NAmE* ˌpɑːl-/ *noun* [U]

pom /pɒm; *NAmE* pɑːm/ *noun* = POMMY

Poma™ /ˈpəʊmə; *NAmE* ˈpoʊmə/ *noun* (*BrE*) = BUTTON LIFT

pom·ade /pəˈmeɪd; -ˈmɑːd/ *noun* (*old-fashioned*) [U, C] a liquid that is put on the hair to make it look shiny and smell nice 髮油

po·man·der /pəˈmændə(r); *NAmE* ˈpoʊmændər/ *noun* a round container filled with dried flowers, leaves, etc. that is used to give a pleasant smell to rooms or clothes 香盒（圓形，盛乾的馨香花葉等）

pom·egran·ate /ˈpɒmɪɡrænɪt; *NAmE* ˈpɑːm-/ *noun* a round fruit with thick smooth skin and red flesh full of large seeds 石榴 ➲ **VISUAL VOCAB** page V30

pom·elo /ˈpɒmələʊ; *NAmE* ˈpɑːməloʊ/ (also **pum·melo**) *noun* (*pl.* **-os**) a large CITRUS fruit that has thick yellow skin and that tastes similar to a GRAPEFRUIT, but sweeter 柚子

pom·mel /ˈpɒml; *NAmE* ˈpɑːml/ *noun* **1** the higher front part of a SADDLE on a horse（馬鞍）鞍橋，鞍頭 **2** the round part on the end of the handle of a SWORD（劍柄頂端的）圓球

ˈpommel horse *noun* a large object on four legs with two handles on top, which GYMNASTS put their hands on and swing their body and legs around 鞍馬

pommy /ˈpɒmi; *NAmE* ˈpɑːmi/ *noun* (*pl.* **-ies**) (also **pom**) (*AustralE, NZE, informal*) an offensive word for a British person（蔑稱）英國人

pomp /pɒmp; *NAmE* pɑːmp/ *noun* [U] the impressive clothes, decorations, music, etc. and traditional customs that are part of an official occasion or ceremony 排場；氣派；盛況：*all the pomp and ceremony of a royal wedding* 王室婚禮的盛大場面與儀式

IDM **ˌpomp and ˈcircumstance** formal and impressive ceremony 隆重的儀式

pom·pom /ˈpɒmpɒm; *NAmE* ˈpɑːmpɑːm/ (also **pom·pon** /ˈpɒmpɒn; *NAmE* ˈpɑːmpɑːn/) *noun* **1** a small ball made of wool, used for decoration, especially on a hat 小絨球（尤用以裝飾帽子）**SYN** **bobble** ➲ **VISUAL VOCAB** page V65 **2** (especially in the US) a large round bunch of strips of plastic, tied to a handle, used by CHEERLEADERS（美國啦啦隊常用的）塑料絲球

P

pom·pous /ˈpɒmpəs; *NAmE* ˈpɑːm-/ *adj.* (*disapproving*) showing that you think you are more important than other people, especially by using long and formal words 虛華的；言辭浮誇的 **SYN** **pretentious**：*a pompous official* 自負的官員 ▸ **pom·pos·ity** /pɒmˈpɒsəti; *NAmE* pɑːmˈpɑːs-/ *noun* [U]：*The prince's manner was informal, without a trace of pomposity.* 王子態度平易謙和，沒有一點傲氣。 **pom·pous·ly** *adv.*

ponce /pɒns; *NAmE* pɑːns/ *noun, verb*
■ ***noun*** (*BrE, informal*) **1** a man who controls one or several PROSTITUTES and the money that they earn 男鴇；拉皮條者 **SYN** **pimp** **2** an offensive word for a man whose appearance and behaviour seem similar to a woman's, or who is thought to be HOMOSEXUAL 娘娘腔的男人；貌似同性戀的男子
■ ***verb***
PHR V **ˌponce aˈbout/aˈround** (usually used in the progressive tenses 通常用於進行時) (*BrE, informal*) to waste time when you are doing sth so that you achieve nothing; to do silly things in a way that looks ridiculous 無事忙；幹些無聊的事

poncey (also **poncy**) /ˈpɒnsi; *NAmE* ˈpɑːnsi/ *adj.* (*BrE, disapproving, informal*) trying to be impressive in a way that is silly and not natural 虛誇的；張揚而做作的：*I don't want to go to some poncey restaurant—I just want something to eat!* 我不想去什麼花裏胡哨的餐館，我只想吃點東西！

pon·cho /ˈpɒntʃəʊ; *NAmE* ˈpɑːntʃoʊ/ *noun* (*pl.* **-os**) a type of coat without sleeves, made from one large piece of cloth with a hole in the middle for the head to go through 龐喬斗篷（在大塊織物正中開領口製成）

pond /pɒnd; *NAmE* pɑːnd/ *noun* a small area of still water, especially one that is artificial 池塘；人工池：*a fish pond* 養魚池 ➲ VISUAL VOCAB pages V2, V19
IDM **across the ˈpond** (*informal*) on the other side of the Atlantic Ocean from Britain/the US 在大西洋彼岸 ➲ more at BIG *adj.*

pon·der /ˈpɒndə(r); *NAmE* ˈpɑːn-/ *verb* [I, T] (*formal*) to think about sth carefully for a period of time 沉思；考慮；琢磨 **SYN** **consider**：**~ (about/on/over sth)** *She pondered over his words.* 她反複琢磨他的話。◇ *They were left to ponder on the implications of the announcement.* 交由他們去琢磨這項宣告的含義。◇ **~ sth** *The senator pondered the question for a moment.* 這位參議員考慮了一下這個問題。◇ **~ whether, what, etc. ...** *They are pondering whether the money could be better used elsewhere.* 他們正在斟酌能否把錢花到其他更適當的地方。◇ **+ speech** *'I wonder why,' she pondered aloud.* "我想知道為什麼。" 她邊想邊說。

pon·der·ous /ˈpɒndərəs; *NAmE* ˈpɑːn-/ *adj.* (*formal*) **1** (*disapproving*) (of speech and writing 言語或文字) too slow and careful; serious and boring 慢條斯理的；遲重的；沉悶乏味的 **SYN** **tedious** **2** moving slowly and heavily; able to move only slowly 緩慢的；笨拙的；笨重的 **SYN** **laboured**：*She watched the cow's ponderous progress.* 她看着牛遲緩地向前走着。 ▸ **pon·der·ous·ly** *adv.* **pon·der·ous·ness** *noun* [U]

ˈpond skater (*BrE*) (*NAmE* **ˈwater strider**) *noun* an insect that moves quickly across the surface of water 黽蝽；水黽

pone /pəʊn; *NAmE* poʊn/ *noun* [U] (*US*) = CORN PONE

pong /pɒŋ; *NAmE* pɔːŋ; pɑːŋ/ *noun* (*BrE, informal*) a strong unpleasant smell 強烈難聞的氣味；臭味；惡臭 ▸ **pong** *verb* [I]：*That cheese pongs!* 那奶酪熏死人了！

pon·tiff /ˈpɒntɪf; *NAmE* ˈpɑːn-/ *noun* (*formal*) the POPE (= the leader of the Roman Catholic Church) 教宗；宗座

pon·tif·ic·al /pɒnˈtɪfɪkl; *NAmE* pɑːn-/ *adj.* (*formal*) connected with a POPE 教宗的；宗座的

pon·tifi·cate *verb, noun*
■ ***verb*** /pɒnˈtɪfɪkeɪt; *NAmE* pɑːn-/ [I] **~ (about/on sth)** (*disapproving*) to give your opinions about sth in a way that shows that you think you are right 自以為是地談論；目空一切地議論
■ ***noun*** /pɒnˈtɪfɪkət; *NAmE* pɑːn-/ the official position or period in office of a POPE 教宗職務（或在任時期）

pon·toon /pɒnˈtuːn; *NAmE* pɑːn-/ *noun* **1** [C] a temporary floating platform built across several boats or hollow structures, especially one used for tying boats to 浮碼頭；浮橋平台 **2** [C] a boat or hollow structure that is one of several used to support a floating platform or bridge（支撐浮橋的）浮筒，躉船：*a pontoon bridge* 浮橋 **3** [U] (*BrE*) = BLACKJACK (1)

pony /ˈpəʊni; *NAmE* ˈpoʊni/ *noun, verb*
■ ***noun*** (*pl.* **-ies**) **1** a type of small horse 小型馬；矮馬 ➲ see also SHETLAND PONY **2** (*BrE, slang*) £25 * 25 英鎊
IDM see DOG *n.*, SHANK
■ ***verb*** (**po·nies**, **pony·ing**, **po·nied**, **po·nied**)
PHR V **ˌpony ˈup sth** (*NAmE, informal*) to pay money for sth 為…付款：*Each guest had to pony up $40 for the meal.* 每位來賓都得為這頓飯付 40 元。

pony·tail /ˈpəʊniteɪl; *NAmE* ˈpoʊ-/ *noun* a bunch of hair tied at the back of the head so that it hangs like a horse's tail 馬尾辮 ➲ VISUAL VOCAB page V60 ➲ compare PIGTAIL

ˈpony-trekking *noun* [U] (*BrE*) the activity of riding PONIES in the countryside for pleasure 騎矮馬兜風（或野遊）：*to go pony-trekking* 騎矮馬出遊

Ponzi scheme /ˈpɒnzi skiːm; *NAmE* ˈpɑːnzi/ *noun* a plan for making money that involves encouraging people to invest by offering them a high rate of interest and using their money to pay earlier INVESTORS. When there are not enough new INVESTORS, people who have recently invested lose their money. 龐氏騙局，非法吸金，老鼠會，種金（指提供高息以吸引人們投資，將得來的錢用於償還之前的投資者，而當沒有足夠的新投資者時，就會給最近的投資者造成損失） **ORIGIN** From Charles Ponzi, who organized the first scheme of this kind in the US in 1919. 源自查爾斯•龐茲。他於 1919 年在美國首次策劃了此類騙局。

poo (also **pooh**) /puː/ (both *BrE*) *noun* [U, C] (also **poop** *NAmE, BrE*) a child's word for the solid waste that is passed through the BOWELS（兒童用語）屎，屁屁 **SYN** **faeces**：*dog poo* 狗屎 ◇ *I want to do a poo!* 我要拉屁屁！ ▸ **poo** (also **pooh**) *verb* [I]

pooch /puːtʃ/ *noun* (*informal, especially NAmE*) a dog 狗

poo·dle /ˈpuːdl/ *noun* **1** a dog with thick curly hair that is sometimes cut into special shapes 鬈毛狗 **2** (*BrE, informal*) a person who is too willing to do what sb else tells them to do 百依百順的人

poof /pʊf/ *noun, exclamation*
■ ***noun*** (also **poof·ter** /ˈpʊftə(r)/) (*BrE, taboo, slang*) an offensive word for a HOMOSEXUAL man（指男同性戀者）假鸞鸞，雞公對
■ ***exclamation*** used when talking about sth disappearing suddenly（描述事物突然消失）嗖的一聲，刺溜一下：*He walked through—and vanished. Poof! Like that.* 他走了過去，然後就嗖的一下子不見了。

pooh /puː/ *exclamation, noun, verb*
■ ***exclamation*** (*especially BrE*) **1** used to express disgust at a bad smell（表示對臭味的厭惡）噗，呸：*It stinks! Pooh!* 好臭！噗！ **2** used to say that you think sb's idea, suggestion, etc. is not very good or that you do not believe what sb has said（表示對別人的意見等不屑一顧或不相信）喊，得了吧：*'I might lose my job for this.' 'Oh, pooh, nobody will care.'* "這下子我可能會丟飯碗了。" "喊，得了吧！誰會在乎！"
■ ***noun, verb*** = POO

ˌpooh-ˈpooh *verb* **~ sth** (*informal*) to say that a suggestion, an idea, etc. is not true or not worth thinking about 說…不真實；對…不屑一顧（或嗤之以鼻）

pool 0‑w /puːl/ *noun, verb*
■ ***noun***
‣ **FOR SWIMMING** 游泳 **1** 0‑w [C] = SWIMMING POOL：*Does the hotel have a pool?* 這家旅館有沒有游泳池？◇ *relaxing by the pool* 在游泳池邊休息 ➲ see also PLUNGE POOL
‣ **OF WATER** 水 **2** 0‑w [C] a small area of still water, especially one that has formed naturally 水坑，水塘，池塘（尤指自然形成的）：*freshwater pools* 淡水池塘 ◇ *a rock*

pool (= between rocks by the sea)（海邊岩石間的）潮水潭

▸ **OF LIQUID/LIGHT** 液體；光 **3** 🔑 [C] **~ (of sth)** a small amount of liquid or light lying on a surface 一灘（液體）；一小片（液體或光）：*The body was lying in a pool of blood.* 屍體倒卧在血泊之中。◇ *a pool of light* 一小片亮光

▸ **GROUP OF THINGS/PEOPLE** 眾人；事物 **4** [C] **~ (of sth)** a supply of things or money that is shared by a group of people and can be used when needed 共用的資源（或資金）：*a pool of cars used by the firm's sales force* 公司銷售人員共用的車輛 ◇ *a pool car* 一輛共用的汽車 **5** [C] **~ (of sth)** a group of people available for work when needed（統稱）備用人員：*a pool of cheap labour* 廉價後備勞力

▸ **GAME** 遊戲 **6** [U] a game for two people played with 16 balls on a table, often in pubs and bars. Players use CUES (= long sticks) to try to hit the balls into pockets at the edge of the table. 普爾；落袋枱球；彈子球；落袋撞球：*a pool table* 普爾球枱 ◇ *to shoot (= play) pool* 打普爾 ➲ **VISUAL VOCAB** page V40 ➲ compare BILLIARDS, SNOOKER *n.* (1)

▸ **FOOTBALL** 足球 **7 the pools** [pl.] = FOOTBALL POOLS：*He does the pools every week.* 他每週都去賭足球普爾。◇ *a pools winner* 賭普爾獲勝者 ➲ see also GENE POOL

■ ***verb*** **~ sth** to collect money, information, etc. from different people so that it can be used by all of them 集中資源（或材料等）：*The students work individually, then pool their ideas in groups of six.* 學生先分頭工作，然後六人一組交流意見。◇ *Police forces across the country are pooling resources in order to solve this crime.* 全國各地警方通力合作以偵破這宗罪案。

pool·room /ˈpuːlruːm; -rʊm/ *noun* (*NAmE*) **1** a place for playing a game of POOL 枱球室 **2** a BETTING SHOP 彩票經銷點；彩票投注站

pool·side /ˈpuːlsaɪd/ *noun* [sing.] the area around a swimming pool 游泳池池邊：*lazing at the poolside* 在游泳池邊消閒 ◇ *a poolside bar* 游泳池邊酒吧

poop /puːp/ *noun, verb*

■ ***noun*** **1** (also **ˈpoop deck**) [C] the raised part at the back end of a ship 船尾樓甲板 ➲ compare STERN *n.* **2** [U] (*especially NAmE*) (*BrE* also **poo**) (*informal*) a child's word for the solid waste that is passed through the BOWELS（兒童用語）屁屁：*dog poop on the sidewalk* 便道上的狗屎 **3** [U] (*old-fashioned, informal, especially NAmE*) information about sth, especially the most recent news 信息；（尤指）最新消息

■ ***verb*** (*NAmE, informal*) **1** [I] to pass solid waste from the BOWELS 拉屎；大便：*The dog just pooped in the kitchen!* 狗剛在廚房拉屎了！ **2** [T] **~ sb (out)** to make sb very tired 累垮（某人）；使筋疲力盡

PHR V **ˌpoop ˈout** to stop working or functioning 停止工作；拋錨；喪失功能

pooped /puːpt/ (also **ˌpooped ˈout**) *adj.* [not before noun] (*informal, especially NAmE*) very tired 疲憊不堪；筋疲力盡

pooper scoop·er /ˈpuːpə skuːpə(r)/ (also **ˈpoop scoop**) *noun* (*informal*) a tool used by dog owners for removing their dogs' solid waste from the streets, parks, etc. 狗糞鏟；狗糞夾

poor 🔑 /pɔː(r); pʊə(r); *NAmE* pɔːr; pʊr/ *adj.* (**poor·er, poor·est**)

▸ **HAVING LITTLE MONEY** 拮据 **1** 🔑 having very little money; not having enough money for basic needs 貧窮的；貧寒的；清貧的：*They were too poor to buy shoes for the kids.* 他們窮得沒錢給孩子買鞋穿。◇ *We aim to help the poorest families.* 我們的目標是接濟最貧困的家庭。◇ *It's among the poorer countries of the world.* 它是世界上的貧窮國家之一。**OPP** rich **2 the poor** *noun* [pl.] people who have very little money 貧困者；窮人：*They provided food and shelter for the poor.* 他們為貧困者提供食物和住所。**OPP** **the rich**

▸ **UNFORTUNATE** 不幸 **3** 🔑 [only before noun] deserving pity and sympathy 可憐的；不幸的；令人同情的：*Have you heard about **poor old** Harry? His wife's left him.* 你聽說了不幸的老哈里的近況嗎？他妻子離他而去了。◇ *It's hungry—the poor little thing.* 它餓了，這可憐的小傢伙。◇ *'I have stacks of homework to do.' 'Oh, **you poor thing**.'* "我有一大堆的作業要做哪。" "唉喲，你好可憐哦。"

Synonyms 同義詞辨析

poor

disadvantaged • needy • impoverished • deprived • penniless • hard up

These words all describe sb who has very little or no money and therefore cannot satisfy their basic needs. 以上各詞均形容人貧窮、貧寒。

poor having very little money; not having enough money for basic needs 指貧窮的、貧寒的、清貧的：*They were too poor to buy shoes for the kids.* 他們窮得沒錢給孩子買鞋穿。

disadvantaged having less money and fewer opportunities than most people in society 指生活條件差的、貧困的、社會地位低下的：*socially disadvantaged sections of the community* 該社區社會地位低下的貧困階層

needy poor 指缺乏生活必需品的、貧困的：*It's a charity that provides help for needy children.* 這是一個為貧困孩子提供援助的慈善機構。

impoverished (*journalism*) poor 指赤貧的、不名一文的：*Thousands of impoverished peasants are desperate to move to the cities.* 成千上萬赤貧的農民急切盼望搬到城裏去。

deprived [usually before noun] without enough food, education, and all the things that are necessary for people to live a happy and comfortable life 指貧窮的、窮困的、窮苦的

POOR, NEEDY, IMPOVERISHED OR DEPRIVED? 用 poor、needy、impoverished 還是 deprived？

Poor is the most general of these words and can be used to describe yourself, another individual person, people as a group, or a country or an area. **Needy** is mostly used to describe people considered as a group: it is not used to talk about yourself or individual people. * poor 在這組詞中最通用，可用以描述自己、另一個人、某個群體、國家或地區。needy 主要用以描述群體，不用以描述自己或個人：*poor/needy children/families* 貧困的孩子／家庭 ◇ ~~*They were too needy to buy shoes for the kids.*~~ **Impoverished** is used, especially in journalism, to talk about poor countries and the people who live there. To talk about poor areas in rich countries, use **deprived**. * impoverished 尤用於新聞，指貧窮國家和生活在貧窮國家的人。指富裕國家的貧困地區用 deprived。

penniless (*literary*) having no money; very poor 指一文不名的、窮困的：*He died penniless in Paris.* 他死於巴黎，死時身無分文。

hard up (*informal*) having very little money, especially for a short period of time 尤指暫時拮据、缺錢：*I was always hard up as a student.* 我當學生時總是很拮据。

PATTERNS

- poor/disadvantaged/needy/impoverished/deprived/penniless/hard-up **people/families**
- poor/disadvantaged/needy/impoverished/deprived **areas**
- poor/disadvantaged/impoverished **countries**
- a(n) poor/disadvantaged/impoverished/deprived **background**

▸ **NOT GOOD** 不好 **4** 🔑 not good; of a quality that is low or lower than expected 劣質的；差的；次的：*the party's poor performance in the election* 該黨在選舉中的表現欠佳 ◇ *to be in poor health* 身體不好 ◇ *It was raining heavily and visibility was poor.* 當時天下着大雨，能見度很低。◇ *poor food/light/soil* 劣質食品；昏暗的光線；貧瘠的土地 ◇ *to have a poor opinion of sb* (= to not think well of sb) 對某人評價很低 **5** 🔑 (of a person 人) not good or skilled at sth 不擅長的；不熟練的：*a poor swimmer* 不擅游泳

P

的人 ◇ *a poor judge of character* 不擅看人的人 ◇ *She's a good teacher but a poor manager.* 她長於教學，卻拙於管理。◇ *a poor sailor* (= sb who easily gets sick at sea) 易暈船的人

▸ **HAVING LITTLE OF STH** 匱乏 **6** ~ **in sth** having very small amounts of sth 缺乏；貧乏；缺少：*a country poor in natural resources* 自然資源貧乏的國家 ◇ *soil poor in nutrients* 養分不足的土壤 **OPP** **rich**

IDM **be/come a poor second, third, etc.** (*especially BrE*) to finish a long way behind the winner in a race, competition, etc. (在體育競賽等中) 遠遠落後 **the ˌpoor man's 'sb/'sth** a person or thing that is similar to but of a lower quality than a particular famous person or thing (比同類的名人顯物) 遜色的人 (或物)；次級貨色：*Sparkling white wine is the poor man's champagne.* 白葡萄汽酒是廉價的香檳。➲ more at ACCOUNT *n.*

poor·house /'pɔːhaʊs; 'pʊə-; *NAmE* 'pʊr-; 'pɔːr-/ (*BrE* also **work·house**) *noun* (in Britain in the past) a building where very poor people were sent to live and given work to do (英國舊時的) 救濟院，濟貧院，勞動救濟所

the 'Poor Law *noun* a group of laws used in Britain in the past to control the help that was given to poor people (英國舊時的) 濟貧法

poor·ly /'pɔːli; 'pʊəli; *NAmE* 'pʊrli; 'pɔːrli/ *adv., adj.*

■ ***adv.*** in a way that is not good enough 糟糕地；不如意；不足 **SYN** **badly**：*a poorly attended meeting* (= at which there are not many people) 寥寥幾個人參加的會議 ◇ *poorly designed* 設計不周的 ◇ *The job is relatively poorly paid.* 相對而言，這工作報酬很低。◇ *Our candidate* ***fared poorly*** *in the election* (= did not get many votes). 我們的候選人在選舉中得票不多。

■ ***adj.*** [not usually before noun] (*BrE, informal*) ill/sick 有病；不適；不舒服：*She felt poorly.* 她感到身體不適。

poor·ness /'pɔːnəs; 'pʊənəs; *NAmE* 'pɔːrnəs; 'pʊrnəs/ *noun* [U] the state of lacking a good quality or feature (優點等的) 匱乏，缺乏，貧乏：*The poorness of the land makes farming impossible.* 土地貧瘠以致無法耕作。

ˌpoor re'lation *noun* something that is not treated with as much respect as other similar things because it is not thought to be as good, important or successful 略遜一籌的事物；不受青睞的事物：*The short story is often considered to be a poor relation to the novel.* 人們通常認為短篇小說遠不如長篇小說受青睞。

poo·tle /'puːtl/ *verb* [I] + **adv./prep.** (*BrE, informal*) to move or travel without any hurry 緩慢地移動 (或行進)：*She pootled along in her old car.* 她開着舊車緩緩而行。

pop /pɒp; *NAmE* pɑːp/ *noun, verb, adj., adv.*

■ ***noun***

▸ **MUSIC** 音樂 **1** (also **'pop music**) [U] popular music of the sort that has been popular since the 1950s, usually with a strong rhythm and simple tunes, often contrasted with rock, SOUL and other forms of popular music 流行音樂，流行樂曲 (通常與搖滾樂、靈樂和其他形式的流行音樂相對)：*rock, pop and soul* 搖滾樂、流行音樂和靈樂 ➲ COLLOCATIONS at MUSIC

▸ **SOUND** 聲音 **2** [C] a short sharp EXPLOSIVE sound (短促清脆的爆裂聲) 砰：*The cork came out of the bottle with a loud pop.* 軟木塞砰的一聲從瓶口迸了出來。

▸ **DRINK** 飲料 **3** [U] (*old-fashioned, informal*) a sweet FIZZY drink (= with bubbles) that is not alcoholic 汽水

▸ **FATHER** 父親 **4** [sing.] (*informal, especially NAmE*) used as a word for 'father', especially as a form of address (尤用作稱呼) 爸，爹：*Hi, Pop!* 喂，爸！

IDM **have/take a 'pop (at sb)** (*BrE, informal*) to attack sb physically or in words 攻擊，抨擊 (某人) **... a pop** (*informal, especially NAmE*) costing a particular amount for each one 每個…錢：*We can charge $50 a pop.* 我們可以每個收費 50 元。

■ ***verb*** **(-pp-)**

▸ **MAKE SOUND** 發聲 **1** [I, T] ~ **(sth)** to make a short EXPLOSIVE sound; to cause sth to make this sound (使) 發砰砰聲：*the sound of corks popping* 瓶塞被拔起時發出的砰砰聲 **2** [T, I] ~ **(sth)** to burst, or make sth burst, with a short EXPLOSIVE sound (使) 爆裂，發爆裂聲：*She jumped as someone popped a balloon behind her.* 有人在她背後弄爆了一個氣球，把她嚇了一跳。

▸ **GO QUICKLY** 速去 **3** [I] + **adv./prep.** (*BrE, informal*) to go somewhere quickly, suddenly or for a short time (突然或匆匆) 去：*I'll pop over and see you this evening.* 我今晚就趕去看你。◇ *Why don't you pop in* (= visit us) *for a drink next time you're in the area?* 下次來到這一帶時，就到我們這兒小酌一杯如何？

▸ **PUT QUICKLY** 迅速放置 **4** [T] ~ **sth/sb** + **adv./prep.** (*informal, especially BrE*) to put sth/sb somewhere quickly, suddenly or for a short time (迅速或突然) 放置：*He popped his head around the door and said hello.* 他從門後探一探頭，打了聲招呼。◇ *I'll pop the books in* (= deliver them) *on my way home.* 我回家時順便把書送過去吧。◇ *Pop your bag on here.* 把你的包放在這上面。

▸ **APPEAR SUDDENLY** 突然出現 **5** [I] + **adv./prep.** to suddenly appear, especially when not expected 突然出現；冷不防冒出：*The window opened and a dog's head popped out.* 窗子打開了，冷不防一隻狗探出頭來。◇ *An idea suddenly popped into his head.* 他突然想到了一個主意。◇ (*computing* 計) *The menu pops up when you click twice on the mouse.* 雙擊鼠標，選單便會彈出來。

▸ **OF EARS** 耳朵 **6** [I] if your ears **pop** when you are going up or down in a plane, etc., the pressure in them suddenly changes (乘飛機等升降時) 耳壓變化；(耳) 脹

▸ **OF EYES** 眼睛 **7** [I] if your eyes **pop** or **pop out**, they suddenly open fully because you are surprised or excited (因激動、驚奇) 張大，睜大，瞪起：*Her eyes nearly popped out of her head when she saw them.* 她一看到他們，眼睛瞪得快要掉出來了。

▸ **TAKE DRUGS** 服藥 **8** [T] ~ **sth** (*informal*) to take a lot of a drug, regularly (經常) 服藥，用毒品：*She's been popping pills for months.* 她大量服藥已有幾個月了。

9 [T] ~ **the hood** (*NAmE*) to open the HOOD/BONNET of a car 打開汽車的引擎蓋

IDM **pop your 'clogs** (*BrE, humorous*) to die 翹辮子；上西天；一命嗚呼 **pop the 'question** (*informal*) to ask sb to marry you 開口求婚

PHR V **ˌpop 'off** (*informal*) to die 上西天；一命嗚呼 **ˌpop sth↔'on** (*BrE, informal*) **1** to put on a piece of clothing 穿 (衣)：*I'll just pop on a sweater and meet you outside.* 我套件毛衣就出來見你。 **2** to turn on a piece of electrical equipment 開啟 (電器)

■ ***adj.*** [only before noun]

▸ **MUSIC/STYLE** 音樂；風格 **1** connected with modern popular music 流行音樂的；通俗風格的：***a pop song*** 流行歌曲 ◇ ***a pop band/group*** 流行音樂樂隊 / 組合 ◇ ***a pop star*** 流行音樂歌星 ◇ ***a pop concert*** 流行音樂會 **2** made in a modern popular style 通俗的；現代的：*pop culture* 通俗文化

■ ***adv.***

IDM **go 'pop** to burst or explode with a sudden short sound 爆裂；爆炸：*The balloon went pop.* 氣球砰地一聲爆了。

pop. *abbr.* population 人口：*pop. 200 000* 人口 20 萬

'pop art (also **Pop Art**) *noun* [U] a style of art, developed in the 1960s, that was based on popular culture and used material such as advertisements, film/movie images, etc. 波普藝術，通俗藝術，大眾藝術 (20 世紀 60 年代興起，以通俗文化為基礎，以廣告和電影形象等為素材)

pop·corn /'pɒpkɔːn; *NAmE* 'pɑːpkɔːrn/ *noun* [U] a type of food made from grains of MAIZE (CORN) that are heated until they burst, forming light whitish balls that are then covered with salt or sugar 爆 (玉) 米花

pope /pəʊp; *NAmE* poʊp/ (often **the Pope**) *noun* the leader of the Roman Catholic Church, who is also the Bishop of Rome 教宗；教皇：*the election of a new pope* 新教宗的選舉 ◇ *Pope Benedict* 教皇本篤 ◇ *a visit from the Pope* 教宗的來訪 ➲ see also PAPACY, PAPAL

IDM **Is the Pope a 'Catholic?** (*humorous*) used to say that there is no doubt that sth is true 這還用問嗎；當然是：*'Will they arrive late?' 'Is the Pope a Catholic?'* "他們會遲到嗎？" "這還用問嗎？"

popery /ˈpəʊpəri; *NAmE* ˈpoʊ-/ *noun* [U] (*taboo*) an offensive way of referring to Roman Catholicism 教宗主義（對羅馬天主教的貶稱）

ˌpope's ˈnose *noun* (*NAmE*) = PARSON'S NOSE

ˈpop-eyed *adj.* (*informal*) having eyes that are wide open, especially because you are very surprised, excited or frightened（因驚恐或激動）瞪大眼睛的，雙目圓睜的

pop·gun /ˈpɒpɡʌn; *NAmE* ˈpɑːp-/ *noun* a toy gun that fires small objects such as CORKS and makes a short sharp noise 玩具氣槍

pop·ish /ˈpəʊpɪʃ; *NAmE* ˈpoʊ-/ *adj.* [usually before noun] (*taboo*, *offensive*) used by some people to describe sb/sth that is connected with Roman Catholicism（某些人用以形容與羅馬天主教有關的人或事物）

pop·lar /ˈpɒplə(r); *NAmE* ˈpɑːp-/ *noun* a tall straight tree with soft wood 楊，楊樹（樹幹高，木質較軟）

pop·lin /ˈpɒplɪn; *NAmE* ˈpɑːp-/ *noun* [U] a type of strong cotton cloth used for making clothes 府綢；毛葛

ˈpop music *noun* = POP *n.* (1)

pop·over /ˈpɒpəʊvə(r); *NAmE* ˈpɑːpoʊvər/ *noun* (*NAmE*) a type of food made from a mixture of eggs, milk and flour which rises to form a hollow shell when it is baked 空心鬆餅，膨鬆餅（將蛋、奶、麵調和後烘焙而成）

poppa /ˈpɒpə; *NAmE* ˈpɑːpə/ *noun* (*NAmE*, *informal*) used by children to talk about or to address their father（兒童用語）爸 ➲ see also PAPA, POP *n.* (4)

pop·pa·dom /ˈpɒpədəm; *NAmE* ˈpɑːp-/ *noun* a type of thin round crisp S Asian bread that is fried in oil and often served with CURRY 印度炸圓麵包（常佐以咖喱）

pop·per /ˈpɒpə(r); *NAmE* ˈpɑːp-/ *noun* (*BrE*) = PRESS STUD

pop·pet /ˈpɒpɪt; *NAmE* ˈpɑːp-/ *noun* (*BrE*, *informal*) used to talk to or about sb you like or love, especially a child 寶貝兒；乖乖；心肝兒

ˌpop psyˈchology *noun* [U] the use by ordinary people of simple or fashionable ideas from PSYCHOLOGY in order to understand or explain people's feelings and emotional problems 大眾心理學（普通人運用心理學中簡單或流行的概念來理解或解釋情感問題）

poppy /ˈpɒpi; *NAmE* ˈpɑːpi/ *noun* (*pl.* **-ies**) a wild or garden plant, with a large delicate flower that is usually red, and small black seeds. OPIUM is obtained from one type of poppy. 罌粟：*poppy fields/seeds* 罌粟田／籽 ➲ VISUAL VOCAB page V11

poppy·cock /ˈpɒpikɒk; *NAmE* ˈpɑːpikɑːk/ *noun* [U] (*old-fashioned*, *informal*) nonsense 廢話；胡說

ˈpop quiz *noun* (*NAmE*) a short test that is given to students without any warning（給學生的）突擊小測驗

Pop·sicle™ /ˈpɒpsɪkl; *NAmE* ˈpɑːp-/ (*NAmE*) (*BrE* **ˌice ˈlolly**, *informal* **lolly**) *noun* a piece of ice flavoured with fruit, served on a stick 冰棍；冰棒

pop·sock /ˈpɒpsɒk; *NAmE* ˈpɑːpsɑːk/ *noun* a short STOCKING that covers the foot and the lower part of the leg to the ankle or knee 女式短襪；中統襪

pop·tas·tic /pɒpˈtæstik; *NAmE* pɑːp-/ *adj.* (*informal*, *especially BrE*) very good 呱呱叫的：*She's the most poptastic pop star of the lot.* 她是這批流行歌星中最棒的。

popu·lace /ˈpɒpjələs; *NAmE* ˈpɑːp-/ (usually **the popu·lace**) *noun* [sing.+sing./pl. v.] (*formal*) all the ordinary people of a particular country or area 平民百姓；民眾：*He had the support of large sections of the local populace.* 他受到當地大部份百姓的擁護。◇ *The populace at large is/are opposed to sudden change.* 民眾普遍反對突然的改變。

popu·lar 🔑 /ˈpɒpjələ(r); *NAmE* ˈpɑːp-/ *adj.*
1 🔑 liked or enjoyed by a large number of people 受喜愛的；受歡迎的；當紅的：*a* ***hugely/immensely popular*** *singer* 一個十分／非常受歡迎的歌手 ◇ *This is one of our most popular designs.* 這是我們最受歡迎的設計之一。◇ *Skiing has become very popular recently.* 滑雪運動最近盛行起來。◇ **~ (with sb)** *These policies are unlikely to* ***prove popular*** *with middle-class voters.* 這些政策不大可能博得中產階級選民的歡心。◇ *I'm not very popular with my parents* (= they are annoyed with me) *at the moment.* 眼下爸媽對我都很不高興。◇ (*ironic*) *'Our dog got into the neighbour's garden again!' 'You'll be popular.'* "我們的狗又鑽進鄰家的花園了！" "你要有好受的了。" **OPP** **unpopular** **2** 🔑 [only before noun] (sometimes *disapproving*) suited to the taste and knowledge of ordinary people 通俗的；大眾化的：***popular music/culture/fiction*** 流行音樂／文化／小說 ◇ *the popular press* 通俗報刊 **3** 🔑 [only before noun] (of ideas, beliefs and opinions 概念、信仰、意見) shared by a large number of people 普遍的；大眾的；流行的：*a popular misconception* 民眾的錯誤觀念 ◇ ***Contrary to popular belief****, women cause fewer road accidents than men.* 與普遍的看法相反，女性交通肇事比男性少。◇ ***Popular opinion*** *was divided on the issue.* 在這個議題上，民眾意見有分歧。◇ *By* ***popular demand****, the tour has been extended by two weeks.* 應大家要求，這次旅遊延長了兩週。 **4** [only before noun] connected with the ordinary people of a country 民眾的；百姓的：*The party still has widespread popular support.* 這個政黨仍得到民眾的廣泛支持。

ˌpopular etyˈmology *noun* = FOLK ETYMOLOGY

ˌpopular ˈfront *noun* a political group or party that has SOCIALIST aims 人民陣線（指有社會主義目標的政治團體或政黨）

popu·lar·ity /ˌpɒpjuˈlærəti; *NAmE* ˌpɑːp-/ *noun* [U] the state of being liked, enjoyed or supported by a large number of people 受歡迎；普及；流行：*the increasing popularity of cycling* 騎自行車運動的日益風行 ◇ *Her novels have* ***gained in popularity*** *over recent years.* 近年來她的小說漸受歡迎。◇ **~ with/among sb** *to* ***win/lose popularity*** *with the students* 受到／不受學生的歡迎

popu·lar·ize (*BrE* also **-ise**) /ˈpɒpjələraɪz; *NAmE* ˈpɑːp-/ *verb* **1 ~ sb/sth** to make a lot of people know about sth and enjoy it 宣傳；宣揚；推廣：*The programme did much to popularize little-known writers.* 這個節目大力宣揚不太知名的作家。 **2 ~ sth** to make a difficult subject easier to understand for ordinary people 使通俗化；使普及：*He spent his life popularizing natural history.* 他畢生致力於普及博物學。 ▶ **popu·lar·iza·tion, -isa·tion** /ˌpɒpjələraɪˈzeɪʃn; *NAmE* ˌpɑːpjələrəˈz-/ *noun* [U]

popu·lar·ly /ˈpɒpjələli; *NAmE* ˈpɑːpjələrli/ *adv.* **1** by a large number of people 普遍地；廣泛地；一般地 **SYN** **commonly**：*a popularly held belief* 大多數人的看法 ◇ *the UN Conference on Environment and Development, popularly known as the 'Earth Summit'* 聯合國環境與發展會議，即一般所稱的"地球高峰會議" **2** by the ordinary people of a country （一國）民眾做出的 **SYN** **democratically**：*a popularly elected government* 民選政府

popu·late /ˈpɒpjuleɪt; *NAmE* ˈpɑːp-/ *verb* **1** [often passive] **~ sth** to live in an area and form its population 居住於；生活於；構成…的人口 **SYN** **inhabit**：*a* ***heavily/densely/sparsely/thinly populated*** *country* 人口密集／稠密／稀疏／稀少的國家 ◇ *The island is populated largely by sheep.* 這個島的主要生物是綿羊。◇ (*figurative*) *the amazing characters that populate her novels* 常見於她小說中的令人驚歎的人物 **2 ~ sth** to move people or animals to an area to live there 遷移；移居；殖民於：*The French began to populate the island in the 15th century.* 法國人於 15 世紀開始遷移到這個島。 **3 ~ sth** (*computing* 計) to add data to a document （給文件）增添數據，輸入數據

popu·la·tion 🔑 /ˌpɒpjuˈleɪʃn; *NAmE* ˌpɑːp-/ *noun*
1 🔑 [C+sing./pl. v., U] all the people who live in a particular area, city or country; the total number of people who live there （地區、國家等的）人口，人口數量：*One third of the world's population consumes/consume two thirds of the world's resources.* 世界上三分之一的人口消耗着全球三分之二的資源。◇ *The entire population of the town was at the meeting.* 全鎮的居民都出席了集會。◇ *countries with ageing populations* 人口老化的國家 ◇ *Muslims make up 55% of the population.* 穆斯林佔人口的 55%。◇ *an increase in population* 人口的增長 ◇ *areas of* ***dense/sparse population*** (= where many/not many people live) 人口稠密／稀少的地區 ◇ *The population is increasing at about 6% per year.* 人口

以每年約 6% 的速度增加。◇ *Japan has a population of nearly 130 million.* 日本有近 1.3 億人口。**2** [C+sing./pl. v.] a particular group of people or animals living in a particular area（統稱）某領域的生物；族群；人口：*the* ***adult/working/rural, etc. population*** *of the country* 一國的成年人口、勞動人口、農村人口等

popu'lation explosion *noun* a sudden large increase in the number of people in an area 人口激增；人口爆炸

popu·lism /ˈpɒpjəlɪzəm; *NAmE* ˈpɑːp-/ *noun* [U] a type of politics that claims to represent the opinions and wishes of ordinary people 平民政治；民粹主義；民意論 ▸ **popu·list** /-ɪst/ *noun*：*a party of populists* 民粹黨 **popu·list** *adj.* [usually before noun]：*a populist leader* 民粹主義領袖

popu·lous /ˈpɒpjələs; *NAmE* ˈpɑːp-/ *adj.* (*formal*) where a large number of people live 人口眾多的；人口密集的：*one of America's most populous states* 美國人口最多的州之一

'pop-up *adj.* [only before noun] **1** (of a book, etc. 書籍等) containing a picture that stands up when the pages are opened 有立體活動圖的：*a pop-up birthday card* 立體生日卡 **2** (of an electric TOASTER 吐司爐) that pushes the bread quickly upwards when it is ready 彈出烤麪包片的 **3** (of a computer menu, etc. 計算機選單等) that can be brought to the screen quickly while you are working on another document 有彈出功能的；能迅速顯示的：*a* ***pop-up menu/window*** 彈出式選單／視窗

por·cel·ain /ˈpɔːsəlɪn; *NAmE* ˈpɔːrs-/ *noun* [U, C] a hard white shiny substance made by baking CLAY and used for making delicate cups, plates and decorative objects; objects that are made of this 瓷；瓷器：*a porcelain figure* 瓷像

porch /pɔːtʃ; *NAmE* pɔːrtʃ/ *noun* **1** a small area at the entrance to a building, such as a house or a church, that is covered by a roof and often has walls 門廊；門廳 ➲ VISUAL VOCAB page V17 **2** (*NAmE*) = VERANDA (1)

por·cine /ˈpɔːsaɪn; *NAmE* ˈpɔːrs-/ *adj.* (*formal*) like a pig; connected with pigs 像豬的；豬的

P

por·cu·pine /ˈpɔːkjupaɪn; *NAmE* ˈpɔːrk-/ *noun* an animal covered with long stiff parts like needles (called QUILLS), which it can raise to protect itself when it is attacked 豪豬；箭豬

pore /pɔː(r)/ *noun, verb*

■ ***noun*** one of the very small holes in your skin that sweat can pass through; one of the similar small holes in the surface of a plant or a rock（皮膚上的）毛孔；（植物的）氣孔；孔隙 ➲ see also POROUS

■ ***verb***

PHR V **'pore over sth** to look at or read sth very carefully 仔細打量；審視；認真研讀；審閱 **SYN** **examine**：*His lawyers are poring over the small print in the contract.* 他的律師們正在審閱合同上的小號字。

pork /pɔːk; *NAmE* pɔːrk/ *noun* [U] meat from a pig that has not been CURED (= preserved using salt or smoke) 豬肉：*roast pork* 烤豬肉 ◇ *pork chops* 豬排 ◇ *a leg of pork* 豬腿肉 ➲ compare BACON, GAMMON, HAM *n.* (1)

'pork barrel *noun* [U] (*NAmE, slang*) local projects that are given a lot of government money in order to win votes; the money that is used 分肥項目，分肥撥款（議員等為爭取選票而促使政府撥款給所屬地區的發展項目）

porker /ˈpɔːkə(r); *NAmE* ˈpɔːrk-/ *noun* a pig that is made fat and used as food 育肥的豬；食用豬

,pork 'pie *noun* [C, U] (*BrE*) a small PIE filled with PORK and usually eaten cold 豬肉餡餅（通常冷吃）

,pork 'scratchings (*BrE*) (*US* **'pork rinds**) *noun* [pl.] crisp pieces of pig skin that are fried and eaten cold, often sold in bags as a SNACK 脆豬皮片（小吃）

porky /ˈpɔːki; *NAmE* ˈpɔːrki/ *noun, adj.*

■ ***noun*** (*pl.* **-ies**) (also **,porky 'pie**) (*BrE, slang*) a statement that is not true; a lie 假話；謊言：*to tell porkies* 編瞎話

■ ***adj.*** (*informal, disapproving*) (of people 人) fat 肥胖的

porn /pɔːn; *NAmE* pɔːrn/ *noun* [U] (*informal*) = PORNOGRAPHY ➲ see also HARD PORN, SOFT PORN

porno /ˈpɔːnəʊ; *NAmE* ˈpɔːrnoʊ/ *adj.* [usually before noun] (*informal*) = PORNOGRAPHIC：*a porno movie* 色情電影

porn·og·raph·er /pɔːˈnɒgrəfə(r); *NAmE* pɔːrˈnɑːg-/ *noun* (*disapproving*) a person who produces or sells pornography 色情作品的製作者（或發行者、銷售者）

porno·graph·ic /ˌpɔːnəˈgræfɪk; *NAmE* ˌpɔːrn-/ (also *informal* **porno**) *adj.* [usually before noun] (*disapproving*) intended to make people feel sexually excited by showing naked people or sexual acts, usually in a way that many other people find offensive 下流的；黃色的；色情的：*pornographic movies/magazines* 黃色電影／雜誌

porn·og·raphy /pɔːˈnɒgrəfi; *NAmE* pɔːrˈnɑːg-/ (also *informal* **porn**) *noun* [U] (*disapproving*) books, magazines, DVDs, etc. that describe or show naked people and sexual acts in order to make people feel sexually excited, especially in a way that many other people find offensive 淫穢品；色情書刊（或影碟等）：*child pornography* 兒童色情作品

por·os·ity /pɔːˈrɒsəti; *NAmE* -ˈrɑːs-/ *noun* [U] (*technical* 術語) the quality or state of being porous 滲透（性）；多孔（性）

por·ous /ˈpɔːrəs/ *adj.* having many small holes that allow water or air to pass through slowly 多孔的；透水的；透氣的：*porous material/rocks/surfaces* 滲透性材料／岩石／表面

por·phy·ria /pɔːˈfɪriə; *NAmE* pɔːrˈf-/ *noun* [U] (*medical* 醫) a disease of the blood that causes mental problems and makes the skin sensitive to light 啉症，卟啉病，紫質症（引發精神症狀和皮膚對光過敏的血液病）

por·poise /ˈpɔːpəs; *NAmE* ˈpɔːrpəs/ *noun* a sea animal that looks like a large fish with a pointed mouth. Porpoises are similar to DOLPHINS but smaller. 鈍吻海豚；鼠海豚

por·ridge /ˈpɒrɪdʒ; *NAmE* ˈpɔːr-/ *noun* [U] **1** (*especially BrE*) (*NAmE* usually **oat·meal**) a type of soft thick white food made by boiling OATS in milk or water, eaten hot, especially for breakfast 麥片粥 **2** (*EAfrE*) a type of thick drink made by boiling flour with water 麪糊；粥

port 🔑 /pɔːt; *NAmE* pɔːrt/ *noun, verb*

■ ***noun*** **1** 🔑 [C] a town or city with a HARBOUR, especially one where ships load and unload goods 港口城市；口岸城市：*fishing ports* 漁港 ◇ *Rotterdam is a major port.* 鹿特丹是一個重要的港口城市。**2** 🔑 [C, U] (*abbr.* **Pt.**) a place where ships load and unload goods or shelter from storms 港口；避風港：*a naval port* 軍港 ◇ *The ship spent four days* ***in port***. 這艘船在港口停泊了四天。◇ *They reached port at last.* 他們終於抵達港口。◇ ***port of entry*** (= a place where people or goods can enter a country) 入境口岸 ➲ see also AIRPORT, FREE PORT, HELIPORT, SEAPORT **3** (also **port 'wine**) [U] a strong sweet wine, usually dark red, that is made in Portugal. It is usually drunk at the end of a meal. 波爾圖葡萄酒（葡萄牙產）**4** [C] a glass of port 一杯波爾圖葡萄酒 **5** [U] the side of a ship or aircraft that is on the left when you are facing forward（船、飛機等的）左舷：*the port side* 左舷 ➲ compare STARBOARD **6** [C] (*computing* 計) a place on a computer where you can attach another piece of equipment, often using a cable（輸出或輸入）端口；出入埠：*the modem port* 調制解調器端口 ➲ VISUAL VOCAB page V66

IDM **any port in a 'storm** (*saying*) if you are in great trouble, you take any help that is offered 慌不擇路；飢不擇食；有病亂投醫

■ ***verb*** **1 ~ sth (to sth)** (*computing* 計) to copy software from one system or machine to another 移植（軟件）**2 ~ sth (to sth)** to continue to use the same number when you change from one phone company to another（更換電話公司時）攜帶（電話號碼）：*how to port your number to a new mobile phone* 如何攜號使用新手機

port·able /ˈpɔːtəbl; *NAmE* ˈpɔːrt-/ *adj., noun*

■ ***adj.*** that is easy to carry or to move 便攜式的；手提的；輕便的：*a portable TV* 手提電視機 ◇ (*figurative*) *a portable loan/pension* (= that can be moved if you change banks, jobs, etc.) 可轉移貸款／養老金 ◇ *portable software* 可移植軟件 ▸ **port·abil·ity** /ˌpɔːtəˈbɪləti; *NAmE* ˌpɔːrt-/ *noun* [U]：*The new light cover increases this model's portability.* 新型的輕質外殼使這種型號攜帶更輕便。

■ *noun* a small type of machine that is easy to carry, especially a computer or a television 便攜機；（尤指）手提電腦，便攜式電視機

port·age /ˈpɔːtɪdʒ; *NAmE* ˈpɔːrt-/ *noun* [U] the act of carrying boats or goods between two rivers （在兩條河之間運送船隻或貨物的）陸上運輸，陸上搬運

Porta-john™ /ˈpɔːtə dʒɒn; *NAmE* ˈpɔːrtə dʒɑːn/ *noun* = PORTAPOTTY (1)

Porta·kabin™ /ˈpɔːtəkæbɪn; *NAmE* ˈpɔːrt-/ *noun* (*BrE*) a small building that can be moved from place to place by a vehicle, designed to be used as a temporary office, etc. 波特卡賓房；移動辦公室；移動房

por·tal /ˈpɔːtl; *NAmE* ˈpɔːrtl/ *noun* **1** [usually pl.] (*formal* or *literary*) a large, impressive gate or entrance to a building 壯觀的大門；豪華的入口 **2** (*computing* 計) a website that is used as a point of entry to the Internet, where information has been collected that will be useful to a person interested in particular kinds of things 門戶網站；入口站點：*a business/news/shopping portal* 商務／新聞／購物門戶網站

Porta·loo™ /ˈpɔːtəluː; *NAmE* ˈpɔːrt-/ (*BrE*) (*NAmE* **portapotty**, **Porta-john™**) *noun* (*pl.* **-oos**) a toilet inside a small light building that can be moved from place to place 波特廬移動式廁所

ˈ**portal vein** (also **hepatic ˈportal vein**) *noun* (*anatomy* 解) a VEIN that takes blood from the stomach and other organs near the stomach to the LIVER 門靜脈

porta·potty (also **Porta Potti™**) /ˈpɔːtə pɒti; *NAmE* ˈpɔːrtəpɑːti/ *noun* (*pl.* **-ies**) **1** (*NAmE*) (*BrE* **Portaloo™**) (*NAmE* also **Porta-john™**) a toilet inside a small light building that can be moved from place to place 移動式廁所 **2** (*BrE*) a toilet that you can take with you when you are travelling 戶外便攜式坐便器

port·cul·lis /pɔːtˈkʌlɪs; *NAmE* pɔːrt-/ *noun* a strong, heavy iron gate that can be raised or let down at the entrance to a castle （城堡入口可升降的）鐵閘門，吊閘門

por·tend /pɔːˈtend; *NAmE* pɔːrˈt-/ *verb* **~ sth** (*formal*) to be a sign or warning of sth that is going to happen in the future, especially sth bad or unpleasant 預兆，預示，預告（尤指壞事） SYN **foreshadow**

por·tent /ˈpɔːtent; *NAmE* ˈpɔːrt-/ *noun* (*literary*) a sign or warning of sth that is going to happen in the future, especially when it is sth unpleasant 預兆；徵兆；先兆；（尤指）惡兆，凶兆 SYN **omen**

por·tent·ous /pɔːˈtentəs; *NAmE* pɔːrˈt-/ *adj.* **1** (*literary*) important as a sign or a warning of sth that is going to happen in the future, especially when it is sth unpleasant 預示（壞事）的；先兆的：*a portentous sign* 不祥的徵兆 **2** (*formal, disapproving*) very serious and intended to impress people 煞有介事的；裝腔作勢的；裝模作樣的 SYN **pompous**：*a portentous remark* 裝腔作勢的言論 ▸ **por·tent·ous·ly** *adv.* **por·tent·ous·ness** *noun* [U]

por·ter /ˈpɔːtə(r); *NAmE* ˈpɔːrt-/ *noun* **1** a person whose job is carrying people's bags and other loads, especially at a train station, an airport or in a hotel （尤指火車站、機場或旅館）行李員，搬運工 ➲ see also KITCHEN PORTER **2** (*BrE*) a person whose job is to move patients from one place to another in a hospital （醫院裏護送病人的）護工 **3** (*BrE*) a person whose job is to be in charge of the entrance to a hotel, large building, college, etc. 門衛；門房：*the night porter* 夜班門衛 ◇ *The hotel porter will get you a taxi.* 旅館的門衛會給你叫出租車的。 ➲ compare DOORMAN **4** (*NAmE*) a person whose job is helping passengers on a train, especially in a SLEEPING CAR （尤指臥鋪車廂的）列車服務員

port·folio /pɔːtˈfəʊliəʊ; *NAmE* pɔːrtˈfoʊlioʊ/ *noun* (*pl.* **-os**) **1** a thin flat case used for carrying documents, drawings, etc. 文件夾；公事包 **2** a collection of photographs, drawings, etc. that you use as an example of your work, especially when applying for a job （求職時用以證明資歷的）作品，整套照片 **3** (*finance* 財) a set of shares owned by a particular person or organization （個人或機構的）投資組合，有價證券組合：*an investment/share portfolio* 投資／股份組合 **4** (*formal, especially BrE*) the particular area of responsibility of a government minister （部長或大臣的）職責，職務：*the defence portfolio* 國防部長職責 ◇ *She resigned her portfolio.* 她辭去了部長職務。 ◇ *He was asked to join as a* ***minister without portfolio*** (= one without responsibility for a particular government department). 他獲邀出任不管部大臣。 **5** the range of products or services offered by a particular company or organization （公司或機構提供的）系列產品，系列服務：*a portfolio of wines* 系列葡萄酒

port·hole /ˈpɔːthəʊl; *NAmE* ˈpɔːrthoʊl/ *noun* a round window in the side of a ship or an aircraft （船、飛機等的）舷窗

por·tico /ˈpɔːtɪkəʊ; *NAmE* ˈpɔːrtɪkoʊ/ *noun* (*pl.* **-oes** or **-os**) (*formal*) a roof that is supported by columns, especially one that forms the entrance to a large building 柱廊；柱廳 ➲ VISUAL VOCAB page V14

por·tion AW /ˈpɔːʃn; *NAmE* ˈpɔːrʃn/ *noun, verb*

■ *noun* **1** one part of sth larger 部份：*a* ***substantial/significant portion*** *of the population* 人口中的一大部份／重要部份 ◇ *Only a small portion of the budget is spent on books.* 購書只佔預算的一小部份。 ◇ *The central portion of the bridge collapsed.* 橋的中段坍塌了。 **2** an amount of food that is large enough for one person （食物的）一份，一客：*a generous portion of meat* 一大份肉 ◇ *She cut the cake into six small portions.* 她把蛋糕切成了六小份。 **3** [usually sing.] a part of sth that is shared with other people 分享的部份；分擔的責任 SYN **share**：*You must accept a portion of the blame for this crisis.* 你必須承擔這次危機的一部份責任。

■ *verb* to divide sth into parts or portions 把…分成若干份（或部份）：**~ sth** *The factory portions and packs over 12 000 meals a day.* 這個工廠每天分裝 12 000 多份飯食。 ◇ **~ sth out** *Land was portioned out among the clans.* 土地已分給了各個家族。

port·ly /ˈpɔːtli; *NAmE* ˈpɔːrt-/ *adj.* [usually before noun] (especially of an older man 尤指年長男子) rather fat 發福的；發胖的 SYN **stout**

port·man·teau /pɔːtˈmæntəʊ; *NAmE* pɔːrtˈmæntoʊ/ *noun, adj.*

■ *noun* (*pl.* **portmanteaus** or **portmanteaux**) (*old-fashioned*) a large heavy suitcase that opens into two parts 兩格式旅行衣箱

■ *adj.* [only before noun] consisting of a number of different items that are combined into a single thing 綜合的；複合式的：*a portmanteau course* 綜合課程 ◇ *'Depression' is a portmanteau condition.* "抑鬱症"是一種綜合症狀。

portˈmanteau word *noun* a word that is invented by combining the beginning of one word and the end of another and keeping the meaning of each. For example *motel* is a portmanteau word that is a combination of *motor* and *hotel*. 縮合詞，合併詞（由一個詞的詞首和另一個詞的詞尾合成）

ˌ**port of ˈcall** *noun* (*pl.* **ports of call**) **1** a port where a ship stops during a journey （航行途中的）停靠港，停泊港 **2** (*informal*) a place where you go or stop for a short time, especially when you are going to several places （旅途中的）落腳處，落腳點：*My first port of call in town was the bank.* 我進城的第一站是銀行。

por·trait /ˈpɔːtreɪt; -trət; *NAmE* ˈpɔːrtrət/ *noun, adj.*

■ *noun* **1** a painting, drawing or photograph of a person, especially of the head and shoulders 肖像；半身畫像；半身照：*He had his portrait painted in uniform.* 他讓人畫了一幅身着制服的畫像。 ◇ *a full-length portrait* 全身畫像 ◇ *a portrait painter* 肖像畫家 ➲ SYNONYMS at PICTURE ➲ COLLOCATIONS at ART ➲ see also SELF-PORTRAIT **2** a detailed description of sb/sth 詳細的描述；描繪 SYN **depiction**：*a portrait of life at the French court* 對法國宮廷生活的詳細描述

■ *adj.* (*computing* 計) (of a page of a document 文件頁面) printed so that the top of the page is one of the shorter sides 豎式的；縱向打印格式的 ➲ compare LANDSCAPE *n.* (3)

P

por·trait·ist /ˈpɔːtreɪtɪst; -trət-; *NAmE* ˈpɔːrtrət-/ *noun* a person who makes portraits 肖像畫家（或攝影師等）

por·trait·ure /ˈpɔːtrətʃə(r); *NAmE* ˈpɔːrt-/ *noun* [U] the art of making portraits; the portraits that are made 畫像技法；人像攝影法；肖像；畫像；照片

por·tray /pɔːˈtreɪ; *NAmE* pɔːrˈt-/ *verb* **1 ~ sb/sth** to show sb/sth in a picture; to describe sb/sth in a piece of writing 描繪；描畫；描寫 SYN **depict** **2 ~ sb/sth (as sb/sth)** to describe or show sb/sth in a particular way, especially when this does not give a complete or accurate impression of what they are like 將…描寫成；給人以某種印象；表現 SYN **represent**: *Throughout the trial, he portrayed himself as the victim.* 在審訊過程中，他始終把自己說成是受害者。 **3 ~ sb/sth** to act a particular role in a film/movie or play 扮演（某角色）SYN **play**: *Her father will be portrayed by Sean Connery.* 肖恩•康納利將飾演她的父親。

por·tray·al /pɔːˈtreɪəl; *NAmE* pɔːrˈt-/ *noun* [C, U] the act of showing or describing sb/sth in a picture, play, book, etc.; a particular way in which this is done 描繪；描述；描寫；展現方式：*The article examines the portrayal of gay men in the media.* 這篇文章剖析了傳媒對男同性戀者的描述。◇ *He is best known for his chilling portrayal of Hannibal Lecter.* 他以飾演令人毛骨悚然的漢尼拔•萊克特而著稱。

Por·tu·guese /ˌpɔːtʃuˈɡiːz; *NAmE* ˌpɔːrt-/ *adj., noun*
- **adj.** from or connected with Portugal 葡萄牙的
- **noun** **1** [C] (*pl.* **Por·tu·guese**) a person from Portugal 葡萄牙人 **2** [U] the language used in Portugal and Brazil and some other countries 葡萄牙語

pose 0‑w AW /pəʊz; *NAmE* poʊz/ *verb, noun*
- **verb** **1** 0‑w [T] **~ sth** to create a threat, problem, etc. that has to be dealt with 造成（威脅、問題等）；引起；產生：*to **pose a threat/challenge/danger/risk*** 構成威脅／挑戰／危險／風險 ◇ *The task poses no special **problems**.* 這項任務不會造成特別的問題。 **2** [T] **~ a question** (*formal*) to ask a question, especially one that needs serious thought 提問；質詢 **3** 0‑w [I] **~ (for sb/sth)** to sit or stand in a particular position in order to be painted, drawn or photographed（為畫像、攝影）擺好姿勢：*The delegates posed for a group photograph.* 代表們擺好姿勢準備拍集體照。 **4** 0‑w [I] **~ as sb** to pretend to be sb in order to trick other people 佯裝；冒充；假扮：*The gang entered the building posing as workmen.* 這夥匪徒冒充工人混進了大樓。 **5** [I] (usually used in the progressive tenses 通常用於進行時) (*disapproving*) to dress or behave in a way that is intended to impress other people 招搖；炫耀；拿姿作態：*I saw him out posing in his new sports car.* 我看見他開着他的嶄新跑車招搖過市。
- **noun** **1** 0‑w a particular position in which sb stands, sits, etc., especially in order to be painted, drawn or photographed（為畫像、拍照等擺的）姿勢：*He adopted a relaxed pose for the camera.* 他擺了個悠閒的姿勢拍照。 **2** 0‑w (*disapproving*) a way of behaving that is not sincere and is only intended to impress other people 裝腔作勢；故作姿態 SYN **affectation** IDM see STRIKE *v.*

poser /ˈpəʊzə(r); *NAmE* ˈpoʊ-/ *noun* **1** (*informal*) a difficult question or problem 難題；困難；棘手的事 SYN **puzzler** **2** (also **pos·eur**) (*disapproving*) a person who behaves or dresses in a way that is intended to impress other people and is not sincere 裝腔作勢的人；裝模作樣的人

pos·eur /pəʊˈzɜː(r); *NAmE* poʊ-/ *noun* = POSER (2)

posey /ˈpəʊzi; *NAmE* ˈpoʊzi/ *adj.* (*informal*) trying to impress other people, especially in a way that is silly or not natural 竭力表現的；虛誇的；張揚而做作的

posh /pɒʃ; *NAmE* pɑːʃ/ *adj.* (**posh·er**, **posh·est**) (*informal*) **1** elegant and expensive 優雅豪華的；富麗堂皇的：*a posh hotel* 豪華旅館 ◇ *You look very posh in your new suit.* 你穿上新套裝顯得雍容華貴。 **2** (*BrE*, sometimes *disapproving*) typical of or used by people who belong to a high social class 上流社會的；上等人的 SYN **stylish**: *a **posh accent/voice*** 上等人的腔調／嗓音 ◇ *They live in the posh part of town.* 他們生活在市內的富人區。◇ *They pay for their children to go to a posh school.* 他們花錢讓子女上貴族學校。 ▶ **posh** *adv.*: (*BrE*) *to talk posh* 談吐高雅

posho /ˈpɒʃəʊ; *NAmE* ˈpɑːʃoʊ/ *noun* **1** [C] (*pl.* **-os**) (*BrE*, *informal*, *disapproving*) a person from a high social class 上等人；貴人 **2** [U] (*EAfrE*) a type of flour made from MAIZE (CORN) 玉米粉：*a posho mill* 玉米粉研磨機

ˈposing pouch *noun* (*BrE*) an item of men's clothing that covers only the GENITALS（只遮蓋生殖器的）一點式男內褲

posit /ˈpɒzɪt; *NAmE* ˈpɑːz-/ *verb* **~ sth | ~ that …** (*formal*) to suggest or accept that sth is true so that it can be used as the basis for an argument or discussion 假設；認定；認為…為實 SYN **postulate**: *Most religions posit the existence of life after death.* 大多數宗教都假定人死後生命仍存在。

pos·ition 0‑w /pəˈzɪʃn/ *noun, verb*
- **noun**
- ▸ PLACE 地方 **1** 0‑w [C] the place where sb/sth is located 位置；地方：*From his position on the cliff top, he had a good view of the harbour.* 他在懸崖之巔，海港景色一覽無餘。◇ *Where would be the best position for the lights?* 這些燈裝在什麼位置最好？ ➲ SYNONYMS at PLACE **2** 0‑w [U] the place where sb/sth is meant to be; the correct place 恰當位置；正確位置：*Is everybody **in position**?* 大家都就位了嗎？◇ *He took up his position by the door.* 他到門邊就位。
- ▸ WAY SB/STH IS PLACED 安置方式 **3** 0‑w [C, U] the way in which sb is sitting or standing, or the way in which sth is arranged（坐或站的）姿態，姿勢；放置方式：*a **sitting/kneeling/lying position*** 坐／跪／臥姿 ◇ *Keep the box in an upright position.* 把盒子豎着放。◇ *Make sure that you are working in a comfortable position.* 工作時一定要保持舒適的姿勢。◇ *My arms were aching so I shifted (my) position slightly.* 我胳膊疼了，所以稍微變了變姿勢。 ➲ see also MISSIONARY POSITION
- ▸ SITUATION 情勢 **4** 0‑w [C, usually sing.] the situation that sb is in, especially when it affects what they can and cannot do 處境；地位；狀況：*to be in a **position of power/strength/authority*** 處於有權力／有實力／有權威的地位 ◇ *What would you do in my position?* 你要是碰到我這樣的情況會怎麼辦？◇ *This put him and his colleagues in a difficult position.* 這使他和他的同事陷於困境。◇ *The company's financial position is not certain.* 這家公司的財務狀況不明朗。◇ **~ to do sth** *I'm afraid I am **not in a position** to help you.* 我恐怕愛莫能助。 ➲ note at SITUATION
- ▸ OPINION 看法 **5** 0‑w [C] **~ (on sth)** an opinion on or an attitude towards a particular subject 觀點；態度；立場：*to **declare/reconsider/shift/change your position*** 表明／重新考慮／轉變／改變立場 ◇ *the party's position on education reforms* 這個黨對教育改革的態度 ◇ *She has made her position very clear.* 她明確表示了自己的立場。◇ *My parents always **took the position** that early nights meant healthy children.* 我的父母總是認為孩子早睡就會身體健康。
- ▸ LEVEL OF IMPORTANCE 重要程度 **6** 0‑w [C, U] a person or organization's level of importance when compared with others 地位；等級：*the position of women in society* 婦女的社會地位 ◇ *the company's dominant position in the world market* 那個公司在全球市場中的主導地位 ◇ *Wealth and position (= high social status) were not important to her.* 財富與地位對她並不重要。
- ▸ JOB 工作 **7** 0‑w [C] (*formal*) a job 職位；職務 SYN **post**: *He held a senior position in a large company.* 他在一家大公司擔任高級職務。◇ *I should like to apply for the position of Sales Director.* 我想申請銷售部主任一職。 ➲ SYNONYMS at JOB
- ▸ IN RACE/COMPETITION 競賽；競爭 **8** [C] a place in a race, competition, or test, when compared to others 名次：*United's 3–0 win moved them up to third position.* 聯隊 3:0 的勝利使他們排名升至第三。
- ▸ IN SPORT 體育運動 **9** [C] the place where sb plays and the responsibilities they have in some team games（隊員的）職責，位置，角色：*What position does he play?* 他打哪個位置？
- ▸ IN WAR 戰爭 **10** [C, usually pl.] a place where a group of people involved in fighting have put men and guns

陣地：*They attacked the enemy positions at dawn.* 黎明時分，他們向敵軍陣地發起進攻。

■ ***verb*** **~ sth** (**+ adv./prep.**) to put sb/sth in a particular position 安裝；安置；使處於 SYN **place**：*Large television screens were positioned at either end of the stadium.* 體育場的兩端安裝了大型電視屏幕。◇ *She quickly positioned herself behind the desk.* 她迅速在桌子後面她的位置上坐好。◇ *The company is now well positioned to compete in foreign markets.* 現在這家公司已準備好在國外市場競爭。▶ **pos·ition·ing** *noun* [U]

pos·ition·al /pəˈzɪʃənəl/ *adj.* [only before noun] (*technical* 術語 or *sport* 體) connected with the position of sb/sth 位置上的；地位上的；職位上的：*The team has made some positional changes because two players are injured.* 因有兩名隊員受傷，這個隊的隊員位置作了調整。

poˈsition paper *noun* a written report from an organization or a government department that explains or recommends a particular course of action（機構或政府部門的）行動報告，施政說明，建議書

posi·tive 🔑 AW /ˈpɒzətɪv; *NAmE* ˈpɑːz-/ *adj.*, *noun*

■ ***adj.***

▸ CONFIDENT 有信心 **1** 🔑 thinking about what is good in a situation; feeling confident and sure that sth good will happen 積極樂觀的；自信的：*a* ***positive attitude/outlook*** 樂觀的態度／前景 ◇ *the power of positive thought* 樂觀思想的力量 ◇ **~** (**about sth**) *She tried to be more positive about her new job.* 她努力更積極地投入新工作。◇ ***On the positive side****, profits have increased.* 從好的方面看，利潤增加了。◇ *The report ended on a positive note.* 報告的結尾顯得很樂觀。OPP **negative**

▸ EFFECTIVE/USEFUL 有效；有用 **2** 🔑 directed at dealing with sth or producing a successful result 積極的；建設性的；朝着成功的：*We must take* ***positive steps*** *to deal with the problem.* 我們必須採取積極步驟處理這個問題。◇ *It will require* ***positive action*** *by all in the industry.* 這將需要業內全體同人和衷共濟。OPP **negative** **3** 🔑 expressing agreement or support 表示贊同的；擁護的：*We've had a very positive response to the idea.* 我們對這個想法反應很好。OPP **negative** **4** 🔑 good or useful 良好的；有助益的；正面的：*to make a positive contribution to a discussion* 在討論中獻計獻策 ◇ *His family have been a very positive influence on him.* 他的家庭對他有十分良好的影響。◇ *Overseas investment has had a positive effect on exports.* 海外投資對出口有積極影響。OPP **negative**

▸ SURE/DEFINITE 確信；肯定 **5** 🔑 [not before noun] (of a person 人) completely sure that sth is correct or true 有絕對把握；確信；肯定：**~** (**about sth**) *I can't be positive about what time it happened.* 我說不準這事是什麼時間發生的。◇ **~** (**that** …) *She was positive that he had been there.* 她確信他曾在場。◇ *'Are you sure?' 'Positive.'* "你敢肯定嗎？" "絕對肯定。" ➲ SYNONYMS at SURE **6** [only before noun] (*informal*) complete and definite 完全的；絕對的 SYN **absolute**：*He has a positive genius for upsetting people.* 他氣人的本事可大呢。◇ *It was a positive miracle that we survived.* 我們能夠生還，完全是個奇跡。**7** 🔑 giving clear and definite proof or information 證據確鑿的；明確的 SYN **conclusive**：*We have no positive evidence that she was involved.* 我們沒有確鑿證據證明她參與其事。◇ (*formal*) *This is* ***proof positive*** *that he stole the money.* 這就是他偷錢的肯定證據。

▸ SCIENTIFIC TEST 科學試驗 **8** 🔑 showing clear evidence that a particular substance or medical condition is present 陽性的；證明…存在的：*a positive pregnancy test* 呈陽性反應的懷孕檢測 ◇ *The athlete* ***tested positive*** *for steroids.* 這個運動員類固醇檢測呈陽性。◇ *to be HIV positive* 艾滋病病毒化驗呈陽性 OPP **negative**

▸ NUMBER/QUANTITY 數目；數量 **9** greater than zero 正數的 OPP **negative**

▸ ELECTRICITY 電 **10** (*technical* 術語) containing or producing the type of electricity that is carried by a PROTON 正電的；正極的：*a* ***positive charge*** 正電荷 ◇ *the* ***positive terminal*** *of a battery* 電池的正極 OPP **negative**

■ ***noun***

▸ GOOD QUALITY 優點 **1** [C, U] a good or useful quality or aspect 優勢；優點：*Take your weaknesses and translate them into positives.* 把你自己的弱點變成優點。

▸ IN PHOTOGRAPHY 攝影 **2** [C] (*technical* 術語) a developed film showing light and dark areas and colours as they actually were, especially one printed from a NEGATIVE 正片

▸ RESULT OF TEST 化驗結果 **3** [C] the result of a test or an experiment that shows that a substance or condition is present 陽性結果（或反應）OPP **negative**

ˌpositive disˌcriminˈation (*BrE*) (also **afˌfirmative ˈaction** *NAmE*, *BrE*) *noun* [U] the practice or policy of making sure that a particular number of jobs, etc. are given to people from groups that are often treated unfairly because of their race, sex, etc. 積極區別對待政策（對因種族、性別等原因遭歧視的群體在就業等方面給予特別照顧）➲ COLLOCATIONS at RACE ➲ compare REVERSE DISCRIMINATION

posi·tive·ly AW /ˈpɒzətɪvli; *NAmE* ˈpɑːz-/ *adv.* **1** used to emphasize the truth of a statement, especially when this is surprising or when it contrasts with a previous statement 絕對地；肯定地：*The instructions were not just confusing, they were positively misleading.* 這些指示不單令人費解，而且肯定會誤導人。**2** in a way that shows you are thinking of the good things about a situation, not the bad 樂觀地；肯定地；積極地：*Very few of those interviewed spoke positively about their childhood.* 接受採訪的人當中，很少有人說他們的童年是快樂的。◇ *Thinking positively is one way of dealing with stress.* 保持樂觀是對付壓力的一種方法。OPP **negatively** **3** in a way that shows you approve of or agree with sth/sb 贊成地；積極地：*Investors reacted positively to news of the takeover.* 投資者對公司收購的消息反應積極。OPP **negatively** **4** in a way that leaves no possibility of doubt 明確地；明白無誤地 SYN **conclusively**：*Her attacker has now been positively identified by police.* 襲擊她的人現在已被警方確認。**5** (*technical* 術語) in a way that contains or produces the type of electricity that is opposite to that carried by an ELECTRON 帶（或產生）正電地：*positively charged protons* 帶正電的質子 OPP **negatively**

ˌpositive ˈvetting *noun* [U, C] (*BrE*) the process of checking everything about a person's background and character when they apply for a job in which they will have to deal with secret information, especially in the CIVIL SERVICE 道德審查（對申請從事保密工作者的背景和品行進行檢查）

posi·tiv·ism /ˈpɒzətɪvɪzəm; *NAmE* ˈpɑːz-/ *noun* [U] a system of philosophy based on things that can be seen or proved, rather than on ideas 實證主義；實證哲學；實證論 ▶ **posi·tiv·ist** /-vɪst/ *noun* **posi·tiv·ist** *adj.*：*a positivist approach* 實證主義方式

posi·tron /ˈpɒzɪtrɒn; *NAmE* ˈpɑːzɪtrɑːn/ *noun* (*physics* 物) a PARTICLE in an atom which has the same mass as an ELECTRON and an equal but positive charge 正電子；陽電子

poss /pɒs; *NAmE* pɑːs/ *adj.* [not before noun] (*BrE*, *informal*) possible 可能：*I'll be there* ***if poss****.* 如果可以，我會去那裏的。◇ *as soon* ***as poss*** 儘快

posse /ˈpɒsi; *NAmE* ˈpɑːsi/ *noun* **1** (*informal*) a group of people who are similar in some way, or who spend time together 一群，一隊，一夥（有共同之處的人）：*a little posse of helpers* 一小夥幫忙的人 **2** (in the US in the past) a group of people who were brought together by a SHERIFF (= an officer of the law) in order to help him catch a criminal（美國舊時由縣治安官調集、協助捉拿罪犯的）地方武裝團隊 **3** (*informal*) a group of young men involved in crime connected with drugs（與毒品有關的）青年犯罪團夥

pos·sess 🔑 /pəˈzes/ *verb* (not used in the progressive tenses 不用於進行時) **1** 🔑 **~ sth** (*formal*) to have or own sth 有；擁有：*He was charged with possessing a shotgun without a licence.* 他被控無照擁有獵槍。◇ *The gallery possesses a number of the artist's early works.* 這家畫廊藏有一些那位畫家的早期作品。**2** 🔑 **~ sth** (*formal*) to have a particular quality or feature 具有（特質）：*I'm afraid he doesn't possess a sense of humour.* 恐怕他沒有什麼幽默感。**3** [usually passive] **~ sb** (*literary*) (of a feeling, an emotion, etc. 感覺、情緒等) to have a powerful effect

P

on sb and control the way that they think, behave, etc. 攫住；支配；控制 **4 ~ sb to do sth** (used in negative sentences and questions 用於否定句和疑問句) to make sb do sth that seems strange or unreasonable 使言行失常：*What possessed him to say such a thing?* 他着了什麼魔竟說出這種話來？

pos·sessed /pəˈzest/ *adj.* [not before noun] **~ (by sth)** (of a person or their mind 人或頭腦) controlled by an evil spirit 着了魔：*She has convinced herself that she is possessed by the devil.* 她確信自己被魔鬼附了身。
IDM **be possessed of sth** (*formal*) to have a particular quality or feature 具有某種品質（或特徵）：*She was possessed of exceptional powers of concentration.* 她有高超的專注能力。 **like a man/woman posˈsessed | like one posˈsessed** with a lot of force or energy 着了魔似的；拚命地；猛烈地：*He flew out of the room like a man possessed.* 他猛然衝出房門，像着了魔似的。

pos·ses·sion 0-n /pəˈzeʃn/ *noun*
▸ **HAVING/OWNING 擁有** **1** 0-n [U] (*formal*) the state of having or owning sth 具有；擁有：*The manuscript is just one of the treasures **in their possession**.* 這部手稿只是他們的珍藏之一。◇ *The gang was caught **in possession of** stolen goods.* 這夥人被逮住，人贓俱獲。◇ *The possession of a passport is essential for foreign travel.* 出國旅行必須持有護照。◇ *On her father's death, she **came into possession of*** (= received) *a vast fortune.* 她父親死後，她繼承了一大筆財產。◇ *You cannot legally **take possession of** the property* (= start using it after buying it) *until three weeks after the contract is signed.* 契約簽署三週以後，你才能合法取得這份產業的所有權。➲ see also VACANT POSSESSION **2** 0-n [C, usually pl.] something that you own or have with you at a particular time 個人財產；私人物品 SYN **belongings**：*personal possessions* 私人物品 ◇ *The ring is one of her most treasured possessions.* 這隻戒指是她最珍貴的財產之一。➲ SYNONYMS at THING
▸ **IN SPORT 體育運動** **3** [U] the state of having control of the ball 控球狀態：*to **win/get/lose possession** of the ball* 贏得／得到／失去對球的控制
▸ **LAW 法律** **4** [U] the state of having illegal drugs or weapons with you at a particular time 持有違禁物；私藏毒品（或武器）：*She was charged with possession.* 她被控持有違禁物品。
▸ **COUNTRY 國家** **5** [C] (*formal*) a country that is controlled or governed by another country 殖民地；託管地；屬地
▸ **BY EVIL SPIRIT 受惡魔控制** **6** [U] the situation when sb's mind is believed to be controlled by the DEVIL or by an evil spirit 鬼魂纏身；着魔
IDM **possession is nine tenths of the ˈlaw** (*saying*) if you already have or control sth, it is difficult for sb else to take it away from you, even if they have the legal right to it 現實佔有，敗一勝九；佔有者在訴訟中總佔上風 ➲ more at FIELD *n.*

pos·ses·sive /pəˈzesɪv/ *adj., noun*
■ ***adj.*** **1 ~ (of/about sb/sth)** demanding total attention or love; not wanting sb to be independent 要求悉心關愛的；佔有慾強的：*Some parents are too possessive of their children.* 有些父母過分要求子女百依百順。 **2 ~ (of/about sth)** not liking to lend things or share things with others 不願分享的；有獨佔慾望的：*Jimmy's very possessive about his toys.* 吉米的玩具誰也碰不得。 **3** [usually before noun] (*grammar* 語法) showing that sth belongs to sb/sth 表示所屬關係的；所有格的：*possessive pronouns* (= yours, theirs, etc.) 所有格代詞 ▸ **pos·ses·sive·ly** *adv.*：*'That's mine!' she said possessively.* "那是我的！" 她霸道地說。 **pos·ses·sive·ness** *noun* [U]：*I couldn't stand his jealousy and possessiveness.* 我受不了他的嫉妒與霸道作風。
■ ***noun*** (*grammar* 語法) **1** [C] a pronoun or a form of a word that expresses the fact that sth belongs to sb/sth 所有格代詞；物主代詞；屬有詞：*'Ours' and 'their' are possessives.* * ours 和 their 是所有格形式。 **2 the possessive** *noun* [sing.] the special form of a word that expresses belonging 所有格 ➲ compare GENITIVE

pos·ses·sor /pəˈzesə(r)/ *noun* (*formal* or *humorous*) a person who owns or has sth 持有人；所有者 SYN **owner**：*He is now **the proud possessor** of a driving licence.* 他現在有了駕駛執照，頗有些飄飄然。

pos·set /ˈpɒsɪt; *NAmE* ˈpɑːs-/ *noun, verb*
■ ***noun*** in the past, a drink made with hot milk and beer or wine 牛奶甜酒（舊時用熱牛奶加啤酒或葡萄酒調製而成）
■ ***verb*** (*BrE*) (**-tt-**, *NAmE* also **-t-**) [I] if a baby **possets**, milk comes back up from its stomach and out through its mouth （嬰兒）漾奶，吐奶

pos·si·bil·ity 0-n /ˌpɒsəˈbɪləti; *NAmE* ˌpɑːs-/ *noun* (*pl.* **-ies**)
1 0-n [U, C] the fact that sth might exist or happen, but is not certain to 可能；可能性：**~ (that ...)** *There is now no possibility that she will make a full recovery.* 她現在已不可能完全康復。◇ **~ (of sth/of doing sth)** *He refused to rule out the possibility of a tax increase.* 他拒絕排除增稅的可能性。◇ *It is not **beyond the bounds of possibility** that we'll all meet again one day.* 我們大家將來有一天再度聚在一起，並非絕不可能。◇ *Bankruptcy is a real possibility if sales don't improve.* 如果銷售情況得不到改善，真有破產的可能。◇ *What had seemed impossible now seemed a **distinct possibility**.* 過去看似不可能的事，現在顯然有可能了。OPP **impossibility** **2** 0-n [C, usually pl.] one of the different things that you can do in a particular situation 可選擇的方法：*to **explore/consider/investigate** a wide range of **possibilities*** 探究／考慮／調查各種可能的情況 ◇ *to **exhaust** all **the possibilities*** 用盡一切可能的手段 ◇ *Selling the house is just one possibility that is open to us.* 賣掉房子只是我們可以選擇的其中一種做法。◇ ***The possibilities are endless.*** 可想的辦法是無窮的。➲ SYNONYMS at OPTION **3** 0-n [C, usually pl.] something that gives you a chance to achieve sth 機會；契機 SYN **opportunity**：*The course offers a range of exciting possibilities for developing your skills.* 這門課程可提供一整套新鮮活潑的技能訓練。 **4 possibilities** [pl.] if sth **has possibilities**, it can be improved or made successful 潛力；改進的餘地 SYN **potential**：*The house is in a bad state of repair but it has possibilities.* 這房子雖亟待修繕，但仍有可資利用的價值。

pos·sible 0-n /ˈpɒsəbl; *NAmE* ˈpɑːs-/ *adj., noun*
■ ***adj.*** **1** 0-n [not usually before noun] that can be done or achieved 可能；能做到（或取得）：***It is possible to** get there by bus.* 可以乘公共汽車到那裏。◇ ***Would it be possible for** me to leave a message for her?* 我可以給她留個話兒嗎？◇ *This wouldn't have been possible without you.* 若沒有你，這事恐怕就辦不成了。◇ *Try to avoid losing your temper **if at all possible*** (= if you can). 盡可能別發脾氣。◇ *Use public transport **whenever possible*** (= when you can). 只要可能，就利用公共交通。◇ *It's just not **physically possible** to finish all this by the end of the week.* 要在本週末完成這一切，這在客觀上是辦不到的。◇ *We spent every possible moment on the beach.* 我們一有時間就到海灘。OPP **impossible** **2** 0-n that might exist or happen but is not certain to 可能存在（或發生）的：*a possible future president* 未來可能當選總統的人 ◇ *the possible side effects of the drug* 這種藥可能產生的副作用 ◇ *Frost is possible, although unlikely, at this time of year.* 每年這個時節都有可能下霜，只是並不常見。◇ *It's just possible that I gave them the wrong directions.* 我也許給他們指錯了方向。◇ *With the possible exception of the Beatles, no other band has become so successful so quickly.* 可能除了披頭士樂隊這個例外，還沒有哪個樂隊如此轉瞬走紅的。➲ LANGUAGE BANK at PERHAPS **3** 0-n reasonable or acceptable in a particular situation 合理的；可接受的：*There are several possible explanations.* 有幾種合理的解釋。 **4** used after adjectives to emphasize that sth is the best, worst, etc. of its type（用於形容詞後表示強調）最…的：*It was the **best possible** surprise anyone could have given me.* 那是我曾感受過的最大驚喜。◇ *Don't leave your packing until the **last possible** moment.* 打點行李不要拖到最後一刻。
IDM **as quickly, much, soon, etc. as ˈpossible** 0-n as quickly, much, soon, etc. as you can 盡量快（或多、早等）：*We will get your order to you as soon as possible.* 我們將會把您的訂貨儘早送達。➲ more at WORLD, WORST *n.*

■ ***noun*** a person or thing that is suitable for a particular job, purpose, etc. and might be chosen 合適的人（或物）；恰當人選（或事項）：*Out of all the people interviewed, there are only five possibles.* 在所有面試過的人中，僅有五個合適的人選。

pos·sibly 0-w /ˈpɒsəbli; *NAmE* ˈpɑːs-/ *adv.*
1 0-w used to say that sth might exist, happen or be true, but you are not certain 可能；或許 SYN **perhaps**：*It was possibly their worst performance ever.* 這也許是他們迄今為止最糟糕的表現。◇ *She found it difficult to get on with her, possibly because of the difference in their ages.* 她覺得很難與她相處，這可能是因為她們年齡上的差距。◇ *'Will you be around next week?' 'Possibly.'* "你下週過來嗎？" "也許吧。" ➲ LANGUAGE BANK at PERHAPS **2** 0-w used to emphasize that you are surprised, annoyed, etc. about sth（強調驚奇、惱怒等）：*You can't possibly mean that!* 你絕不會是那個意思吧！ **3** 0-w used to ask sb politely to do sth（表示委婉的請求）：*Could you possibly open that window?* 請你把那扇窗子打開好嗎？ **4** 0-w used to say that sb will do or has done as much as they can in order to make sth happen 盡量；盡可能：*I will come as soon as I possibly can.* 我會儘快趕來的。◇ *They tried everything they possibly could to improve the situation.* 他們為改善局面用盡了一切辦法。 **5** used with negatives, especially 'can't' and 'couldn't', to say strongly that you cannot do sth or that sth cannot or could not happen or be done（與 can't、couldn't 等否定詞連用，以加強語氣）：*I can't possibly tell you that!* 我絕不會把那件事告訴你的！◇ *You can't possibly carry all those bags.* 你絕拿不了所有這些包包袋袋的。◇ *'Let me buy it for you.' 'That's very kind of you, but I couldn't possibly* (= accept).' "這個，我買給你吧。" "您太客氣了。可我決不能讓您破費呀。"

British/American 英式/美式英語

post / mail

Nouns 名詞

- In *BrE* the official system used for sending and delivering letters, parcels/packages, etc. is usually called the **post**. In *NAmE* it is usually called the **mail**. 郵政系統在英式英語中通常叫做 post，在美式英語中通常稱為 mail：*I'll put an application form in the post/mail for you today.* 我今天會把申請表郵寄給你。◇ *Send your fee by post/mail to this address.* 將費用郵寄到此地址。 **Mail** is sometimes used in *BrE* in such expressions as *the Royal Mail.* 在英式英語中，mail 有時用於 the Royal Mail（皇家郵政）等短語中。 **Post** occurs in *NAmE* in such expressions as *the US Postal Service.* 在美式英語中，post 出現在 the US Postal Service（美國郵政管理局）等短語中。
- In *BrE* **post** is also used to mean the letters, parcels/packages, etc. that are delivered to you. **Mail** is the usual word in *NAmE* and is sometimes also used in *BrE*. 在英式英語中，post 亦指郵件。mail 在美式英語中為常用詞，有時亦用於英式英語：*Was there any post/mail this morning?* 今早有郵件嗎？◇ *I sat down to open my post/mail.* 我坐下來打開我的郵件。

Verbs 動詞

- Compare 比較：*I'll post the letter when I go out.* (*BrE*) 我出門時去寄這封信。（英式英語） and 與 *I'll mail the letter when I go out.* (*NAmE*) 我出門時去寄這封信。（美式英語）

Compounds 複合詞

- Note these words: **postman** (*BrE*), **mailman / mail carrier** (both *NAmE*); **postbox** (*BrE*), **mailbox** (*NAmE*) Some compounds are used in both *BrE* and *NAmE*: **post office**, **postcard**, **mail order**. 注意下列詞彙：郵遞員英式英語為 postman，美式英語為 mailman/mail carrier，郵筒英式英語為 postbox，美式英語為 mailbox。有些複合詞既用於英式英語，也用於美式英語，如 post office（郵局）、postcard（明信片）、mail order（郵購）。

pos·sum /ˈpɒsəm; *NAmE* ˈpɑːsəm/ *noun* (*AustralE, NZE* or *NAmE, informal*) = OPOSSUM
IDM **play ˈpossum** (*informal*) to pretend to be asleep or not aware of sth, in order to trick sb 裝睡；裝蒜；裝傻；裝糊塗

post 0-w /pəʊst; *NAmE* poʊst/ *noun, verb*
■ ***noun***
▸ LETTERS 信函 **1** 0-w (*BrE*) (also **mail** *NAmE, BrE*) [U] the official system used for sending and delivering letters, packages, etc. 郵政；郵遞；郵寄：*I'll send the original to you **by post**.* 我將把原件郵寄給你。◇ *I'll put the information **in the post** to you tomorrow.* 我明天會把資料郵寄給你。◇ *My application **got lost in the post**.* 我的申請書寄丟了。 **2** 0-w (*BrE*) (also **mail** *NAmE, BrE*) [U] letters, packages, etc. that are sent and delivered 郵寄的信函（或包裹等）；郵件：*There was a lot of post this morning.* 今天上午郵件很多。◇ *Have you opened your post yet?* 你拆開你的郵件了沒有？ **3** 0-w (*BrE*) [U, sing.] an occasion during the day when letters, etc. are collected or delivered 收集（或投遞）郵件的時間；郵班：*to **catch/miss the post*** 趕上 / 錯過郵班 ◇ *The parcel came in this morning's post.* 這個包裹是今天上午郵送來的。◇ *Payment should be sent **by return of post*** (= immediately). 請立即付款。
▸ JOB 工作 **4** 0-w [C] a job, especially an important one in a large organization 職位；（尤指）要職 SYN **position**：*an academic/government post* 教學 / 政府職位 ◇ *to **take up a post*** 就職 ◇ *to **resign** (**from**) **a post*** 辭職 ◇ *We will be creating 15 new posts next year.* 明年我們將增設 15 個新職位。◇ *The company has been unable to **fill the post**.* 公司的這個空缺還未能填補。◇ *He has **held the post** for three years.* 他擔任這個職務已經三年了。 ➲ SYNONYMS at JOB **5** (*especially NAmE*) (*BrE* usually **posting**) an act of sending sb to a particular place to do their job, especially for a limited period of time 派駐：*an overseas post* 派駐海外
▸ FOR SOLDIER/GUARD 士兵；警衛 **6** 0-w [C] the place where sb, especially a soldier, does their job 哨所；崗位：*a **police/customs/military post*** 警察崗亭；海關關卡；軍事哨所 ◇ *an observation post* 觀察哨所 ◇ *The guards were ordered not to leave their posts.* 警衛受命不得擅離崗位。 ➲ see also THE LAST POST, STAGING POST, TRADING POST
▸ WOOD/METAL 木頭；金屬 **7** [C] (often in compounds 常構成複合詞) a piece of wood or metal that is set in the ground in a vertical position, especially to support sth or to mark a point 柱；樁；標誌杆：*corner posts* (= that mark the corners of a sports field) 運動場的角杆 ➲ see also BEDPOST, GATEPOST, LAMP POST, SIGNPOST
▸ END OF RACE 速度比賽終點 **8 the post** [sing.] the place where a race finishes, especially in horse racing（尤指賽馬的）終點，終點標誌 ➲ see also FIRST-PAST-THE-POST, WINNING POST
▸ FOOTBALL 足球 **9** [C, usually sing.] = GOALPOST：*The ball hit the post and bounced in.* 球擊在門柱上彈進了球門。
▸ INTERNET 互聯網 **10** (also **post·ing**) [C] (*computing* 計) a message sent to a discussion group on the Internet; a piece of writing that forms part of a BLOG（發送到互聯網討論組的）帖子，信息；博文；網誌文章：*The forum does not allow posts from non-members.* 該論壇不允許非會員發帖。 IDM see DEAF, PILLAR
■ ***verb***
▸ LETTERS 信函 **1** 0-w (*BrE*) (*NAmE* **mail**) [T] to send a letter, etc. to sb by post/mail 寄；郵寄：**~ sth** (**off**) (**to sb**) *Have you posted off your order yet?* 你把訂單寄出去沒有？◇ *Is it OK if I post the cheque to you next week?* 我下週把支票寄給你行不行？◇ **~ sb sth** *Is it OK if I post you the cheque next week?* 我下週寄給你支票可以嗎？ ➲ compare MAIL **2** 0-w (*BrE*) (*NAmE* **mail**) [T] **~ sth** to put a letter, etc. into a POSTBOX 把（信件等）投入郵筒；投遞；郵寄：*Could you post this letter for me?* 請把這封信替我寄了好嗎？
▸ STH THROUGH HOLE 塞入孔中 **3** [T] **~ sth + adv./prep.** to put sth through a hole into a container 把…放入（或塞入）：*Let yourself out and post the keys through the letter box.* 你先出去，再把這些鑰匙塞進信箱吧。

P

▸ **SB FOR JOB** 委派 **4** [T, usually passive] **~ sb + adv./prep.** to send sb to a place for a period of time as part of their job 派駐：*She's been posted to Washington for two years.* 她被派往華盛頓工作兩年。◇ *Most of our employees get posted abroad at some stage.* 我們的大部份雇員都會在某一時期派駐國外。
▸ **SOLDIER/GUARD** 士兵；警衛 **5** [T] **~ sb + adv./prep.** to put sb, especially a soldier, in a particular place so that they can guard a building or area 使駐守；佈置…站崗：*Guards have been posted along the border.* 邊界上已部署了邊防崗哨。
▸ **PUBLIC NOTICE** 公告 **6** [T, often passive] **~ sth + adv./prep.** to put a notice, etc. in a public place so that people can see it 張貼；公佈 SYN **display**：*A copy of the letter was posted on the noticeboard.* 佈告牌上張貼了這封信的內容。
▸ **GIVE INFORMATION** 發佈信息 **7** [T] (*especially NAmE*) to announce sth publicly or officially, especially financial information or a warning 發佈，公佈，宣佈（尤指財經信息或警告）：**~ sth** *The company posted a $1.1 billion loss.* 這家公司公佈了 11 億元的虧損。◇ *A snow warning was posted for Ohio.* 俄亥俄州已發出大雪警報。◇ **~ sb/sth + adj.** *The aircraft and its crew were **posted missing**.* 據報這架飛機和機組人員已失踪。 **8** [T, I] to put information or pictures on a website（在網站上）發佈（信息或圖片）：**~ sth (on sth)** *The results will be posted on the Internet.* 結果將在互聯網上公佈。◇ **~ (on sth)** *The photos have been provided by fans who post on the message board.* 這些照片由那些在留言板上發佈信息的愛好者提供。
▸ **PAY MONEY TO COURT** 向法院交款 **9** [T] **~ bail/(a) bond** (*especially NAmE*) to pay money to a court so that a person accused of a crime can go free until their trial 交付（保釋金）：*She was released after posting $100 cash bond and her driver's license.* 交了 100 元現款保釋金及駕駛執照以後，她獲得保釋了。
IDM **keep sb 'posted (about/on sth)** to regularly give sb the most recent information about sth and how it is developing 定期通報；及時報告

post- /pəʊst; *NAmE* poʊst/ *prefix* (in nouns, verbs and adjectives 構成名詞、動詞和形容詞) after 後；以後：*a postgraduate* 研究生 ◇ *a post-Impressionist* 後印象主義者 ◇ *the post-1945 period* * 1945 年以後的時期 ➲ compare ANTE-, PRE-

post·age /ˈpəʊstɪdʒ; *NAmE* ˈpoʊ-/ *noun* [U] the cost of sending a letter, etc. by post 郵資；郵費：*an increase in postage rates* 郵費的增加 ◇ *How much was the postage on that letter?* 寄那封信要多少錢？◇ (*BrE*) *All prices include **postage and packing**.* 所有的價格都包括郵資和包裝費。◇ (*NAmE*) *All prices include **postage and handling**.* 所有的價格都包括郵資和手續費。

ˈpostage meter *noun* (*NAmE*) = FRANKING MACHINE

ˈpostage stamp *noun* (*formal*) = STAMP *n.* (1)

pos·tal /ˈpəʊstl; *NAmE* ˈpoʊstl/ *adj.* [only before noun] **1** connected with the official system for sending and delivering letters, etc. 郵政的；郵遞的：*your full **postal address*** 你郵政地址的全寫 ◇ *the **postal service/system*** 郵政業務／系統 ◇ *postal charges* 郵費 **2** (*especially BrE*) involving things that are sent by post 郵寄物品的；郵寄的：*postal bookings* 郵寄預訂
IDM **go ˈpostal** (*informal, especially NAmE*) to become very angry 大怒：*He went postal when he found out.* 他發現後勃然大怒。

ˈpostal ballot *noun* (*BrE*) a system of voting on a particular issue in which everyone sends their vote by post 郵寄式投票

ˈpostal code *noun* (*BrE, CanE*) = POSTCODE

ˈpostal order (*BrE*) (also **ˈmoney order** *NAmE, BrE*) *noun* (*abbr.* **PO**) an official document that you can buy at a bank or a post office and send to sb so that they can exchange it for money 郵政匯票

ˈpostal service *noun* **1** a system of collecting and delivering letters, etc. 郵政業務：*a good postal service* 良好的郵政服務 **2 the Postal Service** (*US*) (*BrE* **the ˈPost Office**) the national organization in many countries that is responsible for collecting and delivering letters, etc. 郵政部門；郵政系統

ˈpostal vote (*BrE*) (*US* **ˌabsentee ˈballot**) *noun* a vote in an election that you can send when you cannot be present 郵寄的選票；郵寄投票

post·bag /ˈpəʊstbæg; *NAmE* ˈpoʊst-/ *noun* (*BrE*) **1** (also **mail·bag** *NAmE, BrE*) [usually sing.] all the letters, emails, etc. received by a newspaper, a TV station, a website, or an important person at a particular time or about a particular subject（寄給報紙、電視台、網站、要人等的）公眾來信：*We had a huge postbag on the subject from our readers.* 我們收到了讀者關於這個問題的大量來函。 **2** = MAILBAG (1)

post·box /ˈpəʊstbɒks; *NAmE* ˈpoʊstbɑːks/ (also **ˈletter box**) (both *BrE*) (*NAmE* **mail·box**) *noun* a public box, for example in the street, that you put letters into when you send them 郵筒；郵箱 ➲ picture at LETTER BOX ➲ **VISUAL VOCAB** pages V2, V3 ➲ compare PILLAR BOX

post·card /ˈpəʊstkɑːd; *NAmE* ˈpoʊstkɑːrd/ (also **card**) *noun* a card used for sending messages by post without an envelope, especially one that has a picture on one side 明信片：*colourful postcards of California* 五顏六色的加利福尼亞州明信片 ◇ *Send us a postcard from Venice!* 從威尼斯給我們寄張明信片來！◇ *Send your answers on a postcard to the above address.* 把答案寫在明信片上，寄到上述地址。➲ see also PICTURE POSTCARD

post·code /ˈpəʊstkəʊd; *NAmE* ˈpoʊstkoʊd/ (also **ˈpostal code**) (*BrE, CanE*) (*US* **ˈzip code**) *noun* a group of letters and/or numbers that are used as part of an address so that post/mail can be separated into groups and delivered more quickly 郵政編碼；郵編；郵遞區號

ˌpostcode ˈlottery *noun* [sing.] (*BrE*) a situation in which the amount or type of medical treatment that is provided to people depends on the particular area of the country they live in 郵編幸運醫療（在英國指能得到的醫保程度或方式取決於居住的地區）

post-coital /ˌpəʊst ˈkɔɪtl; ˈkəʊɪtl; *NAmE* ˌpoʊst; ˈkoʊɪtl/ *adj.* [usually before noun] happening or done after SEXUAL INTERCOURSE 性交後發生（或做）的；性交後的

ˌpost-ˈdate *verb* **1 ~ sth** to write a date on a cheque that is later than the actual date so that the cheque cannot be CASHED (= exchanged for money) until that date 把（支票日期）填遲；預填（支票）日期；簽遲日期 ➲ compare BACKDATE (1) **2 ~ sth** to happen, exist or be made at a later date than sth else in the past 發生（或存在、造出）得較晚；發生在…之後 OPP **predate**

post·doc·tor·al /ˌpəʊstˈdɒktərəl; *NAmE* ˌpoʊstˈdɑːk-/ *adj.* [usually before noun] connected with advanced research or study that is done after a PHD has been completed 博士後的

pos·ter /ˈpəʊstə(r); *NAmE* ˈpoʊ-/ *noun* **1** a large notice, often with a picture on it, that is put in a public place to advertise sth 招貼畫；海報 SYN **placard**：*election posters* 選舉海報 ◇ *a poster campaign* (= an attempt to educate people about sth by using posters) 招貼宣傳運動 **2** a large picture that is printed on paper and put on a wall as decoration 巨幅裝飾畫：*posters of her favourite pop stars* 她所喜愛的流行歌星的海報 ➲ **VISUAL VOCAB** page V70 **3** a person who posts a message on a MESSAGE BOARD (= a place on a website where people can read or write messages)（在網絡留言板上）發佈消息的人，張貼信息的人

ˈposter child (also **ˈposter boy**, **ˈposter girl**) *noun* (*especially NAmE*) **1** a child with a particular illness or other problem whose picture appears on a poster advertising an organization that helps children with that illness or problem 出現在慈善海報上的兒童（呼籲捐助有某種病或困難的孩童） **2** (often *humorous*) a person who is seen as representing a particular quality or activity 代表人物；典型：*He is the poster child for incompetent government.* 他是無能政府的典型人物。

poste rest·ante /ˌpəʊst ˈrestɑːnt; *NAmE* ˌpoʊst reˈst-/ (*BrE*) (*NAmE* **ˌgeneral deˈlivery**) *noun* [U] an arrangement in which a post office keeps a person's mail until they go to collect it, used especially when sb is travelling（郵局的）郵件寄存服務

pos·ter·ior /pɒˈstɪəriə(r); *NAmE* pɑːˈstɪr-/ *adj.*, *noun*

■ ***adj.*** [only before noun] (*technical* 術語) located behind sth or at the back of sth 在後面的；在後部的 OPP **anterior**

■ ***noun*** (*humorous*) the part of your body that you sit on; your bottom 臀部；屁股

pos·teri·ori ➲ A POSTERIORI

pos·ter·ity /pɒˈsterəti; *NAmE* pɑːˈs-/ *noun* [U] (*formal*) all the people who will live in the future 後代；後裔；子孫；後世：*Their music has been **preserved for posterity**.* 他們的音樂已為後世保存起來。◇ *Posterity will remember him as a great man.* 後人將會記住他是個偉人。

ˈ**poster paint** *noun* [U, C] a thick paint used especially for children's paintings 廣告顏料

ˌ**post exˈchange** *noun* = PX

ˌ**post-ˈfree** *adj.* [only before noun] (*BrE*) used to describe sth that you can send by post without having to pay anything 免付郵資的 ▸ ˌ**post-ˈfree** *adv.*：*Information will be sent post-free to any interested readers.* 有意索取資料的讀者可免付郵資。

post·grad /ˈpəʊstgræd; *NAmE* ˈpoʊst-/ *noun* (*informal*) a POSTGRADUATE 研究生

post·gradu·ate /ˌpəʊstˈgrædʒuət; *NAmE* ˌpoʊst-/ (also *informal* **post·grad**) *noun* (*especially BrE*) a person who already holds a first degree and who is doing advanced study or research; a GRADUATE student 研究生：*postgraduate students* 研究生 ◇ *a postgraduate course* 研究生課程 ➲ note at STUDENT

ˌ**post-ˈhaste** *adv.* (*literary*) as quickly as you can 儘快；從速：*to depart post-haste* 火速動身

post hoc /ˌpəʊst ˈhɒk; *NAmE* ˌpoʊst ˈhɑːk/ *adj.* (from *Latin*, *formal*) (of an argument, etc. 論點等) happening after the event, especially when one event is the cause of another 以先後為因果的；事後歸因的：*a post hoc explanation* 事後歸因的解釋 ▸ **post hoc** *adv.*

post·hu·mous /ˈpɒstjʊməs; *NAmE* ˈpɑːstʃəməs/ *adj.* [usually before noun] happening, done, published, etc. after a person has died 死後發生（或做、出版等）的：*a posthumous award for bravery* 死後榮膺的英勇獎 ▸ **post·hu·mous·ly** *adv.*

post·ie /ˈpəʊsti; *NAmE* ˈpoʊ-/ *noun* (*BrE*, *informal*) = POSTMAN

ˌ**post-in·ˈdus·trial** *adj.* [only before noun] (of a place or society 地方或社會) no longer relying on heavy industry (= the production of steel, large machinery, etc.) 後工業化的；不再依賴重工業的

post·ing /ˈpəʊstɪŋ; *NAmE* ˈpoʊ-/ *noun* **1** (*especially BrE*) (*NAmE* usually **post**) an act of sending sb to a particular place to do their job, especially for a limited period of time 派駐：*an overseas posting* 派駐海外 **2** = POST *n.* (10)

ˈ**Post-it™** (also ˈ**Post-it note**) *noun* a small piece of coloured, sticky paper that you use for writing a note on, and that can be easily removed 報事貼便條紙；黏膠便條紙；便利貼 ➲ VISUAL VOCAB page V69

post·man /ˈpəʊstmən; *NAmE* ˈpoʊst-/, **post·woman** /ˈpəʊstwʊmən; *NAmE* ˈpoʊst-/ *noun* (*pl.* **-men** /-mən/, **-women** /-wɪmɪn/) (also *informal* **post·ie**) (*especially BrE*) a person whose job is to collect and deliver letters, etc. 郵遞員；郵差 ➲ see also MAILMAN ➲ note at GENDER

ˌ**postman's ˈknock** (*BrE*) (*NAmE* ˈ**post office**) *noun* [U] a children's game in which imaginary letters are exchanged for kisses 郵差敲門遊戲（兒童用假託的信件換取親吻）

post·mark /ˈpəʊstmɑːk; *NAmE* ˈpoʊstmɑːrk/ *noun* an official mark placed over the stamp on a letter, etc. that shows when and where it was posted and makes it impossible to use the stamp again 郵戳 ▸ **post·mark** *verb* [usually passive]：**~ sth** *The card was postmarked Tokyo 9th March.* 明信片上蓋着東京三月九日的郵戳。

post·mas·ter /ˈpəʊstmɑːstə(r); *NAmE* ˈpoʊstmæstər/, **post·mist·ress** /ˈpəʊstmɪstrəs; *NAmE* ˈpoʊst-/ *noun* a person who is in charge of a post office 郵政局長

post·mod·ern /ˌpəʊstˈmɒdn; *NAmE* ˌpoʊstˈmɑːdərn/ *adj.* connected with or influenced by postmodernism 後現代主義的；受後現代主義影響的

post·mod·ern·ism /ˌpəʊstˈmɒdənɪzəm; *NAmE* ˌpoʊstˈmɑːdərn-/ *noun* [U] a style and movement in art, ARCHITECTURE, literature, etc. in the late 20th century that reacts against modern styles, for example by mixing features from traditional and modern styles 後現代主義（20 世紀後期在藝術、建築、文學等方面對抗現代風格，如融合傳統與現代風格）➲ compare MODERNISM ▸ **post·mod·ern·ist** *noun*, *adj.* [usually before noun]

post·modi·fier /ˌpəʊstˈmɒdɪfaɪə(r); *NAmE* ˌpoʊstˈmɑːd-/ *noun* (*grammar* 語法) a word or group of words that describes a noun phrase or restricts its meaning in some way, and is placed after it 後置修飾語；後修飾成分：*In 'the house on the corner', 'on the corner' is a post-modifier.* 在 the house on the corner 中，on the corner 是後置修飾語。➲ compare MODIFIER, PREMODIFIER

post-mortem /ˌpəʊst ˈmɔːtəm; *NAmE* ˌpoʊst ˈmɔːrtəm/ *noun* **1** (also **post-ˌmortem examiˈnation**) a medical examination of the body of a dead person in order to find out how they died 驗屍；屍體解剖 SYN **autopsy**：***to do/conduct/carry out a post-mortem*** 進行剖屍驗證 ◇ **~ on sb** *The post-mortem on the child revealed that she had been poisoned.* 驗屍證明這孩子是被人毒死的。**2 ~** (**on sth**) a discussion or an examination of an event after it has happened, especially in order to find out why it failed 事後反思（或剖析）：*to hold a post-mortem on the party's election defeat* 對該黨競選失敗進行檢討

post-natal /ˌpəʊst ˈneɪtl; *NAmE* ˌpoʊst/ (*BrE*) (*NAmE* **post-partum**) *adj.* [only before noun] connected with the period after the birth of a child 產後的；分娩後的：*post-natal care* 產後護理 ➲ compare ANTENATAL, PRENATAL

ˌ**post-ˌnatal deˈpression** (*BrE*) (*NAmE* ˌ**post-ˌpartum deˈpression**) *noun* [U] a medical condition in which a woman feels very sad and anxious in the period after her baby is born 產後抑鬱（症）

ˈ**post office** 🔑 *noun*

1 🔑 [C] a place where you can buy stamps, send letters, etc. 郵局：*Where's the main post office?* 郵政總局在哪兒？◇ *You can buy your stamps at the post office.* 你可以在郵局買郵票。◇ *a post office counter* 郵局的櫃枱 **2** 🔑 **the ˈPost Office** [sing.] (*abbr.* **PO**) the national organization in many countries that is responsible for collecting and delivering letters, etc. 郵政部門；郵政系統：*He works for the Post Office.* 他在郵政部門工作。**3** (*NAmE*) (*BrE* ˌ**postman's ˈknock**) [U] a children's game in which imaginary letters are exchanged for kisses 郵差敲門遊戲（兒童用假託的信件換取親吻）

ˈ**post office box** *noun* = PO BOX

ˌ**post-ˈop·era·tive** *adj.* [only before noun] (*medical* 醫) connected with the period after a medical operation 手術後的：*post-operative complications/pain/care* 手術後併發症／疼痛／護理

ˌ**post-ˈpaid** *adj.* [only before noun] that you can send free because the charge has already been paid 郵資已付的：*a post-paid envelope* 已付郵資的信封 ▸ ˌ**post-ˈpaid** *adv.*

post-partum /ˌpəʊst ˈpɑːtəm; *NAmE* ˌpoʊst ˈpɑːrtəm/ (*NAmE*) (*BrE* **post-natal**) *adj.* [only before noun] connected with the period after the birth of a child 產後的；分娩後的 ➲ compare ANTENATAL, PRENATAL

ˌ**post-ˌpartum deˈpression** (*NAmE*) (*BrE* ˌ**post-ˌnatal deˈpression**) *noun* [U] a medical condition in which a woman feels very sad and anxious in the period after her baby is born 產後抑鬱（症）

post·pone /pəˈspəʊn; *NAmE* poʊˈspoʊn/ *verb* to arrange for an event, etc. to take place at a later time or date 延遲；延期；展緩 SYN **put off**：**~ sth** *The game has already been postponed three times.* 這場比賽已經三度延期了。◇ **~ sth to/until sth** *We'll have to postpone the meeting until next week.* 我們將不得不把會議推遲到下週舉行。◇ **~ doing sth** *It was an unpopular decision to postpone building the new hospital.* 延遲興建新醫院的決定是不得人心的。➲ compare CANCEL (1) ▸ **post·pone·ment** *noun* [U, C]：*Riots led to the postponement of local elections.* 騷亂致使地方選舉延期了。

P

post·pos·ition /ˌpəʊstpəˈzɪʃn; *NAmE* ˌpoʊst-/ *noun* (*grammar* 語法) a word or part of a word that comes after the word it relates to, for example '-ish' in 'greenish' 後置詞；後置成分 ▸ **post·pos·ition·al** /-ʃənl/ *adj.*

post·pran·dial /ˌpəʊstˈprændiəl; *NAmE* ˌpoʊst-/ *adj.* [usually before noun] (*formal* or *humorous*) happening immediately after a meal 飯後的；餐後的

ˌpost-proˈduc·tion *adj.* [usually before noun] **post-production** work on music or on films/movies is done after recording or filming （音樂或電影製作）錄製之後的，後期的：*post-production editing* 後期剪輯 ▸ **ˌpost-proˈduc·tion** *noun* [U]：*The movie is now in post-production and will be released next month.* 這部電影目前正在進行後期製作，將於下月發行。

ˈpost room *noun* (*BrE*) the department of a company that deals with sending and receiving mail （公司的）郵件收發部，郵件收發室

post·script /ˈpəʊstskrɪpt; *NAmE* ˈpoʊst-/ *noun* **1** (*abbr.* PS) **~ (to sth)** an extra message that you add at the end of a letter after your signature （加於信末的）附言，又及 **2 ~ (to sth)** extra facts or information about a story, an event, etc. that are added after it has finished 補充；補編；後話；跋

ˌpost-ˈsync (also **ˌpost-ˈsynch**) *verb* **~ sth** (*technical* 術語) to add sound to a film/movie after it has been filmed 給（電影）後期配音；為…後期錄音

ˌpost-ˌtraumatic ˈstress disorder *noun* [U] (*medical* 醫) a medical condition in which a person suffers mental and emotional problems resulting from an experience that shocked them very much 創傷後精神緊張性障礙

pos·tu·late *verb, noun*

■ ***verb*** /ˈpɒstjuleɪt; *NAmE* ˈpɑːstʃəl-/ **~ sth | ~ that ...** (*formal*) to suggest or accept that sth is true so that it can be used as the basis for a theory, etc. 假定；假設 **SYN posit**：*They postulated a 500-year lifespan for a plastic container.* 他們假定塑料容器的壽命為 500 年。

■ ***noun*** /ˈpɒstjʊlət; *NAmE* ˈpɑːstʃəl-/ (*formal*) a statement that is accepted as true, that forms the basis of a theory, etc. 假定；假設

P

pos·tural /ˈpɒstʃərəl; *NAmE* ˈpɑːs-/ *adj.* (*formal*) connected with the way you hold your body when sitting or standing （坐、立）姿勢的

pos·ture /ˈpɒstʃə(r); *NAmE* ˈpɑːs-/ *noun, verb*

■ ***noun*** **1** [U, C] the position in which you hold your body when standing or sitting （坐立的）姿勢：*a comfortable/relaxed posture* 舒適的／輕鬆的姿勢 ◇ ***upright/sitting/supine postures*** 直立的／坐着的／仰卧的姿勢 ◇ ***Good posture** is essential when working at the computer.* 用電腦工作時良好的姿勢極其重要。◇ *Back pains can be the result of **bad posture**.* 腰背疼可能是不良姿勢造成的。 **2** [C, usually sing.] your attitude to a particular situation or the way in which you deal with it 態度；看法；立場；處理方式：*The government has adopted an aggressive posture on immigration.* 政府對移民入境採取了強硬的態度。

■ ***verb*** [I] **~ (as sth)** (*formal*) to pretend to be sth that you are not by saying and doing things in order to impress or trick people 故作姿態；裝樣子

pos·tur·ing /ˈpɒstʃərɪŋ; *NAmE* ˈpɑːs-/ *noun* [U, C] (*disapproving*) behaviour that is not natural or sincere but is intended to attract attention or to have a particular effect 做作的舉止；忸怩作態；虛偽表現

post·viral syn·drome /ˌpəʊstˈvaɪrəl sɪndrəʊm; *NAmE* ˌpoʊstˈvaɪrəl sɪndroʊm/ (also **ˌpost viral faˈtigue syndrome**) *noun* [U] a condition that follows a VIRAL infection, in which sb feels extremely weak and tired, and which can last for a long time 病毒後綜合症（受病毒性感染後長時間虛弱疲勞）

ˌpost-ˈwar *adj.* [usually before noun] existing, happening or made in the period after a war, especially the Second World War 戰後的；（尤指）第二次世界大戰以後的：*the post-war years* 戰後的年代

post·woman ➲ POSTMAN

posy /ˈpəʊzi; *NAmE* ˈpoʊzi/ *noun* (*pl.* **-ies**) a small bunch of flowers 小花束

pot 🔑 /pɒt; *NAmE* pɑːt/ *noun, verb*

■ ***noun***

▸ **FOR COOKING** 烹飪 **1** 🔑 [C] a deep round container used for cooking things in 鍋：*pots and pans* 鍋碗瓢盆

▸ **CONTAINER** 容器 **2** 🔑 [C] (*especially BrE*) a container made of glass, CLAY or plastic, used for storing food in （盛食品的）罐，瓶，壺：*a pot of jam* 一罐果醬 ◇ *a yogurt pot* 酸奶瓶 ➲ **VISUAL VOCAB** page V33 **3** 🔑 [C] (especially in compounds 尤用於構成複合詞) a container of various kinds, made for a particular purpose （某種用途的）容器：*a coffee pot* 咖啡壺 ◇ *a pepper pot* 胡椒瓶 ◇ *a teapot* 茶壺 ◇ *Is there any more tea in the pot?* 茶壺裏還有茶嗎？➲ **VISUAL VOCAB** page V25 ➲ see also CHAMBER POT, CHIMNEY POT, FLOWERPOT, LOBSTER POT, MELTING POT, POTTED **4** 🔑 [C] the amount contained in a pot 一罐，一瓶，一壺（的量）：*They drank a pot of coffee.* 他們喝了一壺咖啡。 **5** [C] a bowl, etc. that is made by a POTTER 陶盆；陶罐；碗

▸ **MONEY** 錢 **6 the pot** [sing.] (*especially NAmE*) the total amount of money that is bet in a card game （一局紙牌遊戲的）賭注總額，全部賭注 **7 the pot** [sing.] (*especially NAmE*) all the money given by a group of people in order to do sth together, for example to buy food 湊集的資金；湊合的錢 ➲ see also KITTY (1), (2)

▸ **DRUG** 毒品 **8** [U] (*informal*) = MARIJUANA：*pot smoking* 吸大麻

▸ **SHOT** 發射 **9** [C] = POTSHOT：*He took a pot at the neighbour's cat with his air rifle.* 他用氣槍向鄰居的貓打了一槍。

▸ **IN BILLIARDS, ETC.** 枱球等 **10** [C] (in the game of BILLIARDS, POOL or SNOOKER 枱球、普爾或斯諾克) the act of hitting a ball into one of the pockets around the edge of the table 擊球入袋

▸ **STOMACH** 胃 **11** [C] (*informal*) = POT BELLY at POT-BELLIED

IDM **go to ˈpot** (*informal*) to be spoiled because people are not working hard or taking care of things （因疏懶或忽視）搞砸了，糟蹋了：*Her handwriting's gone to pot since she started using a computer all the time.* 自從她開始完全使用電腦後，她的手寫就荒疏了。 **the pot calling the kettle ˈblack** (*saying, informal*) used to say that you should not criticize sb for a fault that you have yourself 鍋笑壺黑；五十步笑百步；烏鴉說豬黑 **ˌpot ˈluck** when you take **pot luck**, you choose sth or go somewhere without knowing very much about it, but hope that it will be good, pleasant, etc. 碰運氣；撞大運：*It's pot luck whether you get good advice or not.* 能不能得到好的指點那就全靠運氣了。◇ *You're welcome to stay to supper, but you'll have to take pot luck* (= eat whatever is available). 歡迎你留下來吃晚飯，不過你得有什麼就吃什麼了。➲ see also POTLUCK **ˈpots of money** (*BrE, informal*) a very large amount of money 大筆的金錢；巨額款項 ➲ more at GOLD *n.*, MELTING POT, QUART, WATCH *v.*

■ ***verb*** (**-tt-**)

▸ **PLANT** 植物 **1 ~ sth** to put a plant into a FLOWERPOT filled with soil 把…栽入盆中；種盆栽

▸ **IN BILLIARDS, ETC.** 枱球等 **2 ~ sth** (in the games of BILLIARDS, POOL and SNOOKER 枱球、普爾和斯諾克) to hit a ball into one of the pockets (= holes at the corners and edges of the table) 擊（球）入袋 **SYN pocket**：*He potted the black to take a 7–3 lead.* 他把黑球擊入袋中，以 7:3 領先。

▸ **SHOOT** 射擊 **3 ~ sth** to kill an animal or a bird by shooting it 射殺，射獵（飛禽或走獸）➲ see also POTTED

pot·able /ˈpəʊtəbl; *NAmE* ˈpoʊ-/ *adj.* (*formal*) (of water 水) safe to drink 可飲用的；適於飲用的

pot·ash /ˈpɒtæʃ; *NAmE* ˈpɑːt-/ *noun* [U] a chemical containing potassium, used to improve soil for farming and in making soap 鉀鹼

po·tas·sium /pəˈtæsiəm/ *noun* [U] (*symb.* K) a chemical element. Potassium is a soft silver-white metal that exists mainly in COMPOUNDS which are used in industry and farming. 鉀

po·tato 🔑 /pəˈteɪtəʊ; *NAmE* -toʊ/ *noun* [C, U] (*pl.* **-oes**) a round white vegetable with a brown or red skin that grows underground as the root of a plant also called a potato 馬鈴薯；土豆；洋芋：*Will you peel the potatoes for me?* 你給我削土豆皮好不好？◇ ***roast/boiled/baked/fried potatoes*** 烘／煮／烤／炸土豆 ➲ VISUAL VOCAB page V31 ➲ see also COUCH POTATO, HOT POTATO, JACKET (4), MASHED POTATO, MEAT AND POTATOES, MEAT-AND-POTATOES, SMALL POTATOES, SWEET POTATO

po,tato 'crisp (*BrE*), **po'tato chip** (*NAmE*) *noun* = CRISP *n.*, CHIP *n.* (4)

po'tato masher *noun* a kitchen UTENSIL (= tool) for MASHING potatoes 土豆搗泥器；馬鈴薯搗爛器 ➲ VISUAL VOCAB pages V26, V28

,pot-'bellied *adj.* (of people and animals 人或動物) having a large stomach that sticks out 肚子大的；大腹便便的；啤酒肚的 ▸ **,pot 'belly** (also *informal* **pot**) *noun*

pot·boil·er /'pɒtbɔɪlə(r); *NAmE* 'pɑːt-/ *noun* (*disapproving*) a book, a play, etc. that is produced only to earn money quickly 為賺錢創作的書籍（或戲劇等）；營利文藝

'pot-bound (also **'root-bound**) *adj.* (of a plant 植物) having roots that fill the flower pot, with no more room for them to grow 根滿盆的；盆縛的

'pot cheese *noun* [U] (*US*) a type of soft white cheese with lumps in it 大顆粒鬆軟白乾酪

po·teen (also **po·theen**) /pə'tiːn; pə'tʃiːn/ *noun* [U] (*IrishE*) strong alcoholic drink made illegally, usually from potatoes 卜丁酒（愛爾蘭私酒，常用土豆釀製）

po·tency /'pəʊtnsi; *NAmE* 'poʊ-/ *noun* (*pl.* **-ies**) **1** [U, C] the power that sb/sth has to affect your body or mind 影響力；支配力；效力：*the potency of desire* 慾望的支配力 ◇ *If you keep a medicine too long, it may lose its potency.* 藥物存放太久，可能會失去效力。 **2** [U] the ability of a man to have sex （男子）性能力，性機能

po·tent /'pəʊtnt; *NAmE* 'poʊ-/ *adj.* **1** having a strong effect on your body or mind 有強效的；有力的；烈性的；影響身心的：*a potent drug* 猛藥 ◇ *a very potent alcoholic brew* 烈性酒精飲料 ◇ *a potent argument* 有力的論據 **2** powerful 強大的；強有力的：*a potent force* 強大的力量 ➲ see also IMPOTENT ▸ **po·tent·ly** *adv.*

po·ten·tate /'pəʊtnteɪt; *NAmE* 'poʊ-/ *noun* (*literary*, often *disapproving*) a ruler who has a lot of power, especially when this is not restricted by a parliament, etc. 權力大的統治者；（尤指不受國會等約束的）君主，統治者

po·ten·tial 🔑 AW /pə'tenʃl/ *adj.*, *noun*

■ ***adj.*** 🔑 [only before noun] that can develop into sth or be developed in the future 潛在的；可能的 SYN **possible**：*potential customers* 潛在的客戶 ◇ *a potential source of conflict* 潛在的衝突根源 ◇ *a potential prime minister* 未來的首相 ◇ *First we need to identify actual and potential problems.* 首先，我們需要弄清實際的問題和潛在的問題。 ▸ **po·ten·tial·ly** 🔑 AW /-ʃəli/ *adv.*：*a potentially dangerous situation* 有潛在危險的局勢

■ ***noun*** **1** 🔑 [U] the possibility of sth happening or being developed or used 可能性；潛在性：**~ (for)** *the potential for change* 變革的可能性 ◇ **~ (for doing sth)** *The European marketplace offers excellent potential for increasing sales.* 歐洲市場帶來了擴銷的大好機遇。 **2** 🔑 [U] qualities that exist and can be developed 潛力；潛質 SYN **promise**：*All children should be encouraged to **realize their full potential**.* 應當鼓勵所有的兒童充分發揮他們的潛能。◇ *She has great potential as an artist.* 她很有潛質，是一位可造就的藝術家。◇ *He has the potential to become a world-class musician.* 他有潛力成為世界級的音樂家。◇ *The house has a lot of potential.* 這所房子頗具潛力。 **3** [U, C] (*physics* 物) the difference in VOLTAGE between two points in an electric field or CIRCUIT 電位；電勢；電壓

po,tential 'energy *noun* [U] (*physics* 物) the form of energy that an object gains as it is lifted 勢能

po·ten·ti·al·ity /pə,tenʃi'æləti/ *noun* (*pl.* **-ies**) (*formal*) a power or a quality that exists and is capable of being developed 潛力；潛在的可能性：*We often underestimate our potentialities.* 我們常常低估自己的潛力。

po·tenti·om·eter /pə,tenʃi'ɒmɪtə(r); *NAmE* -'ɑːm-/ *noun* **1** a device for measuring differences in electrical POTENTIAL 電勢差計 **2** a device for varying electrical RESISTANCE, used, for example, in volume controls 分壓器

po·theen = POTEEN

pot·hole /'pɒthəʊl; *NAmE* 'pɑːthoʊl/ *noun* **1** a large rough hole in the surface of a road that is formed by traffic and bad weather （路面的）坑窪 **2** a deep hole that is formed in rock, especially by the action of water 岩石中的溶洞；地壺；甌穴

pot·hol·ing /'pɒthəʊlɪŋ; *NAmE* 'pɑːthoʊlɪŋ/ (*BrE*) *noun* [U] = CAVING：*to go potholing* 去探測甌穴 ▸ **pot·holer** *noun* = CAVER

po·tion /'pəʊʃn; *NAmE* 'poʊʃn/ *noun* (*literary*) a drink of medicine or poison; a liquid with magic powers 藥水；毒液；魔水：*a **magic/love potion*** 魔水；春藥飲劑 ◇ (*humorous*) *I've tried all sorts of drugs, creams, pills and potions.* 我已試過各種各樣的藥物、藥膏、藥片和藥水。

potjie /'pɔɪki/ *noun* (*SAfrE*) **1** a round pot, usually with three legs, that is made from CAST IRON and used for cooking food slowly over a fire 波基火鍋，鼎鍋（通常有三足的鑄鐵圓罐燜燒鍋） **2** a meal that is prepared in a pot like this 波基火鍋燉菜：*a chicken potjie* 波基火鍋燉雞

'pot liquor *noun* [U] (*especially US*) the liquid in which meat, fish, or vegetables have been cooked 肉汁；菜滷；高湯

pot·luck /'pɒt'lʌk; *NAmE* pɑːt-/ *noun* (*NAmE*) a meal to which each guest brings some food, which is then shared out among the guests 百味餐（參加者帶食物分享）

'pot plant *noun* (*BrE*) = HOUSE PLANT

pot·pourri /,pəʊpʊ'riː; *NAmE* ,poʊ/ *noun* (from *French*) **1** [U, C] a mixture of dried flowers and leaves used for making a room smell pleasant 百花香（房間薰香用的乾花和葉子的混合物） **2** [sing.] a mixture of various things that were not originally intended to form a group 雜燴；集錦：*a potpourri of tunes* 樂曲集錦

'pot roast *noun* a piece of meat cooked with vegetables in a pot 蔬菜燉肉塊 ▸ **'pot-roast** *verb* **~ sth**

pot·shot /'pɒtʃɒt; *NAmE* 'pɑːtʃɑːt/ (also **pot**) *noun* (*informal*) a shot that sb fires without aiming carefully 亂射；盲目射擊：*Somebody **took a potshot at** him as he drove past.* 他開車經過的時候，有人向他亂開了一槍。◇ (*figurative*) *The newspapers **took** constant **potshots at*** (= criticized) *the president.* 報界經常恣意批評總統。

pot·tage /'pɒtɪdʒ; *NAmE* 'pɑːt-/ *noun* [U] (*old use*) soup or STEW 湯；燉菜

pot·ted /'pɒtɪd; *NAmE* 'pɑːt-/ *adj.* [only before noun] **1** planted in a pot 盆栽的：*potted plants* 盆栽植物 **2** (*BrE*) (of a book, or a story 書籍或故事) in a short simple form 簡本的；縮略的：*a potted history of England* 英格蘭簡史 **3** (*BrE*) **potted** meat or fish has been cooked and preserved in a small container （魚、肉等熟食）罐裝的

pot·ter /'pɒtə(r); *NAmE* 'pɑːt-/ *verb*, *noun*

■ ***verb*** (*BrE*) (*NAmE* **putt·er**) [I] **+ adv./prep.** to do things or move without hurrying, especially when you are doing sth that you enjoy and that is not important 從容做事；欣然從事；漫步；閒蕩：*I spent the day pottering around the house.* 我在家裏逍遙了一天。

■ ***noun*** a person who makes CLAY pots by hand 陶工

,potter's 'wheel *noun* a piece of equipment with a flat disc that goes around, on which potters put wet CLAY in order to shape it into pots 陶鈞（製陶用的轉輪） ➲ VISUAL VOCAB page V41

pot·tery /'pɒtəri; *NAmE* 'pɑːt-/ *noun* (*pl.* **-ies**) **1** [U] pots, dishes, etc. made with CLAY that is baked in an oven, especially when they are made by hand 陶器（尤指手工製的）：*Roman pottery* 羅馬時期的陶器 ◇ *a piece of pottery* 一件陶製品 **2** [U] the CLAY that some dishes and pots are made of 陶土：*a jug made of blue-glazed pottery* 一把藍釉陶壺 **3** [U] the skill of making pots and dishes from CLAY, especially by hand 製陶手藝；製陶技藝：*a pottery class* 陶藝班 ➲ VISUAL VOCAB page V41

P

4 [C] a place where CLAY pots and dishes are made 製陶作坊；陶窰；陶器工廠

ˈpotting compost *noun* [U] good quality soil, used for growing plants in flower pots 盆栽用土

ˈpotting shed *noun* (*BrE*) a small building where seeds and young plants are grown in pots before they are planted outside 盆栽育秧棚

potto /ˈpɒtəʊ; *NAmE* ˈpɑːtoʊ/ *noun* (*pl.* **-os**) an animal like a MONKEY with a pointed face, found in tropical W Africa 樹熊猴，波特懶猴（生活於非洲西部熱帶地區）

potty /ˈpɒti; *NAmE* ˈpɑːti/ *adj., noun*

■ ***adj.*** (*BrE, informal,* becoming *old-fashioned*) (**pot·tier, pot·ti·est**) **1** crazy 發瘋的；瘋狂的：*The kids are driving me potty!* 這群小崽子煩死我了！ **2 ~ about sb/sth** liking sb/sth a lot 喜愛；對…痴迷

■ ***noun*** (*pl.* **-ies**) (*informal*) a bowl that very young children use when they are too small to use a toilet（幼兒的）便盆 ➲ compare CHAMBER POT

ˌpotty-ˈmouthed *adj.* (*informal, especially NAmE*) using rude, offensive language 滿口髒話的；粗口的：*a potty-mouthed comedian* 爆粗口的喜劇演員

ˈpotty-train *verb* **~ sb** to teach a small child to use a potty or toilet 訓練（幼兒）使用便器 ▸ **ˈpotty-trained** *adj.* **ˈpotty-training** *noun* [U]

pouch /paʊtʃ/ *noun* **1** a small bag, usually made of leather, and often carried in a pocket or attached to a belt 小袋子；荷包：*a tobacco pouch* 煙絲荷包 ◇ *She kept her money in a pouch around her neck.* 她把錢裝在脖子上掛的荷包裏。 **2** a large bag for carrying letters, especially official ones 郵袋 ➲ see also DIPLOMATIC POUCH at DIPLOMATIC BAG **3** a pocket of skin on the stomach of some female MARSUPIAL animals, such as KANGAROOS, in which they carry their young（有袋目動物腹部的）育兒袋 ➲ **VISUAL VOCAB** page V12 **4** a pocket of skin in the cheeks of some animals, such as HAMSTERS, in which they store food（某些動物貯存食物的）頰袋，喉囊

pouffe (also **pouf**) /puːf/ (both *BrE*) (*NAmE* **has·sock**) *noun* a large thick CUSHION used as a seat or for resting your feet on（厚實的）坐墊，腳墊

poult·ice /ˈpəʊltɪs; *NAmE* ˈpoʊ-/ *noun* a soft substance spread on a cloth, sometimes heated, and put on the skin to reduce pain or swelling 泥敷劑（塗於敷料上，有時用以熱敷）

poult·ry /ˈpəʊltri; *NAmE* ˈpoʊ-/ *noun* **1** [pl.] chickens, DUCKS and GEESE, kept for their meat or eggs 家禽：*to keep poultry* 飼養家禽 ◇ *poultry farming* 養禽業 ➲ **VISUAL VOCAB** page V12 **2** [U] meat from chickens, DUCKS and GEESE 禽的肉：*Eat plenty of fish and poultry.* 要多吃魚和禽肉。

pounce /paʊns/ *verb* [I] to move suddenly forwards in order to attack or catch sb/sth 猛撲；突襲：*The lion crouched ready to pounce.* 獅子蹲下身，準備猛撲。◇ **~ on/upon sb/sth** *The muggers pounced on her as she got out of the car.* 她一下汽車，劫匪便向她撲上去。◇ *Rooney pounced on the loose ball and scored.* 魯尼對準無人控制的球飛起一腳，破門得分。

PHR V **ˈpounce on/upon sth** to quickly notice sth that sb has said or done, especially in order to criticize it 一眼看出，抓緊機會（以便批評） **SYN** **seize on/upon**：*His comments were pounced upon by the press.* 他的評論立即被新聞界揪住。

pound 🔑 /paʊnd/ *noun, verb*

■ ***noun***

▸ **MONEY** 錢 **1** 🔑 [C] (also *technical* 術語 **ˌpound ˈsterling**) (*symb.* **£**) the unit of money in the UK, worth 100 pence 英鎊（英國貨幣單位，等於 100 便士）：*a ten-pound note* 一張十英鎊的鈔票 ◇ *a pound coin* 一英鎊的硬幣 ◇ *I've spent £25 on food today.* 我今天的餐費花了 25 英鎊。◇ *What would you do if you won a million pounds?* 你要是贏了一百萬英鎊，你想怎麼用？ ➲ see also STERLING *n.* **2** 🔑 [C] the unit of money of several other countries 鎊（英國以外某些國家的貨幣單位） **3 the pound** [sing.] (*finance* 財) the value of the British pound compared with the value of the money of other countries 英鎊與外幣的比值：*the* ***strength/weakness of the pound*** (*against other currencies*) 英鎊強勢／疲軟 ◇ *The pound closed slightly down at $1.534.* 英鎊的匯價略跌，收盤時為 1.534 美元。

▸ **WEIGHT** 重量 **4** 🔑 [C] (*abbr.* **lb**) a unit for measuring weight, equal to 0.454 of a kilogram 磅（重量單位，合 0.454 千克）：*half a pound of butter* 半磅黃油 ◇ *They cost two dollars* ***a pound.*** 這些東西每磅兩元。◇ *I've lost six and a half pounds since I started my diet.* 從節食以來，我體重已減輕了六磅半。

▸ **FOR CARS** 汽車 **5** [C] a place where vehicles that have been parked illegally are kept until their owners pay to get them back 違章停車車輛扣留場

▸ **FOR DOGS** 狗 **6** [C] a place where dogs that have been found in the street without their owners are kept until their owners claim them 失狗收留所

IDM **(have, get, want, etc.) your pound of ˈflesh** the full amount that sb owes you, even if this will cause them trouble or suffering（不顧別人死活要討回）應得的東西 **ORIGIN** From Shakespeare's *Merchant of Venice*, in which the moneylender Shylock demanded a pound of flesh from Antonio's body if he could not pay back the money he borrowed. 源自莎士比亞的《威尼斯商人》。如果安東尼奧不能償還借款，放債者夏洛克就要割他身上的一磅肉抵債。 ➲ more at PENNY, PREVENTION

■ ***verb***

▸ **HIT** 擊打 **1** [I, T] to hit sth/sb hard many times, especially in a way that makes a lot of noise 反復擊打；連續砰砰地猛擊 **SYN** **hammer**：**~ at/against/on sth** *Heavy rain pounded on the roof.* 暴雨啪啪地砸在屋頂上。◇ *Someone was pounding at the door.* 有人在砰砰地敲門。◇ **~ away (at/against/on sth)** *The factory's machinery pounded away day and night.* 工廠的機器晝夜轟隆個不停。◇ **~ sb/sth (with sth)** *She pounded him with her fists.* 她用拳頭一個勁地捶他。 ➲ **SYNONYMS** at BEAT

▸ **WALK NOISILY** 咚咚走動 **2** [I] **+ adv./prep.** to move with noisy steps 咚咚地走：*She pounded along the corridor after him.* 她跟着他在走廊裏咚咚地走過。

▸ **OF HEART/BLOOD** 心臟；血液 **3** [I] to beat quickly and loudly（心臟）狂跳，怦怦地跳：*Her heart was pounding with excitement.* 她激動得心臟怦怦直跳。◇ *The blood was pounding* (= making a beating noise) *in his ears.* 他聽到血液在耳中怦怦搏動的聲音。◇ *Her head began to pound.* 她的頭開始怦怦地抽痛。◇ *a pounding headache* 錘擊般的頭痛

▸ **BREAK INTO PIECES** 粉碎 **4** [T] **~ sth (to/into sth)** to hit sth many times in order to break it into smaller pieces 搗碎；擊碎：*The seeds were pounded to a fine powder.* 籽粒被搗成了細粉。

▸ **ATTACK WITH BOMBS** 轟炸 **5** [T] **~ sth** to attack an area with a large number of bombs over a period of time 狂轟濫炸：*The area is still being pounded by rebel guns.* 這個地區仍然遭受着叛軍炮火的轟擊。

▸ **OF MUSIC** 音樂 **6** [I] **~ (out)** to be played loudly 大聲播放：*Rock music was pounding out from the jukebox.* 自動點唱機高聲播放着搖滾樂。

PHR V **ˌpound sth↔ˈout** to play music loudly on a musical instrument（用樂器）大聲彈奏：*to pound out a tune on the piano* 在鋼琴上用力彈奏曲子

pound·age /ˈpaʊndɪdʒ/ *noun* [U] **1** (*technical* 術語) a charge that is made for every pound in weight of sth, or for every £1 in value 按每磅重量的收費；按每英鎊價值計算的收費 **2** (*informal*) weight 重量：*to carry extra poundage* 超重負載

ˈpound cake (*NAmE*) (*BrE* **Maˈdeira cake**) *noun* [C, U] a plain yellow cake made with eggs, fat, flour and sugar 磅餅

pound·er /ˈpaʊndə(r)/ *noun* (in compounds 構成複合詞) **1** something that weighs the number of pounds mentioned 重…磅的東西：*a three-pounder* (= a fish, for example, that weighs 3lb) 三磅重的東西（如 3 磅重的魚） **2** a gun that fires a SHELL that weighs the number of pounds mentioned 發射…磅炮彈的大炮：*an eighteen-pounder* 發射十八磅炮彈的大炮

pound·ing /ˈpaʊndɪŋ/ *noun* [usually sing.] **1** a very loud repeated noise, such as the sound of sth hitting sth else hard; the sound or the feeling of your heart beating strongly 連續的重擊聲；劇烈的心跳（聲）：*We were*

P

awoken by a pounding at the door. 我們被砰砰的敲門聲吵醒。◇ *There was a pounding in his head.* 他覺得頭嗡嗡直響。 **2** an occasion when sth is hit hard or attacked and severely damaged 遭重創的情景；嚴重破損的情況 **SYN** **battering**： *The boat* ***took a pounding*** *in the gale.* 這條船在狂風中嚴重受損。◇ (*figurative*) *The team* ***took a pounding*** (= were badly defeated). 這支隊遭到慘敗。

ˈpound sign *noun* **1** the symbol (£) that represents a pound in British money 英鎊符號 **2** (*NAmE*) (*BrE* **hash**, **ˈhash sign**) the symbol (#), especially one on a telephone（尤指電話上的）#號

pour /pɔː(r)/ *verb*
1 [T] **~ sth** (+ **adv./prep.**) to make a liquid or other substance flow from a container in a continuous stream, especially by holding the container at an angle 使（液體）連續流出；傾倒；倒出： *Pour the sauce over the pasta.* 把醬汁澆在意大利麪上。◇ *Although I poured it carefully, I still managed to spill some.* 儘管我倒這東西很小心，還是灑了一些。 **2** [I] + **adv./prep.** (of liquid, smoke, light, etc. 液體、煙、光等) to flow quickly in a continuous stream 湧流；傾瀉；噴發： *Tears poured down his cheeks.* 眼淚順着他的面頰簌簌地落下。◇ *Thick black smoke was pouring out of the roof.* 黑色濃煙從屋頂滾滾冒出。 **3** [T, I] to serve a drink by letting it flow from a container into a cup or glass 倒，斟（飲料）： **~ (sth)** *Will you pour the coffee?* 你來倒咖啡好嗎？◇ *Shall I pour?* 我來倒好嗎？◇ **~ sth out** *I was in the kitchen, pouring out drinks.* 我在廚房裏倒飲料。◇ **~ sth for sb** *I've poured a cup of tea for you.* 我給你倒了一杯茶。◇ **~ sb sth** *I've poured you a cup of tea.* 我倒了杯茶給你。 **4** [I, T] when rain **pours** down or when **it's pouring** (**with**) **rain**, rain is falling heavily（雨）傾盆而下；下大雨： **~** (**down**) *The rain continued to pour down.* 大雨嘩嘩地下個不停。◇ *It's pouring outside.* 外面下着瓢潑大雨。◇ (*BrE*) ◇ **~ with rain** *It's pouring with rain.* 大雨滂沱。◇ (*NAmE*) ◇ **~** (**down**) **rain** *It's pouring rain outside.* 外面下着瓢潑大雨。 **5** [I] + **adv./prep.** to come or go somewhere continuously in large numbers 不斷湧向（或湧現） **SYN** **flood**： *Letters of complaint continue to pour in.* 投訴信紛至沓來。◇ *Commuters came pouring out of the station.* 通勤上班者湧出車站。

IDM **pour oil on troubled ˈwater(s)** to try to settle a disagreement or argument 調解爭端；排解糾紛 ➲ more at COLD *adj.*, HEART, RAIN *v.*, SCORN *n.*

PHR V **ˌpour sth ˈinto sth** to provide a large amount of money for sth 向…投入大量金錢；大量投資於： *The government has poured millions into the education system.* 政府在教育上已投資數百萬。 **ˌpour ˈout** when feelings or sb's words **pour out** they are expressed, usually after they have been kept hidden for some time（感情或說話）奔湧，迸發：*The whole story then came pouring out.* 接着，事情的來龍去脈被和盤托出。 **ˌpour sth↔ˈout** to express your feelings or give an account of sth, especially after keeping them or it secret or hidden 毫無保留地表達感情（或思想等）；表露無遺；暢所欲言： *She poured out her troubles to me over a cup of coffee.* 她一面喝着咖啡，一面向我傾吐着她的煩惱。 ➲ related noun OUTPOURING

pout /paʊt/ *verb* [I, T] **~** (**sth**) | **+ speech** if you **pout**, **pout** your lips or if your lips **pout**, you push out your lips, to show you are annoyed or to look sexually attractive（惱怒或性感地）撅嘴： *He pouted angrily.* 他生氣地撅起嘴。◇ *Her lips pouted invitingly.* 她挑逗地撮起雙唇。◇ *models pouting their lips for the camera* 噘唇拍照的模特兒 ▶ **pout** *noun*： *Her lips were set in a pout of annoyance.* 她慍惱地撅起了雙唇。 **pouty** *adj.*： *pouty lips* 撅起的嘴唇

pout·ine /puːˈtiːn/ *noun* [U] (*CanE*) a dish of FRENCH FRIES with melted cheese on top, served with a sauce (usually GRAVY) 肉汁乳酪薯條（以軟乳酪覆蓋，澆肉汁等食用）

pov·erty /ˈpɒvəti; *NAmE* ˈpɑːvərti/ *noun* **1** [U] the state of being poor 貧窮；貧困：*conditions of* ***abject/extreme poverty*** 極度貧窮的狀況◇ *to* ***alleviate/relieve poverty*** 緩解 / 解除貧困◇ *Many elderly people live* ***in poverty***. 許多老年人生活於貧困之中。 ➲ COLLOCATIONS at INTERNATIONAL **2** [U, sing.] a lack of sth; poor quality 貧乏；短缺；劣質： *There is a poverty of colour in her work.* 她的作品缺乏色彩。

the ˈpoverty line (also **the ˈpoverty level** especially in *US*) *noun* [sing.] the official level of income that is necessary to be able to buy the basic things you need such as food and clothes and to pay for somewhere to live 貧困線（政府規定維持最低生活水平所需的收入標準）： *A third of the population is living* ***at or below the poverty line***. 三分之一的人口生活在貧困線或以下。

ˈpoverty-stricken *adj.* extremely poor; with very little money 赤貧的；一貧如洗的

ˈpoverty trap *noun* [usually sing.] a situation in which a person stays poor even when they get a job because the money they receive from the government is reduced 貧困的牢籠（即使找到工作也依舊貧困，因為政府補貼相應減少）

POW /ˌpiː əʊ ˈdʌbljuː; *NAmE* oʊ/ *noun* the abbreviation for PRISONER OF WAR 戰俘，俘虜（全寫為 prisoner of war）： *a POW camp* 戰俘營

pow /paʊ/ *exclamation* used to express the sound of an explosion, a gun firing or sb hitting sb else（爆炸聲、槍聲或打人的聲音）嘭，乒，砰

pow·der /ˈpaʊdə(r)/ *noun, verb*
■ ***noun*** **1** [U, C] a dry mass of very small fine pieces or grains 粉末；細麪： *chilli powder* 辣椒粉◇ *lumps of chalk crushed to (a) fine white powder* 白堊塊被碾成白色細粉◇ *The snow was like powder.* 雪像粉末一樣。◇ *A wide range of cleaning fluids and powders is available.* 有各種各樣的清洗液和去污粉供應。◇ *The mustard is sold* ***in powder form***. 芥末是以粉末狀出售的。 ➲ see also BAKING POWDER, CURRY POWDER, SOAP POWDER, TALCUM POWDER, WASHING POWDER **2** [U] a very fine, soft, dry substance that you can put on your face to make it look smooth and dry 撲面粉；美容粉 ➲ **VISUAL VOCAB** page V60 **3** [U] = GUNPOWDER

IDM **keep your ˈpowder dry** (*old-fashioned*) to remain ready for a possible emergency 時刻準備應急；枕戈待旦；有備無患 **take a ˈpowder** (*NAmE, informal*) to leave suddenly; to run away 突然離開；跑掉；溜掉

■ ***verb*** **~ sth** to put powder on sth 傅粉；抹粉： *She powdered her face and put on her lipstick.* 她往臉上搽了粉，又塗上了口紅。

IDM **powder your ˈnose** (*old-fashioned*) a polite way of referring to the fact that a woman is going to the toilet/bathroom（女士如廁的委婉說法）補妝，淨手： *I'm just going to powder my nose.* 我想去補補妝。

ˌpowder ˈblue *adj.* very pale blue in colour 淺藍色的 ▶ **ˌpowder ˈblue** *noun* [U]

pow·dered /ˈpaʊdəd; *NAmE* -dərd/ *adj.* **1** (of a substance that is naturally liquid 原為液體的物質) dried and made into powder 製成粉狀的；乾燥成粉的： *powdered milk* 奶粉 **2** crushed and made into a powder 研成粉末的： *powdered chalk* 白堊粉 **3** covered with powder 塗粉的；傅粉的： *her powdered cheeks* 她那搽了粉的面頰

ˌpowdered ˈmilk *noun* [U] = MILK POWDER

ˈpowdered sugar *noun* [U] (*US*) = CONFECTIONER'S SUGAR

ˈpowder keg *noun* a dangerous situation that may suddenly become very violent 危險的局面；一觸即發的情勢；火藥桶

ˈpowder puff *noun* a round thick piece of soft material that you use for putting powder on your face 粉撲

ˈpowder room *noun* **1** a polite word for a women's toilet/bathroom in a public building（委婉語）女洗手間，女廁所 **2** (*NAmE*) a small room in a house containing a WASHBASIN and a toilet, usually for guests to use（常為客人用）盥洗室 **SYN** **half-bath**

pow·dery /ˈpaʊdəri/ *adj.* like powder; covered with powder 粉狀的；傅了粉的： *a light fall of powdery snow* 細雪輕輕飄落◇ *powdery cheeks* 傅粉的面頰

power /ˈpaʊə(r)/ *noun, verb*
■ ***noun***
▸ CONTROL 操縱 **1** [U] the ability to control people or things 控制力；影響力；操縱力： **~** (**over sb/sth**) *The*

P

aim is to give people more power over their own lives. 目的是讓人們更能主宰自己的生命。◇ **~ (to do sth)** *He has the power to make things very unpleasant for us.* 他掌握着我們的命運，可以把我們搞得狼狽不堪。◇ *to have sb **in your power*** (= to be able to do what you like with sb) 能支配某人 **2** 🔑 [U] political control of a country or an area 統治；政權：*to **take/seize/lose power*** 掌握 / 奪取 / 失掉政權 ◇ *The present regime has been **in power** for two years.* 現政權已經執政兩年了。◇ *The party **came to power** at the last election.* 這個政黨是在上次大選中當選執政的。◇ *They are hoping to return to power.* 他們希望重掌政權。◇ *a **power struggle** between rival factions within the party* 黨內對立派別之間的權力鬥爭 ➲ COLLOCATIONS at POLITICS ➲ see also BALANCE OF POWER

▸ **ABILITY** 能力 **3** 🔑 [U] (in people 人的) the ability or opportunity to do sth 能力；機會：*It is not **within my power*** (= I am unable or not in a position) *to help you.* 我是愛莫能助啊。◇ *I will **do everything in my power** to help you.* 我將盡全力幫助你。 **4** 🔑 [U] (also **powers** [pl.]) a particular ability of the body or mind（身體、心智的）某種能力：*He had lost the power of speech.* 他喪失了說話能力。◇ *The drug may affect your powers of concentration.* 這種藥可能會影響你的注意力集中。◇ *He had to use all his powers of persuasion.* 他只好使出說服人的全部本領。 **5** **powers** [pl.] all the abilities of a person's body or mind（全部）體力，智力：*At 26, he is **at the height of his powers** and ranked fourth in the world.* * 26 歲時，他處於巔峰狀態，排名世界第四。

▸ **AUTHORITY** 權威 **6** 🔑 [U, C, usually pl.] the right or authority of a person or group to do sth 權力；職權；權勢：**~ (to do sth)** *The Secretary of State has the power to approve the proposals.* 國務卿有權批准這些提案。◇ *The powers of the police must be clearly defined.* 警察的職權必須明確界定。◇ **~ (of sth)** *The president has the power of veto over all new legislation.* 總統有權否決一切新法規。 ➲ see also POWER OF ATTORNEY

▸ **COUNTRY** 國家 **7** 🔑 [C] a country with a lot of influence in world affairs, or with great military strength 有影響力的大國；軍事強國：*world powers* 世界列強 ◇ *an **allied/enemy power*** 同盟國；敵對國 ➲ see also SUPERPOWER

▸ **INFLUENCE** 影響 **8** 🔑 [U] (in compounds 構成複合詞) strength or influence in a particular area of activity 某方面的力量（或影響）；實力：*economic power* 經濟實力 ◇ ***air/sea power*** (= military strength in the air/ at sea) 空中 / 海上軍事力量 ◇ *purchasing power* 購買力 **9** 🔑 [U] the influence of a particular thing or group within society（某事物或社會集團的）影響力，勢力：*the power of the media* 新聞媒體的影響力 ◇ *parent power* 父母的影響力

▸ **ENERGY** 能量 **10** [U] the strength or energy contained in sth 力；力量；能量：*The ship was helpless against the power of the storm.* 那艘船無力抵抗強大的暴風雨。◇ *It was a performance of great power.* 那是巨大能量的作用。 ➲ see also FIREPOWER, STAYING POWER **11** [U] physical strength used in action; physical strength that sb possesses and might use（身體的）力量；體力：*He hit the ball with as much power as he could.* 他用盡全力擊球。◇ *the sheer physical power of the man* 那個男人驚人的體力 **12** 🔑 [U] energy that can be collected and used to operate a machine, to make electricity, etc. 能；能量；動力：***nuclear/wind/solar power*** 核能；風能；太陽能 ◇ *engine power* 發動機的功率 ➲ see also HORSEPOWER

▸ **ELECTRICITY** 電 **13** 🔑 [U] the public supply of electricity 電力供應：*They've switched off the power.* 他們關掉了電源。◇ *a power failure* 停電

▸ **MATHEMATICS** 數學 **14** [C, usually sing.] the number of times that an amount is to be multiplied by itself 乘方；冪：*4 **to the power of** 3 is* 4^3 (= $4 \times 4 \times 4 = 64$). * 4 的 3 次方是 4^3。

▸ **OF LENS** 透鏡 **15** [U] the amount by which a LENS can make objects appear larger 放大倍數；放大率：*the power of a microscope/telescope* 顯微鏡 / 望遠鏡的放大率

▸ **GOOD/EVIL SPIRIT** 善良的 / 邪惡的精靈 **16** [C] a good or evil spirit that controls the lives of others 正義（或邪惡）力量：*the powers of darkness* (= the forces of evil) 黑暗勢力

IDM **do sb a ˈpower of good** (*old-fashioned, informal*) to be very good for sb's physical or mental health 對身心大為有益 **more power to sb's ˈelbow** (*old-fashioned, BrE, informal*) used to express support or encouragement for sb to do sth（表示支持或鼓勵）再加把勁，加油，祝…成功 **the (real) power behind the ˈthrone** the person who really controls an organization, a country, etc. in contrast to the person who is legally in charge 太上皇；幕後操縱者 **the ˌpowers that ˈbe** (often *ironic*) the people who control an organization, a country, etc. 當權派；權力集團 ➲ more at CORRIDOR, SWEEP *v.*

■ ***verb***

▸ **SUPPLY ENERGY** 提供動力 **1** [T, usually passive] **~ sth** to supply a machine or vehicle with the energy that makes it work 驅動，推動（機器或車輛）：*The aircraft is powered by a jet engine.* 這架飛機由噴氣發動機驅動。

▸ **MOVE QUICKLY** 快速移動 **2** [I, T] to move or move sth very quickly and with great power in a particular direction（使）迅猛移動，快速前進：**+ adv./prep.** *He powered through the water.* 他在水中迅速游動。◇ **~ sth + adv./prep.** *She **powered her way** into the lead.* 她迅速用力衝到最前面。◇ *He powered his header past the goalie.* 他用力把球頂過了守門員。

PHR V **ˌpower ˈdown | ˌpower sth↔ˈdown** to stop a machine, especially a computer, by turning off the electricity supply 使（機器）停止工作；關機（尤指計算機）；關閉電源：*We were told to power down at 9.45.* 我們收到通知 9:45 要關閉電源。◇ *Log off or power down your system.* 退出或關閉系統。 OPP **power sth up** ➲ related noun POWER-DOWN **ˌpower sth↔ˈup** to prepare a machine to start working by supplying it with electricity, etc. 給…供電（等）；使（機器）啟動 OPP **power sth down**

ˌpower-assisted ˈsteering *noun* [U] (*BrE*) = POWER STEERING

ˈpower base *noun* the area or the people that provide the main support for a politician or a political party（政治人物或政黨的）權力基礎，後盾

power·boat /ˈpaʊəbəʊt; *NAmE* ˈpaʊərboʊt/ *noun* a fast boat with a powerful engine that is used especially for racing 摩托艇；汽艇；快艇

ˈpower breakfast *noun* a meeting that business people have early in the morning while they eat breakfast（商界人士）早餐會

ˈpower broker *noun* a person who has a strong influence on who has political power in an area 能左右當權者的人；權力經紀人

ˈpower cut (*BrE*) (*NAmE* **ˈpower outage**) *noun* an interruption in the supply of electricity; a period of time when this happens 供電中斷；停電（的一段時間）

ˈpower-down (also **power·down**) *noun* [C, U] a time when a machine or system stops working（機器或系統的）停止運行（時間）：*a power-down of the whole building* 整座大樓的癱瘓 ◇ *The internal clock and date were not stored after power-down.* 內置時鐘和日期在停機之後沒有保存下來。

ˈpower dressing *noun* [U] a style of dressing in which people in business wear formal and expensive clothes to emphasize how important they and their jobs are（為顯示身分的）顯貴穿着，商界要員打扮

powered /ˈpaʊəd; *NAmE* ˈpaʊərd/ *adj.* (usually in compounds 通常構成複合詞) operated by a form of energy such as electricity or by the type of energy mentioned 由…驅動的；電動的：*a powered wheelchair* 電動輪椅 ◇ *a solar-powered calculator* 太陽能電池計算器 ➲ see also HIGH-POWERED

power·ful 🔑 /ˈpaʊəfl; *NAmE* ˈpaʊərfl/ *adj.*
1 🔑 (of people 人) being able to control and influence people and events 有權勢的；有影響力的 SYN **influential**：*an **immensely powerful** organization* 有巨大影響力的組織 ◇ *a rich and powerful man* 一個有錢有勢的人 ◇ *Only the intervention of powerful friends obtained her release.* 經過有影響力的朋友們斡旋她才得以釋放。 **2** 🔑 having great power or force; very effective 強有力的；力量大的；很有效的：*powerful weapons* 威力強大的武器 ◇ *a powerful engine* 大功率引擎 ◇ *a powerful voice* 洪亮的嗓音 **3** 🔑 having a strong effect on your mind or

body（對身心）有強烈作用的，效力大的：*a powerful image/drug/speech* 鮮明的形象；療效顯著的藥物；有力的演說 **4** (of a person or an animal 人或動物) physically strong 健壯的；強壯的 SYN **muscular**：*a powerful body* 健壯的體魄 ◇ *a powerful athlete* 矯健的運動員 ▸ **power·ful·ly** /-fəli/ *adv.*：*a powerfully emotive song* 激動人心的歌曲 ◇ *He is powerfully built* (= he has a large strong body). 他身體魁梧健壯。◇ *She argued powerfully for reform.* 她雄辯滔滔，力主改革。

power·house /ˈpaʊəhaʊs; *NAmE* ˈpaʊərh-/ *noun* **1** a group or an organization that has a lot of power 強大的集團（或組織）：*China has been described as an 'emerging economic powerhouse'.* 中國被稱為"崛起中的經濟強國"。**2** a person who is very strong and full of energy 精力充沛的人；身強力壯的人

power·less /ˈpaʊələs; *NAmE* ˈpaʊərləs/ *adj.* **1** without power to control or to influence sb/sth 無影響力的；無權的 SYN **helpless**：*powerless minorities* 弱勢的少數族群 ◇ *When the enemy attacked, we were completely powerless against them.* 敵人進攻的時候，我們毫無抵禦能力。**2 ~ to do sth** completely unable to do sth 無能為力：*I saw what was happening, but I was powerless to help.* 我眼看着事情發生，卻無力相助。▸ **power·less·ness** *noun* [U]：*a **feeling/sense of powerlessness*** 無能為力的感覺 / 意識

power·lift·ing /ˈpaʊəlɪftɪŋ; *NAmE* ˈpaʊər-/ *noun* [U] the sport of lifting weights in three different ways, in a set order（分三項依次進行的）力量舉重 ▸ **power·lift·er** *noun*

ˈpower line *noun* a thick wire that carries electricity 輸電線；電源線：*overhead power lines* 架空輸電線

ˈpower nap *noun* a short sleep that sb has during the day in order to get back their energy 恢復精力的小睡 ▸ **ˈpower-nap** *verb* [I] (**-pp-**)

ˌpower of atˈtorney *noun* [U, C] (*pl.* **powers of attorney**) (*law* 律) the right to act as the representative of sb in business or financial matters; a document that gives sb this right（商業或金融等事務的）代表權，代理權；授權書；委託書

ˈpower outage (*NAmE*) (*BrE* **ˈpower cut**) *noun* an interruption in the supply of electricity; a period of time when this happens 供電中斷；停電（的一段時間）

ˈpower plant (*BrE* also **ˈpower station**) *noun* a building or group of buildings where electricity is produced 發電廠；發電站

ˈpower play *noun* [U] **1** (in ICE HOCKEY 冰上曲棍球) a situation in which one team has more players than another because a player is off the ice as a punishment 以多打少（隊員被罰下場造成一隊的隊員人數比另一隊為多）**2** a way of behaving that shows or increases a person's power, especially in a relationship 強權行為；高壓行動：*political power play* 政治強權行為

ˈpower point *noun* (*BrE*) = SOCKET (1)

ˈpower politics *noun* [U+sing./pl. v.] a situation in which a country tries to achieve its aims by using or threatening to use its military or economic power against another country 強權政治；強權外交

ˈpower-sharing *noun* [U] a policy or system in which different groups or political parties share responsibility for making decisions, taking political action, etc. 權力分掌（按聯盟成員或政黨分配決策和政治行動等的權力）

ˈpower shower *noun* (*BrE*) a shower that has an electric PUMP to make the water come out fast 電泵淋浴器；強力淋浴器

ˈpower station (*BrE*) (also **ˈpower plant** *NAmE, BrE*) *noun* a building or group of buildings where electricity is produced 發電廠；發電站：*a coal-fired power station* 燃煤火力發電廠 ◇ *a nuclear power station* 核電站

ˈpower steering (*BrE* also **ˌpower-assisted ˈsteering**) *noun* [U] (in a vehicle 車輛) a system that uses power from the engine to help the driver change direction 動力轉向系統

ˈpower-up *noun* **1** [U] the moment when a machine is switched on and starts working（機器的）啟動；開機：*Does the computer beep on power-up?* 電腦開機時有發出"嗶"的響聲嗎？**2** [C] in computer games, an advantage that a character can get if a player wins a certain number of points, for example more strength 威力升級（玩電腦遊戲者贏得一定點數時人物獲得力量提升等）

ˈpower user *noun* (*computing* 計) a user who needs computer products that are fastest and have the most features 需要高性能計算機的用戶

ˈpower walking *noun* [U] the activity of walking very quickly as a form of exercise（為鍛煉而做的）快走，疾走

pow·wow /ˈpaʊwaʊ/ *noun* **1** a meeting of Native Americans 帕瓦儀式（美洲土著一種盛宴和舞蹈儀式）**2** (*informal* or *humorous*) a meeting for discussion 討論會；議事會

pox /pɒks; *NAmE* pɑːks/ *noun* **the pox** [sing.] (*old use*) **1** an infectious disease spread by sexual contact 梅毒 SYN **syphilis 2** = SMALLPOX

poxy /ˈpɒksi; *NAmE* ˈpɑːksi/ *adj.* [only before noun] (*BrE, informal*) if sb describes sth as **poxy**, they think it has little value or importance 無價值的；無足輕重的；雞毛蒜皮的

pp *abbr.* **1 pp.** pages 頁；頁碼：*See pp. 100–117.* 參閱第100–117頁。**2** (also **p.p.**) (*especially BrE*) used in front of a person's name when sb signs a business letter on his/her behalf（信末署名時置於另一人的名字前，表示代其發函）：*pp Chris Baker* (= from Chris Baker, but signed by sb else because Chris Baker is away) 代表克里斯・貝克 **3** (*music* 音) very quietly (from Italian 'pianissimo') 極輕柔地，很弱（源於意大利語 pianissimo）

ppi /ˌpiː piː ˈaɪ/ *abbr.* (*computing* 計) pixels per inch (a measure of the quality of images)（圖像質量度量單位）每英寸像素

PPS /ˌpiː piː ˈes/ *noun* the abbreviation for 'Parliamentary Private Secretary' (a Member of Parliament in Britain who is given the job of helping a minister) 議會私人秘書（全寫為 Parliamentary Private Secretary，協助各大臣工作的議員）

PPV /ˌpiː piː ˈviː/ *abbr.* PAY-PER-VIEW

PR /ˌpiː ˈɑː(r)/ *noun* [U] **1** the abbreviation for PUBLIC RELATIONS 公關，公共關係（全寫為 public relations）：*a **PR department/agency/campaign*** 公關部 / 機構 / 運動 ◇ *The article is very good PR for the theatre.* 這篇文章有助於加強該劇院的公共關係。**2** the abbreviation for PROPORTIONAL REPRESENTATION 比例代表制（全寫為 proportional representation）

prac·tic·able /ˈpræktɪkəbl/ *adj.* (*formal*) able to be done; likely to be successful 可行的；行得通的 SYN **feasible, workable**：*at the earliest practicable opportunity* 在盡可能早的時機 ◇ *as soon as (is) practicable* 儘快 ◇ *The only practicable alternative is to postpone the meeting.* 另外唯一可行的辦法就是推遲會期。◇ *Employers should provide a safe working environment, as far as is reasonably practicable.* 只要條件許可，雇主就須提供安全的工作環境。➲ compare IMPRACTICABLE ▸ **prac·tic·abil·ity** /ˌpræktɪkəˈbɪləti/ *noun* [U]：*We were doubtful about the practicability of the plan.* 我們懷疑這個計劃是否切實可行。**prac·tic·ably** /-əbli/ *adv.*：*Please reply as soon as is practicably possible.* 請儘早回覆。

prac·tical /ˈpræktɪkl/ *adj., noun*

■ *adj.*

▸ CONNECTED WITH REAL THINGS 真實 **1** connected with real situations rather than with ideas or theories 實際的；真實的；客觀存在的：*to have gained **practical experience** of the work* 獲得實際工作經驗 ◇ ***practical advice/help/support*** 切實的忠告 / 幫助 / 支持 ◇ *practical problems* 實際問題 ◇ *There are some obvious practical applications of the research.* 這項研究有一些明顯的實際用途。◇ ***In practical terms**, it means spending less.* 具體點說，那意味着少花些錢。◇ *From a practical point of view, it isn't a good place to live.* 實際一點看，這裏不是理想的住處。➲ compare THEORETICAL

▸ LIKELY TO WORK 可行 **2** (of an idea, a method or a course of action 想法、方法或行動) right or sensible; likely to be successful 切實可行的 SYN **workable**：

P

It wouldn't be practical for us to go all that way just for the weekend. 我們跑那麼遠只為了去度個週末實在很不切實際。**OPP** **impractical**
▸ **USEFUL 有用 3** (of things 東西) useful or suitable 有用的；適用的：*a practical little car, ideal for the city* 適合城市內使用的實用小汽車 **OPP** **impractical**
▸ **SENSIBLE 理智 4** (of a person 人) sensible and realistic 明智的；實事求是的：*Let's be practical and work out the cost first.* 咱們實際一點兒，先計算一下成本費用。**OPP** **impractical**
▸ **GOOD AT MAKING THINGS 長於製作 5** (of a person 人) good at making or repairing things 心靈手巧的；善於製作（或修補）的 **SYN** **handy**：*Bob's very practical. He does all the odd jobs around the house.* 鮑勃心靈手巧，家裏的零活他都包了。
▸ **ALMOST TOTAL 幾乎全部 6** [only before noun] almost complete or total 幾乎完全的；實際上的 **SYN** **virtual**：*She married a practical stranger.* 她等於是嫁了個陌生人。
IDM **for (all) 'practical purposes** used when you are stating what the reality of a situation is 事實上；其實：*There's still another ten minutes of the game to go, but for practical purposes it's already over.* 比賽雖然還有十分鐘，但實際上等於已經結束了。
■ ***noun*** (*BrE, informal*) a lesson or an exam in science or technology in which students have to do or make things, not just read or write about them 實習課；實踐課；實驗考核

prac·ti·cal·ity /ˌpræktɪˈkæləti/ *noun* **1** [U] the quality of being suitable, or likely to be successful 可行性；適用性 **SYN** **feasibility**：*I have doubts about the practicality of their proposal.* 我懷疑他們的建議是否行得通。**2** [U] the quality of being sensible and realistic 實事求是：*I was impressed by her practicality.* 她做事踏實，着實令我讚佩。**3** **practicalities** [pl.] the real facts and circumstances rather than ideas or theories 實際事物；實際情況：*It sounds like a good idea; let's look at the practicalities and work out the costs.* 這個主意聽起來不錯。咱們來看看實際運作，計算一下費用。

P

ˌpractical 'joke *noun* a trick that is played on sb to make them look stupid and to make other people laugh 惡作劇；捉弄人的把戲 ▸ **ˌpractical 'joker** *noun*

prac·tic·al·ly /ˈpræktɪkli/ *adv.* **1** almost; very nearly 幾乎；差不多；很接近 **SYN** **virtually**：*The theatre was practically empty.* 劇院幾乎是空的。◇ *I meet famous people practically every day.* 我幾乎每天都見到名人。◇ *My essay is practically finished now.* 我的論文現在差不多寫完了。◇ *There's practically no difference between the two options.* 這兩種選擇幾乎沒什麼差別。➲ SYNONYMS at ALMOST **2** in a realistic or sensible way; in real situations 實事求是地；實際地：*Practically speaking, we can't afford it.* 實際說來，我們買不起這東西。◇ *It sounds like a good idea, but I don't think it will work practically.* 這個主意聽起來不錯，但我認為它實際上行不通。➲ compare THEORETICALLY at THEORETICAL

ˌpractical 'nurse *noun* (*NAmE*) a nurse with practical experience but less training than a REGISTERED NURSE 經驗護士（有實際經驗，但所受訓練不及註冊護士）

prac·tice /ˈpræktɪs/ *noun, verb*
■ ***noun***
▸ **ACTION NOT IDEAS 實踐 1** [U] action rather than ideas 實踐；實際行動：*the **theory and practice** of teaching* 教學的理論與實踐 ◇ *She's determined to **put** her new ideas **into practice**.* 她決心要把自己的新想法付諸實踐。
▸ **WAY OF DOING STH 做法 2** [U, C] a way of doing sth that is the usual or expected way in a particular organization or situation 通常的做法；慣例；常規：***common/current/standard practice*** 一般 / 現行 / 常規做法 ◇ *guidelines for **good practice*** 優良做法的指導原則 ◇ *a review of pay and **working practices*** 對薪金和工作制度的檢討 ◇ *religious practices* 宗教習俗 ➲ see also BEST PRACTICE, CODE OF PRACTICE, RESTRICTIVE PRACTICES, SHARP PRACTICE at SHARP *adj.* (11)
▸ **HABIT/CUSTOM 習慣；風俗 3** [C] a thing that is done regularly; a habit or a custom 慣常做的事；習慣；習俗：*the German practice of giving workers a say in how their company is run* 德國人在公司經營上給予工人發言權的做法 ◇ *It is his practice to read several books a week.* 他習慣於每週讀幾本書。
▸ **FOR IMPROVING SKILL 提高技巧 4** [U, C] doing an activity or training regularly so that you can improve your skill; the time you spend doing this 訓練；練習（時間）：*conversation practice* 會話練習 ◇ *It takes a lot of practice to play the violin well.* 拉好小提琴需要多加練習。◇ *There's a basketball practice every Friday evening.* 每星期五晚上有籃球訓練。◇ *She does an hour's piano practice every day.* 她每天練一小時鋼琴。➲ see also TEACHING PRACTICE
▸ **OF DOCTOR/LAWYER 醫生；律師 5** [U, C] the work or the business of some professional people such as doctors, dentists and lawyers; the place where they work（醫生、律師的）工作，業務活動，工作地點：*the practice of medicine* 行醫 ◇ *Students should have prior experience of veterinary practice.* 學生應有獸醫工作的經驗。◇ *My solicitor is no longer in practice.* 我的律師已不再執業了。◇ *a successful **medical/dental/law practice*** 成功的診所 / 牙醫診所 / 律師事務所 ➲ see also GENERAL PRACTICE, GROUP PRACTICE, PRIVATE PRACTICE
IDM **in 'practice** in reality 實際上；事實上：*Prisoners have legal rights, but in practice these rights are not always respected.* 囚犯雖有合法的權利，但實際上這些權利常未受到尊重。**be/get/ˌout of 'practice** to be/become less good at doing sth than you were because you have not spent time doing it recently 生疏；荒疏；疏於練習：*Don't ask me to speak French! I'm out of practice.* 可別讓我講法語！我已經生疏了。**ˌpractice makes 'perfect** (*saying*) a way of encouraging people by telling them that if you do an activity regularly and try to improve your skill, you will become very good at it 熟能生巧
■ ***verb*** (*especially US*) = PRACTISE：*to practice the piano every day* 每天練習彈鋼琴 ◇ *The team is practicing for their big game on Friday.* 球隊正在訓練，備戰星期五的重大比賽。◇ *They practiced the dance until it was perfect.* 他們反複練舞，直到盡善盡美為止。◇ *She's practicing medicine in Philadelphia.* 她在費城行醫。

prac·tise (*especially US* **prac·tice**) /ˈpræktɪs/ *verb* **1** [I, T] to do an activity or train regularly so that you can improve your skill 練習；實習；訓練：*You need to practise every day.* 你需要每天練習。◇ **~ for sth** *She's practising for her piano exam.* 她在練習準備鋼琴考試。◇ **~ sth** *I've been practising my serve for weeks.* 我練發球有好幾週了。◇ **~ (sth) on sb/sth** *He usually wants to practise his English on me.* 他通常想跟我練習英語。◇ **~ doing sth** *Practise reversing the car into the garage.* 練習倒車入車庫。**2** [T] **~ sth** (*formal*) to do sth regularly as part of your normal behaviour 經常做；養成…的習慣：*to practise self-restraint/safe sex* 培養自制力；實行安全性行為 ◇ *Do you still practise your religion?* 你還奉行你的宗教信仰嗎？**3** [I, T] to work as a doctor, lawyer, etc. 從事（醫務工作、法律專業等）；執業：*There are over 50 000 solicitors practising in England and Wales.* 英格蘭和威爾士共有 5 萬多名律師執業。◇ **~ as sth** *She practised as a barrister for many years.* 她從事出庭律師工作多年。◇ **~ sth** *He was banned from practising medicine.* 他被禁止行醫。
IDM **ˌpractise what you 'preach** to do the things yourself that you tell other people to do 身體力行；躬行所言；言行一致

prac·tised (*especially US* **-ticed**) /ˈpræktɪst/ *adj.* good at doing sth because you have been doing it regularly 熟練的；老到的；內行的：*She's only 18 but she's already a practised composer.* 她才 18 歲，但已成了老練的作曲家。◇ *It took **a practised eye** to spot the difference.* 只有內行人才能看出其中的差異。◇ **~ in sth** *He has good ideas but he isn't practised in the art of marketing.* 他有好的構想，但推銷技巧卻嫌生嫩。

prac·tis·ing (*especially US* **-ticing**) /ˈpræktɪsɪŋ/ *adj.* [only before noun] taking an active part in a particular religion, profession, etc. 積極履行（信仰上、專業上等）義務的；熱心的；虔誠的：*a practising Christian/teacher* 虔誠的基督徒；熱忱的教師

prac·ti·tion·er AW /præk'tɪʃənə(r)/ *noun* **1** (*technical* 術語) a person who works in a profession, especially medicine or law （尤指醫學或法律界的）從業人員：*dental practitioners* 牙醫 ◇ *a qualified practitioner* 執業者 ➲ see also GENERAL PRACTITIONER **2** (*formal*) a person who regularly does a particular activity, especially one that requires skill 習藝者；專門人才：*one of the greatest practitioners of science fiction* 最了不起的科幻小說家之一

prae·sid·ium (*especially BrE*) = PRESIDIUM

prag·mat·ic /præg'mætɪk/ *adj.* solving problems in a practical and sensible way rather than by having fixed ideas or theories 實用的；講求實效的；務實的 SYN **realistic**：*a pragmatic approach to management problems* 對管理問題採取的務實做法 ▶ **prag·mat·ic·al·ly** /-kli/ *adv.*

prag·mat·ics /præg'mætɪks/ *noun* [U] (*linguistics* 語言) the study of the way in which language is used to express what sb really means in particular situations, especially when the actual words used may appear to mean sth different 語用學，語言實用學（研究語言使用及其和語境的關係）

prag·ma·tism /'prægmətɪzəm/ *noun* [U] (*formal*) thinking about solving problems in a practical and sensible way rather than by having fixed ideas and theories 實用主義；務實思想；實用觀點 ▶ **prag·ma·tist** /-tɪst/ *noun*

prairie /'preəri; *NAmE* 'preri/ *noun* [C, U] a flat wide area of land in N America and Canada, without many trees and originally covered with grass 北美草原；新大陸北部草原（美國北部和加拿大）

'prairie dog *noun* a small brown N American animal of the SQUIRREL family that lives in holes on the prairies 草原犬鼠（生活於北美地穴）

ˌprairie 'oyster *noun* **1** a drink containing raw egg, used as a treatment for a HANGOVER (= the bad feeling sb has the day after drinking too much alcohol) 生雞蛋醒酒湯（用於解除宿醉） **2 prairie oysters** [pl.] (*especially NAmE*) a dish consisting of cooked TESTICLES from a young cow 煮小牛睾丸

'prairie wolf *noun* = COYOTE

praise 🔑 /preɪz/ *noun, verb*

■ ***noun*** [U] **1** 🔑 (also *less frequent* **praises** [pl.]) words that show approval of or admiration for sb/sth 讚揚；稱讚；讚美：*His teachers are* ***full of praise for*** *the progress he's making.* 老師們對他的進步讚不絕口。◇ *She wrote poems* ***in praise of*** *freedom.* 她寫詩謳歌自由。◇ *His latest movie has* ***won high praise from*** *the critics.* 他的最新電影得到了評論家的高度讚揚。◇ *We have* ***nothing but praise*** *for the way they handled the investigation.* 對於他們處理調查的方式我們唯有讚賞。◇ *The team coach singled out two players for special praise.* 教練提出兩名隊員給予特別表揚。◇ *She left with their praises ringing in her ears.* 她離開了，耳邊迴盪着大家的讚美聲。◇ *They always* ***sing his praises*** (= praise him very highly). 他們總是對他大加讚揚。 **2** 🔑 the expression of worship to God（對上帝的）頌揚，讚頌：***hymns/songs of praise*** 讚美詩；頌歌 ◇ *Praise be (to God)!* (= expressing belief or joy) 願主受讚美！ IDM see DAMN *v.*

■ ***verb*** **1** 🔑 to express your approval or admiration for sb/sth 表揚；讚揚；稱讚 SYN **compliment**：**~ sb/sth** *She praised his cooking.* 她稱讚他的烹調技術。◇ **~ sb/sth for sth/for doing sth** *He praised his team for their performance.* 他稱讚了各隊員的表現。◇ **~ sb/sth as sth** *Critics praised the work as highly original.* 評論家稱讚這部作品獨樹一幟。 **2** 🔑 **~ sb** to express your thanks to or your respect for God 頌揚，讚頌（上帝）：*Praise the Lord.* 讚美上帝！◇ *Allah be praised.* 感謝真主！

IDM **praise sb/sth to the 'skies** to praise sb/sth a lot 高度讚揚

praise·worthy /'preɪzwɜːði; *NAmE* -wɜːrði/ *adj.* (*formal*) deserving praise 值得稱讚的；值得表揚的 SYN **commendable**：*a praiseworthy achievement* 值得稱頌的成就

pra·line /'prɑːliːn; 'preɪliːn/ *noun* [U] a sweet substance made of nuts and boiled sugar, often used to fill chocolates 果仁糖（常用來做巧克力糖果的內餡）

pram /præm/ (*BrE*) (*NAmE* **'baby carriage**) *noun* a small vehicle on four wheels for a baby to go out in, pushed by a person on foot 嬰兒車 ➲ picture at PUSHCHAIR

prana /'prɑːnə/ *noun* [U] (in Hindu philosophy) the force that keeps all life in existence （印度教哲學中的）息，生命氣息

prance /prɑːns; *NAmE* præns/ *verb* **1** [I] **+ adv./prep.** to move quickly with exaggerated steps so that people will look at you 闊步行走；神氣地快速走動：*The lead singer was prancing around with the microphone.* 首席歌手手執麥克風，神氣地走來走去。 **2** [I] (of a horse 馬) to move with high steps 騰躍；騰跳

prang /præŋ/ *verb* **~ sth** (*BrE, informal*) to damage a vehicle in an accident 使（汽車）碰撞 ▶ **prang** *noun*

prank /præŋk/ *noun* a trick that is played on sb as a joke 玩笑；惡作劇：*a childish prank* 幼稚的惡作劇 ▶ **prank·ster** /'præŋkstə(r)/ *noun*：*Student pranksters have done considerable damage to the school buildings.* 惡作劇的學生對學校的建築造成相當大的損壞。

praseo·dym·ium /ˌpreɪziəʊ'dɪmiəm; *NAmE* -zioʊ-/ *noun* [U] (*symb.* **Pr**) a chemical element. Praseodymium is a soft silver-white metal used in ALLOYS and to colour glass. 鐠

prat /præt/ *noun* (*BrE, informal*) a stupid person 笨蛋；蠢驢；傻瓜

prate /preɪt/ *verb* [I] **~ (on) (about sth)** (*old-fashioned, disapproving*) to talk too much in a stupid or boring way 胡扯；瞎吹；嘮叨

prat·fall /'prætfɔːl/ *noun* (*especially NAmE*) **1** an embarrassing mistake 丟人現眼；出醜 **2** a fall on your bottom 屁股蹲兒；坐跌

prat·tle /'prætl/ *verb* [I] **~ (on/away) (about sb/sth)** (*old-fashioned*, often *disapproving*) to talk a lot about unimportant things 閒扯；嘮叨：*She prattled on about her children all evening.* 她整個晚上沒完沒了地嘮叨她的孩子們的事。 ▶ **prat·tle** *noun* [U]

prawn /prɔːn/ *noun* [C, U] (*especially BrE*) (*NAmE* usually **shrimp**) a SHELLFISH with ten legs and a long tail, that can be eaten. Prawns turn pink when cooked. 對蝦；大蝦；明蝦 ➲ VISUAL VOCAB page V13

ˌprawn 'cracker *noun* (*BrE*) a small piece of food made from rice flour with a PRAWN flavour, that is fried until it is crisp 蝦片（用米粉製成的蝦味薄片，油炸至酥脆後食用）

praxis /'præksɪs/ *noun* [U] (*philosophy* 哲) a way of doing sth; the use of a theory or a belief in a practical way 做事方法；實踐；實際運用

pray 🔑 /preɪ/ *verb, adv.*

■ ***verb*** **1** 🔑 [I, T] to speak to God, especially to give thanks or ask for help 祈禱；禱告：*They knelt down and prayed.* 他們跪下來禱告。◇ **~ for sb/sth** *I'll pray for you.* 我將為你祈禱。◇ *to pray for peace* 祈求和平 ◇ **~ to sb (for sb/sth)** *She prayed to God for an end to her sufferings.* 她祈求上帝結束她的苦難。◇ **~ (that) …** *We prayed (that) she would recover from her illness.* 我們為她的康復祈禱。◇ **~ to do sth** *He prayed to be forgiven.* 他祈求寬恕。◇ **+ speech** *'Please God don't let it happen,' she prayed.* "請求上帝不要讓這事發生。" 她祈禱說。 **2** 🔑 [I, T] to hope very much that sth will happen 企盼；祈望：**~ (for sth)** *We're praying for good weather on Saturday.* 我們十分企盼星期六是個晴天。◇ **~ that …** *I prayed that nobody would notice my mistake.* 我但願沒人注意到我的錯誤。

■ ***adv.*** (*old use* or *ironic*) used to mean 'please' when you are asking a question or telling sb to do sth （用於詢問或指示）請問，請：*What, pray, is the meaning of this?* 請問，這是什麼意思？◇ *Pray continue.* 請繼續。

pray·er 🔑 /preə(r); *NAmE* prer/ *noun*

1 🔑 [C] **~ (for sb/sth)** words that you say to God giving thanks or asking for help 禱告，祈禱（的內容）：*to say your prayers* 禱告 ◇ *prayers for the sick* 為病人的祈禱 ◇ *He arrived at that very moment, as if* ***in answer to her prayer***. 他就在那一刻到了，好像是她的祈禱應驗了。◇

P

Their ***prayers were answered*** *and the child was found safe and well.* 他們的禱告應驗了：小孩找到了，安然無恙。 ➲ COLLOCATIONS at RELIGION **2** [C] a fixed form of words that you can say when you speak to God 祈禱文；經文：*It was a prayer she had learnt as a child.* 這是她兒時就學會了的祈禱文。 ➲ see also THE LORD'S PRAYER **3** [U] the act or habit of praying 禱告，祈禱（的行為）：*They knelt in prayer.* 他們跪下祈禱。◇ *We believe in the power of prayer.* 我們相信祈禱的力量。 **4 prayers** [pl.] a religious meeting that takes place regularly in which people say prayers 祈禱會；禱告式 **5** [C, usually sing.] a thing that you hope for very much 企盼的事；祈望：*My prayer is that one day he will walk again.* 我的企盼就是有一天他能重新走路。 IDM see WING *n.*

IDM **not have a 'prayer (of doing sth)** to have no chance of succeeding (in doing sth)（做某事）沒有成功的機會

'prayer book *noun* a book that contains prayers, for use in religious services 祈禱書（禮拜時用）

'prayer meeting *noun* a religious meeting when people say prayers to God 禱告會；祈禱會

'prayer rug (also **'prayer mat**) *noun* a small carpet on which Muslims rest their knees when they are saying prayers 祈禱跪墊（穆斯林禱告時用）

'prayer wheel *noun* (in Tibetan Buddhism 藏傳佛教) an object that is turned as a way of saying a prayer or MEDITATING 轉經筒（轉動經筒即表示誦經或冥思）

,praying 'mantis (also **mantis**) *noun* a large green insect that eats other insects. The female praying mantis often eats the male. 螳螂

pre- /priː/ *prefix* (in verbs, nouns and adjectives 構成動詞、名詞和形容詞) before 先於；在…前：*preheat* 預熱 ◇ *precaution* 預防 ◇ *pre-war* 戰前的 ◇ *preseason training* (= before a sports season starts) 賽季前的訓練 ➲ compare ANTE-, POST-

preach /priːtʃ/ *verb* **1** [I, T] to give a religious talk in a public place, especially in a church during a service 佈道，講道（尤指教堂中禮拜時）：*She preached to the congregation about forgiveness.* 她向會眾宣講寬恕的道理。◇ **~ sth** *The minister preached a sermon on the parable of the lost sheep.* 牧師講道時用了亡羊的比喻。 **2** [T, I] to tell people about a particular religion, way of life, system, etc. in order to persuade them to accept it 宣傳，宣揚，宣講（教義、生活方式、體制等）：**~ sth** *to preach the word of God* 傳佈上帝的道 ◇ *He preached the virtues of capitalism to us.* 他向我們宣揚資本主義的優點。◇ **~ (about sth)** *She preached about the benefits of a healthy lifestyle.* 她宣揚了健康生活的好處。 ➲ COLLOCATIONS at RELIGION **3** [I] (*disapproving*) to give sb advice on moral standards, behaviour, etc., especially in a way that they find annoying or boring 說教：*I'm sorry, I didn't mean to preach.* 很抱歉，我並沒有說教的意思。◇ **~ at sb** *You're preaching at me again!* 你又在對我說教了！

IDM **preach to the con'verted** to speak to people in support of views that they already hold 向教徒宣教；教讀書人寫大字 ➲ more at PRACTISE

preach·er /ˈpriːtʃə(r)/ *noun* a person, often a member of the CLERGY, who gives religious talks and often performs religious ceremonies, for example in a church 傳道者；牧師：*a preacher famous for her inspiring sermons* 以發人深省的講道出名的傳道者 ◇ *a lay preacher* (= who is not a priest, etc. but who has been trained to give religious talks) 傳道員

preachy /ˈpriːtʃi/ *adj.* (*informal, disapproving*) trying to give advice or to persuade people to accept an opinion on what is right and wrong 說教的；勸誡的

pre·amble /priˈæmbl; ˈpriːæmbl/ *noun* [C, U] (*formal*) an introduction to a book or a written document; an introduction to sth you say 序言；緒論；導言；前言；開場白：*The aims of the treaty are stated in its preamble.* 條約的宗旨已在序言中說明。◇ *She gave him the bad news* ***without preamble.*** 她開門見山地把壞消息告訴了他。

pre·ar·ranged /ˌpriːəˈreɪndʒd/ *adj.* planned or arranged in advance 預先安排的；預先準備的；預定的 SYN **predetermined**

,pre-'book *verb* [I, T] (*BrE*) to arrange to have sth such as a room, table, seat, or ticket in advance 預訂（房間、餐桌、座位或票等）；預約：*You are advised to pre-book.* 敬請預約。◇ **~ sth** *Accommodation is cheaper if you pre-book it.* 預訂住宿要便宜些。

pre·but·tal /ˈpriːbʌtl/ *noun* [C, U] (*informal*) a statement saying or proving that a criticism is false or unfair before the criticism has actually been made（對尚未出現的指責等的）預先駁斥

pre·can·cer·ous /ˌpriːˈkænsərəs/ *adj.* (*medical* 醫) that will develop into cancer if not treated 癌前的；癌變前的：*precancerous cells* 癌前細胞

pre·car·ious /prɪˈkeəriəs; *NAmE* -ˈker-/ *adj.* **1** (of a situation 情勢) not safe or certain; dangerous 不穩的；不確定的；不保險的；危險的：*He earned a precarious living as an artist.* 作為一個藝術家，他過的是朝不保夕的生活。◇ *The museum is in a financially precarious position.* 這家博物館的財政狀況不穩定。 **2** likely to fall or cause sb to fall 搖搖欲墜的；不穩固的：*That ladder looks very precarious.* 那梯子看來搖搖晃晃的。◇ *The path down to the beach is very precarious in wet weather.* 通往海濱的小路在雨天非常濕滑危險。 ▶ **pre·car·ious·ly** *adv.*：*The economy is precariously close to recession.* 經濟瀕於衰退的邊緣。◇ *He balanced the glass precariously on the arm of his chair.* 他把杯子放在椅子的扶手上，隨時可能摔下。 **pre·car·ious·ness** *noun* [U]

pre·cast /ˌpriːˈkɑːst; *NAmE* -ˈkæst/ *adj.* (of some building materials 某些建築材料) made into blocks ready to use 預製的；預先澆鑄的：*precast concrete slabs* 混凝土預製板

pre·cau·tion /prɪˈkɔːʃn/ *noun* [usually pl.] **1 ~ (against sth)** something that is done in advance in order to prevent problems or to avoid danger 預防措施；預防；防備：*safety precautions* 安全防範措施 ◇ *precautions against fire* 防火措施 ◇ *You must* ***take all reasonable precautions*** *to protect yourself and your family.* 你必須採取一切合理的預防措施，保護自己和家人。◇ *I'll keep the letter* ***as a precaution.*** 我會保存這封信，以防萬一。 **2 precautions** [pl.] a way of referring to CONTRACEPTION 避孕措施：*We didn't* ***take any precautions*** *and I got pregnant.* 我們沒有採取任何避孕措施，所以我懷孕了。 ▶ **pre·cau·tion·ary** /prɪˈkɔːʃənəri; *NAmE* -neri/ *adj.*：*He was kept in the hospital overnight* ***as a precautionary measure.*** 為了謹慎起見，他被安排整晚留院觀察。

pre·cede AW /prɪˈsiːd/ *verb* (*formal*) **1** [T, I] **~ (sb/sth)** to happen before sth or come before sth/sb in order 在…之前發生（或出現）；先於：*the years preceding the war* 戰前的幾年 ◇ *His resignation was preceded by weeks of speculation.* 在他辭職之前，有關的猜測已持續了幾個星期。◇ *She preceded me in the job.* 她是我這工作的前任。◇ *See the preceding chapter.* 請見前一章。 **2** [T] **~ sb + adv./prep.** to go in front of sb 走在…前面：*She preceded him out of the room.* 她先於他走出屋子。

PHR V **pre'cede sth with sth** to do or say sth to introduce sth else 以…開始（或引導）：*She preceded her speech with a vote of thanks to the committee.* 她講話的開頭是對委員會的鳴謝。

pre·ce·dence AW /ˈpresɪdəns/ *noun* [U] **~ (over sb/sth)** the condition of being more important than sb else and therefore coming or being dealt with first 優先；優先權 SYN **priority**：*She had to learn that her wishes did not* ***take precedence over*** *other people's needs.* 她必須懂得自己的願望不能先於別人的需要。◇ *The speakers came on to the platform* ***in order of precedence*** (= the most important one first). 演講人按行輩魚貫上台。

pre·ce·dent AW /ˈpresɪdənt/ *noun* **1** [C, U] an official action or decision that has happened in the past and that is seen as an example or a rule to be followed in a similar situation later 可援用參考的具體例子；實例；範例：*The ruling* ***set a precedent*** *for future libel cases.* 這項裁決為今後的誹謗案提供了判例。 **2** [C, U] a similar action or event that happened earlier 先前出現的事例；前例；先例：*historical precedents* 歷史前例◇*There is no precedent for a disaster of this scale.* 這種規模的災難是空前的。◇*Such protests are **without precedent** in recent history.* 這類抗議事件在近代史上沒有發生過。**3** [U] the way that things have always been done 傳統；常例；常規 **SYN** **tradition**：*to break with precedent* (= to do sth in a different way) 打破常規 ➲ see also UNPRECEDENTED

pre·cept /ˈpriːsept/ *noun* [C, U] (*formal*) a rule about how to behave or what to think（思想、行為的）準則，規範 **SYN** **principle**

pre·cinct /ˈpriːsɪŋkt/ *noun* **1** (*BrE*) a commercial area in a town where cars cannot go 步行商業區：*a **pedestrian/shopping precinct*** 步行 / 購物區 **2** (*NAmE*) one of the parts into which a town or city is divided in order to organize elections 選區 **3** (*NAmE*) a part of a city that has its own police station; the police station in this area 警區；分區警察局；派出所：*Detective Hennessy of the 44th precinct* 第 44 警區的亨尼西警探◇*The murder occurred just a block from the precinct.* 謀殺案就發生在和警察分局相隔一條街的地方。**4** [usually pl.] (*formal*) the area around a place or a building, sometimes surrounded by a wall（建築物等的）外圍，圍牆內區域：*the **cathedral/college precincts*** 大教堂 / 學院周圍◇*within the precincts of the castle* 在城堡的圍牆內

pre·cious /ˈpreʃəs/ *adj., adv.*

■ ***adj.*** **1** rare and worth a lot of money 珍奇的；珍稀的：*a precious vase* 稀世花瓶◇*The crown was set with precious jewels—diamonds, rubies and emeralds.* 王冠上鑲嵌着稀世寶石，有鑽石、紅寶石和綠寶石。➲ see also PRECIOUS METAL, PRECIOUS STONE ➲ SYNONYMS at VALUABLE **2** valuable or important and not to be wasted 寶貴的；珍貴的：*Clean water is a precious commodity in that part of the world.* 在世界的那個地方，潔淨的水是寶貴的東西。◇*You're wasting precious time!* 你在浪費寶貴的時間！**3** loved or valued very much 受珍愛的；被珍惜的 **SYN** **treasured**：***precious memories/possessions*** 珍貴的回憶 / 財物 **4** [only before noun] (*informal*) used to show you are angry that another person thinks sth is very important（表示氣憤）寶貝似的：*I didn't touch your precious car!* 我沒碰你那輛寶貝車！**5** (*disapproving*) (especially of people and their behaviour 尤指人或行為) very formal, exaggerated and not natural in what you say and do 道貌岸然的；矯揉造作的 **SYN** **affected** ▸ **pre·cious·ness** *noun* [U]：*the preciousness of an old friendship* 悠久友誼的可貴◇*His writings reveal an unattractive preciousness of style.* 他的文章流露出不討好的做作風格。

■ ***adv.*** (*informal*) **~ little/few** used to emphasize the fact that there is very little of sth or that there are very few of sth（強調極少或太少）：*There's precious little to do in this town.* 這個鎮上沒有多少可做的事。

ˌprecious ˈmetal *noun* [C, U] a very valuable metal such as gold or silver 貴重金屬

ˌprecious ˈstone (also **stone**) *noun* a rare valuable stone, such as a diamond, that is used in jewellery 寶石 ➲ see also SEMI-PRECIOUS

preci·pice /ˈpresəpɪs/ *noun* a very steep side of a high CLIFF, mountain or rock 懸崖；峭壁 ➲ VISUAL VOCAB page V5：(*figurative*) *The country was now **on the edge of a precipice*** (= very close to disaster). 這個國家現在情勢岌岌可危。➲ see also PRECIPITOUS

pre·cipi·tate *verb, adj., noun*

■ ***verb*** /prɪˈsɪpɪteɪt/ (*formal*) **1 ~ sth** to make sth, especially sth bad, happen suddenly or sooner than it should 使…突然降臨；加速（壞事的發生）**SYN** **bring on, spark off**：*His resignation precipitated a leadership crisis.* 他的辭職立即引發了領導層的危機。**2 ~ sb/sth into sth** to suddenly force sb/sth into a particular state or condition 使突然陷入（某種狀態）：*The assassination of the president precipitated the country into war.* 總統被暗殺使國家驟然陷入戰爭狀態。

■ ***adj.*** /prɪˈsɪpɪtət/ (*formal*) (of an action or a decision 行動或決定) happening very quickly or suddenly and usually without enough care and thought 魯莽的；草率的；倉促的 ▸ **pre·cipi·tate·ly** *adv.*：*to act precipitately* 貿然行事

■ ***noun*** /prɪˈsɪpɪteɪt/ (*chemistry* 化) a solid substance that has been separated from a liquid in a chemical process 沉澱物；析出物質

pre·cipi·ta·tion /prɪˌsɪpɪˈteɪʃn/ *noun* **1** [U] (*technical* 術語) rain, snow, etc. that falls; the amount of this that falls 降水，降水量（包括雨、雪等）：*an increase in annual precipitation* 年降水量的增加 **2** [U, C] (*chemistry* 化) a chemical process in which solid material is separated from a liquid 沉澱；澱析

pre·cipit·ous /prɪˈsɪpɪtəs/ *adj.* (*formal*) **1** very steep, high and often dangerous 陡峭的；險峻的；峭拔的 **SYN** **sheer**：*precipitous cliffs* 險峻的峭壁◇*a precipitous drop at the side of the road* 道路一旁陡降的坡面 **2** sudden and great 突然的；驟然的；急劇的 **SYN** **abrupt**：*a precipitous decline in exports* 出口的急劇下降 **3** done very quickly, without enough thought or care 草率的；倉促的；貿然的 **SYN** **hasty**：*a precipitous action* 貿然行動 ▸ **pre·cipit·ous·ly** *adv.*：*The land dropped precipitously down to the rocky shore.* 地面陡降，下方是佈滿岩石的岸邊。◇*The dollar plunged precipitously.* 美元直線下跌。◇*We don't want to act precipitously.* 我們不想倉促行事。➲ see also PRECIPICE

pre·cis /ˈpreɪsiː; *NAmE* preɪˈsiː/ *noun* [C, U] (*pl.* **pre·cis** /-siːz/) a short version of a speech or a piece of writing that gives the main points or ideas 概要；摘要；大綱 **SYN** **summary**：*to **write/give/make a precis** of a report* 寫 / 提供 / 做一份報告摘要 ▸ **pre·cis** *verb* (**pre·cises** /-siːz/, **pre·cis·ing** /-siːɪŋ/, **pre·cised**, **pre·cised** /-siːd/)：**~ sth** *to precis a scientific report* 寫科研報告摘要

pre·cise 🔑 AW /prɪˈsaɪs/ *adj.*

1 🔑 clear and accurate 準確的；確切的；精確的；明確的 **SYN** **exact**：*precise details/instructions/measurements* 確切的細節；明確的指令；精確的尺寸◇*Can you give a more precise definition of the word?* 你能給這個詞下個更確切的定義嗎？◇*I can be reasonably precise about the time of the incident.* 我可以相當準確地說出這件事發生的時間。**2** 🔑 [only before noun] used to emphasize that sth happens at a particular time or in a particular way（強調時間或方式等）就，恰好：*We were just talking about her when, **at that precise moment**, she walked in.* 我們正談論着她，恰好在這個時候，她走進來了。◇*Doctors found it hard to establish the precise nature of her illness.* 醫生們難以判定她的確切病因。**3** 🔑 taking care to be exact and accurate, especially about small details 細緻的；精細的；認真的；一絲不苟的 **SYN** **meticulous**：*a skilled and precise worker* 熟練而認真的工人◇*small, precise movements* 細微的動作◇(*disapproving*) *She's rather prim and precise.* 她拘謹嚴肅，一絲不苟。

IDM **to be (more) preˈcise** used to show that you are giving more detailed and accurate information about sth you have just mentioned 確切地說；準確地說：*The shelf is about a metre long—well, 98cm, to be precise.* 架子長約一米。嗯，精確地說，是 98 厘米。

pre·cise·ly 🔑 AW /prɪˈsaɪsli/ *adv.*

1 🔑 exactly 準確地；恰好地：*They look precisely the same to me.* 依我看，他們的長相一模一樣。◇*That's precisely what I meant.* 那恰恰是我的意思。◇*It's not clear precisely how the accident happened.* 事故究竟是怎麼發生的不是很清楚。◇*The meeting starts at 2 o'clock precisely.* 會議在兩點整開始。**2** 🔑 accurately; carefully 精確地；細心地；仔細地：*to describe sth precisely* 精確地描述某事物◇*She pronounced the word very slowly and precisely.* 她緩慢而清晰地讀出這個字。**3** 🔑 used to emphasize that sth is very true or obvious（強調真實或明顯）正是，確實：*It's **precisely because** I care about you that I don't like you staying out late.* 正因為我關心你，我才不要你太晚回家。**4** used to emphasize that you agree with a statement, especially because you think it is obvious or is similar to what you have just said（加強同意的語氣）對，的確如此，一點也不錯：*'It's not that easy, is it?' 'No, precisely.'* "事情並不那麼容易吧？" "對，的確不容易。"

P

IDM **more pre'cisely** used to show that you are giving more detailed and accurate information about sth you have just mentioned 更確切地說；更嚴格地說：*The problem is due to discipline, or, more precisely, the lack of discipline, in schools.* 問題出在紀律上，或者更確切地說，是學校缺乏紀律。➲ LANGUAGE BANK at I.E.

pre·ci·sion **AW** /prɪˈsɪʒn/ *noun* [U] the quality of being exact, accurate and careful 精確；準確；細緻 **SYN** **accuracy**：*done with mathematical precision* 以數學般的精準完成的 ◇ *Historians can't estimate the date* ***with any (degree of) precision.*** 歷史學家無法準確估算這個日期。◇ *He chose his words* ***with precision.*** 他用詞確切。◇ ***precision instruments/tools*** 精密儀器 / 工具

pre·clude /prɪˈkluːd/ *verb* (*formal*) to prevent sth from happening or sb from doing sth; to make sth impossible 使行不通；阻止；妨礙；排除：**~ sth** *Lack of time precludes any further discussion.* 由於時間不足，不可能作深入的討論。◇ **~ sb from doing sth** *My lack of interest in the subject precluded me from gaining much enjoyment out of it.* 由於對這個科目缺乏興趣，我沒有從中獲得多少樂趣。◇ **~ (sb) doing sth** *His religious beliefs precluded him/his serving in the army.* 他的宗教信仰不允許他服兵役。

pre·co·cious /prɪˈkəʊʃəs; *NAmE* -ˈkoʊ-/ *adj.* (sometimes *disapproving*) (of a child 兒童) having developed particular abilities and ways of behaving at a much younger age than usual（能力或行為）早熟的：*a precocious child who started her acting career at the age of 5* * 5 歲便開始演藝生涯的超常兒童 ◇ *sexually precocious* 性早熟 ◇ *From an early age she displayed a precocious talent for music.* 她年紀輕輕就表現出不凡的音樂天賦。▶ **pre·co·cious·ly** *adv.*：*a precociously talented child* 有超常天才的兒童 **pre·co·city** /prɪˈkɒsəti; *NAmE* -ˈkɑː-/ (also **pre·co·cious·ness**) *noun* [U]：*his unusual precocity* 他的異常早熟

pre·cog·ni·tion /ˌpriːkɒɡˈnɪʃn; *NAmE* -kɑːɡ-/ *noun* [U] (*formal*) the knowledge that sth will happen in the future, which sb has because of a dream or a sudden feeling 預知，早知，先知（由夢境或突如其來的感覺感知到未來會發生的事）

pre-Columbian /ˌpriː kəˈlʌmbiən/ *adj.* connected with N and S America and their cultures before the arrival of Columbus in 1492 哥倫布到達之前的美洲的；前哥倫布的

pre·con·ceived /ˌpriːkənˈsiːvd/ *adj.* [only before noun] (of ideas, opinions, etc. 思想、觀點等) formed before you have enough information or experience of sth 事先形成的；預想的：*Before I started the job, I had no preconceived notions of what it would be like.* 開始做這工作之前，我並未預想過它的實際情況。

pre·con·cep·tion /ˌpriːkənˈsepʃn/ *noun* [C, usually pl., U] an idea or opinion that is formed before you have enough information or experience 事先形成的觀念；先入之見；預想；成見 **SYN** **assumption**：*a book that will challenge your preconceptions about rural life* 一本改變你對農村生活成見的書 ➲ compare MISCONCEPTION

pre·con·di·tion /ˌpriːkənˈdɪʃn/ *noun* **~ (for/of sth)** something that must happen or exist before sth else can exist or be done 先決條件；前提 **SYN** **prerequisite**：*A ceasefire is an essential precondition for negotiation.* 停火是談判的必要前提。

pre·con·scious /ˌpriːˈkɒnʃəs; *NAmE* -ˈkɑːn-/ *adj.* (*psychology* 心) associated with a part of the mind from which memories and thoughts that have not been REPRESSED can be brought to the surface 前意識的（指能被帶到意識區域的未受壓抑的記憶和思想）

pre·cooked /ˌpriːˈkʊkt/ *adj.* (of food 食物) prepared and partly cooked in advance so that it can be quickly heated and eaten later 預煮的；預先烹調的

pre·cur·sor /priːˈkɜːsə(r); *NAmE* -ˈkɜːrs-/ *noun* **~ (of/to sth)** (*formal*) a person or thing that comes before sb/sth similar and that leads to or influences its development 先驅；先鋒；前身 **SYN** **forerunner**

ˌpre-ˈcut *adj.* cut in advance and ready to use 預先剪切的；經剪切隨時可用的

pre·date /ˌpriːˈdeɪt/ (also **ante·date**) *verb* **~ sth** to be built or formed, or to happen, at an earlier date than sth else in the past 早於；先於…建成（或形成、發生等）：*Few of the town's fine buildings predate the earthquake of 1755.* 該城那些美的建築很少是 1755 年大地震前建成的。**OPP** **post-date**

pre·da·tion /prɪˈdeɪʃn/ *noun* [U] (*technical* 術語) the act of an animal killing and eating other animals（動物的）捕食，捕獵行為

preda·tor /ˈpredətə(r)/ *noun* [C, U] **1** an animal that kills and eats other animals 捕食性動物：*Some animals have no natural predators.* 有些動物沒有天敵。**2** (*disapproving*) a person or an organization that uses weaker people for their own advantage 弱肉強食的人（或機構）；剝削者；掠奪者：*to protect domestic industry from foreign predators* 保護本國工業不受外來剝削

preda·tory /ˈpredətri; *NAmE* -tɔːri/ *adj.* **1** (*technical* 術語) (of animals 動物) living by killing and eating other animals 捕食性的 **2** (of people 人) using weaker people for their own financial or sexual advantage（在金錢或性關係上）欺負弱小的，壓榨他人的：*a predatory insurance salesman* 斂財的保險推銷員 ◇ *a predatory look* 色狼般的眼神

ˌpredatory ˈpricing *noun* [U] (*business* 商) the fact of a business company selling its goods at such a low price that other companies can no longer compete and have to stop selling similar goods 為擠垮對手的大削價；掠奪性定價

pre·de·cease /ˌpriːdɪˈsiːs/ *verb* **~ sb** (*law* 律) to die before sb 先於…去世：*His wife predeceased him.* 他的妻子先於他去世。

pre·de·ces·sor /ˈpriːdɪsesə(r); *NAmE* ˈpredəs-/ *noun* **1** a person who did a job before sb else 前任：*The new president reversed many of the policies of his predecessor.* 新任總統徹底改變了其前任的許多政策。**2** a thing, such as a machine, that has been followed or replaced by sth else 原先的東西；被替代的事物 ➲ compare SUCCESSOR

pre·des·tin·ation /ˌpriːdestɪˈneɪʃn/ *noun* [U] the theory or the belief that everything that happens has been decided or planned in advance by God or by FATE and that humans cannot change it 宿命論；命定說

pre·des·tined /ˌpriːˈdestɪnd/ *adj.* **~ (to do sth)** (*formal*) already decided or planned by God or by FATE 命中注定的；上天安排的：*It seems she was predestined to be famous.* 她好像是命中注定要出名似的。

pre·de·ter·mine /ˌpriːdɪˈtɜːmɪn; *NAmE* -ˈtɜːrm-/ *verb* **~ sth** (*formal*) to decide sth in advance so that it does not happen by chance 預先決定；事先安排：*The sex of the embryo is predetermined at fertilization.* 胚胎的性別早在受精時就決定了。▶ **pre·de·ter·mined** *adj.*：*An alarm sounds when the temperature reaches a predetermined level.* 溫度一達到預設的度數，警報就會響起來。

pre·de·ter·miner /ˌpriːdɪˈtɜːmɪnə(r); *NAmE* -ˈtɜːrm-/ *noun* (*grammar* 語法) a word that can be used before a determiner, such as *all* in *all the students* or *twice* in *twice the price* 前位限定詞，前位限定成分（置於限定詞前，如 all the students 中的 all 和 twice the price 中的 twice）

pre·dica·ment /prɪˈdɪkəmənt/ *noun* a difficult or unpleasant situation, especially one where it is difficult to know what to do 尷尬的處境；困境；窘境 **SYN** **quandary**：*the club's financial predicament* 俱樂部的財政困境 ◇ *I'm in a terrible predicament.* 我的處境十分尷尬。

predi·cate *noun, verb*

■ ***noun*** /ˈpredɪkət/ (*grammar* 語法) a part of a sentence containing a verb that makes a statement about the subject of the verb, such as *went home* in *John went home* 謂語，述語（句子成分，對主語加以陳述，如 John went home 中的 went home）➲ compare OBJECT *n.* (4)

■ ***verb*** /ˈpredɪkeɪt/ (*formal*) **1** [usually passive] **~ sth on/upon sth** to base sth on a particular belief, idea or principle 使基於；使以…為依據：*Democracy is predicated upon the rule of law.* 民主是以法制為基礎的。**2** **~ that ... | ~ sth** to state that sth is true 表明；闡明；斷言：*The article predicates that the market collapse was caused by* *weakness of the dollar.* 這篇文章聲言，市場的崩潰是美元疲軟造成的。

pre·dica·tive /prɪˈdɪkətɪv; *NAmE* ˈpredɪkeɪtɪv/ *adj.* (*grammar* 語法) (of an adjective 形容詞) coming after a verb such as *be, become, get, seem, look*. Many adjectives, for example *old* can be either predicative as in *The man is very old*, or ATTRIBUTIVE as in *an old man*. Some, like *asleep*, can only be predicative. 作表語的，敍述性的（例如 asleep，用於 be、become、get、seem、look 等動詞後；與 attributive 相對）▸ **pre·dica·tive·ly** *adv.*

pre·dict AW /prɪˈdɪkt/ *verb* to say that sth will happen in the future 預言；預告；預報 SYN **forecast**：**~ sth** *a reliable method of predicting earthquakes* 預報地震的可靠方法 ◇ *Nobody could predict the outcome.* 誰也無法預料結果如何。◇ **~ what, whether, etc. …** *It is impossible to predict what will happen.* 預知未來的事是不可能的。◇ **~ (that) …** *She predicted (that) the election result would be close.* 她預言選舉結果將很接近。◇ **it is predicted that …** *It was predicted that inflation would continue to fall.* 據預報，通貨膨脹率將繼續下降。◇ **sb/sth is predicted to do sth** *The trial is predicted to last for months.* 預料審訊將持續數月之久。➲ LANGUAGE BANK at EXPECT

pre·dict·able AW /prɪˈdɪktəbl/ *adj.* **1** if sth is **predictable**, you know in advance that it will happen or what it will be like 可預見的；可預料的：*a predictable result* 可預見的結果 ◇ *The ending of the book was entirely predictable.* 那本書的結局完全是預料得到的。◇ *In March and April, the weather is much less predictable.* 三、四月份的天氣非常不好預測。 **2** (*often disapproving*) behaving or happening in a way that you would expect and therefore boring 意料之中的；老套乏味的：*He's very nice, but I find him rather dull and predictable.* 他為人很不錯，但我覺得他相當呆板乏味。▸ **pre·dict·abil·ity** AW /prɪˌdɪktəˈbɪləti/ *noun* [U] **pre·dict·ably** AW /-əbli/ *adv.*：*Prices were predictably high.* 價格高昂是意料中的事。◇ *Predictably, the new regulations proved unpopular.* 正如所預料，新規定果然不得人心。

pre·dic·tion AW /prɪˈdɪkʃn/ *noun* [C, U] a statement that says what you think will happen; the act of making such a statement 預言；預測；預告：*Not many people agree with the government's prediction that the economy will improve.* 沒有多少人贊同政府認為經濟將會有所改善的預測。◇ *The results of the experiment confirmed our predictions.* 實驗結果證實了我們的預測。◇ *Skilled readers make use of context and prediction.* 閱讀能力強的人會利用上下文及推測來理解文意。◇ *It's difficult to make accurate predictions about the effects on the environment.* 很難準確預測對環境產生的影響。➲ COLLOCATIONS at SCIENTIFIC ➲ LANGUAGE BANK at EXPECT

pre·dict·ive /prɪˈdɪktɪv/ *adj.* [usually before noun] **1** (*formal*) connected with the ability to show what will happen in the future 預測的；預言的；前瞻的：*the predictive power of science* 科學的預測能力 **2** (of a computer program 計算機程序) allowing you to enter text on a computer or a mobile/cell phone more quickly by using the first few letters of each word to predict what you want to say 聯想輸入的（輸入某詞頭幾個字母即可提示該詞）：***predictive text input*** 預設文字輸入 ◇ ***predictive messaging*** 預設信息傳送

pre·dic·tor /prɪˈdɪktə(r)/ *noun* (*formal*) something that can show what will happen in the future 預測器；預示物：*Cholesterol level is not a strong predictor of heart disease in women.* 膽固醇水平在預示女性患心臟病方面並不是一個很準確的因素。

pre·digest·ed /ˌpriːdaɪˈdʒestɪd/ *adj.* (of information 信息) put in a simple form that is easy to understand 簡化的；使易於理解的

pre·di·lec·tion /ˌpriːdɪˈlekʃn; *NAmE* ˌpredlˈek-/ *noun* [usually sing.] **~ (for sth)** (*formal*) if you **have a predilection for** sth, you like it very much 喜愛；偏愛；鍾愛 SYN **liking, preference**

pre·dis·pose /ˌpriːdɪˈspəʊz; *NAmE* -ˈspoʊz/ *verb* (*formal*) **1** to influence sb so that they are likely to think or behave in a particular way 使傾向於；使受…的影響：**~ sb to sth** *He believes that some people are predisposed to criminal behaviour.* 他認為有些人容易犯罪。◇ **~ sb to do sth** *Her good mood predisposed her to enjoy the play.* 她當時興致高，所以一定喜歡那齣戲。 **2 ~ sb to sth** to make it likely that you will suffer from a particular illness 使易於患（某種病）；容易誘發：*Stress can predispose people to heart attacks.* 壓力容易使人心臟病發作。

pre·dis·pos·ition /ˌpriːdɪspəˈzɪʃn/ *noun* [C, U] **~ (to/towards sth)** | **~ (to do sth)** (*formal*) a condition that makes sb/sth likely to behave in a particular way or to suffer from a particular disease 傾向；癖性；（易患某種病的）體質：*a genetic predisposition to liver disease* 易患肝病的遺傳體質

pre·dom·in·ance AW /prɪˈdɒmɪnəns; *NAmE* -ˈdɑːm-/ *noun* **1** [sing.] the situation of being greater in number or amount than other things or people （數量上的）優勢 SYN **preponderance**：*a predominance of female teachers in elementary schools* 小學裏女教師居多的現象 **2** [U] the state of having more power or influence than others 主導地位；支配地位；霸業 SYN **dominance**

pre·dom·in·ant AW /prɪˈdɒmɪnənt; *NAmE* -ˈdɑːm-/ *adj.* **1** most obvious or noticeable 顯著的；明顯的；盛行的：*a predominant feature* 顯著特徵 ◇ *Yellow is the predominant colour this spring in the fashion world.* 黃色是今春時裝界的流行顏色。 **2** having more power or influence than others 佔優勢的；主導的 SYN **dominant**：*a predominant culture* 主流文化

pre·dom·in·ant·ly AW /prɪˈdɒmɪnəntli; *NAmE* -ˈdɑːm-/ (also *less frequent* **pre·dom·in·ate·ly** /prɪˈdɒmɪnətli; *NAmE* -ˈdɑːm-/) *adv.* mostly; mainly 主要地；多數情況下：*She works in a predominantly male environment.* 她在一個男性居多的環境裏工作。➲ LANGUAGE BANK at GENERALLY

pre·dom·in·ate AW /prɪˈdɒmɪneɪt; *NAmE* -ˈdɑːm-/ *verb* **1** [I] to be greater in amount or number than sth/sb else in a place, group, etc.（數量上）佔優勢；以…為主：*a colour scheme in which red predominates* 以紅色為主的色彩組合 ◇ *Women predominated in the audience.* 觀眾以婦女為主。 **2** [I] **~ (over sb/sth)** to have the most influence or importance 佔主導地位；有最大影響（或重要性）：*Private interest was not allowed to predominate over the public good.* 私人利益不得淩駕公眾利益。

ˌpre-eˈclamp·sia *noun* [U] (*medical* 醫) a condition in which a pregnant woman has high BLOOD PRESSURE, which can become serious if it is not treated 先兆子癇，水腫蛋白尿高血壓綜合症（由懷孕引起）

pree·mie /ˈpriːmi/ *noun* (*NAmE, informal*) a PREMATURE baby 早產兒

ˌpre-ˈeminent *adj.* (*formal*) more important, more successful or of a higher standard than others 傑出的；出類拔萃的；卓越的 SYN **outstanding**：*Dickens was pre-eminent among English writers of his day.* 狄更斯在其同時期英國作家中最為出色。▸ **ˌpre-ˈeminence** *noun* [U]：*to achieve pre-eminence in public life* 成為出色的公眾人物

ˌpre-ˈeminent·ly *adv.* to a very great degree; especially 極大地；特別地；格外地

pre-empt /priˈempt/ *verb* **1 ~ sth** to prevent sth from happening by taking action to stop it 預先制止；防止；避免：*A good training course will pre-empt many problems.* 良好的培訓課程會防止許多問題產生。 **2 ~ sb/sth** to do or say sth before sb else does 搶在…之前做（或說）；先發制人：*She was just about to apologize when he pre-empted her.* 她正想道歉，他卻搶先說了。 **3 ~ sth** (*NAmE*) to replace a planned programme on the television 臨時取代（廣播時間表上的節目）：*The scheduled programme will be pre-empted by a special news bulletin.* 預定的節目將臨時換成特別新聞簡報。

pre-emption /priˈempʃn/ *noun* [U] (*business* 商) the opportunity given to one person or group to buy goods, shares, etc. 優先採購；先行購買：*Existing shareholders will have pre-emption rights.* 現有股東將有優先購買權。

pre-emptive /priˈemptɪv/ *adj.* [usually before noun] done to stop sb taking action, especially action that will be

P

harmful to yourself 先發制人的：*a **pre-emptive attack/strike** on the military base* 對軍事基地的搶先進攻／打擊

preen /priːn/ *verb* **1** [T, I] **~ (yourself)** (usually *disapproving*) to spend a lot of time making yourself look attractive and then admiring your appearance 刻意打扮，精心修飾（並自我欣賞）：*Will you stop preening yourself in front of the mirror?* 你別對着鏡子打扮個沒完行不行？ **2** [T] **~ yourself (on sth)** (usually *disapproving*) to feel very pleased with yourself about sth and show other people how pleased you are 顧盼自雄；沾沾自喜；得意揚揚 **3** [I, T] **~ (itself)** (of a bird 鳥) to clean itself or make its feathers smooth with its beak（用喙）整理羽毛

,pre-e'xist *verb* [I] to exist from an earlier time 早先存在；在先出現：*a pre-existing medical condition* 宿疾 ▸ **,pre-e'xistent** *adj.*

pre·fab /ˈpriːfæb/ *noun* (*informal*) a prefabricated building 預製建築：*prefabs built after the war* 戰後修建的預製房屋

pre·fab·ri·cated /ˌpriːˈfæbrɪkeɪtɪd/ *adj.* (especially of a building 尤指建築) made in sections that can be put together later 預製的；用預製構件組裝的 ▸ **pre·fab·ri·ca·tion** /ˌpriːfæbrɪˈkeɪʃn/ *noun* [U]

pref·ace /ˈprefəs/ *noun, verb*

■ ***noun*** an introduction to a book, especially one that explains the author's aims（書的）前言，序言 ➲ compare FOREWORD

■ ***verb*** **1 ~ sth (with sth)** to provide a book or other piece of writing with a preface 為…寫序言：*He prefaced the diaries with a short account of how they were discovered.* 他在前言中簡要敍述了發現日記的經過。 **2 ~ sth by/with sth | ~ sth by doing sth** (*formal*) to say sth before you start making a speech, answering a question, etc. 以…為開端；作…的開場白：*I must preface my remarks with an apology.* 講話前，我必須先表示歉意。

pref·a·tory /ˈprefətri; *NAmE* -tɔːri/ *adj.* [only before noun] (*formal*) acting as a PREFACE or an introduction to sth 序言性的；前言性的；導言性的：*a prefatory note* 卷首語

pre·fect /ˈpriːfekt/ *noun* **1** (in some British schools) an older student with some authority over younger students and some other responsibilities and advantages（某些英國學校中負責維持紀律等的）學長 **2** (also **Prefect**) an officer responsible for an area of local government in some countries, for example France, Italy and Japan（法、意、日等國家的）地方行政長官；省長；縣長

pre·fec·ture /ˈpriːfektʃə(r)/ *noun* an area of local government in some countries, for example France, Italy and Japan（法、意、日等國的）地方行政區域；省；縣

pre·fer 0➡ /prɪˈfɜː(r)/ *verb* (**-rr-**) (not used in the progressive tenses 不用於進行時) to like one thing or person better than another; to choose one thing rather than sth else because you like it better 較喜歡；喜歡…多於…：**~ sth** *'Coffee or tea?' 'I'd prefer tea, thanks.'* "要咖啡還是茶？" "我要茶，謝謝。" ◇ *I much prefer jazz to rock music.* 我喜歡爵士樂遠勝過搖滾樂。◇ *I **would prefer it if** you didn't tell anyone.* 我希望你別告訴任何人。◇ *A local firm is **to be preferred**.* 選一家當地的公司更好。◇ **~ sth + adj.** *I prefer my coffee black.* 我喜歡不加奶的咖啡。◇ **~ to do sth** *The donor prefers to remain anonymous.* 捐贈者希望自己的姓名不被公開。◇ *I prefer not to think about it.* 我不想考慮此事。◇ **~ sb/sth to do sth** *Would you prefer me to stay?* 你願意我留下來嗎？◇ **~ doing sth** *I prefer playing in defence.* 我喜歡打防守。◇ **~ that...** (*formal*) *I would prefer that you did not mention my name.* 我希望你不要說出我的名字。
IDM see CHARGE *n.*

pref·er·able /ˈprefrəbl/ *adj.* more attractive or more suitable; to be preferred to sth 較適合；更可取：**~ (to sth)** *Anything was preferable to the tense atmosphere at home.* 什麼都比家裏的緊張氣氛好。◇ **~ (to doing sth)** *He finds country life **infinitely preferable** to living in the city.* 他覺得鄉村生活比都市生活稱心得多。◇ **~ (to do sth)** *It would be preferable to employ two people, not one.* 雇請兩個人比雇請一個更好。 ▸ **pref·er·ably** /ˈprefrəbli/ *adv.*：*We're looking for a new house, preferably one near the school.* 我們正在找新房子，最好是靠近學校的。

pref·er·ence 0➡ /ˈprefrəns/ *noun*

1 0➡ [U, sing.] **~ (for sb/sth)** a greater interest in or desire for sb/sth than sb/sth else 偏愛；愛好；喜愛：*It's a matter of **personal preference**.* 那是個人的愛好問題。◇ *Many people **expressed a strong preference** for the original plan.* 許多人表示尤為喜歡原計劃。◇ *I can't say that I have any particular preference.* 我說不出自己有什麼特別偏好。◇ *Let's make a list of possible speakers, **in order of preference**.* 咱們按優先順序列出一份可能請到的發言者名單。 **2** 0➡ [C] a thing that is liked better or best 偏愛的事物；最喜愛的東西：*a study of consumer preferences* 消費者偏好調查 ➲ SYNONYMS at CHOICE

IDM **give (a) preference to sb/sth** to treat sb/sth in a way that gives them an advantage over other people or things 給…以優惠；優待：*Preference will be given to graduates of this university.* 這所大學的畢業生會獲得優先考慮。 **in preference to sb/sth** 0➡ rather than sb/sth 而不是：*She was chosen in preference to her sister.* 她被選中了，而不是她妹妹。

pref·er·en·tial /ˌprefəˈrenʃl/ *adj.* [only before noun] giving an advantage to a particular person or group 優先的；優惠的；優待的：*Don't expect to get **preferential treatment**.* 不要指望受到優待。 ▸ **pref·er·en·tial·ly** /-ʃəli/ *adv.*

pre·fer·ment /prɪˈfɜːmənt; *NAmE* ˈfɜːrm-/ *noun* [U] (*formal*) the fact of being given a more important job or a higher rank 晉升；提升 SYN **promotion**

pre·fig·ure /ˌpriːˈfɪɡə(r); *NAmE* -ɡjər/ *verb* **~ sth** (*formal*) to suggest or show sth that will happen in the future 預示；預兆

pre·fix /ˈpriːfɪks/ *noun, verb*

■ ***noun*** **1** (*grammar* 語法) a letter or group of letters added to the beginning of a word to change its meaning, such as *un-* in *unhappy* and *pre-* in *preheat* 前綴，詞首（綴於單詞前以改變其意義的字母或字母組合）➲ compare AFFIX *n.*, SUFFIX **2** a word, letter or number that is put before another 前置代號（置於前面的單詞或字母、數字）：*Car insurance policies have the prefix MC (for motor car).* 汽車保險單標有 MC 代號（表示汽車）。 **3** (*old-fashioned*) a title such as *Dr* or *Mrs* used before a person's name（人名前的）稱謂

■ ***verb*** to add letters or numbers to the beginning of a word or number 在…前面加（字母或數字）：**~ A to B** *American members have the letters US prefixed to their code numbers.* 美國會員的代碼前加了字母 US。◇ **~ B with A** *Their code numbers are prefixed with US.* 他們的代碼前加上了字母 US。

preg·gers /ˈpreɡəz; *NAmE* -ɡərz/ *adj.* [not before noun] (*BrE, informal*) pregnant 懷孕的；懷胎的

preg·nancy /ˈpreɡnənsi/ *noun* [U, C] (*pl.* **-ies**) the state of being pregnant 懷孕；妊娠；孕期：*Many women experience sickness **during pregnancy**.* 許多婦女在懷孕期都會有惡心現象。◇ *a **pregnancy test*** 妊娠化驗 ◇ ***unplanned/unwanted pregnancies*** 意外的／不期的懷孕 ◇ *the increase in teenage pregnancies* 十幾歲少女懷孕率的上升 ➲ COLLOCATIONS at CHILD

preg·nant 0➡ /ˈpreɡnənt/ *adj.*

1 0➡ (of a woman or female animal 婦女或母獸) having a baby or young animal developing inside her/its body 懷孕的；妊娠的：*My wife is pregnant.* 我妻子懷孕了。◇ *I was pregnant with our third child at the time.* 當時我正懷着我們的第三個孩子。◇ *a **heavily pregnant** woman* (= one whose baby is nearly ready to be born) 臨產期孕婦 ◇ *to **get/become pregnant*** 懷孕 ◇ *He got his girlfriend pregnant and they're getting married.* 他讓女友懷孕了，因此他們即將結婚。◇ *She's six months pregnant.* 她懷孕六個月了。 ➲ COLLOCATIONS at CHILD **2 ~ with sth** (*formal*) full of a quality or feeling 飽含；充溢着：*Her silences were pregnant with criticism.* 她的沉默裏充滿了批評之意。

IDM **a pregnant 'pause/'silence** an occasion when nobody speaks, although people are aware that there are feelings or thoughts to express 耐人尋味的停頓；心照不宣的沉默

pre·heat /ˌpriːˈhiːt/ *verb* **~ sth** to heat an oven to a particular temperature before you put food in it to cook 使（烤箱）預熱

pre·hen·sile /prɪˈhensaɪl; *NAmE* -sl/ *adj.* (*technical* 術語) (of a part of an animal's body 動物肢體的一部份) able to hold things 能抓住東西的；纏繞性的： *the monkey's prehensile tail* 猴子能纏住東西的尾巴 ➲ VISUAL VOCAB page V12

pre·his·toric /ˌpriːhɪˈstɒrɪk; *NAmE* -ˈstɔːr-/ *adj.* connected with the time in history before information was written down 史前的；有文字記載以前的；遠古的： *in prehistoric times* 在史前時期 ◇ *prehistoric man/remains/animals/burial sites* 史前人類 / 遺跡 / 動物 / 葬地

pre·his·tory /ˌpriːˈhɪstri/ *noun* **1** [U] the period of time in history before information was written down 史前時期；遠古時期 **2** [sing.] the earliest stages of the development of sth （事物發展的）初期，開始階段，萌芽時期： *the prehistory of capitalism* 資本主義發展的初期

ˌpre-inˈstall *verb* = PRELOAD

pre·judge /ˌpriːˈdʒʌdʒ/ *verb* **~ sth** (*formal*) to make a judgement about a situation before you have all the necessary information 預先判斷；過早判斷： *They took care not to* ***prejudge the issue.*** 他們態度謹慎，不過早對此事下判斷。

preju·dice /ˈpredʒudɪs/ *noun, verb*

■ ***noun*** [U, C] an unreasonable dislike of or preference for a person, group, custom, etc., especially when it is based on their race, religion, sex, etc. 偏見；成見： *a victim of* ***racial prejudice*** 種族偏見的受害者 ◇ *Their decision was based on ignorance and prejudice.* 他們的決定是基於無知和偏見。◇ **~ against sb/sth** *There is little prejudice against workers from other EU states.* 對來自其他歐盟國家的勞工可說並無偏見。◇ **~ in favour of sb/sth** *I must admit to a prejudice in favour of British universities.* 我得承認我對英國大學有所偏愛。 ➲ COLLOCATIONS at RACE

IDM **without ˈprejudice (to sth)** (*law* 律) without affecting any other legal matter 不損害其他權益；無損於合法權利： *They agreed to pay compensation without prejudice* (= without admitting GUILT). 他們同意賠償，但不承認有罪。

■ ***verb*** **1 ~ sb (against sb/sth)** to influence sb so that they have an unfair or unreasonable opinion about sb/sth 使懷有（或產生）偏見 SYN **bias**： *The prosecution lawyers have been trying to prejudice the jury against her.* 控方律師一直力圖使陪審團對她產生偏見。 **2 ~ sth** (*formal*) to have a harmful effect on sth 損害；有損於： *Any delay will prejudice the child's welfare.* 任何延誤都會損及這個孩子的身心健康。

preju·diced /ˈpredʒədɪst/ *adj.* having an unreasonable dislike of or preference for sb/sth, especially based on their race, religion, sex, etc. 有偏見的；帶成見的；偏愛的；偏心的： *Few people will admit to being racially prejudiced.* 很少有人會承認自己有種族偏見。◇ **~ (against/in favour of sb/sth)** *They are prejudiced against older applicants.* 他們對年長一些的申請人抱有成見。◇ (*humorous*) *I think it's an excellent article, but then I'm prejudiced—I wrote it.* 我認為那篇文章相當出色；不過，我有些偏心，那是我寫的嘛！

preju·di·cial /ˌpredʒuˈdɪʃl/ *adj.* **~ (to sth)** (*formal*) harming or likely to harm sb/sth 有害的；不利的；會造成損害的 SYN **damaging**： *developments prejudicial to the company's future* 不利於公司未來發展的新形勢

prel·ate /ˈprelət/ *noun* (*formal*) a priest of high rank in the Christian Church, such as a BISHOP or CARDINAL （基督教會的）教長，高級神長

pre·lim·in·ary AW /prɪˈlɪmɪnəri; *NAmE* -neri/ *adj., noun*

■ ***adj.*** happening before a more important action or event 預備性的；初步的；開始的 SYN **initial**： *After a few preliminary remarks he announced the winners.* 說了幾句開場白之後，他即宣佈優勝者名單。◇ *preliminary results/findings/enquiries* 初步結果 / 發現 / 調查 ◇ *the preliminary rounds of the contest* 預賽 ◇ **~ to sth** *pilot studies preliminary to a full-scale study* 全面研究前的試驗性初步研究

■ ***noun*** (*pl.* **-ies**) **~ (to sth)** a **preliminary** is an action or event that is done in preparation for sth 初步行動（或活動）；預備性措施： *Research will be needed as a preliminary to taking a decision.* 做決定之前需要進行研究。◇ *I'll skip the usual preliminaries and come straight to the point.* 閒話少說，我就直接進入正題。◇ *England was lucky to get through the preliminaries* (= the preliminary stages in a sports competition). 英格蘭隊幸運地通過了預選賽。

pre·load /ˌpriː ˈləʊd; *NAmE* -ˈloʊd/ (also **ˌpre-inˈstall**) *verb* **~ sth** to load sth in advance 預載；預裝： *The PC comes with office software preloaded.* 這台電腦隨機預裝了辦公軟件。 ▶ **pre·load** *noun*

prel·ude /ˈpreljuːd/ *noun* **1** a short piece of music, especially an introduction to a longer piece 序曲；前奏曲 **2 ~ (to sth)** an action or event that happens before another more important one and forms an introduction to it 序幕；前奏；先聲

pre·mar·ital /ˌpriːˈmærɪtl/ *adj.* [only before noun] happening before marriage 婚前的：*premarital sex* 婚前性行為

pre·ma·ture /ˈpremətʃə(r); *NAmE* ˌpriːməˈtʃʊr; -ˈtʊr/ *adj.* **1** happening before the normal or expected time 未成熟的；過早的；提前的： *his premature death at the age of 37* 他 37 歲時早逝 **2** (of a birth or a baby 生產或嬰兒) happening or being born before the normal length of PREGNANCY has been completed 早產的： *The baby was four weeks premature.* 這個嬰兒早產了四週。◇ *a premature birth after only thirty weeks* 懷孕僅三十週的早產 **3** happening or made too soon 草率的；倉促的： *a premature conclusion/decision/judgement* 草率的結論 / 決定 / 判斷 ◇ ***It is premature*** *to talk about success at this stage.* 現階段就談成功尚為時過早。 ▶ **pre·ma·ture·ly** *adv.*： *The child was born prematurely.* 這孩子是早產的。◇ *Her hair became prematurely white.* 她的頭髮過早地蒼白了。

ˈpre-med *noun* (*informal*) **1** [U] (*especially NAmE*) a course or set of classes that students take in preparation for medical school 醫學預科（課程） **2** [C] (*especially NAmE*) a student who is taking classes in preparation for medical school 醫學預科生 **3** [U] = PREMEDICATION

pre·medi·ca·tion /ˌpriːˌmedɪˈkeɪʃn/ (also *informal* **pre-med**) *noun* [U] drugs given to sb in preparation for an operation or other medical treatment 術前用藥；（治療）前驅藥

pre·medi·tated /ˌpriːˈmedɪteɪtɪd/ *adj.* (of a crime or bad action 罪案或惡行) planned in advance 預謀的；事先策劃的： *a premeditated attack* 事先策劃周詳的攻擊 ◇ *The killing had not been premeditated.* 這次殺人不是預謀的。 OPP **unpremeditated** ▶ **pre·medi·ta·tion** /ˌpriːˌmedɪˈteɪʃn/ *noun* [U]

pre·men·strual /ˌpriːˈmenstruəl/ *adj.* happening or experienced before MENSTRUATION 月經前的： *Many women suffer from* ***premenstrual tension/syndrome,*** *causing headaches and depression.* 許多婦女患月經前緊張 / 綜合症，引起頭疼和情緒低落。 ➲ see also PMS

prem·ier /ˈpremiə(r); *NAmE* prɪˈmɪr; -ˈmjɪr/ *adj., noun*

■ ***adj.*** [only before noun] most important, famous or successful 首要的；最著名的；最成功的；第一的： *one of the country's premier chefs* 國家名廚之一 ◇ (*BrE, sport* 體) *the Premier League/Division* 超級聯賽

■ ***noun*** **1** used especially in newspapers, etc. to mean 'prime minister' （尤用於報章等）首相，總理 **2** (in Canada) the first minister of a PROVINCE or TERRITORY （加拿大的）省總理，地方總理

premi·ere /ˈpremieə(r); *NAmE* prɪˈmɪr; -ˈmjɪr/ *noun, verb*

■ ***noun*** the first public performance of a film/movie or play （電影、戲劇的）首次公演，首映： ***the world premiere*** *of his new play* 他的新戲在全世界的首次公演 ◇ *The movie will have its premiere in July.* 這部電影將於七月首映。

■ ***verb*** [T, I] **~ (sth)** to perform a play or piece of music or show a film/movie to an audience for the first time; to be performed or shown to an audience for the first

P

time 首次公演（戲劇、音樂、電影）：*The play was premiered at the Birmingham Rep in 2008.* 這齣戲於 2008 年在伯明翰輪演劇場首次公演。◇ *His new movie premieres in New York this week.* 他的新電影本週在紐約首映。

prem·ier·ship /ˈpremiəʃɪp; *NAmE* prɪˈmɪrʃɪp; -ˈmjɪr-/ *noun* [sing.] **1** the period or position of being prime minister 首相職位（或任期）；總理職位（或任期）：*during Gordon Brown's premiership* 在戈登·布朗的首相任期內 **2** (often **the Premiership**) the football (SOCCER) league in England and Wales which has the best teams in it（英格蘭和威爾士的）足球超級聯賽

prem·ise (*BrE* also *less frequent* **prem·iss**) /ˈpremɪs/ *noun* (*formal*) a statement or an idea that forms the basis for a reasonable line of argument 前提；假定：*the basic premise of her argument* 她的論證的基本前提 ◇ *a false premise* 錯誤的前提 ◇ *His reasoning is based on the premise that all people are equally capable of good and evil.* 他的推理是以人可以為善亦可以為惡為前提的。

prem·ised /ˈpremɪst/ *adj.* **~ on/upon sth** (*formal*) based on a particular idea or belief that is considered to be true 根據，基於（觀點、信念等）：*Traditional economic analysis is premised on the assumption that more is better.* 傳統的經濟分析是以多多益善的設想為依據的。

prem·ises 0→ /ˈpremɪsɪz/ *noun* [pl.] the building and land near to it that a business owns or uses（企業的）房屋建築及附屬場地，營業場所：***business/commercial/industrial premises*** 事務所；商業 / 工業經營場所 ◇ *No alcohol may be consumed **on the premises**.* 場區內禁止飲酒。◇ *Police were called to escort her **off the premises**.* 召來警察護送她離場。 ➲ SYNONYMS at BUILDING

pre·mium /ˈpriːmiəm/ *noun, adj.*

■ ***noun*** **1** an amount of money that you pay once or regularly for an insurance policy 保險費：*a monthly premium of £6.25* 每月 6.25 英鎊的保險費 ➲ SYNONYMS at PAYMENT **2** an extra payment added to the basic rate 額外費用；附加費：*You have to pay a high premium for express delivery.* 快遞須付高額的附加費。◇ *A premium of 10% is paid out after 20 years.* * 20 年後要付清 10% 的額外費用。

IDM **at a ˈpremium** **1** if sth is **at a premium**, there is little of it available and it is difficult to get 稀少；難得：*Space is at a premium in a one-bedroomed apartment.* 單居室公寓的空間是很有限的。 **2** at a higher than normal price 超出平常價；溢價：*Shares are selling at a premium.* 這種股票以高於面值的價格出售。 **put/place/set a premium on sb/sth** to think that sb/sth is particularly important or valuable 重視；珍視

■ ***adj.*** [only before noun] very high (and higher than usual); of high quality 高昂的；優質的：*premium prices/products* 奇高的價格；優質產品

pre·modi·fier /ˌpriːˈmɒdɪfaɪə(r); *NAmE* -ˈmɑːd-/ *noun* (*grammar* 語法) a word, especially an adjective or a noun, that is placed before a noun and describes it or restricts its meaning in some way 前置修飾語；前修飾成分：*In 'a loud noise', the adjective 'loud' is a premodifier.* 在 a loud noise 中，形容詞 loud 是前置修飾語。 ➲ compare MODIFIER, POSTMODIFIER

pre·mon·ition /ˌpriːməˈnɪʃn; ˌprem-/ *noun* a feeling that sth is going to happen, especially sth unpleasant（尤指不祥的）預感：**~ (of sth)** *a premonition of disaster* 大禍臨頭的預感 ◇ **~ (that …)** *He had a premonition that he would never see her again.* 他有一種再也見不到她的預感。 ▶ **pre·moni·tory** /prɪˈmɒnɪtəri; *NAmE* -ˈmɑːnɪtɔːri/ *adj.*：(*formal*) *a premonitory dream* 預兆性的夢

pre·natal /ˌpriːˈneɪtl/ (*especially NAmE*) (*BrE* also **ante·natal**) *adj.* relating to the medical care given to pregnant women 產前的；孕期的 ➲ compare POST-NATAL

pre·nup·tial agreement /priːˌnʌpʃl əˈɡriːmənt/ (also *informal* **pre·nup** /ˈpriːnʌp/) *noun* an agreement made by a couple before they get married in which they say how their money and property is to be divided if they get divorced 婚前協議（關於倘若離婚財產如何分配等）

pre·occu·pa·tion /priˌɒkjuˈpeɪʃn; *NAmE* -ˌɑːk-/ *noun* **1** [U, C] **~ (with sth)** a state of thinking about sth continuously; sth that you think about frequently or for a long time 盤算；思慮；長久思考的事情 SYN **obsession**：*She found his preoccupation with money irritating.* 她對他一心只想着錢感到很厭煩。◇ *His current preoccupation is the appointment of the new manager.* 他目前操心的是新經理的任命。 **2** [U] a mood created by thinking or worrying about sth and ignoring everything else 心事重重；憂心忡忡；全神貫注：*She spoke slowly, in a state of preoccupation.* 她說話慢吞吞的，顯得心事重重。

pre·occu·pied /priˈɒkjupaɪd; *NAmE* -ˈɑːk-/ *adj.* **~ (with sth)** thinking and/or worrying continuously about sth so that you do not pay attention to other things 心事重重；一門心思：*He was too preoccupied with his own thoughts to notice anything wrong.* 他只顧想着心事，沒注意到有什麼不對。

pre·occupy /priˈɒkjupaɪ; *NAmE* -ˈɑːk-/ *verb* (**pre·occu·pies**, **pre·occu·py·ing**, **pre·occu·pied**, **pre·occu·pied**) **~ sb** if sth is **preoccupying** you, you think or worry about it very often or all the time 使日夜思考；使憂心忡忡

pre·or·dained /ˌpriːɔːˈdeɪnd; *NAmE* -ɔːrˈd-/ *adj.* (*formal*) already decided or planned by God or by FATE 命中注定的；上天安排的 SYN **predestined**：*Is everything we do preordained?* 我們做的事都是天意嗎？◇ **~ to do sth** *They seemed preordained to meet.* 他們似乎命中注定要相逢。

ˌpre-ˈowned *adj.* (*NAmE*) not new; owned by sb else before 舊的；二手的；轉手的

prep /prep/ *noun, verb*

■ ***noun*** [U] (*BrE*) (in some private schools) school work that is done at the end of the day after lessons（某些私立學校的）課外作業，備課

■ ***verb*** (**-pp-**) **1** [T, I] (*NAmE, informal*) to prepare (sth) 把…準備好；預備：**~ sth** *Prep the vegetables in advance.* 提前把蔬菜準備好。◇ **~ (for sth)** *They're prepping for college.* 他們正為上大學做準備。 **2** [T] **~ sb** (*technical* 術語) to prepare sb for a medical operation 為（患者）做手術前準備

ˌpre-ˈpacked (also **ˌpre-ˈpackaged**) *adj.* (of goods, especially food 商品，尤指食物) put into packages before being sent to shops/stores to be sold 包裝好的；已包裝的：*pre-packed sandwiches* 預先包裝的三明治

pre·paid /ˌpriːˈpeɪd/ (*BrE* also **ˌpre-ˈpay**) *adj.* paid for in advance 預付款的；資費已付的：*a prepaid mobile phone* 預付話費的移動電話 ◇ *A prepaid envelope is enclosed* (= so you do not have to pay the cost of sending a letter). 內附郵資已付的信封一個。

prep·ar·ation 0→ /ˌprepəˈreɪʃn/ *noun*

1 0→ [U] **~ (for sth)** the act or process of getting ready for sth or making sth ready 準備；預備：*Preparation for the party started early.* 聚會的準備工作很早就開始了。◇ *food preparation* 食物製作 ◇ *Careful preparation for the exam is essential.* 認真準備考試十分必要。◇ *The third book in the series is currently **in preparation**.* 叢書的第三冊現在正準備出版。◇ *The team has been training hard **in preparation for** the big game.* 為備戰這場重要比賽，隊伍一直在嚴格訓練。 **2** 0→ [C, usually pl.] things that you do to get ready for sth or make sth ready 準備工作：**~ (for sth)** *The country is **making preparations** for war.* 這個國家正在備戰。◇ *Was going to college a good preparation for your career?* 上大學是否為你的事業打下了良好基礎？◇ **~ (to do sth)** *We made preparations to move to new offices.* 我們為搬新辦公室做準備。◇ *wedding preparations* 婚禮的籌備工作 **3** [C] a substance that has been specially prepared for use as a medicine, COSMETIC, etc.（醫藥、化妝品等）配製品，製劑：*a pharmaceutical preparation* 藥劑 ◇ *preparations for the hair and skin* 護髮護膚製劑

pre·para·tory /prɪˈpærətri; *NAmE* -tɔːri/ *adj.* (*formal*) done in order to prepare for sth 預備的；籌備的：*preparatory meetings* 預備會議 ◇ *Security checks had been carried out **preparatory to** (= to prepare for) the President's visit.* 為迎接總統來訪，當局已預先進行了安全檢查。

P

pre'paratory school (also **'prep school**) *noun* **1** (in Britain) a private school for children between the ages of 7 and 13 預備學校（英國為準備升入公學者而設的私立小學）➲ compare PUBLIC SCHOOL (1) **2** (in the US) a school, usually a private one, that prepares students for college 預備學校（美國為準備升入高等院校者而設的私立中學）

pre·pare 0‑w /prɪˈpeə(r); *NAmE* -ˈper/ *verb*
1 0‑w [T] to make sth or sb ready to be used or to do sth 使做好準備；把…預備好：**~ sth/sb** *to prepare a report* 撰寫報告 ◇ **~ sth/sb for sb/sth** *A hotel room is being prepared for them.* 正在為他們準備一間旅館客房。◇ *The college prepares students for a career in business.* 這個學院是培養商務人才的。**2** 0‑w [I, T] to make yourself ready to do sth or for sth that you expect to happen 使（自己）有準備；防範：*I had no time to prepare.* 我當時沒時間準備。◇ **~ for sth** *The whole class is working hard preparing for the exams.* 全班都在努力用功準備考試。◇ **~ yourself (for sth)** *The police are preparing themselves for trouble at the demonstration.* 警察正在準備防範示威時可能出現的騷亂。◇ **~ to do sth** *I was preparing to leave.* 我正準備離開。◇ **~ yourself to do sth** *The troops prepared themselves to go into battle.* 部隊準備開赴戰場。**3** 0‑w [T] **~ sth** to make food ready to be eaten 預備（飯菜）；做（飯）：*He was in the kitchen preparing lunch.* 他在廚房做午飯。**4** [T] **~ sth (from sth)** to make a medicine or chemical substance, for example by mixing other substances together 調製，配製（藥品等）：*remedies prepared from herbal extracts* 從草藥提取成分配製的藥物

IDM **prepare the 'ground (for sth)** to make it possible or easier for sth to be achieved（為…）準備條件，鋪路：*The committee will prepare the ground for next month's meeting.* 這個委員會將為下個月的會議做好準備。

pre·pared 0‑w /prɪˈpeəd; *NAmE* -ˈperd/ *adj.*
1 0‑w [not before noun] **~ (for sth)** ready and able to deal with sth 準備好；有所準備：*I was not prepared for all the problems it caused.* 我對這事引起的諸多麻煩毫無防備。◇ *We'll be better prepared next time.* 下次我們會準備得更充分。◇ *When they set out they were well prepared.* 他們出發時有很充分的準備。OPP **unprepared** ➲ see also ILL-PREPARED **2** 0‑w **~ to do sth** willing to do sth 願意：*We are not prepared to accept these conditions.* 我們無意接受這些條件。◇ *How much are you prepared to pay?* 你願意出多少錢？OPP **unwilling** **3** 0‑w done, made, written, etc. in advance 事先做好（或寫好等）的：*The police officer read out a prepared statement.* 那個警察宣讀了一份事先寫好的聲明。

pre·pared·ness /prɪˈpeərɪdnəs; *NAmE* -ˈperd-/ *noun* [U] **~ (to do sth)** (*formal*) the state of being ready or willing to do sth 準備好的狀態；願意：*I was surprised by his preparedness to break the law.* 我對他打算以身試法感到驚訝。◇ *The troops are in a state of preparedness.* 軍隊已進入備戰狀態。

,pre-'pay *adj.* (*BrE*) = PREPAID：*pre-pay phones* 預付電話

pre·pay·ment /ˌpriːˈpeɪmənt/ *noun* [U] payment in advance 預先支付；預付款：*a prepayment plan* 預付款計劃

pre·pon·der·ance /prɪˈpɒndərəns; *NAmE* -ˈpɑːn-/ *noun* [sing.] if there is a **preponderance** of one type of people or things in a group, there are more of them than others 優勢；多數；主體 SYN **predominance**

pre·pon·der·ant /prɪˈpɒndərənt; *NAmE* -ˈpɑːn-/ *adj.* [usually before noun] (*formal*) larger in number or more important than other people or things in a group 主要的；佔多數的；主導的；佔優勢的 ▸ **pre·pon·der·ant·ly** *adv.*

pre·pone /priːˈpəʊn; *NAmE* -poʊn/ *verb* **~ sth** (*IndE, informal*) to move sth to an earlier time than was originally planned 將…提前

prep·os·ition /ˌprepəˈzɪʃn/ *noun* (*grammar* 語法) a word or group of words, such as *in, from, to, out of* and *on behalf of*, used before a noun or pronoun to show place, position, time or method 介詞 ▸ **prep·os·ition·al** /-ʃənl/ *adj.*：*a prepositional phrase* (= a preposition and the noun following it, for example *at night* or *after breakfast*) 介詞短語

pre·pos·sess·ing /ˌpriːpəˈzesɪŋ/ *adj.* (especially after a negative 尤用於否定詞後) (*formal*) attractive in appearance 外表吸引人的；嫵媚的；漂亮的 SYN **appealing**：*He was not a prepossessing sight.* 他長相不怎麼樣。➲ compare UNPREPOSSESSING

pre·pos·ter·ous /prɪˈpɒstərəs; *NAmE* -ˈpɑːs-/ *adj.* (*formal*) **1** completely unreasonable, especially in a way that is shocking or annoying 荒唐的；極不合情理的 SYN **outrageous**：*These claims are absolutely preposterous!* 這些要求簡直荒謬絕倫！**2** unusual in a silly or shocking way 怪誕的；離奇古怪的 SYN **outrageous**：*The band were famous for their preposterous clothes and haircuts.* 這支樂隊以怪異的服裝和髮式而聞名。▸ **pre·pos·ter·ous·ly** *adv.*：*a preposterously expensive bottle of wine* 一瓶天價的葡萄酒

prep·py (also **prep·pie**) /ˈprepi/ *noun* (*pl.* **-ies**) (*NAmE, informal*) a young person who goes or went to an expensive private school and who dresses and acts in a way that is thought to be typical of such a school 預備學校學生，預備學校畢業生（指有私立學校學生派頭的人）▸ **prep·py** (also **prep·pie**) *adj.*：*a preppy image* 私立學校學生形象 ◇ *preppy clothes* 私立學校學生的衣着

pre·pran·dial /ˌpriːˈprændiəl/ *adj.* [only before noun] (*formal* or *humorous*) happening immediately before a meal 餐前的；飯前的：*a preprandial drink* 餐前飲料

,pre-pro'duc·tion *adj.* [usually before noun] done before the process of producing sth, especially a film/movie, begins 生產前的；（尤指電影拍攝）準備期的：*the pre-production script* 開拍前的劇本 ▸ **,pre-pro'duc·tion** *adv.* **,pre-pro'duc·tion** *noun* [U]

'prep school *noun* = PREPARATORY SCHOOL

,pre-'qualify·ing *adj.* [only before noun] relating to a competition or game in which teams or players take part to decide if they are good enough to be in another competition 預選賽的；資格賽的：*players who fail at the pre-qualifying stage* 在預選賽中淘汰掉的選手 ▸ **,pre-'qualifier** *noun*

pre·quel /ˈpriːkwəl/ *noun* a book or a film/movie about events that happened before those in a popular book or film/movie 先篇，前篇，前傳（敍述某流行圖書或電影中的故事之前的事情）：*Fans waited for years for the first Star Wars prequel.* 《星球大戰》的第一部前傳讓影迷期待了多年。➲ compare SEQUEL (1)

Pre-Raphael·ite /ˌpriː ˈræfəlaɪt/ *noun, adj.*
▪ ***noun*** a member of a group of British 19th century artists who painted in a style similar to Italian artists of the 14th and 15th centuries, before the time of Raphael 前拉斐爾派畫家（英國 19 世紀的畫家，風格近似拉斐爾之前的 14、15 世紀意大利畫家）
▪ ***adj.*** **1** connected with or in the style of the Pre-Raphaelites 前拉斐爾派繪畫風格的：*Pre-Raphaelite paintings* 前拉斐爾派風格的繪畫 **2** (especially of a woman 尤指女人) looking like a person in a painting by one of the Pre-Raphaelites, for example with pale skin and long thick dark red hair 似前拉斐爾畫派繪畫中人物的（如皮膚白皙，濃密的深紅色長髮）

,pre-re'cord *verb* **~ sth** to record music, a television programme, etc. in advance, so that it can be broadcast or used later 預先錄製（音樂、電視節目等）

pre·regis·ter /ˌpriːˈredʒɪstə(r)/ *verb* [I] **~ (for sth)** (*especially NAmE*) to register for sth before the usual time or before sth starts 預先註冊；提前登記 ▸ **pre·regis·tra·tion** /ˌpriːredʒɪˈstreɪʃn/ *noun* [U]

pre·requis·ite /ˌpriːˈrekwəzɪt/ *noun* [usually sing.] **~ (for/of/to sth)** (*formal*) something that must exist or happen before sth else can happen or be done 先決條件；前提；必備條件 SYN **precondition**：*A degree is an essential prerequisite for employment at this level.* 學位是做這級工作必備的先決條件。➲ compare REQUISITE *n.* ▸ **pre·requis·ite** *adj.* [only before noun]：*prerequisite knowledge* 必備的知識

P

pre·roga·tive /prɪˈrɒɡətɪv; *NAmE* -ˈrɑːɡ-/ *noun* (*formal*) a right or advantage belonging to a particular person or group because of their importance or social position 特權；優先權：*In many countries education is still the prerogative of the rich.* 在許多國家接受教育仍然是富人的特權。◇ *the **royal prerogative*** (= the special rights of a king or queen) 君主特權

pres·age /ˈpresɪdʒ; prɪˈseɪdʒ/ *verb* **~ sth** (*literary*) to be a warning or sign that sth will happen, usually sth unpleasant 預兆，警示，預言（尤指不祥之事）▸ **pre·sage** /ˈpresɪdʒ/ *noun*: *the first presages of winter* 第一絲冬意

Pres·by·ter·ian /ˌprezbɪˈtɪəriən; *NAmE* -ˈtɪr-/ *noun* a member of a branch of the Christian Protestant Church that is the national Church of Scotland and one of the largest Churches in the US. It is governed by ELDERS who are all equal in rank. 長老派成員（長老會為蘇格蘭國教及美國最大教會之一）▸ **Pres·by·ter·ian** *adj.* **Pres·by·ter·ian·ism** /ˌprezbɪˈtɪəriənɪzəm; *NAmE* -ˈtɪr-/ *noun* [U]

pres·by·tery /ˈprezbɪtri; *NAmE* -teri/ *noun* (*pl.* **-ies**) **1** a local council of the Presbyterian Church 長老部 **2** a house where a Roman Catholic priest lives 本堂神父住宅 **3** part of a church, near the east end, beyond the CHOIR 教堂的聖所

pre·school /ˈpriːskuːl/ *noun* a school for children between the ages of about two and five 幼兒園；幼稚園 SYN **nursery school**

pres·ci·ent /ˈpresiənt/ *adj.* (*formal*) knowing or appearing to know about things before they happen 預知的；先覺的 ▸ **pres·ci·ence** /-əns/ *noun* [U]

pre·scribe /prɪˈskraɪb/ *verb* **1** (of a doctor 醫生) to tell sb to take a particular medicine or have a particular treatment; to write a PRESCRIPTION for a particular medicine, etc. 給…開（藥）；讓…採用（療法）；開（處方）：**~ sth** *Valium is usually prescribed to treat anxiety.* 安定劑通常用於治療焦躁。◇ **~ (sb) sth (for sth)** *He may be able to prescribe you something for that cough.* 他也許能給你開一些咳嗽藥。**2** (of a person or an organization with authority 當局) to say what should be done or how sth should be done 規定；命令；指示 SYN **stipulate**：**~ sth** *The prescribed form must be completed and returned to this office.* 必須把指定的表格填好並交回本辦事處。◇ **~ that …** *Police regulations prescribe that an officer's number must be clearly visible.* 警政制度規定，警察的番號必須清晰可見。◇ **~ which, what, etc. …** *The syllabus prescribes precisely which books should be studied.* 教學大綱明確規定了哪些是必讀的書。

pre·scrip·tion /prɪˈskrɪpʃn/ *noun* **1** [C] **~ (for sth)** an official piece of paper on which a doctor writes the type of medicine you should have, and which enables you to get it from a chemist's shop/drugstore 處方；藥方：*The doctor gave me a prescription for antibiotics.* 醫生給我開了抗生素。◇ (*BrE*) *Antibiotics are only available **on prescription**.* 抗生素只能憑處方購買。◇ (*NAmE*) *Antibiotics are only available **by prescription**.* 抗生素只能憑處方購買。◇ *They are not available without a prescription.* 這些藥沒有處方不能出售。◇ ***prescription drugs/medication(s)*** 處方藥 **2** [C] medicine that your doctor has ordered for you 醫生開的藥：*The pharmacist will make up your prescription.* 藥劑師會給你依處方配藥。◇ *a **prescription charge*** (= in Britain, the money you must pay for a medicine your doctor has ordered for you) 處方藥費 **3** [U] the act of prescribing medicine 開處方；開藥：*The prescription of drugs is a doctor's responsibility.* 開藥是醫生的責任。**4** [C] **~ (for sth)** (*formal*) a plan or a suggestion for making sth happen or for improving it 計劃；建議；秘訣：*a prescription for happiness* 增進幸福的秘訣

pre·scrip·tive /prɪˈskrɪptɪv/ *adj.* **1** (*formal*) telling people what should be done 指定的；規定的：*prescriptive methods of teaching* 灌輸式教學法 **2** (*linguistics*) 語言) telling people how a language should be used, rather than describing how it is used 規定的；規範的 OPP **descriptive** **3** (*technical* 術語) (of rights and institutions 權利和風俗) made legal or acceptable because they have existed for a long time 約定俗成的；相沿成習的：*prescriptive powers* 相沿成習的權力

pre·select /ˌpriːsɪˈlekt/ *verb* **~ sth** to choose sth in advance so it is ready to be used 預先選擇；預先挑選：*You can preselect programmes you want to watch, and program your VCR to record them.* 你可以預選想看的節目並設定錄像機錄下來。

pre·sell /ˌpriːˈsel/ *verb* (**pre·sold**, **pre·sold** /ˌpriːˈsəʊld; *NAmE* -ˈsoʊld/) **1 ~ sth** to help sell a product, service, etc., especially one that is not yet available, by using advertising and other techniques to attract consumers' attention（通過廣告等）提前促銷（尤指未上市的產品、服務等）：*Putting a trial version on your website is a great way of preselling your product.* 將試用版放到網站上是一種很好的提前促銷產品的方式。**2 ~ sth** to sell sth in advance of when it is available 預售：*These farmers presell their crops.* 這些農民預售他們的作物。

pres·ence 0→ /ˈprezns/ *noun*

1 0→ [U] (of a person 人) the fact of being in a particular place 在場；出席：*He hardly seemed to notice my presence.* 他似乎沒有注意到我在場。◇ *Her presence during the crisis had a calming effect.* 危難時她的到來穩定了大家的心情。◇ (*formal*) *Your presence is requested at the meeting.* 務請出席會議。OPP **absence** **2** 0→ [U] (of a thing or a substance 事物或物質) the fact of being in a particular place or thing 存在；出現：*The test can identify the presence of abnormalities in the unborn child.* 這項化驗能鑒定胎兒是否有不正常現象。OPP **absence** **3** [sing.] a group of people, especially soldiers, who have been sent to a place to deal with a particular situation（派遣的）一個隊；（尤指執行任務的）部隊：*The government is maintaining a heavy police presence in the area.* 政府在這地區派駐了大批警察。◇ *a military presence* 駐軍 **4** [C, usually sing.] (*literary*) a person or spirit that you cannot see but that you feel is near 感覺在附近的人（或鬼魂）：*She felt a presence behind her.* 她覺得有什麼東西跟在背後。**5** [U] (*approving*) the quality of making a strong impression on other people by the way you talk or behave 儀態；風度；氣質：*a man of great presence* 風度翩翩的男子

IDM **in the ˈpresence of sb | in sb's ˈpresence** with sb in the same place 在…面前；有…在場：*The document was signed in the presence of two witnesses.* 本文件是有兩位證人見證簽署的。◇ *She asked them not to discuss the matter in her presence.* 她要求他們不要當着她的面討論這個問題。**in the ˈpresence of sth** when sth exists in a particular place 存在…的情況下；有…的存在：*Litmus paper turns red in the presence of an acid.* 石蕊試紙遇到酸就變紅。**make your presence ˈfelt** to do sth to make people very aware of the fact that you are there; to have a strong influence on a group of people or a situation 突顯自己；對（人群或局勢）發揮作用

ˌpresence of ˈmind *noun* [U] the ability to react quickly and stay calm in a difficult or dangerous situation 鎮定；處變不驚；遇事不慌：*The boy **had the presence of mind to** turn off the gas.* 那男孩子鎮定地關掉了煤氣。

pres·ent 0→ *adj.*, *noun*, *verb*

■ ***adj.*** /ˈpreznt/ **1** 0→ [only before noun] existing or happening now 現存的；當前的：*in the present situation* 在當前形勢下 ◇ *the present owner of the house* 現在的房主 ◇ *a list of all club members, **past and present*** 過去和現在的全部會員名單 ◇ *We do not have any more information **at the present time**.* 目前我們沒有進一步的消息。◇ *A few brief comments are sufficient **for present purposes**.* 就當前而言，幾句簡短的話已經足夠了。➲ note at ACTUAL ➲ see also THE PRESENT DAY **2** 0→ [not before noun] **~ (at sth)** (of a person 人) being in a particular place 出現；在場；出席：*There were 200 people present at the meeting.* 有 200 人出席會議。OPP **absent** **3** 0→ [not before noun] **~ (in sth)** (of a thing or a substance 事物或物質) existing in a particular place or thing 存在：*Levels of pollution present in the atmosphere are increasing.* 大氣中的污染程度正在加深。◇ *Analysis showed that traces of arsenic were present in the body.* 分析顯示，屍體中有微量砒霜。OPP **absent**

IDM **all ˌpresent and corˈrect** (*BrE*) (*NAmE* **all present and acˈcounted for**) used to say that all the things or people who should be there are now there 全到無誤；應在場的都在場了 **present company exˈcepted** (*informal*) used after being rude or critical about sb to say that the people you are talking to are not included in the criticism 在座諸位除外；不關這裏的各位

■ **noun** /ˈpreznt/ **1** a thing that you give to sb as a gift 禮物；禮品：***birthday/Christmas/wedding, etc. presents*** 生日、聖誕節、結婚等禮物 ◇ *What can I get him for a birthday present?* 我給他送點什麼生日禮物呢？ **2** (usually **the present**) [sing.] the time now 目前；現在：*You've got to forget the past and start living in the present.* 你必須忘掉過去，開始現在的生活。◇ *I'm sorry he's out* ***at present*** (= now). 很抱歉他這會兒不在。 **3 the present** [sing.] (*grammar* 語法) = THE PRESENT TENSE **IDM** see MOMENT, TIME *n.*

■ **verb** /prɪˈzent/

▸ **GIVE** 給 **1** to give sth to sb, especially formally at a ceremony 把…交給；頒發；授予：**~ sth** *The local MP will start the race and present the prizes.* 當地議員將鳴槍開賽，並頒發獎品。◇ **~ sb with sth** *On his retirement, colleagues presented him with a set of golf clubs.* 在他退休之際，同事們贈給他一套高爾夫球杆。◇ **~ sth to sb** *The sword was presented by the family to the museum.* 這家人把寶劍捐贈給了博物館。

▸ **STH TO BE CONSIDERED** 考慮的事 **2** to show or offer sth for other people to look at or consider 提出；提交：**~ sth** (**to sb**) *The committee will present its final report to Parliament in June.* 委員會將於六月向議會提交最後的報告。◇ **~ sth** (**for sth**) *Eight options were presented for consideration.* 已提出八項備選方案供審議。◇ *Are you presenting a paper at the conference?* 你要在大會上宣讀論文嗎？

▸ **STH IN PARTICULAR WAY** 方式 **3** to show or describe sth/sb in a particular way （以某種方式）展現，顯示，表現：**~ sth** *The company has decided it must present a more modern image.* 公司已決定，必須展現出更加現代的形象。◇ *It is essential that we present a united front* (= show that we all agree). 至關重要的是我們要表現得團結一致。◇ **~ yourself + adv./prep.** *You need to present yourself better.* 你需要更善於展示自己。◇ **~ sth/sb/yourself as sth** *He likes to present himself as a radical politician.* 他喜歡表現出一副激進政治家的樣子。◇ *The article presents these proposals as misguided.* 文章把這些提案評為誤導的產物。

▸ **SB WITH PROBLEM** 麻煩 **4** to cause sth to happen or be experienced 使發生；使經歷：**~ sb with sth** *Your request shouldn't present us with any problems.* 你的請求應該不會給我們造成任何問題。◇ **~ sth** *Use of these chemicals may present a fire risk.* 使用這些化學品有可能導致失火。

▸ **ITSELF** 本身 **5** (of an opportunity, a solution, etc. 機會、答案等) to suddenly happen or become available 突然出現；顯露；產生 **SYN** **arise**：**~ itself** *One major problem did present itself, though.* 不過，確實出現了一個重大問題。◇ *As soon as the opportunity presented itself, she would get another job.* 一有機會，她就會另謀新職。◇ **~ itself to sb** *Thankfully, a solution presented itself to him surprisingly soon.* 謝天謝地，他意外地很快就找到了答案。

▸ **RADIO/TV PROGRAMME** 廣播／電視節目 **6 ~ sth** (*BrE*) to appear in a radio or television programme and introduce the different items in it 主持播放；主持（節目）：*She used to present a gardening programme on TV.* 她曾在電視上主持一個園藝節目。

▸ **PLAY/BROADCAST** 戲劇；廣播 **7 ~ sth** to produce a show, play, broadcast, etc. for the public 上演；公演；推出：*Compass Theatre Company presents a new production of 'King Lear'.* 羅經劇團推出了全新製作的《李爾王》。

▸ **INTRODUCE SB** 介紹 **8 ~ sb** (**to sb**) (*formal*) to introduce sb formally, especially to sb of higher rank or status 正式介紹；引見：*May I present my fiancé to you?* 請允許我向您介紹我的未婚夫。

▸ **YOURSELF** 自己 **9 ~ yourself at, for, in, etc.** (*formal*) to officially appear somewhere 正式出席；蒞臨；出現：*You will be asked to present yourself for interview.* 將請你到場面試。◇ *She was ordered to present herself in court on 20 May.* 她被傳喚於 5 月 20 日出庭。

▸ **EXPRESS STH** 表達 **10 ~ sth** (**to sb**) (*formal*) to offer or express sth in speech or writing （口頭或書面）表達，表示：*Please allow me to present my apologies.* 請允許我致歉。

▸ **CHEQUE/BILL** 支票；賬單 **11 ~ sth** to give sb a cheque or bill that they should pay 交付；提交：*A cheque presented by Mr Jackson was returned by the bank.* 銀行退回了傑克遜先生提交的支票。◇ *The builders presented a bill for several hundred pounds.* 承建商送來了一份數百英鎊的賬單。

IDM **preˌsent ˈarms** (of soldiers 士兵) to hold a RIFLE vertical in front of the body as a mark of respect 持槍敬禮

pre·sent·able /prɪˈzentəbl/ *adj.* **1** looking clean and attractive and suitable to be seen in public 像樣的；體面的：*I must go and* ***make myself presentable*** *before the guests arrive.* 趁客人還沒到，我得去打扮一下好見人。 **2** acceptable 可接受的；符合要求的：*You're going to have to do a lot more work on this essay before it's presentable.* 你的這篇文章還得多加潤飾才能交得出手。

pre·sen·ta·tion /ˌpreznˈteɪʃn; *NAmE* ˌpriːzen-/ *noun*
1 [U] the act of showing sth or of giving sth to sb 提交；授予；頒發；出示：*The trial was adjourned following the presentation of new evidence to the court.* 新證據呈到庭上後，審訊就宣告暫停。◇ *The presentation of prizes began after the speeches.* 講話結束後就開始頒獎了。◇ *The Mayor will* ***make the presentation*** (= hand over the gift) *herself.* 市長將親自頒發禮品。◇ *Members will be admitted* ***on presentation of*** *a membership card.* 會員出示會員證便可入場。 **2** [U] the way in which sth is offered, shown, explained, etc. to others 提出（或展示、解釋等）的方式：*Improving the product's presentation* (= the way it is wrapped, advertised, etc.) *should increase sales.* 改進產品的呈現方式會提高銷售量。◇ *I admire the clear, logical presentation of her arguments.* 我很欣賞她的論證，言辭清晰且有條理。 **3** [C] a meeting at which sth, especially a new product or idea, or piece of work, is shown to a group of people 展示會；介紹會；發佈會：*The sales manager will* ***give a presentation*** *on the new products.* 營銷經理將舉行一次新產品推介會。 ➲ WRITING TUTOR page WT12 **4** [C] the series of computer SLIDES (= images) that accompany the talk when sb gives a presentation at a meeting 幻燈片演示：*I've put my presentation on a memory stick.* 我已經把我的幻燈片演示存在 U 盤裏了。 ➲ WRITING TUTOR page WT12 **5** [C] a ceremony or formal occasion during which a gift or prize is given 頒獎儀式；贈送儀式 **6** [C] a performance of a play, etc. in a theatre （戲劇等的）上演，演出 **7** [C, U] (*medical* 醫) the position in which a baby is lying in the mother's body just before birth （胎兒的）臨產胎位，產式，先露位置

pre·sen·ta·tion·al /ˌpreznˈteɪʃənl; *NAmE* ˌpriːzen-/ *adj.* [only before noun] connected with the act of showing, explaining or offering sth to other people, especially a new product, a policy or a performance 展示的；介紹的；提交的；表演的：*a course on developing presentational skills* 展示技巧訓練課程

the ˌpresent ˈday *noun* [sing.] the situation that exists in the world now, rather than in the past or the future 當代；現代；當今：*a study of European drama, from Ibsen* ***to the present day*** 從易卜生到現代歐洲戲劇的研究 ▸ **ˌpresent-ˈday** *adj.* [only before noun]：*present-day fashions* 現代時裝 ◇ *present-day America* 今日美國

pre·sent·ee·ism /ˌpreznˈtiːɪzəm/ *noun* [U] (*BrE*) the practice of spending more time at your work than you need to according to your contract 超時工作

pre·sent·er /prɪˈzentə(r)/ *noun* **1** (*BrE*) a person who introduces the different sections of a radio or television programme （廣播、電視）節目主持人：*a TV presenter* 電視節目主持人 ➲ see also ANNOUNCER (1), HOST *n.* (3) **2** a person who makes a speech or talks to an audience about a particular subject 演講人；發言人：*conference presenters* 會議發言人 **3** (*NAmE*) a person who gives sb a prize at a ceremony （儀式上的）頒獎人

P

pre·sen·ti·ment /prɪˈzentɪmənt/ *noun* (*formal*) a feeling that sth is going to happen, especially sth unpleasant 預感；（尤指）不祥之感 SYN **foreboding**：*a presentiment of disaster* 大難臨頭的預感

pres·ent·ly /ˈpreznt̬li/ *adv.* **1** (*especially NAmE*) at the time you are speaking or writing; now 此刻；現在；眼下 SYN **currently**：*The crime is presently being investigated by the police.* 警方目前正在調查這起案件。◇ *These are the courses presently available.* 這些就是現有的課程。HELP In this meaning **presently** usually comes before the verb, adjective or noun that it refers to. 作此義時 presently 通常放在所修飾的動詞、形容詞或名詞之前。**2** used to show that sth happened after a short time（表示馬上就已發生了）：*Presently, the door opened again and three men stepped out.* 不久，門又打開了，走出來三個人。HELP In this meaning **presently** usually comes at the beginning of a sentence. 作此義時 presently 通常置於句首。**3** used to show that sth will happen soon（表示即將發生）SYN **shortly**：*She'll be here presently.* 她馬上就會到這兒。HELP In this meaning **presently** usually comes at the end of a sentence. 作此義時 presently 通常置於句末。

British/American 英式/美式英語

presently

- In both *BrE* and *NAmE*, **presently** can mean 'soon' or 'after a short time'. 在英式英語和美式英語中，presently 均含不久、一會兒之意：*I'll be with you presently.* 我一會兒就來。In *NAmE* the usual meaning of **presently** is 'at the present time' or 'now'. 在美式英語中，presently 通常表示目前、現在：*She is presently living in Milan.* 她現住在米蘭。◇ *There is presently no cure for the disease.* 目前這種疾病無藥可醫。This use is becoming more accepted in *BrE*, but **at present** or **currently** are usually used. 此用法在英式英語中正逐漸被接受，不過通常用的還是 at present 或 currently。

P

ˌpresent ˈparticiple *noun* (*grammar* 語法) the form of the verb that in English ends in *-ing* and is used with the verb *to be* to form progressive tenses such as *I was running* or sometimes as an adjective as in *running water* 現在分詞 ➲ compare PAST PARTICIPLE

the ˌpresent ˈperfect *noun* [sing.] (*grammar* 語法) the form of a verb that expresses an action done in a time period up to the present, formed in English with the present tense of *have* and the past participle of the verb, as in *I have eaten* 現在完成時；現在完成式

ˌpresent ˈtense (also **the present**) *noun* [usually sing.] (*grammar* 語法) the form of a verb that expresses an action that is happening now or at the time of speaking 現在時；現在式

pre·ser·va·tion /ˌprezəˈveɪʃn; *NAmE* -zərˈv-/ *noun* [U] **1** the act of keeping sth in its original state or in good condition 保護；維護；保存：*building/environmental/food preservation* 建築物的保養；環境保護；食物的保存◇ *a preservation group/society* 環保團體 / 組織 **2** the act of making sure that sth is kept 保留；維持；保持：*The central issue in the strike was the preservation of jobs.* 罷工的核心問題是工作職位的保留。**3** the degree to which sth has not been changed or damaged by age, weather, etc. 保存的狀況；保養的程度：*The paintings were in an excellent state of preservation.* 這些繪畫保存得非常好。➲ see also SELF-PRESERVATION

pre·ser·va·tion·ist /ˌprezəˈveɪʃənɪst; *NAmE* -zərˈv-/ *noun* a person who works to keep old buildings or areas of the countryside in their original condition and to prevent them from being destroyed 文物保護者；環境保護者

preserˈvation order *noun* (in Britain) a document that makes it illegal to change or destroy a building, a tree or part of the countryside, because of its beauty or historical interest（英國）文物及環境保護令

pre·ser·va·tive /prɪˈzɜːvətɪv; *NAmE* -ˈzɜːrv-/ *noun* [C, U] a substance used to prevent food or wood from decaying 防腐劑；保護劑：*The juice contains no artificial preservatives.* 這種果汁不含人工防腐劑。◇ *(a) wood preservative* 木材防腐劑 ➲ COLLOCATIONS at DIET ▶ **pre·ser·va·tive** *adj.* [only before noun]

pre·serve 0-π /prɪˈzɜːv; *NAmE* -ˈzɜːrv/ *verb, noun*

■ *verb* **1** 0-π **~ sth** to keep a particular quality, feature, etc.; to make sure that sth is kept 保護；維護；保留：*He was anxious to preserve his reputation.* 他急於維護自己的名聲。◇ *Efforts to preserve the peace have failed.* 維護和平的努力失敗了。**2** 0-π [often passive] to keep sth in its original state in good condition 維持…的原狀；保存；保養：**~ sth/sb** *a perfectly preserved 14th century house* 保存完好的 14 世紀宅第◇ (*humorous*) *Is he really 60? He's remarkably* **well preserved**. 他真有 60 歲了嗎？他真會保養啊。◇ **~ sth + adj.** *This vase has been preserved intact.* 這個花瓶保存得完好無損。**3** 0-π **~ sth** to prevent sth, especially food, from decaying by treating it in a particular way 貯存；保鮮：*olives preserved in brine* 鹽水橄欖◇ *Wax polish preserves wood and leather.* 上光蠟可保護木材和皮革。**4** 0-π **~ sb/sth (from sth)** to keep sb/sth alive, or safe from harm or danger 使繼續存活；保護；保全 SYN **save**：*The society was set up to preserve endangered species from extinction.* 成立這個協會是為了保護瀕危物種不致滅絕。➲ compare CONSERVE *v.* (2)

■ *noun* **1** [sing.] **~ (of sb)** an activity, a job, an interest, etc. that is thought to be suitable for one particular person or group of people（某人或群體活動、工作等的）專門領域：*Football is no longer the preserve of men.* 足球再也不是男人的專利了。◇ *in the days when nursing was a female preserve* 在護理工作為女性所專有的時代 **2** [C, usually pl., U] a type of jam made by boiling fruit with a large amount of sugar 果醬 **3** [C, usually pl., U] (*especially BrE*) a type of PICKLE made by cooking vegetables with salt or VINEGAR 醃菜；泡菜 **4** [C] (*NAmE*) = RESERVE (2) **5** [C] an area of private land or water where animals and fish are kept for people to hunt 私人漁獵場（或保留地）

pre·server /prɪˈzɜːvə(r); *NAmE* -ˈzɜːrv-/ *noun* **1** [C] a person who makes sure that a particular situation does not change 保護人；維護者；保存者：*The police are the preservers of law and order.* 警察負責維持治安。**2** [C, U] a substance used to prevent wood from decaying 木材防腐劑 ➲ see also LIFE PRESERVER

pre·set /ˌpriːˈset/ *verb* (**pre·setting**, **pre·set**, **pre·set**) **1** to set the controls of a piece of electrical equipment so that it will start to work at a particular time 預調；預置；給…預定時間：**~ sth to do sth** *You can preset the radiators to come on when you need them to.* 你可以預先調好暖氣，使它在你需要的時候啟動。◇ **~ sth** *to preset TV channels/radio stations* (= to set the controls so that particular channels are selected when you press particular buttons) 預調電視頻道 / 廣播電台 **2** [usually passive] **~ sth** to decide sth in advance 預先決定；事先安排：*They kept to the preset route.* 他們沿着事先規劃的路線前進。

pre·side /prɪˈzaɪd/ *verb* [I] (*formal*) to lead or be in charge of a meeting, ceremony, etc. 主持（會議、儀式等）；擔任（會議）主席：*the presiding judge* 首席法官◇ **~ at/over sth** *They asked if I would preside at the committee meeting.* 他們問我是否會主持委員會會議。◇ (*figurative*) *The party presided over one of the worst economic declines in the country's history* (= it was in power when the decline happened). 該黨執政時期，國家經歷了歷史上最嚴重的經濟衰退。

presi·dency /ˈprezɪdənsi/ *noun* [usually sing.] (*pl.* **-ies**) the job of being president of a country or an organization; the period of time sb holds this job 主席的職位（或任期等）；總統的職位（或任期等）：*the current holder of the EU presidency* 現任歐盟主席◇ *He was a White House official during the Bush presidency.* 他是布什任總統時的白宮官員。

presi·dent 🔑 /ˈprezɪdənt/ *noun*
1 🔑 (also **President**) the leader of a REPUBLIC, especially the US 總統；國家主席： *Several presidents attended the funeral.* 好幾位總統參加了葬禮。◇ *the President of the United States* 美國總統 ◇ *President Obama is due to visit the country next month.* 奧巴馬總統定於下月訪問該國。◇ *Do you have any comment, Mr President?* 總統先生，您有何評論？ ➲ **COLLOCATIONS** at POLITICS **2** 🔑 (also **President**) the person in charge of some organizations, clubs, colleges, etc.（機構、俱樂部、學院等的）負責人，會長，院長，主席： *to be made president of the students' union* 當選學生會主席 **3** 🔑 (*especially NAmE*) the person in charge of a bank or a commercial organization 銀行行長；總經理；董事長；總裁： *the bank president* 銀行行長 ◇ *the president of Columbia Pictures* 哥倫比亞影業公司董事長 ▸ **presi·den·tial** /ˌprezɪˈdenʃl/ *adj.*： *a presidential campaign/candidate/election* 總統競選活動／候選人／選舉 ◇ *a presidential system of government* 總統制政體

ˌpresident-eˈlect *noun* (*pl.* **presidents-elect**) a person who has been elected to be president but who has not yet begun the job 候任總統

Presiˌdential ˌMedal of ˈFreedom *noun* a MEDAL in the US that is the highest award a person can be given during a time of peace 總統自由勳章（美國和平時期授予個人的最高獎章）

ˈPresidents' Day *noun* (in the US) a legal holiday on the third Monday in February, in memory of the birthdays of George Washington and Abraham Lincoln 總統日（美國法定假日，在二月份的第三個星期一，紀念華盛頓和林肯的生日）

pre·sid·ium (also **prae·sid·ium** especially in *BrE*) /prɪˈsɪdiəm/ *noun* a permanent committee that makes important decisions as part of a government or large political organization, especially in COMMUNIST countries（尤指共產主義國家的）常務委員會，主席團

press 🔑 /pres/ *noun, verb*
■ ***noun***
▸ NEWSPAPERS 報章 **1** 🔑 (often **the Press**) [sing.+sing./pl. v.] newspapers and magazines 報章雜誌；報刊；印刷媒體： *the* ***local/national/foreign press*** 地方／全國／外國報刊 ◇ *the* ***popular/tabloid press*** (= smaller newspapers with a lot of pictures and stories of famous people) 通俗報刊；小報 ◇ *The story was reported* ***in the press*** *and on television.* 這件事已在報刊和電視上報道了。◇ *the* ***music/sporting press*** (= newspapers and magazines about music/sport) 音樂／體育報刊 ◇ *Unlike the American, the British press operates on a national scale.* 與美國不同，英國報刊都是行銷全國的。◇ *the* ***freedom of the Press/press freedom*** (= the freedom to report any events and express opinions) 新聞自由 ◇ *The event is bound to attract wide* ***press coverage*** (= it will be written about in many newspapers). 這個事件一定會在各報刊廣泛報道。➲ see also GUTTER PRESS **2** 🔑 **the press, the Press** [sing.+sing./pl. v.] the journalists and photographers who work for newspapers and magazines 記者；新聞工作者；新聞界： *The Press was/were not allowed to attend the trial.* 庭審謝絕新聞採訪。**3** [sing., U] the type or amount of reports that newspapers write about sb/sth 報道；評論： *The airline has* ***had a bad press*** *recently* (= journalists have written unpleasant things about it). 這家航空公司最近受到新聞界的責難。
▸ PUBLISHING/PRINTING 出版；印刷 **4** [C, U] a machine for printing books, newspapers, etc.; the process of printing them 印刷機；印刷： *We were able to watch the books rolling off the presses.* 我們可以看到書本從印刷機上源源不斷地印出。◇ *These prices are correct at the time* ***of going to press.*** 這些價格在付印時是準確無誤的。◇ *a story that is* ***hot off the press*** (= has just appeared in the newspapers) 剛剛見報的新聞報道 ➲ see also PRINTING PRESS, STOP PRESS **5** [C] a business that prints and publishes books 出版社；印刷所： *Oxford University Press* 牛津大學出版社
▸ EQUIPMENT FOR PRESSING 擠壓設備 **6** [C] (especially in compounds 尤用於構成複合詞) a piece of equipment that is used for creating pressure on things, to make them flat or to get liquid from them 壓平機；壓榨機；榨汁機： *a trouser press* 褲腿壓摺機 ◇ *a garlic press* 壓蒜器 ➲ **VISUAL VOCAB** page V26
▸ ACT OF PUSHING 推壓 **7** [C, usually sing.] an act of pushing sth with your hand or with a tool that you are holding 擠壓；推；按： *He gave the bell another press.* 他又按了一下鈴。◇ *Those shirts need a press* (= with an iron). 這些襯衣需要熨一熨。
▸ CROWD 群集 **8** [sing.] a large number of people or things competing for space or movement 擁擠的人群（或大批事物） **SYN** **throng**： *the press of bodies all moving the same way* 擁向同一方向的人群
▸ CUPBOARD 櫥櫃 **9** [C] (*IrishE, ScotE*) a large cupboard, usually with shelves, for holding clothes, books, etc.（分層）大壁櫥，衣櫃，書櫃，碗櫃
■ ***verb***
▸ PUSH/SQUEEZE 推；擠 **1** 🔑 [T, I] to push sth closely and firmly against sth; to be pushed in this way（被）壓，擠，推，施加壓力： **~ sth/sb/yourself against sth** *She pressed her face against the window.* 她把臉貼在窗子上。◇ **~ sth to sth** *He pressed a handkerchief to his nose.* 他用手絹捂住鼻子。◇ **~ sth together** *She pressed her lips together.* 她緊抿着雙唇。◇ **~ against sth** *His body was pressing against hers.* 他的身體緊貼着她。**2** 🔑 [T, I] to push or squeeze part of a device, etc. in order to make it work 按，壓（使啟動）： **~ sth** *to press a button/switch/key* 按下按鈕／開關；按鍵 ◇ **~ sth + adj.** *He pressed the lid firmly shut.* 他把蓋子蓋得緊緊的。◇ (**+ adv./prep.**) *Press here to open.* 請按此處打開。◇ *She pressed down hard on the gas pedal.* 她用力踩下油門踏板。➲ picture at SQUEEZE **3** [T] **~ sth into/onto sth** to put sth in a place by pushing it firmly 將…塞進；把…按入： *He pressed a coin into her hand and moved on.* 他把一枚硬幣塞進她手裏，然後繼續向前走。**4** [T] **~ sth** to squeeze sb's hand or arm, especially as a sign of affection（深情地）緊握（某人的手或臂）**5** [I] **+ adv./prep.** (of people in a crowd 人群) to move in the direction mentioned by pushing（向…）擁擠，推搡着移動： *The photographers pressed around the royal visitors.* 攝影記者們在王室貴賓周圍擠來擠去。◇ (*figurative*) *A host of unwelcome thoughts were pressing in on him.* 一大堆惱人的心事湧上他的心頭。
▸ TRY TO PERSUADE 勸說 **6** [T] to make strong efforts to persuade or force sb to do sth 催促；敦促；逼迫 **SYN** **push, urge**： **~ sb** *If pressed, he will admit that he knew about the affair.* 如果逼問他，他就會承認對此事知情。◇ **~ sb for sth** *The bank is pressing us for repayment of the loan.* 銀行正在催我們償還貸款。◇ **~ sb to do sth** *They are pressing us to make a quick decision.* 他們正催促我們儘快做決定。◇ **~ sb into sth/into doing sth** *Don't let yourself be pressed into doing something you don't like.* 不要勉強自己做不喜歡的事情。
▸ POINT/CLAIM/CASE 觀點；要求；事情 **7** [T] **~ sth** to express or repeat sth with force 堅持；反複強調： *I don't want to* ***press the point***, *but you do owe me $200.* 我不想老提這一點，但你確實欠我 200 元錢。◇ *She is still* ***pressing her claim*** *for compensation.* 她仍然堅持索賠。◇ *They were determined to* ***press their case*** *at the highest level.* 他們決心把事情鬧到最高層。
▸ MAKE FLAT/SMOOTH 弄平 **8** [T] to make sth flat or smooth by using force or putting sth heavy on top 把…壓平；壓扁： **~ sth** *pressed flowers* (= pressed between the pages of a book) 夾在書頁中間壓扁的花 ◇ **~ sth + adj.** *Press the soil flat with the back of a spade.* 用鐵鍬背面把土拍平。**9** [T] **~ sth** to make clothes smooth using a hot iron 熨平；燙平 **SYN** **iron**： *My suit needs pressing.* 我的西服該熨了。
▸ FRUIT/VEGETABLES 蔬果 **10** [T] **~ sth** to squeeze the juice out of fruit or vegetables by using force or weight 把…榨汁；壓榨
▸ METAL 金屬 **11** [T] to make sth from a material, using pressure 把…壓成；壓製： **~ sth** *to press a CD* 壓製一張光盤 ◇ **~ sth from/out of sth** *The car bodies are pressed out of sheets of metal.* 汽車車身是用板金壓製成的。
IDM **ˌpress (the) ˈflesh** (*informal*) (of a famous person or politician 名人或政治人物) to say hello to people by shaking hands 和群眾握手致意 **ˌpress sth ˈhome** to get as much advantage as possible from a situation by

P

attacking or arguing in a determined way 堅持不懈；爭辯到底：*to press home an attack/an argument/a point* 把進攻／論證／論點堅持到底 ◇ *Simon saw she was hesitating and pressed home his advantage.* 西蒙見她猶豫不決，便趁機佔盡優勢。 **,press sb/sth into 'service** to use sb/sth for a purpose that they were not trained or intended for because there is nobody or nothing else available 姑且使用；臨時湊合：*Every type of boat was pressed into service to rescue passengers from the sinking ferry.* 為了營救下沉渡輪上的旅客，各類船隻都被臨時徵用了。 ➲ more at BUTTON *n.*, CHARGE *n.*, PANIC BUTTON

PHR V **,press a'head/'on (with sth)** to continue doing sth in a determined way; to hurry forward 堅決繼續進行；匆忙前進；加緊：*The company is pressing ahead with its plans for a new warehouse.* 這家公司正加緊推動設置新倉庫的計劃。◇ *'Shall we stay here for the night?' 'No, let's press on.'* "我們今晚在這裏住下好嗎？""不，咱們繼續走。" **'press for sth** to keep asking for sth 不斷要求 **SYN** **demand, push for**：*They continued to press for a change in the law.* 他們不斷要求修改這項法律。 **'press sth on sb** to try to make sb accept sth, especially food or drink, although they may not want it 勉強某人接受；促某人吃（或喝）：*She kept pressing cake on us.* 她非要我們吃蛋糕不可。

'press agency *noun* = NEWS AGENCY

'press agent (also *NAmE informal* **flack**) *noun* a person whose job is to supply information and advertising material about a particular actor, musician, theatre, etc. to newspapers, radio or television（劇團等雇用的）廣告宣傳人員

'press box *noun* a special area or a room at a sports ground where sports journalists sit（體育場的）新聞工作室，記者席

'press conference (*especially BrE*) (*NAmE* usually **'news conference**) *noun* a meeting at which sb talks to a group of journalists in order to answer their questions or to make an official statement 記者招待會；新聞發佈會：*to **hold/give a press conference*** 舉行／召開記者招待會

P

'press corps *noun* (*pl.* **press corps**) a group of journalists who work in or go to a particular place to report on an event 記者團；特派記者組

'press cutting (*BrE*) (also **'press clipping** *NAmE, BrE*) *noun* = CUTTING *n.* (1)

pressed /prest/ *adj.* **1** [not before noun] **~ (for sth)** not having enough of sth, especially time or money（時間、資金等）緊缺，短絀：*I'm really pressed for cash at the moment.* 眼下我十分缺錢。 ➲ see also HARD-PRESSED **2** made flat using force or a heavy object 壓平的；壓扁的：*pictures made with pressed flowers* 用壓花製作的畫 ◇ *neatly pressed trousers* 熨得平平整整的西褲

'press gallery *noun* an area in a parliament building or a court for journalists to sit in（議會或法庭的）記者席

'press gang *noun* a group of people who were employed in the past to force men to join the army or navy 抓丁團，拉夫隊（舊時受雇抓人當兵）

'press-gang *verb* **~ sb (into sth/into doing sth)** (*informal*) to force sb to do sth that they do not want to do 迫使自己，勉強別人（做某事）

pres·sie *noun* = PREZZIE

press·ing /ˈpresɪŋ/ *adj., noun*

■ **adj.** [usually before noun] **1** needing to be dealt with immediately 緊急的；急迫的 **SYN** **urgent**：*I'm afraid I have some pressing business to attend to.* 很抱歉，我有些急事需要處理。 **2** difficult to refuse or to ignore 難以推卻的；不容忽視的：*a pressing invitation* 難以推卻的邀請

■ **noun** an object, especially a record, made by using pressure or weight to shape a piece of metal, plastic, etc.; a number of such objects that are made at one time 模壓製品，同批次的模壓產品（尤指唱片）：*The initial pressing of the group's album has already sold out.* 這個樂隊的首批專輯唱片已售罄。

press·man /ˈpresmæn/ *noun* (*pl.* **-men** /-men/) (*BrE, informal*) a journalist 記者；報人；新聞工作者

'press office *noun* the office of a large organization, political party or government department that answers questions from journalists and provides them with information（組織、政黨或政府的）新聞辦公室

'press officer *noun* a person who is in charge of or works for a press office 新聞發言人；新聞發佈官；新聞局長

'press release *noun* an official statement made to journalists by a large organization, a political party or a government department（向媒體發佈的）新聞稿

'press secretary *noun* a person who works for a politician or a political organization and gives information about them to journalists, the newspapers, etc. 新聞秘書

'press stud (also **pop·per**) (both *BrE*) (*NAmE* **snap**) *noun* a type of button used for fastening clothes, consisting of two metal or plastic sections that can be pressed together 摁扣；子母扣 ➲ VISUAL VOCAB page V63

'press-up (*BrE*) (also **'push-up** *NAmE, BrE*) *noun* [usually pl.] an exercise in which you lie on your stomach and raise your body off the ground by pressing down on your hands until your arms are straight 俯卧撑；伏地挺身；掌上壓 ➲ VISUAL VOCAB page V42

pres·sure 0→ /ˈpreʃə(r)/ *noun, verb*

■ **noun**

▸ **WHEN STH PRESSES** 擠壓時 **1** 0→ [U] the force or weight with which sth presses against sth else 壓力；擠壓：*The nurse applied pressure to his arm to stop the bleeding.* 護士壓住他的胳膊止血。◇ *The barriers gave way under the pressure of the crowd.* 擁擠的人群把路障推倒了。

▸ **OF GAS/LIQUID** 氣體；液體 **2** 0→ [U, C] the force produced by a particular amount of gas or liquid in a confined space or container; the amount of this 壓力；壓強：***air/water pressure*** 空氣／水的壓力 ◇ *Check the **tyre pressure*** (= the amount of air in a tyre) *regularly.* 要定期檢查輪胎的氣壓。 ➲ see also BLOOD PRESSURE

▸ **OF ATMOSPHERE** 大氣 **3** 0→ [U] the force of the atmosphere on the earth's surface 大氣壓：*A band of **high/low pressure** is moving across the country.* 一股高／低氣壓正橫越這個國家。 ➲ see also ATMOSPHERIC (1)

▸ **PERSUASION/FORCE** 勸說；強迫 **4** 0→ [U] the act of trying to persuade or to force sb to do sth 催促；要求；呼籲；強迫：**~ (for sth)** *The pressure for change continued to mount.* 改革的呼聲持續高漲。◇ **~ (on sb) (to do sth)** *There is a great deal of pressure on young people to conform.* 年輕人被大力要求守規矩。◇ *The government eventually bowed to **popular pressure*** (= they agreed to do what people were trying to get them to do). 政府最終向群眾的壓力低頭。◇ *Teenagers may find it difficult to resist **peer pressure**.* 青少年可能覺得很難抗拒同儕的壓力。

▸ **STRESS** 緊張 **5** 0→ [U] (also **pressures** [pl.]) difficulties and feelings of anxiety that are caused by the need to achieve or to behave in a particular way 心理壓力；緊張：*She was unable to attend because of the pressure of work.* 由於工作緊張她不能出席。◇ *You need to be able to handle pressure in this job.* 你要能應付這一工作的壓力。◇ *How can anyone enjoy the pressures of city life?* 怎麼會有人喜歡都市生活的壓力呢？

IDM **put 'pressure on sb (to do sth)** to force or to try to persuade sb to do sth 強迫；促使；勸說 **under 'pressure** **1** 0→ if a liquid or a gas is kept **under pressure**, it is forced into a container so that when the container is opened, the liquid or gas escapes quickly（液體或氣體）受壓力，壓縮 **2** 0→ being forced to do sth 被迫：*The director is under increasing pressure to resign.* 主任面對被迫請辭的壓力越來越大。 **3** 0→ made to feel anxious about sth you have to do 承受着（急於完成某事的）壓力：*The team performs well under pressure.* 這個隊在壓力下表現良好。

■ **verb** [often passive] (*especially NAmE*) (*BrE* also **pres·sur·ize**) **~ sb (into sth/into doing sth)** | **~ sb to do sth** to persuade sb to do sth, especially by making them feel that they have to or should do it 逼迫；使迫不得已：*Don't let yourself be pressured into making a hasty decision.* 不要勉強自己倉促做決定。

Synonyms 同義詞辨析

pressure

stress • tension • strain

These are all words for the feelings of anxiety caused by the problems in sb's life. 以上各詞均指生活上的心理壓力、精神緊張。

pressure difficulties and feelings of anxiety that are caused by the need to achieve sth or to behave in a particular way 指為達到某一目標或有某種行為表現而產生的心理壓力、緊張： *She was unable to attend because of the pressures of work.* 由於工作緊張她不能出席。

stress pressure or anxiety caused by the problems in sb's life 指因生活問題引起的精神壓力、心理負擔、緊張： *stress-related illnesses* 與精神壓力有關的疾病

PRESSURE OR STRESS? 用 pressure 還是 stress？

It is common to say that sb *is suffering from stress*, while **pressure** may be the thing that causes **stress**. 承受精神壓力常用 suffer from stress，而 pressure 可指造成壓力（stress）的事物。

tension a feeling of anxiety and stress that makes it impossible to relax 指情緒上的緊張、煩躁： *nervous tension* 神經緊張

strain pressure on sb/sth because they have too much to do or manage; the problems, worry or anxiety that this produces 指壓力、重負、重壓之下出現的問題、擔憂： *I found it a strain looking after four children.* 我覺得照料四個孩子挺累的。

PATTERNS

- to be **under** pressure/stress/strain
- **considerable** pressure/stress/tension/strain
- to **cause** stress/tension/strain
- to **cope with** the pressure/stress/tension/strain
- to **relieve/release** the pressure/stress/tension/strain
- to be **suffering from** stress/tension

ˈpressure cooker *noun* **1** a strong metal pot with a tight lid, that cooks food quickly by steam under high pressure 高壓鍋；壓力鍋 **2** a situation that is difficult or dangerous because people are likely to become anxious or violent 一觸即發的危險局勢；劍拔弩張的形勢

ˈpressure group *noun* a group of people who try to influence the government and ordinary people's opinions in order to achieve the action they want, for example a change in a law 壓力集團（向政府和輿眾施加影響的團體）： *the environmental pressure group 'Greenpeace'* "綠色和平"這個環保壓力集團 ➲ compare ADVOCACY GROUP ➲ see also INTEREST GROUP

ˈpressure hose *noun* a long tube that is strong enough for liquid to pass through it at high pressure 耐壓軟管

ˈpressure point *noun* **1** a place on the surface of the body that is sensitive to pressure, for example where an artery can be pressed against a bone to stop the loss of blood 止血點；壓覺點 **2** a place or situation where there is likely to be trouble 危機地點（或局面）

ˈpressure suit *noun* a suit which can be filled with air, used to protect the person wearing it from low air pressure, for example while flying a plane very high in the atmosphere 增壓服，加壓服（高空飛行等用）

ˈpressure washer *noun* a machine that cleans things by spraying them with water under high pressure 高壓噴洗機

pres·sur·ize (*BrE* also **-ise**) /ˈpreʃəraɪz/ *verb* **1** (*BrE*) (also **pres·sure** *NAmE, BrE*) [often passive] to persuade sb to do sth, especially by making them feel that they have to or should do it 逼迫；使迫不得已： **~ sb (into sth/into doing sth)** *She was pressurized into accepting the job.* 她被迫接受了這份工作。◇ **~ sb to do sth** *He felt that he was being pressurized to resign.* 他覺得被迫要辭職。**2** [usually passive] **~ sth** to keep the air pressure in a SUBMARINE, an aircraft, etc. the same as it is on earth 使（潛艇、飛機等內）保持正常氣壓 ▸ **pres·sur·iza·tion, -isa·tion** /ˌpreʃəraɪˈzeɪʃn; *NAmE* -rəˈz-/ *noun* [U]

pres·tige /preˈstiːʒ/ *noun, adj.*

▪ ***noun*** [U] the respect and admiration that sb/sth has because of their social position, or what they have done 威信；聲望；威望 **SYN status**： *personal prestige* 個人聲望 ◇ *There is a lot of prestige attached to owning a car like this.* 擁有這樣一部汽車會顯得很氣派。◇ *jobs with low prestige* 地位低微的工作

▪ ***adj.*** [only before noun] **1** that brings respect and admiration; important 令人敬仰的；受尊重的；重要的： *a prestige job* 體面的工作 **2** admired and respected because it looks important and expensive 名貴的；貴重的；講究派頭的 **SYN luxurious**： *a prestige car* 豪華的汽車

pres·ti·gious /preˈstɪdʒəs/ *adj.* [usually before noun] respected and admired as very important or of very high quality 有威望的；聲譽高的： *a prestigious award* 赫赫有名的獎項◇ *a prestigious university* 名牌大學

presto /ˈprestəʊ; *NAmE* ˈprestoʊ/ *exclamation, adv., adj., noun*

▪ ***exclamation*** (*NAmE*) (*BrE* **ˌhey ˈpresto**) **1** something that people say when they have just done sth so quickly and easily that it seems to have been done by magic 嘿，瞧（變魔術般迅速而輕鬆地做完某事時所說） **2** something that people say just before they finish a magic trick 變（變魔術完成之前所說）

▪ ***adv., adj.*** (used as an instruction in a piece of music 用作樂曲指示語) very quickly 急板

▪ ***noun*** (*pl.* **-os**) a piece of music that should be performed very quickly 急板樂曲（或樂章、樂段）

pre·sum·ably 🔑 **AW** /prɪˈzjuːməbli; *NAmE* -ˈzuː-/ *adv.* used to say that you think that sth is probably true 很可能；大概；想必是： *Presumably this is where the accident happened.* 這大概就是事故現場。◇ *You'll be taking the car, presumably?* 想必您是要買這輛汽車了？◇ *I couldn't concentrate, presumably because I was so tired.* 我的精神集中不起來，大概是太累了吧。

pre·sume **AW** /prɪˈzjuːm; *NAmE* -ˈzuːm/ *verb* **1** [I, T] to suppose that sth is true, although you do not have actual proof 假設；假定 **SYN assume**： *They are very expensive, I presume?* 我想這些東西很貴吧？◇ *'Is he still abroad?' '**I presume so**.'* "他還在國外嗎？" "我想是吧。" ◇ **~ (that) …** *I presumed (that) he understood the rules.* 我相信他已經明白這些規則。◇ **it is presumed that …** *Little is known of the youngest son; it is presumed that he died young.* 對於最小的兒子一般所知甚少，據推測他已經天亡。◇ **~ sb/sth to be/have sth** *I presumed him to be her husband.* 我料想那就是她丈夫。**2** [T] to accept that sth is true until it is shown not to be true, especially in court（尤指法庭上）推定，假定： **~ sb/sth + adj.** *Twelve passengers are missing, **presumed dead**.* 有十二名旅客失踪，並已推定罹難。◇ *In English law, a person is **presumed innocent** until proved guilty.* 英國法律規定，一個人被證明有罪前假定為無罪。◇ **~ sth** *We must presume innocence until we have proof of guilt.* 在證實一個人有罪之前，我們必須假定其無辜。◇ **~ sb/sth to be/have sth** *We must presume them to be innocent until we have proof of guilt.* 在證實他們有罪之前，我們必須假定其無罪。**3** [T] **~ sth** (*formal*) to accept sth as true or existing and to act on that basis 設定；設想；假設： *The course seems to presume some previous knowledge of the subject.* 這門課程似乎是以具備某些基礎知識為前提的。**4** [I] **~ to do sth** (*formal*) to behave in a way that shows a lack of respect by doing sth that you have no right to do 妄行；越權行事： *I wouldn't presume to tell you how to run your own business.* 我不會僭越去指點你該如何經營你自己的事業。

PHR V **preˈsume on/upon sb/sth** (*formal*) to make use of sb's friendship by asking them for more than you should 利用（友誼）作過分的要求： **~ to do sth** *I felt it would be presuming on our personal relationship to keep asking her for help.* 我覺得總要她幫忙就是利用了我們的私人交情。

P

pre·sump·tion AW /prɪˈzʌmpʃn/ *noun* **1** [C] something that is thought to be true or probable 可能的事；認為真實的事：*There is a general presumption that the doctor knows best.* 一般人都以為醫生最瞭解情況。 **2** [U] (*formal*) behaviour that is too confident and shows a lack of respect for other people 非分的行為；妄自尊大 **3** [U, C] (*law* 律) the act of supposing that sth is true, although it has not yet been proved or is not certain 推定；假定；假設：*Everyone is entitled to the presumption of innocence until they are proved to be guilty.* 在被證明有罪以前，每一個人都應被假定無辜。

pre·sump·tive /prɪˈzʌmptɪv/ *adj.* [usually before noun] (*formal* or *technical* 術語) likely to be true, based on the facts that are available 很可能的；假設的；推斷的 ➲ see also HEIR PRESUMPTIVE

pre·sump·tu·ous AW /prɪˈzʌmptʃuəs/ *adj.* [not usually before noun] too confident, in a way that shows a lack of respect for other people 自負；冒昧；放肆

pre·sup·pose /ˌpriːsəˈpəʊz; *NAmE* -ˈpoʊz/ *verb* (*formal*) **1 ~ sth** to accept sth as true or existing and act on that basis, before it has been proved to be true 姑且認為；假設 SYN **presume**：*Teachers sometimes presuppose a fairly high level of knowledge by the students.* 教師有時候假定學生的知識水平相當高。 **2 ~ that …** | **~ sth** to depend on sth in order to exist or be true 以…為前提；依…而定 SYN **assume**：*His argument presupposes that it does not matter who is in power.* 他的論點前提是誰掌權都無關緊要。

pre·sup·pos·ition /ˌpriːsʌpəˈzɪʃn/ *noun* [C, U] (*formal*) something that you believe to be true and use as the beginning of an argument even though it has not been proved; the act of believing it is true 假設的事情；假定；預設 SYN **assumption**：*theories based on presupposition and coincidence* 基於假設和偶合的理論

ˌpre-ˈtax *adj.* [only before noun] before the tax has been taken away 未扣稅的；稅前的：***pre-tax profits/losses/income*** 稅前利潤／虧損／收入

ˌpre-ˈteach *verb* **~ sth** to teach sth, especially new words, to students before a test or exercise 考試（或練習）前教授（新詞等）；先期教授

ˌpre-ˈteen *noun* a young person of about 11 or 12 years of age（約 11 或 12 歲的）大兒童，小少年；10 歲出頭的兒童 ▸ **ˌpre-ˈteen** *adj.* [usually before noun]：*the pre-teen years* 十歲出頭的幾年

pre·tence (*BrE*) (*NAmE* **pre·tense**) /prɪˈtens; *NAmE* ˈpriːtens/ *noun* **1** [U, sing.] the act of behaving in a particular way, in order to make other people believe sth that is not true 假象；偽裝；虛偽的表現：*Their friendliness was only pretence.* 他們的友善態度只不過是裝出來的。◇ **~ of doing sth** *By the end of the evening she had abandoned all pretence of being interested.* 到晚會快結束時，她已將假裝出來的興趣拋得一乾二淨了。◇ **~ of sth** *He made no pretence of great musical knowledge.* 他未敢妄稱音樂知識豐富。◇ **~ that …** *She was unable to **keep up the pretence** that she loved him.* 她無法繼續假裝愛他了。 **2** [U, C, usually sing.] (*formal* or *literary*) a claim that you have a particular quality or skill 妄稱；自稱；標榜：**~ (to sth)** *a woman with some pretence to beauty* 自詡有幾分姿色的女人 ◇ **~ (to doing sth)** *I **make no pretence to** being an expert on the subject.* 我不敢自詡為這方面的專家。 IDM see FALSE

pre·tend 0-π /prɪˈtend/ *verb, adj.*

■ ***verb*** **1** 0-π [I, T] to behave in a particular way, in order to make other people believe sth that is not true 假裝；佯裝：*I'm tired of having to pretend all the time.* 我討厭老得裝假。◇ *Of course I was wrong; it would be hypocritical to **pretend otherwise**.* 當然是我錯了，混充正確就是虛偽了。◇ **~ (to sb) (that …)** *He pretended to his family that everything was fine.* 他對家人佯稱一切都好。◇ *We pretended (that) nothing had happened.* 我們假裝什麼事情也沒發生。◇ **~ to do sth** *He pretended not to notice.* 他假裝沒注意。◇ *She didn't love him, though she **pretended to**.* 她並不愛他，雖然她裝出愛的樣子。◇ **~ sth** (*formal*) *She pretended an interest she did not feel.* 她毫無興趣卻裝作有。 **2** 0-π [I, T] (especially of children 尤指兒童) to imagine that sth is true as part of a game（在遊戲中）裝扮，扮作，模擬：*They didn't have any real money so they had to pretend.* 他們沒有真錢，就用假的代替。◇ **~ (that) …** *Let's pretend (that) we're astronauts.* 咱們裝扮成太空人吧。 **3** [I, T] (usually used in negative sentences and questions 通常用於否定句和疑問句) to claim to be, do or have sth, especially when this is not true 自詡；自稱；自認為：**~ to sth** *I can't pretend to any great musical talent.* 我不能妄稱自己多有音樂天賦。◇ **~ (that) …** *I don't pretend (that) I know much about the subject, but …* 我不敢說自己對這個主題有多瞭解，但是…◇ **~ to be/do/have sth** *The book doesn't pretend to be a great work of literature.* 這本書並未自封為文學傑作。

■ ***adj.*** [usually before noun] (*informal*) (often used by children 常為兒童用語) not real, imaginary 假裝的；想像的：*pretend cakes* 假糕點

pre·tend·er /prɪˈtendə(r)/ *noun* **~ (to sth)** a person who claims they have a right to a particular title even though other people disagree with them（頭銜的）覬覦者，冒充者

pre·tense (*NAmE*) = PRETENCE

pre·ten·sion /prɪˈtenʃn/ *noun* [C, usually pl., U] **1** the act of trying to appear more important, intelligent, etc. than you are in order to impress other people 虛飾；虛誇：*intellectual pretensions* 裝作有知識 ◇ *The play mocks the pretensions of the new middle class.* 這齣戲諷刺了新中產階級的裝模作樣。◇ *He spoke without pretension.* 他有話直說，不裝相。 **2** a claim to be or to do sth 自命；聲稱；標榜：**~ (to sth/to doing sth)** *a building with no pretensions to architectural merit* 沒有刻意表現建築特色的樓房 ◇ **~ (to do sth)** *The movie makes no pretension to reproduce life.* 這部電影並未標榜重現了真實生活。

pre·ten·tious /prɪˈtenʃəs/ *adj.* (*disapproving*) trying to appear important, intelligent, etc. in order to impress other people; trying to be sth that you are not, in order to impress 炫耀的；虛誇的；自命不凡的：*That's a pretentious name for a dog!* 狗叫這個名字真夠炫的！◇ *It was just an ordinary house—nothing pretentious.* 那只是一座普通的房子，沒有故作特別。◇ *He's so pretentious!* 瞧他那副自命不凡的樣兒！ ➲ compare UNPRETENTIOUS ▸ **pre·ten·tious·ly** *adv.* **pre·ten·tious·ness** *noun* [U]

the pret·er·ite (*NAmE* also **pret·erit**) /ˈpretərət/ *noun* [sing.] (*grammar* 語法) a form of a verb that expresses the past 過去時；過去式

pre·term /ˌpriːˈtɜːm; *NAmE* -ˈtɜːrm/ *adj.* born or happening after a short PREGNANCY, especially one that is less than 37 weeks 早產的，不滿妊娠期的（尤指懷孕少於 37 週的）：*caring for low birthweight and preterm babies* 對體重不足和早產嬰兒的護理 ◇ *a preterm birth/delivery* 早產 ▸ **pre·term** *adv.*：*Babies born preterm are at greater risk of needing hospitalization.* 早產兒更需要入院治療。

pre·ter·nat·ural /ˌpriːtəˈnætʃrəl; *NAmE* -tərˈn-/ *adj.* [only before noun] (*formal*) that does not seem natural; that cannot be explained by natural laws 不尋常的；超自然的；難以解釋的 ▸ **pre·ter·nat·ur·al·ly** *adv.*：*The city was preternaturally quiet.* 這座城市顯得異樣的寧靜。

pre·test /ˈpriːtest/ *noun* a test that you take to find out how much you already know or can do before learning or doing sth（學習或做某事前的）預先測試 ▸ **pre·test** *verb* **~ sb**

pre·text /ˈpriːtekst/ *noun* **~ (for sth/for doing sth)** | **~ (to do sth)** a false reason that you give for doing sth, usually sth bad, in order to hide the real reason; an excuse 藉口；託辭：*The incident was used as a pretext for intervention in the area.* 這次事件成了干涉那個地區的藉口。◇ *He left the party early **on the pretext of** having work to do.* 他藉口有事要處理，早早離開了聚會。 ➲ SYNONYMS at REASON

pret·tify /ˈprɪtifaɪ/ *verb* (**pret·ti·fies**, **pret·ti·fy·ing**, **pret·ti·fied**, **pret·ti·fied**) **~ sth** (usually *disapproving*) to try to make sth pretty, often with the result that it looks worse or false 粉飾，美化（常弄巧成拙）

P

pretty 0-ᴡ /ˈprɪti/ *adv., adj.*
■ ***adv.*** (with adjectives and adverbs 與形容詞和副詞連用) (*rather informal*) **1** 0-ᴡ to some extent; fairly 頗；相當：*I'm pretty sure I'll be going.* 我相當肯定會去的。◇ *The game was pretty good.* 這個遊戲相當不錯。◇ *It's pretty hard to explain.* 這事很難解釋清楚。◇ *I'm going to have to find a new apartment pretty soon.* 我很快就得找個新住處了。➲ note at QUITE **2** 0-ᴡ very 十分；非常；極；很：*That performance was pretty impressive.* 那場表演很出色。◇ *Things are looking pretty good!* 形勢看來很不錯！

IDM **pretty 'much/'well** (*BrE* also **pretty 'nearly**) (*NAmE* also **pretty 'near**) (*informal*) almost; almost completely 幾乎；差不多：*One dog looks pretty much like another to me.* 在我看來，狗長得都差不多。➲ more at SIT

■ ***adj.*** (**pret·tier**, **pret·ti·est**) **1** 0-ᴡ (especially of a woman, or a girl 尤指女子或女孩) attractive without being very beautiful 漂亮的；標致的；嫵媚的；動人的：*a pretty face* 俏麗的臉 ◇ *a pretty little girl* 俊俏的小姑娘 ◇ *You look so pretty in that dress!* 你穿那件連衣裙真漂亮！➲ SYNONYMS at BEAUTIFUL **2** 0-ᴡ (of places or things 地方或事物) attractive and pleasant to look at or to listen to without being large, beautiful or impressive 賞心悅目的；動聽的；美觀的；精緻的：*pretty clothes* 漂亮的衣服 ◇ *a pretty garden* 賞心悅目的花園 ◇ *a pretty name* 優美的名字 ▶ **pret·tily** /ˈprɪtɪli/ *adv.*：(*especially BrE*) *She laughed prettily.* 她的笑聲很迷人。◇ *The rooms are simply but prettily furnished.* 房間都佈置得簡樸而美觀。 **pret·ti·ness** *noun* [U]：*the prettiness of youth* 青春的美好

IDM **as ˌpretty as a 'picture** (*old-fashioned*) very pretty 美麗如畫；非常漂亮 **not just a pretty 'face** (*humorous*) used to emphasize that you have particular skills or qualities 並非徒有其表；不只臉蛋漂亮：*'I didn't know you could play the piano.' 'I'm not just a pretty face, you know!'* "我不知道你還會彈鋼琴呢。" "我可不只是臉蛋兒漂亮，對吧！" **ˌnot a pretty 'sight** (*humorous*) not pleasant to look at 不順眼；有礙觀瞻：*You should have seen him in his swimming trunks—not a pretty sight!* 你應該見識見識他穿游泳褲的樣子，真是一景呢！ **a pretty 'penny** (*old-fashioned*) a lot of money 很多錢；一大筆錢 ➲ more at PASS *n.*

pret·zel /ˈpretsl/ *noun* a crisp salty biscuit in the shape of a knot or stick, often served with drinks at a party 椒鹽捲餅（常作小吃）

pre·vail /prɪˈveɪl/ *verb* (*formal*) **1** [I] **~ (in/among sth)** to exist or be very common at a particular time or in a particular place 普遍存在；盛行；流行：*We were horrified at the conditions prevailing in local prisons.* 地方監獄的普遍狀況讓我們震驚。◇ *Those beliefs still prevail among certain social groups.* 那些觀念在某些社會群體中仍很盛行。 **2** [I] **~ (against/over sth)** (of ideas, opinions, etc. 思想、觀點等) to be accepted, especially after a struggle or an argument 被接受；戰勝；壓倒 **SYN** **triumph**：*Justice will prevail over tyranny.* 正義必將戰勝暴虐。◇ *Fortunately, common sense prevailed.* 幸而理智佔了上風。**3** [I] **~ (against/over sb)** to defeat an opponent, especially after a long struggle （尤指長時間鬥爭後）戰勝，挫敗

PHR V **pre'vail on/upon sb to do sth** to persuade sb to do sth 勸說：*I'm sure he could be prevailed upon to give a talk.* 我相信能說服他來做一次演講。

pre·vail·ing /prɪˈveɪlɪŋ/ *adj.* [only before noun] **1** existing or most common at a particular time 普遍的；盛行的；流行的 **SYN** **current**, **predominant**：*the prevailing economic conditions* 普遍的經濟狀況 ◇ *the attitude towards science prevailing at the time* 當時對科學的流行看法 ◇ *The prevailing view seems to be that they will find her guilty.* 一般人的看法似乎認為她會被判有罪。 **2** the **prevailing wind** in an area is the one that blows over it most frequently （指風）某地區常颳的，盛行的

preva·lent /ˈprevələnt/ *adj.* **~ (among sb)** | **~ (in sb/sth)** (*formal*) that exists or is very common at a particular time or in a particular place 流行的；普遍存在的；盛行的 **SYN** **common**, **widespread**：*a prevalent view* 普遍的觀點 ◇ *These prejudices are particularly prevalent among people living in the North.* 這些偏見在北方人中尤為常見。▶ **preva·lence** /-əns/ *noun* [U]

pre·vari·cate /prɪˈværɪkeɪt/ *verb* [I, T] (+ **speech**) (*formal*) to avoid giving a direct answer to a question in order to hide the truth 支吾搪塞；閃爍其詞；吞吞吐吐 **SYN** **beat about the bush**：*Stop prevaricating and come to the point.* 別吞吞吐吐的，有話快說吧。▶ **pre·vari·ca·tion** /prɪˌværɪˈkeɪʃn/ *noun* [U, C]

pre·vent 0-ᴡ /prɪˈvent/ *verb* to stop sb from doing sth; to stop sth from happening 阻止；阻礙；阻撓：**~ sth/sb** *The accident could have been prevented.* 這次事故本來是可以防止的。◇ **~ sb/sth from doing sth** *He is prevented by law from holding a licence.* 法律不准他持有執照。◇ *Nothing would prevent him from speaking out against injustice.* 什麼都不能阻止他鳴不平。◇ **~ (sb/sth) doing sth** (*BrE*) *Nothing would prevent him/his speaking out against injustice.* 什麼也阻擋不了他為不平之事鳴冤叫屈。▶ **pre·vent·able** /prɪˈventəbl/ *adj.*：*preventable diseases/accidents* 可以防止的疾病／事故

pre·ven·tion /prɪˈvenʃn/ *noun* [U] the act of stopping sth bad from happening 預防；防止；防範：***accident/crime prevention*** 防止事故／犯罪 ◇ *the prevention of disease* 疾病的預防 ◇ *a fire prevention officer* 消防官員

IDM **preˌvention is better than 'cure** (*BrE*) (*US* **an ounce of preˌvention is better than a pound of 'cure**) (*saying*) it is better to stop sth bad from happening rather than try to deal with the problems after it has happened 預防優於補救；防患於未然是上策

pre·vent·ive /prɪˈventɪv/ (also **pre·venta·tive** /prɪˈventətɪv/) *adj.* [only before noun] intended to try to stop sth that causes problems or difficulties from happening 預防性的；防備的：*preventive medicine* 預防醫學 ◇ *The police were able to take preventive action and avoid a possible riot.* 警方及時採取防範措施，避免了可能發生的騷亂。➲ compare CURATIVE

pre·ver·bal /ˌpriːˈvɜːbl; *NAmE* -ˈvɜːrbl/ *adj.* [usually before noun] (*technical* 術語) connected with the time before a child learns to speak （幼兒）前語言期的，習得語言能力前的：*preverbal communication* 前語言交流

pre·view /ˈpriːvjuː/ *noun, verb*
■ ***noun*** **1** an occasion at which you can see a film/movie, a show, etc. before it is shown to the general public 預映；預演；預展：*a press preview* (= for journalists only) 招待新聞界的預展 ◇ *a special preview of our winter fashion collection* 我們冬季時裝系列的特別預展 ➲ see also SNEAK PREVIEW **2** a description in a newspaper or a magazine that tells you about a film/movie, a television programme, etc. before it is shown to the public （報刊上有關電影、電視節目等的）預先評述，預告：*Turn to page 12 for a preview of next week's programmes.* 下週節目預告請見第 12 頁。 **3** (*NAmE*) = TRAILER (4)
■ ***verb*** **1 ~ sth** to see a film/movie, a television programme, etc. before it is shown to the general public and write an account of it for a newspaper or magazine 為（影視節目）寫預評：*The exhibition was previewed in last week's issue.* 本刊上週對展覽作了預評。 **2 ~ sth** (*especially NAmE*) to give sb a short account of sth that is going to happen, be studied, etc. 概述；扼要介紹：*The professor previewed the course for us.* 教授為我們扼要介紹了這門課程。

pre·vi·ous 0-ᴡ **AW** /ˈpriːviəs/ *adj.* [only before noun] **1** 0-ᴡ happening or existing before the event or object that you are talking about 先前的；以往的 **SYN** **prior**：*No previous experience is necessary for this job.* 這一工作無需相關的經驗。◇ *The car has only had one previous owner.* 這輛汽車以前沒換過車主。◇ *She is his daughter from a previous marriage.* 她是他與前妻生的女兒。◇ *I was unable to attend because of a previous engagement.* 我因有約在先，無法出席。◇ *The judge will take into consideration any previous convictions.* 任何前科法官都將予以考慮。 **2** 0-ᴡ immediately before the time you are talking about （時間上）稍前的 **SYN** **preceding**：*I couldn't believe it when I heard the news. I'd only seen him the previous day.* 聽到這消息時，我不敢相信；我就在前一天還見到過他。▶ **pre·vi·ous·ly** 0-ᴡ **AW** *adv.*：*The*

P

building had previously been used as a hotel. 這座樓房早先曾用作旅館。◇ *I had visited them three days previously.* 我之前曾探訪過他們三天。 **pre·vi·ous to** *prep.*: *Previous to this, she'd always been well.* 這以前，她身體一向很好。

ˌpre-ˈwar *adj.* [usually before noun] happening or existing before a war, especially before the Second World War 戰前的；（尤指）第二次世界大戰以前的：*the pre-war years* 戰前的年代 ◇ *pre-war Britain* 戰前的英國

ˌpre-ˈwash *verb, noun*

■ ***verb*** **1 ~ sth** to wash cloth before it is used, or clothing before it is sold 預洗（未使用或待售的布料或衣物） **2 ~ sth** to give clothing an extra wash before the main wash, especially in a machine（衣物主洗之前用洗衣機等）預洗

■ ***noun*** **ˈpre-wash** **1** [C] an extra wash before the main wash（主洗之前的）預洗 **2** [U] a substance which is applied to clothing before washing, in order to make it cleaner（洗滌之前使用的）衣物除漬精

prey /preɪ/ *noun, verb*

■ ***noun*** [U, sing.] **1** an animal, a bird, etc. that is hunted, killed and eaten by another 被捕食的動物；獵物：*The lion will often stalk its prey for hours.* 獅子經常悄然跟踪獵物達幾個小時。◇ ***birds of prey*** (= birds that kill for food) 猛禽 ➲ COLLOCATIONS at LIFE **2** a person who is harmed or tricked by sb, especially for dishonest purposes 受害者；受騙者：*Elderly people are* ***easy prey*** *for dishonest salesmen.* 老年人容易上狡詐推銷員的當。

IDM **be/fall ˈprey to sth** (*formal*) **1** (of an animal 動物) to be killed and eaten by another animal or bird 被捕食；成為獵物 **2** (of a person 人) to be harmed or affected by sth bad 受害；受壞影響

■ ***verb***

IDM **prey on sb's ˈmind** (of a thought, problem, etc. 想法、問題等) to make sb think and worry about it all the time 縈繞心頭；使耿耿於懷

PHR V **ˈprey on/upon sb/sth** **1** (of an animal or a bird 獸或鳥) to hunt and kill another animal for food 捕食；獵獲 **2** to harm sb who is weaker than you, or make use of them in a dishonest way to get what you want 欺凌，坑騙，敲詐（弱者）：*Bogus social workers have been preying on old people living alone.* 冒牌社會福利工作員不斷坑害獨居老人。

prez /prez/ *noun* (*slang*) = PRESIDENT

prez·zie (also **pres·sie**) /ˈprezi/ *noun* (*BrE, informal*) a present that you give sb, for example for their birthday 禮物；禮品

pri·ap·ic /praɪˈæpɪk; *NAmE* also -ˈeɪp-/ *adj.* **1** (*formal*) connected with or like a PENIS（似）陰莖的 **2** (*formal*) connected with male sexual activity 男子性活動的 **3** (*medical* 醫) having a PENIS which is always ERECT (= stiff) 陰莖異常勃起的

pri·ap·ism /ˈpraɪəpɪzəm/ *noun* [U] (*medical* 醫) a condition in which a man's PENIS remains ERECT (= stiff) 陰莖異常勃起

price 0→ /praɪs/ *noun, verb*

■ ***noun*** **1** 0→ [C, U] the amount of money that you have to pay for sth 價格；價錢；物價：*Boat for sale, price £2 000* 小船，售價 2 000 英鎊 ◇ *house/retail/oil/share prices* 房屋 / 零售 / 石油 / 股票價格 ◇ *to charge a* ***high/reasonable/low price*** *for sth* 索要很高 / 適中 / 很低的價格 ◇ *The price of cigarettes is set to rise again.* 香煙又要漲價。◇ *He managed to get a good price for the car.* 他終於把汽車賣了個好價錢。◇ ***rising/falling prices*** 攀升 / 下跌的價格 ◇ *Can you* ***give me a price*** *for the work* (= tell me how much you will charge)? 請問做這件工作要多少錢？◇ *I'm only buying it if it's the* ***right price*** (= a price that I think is reasonable). 只有價錢合理我才會買這東西。◇ *Children over five must pay (the)* ***full price*** *for the ticket.* 五歲以上的兒童須買全票。◇ *How much are these? They don't have a price on them.* 這些東西賣多少錢？它們都沒有標價。◇ *It's amazing how much computers have come down* ***in price*** *over the past few years.* 過去這幾年，電腦的價格大大降低，簡直令人驚訝。◇ ***price rises/increases/cuts*** 價格上升 / 提高 / 降低 ◇ *a price list* 價目表 ➲ see also ASKING PRICE, COST PRICE, CUT-PRICE, HALF-PRICE, LIST PRICE, MARKET PRICE, PURCHASE PRICE, SELLING PRICE **2** 0→ [sing.] the unpleasant things that you must do or experience in order to achieve sth or as a result of achieving sth 代價：**~ (of sth)** *Criticism is part of the price of leadership.* 挨批評是當領導要付出的部份代價。◇ **~ (for sth/for doing sth)** *Loneliness is a* ***high price to pay*** *for independence in your old age.* 孤寂是老年獨自生活要付出的高昂代價。◇ *Giving up his job was* ***a small price to pay*** *for his children's happiness.* 放棄工作是他為子女幸福所付出的小小代價。 **3** [C] (in horse racing 賽馬) the numbers that tell you how much money you will receive if the horse that you bet on wins the race 投注賠率 **SYN** **odds**: *Six to one is a good price for that horse.* 那匹馬有六比一的賠率很不錯。 ➲ see also STARTING PRICE

IDM **at ˈany price** whatever the cost or the difficulties may be 不惜任何代價；無論如何：*We want peace at any price.* 為了爭取和平，我們不惜任何代價。 **at a ˈprice** **1** costing a lot of money 以高價；花大錢：*You can buy strawberries all year round, but at a price.* 草莓一年到頭都買得到，不過很貴。 **2** involving sth unpleasant 付代價：*He'll help you—at a price!* 他會幫助你的，但要付出代價！ **beyond ˈprice** (*formal or literary*) extremely valuable or important 無價的；極寶貴的；極重要的 **everyone has their ˈprice** (*saying*) you can persuade anyone to do sth by giving them more money or sth that they want 重賞之下，必有勇夫；人皆有價；有錢能使鬼推磨 **not at ˈany price** used to say that no amount of money would persuade you to do or to sell sth 無論如何也不；給多少錢也不：*I wouldn't work for her again—not at any price!* 我再也不替她做事了，給多少錢也不做！ **a ˈprice on sb's head** an amount of money that is offered for capturing or killing sb 緝拿（或殺害）某人的懸賞金 **put a ˈprice on sth** to say how much money sth valuable is worth（為貴重物）定價，作價：*They haven't yet put a price on the business.* 他們還沒有給這筆生意開價。◇ *You can't put a price on that sort of loyalty.* 那樣的忠誠是無法用金錢衡量的。 **ˈwhat price ...?** (*BrE, informal*) **1** used to say that you think that sth you have achieved may not be worth all the problems and difficulties it causes（認為得不償失）…不值得，…有什麼用？：*What price fame and fortune?* 名利的代價何其大。 **2** used to say that sth seems unlikely（認為可能性不大）…可能嗎，…不可能吧：*What price England winning the World Cup?* 英格蘭隊奪得世界杯冠軍，這可能嗎？ ➲ more at CHEAP *adj.*, PAY *v.*

■ ***verb*** **1** [usually passive] to fix the price of sth at a particular level 給…定價；為…作價：**~ sth + adv./prep.** *a reasonably priced house* 定價合理的一座房子 ◇ *These goods are priced too high.* 這些貨品定價過高。◇ **~ sth at sth** *The tickets are priced at $100 each.* 每張票定價 100 元。 **2 ~ sth (up)** to write or stick tickets on goods to show how much they cost（在商品上）標價，貼價格標籤 **3 ~ sth** to compare the prices of different types of the same thing 比較…的價格：*We priced various models before buying this one.* 我們比較了多種型號的價格以後才買了這一款。

IDM **price yourself/sth out of the ˈmarket** to charge such a high price for your goods, services, etc. that nobody wants to buy them 因索價過高而無人問津

ˈprice controls *noun* [pl.] (*economics* 經) restrictions that a government puts on the price of goods at particular times, such as when there is not enough of sth, when there is a war, etc.（物品短缺或戰時等的）物價控制，價格管制

ˈprice-fixing *noun* [U] the practice of companies agreeing not to sell goods below a particular price 價格壟斷（公司之間協議不低於某價位銷售貨品）

ˈprice index *noun* = RETAIL PRICE INDEX

price·less /ˈpraɪsləs/ *adj.* **1** extremely valuable or important 無價的；極珍貴的；極重要的：*a priceless collection of antiques* 價值連城的古文物收藏 ◇ *priceless information* 極有價值的信息 ➲ SYNONYMS at VALUABLE **2** (*informal*) extremely amusing 極有趣的：*You should have seen his face—it was priceless!* 你真該見識見識他那副尊容，可笑極了！

Synonyms 同義詞辨析

price

cost • value • expense • worth

These words all refer to the amount of money that you have to pay for sth. 以上各詞均指價值、價錢。

price the amount of money that you have to pay for an item or service 指商品或服務的價格、價錢：*house prices* 房屋價格 ◇ *How much are these? They don't have a price on them.* 這些東西賣多少錢？它們都沒有標價。◇ *I can't afford it **at that price**.* 這樣的價格我付不起。

cost the amount of money that you need in order to buy, make or do sth 指購買、製造某物或做某事所需的成本、費用、花費：*A new computer system has been installed at a cost of £80 000.* 新的計算機系統已安裝，費用為 8 萬英鎊。

value how much sth is worth in money or other goods for which it can be exchanged 指價值：*The winner will receive a prize **to the value of** £1 000.* 獲勝者將得到價值為 1 000 英鎊的獎品。
NOTE Especially in British English, **value** can also mean how much sth is worth compared with its price. 尤其在英式英語中，value 亦含與其價格相比的值、划算程度：*This restaurant is excellent value* (= is worth the money it costs). 這家餐館很合算。

PRICE, COST OR VALUE? 用 price、cost 還是 value？

The **price** is what sb asks you to pay for an item or service. * price 指商品或服務的要價：*to ask/charge a high price* 要價 / 收費高 ◇ ~~*to ask/charge a high cost/value*~~ Obtaining or achieving sth may have a **cost**; the **value** of sth is how much other people would be willing to pay for it. * cost 指獲取某物或達到某目的所需的費用；value 指別人願意為某物付出的價值：*house prices* 房屋價格 ◇ *the cost of moving house* 搬家費用 ◇ *The house now has a market value of one million pounds.* 這棟房子目前的市場價值為 100 萬英鎊。

expense the money that you spend on sth; sth that makes you spend money 指所花費用、花錢的東西、開銷：*The garden was transformed **at great expense**.* 花園改建花了一大筆費用。◇ *Running a car is a big expense.* 養一輛車開銷很大。

worth the financial value of sb/sth 指人或物的價值：*He has a personal net worth of $10 million.* 他有價值 1 千萬元的個人淨資產。NOTE Worth is more often used to mean the practical or moral value of sth. * worth 較常用以指某事物的實際作用或道德意義。

PATTERNS

- the **high** price/cost/value
- the **real/true** price/cost/value/worth
- to **put/set** a price/value **on** sth
- to **increase/reduce** the price/cost/value/expense
- to **raise/double/lower** the price/cost/value
- to **cut** the price/cost

'price tag *noun* a label on sth that shows how much you must pay 價格標籤：(*figurative*) *There is a £2 million price tag on the team's star player.* 這個球隊的明星球員身價為 200 萬英鎊。➲ picture at LABEL

'price war *noun* a situation in which companies or shops/stores keep reducing the prices of their products and services in order to attract customers away from their COMPETITORS 價格戰（以減價來吸引顧客）

pricey /'praɪsi/ *adj.* (**prici·er**, **prici·est**) (*informal*) expensive 昂貴的 ➲ **SYNONYMS** at EXPENSIVE

pri·cing /'praɪsɪŋ/ *noun* [U] the act of deciding how much to charge for sth 定價；作價；計價：*competitive pricing* 有競爭力的定價 ◇ *pricing policy* 定價政策 ➲ see also ROAD PRICING

prick /prɪk/ *verb*, *noun*

■ ***verb*** **1** [T] to make a very small hole in sth with a sharp point 扎；刺；戳：**~ sth** *He pricked the balloon and burst it.* 他把氣球扎爆了。◇ **~ sth with sth** *Prick holes in the paper with a pin.* 用大頭針在紙上扎洞。 **2** [T] **~ sth (on sth)** to make a small hole in the skin so that it hurts or blood comes out 扎破，刺破（皮膚）：*She pricked her finger on a needle.* 她的手指被針扎了。 **3** [I, T] to make sb feel a slight pain as if they were being pricked 使感到刺痛：*He felt a pricking sensation in his throat.* 他感覺喉嚨有點刺痛。◇ **~ sth** *Tears pricked her eyes.* 淚水刺激了她的雙眼。

IDM **prick your 'conscience | your 'conscience pricks you** to make you feel guilty about sth; to feel guilty about sth 喚醒良心；受到良心譴責：*Her conscience pricked her as she lied to her sister.* 她對姐姐撒謊時良心上感到很不安。 **prick (up) your 'ears 1** (of an animal, especially a horse or dog 動物，尤指馬或狗) to raise the ears 豎起耳朵 **2** (also **your 'ears prick up**) (of a person 人) to listen carefully, especially because you have just heard sth interesting 傾耳細聽：*Her ears pricked up at the sound of his name.* 一聽到他的名字她的耳朵就立刻豎了起來。

■ ***noun*** **1** (*taboo, slang*) a PENIS 雞巴；屌 **2** (*taboo, slang*) an offensive word for a stupid or unpleasant man 鳥人；笨蛋：*Don't be such a prick!* 別那麼笨！ **3** an act of making a very small hole in sth with a sharp point 扎；穿刺：*I'm going to give your finger a little prick with this needle.* 我將用這根針在你手指上輕輕扎一下。 **4** a slight pain caused by a sharp point or sth that feels like a sharp point 針刺感；刺痛（感）：*You will feel a tiny prick in your arm.* 你會覺得胳膊上有一點點刺痛。◇ (*figurative*) *He could feel the hot prick of tears in his eyes.* 他眼裏噙着淚水，火辣辣的。

prickle /'prɪkl/ *verb*, *noun*

■ ***verb*** **1** [T, I] **~ (sth)** to give sb an unpleasant feeling on their skin, as if a lot of small sharp points are pushing into it 刺痛；扎疼：*The rough cloth prickled my skin.* 粗布扎我的皮膚。◇ *His moustache prickled when he kissed me.* 他吻我的時候鬍子扎人。 **2** [I] **~ (with sth)** (of skin, eyes, etc. 皮膚、眼睛等) to sting or feel strange and unpleasant because you are frightened, angry, excited, etc. 有刺痛感：*Her eyes prickled with tears.* 淚水刺疼了她的眼睛。◇ *The hairs on the back of my neck prickled when I heard the door open.* 聽到開門聲，我頸後汗毛倒豎。◇ (*figurative*) *He prickled* (= became angry) *at the suggestion that it had been his fault.* 一聽説過錯在他，他馬上火兒了。

■ ***noun*** **1** a small sharp part on the STEM or leaf of a plant or on the skin of some animals（植物的）芒刺，刺；（動物的）皮刺，刺毛：*a cactus covered in prickles* 長滿刺的仙人掌 **2** a slight stinging feeling on the skin 刺癢；輕微的刺痛感：*a prickle of fear/excitement* 恐懼 / 激動的刺癢感

prick·ly /'prɪkli/ *adj.* (**prick·lier**, **prick·li·est**) **1** covered with prickles 多刺的：*a prickly bush* 多刺的灌木 **2** causing you to feel as if your skin is touching sth that is covered with prickles 引起刺痛的；扎疼的；刺癢的：*a prickly feeling* 刺痛感 **3** (*informal*) (of a person 人) easily annoyed or offended 易怒的；愛生氣的 SYN **touchy** **4** (of a decision, an issue, etc. 決定、問題等) difficult to deal with because people have very different ideas about it 棘手的；難處理的；燙手的 SYN **thorny**：*Let's move on to the prickly subject of taxation reform.* 咱們繼續討論下一項稅制改革這個棘手的問題吧。

,prickly 'heat *noun* [U] a skin condition, common in hot countries, that causes small red spots that ITCH 痱子

,prickly 'pear *noun* **1** a type of CACTUS with PRICKLES (= sharp parts like needles), and yellow flowers 仙人果，刺梨（仙人掌屬植物，花黃色） **2** the reddish fruit of the prickly pear that is shaped like a PEAR and can be eaten 仙人果（梨狀，紅色，可食用）

'prick-teaser (also **'prick-tease**) *noun* (*taboo, slang*) = COCK-TEASER

pride 🔑 /praɪd/ *noun*, *verb*

■ ***noun***

▸ **PLEASURE/SATISFACTION** 愉悦；滿足 **1** 🔑 [U, sing.] a feeling of pleasure or satisfaction that you get when you or people who are connected with you have done sth well or own sth that other people admire 自豪；驕傲；得意感：*The sight of her son graduating filled her with pride.* 看到兒子畢業她充滿了自豪。◇ **~ (in sth)** *I take (a) pride in my work.* 我為自己的工作感到驕傲。◇ **~ (in doing sth)** *We take great pride in offering the best service in town.* 我們以能夠提供全城最好的服務而自豪。◇ *I looked* **with pride** *at what I had achieved.* 回顧過去的成就，我感到十分光榮。◇ *Success in sport is a source of national pride.* 體育成就是民族光榮的源泉。➲ SYNONYMS at SATISFACTION **2** [sing.] **the ~ of sth** a person or thing that gives people a feeling of pleasure or satisfaction 值得自豪的人（或事物）：*The new sports stadium is the pride of the town.* 新體育場是這個城市的驕傲。

▸ RESPECT FOR YOURSELF 自尊 **3** 🔑 [U] the feeling of respect that you have for yourself 自尊心；自尊；尊嚴：*Pride would not allow him to accept the money.* 自尊心不容他接受這筆錢。◇ *Her pride was hurt.* 她的自尊心受到了傷害。◇ *Losing his job was a real* **blow to his pride**. 失掉工作對他的自尊是個沉重的打擊。◇ *It's time to* **swallow your pride** (= hide your feelings of pride) *and ask for your job back.* 這時候你應該收起自尊，討回那份工作。 **4** 🔑 [U] (*disapproving*) the feeling that you are better or more important than other people 自負；傲慢：*Male pride forced him to suffer in silence.* 男性的自尊迫使他隱忍不言。➲ see also PROUD

▸ LIONS 獅子 **5** [C+sing./pl. v.] a group of LIONS 獅群

IDM **sb's pride and 'joy** a person or thing that causes sb to feel great pleasure or satisfaction 某人引以為榮的人（或事物） **pride comes/goes before a 'fall** (*saying*) if you have too high an opinion of yourself or your abilities, sth will happen to make you look stupid 驕傲使人失敗 **pride of 'place** the position in which sth is most easily seen, that is given to the most important thing in a particular group 顯要位置；最突出（或最重要）的位置

■ *verb*

PHR V **'pride yourself on sth/on doing sth** [no passive] to be proud of sth 引以為榮；為…而驕傲：*She had always prided herself on her appearance.* 她總是對自己的外貌感到得意。

P

priest 🔑 /priːst/ *noun*

1 🔑 a person who is qualified to perform religious duties and ceremonies in the Roman Catholic, Anglican and Orthodox Churches（天主教、聖公會、東正教的）司祭，神父，司鐸：*a parish priest* 堂區司鐸 ◇ *the ordination of women priests* 女司祭的授職禮 ➲ compare CHAPLAIN, CLERGYMAN, MINISTER *n.* (2), VICAR **2** 🔑 (*feminine* **priest·ess** /ˈpriːstes/) a person who performs religious ceremonies in some religions that are not Christian（非基督教會的）教士，祭司，僧侶

priest·hood /ˈpriːsthʊd/ *noun* **1 the priesthood** [sing.] the job or position of being a priest 牧師（或教士、神父、司鐸）的職位；司祭品：*to enter the priesthood* (= to become a priest) 接受司祭職 ➲ COLLOCATIONS at RELIGION **2** all the priests of a particular religion or country（總稱教會或國家的）全體教士，全體神職人員；司祭團

priest·ly /ˈpriːstli/ *adj.* [usually before noun] connected with a priest; like a priest 神職人員的；像神職人員的

'priest's hole *noun* a secret space in a house where Catholic priests hid in the past at times when Catholicism was against the law in England（舊時天主教在英國屬違法時的）司鐸藏身處

prig /prɪɡ/ *noun* (*disapproving*) a person who behaves in a morally correct way and who shows that they disapprove of what other people do 自命清高的人 ▸ **prig·gish** *adj.* **prig·gish·ness** *noun* [U]

prim /prɪm/ *adj.* (**prim·mer**, **prim·mest**) (*disapproving*) **1** (of a person 人) always behaving in a careful and formal way, and easily shocked by anything that is rude 一本正經的；循規蹈矩的；古板的：*You can't tell her that joke—she's much too* **prim and proper**. 你可別跟她講那個笑話；她這個人古板正經得要命。 **2** formal and neat 正式的；端莊的 SYN **demure**：*a prim suit with a high-necked collar* 端莊的高領西服 ▸ **prim·ly** *adv.*：*'You're not supposed to say that,' she said primly.* "你不該講那樣的話。" 她一本正經地說。

prima ballerina /ˌpriːmə ˌbæləˈriːnə/ *noun* the main woman dancer in a BALLET company（芭蕾舞團的）首席女舞蹈演員

pri·macy AW /ˈpraɪməsi/ *noun* (*pl.* **-ies**) (*formal*) **1** [U] the fact of being the most important person or thing 首要；至高無上：*a belief in the primacy of the family* 家庭至上論 **2** [C] the position of an ARCHBISHOP 總主教職

prima donna /ˌpriːmə ˈdɒnə; *NAmE* ˈdɑːnə/ *noun* **1** the main woman singer in an OPERA performance or an OPERA company（歌劇演出或歌劇團的）首席女歌唱演員，女主角演員 **2** (*disapproving*) a person who thinks they are very important because they are good at sth, and who behaves badly when they do not get what they want 妄自尊大而愛鬧脾氣者；恃才傲物者

prim·aeval *adj.* = PRIMEVAL

prima facie /ˌpraɪmə ˈfeɪʃi/ *adj.* [only before noun] (from *Latin, law* 律) based on what at first seems to be true, although it may be proved false later 基於初步印象的；初步認定的：*prima facie evidence* 初步的證據 ▸ **prima facie** *adv.*：*Prima facie, there is a strong case against him.* 據初步認定，證據對他極其不利。

primal /ˈpraɪml/ *adj.* [only before noun] (*formal*) connected with the earliest origins of life; very basic 原始的；最初的；根源的；根本的 SYN **primeval**：*the primal hunter-gatherer* 原始狩獵採集者 ◇ *a primal urge/fear* 本能的慾望／恐懼

pri·mar·ily 🔑 AW /praɪˈmerəli; *BrE* also ˈpraɪmərəli/ *adv.* mainly 主要地；根本地 SYN **chiefly**：*a course designed primarily for specialists* 主要為專業人員開設的課程 ◇ *The problem is not primarily a financial one.* 這個問題基本上不是財政問題。

pri·mary 🔑 AW /ˈpraɪməri; *NAmE* -meri/ *adj.*, *noun*

■ *adj.* **1** 🔑 [usually before noun] main; most important; basic 主要的；最重要的；基本的 SYN **prime**：*The primary aim of this course is to improve your spoken English.* 這門課的主要目的是提高英語會話能力。◇ *Our primary concern must be the children.* 我們首先要關心的必須是兒童。◇ *Good health care is of primary importance.* 良好的醫療保健是重中之重。 **2** 🔑 [usually before noun] (*formal* or *technical* 術語) developing or happening first; earliest 最初的；最早的：*primary causes* 最初的原因 ◇ *The disease is still in its primary stage.* 這病尚處於初始階段。 **3** 🔑 [only before noun] (*especially BrE*) connected with the education of children between the ages of about five and eleven 初等教育的；小學教育的：*primary teachers* 小學教師 ➲ compare ELEMENTARY (1), SECONDARY (3), TERTIARY

■ *noun* (*pl.* **-ies**) (also **ˌprimary eˈlection**) (in the US) an election in which people in a particular area vote to choose a candidate for a future important election（美國）初選：*the Illinois primary* 伊利諾伊州的初選 ◇ *the presidential primaries* 總統候選人初選

ˌprimary ˈcare (also **ˌprimary ˈhealth care**) *noun* [U] the medical treatment that you receive first when you are ill/sick, for example from your family doctor 最初保健護理；基礎醫療；初始的治療

primary ˌcare phyˈsician *noun* (*abbr.* **PCP**) (*especially NAmE*) a doctor who provides primary care 提供初始治療的醫生；基礎醫療醫師

primary ˌcare proˈvider *noun* (*abbr.* **PCP**) a company or organization that provides primary care 初級保健護理機構；基礎醫療機構

ˌprimary ˈcolour (*especially US* **ˌprimary ˈcolor**) *noun* one of the three colours, red, yellow and blue, that can be mixed together to make all other colours 原色，基色（指能混合成其他各種顏色的紅、黃、藍三色之一）

ˌprimary ˈhealth care *noun* = PRIMARY CARE

ˈprimary industry *noun* [U, C] (*economics* 經) the section of industry that provides RAW MATERIALS to be made into goods, for example farming and MINING 第一產業（指農業、礦業等生產原材料的產業）➲ compare SECONDARY INDUSTRY, TERTIARY INDUSTRY

ˈprimary school *noun* **1** (*BrE*) a school for children between the ages of 5 and 11 小學 **2** (*old-fashioned,*

NAmE) = ELEMENTARY SCHOOL ➲ compare SECONDARY SCHOOL

ˈprimary source *noun* a document, etc. that contains information obtained by research or observation, not taken from other books, etc. 第一手資料；(通過研究或觀察等獲得的)直接材料 ➲ compare SECONDARY SOURCE

ˌprimary ˈstress *noun* [C, U] (*phonetics* 語音) the strongest stress that is put on a syllable in a word or a phrase when it is spoken 主重音；第一重音 ➲ compare SECONDARY STRESS

pri·mate *noun* **1** /ˈpraɪmeɪt/ any animal that belongs to the group of MAMMALS that includes humans, APES and MONKEYS 靈長類；靈長目動物 ➲ VISUAL VOCAB page V12 **2** /ˈpraɪmət; -meɪt/ an ARCHBISHOP (= a priest of very high rank in the Christian Church) 大主教；總主教：*the Primate of all England* (= the Archbishop of Canterbury) 全英格蘭主教長(坎特伯雷大主教)

prime AW /praɪm/ *adj., noun, verb*

■ ***adj.*** [only before noun] **1** main; most important; basic 主要的；首要的；基本的：*My prime concern is to protect my property.* 我最關心的是保護自己的財產。◇ *Winning is not the prime objective in this sport.* 獲勝不是這項體育運動的主要目的。◇ *The care of the environment is of prime importance.* 保護環境是最重要的。◇ *He's the police's* ***prime suspect*** *in this case.* 他是該案中警方的主要懷疑對象。 ➲ SYNONYMS at MAIN **2** of the best quality; excellent 優質的；上乘的；優異的：*prime (cuts of) beef* 上等的牛肉(塊) ◇ *The store has a prime position in the mall.* 這家商店位於購物廣場一個非常理想的位置。 **3 a prime example** of sth is one that is typical of it 典型的；有代表性的：*The building is a prime example of 1960s architecture.* 這座大樓是 20 世紀 60 年代的典型建築。 **4** most likely to be chosen for sth; most suitable 最可能的；首選的；最適宜的：*The house is isolated and a prime target for burglars.* 這座孤零零的房子是盜賊的首選目標。◇ *He's a prime candidate for promotion.* 他是獲得晉升機會的最佳人選。

■ ***noun*** [sing.] the time in your life when you are strongest or most successful 盛年；年富力強的時期；鼎盛時期：*a young woman in her prime* 正當妙齡的女郎 ◇ *He was barely 30 and* ***in the prime of (his) life.*** 他還不滿 30 歲，正是英姿勃發的年華。◇ *These flowers are long* ***past their prime.*** 這些花的鼎盛花期早過了。

■ ***verb*** **1** to prepare sb for a situation so that they know what to do, especially by giving them special information 事先指點；使(某人)做好準備 SYN **brief**：**~ sb (with sth)** *They had been primed with good advice.* 他們事先得到了高人指點。◇ **~ sb (for sth)** *She was ready and primed for action.* 她已胸有成竹、躍躍欲試了。◇ **~ sb to do sth** *He had primed his friends to give the journalists as little information as possible.* 他已經知會他的朋友，盡量少向記者透露消息。 **2 ~ sth** to make sth ready for use or action 把(事物)準備好：*The bomb was primed, ready to explode.* 炸彈已準備好，可隨時引爆。 **3 ~ sth** to prepare wood, metal, etc. for painting by covering it with a special paint that helps the next layer of paint to stay on 在(金屬、木材等上)打底漆

IDM **prime the ˈpump** to encourage the growth of a new or weak business or industry by putting money into it 投資以振興(新的或不景氣的企業或行業)

ˈprime cost (also **ˈfirst cost**) *noun* [C, U] (*business* 商) the cost of sth calculated by adding the cost of materials used to make it and the cost of paying sb to make it, but not including costs that are connected with running a business, such as rent and electricity 主要成本(包括原材料和勞動力)

ˌprime ˈminister 🗝 (also **ˌPrime ˈMinister**) *noun* (*abbr.* **PM**) the main minister and leader of the government in some countries 首相；總理

ˌprime ˈmover *noun* a person or thing that starts sth and has an important influence on its development 發起者；推動者；原動力

ˌprime ˈnumber *noun* (*mathematics* 數) a number that can be divided exactly only by itself and 1, for example 7, 17 and 41 素數，質數(只能被 1 和其自身整除)

primer /ˈpraɪmə(r)/ *noun* **1** [U, C] a type of paint that is put on wood, metal, etc. before it is painted to help the paint to stay on the surface 底漆；底層塗料 **2** [C] /ˈpraɪmə(r); *NAmE* ˈprɪmər/ (*NAmE*) a book that contains basic instructions 初級讀本；入門書：*The President doesn't need a primer on national security.* 總統對於國家安全是不需要讀入門書的。 **3** [C] /ˈpraɪmə(r); *NAmE* ˈprɪmər/ (*old-fashioned*) a book for teaching children how to read, or containing basic facts about a school subject 識字課本；啟蒙讀本

ˈprime rate *noun* (in the US) the lowest rate of interest at which business customers can borrow money from banks (美國銀行的)最優惠貸款利率 ➲ compare BASE RATE

ˈprime time (*BrE* also **ˈpeak time**, **ˌpeak ˈviewing time**) *noun* [U] the time when the greatest number of people are watching television or listening to the radio (廣播、電視的)黃金時間：*prime-time television* 黃金時間的電視節目

pri·meval (also **prim·aeval**) /praɪˈmiːvl/ *adj.* [usually before noun] **1** from the earliest period of the history of the world, very ancient 遠古的；原始的：*primeval forests* 原始森林 **2** (*formal*) (of a feeling, or a desire 感覺或慾望) very strong and not based on reason, as if from the earliest period of human life 出於原始天性的：*primeval urges* 本能的慾望

primi·tive /ˈprɪmətɪv/ *adj., noun*

■ ***adj.*** **1** [usually before noun] belonging to a very simple society with no industry, etc. 原始的；遠古的：*primitive tribes* 原始部落 ◇ *primitive beliefs* 原始的信仰 **2** [usually before noun] belonging to an early stage in the development of humans or animals 原始的；人類或動物發展早期的：*primitive man* 原始人 **3** very simple and old-fashioned, especially when sth is also not convenient and comfortable 發展水平低的；落後的 SYN **crude**：*The methods of communication used during the war were primitive by today's standards.* 按今天的標準，大戰時期使用的通訊方法非常落後。◇ *The facilities on the campsite were very primitive.* 營地的設施非常簡陋。 **4** [usually before noun] (of a feeling or a desire 感覺或慾望) very strong and not based on reason, as if from the earliest period of human life 原始本能的：*a primitive instinct* 原始本能 ▶ **primi·tive·ly** *adv.* **primi·tive·ness** *noun* [U]

■ ***noun*** **1** an artist of the period before the Renaissance; an example of work from this period 文藝復興前的藝術家(或作品) **2** an artist who paints in a very simple style like a child; an example of the work of such an artist 原始派畫家(或作品)

primi·tiv·ism /ˈprɪmɪtɪvɪzəm/ *noun* [U] a belief that simple forms and ideas are the most valuable, expressed as a philosophy or in art or literature (哲學、藝術或文學的)原始主義，尚古主義，原始風格

primo·geni·ture /ˌpraɪməʊˈdʒenɪtʃə(r); *NAmE* -moʊ-/ *noun* [U] **1** (*formal*) the fact of being the first child born in a family 長子身分；長嗣身分 **2** (*law* 律) the system in which the oldest son in a family receives all the property when his father dies 長子繼承權

prim·or·dial /praɪˈmɔːdiəl; *NAmE* -ˈmɔːrdiəl/ *adj.* [usually before noun] (*formal*) **1** existing at or from the beginning of the world 原生的；原始的 SYN **primeval** **2** (of a feeling or a desire 感覺或慾望) very basic 基本的 SYN **primeval**：*primordial impulses* 本能的衝動

primp /prɪmp/ *verb* [I, T] **~ (sth/yourself)** (often *disapproving*) to make yourself look attractive by arranging your hair, putting on make-up, etc. 打扮；修飾

prim·rose /ˈprɪmrəʊz; *NAmE* -roʊz/ *noun* **1** [C] a small wild plant that produces pale yellow flowers in spring 報春花，櫻草(開黃色花) ➲ VISUAL VOCAB page V11 **2** (also **ˌprimrose ˈyellow**) [U] a pale yellow colour 淡黃色 ▶ **prim·rose** (also **ˌprimrose ˈyellow**) *adj.*

IDM **the primrose ˈpath** (*literary*) an easy life that is full of pleasure but that causes you harm in the end 追求享樂(招致惡果)

P

prim·ula /ˈprɪmjələ/ *noun* a type of primrose that is often grown in gardens/yards 報春花屬植物（廣泛栽種於庭園）

Pri·mus™ /ˈpraɪməs/ (also **ˈPrimus stove**) *noun* a small cooker/stove that you can move around that burns oil. It is used especially by people who are camping. 普賴默斯便攜式燃油爐

prince 🔑 /prɪns/ *noun*
1 🔑 a male member of a royal family who is not king, especially the son or grandson of the king or queen 王子；王孫；親王：*the royal princes* 親王 ◇ *the Prince of Wales* 威爾士親王 **2** 🔑 the male ruler of a small country or state that has a royal family; a male member of this family, especially the son or grandson of the ruler（小國的）國王，王室的男性成員，王子，王孫：*Prince Albert of Monaco* 摩納哥親王阿爾伯特 **3** (in some European countries) a NOBLEMAN（某些歐洲國家的）貴族 **4 ~ of/among sth** (*literary*) a man who is thought to be one of the best in a particular field（某一領域的）傑出人物，鉅子，大王：*the prince of comedy* 喜劇大師

ˌPrince ˈCharming *noun* [sing.] (usually *humorous*) a man who seems to be a perfect boyfriend or husband because he is very attractive, kind, etc. 白馬王子；（女子的）夢中情人 **ORIGIN** From the hero of some European fairy tales, for example *Cinderella* and *Sleeping Beauty*. 源自某些歐洲童話如《灰姑娘》和《睡美人》中的男主角。

ˌprince ˈconsort *noun* a title sometimes given to the husband of a queen who is himself a prince 王夫：*Prince Albert, the Prince Consort* 王夫艾伯特親王

prince·ling /ˈprɪnslɪŋ/ *noun* (usually *disapproving*) a prince who rules a small or unimportant country（小國的）國王，國君，大公

prince·ly /ˈprɪnsli/ *adj.* [usually before noun] **1** (usually *ironic*) if you say that an amount of money is **princely**, you are usually saying the opposite and that it is not very large 巨額的；龐大的：*I bought a bike for **the princely sum of** £20!* 我花 20 英鎊巨款買了一輛自行車！ **2** (*old-fashioned, formal*) very grand; generous 雄偉的；堂皇的；慷慨的：*princely buildings* 宏偉的建築 ◇ *a princely gift* 一份豐厚的禮物 **3** connected with a prince; like a prince 王子王孫的；王公貴族的；似王子的

the ˌPrince of ˈDarkness *noun* a name for the DEVIL 黑暗之王（指魔鬼）

the ˌPrince of ˈPeace *noun* a name for Jesus Christ 和平之主（指耶穌基督）

prin·cess 🔑 /ˌprɪnˈses; ˈprɪnses/ *noun*
1 🔑 a female member of a royal family who is not a queen, especially the daughter or granddaughter of the king or queen（除女王或王后外的）王室女成員；（尤指）公主：*the royal princesses* 王室女成員 ◇ *Princess Anne* 安妮公主 **2** 🔑 the wife of a prince 王妃；公貴族夫人：*the Princess of Wales* 威爾士王妃 ◇ *Princess Michael of Kent* 肯特郡邁克爾公爵夫人 **3** (*disapproving*) a young woman who has always been given everything that she wants, and who thinks that she is better than other people（受寵溺而自以為優越的）嬌小姐 **4** (*BrE, informal*) used as a form of address by a man to a girl or young woman（男子對女孩或年輕女子的稱呼）大小姐：*Is something the matter, princess?* 有什麼事嗎，大小姐？

ˌprincess ˈroyal *noun* a title often given to the oldest daughter of a British king or queen 長公主，大公主（英國授予君主長女的稱號）

prin·ci·pal **AW** /ˈprɪnsəpl/ *adj., noun*
■ ***adj.*** [only before noun] most important; main 最重要的；主要的：*The principal reason for this omission is lack of time.* 跳過它的主要原因是時間不足。◇ *New roads will link the principal cities of the area.* 新建道路將連通這個地區的主要城市。➲ **SYNONYMS** at MAIN
■ ***noun*** **1** (*BrE*) the person who is in charge of a college or a university 大學校長；學院院長：*Peter Brown, principal of St John's College* 彼得 • 布朗，聖約翰學院院長 ➲ see also DEAN (3) **2** (*NAmE*) (*BrE* **ˌhead ˈteacher**) a teacher who is in charge of a school 校長：*Principal Ray Smith* 雷 • 史密斯校長 **3** [usually sing.] (*finance* 財) an amount of money that you lend to sb or invest to earn interest 本金；資本 **4** the person who has the most important part in a play, an OPERA, etc. 主要演員；主角 **5** (*technical* 術語) a person that you are representing, especially in business or law（尤指商務或法律事務的）當事人，委託人

ˌprincipal ˈboy *noun* (*BrE*) the main male role in a PANTOMIME, usually played by a woman 英國童話劇男主角（通常由女演員扮演）

prin·ci·pal·ity /ˌprɪnsɪˈpæləti/ *noun* (*pl.* **-ies**) **1** [C] a country that is ruled by a prince 王公治理的國家；公國；侯國：*the principality of Monaco* 摩納哥公國 **2 the Principality** [sing.] (*BrE*) Wales 威爾士

prin·ci·pal·ly **AW** /ˈprɪnsəpli/ *adv.* mainly 主要地 **SYN** **chiefly**：*The book is aimed principally at beginners.* 這本書主要是為初學者編寫的。◇ *No new power stations have been built, principally because of the cost.* 沒有新建的發電站，主要是因為經費問題。

ˌprincipal ˈparts *noun* [pl.] (*grammar* 語法) the forms of a verb from which all the other forms can be made. In English these are the infinitive (for example *swim*), the past tense (*swam*) and the past participle (*swum*).（動詞）主要部份，主要形式（英語中有動詞的不定式、過去時和過去分詞）

prin·ciple 🔑 **AW** /ˈprɪnsəpl/ *noun*
1 🔑 [C, usually pl., U] a moral rule or a strong belief that influences your actions 道德原則；行為準則；規範：*He has high moral principles.* 他很有道德。◇ *I refuse to lie about it; **it's against my principles**.* 我絕不為此事撒謊；那是違背我的原則的。◇ ***Stick to your principles** and tell him you won't do it.* 要恪守自己的原則，告訴他你絕不會幹的。◇ *She refuses to allow her family to help her as **a matter of principle**.* 她不要家人幫忙，對她來説這是個原則問題。◇ *He doesn't invest in the arms industry **on principle**.* 他根據自己的信條，不投資軍火工業。 **2** 🔑 [C] a law, a rule or a theory that sth is based on 法則；原則；原理：*the principles and practice of writing reports* 報告寫作的理論與實踐 ◇ *The principle behind it is very simple.* 其中的原理十分簡單。◇ *There are three fundamental principles of teamwork.* 團隊合作有三個基本原則。◇ *Discussing all these details will get us nowhere; we must get back to **first principles*** (= the most basic rules). 一直談這些細節不會有結果的；我們必須回到根本原則上來。 **3** 🔑 [C] a belief that is accepted as a reason for acting or thinking in a particular way 觀念；（行動、思想的）理由，信條：*the principle that free education should be available for all children* 所有兒童都應該能享受免費教育的觀念 **4** 🔑 [sing.] a general or scientific law that explains how sth works or why sth happens 定律；工作原理：*the principle that heat rises* 熱氣上升的定律
IDM **in ˈprinciple** **1** 🔑 if something can be done **in principle**, there is no good reason why it should not be done although it has not yet been done and there may be some difficulties 原則上；理論上：*In principle there is nothing that a human can do that a machine might not be able to do one day.* 原則上，總會有一天，凡是人能做的事，機器就能做。 **2** 🔑 in general but not in detail 大體上；基本上：*They have agreed to the proposal in principle but we still have to negotiate the terms.* 他們已基本同意了這項提議，但我們還得磋商各項條款。

prin·cipled **AW** /ˈprɪnsəpld/ *adj.* **1** having strong beliefs about what is right and wrong; based on strong beliefs 是非觀念強的；原則性強的；基於堅定信念的：*a principled woman* 堅持原則的女人 ◇ *to take a principled stand against abortion* 採取反墮胎的原則性立場 **OPP** **unprincipled** **2** based on rules or truths 根據規則（或事實）的：*a principled approach to language teaching* 有理論基礎的語言教學法

print 🔑 /prɪnt/ *verb, noun*
■ ***verb***
▸ **LETTERS/PICTURES** 圖文 **1** 🔑 [T, I] **~ (sth)** to produce letters, pictures, etc. on paper using a machine that puts ink on the surface 在紙上印；打印：*Do you want your address printed at the top of the letter?* 你要不要把地址印在信的頂端？◇ *I'm printing a copy of the*

P

document for you. 我正在給你印一份這個文件。◇ *Each card is printed with a different message.* 每張卡片都印着不同的信息。◇ (*computing* 計) *Click on the icon when you want to print.* 你想打印時就點擊一下這個圖標。

▸ **BOOKS/NEWSPAPERS** 書報 **2** [T] **~ sth** to produce books, newspapers, etc. by printing them in large quantities 印刷：*They printed 30 000 copies of the book.* 這本書他們印了 3 萬冊。

▸ **PUBLISH** 出版 **3** [T] **~ sth** to publish sth in printed form 登載；刊登；發表：*The photo was printed in all the national newspapers.* 這張照片被刊登在各全國性報紙上。

▸ **PHOTOGRAPH** 照片 **4** [T] **~ sth** to produce a photograph from a film 洗印；沖洗：*I'm having the pictures developed and printed.* 我已把照片送去沖印。

▸ **WRITE** 書寫 **5** [I, T] to write without joining the letters together 用印刷體寫（字母之間筆畫不相連接）：*In some countries children learn to print when they first go to school.* 在有些國家，兒童剛上學時學習用印刷體書寫。◇ **~ sth** *Print your name and address clearly in the space provided.* 請用印刷體在空白處填寫你的姓名和住址。

▸ **MAKE MARK** 留痕跡 **6** [T] **~ sth (in/on sth)** to make a mark on a soft surface by pressing （在鬆軟的表面）壓印，印出：*The tracks of the large animal were clearly printed in the sand.* 這隻大動物的足跡清晰地印在沙灘上。◇ (*figurative*) *The memory of that day was indelibly printed on his brain.* 那天的記憶永不磨滅地深印在他的腦海裏。

▸ **MAKE DESIGN** 印圖案 **7** [T] to make a design on a surface or cloth by pressing a surface against it which has been coloured with ink or DYE 印（圖案）；印染：*They had printed their own design on the T-shirt.* 他們在 T 恤衫上印了自己設計的圖案。

IDM **the ˌprinted ˈword/ˈpage** what is published in books, newspapers, etc. 印在書報上的文字；書刊文字；印刷品：*the power of the printed word* 書刊文字的力量 ➲ more at LICENCE, WORTH *adj.*

PHR V **ˌprint sth↔ˈoff/ˈout** to produce a document or information from a computer in printed form （從計算機中）打印出 ➲ related noun PRINTOUT

■ ***noun***

▸ **LETTERS/NUMBERS** 文字；數字 **1** [U] letters, words, numbers, etc. that have been printed onto paper 印刷字體：*in* ***large/small/bold print*** 用大號／小號／粗字體 ◇ *The print quality of the new laser printer is superb.* 新激光打印機的打印質量好極了。➲ see also THE SMALL PRINT

▸ **NEWSPAPERS/BOOKS** 書報 **2** [U] used to refer to the business of producing newspapers, magazines and books 印刷行業；出版界：*the print media* 印刷媒體 ◇ *print unions* 出版業工會

▸ **MARK** 痕跡 **3** [C, usually pl.] a mark left by your finger, foot, etc. on the surface of sth 指紋；手印；腳印；足跡：*His prints were found on the gun.* 在槍上發現了他的指紋。➲ see also FINGERPRINT, FOOTPRINT (1)

▸ **PICTURE** 圖片 **4** [C] a picture that is cut into wood or metal then covered with ink and printed onto paper; a picture that is copied from a painting using photography 版畫；（用照相製版法製作的）繪畫複製品：*a framed set of prints* 一組鑲框的版畫 ➲ SYNONYMS at PICTURE ➲ COLLOCATIONS at ART

▸ **PHOTOGRAPH** 照片 **5** [C] a photograph produced from film （用底片洗印的）相片：*How many sets of prints would you like?* 你想洗幾套照片？◇ *a colour print* 一張彩色照片 ➲ SYNONYMS at PHOTOGRAPH

▸ **CLOTH** 織物 **6** [U, C] cotton cloth that has a pattern printed on it; this pattern 印花棉布（或圖案）；花樣：*a cotton print dress* 花布連衣裙 ◇ *a floral print* 花卉圖案 ➲ see also BLUEPRINT

IDM **get into ˈprint** to be published 被出版；被發表：*By the time this gets into print, they'll already have left the country.* 這篇東西發表的時候，他們將已經離開這個國家了。**in print** **1** (of a book 書籍) still available from the company that publishes it 繼續印行 **2** (of a person's work 作品) printed in a book, newspaper, etc. 已刊印；已出版：*It was the first time he had seen his name in print.* 那是他第一次見到自己的名字被刊印出來。**ˌout of ˈprint** (of a book 書籍) no longer available from the company that publishes it 絕版；不再印行

print·able /ˈprɪntəbl/ *adj.* (usually used with a negative 通常與否定詞連用) suitable to be repeated in writing and read by people 適宜刊印（或閱讀）的：*His comment when he heard the news was not printable* (= was very rude). 他聽到這消息時下的評語不宜刊登。**OPP** **unprintable**

ˌprinted ˈcircuit *noun* a CIRCUIT for electricity that uses thin strips of metal instead of wires to carry the current 印刷電路

print·er /ˈprɪntə(r)/ *noun*
1 a machine for printing text on paper, especially one connected to a computer 打印機，印表機（尤指與計算機相連的）：***a colour/laser printer*** 彩色／激光打印機 ➲ VISUAL VOCAB page V69 **2** a person or a company whose job is printing books, etc. 印刷商；印刷工人；印刷公司 **3** **printer's** (*pl.* **printers**) a place where books, etc. are printed 印刷廠

print·ing /ˈprɪntɪŋ/ *noun*
1 [U] the act of producing letters, pictures, patterns, etc. on sth by pressing a surface covered with ink against it 印刷；印刷術：*the invention of printing* 印刷術的發明 ◇ *the printing trade* 印刷業 ◇ *colour printing* 彩色印刷 **2** [C] the act of printing a number of copies of a book at one time （書籍的）一次印刷：*The book is in its sixth printing.* 這本書是第六次印刷了。**3** [U] a type of writing when you write all the letters separately and do not join them together 印刷字體

ˈprinting press *noun* a machine that produces books, newspapers, etc. by pressing a surface covered in ink onto paper 印刷機

print·maker /ˈprɪntmeɪkə(r)/ *noun* an artist who prints pictures or designs 版畫匠；版畫家

ˌprint on deˈmand *noun* (*abbr.* **POD**) [U] a system of printing books only when a customer wants one 按需印刷；隨選印刷：*The titles are available through print on demand.* 這些書刊可按需印刷。◇ *This is a print-on-demand title.* 這是按需印刷的書。

print·out /ˈprɪntaʊt/ *noun* [U, C] a page or set of pages containing information in printed form from a computer （計算機）打印件，打印資料：*a printout of text downloaded from the Internet* 從互聯網下載文本的打印件 ➲ VISUAL VOCAB page V69 ➲ compare READ-OUT

ˈprint run *noun* (*technical* 術語) the number of copies of a book, magazine, etc. printed at one time （書刊等的）一次印數，每次印數

print·works /ˈprɪntwɜːks; *NAmE* -wɜːrks/ *noun* (*pl.* **print·works**) (*BrE*) a factory where patterns are printed on cloth 印染廠；印花廠

prion /ˈpriːɒn; *NAmE* -ɑːn/ *noun* (*biology* 生) a very small unit of PROTEIN that is believed to be the cause of brain diseases such as BSE, CJD and SCRAPIE 普利子，傳染性蛋白質粒子，朊病毒（能導致腦病）

prior **AW** /ˈpraɪə(r)/ *adj.*, *noun*
■ ***adj.*** [only before noun] (*formal*) **1** happening or existing before sth else or before a particular time 先前的；較早的；在前的：*Although not essential, some* ***prior knowledge*** *of statistics is desirable.* 統計學的知識雖非必要，但最好是學過一點。◇ *This information must not be disclosed without* ***prior written consent.*** 未事先徵得書面許可，此消息不得泄露。◇ *Visits are by* ***prior arrangement.*** 參觀需要事先安排。◇ *Please give us* ***prior notice*** *if you need an evening meal.* 需用晚餐者，請預先通知我們。◇ *She will be unable to attend because of a* ***prior engagement.*** 因事先有別的安排，她將不能出席。
2 already existing and therefore more important 優先的；佔先的；較重要的：*They have a* ***prior claim*** *to the property.* 他們有權優先獲得該處房產。**3** **ˈprior to** before sth 在…前面的：*during the week prior to the meeting* 在開會前的一週內
■ ***noun*** (*feminine* **pri·or·ess** /ˈpraɪərəs; *BrE* also ˌpraɪəˈres/) **1** a person who is in charge of a group of MONKS or NUNS living in a PRIORY （小隱修院）上司 **2** (in an

P

ABBEY) a person next in rank below an ABBOT or ABBESS（隱修院）會長，副院長

pri·ori ➲ A PRIORI

pri·ori·tize (*BrE* also **-ise**) AW /praɪˈɒrətaɪz; *NAmE* -ˈɔːr-/ *verb* **1** [T, I] **~ (sth)** to put tasks, problems, etc. in order of importance, so that you can deal with the most important first 按重要性排列；劃分優先順序：*You should make a list of all the jobs you have to do and prioritize them.* 你應該把所有要做的事都列出來，並按輕重緩急排個順序。 **2** [T] **~ sth** (*formal*) to treat sth as being more important than other things 優先處理：*The organization was formed to prioritize the needs of older people.* 這個機構是為優先滿足老年人的需要而成立的。
▸ **pri·ori·tiza·tion**, **-isation** AW /praɪˌɒrətaɪˈzeɪʃn; *NAmE* -ˌɔːrətəˈz-/ *noun* [U]

pri·or·ity 0▬ AW /praɪˈɒrəti; *NAmE* -ˈɔːr-/ *noun* (*pl.* **-ies**)
1 0▬ [C] something that you think is more important than other things and should be dealt with first 優先事項；最重要的事；首要事情：*a **high/low priority*** 重點 / 非重點項目 ◇ *Education is a **top priority**.* 教育是當務之急。◇ *Our **first priority** is to improve standards.* 我們的頭等大事是提高水平。◇ *Financial security was high on his **list of priorities**.* 在他的心目中，財政穩固是十分重要的一環。◇ *You need to **get your priorities right*** (= decide what is important to you). 你需要把自己的事情分出輕重緩急。◇ (*NAmE*) *You need to **get your priorities straight**.* 你需要把個人事情的輕重緩急分清楚。 **2** 0▬ [U] **~ (over sth)** the most important place among various things that have to be done or among a group of people 優先；優先權；重點 SYN **precedence**：*Club members will be **given priority**.* 俱樂部成員享有優先權。◇ *The search for a new vaccine will **take priority over** all other medical research.* 研製新的疫苗將排在其他一切醫學研究之前。◇ *Priority cases, such as homeless families, get dealt with first.* 優先事項，比如無家可歸家庭的問題，得到優先處理。 **3** [U] (*BrE*) the right of a vehicle to go before other traffic at a particular place on a road（車輛的）優先通行權 SYN **right of way**：*Buses have priority at this junction.* 在這個路口，公共汽車有優先通行權。

P

pri·ory /ˈpraɪəri/ *noun* (*pl.* **-ies**) a building where a community of MONKS or NUNS lives, which is smaller and less important than an ABBEY 小修道院

prise (*especially BrE*) (*US* **prize**) /praɪz/ (also **pry** especially in *NAmE*) *verb* to use force to separate sth from sth else 強行使分開；撬開：**~ sth + adv./prep.** *He prised her fingers from the bag and took it from her.* 他掰開她的手指，把她手中的袋子搶走了。◇ **~ sth + adj.** *She used a knife to prise open the lid.* 她用刀把蓋子撬開了。

PHR V **ˌprise sth↔ˈout (of sb)** | **ˈprise sth from sb** to force sb to give you information about sb/sth（向某人）逼問情況；強迫…透露消息

prism /ˈprɪzəm/ *noun* **1** (*geometry* 幾何) a solid figure with ends that are parallel and of the same size and shape, and with sides whose opposite edges are equal and parallel 棱柱體；棱柱 ➲ VISUAL VOCAB page V71 **2** a transparent glass or plastic object, often with ends in the shape of a triangle, which separates light that passes through it into the colours of the RAINBOW 棱鏡；三棱鏡

pris·mat·ic /prɪzˈmætɪk/ *adj.* **1** (*technical* 術語) using or containing a prism; in the shape of a prism 用棱柱體（或棱鏡）的；棱柱形的 **2** (*literary*) (of colours 顏色) formed by a prism; very bright and clear 棱鏡折射的；分光的；絢麗的；五光十色的

prison 0▬ /ˈprɪzn/ *noun*
1 0▬ [C, U] a building where people are kept as a punishment for a crime they have committed, or while they are waiting for trial 監獄；牢獄；看守所 SYN **jail**：*He was **sent to prison** for five years.* 他被關押了五年。◇ *She is **in prison**, awaiting trial.* 她正在拘押候審中。◇ *to **be released from prison*** 被釋放出獄 ◇ *a **maximum-security prison*** 最高度戒備的監獄 ◇ *the **prison population*** (= the total number of prisoners in a country) 在押人數 ◇ *the problem of overcrowding in prisons* 監獄人滿為患的問題 ◇ *Ten prison officers and three inmates needed hospital treatment following the riot.* 騷亂之後，有十名獄警和三名囚犯需入院治療。➲ COLLOCATIONS at JUSTICE ➲ note at SCHOOL **2** 0▬ [U] the system of keeping people in prisons 監禁；關押；關押制度：*the **prison service/system*** 監獄管理機構 / 制度 ◇ *The government insists that 'prison works' and plans to introduce a tougher sentencing policy for people convicted of violent crime.* 政府堅持認為"關押有效"，並計劃對暴力犯罪者實行更嚴厲的判刑政策。 **3** [C] a place or situation from which sb cannot escape 難以脫身的地方（或處境）；牢籠；樊籠：*His hospital room had become a prison.* 他的病房變成了牢籠。

ˈprison camp *noun* a guarded camp where prisoners, especially prisoners of war or political prisoners, are kept 集中營；戰俘營

pris·on·er 0▬ /ˈprɪznə(r)/ *noun*
1 0▬ a person who is kept in prison as a punishment, or while they are waiting for trial 囚犯；犯人；羈押候審者：*The number of prisoners serving life sentences has fallen.* 被判無期徒刑的囚犯數目下降了。◇ *They are demanding the release of all **political prisoners**.* 他們正在要求釋放所有的政治犯。 **2** 0▬ a person who has been captured, for example by an enemy, and is being kept somewhere 被（敵人等）關起來的人；俘虜；戰俘：*He was **taken prisoner** by rebel soldiers.* 他被叛軍俘虜了。◇ *They are **holding** her **prisoner** and demanding a large ransom.* 他們把她劫持了，並索要巨額贖金。◇ (*figurative*) *She is afraid to go out and has become a virtual prisoner in her own home.* 她不敢出門，實際上已成了關在家中的囚犯。

ˌprisoner of ˈconscience *noun* (*pl.* **prisoners of conscience**) a person who is kept in prison because of his or her political or religious beliefs（因政治或宗教信仰）被關押的人；政治犯；宗教犯

ˌprisoner of ˈwar *noun* (*pl.* **prisoners of war**) (*abbr.* **POW**) a person, usually a member of the armed forces, who is captured by the enemy during a war and kept in a prison camp until the war has finished 戰俘；俘虜

ˌprison ˈvisitor *noun* (in Britain) a person who visits people in prison in order to help them, and who does not get paid for doing so（英國）義務探監者，探監義工

prissy /ˈprɪsi/ *adj.* (*informal, disapproving*) too careful to always behave correctly and appearing easily shocked by rude behaviour, etc. 謹小慎微的；大驚小怪的；拘泥謹慎的 SYN **prudish**

pris·tine /ˈprɪstiːn/ *adj.* **1** fresh and clean, as if new 嶄新的；清新的 SYN **immaculate**：*The car is **in pristine condition**.* 這輛汽車是全新的。 **2** not developed or changed in any way; left in its original condition 未開發的；處於原始狀態的 SYN **unspoiled**：*pristine, pollution-free beaches* 沒有污染的原始海灘

pri·thee /ˈprɪðiː/ *exclamation* (*old use*) used when asking sb politely to do sth 請；求您

priv·acy /ˈprɪvəsi; *NAmE* ˈpraɪv-/ *noun* [U] **1** the state of being alone and not watched or disturbed by other people 隱私；私密：*She was longing for some peace and privacy.* 她渴望過清靜的私人生活。◇ *I value my privacy.* 我重視自己的隱私。◇ *He read the letter later **in the privacy of** his own room.* 稍後，他在自己房間裏私下讀了那封信。 **2** the state of being free from the attention of the public 不受公眾干擾的狀態：*freedom of speech and the **right to privacy*** 言論自由與隱私權

pri·vate 0▬ /ˈpraɪvət/ *adj., noun*
■ ***adj.***
▸ **NOT PUBLIC** 非公開 **1** 0▬ [usually before noun] belonging to or for the use of a particular person or group; not for public use 私有的；私用的；自用的：*The sign said, 'Private property. Keep out.'* 標牌上寫着："私人領地，禁止進入。" ◇ *Those are my father's private papers.* 那些都是我父親的私人文件。◇ *The hotel has 110 bedrooms, all with private bathrooms.* 這家旅館有 110 間客房，各有獨立衛生間。

▸ CONVERSATION/MEETING 談話；會晤 **2** 🔑 intended for or involving a particular person or group of people, not for people in general or for others to know about 為一部份人的；私人的；秘密的：*a private conversation* 私人交談 ◇ *They were sharing a private joke.* 他們講着外人聽不懂的笑話。◇ *Senior defence officials held private talks.* 高級防務官員舉行了秘密會談。

▸ FEELINGS/INFORMATION 情感；信息 **3** 🔑 that you do not want other people to know about 內心的；隱秘的；私下的 SYN **secret**：*her private thoughts and feelings* 她私下的想法和感情

▸ NOT OWNED/RUN BY STATE 非國有 **4** 🔑 [usually before noun] owned or managed by an individual person or an independent company rather than by the state 私立的；私營的；民營的：***private banks*** 私營銀行 ◇ *a programme to return many of the state companies to **private ownership*** 把眾多國營公司轉為民營的計劃 OPP **public** **5** 🔑 [only before noun] working or acting for yourself rather than for the state or for a group or company, especially in health or education 個體的，獨立的，私人的（尤指醫療或教育）：*private doctors* 私人醫生 ◇ (*BrE*) *If I can afford it, I think I'll **go private*** (= pay for medical care rather than use the government service). 如果花得起，我想我會自費醫療的。

▸ NOT WORK 非工作 **6** 🔑 [usually before noun] not connected with your work or official position 與工作（或官職）無關的；個人的；私人的：*a politician's **private life*** 政界人物的私生活

▸ QUIET 清靜 **7** 🔑 where you are not likely to be disturbed; quiet 僻靜的；不受打擾的：*Let's go somewhere a bit more private.* 咱們另找個僻靜些的地方吧。OPP **public**

▸ PERSON 人 **8** [usually before noun] not wanting to share thoughts and feelings with other people 不願吐露心思的；內向的；不愛交流思想感情的：*He's a very private person.* 他是個悶葫蘆。

▸ LESSONS 課堂 **9** [usually before noun] given by a teacher, etc. to one person or a small group of people for payment 私人教授的；個別傳授的：*She gives private English lessons at weekends.* 她週末做私人英語家教。

▸ MONEY 錢 **10** that you receive from property or other sources but do not have to earn 由財產增溢的；間接收入的；非勞動所得的：*He has a private income.* 他有一筆私人收入。

▸ **pri·vate·ly** 🔑 *adv.*：*Can we speak privately?* 我們能單獨談談嗎？◇ *In public he supported the official policy, but privately he was sure it would fail.* 他明裏支持這項官方政策，但暗中卻確信它會失敗。◇ *a privately owned company* 私營公司 ◇ *Their children were educated privately.* 他們的子女都是上私立學校的。◇ *She smiled, but privately she was furious.* 她面露微笑，但心裏卻十分氣憤。

■ *noun* **1** [C] (*abbr.* **Pte**) (*BrE*) a soldier of the lowest rank in the army 二等兵，列兵（級別最低的士兵）：*Private (John) Smith* 列兵（約翰·）史密斯 **2** **privates** [pl.] (*informal*) = PRIVATE PARTS

IDM **in 'private** 🔑 with nobody else present 私下地；沒外人在場：*Is there somewhere we can discuss this in private?* 有沒有什麼地方能讓我們單獨談談這件事？ ➲ compare IN PUBLIC at PUBLIC *n.*

,private 'company (also **,private ,limited 'company**) *noun* (*business* 商) a business that may not offer its shares for sale to the public 私營公司；私人持股公司 ➲ compare PUBLIC COMPANY, PLC

,private de'tective (also **,private in'vestigator**) (also *informal* **,private 'eye**) *noun* a DETECTIVE who is not in the police, but who can be employed to find out information, find a missing person, follow sb, etc. 私人偵探

,private 'enterprise *noun* [U] the economic system in which industry or business is owned by independent companies or private people and is not controlled by the government 私營企業；民營企業 ➲ compare FREE ENTERPRISE

,private 'equity *noun* [U] (*finance* 財) investment made in a company, usually a small one, whose shares are not bought and sold by the public（通常指小公司的）私募股權，私人權益資本，私人股權投資

pri·vat·eer /ˌpraɪvəˈtɪə(r); *NAmE* -ˈtɪr/ *noun* a ship used in the past for attacking and stealing from other ships 武裝民船，私掠船（舊時用以攻擊和劫掠其他船隻）

,private 'law *noun* [U] (*law* 律) the part of the law that concerns individual people and their property 私法（涉及個人權益、財產等）

,private 'member *noun* (in the British political system) a member of parliament who is not a minister in the government 普通議員（英國議會中不擔任政府部長職位的議員）

,private 'member's bill *noun* (in the British political system) a law that is suggested by a member of parliament who is not a minister in the government and that is not part of the government's plans（英國政體）非閣僚議員提案

,private 'parts (also *informal* **pri·vates**) *noun* [pl.] a polite way of referring to the sexual organs without saying their names 私處

,private 'patient *noun* (in Britain) a person who is treated by a doctor outside the National Health Service and who pays for their treatment 自費病人（不受英國國民保健服務計劃補助者）

,private 'practice *noun* **1** [U] (of a profession 職業) the fact of working on your own or in a small independent company rather than as an employee of the government or a large company 私人開業：*Most solicitors in England and Wales are **in private practice**.* 英格蘭和威爾士的大多數律師都是私人執業者。 **2** [U, C] (in Britain) the fact of providing medical care outside the National Health Service, which people must pay for; a place providing this care 私人醫生開業，私營醫療院所（不屬於英國國民保健計劃）

,private 'school (also **inde,pendent 'school**) *noun* a school that receives no money from the government and where the education of the students is paid for by their parents 私立學校 ➲ compare PUBLIC SCHOOL (1), STATE SCHOOL (1)

,private 'secretary *noun* **1** a secretary whose job is to deal with the more important and personal affairs of a business person 私人秘書 **2** a CIVIL SERVANT who acts as an assistant to a senior government official 政府高級官員的助理

the ,private 'sector *noun* [sing.] the part of the economy of a country that is not under the direct control of the government（國家經濟的）私營部份 ➲ COLLOCATIONS at ECONOMY ➲ compare THE PUBLIC SECTOR

,private 'soldier *noun* a soldier of the lowest rank 列兵

,private 'view (also **,private 'viewing**) *noun* an occasion when a few people are invited to look at an exhibition of paintings before it is open to the public（局限於少數參觀者的）畫作預展

pri·va·tion /praɪˈveɪʃn/ *noun* [C, usually pl., U] (*formal*) a lack of the basic things that people need for living 貧困；匱乏；艱難 SYN **hardship**：*the privations of poverty* 艱難困苦 ◇ *They endured years of suffering and privation.* 他們飽受多年的煎熬與貧困。

pri·vat·ize (*BrE* also **-ise**) /ˈpraɪvətaɪz/ *verb* ~ **sth** to sell a business or an industry so that it is no longer owned by the government 使私有化；將…私營化 SYN **denationalize** OPP **nationalize** ▸ **pri·vat·iza·tion**, **-isa·tion** /ˌpraɪvətaɪˈzeɪʃn; *NAmE* -təˈz-/ *noun* [U]：*There were fears that privatization would lead to job losses.* 人們擔心私有化會導致失業。

privet /ˈprɪvɪt/ *noun* [U] a bush with small dark green leaves that remain on the bush and stay green all year, often used for garden HEDGES 女貞（常綠灌木，常用作花園綠籬）：*a privet hedge* 女貞樹籬

priv·il·ege /ˈprɪvəlɪdʒ/ *noun, verb*

■ *noun* **1** [C] a special right or advantage that a particular person or group of people has 特殊利益；優惠待遇：*Education should be a universal right and not a privilege.* 教育應當是全民共有的而非少數人獨享的權利。◇ *You*

P

can enjoy all the benefits and privileges of club membership. 你可以享受俱樂部成員的一切福利和優惠。 **2** [U] (*disapproving*) the rights and advantages that rich and powerful people in a society have （有錢有勢者的）特權，特殊待遇： *As a member of the nobility, his life had been one of wealth and privilege.* 身為貴族中的一員，他過着有錢有勢的生活。 **3** [sing.] something that you are proud and lucky to have the opportunity to do 榮幸；榮耀；光榮 **SYN** **honour** ： *I hope to have the privilege of working with them again.* 但願有幸與他們再度合作。 ◇ *It was a great privilege to hear her sing.* 聽她唱歌真是三生有幸。 ➲ SYNONYMS at PLEASURE **4** [C, U] (*technical* 術語) a special right to do or say things without being punished 免責特權： *parliamentary privilege* (= the special right of members of parliament to say particular things without risking legal action) 議會言論免責權

■ ***verb*** **~ sb/sth** (*formal*) to give sb/sth special rights or advantages that others do not have 給予特權；特別優待 **SYN** **favour** ： *education policies that privilege the children of wealthy parents* 特別優遇富家子弟的教育政策

priv·il·eged /ˈprɪvəlɪdʒd/ *adj.* **1** (sometimes *disapproving*) having special rights or advantages that most people do not have 有特權的；受特別優待的： *Those in authority were in a privileged position.* 有地位者自有特權。 ◇ *She comes from a privileged background.* 她出身特權階層。 ◇ *In those days, only* ***a privileged few*** *had the vote.* 在那個時代，只有少數特殊的人才享有選舉權。 **2** [not before noun] having an opportunity to do sth that makes you feel proud 榮幸；幸運 **SYN** **honoured** ： *We are privileged to welcome you as our speaker this evening.* 我們榮幸地歡迎您今晚來講演。 **3** (*law* 律) (of information 信息) known only to a few people and legally protected so that it does not have to be made public 特許保密的 **SYN** **confidential**

privy /ˈprɪvi/ *adj., noun*

■ ***adj.*** (*formal*) **~ to sth** allowed to know about sth secret 准許知情；可參與秘事： *She was not privy to any information contained in the letters.* 她未獲准接觸那些信的內容。

■ ***noun*** (*pl.* **-ies**) (*old-fashioned*) a toilet, especially an outdoor one （戶外）廁所，茅房

P

the ˌPrivy ˈCouncil *noun* [sing.+sing./pl. v.] (in Britain) a group of people who advise the king or queen on political affairs （英國）樞密院 ▸ **ˌPrivy ˈCouncillor** *noun*

the ˌprivy ˈpurse *noun* [sing.] (in Britain) an amount of money that the government gives to the king or queen to pay his or her private expenses plus some official expenses （由英國政府撥的）女王私用金，國王私用金

prize 🔑 /praɪz/ *noun, adj., verb*

■ ***noun*** **1** 🔑 an award that is given to a person who wins a competition, race, etc. or who does very good work 獎；獎賞；獎勵；獎品；獎金： *She was awarded the Nobel Peace prize.* 她獲頒諾貝爾和平獎。 ◇ *He* ***won first prize*** *in the woodwind section.* 他獲得木管樂器組一等獎。 ◇ *There are* ***no prizes for guessing*** (= it is very easy to guess) *who she was with.* 一下子就能猜出她和誰在一起了。 ◇ *I won £500 in* ***prize money***. 我獲得了 500 英鎊的獎金。 ◇ *Win a car in our grand* ***prize draw***! 參加我們的大抽獎，贏取一輛汽車！ ➲ see also CONSOLATION PRIZE **2** something very important or valuable that is difficult to achieve or obtain 難能可貴的事物；難以爭取的重要事物： *World peace is the greatest prize of all.* 世界和平是最可貴的。

■ ***adj.*** [only before noun] **1** (especially of an animal, a flower or a vegetable 尤指動物、花或蔬菜) good enough to win a prize in a competition 好得足以得獎的；應獲獎的： *prize cattle* 能獲獎的牛 **2** being a very good example of its kind 優秀的；典範性的；出類拔萃的： *a prize student* 模範學生 ◇ *He's a* ***prize specimen*** *of the human race!* 他是人中楷模！ ◇ (*informal*) *She's a* ***prize idiot*** (= very silly). 她是十足的蠢豬。

■ ***verb*** **1** [usually passive] to value sth highly 珍視；高度重視 **SYN** **treasure** ： **~ sth** *an era when honesty was prized above all other virtues* 尊誠實為美德之首的時代 ◇ **~ sth for sth** *Oil of cedarwood is* ***highly prized*** *for its use in perfumery.* 雪松油可用於製香水，因此十分珍貴。 **2** (*NAmE*) = PRISE

prized /praɪzd/ *adj.* [only before noun] very valuable to sb 珍貴的；寶貴的： *I lost some of my most* ***prized possessions*** *in the fire.* 大火吞噬了我的一些最珍貴的物品。

prize·fight /ˈpraɪzfaɪt/ *noun* a BOXING competition that is fought for money 職業拳擊賽 ▸ **prize·fight·er** *noun* **prize·fight·ing** *noun* [U]

ˈprize-giving *noun* (*BrE*) a ceremony at which prizes are given to people who have done very good work 頒獎儀式；頒獎典禮

prize·win·ner /ˈpraɪzwɪnə(r)/ *noun* a person who has won a prize 獲獎者；優勝者 ▸ **prize·win·ning** *adj.* [only before noun]： *a prizewinning story* 獲獎故事

pro /prəʊ; *NAmE* proʊ/ *noun, adj., prep.*

■ ***noun*** (*pl.* **pros**) (*informal*) a person who works as a professional, especially in a sport 從事某職業的人；職業運動員；職業選手；老手： *a golf pro* 職業高爾夫球選手 ◇ *He handled the situation like an* ***old pro*** (= sb who has a lot of experience). 他像行家一般處理了這一局面。

IDM **the ˌpros and ˈcons** the advantages and disadvantages of sth 事物的利與弊；支持與反對： *We weighed up the pros and cons.* 我們權衡了利弊得失。

■ ***adj.*** (*especially NAmE*) (in sport 體育運動) professional 職業的；專業的： *a pro wrestler* 職業摔跤手 ◇ *pro football* 職業足球 ◇ *a young boxer who's just* ***turned pro*** 剛轉為職業選手的年輕拳擊手

■ ***prep.*** (*informal*) if sb is **pro** sb/sth, they are in favour of or support that person or thing 贊成；支持： *He has always been pro the environment.* 他一向支持環境保護。 ➲ compare ANTI

pro- /prəʊ; *NAmE* proʊ/ *prefix* (in adjectives 構成形容詞) in favour of; supporting 擁護；支持；親： *pro-democracy* 擁護民主 ➲ compare ANTI- (1)

pro·active /ˌprəʊˈæktɪv; *NAmE* ˌproʊ-/ *adj.* (of a person or policy 人或政策) controlling a situation by making things happen rather than waiting for things to happen and then reacting to them 積極主動的；主動出擊的；先發制人的 ➲ compare REACTIVE (1) ▸ **pro·active·ly** *adv.*

ˌpro-ˈam *adj.* [only before noun] (in sport 體育運動) involving both professional and AMATEUR players 包括職業和業餘選手的： *a pro-am golf tournament* 包括職業和業餘選手參加的高爾夫球錦標賽 ▸ **ˌpro-ˈam** *noun*： *to play in a pro-am* 參加公開賽

prob·abil·ist·ic /ˌprɒbəbɪˈlɪstɪk; *NAmE* ˌprɑːb-/ *adj.* [usually before noun] (*technical* 術語) (of methods, arguments, etc. 方法、論點等) based on the idea that, as we cannot be certain about things, we can base our beliefs or actions on what is probable 基於概率的；或然的；蓋然性的

prob·abil·ity /ˌprɒbəˈbɪləti; *NAmE* ˌprɑːb-/ *noun* (*pl.* **-ies**) **1** [U, C] how likely sth is to happen 可能性；或然性 **SYN** **likelihood** ： *The probability is that prices will rise rapidly.* 物價有可能會迅速上升。 ◇ *There seemed to be a high probability of success.* 成功的幾率似乎很高。 **2** [C] a thing that is likely to happen 很可能發生的事： *A fall in interest rates is a* ***strong probability*** *in the present economic climate.* 在目前的經濟形勢下，降低利率大有可能。 ◇ *It now seems a probability rather than just a possibility.* 這件事似乎十拿九穩，而不是僅有可能。 **3** [C, U] (*mathematics* 數) a RATIO showing the chances that a particular thing will happen 概率；幾率；或然率： *There is a 60% probability that the population will be infected with the disease.* 民眾感染這種疾病的概率為 60%。

IDM **in ˌall probaˈbility** ... it is very likely that 很可能： *In all probability he failed to understand the consequences of his actions.* 他很可能未瞭解到行動的後果。 ➲ more at BALANCE *n.*

prob·able 🔑 /ˈprɒbəbl; *NAmE* ˈprɑːb-/ *adj., noun*

■ ***adj.*** 🔑 likely to happen, to exist or to be true 很可能發生（或存在等）的： *the probable cause/explanation/outcome* 可能的原因／解釋／結果 ◇ ***highly/quite/most probable*** 極其／相當／最可能的 ◇ ***It is probable that*** *the disease has a genetic element.* 這種疾病很可能有遺傳因素。 ➲ compare IMPROBABLE

■ ***noun* ~** (**for sth**) (*especially BrE*) a person or an animal that is likely to win a race or to be chosen for a team 可能獲勝的人（或動物）；可能入選者

prob·ably /ˈprɒbəbli; *NAmE* ˈprɑːb-/ *adv.* used to say that sth is likely to happen or to be true 幾乎肯定；很可能；大概：*You're probably right.* 你很可能是對的。◇ *It'll probably be OK.* 這大概沒有問題。◇ *It was the best known and probably the most popular of her songs.* 這是她最著名的、大概也是她最受歡迎的歌曲。◇ *'Is he going to be there?' 'Probably.'* "他會去那裏嗎？" "大概吧。" ◇ *'Do we need the car?' '**Probably not.**'* "我們需要開車嗎？" "大概不需要吧。" ◇ *As you probably know, I'm going to be changing jobs soon.* 你或許知道，我不久就要換工作了。◇ *The two cases are **most probably** connected.* 這兩樁案件極有可能互相關聯。 ➲ LANGUAGE BANK at PERHAPS

pro·bate /ˈprəʊbeɪt; *NAmE* ˈproʊ-/ *noun, verb*

■ ***noun*** [U] (*law* 律) the official process of proving that a WILL (= a legal document that says what is to happen to a person's property when they die) is valid 遺囑認證；遺囑檢驗

■ ***verb* ~ sth** (*NAmE, law* 律) to prove that a WILL is valid 核實（或檢驗）遺囑

pro·ba·tion /prəˈbeɪʃn; *NAmE* proʊ-/ *noun* [U] **1** (*law* 律) a system that allows a person who has committed a crime not to go to prison if they behave well and if they see an official (called a PROBATION OFFICER) regularly for a fixed period of time 緩刑制；緩刑：*The prisoner was put **on probation**.* 犯人已獲緩刑。◇ *He was given two years' probation.* 他被判緩刑兩年。 **2** a time of training and testing when you start a new job to see if you are suitable for the work 試用期；見習期；考察期：*a period of probation* 試用期 **3** (*NAmE*) a fixed period of time during which a student who has behaved badly or not worked hard must improve their work or their behaviour 試讀，試讀期（為表現未如理想的學生而設） ▸ **pro·ba·tion·ary** /prəˈbeɪʃnri; *NAmE* proʊˈbeɪʃəneri/ *adj.*：*a probationary period* 試用期 ◇ *young probationary teachers* 年輕的見習教師

pro·ba·tion·er /prəˈbeɪʃnə(r); *NAmE* proʊ-/ *noun* **1** a person who is new in a job and is being watched to see if they are suitable 試用員工 **2** a person who is seeing a PROBATION OFFICER because of having committed a crime 緩刑犯

proˈbation officer *noun* a person whose job is to check on people who are on probation and help them 緩刑監督官

probe /prəʊb; *NAmE* proʊb/ *verb, noun*

■ ***verb*** **1** [I, T] to ask questions in order to find out secret or hidden information about sb/sth 盤問；追問；探究 SYN **investigate**：**~ (into sth)** *He didn't like the media probing into his past.* 他不喜歡媒體追問他的過去。◇ **~ sth** *a TV programme that probed government scandals in the 1990s* 追查 20 世紀 90 年代政府醜聞的電視節目 ◇ **+ speech** *'Then what happened?' he probed.* "後來發生了什麼事？" 他追問道。 **2** [T] **~ sth** to touch, examine or look for sth, especially with a long thin instrument（用細長工具）探查，查看：*The doctor probed the wound for signs of infection.* 醫生檢查傷口是否有感染的跡象。◇ *Searchlights probed the night sky.* 探照燈掃視着夜空。

■ ***noun*** **1 ~** (**into sth**) (used especially in newspapers 尤用於報章) a thorough and careful investigation of sth 探究；詳盡調查：*a police probe into the financial affairs of the company* 警方對這家公司的財務進行的詳細調查 **2** (also **ˈspace probe**) a SPACECRAFT without people on board which obtains information and sends it back to earth（不載人）航天探測器，宇宙探測航天器 **3** (*technical* 術語) a long thin metal tool used by doctors for examining inside the body（醫生用的）探針 **4** (*technical* 術語) a small device put inside sth and used by scientists to test sth or record information 探測儀；傳感器；取樣器

prob·ing /ˈprəʊbɪŋ; *NAmE* ˈproʊ-/ *adj.* **1** intended to discover the truth 探查性的；追根究底的：*They asked a lot of **probing questions**.* 他們提了許多盤根問底的問題。 **2** examining sb/sth closely 逼視的；仔細觀察的：*She looked away from his dark probing eyes.* 她轉移目光，避開他那雙盯人的黑眼睛。 ▸ **prob·ing** *noun*：*the journalist's unwanted probings* 記者不受歡迎的追問

pro·biot·ic /ˌprəʊbaɪˈɒtɪk; *NAmE* ˌproʊbaɪˈɑːtɪk/ *adj.* [only before noun] encouraging the growth of bacteria that have a good effect on the body 促進有益菌生長的；益生菌的；益生素的：*probiotic products/yogurt/cheese* 益生菌產品／酸奶／乳酪

prob·ity /ˈprəʊbəti; *NAmE* ˈproʊ-/ *noun* [U] (*formal*) the quality of being completely honest 正直；誠實：*financial probity* 在錢財方面的誠實

prob·lem /ˈprɒbləm; *NAmE* ˈprɑːb-/ *noun, adj.*

■ ***noun*** **1** a thing that is difficult to deal with or to understand 棘手的問題；難題；困難：***big/major/serious problems*** 重大／主要／嚴重的問題 ◇ ***health/family, etc. problems*** 健康、家庭等問題 ◇ ***financial/practical/technical problems*** 財政／實際／技術困難 ◇ *to **address/tackle/solve a problem*** 處理／應付／解決難題 ◇ (*especially NAmE*) *to **fix a problem*** 解決問題 ◇ *the problem of drug abuse* 濫用毒品的問題 ◇ *If he chooses Mary it's bound to **cause problems**.* 如果他選上瑪麗，肯定要招來後患。◇ *Let me know if you have any problems.* 你若有困難就告訴我。◇ *Most students **face the problem** of funding themselves while they are studying.* 大多數學生在求學期間都會面臨經濟來源的問題。◇ *The problem first arose in 2008.* 這個問題首次出現在 2008 年。◇ *Unemployment is a very real problem for graduates now.* 現在，失業對大學畢業生是個實質問題。◇ *It's a nice table! **The only problem is** (**that**) it's too big for our room.* 這張桌子的確不錯！唯一的問題是放在我們的屋子裏太大了。◇ *Stop worrying about their marriage—it isn't your problem.* 別替他們的婚事操心了，那不關你的事。◇ *There's no history of heart problems* (= disease connected with the heart) *in our family.* 我們家族裏沒有心臟病史。◇ *the magazine's **problem page*** (= containing letters about readers' problems and advice about how to solve them) 這本雜誌的解疑專欄 **2** a question that can be answered by using logical thought or mathematics 邏輯題；數學題：*mathematical problems* 數學題 ◇ *to find the answer to the problem* 找出問題的答案

IDM **have a ˈproblem with sth** to disagree with or object to sth 對…有異議；不同意；反對：*I have no problem with you working at home tomorrow.* 你明天在家裏工作，我沒有意見。◇ (*informal*) *We are going to do this my way. **Do you have a problem with that?*** (= showing that you are impatient with the person that you are speaking to) 這件事將按照我的方法來做，你有什麼意見嗎？ **no ˈproblem** (*informal*) **1** (also **not a ˈproblem**) used to show that you are happy to help sb or that sth will be easy to do（表示樂於相助或事情容易做）沒問題：*'Can I pay by credit card?' 'Yes, no problem.'* "我能用信用卡付款嗎？" "行，沒問題。" **2** used after sb has thanked you or said they are sorry for sth（回答別人的道謝或道歉）沒什麼，不客氣，沒關係：*'Thanks for the ride.' 'No problem.'* "謝謝你載我一程。" "不客氣。" **ˌit's/ˌthat's not ˈmy problem** (*informal*) used to show that you do not care about sb else's difficulties 那不關我的事 **that's ˈher/ˈhis/ˈtheir/ˈyour problem** (*informal*) used to show that you think a person should deal with their own difficulties 那是她／他／他們／你自己的問題 **what's your problem?** (*informal*) used to show that you think sb is being unreasonable（認為對方不講道理時說）你怎麼了，你犯啥病啊：*What's your problem?—I only asked if you could help me for ten minutes.* 你有毛病啊？我只是問問你能不能抽十分鐘幫個忙而已。

■ ***adj.*** [only before noun] causing problems for other people 找麻煩的；成問題的；惹亂子的：*She was a **problem child**, always in trouble with the police.* 她曾是個問題兒童，總是給警察惹麻煩。

prob·lem·at·ic /ˌprɒbləˈmætɪk; *NAmE* ˌprɑːb-/ (also *less frequent* **prob·lem·at·ical** /-ɪkl/) *adj.* difficult to deal with or to understand; full of problems; not certain to be successful 造成困難的；產生問題的 OPP **unproblematic**

P

'problem-solving *noun* [U] the act of finding ways of dealing with problems 尋求答案；解決問題

pro bono /ˌprəʊ ˈbəʊnəʊ; *NAmE* ˌproʊ ˈboʊnoʊ/ *adj.* [only before noun] (from *Latin*) (especially of legal work 尤指法律工作) done without asking for payment 無償服務的；公益性的 ▸ **pro bono** *adv.*

pro·bos·cis /prəˈbɒsɪs; *NAmE* -ˈbɑːs-; *NAmE* also -ˈbɑːskɪs/ *noun* (*pl.* **pro·bos·ces** /-siːz/, **pro·bos·cises**) (*technical* 術語) **1** the long FLEXIBLE nose of some animals, such as an ELEPHANT（某些動物的）長鼻子；象鼻 **2** the long thin mouth, like a tube, of some insects（某些昆蟲的）管狀長嘴，針狀吻 **3** (*humorous*) a large human nose（人的）大鼻子

probs /prɒbz; *NAmE* prɑːbz/ *noun* [pl.]
IDM **no 'probs** (*informal*) used to mean 'there is no problem' 沒問題；一定：*I can let you have it by next week. No probs.* 我下週就會給你。沒問題。

pro·caine /ˈprəʊkeɪn; *NAmE* ˈproʊ-/ (also **novo·caine**) *noun* [U] (*medical* 醫) a substance used to stop sb from feeling pain in a particular part of their body, especially by a dentist 普魯卡因（牙醫等用的局部麻醉藥）

pro·ced·ure 0‑w AW /prəˈsiːdʒə(r)/ *noun* **1** 0‑w [C, U] **~ (for sth)** a way of doing sth, especially the usual or correct way（正常）程序，手續，步驟：*maintenance procedures* 維修程序 ◇ ***emergency/safety/disciplinary procedures*** 緊急狀況／安全事務／紀律問題的處理程序 ◇ *to follow **normal/standard/accepted procedure*** 遵循正常的／標準的／認可的步驟 ◇ *Making a complaint is quite a simple procedure.* 申訴的手續相當簡單。 **2** [U] the official or formal order or way of doing sth, especially in business, law or politics（商業、法律或政治上的）程序：***court/legal/parliamentary procedure*** 法庭／司法／議會程序 **3** [C] (*medical* 醫) a medical operation 手術：*to perform a routine surgical procedure* 做常規的外科手術 ▸ **pro·ced·ural** AW /prəˈsiːdʒərəl/ *adj.*：(*formal*) *procedural rules* 程序性規則

pro·ceed 0‑w AW /prəˈsiːd; *NAmE* proʊ-/ *verb* **1** 0‑w [I] **~ (with sth)** to continue doing sth that has already been started; to continue being done 繼續做（或從事、進行）：*We're not sure whether we still want to proceed with the sale.* 我們不確定是否還要繼續減價促銷。 ◇ *Work is proceeding slowly.* 工作進展緩慢。 **2** [I] **~ to do sth** to do sth next, after having done sth else first 接着做；繼而做 SYN **go on**：*He outlined his plans and then proceeded to explain them in more detail.* 他簡單介紹了他的計劃，接着又作了更詳細的解釋。 ◇ (*humorous*) *Having said she wasn't hungry, she then proceeded to order a three-course meal.* 她先說不餓，接着卻要了一份三道菜的大餐。 **3** [I] **+ adv./prep.** (*formal*) to move or travel in a particular direction 行進；前往：*The marchers proceeded slowly along the street.* 遊行者沿着街道緩緩行進。 ◇ *Passengers for Rome should proceed to Gate 32 for boarding.* 前往羅馬的旅客，請到 32 號登機口登機。
PHR V **pro'ceed against sb** (*law* 律) to start a court case against sb 起訴（某人） **pro'ceed from sth** (*formal*) to be caused by or be the result of sth 由…引起；起因於；是…的結果

pro·ceed·ing AW /prəˈsiːdɪŋ/ *noun* (*formal*) **1** [C, usually pl.] **~ (against sb) (for sth)** the process of using a court to settle a disagreement or to deal with a complaint 訴訟；訴訟程序：***bankruptcy/divorce/extradition, etc. proceedings*** 破產、離婚、引渡等訴訟 ◇ *to bring **legal proceedings** against sb* 向某人提起法律訴訟 **2 proceedings** [pl.] an event or a series of actions 事件；過程；一系列行動：*The Mayor will open the proceedings at the City Hall tomorrow.* 明天市長將在市政廳宣佈開幕。 ◇ *We watched the proceedings from the balcony.* 我們從陽台上觀看儀式。 **3 proceedings** [pl.] the official written report of a meeting, etc.（會議等的）正式記錄；公報

pro·ceeds AW /ˈprəʊsiːdz; *NAmE* ˈproʊ-/ *noun* [pl.] **~ (of/from sth)** the money that you receive when you sell sth or organize a performance, etc.; profits（售物或演出等的）收入，收益，進款：*She sold her car and bought a piano with the proceeds.* 她賣掉了汽車，然後用這筆收入買了一架鋼琴。 ◇ *The proceeds of the concert will go to charity.* 這次音樂會的收入將捐給慈善機構。

Language Bank 用語庫

process

Describing a process 描述過程

- This diagram **illustrates the process of** paper-making./This diagram **shows how** paper is made. 這個圖說明了造紙的過程。
- **First/First of all**, logs are delivered to a paper mill, where the bark is removed and the wood is cut into small chips. 首先，原木被運送到造紙廠，在那裏去掉樹皮，然後被切成木片。
- **Next/Second**, the wood chips are pulped, either using chemicals or in a pulping machine. 接下來，用化學品或磨漿機把木片化成漿。
- Pulping breaks down the internal structure of the wood and **enables/allows** the natural oils **to** be removed. 製漿過程使木材的內部結構分解，從而去除木材裏的天然油。
- **Once/After** the wood has been pulped, the pulp is bleached **in order to** remove impurities./… is bleached **so that** impurities **can** be removed. 木材製成漿後，將其漂白以去除雜質。
- **The next stage is to** feed the pulp into the paper machine, where it is mixed with water **and then** poured onto a wire conveyor belt. 下一步便是將紙漿送入製紙機，與水混合後再倒入金屬傳送帶。
- **As** the pulp travels along the conveyor belt, the water drains away. **This causes** the solid material **to** sink to the bottom, forming a layer of paper. 當紙漿沿傳送帶傳送時，水分蒸發，使得固體物質沉到底部，形成一層紙。
- **At this point** the new paper is still wet, **so** it is passed between large heated rollers, which press out the remaining water and **simultaneously** dry the paper./… dry the paper **at the same time**. 這時，新出的紙仍然是濕的，故讓其經過幾個巨大的熱滾筒，擠壓脫水並同時烘乾。
- **The final stage is to** wind the paper onto large rolls./**Finally**, the paper is wound onto large rolls. 最後一步是將紙捲在巨大的捲軸上。

➲ notes at FIRSTLY, LASTLY
➲ Language Banks at CONCLUSION, FIRST

pro·cess[1] 0‑w AW /ˈprəʊses; *NAmE* ˈprɑːses; ˈproʊ-/ *noun, verb* ➲ see also PROCESS[2]

▪ *noun* **1** 0‑w a series of things that are done in order to achieve a particular result（為達到某一目標的）過程；進程：*a consultation process* 磋商過程 ◇ *to begin the difficult process of reforming the education system* 開始改革教育制度的艱難歷程 ◇ *I'm afraid getting things changed will be a slow process.* 做任何改革恐怕都會是個緩慢的過程。 ◇ *mental processes* 思維過程 ◇ *Coming off the drug was a long and painful* (= difficult) *process for him.* 戒毒對他是個漫長、痛苦的過程。 ◇ *Find which food you are allergic to by **a process of elimination**.* 用淘汰法找出你對哪種食物過敏。 ◇ *We're **in the process of** selling our house.* 我們正在出售自家的住宅。 ◇ *I was moving some furniture and I twisted my ankle **in the process*** (= while I was doing it). 我在搬動傢具時把腳給崴了。 ➲ see also PEACE PROCESS **2** 0‑w a series of things that happen, especially ones that result in natural changes（事物發展，尤指自然變化的）過程，步驟，流程：*the ageing process* 老化過程 ◇ *It's a normal part of the **learning process**.* 那是學習過程中的正常現象。 **3** 0‑w a method of doing or making sth, especially one that is used in industry 做事方法；工藝流程；工序：*manufacturing processes* 製造方法

▪ *verb* **1** 0‑w **~ sth** to treat raw material, food, etc. in order to change it, preserve it, etc. 加工；處理：*Most of the food we buy is processed in some way.* 我們買的大部份食

品都用某種方法加工過。◇ *processed cheese* 加工好的乾酪 ◇ *a sewage processing plant* 污水處理廠 **2 ~ sth** to deal officially with a document, request, etc. 審閱，審核，處理（文件、請求等）： *It will take a week for your application to be processed.* 審核你的申請需要一週時間。 **3 ~ sth** (*computing* 計) to perform a series of operations on data in a computer 數據處理 ▸ **pro·cess·ing** AW *noun* [U]： *the food processing industry* 食品加工業 ➲ see also DATA PROCESSING, WORD PROCESSING

pro·cess² /prə'ses/ *verb* [I] **+ adv./prep.** (*formal*) to walk or move along slowly in, or as if in, a procession 列隊行進；緩緩前進 ➲ see also PROCESS¹

pro·ces·sion /prə'seʃn/ *noun* **1** [C, U] a line of people or vehicles that move along slowly, especially as part of a ceremony; the act of moving in this way （人或車輛的）隊列，行列；列隊行進；遊行： *a funeral procession* 送葬的隊列 ◇ *a torchlight procession* 火炬遊行隊伍 ◇ *The procession made its way down the hill.* 隊伍走下山了。◇ *Groups of unemployed people from all over the country marched* ***in procession*** *to the capital.* 來自全國的失業群眾列隊向首都進發。 **2** [C] a number of people who come one after the other （一個接着一個而來的）一隊人，一列人： *A procession of waiters appeared bearing trays of food.* 一長列服務生端着一盤一盤飯菜出現了。

pro·ces·sion·al /prə'seʃənl/ *adj.* [only before noun] used in a procession, especially a religious one; connected with a procession 供（宗教）遊行用的；列隊行進的

pro·ces·sor /'prəʊsesə(r); *NAmE* 'prɑː-; 'proʊ-/ *noun* **1** a machine or person that processes things 加工機（或工人） **2** (*computing* 計) a part of a computer that controls all the other parts of the system 處理器；處理機 SYN **central processing unit** ➲ see also FOOD PROCESSOR, MICROPROCESSOR, WORD PROCESSOR

ˌpro-'choice *adj.* believing that a pregnant woman should be able to choose to have an ABORTION if she wants 提倡墮胎合法的；主張自由選擇人工流產的 ➲ compare ANTI-CHOICE, PRO-LIFE

pro·claim /prə'kleɪm/ *verb* (*formal*) **1** to publicly and officially tell people about sth important 宣佈；宣告；聲明 SYN **declare**： **~ sth** *The president proclaimed a state of emergency.* 總統宣佈了緊急狀態。◇ **~ that ...** *The charter proclaimed that all states would have their own government.* 憲章規定，所有各州皆允建立各自的政府。◇ **~ sb/sth/yourself + noun** *He proclaimed himself emperor.* 他自封為皇帝。◇ **~ sb/sth/yourself to be/have sth** *Steve checked the battery and proclaimed it to be dead.* 史蒂夫檢查了電池後宣佈它沒電了。◇ **~ how, what, etc. ...** *The senator proclaimed how shocked he was at the news.* 那名參議員聲稱他聽到這消息時是多麼的震驚。◇ **+ speech** *'We will succeed,' she proclaimed.* "我們會成功的。" 她宣稱。 **2** to show sth clearly; to be a sign of sth 明確顯示；成為標誌；表明： **~ sth** *This building, more than any other, proclaims the character of the town.* 這座建築比任何其他建築都能代表本城的特色。◇ **~ sb/sth + noun** *His accent proclaimed him a Scot.* 他的口音表明他是蘇格蘭人。◇ **~ sb/sth to be/have sth** *His accent proclaimed him to be a Scot.* 他的口音表明他是蘇格蘭人。

proc·lama·tion /ˌprɒklə'meɪʃn; *NAmE* ˌprɑːk-/ *noun* [C, U] an official statement about sth important that is made to the public; the act of making an official statement 宣言；公告；聲明

pro·cliv·ity /prə'klɪvəti/ *noun* (*pl.* **-ies**) **~ (for sth/for doing sth)** (*formal*) a natural tendency to do sth or to feel sth, often sth bad （常指對壞事的）傾向，癖好 SYN **propensity**： *his sexual/criminal proclivities* 他的性傾向／犯罪傾向 ◇ *the government's proclivity for spending money* 政府花錢的傾向

pro·cras·tin·ate /prəʊ'kræstɪneɪt; *NAmE* proʊ-/ *verb* [I] (*formal, disapproving*) to delay doing sth that you should do, usually because you do not want to do it 拖延；耽擱 ▸ **pro·cras·tin·ation** /prəʊˌkræstɪ'neɪʃn; *NAmE* proʊ-/ *noun* [U]

pro·cre·ate /'prəʊkrieɪt; *NAmE* 'proʊ-/ *verb* [I, T] **~ (sth)** (*formal*) to produce children or baby animals 繁殖；生育；生殖 SYN **reproduce** ▸ **pro·cre·ation** /ˌprəʊkri'eɪʃn; *NAmE* ˌproʊ-/ *noun* [U]： *They believe that sex is primarily for procreation.* 他們認為，性交主要是為了繁衍。

Pro·crus·tean /ˌprəʊ'krʌstiən; *NAmE* ˌproʊ-/ *adj.* (of a system, a set of rules, etc. 體系或系列規章等) treating all people or things as if they are the same, without considering individual differences and in a way that is too strict and unreasonable 強求一致的；一刀切的 ORIGIN From the Greek story of **Procrustes**, a robber who forced people to lie on a bed and made them fit it by stretching their bodies or cutting off part of their legs. 源自有關強盜普洛克路斯忒斯（Procrustes）的希臘傳說，他迫使人們躺在一張牀上並通過拽拉身體或截腿使其適合牀的長度。

proc·tor /'prɒktə(r); *NAmE* 'prɑːk-/ (*NAmE*) (*BrE* **in·vigi·la·tor**) *noun* a person who watches people while they are taking an exam to make sure that they have everything they need, that they keep to the rules, etc. 監考人員 ▸ **proc·tor** (*NAmE*) (*BrE* **in·vigi·late**) *verb* [T, I] **~ (sth)**

proc·ur·ator fis·cal /ˌprɒkjureɪtə 'fɪskl; *NAmE* ˌprɑːkjəreɪtər/ *noun* (*pl.* **proc·ur·ators fis·cal**) (in Scotland) a public official whose job is to decide whether people who are suspected of a crime should be brought to trial （蘇格蘭）地方檢察官

pro·cure /prə'kjʊə(r); *NAmE* -'kjʊr/ *verb* **1** [T] (*formal*) to obtain sth, especially with difficulty （設法）獲得，取得，得到： **~ sth (for sb/sth)** *She managed to procure a ticket for the concert.* 她好不容易弄到一張音樂會入場券。◇ *They procured a copy of the report for us.* 他們為我們弄到了一份報告。◇ **~ sb sth** *They procured us a copy of the report.* 他們給我們弄到了一份報告。 **2** [T, I] **~ (sb)** to provide a PROSTITUTE for sb 誘使（婦女）賣淫： *He was accused of procuring under-age girls.* 他被控唆使未成年女性賣淫。

pro·cure·ment /prə'kjʊəmənt; *NAmE* -'kjʊrm-/ *noun* [U] (*formal*) the process of obtaining supplies of sth, especially for a government or an organization （尤指為政府或機構）採購，購買

P

prod /prɒd; *NAmE* prɑːd/ *verb, noun*

■ *verb* (**-dd-**) **1** [T, I] to push sb/sth with your finger or with a pointed object 戳；杵；捅 SYN **poke**： **~ sb/sth (+ adv./prep.)** *She prodded him in the ribs to wake him up.* 她用手指杵他的肋部把他叫醒。◇ **~ at sb/sth** *He prodded at his breakfast with a fork.* 他拿叉子戳弄着早餐。 **2** [T] **~ sb (into sth/into doing sth)** to try to make sb do sth, especially when they are unwilling 催促；督促；鼓動： *She finally prodded him into action.* 她終於促使他行動起來。

■ *noun* **1** the act of pushing sb with your finger or with a pointed object 戳；杵；捅 SYN **dig**： *She gave him a sharp prod with her umbrella.* 她用雨傘使勁捅了他一下。 **2** (*informal*) an act of encouraging sb or of reminding sb to do sth 催促；鼓勵；提醒： *If they haven't replied by next week, you'll have to call them and* ***give them a prod.*** 如果下週他們還沒答覆，你就得打電話催催他們。 **3** an instrument like a stick that is used for prodding animals （趕牲畜用的）尖棒，刺棒 **4 Prod** (also **Prod·die** /'prɒdi; *NAmE* 'prɑːdi/) (*informal*) an offensive word for a Protestant （貶稱）新教徒

prod·ding /'prɒdɪŋ; *NAmE* 'prɑːd-/ *noun* [U] encouragement to do sth 催促；督促；鼓勵；激勵： *He needed no prodding.* 他不用督促。

prod·igal /'prɒdɪgl; *NAmE* 'prɑːd-/ *adj.* (*formal, disapproving*) too willing to spend money or waste time, energy or materials 浪費的；揮霍的；大手大腳的 SYN **extravagant** ▸ **prod·ig·al·ity** /ˌprɒdɪ'gæləti; *NAmE* ˌprɑːd-/ *noun* [U]

IDM **the/a ˌprodigal ('son)** a person who leaves home and wastes their money and time on a life of pleasure, but who later is sorry about this and returns home 回頭的浪子；改邪歸正的人

pro·di·gious /prə'dɪdʒəs/ *adj.* [usually before noun] (*formal*) very large or powerful and causing surprise or admiration 巨大的；偉大的 SYN **colossal, enormous**：

a prodigious achievement/memory/talent 驚人的成就／記憶力／才華 ◇ *DVDs can store* **prodigious amounts** *of information.* * DVD光盤能夠貯存大量信息。 ▶ **pro·di·gious·ly** *adv.* : *a prodigiously talented musician* 有驚人天賦的音樂家

prod·igy /ˈprɒdədʒi; *NAmE* ˈprɑːd-/ *noun* (*pl.* **-ies**) a young person who is unusually intelligent or skilful for their age （年輕的）天才，奇才，精英；神童： ***a child/an infant prodigy*** 天才兒童；神童 ◇ *a musical prodigy* 音樂奇才

pro·duce 🔑 *verb, noun*

WORD FAMILY
produce *verb*
producer *noun*
production *noun*
productive *adj.* (≠ unproductive)
productively *adv.*
product *noun*
produce *noun*

■ ***verb*** /prəˈdjuːs; *NAmE* -ˈduːs/

▸ **GOODS** 商品 **1** 🔑 **~ sth** to make things to be sold, especially in large quantities 生產；製造 **SYN** **manufacture** : *a factory that produces microchips* 微芯片製造廠 ➲ SYNONYMS at MAKE, PRODUCT ➲ see also MASS-PRODUCE

▸ **MAKE NATURALLY** 自然生產 **2** 🔑 **~ sth** to grow or make sth as part of a natural process; to have a baby or young animal 生長；出產；繁育： *The region produces over 50% of the country's wheat.* 這個地區出產全國 50% 以上的小麥。◇ *Our cat produced kittens last week.* 我家的貓上週生小貓咪了。◇ *Her duty was to produce an heir to the throne.* 她的任務就是生育王位繼承人。

▸ **CREATE WITH SKILL** 巧妙製作 **3** 🔑 **~ sth** to create sth, especially when skill is needed （運用技巧）製作，造出： *She produced a delicious meal out of a few leftovers.* 她用幾樣剩菜烹製出美味的一餐。

▸ **RESULT/EFFECT** 結果；效果 **4** 🔑 **~ sth** to cause a particular result or effect 引起；導致；使產生 **SYN** **bring about** : *A phone call to the manager produced the result she wanted.* 她給經理打了個電話便如願以償。◇ *The drug produces a feeling of excitement.* 這種藥能使人產生興奮的感覺。

▸ **SHOW/BRING OUT** 展示；出示 **5 ~ sth (from/out of sth)** to show sth or make sth appear from somewhere 出示；展現；使出現： *He produced a letter from his pocket.* 他從口袋裏掏出一封信來。◇ *At the meeting the finance director produced the figures for the previous year.* 會上，財務總監出示了前一年的數字。

▸ **PERSON** 人 **6 ~ sb** if a town, country, etc. **produces** sb with a particular skill or quality, the person comes from that town, country, etc. 栽培；培養： *He is the greatest athlete this country has ever produced.* 他是這個國家曾經栽培出來的運動員中最了不起的一個。

▸ **MOVIE/PLAY** 電影；戲劇 **7 ~ sth** to be in charge of preparing a film/movie, play, etc. for the public to see 製作，拍攝（電影、戲劇等）；監督： *She produced a TV series about adopted children.* 她拍了一部描寫收養兒童的電視系列片。

■ ***noun*** /ˈprɒdjuːs; *NAmE* ˈprɑːduːs; ˈproʊ-/ [U] things that have been made or grown, especially things connected with farming 產品；（尤指）農產品： *farm produce* 農產品 ◇ *The shop sells only fresh local produce.* 這家商店只售當地的新鮮農產品。◇ *It says on the label 'Produce of France'.* 標籤上寫着"法國出產"。

pro·du·cer 🔑 /prəˈdjuːsə(r); *NAmE* -ˈduː-/ *noun* **1** 🔑 a person, a company or a country that grows or makes food, goods or materials 生產商；製造商；產地： *French wine producers* 法國葡萄酒釀造商 ◇ *Libya is a major oil producer.* 利比亞是主要石油生產國之一。 ➲ compare CONSUMER **2** 🔑 a person who is in charge of the practical and financial aspects of making a film/movie or a play （電影的）製片人，監製人；舞台監督： *Hollywood screenwriters, actors and producers* 好萊塢的劇作家、演員和製片人 ➲ compare DIRECTOR (3) **3** a person or company that arranges for sb to make a programme for radio or television, or a record, CD, etc. （廣播、電視、唱片等的）製作人，製作公司，監製： *an independent television producer* 獨立電視節目製作人

prod·uct 🔑 /ˈprɒdʌkt; *NAmE* ˈprɑːd-/ *noun* **1** 🔑 [C, U] a thing that is grown or produced, usually for sale 產品；製品： ***dairy/meat/pharmaceutical, etc. products*** 乳製品、肉製品、藥物產品等 ◇ *investment in* ***product development*** 產品開發投資 ◇ *to* ***launch a new product*** *on to the market* 把新產品推向市場 ◇ (*business* 商) *We need new product to sell* (= a new range of products). 我們需要新產品供銷售。 ➲ COLLOCATIONS at BUSINESS ➲ see also END PRODUCT, GROSS NATIONAL PRODUCT **2** 🔑 [C] a thing produced during a natural, chemical or industrial process （自然、化學或工業過程的）產物，生成物，產品： *the products of the reaction* 反應的生成物 ➲ see also BY-PRODUCT, WASTE PRODUCT **3** [C] **~ of sth** a person or thing that is the result of sth 產兒；產物；結果： *The child is the product of a broken home.* 這孩子是一個破裂家庭的產兒。 **4** [C, U] a cream, jelly or liquid that you put on your hair or skin to make it look better 美容（或美髮）用品（指髮乳、髮膠、潤膚霜、潤膚水等）： *This product can be used on wet or dry hair.* 這種美髮用品可用於濕髮或乾髮上。 **5** (*mathematics* 數) [C] a quantity obtained by multiplying one number by another 乘積；積： *The product of 21 and 16 is 336.* * 21 和 16 的乘積是 336。

Synonyms 同義詞辨析

product

goods · commodity · merchandise · produce

These are all words for things that are produced to be sold. 以上各詞均指產品、商品。

product a thing that is produced or grown, usually to be sold 指製造或種植的產品： *to create/develop/launch a new product* 創造／開發／推出新產品

goods things that are produced to be sold 指商品、貨品： *cotton/leather goods* 棉織／皮革商品 ◇ *electrical goods* 電器商品

commodity (*economics*) a product or raw material that can be bought and sold, especially between countries 尤指國家間貿易的商品： *rice, flour and other basic commodities* 稻米、麪粉和其他基本商品

merchandise [U] goods that are bought or sold; things that you can buy that are connected with or advertise a particular event or organization 指商品、貨品、相關商品、指定商品： *official Olympic merchandise* 奧林匹克運動會官方指定商品

GOODS OR MERCHANDISE? 用 goods 還是 merchandise？

Choose **goods** if the emphasis is on what the product is made of or what it is for. 強調商品製作的原料或用途用 goods： *leather/household goods* 皮革商品；家庭用品 Choose **merchandise** if the emphasis is less on the product itself and more on its brand or the fact of buying/selling it. 如果不太強調商品本身，而更強調品牌或交易用 merchandise。

produce [U] things that have been grown or made, especially things connected with farming 尤指農產品，也包括其他種植或製造的產品： *We sell only fresh local produce.* 我們只售當地的新鮮農產品。

PATTERNS

- **consumer/industrial** products/goods/commodities
- **household** products/goods
- **farm** products/produce
- **luxury** products/goods/commodities
- to **sell/market** a product/goods/a commodity/merchandise/produce
- to **export** a product/goods/a commodity/merchandise
- to **buy/purchase** a product/goods/a commodity/merchandise/produce

pro·duc·tion 🔑 /prəˈdʌkʃn/ *noun* **1** 🔑 [U] the process of growing or making food, goods or materials, especially large quantities 生產；製造；

製作：*wheat/oil/car, etc.* ***production*** 小麥、石油、汽車等的生產 ◇ *land available for* ***food production*** 可用於食品生產的土地 ◇ *The new model will be* ***in production*** *by the end of the year.* 新型號將於年底投產。◇ *Production of the new aircraft will start next year.* 新飛機的生產將於明年開始。◇ *The car* ***went out of production*** *in 2007.* 這款汽車已於 2007 年停產。◇ *production costs* 生產成本 ◇ *a production process* 生產工序 ➲ see also MASS PRODUCTION at MASS-PRODUCE **2** 🔑 [U] the quantity of goods that is produced 產量：***a decline/an increase in production*** 產量的下降／上升 ◇ *It is important not to let* ***production levels*** *fall.* 重要的是別讓產量滑落。**3** 🔑 [U] the act or process of making sth naturally（自然的）產生，分泌：*drugs to stimulate the body's production of hormones* 刺激身體分泌荷爾蒙的藥物 **4** 🔑 [C, U] a film/movie, a play or a broadcast that is prepared for the public; the act of preparing a film or a play, etc.（電影、戲劇或廣播節目的）上映，上演，播出，製作：*a new production of 'King Lear'* 新製作的《李爾王》◇ *He wants a career in film production.* 他想從事電影製作。

IDM **on production of sth** (*formal*) when you show sth 經出示（某物）：*Discounts only on production of your student ID card.* 須出示學生證方可打折。

pro'duction line (also **as'sembly line**) *noun* a line of workers and machines in a factory, along which a product passes, having parts made, put together or checked at each stage until the product is finished 生產線；裝配線；流水線：*Cars are checked as they come off the production line.* 汽車下了生產線立即作檢驗。

pro'duction number *noun* a scene in a musical play or a film/movie where a lot of people sing and dance（音樂劇、電影中的）集體歌舞

pro·duct·ive /prə'dʌktɪv/ *adj.* **1** making goods or growing crops, especially in large quantities 生產的；（尤指）多產的：***highly productive*** *farming land* 高產農田 ◇ *productive workers* 高效工人 **OPP** **unproductive** **2** doing or achieving a lot 有效益的；富有成效的 **SYN** **fruitful**：*a productive meeting* 有成效的會議 ◇ *My time spent in the library was very productive.* 我花在圖書館的時間很有收穫。➲ compare COUNTERPRODUCTIVE **3** **~ of sth** (*formal*) resulting in sth or causing sth 引起；導致；喚起：*a play productive of the strongest emotions* 喚起強烈感情的一齣戲 ▸ **pro·duct·ive·ly** *adv.*：*to use land more productively* 更有效地利用土地 ◇ *It's important to spend your time productively.* 重要的是要有效地利用時間。

prod·uct·iv·ity /ˌprɒdʌk'tɪvəti; *NAmE* ˌprɑːd-; ˌproʊd-/ *noun* [U] the rate at which a worker, a company or a country produces goods, and the amount produced, compared with how much time, work and money is needed to produce them 生產率；生產效率：***high/improved/increased productivity*** 高的／提高了的／增長了的生產率 ◇ *Wage rates depend on levels of productivity.* 工資水平取決於生產量的多寡。

ˌproduct 'placement *noun* [U, C] the use of particular products in films/movies or television programmes in order to advertise them 植入式廣告，置入性行銷（為了廣告目的而在電影或電視節目中使用某些產品）

Prof. *abbr.* (in writing 書寫形式) PROFESSOR 教授：*Prof. Mike Harrison* 邁克 • 哈里森教授

prof /prɒf; *NAmE* prɑːf/ *noun* (*informal*) = PROFESSOR：*a college prof* 大學教授

pro·fane /prə'feɪn/ *adj.*, *verb*

▪ ***adj.*** **1** (*formal*) having or showing a lack of respect for God or holy things 褻瀆神靈的；褻聖的：*profane language* 褻瀆上帝的語言 **2** (*technical* 術語) not connected with religion or holy things 非宗教的；世俗的 **SYN** **secular**：*songs of sacred and profane love* 歌唱聖潔與世俗愛情的歌曲

▪ ***verb*** **~ sth** (*formal*) to treat sth holy with a lack of respect 褻瀆神靈；褻聖

pro·fan·ity /prə'fænəti; *NAmE* also proʊ'f-/ *noun* (*pl.* **-ies**) (*formal*) **1** [U] behaviour that shows a lack of respect for God or holy things 褻聖；對神靈的褻瀆 **2** [C, usually pl.] swear words, or religious words used in a way that shows a lack of respect for God or holy things（褻聖的）詛咒語：*He uttered a stream of profanities.* 他髒話連篇。

pro·fess /prə'fes/ *verb* (*formal*) **1** to claim that sth is true or correct, especially when it is not 妄稱；偽稱；聲稱：**~ sth** *She still professes her innocence.* 她仍然聲稱自己無辜。◇ **~ to be/have sth** *I don't profess to be an expert in this subject.* 我不敢自詡為這方面的專家。**2** to state openly that you have a particular belief, feeling, etc. 宣稱；公開表明 **SYN** **declare**：**~ sth** *He professed his admiration for their work.* 他表示欽佩他們的工作。◇ **~ yourself + adj.** *She professed herself satisfied with the progress so far.* 她表示對目前為止的進度很滿意。**3** **~ sth** to belong to a particular religion 信奉，信仰（某一宗教）：*to profess Christianity/Islam/Judaism* 信仰基督教／伊斯蘭教／猶太教

pro·fessed /prə'fest/ *adj.* [only before noun] (*formal*) **1** used to describe a belief or a position that sb has publicly made known 公開表明的：*a professed Christian/anarchist* 公開表明信仰的基督教徒；公開表明立場的無政府主義者 **2** used to describe a feeling or an attitude that sb says they have but which may not be sincere 自稱的；自詡的；假充的：*These, at least, were their professed reasons for pulling out of the deal.* 至少這些是他們自稱退出這宗交易的理由。

pro·fes·sion 🔑 /prə'feʃn/ *noun*

1 🔑 [C] a type of job that needs special training or skill, especially one that needs a high level of education（需要專門技能，尤指需要較高教育水平的某一）行業，職業：*the* ***medical/legal/teaching, etc. profession*** 醫療、法律、教學等專業 ◇ *to* ***enter/go into/join a profession*** 加入一個行業 ◇ (*BrE*) *the* ***caring professions*** (= that involve looking after people) 護理行業 ◇ *He was an electrician* ***by profession.*** 他的職業是電工。◇ *She was at the very top of her profession.* 她是她那個行業中的佼佼者。➲ SYNONYMS at WORK ➲ COLLOCATIONS at JOB **2** 🔑 **the profession** [sing.+sing./pl. v.] all the people who work in a particular type of profession（某）職業界；業內人士；同業；同行；同人：*The legal profession has/have always resisted change.* 法律界向來抗拒變革。**3** **the professions** [pl.] the traditional jobs that need a high level of education and training, such as being a doctor or a lawyer（統稱，指需要較高教育水平的）職業：*employment in industry and the professions* 實業界與專業界的工作 **4** [C] **~ of sth** a statement about what you believe, feel or think about sth, that is sometimes made publicly 聲明；宣稱；表白 **SYN** **declaration**：*a profession of faith* 信仰的表白

pro·fes·sion·al 🔑 **AW** /prə'feʃənl/ *adj.*, *noun*

▪ ***adj.*** **1** 🔑 [only before noun] connected with a job that needs special training or skill, especially one that needs a high level of education 職業的；專業的：*professional qualifications/skills* 專業資格／技能 ◇ *professional standards/practice* 專業水平；行業慣例 ◇ *an opportunity for professional development* 專業進修的機會 ◇ *If it's a legal matter you need* ***to seek professional advice.*** 如果這屬於法律問題，你就需要尋求專業意見了。**2** 🔑 (of people 人) having a job which needs special training and a high level of education 有職業的；專業的：*Most of the people on the course were professional women.* 參加本課程的大多數人是職業女性。**3** 🔑 showing that sb is well trained and extremely skilled 嫻熟的；訓練有素的；精通業務的 **SYN** **competent**：*He dealt with the problem in a highly professional way.* 他處理這個問題非常專業。**OPP** **amateur** **4** 🔑 suitable or appropriate for sb working in a particular profession 職業上的；專業上的：***professional conduct/misconduct*** 職業道德；失職 **OPP** **unprofessional** **5** 🔑 doing sth as a paid job rather than as a hobby 職業性的；專業的；非業餘的：*a professional golfer* 職業高爾夫球運動員 ◇ *After he won the amateur championship he* ***turned professional.*** 他獲得業餘賽冠軍後就轉為職業運動員了。**OPP** **amateur** **6** 🔑 (of sport 體育運動) done as a paid job rather than as a hobby 職業性的；專業的；非業餘的：*the world of professional football* 職業足球界 **OPP** **amateur** ➲ compare NON-PROFESSIONAL

P

■ *noun* **1** 🔑 a person who does a job that needs special training and a high level of education 專門人員；專業人士；專家：*the terms that doctors and other health professionals use* 醫師和其他保健專業人員使用的術語 **2** 🔑 (also *informal* **pro**) a person who does a sport or other activity as a paid job rather than as a hobby 職業運動員；（從事某活動的）專業人員：*a top golf professional* 頂尖高爾夫球職業選手 OPP **amateur** **3** 🔑 (also *informal* **pro**) a person who has a lot of skill and experience 內行；專門人才；技術精湛者；老練的人：*This was clearly a job for a real professional.* 這顯然是真正的專家才能幹的工作。OPP **amateur**

pro,fessional de'velopment day *noun* (*especially CanE*) a day on which classes at schools are cancelled so that teachers can get further training in their subjects 專職進修日，教師發展日（學校停課）

pro,fessional 'foul *noun* (*BrE*) (in sport, especially football (SOCCER) 體育運動，尤指足球) a rule that sb breaks deliberately so that their team can gain an advantage, especially to prevent a player from the other team from scoring a goal 故意犯規

pro·fes·sion·al·ism AW /prəˈfeʃənəlɪzəm/ *noun* [U] **1** the high standard that you expect from a person who is well trained in a particular job 專業水平；專業素質：*We were impressed by the professionalism of the staff.* 職員的專業素質給我們的印象很深。 **2** great skill and ability 精湛的技藝；高超的能力；專長：*the power and professionalism of her performance* 她的表演的感染力和精湛技藝 **3** the practice of using professional players in sport 職業化（在體育運動中使用職業運動員）：*Increased professionalism has changed the game radically.* 職業運動員日益增加，徹底改變了這項運動。

pro·fes·sion·al·ize (*BrE* also **-ise**) /prəˈfeʃənəlaɪz/ *verb* [usually passive] **~ sth** to make an activity more professional, for example by paying people who take part in it 使專業化；使職業化 ▸ **pro·fes·sion·al·iza·tion, -isa·tion** /prə,feʃənəlaɪˈzeɪʃn/ *noun* [U]：*the increasing professionalization of sports* 體育運動的日益職業化

P

pro·fes·sion·al·ly AW /prəˈfeʃənəli/ *adv.* **1** in a way that is connected with a person's job or training 在工作上；在職業上：*You need a complete change, both professionally and personally.* 你需要在工作上和自身兩方面有徹底的改變。 **2** in a way that shows skill and experience 嫻熟地；老練地；內行地：*The product has been marketed very professionally.* 這項產品的推銷一直很講究專業技巧。 **3** by a person who has the right skills and qualifications 專業人員做的；內行人幹的：*The burglar alarm should be professionally installed.* 防盜警報應當由專業人員安裝。 **4** as a paid job, not as a hobby 作為職業；非業餘地：*After the injury, he never played professionally again.* 受傷以後，他再也沒有參加職業比賽。

pro·fes·sor 🔑 /prəˈfesə(r)/ (also *informal* **prof**) *noun* (*abbr.* **Prof.**)
1 🔑 (*especially BrE*) (*NAmE* **'full professor**) a university teacher of the highest rank 教授：*Professor (Ann) Williams*（安•）威廉斯教授 ◇ *a chemistry professor* 化學教授 ◇ *to be appointed Professor of French at Cambridge* 被任命為劍橋大學的法文教授 ◇ *He was made (a) professor at the age of 40.* 他 40 歲時就成為教授。HELP **Full professor** is used to describe a rank of university teacher, and not as a title. * full professor 是大學教師的級別，不用作稱呼。 **2** 🔑 (*NAmE*) a teacher at a university or college（大學的）講師，教員 ➲ compare ASSISTANT PROFESSOR, ASSOCIATE PROFESSOR

pro·fes·sor·ial /,prɒfəˈsɔːriəl; *NAmE* ,prɑːf-/ *adj.* connected with a professor; like a professor 教授的；教授似的：*professorial duties* 教授的職責 ◇ *His tone was almost professorial.* 他說話的口氣簡直像個教授。

pro·fes·sor·ship /prəˈfesəʃɪp; *NAmE* -sərʃ-/ *noun* the rank or position of a university professor 教授的級別（或職位等）：*a visiting professorship* 客座教授職位 ◇ *She was appointed to a professorship in Economics at Princeton.* 她獲聘為普林斯頓大學經濟學教授。

prof·fer /ˈprɒfə(r); *NAmE* ˈprɑːf-/ *verb* (*formal*) **1 ~ sth (to sb)** | **~ sb sth** to offer sth to sb, by holding it out to them 端着（給…）；遞上：*'Try this,' she said, proffering a plate.* "嚐嚐這個吧。" 她端上一盤菜說。 **2** to offer sth such as advice or an explanation 提出，提供（建議、解釋等）：**~ sth (to sb)** *What advice would you proffer to someone starting up in business?* 您對初入商界的人有何建議？◇ **~ sb sth** *What advice would you proffer her?* 您對她有什麼忠告？◇ **~ itself** *A solution proffered itself.* 一個解答自然出現了。

pro·fi·cient /prəˈfɪʃnt/ *adj.* able to do sth well because of training and practice 熟練的；嫻熟的；精通的；訓練有素的：*I'm a reasonably proficient driver.* 我開車的技術還算不錯。◇ **~ in sth/in doing sth** *She's proficient in several languages.* 她精通好幾種語言。◇ **~ at sth/at doing sth** *He's proficient at his job.* 他的工作效率很高。 ▸ **pro·fi·ciency** /-nsi/ *noun* [U]：*to develop proficiency* 提高熟練程度 ◇ *a certificate of language proficiency* 語言水平證書 ◇ **~ in sth/in doing sth** *a high level of oral proficiency in English* 一口流利的英語

pro·file /ˈprəʊfaɪl; *NAmE* ˈproʊ-/ *noun, verb*
■ *noun* **1** the outline of a person's face when you look from the side, not the front 面部的側影；側面輪廓：*his strong profile* 他輪廓清晰的側影 ◇ *a picture of the president **in profile*** 總統的側面畫像 **2** a description of sb/sth that gives useful information 概述；簡介；傳略：*a job/employee profile* 工作／雇員簡介 ◇ *We first build up a detailed profile of our customers and their requirements.* 首先，我們建立起我們的客戶及其需求的詳細資料。◇ *You can update your Facebook profile* (= your description of yourself on a SOCIAL NETWORKING website). 你可以更新你在"臉譜"網站上的個人資料。 **3** the general impression that sb/sth gives to the public and the amount of attention they receive 印象；形象：*The deal will certainly raise the company's international profile.* 這宗交易肯定會提高這家公司的國際形象。 **4** the edge or outline of sth that you see against a background 外形；輪廓：*the profile of the tower against the sky* 天空映襯出塔樓的輪廓
IDM **a ,high/,low 'profile** the amount of attention sb/sth has from the public 惹人／不惹人注目；高／低姿態：*This issue has had a high profile in recent months.* 近幾個月來，這個議題一直是關注的焦點。◇ *I advised her to **keep a low profile** for the next few days* (= not to attract attention). 我建議她未來幾天保持低姿態。
■ *verb* **~ sb/sth** to give or write a description of sb/sth that gives the most important information 扼要介紹；概述；寫簡介：*His career is profiled in this month's journal.* 這期月刊概述了他的工作生涯。

pro·fil·ing /ˈprəʊfaɪlɪŋ; *NAmE* ˈproʊ-/ *noun* [U] the act of collecting useful information about sb/sth so that you can give a description of them or it（有關人或事物的）資料搜集：*customer profiling* 客戶情況彙集 ◇ *offender profiling* 犯人資料收集 ➲ see also RACIAL PROFILING ▸ **pro·fil·er** /ˈprəʊfaɪlə(r); *NAmE* ˈproʊ-/ *noun*

profit 🔑 /ˈprɒfɪt; *NAmE* ˈprɑːfɪt/ *noun, verb*
■ *noun* **1** 🔑 [C, U] the money that you make in business or by selling things, especially after paying the costs involved 利潤；收益；贏利：*a rise/an increase/a drop/a fall in profits* 收益的上升／增長／跌落／下降 ◇ **~ (on sth)** *The company **made a** healthy **profit** on the deal.* 公司在這筆生意中獲利頗豐。◇ **~ (from sth)** *Profit from exports rose 7.3%.* 出口利潤增長了 7.3%。◇ ***Net profit*** (= after you have paid costs and tax) *was up 16.1%.* 純利潤上升了 16.1%。◇ *The sale generated **record profits**.* 這筆生意帶來了創紀錄的收益。◇ *We should be able to sell the house **at a profit**.* 我們賣掉這座房子應該可以獲利。◇ *The agency is voluntary and not run **for profit**.* 這個機構是義務性的，不是為了贏利。OPP **loss** ➲ COLLOCATIONS at BUSINESS **2** [U] (*formal*) the advantage that you get from doing sth 好處；利益；裨益：*Future lawyers could study this text with profit.* 未來的律師研讀這一文本也許會有裨益。
■ *verb* [I, T] (*formal*) to get sth useful from a situation; to be useful to sb or give them an advantage 獲益；得到好處；對…有用（或有益）：**~ (from sth)** *Farmers are profiting from the new legislation.* 新法規使農民受益。◇ **~ (by sth)** *We tried to profit by our mistakes* (= learn

from them). 我們努力從錯誤中吸取教訓。◇ **~ sth** *Many local people believe the development will profit them.* 當地的許多人認為，這項開發將對他們有利。

prof·it·able /ˈprɒfɪtəbl; *NAmE* ˈprɑːf-/ *adj.* **1** that makes or is likely to make money 有利潤的；贏利的：*a highly profitable business* 一家贏利很高的企業 ◇ *It is usually more profitable to sell direct to the public.* 向社會大眾直銷往往獲利較高。➲ SYNONYMS at SUCCESSFUL **2** that gives sb an advantage or a useful result 有益的；有好處的 SYN **rewarding**：*She spent a profitable afternoon in the library.* 她在圖書館待了一個下午，頗有收穫。▶ **prof·it·abil·ity** /ˌprɒfɪtəˈbɪləti; *NAmE* ˌprɑːf-/ *noun* [U]：*to increase profitability* 增加收益 **prof·it·ably** /-əbli/ *adv.*：*to run a business profitably* 把企業經營得有盈餘 ◇ *He spent the weekend profitably.* 他過了一個有收穫的週末。

ˌprofit and ˈloss account *noun* (*business* 商) a list that shows the amount of money that a company has earned and the total profit or loss that it has made in a particular period of time 損益賬

prof·it·eer·ing /ˌprɒfɪˈtɪərɪŋ; *NAmE* ˌprɑːfəˈtɪr-/ *noun* [U] (*disapproving*) the act of making a lot of money in an unfair way, for example by asking very high prices for things that are hard to get 牟取暴利 ▶ **prof·it·eer** *noun*

pro·fit·er·ole /prəˈfɪtərəʊl; *NAmE* -roʊl/ (*especially BrE*) (*NAmE* usually ˌ**cream** ˈ**puff**) *noun* a small cake in the shape of a ball, made of light PASTRY, filled with cream and usually with chocolate on top 奶心巧克力酥球

prof·it·less /ˈprɒfɪtləs; *NAmE* ˈprɑːf-/ *adj.* (*formal*) producing no PROFIT or useful result 無利可圖的；無益的

ˈ**profit-making** *adj.* [usually before noun] (of a company or a business 公司或企業) that makes or will make a profit 贏利的；能賺錢的

ˈ**profit margin** (also **margin**) *noun* (*business* 商) the difference between the cost of buying or producing sth and the price that it is sold for 利潤；利潤幅度；毛利

ˈ**profit-sharing** *noun* [U] the system of dividing all or some of a company's profits among its employees（公司內部的）利潤分成，利潤分配，分紅

ˈ**profit-taking** *noun* [U] (*business* 商) the sale of shares in companies whose value has increased 獲利回吐（股價上升時售出股票）

prof·li·gate /ˈprɒflɪɡət; *NAmE* ˈprɑːf-/ *adj.* (*formal, disapproving*) using money, time, materials, etc. in a careless way 揮霍的；浪費的 SYN **wasteful**：*profligate spending* 恣意揮霍的開支 ▶ **prof·li·gacy** /ˈprɒflɪɡəsi; *NAmE* ˈprɑːf-/ *noun* [U]

ˈ**pro-form** *noun* (*grammar* 語法) a word that depends on another part of the sentence or text for its meaning, for example 'her' in 'I like Ruth but I don't love her.' 替代形式（意義依上下文而定，如 I like Ruth but I don't love her 中的 her）

pro forma /ˌprəʊ ˈfɔːmə; *NAmE* ˌproʊ ˈfɔːrmə/ *adj.* (from *Latin*) [usually before noun] **1** (especially of a document 尤指文件) prepared in order to show the usual way of doing sth or to provide a standard method 按慣例的；慣常的；例行的：*a pro forma letter* 例行的信函 ◇ *pro forma instructions* 常規指示 **2** (of a document 文件) sent in advance 預開的；預先通知性的；形式上的：*a pro forma invoice* (= a document that gives details of the goods being sent to a customer) 形式發票 **3** done because it is part of the usual way of doing sth, although it has no real meaning 流於形式的；擺樣子的：*a pro forma debate* 流於形式的辯論 ▶ **pro forma** *noun*：*I enclose a pro forma for you to complete, sign and return.* 謹附估價單一份，請填好並簽字後寄回。

pro·found /prəˈfaʊnd/ *adj.* **1** very great; felt or experienced very strongly 巨大的；深切的；深遠的：*profound changes in the earth's climate* 地球氣候的巨大變化 ◇ *My father's death had a profound effect on us all.* 父親的去世深深地影響了我們全家。**2** showing great knowledge or understanding 知識淵博的；理解深刻的；深邃的：*profound insights* 精闢的見解 ◇ *a profound book* 深奧的書 **3** needing a lot of study or thought 艱深的；玄奧的：*profound questions about life and death* 生死方面的玄奧問題 **4** (*medical* 醫) very serious; complete 嚴重的；完全的；徹底的：*profound disability* 嚴重殘疾

pro·found·ly /prəˈfaʊndli/ *adv.* **1** in a way that has a very great effect on sb/sth 極大地；深刻地：*We are profoundly affected by what happens to us in childhood.* 童年發生的事深深地影響着我們。**2** (*medical* 醫) very seriously; completely 嚴重地；完全地；徹底地：*profoundly deaf* 完全失聰

pro·fund·ity /prəˈfʌndəti/ *noun* (*pl.* **-ies**) (*formal*) **1** [U] the quality of understanding or dealing with a subject at a very serious level（理解或處理問題的）深刻性，徹底性 SYN **depth**：*He lacked profundity and analytical precision.* 他缺乏深度和分析的精確性。**2** [U] the quality of being very great, serious or powerful 巨大；嚴重；強大：*the profundity of her misery* 她的苦難之深 **3** [C, usually pl.] something that sb says that shows great understanding 深奧的話；意味深長的話：*His profundities were lost on the young audience.* 他語重心長，但年輕的聽眾卻沒有領會。

pro·fuse /prəˈfjuːs/ *adj.* produced in large amounts 大量的；眾多的；豐富的：*profuse apologies/thanks* 一再道歉；千恩萬謝 ◇ *profuse bleeding* 血流如注 ▶ **pro·fuse·ly** *adv.*：*to bleed profusely* 大量出血 ◇ *to apologize profusely* 連連道歉

pro·fu·sion /prəˈfjuːʒn/ *noun* [sing.+sing./pl. v., U] (*formal* or *literary*) a very large quantity of sth 大量；眾多 SYN **abundance**：*a profusion of colours* 色彩斑斕 ◇ *Roses grew* ***in profusion*** *against the old wall.* 老舊牆邊遍生玫瑰。

pro·geni·tor /prəʊˈdʒenɪtə(r); *NAmE* proʊ-/ *noun* (*formal*) **1** a person or thing from the past that a person, animal or plant that is alive now is related to（人或動、植物等的）祖先，祖代 SYN **ancestor**：*He was the progenitor of a family of distinguished actors.* 他是一個著名演藝世家的先輩。**2** a person who starts an idea or a development 創始人；先驅：*the progenitors of modern art* 現代藝術的先驅

pro·geny /ˈprɒdʒəni; *NAmE* ˈprɑːdʒ-/ *noun* [pl.] (*formal* or *humorous*) a person's children; the young of animals and plants 子孫；幼崽；幼獸；幼苗：*He was surrounded by his numerous progeny.* 眾多的子孫簇擁着他。

pro·ges·ter·one /prəˈdʒestərəʊn; *NAmE* -roʊn/ *noun* [U] a HORMONE produced in the bodies of women and female animals which prepares the body to become pregnant and is also used in CONTRACEPTION 黃體酮；孕酮 ➲ compare OESTROGEN, TESTOSTERONE

prog·no·sis /prɒɡˈnəʊsɪs; *NAmE* prɑːɡˈnoʊ-/ *noun* (*pl.* **prog·no·ses** /-siːz/) **1** (*medical* 醫) an opinion, based on medical experience, of the likely development of a disease or an illness（對病情的）預斷，預後 **2** (*formal*) a judgement about how sth is likely to develop in the future 預測；預言；展望 SYN **forecast**：*The prognosis is for more people to work part-time in the future.* 預計將來會有更多人從事兼職工作。▶ **prog·nos·tic** /prɒɡˈnɒstɪk; *NAmE* prɑːɡˈnɑːs-/ *adj.*

prog·nos·ti·ca·tion /prɒɡˌnɒstɪˈkeɪʃn; *NAmE* prɑːɡˌnɑːs-/ *noun* (*formal*) a thing that sb says will happen in the future 預言；預告；預報：*gloomy prognostications* 悲觀的預言

pro·gram 0-π /ˈprəʊɡræm; *NAmE* ˈproʊ-/ *noun, verb*

■ *noun* **1** 0-π (*computing* 計) a set of instructions in CODE that control the operations or functions of a computer 程序；編碼指令；程式：*Load the program into the computer.* 把程序裝入電腦。**2** 0-π (*NAmE*) = PROGRAMME：*an intense training program* 強化培訓方案 ◇ *the university's graduate programs* 大學研究生課程 ◇ *a TV program* 電視節目

■ *verb* (**-mm-**, *NAmE* also **-m-**) **1** 0-π [I, T] (*computing* 計) to give a computer, etc. a set of instructions to make it perform a particular task 編寫程序；設計程式：*In this class, students will learn how to program.* 這節課學生將學習編程。◇ **~ sth (to do sth)** *The computer is programmed to warn users before information is deleted.*

P

這台計算機編程時已設計在信息刪除前提醒用戶。➲ compare PROGRAMME *v.* **2** 🗝 (*NAmE*) = PROGRAMME

pro·gram·mable /ˈprəʊɡræməbl; prəʊˈɡræm-; *NAmE* ˈproʊ-; proʊˈɡ-/ *adj.* (of a computer or electrical device 計算機或電器) able to accept instructions that control how it operates or functions 程控的；可編程序的；可程式化的

pro·gram·mat·ic /ˌprəʊɡrəˈmætɪk; *NAmE* ˌproʊ-/ *adj.* [usually before noun] (*formal*) connected with, suggesting or following a plan 計劃的；有關計劃的；按計劃的：*programmatic reforms* 按計劃進行的改革

pro·gramme 🗝 (*BrE*) (*NAmE* **pro·gram**) /ˈprəʊɡræm; *NAmE* ˈproʊ-/ *noun, verb*

■ ***noun***

▸ **PLAN** 計劃 **1** 🗝 a plan of things that will be done or included in the development of sth 計劃；方案；活動安排：*to launch a research programme* 開展科研計劃 ◇ *a training programme for new staff* 新職員培訓方案 ◇ *a programme of economic reform* 經濟改革方案

▸ **ON TV/RADIO** 電視；廣播 **2** 🗝 something that people watch on television or listen to on the radio 節目：*a news programme* 新聞節目 ◇ *Did you see that programme on India last night?* 昨晚關於印度的那個節目你看了沒有？ ➲ **COLLOCATIONS** at TELEVISION

▸ **FOR PLAY/CONCERT** 戲劇；音樂會 **3** 🗝 a thin book or a piece of paper that gives you information about a play, a concert, etc. 節目單；演出介紹：*a theatre programme* 劇場節目表

▸ **ORDER OF EVENTS** 活動程序 **4** 🗝 an organized order of performances or events （演出或活動的）程序 **SYN** **line-up**：*an exciting musical programme* 一場激動人心的音樂演出 ◇ *a week-long programme of lectures* 持續一週的講座安排 ◇ *What's the programme for* (= what are we going to do) *tomorrow?* 明天安排了什麼活動？

▸ **COURSE OF STUDY** 課程 **5** (*NAmE*) a course of study 課程：*a school programme* 學校課程 ➲ note at COURSE

▸ **OF MACHINE** 機器 **6** a series of actions done by a machine, such as a WASHING MACHINE （機器工作的）程序：*Select a cool programme for woollen clothes.* 洗毛衣要選擇涼水程序。

IDM **get with the ˈprogramme** (*BrE*) (*NAmE* **get with the ˈprogram**) (*informal*) (usually in orders 通常用於命令) used to tell sb that they should change their attitude and do what they are supposed to be doing （讓人改變態度）按計劃行事，做應該做的事

■ ***verb*** [usually passive]

▸ **PLAN** 計劃 **1** 🗝 **~ sth (for sth)** to plan for sth to happen, especially as part of a series of planned events 計劃；規劃；安排：*The final section of road is programmed for completion next month.* 最後一段道路計劃於下月竣工。

▸ **PERSON/ANIMAL** 人；動物 **2** 🗝 **~ sb/sth to do sth** to make a person, an animal, etc. behave in a particular way, so that it happens automatically 訓練；培養：*Human beings are genetically programmed to learn certain kinds of language.* 人類生來有學習某幾種語言的遺傳因素。

▸ **MACHINE** 機器 **3** **~ sth (to do sth)** to give a machine instructions to do a particular task 預調；預設：*She programmed the VCR to come on at eight.* 她把錄像機預調到八點開機。

ˌprogrammed ˈlearning *noun* [U] a method of study in which a subject is divided into very small parts and the student must be successful in one part before he or she can go on to the next 程序化學習，循序漸進學習（按個別學生的進度，分階段預定目標）

pro·gram·mer /ˈprəʊɡræmə(r); *NAmE* ˈproʊ-/ *noun* a person whose job is writing programs for computers （計算機）程序設計員，編程人員，程式設計員

pro·gram·ming /ˈprəʊɡræmɪŋ; *NAmE* ˈproʊ-/ *noun* [U] **1** the process of writing and testing programs for computers （計算機）程序設計，程序編製，編程，程式設計：*a high-level programming language* 高級編程語言 **2** the planning of which television or radio programmes to broadcast （廣播、電視節目的）編排，選編：*politically balanced programming* 政治上均衡報道的節目編選

pro·gress 🗝 *noun, verb*

■ ***noun*** /ˈprəʊɡres; *NAmE* ˈprɑːɡ-; -ɡrəs/ [U] **1** 🗝 the process of improving or developing, or of getting nearer to achieving or completing sth 進步；進展；進程：*to **make progress*** 取得進步 ◇ ***slow/steady/rapid/good progress*** 緩慢的／平穩的／迅速的／良好的進展 ◇ *We have made great progress in controlling inflation.* 我們在抑制通貨膨脹方面取得了巨大進展。◇ ***economic/scientific/technical progress*** 經濟的／科學的／技術的進步 ◇ *They asked for **a progress report** on the project.* 他們索要工程進度報告。 **2** movement forwards or towards a place 前進；行進：*She watched his slow progress down the steep slope.* 她望着他慢慢走下陡坡。◇ *There wasn't much traffic so we made good progress.* 來往車輛不多，所以我們開得很快。

IDM **in progress** 🗝 (*formal*) happening at this time 進行中：*Work on the new offices is now in progress.* 新辦公樓正在施工。◇ *Please be quiet—examination in progress.* 考試正在進行，請安靜。

■ ***verb*** /prəˈɡres/ **1** 🗝 [I] to improve or develop over a period of time; to make progress 進步；改進；進展 **SYN** **advance**：*The course allows students to progress at their own speed.* 本課程允許學生按各自的速度學習。◇ *Work on the new road is progressing slowly.* 新路的修建工作在緩慢進行。 **2** 🗝 [I] + **adv./prep.** (*formal*) to move forward 前進；行進：*The line of traffic progressed slowly through the town.* 車流緩慢地穿過城鎮。◇ (*figurative*) *Cases can take months to progress through the courts.* 案件可能需要好幾個月才能審結。 **3** [I] to go forward in time （時間上）推移，流逝 **SYN** **go on**：*The weather became colder as the day progressed.* 天色越晚，天氣就越冷。

PHR V **proˈgress to sth** to move on from doing one thing to doing sth else 接着做（另一件事）：*She started off playing the recorder and then progressed to the clarinet.* 她起初吹豎笛，進而吹單簧管。

pro·gres·sion /prəˈɡreʃn/ *noun* **1** [U, C] the process of developing gradually from one stage or state to another （進入另一階段的）發展；前進；進程：*opportunities for career progression* 事業發展的機遇 ◇ *the rapid progression of the disease* 病情的迅速發展 ◇ **~ (from sth) (to sth)** *a natural progression from childhood to adolescence* 從童年到青少年的自然過渡 **2** [C] a number of things that come in a series 系列；序列；連續 ➲ see also ARITHMETIC PROGRESSION, GEOMETRIC PROGRESSION

pro·gres·sive /prəˈɡresɪv/ *adj., noun*

■ ***adj.*** **1** in favour of new ideas, modern methods and change 進步的；先進的；開明的：*progressive schools* 開明的學校 **OPP** **retrogressive** **2** happening or developing steadily 穩步的；逐步的；穩定發展的：*a progressive reduction in the size of the workforce* 勞力數量的逐步減少 ◇ *a progressive muscular disease* 逐漸嚴重的肌肉病症 **3** (also **con·tinu·ous**) (*grammar* 語法) connected with the form of a verb (for example *I am waiting* or *It is raining*) that is made from a part of *be* and the present participle. Progressive forms are used to express an action that continues for a period of time. （動詞）進行時的，進行式的 ▸ **pro·gres·siv·ism** *noun* [U]：*political progressivism* 政治進步主義

■ ***noun*** [usually pl.] a person who is in favour of new ideas, modern methods and change 進步人士；開明人士；改革派：*political battles between progressives and conservatives* 改革派與保守派之間的政治鬥爭

pro·gres·sive·ly /prəˈɡresɪvli/ *adv.* (often with a comparative 常與比較級連用) steadily and continuously 持續穩定地；逐步地；愈益：*The situation was becoming progressively more difficult.* 局勢變得愈發困難起來。◇ *The pain got progressively worse.* 疼痛越來越厲害。

prog rock /ˌprɒɡ ˈrɒk; *NAmE* ˌprɑːɡ ˈrɑːk/ (also **proˌgressive ˈrock**) *noun* [U] a style of rock music that includes elements of other kinds of music, including JAZZ 前衛搖滾樂（包括爵士樂等其他音樂元素）

pro·hibit **AW** /prəˈhɪbɪt; *NAmE* also proʊˈh-/ *verb* (*formal*) **1** [often passive] to stop sth from being done or used especially by law （尤指以法令）禁止 **SYN** **forbid**：**~ sth** *a law prohibiting the sale of alcohol* 禁止售酒的法令 ◇ **~ sb from doing sth** *Soviet citizens were prohibited from travelling abroad.* 蘇聯時代國民被禁止出國旅遊。

P

◇ ~ (**sb**) **doing sth** *The policy prohibits smoking on school grounds.* 該政策禁止在校內吸煙。 **2** ~ **sth/sb from doing sth** to make sth impossible to do 阻止；使不可能 **SYN** **prevent**： *The high cost of equipment prohibits many people from taking up this sport.* 昂貴的裝備令許多人對這項運動望而卻步。

pro·hib·ition **AW** /ˌprəʊɪˈbɪʃn; NAmE ˌproʊəˈb-/ *noun* **1** [U] (*formal*) the act of stopping sth being done or used, especially by law （尤指通過法律的）禁止，阻止： *the prohibition of smoking in public areas* 禁止在公共場所吸煙的規定 **2** [C] ~ (**against/on sth**) (*formal*) a law or a rule that stops sth being done or used 禁令；禁律： *a prohibition against selling alcohol to people under the age of 18* 禁止向 18 歲以下青少年售酒的法令 **3 Prohib·ition** [U] (in the US) the period of time from 1920 to 1933 when it was illegal to make and sell alcoholic drinks（1920 至 1933 年美國的）禁酒時期

pro·hib·ition·ist /ˌprəʊɪˈbɪʃənɪst; NAmE ˌproʊəˈb-/ *noun* a person who supports the act of making sth illegal, especially the sale of alcoholic drinks 禁止令擁護者；禁止論者（尤指禁酒主義者）

pro·hibi·tive **AW** /prəˈhɪbətɪv; NAmE also proʊˈh-/ *adj.* **1** (of a price or a cost 價格或費用) so high that it prevents people from buying sth or doing sth 高昂得令人難以承受的；貴得買不起的 **SYN** **exorbitant**： *prohibitive costs* 難以承受的費用 ◇ *The price of property in the city is prohibitive.* 城市的房地產價格令人望而卻步。 **2** preventing people from doing sth by law （以法令）禁止的： *prohibitive legislation* 禁律 **3** (*NAmE*) (of a person taking part in an election or a competition 參加競選或比賽的人) extremely likely to win 極可能獲勝的： *Miami began the day a prohibitive Super Bowl favorite.* 邁阿密隊今天從一開始就表現出是美國橄欖球超級碗大賽的奪冠熱門。 ▸ **pro·hibi·tive·ly** *adv.*： *Car insurance can be prohibitively expensive for young drivers.* 汽車保險費有時高得讓年輕開車人承受不起。

pro·ject 🔑 **AW** *noun, verb*

■ ***noun*** /ˈprɒdʒekt; NAmE ˈprɑːdʒ-/

▸ **PLANNED WORK** 規劃的工作 **1** 🔑 a planned piece of work that is designed to find information about sth, to produce sth new, or to improve sth 生產（或研究等）項目；方案；工程： *a research project* 研究計劃 ◇ *a building project* 建築工程 ◇ *to set up a project to computerize the library system* 開展一個圖書館系統電腦化的項目

▸ **SCHOOL/COLLEGE WORK** 學校的課題 **2** 🔑 a piece of work involving careful study of a subject over a period of time, done by school or college students （大、中學學生的）專題研究： *a history project* 歷史科的專題研究 ◇ *The final term will be devoted to project work.* 最後一學期的時間將全部用於專題研究。

▸ **SET OF AIMS/ACTIVITIES** 方案 **3** a set of aims, ideas or activities that sb is interested in or wants to bring to people's attention 方案；計劃： *The party attempted to assemble its aims into a focussed political project.* 這個黨試圖把訂立的目標綜合為一個政治方案。

▸ **HOUSING** 住房 **4** (*NAmE*) = HOUSING PROJECT： *Going into the projects alone is dangerous.* 隻身進入公房區是危險的。

■ ***verb*** /prəˈdʒekt/

▸ **PLAN** 計劃 **1** 🔑 [T, usually passive] ~ **sth** to plan an activity, a project etc. for a time in the future 規劃；計劃；擬訂方案： *The next edition of the book is projected for publication in March.* 本書的下一版計劃於三月發行。 ◇ *The projected housing development will go ahead next year.* 計劃中的住宅建設將於明年動工。

▸ **ESTIMATE** 估計 **2** 🔑 [T, usually passive] to estimate what the size, cost or amount of sth will be in the future based on what is happening now 預測；預計；推想 **SYN** **forecast**： ~ **sth** *A growth rate of 4% is projected for next year.* 預計明年的增長率為 4%。 ◇ ~ **sth to do sth** *The unemployment rate has been projected to fall.* 據預測失業率將下降。 **HELP** This pattern is usually used in the passive. 此句型通常用於被動語態： **it is projected that** ... *It is projected that the unemployment rate will fall.* 據預測失業率將會下降。

▸ **LIGHT/IMAGE** 光；影像 **3** 🔑 [T] ~ **sth** (**on/onto sth**) to make light, an image, etc. fall onto a flat surface or screen 放映；投射；投影： *Images are projected onto the retina of the eye.* 影像被投射到眼睛的視網膜上。

▸ **STICK OUT** 突出 **4** [I] + **adv./prep.** to stick out beyond an edge or a surface 突出；外伸；伸出 **SYN** **protrude**： *a building with balconies projecting out over the street* 陽台伸出到街上的樓房

▸ **PRESENT YOURSELF** 表現 **5** [T] to present sb/sth/yourself to other people in a particular way, especially one that gives a good impression 展現；表現；確立（好印象）： ~ **sth** *They sought advice on how to project a more positive image of their company.* 他們就如何加強樹立公司的形象徵詢意見。 ◇ *She projects an air of calm self-confidence.* 她表現出鎮定自若的神態。 ◇ ~ **sb/sth/yourself** (**as sb/sth**) *He projected himself as a man worth listening to.* 他裝成很有見地的樣子。

▸ **SEND/THROW UP OR AWAY** 發出；拋射 **6** [T] ~ **sth/sb** (+ **adv./prep.**) to send or throw sth up or away from yourself 投擲；拋射；發送： *Actors must learn to project their voices.* 演員必須學會放開聲音。 ◇ (*figurative*) *the powerful men who would project him into the White House* 能使他平步進入白宮的有力人士

PHR V **proˈject sth onto sb** (*psychology* 心) to imagine that other people have the same feelings, problems, etc. as you, especially when this is not true （不自覺地）把（自己的感覺或問題等）投射到別人身上

pro·ject·ile /prəˈdʒektaɪl; NAmE -tl/ *noun, adj.*

■ ***noun*** (*formal* or *technical* 術語) **1** an object, such as a bullet, that is fired from a gun or other weapon （武器發射的）投射物；槍彈；炮彈 **2** any object that is thrown as a weapon （作為武器的）發射物；導彈

■ ***adj.*** (*formal* or *technical* 術語) very fast and with a lot of force 迅速有力的；猛烈的： *projectile motion* 迅速有力的動作 ◇ *The virus causes projectile* (= sudden and violent) *vomiting.* 該病毒可引起突然的劇烈嘔吐。

pro·jec·tion **AW** /prəˈdʒekʃn/ *noun*

▸ **ESTIMATE** 估計 **1** [C] an estimate or a statement of what figures, amounts, or events will be in the future, or what they were in the past, based on what is happening now 預測；推斷；設想： *to make* ***forward/backward projections*** *of population figures* 推斷未來 / 過去的人口數量 ◇ *Sales have exceeded our projections.* 銷售量超過了我們的預測。

▸ **OF IMAGE** 影像 **2** [U, C] the act of putting an image of sth onto a surface; an image that is shown in this way 投射；放映；投影；放映的影像： *the projection of three-dimensional images on a computer screen* 在電腦屏幕上顯示的立體影像 ◇ *laser projections* 激光影像

▸ **OF SOLID SHAPE** 立體圖形 **3** [C] (*technical* 術語) a solid shape or object as represented on a flat surface 投影圖： *map projections* 投影地圖

▸ **STH THAT STICKS OUT** 突出物 **4** [C] something that sticks out from a surface 突起物；隆起物： *tiny projections on the cell* 細胞上的小尖突出物

▸ **OF VOICE/SOUND** 聲音 **5** [U] the act of making your voice, a sound, etc. AUDIBLE (= able to be heard) at a distance （嗓音或聲音的）發送，傳送，放開： *voice projection* 嗓音的放開

▸ **PSYCHOLOGY** 心理學 **6** [U] the act of imagining that sb else is thinking the same as you and is reacting in the same way 投射（不自覺地把自己的思想等加諸他人）

▸ **OF THOUGHTS/FEELINGS** 思想感情 **7** [C, U] the act of giving a form and structure to inner thoughts and feelings （思想感情的）體現，形象化： *The idea of God is a projection of humans' need to have something greater than themselves.* 人類需要有強於自身的形象；上帝就是這個想法的投射。

pro·jec·tion·ist /prəˈdʒekʃənɪst/ *noun* a person whose job is to show films/movies by operating a PROJECTOR 電影放映員

pro·ject·or /prəˈdʒektə(r)/ *noun* a piece of equipment for projecting photographs, films/movies or computer SLIDES onto a screen 放映機；投影儀 ➲ see also DATA PROJECTOR ➲ **VISUAL VOCAB** pages V69, V70 ➲ see also OVERHEAD PROJECTOR, SLIDE PROJECTOR

P

pro·lapse /ˈprəʊlæps; *NAmE* ˈproʊ-/ *noun* (*medical* 醫) a condition in which an organ of the body has slipped forward or down from its normal position（身體器官的）脱垂，下垂，脱出

prole /prəʊl; *NAmE* proʊl/ *noun* (*old-fashioned, BrE, informal*) an offensive word for a WORKING CLASS person（含冒犯意，指無產階級工人）

pro·le·tar·ian /ˌprəʊləˈteəriən; *NAmE* ˌproʊləˈter-/ *adj.* connected with ordinary people who earn money by working, especially those who do not own any property 無產者的；無產階級的；工人階級的 ➲ compare BOURGEOIS ▸ **pro·le·tar·ian** *noun*

the pro·le·tar·iat /ˌprəʊləˈteəriət; *NAmE* ˌproʊləˈter-/ *noun* [sing.+sing./pl. v.] (*technical* 術語) (used especially when talking about the past 尤用以指過去) the class of ordinary people who earn money by working, especially those who do not own any property 無產階級；工人階級；普羅階級 ➲ compare BOURGEOISIE

ˌpro-ˈlife *adj.* [usually before noun] opposed to ABORTION 反墮胎的；反對人工流產的：*the pro-life movement* 反墮胎運動 ◇ *a pro-life campaigner* 反墮胎運動成員 ➲ compare PRO-CHOICE

pro·lif·er·ate /prəˈlɪfəreɪt/ *verb* [I] to increase rapidly in number or amount 迅速繁殖（或增殖）；猛增 SYN **multiply**：*Books and articles on the subject have proliferated over the last year.* 過去一年以來，論及這一專題的書和文章大量湧現。

pro·lif·er·ation /prəˌlɪfəˈreɪʃn/ *noun* [U, sing.] the sudden increase in the number or amount of sth; a large number of a particular thing 激增；湧現；增殖；大量的事物：*attempts to prevent cancer cell proliferation* 防止癌細胞擴散的努力 ◇ *a proliferation of personal computers* 個人電腦的激增

pro·lif·ic /prəˈlɪfɪk/ *adj.* **1** (of an artist, a writer, etc. 藝術家、作家等) producing many works, etc. 多產的；創作豐富的：*a prolific author* 多產的作家 ◇ *a prolific goalscorer* 傑出射門手 ◇ *one of the most prolific periods in her career* 她的創作生涯中成果最豐的時期之一 **2** (of plants, animals, etc. 植物、動物等) producing a lot of fruit, flowers, young, etc. 豐碩的；多產的；多育的 **3** able to produce enough food, etc. to keep many animals and plants alive 富饒的；富庶的；肥沃的：*prolific rivers* 富饒的河川 **4** existing in large numbers 眾多的；大批的：*a pop star with a prolific following of teenage fans* 擁有大批少男少女歌迷的流行歌星 ▸ **pro·lif·ic·al·ly** *adv.*：*to write prolifically* 著作等身 ◇ *animals that breed prolifically* 多產的動物

pro·lix /ˈprəʊlɪks; *NAmE* ˈproʊ-/ *adj.* (*formal*) (of writing, a speech, etc. 文章、講話等) using too many words and therefore boring 冗長乏味的；繁瑣的；囉嗦的 ▸ **pro·lix·ity** /prəʊˈlɪksəti; *NAmE* proʊ-/ *noun* [U]

pro·logue /ˈprəʊlɒɡ; *NAmE* ˈproʊlɔːɡ; -lɑːɡ/ *noun* a speech, etc. at the beginning of a play, book, or film/movie that introduces it 序言；序幕；開場白 ➲ compare EPILOGUE

pro·long /prəˈlɒŋ; *NAmE* -ˈlɔːŋ; -ˈlɑːŋ/ *verb* **~ sth** to make sth last longer 延長 SYN **extend**：*The operation could prolong his life by two or three years.* 這次手術可使他多活兩三年。◇ *Don't* ***prolong the agony*** (of not knowing sth)—*just tell us who won!* 別賣關子了，快說誰贏了！

pro·longa·tion /ˌprəʊlɒŋˈɡeɪʃn; *NAmE* ˌproʊlɔːŋ-/ *noun* [U, sing.] (*formal*) the act of making sth last longer 延長；延伸：*the artificial prolongation of human life* 對人類壽命的人為的延長

pro·longed /prəˈlɒŋd; *NAmE* -ˈlɔːŋd; -ˈlɑːŋd/ *adj.* continuing for a long time 持久的；長期的：*a prolonged illness* 長期的病 ◇ *a prolonged period of dry weather* 長期的乾旱天氣

prom /prɒm; *NAmE* prɑːm/ *noun* **1** (especially in the US) a formal dance, especially one that is held at a HIGH SCHOOL（尤指美國高中的）正式舞會：*the senior prom* 高年級畢業舞會 **2** (*BrE, informal,* becoming *old-fashioned*) = PROMENADE *n.* (1)：*to walk along the prom* 沿步行道散步 **3** (*BrE*) = PROMENADE CONCERT：*the last night of the proms* 逍遙音樂會的最後夜場

prom·en·ade /ˌprɒməˈnɑːd; *NAmE* ˌprɑːməˈneɪd/ *noun, verb*

▪ ***noun*** **1** (also *informal* **prom**) (both *BrE*, becoming *old-fashioned*) a public place for walking, usually a wide path beside the sea 公共散步場所；（常指）濱海步行大道 **2** (*old-fashioned*) a walk that you take for pleasure or exercise, especially by the sea, in a public park, etc.（尤指在海濱、公園等的）散步，漫步

▪ ***verb*** [I] (*old-fashioned*) to walk up and down in a relaxed way, by the sea, in a public park, etc.（在海濱、公園等）散步，漫步

ˌpromenade ˈconcert (also *informal* **prom**) (both *BrE*) *noun* a concert at which many of the audience stand up or sit on the floor 逍遙音樂會（聽眾可隨意走動）

Pro·me·thean /prəˈmiːθiən/ *adj.* doing things in an individual and original way and showing no respect for authority and rules 勇於開創的；不畏權勢的；不受約束的 ORIGIN From the Greek myth in which **Prometheus**, a Titan, stole fire from the gods and gave it to humans. 源自提坦巨神普羅米修斯（Prometheus）盜取火種送到人間的希臘神話。

pro·me·thium /prəˈmiːθiəm/ *noun* [U] (*symb.* **Pm**) a chemical element. Promethium is a RADIOACTIVE metal that was first produced artificially in a nuclear REACTOR and is found in small amounts in nature. 鉕（放射性化學元素）

prom·in·ence /ˈprɒmɪnəns; *NAmE* ˈprɑːm-/ *noun* [U, sing.] the state of being important, well known or noticeable 重要；突出；卓越；出名：*a young actor who has recently risen to prominence* 最近嶄露頭角的一名年輕演員 ◇ *The newspapers have given undue prominence to the story.* 報章對這件事的報道太多了。◇ *She has achieved a prominence she hardly deserves.* 她實在不配享有這麼大的名聲。

prom·in·ent /ˈprɒmɪnənt; *NAmE* ˈprɑːm-/ *adj.* **1** important or well known 重要的；著名的；傑出的：*a prominent politician* 傑出的政治家 ◇ *He* ***played a prominent part*** *in the campaign.* 他在這次運動中發揮了重要作用。◇ *She was prominent in the fashion industry.* 她曾在時裝界名噪一時。**2** easily seen 顯眼的；顯著的；突出的 SYN **noticeable**：*The church tower was a prominent feature in the landscape.* 教堂的尖塔曾經是此地景觀的重要特色。◇ *The story was given a prominent position on the front page.* 這則報道刊登在頭版的顯著位置。**3** sticking out from sth 突出的；凸現的：*a prominent nose* 高鼻子 ◇ *prominent cheekbones* 突出的顴骨 ▸ **prom·in·ent·ly** *adv.*：*The photographs were prominently displayed on her desk.* 幾張照片擺在她桌子上顯眼的位置。◇ *Problems of family relationships feature prominently in her novels.* 家庭糾葛是她小說的顯著特點。

pro·mis·cu·ous /prəˈmɪskjuəs/ *adj.* (*disapproving*) **1** having many sexual partners 淫亂的；濫交的：*promiscuous behaviour* 淫亂行為 ◇ *a promiscuous lifestyle* 不檢點的生活 ◇ *to be sexually promiscuous* 性生活淫亂 **2** (*formal*) taken from a wide range of sources, especially without careful thought 大雜燴的；雜亂的：*promiscuous reading* 讀書龐雜 ◇ *a stylistically promiscuous piece of music* 一支風格雜亂的樂曲 ▸ **prom·is·cu·ity** /ˌprɒmɪsˈkjuːəti; *NAmE* ˌprɑːməs-/ *noun* [U]：*sexual promiscuity* 淫亂 **prom·is·cu·ous·ly** *adv.*

prom·ise 🔑 /ˈprɒmɪs; *NAmE* ˈprɑːm-/ *verb, noun*

▪ ***verb*** **1** 🔑 [I, T] to tell sb that you will definitely do or not do sth, or that sth will definitely happen 許諾；承諾；答應；保證：**~ (to do sth)** *The college principal promised to look into the matter.* 學院院長答應研究這個問題。◇ *'Promise not to tell anyone!' 'I promise.'* "你要保證不告訴別人！" "我保證。" ◇ *They arrived at 7.30* ***as they had promised.*** 他們按說定的 7:30 到達了。◇ **~ sth** *The government has promised a full investigation into the disaster.* 政府已承諾對這次災難進行全面調查。◇ *I'll see what I can do but* ***I can't promise anything.*** 我會看看我能做什麼，但不能給予任何承諾。◇ **~ (that)** ... *The brochure promised (that) the local food would be superb.* 旅遊指南中保證說當地有上佳的美食。◇ **~ sb (that)** ... *You promised me (that) you'd be home early tonight.*

你曾向我保證今晚會早回家的。◇ **~ sth to sb** *He promised the money to his grandchildren.* 他答應把這筆錢給孫兒孫女們。◇ **~ sb sth** *He promised his grandchildren the money.* 他答應給孫兒孫女們這筆錢。◇ **~ yourself sth** *I've promised myself some fun when the exams are over.* 等考試完了，我打算好好玩玩。◇ **~ (sb) + speech** *'I'll be back soon,' she promised.* "我馬上回來。" 她答應說。 **2** [T] to make sth seem likely to happen; to show signs of sth 使很可能；預示： **it promises to be sth** *It promises to be an exciting few days.* 那可望是興奮刺激的幾天。◇ **~ sth** *There were dark clouds overhead promising rain.* 天上烏雲密佈，預示就要下雨。

IDM **I (can) 'promise you** (*informal*) used as a way of encouraging or warning sb about sth（用於鼓勵或警告）保證，保管： *I can promise you, you'll have a wonderful time.* 我保證你會玩得很痛快。◇ *If you don't take my advice, you'll regret it, I promise you.* 你若不聽我的勸告，保管你會後悔的。 **promise (sb) the 'earth/'moon/'world** (*informal*) to make promises that will be impossible to keep 作出不可能實現的承諾

■ ***noun*** **1** 0-w [C] a statement that tells sb that you will definitely do or not do sth 諾言；許諾；承諾：*to* ***make/keep/break a promise*** 許下 / 信守 / 違背諾言 ◇ **~ (to do sth)** *She kept her promise to visit her aunt regularly.* 她信守諾言，定期去看望姑媽。◇ **~ (of sth)** *The government failed to keep its promise of lower taxes.* 政府未能兌現減稅的承諾。◇ **~ (that ...)** *Do I have your promise that you won't tell anyone about this?* 你保證不把這事告訴任何人嗎？◇ *You haven't gone back on your promise, have you?* 你該不會反悔了吧？ **IDM** see LICK *n.* **2** 0-w [U] a sign that sb/sth will be successful 獲得成功的跡象 **SYN** **potential**： *Her work* ***shows*** *great* ***promise***. 她的作品顯示她大有前途。◇ *He failed to fulfil his* ***early promise***. 他沒有像小時候表現的那樣有出息。◇ *Their future was* ***full of promise***. 他們的前途希望無窮。 **3** [U, sing.] **~ of sth** a sign, or a reason for hope that sth may happen, especially sth good 吉兆；跡象： *The day dawned bright and clear, with the promise of warm, sunny weather.* 拂曉時晴空萬里，預示着温暖晴朗的天氣。

the ˌPromised 'Land *noun* [sing.] a place or situation where you expect to be happy, safe, etc. 福地；樂土；安樂境界

prom·is·ing /'prɒmɪsɪŋ; *NAmE* 'prɑːm-/ *adj.* showing signs of being good or successful 有希望的；有前途的；有出息的： *He was voted the most promising new actor for his part in the movie.* 他因在該電影中扮演的角色而獲評為最有前途的新演員。◇ *The weather doesn't look very promising.* 天氣看起來不會太好。▸ **prom·is·ing·ly** *adv.*： *The day began promisingly with bright sunshine.* 晨曦燦爛，預示了一個大好的晴天。

prom·is·sory note /'prɒmɪsəri nəʊt; *NAmE* 'prɑːm-; noʊt/ *noun* (*technical* 術語) a signed document containing a promise to pay a stated amount of money before a particular date 期票；欠票

promo /'prəʊməʊ; *NAmE* 'proʊmoʊ/ *adj.* [only before noun] (*informal*) connected with advertising (= PROMOTING) sb/sth, especially a new pop record 推銷（新流行唱片等）的；廣告宣傳的： *a promo video* 促銷錄像 ▸ **promo** *noun* (*pl.* **-os**)： *to make pop promos* 做流行音樂促銷

prom·on·tory /'prɒməntri; *NAmE* 'prɑːməntɔːri/ *noun* (*pl.* **-ies**) a long narrow area of high land that goes out into the sea 岬，岬角（深入海中的狹長高地） **SYN** **headland** ➲ VISUAL VOCAB pages V4, V5

pro·mote 0-w AW /prə'məʊt; *NAmE* -'moʊt/ *verb* **1** 0-w **~ sth** to help sth to happen or develop 促進；推動 **SYN** **encourage**： *policies to promote economic growth* 促進經濟增長的政策 ◇ *a campaign to promote awareness of environmental issues* 提高環保意識的運動 **2** 0-w to help sell a product, service, etc. or make it more popular by advertising it or offering it at a special price 促銷；推銷： **~ sth** *The band has gone on tour to promote their new album.* 這個樂隊已開始巡迴宣傳他們的新唱片。◇ **~ sth as sth** *The area is being promoted as a tourist destination.* 這個地區正被推廣為旅遊點。 **3** 0-w [often passive] to move sb to a higher rank or more senior job 提升；晉升： **~ sb** *She worked hard and was soon promoted.* 她工作勤奮，不久就得到提升了。◇ **~ sb (from sth) (to sth)** *He has been promoted to sergeant.* 他已晉升為巡佐。 **OPP** **demote** **4** **~ sth (from sth) (to sth)** to move a sports team from playing with one group of teams to playing in a better group 將（體育運動隊）晉級： *They were promoted to the First Division last season.* 上個賽季他們晉升為甲級隊。 **OPP** **relegate**

pro·moter AW /prə'məʊtə(r); *NAmE* -'moʊ-/ *noun* **1** a person or company that organizes or provides money for an artistic performance or a sporting event （藝術演出或體育比賽的）籌辦人，發起者，贊助者 **2** **~ of sth** a person who tries to persuade others about the value or importance of sth 倡導者；支持者 **SYN** **champion**： *She became a leading promoter of European integration.* 她成為歐洲一體化的主要支持者。

pro·mo·tion 0-w AW /prə'məʊʃn; *NAmE* -'moʊʃn/ *noun*

1 0-w [U, C] **~ (to sth)** a move to a more important job or rank in a company or an organization 提升；提拔；晉升： *Her promotion to Sales Manager took everyone by surprise.* 竟然提拔她當銷售經理，叫每個人都感到意外。◇ *The new job is a promotion for him.* 這一新職務對他是擢升。◇ *a job with excellent* ***promotion prospects*** 有充分晉升機會的職務 ➲ COLLOCATIONS at JOB **2** [U] **~ (to sth)** a move by a sports team from playing in one group of teams to playing in a better group （體育運動隊的）晉級，升級： *the team's promotion to the First Division* 這個球隊晉升為甲級隊 **OPP** **relegation** **3** 0-w [U, C] activities done in order to increase the sales of a product or service; a set of advertisements for a particular product or service 促銷活動；廣告宣傳： *Her job is mainly concerned with sales and promotion.* 她的工作主要是銷售和廣告宣傳方面的。◇ *We are doing a special promotion of Chilean wines.* 我們正在做智利葡萄酒的特別促銷活動。 ➲ see also CROSS-PROMOTION ➲ **SYNONYMS** at ADVERTISEMENT **4** [U] **~ of sth** (*formal*) activity that encourages people to believe in the value or importance of sth, or that helps sth to succeed 推廣；促進： *a society for the promotion of religious tolerance* 一個促進宗教包容的團體

pro·mo·tion·al /prə'məʊʃənl; *NAmE* -'moʊ-/ *adj.* connected with advertising 廣告宣傳的；推銷的： *promotional material* 廣告宣傳資料

prompt 0-w /prɒmpt; *NAmE* prɑːmpt/ *adj.*, *verb*, *noun*, *adv.*

■ ***adj.*** **1** 0-w done without delay 立即的；迅速的；及時的 **SYN** **immediate**： *Prompt action was required as the fire spread.* 由於火勢蔓延，須要立即採取行動。◇ *Prompt payment of the invoice would be appreciated.* 見發票即付款，將不勝感激。 **2** 0-w [not before noun] (of a person 人) acting without delay; arriving at the right time 敏捷；迅速；準時 **SYN** **punctual**： *Please be prompt when attending these meetings.* 參加上述會議，請準時出席。 ▸ **prompt·ness** *noun* [U]

■ ***verb*** **1** 0-w [T] to make sb decide to do sth; to cause sth to happen 促使；導致；激起 **SYN** **provoke**： **~ sth** *The discovery of the bomb prompted an increase in security.* 此次發現炸彈促使當局加強了安全工作。◇ *His speech prompted an angry outburst from a man in the crowd.* 他的講話激起了人群中一男子的憤怒。◇ **~ sb to do sth** *The thought of her daughter's wedding day prompted her to lose some weight.* 對女兒婚期的操心使她消瘦不少。 **2** [T] to encourage sb to speak by asking them questions or suggesting words that they could say 鼓勵，提示，提醒（某人說話）： **~ sb** *She was too nervous to speak and had to be prompted.* 她緊張得說不出話來，只好聽人提示。◇ **~ sb to do sth** (*computing* 計) *The program will prompt you to enter data where required.* 這個程序在必要時將提醒你輸入數據。◇ **~ (sb) + speech** *'And then what happened?' he prompted.* "後來怎樣了？" 他鼓勵對方繼續說下去。 **3** [T, I] **~ (sb)** to follow the text of a play and remind the actors what the words are if they forget their lines 給（演員）提詞

■ ***noun*** **1** a word or words said to an actor, to remind them what to say next when they have forgotten（給演員的）提詞，提示 **2** (*computing* 計) a sign on a computer

P

screen that shows that the computer has finished doing sth and is ready for more instructions 提示符

▪ ***adv.*** exactly at the time mentioned 準時地：*The meeting will begin at ten o'clock prompt.* 會議將於十點鐘準時開始。

prompt·er /ˈprɒmptə(r); *NAmE* ˈprɑːm-/ *noun* a person who prompts actors in a play 提詞人（給演員提示台詞）

prompt·ing /ˈprɒmptɪŋ; *NAmE* ˈprɑːm-/ *noun* [U] (also **promptings** [pl.]) an act of persuading sb to do sth 勸說；催促；督促：*He wrote the letter without further prompting.* 他不用人再催促就寫了信。◇ *Never again would she listen to the promptings of her heart.* 她再也不會衝動行事了。

prompt·ly 🔑 /ˈprɒmptli; *NAmE* ˈprɑːm-/ *adv.* **1** 🔑 without delay 迅速地；立即：*She deals with all the correspondence promptly and efficiently.* 她迅速有效地處理全部來往信件。**2** 🔑 exactly at the correct time or at the time mentioned 及時地；準時地 SYN **punctually**：*They arrived promptly at two o'clock.* 他們於兩點鐘準時到達。**3** (always used before the verb 總置於動詞前) immediately 立即；馬上：*She read the letter and promptly burst into tears.* 她一看信眼淚就奪眶而出。

pro·mul·gate /ˈprɒmlgeɪt; *NAmE* ˈprɑːm-/ *verb* (*formal*) **1** [usually passive] **~ sth** to spread an idea, a belief, etc. among many people 傳播；傳揚；宣傳 **2 ~ sth** to announce a new law or system officially or publicly 宣佈，頒佈，發佈（新法律或體制）▶ **pro·mul·ga·tion** /ˌprɒmlˈgeɪʃn; *NAmE* ˌprɑːm-/ *noun* [U]

prone /prəʊn; *NAmE* proʊn/ *adj.* **1** likely to suffer from sth or to do sth bad 易於遭受；有做（壞事）的傾向 SYN **liable**：**~ to sth** *prone to injury* 容易受傷 ◇ *Working without a break makes you more prone to error.* 連續工作不停歇使人更容易出錯。◇ **~ to do sth** *Tired drivers were found to be particularly prone to ignore warning signs.* 據調查，疲勞駕車時特別容易忽視警示標誌。**2 -prone** (in adjectives 構成形容詞) likely to suffer or do the thing mentioned 有做…傾向的；易於遭受…的：*error-prone* 容易出錯的 ◇ *injury-prone* 容易受傷的 ➲ see also ACCIDENT-PRONE **3** (*formal*) lying flat with the front of your body touching the ground 俯卧的 SYN **prostrate**：*The victim lay prone without moving.* 受害人趴在地上一動不動。◇ *He was found lying in a prone position.* 人們發現他俯卧着。➲ compare SUPINE (1) ▶ **prone·ness** /ˈprəʊnnəs; *NAmE* ˈproʊn-/ *noun* [U]：*proneness to depression* 易消沉傾向

prong /prɒŋ; *NAmE* prɔːŋ/ *noun* **1** each of the two or more long pointed parts of a fork 叉子齒 ➲ VISUAL VOCAB page V22 **2** each of the separate parts of an attack, argument, etc., that move towards a place, subject, etc. from different positions（進攻、論點等的）方面 **3 -pronged** (in adjectives 構成形容詞) having the number or type of prongs mentioned 有…齒的；分…方面的：*a two-pronged fork* 二齒叉 ◇ *a three-pronged attack* 三路進攻

pro·nom·inal /prəʊˈnɒmɪnl; *NAmE* proʊˈnɑːm-/ *adj.* (*grammar* 語法) relating to a pronoun 代詞的；代名詞的

pro·noun /ˈprəʊnaʊn; *NAmE* ˈproʊ-/ *noun* (*grammar* 語法) a word that is used instead of a noun or noun phrase, for example *he, it, hers, me, them*, etc. 代詞，代名詞（代替名詞或名詞詞組的單詞）：*demonstrative/interrogative/possessive/relative pronouns* 指示／疑問／物主／關係代詞 ➲ see also PERSONAL PRONOUN

pro·nounce 🔑 /prəˈnaʊns/ *verb*

> **WORD FAMILY**
> **pronounce** *verb*
> **pronunciation** *noun*
> **unpronounceable** *adj.*
> **mispronounce** *verb*

1 🔑 **~ sth** to make the sound of a word or letter in a particular way 發音；讀（音）：*Very few people can pronounce my name correctly.* 很少人能把我的名字唸正確。◇ *The 'b' in lamb is not pronounced.* * lamb 中的 b 不發音。➲ see also PRONUNCIATION, UNPRONOUNCEABLE **2** (*formal*) to say or give sth formally, officially or publicly 正式宣佈（或公佈、授予等）：**~ sth** *to pronounce an opinion* 發表意見 ◇ *The judge will pronounce sentence today.* 法官將於今天宣判。◇ **~ sb/sth + noun** *She pronounced him the winner of the competition.* 她宣佈他是競賽的優勝者。◇ *I now pronounce you man and wife* (= in a marriage ceremony). 現在正式宣佈你們結為夫妻。◇ **~ sb/sth + adj.** *She was pronounced dead on arrival at the hospital.* 到達醫院時她被宣告已經死亡。◇ **~ sb/sth to be/have sth** *He pronounced the country to be in a state of war.* 他宣佈全國進入戰爭狀態。◇ **~ that ...** *She pronounced that an error had been made.* 她宣稱曾經有個錯誤。◇ **+ speech** *'It's pneumonia,' he pronounced gravely.* "是肺炎。"他沉重地宣佈。

PHR V **proˈnounce for/against sb** (*law* 律) to give a judgement in court for or against sb 作有利（或不利）於…的判決；判…勝訴（或敗訴）：*The judge pronounced for* (= in favour of) *the defendant.* 法官宣佈被告勝訴。**proˈnounce on/upon sth** (*formal*) to state your opinion on sth, or give a decision about sth 就…表態（或做決定）：*The minister will pronounce on further security measures later today.* 今天稍後部長將發表進一步的安全措施。

pro·nounce·able /prəˈnaʊnsəbl/ *adj.* (of sounds or words 聲音或詞語) that can be pronounced 發音的；讀得出的 OPP **unpronounceable**

pro·nounced /prəˈnaʊnst/ *adj.* very noticeable, obvious or strongly expressed 顯著的；很明顯的；表達明確的 SYN **definite**：*He walked with a pronounced limp.* 他走路明顯跛足。◇ *She has very pronounced views on art.* 她有非常明確的藝術觀。

pro·nounce·ment /prəˈnaʊnsmənt/ *noun* **~ (on sth)** (*formal*) a formal public statement 聲明；公告；宣告

pronto /ˈprɒntəʊ; *NAmE* ˈprɑːntoʊ/ *adv.* (*informal*) quickly; immediately 立即；馬上；火速：*I expect to see you back here, pronto!* 我要你立即回到這裏來！

pro·nun·ci·ation 🔑 /prəˌnʌnsiˈeɪʃn/ *noun* **1** 🔑 [U, C] the way in which a language or a particular word or sound is pronounced 發音；讀音：*a guide to English pronunciation* 英語發音指南 ◇ *There is more than one pronunciation of 'garage'.* * garage 的讀音不止一種。**2** 🔑 [sing.] the way in which a particular person pronounces the words of a language（某人的）發音：*Your pronunciation is excellent.* 你的發音好極了。

proof 🔑 /pruːf/ *noun, adj., verb*

▪ ***noun*** **1** 🔑 [U, C] information, documents, etc. that show that sth is true 證據；證明 SYN **evidence**：***positive/conclusive proof*** 確切的／確鑿的證據 ◇ **~ of sth** *Can you provide any **proof of identity**?* 你能提供什麼身分證明嗎？◇ *Keep the receipt as **proof of purchase**.* 保存發票，作為購物證明。◇ *These results are a further proof of his outstanding ability.* 這些成果進一步證明了他的傑出才幹。◇ **~ that ...** *There is no proof that the knife belonged to her.* 沒有證據證明那把刀子是屬於她的。**2** [U] the process of testing whether sth is true or a fact 檢驗；證實：*Is the claim capable of proof?* 這個說法能證明是正確的嗎？➲ see also BURDEN OF PROOF **3** [C] (*mathematics* 數) a way of proving that a statement is true or that what you have calculated is correct 證明；求證；驗算 **4** [C, usually pl.] a copy of printed material which is produced so that mistakes can be corrected 校樣：*She was checking the proofs of her latest novel.* 她正在審閱她的新小說的校樣。**5** [U] a standard used to measure the strength of alcoholic drinks（酒的）標準酒精度

IDM **the proof of the ˈpudding (is in the ˈeating)** (*saying*) you can only judge if sth is good or bad when you have tried it 只有通過體驗才能判斷事物的好壞 ➲ more at LIVING *adj.*

▪ ***adj.*** **1 ~ against sth** (*formal*) that can resist the damaging or harmful effects of sth 能抵禦；能防範；可防護：*The sea wall was not proof against the strength of the waves.* 防波堤擋不住海浪的力量。**2** (in compounds 構成複合詞) that can resist or protect against the thing mentioned 防…的；抗…的：***rainproof/windproof** clothing* 防雨／防風服裝 ◇ *The car has childproof locks on the rear doors.* 汽車後門裝有防止兒童開啟的鎖。◇ *an inflation-proof pension plan* 已考慮通貨膨脹的養老金計劃

▪ ***verb*** **1 ~ sth** to put a special substance on sth, especially cloth, to protect it against water, fire, etc. 給（織物等）做防護處理；使防水（或防火等）：*proofed canvas* 做過防水處理的帆布 **2 ~ sth** to produce a test copy of a piece of printed work so that mistakes can be corrected 印…的校樣：*colour proofing* 印彩色校樣

proof·read /'pru:fri:d/ *verb* (**proof·read**, **proof·read** /-red/) [T, I] **~ (sth)** to read and correct a piece of written or printed work 校閱；校對；勘校：*Has this document been proofread?* 這份文件校對過沒有？ ▶ **proof·read·er** *noun*：*to work as a proofreader for a publishing company* 給一家出版公司當校對員

prop /prɒp; *NAmE* prɑ:p/ *noun*, *verb*

■ ***noun*** **1** a piece of wood, metal, etc. used to support sth or keep it in position 支柱；支撐物：*Rescuers used props to stop the roof of the tunnel collapsing.* 救援人員用支柱防止隧道頂塌陷。◇ *a pit prop* (= one used in a coal mine) 煤礦坑木 **2** a person or thing that gives help or support to sb/sth that is weak 支持者；支柱；後盾 **3** [usually pl.] a small object used by actors during the performance of a play or in a film/movie 道具：*He is responsible for all the stage props and lighting.* 他負責全部舞台道具和燈光。 **4** (also **'prop forward**) (in RUGBY 橄欖球) a player on either side of the front row of a SCRUM 支柱前鋒

IDM **give props to sb** (*informal*) used to say that people should appreciate what sb has done because it is good 對（某人）表示感激（或敬佩）：*I gotta give props to the bass player.* 我得向貝斯手表示感謝。 ORIGIN Props here means 'proper respect or recognition'. 在這裏 props 意為"應得的尊重或認可"。

■ ***verb*** (**-pp-**) to support an object by leaning it against sth, or putting sth under it etc.; to support a person in the same way 支撐：**~ sth/sb/yourself (up) (against sth)** *He propped his bike against the wall.* 他把自行車靠在牆邊。◇ *She propped herself up on one elbow.* 她單肘撐起身子。◇ *He lay propped against the pillows.* 他靠着枕頭躺着。◇ **~ sth + adj.** *The door was propped open.* 門被支開着。

PHR V **,prop sth↔'up** **1** to prevent sth from falling by putting sth under it to support it 撐起；支起 SYN **shore up** **2** (often *disapproving*) to help sth that is having difficulties 幫助；扶持；救濟：*The government was accused of propping up declining industries.* 人們指責政府貼補日趨衰落的產業。

propa·ganda /,prɒpə'gændə; *NAmE* ,prɑ:pə-/ *noun* [U] (usually *disapproving*) ideas or statements that may be false or exaggerated and that are used in order to gain support for a political leader, party, etc. 宣傳；鼓吹：*enemy propaganda* 敵方的宣傳 ◇ *a propaganda campaign* 宣傳運動

propa·gand·ist /,prɒpə'gændɪst; *NAmE* ,prɑ:pə-/ *noun* (*formal*, usually *disapproving*) a person who creates or spreads propaganda 鼓吹者；宣傳者 ▶ **propa·gand·ist** *adj.* [only before noun]：*a propagandist organization* 宣傳機構

propa·gand·ize (*BrE* also **-ise**) /,prɒpə'gændaɪz; *NAmE* ,prɑ:pə-/ *verb* [I, T] **~ (sb/sth)** (*formal*, *disapproving*) to spread PROPAGANDA; to influence people using PROPAGANDA 宣傳；大肆鼓吹

propa·gate /'prɒpəgeɪt; *NAmE* 'prɑ:p-/ *verb* **1** [T] **~ sth** (*formal*) to spread an idea, a belief or a piece of information among many people 傳播；宣傳：*Television advertising propagates a false image of the ideal family.* 電視廣告傳播着理想家庭的一種假象。 **2** [T, I] **~ (sth)** (*technical* 術語) to produce new plants from a parent plant 繁殖；增殖：*The plant can be propagated from seed.* 這種植物可由種子繁殖。◇ *Plants won't propagate in these conditions.* 植物在這種條件下不能繁殖。 ▶ **propa·ga·tion** /,prɒpə'geɪʃn; *NAmE* ,prɑ:p-/ *noun* [U]

prop·aga·tor /'prɒpəgeɪtə(r); *NAmE* 'prɑ:p-/ *noun* a box for propagating plants in （植物）繁殖盒

pro·pane /'prəʊpeɪn; *NAmE* 'proʊ-/ *noun* [U] a gas found in natural gas and PETROLEUM and used as a fuel for cooking and heating 丙烷：*a propane gas cylinder* 丙烷氣鋼瓶

pro·pel /prə'pel/ *verb* (**-ll-**) [often passive] **1 ~ sth (+ adv./prep.)** to move, drive or push sth forward or in a particular direction 推動；驅動；推進：*mechanically propelled vehicles* 機動車輛 ◇ *He succeeded in propelling the ball across the line.* 他成功地把球帶過線。 **2 ~ sb + adv./prep.** to force sb to move in a particular direction or to get into a particular situation 驅使；迫使；推搡：*He was grabbed from behind and propelled through the door.* 有人從後面抓住他，把他推過門去。◇ *Fury propelled her into action.* 怒火驅使她行動起來。 ➲ see also PROPULSION

pro·pel·lant /prə'pelənt/ *noun* [C, U] **1** a gas that forces out the contents of an AEROSOL 噴射劑（如噴霧器中的壓縮氣體） **2** a thing or substance that propels sth, for example the fuel that fires a ROCKET 推進器，推進劑（如發射火箭用）

pro·pel·ler /prə'pelə(r)/ *noun* a device with two or more blades that turn quickly and cause a ship or an aircraft to move forward 螺旋槳（飛機或輪船的推進器） ➲ VISUAL VOCAB page V53

pro,pelling 'pencil *noun* a pencil with a LEAD that can be moved down for writing by turning or pushing the top of the pencil 自動鉛筆；活動鉛筆

pro·pen·sity /prə'pensəti/ *noun* (*pl.* **-ies**) (*formal*) a tendency to a particular kind of behaviour （行為方面的）傾向；習性 SYN **inclination**：**~ (for sth/for doing sth)** *He showed a propensity for violence.* 他表現出暴力傾向。◇ **~ (to do sth)** *She has a propensity to exaggerate.* 她愛言過其實。

proper 0‑w /'prɒpə(r); *NAmE* 'prɑ:p-/ *adj.*

1 0‑w [only before noun] (*especially BrE*) right, appropriate or correct; according to the rules 正確的；恰當的；符合規則的：*We should have had a proper discussion before voting.* 我們本應在表決之前好好討論一下才是。◇ *Please follow the proper procedures for dealing with complaints.* 請按正當手續處理投訴。◇ *Nothing is in its proper place.* 東西都放得亂七八糟。 **2** 0‑w [only before noun] (*BrE*, *informal*) that you consider to be real and of a good enough standard 真正的；像樣的；名副其實的：*Eat some proper food, not just toast and jam!* 吃點正常的食物，別淨吃烤麪包加果醬！◇ *When are you going to get a proper job?* 你打算什麼時候去找一份正經的工作呀？ **3** socially and morally acceptable 符合習俗（或體統）的；正當的；規矩的：*It is* **right and proper** *that parents take responsibility for their children's attendance at school.* 父母負責督促子女上學上課，這是天經地義的事。◇ *The development was planned without proper regard to the interests of local people.* 新開發區的規劃沒有正當考慮當地居民的利益。◇ *He is always perfectly proper in his behaviour.* 他的行為舉止向來是無可挑剔的。 OPP **improper** ➲ see also PROPRIETY **4** [after noun] according to the most exact meaning of the word 嚴格意義上的；狹義的：*The celebrations proper always begin on the last stroke of midnight.* 正式慶典總是在午夜鐘聲的最後一響開始。 **5** [only before noun] (*BrE*, *informal*) complete 完全的；徹底的：*We're in a proper mess now.* 我們現在真是一團糟。 **6 ~ to sth** (*formal*) belonging to a particular type of thing; natural in a particular situation or place 獨具的；天然享有的；特有的：*They should be treated with the dignity proper to all individuals created by God.* 他們應當享有上帝賦予每一個受造物的尊嚴。

IDM **,good and 'proper** (*BrE*, *informal*) completely; thoroughly 完全；徹底：*That's messed things up good and proper.* 這就把事情徹底弄砸了。

,proper 'fraction *noun* (*mathematics* 數) a FRACTION that is less than one, with the bottom number greater than the top number, for example ¼ or ⅜ 真分數

prop·er·ly 0‑w /'prɒpəli; *NAmE* 'prɑ:pərli/ *adv.*

1 0‑w (*especially BrE*) in a way that is correct and/or appropriate 正確地；適當地：*How much money do we need to do the job properly?* 我們需要多少錢才能做好這件事？◇ *The television isn't working properly.* 這台電視機運作不正常。◇ *Make sure the letter is properly addressed.* 一定要正確書寫信上的地址。 **2** 0‑w in a way that is socially or morally acceptable 得體地；恰當地；符合習俗地：*You acted perfectly properly in approaching me first.* 你先來找我是完全對的。◇ *When will these kids learn to behave properly?* 這些孩子何時才能學會規矩些？ OPP **improperly** **3** really; in fact 真正地；實際上：

He had usurped powers that properly belonged to parliament. 他僭越了實際上屬於議會的權力。◇ *The subject is not,* ***properly speaking*** (= really)*, a science.* 嚴格地說，這門學科不是科學。

ˌproper ˈnoun (also **ˌproper ˈname**) *noun* (*grammar* 語法) a word that is the name of a person, a place, an institution, etc. and is written with a capital letter, for example *Tom, Mrs Jones, Rome, Texas, the Rhine, the White House* 專有名詞（人、地、機構等的名稱）➲ compare ABSTRACT NOUN, COMMON NOUN

prop·er·tied /ˈprɒpətid; *NAmE* ˈprɑːpərtid/ *adj.* [only before noun] (*formal*) owning property, especially land 有財產的；（尤指）有地產的

prop·erty 🔑 /ˈprɒpəti; *NAmE* ˈprɑːpərti/ *noun* (*pl.* **-ies**)
1 🔑 [U] a thing or things that are owned by sb; a possession or possessions 所有物；財產；財物：*This building is government property.* 這座大樓是政府的財產。◇ *Be careful not to damage other people's property.* 小心別損及別人的財物。➲ see also INTELLECTUAL PROPERTY, LOST PROPERTY, PUBLIC PROPERTY ➲ **SYNONYMS** at THING **2** 🔑 [U] land and buildings 不動產；房地產：*The price of property has risen enormously.* 房地產的價格大幅上升了。◇ *property prices* 房地產價格 ◇ *a property developer* 房地產開發商 ➲ **SYNONYMS** at BUILDING **3** 🔑 [C] a building or buildings and the surrounding land 房屋及院落；莊園；房地產：*There are a lot of empty properties in the area.* 這個地區有大量的閒置房地產。➲ **SYNONYMS** at BUILDING ➲ **COLLOCATIONS** at HOUSE **4** [C, usually pl.] (*formal*) a quality or characteristic that sth has 性質；特性：*Compare the physical properties of the two substances.* 比較一下這兩種物質的物理特性。◇ *a plant with medicinal properties* 藥用植物

proph·ecy /ˈprɒfəsi; *NAmE* ˈprɑːf-/ *noun* (*pl.* **-ies**) **1** [C] a statement that sth will happen in the future, especially one made by sb with religious or magic powers 預言：*to fulfil a prophecy* (= make it come true) 實現預言 **2** [U] (*formal*) the power of being able to say what will happen in the future 預言能力：*She was believed to have the gift of prophecy.* 據信她有預言的天賦。

proph·esy /ˈprɒfəsaɪ; *NAmE* ˈprɑːf-/ *verb* (**proph·es·ies, proph·esy·ing, proph·es·ied, proph·es·ied**) to say what will happen in the future (done in the past using religious or magic powers) 預告；預言：**~ sth** *to prophesy war* 預言有戰爭 ◇ **~ that …** *She prophesied that she would win a gold medal.* 她預言自己將贏得金牌。◇ **+ speech** *'It will end in disaster,' he prophesied.* "這將以災難而告終。" 他預言道。

prophet /ˈprɒfɪt; *NAmE* ˈprɑːf-/ *noun* **1** [C] (in the Christian, Jewish and Muslim religions) a person sent by God to teach the people and give them messages from God （基督教、猶太教和伊斯蘭教的）先知 **2 the Prophet** [sing.] Muhammad, who founded the religion of Islam 穆罕默德（伊斯蘭教的創始人）**3** [C] a person who claims to know what will happen in the future 預言家；預言者 **4** [C] **~ (of sth)** a person who teaches or supports a new idea, theory, etc. 倡導者；擁護者；鼓吹者：*William Morris was one of the early prophets of socialism.* 威廉 • 莫里斯是社會主義的早期傳播者之一。**5 the Prophets** [pl.] the name used for some books of the Old Testament and the Hebrew Bible 《〈聖經〉舊約》和《希伯來聖經》中的）先知書 **IDM** see DOOM *n.*

proph·et·ess /ˈprɒfɪtes; ˌprɒfɪˈtes; *NAmE* ˈprɑːfətəs/ *noun* a woman who is a prophet (1), (3), (4) 女預言家；女倡導者

proph·et·ic /prəˈfetɪk/ *adj.* (*formal*) **1** correctly stating or showing what will happen in the future 正確預言的；有預見的：*Many of his warnings proved prophetic.* 他的許多警告都證明是有先見之明的。**2** like or connected with a prophet or prophets 預言家的；像預言家的；似先知的：*the prophetic books of the Old Testament* 《〈聖經〉舊約》先知書 ▸ **proph·et·ic·al·ly** /prəˈfetɪkli/ *adv.*

prophy·lac·tic /ˌprɒfɪˈlæktɪk; *NAmE* ˌproʊfəˈlæktɪk/ *adj.*, *noun*
▪ ***adj.*** (*medical* 醫) done or used in order to prevent a disease 預防疾病的：*prophylactic treatment* 預防性治療 ▸ **prophy·lac·tic·al·ly** /-kli/ *adv.*
▪ ***noun*** **1** (*medical* 醫) a medicine, device or course of action that prevents disease 預防性藥物（或器具、措施）**2** (*NAmE, formal*) = CONDOM (1)

prophy·laxis /ˌprɒfɪˈlæksɪs; *NAmE* ˌprɑːf-/ *noun* [U] (*medical* 醫) action that is taken in order to prevent disease（疾病）預防

pro·pin·quity /prəˈpɪŋkwəti/ *noun* [U] (*formal*) the state of being near in space or time（空間或時間上的）臨近，接近 **SYN** **proximity**

pro·piti·ate /prəˈpɪʃieɪt/ *verb* **~ sb** (*formal*) to stop sb from being angry by trying to please them 使息怒 **SYN** **placate**：*Sacrifices were made to propitiate the gods.* 人們供奉祭品以求神靈息怒。▸ **pro·piti·ation** /prəˌpɪʃiˈeɪʃn/ *noun* [U]

pro·piti·atory /prəˈpɪʃiətri; *NAmE* -tɔːri/ *adj.* (*formal*) intended to win back the friendship and approval of an angry or aggressive person 為和解的；為贏回好感的；安撫的：*She saw the flowers as a propitiatory offering.* 在她看來，送花是主動和解的表示。

pro·pi·tious /prəˈpɪʃəs/ *adj.* **~ (for sth/sb)** (*formal*) likely to produce a successful result 吉利的；吉慶的；吉祥的：*It was not a propitious time to start a new business.* 那不是營業開張的吉時佳日。

pro·pon·ent /prəˈpəʊnənt; *NAmE* -ˈpoʊ-/ *noun* **~ (of sth)** (*formal*) a person who supports an idea or course of action 倡導者；支持者；擁護者 **SYN** **advocate**

Language Bank 用語庫

proportion 份額

Describing fractions and proportions
描述分數和份額

- According to this pie chart, **a third of** students' leisure time is spent watching TV. 如餅分圖所示，學生的閒暇時間有三分之一都花在看電視上。
- **One in five** hours is/are spent socializing. 每五個小時中有一個小時花在社交活動上。
- Socializing **accounts for / makes up / comprises** about 20% of leisure time. 社交活動佔去大約百分之二十的閒暇時間。
- Students spend **twice as much** time playing computer games as doing sport. 學生們玩電腦遊戲的時間是做運動時間的兩倍。
- **Three times as many** hours are spent playing computer games as reading. 玩電腦遊戲的時間是閱讀時間的三倍。
- The figure for playing computer games is **three times higher than** the figure for reading. 玩電腦遊戲的時間比閱讀時間多兩倍。
- **The largest proportion of** time is spent playing computer games. 大部份時間都花在玩電腦遊戲上。

➲ note at HALF
➲ Language Banks at EXPECT, FALL, ILLUSTRATE, INCREASE

pro·por·tion 🔑 **AW** /prəˈpɔːʃn; *NAmE* -ˈpɔːrʃn/ *noun*
▸ **PART OF WHOLE 部份** **1** 🔑 [C+sing./pl. v.] a part or share of a whole 部份；份額：*Water covers a large proportion of the earth's surface.* 水覆蓋了地球表面的大部份。◇ *Loam is a soil with roughly equal proportions of clay, sand and silt.* 壤土是由大約等份的黏土、沙和粉砂合成的。◇ *The proportion of regular smokers increases with age.* 經常吸煙者的人口比重隨年齡的增長而上升。◇ *A higher proportion of Americans go on to higher education than is the case in Britain.* 美國人上大學的比例大於英國。
▸ **RELATIONSHIP 關係** **2** 🔑 [U] **~ (of sth to sth)** the relationship of one thing to another in size, amount, etc. 比例；

倍數關係 SYN **ratio**：*The proportion of men to women in the college has changed dramatically over the years.* 近年來，這個學院的男女學生比例出現了劇變。◇ *The basic ingredients are limestone and clay in the proportion 2:1.* 基本成分是石灰石和黏土，比例為 2:1。◇ *The room is very long* ***in proportion to*** (= relative to) *its width.* 這房間的長度比寬度大很多。 **3** [U, C, usually pl.] the correct relationship in size, degree, importance, etc. between one thing and another or between the parts of a whole 正確的比例；均衡；勻稱：*You haven't drawn the figures in the foreground* ***in proportion.*** 你的前景人物畫得不合比例。◇ *The head is* ***out of proportion with*** *the body.* 頭部和身體不成比例。◇ *an impressive building with fine proportions* 比例諧調的雄偉建築物 ◇ *Always try to keep a* ***sense of proportion*** (= of the relative importance of different things). 事有輕重緩急之分，這要常記在心。

▸ **SIZE/SHAPE 大小；形狀 4 proportions** [pl.] the measurements of sth; its size and shape 面積；體積；規模；程度：*This method divides the task into more manageable proportions.* 這個方法把要完成的任務劃分成較為易於操作的步驟。◇ *a food shortage that could soon* ***reach crisis proportions*** 可能會很快達到危機程度的糧食短缺 ◇ *a room of fairly generous proportions* 相當寬敞的屋子

▸ **MATHEMATICS 數學 5** [U] the equal relationship between two pairs of numbers, as in the statement '4 is to 8 as 6 is to 12' 等比關係；比例

IDM **ˌkeep sth in proˈportion** to react to sth in a sensible way and not think it is worse or more serious than it really is 恰當地處事；看待事物恰如其分 **out of (all) proˈportion (to sth)** larger, more serious, etc. in relation to sth than is necessary or appropriate 不相稱；不諧調：*They earn salaries out of all proportion to their ability.* 他們掙的工資與其能力不相稱。◇ *The media have blown the incident up out of all proportion.* 媒體大肆渲染這件事。

Grammar Point 語法説明

proportion

- If **proportion** is used with an uncountable or a singular noun, the verb is generally singular. * proportion 與不可數名詞或單數名詞連用時，動詞一般用單數：*A proportion of the land* ***is*** *used for agriculture.* 一部份土地作農用。
- If **the proportion of** is used with a plural countable noun, or a singular noun that represents a group of people, the verb is usually singular, but with **a (large, small, etc.) proportion of** a plural verb is often used, especially in *BrE*. * the proportion of 與複數可數名詞或單數集合名詞連用時，動詞通常為單數；但如果是 a（large、small 等）proportion of，則常用複數動詞，尤其在英式英語中：*The proportion of small cars on America's roads* ***is*** *increasing.* 美國公路上小型車的比例在逐漸增加。◇ *A high proportion of five-year-olds* ***have*** *teeth in poor condition.* 五歲兒童牙齒不健康的比例高。

pro·por·tion·al AW /prəˈpɔːʃənl; *NAmE* -ˈpɔːrʃ-/ *adj.* **~ (to sth)** of an appropriate size, amount or degree in comparison with sth 相稱的；成比例的；均衡的：*Salary is proportional to years of experience.* 薪金視資歷而定。◇ *to be* ***directly/inversely proportional*** *to sth* 與某事物成正比／反比 ▸ **pro·por·tion·al·ly** AW *adv.*：*Families with children spend proportionally less per person than families without children.* 有子女家庭比無子女家庭的人均開銷相對地少。

pro·por·tion·al·ity /prəˌpɔːʃəˈnæləti; *NAmE* -pɔːrʃ-/ *noun* [U] (*formal*) the principle that an action, a punishment, etc. should not be more severe than is necessary（行動、處罰等的）相稱原則，恰當性

proˌportional ˌrepresenˈtation *noun* [U] (*abbr.* **PR**) a system that gives each party in an election a number of seats in relation to the number of votes its candidates receive 比例代表制（按參選各黨派的得票比例分配席位）➲ compare FIRST-PAST-THE-POST

pro·por·tion·ate AW /prəˈpɔːʃənət; *NAmE* -ˈpɔːrʃ-/ *adj.* **~ (to sth)** (*formal*) increasing or decreasing in size, amount or degree according to changes in sth else 成比例的；相應的；相稱的 SYN **proportional**：*The number of accidents is proportionate to the increased volume of traffic.* 交通事故的數字與交通量的增長成正比。➲ compare DISPROPORTIONATE ▸ **pro·por·tion·ate·ly** AW *adv.*：*Prices have risen but wages have not risen proportionately.* 物價上漲了，但是工資並沒有相應增加。

pro·por·tioned /prəˈpɔːʃənd; *NAmE* -ˈpɔːrʃ-/ *adj.* (used especially after an adverb 尤用於副詞後) having parts that relate in size to other parts in the way that is described 按比例的；有某種比例關係的：*a well-proportioned living room* 比例合理的起居室 ◇ *She was tall and perfectly proportioned.* 她身材高挑且十分勻稱。

pro·posal /prəˈpəʊzl; *NAmE* -ˈpoʊzl/ *noun* **1** [C, U] a formal suggestion or plan; the act of making a suggestion 提議；建議；動議：*to* ***submit/consider/accept/reject a proposal*** 提交／審議／接受／拒絕一項建議 ◇ **~ to do sth** *a proposal to build more office accommodation* 增建辦公樓的建議 ◇ **~ that …** *His proposal that the system should be changed was rejected.* 他提的關於修改制度的建議被拒絕了。◇ **~ for sth** *They judged that the time was right for the proposal of new terms for the trade agreement.* 他們判斷，提出貿易協定新條款的時機成熟了。 **2** [C] an act of formally asking sb to marry you 求婚

pro·pose /prəˈpəʊz; *NAmE* -ˈpoʊz/ *verb*

▸ **SUGGEST PLAN 建議 1** [T] (*formal*) to suggest a plan, an idea, etc. for people to think about and decide on 提議；建議：**~ sth** *The government proposed changes to the voting system.* 政府建議修改表決制度。◇ *What would you propose?* 你想提什麼建議？◇ **~ that …** *She proposed that the book be banned.* 她提議查禁這本書。◇ (*BrE* also) *She proposed that the book should be banned.* 她提議查禁這本書。◇ **it is proposed that …** *It was proposed that the president be elected for a period of two years.* 有人提議選出的主席任期為兩年。◇ **~ doing sth** *He proposed changing the name of the company.* 他建議更改公司的名稱。◇ **it is proposed to do sth** *It was proposed to pay the money from public funds.* 有人提議用公款支付這筆錢。

▸ **INTEND 意欲 2** [T] (*formal*) to intend to do sth 打算；希冀；計劃：**~ to do sth** *What do you propose to do now?* 現在你打算做什麼？◇ **~ doing sth** *How do you propose getting home?* 你打算怎麼回家？

▸ **MARRIAGE 婚姻 3** [I, T] to ask sb to marry you 求婚：*He was afraid that if he proposed she might refuse.* 他擔心他若求婚，她會拒絕。◇ **~ to sb** *She proposed to me!* 她向我求婚了！◇ **~ sth (to sb)** *to propose marriage* 求婚

▸ **AT FORMAL MEETING 正式會議 4** [T] to suggest sth at a formal meeting and ask people to vote on it 提名；提出…供表決：**~ sb (for/as sth)** *I propose Tom Ellis for chairman.* 我提名湯姆•埃利斯做主席。◇ **~ sth** *to* ***propose a motion*** (= to be the main speaker in support of an idea at a formal debate) 提出動議 ➲ compare OPPOSE (1), SECOND[1] *v.*

▸ **SUGGEST EXPLANATION 提出解釋 5** [T] **~ sth** (*formal*) to suggest an explanation of sth for people to consider 提供（解釋）SYN **propound**：*She proposed a possible solution to the mystery.* 她提出了對這個奧秘的一種可能的解答。

IDM **propose a ˈtoast (to sb) | propose sb's ˈhealth** to ask people to wish sb health, happiness and success by raising their glasses and drinking（為某人）祝酒：*I'd like to propose a toast to the bride and groom.* 我提議為新郎新娘的幸福乾杯！

pro·poser /prəˈpəʊzə(r); *NAmE* -ˈpoʊz-/ *noun* a person who formally suggests sth at a meeting 提議人；建議人 ➲ compare SECONDER

prop·os·ition /ˌprɒpəˈzɪʃn; *NAmE* ˌprɑːp-/ *noun, verb*

■ *noun* **1** an idea or a plan of action that is suggested, especially in business 提議，建議，計劃（尤指業務上的）：*I'd like to put a business proposition to you.* 我想向您提個業務上的建議。◇ *He was trying to make it look like an* ***attractive proposition.*** 他正設法使他的計劃顯得

P

吸引人。 **2** a thing that you intend to do; a problem or task to be dealt with 欲做的事；待處理的問題；任務 SYN **matter**： *Getting a work permit in the UK is not always a simple proposition.* 在英國獲得工作許可證往往不是一件簡單的事情。 **3** (also **Proposition**) (in the US) a suggested change to the law that people can vote on （美國）法律修正議案： *How did you vote on Proposition 8?* 對於第 8 項修正案你是怎麼投的票？ **4** (*formal*) a statement that expresses an opinion 見解；主張；觀點： *Her assessment is based on the proposition that power corrupts.* 她的分析是建立在權力使人墮落的觀點上的。 **5** (*mathematics* 數) a statement of a THEOREM, and an explanation of how it can be proved 命題 ▸ **prop·os·ition·al** *adj.*

■ *verb* **~ sb** to say in a direct way to sb that you would like to have sex with them 求歡： *She was propositioned by a strange man in the bar.* 酒吧裏有個陌生男人向她求歡。

pro·pound /prəˈpaʊnd/ *verb* **~ sth** (*formal*) to suggest an idea or explanation of sth for people to consider 提出（主意或解釋）供考慮 SYN **propose, put forward**： *the theory of natural selection, first propounded by Charles Darwin* 查爾斯 • 達爾文首先提出的物競天擇理論

pro·pri·etary /prəˈpraɪətri; *NAmE* -teri/ *adj.* [usually before noun] **1** (of goods 商品) made and sold by a particular company and protected by a REGISTERED TRADEMARK 專賣的；專營的；專利的： *a proprietary medicine* 專賣藥品 ◇ *proprietary brands* 專利品牌 ◇ *a proprietary name* 專利名稱 **2** relating to an owner or to the fact of owning sth 所有的；所有權的： *The company has a proprietary right to the property.* 公司擁有這筆財產的所有權。

pro·pri·etor /prəˈpraɪətə(r)/ *noun* (*formal*) the owner of a business, a hotel, etc. 業主；所有人： *newspaper proprietors* 報業老闆 ▸ **pro·pri·etor·ship** /prəˈpraɪətəʃɪp; *NAmE* -tərʃ-/ *noun* [U] ➲ see also PROPRIETRESS

pro·pri·etor·ial /prəˌpraɪəˈtɔːriəl/ *adj.* (*formal*) relating to an owner or to the fact of owning sth 業主的；所有者的；所有權的： *proprietorial rights* 所有權 ◇ *He laid a proprietorial hand on her arm* (= as if he owned her). 他緊緊攥住她的胳膊不放。 ▸ **pro·pri·etor·ial·ly** *adv.*

pro·pri·etress /prəˈpraɪətres/ *noun* (*old-fashioned*) a woman who owns a business, hotel, etc. 女業主；女所有人 ➲ see also PROPRIETOR ➲ note at GENDER

pro·pri·ety /prəˈpraɪəti/ *noun* (*formal*) **1** [U] moral and social behaviour that is considered to be correct and acceptable 得體的舉止；有分寸的行為： *Nobody questioned the propriety of her being there alone.* 沒人認為她隻身出現在那裏不得體。 OPP **impropriety** **2 the proprieties** [pl.] the rules of correct behaviour 行為規範；禮節；規矩 SYN **etiquette**： *They were careful to observe the proprieties.* 他們恪守規矩。

pro·pul·sion /prəˈpʌlʃn/ *noun* [U] (*technical* 術語) the force that drives sth forward 推動力；推進： ***wind/steam/jet propulsion*** 風力／蒸汽／噴氣推進 ➲ see also PROPEL ▸ **pro·pul·sive** /prəˈpʌlsɪv/ *adj.*

pro rata /ˌprəʊ ˈrɑːtə; *NAmE* ˌproʊ/ *adj.* (from *Latin*, *formal*) (of a payment or share of sth 付款或份額) calculated according to how much of sth has been used, the amount of work done, etc. 按比例的；成比例的；相應的 SYN **proportionate**： *If costs go up, there will be a pro rata increase in prices.* 如果成本增加，價格就會相應上漲。 ▸ **pro rata** *adv.*： *Prices will increase pro rata.* 價格將相應提高。

pro·sa·ic /prəˈzeɪɪk/ *adj.* (usually *disapproving*) **1** ordinary and not showing any imagination 平庸的；沒有詩意（或美感）的 SYN **unimaginative**： *a prosaic style* 平淡的風格 **2** dull; not romantic 平淡的；乏味的；無聊的 SYN **mundane**： *the prosaic side of life* 生活平淡的一面 ▸ **pro·saic·al·ly** /-kli/ *adv.*

pro·scen·ium /prəˈsiːniəm/ *noun* the part of the stage in a theatre that is in front of the curtain 台口（劇場舞台帷幕前的部份）： *a traditional theatre with a* ***proscenium arch*** (= one that forms a frame for the stage where the curtain is opened) 舞台有拱形框架的傳統劇場

pro·scribe /prəˈskraɪb; *NAmE* proʊˈs-/ *verb* **~ sth** (*formal*) to say officially that sth is banned 宣佈禁止： *proscribed organizations* 被查禁的組織 ▸ **pro·scrip·tion** /prəˈskrɪpʃn; *NAmE* proʊˈs-/ *noun* [U, C]

prose /prəʊz; *NAmE* proʊz/ *noun* [U] writing that is not poetry 散文： *the author's clear elegant prose* (= style of writing) 作者清雅的散文

pros·ecute /ˈprɒsɪkjuːt; *NAmE* ˈprɑːs-/ *verb* **1** [T, I] **~ (sb/sth) (for sth/doing sth)** to officially charge sb with a crime in court 起訴；控告；檢舉： *The company was prosecuted for breaching the Health and Safety Act.* 這家公司被控違反《衞生安全條例》。◇ *Trespassers will be prosecuted* (= a notice telling people to keep out of a particular area). 閒人莫入，違者必究。◇ *The police decided not to prosecute.* 警方決定不予起訴。 **2** [I, T] **~ (sb)** to be a lawyer in a court case for a person or an organization that is charging sb with a crime 擔任控方律師： *the* ***prosecuting counsel/lawyer/attorney*** 原告律師 ◇ *James Spencer, prosecuting, claimed that the witness was lying.* 原告律師詹姆斯 • 斯潘塞指稱證人在撒謊。 **3** [T] **~ sth** (*formal*) to continue taking part in or doing sth 繼續從事（或參與）： *They had overwhelming public support to prosecute the war.* 絕大多數民眾支持他們繼續這場戰爭。

pros·ecu·tion /ˌprɒsɪˈkjuːʃn; *NAmE* ˌprɑːs-/ *noun* **1** [U, C] the process of trying to prove in court that sb is guilty of a crime (= of prosecuting them); the process of being officially charged with a crime in court 起訴；檢舉；訴訟： *Prosecution for a first minor offence rarely leads to imprisonment.* 因初犯輕罪被控者很少被判監禁。◇ *He threatened to bring a private prosecution against the doctor.* 他威脅要對醫生提起民事訴訟。 ➲ COLLOCATIONS at JUSTICE **2 the prosecution** [sing.+sing./pl. v.] a person or an organization that prosecutes sb in court, together with the lawyers, etc. 原告，控方（包括原告和原告律師等）： *He was a* ***witness for the prosecution.*** 他是原告證人。◇ *The prosecution has/have failed to prove its/their case.* 控方未能證明所控屬實。◇ *defence and prosecution* 被告和原告 ◇ *a prosecution lawyer* 控方律師 **3** [U] (*formal*) the act of making sth happen or continue 實施；從事；繼續進行

pros·ecu·tor /ˈprɒsɪkjuːtə(r); *NAmE* ˈprɑːs-/ *noun* **1** a public official who charges sb officially with a crime and prosecutes them in court 公訴人；檢察官： *the* ***public/state prosecutor*** 公訴人；州檢察官 **2** a lawyer who leads the case against a DEFENDANT in court 原告律師；控方律師

pros·elyt·ize (*BrE* also **-ise**) /ˈprɒsələtaɪz; *NAmE* ˈprɑːs-/ *verb* [I] (*formal*, often *disapproving*) to try to persuade other people to accept your beliefs, especially about religion or politics 使（在宗教、政治等方面）歸附

ˈprose poem *noun* a piece of writing that uses the language and ideas associated with poetry, but is not in VERSE form 散文詩

ˈpro shop *noun* a shop/store at a GOLF club that sells or repairs golf equipment, usually run by a professional player who works at that club（高爾夫球俱樂部中通常由職業球員經營的）球具店

pros·ody /ˈprɒsədi; *NAmE* ˈprɑːs-/ *noun* [U] **1** (*technical* 術語) the patterns of sounds and rhythms in poetry; the study of this 韻律；韻律學 **2** (*phonetics* 語音) the part of PHONETICS which is concerned with stress and INTONATION as opposed to individual speech sounds 重音和語調模式；韻律結構 ▸ **pro·sodic** /prəʊˈsɒdɪk; *NAmE* prəˈsɑːdɪk/ *adj.*

pro·spect 0-w AW *noun, verb*

■ *noun* /ˈprɒspekt; *NAmE* ˈprɑːs-/ **1** 0-w [U, sing.] the possibility that sth will happen 可能性；希望： **~ (of sth/of doing sth)** *There is no immediate prospect of peace.* 短期內沒有和平的可能。◇ *A place in the semi-finals is* ***in prospect*** (= likely to happen). 可望爭得半決賽權。◇ **~ (that ...)** *There's a reasonable prospect that his debts will be paid.* 可以合理地預期他會償還債務。 **2** 0-w [sing.] an idea of what might or will happen in the future 前景；展望；設想： *an exciting prospect* 令人興奮的前景 ◇

Travelling alone around the world is a daunting prospect. 想像着隻身走遍世界頗令人心悸。◇ **~ (of sth/of doing sth)** *The prospect of becoming a father filled him with alarm.* 一想到將為人父他就滿懷憂思。 **3** 🔑 **prospects** [pl.] the chances of being successful 成功的機會；前景；前途： *good* ***job/employment/career prospects*** 美好的工作 / 就業 / 事業前途 ◇ *At 25 he was an unemployed musician with no prospects.* * 25 歲的他是個沒有工作、前途渺茫的樂師。◇ **~ for sth** *Long-term prospects for the economy have improved.* 長期的經濟前景已有所改善。◇ **~ of sth** *What are the prospects of promotion in this job?* 做這份工作有多少晉升的機會？ **4** [C] **~ (for sth)** a person who is likely to be successful in a competition （競賽中的）有望獲勝者： *She is one of Canada's best prospects for a gold medal.* 她是加拿大最有希望奪金的選手之一。 **5** [C] (*formal*) a wide view of an area of land, etc. 風景；景色： *a delightful prospect of the lake* 令人心曠神怡的湖上風光

■ ***verb*** /prəˈspekt; *NAmE* ˈprɑːspekt/ [I] **~ (for sth)** to search an area for gold, minerals, oil, etc. 探礦；勘探： *Thousands moved to the area to prospect for gold.* 數以千計的人湧入那個地區淘金。◇ (*figurative*) *to prospect for new clients* 尋找新客戶

pro·spect·ive AW /prəˈspektɪv/ *adj.* [usually before noun] **1** expected to do sth or to become sth 有望的；可能的；預期的；潛在的 SYN **potential**： *a prospective buyer* 可能的買主 **2** expected to happen soon 即將發生的；行將來臨的 SYN **forthcoming**： *They are worried about prospective changes in the law.* 他們擔心即將修改法律。

pro·spect·or /prəˈspektə(r); *NAmE* ˈprɑːspektər/ *noun* a person who searches an area for gold, minerals, oil, etc. 勘探者；探礦者

pro·spec·tus /prəˈspektəs/ *noun* **1** a book or printed document that gives information about a school, college, etc. in order to advertise it （學校的）簡章，簡介 **2** (*business* 商) a document that gives information about a company's shares before they are offered for sale （企業的）招股章程，募股章程

pros·per /ˈprɒspə(r); *NAmE* ˈprɑːs-/ *verb* [I] to develop in a successful way; to be successful, especially in making money 繁榮；興旺；成功；發達 SYN **thrive**

pros·per·ity /prɒˈsperəti; *NAmE* prɑːˈs-/ *noun* [U] the state of being successful, especially in making money 興旺；繁榮；成功；昌盛 SYN **affluence**： *Our future prosperity depends on economic growth.* 我們未來的繁榮昌盛依賴經濟的發展。◇ *The country is enjoying a period of* ***peace and prosperity***. 國家正值太平盛世。

pros·per·ous /ˈprɒspərəs; *NAmE* ˈprɑːs-/ *adj.* (*formal*) rich and successful 繁榮的；成功的；興旺的 SYN **affluent**： *prosperous countries* 繁榮的國家 ➲ SYNONYMS at RICH

pro·state /ˈprɒsteɪt; *NAmE* ˈprɑːs-/ (also **ˈprostate gland**) *noun* a small organ in men, near the BLADDER, that produces a liquid in which SPERM is carried 前列腺

pros·thesis /prɒsˈθiːsɪs; *NAmE* prɑːs-/ *noun* (*pl.* **pros·theses** /-ˈθiːsiːz/) (*medical* 醫) an artificial part of the body, for example a leg, an eye or a tooth 假體（如假肢、假眼或假牙）▸ **pros·thet·ic** /prɒsˈθetɪk; *NAmE* prɑːs-/ *adj.*： *a prosthetic arm* 假臂

pros·thet·ics /prɒsˈθetɪks; *NAmE* prɑːs-/ *noun* **1** [pl.] artificial parts of the body 假體（人造的身體部份）；義肢 **2** [U] the activity of making or attaching artificial body parts 假體製作（或安裝）；義肢製作（或安裝）

pros·ti·tute /ˈprɒstɪtjuːt; *NAmE* ˈprɑːstətuːt/ *noun, verb*

■ ***noun*** a person who has sex for money 賣淫者；娼妓；妓女；男妓

■ ***verb*** **1 ~ sth/yourself** to use your skills, abilities, etc. to do sth that earns you money but that other people do not respect because you are capable of doing sth better 濫用才能；糟蹋自己： *Many felt he was prostituting his talents by writing Hollywood scripts.* 許多人覺得他給好萊塢寫劇本是濫用自己的才華。 **2 ~ yourself** to work as a prostitute 賣淫；出賣肉體

pros·ti·tu·tion /ˌprɒstɪˈtjuːʃn; *NAmE* ˌprɑːstəˈtuːʃn/ *noun* [U] **1** the work of a prostitute 賣淫；為娼；當男妓： *Many women were forced into prostitution.* 許多婦女被迫為娼。◇ *child prostitution* 兒童賣淫 **2 ~ of sth** (*formal*) the use of your abilities on sth of little value 才能的濫用（或糟蹋）

pros·trate *adj., verb*

■ ***adj.*** /ˈprɒstreɪt; *NAmE* ˈprɑːs-/ (*formal*) **1** lying on the ground and facing downwards 俯卧的；趴着的；俯伏的： *They fell prostrate in worship.* 他們拜倒在地。◇ *He stumbled over Luke's prostrate body.* 他絆倒在盧克俯卧的身軀上。 **2 ~ (with sth)** so shocked, upset, etc. that you cannot do anything 給（悲傷等）壓倒： *She was* ***prostrate with grief*** *after her son's death.* 她因喪子悲痛欲絕。

■ ***verb*** /prɒˈstreɪt; *NAmE* ˈprɑːstreɪt/ **1 ~ yourself** to lie on your front with your face looking downwards, especially as an act of worship 俯伏；拜倒 **2** [usually passive] **~ sb** to make sb feel weak, shocked, and unable to do anything 使一籌莫展；使無能為力 SYN **overcome**： *He was expecting to find her prostrated by the tragedy.* 他以為這場悲劇會使她一蹶不振。◇ *For months he was* ***prostrated with grief***. 他好幾個月都悲痛不已。

pros·tra·tion /prɒˈstreɪʃn; *NAmE* prɑːˈs-/ *noun* [U] (*formal*) **1** extreme physical weakness 筋疲力盡；極度虛弱；虛脱： *a state of prostration brought on by the heat* 暑熱導致的虛脱狀態 **2** the action of lying with your face downwards, especially in worship 拜倒；俯伏

prot·ac·tin·ium /ˌprəʊtækˈtɪniəm; *NAmE* ˌproʊ-/ *noun* [U] (*symb.* **Pa**) a chemical element. Protactinium is a RADIOACTIVE metal found naturally when URANIUM decays. 鏷（放射性化學元素）

prot·ag·on·ist /prəˈtægənɪst/ *noun* (*formal*) **1** the main character in a play, film/movie or book （戲劇、電影、書的）主要人物，主人公，主角 ➲ compare HERO (2) **2** one of the main people in a real event, especially a competition, battle or struggle （比賽、鬥爭中的）主要人物，主要參與者 **3** an active supporter of a policy or movement, especially one that is trying to change sth （政策、運動的）倡導者，擁護者 SYN **champion**： *a leading protagonist of the conservation movement* 資源保護運動的急先鋒

pro·tea /ˈprəʊtiə; *NAmE* ˈproʊ-/ *noun* **1** a type of bush found in South Africa with large flowers with thick orange or pink outer leaves 普羅蒂亞木（南非灌木，開外層花瓣為橙色或粉紅色的大花） **2** the flower itself, which is one of South Africa's national symbols 普羅蒂亞花，帝王花（南非國花）

pro·tean /ˈprəʊtiən; prəʊˈtiːən; *NAmE* ˈproʊ-; proʊˈt-/ *adj.* (*literary*) able to change quickly and easily 多變的；易變的；變幻無常的： *a protean character* 多變的性格

pro·te·ase /ˈprəʊtieɪz; *NAmE* ˈproʊ-/ *noun* (*biology* 生) a substance in the body that breaks down PROTEINS and PEPTIDES 蛋白（水解）酶

pro·tect 🔑 /prəˈtekt/ *verb* **1** 🔑 [T, I] to make sure that sb/sth is not harmed, injured, damaged, etc. 保護；防護： **~ sb/sth/yourself (against/from sth)** *Troops have been sent to protect aid workers against attack.* 已經派出部隊保護援助工作人員免遭襲擊。◇ *They huddled together to protect themselves from the wind.* 他們擠在一起，免受風吹。◇ *Each company is fighting to protect its own commercial interests.* 每家公司都在奮力保護自己的商業利益。◇ **~ (against/from sth)** *a paint that helps protect against rust* 防銹漆 **2** 🔑 [T, usually passive] **~ sth** to introduce laws that make it illegal to kill, harm or damage a particular animal, area of land, building, etc. （制訂法律）保護： *a protected area/species* 受保護的地區 / 物種 **3** [T, usually passive] **~ sth** to help an industry in your own country by taxing goods from other countries so that there is less competition （通過徵關税）保護（國內企業）；實行貿易保護： *protected markets* 受保護的市場 **4** [T, I] **~ (sb/sth) (against sth)** to provide sb/sth with insurance against fire, injury, damage, etc. 投保；為…買保險： *Many policies do not protect you against personal injury.* 許多保單都列明不保障人身傷害。

P

pro·tec·tion 🗝 /prəˈtekʃn/ *noun*
1 🗝 [U] **~ (for/of sb/sth) (against/from sth)** the act of protecting sb/sth; the state of being protected 保護；防衛：*Wear clothes that provide adequate protection against the wind and rain.* 穿上足以防風雨的衣服。◇ *He asked to be put* ***under*** *police* ***protection.*** 他請求警方保護。◇ *the conservation and protection of the environment* 環境的維護與保護 ◇ ***data protection*** *laws* 數據保護法 **2** 🗝 [C] **~ (against sth)** a thing that protects sb/sth against sth 保護物；護身符：*They wore the charm as a protection against evil spirits.* 他們戴着護身符以驅邪。**3** [U] **~ (against sth)** insurance against fire, injury, damage, etc. 保險：*Our policy offers complete protection against fire and theft.* 我們的保單全面承保火災及盜竊風險。**4** [U] the system of helping an industry in your own country by taxing foreign goods 貿易保護；關稅保護制：*The government is ready to introduce protection for the car industry.* 政府準備對汽車工業實行貿易保護。**5** [U] the system of paying criminals so that they will not attack your business or property（付給犯罪分子以求平安的）保護費：*to pay* ***protection money*** 交保護費 ◇ *to run a* ***protection racket*** 幹敲詐保護費的勾當

pro·tec·tion·ism /prəˈtekʃənɪzəm/ *noun* [U] the principle or practice of protecting a country's own industry by taxing foreign goods（貿易）保護主義 ▶ **pro·tec·tion·ist** /-ʃənɪst/ *adj.*：*protectionist policies* 貿易保護政策

pro·tect·ive /prəˈtektɪv/ *adj.* **1** [only before noun] providing or intended to provide protection 保護的；防護的：*Workers should wear full* ***protective clothing.*** 工人應該穿着全套防護服。◇ *a protective layer of varnish* 清漆防護層 ◇ *a protective barrier against the sun's rays* 防曬層 **2** having or showing a wish to protect sb/sth 出於（對…的）保護：**~ (towards sb/sth)** *She had been fiercely protective towards him as a teenager.* 他十幾歲時，她曾極力呵護他。◇ **~ (of sb/sth)** *He was extremely protective of his role as advisor.* 他極力保護自己的顧問角色。◇ *He put a protective arm around her shoulders.* 他呵護地用胳膊摟住她的肩膀。◇ *Parents can easily become over-protective of their children* (= want to protect them too much). 父母容易過度保護孩子。**3** intended to give an advantage to your own country's industry 貿易保護的；實行關稅保護的：*protective tariffs* 保護性關稅 ▶ **pro·tect·ive·ly** *adv.*：*She clutched her bag protectively.* 她用力抓緊護着自己的提包。**pro·tect·ive·ness** *noun* [U]

proˌtective ˈcustody *noun* [U] the state of being kept in prison for your own safety 保護性拘留；保護性監禁

pro·tect·or /prəˈtektə(r)/ *noun* a person, an organization or a thing that protects sb/sth 保護人（或組織、裝置等）：*I regarded him as my friend and protector.* 我視他為我的朋友和保護者。◇ *the company's image as a protector of the environment* 這個公司作為環境保護者的形象 ◇ *Hard hats and ear protectors are provided.* 提供了安全帽和護耳。

pro·tect·or·ate /prəˈtektərət/ *noun* **1** [C] a country that is controlled and protected by a more powerful country 受保護國；受保護領地 ➲ compare COLONY (1) **2** [U] the state or period of being controlled and protected by another country（一國對另一國的）保護關係

pro·tégé (*feminine* **pro·té·gée**) /ˈprɒtəʒeɪ; *NAmE* ˈproʊt-/ *noun* (from *French*) a young person who is helped in their career and personal development by a more experienced person 受提攜的後進：*a protégé of the great violinist Yehudi Menuhin* 偉大的小提琴家耶胡迪•梅紐因的門生

pro·tein /ˈprəʊtiːn; *NAmE* ˈproʊ-/ *noun* [C, U] a natural substance found in meat, eggs, fish, some vegetables, etc. There are many different proteins and they are an essential part of what humans and animals eat to help them grow and stay healthy. 蛋白質：*essential proteins and vitamins* 必不可少的蛋白質和維生素 ◇ *protein deficiency* 蛋白質缺乏 ◇ *Peas, beans and lentils are a good source of vegetable protein.* 豌豆、豆莢和扁豆是植物蛋白質的豐富來源。

pro tem /ˌprəʊ ˈtem; *NAmE* ˌproʊ/ *adv.* (from *Latin*) for now, but not for a long time 暫時；臨時 SYN **temporarily**：*A new manager will be appointed pro tem.* 將臨時任命一位新經理。▶ **pro tem** *adj.*：*A pro tem committee was formed from existing members.* 由現有的委員組成了一個臨時委員會。

pro·test 🗝 *noun, verb*
■ ***noun*** 🗝 /ˈprəʊtest; *NAmE* ˈproʊ-/ [U, C] the expression of strong disagreement with or opposition to sth; a statement or an action that shows this 抗議；抗議書（或行動）；反對：*The director resigned* ***in protest*** *at the decision.* 主任辭職以示抗議這項決定。◇ *The announcement* ***raised a storm of protest.*** 這個聲明引起了一場抗議風潮。◇ *a protest march* 抗議遊行 ◇ *She accepted the charge* ***without protest.*** 她一聲未吭地接受了指控。◇ **~ (against sth)** *The workers staged a protest against the proposed changes in their contracts.* 工人們發起抗議，反對擬議中的對他們合同的修改。◇ *The building work will go ahead, despite protests from local residents.* 儘管當地居民反對，建築工程將照樣進行。◇ *The riot began as a peaceful protest.* 暴亂是從一場和平抗議開始的。
IDM **under ˈprotest** unwillingly and after expressing disagreement 無奈地；不服氣地；不甘心地：*She wrote a letter of apology but only under protest.* 她無奈之下寫了一封致歉信。
■ ***verb*** /prəˈtest; *NAmE* also ˈproʊ-/ **1** 🗝 [I, T] to say or do sth to show that you disagree with or disapprove of sth, especially publicly （公開）反對；抗議：**~ (about/against/at sth)** *Students took to the streets to protest against the decision.* 學生們走上街頭，抗議這項決定。◇ *The victim's widow protested at the leniency of the sentence.* 受害人的遺孀抗議判決太輕。◇ *There's no use protesting, I won't change my mind.* 抗議沒有用，我決不改變主意。◇ **~ sth** (*NAmE*) *They fully intend to protest the decision.* 他們決意反對這項決定。➲ SYNONYMS at COMPLAIN **2** [T] to say firmly that sth is true, especially when you have been accused of sth or when other people do not believe you 堅決地表示；申辯：**~ sth** *She has always* ***protested her innocence.*** 她一直堅持說自己是無辜的。◇ **~ that …** *He protested that the journey was too far by car.* 他堅持說路途太遠，不宜開汽車去。◇ **+ speech** *'That's not what you said earlier!' Jane protested.* "你當初不是這麼說的！"簡爭辯說。

Prot·est·ant /ˈprɒtɪstənt; *NAmE* ˈprɑːt-/ *noun* a member of a part of the Western Christian Church that separated from the Roman Catholic Church in the 16th century 新教教徒（16 世紀脱離羅馬天主教）：*He's a Protestant.* 他是新教教徒。▶ **Prot·est·ant** *adj.*：*The majority of the population is Protestant.* 這裏的人大多數都信奉新教。◇ *a Protestant church/country* 新教教堂/國家 **Prot·est·ant·ism** /ˈprɒtɪstəntɪzəm; *NAmE* ˈprɑːt-/ *noun* [U]

ˌProtestant ˈethic (also **ˌProtestant ˈwork ethic**) *noun* [sing.] the idea that a person has a duty to work hard and spend their time and money in a careful, responsible way, sometimes thought to be typical of Protestants 新教倫理，新教工作道德（強調勤奮工作、有效利用時間與節儉）

pro·test·ation /ˌprɒtəˈsteɪʃn; *NAmE* ˌprɑːt-/ *noun* [C, U] (*formal*) a strong statement that sth is true, especially when other people do not believe you 鄭重的聲明；堅決的表示：*She repeated her protestation of innocence.* 她再度強調自己是清白的。◇ *Despite his protestation to the contrary, he was extremely tired.* 儘管他極力否認，但他確實筋疲力盡了。

pro·test·er /prəˈtestə(r)/ *noun* a person who makes a public protest （公開）抗議者，反對者 SYN **demonstrator**：*Thousands of protesters marched through the city.* 數千人遊行抗議，走過全城。

proto- /ˈprəʊtəʊ; *NAmE* ˈproʊtoʊ/ *combining form* (in nouns and adjectives 構成名詞和形容詞) original; from which others develop 原始的；最初的：*prototype* 原型 ◇ *proto-modernist painters* 原始現代派畫家

proto·col AW /ˈprəʊtəkɒl; *NAmE* ˈproʊtəkɔːl; -kɑːl/ *noun* **1** [U] a system of fixed rules and formal behaviour used at official meetings, usually between governments 禮儀；外交禮節：*a breach of protocol* 違反外交禮節 ◇ *the* *protocol of diplomatic visits* 外交訪問的禮儀 **2** [C] (*technical* 術語) the first or original version of an agreement, especially a TREATY between countries, etc.; an extra part added to an agreement or TREATY 條約草案；議定書；（協議或條約的）附件：*the first Geneva Protocol* 《日內瓦四公約》第一議定書 ◇ *It is set out in a legally binding protocol which forms part of the treaty.* 這在有法律約束力的、屬於條約一部份的附件中有說明。**3** [C] (*computing* 計) a set of rules that control the way data is sent between computers（數據傳遞的）協議，規程，規約 **4** [C] (*technical* 術語) a plan for performing a scientific experiment or medical treatment 科學實驗計劃；醫療方案

ˌProto-ˌIndo-ˌEuroˈpean *noun* [U] the ancient language on which all Indo-European languages are thought to be based. There are no written records of Proto-Indo-European, but experts have tried to construct it from the evidence of modern languages. 原始印歐語（據信為所有印歐語言之源頭）

pro·ton /ˈprəʊtɒn; *NAmE* ˈproʊtɑːn/ *noun* (*physics* 物) a very small piece of matter (= a substance) with a positive electric charge that forms part of the NUCLEUS (= central part) of an atom 質子 ➲ see also ELECTRON, NEUTRON

proto·plasm /ˈprəʊtəplæzəm; *NAmE* ˈproʊ-/ *noun* [U] (*biology* 生) a clear substance like jelly which forms the living part of an animal or plant cell 原生質 ➲ compare CYTOPLASM

proto·type /ˈprəʊtətaɪp; *NAmE* ˈproʊ-/ *noun* **~** (**for/of sth**) the first design of sth from which other forms are copied or developed 原型；雛形；最初形態：*the prototype of the modern bicycle* 現代自行車的雛形 ▸ **proto·typ·ical** /ˌprəʊtəˈtɪpɪkl; *NAmE* ˌproʊ-/ *adj.*

proto·zoan /ˌprəʊtəˈzəʊən; *NAmE* ˌproʊtəˈzoʊən/ *noun* (*pl.* **proto·zoans** or **proto·zoa** /-ˈzəʊə; *NAmE* -ˈzoʊə/) (*biology* 生) a very small living thing, usually with only one cell, that can only be seen under a MICROSCOPE 單細胞生物；原生動物 ▸ **proto·zoan** *adj.*

pro·tract·ed /prəˈtræktɪd; *NAmE* also proʊˈt-/ *adj.* (*formal*) lasting longer than expected or longer than usual 延長的；拖延的；持久的 SYN **prolonged**：***protracted delays/disputes/negotiations*** 持久的延誤／爭論／談判

pro·tract·or /prəˈtræktə(r); *NAmE* also proʊˈt-/ *noun* an instrument for measuring and drawing angles, usually made from a half circle of clear plastic with degrees (0° to 180°) marked on it 量角器；分度規 ➲ VISUAL VOCAB page V70

pro·trude /prəˈtruːd; *NAmE* proʊ-/ *verb* [I] (*formal*) to stick out from a place or a surface 突出；伸出；鼓出：*protruding teeth* 齙牙 ◇ **~ from sth** *He hung his coat on a nail protruding from the wall.* 他把上衣掛在凸出牆面的一根釘子上。

pro·tru·sion /prəˈtruːʒn; *NAmE* proʊˈt-/ *noun* [C, U] (*formal*) a thing that sticks out from a place or surface; the fact of doing this 突出物；凸起；伸出：*a protrusion on the rock face* 岩石表面的突起部份

pro·tu·ber·ance /prəˈtjuːbərəns; *NAmE* proʊˈtuː-/ *noun* (*formal*) a round part that sticks out from a surface 突出物；隆起部份 SYN **bulge**

pro·tu·ber·ant /prəˈtjuːbərənt; *NAmE* proʊˈtuː-/ *adj.* (*formal*) curving or swelling out from a surface 隆起的；鼓出的；凸起的 SYN **bulging**：*protuberant eyes* 凸出的眼睛

proud 0‑w /praʊd/ *adj.*, *adv.*

■ *adj.* (**proud·er**, **proud·est**)

▸ PLEASED 滿意 **1** 0‑w feeling pleased and satisfied about sth that you own or have done, or are connected with 驕傲的；自豪的；得意的；滿足的：*proud parents* 自豪的父母 ◇ *the* ***proud owner*** *of a new car* 得意揚揚的新汽車主人 ◇ **~ of sb/sth/yourself** *Your achievements are* ***something to be proud of.*** 你的成就是值得驕傲的。◇ *He was proud of himself for not giving up.* 他為自己沒有放棄而深感自豪。◇ **~ to be/have sth** *I feel very proud to be a part of the team.* 能成為隊中的一員我感到十分榮幸。◇ **~ that ...** *She was proud that her daughter had so much talent.* 女兒這麼有天賦令她喜不自勝。➲ see also HOUSE-PROUD ➲ SYNONYMS at GLAD **2** 0‑w [only before noun] causing sb to feel pride 引以為榮的；令人自豪的：*This is the proudest moment of my life.* 這是我生命中最榮耀的時刻。◇ *The car had been his* ***proudest possession.*** 這輛汽車是他最引以自豪的財產。

▸ FEELING TOO IMPORTANT 自負 **3** 0‑w (*disapproving*) feeling that you are better and more important than other people 傲慢的；驕傲自大的 SYN **arrogant**：*She was too proud to admit she could be wrong.* 她自視甚高，不願承認自己也會有錯。

▸ HAVING SELF-RESPECT 自尊的 **4** 0‑w having respect for yourself and not wanting to lose the respect of others 自尊的；自重的：*They were a proud and independent people.* 他們是一個獨立自主的民族。◇ *Don't be too proud to ask for help.* 不要自尊心太強而羞於求人幫忙。

▸ BEAUTIFUL/TALL 秀麗；頎長 **5** (*literary*) beautiful, tall and impressive 秀麗的；挺拔的；壯觀的：*The sunflowers stretched tall and proud to the sun.* 向日葵在陽光中亭亭玉立。➲ see also PRIDE

■ *adv.*

IDM **do sb ˈproud** (*old-fashioned*, *BrE*) to treat sb very well by giving them a lot of good food, entertainment, etc. 盛情款待；給某人隆重禮遇 **do yourself/sb ˈproud** to do sth that makes you proud of yourself or that makes other people proud of you 做令自己風光（或自豪）的事；做贏得讚譽的事

proud·ly 0‑w /ˈpraʊdli/ *adv.*

1 0‑w in a way that shows that sb is proud of sth 得意地；自豪地；驕傲地：*She proudly displayed her prize.* 她得意地展示所獲的獎品。**2** (*literary*) in a way that is large and impressive 雄偉地；壯觀地；高大地：*The Matterhorn rose proudly in the background.* 馬特峰巍然屹立在背景中。

prov·able /ˈpruːvəbl/ *adj.* that can be shown to be true 可以證明的；能證實的 SYN **verifiable**

prove 0‑w /pruːv/ *verb* (**proved**, **proved** or **proved**, **proven** /ˈpruːvn/ (especially in *NAmE*)) HELP In *BrE* **proved** is the more common form. Look also at **proven**. 英式英語中 proved 是較常見的形式。另見 proven。

> **WORD FAMILY**
> **prove** *verb* (≠ disprove)
> **proof** *noun*
> **proven** *adj.* (≠ unproven)

▸ SHOW STH IS TRUE 證明 **1** 0‑w [T] to use facts, evidence, etc. to show that sth is true 證明；證實：**~ sth** *They hope this new evidence will prove her innocence.* 他們希望這一新證據能證明她無罪。◇ *'I know you're lying.' 'Prove it!'* "我知道你在撒謊。" "拿出證據來！" ◇ *He felt he needed to* ***prove his point*** (= show other people that he was right). 他覺得有必要證明自己的想法是對的。◇ *Are you just doing this to* ***prove a point?*** 你這麼做就是為證明自己對嗎？◇ ***What are you trying to prove?*** 你想證明什麼？◇ *I certainly* ***don't have anything to prove***—*my record speaks for itself.* 我固然無以為證，但我的紀錄可說明一切。◇ **~ sth to sb** *Just give me a chance and I'll prove it to you.* 只要給我個機會，我會證明給你看。◇ **~ (that) ...** *This proves (that) I was right.* 這證明我是對的。◇ **~ sb/sth/yourself + adj./noun** *She was determined to prove everyone wrong.* 她決心證明大家都錯了。◇ *In this country, you are innocent until proved guilty.* 在這個國家，一個人在被證明有罪之前是清白的。◇ **~ sb/sth/yourself to be/have sth** *You've just proved yourself to be a liar.* 你恰恰證明了自己是撒謊者。◇ **~ what, how, etc. ...** *This just proves what I have been saying for some time.* 這恰好證實了我長久以來所說的。◇ **it is proved that ...** ***Can it be proved that*** *he did commit these offences?* 能證明他確實犯了這些罪嗎？OPP **disprove** ➲ LANGUAGE BANK at EVIDENCE ➲ see also PROOF *n.* (1)

▸ BE 是 **2** 0‑w *linking verb* if sth **proves** dangerous, expensive, etc. or if it **proves to be** dangerous, etc., you discover that it is dangerous, etc. over a period of time 後來被發現是；最終顯現為 SYN **turn out**：**+ adj.** *The opposition proved too strong for him.* 這個對手過於強勁，使得他難以招架。◇ **+ noun** *Shares in the industry proved a poor investment.* 事實證明投資這個行業的股票是一個失敗。◇ **~ to be sth** *The promotion proved to be a*

P

turning point in his career. 這次提升最後成了他職業生涯的一個轉折點。

▸ YOURSELF 自己 **3** 🔑 [T] **~ yourself (to sb)** to show other people how good you are at doing sth or that you are capable of doing sth 展現，展示，顯示（自己的才能）：*He constantly feels he has to prove himself to others.* 他時常覺得自己必須向人一展身手。 **4** [T] **~ yourself + adj/noun | ~ yourself to be sth** to show other people that you are a particular type of person or that you have a particular quality 顯示（自己）是；向人證明（自己）是：*He proved himself determined to succeed.* 他向人證明了自己不達目的不罷休。

▸ OF BREAD 麪包 **5** [I] to swell before being baked because of the action of YEAST 發酵 SYN **rise** IDM see EXCEPTION

proven /ˈpruːvn; ˈprəʊvn; *NAmE* ˈproʊ-/ *adj.* [only before noun] tested and shown to be true 被證明的；已證實的：*a student of proven ability* 確有才華的學生 ◇ *It is a proven fact that fluoride strengthens growing teeth.* 氟化物可以強化生長中的牙齒，這是已證明的事實。 ➲ see also PROVE *v.* OPP **unproven**

IDM **not ˈproven** (in Scottish law 蘇格蘭法律) a VERDICT (= decision) at a trial that there is not enough evidence to show that sb is guilty or innocent, and that they must be set free 證據不足（不予起訴）

prov·en·ance /ˈprɒvənəns; *NAmE* ˈprɑːv-/ *noun* [U, C] (*technical* 術語) the place that sth originally came from 發源地；起源；出處 SYN **origin**：*All the furniture is of English provenance.* 所有這些傢具都是英國貨。 ◇ *There's no proof about the provenance of the painting* (= whether it is genuine or not). 這幅畫的真偽無法鑒別。

ˈpro-verb *noun* (*grammar* 語法) a verb that depends on another verb for its meaning for example 'do' in 'she likes chocolate and so do I.' 代動詞（意義依另一動詞而定，如 She likes chocolate and so do I 中的 do）

prov·erb /ˈprɒvɜːb; *NAmE* ˈprɑːvɜːrb/ *noun* a well-known phrase or sentence that gives advice or says sth that is generally true, for example 'Waste not, want not.' 諺語；格言

P

pro·verb·ial /prəˈvɜːbiəl; *NAmE* -ˈvɜːrb-/ *adj.* **1** [only before noun] used to show that you are referring to a particular proverb or well-known phrase 諺語的；諺語表達的；如諺語所說的：*Let's not count our proverbial chickens.* 我們還是不要過分樂觀。 **2** [not usually before noun] well known and talked about by a lot of people 眾所周知；著名 SYN **famous**：*Their hospitality is proverbial.* 他們的熱情好客人人皆知。 ▸ **pro·verbi·al·ly** /-biəli/ *adv.*

pro·vide 🔑 /prəˈvaɪd/ *verb*

1 🔑 to give sth to sb or make it available for them to use 提供；供應；給予 SYN **supply**：**~ sth** *The hospital has a commitment to provide the best possible medical care.* 這家醫院承諾要提供最好的醫療服務。 ◇ *The report was not expected to provide any answers.* 不要指望這個報告能提供什麼答案。 ◇ *Please answer questions in the space provided.* 請在留出的空白處答題。 ◇ **~ sth for sb** *We are here to provide a service for the public.* 我們來這裏是為公眾服務。 ◇ **~ sb with sth** *We are here to provide the public with a service.* 我們來這裏是為公眾服務。 ◇ **~ sth to sb** *The charity aims to provide assistance to people in need.* 這家慈善機構的宗旨是向貧困者提供幫助。 **2** **~ that ...** (*formal*) (of a law or rule 法律或規則) to state that sth will or must happen 規定 SYN **stipulate**：*The final section provides that any work produced for the company is thereafter owned by the company.* 最後一節規定，此後為公司創作的一切作品均為本公司所有。 ➲ see also PROVISION

PHR V **proˈvide against sth** (*formal*) to make preparations to deal with sth bad or unpleasant that might happen in the future 預防；防備 **proˈvide for sb** to give sb the things that they need to live, such as food, money and clothing 提供生活所需 **proˈvide for sth** (*formal*) **1** to make preparations to deal with sth that might happen in the future 為…做好準備 **2** (of a law, rule, etc. 法律、規定等) to make it possible for sth to be done 作出規定；使有據可依；使可以做：*The legislation provides for the detention of suspected terrorists for up to seven days.* 法律規定，對嫌疑恐怖分子最多可拘留七天。

pro·vided 🔑 /prəˈvaɪdɪd/ (also **pro·vid·ing**) *conj.* **~ (that) ...** used to say what must happen or be done to make it possible for sth else to happen 如果；假如；在…條件下 SYN **if**：*We'll buy everything you produce, provided of course the price is right.* 當然了，倘若價格合適，我們將採購你們的全部產品。 ◇ *Provided that you have the money in your account, you can withdraw up to £100 a day.* 只要賬戶存款足夠，每天可提取不超過 100 英鎊。

provi·dence /ˈprɒvɪdəns; *NAmE* ˈprɑːv-/ (also **Providence**) *noun* [U] (*formal*) God, or a force that some people believe controls our lives and the things that happen to us, usually in a way that protects us 上帝；蒼天；天祐 SYN **fate**：*to trust in divine providence* 相信上蒼 IDM see TEMPT

provi·dent /ˈprɒvɪdənt; *NAmE* ˈprɑːv-/ *adj.* (*formal*) careful in planning for the future, especially by saving money 精打細算的；未雨綢繆的 SYN **prudent** OPP **improvident**

provi·den·tial /ˌprɒvɪˈdenʃl; *NAmE* ˌprɑːv-/ *adj.* (*formal*) lucky because it happens at the right time, but without being planned 天緣巧合的；及時的；適時的 SYN **timely** ▸ **provi·den·tial·ly** /-ʃəli/ *adv.*

pro·vider /prəˈvaɪdə(r)/ *noun* a person or an organization that supplies sb with sth they need or want 供應者；提供者；供養人：*training providers* 提供訓練的人 ◇ *We are one of the largest providers of employment in the area.* 我們是本地區最大的雇主之一。 ◇ *The eldest son is the family's sole provider* (= the only person who earns money). 這家的長子是唯一養家餬口的人。 ➲ see also SERVICE PROVIDER

pro·vid·ing 🔑 /prəˈvaɪdɪŋ/ *conj.* = PROVIDED

prov·ince /ˈprɒvɪns; *NAmE* ˈprɑːv-/ *noun* **1** [C] one of the areas that some countries are divided into with its own local government 省份；（某些國家的）一級行政區：*the provinces of Canada* 加拿大各省 **2** **the provinces** [pl.] (*BrE*) all the parts of a country except the capital city 首都以外的地區：*The show will tour the provinces after it closes in London.* 倫敦的演出結束後，將到全國各地巡迴演出。 ◇ *a shy young man from the provinces* 靦腆的外地男青年 **3** [sing.] (*formal*) a person's particular area of knowledge, interest or responsibility 知識（或興趣、職責）範圍；領域：*Such decisions are normally the province of higher management.* 這類決定一般屬於高層管理的職責範圍。 ◇ *I'm afraid the matter is* **outside my province** (= I cannot or need not deal with it). 很抱歉，這事不歸我管。

pro·vin·cial /prəˈvɪnʃl/ *adj., noun*

■ **adj.** **1** [only before noun] connected with one of the large areas that some countries are divided into, with its own local government 省的；一級行政區的：***provincial assemblies/elections*** 省議會；省選舉 **2** [only before noun] (sometimes *disapproving*) connected with the parts of a country that do not include the capital city 都城以外的；首都以外的：*a provincial town* 首都以外的城鎮 **3** (*disapproving*) unwilling to consider new or different ideas or things 心胸狹隘的；守舊的；迂腐的 SYN **narrow-minded** ▸ **pro·vin·cial·ly** /-ʃəli/ *adv.*

■ **noun** (often *disapproving*) a person who lives in or comes from a part of the country that is not near the capital city 都城以外的人；鄉巴佬；外鄉人

pro·vin·cial·ism /prəˈvɪnʃəlɪzəm/ *noun* [U] (*disapproving*) the attitude of people who are unwilling to consider new or different ideas or things 胸襟狹隘；陳腐態度；排外主義

ˈproving ground *noun* a place where sth such as a new machine, vehicle or weapon can be tested 實驗場；試驗地：*It's an ideal proving ground for the new car.* 這裏是個理想的新車試驗場。 ◇ (*figurative*) *The club is the proving ground for young boxers.* 這個俱樂部是年輕拳擊手的搖籃。

pro·vi·sion /prəˈvɪʒn/ *noun, verb*

■ **noun** **1** [U, C, usually sing.] the act of supplying sb with sth that they need or want; sth that is supplied 提供；

供給；給養；供應品：*housing provision* 住房供應 ◇ *The government is responsible for the provision of health care.* 政府負責提供醫療服務。◇ *There is no provision for anyone to sit down here.* 這裏沒有可坐的地方。◇ *The provision of specialist teachers is being increased.* 當局正在增加設置專門師資。 **2** [U, C] **~ for sb/sth** preparations that you make for sth that might or will happen in the future （為將來做的）準備：*He had already* ***made provisions for*** (= planned for the financial future of) *his wife and children before the accident.* 意外事故發生之前，他已為妻子、兒女做好了經濟安排。◇ *You should* ***make provision for*** *things going wrong.* 你要採取措施，以防不測。 **3 provisions** [pl.] supplies of food and drink, especially for a long journey 飲食供應；（尤指旅途中的）糧食 **4** [C] a condition or an arrangement in a legal document （法律文件的）規定，條款：*Under the provisions of the lease, the tenant is responsible for repairs.* 按契約規定，房客負責房屋維修。 ➲ see also PROVIDE

■ ***verb*** [often passive] **~ sb/sth** (**with sth**) (*formal*) to supply sb/sth with enough of sth, especially food, to last for a particular period of time 為…提供所需物品（尤指食物）

pro·vi·sion·al /prəˈvɪʒənl/ *adj.* **1** arranged for the present time only and likely to be changed in the future 臨時的；暫時的 SYN **temporary**：*a provisional government* 臨時政府 ◇ *provisional arrangements* 暫時性安排 **2** arranged, but not yet definite 暫定的：*The booking is only provisional.* 這只是暫定的預訂。 ▶ **pro·vi·sion·al·ly** /-nəli/ *adv.*：*The meeting has been provisionally arranged for Friday.* 會議暫定於星期五舉行。

pro,visional ˈlicence (*BrE*) (*NAmE* **ˈlearner's permit**) *noun* an official document that you must have when you start to learn to drive 實習駕駛執照；學員駕照

pro·viso /prəˈvaɪzəʊ; *NAmE* -zoʊ/ *noun* (*pl.* **-os**) (*formal*) a condition that must be accepted before an agreement can be made 限制條款；附文；但書 SYN **provision**：*Their participation is subject to a number of important provisos.* 他們的參與受一些重要條款的限制。◇ *He agreed to their visit* ***with the proviso that*** *they should stay no longer than one week.* 他同意他們來做客，但條件是逗留不得超過一週。

pro·voca·teur /prəˌvɒkəˈtɜː(r); *NAmE* -ˌvɑːkə-/ *noun* = AGENT PROVOCATEUR

pro·voca·tion /ˌprɒvəˈkeɪʃn; *NAmE* ˌprɑːv-/ *noun* [U, C] the act of doing or saying sth deliberately in order to make sb angry or upset; something that is done or said to cause this 挑釁；刺激；激怒：*He reacted violently only* ***under provocation***. 只因為被激怒，他才暴力相向。◇ *The terrorists can strike at any time* ***without provocation***. 恐怖分子可能無緣無故地隨時攻擊。◇ *She bursts into tears* ***at the slightest provocation***. 稍一招惹，她就大哭起來。◇ *So far the police have refused to respond to their provocations.* 截至目前為止，警方並未對他們的挑釁作出反應。

pro·voca·tive /prəˈvɒkətɪv; *NAmE* -ˈvɑːkə-/ *adj.* **1** intended to make people angry or upset; intended to make people argue about sth 挑釁的；煽動性的；激起爭端的：*a provocative remark* 煽動性的言論 ◇ *He doesn't really mean that—he's just being deliberately provocative.* 他不是真有此意，只不過是存心挑逗一下罷了。 **2** intended to make sb sexually excited 引誘的；激起性慾的：*a provocative smile* 撩人的一笑 ▶ **pro·voca·tive·ly** *adv.*

pro·voke /prəˈvəʊk; *NAmE* -ˈvoʊk/ *verb* **1 ~ sth** to cause a particular reaction or have a particular effect 激起；引起；引發：*The announcement provoked a storm of protest.* 這個聲明激起了抗議的風潮。◇ *The article was intended to provoke discussion.* 這篇文章旨在引發討論。◇ *Dairy products may provoke allergic reactions in some people.* 乳製品可能會引起某些人的過敏反應。 **2 ~ sb** (**into sth/into doing sth**) | **~ sb to do sth** to say or do sth that you know will annoy sb so that they react in an angry way 挑釁；激怒；刺激 SYN **goad**：*The lawyer claimed his client was provoked into acts of violence by the defendant.* 律師聲稱，他的當事人是受到被告的挑釁才採取暴力行動的。◇ *Be careful what you say—he's easily provoked.* 說話要小心，他這個人一惹就火兒。

prov·ost /ˈprɒvəst; *NAmE* ˈproʊvoʊst/ (also **Provost**) *noun* **1** (in Britain) the person in charge of a college at some universities （英國某些大學的）學院院長 **2** (in the US) a senior member of the staff who organize the affairs of some universities （美國某些大學的）教務長 **3** (in Scotland) the head of a council in some towns, cities and districts （蘇格蘭的）市長，鎮長，區長 ➲ compare MAYOR (1) **4** the head of a group of priests belonging to a particular CATHEDRAL 座堂主任；教區長

prow /praʊ/ *noun* (*formal* or *literary*) the pointed front part of a ship or boat 船頭

prow·ess /ˈpraʊəs/ *noun* [U] (*formal*) great skill at doing sth 非凡的技能；高超的技藝；造詣：*academic/sporting prowess* 學術 / 體育運動造詣

prowl /praʊl/ *verb, noun*

■ ***verb*** **1** [I, T] (+ **adv./prep.**) | **~ sth** (of an animal 動物) to move quietly and carefully around an area, especially when hunting 潛行（為捕獵等）：*The tiger prowled through the undergrowth.* 老虎悄然穿過矮樹叢。 **2** [I, T] (+ **adv./prep.**) | **~ sth** to move quietly and carefully around an area, especially with the intention of committing a crime 潛行（圖謀不軌等）：*A man was seen prowling around outside the factory just before the fire started.* 就在起火之前，有人看到一個男子在工廠外踱來踱去。 **3** [T, I] **~ sth** | (+ **adv./prep.**) to walk around a room, an area, etc., especially because you are bored, anxious, etc., and cannot relax （因無聊、焦躁等）徘徊，走來走去：*He prowled the empty rooms of the house at night.* 夜裏，他在家中的空屋子裏踱來踱去。

■ ***noun***

IDM **(be/go) on the ˈprowl** (of an animal or a person 人或動物) moving quietly and carefully, hunting or looking for sth 悄然潛行（以捕獵或尋找）：*There was a fox on the prowl near the chickens.* 有一隻狐狸在雞群附近徘徊。◇ *an intruder on the prowl* 一個躡足潛入的人

prowl·er /ˈpraʊlə(r)/ *noun* a person who follows sb or who moves around quietly outside their house, especially at night, in order to frighten them, harm them or steal sth from them （圖謀不軌的）潛行者

prox·imal /ˈprɒksɪməl; *NAmE* ˈprɑːk-/ *adj.* (*anatomy* 解) located towards the centre of the body 近端的；近身體中心的

prox·im·ate /ˈprɒksɪmət; *NAmE* ˈprɑːk-/ *adj.* [usually before noun] (*technical* 術語) nearest in time, order, etc. to sth （時間、順序等）最接近的，最鄰近的

prox·im·ity /prɒkˈsɪməti; *NAmE* prɑːk-/ *noun* [U] **~ (of sb/sth) (to sb/sth)** (*formal*) the state of being near sb/sth in distance or time （時間或空間）接近，鄰近，靠近：*a house* ***in the proximity of*** (= near) *the motorway* 靠近高速公路的一座房子 ◇ *The proximity of the college to London makes it very popular.* 這所學院因靠近倫敦而備受歡迎。◇ *The area has a number of schools* ***in close proximity*** *to each other.* 這個地區有許多學校比鄰而立。◇ *the death of two members of her family in close proximity* 她的兩個親人在短時間內的相繼去世

proxy /ˈprɒksi; *NAmE* ˈprɑːksi/ *noun* (*pl.* **-ies**) **1** [U] the authority that you give to sb to do sth for you, when you cannot do it yourself 代理權；代表權：*You can vote either in person or* ***by proxy***. 你可以親自投票或請人代理。◇ ***a proxy vote*** 由他人代投的票 **2** [C, U] a person who has been given the authority to represent sb else 代理人；受託人；代表：*Your proxy will need to sign the form on your behalf.* 你的代理人將須代表你在表格上簽字。◇ *They were like proxy parents to me.* 他們待我如同父母。◇ **~ for sb** *She is acting as proxy for her husband.* 她做她丈夫的代表。 **3** [C] **~ for sth** (*formal* or *technical* 術語) something that you use to represent sth else that you are trying to measure or calculate （測算用的）代替物，指標：*The number of patients on a doctor's list was seen as a good proxy for assessing how hard they work.* 醫生診單上的病人數被看作是衡量他們工作努力程度的可靠指標。

Pro·zac™ /ˈprəʊzæk; *NAmE* ˈproʊ-/ *noun* [C, U] a drug used to treat the illness of DEPRESSION 百憂解，鹽酸氟西汀（抗抑鬱藥）：*She's been* ***on Prozac*** *for two years.* 她服用百憂解已經兩年了。

P

prude /pruːd/ *noun* (*disapproving*) a person that you think is too easily shocked by things connected with sex 正經過度的人；對性問題大驚小怪者；談性色變者

pru·dent /ˈpruːdnt/ *adj.* (*formal*) sensible and careful when you make judgements and decisions; avoiding unnecessary risks 謹慎的；慎重的；精明的：*a prudent businessman* 精明的商人 ◇ *a prudent decision/investment* 審慎的決定／投資 ◇ *It might be more prudent to get a second opinion before going ahead.* 行動之前再徵求一下意見也許更為慎重。**OPP imprudent** ▸ **pru·dence** /-dns/ *noun* [U] (*formal*) ➲ SYNONYMS at CARE **pru·dent·ly** *adv.*

prud·ery /ˈpruːdəri/ *noun* [U] (*formal, disapproving*) the attitude or behaviour of people who seem very easily shocked by things connected with sex 談性色變的態度（或行為）；（對性問題的）大驚小怪，假正經

prud·ish /ˈpruːdɪʃ/ *adj.* (*disapproving*) very easily shocked by things connected with sex （對性問題）大驚小怪的，迂腐守舊的，偽善的 **SYN strait-laced** ▸ **prud·ish·ness** *noun* [U]

prune /pruːn/ *noun, verb*

■ ***noun*** a dried PLUM that is often eaten cooked 乾梅子；西梅乾；李子乾：*stewed prunes* 燉梅脯

■ ***verb*** **1** to cut off some of the branches from a tree, bush, etc. so that it will grow better and stronger 修剪樹枝；打杈：**~ sth** *When should you prune apple trees?* 蘋果樹應該什麼時候剪枝？◇ *He pruned the longer branches off the tree.* 他把較長的樹枝剪掉了。◇ **~ sth back** *The hedge needs pruning back.* 樹籬需要修剪了。**2 ~ sth (back)** to make sth smaller by removing parts; to cut out parts of sth 裁減；削減；精簡：*Staff numbers have been pruned back to 175.* 員工的數量已精簡到 175 人。◇ *Prune out any unnecessary details.* 把無關緊要的細節統統刪掉。▸ **prun·ing** *noun* [U]：*All roses require annual pruning.* 玫瑰都要年年修剪。◇ *The company would benefit from a little pruning here and there.* 公司如能處處精簡一點，必將獲益。

pruri·ent /ˈprʊəriənt; *NAmE* ˈprʊr-/ *adj.* (*formal, disapproving*) having or showing too much interest in things connected with sex 好色的；下作的；淫褻的 ▸ **pruri·ence** /-əns/ *noun* [U]

Prus·sian blue /ˌprʌʃn ˈbluː/ *noun* [U] a deep blue colour used in paints 普魯士藍；深藍色

pry /praɪ/ *verb* (**pries**, **pry·ing**, **pried**, **pried** /praɪd/) **1** [I] **~ (into sth)** to try to find out information about other people's private lives in a way that is annoying or rude 探聽，打聽，探查（隱私）：*I'm sick of you prying into my personal life!* 我討厭你刺探我的私生活！◇ *I'm sorry. I didn't mean to pry.* 對不起，我並不想刺探別人的私事。◇ *She tried to keep the children away from* ***the prying eyes*** *of the world's media.* 她盡量使孩子們躲開世界上媒體獵奇的目光。**2** (*especially NAmE*) = PRISE

PS /ˌpiː ˈes/ *noun* something written at the end of a letter to introduce some more information or sth that you have forgotten. PS is the abbreviation for 'postscript'. 附言，又及（全寫為 postscript，用於信末）：*PS Could you send me your fax number again?* 又及：請再把您的傳真號碼發給我好嗎？◇ *She added a PS asking me to water the plants.* 她加了一句附言，要我澆花。

psalm /sɑːm/ *noun* a song, poem or prayer that praises God, especially one in the Bible（《聖經》中的）聖詠；讚美詩；讚美歌：*the Book of Psalms*《〈聖經〉詩篇》

psal·ter /ˈsɔːltə(r)/ *noun* a book containing a collection of songs and poems, (called PSALMS), with their music, that is used in a church 聖詠集；詩篇集

PSAT /ˌpiː es eɪ ˈtiː/ *noun* (in the US) the abbreviation for 'Preliminary Scholastic Aptitude Test' (a test taken by HIGH SCHOOL students in order to prepare for the SAT) 初級學業能力傾向測驗（全寫為 Preliminary Scholastic Aptitude Test，美國中學生為備考學業能力傾向測驗而參加的考試）

pseph·ology /siˈfɒlədʒi; *NAmE* -ˈfɑːl-/ *noun* [U] the study of how people vote in elections 選舉學 ▸ **pseph·olo·gist** /siˈfɒlədʒɪst; *NAmE* -ˈfɑːl-/ *noun*

pseud /suːd; *BrE* also sjuːd/ *noun* (*BrE, informal, disapproving*) a person who pretends to know a lot about a particular subject in order to impress other people 假博士；冒牌學問家 ▸ **pseud** *adj.*

pseudo- /ˈsuːdəʊ; ˈsjuː-; *NAmE* ˈsuːdoʊ/ *combining form* (in nouns, adjectives and adverbs 構成名詞、形容詞和副詞) not genuine; false or pretended 假的；偽的；冒牌的：*pseudo-intellectual* 假知識分子 ◇ *pseudo-science* 偽科學

pseudo·nym /ˈsuːdənɪm; *BrE* also ˈsjuː-/ *noun* a name used by sb, especially a writer, instead of their real name 假名；化名；筆名：*She writes* ***under a pseudonym.*** 她用筆名寫作。➲ compare PEN-NAME ▸ **pseud·onym·ous** /suːˈdɒnɪməs; sjuː-; *NAmE* suːˈdɑːn-/ *adj.*

PSHE /ˌpiː es eɪtʃ ˈiː/ *noun* [U] the abbreviation for 'personal, social and health education' (a subject taught in British schools that deals with a person's emotional and social development and discusses such issues as health, sex, drugs and relationships with other people) 個人、社會及健康教育（全寫為 personal, social and health education，英國學校課程）**HELP** In secondary schools the subject also includes 'economic education' that deals with managing personal finances. 在中學該課程還包括涉及個人財務管理的"理財教育"。

psi /psaɪ; saɪ/ *noun* the 23rd letter of the Greek alphabet (Ψ, ψ) 希臘字母表的第 23 個字母

p.s.i. /ˌpiː es ˈaɪ/ *abbr.* pounds per square inch (used for giving the pressure of tyres, etc.) 磅／平方英寸（胎壓等的單位）

psit·ta·cosis /ˌsɪtəˈkəʊsɪs; *NAmE* -ˈkoʊ-/ *noun* [U] (*medical* 醫) a disease of birds, especially PARROTS, which causes PNEUMONIA (= a disease of the lungs) in humans 鸚鵡熱，鳥熱（可傳染人類引起肺炎）

psor·ia·sis /səˈraɪəsɪs/ *noun* [U] (*medical* 醫) a skin disease that causes rough red areas where the skin comes off in small pieces 牛皮癬；銀屑病

psst /pst/ *exclamation* the way of writing the sound people say when they want to attract sb's attention quietly（書寫形式，表示輕聲引人注意的聲音）嘶，嘘：*Psst! Let's get out now before they see us!* 嘘！咱們現在趁別人沒看見時走吧！

PST /ˌpiː es ˈtiː/ *abbr.* **1** PACIFIC STANDARD TIME **2** provincial sales tax (a tax that is added to the price of goods in some parts of Canada)（加拿大部份地區徵收的）省銷售税

psych /saɪk/ *verb*

PHR V **ˌpsych sb↔ˈout (of sth)** (*informal*) to make an opponent feel less confident by saying or doing things that make you seem better, stronger, etc. than them 使（對手）心虛；震懾（對手）**ˌpsych sb/yourself ˈup (for sth)** (*informal*) to prepare sb/yourself mentally for sth difficult or unpleasant 為（困難或不快的事）做好思想準備：*I'd got myself all psyched up for the interview and then it was called off at the last minute.* 我為這次面試做好了萬全的心理準備，可最後它臨時取消了。➲ see also PSYCHED

psy·che /ˈsaɪki/ *noun* (*formal*) the mind; your deepest feelings and attitudes 靈魂；心靈；精神；心態：*the human psyche* 人的心靈 ◇ *She knew, at some deep level of her psyche, that what she was doing was wrong.* 她在內心深處還是知道自己當時正在做錯誤的事。

psyched /saɪkt/ *adj.* [not before noun] (*informal, especially NAmE*) excited, especially about sth that is going to happen 興奮；殷切期待

psy·che·delia /ˌsaɪkəˈdiːliə/ *noun* [U] music, art, fashion, etc. that is created as a result of the effects of psychedelic drugs（迷幻藥物作用下創作的）迷幻音樂，迷幻藝術，迷幻文化

psy·che·del·ic /ˌsaɪkəˈdelɪk/ *adj.* [usually before noun] **1** (of drugs 藥物) causing the user to see and hear things that are not there or that do not exist (= to HALLUCINATE) 引起幻覺的；使人精神恍惚的 **2** (of art, music, clothes, etc. 藝術、音樂、服裝等) having bright colours, strange sounds, etc. like those that are experienced when taking psychedelic drugs 產生迷幻效果的

psy·chi·at·ric /ˌsaɪkiˈætrɪk/ *adj.* relating to PSYCHIATRY or to mental illness 精神病的；精神病學的：*a psychiatric hospital/nurse* 精神病醫院 / 護理人員 ◇ *psychiatric treatment* 精神病治療 ◇ *psychiatric disorders* 精神紊亂 ➲ compare MENTAL (2)

psych·iatrist /saɪˈkaɪətrɪst/ *noun* a doctor who studies and treats mental illnesses 精神病學家；精神科醫生

psych·iatry /saɪˈkaɪətri/ *noun* [U] the study and treatment of mental illness 精神病學；精神病治療

psy·chic /ˈsaɪkɪk/ *adj., noun*

■ ***adj.*** **1** (also *less frequent* **psych·ical** /ˈsaɪkɪkl/) connected with strange powers of the mind and not able to be explained by natural laws 關於通靈的；超自然的 SYN **paranormal**：*psychic energy/forces/phenomena/powers* 超自然的能量；超自然力量；超自然的現象；心靈力 ◇ *psychic healing* 心靈治療法 **2** (of a person 人) seeming to have strange mental powers and to be able to do things that are not possible according to natural laws 有特異功能的；通靈的：*She claims to be psychic and helps people to contact the dead.* 她自稱有通靈術，能幫助活人與死者溝通。◇ *How am I supposed to know—I'm not psychic!* 我怎麼會知道呢，我又沒有特異功能！ **3** (also *less frequent* **psych·ical**) (*formal*) connected with the mind rather than the body 心靈的；靈魂的 ▸ **psych·ic·al·ly** /-kli/ *adv.*

■ ***noun*** a person who claims to have strange mental powers so that they can do things that are not possible according to natural laws, such as predicting the future and speaking to dead people （自稱）有特異功能的人，有通靈術的人

psy·cho /ˈsaɪkəʊ; *NAmE* -koʊ/ *noun* (*pl.* **-os**) (*informal*) a person who is mentally ill and who behaves in a very strange violent way 精神病患者；精神病人 ▸ **psy·cho** *adj.*

psycho- /ˈsaɪkəʊ; *NAmE* -koʊ/ (also **psych-**) *combining form* (in nouns, adjectives and adverbs 構成名詞、形容詞和副詞) connected with the mind 精神的；靈魂的；心靈的；心理的：*psychology* 心理學 ◇ *psychiatric* 精神病學的

psy·cho·active /ˌsaɪkəʊˈæktɪv; *NAmE* -koʊ-/ *adj.* (*technical* 術語) (of a drug 藥) affecting the mind 作用於精神的

psy·cho·ana·lyse (*BrE*) (*NAmE* **-yze**) /ˌsaɪkəʊˈænəlaɪz; *NAmE* -koʊ-/ (also **ana·lyse**, **ana·lyze**) *verb* **~ sb** to treat or study sb using psychoanalysis 對…進行精神分析（或治療）；對…做心理分析（或治療）

psy·cho·analy·sis /ˌsaɪkəʊəˈnæləsɪs; *NAmE* -koʊə-/ (also **an·aly·sis**) *noun* [U] a method of treating sb who is mentally ill by asking them to talk about past experiences and feelings in order to try to find explanations for their present problems 精神分析（或療法）；心理分析（或療法） ▸ **psy·cho·ana·lyt·ic** /ˌsaɪkəʊˌænəˈlɪtɪk; *NAmE* -koʊ-/ *adj.* [only before noun]：*a psychoanalytic approach* 精神分析法 **psy·cho·ana·lyt·ic·al·ly** /-ɪkli/ *adv.*

psy·cho·ana·lyst /ˌsaɪkəʊˈænəlɪst; *NAmE* -koʊ-/ (also **ana·lyst**) *noun* a person who treats patients using psychoanalysis 精神分析學家（或醫生）

psy·cho·bab·ble /ˈsaɪkəʊbæbl; *NAmE* -koʊ-/ *noun* [U] (*informal, disapproving*) the language that people use when they talk about feelings and emotional problems, that sounds very scientific, but really has little meaning 心理學囈語（談論感情問題時使用的用詞非常專門但意思空洞的語言）

psy·cho·drama /ˈsaɪkəʊdrɑːmə; *NAmE* -koʊ-/ *noun* **1** a way of treating people who are mentally ill by encouraging them to act events from their past to help them understand their feelings 心理劇療法，精神表演療法（重演舊事以幫助精神病患者瞭解自己） **2** a play or film/movie that makes the minds and feelings of the characters more important than the events 心理戲劇，心理電影（着重人物心理）

psy·cho·kin·esis /ˌsaɪkəʊkɪˈniːsɪs; -kaɪˈn-; *NAmE* -koʊ-/ *noun* [U] the act of moving an object by using the power of the mind 心靈致動，傳心致動（精神集中於物體使之移動）

psy·cho·lin·guis·tics /ˌsaɪkəʊlɪŋˈɡwɪstɪks; *NAmE* -koʊ-/ *noun* [U] the study of how the mind processes and produces language 心理語言學 ▸ **psy·cho·lin·guis·tic** /ˌsaɪkəʊlɪŋˈɡwɪstɪk; *NAmE* -koʊ-/ *adj.*

psy·cho·logic·al AW /ˌsaɪkəˈlɒdʒɪkl; *NAmE* -ˈlɑːdʒ-/ *adj.* **1** [usually before noun] connected with a person's mind and the way in which it works 心靈的；心理的；精神上的：*the psychological development of children* 兒童的心理發展 ◇ *Abuse can lead to both psychological and emotional problems.* 虐待可造成心理和情緒上的問題。◇ *Her symptoms are more psychological than physical* (= imaginary rather than real). 她的病症是臆想的，而不是真實的。◇ *Victory in the last game gave them **a psychological advantage** over their opponents.* 上一場比賽的勝利使他們比對手有心理優勢。◇ *a psychological novel* (= one that examines the minds of the characters) 心理小說 **2** [only before noun] connected with the study of PSYCHOLOGY 心理學的；關於心理學的：*psychological research* 心理學研究 ▸ **psy·cho·logic·al·ly** AW /-kli/ *adv.*：*psychologically harmful* 精神上有害的 ◇ *Psychologically, the defeat was devastating.* 就心理而言，這次失敗是致命的。

IDM **the ˌpsychological ˈmoment** the best time to do sth in order for it to be successful 最佳時機；最適當時機

ˌpsychological ˈwarfare *noun* [U] things that are said and done in order to make an opponent believe that they cannot win a war, a competition, etc. 心理戰

psych·olo·gist AW /saɪˈkɒlədʒɪst; *NAmE* -ˈkɑːl-/ *noun* a scientist who studies and is trained in psychology 心理學家；心理學研究者：*an educational psychologist* 教育心理學家 ◇ *a clinical psychologist* (= one who treats people with mental DISORDERS or problems) 心理醫生

psych·ology AW /saɪˈkɒlədʒi; *NAmE* -ˈkɑːl-/ *noun* **1** [U] the scientific study of the mind and how it influences behaviour 心理學：***social/educational/child psychology*** 社會 / 教育 / 兒童心理學 ➲ compare POP PSYCHOLOGY **2** [sing.] the kind of mind that sb has that makes them think or behave in a particular way 心理；心理特徵：*the psychology of small boys* 小男孩的心理特徵 **3** [sing.] how the mind influences behaviour in a particular area of life 心理影響：*the psychology of interpersonal relationships* 人際關係的心理影響

psy·cho·met·ric /ˌsaɪkəˈmetrɪk/ *adj.* [only before noun] (*technical* 術語) used for measuring mental abilities and processes 心理測量的；精神測定的：*psychometric testing* 心理測試

psy·cho·path /ˈsaɪkəpæθ/ *noun* a person suffering from a serious mental illness that causes them to behave in a violent way towards other people 精神變態者；精神病患者 ▸ **psy·cho·path·ic** /ˌsaɪkəˈpæθɪk/ *adj.*：*a psychopathic disorder/killer* 精神錯亂；精神變態殺人者

psy·cho·path·ology /ˌsaɪkəʊpəˈθɒlədʒi; *NAmE* -koʊpəˈθɑːl-/ *noun* **1** [U] the scientific study of mental DISORDERS 精神病理學；心理病理學 **2** [C] a DISORDER that affects sb's mind or their behaviour 精神機能障礙

psych·osis /saɪˈkəʊsɪs; *NAmE* -ˈkoʊ-/ *noun* [C, U] (*pl.* **psych·oses** /-siːz/) a serious mental illness that affects the whole personality 精神病 ➲ see also PSYCHOTIC

psy·cho·somat·ic /ˌsaɪkəʊsəˈmætɪk; *NAmE* -koʊ-/ *adj.* **1** (of an illness 疾病) caused by mental problems, such as stress and worry, rather than physical problems 由心理負擔導致的；由精神壓力引起的 **2** (*technical* 術語) connected with the relationship between the mind and the body 身心的

psy·cho·ther·apy /ˌsaɪkəʊˈθerəpi; *NAmE* -koʊ-/ (also **ther·apy**) *noun* [U] the treatment of mental illness by discussing sb's problems with them rather than by giving them drugs 心理治療；精神治療 ▸ **psy·cho·ther·ap·ist** /-pɪst/ (also **ther·ap·ist**) *noun*

psych·ot·ic /saɪˈkɒtɪk; *NAmE* -ˈkɑːt-/ *noun* (*medical* 醫) a person suffering from severe mental illness 精神病患者 ▸ **psych·ot·ic** *adj.*：*a psychotic disorder/illness* 精神錯亂；精神病 ◇ *a psychotic patient* 精神病患者 ➲ see also PSYCHOSIS ➲ **SYNONYMS** at MENTALLY

P

psy·cho·trop·ic /ˌsaɪkəˈtrəʊpɪk; *NAmE* -ˈtroʊpɪk/ *adj.* [usually before noun] (*medical* 醫) relating to drugs or substances that affect a person's mental state（藥物等）精神（類）的：*psychotropic medication/drugs* 精神藥物

PT /ˌpiː ˈtiː/ *abbr.* **1** (*BrE*) physical training (sport and physical exercise that is taught in schools, in the army, etc.) 體育；體格訓練 **2** (also **P/T**) (in writing) PART-TIME（書寫形式）部份時間的，兼職的：*The course is 1 year FT, 2 years PT.* 這門課程全讀生修一年，半讀生修兩年。

pt (also **pt.** especially in *NAmE*) *abbr.* **1** part 部份：*Shakespeare's Henry IV Pt 2* 莎士比亞《亨利四世》下篇 **2** pint 品脫 **3** point 得分；點：*The winner scored 10 pts.* 獲勝者得了 10 分。 **4 Pt.** (especially on a map) port（尤用於地圖）港口：*Pt. Moresby* 莫爾茲比港

PTA /ˌpiː tiː ˈeɪ/ *noun* the abbreviation for 'parent-teacher association' (a group run by parents and teachers in a school that organizes social events and helps the school in different ways) 家長教師聯誼會，家長教師會（全寫為 parent-teacher association）

ptar·migan /ˈtɑːmɪɡən; *NAmE* ˈtɑːrm-/ *noun* a type of GROUSE (= a bird with a fat body and feathers on its legs), found in mountain areas and in Arctic regions 雷鳥（棲息於山區和北極地區）

Pte *abbr.* (*BrE*) (in writing) PRIVATE（書寫形式）二等兵：*Pte Jim Hill* 二等兵吉姆・希爾

ptero·dac·tyl /ˌterəˈdæktɪl/ *noun* a flying REPTILE that lived millions of years ago 翼指龍（數百萬年前的飛行爬行動物）

PTO /ˌpiː tiː ˈəʊ; *NAmE* ˈoʊ/ *abbr.* (*BrE*) please turn over (written at the bottom of a page to show that there is more on the other side)（頁末字樣）請見下頁，見反面

Pty *abbr.* proprietary (used in the names of some companies in Australia and South Africa) 公司（用於澳大利亞和南非的一些公司名稱）：*Computer Software Packages Pty Ltd* 電腦軟件包有限公司

P

pub 🔑 /pʌb/ (also *formal* ˌ**public** ˈ**house**) (both *BrE*) *noun* a building where people go to drink and meet their friends. Pubs serve alcoholic and other drinks, and often also food. 酒吧；酒館：*They've gone down the pub for a drink.* 他們下酒館喝酒去了。◇ *a pub lunch* 酒館供的午餐 ◇ *the landlord of the local pub* 當地酒館的老闆 ➲ **VISUAL VOCAB** page V15

ˈ**pub crawl** *noun* (*BrE*, *informal*) a visit to several pubs, going straight from one to the next, drinking at each of them 挨店喝酒；串酒館

pube /pjuːb/ *noun* [usually pl.] (*informal*) a pubic hair 陰毛

pu·berty /ˈpjuːbəti; *NAmE* -bərti/ *noun* [U] the period of a person's life during which their sexual organs develop and they become capable of having children 青春期：*to reach puberty* 進入青春期 ➲ **COLLOCATIONS** at AGE ➲ see also ADOLESCENCE

pubes /ˈpjuːbiːz/ *noun* (*pl.* **pubes**) the lower front part of the body, above the legs, covered by hair in adults 恥骨區

pu·bes·cent /pjuːˈbesnt/ *adj.* [usually before noun] (*formal*) in the period of a person's life when they are changing physically from a child to an adult 青春期的；到達發育期的

pubic /ˈpjuːbɪk/ *adj.* [only before noun] connected with the part of a person's body near their sexual organs 陰部的：*pubic hair* 陰毛 ◇ *the pubic bone* 恥骨

pubis /ˈpjuːbɪs/ *noun* (*pl.* **pubes** /-biːz/) one of the two bones that form the sides of the PELVIS 恥骨

pub·lic 🔑 /ˈpʌblɪk/ *adj.*, *noun*

■ ***adj.***

▸ **OF ORDINARY PEOPLE** 普通人 **1** 🔑 [only before noun] connected with ordinary people in society in general 平民的；大眾的；公眾的；百姓的：*The campaign is designed to increase public awareness of the issues.* 這場運動旨在提高民眾對這些問題的認識。◇ *Levels of waste from the factory may be a danger to public health.* 工廠排出廢棄物的含量可能危及大眾的健康。◇ *Why would the closure of hospitals be **in the public interest*** (= useful to ordinary people)? 關閉醫院怎麼會對民眾有利呢？◇ *The government had to bow to public pressure.* 政府不得不向公眾的壓力低頭。

▸ **FOR EVERYONE** 公眾 **2** 🔑 [only before noun] provided, especially by the government, for the use of people in general 公共的；公立的：*a public education system* 公共教育體系 ◇ *a public library* 公共圖書館 **OPP** **private**

▸ **OF GOVERNMENT** 政府 **3** 🔑 [only before noun] connected with the government and the services it provides 政府的；有關政府所提供服務的：***public money/spending/funding/expenditure*** 公款；公共開支；政府撥款；政府開支 ◇ *He spent much of his career in **public office*** (= working in the government). 他的事業生涯中大部份時間從事政府工作。◇ (*BrE*) *the **public purse*** (= the money that the government can spend) 國庫 ◇ *The rail industry is no longer in **public ownership*** (= controlled by the government). 鐵路業不再歸國有了。 **OPP** **private**

▸ **SEEN/HEARD BY PEOPLE** 公開 **4** 🔑 known to people in general 人人皆知的；公開的：*a **public figure*** (= a person who is well known because they are often on the television, radio, etc.) 公眾人物 ◇ *Details of the government report have not yet been **made public**.* 政府報告的細節尚未公佈。◇ *She entered **public life*** (= started a job in which she became known to the public) *at the age of 25.* 她 25 歲時開始了面對公眾的工作。 **5** 🔑 open to people in general; intended to be seen or heard by people in general 公諸於眾的；公開的：*a public apology* 公開的道歉 ◇ *The painting will be put on **public display** next week.* 這幅畫將於下週公開展出。◇ *This may be the band's last **public appearance** together.* 這可能是這個樂隊最後一次全體公開亮相。

▸ **PLACE** 地方 **6** 🔑 where there are a lot of people who can see and hear you 公開場合的；大庭廣眾的：*Let's go somewhere a little less public.* 咱們找一個僻靜些的地方吧。 **OPP** **private**

▸ **pub·lic·ly** 🔑 /-kli/ *adv.*：*a publicly owned company* 股票上市公司 ◇ *He later publicly apologized for his comments.* 後來他對自己的言論作了公開道歉。◇ *This information is not publicly available.* 這個消息沒有對外公開。

IDM **go** ˈ**public** **1** to tell people about sth that is a secret 公之於世；公開（秘密等） **2** (of a company 公司) to start selling shares on the STOCK EXCHANGE 上市；公開出售股份 **in the public** ˈ**eye** well known to many people through newspapers and television（通過報紙、電視）讓公眾熟知的，廣為人知的：*She doesn't want her children growing up in the public eye.* 她不想讓子女在眾人矚目中成長。 ➲ more at KNOWLEDGE

■ ***noun*** [sing.+sing./pl. v.]

▸ **ORDINARY PEOPLE** 普通人 **1** 🔑 **the public** ordinary people in society in general 平民；百姓；民眾：*The palace is now **open to the public**.* 這座宮殿現在向大眾開放了。◇ *There have been many complaints from **members of the public**.* 現在已有大量的民眾投訴。◇ *The public has/have a right to know what is contained in the report.* 民眾有權瞭解報告的內容。 ➲ see also THE GENERAL PUBLIC

▸ **GROUP OF PEOPLE** 民眾 **2** a group of people who share a particular interest or who are involved in the same activity 志趣相同（或從事同一類活動）的群體：*the theatre-going public* 愛看戲的民眾 ◇ *She knows how to keep her public* (= for example, the people who buy her books) *satisfied.* 她知道如何迎合受眾的興趣。

IDM **in** ˈ**public** 🔑 when other people, especially people you do not know, are present 公開地；在別人（尤指生人）面前：*She doesn't like to be seen in public without her make-up on.* 她不願意未化妝就公開露面。 ➲ compare IN PRIVATE at PRIVATE *n.* ➲ more at WASH *v.*

ˌ**public** ˈ**access** *noun* [U] **1** the right of people in general to go into particular buildings or areas of land or to obtain particular information（進入公共場所的）大眾通行權；（對信息的）公眾知情權，公眾使用權：*public access to the countryside* 公眾使用郊野的權利 **2** (in the US and some other countries) the right of people in general to use television or radio channels to present their own programmes（美國及其他一些國家的）公共頻道播送：*a public access channel* 公共頻道

ˌpublic adˈdress system *noun* (*abbr.* **PA system**) an electronic system that uses MICROPHONES and LOUDSPEAKERS to make music, voices, etc. louder so that they can be heard by everyone in a particular place or building 擴音系統

ˌpublic afˈfairs *noun* [pl.] issues and questions about social, economic, political or business activities, etc. that affect ordinary people in general 公共事務

pub·li·can /ˈpʌblɪkən/ *noun* **1** (*BrE, formal*) a person who owns or manages a pub 酒館老闆（或經理） **2** (*AustralE, NZE*) a person who owns or manages a hotel 旅館老闆（或經理）

pub·li·ca·tion 0-w AW /ˌpʌblɪˈkeɪʃn/ *noun*
1 0-w [U, C] the act of printing a book, a magazine, etc. and making it available to the public; a book, a magazine, etc. that has been published （書刊等的）出版，發行；出版物：*the publication date* 出版日期 ◇ *the publication of his first novel* 他首部小說的出版 ◇ *specialist publications* 專業出版物 **2** 0-w [U] the act of printing sth in a newspaper, report, etc. so that the public knows about it 發表；刊登；公佈：*a delay in the publication of the exam results* 考試成績的延期公佈 ◇ *The newspaper continues to defend its publication of the photographs.* 這家報紙繼續為刊登這些照片辯護。

ˌpublic ˈbar *noun* (in Britain) a bar in a pub with simple or less comfortable furniture than the other bars（英國酒館中的）廉價酒吧，大眾酒吧 ➲ compare LOUNGE BAR

ˌpublic ˈcompany (also **ˌpublic ˌlimited ˈcompany**) (both *BrE*) (*NAmE* **ˌpublic corpoˈration**) *noun* (*abbr.* **plc, PLC**) a company that sells shares in itself to the public 公開招股公司；公開股份有限公司

ˌpublic conˈvenience *noun* (*BrE, formal*) a public building containing toilets that are provided for anyone to use 公共廁所

ˌpublic corpoˈration *noun* **1** (*NAmE*) (*BrE* **ˌpublic ˈcompany, ˌpublic ˌlimited ˈcompany**) a company that sells shares in itself to the public 公開招股公司；上市公司 **2** (*BrE*) an organization that is owned by the government and that provides a national service 公營機構；國有化公司

ˌpublic deˈfender *noun* (*law* 律) (in the US) a lawyer who is paid by the government to defend people in court if they cannot pay for a lawyer themselves（美國）公設辯護人，公設辯護律師

ˌpublic ˈdomain *noun* [sing.] something that is in the **public domain** is available for everyone to use or to discuss and is not secret （用於不受版權保護的財產）公有領域，公有產業：*The information has been placed in the public domain.* 這資料不受版權保護。◇ *public domain software* 無版權軟件

ˌpublic ˈenemy *noun* a person who has done, or is believed to have done, a very bad thing, especially sth that is harmful to society 人民公敵；社會公敵：*public enemy number one* (= the person or thing that is most frightening or that is most hated) 頭號公敵（最可怕或最可惡的人或事物）

ˌpublic ˈholiday *noun* a day on which most of the shops/stores, businesses and schools in a country are closed, often to celebrate a particular event 公共假日；公休日 ➲ compare BANK HOLIDAY

ˌpublic ˈhouse *noun* (*BrE, formal*) = PUB

ˌpublic ˈhousing *noun* [U] (in the US) houses and flats/apartments that are built by the government for people who do not have enough money to pay for private accommodation（美國政府為低收入者修建的）公共住房

pub·li·cist /ˈpʌblɪsɪst/ *noun* a person whose job is to make sth known to the public, for example a new product, actor, etc. 推介人員；宣傳員；廣告人員

pub·li·city 0-w /pʌbˈlɪsəti/ *noun* [U]
1 0-w the attention that is given to sb/sth by newspapers, television, etc.（媒體的）關注，宣傳，報道：***good/bad/adverse publicity*** 有利的／不利的／反面的報道 ◇ *There has been a great deal of publicity surrounding his disappearance.* 他的失踪已為傳媒廣泛報道。◇ *The trial took place amid* ***a blaze of*** (= a lot of) *publicity.* 審訊在全面曝光的情況下進行。 **2** 0-w the business of attracting the attention of the public to sth/sb; the things that are done to attract attention 宣傳業；廣告宣傳工作；傳播工作：*She works in publicity.* 她從事宣傳工作。◇ *There has been a lot of advance publicity for her new film.* 她的新電影尚未上映即大加宣傳。◇ *publicity material* 宣傳材料 ◇ *a* ***publicity campaign*** 宣傳運動 ◇ *The band dressed up as the Beatles as a* ***publicity stunt.*** 樂隊扮作披頭士樂隊作為宣傳噱頭。 ➲ SYNONYMS at ADVERTISEMENT

pub·li·cize (*BrE* also **-ise**) /ˈpʌblɪsaɪz/ *verb* **~ sth** to make sth known to the public; to advertise sth 宣傳；推廣；宣揚；傳播：*They flew to Europe to publicize the plight of the refugees.* 他們飛往歐洲報道難民的慘狀。◇ *a* ***much/highly/widely publicized*** *speech* (= that has received a lot of attention on television, in newspapers, etc.) 一篇受到媒體廣泛報道的講話 ◇ *He was in London publicizing his new biography of Kennedy.* 他在倫敦推銷他新出版的肯尼迪傳。

ˌpublic ˌlimited ˈcompany *noun* (*BrE*) (*abbr.* **plc**) = PUBLIC COMPANY

ˌpublic ˈnuisance *noun* **1** [sing., U] (*law* 律) an illegal act that causes harm to people in general 公害；妨害大眾的行為：*He was charged with committing (a) public nuisance.* 他被控妨害公眾利益。 **2** [C, usually sing.] (*informal*) a person or thing that annoys a lot of people 妨害大眾的人（或事物）；公害；蠹蟲

ˌpublic oˈpinion *noun* [U] the opinions that people in society have about an issue 輿論；民意：*The media has a powerful influence on public opinion.* 傳媒對於輿論有很大的影響。

ˌpublic ˈproperty *noun* [U] **1** (*law* 律) land, buildings, etc. that are owned by the government and can be used by everyone 公共財產；公產；公物 **2** a person or thing that everyone has a right to know about 公眾人物；公眾有權瞭解的人（或事情）：*Sophie became public property when she married into the royal family.* 索菲嫁入王室後，即成為公眾人物。

ˌpublic ˈprosecutor *noun* (*BrE*) a lawyer who works for the government and tries to prove people guilty in court 公訴人；檢察官 ➲ see also DISTRICT ATTORNEY

ˌpublic reˈlations *noun* **1** [U] (*abbr.* **PR**) the business of giving the public information about a particular organization or person in order to create a good impression 公關工作（或活動）：*She works in public relations.* 她從事公關工作。◇ *a public relations exercise* 一項公關活動 **2** [pl.] the state of the relationship between an organization and the public 公共關係：*Sponsoring the local team is good for public relations.* 贊助當地球隊有利於公共關係。

ˌpublic ˈschool *noun* [C, U] **1** (in Britain, especially in England) a private school for young people between the ages of 13 and 18, whose parents pay for their education. The students often live at the school while they are studying. 公學（在英國，尤其是英格蘭，為 13 到 18 歲青少年開辦的私立付費學校，學生常寄宿）：*He was educated at (a) public school.* 他出身英國公學。 ➲ compare PREPARATORY SCHOOL (1), PRIVATE SCHOOL **2** **ˈpublic school** (in the US, Australia, Scotland and other countries) a free local school paid for by the government （美國、澳大利亞、蘇格蘭及其他國家的）免費公立學校 ➲ compare STATE SCHOOL (1)

the ˌpublic ˈsector *noun* [sing.] (*economics* 經) the part of the economy of a country that is owned or controlled by the government 公營部門；公共部門 ➲ compare THE PRIVATE SECTOR

ˌpublic ˈservant *noun* a person who is employed by the state or in local government or who is an elected representative 公務員；公僕：*pay increases for public servants* 公務員的加薪 ◇ *a long and outstanding career as a public servant* 任公務員時間長且表現優秀

ˌpublic ˈservice *noun* **1** [C] a service such as transport or health care that a government or an official organization provides for people in general in a particular

P

society 公共事業；公營事業： *to improve public services in the area* 改進本地區的公用事業 ◇ *a public service broadcast* 公營廣播 **2** [C, U] something that is done to help people rather than to make a profit 公益事業（或服務）： *to perform a public service* 從事一項公益服務 **3** [U] the government and government departments 政府；政府部門： *to work in public service* 在政府機關工作 ◇ *public service workers* 公務人員

ˌpublic ˈservice broadcasting *noun* [U] radio and television programmes broadcast by organizations such as the BBC in Britain that are independent of government but are financed by public money 公共服務廣播（由英國廣播公司等受公款資助的非政府獨立機構播放的節目）

ˌpublic-ˈspirit·ed *adj.* willing to do things that will help other people in society 有公益精神的；熱心公益的；助人為樂的： *a public-spirited act* 助人為樂的行為 ◇ *That was very public-spirited of you.* 你那樣做真是熱心公益啊！ ▶ **ˌpublic ˈspirit** *noun* [U]

ˌpublic ˈtelevision *noun* [U] (*NAmE*) a television service that shows mainly EDUCATIONAL programmes and is paid for by the government, the public and some companies 大眾文化教育電視（由政府、公眾以及某些公司贊助）

ˌpublic ˈtransport (*BrE*) (*NAmE* **ˌpublic transporˈtation**) *noun* [U] the system of buses, trains, etc. provided by the government or by companies, which people use to travel from one place to another 公共交通；公交制度： *to **travel on/by public transport*** 乘公交車 ◇ *Most of us use public transport to get to work.* 我們大多數人都乘公共交通工具上班。 ➲ COLLOCATIONS at TOWN ➲ VISUAL VOCAB page V8

ˌpublic uˈtility *noun* (*formal*) a private company that must obey government rules, that supplies essential services such as gas, water and electricity to the public 公用事業（公司）

P

ˌpublic ˈworks *noun* [pl.] building work, such as that of hospitals, schools and roads, that is paid for by the government 公共工程（或建設）

pub·lish 0‑ AW /ˈpʌblɪʃ/ *verb*
1 0‑ [T] ~ sth to produce a book, magazine, CD-ROM, etc. and sell it to the public 出版；發行： *The first edition was published in 2007.* 第一版於 2007 年發行。◇ *He works for a company that publishes reference books.* 他在一家參考書出版公司工作。◇ *Most of our titles are also published on CD-ROM.* 我們的大部份書籍也製成光盤發行。 **2** 0‑ [T] ~ sth to print a letter, an article, etc. in a newspaper or magazine （在報刊）發表，刊登，登載： *Pictures of the suspect were published in all the daily papers.* 嫌疑人的照片刊登在各家日報上了。 **3** 0‑ [T] ~ sth to make sth available to the public on the Internet （在互聯網上）發表，公佈： *The report will be published on the Internet.* 報告將在互聯網上公佈。 **4** 0‑ [T, I] ~ (**sth**) (of an author 作者) to have your work printed and sold to the public 發表（作品）；使（作品）出版： *She hasn't published anything for years.* 她好幾年沒有發表作品了。◇ *University teachers are under pressure to publish.* 大學教師有不得不發表作品的壓力。 **5** [T] ~ sth (*formal*) to make official information known to the public 公佈；發佈 SYN **release** : *The findings of the committee will be published on Friday.* 委員會的調查結果將於星期五公佈。

pub·lish·er AW /ˈpʌblɪʃə(r)/ *noun* a person or company that prepares and prints books, magazines, newspapers or electronic products and makes them available to the public 出版人（或機構）；發行人（或機構）

pub·lish·ing 0‑ AW /ˈpʌblɪʃɪŋ/ *noun* [U]
the profession or business of preparing and printing books, magazines, CD-ROMs, etc. and selling or making them available to the public 出版（業）；發行（業）： *a publishing house* (= company) 出版社 ➲ see also DESKTOP PUBLISHING

puce /pjuːs/ *adj.* reddish-purple in colour 紫紅色的： *His face was puce with rage.* 他氣得臉色發紫。 ▶ **puce** *noun* [U]

puck /pʌk/ *noun* **1** a hard flat rubber disc that is used as a ball in ICE HOCKEY （冰球運動使用的）冰球 ➲ VISUAL VOCAB page V44 **2** (*computing* 計) a pointing device that looks like a computer mouse and is used to control the movement of the CURSOR on a computer screen 定標器；光標定位器；手持游標器

puck·er /ˈpʌkə(r)/ *verb* [I, T] ~ (**sth**) (**up**) to form or to make sth form small folds or lines 皺起；使起褶子；噘起： *His **face puckered**, and he was ready to cry.* 他的臉一皺，像要哭了。◇ *She puckered her lips.* 她噘起嘴唇。◇ *puckered fabric* 有褶皺的織物

puck·ish /ˈpʌkɪʃ/ *adj.* [usually before noun] (*literary*) enjoying playing tricks on other people 頑皮的；淘氣的；愛惡作劇的 SYN **mischievous**

pud /pʊd/ *noun* (*BrE, informal*) = PUDDING

pud·ding /ˈpʊdɪŋ/ (*BrE, informal* **pud**) *noun* [U, C] **1** (*BrE*) a sweet dish eaten at the end of a meal （餐末的）甜食，甜點： *What's for pudding?* 有什麼甜點？◇ *I haven't made a pudding today.* 我今天沒做甜點。 SYN **afters, dessert, sweet** **2** (*BrE*) a hot sweet dish, often like a cake, made from flour, fat and eggs with fruit, jam, etc. in or on it 熱布丁糕（用麵粉、油、蛋製作，加水果、果醬等）： *treacle pudding* 糖漿布丁 ◇ *bread and butter pudding* (= made with bread, butter and milk) 麵包黃油布丁 ➲ see also CHRISTMAS PUDDING, RICE PUDDING, SPONGE PUDDING, SUMMER PUDDING **3** (*BrE*) a hot dish like a PIE with soft PASTRY made from flour, fat and eggs and usually filled with meat 熱布丁餅（用麵粉、油、蛋製作，通常用肉填充）： *a steak and kidney pudding* 牛肉腰子布丁 **4** (*especially NAmE*) a cold DESSERT (= a sweet dish) like cream flavoured with fruit, chocolate, etc. 冷布丁（有水果、巧克力等口味）： *chocolate pudding* 巧克力布丁 ➲ see also BLACK PUDDING, YORKSHIRE PUDDING IDM see OVER-EGG, PROOF *n.*

ˈpudding basin *noun* (*BrE*) a deep round bowl that is used for mixing food or for cooking puddings in （調拌食物的）深盆；布丁蒸盤

pud·dle /ˈpʌdl/ *noun* a small amount of water or other liquid, especially rain, that has collected in one place on the ground 水窪；小水坑；（尤指）雨水坑

pu·denda /pjuːˈdendə/ *noun* [pl.] (*old-fashioned, formal*) the sexual organs that are outside the body, especially those of a woman 陰部；（尤指）女陰

pudgy /ˈpʌdʒi/ (*BrE* also **podgy**) *adj.* (*informal*, usually *disapproving*) slightly fat 微胖的

Pue·blo /ˈpwebləʊ; *NAmE* -loʊ/ *noun* (*pl.* **Pue·blo** or **Pue·blos**) *noun* a member of a group of Native American people who live in the US states of Arizona and New Mexico 普韋布洛人（美洲土著，居於美國亞利桑那州和新墨西哥州）

pue·blo /ˈpwebləʊ; *NAmE* -bloʊ/ *noun* (*pl.* **-os**) (from *Spanish*) a town or village in Latin America or the south-western US, especially one with traditional buildings 普韋布洛村落（在拉丁美洲或美國西南部，尤指有傳統房屋建築）

pu·er·ile /ˈpjʊəraɪl; *NAmE* ˈpjʊrəl/ *adj.* (*disapproving*) silly; suitable for a child rather than an adult 愚蠢的；幼稚的；孩子氣的 SYN **childish**

puff /pʌf/ *verb, noun*
■ *verb* **1** [I, T] to smoke a cigarette, pipe, etc. 吸，抽（香煙、煙斗等）： ~ (**at/on sth**) *He puffed* (*away*) *on his pipe.* 他（一口一口地）吸着煙斗。◇ ~ **sth** *I sat puffing my cigar.* 我坐着抽雪茄。 **2** [T, I] to make smoke or steam blow out in clouds; to blow out in clouds 使噴出，冒出（煙或蒸汽）： ~ **sth** (**out**) *Chimneys were puffing out clouds of smoke.* 煙囱冒着滾滾濃煙。◇ ~ (**out**) *Steam puffed out.* 蒸汽向外噴出。 **3** [I, T] (+ **speech**) (*informal*) to breathe loudly and quickly, especially after you have been running 急促喘息；氣喘吁吁 SYN **gasp** : *I was starting to puff a little from the climb.* 爬坡弄得我有點喘息起來。 ➲ see also PUFFED, PUFFED OUT at PUFFED **4** [I] + **adv./prep.** to move in a particular direction, sending out small clouds of smoke

or steam 噴着汽（或煙）移動： *The train puffed into the station.* 火車噴着蒸汽駛進車站。
IDM **be puffed up with 'pride, etc.** to be too full of pride, etc. 自滿；自負 **ˌpuff and 'pant** (also **ˌpuff and 'blow**, *informal*) to breathe quickly and loudly through your mouth after physical effort 氣喘吁吁；呼哧呼哧地喘 ➲ more at HUFF *v.*
PHR V **ˌpuff sth↔'out** to make sth bigger and rounder, especially by filling it with air 吹脹；使鼓起來： *She puffed out her cheeks.* 她鼓起了腮幫子。 **ˌpuff 'up** | **ˌpuff sth↔'up** to swell or to make sth swell 膨脹；使膨脹： *Her cheeks puffed up.* 她的腮幫子鼓了起來。◇ *The frog puffed itself up.* 這隻青蛙脹得鼓鼓的。
■ ***noun*** **1** [C] an act of breathing in sth such as smoke from a cigarette, or drugs 吸，抽（把氣體經口或鼻引到體內的動作）： *He had a few puffs at the cigar.* 他吸了幾口雪茄。◇ *Take two puffs from the inhaler every four hours.* 每隔四小時從吸藥器中吸兩口藥。 **2** [C] a small amount of air, smoke, etc. that is blown from somewhere（煙、氣等的）一縷，少量： *a puff of wind* 一絲清風◇ *Puffs of white smoke came from the chimney.* 煙囱冒出了裊裊白煙。◇ *Any chance of success seemed to vanish in a puff of smoke* (= to disappear quickly). 成功的機會猶如一縷青煙，瞬息即逝。 **3** [C] a hollow piece of light PASTRY that is filled with cream, jam, etc. 千層酥；奶油酥；泡芙 ➲ see also CREAM PUFF (1) **4** (*NAmE* also **'puff piece**) [C] (*informal, usually disapproving*) a piece of writing or speech that praises sb/sth too much 吹捧的文章（或講話） **5** [U] (*informal, especially BrE*) breath 呼吸；喘息： *The hill was very steep and I soon* ***ran out of puff.*** 山坡陡峭，我很快就氣喘吁吁了。 ➲ see also POWDER PUFF

puff·ball /ˈpʌfbɔːl/ *noun* a FUNGUS with a round brown head, that bursts when it is ready to release its seeds 馬勃（菌）

puffed /pʌft/ (also **ˌpuffed 'out**) *adj.* [not before noun] (*BrE, informal*) breathing quickly and with difficulty because you have been having a lot of physical exercise 氣喘吁吁；上氣不接下氣

puff·er /ˈpʌfə(r)/ *noun* **1** (*informal*) = INHALER **2** = PUFFERFISH

puff·er·fish /ˈpʌfəfɪʃ; *NAmE* -fərf-/ *noun* (*pl.* **puffer·fish** or **puffer·fishes**) (also **puff·er**) a poisonous fish that lives in warm seas and fills with air when it is in danger 河豚

puf·fin /ˈpʌfɪn/ *noun* a black and white bird with a large, brightly coloured beak that lives near the sea, common in the N Atlantic 角嘴海雀，海鸚（常見於北大西洋，喙大而色豔） ➲ VISUAL VOCAB page V12

ˌpuff 'pastry *noun* [U] a type of light PASTRY that forms many thin layers when baked, used for making PIES, cakes, etc. 千層酥麪糰；油酥麪糰

'puff piece *noun* (*NAmE*) = PUFF (4)

ˌpuff 'sleeve (also **ˌpuffed 'sleeve**) *noun* a type of sleeve on a piece of clothing that fits close to the body at the shoulder and the lower edge and is wider in the middle, forming a round shape 泡泡袖

puffy /ˈpʌfi/ *adj.* (**puff·ier**, **puffi·est**) **1** (of eyes, faces, etc. 眼睛、面部等) looking swollen (= larger, rounder, etc. than usual) 鼓脹的；腫脹的： *Her eyes were puffy from crying.* 她眼睛都哭腫了。 **2** (of clouds, etc. 雲等) looking soft, round and white 鬆軟潔白的；白絨團狀的 ▸ **puf·fi·ness** *noun* [U]

pug /pʌɡ/ *noun* a small dog with short hair and a wide flat face with deep folds of skin 哈巴狗

pu·gil·ist /ˈpjuːdʒɪlɪst/ *noun* (*old-fashioned*) a BOXER 拳擊手 ▸ **pu·gil·ism** /-lɪzəm/ *noun* [U] **pu·gil·is·tic** /ˌpjuːdʒɪˈlɪstɪk/ *adj.*

pug·na·cious /pʌɡˈneɪʃəs/ *adj.* (*formal*) having a strong desire to argue or fight with other people 愛爭執的；好鬥的；愛滋事的 **SYN** **bellicose** ▸ **pug·na·cious·ly** *adv.* **pug·na·city** /pʌɡˈnæsəti/ *noun* [U]

puis·sance /ˈpwiːsɒ̃s; *NAmE* ˈpwɪsəns/ *noun* **1** **Puis·sance** [sing.] a competition in SHOWJUMPING to test a horse's ability to jump high fences（馬的）越障能力測試賽 **2** [U] (*literary*) great power or influence 大權；權勢；影響力

puja /ˈpuːdʒɑː/ *noun* **1** a Hindu ceremony of worship 普闍（印度教的禮拜） **2** an OFFERING (= a gift that is given to a god) at the ceremony 普闍祭品；印度教禮拜祭品

pu·jari /puːˈdʒɑːri/ *noun* a Hindu priest 印度教祭司

puke /pjuːk/ *verb* [I, T] **~ (sth) (up)** (*informal*) to VOMIT 吐；嘔吐： *The baby puked all over me this morning.* 寶寶今天早上吐了我一身。◇ *That guy makes me puke!* (= makes me angry) 那個傢伙氣死我了！◇ *I puked up my dinner.* 我把吃的飯都吐了。 ▸ **puke** *noun* [U]： *to be covered in puke* 到處是吐的東西

pukka /ˈpʌkə/ *adj.* (*BrE*) **1** (*old-fashioned*) genuine; not a copy; appropriate in a particular social situation 真品的；適用於社交場合的 **2** (*informal*) of very good quality 高質量的；上等的；一流的

pul·chri·tude /ˈpʌlkrɪtjuːd; *NAmE* also -tuːd/ *noun* [U] (*literary*) beauty 美麗；標致

Pul·it·zer Prize /ˈpʊlɪtzə(r); *NAmE* also ˈpjuːl-/ *noun* [C, usually sing.] in the US, one of 13 prizes that are given each year for excellent work in literature, music, or JOURNALISM 普利策獎（美國年度獎，頒發給文學、音樂或新聞業等 13 個領域的優秀作品）

pull 🔑 /pʊl/ *verb, noun*
■ ***verb***
▸ **MOVE/REMOVE STH** 移動／挪走某物 **1** 🔑 [I, T] to hold sth firmly and use force in order to move it or try to move it towards yourself 拉；拽；扯；拖： *You push and I'll pull.* 你推，我拉。◇ *Don't pull so hard or the handle will come off.* 別太使勁拉，不然把手會脱落。◇ **~ at/on sth** *I pulled on the rope to see if it was secure.* 我抻了抻繩子看看是否牢固。◇ **~ sth** *Stop pulling her hair!* 別揪她頭髮！◇ **~ sb/sth + adv./prep.** *She pulled him gently towards her.* 她把他輕輕地拉到身邊。◇ **~ sth + adj.** *Pull the door shut.* 把門拉上。 **2** 🔑 [T] **~ sth (+ adv./prep.)** to remove sth from a place by pulling 拔出；抽出： *Pull the plug out.* 把插頭拔掉。◇ *She pulled off her boots.* 她脱下了靴子。◇ *He pulled a gun on me* (= took out a gun and aimed it at me). 他拔出槍來指着我。 **3** 🔑 [T] **~ sb/sth + adv./prep.** to move sb/sth in a particular direction by pulling（向某方向）拖，拉動： *Pull your chair nearer the table.* 把你的椅子再往桌子拉近些。◇ *He pulled on his sweater.* 他套上了毛衣。◇ *She took his arm and pulled him along.* 她抓起他的胳膊，拉着他往前走。 **4** 🔑 [T] **~ sth** to hold or be attached to sth and move it along behind you 將…拖在身後；拉；牽引： *In this area oxen are used to pull carts.* 這個地區用牛拉車。
▸ **BODY** 身體 **5** 🔑 [I, T] to move your body or a part of your body in a particular direction, especially using force 扭轉；移開；抽回： **+ adv./prep.** *He tried to kiss her but she pulled away.* 他想吻她，但她卻扭開了身子。◇ **~ sth/yourself + adv./prep.** *The dog snapped at her and she quickly pulled back her hand.* 那狗要咬她，她馬上把手縮了回來。◇ **~ sth/yourself + adj.** *John pulled himself* ***free*** *and ran off.* 約翰脱身跑掉了。
▸ **CURTAINS** 簾；幔 **6** 🔑 [T] **~ sth** to open or close curtains, etc. 拉上；收攏 **SYN** **draw**： *Pull the curtains—it's dark outside.* 外邊天黑了，把窗簾拉上。
▸ **MUSCLE** 肌肉 **7** 🔑 [T] **~ sth** to damage a muscle, etc. by using too much force 拉傷；扭傷；抻： *to* ***pull a muscle/ligament/tendon*** 扭傷肌肉／肌腱／韌帶 ➲ **SYNONYMS** at INJURE
▸ **SWITCH** 開關 **8** 🔑 [T] **~ sth** to move a switch, etc. towards yourself or down in order to operate a machine or piece of equipment 扳動；拉；扣： *Pull the lever to start the motor.* 拉動手柄啟動馬達。◇ *Don't pull the trigger!* 別扣扳機！
▸ **VEHICLE/ENGINE** 車輛；引擎 **9** [I, T] **~ (sth) to the right/the left/one side** to move or make a vehicle move sideways（使車輛）轉向，打斜： *The wheel is pulling to the left.* 方向盤正在向左打。◇ *She pulled the car to the right to avoid the dog.* 她把汽車向右一閃，好躲開那條狗。 **10** [I] (of an engine 發動機) to work hard and use a lot of power 吃力地運轉： *The old car pulled hard as we*

P

drove slowly up the hill. 老舊的汽車吃力地向前爬，把我們緩緩地拖上了山坡。

▸ **BOAT** 小船 **11** [I, T] **~ (sth)** (+ **adv./prep.**) to use OARS to move a boat along 划；划動：*They pulled towards the shore.* 他們向岸邊划去。

▸ **CROWD/SUPPORT** 群眾；支持 **12** [T] **~ sb/sth (in)** to attract the interest or support of sb/sth 吸引；博取：*They pulled in huge crowds on their latest tour.* 最近巡迴演出時，他們吸引了大批觀眾。

▸ **ATTRACT SEXUALLY** 吸引異性 **13** [T, I] **~ (sb)** (*BrE, informal*) to attract sb sexually 吸引異性：*He can still pull the girls.* 他仍然能讓姑娘們着迷。◇ *She's hoping to pull tonight.* 她希望今晚手采迷人。

▸ **TRICK/CRIME** 計謀；罪行 **14** [T] **~ sth** (*informal*) to succeed in playing a trick on sb, committing a crime, etc.（要手腕）得逞；犯下（罪行）：*He's pulling some sort of trick on you.* 他在耍花招騙你呢。

▸ **CANCEL** 撤銷 **15** [T] **~ sth** (*informal*) to cancel an event; to stop showing an advertisement, etc. 取消，撤銷（活動、廣告等）：*The gig was pulled at the last moment.* 特約演奏臨時取消了。

IDM **pull a 'fast one (on sb)** (*slang*) to trick sb 矇騙；捉弄 **pull in different/opposite di'rections** to have different aims that cannot be achieved together without causing problems 目標迥異；各行其是 **pull sb's 'leg** (*informal*) to play a joke on sb, usually by making them believe sth that is not true 捉弄；和…開玩笑 **pull the 'other one (—it's got 'bells on)** (*BrE, informal*) used to show that you do not believe what sb has just said（表示不相信對方的話）別打哈哈了 **pull out all the 'stops** (*informal*) to make the greatest effort possible to achieve sth 竭盡全力；費九牛二虎之力 **pull the 'plug on sb/sth** (*informal*) to put an end to sb's project, a plan, etc. 阻止；制止；終止 **pull your 'punches** (*informal*) (usually used in negative sentences 通常用於否定句) to express sth less strongly than you are able to, for example to avoid upsetting or shocking sb 言辭婉轉；委婉表示：*Her articles certainly don't pull any punches.* 她的文章確實一針見血。 **pull sth/a ,rabbit out of the 'hat** (*informal*) to suddenly produce sth as a solution to a problem 突然提出解決方法；突施妙計 **pull 'rank (on sb)** to make use of your place or status in society or at work to make sb do what you want 憑藉地位指使（某人）；弄權 **pull the rug (out) from under sb's 'feet** (*informal*) to take help or support away from sb suddenly 突然停止幫助（或支援） **pull your 'socks up** (*BrE, informal*) to try to improve your performance, work, behaviour, etc. 力求做好；努力向上：*You're going to have to pull your socks up.* 你可得加把勁兒了。 **pull 'strings (for sb)** (*NAmE* also **pull 'wires**) (*informal*) to use your influence in order to get an advantage for sb 憑影響（為某人）謀利益；（為某人）活動，走後門 **pull the 'strings** to control events or the actions of other people 幕後操縱；暗中控制 **,pull up 'stakes** (*NAmE*) (*BrE* **,up 'sticks**) to suddenly move from your house and go to live somewhere else 突然遷居 **pull your 'weight** to work as hard as everyone else in a job, an activity, etc. 盡本分；盡職責 **pull the 'wool over sb's eyes** (*informal*) to try to trick sb; to hide your real actions or intentions from sb 蒙蔽某人；欺騙某人 ➲ more at BOOTSTRAP, FACE *n.*, HORN *n.*, PIECE *n.*, SHRED *n.*

PHR V **,pull a'head (of sb/sth)** to move in front of sb/sth 搶先；領先：*The cyclists were together until the bend, when Tyler pulled ahead.* 自行車選手們原本膠着在一起，直到轉彎處泰勒才超前領先。 **,pull sb/sth a'part** to separate people or animals that are fighting 分開，拉開（打鬥的人或動物） **,pull sth a'part** 🔑 to separate sth into pieces by pulling different parts of it in different directions 拆散；拆卸 **'pull at sth** = PULL ON STH **,pull a'way (from sth)** (of a vehicle 車輛) to start moving 開動：*They waved as the bus pulled away.* 公共汽車開動時他們揮手告別。 **,pull 'back 1** (of an army 軍隊) to move back from a place 撤退；撤離 **SYN** **withdraw 2** to decide not to do sth that you were intending to do, because of possible problems 退出；退卻 **SYN** **withdraw**：*Their sponsors pulled back at the last minute.* 他們的贊助人臨時打了退堂鼓。 **,pull sb↔'back** to make an army move back from a place 撤回部隊；撤兵 **,pull 'back | ,pull sth↔'back** (*sport* 體) to improve a team's position in a game（比賽中）挽回局勢，翻盤，扳回：*Rangers pulled back to 4–3.* 流浪隊以 4:3 反敗為勝。◇ *They pulled back a goal just before half-time.* 在上半場臨結束時，他們扳回一球。 **,pull sb 'down** (*especially US*) to make sb less happy, healthy or successful 使掃興；貶低某人 **,pull sth↔'down 1** 🔑 to destroy a building completely 搗毀，拆毀，摧毀（建築物）**SYN** **demolish 2** = PULL STH IN **,pull sb↔'in** (*informal*) to bring sb to a police station in order to ask them questions about a crime 拘留（問話） **,pull sth↔'in/'down** (*informal*) to earn the large amount of money mentioned 賺（大筆錢）**SYN** **make**：*I reckon she's pulling in over $100 000.* 我估計她要賺 10 多萬。 **,pull 'in (to sth)** 🔑 **1** (of a train 火車) to enter a station and stop 進站停靠 **2** (*BrE*) (of a vehicle or its driver 車輛或司機) to move to the side of the road or to the place mentioned and stop 駛向路邊（或某處）停靠：*The police car signalled to us to pull in.* 警車發出信號，要我們駛向路邊停靠。 **,pull 'off | ,pull 'off sth** 🔑 (of a vehicle or its driver 車輛或司機) to leave the road in order to stop for a short time 駛向路邊短暫停車 **,pull sth↔'off** (*informal*) to succeed in doing sth difficult 做成，完成（困難的事情）：*We pulled off the deal.* 我們做成了這筆交易。◇ *I never thought you'd pull it off.* 我真沒想到你把這事辦成了。 **'pull on/at sth** to take long deep breaths from a cigarette, etc. 猛吸，狠抽（香煙等） **,pull 'out** 🔑 (of a vehicle or its driver 車輛或司機) to move away from the side of the road, etc. 駛離路邊；駛出：*A car suddenly pulled out in front of me.* 一輛汽車突然由路邊衝到我前面。 **,pull 'out (of sth)** **1** 🔑 (of a train 火車) to leave a station 駛離車站；出站 **2** 🔑 to move away from sth or stop being involved in it 脫離；退出 **SYN** **withdraw**：*The project became so expensive that we had to pull out.* 這個項目變得耗資巨大，我們只得退出。 **,pull sb/sth 'out (of sth)** 🔑 to make sb/sth move away from sth or stop being involved in it 使脫離；使退出 **SYN** **withdraw**：*They are pulling their troops out of the war zone.* 他們正從戰區撤出軍隊。➲ related noun PULL-OUT **,pull 'over** 🔑 (of a vehicle or its driver 車輛或司機) to move to the side of the road in order to stop or let sth pass 駛向路邊；向路邊停靠（或讓車） **,pull sb/sth↔'over** 🔑 (of the police 警察) to make a driver or vehicle move to the side of the road 令（司機或車輛）停靠路邊 **,pull 'through | ,pull 'through sth 1** 🔑 to get better after a serious illness, operation, etc.（大病、手術等後）康復，痊癒：*The doctors think she will pull through.* 醫生相信她將康復。 **2** to succeed in doing sth very difficult 完成，做成（十分困難的事）：*It's going to be tough but we'll pull through it together.* 這件事會很棘手，但我們將協力把它完成。 **,pull sb 'through | ,pull sb 'through sth 1** to help sb get better after a serious illness, operation, etc. 幫…復原（或康復） **2** to help sb succeed in doing sth very difficult 協助…完成（十分困難的事）：*I relied on my instincts to pull me through.* 我全靠本能闖了過來。 **,pull to'gether** to act, work, etc. together with other people in an organized way and without fighting 齊心協力；通力合作 **,pull yourself to'gether** 🔑 to take control of your feelings and behave in a calm way 使自己鎮定自若（或冷靜）：*Stop crying and pull yourself together!* 別哭了，振作起來！ **,pull 'up** 🔑 (of a vehicle or its driver 車輛或司機) to stop 停車；停止：*He pulled up at the traffic lights.* 他在紅綠燈處停了車。 **,pull sb 'up** (*BrE, informal*) to criticize sb for sth that they have done wrong 訓斥；斥責

■ ***noun***

▸ **TRYING TO MOVE STH** 試圖移動 **1** 🔑 [C] an act of trying to make sth move by holding it firmly and bringing it towards you 拉；拽；扯：*I gave the door a sharp pull and it opened.* 我猛地一拉，門開了。

▸ **PHYSICAL FORCE** 自然力 **2** 🔑 [sing.] **the ~ (of sth)** a strong physical force that makes sth move in a particular direction 力；引力；磁力：*the earth's gravitational pull* 地球的引力

▸ **ATTRACTION** 吸引 **3** 🔑 [C, usually sing.] **the ~ (of sth)** the fact of sth attracting you or having a strong effect on you 吸引力；誘惑；影響：*The magnetic pull of the city was hard to resist.* 都市的強大魅力難以抗拒。

P

▸ **INFLUENCE** 影響 **4** [U] (*informal*) power and influence over other people（對他人的）影響，影響力：*people who have a lot of pull with the media* 能左右傳媒的人物
▸ **ON CIGARETTE/DRINK** 香煙；飲料 **5** [C] ~ (**at/on sth**) an act of taking a deep breath of smoke from a cigarette, etc. or a deep drink of sth 深吸；大口喝：*She* ***took a long pull*** *on her cigarette.* 她深深地吸了口煙。
▸ **WALK UP HILL** 登山 **6** [C, usually sing.] (*BrE*) a difficult walk up a steep hill 艱難攀登：*It's* ***a long pull*** *up to the summit.* 登上山頂要攀爬很久。
▸ **MUSCLE INJURY** 肌肉損傷 **7** [C] an injury to a muscle caused by using too much force 拉傷；扭傷
▸ **HANDLE/ROPE** 手柄；繩索 **8** [C] (especially in compounds 尤用於構成複合詞) something such as a handle or rope that you use to pull sth 拉手；拉繩；拉環：***a bell/door pull*** 鐘繩；門把手 ➲ see also RING PULL

IDM **on the 'pull** (*BrE, slang*) (of a person 人) trying to find a sexual partner 尋覓性伴侶

Synonyms 同義詞辨析

pull

drag • draw • haul • tow • tug

These words all mean to move sth in a particular direction, especially towards or behind you. 以上各詞均含拖、拉、拽之意。

pull to hold sth and move it in a particular direction; to hold or be attached to a vehicle and move it along behind you 指向某方向拖、拉、牽引：*Pull the chair nearer the table.* 把椅子再往桌子拉近些。◇ *They use oxen to pull their carts.* 他們用牛拉車。

drag to pull sb/sth in a particular direction or behind you, usually along the ground, and especially with effort 通常指使勁在地上拖、拉、拽：*The sack is too heavy to lift—you'll have to drag it.* 這麻袋太重了，提不起來。你得拖着走。

draw (*formal*) to move sb/sth by pulling them/it gently; to pull a vehicle such as a carriage 指拖動、拉動、牽引、拖車：*I drew my chair closer to the fire.* 我把椅子向火旁拉近了點。◇ ***a horse-drawn*** *carriage* 馬車

haul to pull sb/sth to a particular place with a lot of effort 指用力拖、拉、拽：*Fishermen were hauling in their nets.* 漁民在拉網。

DRAG OR HAUL? 用 drag 還是 haul？

You usually **drag** sth behind you along the ground; you usually **haul** sth towards you, often upwards towards you. **Dragging** sth often needs effort, but **hauling** sth always does. * drag 通常指在身後沿地上拖，haul 通常指由下往上地朝自己拉、拽。drag 常需要用力，而 haul 總是要用力。

tow to pull a car, boat or light plane behind another vehicle, using a rope or chain 指用繩索拖、拉、牽引（汽車、船或輕型飛機）：*Our car was towed away by the police.* 我們的汽車被警察拖走了。

tug to pull sb/sth hard in a particular direction 指朝某一方向用力拖、拉、拽：*She tried to escape but he tugged her back.* 她試圖逃跑，但他把她拽了回來。

PATTERNS

- to pull/drag/draw/haul/tow/tug sb/sth **along/down/towards** sth
- to pull/drag/draw/haul/tow sb/sth **behind you**
- to pull/drag/draw/haul a **cart/sledge**
- to pull/draw a **coach/carriage**
- to pull/haul/tow a **truck**
- **horses** pull/draw/haul sth
- **dogs** pull/drag/haul sth

pull·back /ˈpʊlbæk/ *noun* **1** an act of taking soldiers away from an area 撤兵；撤回部隊 **2** a time when prices are reduced, or when fewer people want to buy sth 價格下跌；需求減少

'pull date (*US*) (*BrE* **'sell-by date**) *noun* the date printed on food packages, etc. after which the food must not be sold（食品等的）最遲銷售日期，保質期

'pull-down *adj.* **1** designed to be used by being pulled down 下拉式的；拉下使用的：*a pull-down bed* 下拉式牀 **2** ~ **menu** (*computing* 計) a list of possible choices that appears on a computer screen below a menu title 下拉式選單；下拉選項屏；下拉選單 ➲ VISUAL VOCAB page V67

ˌpulled 'pork *noun* [U] meat from a pig that is cooked very slowly, often with smoke, until it is so soft you can pull it into small pieces with your hands 手撕豬肉（慢火烹至鬆軟，常熏製）

pul·let /ˈpʊlɪt/ *noun* a young chicken, especially one that is less than one year old（尤指未滿一年的）小母雞

pul·ley /ˈpʊli/ *noun* a wheel or set of wheels over which a rope or chain is pulled in order to lift or lower heavy objects 滑輪；滑輪組；滑車：*a system of ropes and pulleys* 繩索滑輪系統 ➲ picture at BLOCK AND TACKLE

'pulling power (*BrE*) (*NAmE* **'drawing power**) *noun* [U] the ability of sb/sth to attract people 吸引力；誘惑力

Pull·man /ˈpʊlmən/ *noun* (*pl.* **Pull·mans**) a type of very comfortable coach/car on a train 普爾曼豪華火車車廂

'pull-out *noun, adj.*

▪ ***noun*** **1** a part of a magazine, newspaper, etc. that can be taken out easily and kept separately（報刊等的）可取出插頁：*an eight-page pull-out on health* 八頁的保健插頁 ◇ *a pull-out guide* 活頁指南 **2** an act of taking an army away from a particular place; an act of taking an organization out of a system（軍隊的）轉移，撤離；（機構的）撤銷

▪ ***adj.*** [only before noun] (*especially NAmE*) a **pull-out** bed, couch, etc. can be kept hidden when not in use and pulled out when it is needed（牀、沙發等）抽拉式的，伸縮的

pull·over /ˈpʊləʊvə(r); *NAmE* -oʊ-/ *noun* (*especially BrE*) a knitted piece of clothing made of wool or cotton for the upper part of the body, with long sleeves and no buttons 套頭毛衣；套衫 **SYN** **jumper, sweater**

'pull tab (also **tab**) (both *NAmE*) (*BrE* **'ring pull**) *noun* a small piece of metal with a ring attached which is pulled to open cans of food, drink, etc.（易拉罐等的）拉環；易拉環 ➲ VISUAL VOCAB page V33

pul·lu·late /ˈpʌljuleɪt/ *verb* (*formal*) **1** [I] to breed or spread quickly 迅速繁殖；大量擴散 **2** [I] to be full of life or activity 充滿生機；生機勃勃；生機盎然 ▸ **pul·lu·lat·ing** *adj.*：*a pullulating mass of people* 活躍的人群

'pull-up (also **'chin-up** especially in *NAmE*) *noun* [usually pl.] an exercise in which you hold onto a high bar above your head and pull yourself up towards it 引體向上（單槓運動）

pul·mon·ary /ˈpʌlmənəri; *NAmE* -neri/ *adj.* [only before noun] (*medical* 醫) connected with the lungs 肺的；肺部的；與肺有關的

pulp /pʌlp/ *noun, verb, adj.*

▪ ***noun*** **1** [sing., U] a soft wet substance that is made especially by crushing sth 漿狀物：*Cook the fruit gently until it forms a pulp.* 用文火把水果煮爛。◇ *His face had been* ***beaten to a pulp*** (= very badly beaten). 他的臉被打得稀巴爛。 **2** [U] a soft substance that is made by crushing wood, cloth or other material and then used to make paper 紙漿：***paper/wood pulp*** 紙漿；木漿 **3** [U] the soft part inside some fruit and vegetables（瓜果等的）肉質部份，髓 **SYN** **flesh** ▸ **pulpy** *adj.*：*Cook the fruit slowly until soft and pulpy.* 把水果慢慢地煮成軟糊狀。

▪ ***verb*** ~ **sth** to crush or beat sth so that it becomes soft and wet 將…搗成漿：*Unsold copies of the novel had to be pulped.* 沒賣出去的小說只好化成紙漿。◇ *pulped fruit* 果泥

▪ ***adj.*** [only before noun] (of books, magazines, etc. 書刊等) badly written and often intended to shock people 粗製濫造的；庸俗刺激的：*pulp fiction* 粗製濫造的小說

P

pul·pit /ˈpʊlpɪt/ *noun* a small platform in a church that is like a box and is high above the ground, where a priest, etc. stands to speak to the people（教堂中的）小講壇

pul·sar /ˈpʌlsɑː(r)/ *noun* (*astronomy* 天) a star that cannot be seen but that sends out regular rapid radio signals 脈衝星 ➲ compare QUASAR

pul·sate /pʌlˈseɪt; *NAmE* ˈpʌlseɪt/ *verb* **1** [I] to make strong regular movements or sounds 有規律地跳動（或發聲）；均勻震動；搏動：*pulsating rhythms* 均勻的節奏 ◊ *a pulsating headache* 陣陣的頭痛 ◊ *Lights were pulsating in the sky.* 天空有閃爍的光。 **2** [I] to be full of excitement or energy 洋溢，充滿（激情或活力） **SYN** **buzz**：*a pulsating game* 令人興奮的遊戲 ◊ **~ with sth** *The streets were pulsating with life.* 街上生機勃勃。
▸ **pul·sa·tion** /pʌlˈseɪʃn/ *noun* [C, U]

pulse /pʌls/ *noun, verb*
■ *noun* **1** [usually sing.] the regular beat of blood as it is sent around the body, that can be felt in different places, especially on the inside part of the wrist; the number of times the blood beats in a minute 脈搏；脈率：*a* ***strong/weak pulse*** 強／弱脈搏 ◊ *an abnormally high pulse rate* 異常高的脈率 ◊ *The doctor* ***took/felt my pulse.*** 醫生給我量了脈搏／把了脈。◊ *Fear sent her* ***pulse racing*** (= made it beat very quickly). 她嚇得脈搏急速跳動。 **2** a strong regular beat in music 強勁的音樂節拍 **SYN** **rhythm**：*the throbbing pulse of the drums* 陣陣強勁的鼓點 **3** a single short increase in the amount of light, sound or electricity produced by a machine, etc. 脈衝：*pulse waves* 脈衝波 ◊ *sound pulses* 聲脈衝 **4 pulses** [pl.] the seeds of some plants that are eaten as food, such as PEAS and LENTILS 豆果果實；莢果；豆子 **IDM** see FINGER *n.*
■ *verb* **1** [I] to move, beat or flow with strong regular movements or sounds 搏動；跳動；震動 **SYN** **throb**：*A vein pulsed in his temple.* 他太陽穴上的靜脈在搏動。◊ *the pulsing rhythm of the music* 這樂曲的強烈節奏 **2** [I] **~ (with sth)** to be full of a feeling such as excitement or energy 洋溢着；充滿（激情等） **SYN** **buzz**：*The auditorium pulsed with excitement.* 禮堂裏洋溢着熱烈的氣氛。

pul·ver·ize (*BrE* also **-ise**) /ˈpʌlvəraɪz/ *verb* **1 ~ sth** (*formal*) to crush sth into a fine powder 粉碎；將…磨成粉 **2 ~ sb/sth** (*informal, especially BrE*) to defeat or destroy sb/sth completely 徹底擊敗（或戰勝）；摧毀 **SYN** **crush**：*We pulverized the opposition.* 我們徹底擊敗了反對派。

puma /ˈpjuːmə; *NAmE* ˈpuːmə/ (*especially BrE*) (*NAmE* usually **cou·gar**) (*NAmE* also **ˈmountain lion**, **pan·ther**) *noun* a large American wild animal of the cat family, with yellowish-brown or greyish fur 美洲獅

pum·ice /ˈpʌmɪs/ (also **ˈpumice stone**) *noun* [U] a type of grey stone that comes from VOLCANOES and is very light in weight. It is used in powder form for cleaning and polishing, and in pieces for rubbing on the skin to make it softer. 浮岩，浮石（一種火山玻璃，其粉末用於清潔拋光以及使皮膚光滑）

pum·mel /ˈpʌml/ *verb* (**-ll-**, *US* **-l-**) [T, I] to keep hitting sb/sth hard, especially with your FISTS (= tightly closed hands) 連續猛擊；反複拳打；捶打：**~ sb/sth (with sth)** *He pummelled the pillow with his fists.* 他用雙拳不停地捶打枕頭。◊ (*figurative*) *She pummelled* (= strongly criticized) *her opponents.* 她嚴厲抨擊了對手。◊ **~ (at sth)** *Her fists pummelled at his chest.* 她用拳頭連連捶打他的胸膛。

pum·melo /ˈpʌmələʊ; *NAmE* -loʊ/ *noun* = POMELO

pump /pʌmp/ *noun, verb*
■ *noun* **1** a machine that is used to force liquid, gas or air into or out of sth 抽水機；泵；打氣筒：*She washed her face at the pump in front of the inn.* 她在客棧前的水泵旁洗了洗臉。◊ (*BrE*) *a petrol pump* 汽油泵 ◊ (*NAmE*) *a gas pump* 煤氣泵 ◊ *a* ***foot/hand pump*** (= that you work by using your foot or hand) 腳踏／手搖泵 ◊ *a bicycle pump* 自行車打氣筒 ➲ **VISUAL VOCAB** pages V23, V51 ➲ see also STOMACH PUMP **2** (*BrE*) = PLIMSOLL **3** (*especially NAmE*) (*BrE* **ˈcourt shoe**) a woman's formal shoe that is plain and does not cover the top part of the foot 無帶低幫女鞋，無帶半高跟女鞋（正式場合穿的一種女鞋） ➲ **VISUAL VOCAB** page V64 **4** (*BrE*) a woman's light soft flat shoe worn for dancing or exercise; a similar style of shoe worn as a fashion item 輕軟舞鞋，休閒女鞋（女子跳舞、運動時穿或用作時裝）：*ballet pumps* 芭蕾舞鞋 ➲ **VISUAL VOCAB** page V64 **IDM** see HAND *n.*, PRIME *v.*
■ *verb* **1** [T, I] to make water, air, gas, etc. flow in a particular direction by using a pump or sth that works like a pump 用泵（或泵樣器官等）輸送：**~ (sth) (+ adv./prep.)** *The engine is used for pumping water out of the mine.* 這台發動機是用來從礦井中抽水的。◊ *The heart pumps blood around the body.* 心臟把血液輸送到全身。◊ **~ sth + adj.** *The lake had been pumped dry.* 湖水已被抽乾。 **2** [I] **+ adv./prep.** (of a liquid 液體) to flow in a particular direction as if it is being forced by a pump 湧出；湧流；奔流：*Blood was pumping out of his wound.* 血從他的傷口噴出。 **3** [T] **~ sth (+ adv./prep.)** to move sth quickly up and down or in and out 上下（或內外）快速搖動；急速搖晃：*He kept pumping my hand up and down.* 他不停地搖動着我的手。◊ *I pumped the handle like crazy.* 我拚命地來回搖動手柄。 **4** [I] to move quickly up and down or in and out 快速上下（或內外）運動：*She sprinted for the line, legs pumping.* 她雙腿緊蹬，奔向終點線。◊ *My heart was pumping with excitement.* 我激動得心裏怦怦直跳。 **5** [T] **~ sb (for sth)** (*informal*) to try to get information from sb by asking them a lot of questions 盤問；追問；一再探問：*See if you can pump him for more details.* 看你能不能向他再探問出些細節來。
IDM **pump ˈbullets, ˈshots, etc. into sb** to fire a lot of bullets into sb 向…連續發射 **pump sb full of sth** to fill sb with sth, especially drugs 給…大量（服用藥物等）：*They pumped her full of painkillers.* 他們淨讓她服止痛藥。 **pump ˈiron** (*informal*) to do exercises in which you lift heavy weights in order to make your muscles stronger 舉重（鍛煉） **pump sb's ˈstomach** to remove the contents of sb's stomach using a pump, because they have swallowed sth harmful 給…洗胃
PHR V **ˌpump sth ˈinto sth | ˌpump sth ˈin** to put a lot of money into sth 向…大量投資；注入大量資金：*He pumped all his savings into the business.* 他把全部積蓄都投入了該企業。 **ˌpump sth ˈinto sb** to force a lot of sth into sb 強行向…灌輸：*It's difficult to pump facts and figures into tired students.* 把事實和數字硬灌輸給疲憊的學生太難了。 **ˌpump sth↔ˈout** (*informal*) to produce sth in large amounts 大量生產（或製造）：*loudspeakers pumping out rock music* 大播搖滾樂的擴音器 ◊ *Our cars pump out thousands of tonnes of poisonous fumes every year.* 我們的汽車每年排放出數千噸的有毒尾氣。 **ˌpump sb↔ˈup** [usually passive] to make sb feel more excited or determined 給（某人）打氣；鼓勵 **ˌpump sth↔ˈup** **1** to fill a tyre, etc. with air using a pump 為（輪胎等）充氣；打氣 **2** (*informal*) to increase the amount, value or volume of sth 增加…的量（或價值、體積等）；提高：*Interest rates were pumped up last week.* 上週利率提高了。

ˈpump-action *adj.* [only before noun] (of a gun or other device 槍或其他設備) worked by quickly pulling or pressing part of it in and out or up and down 唧筒式的；壓動式的：*a pump-action shotgun* 唧筒式獵槍 ◊ *a pump-action spray* 手壓式噴霧器

pum·per·nickel /ˈpʌmpənɪkl; *NAmE* -pərn-/ *noun* [U] (from *German*) a type of heavy dark brown bread made from RYE, originally from Germany and often sold in slices 黑麥粗麵包（源於德國，常切片出售）

pump·kin /ˈpʌmpkɪn/ *noun* [U, C] a large round vegetable with thick orange skin. The seeds can be dried and eaten and the soft flesh can be cooked as a vegetable or in sweet PIES. 南瓜；南瓜大果：*Pumpkin pie is a traditional American dish served on Thanksgiving.* 南瓜餡餅是美國傳統的感恩節食物。 ➲ **VISUAL VOCAB** page V31

ˈpump-priming *noun* [U] the act of investing money to encourage growth in an industry or a business, especially by a government（政府）注資刺激經濟

ˈpump room *noun* (especially in the past) the room at a SPA where people go to drink the special water （尤指舊時設在礦泉地的）礦泉水供應室

pun /pʌn/ *noun, verb*

▪ ***noun*** **~ (on sth)** the clever or humorous use of a word that has more than one meaning, or of words that have different meanings but sound the same 雙關語：*We're banking on them lending us the money—no pun intended!* 我們正指望他們借給我們錢呢 —— bank 絕無雙關之意！ ➲ compare WORDPLAY

▪ ***verb*** (-nn-) [I] to make a pun 使用雙關語

Punch /pʌntʃ/ *noun* IDM see PLEASED

punch 0‑ /pʌntʃ/ *verb, noun*

▪ ***verb*** **1** 0‑ to hit sb/sth hard with your FIST (= closed hand) 拳打；以拳痛擊：**~ sb/sth** *He was kicked and punched as he lay on the ground.* 他倒在地上，被拳打腳踢。◇ *He was* ***punching the air*** *in triumph.* 他得意揚揚地揮舞着拳頭。◇ **~ sb/sth in/on sth** *She punched him on the nose.* 她一拳打中了他的鼻子。 **2** to make a hole in sth with a PUNCH *n.* (3) or some other sharp object 給…打孔；（用打孔器等）打孔：**~ sth** *to punch a time card* 在記時卡上打孔◇ **~ sth in/through sth** *The machine punches a row of holes in the metal sheet.* 機器在金屬薄板上衝出一排孔。 **3 ~ sth** to press buttons or keys on a computer, telephone, etc. in order to operate it 按（鍵）；壓（按鈕）：*I punched the button to summon the elevator.* 我按電鈕叫電梯。 ▸ **punch·er** *noun*：*He's one of boxing's strongest punchers.* 他是拳壇的鐵榔頭之一。

IDM **ˌpunch above your ˈweight** to be or try to be more successful than others in doing sth that normally requires more skill, experience, money, etc. than you have 超常發揮取勝；以小搏大：*This player seems to be able to constantly punch above his weight.* 這名選手似乎總有本事擊敗實力比他強的對手。

PHR V **ˌpunch ˈin/ˈout** (*NAmE*) to record the time you arrive at/leave work by putting a card into a special machine 用記時卡登錄（上、下班）時間；刷記時卡 ➲ see also CLOCK IN/ON at CLOCK *v.*, CLOCK OUT/OFF at CLOCK *v.* **ˌpunch sth↔ˈin | ˌpunch sth ˈinto sth** to put information into a computer by pressing the keys 將（信息）鍵入計算機：*He punched in the security code.* 他把密碼輸入電腦。 **ˌpunch sb ˈout** (*NAmE, informal*) to hit sb so hard that they fall down 將某人擊倒 **ˌpunch sth↔ˈout 1** to press a combination of buttons or keys on a computer, telephone, etc. 按鍵（輸入號碼等）：*He picked up the telephone and punched out his friend's number.* 他拿起電話，撥打朋友的電話號碼。 **2** to make a hole in sth or knock sth out by hitting it very hard 在…上打孔；打掉：*I felt as if all my teeth had been punched out.* 我覺得好像我滿口牙齒都被打掉了。 **3** to cut sth from paper, wood, metal, etc. with a special tool 衝壓

▪ ***noun*** **1** 0‑ [C] a hard hit made with the FIST (= closed hand) 重拳擊打；用力的捶打：*a punch in the face* 打在臉上的一記重拳◇ *Hill* ***threw a punch*** *at the police officer.* 希爾對警察揮了一拳。◇ *a knockout punch* 將對手擊倒的一拳◇ *He shot out his right arm and* ***landed a punch*** *on Lorrimer's nose.* 他突然掄起右臂，一拳打在洛里默的鼻子上。 **2** [U] the power to interest people 吸引力：*It's a well-constructed crime story, told with speed and punch.* 這篇描寫犯罪的故事構思精巧，情節緊湊，引人入勝。 **3** [C] a tool or machine for cutting holes in paper, leather or metal 打孔機；穿孔器；衝牀：*a hole punch* 打孔器 ➲ VISUAL VOCAB page V69 **4** [U] a hot or cold drink made by mixing water, fruit juice, spices, and usually wine or another alcoholic drink 潘趣酒，賓治酒（用水、果汁、香料及葡萄酒或其他酒類勾兑成的冷或熱的飲料） IDM see BEAT *v.*, PACK *v.*, PULL *v.*, ROLL *v.*

Punch and Judy show /ˌpʌntʃ ən ˈdʒuːdi ʃəʊ; *NAmE* ʃoʊ/ *noun* (in Britain) a traditional type of entertainment for children in which PUPPETS are used to tell stories about Punch, who is always fighting with his wife Judy 《龐奇和朱迪》傀儡戲（英國傳統木偶劇，講述總和妻子朱迪打鬧的龐奇的故事）

punch·bag /ˈpʌntʃbæɡ/ (*BrE*) (*NAmE* **ˈpunching bag**) *noun* a heavy leather bag, hung on a rope, which is punched, especially by BOXERS as part of training, or as a form of exercise 沙袋（懸吊式，用於拳擊訓練）

punch·ball /ˈpʌntʃbɔːl/ *noun* a heavy leather ball, fixed on a spring, which is punched, especially by BOXERS as a part of training, or as a form of exercise 梨球（用彈簧等固定，用於拳擊訓練）

punch·bowl /ˈpʌntʃbəʊl; *NAmE* -boʊl/ *noun* a bowl used for serving PUNCH *n.* (4) 潘趣酒碗

punch·card /ˈpʌntʃkɑːd; *NAmE* -kɑːrd/ (also **ˌpunched ˈcard**) *noun* a card on which, in the past, information was recorded as lines of holes and used for giving instructions, etc. to computers and other machines 穿孔卡（舊時把信息打成一排排的小孔，用以將指令輸入計算機等）

ˈpunch-drunk (also **ˌslap-ˈhappy** especially in *NAmE*) *adj.* **1** (of a BOXER 拳擊手) confused as a result of being punched on the head many times 被擊暈的；暈頭轉向的 **2** unable to think clearly; in a confused state 思維混亂的；糊塗的

ˈpunching bag (*NAmE*) (*BrE* **punch·bag**) *noun* a heavy leather bag, hung on a rope, which is punched, especially by BOXERS as part of training, or as a form of exercise （用於拳擊訓練的懸吊式）沙袋

punch·line /ˈpʌntʃlaɪn/ (also *NAmE informal* **ˈtag line**) *noun* the last few words of a joke that make it funny （笑話最後的）妙趣橫生的語句，妙語；畫龍點睛之語

ˈpunch-up *noun* (*BrE, informal*) a physical fight 打架；鬥毆；動拳腳 SYN **brawl**

punchy /ˈpʌntʃi/ *adj.* (**punch·ier**, **punchi·est**) (of a speech, song, etc. 演説、歌曲等) having a strong effect because it expresses sth clearly in only a few words 簡潔有力的；言簡意賅的；簡煉的

punc·tili·ous /pʌŋkˈtɪliəs/ *adj.* (*formal*) very careful to behave correctly or to perform your duties exactly as you should 一絲不苟的；循規蹈矩的：*a punctilious host* 一絲不苟的主人 ▸ **punc·tili·ous·ly** *adv.* **punc·tili·ous·ness** *noun* [U]

punc·tual /ˈpʌŋktʃuəl/ *adj.* happening or doing sth at the arranged or correct time; not late 按時的；準時的；守時的：*She has been reliable and punctual.* 她一直可靠守時。◇ *a punctual start at 9 o'clock* * 9 點鐘準時開始 ▸ **punc·tu·al·ity** /ˌpʌŋktʃuˈæləti/ *noun* [U] **punc·tu·al·ly** /ˈpʌŋktʃuəli/ *adv.*：*They always pay punctually.* 他們一向按時付款。

punc·tu·ate /ˈpʌŋktʃueɪt/ *verb* **1** [T, often passive] **~ sth (with sth)** to interrupt sth at intervals 不時打斷：*Her speech was punctuated by bursts of applause.* 她的講演不時被陣陣掌聲打斷。 **2** [I, T] **~ (sth)** to divide writing into sentences and phrases by using special marks, for example commas, question marks, etc. 給…加標點符號

punc·tu·ation /ˌpʌŋktʃuˈeɪʃn/ *noun* [U] the marks used in writing that divide sentences and phrases; the system of using these marks 標點符號；標點符號用法

ˌpunctuˈation mark *noun* a sign or mark used in writing to divide sentences and phrases 標點符號

punc·ture /ˈpʌŋktʃə(r)/ *noun, verb*

▪ ***noun*** **1** (*BrE*) a small hole in a tyre made by a sharp point （輪胎上刺破的）小孔，小洞：*I had a puncture on the way and arrived late.* 我在路上扎破了輪胎，所以遲到了。 ➲ see also FLAT *n.* (6) **2** a small hole, especially in the skin, made by a sharp point （尤指皮膚上被刺破的）扎孔；刺傷

▪ ***verb*** **1** [T, I] **~ (sth)** to make a small hole in sth; to get a small hole 在…上扎孔（或穿孔）；（被）刺破：*to puncture a tyre* 扎破輪胎◇ *She was taken to the hospital with broken ribs and a punctured lung.* 她肋骨骨折、肺部穿孔，被送往醫院。◇ *One of the front tyres had punctured.* 一個前輪被扎破了。 **2** [T] **~ sth** to suddenly make sb feel less confident, proud, etc. 使突然泄氣；挫傷（鋭氣等）：*to puncture sb's confidence* 打擊某人的信心

pun·dit /ˈpʌndɪt/ *noun* **1** a person who knows a lot about a particular subject and who often talks about it in public 行家；權威；專家 SYN **expert** **2** = PANDIT

P

pun·gent /ˈpʌndʒənt/ *adj.* **1** having a strong taste or smell 味道（或氣味）強烈的；刺激性的：*the pungent smell of burning rubber* 燒橡膠的刺鼻氣味 ➲ **SYNONYMS** at BITTER **2** direct and having a strong effect 說穿的；一語道破的；一針見血的：*pungent criticism* 一針見血的批評 ▸ **pun·gency** /-nsi/ *noun* [U] **pun·gent·ly** *adv.*

pun·ish 🗝 /ˈpʌnɪʃ/ *verb*
1 🗝 to make sb suffer because they have broken the law or done sth wrong 處罰；懲罰：**~ sb** *Those responsible for this crime will be severely punished.* 犯下這宗罪行的人將受到嚴厲懲罰。◇ *My parents used to punish me by not letting me watch TV.* 過去我父母常以不讓我看電視來懲罰我。◇ **~ sb for sth/for doing sth** *He was punished for refusing to answer their questions.* 他拒不回答他們的問題，受到了懲罰。**2 ~ sth (by/with sth)** to set the punishment for a particular crime 對…判罪；判定…的處罰方式：*In those days murder was always punished with the death penalty.* 那個時候，謀殺總是判死罪。**3 ~ yourself (for sth)** to blame yourself for sth that has happened 責怪（自己）；自責

pun·ish·able /ˈpʌnɪʃəbl/ *adj.* **~ (by/with sth)** (of a crime 罪行) that can be punished, especially by law 可以懲罰的；可以處罰的；（尤指）應法辦的：*a crime punishable by/with imprisonment* 可判監禁的罪行 ◇ *Giving false information to the police is a punishable offence.* 向警方謊報情況是應受懲處的罪行。

pun·ish·ing /ˈpʌnɪʃɪŋ/ *adj.* [usually before noun] long and difficult and making you work hard so you become very tired 艱難持久的；令人筋疲力盡的：*The President has a punishing schedule for the next six months.* 總統今後六個月的工作日程十分繁忙。

pun·ish·ment 🗝 /ˈpʌnɪʃmənt/ *noun*
1 🗝 [U, C] an act or a way of punishing sb 懲罰；處罰；刑罰：*to* ***inflict/impose/mete out punishment*** 予以懲罰 ◇ **~ (for sth)** *What is the punishment for murder?* 謀殺應處以什麼刑罰？◇ *There is little evidence that harsher punishments deter any better than more lenient ones.* 甚少證據顯示嚴懲比寬待更能遏止犯罪。◇ *The punishment should fit the crime.* 罰宜當罪。◇ *He was sent to his room* ***as a punishment***. 他被罰回到他的房間。➲ see also CAPITAL PUNISHMENT, CORPORAL PUNISHMENT **2** [U] rough treatment 粗暴對待；虐待：*The carpet by the door takes the most punishment.* 門邊的地毯磨損得最厲害。

pu·ni·tive /ˈpjuːnətɪv/ *adj.* [usually before noun] (*formal*) **1** intended as punishment 懲罰性的；刑罰的；處罰的：*There are calls for more* ***punitive measures*** *against people who drink and drive.* 有人呼籲對酒後駕車的人要有更具處罰性的措施。◇ (*NAmE*) *He was awarded* ***punitive damages*** (= in a court of law). 法庭判給他處罰性的損害賠償。**2** very severe and that people find very difficult to pay（租稅等）苛刻的：*punitive taxes* 懲罰性徵稅 ▸ **pu·ni·tive·ly** *adv.*

Pun·jabi /pʊnˈdʒɑːbi/ *noun* **1** [C] a person from the Punjab area in NW India and Pakistan 旁遮普人（印度西北部和巴基斯坦的旁遮普地區的人）**2** [U] the language of people from the Punjab 旁遮普語 ▸ **Pun·jabi** *adj.*

punk /pʌŋk/ *noun* **1** (also **ˌpunk ˈrock**) [U] a type of loud and aggressive rock music popular in the late 1970s and early 1980s 鬅客搖滾樂，龐克搖滾樂（流行於 20 世紀 70 年代後期和 80 年代初期）：*a punk band* 鬅客搖滾樂隊 **2** (also **ˌpunk ˈrocker**) [C] a person who likes punk music and dresses like a punk musician, for example by wearing metal chains, leather clothes and having brightly coloured hair 鬅客搖滾樂迷：*a punk haircut* 鬅客髮式 **3** [C] (*informal, especially NAmE*) a young man or boy who behaves in a rude or violent way 小流氓；小混混；小阿飛 **SYN** **lout**

pun·kah /ˈpʌŋkə; -kɑː/ *noun* **1** (*IndE*) an electric fan 電風扇 **2** (in India in the past) a large cloth fan that hung from the ceiling and that was moved by pulling a string 拉風（印度舊時懸掛於天花板用繩子拉動的布屏風扇）

pun·net /ˈpʌnɪt/ *noun* (*BrE*) a small box or BASKET that soft fruit is often sold in（盛軟質水果的）小果盒，小果籃 ➲ **VISUAL VOCAB** page V33

pun·ster /ˈpʌnstə(r)/ *noun* a person who often makes PUNS 愛說雙關語的人

punt¹ /pʌnt/ *noun, verb* ➲ see also PUNT²
■ ***noun*** **1** a long shallow boat with a flat bottom and square ends which is moved by pushing the end of a long pole against the bottom of a river 方頭平底船（用篙撐）➲ **VISUAL VOCAB** page V55 **2** (*BrE, informal*) a bet 賭博；打賭：*The investment is little more than a punt.* 這項投資無異於一場賭博。**3** (in RUGBY or AMERICAN FOOTBALL 橄欖球或美式足球) a long kick made after dropping the ball from your hands（踢）淩空長球，脫手球
■ ***verb*** **1** [I, T] **~ (sth) (+ adv./prep.)** to travel in a punt, especially for pleasure 乘方頭平底船航行（尤指遊覽）：*We spent the day punting on the river.* 我們乘方頭平底小船在河上遊覽了一天。◇ *to go punting* 坐方頭平底船遊玩 **2** [T] **~ sth (+ adv./prep.)** to kick a ball hard so that it goes a long way, sometimes after it has dropped from your hands and before it reaches the ground 踢淩空長球；踢脫手球

punt² /pʊnt/ *noun* the former unit of money in the Republic of Ireland (replaced in 2002 by the euro) 愛爾蘭鎊（愛爾蘭共和國以前的貨幣單位，於 2002 年為歐元所取代）➲ see also PUNT¹

punt·er /ˈpʌntə(r)/ *noun* (*BrE, informal*) **1** a person who buys or uses a particular product or service 顧客；主顧；客戶 **SYN** **customer**：*It's important to keep the punters happy.* 重要的是讓顧客滿意。**2** a person who gambles on the result of a horse race 賭馬的人

puny /ˈpjuːni/ *adj.* (**puni·er**, **puni·est**) (*disapproving*) **1** small and weak 弱小的；孱弱的 **SYN** **feeble**：*The lamb was a puny little thing.* 羊羔瘦小孱弱。**2** not very impressive 不起眼的；可憐的；微不足道的：*They laughed at my puny efforts.* 他們嘲笑我微不足道的努力。

pup /pʌp/ *noun* **1** = PUPPY **2** a young animal of various SPECIES (= types) 幼小動物：*a seal pup* 一隻小海豹
IDM **sell sb/buy a pup** (*old-fashioned, BrE, informal*) to sell sb or be sold sth that has no value or is worth much less than the price paid 賣給…（或買到）偽劣貨

pupa /ˈpjuːpə/ *noun* (*pl.* **pupae** /ˈpjuːpiː/) an insect in the stage of development between a LARVA and an adult insect 蛹 ➲ compare CHRYSALIS ▸ **pupal** /ˈpjuːpəl/ *adj.* [usually before noun]

pu·pate /pjuːˈpeɪt; *NAmE* ˈpjuːpeɪt/ *verb* [I] (*biology* 生) to develop into a pupa 化蛹；變成蛹

pupil 🗝 /ˈpjuːpl/ *noun*
1 🗝 (*especially BrE*, becoming *old-fashioned*) a person who is being taught, especially a child in a school 學生；（尤指）小學生：*How many pupils does the school have?* 這所小學有多少學生？◇ *She now teaches only private pupils.* 她現在只當私人教師。➲ **SYNONYMS** at STUDENT **2** 🗝 a person who is taught artistic, musical, etc. skills by an expert 弟子；門生；門徒：*The painting is by a pupil of Rembrandt.* 這幅畫為倫勃朗的一位弟子所作。**3** the small round black area at the centre of the eye 瞳孔；眸子；瞳人：*Her pupils were dilated.* 她的瞳孔擴大了。➲ **VISUAL VOCAB** page V59 ➲ compare IRIS (1)

pu·pil·lage (*especially US* **pu·pil·age**) /ˈpjuːpɪlɪdʒ/ *noun* [U, C, sing.] **1** (*formal*) a period during which you are a student, especially when you are being taught by a particular person 學生時期（尤指接受某人教育）**2** (*BrE*) a period during which a lawyer trains to become a BARRISTER by studying with a qualified barrister; the system which allows this training 大律師見習期（或制度）；大律師實習期（或制度）

pup·pet /ˈpʌpɪt/ *noun* **1** a model of a person or an animal that can be made to move, for example by pulling strings attached to parts of its body or by putting your hand inside it. A puppet with strings is also called a MARIONETTE. 木偶：*a hand puppet* 手套式木偶 ◇ *a puppet show* 木偶表演 ➲ see also GLOVE PUPPET **2** (usually *disapproving*) a person or group whose actions are controlled by another 傀儡：*The occupying forces set up a* ***puppet government***. 佔領軍建立了一個傀儡政府。

pup·pet·eer /ˌpʌpɪˈtɪə(r); *NAmE* -ˈtɪr/ *noun* a person who performs with puppets 演木偶戲的人；操縱木偶的人

pup·pet·ry /ˈpʌpɪtri/ *noun* [U] the art and skill of making and using puppets 木偶製作（或表演）藝術

puppy /ˈpʌpi/ *noun* (*pl.* **-ies**) (also **pup**) **1** a young dog 小狗；幼犬：*a litter of puppies* 一窩小狗 ◇ *a Labrador puppy* 拉布拉多小狗 **2** (*old-fashioned, informal*) a proud or rude young man 傲慢小子；自負無禮的青年

ˈ**puppy fat** (*BrE*) (*NAmE* ˈ**baby fat**) *noun* [U] fat on a child's body that disappears as the child grows older 小兒虛胖（長大後消失）

ˈ**puppy love** *noun* [U] feelings of love that a young person has for sb else and that adults do not think is very serious 青少年的初戀；少年不成熟的戀愛

ˈ**pup tent** *noun* (*NAmE*) a small tent for two people 三角形小帳篷

pur·chase 0→ AW /ˈpɜːtʃəs; *NAmE* ˈpɜːrtʃəs/ *noun, verb*

■ *noun* (*formal*) **1** 0→ [U, C] the act or process of buying sth 購買；採購：*to* ***make a purchase*** (= buy sth) 採購 ◇ *Keep your receipt as* ***proof of purchase***. 保存好收據作為購貨憑證。◇ *The company has just announced its £27 million purchase of Park Hotel.* 這家公司剛剛宣佈以 2 700 萬英鎊買下了帕克酒店。➲ COLLOCATIONS at SHOPPING ➲ see also HIRE PURCHASE **2** 0→ [C] something that you have bought 購買的東西；購買項目：*major purchases, such as a new car* 新汽車之類的巨額購買項目 ◇ *If you are not satisfied with your purchase we will give you a full refund.* 所購之物若不合意，我們將全額退款。**3** [U, sing.] (*technical* 術語) a firm hold on sth with the hands or feet, for example when you are climbing 握緊；抓牢；蹬穩 SYN **grip**：*She tried to get a purchase on the slippery rock.* 她設法抓牢光滑的岩石。

■ *verb* 0→ **~ sth** (**from sb**) (*formal*) to buy sth 買；購買；採購：*The equipment can be purchased from your local supplier.* 這種設備可從您當地的供應商購買。◇ *They purchased the land for $1 million.* 他們以 100 萬元買下了這塊土地。◇ (*figurative*) *Victory was purchased* (= achieved) *at too great a price.* 這次勝利的代價太大了。

ˈ**purchase price** *noun* [usually sing.] (*formal*) the price that is paid for sth you buy 買價

pur·chaser AW /ˈpɜːtʃəsə(r); *NAmE* ˈpɜːrtʃ-/ *noun* (*formal*) a person who buys sth 購買人；採購人員；買主 ➲ compare BUYER (1)

pur·chas·ing AW /ˈpɜːtʃəsɪŋ; *NAmE* ˈpɜːrtʃ-/ *noun* [U] (*business* 商) the activity of buying things, especially for a company 購買；採購

ˈ**purchasing power** *noun* [U] **1** money that people have available to buy goods with （人民的）購買力 **2** the amount that a unit of money can buy （貨幣的）購買力：*the peso's purchasing power* 比索的購買力

pur·dah /ˈpɜːdə; *NAmE* ˈpɜːrdə/ *noun* [U] the system in some Muslim societies by which women live in a separate part of a house or cover their faces so that men do not see them （某些穆斯林社會的）深閨制度：*to be* ***in purdah*** 不公開露面 ◇ *He kept his daughters in virtual purdah.* 他讓女兒們恪守深閨的習俗。

pure 0→ /pjʊə(r); *NAmE* pjʊr/ *adj.* (**purer** /ˈpjʊərə(r); *NAmE* ˈpjʊr-/, **purest** /ˈpjʊərɪst; *NAmE* ˈpjʊr-/)

▸ NOT MIXED 純的 **1** 0→ [usually before noun] not mixed with anything else; with nothing added 純的；純淨的；純粹的：***pure gold/silk, etc.*** 純金、真絲等 ◇ *These shirts are* ***100% pure*** *cotton.* 這些襯衫是 100% 的純棉。◇ *Classical dance* ***in its purest form*** *requires symmetry and balance.* 純正的古典舞蹈要求對稱與平衡。◇ *One movie is classified as pure art, the other as entertainment.* 一部電影被列為純藝術片，另一部被列為娛樂片。

▸ CLEAN 潔淨 **2** 0→ clean and not containing any harmful substances 乾淨的；不含有害物質的：*a bottle of pure water* 一瓶純淨水 ◇ *The air was sweet and pure.* 空氣清新而純淨。OPP **impure**

▸ COMPLETE 完全 **3** 0→ [only before noun] complete and total 完全的；純粹的：*They met by pure chance.* 他們相遇純屬偶然。◇ *She laughed with pure joy.* 她由衷地笑起來。

▸ COLOUR/SOUND/LIGHT 色；聲；光 **4** 0→ very clear; perfect 清晰的；純正的：*beaches of pure white sand* 潔白的沙灘 ◇ *a pure voice* 純淨的嗓音

▸ MORALLY GOOD 純良 **5** without evil thoughts or actions, especially sexual ones; morally good 純真的；無邪的；貞潔的；正派的：*to lead a pure life* 過純潔的生活 ◇ *His motives were pure.* 他動機純正。◇ (*literary*) *to be pure in body and mind* 身心純潔 OPP **impure**

▸ SUBJECT YOU STUDY 學科 **6** [only before noun] concerned with increasing knowledge of the subject rather than with using knowledge in practical ways 純理論的；非應用的：*pure mathematics* 純粹數學 ◇ *technology as opposed to pure science subjects* 相對於純理論學科的技術 ➲ compare APPLIED

▸ BREED/RACE 品種；種族 **7** not mixed with any other breed or race, etc. 血統純的；純種的：*These cattle are one of the purest breeds in Britain.* 這些牛是英國最純的品種之一。➲ see also PURE-BRED ➲ see also PURIFY, PURITY

IDM ˌ**pure and** ˈ**simple** used after the noun that it refers to in order to emphasize that there is nothing but the thing you have just mentioned involved in sth （用於名詞後表示強調）純粹，全然：*It's laziness, pure and simple.* 這全然是懶惰。

ˈ**pure-bred** *adj.* (of an animal 動物) born from parents of the same breed, not from a mix of two or more breeds 純種的

purée /ˈpjʊəreɪ; *NAmE* pjʊˈreɪ/ *noun, verb*

■ *noun* [U, C] food in the form of a thick liquid made by crushing fruit or cooked vegetables in a small amount of water （用水果、熟的蔬菜壓成的）醬，糊，泥：*apple purée* 蘋果泥

■ *verb* (**pur·éed**, **pur·éed**) **~ sth** to make food into a purée 把（食物）研成糊狀

pure·ly 0→ /ˈpjʊəli; *NAmE* ˈpjʊrli/ *adv.* only; completely 僅僅；完全：*I saw the letter purely by chance.* 我看見這封信純屬偶然。◇ *The charity is run on a purely voluntary basis.* 這個慈善團體完全是義務性質的。◇ *She took the job* ***purely and simply*** *for the money.* 她做這份工作圖的就是錢。

pur·ga·tive /ˈpɜːɡətɪv; *NAmE* ˈpɜːrɡ-/ *noun* a substance, especially a medicine, that causes your BOWELS to empty 瀉藥；通便藥物 ▸ **pur·ga·tive** *adj.*

pur·ga·tory /ˈpɜːɡətri; *NAmE* ˈpɜːrɡətɔːri/ *noun* [U] **1** (usually **Purgatory**) (in Roman Catholic teaching 羅馬天主教教義) a place or state in which the souls of dead people suffer for the bad things they did when they were living, so that they can become pure enough to go to heaven 煉獄 **2** (*informal, humorous*) any place or state of suffering 受難的處所（或狀態）；懲戒所；折磨；磨難 SYN **hell**：*Getting up at four o'clock every morning is sheer purgatory.* 每天早上四點起牀簡直是活受罪。

purge /pɜːdʒ; *NAmE* pɜːrdʒ/ *verb, noun*

■ *verb* **1** to remove people from an organization, often violently, because their opinions or activities are unacceptable to the people in power 清除，清洗（組織中的異己分子）：**~ sth** (**of sb**) *His first act as leader was to purge the party of extremists.* 他當上領導的第一件事就是清除黨內的極端分子。◇ **~ sb** (**from sth**) *He purged extremists from the party.* 他把極端分子清除出黨。**2** (*formal*) to make yourself/sb/sth pure, healthy or clean by getting rid of bad thoughts or feelings 淨化（心靈、風氣等）；滌蕩（污穢）：**~ yourself/sb/sth** (**of sth**) *We need to purge our sport of racism.* 我們必須消除體育界的種族主義。◇ **~ sth** (**from sth**) *Nothing could purge the guilt from her mind.* 她內心的愧疚是無法消除的。

■ *noun* the act of removing people, often violently, from an organization because their views are unacceptable to the people who have power （對異己的）清洗，清除，暴力剷除

puri·fier /ˈpjʊərɪfaɪə(r); *NAmE* ˈpjʊr-/ *noun* a device that removes substances that are dirty, harmful or not wanted 清潔器；淨化器： *an air/water purifier* 空氣/水淨化器

pur·ify /ˈpjʊərɪfaɪ; *NAmE* ˈpjʊr-/ *verb* (**puri·fies**, **puri·fy·ing**, **puri·fied**, **puri·fied**) **1 ~ sth** to make sth pure by removing substances that are dirty, harmful or not wanted 使（某物）潔淨；淨化： *One tablet will purify a litre of water.* 一顆丸即可淨化一升水。 **2 ~ sb/sth/yourself** to make sb pure by removing evil from their souls 洗滌（思想）；淨化（心靈）： *Hindus purify themselves by bathing in the river Ganges.* 印度教徒在恒河中浸泡藉以滌罪。 **3 ~ sth (from sth)** (*technical* 術語) to take a pure form of a substance out of another substance that contains it 提純；精煉 ▸ **puri·fi·ca·tion** /ˌpjʊərɪfɪˈkeɪʃn; *NAmE* ˌpjʊr-/ *noun* [U]： *a water purification plant* 濾水廠

Pu·rim /ˈpʊərɪm; pʊˈriːm; *NAmE* ˈpʊr-/ *noun* [U] a Jewish festival that is celebrated in the spring 普林節，普珥節（猶太教春季的節日）

pur·ist /ˈpjʊərɪst; *NAmE* ˈpjʊr-/ *noun* a person who thinks things should be done in the traditional way and who has strong opinions on what is correct in language, art, etc.（語言、藝術等方面的）純粹主義者，正統主義者 ▸ **pur·ism** /ˈpjʊərɪzəm; *NAmE* ˈpjʊr-/ *noun* [U]

pur·itan /ˈpjʊərɪtən; *NAmE* ˈpjʊr-/ *noun, adj.*

■ ***noun*** **1** (usually *disapproving*) a person who has very strict moral attitudes and who thinks that pleasure is bad 禁慾者；苦行者 **2 Puritan** a member of a Protestant group of Christians in England in the 16th and 17th centuries who wanted to worship God in a simple way 清教徒（屬於 16 和 17 世紀的英國教會）

■ ***adj.*** **1 Puritan** connected with the Puritans and their beliefs 清教徒的；清教主義的；禁慾的；苦行的 **2** = PURITANICAL

pur·it·an·ical /ˌpjʊərɪˈtænɪkl; *NAmE* ˌpjʊr-/ (also **pur·itan**) *adj.* (usually *disapproving*) having very strict moral attitudes 清教徒式的；道德極嚴格的： *Their parents had a puritanical streak and didn't approve of dancing.* 他們的父母管教頗嚴格，不贊成跳舞。

P

pur·itan·ism /ˈpjʊərɪtənɪzəm; *NAmE* ˈpjʊr-/ *noun* [U] **1 Puritanism** the beliefs and practices of the Puritans 清教主義；清教徒的教義和行為 **2** very strict moral attitudes 十分嚴格的道德觀

pur·ity /ˈpjʊərəti; *NAmE* ˈpjʊr-/ *noun* [U] the state or quality of being pure 純潔；純淨；純粹： *The purity of the water is tested regularly.* 水的純度定期檢測。◇ *spiritual purity* 心靈純潔 **OPP** **impurity**

purl /pɜːl; *NAmE* pɜːrl/ *noun* [U] a STITCH used in knitting（編織的）反針，倒針 ▸ **purl** *verb* [I]

pur·lieus /ˈpɜːljuːz; *NAmE* ˈpɜːrluːz/ *noun* [pl.] (*literary*) the area near or surrounding a place 臨近地區；周圍地區

pur·loin /pɜːˈlɔɪn; ˈpɜːlɔɪn; *NAmE* pɜːrˈl-; ˈpɜːrl-/ *verb* **~ sth (from sb/sth)** (*formal* or *humorous*) to steal sth or use it without permission 偷竊；擅自使用

pur·ple 🗝 /ˈpɜːpl; *NAmE* ˈpɜːrpl/ *adj.*

1 🗝 having the colour of blue and red mixed together 紫色的： *a purple flower* 紫色的花 ◇ *His face was purple with rage.* 他氣得臉色發紫。 **2 ~ prose/passage** writing or a piece of writing that is too grand in style 華麗的文辭；雕琢的章句 ▸ **pur·ple** 🗝 *noun* [U, C]： *She was dressed in purple.* 她穿一身紫色衣裳。

ˌPurple ˈHeart *noun* a MEDAL given to a member of the armed forces of the US who has been wounded in battle（美國授予作戰負傷軍人的）紫心勳章

ˈpurple patch *noun* (*BrE*) a period of success or good luck 成功的時期；鴻運

pur·plish /ˈpɜːpəlɪʃ; *NAmE* ˈpɜːrp-/ *adj.* similar to purple in colour 帶紫色的；發紫的： *purplish lips* 發紫的嘴唇

pur·port *verb, noun*

■ ***verb*** /pəˈpɔːt; *NAmE* pərˈpɔːrt/ **~ to be/have sth** (*formal*) to claim to be sth or to have done sth, when this may not be true 自稱；標榜 **SYN** **profess**： *The book does not purport to be a complete history of the period.* 本書無意標榜為那個時期的全史。

■ ***noun*** /ˈpɜːpɔːt; *NAmE* ˈpɜːrpɔːrt/ [sing.] **the ~ of sth** (*formal*) the general meaning of sth 主要意思；大意；主旨

Synonyms 同義詞辨析

purpose

aim • intention • plan • point • idea

These are all words for talking about what sb/sth intends to do or achieve. 以上各詞均指意圖、目的、目標。

purpose what sth is supposed to achieve; what sb is trying to achieve 指目的、目標： *Our campaign's main purpose is to raise money.* 我們這次活動的主要目的是募款。

aim what sb is trying to achieve; what sth is supposed to achieve 指目標、目的： *She went to London with the aim of finding a job.* 她去倫敦是為了找工作。◇ *Our main aim is to increase sales in Europe.* 我們的主要目標是增加在歐洲的銷售量。

PURPOSE OR AIM? 用 purpose 還是 aim？

Your **purpose** for doing something is your reason for doing it; your **aim** is what you want to achieve. **Aim** can suggest that you are only trying to achieve sth; **purpose** gives a stronger sense of achievement being certain. **Aim** can be *sb's aim* or *the aim of sth*. **Purpose** is more usually *the purpose of sth*: you can talk about *sb's purpose* but that is more formal. * purpose 指做某事的原因，aim 指要達到的目的。aim 可以指嘗試達到目的，purpose 含有要成就某事的強烈感覺。aim 可指某人的目的（sb's aim），也可指某事的目的（the aim of sth），purpose 更常指做某事的原因（the purpose of sth），也可指某人的目的（sb's purpose），但這樣用較正式。

intention what you intend to do 指打算、計劃、意圖： *I have no intention of going to the wedding.* 我無意去參加婚禮。◇ *She's full of **good intentions** but they rarely work out.* 她雖然處處出於善意，卻很少產生效果。

plan what you intend to do or achieve 指計劃、打算： *There are no plans to build new offices.* 現在沒有建新辦公樓的計劃。

INTENTION OR PLAN? 用 intention 還是 plan？

Your **intentions** are what you want to do, especially in the near future; your **plans** are what you have decided or arranged to do, often, but not always, in the longer term. * intention 尤指近期的打算、意圖；plan 通常但不總是指較長遠的計劃、安排。

point (*rather informal*) the purpose or aim of sth 指意圖、目的、理由： ***What's the point** of all this violence?* 這些暴行的意圖何在？◇ *The point of the lesson is to compare the two countries.* 本課的目的是比較這兩個國家。

idea (*rather informal*) the purpose of sth; sb's aim 指目的、意圖： *The whole idea of going was so that we could meet her new boyfriend.* 我們去的唯一目的就是要見她的新男朋友。◇ ***What's the idea** behind this?* 這背後的目的是什麼？

POINT OR IDEA? 用 point 還是 idea？

Point is a more negative word than **idea.** If you say *What's the point ...?* you are suggesting that there is no point; if you say *What's the idea ... ?* you are genuinely asking a question. **Point**, but not **idea**, is used to talk about things you feel annoyed or unhappy about. * point 比 idea 有更多的否定含義：what's the point ...? 暗指毫無意義；what's the idea ...? 用於真正詢問目的。用 point 而非 idea 表示對所談論的事情感到不快： ~~*There's no idea in ...*~~ ◇ ~~*I don't see the idea of ...*~~

PATTERNS

- **with** the purpose/aim/intention/idea **of** doing sth
- sb's intention/plan **to do sth**
- to **have** a(n) purpose/aim/intention/plan/point
- to **achieve/fulfil** a(n) purpose/aim

pur·port·ed /pə'pɔ:tɪd; *NAmE* pər'pɔ:rt-/ *adj.* [only before noun] (*formal*) that has been stated to have happened or to be true, when this might not be the case 據稱的；傳言的： *the scene of the purported crime* 傳聞中的罪案發生地點 ▶ **pur·port·ed·ly** *adv.* : *a letter purportedly written by Mozart* 一封據傳是莫扎特的親筆信

pur·pose /'pɜ:pəs; *NAmE* 'pɜ:rpəs/ *noun*
1 [C] the intention, aim or function of sth; the thing that sth is supposed to achieve 意圖；目的；用途；目標： *Our campaign's main purpose is to raise money.* 我們這次活動的主要目的就是募款。◇ *The purpose of the book is to provide a complete guide to the university.* 本書旨在全面介紹這所大學。◇ *A meeting was called* ***for the purpose of*** *appointing a new treasurer.* 為任命新司庫而召開了一次會議。◇ *The experiments* ***serve no useful purpose*** (= are not useful). 這些實驗毫無用處。◇ *The building is used for religious purposes.* 這座建築是用於宗教活動的。 **2** **purposes** [pl.] what is needed in a particular situation 情勢的需要： *These gifts count as income for tax purposes.* 這些贈與物品視為應課稅收入。◇ ***For the purposes of*** *this study, the three groups have been combined.* 為了這項研究工作，三個小組業已合併。 **3** [C, U] meaning that is important and valuable to you 重要意義；有價值的意義： *Volunteer work gives her life (****a sense of****)* ***purpose****.* 做志願工作使她的生活有了意義。 **4** [U] the ability to plan sth and work successfully to achieve it 意志；毅力；決心 SYN **determination** : *He has enormous confidence and* ***strength of purpose****.* 他信心十足，意志堅強。 ➲ see also CROSS PURPOSES
IDM **on 'purpose** not by accident; deliberately 故意；有意地： *He did it on purpose, knowing it would annoy her.* 他明知會激怒她，卻故意那麼做。 **to little/no 'purpose** (*formal*) with little/no useful effect or result 作用不大；徒勞 ➲ more at INTENT *n.*, PRACTICAL *adj.*

,purpose-'built *adj.* (*BrE*) designed and built for a particular purpose 特別建造的；專門設置的

pur·pose·ful /'pɜ:pəsfl; *NAmE* 'pɜ:rp-/ *adj.* having a useful purpose; acting with a clear aim and with determination 有意義的；有目的的；堅毅的；果斷的： *Purposeful work is an important part of the regime for young offenders.* 使從事有意義的勞動是管理少年犯的重要一環。◇ *She looked purposeful and determined.* 她看來胸有成竹、意志堅定。 ▶ **pur·pose·ful·ly** /-fəli/ *adv.* **pur·pose·ful·ness** *noun* [U]

pur·pose·less /'pɜ:pəsləs; *NAmE* 'pɜ:rp-/ *adj.* having no meaning, use or clear aim 無目的的；無用的；無意義的 SYN **meaningless**, **pointless** : *purposeless destruction* 盲目的破壞

pur·pose·ly /'pɜ:pəsli; *NAmE* 'pɜ:rp-/ *adv.* on purpose; deliberately 故意地；蓄意地： *He sat down, purposely avoiding her gaze.* 他坐了下來，有意避開她的目光。

pur·pos·ive /'pɜ:pəsɪv; *NAmE* 'pɜ:rp-/ *adj.* (*formal*) having a clear and definite purpose 目標明確的；有目的的 SYN **purposeful**

purr /pɜ:(r)/ *verb* **1** [I] when a cat **purrs**, it makes a low continuous sound in the throat, especially when it is happy or comfortable （貓）發出呼嚕聲，愜意地打呼嚕 **2** [I] (of a machine or vehicle 機器或機動車) to make a low continuous sound; to move making such a sound 轟隆作響；轟鳴着移動： *a purring engine* 轟隆作響的發動機◇ *The car purred away.* 汽車咕隆着開走了。 **3** [I, T] (+ **speech**) to speak in a low and gentle voice, for example to show you are happy or satisfied, or because you want to attract sb or get them to do sth （愉快或滿意地）低沉柔和地講話；輕聲招呼： *He was purring with satisfaction.* 他滿足地輕聲低語。 ▶ **purr** (also **pur·ring**) *noun* [sing.] : *the purr of a cat/a car engine* 貓發出的呼嚕聲；汽車發動機的隆隆聲

purse /pɜ:s; *NAmE* pɜ:rs/ *noun, verb*
■ ***noun*** **1** [C] (*especially BrE*) a small bag made of leather, plastic, etc. for carrying coins and often also paper money, cards, etc., used especially by women 錢包，皮夾子（尤指女用的）： *I took a coin out of my purse and gave it to the child.* 我從錢包取出一枚硬幣給那個小孩。 ➲ VISUAL VOCAB page V64 ➲ compare CHANGE PURSE, WALLET (1) **2** [C] (*NAmE*) = HANDBAG **3** [sing.] the amount of money that is available to a person, an organization or a government to spend 資金；財源；備用款： *We have holidays to suit every purse.* 我們有適合不同消費計劃的度假安排。◇ *Should spending on the arts be met out of the* ***public purse*** (= from government money)? 花在藝術活動的開支應該由政府支付嗎？ **4** [C] (*sport* 體) a sum of money given as a prize in a BOXING match （拳擊賽的）獎金 IDM see SILK
■ ***verb*** **~ your lips** to form your lips into a small tight round shape, for example to show disapproval 噘嘴，撮起嘴唇（以表示反對等）

purs·er /'pɜ:sə(r); *NAmE* 'pɜ:rs-/ *noun* an officer on a ship who is responsible for taking care of the passengers, and for the accounts （輪船上的）事務長

the 'purse strings *noun* [pl.] a way of referring to money and how it is controlled or spent 資金（或支出）的管理： *Who* ***holds the purse strings*** *in your house?* 你們家裏誰管錢？◇ *The government will have to* ***tighten the purse strings*** (= spend less). 政府將不得不緊縮開支。

pur·su·ance /pə'sju:əns; *NAmE* pər'su:-/ *noun*
IDM **in pursuance of sth** (*formal* or *law* 律) in order to do sth; in the process of doing sth 為了；在…過程中： *They may need to borrow money in pursuance of their legal action.* 他們在訴訟過程中可能需要借貸。

pur·su·ant /pə'sju:ənt; *NAmE* pər'su:-/ *adj.* **~ to sth** (*formal* or *law* 律) according to or following sth, especially a rule or law 依照，根據，按照（尤指規則或法律） SYN **in accordance with**

pur·sue AW /pə'sju:; *NAmE* pər'su:/ *verb* (*formal*)
1 **~ sth** to do sth or try to achieve sth over a period of time 追求；致力於；執行；貫徹： *to* ***pursue a goal/an aim/an objective*** 追求目標；貫徹宗旨；實現目標◇ *We intend to pursue this policy with determination.* 我們準備堅決貫徹這項政策。◇ *She wishes to pursue a medical career.* 她希望從事醫學工作。 **2** **~ sth | + speech** to continue to discuss, find out about or be involved in sth 繼續探討（或追究、從事）： *to pursue legal action* 進行訴訟◇ *We have decided not to pursue the matter.* 我們決定不再追究這件事。 **3** **~ sb/sth** to follow or chase sb/sth, especially in order to catch them 追逐；跟踪；追趕： *She left the theatre, hotly pursued by the press.* 她離開劇場，被記者窮追不捨。◇ *Police pursued the car at high speed.* 警察高速追趕那輛汽車。

pur·suer /pə'sju:ə(r); *NAmE* pər'su:-/ *noun* a person who is following or chasing sb 追趕者；追尋者；追捕者

pur·suit AW /pə'sju:t; *NAmE* pər'su:t/ *noun* **1** [U] **~ of sth** the act of looking for or trying to find sth 追求；尋找： *the* ***pursuit of happiness/knowledge/profit*** 對幸福／知識／利潤的追求◇ *She travelled the world* ***in pursuit of*** *her dreams.* 她走遍天下，追尋她的夢想。 **2** [U] the act of following or chasing sb 追趕；跟踪；追捕： *We drove away with two police cars* ***in pursuit*** (= following). 我們駕車離開，後面有兩輛警車跟着追趕。◇ *I galloped off on my horse with Rosie* ***in hot pursuit*** (= following quickly behind). 我縱馬而去，羅西緊追不捨。 **3** [C, usually pl.] something that you give your time and energy to, that you do as a hobby 事業；消遣；愛好 SYN **hobby**, **pastime** : ***outdoor/leisure/artistic pursuits*** 戶外活動；休閒活動；藝術愛好

puru·lent /'pjʊərələnt; *NAmE* 'pjʊr-/ *adj.* (*medical* 醫) containing or producing PUS 化膿的；流膿的： *a purulent discharge from the wound* 從傷口中流出的膿

pur·vey /pə'veɪ; *NAmE* pər'veɪ/ *verb* **~ sth** (*formal*) to supply food, services or information to people 提供，供應（食物、服務或信息）

pur·vey·or /pə'veɪə(r); *NAmE* pər'v-/ *noun* (*formal*) a person or company that supplies sth 提供者；供應商；供應公司

pur·view /'pɜ:vju:; *NAmE* 'pɜ:rv-/ *noun* [U]
IDM **within/outside the purview of sth** (*formal*) within/outside the limits of what a person, an organization, etc. is responsible for; (not) dealt with by a document, law, etc. 在（個人或組織等的）權限之內／外；在（文件、法律等的）範圍之內／之外

P

pus /pʌs/ *noun* [U] a thick yellowish or greenish liquid that is produced in an infected wound 膿

push 🗝 /pʊʃ/ *verb, noun*

■ *verb*

▸ **USING HANDS/ARMS/BODY 用手／胳膊／身體 1** 🗝 [I, T] to use your hands, arms or body in order to make sb/sth move forward or away from you; to move part of your body into a particular position 推動（人或物）；移動（身體部位）：*We pushed and pushed but the piano wouldn't move.* 我們推了又推，但鋼琴一動不動。◇ *Push hard when I tell you to.* 我叫你推時，你就使勁推。◇ *You push and I'll pull.* 你推，我拉。◇ **~ at sth** *She pushed at the door but it wouldn't budge.* 她推了推門，但門紋絲不動。◇ **~ sth** *He walked slowly up the hill pushing his bike.* 他推着自行車緩緩爬上山。◇ **~ sb/sth + adv./prep.** *She pushed the cup towards me.* 她把杯子推向我這邊。◇ *He pushed his chair back and stood up.* 他向後挪挪椅子，站了起來。◇ *He tried to kiss her but she pushed him away.* 他想吻她，但她把他推開了。◇ *She pushed her face towards him.* 她把臉湊近了他。◇ **~ sth + adj.** *I pushed the door open.* 我推開了門。**2** 🗝 [I, T] to use force to move past sb/sth using your hands, arms, etc. 推進（道路）；擠開：*People were* ***pushing and shoving*** *to get to the front.* 人們推推搡搡，向最前面擠。◇ **+ adv./prep.** *The fans pushed against the barrier.* 球迷們推擠着路障。◇ **~ your way + adv./prep.** *Try and push your way through the crowd.* 試着從人群中擠過去。

▸ **AFFECT STH 影響 3** 🗝 [T] **~ sth + adv./prep.** to affect sth so that it reaches a particular level or state 推動；促使（達到某程度或狀態）：*This development could push the country into recession.* 這種發展趨勢可能使國家陷入蕭條。◇ *The rise in interest rates will push prices up.* 利率的提高將促使價格上揚。

▸ **SWITCH/BUTTON 開關；按鈕 4** 🗝 [T] **~ sth** to press a switch, button, etc., for example in order to make a machine start working 按；揿；摁：*I pushed the button for the top floor.* 我按了到頂層的按鈕。

▸ **PERSUADE 勸說 5** 🗝 [T] to persuade or encourage sb to do sth that they may not want to do 說服；勸解；鼓勵；敦勸：**~ sb (into sth/into doing sth)** *My teacher pushed me into entering the competition.* 我的老師勸我參加比賽。◇ **~ sb to do sth** *No one pushed you to take the job, did they?* 誰也沒推着你接受這份工作，對不對？

▸ **WORK HARD 辛勤工作 6** 🗝 [T] **~ sb/yourself** to make sb work hard 鞭策；督促：*The music teacher really pushes her pupils.* 這個音樂老師對學生督促得很嚴。◇ *Lucy should push herself a little harder.* 露西應該鞭策自己多加把勁了。

▸ **PUT PRESSURE ON SB 施壓 7** [T] **~ sb (+ adv./prep.)** (*informal*) to put pressure on sb and make them angry or upset 迫使…生氣（或不安）：*Her parents are very tolerant, but sometimes she pushes them too far.* 她的父母十分寬容，但她有時也讓他們忍無可忍。

▸ **NEW IDEA/PRODUCT 新主意／產品 8** [T] **~ sth** (*informal*) to try hard to persuade people to accept or agree with a new idea, buy a new product, etc. 力勸…接受；推銷：*The interview gave him a chance to push his latest movie.* 這次採訪使他有機會推銷他的新電影。◇ *She didn't want to* ***push the point*** *any further at that moment.* 當時她不想繼續強調那個觀點。

▸ **SELL DRUGS 販毒 9** [T] **~ sth** (*informal*) to sell illegal drugs 販賣毒品

▸ **OF ARMY 軍隊 10** [I] **+ adv./prep.** to move forward quickly through an area 挺進；推進：*The army pushed (on) towards the capital.* 軍隊向首都挺進。

IDM **be ˌpushing ˈ40, ˈ50, etc.** (*informal*) to be nearly 40, 50, etc. years old 接近40歲（或50歲等） **be ˌpushing up (the) ˈdaisies** (*old-fashioned, humorous*) to be dead and in a grave 葬入地下；正忙着滋養墳上黃花 **push the ˈboat out** (*BrE, informal*) to spend a lot of money on enjoying yourself or celebrating sth 揮霍享樂；鋪張慶賀 **SYN** **splash out** **ˈpush the envelope** (*informal*) to go beyond the limits of what is allowed or thought to be possible 超越界線；突破：*He is a performer who consistently pushes the envelope of TV comedy.* 他是一個在電視喜劇表演中不斷尋求突破的演員。 **push your ˈluck | ˈpush it/things** (*informal*) to take a risk because you have successfully avoided problems in the past（由於過去的成功過關）再冒一次險，繼續碰運氣：*You didn't get caught last time, but don't push your luck!* 上次沒被逮住，但你不要再心存僥幸了！ **push sth to the back of your ˈmind** to try to forget about sth unpleasant 刻意忘掉（不愉快的事）；把…丟到腦後：*I tried to push the thought to the back of my mind.* 我盡量把這個念頭忘掉。➲ more at BUTTON *n.*, PANIC BUTTON

PHR V **ˌpush sb aˈbout/aˈround** 🗝 to give orders to sb in a rude or unpleasant way 粗暴命令；任意擺佈 **ˌpush aˈhead/ˈforward (with sth)** 🗝 to continue with a plan in a determined way 毅然推行（計劃）：*The government is pushing ahead with its electoral reforms.* 政府正堅定地推行選舉改革。 **ˌpush sth↔ˈaside** to avoid thinking about sth 不考慮；不去想：*He pushed aside the feelings of fear.* 他排除了恐懼。 **ˌpush sth ˈback** to make the time or date of a meeting, etc. later than originally planned 推遲；延遲：*The start of the game was pushed back from 2 p.m. to 4 p.m.* 比賽從午後兩點延遲到4點才開始。 **ˈpush for sth | ˈpush sb for sth** to repeatedly ask for sth or try to make sth happen because you think it is very important（向某人）反複要求，施壓爭取…：*The pressure group is pushing for a ban on GM foods.* 壓力集團正強烈要求取締轉基因食品。◇ *I'm going to have to push you for an answer.* 我將不得不催促你答覆了。 **ˌpush ˈforward** to continue moving or travelling somewhere, especially when it is a long distance or difficult 繼續前進；繼續跋涉 **ˌpush yourself/sb ˈforward** to make other people think about and notice you or sb else 使引人注目；使出風頭；突顯：*She had to push herself forward to get a promotion.* 她必須努力表現自己以求得升遷機會。 **ˌpush ˈin** (*BrE*) (*NAmE* **ˌcut ˈin**) to go in front of other people who are waiting 加塞兒；插隊 **ˌpush ˈoff 1** (*BrE, informal*) used to tell sb rudely to go away 滾開；一邊去：*Hey, what are you doing? Push off!* 嘿，你在幹什麼？滾開！ **2** to move away from land in a boat, or from the side of a swimming pool, etc.（乘船）離岸；離開（游泳池邊等） **ˌpush ˈon** to continue with a journey or an activity 繼續前進（或進行活動）：*We rested for a while then pushed on to the next camp.* 我們休息了一會，然後繼續朝下一個營地邁進。 **ˌpush sb↔ˈout** to make sb leave a place or an organization 驅逐；開除 **ˌpush sb/sth↔ˈout** to make sth less important than it was; to replace sth 減少…的重要性；使失勢；替換 **ˌpush sth↔ˈout** to produce sth in large quantities 大量生產：*factories pushing out cheap cotton shirts* 大量生產廉價棉襯衣的工廠 **ˌpush sb/sth ˈover** to make sb/sth fall to the ground by pushing them 推倒；推翻：*Sam pushed me over in the playground.* 薩姆在運動場上把我推倒了。➲ see also PUSHOVER **ˌpush sth↔ˈthrough** to get a new law or plan officially accepted 使通過；使得到批准：*The government is pushing the changes through before the election.* 政府正努力推動，要在選舉前促成這些變革。

■ *noun*

▸ **USING HANDS/ARMS/BODY 用手／胳膊／身體 1** 🗝 an act of pushing sth/sb 推；搡：*She gave him a gentle push.* 她輕輕地推了他一下。◇ *The car won't start. Can you give it a push?* 汽車發動不起來。你推一下好不好？◇ ***At the push of a button*** (= very easily) *he could get a whole list of names.* 他一按鍵就能得到完整的名單。

▸ **OF ARMY 軍隊 2** 🗝 a large and determined military attack 進攻；攻勢；挺進：*a final push against the enemy* 對敵軍的最後猛攻 ◇ (*figurative*) *The firm has begun a major push into the European market.* 這家公司已展開了對歐洲市場的重大攻勢。

▸ **EFFORT 努力 3** 🗝 **~ for sth** a determined effort to achieve sth 矢志的追求；堅定的努力：*The push for reform started in 2007.* 推行改革的努力始於2007年。**4** 🗝 encouragement to do sth 鼓勵；激勵：*He wants to open his own business, but needs a push in the right direction to get him started.* 他想創業，但還需要適當的鼓勵助他起步。

IDM **at a ˈpush** (*BrE, informal*) used to say that sth is possible, but only with difficulty 不得已時；為難地；勉強地：*We can provide accommodation for six people at a*

push. 我們勉強可以安排六個人住宿。 **give sb/get the 'push 1** (*BrE, informal*) to dismiss sb/to be dismissed from your job （被）解雇，炒魷魚 SYN **be fired/fire sb**： *They gave him the push after only six weeks.* 他只幹了六週就被開除了。 **2** (*BrE, informal*) to end a romantic relationship with sb; to be told that a romantic relationship with sb is over 與某人結束戀愛關係；把（戀人）甩掉；被甩： *He was devastated when his girlfriend gave him the push.* 女友把他甩了，他感到極度沮喪。 **when ˌpush comes to 'shove** (*informal*) when there is no other choice; when everything else has failed 別無選擇時；須孤注一擲時

push·back /ˈpʊʃbæk/ *noun* [U] (*especially NAmE*) opposition or resistance to a plan, an idea or a change 反對；抵制；反彈： *The plan was abandoned because the pushback from the military was so strong.* 由於軍方強烈反對，這一計劃中止了。

push·bike /ˈpʊʃbaɪk/ *noun* (*old-fashioned, BrE*) a bicycle 自行車；腳踏車

'push-button *adj.* [only before noun] operated by pressing buttons with your fingers 按鍵式的；用按鈕操作的： *a push-button phone* 按鍵式電話 ▸ **'push-button** *noun*

pushchair (*BrE*)
stroller (*NAmE*)
摺疊式幼兒小推車

pram (*BrE*)
baby carriage (*NAmE*)
嬰兒車

carrycot (*BrE*)
手提式嬰兒牀

push·chair /ˈpʊʃtʃeə(r); *NAmE* -tʃer/ (*BrE*) (*NAmE* **stroll·er**) *noun* a small folding seat on wheels in which a small child sits and is pushed along 摺疊式幼兒小推車 ➲ compare BUGGY (2)

pushed /pʊʃt/ *adj.* [not before noun] (*informal*) **1 ~ (to do sth)** having difficulty doing sth 有困難；難於；有難處： *You'll be **hard pushed** to finish this today.* 要你今天做完這件事會很難。 **2 ~ for sth** not having enough of sth 短缺；缺乏： *to **be pushed for money/time*** 缺少資金/時間 **3** busy 忙碌： *I know you're pushed, but can you make tomorrow's meeting?* 我知道你很忙，可是你能不能參加明天的會議？

push·er /ˈpʊʃə(r)/ *noun* (*informal*) a person who sells illegal drugs 販毒者；毒品販子： *drug pushers* 毒品販子 ➲ see also PAPER-PUSHER, PEN-PUSHER

push·over /ˈpʊʃəʊvə(r); *NAmE* -oʊ-/ *noun* (*informal*) **1** a thing that is easy to do or win 輕易的事；容易獲得的勝利： *The game will be a pushover.* 贏這場比賽將會是輕而易舉的事。 **2** a person who is easy to persuade or influence 容易說服的人；耳軟心活的人；好說話的人： *I don't think she'll agree—she's no pushover.* 我想她不會同意，她可不好說話。

push·pin /ˈpʊʃpɪn/ *noun* (*NAmE*) a type of DRAWING PIN with a coloured plastic head that is not flat 彩頭圖釘；撳釘 ➲ VISUAL VOCAB page V69

'push poll *noun* (*politics* 政) a way of trying to influence the way people vote by giving them information, often sth bad about an opposing candidate, while seeming to be asking their opinion 導向性民意調查，引導式民調（旨在影響選民投票的調查，常提供有關對手的負面信息） ▸ **'push polling** *noun* [U]： *allegations of push polling* 關於導向性民意調查的指控

'push-start *verb* **~ sth** (*especially BrE*) to push a vehicle in order to make the engine start 推車啟動（發動機） ▸ **'push-start** *noun* ➲ see also KICK-START

'push technology *noun* [U] (*computing* 計) a service that allows Internet users to keep receiving the particular type of information that they describe by completing a form 推送技術（用戶能不斷接收所選擇的某類互聯網信息）

'push-up (*especially NAmE*) (*BrE* also **'press-up**) *noun* [usually pl.] an exercise in which you lie on your stomach and raise your body off the ground by pressing down on your hands until your arms are straight 俯卧撐；伏地挺身；掌上壓 ➲ VISUAL VOCAB page V42

pushy /ˈpʊʃi/ *adj.* (**push·ier**, **pushi·est**) (*informal, disapproving*) trying hard to get what you want, especially in a way that seems rude 執意強求的；死纏硬磨的： *a pushy salesman* 糾纏不休的推銷員 ▸ **pushi·ness** *noun* [U]

pu·sil·lan·im·ous /ˌpjuːsɪˈlænɪməs/ *adj.* (*formal*) frightened to take risks 膽怯的；怯懦的 SYN **cowardly**

puss /pʊs/ *noun* **1** (*especially BrE*) used when you are calling or talking to a cat （用於喚貓或對貓說話）咪咪，貓咪 **2** (*informal, especially NAmE*) a person's face or mouth （人的）臉，嘴

pussy /ˈpʊsi/ *noun* (*pl.* **-ies**) **1** a child's word for a cat （兒童用語）貓咪 **2** (*taboo, slang*) the female sexual organs, especially the VULVA 屄；女陰

pussy·cat /ˈpʊsikæt/ *noun* (*informal*) **1** a child's word for a cat （兒童用語）貓咪 **2** a person who is kind and friendly, especially when you would not expect them to be like this （尤指不可貌相的）和藹可親的人： *He's just a pussycat really, once you get to know him.* 你瞭解他以後就會發現他實在和藹可親。

pussy·foot /ˈpʊsifʊt/ *verb* [I] **~ (about/around)** (*informal, usually disapproving*) to be careful or anxious about expressing your opinion in case you upset sb （說話）態度曖昧，小心翼翼

'pussy willow *noun* a small tree with flowers in spring that are like soft fur 飛絮柳；（尤指）褪色柳

pus·tule /ˈpʌstjuːl; *NAmE* -tʃuːl/ *noun* (*formal* or *medical* 醫) a spot on the skin containing PUS 膿疱

P

put 0‑ /pʊt/ *verb* (**put·ting**, **put**, **put**)
▸ **IN PLACE/POSITION** 處所；位置 **1** 0‑ **~ sth + adv./prep.** to move sth into a particular place or position 放；安置： *Put the cases down there, please.* 請把箱子擱在那邊。 ◇ *Did you put sugar in my coffee?* 你在我的咖啡裏放糖了沒有？ ◇ *Put your hand up if you need more paper.* 若有人還要紙，請舉手。 **2** 0‑ **~ sth + adv./prep.** to move sth into a particular place or position using force 猛推；用力插入： *He put his fist through a glass door.* 他把拳頭伸進了玻璃門。 **3** 0‑ **~ sb/sth + adv./prep.** to cause sb/sth to go to a particular place 將…送往；使…前往： *Her family put her into a nursing home.* 她的家人把她送進了一家療養院。 ◇ *It was the year the Americans put a man on the moon.* 那是美國人把人送上月球的那一年。
▸ **ATTACH** 附着 **4** 0‑ **~ sth + adv./prep.** to attach or fix sth to sth else 使與…連接；安裝： *We had to put new locks on all the doors.* 我們只好把所有的門都安上新鎖。
▸ **WRITE** 寫 **5** 0‑ **~ sth (+ adv./prep.)** to write sth or make a mark on sth （在…上）書寫，記，做標記： *Put your name here.* 在這裏填上姓名。 ◇ *Friday at 11? I'll put it in my diary.* 星期五 11 點？我要把它記在記事本裏。 ◇ *I couldn't read what she had put.* 她寫的什麼我辨認不出來。
▸ **INTO STATE/CONDITION** 狀態；情況 **6** 0‑ **~ sb/sth + adv./prep.** to bring sb/sth into the state or condition mentioned 使處於（某狀態或情況）： *I was put in charge of the office.* 他們讓我負責管理這個辦公室。 ◇ *The incident put her in a bad mood.* 這件事弄得她心情很不好。 ◇ ***Put yourself in my position.** What would you have done?* 你設身處地為我想想，你會怎麼辦？ ◇ *I tried to **put the matter into perspective**.* 我盡量正確評估一下這個問題。 ◇ *Don't go **putting yourself at risk**.* 當心不可冒什麼風險。 ◇ *It was time to **put** their suggestion **into practice**.* 那時就該把他們的建議付諸實施了。 ◇ *This new injury will **put him out of action** for several weeks.* 這次的新傷將使他幾週無法動彈。

▸ **AFFECT SB/STH** 影響某人／某事物 **7** **~ sth on/onto/to sth** to make sb/sth feel sth or be affected by sth 使感覺到；使受到…的影響：*Her new job has put a great strain on her.* 她的新工作使她感到負擔很重。◇ *They **put pressure on** her to resign.* 他們向她施加壓力，讓她自行辭職。◇ *It's time you **put a stop to** this childish behaviour.* 這種孩子氣的行為你該收斂了。

▸ **GIVE VALUE/RANK** 釐定；劃定 **8** **~ sth on sth** to give or attach a particular level of importance, trust, value, etc. to sth 給予（重視、信任、價值等）：*Our company puts the emphasis on quality.* 我們公司重視質量。◇ *He put a limit on the amount we could spend.* 他規定了我們開銷的數額。 **9** **~ sb/sth + adv./prep.** to consider sb/sth to belong to the class or level mentioned 把…視為（或列為）：*I'd put her in the top rank of modern novelists.* 我認為她應屬於一流的當代小說家。

▸ **EXPRESS** 表述 **10** **~ sth + adv./prep.** to express or state sth in a particular way 說；表達：*She put it very tactfully.* 她的話說得很巧妙。◇ ***Put simply**, we accept their offer or go bankrupt.* 簡單地說吧，我們要麼接受他們的條件，要麼破產。◇ *I was, **to put it mildly**, annoyed* (= I was extremely angry). 說得溫和點兒，我相當惱火。◇ *He was too trusting—or, **to put it another way**, he had no head for business.* 他太輕信人了。或者換個說法，他沒有商業頭腦。◇ *The meat was—**how shall I put it?**—a little overdone.* 這肉嘛，怎麼說呢，做得稍微老了點兒。◇ *As T.S. Eliot puts it ...* 正如 T • S • 艾略特所說…◇ *She had never tried to **put** this feeling **into words**.* 她從未試圖把這種感情說出來。◇ *Can you help me put this letter into good English, please?* 請問你能幫我用通順的英語來表達這信的內容嗎？

▸ **IN SPORT** 體育運動 **11** **~ sth** to throw the SHOT 推（鉛球）

IDM Most idioms containing **put** are at the entries for the nouns and adjectives in the idioms, for example **put your foot in it** is at **foot**. 大多數含 put 的習語，都可在該等習語中的名詞及形容詞相關詞條找到，如 put your foot in it 在詞條 foot 下。 **put it a'bout** (*BrE, informal*) to have many sexual partners 浪蕩胡為；亂搞男女關係 **I wouldn't put it 'past sb (to do sth)** (*informal*) used to say that you think sb is capable of doing sth wrong, illegal, etc. 我看…幹得出（錯的、違法的等事） **put it to sb that ...** to suggest sth to sb to see if they can argue against it 與…挑明；對…提出：*I put it to you that you are the only person who had a motive for the crime.* 我跟你說白了，你是唯一有作案動機的人。 **put one 'over on sb** (*informal*) to persuade sb to believe sth that is not true 矇騙；誘騙：*Don't try to put one over on me!* 你甭想矇我！ **put sb 'through it** (*informal, especially BrE*) to force sb to experience sth difficult or unpleasant 折磨；讓…難堪：*They really put me through it* (= asked me difficult questions) *at the interview.* 面試的時候，他們真把我折騰了一番。 **put to'gether** used when comparing or contrasting sb/sth with a group of other people or things to mean 'combined' or 'in total'（用於與一組人或事物作比較）合計，總和，合起來：*Your department spent more last year than all the others put together.* 去年，你們部門的開支比其他所有部門合起來都多。 **,put up or 'shut up** (*especially BrE*) used to tell sb to stop just talking about sth and actually do it, show it, etc. 要麼拿出實際行動來，要麼就閉嘴；動點兒真格的，別光耍嘴皮子

PHR V **,put sth↔a'bout** (*BrE, informal*) to tell a lot of people news, information, etc. that may be false 散佈，傳播（不實的消息等）：**put it about that ...** *Someone's been putting it about that you plan to resign.* 有人傳說你打算辭職。

'put sth above sth = PUT STH BEFORE STH

,put yourself/sth↔a'cross/'over (to sb) to communicate your ideas, feelings, etc. successfully to sb 交流，溝通（思想、感情等）：*She's not very good at putting her views across.* 她不大善於表達自己的觀點。

,put sth↔a'side **1** to ignore or forget sth, usually a feeling or difference of opinion 忽視；不理睬；忘記 **SYN** **disregard**：*They decided to put aside their differences.* 他們決定擱置雙方的分歧。 **2** to save sth or keep it available to use 儲存；保留：*We put some money aside every month for our retirement.* 我們每月都存一些錢供退休後使用。◇ *I put aside half an hour every day to write my diary.* 我每天留出半個小時寫日記。

'put sb/sth at sth to calculate sb/sth to be a particular age, weight, amount, etc. 估計；計算：*The damage to the building is put at over $1 million.* 對這座建築物造成的損壞估計超過 100 萬元。

,put sb↔a'way [often passive] (*informal*) to send sb to prison, to a mental hospital, etc. 把某人送入監獄（或精神病院等） **,put sth↔a'way** **1** to put sth in the place where it is kept because you have finished using it 將…收起；把…放回原處：*I'm just going to put the car away* (= in the garage). 我正打算把汽車開進車庫。 **2** to save money to spend later 積蓄；攢錢：*She has a few thousand dollars put away for her retirement.* 她為退休生活積攢了幾千元錢。 **3** (*informal*) to eat or drink large quantities of sth 猛吃；猛喝；胡吃海塞：*He must have put away a bottle of whisky last night.* 昨晚他準是喝了一整瓶威士忌。

,put sth↔'back **1** to return sth to its usual place or to the place where it was before it was moved 將…放回：*If you use something, put it back!* 用過的東西要放回原處！ **2** to move sth to a later time or date 推遲；延遲 **SYN** **postpone**：*The meeting has been put back to next week.* 這次會議已延期到下週了。 **3** to cause sth to be delayed 拖延；延緩；使延遲：*Poor trading figures put back our plans for expansion.* 貿易額不佳延緩了我們的拓展計劃。 **4** to move the hands of a clock so that they show the correct earlier time 向後撥，撥慢（鐘錶指針）：*Remember to put your clocks back tonight* (= because the time has officially changed). 記住今晚把時鐘撥回去。

'put sth before/above sth to treat sth as more important than sth else 把…看得比…重要

,put sth be'hind you to try to forget about an unpleasant experience and think about the future 把某事置諸腦後

,put sth↔'by (*especially BrE*) (also **,put sth↔a'side**) to save money for a particular purpose 攢錢；積蓄：*I'm putting by part of my wages every week to buy a bike.* 我每個星期把一部份工資存起來準備買輛自行車。

,put 'down (of an aircraft or its pilot 飛機或飛行員) to land 降落；着陸：*He put down in a field.* 他降落在一塊田裏。 **,put sb↔'down** (*informal*) to make sb look or feel stupid, especially in front of other people 使（當眾）出醜；使出洋相；讓某人現眼 ➲ related noun PUT-DOWN **,put sth↔'down** **1** to stop holding sth and place it on a table, shelf, etc. 擱在（桌子上等）；放下：*Put that knife down before you hurt somebody!* 把刀子放下，別傷着人！◇ *It's a great book. **I couldn't put it down.*** 這本書棒極了。我是愛不釋手啊。◇ (*BrE*) *She put the phone down on me* (= ended the call before I had finished speaking). 她沒等我把話說完就掛了線。 ➲ see also UNPUTDOWNABLE **2** to write sth; to make a note of sth 寫下；（用筆等）記下：*The meeting's on the 22nd. Put it down in your diary.* 會議日期是 22 號。把它記在你的記事本裏。 **3** to pay part of the cost of sth 下訂金；付部份費用：*We put a 5% deposit down on the house.* 我們給這所房子交了 5% 的訂金。 **4** to stop sth by force 鎮壓；平定 **SYN** **crush**：*to put down a rebellion* 平定叛亂 ◇ *The military government is determined to put down all opposition.* 軍政府決心鎮壓一切反對勢力。 **5** [often passive] to kill an animal, usually by giving it a drug, because it is old or sick 藥死（衰老或有病的動物）；人道毀滅：*We had to have our cat put down.* 我們只得用藥結束了貓的生命。 **6** (*BrE*) to put a baby to bed 安置（嬰兒）入睡：*Can you be quiet—I've just put the baby down.* 請安靜點。我剛哄小孩睡着了。 **7** to present sth formally for discussion by a parliament or committee 將…提請（議會或委員會）審議 **SYN** **table**：*to put down a motion/an amendment* 提交一項動議／修正案 **,put sb 'down as sth** to consider or judge sb to be a particular type of person 把某人視為（或看作）：*I'd put them both down as retired teachers.* 我看他們倆都是退休教師。 **,put sb 'down for sth** to put sb's name on a list, etc. for sth 登記；註冊；列入（名單等）：*Put me down for three tickets for Saturday.* 給我登記預訂三張星期六的票。◇ *They've put their son down for the local school.* 他們已經給兒子報名上當地的學校。 **'put sth**

down to sth to consider that sth is caused by sth 把…歸因於 **SYN attribute**： *What do you put her success down to?* 你認為她是靠什麼成功的？

ˌput sth↔ˈforth (*formal*) = PUT STH OUT (9)

ˌput yourself/sb↔ˈforward to suggest yourself/sb as a candidate for a job or position 推薦；薦舉： *Can I put you/your name forward for club secretary?* 我推薦你／提名你任俱樂部秘書好不好？ **ˌput sth↔ˈforward 1** to move sth to an earlier time or date 將…提前： *We've put the wedding forward by one week.* 我們已把婚禮提前了一週。 **2** to move the hands of a clock to the correct later time 向前撥，撥快（時鐘指針）： *Remember to put your clocks forward tonight* (= because the time has officially changed). 記住今晚把時鐘指針往前撥。 **3** to suggest sth for discussion 提出；提議；建議： *to put forward a suggestion* 提出建議

ˌput sb↔ˈin to elect a political party to govern a country 選舉（政黨）執政： *Who will the voters put in this time?* 這次選民會選誰執政呢？ **ˌput sth↔ˈin 1** to fix equipment or furniture into position so that it can be used 安裝 **SYN install**： *We're having a new shower put in.* 我們要安裝新淋浴設備。 **2** to include sth in a letter, story, etc. 把…寫進（信函、故事等）；添上；插入 **3** to interrupt another speaker in order to say sth 打斷；插話： *Could I put in a word?* 我可以插句話嗎？◇ **+ speech** *'But what about us?' he put in.* "那我們怎麼辦？"他插嘴說。 **4** to officially make a claim, request, etc. 正式提出（要求等）： *The company has put in a claim for damages.* 這家公司已提出賠償損失的要求。 **5 ~ a (...) performance** to give a performance of sth, especially one of a particular kind 表演： *All the actors put in great performances.* 所有演員都表演得非常好。 **6** (also **ˈput sth into sth**) to spend a lot of time or make a lot of effort doing sth 花費，耗費，投入（時間、心思等）： *She often puts in twelve hours' work a day.* 她時常每天工作十二個小時。◇ **~ doing sth** *He's putting a lot of work into improving his French.* 他正下功夫提高他的法語水平。 ➲ related noun INPUT **7** (also **ˈput sth into sth**) to use or give money 投入，投放（資金等）： **~ doing sth** *He's put all his savings into buying that house.* 他把所有的積蓄都用來買那所房子了。 **ˌput ˈin (at ...) | ˈput into ...** (of a boat or its sailors 船或水手) to enter a port 進港；入港： *They put in at Lagos for repairs.* 他們駛入拉各斯港進行維修。 **OPP put out (to .../from ...)** **ˌput ˈin for sth** (*especially BrE*) to officially ask for sth 申請： *Are you going to put in for that job?* 你想申請那份工作嗎？ **ˌput yourself/sb/sth ˈin for sth** to enter yourself/sb/sth for a competition 報名，給…登記（參加競賽）

ˌput sth ˈinto sth 1 to add a quality to sth 將…注入；使融入： *He put as much feeling into his voice as he could.* 他盡可能把感情融進他的聲音。 **2** = PUT STH IN (6), (7)

ˌput sb↔ˈoff 1 to cancel a meeting or an arrangement that you have made with sb 取消，撤銷（與某人的會晤或安排）： *It's too late to put them off now.* 現在已來不及取消與他們的安排了。 **2** to make sb dislike sb/sth or not trust them/it 使反感；使疏遠；使不信任： *She's very clever but her manner does tend to put people off.* 她人很精明，但態度令人反感。◇ *Don't be put off by how it looks—it tastes delicious.* 別看外表就討厭它，這東西味道可美哩。 ➲ see also OFF-PUTTING **3** (also **ˌput sb ˈoff sth**) to disturb sb who is trying to give all their attention to sth that they are doing 攪擾；使分神： *Don't put me off when I'm trying to concentrate.* 別在我要集中精神時打擾我。◇ *The sudden noise put her off her game.* 突然的嘈雜聲干擾了她的比賽。 **4** (*BrE*) (of a vehicle or its driver 車輛或司機) to stop in order to allow sb to leave 停車卸（客）；讓…下車： *I asked the bus driver to put me off at the station.* 我請公共汽車司機讓我在火車站下車。 **ˌput sb ˈoff sth/sb** to make sb lose interest in or enthusiasm for sth/sb 使失去興趣（或熱情）： *He was put off science by bad teaching.* 老師教得不好使他失去了對理科的興趣。◇ **~ doing sth** *The accident put her off driving for life.* 那場事故讓她一生都不想開車了。 **ˌput sth↔ˈoff** to change sth to a later time or date 推遲；延遲 **SYN postpone, delay**： *We've had to put off our wedding until September.* 我們只得把婚期推遲到九月。◇ **~ doing sth** *He keeps putting off going to the dentist.* 他把看牙醫的事一拖再拖。

ˌput sb ˈon to give sb the telephone so that they can talk to the person at the other end 讓某人聽電話： *Hi, Dad—can you put Nicky on?* 你好，爸爸。你讓尼基接電話好嗎？ **ˌput sth↔ˈon 1** to dress yourself in sth 穿上；戴上： *Hurry up! Put your coat on!* 快點！把外衣穿上！ **OPP take off 2** to apply sth to your skin, face, etc. 抹；搽；擦；塗： *She's just putting on her make-up.* 她正在化妝呢。 **3** to switch on a piece of equipment 開動；發動；使運行： *I'll put the kettle on for tea.* 我來燒壺水好沏茶。◇ *She put on the brakes suddenly.* 她突然踩了剎車。 **4** to make a tape, CD, DVD, etc. begin to play 播放（磁帶、CD、DVD 等）： *Do you mind if I put some music on?* 我放點音樂你不介意吧？◇ *He put some jazz on the stereo.* 他用立體聲音響播放了一點爵士樂。 **5** to become heavier, especially by the amount mentioned 增加（若干）體重；發胖 **SYN gain**： *She looks like she's* **put on weight**. 她似乎發胖了。◇ *He must have put on several kilos.* 他體重一定增加了好幾公斤。 **6** (*BrE*) to provide sth specially 專門提供： *The city is putting on extra buses during the summer.* 今年夏天，這城市將額外增開公共汽車。 **7** to produce or present a play, a show, etc. 舉辦；上演；展出： *The local drama club is putting on 'Macbeth'.* 當地的劇社正在演出《麥克佩斯》。 **8** to pretend to have a particular feeling, quality, way of speaking, etc. 裝作；假裝： *He put on an American accent.* 他假操着一口美國腔。◇ *I don't think she was hurt. She was just* **putting it on**. 我想她沒有受傷。她只是在裝樣子。 **ˌput sth ˈon sth 1** to add an amount of money or a tax to the cost of sth 在（價格等）上加某金額（或稅額）： *The government has put ten pence on the price of twenty cigarettes.* 政府在每二十支香煙的價格上加徵了十便士的稅款。 **2** to bet money on sth 把錢押在；下賭注： *I've never put money on a horse.* 我從未賭過馬。◇ *I put £5 on him to win.* 我在他身上押 5 英鎊賭他贏。

ˌput sb ˈonto sb/sth 1 to tell the police, etc. about where a criminal is or about a crime 向（警方等）揭發，告發，舉報： *What first put the police onto the scam?* 警方當初怎麼得知這個騙局的？ **2** to tell sb about sb/sth that they may like or find useful 告訴；提供信息： *Who put you onto this restaurant—it's great!* 誰告訴你這家餐館的？真棒極了！

ˌput ˈout (for sb) (*NAmE, slang*) to agree to have sex with sb 同意性交 **ˌput yourself ˈout (for sb)** (*informal*) to make a special effort to do sth for sb 特意（為某人）費事： *Please don't put yourself out on my account.* 請別特意為我費事了。 **ˌput sb ˈout 1** to cause sb trouble, extra work, etc. 給某人添麻煩（或增加額外工作等） **SYN inconvenience**： *I hope our arriving late didn't put them out.* 但願我們遲到沒有給人家添麻煩。 **2 be put out** to be upset or offended 煩惱；生氣： *He looked really put out.* 看來他真生氣了。 **3** to make sb unconscious 使昏迷；使失去知覺： *These pills should put him out for a few hours.* 這些藥片會使他昏迷幾個小時。 **ˌput sth↔ˈout 1** to take sth out of your house and leave it, for example for sb to collect 將…扔到外面；清理掉；扔掉： (*BrE*) *to put the rubbish out* 倒垃圾◇ (*NAmE*) *to put the garbage/trash out* 倒垃圾 **2** to place sth where it will be noticed and used 把…擺好；預備好（物品）： *Have you put out clean towels for the guests?* 你為客人預備好乾淨毛巾沒有？ **3** to stop sth from burning or shining 熄滅；撲滅： *to put out a candle/cigarette/light* 熄滅蠟燭／香煙／燈火◇ *Firefighters soon put the fire out.* 消防人員很快把火撲滅了。 **4** to produce sth, especially for sale 生產；製造： *The factory puts out 500 new cars a week.* 這家工廠每週生產 500 輛新汽車。 ➲ related noun OUTPUT **5** to publish or broadcast sth 出版；廣播；公佈： *Police have put out a description of the man they wish to question.* 警方公佈了他們想要訊問的那名男子的特徵。 **6** to give a job or task to a worker who is not your employee or to a company that is not part of your own group or organization 把（工作）外包： *A lot of the work is put out to freelancers.* 許多工作都外包給自由職業者了。 **7** to make a figure, result, etc. wrong 使出差錯： *The rise in interest rates put our estimates out by several thousands.* 利率上升使我們的估算差了好幾千。 **8** to push a bone out of its normal position 使脫臼

P

SYN **dislocate**：*She fell off her horse and put her shoulder out.* 她落下馬來，造成肩關節脫位。**9** (also *formal* **ˌput sth↔ˈforth**) to develop or produce new leaves, SHOOTS, etc. 長出（葉、芽等）；抽芽 **ˌput ˈout (to …/from …)** (of a boat or its sailors 船或水手) to leave a port 離港；起航：*to put out to sea* 起航出海◇*We put out from Liverpool.* 我們從利物浦起航。OPP **put in (at …)**

ˌput yourself/sth ˈover (to sb) = PUT YOURSELF/STH ACROSS (TO SB)

ˌput sth↔ˈthrough to continue with and complete a plan, programme, etc. 完成；達成；使成功：*We managed to put the deal through.* 我們設法做成了這筆生意。**ˌput sb ˈthrough sth 1** to make sb experience sth very difficult or unpleasant 使經受（磨練、痛苦）；折磨：*You have put your family through a lot recently.* 最近你讓家人受了不少苦。**2** to arrange or pay for sb to attend a school, college, etc. 安排某人上（學）；供某人上（學）：*He put all his children through college.* 他把子女都送進了大學。**ˌput sb/sth ˈthrough (to sb/…)** ⊶ to connect sb by telephone 給…接通（電話）；把…接到：*Could you put me through to the manager, please?* 請幫我找經理接一下電話好嗎？

ˈput sb to sth to cause sb trouble, difficulty, etc. 給某人添麻煩（或增加困難等）：*I hope we're not putting you to too much trouble.* 希望我們沒有給你添太多的麻煩。**ˈput sth to sb 1** to offer a suggestion to sb so that they can accept or reject it 給…提出（建議）：*Your proposal will be put to the board of directors.* 你的建議將提交董事會裁決。**2** to ask sb a question 提問：*The audience is now invited to put questions to the speaker.* 現在請聽眾向講演者提問。

ˌput sth↔toˈgether ⊶ to make or prepare sth by fitting or collecting parts together 組裝；組織；彙集：*to put together a model plane/an essay/a meal* 組裝飛機模型；構思文章；準備飯菜◇*I think we can put together a very strong case for the defence.* 我想我們能夠為辯方整理出十分有力的論據。

ˈput sth towards sth to give money to pay part of the cost of sth 為…湊錢：*Here's $100 to put towards your ski trip.* 這是 100 元，補助你去滑雪用。

ˌput ˈup sth 1 to show a particular level of skill, determination, etc. in a fight or contest（在戰鬥、競賽中）顯示，表現：*They surrendered without putting up much of a fight.* 他們沒怎麼抵抗就投降了。◇*The team put up a great performance* (= played very well). 這個隊表現好極了。**2** to suggest an idea, etc. for other people to discuss 提出（意見等）：*to put up an argument/a case/a proposal* 提出論據／事實／建議 **ˌput sb↔ˈup 1** ⊶ to let sb stay at your home 留某人住在家中：*We can put you up for the night.* 今晚我們可以留你過夜。**2** to suggest or present sb as a candidate for a job or position 推薦；提名：*The Green Party hopes to put up more candidates in the next election.* 綠黨希望在下屆大選中推出更多的候選人。**ˌput sth↔ˈup 1** ⊶ to raise sth or put it in a higher position 提升；使升高：*to put up a flag* 升旗◇*She's put her hair up.* 她把頭髮挽在頭上。**2** ⊶ to build sth or place sth somewhere 建造；搭建；豎立：*to put up a building/fence/memorial/tent* 蓋樓房；架籬笆；修紀念碑；搭帳篷 ➲ SYNONYMS at BUILD **3** ⊶ to fix sth in a place where it will be seen 置…於明顯處；張貼 SYN **display**：*to put up a notice* 貼出通知 **4** ⊶ to raise or increase sth 提高；增加：*They've put up the rent by £20 a month.* 他們把每月的租金提高了 20 英鎊。**5** to provide or lend money 提供，借出（資金）：*A local businessman has put up the £500 000 needed to save the club.* 一位當地的商人拿出了拯救該俱樂部所需的 50 萬英鎊。**ˌput ˈup (at …)** (*especially BrE*) to stay somewhere for the night 投宿；（在…）過夜：*We put up at a motel.* 我們晚間住在一家汽車旅館。**ˌput ˈup for sth | ˌput yourself ˈup for sth** to offer yourself as a candidate for a job or position 自薦為…的候選人；參與甄選：*She is putting up for election to the committee.* 她正在參加委員會委員的競選。**ˌput sb ˈup to sth** (*informal*) to encourage or persuade sb to do sth wrong or stupid 慫恿；攛掇；唆使：*Some of the older boys must have put him up to it.* 那件事準是一些大孩子慫恿他幹的。

ˌput ˈup with sb/sth ⊶ to accept sb/sth that is annoying, unpleasant, etc. without complaining 容忍；忍受 SYN **tolerate**：*I don't know how she puts up with him.* 我不明白她怎麼受得了他。◇*I'm not going to put up with their smoking any longer.* 我再也不能容忍他們抽煙了。

pu·ta·tive /ˈpjuːtətɪv/ *adj.* [only before noun] (*formal* or *law* 律) believed to be the person or thing mentioned 推定的；認定的；公認的 SYN **presumed**：*the putative father of this child* 這孩子的推定的父親

ˈput-down *noun* (*informal*) a remark or criticism that is intended to make sb look or feel stupid 令人難堪的話；噎人的話

ˈput-on *noun* [usually sing.] (*NAmE*) something that is done to trick or cheat people 假象；騙局

pu·tong·hua /puːˈtʊŋhwɑː/ *noun* [U] the standard spoken form of modern Chinese, based on the form spoken in Beijing 普通話（以北京話為基礎的標準現代漢語口語）➲ compare MANDARIN (3)

pu·tre·fac·tion /ˌpjuːtrɪˈfækʃn/ *noun* [U] (*formal*) the process of decaying, especially that of a dead body 腐爛；（屍體）腐化

pu·trefy /ˈpjuːtrɪfaɪ/ *verb* (**pu·tre·fies**, **pu·tre·fy·ing**, **pu·tre·fied**, **pu·tre·fied**) [I] (*formal*) to decay and smell very bad 腐爛；腐化 SYN **rot**

pu·trid /ˈpjuːtrɪd/ *adj.* **1** (of dead animals or plants 死的動植物) decaying and therefore smelling very bad 腐爛的；腐臭的 SYN **foul**：*the putrid smell of rotten meat* 爛肉的臭味 **2** (*informal*) very unpleasant 令人厭惡（或惡心）的：*a putrid pink colour* 難看的粉紅色

putsch /pʊtʃ/ *noun* (from *German*) a sudden attempt to remove a government by force 政變；武力奪取政權

putt /pʌt/ *verb* [I, T] ~ (**sth**) (in GOLF 高爾夫球) to hit the ball gently when it is on the short grass near the hole, so that it rolls across the ground a short distance into or towards the hole 輕擊；推球入洞 ▸ **putt** *noun*

putt·er /ˈpʌtə(r)/ *verb, noun*

■ *verb* **1** [I] (*BrE*) (of a boat or vehicle 船或車輛) to make a repeated low sound as it moves slowly 嘟嘟（或咕嚕）作響：*the puttering of the engine as it reduced speed* 發動機減速時的咕嚕聲 **2** (*NAmE*) (*BrE* **pot·ter**) [I] (+ **adv./prep.**) to do things or move without hurrying, especially when you are doing sth that you enjoy and that is not important 從容做事；欣然從事；漫步；閒蕩：*I spent the morning puttering around the house.* 我在家磨蹭了一上午。

■ *noun* (in the game of GOLF 高爾夫球運動) the type of CLUB that is used for putting (= hitting the ball short distances) 輕擊球杆

ˈputting green *noun* a small GOLF COURSE on an area of smooth short grass where people can practise PUTTING（高爾夫球的）輕擊區；（練習輕擊的）小型高爾夫球場

putty /ˈpʌti/ *noun* [U] a soft sticky substance that becomes hard when it is dry and that is used for fixing glass into window frames（窗用）油灰

IDM **(like) putty in sb's ˈhands** easily controlled or influenced by another person（像）某人手中的麪糰；任某人擺佈；易受某人的影響：*She'll persuade him. He's like putty in her hands.* 她會說服他的。他就像她手裏的麪糰一樣。

ˌput-up ˈjob *noun* [usually sing.] (*BrE, informal*) a plan or an event that has been arranged secretly in order to trick or cheat sb 騙局；障眼法

ˌput-upon *adj.* treated in an unfair way by sb because they take advantage of your kindness or willingness to do things 被佔便宜的；被利用的：*his much put-upon wife* 他那飽受委屈的妻子

putz /pʌts/ *verb, noun*

■ *verb* [I] ~ **around** (*NAmE, informal*) to waste time not doing anything useful or important 閒蕩；遊手好閒

■ *noun* (*NAmE, informal*) a stupid person 笨蛋；傻瓜

puz·zle /ˈpʌzl/ *noun, verb*

■ *noun* **1** a game, etc. that you have to think about carefully in order to answer it or do it 謎；智力遊戲：*a crossword puzzle* 縱橫字謎◇*a book of puzzles for* *children* 兒童謎語書 ➲ VISUAL VOCAB page V39 **2** (*especially NAmE*) = JIGSAW (1) **3** [usually sing.] something that is difficult to understand or explain 不解之謎；疑問 SYN **mystery**

■ *verb* **~ sb** to make sb feel confused because they do not understand sth 迷惑；使困惑 SYN **baffle**：*What puzzles me is why he left the country without telling anyone.* 令我不解的是，他為什麼悄悄地離開了這個國家。▸ **puzzling** /ˈpʌzlɪŋ/ *adj.*： *one of the most puzzling aspects of the crime* 這樁罪案最費解的一面

PHR V **ˈpuzzle over/about sth** to think hard about sth in order to understand or explain it 苦苦思索；仔細琢磨 **ˌpuzzle sth↔ˈout** to find the answer to a difficult or confusing problem by thinking carefully 琢磨出…的答案 SYN **work out**： **~ why, what, etc. …** *He was trying to puzzle out why he had been brought to the house.* 他想弄明白自己為何被帶到這所房子。

puz·zled /ˈpʌzld/ *adj.* unable to understand sth or the reason for sth 困惑的；迷惑不解的 SYN **baffled**： *She had a **puzzled look** on her face.* 她滿臉困惑的表情。◇ *Scientists are puzzled as to why the whale had swum to the shore.* 科學家們感到不解：為什麼這頭鯨游到海岸上來。◇ *He looked puzzled so I repeated the question.* 他好像沒聽懂，於是我把問題又重複了一遍。

puzzle·ment /ˈpʌzlmənt/ *noun* [U] (*formal*) a feeling of being confused because you do not understand sth 迷惘；困惑： *She frowned in puzzlement.* 她迷惑地蹙着眉。

puz·zler /ˈpʌzlə(r)/ *noun* (*informal*) something that makes you feel confused 費解的事；謎團 SYN **poser**

PVC /ˌpiː viː ˈsiː/ *noun* [U] a strong plastic material used for a wide variety of products, such as clothing, pipes, floor coverings, etc. 聚氯乙烯（用於服裝、管材、地板鋪料等）

PVR /ˌpiː viː ˈɑː(r)/ *noun* (*BrE*) a device that records video onto a hard disk or other memory device, using digital technology (the abbreviation for 'personal video recorder') 個人視頻錄像機，數位硬碟錄影機（全寫為 personal video recorder，用數字技術將視頻錄製到硬盤等存貯器的裝置） SYN **DVR**

p.w. *abbr.* (*BrE*) per week 每週： *Rent is £100 p.w.* 租金為每週 100 英鎊。

PX /ˌpiː ˈeks/ (*pl.* **PXs** /ˌpiː ˈeksɪz/) *noun* post exchange (a shop/store at a US military base that sells food, clothes and other things)（美軍軍營內）軍人服務社，小賣部

pye-dog (also **pie-dog**, **pi-dog**) /ˈpaɪ dɒg; *NAmE* dɔːg/ (also **paˈriah dog**) *noun* (especially in Asia) a dog that has no owner or home and is of no particular breed（尤指亞洲的）無主野狗，流浪狗

pygmy (also **pigmy**) /ˈpɪgmi/ *noun, adj.*

■ *noun* (*pl.* **-ies**) **1 Pygmy** a member of a race of very short people living in parts of Africa and SE Asia 俾格米人（生活於非洲和東南亞部份地區，身材矮小） **2** (*disapproving*) a very small person or thing or one that is weak in some way 矮小的人（或物）；侏儒；弱小者： *He regarded them as intellectual pygmies.* 他把他們視為智力低弱的人。

■ *adj.* [only before noun] used to describe a plant or SPECIES (= type) of animal that is much smaller than other similar kinds （比同類動植物）小得多的，矮小的，微小的： *a pygmy shrew* 倭鼩鼱

py·jama /pəˈdʒɑːmə; *NAmE* -ˈdʒæm-/ *noun* loose trousers/pants tied at the waist and worn by men or women in some Asian countries （一些亞洲國家男女圍腰而繫的）寬鬆褲： *He was dressed in a pyjama and kurta, ideal for a summer evening.* 他穿着寬鬆褲和庫爾塔衫，是夏日夜晚的理想穿着。

py·ja·mas (*especially US* **pa·ja·mas**) /pəˈdʒɑːməz; *NAmE* -ˈdʒæm-/ *noun* [pl.] a loose jacket and trousers/pants worn in bed （一套）睡衣褲： *a pair of pyjamas* 一套睡衣 ➲ VISUAL VOCAB page V63 ▸ **py·jama** (*especially US* **pa·jama**) *adj.* [only before noun]： *pyjama bottoms* 睡褲 IDM see CAT

pylon /ˈpaɪlən; *NAmE* also -lɑːn/ *noun* a tall metal structure that is used for carrying electricity wires high above the ground 電纜塔

pyra·mid /ˈpɪrəmɪd/ *noun* **1** a large building with a square or TRIANGULAR base and sloping sides that meet in a point at the top. The ancient Egyptians built stone pyramids as places to bury their kings and queens.（古埃及的）金字塔 ➲ VISUAL VOCAB page V15 **2** (*geometry* 幾何) a solid shape with a square or TRIANGULAR base and sloping sides that meet in a point at the top 錐體；稜錐體 ➲ VISUAL VOCAB page V71 **3** an object or a pile of things that has the shape of a pyramid 金字塔形的物體（或一堆東西）： *a pyramid of cans in a shop window* 商店櫥窗中擺成金字塔形的罐頭 **4** an organization or a system in which there are fewer people at each level as you get near the top 金字塔式的組織（或系統）： *a management pyramid* 金字塔式管理系統 ▸ **pyr·am·idal** /ˈpɪrəmɪdl/ *adj.*

ˌpyramid ˈselling *noun* [U] a way of selling things in which sb buys the right to sell a company's goods and then sells the goods to other people. These other people sell the goods again to others. 金字塔式銷售；寶塔式營銷

pyre /ˈpaɪə(r)/ *noun* a large pile of wood on which a dead body is placed and burned in a funeral ceremony （火葬用的）柴堆

pyr·eth·rum /paɪˈriːθrəm/ *noun* **1** [C] a type of flower grown especially in Kenya 除蟲菊（尤見於肯尼亞） **2** [U] a substance made from this flower and used for killing insects 除蟲菊殺蟲劑

Pyrex™ /ˈpaɪreks/ *noun* [U] a type of hard glass that does not break at high temperatures, and is often used to make dishes for cooking food in 派萊克斯耐高溫玻璃（常用以製造炊具）

pyr·ites /paɪˈraɪtiːz; *NAmE* pəˈr-/ *noun* [U] a shiny yellow mineral that is made up of SULPHUR and a metal such as iron 硫化礦物；黃鐵礦： ***iron/copper pyrites*** 黃鐵礦；黃銅礦

pyro·mania /ˌpaɪrəʊˈmeɪniə; *NAmE* ˌpaɪroʊ-/ *noun* [U] (*technical* 術語) a mental illness that causes a strong desire to set fire to things 縱火狂

pyro·maniac /ˌpaɪrəʊˈmeɪniæk; *NAmE* ˌpaɪroʊ-/ *noun* **1** (*technical* 術語) a person who suffers from pyromania 縱火狂患者 **2** (*informal, humorous*) a person who enjoys making or watching fires 愛玩火（或看火）的人

pyro·tech·nics /ˌpaɪrəˈteknɪks/ *noun* **1** [U+sing./pl. v.] (*technical* 術語) FIREWORKS or a display of FIREWORKS 煙花；煙火的施放 **2** [pl.] (*formal*) a clever and complicated display of skill, for example by a musician, writer or speaker （音樂家、作家、演講者等的）技巧的展示： *guitar pyrotechnics* 吉他演奏技巧的展示 ▸ **pyro·tech·nic** *adj.* [usually before noun]

Pyr·rhic vic·tory /ˌpɪrɪk ˈvɪktəri/ *noun* a victory that is not worth winning because the winner has suffered or lost so much in winning it 得不償失的勝利；以慘重代價換取的勝利 ORIGIN From **Pyrrhus**, the king of Epirus who defeated the Romans in 279BC but lost many of his own men. 源自伊庇魯斯國王皮洛士，他於公元前 279 年打敗羅馬人，但自己的部隊也傷亡慘重。

Py·thag·oras' the·orem /paɪˈθægərəsɪz θɪərəm; *NAmE* θiːə-; θɪr-/ (*NAmE* **Py·thag·orean the·orem** /paɪˌθægəˈriːən θɪərəm; *NAmE* also pə-; θiːə-; θɪr-/) *noun* (*geometry* 幾何) the rule that, in a RIGHT-ANGLED TRIANGLE/RIGHT TRIANGLE, the SQUARE *n.* (4) of the HYPOTENUSE (= the side opposite the right angle) is equal to the squares of the other two sides added together 勾股定理；畢達哥拉斯定理；畢式定理

py·thon /ˈpaɪθən; *NAmE* -θɑːn/ *noun* a large tropical snake that kills animals for food by winding its long body around them and crushing them 蟒；蚺蛇

Q q

Q /kjuː/ *noun, abbr.*

■ ***noun*** (also **q**) [C, U] (*pl.* **Qs, Q's, q's** /kjuːz/) the 17th letter of the English alphabet 英語字母表的第 17 個字母：*'Queen' begins with (a) Q/'Q'.* * queen 一詞以字母 q 開頭。➲ see also Q-TIP

■ ***abbr.*** question 問題；疑問 **IDM** see MIND *v.*

Qa·ba·lah = KABBALAH

QC /ˌkjuː ˈsiː/ *noun* (in Britain) the highest level of BARRISTER, who can speak for the government in court. QC is the abbreviation for 'Queen's Counsel' and is used when there is a queen in Britain.（英國）王室法律顧問，御用大律師（全寫為 Queen's Counsel，女王在位時使用）➲ compare KC

QED (*BrE*) (also **Q.E.D.** *US, BrE*) /ˌkjuː iː ˈdiː/ *abbr.* that is what I wanted to prove and I have proved it (from Latin 'quod erat demonstrandum') 證明完畢，證訖（源自拉丁文 quod erat demonstrandum）

qib·lah (also **qibla**, **kibla**) /ˈkɪblə/ *noun* [sing.] the direction of the Kaaba (the holy building at Mecca), towards which Muslims turn when they are PRAYING 吉布拉，天房方向（即麥加天房克爾白的方向，為穆斯林朝拜方向）

qt *abbr.* (in writing) QUART（書寫形式）夸脫

ˈQ-tip™ *noun* (*NAmE*) = COTTON BUD

qua /kweɪ; kwɑː/ *prep.* (from *Latin, formal*) as sth; in the role of sth 作為；以…身分：*The soldier acted qua soldier, not as a human being.* 那名士兵當時以軍人的身分行事，而不是以一般人的身分。➲ see also SINE QUA NON

quack /kwæk/ *noun, verb*

■ ***noun*** **1** the sound that a DUCK makes（鴨子的）呱呱聲，嘎嘎聲 **2** (*informal, disapproving*) a person who dishonestly claims to have medical knowledge or skills 江湖郎中；冒牌醫生；庸醫：*quack doctors* 庸醫 ◇ *I've got a check-up with the quack* (= the doctor) *next week.* 我下週要到庸醫那裏檢查身體。

■ ***verb*** [I] when a DUCK **quacks**, it makes the noise that is typical of ducks（鴨子）嘎嘎叫，呱呱叫

quack·ery /ˈkwækəri/ *noun* [U] the methods or behaviour of sb who pretends to have medical knowledge 江湖醫術；庸醫行徑

quad /kwɒd; *NAmE* kwɑːd/ *noun* **1** = QUADRANGLE **2** = QUADRUPLET ➲ see also QUADS

ˈquad bike (*BrE*) (*NAmE* **ˌfour-ˈwheeler**) *noun* a motorcycle with four large wheels, used for riding over rough ground, often for fun 四輪摩托車（常用於娛樂）➲ VISUAL VOCAB page V51 ➲ see also ATV

quad·ran·gle /ˈkwɒdræŋgl; *NAmE* ˈkwɑːd-/ *noun* (*formal*) (also rather *informal* **quad**) an open square area that has buildings all around it, especially in a school or college 四方院子（四周有建築，常見於校園）

quad·ran·gu·lar /kwɒˈdræŋgjələ(r); *NAmE* kwɑːˈd-/ *adj.* **1** (*geometry* 幾何) (of a shape 形狀) having four sides and flat rather than solid 四角形的 **2** (of a sporting competition 體育比賽) involving four teams or individuals who each compete against all the others 四隊（或四人）參加的；四方角逐的

quad·rant /ˈkwɒdrənt; *NAmE* ˈkwɑːd-/ *noun* **1** (*geometry* 幾何) a quarter of a circle or of its CIRCUMFERENCE (= the distance around it) 四分之一圓（或圓周）；象限 ➲ VISUAL VOCAB page V71 **2** an instrument for measuring angles, especially to check your position at sea or to look at stars 象限儀，四分儀（常用於測量海上方位或觀看星辰）

quadra·phon·ic (also **quadro·phon·ic**) /ˌkwɒdrəˈfɒnɪk; *NAmE* ˌkwɑːdrəˈfɑːn-/ *adj.* (of a system of recording or broadcasting sound 錄音或廣播系統) coming from four different SPEAKERS at the same time 四聲道的；四軌錄放音的 ➲ compare MONO, STEREO (2)

quad·rat·ic /kwɒˈdrætɪk; *NAmE* kwɑːˈd-/ *adj.* (*mathematics* 數) involving an unknown quantity that is multiplied by itself once only 平方的；二次方的：*a quadratic equation* 二次方程式

quadri- /ˈkwɒdrɪ-; *NAmE* ˈkwɑːd-/ (also **quadr-**) *combining form* (in nouns, adjectives and adverbs 構成名詞、形容詞和副詞) four; having four 四；四…的：*quadrilateral* 四邊形 ◇ *quadruplet* 四胞胎之一

quad·ri·ceps /ˈkwɒdrɪseps; *NAmE* ˈkwɑːd-/ *noun* (*pl.* **quad·ri·ceps**) (also *informal* **quads**) (*anatomy* 解) the large muscle at the front of the THIGH 四頭肌

quad·ri·lat·eral /ˌkwɒdrɪˈlætərəl; *NAmE* ˌkwɑːd-/ *noun* (*geometry* 幾何) a flat shape with four straight sides 四邊形 ➲ VISUAL VOCAB page V71 ▸ **quad·ri·lat·eral** *adj.*

quad·rille /kwəˈdrɪl/ *noun* a dance for four or more couples in a square, popular in the past 方陣舞，卡德利爾舞（過去流行，由四對或以上的男女構成方陣）

quad·ril·lion /kwɒˈdrɪljən; *NAmE* kwɑːˈd-/ *number* the number 10^{15}, or 1 followed by 15 zeros 千的五次冪

quadri·ple·gic /ˌkwɒdrɪˈpliːdʒɪk; *NAmE* ˌkwɑːd-/ *noun* a person who is permanently unable to use their arms and legs 四肢癱瘓者 ▸ **quadri·ple·gic** *adj.* **quadri·ple·gia** /ˌkwɒdrɪˈpliːdʒə; *NAmE* ˌkwɑːd-/ *noun* [U]

quadro·phon·ic *adj.* = QUADRAPHONIC

quad·ru·ped /ˈkwɒdruped; *NAmE* ˈkwɑːd-/ *noun* (*technical* 術語) any creature with four feet 四足動物 ➲ compare BIPED

quad·ru·ple *verb, adj., det.*

■ ***verb*** /kwɒˈdruːpl; *NAmE* kwɑːˈd-/ [I, T] **~ (sth)** to become four times bigger; to make sth four times bigger（使）變為四倍：*Sales have quadrupled in the last five years.* 在過去五年中，銷售額已增長至四倍。

■ ***adj.*** [only before noun], ***det.*** /ˈkwɒdrʊpl; *NAmE* kwɑːˈdruːpl/ **1** consisting of four parts, people or groups 由四部份（或人、群體）構成的；四方面的：*a quadruple alliance* 四方聯盟 **2** being four times as much or as many 四倍的：*a quadruple whisky* 一份四倍的威士忌 ◇ *This year we produced quadruple the amount produced in 2008.* 我們今年的產量是 2008 年的四倍。

quad·ru·plet /ˈkwɒdrʊplət; kwɒˈdruːplət; *NAmE* kwɑː-/ (also **quad**) *noun* one of four children born at the same time to the same mother 四胞胎之一

quads /kwɒdz/ *noun* [pl.] (*informal*) = QUADRICEPS

quaff /kwɒf; *NAmE* kwæf; kwɑːf/ *verb* **~ sth** (*old-fashioned* or *literary*) to drink a large amount of sth quickly 豪飲；痛飲；開懷暢飲

quag·mire /ˈkwægmaɪə(r); *BrE* also ˈkwɒg-/ *noun* **1** an area of soft wet ground 泥淖；濕地；泥沼 **SYN** **bog** (1) **2** a difficult or dangerous situation 困境；險境 **SYN** **morass** (2)

quail /kweɪl/ *noun, verb*

■ ***noun*** [C, U] (*pl.* **quails** or **quail**) a small brown bird, whose meat and eggs are used for food; the meat of this bird 鵪鶉；鵪鶉肉

■ ***verb*** [I] **~ (at/before sb/sth)** (*literary*) to feel frightened or to show that you are frightened 感覺（或顯出）恐懼；膽怯；畏縮

quaint /kweɪnt/ *adj.* attractive in an unusual or old-fashioned way 新奇有趣的；古色古香的：*quaint old customs* 稀奇的古老習俗 ◇ *a quaint seaside village* 古樸典雅的海濱村莊 ▸ **quaint·ly** *adv.* **quaint·ness** *noun* [U]

quake /kweɪk/ *verb, noun*

■ ***verb*** **1** [I] **~ (with sth)** (of a person 人) to shake because you are very frightened or nervous（因恐懼或緊張）發抖，顫抖，哆嗦 **SYN** **tremble**：*Quaking with fear, Polly slowly opened the door.* 波利嚇得直發抖，慢慢地打開了門。**2** [I] (of the earth or a building 地面或建築物) to move or shake violently 震動；顫動：*The ground quaked as the bomb exploded.* 炸彈爆炸時，地面都震動了。

■ ***noun*** (*informal*) = EARTHQUAKE

Quaker /ˈkweɪkə(r)/ *noun* a member of the Society of Friends, a Christian religious group that meets without any formal ceremony and is strongly opposed to violence and war 貴格會教徒，公誼會教徒（屬於基督教派，廢除禮儀，反對暴力和戰爭）▶ **Quaker** *adj.*: *a Quaker school* 貴格會學校

quali·fi·ca·tion /ˌkwɒlɪfɪˈkeɪʃn; *NAmE* ˌkwɑːl-/ *noun*
1 [C, usually pl.] (*BrE*) an exam that you have passed or a course of study that you have successfully completed（通過考試或學習課程取得的）資格，學歷：***academic/educational/professional/vocational qualifications*** 學術／教育／專業／職業資歷 ◇ *a* ***nursing/teaching, etc. qualification*** 護理、教學等資格 ◇ *He left school with no* ***formal qualifications***. 他沒有獲得正式學歷就離校了。◇ *to* ***acquire/gain/get/obtain/have/hold qualifications*** 獲得／取得／得到／拿到／擁有／持有資格 ◇ *In this job, experience counts for more than* ***paper qualifications***. 擔任這項工作，經驗比文憑更重要。➲ COLLOCATIONS at EDUCATION **2** [C] a skill or type of experience that you need for a particular job or activity（通過經驗或具備技能而取得的）資格，資歷：*Previous teaching experience is a necessary qualification for this job.* 過往的教學經驗是擔任這項工作的必備條件。**3** [C, U] information that you add to a statement to limit the effect that it has or the way it is applied 限定條件 SYN **proviso**: *I accept his theories, but not without certain qualifications.* 我接受他的理論，但並非毫無保留。◇ *The plan was approved without qualification.* 這項計劃獲得無條件批准。**4** [U] the fact of passing an exam, completing a course of training or reaching the standard necessary to do a job or take part in a competition 獲得資格；合格；達到標準：*Nurses in training should be given a guarantee of employment following qualification.* 接受培訓的護士取得資格後應有工作保障。◇ *A victory in this game will earn them qualification for the World Cup.* 這場比賽的勝利將使他們取得世界杯的參賽資格。

quali·fied /ˈkwɒlɪfaɪd; *NAmE* ˈkwɑːl-/ *adj.*
1 having passed the exams or completed the training that are necessary in order to do a particular job; having the experience to do a particular job 具備…的學歷（或資歷）：*a* ***qualified accountant/teacher, etc.*** 取得執業資格的會計師、教師等 ◇ *to be* ***highly/suitably/fully qualified*** 十分／正好／完全符合資格 ◇ **~ for sth** *She's extremely* ***well qualified*** *for the job.* 她完全符合擔任這項工作的條件。**2** [not before noun] **~ (to do sth)** having the practical knowledge or skills to do sth 具備…的知識（或技能）；符合資格：*I don't know much about it, so I don't feel qualified to comment.* 關於此事我所知不多，所以覺得沒資格評論。**3** [usually before noun] (of approval, support, etc. 贊同、支持等) limited in some way 有限度的；有保留的；有條件的：*The plan was given only qualified support.* 這項計劃只得到有限度的支持。◇ *The project was only a* ***qualified success***. 這個項目只取得了一般的效益。

quali·fier /ˈkwɒlɪfaɪə(r); *NAmE* ˈkwɑːl-/ *noun* **1** a person or team that has defeated others in order to enter a particular competition（擊敗對手取得進入某競賽資格的）參賽者，參賽隊伍 **2** a game or match that a person or team has to win in order to enter a particular competition 預選賽；資格賽；外圍賽：*a World Cup qualifier* 世界杯預選賽 **3** (*grammar* 語法) a word, especially an adjective or adverb, that describes another word in a particular way 修飾詞（尤指形容詞或副詞）：*In 'the open door', 'open' is a qualifier, describing the door.* 在 the open door 中，open 是修飾詞，描述 door。

quali·fy /ˈkwɒlɪfaɪ; *NAmE* ˈkwɑːl-/ *verb* (**quali·fies, quali·fy·ing, quali·fied, quali·fied**)
▸ **FOR JOB** 工作 **1** [I] to reach the standard of ability or knowledge needed to do a particular job, for example by completing a course of study or passing exams 取得資格（或學歷）；合格：*How long does it take to qualify?* 需要多長時間才能取得資格？◇ **~ as sth** *He qualified as a doctor last year.* 他去年獲得了醫生的資格。
▸ **GIVE SKILLS/KNOWLEDGE** 傳授技能／知識 **2** [T] to give sb the skills and knowledge they need to do sth 使合格；使具備資格：**~ sb (for sth)** *This training course will qualify you for a better job.* 本培訓課程將使你能勝任更好的工作。◇ **~ sb to do sth** *The test qualifies you to drive heavy vehicles.* 通過這一考試就有資格駕駛重型車輛。
▸ **HAVE/GIVE RIGHT** 有／賦予權利 **3** [I, T] to have or give sb the right to do sth 有權，使有權（做某事）：**~ (for sth)** *If you live in the area, you qualify for a parking permit.* 你若在本地區居住，就有權領取停車許可證。◇ *To qualify, you must have lived in this country for at least three years.* 你必須在這個國家居住至少三年才能享有此權利。◇ **~ sb (for sth)** *Paying a fee doesn't automatically qualify you for membership.* 交納會費並不能使你自動成為會員。
▸ **FOR COMPETITION** 競賽 **4** [I] to be of a high enough standard to enter a competition; to defeat another person or team in order to enter or continue in a competition 達標；獲得參賽資格：*He failed to qualify.* 他未能獲得參賽資格。◇ **~ for sth** *They qualified for the World Cup.* 他們取得世界杯的參賽資格。
▸ **FIT DESCRIPTION** 名副其實 **5** [I, T] to have the right qualities to be described as a particular thing 符合，配得上（某稱號、名稱等）：**~ (as sth)** *Do you think this dress qualifies as evening wear?* 你看這連衣裙適合作晚禮服嗎？◇ **~ sth (as sth)** *It's an old building, but that doesn't qualify it as an ancient monument!* 這是一座老建築，但不足以稱為古跡。
▸ **STATEMENT** 陳述 **6** [T] **~ sth | ~ what ...** to add sth to a previous statement to make the meaning less strong or less general 使所說的話語氣減弱（或更具體等）：*I want to qualify what I said earlier—I didn't mean he couldn't do the job, only that he would need supervision.* 我想具體說明一下我原先的話，我沒有說他不能擔任這工作，只是說他需要指導。
▸ **GRAMMAR** 語法 **7** [T] **~ sth** (of a word 單詞) to describe another word in a particular way 修飾；限定：*In 'the open door', 'open' is an adjective qualifying 'door'.* 在 the open door 中，open 是修飾 door 的形容詞。

quali·ta·tive AW /ˈkwɒlɪtətɪv; *NAmE* ˈkwɑːləteɪt-/ *adj.* [usually before noun] connected with how good sth is, rather than with how much of it there is 質量的；定性的；性質的：***qualitative analysis/research*** 定性分析／研究 ◇ *There are qualitative differences between the two products.* 這兩種產品質量上有差別。➲ compare QUANTITATIVE ▶ **quali·ta·tive·ly** AW *adv.*: *qualitatively different* 性質上不同的

qual·ity /ˈkwɒləti; *NAmE* ˈkwɑːl-/ *noun, adj.*
■ *noun* (*pl.* **-ies**) **1** [U, C] the standard of sth when it is compared to other things like it; how good or bad sth is 質量；品質：*to* ***be of good/poor/top quality*** 質量好／差／上乘 ◇ *goods of a* ***high quality*** 優質商品 ◇ *high-quality goods* 優質商品 ◇ *a decline in water quality* 水質的下降 ◇ *When costs are cut product quality suffers.* 一降低成本，產品質量就會受到影響。◇ *Their* ***quality of life*** *improved dramatically when they moved to France.* 他們移居法國以後，生活質量大大提高。**2** [U] a high standard 上乘；優質；高標準 SYN **excellence**: *contemporary writers* ***of quality*** 當代的優秀作家 ◇ *We aim to provide quality at reasonable prices.* 我們的宗旨是質量上乘、價格合理。**3** [C] a thing that is part of a person's character, especially sth good（尤指好的）人品，素質，品德：***personal qualities*** *such as honesty and generosity* 誠實、寬容等個人品質 ◇ *to have* ***leadership qualities*** 具有領導素質 **4** [C, U] a feature of sth, especially one that makes it different from sth else 特徵；特質；特色：*the special quality of light and shade in her paintings* 她繪畫中的明、暗特徵 **5** [C] (*BrE*) = QUALITY NEWSPAPER
■ *adj.* **1** [only before noun] used especially by people trying to sell goods or services to say that sth is of a high quality 優質的；高質量的：*We specialize in quality furniture.* 我們專營高檔傢具。◇ *quality service at a competitive price* 質優價廉的服務 **2** (*BrE, slang*) very good 蓋帽兒了；棒極了：*'What was the film like?' 'Quality!'* "這部電影怎麼樣？" "棒極了！"

ˌquality asˈsurance *noun* [U] the practice of managing the way goods are produced or services are provided to make sure they are kept at a high standard 質量保證

ˈquality control *noun* [U] the practice of checking goods as they are being produced, to make sure that they are of a high standard 質量管理

ˌquality ˈnewspaper (also *less frequent* **qual·ity**) *noun* (*BrE*) a newspaper that is intended for people who are intelligent and educated（供有品位者閱讀的）高質量報紙 ➲ compare TABLOID *n.* (2)

ˈquality time *noun* [U] time spent giving your full attention to sb, especially to your children after work 優質時間（尤指下班後全心照顧子女等的時間）

qualm /kwɑːm; kwɔːm/ *noun* [usually pl.] **~ (about sth)** a feeling of doubt or worry about whether what you are doing is right（對自己行為的）顧慮，不安 SYN **misgiving**：*He had been working very hard so he had* ***no qualms about*** *taking a few days off.* 他一直辛勤工作，所以休息幾天他覺得心安理得。

quan·dary /ˈkwɒndəri; *NAmE* ˈkwɑːn-/ *noun* [usually sing.] (*pl.* **-ies**) the state of not being able to decide what to do in a difficult situation 困惑；進退兩難；困窘 SYN **dilemma**：*George was* ***in a quandary****—should he go or shouldn't he?* 喬治猶豫不定，拿不準是該去還是不該去。

quango /ˈkwæŋɡəʊ; *NAmE* -ɡoʊ/ *noun* (*pl.* **-os**) (often *disapproving*) (in Britain) an organization dealing with public matters, started by the government, but working independently and with its own legal powers（英國）半獨立政府機構

quanta *pl.* of QUANTUM

quan·ti·fier /ˈkwɒntɪfaɪə(r); *NAmE* ˈkwɑːn-/ *noun* (*grammar* 語法) a determiner or pronoun that expresses quantity, for example 'all' or 'both' 數量詞；數量修飾語；量詞

quan·tify /ˈkwɒntɪfaɪ; *NAmE* ˈkwɑːn-/ *verb* (**quan·ti·fies, quan·ti·fy·ing, quan·ti·fied, quan·ti·fied**) **~ sth** to describe or express sth as an amount or a number 以數量表述；量化：*The risks to health are impossible to quantify.* 健康的風險是無法用數量表示的。▸ **quan·ti·fi·able** *adj.*：*quantifiable data* 可量化的資料 **quan·ti·fi·ca·tion** /ˌkwɒntɪfɪˈkeɪʃn; *NAmE* ˌkwɑːn-/ *noun* [U]

Q

quan·ti·ta·tive /ˈkwɒntɪtətɪv; *NAmE* ˈkwɑːntəteɪt-/ *adj.* connected with the amount or number of sth rather than with how good it is 數量的；量化的；定量性的：***quantitative analysis/research*** 定量分析／研究 ◇ *There is no difference between the two in quantitative terms.* 兩者在數量上毫無差別。➲ compare QUALITATIVE ▸ **quan·ti·ta·tive·ly** *adv.*

quan·tity 0‑w /ˈkwɒntəti; *NAmE* ˈkwɑːn-/ *noun* (*pl.* **-ies**) **1** 0‑w [C, U] an amount or a number of sth 數量；數額；數目：*a* ***large/small quantity*** *of sth* 大量／小量的某物 ◇ ***enormous/vast/huge quantities*** *of food* 大量的食物 ◇ *a product that is cheap to produce* ***in large quantities*** 可以大批廉價生產的產品 ◇ *Is it available in sufficient quantity?* 這東西能不能足量供應？ **2** 0‑w [U] the measurement of sth by saying how much of it there is 量；數量：*The data is limited in terms of both quality and quantity.* 這份資料在質量和數量上都很有限。 **3** 0‑w [C, U] a large amount or number of sth 大量；大批；眾多；大宗：*The police found a quantity of drugs at his home.* 警察在他家發現了大量毒品。◇ *It's cheaper to buy goods* ***in quantity****.* 大量購物比較便宜。◇ *I was overwhelmed by the sheer quantity of information available.* 單是已有的信息量就大得令我不知所措。 IDM see UNKNOWN

ˈquantity surveyor *noun* (*BrE*) a person whose job is to calculate the quantity of materials needed for building sth, how much it will cost and how long it will take（建築）估算師，估算員

quan·tum /ˈkwɒntəm; *NAmE* ˈkwɑːn-/ *noun* (*pl.* **quanta** /-tə/) (*physics* 物) a very small quantity of ELECTROMAGNETIC energy 量子

ˌquantum ˈleap (also *less frequent* **ˌquantum ˈjump**) *noun* a sudden, great and important change, improvement or development 突變；巨變；飛躍

ˌquantum meˈchanics *noun* [U] (*physics* 物) the branch of MECHANICS that deals with movement and force in pieces of matter smaller than atoms 量子力學

ˈquantum theory *noun* [U] (*physics* 物) a theory based on the idea that energy exists in units that cannot be divided 量子論

quar·an·tine /ˈkwɒrəntiːn; *NAmE* ˈkwɔːr-/ *noun, verb*

■ ***noun*** [U] a period of time when an animal or a person that has or may have a disease is kept away from others in order to prevent the disease from spreading（為防傳染的）隔離期，檢疫：*The dog was kept* ***in quarantine*** *for six months.* 這條狗被檢疫隔離了六個月。◇ *quarantine regulations* 檢疫的規定

■ ***verb*** **~ sth/sb** to put an animal or a person into quarantine（對動物或人）進行檢疫，隔離

quark /kwɑːk; *NAmE* kwɑːrk/ *noun* **1** [C] (*physics* 物) a very small part of matter (= a substance). There are several types of quark and it is thought that PROTONS, NEUTRONS, etc. are formed from them. 夸克（據信構成質子、中子等的細小粒子） **2** [U] a type of soft cheese from central Europe, similar to CURD CHEESE 夸克乾酪；軟（質）乾酪

quar·rel /ˈkwɒrəl; *NAmE* ˈkwɔːr-; ˈkwɑːr-/ *noun, verb*

■ ***noun*** **1** [C] **~ (with sb/between A and B) (about/over sth)** an angry argument or disagreement between people, often about a personal matter 口角；爭吵；拌嘴：*a family quarrel* 家庭紛爭 ◇ *He did not mention the quarrel with his wife.* 他沒有提起和妻子的爭吵。◇ *They had a quarrel about money.* 他們為錢吵了一架。◇ *Were you at any time aware of a quarrel between the two of them?* 你有沒有察覺到他倆拌過嘴？ **2** [U] **~ (with sb/sth)** (especially in negative sentences 尤用於否定句) a reason for complaining about sb/sth or for disagreeing with sb/sth 抱怨（或不贊成）的理由：*We* ***have no quarrel with*** *his methods.* 我們沒有理由不贊成他的方法。 IDM see PICK *v.*

■ ***verb*** (**-ll-**, *US* **-l-**) [I] to have an angry argument or disagreement 爭吵；吵嘴；吵架：*My sister and I used to quarrel all the time.* 我和妹妹過去老是吵架。◇ **~ (with sb) (about/over sth)** *She quarrelled with her brother over their father's will.* 她和弟弟因父親遺囑的事起了爭執。

PHR V **ˈquarrel with sb/sth** to disagree with sb/sth 不贊同；反對：*Nobody could quarrel with your conclusions.* 你的結論無可辯駁。

quar·rel·some /ˈkwɒrəlsəm; *NAmE* ˈkwɔːr-; ˈkwɑːr-/ *adj.* (of a person 人) liking to argue with other people 愛爭吵的；好與人口角的 SYN **argumentative**

quarry /ˈkwɒri; *NAmE* ˈkwɔːri; ˈkwɑːri/ *noun, verb*

■ ***noun*** (*pl.* **-ies**) **1** [C] a place where large amounts of stone, etc. are dug out of the ground 採石場：*a slate quarry* 板岩採石廠 ◇ *the site of a disused quarry* 廢棄的採石場 ➲ compare MINE *n.* (1) **2** [sing.] an animal or a person that is being hunted or followed 被追獵的動物（或人）；追捕的對象；獵物 SYN **prey**：*The hunters lost sight of their quarry in the forest.* 獵人在森林裏看不見他們的獵物了。◇ *The photographers pursued their quarry through the streets.* 攝影師滿街捕捉拍攝對象。

■ ***verb*** (**quar·ries, quarry·ing, quar·ried, quar·ried**) [T, I] to take stone, etc. out of a quarry 從（採石場）採（石等）：**~ sth (from/out of sth)** *The local rock is quarried from the hillside.* 當地的石頭都是從那片山坡開採的。◇ **~ (for) sth** *The area is being quarried for limestone.* 這地方正在開採石灰石。▸ **quarry·ing** *noun* [U]：*There has been quarrying in the area for centuries.* 這地方的採石業已有幾百年了。

ˈquarry tile *noun* a floor TILE made from stone that has not been GLAZED（未上釉的）崗石地磚；缸磚

quart /kwɔːt; *NAmE* kwɔːrt/ *noun* (*abbr.* **qt**) a unit for measuring liquids, equal to 2 pints or about 1.14 litres in the UK and Canada, and 0.94 of a litre in the US 夸脫（液量單位，在英國和加拿大等於 2 品脫或 1.14 升，在美國等於 0.94 升）

IDM **put a quart into a pint ˈpot** (*BrE*) to put sth into a space that is too small for it 將…置於容不下之處

quar·ter 0-ᵣ /'kwɔːtə(r); *NAmE* 'kwɔːrt-/ *noun, verb*

■ ***noun***

▸ **1 OF 4 PARTS 四分之一** **1** 0-ᵣ (also **fourth** especially in *NAmE*) [C] one of four equal parts of sth 四等份之一：*a quarter of a mile* 四分之一英里 ◇ *The programme lasted an hour and a quarter.* 這個節目歷時一小時十五分鐘。◇ *Cut the apple into quarters.* 把蘋果切成四瓣。◇ *The theatre was about three quarters full.* 劇場大約坐了四分之三的人。➲ note at HALF

▸ **15 MINUTES * 15 分鐘** **2** 0-ᵣ [C] a period of 15 minutes either before or after every hour（正點之前或之後的）15 分鐘，一刻鐘：*It's (a) quarter to four now—I'll meet you at (a) quarter past.* 現在是差一刻四點，我會在四點一刻和你碰面。◇ (*NAmE* also) *It's quarter of four now—I'll meet you at quarter after.* 現在是三點四十五分，我將在四點十五分和你碰面。

▸ **3 MONTHS * 3 個月** **3** [C] a period of three months, used especially as a period for which bills are paid or a company's income is calculated 三個月時間；季度；季

▸ **PART OF TOWN 城區** **4** [C, usually sing.] a district or part of a town 城鎮的區（或一部份）：*the Latin quarter* 拉丁區 ◇ *the historic quarter of the city* 具有歷史意義的城區

▸ **PERSON/GROUP 個人；群體** **5** [C] a person or group of people, especially as a source of help, information or a reaction（尤指能提供幫助、信息或作出反應的）個人，群體：*Support for the plan came from an unexpected quarter.* 支持這一計劃的是沒料想到的一方。◇ *The news was greeted with dismay* ***in some quarters***. 有一部份人對這條消息感到泄氣。

▸ **25 CENTS * 25 分錢** **6** [C] a coin of the US and Canada worth 25 cents（美國和加拿大的）25 分硬幣

▸ **ROOMS TO LIVE IN 住房** **7** **quarters** [pl.] rooms that are provided for soldiers, servants, etc. to live in（供士兵、僕人等居住的）營房，宿舍，住房：*We were moved to more comfortable* ***living quarters***. 我們搬進了較舒適的住處。◇ ***married quarters*** 已婚軍人宿舍

▸ **OF MOON 月亮** **8** [C] the period of time twice a month when we can see a quarter of the moon 半圓的月相；上弦（或下弦）月：*The moon is in its first quarter.* 月亮正處於上弦。

▸ **IN SPORT 體育運動** **9** [C] one of the four periods of time into which a game of AMERICAN FOOTBALL is divided（美式足球的）一節，一局

▸ **WEIGHT 重量** **10** [C] (*BrE*) a unit for measuring weight, a quarter of a pound; 4 OUNCES 夸特（重量單位，¼ 磅；4 盎司）**11** [C] a unit for measuring weight, 28 pounds in the UK or 25 pounds in the US; a quarter of a HUNDREDWEIGHT 夸特（重量單位，英國為 28 磅，美國為 25 磅；四分之一英擔）

▸ **PITY 憐憫** **12** [U] (*old-fashioned* or *literary*) pity that sb shows towards an enemy or opponent who is in their power（對掌控中的敵人或對手的）慈悲，同情 **SYN** **mercy**：*His rivals knew that they could expect no quarter from such a ruthless adversary.* 他的競爭者明白，不能期望從如此殘忍的對手發善心。**IDM** see CLOSE² *adj.*

■ ***verb***

▸ **DIVIDE INTO 4 分為 4 份** **1** **~ sth** to cut or divide sth into four parts 把…切成（或分成）四部份：*She peeled and quartered an apple.* 她削去蘋果皮，把蘋果切成四瓣。

▸ **PROVIDE ROOMS 提供房間** **2** **~ sb (+ adv./prep.)** (*formal*) to provide sb with a place to eat and sleep 給…提供食宿：*The soldiers were quartered in the town.* 士兵在鎮裏宿營。

quar·ter·back /'kwɔːtəbæk; *NAmE* 'kwɔːrtərbæk/ *noun, verb*

■ ***noun*** (in AMERICAN FOOTBALL 美式足球) the player who directs the team's attacking play and passes the ball to other players at the start of each attack（指揮進攻的）四分衛，樞紐前衛

■ ***verb*** **1** [I] (in AMERICAN FOOTBALL 美式足球) to play as a quarterback 打四分衛；擔任樞紐前衛 **2** [T] **~ sth** to direct or organize sth 指揮；組織

'quarter day *noun* (*BrE*, *technical* 術語) the first day of a QUARTER (= a period of three months) on which payments must be made, for example at the STOCK EXCHANGE 季度結算日（季度的第一天，證券等的清賬日）

quar·ter·deck /'kwɔːtədek; *NAmE* 'kwɔːrtərdek/ *noun* a part of the upper level of a ship, at the back, that is used mainly by officers 上層後甲板區（主要供軍官使用）

,quarter-'final *noun* (in sports or competitions 體育運動或競賽) one of the four games or matches to decide the players or teams for the SEMI-FINALS of a competition 四分之一決賽；半準決賽

'Quarter Horse *noun* (*NAmE*) a small breed of horse that can run very fast over short distances 四分之一英里賽馬（美國一種在短距離內能疾跑的矮種馬）

quar·ter·ly /'kwɔːtəli; *NAmE* 'kwɔːrtərli/ *adj., adv., noun*

■ ***adj.*** produced or happening every three months 季度的；每季的：*a quarterly meeting of the board* 董事會的季度會議 ▸ **quar·ter·ly** *adv.*：*to pay the rent quarterly* 按季付租金

■ ***noun*** (*pl.* **-ies**) a magazine, etc. published four times a year 季刊

quar·ter·mas·ter /'kwɔːtəmɑːstə(r); *NAmE* 'kwɔːrtərmæs-/ *noun* an officer in the army who is in charge of providing food, uniforms and accommodation 軍需官；軍需主任

'quarter note (*NAmE*) (*BrE* **crot·chet**) *noun* (*music* 音) a note that lasts half as long as a MINIM/HALF NOTE 四分音符 ➲ picture at MUSIC

'quarter sessions *noun* [pl.] (in England, in the past) a court with limited powers that was held every three months（英格蘭舊時每季開庭一次的）季審法院，季審法庭

'quarter-tone *noun* (*music* 音) a quarter of a TONE on a musical SCALE, for example half of the INTERVAL (= the difference) between the notes E and F 四分音

quar·tet /kwɔː'tet; *NAmE* kwɔːr'tet/ *noun* **1** [C+sing./pl. v.] a group of four musicians or singers who play or sing together 四重奏樂團；四重唱組合：*the Amadeus Quartet* 阿瑪迪厄斯四重奏樂隊 **2** [C] a piece of music for four musicians or singers 四重奏（曲）；四重唱（曲）：*a Beethoven string quartet* 貝多芬弦樂四重奏曲 **3** [C+sing./pl. v.] a set of four people or things 四人組；四件套；四部曲：*the last in a quartet of novels* 四部曲小說的最後一部

quar·tile /'kwɔːtaɪl; *NAmE* 'kwɔːrt-; -tl/ *noun* (*statistics* 統計) one of four equal groups into which a set of things can be divided according to the DISTRIBUTION of a particular VARIABLE 四分位數；四分位值：*women in the fourth quartile of height* (= the shortest 25% of women) 身高在第四個四分位值的婦女（即最矮的 25% 婦女）➲ compare QUINTILE

quarto /'kwɔːtəʊ; *NAmE* 'kwɔːrtoʊ/ *noun* (*pl.* **-os**) (*technical* 術語) **1** [U] a size of page made by folding a standard sheet of paper twice to make eight pages 四開（標準印張的四分之一大小）**2** [C] a book with pages in quarto size 四開本圖書

quartz /kwɔːts; *NAmE* kwɔːrts/ *noun* [U] a hard mineral, often in CRYSTAL form, that is used to make very accurate clocks and watches 石英

qua·sar /'kweɪzɑː(r)/ *noun* (*astronomy* 天) a large object like a star, that is far away and that shines very brightly and occasionally sends out strong radio signals 類星體 ➲ compare PULSAR

quash /kwɒʃ; *NAmE* kwɔːʃ; kwɑːʃ/ *verb* **1** **~ sth** (*BrE*, *law* 律) to officially say that a decision made by a court is no longer valid or correct 宣佈（法庭的裁決）無效；撤銷（判決）**SYN** **overturn**：*His conviction was later quashed by the Court of Appeal.* 後來，上訴法院撤銷了對他的判決。**2** **~ sth** to take action to stop sth from continuing 制止；阻止；平息 **SYN** **suppress**：*The rumours were quickly quashed.* 流言很快被制止了。

quasi- /'kweɪzaɪ; -saɪ; 'kwɑːzi/ *combining form* (in adjectives and nouns 構成形容詞和名詞) **1** that appears to be sth but is not really so 類似：*a quasi-scientific explanation* 類似科學的解釋 **2** partly; almost 半；準：*a quasi-official body* 半官方機構

Q

quat·er·cen·ten·ary /ˌkwætəsenˈtiːnəri; NAmE -tərsenˈteneri/ *noun* (*pl.* **-ies**) a 400th anniversary * 400 週年紀念： *to celebrate the quatercentenary of Shakespeare's birth* 慶祝莎士比亞誕辰 400 週年

quat·rain /ˈkwɒtreɪn; NAmE ˈkwɑːt-/ *noun* (*technical* 術語) a poem or VERSE of a poem that has four lines 四行詩；四行的詩節

qua·ver /ˈkweɪvə(r)/ *verb, noun*

■ ***verb*** [I, T] (+ **speech**) if sb's voice **quavers**, it is unsteady, usually because the person is nervous or afraid（嗓音因緊張或害怕等）顫抖，顫動： *'I'm not safe here, am I?' she asked in a quavering voice.* "我在這裏不安全吧？" 她用顫抖的聲音問道。 ▸ **qua·very** /ˈkweɪvəri/ *adj.*： *a quavery voice* 顫抖的嗓音

■ ***noun*** **1** (*BrE*) (*NAmE* **ˈeighth note**) (*music* 音) a note that lasts half as long as a CROTCHET/QUARTER NOTE 八分音符 ➲ picture at MUSIC **2** [usually sing.] a shaking sound in sb's voice 顫抖的嗓音

quay /kiː/ *noun* a platform in a HARBOUR where boats come in to load, etc. 碼頭；埠頭： *A crowd was waiting on the quay.* 有一群人在碼頭上等着。 ➲ VISUAL VOCAB page V5

quay·side /ˈkiːsaɪd/ *noun* [usually sing.] a quay and the area near it 碼頭邊： *crowds waiting **on/at the quayside** to welcome them* 等在碼頭邊歡迎他們的人群

queasy /ˈkwiːzi/ *adj.* **1** feeling sick; wanting to VOMIT 惡心的；欲吐的 SYN **nauseous** **2** slightly nervous or worried about sth 稍感緊張的；略有不安的；心神不定的 ▸ **queas·ily** *adv.* **queasi·ness** *noun* [U]

Que·chua /ˈketʃwə/ *noun* [U] a language originally spoken by the Quechua people of S America, now spoken in Peru, Bolivia, Chile, Colombia and Ecuador 克丘亞語，奇楚瓦語（原為南美克丘亞人的語言，現在秘魯、玻利維亞、智利、哥倫比亞和厄瓜多爾使用）

queen 🔑 /kwiːn/ *noun*

▸ FEMALE RULER 女統治者 **1** 🔑 the female ruler of an independent state that has a royal family 女王；女酋長；女首領： ***to be crowned queen*** 加冕為女王 ◇ *kings and queens* 國王和女王 ◇ *the Queen of Norway* 挪威女王 ◇ *Queen Victoria* 維多利亞女王 **2** 🔑 (also **ˌqueen ˈconsort**) the wife of a king 王后

▸ BEST IN GROUP 出類拔萃 **3 ~ (of sth)** a woman, place or thing that is thought to be one of the best in a particular group or area（某領域的）王后，精髓，精華：*the queen of fashion* 時裝之最 ◇ *a movie queen* 影后 ◇ *Venice, queen of the Adriatic* 威尼斯，亞得里亞海的明珠

▸ AT FESTIVAL 節日 **4** a woman or girl chosen to perform official duties at a festival or celebration（節日或慶典活動中當選的）履行職責的女子： *a carnival queen* 狂歡節小姐 ◇ *a May queen* (= at a festival to celebrate the coming of spring) 五朔節王后 ◇ *a homecoming queen* 返校節王后 ➲ see also BEAUTY QUEEN

▸ IN CHESS 國際象棋 **5** the most powerful piece used in the game of CHESS that can move any number of squares in any direction 后 ➲ VISUAL VOCAB page V38

▸ IN CARDS 紙牌 **6** a PLAYING CARD with the picture of a queen on it 王后（牌） ➲ VISUAL VOCAB page V37

▸ INSECT 昆蟲 **7** a large female insect that lays eggs for the whole group（為群體產卵的）雌性昆蟲，王；后： *a queen bee* 蜂王

▸ HOMOSEXUAL 同性戀 **8** (*informal, taboo*) an offensive word for a male HOMOSEXUAL who behaves like a woman（女性化的男同性戀者貶稱）王后，假娘兒們

IDM see EVIDENCE, UNCROWNED

ˌqueen ˈbee *noun* **1** a female BEE that produces eggs for the whole group of bees in a HIVE 蜂王；后蜂 ➲ compare DRONE *n.* (3), WORKER (4) **2** a woman who behaves as if she is the most important person in a particular place or group 女強人；大姐大

queen·ly /ˈkwiːnli/ *adj.* of, like or suitable for a queen 女王的；似女王的；適於女王的

ˌqueen ˈmother *noun* a title given to the wife of a king who has died and who is the mother of the new king or queen 太后；皇太后；王太后： *Queen Elizabeth, the Queen Mother* 王太后伊麗莎白女王

ˌQueen's ˈBench (also **ˌQueen's ˈBench Division**) *noun* [sing.] part of the UK High Court（英國高等法院的）（女）王座法庭

Queens·berry Rules /ˌkwiːnzbəri ˈruːlz; NAmE -beri/ *noun* [pl.] **1** the standard rules of BOXING 昆斯伯里規則（拳擊比賽的標準規則） **2** the rules of polite and acceptable behaviour 禮貌行為準則

ˌQueen's ˈCounsel *noun* = QC

the ˌQueen's ˈEnglish *noun* [U] (*old-fashioned*) the English language as written and spoken correctly by educated people in the UK 標準英語；規範英語 HELP 'The Queen's English' is used when the United Kingdom has a queen, and 'the King's English' when it has a king. 英國女王在位時用 the Queen's English，國王在位時用 the King's English。

ˌQueen's ˈevidence *noun* [U] (*BrE*) if a criminal **turns Queen's evidence**, he or she gives evidence against the people who committed a crime with him or her（刑事被告向法庭提供的）對同案犯不利的證據

ˈqueen-size (also **ˈqueen-sized**) *adj.* (*NAmE*) (of beds, sheets, etc. 牀、牀單等) larger than a standard size but not as big as KING-SIZE 次特大號的；大號的

the ˌQueen's ˈSpeech *noun* [sing.] in the UK, a statement read by the Queen at the start of a new Parliament, which contains details of the government's plans 女王施政演說（英國新一屆議會開始時由女王宣讀，內容包括政府施政詳情）

queer /kwɪə(r); NAmE kwɪr/ *adj., noun, verb*

■ ***adj.*** (**queer·er, queer·est**) **1** (*old-fashioned*) strange or unusual 奇怪的；反常的 SYN **odd**： *His face was a queer pink colour.* 他滿臉奇怪的粉紅色。 **2** (*taboo, slang*) an offensive way of describing a HOMOSEXUAL, especially a man, which is, however, also used by some homosexuals about themselves 娘兒們似的；妖裏妖氣的 IDM see AN ODD/A QUEER FISH at FISH *n.*

■ ***noun*** (*taboo, slang*) an offensive word for a HOMOSEXUAL, especially a man, which is, however, also used by some homosexuals about themselves 同性戀者；假娘兒們；賽妖婆

■ ***verb***

IDM **queer sb's ˈpitch | queer the ˈpitch (for sb)** (*BrE, informal*) to spoil sb's plans or their chances of getting sth 破壞…的計劃（或機會）

queer·ly /ˈkwɪəli; NAmE ˈkwɪrli/ *adv.* in a strange or unusual way 奇怪地；反常地： *He looked at me queerly.* 他異樣地望着我。

quell /kwel/ *verb* (*formal*) **1 ~ sth/sb** to stop sth such as violent behaviour or protests 制止；平息；鎮壓： *Extra police were called in to quell the disturbances.* 已調集了增援警力來平定騷亂。 ◇ (*figurative*) *She started to giggle, but Bob quelled her with a look.* 她格格地笑了起來，但鮑勃用眼色制止了她。 **2 ~ sth** to stop or reduce strong or unpleasant feelings 消除；緩解，減輕（強烈或不快的感情） SYN **calm**： *to quell your fears* 消除恐懼

quench /kwentʃ/ *verb* **1 ~ your thirst** to drink so that you no longer feel thirsty 解（渴）；止（渴） SYN **slake** **2 ~ sth** (*formal*) to stop a fire from burning 撲滅；熄滅 SYN **extinguish**： *Firemen tried to quench the flames raging through the building.* 消防隊員奮力撲救大樓中熊熊的火焰。

queru·lous /ˈkwerələs; -rjə-/ *adj.* (*formal, disapproving*) complaining; showing that you are annoyed 抱怨的；顯得惱怒的 SYN **peevish** ▸ **queru·lous·ly** *adv.*

query /ˈkwɪəri; NAmE ˈkwɪri/ *noun, verb*

■ ***noun*** (*pl.* **-ies**) **1** a question, especially one asking for information or expressing a doubt about sth 疑問；詢問： *Our assistants will be happy to answer your queries.* 我們的助理很樂意回答諸位的問題。 ◇ *If you have a query about your insurance policy, contact our helpline.* 若對保險單有疑問，請撥打我們的咨詢熱線。 **2** a question mark to show that sth has not been finished or decided 問號： *Put a query against Jack's name—I'm not sure if he's coming.* 在傑克的名字旁邊打個問號，我不確定他是否會來。

■ *verb* (**quer·ies**, **query·ing**, **quer·ied**, **quer·ied**) **1 ~ sth | ~ what, whether, etc. ...** to express doubt about whether sth is correct or not 懷疑；表示疑慮：*We queried the bill as it seemed far too high.* 賬單上的費用似乎太高了，我們對此表示懷疑。◇ *I'm not in a position to query their decision.* 我無權懷疑他們的決定。 **2 + speech** to ask a question 詢問：*'Who will be leading the team?' queried Simon.* "由誰當隊長呢？"西蒙問道。

'query language *noun* [C, U] (*computing* 計) a system of words and symbols that you type in order to ask a computer to give you information 查詢語言

quest /kwest/ *noun, verb*

■ *noun* **~ (for sth)** (*formal* or *literary*) a long search for sth, especially for some quality such as happiness 探索，尋找，追求（幸福等）：*the quest for happiness/knowledge/truth* 對幸福 / 知識 / 真理的追求 ◇ *He set off* ***in quest of*** *adventure.* 他出行探險去了。

■ *verb* [I] **~ (for sth)** (*formal* or *literary*) to search for sth that is difficult to find 探索；探求

ques·tion 🔑 /'kwestʃən/ *noun, verb*

■ *noun* **1** 🔑 [C] a sentence, phrase or word that asks for information 問題；疑問：*to* ***ask/answer a question*** 提出 / 回答問題 ◇ ***The question is,*** *how much are they going to pay you?* 問題是，他們打算付給你多少錢？◇ (*formal*) ***The question arises*** *as to whether or not he knew of the situation.* 問題是，他對局勢是否瞭解。◇ *The key question of what caused the leak remains unanswered.* 泄漏究竟是怎麼造成的，這一關鍵問題仍未得到答案。◇ (*formal*) *He* ***put a question to*** *the minister about the recent reforms.* 他就最近的改革措施向部長提了一個問題。◇ *I hope the police don't ask any* ***awkward questions.*** 我希望警方不要提出難應付的問題。◇ *In an interview try to ask* ***open questions*** *that don't just need 'Yes' or 'No' as an answer.* 在面試中要盡量問易於發揮的問題，不要讓對方回答"是"或"否"便了事。 **2** 🔑 [C] a task or request for information that is intended to test your knowledge or understanding, for example in an exam or a competition 考題；試題：*Question 3 was very difficult.* 第 3 題難極了。◇ *In the exam there's sure to be* ***a question on*** *energy.* 考試時準有關於能量的題目。 **3** 🔑 [C] **~ (of sth)** a matter or topic that needs to be discussed or dealt with（待討論或處理的）事情，議題，課題：*Let's look at the question of security.* 咱們來看一下保安問題。◇ *The question which needs to be addressed is one of funding.* 需要面對的是資金問題。◇ *Which route is better remains* ***an open question*** (= it is not decided). 哪條路線較好還沒有定論。 **4** [U] doubt or confusion about sth 懷疑；困惑：*Her honesty is* ***beyond question.*** 她的誠實是毋庸置疑的。◇ *His suitability for the job is* ***open to question.*** 他是否適合擔任這工作還需要考慮。◇ *Her version of events was accepted* ***without question.*** 她對事情的陳述沒有受到任何質疑就被接受了。

IDM **bring/throw sth into 'question** to cause sth to become a matter for doubt and discussion 引起有關…的懷疑（或議論）：*This case brings into question the whole purpose of the law.* 這宗案件引起了對整個法律宗旨的懷疑。 **come into 'question** to become a matter for doubt and discussion 成為懷疑（或討論）的對象 **,good 'question!** (*informal*) used to show that you do not know the answer to a question（表示不知道答案）問得好：*'How much is all this going to cost?' 'Good question!'* "這一切得花多少錢？""問得好！" **in 'question 1** 🔑 that is being discussed 討論（或議論）中的：*On the day in question we were in Cardiff.* 在所說的那一天，我們在加的夫。 **2** 🔑 in doubt; uncertain 有疑問；不確定：*The future of public transport is not in question.* 公共交通的未來發展是不容置疑的。 **just/merely/only a question of (sth/doing sth)** 🔑 used to say that sth is not difficult to predict, explain, do, etc. 只不過是…的問題（指不難預料、解釋、做等的事情）：*It's merely a question of time before the business collapses.* 這家企業的倒閉只是時間問題。◇ *It's just a question of deciding what you really want.* 那只是個確定你真正想要什麼的問題。 **out of the 'question** 🔑 impossible or not allowed and therefore not worth discussing 不可能；不允許；不值得討論：*Another trip abroad this year is out of the question.* 今年再度出國是絕無可能的。 **there is/was no question of (sth happening/sb doing sth)** 🔑 there is/was no possibility of sth（某事）是不可能的：*There was no question of his/him cancelling the trip so near the departure date.* 離出發日期這麼近，他不可能取消行程。 ➲ more at BEG, CALL *v.*, MOOT *adj.*, POP *v.*

■ *verb* **1** 🔑 **~ sb (about/on sth) | + speech** to ask sb questions about sth, especially officially 正式提問；質詢；問：*She was arrested and questioned about the fire.* 她被拘留訊問有關火災的事情。◇ *The students were questioned on the books they had been studying.* 學生被問到有關他們所學課本內容的問題。◇ *Over half of those questioned said they rarely took any exercise.* 被問到的人有一半以上說他們很少鍛煉身體。 **2** 🔑 to have or express doubts or suspicions about sth 表示疑問；懷疑：**~ sth** *I just accepted what he told me. I never thought to question it.* 他說什麼我就相信什麼。我從未想過要去懷疑它。◇ *No one has ever questioned her judgement.* 對她的判斷從沒有人表示過懷疑。◇ **~ whether, what, etc. ...** *He questioned whether the accident was solely the truck driver's fault.* 他懷疑事故是否應把責任全歸咎於卡車司機一個人。

ques·tion·able /'kwestʃənəbl/ *adj.* **1** that you have doubts about because you think it is not accurate or correct 可疑的；有問題的；未必準確（或正確）的 SYN **debatable**：*The conclusions that they come to are highly questionable.* 他們得出的結論大有問題。◇ ***It is questionable whether*** *this is a good way of solving the problem.* 這未必是一個解決問題的好辦法。 **2** likely to be dishonest or morally wrong 可能不誠實（或不道德）的；別有用心的 SYN **suspect**：*Her motives for helping are questionable.* 她幫忙的動機令人生疑。 ▶ **ques·tion·ably** /-əbli/ *adv.*

ques·tion·er /'kwestʃənə(r)/ *noun* a person who asks questions, especially in a broadcast programme or a public debate（廣播節目或公開辯論等的）提問人

ques·tion·ing /'kwestʃənɪŋ/ *noun, adj.*

■ *noun* [U] the activity of asking sb questions 提問；詢問；盤問：*He was taken to the police station for questioning.* 他被帶到警察局盤問。◇ *They faced some hostile questioning over the cost of the project.* 關於這個項目的費用，他們面臨着咄咄逼人的盤問。

■ *adj.* showing that you need information, or that you have doubts 詢問的；表示懷疑的：*a questioning look* 懷疑的目光 ◇ *She raised a questioning eyebrow.* 她懷疑地皺起眉頭。 ▶ **ques·tion·ing·ly** *adv.*

'question mark *noun* the mark (?) used in writing after a question 問號

IDM **a 'question mark over/against sth** used to say that sth is not certain 對…的疑問；畫在…上的問號：*There's still a big question mark hanging over his future with the team.* 他在隊中的前途還是個大問號。

'question master (also **quiz·master**) *noun* (both *BrE*) a person who asks the questions in a QUIZ, especially on television or the radio（問答比賽的）提問者；問答節目主持人

ques·tion·naire /,kwestʃə'neə(r); *NAmE* -'ner/ *noun* **~ (on/about sth)** a written list of questions that are answered by a number of people so that information can be collected from the answers 調查表；問卷：*to complete a questionnaire* 填好問卷 ◇ (*BrE*) *to fill in a questionnaire* 填調查表 ◇ (*especially NAmE*) *to fill out a questionnaire* 填調查表

'question tag (also **'tag question**) *noun* (*grammar* 語法) a phrase such as *isn't it?* or *don't you?* that you add to the end of a statement in order to turn it into a question or check that the statement is correct, as in *You like mushrooms, don't you?* 附加疑問成分，反意疑問成分（綴於陳述句之後，以將其變為問句或核實原句的正確性）

queue /kjuː/ *noun, verb*

■ *noun* **1** (*BrE*) (*NAmE* **line**) a line of people, cars, etc. waiting for sth or to do sth（人、汽車等的）隊，行列：*the bus queue* 排隊等候公共汽車的人 ◇ *I had to join a queue for the toilets.* 我只得排隊等着上廁所。◇ *How long were you* ***in the queue?*** 你排多長時間隊了？◇ *There was a queue of traffic waiting to turn right.* 有一長列車輛等着右轉彎。 ➲ COLLOCATIONS at SHOPPING **2** (*computing*

Q

計) a list of items of data stored in a particular order (貯存的數據)隊列 **IDM** see JUMP *v.*

■ ***verb*** (**queu·ing** or **queue·ing**) **1** [I] (*BrE*) **~ (up)** (**for sth**) to wait in a line of people, vehicles, etc. in order to do sth, get sth or go somewhere (人、車等)排隊等候：*We had to queue up for an hour for the tickets.* 我們只得排一個小時的隊買票。◇ *Queue here for taxis.* 等出租車在這裏排隊。**2** [T, I] **~ (sth)** (*computing* 計) to add tasks to other tasks so that they are ready to be done in order; to come together to be done in order (使)排隊；列隊等待：*The system queues the jobs before they are processed.* 這系統先把任務排列再進行處理。

PHR V **be ˌqueuing ˈup (for sth/to do sth)** if people are said to be **queuing up** for sth or to do sth, a lot of them want to have it or do it 排長隊等待；趨之若鶩：*Italian football clubs are queuing up to sign the young star.* 意大利的足球俱樂部都搶着要與這個年輕球星簽約。

ˈqueue-jumping *noun* [U] (*BrE*) a situation in which a person moves to the front of a queue to get served before other people who have been waiting longer 插隊；加塞

quib·ble /ˈkwɪbl/ *verb, noun*

■ ***verb*** [I] **~ (about/over sth)** to argue or complain about a small matter or an unimportant detail (為小事)爭論，發牢騷；斤斤計較；吹毛求疵：*It isn't worth quibbling over such a small amount.* 不值得為這樣的小數目斤斤計較。

■ ***noun*** a small complaint or criticism, especially one that is not important (無足輕重的)抱怨，牢騷，小意見：*minor quibbles* 小牢騷

quiche /kiːʃ/ *noun* [C, U] an open PIE filled with a mixture of eggs and milk with meat, vegetables, cheese, etc. (以蛋、奶和肉、蔬菜、乾酪做餡的)開口餡餅 ➲ compare FLAN *n.* (1), TART *n.* (1)

quick 🔑 /kwɪk/ *adj., adv., noun*

■ ***adj.*** (**quick·er**, **quick·est**) **1** 🔑 done with speed; taking or lasting a short time 快的；迅速的；時間短暫的：*She gave him a quick glance.* 她迅速掃了他一眼。◇ *These cakes are very quick and easy to make.* 這些糕餅做起來又快又簡單。◇ *Would you like a quick drink?* 你要不要小飲一杯？◇ *The doctor said she'd make a quick recovery.* 醫生說她很快就能康復。◇ *It's quicker by train.* 坐火車比較快。◇ *Are you sure this is the quickest way?* 你確信這是最快捷的方法嗎？◇ *Have you finished already? That was quick!* 你已經做完了？真快呀！◇ *His quick thinking saved her life.* 他敏捷的思考救了她一命。◇ *He fired three shots **in quick succession**.* 他瞬間連發三槍。➲ see also DOUBLE QUICK **2** 🔑 moving or doing sth fast 敏捷的；迅速的：*a quick learner* 學習得快的人 ◇ **~ (to do sth)** *The kids were quick to learn.* 那些孩子學東西很快。◇ *She was quick* (= too quick) *to point out the mistakes I'd made.* 她總迫不及待地挑我的錯。◇ *Her quick hands suddenly stopped moving.* 她敏捷的雙手突然停下不動了。◇ *Try to **be quick**! We're late already.* 你盡量快點！我們已經晚了。◇ *Once again, his **quick wits*** (= quick thinking) *got him out of an awkward situation.* 他的急智使他再次擺脫了窘境。◇ (*NAmE, informal*) *He's a **quick study*** (= he learns quickly). 他學東西特別快。**3** 🔑 [only before noun] happening very soon or without delay 迅速的；立竿見影的：*We need to make a quick decision.* 我們需要當機立斷。◇ *The company wants quick results.* 這公司要立竿見影的成果。➲ **SYNONYMS** at FAST

IDM **to have a quick ˈtemper** to become angry easily 性子急；容易發脾氣 **ˌquick and ˈdirty** (*informal*) used to describe sth that is usually complicated, but is being done quickly and simply in this case 權宜處理；機動安排：*Read our quick-and-dirty guide to creating a website.* 閱讀一下我們的建立網站便捷指南。➲ more at BUCK *n.*, DRAW *n.*, MARK *n.*, UPTAKE

■ ***adv.*** (**quick·er**, **quick·est**) **1** quickly; fast 迅速地；快速地：*Come as quick as you can!* 你儘快過來吧！◇ *Let's see who can get there quickest.* 咱們看看誰最先到達。◇ *It's another of his schemes to **get rich quick**.* 那是他迅速致富的另一種計謀。**2** **quick-** (in adjectives 構成形容詞) doing the thing mentioned quickly 敏捷的；迅速的：*quick-thinking* 才思敏捷的 ◇ *quick-growing* 生長迅速的

IDM **(as) quick as a ˈflash** very quickly 極快；神速；旋即：*Quick as a flash she was at his side.* 她旋即來到他身邊。

■ ***noun*** **the quick** [sing.] the soft, sensitive flesh that is under your nails (指甲下的)活肉：*She has bitten her nails down to the quick.* 她咬指甲都咬到了活肉。

IDM **cut sb to the ˈquick** to upset sb very much by doing or saying sth unkind (以惡意的言行)深深傷害別人，把…傷害到家

Which Word? 詞語辨析

quick / quickly / fast

- **Quickly** is the usual adverb from **quick**. * quickly 為源自 quick 的常用副詞：*I quickly realized that I was on the wrong train.* 我很快意識到我坐錯了火車。◇ *My heart started to beat more quickly.* 我的心開始跳得快起來。
- **Quick** is sometimes used as an adverb in very informal language, especially as an exclamation. 在日常用語中，quick 有時用作副詞，尤作感歎語：*Come on! Quick! They'll see us!* 快點吧！快！他們會看見我們的！ **Quicker** is used more often. * quicker 更常用：*My heart started to beat much quicker.* 我的心開始跳得快了很多。◇ *The quicker I get you away from here, the better.* 我越快送你離開此地越好。
- **Fast** is more often used when you are talking about the speed that somebody or something moves at. 指某人或某物移動的速度多用 fast：*How fast can a cheetah run?* 獵豹奔跑的速度有多快？◇ *Can't you drive any faster?* 你難道不能開快點兒？◇ ~~*You're driving too quickly.*~~ There is no word **fastly**. 沒有 fastly 這個詞。

quick·en /ˈkwɪkən/ *verb* (*formal*) **1** [I, T] to become quicker or make sth quicker (使)加快，加速：*She felt her heartbeat quicken as he approached.* 隨着他的走近，她覺得自己的心跳加速了。◇ **~ sth** *He quickened his pace to catch up with them.* 他加快腳步趕上他們。**2** [I, T] **~ (sth)** to become more active; to make sth more active 變得更活躍；使更活躍：*His interest quickened as he heard more about the plan.* 他越聽這個計劃越覺得感興趣。

ˌquick-ˈfire *adj.* [only before noun] (of a series of things 一系列) done or said very fast, one after the other 一個接一個的；連珠炮似的：*a series of quick-fire questions* 一連串連珠炮似的問題

quickie /ˈkwɪki/ *noun* (*informal*) **1** a thing that only takes a short time 簡短的事；短暫的事：*I've got a question—it's just a quickie.* 我有個問題，一個簡短的問題。◇ *a quickie divorce* 神速的離婚 **2** a sexual act that takes a very short time 瞬間完事的性交

quick·lime /ˈkwɪklaɪm/ *noun* [U] = LIME (1)

quick·ly 🔑 /ˈkwɪkli/ *adv.*

1 🔑 fast 迅速地；很快地：*She walked quickly away.* 她迅速走開了。◇ *We'll repair it as quickly as possible.* 我們會儘快把它修好的。◇ *The last few weeks have **gone quickly*** (= the time seems to have passed quickly). 最近的幾個星期過得很快。**2** 🔑 soon; after a short time 不久；立即：*He replied to my letter very quickly.* 他立即答覆了我的信。◇ *It quickly became clear that she was dying.* 很快就看得出她當時已生命垂危。➲ note at QUICK

quick·ness /ˈkwɪknəs/ *noun* [U] the quality of being fast, especially at thinking, etc. 機智；機敏；敏捷：*She was known for the quickness of her wit.* 她以頭腦靈活見稱。◇ *He amazes me with his quickness and eagerness to learn.* 他敏思好學，令我驚訝。

ˈquick one *noun* (*BrE, informal*) a drink, usually an alcoholic one, taken quickly 一飲而盡的飲料(通常指酒)；小酌

quick·sand /ˈkwɪksænd/ *noun* [U] (also **quicksands** [pl.]) **1** deep wet sand that you sink into if you walk on it 流沙

2 a situation that is dangerous or difficult to escape from 難以擺脫的困境；危險局面

quick·sil·ver /ˈkwɪksɪlvə(r)/ *noun, adj.*
■ ***noun*** [U] (*old use*) = MERCURY
■ ***adj.*** [only before noun] (*literary*) changing or moving very quickly 變化（或移動）極快的；瞬息萬變的：*his quicksilver temperament* 他那喜怒無常的性情

quick·step /ˈkwɪkstep/ *noun* a dance for two people together, with a lot of fast steps; a piece of music for this dance 雙人快步舞；雙人快步舞曲

ˌquick-ˈtempered *adj.* likely to become angry very quickly 火爆脾氣的；急性子的：*a quick-tempered woman* 急性子的女人

ˌquick-ˈwitted *adj.* able to think quickly; intelligent 聰穎的；機敏的；機智的：*a quick-witted student/response* 機敏的學生／反應 OPP **slow-witted**

quid /kwɪd/ *noun* (*pl.* **quid**) (*BrE, informal*) one pound in money 一英鎊：*Can you lend me five quid?* 你借給我五英鎊行嗎？
IDM **not the full ˈquid** (*AustralE, NZE, informal*) not very intelligent 不聰明；悟性差 **quids ˈin** in a position of having made a profit, especially a good profit 獲得利潤；獲厚利

quid pro quo /ˌkwɪd prəʊ ˈkwəʊ; *NAmE* proʊ ˈkwoʊ/ *noun* [sing.] (from *Latin*) a thing given in return for sth else 報償；回報

qui·es·cent /kwiˈesnt/ *adj.* **1** (*formal*) quiet; not active 沉寂的；靜態的 **2** (*medical* 醫) (of a disease, etc. 疾病等) not developing, especially when this is probably only a temporary state 靜止狀態的 SYN **dormant** ▸ **qui·es·cence** /-sns/ *noun* [U]

quiet 0ᵛ /ˈkwaɪət/ *adj., noun, verb*
■ ***adj.*** (**quiet·er, quiet·est**) **1** 0ᵛ making very little noise 輕聲的；輕柔的；安靜的：*her quiet voice* 她那輕柔的聲音 ◇ *a quieter, more efficient engine* 一台聲音更小、效率更高的發動機 ◇ *Could you keep the kids quiet while I'm on the phone?* 我在打電話，你讓孩子們安靜點好嗎？◇ *He **went** very **quiet** (= did not say much) so I knew he was upset.* 他沉默不語了，所以我知道他很煩惱。◇ *'**Be quiet,**' said the teacher.* "安靜點！"老師說道。◇ *She crept downstairs **(as) quiet as a mouse**.* 她躡手躡腳，悄聲下了樓。 **2** 0ᵛ without many people or much noise or activity 僻靜的；寂靜的；清靜的：*a quiet street* 寂靜的街道 ◇ *They lead a quiet life.* 他們過着平靜的生活。◇ *Business is usually quieter at this time of year.* 每年這個時節，生意往往比較清淡。◇ *They had a quiet wedding.* 他們舉行了不事鋪張的婚禮。 **3** 0ᵛ not disturbed; peaceful 清靜的；平靜的；恬靜的：*to have a quiet drink* 悠閒地飲酒 ◇ *I was looking forward to a quiet evening at home.* 我盼着在家過個恬靜的夜晚。 **4** 0ᵛ (of a person 人) tending not to talk very much 寡言少語的；文靜的：*She was quiet and shy.* 她文靜而又靦腆。 **5** (of a feeling or an attitude 感情或態度) definite but not expressed in an obvious way 克制的；穩重的；不張揚的：*He had an air of quiet authority.* 他神態威嚴穩重。 ▸ **quiet·ly** 0ᵛ *adv.*：*to speak/move quietly* 輕輕地說話／移動 ◇ *I spent a few hours quietly relaxing.* 我怡然自得地輕鬆了幾個小時。◇ *He is **quietly confident** that they can succeed (= he is confident, but he is not talking about it too much).* 他心裏相信他們能成功。◇ *a **quietly-spoken** woman* 話語輕柔的女人 **quiet·ness** *noun* [U]：*the quietness of the countryside* 鄉村的恬靜 ◇ *His quietness worried her.* 他的沉默不語令她不安。
IDM **keep quiet about sth | keep sth quiet** 0ᵛ to say nothing about sth; to keep sth secret 對…守口如瓶；不聲張；保密：*I've decided to resign but I'd rather you kept quiet about it.* 我已決定辭職，但希望你不要聲張出去。
■ ***noun*** [U] the state of being calm and without much noise 寧靜；寂靜；平靜；安靜：*the quiet of his own room* 他自己房間的寧靜 ◇ *the quiet of the early morning* 清晨的寂靜 ◇ *I go to the library for a little **peace and quiet**.* 我到圖書館去清靜一下。
IDM **on the ˈquiet** without telling anyone 悄悄地 SYN **secretly**
■ ***verb*** [I, T] (*especially NAmE*) to become calmer or less noisy; to make sb/sth calmer or less noisy（使）平靜，安靜 SYN **calm (sb) down**：**~ (down)** *The demonstrators quieted down when the police arrived.* 警察一到示威者便安靜了下來。◇ **~ sb/sth (down)** *He's very good at quieting the kids.* 他很懂得如何讓孩子們安靜下來。

quiet·en /ˈkwaɪətn/ *verb* [I, T] **~ (sb/sth) (down)** (*BrE*) to become calmer or less noisy; to make sb/sth calmer or less noisy（使）安靜下來，平靜些：*The chatter of voices gradually quietened.* 唧唧喳喳的聲音漸漸地平靜了。◇ *Things seem to have quietened down a bit this afternoon* (= we are not so busy, etc.). 今天下午，事情似乎平靜些了。

quiet·ism /ˈkwaɪətɪzəm/ *noun* [U] (*formal*) an attitude to life which makes you calmly accept things as they are rather than try to change them 淡泊；無為沉靜；安之若素 ▸ **quiet·ist** /-ɪst/ *noun, adj.*

quiet·ude /ˈkwaɪətjuːd; *NAmE* -tuːd/ *noun* [U] (*literary*) the state of being still and quiet 平靜；寂靜；寧靜；靜謐 SYN **calm**

quie·tus /kwaɪˈiːtəs/ *noun* [C, U] (*literary*) **1** death, or sth that causes death, considered as a welcome end to life 寂滅，解脫（指人生的完結或讓人生得以完結的事物） **2** something that makes a person or situation calm 有平靜（或緩解）作用的東西

quiff /kwɪf/ *noun* (*especially BrE*) a piece of hair at the front of the head that is brushed upwards and backwards 額髮（額前向上梳的一綹頭髮）

quill /kwɪl/ *noun* **1** (also **ˈquill feather**) a large feather from the wing or tail of a bird 翎（鳥的翅膀或尾部的大羽毛） **2** (also **ˌquill ˈpen**) a pen made from a quill feather 翎筆；羽管筆 **3** one of the long sharp stiff SPINES on a PORCUPINE（豪豬的）棘刺

quilt /kwɪlt/ *noun* **1** a decorative cover for a bed, made of two layers with soft material between them 加襯芯牀罩：*a patchwork quilt* 拼縫牀罩 ➲ VISUAL VOCAB page V23 **2** (*BrE*) = DUVET ➲ compare COMFORTER (2)

quilt·ed /ˈkwɪltɪd/ *adj.* (of clothes, etc. 衣服等) made of two layers of cloth with soft material between them, held in place by lines of STITCHES 絮棉的；加襯芯的：*a quilted jacket* 棉襖

quilt·ing /ˈkwɪltɪŋ/ *noun* [U] the work of making a QUILT; cloth that is used for this（被子的）絎縫，衲縫；被褥料

quin /kwɪn/ *noun* (*BrE, informal*) = QUINTUPLET

quince /kwɪns/ *noun* a hard bitter yellow fruit used for making jam, etc. It grows on a tree, also called a quince. 榲桲（果實金黃有澀味，可製果醬）：*quince jelly* 榲桲果凍 ◇ *a flowering quince* 開花的榲桲

quin·cen·ten·ary /ˌkwɪnsenˈtiːnəri; *NAmE* -senˈteneri/ *noun* (*pl.* **-ies**) a 500th anniversary * 500 週年紀念：*the quincentenary of Columbus's voyage to America* 哥倫布航海到達美洲的 500 週年紀念日

quin·ine /kwɪˈniːn; ˈkwɪniːn; *NAmE* also ˈkwaɪnaɪn/ *noun* [U] a drug made from the BARK of a S American tree, used in the past to treat MALARIA 奎寧，金雞納霜（過去用於治療瘧疾）

qui·noa /ˈkiːnwɑː; *BrE* also kiˈnəʊə; *NAmE* also kiˈnoʊə/ *noun* [U] a South American plant, grown for its seeds, used as food and to make alcoholic drinks; the seeds of the quinoa plant 昆諾阿藜，藜麥（產於南美，籽實用作食物和釀酒）；昆諾阿藜籽；藜麥籽

quint /kwɪnt/ *noun* (*NAmE, informal*) = QUINTUPLET

quint·es·sence /kwɪnˈtesns/ *noun* [sing.] **the ~ of sth** (*formal*) **1** the perfect example of sth 典範；範例：*It was the quintessence of an English manor house.* 那是典型的英式莊園宅第。 **2** the most important features of sth 精髓；精華 SYN **essence**：*a painting that captures the quintessence of Viennese elegance* 一幅薈萃維也納典雅之最的繪畫 ▸ **quint·es·sen·tial** /ˌkwɪntɪˈsenʃl/ *adj.*：*He was the quintessential tough guy.* 他是個典型的硬漢子。 **quint·es·sen·tial·ly** /-ʃəli/ *adv.*

quin·tet /kwɪnˈtet/ *noun* **1** [C+sing./pl. v.] a group of five musicians or singers who play or sing together 五重奏樂團；五重唱組合：*the Miles Davis Quintet* 戴維斯五重奏

Q

樂團 **2** [C] a piece of music for five musicians or singers 五重奏（曲）；五重唱（曲）：*a string quintet* 弦樂五重奏曲

quin·tile /ˈkwɪntaɪl/ *noun* (*statistics* 統計) one of five equal groups into which a set of things can be divided according to the DISTRIBUTION of a particular VARIABLE 五分位數；五分位值：*men in the first quintile of weight* (= the heaviest 20% of men) 體重在第一個五分位組的男性（即最重的 20% 男性）➲ compare QUARTILE

quin·tu·ple /ˈkwɪntjʊpl; kwɪnˈtjuːpl; *NAmE* also -ˈtuːpl/ *adj., det., verb*

■ ***adj.*** [only before noun], ***det.*** **1** consisting of five parts, people, or groups 由五部份（或人、群體）構成的；五方面的 **2** being five times as much or as many 五倍的

■ ***verb*** [I, T] **~ (sth)** to become five times bigger; to make sth five times bigger （使）成為五倍：*Sales have quintupled over the past few years.* 過去幾年中銷售量較原來的增加了四倍。

quin·tu·plet /ˈkwɪntʊplət; kwɪnˈtjuːplət; -ˈtʌpl-/ (also *BrE, informal* **quin**) (also *NAmE, informal* **quint**) *noun* one of five children born at the same time to the same mother 五胞胎之一

quip /kwɪp/ *noun, verb*

■ ***noun*** a quick and clever remark 俏皮話；妙語：*to make a quip* 說俏皮話

■ ***verb*** (**-pp-**) **+ speech** to make a quick and clever remark 講俏皮話；譏諷；嘲弄；打趣

quire /ˈkwaɪə(r)/ *noun* (*old-fashioned*) four sheets of paper folded to make eight LEAVES (= 16 pages) 對摺的四張紙（有 16 頁）

quirk /kwɜːk; *NAmE* kwɜːrk/ *noun, verb*

■ ***noun*** **1** an aspect of sb's personality or behaviour that is a little strange 怪異的性格（或行為）；怪癖 SYN **peculiarity** **2** a strange thing that happens, especially by accident （尤指偶發的）怪事，奇事：*By a strange* ***quirk of fate*** *they had booked into the same hotel.* 真是天緣奇遇，他們住進了同一家旅館。▸ **quirky** *adj.*：*a quirky sense of humour* 怪異的幽默感

■ ***verb*** [T, I] **~ (sth)** (*especially NAmE*) to twist your mouth or eyebrows suddenly; (of your mouth or eyebrows) to move in this way 突然扭曲（嘴或眉毛）；撇嘴；揚眉；皺眉：*David quirked an eyebrow and smirked slightly.* 戴維突然揚了揚眉毛，輕輕地傻笑了一下。◇ *Her lips quirked suddenly.* 她的嘴唇突然抽動了一下。

Q

quis·ling /ˈkwɪzlɪŋ/ *noun* (*disapproving*) a person who helps an enemy that has taken control of his or her country 賣國賊；內奸 SYN **collaborator**

quit 🔑 /kwɪt/ *verb* (**quit·ting, quit, quit**) (*BrE* also **quit·ting, quit·ted, quit·ted**)

1 🔑 [I, T] (*informal*) to leave your job, school, etc. 離開（工作職位、學校等）；離任；離校：*If I don't get more money I'll quit.* 不給我加薪我就辭職。◇ **~ as sth** *He has decided to quit as manager of the team.* 他已決定辭掉球隊經理的職務。◇ **~ sth** *He quit the show last year because of bad health.* 去年他因身體欠佳而退出了表演。◇ (*NAmE*) *She quit school at 16.* 她 16 歲退學。 **2** 🔑 [T, I] (*informal, especially NAmE*) to stop doing sth 停止；戒掉：**~ doing sth** *I've quit smoking.* 我戒了煙。◇ **~ (sth)** *Just quit it!* 你就罷手吧！◇ *We only just started. We're not going to quit now.* 我們才剛剛開始，現在決不放棄。 **3** [T, I] **~ (sth)** to leave the place where you live 離開，遷出，搬離（住處）：*We decided it was time to quit the city.* 當時我們決定，該離開城市生活了。◇ *The landlord gave them all* ***notice to quit.*** 房東通知他們都搬出去。 **4** 🔑 [I, T] **~ (sth)** to close a computer program or application 關閉，退出（計算機程序等）

quite 🔑 /kwaɪt/ *adv.*

1 🔑 (*BrE*) (not used with a negative 不與否定詞連用) to some degree 頗；相當；某種程度上 SYN **fairly, pretty**：*quite big/good/cold/warm/interesting* 相當大／好／冷／暖和／有趣 ◇ *He plays quite well.* 他表現得相當好。◇ ***I quite like*** *opera.* 我很喜歡歌劇。 HELP When **quite** is used with an adjective before a noun, it comes before *a* or *an*. * quite 同形容詞連用修飾名詞時，置於 a 或 an 之前。You can say 可以說：*It's quite a small house* or 或：*Their house is quite small*；but not 但不說：~~*It's a quite small house.*~~ **2** 🔑 (*BrE*) to the greatest possible degree 完全；十分；非常；徹底 SYN **completely, absolutely, entirely**：*quite delicious/amazing/empty/perfect* 非常美味／驚人／空／出眾 ◇ *This is quite a different problem.* 這是個截然不同的問題。◇ ***I'm quite happy*** *to wait for you here.* 我非常高興在此等候您。◇ *Flying is* ***quite the best*** *way to travel.* 航空絕對是最佳旅行方式。◇ *It wasn't quite as simple as I thought it would be.* 這事不完全像我想的那麼簡單。◇ ***Quite frankly,*** *I don't blame you.* 坦白說，我並不怪你。◇ *I've had* ***quite enough*** *of your tantrums.* 我已經受夠了你那臭脾氣！◇ *Are you* ***quite sure?*** 你有十足把握嗎？◇ ***I quite agree.*** 我完全同意。◇ *I don't quite know what to do next.* 我不太清楚下一步該怎麼辦。◇ ***Quite apart from*** *all the work, he had financial problems.* 即便不理會所有那些工作的事情，他還有財政困難。◇ *The theatre was* ***not quite*** (= was almost) *full.* 劇場並未完全滿座。◇ *It's like being in the Alps, but not quite.* 那好像是在阿爾卑斯山，但又不盡然。◇ *'I almost think she prefers animals to people.'* ***'Quite right too,'*** *said Bill.* "我簡直認為她喜愛動物勝過喜愛人。""沒錯兒。"比爾說道。◇ *'I'm sorry to be so difficult.'* ***'That's quite all right.'*** "對不起，我太為難你了。""沒關係。" **3** 🔑 to a great degree; very; really 在很大程度上；很；的確：*You'll be quite comfortable here.* 你在這裏會很舒服的。◇ *I can see it quite clearly.* 我能清清楚楚地看見它。◇ (*NAmE*) *'You've no intention of coming back?' 'I'm quite sorry, but no, I have not.'* "你不打算回來了嗎？""是的。非常抱歉，我不想回來了。" **4** (also *formal* **quite so**) (*BrE*) used to agree with sb or show that you understand them （表示贊同或理解）對，正是：*'He's bound to feel shaken after his accident.' 'Quite.'* "那次事故之後，他一定是像驚弓之鳥。""可不是。"

IDM **ˈquite a/the sth** (also *informal* **ˈquite some sth**) used to show that a person or thing is particularly impressive or unusual in some way （強調在某方面很突出）：*She's quite a beauty.* 她可是個大美人啊。◇ *We found it quite a change when we moved to London.* 我們搬到倫敦後，感覺生活變化很大。◇ *He's quite the little gentleman, isn't he?* 他真是個小紳士，不是嗎？◇ *It must be quite some car.* 那輛汽車肯定很了不得。 **quite a ˈlot (of sth)** 🔑 (also *BrE, informal* **quite a ˈbit**) a large number or amount of sth 大量；許多；眾多：*They drank quite a lot of wine.* 他們喝了好多酒。 **ˈquite some sth** **1** a large amount of sth 大量；眾多：*She hasn't been seen for quite some time.* 好久沒人看見她了。 **2** (*informal*) = QUITE A/THE STH ➲ more at CONTRARY[1] *n.*, FEW *pron.*

quits /kwɪts/ *adj.*

IDM **be quits (with sb)** (*informal*) when two people **are quits**, they do not owe each other anything, especially money 互不相欠；兩清：*I'll give you £5 and then we're quits.* 我給你 5 英鎊，那樣我們就兩清了。➲ more at CALL *v.*, DOUBLE *n.*

quit·ter /ˈkwɪtə(r)/ *noun* (often *disapproving*) a person who gives up easily and does not finish a task they have started 有始無終的人；虎頭蛇尾的人；半途而廢者

quiver /ˈkwɪvə(r)/ *verb, noun*

■ ***verb*** [I] to shake slightly; to make a slight movement 輕微顫動；抖動；抽動；哆嗦 SYN **tremble**：*Her lip quivered and then she started to cry.* 她嘴唇微微一顫就哭了起來。

■ ***noun*** **1** an emotion that has an effect on your body; a slight movement in part of your body 強烈感情；哆嗦；微顫；抖動：*He felt a quiver of excitement run through him.* 他內心激動得全身一陣哆嗦。◇ *Jane couldn't help the quiver in her voice.* 簡不禁聲音顫抖。 **2** a case for carrying arrows 箭筒；箭套

qui vive /ˌkiː ˈviːv/ *noun*

IDM **on the qui ˈvive** paying close attention to a situation, in case sth happens 密切注意着；警惕：*He's always on the qui vive for a business opportunity.* 他經常密切關注商機。

quix·ot·ic /kwɪkˈsɒtɪk; *NAmE* -ˈsɑːtɪk/ *adj.* (*formal*) having or involving ideas or plans that show imagination but are usually not practical 想入非非的；異想天開的；堂吉訶德式的 ORIGIN From the character Don Quixote in the novel by Miguel de Cervantes, whose adventures are a result of him trying to achieve or obtain things that are impossible. 源自米蓋爾 • 塞萬提斯的作品《堂吉訶德》，其主人公堂吉訶德為了實現不切實際的理想而到處歷險。

quiz /kwɪz/ *noun, verb*

■ ***noun*** (*pl.* **quiz·zes**) **1** a competition or game in which people try to answer questions to test their knowledge 知識競賽；智力遊戲：*a general knowledge quiz* 常識問答競賽 ◊ *a television quiz show* 電視智力遊戲節目 **2** (*especially NAmE*) an informal test given to students 小測驗：*a reading comprehension quiz* 閱讀理解小測驗 ➲ see also POP QUIZ ➲ note at EXAM

■ ***verb*** (-zz-) **1** to ask sb a lot of questions about sth in order to get information from them 盤問；查問；詢問；訊問 SYN **question**：**～ sb** (**about sb/sth**) *Four men are being quizzed by police about the murder.* 警察就這宗謀殺案正在盤問四個男子。◊ **～ sb** (**on/over sth**) *We were quizzed on our views about education.* 我們被徵詢對教育的看法。 **2 ～ sb** (*NAmE*) to give students an informal test 測驗（學生）：*You will be quizzed on chapter 6 tomorrow.* 明天將考你們第 6 章。

quiz·master /ˈkwɪzmɑːstə(r); *NAmE* -mæs-/ *noun* = QUESTION MASTER

quiz·zical /ˈkwɪzɪkl/ *adj.* (of an expression 表情) showing that you are slightly surprised or amused 詫異的；感到好笑的：*a quizzical expression* 詫異的表情 ▸ **quiz·zi·cal·ly** /-kli/ *adv.*：*She looked at him quizzically.* 她疑惑地望着他。

quoit /kɔɪt; kwɔɪt/ *noun* **1** [C] a ring that is thrown onto a small post in the game of quoits（投環遊戲用的）環，圈 **2 quoits** [U] a game in which rings are thrown onto a small post 投環（將圈投向標棍的遊戲）

Quonset hut™ /ˈkwɒnset hʌt; *NAmE* ˈkwɑːn-/ (*NAmE*) (*BrE* **Nis·sen hut**) *noun* a shelter made of metal with curved walls and roof 尼森式半筒形鐵皮屋

quor·ate /ˈkwɔːrət; -ət/ *adj.* (*BrE, technical* 術語) a meeting that is **quorate** has enough people present for them to make official decisions by voting（會議）夠法定人數的 OPP **inquorate**

Quorn™ /kwɔːn; *NAmE* kwɔːrn/ *noun* [U] a substance made from a type of FUNGUS, used in cooking instead of meat 闊恩素肉（用一種真菌製成）

quorum /ˈkwɔːrəm/ *noun* [sing.] the smallest number of people who must be at a meeting before it can begin or decisions can be made（會議的）法定人數

quota /ˈkwəʊtə; *NAmE* ˈkwoʊtə/ *noun* **1** [C] the limited number or amount of people or things that is officially allowed 定額；限額；配額：*to introduce a strict import quota on grain* 嚴格限制穀物進口量 ◊ *a quota system for accepting refugees* 接收難民的限額制度 **2** [C] an amount of sth that sb expects or needs to have or achieve 定量；定額；指標：*I'm going home now—I've done my quota of work for the day.* 我現在要回家了。我已完成了今天的工作量。**3** [sing.] (*politics* 政) a fixed number of votes that a candidate needs in order to be elected（候選人當選所需的）規定票數，最低票數：*He was 76 votes short of the quota.* 他比規定當選票數少了 76 票。

quot·able /ˈkwəʊtəbl; *NAmE* ˈkwoʊ-/ *adj.* (of a statement 話語) interesting or amusing and worth repeating 值得（或適合）引用的

quota·tion AW /kwəʊˈteɪʃn; *NAmE* kwoʊ-/ *noun* **1** (rather *formal*) (also rather *informal* **quote**) [C] a group of words or a short piece of writing taken from a book, play, speech, etc. and repeated because it is interesting or useful 引語；引文；語錄：*The book began with a quotation from Goethe.* 這本書一開頭引用了歌德的雋語。◊ *a dictionary of quotations* 引語詞典 ➲ see also MISQUOTATION at MISQUOTE *v.* **2** [U] the act of repeating sth interesting or useful that another person has written or said 引用；引述；引證：*The writer illustrates his point by quotation from a number of sources.* 作者旁徵博引以證明自己的觀點。 **3** [C] (rather *formal*) (also rather *informal* **quote**) a statement of how much money a particular piece of work will cost 報價；估價 SYN **estimate**：*You need to get a written quotation before they start work.* 你得在他們開工之前拿到報價單。 **4** [C] (*finance* 財) a

statement of the current value of goods or shares（貨物或股票的）行情，市價，牌價：*the latest quotations from the Stock Exchange* 股票交易所的最新行情

quoˈtation marks (also **quotes**, **ˈspeech marks**) (*BrE* also **in·vert·ed commas**) *noun* [pl.] a pair of marks (' ') or (" ") placed around a word, sentence, etc. to show that it is what sb said or wrote, that it is a title or that you are using it in an unusual way 引號

Which Word? 詞語辨析

quite / fairly / rather / pretty

Look at these examples 看下列例句：

- *The exam was fairly difficult.* 這場考試頗難。
- *The exam was quite difficult.* 這場考試相當難。
- *The exam was rather difficult.* 這場考試十分難。
- **Quite** is a little stronger than **fairly**, and **rather** is a little stronger than **quite**. **Rather** is not very common in *NAmE*; **pretty** has the same meaning and this is used in informal *BrE* too. * quite 比 fairly 詞義稍強，而 rather 又比 quite 詞義稍強。在美式英語中，rather 不太常用。pretty 與上述詞含義相同，也用於非正式英式英語：*The exam was pretty difficult.* 這場考試相當難。
- In *BrE* **quite** has two meanings. 在英式英語中，quite 含義有二：*I feel quite tired today* (= fairly tired). 今天我感到相當累。 With adjectives that describe an extreme state ('non-gradable' adjectives) it means 'completely' or 'absolutely'. 與表示極端狀態的形容詞（即非等級形容詞）連用，意為完全地、絕對地：*I feel quite exhausted.* 我感到筋疲力盡。 With some adjectives, both meanings are possible. The speaker's stress and intonation will show you which is meant. 與某些形容詞連用，兩種含義均有可能，究竟屬於哪一種由說話者的重音和語調決定：*Your essay is ˈquite good* (= fairly good—it could be better). 你的文章還不錯（挺好，不過還可以更好）；*Your essay is quite ˈgood* (= very good, especially when this is unexpected). 你的文章簡直太好了（非常好，尤指出乎意料）。
- In *NAmE* **quite** usually means something like 'very', not 'fairly' or 'rather'. **Pretty** is used instead for this sense. 在美式英語中，quite 通常含 very 之意，而非 fairly 或 rather。表示後一種意思用 pretty。

Q

quote 0⁻ʷ AW /kwəʊt; *NAmE* kwoʊt/ *verb, noun*

■ ***verb***

▸ **REPEAT EXACT WORDS** 引述 **1** 0⁻ʷ [T, I] to repeat the exact words that another person has said or written 引用；引述：**～ sth** (**from sb/sth**) *He quoted a passage from the minister's speech.* 他引用了部長的一段講話。◊ *to quote Shakespeare* 引用莎士比亞的話 ◊ *Quote this reference number in all correspondence.* 請在所有函件中標明這個編號。◊ **～** (**sb**) (**as doing sth**) *The President was* **quoted** *in the press* **as saying** *that he disagreed with the decision.* 報刊援引總統的話，說他不贊成這項決定。◊ *'It will all be gone tomorrow.'* **'Can I quote you on that?'** "明天一切將煙消雲散。" "這是你說的，我能引用你的話嗎？" ◊ **Don't quote me on this** (= this is not an official statement), *but I think he is going to resign.* 不要說這話是我說的，但我想他打算辭職。◊ *She said, and I quote, 'Life is meaningless without love.'* 我援引她曾說過的話："人生無愛一場空。" ◊ **+ speech** *'The man who is tired of London is tired of life,' he quoted.* "厭倦倫敦等於厭倦生活。" 他引述道。 ➲ see also MISQUOTE

▸ **GIVE EXAMPLE** 舉例 **2** [T] **～** (**sb**) **sth** to mention an example of sth to support what you are saying 舉例說明：*Can you quote me an instance of when this happened?* 你能否給我舉例說明一下這事發生的時間？ ➲ SYNONYMS at MENTION

▸ **GIVE PRICE** 報價 **3** [T, I] **～** (**sb**) (**sth**) (**for sth/for doing sth**) to tell a customer how much money you will charge them for a job, service or product 開價；出價；報價：

They quoted us £300 for installing a shower unit. 他們向我們開價 300 英鎊安裝淋浴設備。 **4** [T] **~ sth (at sth)** (*finance* 財) to give a market price for shares, gold or foreign money 為（股票，黃金或外匯）報價：*Yesterday the pound was quoted at $1.8285, unchanged from Monday.* 昨天英鎊報價為 1.8285 美元，這個價格從星期一以來未變。 **5** [T] **~ sth** (*finance* 財) to give the prices for a business company's shares on a STOCK EXCHANGE 為（企業的股份）上市，掛牌：*Several football clubs are now quoted on the Stock Exchange.* 目前有幾家足球俱樂部在股票交易所上市。

IDM **'quote (... 'unquote)** (*informal*) used to show the beginning (and end) of a word, phrase, etc. that has been said or written by sb else （用於引文的開始和結尾）引文起…引文止：*It was quote, 'the hardest decision of my life', unquote, and one that he lived to regret.* 那是，原話起，"我一生最難作出的決定"，原話止，而且是他終生悔恨的決定。

■ ***noun*** (rather *informal*)

▸ EXACT WORDS 原話 **1** = QUOTATION (1)：*The essay was full of quotes.* 這篇文章滿篇皆是引語。

▸ PRICE 價格 **2** = QUOTATION (3)：*Their quote for the job was way too high.* 他們給這項工作開價太高了。

▸ PUNCTUATION 標點符號 **3 quotes** [pl.] = QUOTATION MARKS：*If you take text from other sources, place it* ***in quotes****.* 引用其他來源的資料要放在引號裏。

quoth /kwəʊθ; *NAmE* kwoʊθ/ *verb* **+ speech** (*old use* or *humorous*) used meaning 'said' before 'I', 'he' or 'she' （用於 I、he 或 she 之前）說過，言道

quo·tid·ian /kwɒ'tɪdiən; kwəʊ't-; *NAmE* kwoʊ-/ *adj.* (*formal*) ordinary; typical of what happens every day 尋常的；普通的；司空見慣的 SYN **day-to-day**

quo·tient /'kwəʊʃnt; *NAmE* 'kwoʊ-/ *noun* (*mathematics* 數) a number which is the result when one number is divided by another 商（除法所得的結果） ➲ see also INTELLIGENCE QUOTIENT

Qur'an = KORAN

q.v. /ˌkju: 'vi:/ *abbr.* used in books to tell a reader that there is more information in another part of the book (from Latin 'quod vide') 見該項，參見該條（源自拉丁文 quod vide）

QWERTY /'kwɜ:ti; *NAmE* 'kwɜ:rti/ *adj.* [usually before noun] (of a keyboard on a computer or TYPEWRITER 計算機或打字機鍵盤) with the keys arranged in the usual way with Q, W, E, R, T and Y on the left of the top row of letters 標準鍵盤的，傳統鍵盤的（Q、W、E、R、T 和 Y 各鍵分佈在左側上排）

Q

Rr

R /ɑː(r)/ *noun, abbr.*

■ ***noun*** (also **r**) [C, U] (*pl.* **Rs**, **R's**, **r's** /ɑːz; *NAmE* ɑːrz/) the 18th letter of the English alphabet 英語字母表的第 18 個字母： *'Rose' begins with (an) R/'R'.* * rose 一詞以字母 r 開頭。 IDM see THREE

■ ***abbr.*** **1** (*BrE*) Queen; King (from Latin 'Regina'; 'Rex') 女王，國王（源自拉丁語 Regina、Rex）： *Elizabeth R.* 伊麗莎白女王 **2** **R.** (especially on maps) River（尤用於地圖）河，江： *R. Trent* 特倫特河 **3** (also **R.** especially in *NAmE*) (in politics in the US 美國政治) REPUBLICAN 共和黨人；共和黨黨員 **4** (*BrE*) Royal（用於服務於國王或女王或受其贊助的組織名稱）王室的，皇家的： *the RAC* (= Royal Automobile Club) 英國皇家汽車俱樂部 **5** (*NAmE*) the abbreviation for 'restricted' (a label for a film/movie that is not suitable for people under the age of 17 to see without an adult present) 限制級的（全寫為 restricted，未滿 17 歲者無成人陪同不宜觀看的電影的標記） ➲ see also R & B, R & D

rabbi /ˈræbaɪ/ *noun* a Jewish religious leader or a teacher of Jewish law 拉比，辣彼（猶太教經師或神職人員）： *the Chief Rabbi* (= the leader of Jewish communities in a particular country) 首席拉比◇ *Rabbi Sacks* 薩克斯拉比

rab·bin·ical /rəˈbɪnɪkl/ (also **rab·bin·ic**) *adj.* connected with rabbis or Jewish law or teaching 猶太教教士（或法規、教義）的

rabbit 兔

hare 野兔

rab·bit /ˈræbɪt/ *noun, verb*

■ ***noun*** **1** [C] a small animal with soft fur, long ears and a short tail. Rabbits live in holes in the ground or are kept as pets or for food. 兔；野兔： *a rabbit hutch* 兔籠 ➲ compare HARE **2** [U] meat from a rabbit 兔肉 IDM see PULL *v.*

■ ***verb*** [I] **go rabbiting** to hunt or shoot rabbits 獵兔；捕兔 PHR V **ˌrabbit ˈon (about sb/sth)** (*BrE, informal, disapproving*) to talk continuously about things that are not important or interesting 沒完沒了地說廢話；閒扯 SYN **chatter**

ˈrabbit warren (also **war·ren**) *noun* **1** a system of holes and underground tunnels where wild rabbits live 野兔繁殖區（由地下交錯相連的洞穴組成） **2** (*disapproving*) a building or part of a city with many narrow passages or streets 有許多狹小通道的建築；街道狹窄而密集的城區

rab·ble /ˈræbl/ *noun* [sing.+sing./pl. v.] (*disapproving*) **1** a large group of noisy people who are or may become violent 烏合之眾；聚眾的暴民 SYN **mob**： *a drunken rabble* 醉酒鬧事的人群 **2** **the rabble** ordinary people or people who are considered to have a low social position 賤民；下等人 SYN **the masses**： *a speech that appealed to the rabble* 煽動賤民的演講

ˈrabble-rouser *noun* a person who makes speeches to crowds of people intending to make them angry or excited, especially for political aims 煽動民眾者 ▸ **ˈrabble-rousing** *adj.* **ˈrabble-rousing** *noun* [U]

Rabe·lais·ian /ˌræbəˈleɪziən; -ˈleɪʒn/ *adj.* dealing with sex and the human body in a rude but humorous way 拉伯雷風格的；粗俗幽默的 ORIGIN From the French writer François Rabelais, whose works dealt with sex and the body in this way. 源自作品對性和人體作粗俗幽默描繪的法國作家弗朗索瓦·拉伯雷。

rabid /ˈræbɪd; ˈreɪb-/ *adj.* **1** [usually before noun] (*disapproving*) (of a type of person 某類人) having very strong feelings about sth and acting in an unacceptable way 極端的；瘋狂的： *rabid right-wing fanatics* 極端的右翼狂熱分子◇ *the rabid tabloid press* 偏激的小報新聞界 **2** [usually before noun] (*disapproving*) (of feelings or opinions 感情或看法) violent or extreme 激烈的；極端的： *rabid speculation* 非理性推斷 **3** suffering from rabies 患狂犬病的： *a rabid dog* 瘋狗 ▸ **rabid·ly** *adv.*

ra·bies /ˈreɪbiːz/ *noun* [U] a disease of dogs and other animals that causes MADNESS and death. Infected animals can pass the disease to humans by biting them. 狂犬病；恐水症

RAC /ˌɑːr eɪ ˈsiː/ *abbr.* Royal Automobile Club (a British organization which provides services for car owners)（英國）皇家汽車俱樂部

rac·coon (also **ra·coon**) /rəˈkuːn; *NAmE* ræ-/ *noun* **1** [C] a small N American animal with greyish-brown fur, black marks on its face and a thick tail 浣熊；北美浣熊 **2** [U] the fur of the raccoon 浣熊的毛皮

race 0-w /reɪs/ *noun, verb*

■ ***noun***

▸ COMPETITION 競賽 **1** 0-w [C] **~ (between A and B)** | **~ (against sb)** a competition between people, animals, vehicles, etc. to see which one is the faster or fastest 賽跑；速度競賽： *a race between the two best runners of the club* 俱樂部中兩名最佳選手的賽跑◇ *Who **won the race**?* 誰贏了賽跑？◇ *He's already in training for the big race against Bailey.* 為了跟貝利決一雌雄，他已經着手訓練了。◇ *Their horse came third in the race last year.* 他們的馬在去年的比賽中獲得了第三名。◇ *a **boat/horse/road, etc. race*** 划船比賽、賽馬、公路賽等◇ *a five-kilometre race* 五公里賽跑◇ *Shall we **have a race** to the end of the beach?* 咱們比賽跑到海灘那一頭，好嗎？ ➲ see also DRAG RACE, HORSE RACE **2** 0-w [sing.] a situation in which a number of people, groups, organizations, etc. are competing, especially for political power or to achieve sth first 競爭；角逐： **~ (for sth)** *the race for the presidency* 總統競選◇ **~ (to do sth)** ***The race is on*** (= has begun) *to find a cure for the disease.* 人們開始爭相尋找這種疾病的療法。 ➲ see also RAT RACE

▸ FOR HORSES 馬 **3** **the races** [pl.] a series of horse races that happen at one place on a particular day 賽馬會： *to go to the races* 去參加賽馬會

▸ PEOPLE 人 **4** 0-w [C, U] one of the main groups that humans can be divided into according to their physical differences, for example the colour of their skin 人種；種族： *the **Caucasian/Mongolian, etc. race*** 白種人、蒙古人種等◇ *people of **mixed race*** 混合種族的人◇ *This custom is found in people of all races throughout the world.* 這一習俗在全世界各種族中都有。◇ *legislation against discrimination on the grounds of race or sex* 反對種族和性別歧視的立法 **5** [C] a group of people who share the same language, history, culture, etc. 民族： *the Nordic races* 北歐日耳曼民族◇ *He admired Canadians as a hardy and determined race.* 他敬佩加拿大人，因為他們是吃苦耐勞、意志堅定的民族。 ➲ see also HUMAN RACE

▸ ANIMALS/PLANTS 動植物 **6** [C] a breed or type of animal or plant 種；屬；類；族： *a race of cattle* 一種牛

IDM **a ˌrace against ˈtime/the ˈclock** a situation in which you have to do sth or finish sth very fast before it is too late 和時間賽跑；搶時間；爭分奪秒 ➲ more at HORSE *n.*

■ *verb*

▸ **COMPETE** 競賽 **1** 🔑 [I, T] to compete against sb/sth to see who can go faster or the fastest, do sth first, etc.; to take part in a race or races （和…）比賽；參加比賽：**~ (against sb/sth)** *Who will he be racing against in the next round?* 下一輪他和誰比賽？◇ *They raced to a thrilling victory in the relay.* 他們在接力賽中取得了激動人心的勝利。◇ *She'll be racing for the senior team next year.* 明年她將參加高級組別的比賽。◇ **~ sb/sth** *We raced each other back to the car.* 我們爭先恐後地跑回汽車那兒。◇ **~ to do sth** *Television companies are racing to be the first to screen his life story.* 幾家電視公司爭着將他的生平搶先搬上熒屏。 **2** [T] **~ sth** to make an animal or a vehicle compete in a race 使比賽；讓…參加速度比賽：*to race dogs/horses/pigeons* 賽狗；賽馬；賽鴿 ◇ *to race motorbikes* 賽摩托車

▸ **MOVE FAST** 快速運動 **3** 🔑 [I, T] to move very fast; to move sb/sth very fast （使）快速移動，快速運轉：**+ adv./prep.** *He raced up the stairs.* 他飛快地衝上樓去。◇ *The days seemed to race past.* 日子似乎很快就過去了。◇ **~ sb/sth + adv./prep.** *The injured man was raced to the hospital.* 受傷者被迅速送往醫院。◇ *She raced her car through the narrow streets of the town.* 她開着車在小鎮狹窄的街道上飛快地穿行。

▸ **OF HEART/MIND/THOUGHTS** 心；頭腦；思想 **4** [I] to function very quickly because you are afraid, excited, etc. （因為害怕、興奮等）急速跳動，快速轉動：*My mind raced as I tried to work out what was happening.* 我拚命地轉動腦筋，想搞清楚發生了什麼事。◇ *She took a deep breath to calm her racing pulse.* 她深深地吸了口氣，想使急速跳動的脈搏平靜下來。

▸ **OF ENGINE** 發動機 **5** [I] to run too fast 運轉過快；空轉：*The truck came to rest against a tree, its engine racing.* 卡車在一棵樹旁停了下來，引擎空轉着。

'race car (*NAmE*) (*BrE* **'racing car**) *noun* a car that has been specially designed for motor racing 賽車

'race card *noun*

IDM **play the 'race card** (*disapproving*) to criticize people who belong to different races in a way that is meant to make other people feel opposed to them and to gain you a political advantage, especially during an election 打種族牌

Collocations 詞語搭配

Race and immigration 種族與移民

Prejudice and racism 偏見與種族歧視

- **experience/encounter** racism/discrimination/prejudice/anti-semitism 經歷／遭遇種族歧視／歧視／偏見／反猶太主義
- **face/suffer** persecution/discrimination 面臨／遭受迫害／歧視
- **fear/escape from/flee** racial/political/religious persecution 懼怕／逃離種族／政治／宗教迫害
- **constitute/be a form of** racial/race discrimination 構成／是一種種族歧視
- **reflect/reveal/show/have** a racial/cultural bias 反映出／揭示出／表現出／具有種族／文化偏見
- **be biased/be prejudiced against** (*especially BrE*) black people/(*both especially NAmE*) people of color/African Americans/Asians/Africans/Indians, etc. 對黑人／有色人種／非裔美國人／亞洲人／非洲人／印度人等有偏見
- **discriminate against** minority groups/minorities 歧視少數群體／少數民族
- **perpetuate/conform to/fit/defy** a common/popular/traditional/negative stereotype 固守／遵從／符合／藐視普遍的／流行的／傳統的／負面的模式化觀念
- **overcome/be blinded by** deep-seated/racial/(*especially NAmE*) race prejudice 克服根深蒂固的／種族的偏見；被根深蒂固的／種族的偏見所蒙蔽
- **entrench/perpetuate** racist attitudes 固守種族主義的態度
- **hurl/shout** (*especially BrE*) racist abuse; (*especially NAmE*) a racist/racial/ethnic slur 高聲地進行種族污辱
- **challenge/confront** racism/discrimination/prejudice 拒絕接受／對抗種族主義／歧視／偏見
- **combat/fight** (**against**)/**tackle** blatant/overt/covert/subtle/institutional/systemic racism 防止／反對／處理公然的／公開的／隱蔽的／微妙的／制度性的種族歧視

Race and society 種族和社會

- **damage/improve** (*especially BrE*) race relations 破壞／改善種族關係
- **practise**/(*especially US*) **practice** (racial/religious) tolerance/segregation 實行（種族／宗教）容忍／隔離政策
- **bridge/break down/transcend** cultural/racial barriers 消除／打破／超越文化／種族隔閡
- **encourage/promote** social integration 鼓勵／促進社會融合
- **outlaw/end** discrimination/slavery/segregation 取締／終止歧視／奴隸制／種族隔離
- **promote/embrace/celebrate** cultural diversity 促進／欣然接納／頌揚文化多樣性
- **conform to/challenge/violate** (accepted/established/prevailing/dominant) social/cultural norms 遵循／挑戰／違背（公認的／確立的／盛行的／佔支配地位的）社會／文化規範
- **live in** a multicultural society 生活在多元文化社會
- **attack/criticize** multiculturalism 攻擊／批評多元文化主義
- **fight for/struggle for/promote** racial equality 為種族平等而鬥爭；促進種族平等
- **perpetuate/reinforce** economic and social inequality 延續／加劇經濟和社會的不平等
- **introduce/be for/be against** (*BrE*) positive discrimination/(*especially NAmE*) affirmative action 推行／支持／反對積極性區別對待政策
- **support/be active in/play a leading role in** the civil rights movement 支持／積極參與／領導民權運動

Immigration 移居

- **control/restrict/limit/encourage** immigration 控制／限制／鼓勵外來移民
- **attract/draw** a wave of immigrants 吸引一批外來移民
- **assist/welcome** refugees 援助／欣然接受難民
- **house/shelter** refugees and asylum seekers 安置／庇護難民和尋求政治避難者
- **smuggle** illegal immigrants into the UK 偷運非法移民到英國
- **deport/repatriate** illegal immigrants/failed asylum seekers 驅逐／遣返非法移民／尋求政治避難失敗者
- **assimilate/integrate** new immigrants 同化／融合新移民
- **employ/hire** migrant workers 雇用流動工人
- **exploit/rely on** (cheap/illegal) immigrant labour/(*especially US*) labor 剝削／依賴（廉價的／非法的）移民勞動力
- **apply for/gain/obtain/be granted/be denied** (full) citizenship 申請／獲得／准予／未准予（完全的）公民身份
- **have/hold** dual citizenship 持有雙重國籍

R

race·card /ˈreɪskɑːd; *NAmE* -kɑːrd/ *noun* (*BrE*) a list of all the horse races at a particular event （賽馬）賽程表

race·course /ˈreɪskɔːs; *NAmE* -kɔːrs/ (*BrE*) (*NAmE* **race·track**) *noun* a track where horses race and the buildings, etc. that are connected with it 賽馬跑道；賽馬場 ➲ VISUAL VOCAB page V46

race·goer /ˈreɪsɡəʊə(r); *NAmE* -ɡoʊ-/ *noun* (*BrE*) a person who goes to horse races 觀看賽馬的人

race·horse /ˈreɪshɔːs; *NAmE* -hɔːrs/ *noun* a horse that is bred and trained to run in races 賽馬用的馬 ➲ VISUAL VOCAB page V46

ˈrace meeting *noun* (*BrE*) a series of races, especially for horses, held at one course over one day or several days 比賽大會；（尤指）賽馬大會

racer /ˈreɪsə(r)/ *noun* **1** a person or an animal that competes in races 參賽的人（或動物）： *Italy's champion downhill racer* 意大利的山坡速降滑雪冠軍 **2** a car, boat, etc. designed for racing 專供比賽用的車輛（或小艇等）；賽車；賽艇： *an ocean racer* 海上賽艇

ˌrace reˈlations *noun* [pl.] the relationships between people of different races who live in the same community 種族關係

ˈrace riot *noun* violent behaviour between people of different races living in the same community 種族騷亂；種族暴亂

race·track /ˈreɪstræk/ *noun* **1** a track for races between runners, cars, bicycles, etc. 跑道；賽道： *You can't cross the road—it's like a racetrack.* 那條馬路像賽車道一樣，讓人無法橫越。 **2** (*NAmE*) (*BrE* **race·course**) a track where horses race and the buildings, etc. that are connected with it 賽馬跑道；賽馬場 ➲ VISUAL VOCAB page V46

race·way /ˈreɪsweɪ/ *noun* (*NAmE*) a track for racing cars or horses 賽車道；賽馬跑道

ra·cial /ˈreɪʃl/ *adj.* **1** [only before noun] happening or existing between people of different races 種族的；種族間的： ***racial hatred/prejudice/tension/violence*** 種族仇恨／偏見；種族間的緊張狀況／暴力 ◇ *racial equality* 種族平等 ◇ *They have pledged to end **racial discrimination** in areas such as employment.* 他們已經保證在諸如就業等方面停止種族歧視。 **2** [usually before noun] connected with a person's race 人種的；種族的： *racial minorities* 少數民族 ◇ *a person's **racial origin*** 某人的種族背景 ▸ **ra·cial·ly** /-ʃəli/ *adv.* ： *The attacks were not racially motivated.* 襲擊事件不是由種族原因引起的。 ◇ *racially mixed schools* 不分種族的學校

ra·cial·ism /ˈreɪʃəlɪzəm/ *noun* [U] (*old-fashioned, BrE*) = RACISM

ra·cial·ist /ˈreɪʃəlɪst/ *noun, adj.* (*old-fashioned, BrE*) = RACIST

ˌracial ˈprofiling *noun* [U] (*NAmE*) the fact of police officers, etc. suspecting that sb has committed a crime based on the colour of their skin or their race rather than on any evidence 種族形象定性（指警察等因膚色或種族而不是證據懷疑人犯罪）

ra·cing 0➡ /ˈreɪsɪŋ/ *noun* [U]
1 0➡ (also **ˈhorse racing**) the sport of racing horses 賽馬： *a racing stable* 賽馬馬廄 ➲ see also FLAT RACING
2 0➡ (usually in compounds 通常構成複合詞) any sport that involves competing in races 速度比賽： ***motor/yacht/greyhound, etc. racing*** 摩托車賽、快艇賽、賽狗等 ◇ *a racing driver* 賽車選手 ➲ see also DRAG RACING

ˈracing car (*BrE*) (*NAmE* **ˈrace car**) *noun* a car that has been specially designed for motor racing 賽車

ˌracing ˈcertainty *noun* (*BrE, informal*) a thing that is certain to happen 必然發生的事；確定無疑的事： *It's a racing certainty that the vote will go against him.* 投票將對他不利，這是板上釘釘的事。

ra·cism /ˈreɪsɪzəm/ *noun* [U] (*disapproving*) **1** the unfair treatment of people who belong to a different race; violent behaviour towards them 種族歧視；種族迫害： *a victim of racism* 種族歧視的受害者 ◇ *ugly outbreaks of racism* 危險的種族迫害事件 ➲ COLLOCATIONS at RACE **2** the belief that some races of people are better than others 種族主義；種族偏見： *irrational racism* 不理性的種族主義 ▸ **ra·cist** /ˈreɪsɪst/ *noun* ： *He's a racist.* 他是個種族主義者。 **ra·cist** *adj.* ： *racist thugs* 種族主義暴徒 ◇ *racist attitudes/attacks/remarks* 種族主義的態度／攻擊／言論

rack /ræk/ *noun, verb*

■ ***noun*** **1** (often in compounds 常構成複合詞) a piece of equipment, usually made of metal or wooden bars, that is used for holding things or for hanging things on 支架；架子： *a **vegetable/wine/plate/toast rack*** 蔬菜架；酒瓶架；盤碟架；麵包片架 ◇ *I looked through a rack of clothes at the back of the shop.* 我看遍了掛在商店儘裏面的一架子衣服。 ➲ VISUAL VOCAB pages V21, V70 ➲ see also LUGGAGE RACK, ROOF RACK **2** (usually **the rack**) an instrument of TORTURE, used in the past for punishing and hurting people. Their arms and legs were tied to the wooden frame and then pulled in opposite directions, stretching the body. （舊時的）拉肢刑具 **3 ~ of lamb/pork** a particular piece of meat that includes the front RIBS and is cooked in the oven （羊、豬等帶前肋的）頸脊肉 **4** a part of a machine that consists of a bar with parts that a wheel or gear can fit into （機器的）齒條，齒軌

IDM **go to ˌrack and ˈruin** to get into a bad condition 變得一團糟： *They let the house go to rack and ruin.* 這房子越來越破舊，他們也不管。 **ˌoff the ˈrack** (*NAmE*) (*BrE* **ˌoff the ˈpeg**) (of clothes 衣服) made to a standard average size and not made especially to fit you 成品的；現成的 **on the ˈrack** feeling extreme pressure, anxiety or pain 倍感壓力；焦慮萬分；痛苦不堪

■ ***verb*** (also *less frequent* **wrack**) [often passive] **~ sb/sth** to make sb suffer great physical or mental pain 使痛苦不堪；使受折磨： *to be racked with/by guilt* 深感內疚 ◇ *Her face was racked with pain.* 她滿臉痛苦。 ◇ *Violent sobs racked her whole body.* 劇烈的抽泣使她全身都難受。 ◇ (*BrE*) *a racking cough* 劇烈的咳嗽

IDM **rack your ˈbrain(s)** to think very hard or for a long time about sth 絞盡腦汁；冥思苦想： *She racked her brains, trying to remember exactly what she had said.* 她絞盡腦汁，想要回憶起她到底說過些什麼話。

PHR V **ˌrack ˈup sth** (*especially NAmE*) to collect sth, such as profits or losses in a business, or points in a competition 累積；聚集（某物）；累計（得分）： *The company racked up $200 million in losses in two years.* 公司兩年內損失累計達 2 億元。 ◇ *In ten years of boxing he racked up a record 176 wins.* 在十年的拳擊生涯中，他累計獲勝 176 次，創下紀錄。

R

racket /ˈrækɪt/ *noun* **1** [sing.] (*informal*) a loud unpleasant noise 喧譁；吵鬧 SYN **din**：*Stop making that terrible racket!* 別吵啦！ **2** [C] (*informal*) a dishonest or illegal way of getting money 詐騙；勒索：*a **protection/extortion/drugs, etc. racket*** 收取保護費、敲詐、販毒等勾當 **3** (also **rac·quet**) [C] a piece of sports equipment used for hitting the ball, etc. in the games of TENNIS, SQUASH or BADMINTON. It has an OVAL frame, with strings stretched across and down it.（網球、羽毛球等的）球拍 ➲ VISUAL VOCAB page V45 ➲ compare BAT *n.* (1) **4 rackets, racquets** [U] a game for two or four people, similar to SQUASH, played with rackets and a small hard ball in a COURT with four walls 牆網球

rack·et·eer /ˌrækəˈtɪə(r); *NAmE* -ˈtɪr/ *noun* (*disapproving*) a person who makes money through dishonest or illegal activities 詐騙者；非法獲取錢財者 ▸ **rack·et·eer·ing** *noun* [U]

ˈrack rate *noun* (*especially NAmE*) the standard price of a hotel room（旅館的）標準房租，原定房租

ra·con·teur /ˌrækɒnˈtɜː(r); *NAmE* -kɑːn-/ *noun* a person who is good at telling stories in an interesting and amusing way 善於講故事的人

ra·coon = RACCOON

rac·quet = RACKET (3)

rac·quet·ball /ˈrækɪtbɔːl/ *noun* [U] a game played especially in the US by two or four players on a COURT with four walls, using RACKETS and a small hollow rubber ball 美式牆網球（二人或四人對壘，場地四面有牆，使用球拍和空心小橡皮球）

racy /ˈreɪsi/ *adj.* (**raci·er**, **raci·est**) having a style that is exciting and amusing, sometimes in a way that is connected with sex（風格）活潑的；不雅的：*a racy novel* 帶葷的小說

rad /ræd/ *adj., noun*
■ ***adj.*** (*old-fashioned, slang, especially NAmE*) very good 非常棒的；精彩的
■ ***noun*** (*physics* 物) a unit for measuring the effect of RADIATION 拉德，雷得（輻射吸收劑量單位）

radar /ˈreɪdɑː(r)/ *noun* [U] a system that uses radio waves to find the position and movement of objects, for example planes and ships, when they cannot be seen 雷達：*They located the ship by radar.* 他們通過雷達確定了船隻的位置。◇ *a radar screen* 雷達顯示屏 ➲ compare SONAR
IDM **below/under the ˈradar** used to say that people are not aware of sth 在視線以外的；未引起注意的：*Experts say a lot of corporate crime stays under the radar.* 專家說許多公司犯罪還沒有為人所注意到。 **on/off the ˈradar screen** used to say that people's attention is on or not on sth 受/不受人關注：*The issue of terrorism is back on the radar screen.* 恐怖主義問題重新受人關注。 ➲ more at BUBBLE *v.*

ˈradar trap *noun* (*BrE*) = SPEED TRAP

rad·dled /ˈrædld/ *adj.* (*BrE*) (of a person, their face, etc. 人、面容等) looking very tired 疲勞的；疲倦的 SYN **worn**

ra·dial /ˈreɪdiəl/ *adj., noun*
■ ***adj.*** having a pattern of lines, etc. that go out from a central point towards the edge of a circle 放射狀的；輻射狀的：*the radial pattern of public transport facilities* 呈輻射狀分佈的公共交通設施 ▸ **ra·di·al·ly** /-iəli/ *adv.*
■ ***noun*** (*BrE* also ˌ**radial ˈtyre**) (*NAmE* also ˌ**radial ˈtire**) a car tyre with strong parts inside that point away from the outside part and make the tyre stronger and safer 輻射式輪胎；子午線輪胎

ra·dian /ˈreɪdiən/ *noun* (*geometry* 幾何) a unit used to measure an angle, equal to the angle at the centre of a circle whose ARC is the same length as the circle's RADIUS 弧度

ra·di·ance /ˈreɪdiəns/ *noun* [U] **1** a special bright quality that shows in sb's face, for example because they are very happy or healthy 容光煥發；紅光滿面 **2** warm light shining from sth（散發出來的）光輝

ra·di·ant /ˈreɪdiənt/ *adj.* **1** showing great happiness, love or health 喜氣洋洋的；容光煥發的；面色紅潤的：*a radiant smile* 喜氣洋洋的微笑 ◇ *The bride looked radiant.* 新娘看上去滿面春風。◇ **~ with sth** *She was radiant with health.* 她身體健康，容光煥發。 **2** giving a warm bright light 燦爛的；光芒四射的：*The sun was radiant in a clear blue sky.* 湛藍的天空陽光燦爛。 **3** [only before noun] (*technical* 術語) sent out in RAYS from a central point 輻射的；放射的：*the **radiant heat/energy** of the sun* 太陽的輻射熱/輻射能 ▸ **ra·di·ant·ly** *adv.*：*radiantly happy* 喜氣洋洋 ◇ *He smiled radiantly.* 他喜笑顏開。

ra·di·ate /ˈreɪdieɪt/ *verb* **1** [T, I] **~ (sth) | ~ (from sb)** if a person **radiates** a particular quality or emotion, or if it **radiates** from them, people can see it very clearly（使品質或情感）顯出，流露：*He radiated self-confidence and optimism.* 他顯得自信樂觀。 **2** [I, T] **~ (from sth) | ~ (sth)** if sth **radiates** heat, light or energy or heat, etc. **radiates** from it, the heat is sent out in all directions（使熱、光、能量）輻射，放射，發散 SYN **give (sth) off**：*Heat radiates from the stove.* 爐子的熱力向外散發。 **3** [I] **+ adv./prep.** (of lines, etc. 直線等) to spread out in all directions from a central point 自中心輻射出；向周圍伸展：*Five roads radiate from the square.* 五條道路由廣場向外延伸。◇ *The pain started in my stomach and radiated all over my body.* 我起初只是肚子疼，後來全身都疼。

ra·di·ation /ˌreɪdiˈeɪʃn/ *noun* **1** [U, C] powerful and very dangerous RAYS that are sent out from RADIOACTIVE substances 輻射；放射線：*high **levels/doses of radiation** that damage cells* 損害細胞的高強度輻射 ◇ *the link between exposure to radiation and childhood cancer* 接觸輻射與兒童惡性腫瘤之間的聯繫 ◇ *a radiation leak from a nuclear power station* 核電站的輻射泄漏 ◇ *radiation sickness* 輻射病 ◇ *the radiations emitted by radium* 鐳釋放出的放射線 **2** [U] heat, energy, etc. that is sent out in the form of RAYS 輻射的熱（或能量等）：*ultraviolet radiation* 紫外線輻射 ◇ *electromagnetic radiation from power lines* 輸電線的電磁輻射 **3** (also ˌ**radiˈation therapy**) [U] the treatment of cancer and other diseases using radiation 放射療法 ➲ compare CHEMOTHERAPY, RADIOTHERAPY

ra·di·ator /ˈreɪdieɪtə(r)/ *noun* **1** a hollow metal device for heating rooms. Radiators are usually connected by pipes through which hot water is sent. 散熱器；暖氣片：*a central heating system with a radiator in each room* 每個房間都配有一個散熱器的中央供暖系統 ➲ VISUAL VOCAB page V21 **2** a device for cooling the engine of a vehicle or an aircraft（車輛或飛機發動機的）冷卻器，水箱

rad·ical AW /ˈrædɪkl/ *adj., noun*
■ ***adj.*** [usually before noun] **1** concerning the most basic and important parts of sth; thorough and complete 根本的；徹底的；完全的 SYN **far-reaching**：*the need for **radical changes** in education* 對教育進行徹底變革的需要 ◇ *demands for radical reform of the law* 徹底改變法律的要求 ◇ *radical differences between the sexes* 兩性間的根本差異 **2** new, different and likely to have a great effect 全新的；不同凡響的：*radical ideas* 不同凡響的觀點 ◇ *a radical solution to the problem* 解決問題的全新方法 ◇ *radical proposals* 有創見的建議 **3** in favour of thorough and complete political or social change 激進的；極端的：*the radical wing of the party* 黨內的激進派 ◇ *radical politicians/students/writers* 激進的政治人物/學生/作家 **4** (*old-fashioned, NAmE, slang*) very good 很好；非常好 ▸ **rad·ic·al·ly** AW /-kli/ *adv.*：*The new methods are radically different from the old.* 新的方法迥然不同於舊的方法。◇ *Attitudes have changed radically.* 態度發生了根本的變化。
■ ***noun*** **1** a person with radical opinions 激進分子：*political radicals* 政治激進分子 **2** (*chemistry* 化) a group of atoms that behave as a single unit in a number of COMPOUNDS 游離基；自由基 ➲ see also FREE RADICAL

ˌ**radical ˈchic** *noun* [U] fashionable LEFT-WING views; the people, behaviour and way of life connected with these views 時髦的左派觀點；時髦左派（或行為、生活方式）

rad·ic·al·ism /ˈrædɪkəlɪzəm/ *noun* [U] belief in RADICAL ideas and principles 激進主義

R

rad·ic·al·ize (*BrE* also **-ise**) /ˈrædɪkəlaɪz/ *verb* **~ sb/sth** to make people more willing to consider new and different policies, ideas, etc.; to make people more RADICAL in their political opinions 使人趨於考慮新而不同的政策（或觀點等）；使激進：*Recent events have radicalized opinion on educational matters.* 最近發生的事使人們對教育的看法有了全新的改變。

rad·icchio /ræˈdiːkiəʊ; *NAmE* -kioʊ/ *noun* [U] a type of CHICORY (= a leaf vegetable) with dark red leaves 紫葉菊苣

radii *pl.* of RADIUS

radio 🔑 /ˈreɪdiəʊ; *NAmE* -oʊ/ *noun, verb*

■ ***noun*** **1** 🔑 (often **the radio**) [U, sing.] the activity of broadcasting programmes for people to listen to; the programmes that are broadcast 無線電廣播；無線電廣播節目：*The interview was broadcast **on radio** and television.* 廣播和電視都報道了這次會見。◇ *The play was written specially for radio.* 這齣戲是專為無線電廣播而寫的。◇ ***I listen to the radio** on the way to work.* 我在上班的路上聽廣播。◇ *Did you hear the interview with him **on the radio**?* 你有沒有在廣播裏聽到採訪他的情況？◇ ***local/national radio*** 地方／國家無線電廣播 ◇ ***a radio programme/station*** 廣播節目／電台 **2** 🔑 [C] a piece of equipment used for listening to programmes that are broadcast to the public 收音機：*to **turn the radio on/off*** 打開／關上收音機 ◇ *a car radio* 汽車收音機 ◇ *a radio cassette player* 盒式收音放音機 ➲ see also CLOCK RADIO **3** 🔑 [U] the process of sending and receiving messages through the air using ELECTROMAGNETIC waves 無線電傳送；無線電通信：*He was unable to contact Blake **by radio**.* 他未能通過無線電和布萊克取得聯繫。◇ *to keep in **radio contact*** 保持無線電聯繫 ◇ ***radio signals/waves*** 無線電信號／電波 **4** 🔑 [C] a piece of equipment, for example on ships or planes, for sending and receiving radio signals 無線電收發報機：*to hear a gale warning on/over the ship's radio* 用船上的無線電收發報機接聽大風警報

■ ***verb*** (**ra·dio·ing**, **ra·dioed**, **ra·dioed**) [I, T] **~ (sth)** | **~ that ...** to send a message to sb by radio（用無線電）發送，傳送：*The police officer radioed for help.* 警察用無線電呼救。◇ *The warning was radioed to headquarters.* 通過無線電向總部發出了警報。

radio- /ˈreɪdiəʊ; *NAmE* -oʊ/ *combining form* (in nouns, adjectives and adverbs 構成名詞、形容詞和副詞) **1** connected with radio waves or broadcasting 無線電波的；無線電廣播的：*radio-controlled* 無線電遙控的 **2** connected with RADIOACTIVITY 放射的；輻射的：*radiotherapy* 放射療法

radio·active /ˌreɪdiəʊˈæktɪv; *NAmE* -oʊˈæk-/ *adj.* sending out harmful RADIATION caused when the NUCLEI (= central parts) of atoms are broken up 放射性的；有輻射的 ▸ **radio·activ·ity** /ˌreɪdiəʊækˈtɪvəti; *NAmE* -oʊæk-/ *noun* [U]：*the study of radioactivity* 放射性研究 ◇ *a rise in the level of radioactivity* 輻射強度的增加

ˌradio aˈstronomy *noun* [U] the part of ASTRONOMY that studies radio waves sent out by objects in space 射電天文學；電波天文學

ˈradio button *noun* (*computing* 計) a small circle that you click on in order to make a particular choice. The radio button is then marked with a dot to show that it has been selected. 單選按鈕

radio·car·bon /ˌreɪdiəʊˈkɑːbən; *NAmE* -oʊˈkɑːrb-/ *noun* [U] (*technical* 術語) a RADIOACTIVE form of CARBON that is present in the materials of which living things are formed, used in CARBON DATING 放射性碳（碳的放射性同位素，用以測定物體的年代）：*radiocarbon analysis* 放射性碳分析

ˌradiocarbon ˈdating *noun* [U] (*formal*) = CARBON DATING

radio·chem·is·try /ˌreɪdiəʊˈkemɪstri; *NAmE* -oʊˈk-/ *noun* [U] the area of chemistry which is concerned with RADIOACTIVE substances 放射化學 ▸ **radio·chem·ical** /ˌreɪdiəʊˈkemɪkl; *NAmE* -oʊˈk-/ *adj.*

ˌradio-conˈtrolled *adj.* controlled from a distance by radio signals 無線電操縱的；無線電遙控的

radi·og·raph·er /ˌreɪdiˈɒgrəfə(r); *NAmE* -ˈɑːg-/ *noun* a person working in a hospital whose job is to take X-RAY photographs or to use X-RAYS to treat some illnesses, such as cancer * X 光攝影師；放射治療師

radi·og·raphy /ˌreɪdiˈɒgrəfi; *NAmE* -ˈɑːg-/ *noun* [U] the process or job of taking X-RAY photographs * X 光照相

radio·iso·tope /ˌreɪdiəʊˈaɪsətəʊp; *NAmE* ˌreɪdioʊˈaɪsətoʊp/ *noun* (*chemistry* 化) a form of a chemical element which sends out RADIATION 放射性同位素

radi·olo·gist /ˌreɪdiˈɒlədʒɪst; *NAmE* -ˈɑːlə-/ *noun* a doctor who is trained in radiology 放射科醫生；X 光科的醫生

radi·ology /ˌreɪdiˈɒlədʒi; *NAmE* -ˈɑːlə-/ *noun* [U] the study and use of different types of RADIATION in medicine, for example to treat diseases 放射學；放射醫療

radio·met·ric /ˌreɪdiəʊˈmetrɪk; *NAmE* -dioʊ-/ *adj.* relating to a measurement of RADIOACTIVITY 輻射度測量的 ▸ **radio·met·ric·ally** /-ɪkli/ *adv.*：*These rocks have been dated radiometrically at two billion years old.* 經輻射能探測，這些岩石於 20 億年前形成。

ˌradio-ˈtelephone *noun* a telephone that works by sending and receiving radio signals, used especially in cars, boats, etc. 無線電話

ˌradio ˈtelescope *noun* a piece of equipment that receives radio waves from space and is used for finding stars and the position of SPACECRAFT, etc. 射電望遠鏡

radio·ther·apy /ˌreɪdiəʊˈθerəpi; *NAmE* -oʊˈθe-/ *noun* [U] the treatment of disease by RADIATION 放射療法：*a course of radiotherapy* 放射療程 ➲ compare CHEMOTHERAPY ▸ **radio·thera·pist** *noun*

ˈradio wave *noun* a low-energy ELECTROMAGNETIC wave, especially when used for long-distance communication 無線電波

rad·ish /ˈrædɪʃ/ *noun* [C, U] a small crisp red or white root vegetable with a strong taste, eaten raw in salads 櫻桃蘿蔔：*a bunch of radishes* 一把櫻桃蘿蔔 ➲ VISUAL VOCAB page V31

ra·dium /ˈreɪdiəm/ *noun* [U] (*symb.* **Ra**) a chemical element. Radium is a white RADIOACTIVE metal used in the treatment of diseases such as cancer. 鐳

ra·dius /ˈreɪdiəs/ *noun* (*pl.* **radii** /ˈreɪdiaɪ/) **1** a straight line between the centre of a circle and any point on its outer edge; the length of this line 半徑（長度）➲ VISUAL VOCAB page V71 ➲ compare DIAMETER (1) **2** a round area that covers the distance mentioned from a central point 半徑範圍；周圍：*They deliver to within a 5-mile radius of the store.* 他們對距離店鋪 5 英里的範圍內送貨上門。 **3** (*anatomy* 解) the shorter bone of the two bones in the lower part of the arm between the elbow and the wrist, on the same side as the thumb 橈骨 ➲ VISUAL VOCAB page V59 ➲ see also ULNA

radon /ˈreɪdɒn; *NAmE* -dɑːn/ *noun* [U] (*symb.* **Rn**) a chemical element. Radon is a RADIOACTIVE gas used in the treatment of diseases such as cancer. 氡（放射性化學元素）

RAF /ˌɑːr eɪ ˈef; *or, in informal use,* ræf/ *abbr.* Royal Air Force (the British AIR FORCE)（英國）皇家空軍：*He was an RAF pilot.* 他是皇家空軍飛行員。

Raf·fer·ty's rules /ˈræfətiz ruːlz; *NAmE* -fərt-/ *noun* [pl.] (*AustralE, NZE, informal*) no rules at all 毫無章法；全無規則

raf·fia /ˈræfiə/ *noun* [U] soft material that looks like string and is made from the leaves of a type of PALM tree, used for making BASKETS, MATS, etc. or for tying things 酒椰葉纖維（由酒椰棕櫚樹葉製成，用於編籃子、墊子或捆紮東西等）

raff·ish /ˈræfɪʃ/ *adj.* (of sb's behaviour, clothes, etc. 人的行為、衣着等) not very acceptable according to some social standards, but interesting and attractive 放蕩不羈的

raf·fle /ˈræfl/ *noun, verb*

■ ***noun*** a way of making money for a particular project or organization. People buy tickets with numbers on them

R

and some of these numbers are later chosen to win prizes. 抽彩 ➲ compare LOTTERY (1)

■ *verb* **~ sth** to give sth as a prize in a raffle 在抽彩中獎以（物品）

raft /rɑːft; *NAmE* ræft/ *noun* **1** a flat structure made of pieces of wood tied together and used as a boat or floating platform 木排；筏 **2** a small boat made of rubber or plastic that is filled with air 橡皮艇；充氣船：*an inflatable raft* 充氣橡皮筏 **3** [usually sing.] **~ of sth** (*informal*) a large number or amount of sth 大量；許多：*a whole raft of new proposals* 大量新的提議

raft·er /ˈrɑːftə(r); *NAmE* ˈræf-/ *noun* [C, usually pl.] one of the sloping pieces of wood that support a roof 椽子

raft·ing /ˈrɑːftɪŋ; *NAmE* ˈræft-/ *noun* [U] the sport or activity of travelling down a river on a RAFT 皮划艇運動：*We went* ***white-water rafting*** *on the Colorado River.* 我們到科羅拉多河湍急的河水中划皮划艇。➲ VISUAL VOCAB page V50

rag /ræɡ/ *noun, verb*

■ *noun* **1** [C, U] a piece of old, often torn, cloth used especially for cleaning things 抹布；破布 ➲ see also GLAD RAGS **2** [C] (*informal, disapproving*) a newspaper that you believe to be of low quality 質量低劣的報紙；小報：*the local rag* 地方小報 **3** [C] a piece of RAGTIME music 雷格泰姆樂曲 **4** (*BrE*) [U, C] an event or a series of events organized by students each year to raise money for charity（學生每年組織的）慈善募捐活動：*rag week* 學生募捐週

IDM **in ˈrags** wearing very old torn clothes 衣衫襤褸；穿得破舊：*The children were dressed in rags.* 孩子們穿着破衣爛衫。**(from) ˌrags to ˈriches** from being extremely poor to being very rich 從赤貧到巨富：*a rags-to-riches story* 窮人發跡史 ◇ *Hers was a classic tale of rags to riches.* 她的經歷是從赤貧到富有的一個典型例子。**ˌlose your ˈrag** (*BrE, informal*) to get angry 發怒；生氣 ➲ more at RED *adj.*

■ *verb* (**-gg-**) **~ sb (about sth)** (*old-fashioned, BrE*) to laugh at and/or play tricks on sb 嘲笑；捉弄 SYN **tease**

PHR V **ˈrag on sb** (*NAmE, informal*) to complain to sb about their behaviour, work, etc. 向某人抱怨（或埋怨、發牢騷）

raga /ˈrɑːɡə/ *noun* a traditional pattern of notes used in Indian music; a piece of music based on one of these patterns 拉伽（印度音樂中的傳統曲調）；拉伽曲

raga·muf·fin (also **ragga·muf·fin**) /ˈræɡəmʌfɪn/ *noun* **1** [C] a person, usually a child, who is wearing old clothes that are torn and dirty 衣着破舊骯髒的人（尤指兒童）**2** [C] (*especially BrE*) a person who likes or performs RAGGA music 雷戈音樂愛好者；雷戈音樂表演者 **3** [U] = RAGGA

ˌrag-and-ˈbone man *noun* (*BrE*) (especially in the past) a man who travels around buying things that people no longer want and selling them to other people（尤指舊時）沿街買賣舊貨的行販

rag·bag /ˈræɡbæɡ/ *noun* [sing.] a collection of things that appear to have little connection with each other 大雜燴；雜七雜八的東西：*a ragbag of ideas* 雜亂無章的觀點

ˌrag ˈdoll *noun* a soft DOLL made from pieces of cloth 碎布製玩偶；布娃娃 ➲ VISUAL VOCAB page V37

rage /reɪdʒ/ *noun, verb*

■ *noun* **1** [U, C] a feeling of violent anger that is difficult to control 暴怒；狂怒：*His face was dark with rage.* 他氣得面色鐵青。◇ *to* ***be shaking/trembling/speechless with rage*** 氣憤得發抖／戰慄／說不出話來 ◇ *Sue stormed out of the room* ***in a rage.*** 蘇怒氣沖沖地走出了房間。◇ *He* ***flies into a rage*** *if you even mention the subject.* 你只要一提起這個話題，他就會暴跳如雷。**2** [U] (in compounds 構成複合詞) anger and violent behaviour caused by a particular situation（某情況引起的）憤怒，暴力行為：*a case of trolley rage in the supermarket* 超市裏一起由手推車引起的暴力事件 ➲ see also ROAD RAGE

IDM **be all the ˈrage** (*informal*) to be very popular and fashionable 十分流行；成為時尚；風靡一時

■ *verb* **1** [I, T] to show that you are very angry about sth or with sb, especially by shouting 發怒；怒斥 SYN **rail** : **~ (at/against/about sb/sth)** *He raged against the injustice of it all.* 這一切不公正使他大發怒火。◇ **+ speech** *'That's unfair!' she raged.* "這不公平！" 她憤怒地喊道。**2** [I] **~ (on)** (of a storm, a battle, an argument, etc. 暴風雨、戰鬥、爭論等) to continue in a violent way 猛烈地繼續；激烈進行：*The riots raged for three days.* 暴亂持續了三天。◇ *The blizzard was still raging outside.* 外面暴風雪仍在肆虐。**3** [I] **(+ adv./prep.)** (of an illness, a fire, etc. 疾病、火焰等) to spread very quickly 迅速蔓延；快速擴散：*Forest fires were raging out of control.* 森林大火迅速蔓延，無法控制。◇ *A flu epidemic raged through Europe.* 流感在整個歐洲肆虐。**4** [I] (*AustralE, NZE, slang*) to go out and enjoy yourself 外出玩個痛快；出去作樂

ragga /ˈræɡə/ (also **ragga·muf·fin**, **raga·muf·fin**) *noun* [U] a type of dance music from the West Indies that contains features of REGGAE and HIP HOP 雷戈（一種源自西印度群島的舞曲，帶有雷蓋和嘻哈的特徵）

ragga·muf·fin = RAGAMUFFIN

rag·ged /ˈræɡɪd/ *adj.* **1** (of clothes 衣服) old and torn 破舊的；襤褸的 SYN **shabby** **2** (of people 人) wearing old or torn clothes 衣衫襤褸的；破衣爛衫的：*ragged children* 衣衫襤褸的孩子們 **3** having an outline, an edge or a surface that is not straight or even（輪廓線、邊緣或表面）粗糙的，參差不齊的，不規則的：*ragged clouds* 形狀不規則的雲 ◇ *a ragged coastline* 彎彎曲曲的海岸線 **4** not smooth or controlled 不流暢的；不受控制的：*I could hear the sound of his ragged breathing.* 我聽到他那急促的呼吸聲。◇ *Their performance was still very ragged.* 他們的表演仍然很粗糙。**5** (*informal*) very tired, especially after physical effort 精疲力竭的；疲憊的 ▸ **rag·ged·ly** *adv.*：*raggedly dressed* 衣着破舊 ◇ *She was breathing raggedly.* 她急促地呼吸着。**rag·ged·ness** *noun* [U]

IDM **ˌrun sb ˈragged** (*informal*) to make sb do a lot of work or make a big effort so that they become tired 使某人疲於奔命

ra·ging /ˈreɪdʒɪŋ/ *adj.* [only before noun] **1** (of feelings or emotions 感覺或情緒) very strong 強烈的：*a raging appetite/thirst* 極強的食慾；口渴難耐 ◇ *raging jealousy* 強烈的忌妒心 **2** (of natural forces 自然力) very powerful 極其強大的；猛烈的：*a raging storm* 狂風暴雨 ◇ *The stream had become a raging torrent.* 小河變成了一條洶湧的急流。◇ *The building was now a raging inferno.* 這座大樓現在正烈焰熊熊。**3** (of a pain or an illness 疼痛或疾病) very strong or painful 很嚴重的；很痛苦的：*a raging headache* 劇烈的頭痛 **4** very serious and causing strong feelings 嚴重的；激發強烈感情的：*His speech has provoked a raging debate.* 他的演講激起了激烈的爭論。

rag·lan /ˈræɡlən/ *adj.* [only before noun] **1** (of a sleeve 衣袖) sewn to the front and back of a coat, sweater, etc. in a line that slopes down from the neck to under the arm 插肩的 **2** (of a coat, sweater, etc. 大衣、毛衣等) having raglan sleeves 有插肩袖的

ra·gout /ræˈɡuː; ˈræɡuː/ *noun* [C, U] (from *French*) a hot dish of meat and vegetables boiled together with various spices（加入各種香料的）蔬菜燉肉

rag·tag /ˈræɡtæɡ/ *adj.* [usually before noun] (*informal*) (of a group of people or an organization 一群人或某組織) not well organized; giving a bad impression 組織散漫的；雜亂的；給人印象差的：*a ragtag band of rebels* 一隊叛亂的烏合之眾

rag·time /ˈræɡtaɪm/ *noun* [U] an early form of JAZZ, especially for the piano, first played by African American musicians in the early 1900s 雷格泰姆音樂（早期爵士音樂，多在鋼琴上演奏，20 世紀初由非洲裔美國音樂家發展而成）

the ˈrag trade *noun* [sing.] (*old-fashioned, informal*) the business of designing, making and selling clothes 服裝業；服裝生意

rag·weed /ˈræɡwiːd/ *noun* [U] a N American plant with small green flowers that contain a lot of POLLEN, which causes HAY FEVER in some people 豚草（北美植物，其綠色小花含大量花粉，可引起枯草熱）

rag·wort /ˈrægwɜːt; *NAmE* -wɜːrt/ *noun* [U] a wild plant with yellow flowers, poisonous to cows and horses 千里光，狗舌草（開黃色小花，能毒害牛馬）

raid /reɪd/ *noun*, *verb*

■ **noun** **1** **~ (on sth)** a short surprise attack on an enemy by soldiers, ships or aircraft 突然襲擊：*They carried out a bombing raid on enemy bases.* 他們突然出擊，轟炸了敵軍的基地。➲ COLLOCATIONS at WAR ➲ see also AIR RAID **2** **~ (on sth)** a surprise visit by the police looking for criminals or for illegal goods or drugs 突擊檢查；突然搜查：*They were arrested during a* ***dawn raid***. 在一次清晨的突擊搜查中，他們都被捕了。**3** **~ (on sth)** an attack on a building, etc. in order to commit a crime 搶劫；打劫：*an armed bank raid* 一起持械搶劫銀行案 ➲ see also RAM-RAIDING

■ **verb** **1** **~ sth** (of police 警察) to visit a person or place without warning to look for criminals, illegal goods, drugs, etc. 突擊搜捕；突然搜查 **2** **~ sth** (of soldiers, fighting planes, etc. 戰士、殲擊機等) to attack a place without warning 突襲；偷襲：*Villages along the border are regularly raided.* 邊境附近的村莊經常遭受突襲。◇ *a* ***raiding party*** (= a group of soldiers, etc. that attack a place) 突襲小分隊 **3** **~ sth** to enter a place, usually using force, and steal from it 劫掠；打劫 SYN **plunder**, **ransack**：*Many treasures were lost when the tombs were raided in the last century.* 上世紀這些墳墓遭到偷盜，很多財寶都失踪了。◇ (*humorous*) *I caught him raiding the fridge again* (= taking food from it). 我撞見他又在掃盪冰箱裏的食物。

raid·er /ˈreɪdə(r)/ *noun* a person who makes a criminal raid on a place 襲擊者；搶劫者：***armed/masked raiders*** 武裝／蒙面襲擊者

rail 🔑 /reɪl/ *noun*, *verb*

■ **noun** **1** 🔑 [C] a wooden or metal bar placed around sth as a barrier or to provide support 欄杆；扶手；圍欄：*She leaned on the ship's rail and gazed out to sea.* 她靠着船上的護欄，凝望大海。➲ see also GUARD RAIL, HANDRAIL **2** 🔑 [C] a bar fixed to the wall for hanging things on（固定在牆上用以掛物品的）横杆：*a picture/curtain/towel rail* 掛圖畫／窗簾／毛巾用的横杆 ➲ VISUAL VOCAB page V23 **3** 🔑 [C, usually pl.] each of the two metal bars that form the track that trains run on 鐵軌；軌道 ➲ VISUAL VOCAB page V58 **4** 🔑 [U] (often before another noun 常用於另一名詞前) railways/railroads as a means of transport 鐵路；鐵道：*to travel* ***by rail*** 乘火車 ◇ *rail travel/services/fares* 鐵路旅行／服務／車費 ◇ *a rail link/network* 鐵路連接；鐵路網

IDM **get back on the ˈrails** (*informal*) to become successful again after a period of failure, or to begin functioning normally again 恢復常軌；東山再起 **go off the ˈrails** (*informal*) **1** to start behaving in a strange or unacceptable manner, for example, drinking a lot or taking drugs 舉止怪異；行為出軌 **2** to lose control and stop functioning correctly 失去控制；無法正常運行：*The company has gone badly off the rails in recent years.* 這家公司最近幾年已經陷於嚴重癱瘓。➲ more at JUMP *v.*

■ **verb** [I, T] **~ (at/against sth/sb)** | **+ speech** (*formal*) to complain about sth/sb in a very angry way 怒斥；責罵；抱怨 SYN **rage**：*She railed against the injustice of it all.* 她大罵此事太不公正。

PHR V **ˌrail sth ˈin/ˈoff** to separate an area or object from others by placing rails around it 用圍欄圍住；用圍欄隔開

rail·car /ˈreɪlkɑː(r)/ *noun* = CAR (2)

rail·card /ˈreɪlkɑːd; *NAmE* -kɑːrd/ *noun* (*BrE*) a card that allows sb to travel by train at a reduced price 火車通行優惠卡

rail·head /ˈreɪlhed/ *noun* (*technical* 術語) the point at which a railway/railroad ends 鐵路終點站；鐵路末端

rail·ing /ˈreɪlɪŋ/ *noun* [C, usually pl.] a fence made of vertical metal bars; one of these bars 金屬圍欄；金屬欄杆：*iron railings* 鐵欄杆 ◇ *I chained my bike to the park railings.* 我用鏈子把自行車鎖在公園的圍欄上了。◇ *She leaned out over the railing.* 她靠在欄杆上探出身去。➲ VISUAL VOCAB pages V2, V3

rail·lery /ˈreɪləri/ *noun* [U] (*formal*) friendly joking about a person 善意的玩笑；戲謔；逗趣

rail·man /ˈreɪlmən/ *noun* (*pl.* **-men** /-mən/) (*BrE*) = RAILWAYMAN

rail·road 🔑 /ˈreɪlrəʊd; *NAmE* -roʊd/ *noun*, *verb*

■ **noun** (*NAmE*) (*BrE* **rail·way**) **1** 🔑 (*BrE* also **ˈrailway line**) a track with rails on which trains run 鐵路；鐵道：*railroad tracks* 鐵路軌道 **2** 🔑 a system of tracks, together with the trains that run on them, and the organization and people needed to operate them 鐵路系統；鐵路公司；鐵道部門：*This town got a lot bigger when the railroad came in the 1860s.* 自從 19 世紀 60 年代通了火車之後，這座城鎮變大了許多。

■ **verb** **1** **~ sb (into sth/into doing sth)** to force sb to do sth before they have had enough time to decide whether or not they want to do it 迫使…倉促行事；強迫…做 SYN **bulldoze** **2** **~ sth (through/through sth)** to make a group of people accept a decision, law, etc. quickly by putting pressure on them 強使（決定、法律等）草率通過：*The bill was railroaded through the House.* 議院不得已草率通過了這項提案。**3** **~ sb** (*NAmE*) to decide that sb is guilty of a crime, without giving them a fair trial 輕率判處

ˈrailroad crossing (*NAmE*) (*BrE* **ˌlevel ˈcrossing**) *noun* a place where a road crosses a railway/railroad line（公路與鐵路交匯的）道口，平面交叉，平交道

rail·road·er /ˈreɪlrəʊdə(r); *NAmE* -roʊd-/ (*NAmE*) (*BrE* **rail·way·man**, **rail·man**) *noun* a person who works for a rail company 鐵路工人；鐵路員工

rail·way 🔑 /ˈreɪlweɪ/ (*BrE*) (*NAmE* **rail·road**) *noun*

1 🔑 (*BrE* also **ˈrailway line**) a track with rails on which trains run 鐵路；鐵道：*The railway is still under construction.* 這條鐵路仍在建設之中。◇ *a disused railway* 被廢棄的鐵路 **2** 🔑 a system of tracks, together with the trains that run on them, and the organization and people needed to operate them 鐵路公司；鐵道部門；鐵路系統：*Her father worked on the railways.* 她父親在鐵路部門工作。◇ ***a railway station/worker/company*** 火車站；鐵路工人／公司 ◇ *the Midland Railway* 米德蘭鐵路公司 ◇ *a model railway* 鐵路模型

rail·way·man /ˈreɪlweɪmən/ *noun* (*pl.* **-men** /-mən/) (also **rail·man**) (both *BrE*) (*NAmE* **rail·road·er**) a person who works for a rail company 鐵路工人；鐵路員工

rai·ment /ˈreɪmənt/ *noun* [U] (*old use*) clothing 衣服；服裝

rain 🔑 /reɪn/ *noun*, *verb*

■ **noun** **1** 🔑 [U, sing.] water that falls from the sky in separate drops 雨；雨水：*There will be rain in all parts tomorrow.* 明天，各地區都會有雨。◇ *Rain is forecast for the weekend.* 預報週末有雨。◇ *Don't go out* ***in the rain***. 下雨呢，別出去了。◇ *It's* ***pouring with rain*** (= raining very hard). 大雨傾盆。◇ ***heavy/torrential/driving rain*** 大雨；傾盆大雨 ◇ *The rain poured down.* 雨瓢潑而下。◇ ***It looks like rain*** (= as if it is going to rain). 好像要下雨。◇ *A light rain began to fall.* 開始下小雨。◇ *I think I felt a drop of rain.* 我好像感覺到掉雨點兒了。➲ COLLOCATIONS at WEATHER ➲ see also ACID RAIN, RAINY **2** **the rains** [pl.] the season of heavy continuous rain in tropical countries（熱帶地區的）雨季：*The rains come in September.* 雨季九月份開始。**3** [sing.] **~ of sth** a large number of things falling from the sky at the same time 雨點般降落的東西：***a rain of arrows/stones*** 箭密如雨；鋪天蓋地而來的石頭

IDM **come ˌrain, come ˈshine** | **(come) ˌrain or ˈshine** whether there is rain or sun; whatever happens 不論是雨或是晴；不管發生什麼事：*He goes jogging every morning, rain or shine.* 他每天早晨出去跑步，風雨無阻。➲ more at RIGHT *adj.*

■ **verb** **1** 🔑 [I] when **it rains**, water falls from the sky in drops 下雨：*Is it raining?* 下雨了嗎？◇ *It had been raining hard all night.* 大雨下了一整夜。◇ *It hardly rained at all last summer.* 去年夏天幾乎沒怎麼下雨。◇ *It started to rain.* 開始下雨了。**2** [I, T] to fall or to make sth fall on sb/sth in large quantities（使）大量降落，雨點般落下：**~ (down) (on sb/sth)** *Bombs rained (down) on the city's streets.* 炸彈雨點兒似地落在這座城市的街

R

道上。◇ *Falling debris rained on us from above.* 碎片從上面像雨點兒一樣落在我們身上。◇ *He covered his face as the blows rained down on him* (= he was hit repeatedly). 他在遭到雨點般的擊打時護住了自己的臉。◇ **~ sth (down) (on sb/sth)** *The volcano erupted, raining hot ash over a wide area.* 火山噴發，將熾熱的火山灰灑落在一大片地域上。

IDM **be raining cats and 'dogs** (*informal*) to be raining heavily 下傾盆大雨 **it never rains but it 'pours** (*BrE*) (*NAmE* **when it rains, it 'pours**) (*saying*) used to say that when one bad thing happens to you, other bad things happen soon after 不雨則已，一雨傾盆；禍不單行 **,rain on sb's 'parade** (*NAmE, informal*) to spoil sth for sb 煞風景；破壞原定的計劃

PHR V **be ,rained 'off** (*BrE*) (*NAmE* **be ,rained 'out**) (of an event 賽事) to be cancelled or to have to stop because it is raining 因雨取消（或中斷）：*The game has been rained off again.* 比賽又一次因雨而被取消。

Vocabulary Building 詞彙擴充

Rain and storms 雨和暴風雨

Rain 雨

- **Drizzle** is fine light rain. * drizzle 指毛毛細雨。
- A **shower** is a short period of rain. * shower 指陣雨。
- A **downpour** or a **cloudburst** is a heavy fall of rain that often starts suddenly. * downpour 或 cloudburst 指傾盆大雨、大暴雨、驟雨。
- When it is raining very hard you can say that it is **pouring**. In informal *BrE* you can also say that it is **bucketing down** or **chucking it down**. 大雨傾盆可用 it is pouring。非正式英式英語亦可用 it is bucketing down 或者 it is chucking it down。 You can also say 還可說： **The heavens opened.**

Storms 暴風雨

- A **cyclone** and a **typhoon** are types of violent tropical storms with very strong winds. * cyclone 指氣旋，typhoon 指颱風。
- A **hurricane** has very strong winds and is usually at sea. * hurricane 通常指海上的颶風。
- A **monsoon** is a period of very heavy rain in particular countries, or the wind that brings this rain. * monsoon 指某些國家的雨季、季節性暴雨或帶來暴雨的季風。
- A **squall** is a sudden strong, violent wind, usually in a rain or snow storm. * squall 通常指在暴風雨或暴風雪中突起的颮。
- A **tornado** (or *informal* **twister**) has very strong winds which move in a circle, often with a long narrow cloud. * tornado（或非正式用語 twister）指龍捲風。
- A **whirlwind** moves very fast in a spinning movement and causes a lot of damage. * whirlwind 指旋風。
- A **blizzard** is a snow storm with very strong winds. * blizzard 指暴風雪。
- **Tempest** is used mainly in literary language to describe a violent storm. * tempest 主要為文學用語，指暴風雨、風暴、暴風雪。

R

'rain barrel (*NAmE*) (*BrE* **'water butt**) *noun* a large BARREL for collecting rain as it flows off a roof（屋簷下的）雨水桶 ➲ **VISUAL VOCAB** page V19

rain·bow /ˈreɪnbəʊ; *NAmE* -boʊ/ *noun* a curved band of different colours that appears in the sky when the sun shines through rain 虹；彩虹：*all the colours of the rainbow* 彩虹的各種顏色

,rainbow coa'lition *noun* a political group formed by different parties who agree to work together, especially one that includes one or more very small parties（由不同政黨組成，尤指包括小黨派的）彩虹聯盟

,rainbow 'nation *noun* [usually sing.] (*approving*) a name used to describe the people of South Africa because of their many races and cultures 彩虹之國（指南非，因其多種族、多文化而得名）

,rainbow 'trout *noun* [C, U] type of TROUT (= a fish that is often eaten as food, and often caught in the sport of fishing) 虹鱒

'rain check *noun* (*especially NAmE*) a ticket that can be used later if a game, show, etc. is cancelled because of rain（比賽、演出等因雨取消時）可延期使用的票

IDM **take a rain check (on sth)** (*informal, especially NAmE*) to refuse an offer or invitation but say that you might accept it later（婉辭邀請）下次吧，以後再說：*'Are you coming for a drink?' 'Can I take a rain check?—I must get this finished tonight.'* "你來喝一杯吧？""下次吧，好嗎？今晚我得把這項工作做完。"

rain·coat /ˈreɪnkəʊt; *NAmE* -koʊt/ *noun* a long light coat that keeps you dry in the rain 雨衣 ➲ **VISUAL VOCAB** page V61

'rain date *noun* (*NAmE*) an alternative date when an event will take place if it has to be cancelled on the original date because of rain 遇雨改期日：*July 15 is our annual fun day (rain date July 22).* * 7 月 15 日是我們一年一度的遊樂日（遇雨則改至 7 月 22 日）。

rain·drop /ˈreɪndrɒp; *NAmE* -drɑːp/ *noun* a single drop of rain 雨點；雨滴

rain·fall /ˈreɪnfɔːl/ *noun* [U, sing.] the total amount of rain that falls in a particular area in a particular amount of time; an occasion when rain falls 降雨量；下雨：*There has been below average rainfall this month.* 這個月的降雨低於平均降雨量。◇ *an average annual rainfall of 10 cm* * 10 厘米的年平均降雨量

rain·for·est /ˈreɪnfɒrɪst; *NAmE* -fɔːr-; -fɑːr-/ *noun* [C, U] a thick forest in tropical parts of the world that have a lot of rain（熱帶）雨林：*the Amazon rainforest* 亞馬孫雨林 ➲ compare CLOUD FOREST

rain·maker /ˈreɪnmeɪkə(r)/ *noun* **1** (*especially NAmE, business* 商) a person who makes a business grow and become successful 使公司生意興隆的人；成功的企業家 **2** a person who is believed to have the power to make rain fall, especially among Native Americans（尤指印第安人的）求雨法師

rain·out /ˈreɪnaʊt/ *noun* (*NAmE*) an occasion when bad weather prevents an event from starting or finishing 因雨取消；因雨中止

rain·proof /ˈreɪnpruːf/ *adj.* that can keep rain out 防雨的：*a rainproof jacket* 防雨夾克

rain·storm /ˈreɪnstɔːm; *NAmE* -stɔːrm/ *noun* a heavy fall of rain 暴風雨

rain·water /ˈreɪnwɔːtə(r); *NAmE* also -wɑːtər/ *noun* [U] water that has fallen as rain 雨水：*a barrel for collecting rainwater* 接雨水的桶

rainy /ˈreɪni/ *adj.* (**rain·ier**, **rain·iest**) having or bringing a lot of rain 陰雨的；多雨的：*a rainy day* 陰雨天 ◇ *the rainy season* 多雨季節 ◇ *the rainiest place in Britain* 英國最多雨的地區

IDM **save, keep, etc. sth for a ,rainy 'day** to save sth, especially money, for a time when you will really need it 有備無患；未雨綢繆

raise 🔑 /reɪz/ *verb, noun*

■ *verb*

▸ **MOVE UPWARDS** 提升 **1** 🔑 **~ sth** to lift or move sth to a higher level 提升；舉起；提起：*She raised the gun and fired.* 她舉槍射擊。◇ *He raised a hand in greeting.* 他揚起手表示問候。◇ *She raised her eyes from her work.* 她停下工作，抬起頭看了看。**OPP** **lower** ➲ note at RISE **2** 🔑 **~ sth/sb/yourself** (+ **adv./prep.**) to move sth/sb/yourself to a vertical position（使）直立，站立：*Somehow we managed to raise her to her feet.* 不管怎樣，我們終於讓她站了起來。◇ *He raised himself up on one elbow.* 他用一隻胳膊肘支起身子。**OPP** **lower**

▸ **INCREASE** 增加 **3** 🗝 **~ sth (to sth)** to increase the amount or level of sth 增加，提高（數量、水平等）：*to* ***raise*** ***salaries/prices/taxes*** 提高薪水／價格／稅金 ◇ *They raised their offer to $500.* 他們將出價抬高到 500 元。◇ *How can we raise standards in schools?* 我們怎樣才能提高學校的水平？◇ *Don't tell her about the job until you know for sure—we don't want to* ***raise her hopes*** (= make her hope too much). 沒確定之前別告訴她工作的事，我們不想讓她期望過高。◇ *I've never heard him even* ***raise his voice*** (= speak louder because he was angry). 我甚至從沒聽到他提高過嗓門兒。

▸ **COLLECT MONEY/PEOPLE** 籌募錢財；徵集人員 **4** 🗝 **~ sth** to bring or collect money or people together; to manage to get or form sth 籌募；徵集；召集；組建：*to raise a loan* 籌集貸款 ◇ *We are* ***raising money*** *for charity.* 我們在進行慈善募捐。◇ *He set about* ***raising an army***. 他着手組建一支部隊。➲ see also FUND-RAISER

▸ **MENTION SUBJECT** 提出課題 **5** 🗝 **~ sth** to mention sth for people to discuss or sb to deal with 提及；提起（課題）**SYN** **broach**：*The book* ***raises*** *many important* ***questions***. 這本書談到了許多重要問題。◇ *I'm glad you* ***raised the subject*** *of money.* 我很高興你提到了錢。

▸ **CAUSE** 引起 **6 ~ sth** to cause or produce sth; to make sth appear 引起；導致；使出現：*to raise doubts in people's minds* 引起人們的懷疑 ◇ *The plans for the new development have raised angry protests from local residents.* 新的開發計劃惹得當地居民憤怒抗議。◇ *It wasn't an easy audience but he* ***raised a laugh*** *with his joke.* 雖然這些觀眾很難逗樂，但他的笑話還是引起了一陣笑聲。◇ *It had been a difficult day but she managed to* ***raise a smile***. 儘管這一天很不順利，但她還是努力露出笑容。◇ *The horses' hooves raised a cloud of dust.* 馬蹄翻飛，揚起一片塵土。➲ see also CURTAIN-RAISER, FIRE-RAISER

▸ **CHILD/ANIMAL** 孩子；動物 **7** 🗝 (*especially NAmE*) to care for a child or young animal until it is able to take care of itself 撫養；養育；培養：**~ sb/sth** *They were both raised in the South.* 他們倆都是在南方長大的。◇ *kids raised on a diet of hamburgers* 吃漢堡包長大的孩子 ◇ **~ sb/sth as sth | ~ sb/sth + noun** *They raised her (as) a Catholic.* 他們把她培養成為天主教徒。◇ *I was* ***born and raised*** *a city boy.* 我是個在都市裏成長的男孩子。➲ compare BRING UP

▸ **FARM ANIMALS/CROPS** 牲畜；農作物 **8 ~ sth** to breed particular farm animals; to grow particular crops 飼養；培育；種植：*to raise cattle/corn* 養牛；種植玉米

▸ **END STH** 終止 **9 ~ sth** to end a restriction on sb/sth 終止，解除（約束）：*to* ***raise a blockade/a ban/an embargo/a siege*** 解除封鎖／禁令／禁運／包圍

▸ **ON RADIO/PHONE** 無線電；電話 **10 ~ sb** to contact sb and speak to them by radio or telephone（通過無線電或電話）與…取得聯繫，和…通話：*We managed to raise him on his mobile phone.* 我們打他的移動電話，總算找到了他。

▸ **DEAD PERSON** 死人 **11 ~ sb (from sth)** to make sb who has died come to life again 使起死回生；使復活 **SYN** **resurrect**：*Christians believe that God raised Jesus from the dead.* 基督教徒相信上帝讓耶穌死而復生。

▸ **IN CARD GAMES** 紙牌遊戲 **12 ~ sb sth** to make a higher bet than another player in a card game 在（另一玩牌人）基礎上加注：*I'll raise you another hundred dollars.* 我比你再加 100 元。

▸ **MATHEMATICS** 數學 **13 ~ sth to the power of sth** to multiply an amount by itself a particular number of times 使自乘（若干次）：*3 raised to the power of 3 is 27 (= 3 × 3 × 3).* * 3 的三次方等於 27。

IDM **raise a/your 'hand against/to sb** to hit or threaten to hit sb 打人；威脅要打人 **raise the 'bar** to set a new, higher standard of quality or performance 提高標準：*The factory has raised the bar on productivity, food safety and quality.* 工廠提高了在生產力、食品安全和質量方面的標準。**OPP** **lower the bar** ➲ compare SET THE BAR at BAR *n.* **raise your 'eyebrows (at sth)** [often passive] to show that you disapprove of or are surprised by sth 揚起眉毛（表示不贊同或驚訝）：*Eyebrows were raised when he arrived without his wife.* 他沒有和妻子一起來，大家都很驚訝。**raise your 'glass (to sb)** to hold up your glass and wish sb happiness, good luck, etc. before you drink 舉杯祝酒 **raise 'hell** (*informal*) to protest angrily, especially in a way that causes trouble for sb 憤怒抗議；（尤指）大吵大鬧 **raise the 'roof** to produce or make sb produce a lot of noise in a building, for example by shouting or CHEERING（在屋內）大聲喧鬧，鬧翻天 **raise sb's 'spirits** to make sb feel more cheerful or brave 使振奮；使鼓起勇氣 **SYN** **cheer sb up** ➲ more at ANTE, HACKLES, LIFT *v.*, SIGHT *n.*, TEMPERATURE

PHR V **'raise sth to sb/sth** to build or place a statue, etc. somewhere in honour or memory of sb/sth（為…）建造，樹立（塑像等）：*The town raised a memorial to those killed in the war.* 這座小鎮為戰爭中犧牲的人樹立了一座紀念碑。

■ ***noun*** 🗝 (*NAmE*) (*BrE* **rise**) an increase in the money you are paid for the work you do 加薪；工資增長

raised /reɪzd/ *adj.* **1** higher than the area around 凸起的：*a raised platform* 凸起的平台 **2** at a higher level than normal 提高的；升高的：*the sound of raised voices* 提高嗓門的說話聲 ◇ *Smokers often have raised blood pressure.* 吸煙者往往血壓高。

rai·sin /ˈreɪzn/ *noun* a dried GRAPE, used in cakes, etc. 葡萄乾

rais·ing /ˈreɪzɪŋ/ *noun* [U, sing.] the act of raising sth 增加；提高：*consciousness raising* 覺悟的提高 ◇ *a raising of standards in schools* 學校水平的提高 ➲ see also FUND-RAISING

rai·son d'être /ˌreɪzɒ̃ ˈdetrə; *NAmE* ˌreɪzɔːn/ *noun* [sing.] (from *French*) the most important reason for sb's/sth's existence 存在的理由：*Work seems to be her sole raison d'être.* 工作似乎成了她生存的唯一理由。

raita /ˈraɪtə/ *noun* [U] a S Asian dish of finely chopped raw vegetables mixed with YOGURT（南亞）酸奶色拉，優格沙拉

the Raj /rɑːdʒ; rɑːʒ/ *noun* [sing.] British rule in India before 1947（1947 年前）英國對印度的統治

raja (also *less frequent* **rajah**) /ˈrɑːdʒə/ *noun* an Indian king or prince who ruled over a state in the past（舊時印度的）邦主，王公

rake /reɪk/ *noun, verb*

■ ***noun*** **1** [C] a garden tool with a long handle and a row of metal points at the end, used for gathering fallen leaves and making soil smooth 耙子；耙狀工具 ➲ **VISUAL VOCAB** page V16 **2** [C] (*old-fashioned*) a man, especially a rich and fashionable one, who is thought to have low moral standards, for example because he drinks or gambles a lot or has sex with a lot of women 浪蕩的男人；花花公子 **3** [sing.] (*technical* 術語) the amount by which sth, especially the stage in a theatre, slopes 傾斜度（尤指劇院舞台的）

■ ***verb*** **1** [T, I] to pull a rake over a surface in order to make it level or to remove sth 耙；梳理：**~ (sth) (+ adv./prep.)** *The leaves had been raked into a pile.* 樹葉已經用耙子攏成了一堆。◇ (*figurative*) *She raked a comb through her hair.* 她用梳子梳理頭髮。◇ **~ sth + adj.** *First rake the soil smooth.* 首先把地耙平。**2** [T] **~ sth (with sth)** to point a camera, light, gun, etc. at sb/sth and move it slowly from one side to the other 掃視；掠過；掃射：*They raked the streets with machine-gun fire.* 他們用機槍在街上掃射。◇ *Searchlights raked the grounds.* 探照燈從場地上掠過。**3** [I] **+ adv./prep.** to search a place carefully for sth 搜尋；搜索：*She raked around in her bag for her keys.* 她在包裏到處找鑰匙。**4** [T, I] **~ (sth)** to scratch the surface of sth with a sharp object, especially your nails 擦；刮；搔；抓

IDM **rake sb over the 'coals** (*NAmE*) (*BrE* **haul sb over the 'coals**) to criticize sb severely because they have done sth wrong 嚴厲訓斥（或斥責）某人

PHR V **ˌrake 'in sth** (*informal*) to earn a lot of money, especially when it is done easily 賺大錢（尤指輕易地）：*The movie raked in more than $300 million.* 這部電影輕易地賺了 3 億多元。◇ *She's been* ***raking it in*** *since she started her new job.* 她自從開始新的工作以來，已經賺了很多錢。**ˌrake 'over sth** (*informal, disapproving*) to examine sth that happened in the past in great detail and keep talking about it, when it should be forgotten 重提往日某事：*She had no desire to rake over the past.*

R

她不想舊事重提。ˌ**rake sth↔ˈup** (*informal, disapproving*) to mention sth unpleasant that happened in the past and that other people would like to forget 重翻舊賬

raked /reɪkt/ *adj.* (*technical* 術語) placed on a slope 傾斜的；置於斜坡上的：*raked seating* 階梯式座位

ˈ**rake-off** *noun* (*informal*) a share of profits, especially from dishonest or illegal activity 佣金，回扣（尤指不正當或非法所得）

raki /ˈrɑːki; rəˈkiː/ *noun* [U, C] a strong alcoholic drink from eastern Europe and the Middle East 拉克酒（產於東歐和中東）

rak·ish /ˈreɪkɪʃ/ *adj.* **1** (of a man 男人) acting like a RAKE (= in an immoral, etc. way) 放蕩的；肆無忌憚的 **SYN dissolute 2** if you wear a hat at a **rakish angle**, it is not straight on your head and it makes you look relaxed and confident （把帽子）瀟灑地歪戴着的 **SYN jaunty** ▸ **rak·ish·ly** *adv.*

rally /ˈræli/ *noun, verb*

▪ *noun* **1** [C] a large public meeting, especially one held to support a particular idea or political party 公眾集會，群眾大會（尤指支持某信念或政黨的）：*to* ***attend/hold a rally*** 參加 / 召集大會 ◇ *a* ***peace/protest, etc. rally*** 和平集會、抗議集會等 ◇ *a* ***mass rally*** *in support of the strike* 支持罷工的群眾大會 ➲ see also PEP RALLY **2** [C] (*BrE*) a race for cars, motorcycles, etc. over public roads（汽車、摩托車等的）拉力賽：*the Monte Carlo rally* 蒙特卡羅公路汽車賽 ◇ *rally driving* 公路賽車 **3** [C] (in TENNIS and similar sports 網球及類似項目) a series of hits of the ball before a point is scored （爭奪一分的）往返拍擊；對打 **4** [sing.] (in sport or on the Stock Exchange 體育運動或證券交易) an act of returning to a strong position after a period of difficulty or weakness 振作；止跌回升 **SYN recovery**：*After a furious late rally, they finally scored.* 他們後來狀態恢復迅速，終於得分了。◇ *a rally in shares on the stock market* 證券市場股票的止跌回升

▪ *verb* (**ral·lies, rally·ing, ral·lied, ral·lied**) **1** [I, T] to come together or bring people together in order to help or support sb/sth 召集；集合：**~ (around/behind/to sb/sth)** *The cabinet rallied behind the Prime Minister.* 內閣團結一致支持首相。◇ *Many national newspapers rallied to his support.* 許多全國性報紙一致對他表示支持。◇ **~ sb/sth (around/behind/to sb/sth)** *They have rallied a great deal of support for their campaign.* 他們為競選活動徵得了大量的支持。 **2** [I] to become healthier, stronger, etc. after a period of illness, weakness, etc. 復原；恢復健康；振作精神 **SYN recover**：*He never really rallied after the operation.* 手術後，他根本沒有真正康復。◇ *The champion rallied to win the second set 6–3.* 冠軍選手振作精神，以 6:3 贏下第二局。 **3** [I] (*finance* 財) (especially of share prices or a country's money 尤指股票價格或貨幣) to increase in value after falling in value 價格回升；跌後回升 **SYN recover**：*The company's shares had rallied slightly by the close of trading.* 這家公司的股票價格在收盤前略有回升。◇ *The pound rallied against the dollar.* 英鎊對美元的比值回升了。

PHR V ˌ**rally ˈround/aˈround** | ˌ**rally ˈround/aˈround sb** (of a group of people 一群人) to work together in order to help sb who is in a difficult or unpleasant situation 團結在一起

rally·cross /ˈrælikrɒs; *NAmE* -krɔːs; -krɑːs/ *noun* [U] a form of motor racing in which cars are driven both over rough ground and on roads 汽車越野賽 ➲ compare AUTOCROSS

ˈ**rallying cry** *noun* a phrase or an idea that is used to encourage people to support sb/sth（團結眾人的）戰鬥口號，信念

ˈ**rallying point** *noun* a person, a group, an event, etc. that makes people come together in support of sth 有感召力的人（或團體、事件等）；號召力

RAM /ræm/ *noun* [U] the abbreviation for 'random-access memory' (computer memory in which data can be changed or removed and can be looked at in any order) 內存，隨機存貯器，隨時存取記憶體（全寫為 random-access memory）：*256 megabytes of RAM* * 256 兆的內存

ram /ræm/ *verb, noun*

▪ *verb* (**-mm-**) **1 ~ sth** (of a vehicle, a ship, etc. 汽車、輪船等) to drive into or hit another vehicle, ship, etc. with force, sometimes deliberately 和…相撞；撞擊：*Two passengers were injured when their taxi was rammed from behind by a bus.* 公共汽車從後面撞來，出租車上的兩位乘客因此受了傷。 **2 ~ sth + adv./prep.** to push sth somewhere with force 塞進；擠進：*She rammed the key into the lock.* 她將鑰匙塞進鎖眼。◇ (*figurative*) *The spending cuts had been rammed through Congress.* 削減開支一事在國會強行通過。

IDM ˌ**ram sth↔ˈhome** (*especially BrE*) to emphasize an idea, argument, etc. very strongly to make sure people listen to it 強調（想法、論點等）以使人接受 ➲ more at THROAT

PHR V ˌ**ram ˈinto sth** | ˌ**ram sth ˈinto sth** to hit against sth or to make sth hit against sth with force 猛烈撞擊；使猛烈撞上另一物：*He rammed his truck into the back of the one in front.* 他把卡車驀地撞到前一輛卡車的車尾上。

▪ *noun* **1** a male sheep 公羊 ➲ compare EWE **2** a part in a machine that is used for hitting sth very hard or for lifting or moving things 夯錘；撞擊裝置：*hydraulic rams* 水力夯錘 ➲ see also BATTERING RAM

Ram·adan /ˈræmədæn; ˌræməˈdæn/ *noun* [U, C] the 9th month of the Muslim year, when Muslims do not eat or drink between DAWN and SUNSET 回曆九月，齋月，萊麥丹月（齋月期間，穆斯林從破曉到日落禁食）

ram·ble /ˈræmbl/ *verb, noun*

▪ *verb* **1** [I] **+ adv./prep.** (*especially BrE*) to walk for pleasure, especially in the countryside 漫遊，漫步，閒逛（尤指在鄉間）：*We spent the summer rambling in Ireland.* 我們花了一個夏天漫遊愛爾蘭。 **2** [I] to talk about sb/sth in a confused way, especially for a long time 漫談；閒聊；瞎扯：*He had lost track of what he was saying and began to ramble.* 他忘了原先的話題，開始瞎扯起來。◇ **~ (on) (about sb/sth)** *What is she rambling on about now?* 她在東拉西扯些什麼呀？ **3** [I] (**+ adv./prep.**) (of plants 植物) to grow in many different directions, especially over other plants or objects 蔓生；攀附生長：*Climbing plants rambled over the front of the house.* 攀緣植物貼着房子正面的牆到處長。➲ see also RAMBLING

▪ *noun* **1** (*especially BrE*) a long walk for pleasure 漫步；散步：*to go for a ramble in the country* 去鄉間散步 **2** a long confused speech or piece of writing 雜亂無章的長篇大論：*She went into a long ramble about the evils of television.* 她開始東拉西扯地大談電視的弊端。

ram·bler /ˈræmblə(r)/ *noun* **1** (*especially BrE*) a person who walks in the countryside for pleasure, especially as part of an organized group 漫步者；（尤指）有組織的鄉間漫步者 **2** a plant, especially a ROSE, that grows up walls, fences, etc. 蔓生植物

ram·bling /ˈræmblɪŋ/ *adj., noun*

▪ *adj.* **1** (of a building 建築物) spreading in various directions with no particular pattern 向四處延伸的；規劃凌亂的 **SYN sprawling 2** (of a speech or piece of writing 講話或文章) very long and confused 冗長而含糊的；不切題的 **SYN incoherent**：*a rambling letter* 不知所云的長信 **3** (of a plant 植物) growing or climbing in all directions, for example up a wall 蔓生的；攀緣生長的：*a rambling rose* 蔓生的薔薇

▪ *noun* **1** [U] (*BrE*) the activity of walking for pleasure in the countryside 鄉間漫步 **2 ramblings** [pl.] speech or writing that continues for a long time without saying much and seems very confused 漫無目的的講話；長而離題的文章：*the ramblings of a madman* 瘋子的胡言亂語

Rambo /ˈræmbəʊ; *NAmE* -boʊ/ *noun* (*informal*) a very strong and aggressive man 強壯好鬥的男子；猛男 **ORIGIN** From the name of the main character in David Morrell's novel *First Blood*, which was made popular in three films/movies in the 1980s. 源自戴維・莫雷爾的小說《第一滴血》中主人公蘭博的名字，據此改編的三部電影在 20 世紀 80 年代風靡一時。

ram·bunc·tious /ræmˈbʌŋkʃəs/ *adj.* (*informal, especially NAmE*) = RUMBUSTIOUS

ram·bu·tan /ræmˈbuːtn/ *noun* a red tropical fruit with soft pointed parts on its skin and a slightly sour taste 紅毛丹（熱帶水果，味略酸）

ram·ekin /ˈræməkɪn/ *noun* a small dish for baking and serving food for one person（一人份的）小盤子（用於烤製和盛放食物）➲ VISUAL VOCAB page V26

ram·ifi·ca·tion /ˌræmɪfɪˈkeɪʃn/ *noun* [usually pl.] one of the large number of complicated and unexpected results that follow an action or a decision（眾多複雜而又難以預料的）結果，後果 **SYN complication**：*These changes are bound to have widespread social ramifications.* 這些變化注定會造成許多難以預料的社會後果。

ramp /ræmp/ *noun, verb*

■ ***noun* 1** a slope that joins two parts of a road, path, building, etc. when one is higher than the other 斜坡；坡道：*Ramps should be provided for wheelchair users.* 應該給輪椅使用者提供坡道。 **2** (*NAmE*) (*BrE* **ˈslip road**) a road used for driving onto or off a major road such as a MOTORWAY or INTERSTATE（進出高速公路等的）支路，引路：*a freeway exit ramp* 高速公路的出口坡道 ➲ see also OFF-RAMP, ON-RAMP **3** a slope or set of steps that can be moved, used for loading a vehicle or getting on or off a plane（裝車或上下飛機的）活動梯，活動坡道：*a loading ramp* 裝貨用的活動坡道 **4** (*IndE*) the long stage that models walk on during a fashion show（時裝模特走秀的）T 型台 **SYN catwalk, runway**

■ ***verb***

PHR V **ˌramp sth↔ˈup** to make sth increase in amount 使…的數量增加

ram·page *noun, verb*

■ ***noun*** /ˈræmpeɪdʒ/ [usually sing.] a sudden period of wild and violent behaviour, often causing damage and destruction 暴跳如雷；狂暴行為：*Gangs of youths **went on the rampage** in the city yesterday.* 成群結夥的年輕人昨天在城裏橫衝直撞。

■ ***verb*** /ræmˈpeɪdʒ; ˈræmpeɪdʒ/ [I] **+ adv./prep.** (of people or animals 人或動物) to move through a place in a group, usually breaking things and causing damage 橫衝直撞 **SYN run amok**：*a herd of rampaging elephants* 一群橫衝直撞的大象

ram·pant /ˈræmpənt/ *adj.* **1** (of sth bad 壞事) existing or spreading everywhere in a way that cannot be controlled 泛濫的；猖獗的 **SYN unchecked**：*rampant inflation* 失控的通脹 ◇ *Unemployment is now rampant in most of Europe.* 在歐洲的大部份地區，失業問題難以控制。 **2** (of plants 植物) growing thickly and very fast in a way that cannot be controlled 瘋長的 ▸ **ram·pant·ly** *adv.*

ram·part /ˈræmpɑːt; *NAmE* -pɑːrt/ *noun* [usually pl.] a high wide wall of stone or earth with a path on top, built around a castle, town, etc. to defend it 壁壘；城牆

ˈram-raiding *noun* [U] (*BrE*) the crime of driving a vehicle into a shop/store window in order to steal goods 飆車搶劫（指駕車闖入商店行竊）▸ **ˈram-raid** *noun* **ˈram-raid** *verb* **~ sth** **ˈram-raider** *noun*

ram·rod /ˈræmrɒd; *NAmE* -rɑːd/ *noun* a long straight piece of iron used in the past to push EXPLOSIVE into a gun（舊時用以將火藥推進槍支的）推彈杆，通條

IDM **ˌramrod ˈstraight | (as) straight as a ˈramrod** (of a person 人) with a very straight back and looking serious and formal 腰桿筆直的；挺立的

ram·shackle /ˈræmʃækl/ *adj.* **1** (of buildings, vehicles, furniture, etc. 建築物、車輛、傢具等) in a very bad condition and needing repair 搖搖欲墜的；破爛不堪的 **SYN tumbledown 2** (of an organization or a system 組織或體制) badly organized or designed and not likely to last very long 組織鬆散（而不能持久）的；行將瓦解的 **SYN rickety**

ran *past tense* of RUN

ranch /rɑːntʃ; *NAmE*ræntʃ/ *noun* a large farm, especially in N America or Australia, where cows, horses, sheep, etc. are bred 牧場，大農場（尤指北美或澳大利亞的）：*a **cattle/sheep ranch*** 牧牛場；牧羊場 ◇ ***ranch hands*** (= the people who work on a ranch) 牧場工人 ➲ see also DUDE RANCH

ranch·er /ˈrɑːntʃə(r); *NAmE* ˈræntʃər/ *noun* a person who owns, manages or works on a ranch 大農場（或牧場）主；大農場（或牧場）工人：*a cattle rancher* 牧牛場主

ˈranch house *noun* **1** a house on a ranch 農場莊園；牧場住宅 **2** (*NAmE*) a house built all on one level, that is very wide but not very deep from front to back and has a roof that is not very steep 平房住宅（矮屋頂單層，開敞長方形）➲ compare BUNGALOW (1) ➲ VISUAL VOCAB page V16

ranch·ing /ˈrɑːntʃɪŋ; *NAmE* ˈræntʃɪŋ/ *noun* [U] the activity of running a RANCH 牧場經營；農場經營：***cattle/sheep ranching*** 牧牛／牧羊場的經營

ran·cid /ˈrænsɪd/ *adj.* if food containing fat is **rancid**, it tastes or smells unpleasant because it is no longer fresh（含油食品）變質的，變味的，哈喇的

ran·cour (*US* **ran·cor**) /ˈræŋkə(r)/ *noun* [U] (*formal*) feelings of hatred and a desire to hurt other people, especially because you think that sb has done sth unfair to you 怨恨；怨毒 **SYN bitterness**：*She learned to accept criticism **without rancour**.* 她學會了坦然接受批評而不懷恨在心。 ▸ **ran·cor·ous** /ˈræŋkərəs/ *adj.*：*a rancorous legal battle* 充滿敵意的法律爭端

rand /rænd; *in South Africa, commonly* rɑːnt/ *noun* (*pl.* **rand**) **1** [C] the unit of money in the Republic of South Africa 蘭特（南非共和國貨幣單位） **2 the Rand** [sing.] (in South Africa) a large area around Johannesburg where gold is mined and where there are many cities and towns 蘭德（南非約翰內斯堡周圍的金礦區）

R & B /ˌɑːr ən ˈbiː/ *abbr.* RHYTHM AND BLUES

R & D /ˌɑːr ən ˈdiː/ *abbr.* RESEARCH AND DEVELOPMENT

ran·dom **AW** /ˈrændəm/ *adj., noun*

■ ***adj.* 1** [usually before noun] done, chosen, etc. without sb deciding in advance what is going to happen, or without any regular pattern 隨機的，隨意的（非事先決定或不規則）：*the random killing of innocent people* 對無辜者的隨意殺戮 ◇ *a **random sample/selection*** (= in which each thing has an equal chance of being chosen) 隨機抽樣／選擇 ◇ *The information is processed in a random order.* 信息是按隨機順序處理的。◇ (*informal*) *He grabbed a pair of random jeans and an old red shirt.* 他抓了一條隨意拿到的牛仔褲和一件舊的紅襯衫。◇ *She dodged the random items that were on the concrete floor.* 她避開了混凝土地上隨意散放的物品。 **2** [only before noun] (*informal*) (especially of a person 尤指人) not known or not identified 不認識的；辨認不出的：*Some random guy gave me a hundred bucks.* 有個陌生男人給了我 100 美元。 **3** (*informal*) a thing or person that is **random** is strange and does not make sense, often in a way that amuses or interests you（人或物）與眾不同的，出人意料的，不可思議的：*Mom, you are so random!* 媽媽，你太不可思議了！◇ *The humour is great because it's just so random and unhinged from reality.* 幽默之妙在於它如此的出人意料又不受現實的束縛。 ▸ **ran·dom·ly** **AW** *adv.*：*The winning numbers are randomly selected by computer.* 獲獎號碼是由電腦隨機選取的。◇ *My phone seems to switch itself off randomly.* 我的手機好像隨時自動關機。 **ran·dom·ness** **AW** *noun* [U]：*It introduced an element of randomness into the situation.* 這就為形勢增加了一種不確定因素。

■ ***noun***

IDM **at ˈrandom** without deciding in advance what is going to happen, or without any regular pattern 隨意；隨機：*She opened the book at random* (= not at any particular page) *and started reading.* 她隨意翻開書就看了起來。◇ *The terrorists fired into the crowd at random.* 恐怖分子胡亂地向人群開槍。◇ *Names were chosen at random from a list.* 名字是從名單中隨便點的。

ˌrandom ˈaccess *noun* [U] (*computing* 計) the ability in a computer to go straight to data items without having to read through items stored previously 隨機存取；隨機訪問

ˌrandom-ˌaccess ˈmemory *noun* [U] (*computing* 計) = RAM

ran·dom·ize (*BrE* also **-ise**) /ˈrændəmaɪz/ *verb* **~ sth** (*technical* 術語) to use a method in an experiment, a piece of research, etc. that gives every item an equal chance of being considered; to put things in a RANDOM order 使隨機化；（使）作任意排列

R & R /ˌɑːr ən ˈɑː(r)/ *abbr.* **1** rest and recreation (doing things for enjoyment rather than working) 休閒娛樂 **2** (*medical* 醫) rescue and resuscitation 急救與復蘇；救生

randy /ˈrændi/ *adj.* (**ran·dier**, **ran·di·est**) (*BrE, informal*) sexually excited 性興奮的；性慾衝動的： *to feel/get randy* 感到性衝動

ranee = RANI

rang *past tense of* RING

range AW /reɪndʒ/ *noun, verb*

■ *noun*

▸ VARIETY 種類 **1** [C, usually sing.] **~ (of sth)** a variety of things of a particular type 一系列： *The hotel offers **a wide range of** facilities.* 這家酒店提供各種各樣的設施。◇ *There is **a full range of** activities for children.* 這裏有給孩子們提供的各種活動。

▸ LIMITS 界限 **2** [C, usually sing.] the limits between which sth varies （變動或浮動的）範圍，界限，區域： *Most of the students are in the 17-20 **age range**.* 大多數學生都是在 17 至 20 歲的年齡範圍內。◇ *There will be an increase **in the range of** 0 to 3 per cent.* 將會有 0 到 3 個百分點的增長幅度。◇ *It's difficult to find a house in our **price range*** (= that we can afford). 在我們的價格範圍以內，很難找到房子。◇ *This was **outside the range of his experience**.* 這超出了他的閱歷。

▸ OF PRODUCTS 產品 **3** [C] a set of products of a particular type 類；種： *our new range of hair products* 我們的新的頭髮產品系列 ➲ see also MID-RANGE, TOP OF THE RANGE

▸ DISTANCE 距離 **4** [C, U] the distance over which sth can be seen or heard 視覺（或聽覺）範圍： *The child was now out of her **range of vision*** (= not near enough for her to see). 這孩子已經走出了她的視線。 **5** [C, U] the distance over which a gun or other weapon can hit things 射程；射擊距離： *These missiles have a range of 300 miles.* 這些導彈的射程為 300 英里。➲ see also CLOSE-RANGE, LONG-RANGE, SHORT-RANGE **6** [C] the distance that a vehicle will travel before it needs more fuel （車輛）加一次油可行的路程

▸ OF MOUNTAINS 山 **7** [C] a line or group of mountains or hills 山脈： *the great mountain range of the Alps* 雄偉的阿爾卑斯山脈 ➲ VISUAL VOCAB pages V4, V5

▸ FOR SHOOTING 射擊 **8** [C] an area of land where people can practise shooting or where bombs, etc. can be tested 靶場；射擊場；炸彈試驗場： *a shooting range* 射擊場 ➲ see also DRIVING RANGE, RIFLE RANGE

▸ OVEN 爐子 **9** [C] a large piece of equipment that can burn various fuels and is kept hot all the time, used for cooking, especially in the past （尤指舊時的）爐灶 **10** (*NAmE*) = STOVE： *Cook the meat on a low heat on top of the range.* 把肉放在爐灶上用文火燉着。

▸ FOR COWS 乳牛 **11 the range** [sing.] (*NAmE*) a large open area for keeping cows, etc. 牧場；乳牛場 ➲ see also FREE-RANGE

IDM **in/within ˈrange (of sth)** near enough to be reached, seen or heard 在可及的範圍內；在視覺（或聽覺）範圍內： *He shouted angrily at anyone within range.* 他看見誰就對誰吼叫。 **out of ˈrange (of sth)** too far away to be reached, seen or heard 超出…的範圍；在視覺（或聽覺）範圍之外： *The cat stayed well out of range of the children.* 這隻貓離孩子們遠遠的。

■ *verb*

▸ VARY 變化 **1** [I] to vary between two particular amounts, sizes, etc., including others between them （在一定的範圍內）變化，變動： **~ from A to B** *to **range in size/length/price** from A to B* 尺寸／長度／價格在 A 到 B 間變動 ◇ *Accommodation ranges from tourist class to luxury hotels.* 住宿檔次從經濟旅館至豪華酒店不等。◇ **~ between A and B** *Estimates of the damage range between $1 million and $5 million.* 估計損失在 100 萬到 500 萬元之間。 **2** [I] to include a variety of different things in addition to those mentioned 包括（從…到…）之間的各類事物： **~ from A to B** *She has had a number of different jobs, ranging from chef to swimming instructor.* 她做過許多不同的工作，從廚師到游泳教練。◇ **+ adv./prep.** *The conversation ranged widely* (= covered a lot of different topics). 談話所涉及的範圍很廣。➲ see also WIDE-RANGING

▸ ARRANGE 安排 **3** [T, usually passive] **~ sb/sth/yourself + adv./prep.** (*formal*) to arrange people or things in a particular position or order（按一定位置或順序）排列，排序： *The delegates ranged themselves around the table.* 代表依次在桌子周圍就座。◇ *Spectators were ranged along the whole route of the procession.* 旁觀者排列在整個遊行路線的兩側。

▸ MOVE AROUND 徘徊 **4** [I, T] to move around an area 徘徊；漫步；四處移動： **+ adv./prep.** *He ranges far and wide in search of inspiration for his paintings.* 他四處漫步，尋找繪畫的靈感。◇ **~ sth** *Her eyes ranged the room.* 她的目光在屋子裏來回掃視。

PHR V **ˌrange yourself/sb aˈgainst/ˈwith sb/sth** [usually passive] to join with other people to oppose or support sb/sth （使）結夥反對／支持…： *The whole family seemed ranged against him.* 全家人好像在合夥對付他。 **ˈrange over sth** to include a variety of different subjects 涉及；包括： *His lecture ranged over a number of topics.* 他的講座涉及許多話題。

range·find·er /ˈreɪndʒfaɪndə(r)/ *noun* an instrument for estimating how far away an object is, used with a camera or gun （照相機、槍炮的）測距儀

ran·ger /ˈreɪndʒə(r)/ *noun* **1** a person whose job is to take care of a park, a forest or an area of countryside 園林管理員；護林人 **2 Ranger (Guide)** a girl who belongs to the part of the Guide Association in Britain for girls between the ages of 14 and 19 （英國 14 至 19 歲的）女童子軍 **3 Ranger** (*US*) a soldier who is trained to make quick attacks in enemy areas （接受突襲敵戰區訓練的）突擊隊員，特別行動隊隊員 ➲ compare COMMANDO

rangy /ˈreɪndʒi/ *adj.* (of a person or an animal 人或動物) having long thin arms and/or legs 四肢瘦長的

rani (also **ranee**) /ˈrɑːniː; rɑːˈniː/ *noun* an Indian queen; the wife of a RAJA 印度土邦女邦主；印度邦主（或王公）之妻

rank /ræŋk/ *noun, verb, adj.*

■ *noun*

▸ POSITION IN ORGANIZATION/ARMY, ETC. 級別 **1** [U, C] the position, especially a high position, that sb has in a particular organization, society, etc. （尤指較高的）地位，級別： *She was not used to mixing with people of high social rank.* 她不習慣和社會地位很高的人交往。◇ *He **rose through the ranks** to become managing director.* 他級級攀升，當上了常務董事。◇ *Within months she was elevated to ministerial rank.* 不出幾個月，她就被提升至部級。➲ see also RANKING *n.* (1) **2** [C, U] the position that sb has in the army, navy, police, etc. 軍銜；軍階；警銜： *He was soon promoted to the rank of captain.* 他很快被提升至上尉軍階。◇ *officers of **junior/senior rank*** 低級／高級軍階的軍官 ◇ *a campaign to attract more women into the military ranks* 吸引更多的女性擔任各級軍官的運動 ◇ *officers, and **other ranks*** (= people who are not officers) 軍官及士兵 ◇ *The colonel was stripped of his rank* (= was given a lower position, especially as a punishment). 那名上校被降職了。 **3 the ranks** [pl.] the position of ordinary soldiers rather than officers 普通士兵： *He served in the ranks for most of the war.* 戰爭期間，他大部份時間都在部隊服役。◇ *He **rose from the ranks*** (= from being an ordinary soldier) *to become a warrant officer.* 他從普通士兵升至准尉。

▸ QUALITY 質量 **4** [sing.] the degree to which sb/sth is of high quality 等級；級別： *a painter **of the first rank*** 一流的畫家 ◇ *Britain is no longer **in the front rank of** world powers.* 英國再也不是位於前列的世界強國。◇ *The findings are arranged **in rank order** according to performance.* 這些研究結果是根據性能等級排列的。

▸ MEMBERS OF GROUP 成員 **5 the ranks** [pl.] the members of a particular group or organization （團體或組織的）成員： *We have a number of international players in our ranks.* 我們的隊員中有好幾個國際選手。◇ *At 50, he was* forced to **join the ranks of** the unemployed. 他 50 歲時被迫加入了失業行列。◇ *There were serious divisions within the party's own ranks.* 這個黨內部存在着嚴重對立的派別。

▸ **LINE/ROW 行；列** **6** [C] a line or row of soldiers, police, etc. standing next to each other（警察、士兵等的）隊列，行列：*They watched as ranks of marching infantry passed the window.* 他們看着步兵列隊從窗前走過。**7** [C] a line or row of people or things 排；行；列：*massed ranks of spectators* 聚集起來的旁觀者的行列 ◇ *The trees grew **in serried ranks*** (= very closely together). 樹木一排靠一排地生長。➲ see also TAXI RANK

IDM break 'ranks **1** (of soldiers, police, etc. 士兵、警察等) to fail to remain in line 掉隊；未保持隊形 **2** (of the members of a group 成員) to refuse to support the group or the organization of which they are members 不支持所屬團體（或組織）➲ more at CLOSE[1] *v.*, PULL *v.*

■ ***verb*** (not used in the progressive tenses 不用於進行時)

▸ **GIVE POSITION 分等級** **1** 🔑 [T, I] to give sb/sth a particular position on a scale according to quality, importance, success, etc.; to have a position of this kind 把…分等級；屬於某等級：**~ sb/sth (+ adv./prep.)** *The tasks have been ranked in order of difficulty.* 按照困難程度對工作進行了分類。◇ *She is currently the highest ranked player in the world.* 她是目前居全球榜首的運動員。◇ ***top-ranked** players* 一流的選手 ◇ **~ sb/sth as sth** *Voters regularly rank education as being more important than defence.* 投票者通常認為教育比國防更重要。◇ **~ (sb/sth) + adj.** *At the height of her career she ranked second in the world.* 在她事業的頂峰時期，她排名世界第二位。◇ **~ sb/sth + noun** *The university is ranked number one in the country for engineering.* 在工程學領域上，這所大學位居本國第一。◇ **~ as sth** *It certainly doesn't rank as his greatest win.* 這肯定算不上他最大的勝利。◇ **(+ adv./prep.)** *The restaurant ranks among the finest in town.* 這家飯店屬於城裏最好的。◇ *This must rank with* (= be as good as) *the greatest movies ever made.* 這部影片一定可與史上最優秀的影片相媲美。◇ (*NAmE*) *You just don't rank* (= you're not good enough). 你還不夠等級。

▸ **PUT IN LINE/ROW 排列；排成行** **2** [T, usually passive] **~ sth** to arrange objects in a line or row 排列；使排成行

■ ***adj.*** **1** having a strong unpleasant smell 難聞的；惡臭的：*The house was full of the rank smell of urine.* 這屋子裏到處有一股尿的臊味。**2** [only before noun] used to emphasize a particular quality, state, etc.（強調質量、狀況等）極端的，糟糕的：*an example of rank stupidity* 極端愚蠢的例子 ◇ *The winning horse was a **rank outsider**.* 獲勝的這匹馬，本來誰也沒指望它能獲勝。**3** (of plants, etc. 植物) growing too thickly 瘋長的

the ˌrank and 'file *noun* [sing.+sing./pl. v.] **1** the ordinary soldiers who are not officers 普通士兵 **2** the ordinary members of an organization 普通成員：*the rank and file of the workforce* 普通勞動力 ◇ *rank-and-file members* 普通成員

'rank correlation *noun* [U] (*statistics* 統計) a method for finding to what extent two sets of numbers, each arranged in order, are connected or have an effect on each other 秩相關；等級相關

rank·ing /ˈræŋkɪŋ/ *noun, adj.*

■ ***noun*** **1** the position of sb/sth on a scale that shows how good or important they are in relation to other similar people or things, especially in sport 地位，排名，排位（尤指在體育運動中）：*He has improved his ranking this season from 67th to 30th.* 本賽季他將自己的排名從第 67 位提高到了第 30 位。◇ *She has retained her No.1 world ranking.* 她保住了自己世界第一的排名。**2 the rankings** [pl.] an official list showing the best players of a particular sport in order of how successful they are（某項體育運動的）最佳運動員排名表

■ ***adj.*** **1** (*especially NAmE*) having a high or the highest rank in an organization, etc. 地位高的；高級的；最高級的：*a ranking diplomat* 高級外交官 ◇ *He was the **ranking officer*** (= the most senior officer present at a particular time). 當時他是最高官員。**2** (in compounds 構成複合詞) having the particular rank mentioned …級別的；…等級的：*high-ranking/low-ranking police officers* 高／低級別的警官 ◇ *a top-ranking player* 頂尖級選手

ran·kle /ˈræŋkl/ *verb* [I, T] if sth such as an event or a remark **rankles**, it makes you feel angry or upset for a long time 使人耿耿於懷（或怨恨不已、痛苦不已）：**~ (sb)** *Her comments still rankled.* 她的評價仍然讓人耿耿於懷。◇ **~ with sb** *His decision to sell the land still rankled with her.* 他要把地賣掉的決定仍然使她痛心。

ran·sack /ˈrænsæk/ *verb* **~ sth (for sth)** to make a place untidy, causing damage, because you are looking for sth 洗劫；（為找東西）把…翻騰得亂七八糟 **SYN turn upside down**：*The house had been ransacked by burglars.* 這房子遭到了盜賊的洗劫。

ran·som /ˈrænsəm/ *noun, verb*

■ ***noun*** [C, U] money that is paid to sb so that they will set free a person who is being kept as a prisoner by them 贖金：*The kidnappers demanded a ransom of £50 000 from his family.* 綁架者向他的家人索要贖金 5 萬英鎊。◇ *a **ransom demand/note*** 索要贖金的要求／通知 ◇ *ransom money* 贖金 ◇ *They are refusing to pay ransom for her release.* 他們拒絕支付贖金來解救她。

IDM hold sb to 'ransom **1** to keep sb as a prisoner and demand that other people pay you an amount of money before you set them free 將…綁票 **2** (*disapproving*) to take action that puts sb in a very difficult situation in order to force them to do what you want 脅迫；要挾 ➲ more at KING

■ ***verb*** **~ sb** to pay money to sb so that they will set free the person that they are keeping as a prisoner（為某人）交付贖金：*The kidnapped children were all ransomed and returned home unharmed.* 被綁架的兒童在贖金交付後均安然回到家中。

rant /rænt/ *verb* [I, T] **~ (on) (about sth)** | **~ at sb** | **+ speech** (*disapproving*) to speak or complain about sth in a loud and/or angry way 怒吼；咆哮；大聲抱怨 ▸ **rant** *noun*

IDM ˌrant and 'rave (*disapproving*) to show that you are angry by shouting or complaining loudly for a long time 氣憤地大叫大嚷；大聲吵鬧

rant·ings /ˈræntɪŋz/ *noun* [pl.] loud or angry comments or speeches that continue for a long time（長時間的）怒氣沖沖的厲聲斥責

rap /ræp/ *noun, verb*

■ ***noun*** **1** [C] a quick sharp hit or knock 叩擊；快速的敲擊：*There was a sharp rap on the door.* 有人在重重地急促敲門。**2** [U] a type of popular music with a fast strong rhythm and words which are spoken fast, not sung 說唱音樂，饒舌音樂（節奏快而強，配有快速唸白的流行音樂）：*a **rap song/artist*** 說唱歌曲／歌手 **3** [C] a rap song 說唱歌；快板歌；饒舌歌 **4** [C] (*NAmE, informal*) a criminal CONVICTION (= the fact of being found guilty of a crime) 罪責；罪名；判刑：*a police **rap sheet*** (= a record of the crimes sb has committed) 判刑記錄 **5** [sing.] (*NAmE, informal*) an unfair judgement on sth or sb 不公正的判決；苛評：*He denounced the criticisms as 'just one **bum rap** after another.'* 他譴責這樣的批評"只不過是一次又一次的橫加指斥"。◇ *Wolves **get a bad rap**, says a woman who owns three.* "狼的名聲不好，這是不公正的。"一名養着三隻狼的女人說。

IDM (give sb/get) a rap on/over/across the 'knuckles (*informal*) (to give sb/receive) strong criticism for sth（給某人以／受到）嚴厲譴責，厲聲訓斥：*We got a rap over the knuckles for being late.* 我們因為遲到而受到嚴厲訓斥。**take the 'rap (for sb/sth)** (*informal*) to be blamed or punished, especially for sth you have not done（無辜）受罰；背黑鍋 **SYN take the blame**：*She was prepared to take the rap for the shoplifting, though it had been her sister's idea.* 儘管在商店偷東西是她妹妹的主意，可她甘願為此受罰。➲ more at BEAT *v.*

■ ***verb*** **(-pp-)** **1** [I, T] to hit a hard object or surface several times quickly, making a noise 敲擊；擊打：**(+ adv./prep.)** *She rapped angrily on the door.* 她怒氣沖沖地敲着門。◇ **~ sth (+ adv./prep.)** *He rapped the table with his pen.* 他用鋼筆敲了敲桌子。**2** [T] **~ sth (out)** | **+ speech** to say sth suddenly and quickly in a loud, angry way 突然大聲說出；突然厲聲說出：*He walked through the store, rapping out orders to his staff.* 他在商店裏一邊走一邊對他的員工大聲發號施令。**3** [T] **~ sb/sth (for sth/for doing sth)** (used mainly in newspapers 主要用於報章) to

R

criticize sb severely, usually publicly （公開地）嚴厲批評，嚴加指責：*Some of the teachers were rapped for poor performance.* 一些老師因為表現差勁而受到嚴厲批評。 **4** [I, T] ~ (sth) (*music* 音) to say the words of a rap（說唱歌中）唸白；唱饒舌歌 ➲ see also RAPPER

IDM ˌrap sb on/over the ˈknuckles | rap sb's ˈknuckles to criticize sb for sth 批評；指責

ra·pa·cious /rəˈpeɪʃəs/ *adj.* (*formal, disapproving*) wanting more money or goods than you need or have a right to 貪婪的；貪慾的；強取的 **SYN** **grasping** ▸ **ra·pa·cious·ly** *adv.* **rap·acity** /rəˈpæsəti/ *noun* [U]：*the rapacity of landowners seeking greater profit* 土地擁有者牟取更大利益的貪婪

rape /reɪp/ *verb, noun*

■ ***verb*** ~ **sb** to force sb to have sex with you when they do not want to by threatening them or using violence 強姦；強暴 ➲ see also RAPIST

■ ***noun*** **1** [U, C] the crime of forcing sb to have sex with you, especially using violence 強姦罪；強姦案：*He was charged with rape.* 他被控犯了強姦罪。◇ *a rape victim* 強姦案的受害者 ◇ *an increase in the number of reported rapes* 強姦案報案數字的增加 ➲ see also DATE RAPE, RAPIST **2** [sing.] ~ (**of sth**) (*literary*) the act of destroying or spoiling an area in a way that seems unnecessary 肆意損壞；肆意糟蹋；蹂躪 **3** (also ˌ**oilseed** ˈ**rape**) [U] a plant with bright yellow flowers, grown as food for farm animals and for its seeds that are used to make oil 油菜

rape·seed /ˈreɪpsiːd/ [U] seeds of the rape plant, used mainly for cooking oil 油菜籽 ➲ see also CANOLA

rapid 0-ᵂ /ˈræpɪd/ *adj.*

1 0-ᵂ [usually before noun] happening in a short period of time 瞬間的；短時間內發生的：***rapid change/expansion/growth*** 迅速的改變／擴張／增長 ◇ *a* ***rapid rise/decline*** *in sales* 銷售額的急劇上升／下降 ◇ *The patient made a* ***rapid recovery****.* 病人很快恢復了健康。 **2** 0-ᵂ done or happening very quickly 迅速的；快速的；快捷的：*a* ***rapid pulse/heartbeat*** 急促的脈搏／心跳 ◇ *The guard fired four shots in rapid succession.* 衛兵接連開了四槍。◇ *The disease is spreading at a rapid rate.* 這種疾病正在迅速蔓延。 ➲ SYNONYMS at FAST ▸ **rap·id·ity** /rəˈpɪdəti/ *noun* [U]：*the rapidity of economic growth* 經濟增長的高速度 ◇ *The disease is spreading with alarming rapidity.* 這種疾病正在以令人吃驚的速度蔓延。 **rap·id·ly** 0-ᵂ *adv.*：*a rapidly growing economy* 迅速增長的經濟 ◇ *Crime figures are rising rapidly.* 犯罪數字正在迅速上升。

R

ˌ**rapid-ˈfire** *adj.* [only before noun] **1** (of questions, comments, etc. 問題、評論等) spoken very quickly, one after the other 連珠炮似的；接二連三的 **2** (of a gun 槍炮) able to shoot bullets very quickly, one after the other 速射的；連續發射的

ˌ**rapid-reˈsponse** *adj.* [only before noun] having the necessary training and equipment to be able to act quickly when there is an emergency such as an accident, an attack or a natural disaster 快速反應的（指訓練有素、配有必要裝備，能夠快速應對緊急情況的）：*a UN rapid-response unit* 聯合國快速反應小組 ◇ *rapid-response systems for early detection of the virus* 盡早發現病毒的快速反應體系

rapids /ˈræpɪdz/ *noun* [pl.] part of a river where the water flows very fast, usually over rocks（河的）急流；湍急的河水：*to* ***shoot the rapids*** (= to travel quickly over them in a boat) 穿越急流

ˌ**rapid ˈtransit** *noun* [U] (*especially NAmE*) the system of fast public transport in cities, especially the SUBWAY（城市）高速交通系統；（尤指）地鐵 ➲ see also TRANSIT (3)

ra·pier /ˈreɪpiə(r)/ *noun* a long thin light SWORD that has two sharp edges 輕巧細長的雙刃劍：(*figurative*) *rapier wit* (= very quick and sharp) 敏銳的才思

rap·ist /ˈreɪpɪst/ *noun* a person who forces sb to have sex when they do not want to (= RAPES them) 強姦犯；強姦者

rap·pel /ræˈpel/ (*NAmE*) (*BrE* **ab·seil**) *verb* (**-ll-**) [I] ~ (**down, off, etc. sth**) to go down a steep CLIFF or rock while attached to a rope, pushing against the slope or rock with your feet 繞繩下降（用繩纏繞着身體，雙腳蹬陡坡或峭壁自己放繩下滑） ➲ VISUAL VOCAB page V49 ▸ **rap·pel** (*NAmE*) (*BrE* **ab·seil**) *noun*

rap·per /ˈræpə(r)/ *noun* a person who speaks the words of a RAP song 說唱歌手；饒舌歌手

rap·port /ræˈpɔː(r)/ *noun* [sing., U] ~ (**with sb**) | ~ (**between A and B**) a friendly relationship in which people understand each other very well 親善；融洽；和諧：*She understood the importance of establishing a close rapport with clients.* 她懂得與客戶建立密切和諧的關係的重要性。

rap·por·teur /ˌræpɔːˈtɜː(r); *NAmE* -pɔːrˈt-/ *noun* (from *French, technical* 術語) a person officially chosen by an organization to investigate a problem and report on it 特派調查員：*the UN special rapporteur on human rights* 聯合國人權問題特派調查員

rap·proche·ment /ræˈprɒʃmɒ̃; ræˈprəʊʃmɒ̃; *NAmE* ˌræproʊʃˈmɑːn; -prɑːʃ-/ *noun* [sing., U] (from *French, formal*) a situation in which the relationship between two countries or groups of people becomes more friendly after a period during which they were enemies 友好關係的恢復；和解：~ (**with sb**) *policies aimed at bringing about a rapprochement with China* 旨在與中國恢復友好關係的政策 ◇ ~ (**between A and B**) *There now seems little chance of rapprochement between the warring factions.* 目前，敵對雙方和解的可能性似乎很渺茫。

rapt /ræpt/ *adj.* so interested in one particular thing that you are not aware of anything else 全神貫注的；專心致志的：*a rapt audience* 聽得入神的聽眾 ◇ *She listened to the speaker with rapt attention.* 她全神貫注地聽演講者講話。 ▸ **rapt·ly** *adv.*

rap·tor /ˈræptə(r)/ *noun* (*technical* 術語) any BIRD OF PREY (= a bird that kills other creatures for food) 猛禽；攫禽

rap·ture /ˈræptʃə(r)/ *noun* [U] (*formal*) a feeling of extreme pleasure and happiness 狂喜；歡天喜地；興高采烈 **SYN** **delight**：*Charles listened with rapture to her singing.* 查爾斯興致勃勃地聽她演唱。◇ *The children gazed at her in rapture.* 孩子們欣喜若狂地看着她。

IDM **be in, go into, etc. ˈraptures** (**about/over sb/sth**) to feel or express extreme pleasure or enthusiasm for sb/sth 感到（或顯得）極為高興；熱情至極：*The critics went into raptures about her performance.* 評論家們對她的表演讚不絕口。◇ *The last minute goal sent the fans into raptures.* 最後一刻的進球使得球迷們欣喜若狂。

rap·tur·ous /ˈræptʃərəs/ *adj.* [usually before noun] expressing extreme pleasure or enthusiasm for sb/sth 興高采烈的；狂喜的；熱烈的 **SYN** **ecstatic**：*rapturous applause* 熱烈的鼓掌歡呼 ➲ SYNONYMS at EXCITED ▸ **rap·tur·ous·ly** *adv.*

rare 0-ᵂ /reə(r); *NAmE* rer/ *adj.* (**rarer, rar·est**)

1 0-ᵂ not done, seen, happening, etc. very often 稀少的；稀罕的：*a rare disease/occurrence/sight* 罕見的疾病／事件；難得一見的事物 ◇ ~ (**for sb/sth to do sth**) *It's extremely rare for it to be this hot in April.* 四月份就這樣炎熱是極其罕見的。◇ ~ (**to do sth**) *It is rare to find such loyalty these days.* 這樣忠心耿耿，在今天非常少見。◇ ***On the rare occasions when*** *they met he hardly even dared speak to her.* 彼此難得相見，他還幾乎不敢跟她說話。◇ *It was a rare* (= very great) *honour to be made a fellow of the college.* 成為這所學院的研究員是極大的榮譽。 **2** 0-ᵂ existing only in small numbers and therefore valuable or interesting 稀罕的；珍貴的：*a rare book/coin/stamp* 珍貴的書／硬幣／郵票 ◇ *a rare breed/plant* 珍奇物種／植物 ◇ *This species is extremely rare.* 這一物種極為罕見。 **3** (of meat 肉) cooked for only a short time so that the inside is still red 半熟的；半生的 ➲ compare WELL DONE ➲ see also RARITY

rare·bit /ˈreəbɪt; *NAmE* ˈrerbɪt/ *noun* = WELSH RAREBIT

rar·efied /ˈreərɪfaɪd; *NAmE* ˈreræf-/ *adj.* [usually before noun] **1** (often *disapproving*) understood or experienced by only a very small group of people who share a particular area of knowledge or activity 高深精妙的；曲高和寡的：*the rarefied atmosphere of academic life*

陽春白雪的學術生活氛圍 **2** (of air 空氣) containing less OXYGEN than usual 稀薄的；含氧量低的

ˈrare gas *noun* (*chemistry* 化) = NOBLE GAS

rare·ly /ˈreəli; *NAmE* ˈrerli/ *adv.* not very often 罕有；很少；不常：*She is rarely seen in public nowadays.* 如今在公共場所很少能見到她。◇ *We rarely agree on what to do.* 我們很少在要做的事情上看法一致。◇ *a rarely-performed play* 一部很少上演的戲劇 ◇ (*formal*) *Rarely has a debate attracted so much media attention.* 很少有辯論吸引這麼多媒體關注。

rar·ing /ˈreərɪŋ; *NAmE* ˈrer-/ *adj.* **~ to do sth** (*informal*) very enthusiastic about starting to do sth 熱切；渴望：*The new recruits arrived early, all dressed up and* ***raring to go*** (= to start). 新兵早早地就到了，都穿得整整齊齊，盼着出發。◇ *She is raring to get back to work after her operation.* 動完了手術，她渴望回到工作崗位上去。

rar·ity /ˈreərəti; *NAmE* ˈrer-/ *noun* (*pl.* **-ies**) **1** [C] a person or thing that is unusual and is therefore often valuable or interesting 珍品；稀有物：*Women are still something of a rarity in senior positions in business.* 在商界位居高職的女性仍然十分罕見。◇ *His collection of plants contains many rarities.* 他收藏的植物包括許多稀有品種。**2** (also *less frequent* **rare·ness**) [U] the quality of being rare 稀有；罕見：*The value of antiques will depend on their condition and rarity.* 古董的價值依它們的保存狀況和稀有程度而定。

ras·cal /ˈrɑːskl; *NAmE* ˈræskl/ *noun* **1** (*humorous*) a person, especially a child or man, who shows a lack of respect for other people and enjoys playing tricks on them 無賴；壞蛋；淘氣鬼：*Come here, you little rascal!* 過來，你這個小壞蛋！**2** (*old-fashioned*) a dishonest man 不誠實的人 ▶ **ras·cal·ly** *adj.* (*old-fashioned*)

rash /ræʃ/ *noun, adj.*

■ ***noun*** **1** [C, usually sing.] an area of red spots on a person's skin, caused by an illness or a reaction to sth 皮疹；疹：*I woke up covered in a rash.* 我醒來時長了一身皮疹。◇ *I* ***come out in a rash*** (= a rash appears on my skin) *if I eat chocolate.* 我一吃巧克力就長皮疹。◇ *The sun* ***brought her out in*** (= caused) *an itchy rash.* 太陽曬了她一身痱子。◇ *a* ***heat rash*** (= caused by heat) 痱子 ➲ compare SPOT *n.* (3) **2** [sing.] **~ (of sth)** a lot of sth; a series of unpleasant things that happen over a short period of time 大量；許多；（湧現的）令人不快的事物 **SYN** **spate**：*a rash of movies about life in prison* 大量關於監獄生活的電影 ◇ *There has been a rash of burglaries in the area over the last month.* 近一個月這一帶發生了很多起入室行竊案。

■ ***adj.*** (of people or their actions 人或行為) doing sth that may not be sensible without first thinking about the possible results; done in this way 輕率的；魯莽的 **SYN** **impulsive**, **reckless**：*a rash young man* 魯莽的年輕人 ◇ **~ (to do sth)** *It would be rash to assume that everyone will agree with you on this.* 你要是認為在這件事上誰都會同意你的看法，那就太欠考慮了。◇ *Think twice before doing anything rash.* 不要草率行事，要三思而行。◇ *This is what happens when you make rash decisions.* 這就是你貿然作決定的後果。▶ **rash·ly** *adv.*：*She had rashly promised to lend him the money.* 她輕率地答應借錢給他。**rash·ness** *noun* [U]：*He bitterly regretted his rashness.* 他對自己的莽撞極其後悔。

rasher /ˈræʃə(r)/ *noun* (*especially BrE*) a thin slice of BACON (= meat from the back or sides of a pig) 火腿薄片

rasp /rɑːsp; *NAmE* ræsp/ *noun, verb*

■ ***noun*** **1** [sing.] a rough unpleasant sound 刺耳的聲音；刮擦聲 **2** [C] a metal tool with a long blade covered with rows of sharp points, used for making rough surfaces smooth 銼；銼刀

■ ***verb*** **1** [T, I] to say sth in a rough unpleasant voice 用刺耳的聲音說 **SYN** **croak**：**+ speech** *'Where have you been?' she rasped.* "你去哪兒啦？" 她尖聲問道。◇ **~ (sth) (out)** *He rasped out some instructions.* 他粗聲粗氣地發出指令。**2** [I] to make a rough unpleasant sound 發出刺耳的聲音；發出刮擦聲 **SYN** **grate**：*a rasping cough/voice* 刺耳的咳嗽聲／嗓音 **3** [T] **~ sth** to rub a surface with a rasp or with sth rough that works or feels like a rasp 用銼刀銼；用粗糙的東西磨擦：*The wind rasped his face.* 寒風刺疼了他的臉。

rasp·berry /ˈrɑːzbəri; *NAmE* ˈræzberi/ *noun* (*pl.* **-ies**) **1** a small dark red soft fruit that grows on bushes 覆盆子；山莓；懸鉤子：*raspberry jam* 山莓醬 ➲ VISUAL VOCAB page V30 **2** (*NAmE* also **ˌBronx ˈcheer**) (*informal*) a rude sound made by sticking out the tongue and blowing（將舌頭伸出並吹氣而發出的粗魯的聲音）呸聲，噓聲：*to blow a raspberry at sb* 對某人發出噓聲

raspy /ˈrɑːspi; *NAmE* ˈræspi/ *adj.* (of sb's voice 嗓音) having a rough sound, as if the person has a sore throat 沙啞刺耳的 **SYN** **croaky**

Ras·ta·far·ian /ˌræstəˈfeəriən; *NAmE* -ˈfer-/ (also *informal* **Rasta**) *noun* a member of a Jamaican religious group which worships the former Emperor of Ethiopia, Haile Selassie, and which believes that black people will one day return to Africa. Rastafarians often wear DREADLOCKS and have other distinguishing patterns of behaviour and dress. 拉斯塔法里教徒（牙買加一教派成員。崇拜前埃塞俄比亞皇帝海爾·塞拉西，並認為黑人將返回非洲大陸）▶ **Ras·ta·far·ian** (also *informal* **Rasta**) *adj.* **Ras·ta·far·ian·ism** *noun* [U]

ras·ter·ize (*BrE* also **-ise**) /ˈræstəraɪz/ (also **rip**) *verb* **~ sth** (*computing* 計) to change text or images into a form in which they can be printed 將（文本或圖像）光柵化；將…轉換為打印形式

rat /ræt/ *noun, verb*

■ ***noun*** **1** a small animal with a long tail, that looks like a large mouse, usually considered a PEST (= an animal which is disliked because it destroys food or spreads disease) 老鼠；耗子：*rat poison* 老鼠藥 ➲ compare RUG RAT **2** (*informal, disapproving*) an unpleasant person, especially one who is not loyal or who tricks sb 討厭的人；卑鄙的小人；騙子 **IDM** see SINK *v.*, SMELL *v.*

■ ***verb*** (**-tt-**)

PHR V **ˈrat on sb** (*NAmE* also **rat sb out (to sb)**) (*informal, disapproving*) to tell sb in authority about sth wrong that sb else has done 泄漏秘密；告密：*Where I come from, you don't rat on your friends.* 在我的老家，誰都不出賣朋友。**ˈrat on sth** (*BrE, informal*) to not do sth that you have agreed or promised to do 背棄做某事的諾言 **SYN** **renege**：*The government is accused of ratting on its promises to the unemployed.* 政府被指責對失業者背信棄義。**rat sb↔out (to sb)** (*especially NAmE, informal, disapproving*) = RAT ON SB：*Someone ratted us out to the police.* 有人向警方告發了我們。

rata ➲ PRO RATA

ˈrat-arsed *adj.* (*BrE, slang*) extremely drunk 爛醉如泥的

ˌrat-a-tat-ˈtat *noun* [sing.] = RAT-TAT

rata·touille /ˌrætəˈtuːi; -ˈtwiː/ *noun* [U, C] a dish of onions, PEPPERS, AUBERGINES/EGGPLANTS, COURGETTES/ZUCCHINI and tomatoes cooked together 蔬菜雜燴，炖燜蔬菜（用洋蔥、辣椒、茄子、小胡瓜以及番茄一同烹製）

rat·bag /ˈrætbæg/ *noun* (*BrE, slang*) an unpleasant or disgusting person 討厭的人；令人厭煩的人

ratchet 棘輪

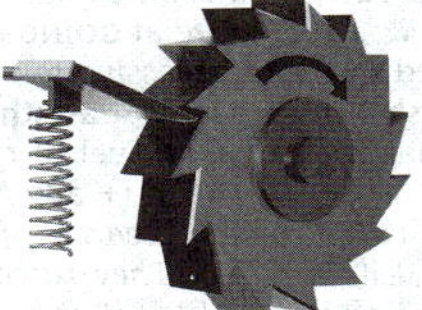

ratchet /ˈrætʃɪt/ *noun, verb*

■ ***noun*** a wheel or bar with teeth along the edge and a metal piece that fits between the teeth, allowing movement in one direction only（防止倒轉的）棘輪，棘齒

R

■ *verb*

PHR V ˌ**ratchet (sth)↔ˈup** to increase, or make sth increase, repeatedly and by small amounts（使）逐漸小幅增長：*Overuse of credit cards has ratcheted up consumer debt to unacceptable levels.* 濫用信用卡使消費債務逐漸增加到了難以接受的地步。

rate 0-π /reɪt/ *noun, verb*

■ *noun* **1** 0-π [C] a measurement of the speed at which sth happens 速度；進度：*Most people walk at an average rate of 5 kilometres an hour.* 大多數人步行的平均速度為每小時 5 公里。◇ *The number of reported crimes is increasing at an alarming rate.* 報警案件的數量正在以驚人的速度增長。◇ *Figures published today show another fall in the rate of inflation.* 今天公佈的數字表明通貨膨脹速度又一次下降。◇ *At the rate you work, you'll never finish!* 以你工作的速度，你永遠也做不完！ **2** 0-π [C] a measurement of the number of times sth happens or exists during a particular period 比率；率：*Local businesses are closing* ***at a/the rate of*** *three a year.* 地方企業正在以每年三家的速度關閉。◇ *a* ***high/low/rising rate*** *of unemployment* 高／低／不斷增長的失業率◇ *the annual* ***crime/divorce rate*** 年犯罪／離婚率◇ *His pulse rate dropped suddenly.* 他的脈搏速率突然下降。◇ *a high* ***success/failure rate*** 很高的成功／失敗率 ➲ see also BIRTH RATE, DEATH RATE **3** [C] a fixed amount of money that is charged or paid for sth 價格；費用：***advertising/insurance/postal, etc. rates*** 廣告費、保險費、郵費等◇ *a* ***low/high*** *hourly* ***rate of pay*** 按小時支付的低／高報酬◇ *We offer special* ***reduced rates*** *for students.* 我們對學生有特惠價格。◇ *a* ***fixed-rate*** *mortgage* (= one in which the amount of money paid back each month is fixed for a particular period) 定額償還按揭貸款◇ *the basic rate of tax* (= the lowest amount that is paid by everyone) 基本稅額◇ ***exchange/interest rates*** 兌換／利息率◇ ***rates of exchange/interest*** 兌換／利息率 ➲ see also BASE RATE, FLAT RATE, RACK RATE **4** **rates** [pl.] (in Britain) a tax paid by businesses to a local authority for land and buildings that they use and in the past also paid by anyone who owned a house（英國地方政府徵收的）房地產稅，房產稅 ➲ **SYNONYMS** at TAX ➲ see also FIRST-RATE, SECOND-RATE, THIRD-RATE

IDM **at ˈany rate** (*informal*) **1** used to say that a particular fact is true despite what has happened in the past or what may happen in the future（強調事情的真實性）無論如何，不管怎樣：*Well, that's one good piece of news at any rate.* 不管怎麼說，這是個好消息。◇ *I may be away on business next week but at any rate I'll be back by Friday.* 我下週可能要出差，但無論如何，我最晚星期五回來。 **2** used to show that you are being more accurate about sth that you have just said（表示說得更加確切）不管怎樣，至少：*He said he'll be coming tomorrow. At any rate, I think that's what he said.* 他說他明天要來。至少，我認為他是這麼說的。 **3** used to show that what you have just said is not as important as what you are going to say（強調下文）總而言之，反正：*There were maybe 60 or 70 people there. At any rate, the room was packed.* 那裏也許有六七十人吧。反正屋子裏擠得嚴嚴實實。 **at a rate of ˈknots** (*BrE, informal*) very quickly 飛快地；迅速地 **at ˈthis/ˈthat rate** (*informal*) used to say what will happen if a particular situation continues to develop in the same way 照此情形；如此下去：*At this rate, we'll soon be bankrupt.* 照此情形，我們很快就會破產。➲ more at GOING *adj.*

■ *verb* (not used in the progressive tenses 不用於進行時) **1** 0-π [T, I] **~ sb/sth (as) sth | ~ as sth** to have or think that sb/sth has a particular level of quality, value, etc. 評估；評價；估價：**~ sb/sth (+ adv./prep.)** *The university is* ***highly rated*** *for its research.* 這所大學因其研究工作而受到高度評價。◇ *They rated him highly as a colleague.* 作為同事，他們對他評價甚高。◇ **~ sb/sth + adj.** *Voters continue to rate education high on their list of priorities.* 選民繼續把教育看作是頭等重要的大事。◇ **~ sb/sth (as) sth | ~ sb/sth + noun** *The show was rated (as) a success by critics and audiences.* 評論家和觀眾都認為這次演出是成功的。◇ **~ as sth** *The match rated as one of their worst defeats.* 這次比賽可以說是他們最為慘重的一次失敗。◇ **+ adj.** *I'm afraid our needs do not rate very high with this administration.* 我們的需求恐怕不會受到這屆政府的高度重視。 **2** [T] **~ sth** (*informal*) to think that sb/sth is good 認為…是好的；看好：*What did you think of the movie? I didn't rate it myself.* 你覺得這部電影怎麼樣？我個人認為不怎麼樣。 **3** 0-π [T, usually passive] to place sb/sth in a particular position on a scale in relation to similar people or things 劃分等級；分等 SYN **rank**：**~ sb/sth (+ adv./prep.)** *The schools were rated according to their exam results.* 這些學校是按考試成績排名次的。◇ *a top-rated programme* 一級項目◇ **~ sb/sth + noun** *She is currently rated number two in the world.* 她目前排名世界第二。 **4** [T] **~ sth** to be good, important, etc. enough to be treated in a particular way 值得，配得上（某種對待）SYN **merit**：*The incident didn't even* ***rate*** ***a mention*** *in the press.* 這件事在報紙上連提都不值得一提。 **5** [T, usually passive] **~ sth (+ noun)** to state that a film/movie or video is suitable for a particular audience 對（電影或錄像片）分級 ➲ see also X-RATED, ZERO-RATED

ˈ**rate cap** *noun* (in the US) a limit placed on the amount of interest banks, etc. may charge（美國）利息限額

Synonyms 同義詞辨析

rate

charge • fee • rent • fine • fare • toll • rental

These are all words for an amount of money that is charged or paid for sth. 以上各詞均指所收取或付出的費用。

rate a fixed amount of money that is asked or paid for sth 指所索取或付出的價格、費用：*a low hourly rate of pay* 按小時支付的低報酬◇ *interest rates* 利息率

charge an amount of money that is asked for goods or services 指商品或服務的要價、收費：*an admission charge* 入場費

fee (*rather formal*) an amount of money that you have to pay for professional advice or services, to go to a school or college, or to join an organization 指專業服務費、咨詢費、學費、會費：*legal fees* 訴訟費◇ *an annual membership fee* 年度會費

rent an amount of money that you regularly have to pay for use of a building or room 指房屋租金

NOTE In American English, **rent** can be used to mean **rental**. 在美式英語中，rent 可用以表示 rental（租金）：*The weekly rent on the car was over $300.* 這輛汽車每週的租金是 300 多元。

fine a sum of money that must be paid as punishment for breaking a law or rule 指罰金、罰款：*a parking fine* 違規停車罰款

fare the money that you pay to travel by bus, plane, taxi, etc. 指乘坐車、船、飛機等的費用

toll an amount of money that you have to pay to use a particular road or bridge 指道路、橋梁的通行費

rental an amount of money that you have to pay to use sth for a particular period of time 指租金

RENT OR RENTAL? 用 rent 還是 rental？

In British English **rent** is only money paid to use a building or room: for other items use **rental**. In American English **rent** can be used for both, but **rental** is still more common for other items. 在英式英語中，rent 只指房屋租金，其他物品的租金用 rental。在美式英語中，rent 可指以上兩種租金，但指其他物品的租金，rental 仍然較通用。

PATTERNS

- (a) rate/charge/fee/rent/fine/fare/toll/rental **for** sth
- (a) rate/charge/fee/rent/toll/rental **on** sth
- **at** a rate/charge/fee/rent/fare/rental of …
- **for** a charge/fee
- to **pay** (a) rate/charge/fee/rent/fine/fare/toll/rental
- to **charge** (a) rate/fee/rent/fare/toll/rental

rate·pay·er /ˈreɪtpeɪə(r)/ *noun* (in Britain in the past) a person who paid taxes to the local authority on the buildings and land they owned（英國舊時的）地方税納税人

ra·ther /ˈrɑːðə(r); *NAmE* ˈræðər/ *adv., exclamation*

■ ***adv.*** **1** used to mean 'fairly' or 'to some degree', often when you are expressing slight criticism, disappointment or surprise（常用於表示輕微的批評、失望或驚訝）相當，在某種程度上：*The instructions were rather complicated.* 這些説明相當複雜。◇ *She fell and hurt her leg rather badly.* 她跌倒了，腿傷得相當重。◇ *I didn't fail the exam; in fact I did rather well!* 我沒有考不及格，事實上，我考得不錯！◇ *It was a rather difficult question.* 這是個相當難的問題。◇ *It was* ***rather a*** *difficult question.* 這真是個難題。◇ *He looks rather like his father.* 他看上去很像他的父親。◇ *The patient has responded to the treatment rather better than expected.* 病人對治療的反應比預想的好得多。◇ *He was conscious that he was talking* ***rather too*** *much.* 他意識到他説得實在太多了。➲ note at QUITE **2** used with a verb to make a statement sound less strong（與動詞連用以減弱語氣）有點兒，稍微：*I rather suspect we're making a mistake.* 我有點兒懷疑我們正在犯錯誤。◇ *We were rather hoping you'd be able to do it by Friday.* 我們希望你最好能在星期五之前做這件事。**3** used to correct sth you have said, or to give more accurate information（糾正所説的話或提供更確切的信息）更確切地講，更準確地説：*She worked as a secretary, or rather, a personal assistant.* 她當了秘書；確切地講，是私人助理。◇ *In the end he had to walk—or rather run—to the office.* 最後他不得不走着，應該説是跑着，去辦公室。➲ **LANGUAGE BANK** at I.E. **4** used to introduce an idea that is different or opposite to the idea that you have stated previously（提出不同或相反的觀點）相反，反而，而是：*The walls were not white, but rather a sort of dirty grey.* 牆面不是白的，而是灰不溜秋的。

IDM **rather you, him, etc. than ˈme** (*informal*) used for saying that you would not like to do sth that another person is going to do（表明不想做別人要去做的事）：*'I'm going climbing tomorrow.' 'Rather you than me!'* "我明天去爬山。" "你去吧，我可不去！" **rather than** instead of sb/sth 而不是：*I think I'll have a cold drink rather than coffee.* 我想要冷飲，不要咖啡。◇ *Why didn't you ask for help, rather than trying to do it on your own?* 你幹嗎非得自己幹，而不請人幫忙？ **would rather ... (than)** (usually reduced to *'d rather* 通常縮寫為 'd rather) would prefer to 寧願；更喜歡：*She'd rather die than give a speech.* 她寧願死也不願意演講。◇ *'Do you want to come with us?' 'No, I'd rather not.'* "你想跟我們一起來嗎？" "不，我不想去。" ◇ *Would you rather walk or take the bus?* 你比較喜歡步行還是坐公共汽車？◇ *'Do you mind if I smoke?' 'Well, I'd rather you didn't.'* "你介意我抽煙嗎？" "嗯，最好別抽。"

■ ***exclamation*** /*also* ˌrɑːˈðɜː(r)/ (*old-fashioned, BrE*) used to agree with sb's suggestion（表示同意某人的提議）：*'How about a trip to the beach?' 'Rather!'* "去海邊旅遊怎麼樣？" "太好了！"

rat·ify /ˈrætɪfaɪ/ *verb* (**rati·fies**, **rati·fy·ing**, **rati·fied**, **rati·fied**) **~ sth** to make an agreement officially valid by voting for or signing it 正式批准；使正式生效：*The treaty was ratified by all the member states.* 這個條約得到了所有成員國的批准。▸ **rati·fi·ca·tion** /ˌrætɪfɪˈkeɪʃn/ *noun* [U]

rat·ing /ˈreɪtɪŋ/ *noun* **1** [C] a measurement of how good, popular, important, etc. sb/sth is, especially in relation to other people or things 等級；級別：*The poll gave a popular approval rating of 39% for the President.* 民意調查表明民眾對總統的支持率為 39%。◇ *Education has been given a high-priority rating by the new administration.* 新一屆政府將教育放在了高度優先的地位。➲ see also CREDIT RATING **2** **the ratings** [pl.] a set of figures that show how many people watch or listen to a particular television or radio programme, used to show how popular a programme is 收視率；收聽率：*The show has gone up in the ratings.* 這個節目的收視率上升了。➲ **COLLOCATIONS** at TELEVISION **3** [C] a number or letter that shows which groups of people a particular film/movie is suitable for 表示電影分級的數字（或字母）；電影的等級：*The film was given a 15 rating by British censors.* 英國審査員將這部電影定為 15 歲以上級。◇ *The movie carries an R rating.* 這部電影帶有限制級 R 的標誌。**4** [C] (*BrE*) a sailor in the navy who is not an officer 海軍士兵；水手

ratio **AW** /ˈreɪʃiəʊ; *NAmE* -oʊ/ *noun* (*pl.* **-os**) **~ (of A to B)** the relationship between two groups of people or things that is represented by two numbers showing how much larger one group is than the other 比率；比例：*What is the ratio of men to women in the department?* 這個部門的男女比例是多少？◇ *The school has a very high teacher-student ratio.* 這所學校的師生比例很高。◇ *The ratio of applications to available places currently stands at 100:1.* 目前，申請人數和錄取名額的比例為 100:1。

rati·ocin·ation /ˌrætiˌɒsɪˈneɪʃn; *NAmE* ˌreɪʃioʊ-/ *noun* [U] (*formal*) the process of thinking or arguing about sth in a logical way 推理；推論

ra·tion /ˈræʃn/ *noun, verb*

■ ***noun*** **1** [C] a fixed amount of food, fuel, etc. that you are officially allowed to have when there is not enough for everyone to have as much as they want, for example during a war（食品、燃料等短缺時的）配給量，定量：*the weekly butter ration* 每週的黃油配給量 **2** **rations** [pl.] a fixed amount of food given regularly to a soldier or to sb who is in a place where there is not much food available（給戰士或食品短缺地區的人提供的）定量口糧：*We're* ***on short rations*** (= allowed less than usual) *until fresh supplies arrive.* 在新的補給到達之前，我們的口糧定量不足。◇ *Once these latest rations run out, the country will again face hunger and starvation.* 最後這批口糧一旦用完，國家又要面臨饑荒。**3** [sing.] **~ (of sth)** an amount of sth that is thought to be normal or fair 正常量；合理的量：*As part of the diet, allow yourself a small daily ration of sugar.* 作為飲食的一部份，每天要攝入少量的糖。◇ *I've had my ration of problems for one day—you deal with it!* 我手頭的問題已經夠我忙活一天的了，你來處理這件事吧！

■ ***verb*** [often passive] to limit the amount of sth that sb is allowed to have, especially because there is not enough of it available 限定…的量；定量供應；配給：**~ sth** *Eggs were rationed during the war.* 戰爭期間，雞蛋限量供應。◇ **~ sb to sth** *The villagers are rationed to two litres of water a day.* 村民每天的用水量限定為兩升。➲ see also RATIONING

ra·tion·al **AW** /ˈræʃnəl/ *adj.* **1** (of behaviour, ideas, etc. 行為、思想等) based on reason rather than emotions 合理的；理性的；明智的：*a rational argument/choice/decision* 合理的論點／選擇／決定 ◇ *rational analysis/thought* 有道理的分析／思考 ◇ *There is no rational explanation for his actions.* 對他的所作所為無法作出合理的解釋。**2** (of a person 人) able to think clearly and make decisions based on reason rather than emotions 理智的；清醒的 **SYN** **reasonable**：*No rational person would ever behave like that.* 有頭腦的人都不會這樣做。**OPP** **irrational** ▸ **ra·tion·al·ity** **AW** /ˌræʃəˈnæləti/ *noun* [U]：*the rationality of his argument* 他的論點的合理性 **ra·tion·al·ly** **AW** /ˈræʃnəli/ *adv.*：*to act/behave/think rationally* 行動／舉止／思考合情合理 ◇ *She argued her case calmly and rationally.* 她冷靜而又理智地為她的情況辯解。

ra·tion·ale /ˌræʃəˈnɑːl; *NAmE* -ˈnæl/ *noun* **~ (behind/for/of sth)** (*formal*) the principles or reasons which explain a particular decision, course of action, belief, etc. 基本原理；根本原因 **SYN** **reason**：*What is the rationale behind these new exams?* 這些新考試的理論依據是什麼？

ra·tion·al·ism **AW** /ˈræʃnəlɪzəm/ *noun* [U] (*philosophy* 哲) the belief that all behaviour, opinions, etc. should be based on reason rather than on emotions or religious beliefs 理性主義；唯理論

ra·tion·al·ist /ˈræʃnəlɪst/ *noun* a person who believes in rationalism 理性主義者；唯理論者 ▸ **ra·tion·al·ist** (also **ra·tion·al·is·tic** /ˌræʃnəˈlɪstɪk/) *adj.* [usually before noun]：*a rationalistic position* 理性主義立場

R

ra·tion·al·ize (*BrE* also **-ise**) **AW** /ˈræʃnəlaɪz/ *verb* **1** [T, I] **~ (sth)** to find or try to find a logical reason to explain why sb thinks, behaves, etc. in a way that is difficult to understand 對…進行理性的解釋；對…加以科學的說明：*an attempt to rationalize his violent behaviour* 對他的暴力行為作出合理解釋的嘗試 **2** [T, I] **~ (sth)** (*BrE*) to make changes to a business, system, etc. in order to make it more efficient, especially by spending less money 使合理化；進行合理化改革；使有經濟效益：*Twenty workers lost their jobs when the department was rationalized.* 在部門的合理化改革中，有二十名工人失業。➲ SYNONYMS at CUT ▸ **ra·tion·al·iza·tion, -isa·tion** **AW** /ˌræʃnəlaɪˈzeɪʃn; *NAmE* -ləˈz-/ *noun* [U, C]：*No amount of rationalization could justify his actions.* 無論怎麼解釋，他的行為都不能說是正當的。◇ *a need for rationalization of the industry* 對這一行業進行合理化改革的必要性

ˌrational ˈnumber *noun* (*mathematics* 數) a number that can be expressed as the RATIO of two whole numbers 有理數

ra·tion·ing /ˈræʃənɪŋ/ *noun* [U] the policy of limiting the amount of food, fuel, etc. that people are allowed to have when there is not enough for everyone to have as much as they want 定量配給政策；配給制

ˈrat pack *noun* [sing.+sing./pl. v.] (*BrE, disapproving*) journalists and photographers who follow famous people around in a way which makes their lives unpleasant 鼠幫（指追蹤騷擾名人的新聞或攝影記者）

the ˈrat race *noun* [sing.] (*disapproving*) the way of life of people living and working in a large city where people compete in an aggressive way with each other in order to be more successful, earn more money, etc.（大城市裏為財富、權力等的）瘋狂競爭，你死我活的競爭 ➲ COLLOCATIONS at TOWN

ˈrat run *noun* (*BrE, informal*) a small road, especially one with houses on it, used by drivers during busy times when the main roads are full of traffic（開車者在高峰時段為避開擁擠的大路而行駛其間的）小街

rats /ræts/ *exclamation* (*informal*) used to show that you are annoyed about sth（表示氣惱）該死，可惡：*Rats! I forgot my glasses.* 該死！我忘了帶眼鏡。

rat·tan /ræˈtæn/ *noun* [U] a SE Asian climbing plant with long thin strong STEMS used especially for making furniture 藤（東南亞蔓生植物，莖幹多用於做傢具）：*a rattan chair* 藤椅

ˌrat-ˈtat (also **ˌrat-a-tat-ˈtat**) *noun* [sing.] the sound of knocking, especially on a door（敲擊聲，尤指敲門聲）吧噠，噠噠

rat·tle /ˈrætl/ *verb, noun*

■ **verb** (*informal*) **1** [I, T] **~ (sth)** to make a series of short loud sounds when hitting against sth hard; to make sth do this （使）發出咔噠咔噠的聲音：*Every time a bus went past, the windows rattled.* 每逢公共汽車經過這裏，窗戶都格格作響。 **2** [I] **+ adv./prep.** (of a vehicle 車輛) to make a series of short loud sounds as it moves somewhere（運行時）發出連續短促的高聲：*A convoy of trucks rattled by.* 卡車隊隆隆駛過。 **3** [T] **~ sb** to make sb nervous or frightened 使緊張；使恐懼 **SYN** **unnerve**：*He was clearly rattled by the question.* 這個問題顯然令他感到緊張。➲ see also SABRE-RATTLING

IDM **ˌrattle sb's ˈcage** (*informal*) to annoy sb 騷擾；使惱怒：*Who's rattled his cage?* 誰惹他生氣了？

PHR V **ˌrattle aˈround** | **ˌrattle aˈround sth** (*informal*) to be living, working, etc. in a room or building that is too big 在空蕩的大房子裏居住（或工作等）：*She spent the last few years alone, rattling around the old family home.* 她在世的最後幾年，一個人居住在空空蕩蕩的老宅子裏。**ˌrattle sth↔ˈoff** to say sth from memory without having to think too hard 脫口而出；不假思索地說出：*She can rattle off the names of all the presidents of the US.* 她可以不假思索地說出所有美國總統的名字。**ˌrattle ˈon (about sth)** (*informal*) to talk continuously about sth that is not important or interesting, especially in an annoying way 對…喋喋不休

■ **noun** **1** (also **rat·tling**) [usually sing.] a series of short loud sounds made when hard objects hit against each other 一連串短促尖厲的撞擊聲；咔噠聲：*the rattle of gunfire* 轟隆轟隆的炮火聲 ◇ *From the kitchen came a rattling of cups and saucers.* 從廚房裏傳來叮叮噹噹杯盤相碰的聲音。➲ see also DEATH RATTLE **2** a baby's toy that makes a series of short loud sounds when it is shaken 撥浪鼓 **3** (*BrE*) a wooden object that is held in one hand and makes a series of short loud sounds when you spin it round, used, for example, by people watching a sports game 響板（在體育比賽等中觀眾用來助陣）

rattle·snake /ˈrætlsneɪk/ (also *informal* **rat·tler** /ˈrætlə(r)/) *noun* a poisonous American snake that makes a noise like a rattle with its tail when it is angry or afraid 響尾蛇（產於美洲）

rat·tling /ˈrætlɪŋ/ *adv.* **~ good** (*old-fashioned, BrE*) very good 很；非常：*This book is a rattling good read.* 這是一本非常好的讀物。

ratty /ˈræti/ *adj.* **1** (*BrE, informal*) becoming angry very easily 易怒的；暴躁的 **SYN** **grumpy, irritable**：*He gets ratty if he doesn't get enough sleep.* 他要是睡眠不足動不動就發脾氣。 **2** (*NAmE, informal*) in bad condition 糟糕的；狀況差的 **SYN** **shabby**：*long ratty hair* 亂蓬蓬的長髮 ◇ *a ratty old pair of jeans* 破舊的牛仔褲 **3** looking like a RAT 像鼠的

rau·cous /ˈrɔːkəs/ *adj.* sounding loud and rough 刺耳的；尖厲的：*raucous laughter* 刺耳的笑聲 ◇ *a raucous voice* 沙啞的聲音 ◇ *a group of raucous young men* 一群吵鬧的年輕人 ▸ **rau·cous·ly** *adv.* **rau·cous·ness** *noun* [U]

raunchy /ˈrɔːntʃi/ *adj.* (*informal*) **1** intended to be sexually exciting 淫穢的；下流的 **SYN** **sexy**：*a raunchy magazine* 色情雜誌 ◇ *Their stage act is a little too raunchy for television.* 他們的舞台表演有點兒太淫穢了，不適合上電視。 **2** (*NAmE*) looking dirty and untidy 骯髒的；邋遢的：*a raunchy old man* 邋遢的老頭子

rav·age /ˈrævɪdʒ/ *verb* [usually passive] **~ sth** to damage sth badly 毀壞；損壞；嚴重損害 **SYN** **devastate**：*a country ravaged by civil war* 遭受內戰重創的國家

rav·ages /ˈrævɪdʒɪz/ *noun* [pl.] **the ~ of sth** (*formal*) the destruction caused by sth 破壞；損害；毀壞：*the ravages of war* 戰爭造成的災難 ◇ *Her looks had not survived* ***the ravages of time.*** 她的容顏未能幸免於歲月的摧殘。

rave /reɪv/ *verb, noun*

■ **verb** **1** [I, T] **~ (about sb/sth)** | **+ speech** to talk or write about sth in a very enthusiastic way 熱烈談論（或書寫）；（熱情洋溢地）奮筆疾書：*The critics raved about his performance in 'Hamlet'.* 評論家們熱情讚揚了他在《哈姆雷特》中的表演。 **2** [I, T] **~ (at sb)** | **+ speech** to shout in a loud and emotional way at sb because you are angry with them 咆哮；怒吼：*She was shouting and raving at them.* 她衝着他們大喊大叫。 **3** [I, T] **~ (at sb)** | **+ speech** to talk or shout in a way that is not logical or sensible 瞎扯；胡說八道：*He wandered the streets raving at passers-by.* 他在街上閒逛，跟過路的人瞎扯。

IDM see RANT

■ **noun** **1** (in Britain) a large party, held outside or in an empty building, at which people dance to fast electronic music and often take illegal drugs（英國）狂歡晚會：*an all-night rave* 通宵狂歡晚會 **2** (*NAmE*) = RAVE REVIEW

ravel /ˈrævl/ *verb* (**-ll-**, *US* **-l-**) **~ sth** to make a situation or problem more complicated 使更複雜；使更紛亂

PHR V **ravel sth↔out** to open sth which has become twisted or which contains knots 拆開（纏結的東西）；解開…的結 **SYN** **unravel**：(*figurative*) *He was trying to ravel out the complicated series of events that had led to this situation.* 他那時正試圖把導致這一局面的一系列複雜事件理出個頭緒來。

raven /ˈreɪvn/ *noun, adj.*

■ **noun** a large bird of the CROW family, with shiny black feathers and a rough unpleasant cry 渡鴉（羽毛黑色，鳴聲刺耳）

■ **adj.** [only before noun] (*literary*) (of hair 毛髮) shiny and black 烏黑光亮的：*raven-haired* 毛髮烏黑光亮的

R

raven·ing /ˈrævənɪŋ/ *adj.* (*literary*) (especially of animals 尤指動物) aggressive and hungry 兇猛的；飢餓而富攻擊性的：*He says the media are ravening wolves.* 他說媒體就如同餓狼一般。

rav·en·ous /ˈrævənəs/ *adj.* **1** (of a person or an animal 人或動物) extremely hungry 極其飢餓的 SYN **starving**：*What's for lunch? I'm absolutely ravenous.* 午飯吃什麼？我餓死了。 **2** [only before noun] (of HUNGER 飢餓) very great 嚴重的；十分的：*a ravenous appetite* 極強的食慾 ▸ **rav·en·ous·ly** *adv.*

raver /ˈreɪvə(r)/ *noun* (*BrE, informal*) **1** (often *humorous*) a person who likes going out and who has an exciting social life 喜歡社交活動的人；喜歡尋歡作樂的人 **2** a person who goes to RAVES 參加狂歡聚會的人

ˌrave reˈview (*NAmE* also **rave**) *noun* an article in a newspaper or magazine that is very enthusiastic about a particular film/movie, book, etc. 熱情洋溢的評論文章

ˈrave-up *noun* (*old-fashioned, BrE, informal*) a lively party or celebration 狂歡聚會；熱鬧的慶典

rav·ine /rəˈviːn/ *noun* a deep, very narrow valley with steep sides 溝壑；溪谷

rav·ing /ˈreɪvɪŋ/ *adj., adv.*

■ **adj.** [only before noun] **1** (of a person 人) talking or behaving in a way that shows they are crazy 狂亂的；語無倫次的；瘋瘋癲癲的：*The man's a raving lunatic.* 那個男子是個語無倫次的瘋子。 **2** used to emphasize a particular state or quality（強調某狀態或品質）：*She's no raving beauty.* 她根本算不上漂亮。

■ **adv.**

IDM **(stark) raving ˈmad/ˈbonkers** (*informal*) completely crazy 十分瘋狂；徹底瘋狂

rav·ings /ˈreɪvɪŋz/ *noun* [pl.] words that have no meaning, spoken by sb who is crazy 瘋話；胡言亂語：*He dismissed her words as the ravings of a hysterical woman.* 他不理睬她的話，認為那是一個歇斯底里的女人的胡言亂語。

ravi·oli /ˌræviˈəʊli; *NAmE* -ˈoʊli/ *noun* [U] PASTA in the shape of small squares filled with meat, cheese, etc., usually served with a sauce 意大利方形餃（以肉、奶酪等為餡，通常佐以醬汁食用）

rav·ish /ˈrævɪʃ/ *verb* (*literary*) **1** **~ sb** (of a man 男子) to force a woman to have sex 強暴；強姦 SYN **rape** **2** [usually passive] **~ sb** to give sb great pleasure 使狂喜；使銷魂

rav·ish·ing /ˈrævɪʃɪŋ/ *adj.* extremely beautiful 極其美麗的 SYN **gorgeous**：*a ravishing blonde* 迷人的金髮女郎 ▸ **rav·ish·ing·ly** *adv.*：*ravishingly beautiful* 異常美麗

raw 🔑 /rɔː/ *adj., noun*

■ **adj.**

▸ **FOOD** 食物 **1** 🔑 not cooked 生的；未烹製的；未煮的：*raw meat* 生肉 ◇ *These fish are often eaten raw.* 這些魚常常生吃。

▸ **MATERIALS** 材料 **2** [usually before noun] in its natural state; not yet changed, used or made into sth else 未經加工的；自然狀態的：*raw sugar* 原糖

▸ **INFORMATION** 信息 **3** [usually before noun] not yet organized into a form in which it can be easily used or understood 未經處理的；未經分析的；原始的：*This information is only **raw data** and will need further analysis.* 這些資料只是原始數據，還需要進一步分析。

▸ **EMOTIONS/QUALITIES** 情感；品質 **4** [usually before noun] powerful and natural; not controlled or trained 未經訓練的；粗獷的：*songs full of raw emotion* 充滿原始情感的歌曲 ◇ *He started with nothing but raw talent and determination.* 他起初一無所有，只有天生的才能和決心。

▸ **PART OF BODY** 身體部位 **5** red and painful because the skin has been damaged 紅腫疼痛的；皮膚破損的；擦傷的：*There were raw patches on her feet where the shoes had rubbed.* 她的雙腳被鞋子磨破了好幾塊皮。 ➲ SYNONYMS at PAINFUL

▸ **PERSON** 人 **6** [usually before noun] new to a job or an activity and therefore without experience or skill 工作生疏的；不熟練的；無經驗的：*a raw beginner* 沒有經驗的新手 ◇ *raw recruits* (= for example, in the army) 未經訓練的新兵

▸ **WEATHER** 天氣 **7** very cold 寒冷的；嚴寒的：*a raw north wind* 寒冷的北風 ◇ *It had been a wet raw winter.* 那是一個寒冷潮濕的冬天。

▸ **DESCRIPTION** 描述 **8** honest, direct and sometimes shocking 真實的；反映真實情況的：*a raw portrayal of working-class life* 工人階級生活的真實寫照 ◇ (*NAmE*) *raw language* (= containing many sexual details) 粗魯的語言 ▸ **raw·ness** *noun* [U]

IDM **a raw ˈdeal** the fact of sb being treated unfairly 不公平的待遇；不公正的對待：*Older workers often get a raw deal.* 年紀大的工人經常受到不公正的對待。

■ ***noun***

IDM **catch/touch sb on the ˈraw** (*BrE*) to upset sb by reminding them of sth they are particularly sensitive about 觸到某人的痛處；揭某人的瘡疤 **in the ˈraw** **1** in a way that does not hide the unpleasant aspects of sth 質樸的；不加掩飾的：*He spent a couple of months on the streets to experience life in the raw.* 他花了幾個月時間走街串巷，體驗真實的生活。 **2** (*especially NAmE*) with no clothes on 赤條條；赤身裸體；一絲不掛 SYN **naked** ➲ more at NERVE *n.*

raw·hide /ˈrɔːhaɪd/ *noun* [U] natural leather that has not had any special treatment 生皮；未經加工的皮革

Rawl·plug™ /ˈrɔːlplʌg/ *noun* (also **ˈwall plug**) (both *BrE*) (*NAmE* **ˈwall anchor**) a small plastic tube, closed at one end, that you put into a wall to hold a screw 羅威套管（塑料螺釘栓）

ˌraw maˈterial *noun* [C, U] a basic material that is used to make a product 原料：*We have had problems with the supply of raw materials to the factory.* 我們在工廠的原料供應方面遇到過問題。◇ *These trees provide the raw material for high-quality paper.* 這些樹是製造優質紙張的原料。◇ (*figurative*) *The writer uses her childhood as raw material for this novel.* 作者將她的童年時代作為這部小說的素材。

ray /reɪ/ *noun* **1** a narrow line of light, heat or other energy 光線；（熱或其他能量的）射線：*the sun's rays* 太陽的光線 ◇ *ultraviolet rays* 紫外線 ◇ *The windows were shining in the reflected rays of the setting sun.* 窗戶上閃耀着落日的餘暉。 ➲ see also COSMIC RAYS, GAMMA RAYS at GAMMA RADIATION, X-RAY **2** **~ of sth** a small amount of sth good or of sth that you are hoping for（好事或所希望事物的）一點，少量 SYN **glimmer**：*There was just one small **ray of hope**.* 只有一絲希望。 **3** a sea fish with a large broad flat body and a long tail, that is used for food 魟，鰩（扁體長尾，可食用） **4** (also **re**) (*music* 音) the second note of a MAJOR SCALE 大調音階的第 2 音

IDM **a ˌray of ˈsunshine** (*informal*) a person or thing that makes life brighter or more cheerful 給人帶來快樂的人（或事物） **catch/get/grab some ˈrays** (*informal*) to sit or lie in the sun, especially in order to get a SUNTAN 曬太陽；沐日光浴

ˈray gun *noun* (in SCIENCE FICTION stories) a gun that kills or injures people by sending out harmful rays（科幻小說中的）死光槍，射線槍，雷射槍

rayon /ˈreɪɒn; *NAmE* -ɑːn/ *noun* [U] a FIBRE made from CELLULOSE; a smooth material made from this, used for making clothes 人造絲；人造絲織品

raze /reɪz/ *verb* [usually passive] **~ sth** to completely destroy a building, town, etc. so that nothing is left 徹底摧毀；將…夷為平地：*The village was **razed to the ground**.* 這座村莊被夷為平地。

razor /ˈreɪzə(r)/ *noun* an instrument that is used for shaving 剃鬚刀；刮臉刀：*an electric razor* 電動剃鬚刀 ◇ *a **cut-throat/safety/disposable razor*** 開式／保險／一次性剃刀 ➲ VISUAL VOCAB page V24 ➲ compare SHAVER

IDM **be on the ˈrazor's edge** | **be on a ˈrazor edge** to be in a difficult situation where any mistake may be very dangerous 處於非常危險的困境；境況岌岌可危

razor·bill /ˈreɪzəbɪl; *NAmE* -zərb-/ *noun* a black and white bird with a beak that looks like an old-fashioned RAZOR, found in the N Atlantic and the Baltic Sea 刀嘴海雀（產於北大西洋和波羅的海）

R

'razor blade *noun* a thin sharp piece of metal that is used in a razor, especially one that can be thrown away when it is no longer sharp（尤指可更換的）剃鬚刀刀片 ➲ picture at BLADE

,razor-'sharp *adj.* **1** extremely sharp 極鋒利的：*razor-sharp teeth* 十分鋒利的牙齒 **2** showing that sb is extremely intelligent 極其敏銳的：*a razor-sharp mind* 極敏銳的頭腦

,razor-'thin *adj.* (*NAmE*) (of a victory in an election, etc. 選舉等的勝利) won by a very small number of votes 以微弱優勢取勝的；險勝的

'razor wire *noun* [U] strong wire with sharp blades sticking out, placed on top of walls and around areas of land to keep people out 尖利鐵絲網，刺鋼絲（牆頭及土地周圍防護用）

razz /ræz/ *verb* **~ sb** (*old-fashioned, NAmE, informal*) to TEASE sb by saying or doing things to make people laugh at them 嘲弄；戲弄

raz·zle /'ræzl/ *noun*

IDM **be/go (out) on the razzle** (*BrE, informal*) to go out drinking, dancing and enjoying yourself 出外縱飲狂歡；外出尋歡作樂

razz·ma·tazz /,ræzmə'tæz/ (also **raz·za·ma·tazz** /,ræzəmə'tæz/) (also **,razzle-'dazzle**) *noun* [U] (*informal*) a lot of noisy exciting activity that is intended to attract people's attention 令人眼花繚亂的活動：*The documentary focuses on the razzmatazz of an American political campaign.* 這部紀錄影片着重展現出一場美國政治運動令人眼花繚亂的一面。

RC /,ɑː 'siː; *NAmE* ,ɑːr/ *abbr.* ROMAN CATHOLIC 天主教

RCMP /,ɑː siː em 'piː; *NAmE* ,ɑːr/ *abbr.* Royal Canadian Mounted Police (the national police force of Canada) 皇家加拿大騎警隊（加拿大的國家警力）

Rd (also **Rd.** especially in *NAmE*) *abbr.* (used in written addresses) Road（用於書面地址）路：*12 Ashton Rd* 阿什頓路 12 號

RDA /,ɑː diː 'eɪ; *NAmE* ,ɑːr/ *abbr.* recommended daily allowance (the amount of a chemical, for example a VITAMIN or a mineral, which you should have every day)（維生素或礦物質等的）建議每日攝取量

RE /,ɑːr 'iː/ *noun* [U] the abbreviation for religious education (a school subject in which students learn about different religions) 宗教教育（全寫為 religious education，學校裏講授不同宗教知識的課程）：*an RE teacher* 宗教教育科老師

re¹ /reɪ/ = RAY (4)

re² /riː/ *prep.* used at the beginning of a business letter, etc. to introduce the subject that it is about; used on an email that you are sending as a reply（用於商業信函等開頭介紹主題或回覆電子郵件）關於，事由：*Re your letter of 1 September …* 關於你 9 月 1 日的來信…◇ *Re: travel expenses* 回覆：旅行開支

re- 🔑 /riː/ *prefix*
(in verbs and related nouns, adjectives and adverbs 構成動詞及相關的名詞、形容詞和副詞) again 又；再；重新：*reapply* 再申請 ◇ *reincarnation* 再生 ◇ *reassuring* 使人放心的

reach 🔑 /riːtʃ/ *verb, noun*

■ *verb*

▸ **ARRIVE** 到達 **1** 🔑 [T] **~ sth/sb** to arrive at the place that you have been travelling to 到達；抵達：*They didn't reach the border until after dark.* 他們天黑以後才到達邊境。◇ *I hope this letter reaches you.* 我希望你能收到這封信。 **2** 🔑 [T] **~ sb** to come to sb's attention 引起…的注意：*The rumours eventually reached the President.* 傳聞最終引起了總統的注意。

▸ **LEVEL/SPEED/STAGE** 水平；速度；階段 **3** 🔑 [T] **~ sth** to increase to a particular level, speed, etc. over a period of time 增加到，提升到（某一水平、速度等）：*The conflict has now reached a new level of intensity.* 衝突現在已經達到了新的激烈程度。◇ *Daytime temperatures can reach 40°C.* 白天的氣温可以達到 40 攝氏度。 **4** 🔑 [T] **~ sth** to arrive at a particular point or stage of sth after a period of time 達到（某點）；進入（某階段）：*He first reached the finals in 2008.* 他於 2008 年第一次進入決賽。◇ *The negotiations have reached deadlock.* 談判陷入僵局。

▸ **ACHIEVE AIM** 實現目標 **5** 🔑 [T] **~ sth** to achieve a particular aim 實現；達到 SYN **arrive at**：*to reach a **conclusion/decision/verdict/compromise*** 得出結論；作出決定／裁決／妥協 ◇ *Politicians again failed to **reach an agreement**.* 政治家們又一次沒有達成一致。 ➲ see also FAR-REACHING

▸ **WITH HAND/ARM** 用手／手臂 **6** 🔑 [I, T] to stretch your hand towards sth in order to touch it, pick it up, etc. 伸；伸手：**+ adv./prep.** *She reached inside her bag for a pen.* 她把手伸到包裏掏鋼筆。◇ **~ sth + adv./prep.** *He reached out his hand to touch her.* 他伸出手去摸她。 **7** 🔑 [I, T] to be able to stretch your hand far enough in order to touch sth, pick sth up, etc. 能伸到；夠得着：(**+ adv./prep.**) *'Grab the end of the rope.' 'I can't reach that far!'* "抓住繩子頭。" "我夠不着！" ◇ **~ sth** *Can you reach the light switch from where you're sitting?* 從你坐的地方夠得着燈的開關嗎？ **8** [T] to stretch your hand out or up in order to get sth for sb 伸手取（物）；傳遞：**~ sth (down) for sb** *Can you reach that box down for me?* 你幫我把那個盒子拿下來好嗎？◇ **~ sb (down) sth** *Can you reach me down that box?* 你幫我把那個盒子拿下來好嗎？

▸ **BE LONG ENOUGH** 夠長 **9** 🔑 [I, T] to be big enough, long enough, etc. to arrive at a particular point（大或長等）足夠達到：**+ adv./prep.** *The carpet only reached halfway across the room.* 地毯只夠覆蓋半間屋。◇ **~ sth** *Is the cable long enough to reach the socket?* 電線夠得着插座嗎？

▸ **CONTACT SB** 聯繫 **10** [T] **~ sb** to communicate with sb, especially by telephone（尤指用電話）聯繫，與…取得聯繫：*Do you know where I can reach him?* 你知道我在哪兒能跟他聯繫上嗎？

▸ **BE SEEN/HEARD BY SB** 被看到／聽到 **11** [T] **~ sb** to be seen or heard by sb 被…看到（或聽到）：*Through television and radio we are able to reach a wider audience.* 通過電視和收音機，我們能夠為更加廣泛的觀眾和聽眾所熟悉。

IDM **reach for the 'stars** to try to be successful at sth that is difficult 有九天攬月之志；努力完成壯舉 ➲ more at EAR

PHR V **,reach 'out to sb** to show sb that you are interested in them and/or want to help them 表示對某人感興趣；表示願意提供援助：*The church needs to find new ways of reaching out to young people.* 教會需要尋找新途徑來為年輕人提供幫助。

■ *noun*

▸ **OF ARMS** 手臂 **1** [sing., U] the distance over which you can stretch your arms to touch sth; the distance over which a particular object can be used to touch sth else 手臂展開的長度；臂展：*As a boxer, his long reach gives him a significant advantage.* 作為拳擊運動員，他出拳距離長是他很大的優勢。◇ *The shot was well **beyond the reach of** the goalkeeper.* 這次射門使守門員鞭長莫及。◇ *Cleaning fluids should be kept **out of the reach of** children.* 洗滌劑應該放在兒童夠不到的地方。◇ *He lashed out angrily, hitting anyone **within his reach**.* 他氣急敗壞，見人就打。◇ *Use shears with a long reach for cutting high hedges.* 用長柄大剪刀修剪高樹籬。

▸ **OF POWER/INFLUENCE** 權力；影響 **2** [sing., U] the limit to which sb/sth has the power or influence to do sth 波及範圍；影響範圍：*Such matters are **beyond the reach of** the law.* 這樣的事情不受法律的保護。◇ *Victory is now **out of her reach**.* 勝利現在對於她來説遙不可及。◇ *The basic model is priced well **within the reach of** most people.* 基本款式的定價大多數人都完全負擔得起。◇ *The company has now overtaken IBM in terms of size and reach.* 在規模和影響範圍上，這家公司已經超越了國際商用機器。

▸ **OF RIVER** 河流 **3** [C, usually pl.] a straight section of water between two bends on a river 河段；直水道：*the **upper/lower reaches** of the Nile* (= the part that is furthest from/nearest to the sea) 尼羅河上游／下游

▸ **PLACE FAR FROM CENTRE** 邊緣 **4 reaches** [pl.] **the outer, further, etc. ~ of sth** the parts of an area or a place that are a long way from the centre 邊緣地帶；邊遠地區：*the outer reaches of space* 外層太空 ◇ (*figurative*) *an exploration of the deepest reaches of the human mind* 對人類思想最深處的探索

▸ SECTIONS OF ORGANIZATION 組織部門 **5 reaches** [pl.] **the higher, lower, etc. ~ of sth** the higher, etc. sections of an organization, a system, etc. （組織、體制等的）領域，部門：*There are still few women in the upper reaches of the civil service.* 在高級別公務員中，女性仍然寥寥無幾。◇ *Many clubs in the lower reaches of the league are in financial difficulty.* 聯合會下層的許多俱樂部都處於財政困難之中。

IDM **within (easy) ˈreach (of sth)** close to sth 很接近；靠近：*The house is within easy reach of schools and sports facilities.* 這房子距離學校和體育設施都很近。

reach·able /ˈriːtʃəbl/ *adj.* [not before noun] that is possible to reach 可及；可到達；夠得到：*The farm is only reachable by car.* 那個農場只能開車去。

re·acquaint /ˌriːəˈkweɪnt/ *verb* **~ sb/yourself with sth** to let sb/yourself find out about sth again or get used to sth again（使）重新瞭解；（使）再熟悉：*I'll need to reacquaint myself with this program—it's a long time since I've used it.* 我得再熟悉一下這個程序，我已經很長時間沒用了。

react 0-w AW /riˈækt/ *verb*
1 0-w [I] **~ (to sth)** **(by doing sth)** to change or behave in a particular way as a result of or in response to sth 起反應；（對…）作出反應；回應：*Local residents have reacted angrily to the news.* 當地居民對這一消息表示憤怒。◇ *I nudged her but she didn't react.* 我用胳膊肘捅了她一下，可她沒有反應。◇ *You never know how he is going to react.* 你根本不知道他會作何反應。◇ *The market reacted by falling a further two points.* 股市的反應是再下跌兩個百分點。 **2** 0-w [I] **(+ adv./prep.)** to become ill/sick after eating, breathing, etc. a particular substance（對食物等）有不良反應，過敏：*People can react badly to certain food additives.* 人們對某些食品添加劑可能會嚴重過敏。 **3** [I] **~ (with sth)** | **~ (together)** (*chemistry* 化) (of substances 物質) to experience a chemical change when coming into contact with another substance 起化學反應；發生化學變化：*Iron reacts with water and air to produce rust.* 鐵和水及空氣發生反應產生鐵銹。

PHR V **reˌact aˈgainst sb/sth** to show dislike or opposition in response to sth, especially by deliberately doing the opposite of what sb wants you to do 反對；反抗：*He reacted strongly against the artistic conventions of his time.* 他強烈反對當時的藝術俗套。

react·ance /riˈæktəns/ *noun* [U, C] (*physics* 物) (*symb.* X) the opposition of a piece of electrical equipment, etc. to the flow of an ALTERNATING CURRENT 電抗 ➲ compare RESISTANCE (5)

react·ant /riˈæktənt/ *noun* (*chemistry* 化) a substance that takes part in and is changed by a chemical reaction 反應物

re·action 0-w AW /riˈækʃn/ *noun*

▸ TO EVENT/SITUATION 對於事件／局勢 **1** 0-w [C, U] **~ (to sb/sth)** what you do, say or think as a result of sth that has happened 反應；回應：*What was his reaction to the news?* 他對這消息有何反應？◇ *My* ***immediate reaction*** *was one of shock.* 我當即的反應是大吃一驚。◇ *A spokesman said the changes were not* ***in reaction to*** *the company's recent losses.* 一位發言人說，這些變動不是針對公司最近的損失而作出的反應。◇ *There has been a* ***mixed reaction*** *to her appointment as director.* 對她獲任命為主管一事，人們的反應各不相同。◇ *The decision provoked an angry reaction from local residents.* 這個決定引起了當地居民的憤怒抗議。◇ *I tried shaking him but there was no reaction.* 我試着搖了搖他，但他一動不動。

▸ CHANGE IN ATTITUDES 態度的改變 **2** 0-w [C, usually sing., U] **~ (against sth)** a change in people's attitudes or behaviour caused by disapproval of the attitudes, etc. of the past（對舊觀念等的）抗拒：*The return to traditional family values is a reaction against the permissiveness of recent decades.* 傳統家庭價值觀的恢復是對近幾十年來放縱自由的一種改變。

▸ TO DRUGS 藥物 **3** 0-w [C, U] a response by the body, usually a bad one, to a drug, chemical substance, etc. 生理反應；副作用：*to have an* ***allergic reaction*** *to a drug* 對某藥物有過敏反應

▸ TO DANGER 對於危險 **4** 0-w **reactions** [pl.] the ability to move quickly in response to sth, especially if in danger 反應能力：*a skilled driver with quick reactions* 反應敏捷的熟練司機

▸ SCIENCE 科學 **5** 0-w [C, U] (*chemistry* 化) a chemical change produced by two or more substances acting on each other 化學反應：*a* ***chemical/nuclear reaction*** 化學／核反應 ➲ see also CHAIN REACTION (1) **6** [U, C] (*physics* 物) a force shown by sth in response to another force, which is of equal strength and acts in the opposite direction 反作用力

▸ AGAINST PROGRESS 反對發展 **7** [U] opposition to social or political progress or change 反對；反動；阻礙：*The forces of reaction made change difficult.* 反動勢力使得改革舉步維艱。

re·ac·tion·ary AW /riˈækʃənri; *NAmE* -neri/ *noun* (*pl.* **-ies**) (*disapproving*) a person who is opposed to political or social change 反動分子；反對政治（或社會）變革者 ▸ **re·ac·tion·ary** *adj.*：*a reactionary government* 反動的政府

re·acti·vate AW /riˈæktɪveɪt/ *verb* **~ sth** to make sth start working or happening again after a period of time 使恢復活動；使重新出現 ▸ **re·acti·va·tion** AW /riˌæktɪˈveɪʃn/ *noun* [U]

re·act·ive AW /riˈæktɪv/ *adj.* **1** (*formal*) showing a reaction or response 反應的；有反應的；回應的：*The police presented a reactive rather than preventive strategy against crime.* 警方對付犯罪的辦法，不是事先加以防範，而是事後作出反應。➲ compare PROACTIVE **2** (*chemistry* 化) tending to show chemical change when mixed with another substance 能起化學反應的；易反應的：*highly reactive substances* 很容易起反應的物質

re·activ·ity /ˌriːækˈtɪvɪti/ *noun* (*chemistry* 化) the degree to which sth reacts, or is likely to react 反應性：*Oxygen has high reactivity.* 氧的反應性很高。

re·act·or AW /riˈæktə(r)/ (also **ˌnuclear reˈactor**) *noun* a large structure used for the controlled production of nuclear energy 核反應堆；反應器

read 0-w *verb* /riːd/ *noun* /riːd/ *adj.* /red/

■ *verb* /riːd/ **(read, read** /red/**)**

▸ WORDS/SYMBOLS 文字；符號 **1** 0-w [I, T] (not used in the progressive tenses 不用於進行時) to look at and understand the meaning of written or printed words or symbols 識字；閱讀；讀懂：*She's still learning to read.* 她還在學習識字。◇ *Some children can read and write before they go to school.* 有些孩子在上學前就會看書寫字了。◇ **~ sth** *I can't read your writing.* 我看不懂你的筆跡。◇ *Can you read music?* 你能讀懂樂譜嗎？◇ *I'm trying to read the map.* 我正看地圖。 **2** 0-w [I, T] to go through written or printed words, etc. in silence or speaking them to other people 讀；朗讀：*I'm going to go to bed and read.* 我要上牀看書去。◇ **~ to sb/yourself** *He liked reading to his grandchildren.* 他喜歡唸書給孫子孫女聽。◇ **~ sth** *to read a book/a magazine/the newspaper* 讀書；看雜誌／報紙◇ *Have you read any Steinbeck* (= novels by him)? 你讀過斯坦貝克的小說嗎？◇ *He read the poem aloud.* 他朗讀了這首詩。◇ **~ sth to sb/yourself** *Go on—read it to us.* 唸吧，唸給我們聽聽。◇ **~ sb sth** *She read us a story.* 她給我們讀了個故事。➲ see also PROOFREAD

▸ DISCOVER BY READING 讀到 **3** 0-w [I, T] (not used in the progressive tenses 不用於進行時) to discover or find out about sb/sth by reading 讀到；查閱到：**~ about/of sth** *I read about the accident in the local paper.* 我在當地的報紙上看到了這次事故。◇ **~ that …** *I read that he had resigned.* 我看到了他辭職的消息。◇ **~ sth** *Don't believe everything you read in the papers.* 報上看到的東西，不能盡信。

▸ SB'S MIND/THOUGHTS 思想；想法 **4** [T] **~ sb's mind/thoughts** to guess what sb else is thinking 猜測；揣摩

▸ SB'S LIPS 嘴唇 **5** [T] **~ sb's lips** to look at the movements of sb's lips to learn what they are saying 觀唇辨意；

R

讀唇語 ➲ see also LIP-READ

▸ **UNDERSTAND 理解** **6** [T] to understand sth in a particular way 懂得；理解 **SYN** **interpret**：**~ sth** *How do you read the present situation?* 你對目前的形勢有何看法？◇ **~ sth as sth** *Silence must not always be read as consent.* 不能總是將沉默理解為同意。

▸ **OF A PIECE OF WRITING 書寫的東西** **7** [T] **+ speech** to have sth written on it; to be written in a particular way 寫着；寫成：*The sign read 'No admittance'.* 告示牌上寫着"禁止入內"。◇ *I've changed the last paragraph. It now reads as follows …* 我已經修改了最後一段。現在是這樣寫的… **8** [I] **+ adv./prep.** to give a particular impression when read 讀起來（給人以某種印象）：*Generally, the article reads very well.* 一般而言，這篇文章讀起來很不錯。◇ *The poem reads like* (= sounds as if it is) *a translation.* 這首詩讀起來像是譯文。

▸ **MEASURING INSTRUMENT 測量儀器** **9** [T] **~ sth** (of measuring instruments 測量儀器) to show a particular weight, pressure, etc. 讀數為；顯示：*What does the thermometer read?* 溫度計的讀數是多少？ **10** [T] **~ sth** to get information from a measuring instrument 看讀數：*A man came to read the gas meter.* 一個男子來查了煤氣表。

▸ **HEAR 聽** **11** [T] **~ sb** to hear and understand sb speaking on a radio set 聽到，聽明白（用無線電機講的話）：*'Do you read me?' 'I'm reading you loud and clear.'* "你聽得見我的話嗎？""聽見了，你的聲音又大又清楚。"

▸ **REPLACE WORD 替換文字** **12** [T] **~ A for B | ~ B as A** to replace one word, etc. with another when correcting a text 替換；將…改為：*For 'madam' in line 3 read 'madman'.* 第3行中的madam應為madman。

▸ **SUBJECT AT UNIVERSITY 大學課程** **13** [T, I] (*BrE*, rather *old-fashioned*) to study a subject, especially at a university 學習；攻讀；主修：**~ sth** *I read English at Oxford.* 我在牛津攻讀英語。◇ **~ for sth** *She's reading for a law degree.* 她在攻讀法學學位。

▸ **COMPUTING 計算機技術** **14** [T] (of a computer or the person using it 計算機或計算機使用者) to take information from a disk 讀盤；從磁盤提取信息：**~ sth** *My computer can't read the CD-ROM you sent.* 我的電腦不能讀你送來的光盤。◇ **~ sth into sth** *to read a file into a computer* 把文件讀入電腦

IDM **ˌread between the ˈlines** to look for or discover a meaning in sth that is not openly stated 領悟隱含的意義；看出言外之意：*Reading between the lines, I think Clare needs money.* 斟酌一下她的言外之意，我覺得克萊爾需要錢。 **ˌread sb like a ˈbook** to understand easily what sb is thinking or feeling 輕易地瞭解某人的想法（或感受）；看透某人 **ˌread my ˈlips** (*informal*) used to tell sb to listen carefully to what you are saying 請聽清楚；請注意聽：*Read my lips: no new taxes* (= I promise there will be no new taxes). 注意聽我說：不會徵新稅。 **ˌread (sb) the ˈRiot Act** (*BrE*) to tell sb with force that they must not do sth 警告（某人）不得做某事 **ORIGIN** From an Act of Parliament passed in 1715 to prevent riots. It made it illegal for a group of twelve or more people to refuse to split up if they were ordered to do so and part of the Act was read to them. 源自1715年通過的防止暴亂的議會法案。法案規定如果十二名或以上的人集結，在宣佈解散命令並宣讀相關條文後仍拒絕解散，則視為非法。 **ˌtake it/sth as ˈread** (*BrE*) to accept sth without discussing it 直接認定為；不經討論即認可：*Can we take it as read that you want the job?* 我們能不能認為你想要這份工作？

PHR V **ˌread sth↔ˈback** to read a message, etc. to others in order to check that it is correct 讀出（以便核對） **ˌread sth ˈinto sth** to think that sth means more than it really does 把本沒有的意思加進去解釋；對…作過多的理解：*Don't read too much into what she says.* 不要在她的話裏加進太多自己的理解。 **ˌread ˈon** to continue reading 繼續讀；接着讀：*That's the story so far. Now read on …* 故事就講到這裏。現在接着讀… **ˌread sth↔ˈout** 🔑 to read sth using your voice, especially to other people（尤指向別人）讀，朗讀 **ˌread sth↔ˈover/ˈthrough** 🔑 to read sth carefully from beginning to end to look for mistakes or check details 認真通讀；仔細核對 **ˌread sth↔ˈup | ˌread ˈup on sb/sth** to read a lot about a subject（就某課題）廣泛閱讀，博覽群書：*I'll need to read up on the case before the meeting.* 在開會前，我需要看一些有關這件事的材料。

■ *noun* /riːd/ [sing.] (*informal*) **1** (*especially BrE*) an act or a period of reading sth 閱讀；讀書：*I was having a quiet read when the phone rang.* 我在靜靜地看書，忽然電話鈴響了。 **2 a good, interesting, etc. ~** a book, an article, etc. that is good, etc. 好的（或有意思等的）讀物；好書（或文章等）：*His thrillers are always a gripping read.* 他的驚險小說向來引人入勝。

■ *adj.* /red/ (used after an adverb 用於副詞後) (of a person 人) having knowledge that has been gained from reading books, etc. 博學的；熟知的；精通的：*She's very widely read in law.* 她在法律方面知識淵博。➲ see also WELL READ

read·able /ˈriːdəbl/ *adj.* **1** (of a book, an article, etc. 書、文章等) that is easy, interesting and enjoyable to read 可讀性強的；通俗易懂的 **2** (of written or printed words 書寫的或印刷文字) clear and easy to read 清晰可辨的；易於識讀的 **SYN** **legible** ➲ see also MACHINE-READABLE ▸ **read·abil·ity** /ˌriːdəˈbɪləti/ *noun* [U]

re·address /ˌriːəˈdres/ *verb* **~ sth** to change the address written on an envelope because the person the letter is for does not live at the address it has been delivered to 更改（郵件）上的地址

read·er 🔑 /ˈriːdə(r)/ *noun*

1 🔑 a person who reads, especially one who reads a lot or in a particular way 讀者；讀書…的人；閱讀量大的人：*an avid reader of science fiction* 科幻小說迷 ◇ *a* ***fast/slow reader*** 讀書快／慢的人 ◇ *The reader is left to draw his or her own conclusions.* 讀者需要自己去得出結論。➲ COLLOCATIONS at LITERATURE **2** 🔑 a person who reads a particular newspaper, magazine, etc.（報刊雜誌等的）讀者：*readers' letters* 讀者來信 ◇ *Are you a 'Times' reader?* 你是《泰晤士報》的讀者嗎？ **3** an easy book that is intended to help people learn to read their own or a foreign language 簡易讀物；讀本：*a series of graded English readers* 一系列分級英語讀物 **4** (usually **Reader**) a senior teacher at a British university just below the rank of a professor 準教授（英國大學教師，僅次於教授）：*She is Reader in Music at Edinburgh.* 她是愛丁堡大學的音樂準教授。 **5** (*computing* 計) an electronic device that reads data stored in one form and changes it into another form so that a computer can perform operations on it 電子閱讀器；電子識讀機 **6** (*technical* 術語) a machine that produces on a screen a large image of a text stored on a MICROFICHE or MICROFILM 縮微軟片閱讀機 ➲ see also MIND-READER, NEWSREADER

read·er·ship /ˈriːdəʃɪp; *NAmE* -dərʃ-/ *noun* **1** [usually sing.] the number or type of people who read a particular newspaper, magazine, etc.（統稱某報刊雜誌等的）讀者：*a readership of around 10 000* * 1 萬左右的讀者人數 ◇ *In its new format, the magazine hopes to attract a much wider readership.* 這份雜誌希望以新的版式吸引更多的讀者。 **2** (usually **Readership**) **~ (in sth)** (*BrE*) the position of a READER at a university（英國大學）準教授職位

read·ily /ˈredɪli/ *adv.* **1** quickly and without difficulty 快捷地；輕而易舉地；便利地 **SYN** **freely**：*All ingredients are* ***readily available*** *from your local store.* 所有的原料都可以方便地從你當地的商店買到。 **2** in a way that shows you do not object to sth 欣然地；樂意地 **SYN** **willingly**：*Most people readily accept the need for laws.* 大多數人都毫不遲疑地認為法律是必要的。

ˈread-in *noun* **1** [U, C] (*computing* 計) the entry of data into a computer or onto a disk（數據的）讀入，錄入 **2** [C] (*NAmE*) an organized event when people come to a place to read books together 讀書會

readi·ness /ˈredinəs/ *noun* **1** [U] **~ (for sth)** the state of being ready or prepared for sth 準備就緒：*Everyone has doubts about their readiness for parenthood.* 對於自己是否準備好了為人父母，人人都會感到疑慮。 **2** [U, sing.] **~ (of sb) (to do sth)** the state of being willing to do sth 願意；樂意：*Over half the people interviewed expressed their readiness to die for their country.* 半數以上接受採訪的人都表示願意為國獻身。

read·ing 0-**π** /ˈriːdɪŋ/ *noun*

▸ **ACTIVITY 活動** **1** 0-**π** [U] the activity of sb who reads 閱讀；讀書活動：*My hobbies include reading and painting.* 我的業餘愛好包括讀書和繪畫。◇ *He needs more help with his reading.* 他在閱讀方面需要更多的幫助。◇ *Are you any good at map reading?* 你會看地圖嗎？◇ ***reading glasses*** (= worn when reading) 讀書用的眼鏡 ◇ *a* ***reading lamp/light*** (= one that can be moved to shine light onto sth that you are reading) 供閱讀用的燈 **2** [sing.] an act of reading sth 閱讀；宣讀：*A closer* (= more detailed) *reading of the text reveals just how desperate he was feeling.* 細讀此文就會看出他當時感到多麼絕望。

▸ **BOOKS/ARTICLES 書；文章** **3** 0-**π** [U] books, articles, etc. that are intended to be read 讀本；讀物；閱讀材料：***reading matter/material*** 閱讀材料 ◇ *a series of* ***reading books*** *for children* 一套兒童讀物 ◇ *a* ***reading list*** (= a list of books, etc. that students are expected to read for a particular subject) 閱讀書目 ◇ ***further reading*** (= at the end of a book, a list of other books that give more information about the same subject) 其他閱讀參考材料 ◇ *The report makes for interesting reading* (= it is interesting to read). 這篇報道讀起來很有意思。◇ *The article is not exactly* ***light reading*** (= it is not easy to read). 這篇文章讀起來並不輕鬆。

▸ **WAY OF UNDERSTANDING 理解方法** **4** [C] **~ (of sth)** the particular way in which you understand a book, situation, etc. 理解方法；解讀方法 **SYN** **interpretation**：*a literal reading of the text* 對文本的字面理解 ◇ *My own reading of events is less optimistic.* 我本人對事態的看法不怎麼樂觀。

▸ **MEASUREMENT 度量** **5** 0-**π** [C] the amount or number shown on an instrument used for measuring sth（儀表的）讀數：*Meter readings are taken every three months.* 每三個月查一次表。

▸ **EVENT 活動** **6** [C] an event at which sth is read to an audience for entertainment; a piece of literature that is read at such an event 讀書會；朗誦會；朗誦的作品：*a poetry reading* 詩歌朗誦會 ◇ *The evening ended with a reading from her latest novel.* 晚會最後朗誦了一段她的最新小說。

▸ **FROM BIBLE《聖經》** **7** [C] a short section from the Bible that is read to people as part of a religious service（在禮拜儀式中朗讀的）《聖經》章節：*The reading today is from the Book of Daniel.* 今天朗讀的經文選自《但以理書》。

▸ **IN PARLIAMENT 議會** **8** [C] one of the stages during which a BILL (= a proposal for a new law) must be discussed and accepted by a parliament before it can become law 議案宣讀（法案在成為法律前須經議會討論通過的步驟）

ˈreading age *noun* a person's ability to read, measured by comparing it with the average ability of children of a particular age 閱讀年齡；某一年齡段的閱讀能力：*a 30-year-old man with a reading age of eight* 閱讀能力相當於八歲兒童的 30 歲男子

ˈreading group *noun* = BOOK GROUP

ˈreading room *noun* a room in a library, club, etc. where people can read or study 閱覽室

re·adjust **AW** /ˌriːəˈdʒʌst/ *verb* **1** [I] to get used to a changed or new situation 重新適應；再適應：*Children are highly adaptable—they just need time to readjust.* 兒童的適應能力很強，他們只是需要時間重新適應。◇ **~ to sth/doing sth** *Once again he had to readjust to living alone.* 他又一次不得不重新適應單獨居住。**2** [T] **~ sth** to change or move sth slightly 稍作改變；微調：*She got out of the car and readjusted her dress.* 她下了車，稍稍整了整裙子。▸ **re·adjust·ment** **AW** *noun* [C, U]：*He has made a number of readjustments to his technique.* 他對自己的技術作了不少調整。◇ *a painful period of readjustment* 痛苦的適應期

re·admit /ˌriːədˈmɪt/ *verb* (**-tt-**) [often passive] **1 ~ sb (to sth)** to allow sb to join a group, an organization or an institution again 重新接納；允許再次加入 **2 ~ sb (to sth)** to take sb into a hospital again after they had been allowed to leave 再次接收…住院：*He was readmitted only a week after being discharged.* 他出院僅一個星期又再次住院。▸ **re·admis·sion** /ˌriːədˈmɪʃn/ *noun* [U, C] **~ (to sth)**

ˌread-only ˈmemory *noun* [U] (*computing* 計) = ROM

ˈread-out *noun* (*computing* 計) a display of information on a computer screen 讀出 ➲ compare PRINTOUT

ˈread-through *noun* an occasion when the words of a play are spoken by members of a theatre group, before they begin practising acting it（劇組排演之前的）對台詞

ˌre-ˈadvertise *verb* [T, I] **~ (sth)** to advertise sth again, especially a job 再做廣告；再登（招聘）廣告

ready 0-**π** /ˈredi/ *adj., verb, adv., noun*

■ *adj.* (**read·ier**, **readi·est**)

▸ **PREPARED/AVAILABLE 準備好；可利用** **1** 0-**π** [not before noun] fully prepared for what you are going to do 準備好；準備完畢：*Are you nearly ready?* 你快準備好了嗎？◇ *'Shall we go?' 'I'm* ***ready when you are!****'* "我們可以走了嗎？" "我準備好了，就等你了！" ◇ **~ for sth** *I'm just* ***getting*** *the kids* ***ready*** *for school.* 我正在讓孩子們準備好去上學。◇ *I was twenty years old and* ***ready for anything.*** 我當時二十歲，什麼都願意去做。◇ **~ to do sth** *Right, we're ready to go.* 好，我們準備好了，可以走了。◇ *Volunteers were* ***ready and waiting*** *to pack the food in boxes.* 志願者已經準備完畢，等着將食物裝箱。**2** 0-**π** [not before noun] completed and available to be used 已完成；準備好；可利用：*Come on, dinner's ready!* 快過來，飯準備好了！◇ *The new building should be ready by 2015.* 這座新大樓應該能在 2015 年前交付使用。◇ **~ for sth** *Can you help me* ***get*** *everything* ***ready*** *for the party?* 你能不能幫我把這次聚會準備妥當？◇ **~ to do sth** *The contract will be ready to sign in two weeks.* 這份合同兩週後即可簽字。**3** available to be used easily and immediately 方便使用的；現成的：*All the relevant records are easily available* ***ready to hand.*** 所有相關記錄都在手邊，用起來很方便。◇ *a ready supply of wood* 現成的木材供應 ◇ *a ready source of income* 現成的收入來源 ➲ see also READILY, READINESS, ROUGH-AND-READY

▸ **WILLING 情願** **4** [not before noun] willing and quick to do or give sth 願意迅速做某事（或給某物）；急於行動：**~ for sth** *I was very angry and ready for a fight.* 我非常生氣，想打一架。◇ **~ with sth** *She's always ready with advice.* 她總是樂於提出建議。◇ **~ to do sth** *He's always ready to help his friends.* 他總是樂意幫助朋友。◇ *Don't be so ready to believe the worst about people.* 不要總把人往壞處想。

▸ **LIKELY TO DO STH 可能做某事** **5 ~ to do sth** likely to do sth very soon 馬上要，很可能即將（做某事）**SYN** **on the point of**：*She looked ready to collapse at any minute.* 她看樣子隨時都會倒下。

▸ **NEEDING STH 需要某事物** **6 ~ for sth** needing sth as soon as possible 急需；需儘快得到：*Right, I'm ready for bed.* 對，我現在就想睡覺。◇ *After the long walk, we were all ready for a drink.* 長途步行之後，我們大家急需喝水。

▸ **QUICK/CLEVER 機敏；聰明** **7** [only before noun] quick and clever 聰明的；機敏的：*She has great charm and a ready wit.* 她光彩照人，頭腦機敏。

IDM **make ˈready (for sth)** (*formal*) to prepare 準備：*to make ready for the President's visit* 為總統來訪作準備 **ready, steady, ˈgo!** (*BrE*) (also **(get) ready, (get) set, ˈgo** *NAmE, BrE*) what you say to tell people to start a race（賽跑口令）各就位，預備，跑！**ˌready to ˈroll** (*informal*) ready to start 準備開始；就要開始

■ *verb* (**read·ies**, **ready·ing**, **read·ied**, **read·ied**) **~ sb/yourself/sth (for sth)** | **~ sb/yourself/sth (to do sth)** (*formal*) to prepare sb/yourself/sth for sth 做好…的準備；（為…）做好準備：*Western companies were readying themselves for the challenge from Eastern markets.* 西方的公司正在為迎接來自東方市場的挑戰作準備。

■ *adv.* (used before a past participle, especially in compounds 用於過去分詞前，尤用於構成複合詞) already done 已做完；已完成：*ready-cooked meals* 現成的飯菜 ◇ *The concrete was ready mixed.* 混凝土是攪拌好的。

■ *noun* **the ready** [sing.] (also **read·ies** [pl.]) (*BrE, informal*) money that you can use immediately 現錢

IDM **at the ˈready** available to be used immediately 隨時可用；即可使用：*We all had our cameras at the ready.* 我們都準備好了照相機。

ˌready-ˈmade *adj.* **1** prepared in advance so that you can eat or use it immediately 預製的；已做好的；現成的： *ready-made pastry* 預製的油酥麪糰 **2** (*old-fashioned*) (especially of clothes 尤指衣服) made in standard sizes, not to the measurements of a particular customer 標準尺碼的；現成的；成品的： *a ready-made suit* 成品套裝 **3** already provided for you so you do not need to produce or think about it yourself 已有的；現成的： *When he married her he also took on a ready-made family.* 他和她結婚，就接過來一個現成的家庭。

ˌready ˈmeal *noun* (*BrE*) a meal that you buy already prepared and which only needs to be heated before you eat it 預製餐（加熱即可食用）

ˌready-ˈmixed *adj.* already mixed and ready to use 預拌的；預先調製的： *ready-mixed concrete* 預拌混凝土

ˌready ˈmoney (also **ˌready ˈcash**) *noun* [U] (*informal*) money in the form of coins and notes that you can spend immediately 現金；現錢

ˌready-to-ˈwear *adj.* (of clothes 衣服) made in standard sizes, not to the measurements of a particular customer 標準尺寸的；現成的

re·affirm /ˌriːəˈfɜːm; *NAmE* -ˈfɜːrm/ *verb* **~ sth** to state sth again in order to emphasize that it is still true 重申；再次確定 ▸ **re·affirm·ation** /ˌriːˌæfəˈmeɪʃn; *NAmE* -fərˈm-/ *noun* [C, U]

re·affor·estation /ˌriːəˌfɒrɪˈsteɪʃn; *NAmE* -ˌfɔːr-/ *noun* [U] (*BrE, technical* 術語) = REFORESTATION

re·agent /riˈeɪdʒənt/ *noun* (*chemistry* 化) a substance used to cause a chemical reaction, especially in order to find out if another substance is present 試劑

real 🔑 /ˈriːəl; *BrE* usually rɪəl/ *adj., adv.*

■ ***adj.***

▸ **EXISTING/NOT IMAGINED** 存在；真實 **1** 🔑 actually existing or happening and not imagined or pretended 真實的；實際存在的；非憑空想像的： *It wasn't a ghost; it was a real person.* 那不是鬼魂，是實實在在的人。◇ *pictures of animals, both real and mythological* 現實和神話中的動物圖片 ◇ *In the movies guns kill people instantly, but it's not like that* ***in real life****.* 電影中，槍能使人在瞬間斃命，而實際情況並非如此。◇ *Politicians seem to be out of touch with* ***the real world****.* 政治家們似乎不接觸現實世界。◇ *The growth of violent crime is a very real problem.* 暴力犯罪的增長是個非常實際的問題。◇ *There's no real possibility of them changing their minds.* 他們實際上不可能改變主意。◇ *We have a real chance of success.* 我們確實有獲得成功的機會。

▸ **TRUE/GENUINE** 確實；真正 **2** 🔑 genuine and not false or artificial 真的；正宗的；非假冒的；非人工的： *Are those real flowers?* 那些是真花嗎？◇ *real leather* 真皮 **3** 🔑 [only before noun] actual or true, rather than what appears to be true 真正的；確實的；真實的： *Tell me the real reason.* 告訴我真正的理由。◇ *Bono's real name is Paul Hewson.* 博諾的真實姓名是保羅 • 休森。◇ *See the real Africa on one of our walking safaris.* 參加一次我們的觀察野獸徒步旅行，實地看一看非洲吧。◇ *I couldn't resist the opportunity to meet a* ***real live*** *celebrity.* 我不想錯過見到名人真人的機會。 **4** 🔑 [only before noun] having all the important qualities that it should have to deserve to be called what it is called 真正的；名副其實的： *She never had any real friends at school.* 在學校，她從來沒有交過真正的朋友。◇ *his first real kiss* 他真正的初吻 ◇ *I had no real interest in politics.* 我對政治興趣不大。◇ *He was making a real effort to be nice to her.* 他費盡心思地對她好。◇ *She has not shown any real regret for what she did.* 她對自己做過的事還沒有表現出真正後悔的樣子。

▸ **FOR EMPHASIS** 強調 **5** 🔑 [only before noun] used to emphasize a state or quality（強調狀態或品質）： *He looks a real idiot.* 他看上去像個十足的白痴。◇ *This accident could have produced a real tragedy.* 這次事故差一點造成一場慘劇。◇ *Her next play was a real contrast.* 她的下一部戲是個鮮明的對比。

▸ **MONEY/INCOME** 錢；收入 **6** [only before noun] when the effect of such things as price rises on the power of money to buy things is included in the sums 實際的（已按物價指數等調整）；按購買力衡量的： *Real wage costs have risen by 10% in the past year.* 在過去的一年裏，實際工資成本增加了 10%。◇ *This represents a reduction of 5%* ***in real terms****.* 這相當於實際減少了 5%。

IDM **for ˈreal** genuine or serious 真實的；嚴肅的： *This is not a fire drill—it's for real.* 這不是救火演習，是真失火了。◇ (*NAmE*) *He managed to convince voters that he was for real.* 他使得投票者相信了他是嚴肅認真的。 **get ˈreal!** (*informal*) used to tell sb that they are behaving in a stupid or unreasonable way 現實點吧；別傻了 **keep it ˈreal** (*informal*) to act in an honest and natural way 做事質樸、誠實 **the ˌreal ˈthing** (*informal*) the genuine thing 真品；真正的事物： *Are you sure it's the real thing* (= love), *not just infatuation?* 你能確定這是真愛，而非一時痴迷？ ➲ more at MCCOY, POWER *n.*

■ ***adv.*** (*NAmE, ScotE, informal*) very 非常；很： *That tastes real good.* 味道好極了。◇ *He's a real nice guy.* 他是個非常好的人。◇ *I'm real sorry.* 我很抱歉。

ˌreal ˈale *noun* [U, C] (*BrE*) a type of beer that is made and stored in the traditional way（按傳統方法製作和貯存的）啤酒

ˈreal estate *noun* [U] (*especially NAmE*) **1** (also **realty**) property in the form of land or buildings 房地產；不動產： *My father sold real estate.* 我父親經營過房地產。 ➲ COLLOCATIONS at HOUSE **2** the business of selling houses or land for building 房地產業；房地產銷售業： *to work in real estate* 經營房地產

ˈreal estate agent (also **Real·tor™**) (both *NAmE*) (*BrE* **eˈstate agent**) *noun* a person whose job is to sell houses and land for people 房地產經紀人

realia /reɪˈɑːliə; riˈeɪliə/ *noun* [U] ordinary objects used in a class for teaching purposes 實物教具（用於教學的日常用品）

re·align /ˌriːəˈlaɪn/ *verb* **1 ~ sth** to change the position or direction of sth slightly 調整位置（或方向）： *The road was realigned to improve visibility.* 道路做了調整，視野清晰了。 **2 ~ sth** to make changes to sth in order to adapt it to a new situation 對…進行調整；使適應新形勢： *The company has been forced to realign its operations in the area.* 公司被迫對這一領域的經營作了調整。 **3 ~ yourself** (**with sb/sth**) to change your opinions, policies, etc. so that they are the same as those of another person, group, etc. 改變觀點，改變策略（以與別人相同）： *The rebel MPs have realigned themselves with the opposition party.* 幾個造反的下院議員已與反對派站在一起。 ▸ **re·align·ment** *noun* [U, C]: **~** (**of sth**) *the realignment of personal goals* 個人目標的調整 ◇ *political realignments* 政治改組

real·ism /ˈriːəlɪzəm; *BrE* also ˈrɪəl-/ *noun* [U] **1** a way of seeing, accepting and dealing with situations as they really are without being influenced by your emotions or false hopes 務實作風；現實主義方式： *There was a new mood of realism among the leaders at the peace talks.* 參加和平談判的領導人之間有着一種務實的新氣氛。 **2** (of novels, paintings, films/movies, etc. 小說、繪畫、電影等) the quality of being very like real life 現實性；逼真 **3** (also **Realism**) a style in art or literature that shows things and people as they are in real life（文藝的）現實主義風格，現實主義 ➲ compare IDEALISM, ROMANTICISM (1)

real·ist /ˈriːəlɪst; *BrE* also ˈrɪə-/ *noun* **1** a person who accepts and deals with a situation as it really is and does not try to pretend that it is different 現實主義者；務實的人： *I'm a realist—I know you can't change people overnight.* 我是個務實的人，我知道人不可能一夜之間被改變。 **2** a writer, painter, etc. whose work represents things as they are in real life 現實主義作家（或畫家等）

real·is·tic 🔑 /ˌriːəˈlɪstɪk; *BrE* also ˌrɪə-/ *adj.*

1 🔑 accepting in a sensible way what it is actually possible to do or achieve in a particular situation 現實的；實際的；實事求是的： *a realistic assessment* 實事求是的評估 ◇ *We have to* ***be realistic*** *about our chances of winning.* 我們必須實事求是地估計我們獲勝的可能性。◇ *It is not realistic to expect people to spend so much money.* 期望人們花那麼多的錢是不實際的。 **2** 🔑 sensible and appropriate; possible to achieve 明智的；恰如其分的；能夠實現的 SYN **feasible, viable**：*We must set realistic goals.* 我們必須制訂可實現的目標。◇ *a realistic target* 切實的目標 ◇ *to pay a realistic salary* 支付合理的薪水 **3** representing things as they are in real life 逼真的；栩栩如生的：*a realistic drawing* 逼真的繪畫 ◇ *We try to make these training courses as realistic as possible.* 我們努力使這些訓練課程盡可能地貼近實際情況。OPP **unrealistic**

real·is·tic·al·ly /ˌriːəˈlɪstɪkli; *BrE* also ˌrɪə-/ *adv.* **1** used to say what you think can actually be achieved in a particular situation（表明你認為實際實現的可能性）如實地，實際地：*Realistically, there is little prospect of a ceasefire.* 實事求是地講，停火的希望很渺茫。 **2** in a way that shows sb accepts in a sensible way what it is actually possible to do or achieve 切合實際地；明智地：*How many can you realistically hope to sell?* 實事求是地講，你希望能賣出多少？◇ *Kate spoke realistically about the task ahead.* 凱特如實地談了面臨的任務。 **3** in a way that represents things as they are in real life 逼真地；栩栩如生地：*a fireplace with realistically glowing coals* 有逼真的爐火亮光的壁爐

real·ity /riˈæləti/ *noun* (*pl.* **-ies**)
1 [U] the true situation and the problems that actually exist in life, in contrast to how you would like life to be 現實；實際情況：*She refuses to* **face reality**. 她不肯面對現實。◇ *You're* **out of touch with reality**. 你脫離了現實。◇ *The reality is that there is not enough money to pay for this project.* 實際情況是沒有足夠的錢花在這個項目上。 **2** [C] a thing that is actually experienced or seen, in contrast to what people might imagine 事實；實際經歷；見到的事物：*the* **harsh realities of** *life* 嚴峻的生活現實 ◇ *This decision reflects the realities of the political situation.* 這一決定反映了政治形勢的真實情況。◇ *Will time travel ever* **become a reality**? 時光旅行真的會成為現實嗎？ **3** [U] **~ television/TV/shows/series/contestants** television/shows, etc. that use real people (not actors) in real situations, presented as entertainment 真人秀節目：*a reality TV star* 一個真人秀電視明星 ◇ *the reality show 'Big Brother'* 真人秀節目"老大哥"
IDM **in reˈality** used to say that a situation is different from what has just been said or from what people believe 實際上；事實上：*Outwardly she seemed confident but in reality she felt extremely nervous.* 表面上看，她顯得信心十足，而實際上她緊張得要命。➲ see also VIRTUAL REALITY

reˈality check *noun* [usually sing.] (*informal*) an occasion when you are reminded of how things are in the real world, rather than how you would like things to be（提醒人面對現實而不再想當然的）實際檢驗

reˌality TˈV *noun* [U] television shows that are based on real people (not actors) in real situations, presented as entertainment（電視）真人秀

real·iz·able (*BrE* also **-is·able**) /ˈriːəlaɪzəbl; *BrE* also ˈrɪə-/ *adj.* **1** possible to achieve or make happen 可實現的；可實行的 SYN **achievable**：*realizable objectives* 可實現的目標 **2** that can be sold and turned into money 可兌現的；可變為現金的：*realizable assets* 流動資產

real·iza·tion (*BrE* also **-isa·tion**) /ˌriːəlaɪˈzeɪʃn; ˌrɪəl-; *NAmE* ˌriːələˈz-/ *noun* **1** [U, sing.] the process of becoming aware of sth 認識；領會；領悟 SYN **awareness**：**~ (of sth)** *the sudden realization of what she had done* 突然意識到她自己究竟幹了些什麼 ◇ **~ (that ...)** *There is a growing realization that changes must be made.* 越來越多的人認識到改革勢在必行。 **2** [U] **~ (of sth)** the process of achieving a particular aim, etc.（目標等的）實現 SYN **achievement**：*It was the realization of his greatest ambition.* 這就實現了他的宏偉抱負。 **3** [U] **~ of your assets** (*formal*) the act of selling sth that you own, such as property, in order to get the money that you need for sth 變賣；兌換成現金 **4** [U, C] **~ (of sth)** (*formal*) the act of producing a sound, play, design, etc.; or the thing that is produced 發聲；（戲劇）演出；設計成果

real·ize (*BrE* also **-ise**) /ˈriːəlaɪz; *BrE* also ˈrɪəl-/ *verb*
▸ **BE/BECOME AWARE** 察覺 **1** [T, I] (not used in the progressive tenses 不用於進行時) to understand or become aware of a particular fact or situation 理解；領會；認識到；意識到：**~ (that) ...** *I didn't realize (that) you were so unhappy.* 我沒有察覺到你那麼不開心。◇ *The moment I saw her, I realized something was wrong.* 我一看到她，就覺得不太對勁。◇ **~ how, what, etc. ...** *I don't think you realize how important this is to her.* 我認為你沒有意識到這對她是多麼重要。◇ **~ (sth)** *I hope you realize the seriousness of this crime.* 我希望你能認識到這一罪行的嚴重性。◇ *Only later did she realize her mistake.* 只是到了後來她才意識到自己的錯誤。◇ *The situation was more complicated than they had at first realized.* 形勢比他們最初意識到的更為複雜。◇ *They managed to leave without any of us realizing.* 我們誰也沒注意，他們悄悄走了。◇ **it is realized that ...** *There was a cheer when it was realized that everyone was safely back.* 人們意識到大家都已平安歸來的時候便發出了一陣歡呼聲。
▸ **ACHIEVE STH** 實現 **2** [T] **~ sth** to achieve sth important that you very much want to do 實現；將…變為現實：*She never realized her ambition of becoming a professional singer.* 她從未能實現成為一名職業歌手的志向。◇ *We try to help all students* ***realize their full potential*** (= be as successful as they are able to be). 我們努力幫助所有的學生充分發揮他們的潛力。
▸ **HAPPEN** 發生 **3** [T, usually passive] **~ sth** if sb's fears **are realized**, the things that they are afraid will happen, do happen（所擔心的事）發生，產生：*His worst fears were realized when he saw that the door had been forced open.* 他一看門被撬了，就知道最擔心的事還是發生了。
▸ **SELL** 出售 **4** [T] **~ your assets** (*formal*) to sell things that you own, for example property, in order to get the money that you need for sth 把（財產等）變賣，變現 SYN **convert** **5** [T] **~ sth** (*formal*) (of goods, etc. 貨品等) to be sold for a particular amount of money 以…價格賣出 SYN **make**：*The paintings realized $2 million at auction.* 這些繪畫在拍賣會上以 200 萬元賣出。
▸ **MAKE STH REAL** 使成為現實 **6** [T] **~ sth** (*formal*) to produce sth that can be seen or heard, based on written information or instructions 把（概念等）具體表現出來：*The stage designs have been beautifully realized.* 舞台設計得到了完美的體現。

ˌreal-ˈlife *adj.* [only before noun] actually happening or existing in life, not in books, stories or films/movies 真實的；實際發生的；現實生活中的：*a novel based on real-life events* 以真實事件為素材的小說 ◇ *a real-life Romeo and Juliet* 現實生活中的羅密歐與朱麗葉 OPP **fictional**

re·allo·cate /ˌriːˈæləkeɪt/ *verb* **~ sth (to sb/sth)** to change the way money or materials are shared between different people, groups, projects, etc. 重新分配；再分配 SYN **redistribute** ▸ **re·allo·ca·tion** /ˌriːˌæləˈkeɪʃn/ *noun* [U]

real·ly /ˈriːəli; *BrE* also ˈrɪəli/ *adv.*
1 used to say what is actually the fact or the truth about sth（表明事實或真相）事實上，真正地，真實地：*What do you really think about it?* 你到底對這事怎麼看？◇ *Tell me what really happened.* 告訴我究竟發生了什麼事。◇ *They are not really my aunt and uncle.* 其實他們並不是我的姑姑和姑父。◇ *I can't believe I am really going to meet the princess.* 我不敢相信我真的要去見公主。 **2** used to emphasize sth you are saying or an opinion you are giving（強調觀點等）確實，的確：*I want to help, I really do.* 我想幫忙，真的。◇ *Now I really must go.* 我確實得走了。◇ *I really don't mind.* 我一點都不在意。◇ *He really likes you.* 他的確喜歡你。◇ ***I really and truly*** *am in love this time.* 我這一次確確實實是在戀愛。 **3** used to emphasize an adjective or adverb（加強形容詞或副詞的語氣）：*a really hot fire* 好熱的爐子 ◇ *I'm really sorry.* 我十分抱歉。 **4** used, often in negative sentences, to reduce the force of sth you are saying（常用於否定句以減弱語氣）：*I don't really agree with that.* 對此我不太贊同。◇ *It doesn't really matter.* 沒什麼關係。◇ *'Did you enjoy the book?' '****Not really.****'* (= 'no' or 'not very much') "你喜歡那本書嗎？""不怎麼喜歡。" HELP The position of **really** can change the meaning of the sentence. **I don't really know** means that you are not sure about something; **I really don't know** emphasizes that you do not know. (Look at

R

sense 2.) * really 的位置會改變句子的意思。I don't really know 的意思是對某事沒有把握；而 I really don't know 則強調不知道。（見第 2 義） **5** used in questions and negative sentences when you want sb to say 'no'（用於疑問句和否定句，期望對方給以否定的答覆）: *Do you really expect me to believe that?* 你真以為我會相信嗎？◇ *I don't really need to go, do I?* 我並不一定非要去，對吧？ **6** used to express interest in or surprise at what sb is saying（答話時表示感興趣或驚訝）: *'We're going to Japan next month.' 'Oh, really?'* "我們下個月要去日本。""哦，真的嗎？" ◇ *'She's resigned.' 'Really? Are you sure?'* "她辭職了。""真的？你肯定嗎？" **7** used to show that you disapprove of sth sb has done（表示不贊同某人所為）: *Really, you could have told us before.* 真是的，其實你大可事先跟我們說一聲的。

realm /relm/ *noun* **1** an area of activity, interest, or knowledge 領域；場所: *in the realm of literature* 在文學領域內 ◇ *At the end of the speech he seemed to be moving* ***into the realms of*** *fantasy.* 講話的最後，他似乎進入了虛幻的境地。 **2** (*formal*) a country ruled by a king or queen 王國 SYN **kingdom**: *the defence of the realm* 王國的防衛

IDM **beyond/within the realms of possibility** not possible/possible 超出／在可能範圍: *A successful outcome is not beyond the realms of possibility.* 最後取得成功並非沒有可能。

ˌreal ˈnumber *noun* (*mathematics* 數) any number that is not an IMAGINARY NUMBER 實數 ➲ compare COMPLEX NUMBER

real·poli·tik /reɪˈɑːlpɒlɪtiːk; *NAmE* -pɑːl-/ *noun* [U] (from *German*) a system of politics that is based on the actual situation and needs of a country or political party rather than on moral principles 現實政治；實用政治；實力政策

ˈreal tennis (*BrE*) (*NAmE* **ˈcourt tennis**) (*AustralE* **ˈroyal tennis**) *noun* [U] an old form of tennis played inside a building with a hard ball 庭院網球（使用硬球的舊式室內網球運動）

ˌreal ˈtime *noun* [U] (*computing* 計) the fact that there is only a very short time between a computer system receiving information and dealing with it 實時: *To make the training realistic the simulation operates* ***in real time.*** 為使訓練真實，模擬是實時運行的。◇ *real-time missile guidance systems* 實時導彈導航系統

real·tone /ˈriːəltəʊn; *BrE* usually ˈrɪəl-; *NAmE* -toʊn/ *noun* (*BrE*) a part of a song or other recording that is used as the sound a MOBILE/CELL PHONE makes when it rings 原音鈴聲（使用歌曲等錄音片段的手機鈴聲）: *Get the top realtones from the best artists delivered instantly to your mobile.* 即時取得一流歌手的最佳原音手機鈴聲。

Real·tor™ (also **real·tor**) /ˈriːəltə(r)/ *noun* (*NAmE*) = REAL ESTATE AGENT

realty /ˈriːəlti/ *noun* [U] (*especially NAmE*) = REAL ESTATE

ˈreal-world *adj.* existing in the real world and not specially invented for a particular purpose 存在於現實世界的；真實的: *Teachers need to prepare their students to deal with real-world situations outside the classroom.* 教師應該讓學生做好應對課堂以外的現實世界的準備。

ream /riːm/ *noun, verb*

■ ***noun*** **1** **reams** [pl.] (*informal*) a large quantity of writing 大量的文字（或寫作）: *She wrote reams in the exam.* 她在考試中寫得很多。 **2** [C] (*technical* 術語) 500 sheets of paper 令（紙張的記數單位，等於 500 張）

■ ***verb*** **~ sb** (*NAmE, informal*) to treat sb unfairly or cheat them 不公平地對待；欺騙: *We got reamed on that deal.* 那筆交易我們上當受騙了。

PHR V **ˌream sb↔ˈout** (*NAmE, informal*) to criticize sb strongly because they have done sth wrong 訓斥；斥責；責罵

re·ani·mate /riˈænɪmeɪt/ *verb* **~ sb/sth** (*formal*) to give sb/sth new life or energy 賦予新的生命；使重新充滿活力

reap /riːp/ *verb* **1** [T] **~ sth** to obtain sth, especially sth good, as a direct result of sth that you have done 取得（成果）；收獲: *They are now reaping the rewards of all their hard work.* 現在，他們的全部辛勞都得到了回報。 **2** [I, T] **~ (sth)** to cut and collect a crop, especially WHEAT, from a field 收割（莊稼）；收穫 SYN **harvest**

IDM **reap a/the ˈharvest** (*BrE*) to benefit or suffer as a direct result of sth that you have done 享受成果；承擔後果；種瓜得瓜，種豆得豆 **you ˌreap what you ˈsow** (*saying*) you have to deal with the bad effects or results of sth that you originally started 種瓜得瓜，種豆得豆

reap·er /ˈriːpə(r)/ *noun* a person or a machine that cuts and collects crops on a farm 收割者；收割機 ➲ see also THE GRIM REAPER

re·appear /ˌriːəˈpɪə(r); *NAmE* -ˈpɪr/ *verb* [I] to appear again after not being heard of or seen for a period of time 再次出現；重新出現: *She went upstairs and did not reappear until morning.* 她上了樓，直到第二天早晨才再次露面。 ▸ **re·appear·ance** /-rəns/ *noun* [U, sing.]

re·apply /ˌriːəˈplaɪ/ *verb* (**re·applies, re·apply·ing, re·applied, re·applied**) **1** [T] **~ sth** to put another layer of a substance on a surface 再敷一層；再塗一層: *Sunblock should be reapplied every hour.* 防曬霜應每隔一小時再抹一次。 **2** [I] **~ (for sth)** to make another formal request for sth 重新申請；再次申請: *Previous applicants for the post need not reapply.* 申請過這個職位的人不需重新申請。 **3** [T] **~ sth** to use sth again, especially in a different situation（尤指在不同場合）再利用: *Students are taught a number of skills that can be reapplied throughout their studies.* 教給學生一些方法，讓他們在整個學習過程中可以反複使用。

re·appoint /ˌriːəˈpɔɪnt/ *verb* **~ sb (as) sth | ~ sb + noun | ~ sb (to sth)** to give sb the job that they used to have in the past 使恢復職位；使回到原崗位: *After the trial he was reappointed (as) treasurer.* 審理過後，他被重新任命為財務主管。 ▸ **re·appoint·ment** *noun* [U]

re·appraisal /ˌriːəˈpreɪzl/ *noun* [C, usually sing., U] the act of examining sth again to see if it needs to be changed 重新檢查；重新評價 SYN **reassessment**

re·appraise /ˌriːəˈpreɪz/ *verb* **~ sth/sb** (*formal*) to think again about the value or nature of sth/sb to see if your opinion about it/them should be changed 重新評估；重新評價 SYN **reassess**

rear 0‑ /rɪə(r); *NAmE* rɪr/ *noun, adj., verb*

■ ***noun*** **1** 0‑ (usually **the rear**) [sing.] the back part of sth 後部: *A trailer was attached to the rear of the truck.* 卡車後面掛了一輛拖車。◇ *There are toilets at both* ***front and rear*** *of the plane.* 飛機前後艙都有洗手間。◇ *A high gate blocks the only entrance* ***to the rear.*** 一座高大的門擋住了通往後面的唯一入口。 ➲ note at BACK **2** (also **ˌrear ˈend**) [C, usually sing.] (*informal*) the part of the body that you sit on 屁股；臀部 SYN **bottom**: *a kick in the rear* 踢了一下屁股

IDM **ˌbring up the ˈrear** to be at the back of a line of people, or last in a race 站在隊尾；落在最後；殿後

■ ***adj.*** 0‑ [only before noun] at or near the back of sth 後面的；後部的: *front and rear windows* 前面和後面的窗戶 ◇ *the rear entrance of the building* 大樓的後門

■ ***verb*** **1** [T] **~ sb/sth** [often passive] to care for young children or animals until they are fully grown 撫養；養育；培養 SYN **bring sb up, raise**: *She reared a family of five on her own.* 她一個人養活五口人。 **2** [T] **~ sth** to breed or keep animals or birds, for example on a farm 飼養: *to rear cattle* 養牛 **3** [I] **~ (up)** (of an animal, especially a horse 動物，尤指馬) to raise itself on its back legs, with the front legs in the air 用後腿直立: *The horse reared, throwing its rider.* 這匹馬後腿直立，將騎手摔下。 **4** [I] **~ (up)** (of sth large 大的東西) to seem to lean over you, especially in a threatening way（尤指可怖地）巍然聳立: *The great bulk of the building reared up against the night sky.* 夜幕下，巨大的高樓顯得陰森森的。

IDM **sth rears its (ugly) ˈhead** if sth unpleasant **rears its head** or **rears its ugly head**, it appears or happens（討厭的事情）出現，發生

PHR V **ˈrear sb/sth on sth** [usually passive] to give a person or an animal a particular type of food,

R

entertainment, etc. while they are young （用…）餵養；（以…）娛樂，培養：*I was the son of sailors and reared on stories of the sea.* 我是水手的兒子，是聽海的故事長大的。

Synonyms 同義詞辨析

reason

explanation • grounds • basis • excuse • motive • justification • pretext

These are all words for a cause or an explanation for sth that has happened or that sb has done. 以上各詞均指事情發生或做某事的原因、理由、解釋。

reason a cause or an explanation for sth that has happened or that sb has done; a fact that makes it right or fair to do sth 指某事發生或做某事的原因、理由、解釋、正當理由、道理：*He said no but he didn't give a reason.* 他說不行，但沒有說明原因。

explanation a statement, fact or situation that tells you why sth has happened; a reason given for sth 指解釋、說明、闡述：*The most likely explanation is that his plane was delayed.* 最可能的解釋是他的飛機晚點了。◇ *She left the room abruptly without explanation.* 她未作解釋就突然離開了房間。

grounds (*rather formal*) a good or true reason for saying, doing or believing sth 指說、做或相信某事的充分理由、根據：*You have no grounds for complaint.* 你沒有理由抱怨。

basis (*rather formal*) the reason why people take a particular action 指原因、緣由：*On what basis will this decision be made?* 將基於何種原因作出這一決定呢？

excuse a reason, either true or invented, that you give to explain or defend your behaviour; a good reason that you give for doing sth that you want to do for other reasons 指為自己行為所作的辯護、藉口、理由：*Late again! What's your excuse this time?* 又遲到了！你這次有什麼藉口？◇ *It gave me an excuse to take the car.* 這使我有理由開車去了。

motive a reason that explains sb's behaviour 指動機、原因：*There seemed to be no motive for the murder.* 這起謀殺案看不出有什麼動機。

justification (*rather formal*) a good reason why sth exists or is done 指事物存在或做某事的正當理由：*I can see no possible justification for any further tax increases.* 我看不出還能提出什麼理由來加稅了。

GROUNDS OR JUSTIFICATION? 用 grounds 還是 justification？

Justification is used to talk about finding or understanding reasons for actions, or trying to explain why it is a good idea to do sth. It is often used with words like *little, no, some, every, without*, and *not any*. * justification 用於找出或明白做事的理由，或解釋要做的事，常與 little、no、some、every、without 和 not any 等詞連用。 **Grounds** is used more for talking about reasons that already exist, or that have already been decided, for example by law. * grounds 多用於已存在的原因或已決定的（法律等）根據：*moral/ economic grounds* 道德／經濟原因

pretext (*rather formal*) a false reason that you give for doing sth, usually sth bad, in order to hide the real reason 指為掩蓋做某事（通常為不好的事）的真正理由而找的藉口、託辭：*He left the party early on the pretext of having to work.* 他藉口有事要處理，早早離開了聚會。

PATTERNS

- (a/an) reason/explanation/grounds/basis/excuse/ motive/justification/pretext **for** sth
- the reason/motive **behind** sth
- **on the** grounds/basis/pretext **of/that** ...
- (a) **good/valid** reason/explanation/grounds/excuse/ motive/justification

ˌrear ˈadmiral *noun* an officer of very high rank in the navy 海軍少將：*Rear Admiral Baines* 海軍少將貝恩斯

ˈrear-end *verb* **~ sth/sb** (*informal, especially NAmE*) (of a vehicle or driver 車輛或駕駛員) to drive into the back of another vehicle 撞上（前車的尾部）

rear·guard /ˈrɪəɡɑːd; *NAmE* ˈrɪrɡɑːrd/ *noun* (usually **the rearguard**) [sing.+sing./pl. v.] a group of soldiers that protect the back part of an army especially when the army is RETREATING after it has been defeated 後衛部隊 **OPP** **vanguard**

ˌrearguard ˈaction *noun* [usually sing.] a struggle to change or stop sth even when it is not likely that you will succeed 頑抗到底；最後掙扎：*They have been **fighting a rearguard action** for two years to stop their house being demolished.* 兩年來，為了不讓他們的房子被拆除，他們一直在頑強抗爭。

rear·ing /ˈrɪərɪŋ; *NAmE* ˈrɪrɪŋ/ *noun* [U] **1** the process of caring for children as they grow up, teaching them how to behave as members of society 撫養；養育；培養 **2** the process of breeding animals or birds and caring for them as they grow 飼養：*livestock rearing* 家畜飼養

rearm /riˈɑːm; *NAmE* -ˈɑːrm/ *verb* [I, T] to obtain, or supply sb with, new or better weapons, armies, etc. 重新武裝；重新裝備：*The country was forbidden to rearm under the terms of the treaty.* 根據條約規定，這個國家不允許重新武裝。◇ **~ sb** *Rebel troops were being rearmed.* 叛軍在進行重新裝備。▶ **re·arma·ment** /riˈɑːməmənt; *NAmE* -ˈɑːrm-/ *noun* [U]

rear·most /ˈrɪəməʊst; *NAmE* ˈrɪrmoʊst/ *adj.* (*formal*) furthest back 最靠後的；最後面的：*the rearmost section of the aircraft* 飛機的最後部

re·arrange /ˌriːəˈreɪndʒ/ *verb* **1 ~ sth** to change the position or order of things; to change your position 重新排列；改變位置：*We've rearranged the furniture in the bedroom.* 我們重新擺放了臥室裏的傢具。◇ *She rearranged herself in another pose.* 她重新擺了個姿勢。 **2 ~ sth** to change the time, date or place of an event 重新安排；改變時間（或日期、地點） **SYN** **reschedule**：*Can we rearrange the meeting for next Tuesday at 2?* 我們把會議改到下週二下午兩點好嗎？ ▶ **re·arrange·ment** *noun* [C, U]

ˌrear-view ˈmirror *noun* a mirror in which a driver can see the traffic behind 後視鏡 ➲ VISUAL VOCAB page V42

rear·ward /ˈrɪəwəd; *NAmE* ˈrɪrwərd/ *adj.* (*formal*) at or near the back of sth 後面的；後部的：*rearward seats* 後面的座位

ˌrear-wheel ˈdrive *noun* [U] a system in which power from the engine is sent to the back wheels of a vehicle 後輪驅動（系統） ➲ compare FRONT-WHEEL DRIVE

rea·son 0-ᴡ /ˈriːzn/ *noun, verb*

■ *noun* **1** 0-ᴡ [C] a cause or an explanation for sth that has happened or that sb has done 原因；理由；解釋：**~ (why ...)** *I'd like to know the reason why you're so late.* 我想知道你為什麼遲到那麼長時間。◇ *Give me **one good reason** why I should help you.* 我為什麼要幫你？給我一個充分的理由。◇ **~ (that ...)** *We aren't going for the **simple reason** that we can't afford it.* 我們不去，只是因為我們負擔不起。◇ **~ (for sth)** *She gave no reasons for her decision.* 她沒有對她的決定作出任何解釋。◇ **~ (for doing sth)** *I have no particular reason for doubting him.* 我沒有什麼特別的理由懷疑他。◇ *He said no but he didn't **give a reason**.* 他說不行，但沒有說明原因。◇ ***For some reason*** (= one that I don't know or don't understand) *we all have to come in early tomorrow.* 出於某種原因，我們大家明天都不得不早點來。◇ *The man attacked me **for no apparent reason**.* 那個人不知何故攻擊我。◇ *She resigned for **personal reasons**.* 她出於個人原因而辭職。◇ ***For reasons of** security the door is always kept locked.* 為了保證安全，門總是鎖着的。◇ *He wants to keep them all in his office **for reasons best known to himself**.* 他想把他們都留在他的辦公室裏，原因只有他自己知道。◇ *people who, **for whatever reason**, are unable to support themselves* 那些因為種種原因不能自立的人 ◇ *'Why do you*

R

*want to know?' **'No reason.'*** (= I do not want to say why.) "你為什麼想知道？" "不為什麼。" ◇ *'Why did she do that?' 'She must **have her reasons.**'* (= secret reasons which she does not want to tell) "她為什麼那麼做？" "她一定有她的理由。" ◇ (*formal*) *He was excused* **by reason of** (= because of) *his age.* 他因為其年齡而得到原諒。 ➲ LANGUAGE BANK at THEREFORE **2** 🔑 [U] a fact that makes it right or fair to do sth 正當理由；道理；情理：**~ (to do sth)** *They have reason to believe that he is lying.* 他們有理由認為他是在撒謊。 ◇ *We **have every reason*** (= have very good reasons) *to feel optimistic.* 我們完全有理由感到樂觀。 ◇ **~ (why …)** *There is no reason why we should agree to this.* 我們沒有理由同意這點。 ◇ **~ (for sth/for doing sth)** *This result gives us **all the more reason** for optimism.* 這個結果使我們更有理由保持樂觀。 ◇ *She complained, **with reason*** (= rightly), *that she had been underpaid.* 她抱怨給她的報酬太低，是有道理的。 **3** 🔑 [U] the power of the mind to think in a logical way, to understand and have opinions, etc. 思考力；理解力；理性：*Only human beings are capable of reason* (= of thinking in a logical way, etc.). 只有人類才有理性思考的能力。 ◇ *to lose your reason* (= become mentally ill) 喪失理智 **4** 🔑 [U] what is possible, practical or right 道理；情理；明智：*I can't get her to **listen to reason**.* 我沒法跟她講道理。 ◇ *Why can't they **see reason**?* 他們為什麼不明事理？ ◇ *to be open to reason* (= to be willing to accept sensible advice) 願意聽好言相勸 ◇ *He's looking for a job and he's willing to do anything **within reason**.* 他在尋找工作，而且只要是正當的事他都願意做。

IDM **it ˌstands to ˈreason** (*informal*) it must be clear to any sensible person who thinks about it 這是人人都清楚的；這是明擺着的：*It stands to reason that they'll leave if you don't pay them enough.* 這是明擺着的，你不給他們足夠的報酬，他們就走人。 ➲ more at RHYME *n.*

■ *verb* **1** [T, I] **~ (that …)** | **+ speech** to form a judgement about a situation by considering the facts and using your power to think in a logical way 推理；推論；推斷：*She reasoned that she must have left her bag on the train.* 她斷定準是把包落在火車上了。 ◇ *They couldn't fire him, he reasoned. He was the only one who knew how the system worked.* 他推斷他們不會解雇他。他是唯一知道這套系統如何運轉的人。 **2** [I] to use your power to think and understand 思考；理解：*the human ability to reason* 人的思考能力

R

PHR V **ˌreason sth ˈout** to try and find the answer to a problem by using your power to think in a logical way 通過思考想出對策 **SYN** **figure out** **ˈreason with sb** to talk to sb in order to persuade them to be more sensible 和某人講道理；規勸：*I tried to reason with him, but he wouldn't listen.* 我盡量跟他講道理，可他就是不聽。

rea·son·able 🔑 /ˈriːznəbl/ *adj.*
1 🔑 **~ (to do sth)** fair, practical and sensible 公平的；合理的；有理由的；明智的：***It is reasonable** to assume that he knew beforehand that this would happen.* 有理由認為他事先就知道會發生這樣的事。 ◇ ***Be reasonable!** We can't work late every night.* 要講道理呀！我們不能每天晚上都幹得很晚呀。 ◇ *Any reasonable person would have done exactly as you did.* 任何有頭腦的人都會完全像你那樣去做的。 ◇ *The prosecution has to prove **beyond reasonable doubt** that he is guilty of murder.* 控方必須毫無疑義地證明他犯有謀殺罪。 **OPP** **unreasonable** **2** 🔑 acceptable and appropriate in a particular situation 可以接受的；合乎情理的；公道的：*He made us a reasonable offer for the car.* 他給我們出的車價公平合理。 ◇ *You must submit your claim within a reasonable time.* 你必須在適當的時間內提出要求。 **3** 🔑 (of prices 價格) not too expensive 不太貴的；公道的 **SYN** **fair**：*We sell good quality food at reasonable prices.* 我們以公道的價格出售優質食品。 ➲ SYNONYMS at CHEAP **4** 🔑 [usually before noun] fairly good, but not very good 不錯的；還算好的；過得去的 **SYN** **average**：*a reasonable standard of living* 還算不錯的生活水平 ◇ *The hotel was reasonable, I suppose* (= but not excellent). 我覺得這家酒店還可以。 ▸ **rea·son·able·ness** *noun* [U]

rea·son·ably 🔑 /ˈriːznəbli/ *adv.*
1 🔑 to a degree that is fairly good but not very good 尚可；過得去：*The instructions are reasonably straightforward.* 用法說明還算簡單易懂。 ◇ *She seems reasonably happy in her new job.* 她在新的工作崗位上好像還挺開心。 **2** 🔑 in a logical and sensible way 合乎邏輯地；明智地；通情達理地：*We tried to discuss the matter calmly and reasonably.* 我們試圖冷靜且通情達理地來討論這個問題。 **3** 🔑 in a fair way 公平合理地；適度地：*He couldn't reasonably be expected to pay back the loan all at once.* 公平合理地講，不可能指望他一下子歸還全部借款。 ◇ *The apartments are **reasonably priced*** (= not too expensive). 這些單元住宅價格合理。

rea·soned /ˈriːzənd/ *adj.* [only before noun] (of an argument, opinion, etc. 論點、意見等) presented in a logical way that shows careful thought 合乎邏輯的；縝密的

rea·son·ing /ˈriːzənɪŋ/ *noun* [U] the process of thinking about things in a logical way; opinions and ideas that are based on logical thinking 推想；推理；理性的觀點；論證：*What is **the reasoning behind** this decision?* 作出這個決定的依據是什麼？ ◇ *This **line of reasoning** is faulty.* 這樣的思路有問題。

re·assem·ble /ˌriːəˈsembl/ *verb* **1** [T] **~ sth** to fit the parts of sth together again after it has been taken apart 重新裝配（或組裝）：*We had to take the table apart and reassemble it upstairs.* 我們只好先把桌子拆開，到樓上再組裝起來。 **2** [I] to meet together again as a group after a break 重新集結；再次集合：*The class reassembled after lunch.* 午飯後，全班同學又集合起來。

re·assert /ˌriːəˈsɜːt; *NAmE* -ˈsɜːrt/ *verb* **1 ~ sth** to make other people recognize again your right or authority to do sth, after a period when this has been in doubt 重申；堅持：*She found it necessary to reassert her position.* 她覺得有必要重申她的立場。 **2 ~ itself** to start to have an effect again, after a period of not having any effect 重新發揮作用：*He thought about giving up his job, but then common sense reasserted itself.* 他曾想放棄這份工作，但後來還是理智佔了上風。 **3** to state again, clearly and firmly, that sth is true 再次斷言；再次聲明：**~ that …** *He reasserted that all parties should be involved in the talks.* 他再次聲明各方均應參加會談。 ◇ **~ sth** *Traditional values have been reasserted.* 傳統價值再次得到肯定。 ▸ **re·asser·tion** *noun* [sing., U]

re·assess **AW** /ˌriːəˈses/ *verb* **~ sth** to think again about sth to decide if you need to change your opinion of it 重新考慮；再次評價 **SYN** **reappraise** ▸ **re·assess·ment** **AW** *noun* [U, C]

re·assign **AW** /ˌriːəˈsaɪn/ *verb* [often passive] **1 ~ sb (to sth)** to give sb a different duty, position, or responsibility 重新委派，再次指派（任務、職位、責任等）：*After his election defeat he was reassigned to the diplomatic service.* 落選之後，他又被派到外交部門工作。 **2 ~ sth (to sb/sth)** to give sth to a different person or organization; to change the status of sth 重新分配…（給某人或機構）；重新指定：*The case was reassigned to a different court.* 這樁案件已交由另一法院審理。 ▸ **re·assign·ment** *noun* [U]

re·assur·ance /ˌriːəˈʃʊərəns; -ˈʃɔːr-; *NAmE* -ˈʃʊr-/ *noun* **1** [U] **~ (that …)** the fact of giving advice or help that takes away a person's fears or doubts（能消除疑慮等的）肯定，保證：*to **give/provide/offer reassurance*** 表明肯定的態度 **2** [C] **~ (that …)** something that is said or done to take away a person's fears or doubts 能消除疑慮的說話（或行動）；保證：*We have been given reassurances that the water is safe to drink.* 我們得到保證說這水適合飲用。

re·assure /ˌriːəˈʃʊə(r); -ˈʃɔː(r); *NAmE* -ˈʃʊr/ *verb* to say or do sth that makes sb less frightened or worried 使…安心；打消…的疑慮 **SYN** **set sb's mind at rest**：**~ sb (about sth)** *They tried to reassure her, but she still felt anxious.* 他們設法讓她放心，可她還是焦慮不安。 ◇ **~ sb that …** *The doctor reassured him that there was nothing seriously wrong.* 醫生安慰他說，沒什麼嚴重的病。

re·assur·ing /ˌriːəˈʃʊərɪŋ; -ˈʃɔːr-; *NAmE* -ˈʃʊr-/ *adj.* making you feel less worried or uncertain about sth 令人感到寬慰的；令人放心的：*a reassuring smile* 使人信心倍增的微笑 ◇ ***It's reassuring** (to know) **that** we've got* *the money if necessary.* 我們有了應急的錢，這就不必擔心了。 ▸ **re·assur·ing·ly** *adv.*

re·awaken /ˌriːəˈweɪkən/ *verb* **~ sth** to make you feel a particular emotion again or to make you remember sth again 勾起，喚起，再次引發（感情、回憶等） SYN **rekindle** : *The place reawakened childhood memories.* 這地方喚起了童年的回憶。

re·bar·ba·tive /rɪˈbɑːbətɪv; *NAmE* -ˈbɑːrb-/ *adj.* (*formal*) not attractive 無吸引力的；令人厭惡的 SYN **objectionable**

re·bate /ˈriːbeɪt/ *noun* **1** an amount of money that is paid back to you because you have paid too much 退還款： *a tax rebate* 退還稅款 **2** an amount of money that is taken away from the cost of sth, before you pay for it 回扣，返還（退還的部份貨價）；折扣 SYN **discount** : *Buyers are offered a cash rebate.* 購買者享受現金回扣。

rebel *noun, verb*

■ ***noun*** /ˈrebl/ **1** a person who fights against the government of their country 反政府的人；叛亂者；造反者： *rebel forces* 叛亂武裝 ◇ *Armed rebels advanced towards the capital.* 武裝叛亂分子向首都推進。 **2** a person who opposes sb in authority over them within an organization, a political party, etc. 反抗權威者 **3** a person who does not like to obey rules or who does not accept normal standards of behaviour, dress, etc. 叛逆者；不守規矩者： *I've always been the rebel of the family.* 我在家裏向來是個叛逆者。

■ ***verb*** /rɪˈbel/ (**-ll-**) [I] **~** (**against sb/sth**) to fight against or refuse to obey an authority, for example a government, a system, your parents, etc. 造反；反抗；背叛： *He later rebelled against his strict religious upbringing.* 他後來背叛了他所受的嚴格的宗教教育。 ◇ *Most teenagers find something to rebel against.* 大多數青少年都有反抗意識。

re·bel·lion /rɪˈbeljən/ *noun* **~** (**against sb/sth**) **1** [U, C] an attempt by some of the people in a country to change their government, using violence 謀反；叛亂；反叛 SYN **uprising** : *The north of the country rose in rebellion against the government.* 這個國家的北方地區發生了反對政府的叛亂。 ◇ *The army put down the rebellion.* 軍隊鎮壓了叛亂。 ➲ COLLOCATIONS at WAR **2** [U, C] opposition to authority within an organization, a political party, etc. （對權威的）反抗，不服從： (*a*) *back-bench rebellion* 下院普通議員的反對 **3** [U] opposition to authority; being unwilling to obey rules or accept normal standards of behaviour, dress, etc. 不順從；叛逆： *teenage rebellion* 青少年的叛逆

re·bel·li·ous /rɪˈbeljəs/ *adj.* **1** unwilling to obey rules or accept normal standards of behaviour, dress, etc. 反叛的；叛逆的；桀驁不馴的： *rebellious teenagers* 叛逆的青少年 ◇ *He has always had* ***a rebellious streak.*** 他總是有點叛逆。 **2** opposed to the government of a country; opposed to those in authority within an organization 叛亂的；造反的；反對權威的： *rebellious cities/factions* 叛亂的城市；反對派別 ▸ **re·bel·li·ous·ly** *adv.* : *'I don't care!' she said rebelliously.* "我不在乎！" 她桀驁不馴地說道。 **re·bel·li·ous·ness** *noun* [U]

re·birth /ˌriːˈbɜːθ; *NAmE* -ˈbɜːrθ/ *noun* [U, sing.] **1** a period of new life, growth or activity 新生；復活；復興： *the seasonal cycle of death and rebirth* 春榮冬枯的季節循環 **2** a spiritual change when a person's faith becomes stronger or they convert to another religion（信仰加強或皈依另一宗教後精神上的）新生，再生

re·birth·ing /ˌriːˈbɜːθɪŋ; *NAmE* -ˈbɜːrθ-/ *noun* [U] a type of PSYCHOTHERAPY that involves reproducing the experience of being born using controlled breathing 呼吸重生法，再生療法（通過控制呼吸重新體驗出生的心理療法）

re·boot /ˌriːˈbuːt/ *verb* [T, I] **~** (**sth**) (*computing* 計) if you **reboot** a computer or it **reboots**, you switch it off and then start it again immediately 重新啟動

re·born /ˌriːˈbɔːn; *NAmE* -ˈbɔːrn/ *verb, adj.*

■ ***verb*** **be reborn** (used only in the passive without *by* 僅用於不帶 by 的被動語態) **1** to become active or popular again 復興；再次流行 **2** to be born again 再生；輪迴： *If you were reborn as an animal, which animal would you be?* 如果你轉世成為動物，你願意做哪種動物？

■ ***adj.*** **1** having become active again 重生的；復興的： *a reborn version of social democracy* 一種社會民主主義的翻版 **2** having experienced a complete spiritual change（精神上）再生的，新生的： *reborn evangelical Christians* 獲得再生的福音教會信徒 ➲ see also BORN-AGAIN

re·bound *verb, noun*

■ ***verb*** /rɪˈbaʊnd/ **1** [I] **~** (**from/off sth**) to BOUNCE back after hitting sth 彈回；反彈： *The ball rebounded from the goalpost and Podolski headed it in.* 球從門柱彈回，波多爾斯基頭球破門。 **2** [I] **~** (**on sb**) (*formal*) if sth that you do **rebounds** on you, it has an unpleasant effect on you, especially when the effect was intended for sb else 報應；反作用於 SYN **backfire** **3** [I] (*business* 商) (of prices, etc. 價格等) to rise again after they have fallen 回升；反彈 SYN **bounce back**

■ ***noun*** /ˈriːbaʊnd/ **1** (*sport* 體) a ball that hits sth and BOUNCES back 反彈球；回彈球 **2** (in BASKETBALL 籃球) the act of catching the ball after a player has thrown it at the BASKET and has not scored a point 搶斷籃板球 **3** (*business* 商) a positive reaction that happens after sth negative 復興；振作

IDM **on the 'rebound** while you are sad and confused, especially after a relationship has ended（尤指關係破裂之後）在傷心困惑之時

re·brand /ˌriːˈbrænd/ *verb* **~ sth/yourself** to change the image of a company or an organization or one of its products or services, for example by changing its name or by advertising it in a different way 重塑…的形象（如通過改變名稱或廣告）；將…重塑： *In the 1990s the Labour Party rebranded itself as New Labour.* 工黨於 20 世紀 90 年代重塑形象，改稱新勞工黨。 ▸ **re·brand·ing** *noun* [sing., U] : *a rebranding exercise* 重塑形象的活動 ◇ *a £5 million rebranding* 投資 500 萬英鎊的形象重塑工程

re·buff /rɪˈbʌf/ *noun* (*formal*) an unkind refusal of a friendly offer, request or suggestion 粗暴回絕；生硬的拒絕 SYN **rejection** : *Her offer of help was met with a sharp rebuff.* 她主動幫忙，卻遭到斷然拒絕。 ▸ **re·buff** *verb* : **~ sth** *They rebuffed her request for help.* 他們拒絕了她的請求，不給她幫助。

re·build /ˌriːˈbɪld/ *verb* (**re·built**, **re·built** /ˌriːˈbɪlt/) **1 ~ sth** to build or put sth together again 重建；重組；重新裝配： *After the earthquake, the people set about rebuilding their homes.* 地震過後，人們開始重建家園。 ◇ *He rebuilt the engine using parts from cars that had been scrapped.* 他用廢棄的汽車零件重新組裝了發動機。 **2 ~ sth** to make sth/sb complete and strong again 使復原；使恢復： *When she lost her job, she had to* ***rebuild her life*** *completely.* 她丟了工作以後，不得不徹底重新安排自己的生活。 ◇ *attempts to rebuild the shattered post-war economy* 為恢復支離破碎的戰後經濟所作的嘗試

re·buke /rɪˈbjuːk/ *verb* [often passive] **~ sb** (**for sth/for doing sth**) (*formal*) to speak severely to sb because they have done sth wrong 指責；批評 SYN **reprimand** : *The company was publicly rebuked for having neglected safety procedures.* 公司因忽略了安全措施而受到公開批評。 ▸ **re·buke** *noun* [C, U] : *He was silenced by her stinging rebuke.* 她的尖銳批評使他啞口無言。

rebus 字畫謎

to be or not to be

rebus /ˈriːbəs/ *noun* a combination of pictures and letters which represent a word or phrase whose meaning has to be guessed（以圖畫和字母混合構成的）圖形字迷

R

rebut /rɪˈbʌt/ *verb* (-tt-) **~ sth** (*formal*) to say or prove that a statement or criticism is false 反駁；駁斥；證明（言論等）錯誤 SYN **refute** ▸ **re·but·tal** /-tl/ *noun* [C, U]：*The accusations met with a firm rebuttal.* 這些指控受到了堅決的駁斥。

re·cal·ci·trant /rɪˈkælsɪtrənt/ *adj.* (*formal*) unwilling to obey rules or follow instructions; difficult to control 不守規章的；不服從指揮的；桀驁不馴的；難以控制的 ▸ **re·cal·ci·trance** /-əns/ *noun* [U]

re·call *verb, noun*

■ *verb* /rɪˈkɔːl/ **1** [T, I] (*formal*) (not used in the progressive tenses 不用於進行時) to remember sth 記起；回憶起；回想起 SYN **recollect**：**~ sth** *She could not recall his name.* 她想不起他的名字。◇ **(+ adv./prep.)** *If I recall correctly, he lives in Luton.* 如果我沒記錯的話，他住在盧頓。◇ **~ (sb/sth) doing sth** *I can't recall meeting her before.* 我想不起來以前曾經見過她。◇ **~ that** ... *He recalled that she always came home late on Wednesdays.* 他回想起她星期三總是很晚回家。◇ **~ what, when, etc.** ... *Can you recall exactly what happened?* 你能記起到底發生了什麼事嗎？◇ **+ speech** *'It was on a Thursday in March,' he recalled.* "那是三月份的一個星期四。"他回憶道。 **2** [T] **~ sth** (not used in the progressive tenses 不用於進行時) to make sb think of sth 使想起；使想到；勾起 SYN **evoke**：*The poem recalls Eliot's 'The Waste Land'.* 這首詩令人想起艾略特的《荒原》。 **3** [T] to order sb to return 召回：**~ sb** *Both countries recalled their ambassadors.* 兩個國家都召回了各自的大使。◇ **~ sb to sth** *He was recalled to military duty.* 他被召回執行軍事任務。◇ *They have both been recalled to the Welsh squad* (= selected as members of the team after a time when they were not selected). 他們倆都被重新召回了威爾士人隊。 **4** [T] **~ sth** to ask for sth to be returned, often because there is sth wrong with it 收回（殘損貨品等）：*The company has recalled all the faulty hairdryers.* 公司回收了所有有瑕疵的吹風機。

■ *noun* /rɪˈkɔːl; ˈriːkɔːl/ **1** [U] the ability to remember sth that you have learned or sth that has happened in the past 記憶力；記性：*She has amazing powers of recall.* 她有驚人的記憶力。◇ *to have* ***instant recall*** (= to be able to remember sth immediately) 有快速記憶的能力 ◇ *to have* ***total recall*** (= to be able to remember all the details of sth) 記得所有細節 **2** [sing.] an official order or request for sb/sth to return, or for sth to be given back 召回令；回歸請求；回收令：*Thomas's recall to the Welsh team* 讓托馬斯回歸威爾士隊的要求

IDM **beyond reˈcall** impossible to bring back to the original state; impossible to remember 不可恢復；想不起來；記不住

re·cant /rɪˈkænt/ *verb* [T, I] **~ (sth)** (*formal*) to say, often publicly, that you no longer have the same belief or opinion that you had before 公開宣佈放棄（原先的信仰、觀點等） ▸ **re·can·ta·tion** /ˌriːkænˈteɪʃn/ *noun* [C, U]

recap /ˈriːkæp/ *verb, noun*

■ *verb* (-pp-) [I, T] **~ (on sth)** | **~ sth** | **~ what, where, etc.** ... = RECAPITULATE：*Let me just recap on what we've decided so far.* 讓我來概括一下到目前為止我們所作的決定吧。

■ *noun* = RECAPITULATION

re·cap·itu·late /ˌriːkəˈpɪtʃuleɪt/ *verb* (*formal*) (also **recap**) [I, T] **~ (on sth)** | **~ sth** | **~ what, where, etc.** ... to repeat or give a summary of what has already been said, decided, etc. 重述；概括：*To recapitulate briefly, the three main points are these ...* 簡要概括起來，主要有這樣三點… ▸ **re·cap·itu·la·tion** /ˌriːkəpɪtʃuˈleɪʃn/ *noun* [C, U] (*formal*) (also **recap**)

re·cap·ture /ˌriːˈkæptʃə(r)/ *verb* **1 ~ sth** to win back a place, position, etc. that was previously taken from you by an enemy or a rival 贏回；奪回：*Government troops soon recaptured the island.* 政府的軍隊很快奪回了這個島。 **2 ~ sb/sth** to catch a person or an animal that has escaped 抓回；再次捕獲 **3 ~ sth** to bring back a feeling or repeat an experience that you had in the past 回憶；再體驗；重溫：*He was trying to recapture the happiness of his youth.* 他在努力回憶年輕時的快樂。 ▸ **re·cap·ture** *noun* [U]：*the recapture of towns occupied by the rebels* 奪回被叛軍佔領的城鎮

re·cast /ˌriːˈkɑːst; *NAmE* -ˈkæst/ *verb* (**re·cast**, **re·cast**) **1 ~ sth (as sth)** to change sth by organizing or presenting it in a different way 改動；重組；改寫：*She recast her lecture as a radio talk.* 她把講稿修改成了一篇廣播講話。 **2 ~ sb (as sth)** to change the actors or the role of a particular actor in a play, etc. 重新安排（演員陣容）；改變（演員角色）

recce /ˈreki/ *noun* (*BrE, informal*) = RECONNAISSANCE：*to do a quick recce of an area* 對一地區進行快速偵察

re·cede /rɪˈsiːd/ *verb* **1** [I] to move gradually away from sb or away from a previous position 逐漸遠離；漸漸遠去：*The sound of the truck receded into the distance.* 卡車的聲音漸漸在遠處消失了。◇ *She watched his receding figure.* 她看着他的身影漸漸遠去。 **2** [I] (especially of a problem, feeling or quality 尤指問題、感覺或特質) to become gradually weaker or smaller 逐漸減弱；慢慢變小：*The prospect of bankruptcy has now receded* (= it is less likely). 破產的可能性現已減少了。◇ *The pain was receding slightly.* 疼痛正在一點一點地減弱。 **3** [I] (of hair 頭髮) to stop growing at the front of the head （頭頂前部）頭髮停止生長，變禿：*a middle-aged man with* ***receding hair/a receding hairline*** 髮際後移的中年男子 ➲ VISUAL VOCAB page V60 **4** [I] **a ~ chin** a chin that slopes backwards towards the neck 向後縮的下巴

re·ceipt /rɪˈsiːt/ *noun*

1 (*NAmE* also **ˈsales slip**) [C] **~ (for sth)** a piece of paper that shows that goods or services have been paid for 收據；收條：*Can I have a receipt, please?* 請給我開個收據，好嗎？◇ *to make out* (= write) *a receipt* 寫收據 ➲ COLLOCATIONS at SHOPPING **2** [U] **~ (of sth)** (*formal*) the act of receiving sth 接收；收到：*to acknowledge receipt of a letter* 簽收信件 ◇ *The goods will be dispatched* ***on receipt of*** *an order form.* 訂單一到即發貨。◇ *Are you* ***in receipt of*** *any state benefits?* 你目前是否享有政府補助金？ **3 receipts** [pl.] (*business* 商) money that a business, bank or government receives （企業、銀行、政府等）收到的款項，收入：***net/gross receipts*** 淨收入；總收入

re·ceiv·able /rɪˈsiːvəbl/ *adj.* (*business* 商) (usually following a noun 通常用於名詞後) (of bills, accounts, etc. 票據、賬目等) for which money has not yet been received 應收款的：*accounts receivable* 應收賬款

re·ceiv·ables /rɪˈsiːvəblz/ *noun* [pl.] (*business* 商) money that is owed to a business 應收款項

re·ceive /rɪˈsiːv/ *verb*

▸ GET/ACCEPT 得到；接受 **1** [T] (rather *formal*) to get or accept sth that is sent or given to you 拿到；接到；收到：**~ sth** *to receive a letter/present/phone call* 收到信/禮物；接到電話 ◇ *to receive information/payment/thanks* 接收信息/付款；受到感謝 ◇ **~ sth from sb/sth** *He received an award for bravery from the police service.* 他以其勇敢行為受到警務部門的嘉獎。

▸ TREATMENT/INJURY 待遇；傷害 **2** [T] to experience or be given a particular type of treatment or an injury 體驗；受到（某種待遇或傷害）：**~ sth from sb** *We received a warm welcome from our hosts.* 我們受到了主人的熱情歡迎。◇ **~ sth** *Emergency cases will receive professional attention immediately.* 急診病人將立即得到診治。◇ *to receive severe injuries* 受重傷

▸ REACT TO STH 作出反應 **3** [T, usually passive] to react to sth new, in a particular way 對…作出反應：**~ sth + adv./prep.** *The play was* ***well received*** *by the critics.* 劇評家對這齣戲反應良好。◇ **~ sth with sth** *The statistics were received with concern.* 這些統計數字受到了關注。

▸ GUESTS 客人 **4** [T, often passive] **~ sb (with sth)** | **~ sb (as sth)** (*formal*) to welcome or entertain a guest, especially formally 接待；歡迎；招待：*He was received as an honoured guest at the White House.* 他在白宮受到貴賓的禮遇接待。

▸ AS MEMBER OF STH 成員 **5** [T] **~ sb (into sth)** (*formal*) to officially recognize and accept sb as a member of a group 接納；允許加入：*Three young people were received into the Church at Easter.* 復活節時有三位年輕人入教。

▸ TV/RADIO 電視；收音機 **6** [T] **~ sth** to change broadcast signals into sounds or pictures on a television, radio, etc. 接收；收看；收聽：*to receive programmes via*

satellite 通過衛星收看節目 **7** [T] **~ sth/sb** to be able to hear a radio message that is being sent by sb 接收到，收聽到（無線電訊號）：*I'm receiving you loud and clear.* 我聽得到你的聲音，又清晰，又響亮。
▸ **STOLEN GOODS 贓物 8** [T, I] **~ (sth)** (*especially BrE*) to buy or accept goods that you know have been stolen 購買，接受（贓物）
▸ **IN SPORT 體育運動 9** [I, T] **~ (sth)** (in TENNIS, etc. 網球等) to be the player that the SERVER hits the ball to 接（發球）：*She won the toss and chose to receive.* 她猜中了擲幣結果，選擇接發球。
IDM **be at/on the re'ceiving end (of sth)** (*informal*) to be the person that an action, etc. is directed at, especially an unpleasant one 承受不愉快之事：*She found herself on the receiving end of a great deal of criticism.* 她發現自己遭到眾多的批評。

re·ceived /rɪ'siːvd/ *adj.* [only before noun] (*formal*) accepted by most people as being correct 被承認的；被一致認可的：*The* ***received wisdom*** *is that they cannot win.* 大家一致認為他們不會贏。IDM see WISDOM

re,ceived pronunci'ation *noun* [U] = RP

re·ceiver /rɪ'siːvə(r)/ *noun* **1** the part of a telephone that you hold close to your mouth and ear 聽筒；受話器：*to* ***pick up/lift/put down/replace the receiver*** 拿起／放回聽筒 ➲ COLLOCATIONS at PHONE ➲ compare HANDSET (1) **2** a piece of radio or television equipment that changes broadcast signals into sound or pictures 無線電接收機；收音機；電視機：*a satellite receiver* 衛星信號接收機 ➲ compare TRANSMITTER (1) **3** (*BrE* also **of,ficial re'ceiver**) (*law* 律) a person who is chosen by a court to be in charge of a company that is BANKRUPT（破產公司的）財產管理人，官方接管人：*to call in the receivers* 申請委派官方接管人 **4** a person who receives sth 接收者：*Molly's more of a giver than a receiver.* 莫利是捐贈者而不是接收者。**5** a person who buys or accepts stolen goods, knowing that they have been stolen 購買（或接受）贓物的人 **6** (in AMERICAN FOOTBALL 美式足球) a player who plays in a position in which the ball can be caught when it is being passed forward 前傳球接球手；直傳球接球手

re·ceiv·er·ship /rɪ'siːvəʃɪp; *NAmE* -vərʃ-/ *noun* [U] (*law* 律) the state of a business being controlled by an official receiver because it has no money 破產管理；破產產業接管

re·cent 0━ /'riːsnt/ *adj.* [usually before noun] that happened or began only a short time ago 近來的；新近的：*a recent development/discovery/event* 近來的發展／發現／事件 ◇ *his most recent visit to Poland* 他最近到波蘭的訪問 ◇ *There have been many changes* ***in recent years***. 近幾年發生了許多變化。

re·cent·ly 0━ /'riːsntli/ *adv.* not long ago 不久前；最近：*We received a letter from him recently.* 我們不久以前收到了他的一封信。◇ *Until recently they were living in York.* 他們不久以前還住在約克。◇ *I haven't seen them recently* (= it is some time since I saw them). 我近來沒見過他們。◇ *Have you used it recently* (= in the recent past)? 你最近用過它嗎？

re·cep·tacle /rɪ'septəkl/ *noun* **1 ~ (for sth)** (*formal*) a container for putting sth in 容器：(*figurative*) *The seas have been used as a receptacle for a range of industrial toxins.* 海洋成了各種有毒工業廢料的大容器。**2** (*NAmE*) = OUTLET (5)

re·cep·tion 0━ /rɪ'sepʃn/ *noun*
1 0━ [U] (*especially BrE*) the area inside the entrance of a hotel, an office building, etc. where guests or visitors go first when they arrive 接待處；接待區：*the reception area* 接待區 ◇ *We arranged to meet* ***in reception*** *at 6.30.* 我們約定 6:30 在接待處會面。◇ *You can leave a message* ***with reception***. 你可以在接待處留個口信。◇ (*NAmE, BrE*) *the reception desk* 接待處 ➲ compare FRONT DESK **2** 0━ [C] a formal social occasion to welcome sb or celebrate sth 接待儀式；歡迎會；招待會：*a wedding reception* 結婚喜筵 **3** 0━ [sing.] the type of welcome that is given to sb/sth 歡迎；接受：*Her latest album has met with a* ***mixed reception*** *from fans.* 她的最新唱片在歌迷之間反響不一。◇ *Delegates gave him a* ***warm reception*** *as he called for more spending on education.* 由於他呼籲增加教育經費，代表們向他報以熱烈的歡迎。**4** 0━ [U] the quality of radio and television signals that are broadcast（無線電和電視信號的）接收效果：***good/bad reception*** 良好的／差的接收效果 ◇ *There was very poor reception on my phone.* 我的電話接收效果很差。**5** [U] the act of receiving or welcoming sb 接納；接待；迎接：*the reception of refugees from the war zone* 接納交戰地區來的難民

re'ception centre (*NAmE* **re'ception center**) *noun* **1** a place where people can get information or advice 接待處；接待室：*The museum is building a new reception centre for visitors.* 博物館正在修建新的來賓接待室。**2** a place where people, for example those without a home, can get help and temporary accommodation 收容所；救助站：*a reception centre for refugees* 難民救助站

re'ception class *noun* (in Britain) the first class at school for children aged 4 or 5（英國學校為 4 至 5 歲兒童開設的）預備班，啟蒙班

re·cep·tion·ist /rɪ'sepʃənɪst/ *noun* a person whose job is to deal with people arriving at or telephoning a hotel, an office building, a doctor's SURGERY, etc. 接待員

re'ception room *noun* (*BrE*) (used especially when advertising houses for sale) a room in a house where people can sit, for example a living room or DINING ROOM（尤用於售房廣告中的）接待室；會客室

re·cep·tive /rɪ'septɪv/ *adj.* **~ (to sth)** willing to listen to or to accept new ideas or suggestions（對新觀點、建議等）願意傾聽的，樂於接受的 SYN **responsive**：*She was always receptive to new ideas.* 她總是願意接受新觀點。◇ *He gave an impressive speech to a receptive audience.* 他做了一次感人的講演，聽眾深受感動。▸ **re·cep·tive·ness**, **re·cep·tiv·ity** /,riːsep'tɪvəti/ *noun* [U]：*receptivity to change* 對變化的適應能力

re·cep·tor /rɪ'septə(r)/ *noun* (*biology* 生) a sense organ or nerve ending in the body that reacts to changes such as heat or cold and makes the body react in a particular way 感受器；受體

re·cess *noun, verb*
■ ***noun*** /rɪ'ses; 'riːses/ **1** [C, U] a period of time during the year when the members of a parliament, committee, etc. do not meet 休會期 **2** [C] a short break in a trial in court 休庭：*The judge called a short recess.* 法官宣佈短暫休庭。**3** (*NAmE*) (*BrE* **break**, **'break time**) [U] a period of time between lessons at school 課間休息 **4** [C] a part of a wall that is set further back than the rest of the wall, forming a space 壁龕；壁櫥；凹室 SYN **alcove**：*a recess for books* 放書的壁櫥 **5** [C, usually pl.] the part of a place that is furthest from the light and hard to see or get to 隱蔽處；幽深處：*He stared into the dark recesses of the room.* 他盯着房間裏黑暗的角落。◇ (*figurative*) *The doubt was still there, in the deep recesses of her mind.* 在她的內心深處依然存有疑慮。
■ ***verb*** /rɪ'ses/ [often passive] **1** [T, I] **~ (sth)** (*NAmE*) to take or to order a recess 休會；暫停；宣佈暫停：*The hearing was recessed for the weekend.* 聽證會週末暫停。**2** [T] **~ sth (in/into sth)** to put sth in a position that is set back into a wall, etc. 把…放進壁龕（或壁櫥）；將…嵌入牆壁：*recessed shelves* 凹進牆壁的格子架

re·ces·sion /rɪ'seʃn/ *noun* **1** [C, U] a difficult time for the economy of a country, when there is less trade and industrial activity than usual and more people are unemployed 經濟衰退；經濟萎縮：*the impact of the current recession on manufacturing* 時下經濟萎縮對製造業的影響 ◇ *The economy is* ***in deep recession***. 經濟正處於嚴重的衰退之中。◇ *policies to pull the country out of recession* 引導國家走出經濟萎縮的政策 ➲ COLLOCATIONS at ECONOMY **2** [U] (*formal*) the movement backwards of sth from a previous position 退後；撤回：*the gradual recession of the floodwater* 洪水的漸漸消退

re·ces·sion·ary /rɪ'seʃnri; *NAmE* -neri/ *adj.* [only before noun] connected with a recession or likely to cause one 經濟衰退（或萎縮）的

R

re·ces·sive /rɪˈsesɪv/ *adj.* (*biology* 生) a **recessive** physical characteristic only appears in a child if it has two GENES for this characteristic, one from each parent. It does not appear if a DOMINANT gene is also present. 隱性的

re·charge /ˌriːˈtʃɑːdʒ; *NAmE* -ˈtʃɑːrdʒ/ *verb* **1** [T, I] **~ (sth)** to fill a battery with electrical power; to be filled with electrical power 給（電池）充電；充電：*He plugged his razor in to recharge it.* 他把剃刀插在插座上，給它充電。◇ *The drill takes about three hours to recharge.* 鑽機充一次電大約要三個小時。 **2** [I] (*informal*) to get back your strength and energy by resting for a time 恢復體力；恢復精力；休整：*We needed the break in order to recharge.* 我們需要休息一下以恢復體力。▸ **re·charge·able** *adj.*：*rechargeable batteries* 可充電電池

IDM **recharge your 'batteries** to get back your strength and energy by resting for a while 養精蓄銳；休整

re·cher·ché /rəˈʃeəʃeɪ; *NAmE* ˌrəʃerˈʃeɪ/ *adj.* (from *French, formal*, usually *disapproving*) unusual and not easy to understand, chosen in order to impress people 故作艱深的；矯揉造作的

re·cid·iv·ist /rɪˈsɪdɪvɪst/ *noun* (*formal*) a person who continues to commit crimes, and seems unable to stop, even after being punished 慣犯；累犯者 ▸ **re·cid·iv·ism** /-ɪzəm/ *noun* [U]

re·cipe /ˈresəpi/ *noun* **1 ~ (for sth)** a set of instructions that tells you how to cook sth and the INGREDIENTS (= items of food) you need for it 烹飪法；食譜：*a recipe for chicken soup* 雞湯的做法 ◇ *vegetarian recipes* 素菜食譜 ◇ *a recipe book* 烹飪書 **2 ~ for sth** a method or an idea that seems likely to have a particular result 方法；秘訣；訣竅 **SYN** **formula**：*His plans are **a recipe for disaster**.* 他的計劃後患無窮。◇ *What's her recipe for success?* 她成功的秘訣是什麼？

re·cipi·ent /rɪˈsɪpiənt/ *noun* (*formal*) a person who receives sth 受方；接受者：*recipients of awards* 領獎者

re·cip·ro·cal /rɪˈsɪprəkl/ *adj.* involving two people or groups who agree to help each other or behave in the same way to each other 互惠的；相應的：*The two colleges have a reciprocal arrangement whereby students from one college can attend classes at the other.* 兩所學院有一項互惠協定，允許學生在院際間選課。▸ **re·cip·ro·cal·ly** /-kli/ *adv.*

R

re'ciprocal verb *noun* (*grammar* 語法) a verb that expresses the idea of an action that is done by two or more people or things to each other, for example 'kiss' in the sentence 'Paul and Claire kissed.' 相互動詞，交互動詞（如 Paul and Claire kissed 中的 kiss）

re·cip·ro·cate /rɪˈsɪprəkeɪt/ *verb* **1** [T, I] to behave or feel towards sb in the same way as they behave or feel towards you 回報；回應：**~ sth (with sth)** *Her passion for him was not reciprocated.* 她對他的熱情沒有得到回應。◇ *He smiled but his smile was not reciprocated.* 他露出微笑，可他的微笑沒有得到回應。◇ **~ (with sth)** *I wasn't sure whether to laugh or to reciprocate with a remark of my own.* 我不知道是該笑一笑還是該說點什麼作為回應。 **2** [I] (*technical* 術語) to move backwards and forwards in a straight line 沿直線往復移動：*a reciprocating action* 往復運動 ▸ **re·cip·ro·ca·tion** /rɪˌsɪprəˈkeɪʃn/ *noun* [U]

reci·procity /ˌresɪˈprɒsəti; *NAmE* -ˈprɑːs-/ *noun* [U] (*formal*) a situation in which two people, countries, etc. provide the same help or advantages to each other 互惠；互助；互換

re·cital /rɪˈsaɪtl/ *noun* **1** a public performance of music or poetry, usually given by one person or a small group 音樂演奏會；詩歌朗誦會：*to give a piano recital* 舉辦鋼琴演奏會 ➲ COLLOCATIONS at MUSIC **2** a spoken description of a series of events, etc. that is often long and boring（口述）逐一列舉；贅述

reci·ta·tion /ˌresɪˈteɪʃn/ *noun* **1** [C, U] an act of saying a piece of poetry or literature that you have learned to an audience 朗誦；朗讀 **2** [C] an act of talking or writing about a series of things 逐一列舉；逐個敘述：*She continued her recitation of the week's events.* 她接着逐一講述這一週發生的事。

reci·ta·tive /ˌresɪtəˈtiːv/ *noun* [C, U] (*music* 音) a passage in an OPERA or ORATORIO that is sung in the rhythm of ordinary speech with many words on the same note（歌劇或清唱劇中的）宣敍調，朗誦調

re·cite /rɪˈsaɪt/ *verb* **1** [T, I] **~ (sth) (to sb)** | **~ what ...** | **+ speech** to say a poem, piece of literature, etc. that you have learned, especially to an audience（尤指對聽眾）背誦，吟誦，朗誦：*Each child had to recite a poem to the class.* 每個孩子都得在班上背誦一首詩。 **2** [T] **~ sth (to sb)** | **~ what ...** | **+ speech** to say a list or series of things（口頭）列舉；逐一講述：*They recited all their grievances to me.* 他們把所受的委屈都告訴了我。◇ *She could recite a list of all the kings and queens.* 她能一一說出所有的國王和王后的名字。

reck·less /ˈrekləs/ *adj.* showing a lack of care about danger and the possible results of your actions 魯莽的；不計後果的；無所顧忌的 **SYN** **rash**：*He showed a **reckless disregard for** his own safety.* 他對個人安危全然無所顧忌。◇ *She was a good rider, but reckless.* 她是個好騎手，但太魯莽。◇ *He had always been reckless with money.* 他花錢總是大手大腳。◇ *to cause death by **reckless driving*** 魯莽駕駛造成死亡 ▸ **reck·less·ly** *adv.*：*He admitted driving recklessly.* 他承認魯莽駕駛。 **reck·less·ness** *noun* [U]

reckon 🔑 /ˈrekən/ *verb*

1 🔑 [T, I] **~ (that) ...** (*informal, especially BrE*) to think sth or have an opinion about sth 想；認為：*I reckon (that) I'm going to get that job.* 我認為我會得到那份工作。◇ *He'll be famous one day. **What do you reckon** (= do you agree)?* 總有一天，他會成為名人的。你覺得呢？◇ *It's worth a lot of money, I reckon.* 我想這值很多錢。◇ *'They'll never find out.' '**You reckon?**' (= I think you may be wrong about that.)* "他們永遠不會發現。" "是嗎？" ➲ SYNONYMS at THINK **2** 🔑 **be reckoned** [T] (not used in the progressive tenses 不用於進行時) to be generally considered to be sth 被普遍認為是；被看作是：**~ to be/have sth** *Children are reckoned to be more sophisticated nowadays.* 人們認為今天的孩子比過去世故。◇ **+ noun/adj.** *It was generally reckoned a success.* 大家都認為那是一次成功。 **3** [T] **~ to do sth** (*BrE, informal*) to expect to do sth 料想；預計；指望：*We reckon to finish by ten.* 我們預計十點鐘以前結束。 **4** [T] to calculate an amount, a number, etc. 估算；估計；計算：**~ sth (at sth)** *The age of the earth is reckoned at about 4 600 million years.* 估計地球的年齡大約為 46 億年。◇ **~ (that) ...** *They reckon (that) their profits are down by at least 20%.* 他們估計利潤至少下降了 20%。◇ **be reckoned to do sth** *The journey was reckoned to take about two hours.* 路上估計要花大約兩個小時。 **IDM** see NAME *n.*

PHR V **'reckon on sth** 🔑 to expect sth to happen or to rely on sth happening 指望；依賴：*They hadn't reckoned on a rebellion.* 他們沒有料到會發生叛亂。◇ **~ doing sth** *We'd reckoned on having good weather.* 我們原指望會有好天氣。 **ˌreckon sth↔'up** (*especially BrE*) to calculate the total amount or number of sth 統計；合計：*He reckoned up the cost of everything in his mind.* 他在腦子裏把所有費用都合計了一下。 **'reckon with sb/sth 1** [usually passive] to consider or treat sb/sth as a serious opponent, problem , etc. 重視；認真處理：*They were already a political force **to be reckoned with**.* 他們已經成為一支不容忽視的政治力量。 **2** (usually used in negative sentences 通常用於否定句) to consider sth as a possible problem that you should be prepared for 把（可能出現的問題）考慮進去 **SYN** **take sth into account**：**~ doing sth** *I didn't reckon with getting caught up in so much traffic.* 我沒有考慮到塞車會這麼嚴重。 **'reckon without sb/sth** (*especially BrE*) to not consider sb/sth as a possible problem that you should be prepared for 沒考慮到；不把…算在內 **SYN** **not take sth into account**：*They had reckoned without the determination of the opposition.* 他們沒料到會遭到堅決反對。

reck·on·ing /ˈrekənɪŋ/ *noun* **1** [U, C] the act of calculating sth, especially in a way that is not very exact 估計；估算；計算：***By my reckoning** you still owe me £5.* 我算計着，你還欠我 5 英鎊。 **2** [C, usually sing., U] a time when sb's actions will be judged to be right or wrong and they may be punished 最後審判日；算總賬：*In the* ***final reckoning*** *truth is rewarded.* 在最後算總賬的時候，真實情況最沾光。◇ *Officials concerned with environmental policy predict that* ***a day of reckoning*** *will come.* 關心環境政策的官員們預言總有一天人們會受到報應。

IDM in/into/out of the 'reckoning (*especially BrE*) (especially in sport 尤用於體育運動) among/not among those who are likely to win or be successful 有（或沒有）獲勝的可能

re·claim /rɪˈkleɪm/ *verb* **1** to get sth back or to ask to have it back after it has been lost, taken away, etc. 取回；拿回；要求歸還：**~ sth** *You'll have to go to the police station to reclaim your wallet.* 你得到警察局去領回你的錢包。◇ **~ sth from sb/sth** *The team reclaimed the title from their rivals.* 這個隊從對手手中奪回了冠軍。⊃ see also BAGGAGE RECLAIM **2 ~ sth** (**from sth**) to make land that is naturally too wet or too dry suitable to be built on, farmed, etc. 開墾，利用，改造（荒地）：*The site for the airport will be reclaimed from the swamp.* 這片濕地將會被開發來建機場。◇ *reclaimed marshland* 被開發利用的沼澤地 **3** [usually passive] **~ sth** if a piece of land **is reclaimed by** desert, forest, etc., it turns back into desert, etc. after being used for farming or building 重新變為沙漠（或森林等）；沙化；荒漠化；拋荒 **4 ~ sth** (**from sth**) to obtain materials from waste products so that they can be used again 回收（廢品中有用的東西）⊃ see also RECYCLE **5 ~ sb** (**from sth**) to rescue sb from a bad or criminal way of life 挽救；感化；使糾正；使悔過自新 ▸ **rec·lam·ation** /ˌrekləˈmeɪʃn/ *noun* [U]：*land reclamation* 土地開墾

re·clas·sify /ˌriːˈklæsɪfaɪ/ *verb* (**re·clas·si·fies, re·clas·si·fy·ing, re·clas·si·fied, re·clas·si·fied**) **~ sth** to put sth in a different class or category 將…重新分類；將…重新歸類：*The drug is to be reclassified after trials showed it to be more harmful than previously thought.* 試驗顯示這種藥比先前想像的危害更大，要重新歸類。

re·cline /rɪˈklaɪn/ *verb* **1** [I] **~** (**against/in/on sth**) (*formal*) to sit or lie in a relaxed way, with your body leaning backwards 斜倚；斜躺；向後倚靠：*She was reclining on a sofa.* 她倚靠在沙發上。◇ *a reclining figure* (= for example in a painting) 半躺着的人像 **2** [I, T] **~** (**sth**) when a seat **reclines** or when you **recline** a seat, the back of it moves into a comfortable sloping position（使座椅靠背）向後傾：*a reclining chair* 躺椅

re·cliner /rɪˈklaɪnə(r)/ (also **re'cliner chair**) *noun* (*especially NAmE*) a soft comfortable chair with a back that can be pushed back at an angle so that you can lean back in it（可調式）躺椅 ⊃ VISUAL VOCAB page V21

re·cluse /rɪˈkluːs; *NAmE* ˈrekluːs/ *noun* a person who lives alone and likes to avoid other people 隱居者；喜歡獨處的人：*to lead the life of a recluse* 過隱居的生活 ▸ **re·clu·sive** /rɪˈkluːsɪv/ *adj.*：*a reclusive millionaire* 深居簡出的富翁

rec·og·ni·tion 0-w /ˌrekəgˈnɪʃn/ *noun*

1 0-w [U] the act of remembering who sb is when you see them, or of identifying what sth is 認出；認識；識別：*He glanced briefly towards her but there was no sign of recognition.* 他瞥了她一眼，但似乎沒認出她來。◇ *the automatic recognition of handwriting and printed text by computer* 計算機對手寫和印刷文本的自動識別 **2** 0-w [sing., U] **~** (**that** ...) the act of accepting that sth exists, is true or is official 承認；認可：*a growing recognition that older people have potential too* 越來越多的人認識到老年人也是有潛力的 ◇ *There is a general recognition of the urgent need for reform.* 人們普遍認為迫切需要改革。◇ *to seek* ***international/official/formal recognition*** *as a sovereign state* 尋求國際上的／官方／正式的承認，承認它是一個主權國家 **3** 0-w [U] **~** (**for sth**) public praise and reward for sb's work or actions 讚譽；賞識；獎賞：*She gained only minimal recognition for her work.* 她的工作僅僅得到極少的讚譽。◇ *He received the award* ***in recognition of*** *his success over the past year.* 他受到了獎勵，這是對他過去一年的成績的肯定。

IDM to change, alter, etc. beyond/out of (**all**) **recog'nition** to change so much that you can hardly recognize it 變得面目全非；滄海桑田：*The town has changed beyond recognition since I was last here.* 自從我上次離開這裏以來，這座小鎮已經變得讓人認不出來了。

rec·og·niz·able (*BrE* also **-is·able**) /ˈrekəgnaɪzəbl; ˌrekəgˈnaɪzəbl/ *adj.* **~** (**as sth/sb**) easy to know or identify 容易認出的；易於識別的：*The building was easily recognizable as a prison.* 很容易看出這座建築是所監獄。◇ *After so many years she was still instantly recognizable.* 過了這麼多年，還是一眼就能認出她。**OPP unrecognizable** ▸ **rec·og·niz·ably, -is·ably** /-əbli/ *adv.*

rec·og·niz·ance (*BrE* also **-sance**) /rɪˈkɒgnɪzəns; *NAmE* -ˈkɑːg-/ *noun* [U] (*law* 律) a promise by sb who is accused of a crime to appear in court on a particular date; a sum of money paid as a guarantee of this promise 保證書；具結；保釋金；保證金

rec·og·nize (*BrE* also **-ise**) 0-w /ˈrekəgnaɪz/ *verb* (not used in the progressive tenses 不用於進行時)

1 0-w to know who sb is or what sth is when you see or hear them, because you have seen or heard them or it before 認識；認出；辨別出：**~ sb/sth** *I recognized him as soon as he came in the room.* 他一進屋我就認出了他。◇ *Do you recognize this tune?* 你能聽出這是哪支曲子嗎？◇ **~ sb/sth by/from sth** *I recognized her by her red hair.* 我從她的紅頭髮認出了她。⊃ SYNONYMS at IDENTIFY **2** 0-w to admit or to be aware that sth exists or is true 承認；意識到 **SYN acknowledge**：**~ sth** *They recognized the need to take the problem seriously.* 他們承認需要嚴肅對待這個問題。◇ **~ sth as sth** *Drugs were not recognized as a problem then.* 那時候還沒有把毒品看成嚴重問題。◇ **~ how, what, etc.** ... *Nobody recognized how urgent the situation was.* 當時沒有人意識到形勢有多麼緊急。◇ **~ that** ... *We recognized that the task was not straightforward.* 我們意識到這個任務並非輕而易舉。◇ **it is recognized that** ... *It was recognized that this solution could only be temporary.* 人們意識到這只是個臨時的解決方案。◇ **~ sb/sth to be/have sth** *Drugs were not recognized to be a problem then.* 那時候毒品問題還沒有受到重視。⊃ SYNONYMS at ADMIT **3** 0-w to accept and approve of sb/sth officially（正式）認可，接受，贊成：**~ sb/sth** (**as sth**) *recognized qualifications* 獲得承認的資格 ◇ *The UK has refused to recognize the new regime.* 英國已拒絕承認這個新的政權。◇ **be recognized to be/have sth** *He is recognized to be their natural leader.* 人們都承認他是他們的當然領袖。**4** 0-w **be recognized** (**as sth**) to be thought of as very good or important by people in general 讚賞；賞識；看重；公認：*The book is now recognized as a classic.* 這本書現在是一部公認的經典著作。◇ *She's a recognized authority on the subject.* 她在這個學科上被奉為權威。**5 ~ sb/sth** to give sb official thanks for sth that they have done or achieved 正式向…致謝；正式感謝：*His services to the state were recognized with the award of a knighthood.* 他被封為爵士，以表彰他對國家的貢獻。

re·coil *verb, noun*

■ ***verb*** /rɪˈkɔɪl/ **1** [I] to move your body quickly away from sb/sth because you find them or it frightening or unpleasant 退縮；畏縮 **SYN flinch**：**~** (**from sb/sth**) *She recoiled from his touch.* 她躲開他的觸摸。◇ **~** (**at sth**) *He* ***recoiled in horror*** *at the sight of the corpse.* 他一見到屍體就嚇得往後縮了。**2** [I] **~** (**from sth/from doing sth**) | **~** (**at sth**) to react to an idea or a situation with strong dislike or fear 對…作出厭惡（或恐懼）的反應 **SYN shrink**：*She recoiled from the idea of betraying her own brother.* 背叛自己親兄弟的這個想法使她感到恐懼。**3** [I] (of a gun 槍炮) to move suddenly backwards when you fire it 反衝；產生後坐力

■ ***noun*** /ˈriːkɔɪl/ [U, sing.] a sudden movement backwards, especially of a gun when it is fired 反衝；（尤指槍炮的）後坐力

rec·ol·lect /ˌrekəˈlekt/ *verb* [T, I] (not used in the progressive tenses 不用於進行時) (rather *formal*) to remember sth, especially by making an effort to remember it 記起；回憶起；記得 **SYN recall**：**~** (**sth**) *She could no longer recollect the details of the letter.* 她想不起那封信的細節了。◇ *As far as I can recollect, she*

R

wasn't there on that occasion. 據我回憶，當時她不在場。◇ **~ what, how, etc.** … *I don't recollect what he said.* 我不記得他說過什麼。◇ **~ that** … *I recollect that we were all gathered in the kitchen.* 我記得當時我們都被召集到廚房裏。◇ **~ (sb/sth) doing sth** *I recollect him/his saying that it was dangerous.* 我記得他說那很危險。◇ **+ speech** *'It was just before the war,' she recollected.* "那是在戰爭即將發生之前。" 她回憶道。

rec·ol·lec·tion /ˌrekəˈlekʃn/ *noun* (*formal*) **1** [U] the ability to remember sth; the act of remembering sth 記憶力；回憶；記憶 **SYN** **memory**：**~ (of doing sth)** *I **have no recollection of** meeting her before.* 我不記得以前見過她。◇ **~ (of sth)** *My recollection of events differs from his.* 我記憶中的情況和他的不一樣。◇ ***To the best of my recollection*** (= if I remember correctly) *I was not present at that meeting.* 如果我沒記錯的話，我沒有出席那次會議。 **2** [C] a thing that you remember from the past 往事；回憶的事 **SYN** **memory**：*to have a **clear/vivid/dim/vague recollection** of sth* 對某事的記憶清晰／歷歷在目／模糊不清／依稀如煙

re·com·mence **AW** /ˌriːkəˈmens/ *verb* [I, T] (*formal*) to begin again; to start doing sth again 重新開始；再次開始：*Work on the bridge will recommence next month.* 下個月將重新開始這座橋的建造工作。◇ **~ (doing) sth** *The two countries agreed to recommence talks the following week.* 兩國同意於隨後的一週重新開始會談。

rec·om·mend 🗝 /ˌrekəˈmend/ *verb*
1 🗝 to tell sb that sth is good or useful, or that sb would be suitable for a particular job, etc. 推薦；舉薦；介紹：**~ sb/sth** *Can you recommend a good hotel?* 你能推薦一家好的旅館嗎？◇ **~ sb/sth (to sb) (for/as sth)** *I recommend the book to all my students.* 我向我所有的學生都推薦這本書。◇ *She was recommended for the post by a colleague.* 她獲得同事推薦到這個崗位。◇ *The hotel's new restaurant comes **highly recommended*** (= a lot of people have praised it). 這家酒店的新餐廳得到了人們的極力推薦。 **2** 🗝 to advise a particular course of action; to advise sb to do sth 勸告；建議：**~ sth** *The report recommended a 10% pay increase.* 報告提議工資增加 10%。◇ *It is dangerous to exceed the recommended dose.* 超過建議使用的劑量會有危險。◇ *a recommended price of $50* 建議售價 50 元 ◇ **~ (that)** … *I recommend (that) he see a lawyer.* 我建議他去找個律師。◇ (*BrE* also) *I recommend (that) he should see a lawyer.* 我建議他去找個律師。◇ **it is recommended that** … *It is strongly recommended that the machines should be checked every year.* 強烈建議每年都要檢查機器。◇ **~ sb to do sth** *We'd recommend you to book your flight early.* 我們建議你早點兒預訂航班。◇ **~ (sb) doing sth** *He recommended reading the book before seeing the movie.* 他建議先看這本書，再去看這部電影。◇ **~ how, what, etc.** … *Can you recommend how much we should charge?* 我們該收多少錢，你能給個建議嗎？ **3 ~ sb/sth (to sb)** to make sb/sth seem attractive or good 使顯得吸引人；使受歡迎 **SYN** **commend**：*This system has **much to recommend it**.* 這套系統有很多可取之處。

rec·om·men·da·tion /ˌrekəmenˈdeɪʃn/ *noun* **1** [C] an official suggestion about the best thing to do 正式建議；提議：*to accept/reject a recommendation* 接受／拒絕一項建議◇ **~ (to sb) (for/on/about sth)** *The committee **made recommendations** to the board on teachers' pay and conditions.* 委員會就教師的工資和工作條件問題向董事會提出建議。◇ *I had the operation **on the recommendation of** my doctor.* 我根據醫生的建議做了手術。 **2** [U, C] the act of telling sb that sth is good or useful or that sb would be suitable for a particular job, etc. 推薦；介紹：*We chose the hotel **on their recommendation*** (= because they recommended it). 我們根據他們的推薦選了這家酒店。◇ *It's best to find a builder through **personal recommendation**.* 最好通過私人介紹尋找施工人員。◇ *Here's a list of my top CD recommendations.* 這是我認為最值得推薦的 CD 的清單。 **3** [C] (*especially NAmE*) a formal letter or statement that sb would be suitable for a particular job, etc. 推薦信；求職介紹信 **SYN** **testimonial**

Synonyms 同義詞辨析

recommend

advise • advocate • urge

These words all mean to tell sb what you think they should do in a particular situation. 以上各詞均含勸告、建議之意。

recommend to tell sb what you think they should do in a particular situation; to say what you think the price or level of sth should be 指勸告、建議（應對方法、售價、水平等）：*We'd recommend you to book your flight early.* 我們建議你早點兒預訂航班。◇ *a recommended price of $50* 建議售價 50 元

advise to tell sb what you think they should do in a particular situation 指勸告、忠告、建議：*I'd advise you not to tell him.* 我勸你別告訴他。

RECOMMEND OR ADVISE? 用 recommend 還是 advise？

Advise is a stronger word than **recommend** and is often used when the person giving the advice is in a position of authority. * advise 語氣較 recommend 強烈，通常指權威人士的忠告：*Police are advising fans without tickets to stay away.* 警察正在告誡沒有票的球迷離去。◇ ~~*Police are recommending fans without tickets to stay away.*~~ *I advise you* … can suggest that you know better than the person you are advising: this may cause offence if they are your equal or senior to you. *I recommend* … mainly suggests that you are trying to be helpful and is less likely to cause offence. **Recommend** is often used with more positive advice to tell sb about possible benefits and **advise** with more negative advice to warn sb about possible dangers. * I advise you 暗含提出忠告者比對方更瞭解情況，如果對方處於同等或更高的地位就可能引起反感。I recommend 主要含試圖幫助之意，不大可能引起反感。recommend 多指正面的建議，告知某人可能得到的益處；advise 多指反面告誡，警告某人可能產生的危險：~~*He advised reading the book before seeing the movie.*~~ ◇ ~~*I would recommend against going out on your own.*~~

advocate (*formal*) to support or recommend sth publicly 指擁護、公開支持、提倡：*The group does not advocate the use of violence.* 該團體不支持使用暴力。

urge (*formal*) to recommend sth strongly 指大力推薦、竭力主張：*The situation is dangerous and the UN is urging caution.* 局勢岌岌可危，聯合國力主謹慎行事。

PATTERNS

- to recommend/advise/advocate/urge **that** …
- **It is** recommended/advised/advocated/urged **that** …
- to recommend/advise/urge **sb to do sth**
- to recommend/advise/advocate **doing sth**
- to **strongly** recommend/advise/advocate sb/sth

rec·om·pense /ˈrekəmpens/ *noun, verb*
■ *noun* [U] **~ (for sth/sb)** (*formal*) something, usually money, that you are given because you have suffered in some way, or as a payment for sth 賠償；補償；報酬：*There must be adequate recompense for workers who lose their jobs.* 必須給失業的工人足夠的補償。◇ *I received $1 000 **in recompense** for loss of earnings.* 我得到了 1 000 元的收入損失賠償。
■ *verb* **~ sb (for sth)** (*formal*) to do sth for sb or give them a payment for sth that they have suffered 給…以補償；賠償 **SYN** **compensate**：*There was no attempt to recompense the miners for the loss of their jobs.* 沒有人有意向失業礦工給予補償。

recon /ˈriːkɒn; *NAmE* riˈkɑːn/ *noun* [C, U] (*US, informal*) = RECONNAISSANCE

rec·on·cile /ˈrekənsaɪl/ *verb* (*formal*) **1 ~ sth (with sth)** to find an acceptable way of dealing with two or more ideas, needs, etc. that seem to be opposed to each other 使和諧一致；調和；使配合：*an attempt to reconcile* the need for industrial development with concern for the environment 協調工業發展的需要和環境保護之間關係的努力 ◇ *It was hard to reconcile his career ambitions with the needs of his children.* 他很難兼顧事業上的抱負和孩子們的需要。 **2** [usually passive] to make people become friends again after an argument or a disagreement 使和解；使和好如初： **~ sb** *The pair were reconciled after Jackson made a public apology.* 傑克遜公開道歉之後，這兩個人又言歸於好了。 ◇ **~ sb with sb** *He has recently been reconciled with his wife.* 他最近已經和妻子和好了。 **3 ~ sb/yourself (to sth)** to make sb/yourself accept an unpleasant situation because it is not possible to change it 將就；妥協 **SYN resign yourself to**： *He could not reconcile himself to the prospect of losing her.* 他一想到有可能失去她，就覺得難以忍受。 ▸ **rec·on·cil·able** /ˌrekənˈsaɪləbl/ *adj.*

rec·on·cili·ation /ˌrekənsɪliˈeɪʃn/ *noun* **1** [sing., U] **~ (between A and B) | ~ (with sb)** an end to a disagreement and the start of a good relationship again 調解；和解： *Their change of policy brought about a reconciliation with Britain.* 他們的政策改變促成了與英國的和解。 **2** [U] **~ (between A and B) | ~ (with sth)** the process of making it possible for two different ideas, facts, etc. to exist together without being opposed to each other 協調；和諧一致：*the reconciliation between environment and development* 環境保護與發展之間的協調

rec·on·dite /ˈrekəndaɪt/ *adj.* (*formal*) not known about or understood by many people 深奧的；晦澀的 **SYN obscure**

re·con·di·tion /ˌriːkənˈdɪʃn/ *verb* [often passive] **~ sth** to repair a machine so that it is in good condition and works well 修復（機器）；使（機器）恢復正常運轉 **SYN overhaul**

re·con·fig·ure /ˌriːkənˈfɪɡə(r); *NAmE* -ˈfɪɡjər/ *verb* **~ sth** to make changes to the way that sth is arranged to work, especially computer equipment or a program 重新配置（計算機設備等）；重新設定（程序等）： *You may need to reconfigure the firewall if you add a new machine to your network.* 如果在網絡中增加新計算機，可能就得重新設定防火牆。

re·con·firm /ˌriːkənˈfɜːm; *NAmE* -ˈfɜːrm/ *verb* **~ sth** to check again that sth is definitely correct or as previously arranged 再確認；再確定： *You have to reconfirm your flight 24 hours before travelling.* 你必須在乘飛機之前 24 小時再次確認你的航班。

re·con·nais·sance /rɪˈkɒnɪsns; *NAmE* -ˈkɑːn-/ (also *BrE informal* **recce**) (also *US informal* **recon**) *noun* [C, U] the activity of getting information about an area for military purposes, using soldiers, planes, etc. 偵察： *to make an aerial reconnaissance of the island* 對這座島進行空中偵察 ◇ *Time spent on reconnaissance is seldom wasted.* 花在偵察上的時間很少會白費。 ◇ *a reconnaissance aircraft/mission/satellite* 偵察飛機／任務／衞星 ➲ COLLOCATIONS at WAR

re·con·nect /ˌriːkəˈnekt/ *verb* [T, I] to connect sth again; to connect to sth again 再連接；再接合： **~ sth (to sth)** *I replaced the taps and reconnected the water supply.* 我更換了水龍頭，再次接通了自來水。 ◇ **~ (to sth)** *Once you have removed the virus it is safe to reconnect to the Internet.* 病毒一消除，就可以安全地重新連接互聯網。

rec·on·noitre (*especially US* **-ter**) /ˌrekəˈnɔɪtə(r); *NAmE* also ˌriːkə-/ *verb* [I, T] **~ (sth)** to get information about an area, especially for military purposes, by using soldiers, planes, etc. 偵察；勘察；觀測

re·con·quer /ˌriːˈkɒŋkə(r); *NAmE* -ˈkɑːŋ-/ *verb* **~ sth** to take control again of a country or city by force, after having lost it 重新佔領（國家或城市）；再征服；奪回

re·con·sider /ˌriːkənˈsɪdə(r)/ *verb* [T, I] **~ (sth) | ~ what, how, etc. …** to think about sth again, especially because you might want to change a previous decision or opinion 重新考慮；重新審議： *to **reconsider** your **decision/position*** 重新考慮你的決定／立場 ◇ *Recent information may persuade the board to reconsider.* 最近得到的信息也許會使董事會重新考慮。 ▸ **re·con·sid·er·ation** /ˌriːkənˌsɪdəˈreɪʃn/ *noun* [U, sing.]

re·con·sti·tute /ˌriːˈkɒnstɪtjuːt; *NAmE* -ˈkɑːnstətuːt/ *verb* **1 ~ sth/itself (as sth)** (*formal*) to form an organization or a group again in a different way 重組；重新設立： *The group reconstituted itself as a political party.* 這個團體重新組建為一個政黨。 **2** [usually passive] **~ sth** to bring dried food, etc. back to its original form by adding water 使（脫水食物等）恢復原狀；使還原 ▸ **re·con·sti·tu·tion** /ˌriːˌkɒnstɪˈtjuːʃn; *NAmE* -ˌkɑːnstəˈtuːʃn/ *noun* [U]

re·con·struct **AW** /ˌriːkənˈstrʌkt/ *verb* **1 ~ sth (from sth)** to build or make sth again that has been damaged or that no longer exists 修復；重建；重造： *They have tried to reconstruct the settlement as it would have been in Iron Age times.* 他們已試着按鐵器時代的樣子重建這個小村落。 **2 ~ sth** to be able to describe or show exactly how a past event happened, using the information you have gathered 重現描述；使重現： *Investigators are trying to reconstruct the circumstances of the crash.* 調查人員正試圖重現撞車時的情形。

re·con·struc·tion **AW** /ˌriːkənˈstrʌkʃn/ *noun* **1** [U] the process of changing or improving the condition of sth or the way it works; the process of putting sth back into the state it was in before 重建；改造；復原： *the post-war reconstruction of Germany* 德國的戰後重建 ◇ *a reconstruction period* 重建時期 **2** [U] the activity of building again sth that has been damaged or destroyed 修復；修理： *the reconstruction of the sea walls* 海堤的修復 **3** [C] a copy of sth that no longer exists 重現： *The doorway is a 19th century reconstruction of Norman work.* 門廊是 19 世紀時模仿諾曼式建築修建的。 **4** [C] a short film showing events that are known to have happened, made in order to try and get more information or better understanding, especially about a crime 再現（犯罪過程等的）影片： *Last night police staged a reconstruction of the incident.* 昨天晚上，警方放映了再現事故經過的影片。 **5 Reconstruction** [U] (in the US) the period after the Civil War when the southern states returned to the US and laws were passed that gave rights to African Americans 重建時期（美國南北戰爭後南方各州重新加入聯邦）

re·con·struct·ive /ˌriːkənˈstrʌktɪv/ *adj.* [only before noun] (of medical treatment 醫療) that involves RECONSTRUCTING part of a person's body because it has been badly damaged or because the person wants to change its shape 修復的；整形的；復原的： *reconstructive surgery* 整形手術

re·con·vene /ˌriːkənˈviːn/ *verb* [I, T] **~ (sth)** if a meeting, parliament, etc. **reconvenes** or if sb **reconvenes** it, it meets again after a break 重新集合；重新召集

re·cord 🔑 *noun, verb*

■ ***noun*** /ˈrekɔːd; *NAmE* ˈrekərd/

▸ WRITTEN ACCOUNT 書面記錄 **1** 🔑 [C] **~ (of sth)** a written account of sth that is kept so that it can be looked at and used in the future 記錄；記載： *You should **keep a record** of your expenses.* 你應該記下你的各項開支。 ◇ ***medical/dental records*** 病歷；牙科病歷 ◇ *Last summer was the wettest **on record**.* 去年夏天是有記錄以來降雨量最多的。 ◇ *It was the worst flood **since records began**.* 這是有記錄以來最嚴重的水災。

▸ MUSIC 音樂 **2** 🔑 [C] a thin round piece of plastic on which music, etc. is recorded 唱片： *to **play a record*** 播放唱片 ◇ *a **record collection*** 收藏的唱片 ➲ see also VINYL (2) **3** [C] a piece or collection of music released as a record, or on CD, the Internet, etc. 唱片；專輯： *a **record company*** (= one which produces and sells records) 唱片公司 ◇ *During her career Billie Holiday made over 100 records.* 比利 • 哈樂黛在她的事業生涯中錄製了 100 多張唱片。 ◇ *His new record is available on CD or as a download.* 他的新專輯可以通過購買 CD 或從網上下載獲得。 ➲ COLLOCATIONS at MUSIC ➲ see also ALBUM (2)

▸ HIGHEST/BEST 最高；最好 **4** 🔑 [C] the best result or the highest or lowest level that has ever been reached, especially in sport （尤指體育運動中最高或最低的）紀錄： *She **holds the world record** for the 100 metres.* 她保持着 100 米的世界紀錄。 ◇ *to **break the record*** (= to achieve a better result than there has ever been before) 破紀錄 ◇ *to **set a new record*** 刷新紀錄 ◇ *There was a **record number** of candidates for the post.* 這個職

位的候選人數量空前。◇ *I got to work in **record time**.* 我以歷來最快的速度趕到單位上班。◇ *record profits* 創紀錄的利潤◇ *Unemployment has reached a **record high*** (= the highest level ever). 失業數字已經達到了最高紀錄。

▸ OF SB/STH'S PAST 過去 **5** [sing.] **~ (on sth)** the facts that are known about sb/sth's past behaviour, character, achievements, etc. （有關過去的）事實；記錄；經歷；功過：*The report criticizes the government's record on housing.* 這份報告批評了政府在住房問題上的所作所為。◇ *The airline has a good **safety record**.* 這家航空公司的安全紀錄一向很好。◇ *He has an impressive record of achievement.* 他所取得的一系列成就令人讚歎。➲ see also TRACK RECORD

▸ OF CRIMES 罪行 **6** (also ˌ**criminal** ˈ**record**) [C] the fact of having committed crimes in the past 前科；犯罪記錄：*Does he have a record?* 他有沒有前科？

IDM **(just) for the** ˈ**record** **1** used to show that you want what you are saying to be officially written down and remembered （希望載入正式記錄）（僅）供記錄 **2** used to emphasize a point that you are making, so that the person you are speaking to takes notice （強調要點以引起注意）：*And, for the record, he would be the last person I'd ask.* 需要強調的是，他是我最不願意去找的人。ˌ**off the** ˈ**record** if you tell sb sth **off the record**, it is not yet official and you do not want them to repeat it publicly 非正式的；私下的；不得發表的 **put/place sth on (the)** ˈ**record | be/go on (the)** ˈ**record (as saying …)** to say sth publicly or officially so that it may be written down and repeated 公開發表（意見等）：*He didn't want to go on the record as either praising or criticizing the proposal.* 他不想公開讚揚或批評這項提議。**put/set the** ˈ**record straight** to give people the correct information about sth in order to make it clear that what they previously believed was in fact wrong 陳述真相；糾正誤解 ➲ more at MATTER *n.*

■ *verb* /rɪˈkɔːd; *NAmE* rɪˈkɔːrd/

▸ KEEP ACCOUNT 做記錄 **1** [T] to keep a permanent account of facts or events by writing them down, filming them, storing them in a computer, etc. 記錄；記載：**~ sth** *Her childhood is recorded in the diaries of those years.* 她的童年生活都記在當年的日記裏。◇ *You should record all your expenses during your trip.* 你應該記下你一路上的所有開支。◇ **~ how, what, etc. …** *His job is to record how politicians vote on major issues.* 他的工作就是要記錄政治人物是如何對重大問題投票的。◇ **~ that …** *She recorded in her diary that they crossed the Equator on 15 June.* 她在日記中記載他們是在 6 月 15 日橫越赤道的。◇ **it is recorded that …** *It is recorded that, by the year 630, four hundred monks were attached to the monastery.* 據記載，到了 630 年有 400 個僧侶隸屬該寺院。

▸ MAKE COPY 複製 **2** [T, I] to make a copy of music, a film/movie, etc. by storing it on tape or a disc so that you can listen to or watch it again 錄製；錄（音）；錄（像）：**~ (sth)** *Did you remember to record that programme for me?* 你記得為我錄下那個節目了嗎？◇ *a recorded concert* 錄製的音樂會◇ *Tell me when the tape starts recording.* 磁帶開始錄製時告訴我一聲。◇ **~ sb/sth doing sth** *He recorded the class rehearsing before the performance.* 他錄下了演出前班級的排練。

▸ MUSIC 音樂 **3** [T, I] **~ (sth)** to perform music so that it can be copied onto and kept on tape 演奏音樂供錄製；灌（唱片）：*The band is back in the US recording their new album.* 樂隊回美國錄製新唱片去了。

▸ MAKE OFFICIAL STATEMENT 正式聲明 **4** [T] **~ sth | ~ that …** to make an official or legal statement about sth 發表正式（或法律方面的）聲明；申明：*The coroner recorded a verdict of accidental death.* 驗屍官判定這是一次意外死亡。

▸ OF MEASURING INSTRUMENT 測量儀器 **5** [T] **~ sth | ~ what, how, etc. …** to show a particular measurement or amount 標明；顯示：*The thermometer recorded a temperature of 40°C.* 溫度計顯示氣溫達到了 40 攝氏度。

ˈ**record-breaker** *noun* a person or thing that achieves a better result or higher level than has ever been achieved before 打破紀錄者 ▸ ˈ**record-breaking** *adj.* [only before noun]: *a record-breaking jump* 打破紀錄的一跳

reˌcorded deˈlivery (*BrE*) (*NAmE* ˌ**certified** ˈ**mail**) *noun* [U] a method of sending a letter or package in which the person sending it gets an official note to say it has been posted and the person receiving it must sign a form when it is delivered 掛號郵寄：*I'd like to send this (by) recorded delivery.* 這個郵件要掛號。➲ compare REGISTERED MAIL

re·cord·er /rɪˈkɔːdə(r); *NAmE* -ˈkɔːrd-/ *noun* **1** (in compounds 構成複合詞) a machine for recording sound or pictures or both 錄音機；錄像機；錄影機：*a tape/cassette/video/DVD recorder* 磁帶 / 盒式錄音機；錄像機；DVD 錄像機 ➲ see also FLIGHT RECORDER **2** a musical instrument in the shape of a pipe that you blow into, with holes that you cover with your fingers 豎笛；直笛 ➲ VISUAL VOCAB page V34 **3** a judge in a court in some parts of Britain and the US （英國和美國某些地區的）法院法官，法官 **4** a person who keeps a record of events or facts 記錄員；書記員

ˈ**record holder** *noun* a person who has achieved the best result that has ever been achieved in a sport 紀錄保持者

re·cord·ing /rɪˈkɔːdɪŋ; *NAmE* -ˈkɔːrd-/ *noun* **1** [C] sound or pictures that have been recorded on CD, DVD, video, etc. 錄製的音像；錄音；視頻；錄像：*a video recording of the wedding* 婚禮的錄像 **2** [U] the process of making a record, film/movie, radio or television show, etc. 錄製：*during the recording of the show* 在錄製這場表演期間◇ ***recording equipment*** 錄製設備◇ ***a recording studio*** 錄音室◇ *the **recording industry*** (= the industry that records and sells music) 唱片業 **3** [U] the process or act of writing down and storing information for official purposes （正式的）記錄，記載：*the recording of financial transactions* 關於金融交易的記載

re·cord·ist /rɪˈkɔːdɪst; *NAmE* -ˈkɔːrd-/ *noun* a person whose job is making sound recordings, especially in a recording studio （尤指錄音棚的）錄音員，錄音師

ˈ**record player** *noun* a piece of equipment for playing records in order to listen to the music, etc. on them 唱機

re·count¹ /rɪˈkaʊnt/ *verb* (*formal*) to tell sb about sth, especially sth that you have experienced 講述，敍述（親身經歷）：**~ sth (to sb)** *She was asked to recount the details of the conversation to the court.* 她被要求向法庭陳述談話細節。◇ **~ what, how, etc. …** *They recounted what had happened during those years.* 他們敍述了那些年裏發生的事。◇ **+ speech** *'It was before the war,' he recounted.* "那是在戰前。"他敍述道。

re·count² /ˌriːˈkaʊnt/ *verb* **~ sth** to count sth again, especially votes 重數；重新清點（選票）▸ **re·count** /ˈriːkaʊnt/ *noun*: *The defeated candidate demanded a recount.* 落選的候選人要求重新計票。

re·coup /rɪˈkuːp/ *verb* **~ sth** (*formal*) to get back an amount of money that you have spent or lost 收回（成本）；彌補（虧損）**SYN** **recover**: *We hope to recoup our initial investment in the first year.* 我們希望我們的前期投資在第一年就能賺回來。

re·course /rɪˈkɔːs; *NAmE* ˈriːkɔːrs/ *noun* [U] (*formal*) the fact of having to, or being able to, use sth that can provide help in a difficult situation 依靠；依賴；求助：*Your only recourse is legal action.* 你的唯一依靠就是訴諸法律。◇ *She made a complete recovery **without recourse to** surgery.* 她未做手術就完全恢復了健康。◇ *The government, when necessary, **has recourse to** the armed forces.* 政府在必要時可以動員軍隊。

re·cover **AW** /rɪˈkʌvə(r)/ *verb*

▸ FROM ILLNESS 從疾病中 **1** [I] **~ (from sth)** to get well again after being ill/sick, hurt, etc. 恢復健康；康復；痊癒：*He's still recovering from his operation.* 手術後，他仍在康復之中。

▸ FROM STH UNPLEASANT 從不愉快的事中 **2** [I] **~ (from sth)** to return to a normal state after an unpleasant or unusual experience or a period of difficulty 復原；恢復常態：*It can take many years to recover from the death of a loved one.* 從心愛的人去世的痛苦中恢復過來可能要

R

花很多年。◇ *The economy is at last beginning to recover.* 經濟終於開始復蘇了。

▸ **MONEY 錢 3** [T] **~ sth (from sb/sth)** to get back the same amount of money that you have spent or that is owed to you 全額收回；追回 **SYN recoup**：*He is unlikely to ever recover his legal costs.* 他不大可能收回他的訴訟費用了。

▸ **STH LOST/STOLEN 丟失／失竊的東西 4** [T] to get back or find sth that was lost, stolen or missing 找回；尋回；找到：**~ sth** *The police eventually recovered the stolen paintings.* 警方最終找回了失竊的油畫。◇ **~ sth from sb/sth** *Six bodies were recovered from the wreckage.* 從殘骸中找到了六具屍體。

▸ **POSITION/STATUS 位置；地位 5** [T] **~ sth** to win back a position, level, status, etc. that has been lost 贏回；重新獲得 **SYN regain**：*The team recovered its lead in the second half.* 下半場這支隊再次領先。

▸ **SENSES/EMOTIONS 感覺；情感 6** [T] to get back the use of your senses, control of your emotions, etc. 恢復；重新控制 **SYN regain**：**~ sth** *It took her a few minutes to* ***recover consciousness.*** 過了幾分鐘她才恢復知覺。◇ *to recover your sight* 恢復視力 ◇ **~ yourself** *She seemed upset but quickly recovered herself.* 她顯得心煩意亂，但很快靜下心來。

▸ **re·covered** **AW** *adj.* [not before noun]：*She is now fully recovered from her injuries.* 她現在已經完全從傷痛中恢復過來了。

re-cover /ˌriː ˈkʌvə(r)/ *verb* **~ sth** to put a new cover on sth 重新遮蓋

re·cov·er·able **AW** /rɪˈkʌvərəbl/ *adj.* **1** that you can get back after it has been spent or lost 可收回的；可重新獲得的：*Travel expenses will be recoverable from the company.* 差旅費用可到公司報銷。 **2** that can be obtained from the ground 可開採的：*recoverable oil reserves* 可開採的石油資源

re·cov·ery **AW** /rɪˈkʌvəri/ *noun* (*pl.* **-ies**) **1** [U, C, usually sing.] **~ (from sth)** the process of becoming well again after an illness or injury 恢復；痊癒：*My father has* ***made a full recovery*** *from the operation.* 我父親手術後已完全康復了。◇ *to make* ***a remarkable/quick/speedy/slow, etc. recovery*** 恢復顯著、很快、迅速、緩慢等 ◇ *She is* ***on the road to*** (= making progress towards) ***recovery.*** 她正在康復之中。 **2** [U, C, usually sing.] **~ (in sth)** the process of improving or becoming stronger again 改善；回升；復蘇：*The government is forecasting an* ***economic recovery.*** 政府預測經濟會復蘇。◇ *a recovery in consumer spending* 消費支出的回升 ◇ *The economy is showing signs of recovery.* 經濟呈現出復蘇的跡象。 **3** [U] **~ (of sth)** the action or process of getting sth back that has been lost or stolen 取回；收回；復得：*There is a reward for information leading to the recovery of the missing diamonds.* 凡能為找回丟失的鑽石提供線索者可獲獎賞。 **4** [U] (also **reˈcovery room** [C]) the room in a hospital where patients are kept immediately after an operation（供剛做完手術的病人使用的）監護室

reˈcovery position *noun* [sing.] a position lying on the side, with the arms and legs carefully placed, that helps a person who is not conscious to breathe 復原臥位，復原體位（側臥、四肢穩當放置，以利於昏迷者呼吸）

rec·re·ant /ˈrekriənt/ *adj.* (*literary*) not brave 怯懦的 **SYN cowardly**

re·create **AW** /ˌriːkriˈeɪt/ *verb* **~ sth** to make sth that existed in the past exist or seem to exist again 再現；再創造：*The movie recreates the glamour of 1940s Hollywood.* 這部電影再現了 20 世紀 40 年代好萊塢的輝煌。 ▸ **re·cre·ation** /-ˈeɪʃn/ *noun* [C, U]：*The writer attempts a recreation of the sights and sounds of his childhood.* 作家試圖再現他童年的所見所聞。

rec·re·ation /ˌrekriˈeɪʃn/ *noun* **1** [U] the fact of people doing things for enjoyment, when they are not working 娛樂；消遣：*the need to improve facilities for leisure and recreation* 改進消遣娛樂設施之必要 ◇ *the increasing use of land for recreation* 把越來越多的土地用於娛樂 **2** [C] (*BrE*) a particular activity that sb does when they are not working 娛樂活動；遊戲 **SYN hobby, pastime**：*His recreations include golf, football and shooting.* 他的娛樂活動包括打高爾夫球、踢足球和射擊。 ➲ **SYNONYMS** at ENTERTAINMENT

rec·re·ation·al /ˌrekriˈeɪʃənl/ *adj.* connected with activities that people do for enjoyment when they are not working 娛樂的；消遣的：*recreational activities/facilities* 娛樂活動／設施 ◇ *These areas are set aside for public recreational use.* 這些地方已經劃出來用於公共娛樂。

recreˈational vehicle (*NAmE*) (*BrE* **camp·er, ˈcamper van**) (also **motor·home** *NAmE, BrE*) *noun* (*abbr.* **RV**) a large vehicle designed for people to live and sleep in when they are travelling 野營車，旅行房車（供旅行時居住）➲ **VISUAL VOCAB** page V58

recreˈation ground *noun* (*BrE*) an area of land used by the public for sports and games 公共娛樂場

recreˈation room (also *NAmE, informal* **ˈrec room**) *noun* **1** a room in a school, a hospital, an office building, etc. in which people can relax, play games, etc.（學校、醫院、辦公樓等處的）娛樂室，活動室 **2** (*NAmE*) a room in a private house used for games, entertainment, etc.（私人住宅裏的）康樂室

re·crim·in·ation /rɪˌkrɪmɪˈneɪʃn/ *noun* [C, usually pl., U] an angry statement that sb makes accusing sb else of sth, especially in response to a similar statement from them 指責；反訴；反控：*bitter recriminations* 激烈的反訴 ◇ *We spent the rest of the evening in mutual recrimination.* 我們後來一晚上都在相互指責。 ▸ **re·crim·in·atory** /rɪˈkrɪmɪnətri; *NAmE* -tɔːri/ *adj.*

rec room /ˈrek ruːm; *NAmE* rʊm/ *noun* (*NAmE, informal*) = RECREATION ROOM

re·cru·desce /ˌriːkruːˈdes/ *verb* [I] (*formal*) to happen again 再發生；復發 **SYN recur** ▸ **re·cru·des·cence** /ˌriːkruːˈdesns/ *noun* [U] **re·cru·des·cent** /ˌriːkruːˈdesnt/ *adj.*

re·cruit /rɪˈkruːt/ *verb, noun*

▪ *verb* **1** [T, I] **~ (sb) (to sth)** | **~ sb to do sth** to find new people to join a company, an organization, the armed forces, etc. 吸收（新成員）；徵募（新兵）：*The police are trying to recruit more officers from ethnic minorities.* 警察機關正試圖從少數民族中徵募更多的新警員。◇ *They recruited several new members to the club.* 他們吸收了幾名新成員進入俱樂部。◇ *He's responsible for recruiting at all levels.* 他負責各個層次的徵募工作。 ➲ **COLLOCATIONS** at JOB **2** [T] **~ sb to do sth** to persuade sb to do sth, especially to help you 動員…（提供幫助）：*We were recruited to help peel the vegetables.* 我們被找來幫着給蔬菜去皮。 **3** [T] **~ sth** to form a new army, team, etc. by persuading new people to join it（通過招募）組成，組建：*to recruit a task force* 組建特遣部隊 ▸ **re·cruit·er** *noun* **re·cruit·ment** *noun* [U]：*the recruitment of new members* 新成員的招募 ◇ *a recruitment drive* 徵兵運動

▪ *noun* **1** a person who has recently joined the armed forces or the police 新兵；新警員：*the training of new recruits* 新兵訓練 ◇ *He spoke of us scornfully as* ***raw recruits*** (= people without training or experience). 他輕蔑地稱我們是新兵娃娃。 **2** a person who joins an organization, a company, etc. 新成員：*attempts to attract new recruits to the nursing profession* 吸引新成員參加護理工作的努力

rec·tal /ˈrektəl/ *adj.* (*anatomy* 解) relating to the RECTUM 直腸的

rect·angle /ˈrektæŋgl/ *noun* a flat shape with four straight sides, two of which are longer than the other two, and four angles of 90° 長方形；矩形 ➲ **VISUAL VOCAB** page V71 ▸ **rect·angu·lar** /rekˈtæŋgjələ(r)/ *adj.*

rect·ify /ˈrektɪfaɪ/ *verb* (**rec·ti·fies, rec·ti·fy·ing, rec·ti·fied, rec·ti·fied**) **~ sth** (*formal*) to put right sth that is wrong 矯正；糾正；改正 **SYN correct**：*to rectify a fault* 改正缺點 ◇ *We must take steps to rectify the situation.* 我們一定要採取措施整頓局面。 ▸ **rec·ti·fi·able** /ˌrektɪˈfaɪəbl/ *adj.*：*The damage will be easily rectifiable.* 所受損壞很容易修復。 **rec·ti·fi·ca·tion** /ˌrektɪfɪˈkeɪʃn/ *noun* [U]

rec·ti·lin·ear /ˌrektɪˈlɪniə(r)/ *adj.* (*technical* 術語) **1** in a straight line 直線的；筆直的：*rectilinear motion* 直線運動 **2** having straight lines 有直線的：*rectilinear forms* 直線圖形

R

rec·ti·tude /ˈrektɪtjuːd; *NAmE* -tuːd/ *noun* [U] (*formal*) the quality of thinking or behaving in a correct and honest way 公正；正直；誠實 SYN **uprightness**

recto /ˈrektəʊ; *NAmE* -toʊ/ *noun* (*pl.* **-os**) (*technical* 術語) the page on the right side of an open book （打開的書的）右頁 OPP **verso**

rec·tor /ˈrektə(r)/ *noun* **1** an Anglican priest who is in charge of a particular area, (called a PARISH). In the past a rector received an income directly from this area. （聖公會的）教區牧師，堂區主持人 ➲ compare VICAR **2** (in Britain) the head of certain universities, colleges or schools （英國某些學校的）校長

rec·tory /ˈrektəri/ *noun* (*pl.* **-ies**) a house where the rector of a church lives, or lived in the past 堂區主持人的住宅

rec·tum /ˈrektəm/ *noun* (*pl.* **rec·tums** or **recta** /ˈrektə/) (*anatomy* 解) the end section of the tube where food waste collects before leaving the body through the ANUS 直腸 ➲ VISUAL VOCAB page V59

re·cum·bent /rɪˈkʌmbənt/ *adj.* [usually before noun] (*formal*) (of a person's body or position 人的身體或姿勢) lying down 躺倒的；躺着的 SYN **reclining**

re·cu·per·ate /rɪˈkuːpəreɪt/ *verb* (*formal*) **1** [I] ~ (**from sth**) to get back your health, strength or energy after being ill/sick, tired, injured, etc. 康復；恢復；恢復健康 SYN **recover**：*He's still recuperating from his operation.* 他動了手術，還在恢復。 **2** [T] ~ **sth** to get back money that you have spent or lost 收回；挽回（損失） SYN **recoup, recover**：*He hoped to recuperate at least some of his losses.* 他希望至少挽回一部份損失。 ▸ **re·cu·per·ation** /rɪˌkuːpəˈreɪʃn/ *noun* [U]：*It was a period of rest and recuperation.* 那是一段休養的時間。

re·cu·pera·tive /rɪˈkuːpərətɪv/ *adj.* (*formal*) helping you to get better after you have been ill/sick, very tired, etc. 有助於恢復的

recur /rɪˈkɜː(r)/ *verb* (**-rr-**) [I] to happen again or a number of times 再發生；反復出現：*This theme recurs several times throughout the book.* 這一主題在整部書裏出現了好幾次。◇ *a **recurring illness/problem/nightmare, etc.*** 反複發作的疾病、反複出現的問題、一再出現的噩夢等

re·cur·rence /rɪˈkʌrəns; *NAmE* -ˈkɜːr-/ *noun* [C, usually sing., U] if there is **a recurrence of** sth, it happens again 重現；復發：*attempts to prevent a recurrence of the problem* 防止問題再次發生的努力

re·cur·rent /rɪˈkʌrənt; *NAmE* -ˈkɜːr-/ *adj.* that happens again and again 反複出現的；重複發生的：*recurrent infections* 重複感染 ◇ *Poverty is a **recurrent theme** in her novels.* 貧窮是她的小說中慣有的主題。

re·cur·sion /rɪˈkɜːʃn; *NAmE* -ˈkɜːrʒn/ *noun* [U] (*mathematics* 數) the process of repeating a FUNCTION, each time applying it to the result of the previous stage 遞歸；遞迴

re·cur·sive /rɪˈkɜːsɪv; *NAmE* -ˈkɜːrs-/ *adj.* (*technical* 術語) involving a process that is applied repeatedly 遞歸的；循環的；遞迴的

re·cus·ant /ˈrekjʊzənt; *NAmE* rəˈkjuːzənt/ *noun* (*formal*) a person who refuses to do what a rule or person in authority says they should do 不服從的人；反抗者 ▸ **re·cus·ancy** /ˈrekjʊzənsi/ *noun* [U]

re·cyc·lable /ˌriːˈsaɪkləbl/ *adj.* able to be RECYCLED 可回收利用的；可再循環的

re·cycle /ˌriːˈsaɪkl/ *verb* **1** ~ **sth** to treat things that have already been used so that they can be used again 回收利用；再利用：*Denmark recycles nearly 85% of its paper.* 丹麥的紙張回收率接近 85%。◇ *recycled paper* 再生紙 ➲ COLLOCATIONS at ENVIRONMENT **2** ~ **sth** to use the same ideas, methods, jokes, etc. again 再次應用，重新使用（概念、方法、玩笑等）：*He recycled all his old jokes.* 他把那些老掉牙的笑話又說了一遍。 ▸ **re·cyc·ling** *noun* [U]：*the recycling of glass* 玻璃的回收利用 ◇ *a recycling plant* 廢品回收加工廠 ➲ VISUAL VOCAB page V8

red 0→ /red/ *adj.*, *noun*

■ *adj.* (**red·der, red·dest**) **1** 0→ having the colour of blood or fire 紅的；紅色的：*a red car* 紅色的汽車 ◇ *The lights (= traffic lights) changed to red before I could get across.* 我還沒來得及通過，紅燈又亮了。 **2** (of the eyes 眼睛) BLOODSHOT (= with thin lines of blood in them) or surrounded by red or very pink skin 充血的；佈滿血絲的；紅腫的：*Her eyes were red from crying.* 她的眼睛都哭紅了。 **3** 0→ (of the face 臉) bright red or pink, especially because you are angry, embarrassed or ashamed 漲紅的；通紅的：*He stammered something and went very red in the face.* 他結結巴巴地說了些什麼，臉漲得通紅。◇ (*BrE*) *She went **red as a beetroot**.* 她的臉漲得通紅。◇ (*NAmE*) *She went **red as a beet**.* 她的臉漲得通紅。 **4** 0→ (of hair or an animal's fur 頭髮或動物的毛皮) reddish-brown in colour 紅褐色的：*a red-haired girl* 紅髮女孩 ◇ *red deer* 赤鹿 ➲ see also REDHEAD **5** (*informal*, *politics* 政) (sometimes *disapproving*) having very LEFT-WING political opinions 激進的；革命的；左翼的 ➲ compare PINK *adj.* (3) **6** (*politics* 政) (of an area in the US) having more people who vote for the REPUBLICAN candidate than the DEMOCRATIC one （美國地區）紅色的（支持共和黨候選人多於民主黨候選人）：*red states/counties* 紅州；紅縣 OPP **blue** ▸ **red·ness** *noun* [U, sing.]：*You may notice redness and swelling after the injection.* 注射後會出現紅腫。

IDM **red in ˌtooth and ˈclaw** involving opposition or competition that is violent and without pity 殘酷無情；血淋淋；決不寬容：*nature, red in tooth and claw* 殘酷無情的大自然 **a red rag to a ˈbull** (*BrE*) (*NAmE* **like waving a red flag in front of a ˈbull**) something that is likely to make sb very angry 鬥牛的紅布；激起人怒火的事物 ➲ more at PAINT *v.*

■ *noun* **1** 0→ [C, U] the colour of blood or fire 紅色：*She often wears red.* 她經常穿紅色的衣服。◇ *the reds and browns of the woods in the fall (= of the leaves)* 秋天樹林呈現的紅色和褐色 ◇ *I've marked the corrections in red (= in red ink).* 我已經用紅筆把改正之處標出。◇ *The traffic lights were on red.* 當時是亮紅燈。 **2** [U, C] red wine 紅葡萄酒：*Would you prefer red or white?* 你喜歡喝紅葡萄酒還是白葡萄酒？◇ *an Italian red* 一杯意大利紅葡萄酒 **3** [C] (*informal*, *disapproving*, *politics* 政) a person with very LEFT-WING political opinions 左翼人士；激進分子 ➲ compare PINKO

IDM **be in the ˈred** (*informal*) to owe money to your bank because you have spent more than you have in your account 負債；虧空：*The company has plunged $37 million into the red.* 公司負債已達 3 700 萬元。 ➲ compare BE IN THE BLACK **see ˈred** (*informal*) to become very angry 大發脾氣；大怒

re·dact /rɪˈdækt/ *verb* ~ **sth** (**from sth**) to remove information from a document because you do not want the public to see it 刪除，去掉，輯除（不願公諸於眾的信息）：*All sensitive personal information has been redacted from the public documents.* 所有敏感的個人信息都從公開文件中刪掉了。 ▸ **re·dac·tion** /rɪˈdækʃn/ *noun* [C, U]

ˌred ˈadmiral *noun* a BUTTERFLY (= a flying insect with large brightly coloured wings) that has black wings with bright red marks on them 大西洋赤蛺蝶

ˌred aˈlert *noun* [U, sing.] a situation in which you are prepared for sth dangerous to happen; a warning of this 緊急戒備狀態；緊急警報：*Following the bomb blast, local hospitals have been **put on red alert**.* 炸彈爆炸之後，當地醫院一直處於戒備狀態。

ˌred ˈblood cell (also **ˈred cell**) (also *biology* 生 **eryth·ro·cyte**) *noun* any of the red-coloured cells in the blood, that carry OXYGEN 紅細胞；紅血球

ˌred-ˈblooded *adj.* [usually before noun] (*informal*) full of strength and energy, often sexual energy 充滿活力的；性慾旺盛的 SYN **virile**：*red-blooded young males* 血氣方剛的年輕男子

ˌred ˈbox *noun* (*BrE*) a box used by a government minister to hold official documents （英國大臣用的）公文匣

red·breast /ˈredbrest/ *noun* (*literary*) a ROBIN 知更鳥

ˈred-brick *adj.* [usually before noun] **1** (of buildings, walls, etc. 建築物、牆壁等) built with bricks of a reddish-brown colour 用紅磚建成的：*red-brick cottages* 紅磚建成的村舍 **2** (becoming *old-fashioned*) (of universities in Britain 英國大學) built in the late 19th or early 20th century, in contrast to older universities, such as Oxford and Cambridge 建於 19 世紀末 20 世紀初的（與更為古老的大學如牛津和劍橋形成對照）➲ compare OXBRIDGE

red·cap /ˈredkæp/ *noun* **1** (*BrE*) a member of the MILITARY POLICE 憲兵 **2** (*NAmE*) a railway/railroad PORTER 鐵路搬運工

ˌred ˈcard *noun* (in football (SOCCER) 足球) a card shown by the REFEREE to a player who has broken the rules of the game and is not allowed to play for the rest of the game 紅牌（裁判員判罰犯規球員不能繼續比賽）➲ compare YELLOW CARD

ˌred ˈcarpet (usually **the red carpet**) *noun* [sing.] a strip of red carpet laid on the ground for an important visitor to walk on when he or she arrives（為迎接貴賓鋪的）紅地毯：*I didn't expect to be given **the red carpet treatment**!* 我可沒想到會受到隆重接待！

ˈred cell *noun* = RED BLOOD CELL

ˌred ˈcent *noun* [sing.] (*NAmE*) (especially after a negative 尤用於否定詞後) a very small amount of money 很少的錢：*I didn't get a red cent for all my work.* 我做了那麼多工作，可一分錢也沒得到。

red·coat /ˈredkəʊt; *NAmE* -koʊt/ *noun* **1** a British soldier in the past （舊時的）英國士兵 **2** (in Britain) a worker at a HOLIDAY CAMP who entertains and helps guests （英國的）度假營地招待員，度假營地服務員

the ˌRed ˈCrescent *noun* [sing.] the name used by national branches in Muslim countries of the International Movement of the Red Cross and the Red Crescent, an organization that takes care of people suffering because of war or natural disasters 紅新月會（穆斯林國家中類似於紅十字會的組織）

the ˌRed ˈCross *noun* [sing.] an international organization that takes care of people suffering because of war or natural disasters. Its full name is the International Movement of the Red Cross and the Red Crescent. 紅十字會

red·cur·rant /ˌredˈkʌrənt; ˈredkʌrənt; *NAmE* -kɜːr-/ *noun* a very small red BERRY that grows in bunches on a bush and can be eaten 紅醋栗：*redcurrant jelly* 紅醋栗果子凍 ◇ *a redcurrant bush* 紅醋栗樹叢

ˌred ˈdeer *noun* (*pl.* **red deer**) a DEER with large ANTLERS (= horns shaped like branches), which has a reddish-brown coat in summer 馬鹿；赤鹿

red·den /ˈredn/ *verb* [I, T] **~ (sth)** to become red; to make sth red （使）變紅：*The sky was reddening.* 天空紅霞映照。◇ *He could feel his face reddening with embarrassment.* 他感到自己因為尷尬而臉紅了。◇ *He stared at her and she reddened.* 他盯着她看，弄得她臉都紅了。

red·dish /ˈredɪʃ/ *adj.* fairly red in colour 微紅的；略帶紅色的

ˌred ˈdwarf *noun* (*astronomy* 天) a small, old star that is not very hot 紅矮星

re·dec·or·ate /ˌriːˈdekəreɪt/ *verb* [I, T] to put new paint and/or paper on the walls of a room or house （用塗料或壁紙）重新裝飾，再次裝修：*We've just redecorated.* 我們剛剛重新裝修過。◇ **~ sth** *The house has been fully redecorated.* 這房子已經徹底重新裝修過了。▸ **re·dec·or·ation** /ˌriːˌdekəˈreɪʃn/ *noun* [U]

re·deem /rɪˈdiːm/ *verb* **1 ~ sb/sth** to make sb/sth seem less bad 補救；彌補；掩飾…之不足 **SYN** **compensate for**：*The excellent acting wasn't enough to redeem a weak plot.* 精彩的表演不足以掩蓋情節的拙劣。◇ *The only **redeeming feature** of the job* (= good thing about it) *is the salary.* 這份工作唯一的可取之處就是它的工資。➲ SYNONYMS at SAVE **2 ~ yourself** to do sth to improve the opinion that people have of you, especially after you have done sth bad 挽回影響；改變印象；維護：*He has a chance to redeem himself after last week's mistakes.* 他有機會彌補上星期犯下的錯誤。 **3 ~ sb** (in Christianity 基督教) to save sb from the power of evil 拯救；救贖：*Jesus Christ came to redeem us from sin.* 耶穌基督來將我們從罪惡中拯救出來。 **4 ~ sth** to pay the full sum of money that you owe sb; to pay a debt 償清；付清：*to redeem a loan/mortgage* 清償貸款／按揭貸款 **5 ~ sth** to exchange sth such as shares or VOUCHERS for money or goods 兑換；兑現：*This voucher can be redeemed at any of our branches.* 這票據在我們的任一分支機構都可以兑換。 **6 ~ sth** to get back a valuable object from sb by paying them back the money you borrowed from them in exchange for the object 贖回：*He was able to redeem his watch from the pawnshop.* 他得以從當鋪贖回他的錶。 **7 ~ a pledge/promise** (*formal*) to do what you have promised that you will do 履行，遵守（諾言）

re·deem·able /rɪˈdiːməbl/ *adj.* **~ (against sth)** that can be exchanged for money or goods 可兑换的；可交換的：*These vouchers are redeemable against any future purchase.* 這些禮券可在以後購物時兑換使用。

the Re·deem·er /rɪˈdiːmə(r)/ *noun* [sing.] (*literary*) Jesus Christ 救世主耶穌基督

re·define **AW** /ˌriːdɪˈfaɪn/ *verb* to change the nature or limits of sth; to make people consider sth in a new way 改變…的本質（或界限）；重新定義；使重新考慮：**~ sth** *The new constitution redefined the powers of the president.* 新憲法重新規定了總統的職權。◇ **~ what, how, etc. …** *We need to redefine what we mean by democracy.* 我們需要重新考慮我們對民主的理解。 ▸ **re·def·in·ition** /ˌriːdefɪˈnɪʃn/ *noun* [U, C]

re·demp·tion /rɪˈdempʃn/ *noun* [U] **1** (*formal*) the act of saving or state of being saved from the power of evil; the act of REDEEMING 拯救；救贖：*the redemption of the world from sin* 將世界從罪惡中拯救出來 **2** (*finance* 財) the act of exchanging shares for money (= of REDEEMING them) 贖回（股票等）
IDM **beyond/past reˈdemption** too bad to be saved or improved 無法挽救；不可救藥

re·demp·tive /rɪˈdemptɪv/ *adj.* (*formal*) that saves you from the power of evil 救贖的；拯救的：*the redemptive power of love* 愛情的救贖力量

re·deploy /ˌriːdɪˈplɔɪ/ *verb* to move sb/sth to a new position or job 調配；重新部署：**~ sb/sth** *Our troops are to be redeployed elsewhere.* 我們的部隊將被重新部署到其他地區。◇ **~ sb/sth to sth** *Most of the employees will be redeployed to other parts of the company.* 大多數雇員將被調配到公司的其他部門。 ▸ **re·deploy·ment** *noun* [U]：*the redeployment of staff/resources* 員工／資源的重新配置

re·design /ˌriːdɪˈzaɪn/ *verb* **~ sth** to design sth again, in a different way 重新設計 ▸ **re·design** *noun* [U, C]

re·develop /ˌriːdɪˈveləp/ *verb* [T, I] **~ (sth)** to change an area by building new roads, houses, factories, etc. 改造；重新建設：*The city has plans to redevelop the site.* 這個城市計劃重新建設這個地方。 ▸ **re·devel·op·ment** *noun* [U]：*inner-city redevelopment* 市中心貧民區的改造

ˈred-eye *noun* **1** (also **ˌred-eye ˈflight**) [C] (*informal, especially NAmE*) a flight in a plane at night, on which you cannot get enough sleep 夜間航班；紅眼夜航：*We took the red-eye to Boston.* 我們乘坐夜間航班飛到波士頓。 **2** [U] the appearance of having red eyes that people sometimes have in photographs taken using flash（因使用閃光燈照相而在照片上出現的）紅眼

ˌred-ˈfaced *adj.* with a red face, especially because you are embarrassed or angry 臉色漲紅的；紅臉的

ˌred ˈflag *noun* **1** a flag used to warn people of danger 示警紅旗 **2** a red flag as a symbol of revolution or COMMUNISM（象徵革命或共產主義的）紅旗

ˌred ˈgiant *noun* (*astronomy* 天) a large star towards the end of its life that is relatively cool and gives out a reddish light 紅巨星

ˌred-ˈhanded *adj.* **IDM** see CATCH *v.*

red·head /ˈredhed/ *noun* (sometimes *offensive*) a person who has red hair 紅髮人 ➲ compare BLONDE, BRUNETTE ▸ **ˌred-ˈheaded** *adj.*：*a red-headed girl* 紅髮女孩

ˌred ˈherring *noun* an unimportant fact, idea, event, etc. that takes people's attention away from the important ones 轉移注意力的次要事實（或想法、事件等） **ORIGIN** From the custom of using the smell of a

R

smoked, dried herring (which was red) to train dogs to hunt. 源自用（紅色）熏乾鯡魚的氣味訓練狗狩獵的做法。

ˌred-ˈhot *adj.* **1** (of metal or sth burning 金屬或燃燒物) so hot that it looks red 熾熱的；赤熱的；熱得發紅的：*Red-hot coals glowed in the fire.* 熾熱的煤炭在爐子裏發光。 **2** showing strong feeling 激烈的；強烈的：*her red-hot anger* 她的暴怒 **3** (*informal*) new, exciting and of great interest to people 熱門的：*a red-hot issue* 熱點問題 **4** used to describe the person, animal or team that is considered almost certain to win a race, etc. 幾乎一定能獲勝的人（或動物、運動隊）：*The race was won by the* ***red-hot favourite.*** 奪標呼聲最高的選手獲得了比賽的勝利。

re·dial /ˌriːˈdaɪəl/ *verb, noun*

■ ***verb*** (**-ll-**, *NAmE* **-l-**) **1** [I, T] **~ (sth)** to call a telephone number again by pressing all of the individual numbers again 按鍵逐一重撥（電話號碼） **2** [I] to call a telephone number again, using the button that automatically calls the last number that was called 按鍵自動重撥（電話號碼）；按重撥鍵

■ ***noun*** **1** [U] the ability to redial a telephone number automatically 自動重撥功能 **2** (also **ˈredial button**) [sing.] the button that automatically calls the last number that was called 自動重撥按鈕；重撥鍵

redid *past tense of* REDO

ˌRed ˈIndian (also **red·skin**) *noun* (*old-fashioned, taboo*) a very offensive word for a Native American （蔑稱）印第安人

re·dir·ect /ˌriːdəˈrekt; -dɪ-; -daɪ-/ *verb* **1 ~ sth (to sth)** to use sth, for example money, in a different way or for a different purpose （以新的方式或目的）重新使用：*Resources are being redirected to this important new project.* 為這一重要的新項目重新調配了資源。 **2 ~ sth (to sth)** to send sth to a different address or in a different direction 改寄；改變投遞方向：*Enquiries on this matter are being redirected to the press office.* 詢問此事的信件轉到新聞處。◇ *Make sure you get your mail redirected to your new address.* 注意一定要讓你的郵件改投到你的新住址。 ▸ **re·dir·ec·tion** *noun* [sing., U]：*a sudden redirection of economic policy* 經濟政策的突然轉變◇ *the redirection of mail* 郵件改投

re·dis·cover /ˌriːdɪˈskʌvə(r)/ *verb* **~ sth** to find again sth that had been forgotten or lost 重新發現；重新找到 ▸ **re·dis·cov·ery** /ˌriːdɪˈskʌvəri/ *noun* [U, C] (*pl.* **-ies**)

re·dis·trib·ute AW /ˌriːdɪˈstrɪbjuːt; ˌriːˈdɪs-/ *verb* **~ sth (from sb/sth) (to sb/sth)** to share sth out among people in a different way 重新分配：*Wealth needs to be redistributed from the rich to the poor.* 需要將財富從富人那裏重新分給窮人。 ▸ **re·dis·tri·bu·tion** AW /ˌriːdɪstrɪˈbjuːʃn/ *noun* [U, sing.]：*the redistribution of wealth* 財富的重新分配 **re·dis·tribu·tive** /ˌriːdɪˈstrɪbjətɪv/ *adj.*

re·dis·trict /ˌriːˈdɪstrɪkt/ *verb* [T, I] **~ (sth)** (*US*) to change the official borders between districts （把…）重新劃區

ˌred-ˈletter day *noun* an important day, or a day that you will remember, because of sth good that happened then 重要紀念日；喜慶日 ORIGIN From the custom of using red ink to mark holidays and festivals on a calendar. 源自在日曆上用紅色標示假日和節日的習慣。

ˌred ˈlight *noun* a signal telling the driver of a vehicle to stop 紅燈（示意車輛停下的信號）：*to go through a red light* (= not stop at one) 闖紅燈

ˌred-ˈlight district *noun* a part of a town where there are many PROSTITUTES 紅燈區

red ˈline *noun* an issue or a demand that one person or group refuses to change their opinion about during a disagreement or NEGOTIATIONS （爭論或談判中）拒絕改變立場的問題（或要求）：*The issue of sovereignty is a red line that cannot be crossed.* 主權問題是一條不能跨越的紅線。

ˌred ˈmeat *noun* [U] meat that is dark brown in colour when it has been cooked, such as beef and LAMB 紅肉（指牛肉、羊肉等） ➲ compare WHITE MEAT (1)

red·neck /ˈrednek/ *noun* (*informal*) an offensive word for a person who lives in a country area of the US, has little education and has strong conservative political opinions 鄉巴佬，紅脖子（對美國受教育不多且政治觀點保守的鄉下人的貶稱）

redo /ˌriːˈduː/ *verb* (**re·does** /-ˈdʌz/, **redid** /-ˈdɪd/, **re·done** /-ˈdʌn/) **~ sth** to do sth again or in a different way 重做；換一種方式做：*A whole day's work had to be redone.* 一整天的工作都必須重做。◇ *We've just redone the bathroom* (= decorated it again). 我們剛剛重新裝修了浴室。

redo·lent /ˈredələnt/ *adj.* [not before noun] **~ of/with sth** (*literary*) **1** making you think of the thing mentioned 使人想到；使人聯想起：*an atmosphere redolent of the sea and ships* 讓人聯想起大海和船隻的氛圍 **2** smelling strongly of the thing mentioned 有…的強烈氣味：*a kitchen redolent with the smell of baking* 瀰漫着烘焙氣味的廚房 ▸ **redo·lence** /-əns/ *noun* [U]

re·double /ˌriːˈdʌbl/ *verb* **~ sth** to increase sth or make it stronger 加倍；增加；加強：*The leading banks are expected to* ***redouble their efforts*** *to keep the value of the dollar down.* 人們希望各大銀行加倍努力以保持美元的低價位。◇ *redoubled enthusiasm* 倍加熱情

re·doubt /rɪˈdaʊt/ *noun* **1** (*literary*) a place or situation in which sb/sth is protected when they are being attacked or threatened 藏身之所；堡壘 **2** a small building from which soldiers can fight and defend themselves 掩體；防禦工事

re·doubt·able /rɪˈdaʊtəbl/ *adj.* (*formal*) if a person is **redoubtable**, they have very strong qualities that make you respect them and perhaps feel afraid of them 令人敬畏的；可敬的 SYN **formidable**

re·dound /rɪˈdaʊnd/ *verb*

PHR V **reˈdound to sth** (*formal*) to improve the impression that people have of you 改進，提高（印象）：*Their defeat redounds to the glory of those whom they attacked.* 他們的失敗提高了那些受到他們攻擊的人的聲譽。

ˌred ˈpanda *noun* = PANDA (2)

ˌred ˈpepper *noun* **1** [C, U] a hollow red fruit that is eaten, raw or cooked, as a vegetable 辣椒 **2** [U] (*especially NAmE*) = CAYENNE

re·draft AW /ˌriːˈdrɑːft; *NAmE* -ˈdræft/ *verb* **~ sth** to write an article, a letter, etc. again in order to improve it or make changes 改寫；重新起草 ▸ **ˈre·draft** *noun*

re·draw /ˌriːˈdrɔː/ *verb* (**re·drew** /-ˈdruː/, **re·drawn** /-ˈdrɔːn/) **~ sth** to make changes to sth such as the borders of a country or region, a plan, an arrangement, etc. 重新描繪，修改（邊界、計劃、安排等）：*After the war the map of Europe was redrawn.* 戰後，歐洲版圖被重新劃定。◇ *to* ***redraw the boundaries*** *between male and female roles in the home* 重新劃分兩性在家庭中所扮演的角色

re·dress *verb, noun*

■ ***verb*** /rɪˈdres/ **~ sth** (*formal*) to correct sth that is unfair or wrong 糾正；矯正；改正 SYN **put right**：*to redress an injustice* 糾正不公

IDM **redress the ˈbalance** to make a situation equal or fair again 恢復公平合理的情況；恢復平衡

■ ***noun*** /rɪˈdres; ˈriːdres/ [U] **~ (for/against sth)** (*formal*) payment, etc. that you should get for sth wrong that has happened to you or harm that you have suffered 賠款；損失賠償 SYN **compensation**：*to seek legal redress for unfair dismissal* 因横遭解雇而提起賠償訴訟◇ *to have little prospect of redress* 幾乎沒有獲賠的希望

red·skin /ˈredskɪn/ *noun* (*old-fashioned, taboo, offensive*) = RED INDIAN

ˌred ˈtape *noun* [U] (*disapproving*) official rules that seem more complicated than necessary and prevent things from being done quickly 繁文縟節；官僚作風 ORIGIN From the custom of tying up official documents with red or pink tape. 源自用紅色或粉紅色的帶子捆紮公文的習俗。

ˈred-top *noun* (*BrE, informal*) a British TABLOID newspaper, whose name is in red at the top of the front page （英國的）紅頭通俗小報

re·duce 0‑ᴡ /rɪˈdjuːs; *NAmE* -ˈduːs/ *verb*
1 0‑ᴡ [T] to make sth less or smaller in size, quantity, price, etc. 減少，縮小（尺寸、數量、價格等）：**~ sth** *Reduce speed now* (= on a sign). 減速行駛。◇ *Giving up smoking reduces the risk of heart disease.* 戒煙會減少得心臟病的風險。◇ **~ sth by sth** *Costs have been reduced by 20% over the past year.* 過去一年，成本支出已經減少了20%。◇ **~ sth (from sth) (to sth)** *The number of employees was reduced from 40 to 25.* 雇員人數從 40 人減少到了 25 人。◇ *The skirt was reduced to £10 in the sale.* 在大減價期間，這條裙子減價到 10 英鎊。**2** [T, I] **~ (sth)** if you **reduce** a liquid or a liquid **reduces**, you boil it so that it becomes less in quantity （使）蒸發 **3** [I] (*NAmE, informal*) to lose weight by limiting the amount and type of food that you eat 減輕體重；節食：*a reducing plan* 節食計劃 **4** [T] **~ sth** (*chemistry* 化) to add one or more ELECTRONS to a substance or to remove OXYGEN from a substance 使還原；去氧；脱氧 ➲ compare OXIDIZE
IDM **re,duced 'circumstances** the state of being poorer than you were before. People say 'living in reduced circumstances' to avoid saying 'poor'. （委婉說法，與 poor 同義）境況不濟
PHR V **re'duce sb/sth (from sth) to sth/to doing sth** [usually passive] to force sb/sth into a particular state or condition, usually a worse one 使陷入（更壞的）境地；使淪落；使陷入窘境：*a beautiful building reduced to rubble* 已化為殘垣斷壁的漂亮建築 ◇ *She was* ***reduced to tears*** *by their criticisms.* 他們的批評使她流下了眼淚。◇ *They were reduced to begging in the streets.* 他們淪落到沿街乞討。 **re'duce sth to sth** to change sth to a more general or more simple form 將…概括成（或簡化為）：*We can reduce the problem to two main issues.* 我們可以將這個問題概括成兩個要點。

re·du·cible /rɪˈdjuːsəbl; *NAmE* -ˈduːs-/ *adj.* **~ to sth** (*formal*) that can be described or considered simply as sth 可以簡化的：*The problem is not reducible to one of money.* 這個問題不能簡單地看作是錢的問題。

re·duc·tio ad ab·sur·dum /rɪˌdʌktiəʊ æd æbˈsɜːdəm; *NAmE* rɪˌdʌktioʊ æd æbˈsɜːrdəm/ *noun* [U, C] (*philosophy* 哲) (from *Latin*) a method of proving that sth is not true by showing that its result is not logical or sensible 歸謬法

re·duc·tion 0‑ᴡ /rɪˈdʌkʃn/ *noun*
1 0‑ᴡ [C, U] **~ (in sth)** an act of making sth less or smaller; the state of being made less or smaller 減少；縮小；降低：*a 33% reduction in the number of hospital beds available* 醫院的牀位減少 33% ◇ *There has been some reduction in unemployment.* 失業人數有所減少。◇ *a* ***slight/significant/substantial/drastic reduction*** *in costs* 成本的略微／顯著／大幅度／急劇降低 **2** 0‑ᴡ [C] an amount of money by which sth is made cheaper 減價；折扣：*There are reductions for children sharing a room with two adults.* 孩子和兩個大人合住一間房可以打折。**3** [C] a copy of a photograph, map, picture, etc. that is made smaller than the original one （照片、地圖、圖片等的）縮圖，縮版 OPP **enlargement** **4** [U, C] (*chemistry* 化) the fact of adding one or more ELECTRONS to a substance or of removing OXYGEN from a substance 還原；去氧；脱氧 ➲ compare OXIDATION

re·duc·tion·ism /rɪˈdʌkʃənɪzəm/ *noun* [U] (*formal*, often *disapproving*) the belief that complicated things can be explained by considering them as a combination of simple parts 簡化論；簡單化理論；還原論 ▶ **re·duc·tion·ist** /-ɪst/ *adj.*, *noun*

re·duc·tive /rɪˈdʌktɪv/ *adj.* (*formal*, often *disapproving*) that tries to explain sth complicated by considering it as a combination of simple parts 簡化論的；簡化法的；以簡釋繁的；還原論的

re·dun·dancy /rɪˈdʌndənsi/ *noun* (*pl.* **-ies**) **1** [U, C, usually pl.] (*BrE*) the situation when sb has to leave their job because there is no more work available for them （因勞動力過剩而造成的）裁員，解雇：*Thousands of factory workers are facing redundancy.* 數千名工廠工人面臨裁汰。◇ *to accept/take* ***voluntary redundancy*** (= to offer to leave your job) 接受自願裁汰 ◇ *the threat of* ***compulsory redundancies*** 強制裁員的威脅 ◇ *redundancy payments* 裁員補償 ➲ COLLOCATIONS at UNEMPLOYMENT ➲ see also LAY-OFF (1) **2** [U] (*formal* or *technical* 術語) the state of not being necessary or useful 多餘；贅贅：*Natural language is characterized by redundancy* (= words are used that are not really necessary for sb to understand the meaning). 自然語言的特點是繁複。

re·dun·dant /rɪˈdʌndənt/ *adj.* **1** (*BrE*) (of a person 人) without a job because there is no more work available for you in a company 被裁減的：*to be* ***made redundant*** *from your job* 成為冗員而被裁減 ◇ *redundant employees* 受裁汰的員工 ➲ COLLOCATIONS at UNEMPLOYMENT **2** not needed or useful 多餘的；不需要的：*The picture has too much redundant detail.* 這幅畫中不必要的細節太多。▶ **re·dun·dant·ly** *adv.*

re·du·pli·cate /ˌriːˈdjuːplɪkeɪt; *NAmE* -ˈduː-/ *verb* [I, T] **~ (sth/itself)** to make a copy of sth in order to form another of the same kind 複製；加倍：*These cells are able to reduplicate themselves.* 這些細胞能自我複製。

ˌred ˈwine *noun* **1** [U, C] wine that gets its red colour from the skins of the GRAPES 紅葡萄酒 **2** [C] a glass of red wine 一杯紅葡萄酒 ➲ compare ROSÉ, WHITE WINE

red·wood /ˈredwʊd/ *noun* **1** [C] a very tall type of tree that grows especially in California and Oregon 紅杉，紅木（多生長於加利福尼亞州和俄勒岡州）：*giant redwoods* 巨大的紅杉樹 **2** [U] the reddish wood of the redwood tree 紅杉木

ˈred zone *noun* [sing.] (in AMERICAN FOOTBALL 美式足球) the area within 20 YARDS of a team's GOAL LINE 禁區（距離球門線 20 碼以內的區域）

ˌre-ˈecho *verb* [I, T] to be repeated many times; to repeat sth many times 反複回響；一再重複：*Their shouts re-echoed through the darkness.* 他們的喊聲迴盪在黑暗中。◇ *Her words re-echoed in his mind.* 她的話縈繞在他的腦海中。◇ **~ sth** *He has constantly re-echoed the main theme of his acceptance speech: 'We want to be proud again!'.* 他一再重申他接受提名時那篇演說的主題："我們要重新輝煌！"

reed /riːd/ *noun* **1** a tall plant like grass with a hollow STEM that grows in or near water 蘆葦：*reed beds* (= where they grow) 蘆葦蕩 ➲ VISUAL VOCAB pages V3, V11 **2** a small thin piece of CANE, metal or plastic in some musical instruments such as the OBOE or the CLARINET that moves very quickly when air is blown over it, producing a sound 簧舌，簧片（金屬或塑料製成，用於雙簧管、單簧管等吹奏樂器）➲ VISUAL VOCAB page V34

ˌre-ˈeducate *verb* **~ sb** to teach sb to think or behave in a new or different way 再教育；重新教育 ▶ **ˌre-eduˈcation** *noun* [U]

reedy /ˈriːdi/ *adj.* [usually before noun] **1** (of a voice or sound 嗓音或聲響) high and not very pleasant 尖利刺耳的 **2** full of reeds 蘆葦叢生的；長滿蘆葦的：*reedy river banks* 蘆葦叢生的河岸

reef /riːf/ *noun, verb*
■ *noun* **1** a long line of rocks or sand near the surface of the sea 礁；礁脈：*a coral reef* 珊瑚礁 ➲ VISUAL VOCAB page V5 **2** a part of a sail that can be tied or rolled up to make the sail smaller in a strong wind 縮帆部；帆的可收縮部
■ *verb* **~ sth** (*technical* 術語) to make a sail smaller by tying or rolling up part of it 收帆；捲起縮帆部；疊起縮帆部

reef·er /ˈriːfə(r)/ *noun* **1** (also **ˈreefer jacket**) a short thick jacket made of wool, usually dark blue, with two rows of buttons 雙排扣厚毛上衣（通常為深藍色）**2** (*old-fashioned, slang*) a cigarette containing MARIJUANA 大麻香煙

ˈreef knot (*especially BrE*) (*NAmE* usually **ˈsquare knot**) *noun* a type of double knot that will not come undone easily 平結，方結（不易解開）

reek /riːk/ *verb, noun*
■ *verb* **1** [I] **~ (of sth)** to smell very strongly of sth unpleasant 散發臭氣；發出難聞的氣味：*His breath reeked of tobacco.* 他滿嘴煙臭味。**2** [I] **~ (of sth)** (*disapproving*) to suggest very strongly that sth unpleasant or

R

suspicious is involved in a situation 明顯帶有，強烈地意味着（令人不快或起疑的特性）：*Her denials reeked of hypocrisy.* 她那樣否認顯然很虛偽。

■ **noun** [sing.] a strong unpleasant smell 惡臭；難聞的氣味 SYN **stench**

reel /riːl/ *noun, verb*

■ **noun 1** (*especially BrE*) (also **spool** especially in *NAmE*) a round object around which you wind such things as thread, wire or film; a reel together with the film, wire, thread, etc. that is wound around it 捲軸；捲盤；捲筒；一捲膠捲（或金屬絲、線等）：*a cotton reel* 棉線軸◇ *a reel on a fishing rod* 釣魚竿上的繞線輪◇ *reels of magnetic tape* 磁帶盤◇ *a new reel of film* 一捲新的膠捲◇ *The hero was killed in the final reel* (= in the final part of the film/movie). 主人公在電影的結尾部份被殺。➲ VISUAL VOCAB page V41 **2** a fast Scottish, Irish or American dance, usually for two or four couples; a piece of music for this dance 里爾舞（流行於蘇格蘭、愛爾蘭或美國的一種輕快舞蹈，通常由兩對或四對表演）；里爾舞曲

■ **verb 1** [I] **(+ adv./prep.)** to move in a very unsteady way, for example because you are drunk or have been hit 踉蹌；搖搖晃晃地挪動；蹣跚 SYN **stagger**：*I punched him on the chin, sending him reeling backwards.* 我一拳擊中他的下巴，打得他向後打了個趔趄。 **2** [I] **~ (at/from/with sth)** to feel very shocked or upset about sth 感到震驚；感覺心煩意亂：*I was still reeling from the shock.* 我嚇得依然暈頭轉向。 **3** [I] to seem to be spinning around and around 似乎在不停旋轉；彷彿天旋地轉：*When he opened his eyes, the room was reeling.* 他睜開眼睛時，房間似乎在不停地旋轉。

PHR V **ˌreel sth↔ˈin/ˈout** to wind sth on/off a reel 往捲軸上繞起；從捲軸上放開：*I slowly reeled the fish in.* 我慢慢地收捲魚線，將魚釣起。 **ˌreel sth↔ˈoff** to say or repeat sth quickly without having to stop or think about it 一口氣說出；滔滔不絕地講（或重複）：*She immediately reeled off several names.* 她立即一口氣說出了好幾個名字。

ˌre-eˈlect *verb* **~ sb (to sth)** to elect sb again 再次選舉；再度選上：**~ sb (to sth)** *She was re-elected to parliament.* 她再次當選為議員。◇ **~ sb (as) sth | ~ sb + noun** *The committee voted to re-elect him (as) chairman.* 委員會投票再次選舉他擔任主席。▸ **ˌre-eˈlection** *noun* [U]：(*BrE*) *to stand for re-election* 二度參選◇ (*NAmE*) *to run for re-election* 爭取再次當選

ˌre-eˈmerge *verb* [I] to appear somewhere again （在某處）又出現，再出現：*The cancer may re-emerge years later.* 癌症可能在多年之後復發。

ˌre-eˈnact *verb* **~ sth** to repeat the actions of a past event 重做；再次進行：*Members of the English Civil War Society will re-enact the battle.* 英國內戰協會的成員將再次展現那場戰爭。▸ **ˌre-eˈnactment** *noun*

ˌre-ˈenter *verb* [T, I] **~ (sth)** to return to a place or to an area of activity that you used to be in 再次進入；重返；重操（舊業）

ˌre-ˈentry *noun* [U] **~ (into sth) 1** the act of returning to a place or an area of activity that you used to be in 再次進入；重返；重操舊業：*She feared she would not be granted re-entry into Britain.* 她擔心不會獲准再次踏足英國。◇ *a re-entry programme for nurses* (= for nurses returning to work after a long time doing sth else) 讓護士重返崗位的方案 **2** the return of a SPACECRAFT into the earth's atmosphere （太空飛行器的）重返地球大氣層

ˌre-eˈvaluate AW *verb* **~ sth** to think about sth again, especially in order to form a new opinion about it 重新考慮；再評價；再評估 ▸ **ˌre-evaluˈation** AW *noun* [C, U]

reeve /riːv/ *noun* a law officer in England in the past （英格蘭舊時的）地方治安官

ˌre-eˈxamine *verb* **~ sth** to examine or think about sth again, especially because you may need to change your opinion 再次檢查；重新考慮 SYN **reassess**：*All the evidence needs to be re-examined.* 所有的證據都需要重新審核。▸ **ˌre-eˈxaminˑation** *noun* [U, sing.]

ref /ref/ *noun, verb* (*informal*)

■ **noun** = REFEREE *n.* (1)：*The game's not over till the ref blows the whistle.* 裁判吹響哨子，比賽才算結束。

■ **verb (-ff-) ~ sth** = REFEREE *v.* (1)：*The game was badly reffed.* 這場比賽的裁判糟透了。

ref. /ref/ *abbr.* reference (used especially in business as a way of identifying sth such as a document) 文件編號（尤用於商業文件分類）：*our ref.: 3498* 我方編號：3498

re·fec·tory /rɪˈfektri/ *noun* (*pl.* **-ies**) a large room in which meals are served, especially in a religious institution and in some schools and colleges in Britain （尤指英國教會團體和學校的）食堂，餐廳

refer 0‑w /rɪˈfɜː(r)/ *verb* (**-rr-**)

PHR V **reˈfer to sb/sth (as sth)** 0‑w to mention or speak about sb/sth 提到；談及；說起：*The victims were not referred to by name.* 沒有提到受害人的姓名。◇ *Her mother never referred to him again.* 她的母親再也沒有提起過他。◇ *You know who I'm referring to.* 你知道我指的是誰。◇ *She always referred to Ben as 'that nice man'.* 她總是稱本為"那個大好人"。◇ *I promised not to refer to the matter again.* 我答應過再也不提這事了。➲ SYNONYMS at MENTION **reˈfer to sb/sth 1** 0‑w to describe or be connected to sb/sth 描述；涉及；與…相關：*The star refers to items which are intended for the advanced learner.* 標有星號的項目是給高階學習者的。◇ *The term 'Arts' usually refers to humanities and social sciences.* * arts 一詞通常指人文和社會科學。◇ *This paragraph refers to the events of last year.* 這一段說的是去年發生的事。➲ LANGUAGE BANK at DEFINE **2** 0‑w to look at sth or ask a person for information 查閱；參考；徵詢 SYN **consult**：*You may refer to your notes if you want.* 如果需要，可以查閱筆記。◇ *to refer to a dictionary* 查詞典 **reˈfer sb/sth to sb/sth** to send sb/sth to sb/sth for help, advice or a decision 讓（某人）求助於…；把（某事）移交給…：*My doctor referred me to a specialist.* 我的醫生讓我去找一位專家診治。◇ *The case was referred to the Court of Appeal.* 這個案子被送交到上訴法院。◇ (*formal*) *May I refer you to my letter of 14 May?* 你查看一下我 5 月 14 日給你的信好嗎？

re·fer·able /rɪˈfɜːrəbl; ˈrefrəbl/ *adj.* **~ to sth** (*formal*) that can be related to sth else 可與…相關的：*These symptoms may be referable to virus infection rather than parasites.* 這些症狀也許是由病毒感染引起的，而與寄生蟲無關。

ref·er·ee /ˌrefəˈriː/ *noun, verb*

■ **noun 1** (also *informal* **ref**) the official who controls the game in some sports （某些體育比賽的）裁判，裁判員：*He was sent off for arguing with the referee.* 他因為和裁判發生爭執而被罰出場。➲ compare UMPIRE **2** (*BrE*) a person who gives information about your character and ability, usually in a letter, for example when you are applying for a job 介紹人；推薦人 **3** a person who is asked to settle a disagreement 仲裁員；調解人：*to act as a referee between the parties involved* 充當相關各方的調解人 **4** a person who reads and checks the quality of a technical article before it is published （專業性文章的）審閱人，鑒定專家

■ **verb 1** (also *informal* **ref**) [I, T] to act as the referee in a game 擔任裁判；裁判：*a refereeing decision* 裁判決定 ◇ **~ sth** *Who refereed the final?* 那場決賽誰是裁判？ **2** [T] **~ sth** to read and check the quality of a technical article before it is published 審閱，鑒定（專業性文章）

referee's assistant *noun* = ASSISTANT REFEREE

ref·er·ence 0‑w /ˈrefrəns/ *noun, verb*

■ **noun**

▸ **MENTIONING SB/STH** 提及 **1** 0‑w [C, U] **~ (to sb/sth)** a thing you say or write that mentions sb/sth else; the act of mentioning sb/sth 說到（或寫到）的事；提到；談及；涉及：*The book is full of references to growing up in India.* 這本書談到許多在印度怎樣長大成人的事。◇ *She made no reference to her illness but only to her future plans.* 她沒有提到她的病，只說了說她未來的計劃。◇ *the President's passing reference to* (= brief mention of) *the end of the war* 總統對戰爭的結束一語帶過

▸ **LOOKING FOR INFORMATION** 查詢信息 **2** 0‑w [U] the act of looking at sth for information 參考；查詢；查閱：*Keep the list of numbers near the phone for easy reference.*

把電話號碼表放在電話旁邊，方便查找。◇ *I wrote down the name of the hotel **for future reference*** (= because it might be useful in the future). 我記下了這家酒店的名字，以後也許用得着。◇ *The library contains many popular **works of reference*** (= reference books). 這家圖書館藏有許多常用的參考書。

▸ **ASKING FOR ADVICE** 徵求意見 **3** [U] **~ (to sb/sth)** (*formal*) the act of asking sb for help or advice（幫助或意見的）徵求，徵詢：*The emergency nurse can treat minor injuries without reference to a doctor.* 急救護士不必徵求醫生的意見就可處理輕傷。

▸ **NUMBER/WORD/SYMBOL** 數字；文字；符號 **4** 🔑 [C] (*abbr.* **ref.**) a number, word or symbol that shows where sth is on a map, or where you can find a piece of information（為方便查詢所用的）標記，標識，編號：*The map reference is Y4.* 地圖編號為 Y4。◇ *Please quote your **reference number** when making an enquiry.* 查詢時請報出參考編號。

▸ **FOR NEW JOB** 找工作 **5** 🔑 [C] a letter written by sb who knows you, giving information about your character and abilities, especially to a new employer 推薦信；介紹信：*We will **take up references** after the interview.* 我們在面試之後收推薦信。**6** [C] a person who agrees to write a reference, for you, for example when you are applying for a job 推薦人；介紹人 SYN **referee**：*My previous boss will act as a reference for me.* 我的前任上司將做我的推薦人。

▸ **IN BOOK** 書籍 **7** 🔑 [C] a note in a book that tells you where a particular piece of information comes from 參考書目：*There is a list of references at the end of each chapter.* 每一章的後面都有一組參考書目。➲ WRITING TUTOR page WT11 ➲ see also CROSS REFERENCE, FRAME OF REFERENCE, TERMS OF REFERENCE

IDM **in/with reference to** 🔑 (*formal*) used to say what you are talking or writing about（所述內容）關於：*With reference to your letter of July 22 ...* 關於你 7 月 22 日的來信⋯

■ **verb ~ sth** (*formal*) to refer to sth; to provide a book, etc. with references 查閱；參考；給（書等）附參考資料：*Each chapter is referenced, citing literature up to 2008.* 每一章都附有參考書目，引用文獻近至 2008 年。

ˈreference book *noun* a book that contains facts and information, that you look at when you need to find out sth particular 參考書；工具書

ˈreference library *noun* a library containing books that can be read in the library but cannot be borrowed 參考圖書館，工具書閱覽室（藏書僅供查閱，不外借）➲ compare LENDING LIBRARY

ˈreference point *noun* a standard by which sth can be judged or compared 參比點；參照標準

ref·er·en·dum /ˌrefəˈrendəm/ *noun* (*pl.* **ref·er·en·dums** or **ref·er·enda**) [C, U] **~ (on sth)** an occasion when all the people of a country can vote on an important issue 全民投票；全民公決：*Switzerland decided to **hold a referendum** on joining the EU.* 瑞士決定就加入歐盟問題舉行全民投票。◇ *The changes were approved by referendum.* 全民投票贊同這些變革。➲ COLLOCATIONS at VOTE ➲ note at ELECTION

re·fer·ral /rɪˈfɜːrəl/ *noun* [U, C] **~ (to sb/sth)** the act of sending sb who needs professional help to a person or place that can provide it 送交，轉送，轉介（到能提供專門幫助的人或地方那裏）：*illnesses requiring referral to hospitals* 需要送到醫院就診的疾病 ◇ *to make a referral* 送交

re·fill *verb, noun*

■ **verb** /ˌriːˈfɪl/ **~ sth (with sth)** to fill sth again 再裝滿；重新裝滿：*He refilled her glass.* 他又給她斟滿了一杯。▸ **re·fill·able** /ˌriːˈfɪləbl/ *adj.*：*a refillable gas cylinder* 可重新灌注的煤氣罐

■ **noun** /ˈriːfɪl/ **1** another drink of the same type 又一份同種飲料：*Would you like a refill?* 您要再來一杯嗎？ **2** an amount of sth, sold in a cheap container, that you use to fill up a more expensive container that is now empty 補充裝材料（用以補充產品容器內用完的物品）

re·fi·nance /ˌriːˈfaɪnæns/ *verb* [T, I] **~ (sth)** (*finance* 財) to borrow money in order to pay a debt 再籌資金，再融資（以償還債務）

re·fine AW /rɪˈfaɪn/ *verb* **1 ~ sth** to make a substance pure by taking other substances out of it 精煉；提純；去除雜質：*the process of refining oil/sugar* 煉油的／煉糖的工序 **2 ~ sth** to improve sth by making small changes to it 改進；改善；使精練

re·fined AW /rɪˈfaɪnd/ *adj.* **1** [usually before noun] (of a substance 物質) made pure by having other substances taken out of it 精煉的；提純的；精製的：*refined sugar* 精製糖 **2** (of a person 人) polite, well educated and able to judge the quality of things; having the sort of manners that are considered typical of a high social class 有禮貌的；優雅的；有教養的 SYN **cultured, genteel** OPP **unrefined**

re·fine·ment AW /rɪˈfaɪnmənt/ *noun* **1** [C] a small change to sth that improves it（精細的）改進，改善 SYN **enhancement**：*This particular model has a further refinement.* 這一款式又有了進一步的改進。**2** [C] **~ of sth** a thing that is an improvement on an earlier, similar thing 改良品；經過改進的東西：*The new plan is a refinement of the one before.* 新計劃比原計劃有改進。**3** [U] the process of improving sth or of making sth pure 精煉；提煉；提純：*the refinement of industrial techniques* 工業技術的進一步提高 ◇ *the refinement of uranium* 鈾的提煉 **4** [U] the quality of being polite and well educated and able to judge the quality of things; the state of having the sort of manners that are considered typical of a high social class 優雅；禮貌；有教養 SYN **gentility**：*a person of considerable refinement* 很有教養的人 ◇ *an atmosphere of refinement* 優雅的氣氛

re·finer /rɪˈfaɪnə(r)/ *noun* a person or company that refines substances such as sugar or oil 從事精煉加工的人（或公司）；煉製者：*oil refiners* 煉油公司

re·finery /rɪˈfaɪnəri/ *noun* (*pl.* **-ies**) a factory where a substance such as oil is REFINED (= made pure) 精煉廠；提煉廠；精製廠

refit /ˌriːˈfɪt/ *verb* (**-tt-**) **~ sth** to repair or fit new parts, equipment, etc. to sth 整修；給⋯安裝新配件；改裝：*He spent £70 000 refitting his yacht.* 他花了 7 萬英鎊整修他的遊艇。▸ **refit** /ˈriːfɪt/ *noun*：*The ship has undergone a complete refit.* 這條船已經全面整修了。

re·flate /ˌriːˈfleɪt/ *verb* [T, I] **~ (sth)** (*economics* 經) to increase the amount of money that is used in a country, usually in order to increase the demand for goods 通貨再膨脹，通貨復脹（增加貨幣供應以刺激對商品等的需求）➲ compare DEFLATE (3), INFLATE (3) ▸ **re·fla·tion** /ˌriːˈfleɪʃn/ *noun* [U] **re·fla·tion·ary** /ˌriːˈfleɪʃnri; *NAmE* -neri/ *adj.*：*reflationary policies* 通貨復脹政策

re·flect 🔑 /rɪˈflekt/ *verb*

1 🔑 [T, usually passive] **~ sb/sth (in sth)** to show the image of sb/sth on the surface of sth such as a mirror, water or glass 反映；映出（影像）：*His face was reflected in the mirror.* 他的臉映照在鏡子裏。◇ *She could see herself reflected in his eyes.* 她在他的眼中看到了自己的樣子。**2** 🔑 [T] **~ sth** to throw back light, heat, sound, etc. from a surface 反射（聲、光、熱等）：*The windows reflected the bright afternoon sunlight.* 窗戶反射着午後明媚的陽光。◇ *When the sun's rays hit the earth, a lot of the heat is reflected back into space.* 太陽光線照射到地球時，大量的熱力被反射回太空。**3** 🔑 [T] **~ sth** to show or be a sign of the nature of sth or of sb's attitude or feeling 顯示，表明，表達（事物的自然屬性或人們的態度、情感等）：*Our newspaper aims to reflect the views of the local community.* 本報的宗旨是表達當地人民的心聲。**4** 🔑 [I, T] to think carefully and deeply about sth 認真思考；沉思：*Before I decide, I need time to reflect.* 在作出決定以前，我需要時間認真考慮考慮。◇ **~ on/upon sth** *She was left to reflect on the implications of her decision.* 由她來考慮她這個決定會有什麼後果。◇ **~ that ...** *On the way home he reflected that the interview had gone well.* 回家的路上，他琢磨着這次面試非常順利。◇ **~ how, what, etc. ...** *She reflected how different it could have been.* 她琢磨着那件事本可以有多大的不同。◇ **+ speech** *'It could all have been so different,' she reflected.* "那件事本可以如此完全不同的。" 她思索着。

R

IDM **reflect well, badly, etc. on sb/sth** to make sb/sth appear to be good, bad, etc. to other people 使給人以好的（或壞的等）印象：*This incident reflects badly on everyone involved.* 這一事件給所有相關人士都造成了惡劣影響。

re·flect·ance /rɪˈflektəns/ *noun* [U, C] (*physics* 物) a measure of how much light is reflected off a surface, considered as a part of the total light that shines onto it（光的）反射比

re,flected 'glory *noun* [U] (*disapproving*) admiration or praise that is given to sb, not because of sth that they have done, but because of sth that sb connected with them has done 仰仗別人而得的榮耀：*She basked in the reflected glory of her daughter's success.* 她盡情地享受她女兒的成功帶給她的榮耀。

re·flec·tion (*BrE* also *old-fashioned* **re·flex·ion**) /rɪˈflekʃn/ *noun* **1** [C] an image in a mirror, on a shiny surface, on water, etc. 映像；映照出的影像：*He admired his reflection in the mirror.* 他欣賞着自己在鏡中的影像。 **2** [U] the action or process of sending back light, heat, sound, etc. from a surface（聲、光、熱等的）反射 **3** [C] a sign that shows the state or nature of sth 反映；顯示；表達：*Your clothes are often a reflection of your personality.* 穿着常常反映出一個人的個性。◇ *The increase in crime is a sad* ***reflection on*** (= shows sth bad about) *our society today.* 犯罪上升遺憾地反映了當今社會不太好的一面。 **4** [U] careful thought about sth, sometimes over a long period of time 沉思；深思；審慎的思考：*She decided* ***on reflection*** *to accept his offer after all.* 經過審慎的思考，她還是決定接受他的提議。◇ *A week off would give him time for reflection.* 歇上一週會使他有時間考慮考慮。 **5** [C, usually pl.] your written or spoken thoughts about a particular subject or topic（關於某課題的）思考，回憶：*a book of her reflections on childhood* 一本關於她童年生活的回憶錄 **6** [C] an account or a description of sth 記錄；描述：*The article is an accurate reflection of events that day.* 這篇文章準確地記錄了那天發生的事。 **IDM** see MATURE *adj.*

re·flect·ive /rɪˈflektɪv/ *adj.* **1** (*formal*) thinking deeply about things 沉思的；深思的 **SYN** **thoughtful**：*a quiet and reflective man* 文靜而愛沉思的男子 **2 reflective** surfaces send back light or heat（指物體表面）反射熱的，反光的：*reflective car number plates* 反光的汽車牌照 ◇ *On dark nights children should wear reflective clothing.* 在漆黑的夜晚，兒童應該穿反光的衣服。 **3 ~ of sth** typical of a particular situation or thing; showing the state or nature of sth 典型的；代表性的；體現狀態（或本質）的：*His abilities are not reflective of the team as a whole.* 他的能力並不代表整隊的水平。◇ *Everything you do or say is reflective of your personality.* 你的一言一行都體現你的個性。 ▸ **re·flect·ive·ly** *adv.*：*She sipped her wine reflectively.* 她一邊品酒，一邊沉思。

re·flect·ivity /ˌriːflekˈtɪvəti; rɪˌflek-/ *noun* [U] (*physics* 物) the degree to which a material reflects light or RADIATION（材料對光或輻射的）反射率

re·flect·or /rɪˈflektə(r)/ *noun* **1** a surface that reflects light 反光面 **2** a small piece of special glass or plastic that is put on a bicycle, or on clothing, so that it can be seen at night when light shines on it（夜間光線照射後能反光的）反光玻璃（或塑料），反光體 ➲ VISUAL VOCAB page V51

re·flex /ˈriːfleks/ *noun* an action or a movement of your body that happens naturally in response to sth and that you cannot control; sth that you do without thinking 反射動作；本能反應；反射作用：*The doctor tested her reflexes.* 醫生檢測了她的反射動作。◇ *to have* ***quick/slow reflexes*** 反射動作快／慢 ◇ *a* ***reflex response/reaction*** 反射性反應 ◇ *Only the goalkeeper's reflexes* (= his ability to react quickly) *stopped the ball from going in.* 只是因為守門員反應迅速，球才沒有進。◇ *Almost as a* ***reflex action****, I grab my pen as the phone rings.* 幾乎是一種本能反應，電話鈴一響，我就抓起筆。

,reflex 'angle *noun* an angle of more than 180° 優角（大於 180 度的角）➲ VISUAL VOCAB page V71 ➲ compare ACUTE ANGLE, OBTUSE ANGLE, RIGHT ANGLE

re·flex·ion (*BrE*) = REFLECTION

re·flex·ive /rɪˈfleksɪv/ *adj.* a **reflexive** word or form of a word shows that the action of the verb affects the person who performs the action（詞或詞形）反身的：*In 'He cut himself', 'cut' is a reflexive verb and 'himself' is a reflexive pronoun.* 在 He cut himself 一句中，cut 是反身動詞，himself 是反身代詞。

re·flex·ology /ˌriːflekˈsɒlədʒi; *NAmE* ˌriːflekˈsɑːl-/ *noun* [U] a type of alternative treatment in which sb's feet are rubbed in a particular way in order to heal other parts of their body or to make them feel mentally relaxed 反射療法（通過腳部按摩治療身體其他部位疾病或鬆弛神經）▸ **re·flex·olo·gist** *noun*

re·float /ˌriːˈfləʊt; *NAmE* -ˈfloʊt/ *verb* **~ sth** to make a boat or ship float again, for example after it has become stuck on the bottom in shallow water 使（擱淺船隻）再浮起

re·flow /ˈriːfləʊ; *NAmE* -floʊ/ *noun* [U] (*technical* 術語) **1** a method of joining metals together by heating and melting SOLDER (= a soft metal mixture) 軟熔焊接 **2** the fact of changing text on a computer screen so that it takes more or less space 文檔重整，頁面重排（調整文本在計算機屏幕上的顯示密度）

re·focus **AW** /ˌriːˈfəʊkəs; *NAmE* -ˈfoʊ-/ *verb* **1** [I, T] to give attention, effort, etc. to sth new or different 將（注意力、精力等）轉向；調整…的重點：**~ (on/upon sb/sth)** *Policy must refocus on people instead of places.* 政策重心必須改變，針對人而非地方。◇ **~ sth (on/upon sb/sth)** *We need to refocus attention on the real issues facing this country.* 我們需要將注意力轉向國家所面臨的實際問題。 **2** [I, T] (of your eyes, a camera, etc. 眼睛、相機等) to adapt or be adjusted again so that things can be seen clearly; to adjust sth again so that you can see things clearly（使）重新聚焦；調整…的焦距

re·for·est·ation /ˌriːfɒrɪˈsteɪʃn; *NAmE* -fɔːr-; -fɑːr-/ (*BrE* also **re·affor·est·ation**) *noun* [U] (*technical* 術語) the act of planting new trees in an area where there used to be a forest 重新造林 ➲ VISUAL VOCAB page V8 ➲ compare DEFORESTATION

re·form 0━ /rɪˈfɔːm; *NAmE* rɪˈfɔːrm/ *verb, noun*

■ *verb* **1** 0━ [T] **~ sth** to improve a system, an organization, a law, etc. by making changes to it 改革；改進；改良：*proposals to reform the social security system* 改革社會保險體制的建議 ◇ *The law needs to be reformed.* 法律需要進行改革。 **2** 0━ [I, T] to improve your behaviour; to make sb do this（使）改正，改造（行為）；（使）悔改：*He has promised to reform.* 他許諾要改過自新。◇ **~ sb** *She thought she could reform him.* 她覺得她可以使他洗心革面。 ▸ **re·formed** *adj.*：*a reformed character* 改過自新的人

■ *noun* 0━ [U, C] change that is made to a social system, an organization, etc. in order to improve or correct it 改革；變革；改良；改善：*a government committed to reform* 致力於改革的政府 ◇ ***economic/electoral/constitutional, etc. reform*** 經濟、選舉、憲法等改革 ◇ *the reform of the educational system* 教育體制的改革 ◇ *reforms in education* 教育改革 ◇ ***far-reaching/major/sweeping reforms*** 意義深遠的／重大的／徹底的變革

,re-'form *verb* [I, T] to form again or form sth again, especially into a different group or pattern 再次形成；重新組成：*The band is re-forming after 23 years.* * 23 年後，這個樂隊又在重新組建。◇ **~ sth** *The party has recently been re-formed.* 這個政黨最近進行了重新組合。

re·format /ˌriːˈfɔːmæt; *NAmE* -ˈfɔːr-/ *verb* (-tt-) **~ sth** (*computing* 計) to give a new FORMAT to a computer disk 使重新格式化

ref·or·ma·tion /ˌrefəˈmeɪʃn; *NAmE* -fərˈm-/ *noun* **1** [U] (*formal*) the act of improving or changing sb/sth 改革；改進；變革 **2 the Reformation** [sing.] new ideas in religion in 16th century Europe that led to attempts to reform the Roman Catholic Church and to the forming of the Protestant Churches; the period of time when these changes were taking place 宗教改革（歐洲 16 世紀改革羅馬天主教從而導致新教的產生）；宗教改革時期

re·forma·tory /rɪˈfɔːmətri; *NAmE* rɪˈfɔːrmətɔːri/ *noun* (*pl.* -ies) (also **re'form school**) (*NAmE*) (*old-fashioned* in

R

BrE) a type of school that young criminals are sent to instead of prison 少年犯管教所；青少年教養院

Re'formed 'Church *noun* [sing.] a church that has accepted the principles of the REFORMATION, especially a Calvinist one（基督教）新教教會歸正會，歸正宗（尤指加爾文教派）

re·form·er /rɪ'fɔːmə(r); *NAmE* -'fɔːrm-/ *noun* a person who works to achieve political or social change 改革者；改良者；改造者

re·form·ist /rɪ'fɔːmɪst; *NAmE* -'fɔːrm-/ *adj.* wanting or trying to change political or social situations 主張改革的；改革派的；改良主義的 ▸ **re·form·ist** *noun*

re·for·mu·late AW /ˌriː'fɔːmjuleɪt; *NAmE* -'fɔːrm-/ *verb* **1 ~ sth** to create or prepare sth again 再制訂；再規劃；再準備：*It is never too late to reformulate your goals.* 重訂目標決不會為時過晚。 **2 ~ sth** to say or express sth in a different way 換種方式說（或表達）：*Let me try to reformulate the problem.* 讓我換個角度談談這個問題吧。 ▸ **re·for·mu·la·tion** AW /ˌriːˌfɔːmju'leɪʃn; *NAmE* -ˌfɔːrm-/ *noun* [U, C]

re·fract /rɪ'frækt/ *verb* **~ sth** (*physics* 物) (of water, air, glass, etc. 水、空氣、玻璃等) to make light change direction when it goes through at an angle 使（光線）折射；使產生折射：*Light is refracted when passed through a prism.* 光通過稜鏡時產生折射。 ▸ **re·frac·tion** /rɪ'frækʃn/ *noun* [U]

re·fract·ive /rɪ'fræktɪv/ *adj.* (*physics* 物) causing, caused by or relating to refraction（由）折射引起的；折射的

reˌfractive 'index *noun* (*physics* 物) a measurement of how much an object or a substance refracts light 折射率

re·fract·om·eter /ˌrɪfræk'tɒmɪtə(r); *NAmE* -'tɑːm-/ *noun* (*physics* 物) an instrument for measuring a refractive index 折射計

re·fract·or /rɪ'fræktə(r)/ *noun* (*physics* 物) something such as a LENS which REFRACTS light (= causes it to change direction) 折射器；折射透鏡

re·frac·tory /rɪ'fræktəri/ *adj.* **1** (*formal*) (of a person 人) difficult to control; behaving badly 難以駕馭的；行為乖戾的 **2** (*medical* 醫) (of a disease or medical condition 疾病) difficult to treat or cure 難以診治的；難以治癒的

re·frain /rɪ'freɪn/ *verb, noun*

■ *verb* [I] (*formal*) to stop yourself from doing sth, especially sth that you want to do 克制；節制；避免 SYN **desist from**：**~ (from sth)** *Please refrain from smoking.* 請勿吸煙。◇ **~ (from doing sth)** *He has refrained from criticizing the government in public.* 他克制住了自己，沒有在公開場合批評政府。

■ *noun* **1** a comment or complaint that is often repeated 經常重複的評價（或抱怨）：*Complaints about poor food in schools have become a familiar refrain.* 抱怨學校飯菜差已是耳熟能詳的老調了。 **2** the part of a song or a poem that is repeated after each VERSE 副歌；疊歌；迭句 SYN **chorus**

re·fresh /rɪ'freʃ/ *verb* **1** [T] **~ sb/yourself** to make sb feel less tired or less hot 使恢復精力；使涼爽：*The long sleep had refreshed her.* 一場酣睡使她重又精力充沛。◇ *He refreshed himself with a cool shower.* 他沖了個涼水澡涼快涼快。 **2** [T] **~ sth** (*informal, especially NAmE*) to fill sb's glass or cup again 重新斟滿：*Let me refresh your glass.* 我給你再斟一杯吧。 **3** [T] **~ your/sb's memory** to remind yourself/sb of sth, especially with the help of sth that can be seen or heard 提醒；提示；使想起 SYN **jog**：*He had to refresh his memory by looking at his notes.* 他不得不靠看筆記來提醒自己。 **4** [T, I] **~ (sth)** (*computing* 計) to get the most recent information, for example on an Internet page, by clicking on a button on the screen 刷新；更新；重新整理：*Click here to refresh this document.* 點擊此處以刷新文件。◇ *The page refreshes automatically.* 頁面會自動更新。

re'fresher course (also **re·fresh·er** especially in *NAmE*) *noun* a short period of training to improve your skills or to teach you about new ideas and developments in your job 進修課程

re·fresh·ing /rɪ'freʃɪŋ/ *adj.* **1** pleasantly new or different 令人耳目一新的；別具一格的：*It made a* ***refreshing change*** *to be taken seriously for once.* 總算有一次受到認真對待，這變化真是令人耳目一新。 **2** making you feel less tired or hot 使人精力充沛的；使人涼爽的：*a* ***refreshing drink/shower*** 提神的飲料／淋浴 ▸ **re·fresh·ing·ly** *adv.*：*refreshingly different* 煥然一新 ◇ *The house was refreshingly cool inside.* 屋內清涼宜人。

re·fresh·ment /rɪ'freʃmənt/ *noun* **1 refreshments** [pl.] drinks and small amounts of food that are provided or sold to people in a public place or at a public event（在公共活動場所供應或銷售的）飲料，小食：*Light refreshments will be served during the break.* 中間休息時有點心供應。 **2** [U] (*formal*) food and drink 食物和飲料：*In York we had a short stop for refreshment.* 在約克，我們稍作停留，吃了點東西。◇ *Can we offer you some refreshment?* 您要吃點什麼嗎？◇ *a* ***refreshment room/kiosk/tent*** 小吃部；飲食亭；活動小吃攤 ◇ (*humorous*) ***liquid refreshment*** (= alcoholic drink) 酒 **3** [U] (*formal*) the fact of making sb feel stronger or less tired or hot 恢復活力；煥發精神：*a place to rest and find refreshment for mind and body* 休息和恢復身心的場所

refried beans /ˌriːfraɪd 'biːnz/ *noun* [pl.] BEANS that have been boiled and fried in advance and are heated again when needed, used especially in Mexican cooking（墨西哥）煎豆泥，炒豆

re·friger·ate /rɪ'frɪdʒəreɪt/ *verb* **~ sth** (*formal*) to make food, etc. cold in order to keep it fresh or preserve it 使冷卻；使變冷；冷藏：*Once opened, this product should be kept refrigerated.* 本產品開封後應冷藏。◇ *a* ***refrigerated lorry/truck*** 冷藏卡車 ▸ **re·friger·ation** /rɪˌfrɪdʒə'reɪʃn/ *noun* [U]：*Keep all meat products under refrigeration.* 把所有的肉製品都冷藏起來。

re·friger·ator 0‑ /rɪ'frɪdʒəreɪtə(r)/ *noun* (*formal* or *NAmE*) = FRIDGE：*This dessert can be served straight from the refrigerator.* 這甜點從冰箱裏拿出後即可食用。 ➲ VISUAL VOCAB page V25

re·fuel /ˌriː'fjuːəl/ *verb* (**-ll-**, *US* **-l-**) [T, I] **~ (sth)** to fill sth, especially a plane, with fuel in order to continue a journey; to be filled with fuel（尤指給飛機）補充燃料，加燃料；加油：*to refuel a plane* 給飛機加油 ◇ *The planes needed to refuel before the next mission.* 這些飛機需要添加燃料才能再次飛行。◇ *a refuelling stop* 加油停留

ref·uge /'refjuːdʒ/ *noun* **1** [U] shelter or protection from danger, trouble, etc. 庇護；避難：*A further 300 people have* ***taken refuge*** *in the US embassy.* 又有 300 人在美國大使館避難。◇ **~ (from sb/sth)** *They were forced to* ***seek refuge*** *from the fighting.* 他們被迫尋求庇護，以躲避戰爭。◇ *a place of refuge* 避難所 ◇ *As the situation at home got worse she increasingly took refuge in her work.* 隨着家庭情況的惡化，她越來越在工作中尋求慰藉。 **2** [C] **~ (from sb/sth)** a place, person or thing that provides shelter or protection for sb/sth 避難所；庇護者；慰藉：*He regarded the room as a refuge from the outside world.* 他把這個屋子當作是逃避外界的避難所。◇ *a wetland refuge for birds* 濕地鳥類保護區 **3** [C] a building that provides a temporary home for people in need of shelter or protection from sb/sth 收容所；避難所：*a women's refuge* 婦女收容所 ◇ *a refuge for the homeless* 無家可歸者的收容所 **4** (*BrE*) = TRAFFIC ISLAND

refu·gee /ˌrefju'dʒiː/ *noun* a person who has been forced to leave their country or home, because there is a war or for political, religious or social reasons 避難者；逃亡者；難民：*a steady flow of refugees from the war zone* 從交戰地區不斷湧出的難民 ◇ ***political/economic refugees*** 政治避難者；由於經濟危機而造成的難民 ◇ *a* ***refugee camp*** 難民營 ➲ COLLOCATIONS at RACE, WAR

re·ful·gent /rɪ'fʌldʒənt/ *adj.* (*formal*) very bright 十分明亮的；輝耀的

re·fund *noun, verb*

■ *noun* /'riːfʌnd/ a sum of money that is paid back to you, especially because you paid too much or because you returned goods to a shop/store 退款；返還款；償還金額：*a tax refund* 稅金退款 ◇ *to* ***claim/demand/receive a refund*** 要求／接受退款 ◇ *If there is a delay of 12 hours*

R

or more, you will receive a **full refund** of the price of your trip. 如果耽擱達到或超過 12 小時，你會得到旅費全額退款。➲ COLLOCATIONS at SHOPPING

■ *verb* /rɪˈfʌnd/ to give sb their money back, especially because they have paid too much or because they are not satisfied with sth they bought 退還；退（款）；償付 SYN **reimburse**：**～ sth** *Tickets cannot be exchanged or money refunded.* 門票不可退換。◇ **～ sth to sb** *We will refund your money to you in full if you are not entirely satisfied.* 如果你並不感到完全滿意，我們會退還全部金額。◇ **～ sb sth** *We will refund you your money in full.* 我們會退還你所有的錢。▸ **re·fund·able** *adj.*： *a refundable deposit* 可退還的保證金 ◇ *Tickets are not refundable.* 不能退票。

re·fur·bish /ˌriːˈfɜːbɪʃ; *NAmE* -ˈfɜːrb-/ *verb* **～ sth** to clean and decorate a room, building, etc. in order to make it more attractive, more useful, etc. 再裝修；清理裝修 ➲ COLLOCATIONS at DECORATE ▸ **re·fur·bish·ment** *noun* [U, C]： *The hotel is closed for refurbishment.* 酒店停業整修。

re·fusal 🔑 /rɪˈfjuːzl/ *noun* [U, C] an act of saying or showing that you will not do, give or accept sth 拒絕；回絕：**～ (of sth)** *the refusal of a request/an invitation/an offer* 拒絕請求／邀請／建議 ◇ *a* ***blunt/flat/curt refusal*** 率直的／斷然的／粗率的拒絕 ◇ **～ to do sth** *His refusal to discuss the matter is very annoying.* 他拒絕商量這件事，令人很惱火。➲ see also FIRST REFUSAL

re·fuse¹ 🔑 /rɪˈfjuːz/ *verb* **1** 🔑 [I, T] to say that you will not do sth that sb has asked you to do 拒絕；回絕： *Go on, ask her; she can hardly refuse.* 去吧，去求她，她不大會拒絕。◇ **～ to do sth** *He* ***flatly refused*** *to discuss the matter.* 他斷然拒絕商討這件事。◇ *She refused to accept that there was a problem.* 她拒不承認有問題存在。 **2** 🔑 [T] **～ sth** to say that you do not want sth that has been offered to you 推卻；回絕 SYN **turn down**： *I politely refused their invitation.* 我禮貌地回絕了他們的邀請。◇ *The job offer was simply too good to refuse.* 這個工作機會太好了，簡直無法推掉。 **3** 🔑 [T] to say that you will not allow sth; to say that you will not give or allow sb sth that they want or need 不准許；拒絕給（所需之物） SYN **deny**：**～ sth** *The bank refused his demand for a full refund.* 銀行拒絕了他全額退款的要求。◇ *The authorities refused permission for the new housing development.* 當局不允許新住宅開發。◇ **～ sb sth** *They refused him a visa.* 他們拒絕給他簽證。◇ *She would never refuse her kids anything.* 她對孩子百依百順。

R

re·fuse² /ˈrefjuːs/ *noun* [U] (*formal*) waste material that has been thrown away 廢棄物；垃圾 SYN **rubbish/garbage**： ***domestic/household refuse*** 家裏的／生活垃圾 ◇ *the city refuse dump* 城市垃圾場 ◇ ***refuse collection/disposal*** 垃圾收集／處理 ➲ note at RUBBISH

ˈrefuse collector (*BrE*) (*NAmE* **ˈgarbage collector**) *noun* (*formal*) = DUSTMAN

re·fuse·nik /rɪˈfjuːznɪk/ *noun* a person who refuses to obey an order or law as a protest 拒絕服從指令（或法規）的人；反抗者；抗議者

re·fute /rɪˈfjuːt/ *verb* (*formal*) **1 ～ sth** to prove that sth is wrong 駁斥；批駁 SYN **rebut**：*to* ***refute an argument/a theory, etc.*** 駁斥一個論點、理論等 **2 ～ sth** to say that sth is not true or fair 反駁；否認 SYN **deny**：*She refutes any suggestion that she behaved unprofessionally.* 誰要是表示她不在行，她都予以反駁。▸ **re·fut·able** /-əbl/ *adj.* **refu·ta·tion** /ˌrefjuˈteɪʃn/ *noun* [C, U]： *a refutation of previously held views* 對過去所堅持的觀點的駁斥

reg /redʒ/ *abbr.* (*BrE, informal*) REGISTRATION： *a V reg car* (= a car with 'V' in its REGISTRATION NUMBER, showing the year that it was registered) 汽車牌照號碼含 V 的汽車

re·gain /rɪˈɡeɪn/ *verb* **1 ～ sth** to get back sth you no longer have, especially an ability or a quality 重新獲得，恢復（能力或品質等）： *I struggled to regain some dignity.* 我努力恢復自己的一點兒尊嚴。◇ *The party has regained control of the region.* 這一政黨重新獲得了這個地區的控制權。◇ *She paused on the edge, trying to* ***regain her balance.*** 她在邊緣上暫停下來，努力恢復平衡。◇ *He did not* ***regain consciousness*** (= wake up after being unconscious) *for several days.* 他好幾天都沒有恢復知覺。 **2 ～ sth** (*literary*) to get back to a place that you have left 回到（原位）；返回： *They finally managed to regain the beach.* 他們最後終於回到了海灘。

regal /ˈriːɡl/ *adj.* typical of a king or queen, and therefore impressive 帝王的；王室的；豪華的： *regal power* 王權 ◇ *the regal splendour of the palace* 帝王宮殿之豪華氣派 ◇ *She dismissed him with a regal gesture.* 她以尊貴的動作示意讓他離開。➲ compare ROYAL *adj.* (1) ▸ **re·gal·ly** /-ɡəli/ *adv.*

re·gale /rɪˈɡeɪl/ *verb*

PHR V **reˈgale sb with sth** to amuse or entertain sb with stories, jokes, etc.（通過講故事或說笑話等）愉悅，使高興： *He regaled us with tales of his days as a jazz pianist.* 他給我們講述他當爵士樂鋼琴師時的事，逗我們開心。

re·galia /rɪˈɡeɪliə/ *noun* [U] the special clothes that are worn or objects that are carried at official ceremonies（正式場合上的）特別服飾，特別物品

re·gard 🔑 /rɪˈɡɑːd; *NAmE* rɪˈɡɑːrd/ *verb, noun*

■ *verb* **1** 🔑 to think about sb/sth in a particular way 將…認為；把…視為；看待：**～ sb/sth (+ adv./prep.)** *Her work is very highly regarded.* 她的工作受到高度評價。◇ **～ sb/sth/yourself as sth** *Capital punishment was regarded as inhuman and immoral.* 死刑過去被認為是非人道且不道德的。◇ *He regards himself as a patriot.* 他自認為是個愛國者。◇ *She is* ***widely regarded*** *as the current leader's natural successor.* 人們普遍認為她是現任領導的當然繼任者。 **2** 🔑 **～ sb/sth (+ adv./prep.)** (*formal*) to look at sb/sth, especially in a particular way（尤指以某種方式）注視，凝視 SYN **contemplate**： *He regarded us suspiciously.* 他以懷疑的眼光看着我們。

IDM **as regards sb/sth** 🔑 (*formal*) concerning or in connection with sb/sth 關於；至於： *I have little information as regards her fitness for the post.* 至於說她是否適合這個職位，我無可奉告。◇ *As regards the first point in your letter …* 關於你信中所提到的第一點…

■ *noun* **1** 🔑 [U] (*formal*) attention to or thought and care for sb/sth 注意；關注；關心：**～ for sb/sth** *to do sth* ***with scant/little/no regard for sb/sth*** 做事不怎麼／幾乎不／根本不顧及某人／某事物 ◇ *to* ***have/pay/show little regard*** *for other people's property* 不大愛惜別人的財物 ◇ **～ to sb/sth** *He was driving* ***without regard to*** *speed limits.* 他開着車，根本不理會速度限制。◇ *Social services should* ***pay proper regard*** *to the needs of inner-city areas.* 社會服務機構應該對市中心貧民區的需要給予應有的關注。 **2** 🔑 [U] (*formal*) respect or admiration for sb 尊重；尊敬；敬佩： *He* ***held her in high regard*** (= had a good opinion of her). 他對她非常敬重。◇ **～ for sb/sth** *I had great regard for his abilities.* 我非常敬佩他的能力。 **3 regards** [pl.] used to send good wishes to sb at the end of a letter, or when asking sb to give your good wishes to another person who is not present（用於信函結尾或轉達問候）致意，問候： *With kind regards, Yours …* 謹此致意，…敬上 ◇ *Give your brother my regards when you see him.* 看到你哥哥時，代我向他問好。

IDM **have reˈgard to sth** (*law* 律) to remember and think carefully about sth 記住；記起；仔細考慮： *It is always necessary to have regard to the terms of the contract.* 記住合同條款總是必要的。 **in this/that reˈgard** (*formal*) concerning what has just been mentioned 在這方面；在這一點上： *I have nothing further to say in this regard.* 在這方面，我沒什麼要說的了。 **in/with regard to sb/sth** (*formal*) concerning sb/sth 關於；至於： *a country's laws in regard to human rights* 一個國家關於人權的法律 ◇ *The company's position with regard to overtime is made clear in their contracts.* 公司關於加班的立場在合同中有明確說明。➲ more at AS *conj.*

re·gard·ing 🔑 /rɪˈɡɑːdɪŋ; *NAmE* -ˈɡɑːrd-/ *prep.* concerning sb/sth; about sb/sth 關於；至於： *She has said nothing regarding your request.* 關於你的要求，她什麼也沒說。◇ *Call me if you have any problems regarding* *your work.* 你如果還有什麼工作方面的問題就給我打電話。

re·gard·less /rɪˈɡɑːdləs; *NAmE* -ˈɡɑːrd-/ *adv.* paying no attention, even if the situation is bad or there are difficulties 不顧；不加理會：*The weather was terrible but we **carried on regardless**.* 天氣非常惡劣，但我們並不理會，照常進行。

reˈgardless of *prep.* paying no attention to sth/sb; treating sth/sb as not being important 不管；不顧；不理會：*The club welcomes all new members regardless of age.* 俱樂部對所有新成員不分年齡一律歡迎。◇ *He went ahead and did it, regardless of the consequences.* 他說幹就幹了，沒有考慮後果。◇ *The amount will be paid to everyone regardless of whether they have children or not.* 不管有沒有孩子，每個人都會得到相同的金額。

re·gatta /rɪˈɡætə/ *noun* a sporting event in which races between ROWING BOATS or SAILING BOATS are held 賽艇會；划船比賽

Re·gency /ˈriːdʒənsi/ *adj.* [usually before noun] of or in the style of the period 1811–20 in Britain, when George, Prince of Wales, was REGENT (= ruled the country in place of the king, his father) 攝政時期的，攝政時期的風格的（英國 1811–1820 年間，威爾士親王喬治任攝政王，代替父親管理國家）：*Regency architecture* 攝政時期風格的建築

re·gency /ˈriːdʒənsi/ *noun* (*pl.* -ies) a period of government by a REGENT (= a person who rules a country in place of the king or queen) 攝政期；攝政

re·gen·er·ate /rɪˈdʒenəreɪt/ *verb* **1** [T] **~ sth** to make an area, institution, etc. develop and grow strong again 使振興；使復興；發展壯大：*The money will be used to regenerate the commercial heart of the town.* 這筆錢將用來發展壯大市鎮的商業中心。 **2** [I, T] (*biology* 生) to grow again; to make sth grow again 再生；使再生：*Once destroyed, brain cells do not regenerate.* 腦細胞一旦遭到破壞，就不能再生。◇ **~ sth/itself** *If the woodland is left alone, it will regenerate itself in a few years.* 如果林地不受干擾，幾年後就會再生。 ▸ **re·gen·er·ation** /rɪˌdʒenəˈreɪʃn/ *noun* [U]：*economic regeneration* 經濟復興 ◇ *the regeneration of cells in the body* 身體細胞的再生 **re·gen·era·tive** /rɪˈdʒenərətɪv/ *adj.*：*the regenerative powers of nature* 大自然的再生力

re·gent /ˈriːdʒənt/ (also **Regent**) *noun* a person who rules a country because the king or queen is too young, old, ill/sick, etc. 攝政者；攝政王：*to act as regent* 擔任攝政王 ▸ **re·gent** (also **Regent**) *adj.* [after noun]：*the Prince Regent* 攝政王

reg·gae /ˈreɡeɪ/ *noun* [U] a type of popular music with strong rhythms, developed in Jamaica in the 1960s 雷蓋，雷鬼（20 世紀 60 年代於牙買加興起的一種節奏強勁的流行音樂）

reggo = REGO

regi·cide /ˈredʒɪsaɪd/ *noun* [U, C] (*formal*) the crime of killing a king or queen; a person who is guilty of this crime 弒君罪；弒君者

re·gime AW /reɪˈʒiːm/ *noun* **1** a method or system of government, especially one that has not been elected in a fair way（尤指未通過公正選舉的）統治方式，統治制度，政權，政體：*a **fascist/totalitarian/military, etc. regime*** 法西斯、極權主義、軍事等政權 ◇ *an **oppressive/brutal regime*** 壓迫民眾的 / 殘暴的政權 ➲ COLLOCATIONS at POLITICS **2** a method or system of organizing or managing sth 組織方法；管理體制：*Our tax regime is one of the most favourable in Europe.* 我們的稅收管理體制是歐洲最受歡迎的稅收體制之一。 **3** = REGIMEN：*a dietary regime* 飲食規則

regi·men /ˈredʒɪmən/ (also **re·gime**) *noun* (*medical* 醫 or *formal*) a set of rules about food and exercise or medical treatment that you follow in order to stay healthy or to improve your health 生活規則；養生之道；養生法

regi·ment /ˈredʒɪmənt/ *noun* [C+sing./pl. v.] **1** a large group of soldiers that is commanded by a COLONEL

Synonyms 同義詞辨析

regard

call • find • consider • see • view

These words all mean to think about sb/sth in a particular way. 以上各詞均含認為、視為、看待之意。

regard to think of sb/sth in a particular way 指認為、視為、看待：*He seemed to regard the whole thing as a joke.* 他大概是把整件事當成玩笑。

call to say that sb/sth has particular qualities or characteristics 指認為…是、把…看作：*I wouldn't call German an easy language.* 我並不認為德語是一門容易學的語言。

find to have a particular feeling or opinion about sth 指認為、感到：*You may find your illness hard to accept.* 你可能覺得難以相信自己患病。

consider to think of sb/sth in a particular way 指認為、視為、覺得：*Who do you consider (to be) responsible for the accident?* 你認為誰對這個事故負有責任？

REGARD OR CONSIDER? 用 regard 還是 consider？

These two words have the same meaning, but they are used in different patterns and structures. In this meaning **consider** must be used with a complement or clause: you can *consider sb/sth to be sth* or *consider sb/sth as sth*, although very often the *to be* or *as* is left out. 上述兩詞意義相同，但用於不同的句型和結構。用於此義時，consider 必須與補語或從句連用，可說 consider sb/sth to be sth 或 consider sb/sth as sth，不過 to be 或 as 常常省略不用：*He considers himself an expert.* 他認為自己是專家。◇ *They are considered a high-risk group.* 他們被視為高風險群體。 You can also *consider that sb/sth is sth* and again, the *that* can be left out. 用 consider that sb/sth is sth 亦可，that 同樣可以省略。 **Regard** is used in a narrower range of structures. The most frequent structure is *regard sb/sth as sth*; the *as* cannot be left out. * regard 可用的句型結構較少，最常用的結構是 regard sb/sth as sth，但 as 不可省略：~~*I regard him a close friend.*~~ You cannot 不能說：~~*regard sb/sth to be sth*~~ or 或 ~~*regard that sb/sth is sth*~~. However, **regard** (but not **consider** in this meaning) can also be used without a noun or adjective complement but with just an object and adverb (*sb/sth is highly regarded*) or adverbial phrase (*regard sb/sth with suspicion/jealousy/admiration*). 不過，regard 亦可不跟名詞或形容詞補語連用，只跟賓語和副詞（如 sb/sth is highly regarded）或副詞短語（如 regard sb/sth with suspicion/jealousy/admiration）連用；consider 則不能這樣用。

see to have an opinion of sth 指認為、看待：*Try to see things from her point of view.* 設法從她那個角度去看問題。

view to think of sb/sth in a particular way 指視為、認為、看待：*How do you view your position within the company?* 你如何看待你自己在公司中的位置？ NOTE **View** has the same meaning as **regard** and **consider** but is slightly less frequent and slightly less formal. The main structures are *view sb/sth as sb/sth* (you cannot leave out the *as*) and *view sb/sth with sth*. * view 與 regard、consider 意義相同，但較不常用，也較非正式。主要結構有 view sb/sth as sb/sth（as 不能省略）和 view sb/sth with sth。

PATTERNS

- to regard/consider/see/view sb/sth **as** sth
- to regard/consider/see/view sb/sth **from** a particular point of view
- to find/consider sb/sth **to be** sth
- **generally/usually** regarded/considered/seen/viewed as sth
- to regard/consider/view sb/sth **favourably/unfavourably**

（軍隊的）團 **2** (*formal*) a large number of people or things 一大群人（或事物）

regi·men·tal /ˌredʒɪˈmentl/ *adj.* [only before noun] connected with a particular regiment of soldiers 團的；團隊的：*a regimental flag* 團旗 ◇ *regimental headquarters* 團指揮部

regi·ment·ed /ˈredʒɪmentɪd/ *adj.* (*disapproving*) **1** involving strict discipline and/or organization 非常嚴格的；死板的：*The school imposes a very regimented lifestyle on its students.* 學校將非常死板的生活方式強加給學生。**2** arranged in strict groups, patterns, etc. 嚴格規劃的；排列整齊的：*regimented lines of trees* 排列整齊的樹木 ▸ **regi·men·ta·tion** /ˌredʒɪmenˈteɪʃn/ *noun* [U]：*She rebelled against the regimentation of school life.* 她曾反抗刻板的學校生活。

Re·gina /rɪˈdʒaɪnə/ *noun* [U] (*BrE, formal*, from *Latin*) a word meaning 'queen', used, for example, in the titles of legal cases which are brought by the state when there is a queen in Britain 女王（英國女王在位時用於政府訴訟案案目等）：*Regina v Jones* 女王訴瓊斯案 ➲ compare REX

re·gion 🔑 AW /ˈriːdʒən/ *noun*
1 🔑 [C] a large area of land, usually without exact limits or borders（通常界限不明的）地區，區域，地方：*the* ***Arctic/tropical/desert, etc. regions*** 北極、熱帶、沙漠等地區 ◇ *one of the most densely populated regions of North America* 北美人口最為稠密的地區之一 **2** 🔑 [C] one of the areas that a country is divided into, that has its own customs and/or its own government 行政區：*the Basque region of Spain* 西班牙的巴斯克區 **3 the regions** [pl.] (*BrE*) all of a country except the capital city（一國除首都以外的）全部地區，所有區域 **4** [C] a part of the body, usually one that has a particular character or problem（通常指有某種特性或問題的）身體部位：*pains in the abdominal region* 腹部的疼痛
IDM **in the region of** used when you are giving a number, price, etc. to show that it is not exact（表示不確切的數字等）大約，差不多 SYN **approximately**：*He earns somewhere in the region of €50 000.* 他大約賺 5 萬歐元。

re·gion·al 🔑 AW /ˈriːdʒənl/ *adj.* [usually before noun] of or relating to a region 地區的；區域的；地方的：*regional variations in pronunciation* 發音的地區差異 ◇ *the conflict between regional and national interests* 地方利益和國家利益的衝突 ◇ *regional councils/elections/newspapers* 地方議會／選舉／報紙 ▸ **re·gion·al·ly** AW /-nəli/ *adv.*：*regionally based television companies* 地方經營的電視公司

re·gion·al·ism /ˈriːdʒənəlɪzəm/ *noun* **1** [C] a feature of a language that exists in a particular part of a country, and is not part of the standard language（語言的）地域特徵，地域性 **2** [U] the desire of the people who live in a particular region of a country to have more political and economic independence 地方分權主義；地域主義

regis·ter 🔑 AW /ˈredʒɪstə(r)/ *verb, noun*
■ *verb*
▸ **PUT NAME ON LIST** 登記姓名 **1** 🔑 [T, I] to record your/sb's/sth's name on an official list 登記；註冊：**~ sth** *to* ***register a birth/marriage/death*** 登記出生／結婚／死亡 ◇ *to* ***register a company/trademark*** 註冊公司／商標 ◇ **~ sth in sth** *The ship was registered in Panama.* 這艘船是在巴拿馬註冊的。◇ **~ sb + adj.** | **~ (sb) as sth** *She is officially registered (as) disabled.* 她正式登記為傷殘者。◇ **~ (with sb/sth)** *to register with a doctor* 向醫生登記 ◇ **~ (at/for sth)** *to register at a hotel* 在旅館登記
▸ **GIVE OPINION PUBLICLY** 公開發表意見 **2** [T] **~ sth** (*formal*) to make your opinion known officially or publicly（正式地或公開地）發表意見，提出主張：*China has registered a protest over foreign intervention.* 中國對外國干涉正式提出了抗議。
▸ **ON MEASURING INSTRUMENT** 測量儀器 **3** 🔑 [I] (+ **noun**) if a measuring instrument **registers** an amount or sth **registers** an amount on a measuring instrument, the instrument shows or records that amount 顯示（讀數）；記錄：*The thermometer registered 32°C.* 溫度計顯示讀數為 32 攝氏度。◇ *The earthquake registered 3 on the Richter scale.* 地震震級為里氏 3 級。◇ *The stock exchange has registered huge losses this week.* 本週證券交易遭到重創。
▸ **SHOW FEELING** 表達情感 **4** [T, no passive, I] **~ (sth)** (*formal*) to show or express a feeling 流露出；顯得；表達出：*Her face registered disapproval.* 她臉上流露出不贊同的神色。◇ *Shock registered on everyone's face.* 人人都面露震驚之色。
▸ **NOTICE STH** 注意到 **5** [T, no passive, I] (often used in negative sentences 常用於否定句) **~ (sth)** to notice sth and remember it; to be noticed 注意到；記住；受到注意：*He barely registered our presence.* 他幾乎沒有注意到我們在場。◇ *I told her my name, but it obviously didn't register.* 我把名字告訴了她，但她顯然沒有在意。
▸ **LETTER/PACKAGE** 郵件 **6** [T, usually passive] **~ sth** to send sth by mail, paying extra money to protect it against loss or damage 把…掛號郵寄：*Can I register this, please?* 請給我把這個掛號郵寄。◇ *a registered letter* 掛號信
■ *noun*
▸ **LIST OF NAMES** 名單 **1** 🔑 [C] an official list or record of names, items, etc.; a book that contains such a list 登記表；註冊簿；登記簿：*a* ***parish register*** (= of births, marriages and deaths) 教區登記簿 ◇ *to be on the* ***electoral register/register of voters*** 成為登記在冊的選民 ◇ *Could you sign the* ***hotel register*** *please, sir?* 先生，請在旅館登記簿上簽字好嗎？◇ (*BrE*) *The teacher* ***called the register*** (= checked who was present at school). 老師點了名。
▸ **OF VOICE/INSTRUMENT** 嗓音；樂器 **2** [C] the range, or part of a range, of a human voice or a musical instrument 聲區；音區：*in the* ***upper/middle/lower register*** 在高／中／低聲區
▸ **OF WRITING/SPEECH** 書面語；口語 **3** [C, U] (*linguistics* 語言) the level and style of a piece of writing or speech, that is usually appropriate to the situation that it is used in（適合特定場合使用的）語體風格，語域：*The essay suddenly switches from a formal to an informal register.* 這篇文章的語體風格突然從正式轉為非正式。
▸ **FOR HOT/COLD AIR** 冷／熱空氣 **4** [C] (*NAmE*) an opening, with a cover that you can have open or shut, that allows hot or cold air from a heating or cooling system into a room（供暖或製冷設備的）調風口，節氣門 ➲ compare VENT *n.* (1)
▸ **MACHINE** 機器 **5** [C] (*NAmE*) = CASH REGISTER

ˌregistered ˈmail (*BrE* also **ˌregistered ˈpost**) *noun* [U] a method of sending a letter or package in which the person sending it can claim money if it arrives late or is lost or damaged 掛號郵寄 ➲ compare RECORDED DELIVERY

ˌregistered ˈnurse *noun* (*abbr.* RN) **1** (*NAmE*) a nurse who has a degree in NURSING and who has passed an exam to be allowed to work in a particular state 註冊護士 **2** (*BrE*) a nurse who has an official qualification 合格的護士；註冊護士

ˌregistered ˈtrademark *noun* (*symb.* ®) the sign or name of a product, etc. that is officially recorded and protected so that nobody else can use it 註冊商標

ˈregister office *noun* the official way of referring to a REGISTRY OFFICE 戶籍登記處

regis·trar /ˌredʒɪˈstrɑː(r); ˈredʒɪstrɑː(r)/ *noun* **1** a person whose job is to keep official records, especially of births, marriages and deaths 登記員；戶籍管理員 **2** the senior officer who organizes the affairs of a college or university（大學的）教務長，教務主任，註冊主任 **3** a doctor working in a British hospital who is training to become a specialist in a particular area of medicine（英國醫院的）專科住院醫生：*a paediatric registrar* 兒科住院醫生 ➲ compare CONSULTANT, RESIDENT *n.* (3)

regis·tra·tion AW /ˌredʒɪˈstreɪʃn/ *noun* **1** [U, C] the act of making an official record of sth/sb 登記；註冊；掛號：*the registration of letters and parcels* 信件和包裹的掛號 ◇ *the registration of students for a course* 學生的選課登記 ◇ *registration fees* 註冊費 ◇ *vehicle registrations* 車輛登記 ◇ *the registration of a child's birth* 嬰兒出生登記

2 [U, C] a document showing that an official record has been made of sth 登記文檔；註冊項目 ➲ compare LOGBOOK (1) **3** [C] (*BrE*) = REGISTRATION NUMBER **4** [U] (*BrE*) the time when a teacher looks at the list of students on the class register and checks that the students are present（教師對上課學生的）點名

regi'stration number (also **regis·tra·tion**) (both *BrE*) (*NAmE* **'license (plate) number**) *noun* the series of letters and numbers that are shown on a NUMBER PLATE at the front and back of a vehicle to identify it 車輛的登記號碼；牌照號碼

regis·try /'redʒɪstri/ *noun* (*pl.* **-ies**) a place where registers are kept 登記處；註冊處

'registry office (also **'register office**) *noun* (in Britain) a place where CIVIL marriages (= that do not involve a religious ceremony) are performed and where records of births, marriages and deaths are made 戶籍登記處（在英國可舉辦不涉及宗教儀式的婚禮，並負責登記出生及婚喪等事項）: *to get married in/at a registry office* 在戶籍登記處舉行婚禮

rego (also **reggo**) /'redʒəʊ; *NAmE* -oʊ/ *noun* (*pl.* **-os**) (*AustralE, NZE, informal*) a REGISTRATION for a car, etc. 機動車輛的註冊

re·gress /rɪ'ɡres/ *verb* [I] **~ (to sth)** (*formal*, usually *disapproving*) to return to an earlier or less advanced form or way of behaving 倒退；回歸；退化

re·gres·sion /rɪ'ɡreʃn/ *noun* [U, C] **~ (to sth)** the process of going back to an earlier or less advanced form or state 倒退；回歸；退化

re·gres·sive /rɪ'ɡresɪv/ *adj.* **1** becoming or making sth less advanced 退化的；倒退的；退步的: *The policy has been condemned as a regressive step.* 這項政策被認為是一種倒退而受到譴責。 **2** (*technical* 術語) (of taxes 稅收) having less effect on the rich than on the poor 遞減的（對富人的影響比對窮人的小）

re·gret 🔑 /rɪ'ɡret/ *verb, noun*

■ *verb* (**-tt-**) **1** 🔑 to feel sorry about sth you have done or about sth that you have not been able to do 感到遺憾；惋惜；懊悔: **~ sth** *If you don't do it now, **you'll** only **regret it**.* 你如果現在不做，以後一定會後悔的。◇ *The decision could be one he **lives to regret**.* 這一決定也許會令他終身遺憾。◇ *'I've had a wonderful life,' she said, 'I don't regret a thing.'* "我一輩子生活得很好，" 她說，"我沒什麼可遺憾的。" ◇ **~ doing sth** *He **bitterly regretted** ever having mentioned it.* 他非常懊悔提起那件事。◇ **~ what, how, etc. ...** *I **deeply regret** what I said.* 我非常後悔說了那些話。◇ **~ that ...** *I regret that I never got to meet him in person.* 很遺憾我始終沒能見到他本人。 **2** 🔑 (*formal*) used to say in a polite or formal way that you are sorry or sad about a situation（有禮貌地或正式地表示抱歉、痛惜或悲傷）: **~ sth** *The airline regrets any inconvenience.* 航空公司對所造成的任何不便表示歉意。◇ **~ that ...** *I regret that I am unable to accept your kind invitation.* 很遺憾，我不能接受你的友好邀請。◇ **~ to do sth** *We regret to inform you that your application has not been successful.* 我們很遺憾地通知您，您的申請未通過。◇ **it is regretted that ...** ***It is to be regretted that** so many young people leave school without qualifications.* 遺憾的是那麼多年輕人不能畢業。

■ *noun* 🔑 [U, C] a feeling of sadness or disappointment that you have because of sth that has happened or sth that you have done or not done 痛惜；懊悔；遺憾；失望: *It is **with great regret** that I accept your resignation.* 接受你的辭呈，我感到非常遺憾。◇ *She **expressed her regret at** the decision.* 她對這個決定表示失望。◇ ***a pang/twinge of regret*** 一陣痛悔之情 ◇ ***I have no regrets** about leaving Newcastle* (= I do not feel sorry about it). 我一點也不後悔離開紐卡斯爾。◇ *What is your greatest regret* (= the thing that you are most sorry about doing or not doing)? 你最大的遺憾是什麼？◇ *He gave up teaching in 2009, **much to the regret of** his students.* 他於 2009 年放棄了教學，這使他的學生深感遺憾。

re·gret·ful /rɪ'ɡretfl/ *adj.* feeling or showing sadness or disappointment because of sth that has happened or sth that you have done or not done 後悔的；失望的；令人惋惜的；遺憾的 SYN **rueful**: *a regretful look* 失望的眼神

re·gret·ful·ly /rɪ'ɡretfəli/ *adv.* **1** in a way that shows you are sad or disappointed about sth 遺憾地；痛惜地；失望地；懊悔地: *'I'm afraid not,' he said regretfully.* 他遺憾地說："恐怕不行。" ◇ *Emma shook her head regretfully.* 埃瑪遺憾地搖了搖頭。 **2** used to show that you are sorry that sth is the case and you wish the situation were different 遺憾的是；十分遺憾 SYN **regrettably**: *Regretfully, mounting costs have forced the museum to close.* 遺憾的是，成本不斷增加，博物館不得不關閉。

Which Word? 詞語辨析

regretfully / regrettably

- **Regretfully** and **regrettably** can both be used as sentence adverbs to show that you are sorry about something and wish the situation were different. * regretfully 和 regrettably 均可用作副詞，修飾整個句子，表示非常抱歉、遺憾、惋惜: *Regretfully, some jobs will be lost.* 遺憾的是有些工作將會被裁。◇ *Regrettably, some jobs will be lost.* 令人遺憾的是有些工作將會被裁。
- **Regretfully** can also be used to mean 'in a way that shows you are sad or disappointed about something'. * regretfully 亦可指懊喪、沮喪: *He sighed regretfully.* 他懊喪地歎了口氣。

re·gret·table /rɪ'ɡretəbl/ *adj.* **~ (that ...)** (*formal*) that you are sorry about and wish had not happened 令人惋惜的；可惜的；令人遺憾的: ***It is regrettable that** the police were not informed sooner.* 遺憾的是沒有早些報警。◇ *The loss of jobs is highly regrettable.* 失去工作非常令人遺憾。 ▶ **re·gret·tably** /-əbli/ *adv.*: *Regrettably, crime has been increasing in this area.* 令人遺憾的是這一地區的犯罪率在不斷上升。

re·group /ˌriː'ɡruːp/ *verb* **1** [T, I] **~ (sth) (for sth)** to arrange the way people or soldiers work together in a new way, especially in order to continue fighting or attacking sb 重組；重編: *They regrouped their forces and renewed the attack.* 他們重新聚集兵力，再次發動進攻。◇ *After its election defeat, the party needs to regroup.* 選舉失敗後，這個黨需要改組。 **2** [I] (of a person 人) to return to a normal state after an unpleasant experience or a period of difficulty, and become ready to make an effort again with new enthusiasm or strength 重整旗鼓；重新部署: *Summer is a time to relax, regroup and catch up on all those things you've been putting off all year.* 夏天是休養整頓、並處理一年中積壓事務的時候。

regu·lar 🔑 /'reɡjələ(r)/ *adj., noun*

■ *adj.*

▸ FOLLOWING PATTERN 規律 **1** 🔑 following a pattern, especially with the same time and space in between each thing and the next 規則的；有規律的；間隙均勻的；定時的: *regular breathing* 均勻的呼吸 ◇ ***a regular pulse/heartbeat*** 正常的脈搏 / 心跳 ◇ *A light flashed **at regular intervals**.* 一盞燈有規律地閃着亮光。◇ *There is a regular bus service to the airport.* 有公共汽車定時開往機場。◇ ***regular meetings/visits*** 定期會議 / 訪問 ◇ *The equipment is checked **on a regular basis**.* 設備定期進行檢查。 OPP **irregular**

▸ FREQUENT 頻繁 **2** 🔑 done or happening often 頻繁的；經常做（或發生）的: *Do you take regular exercise?* 你經常鍛煉嗎？◇ *Domestic violence is a regular occurrence in some families.* 在某些家庭中，家庭暴力是常事。 OPP **irregular** **3** 🔑 [only before noun] (of people 人) doing the same thing or going to the same place often 經常做某事的；常去某地的: *our regular customers* 老主顧 ◇ *regular offenders* (= against the law) 慣犯 ◇ *He was a regular visitor to her house.* 他是她家的常客。

▸ USUAL 通常 **4** 🔑 [only before noun] usual 通常的；平常的；慣常的: *I couldn't see my regular doctor today.* 我今天找不到平常給我看病的醫生。◇ *On Monday he would*

R

have to return to his regular duties. 星期一，他就得回去正常上班了。◇ *It's important to follow the regular procedure.* 按照慣常的程序行事是很重要的。

▸ **EVEN** 勻稱 **5** having an even shape 均勻的；端正的；齊整的： *a face with regular features* 五官端正的臉龐 ◇ *a regular geometric pattern* 正幾何圖形 **OPP irregular**

▸ **PERMANENT** 持久 **6** lasting or happening over a long period 持久的；穩定的；固定的： *a regular income* 固定的收入 ◇ *She couldn't find any regular employment.* 她找不到任何固定工作。

▸ **STANDARD SIZE** 標準尺寸 **7** (*especially NAmE*) of a standard size 標準尺寸的；中等大小的；中號的： *Regular or large fries?* 中號的還是大號的炸薯條？

▸ **ORDINARY** 普通 **8** [only before noun] (*especially NAmE*) ordinary; without any special or extra features 普通的；平凡的： *Do you want regular or diet cola?* 你要普通的還是低熱量的可樂？ ◇ (*approving*) *He's just a regular guy who loves his dog.* 他也不過是個十分疼愛自己狗兒的平凡人。

▸ **SOLDIER** 士兵 **9** [only before noun] belonging to or connected with the permanent armed forces or police force of a country 常備軍的；正規軍的： *a* ***regular army/soldier*** 正規軍；正規軍士兵 **OPP irregular**

▸ **GRAMMAR** 語法 **10** (especially of verbs or nouns 尤指動詞或名詞) changing their form in the same way as most other verbs and nouns 規則的；按規則變化的： *The past participle of regular verbs ends in '-ed'.* 規則動詞的過去分詞以 -ed 結尾。 **OPP irregular**

▸ **FOR EMPHASIS** 強調 **11** (*informal*) used for emphasis to show that sb/sth is an exact or clear example of the thing mentioned 完全的；徹底的： *The whole thing was a regular disaster.* 整個事情完全是一場災難。

IDM **(as) regular as 'clockwork** very regularly; happening at the same time in the same way 非常有規律；極有規律： *He is home by six every day, regular as clockwork.* 他每天 6 點前必定準時回到家。

■ ***noun***

▸ **CUSTOMER** 顧客 **1** a customer who often goes to a particular shop/store, pub, restaurant, etc. 常客；老主顧： *He's one of our regulars.* 他是我們的一位老主顧。

▸ **MEMBER OF TEAM** 隊員 **2** a person who often plays in a particular team, takes part in a particular television show, etc. 主力（或正式）隊員；（電視節目的）固定主持人；經常參加某項活動的人： *We are missing six first-team regulars because of injury.* 我們有六位一線主力隊員因傷不能出場。

▸ **SOLDIER** 士兵 **3** a professional soldier who belongs to a country's permanent army 正規軍人；職業軍人

re·gu·lar·ity /ˌregjuˈlærəti/ *noun* **1** [U] the fact that the same thing happens again and again, and usually with the same length of time between each time it happens 規律性；經常性： *Aircraft passed overhead* ***with monotonous regularity.*** 飛機一次又一次反復從頭頂飛過。 **2** [U] the fact that sth is arranged in an even way or in an organized pattern 勻稱；端正；有規則的分佈： *the striking regularity of her features* 她的五官非常端正 **3** [C] a thing that has a pattern to it 有規則的東西；有規律的事物： *They had observed regularities in the behaviour of the animals.* 他們曾觀察過這些動物的習性。 ➲ compare IRREGULARITY

regu·lar·ize (*BrE* also **-ise**) /ˈregjələraɪz/ *verb* **~ sth** to make a situation that already exists legal or official 使合法化；使正式存在： *Illegal immigrants were given the opportunity to regularize their position.* 非法移民得到了使其身分合法化的機會。

regu·lar·ly /ˈregjələli; *NAmE* -lərli/ *adv.* **1** at regular intervals or times 有規律地；間隙均勻地： *We meet regularly to discuss the progress of the project.* 我們定期會面，討論工程進展情況。 **2** often 經常： *I go there quite regularly.* 我經常去那兒。 **3** in an even or balanced way 均勻地；勻稱地： *The plants were spaced regularly, about 50 cm apart.* 這些植株分佈均勻，間距大約為 50 厘米。

regu·late **AW** /ˈregjuleɪt/ *verb* **1** [T, I] **~ (sth)** to control sth by means of rules（用規則條例）約束，控制，管理： *The activities of credit companies are regulated by law.* 信貸公司的業務受法律的制約。◇ *It is up to the regulating authority to put the measures into effect.* 應該由管理部門落實這些措施。 **2** [T] **~ sth** to control the speed, pressure, temperature, etc. in a machine or system 調節，控制（速度、壓力、溫度等）： *This valve regulates the flow of water.* 這個閥門調節水流。

regu·la·tion **AW** /ˌregjuˈleɪʃn/ *noun, adj.*

■ ***noun*** **1** [C, usually pl.] an official rule made by a government or some other authority 章程；規章制度；規則；法規： *too many* ***rules and regulations*** 過多的規章制度 ◇ ***fire/safety/building, etc. regulations*** 防火條例、安全規章、建築法規等 ◇ *to comply with the regulations* 遵守章程 ◇ ***Under the new regulations*** *spending on office equipment will be strictly controlled.* 根據新的規定，辦公設備開支將受到嚴格控制。◇ *the strict regulations governing the sale of weapons* 關於武器銷售的嚴格規定 **2** [U] controlling sth by means of rules（運用規則條例的）管理，控制： *the voluntary regulation of the press* 新聞出版業的自律

■ ***adj.*** [only before noun] that must be worn or used according to the official rules 規定的；必須穿戴的；必須使用的： *in regulation uniform* 穿着規定的制服

regu·la·tor **AW** /ˈregjuleɪtə(r)/ *noun* **1** a person or an organization that officially controls an area of business or industry and makes sure that it is operating fairly（某行業等的）監管者，監管機構 **2** a device that automatically controls sth such as speed, temperature or pressure（速度、溫度、壓力的）自動調節器

regu·la·tory **AW** /ˈregjələtəri; *NAmE* -tɔːri/ *adj.* [usually before noun] having the power to control an area of business or industry and make sure that it is operating fairly（對工商業）具有監管權的，監管的： ***regulatory bodies/authorities/agencies*** 監管部門／機構

re·gur·gi·tate /rɪˈɡɜːdʒɪteɪt; *NAmE* -ˈɡɜːrdʒ-/ *verb* **1 ~ sth** (*formal*) to bring food that has been swallowed back up into the mouth again 使（嚥下的食物）返回到口中；反芻 **2 ~ sth** (*disapproving*) to repeat sth you have heard or read without really thinking about it or understanding it 照搬；照本宣科 ▸ **re·gur·gi·ta·tion** /rɪˌɡɜːdʒɪˈteɪʃn; *NAmE* -ˌɡɜːrdʒ-/ *noun* [U]

rehab /ˈriːhæb/ *noun* [U] (*especially NAmE*) the process of helping to cure sb who has a problem with drugs or alcohol（吸毒或酗酒者的）康復： *to go into rehab* 進行康復治療 ◇ *a rehab clinic* 康復診所

re·habili·tate /ˌriːəˈbɪlɪteɪt/ *verb* **1 ~ sb** to help sb to have a normal, useful life again after they have been very ill/sick or in prison for a long time 使（重病患者）康復；使（長期服刑者）恢復正常生活： *a unit for rehabilitating drug addicts* 幫助吸毒者恢復正常生活的機構 **2 ~ sb (as sth)** to begin to consider that sb is good or acceptable after a long period during which they were considered bad or unacceptable 恢復…的名譽；給…平反昭雪： *He played a major role in rehabilitating Magritte as an artist.* 他對恢復瑪格里特藝術家的名譽起了重要的作用。 **3 ~ sth** to return a building or an area to its previous good condition 使（建築物或地區）恢復原狀；修復 ▸ **re·habili·ta·tion** /ˌriːəˌbɪlɪˈteɪʃn/ *noun* [U]： *a drug rehabilitation centre* 吸毒者康復中心 ◇ *the rehabilitation of the steel industry* 鋼鐵工業的復興

re·hash /ˌriːˈhæʃ/ *verb* **~ sth** (*disapproving*) to arrange ideas, pieces of writing or pieces of film into a new form but without any great change or improvement（稍微改動）重新推出；以新形式表達舊內容： *He just rehashes songs from the 60s.* 他只是把 60 年代的歌曲稍加改編而已。 ▸ **re·hash** /ˈriːhæʃ/ *noun* [sing.]： (*disapproving*) *The movie is just a rehash of the best TV episodes.* 這部電影不過是把電視劇裏最精彩的幾集改編了一下。

re·hear /ˌriːˈhɪə(r); *NAmE* -ˈhɪr/ *verb* (**re·heard**, **re·heard** /ˌriːˈhɜːd; *NAmE* -ˈhɜːrd/) **~ sth** (*law* 律) to hear or consider again a case in court 復審，再審（案件）

re·hear·ing /ˌriːˈhɪərɪŋ; *NAmE* -ˈhɪr-/ *noun* (*law* 律) an opportunity for a case to be heard or considered again in court（法庭對案件的）復審，再審

re·hearsal /rɪˈhɜːsl; *NAmE* rɪˈhɜːrsl/ *noun* **1** [C, U] time that is spent practising a play or piece of music in preparation for a public performance 排演；排練： *to* ***have***

a rehearsal 進行排練 ◇ *We only had six days of rehearsal.* 我們只有六天的排練時間。◇ *Our new production of 'Hamlet' is currently* ***in rehearsal****.* 我們的新版《哈姆雷特》正在排練之中。◇ *a rehearsal room* 排練房 ➲ see also DRESS REHEARSAL **2** [C, usually sing.] **~ (for sth)** an experience or event that helps to prepare you for sth that is going to happen in the future 預演；演習：*These training exercises are designed to be a rehearsal for the invasion.* 這些訓練是為了入侵而進行的演習。**3** [C, usually sing.] **~ of sth** (*formal*) the act of repeating sth that has been said before 複述；重複；敘述：*We listened to his lengthy rehearsal of the arguments.* 我們聽着他沒完沒了地重複他的論點。

re·hearse /rɪˈhɜːs; *NAmE* rɪˈhɜːrs/ *verb* **1** [I, T] to practise or make people practise a play, piece of music, etc. in preparation for a public performance 排練；排演：**~ (for sth)** *We were given only two weeks to rehearse.* 只給了我們兩個星期排練。◇ **~ sth/sb** *Today, we'll just be rehearsing the final scene.* 今天，我們只排演最後一幕。◇ *The actors were poorly rehearsed.* 演員排練得不夠。**2** [T] **~ sth** to prepare in your mind or practise privately what you are going to do or say to sb 默誦；背誦；默默地練習：*She walked along rehearsing her excuse for being late.* 她一邊走一邊默誦着她遲到的託辭。**3** [T] **~ sth** (*formal*, usually *disapproving*) to repeat ideas or opinions that have often been expressed before 照搬；重複

re·heat /ˌriːˈhiːt/ *verb* **~ sth** to heat cooked food again after it has been left to go cold 重新加熱（涼了的熟食）

re·home /ˌriːˈhəʊm; *NAmE* -ˈhoʊm/ *verb* **~ sth** to find a new owner for a pet, especially a dog or cat, usually after caring for it for a time 為（狗、貓等寵物）找新家：*The organization rescues stray dogs and rehomes them.* 這個組織救助流浪狗，並給它們找新主人。

re·house /ˌriːˈhaʊz/ *verb* **~ sb** to provide sb with a different home to live in 給…重新安排住房：*Thousands of earthquake victims are still waiting to be rehoused.* 數千名地震災民仍在等待安排新住處。

reign /reɪn/ *noun, verb*

▪ ***noun*** **1** the period during which a king, queen, EMPEROR, etc. rules 君主統治時期：***in/during the reign*** *of Charles II* 在查理二世統治期間 **2** the period during which sb is in charge of an organization, a team, etc. 任期；當政期

▪ ***verb*** **1** [I] to rule as king, queen, EMPEROR, etc. 統治；當政；為王；為君：*the reigning monarch* 當政的君主 ◇ *Queen Victoria reigned from 1837 to 1901.* 維多利亞女王自 1837 年至 1901 年在位。◇ **~ over sb/sth** *Herod reigned over Palestine at that time.* 那時，希律王統治巴勒斯坦。**2** [I] **~ (over sb/sth)** to be the best or most important in a particular situation or area of skill 成為最佳；成為最重要的：*the reigning champion* 冠軍稱號的保持者 ◇ *In the field of classical music, he still* ***reigns supreme****.* 在古典音樂領域，他仍然是最為傑出的。**3** [I] (*literary*) (of an idea, a feeling or an atmosphere 想法、情感或氛圍) to be the most obvious feature of a place or moment 盛行；成為最顯著的：*At last* ***silence reigned*** (= there was complete silence). 最後，萬籟俱寂。

re·ig·nite /ˌriːɪɡˈnaɪt/ *verb* [I, T] to start burning again; to make sth start burning again （使）重新燃燒；再點燃：*The oven burners reignite automatically if blown out.* 烤爐的火如果吹滅了會自動再點燃。◇ **~ sth** *You may need to reignite the pilot light.* 你得重新點燃長明火。◇ (*figurative*) *Their passion was reignited by a romantic trip to Venice.* 去威尼斯的浪漫之旅重新燃起了他們的激情。

ˌreign of ˈterror *noun* (*pl.* **reigns of terror**) a period during which there is a lot of violence and many people are killed by the ruler or people in power 恐怖統治時期

reiki /ˈreɪki/ *noun* [U] (from *Japanese*) a method of healing based on the idea that energy can be directed into a person's body by touch 靈氣療法（通過觸摸向人體內輸送能量）

re·im·burse /ˌriːɪmˈbɜːs; *NAmE* -ˈbɜːrs/ *verb* (*formal*) to pay back money to sb which they have spent or lost 償還；補償：**~ sth** *We will reimburse any expenses incurred.* 我們將付還所有相關費用。◇ **~ sb (for sth)** *You will be reimbursed for any loss or damage caused by our company.* 如我公司給您造成損失或有所損壞，您都將得到賠償。▶ **re·im·burse·ment** *noun* [U]

rein /reɪn/ *noun, verb*

▪ ***noun*** **1** [C, usually pl.] a long narrow leather band that is attached to a metal bar in a horse's mouth (= a BIT) and is held by the rider in order to control the horse 韁繩：*She pulled gently on the reins.* 她輕輕地拉着韁繩。**2 reins** [pl.] (*BrE*) strips of leather, etc. worn by a small child and held by an adult in order to stop the child from walking off and getting lost（成人攜帶幼兒以防走失的）保護帶 **3 the reins** [pl.] the state of being in control or the leader of sth 控制；主宰；掌管：*It was time to* ***hand over the reins*** *of power* (= to give control to sb else). 是該讓權的時候了。◇ *The vice-president was forced to* ***take up the reins*** *of office.* 副總統被迫走馬上任。

IDM **give/allow sb/sth free/full ˈrein | give/allow free/full ˈrein to sth** to give sb complete freedom of action; to allow a feeling to be expressed freely 對…不加約束；放任自由；充分表達（感情）：*The designer was given free rein.* 設計者可以自由發揮。◇ *The script allows full rein to her larger-than-life acting style.* 劇本允許她充分展現她那誇張的表演風格。➲ more at TIGHT *adj.*

▪ ***verb***

PHR V **ˌrein sb/sth↔ˈback | ˌrein sth↔ˈin** **1** to start to control sb/sth more strictly 嚴格控制；加強管理 **SYN** **check**：*We need to rein back public spending.* 我們需要嚴格控制公共開銷。◇ *She kept her emotions tightly reined in.* 她盡量克制着自己的感情。**2** to stop a horse or make it go more slowly by pulling back the reins 用韁繩勒馬

re·incar·nate /ˌriːɪnˈkɑːneɪt; *NAmE* -ˈkɑːrn-/ *verb* [often passive, T, I] **~ (sb/sth) (in/as sb/sth)** to be born again in another body after you have died; to make sb be born again in this way 使投胎；轉世；使再生：*They believe humans are reincarnated in animal form.* 他們相信人死後轉生為動物。

re·incar·na·tion /ˌriːɪnkɑːˈneɪʃn; *NAmE* -kɑːrˈn-/ *noun* **1** [U] the belief that after sb's death their soul lives again in a new body 轉世說 ➲ COLLOCATIONS at RELIGION **2** [C, usually sing.] a person or an animal whose body contains the soul of a dead person（靈魂的）轉世化身，化身

rein·deer /ˈreɪndɪə(r); *NAmE* -dɪr/ *noun* (*pl.* **rein·deer** or **rein·deers**) a large DEER with long ANTLERS (= horns shaped like branches), that lives in cold northern regions 馴鹿：*herds of reindeer* 馴鹿群

re·inforce **AW** /ˌriːɪnˈfɔːs; *NAmE* -ˈfɔːrs/ *verb* **1 ~ sth** to make a feeling, an idea, etc. stronger 加強；充實；使更強烈：*Such jokes tend to reinforce racial stereotypes.* 這樣的笑話往往進一步加深對種族的模式化觀念。◇ *The climate of political confusion has only reinforced the country's economic decline.* 政局混亂只會加速國家經濟的衰退。◇ *Success in the talks will reinforce his reputation as an international statesman.* 談判成功將會增強他作為國際政治家的聲望。**2 ~ sth** to make a structure or material stronger, especially by adding another material to it 加固；使更結實：*All buildings are now reinforced to withstand earthquakes.* 所有建築現都已加固，以抗地震。◇ *reinforced steel* 增強鋼材 **3 ~ sth** to send more people or equipment in order to make an army, etc. stronger 給…加強力量（或裝備）；使更強大：*The UN has undertaken to reinforce its military presence along the borders.* 聯合國已經着手增強邊境駐軍。

ˌreinforced ˈconcrete *noun* [U] concrete with metal bars or wires inside to make it stronger 鋼筋混凝土

re·inforce·ment **AW** /ˌriːɪnˈfɔːsmənt; *NAmE* -ˈfɔːrs-/ *noun* **1 reinforcements** [pl.] extra soldiers or police officers who are sent to a place because more are needed 援軍；增援警力：*to send in reinforcements* 派出增援部隊 **2** [U, sing.] the act of making sth stronger, especially a feeling or an idea（感情或思想等的）鞏固，加強，強化

re·instate /ˌriːɪnˈsteɪt/ *verb* **1 ~ sb/sth (in/as sth)** to give back a job or position that had been taken away from sb 使恢復原職；使重返崗位：*He was reinstated in his post.* 他重新回到了自己的崗位。 **2 ~ sth (in/as sth)** to return sth to its previous position or status 把…放回原處；使恢復原狀 SYN **restore**：*There have been repeated calls to reinstate the death penalty.* 不斷有人呼籲恢復死刑。 ▸ **re·instate·ment** *noun* [U]

re·insur·ance /ˌriːɪnˈʃʊərəns; -ˈʃɔːr-; *NAmE* -ˈʃʊr-/ *noun* [U] (*finance* 財) the practice of one insurance company buying insurance from another company against any losses that result from claims that are made against it 再保險，分保保險（指一保險公司向其他公司購買保險以減少索賠損失）

re·inter·pret AW /ˌriːɪnˈtɜːprɪt; *NAmE* -ˈtɜːrp-/ *verb* **~ sth** to interpret sth in a new or different way 重新解釋；重新詮釋 ▸ **re·inter·pret·ation** AW /ˌriːɪnˌtɜːprɪˈteɪʃn; *NAmE* -ˌtɜːrp-/ *noun* [C, U]

re·intro·duce /ˌriːɪntrəˈdjuːs; *NAmE* -ˈduːs/ *verb* **1 ~ sth** to start to use sth again 再次使用；重新引入 SYN **bring back**：*to reintroduce the death penalty* 恢復死刑 ◇ *plans to reintroduce trams to the city* 市內重新使用有軌電車的計劃 **2 ~ sth** to put a type of animal, bird or plant back into a region where it once lived 將…放歸自然棲息地 ▸ **re·intro·duc·tion** *noun* [U, C]

re·invent /ˌriːɪnˈvent/ *verb* **~ sth/yourself (as sth)** to present yourself/sth in a new form or with a new image 以新形象示人；以新形式出現：*The former wild man of rock has reinvented himself as a respectable family man.* 過去的那位搖滾狂人已經改變形象，成了一位體面的愛家的男人。

IDM **reinvent the wheel** to waste time creating sth that already exists and works well 重複發明；無謂地重複；浪費時間做無用功

re·invest AW /ˌriːɪnˈvest/ *verb* [T, I] **~ (sth)** to put profits that have been made on an investment back into the same investment or into a new one 再投資；把（利潤）用於再投資 ▸ **re·invest·ment** AW *noun* [U, C]

re·in·vig·or·ate /ˌriːɪnˈvɪɡəreɪt/ *verb* **~ sth/sb** to give new energy or strength to sth/sb 給…增添精力（或力量）；使再振作：*We need to reinvigorate the economy of the area.* 我們需要給這個地區的經濟注入新的活力。◇ *I felt reinvigorated after a rest and a shower.* 我休息了一會兒，沖了個淋浴，感到精神煥發。

re·issue /ˌriːˈɪʃuː/ *verb, noun*

■ *verb* **~ sth (as sth)** to publish or produce again a book, record, etc. that has not been available for some time 重新發行；再版：*old jazz recordings reissued on CD* 以激光唱片重新發行的老爵士樂 ◇ *The novel was reissued in paperback.* 這本小說重新發行了平裝本。

■ *noun* an old book or record that has been published or produced again after not being available for some time 再版書；重新發行的唱片（或其他錄製品）

re·iter·ate /riˈɪtəreɪt/ *verb* (*formal*) to repeat sth that you have already said, especially to emphasize it 反複地說；重申：**~ sth** *to reiterate an argument/a demand/an offer* 重申論點；重複一項要求／建議 ◇ **~ that …** *Let me reiterate that we are fully committed to this policy.* 我再說一遍，我們對這項政策是全力以赴、堅定不移的。◇ **+ speech** *'I said "money",' he reiterated.* "我說的是'錢'。"他重申道。 ▸ **re·iter·ation** /riˌɪtəˈreɪʃn/ *noun* [sing.]：*a reiteration of her previous statement* 重申她說過的話

re·ject 🔑 AW *verb, noun*

■ *verb* /rɪˈdʒekt/

▸ ARGUMENT/IDEA/PLAN 論點；想法；計劃 **1** 🔑 **~ sth** to refuse to accept or consider sth 拒絕接受；不予考慮：*to reject an argument/a claim/a decision/an offer/a suggestion* 拒絕接受一個論點／一項要求／一個決定／一項提議／一個建議 ◇ *The prime minister rejected any idea of reforming the system.* 首相對任何改革體制的想法都不予考慮。◇ *The proposal was **firmly rejected**.* 這項提議被斷然否決。◇ *All our suggestions were **rejected out of hand**.* 我們所有的建議都被一口拒絕了。

▸ SB FOR JOB 找工作者 **2** 🔑 **~ sb** to refuse to accept sb for a job, position, etc. 拒收；不錄用；拒絕接納：*Please reject the following candidates …* 請排除以下候選人… ◇ *I've been rejected by all the universities I applied to.* 所有我申請的大學都沒有錄取我。

▸ NOT USE/PUBLISH 不用；不出版 **3** 🔑 **~ sth** to decide not to use, sell, publish, etc. sth because its quality is not good enough（因質量差）不用，不出售，不出版：*Imperfect articles are rejected by our quality control.* 我們嚴把質量關，不完美的物件都被退回。

▸ NEW ORGAN 新器官 **4** 🔑 **~ sth** (of the body 身體) to not accept a new organ after a TRANSPLANT operation, by producing substances that attack the organ 排斥；排異（移植的器官）

▸ NOT LOVE 不愛 **5** 🔑 **~ sb/sth** to fail to give a person or an animal enough care or affection 不夠關心；慢待：*The lioness rejected the smallest cub, which died.* 母獅不理會最小的幼獅，任由它死去。◇ *When her husband left home she felt rejected and useless.* 丈夫離家後，她覺得遭到了拋棄，且認為自己一無是處。 ▸ **re·jec·tion** AW /rɪˈdʒekʃn/ *noun* [U, C]：*Her proposal met with unanimous rejection.* 她的建議遭到一致否決。◇ *a rejection letter* (= a letter in which you are told, for example, that you have not been accepted for a job) 回絕信 ◇ *painful feelings of rejection* 受冷落的痛苦感受

■ *noun* /ˈriːdʒekt/

▸ STH THAT CANNOT BE USED 無用之物 **1** something that cannot be used or sold because there is sth wrong with it 廢品；次品

▸ PERSON 人 **2** a person who has not been accepted as a member of a team, society, etc. 不合格者；被剔除者；被拒收者：*one of society's rejects* 一名社會棄兒

rejig /ˌriːˈdʒɪɡ/ *verb* (**-gg-**) (*BrE*) (*US* **rejig·ger** /ˌriːˈdʒɪɡə(r)/) **~ sth** (*informal*) to make changes to sth; to arrange sth in a different way 更改；重新安排；重新佈置

re·joice /rɪˈdʒɔɪs/ *verb* [I, T] (*formal*) to express great happiness about sth 非常高興；深感欣喜：*When the war ended, people finally had cause to rejoice.* 戰爭結束，人們終於可以歡欣鼓舞了。◇ **~ at/in/over sth** *The motor industry is rejoicing at the cut in car tax.* 汽車工業對汽車減稅感到非常高興。◇ **~ to do sth** *They rejoiced to see their son well again.* 他們看到兒子恢復了健康，無比高興。◇ **~ that …** *I rejoice that justice has prevailed.* 我非常高興正義得到伸張。

IDM **rejoice in the name of …** (*BrE, humorous*) to have a name that sounds funny 有個滑稽的名字：*He rejoiced in the name of Owen Owen.* 他有個滑稽的名字叫歐文•歐文。

re·joi·cing /rɪˈdʒɔɪsɪŋ/ *noun* [U] (also **rejoicings** [pl.]) the happy celebration of sth 喜慶；歡慶：*a time of great rejoicing* 盡情歡慶的時光

re·join¹ /ˌriːˈdʒɔɪn/ *verb* [T, I] **~ (sb/sth)** to join sb/sth again after leaving them 重新加入；和…重新在一起：*to rejoin a club* 重新加入俱樂部 ◇ *She turned off her phone and rejoined them at the table.* 她關掉電話，再回到餐桌旁和他們坐在一起。◇ *The path goes through a wood before rejoining the main road.* 這條小路穿過一片樹林後與大路交匯。

re·join² /rɪˈdʒɔɪn/ *verb* **+ speech | ~ that …** (*formal*) to say sth as an answer, especially sth quick, critical or amusing 回答；反駁 SYN **retort**：*'You're wrong!' she rejoined.* "你錯了！"她反駁道。

re·join·der /rɪˈdʒɔɪndə(r)/ *noun* [usually sing.] (*formal*) a reply, especially a quick, critical or amusing one 回答；反駁 SYN **retort**

re·ju·ven·ate /rɪˈdʒuːvəneɪt/ *verb* **~ sb/sth** to make sb/sth look or feel younger or more lively 使年輕；使更有活力 ▸ **re·ju·ven·ation** /rɪˌdʒuːvəˈneɪʃn/ *noun* [U, sing.]

re·kin·dle /ˌriːˈkɪndl/ *verb* **~ sth** (*formal*) to make sth become active again 使重新活躍；使復蘇 SYN **reawaken**：*to rekindle feelings/hopes* 再次引發感情；重新點燃希望

re·lapse *noun, verb*

■ *noun* /rɪˈlæps; ˈriːlæps/ [C, U] the fact of becoming

R

ill/sick again after making an improvement 舊病復發：*to **have/suffer a relapse*** 舊病復發 ◇ *a risk of relapse* 舊病復發的危險

■ ***verb*** /rɪˈlæps/ [I] **~ (into sth)** to go back into a previous condition or into a worse state after making an improvement 退回原狀；（好轉後）再倒退：*They relapsed into silence.* 他們又都沉默不語。◇ *He relapsed into his old bad habits.* 他重染惡習。◇ *Two days after leaving the hospital she relapsed into a coma.* 出院兩天後，她再度昏迷。

re·late /rɪˈleɪt/ *verb*

1 show or make a connection between two or more things 聯繫；使有聯繫；把…聯繫起來 SYN **connect**：**~ sth** *I found it difficult to relate the two ideas in my mind.* 我覺得很難把這兩種想法聯繫在一起。◇ **~ A to B** *In the future, pay increases will be related to productivity.* 以後，工資的增加將和業績掛鈎。 **2** (*formal*) to give a spoken or written report of sth; to tell a story 敍述；講述；講（故事）：**~ sth** *She relates her childhood experiences in the first chapters.* 在開始的幾章中，她描述了自己童年的經歷。◇ **~ sth to sb** *He related the facts of the case to journalists.* 他給記者們講述了這件事的實際情況。◇ **~ how, what, etc. …** *She related how he had run away from home as a boy.* 她追述了他小時候是如何離家出走的。◇ **~ that …** *The story relates that an angel appeared and told him to sing.* 這個故事講述一個天使現身，叫他唱歌。

PHR V **reˈlate to sth/sb** **1** to be connected with sth/sb; to refer to sth/sb 涉及；與…相關；談到：*We shall discuss the problem as it relates to our specific case.* 我們應針對我們的具體情況來討論這個問題。◇ *The second paragraph relates to the situation in Scotland.* 第二段談到蘇格蘭的形勢。**2** to be able to understand and have sympathy with sb/sth 能夠理解並同情；瞭解；體恤 SYN **empathize with**：*Many adults can't relate to children.* 許多成年人並不瞭解兒童的想法。◇ *Our product needs an image that people can relate to.* 我們的產品需要一個大家能理解的形象。

re·lated /rɪˈleɪtɪd/ *adj.*

1 **~ (to sth/sb)** connected with sth/sb in some way 相關的；有聯繫的：*Much of the crime in this area is related to drug abuse.* 這一地區的許多犯罪都與濫用藥物有關。◇ *These problems are **closely related.*** 這些問題都是密切相關的。◇ *a **related issue/question*** 相關的課題／問題 ◇ *a stress-related illness* 壓力導致的疾病 **2** **~ (to sth/sb)** in the same family 屬同一家族的；有親屬關係的：*Are you related to Margaret?* 你與瑪格麗特是一家人嗎？◇ *We're distantly related.* 我們是遠親。 **3** **~ (to sth)** belonging to the same group 屬於同一種類的；同一組別的：*related languages* 同系語言 ◇ *The llama is related to the camel.* 美洲駝和駱駝是親緣物種。 OPP **unrelated**

▸ **re·lated·ness** *noun* [U]

re·la·tion /rɪˈleɪʃn/ *noun*

1 **relations** [pl.] the way in which two people, groups or countries behave towards each other or deal with each other（人、團體、國家之間的）關係，聯繫，交往：***diplomatic/international/foreign relations*** 外交／國際／對外關係 ◇ *US-Chinese relations* 美中關係 ◇ *teacher-pupil relations* 師生關係 ◇ **~ (with sb/sth)** *Relations with neighbouring countries are under strain at present.* 目前，與鄰國的關係正處於緊張狀態。◇ **~ (between A and B)** *We seek to improve relations between our two countries.* 我們尋求改進我們兩國間的關係。◇ (*formal*) *to have **sexual relations*** (= to have sex) 發生性關係 ➲ COLLOCATIONS at INTERNATIONAL ➲ see also INDUSTRIAL RELATIONS, PUBLIC RELATIONS, RACE RELATIONS **2** [U, C] the way in which two or more things are connected（事物之間的）關係，關聯，聯繫：**~ between A and B** *the relation between rainfall and crop yields* 降雨量和農作物產量之間的關係 ◇ **~ to sth** *the relation of the farmer to the land* 農民和土地的關係 ◇ *The fee they are offering **bears no relation to** the amount of work involved.* 他們支付的酬金和所需的工作量無關。◇ (*formal*) *I have some comments to make **in relation to*** (= concerning) *this matter.* 關於這件事我有幾點看法。◇ *Its brain is small **in relation to*** (= compared with) *its body.* 和它的身體相比，它的大腦很小。 **3** [C] a person who is in the same family as sb else 親戚；親屬 SYN **relative**：*a **close/near/distant relation** of mine* 我的一位近親／遠親 ◇ *a relation by marriage* 姻親 ◇ *a party for friends and relations* 親戚朋友的聚會 ◇ *He's called Brady too, but we're **no relation*** (= not related). 他也叫布雷迪，但我們不是親戚。◇ *Is he any relation to you?* 他是你的什麼親戚嗎？➲ see also BLOOD RELATION, POOR RELATION

re·la·tion·al /rɪˈleɪʃənl/ *adj.* (*formal* or *technical* 術語) existing or considered in relation to sth else 有關的；相關的

reˌlational ˈdatabase *noun* (*computing* 計) a DATABASE that recognizes relationships between different pieces of information 關係數據庫；關聯式資料庫

re·la·tion·ship /rɪˈleɪʃnʃɪp/ *noun*

1 [C] the way in which two people, groups or countries behave towards each other or deal with each other（人、團體、國家之間的）關係，聯繫：**~ (between A and B)** *The relationship between the police and the local community has improved.* 警察和當地民眾之間的關係已經得到改善。◇ **~ (with sb)** *She has a very **close relationship** with her sister.* 她和她妹妹非常親密。◇ *I have established a good **working relationship** with my boss.* 我與老闆已經建立起良好的工作關係。◇ *a master-servant relationship* 主僕關係 ➲ see also LOVE-HATE RELATIONSHIP **2** [C] **~ (between A and B)** | **~ (with sb)** a loving and/or sexual friendship between two people 情愛關係；性愛關係：*Their affair did not develop into a lasting relationship.* 他們的曖昧關係未能發展成為持久的愛情。◇ *She's had a series of miserable relationships.* 她經歷了一次又一次的戀愛波折。◇ *Are you **in a relationship**?* 你在戀愛嗎？ **3** [C, U] the way in which two or more things are connected（事物之間的）關聯，聯繫，關係：**~ (between A and B)** *the relationship between mental and physical health* 精神健康和身體健康之間的關係 ◇ **~ (to sth)** *This comment **bore no relationship to** the subject of our conversation.* 這個意見與我們所談論的話題毫不相干。◇ *People alter their voices **in relationship to** background noise.* 人們根據環境噪音的大小調節自己的聲音。 **4** [C, U] the way in which a person is related to sb else in a family 血緣關係；姻親關係：*a father-son relationship* 父子關係 ◇ **~ between A and B** *I'm not sure of the exact relationship between them—I think they're cousins.* 我不太清楚他們之間的確切關係，我想他們是表親吧。

rela·tive /ˈrelətɪv/ *adj., noun*

■ ***adj.*** **1** considered and judged by being compared with sth else 相比較而言的；比較的：*the **relative merits** of the two plans* 相比較之下兩個計劃顯出的優點 **2** **~ (to sth)** considered according to its position or connection with sth else 相對的；相關聯的：*the position of the sun relative to the earth* 太陽與地球的相對位置 **3** [only before noun] that exists or that has a particular quality only when compared with sth else 相比之下存在（或有）的 SYN **comparative**：*They now live in relative comfort* (= compared with how they lived before). 他們現在過得比較舒適。◇ *Given the failure of the previous plan, this turned out to be a relative success.* 由於前面那個計劃失敗了，這個計劃是比較成功的。◇ ***It's all relative*** *though, isn't it? We never had any money when I was a kid and $500 was a fortune to us.* 不過，一切都是相對的，是不是？我小的時候，我們根本沒有錢，500 塊錢對於我們來說就是很大的一筆錢了。➲ compare ABSOLUTE **4** **~ to sth** (*formal*) having a connection with sth; referring to sth 關於（或涉及）…的：*the facts relative to the case* 與這個案件有關的事實 **5** (*grammar* 語法) referring to an earlier noun, sentence or part of a sentence（指代前面的名詞、句子或句子的一部份）：*In 'the man who came', 'who' is a **relative pronoun** and 'who came' is a **relative clause**.* 在 the man who came 中，who 是關係代詞，而 who came 是關係從句。

■ ***noun*** **1** a person who is in the same family as sb else 親戚；親屬 SYN **relation**：*a **close/distant relative*** 近／遠親 ◇ *her friends and relatives* 她的親友 **2** a thing that belongs to the same group as sth else 同類事物：

R

The ibex is a distant relative of the mountain goat. 北山羊與石山羊有較遠的親緣關係。

,relative atomic 'mass (also **a,tomic 'mass**, **a,tomic 'weight**) *noun* (*chemistry* 化) the average MASS of all the naturally occurring atoms of a chemical element 相對原子質量

,relative 'density (also **spe,cific 'gravity**) *noun* [U] (*chemistry* 化) the mass of a substance divided by the mass of the same volume of water or air 相對密度

rela·tive·ly 0-w /ˈrelətɪvli/ *adv.*
to a fairly large degree, especially in comparison to sth else 相當程度上；相當地；相對地：*I found the test relatively easy.* 我覺得這次測驗比較容易。◇ *We had relatively few applications for the job.* 申請我們這項工作的人相對較少。◇ *Lack of exercise is also a risk factor for heart disease but it's relatively small when compared with the others.* 缺乏鍛煉也是導致心臟病的一個因素。但和其他因素相比，這方面的危險較小。
IDM **'relatively speaking** used when you are comparing sth with all similar things（和所有類似事物比較）相對而言：*Relatively speaking, these jobs provide good salaries.* 相對來說，這些工作報酬都不低。

rela·tiv·ism /ˈrelətɪvɪzəm/ *noun* [U] (*formal*) the belief that truth is not always and generally valid, but can be judged only in relation to other things, such as your personal situation 相對主義（認為真理並非絕對的，只能根據其他事物加以判斷）▸ **rela·tiv·ist** *adj.*：*a relativist view* 相對主義觀點 **rela·tiv·ist** *noun*

rela·tiv·ity /ˌreləˈtɪvəti/ *noun* [U] **1** (*physics* 物) Einstein's theory of the universe based on the principle that all movement is relative and that time is a fourth DIMENSION related to space 相對論 **2** (*formal*) the state of being relative and only able to be judged when compared with sth else 相對性

re·launch /ˌriːˈlɔːntʃ/ *verb* **~ sth** to start or present sth again in a new or different way, especially a product for sale 重新推出；重新發佈 ▸ **re·launch** /ˈriːlɔːntʃ/ *noun*

relax 0-w **AW** /rɪˈlæks/ *verb*
1 0-w [I] to rest while you are doing sth enjoyable, especially after work or effort 放鬆；休息 **SYN** **unwind**：*Just relax and enjoy the movie.* 休息休息，看看電影吧。◇ *I'm going to spend the weekend just relaxing.* 這個週末，我什麼也不幹，就是休息。◇ **~ with sth** *When I get home from work I like to relax with the newspaper.* 我下班回到家裏，喜歡看看報紙，放鬆一下。 **2** 0-w [I, T] **~ (sb)** to become or make sb become calmer and less worried 寬慰；（使）冷靜，放心，鎮定：*I'll only relax when I know you're safe.* 我只有知道你安然無恙才會放心。◇ *Relax! Everything will be OK.* 別着急！一切都會好的。 **3** 0-w [I, T] to become or make sth become less tight or stiff（使）放鬆，鬆懈；鬆開：*Allow your muscles to relax completely.* 讓你的肌肉完全放鬆。◇ **~ sth** *The massage relaxed my tense back muscles.* 按摩使得我背部緊張的肌肉鬆弛下來。◇ *He* ***relaxed his grip*** *on her arm.* 他本來抓着她的胳膊，現在鬆開了手。◇ (*figurative*) *The dictator refuses to relax his grip on power.* 獨裁者拒絕放鬆對權力的控制。 **4** 0-w [T] **~ sth** to allow rules, laws, etc. to become less strict 放寬（限制等）：*The council has relaxed the ban on dogs in city parks.* 委員會已經放寬了對帶狗到市內公園裏去的禁令。 **5** [T] **~ sth** to allow your attention or effort to become weaker 放鬆精神（或思想）：*You cannot afford to relax your concentration for a moment.* 你必須集中精力，一刻都不能鬆懈。

re·lax·ant /rɪˈlæksənt/ *noun* (*medical* 醫) a drug that is used to make the body relax 鬆弛劑：*a muscle relaxant* 肌肉鬆弛劑

re·lax·ation **AW** /ˌriːlækˈseɪʃn/ *noun* **1** [U] ways of resting and enjoying yourself; time spent resting and enjoying yourself 放鬆；休息；消遣；用於放鬆消遣的時間：*I go hill-walking for relaxation.* 我要是想放鬆一下，就到山上走走。◇ *a few days of relaxation* 幾天的休息時間 ◇ *relaxation techniques* 休息的方法 ➲ **SYNONYMS** at ENTERTAINMENT **2** [C] something pleasant you do in order to rest, especially after you have been working 休閒活動；娛樂活動：*Fishing is his favourite relaxation.* 釣魚是他最喜歡的消遣活動。 **3** [U, C, usually sing.] the act of making a rule or some form of control less strict or severe（對規章制度的）放寬，放鬆：*the relaxation of foreign currency controls* 對外匯管制的放寬 ◇ *a relaxation of travel restrictions* 旅遊限制的放寬

re·laxed 0-w **AW** /rɪˈlækst/ *adj.*
1 0-w **~ (about sth)** (of a person 人) calm and not anxious or worried 放鬆的；冷靜的；鎮定的：*He appeared relaxed and confident before the match.* 比賽前，他顯得鎮定而自信。◇ *She had a very relaxed manner.* 她的舉止特別自然。 **2** 0-w (of a place 地方) calm and informal 安靜的；自在的：*a family-run hotel with a* ***relaxed atmosphere*** 家庭經營的旅店，氣氛自由隨便 **3** 0-w **~ (about sth)** not caring too much about discipline or making people follow rules 不加以拘束的 **SYN** **laid-back**：*I take a fairly* ***relaxed attitude*** *towards what the kids wear to school.* 孩子穿什麼上學，我覺得無所謂。

re·lax·ing 0-w **AW** /rɪˈlæksɪŋ/ *adj.*
helping you to rest and become less anxious 有助於休息的；令人放鬆的；輕鬆的：*a relaxing evening with friends* 和朋友在一起的輕鬆夜晚

relay *verb, noun*
■ ***verb*** /ˈriːleɪ; rɪˈleɪ/ **1 ~ sth (to sb)** to receive and send on information, news, etc. to sb 轉發（信息、消息等）：*He relayed the message to his boss.* 他將這個消息轉給了他的老闆。◇ *Instructions were relayed to him by phone.* 通過電話將指令轉達給了他。 **2 ~ sth (to sb)** to broadcast television or radio signals 播放，轉播（電視或廣播訊號）：*The game was relayed by satellite to audiences all over the world.* 這場比賽通過衛星向全世界的觀眾進行了轉播。
■ ***noun*** /ˈriːleɪ/ **1** (also **'relay race**) a race between teams in which each member of the team runs or swims one section of the race 接力賽：*the 4 × 100m relay* * 4 × 100 米接力賽 ◇ *a relay team* 接力隊 ◇ *the sprint relay* 短跑接力賽 **2** a fresh set of people or animals that take the place of others that are tired or have finished a period of work 接班的人（或動物）；輪換者：*Rescuers worked* ***in relays*** *to save the trapped miners.* 救援人員輪班營救受困的礦工。 **3** an electronic device that receives radio or television signals and sends them on again with greater strength 中繼設備：*a relay station* 中繼站

re·lease 0-w **AW** /rɪˈliːs/ *verb, noun*
■ ***verb***
▸ **SET SB/STH FREE** 釋放 **1** 0-w to let sb/sth come out of a place where they have been kept or trapped 釋放；放出；放走：**~ sb/sth** *to* ***release a prisoner/hostage*** 釋放囚犯／人質 ◇ **~ sb/sth from sth** *Firefighters took two hours to release the driver from the wreckage.* 消防隊員花了兩個小時將司機從汽車殘骸中救出來。
▸ **STOP HOLDING STH** 鬆開 **2** 0-w **~ sth** to stop holding sth or stop it from being held so that it can move, fly, fall, etc. freely 放開；鬆開；使自由移動（或飛翔、降落等）**SYN** **let go, let loose**：*He refused to release her arm.* 他不肯放開她的胳膊。◇ *10 000 balloons were released at the ceremony.* 典禮上放飛了一萬個氣球。◇ *Intense heat is released in the reaction.* 反應過程中產生高熱。
▸ **FEELINGS** 情感 **3** 0-w **~ sth** to express feelings such as anger or worry in order to get rid of them 發泄；宣泄：*She burst into tears, releasing all her pent-up emotions.* 她放聲大哭，發泄出全部鬱積起來的情感。
▸ **FREE SB FROM DUTY** 免除職責 **4** to free sb from a duty, responsibility, contract, etc. 免除，解除（某人的職責、責任、合同等）；解雇：**~ sb** *The club is releasing some of its older players.* 俱樂部正在解聘一些老隊員。◇ **~ sb from sth** *The new law released employers from their obligation to recognize unions.* 新的法律免除了雇主承認工會的義務。
▸ **PART OF MACHINE** 機器部件 **5** 0-w **~ sth** to remove sth from a fixed position, allowing sth else to move or function 鬆開；拉開：*to* ***release the clutch/handbrake/switch, etc.*** 鬆開離合器、手閘、開關等
▸ **MAKE LESS TIGHT** 使不緊張 **6 ~ sth** to make sth less tight 使不緊張；使鬆弛；放鬆：*You need to release the tension in these shoulder muscles.* 你需要放鬆肩部肌肉。
▸ **MAKE AVAILABLE** 使可獲得 **7** 0-w **~ sth** to make sth available to the public 公開；公佈；發佈：*Police have*

released no further details about the accident. 關於這次事故，警方沒有透露更多的細節。◇ *to release a movie/book/CD* 發行電影／書／CD ◇ *new products released onto the market* 投放到市場的新產品 **8 ~ sth** to make sth available that had previously been restricted 開放；放開；解禁：*The new building programme will go ahead as soon as the government releases the funds.* 政府一撥放資金，新的建築項目就動工。

■ **noun**

▸ **SETTING SB/STH FREE** 釋放 **1** [U, sing.] **~ (of sb) (from sth)** the act of setting a person or an animal free; the state of being set free 釋放；獲釋：*The government has been working to secure the release of the hostages.* 政府一直在努力爭取使人質獲釋。◇ *She can expect an early release from prison.* 她有望早一點出獄。

▸ **MAKING STH AVAILABLE** 使可得到 **2** [U, sing.] the act of making sth available to the public 公開；發行；發佈：*The new software is planned for release in April.* 新軟件計劃四月份發行。◇ *The movie* **goes on** *general* **release** (= will be widely shown in cinemas/movie theaters) *next week.* 這部電影將於下週公開發行。 **3** [C] a thing that is made available to the public, especially a new CD or film/movie 新發行的東西；（尤指）新唱片，新電影：*the latest new releases* 最新發行的產品

▸ **OF GAS/CHEMICAL** 氣體；化學品 **4** [U, C] the act of letting a gas, chemical, etc. come out of the container where it has been safely held 排放；泄漏；滲漏：*the release of carbon dioxide into the atmosphere* 二氧化碳向大氣層的排放 ◇ *to monitor radiation releases* 控制輻射的釋放

▸ **FROM UNPLEASANT FEELING** 不愉快的感覺 **5** [U, sing.] the feeling that you are free from pain, anxiety or some other unpleasant feeling 解脫；輕鬆感：*a sense of release after the exam* 考試後的解脫感 ◇ *I think her death was a merciful release.* 我認為她的死是一種幸運的解脫。 ➲ see also PRESS RELEASE

rele·gate /ˈrelɪɡeɪt/ *verb* **1 ~ sb/sth (to sth)** to give sb a lower or less important position, rank, etc. than before 使貶職；使降級；降低…的地位：*She was then relegated to the role of assistant.* 隨後她被降級做助手了。◇ *He relegated the incident to the back of his mind.* 他將這件事拋到了腦後。 **2** [usually passive] **~ sth** (*especially BrE*) to move a sports team, especially a football (SOCCER) team, to a lower position within an official league 使（運動隊，尤指足球隊）降級；使降組 OPP **promote** ▸ **rele·ga·tion** /ˌrelɪˈɡeɪʃn/ *noun* [U]：*teams threatened with relegation* 受降級威脅的球隊

re·lent /rɪˈlent/ *verb* (*formal*) **1** [I] to finally agree to sth after refusing 終於答應；不再拒絕 SYN **give in**：*'Well, just for a little while then,' she said, finally relenting.* "好吧，不過只能待一會兒。" 她最後終於答應了。 **2** [I] to become less determined, strong, etc. 變緩和；變溫和；減弱：*After two days the rain relented.* 兩天後，雨勢減弱了。◇ *The police will not relent in their fight against crime.* 警方將繼續嚴厲打擊犯罪活動。

re·lent·less /rɪˈlentləs/ *adj.* **1** not stopping or getting less strong 不停的；持續強烈的；不減弱的 SYN **unrelenting**：*her* **relentless pursuit of** *perfection* 她對完美的不懈追求 ◇ *The sun was relentless.* 太陽還是那麼熱。 **2** refusing to give up or be less strict or severe 不放棄的；嚴格的；苛刻的；無情的：*a relentless enemy* 殘酷的敵人 ▸ **re·lent·less·ly** *adv.*

rele·vant AW /ˈreləvənt/ *adj.* **1** closely connected with the subject you are discussing or the situation you are thinking about 緊密相關的；切題的：*a relevant suggestion/question/point* 相關的提議／問題／觀點 ◇ *Do you have the relevant experience?* 你有相關的經驗嗎？◇ **~ to sth/sb** *These comments are not directly relevant to this inquiry.* 這些意見與這項調查沒有直接聯繫。 OPP **irrelevant 2 ~ (to sth/sb)** having ideas that are valuable and useful to people in their lives and work 有價值的；有意義的：*Her novel is still relevant today.* 她的小說今天仍有現實意義。 ▸ **rele·vance** AW /-əns/ *noun* [U]：*I don't see the relevance of your question.* 我不懂你這個問題有什麼意義。◇ *What he said has no direct relevance to the matter in hand.* 他所說的話與眼下的事沒有直接關係。◇ *a classic play of contemporary relevance* 在當代仍有價值的古典戲劇 **rele·vant·ly** *adv.*：*The applicant has experience in teaching and, more relevantly, in industry.* 這名申請者有教學經驗，更重要的是，還有行業經驗。

re·li·able AW /rɪˈlaɪəbl/ *adj.* **1** that can be trusted to do sth well; that you can rely on 可信賴的；可依靠的 SYN **dependable**：*We are looking for someone who is reliable and hard-working.* 我們在物色可靠而又勤奮的人。◇ *a reliable friend* 可信賴的朋友 ◇ *My car's not as reliable as it used to be.* 我的車不像過去那樣靠得住了。 **2** that is likely to be correct or true 真實可信的；可靠的：*Our information comes from a reliable source.* 我們的消息來源可靠。◇ *a reliable witness* 可信的目擊證人 OPP **unreliable** ▸ **re·li·abil·ity** AW /rɪˌlaɪəˈbɪləti/ *noun* [U]：*The incident cast doubt on her motives and reliability.* 這件事使人懷疑她有何動機，以及她是否可靠。◇ *The reliability of these results has been questioned.* 這些結果的可信程度已受到質疑。 **re·li·ably** AW /-əbli/ *adv.*：*I am* **reliably informed** (= told by sb who knows the facts) *that the company is being sold.* 有可靠知情人告訴我公司要被賣掉。

re·li·ance AW /rɪˈlaɪəns/ *noun* [U, sing.] **~ (on/upon sb/sth)** the state of needing sb/sth in order to survive, be successful, etc.; the fact of being able to rely on sb/sth 依賴；依靠；信任 SYN **dependence**：*Heavy reliance on one client is risky when you are building up a business.* 創業時過分依賴某一個客戶是有風險的。◇ *Such learning methods encourage too great a reliance upon the teacher.* 這樣的學習方法會造成對老師的過分依賴。◇ *The study programme concentrates more on group work and* **places** *less* **reliance on** (= depends less on) *lectures.* 這個課程較注重小組活動而不倚重講座。◇ *I wouldn't* **place** *too much* **reliance on** (= trust) *these figures.* 我不會太相信這些數字的。

re·li·ant AW /rɪˈlaɪənt/ *adj.* **~ on/upon sb/sth** needing sb/sth in order to survive, be successful, etc. 依賴性的；依靠的 SYN **dependent**：*The hostel is heavily reliant upon charity.* 這家收容所在很大程度上依賴贊助。 ➲ see also SELF-RELIANT

relic /ˈrelɪk/ *noun* **1 ~ (of/from sth)** an object, a tradition, a system, etc. that has survived from the past 遺物；遺跡；遺風；遺俗：*The building stands as the last remaining relic of the town's cotton industry.* 這座建築物是小鎮棉紡業僅存的遺跡。◇ *Videotapes may already seem like relics of a bygone era.* 錄像帶似乎已成為過去時代的遺物。 **2** a part of the body or clothing of a holy person, or sth that they owned, that is kept after their death and respected as a religious object 聖髑；聖骨；聖人遺物：*holy relics* 聖人遺物

re·lief /rɪˈliːf/ *noun*

▸ **REMOVAL OF ANXIETY/PAIN** 焦慮／痛苦的消除 **1** [U, sing.] the feeling of happiness that you have when sth unpleasant stops or does not happen （不快過後的）寬慰，輕鬆；解脫：*a sense of relief* 解脫感 ◇ *We all* **breathed a sigh of relief** *when he left.* 他走了以後，我們大家都如釋重負地鬆了口氣。◇ *She sighed with relief.* 她鬆了口氣。◇ *Much* **to my relief** *the car was not damaged.* 令我非常慶幸的是車並沒有損壞。◇ *News of their safety came as a great relief.* 他們平安的消息給大家帶來了巨大的安慰。◇ *It was a relief to be able to talk to someone about it.* 能和別人談談這件事，感到舒心多了。◇ ***What a relief!*** 可輕鬆了！ **2** [U] **~ (from/of sth)** the act of removing or reducing pain, anxiety, etc. （焦慮、痛苦等的）減輕，消除，緩和：*modern methods of* **pain relief** 現代消除疼痛的辦法 ◇ *the relief of suffering* 痛苦的消除

▸ **HELP** 幫助 **3** [U] food, money, medicine, etc. that is given to help people in places where there has been a war or natural disaster （給災區或交戰地區人民提供的）救濟，救援物品 SYN **aid**：***famine relief*** 饑荒救濟物資 ◇ *a* ***relief agency/organization/worker*** 救助機構／組織／工作者 **4** [U] (*especially NAmE*) financial help given by the government to people who need it 救濟金

▸ **ON TAX** 稅收 **5** [U] = TAX RELIEF：*relief on mortgage interest payments* 支付按揭利息的稅收減免

▸ **STH DIFFERENT** 變化 **6** [U, sing.] something that is interesting or enjoyable that replaces sth boring, diffi-

R

cult or unpleasant for a short period of time（暫時替代單調乏味事物的）調劑，輕鬆場面：*a few moments of **light relief** in an otherwise dull performance* 沉悶的表演中幾處輕鬆的情節 ◇ *There was little **comic relief** in his speech.* 他的演講少有輕鬆幽默的地方。◇ **~ from sth** *The calm of the countryside came as a welcome relief from the hustle and bustle of city life.* 離開喧囂忙碌的城市生活，來到寧靜的鄉村，是一種令人愉快的調劑。
▸ **WORKERS** 工人 **7** [C+sing./pl. v.] (often used as an adjective 常用作形容詞) a person or group of people that replaces another when they have finished working for the day or when they are sick 替班者；接替人；換班者：*The next crew relief comes on duty at 9 o'clock.* 下一批換班的員工 9 點鐘接班。◇ *relief drivers* 換班的司機
▸ **FROM ENEMY** 從敵人手中 **8** [sing.] **~ of …** the act of freeing a town, etc. from an enemy army that has surrounded it（被困城鎮等的）解困，解圍
▸ **IN ART** 藝術 **9** [U, C] a way of decorating wood, stone, etc. by cutting designs into the surface of it so that some parts stick out more than others; a design that is made in this way 浮雕；浮雕法；浮雕作品：*The column was decorated **in high relief** (= with designs that stick out a lot) with scenes from Greek mythology.* 柱子上飾有描述希臘神話中的場面的高浮雕。◇ *The bronze doors are covered with sculpted reliefs.* 青銅門上覆有浮雕。
➲ VISUAL VOCAB page V14
▸ **MAKING STH NOTICEABLE** 使醒目 **10** [U] the effect of colours, light, etc. that makes an object more noticeable than others around it（光和色彩等產生的）醒目效果；醒目；光彩奪目：*The snow-capped mountain stood out **in sharp relief** against the blue sky.* 冰雪覆蓋的高山在藍天的映襯下格外醒目。**11** [U] the quality of a particular situation, problem, etc. that makes it more noticeable than before 突出的品質；令人注目的特徵：*Their differences have been **thrown into sharp relief** by the present crisis.* 目前的危機使得他們的分歧更加引人注目。

re'lief map *noun* a map that uses various colours, etc. to show the different heights of hills, valleys, etc.（用不同顏色表示地勢高低的）地形圖，地勢圖，地貌圖

re'lief road *noun* (*BrE*) a road that vehicles can use to avoid an area of heavy traffic, especially a road built for this purpose（交通高峰時減緩擁擠的）疏導路，旁道

re·lieve /rɪ'liːv/ *verb* **1 ~ sth** to remove or reduce an unpleasant feeling or pain 解除，減輕，緩和（不快或痛苦）：*to relieve the symptoms of a cold* 減輕感冒的症狀 ◇ *to **relieve anxiety/guilt/stress*** 消除焦慮／內疚；緩解壓力 ◇ *Being able to tell the truth at last seemed to relieve her.* 最後能夠講出真話似乎使她感到輕鬆。**2 ~ sth** to make a problem less serious 減輕（問題的嚴重性）；緩和；緩解 SYN **alleviate**：*efforts to relieve poverty* 緩解貧困的努力 ◇ *to relieve traffic congestion* 緩解交通擁擠 **3 ~ sth** to make sth less boring, especially by introducing sth different 調劑；使有趣：*We played cards to relieve the boredom of the long wait.* 長時間等待實在無聊，我們就打撲克來解悶兒。◇ *The black and white pattern is relieved by tiny coloured flowers.* 五彩繽紛的小花使得黑白圖案不那麼單調。**4 ~ sb** to replace sb who is on duty 接替；給…換班：*to relieve a sentry* 換崗 ◇ *You'll be relieved at six o'clock.* 六點鐘有人來換你的班。**5 ~ sth** to free a town, etc. from an enemy army that has surrounded it 將（城鎮從敵人的圍困中）解圍 **6 ~ yourself** a polite way of referring to going to the toilet（去廁所的一種委婉說法）方便，解手：*I had to relieve myself behind a bush.* 我只好在樹叢後面方便了一下。

PHR V **re'lieve sb of sth** **1** to help sb by taking sth heavy or difficult from them 替…拿重物；幫助…減輕（負擔）：*Let me relieve you of some of your bags.* 我來幫你拿幾個袋子吧。◇ *The new secretary will relieve us of some of the paperwork.* 新來的秘書會減輕我們文案工作的一些負擔。**2** (*informal, ironic*) to steal sth from sb 偷竊；竊取：*A boy with a knife relieved him of his wallet.* 一個持刀的傢伙偷了他的錢包。**3** to dismiss sb from a job, position, etc. 開除；解除；解除…的職務：*General Beale was relieved of his command.* 比爾將軍被解除了指揮權。

re·lieved /rɪ'liːvd/ *adj.* feeling happy because sth unpleasant has stopped or has not happened; showing this 感到寬慰的；放心的；顯得開心的：*She sounded relieved.* 她聽上去很放心。◇ **~ (to see, hear, find, etc. sth)** *You'll be relieved to know your jobs are safe.* 現在知道你們的工作保住了，可以放心了。◇ **~ (that …)** *I'm just relieved that nobody was hurt.* 誰都沒有受傷，我深感寬慰。◇ *They exchanged relieved glances.* 他們如釋重負地彼此看了看。➲ SYNONYMS at GLAD

re·li·gion 0-w /rɪ'lɪdʒən/ *noun*
1 0-w [U] the belief in the existence of a god or gods, and the activities that are connected with the worship of them 宗教；宗教信仰：*Is there always a conflict between science and religion?* 科學和宗教信仰之間是否永遠存在着衝突？**2** 0-w [C] one of the systems of faith that are based on the belief in the existence of a particular god or gods 宗教；教派：*the Jewish religion* 猶太教 ◇ *Christianity, Islam and other world religions* 基督教、伊斯蘭教和其他世界性宗教 ◇ *The law states that everyone has the right to practise their own religion.* 法律規定每個人都有信仰宗教的權利。**3** [sing.] a particular interest or influence that is very important in your life 特別的興趣；重大的影響：*For him, football is an absolute religion.* 對於他來說，足球就是他至高無上的追求。

IDM **get re'ligion** (*informal, disapproving*) to suddenly become interested in religion 突然有了信仰；突然對宗教感興趣

re·ligi·os·ity /rɪˌlɪdʒi'ɒsəti; *NAmE* -'ɑːsəti/ *noun* [U] (*formal*, sometimes *disapproving*) the state of being religious or too religious 篤信宗教；過度的宗教熱忱

re·li·gious 0-w /rɪ'lɪdʒəs/ *adj.*
1 0-w [only before noun] connected with religion or with a particular religion 宗教信仰的；宗教的：***religious beliefs/faith*** 宗教信仰；信德 ◇ ***religious education*** (= education about religion) 宗教教育 ◇ ***religious instruction*** (= instruction in a particular religion) 教義講授 ◇ *religious groups* 宗教團體 ◇ *objects which have a religious significance* 聖物 **2** 0-w (of a person 人) believing strongly in the existence of a god or gods 篤信宗教的；虔誠的 SYN **devout**：*His wife is very religious.* 她的妻子非常虔誠。▸ **re·li·gious·ness** *noun* [U]

re·li·gious·ly /rɪ'lɪdʒəsli/ *adv.* **1** very carefully or regularly 十分認真地；審慎地；很有規律地：*She followed the instructions religiously.* 她非常認真地按照說明操作。**2** in a way that is connected with religion 與宗教相關地；虔誠地：*Were you brought up religiously?* 你是在宗教的氛圍中長大的嗎？

re·lin·quish /rɪ'lɪŋkwɪʃ/ *verb* (*formal*) to stop having sth, especially when this happens unwillingly（尤指不情願地）放棄 SYN **give up**：**~ sth** *He was forced to relinquish control of the company.* 他被迫放棄對公司的控制權。◇ *They had relinquished all hope that she was alive.* 他們已經完全不指望她還活着了。◇ **~ sth to sb** *She relinquished possession of the house to her sister.* 她將房子讓給了她的妹妹。

reli·quary /'relɪkwəri; *NAmE* -kweri/ *noun* (*pl.* **-ies**) a container in which a RELIC of a holy person is kept 聖髑盒；盛放聖人遺物的容器

rel·ish /'relɪʃ/ *verb, noun*
■ *verb* to get great pleasure from sth; to want very much to do or have sth 享受；從…獲得樂趣；渴望；喜歡 SYN **enjoy**：**~ sth** *to relish a fight/challenge/debate* 喜歡鬥爭／挑戰／爭辯 ◇ *to relish the idea/thought of sth* 欣賞某觀點／想法 ◇ *I **don't relish the prospect** of getting up early tomorrow.* 我可不願意明天早上早起。◇ **~ (sb/sth) doing sth** *Nobody relishes cleaning the oven.* 沒有人願意清理烤爐。
■ *noun* **1** [U] great enjoyment or pleasure 享受；樂趣：*She savoured the moment **with obvious relish**.* 她顯然津津有味地回味着那一刻。**2** [U, C] a cold thick spicy sauce made from fruit and vegetables that have been boiled, that is served with meat, cheese, etc. 風味佐料（用水果和蔬菜煮後製成的冷稠辛辣醬汁）

re·live /ˌriː'lɪv/ *verb* **~ sth** to experience sth again, especially in your imagination（尤指在想像中）再次體驗，

R

重温；回味：*He relives the horror of the crash every night in his dreams.* 每天晚上他都會夢見那次撞車的可怕情景。

rel·lie /ˈreli/ *noun* (*AustralE, NZE, informal*) a relative 親戚；親眷：*All the rellies will be at the party.* 所有親戚都會來參加聚會。

re·load /ˌriːˈləʊd; *NAmE* -ˈloʊd/ *verb* **1** [I, T] **~ (sth)** to put more bullets into a gun, more film into a camera, etc. 給…再裝填（子彈或膠捲等） **2** [T] **~ sth** to put data or a program into the memory of a computer again 給（計算機）重新裝入（數據或程序） **3** [T] **~ sth** to fill a container, vehicle, machine, etc. again 再裝滿（容器、車輛、機器等）

re·locate AW /ˌriːləʊˈkeɪt; *NAmE* ˌriːˈloʊkeɪt/ *verb* [I, T] (especially of a company or workers 尤指公司或工人) to move or to move sb/sth to a new place to work or operate （使）搬遷，遷移：*The firm may be forced to relocate from New York to Stanford.* 公司也許會被迫從紐約遷移到斯坦福。◇ **~ sth** *The company relocated its head office to Stanford.* 公司將總部遷到了斯坦福。 ▸ **re·loca·tion** AW /ˌriːləʊˈkeɪʃn; *NAmE* ˌriːloʊ-/ *noun* [U]：*relocation costs* 搬遷費用

re·luc·tant AW /rɪˈlʌktənt/ *adj.* hesitating before doing sth because you do not want to do it or because you are not sure that it is the right thing to do 不情願的；勉強的：*reluctant agreement* 勉強同意 ◇ **~ (to do sth)** *She was reluctant to admit she was wrong.* 她不願承認自己有錯。◇ *He finally gave a reluctant smile.* 他最後露出了一絲無可奈何的微笑。◇ *a* ***reluctant hero*** (= a person who does not want to be called a hero) 不情願做英雄的英雄 ▸ **re·luc·tance** AW /-əns/ *noun* [U, sing.]：**~ (to do sth)** *There is still some reluctance on the part of employers to become involved in this project.* 雇主們仍然不太願意涉足這項計劃。◇ *They finally agreed to our terms with a certain reluctance.* 他們最終有點勉強地同意了我們的條件。 **re·luc·tant·ly** AW *adv.*：*We reluctantly agreed to go with her.* 我們勉強答應跟她一起去。

rely 🔑 AW /rɪˈlaɪ/ *verb* (**re·lies**, **rely·ing**, **re·lied**, **re·lied**)

> **WORD FAMILY**
> rely *verb*
> reliable *adj.* (≠ unreliable)
> reliably *adv.*
> reliability *noun* (≠ unreliability)
> reliance *noun*

PHR V **reˈly on/upon sb/sth** **1** 🔑 to need or depend on sb/sth 依賴；依靠：*As babies, we rely entirely on others for food.* 在嬰兒時期，我們完全依賴別人餵食。◇ **~ to do sth** *These days we rely heavily on computers to organize our work.* 現在，我們在很大程度上依賴電腦來安排我們的工作。◇ **~ doing sth** *The industry relies on the price of raw materials remaining low.* 這一產業靠的是原料便宜，不漲價。 **2** 🔑 to trust or have faith in sb/sth 信任；信賴：*You should rely on your own judgement.* 你應該相信你自己的判斷。◇ **~ to do sth** *You can rely on me to keep your secret.* 你可以相信我一定會為你保守秘密。◇ *He*

Collocations 詞語搭配

Religion 宗教

Being religious 篤信宗教的

- **believe in** God/Christ/Allah/free will/predestination/heaven and hell/an afterlife/reincarnation 信仰上帝／耶穌基督／真主／自由意志／宿命論／天堂與地獄／來生／轉世說
- **be/become** a believer/an atheist/an agnostic/a Christian/Muslim/Hindu/Buddhist, etc. 是／成為信徒／無神論者／不可知論者／基督徒／穆斯林／印度教教徒／佛教徒等
- **convert to/practise/**(*especially US*) **practice** a religion/Buddhism/Catholicism/Christianity/Islam/Judaism, etc. 皈依／信奉宗教／佛教／天主教／基督教／伊斯蘭教／猶太教等
- **go to** church/(*NAmE*) temple (= the synagogue) 去教堂／會堂做禮拜
- **go to** the local church/mosque/synagogue/gurdwara 去當地的教堂／清真寺／猶太教會堂／謁師所做禮拜
- **belong to** a church/a religious community 是教堂／宗教團體的成員
- **join/enter** the church/a convent/a monastery/a religious sect/the clergy/the priesthood 成為牧師／女修道士／僧侶／宗教人員／神職人員／司祭
- **praise/worship/obey/serve/glorify** God 讚美／敬拜／遵從／侍奉／頌揚上帝

Celebrations and ritual 慶典與儀式

- **attend/hold/conduct/lead** a service 參加／舉行／組織／主持禮拜儀式
- **perform** a ceremony/a rite/a ritual/a baptism/the Hajj/a mitzvah 舉行典禮／儀式／宗教儀式／洗禮／朝覲／受戒儀式
- **carry out/perform** a sacred/burial/funeral/fertility/purification rite 舉行宗教／安葬／葬禮／豐收／淨化儀式
- **go on/make** a pilgrimage 前往朝聖
- **celebrate** Christmas/Easter/Eid/Ramadan/Hanukkah/Passover/Diwali 慶祝聖誕節／復活節／開齋節／齋月／修殿節／逾越節／排燈節
- **observe/break** the Sabbath/a fast/Ramadan 守／不守安息日／齋戒／齋月
- **deliver/preach/hear** a sermon 傳道；講道；聽佈道
- **lead/address** the congregation 帶領會眾；對會眾發表演講
- **say/recite** a prayer/blessing 念誦／背誦經文；祝禱

Religious texts and ideas 宗教經文與思想

- **preach/proclaim/spread** the word of God/the Gospel/the message of Islam 傳佈／頌揚／傳播上帝的話／《福音》／伊斯蘭教義
- **study/follow** the dharma/the teachings of Buddha 研究／遵循達摩／佛教教義
- **read/study/understand/interpret** scripture/the Bible/the Koran/the gospel/the Torah 閱讀／研究／理解／闡釋經文／《聖經》／《古蘭經》／《福音》／托拉
- **be based on/derive from** divine revelation 基於／來源於上帝的啟示
- **commit/consider sth** heresy/sacrilege 犯異端／瀆聖罪；認為…是異端邪說／褻瀆聖物

Religious belief and experience 宗教信仰與體驗

- **seek/find/gain** enlightenment/wisdom 尋求／找到／獲得啟迪／智慧
- **strengthen/lose** your faith 增強／失去信德
- **keep/practise/practice/abandon** the faith 忠於／踐行／放棄信仰
- **save/purify/lose** your soul 拯救／淨化／失去靈魂
- **obey/follow/keep/break/violate** a commandment/Islamic law/Jewish law 服從／遵循／恪守／違反／褻瀆誡條／伊斯蘭教法／猶太教法
- **be/accept/do** God's will 是／接受／踐行上帝的旨意
- **receive/experience** divine grace 得到／感受神的恩寵
- **achieve/attain** enlightenment/salvation/nirvana 獲得啟迪／拯救／涅槃
- **undergo** a conversion/rebirth/reincarnation 經歷皈依／重生／轉世化身
- **hear/answer** a prayer 聆聽／回應禱告
- **commit/confess/forgive** a sin 犯罪；懺悔；寬恕罪過
- **do/perform** penance 進行補贖

can't be relied on to tell the truth. 不能指望他說真話。 ➲ SYNONYMS at TRUST

REM /ˌɑːr iː ˈem/ *abbr.* rapid eye movement (describes a period of sleep during which you dream and your eyes make many small movements) 快速眼動（夜間做夢時眼睛快速而細微的移動）

re·made *past tense, past part.* of REMAKE

re·main /rɪˈmeɪn/ *verb* (rather *formal*) (not usually in the progressive tenses 通常不用於進行時) **1** *linking verb* to continue to be sth; to be still in the same state or condition 仍然是；保持不變： **+ adj.** *to remain silent/standing/seated/motionless* 依然沉默／站着／坐着／一動不動 ◇ *Train fares are likely to remain unchanged.* 火車票價很可能會保持不變。◇ ***It remains** true that sport is about competing well, not winning.* 體育重在勇於競爭而非獲勝，一向如此。◇ **+ noun** *In spite of their quarrel, they remain the best of friends.* 儘管有過爭吵，他們仍是最好的朋友。◇ *He will remain (as) manager of the club until the end of his contract.* 他將繼續擔任俱樂部經理，直至合同期滿。 **2** [I] to still be present after the other parts have been removed, used, etc.; to continue to exist 剩餘；遺留；繼續存在： *Very little of the house remained after the fire.* 火災之後，這座房子所剩無幾。◇ *There were only ten minutes remaining.* 只剩下十分鐘了。 **3** [I] **~ (to do sth)** to still need to be done, said, or dealt with 仍需去做（或說、處理）： *Much remains to be done.* 還有很多事要去做。◇ ***It remains to be seen** (= it will only be known later) whether you are right.* 你說得對不對還有待證實。◇ ***There remained** one significant problem.* 還有一個非常重要的問題。◇ *Questions remain about the president's honesty.* 總統是否誠實，還有許多疑問。◇ *I feel sorry for her, but **the fact remains** (**that**) she lied to us.* 我為她感到難過，可事實是她對我們撒了謊。 ➲ LANGUAGE BANK at NEVERTHELESS **4** [I] **+ adv./prep.** to stay in the same place; to not leave 逗留；不離去： *They remained in Mexico until June.* 他們在墨西哥一直待到六月。◇ *The plane remained on the ground.* 飛機仍未起飛。◇ *She left, but I remained behind.* 她走了，而我留了下來。 IDM see ALOOF

re·main·der /rɪˈmeɪndə(r)/ *noun, verb*

■ *noun* **1** (usually **the remainder**) [sing.+sing./pl. v.] the remaining people, things or time 其他人員；剩餘物；剩餘時間 SYN **the rest**： *I kept some of his books and gave away the remainder.* 我保留了一些他的書，其他的都送人了。 HELP When **the remainder** refers to a plural noun, the verb is plural. * remainder 作複數名詞時，動詞用複數： *Most of our employees work in New York; the remainder are in London.* **2** [C, usually sing.] (*mathematics* 數) the numbers left after one number has been SUBTRACTED from another, or one number has been divided into another 差數；餘數： *Divide 2 into 7, and the answer is 3, remainder 1.* * 7 除以 2，商 3 餘 1。 ➲ compare DIVISOR **3** [C] a book that has been remaindered 廉價出售的圖書；滯銷圖書

■ *verb* [I, T, usually passive] **~ (sth)** to sell books at a reduced price 廉價出售（書）

re·main·ing /rɪˈmeɪnɪŋ/ *adj.* [only before noun] still needing to be done or dealt with 仍需做的；還需處理的： *The remaining twenty patients were transferred to another hospital.* 其餘的二十名病人給轉送到另一家醫院去了。◇ *Any remaining tickets for the concert will be sold on the door.* 其餘門票均於音樂會時即場發售。 ➲ see also REMAIN

re·mains /rɪˈmeɪnz/ *noun* [pl.]

1 **~ (of sth)** the parts of sth that are left after the other parts have been used, eaten, removed, etc. 剩餘物；殘留物；剩飯菜： *She fed the remains of her lunch to the dog.* 她把剩下的午飯餵狗了。 **2** the parts of ancient objects and buildings that have survived and are discovered in the present day 古代遺物；古跡；遺跡；遺址： *prehistoric remains* 史前遺跡 ◇ *the remains of a Roman fort* 羅馬要塞的遺址 **3** (*formal*) the body of a dead person or animal 遺體；遺骸： *They had discovered **human remains**.* 他們發現過人類遺骸。

re·make *noun, verb*

■ *noun* /ˈriːmeɪk/ a new or different version of an old film/movie or song（電影或歌曲的）新版，改編版

■ *verb* /ˌriːˈmeɪk/ (**re·made**, **re·made** /-ˈmeɪd/) **~ sth** to make a new or different version of sth such as an old film/movie or song; to make sth again 重新製作，改編（電影或歌曲等）；重做： *'The Seven Samurai' was remade in Hollywood as 'The Magnificent Seven'.*《七武士》在好萊塢被重新製作成為《七俠蕩寇誌》。

re·mand /rɪˈmɑːnd; *NAmE* -ˈmænd/ *verb, noun*

■ *verb* [usually passive] **~ sb (+ adv./prep.)** to send sb away from a court to wait for their trial which will take place at a later date 將（嫌疑人）還押候審： *The two men were charged with burglary and **remanded in custody*** (= sent to prison until their trial). 兩名男子被控入室偷竊而被還押候審。◇ *She was **remanded on bail*** (= allowed to go free until the trial after leaving a sum of money with the court). 她獲准取保候審。

■ *noun* [U] (*BrE*) the process of keeping sb in prison while they are waiting for their trial 還押；押候： *He is currently being held **on remand**.* 他正被還押候審。◇ *a remand prisoner* 還押罪犯

reˈmand centre *noun* (*BrE*) a place where young people are sent when they are accused of a crime and are waiting for their trial 青少年拘留所

re·mark /rɪˈmɑːk; *NAmE* -ˈmɑːrk/ *noun, verb*

■ *noun* **1** [C] something that you say or write which expresses an opinion, a thought, etc. about sb/sth 談論；言論；評述 SYN **comment**： *to make a remark* 發表評論 ◇ *He made a number of rude remarks about the food.* 關於這裏的食物他說了許多無禮的評論。◇ *What exactly did you mean by that last remark?* 你最後那句話究竟是什麼意思？ ➲ SYNONYMS at STATEMENT **2** [U] (*old-fashioned* or *formal*) the quality of being important or interesting enough to be noticed 引人注目；顯耀 SYN **note**： *The exhibition contains nothing that is worthy of remark.* 這次展覽沒有任何值得看的東西。

■ *verb* [I, T] to say or write a comment about sth/sb 說起；談論；評論 SYN **comment**： **~ on/upon sth/sb** *The judges remarked on the high standard of entries for the competition.* 眾評委說參賽作品水準很高。◇ **~ how …** *She remarked how tired I was looking.* 她說我看上去顯得特別累。◇ **+ speech** *'It's much colder than yesterday,' he remarked casually.* "今天比昨天冷多了。" 他漫不經心地說。◇ **~ that …** *Critics remarked that the play was not original.* 評論家們指出這部戲劇缺乏創意。◇ **be remarked on** *The similarities between the two have often been remarked on.* 人們經常談到兩者的相似之處。 ➲ SYNONYMS at COMMENT

re·mark·able /rɪˈmɑːkəbl; *NAmE* -ˈmɑːrk-/ *adj.* unusual or surprising in a way that causes people to take notice 非凡的；奇異的；顯著的；引人注目的 SYN **astonishing**： *a remarkable achievement/career/talent* 非凡的成就／事業／才能 ◇ *She was a truly remarkable woman.* 她是一位真正非同凡響的女人。◇ **~ for sth** *The area is remarkable for its scenery.* 這一地區以其優美的景色而引人矚目。◇ **~ that …** *It is remarkable that nobody noticed sooner.* 過去竟然沒有人發現，真有意思。 OPP **unremarkable** ▸ **re·mark·ably** /-əbli/ *adv.*： *The car is in remarkably good condition for its age.* 就車齡而論，這輛車的狀況好極了。◇ *Remarkably, nobody was killed.* 竟然沒有死人，真是萬幸。

re·marry /ˌriːˈmæri/ *verb* (**re·mar·ries**, **re·marry·ing**, **re·mar·ried**, **re·mar·ried**) [I] to marry again after being divorced or after your husband or wife has died 再婚 ▸ **re·mar·riage** /ˌriːˈmærɪdʒ/ *noun* [U, C]

re·mas·ter /ˌriːˈmɑːstə(r); *NAmE* -ˈmæs-/ *verb* **~ sth** to make a new MASTER copy of a recording in order to improve the sound quality 重新錄製（唱片母帶）： *All the tracks have been **digitally remastered** from the original tapes.* 所有的曲子都已經從原始錄音帶轉錄到了數碼母帶上。

re·match /ˈriːmætʃ/ *noun* [usually sing.] a match or game played again between the same people or teams, especially because neither side won the first match or game（尤指因首輪未決出勝負）重賽，複賽

re·medi·able /rɪˈmiːdiəbl/ *adj.* (*formal*) that can be solved or cured 可解決的；可治癒的 **SYN** **curable**：*remediable problems/diseases* 可以解決的問題；可治癒的疾病

re·med·ial /rɪˈmiːdiəl/ *adj.* [only before noun] **1** aimed at solving a problem, especially when this involves correcting or improving sth that has been done wrong 旨在解決問題的；補救的；糾正的：*remedial treatment* (= for a medical problem) 治療 ◇ ***Remedial action** must be taken now.* 現在必須進行補救。 **2** connected with school students who are slower at learning than others（為後進學生）補習的，輔導的：*remedial education* 補習教育 ◇ *a remedial class* 補習班

re·me·di·ation /rɪˌmiːdiˈeɪʃn/ *noun* [U] (*NAmE*) the process of improving sth or correcting sth that is wrong, especially changing or stopping damage to the environment 補救；糾正；（尤指對環境破壞的）整改，制止：*remediation of contaminated soil* 受污染土壤的改善 ▸ **remediate** /rɪˈmiːdieɪt/ *verb*：**~ sth** (*NAmE*) *The problems need to be detected and remediated quickly.* 這些問題得迅速查明並加以糾正。

rem·edy /ˈremədi/ *noun, verb*

■ ***noun*** (*pl.* **-ies**) **1** a way of dealing with or improving an unpleasant or difficult situation 處理方法；改進措施；補償 **SYN** **solution**：**~ (for sth)** *There is no simple remedy for unemployment.* 失業問題沒有簡單的解決辦法。◇ **~ (to sth)** *There are a number of possible remedies to this problem.* 這個問題有許多可能採取的解決辦法。 **2** a treatment or medicine to cure a disease or reduce pain that is not very serious 療法；治療；藥品：*a herbal remedy* 草藥 ◇ **~ for sth** *an excellent home remedy for sore throats* 治療咽喉疼痛的極佳的家庭療法 **3 ~ (against sth)** (*law* 律) a way of dealing with a problem, using the processes of the law（通過法律程序的）解決方法，救濟 **SYN** **redress**：*Holding copyright provides the only legal remedy against unauthorized copying.* 持有版權是反對盜版的唯一法律手段。

■ ***verb*** (**rem·ed·ies**, **rem·edy·ing**, **rem·ed·ied**, **rem·ed·ied**) **~ sth** to correct or improve sth 改正；糾正；改進 **SYN** **put right**：*to remedy a problem* 解決問題 ◇ *This situation is easily remedied.* 這種情形易於補救。

re·mem·ber 0‑ /rɪˈmembə(r)/ *verb* (not usually used in the progressive tenses 通常不用於進行時)

▸ **SB/STH FROM THE PAST** 過去的人／事物 **1** 0‑ [T, I] to have or keep an image in your memory of an event, a person, a place, etc. from the past 回想起；記得；記起：**~ (sb/sth)** *This is Carla. Do you remember her?* 這位是卡拉。你記得她嗎？◇ *I don't remember my first day at school.* 我已經忘了第一天上學的情景。◇ *He still remembered her as the lively teenager he'd known years before.* 他記憶中的她依然是他多年以前認識的那個活潑的少女。◇ ***As far as I can remember**, this is the third time we've met.* 我記得這是我們第三次會面了。◇ **~ doing sth** *Do you remember switching the lights off before we came out?* 你記得我們出來之前關燈了嗎？◇ ***I vaguely remember** hearing him come in.* 我隱約記得聽到他進來。◇ **~ sb/sth doing sth** *I can still vividly remember my grandfather teaching me to play cards.* 爺爺教我打紙牌的情景我記憶猶新。◇ (*formal*) *I can't remember his taking a single day off work.* 我不記得他請過一天假。◇ **~ (that)** … *I remember (that) we used to go and see them most weekends.* 我記得我們過去經常在週末去看望他們。

▸ **FACT/INFORMATION** 事實；信息 **2** 0‑ [T, I] to bring back to your mind a fact, piece of information, etc. that you knew 想起；記起：**~ (sth)** *I'm sorry—I can't remember your name.* 對不起，我想不起你的名字了。◇ *You were going to help me with this. Remember?* 你說要幫着我做的。記得嗎？◇ **~ how, what, etc.** … *Can you remember how much money we spent?* 你能回憶起我們花了多少錢嗎？◇ **~ (that)** … *Remember that we're going out tonight.* 別忘了我們今天晚上要出去。 **3** 0‑ [T] to keep an important fact in your mind 記住；把…牢記在心：**~ (that)** … *Remember (that) you may feel sleepy after taking the pills.* 記住，吃了這些藥片之後，你會覺得犯睏。◇ **it is remembered that** … ***It should be remembered that** the majority of accidents happen in the home.* 不要忘記大多數事故都是在家裏發生的。

▸ **STH YOU HAVE TO DO** 必做之事 **4** 0‑ [T] to not forget to do sth; to actually do what you have to do 記着，不忘（去做）；動手做（必須做的事）：**~ to do sth** *Remember to call me when you arrive!* 你到了之後別忘了給我打電話！◇ **~ sth** *Did you remember your homework* (= to bring it)*?* 你記得帶家庭作業了嗎？ **HELP** Notice the difference between **remember doing sth** and **remember to do sth**: *I remember posting the letter* means 'I have an image in my memory of doing it'; *I remembered to post the letter* means 'I didn't forget to do it.' 注意 remember doing sth 和 remember to do sth 之間的區別：I remember posting the letter 的意思是"我記得把信寄出去了"；I remembered to post the letter 的意思是"我沒有忘記要寄信"。

▸ **IN PRAYERS** 祈禱時 **5** [T] **~ sb** to think about sb with respect, especially when saying a prayer 紀念；緬懷；思念 **SYN** **commemorate**：*a church service to remember the war dead* 紀念戰爭死難者的教堂禮拜儀式

▸ **GIVE PRESENT** 送禮 **6** [T] **~ sb/sth** to give money, a present, etc. to sb/sth 給…送錢（或禮品等）：*My aunt always remembers my birthday* (= by sending a card or present). 我姨媽在我的生日總要送我禮物。◇ *His grandfather remembered him* (= left him money) *in his will.* 他爺爺在遺囑中給他留下了一筆錢。

IDM **be reˈmembered for sth** | **be reˈmembered as sth** to be famous or known for a particular thing that you have done in the past 因某事而成名（或名留青史）：*He is best remembered as the man who brought jazz to England.* 他因為將爵士音樂傳到英國而為人們所熟知。

PHR V **reˈmember me to sb** (*especially BrE*) used to ask sb to give your good wishes to sb else 代我問候某人：*Remember me to your parents.* 代我向你的父母問好。

re·mem·brance /rɪˈmembrəns/ *noun* **1** [U] the act or process of remembering an event in the past or a person who is dead 紀念；記憶；回憶：*A service was held **in remembrance of** local soldiers killed in the war.* 為當地陣亡的戰士舉行了紀念儀式。◇ *a remembrance service* 紀念儀式 ◇ (*formal*) *He smiled at the remembrance of their first kiss.* 他想起了他們的初吻，露出了微笑。 **2** [C] (*formal*) an object that causes you to remember sb/sth; a memory of sb/sth 紀念品；紀念物；一段記憶：*The cenotaph stands as a remembrance of those killed during the war.* 矗立着的紀念碑是對戰爭中死難者的紀念。

ReˌmembranceˈSunday (also **Reˈmembrance Day**) *noun* the Sunday nearest to the 11 November on which those killed in war, especially the wars of 1914–18 and 1939–45, are remembered in ceremonies and church services in Britain and some other countries 陣亡將士紀念日（最接近 11 月 11 日的星期天。英國和其他一些國家在這一天為戰爭中的死難者，尤為兩次世界大戰中的陣亡者舉行紀念儀式和宗教儀式）➲ see also MEMORIAL DAY, VETERANS DAY

re·mind 0‑ /rɪˈmaɪnd/ *verb* **~ sb (about/of sth)** to help sb remember sth, especially sth important that they must do 提醒；使想起：**~ sb** *I'm sorry, I've forgotten your name. Can you remind me?* 對不起，我忘了你的名字。提醒我一下好嗎？◇ ***That*** (= what you have just said, done, etc.) ***reminds me**, I must get some cash.* 這倒提醒了我，我得帶上一些現金。◇ *'You need to finish that essay.' '**Don't remind me*** (= I don't want to think about it).' "你要完成那篇論文。" "別提啦！" ◇ *'Don't forget the camera.' 'Remind me about it nearer the time.'* "別忘了帶相機。" "到時候再提醒我一下。" ◇ **~ sb to do sth** *Remind me to phone Alan before I go out.* 提醒我在出去之前給艾倫打電話。◇ **~ sb (that)** … *Passengers are reminded (that) no smoking is allowed on this train.* 乘客們請注意，本次列車禁止吸煙。◇ **~ sb what, how, etc.** … *Can someone remind me what I should do next?* 誰能告訴我下一步該做什麼？◇ **~ sb + speech** *'You had an accident,' he reminded her.* 他提醒她道："你出過一次事故了。"

PHR V **reˈmind sb of sb/sth** 0‑ if sb/sth **reminds** you of sb/sth else, they make you remember or think about the other person, place, thing, etc. because they are similar

R

in some way 使想起（類似的人、地方、事物等）：*You remind me of your father when you say that.* 你說這樣的話，使我想起了你的父親。◇ *That smell reminds me of France.* 這股氣味使我想起了法國。

re·mind·er /rɪˈmaɪndə(r)/ *noun* **1** ~ **(of sb/sth)** | ~ **(that …)** something that makes you think about or remember sb/sth, that you have forgotten or would like to forget 引起回憶的事物；提醒人的事物：*The sheer size of the cathedral is a* ***constant reminder*** *of the power of religion.* 大教堂的宏大規模使人時刻領略到宗教的威嚴。◇ *The incident* ***served as a*** *timely* ***reminder*** *of just how dangerous mountaineering can be.* 這次事故及時地提醒了人們登山運動有可能會很危險。 **2** a letter or note informing sb that they have not done sth（告知該做某事的）通知單，提示信

rem·in·isce /ˌremɪˈnɪs/ *verb* [I] ~ **(about sth/sb)** to think, talk or write about a happy time in your past 回憶，追憶，緬懷（昔日的快樂時光）：*We spent a happy evening reminiscing about the past.* 我們一晚上回憶往事，感到很愉快。

rem·in·is·cence /ˌremɪˈnɪsns/ *noun* **1** [C, usually pl.] a spoken or written description of sth that sb remembers about their past life 懷舊的談話；回憶錄 SYN **memory**：*The book is a collection of his reminiscences about the actress.* 這本書輯錄了他對那位女演員的回憶。◇ *reminiscences of a wartime childhood* 戰時童年生活的回憶錄 **2** [U] the act of remembering things that happened in the past 回憶；追憶 SYN **recollection 3** [C, usually pl.] something that reminds you of sth similar 使人想起類似事物的東西；引起聯想的相似事物：*Her music is full of reminiscences of African rhythms.* 她的音樂使人一下子聯想到非洲音樂的節奏。

rem·in·is·cent /ˌremɪˈnɪsnt/ *adj.* **1** ~ **of sb/sth** reminding you of sb/sth 使回憶起（人或事）：*The way he laughed was strongly reminiscent of his father.* 他笑的樣子讓人很容易想起他的父親。 **2** [only before noun] (*formal*) showing that you are thinking about the past, especially in a way that causes you pleasure 回憶過去的；懷舊的；緬懷往事的：*a reminiscent smile* 追憶往事時露出的微笑

re·miss /rɪˈmɪs/ *adj.* [not before noun] (*formal*) not giving sth enough care and attention 疏忽；懈怠；玩忽職守 SYN **negligent**：~ **(of sb)** (**to do sth**) *It was remiss of them not to inform us of these changes sooner.* 他們粗心大意，沒有早一些通知我們這些變化。◇ ~ **(in sth/in doing sth)** *She had clearly been remiss in her duty.* 她在工作中顯然馬馬虎虎。

R

re·mis·sion /rɪˈmɪʃn/ *noun* [U, C] **1** a period during which a serious illness improves for a time and the patient seems to get better（重病的）緩解期，減輕期：*The patient has been* ***in remission*** *for the past six months.* 在過去的六個月中，病人的病情已經有所緩解。◇ *The symptoms reappeared after only a short remission.* 短暫的康復之後，症狀再次出現。 **2** (*BrE*) a reduction in the amount of time sb spends in prison, especially because they have behaved well 減刑；減少服刑時間 **3** (*formal*) an act of reducing or cancelling the amount of money that sb has to pay（應付費用的）減少，免除：*New businesses may qualify for tax remission.* 新的企業有資格享受稅收減免。◇ *There is a partial remission of fees for overseas students.* 對留學生可以減免部份費用。

remit *noun, verb*

■ ***noun*** /ˈriːmɪt; rɪˈmɪt/ [usually sing.] ~ **(of sb/sth)** | ~ **(to do sth)** (*BrE*) the area of activity over which a particular person or group has authority, control or influence 職權範圍；控制範圍；影響範圍：*Such decisions are* ***outside the remit*** *of this committee.* 這樣的決定超出了委員會的職權範圍。◇ *In future, staff recruitment will* ***fall within the remit*** *of the division manager.* 以後招募新員工將屬於部門經理的職責。◇ *a remit to report on medical services* 報告醫療服務情況的權限

■ ***verb*** /rɪˈmɪt/ (**-tt-**) (*formal*) **1** to send money, etc. to a person or place 匯付；匯款 SYN **forward**：~ **sth** *to remit funds* 匯寄資金 ◇ ~ **sth to sb** *Payment will be remitted to you in full.* 報酬將會全額匯寄給你。 **2** ~ **sth** to cancel or free sb from a debt, duty, punishment, etc. 免除，赦免（債務、職責、懲罰等）SYN **cancel**：*to remit a fine* 免除罰金 ◇ *to remit a prison sentence* 免除徒刑 ➲ see also UNREMITTING

PHR V **re'mit sth to sb** [usually passive] (*law* 律) to send a matter to an authority so that a decision can be made 將…提交（權力部門以便作出決定）：*The case was remitted to the Court of Appeal.* 這個案件被提交給了上訴法院。

re·mit·tance /rɪˈmɪtns/ *noun* **1** [C] (*formal*) a sum of money that is sent to sb in order to pay for sth 匯款金額：*Please return the completed form with your remittance.* 請將填好的表格連同匯款寄回。 **2** [U] the act of sending money to sb in order to pay for sth 匯付；匯款 SYN **payment**：*Remittance can be made by cheque or credit card.* 可通過支票或信用卡匯款。

remix /ˌriːˈmɪks/ *verb* ~ **sth** to make a new version of a recorded piece of music by using a machine to arrange the separate parts of the recording in a different way, add new parts, etc. 合成，再混合（音樂錄音）▸ **remix** /ˈriːmɪks/ (also **mix**) *noun* **re·mixer** *noun*：*the skills of remixer Tom Moulton* 合成音樂錄音師湯姆・莫爾頓的技藝

rem·nant /ˈremnənt/ *noun* **1** [usually pl.] a part of sth that is left after the other parts have been used, removed, destroyed, etc. 殘餘部份；剩餘部份 SYN **remains**：*The woods are remnants of a huge forest which once covered the whole area.* 這片樹林只是剩下的一部份，原來這一帶是一大片森林。 **2** a small piece of cloth that is left when the rest has been sold（織物的）零頭，零料；布頭

re·model /ˌriːˈmɒdl; *NAmE* -ˈmɑːdl/ *verb* (**-ll-**, *especially US* **-l-**) ~ **sth** to change the structure or shape of sth 改變…的結構（或形狀）

re·mold (*NAmE*) = REMOULD

rem·on·strance /rɪˈmɒnstrəns; *NAmE* -ˈmɑːn-/ *noun* [C, U] (*formal*) a protest or complaint 抗議；抱怨

rem·on·strate /ˈremənstreɪt; *NAmE* rɪˈmɑːnstreɪt/ *verb* [I, T] ~ **(with sb) (about sth)** | **+ speech** (*formal*) to protest or complain about sth/sb 抗議；抱怨；埋怨：*They remonstrated with the official about the decision.* 他們就這一決定向這位官員提出了抗議。

re·morse /rɪˈmɔːs; *NAmE* rɪˈmɔːrs/ *noun* [U] the feeling of being extremely sorry for sth wrong or bad that you have done 懊悔；非常遺憾；自責：*I felt guilty and full of remorse.* 我感到內疚，並且非常懊悔。◇ ~ **for sth/for doing sth** *He was filled with remorse for not believing her.* 他因為沒有相信她而懊悔不已。▸ **re·morse·ful** /-fl/ *adj.* **re·morse·ful·ly** /-fəli/ *adv.*

re·morse·less /rɪˈmɔːsləs; *NAmE* -ˈmɔːrs-/ *adj.* **1** (especially of an unpleasant situation 尤指不愉快的情形) seeming to continue or become worse in a way that cannot be stopped 持續惡化的 SYN **relentless**：*the remorseless increase in crime* 犯罪的持續增長 **2** cruel and having or showing no pity for other people 殘酷的；無情的；無同情心的 SYN **merciless**：*a remorseless killer* 殘酷的殺手 ▸ **re·morse·less·ly** *adv.*

re·mort·gage /ˌriːˈmɔːɡɪdʒ; *NAmE* -ˈmɔːrɡ-/ *verb* [I, T] ~ **(sth)** to arrange a second MORTGAGE on your house or apartment, or to increase or change your first one 再按揭；轉按揭 ▸ **re·mort·gage** *noun*

re·mote 0→ /rɪˈməʊt; *NAmE* rɪˈmoʊt/ *adj., noun*

■ ***adj.*** (**re·moter**, **re·mot·est**)

▸ PLACE 地點 **1** 0→ far away from places where other people live 偏遠的；偏僻的 SYN **isolated**：*a remote beach* 偏遠的海灘 ◇ *one of the remotest areas of the world* 世界上最荒僻的地區之一 ◇ ~ **from sth** *The farmhouse is remote from any other buildings.* 這家農舍附近沒有別的房屋。

▸ TIME 時間 **2** 0→ [only before noun] far away in time 遙遠的；久遠的 SYN **distant**：*in the* ***remote past/future*** 在遙遠的過去／將來 ◇ *a* ***remote ancestor*** (= who lived a long time ago) 遠祖

▸ RELATIVES 親戚 **3** [only before noun] (of people 人) not closely related 關係較遠的；遠親的 SYN **distant**：*a remote cousin* 遠房表親

▸ **COMPUTER/SYSTEM** 計算機；系統 **4** that you can connect to from far away, using an electronic link 遠程的；遠程連接的：*a **remote terminal/database*** 遠程終端 / 數據庫
▸ **DIFFERENT** 不同 **5 ~ (from sth)** very different from sth 相差很大的；極不相同的：*His theories are somewhat remote from reality.* 他的理論有點兒脱離現實。
▸ **NOT FRIENDLY** 不友好 **6** (of people or their behaviour 人或行為) not very friendly or interested in other people 不很友好的；冷漠的 **SYN** **aloof, distant**
▸ **VERY SMALL** 微小 **7** not very great 細微的；微小的 **SYN** **slight**：*There is still a **remote chance** that they will find her alive.* 他們仍然有一線希望能把她活着找到。◇ *I don't have **the remotest idea** what you're talking about.* 你在説什麼我一點都不懂。
▸ **re·mote·ness** *noun* [U]：*the geographical remoteness of the island* 這座島地理位置偏遠 ◇ *His remoteness made her feel unloved.* 他的冷漠使她覺得他不愛她。
■ *noun* (*informal*) = REMOTE CONTROL (2)

re,mote 'access *noun* [U] the use of a computer system, etc. that is in another place, that you can connect to when you are far away, using an electronic link 遠程存取；遠程訪問

re,mote con'trol *noun* **1** [U] the ability to operate a machine from a distance using radio or electrical signals 遙控：*It works **by remote control**.* 它通過遙控工作。◇ *a remote-control camera* 遙控攝像機 **2** (also *informal* **re·mote**, **zap·per**) [C] a device that allows you to operate a television, etc. from a distance 遙控器：*I can't find the remote control.* 我找不到遙控器。➲ VISUAL VOCAB page V21 ▸ **re,mote-con'trolled** *adj.*：*remote-controlled equipment* 可遙控的設備

re·mote·ly /rɪ'məʊtli; *NAmE* -'moʊt-/ *adv.* **1** (usually in negative sentences 通常用於否定句) to a very slight degree 微弱地；細微地；程度很低地 **SYN** **slightly**：*It wasn't even remotely funny* (= it wasn't at all funny). 這一點也不好笑。◇ *The two incidents were only remotely connected.* 兩次事件之間無甚關聯。**2** from a distance 遠程地：*remotely operated* 遠程操作的 **3** far away from places where other people live 在偏僻地方：*The church is remotely situated on the north coast of the island.* 教堂位於這個島偏僻的北部海岸。

re,mote 'sensing *noun* [U] the use of SATELLITES to search for and collect information about the earth 遙感；遙測

re·mould (*especially US* **re·mold**) /,riː'məʊld; *NAmE* -'moʊld/ *verb* **~ sth** (*formal*) to change sth such as an idea, a system, etc. 更新，改變（想法、系統等）：*attempts to remould policy to make it more acceptable* 力圖改變政策以使其易於為人們所接受

re·mount /,riː'maʊnt/ *verb* **1** [I, T] **~ (sth)** to get on a horse, bicycle, etc. again after getting off it or falling off it 再次騎上，重新跨上（馬、自行車等）**2** [T] **~ sth** to organize and begin sth a second time 再次組織；重新開始

re·mov·able **AW** /rɪ'muːvəbl/ *adj.* [usually before noun] that can be taken off or out of sth 可去除的；可取出的 **SYN** **detachable**

re·moval **AW** /rɪ'muːvl/ *noun*
1 [U] **~ (of sb/sth)** the act of taking sb/sth away from a particular place 移動；調動；去除：*Clearance of the site required the removal of a number of trees.* 清理這一場所需要移走不少樹。◇ *the removal of a tumour* 腫瘤切除 **2** [U] **~ (of sth)** the act of getting rid of sth 除去；消除；清除：*stain removal* 清除污漬 ◇ *the removal of trade barriers* 貿易壁壘的消除 **3** [U] **~ (of sb)** the act of dismissing sb from their job 免職；解職 **SYN** **dismissal**：*events leading to the removal of the president from office* 導致總統下台的一些事件 **4** [C] (*BrE*) an act of taking furniture, etc. from one house to another 搬遷；遷移：*house removals* 搬家 ◇ ***a removal company/firm*** 搬家公司 ◇ *When are the removal men coming?* 搬家工人什麼時候到？

re'moval van (also **'furniture van**) (both *BrE*) (*NAmE* **'moving van**) *noun* a large van used for moving furniture from one house to another 搬家卡車

re·move **AW** /rɪ'muːv/ *verb, noun*
■ *verb* **1** to take sth/sb away from a place 移開；拿開；去掉；從…機構開除：**~ sth/sb** *Illegally parked vehicles will be removed.* 非法停放的車輛將被拖走。◇ **~ sth/sb from sth/sb** *He removed his hand from her shoulder.* 他將手從她的肩膀上拿開。◇ *Three children were removed from the school for persistent bad behaviour.* 三個孩子因持續行為不檢被學校開除。**2** **~ sth** to take off clothing, etc. from the body 脱去（衣服等）；摘下：*She removed her glasses and rubbed her eyes.* 她摘下眼鏡，揉了揉眼睛。**3** to get rid of sth unpleasant, dirty, etc.; to make sth disappear 去除，排除（污漬、不愉快的事物等）；使消失：**~ sth** *She has had the tumour removed.* 她已經將腫瘤切除了。◇ *to remove problems/obstacles/objections* 解決問題；排除障礙；消除異議 ◇ **~ sth from sb/sth** *The news removed any doubts about the company's future.* 這個消息消除了一切有關公司前景的疑慮。**4** **~ sb from sth** to dismiss sb from their position or job 免除，解除（職務等）：*The elections removed the government from power.* 這次選舉使得政府倒台。
IDM **once, twice, etc. re'moved** (of a cousin 堂親或表親) belonging to a different generation 隔代的：*He's my cousin's son so he's my first cousin once removed.* 他是我表兄的兒子，所以他是我隔了一代的表親。**be far/further/furthest removed from sth** to be very different from sth; to not be connected with sth 與…大相逕庭；與…不相干：*Many of these books are far removed from the reality of the children's lives.* 很多這樣的書都遠遠地脱離了孩子們的現實生活。
■ *noun* [C, U] (*formal*) an amount by which two things are separated 距離；差距；間距：*Charlotte seemed to be living **at one remove** from reality.* 夏洛特好像生活在現實之外。

re·mover /rɪ'muːvə(r)/ *noun* **1** [U, C] (usually in compounds 通常構成複合詞) a substance used for getting rid of marks, paint, etc. 清除劑：*nail varnish remover* 指甲油清除劑 ◇ *stain remover* 去污劑 ➲ see also STAPLE REMOVER **2** [usually pl.] (*BrE*) a person or company whose job is to take furniture, etc. from one house to another 搬家工人；搬家公司：*a firm of removers* 搬家公司

re·mu·ner·ate /rɪ'mjuːnəreɪt/ *verb* [usually passive] **~ sb (for sth)** (*formal*) to pay sb for work that they have done 酬勞；付酬給

re·mu·ner·ation /rɪ,mjuːnə'reɪʃn/ *noun* [U, C] (*formal*) an amount of money that is paid to sb for the work they have done 酬金；薪水；報酬

re·mu·nera·tive /rɪ'mjuːnərətɪv/ *adj.* [usually before noun] (*formal*) paying a lot of money 報酬豐厚的：*remunerative work* 報酬很高的工作

REN /,ɑːr iː 'en/ *abbr.* registered enrolled nurse （已登記）註冊護士

re·nais·sance /rɪ'neɪsns; *NAmE* 'renəsɑːns/ *noun* [sing.] **1 the Renaissance** the period in Europe during the 14th, 15th and 16th centuries when people became interested in the ideas and culture of ancient Greece and Rome and used these influences in their own art, literature, etc. 文藝復興時期（歐洲 14、15 和 16 世紀時，人們以古希臘羅馬的思想文化來繁榮文學藝術）：*Renaissance art* 文藝復興時期的藝術 **2** a situation when there is new interest in a particular subject, form of art, etc. after a period when it was not very popular （某一學科或藝術形式等衰落後的）復興 **SYN** **revival**：*to experience a renaissance* 經歷復興

Re,naissance 'man *noun* a person who is good at a lot of things and has a lot of interests, especially writing and painting 文藝復興人，全才人（尤指寫作和繪畫方面多才多藝的人）

renal /'riːnl/ *adj.* [usually before noun] (*medical* 醫) relating to or involving the KIDNEYS 腎臟的；與腎臟相關的：*renal failure* 腎衰竭

re·name /,riː'neɪm/ *verb* to give sb/sth a new name 重新命名；給…改名：**~ sth** *to rename a street* 給一條

街道改名 ◇ **~ sth + noun** *Leningrad was renamed St Petersburg.* 列寧格勒被重新命名為聖彼得堡。

re·nas·cence /rɪˈnæsns; -ˈneɪ-/ *noun* [U, sing.] (*formal*) a situation in which there is new interest in a particular subject, form of art, etc. after a period when it was not very popular 復興；再度流行 ▸ **re·nas·cent** /rɪˈnæsnt; -ˈneɪ-/ *adj.*: *renascent fascism* 死灰復燃的法西斯主義

rend /rend/ *verb* (**rent**, **rent** /rent/) **~ sth** (*old use* or *literary*) to tear sth apart with force or violence 撕開；撕碎：*They rent their clothes in grief.* 他們在悲痛之中扯碎了自己的衣服。◇ (*figurative*) *a country rent in two by civil war* 被內戰一分為二的國家 ◇ (*figurative*) *Loud screams rent the air.* 高聲的尖叫劃破了天空。➲ see also HEART-RENDING

ren·der /ˈrendə(r)/ *verb*

▸ **CAUSE SB/STH TO BE STH** 使成為 **1 ~ sb/sth + adj.** (*formal*) to cause sb/sth to be in a particular state or condition 使成為；使變得；使處於某狀態 **SYN** **make**：*to render sth harmless/useless/ineffective* 使某事物無害 / 無用 / 無效 ◇ *Hundreds of people were rendered homeless by the earthquake.* 成百上千的人因為地震而無家可歸。

▸ **GIVE HELP** 提供幫助 **2** (*formal*) to give sb sth, especially in return for sth or because it is expected 給予；提供；回報：**~ sth to sb/sth** *They rendered assistance to the disaster victims.* 他們給災民提供了援助。◇ *to render a service to sb* 給某人提供服務 ◇ **~ sb sth** *to render sb a service* 為某人服務 ◇ **~ sth** *It was payment* ***for services rendered.*** 這是服務酬金。

▸ **PRESENT STH** 提交 **3 ~ sth** (*formal*) to present sth, especially when it is done officially 遞交；呈獻；提交 **SYN** **furnish**：*The committee was asked to render a report on the housing situation.* 要求委員會提交一份有關住房情況的報告。

▸ **EXPRESS/PERFORM** 表達；表演 **4 ~ sth** (*formal*) to express or perform sth 表達；表演；演示：*He stood up and rendered a beautiful version of 'Summertime'.* 他站起來表演了一段優美的《夏日時光》。◇ *The artist has rendered the stormy sea in dark greens and browns.* 畫家用了深綠色和棕色來表現波濤洶湧的大海。

▸ **TRANSLATE** 翻譯 **5** to express sth in a different language（用不同的語言）表達；翻譯；把…譯成 **SYN** **translate**：**~ sth (as sth)** *The Italian phrase can be rendered as 'I did my best'.* 這個意大利語的短語可以譯為"我盡力了"。◇ **~ sth (into sth)** *It's a concept that is difficult to render into English.* 這個概念難以用英語來表達。

▸ **WALL** 牆壁 **6 ~ sth** (*BrE, technical* 術語) to cover a wall with a layer of PLASTER or CEMENT 粉刷；給（牆壁）抹灰

▸ **MELT** 化開 **7 ~ sth (down)** to make fat liquid by heating it; to melt sth 將（脂肪）熬成油；熔化

ren·der·ing /ˈrendərɪŋ/ *noun* **1** [C] the performance of a piece of music, a role in a play, etc.; the particular way in which sth is performed 演奏；扮演；表演 **SYN** **interpretation, rendition**：*her dramatic rendering of Lady Macbeth* 她飾演麥克佩斯夫人的生動表演 **2** [C] a piece of writing that has been translated into a different language; the particular way in which it has been translated 翻譯作品；翻譯：*a faithful rendering of the original text* 對原文的忠實翻譯 **3** [U, C] (*technical* 術語) a layer of PLASTER or CEMENT that is put on a brick or stone wall in order to make it smooth（抹在牆上的）一層灰泥

ren·dez·vous /ˈrɒndɪvuː; -deɪ-; *NAmE* ˈrɑːn-/ *noun, verb*

■ *noun* (*pl.* **ren·dez·vous** /-vuːz/) (from *French*) **1 ~ (with sb)** an arrangement to meet sb at a particular time and place 約會 **2** a place where people have arranged to meet 約會地點 **3** a bar, etc. that is a popular place for people to meet（酒吧等）熱門聚會場所，聚會處：*a lively Paris rendezvous* 巴黎一個很熱鬧的公共場所

■ *verb* (**ren·dez·voused** /-vuːd/, **ren·dez·voused**) [I] **~ (with sb)** (from *French*) to meet at a time and place that have been arranged in advance（在約定的時間和地點）會面，相會，集合

ren·di·tion /renˈdɪʃn/ *noun* **1** [C] the performance of sth, especially a song or piece of music; the particular way in which it is performed 表演；演唱；演奏 **SYN** **interpretation 2** (also **ex,traordinary ren'dition**) [U] (especially in the US) the practice of sending foreign suspects to be questioned in another country where the laws about the treatment of prisoners are less strict（尤指在美國）非常規引渡（將外籍嫌疑犯引渡到其他對待囚犯較寬鬆的國家受審）

rene·gade /ˈrenɪɡeɪd/ *noun* (*formal, disapproving*) **1** (often used as an adjective 常用作形容詞) a person who leaves one political, religious, etc. group to join another that has very different views 變節者；叛徒；背叛者；叛教者 **2** a person who opposes and lives outside a group or society that they used to belong to 叛逆者 **SYN** **outlaw**

re·nege /rɪˈniːɡ; rɪˈneɪɡ/ *verb* [I] **~ (on sth)** (*formal*) to break a promise, an agreement, etc. 違背（諾言）；背信棄義；食言 **SYN** **go back on**：*to* ***renege on a deal/debt/contract, etc.*** 違背協定、賴債、違背合約等

renew /rɪˈnjuː; *NAmE* -ˈnuː/ *verb* **1 ~ sth** to begin sth again after a pause or an interruption 重新開始；中止後繼續 **SYN** **resume**：*The army renewed its assault on the capital.* 軍隊重新發動對首都的攻擊。◇ *We have to renew our efforts to attract young players.* 我們只好重新開始努力吸引年輕隊員。◇ *The annual dinner is a chance to renew acquaintance with old friends.* 一年一度的聚餐會是與老朋友敘舊的好機會。**2 ~ sth** to make sth valid for a further period of time 使繼續有效；延長…的期限：*to* ***renew a licence/lease/subscription/contract, etc.*** 延長執照的期限、續簽租約、續訂、續簽合約等 ◇ *How do I go about renewing my passport?* 我該如何去續簽護照？◇ *I'd like to renew these library books* (= arrange to borrow them for a further period of time). 我想續借這幾本圖書館的書。**3 ~ sth** to emphasize sth by saying or stating it again 重申；重複強調 **SYN** **reiterate, repeat**：*to* ***renew an appeal/a request/a complaint, etc.*** 再次呼籲、請求、投訴等 ◇ *Community leaders have renewed calls for a peaceful settlement.* 社區領導人再次呼籲要和平解決。◇ *The project is to go ahead following renewed promises of aid from the UN.* 在得到聯合國重申提供幫助的承諾以後，這個項目將着手進行。**4 ~ sth** to change sth that is old or damaged and replace it with sth new of the same kind 更新；更換：*The wiring in your house should be renewed every ten to fifteen years.* 你家裏的電線應該每十到十五年更新一次。

re·new·able /rɪˈnjuːəbl; *NAmE* -ˈnuː-/ *adj.* **1** [usually before noun] (of energy and natural resources 能源和自然資源) that is replaced naturally or controlled carefully and can therefore be used without the risk of finishing it all 可更新的；可再生的；可恢復的：*renewable sources of energy such as wind and solar power* 像風力和太陽能這種用之不竭的能源 ➲ COLLOCATIONS at ENVIRONMENT **2** (of a contract, ticket, etc. 合同、票等) that can be made valid for a further period of time after it has finished 可延長有效期的；可展期的；可續訂的：*a renewable lease* 可展期的租約 ◇ *The work permit is not renewable.* 這份工作許可證不能延期。**OPP** **non-renewable**

re·new·ables /rɪˈnjuːəblz; *NAmE* -ˈnuː-/ *noun* [pl.] types of energy that can be replaced naturally such as energy produced from wind or water 可再生能源：*renewables such as hydroelectricity and solar energy* 水力發電和太陽能之類的可再生能源 ◇ *investment in renewables* 對可再生能源的投資 **HELP** **Renewables** are more commonly referred to as **renewable energy** (**sources**). * renewables 更常見的說法是 renewable energy (sources)。➲ COLLOCATIONS at ENVIRONMENT

re·newal /rɪˈnjuːəl; *NAmE* -ˈnuːəl/ *noun* [U, C] **1 ~ (of sth)** a situation in which sth begins again after a pause or an interruption 恢復；更新；重新開始：*a renewal of interest in traditional teaching methods* 對傳統教學法重新產生興趣 **2** the act of making a contract, etc. valid for a further period of time after it has finished（對合同等的）有效期延長，展期，續訂，更新：*The lease comes* ***up for renewal*** *at the end of the month.* 本租約到月底需要辦理展期。◇ *the renewal date* 更新日期 **3** a situation in which sth is replaced, improved or made more successful 更新；改進；復興；振興：*economic renewal*

R

經濟復興 ◇ ***urban renewal*** (= the act of improving the buildings, etc. in a particular area) 市區改造

re·newed /rɪˈnjuːd; *NAmE* rɪˈnuːd/ *adj.* [usually before noun] happening again with increased interest or strength 再次發生的；再次興起的；更新的：*Renewed fighting has been reported on the border.* 據報道，在邊境地區戰火重燃。◇ *with renewed enthusiasm* 以重燃的熱情

ren·min·bi /ˈrenmɪnbi/ *noun* (*pl.* **ren·min·bi**) **1 the renminbi** [sing.] the money system of China 人民幣（中國幣制）**2** = YUAN

ren·net /ˈrenɪt/ *noun* [U] a substance that makes milk thick and sour and is used in making cheese 凝乳酶（使牛奶或乾酪凝結的物質）

re·nounce /rɪˈnaʊns/ *verb* (*formal*) **1 ~ sth** to state officially that you are no longer going to keep a title, position, etc. 聲明放棄；宣佈放棄 SYN **give up**：*to* ***renounce a claim/title/privilege/right*** 宣佈放棄要求／頭銜／特權／權利 **2 ~ sth** to state publicly that you no longer have a particular belief or that you will no longer behave in a particular way 宣佈與…決裂；宣佈摒棄：*to* ***renounce ideals/principles/beliefs, etc.*** 宣佈放棄理想、原則、信仰等 ◇ *a joint declaration renouncing the use of violence* 聲明放棄使用暴力的聯合宣言 **3 ~ sb/sth** to state publicly that you no longer wish to have a connection with sb/sth because you disapprove of them 宣佈斷絕與…的關係 SYN **disown**：*He had renounced his former associates.* 他已經宣佈與過去的夥伴拆夥。➲ see also RENUNCIATION

reno·vate /ˈrenəveɪt/ *verb* **~ sth** to repair and paint an old building, a piece of furniture, etc. so that it is in good condition again 修復；翻新；重新粉刷 ➲ COLLOCATIONS at DECORATE ▸ **reno·va·tion** /ˌrenəˈveɪʃn/ *noun* [U, C, usually pl.]：*buildings in need of renovation* 需要重新裝修的大樓 ◇ *There will be extensive renovations to the hospital.* 這所醫院將進行大規模的翻修。

re·nown /rɪˈnaʊn/ *noun* [U] (*formal*) fame and respect because of sth you have done that people admire 名譽；聲望：*He* ***won renown as*** *a fair judge.* 他贏得了公平裁判的榮譽。◇ *a pianist* ***of some/international/ great*** *renown* 具有一定／國際／相當知名度的鋼琴家

re·nowned /rɪˈnaʊnd/ *adj.* famous and respected 有名的；聞名的；受尊敬的 SYN **celebrated, noted**：*a renowned author* 著名的作家 ◇ **~ as sth** *It is renowned as one of the region's best restaurants.* 這是本地區最好的飯店之一。◇ **~ for sth** *She is renowned for her patience.* 她的耐心是出了名的。

rent 0‑ /rent/ *noun, verb* ➲ see also REND *v.*

■ ***noun*** **1** 0‑ [U, C] an amount of money that you regularly pay so that you can use a house, etc. 租金：*How much rent do you pay for this place?* 你租這個地方的租金是多少？◇ *The landlord has put the rent up again.* 房東又提高房租了。◇ *a month's rent in advance* 預付的月租金 ◇ *a* ***high/low/fair rent*** 高的／低的／合理的租金 ◇ (*BrE*) *a rent book* (= used to record payments of rent) 租金登記簿 ➲ SYNONYMS at RATE ➲ COLLOCATIONS at HOUSE ➲ compare HIRE *n.* (1) **2** [U, C] (*especially NAmE*) = RENTAL (1) **3** [C] (*formal*) a torn place in a piece of material or clothing 破裂處；裂口；撕裂

IDM **for rent** 0‑ (*especially NAmE*) (especially on printed signs 尤用於告示) available to rent 出租；招租

■ ***verb*** **1** 0‑ [T, I] to regularly pay money to sb so that you can use sth that they own, such as a house, some land, a machine, etc. 租用，租借（房屋、土地、機器等）：**~ (sth)** *to live in* ***rented accommodation/housing/ property*** 住在租來的住所裏 ◇ **~ sth from sb** *Who do you rent the land from?* 你從誰那裏租用的土地？ **2** 0‑ [T] to allow sb to use sth that you own such as a house or some land in exchange for regular payments 出租；將…租給：**~ sth (out) (to sb)** *He rents rooms in his house to students.* 他把家中的房間租給學生。◇ *The land is rented out to other farmers.* 這片土地租給別的農民了。◇ *She agreed to rent the room to me.* 她同意將這個房間租給我。◇ **~ sb sth** *She agreed to rent me the room.* 她同意租給我這個房間。 **3** 0‑ [T] **~ sth** (*especially NAmE*) to pay money to sb so that you can use sth for a short period of time （短期）租用，租借：*We rented a car for the week and explored the area.* 我們租了一個星期的車探索這個地區。◇ *Shall we rent a movie this evening?* 我們今天晚上租電影看好嗎？ ➲ compare HIRE *v.* (1) **4** [I] (*NAmE*) to be available for sb to use if they pay a particular amount of money 以…出租；租金為：*The apartment rents for $500 a month.* 這套房間每月租金為 500 元。

British/American 英式/美式英語

rent / hire / let

Verbs 動詞

- You can **hire** something for a short period of time (*BrE* only), but **rent** something for a longer period. 短期租用可用 hire（僅用於英式英語），較長時間的租用則用 rent：*We can hire bikes for a day to explore the town.* 我們可租用自行車一天來遊覽這城鎮。◇ *We don't own our TV, we rent it.* 我們沒有自己的電視機，這是租的。
- In *NAmE*, **rent** is always used. It is sometimes now used in *BrE* instead of **hire**, too. 美式英語總是用 rent，現在英式英語有時也用 rent 代替 hire。
- The owners of a thing can **hire** it **out** for a short period (*BrE*). 物主短期租出某物可用 hire out（英式英語）：*Do you hire out bikes?* 你們出租自行車嗎？ Or they can **rent** (**out**)/**let** (**out**) a building, etc. 出租房屋等可用 rent (out)/let (out)：*We rent out rooms in our house to students.* 我們把住宅裏的房間出租給學生。
- Outside a building you could see 在建築物外可看到：*To let* (*BrE*) 招租 ◇ *For rent* (*especially NAmE*) 招租
- To **hire** can also mean to employ somebody, especially in *NAmE*. * hire 亦含雇用之意，尤其在美式英語中：*We hired a new secretary.* 我們雇了一名新秘書。

➲ see also LEASE *v.*

Nouns 名詞

- The amount of money that you pay to rent something is **rent** or **rental** (more formal). When you hire something you pay a **hire charge** (*BrE*). 較長時間租用的租金為 rent 或 rental（較正式）。短期租借費用為 hire charge（英式英語）。On a sign outside a shop you might see 在商店外的標牌上可看到：*Bikes for hire* (*BrE*) 出租自行車

➲ see also LET, LEASE, HIRE *n.*

ˈrent-a- *combining form* (*informal*, often *humorous*) (in nouns and adjectives 構成名詞和形容詞) showing that the thing mentioned can be hired/rented 出租；可雇用：*rent-a-car* 租用汽車 ◇ *rent-a-crowd* 可雇用的人手

ren·tal /ˈrentl/ *noun* **1** (also **rent** especially in *NAmE*) [U, C, usually sing.] the amount of money that you pay to use sth for a particular period of time 租金：*Telephone charges include line rental.* 電話費包括線路租用費。➲ SYNONYMS at RATE **2** [U] the act of renting sth or an arrangement to rent sth 出租；租賃；招租：*the world's largest car rental company* 世界最大的汽車租賃公司 ◇ *DVD rental* * DVD 出租 ◇ (*especially NAmE*) *a rental car* 供出租的汽車 ◇ *a minimum rental period of three months* 三個月的最低租用期 ➲ compare HIRE *v.* (1) **3** [C] (*especially NAmE*) a house, car, or piece of equipment that you can rent 租用的房屋（或汽車、設備等）：*'Is this your own car?' 'No, it's a rental.'* "這是你自己的車嗎？" "不，是租來的。"

ˈrent boy *noun* (*BrE*) a young male PROSTITUTE 年輕的男妓

rent·ed 0‑ /ˈrentɪd/ *adj.* that you pay rent for 租用的；租借的：*a rented studio* 租來的工作室

R

rent·er /ˈrentə(r)/ *noun* **1** a person who rents sth 承租人；租用人；租戶：*house buyers and renters* 房屋的買主和租戶 **2** (*NAmE*) a person or an organization that provides sth for people to rent 出租人；出租機構：*the nation's biggest automobile renter* 全國最大的汽車出租公司

ˌrent-ˈfree *adj.* for which no rent is paid 免租金的；不收租金的：*rent-free housing* 不收租金的住房 ▸ **ˌrent-ˈfree** *adv.*

ren·tier /ˈrɒntieɪ; *NAmE* ˈrɑːntjeɪ/ *noun* (*technical* 術語) a person who lives from money earned from property and investments 靠房地產和投資生活的人；吃息族

re·nun·ci·ation /rɪˌnʌnsiˈeɪʃn/ *noun* (*formal*) **1** [U, C] an act of stating publicly that you no longer believe sth or that you are giving sth up 聲明摒棄；宣佈放棄：*the renunciation of violence* 放棄使用暴力的聲明 **2** [U] the act of rejecting physical pleasures, especially for religious reasons 棄絕物質享受；克己；禁慾 SYN **self-denial** ➲ see also RENOUNCE

re·occur AW /ˌriːəˈkɜː(r)/ *verb* (**-rr-**) [I] to happen again or a number of times 重新（再次或多次）發生；反複出現 SYN **recur**

re·of·fend /ˌriːəˈfend/ *verb* [I] to commit a crime again 再犯罪；再犯法：*Without help, many released prisoners will reoffend.* 如果得不到幫助，很多獲得釋放的囚犯就會重蹈覆轍。▸ **re·of·fend·er** /ˌriːəˈfendə(r)/ *noun*

re·open /riˈəʊpən; *NAmE* -ˈoʊ-/ *verb* **1** [T, I] **~ (sth)** to open a shop/store, theatre, etc. again, or to be opened again, after being closed for a period of time 重新開業；重新開放（商店、劇場等）：*The school was reopened just two weeks after the fire.* 火災之後僅兩個星期，這所學校就重新開學了。◇ *The store will reopen at 9 a.m. on 2 January.* 商店將於元月 2 號上午 9 點重新開業。**2** [T, I] **~ (sth)** to deal with or begin sth again after a period of time; to start again after a period of time 重新處理；再次開始；恢復：*to reopen a discussion* 重新開始討論 ◇ *The police have decided to reopen the case.* 警方已經決定重新調查這個案子。◇ *Management have agreed to reopen talks with the union.* 資方已經同意和工會重新談判。◇ *The trial reopened on 6 March.* 審判在 3 月 6 日再次進行。▸ **re·open·ing** /riˈəʊpənɪŋ; *NAmE* -ˈoʊ-/ *noun* [U, sing.]

IDM **reˌopen old ˈwounds** to remind sb of sth unpleasant that happened or existed in the past 揭舊瘡疤

R

re·order /riˈɔːdə(r); *NAmE* -ˈɔːrd-/ *verb* **1** [T, I] **~ (sth)** to ask sb to supply you with more of a product 再訂購；追加訂購：*Please quote this reference number when reordering stock.* 再次訂貨時請提供這個編號。**2** [T] **~ sth** to change the order in which sth is arranged 重新佈置；重新排列

re·organ·ize (*BrE* also **-ise**) /riˈɔːgənaɪz; *NAmE* -ˈɔːrg-/ *verb* [T, I] **~ (sth)** to change the way in which sth is organized or done 重新組織；改組；整頓 ▸ **re·organ·iza·tion, -isa·tion** /riˌɔːgənaɪˈzeɪʃn; *NAmE* -ˌɔːrgənəˈz-/ *noun* [U, C]：*the reorganization of the school system* 學校體制的整頓

re·ori·ent AW /riˈɔːrient/ *verb* **1** **~ sb/sth (to/towards/away from sb/sth)** to change the focus or direction of sb/sth 改變…的重點（或方向）：*Other governments may reorient their foreign policies away from the United States.* 其他政府可能調整他們的外交政策，不再以美國為重點。**2** **~ yourself** to find your position again in relation to your surroundings 給（自己）重新定位 ▸ **re·orien·ta·tion** AW /riˌɔːriənˈteɪʃn/ *noun* [U]

Rep. *abbr.* (in American politics 美國政治) **1** REPRESENTATIVE 眾議院議員 **2** REPUBLICAN 共和黨人；共和黨黨員

rep /rep/ *noun* (*informal*) **1** [C] = SALES REPRESENTATIVE, REPRESENTATIVE *n.* (2) **2** [C] a person who speaks officially for a group of people, especially at work 代表；發言人：*a union rep* 工會代表 **3** [U] (*informal*) the abbreviation for REPERTORY 保留劇目輪演（全寫為 repertory）

re·pack·age /riːˈpækɪdʒ/ *verb* **1** **~ sth** to change the boxes, bags, etc. in which a product is sold 改變（產品）包裝；重新包裝 **2** **~ sth** to present sth in a new way 改變…的形象：*She earns more since she repackaged herself as a business consultant.* 自從把自己重新包裝成商業顧問以來，她的收入增加了。

re·paid *past tense, past part.* of REPAY

re·pair 🔑 /rɪˈpeə(r); *NAmE* -ˈper/ *verb, noun*

■ *verb* **1** 🔑 **~ sth** to restore sth that is broken, damaged or torn to good condition 修理；修補；修繕：*to repair a car/roof/road/television* 修理汽車／屋頂／道路／電視 ◇ *It's almost 15 years old. It isn't worth **having it repaired**.* 這東西差不多 15 年了。不值得送去修了。**2** 🔑 **~ sth** to say or do sth in order to improve a bad or unpleasant situation 補救；糾正；彌補 SYN **put right**：*It was too late to repair the damage done to their relationship.* 太晚了，無法彌補他們的關係所遭受的創傷了。▸ **re·pair·er** *noun*：*TV repairers* 電視機修理工

PHR V **reˈpair to …** (*formal* or *humorous*) to go to a particular place 去（某地）

■ *noun* 🔑 [C, U] an act of repairing sth 修理；修補；修繕：*They agreed to pay the costs of any repairs.* 他們答應支付所有的修理費。◇ *I took my bike in **for repair**.* 我把自行車送去修了。◇ *The building was **in need of repair**.* 這座大樓需要維修了。◇ *a TV repair shop* 電視機修配店 ◇ *The car was damaged **beyond repair*** (= it was too badly damaged to be repaired). 汽車損壞嚴重，無法修復。◇ *The hotel is currently **under repair*** (= being repaired). 這家酒店正在維修。◇ *The bridge will remain closed until essential **repair work** has been carried out.* 在基本修繕工作完成之前，這座橋暫時關閉。

IDM **in good, bad, etc. reˈpair | in a good, bad, etc. state of reˈpair** (*formal*) in good, etc. condition 狀況良好（或不佳等）

re·pair·able /rɪˈpeərəbl; *NAmE* -ˈper-/ *adj.* [not usually before noun] that can be repaired 可修理；可修繕；可修補 OPP **irreparable**

re·pair·man /rɪˈpeəmæn; *NAmE* -ˈperm-/ *noun* (*pl.* **-men** /-men/) (also **re·pair·er** especially in *BrE*) a person whose job is to repair things 修理工：*a TV repairman* 電視機修理工

rep·ar·ation /ˌrepəˈreɪʃn/ *noun* (*formal*) **1** **reparations** [pl.] money that is paid by a country that has lost a war, for the damage, injuries, etc. that it has caused （戰敗國的）賠款 **2** [U] the act of giving sth to sb or doing sth for them in order to show that you are sorry for suffering that you have caused 賠償；彌補；補償：*Offenders should be forced to **make reparation to** the community.* 應該強迫違法犯罪分子對社會作出補償。

rep·ar·tee /ˌrepɑːˈtiː; *NAmE* -ɑːrˈtiː/ *noun* [U] clever and amusing comments and replies that are made quickly 機智而又巧妙的應對（或回答）

re·past /rɪˈpɑːst; *NAmE* -ˈpæst/ *noun* (*old-fashioned* or *formal*) a meal 餐；飯菜

re·pat·ri·ate /ˌriːˈpætrieɪt; *NAmE* -ˈpeɪt-/ *verb* **1** **~ sb** (*formal*) to send or bring sb back to their own country 遣送回國；遣返：*The refugees were forcibly repatriated.* 難民被強制遣送回國。**2** **~ sth** (*business* 商) to send money or profits back to your own country 寄（錢）回國；將（利潤）調回本國 ▸ **re·pat·ri·ation** /ˌriːˌpætriˈeɪʃn; *NAmE* -ˌpeɪt-/ *noun* [U, C]：*the repatriation of immigrants/profits* 遣返移民；調回利潤 ◇ *a voluntary repatriation programme* 自願遣返計劃

repay /rɪˈpeɪ/ *verb* (**re·paid, re·paid** /rɪˈpeɪd/) **1** to pay back the money that you have borrowed from sb 歸還；償還；清償：**~ sth** *to **repay a debt/loan/mortgage*** 償還債務／貸款／按揭貸款 ◇ *I'll repay the money I owe them next week.* 我將在下個星期償還欠他們的錢。◇ **~ sth to sb** *The advance must be repaid to the publisher if the work is not completed on time.* 如果作品沒有按時完成，預付款必須返還給出版商。◇ **~ sb** *When are you going to repay them?* 你什麼時候把錢還給他們？◇ **~ sb sth** *I fully intend to repay them the money that they lent me.* 我非常想把他們借給我的錢還給他們。**2** to give sth to sb or do sth for them in return for sth that they have done for you 酬報；報答 SYN **recompense**：**~ sb (for sth)** *How can I ever repay you for your generosity?* 你對

我這樣慷慨，我怎麼才能報答你呢？◇ **~ sth (with sth)** *Their trust was repaid with fierce loyalty.* 他們的信任獲得的回報是忠心耿耿。 **3 ~ sth** (*BrE, formal*) if sth **repays** your attention, interest, study, etc., it is worth spending time to look at it, etc. 值得：*The report repays careful reading.* 這份報告值得仔細閱讀。

re·pay·able /rɪˈpeɪəbl/ *adj.* that can or must be paid back 可償還的；必須償還的；應回報的：*The loan is repayable in monthly instalments.* 這筆借款能以按月攤付的方式償還。

re·pay·ment /rɪˈpeɪmənt/ *noun* **1** [U] the act of paying back money that you have borrowed from a bank, etc. 歸還借款；償還債務：*The loan is due for repayment by the end of the year.* 這筆借款要在年底還清。 **2** [C, usually pl.] (*BrE*) a sum of money that you pay regularly to a bank, etc. until you have returned all the money that you owe 按期償還的款項；分期償還額：*We were unable to **meet** (= pay) **the repayments** on the loan.* 我們無法支付貸款的分期償還額。◇ *mortgage repayments* 按揭貸款的償還款項 ➲ SYNONYMS at PAYMENT ➲ COLLOCATIONS at FINANCE

re'payment mortgage *noun* (*BrE*) a type of MORTGAGE in which you pay regular sums of money to the bank, etc. until you have returned all the money and interest that you owe 固定償還期按揭 ➲ compare ENDOWMENT MORTGAGE

re·peal /rɪˈpiːl/ *verb* **~ sth** if a government or other group or person with authority **repeals** a law, that law is no longer valid 廢除，撤銷，廢止（法規） ▶ **re·peal** *noun* [U]

re·peat 🔑 /rɪˈpiːt/ *verb, noun*

WORD FAMILY
repeat *verb, noun*
repeatable *adj.*
(≠ unrepeatable)
repeated *adj.*
repeatedly *adv.*
repetition *noun*
repetitive *adj.*
repetitious *adj.*

■ ***verb***

▸ **SAY/WRITE AGAIN** 重複說／寫 **1** 🔑 [T] to say or write sth again or more than once 重複；重說；重寫：**~ sth** *to repeat a question* 重複一遍問題 ◇ *I'm sorry—could you repeat that?* 對不起，你可以再說一遍嗎？◇ *She kept repeating his name softly over and over again.* 她輕輕地一遍又一遍地重複着他的名字。◇ *The opposition have been repeating their calls for the president's resignation.* 反對派一再要求總統辭職。◇ **~ yourself** *Do say if I'm repeating myself* (= if I have already said this). 如果我在重複自己說過的話，請直言。◇ **~ that ...** *He's fond of repeating that the company's success is all down to him.* 他老愛說公司的成功全都歸功於他。

▸ **DO AGAIN** 重做 **2** 🔑 [T, I] **~ (sth)** to do or produce sth again or more than once 重做；重新推出；重複：*to repeat a mistake/a process/an exercise* 重複一個錯誤／過程；反複練習 ◇ *The treatment should be repeated every two to three hours.* 這種治療方法應該每隔兩到三小時重複一次。◇ *They are hoping to repeat last year's victory.* 他們希望重複去年的勝利。◇ *These offers are unlikely to be repeated.* 這樣的出價不大可能再有了。◇ *The programmes will be repeated next year.* 明年將繼續開設這些課程。◇ *to **repeat the class/year/grade*** (= in a school, to take the class/year/grade again) 重修這門課；重讀一年；留級 ◇ *Lift and lower the right leg 20 times. Repeat with the left leg.* 將右腿提放 20 次，換左腿重複一樣的動作。

▸ **HAPPEN AGAIN** 再次發生 **3** 🔑 [T, I] **~ (sth/itself)** to happen more than once in the same way 重複發生；再次發生：*History has a strange way of repeating itself.* 歷史會奇怪地重演。◇ *a repeating pattern/design* 重複出現的圖案／設計

▸ **WHAT SB ELSE SAID** 他人的話 **4** 🔑 [T] to tell sb sth that you have heard or been told by sb else 轉述；轉告：**~ sth to sb** *I don't want you to repeat a word of this to anyone.* 這些話你一個字也不要告訴別人。◇ **~ sth** *The rumour has been widely repeated in the press.* 報界廣泛轉載了這一傳聞。 **5** 🔑 [T] to say sth that sb else has said, especially in order to learn it 複述，跟讀（尤指為學習）：**~ sth (after sb)** *Listen and repeat each sentence after me.* 先聽再跟着我朗讀每個句子。◇ **~ what ...** *Can you repeat what I've just said word for word?* 你能一字不差地複述我剛才說過的話嗎？◇ **+ speech** *'Are you really sure?' she repeated.* "你真的很肯定嗎？" 她重複問道。

▸ **OF FOOD** 食物 **6** [I] **~ (on sb)** (*BrE, informal*) if food **repeats**, you can taste it for some time after you have eaten it 留有餘味：*Do you find that onions repeat on you?* 你是不是覺得吃了洋蔥嘴裏老有一股味兒？

▸ **FOR EMPHASIS** 強調 **7** 🔑 [I, T] used to emphasize sth that you have already said（強調說過的話）再說一遍：*The claims are, I repeat, totally unfounded.* 我再說一遍，這些說法是毫無根據的。◇ **~ sth** *I am not, repeat not, travelling in the same car as him!* 我不會，再說一遍，是不會和他坐同一輛車的！

■ ***noun*** **1** a television or radio programme that has been broadcast before 重播的電視（或廣播）節目：*'Is it a new series?' 'No, a repeat.'* "這是新播出的連續劇嗎？" "不，是重播的。" **2** an event that is very similar to sth that happened before 重演的事物；重複的事件：*A repeat of the 1906 earthquake could kill up to 11 000 people.* 如果再次發生 1906 年的地震，可能會有多達 11 000 人死亡。◇ *She didn't want a **repeat performance** of what had happened the night before.* 她不想讓前一天晚上的事件重演。◇ (*business* 商) *a **repeat order*** (= for a further supply of the same goods) 續訂貨單 **3** (*music* 音) a passage that is repeated 重複段；反複部份

re·peat·able /rɪˈpiːtəbl/ *adj.* [not usually before noun] **1** (of a comment, etc. 評論等) (usually in negative sentences 通常用於否定句) polite and not offensive 有禮貌；不冒犯人：*His reply was not repeatable.* 他的回答不便重複。 **2** that can be repeated 可重複 OPP **unrepeatable**

re·peated 🔑 /rɪˈpiːtɪd/ *adj.* [only before noun] happening, said or done many times 重複的；反複發生的：*repeated absences from work* 一再曠工 ▶ **re·peat·ed·ly** 🔑 *adv.*：*The victim had been stabbed repeatedly in the chest.* 受害者胸部多處被刺傷。

re·peat·er /rɪˈpiːtə(r)/ *noun* (*technical* 術語) a gun that you can fire several times without having to load it again 連發槍；轉輪手槍

repel /rɪˈpel/ *verb* (**-ll-**) **1** [T] **~ sb/sth** (*formal*) to successfully fight sb who is attacking you, your country, etc. and drive them away 擊退；驅逐：*to **repel an attack/invasion/invader*** 擊退進攻／入侵；驅逐入侵者 ◇ *Troops repelled an attempt to infiltrate the south of the island.* 部隊挫敗了對該島南部的潛入企圖。◇ (*figurative*) *The reptile's prickly skin repels nearly all of its predators.* 這種爬行動物渾身是刺，幾乎所有的捕食者都退避三舍。 **2** [T] **~ sth** to drive, push or keep sth away 推開；趕走；驅除：*a cream that repels insects* 驅除昆蟲的乳劑 ◇ *The fabric has been treated to repel water.* 這種織物進行過防水處理。 **3** [T] **~ sb** (not used in the progressive tenses 不用於進行時) to make sb feel horror or disgust 使恐懼；使厭惡 SYN **disgust, repulse**：*I was repelled by the smell.* 這種氣味讓我惡心。 **4** [T, I] **~ (sth)** (*technical* 術語) if one thing **repels** another, or if two things **repel** each other, an electrical or MAGNETIC force pushes them apart 排斥；相斥：*Like poles repel each other.* 同極相斥。 OPP **attract** ➲ see also REPULSION, REPULSIVE

re·pel·lent /rɪˈpelənt/ *adj., noun*

■ ***adj.*** **1 ~ (to sb)** (*formal*) very unpleasant; causing strong dislike 使人反感的；令人厭惡的 SYN **repulsive**：*Their political ideas are repellent to most people.* 他們的政治觀點令大多數人反感。 **2** (in compounds 構成複合詞) not letting a particular substance, especially water, pass through it 防…的；隔絕…的：*water-repellent cloth* 防水布

■ ***noun*** [U, C] **1** a substance that is used for keeping insects away from you 驅蟲劑：*(an) insect repellent* 驅蟲劑 **2** a substance that is used on cloth, stone, etc. to prevent water from passing through it 防水劑：*(a) water repellent* 防水劑

re·pent /rɪˈpent/ *verb* [I, T] (*formal*) to feel and show that you are sorry for sth bad or wrong that you have done 後悔；悔過；懺悔：*God welcomes the sinner who repents.* 上帝歡迎悔過的罪人。◇ **~ of sth** *She had repented of what she had done.* 她對自己所做的事深感懊悔。◇ **~ sth**

He came to repent his hasty decision (= wished he had not taken it). 他開始後悔自己的草率決定。

re·pent·ance /rɪˈpentəns/ *noun* [U] ~ (**for sth**) (*formal*) the fact of showing that you are sorry for sth wrong that you have done 後悔；懊悔；悔過；懺悔 SYN **contrition, remorse**：*He shows no sign of repentance.* 他毫無悔意。

re·pent·ant /rɪˈpentənt/ *adj.* (*formal*) feeling or showing that you are sorry for sth wrong that you have done 後悔的；悔過的；表示悔改的 SYN **contrite, remorseful** OPP **unrepentant**

re·per·cus·sion /ˌriːpəˈkʌʃn; *NAmE* -pərˈk-/ *noun* [usually pl.] an indirect and usually bad result of an action or event that may happen some time afterwards （間接的）影響，反響，惡果 SYN **consequence**：*The collapse of the company will **have repercussions** for the whole industry.* 這家公司的垮台將會給整個行業造成間接的負面影響。 ➲ SYNONYMS at RESULT

rep·er·toire /ˈrepətwɑː(r); *NAmE* -pərt-/ *noun* **1** (also *formal* **rep·er·tory**) all the plays, songs, pieces of music, etc. that a performer knows and can perform （總稱某人的）可表演項目：*a pianist with a wide repertoire* 能演奏很多曲子的鋼琴師 **2** all the things that a person is able to do （某人的）全部才能，全部本領：*a young child's growing verbal repertoire* 小孩不斷增長的語言表達能力

rep·er·tory /ˈrepətri; *NAmE* ˈrepərtɔːri/ *noun* **1** (also *informal* **rep**) [U] the type of work of a theatre company in which different plays are performed for short periods of time 保留劇目輪演：*an actor in repertory* 參加輪演劇目的演員 ◇ *a repertory company* 輪演劇目劇團 **2** [C] (*formal*) = REPERTOIRE (1)

repe·ti·tion /ˌrepəˈtɪʃn/ *noun* **1** [U, C] the fact of doing or saying the same thing many times 重複；重做；重說：*learning by repetition* 通過重複來學習 **2** [C] a thing that has been done or said before 重做的事；重說的話：*We do not want to see a repetition of last year's tragic events.* 我們不想看到去年的悲劇重演。

repe·ti·tious /ˌrepəˈtɪʃəs/ *adj.* (often *disapproving*) involving sth that is often repeated 重複的；一再的；反反複複的：*a long and repetitious speech* 冗長重複的講話 ▶ **repe·ti·tious·ly** *adv.* **repe·ti·tious·ness** *noun*

R

re·peti·tive /rɪˈpetətɪv/ *adj.* **1** saying or doing the same thing many times, so that it becomes boring 重複乏味的 SYN **monotonous**：*a repetitive task* 重複乏味的工作 **2** repeated many times 多次重複的：*a repetitive pattern of behaviour* 重複的行為模式 ▶ **re·peti·tive·ly** *adv.* **re·peti·tive·ness** *noun* [U]

re·phrase /ˌriːˈfreɪz/ *verb* ~ **sth** to say or write sth using different words in order to make the meaning clearer 改口說，改變詞句（以使意思更清楚）

re·place 0‑ /rɪˈpleɪs/ *verb*

1 0‑ **sth/sb** to be used instead of sth/sb else; to do sth instead of sb/sth else 代替；取代 SYN **take over from**：*The new design will eventually replace all existing models.* 新的設計最終將會取代所有現有的型號。◇ *Teachers will never be replaced by computers in the classroom.* 課堂上電腦永遠不會取代老師。 **2** 0‑ to remove sb/sth and put another person or thing in their place （用…）替換；（以…）接替：~ **sb/sth** *He will be difficult to replace when he leaves.* 他離職時，他的位置很難找到人接替。◇ ~ **sb/sth with/by sb/sth** *It is not a good idea to miss meals and replace them with snacks.* 不吃正餐，改吃點心，這不是什麼好主意。 **3** 0‑ ~ **sth** to change sth that is old, damaged, etc. for a similar thing that is newer or better 更換；更新：*All the old carpets need replacing.* 所有的舊地毯都需要更換。◇ *You'll be expected to replace any broken glasses.* 玻璃杯如有損壞，要負責賠償。 **4** 0‑ ~ **sth** (+ **adv./prep.**) to put sth back in the place where it was before 把…放回原處：*I replaced the cup carefully in the saucer.* 我小心翼翼地將杯子放回茶碟。◇ *to replace the handset* (= after using the telephone) 放回電話聽筒

re·place·able /rɪˈpleɪsəbl/ *adj.* that can be replaced 可替換的；可代替的 OPP **irreplaceable**

re·place·ment /rɪˈpleɪsmənt/ *noun* **1** [U] the act of replacing one thing with another, especially sth that is newer or better 替換；更換：*the replacement of worn car parts* 汽車上舊零件的更換 ◇ *replacement windows* 新換的窗子 **2** [C] a thing that replaces sth, especially because the first thing is old, broken, etc. 替代品；替換物：*a hip replacement* 人工髖關節 **3** [C] ~ (**for sb**) a person who replaces another person in an organization, especially in their job （尤指工作中的）接替者，替代者：*We need to find a replacement for Sue.* 我們需要找一個替代蘇的人。

re·play *noun, verb*

■ ***noun*** /ˈriːpleɪ/ **1** (*sport* 體) a game that is played again because neither side won in the previous game （由於未決出勝負而進行的）重賽 **2** the playing again of a short section of a film/movie, tape, etc. especially to look at or listen to sth more carefully （錄像、錄音等的）重放，重演，重播：*We watched a replay of the wedding on DVD.* 我們看了婚禮 DVD 錄像的重放。 ➲ see also ACTION REPLAY **3** (*informal*) something that is repeated or happens in exactly the same way as it did before 重演的事物；重複出現的事物：*This election will not be a replay of the last one.* 這次選舉將不會是上一次的重演。

■ ***verb*** /ˌriːˈpleɪ/ **1** [usually passive] ~ **sth** to play a sports game again because neither team won the first game （因勝負未決）重賽 **2** ~ **sth** to play again sth that has been recorded on tape, film, etc. 重新播放（錄像、錄音等）：*The police replayed footage of the accident over and over again.* 警察一遍又一遍地重放事故的片段。◇ (*figurative*) *He replayed the scene in his mind.* 他再次回想起當時的情景。

re·plen·ish /rɪˈplenɪʃ/ *verb* ~ **sth** (**with sth**) (*formal*) to make sth full again by replacing what has been used 補充；重新裝滿 SYN **top up**：*to replenish food and water supplies* 補充食物和水的供應 ◇ *Allow me to replenish your glass.* 讓我再給您斟滿。 ▶ **re·plen·ish·ment** *noun* [U]

re·plete /rɪˈpliːt/ *adj.* **1** [not before noun] ~ (**with sth**) (*formal*) filled with sth; with a full supply of sth 充滿；充足：*literature replete with drama and excitement* 充滿緊張刺激情節的文學作品 **2** (*old-fashioned* or *formal*) very full of food 很飽；飽食

rep·lica /ˈreplɪkə/ *noun* a very good or exact copy of sth 複製品；仿製品：*a replica of the Eiffel Tower* 埃菲爾鐵塔模型 ◇ *The weapon used in the raid was a replica.* 搶劫案中使用的武器是一件仿製品。◇ *replica guns* 仿製的槍支

rep·li·cate /ˈreplɪkeɪt/ *verb* **1** [T] ~ **sth** (*formal*) to copy sth exactly 複製；（精確地）仿製 SYN **duplicate**：*Subsequent experiments failed to replicate these findings.* 後來的實驗沒有得出同樣的結果。 **2** [T, I] ~ (**itself**) (*technical* 術語) (of a virus or a MOLECULE 病毒或分子) to produce exact copies of itself 再造；再生；自我複製：*The drug prevents the virus from replicating itself.* 這種藥能防止病毒複製。 ▶ **rep·li·ca·tion** /ˌreplɪˈkeɪʃn/ *noun* [U, C]

reply 0‑ /rɪˈplaɪ/ *verb, noun*

■ ***verb*** (**re·plies**, **re·ply·ing**, **re·plied**, **re·plied**) **1** 0‑ [I, T] to say or write sth as an answer to sb/sth 回答；答覆：~ (**to sb/sth**) (**with sth**) *to reply to a question/an advertisement* 回答問題；回應廣告 ◇ *He never replied to any of my letters.* 他從來沒給我回過信。◇ *She only replied with a smile.* 她只是報以微笑。◇ + **speech** *'I won't let you down,' he replied confidently.* 他信心十足地答道："我不會讓你失望的。"◇ ~ **that** ... *The senator replied that he was not in a position to comment.* 參議員回答說他不宜發表評論。 ➲ note at ANSWER **2** [I] ~ (**to sth**) (**with sth**) to do sth as a reaction to sth that sb has said or done 回應；作出反應：*The terrorists replied to the government's statement with more violence.* 恐怖分子以更多的暴力事件來回應政府的聲明。

■ ***noun*** 0‑ [C, U] an act of replying to sth/sb in speech, writing or by some action 回答；答覆：*We had over 100 replies to our advertisement.* 我們的廣告收到了 100 多個回應。◇ *I asked her what her name was but she **made no reply**.* 我問她叫什麼名字，但她沒有回答。◇ (*formal*) *I am writing **in reply to** your letter of 16 March.*

* 3 月 16 日來函收悉，現答覆如下。◇ (*BrE*) ***a reply-paid envelope*** (= on which you do not have to put a stamp because it has already been paid for) 郵資已付信封 ◇ (*BrE*) *Morocco scored four goals without reply to win the game.* 摩洛哥隊在一球未失的情況下連入四球，贏得了這場比賽。 ➲ note at ANSWER

repo man /ˈriːpəʊ mæn; *NAmE* ˈriːpoʊ/ *noun* (*NAmE, informal*) a person whose job is to REPOSSESS (= take back) goods from people who still owe money for them and cannot pay（向拖欠貨款者追回商品的）商品收回員

Synonyms 同義詞辨析

report

story • account • version

These are all words for a written or spoken account of events. 以上各詞均指對所發生事情的記述、講述。

report a written or spoken account of an event, especially one that is published or broadcast 尤指刊登或廣播的報道： *Are these newspaper reports true?* 報紙上這些報道屬實嗎？

story an account, often spoken, of what happened to sb or of how sth happened; a report of events in a newspaper, magazine or news broadcast 常指對所發生事情的口頭敍述、描述、（新聞）報道： *It was many years before the full story was made public.* 許多年之後，事情的全貌才公之於眾。 ◇ *the front-page story* 頭版報道

account a written or spoken description of sth that has happened 指對所發生事情的書面或口頭描述、敍述、報告： *She gave the police a full account of the incident.* 她向警方詳盡地敍述了所發生的事情。

REPORT OR ACCOUNT? 用 report 還是 account？

A **report** is always of recent events, especially news. An **account** may be of recent or past events.
* report 總是指對最新事情的報道，尤指新聞報道。account 可指對最近的或過去的事情的敍述。

version a description of an event from the point of view of a particular person or group of people 指特定的人或群體對某事的描述、說法： *She gave us her version of what had happened that day.* 她從她的角度向我們描述了那天發生的事情。

PATTERNS

- a report/story **about** sth
- a **brief/short** report/story/account
- a **full** report/story/account/version
- a **news** report/story
- **to give** a(n) report/account/version

re·port 🔑 /rɪˈpɔːt; *NAmE* rɪˈpɔːrt/ *verb, noun*

▪ ***verb***

▸ **GIVE INFORMATION** 提供信息 **1** 🔑 [T, I] to give people information about sth that you have heard, seen, done, etc. 彙報；報告；通報： **~ sth (to sb)** *The crash happened seconds after the pilot reported engine trouble.* 飛行員報告發動機有故障後幾秒鐘飛機就墜毀了。 ◇ *Call me urgently if you have anything to report.* 如果有什麼事要向我彙報，立即給我打電話。 ◇ **~ (on sth) (to sb)** *The committee will report on its research next month.* 委員會下個月將彙報他們的研究情況。 ◇ **~ (sb/sth) doing sth** *The neighbours reported seeing him leave the building around noon.* 鄰居們說在中午時分看見他離開大樓。 ◇ **~ sb/sth + adj.** *The doctor reported the patient fully recovered.* 醫生說這位病人已經完全康復。 ◇ **~ sb/sth as sth/as doing sth** *The house was reported as being in excellent condition.* 報告說明這房子的狀況極佳。 ◇ **be reported to be/have sth** *The house was reported to be in excellent condition.* 報告說明這房子的狀況極佳。 ◇ **~ (that) …** *Employers reported that graduates were deficient in writing and problem-solving skills.* 雇主反映畢業生缺乏寫作和解決問題的技能。 ◇ **~ what, how, etc. …** *She failed to report what had occurred.* 她對發生的事情沒有報告。 ◇ **+ speech** *'The cabin's empty,' he reported back.* "小屋是空的。" 他彙報說。

▸ **NEWS/STORY** 新聞；事件 **2** 🔑 [T, I] to present a written or spoken account of an event in a newspaper, on television, etc. 報道；公佈；發表；宣佈： **~ sth** *The stabbing was reported in the local press.* 當地的新聞媒體報道了刺殺事件。 ◇ **it is reported that …** *It was reported that several people had been arrested.* 據報道已有數人被捕。 ◇ **~ that …** *The TV news reported that several people had been arrested.* 據電視新聞報道，已有數人被捕。 ◇ **~ (on sth)** *She reports on royal stories for the BBC.* 她為英國廣播公司做有關王室活動的報道。 **3** 🔑 **be reported** [T] used to show that sth has been stated, and you do not know if it is true or not（不知傳言是否確鑿）據說，傳聞： **~ to do sth** *She is reported to earn over $10 million a year.* 據傳她一年掙 1 000 多萬元。 ◇ **~ as doing sth** *The President is reported as saying that he needs a break.* 據傳總統說他需要休息一下。 ◇ **it is reported that …** ***It was reported that*** *changes were being considered.* 有傳言說改革措施正在醞釀之中。

▸ **CRIME/ACCIDENT, ETC.** 犯罪或事故等 **4** 🔑 [T] to tell a person in authority about a crime, an accident, an illness, etc. or about sth bad that sb has done 舉報；告發： **~ sth (to sb)** *Have you reported the accident to the police yet?* 你將這次事故報警了嗎？ ◇ *a decrease in the number of reported cases of AIDS* 報告的艾滋病病例數量的減少 ◇ **~ sb (to sb) (for sth/for doing sth)** *He's already been reported twice for arriving late.* 他因為遲到已經兩次被告發。 ◇ **~ sb/sth + adj.** *She has reported her daughter missing.* 女兒失踪，她已經向警方報案。

▸ **ARRIVE** 到達 **5** 🔑 [I] **~ (to sb/sth) (for sth)** to tell sb that you have arrived, for example for work or for a meeting with sb 報到： *You should report for duty at 9.30 a.m.* 你應該在上午 9:30 報到上班。 ◇ *All visitors must report to the reception desk on arrival.* 所有訪客到達後務必在接待處報到。

PHR V **reˌport ˈback** to return to a place, especially in order to work again 回歸；返回；（尤指）回到工作崗位： *Take an hour for lunch and report back at 2.* 花一個小時吃午飯，兩點鐘返回。 **reˌport ˈback (on sth) (to sb)** to give sb information about sth that they have asked you to find out about 彙報（所需信息）；反饋： *Find out as much as you can about him and report back to me.* 盡量查找有關他的資料，向我彙報。 ◇ *One person in the group should be prepared to report back to the class on your discussion.* 一名組員應準備向全班彙報你們的討論情況。 ◇ **~ that …** *They reported back that no laws had actually been broken.* 他們彙報說並沒有真正發生違法的事。 **reˈport to sb** (not used in the progressive tenses 不用於進行時) (*business* 商) if you **report to** a particular manager in an organization that you work for, they are officially responsible for your work and tell you what to do 對…負責；隸屬；從屬

▪ ***noun***

▸ **OF NEWS** 新聞 **1** 🔑 **~ (on/of sth)** a written or spoken account of an event, especially one that is published or broadcast 報道： *Are these newspaper reports true?* 報紙上這些報道屬實嗎？ ◇ *a weather report* 天氣預報

▸ **INFORMATION** 信息 **2** 🔑 **~ (on sth)** a spoken or written description of sth containing information that sb needs to have 彙報；報告；記述： *a police/medical report* 警方的 / 醫療報告 ◇ *Can you give us a progress report?* 你可以給我們提供進度報告嗎？

▸ **OFFICIAL STUDY** 研究 **3** 🔑 **~ (on sth)** an official document written by a group of people who have examined a particular situation or problem 調查報告：*The committee will publish their report on the health service in a few weeks.* 委員會將在幾週內發表他們對公共醫療服務的調查報告。 ➲ WRITING TUTOR page WT18

▸ **STORY** 傳說 **4** 🔑 a story or piece of information that may or may not be true 傳聞： *I don't believe these reports of UFO sightings.* 我不相信這些有關目擊不明飛行物的傳言。 ◇ *There are unconfirmed reports of a shooting in the capital.* 有未經證實的傳言說在首都發生了槍擊事件。

▸ **ON STUDENT'S WORK** 學生的學習 **5** (*BrE*) (*NAmE* **reˈport card**) a written statement about a student's work at

R

school, college, etc. 成績報告單： *a school report* 學生成績報告單 ◇ *to get a* ***good/bad report*** 成績優異／欠佳

▸ EMPLOYEE 雇員 **6** (*BrE, business* 商) an employee whose work is the responsibility of a particular manager（某個主管的）下屬： *a weekly meeting with my direct reports* 同我的直接下屬一起開的週會

▸ OF GUN 槍炮 **7** the sound of an explosion or of a gun being fired 爆炸聲；射擊聲 SYN **bang, blast**： *a loud report* 巨大的爆炸聲

IDM **of bad/good reˈport** (*formal*) talked about by people in a bad/good way 名聲壞／好

re·por·tage /rɪˈpɔːtɪdʒ; ˌrepɔːˈtɑːʒ; *NAmE* rɪˈpɔːrt-; ˌrepɔːrˈt-/ *noun* [U] (*formal*) the reporting of news or the typical style in which this is done in newspapers, or on TV and radio 新聞報道；報道風格；報道文體

re·port·ed·ly /rɪˈpɔːtɪdli; *NAmE* -ˈpɔːrt-/ *adv.* according to what some people say 據說；據報道；據傳聞： *The band have reportedly decided to split up.* 據說這個樂隊已經決定解散。

reˌported ˈquestion *noun* (*grammar* 語法) = INDIRECT QUESTION

reˌported ˈspeech (also **ˌindirect ˈspeech**) *noun* [U] (*grammar* 語法) a report of what sb has said that does not use their exact words 間接引語；間接敍述法： *In reported speech, 'I'll come later' becomes 'He said he'd come later'.* 在間接引語中，I'll come later 變為 He said he'd come later。

re·port·er /rɪˈpɔːtə(r); *NAmE* -ˈpɔːrt-/ *noun* a person who collects and reports news for newspapers, radio or television 記者；通訊員： *a reporter from the New York Times*《紐約時報》的記者 ◇ *a crime reporter* 報道罪案的記者 ➲ compare JOURNALIST ➲ see also CUB REPORTER

re·port·ing /rɪˈpɔːtɪŋ; *NAmE* -ˈpɔːrt-/ *noun* [U] the presenting and writing about news on television and radio, and in newspapers 新聞報道： *accurate/balanced/objective reporting* 準確的／公正的／客觀的新聞報道 ◇ (*BrE*) ***Reporting restrictions*** *on the trial have been lifted* (= it can now legally be reported). 對報道這次審訊的限制已經撤銷。

re·pose /rɪˈpəʊz; *NAmE* rɪˈpoʊz/ *noun, verb*

■ ***noun*** [U] (*literary*) a state of rest, sleep or feeling calm 休息；睡眠；平靜；鎮靜

■ ***verb*** (*literary*) **1** [I] **+ adv./prep.** (of an object 物體) to be or be kept in a particular place 位於；被擱置在 **2** [I] **+ adv./prep.** (of a person 人) to lie or rest in a particular place 躺；休息

re·posi·tory /rɪˈpɒzətri; *NAmE* rɪˈpɑːzətɔːri/ *noun* (*pl.* **-ies**) (*formal*) **1** a place where sth is stored in large quantities 倉庫；貯藏室；存放處 **2** a person or book that is full of information 學識淵博的人；智囊；知識寶典： *My father is a repository of family history.* 我的父親對家族史無所不知。

re·pos·sess /ˌriːpəˈzes/ *verb* [usually passive] **~ sth** to take back property or goods from sb who has arranged to buy them but who still owes money for them and cannot pay（因買者未如期付款）收回（商品、房地產等）： (*BrE*) *First I lost my job, then my house was repossessed.* 我先是失去了工作，後來房子又被收回。 HELP In *NAmE*, when a bank takes possession of sb's house because they cannot afford to pay the money they owe on it, the usual word is **foreclose**, but **repossess** is used in other contexts. 因房主付不出房貸致使銀行收回房子的所有權，美式英語常用 foreclose，而 repossess 則用於其他場合。 ➲ COLLOCATIONS at HOUSE ➲ compare FORECLOSE (1)

re·pos·ses·sion /ˌriːpəˈzeʃn/ *noun* **1** [U, C] the act of repossessing property, goods, etc.（財產、商品等的）收回： *families threatened with repossession* 受到房子將被收回威脅的家庭 ◇ *a repossession order* 物品收回令 **2** [C] a house, car, etc. that has been repossessed 被收回的房子（或汽車等）： *Auctions are the best place for buying repossessions.* 拍賣會是購買被收回商品的最佳地方。

R

rep·re·hen·sible /ˌreprɪˈhensəbl/ *adj.* (*formal*) morally wrong and deserving criticism 不道德的；應受指責的；應受譴責的 SYN **deplorable**

rep·re·sent 🔑 /ˌreprɪˈzent/ *verb*

▸ ACT/SPEAK FOR SB 為某人做／說 **1** 🔑 [often passive] **~ sb/sth** to be a member of a group of people and act or speak on their behalf at an event, a meeting, etc. 代表： *The competition attracted over 500 contestants representing 8 different countries.* 這次比賽吸引了代表 8 個不同國家的 500 多名參賽者。◇ *Local businesses are well represented on the committee* (= there are a lot of people from them on the committee). 委員會中有許多地方企業的代表。◇ *The President was represented at the ceremony by the Vice-President.* 副總統代表總統出席了這次慶典。 **2** 🔑 **~ sb/sth** to act or speak officially for sb and defend their interests 作為…的代言人；維護…的利益： *The union represents over 200 000 teachers.* 工會代表着 20 餘萬名教師的利益。◇ *The association was formed to* ***represent the interests of*** *women artists.* 成立這個協會是為了維護女性藝術家的利益。◇ *Ms Dale is representing the defendant* (= is his/her lawyer) *in the case.* 在這個案件當中，戴爾女士為被告作辯護。

▸ BE EQUAL TO 等於 **3** 🔑 *linking verb* **+ noun** (not used in the progressive tenses 不用於進行時) to be sth 等於；相當於；意味着 SYN **constitute**： *This contract represents 20% of the company's annual revenue.* 這份合約相當於公司 20% 的年收入。◇ *This decision represents a significant departure from previous policy.* 這個決定意味着在很大程度上脫離了原先的政策。

▸ BE EXAMPLE OF 成為例證 **4** 🔑 [no passive] **~ sth** to be an example or expression of sth 成為…實例；成為典型；體現 SYN **be typical of**： *a project representing all that is good in the community* 體現着社區中一切美好形象的工程 ◇ *Those comments do not represent the views of us all.* 這些言論不足以體現我們所有人的看法。

▸ BE SYMBOL 成為象徵 **5** 🔑 **~ sth** (not used in the progressive tenses 不用於進行時) to be a symbol of sth 作為…的象徵；代表 SYN **symbolize**： *Each colour on the chart represents a different department.* 圖表中的每一種顏色都代表一個不同的部門。◇ *Wind direction is represented by arrows.* 風向是用箭頭表示的。

▸ IN PICTURE 圖畫 **6** 🔑 **~ sb/sth** (**as sb/sth**) | **~ sb/sth doing sth** (*formal*) to show sb/sth, especially in a picture 展示；描繪 SYN **depict**： *The carvings represent a hunting scene.* 這些雕刻作品描繪了一幅狩獵的場面。◇ *The results are represented in fig.3 below.* 結果如下面的圖 3 所示。

▸ DESCRIBE 描述 **7 ~ sb** (**as sth**) (*formal*) to present or describe sb/sth in a particular way, especially when this may not be fair（尤指不公平地）展現，描述，表現： *The king is represented as a villain in the play.* 劇中國王的形象是一個惡棍。◇ *The risks were represented as negligible.* 他們把風險說得微不足道。

▸ MAKE FORMAL STATEMENT 正式聲明 **8 ~ sth** (**to sb**) | **~ that …** (*formal*) to make a formal statement to sb in authority to make your opinions known or to protest 正式提出（意見、抗議等）： *They represented their concerns to the authorities.* 他們向當局陳述了他們關心的問題。

re-present /ˌriː prɪˈzent/ *verb* **~ sth** to give, show or send sth again, especially a cheque, bill, etc. that has not been paid（尤指未支付的支票、賬單等）再給予，再呈上，再遞上

rep·re·sen·ta·tion /ˌreprɪzenˈteɪʃn/ *noun* **1** [U, C] the act of presenting sb/sth in a particular way; something that shows or describes sth 表現；描述；描繪；表現形式 SYN **portrayal**： *the negative representation of single mothers in the media* 媒體對單身母親的負面描述 ◇ *The snake swallowing its tail is a representation of infinity.* 蛇含其尾表示無窮無盡。 **2** [U] the fact of having representatives who will speak or vote for you or on your behalf 有代理人；代表；維護；支持： *The green movement lacks effective representation in Parliament.* 環境保護運動在議會中缺乏有力的支持者。◇ *The accused was not allowed legal representation.* 沒有允許被告請律師。 ➲ see also PROPORTIONAL REPRESENTATION **3 representations** [pl.] (*formal, especially BrE*) formal statements made to sb in authority, especially in order to make your opinions known or to protest 陳述；抗議：*We have* ***made representations to*** *the prime minister, but without success.* 我們同首相進行交涉，但沒有效果。

rep·re·sen·ta·tion·al /ˌreprɪzenˈteɪʃnl/ *adj.* **1** (*technical* 術語) (especially of a style of art or painting 尤指藝術或繪畫風格) trying to show things as they really are 具象派的 ➲ compare ABSTRACT *adj.* (3) **2** involving the act of representing sb/sth 代表性的：*local representational democracy* 地方代議民主政體

rep·re·sen·ta·tive 🔑 /ˌreprɪˈzentətɪv/ *noun, adj.*

▪ ***noun*** **~ (of sb/sth)** **1** 🔑 a person who has been chosen to speak or vote for sb else or on behalf of a group 代表：*a representative of the UN* 聯合國代表 ◇ *our elected representatives in government* 政府中我們選舉產生的代表 ◇ *a union representative* 工會代表 ◇ *The committee includes representatives from industry.* 這個委員會包括產業界的代表。 **2** 🔑 (also *informal* **rep**) a person who works for a company and travels around selling its products 銷售代表；銷售代理；代銷人：*a sales representative* 銷售代表 ◇ *She's our representative in France.* 她是我們公司駐法國的銷售代表。 **3** 🔑 a person chosen to take the place of sb else 代表；代表他人者：*He was the Queen's representative at the ceremony.* 他代表女王出席了慶典。 **4** 🔑 a person who is typical of a particular group 典型人物；代表性人物：*The singer is regarded as a representative of the youth of her generation.* 這位歌手被看作是她那一代年輕人的典型代表。 **5 Representative** (*abbr.* **Rep.**) (in the US) a member of the House of Representatives, the Lower House of Congress; a member of the House of Representatives in the lower house of a state parliament （美國）眾議院議員

▪ ***adj.*** **1** 🔑 **~ (of sb/sth)** typical of a particular group of people 典型的；有代表性的：*Is a questionnaire answered by 500 people* ***truly representative*** *of the population as a whole?* 由 500 人參加的問卷調查能真正代表所有民眾嗎？ **2** 🔑 [usually before noun] containing or including examples of all the different types of people or things in a large group 代表各類人（或事物）的：*a* ***representative sample*** *of teachers* 各類教師的代表 **3** 🔑 **~ (of sth)** able to be used as a typical example of sth 可作為典型（或示例）的：*The painting is not representative of his work of the period.* 這幅畫不是他在那個時期的代表作。 **4** (of a system of government, etc. 政治體制等) consisting of people who have been chosen to speak or vote on behalf of the rest of a group 由代表組成的；代議制的：*a representative democracy* 代議制民主政體 **OPP unrepresentative**

re·press /rɪˈpres/ *verb* **1 ~ sth** to try not to have or show an emotion, a feeling, etc. 克制；壓抑；抑制 **SYN control**：*to repress a smile* 忍住不笑 ◇ *He burst in, making no effort to repress his fury.* 他衝了進來，毫不掩飾自己的憤怒。 **2** [often passive] **~ sb/sth** to use political and/or military force to control a group of people and restrict their freedom 壓制；鎮壓 **SYN put down, suppress**

re·pressed /rɪˈprest/ *adj.* **1** (of a person 人) having emotions or desires that are not allowed to be expressed 壓抑的；克制的 **2** (of emotions 情感) not expressed openly 受壓抑的；被抑制的：*repressed anger* 被抑制的怒氣

re·pres·sion /rɪˈpreʃn/ *noun* [U] **1** the act of using force to control a group of people and restrict their freedom 壓制；鎮壓：*government repression* 政府的壓制 **2** the act of controlling strong emotions and desires and not allowing them to be expressed so that they no longer seem to exist 抑制；克制；壓抑：*sexual repression* 性壓抑

re·pres·sive /rɪˈpresɪv/ *adj.* **1** (of a system of government 政治體制) controlling people by force and restricting their freedom 壓制的；專制的；嚴厲的 **SYN dictatorial, tyrannical**：*a* ***repressive regime/measure/law*** 實行高壓政策的政權；鎮壓措施；嚴厲的法律 **2** controlling emotions and desires and not allowing them to be expressed 壓抑的；抑制的；克制的 ▸ **re·pres·sive·ly** *adv.* **re·pres·sive·ness** *noun* [U]

re·prieve /rɪˈpriːv/ *verb, noun*

▪ ***verb*** [usually passive] (not usually used in the progressive tenses 通常不用於進行時) **1 ~ sb** to officially cancel or delay a punishment for a prisoner who is CONDEMNED to death 撤銷…的死刑；緩期執行…的死刑：*a reprieved murderer* 被判死刑而暫緩執行的殺人犯 **2 ~ sth** to officially cancel or delay plans to close sth or end sth 取消關閉；暫緩終止：*70 jobs have been reprieved until next April.* 有 70 個職位暫時保留到明年四月份。

▪ ***noun*** [usually sing.] **1** an official order stopping a punishment, especially for a prisoner who is CONDEMNED to death 刑罰終止令；（尤指）死刑緩刑令 **SYN stay of execution** **2** a delay before sth bad happens 延緩；緩解：*Campaigners have won a reprieve for the hospital threatened with closure.* 活動家們為這家受關閉威脅的醫院贏得了喘息的機會。

rep·ri·mand /ˈreprɪmɑːnd; *NAmE* -mænd/ *verb* **~ sb (for sth)** | **+ speech** (*formal*) to tell sb officially that you do not approve of them or their actions 申斥；訓斥；斥責 **SYN rebuke**：*The officers were severely reprimanded for their unprofessional behaviour.* 軍官們因違反專業操守而受到了嚴厲的斥責。 ▸ **rep·ri·mand** *noun* [C, U]：*He received a severe reprimand for his behaviour.* 他的行為受到了譴責。

re·print *verb, noun*

▪ ***verb*** /ˌriːˈprɪnt/ [usually passive] **~ sth** to print more copies of a book, an article, etc. with few or no changes 重印

▪ ***noun*** /ˈriːprɪnt/ **1** an act of printing more copies of a book because all the others have been sold 重印；再版 **2** a book that has been reprinted 再版本；重印本

re·prisal /rɪˈpraɪzl/ *noun* [C, U] a violent or aggressive act towards sb because of sth bad that they have done towards you 報復；報復行動 **SYN retaliation**：*They did not want to give evidence for fear of reprisals.* 他們因為害怕報復而不想提供證據。 ◇ *They shot ten hostages* ***in reprisal for*** *the assassination of their leader.* 他們的首領遭到暗殺。為了報復，他們槍殺了十名人質。 ➲ COLLOCATIONS at WAR

re·prise /rɪˈpriːz/ *noun* [usually sing.] a repeated part of sth, especially a piece of music 重複部份；（尤指）樂曲的重複部份，重奏

repro /ˈriːprəʊ; *NAmE* -proʊ/ *adj., noun*

▪ ***adj.*** (*informal*) copied, especially from a style that was originally made in the past （尤指按古典風格）複製的，仿製的：*Victorian repro furniture* 仿製的維多利亞式傢具

▪ ***noun*** **1** [C, U] something that is copied from a style that was originally made in the past 仿古物品 **2** [U] = REPROGRAPHICS

re·proach /rɪˈprəʊtʃ; *NAmE* -ˈproʊtʃ/ *noun, verb*

▪ ***noun*** (*formal*) **1** [U] blame or criticism for sth you have done 責備；批評：*His voice was full of reproach.* 他的話完全是一種責備的語氣。 ◇ *The captain's behaviour is* ***above/beyond reproach*** (= you cannot criticize it). 隊長的行為無可厚非。 **2** [C] a word or remark expressing blame or criticism 責備的話語；批評的言辭：*He listened to his wife's bitter reproaches.* 他聽着妻子嚴厲的責備。 **3** [U] a state of shame or loss of honour 羞恥；沒面子；丟臉：*Her actions brought reproach upon herself.* 她的舉動使她很丟面子。 **4** [sing.] **~ (to sb/sth)** a person or thing that brings shame on sb/sth（給…）帶來羞辱的人（或事）；（使…）丟臉的人（或事） **SYN discredit**：*Such living conditions are a reproach to our society.* 這樣的生活條件是我們這個社會的恥辱。

▪ ***verb*** (*formal*) **1 ~ sb (for sth/for doing sth)** | **~ sb (with sth/with doing sth)** | **~ (sb) + speech** to blame or criticize sb for sth that they have done or not done, because you are disappointed in them 責備；指責；批評：*She was reproached by colleagues for leaking the story to the press.* 她因為將這件事透露給新聞媒體而受到同事的指責。 **2 ~ yourself (for sth/for doing sth)** | **~ yourself (with sth)** to feel guilty about sth that you think you should have done in a different way 自責；（為…）感到內疚：*He reproached himself for not telling her the truth.* 他因為沒有告訴她真相而自責。

re·proach·ful /rɪˈprəʊtʃfl; *NAmE* -ˈproʊtʃ-/ *adj.* expressing blame or criticism 表示責備（或批評）的：

R

a reproachful look 責備的目光 ▸ **re·proach·ful·ly** /-fəli/ *adv.*

rep·ro·bate /ˈreprəbeɪt/ *noun* (*formal* or *humorous*) a person who behaves in a way that society thinks is immoral 墮落的人；不道德的人 ▸ **rep·ro·bate** *adj.* [only before noun]

re·pro·cess /ˌriːˈprəʊses; *NAmE* riːˈprɑːses; -ˈproʊ-/ *verb* **~ sth** to treat waste material so that it can be used again 再加工（廢品）：*All these countries reprocess nuclear fuel.* 這些國家均對核燃料進行後處理。

re·pro·duce 0→ /ˌriːprəˈdjuːs; *NAmE* -ˈduːs/ *verb* **1** 0→ [T] **~ sth** to make a copy of a picture, piece of text, etc. 複製：*It is illegal to reproduce these worksheets without permission from the publisher.* 未經出版者許可翻印這些習題是違法的。◇ *The photocopier reproduces colours very well.* 這台複印機複製的色彩效果很好。 **2** 0→ [T] **~ sth** to produce sth again; to make sth happen again in the same way 再生產；再製造；使再次發生；再現：*The atmosphere of the novel is successfully reproduced in the movie.* 小說的氛圍在電影中成功得到再現。 **3** 0→ [I, T] if people, plants, animals, etc. **reproduce** or **reproduce themselves**, they produce young 繁殖；生育：*Most reptiles reproduce by laying eggs on land.* 大多數爬行動物通過在陸地產卵進行繁殖。◇ **~ itself** *cells reproducing themselves* (= making new ones) 自我繁殖的細胞 ▸ **re·pro·du·cible** /-əbl/ *adj.*

re·pro·duc·tion /ˌriːprəˈdʌkʃn/ *noun* **1** [U] the act or process of producing babies, young animals or plants 生殖；繁殖：*sexual reproduction* 有性生殖 **2** [U] the act or process of producing copies of a document, book, picture, etc. 複製；再版：*Use a black pen on white paper to ensure good reproduction.* 用白紙黑筆，以確保複印清晰。 **3** [U] the process of recording sounds onto tapes, CDs, DVDs, etc.（聲音的）複製，錄製：*Digital recording gives excellent sound reproduction.* 數碼錄音的聲音效果極佳。 **4** [C] a thing that has been reproduced, especially a copy of a work of art（尤指藝術品的）複製品：*a catalogue with colour reproductions of the paintings for sale* 待售畫作的彩色圖樣目錄 ◇ *reproduction furniture* (= furniture made as a copy of an earlier style) 仿製的舊式傢具

re·pro·duct·ive /ˌriːprəˈdʌktɪv/ *adj.* [only before noun] connected with reproducing babies, young animals or plants 生殖的；繁殖的：*reproductive organs* 生殖器官

repro·graph·ics /ˌriːprəˈɡræfɪks/ (also *informal* **repro**) *noun* [U] (*technical* 術語) the science and practice of copying documents and pictures for publishing, etc. 複印術；複製術

re·proof /rɪˈpruːf/ *noun* (*formal*) **1** [U] blame or disapproval 責備；譴責；非難：*His words were a mixture of pity and reproof.* 他的話裏既有同情也有責備。 **2** [C] a remark that expresses blame or disapproval 責備的話語；非難的言辭 **SYN** **rebuke**：*She received a mild reproof from the teacher.* 她受到了老師溫和的責備。

re·prove /rɪˈpruːv/ *verb* **~ sb (for sth/for doing sth)** | **~ (sb) + speech** (*formal*) to tell sb that you do not approve of sth that they have done 指責；責備；非難 **SYN** **rebuke**：*He reproved her for rushing away.* 他責備她不該匆匆離去。 ▸ **re·prov·ing** *adj.* [usually before noun]：*a reproving glance* 責備的目光 **re·prov·ing·ly** *adv.*

rep·tile /ˈreptaɪl; *NAmE* also -tl/ *noun* any animal that has cold blood and skin covered in SCALES, and that lays eggs. Snakes, CROCODILES and TORTOISES are all reptiles. 爬行動物 ➲ VISUAL VOCAB page V13 ➲ compare AMPHIBIAN ▸ **rep·til·ian** /repˈtɪliən/ *adj.*：*our reptilian ancestors* 我們像爬蟲一樣的祖先 ◇ (*figurative*) *He licked his lips in an unpleasantly reptilian way.* 他惡心地像爬蟲般舔着他的嘴唇。

re·pub·lic /rɪˈpʌblɪk/ *noun* a country that is governed by a president and politicians elected by the people and where there is no king or queen 共和國；共和政體：*newly independent republics* 新獨立的共和國 ◇ *the Republic of Ireland* 愛爾蘭共和國 ➲ compare MONARCHY (2)

re·pub·lic·an /rɪˈpʌblɪkən/ *noun, adj.*

■ ***noun*** **1** a person who supports a form of government with a president and politicians elected by the people with no king or queen 擁護共和政體的人；共和主義者 ➲ compare ROYALIST **2 Republican** (*abbr.* **R**, **Rep.**) a member or supporter of the Republican Party of the US（美國）共和黨黨員，共和黨的支持者 ➲ compare DEMOCRAT (2) **3 Republican** a person from Northern Ireland who believes that Northern Ireland should be part of the Republic of Ireland and not part of the United Kingdom 北愛爾蘭共和主義者（認為北愛爾蘭應脫離英國回歸愛爾蘭共和國）➲ compare LOYALIST (2)

■ ***adj.*** **1** connected with or like a republic; supporting the principles of a republic 共和國的；共和政體的；擁護共和政體的：*a republican government/movement* 共和政體／運動 **2** (also **Republican**) (*abbr.* **R**, **Rep.**) connected with the Republican Party in the US（美國）共和黨的 **3** (also **Republican**) connected with or supporting the Republicans in Northern Ireland 北愛爾蘭共和主義者的；支持北愛爾蘭共和主義者的 ▸ **re·pub·lic·an·ism** (also **Re·pub·lic·an·ism**) *noun* [U]：*a strong commitment to Republicanism* 對共和主義的強烈的信念

the Re'publican Party *noun* [sing.] one of the two main political parties in the US, usually considered to support conservative views, and to want to limit the power of central government（美國）共和黨 ➲ compare DEMOCRATIC PARTY

re·pudi·ate /rɪˈpjuːdieɪt/ *verb* (*formal*) **1 ~ sth** to refuse to accept sth 拒絕；不接受；回絕 **SYN** **reject**：*to repudiate a suggestion* 拒絕一項建議 **2 ~ sth** to say officially and/or publicly that sth is not true（正式地）否認，駁斥 **SYN** **deny**：*to repudiate a report* 駁斥一份報告 **3 ~ sb** (*old-fashioned*) to refuse to be connected with sb any longer 拒絕與…往來；斷絕同…的關係 **SYN** **disown**：*He repudiated his first wife and married her sister.* 他和第一個妻子離了婚，又娶了她的妹妹。 ▸ **re·pudi·ation** /rɪˌpjuːdiˈeɪʃn/ *noun* [U]

re·pudi·atory /rɪˈpjuːdiətri; *NAmE* -tɔːri/ *adj.* (*law* 律) relating to a situation in which sb refuses to do sth that they are legally required to do 拒絕履行法律義務的

re·pug·nance /rɪˈpʌɡnəns/ *noun* [U] (*formal*) a strong feeling of dislike or disgust about sth 嫌惡；惡心；強烈的反感 **SYN** **repulsion**：*She was trying to overcome her physical repugnance for him.* 她努力克制對他非常強烈的反感。

re·pug·nant /rɪˈpʌɡnənt/ *adj.* [not usually before noun] (*formal*) making you feel strong dislike or disgust 使十分嫌惡；使反感；不得人心 **SYN** **repulsive**：*We found his suggestion absolutely repugnant.* 我們覺得他的建議絕對不得人心。◇ **~ to sb** *The idea of eating meat was repugnant to her.* 一想到吃肉她就想吐。

re·pulse /rɪˈpʌls/ *verb* (*formal*) **1** [usually passive] **~ sb** to make sb feel disgust or strong dislike 使厭惡；使反感 **SYN** **repel**：*I was repulsed by the horrible smell.* 這種可怕的氣味讓我惡心。 **2 ~ sb/sth** to fight sb who is attacking you and drive them away 擊退；打垮；驅逐 **SYN** **repel**：*to repulse an attack/invasion/offensive* 擊退一次進攻／入侵／攻勢 **3 ~ sb/sth** to refuse to accept sb's help, attempts to be friendly, etc. 拒絕接受；回絕 **SYN** **reject**：*Each time I tried to help I was repulsed.* 每次我想要幫忙都遭到了拒絕。◇ *She repulsed his advances.* 她拒絕了他的追求。

re·pul·sion /rɪˈpʌlʃn/ *noun* [U] **1** a feeling of very strong dislike of sth that you find extremely unpleasant 嫌惡感；強烈的反感；憎惡 **2** (*physics* 物) the force by which objects tend to push each other away 排斥力；斥力：*the forces of attraction and repulsion* 引力和斥力 ➲ see also REPEL ➲ compare ATTRACTION (4)

re·pul·sive /rɪˈpʌlsɪv/ *adj.* **1** causing a feeling of strong dislike; very unpleasant 令人厭惡的；令人反感的；十分討厭的 **SYN** **disgusting**：*a repulsive sight/smell/habit* 令人厭惡的情景／氣味／習慣 ◇ *What a repulsive man!* 這個人真討厭！ ➲ SYNONYMS at DISGUSTING **2** (*physics* 物) causing repulsion (= a force that pushes away) 引起

排斥的；斥力的： *repulsive forces* 斥力 ▸ **re·pul·sive·ly** *adv.*： *repulsively ugly* 極其醜陋

re·pur·pose /ˌriːˈpɜːpəs; *NAmE* -ˈpɜːrp-/ *verb* **~ sth** to change sth slightly in order to make it suitable for a new purpose（為適合新用途）對…稍加修改，略微改動

rep·ut·able /ˈrepjətəbl/ *adj.* that people consider to be honest and to provide a good service 聲譽好的；值得信賴的 SYN **respected**： *a reputable dealer/company/supplier* 可信賴的交易商／公司／供應商 ➲ compare DISREPUTABLE

repu·ta·tion /ˌrepjuˈteɪʃn/ *noun* [C, U] the opinion that people have about what sb/sth is like, based on what has happened in the past 名譽；名聲： *to* ***earn/establish/build a reputation*** 贏得／確立／樹立聲譽◇ *to have* ***a good/bad reputation*** 有好／壞名聲◇ **~ (as sth)** *She soon acquired a reputation as a first-class cook.* 她不久就獲得了一級廚師的榮譽。◇ **~ (for sth/for doing sth)** *I'm aware of Mark's reputation for being late.* 我知道馬克遲到是出了名的。◇ *to damage/ruin sb's reputation* 有損／毀壞某人的名聲◇ *The weather in England is* ***living up to its reputation*** (= is exactly as expected). 英國的天氣完全就如人們所說的那樣。

re·pute /rɪˈpjuːt/ *noun* [U] (*formal*) the opinion that people have of sb/sth 名譽；名聲 SYN **reputation**： *She is a writer of international repute.* 她是一位享有國際聲譽的作家。◇ *My parents were artists* ***of (some) repute*** (= having a very good reputation). 我的雙親是具有（一定）知名度的藝術家。

re·puted /rɪˈpjuːtɪd/ *adj.* [not usually before noun] generally thought to be sth or to have done sth, although this is not certain 所謂；普遍認為；號稱 SYN **rumoured**： **~ (to be sth)** *He is reputed to be the best heart surgeon in the country.* 他號稱是這個國家最好的心臟外科醫生。◇ **~ (to have done sth)** *The house is wrongly reputed to have been the poet's birthplace.* 這所房子被誤以為是詩人的出生地。◇ *She sold her share of the company for a reputed £7 million.* 她的公司股份據說賣了 700 萬英鎊。 ▸ **re·puted·ly** *adv.*

re·quest /rɪˈkwest/ *noun, verb*

■ ***noun*** **~ (for sth)** | **~ (that ...)** **1** the action of asking for sth formally and politely（正式或禮貌的）要求，請求： *They made a request for further aid.* 他們要求再給一些幫助。◇ *He was there* ***at the request of his manager/at his manager's request*** (= because his manager had asked him to go). 他按照經理的請求到了那裏。◇ *The writer's name was withheld* ***by request*** (= because the writer asked for this to be done). 按照作者的要求，姓名不予公佈。◇ *Catalogues are available* ***on request.*** 目錄可以索取。 **2** a thing that you formally ask for 要求的事： *My request was granted.* 我的要求得到了滿足。◇ *a radio request programme* (= a programme of music, songs, etc. that people have asked for) 電台點播節目

■ ***verb*** (*formal*) to ask for sth or ask sb to do sth in a polite or formal way（禮貌或正式地）請求，要求： **~ sth (from sb)** *She requested permission to film at the White House.* 她申請准予在白宮拍攝。◇ *You can request a free copy of the leaflet.* 你可以索要一份免費的宣傳單。◇ **~ sb to do sth** *You are requested not to smoke in the restaurant.* 請不要在餐館裏吸煙。◇ **~ that ...** *She requested that no one be told of her decision until the next meeting.* 她要求下次開會前不要向任何人透露她的決定。◇ (*BrE* also) *She requested that no one should be told of her decision.* 她要求不要向任何人透露她的決定。◇ **+ speech** *'Please come with me,' he requested.* "請跟我來。"他要求道。

reˈquest stop *noun* (*BrE*) a BUS STOP where buses stop only if sb signals to the driver that they want the bus to stop（公共汽車的）揚招站

re·quiem /ˈrekwiəm; -iem/ (also **ˌrequiem ˈmass**) *noun* **1** a Christian ceremony for a person who has recently died, at which people say prayers for his or her soul（基督教）追思彌撒，安魂彌撒 **2** a piece of music for this ceremony 安魂曲

re·quire AW /rɪˈkwaɪə(r)/ *verb* (not usually used in the progressive tenses 通常不用於進行時) (*formal*) **1** to need sth; to depend on sb/sth 需要；依靠；依賴： **~ sth** *These pets require a lot of care and attention.* 這些寵物需要悉心照顧。◇ *This condition requires urgent treatment.* 這種情況得緊急處理。◇ *Do you require anything else?* (= in a shop/store, for example) 你還需要什麼嗎？◇ **~ sb/sth to do sth** *True marriage requires us to show trust and loyalty.* 真正的婚姻有賴於我們表現出信任與忠誠。◇ **~ that ...** *The situation required that he be present.* 這種情形需要他在場。◇ (*BrE* also) *The situation required that he should be present.* 這種情形需要他在場。◇ **~ doing sth** *Lentils do not require soaking before cooking.* 小扁豆在烹飪前不必浸泡。 **2** [often passive] to make sb do or have sth, especially because it is necessary according to a particular law or set of rules 使做（某事）；使擁有（某物）；（尤指根據法規）規定： **~ sth** *The wearing of seat belts is required by law.* 法律規定必須繫安全帶。◇ *'Hamlet' is* ***required reading*** (= must be read) *for this course.* 《哈姆雷特》是這門課程的指定讀物。◇ *Several students failed to reach the required standard.* 有幾名學生沒有達到規定的標準。◇ **~ sth of sb** *What exactly is required of a receptionist* (= what are they expected to do)? 接待員的職責到底是什麼？◇ **~ sb to do sth** *All candidates will be required to take a short test.* 所有候選者都要參加一次小測驗。◇ **~ that ...** *We require that you comply with the following rules: ...* 我們要求你遵守以下規則：… ➲ SYNONYMS at DEMAND

re·quire·ment AW /rɪˈkwaɪəmənt; *NAmE* -ˈkwaɪərm-/ *noun* (*formal*) **1** (usually **requirements**) [pl.] something that you need or want 所需的（或所要的）東西： *the basic requirements of life* 基本生活所需◇ *a software package to* ***meet your requirements*** 滿足你需要的軟件包◇ *Our immediate requirement is extra staff.* 我們亟須增加人手。◇ *These goods are* ***surplus to requirements*** (= more than we need). 這些貨物超過了我們的需要。 **2** something that you must have in order to do sth else 必要條件；必備的條件： *to* ***meet/fulfil/satisfy the requirements*** 符合／滿足必備的條件◇ *What is the minimum entrance requirement for this course?* 這門課程的基本入學條件是什麼？

requis·ite /ˈrekwɪzɪt/ *adj., noun*

■ ***adj.*** [only before noun] (*formal*) necessary for a particular purpose 必需的；必備的；必不可少的： *She lacks the requisite experience for the job.* 她缺少做這份工作所必需的經驗。

■ ***noun*** (*formal*) something that you need for a particular purpose 必需的事物： *toilet requisites* (= soap, TOOTHPASTE, etc.) 洗漱用品◇ **~ for/of sth** *A university degree has become a requisite for entry into most professions.* 大學學位已經成為在大多數行業謀職的必要條件。 ➲ compare PREREQUISITE

requi·si·tion /ˌrekwɪˈzɪʃn/ *noun, verb*

■ ***noun*** [C, U] a formal, official written request or demand for sth 正式要求；徵用；需要： *the requisition of ships by the government* 政府對船隻的徵用◇ *a* ***requisition form/order*** 申領表；徵用令

■ ***verb*** **~ sth** to officially demand the use of a building, vehicle, etc., especially during a war or an emergency（尤指戰時或緊急狀態時）徵用： *The school was requisitioned as a military hospital.* 學校被徵用作為軍用醫院。

re·quite /rɪˈkwaɪt/ *verb* **~ sth** (*formal*) to give sth such as love, kindness, a favour, etc. in return for what sb has given you 回報，報以（友愛、善意等）： *requited love* 得到回報的愛 ➲ compare UNREQUITED

ˌre-ˈroute *verb* **~ sth** to change the route that a road, vehicle, telephone call, etc. normally follows 改變…的路線

rerun *noun, verb*

■ ***noun*** /ˈriːrʌn/ **1** a television programme that is shown again 重播的電視節目： *reruns of old TV shows* 老電視節目的重播 **2** an event, such as a race or competition, that is held again 重新舉行的事；重新賽跑；重賽 **3** something that is done in the same way as sth in the past 重演；再現： *We wanted to avoid a rerun of last year's disastrous trip.* 我們想避免去年那種悲慘旅行再度出現。

R

■ *verb* /ˌriːˈrʌn/ (**re·run·ning**, **reran** /ˌriːˈræn/, **rerun**) **1 ~ sth** to show a film/movie, television programme, etc. again 重演；重播；重放；重映 **2 ~ sth** to do sth again in a similar way （以相同的方式）重做，再次進行：*to rerun an experiment* 重新做實驗 **3 ~ sth** to run a race again 重新進行（賽跑等）

re·sale /ˈriːseɪl; ˌriːˈseɪl/ *noun* [U] the sale to another person of sth that you have bought 轉賣；轉售：*the resale value of a car* 汽車的轉賣價格

re·sched·ule AW /ˌriːˈʃedjuːl; *NAmE* ˌriːˈskedʒuːl/ *verb* **1 ~ sth (for/to sth)** | **~ sth to do sth** to change the time at which sth has been arranged to happen, especially so that it takes place later 將…改期；修改…的時間表；重新安排：*The meeting has been rescheduled for next week.* 會議改期到下週舉行。 **2 ~ sth** (*finance* 財) to arrange for sb to pay back money that they have borrowed at a later date than was originally agreed 推遲還款；延期還款 ▸ **re·sched·ul·ing** *noun* [U, sing.]

re·scind /rɪˈsɪnd/ *verb* **~ sth** (*formal*) to officially state that a law, contract, decision, etc. is no longer valid 廢除；取消；撤銷 SYN **revoke**

re·scis·sion /rɪˈsɪʒn/ *noun* (*formal*) the act of cancelling or ending a law, an order, or an agreement 廢除；取消；撤銷

res·cue 🔑 /ˈreskjuː/ *verb, noun*

■ *verb* 🔑 to save sb/sth from a dangerous or harmful situation 營救；援救；搶救：**~ sb/sth from sth/sb** *He rescued a child from drowning.* 他救起了一名落水兒童。◇ *The house was rescued from demolition.* 這所房子保住了，可以不拆。◇ *You rescued me from an embarrassing situation.* 我正感到尷尬，你為我解了圍。◇ **~ sb/sth** *They were eventually rescued by helicopter.* 他們最後被直升機救走了。◇ **~ sb/sth + adj.** *She had despaired of ever being rescued alive.* 她那時對獲救生還已經絕望了。➲ SYNONYMS at SAVE ▸ **res·cuer** *noun*

■ *noun* **1** 🔑 [U] the act of saving sb/sth from a dangerous or difficult situation; the fact of being saved 救援；營救；搶救；獲救：*We had given up hope of rescue.* 我們那時已經放棄了獲救的希望。◇ *A wealthy benefactor* ***came to their rescue*** *with a generous donation.* 一位富有的贊助人慷慨解囊挽救了他們。◇ *a* ***rescue attempt/operation*** 一次營救行動 ◇ *a* ***mountain rescue*** *team* 登山救援隊 ◇ ***rescue workers/boats/helicopters*** 救援人員／船隻／直升機 **2** 🔑 [C] an occasion when sb/sth is saved from a dangerous or difficult situation 營救行動：*Ten fishermen were saved in a daring sea rescue.* 在一次驚心動魄的海上營救行動中，十名漁民獲救。

R

re·search 🔑 AW *noun, verb*

■ *noun* 🔑 /rɪˈsɜːtʃ; ˈriːsɜːtʃ; *NAmE* -sɜːrtʃ/ [U] (also **re·searches** [pl.]) especially in *BrE*) a careful study of a subject, especially in order to discover new facts or information about it 研究；調查；探索：***medical/historical/scientific, etc. research*** 醫學、歷史、科學等研究 ◇ *to* ***do/conduct/undertake research*** 做／從事／進行研究 ◇ **~ (into/on sth/sb)** *He has carried out extensive research into renewable energy sources.* 他已經對再生能源進行了廣泛研究。◇ *Recent research on deaf children has produced some interesting findings about their speech.* 對失聰兒童的最新研究已經在說話方面取得了一些令人關注的結果。◇ *What have their researches shown?* 他們的研究證明了什麼？◇ *a* ***research project/grant/student*** 研究項目／經費；研究生 ◇ *I've done some research to find out the cheapest way of travelling there.* 我查閱了一番，想找到去那裏最省錢的方式。➲ COLLOCATIONS at SCIENTIFIC ➲ see also MARKET RESEARCH, OPERATIONAL RESEARCH

■ *verb* 🔑 /rɪˈsɜːtʃ; *NAmE* -ˈsɜːrtʃ/ [I, T] to study sth carefully and try to discover new facts about it 研究；探討；調查：**~ (into/in/on sth)** *They're researching into ways of improving people's diet.* 他們在研究如何改進人們飲食的方法。◇ **~ sth** *to research a problem/topic/market* 研究一個問題／課題／市場 ◇ *She's in New York researching her new book* (= finding facts and information to put in it). 她在紐約為她的新書搜集材料。◇ **~ how, what, etc. …** *We have to research how the product will actually be used.* 我們必須研究該產品的實際使用方法。 ▸ **re·search·er** AW *noun*

reˌsearch and deˈvelopment *noun* [U] (*abbr.* **R & D**) (in industry, etc.) work that tries to find new products and processes or to improve existing ones 研究和開發

re·sect /rɪˈsekt/ *verb* **~ sth** (*medical* 醫) to cut out part of an organ or a piece of TISSUE from the body 切除（部份器官或組織） ▸ **re·sec·tion** /rɪˈsekʃn/ *noun* [U, C]

re·sell /ˌriːˈsel/ *verb* (**re·sold**, **re·sold** /ˌriːˈsəʊld; *NAmE* -ˈsoʊld/) **~ sth** to sell sth that you have bought 轉售；轉賣：*He resells the goods at a profit.* 他轉賣貨品贏利。

re·sem·blance /rɪˈzembləns/ *noun* [C, U] the fact of being or looking similar to sb/sth 相似；相像 SYN **likeness**：*a* ***striking/close/strong resemblance*** 明顯的／不小的／顯著的相似之處 ◇ *family resemblances* 親緣相似 ◇ **~ to sb/sth** *She* ***bears an uncanny resemblance*** *to Dido.* 她跟迪多長得像極了。◇ *The movie* ***bears little resemblance to*** *the original novel.* 電影和原著相去甚遠。◇ **~ between A and B** *The resemblance between the two signatures was remarkable.* 兩個簽名的相似之處非常明顯。

re·sem·ble /rɪˈzembl/ *verb* [no passive] (not used in the progressive tenses 不用於進行時) **~ sb/sth** to look like or be similar to another person or thing 看起來像；顯得像；像：*She closely resembles her sister.* 她和她姐姐很像。◇ *So many hotels resemble each other.* 許多酒店看上去都差不多。◇ *The plant resembles grass in appearance.* 這種植物的外形像草。

re·sent /rɪˈzent/ *verb* to feel bitter or angry about sth, especially because you feel it is unfair 憤恨；感到氣憤；憤憤不平：**~ sth/sb** *I deeply resented her criticism.* 我對她的批評感到非常氣憤。◇ **~ doing sth** *He bitterly resents being treated like a child.* 他十分厭惡被別人當孩子對待。◇ **~ sb doing sth** *She resented him making all the decisions.* 她討厭什麼事都要聽他的。◇ (*formal*) *She resented his making all the decisions.* 她討厭什麼事都要聽他的。

re·sent·ful /rɪˈzentfl/ *adj.* feeling bitter or angry about sth that you think is unfair 感到氣憤的；憎恨的；憤慨的：*a resentful look* 充滿怨恨的眼神 ◇ **~ of/at/about sth** *They seemed to be resentful of our presence there.* 他們好像對我們在那裏露面很生氣。◇ *She was resentful at having been left out of the team.* 她對被運動隊淘汰感到氣憤。 ▸ **re·sent·ful·ly** /-fəli/ *adv.*

re·sent·ment /rɪˈzentmənt/ *noun* [U, sing.] a feeling of anger or unhappiness about sth that you think is unfair 憤恨；怨恨：*to* ***feel/harbour/bear resentment towards/against*** *sb* 對某人感到／深懷／有怨恨 ◇ *She could not conceal the deep resentment she felt at the way she had been treated.* 受到那樣的待遇，她無法掩藏內心強烈的憤恨。

re·ser·va·tion 🔑 /ˌrezəˈveɪʃn; *NAmE* -zərˈv-/ *noun* **1** 🔑 [C] an arrangement for a seat on a plane or train, a room in a hotel, etc. to be kept for you 預訂；預約：*I'll call the restaurant and* ***make a reservation***. 我要給餐廳打個電話預訂座位。◇ *We have a reservation in the name of Grant.* 我們是以格蘭特的名字預訂的。➲ COLLOCATIONS at RESTAURANT ➲ compare BOOKING (1) **2** 🔑 [C, U] a feeling of doubt about a plan or an idea 保留意見；疑惑 SYN **misgiving**：*I have serious* ***reservations*** *about his ability to do the job.* 我非常懷疑他有沒有能力勝任這項工作。◇ *They support the measures* ***without reservation*** (= completely). 他們毫無保留地支持這些措施。 **3** (also **re·serve**) [C] an area of land in the US that is kept separate for Native Americans to live in （美國為美洲土著居民劃出的）居留地 **4** [U] = RESERVATION POLICY ➲ see also CENTRAL RESERVATION

reserˈvation policy (also **re·ser·va·tion**) *noun* [U] (in India) the policy of keeping a certain percentage of jobs or places in schools, colleges, etc. for people who are members of SCHEDULED CASTES, SCHEDULED TRIBES or other BACKWARD CLASSES 預留政策（印度為落後階層成員保留一定數目的職位或入學名額等）

re·serve 🔑 /rɪˈzɜːv; *NAmE* rɪˈzɜːrv/ *verb, noun*

■ *verb* **1** 🔑 to ask for a seat, table, room, etc. to be available for you or sb else at a future time 預訂，預約（座位、席位、房間等） SYN **book**：**~ sth for sb/sth** *I'd* *like to reserve a table for three for eight o'clock.* 我想預訂八點鐘供三人用餐的桌位。◇ **~ sth** *I've reserved a room in the name of Jones.* 我以瓊斯的名字預訂了一個房間。➲ compare BOOK *v.* (1) **2** 🔑 to keep sth for sb/sth, so that it cannot be used by any other person or for any other reason 保留；預留：**~ sth for sb/sth** *These seats are reserved for special guests.* 這些座位是留給貴賓的。◇ **~ sth** *I'd prefer to* **reserve** (**my**) **judgement** (= not make a decision) *until I know all the facts.* 在瞭解全部事實之前我不想發表意見。**3 ~ sth** to have or keep a particular power 擁有，保持，保留（某種權利）：*The management* **reserves the right** *to refuse admission.* 管理部門有權拒絕接收。◇ (*law* 律) ***All rights reserved.*** (= nobody else can publish or copy this) 版權所有

■ ***noun***

▸ **SUPPLY** 補給 **1** 🔑 [C, usually pl.] a supply of sth that is available to be used in the future or when it is needed 儲備（量）；貯藏（量）：*large oil and gas reserves* 大量的石油和天然氣貯藏量 ◇ *He discovered unexpected reserves of strength.* 他出乎意料地發現還有體力。◇ *reserve funds* 儲備金

▸ **PROTECTED LAND** 受保護土地 **2** 🔑 (*NAmE* also **pre·serve**) [C] a piece of land that is a protected area for animals, plants, etc. （動植物）保護區；自然保護區：*a wildlife reserve* 野生動植物保護區 ➲ see also GAME RESERVE, NATURE RESERVE **3** [C] = RESERVATION (3)

▸ **QUALITY/FEELING** 品質；情感 **4** 🔑 [U] the quality that sb has when they do not talk easily to other people about their ideas, feelings, etc. 內向；寡言少語；矜持 SYN **reticence**：*She found it difficult to make friends because of her natural reserve.* 她因天性矜持很難交到朋友。**5** [U] (*formal*) a feeling that you do not want to accept or agree to sth, etc. until you are quite sure that it is all right to do so 謹慎；保留：*Any contract should be treated* **with reserve** *until it has been checked.* 任何契約在經過核實之前都應謹慎對待。◇ *She trusted him* **without reserve** (= completely). 她完全信任他。

▸ **IN SPORT** 體育運動 **6** [C] an extra player who plays in a team when one of the other players is injured or not available to play 替補隊員；後備隊員 **7 the reserves** [pl.] a team that is below the level of the main team 替補隊；預備隊；後備隊

▸ **MILITARY FORCE** 軍隊 **8 the reserve** [sing.] (also **the reserves** [pl.]) an extra military force, etc. that is not part of a country's regular forces, but is available to be used when needed 預備役部隊；後備部隊：*the army reserve(s)* 預備役部隊 ◇ *the reserve police* 預備役警察

▸ **PRICE** 價格 **9** (also **re'serve price**) [C] (*BrE*) the lowest price that sb will accept for sth, especially sth that is sold at an AUCTION （尤指拍賣中的）底價，最低價

IDM **in re'serve** available to be used in the future or when needed 儲備；備用：*The money was being* **kept in reserve** *for their retirement.* 他們把錢存着以備退休後使用。◇ *200 police officers were* **held in reserve**. * 200 名警察隨時待命。

re·served /rɪ'zɜːvd; *NAmE* rɪ'zɜːrvd/ *adj.* (of a person or their character 人或性格) slow or unwilling to show feelings or express opinions 內向的；寡言少語的；矜持的 SYN **shy** ➲ compare UNRESERVED

re·serv·ist /rɪ'zɜːvɪst; *NAmE* -'zɜːrv-/ *noun* a soldier, etc. who is a member of the RESERVES (= a military force that can be used in an emergency) 預備役軍人；後備軍戰士

res·er·voir /'rezəvwɑː(r); *NAmE* 'rezərv-/ *noun* **1** a natural or artificial lake where water is stored before it is taken by pipes to houses, etc. 水庫；蓄水池 **2** (*formal*) a large amount of sth that is available to be used （大量的）貯備，貯藏 **3** (*technical* 術語) a place in an engine or a machine where a liquid is kept before it is used 貯液槽

reset /ˌriː'set/ *verb* (**re·set·ting**, **reset**, **reset**) **1 ~ sth** (**to sth**) | **~ sth to do sth** to change a machine, an instrument or a control so that it gives a different time or number or is ready to use again 調整；重新設置：*You need to reset your watch to local time.* 你需要把錶調整到當地時間。**2** [often passive] **~ sth** to place sth in the correct position again 重新安置；將…恢復原位：*to reset a broken bone* 重接斷骨

re·set·tle /ˌriː'setl/ *verb* **1** [T, I] **~** (**sb**) to help people go and live in a new country or area; to go and live in a new country or area 幫助…定居他國（或別的地區）；到他國（或別的地區）定居：*Many of the refugees were resettled in Britain and Canada.* 許多難民被安置到英國和加拿大。**2** [T] **~ sth** to start to use an area again as a place to live 使再次成為定居點：*The region was only resettled 200 years later.* 這一地區 200 年以後才重新有人居住。**3** [I, T] **~** (**yourself**) to make yourself comfortable in a new position 重感舒適：*The birds flew around and then resettled on the pond.* 鳥兒飛來飛去，然後落在池塘邊上。▸ **re·set·tle·ment** *noun* [U]：*the resettlement of refugees* 難民的重新安置 ◇ *a resettlement agency* 重新安置服務機構

re·shape /ˌriː'ʃeɪp/ *verb* **~ sth** to change the shape or structure of sth 改變…的形狀（或結構）；重塑；改組

re·shuf·fle /ˌriː'ʃʌfl/ (also *less frequent* **shuf·fle**) *verb* [T, I] **~** (**sth**) to change around the jobs that a group of people do, for example in a government 改組；進行崗位調整；更改職責配置：*The Prime Minister eventually decided against reshuffling the Cabinet.* 首相最終決定反對改組內閣。▸ **re·shuf·fle** /'riːʃʌfl/ *noun*：*a Cabinet reshuffle* 內閣改組

res·ide AW /rɪ'zaɪd/ *verb* [I] **+ adv./prep.** (*formal*) to live in a particular place 居住在；定居於：*He returned to Britain in 1939, having resided abroad for many years.* 他在國外居住多年以後，於 1939 年回到了英國。

PHR V **re'side in sb/sth** to be in sb/sth; to be caused by sth 在於；由…造成（或引起）：*The source of the problem resides in the fact that the currency is too strong.* 問題的根源在於貨幣過於堅挺。**re'side in/with sb/sth** (of a power, a right, etc. 權力、權利等) to belong to sb/sth 屬於；隸屬於 SYN **be vested in**：*The ultimate authority resides with the board of directors.* 最高權力屬於董事會。

resi·dence AW /'rezɪdəns/ *noun* (*formal*) **1** [C] a house, especially a large or impressive one 住所；住房；（尤指）宅第，豪宅：*a desirable family residence for sale* (= for example, in an advertisement) 待售的理想家居 ◇ *10 Downing Street is the British Prime Minister's* ***official residence***. 唐寧街 10 號是英國首相的官邸。**2** [U] the state of living in a particular place 居住；定居：*They were not able to* **take up residence** *in their new home until the spring.* 他們到第二年春天才住進了新家。◇ *Please state your occupation and* **place of residence**. 請說明你的職業和住址。◇ *The flag flies when the Queen is* **in residence**. 女王駐蹕在這裏時有國旗飄揚。➲ see also HALL OF RESIDENCE **3** (also **resi·dency**) [U] permission to live in a country that is not your own （在他國的）居住權，居留許可：*They have been denied residence in this country.* 這個國家不給他們居住資格。◇ *a residence permit* 居留許可證

IDM **in 'residence** having an official position in a particular place such as a college or university （在大學等處）有正式職位，常駐：*a writer in residence* 常駐作家

resi·dency /'rezɪdənsi/ *noun* (*pl.* **-ies**) (*formal*) **1** [U] = RESIDENCE (3)：*She has been granted permanent residency in Britain.* 她獲准在英國永久居住。**2** [U, C] the period of time that an artist, a writer or a musician spends working for a particular institution （藝術家、作家、音樂家為某機構工作的）駐留時間，駐留期 **3** [U] the state of living in a particular place 居住；定居：*a residency requirement for students* 要求學生住校 **4** [U, C] (*especially NAmE*) the period of time when a doctor working in a hospital receives special advanced training 高級專科住院醫生實習期 **5** (also **resi·dence**) [C] the official house of sb such as an AMBASSADOR 官邸

resi·dent 🔑 AW /'rezɪdənt/ *noun, adj.*

■ ***noun*** **1** 🔑 a person who lives in a particular place or who has their home there 居民；住戶：*a resident of the United States* 美國的居民 ◇ *There were confrontations between local residents and the police.* 當地居民和警察之間有過衝突。**2** 🔑 (*formal*) a person who is staying in a hotel （旅館的）住宿者，旅客，房客：*The hotel*

R

restaurant is open to non-residents. 旅店的餐館對外開放。 **3** a doctor working in a hospital in the US who is receiving special advanced training（美國的）高級專科住院實習醫生 ➲ compare REGISTRAR (3)

■ *adj.* living in a particular place（在某地）居住的：*the town's resident population* (= not tourists or visitors) 鎮上的居民 ◊ *to be resident abroad/in the US* 住在國外／美國 ◊ *Tom's our* ***resident expert*** (= our own expert) *on foreign movies.* 湯姆是我們的外國電影常駐專家。

ˌresident ˈalien *noun* (*NAmE, law* 律) a person from another country who has permission to stay in the US（獲准在美國居留的）外籍居民，外僑

resi·den·tial AW /ˌrezɪˈdenʃl/ *adj.* [usually before noun] **1** (of an area of a town 城市中的地區) suitable for living in; consisting of houses rather than factories or offices 適合居住的；住宅的：*a quiet residential area* 安靜的住宅區 **2** (of a job, a course, etc. 工作、課程等) requiring a person to live at a particular place; offering living accommodation 需要在某地居住的；提供住宿的：*a residential language course* 需要住校的語言課程 ◊ *a residential home for the elderly* 老人院 ◊ *residential care for children* 提供食宿的兒童福利院服務

ˈresidents' association *noun* a group of people who live in a particular area and join together to discuss the problems of that area 居民委員會；居民聯合會

re·sidual /rɪˈzɪdjuəl; *NAmE* -dʒu-/ *adj.* [only before noun] (*formal*) remaining at the end of a process 剩餘的；殘留的 SYN **outstanding**：*There are still a few residual problems with the computer program.* 電腦程序還有一些殘留問題。

re·sidu·ary /rɪˈzɪdjuəri; *NAmE* -dʒueri/ *adj.* **1** (*law* 律) remaining from the money and property left by a person who has died after all debts, gifts, etc. have been paid 剩餘遺產的 **2** (*technical* 術語) remaining at the end of a process 剩餘的；殘留的

resi·due /ˈrezɪdjuː; *NAmE* -duː/ *noun* **1** a small amount of sth that remains at the end of a process 剩餘物；殘留物；殘渣：*pesticide residues in fruit and vegetables* 殘留在水果和蔬菜中的殺蟲劑 **2** (*law* 律) the part of the money, property, etc. of a person who has died that remains after all the debts, gifts, etc. have been paid 剩餘遺產：*The residue of the estate was divided equally among his children.* 剩餘遺產被他的孩子平分了。

re·siduum /rɪˈzɪdjuəm/ *noun* (*pl.* **re·sidua** /-djuə/) (*technical* 術語) something that remains after a reaction or process has taken place（化學反應的）殘基，殘渣，殘留物；（某種進程的）殘體

re·sign /rɪˈzaɪn/ *verb* [I, T] to officially tell sb that you are leaving your job, an organization, etc. 辭職；辭去（某職務）：**~ (as sth)** *He resigned as manager after eight years.* 八年後，他辭去了經理的職務。◊ **~ (from sth)** *Two members resigned from the board in protest.* 董事會的兩名成員辭職以示抗議。◊ **~ sth** *My father resigned his directorship last year.* 我父親去年辭去了董事的職務。

PHR V **reˈsign yourself to sth** to accept sth unpleasant that cannot be changed or avoided 聽任；只好接受；順從：*She resigned herself to her fate.* 她只好聽天由命了。◊ **~ doing sth** *We had to resign ourselves to making a loss on the sale.* 我們只好接受銷售造成的虧損。

res·ig·na·tion /ˌrezɪɡˈneɪʃn/ *noun* **1** [U, C] the act of giving up your job or position; the occasion when you do this 辭職：*a letter of resignation* 辭職信 ◊ *There were calls for her resignation from the board of directors.* 有人要求她辭去董事會中的職務。◊ *Further resignations are expected.* 預計還會有人辭職。 ➲ COLLOCATIONS at JOB **2** [C] a letter, for example to your employers, to say that you are giving up your job or position 辭職信；辭呈：*to* ***offer/hand in/tender your resignation*** 呈遞／上交／提交辭職信 ◊ *We haven't received his resignation yet.* 我們還沒有收到他的辭呈。 **3** [U] patient willingness to accept a difficult or unpleasant situation that you cannot change 順從；聽任：*They accepted their defeat with resignation.* 他們無可奈何地承認失敗。

re·signed /rɪˈzaɪnd/ *adj.* being willing to calmly accept sth unpleasant or difficult that you cannot change 逆來順受的；順從的：*a resigned sigh* 無可奈何的歎息 ◊ **~ to sth/doing sth** *He was resigned to never seeing his birthplace again.* 他認命了，甘願永不再去他的出生地。 ▸ **re·sign·ed·ly** /-nɪdli/ *adv.*：*'I suppose you're right,' she said resignedly.* "看來你的話是對的。"她無奈地說。

re·sili·ence /rɪˈzɪliəns/ (also *less frequent* **re·sili·ency** /-nsi/) *noun* [U] **1** the ability of people or things to feel better quickly after sth unpleasant, such as shock, injury, etc. 快速恢復的能力；適應力 **2** the ability of a substance to return to its original shape after it has been bent, stretched or pressed 還原能力；彈力

re·sili·ent /rɪˈzɪliənt/ *adj.* **1** able to feel better quickly after sth unpleasant such as shock, injury, etc. 可迅速恢復的；有適應力的：*He'll get over it—young people are amazingly resilient.* 他會克服的，年輕人的適應力驚人。 **2** (of a substance 物質) returning to its original shape after being bent, stretched, or pressed 有彈性（或彈力）的；能復原的 ▸ **re·sili·ent·ly** *adv.*

resin /ˈrezɪn; *NAmE* ˈrezn/ *noun* [C, U] **1** a sticky substance that is produced by some trees and is used in making VARNISH, medicine, etc. 樹脂 **2** an artificial substance similar to resin, used in making plastics 合成樹脂 ▸ **res·in·ous** /ˈrezɪnəs; *NAmE* ˈrezənəs/ *adj.*：*the resinous scent of pine trees* 松脂的香氣

re·sist /rɪˈzɪst/ *verb*

1 [T, I] to refuse to accept sth and try to stop it from happening 抵制；阻擋 SYN **oppose**：**~ (sth)** *to resist change* 抵制變革 ◊ *They are determined to resist pressure to change the law.* 他們決心頂住要求改革法律的壓力。◊ **~ doing sth** *The bank strongly resisted cutting interest rates.* 銀行強烈反對降低利率。 **2** [I, T] to fight back when attacked; to use force to stop sth from happening 反抗；回擊；抵抗：*He tried to pin me down, but I resisted.* 他試圖制伏我，但我奮力反抗。◊ **~ sth** *She was charged with* ***resisting arrest.*** 她被控拒捕。 **3** [T, I] (usually in negative sentences 通常用於否定句) to stop yourself from having sth you like or doing sth you very much want to do 忍住；抵擋：**~ (sth)** *I finished the cake. I* ***couldn't resist it.*** 我忍不住把整塊蛋糕都吃了。◊ *I found the temptation to miss the class too hard to resist.* 我抵擋不住逃課的誘惑。◊ **~ doing sth** *He couldn't resist showing off his new car.* 他忍不住炫耀起了他的新車。 **4** [T] **~ sth** to not be harmed or damaged by sth 使不受…的傷害；抗（傷害）：*A healthy diet should help your body resist infection.* 健康飲食有助於身體抗感染。 ◊ *This new paint is designed to resist heat.* 這種新油漆具有耐熱性。

re·sist·ance /rɪˈzɪstəns/ *noun*

1 [U, sing.] dislike of or opposition to a plan, an idea, etc.; refusal to obey 反對；抵制；抗拒：*As with all new ideas it met with resistance.* 和所有的新觀念一樣，它受到了抵制。◊ **~ to sb/sth** *There has been a lot of resistance to this new law.* 這項新的法規已經遇到很多的抵制。◊ *Resistance to change has nearly destroyed the industry.* 對變革的抵制幾乎毀了這個行業。 **2** [U, sing.] the act of using force to oppose sb/sth 抵抗；反抗：*armed resistance* 武裝反抗 ◊ *The defenders* ***put up a strong resistance.*** 保衞者頑強地抵抗。◊ **~ to sb/sth** *The demonstrators* ***offered*** *little or no* ***resistance*** *to the police.* 示威者幾乎沒有對警察作任何反抗。 **3** [U, sing.] **~ (to sth)** the power not to be affected by sth 抗力；抵抗力：*AIDS lowers the body's resistance to infection.* 艾滋病降低了身體的抗感染能力。 **4** [U, sing.] **~ (to sth)** a force that stops sth moving or makes it move more slowly 阻力：***wind/air resistance*** (= in the design of planes or cars) 風阻；空氣阻力 **5** [U, C] (*physics* 物) (*symb.* **R**) the opposition of a substance or device to the flow of an electrical current 電阻 ➲ compare REACTANCE **6** (often **the Resistance**) [sing.+sing./pl. v.] a secret organization that resists the authorities, especially in a country that an enemy has control of（尤指敵佔區的）秘密抵抗組織：*resistance fighters* 秘密抵抗戰士 IDM see LINE *n.*

re·sist·ant /rɪˈzɪstənt/ *adj.* **1 ~ (to sth)** not affected by sth; able to resist sth 抵抗的；有抵抗力的：*plants that are resistant to disease* 抗病植株 **2 ~ (to sth)** opposing sth and trying to stop it happening 抵制的；阻止的：*Elderly people are not always resistant to change.* 上了年紀的人並不總是抵制變革。 **3 -resistant** (in adjectives 構成形容詞) not damaged by the thing mentioned 抗…的；耐…的：*disease-resistant plants* 抗病植株 ◇ *fire-resistant materials* 耐火材料 ➲ see also HEAT-RESISTANT, WATER-RESISTANT

re·sist·er /rɪˈzɪstə(r)/ *noun* a person who resists sb/sth 抵制者；抗拒者；反抗者

re·sist·ible /rɪˈzɪstəbl/ *adj.* that can be resisted 可抵制的；可抗拒的 OPP **irresistible**

re·sist·ive /rɪˈzɪstɪv/ *adj.* **1** able to survive or cope with the action or effect of sth 抗…的；耐…的 **2** (*physics* 物) relating to electrical resistance 電阻的 ▸ **re·sist·iv·ity** /ˌrɪzɪˈstɪvɪti/ *noun* [U, C]

re·sis·tor /rɪˈzɪstə(r)/ *noun* (*physics* 物) a device that has RESISTANCE to an electric current in a CIRCUIT 電阻器

resit /ˌriːˈsɪt/ *verb* (**re·sit·ting**, **resat**, **resat** /ˌriːˈsæt/) (also **re·take**) [T, I] **~ (sth)** (*BrE*) to take an exam or a test again, usually after failing it the first time 重考；(通常指)補考 ▸ **resit** /ˈriːsɪt/ (also **re·take**) *noun*：*Students are only allowed one resit.* 學生只有一次補考機會。

re·size /ˌriːˈsaɪz/ *verb* **~ sth** to make sth bigger or smaller, especially an image on a computer screen 改變（尤指計算機圖像等）的大小

re·skill /ˌriːˈskɪl/ *verb* [I, T] **~ (sb)** to learn new skills so that you can do a new job; to teach sb new skills (為新工作)學習新技能；教(某人)新技能

reso·lute /ˈrezəluːt/ *adj.* having or showing great determination 堅決的；有決心的 SYN **determined**：*resolute leadership* 堅定的領導 ◇ *He became even more resolute in his opposition to the plan.* 他甚至更堅決地反對這個計劃。 OPP **irresolute** ▸ **reso·lute·ly** *adv.*：*They remain resolutely opposed to the idea.* 他們仍然堅決反對這種觀點。 **reso·lute·ness** *noun* [U]

reso·lution AW /ˌrezəˈluːʃn/ *noun* **1** [C] a formal statement of an opinion agreed on by a committee or a council, especially by means of a vote 決議；正式決定：*to **pass/adopt/carry a resolution*** 通過一項決議 **2** [U, sing.] the act of solving or settling a problem, disagreement, etc. (問題、分歧等的)解決，消除 SYN **settlement**：*The government is pressing for an early resolution of the dispute.* 政府正在不斷敦促早日解決這起糾紛。 **3** [U] the quality of being resolute or determined 堅定；堅決；有決心 SYN **resolve**：*The reforms owe a great deal to the resolution of one man.* 這些改革主要歸功於一個人的堅定決心。 **4** [C] **~ (to do sth)** a firm decision to do or not to do sth 決心；決定：*She **made a resolution** to visit her relatives more often.* 她決定要多探望親戚。◇ *Have you made any **New Year's resolutions*** (= for example, to give up smoking from 1 January)? 你有什麼新年計劃嗎？ **5** [U, sing.] the power of a computer screen, printer, etc. to give a clear image, depending on the size of the dots that make up the image 清晰度；析像；分辨率；解像度：*high-resolution graphics* 高清晰度的圖形

re·solve 0-w AW /rɪˈzɒlv; *NAmE* rɪˈzɑːlv; rɪˈzɔːlv/ *verb*, *noun*

■ *verb* (*formal*) **1** 0-w [T] **~ sth/itself** to find an acceptable solution to a problem or difficulty 解決（問題或困難） SYN **settle**：*to **resolve an issue/a dispute/a conflict/a crisis*** 解決問題/爭端/衝突/危機 ◇ *Both sides met in order to try to resolve their differences.* 雙方會晤以努力解決分歧。 **2** [T, I] to make a firm decision to do sth 決心；決定：**~ to do sth** *He resolved not to tell her the truth.* 他決定不告訴她真相。◇ **~ (that)** … *She resolved (that) she would never see him again.* 她決心再也不見他了。◇ **~ on sth/on doing sth** *We had resolved on making an early start.* 我們已經決定早點動身。 **3** [T] (of a committee, meeting, etc. 委員會、會議等) to reach a decision by means of a formal vote (經正式投票)作出決定，作出決議；表決：**it is resolved that** … *It was resolved that the matter be referred to a higher authority.* 經過表決決定把這件事提交給上級主管部門。◇ **~ that** … *They resolved that the matter be referred to a higher authority.* 他們經過表決，決定把這件事提交給上級主管部門。◇ **~ to do sth** *The Supreme Council resolved to resume control over the national press.* 最高委員會決定重新接管對國家新聞機構的控制。

PHR V **re'solve into sth** | **re'solve sth into sth** **1** to separate or to be separated into its parts (使)分解為：*to resolve a complex argument into its basic elements* 把一個複雜的論點分解成幾個基本要點 **2** (of sth seen or heard at a distance 遠處景物、響聲等) to gradually turn into a different form when it is seen or heard more clearly 逐漸變為(另一種形式)；顯現(為)：*The orange light resolved itself into four lanterns.* 橙色的光亮逐漸變成了四盞燈。 **3** to gradually become or be understood as sth 逐步變成；逐漸被理解為：*The discussion eventually resolved itself into two main issues.* 討論後來集中在兩大主要議題上。

■ *noun* [U] (*formal*) strong determination to achieve sth 決心；堅定的信念 SYN **resolution**：*The difficulties in her way merely strengthened her resolve.* 她所遇到的困難只是讓她更加堅定。◇ **~ to do sth** *The government reiterated its resolve to uncover the truth.* 政府重申一定要查個水落石出。

re·solved /rɪˈzɒlvd; *NAmE* rɪˈzɑːlvd; rɪˈzɔːlvd/ *adj.* [not before noun] **~ (to do sth)** (*formal*) determined 下定決心；堅定：*I was resolved not to see him.* 我決意不見他。

res·on·ance /ˈrezənəns/ *noun* **1** [U] (*formal*) (of sound 聲音) the quality of being resonant 洪亮；響亮：*Her voice had a strange and thrilling resonance.* 她的聲音洪亮，有一種奇特的震撼人心的效果。 **2** [C, U] (*technical* 術語) the sound or other VIBRATION produced in an object by sound or VIBRATIONS of a similar FREQUENCY from another object 共鳴；回響；共振 **3** [U, C] (*formal*) (in a piece of writing, music, etc. 文章、樂曲等) the power to bring images, feelings, etc. into the mind of the person reading or listening; the images, etc. produced in this way 激發聯想的力量；引起共鳴的力量；引起的聯想(或共鳴)

res·on·ant /ˈrezənənt/ *adj.* **1** (*formal*) (of sound 聲音) deep, clear and continuing for a long time 嘹亮的；響亮的；回響的；悠揚的：*a deep resonant voice* 深沉而響亮的聲音 **2** (*technical* 術語) causing sounds to continue for a long time 共振的；諧振的；共鳴的 SYN **resounding**：*resonant frequencies* 諧振頻率 **3** (*literary*) having the power to bring images, feelings, memories, etc. into your mind 引起聯想的；產生共鳴的：*a poem filled with resonant imagery* 充滿了讓人浮想聯翩的意象的詩歌 ▸ **res·on·ant·ly** *adv.*

res·on·ate /ˈrezəneɪt/ *verb* (*formal*) **1** [I] (of a voice, an instrument, etc. 嗓音、樂器等) to make a deep, clear sound that continues for a long time 產生共鳴；發出回響；迴盪 **2** [I] (of a place 地方) to be filled with sound; to make a sound continue longer (使)回響，起回聲 SYN **resound**：*a resonating chamber* 產生回音的房間 ◇ **~ with sth** *The room resonated with the chatter of 100 people.* 屋裏會合着 100 人唧唧喳喳的聲音。 **3** [I] **~ (with sb/sth)** to remind sb of sth; to be similar to what sb thinks or believes 使產生聯想；引起共鳴；和…的想法（或觀念）類似：*These issues resonated with the voters.* 這些問題引起了投票者的共鳴。

PHR V **'resonate with sth** (*literary*) to be full of a particular quality or feeling 充滿：*She makes a simple story resonate with complex themes and emotions.* 她使一部情節簡單的小說充滿了複雜的主題和情感。

res·on·ator /ˈrezəneɪtə(r)/ *noun* (*technical* 術語) a device for making sound louder and stronger, especially in a musical instrument 共鳴器；共鳴箱

re·sort 0-w /rɪˈzɔːt; *NAmE* rɪˈzɔːrt/ *noun*, *verb*

■ *noun* **1** 0-w [C] a place where a lot of people go on holiday/vacation 旅遊勝地；度假勝地：***seaside/ski/mountain, etc. resorts*** 海濱、滑雪、山區等旅遊勝地 ◇ (*BrE*) *a popular **holiday resort*** 受歡迎的度假勝地 ◇ *the resort town of Byron Bay* 人們經常光顧的拜倫貝城 ➲ COLLOCATIONS at TRAVEL **2** [U] **~ to sth** the act of using sth, especially sth bad or unpleasant, because nothing else is possible 訴諸；求助；採取 SYN **recourse**：*There are hopes that the conflict can be resolved **without resort to** violence.* 衝突有望不需要訴諸武力而得到解決。

R

3 the **first/last/final ~** the first or last course of action that you should or can take in a particular situation 應急措施；可首先（或最後）採取的手段：*Strike action should be regarded* ***as a last resort****, when all attempts to negotiate have failed.* 罷工應該是最後一着，在所有的談判努力都告失敗時才使用。◇ ***In the last resort*** (= in the end) *everyone must decide for themselves.* 最後人人都得自己作決定。

■ ***verb***

PHR V **re'sort to sth** to make use of sth, especially sth bad, as a means of achieving sth, often because there is no other possible solution 訴諸；求助於；依靠 **SYN** **have recourse to**：*They felt obliged to resort to violence.* 他們覺得有必要訴諸暴力。◇ **~ doing sth** *We may have to resort to using untrained staff.* 我們也許只能使用未受過訓練的員工了。

re·sound /rɪ'zaʊnd/ *verb (formal)* **1** [I] **~ (through sth)** (of a sound, voice, etc. 聲音、噪音等) to fill a place with sound 回響；迴盪：*Laughter resounded through the house.* 笑聲在屋裏迴盪。◇ *(figurative) The tragedy resounded around the world.* 悲劇的反響波及全世界。**2** [I] **~ (with/to sth)** (of a place 地方) to be filled with sound 迴盪着聲音；回響着聲音：*The street resounded to the thud of marching feet.* 街道上迴盪着行進步伐的鏗鏘聲。

re·sound·ing /rɪ'zaʊndɪŋ/ *adj.* [only before noun] **1** very great 巨大的；令人矚目的 **SYN** **emphatic**：*a* ***resounding victory/win/defeat*** 巨大的勝利／成功／失敗◇ *The evening was* ***a resounding success.*** 晚會辦得非常圓滿。**2** (of a sound 聲音) very loud and continuing for a long time 響亮的；嘹亮的；回響的 **SYN** **resonant** ▸ **re·sound·ing·ly** *adv.*

re·source **AW** /rɪ'sɔːs; -'zɔːs; *NAmE* 'riːsɔːrs; rɪ'sɔːrs/ *noun, verb*

■ ***noun*** **1** [C, usually pl.] a supply of sth that a country, an organization or a person has and can use, especially to increase their wealth 資源；財力：*the exploitation of minerals and other* ***natural resources*** 礦產和其他自然資源的開發◇ *We do not have the resources (= money) to update our computer software.* 我們沒有錢來更新我們的電腦軟件。◇ *We must make the most efficient use of the available financial resources.* 我們必須最有效地利用現有財力。◇ *We agreed to* ***pool our resources*** (= so that everyone gives sth). 我們同意把我們的資財集中起來。➲ COLLOCATIONS at ENVIRONMENT ➲ see also HUMAN RESOURCES **2** [C] something that can be used to help achieve an aim, especially a book, equipment, etc. that provides information for teachers and students 有助於實現目標的東西；資料：*The database could be used as a teaching resource in colleges.* 該數據庫可用作大學裏的一種教學輔助工具。◇ *Time is your most valuable resource, especially in examinations.* 時間是你最寶貴的東西，尤其是在考試中。◇ *resource books for teachers* 教師參考書 **3 resources** [pl.] personal qualities such as courage and imagination that help you deal with difficult situations 勇氣；才智；謀略：*He has no inner resources and hates being alone.* 他沒有什麼內在精神寄託，因而害怕孤獨。

■ ***verb*** **~ sth** to provide sth with the money or equipment that is needed 向…提供資金（或設備）：*Schools in the area are still inadequately resourced.* 本地區的學校仍然沒有足夠的資源。

re·source·ful **AW** /rɪ'sɔːsfl; -'zɔːs-; *NAmE* -'sɔːrs-/ *adj.* *(approving)* good at finding ways of doing things and solving problems, etc. 機敏的；足智多謀的；隨機應變的 **SYN** **enterprising** ▸ **re·source·ful·ly** /-fəli/ *adv.* **re·source·ful·ness** *noun* [U]

re·spect /rɪ'spekt/ *noun, verb*

■ ***noun*** **1** [U, sing.] **~ (for sb/sth)** a feeling of admiration for sb/sth because of their good qualities or achievements 尊敬；敬意；尊重：*I have the greatest respect for your brother.* 我非常尊敬你的哥哥。◇ *A two-minute silence was held as a* ***mark of respect****.* 人們靜默兩分鐘以示尊敬。◇ *A deep mutual respect and understanding developed between them.* 他們之間產生了深切的相互尊重和理解。➲ see also SELF-RESPECT **OPP** **disrespect** **2** [U, sing.] **~ (for sb/sth)** polite behaviour towards or care for sb/sth that you think is important 重視；尊重；維護：*to show a lack of respect for authority* 蔑視權威◇ *He has no respect for her feelings.* 他根本不尊重她的感情。◇ *Everyone has a right to be* ***treated with respect****.* 人人有權受到尊重。**OPP** **disrespect** **3** [C] a particular aspect or detail of sth （事物的）方面，細節：***In this respect*** *we are very fortunate.* 在這方面，我們是很幸運的。◇ *There was one respect, however, in which they differed.* 然而，他們在一點上有分歧。

IDM **in respect of sth** *(formal or business 商)* **1** concerning 關於；就…而言：*A writ was served on the firm in respect of their unpaid bill.* 公司由於欠賬而收到了傳票。**2** in payment for sth 作為…的報酬：*money received in respect of overtime worked* 得到的加班費 **with re'spect** | **with all due re'spect** *(formal)* used when you are going to disagree, usually quite strongly, with sb （通常在表示強烈不同意之前說）恕我直言：*With all due respect, the figures simply do not support you on this.* 恕我直言，這些數字根本不能支持你的觀點。**with respect to sth** *(formal or business 商)* concerning 關於；就…而言：*The two groups were similar with respect to income and status.* 這兩組在收入和地位方面是相似的。➲ more at DUE *adj.*, PAY *v.*

■ ***verb*** **1** (not usually used in the progressive tenses 通常不用於進行時) to have a very good opinion of sb/sth; to admire sb/sth 尊敬；尊重；仰慕：**~ sb/sth** *I respect Jack's opinion on most subjects.* 在大多數事情上，我尊重傑克的意見。◇ *a much loved and* ***highly respected*** *teacher* 備受愛戴和尊敬的老師◇ **~ sb/sth for sth** *She had always been honest with me, and I respect her for that.* 她一直對我很誠實。我非常敬重她這一點。**2** **~ sth** to be careful about sth; to make sure you do not do sth that sb would consider to be wrong 慎重對待；謹慎從事；尊重：*to respect other people's property* 不侵犯別人的財產◇ *She promised to respect our wishes.* 她保證尊重我們的願望。◇ *He doesn't respect other people's right to privacy.* 他不尊重別人的隱私權。**3** **~ sth** to agree not to break a law, principle, etc. 遵守；不損害；不違背：*The new leader has promised to respect the constitution.* 新的領導人承諾遵守憲法。

re·spect·abil·ity /rɪˌspektə'bɪləti/ *noun* [U] the fact of being considered socially acceptable 體面；名望；得體

re·spect·able /rɪ'spektəbl/ *adj.* **1** considered by society to be acceptable, good or correct 體面的；得體的；值得尊敬的：*a highly respectable neighbourhood* 非常體面的城區◇ *a respectable married man* 正派的已婚男子◇ *Go and make yourself look respectable.* 去把自己弄得體面點兒。**OPP** **disreputable** **2** fairly good; that there is not reason to be ashamed of 相當好的；不丟面子的 **SYN** **acceptable**：*a perfectly respectable result* 非常好的結果 ▸ **re·spect·ably** *adv.*：*respectably dressed* 穿得體面

re·spect·er /rɪ'spektə(r)/ *noun*

IDM **be no respecter of 'persons** to treat everyone in the same way, without being influenced by their importance, wealth, etc. 平等待人；一視同仁

re·spect·ful /rɪ'spektfl/ *adj.* showing or feeling respect 表示敬意的；尊敬的：*The onlookers stood at a respectful distance.* 旁觀者站在一定的距離之外，以示尊敬。◇ *We were brought up to be respectful of authority.* 我們從小就學會了尊重權威。**OPP** **disrespectful** ▸ **re·spect·ful·ly** /-fəli/ *adv.*：*He listened respectfully.* 他恭敬地聽着。

re·spect·ing /rɪ'spektɪŋ/ *prep. (formal)* concerning 關於 **SYN** **with respect to**：*information respecting the child's whereabouts* 關於孩子下落的消息

re·spect·ive /rɪ'spektɪv/ *adj.* [only before noun] belonging or relating separately to each of the people or things already mentioned 分別的；各自的：*They are each recognized specialists in their respective fields.* 他們在各自的領域都被視為專家。◇ *the respective roles of men and women in society* 男女在社會中各自的角色

re·spect·ive·ly /rɪ'spektɪvli/ *adv.* in the same order as the people or things already mentioned 分別；各自；順序為；依次為：*Julie and Mark, aged 17 and 19 respectively* 朱莉和馬克，年齡分別為 17 歲和 19 歲

res·pir·ation /ˌrespə'reɪʃn/ *noun* [U] *(formal)* the act of breathing 呼吸：*Blood pressure and respiration are also*

R

recorded. 血壓和呼吸也做了記錄。➲ see also ARTIFICIAL RESPIRATION

res·pir·ator /ˈrespəreɪtə(r)/ *noun* **1** a piece of equipment that makes it possible for sb to breathe over a long period when they are unable to do so naturally 人工呼吸器：*She was **put on a respirator**.* 給她戴上了人工呼吸器。 **2** a device worn over the nose and mouth to allow sb to breathe in a place where there is a lot of smoke, gas, etc. 防毒面具；口罩；面罩

re·spira·tory /rəˈspɪrətri; ˈrespərətri; *NAmE* ˈrespərətɔːri/ *adj.* connected with breathing 呼吸的：*the respiratory system* 呼吸系統 ◇ *respiratory diseases* 呼吸道疾病

re·spire /rɪˈspaɪə(r)/ *verb* [I] (*technical* 術語) to breathe 呼吸

res·pir·om·eter /ˌrespɪˈrɒmɪtə(r); *NAmE* -ˈrɑːm-/ *noun* (*medical* 醫) a piece of equipment for measuring how much air sb's lungs will hold 呼吸計；呼吸測定計

res·pite /ˈrespaɪt; *NAmE* ˈrespɪt/ *noun* [sing., U] **1 ~ (from sth)** a short break or escape from sth difficult or unpleasant 暫停；暫緩：*The drug brought a brief respite from the pain.* 藥物暫時緩解了疼痛。◇ *There was no respite from the suffocating heat.* 悶熱的天氣根本沒有緩解。◇ *She continued to work without respite.* 她連續工作，沒有休息。◇ ***respite care*** (= temporary care arranged for old, mentally ill, etc. people so that the people who usually care for them can have a rest) 暫時託管（為老人或病人提供短期照料以使長期照顧者獲得短暫休息）➲ SYNONYMS at REST **2** a short delay allowed before sth difficult or unpleasant must be done 短暫的延緩；喘息 SYN **reprieve**：*His creditors agreed to give him a temporary respite.* 他的債權人同意給他一個喘息的機會。

re·splen·dent /rɪˈsplendənt/ *adj.* **~ (in sth)** (*formal* or *literary*) brightly coloured in an impressive way 輝煌的；燦爛的；華麗的：*He glimpsed Sonia, resplendent in a red dress.* 他瞥了索尼亞一眼，見她一身紅衣，光彩照人。▸ **re·splen·dent·ly** *adv.*

re·spond 🔑 AW /rɪˈspɒnd; *NAmE* rɪˈspɑːnd/ *verb* **1** 🔑 [I, T] (rather *formal*) to give a spoken or written answer to sb/sth（口頭或書面）回答，回應 SYN **reply**：*I asked him his name, but he didn't respond.* 我問他叫什麼名字，可他沒回答。◇ **~ (to sb/sth) (with sth)** *She never responded to my letter.* 她從來沒給我回過信。◇ **+ speech** *'I'm not sure,' she responded.* "我不肯定。" 她答道。◇ **~ that ...** *When asked about the company's future, the director responded that he remained optimistic.* 問到公司的未來的時候，經理回答說他依然樂觀。➲ note at ANSWER **2** 🔑 [I] **~ (to sth) (with sth/by doing sth)** to do sth as a reaction to sth that sb has said or done 作出反應；響應 SYN **react**：*How did they respond to the news?* 他們對這則消息有什麼反應？◇ *The government responded by banning all future demonstrations.* 政府的反應是今後禁止一切示威活動。 **3** 🔑 [I] **~ (to sth/sb)** to react quickly or in the correct way to sth/sb 反應靈敏；作出正確反應：*The car responds very well to the controls.* 這輛汽車操縱自如。◇ *You can rely on him to respond to a challenge.* 你可以信賴他，他懂得應付挑戰。 **4** [I] **~ (to sth)** to improve as a result of a particular kind of treatment 有改進；見起色；顯出效果：*The infection did not respond to the drugs.* 這些藥物對感染沒有起作用。

re·spond·ent AW /rɪˈspɒndənt; *NAmE* -ˈspɑːnd-/ *noun* **1** a person who answers questions, especially in a survey 回答問題的人；（尤指）調查對象：*60% of the respondents agreed with the suggestion.* 回覆調查的人中 60% 同意這項建議。 **2** (*law* 律) a person who is accused of sth 被告

re·sponse 🔑 AW /rɪˈspɒns; *NAmE* rɪˈspɑːns/ *noun* **1** 🔑 [C, U] a spoken or written answer（口頭的或書面的）回答，答覆：*She made no response.* 她沒作任何回答。◇ **~ to sb/sth** ***In response to** your enquiry ...* 茲回覆閣下詢問⋯◇ *I received an encouraging response to my advertisement.* 我的廣告有了令人鼓舞的回應。 **2** 🔑 [C, U] a reaction to sth that has happened or been said 反應；響應：*The news provoked an angry response.* 這條消息引起了人們的憤怒。◇ *a positive response* 積極的反應 ◇ *I knocked on the door but there was no response.* 我敲了門，可是沒有回應。◇ **~ (to sb/sth)** *The product was developed **in response to** customer demand.* 這種產品是為了滿足顧客的需要而開發的。◇ *We sent out over 1 000 letters but the **response rate** has been low* (= few people replied). 我們寄出了 1 000 多封信，但回信寥寥。 **3** [C, usually pl.] **~ (to sb/sth)** a part of a church service that the people sing or speak as an answer to the part that the priest sings or speaks（禮拜儀式中的）答唱詠，啟應經

resˈponse time *noun* the length of time that a person or system takes to react to sth 反應時間；回應時間：*The average response time to emergency calls was 9 minutes.* 緊急呼叫的平均回應時間是 9 分鐘。

re·spon·si·bil·ity 🔑 /rɪˌspɒnsəˈbɪləti; *NAmE* -ˌspɑːn-/ *noun* (*pl.* **-ies**)
1 🔑 [U, C] a duty to deal with or take care of sb/sth, so that you may be blamed if sth goes wrong 責任；負責：**~ (for sth)** *We are recruiting a sales manager with responsibility for the European market.* 我們正在招聘負責歐洲市場的銷售經理。◇ **~ (for doing sth)** *They have responsibility for ensuring that the rules are enforced.* 他們有責任確保制度的執行。◇ **~ (to do sth)** *It is their responsibility to ensure that the rules are enforced.* 他們有責任確保制度的執行。◇ *parental rights and responsibilities* 父母的權利和義務 ◇ *to **take/assume** overall **responsibility** for personnel* 對職員全面負責 ◇ *I don't feel ready **to take on** new **responsibilities**.* 我還沒準備好承擔新的責任。◇ *to be in a **position of responsibility*** 身居要位 ◇ *I did it **on my own responsibility*** (= without being told to and being willing to take the blame if it had gone wrong). 我做的這件事，由我自己負責。 **2** 🔑 [U] **~ (for sth)** blame for sth bad that has happened 事故責任：*The bank refuses to **accept responsibility** for the mistake.* 銀行拒絕為這一錯誤承擔責任。◇ *Nobody has **claimed responsibility** for the bombing.* 沒有人聲稱對爆炸事件負責。➲ see also DIMINISHED RESPONSIBILITY
3 🔑 [U, C] a duty to help or take care of sb because of your job, position, etc. 職責；義務；任務：**~ (to/towards sb)** *She feels a strong **sense of responsibility** towards her employees.* 她對自己的雇員有很強的責任感。◇ **~ (to do sth)** *I think we have a **moral responsibility** to help these countries.* 我認為我們在道義上有責任幫助這些國家。

re·spon·sible 🔑 /rɪˈspɒnsəbl; *NAmE* -ˈspɑːn-/ *adj.*
▸ **HAVING JOB/DUTY** 有工作／職責 **1** 🔑 having the job or duty of doing sth or taking care of sb/sth, so that you may be blamed if sth goes wrong 有責任；負責；承擔義務：**~ (for doing sth)** *Mike is responsible for designing the entire project.* 邁克負責設計全部工程。◇ **~ (for sb/sth)** *Even where parents no longer live together, they each continue to be responsible for their children.* 即使父母不再共同生活，他們也要分別對子女負責。
▸ **CAUSING STH** 引起某事 **2** 🔑 **~ (for sth)** being able to be blamed for sth 應受責備；有責任：*Who's responsible for this mess?* 是誰弄得這麼亂？◇ *Everything will be done to bring those responsible to justice.* 將竭盡全力把罪魁禍首繩之以法。◇ *He is mentally ill and cannot **be held responsible** for his actions.* 他有精神病，不能對自己的行為負責。 **3** 🔑 **~ (for sth)** being the cause of sth 作為原因；成為起因：*Cigarette smoking is responsible for about 90% of deaths from lung cancer.* 因患肺癌而死亡者，約 90% 是吸煙所致。
▸ **TO SB IN AUTHORITY** 對主管者 **4** 🔑 **~ to sb/sth** having to report to sb/sth with authority or in a higher position and explain to them what you have done（向主管者或上級）承擔責任：*The Council of Ministers is responsible to the Assembly.* 內閣須向議會負責。
▸ **RELIABLE** 可靠 **5** 🔑 (of people or their actions or behaviour 人或行為舉止) that you can trust and rely on 可信任的；可信賴的；可靠的 SYN **conscientious**：*Clare has a mature and responsible attitude to work.* 克萊爾對待工作成熟而可信賴。OPP **irresponsible**
▸ **JOB** 工作 **6** 🔑 [usually before noun] needing sb who can be trusted and relied on; involving important duties 責任重大的；需要可靠的人負責的：*a **responsible job/position*** 責任重大的工作／崗位

R

re·spon·sibly /rɪˈspɒnsəbli; *NAmE* -ˈspɑːn-/ *adv.* in a sensible way that shows you can be trusted 明事理地；認真負責地；可信賴地：*to act responsibly* 辦事認真負責 **OPP** **irresponsibly**

re·spon·sive **AW** /rɪˈspɒnsɪv; *NAmE* -ˈspɑːn-/ *adj.* **1** [not usually before noun] **~ (to sb/sth)** reacting quickly and in a positive way 反應敏捷；反應積極：*Firms have to be responsive to consumer demand.* 公司必須對顧客的需求作出積極反應。◇ *a flu virus that is not responsive to treatment* 治療無效的流感病毒 **2 ~ (to sb/sth)** reacting with interest or enthusiasm 反應熱烈的；熱情的 **SYN** **receptive**：*The club is responsive to new ideas.* 俱樂部對新的想法都表示歡迎。◇ *a responsive and enthusiastic audience* 反應熱烈又熱情的觀眾 **OPP** **unresponsive** ▸ **re·spon·sive·ly** *adv.* **re·spon·sive·ness** **AW** *noun* [U]：*a lack of responsiveness to client needs* 對客戶的需要反應冷淡

re·spray /ˌriːˈspreɪ/ *verb* **~ sth** to change the colour of sth, especially a car, by painting it with a spray 再噴漆；再噴塗 ▸ **re·spray** /ˈriːspreɪ/ *noun* [usually sing.]

Synonyms 同義詞辨析

rest

break • respite • time out • breathing space

These are all words for a short period of time spent relaxing. 以上各詞均表示短暫的休息。

rest a period of relaxing, sleeping or doing nothing after a period of activity 指休息、睡眠：*We stopped for a well-earned rest.* 我們停下來作個應有的休息。

break a short period of time when you stop what you are doing and rest or eat 指間歇、休息：*Let's take a break.* 咱們休息一會兒吧。**NOTE** In British English **break** is a period of time between lessons at school. The North American English word is **recess**. 在英式英語中，break 指課間休息。美式英語表示此義用 recess。

respite a short break from sth difficult or unpleasant 指從困境或不愉快、不舒適的狀態中得到暫緩、暫停：*The drug brought a brief respite from the pain.* 藥物暫時緩解了疼痛。

time out (*informal, especially NAmE*) time for resting or relaxing away from your usual work or studies 指暫停工作或學習的時間：*Take time out to relax by the pool.* 去游泳池邊歇一歇吧。

breathing space a short rest in the middle of a period of mental or physical effort 指腦力或體力活動期間的短暫休息、喘息時間：*This delay gives the party a breathing space in which to sort out its policies.* 這一延誤使該黨有了喘息之機來釐定其政策。

PATTERNS

- (a) rest/break/respite/time out **from** sth
- to **have/take** (a) rest/break/time out
- to **give sb** (a) rest/break/respite/breathing space

rest 🔑 /rest/ *noun, verb*

■ *noun*

▸ **REMAINING PART/PEOPLE/THINGS 剩餘的部份／人／事物** **1** 🔑 [sing.] **the ~ (of sth)** the remaining part of sth 剩餘部份；殘留；其餘：*I'm not doing this job for the rest of my life.* 我不會一輩子幹這種工作。◇ *How would you like to spend the rest of the day?* 後半天你打算怎麼過？◇ *Take what you want and throw the rest away.* 把你想要的拿走，其餘的丟掉。 **2** 🔑 [pl.] **the ~ (of sth)** the remaining people or things; the others 其餘的人；其他事物；其他：*Don't blame Alex. He's human, like the rest of us.* 不要責怪亞歷克斯。他和我們大家一樣，也是人。◇ *The first question was difficult, but the rest were pretty easy.* 第一個問題很難，但其餘的都相當簡單。

▸ **PERIOD OF RELAXING 休息時間** **3** 🔑 [C, U] a period of relaxing, sleeping or doing nothing after a period of activity 休息時間；睡眠時間：*I had a good night's rest.* 我睡了一宿好覺。◇ *We stopped for a well-earned rest.* 我們停下來作個應有的休息。◇ **~ (from sth)** *to* **have/take a rest** *from all your hard work* 放下繁重的工作，休息一下 ◇ *Try to* **get some rest**—*you have a busy day tomorrow.* 休息一下吧，你明天還要忙一天呢。◇ *There are no matches tomorrow, which is a* **rest day**, *but the tournament resumes on Monday.* 明天是休息日，沒有比賽，但星期一繼續比賽。

▸ **SUPPORT 支撐物** **4** [C] (often in compounds 常構成複合詞) an object that is used to support or hold sth 支撐物；支架；基座；托：*an armrest* (= for example on a seat or chair) 座椅扶手 ➲ VISUAL VOCAB page V30

▸ **IN MUSIC 音樂** **5** [C, U] a period of silence between notes; a sign that shows a rest between notes 休止；休止符 ➲ picture at MUSIC

IDM **and (all) the ˈrest (of it)** (*informal*) used at the end of a list to mean everything else that you might expect to be on the list （列舉時用）諸如此類，等等：*He wants a big house and an expensive car and all the rest of it.* 他想要大房子、豪華汽車，如此等等。 **and the ˈrest** (*informal*) used to say that the actual amount or number of sth is much higher than sb has stated （比所說的）還要多；遠不止此數：*'It cost 250 pounds …' 'And the rest, and the rest!'* "這要花 250 英鎊…" "不止這些，不止這些！" **at ˈrest** **1** (*technical* 術語) not moving 靜止；不動：*At rest the insect looks like a dead leaf.* 這種昆蟲不動時看上去像一片枯葉。 **2** dead and therefore free from trouble or anxiety. People say 'at rest' to avoid saying 'dead'. （委婉說法，與 dead 同義）安息，長眠：*She now* **lies at rest** *in the churchyard.* 她現在長眠在教堂墓地裏。 **come to ˈrest** to stop moving 停止移動；不再移動：*The car crashed through the barrier and came to rest in a field.* 汽車闖過護欄，在一塊田裏停了下來。◇ *His eyes came to rest on Clara's face.* 他的目光停留在克拉拉的臉上。 **for the ˈrest** (*BrE, formal*) apart from that; as far as other matters are concerned 除此之外；至於其他：*The book has some interesting passages about the author's childhood. For the rest, it is extremely dull.* 這本書中關於作者童年的一些章節倒還有意思。除此之外，便無聊至極。 **give it a ˈrest** (*informal*) used to tell sb to stop talking about sth because they are annoying you 不要再提（惱人的事）了 **give sth a ˈrest** (*informal*) to stop doing sth for a while 暫停；暫時不做 **lay sb to ˈrest** to bury sb. People say 'to lay sb to rest' to avoid saying 'to bury' sb. （委婉說法，與 bury 同義）安葬：*George was laid to rest beside his parents.* 喬治被安葬在他父母墓旁。 **lay/put sth to ˈrest** to stop sth by showing it is not true （通過揭穿假象）平息，使停止：*The announcement finally laid all the speculation about their future to rest.* 通告最終消除了一切有關他們的未來的推測。 **the rest is ˈhistory** used when you are telling a story to say that you do not need to tell the end of it, because everyone knows it already 結局是盡人皆知的；結果如何不必贅述 ➲ more at MIND *n.*, WICKED *n.*

■ *verb*

▸ **RELAX 放鬆** **1** 🔑 [I, T] to relax, sleep or do nothing after a period of activity or illness; to not use a part of your body for some time 休息；放鬆：*The doctor told me to rest.* 醫生叫我休息。◇ *I can* **rest easy** (= stop worrying) *knowing that she's safely home.* 知道她安然無恙地回到家裏，我就可以放心了。◇ (*figurative*) *He* **won't rest** (= will never be satisfied) *until he finds her.* 他非得找到她才會安心。◇ **~ sth** *Rest your eyes every half an hour.* 每過半小時讓眼睛休息一下。➲ see also RESTED

▸ **SUPPORT 支撐** **2** 🔑 [T, I] to support sth by putting it on or against sth; to be supported in this way （被）支撐；（使）倚靠；托：**~ sth + adv./prep.** *Rest your head on my shoulder.* 把頭靠在我肩上。◇ *He rested his chin in his hands.* 他雙手托着下巴。◇ **+ adv./prep.** *His chin rested on his hands.* 他雙手托着下巴。◇ *Their bikes were resting against the wall.* 他們的自行車靠在牆上。

▸ **BE LEFT 被擱置** **3** [I] if you let a matter **rest**, you stop discussing it or dealing with it 被擱置；中止：*The matter cannot rest there—I intend to sue.* 這件事不能就此了結，我打算提出訴訟。

R

▸ **BE BURIED** 被埋葬 **4** [I] **+ adv./prep.** to be buried. People say 'rest' to avoid saying 'be buried' (委婉說法，與 be buried 同義）安息，長眠：*She rests beside her husband in the local cemetery.* 在當地的墓地裏，她長眠在她丈夫的墓旁。◇ *May he **rest in peace**.* 願他安息吧。➲ see also RIP (1)

IDM **rest as'sured (that ...)** (*formal*) used to emphasize that what you say is true or will definitely happen（強調所言確鑿無誤）儘管放心：*You may rest assured that we will do all we can to find him.* 你就放心吧，我們會千方百計找到他。 **,rest your 'case** **1** **I rest my case** (sometimes *humorous*) used to say that you do not need to say any more about sth because you think that you have proved your point 我的論證到此為止（已經足夠） **2** (*law* 律) used by lawyers in court to say that they have finished presenting their case（律師在法庭上）對案情陳述完畢：*The prosecution rests its case.* 控方對案情陳述完畢。➲ more at EASY *adv.*, GOD, LAUREL

PHR V **'rest on/upon sb/sth** **1** to depend or rely on sb/sth 依靠；依賴：*All our hopes now rest on you.* 現在所有的希望都寄託在你的身上。 **2** to look at sb/sth 凝視；凝望：*Her **eyes rested on** the piece of paper in my hand.* 她的目光落在我手裏的一張紙上。 **'rest on sth** to be based on sth 基於；以…為基礎：*The whole argument rests on a false assumption.* 整個論點都是基於一個錯誤的假設。 **'rest with sb (to do sth)** (*formal*) if **it rests with sb to do sth**, it is their responsibility to do it 是…的責任（或分內的事）：***It rests with** management to justify their actions.* 管理部門應當為他們的行動說出個道理來。◇ *The final decision rests with the doctors.* 要由醫生作出最後決定。

'rest area, 'rest stop *noun* (*NAmE*) an area beside an important road where people can stop their cars to rest, eat food, etc.（主要幹道旁的）停車休息區，休息站 ➲ compare LAY-BY (1)

re·start /ˌriːˈstɑːt; *NAmE* -ˈstɑːrt/ *verb* [I, T] **~ (sth)** to start again, or to make sth start again, after it has stopped（使）重新開始：*to restart a game* 重新開始遊戲 ◇ *The doctors struggled to restart his heart.* 醫生竭力重新起搏他的心臟。 ▸ **re·start** /ˈriːstɑːt; *NAmE* -stɑːrt/ *noun*

re·state /ˌriːˈsteɪt/ *verb* **~ sth** (*formal*) to say sth again or in a different way, especially so that it is more clearly or strongly expressed 重申；重新表述 ▸ **re·state·ment** *noun* [U]

res·taur·ant 0┳ /ˈrestrɒnt; *NAmE* -trɑːnt; -tərɑːnt/ *noun*
a place where you can buy and eat a meal 餐館；餐廳：*an Italian restaurant* 一家意大利餐館 ◇ *We had a meal in a restaurant.* 我們在餐廳吃了頓飯。◇ *We went out to a restaurant to celebrate.* 我們到一家餐廳裏慶祝了一番。◇ *a restaurant owner* 餐館老闆 ◇ *a self-service restaurant* 自助餐館 ➲ compare CAFE (1)

'restaurant car *noun* (*BrE*) = DINING CAR

res·taura·teur /ˌrestərəˈtɜː(r)/ *noun* (*formal*) a person who owns and manages a restaurant 餐館老闆；餐廳經理

'rest cure *noun* a period spent resting or relaxing in order to improve your physical or mental health 休養療法；靜養法

rest·ed /ˈrestɪd/ *adj.* feeling healthy and full of energy because you have had a rest 休息後精力恢復（或精神振作）的：*I awoke feeling rested and refreshed.* 我睡醒後感覺精力充沛，神清氣爽。➲ see also REST *v.* (1)

rest·ful /ˈrestfl/ *adj.* that makes you feel relaxed and peaceful 閒適寧靜的；使人感到悠閒的 **SYN** **calming**：*a hotel with a restful atmosphere* 氣氛閒適幽雅的旅館

'rest home *noun* a place where old or sick people are cared for 養老院；療養院；休養所

'rest house *noun* (in parts of Asia and Africa) a house or HUT that you can pay to stay in like a hotel room, especially in wild country（亞洲和非洲部份地區，尤指野外的）客棧，旅舍

'resting place *noun* **1** a grave. People say 'resting place' to avoid saying 'grave'.（委婉說法，與 grave 同義）墳墓，安息處：*her **final/last resting place*** 她的安息處 **2** a place where you can rest 休息處

Collocations 詞語搭配

Restaurants 餐館

Eating out 去餐館吃飯

- **eat (lunch/dinner)/dine/meet** at/in a restaurant 在一家餐館吃（午／晚）飯／進餐／碰面
- **go (out)/take sb (out)** for lunch/dinner/a meal 去／帶某人去（外面）吃午飯／吃晚飯／用餐
- **have** a meal with sb 與某人一起吃飯
- **make/have** a reservation (in/under the name of Yamada)（以山田的名字）預訂座位
- **reserve/**(*especially BrE*) **book** a table for six 預訂一張坐六人的桌子
- **ask for/request** a table for two/a table by the window 要一張兩人桌／靠窗的桌子

In the restaurant 在餐館

- **wait** to be seated 等待就座
- **show sb** to their table 把某人引到桌旁
- **sit** in the corner/by the window/at the bar/at the counter 坐在角落／窗邊／吧枱邊／櫃枱邊
- **hand sb/give sb** the menu/wine list 把菜單／酒水單遞給某人
- **open/read/study/peruse** the menu 打開／看／仔細看菜單
- the restaurant **has** a three-course set menu/a children's menu/an extensive wine list 這餐館有一個三道菜的套餐／兒童菜單／豐富的酒水單
- **taste/sample/try** the wine 品嚐葡萄酒
- the waiter **takes** your order 服務生幫你點餐
- **order/choose/have** the soup of the day/one of the specials/the house (*BrE*) speciality/(*especially NAmE*) specialty 點當日例湯／一道特色菜／餐館特色菜
- **serve/finish** the first course/the starter/the main course/dessert/coffee 端上／吃完第一道菜／開胃菜／主菜／甜點；端上／喝完咖啡
- **complain about** the food/the service/your meal 抱怨食物／服務／飯菜不好
- **enjoy** your meal 享用飯菜

Paying 結賬

- **pay/ask for** (*especially BrE*) the bill/(*NAmE*) the check 付賬；要求結賬
- **pay for/treat sb to** dinner/lunch/the meal 付晚飯／午飯／飯錢；請某人吃晚飯／午飯／飯
- service **is (not) included** 不含服務費
- **give sb/leave (sb)** a tip 給某人小費

res·ti·tu·tion /ˌrestɪˈtjuːʃn; *NAmE* -ˈtuː-/ *noun* [U] **~ (of sth) (to sb/sth)** **1** (*formal*) the act of giving back sth that was lost or stolen to its owner 歸還（真正物主）；歸還（贓物等） **SYN** **restoration** **2** (*law* 律) payment, usually money, for some harm or wrong that sb has suffered 賠償；補償；（通常指）賠款

rest·ive /ˈrestɪv/ *adj.* (*formal*) unable to stay still, or unwilling to be controlled, especially because you feel bored or not satisfied 難駕馭的；焦躁不安的；不耐煩的 ▸ **rest·ive·ness** *noun* [U]

rest·less /ˈrestləs/ *adj.* **1** unable to stay still or be happy where you are, because you are bored or need a change 坐立不安的；不耐煩的：*The audience was becoming restless.* 觀眾開始不耐煩了。◇ *After five years in the job, he was beginning to feel restless.* 這份工作幹了五年以後，他開始厭煩了。 **2** without real rest or sleep 沒有真正休息的；沒有睡眠的 **SYN** **disturbed**：*a restless night* 不眠之夜 ▸ **rest·less·ly** *adv.*：*He moved*

R

restlessly from one foot to the other. 他的兩隻腳不停地倒替着。 **rest·less·ness** *noun* [U]: *the restlessness of youth* 年輕人的躁動

re·stock /ˌriːˈstɒk; *NAmE* -ˈstɑːk/ *verb* [T, I] **~ (sth) (with sth)** to fill sth with new or different things to replace those that have been used, sold, etc.; to get a new supply of sth 更新（舊物品）；補充（貨源）；再補給

res·tor·ation AW /ˌrestəˈreɪʃn/ *noun* **1** [U, C] the work of repairing and cleaning an old building, a painting, etc. so that its condition is as good as it originally was 整修；修復： *The palace is closed* ***for restoration.*** 王宮因整修而停止開放。◇ *restoration work* 修復工作 **2** [U, C] **~ of sth** the act of bringing back a system, a law, etc. that existed previously （規章制度等的）恢復： *the restoration of democracy/the monarchy* 民主制度／君主政體的恢復 **3** [U] **~ (of sth)** the act of returning sth to its correct place, condition or owner 復原；復位；回歸；歸還： *the restoration of the Elgin marbles to Greece* 埃爾金大理石雕像之交還希臘 **4 the Restoration** [sing.] the time in Britain after 1660 when, following a period with no king or queen, Charles II became king 王政復辟時期（1660 年，英國經歷了一段無王時期後，查理二世登基為王）： *Restoration comedy/poetry* (= written during and after this time) 王政復辟時期的喜劇／詩歌

re·stora·tive /rɪˈstɔːrətɪv/ *adj., noun*

■ ***adj.*** **1** *(formal)* making you feel strong and healthy again 恢復健康的；促使康復的： *the restorative power of fresh air* 新鮮空氣的康復功效 **2** *(medical* 醫) connected with treatment that repairs the body or a part of it 整容的；整形的： ***restorative dentistry/surgery*** 整形牙科／外科

■ ***noun*** *(old-fashioned)* a thing that makes you feel better, stronger, etc. 有助恢復健康的事物；滋補品

re·store 🔑 AW /rɪˈstɔː(r)/ *verb*

1 🔑 **~ sth (to sb)** to bring back a situation or feeling that existed before 恢復（某種情況或感受）： *The measures are intended to restore public confidence in the economy.* 這些舉措旨在恢復公眾對經濟的信心。◇ ***Order was quickly restored*** *after the riots.* 暴亂過後秩序很快得到了恢復。◇ *Such kindness restores your faith in human nature* (= makes you believe most people are kind). 這樣的善心使人又一次感到人性善良。◇ *The operation restored his sight* (= made him able to see again). 手術使他恢復了視力。 **2** 🔑 **~ sb/sth to sth** to bring sb/sth back to a former condition, place or position 使復原；使復位；使復職： *He is now fully restored to health.* 他現在完全恢復了健康。◇ *We hope to* ***restore*** *the garden* ***to its former glory*** (= make it as beautiful as it used to be). 我們想把這花園變得和過去一樣美麗。 **3** 🔑 **~ sth** to repair a building, work of art, piece of furniture, etc. so that it looks as good as it did originally 修復；整修；使復原： *Her job is restoring old paintings.* 她的工作是修復舊畫。 **4 ~ sth** to bring a law, tradition, way of working, etc. back into use 重新採用（或實施）；恢復 SYN **reintroduce**: *to restore ancient traditions* 恢復古老的傳統 ◇ *Some people argue that the death penalty should be restored.* 有些人主張恢復死刑。 **5 ~ sth (to sb/sth)** *(formal)* to give sth that was lost or stolen back to sb 歸還（失物、贓款等）： *The police have now restored the painting to its rightful owner.* 警察已經把這幅油畫歸還給了它的合法主人。

re·storer /rɪˈstɔːrə(r)/ *noun* a person whose job is to repair old buildings, works of art, etc. so that they look as they did when new 做修復工作的人

re·strain AW /rɪˈstreɪn/ *verb* **1** to stop sb/sth from doing sth, especially by using physical force （尤指用武力）制止，阻止，管制： **~ sb/sth** *The prisoner had to be restrained by the police.* 警方只好強行制住囚犯。◇ *He placed a restraining hand on her arm.* 他拉住她的胳膊制止她。◇ **~ sb/sth from sth/from doing sth** *They have obtained an injunction restraining the company from selling the product.* 他們已經得到阻止這家公司出售這一產品的禁銷令。 **2** to stop yourself from feeling an emotion or doing sth that you would like to do 約束（自己）；控制（自己）；忍住： **~ sth** *John managed to restrain his anger.* 約翰努力壓制住自己的怒氣。◇ **~ yourself (from sth/from doing sth)** *She had to restrain herself from crying out in pain.* 她只得忍住疼痛，不哭出來。 **3 ~ sth** to stop sth that is growing or increasing from becoming too large 抑制；控制 SYN **keep under control**: *The government is taking steps to restrain inflation.* 政府正在採取措施控制通貨膨脹。

re·strained AW /rɪˈstreɪnd/ *adj.* **1** showing calm control rather than emotion 克制的；有節制的： *her restrained smile* 她克制的微笑 **2** not too brightly coloured or decorated 不豔麗的；樸素的 SYN **discreet**: *The costumes and lighting in the play were restrained.* 這齣戲的服裝和燈光都很樸實。

re'straining order *noun* **~ (against sb)** *(especially NAmE)* an official order given by a judge which demands that sth must or must not be done. A restraining order does not require a trial in court but only lasts for a limited period of time. 限制令 ➲ compare INJUNCTION (1)

re·straint AW /rɪˈstreɪnt/ *noun* **1** [C, usually pl.] **~ (on sb/sth)** a rule, a fact, an idea, etc. that limits or controls what people can do 約束力；管制措施；制約因素： *The government has imposed export restraints on some products.* 政府對一些產品實行了出口控制。➲ SYNONYMS at LIMIT **2** [U] the act of controlling or limiting sth because it is necessary or sensible to do so 控制；限制： *wage restraint* 限制工資增長 **3** [U] the quality of behaving calmly and with control 克制；抑制；約束 SYN **self-control**: *The police appealed to the crowd for restraint.* 警方呼籲群眾保持克制。◇ *He* ***exercised*** *considerable* ***restraint*** *in ignoring the insults.* 他克制住了自己，沒去理會種種侮辱。 **4** [U] *(formal)* the use of physical force to control sb who is behaving in a violent way （武力）阻止，制止，制伏： *the physical restraint of prisoners* 對囚犯的人身限制 **5** [C] *(formal)* a type of SEAT BELT or safety device 座椅安全帶；安全裝置： *Children must use an approved child restraint or adult seat belt.* 兒童必須使用經過認可的兒童安全帶或成人座椅安全帶。

re·strict 🔑 AW /rɪˈstrɪkt/ *verb*

1 🔑 to limit the size, amount or range of sth 限制，限定（數量、範圍等）： **~ sth to sth** *Speed is restricted to 30 mph in towns.* 在城裏車速不得超過每小時 30 英里。◇ *We restrict the number of students per class to 10.* 我們將每個班的學生人數限定為 10 人。◇ **~ sth** *Fog severely restricted visibility.* 濃霧嚴重影響了能見度。◇ *Having small children tends to restrict your freedom.* 有了小孩往往會限制你的自由。 **2** 🔑 **~ sth** to stop sb/sth from moving or acting freely 束縛；妨礙；阻礙 SYN **impede**: *The long skirt restricted her movements.* 長裙妨礙了她的行動。 **3** 🔑 **~ sth (to sb)** to control sth with rules or laws （以法規）限制： *Access to the club is restricted to members only.* 俱樂部僅對會員開放。 **4 ~ yourself/sb (to sth/to doing sth)** to allow yourself or sb to have only a limited amount of sth or to do only a particular kind of activity 約束；管束： *I restrict myself to one cup of coffee a day.* 我限制自己每天只喝一杯咖啡。

re·stricted 🔑 AW /rɪˈstrɪktɪd/ *adj.*

1 🔑 limited or small in size or amount （大小或數量）有限的，很小的： *a restricted space* 有限的空間 ◇ *a restricted range of foods* 有限的食物種類 **2** 🔑 limited in what you are able to do （指能做的事）有限的，受限制的： *In those days women led fairly restricted lives.* 那時，婦女過着相當受限制的生活。◇ *Her vision is restricted in one eye.* 她只有一隻眼睛有視力。 **3** 🔑 controlled by rules or laws 受（法規）制約的；受控制的；受約束的： *to allow children only restricted access to the Internet* 只允許兒童有限地接觸互聯網 ◇ *(BrE) a restricted area* (= controlled by laws about speed or parking) （車速或停車）限制區 ◇ *The tournament is* ***restricted to*** *players under the age of 23.* 這次比賽只允許 23 歲以下的選手參加。 **4** [usually before noun] (of a place 地方) only open to people with special permission, especially because it is secret or dangerous 不對公眾開放的： *to enter a restricted zone* 進入禁區 **5** *(BrE)* officially secret and only available to people with special permission 保密的；限於內部傳閱的 SYN **classified**: *a restricted document* 保密文件 OPP **unrestricted**

R

re·stric·tion 0-w AW /rɪˈstrɪkʃn/ *noun*
1 0-w [C] a rule or law that limits what you can do or what can happen 限制規定；限制法規：*import/speed/travel, etc. restrictions* 進口、速度、旅行等限制 ◇ **~ on sth** *to impose/place a restriction on sth* 對某事實行限制 ◇ *The government has agreed to* **lift restrictions** *on press freedom.* 政府已經同意撤銷對新聞自由的限制。➲ SYNONYMS at LIMIT **2** [U] the act of limiting or controlling sb/sth 限制；約束：*sports clothes that prevent any restriction of movement* 寬鬆的運動服 **3** [C] a thing that limits the amount of freedom you have 制約因素：*the restrictions of a prison* 監獄的種種約束

re·strict·ive AW /rɪˈstrɪktɪv/ *adj.* **1** preventing people from doing what they want 限制性的；約束的：*restrictive laws* 限制性法規 **2** (also **defining**) (*grammar* 語法) (of RELATIVE CLAUSES 關係從句) explaining which particular person or thing you are talking about rather than giving extra information about them. In 'The books which are on the table are mine', 'which are on the table' is a restrictive relative clause. 限制性的 ➲ compare NON-RESTRICTIVE ▸ **re·strict·ive·ly** AW *adv.*

reˌstrictive ˈpractices *noun* [pl.] (*especially BrE, often disapproving*) agreements or ways of working that limit the freedom of workers or employers in order to prevent competition or to protect people's jobs 限制競爭協議，限制競爭的行為（限制工人或雇主的自由，以防止競爭，保護就業）

re·string /ˌriːˈstrɪŋ/ *verb* (**restrung**, **restrung** /ˌriːˈstrʌŋ/) **~ sth** to fit new strings on a musical instrument such as a GUITAR or VIOLIN, or on a sports RACKET 給（樂器或球拍）重新裝弦

rest·room /ˈrestruːm; -rʊm/ *noun* (*NAmE*) a room with a toilet in a public place, such as a theatre or restaurant（公共場所的）盥洗室，洗手間；公共廁所

re·struc·ture AW /ˌriːˈstrʌktʃə(r)/ *verb* [T, I] **~ (sth)** to organize sth such as a system or a company in a new and different way 調整結構；改組；重建 ▸ **re·struc·tur·ing** AW *noun* [U, C, usually sing.]

re·sult 0-w /rɪˈzʌlt/ *noun, verb*

■ *noun*

▸ CAUSED BY STH 由某事引起 **1** 0-w [C, U] **~ (of sth)** a thing that is caused or produced because of sth else 後果；結果：*She died* **as a result of** *her injuries.* 她由於受傷而死亡。◇ *The failure of the company was a direct result of bad management.* 公司衰敗的直接原因是經營不善。◇ *He made one big mistake, and, as a result, lost his job.* 他犯了個大錯，結果丟了工作。◇ *The farm was flooded,* **with the result that** *most of the harvest was lost.* 農場被淹，收成損失了一大半。◇ *The* **end result** (= the final one) *of her hard work was a place at medical school.* 她勤奮苦讀，終於進了醫學院。◇ *This book is the result of 25 years of research.* 這本書是 25 年研究的結晶。➲ LANGUAGE BANK at BECAUSE, CONSEQUENTLY

▸ OF GAME/ELECTION 比賽；選舉 **2** 0-w [C] **~ (of sth)** the final score or the name of the winner in a sports event, competition, election, etc. 結果（包括比分、得票、獲勝者或當選者名單等）：*They will announce the result of the vote tonight.* 今晚他們將宣佈投票結果。◇ *the election results* 選舉結果 ◇ *the football results* 足球比賽的結果 **3** [C, usually sing.] (*BrE, informal*) a victory or a success, especially in a game of football (SOCCER)（尤指足球比賽的）勝利，勝局：*We badly need to* **get a result** *from this match.* 這場比賽我們非贏不可。

▸ OF EXAM 考試 **4** 0-w [C, usually pl.] (*BrE*) the mark/grade you get in an exam or in a number of exams 得分；成績：*Have you had your results yet?* 你知道考試成績了嗎？

▸ OF TEST/RESEARCH 測試；研究 **5** 0-w [C] **~ (of sth)** the information that you get from a scientific test or piece of research 結果；成果：*the result of an experiment* 實驗結果 ➲ COLLOCATIONS at SCIENTIFIC

▸ SUCCESS 成功 **6** 0-w **results** [pl.] things that are achieved successfully 成功實現的事；成果；成效：*The project is beginning to show results.* 這項工程開始顯出成效。◇ *a coach who knows how to get results from his players* 善於調動隊員獲取成功的教練

■ *verb* 0-w [I] **~ (from sth)** to happen because of sth else that happened first（因…）發生；（隨…）產生：*job losses resulting from changes in production* 生產革新造成的失業 ◇ *When water levels rise, flooding results.* 水位上升，就會發生洪水。◇ *It was a large explosion and the resulting damage was extensive.* 爆炸相當劇烈，造成的破壞範圍很大。

PHR V **reˈsult in sth** 0-w to make sth happen 造成；導致 SYN **lead to**：*The cyclone has resulted in many thousands of deaths.* 颶風已經造成了成千上萬的人死亡。◇ **~ sb/sth doing sth** *These policies resulted in many elderly people suffering hardship.* 這些政策使得許多老人飽受困苦。➲ LANGUAGE BANK at CAUSE

Synonyms 同義詞辨析

result

consequence • outcome • repercussion

These are all words for a thing that is caused because of sth else. 以上各詞均表示後果、結果。

result a thing that is caused or produced by sth else 指後果、結果：*She died as a result of her injuries.* 她因傷死亡。◇ *This book is the result of 25 years of research.* 這本書是 25 年研究的成果。

consequence (*rather formal*) a result of sth that has happened, especially a bad result 尤指不好的結果、後果：*This decision could have serious consequences for the industry.* 這項決定可能對該行業造成嚴重後果。NOTE **Consequences** is used most frequently to talk about possible negative results of an action. It is commonly used with such words as *adverse, dire, disastrous, fatal, harmful, negative, serious, tragic* and *unfortunate*. Even when there is no adjective, **consequences** often suggests negative results. * consequence 最常用以指某種行為可能產生的負面結果，常與 adverse、dire、disastrous、fatal、harmful、negative、serious、tragic、unfortunate 等詞連用。即使沒有形容詞修飾，consequence 也常含負面結果之意。

outcome the result of an action or process 指行動或過程的結果、效果：*We are waiting to hear the final outcome of the negotiations.* 我們在等待談判的最終結果。

RESULT OR OUTCOME? 用 result 還是 outcome？

Result is often used to talk about things that are caused directly by sth else. * result 常指由另一事物直接導致的結果：*Aggression is often the result of fear.* 好鬥情緒通常是恐懼所致。**Outcome** is more often used to talk about what happens at the end of a process when the exact relation of cause and effect is less clear. * outcome 較常指某一過程完結時的結果，此時，原因和結果之間的確切關係已不太明顯：~~*Aggression is often the outcome of fear.*~~ **Result** is often used after an event to talk about what happened. **Outcome** is often used before an action or process to talk about what is likely to happen. * result 通常是在事情過去之後談及其結果，outcome 通常是在行動或過程之前談及其可能產生的結果。

repercussion (*rather formal*) an indirect and usually bad result of an action or event that may happen some time afterwards 指一段時間後出現的間接的影響，通常指不良反響、惡果

PATTERNS

- to have consequences/repercussions **for** sb/sth
- **with** the result/consequence/outcome **that** …
- a/the **possible** result/consequences/outcome/repercussions
- a(n)/the **likely/inevitable** result/consequences/outcome
- (a) **negative** results/consequences/outcome/repercussions
- **far-reaching/serious** results/consequences/repercussions
- to **have** a result/consequences/an outcome/repercussions

R

re·sult·ant /rɪˈzʌltənt/ *adj.* [only before noun] (*formal*) caused by the thing that has just been mentioned 因而發生的；因此而產生的：*the growing economic crisis and resultant unemployment* 不斷加劇的經濟危機以及由此而產生的失業

re·sulta·tive /rɪˈzʌltətɪv/ *adj.* (*grammar* 語法) (of verbs, conjunctions or clauses 動詞、連詞或從句) expressing or relating to the result of an action 表示結果的；結果性的；結果格的

re·sume /rɪˈzjuːm; *NAmE* -ˈzuːm/ *verb* (*formal*) **1** [T, I] if you **resume** an activity, or if it **resumes**, it begins again or continues after an interruption 重新開始；（中斷後）繼續：**~ (sth)** *to* ***resume talks/negotiations*** 重新進行會談 / 談判 ◊ *She resumed her career after an interval of six years.* 經過六年的間歇之後她又重新上崗。◊ *The noise resumed, louder than before.* 噪聲再起，比先前更大。◊ **~ doing sth** *He got back in the car and resumed driving.* 他回到車上，繼續開車。 **2** [T] **~ your seat/place/position** to go back to the seat or place that you had before 回到（原來的座位、地方或位置）

ré·sumé /ˈrezjumeɪ; *NAmE* ˈrezəmeɪ/ *noun* **1 ~ (of sth)** a short summary or account of sth 摘要；概述；概要：*a brief résumé of events so far* 到目前為止事件的概述 **2** (*NAmE*) (*BrE* **cur·ricu·lum vitae**) a written record of your education and the jobs you have done, that you send when you are applying for a job （求職用的）履歷，簡歷 ➲ WRITING TUTOR page WT46

re·sump·tion /rɪˈzʌmpʃn/ *noun* [sing., U] **~ (of sth)** (*formal*) the act of beginning sth again after it has stopped 重新開始；繼續進行；恢復：*We are hoping for an early resumption of peace talks.* 我們企盼着早日恢復和談。

re·sup·ply /ˌriːsəˈplaɪ/ *verb* **~ sb (with sth)** to give sb new supplies of sth they need; to give sth to sb again in a different form 向…再供給（所需物品）；（以另一形式）重新提供 ▸ **re·supply** *noun*

re·sur·face /ˌriːˈsɜːfɪs; *NAmE* -ˈsɜːrf-/ *verb* **1** [I] to come to the surface again after being underwater or under the ground 再次浮出，再次露出（水面或地面）：*The submarine resurfaced.* 潛艇重新浮出水面。◊ (*figurative*) *All the old hostilities resurfaced when they met again.* 他們再次碰面時，過去的種種敵意又都冒了出來。 **2** [T] **~ sth** to put a new surface on a road, path, etc. 重鋪路面

re·sur·gence /rɪˈsɜːdʒəns; *NAmE* -ˈsɜːrdʒ-/ *noun* [sing., U] the return and growth of an activity that had stopped 復蘇；復興

re·sur·gent /rɪˈsɜːdʒənt; *NAmE* -ˈsɜːrdʒ-/ *adj.* [usually before noun] (*formal*) becoming stronger or more popular again 復興的；恢復生機活力的；再度流行的

res·ur·rect /ˌrezəˈrekt/ *verb* **1 ~ sth** to bring back into use sth, such as a belief, a practice, etc., that had disappeared or been forgotten 重新應用；恢復使用；使復興 SYN **revive** **2 ~ sb** to bring a dead person back to life 起死回生；使復活 SYN **raise from the dead**

res·ur·rec·tion /ˌrezəˈrekʃn/ *noun* **1 the Resurrection** [sing.] (in the Christian religion 基督教) the time when Jesus Christ returned to life again after his death; the time when all dead people will become alive again, when the world ends 耶穌復活；（世界末日）所有亡者復活 **2** [U, sing.] a new beginning for sth which is old or which had disappeared or become weak 復蘇；復興

re·sus·ci·tate /rɪˈsʌsɪteɪt/ *verb* **~ sb/sth** to make sb start breathing again or become conscious again after they have almost died 使蘇醒；使恢復知覺 SYN **revive**：*He had a heart attack and all attempts to resuscitate him failed.* 他的心臟病發作，所有搶救他的努力都失敗了。◊ (*figurative*) *efforts to resuscitate the economy* 重振經濟的努力 ▸ **re·sus·ci·ta·tion** /rɪˌsʌsɪˈteɪʃn/ *noun* [U]：*frantic attempts at resuscitation* 盡一切努力使人復蘇 ➲ see also MOUTH-TO-MOUTH RESUSCITATION

re·tail¹ /ˈriːteɪl/ *noun, adv., verb* ➲ see also RETAIL²

■ ***noun*** [U] the selling of goods to the public, usually through shops/stores 零售：*The recommended retail price is £9.99.* 建議零售價為 9.99 英鎊。◊ *department stores and other* ***retail outlets*** 百貨商店和其他零售渠道 ◊ *the* ***retail trade*** 零售業 ➲ compare WHOLESALE (1) ▸ **re·tail** *adv.*：*to* ***buy/sell retail*** (= in a shop/store) 零買；零賣

■ ***verb*** **1** [T] **~ sth** to sell goods to the public, usually through shops/stores 零售：*The firm manufactures and retails its own range of sportswear.* 公司生產並零售自己的運動服裝系列。 **2** [I] **~ at/for sth** (*business* 商) to be sold at a particular price 以…價格銷售：*The book retails at £14.95.* 這本書的零售價為 14.95 英鎊。

re·tail² /rɪˈteɪl/ *verb* **~ sth (to sb)** (*formal*) to tell people about sth, especially about a person's behaviour or private life 詳說，述說（尤指別人的事情） SYN **recount**：*She retailed the neighbours' activities with relish.* 她饒有興趣地對鄰居們的活動說三道四。➲ see also RETAIL¹

re·tail·er /ˈriːteɪlə(r)/ *noun* a person or business that sells goods to the public 零售商；零售店

re·tail·ing /ˈriːteɪlɪŋ/ *noun* [U] the business of selling goods to the public, usually through shops/stores 零售業：*career opportunities in retailing* 零售業的職業機會 ➲ compare WHOLESALING

ˈretail park *noun* (*BrE*) an area containing a group of large shops/stores, located outside a town （城郊）零售商業區

ˌretail ˈprice index (also **ˈprice index**) *noun* [sing.] (*abbr.* **RPI**) (in Britain) a list of the prices of some ordinary goods and services which shows how much these prices change each month （英國）零售物價指數 ➲ see also CONSUMER PRICE INDEX

ˌretail ˈtherapy *noun* [U] (usually *humorous*) the act of going shopping and buying things in order to make yourself feel more cheerful 購物療法（對花錢買樂這一做法的戲稱）：*I was ready for a little retail therapy.* 我準備去接受一下購物治療。➲ COLLOCATIONS at SHOPPING

re·tain 🔑 AW /rɪˈteɪn/ *verb* (rather *formal*)

1 🔑 **~ sth** to keep sth; to continue to have sth 保持；持有；保留；繼續擁有 SYN **preserve**：*to retain your independence* 保持獨立 ◊ *He struggled to retain control of the situation.* 他曾努力保持對局勢的控制。◊ *The house retains much of its original charm.* 這所房子保留了許多原有的魅力。◊ *She retained her tennis title for the third year.* 她第三年保住了網球冠軍的頭銜。 **2** 🔑 **~ sth** to continue to hold or contain sth 保持；繼續容納：*a soil that retains moisture* 保持水分的土壤 ◊ *This information is no longer retained within the computer's main memory.* 這些數據不再保留在計算機的主存貯器中。◊ (*figurative*) *She has a good memory and finds it easy to retain facts.* 她記憶力好，很容易記住事情。 **3 ~ sb/sth** (*law* 律) if a member of the public **retains** sb such as a lawyer, he or she pays money regularly or in advance so the lawyer, etc. will do work for him or her 聘請（律師等）：*a retaining fee* 給所委託律師的預付辯護費 ◊ *to retain the services of a lawyer* 聘定律師 ➲ see also RETENTION, RETENTIVE

re·tain·er AW /rɪˈteɪnə(r)/ *noun* **1** a sum of money that is paid to sb to make sure they will be available to do work when they are needed （聘請律師等的）預付費用，保留金：*The agency will pay you a monthly retainer.* 代理機構將會每月付給你聘用金。 **2** (*BrE*) a small amount of rent that you pay for a room, etc. when you are not there in order to keep it available for your use （為保留租房而付的）租房訂金 **3** (*NAmE*) a device that keeps a person's teeth straight after they have had ORTHODONTIC treatment with BRACES（牙齒）固位體，保持器 **4** (*old-fashioned*) a servant, especially one who has been with a family for a long time （尤指服務多年的）僕人，家僕

re·tain·ing /rɪˈteɪnɪŋ/ *adj.* [only before noun] (*technical* 術語) intended to keep sth in the correct position 固定的；矯正的：*a* ***retaining wall*** (= one that keeps the earth or water behind it in position) 擋土牆；擋水牆

re·take *verb, noun*

■ ***verb*** /ˌriːˈteɪk/ (**re·took** /-ˈtʊk/, **re·taken** /-ˈteɪkən/) **1 ~ sth** (especially of an army 尤指部隊) to take control of sth such as a town again 收復（失地）；恢復控制：

Government forces moved in to retake the city. 政府軍開進城市，以恢復對它的控制。◇ (*figurative*) *Moore fought back to retake the lead later in the race.* 後來穆爾奮力反擊，重新奪回了比賽中的領先地位。 **2** = RESIT
■ **noun** /ˈriːteɪk/ **1** the act of filming a scene in a film/movie again, because it was not right before 重拍（電影鏡頭） **2** = RESIT *n.* at RESIT

re·tali·ate /rɪˈtælieɪt/ *verb* [I] to do sth harmful to sb because they have harmed you first 報復；反擊；復仇 **SYN** **take revenge**：**~ (against sb/sth)** *to retaliate against an attack* 對攻擊進行還擊 ◇ **~ (by doing sth/with sth)** *The boy hit his sister, who retaliated by kicking him.* 男孩打了他妹妹，妹妹則回敬了他一腳。 ▸ **re·tali·atory** /rɪˈtæliətri; *NAmE* -tɔːri/ *adj.*：*retaliatory action* 報復行動

re·tali·ation /rɪˌtæliˈeɪʃn/ *noun* [U] **~ (against sb/sth) (for sth)** action that a person takes against sb who has harmed them in some way 報復 **SYN** **reprisal**：*retaliation against UN workers* 對聯合國工作人員的報復 ◇ *The shooting may have been* ***in retaliation for*** *the arrest of the terrorist suspects.* 槍擊事件可能是對逮捕嫌疑恐怖分子進行的報復行動。

re·tard *verb, noun*
■ **verb** /rɪˈtɑːd; *NAmE* rɪˈtɑːrd/ **~ sth** (*formal*) to make the development or progress of sth slower 阻礙；減緩；使放慢速度 **SYN** **delay, slow down**：*The progression of the disease can be retarded by early surgery.* 早期手術可以抑制病情的發展。 ▸ **re·tard·ation** /ˌriːtɑːˈdeɪʃn; *NAmE* ˌriːtɑːrˈd-/ *noun* [U]：*Many factors can lead to growth retardation in unborn babies.* 許多因素可以導致胎兒發育遲緩。
■ **noun** /ˈriːtɑːd; *NAmE* ˈriːtɑːrd/ (*taboo, slang*) an offensive way of describing sb who is not intelligent or who has not developed normally 遲鈍的人；弱智

re·tard·ed /rɪˈtɑːdɪd; *NAmE* -ˈtɑːrd-/ *adj.* (*old-fashioned, offensive*) less developed mentally than is normal for a particular age 遲鈍的；弱智的；智力發育遲緩的 **SYN** **backward**

retch /retʃ/ *verb* [I] to make sounds and movements as if you are VOMITING although you do not actually do so 乾嘔；乾噦：*The smell made her retch.* 這氣味讓她噁心。

re·tell /ˌriːˈtel/ *verb* (**re·told, re·told** /-ˈtəʊld; *NAmE* -ˈtoʊld/) **~ sth** to tell a story again, often in a different way （通常以不同的方式）複述，重新講述

re·ten·tion **AW** /rɪˈtenʃn/ *noun* [U] (*formal*) **1** the action of keeping sth rather than losing it or stopping it 保持；維持；保留：*The company needs to improve its training and retention of staff.* 公司需要改進對員工的培訓和留用工作。 **2** the action of keeping liquid, heat, etc. inside sth rather than letting it escape （液體、熱量等的）保持，阻滯：*Eating too much salt can cause fluid retention.* 食鹽過多會導致體液瀦留。 **3** the ability to remember things 記憶力；記性：*Visual material aids the retention of information.* 直觀材料有助於加強記憶。 ➲ see also RETAIN

re·ten·tive **AW** /rɪˈtentɪv/ *adj.* (of the memory 記憶力) able to store facts and remember things easily 有記性的；記憶力強的 ➲ see also RETAIN (2)

re·test /ˌriːˈtest/ *verb* **~ sb/sth** to test sb/sth again 再測驗；再測試；重新試驗：*Subjects were retested one month later.* 受實驗者一個月後再次接受測試。

re·think /ˌriːˈθɪŋk/ *verb* (**re·thought, re·thought** /-ˈθɔːt/) [T, I] **~ (sth)** to think again about an idea, a course of action, etc., especially in order to change it 重新考慮：*to rethink a plan* 重新考慮一項計劃 ▸ **re·think** /ˈriːθɪŋk/ (also **re·think·ing**) *noun* [sing.]：*a* ***radical rethink*** *of company policy* 對公司政策的徹底反思

reti·cent /ˈretɪsnt/ *adj.* (*formal*) unwilling to tell people about things 寡言少語；不願與人交談；有保留 **SYN** **reserved, uncommunicative**：*She was shy and reticent.* 她羞怯而寡言少語。◇ **~ about sth** *He was extremely reticent about his personal life.* 他對自己的私人生活諱莫如深。 ▸ **reti·cence** /-sns/ *noun* [U]

re·ticu·la·ted /rɪˈtɪkjuleɪtɪd/ *adj.* (*technical* 術語) built, arranged or marked like a net or network, with many small squares or sections 網狀（結構）的；網絡狀的

reti·cule /ˈretɪkjuːl/ *noun* (*old use* or *humorous*) a woman's small bag, usually made of cloth and with a string that can be pulled tight to close it （女用）收口手提包

ret·ina /ˈretɪnə; *NAmE* ˈretənə/ *noun* (*pl.* **ret·inas** or **ret·inae** /-niː/) a layer of TISSUE at the back of the eye that is sensitive to light and sends signals to the brain about what is seen 視網膜 ➲ **VISUAL VOCAB** page V59 ▸ **ret·inal** /ˈretɪnl/ *adj.* [usually before noun]

ret·inue /ˈretɪnjuː; *NAmE* ˈretənuː/ *noun* [C+sing./pl. v.] a group of people who travel with an important person to provide help and support 隨行人員；扈從 **SYN** **entourage**

re·tire 0-w /rɪˈtaɪə(r)/ *verb*
▸ **FROM JOB** 工作 **1** 0-w [I, T] to stop doing your job, especially because you have reached a particular age or because you are ill/sick; to tell sb they must stop doing their job （令）退職；（使）退休：**~ (from sth)** *She was forced to retire early from teaching because of ill health.* 她由於身體不好而被迫早早地從教學崗位上退休。◇ *The company's official retiring age is 65.* 公司正式的退休年齡為 65 歲。◇ **~ to sth** *My dream is to retire to a villa in France.* 我的夢想是退休後在法國住上一棟別墅。◇ **~ as sth** *He has no plans to retire as editor of the magazine.* 他還不打算從雜誌編輯的位子上退休。◇ **~ sb** *She was retired on medical grounds.* 她由於健康原因被安排退休了。
▸ **IN SPORT** 體育運動 **2** [I] to stop competing during a game, race, etc., usually because you are injured （因傷）退出（比賽等）：**~ (from sth)** *She fell badly, spraining her ankle, and had to retire.* 她摔得很重，扭傷了腳踝，只好退出比賽。◇ **+ adj.** *He retired hurt in the first five minutes of the game.* 比賽才開始五分鐘，他就因傷退場。
▸ **FROM/TO A PLACE** 地點 **3** [I] (*formal*) to leave a place, especially to go somewhere quieter or more private 離開（尤指去僻靜處）：*The jury retired to consider the evidence.* 陪審團退庭對證據進行評判。◇ **~ to sth** *After dinner he likes to retire to his study.* 晚飯後，他喜歡躲到書房裏去。
▸ **OF ARMY** 軍隊 **4** [I] (*formal*) to move back from a battle in order to organize your soldiers in a different way 撤離，撤退（以進行休整）
▸ **GO TO BED** 睡覺 **5** [I] (*literary*) to go to bed 睡覺；就寢：*I retired late that evening.* 那天晚上我睡得晚。
▸ **IN BASEBALL** 棒球 **6** [T] **~ sb** to make a player or team have to stop their turn at BATTING 使（擊球員、擊球方）出局：*He retired twelve batters in a row.* 他一連使十二個擊球手出局。

re·tired 0-w /rɪˈtaɪəd; *NAmE* rɪˈtaɪərd/ *adj.* having retired from work 已退休的；已退職的：*a retired doctor* 退休醫生 ◇ *Dad is retired now.* 爸爸現在已經退休了。

re·tir·ee /rɪˌtaɪəˈriː/ *noun* (*NAmE*) a person who has stopped working because of their age 退休人員；退休者

re·tire·ment 0-w /rɪˈtaɪəmənt; *NAmE* -ˈtaɪərm-/ *noun*
1 0-w [U, C] the fact of stopping work because you have reached a particular age; the time when you do this 退休；退職；退休年齡：*At 60, he was now approaching retirement.* 他 60 歲了，就要退休了。◇ *Susan is going to* ***take early retirement*** (= retire before the usual age). 蘇珊要提前退休。◇ *retirement age* 退休年齡 ◇ *a retirement pension* 退休金 ➲ **COLLOCATIONS** at JOB **2** 0-w [U, sing.] the period of your life after you have stopped work at a particular age 退休生活：*to provide for retirement* 為退休生活作準備 ◇ *We all wish you a long and happy retirement.* 我們大家祝願你的退休生活長久而幸福。◇ *Up to a third of one's life is now being spent* ***in retirement.*** 現在人們一生中能有三分之一的時間過退休生活。 ➲ **COLLOCATIONS** at AGE **3** 0-w [U] **~ (from sth)** the act of stopping a particular type of work, especially in sport, politics, etc. （尤指從體育、政治等方面的）退出，引退，退職：*He announced his retirement from football.* 他宣佈退出足球運動。◇ *She* ***came out of retirement*** *to win two gold*

R

medals at the championships. 她復出後在錦標賽上贏得了兩枚金牌。

re'tirement home (*BrE* also **,old 'people's home**) *noun* a place where old people live and are cared for 養老院；敬老院

re'tirement plan *noun* (*NAmE*) = PENSION PLAN

re·tir·ing /rɪ'taɪərɪŋ/ *adj.* preferring not to spend time with other people 不愛與人交往的 SYN **shy**: *a quiet, retiring man* 話少而又靦腆的男子

re·told *past tense, past part.* of RETELL

re·tool /ˌriː'tuːl/ *verb* **1** [T, I] **~ (sth)** to replace or change the machines or equipment in a factory so that it can produce new or better goods 更換，重新裝配（機器設備） **2** [T] **~ sth** (*NAmE, informal*) to organize sth in a new or different way 重新安排；重組

re·tort /rɪ'tɔːt; *NAmE* rɪ'tɔːrt/ *verb, noun*

■ *verb* to reply quickly to a comment, in an angry, offended or humorous way（生氣或幽默地）反駁，回嘴：**+ speech** *'Don't be ridiculous!' Pat retorted angrily.* "別荒唐了！"帕特生氣地回答道。◇ **~ that ...** *Sam retorted that it was my fault as much as his.* 薩姆反駁說我和他同樣有錯。

■ *noun* **1** a quick, angry or humorous reply（生氣或幽默的）回應，反駁 SYN **rejoinder, riposte**: *She bit back (= stopped herself from making) a sharp retort.* 她克制住了自己，沒有尖刻地反駁。 **2** a closed bottle with a long narrow bent SPOUT that is used in a laboratory for heating chemicals 曲頸甑；曲頸瓶；蒸餾器 ➲ VISUAL VOCAB page V70

re·touch /ˌriː'tʌtʃ/ *verb* **~ sth** to make small changes to a picture or photograph so that it looks better 修飾，修整（圖片或照片等）

re·trace /rɪ'treɪs/ *verb* **1 ~ sth** to go back along exactly the same path or route that you have come along 沿原路返回；折回：*She turned around and began to* ***retrace her steps*** *towards the house.* 她轉身沿原路向那棟房子走去。 **2 ~ sth** to make the same trip that sb else has made in the past 重走（別人走過的路線）：*They are hoping to retrace the epic voyage of Christopher Columbus.* 他們期待着沿哥倫布的壯麗航程進行一次航行。 **3 ~ sth** to find out what sb has done or where they have been 追溯；找出；回顧：*Detectives are trying to retrace her movements on the night she disappeared.* 偵探試圖查出她失踪當晚的行踪。

re·tract /rɪ'trækt/ *verb* **1** [T] **~ sth** (*formal*) to say that sth you have said earlier is not true or correct or that you did not mean it 撤銷，收回（說過的話）：*He made a false confession which he later retracted.* 他作了假供詞，後來又翻供。◇ *They tried to persuade me to retract my words.* 他們試圖說服我收回我的話。 **2** [T] **~ sth** (*formal*) to refuse to keep an agreement, a promise, etc. 撤回，收回（協議、承諾等）：*to retract an offer* 撤銷建議 **3** [I, T] (*technical* 術語) to move back into the main part of sth; to pull sth back into the main part of sth 縮回；拉回：*The animal retracted into its shell.* 這隻動物縮回到自己的殼裏。◇ **~ sth** *The undercarriage was fully retracted.* 起落架被完全收起。

re·tract·able /rɪ'træktəbl/ *adj.* that can be moved or pulled back into the main part of sth 可縮進的；可拉回的：*a knife with a retractable blade* 彈簧刀

re·trac·tion /rɪ'trækʃn/ *noun* (*formal*) **1** [C] a statement saying that sth you previously said or wrote is not true 撤銷；收回：*He demanded a full retraction of the allegations against him.* 他要求完全收回針對他的言論。 **2** [U] (*technical* 術語) the act of pulling sth back (= of retracting it) 收回；拉回：*the retraction of a cat's claws* 貓爪子的回縮

re·train /ˌriː'treɪn/ *verb* [I, T] to learn, or to teach sb, a new type of work, a new skill, etc.（接受）重新培養，再教育，再培訓：**~ (sb) (as sth)** *She retrained as a teacher.* 她接受了教師再培訓。◇ **~ sb to do sth** *Staff have been retrained to use the new technology.* 為使員工學會運用新技術，對他們進行了再培訓。 ▶ **re·train·ing** *noun* [U]

re·tread /'riːtred/ *noun* **1** a tyre made by putting a new rubber surface on an old tyre 翻新的舊輪胎 **2** (*NAmE, disapproving*) a book, film/movie, song, etc. that contains ideas that have been used before（書籍、電影、歌曲等的）翻版

re·treat /rɪ'triːt/ *verb, noun*

■ *verb*

▸ FROM DANGER/DEFEAT 過險；失敗 **1** [I] to move away from a place or an enemy because you are in danger or because you have been defeated 退卻；撤退：*The army was forced to retreat after suffering heavy losses.* 部隊因傷亡慘重被迫撤退。◇ *We retreated back down the mountain.* 我們從山上撤了下來。OPP **advance**

▸ MOVE AWAY/BACK 離開；退後 **2** [I] to move away or back 離開；離去；退去；後退 SYN **recede**: *He watched her retreating figure.* 他看着她的身影漸漸遠去。◇ *The flood waters slowly retreated.* 洪水慢慢地消退。

▸ CHANGE DECISION 改變決定 **3** [I] **+ adv./prep.** to change your mind about sth because of criticism or because a situation has become too difficult（由於受到批評或遇到極大困難）改變主意，退縮 SYN **back off**: *The government had retreated from its pledge to reduce class sizes.* 政府已經改變了縮小班級規模的承諾。

▸ TO QUIET PLACE 到僻靜處 **4** [I] (**+ adv./prep.**) to escape to a place that is quieter or safer 隱退；逃避；躲避 SYN **retire**: *Bored with the conversation, she retreated to her bedroom.* 她厭倦了這樣的交談，躲進了自己的卧室。◇ (*figurative*) *He retreated into a world of fantasy.* 他遁入了幻想世界。

▸ FINANCE 金融 **5** [I] **+ noun** to lose value 跌價：*Share prices retreated 45p to 538p.* 這股票價格下跌 45 便士，降到了 538 便士。

■ *noun*

▸ FROM DANGER/DEFEAT 過險；失敗 **1** [C, usually sing., U] a movement away from a place or an enemy because of danger or defeat 撤退；退卻：*Napoleon's retreat from Moscow* 拿破崙從莫斯科的撤退 ◇ *The army was* ***in full retreat*** (= retreating very quickly). 部隊全線撤退。◇ *to* ***sound the retreat*** (= to give a loud signal for an army to move away) 發出撤退信號 ➲ COLLOCATIONS at WAR

▸ ESCAPE 逃跑 **2** [C, usually sing., U] **~ (from/into sth)** an act of trying to escape from a particular situation to one that you think is safer or more pleasant 逃避；退避；躲避 SYN **escape**: *Is watching television a retreat from reality?* 看電視是對現實的一種逃避嗎？

▸ CHANGE OF DECISION 改變決定 **3** [C, usually sing.] an act of changing a decision because of criticism or because a situation has become too difficult（由於批評或環境過於惡劣）改變決定，退縮：*The Senator made an embarrassing retreat from his earlier position.* 這位參議員很尷尬地改變了他早先的立場。

▸ QUIET PLACE 安靜的地方 **4** [C] a quiet, private place that you go to in order to get away from your usual life 僻靜處；隱居處：*a country retreat* 鄉間幽靜的住所 **5** [U, C] a period of time when sb stops their usual activities and goes to a quiet place for prayer and thought; an organized event when people can do this 靜修期間（或活動）：*He went into retreat and tried to resolve the conflicts within himself.* 他去靜修並試圖調節自己內心的矛盾。◇ *to go on a Buddhist retreat* 去參加佛教的靜修 IDM see BEAT *v.*

re·trench /rɪ'trentʃ/ *verb* **1** [I] (*formal*) (of a business, government, etc. 企業、政府等) to spend less money; to reduce costs 節約；緊縮開支 **2** [T] **~ sb** (*AustralE, NZE, SAfrE*) to tell sb that they cannot continue working for you 縮減（人員） ➲ COLLOCATIONS at UNEMPLOYMENT ▶ **re·trench·ment** *noun* [U, C]: *a period of retrenchment* 開支緊縮時期

re·trial /ˌriː'traɪəl; 'riːtraɪəl/ *noun* [usually sing.] a new trial of a person whose criminal offence has already been judged once in court 復審；再審

ret·ri·bu·tion /ˌretrɪ'bjuːʃn/ *noun* [U] **~ (for sth)** (*formal*) severe punishment for sth seriously wrong that sb has done 嚴懲；懲罰；報應：*People are seeking retribution for the latest terrorist outrages.* 人們在設法對恐怖分子最近的暴行進行嚴懲。◇ *fear of divine retribution* (= punishment from God) 對上帝的懲罰的畏懼 ▶ **re·tribu·tive**

/rɪˈtrɪbjətɪv/ *adj.* [usually before noun]：*retributive justice* 因果報應

re·trieval /rɪˈtriːvl/ *noun* [U] **1** (*formal*) the process of getting sth back, especially from a place where it should not be 取回；索回 SYN **recovery**：*The ship was buried, beyond retrieval, at the bottom of the sea.* 船已葬身海底，無法打撈。◇ (*figurative*) *By then the situation was* ***beyond retrieval*** (= impossible to put right). 到那時，局勢已無法挽回。 **2** (*computing* 計) the process of getting back information that is stored on a computer 數據檢索：*methods of* ***information retrieval*** 數據檢索方法

re·trieve /rɪˈtriːv/ *verb* **1** (*formal*) to bring or get sth back, especially from a place where it should not be 取回；索回 SYN **recover**：**~ sth from sb/sth** *She bent to retrieve her comb from the floor.* 她彎腰從地上撿起她的梳子。◇ **~ sth** *The police have managed to retrieve some of the stolen money.* 警方已經追回了部份被盜錢款。 **2** (*computing* 計) to find and get back data or information that has been stored in the memory of a computer 檢索數據：**~ sth from sb/sth** *to retrieve information from the database* 從數據庫檢索資料 ◇ **~ sth** *The program allows you to retrieve items quickly by searching under a keyword.* 這個程序通過關鍵詞進行搜索，能讓你迅速獲取數據項。 **3 ~ sth** to make a bad situation better; to get back sth that was lost 扭轉頹勢；挽回；找回：*You can only* ***retrieve the situation*** *by apologizing.* 你只有道歉才能挽回這個局面。 ▸ **re·triev·able** /rɪˈtriːvəbl/ *adj.* OPP **irretrievable**

re·triever /rɪˈtriːvə(r)/ *noun* a large dog used in hunting to bring back birds that have been shot 尋回犬 ➲ see also GOLDEN RETRIEVER

retro /ˈretrəʊ; *NAmE* -troʊ/ *adj.* using styles or fashions from the recent past （時裝款式等）前不久剛流行過的，再度流行的，回歸的：*the current Seventies retro trend* 當前回歸七十年代的流行趨勢

retro- /ˈretrəʊ; *NAmE* -troʊ/ *prefix* (in nouns, adjectives and adverbs 構成名詞、形容詞和副詞) back or backwards 後；向後：*retrograde* 倒退的 ◇ *retrospectively* 回顧地

retro·active /ˌretrəʊˈæktɪv; *NAmE* -troʊ-/ *adj.* (*formal*) = RETROSPECTIVE *adj.* (2) ▸ **retro·active·ly** *adv.*：*The ruling should be applied retroactively.* 這一裁決應該具有追溯效力。

retro·fit /ˈretrəʊfɪt; *NAmE* -troʊ-/ *verb* (**-tt-**) **~ sth** to put a new piece of equipment into a machine that did not have it when it was built; to provide a machine with a new part, etc. 給機器設備裝配（新部件）；翻新；改型：*Voice recorders were retrofitted into planes already in service.* 錄音設備安在了正在服役的飛機上。◇ *They retrofitted the plane with improved seating.* 他們在飛機上安裝了經過改良的座椅。 ▸ **retro·fit** *noun*

retro·flex /ˈretrəfleks/ *adj.* **1** (*medical* 醫) (of a part of the body 身體部位) turned backwards 向後彎曲的；後屈的；反曲的 **2** (*phonetics* 語音) (of a speech sound 語音) produced with the end of the tongue turned up against the hard PALATE 捲舌的

retro·grade /ˈretrəgreɪd/ *adj.* (*formal, disapproving*) (of an action 行為) making a situation worse or returning to how sth was in the past 倒退的；退化的；退步的：*The closure of the factory is* ***a retrograde step.*** 工廠的關閉是一大退步。

retro·gres·sive /ˌretrəˈgresɪv/ *adj.* (*formal, disapproving*) returning to old-fashioned ideas or methods instead of making progress 倒退的；退化的 OPP **progressive**

retro·spect /ˈretrəspekt/ *noun*
IDM **in retrospect** thinking about a past event or situation, often with a different opinion of it from the one you had at the time 回顧；回想；追溯往事：*In retrospect, I think that I was wrong.* 回首往事，我覺得當時我錯了。◇ *The decision seems extremely odd, in retrospect.* 回想起來，這個決定顯得極其荒謬。

retro·spec·tion /ˌretrəˈspekʃn/ *noun* [U] (*formal*) thinking about past events or situations 回顧；回憶

retro·spect·ive /ˌretrəˈspektɪv/ *adj., noun*
■ ***adj.*** **1** thinking about or connected with sth that happened in the past 回顧的；涉及以往的 **2** (also *less frequent, formal* **retro·active**) (of a new law or decision 新的法律或決定) intended to take effect from a particular date in the past rather than from the present date 有追溯效力的；溯及既往的：*retrospective legislation* 有追溯效力的法律 ◇ *retrospective pay awards* 有追溯效力的加薪 ▸ **retro·spect·ive·ly** *adv.*：*She wrote retrospectively about her childhood.* 她追述了自己的童年生活。◇ *The new rule will be applied retrospectively.* 新的規定將具有追溯效力。
■ ***noun*** a public exhibition of the work that an artist has done in the past, showing how his or her work has developed （藝術家作品）回顧展

retro·virus /ˈretrəʊvaɪrəs; *NAmE* ˈretroʊ-/ *noun* any of a group of viruses that includes HIV. Retroviruses multiply by making changes to DNA. 反轉錄病毒，逆轉錄病毒（如人類免疫缺損病毒） ➲ see also ANTIRETROVIRAL

retry /ˌriːˈtraɪ/ *verb* (**re·tries, re·try·ing, re·tried, re·tried**) **1** [T] **~ sb/sth** to examine a person or case again in court 復審；重新審理 **2** [I] to make another attempt to do sth, especially on a computer （尤指在計算機上）重試

ret·sina /retˈsiːnə/ *noun* [U, C] a type of red or white wine from Greece that is given a special flavour with RESIN (1) 松香味希臘葡萄酒

re·turn 0-w /rɪˈtɜːn; *NAmE* rɪˈtɜːrn/ *verb, noun*
■ ***verb***
▸ **COME/GO BACK** 回來；回去 **1** 0-w [I] to come or go back from one place to another 回來；回去；返回：*I waited a long time for him to return.* 我等他回來等了很長時間。◇ **~ (to ...) (from ...)** *She's returning to Australia tomorrow after six months in Europe.* 她在歐洲逗留了六個月，明天要返回澳大利亞了。◇ *I returned from work to find the house empty.* 我下班回來，發現屋裏空無一人。◇ *When did she return home from the trip?* 她是什麼時候旅行回來的？
▸ **BRING/GIVE BACK** 拿回；歸還 **2** 0-w [T] to bring, give, put or send sth back to sb/sth 帶回；送回；放回；退還：**~ sb/sth to sb/sth** *We had to return the hairdryer to the store because it was faulty.* 我們不得不將吹風機退回商店，因為它有殘損。◇ *I must return some books to the library.* 我得把一些書還給圖書館。◇ **~ sth** *Don't forget to return my pen!* 別忘了把鋼筆還給我！◇ **~ sb/sth + adj.** *I returned the letter unopened.* 我原封不動地將信退了回去。
▸ **OF FEELING/QUALITY** 感覺；特質 **3** 0-w [I] to come back again 恢復；重現 SYN **reappear, resurface**：*The following day the pain returned.* 第二天又疼起來了。◇ *Her suspicions returned when things started going missing again.* 發現又有東西丟失的時候，她又懷疑起來。
▸ **TO PREVIOUS SUBJECT/ACTIVITY** 先前的話題／活動 **4** 0-w [I] **~ (to sth)** to start discussing a subject you were discussing earlier, or doing an activity you were doing earlier 重提；重新開始做：*He returns to this topic later in the report.* 他在報告中後來又提到這個話題。◇ *She looked up briefly then returned to her sewing.* 她抬頭看了一眼，又接着做她的針線活兒。◇ *The doctor may allow her to* ***return to work*** *next week.* 醫生也許會允許她下週回去上班。
▸ **TO PREVIOUS STATE** 先前的狀態 **5** 0-w [I] **~ to sth** to go back to a previous state 恢復；回復：*Train services have* ***returned to normal*** *after the strike.* 罷工過後，列車運營已經恢復正常。
▸ **DO/GIVE THE SAME** 回報 **6** [T] **~ sth** to do or give sth to sb because they have done or given the same to you first; to have the same feeling about sb that they have about you 回報；回應：*to return a favour/greeting/stare* 報恩；回應問候；回瞪一眼 ◇ *She phoned him several times but he was too busy to* ***return her call.*** 她給他打了幾次電話，但他太忙，不能給她回電話。◇ *It's time we* ***returned their invitation*** (= invite them to sth as they invited us to sth first). 該我們回請他們了。◇ *He did not return her love.* 他沒有回報她的愛。◇ *'You were both wonderful!' 'So were you!' we said,* ***returning the compliment.*** "你們倆太棒了！" "你也一樣啊！" 我們

R

也稱讚道。◇ *to* ***return fire*** (= to shoot at sb who is shooting at you) 用槍炮還擊

▸ **IN TENNIS** 網球 **7** [T] **~ sth** to hit the ball back to your opponent during a game 回擊；擊回：*to return a service/shot* 擊回發球／抽球

▸ **A VERDICT** 裁決 **8** [T] **~ a verdict** to give a decision about sth in court 宣告（裁決）：*The jury returned a verdict of not guilty.* 陪審團宣告了無罪的判決。

▸ **ELECT POLITICIAN** 選政治人物 **9** [T, usually passive] **~ sb** (**to sth**) | **~ sb** (**as sth**) (*BrE*) to elect sb to a political position 選舉；選出；推舉

▸ **PROFIT/LOSS** 利潤；損失 **10** [T] **~ sth** (*business* 商) to give or produce a particular amount of money as a profit or loss 帶來，產生（利潤或損失）：*to return a high rate of interest* 有很高的利息回報 ◇ *Last year the company returned a loss of £157 million.* 去年，公司的虧損達 1.57 億英鎊。

■ ***noun***

▸ **COMING BACK** 回來 **1** ⊶ [sing.] **~** (**to** …) (**from** …) the action of arriving in or coming back to a place that you were in before 回來；歸來；返回：*He was met by his brother* ***on his return*** *from Italy.* 他從意大利回來的時候，是他弟弟去接他的。◇ *I saw the play on its return to Broadway.* 這部戲重回百老匯時我看過了。◇ *on the* ***return flight/journey/trip*** 在返回的航班／旅程／路程上

▸ **GIVING/SENDING BACK** 歸還；退回 **2** ⊶ [U, sing.] the action of giving, putting or sending sth/sb back 歸還；放回；退回：*We would appreciate the prompt return of books to the library.* 若能及時將圖書歸還給圖書館，我們將不勝感激。◇ *The judge ordered the return of the child to his mother.* 法官命令將孩子送還他的母親。◇ *Write your* ***return address*** (= the address that a reply should be sent to) *on the back of the envelope.* 請在信封的背面寫明回信地址。

▸ **OF FEELING/STATE** 感覺；狀況 **3** ⊶ [sing.] **~** (**of sth**) the situation when a feeling or state that has not been experienced for some time starts again 重現；恢復 SYN **reappearance**：*the return of spring* 春之歸來 ◇ *a return of my doubts* 我的疑心又起

▸ **TO PREVIOUS SITUATION/ACTIVITY** 先前的情況／活動 **4** ⊶ [sing.] **~ to sth** the action of going back to an activity or a situation that you used to do or be in 恢復；返回：*his return to power* 他的重新掌權 ◇ *They appealed for* ***a return to work*** (= after a strike). 他們呼籲復工。

▸ **PROFIT** 利益 **5** [U, C] the amount of profit that you get from sth 回報；收益；利潤 SYN **earnings, yield**：*a high* ***rate of return*** *on capital* 資本的高回報率 ◇ *farmers seeking to improve returns from their crops* 尋求提高農作物利潤的農民

▸ **OFFICIAL REPORT** 正式報告 **6** [C] an official report or statement that gives particular information to the government or another body 報告；陳述；申報：*census returns* 人口普查報告 ◇ *election returns* (= the number of votes for each candidate in an election) 選舉結果報告 ➲ see also TAX RETURN

▸ **TICKET** 票 **7** [C] (*BrE*) = RETURN TICKET：*'Brighton, please.' 'Single or return?'* "我要一張到布賴頓的票。" "單程的還是往返的？" ◇ *A return is cheaper than two singles.* 一張往返票比兩張單程票便宜。◇ *the return fare to London* 到倫敦的往返票價 ➲ see also DAY RETURN **8** [C] a ticket for the theatre or a sports game that was bought by sb but is given back to be sold again 退票

▸ **ON COMPUTER** 計算機 **9** [U] (also **re'turn key** [C]) the button that you press on a computer when you reach the end of an instruction, or to begin a new line 返回鍵；回車鍵；結束鍵：*To exit this option, press return.* 要退出這個選項，就按返回鍵。

▸ **IN TENNIS** 網球 **10** [C] (in TENNIS and some other sports 網球和其他一些運動) the action of hitting the ball, etc. back to your opponent 擊回球：*a powerful* ***return of serve*** 有力的迎擊發球

IDM **by re'turn (of 'post)** (*BrE*) using the next available post; as soon as possible 由下一班郵遞；儘快：*Please reply by return of post.* 請即賜覆。 **in re'turn (for sth)** **1** ⊶ as a way of thanking sb or paying them for sth they have done 作為（對…的）回報：*Can I buy you lunch in return for your help?* 感謝你幫忙，我請你吃午飯好嗎？ **2** ⊶ as a response or reaction to sth 作為回應：*I asked her opinion, but she just asked me a question in return.* 我徵求她的意見，她卻只是反問了我一句。➲ more at HAPPY, POINT *n.*, SALE *n.*

Synonyms 同義詞辨析

return

come back • go back • get back • turn back

These words all mean to come or go back from one place to another. 以上各詞均含回來、回去、返回之意。

return to come or go back from one place to another 指回來、回去、返回：*I waited a long time for him to return.* 我等他回來等了很長時間。NOTE **Return** is slightly more formal than the other words in this group, and is used more often in writing or formal speech. * return 較本組其他的詞稍為正式，較常用於書面語或正式場合中。

come back to return 指回來、返回 NOTE **Come back** is usually used from the point of view of the person or place that sb returns to. * come back 通常指回到說話人處或所在的地方：*Come back and visit again soon!* 請早點兒再回來探訪！

go back to return to the place you recently or originally came from or that you have been to before 指回去、返回 NOTE **Go back** is usually used from the point of view of the person who is returning. * go back 通常是從要返回者的角度來說：*Do you ever want to go back to China?* 你想回中國去嗎？

get back to arrive back somewhere, especially at your home or the place where you are staying 指返回、回去，尤指回家：*What time did you get back last night?* 你昨晚是什麼時候回家的？

turn back to return the way that you came, especially because sth stops you from continuing 指原路返回、往回走，尤指因某事阻止而不能繼續前進：*The weather got so bad that we had to turn back.* 天氣變得非常惡劣，我們不得不循原路折回。

PATTERNS

- to return/come back/go back/get back **to/from/with** sth
- to return/come back/go back/get back/turn back **again**
- to return/come back/go back/get back **home/to work**
- to return/come back/get back **safely**

re·turn·able /rɪˈtɜːnəbl; *NAmE* -ˈtɜːrn-/ *adj.* **1** (*formal*) that can or must be given back after a period of time 可退還的；應歸還的；必須交還的：*A returnable deposit is payable on arrival.* 抵達時應支付可退還押金。◇ *The application form is returnable not later than 7th June.* 申請表應不遲於 6 月 7 日交回。 **2** (of bottles and containers 瓶子和容器) that can be taken back to a shop/store in order to be used again 可退回的；可回收的 OPP **non-returnable**

re·turn·ee /rɪˌtɜːˈniː; *NAmE* rɪˌtɜːrˈniː/ *noun* [usually pl.] (*especially NAmE*) a person who returns to their own country, after living in another country 回國的人；歸國者

re·turn·er /rɪˈtɜːnə(r); *NAmE* -ˈtɜːrn-/ *noun* (*BrE*) a person who goes back to work after not working for a long time 重返工作崗位者；再就業者

re'turning officer *noun* (*BrE*) an official in a particular area who is responsible for arranging an election and announcing the result 地方選舉監察官

re,turn 'match (also **re,turn 'game**) *noun* (*especially BrE*) a second match or game between the same two

R

players or teams（相同對手間的）第二回合比賽，再度交鋒

re,turn 'ticket (also **re·turn**) (both *BrE*) (*NAmE* **,round-trip 'ticket**) *noun* a ticket for a journey to a place and back again 往返票

re,turn 'visit *noun* a trip to a place that you have been to once before, or a trip to see sb who has already come to see you 重遊；回訪：*This hotel is worth a return visit.* 這家旅店值得再次光顧。◇ *The US president* ***is making a return visit*** *to Moscow.* 美國總統正在對莫斯科進行回訪。

re·unify /ˌriː'juːnɪfaɪ/ *verb* (**re·uni·fies**, **re·uni·fy·ing**, **re·uni·fied**, **re·uni·fied**) [often passive] **~ sth** to join together two or more regions or parts of a country so that they form a single political unit again 重新統一 ▸ **re·uni·fi·ca·tion** /ˌriːˌjuːnɪfɪ'keɪʃn/ *noun* [U]：*the reunification of Germany* 德國的重新統一

re·union /riː'juːniən/ *noun* **1** [C] a social occasion or party attended by a group of people who have not seen each other for a long time 重逢；團聚；聚會：*a family reunion* 家人團聚 ◇ *the school's annual reunion* 一年一度的校友聯歡會 ◇ *a reunion of the class of '85* * 85 屆同學聚會 **2** [C, U] **~ (with sb)** | **~ (between A and B)** the act of people coming together after they have been apart for some time 相聚；團圓：*an emotional reunion between mother and son* 母子團圓的激動場面 ◇ *Christmas is a time of reunion.* 聖誕節是團聚的日子。**3** [U] the action of becoming a single group or organization again 重新結合；再度聯合：*the reunion of the Church of England with the Church of Rome* 英國國教和羅馬天主教的再度聯合

re·unite /ˌriːjuː'naɪt/ *verb* [T, I] **1** [usually passive] to bring two or more people together again after they have been separated for a long time; to come together again（使）重逢，再次相聚：**~ A with/and B** *Last night she was reunited with her children.* 昨天晚上，她和她的子女再度團聚。◇ **~ (sb)** *The family was reunited after the war.* 戰爭過後，一家人又相聚了。◇ *There have been rumours that the band will reunite for a world tour.* 有傳言説這個樂隊將再度聚集作一次環球演出。 **2 ~ (sth)** to join together again separate areas or separate groups within an organization, a political party, etc.; to come together again（使）再結合，再聯合：*As leader, his main aim is to reunite the party.* 作為領導，他的主要目標就是要使黨內各派團結起來。

re·us·able /ˌriː'juːzəbl/ *adj.* that can be used again 可重複使用的；可再次使用的：*reusable plastic bottles* 可重複使用的塑料瓶

reuse /ˌriː'juːz/ *verb* **~ sth** to use sth again 再次使用；重複使用：*Please reuse your envelopes.* 信封請重複利用。▸ **reuse** /ˌriː'juːs/ *noun* [U]

Rev. (*BrE* also **Revd**) *abbr.* (used before a name) REVEREND（尊稱神職人員）尊敬的，可敬的：*Rev. Jesse Jackson* 尊敬的傑西 • 傑克遜牧師

rev /rev/ *verb, noun*

■ ***verb*** (**-vv-**) [T, I] **~ (sth) (up)** when you **rev** an engine or it **revs**, it runs quickly（使）快速運轉：*The taxi driver revved up his engine.* 出租車司機把發動機發動起來。◇ *I could hear the car revving outside.* 我聽到外面汽車發動的聲音。

■ ***noun*** (*informal*) a complete turn of an engine, used when talking about an engine's speed（發動機的轉速）一次旋轉 SYN **revolution**：*4 000 revs per minute* 每分鐘 4 000 轉 ◇ *The needle on the rev counter soared.* 轉數指針快速上升。➲ VISUAL VOCAB page V52

re·value /ˌriː'væljuː/ *verb* **1** [T] **~ sth** to estimate the value of sth again, especially giving it a higher value 重新評價，重新評估（尤指給予更高評價） **2** [T, I] **~ (sth)** to increase the value of the money of a country when it is exchanged for the money of another country 提高（貨幣的）兑換價；使（貨幣）升值：*The yen is to be revalued.* 日元的兑換價將調高。OPP **devalue** ▸ **re·valu·ation** /ˌriːˌvælju'eɪʃn/ *noun* [U, C, usually sing.]：*the revaluation of the pound* 英鎊的升值

re·vamp /ˌriː'væmp/ *verb* **~ sth** to make changes to the form of sth, usually to improve its appearance 改變；修改；（通常指）改進外觀，翻新 ▸ **re·vamp** /'riːvæmp/ *noun* [sing.]

re·vanch·ism /rɪ'væntʃɪzəm; -'vænʃ-/ *noun* [U] a policy of attacking sb who has attacked you, especially by a country in order to get back land（尤指國家為收復失地的）復仇主義

re·veal 0➡ AW /rɪ'viːl/ *verb*

1 0➡ to make sth known to sb 揭示；顯示；透露 SYN **disclose**：**~ sth (to sb)** *to reveal a secret* 泄露一條秘密 ◇ *Details of the murder were revealed by the local paper.* 地方報紙披露了謀殺的細節。◇ **~ (that) ...** *The report reveals (that) the company made a loss of £20 million last year.* 報告顯示，公司去年虧損 2 000 萬英鎊。◇ **it is revealed that ...** *It was revealed that important evidence had been suppressed.* 據透露，重要的證據被隱瞞了。◇ **~ how, what, etc. ...** *Officers could not reveal how he died.* 警察們不能透露他的死因。◇ **~ sb/sth to be/have sth** *Salted peanuts were recently revealed to be the nation's favourite snack.* 最近發現，鹹味花生是該國最受人喜愛的小吃。➲ LANGUAGE BANK at EVIDENCE **2** 0➡ to show sth that previously could not be seen 顯出；露出；展示 SYN **display**：**~ sth** *He laughed, revealing a line of white teeth.* 他笑了起來，露出一排潔白的牙齒。◇ *The door opened to reveal a cosy little room.* 房門打開，一間温暖舒適的小屋展現在眼前。◇ **~ yourself** *She crouched in the dark, too frightened to reveal herself.* 她蜷縮在黑暗中，嚇得不敢露面。➲ see also REVELATION (1), (2), REVELATORY

re,vealed re'ligion *noun* [U, C] religion that is based on a belief that God has shown himself 啟示宗教，天啟教（以神的啟示為信仰基礎）

re·veal·ing AW /rɪ'viːlɪŋ/ *adj.* **1** giving you interesting information that you did not know before 揭露真相的；發人深省的：*The document provided a revealing insight into the government's priorities.* 這份文件使人看出政府的輕重緩急是怎樣安排的。◇ *The answers the children gave were extremely revealing.* 孩子們所給的答案極其發人深省。 **2** (of clothes 衣服) allowing more of sb's body to be seen than usual 暴露的；使身體過分裸露的：*a revealing blouse* 暴露的女式襯衫 ▸ **re·veal·ing·ly** *adv.*：*He spoke revealingly about his problems.* 他坦率地談論他的問題。

re·veille /rɪ'væli; *NAmE* 'revəli/ *noun* [U] a tune that is played to wake soldiers in the morning; the time when it is played（軍隊的）起牀號，起牀時間

revel /'revl/ *verb, noun*

■ ***verb*** (**-ll-**, *US* **-l-**) [I] to spend time enjoying yourself in a noisy, enthusiastic way 狂歡作樂 SYN **make merry**

PHR V **'revel in sth** to enjoy sth very much 陶醉於；着迷於；縱情於：*She was clearly revelling in all the attention.* 顯而易見，她對大家的關注感到十分高興。◇ **~ doing sth** *Some people seem to revel in annoying others.* 有些人好像總是喜歡惹人煩。

■ ***noun*** [usually pl.] (*literary*) noisy celebrations 狂歡；喧鬧的慶典

reve·la·tion AW /ˌrevə'leɪʃn/ *noun* **1** [C] **~ (about/concerning sth)** | **~ (that ...)** a fact that people are made aware of, especially one that has been secret and is surprising 被暴露的真相；被曝光的秘聞 SYN **disclosure**：***startling/sensational revelations*** *about her private life* 對她的私生活令人吃驚的／譁眾取寵的揭露 **2** [U] **~ (of sth)** the act of making people aware of sth that has been secret 披露；揭露 SYN **disclosure**：*The company's financial problems followed the revelation of a major fraud scandal.* 重大的欺詐醜聞被揭露之後，公司隨之出現了財政問題。 **3** [C, U] something that is considered to be a sign or message from God（上帝的）啟示 ➲ COLLOCATIONS at RELIGION ➲ see also REVEAL (1)

IDM **come as/be a revelation (to sb)** to be a completely new or surprising experience; to be different from what was expected 讓人大開眼界；令人耳目一新；出乎意料

rev·ela·tory /ˌrevə'leɪtəri; *NAmE* 'revələtɔːri/ *adj.* (*formal*) making people aware of sth that they did not know before 啟發性的；啟迪人的：*a revelatory insight* 有啟發作用的見解 ➲ see also REVEAL (2)

R

rev·el·ler (US **rev·el·er**) /ˈrevələ(r)/ *noun* a person who is having fun in a noisy way, usually with a group of other people and often after drinking alcohol （醉酒）狂歡者

rev·el·ry /ˈrevlri/ *noun* [U] (also **rev·el·ries** [pl.]) noisy fun, usually involving a lot of eating and drinking 狂歡作樂 SYN **festivity**, **merrymaking**：*We could hear sounds of revelry from next door.* 我們聽到隔壁縱飲狂歡的聲音。◇ *New Year revelries* 新年狂歡

re·venge /rɪˈvendʒ/ *noun, verb*

■ **noun** [U] **1** something that you do in order to make sb suffer because they have made you suffer 報復；報仇：*He swore to* ***take*** *(****his****)* ***revenge on*** *his political enemies.* 他發誓要報復他的政敵。◇ *She is* ***seeking revenge for*** *the murder of her husband.* 丈夫遭到謀殺，她在尋找機會報仇。◇ *The bombing was* ***in revenge for*** *the assassination.* 爆炸事件是對暗殺行為的報復。◇ *an act of revenge* 報復行動 ◇ ***revenge attacks/killings*** 報復性的進攻／殺戮 **2** (*sport* 體) the defeat of a person or team that defeated you in a previous game （曾經失敗一方的）雪恥，打敗對手：*The team wanted to get revenge for their defeat earlier in the season.* 球隊想要為這個賽季早先的失敗雪恥。

■ **verb**

PHR V **re'venge yourself on sb | be re'venged on sb** (*literary*) to punish or hurt sb because they have made you suffer 報復；向（某人）報仇：*She vowed to be revenged on them all.* 她發誓一定要報復他們所有的人。➲ note at AVENGE

rev·enue AW /ˈrevənjuː; *NAmE* -nuː/ *noun* [U] (also **revenues** [pl.]) the money that a government receives from taxes or that an organization, etc. receives from its business 財政收入；稅收收入；收益 SYN **receipts**：*a shortfall in tax revenue* 稅收收入不足 ◇ *a slump in oil revenues* 石油收入的下跌 ◇ *The company's annual revenues rose by 30%.* 公司的年收入增加了30%。➲ COLLOCATIONS at BUSINESS ➲ see also INLAND REVENUE

ˌRevenue and ˈCustoms *noun* = HM REVENUE AND CUSTOMS

re·verb /ˈriːvɜːb; rɪˈvɜːb; *NAmE* -vɜːrb/ *noun* [U] a sound effect that can be adjusted by electronic means to give music more or less of an ECHO 混響（效果）

R

re·ver·ber·ate /rɪˈvɜːbəreɪt; *NAmE* -ˈvɜːrb-/ *verb* **1** [I] (of a sound 聲音) to be repeated several times as it is reflected off different surfaces 回響；迴盪 SYN **echo**：*Her voice reverberated around the hall.* 她的聲音在大廳裏迴盪。**2** [I] **~ (with/to sth)** (of a place 地方) to seem to shake because of a loud noise （由於強大的噪音）震顫，搖晃：*The hall reverberated with the sound of music and dancing.* 音樂和舞蹈的聲音使得整個大廳似乎都在震顫。**3** [I] (*formal*) to have a strong effect on people for a long time or over a large area 有長久深刻的影響；產生廣泛影響：*Repercussions of the case continue to reverberate through the financial world.* 這件事持續影響着整個金融界。

re·ver·ber·ation /rɪˌvɜːbəˈreɪʃn; *NAmE* -ˌvɜːrb-/ *noun* **1** [C, usually pl., U] a loud noise that continues for some time after it has been produced because of the surfaces around it 回響；回聲；反響 SYN **echo** **2 reverberations** [pl.] the effects of sth that happens, especially unpleasant ones that spread among a large number of people 影響；（尤指）廣泛的消極影響 SYN **repercussion**

re·vere /rɪˈvɪə(r); *NAmE* rɪˈvɪr/ *verb* [usually passive] **~ sb (as sth)** (*formal*) to feel great respect or admiration for sb/sth 尊敬；崇敬 SYN **idolize**

rev·er·ence /ˈrevərəns/ *noun* [U] **~ (for sb/sth)** (*formal*) a feeling of great respect or admiration for sb/sth 尊敬；崇敬：*The poem conveys his deep reverence for nature.* 這首詩表達了他對大自然的深深崇敬之情。

rev·er·end /ˈrevərənd/ *adj.* [only before noun] **Reverend** (*abbr.* **Rev.**) the title of a member of the clergy that is also sometimes used to talk to or about one （尊稱神職人員）尊敬的，可敬的：*the Reverend Charles Dodgson* 尊敬的查爾斯・道奇森牧師 ◇ *Good morning, Reverend.* 早安，神父。➲ see also RIGHT REVEREND

ˌReverend ˈMother *noun* a title of respect used when talking to or about a MOTHER SUPERIOR (= the head of a female religious community) （對女修道院院長的尊稱）可敬的修女

rev·er·ent /ˈrevərənt/ *adj.* (*formal*) showing great respect and admiration 非常尊敬的；深表崇敬的 SYN **respectful** ▸ **rev·er·ent·ly** *adv.*

rev·er·en·tial /ˌrevəˈrenʃl/ *adj.* (*formal*) full of respect or admiration 充滿敬意的；恭敬的；滿懷崇敬的：*His name was always mentioned in almost reverential tones.* 人們每次提起他的名字，語調中幾乎總是充滿了敬意。▸ **rev·er·en·tial·ly** /-ʃəli/ *adv.*：*She lowered her voice reverentially.* 她恭敬地放低了聲音。

rev·erie /ˈrevəri/ *noun* [C, U] (*formal*) a state of thinking about pleasant things, almost as though you are dreaming 幻想；白日夢；夢想 SYN **daydream**：*She was jolted out of her reverie as the door opened.* 門一開就把她從幻想中驚醒。

re·vers /rɪˈvɪə(r); *NAmE* rɪˈvɪr/ *noun* (*pl.* **re·vers** /-ˈvɪəz; *NAmE* -ˈvɪrz/) (*technical* 術語) the edge of a coat, jacket, etc. that is turned back so that you see the opposite side of it, especially at the LAPEL （衣服的）翻邊，翻口；（尤指）翻領

re·ver·sal AW /rɪˈvɜːsl; *NAmE* rɪˈvɜːrsl/ *noun* **1** [C, U] **~ (of sth)** a change of sth so that it is the opposite of what it was 顛倒；徹底轉變；反轉；倒置：*a* ***complete/dramatic/sudden reversal*** *of policy* 政策的全面／劇烈／突然轉變 ◇ *the reversal of a decision* 相反的決定 ◇ *The government suffered a total* ***reversal of fortune(s)*** *last week.* 上星期，政府的命運發生了逆轉。**2** [C] a change from being successful to having problems or being defeated 倒退；逆轉；退步；轉勝為敗：*the team's recent reversal* 球隊最近的失敗 ◇ *The company's financial problems were only a temporary reversal.* 公司的財務問題只是暫時的挫折。**3** [C, U] an exchange of positions or functions between two or more people （位置或功能的）轉換，交換：*It's a complete* ***role reversal/reversal of roles*** (= for example when a husband cares for the house and children while the wife works). 這是一種徹底的角色轉換。

re·verse 0→ AW /rɪˈvɜːs; *NAmE* rɪˈvɜːrs/ *verb, noun, adj.*

■ **verb**

▸ **CHANGE TO OPPOSITE** 轉化為對立面 **1** 0→ [T] **~ sth** to change sth completely so that it is the opposite of what it was before 顛倒；徹底轉變；使完全相反：*to reverse a procedure/process/trend* 徹底改變程序／過程／趨勢 ◇ *The government has failed to reverse the economic decline.* 政府未能扭轉經濟滑坡的趨勢。◇ *It is sometimes possible to arrest or reverse the disease.* 有時可以阻止病情發展或使病情徹底好轉。**2** 0→ [T] **~ sth** to change a previous decision, law, etc. to the opposite one 撤銷，廢除（決定、法律等）SYN **revoke**：*The Court of Appeal reversed the decision.* 上訴法庭撤銷了這項裁決。**3** 0→ [T] **~ sth** to turn sth the opposite way around or change the order of sth around 使反轉；使次序顛倒：*Writing is reversed in a mirror.* 鏡子裏的字是反的。◇ *You should reverse the order of these pages.* 你該把這幾頁的順序顛倒過來。

▸ **EXCHANGE TWO THINGS** 交換 **4** 0→ [T] **~ sth** to exchange the positions or functions of two things 交換（位置或功能）：*It felt as if we had reversed our roles of parent and child.* 感覺就像我們父母和孩子交換了角色。◇ *She used to work for me, but our situations are now reversed.* 過去她為我工作，而現在我們的地位對調了。

▸ **YOURSELF** 自己 **5** [T] **~ yourself (on sth)** (*NAmE*) to admit you were wrong or to stop having a particular position in an argument 承認錯誤；放棄（立場）：*He has reversed himself on a dozen issues.* 他已經不再堅持自己在一系列問題上的立場。

▸ **VEHICLE** 車輛 **6** 0→ [I, T] (*especially BrE*) when a vehicle or its driver **reverses** or the driver **reverses** a vehicle, the vehicle goes backwards （使）倒退行駛；倒車：*He reversed around the corner.* 他倒車轉過拐角。◇ *She reversed into a parking space.* 她將車倒着開進停車位。

◇ *Caution! This truck is reversing.* 小心！卡車在倒車。◇ **~ sth** *Now reverse the car.* 現在倒車。➲ compare BACK *v.* (1)

▸ **TELEPHONE CALL** 打電話 **7** [T] **~ (the) charges** (*BrE*) to make a telephone call that will be paid for by the person you are calling, not by you 打對方付費的電話：*I want to reverse the charges, please.* 勞駕，我想打一個由受話人付費的電話。➲ see also COLLECT *adj.*

■ ***noun***

▸ **OPPOSITE** 相反 **1** **the reverse** [sing.] the opposite of what has just been mentioned 相反的情況（或事物）：*This problem is the reverse of the previous one.* 這個問題和上一個問題相反。◇ *Although I expected to enjoy living in the country, in fact* ***the reverse is true.*** 儘管我原以為會喜歡鄉村生活，但實際情況正好相反。◇ *In the south, the reverse applies.* 在南方，情況相反。◇ *It wasn't easy to persuade her to come—****quite the reverse.*** 說服她過來不容易，實在太難了。

▸ **BACK** 後面 **2** **the reverse** [sing.] the back of a coin, piece of material, piece of paper, etc. 後面；背面；反面

▸ **IN VEHICLE** 車輛 **3** (also **re,verse 'gear**) [U] the machinery in a vehicle used to make it move backwards 倒擋：***Put*** *the car* ***in/into reverse.*** 汽車掛上倒擋。

▸ **LOSS/DEFEAT** 損失；失敗 **4** [C] (*formal*) a loss or defeat; a change from success to failure 損失；失敗；倒退 SYN **setback**：*Property values have suffered another reverse.* 房地產價值再次遭受損失。◇ *a damaging political reverse* 具有破壞性的政治倒退

IDM **in re'verse** in the opposite order or way 反向；相反 SYN **backwards**：*The secret number is my phone number in reverse.* 這個密碼是我的電話號碼的逆序排列。◇ *We did a similar trip to you, but in reverse.* 我們走了和你相似的旅程，但方向相反。 **go/put sth into re'verse** to start to happen or to make sth happen in the opposite way （使）出現逆轉，轉化為對立面：*In 2008 economic growth went into reverse.* * 2008 年，經濟增長發生了逆轉。

■ ***adj.*** [only before noun]

▸ **OPPOSITE** 相反 **1** opposite to what has been mentioned 相反的；反面的；反向的：*to travel in the reverse direction* 向相反方向行進 ◇ *The winners were announced* ***in reverse order*** (= the person in the lowest place was announced first). 獲勝者是按逆序宣佈的。◇ *The experiment had the reverse effect to what was intended.* 實驗的結果與原來的意圖相反。

▸ **BACK** 後面 **2** opposite to the front 背面的；反面的；後面的：*Iron the garment on the reverse side.* 這件衣服要從反面熨。

re,verse-'charge *adj.* a **reverse-charge** telephone call is paid for by the person who receives the call, not by the person who makes it （電話）由受話方付費的，對方付費的 ▸ **re,verse-'charge** *adv.*：*I didn't have any money so I had to call reverse-charge.* 我那時沒錢，所以只好打對方付費電話。

re,verse discrimi'nation *noun* [U] (*disapproving*) the practice or policy of making sure that a particular number of jobs, etc. are given to people from groups that are often treated unfairly because of their race, sex, etc. 反向區別對待，反向歧視，逆向歧視（對因種族、性別等原因遭受歧視的群體在就業等方面給予特別照顧） HELP The term **reverse discrimination** is nearly always used in a disapproving way; to describe this policy in a way that is not necessarily disapproving use **positive discrimination** or **affirmative action**. * reverse discrimination 這個術語幾乎總是用於貶義；不一定含貶義的說法是 positive discrimination 或 affirmative action。

re,verse engi'neering *noun* [U] the copying of another company's product after examining it carefully to find out how it is made 逆向工程，倒序製造（研究另一家公司產品的製造後加以仿製）

re·vers·ible AW /rɪˈvɜːsəbl; *NAmE* -ˈvɜːrs-/ *adj.* **1** (of clothes, materials, etc. 衣服、材料等) that can be turned inside out and worn or used with either side showing 可翻轉的；可兩面穿的；正反兩用的：*a reversible jacket* 可兩面穿的夾克 **2** (of a process, an action or a disease 步驟、行動或疾病) that can be changed so that sth returns to its original state or situation 可逆的；可恢復原狀的；可醫治的：*Is the trend towards privatization reversible?* 私有化趨勢可能逆轉嗎？◇ *reversible kidney failure* 可醫治的腎衰竭 OPP **irreversible** ▸ **re·vers·ibil·ity** /rɪˌvɜːsəˈbɪləti; *NAmE* -ˌvɜːrs-/ *noun* [U]

re'versing light (*BrE*) (*NAmE* **'backup light**) *noun* a white light at the back of a vehicle that comes on when the vehicle moves backwards 倒車燈

re·ver·sion /rɪˈvɜːʃn; *NAmE* rɪˈvɜːrʒn/ *noun* **1** [U, sing.] **~ (to sth)** (*formal*) the act or process of returning to a former state or condition 倒退；回復；回歸：*a reversion to traditional farming methods* 傳統耕作方法的回歸 **2** [U, C] (*law* 律) the return of land or property to sb （土地或財產的）歸還，歸屬原主：*the reversion of Hong Kong to China* 香港回歸中國 **3** (*NAmE, law* 律) = LEASEBACK

re·vert /rɪˈvɜːt; *NAmE* rɪˈvɜːrt/ *verb* [I] (**+ adv./prep.**) (*IndE*, rather *formal*) to reply 回覆：*Excellent openings—kindly revert with your updated CV.* 絕佳招聘職位，請回信寄來您的最新簡歷。

PHR V **re'vert to sb/sth** (*law* 律) (of property, rights, etc. 財產、權利等) to return to the original owner again 歸還；歸屬 ➲ see also REVERSION **re'vert to sth** (*formal*) **1** to return to a former state; to start doing sth again that you used to do in the past 回復；恢復：*After her divorce she reverted to her maiden name.* 離婚以後，她重新用起娘家的姓氏。◇ *His manner seems to have reverted to normal.* 他的舉止好像已經恢復了正常。◇ *Try not to revert to your old eating habits.* 盡力不要恢復你過去的飲食習慣。 **2** to return to an earlier topic or subject 重提，回到，恢復（先前的話題或主題）：*So, to revert to your earlier question ...* 那麼，回到你先前所提的問題…◇ *The conversation kept reverting to the events of March 6th.* 談話一再回到 3 月 6 日所發生的事件上來。

re·vet·ment /rɪˈvetmənt/ *noun* (*technical* 術語) stones or other material used to make a wall stronger, hold back a bank of earth, etc. 護牆；護坡；擋土牆

re·view /rɪˈvjuː/ *noun, verb*

■ ***noun*** **1** [U, C] an examination of sth, with the intention of changing it if necessary 評審，審查，檢查，檢討（以進行必要的修改）：*the government's review of its education policy* 政府對其教育政策的檢討 ◇ *The case is* ***subject to*** *judicial* ***review.*** 這個案子必須接受司法審查。◇ *His parole application is* ***up for review*** *next week.* 他的假釋申請下週審查。◇ *The terms of the contract are* ***under review.*** 合同條文正在審議。◇ *a* ***pay/salary review*** 薪酬審定 ◇ *a* ***review body/date/panel*** 評審機關／日期／小組 **2** [C, U] a report in a newspaper or magazine, or on the Internet, television or radio, in which sb gives their opinion of a book, play, film/movie, etc.; the act of writing this kind of report （對書、戲劇、電影等的）評介，評論：*a book review* 書評 ◇ *the reviews* (*page*) *in the papers* 報紙的評論版 ◇ ***good/bad/mixed/rave reviews*** *in the national press* 全國性報刊上良好的／不好的／譭譽參半的／高度讚譽的評論 ◇ *He submitted his latest novel for review.* 他提交了自己的最新小說供評論。➲ **COLLOCATIONS** at LITERATURE ➲ **WRITING TUTOR** page WT31 **3** [C] a report on a subject or on a series of events 報告；彙報；述評；回顧：*a review of customer complaints* 有關消費者種種不滿的彙報 ◇ *to publish a review of recent cancer research* 發表有關最近癌症研究的報告 **4** [C] (*formal*) a ceremony that involves an official INSPECTION of soldiers, etc. by an important visitor 閱兵式；檢閱 **5** [C] (*NAmE*) a lesson in which you look again at sth you have studied, especially in order to prepare for an exam （尤指為準備考試的）溫習課，複習課

■ ***verb*** **1** **~ sth** to carefully examine or consider sth again, especially so that you can decide if it is necessary to make changes 復查；重新考慮 SYN **reassess**：*to review the evidence* 復查證據 ◇ *The government will review the situation later in the year.* 政府將在今年晚些時候對形勢重新加以研究。➲ **SYNONYMS** at EXAMINE **2** **~ sth** to think about past events, for example to try to understand why they happened 回顧；反思 SYN **take stock of**：*to review your failures and triumphs* 回顧自己的成功和失敗 ◇ *She had been reviewing*

R

the previous week on her way home. 她在回家的路上對前一個星期進行了回顧。 **3** 🔑 **~ sth** to write a report of a book, play, film/movie, etc. in which you give your opinion of it 寫（關於書籍、戲劇、電影等的）評論；評介：*The play was reviewed in the national newspapers.* 全國性報紙都對這部戲劇作了評論。 **4 ~ sb/sth** to make an official INSPECTION of a group of soldiers, etc. in a military ceremony 檢閱（部隊） **5** 🔑 **~ sth** (*especially NAmE*) to look again at sth you have studied, especially in order to prepare for an exam（尤指為準備考試而）温習，複習 **6** 🔑 **~ sth** (*especially NAmE*) to check a piece of work to see if there are any mistakes 校閱；審核

re·view·er /rɪˈvjuːə(r)/ *noun* **1** a person who writes reviews of books, films/movies or plays 評論家；評論撰寫者 **2** a person who examines or considers sth carefully, for example to see if any changes need to be made 檢查者；審查者

re·vile /rɪˈvaɪl/ *verb* [usually passive] **~ sb** (**for sth/for doing sth**) (*formal*) to criticize sb/sth in a way that shows how much you dislike them 辱罵；斥責

re·vise 🔑 AW /rɪˈvaɪz/ *verb*
1 🔑 [T] **~ sth** to change your opinions or plans, for example because of sth you have learned 改變，修改（意見或計劃）：*I can see I will have to revise my opinions of his abilities now.* 我明白我現在不得不改變對他的能力的看法了。◇ *The government may need to revise its policy in the light of this report.* 政府可能需要根據這份報告改變其政策。 **2** 🔑 [T] **~ sth** to change sth, such as a book or an estimate, in order to correct or improve it 修改，修訂（書、估算等）：*a revised edition of a textbook* 課本的修訂版 ◇ *I'll prepare a revised estimate for you.* 我會給你一份經過修正的估價單。◇ *We may have to revise this figure upwards.* 我們也許要將這個數字往上調一調。 **3** 🔑 [I, T] (*BrE*) to prepare for an exam by looking again at work that you have done 複習；温習：*I spent the weekend revising for my exam.* 我花了整個週末複習備考。◇ *I can't come out tonight. I have to revise.* 我今晚不能出去。我得複習。◇ **~ sth** *I'm revising Geography today.* 我今天複習地理。

re·vi·sion 🔑 AW /rɪˈvɪʒn/ *noun*
1 🔑 [C] a change or set of changes to sth（一項、一輪等）修訂，修改：*He made some minor revisions to the report before printing it out.* 把報告打印出來之前，他做了一些小的修改。 **2** 🔑 [U, C] the act of changing sth, or of examining sth with the intention of changing it 修訂，修改（的進行）：*a system in need of revision* 需要更新的系統 ◇ *a revision of trading standards* 貿易標準的修改 **3** 🔑 [U] (*BrE*) the process of learning work for an exam 複習；温習：*Have you started your revision yet?* 你開始複習了嗎？ ➲ COLLOCATIONS at EDUCATION

re·vi·sion·ism /rɪˈvɪʒənɪzəm/ *noun* [U] (*politics* 政) (often *disapproving*) ideas that are different from, and want to change, the main ideas or practices of a political system, especially MARXISM 修正主義 ▸ **re·vi·sion·ist** /-ʒənɪst/ *noun*：*bourgeois revisionists* 資產階級修正主義者 **re·vi·sion·ist** /-ʒənɪst/ *adj.*：*revisionist historians* 修正主義歷史學家

re·visit /ˌriːˈvɪzɪt/ *verb* **1 ~ sth** to visit a place again, especially after a long period of time 再訪；重遊 **2 ~ sth** to return to an idea or a subject and discuss it again 重提；再次討論：*It's an idea that may be worth revisiting at a later date.* 這個觀點值得以後進一步探討。

re·vit·al·ize (*BrE* also **-ise**) /ˌriːˈvaɪtəlaɪz/ *verb* **~ sth** to make sth stronger, more active or more healthy 使更強壯；使恢復生機（或健康）：*measures to revitalize the inner cities* 讓市中心更加繁榮的措施 ▸ **re·vit·al·iza·tion, -isa·tion** /ˌriːˌvaɪtəlaɪˈzeɪʃn; *NAmE* -ləˈz-/ *noun* [U]：*the revitalization of the steel industry* 鋼鐵工業的振興

re·vival /rɪˈvaɪvl/ *noun* **1** [U, C] an improvement in the condition or strength of sth（狀況或力量的）進步，振興，復蘇：*the revival of trade* 貿易振興 ◇ *an economic revival* 經濟復蘇 ◇ *a* **revival of interest** *in folk music* 對民間音樂的興趣的恢復 **2** [C, U] the process of sth becoming or being made popular or fashionable again 復興；再流行：*a religious revival* 宗教的奮興 ◇ *Jazz is enjoying a revival.* 爵士音樂再度盛行。 **3** [C] a new production of a play that has not been performed for some time（戲劇的）重演：*a revival of Peter Shaffer's 'Equus'* 彼得•謝弗的《馬》的重演

re·vival·ism /rɪˈvaɪvəlɪzəm/ *noun* [U] **1** the process of creating interest in sth again, especially religion（尤指宗教的）奮興運動 **2** the practice of using ideas, designs, etc. from the past 復興；復古：*revivalism in architecture* 建築的復古

re·vival·ist /rɪˈvaɪvəlɪst/ *noun* a person who tries to make sth popular again 推動復興者；復興運動倡導者 ▸ **re·vival·ist** *adj.*：*revivalist movements* 復興運動 ◇ *a revivalist preacher* 宗教奮興佈道者

re·vive /rɪˈvaɪv/ *verb* **1** [I, T] to become, or to make sb/sth become, conscious or healthy and strong again（使）蘇醒，復活：*The flowers soon revived in water.* 這些花見了水很快就活過來了。◇ *The economy is beginning to revive.* 經濟開始復蘇。◇ **~ sb/sth** *The paramedics couldn't revive her.* 護理人員無法使她蘇醒。◇ *This movie is intended to revive her flagging career.* 這部電影意在使她漸趨衰敗的事業再現輝煌。 **2** [T] **~ sth** to make sth start being used or done again 重新使用；使重做：*This quaint custom should be revived.* 應該恢復這一獨特的風俗。◇ *She has been trying to revive the debate over equal pay.* 她一直在設法再次展開同工同酬的辯論。 **3** [T] **~ sth** to produce again a play, etc. that has not been performed for some time 重新上演：*This 1930s musical is being revived at the National Theatre.* 這部 20 世紀 30 年代的音樂劇正在國家劇院重新上演。 ➲ see also REVIVAL

re·viv·ify /ˌriːˈvɪvɪfaɪ/ *verb* (**re·vivi·fies**, **re·vivi·fy·ing**, **re·vivi·fied**, **re·vivi·fied**) **~ sth** (*formal*) to give new life or health to sth 使獲得新生；使復活；使再生；使恢復健康 SYN **revitalize**

revo·ca·tion /ˌrevəˈkeɪʃn/ *noun* [U, C] (*formal*) the act of cancelling a law, etc.（法律等的）撤銷，廢除：*the revocation of planning permission* 建築許可的撤銷

re·voke /rɪˈvəʊk; *NAmE* -ˈvoʊk/ *verb* **~ sth** (*formal*) to officially cancel sth so that it is no longer valid 取消；廢除；使無效

re·volt /rɪˈvəʊlt; *NAmE* -ˈvoʊlt/ *noun, verb*
■ ***noun*** [C, U] a protest against authority, especially that of a government, often involving violence; the action of protesting against authority（尤指針對政府的）反抗，違抗；起義；叛亂 SYN **uprising**：*the Peasants' Revolt of 1381* * 1381 年的農民起義 ◇ *to* ***lead/stage a revolt*** 領導 / 發動起義 ◇ *The army quickly crushed the revolt.* 軍隊很快鎮壓了叛亂。◇ *the biggest back-bench revolt this government has ever seen* 本屆政府所遭遇到的規模最大的一次普通下院議員的反抗 ◇ *Attempts to negotiate peace ended in armed revolt.* 和談的努力最後以武裝叛亂告終。◇ (*formal*) *The people rose* ***in revolt.*** 人民奮起反抗。 ➲ COLLOCATIONS at WAR ➲ see also REVOLUTION (1)
■ ***verb*** **1** [I] to take violent action against the people in power 反抗，反叛（當權者） SYN **rebel, rise up**：*The peasants threatened to revolt.* 農民威脅說要造反。◇ **~ against sb/sth** *Finally the people revolted against the military dictatorship.* 人民最終起來反抗軍事獨裁。 **2** [I] **~** (**against sth**) to behave in a way that is the opposite of what sb expects of you, especially in protest 叛逆；違抗 SYN **rebel**：*Teenagers often revolt against parental discipline.* 青少年常常不遵從父母的條條框框。 **3** [T] **~ sb** to make you feel horror or disgust 使驚駭；令人厭惡 SYN **disgust**：*All the violence in the movie revolted me.* 電影裏的各種暴力場面令我非常震驚。◇ *The way he ate his food revolted me.* 他吃飯的樣子讓我感到惡心。 ➲ see also REVULSION

re·volt·ing /rɪˈvəʊltɪŋ; *NAmE* -ˈvoʊlt-/ *adj.* extremely unpleasant 令人作嘔的；極其討厭的 SYN **disgusting**：*a revolting smell* 令人作嘔的氣味 ◇ *a revolting little man* 可惡的傢伙 ➲ SYNONYMS at DISGUSTING ▸ **re·volt·ing·ly** *adv.*：*She's revoltingly overweight.* 她胖得讓人難以忍受。

revo·lu·tion 🔑 AW /ˌrevəˈluːʃn/ *noun*
1 🔑 [C, U] an attempt, by a large number of people, to change the government of a country, especially by violent action 革命：*a socialist revolution* 社會主義革命

◇ *the outbreak of the French Revolution in 1789* * 1789 年法國大革命的爆發 ◇ *to start a revolution* 發動一場革命 ◇ *a country on the brink of revolution* 即將發生革命的國家 ➲ COLLOCATIONS at POLITICS ➲ see also COUNTER-REVOLUTION, REVOLT **2** 🗝 [C] a great change in conditions, ways of working, beliefs, etc. that affects large numbers of people 巨變；大變革： *a **cultural/social/scientific, etc. revolution*** 文化、社會、科學等的重大變革 ◇ **~ in sth** *A revolution in information technology is taking place.* 信息技術正在發生巨變。 ➲ see also INDUSTRIAL REVOLUTION **3** [C, U] **~ (around/on sth)** a complete CIRCULAR movement around a point, especially of one planet around another （環繞中心點的）旋轉；（尤指）天體運行： *the revolution of the earth around the sun* 地球環繞太陽的公轉 ➲ see also REVOLVE **4** (also *informal* **rev**) [C] a CIRCULAR movement made by sth fixed to a central point, for example in a car engine 旋轉；繞軸旋轉： *rotating at 300 **revolutions per minute*** 以每分鐘 300 轉的速度旋轉

revo·lu·tion·ary AW /ˌrevəˈluːʃənəri; *NAmE* -neri/ *adj.*, *noun*

■ ***adj.*** **1** [usually before noun] connected with political revolution 革命的： *a revolutionary leader* 革命領袖 ◇ *revolutionary uprisings* 革命起義 **2** involving a great or complete change 徹底變革的；巨變的： *a **revolutionary idea*** 獨出心裁的想法 ◇ *a time of rapid and **revolutionary change*** 迅速劇烈變革的時期

■ ***noun*** (*pl.* **-ies**) a person who starts or supports a revolution, especially a political one （支持）改革者；（尤指）革命者，革命支持者： *socialist revolutionaries* 社會主義革命者

revo·lu·tion·ize (*BrE* also **-ise**) AW /ˌrevəˈluːʃənaɪz/ *verb* **~ sth** to completely change the way that sth is done 徹底改變；完全變革： *Aerial photography has revolutionized the study of archaeology.* 航空攝影已經給考古學研究帶來了一場革命。

re·volve /rɪˈvɒlv; *NAmE* rɪˈvɑːlv; rɪˈvɔːlv/ *verb* [I] to go in a circle around a central point 旋轉；環繞；轉動： *The fan revolved slowly.* 電扇緩慢地轉動着。 ◇ *The earth revolves on its axis.* 地球環繞自身的軸心轉動。

PHR V **reˈvolve around/round sth** to move around sth in a circle 繞…旋轉（或做圓周運動）： *The earth revolves around the sun.* 地球繞太陽公轉。 **reˈvolve around/round sb/sth** to have sb/sth as the main interest or subject 圍繞；以…為中心；將…作為主要興趣（或主題）： *His whole life revolves around surfing.* 他一生都在做與衝浪相關的事。 ◇ *She thinks that the world revolves around her.* 她以為整個世界都以她為中心。 ◇ *The discussion revolved around the question of changing the club's name.* 討論的中心問題是改變俱樂部的名稱。

re·volver /rɪˈvɒlvə(r); *NAmE* -ˈvɑːl-; -ˈvɔːl-/ *noun* a small gun that has a container for bullets that turns around so that shots can be fired quickly without having to stop to put more bullets in 左輪手槍

re·volv·ing /rɪˈvɒlvɪŋ; *NAmE* -ˈvɔːl-; -ˈvɑːl-/ *adj.* [usually before noun] able to turn in a circle 旋轉的： *a revolving chair* 轉椅 ◇ *The theatre has a revolving stage.* 劇院有一個旋轉舞台。

ˌrevolving ˈdoor *noun* **1** a type of door in an entrance to a large building that turns around in a circle as people go through it 旋轉門 **2** used to talk about a place or an organization that people enter and then leave again very quickly 中轉門（指人們進入後很快又離開的地方或機構）： *The company became a revolving-door workplace.* 這家公司成了工作的中轉站。

revue /rɪˈvjuː/ *noun* [C, U] a show in a theatre, with songs, dances, jokes, short plays, etc., often about recent events 時事諷刺劇；活報劇

re·vul·sion /rɪˈvʌlʃn/ *noun* [U, sing.] **~ (at/against/from sth)** (*formal*) a strong feeling of disgust or horror 嫌惡；惡心；驚恐 SYN **repugnance**： *She felt a deep sense of revulsion at the violence.* 她對這一暴行深惡痛絕。 ◇ *I started to feel a revulsion against their decadent lifestyle.* 我對他們那腐朽的生活方式開始感到厭惡。 ◇ *Most people viewed the bombings **with revulsion**.* 大多數人對爆炸事件表現出驚恐不安。 ➲ see also REVOLT *v.* (3)

re·ward 🗝 /rɪˈwɔːd; *NAmE* rɪˈwɔːrd/ *noun*, *verb*

■ ***noun*** **1** 🗝 [C, U] a thing that you are given because you have done sth good, worked hard, etc. 獎勵；回報；報酬： *a financial reward* 經濟獎勵 ◇ **~ (for sth/for doing sth)** *a reward for good behaviour* 優秀行為獎 ◇ *You deserve a reward for being so helpful.* 你幫了這麼大的忙，理應受到獎勵。 ◇ *Winning the match was **just reward** for the effort the team had made.* 贏得比賽的勝利是全隊付出努力應得的回報。 ◇ *The company is now **reaping the rewards** of their investments.* 公司正在收獲他們的投資回報。 **2** 🗝 [C] an amount of money that is offered to sb for helping the police to find a criminal or for finding sth that is lost 賞格；懸賞金： *A £100 reward has been offered for the return of the necklace.* 已懸賞 100 英鎊找尋項鏈。 IDM see VIRTUE

■ ***verb*** 🗝 [often passive] to give sth to sb because they have done sth good, worked hard, etc. 獎勵；獎賞；給以報酬： **~ sb for sth** *She was rewarded for her efforts with a cash bonus.* 她因自己所作的努力而得到一筆獎金。 ◇ **~ sb for doing sth** *He rewarded us handsomely* (= with a lot of money) *for helping him.* 對於我們的幫助，他大加酬謝。 ◇ **~ sb with sth** *She started singing to the baby and was rewarded with a smile.* 她開始給孩子唱歌，孩子則報以微笑。 ◇ **~ sb/sth** *Our patience was finally rewarded.* 我們的耐心最終得到了回報。

re·ward·ing /rɪˈwɔːdɪŋ; *NAmE* -ˈwɔːrd-/ *adj.* **1** (of an activity, etc. 活動等) worth doing; that makes you happy because you think it is useful or important 值得做的；有益的： *a rewarding experience/job* 有益的經歷 / 工作 ➲ SYNONYMS at SATISFYING **2** producing a lot of money 報酬高的 SYN **profitable**： *Teaching is not very financially rewarding* (= is not very well paid). 教書不會有很高的報酬。 OPP **unrewarding**

re·wind /ˌriːˈwaɪnd/ *verb* (**re·wound**, **re·wound** /-ˈwaʊnd/) [T, I] **~ (sth)** to make a tape in a CASSETTE player, etc. go backwards 重繞（磁帶等）；倒帶；倒片

re·wire /ˌriːˈwaɪə(r)/ *verb* **~ sth** to put new electrical wires into a building or piece of equipment 給（建築物或設備）換新電線

re·word /ˌriːˈwɜːd; *NAmE* -ˈwɜːrd/ *verb* **~ sth** to write sth again using different words in order to make it clearer or more acceptable 改寫；修改措辭 ▸ **re·word·ing** *noun* [C, U]

re·work /ˌriːˈwɜːk; *NAmE* -ˈwɜːrk/ *verb* **~ sth** to make changes to sth in order to improve it or make it more suitable 修改；重做；再加工 ▸ **re·work·ing** *noun* [C, U]： *The movie is a reworking of the Frankenstein story.* 這部電影是根據弗蘭肯斯坦科學怪人的故事改編的。

re·writ·able /ˌriːˈraɪtəbl/ *adj.* (*computing* 計) able to be used again for different data 可重寫的： *a rewritable CD* 可重寫光盤

re·write /ˌriːˈraɪt/ *verb* (**re·wrote** /-ˈrəʊt; *NAmE* -ˈroʊt/, **re·writ·ten** /-ˈrɪtn/) **~ sth** to write sth again in a different way, usually in order to improve it or because there is some new information 重寫；改寫： *I intend to rewrite the story for younger children.* 我想為年紀更小的孩子改寫這篇故事。 ◇ *This essay will have to be completely rewritten.* 這篇文章得全部重寫。 ◇ *an attempt to **rewrite history*** (= to present historical events in a way that shows or proves what you want them to) 改寫歷史的企圖 ▸ **re·write** /ˈriːraɪt/ *noun*

Rex /reks/ *noun* [U] (*BrE*, *formal*, from *Latin*) a word meaning 'king', used, for example, in the titles of legal cases brought by the state when there is a king in Britain 國王（英國國王在位時用於政府訴訟案案目等）： *Rex v Jones* 國王訴瓊斯案 ➲ compare REGINA

RGN /ˌɑː dʒiː ˈen; *NAmE* ˌɑːr dʒiː ˈen/ *abbr.* (*BrE*) registered general nurse 註冊全科護士

r.h. *abbr.* (in writing) RIGHT HAND （書寫形式）右手

rhap·sod·ize (*BrE* also **-ise**) /ˈræpsədaɪz/ *verb* [I, T] **~ (about/over sth)** | **+ speech** (*formal*) to talk or write with great enthusiasm about sth 熱情地談論（或寫） SYN **go into raptures about**

R

rhap·sody /ˈræpsədi/ *noun* (*pl.* **-ies**) **1** (often in titles 常用於標題) a piece of music that is full of feeling and is not regular in form 狂想曲：*Liszt's Hungarian Rhapsodies* 李斯特的《匈牙利狂想曲》 **2** (*formal*) the expression of great enthusiasm or happiness in speech or writing（言語或文字的）狂熱表達，充滿欣喜的表達 ▸ **rhap·sodic** /ræpˈsɒdɪk; NAmE -ˈsɑːdɪk/ *adj.*

rhea /ˈriːə/ *noun* a large S American bird that does not fly 美洲鴕鳥；鶆䴈

rheme /riːm/ *noun* (*linguistics* 語言) the part of a sentence or clause that adds new information to what the reader or audience already knows 表位，述位（提供新信息的句子成分）➲ compare THEME *n.* (5)

rhe·nium /ˈriːniəm/ *noun* [U] (*symb.* **Re**) a chemical element. Rhenium is a rare silver-white metal that exists naturally in the ORES of MOLYBDENUM and some other metals. 錸

rhe·sus factor /ˈriːsəs fæktə(r)/ *noun* [sing.] (*medical* 醫) a substance present in the red blood cells of around 85% of humans. Its presence (**rhesus positive**) or absence (**rhesus negative**) can be dangerous for babies when they are born and for people having BLOOD TRANSFUSIONS. * Rh（血型）因子；獼因子；恆河猴因子

rhe·sus monkey /ˈriːsəs mʌŋki/ *noun* a small S Asian MONKEY, often used in scientific experiments 恆河猴（一種南亞獼猴，常用於科學實驗）

rhet·oric /ˈretərɪk/ *noun* [U] **1** (*formal*, often *disapproving*) speech or writing that is intended to influence people, but that is not completely honest or sincere 華而不實的言語；花言巧語：*the rhetoric of political slogans* 政治口號的虛華辭藻 ◇ *empty rhetoric* 空洞的花言巧語 **2** (*formal*) the skill of using language in speech or writing in a special way that influences or entertains people 修辭技巧；修辭 SYN **eloquence, oratory**

rhet·oric·al /rɪˈtɒrɪkl; NAmE -ˈtɔːr-/ *adj.* **1** (of a question 問題) asked only to make a statement or to produce an effect rather than to get an answer 反問的；反詰的：*'Don't you care what I do?' he asked, but it was a* ***rhetorical question.*** "我做什麼，難道你不關心嗎？" 他問道，可那是個反問。 **2** (*formal*, often *disapproving*) (of a speech or piece of writing 言語或文章) intended to influence people, but not completely honest or sincere 辭藻華麗的；虛誇的；花言巧語的 **3** (*formal*) connected with the art of RHETORIC 修辭的；修辭性的；帶有修辭色彩的：*the use of rhetorical devices such as metaphor and irony* 諸如暗喻和反諷等修辭手法的運用 ▸ **rhet·oric·al·ly** /-kli/ *adv.*：*'Do you think I'm stupid?' she asked rhetorically.* "你以為我是傻瓜？" 她反問道。◇ *a rhetorically structured essay* 講究修辭結構的文章

rhet·or·ician /ˌretəˈrɪʃn/ *noun* (*technical* 術語) a person who is skilled in the art of formal rhetoric 修辭學家

rheu,matic 'fever *noun* [U] a serious disease that causes fever with swelling and pain in the joints 風濕熱

rheuma·tism /ˈruːmətɪzəm/ *noun* [U] a disease that makes the muscles and joints painful, stiff and swollen 風濕（病） ▸ **rheum·at·ic** /ruˈmætɪk/ *adj.*：*rheumatic pains* 風濕痛

rheuma·toid arth·ritis /ˌruːmətɔɪd ɑːˈθraɪtɪs; NAmE ɑːrˈθ-/ *noun* [U] (*medical* 醫) a disease that gets worse over a period of time and causes painful swelling and permanent damage in the joints of the body, especially the fingers, wrists, feet and ankles 類風濕性關節炎

rheuma·tol·ogy /ˌruːməˈtɒlədʒi; NAmE -ˈtɑːl-/ *noun* [U] the study of the diseases of joints and muscles, such as RHEUMATISM and ARTHRITIS 風濕病學

rheumy /ˈruːmi/ *adj.* (of the eyes 眼睛) containing a lot of water 充水的；充滿黏液的

rhine·stone /ˈraɪnstəʊn; NAmE -stoʊn/ *noun* a clear stone that is intended to look like a diamond, used in cheap jewellery 萊茵石（用於仿鑽石首飾）

rhin·itis /raɪˈnaɪtɪs/ *noun* [U] (*medical* 醫) a condition in which the inside of the nose becomes swollen and sore, caused by an infection or an ALLERGY 鼻炎（感染或過敏引起）

rhino /ˈraɪnəʊ; NAmE -noʊ/ *noun* (*pl.* **-os**) (*informal*) = RHINOCEROS：*black/white rhino* 黑／白犀牛 ◇ *rhino horn* 犀牛角

rhi·noceros /raɪˈnɒsərəs; NAmE -ˈnɑːs-/ *noun* (*pl.* **rhi·noceros** or **rhi·nocer·oses**) (also *informal* **rhino**) a large heavy animal with very thick skin and either one or two horns on its nose, that lives in Africa and Asia 犀，犀牛（棲於非洲和亞洲）

rhi·zome /ˈraɪzəʊm; NAmE -zoʊm/ *noun* (*technical* 術語) the thick STEM of some plants, such as IRIS and MINT, that grows along or under the ground and has roots and STEMS growing from it 根莖；根狀莖

rho /rəʊ; NAmE roʊ/ *noun* the 17th letter of the Greek alphabet (Ρ, ρ) 希臘字母表的第 17 個字母

Rhodes scholar /ˌrəʊdz ˈskɒlə(r); NAmE ˌroʊdz ˈskɑːl-/ *noun* a student from the US, Germany or the Commonwealth who is given a SCHOLARSHIP to study in Britain at Oxford University from a fund that was started by Cecil Rhodes in 1902 獲羅得斯獎學金的學生（羅得斯基金由塞西爾•羅得斯於 1902 年設立，為美國、德國或英聯邦國家的學生提供到英國牛津大學學習的獎學金）

rho·dium /ˈrəʊdiəm; NAmE ˈroʊ-/ *noun* [U] (*symb.* **Rh**) a chemical element. Rhodium is a hard silver-white metal that is usually found with PLATINUM. 銠

rhodo·den·dron /ˌrəʊdəˈdendrən; NAmE ˌroʊ-/ *noun* a bush with large red, purple, pink or white flowers 杜鵑花

rhom·boid /ˈrɒmbɔɪd; NAmE ˈrɑːm-/ *noun* (*geometry* 幾何) a flat shape with four straight sides, with only the opposite sides and angles equal to each other 長菱形 ➲ VISUAL VOCAB page V71

rhom·bus /ˈrɒmbəs; NAmE ˈrɑːm-/ *noun* (*geometry* 幾何) a flat shape with four equal sides and four angles which are not 90° 菱形 ➲ VISUAL VOCAB page V71

rho·tic /ˈrəʊtɪk; NAmE ˈroʊ-/ *adj.* (*phonetics* 語音) (of an accent 口音) pronouncing the /r/ after a vowel in words like *car*, *early*, etc. General American and Scottish accents are rhotic. * r 化的； r 類音的

rhu·barb /ˈruːbɑːb; NAmE -bɑːrb/ *noun* [U] **1** the thick red STEMS of a garden plant, also called rhubarb, that are cooked and eaten as a fruit 大黃；大黃莖；餡餅菜：*rhubarb pie* 大黃餡餅 **2** a word that a group of actors repeat on stage to give the impression of a lot of people talking at the same time（演員們為了製造人聲嘈雜的效果而重複說的詞）

rhumba = RUMBA

rhyme /raɪm/ *noun, verb*

■ ***noun*** **1** [C] a word that has the same sound or ends with the same sound as another word 押韻詞；同韻詞：*Can you think of a rhyme for 'beauty'?* 你能想出和 beauty 押韻的詞嗎？ **2** [C] a short poem in which the last word in the line has the same sound as the last word in another line, especially the next one 押韻的短詩：*children's rhymes and stories* 兒歌和童話 ➲ see also NURSERY RHYME **3** [U] the use of words in a poem or song that have the same sound, especially at the ends of lines 押韻；韻詞的應用：*a poem written* ***in rhyme*** 押韻的詩 ◇ *the poet's use of rhyme* 詩人對韻的運用

IDM **there's no ˌrhyme or ˈreason to/for sth | without ˌrhyme or ˈreason** if there is **no rhyme or reason to sth** or it happens **without rhyme or reason**, it happens in a way that cannot be easily explained or understood 毫無道理；無規律可循；莫名其妙

■ ***verb*** **1** [I] **~ (with sth)** if two words, syllables, etc. **rhyme**, or if one **rhymes** with the other, they have or end with the same sound（詞或音節）押韻，和…同韻：*'Though' rhymes with 'low'.* * though 和 low 押韻。◇ *'Tough' and 'through' don't rhyme.* * tough 和 through 不押韻。◇ *rhyming couplets* 同韻偶句 **2** [T] **~ sth (with sth)** to put words that sound the same together, for example when you are writing poetry 使押韻：*You can rhyme 'girl' with 'curl'.* 你可以用 girl 和 curl 押韻。 **3** [I] (of a poem 詩歌) to have lines that end with the same sound 押句尾韻：*I prefer poems that rhyme.* 我喜歡句尾押韻的詩。

ˈrhyming slang *noun* [U] a way of talking in which you use words or phrases that rhyme with the word you mean, instead of using that word. For example in COCKNEY rhyming slang 'apples and pears' means 'stairs'. 同韻俚語（以同韻的詞或短語替代另一個詞，如倫敦土話中用 apples and pears 代替 stairs）

rhythm 🔑 /ˈrɪðəm/ *noun* [U, C] **1** 🔑 a strong regular repeated pattern of sounds or movements 節奏；韻律；律動：*to dance to the rhythm of the music* 隨着音樂的節奏跳舞 ◇ *music with **a fast/slow/steady rhythm*** 節奏快的／慢的／平穩的音樂 ◇ *jazz rhythms* 爵士樂的節奏 ◇ *He can't seem to play **in rhythm**.* 他的演奏好像不合節拍。◇ *The boat rocked up and down **in rhythm with** the sea.* 小船隨着海浪起伏有致。◇ *the rhythm of her breathing* 她的呼吸節奏 ◇ *a dancer with a **natural sense of rhythm*** (= the ability to move in time to a fixed beat) 天生節奏感很強的舞蹈者 **2** a regular pattern of changes or events 規則變化；規律；節律：*the rhythm of the seasons* 四季的更迭 ◇ ***biological/body rhythms*** 生物／人體節律 ➲ see also BIORHYTHM

ˌrhythm and ˈblues *noun* [U] (*abbr.* **R & B**) a type of music that is a mixture of BLUES and JAZZ and has a strong rhythm 節奏布魯斯，節奏藍調（由布魯斯和爵士樂綜合而成的節奏感很強的音樂）

ˌrhythm guiˈtar *noun* [U] a GUITAR style that consists mainly of CHORDS played with a strong rhythm 節奏吉他 ➲ compare LEAD GUITAR

rhyth·mic /ˈrɪðmɪk/ (also *less frequent* **rhyth·mic·al** /ˈrɪðmɪkl/) *adj.* having a regular pattern of sounds, movements or events 有節奏（或規律）的；節奏分明的：*music with a fast, rhythmic beat* 節奏快的音樂 ◇ *the rhythmic ticking of the clock* 時鐘有節奏的滴答聲 ▸ **rhyth·mic·al·ly** /-kli/ *adv.*

the ˈrhythm method *noun* [sing.] a method of avoiding getting pregnant that involves a woman only having sex during the time of the month when she is unlikely to get pregnant 安全期避孕法

ˈrhythm section *noun* the part of a band that supplies the rhythm, usually consisting of drums, BASS, and sometimes piano 樂隊的節奏樂器組（通常由鼓、低音提琴，有時還有鋼琴組成）

ria /ˈriːə/ *noun* (*technical* 術語) a long narrow area of water formed when a river valley floods 溺河（河谷泛濫形成的狹長水域）

rib /rɪb/ *noun, verb*

■ *noun* **1** [C] any of the curved bones that are connected to the SPINE and surround the chest 肋骨：*a **broken/bruised/cracked rib*** 折斷的／挫傷的／斷裂的肋骨 ◇ *Stop **poking me in the ribs!*** 別捅我的腰！➲ VISUAL VOCAB page V59 ➲ see also RIBCAGE **2** [U, C] a piece of meat with one or more bones from the ribs of an animal 排骨 ➲ see also SPARE RIB **3** [C] a curved piece of wood, metal or plastic that forms the frame of a boat, roof, etc. and makes it stronger （船或屋頂等的）肋拱，肋材 **4** [U, C] a way of knitting that produces a pattern of vertical lines in which some are higher than others （織物的）凸條花紋，羅紋：*a rib cotton sweater* 一件羅紋棉毛衫 IDM see DIG *v.*

■ *verb* (**-bb-**) **~ sb (about/over sth)** (*old-fashioned, informal*) to laugh at sb and make jokes about them, but in a friendly way 嘲笑；逗弄；開（某人的）玩笑 SYN **tease**

rib·ald /ˈrɪbld; ˈraɪbɔːld/ *adj.* (of language or behaviour 言語或行為) referring to sex in a rude but humorous way 猥褻詼諧的

rib·ald·ry /ˈrɪbldri; ˈraɪb-/ *noun* [U] language or behaviour that refers to sex in a rude but humorous way 猥褻詼諧的言語（或行為）

ribbed /rɪbd/ *adj.* (especially of material for clothes 尤指衣料) having raised lines 有棱紋的：*a ribbed sweater* 有棱紋的毛衣

rib·bing /ˈrɪbɪŋ/ *noun* [U] **1** a pattern of raised lines in knitting or on a surface （織物或物體表面的）棱紋，凸條圖案 **2** (*old-fashioned, informal*) the act of making fun of sb in a friendly way 開玩笑；取笑；逗弄 SYN **teasing**

rib·bon /ˈrɪbən/ *noun* **1** [U, C] a narrow strip of material, used to tie things or for decoration （用於捆綁或裝飾的）帶子；絲帶：*a present tied with yellow ribbon* 繫着黃絲帶的禮物 ◇ *lengths of velvet ribbon* 一段段天鵝絨帶子 ◇ *She was wearing two blue silk ribbons in her hair.* 她的頭髮上繫着兩根藍色絲帶。➲ picture at ROPE **2** [C] something that is long and narrow in shape 帶狀物；狹長的東西：*The road was a ribbon of moonlight.* 這條路在月光下如同一條緞帶。**3** [C] a ribbon in special colours, or tied in a special way, that is given to sb as a prize or as a military honour, or that is worn by sb to show that they belong to a particular political party 綬帶；勳帶 ➲ compare ROSETTE (1) **4** [C] a long strip of material containing ink that you put into TYPEWRITERS and some computer printers （打字機或打印機的）色帶 IDM **cut/tear, etc. sth to ˈribbons** to cut/tear, etc. sth very badly （將某物）撕扯得粉碎，切成碎片

ˈribbon development *noun* [C, U] (*BrE, technical* 術語) houses that are built along a main road leading out of a village or town; the building of houses in this position 帶狀發展（村、鎮沿公路延伸出的房屋）；帶狀房屋建設

ˈribbon lake *noun* (*technical* 術語) a long narrow lake 帶狀湖

rib·cage /ˈrɪbkeɪdʒ/ *noun* the structure of curved bones (called RIBS), that surrounds and protects the chest 肋廓；胸廓；胸腔 ➲ VISUAL VOCAB page V59

ˈrib-eye (also **ˌrib-eye ˈsteak**) *noun* a piece of beef which is cut from outside the RIBS 牛裏脊肉；裏脊牛排

ribo·fla·vin /ˌraɪbəˈfleɪvɪn/ *noun* [U] a VITAMIN which is important for producing energy, found in milk, LIVER, eggs and green vegetables 核黃素；維生素 B_2；維他命 B_2

ˈrib-tickler *noun* (*informal*) a funny joke or story 笑話；惹人發笑的故事 ▸ **ˈrib-tickling** *adj.*

rice 🔑 /raɪs/ *noun* [U] short, narrow white or brown grain grown on wet land in hot countries as food; the plant that produces this grain 大米；稻米；稻：*a grain of rice* 一粒大米 ◇ ***boiled/steamed/fried rice*** 米飯；蒸飯；炒飯 ◇ ***long-/short-grain rice*** 長粒／短粒稻米 ◇ ***brown rice*** (= without its outer covering removed) 糙米 ◇ ***rice paddies*** (= rice fields) 稻田 ➲ VISUAL VOCAB page V32

rice·paper /ˈraɪspeɪpə(r)/ *noun* [U] a type of very thin paper made from tropical plants, used as a base for some types of cake 米紙（用熱帶植物製作的薄紙，用作糕餅墊底）

ˌrice ˈpudding *noun* [U, C] a DESSERT (= a sweet dish) made from rice cooked with milk and sugar 大米布丁

rich 🔑 /rɪtʃ/ *adj.* (**rich·er**, **rich·est**)

▸ WITH A LOT OF MONEY 錢多 **1** 🔑 having a lot of money or property 富有的；富裕的：*one of the richest women in the world* 世界上最富有的女人之一 ◇ *Nobody gets rich from writing nowadays.* 如今沒有人能靠寫作致富。◇ (*slang*) *to be **filthy/stinking*** (= extremely) ***rich*** 富得流油 OPP **poor** **2 the rich** *noun* [pl.] people who have a lot of money or property 富人；有錢人：*It's a favourite resort for the rich and famous.* 這是富人和名流最喜歡去度假的地方。OPP **the poor** **3** 🔑 (of a country 國家) producing a lot of wealth so that many of its people can live at a high standard 富庶的；富饒的：*the richest countries/economies/nations* 最富有的國家／經濟體／國家 OPP **poor**

▸ FULL OF VARIETY 豐富多彩 **4** 🔑 very interesting and full of variety 非常有趣的；豐富多彩的：*the region's rich history and culture* 這個地區豐富多彩的歷史和文化 ◇ *She leads a rich and varied life.* 她過着豐富多彩的生活。

▸ CONTAINING/PROVIDING STH 含有；提供 **5** 🔑 **~ (in sth)** (often in compounds 常構成複合詞) containing or providing a large supply of sth 大量含有（或提供）…的：*Oranges are rich in vitamin C.* 橘子含有豐富的維生素 C。◇ *The area is rich in wildlife.* 這個地區的野生動植物很多。◇ *His novels are a rich source of material for the movie industry.* 他的小說為電影業提供了大量素材。◇ *iron-rich rocks* 富含鐵的岩石 OPP **poor**

R

▸ **FOOD 食物 6** containing a lot of fat, butter, eggs, etc. and making you feel full quickly 油膩的：*a rich creamy sauce* 味道很濃的奶油沙司 ◇ *a rich chocolate cake* 很油膩的巧克力蛋糕

▸ **SOIL 土壤 7** containing the substances that make it good for growing plants in 肥沃的；豐產的 **SYN fertile**：*a rich well-drained soil* 排水性能好的沃土 **OPP poor**

▸ **COLOURS/SOUNDS 色彩；聲音 8** (of colours, sounds, smells and tastes 顏色、聲音、氣味和味道) strong or deep; very beautiful or pleasing 強烈的；深的；低沉的；美好的；宜人的：*rich dark reds* 濃重的深紅色

▸ **EXPENSIVE 昂貴 9** (*literary*) expensive and beautiful 華麗而昂貴的 **SYN sumptuous**：*The rooms were decorated with rich fabrics.* 這些屋子裝飾着華麗昂貴的織物。

▸ **CRITICISM 批評 10** (*informal, especially BrE*) used to say that a criticism sb makes is surprising and not reasonable, because they have the same fault（表示某人所作的批評是無稽之談，因為他們本身也有同樣的問題）：*Me? Lazy? That's rich, coming from you!* 我？懶？你這麼說，實在可笑！➲ compare RICHNESS **IDM** see STRIKE *v.*

riches /ˈrɪtʃɪz/ *noun* [pl.] large amounts of money and valuable or beautiful possessions 財富；財產：*a career that brought him fame and riches* 使他名利雙收的事業 ◇ *material riches* 物質財富 **IDM** see EMBARRASSMENT, RAG *n.*

rich·ly /ˈrɪtʃli/ *adv.* **1** in a beautiful and expensive manner 富麗堂皇地：*a richly decorated room* 裝飾得富麗堂皇的房間 **2** used to express the fact that sth has a pleasant strong colour, taste or smell（色彩）鮮豔富麗地；（口味）醇美地；（氣味）濃郁芬芳地：*a richly flavoured sauce* 味道很濃的沙司 ◇ *The polished floor glowed richly.* 光潔無瑕的地板十分明亮。**3** in a generous way 慷慨地；大方地：*She was richly rewarded for all her hard work.* 她一向勤勞苦幹，得到了豐厚的回報。**4** in a way that people think is right and good 恰如其分地；理所當然地；完全地 **SYN thoroughly**：***richly deserved** success* 理應取得的成功 ◇ *richly earned respect* 理應受到的尊敬 **5** used to express the fact that the quality or thing mentioned is present in large amounts（表明品質突出或物質豐富）：*richly varied countryside* 各地情況迥異的鄉村 ◇ *a richly atmospheric novel* 氛圍渲染得很強烈的小說

rich·ness /ˈrɪtʃnəs/ *noun* [U] the state of being rich in sth, such as colour, minerals or interesting qualities 豐富；富饒；濃烈：*the richness and variety of marine life* 海洋生物的豐富多樣 ➲ compare WEALTH (3)

the Rich·ter scale /ˈrɪktə skeɪl; *NAmE* ˈrɪktər/ *noun* [sing.] a system for measuring how strong an EARTHQUAKE is 里氏震級，里克特震級（測量地震強度的標準）：*an earthquake measuring 7.3 on the Richter scale* 里氏 7.3 級的地震

ricin /ˈraɪsɪn/ *noun* [U] a very poisonous substance obtained from the seeds of the CASTOR OIL plant 蓖麻毒素；蓖麻毒蛋白

rick /rɪk/ *noun, verb*

■ ***noun*** a large pile of HAY or STRAW that is built in a regular shape and covered to protect it from rain 乾草堆；草垛

■ ***verb* ~ sth** (*BrE*) to injure a part of your body by twisting it suddenly 扭傷 **SYN sprain**

rick·ets /ˈrɪkɪts/ *noun* [U] a disease of children caused by a lack of good food that makes the bones become soft and badly formed, especially in the legs 佝僂病

rick·ety /ˈrɪkəti/ *adj.* not strong or well made; likely to break 不結實的；不穩固的；易折斷的：*a rickety chair* 搖搖晃晃的椅子

rick·shaw /ˈrɪkʃɔː/ *noun* a small light vehicle with two wheels used in some Asian countries to carry passengers. The rickshaw is pulled by sb walking or riding a bicycle. 人力車；黃包車

rico·chet /ˈrɪkəʃeɪ; *BrE* also -ʃet/ *verb, noun*

■ ***verb*** (**rico·chet·ing** /ˈrɪkəʃeɪɪŋ/, **rico·cheted**, **rico·cheted** /ˈrɪkəʃeɪd/, *BrE* also **rico·chet·ting** /ˈrɪkəʃetɪŋ/, **rico·chet·ted**, **rico·chet·ted** /ˈrɪkəʃetɪd/) [I] + **adv./prep.** (of a moving object 運動的物體) to hit a surface and come off it fast at a different angle 彈開；反彈出去：*The bullet ricocheted off a nearby wall.* 子彈從附近的一面牆上彈飛了。

■ ***noun* 1** [C] a ball, bullet or stone that ricochets 彈回的球（或子彈、石頭）：*A woman protester was killed by a ricochet (bullet).* 一位女抗議者被跳彈擊中身亡。**2** [U] the action of ricocheting 彈回；反彈；彈開：*the ricochet of bricks and bottles off police riot shields* 砸在警察防暴盾牌上的磚塊和瓶子彈回來

ric·tus /ˈrɪktəs/ *noun* (*formal*) a wide twisted or smiling mouth that does not look natural or relaxed 扭曲（或怪笑）的嘴；齜牙咧嘴

Synonyms 同義詞辨析

rich

wealthy • prosperous • affluent • well off • comfortable

These words all describe sb/sth that has a lot of money, property or valuable possessions. 以上各詞均用以形容人富有或地方富饒。

rich (of a person) having a lot of money, property or valuable possessions; (of a country or city) producing a lot of wealth so that many of its people can live at a high standard 指（人）富有的、富裕的，（國家或城市）富庶的、富饒的

wealthy rich 指富有的、富饒的

RICH OR WEALTHY? 用 rich 還是 wealthy？

There is no real difference in meaning between these two words. Both are very frequent, but **rich** is more frequent and can be used in some fixed phrases where **wealthy** cannot. 上述兩詞在意義上無實質性區別。兩詞均很常用，不過 rich 更常用，並用於一些固定短語中，wealthy 則不能：~~*He's stinking/filthy wealthy.*~~ ◇ ~~*It's a favourite resort for the wealthy and famous.*~~

prosperous (*rather formal*) rich and successful 指繁榮的、成功的、興旺的

affluent (*rather formal*) rich and with a good standard of living 指富裕的：*affluent Western countries* 富裕的西方國家

PROSPEROUS OR AFFLUENT? 用 prosperous 還是 affluent？

Both **prosperous** and **affluent** are used to talk about people and places. **Prosperous** is used much more than **affluent** to talk about times and periods. **Affluent** is often used to contrast rich people or societies with poor ones. Being **prosperous** is nearly always seen as a good thing. * prosperous 和 affluent 均用以指人和地方。prosperous 較 affluent 更常用以指時期或時代。affluent 常用於人或社會的貧富對比，prosperous 幾乎總是被視為好事：*It's good to see you looking so prosperous.* 看到你成功的樣子真是令人高興。◇ ~~*It's good to see you looking so affluent.*~~

well off (often used in negative sentences) rich（常用於否定句中）指富裕、有錢：*His family is not very well off.* 他家境不太寬裕。**NOTE** The opposite of **well off** is **badly off**, but this is not very frequent; it is more common to say that sb is *not well off*. * well off 的反義詞為 badly off，但不常用；指人不寬裕較常用 not well off。

comfortable having enough money to buy what you want without worrying about the cost 指富裕、寬裕：*They're not millionaires, but they're certainly very comfortable.* 他們雖不是百萬富翁，但也很富裕。

PATTERNS

- a(n) rich/wealthy/prosperous/affluent/well-off **family**
- a rich/wealthy/prosperous/well-off **man/woman**
- a(n) rich/wealthy/prosperous/affluent **country/city**

rid /rɪd/ *verb* (**rid·ding**, **rid**, **rid**)

IDM **be 'rid of sb/sth** (*formal*) to be free of sb/sth that has been annoying you or that you do not want 擺脱：*She wanted to be rid of her parents and their authority.* 她想擺脱父母及其權威的束縛。◇ *I was glad to be rid of the car when I finally sold it.* 把車賣掉時，我很慶幸終於脱手了。◇ (*BrE*) *He was a nuisance and we're all* ***well rid of*** *him* (= we'll be much better without him). 他這人很討厭，沒有他我們都會舒服得多。 **get 'rid of sb/sth** to make yourself free of sb/sth that is annoying you or that you do not want; to throw sth away 擺脱；丟棄；扔掉：*Try and get rid of your visitors before I get there.* 在我到達之前，想辦法把你的客人打發走。◇ *The problem is getting rid of nuclear waste.* 問題是如何處理核廢料。◇ *I can't get rid of this headache.* 我這頭疼老是不好。◇ *We got rid of all the old furniture.* 我們扔掉了所有的舊傢具。 ➲ more at WANT *v.*

PHR V **'rid sb/sth of sb/sth** (*formal*) to remove sth that is causing a problem from a place, group, etc. 去除；清除：*Further measures will be taken to rid our streets of crime.* 將採取進一步的措施來防止街頭犯罪。 **'rid yourself of sb/sth** (*formal*) to make yourself free from sb/sth that is annoying you or causing you a problem 擺脱；從…中解脱：*to rid yourself of guilt* 擺脱內疚 ◇ *He wanted to rid himself of the burden of the secret.* 他想把秘密説出來，讓自己得到解脱。

rid·dance /ˈrɪdns/ *noun* [U]

IDM **good 'riddance (to sb/sth)** an unkind way of saying that you are pleased that sb/sth has gone（不友善的話，表示很高興某人或某物已離開）：*'Goodbye and good riddance!' she said to him angrily as he left.* 他離去時，她氣憤地衝着他説："再見吧，早走早好！"

rid·den /ˈrɪdn/ *adj.* (usually in compounds 通常構成複合詞) full of a particular unpleasant thing 充滿（某種不良事物）的；滿是…的：*a disease-ridden slum* 疾病流行的貧民窟 ◇ *a class-ridden society* 等級森嚴的社會 ◇ *She was guilt-ridden at the way she had treated him.* 她為過去曾那樣對待他而深感內疚。◇ *She was ridden with guilt.* 她深感歉疚。 ➲ see also RIDE *v.*

rid·dle /ˈrɪdl/ *noun, verb*

■ ***noun*** **1** a question that is difficult to understand, and that has a surprising answer, that you ask sb as a game 謎；謎語：*Stop* ***talking in riddles*** (= saying things that are confusing)—*say what you mean.* 別拐彎抹角了，有話直説。◇ *to solve the riddle of the Sphinx* 解開斯芬克斯之謎 **2** a mysterious event or situation that you cannot explain 神秘事件；無法解釋的情況 **SYN** **mystery**：*the riddle of how the baby died* 嬰兒死亡之謎

■ ***verb*** [usually passive] **~ sb/sth (with sth)** to make a lot of holes in sb/sth 使佈滿窟窿：*The car was* ***riddled with bullets.*** 這輛車被子彈打得千瘡百孔。

IDM **be 'riddled with sth** to be full of sth, especially sth bad or unpleasant 充滿；充斥：*His body was riddled with cancer.* 癌瘤遍佈他的全身。◇ *Her typing was slow and riddled with mistakes.* 她打字很慢而且錯誤百出。

ride /raɪd/ *verb, noun*

■ ***verb*** (**rode** /rəʊd; *NAmE* roʊd/, **rid·den** /ˈrɪdn/)

▸ **HORSE** 馬 **1** [I, T] to sit on a horse, etc. and control it as it moves 駕馭馬匹；騎馬：*I learnt to ride as a child.* 我小時候就學會了騎馬。◇ **+ adv./prep.** *They rode along narrow country lanes.* 他們騎馬走在狹窄的鄉村小路上。◇ *He was riding on a large black horse.* 他騎在一匹高大的黑馬上。◇ **~ sth** *She had never ridden a horse before.* 她以前從沒騎過馬。◇ *He's ridden six winners so far this year* (= in horse racing). 他今年到目前為止已六次在賽馬中奪標。 **2** **go riding** (*BrE*) (*NAmE* **go 'horseback riding**) [I] to spend time riding a horse for pleasure 騎馬（消遣）：*How often do you go riding?* 你多長時間騎一次馬？

▸ **BICYCLE/MOTORCYCLE** 自行車；摩托車 **3** [T, I] to sit on and control a bicycle, motorcycle, etc. 騎；駕駛：**~ sth (+ adv./prep.)** *The boys were riding their bikes around the streets.* 男孩子們騎着自行車在街上兜風。◇ *He rode a Harley Davidson.* 他騎着一輛哈雷 • 戴維森摩托車。◇ **(+ adv./prep.)** *The ground there is too rough to ride over.* 那裏地面高低不平，無法騎車。

▸ **IN VEHICLE** 車輛 **4** [I, T] to travel in a vehicle, especially as a passenger 搭乘；乘坐：**(+ adv./prep.)** *I walked back while the others rode in the car.* 別人都乘車，而我是走回來的。◇ **~ sth (+ adv./prep.)** (*NAmE*) *to* ***ride the subway/an elevator, etc.*** 乘地鐵、電梯等 ◇ *She rode the bus to school every day.* 她每天乘公共汽車去上學。

▸ **ON WATER/AIR** 在水面／空中 **5** [I, T] to float or be supported on water or air 漂浮；飄浮：**(+ adv./prep.)** *We watched the balloon riding high above the fields.* 我們看着氣球高高地飄浮在田野上空。◇ **~ sth** *surfers riding the waves* 踏浪而行的衝浪者

▸ **GO THROUGH AREA** 穿越 **6** [T] **~ sth** to go through or over an area on a horse, bicycle, etc.（騎馬、自行車等）穿越，翻越：*We rode the mountain trails.* 我們騎着馬走在山裏的小路上。

▸ **CRITICIZE** 批評 **7** [T] **~ sb** (*NAmE*) to criticize or TEASE sb in an annoying way 數落；嘲弄：*Why is everybody riding me today?* 怎麼今天大家都拿我取笑？

IDM **be riding for a 'fall** to be doing sth that involves risks and that may end in disaster 做事莽撞；做招致風險的事 **be riding 'high** to be successful or very confident 獲得成功；信心十足 **let sth 'ride** to decide to do nothing about a problem that you know you may have to deal with later 決定對…不立即採取行動 **ride the crest of sth** to enjoy great success or support because of a particular situation or event（因某種情況）處於鼎盛時期：*The band is riding the crest of its last tour.* 樂隊正處於最近這次巡迴演出後的頂峰狀態。 **ride 'herd on sb/sth** (*NAmE, informal*) to keep watch or control over sb/sth 監視；對某人／某物嚴加控制：*police riding herd on crowds of youths on the streets* 警方監視着街上成群結隊的年輕人 **ride 'shotgun** (*NAmE, informal*) to ride in the front passenger seat of a car or truck 坐在車的前排座位上 **ride a/the wave of sth** to enjoy or be supported by the particular situation or quality mentioned 受益於某事；乘…之勢：*Schools are riding a wave of renewed public interest.* 各校重新受益於公眾的關注。 ➲ more at WISH *n.*

PHR V **'ride on sth** (usually used in the progressive tenses 通常用於進行時) to depend on sth 依賴於；依靠：*My whole future is riding on this interview.* 我的未來全靠這次面試了。 **ˌride sth↔'out** to manage to survive a difficult situation or time without having to make great changes 安然渡過（難關）；經受得住 **ˌride 'up** (of clothing 衣服) to move gradually upwards, out of position 慢慢向上移動；漸漸縮上去：*Short skirts tend to ride up when you sit down.* 坐下來的時候，短裙就會往上收。

■ ***noun***

▸ **IN VEHICLE** 車輛 **1** a short journey in a vehicle, on a bicycle, etc.（乘車或騎車的）短途旅程：*a train ride through beautiful countryside* 乘火車穿越美麗鄉村的旅程 ◇ *It's a ten-minute bus ride from here to town.* 從這裏到鎮上乘公共汽車要花十分鐘。◇ *Steve* ***gave me a ride*** *on his motorbike.* 史蒂夫用摩托車捎了我一程。◇ *We* ***went for a ride*** *on our bikes.* 我們騎自行車出去兜了一圈。◇ *a bike ride* 騎自行車出行 **2** (*NAmE*) (*BrE* **lift**) a free ride in a car, etc. to a place you want to get to 免費搭車；搭便車：*She hitched a ride to the station.* 她搭便車去車站。◇ *We managed to get a ride into town when we missed the bus.* 我們沒趕上公共汽車，就設法搭了一輛便車去城裏。 **3** the kind of journey you make in a car, etc.（乘坐汽車等的）旅行：*a* ***smooth/comfortable/bumpy, etc. ride*** 順利、舒適、顛簸等的旅途 ◇ (*figurative*) *The new legislation faces* ***a bumpy ride*** (= will meet with opposition and difficulties). 新的法規前路崎嶇。

▸ **ON HORSE** 馬 **4** a short journey on a horse, etc.（騎馬等的）短途旅程：*a pony ride* 騎一會兒小馬 ◇ *The kids had a ride on an elephant at the zoo.* 在動物園裏，孩子們騎着大象走了一圈。◇ *He goes for a ride most mornings.* 他上午經常騎馬出去兜一圈。

▸ **AT FUNFAIR** 遊樂場 **5** a large machine at a FUNFAIR or AMUSEMENT PARK that you ride on for fun or excitement; an occasion when you go on one of these 供乘騎的遊樂設施；乘坐（遊樂設施）：*The rides are free.* 免費乘坐。◇ *a roller coaster ride* 坐一趟過山車

IDM **come/go along for the 'ride** (*informal*) to join in an activity for pleasure but without being seriously interested in it 隨大溜；湊湊熱鬧；逢場作戲 **have a**

rough/an easy 'ride | give sb a rough/an easy 'ride (*informal*) to experience/not experience difficulties when you are doing sth; to make things difficult/easy for sb（使）舉步維艱（或一帆風順）: *He will be given a rough ride at the party conference.* 在黨員大會上他會很難過這一關。 **take sb for a 'ride** (*informal*) to cheat or trick sb 欺騙；愚弄: *It's not a pleasant feeling to discover you've been taken for a ride by someone you trusted.* 發現被你信任的人騙了，心裏很不是滋味。 ➲ more at FREE *adj.*

'ride-off *noun* (*NAmE*) = JUMP-OFF

rider 🗝 /ˈraɪdə(r)/ *noun*
1 🗝 a person who rides a horse, bicycle or motorcycle 騎手；騎馬（或自行車、摩托車）的人: *Three riders* (= people riding horses) *were approaching.* 三個騎馬的人越來越近。◇ *horses and their riders* 馬匹及其騎手 ◇ *She's an experienced rider.* 她是位有經驗的騎手。◇ *a motorcycle dispatch rider* 騎摩托車的通信員 ➲ VISUAL VOCAB page V46 **2** ~ (**to sth**) an extra piece of information that is added to an official document 公文的附加材料；附文

ridge /rɪdʒ/ *noun, verb*
■ ***noun*** **1** a narrow area of high land along the top of a line of hills; a high pointed area near the top of a mountain 山脊；山脈: *walking along the ridge* 沿着山脊行走 ◇ *the north-east ridge of Mount Everest* 珠穆朗瑪峰的東北部 ➲ VISUAL VOCAB page V4 **2** a raised line on the surface of sth; the point where two sloping surfaces join 隆起；脊；壟: *The ridges on the soles of my boots stopped me from slipping.* 我靴子底上有隆起的紋路，使我沒有滑倒。◇ *the ridge of the roof* 屋脊 ➲ VISUAL VOCAB page V17 **3** [usually sing.] ~ (**of high pressure**) (*technical* 術語) a long narrow area of high pressure in the atmosphere（大氣層的）高壓脊，高壓帶 ➲ compare TROUGH (3)
■ ***verb*** [usually passive] ~ **sth** to make narrow raised lines or areas on the surface of sth 使隆起；使形成脊狀

ridged /rɪdʒd/ *adj.* (of an object or area 物體或地區) with raised lines on the surface 有隆凸線條的；有埂子的

'ridge tent (*BrE*) (also **'A-frame tent** *BrE, NAmE*) *noun* a tent which forms an upside-down V shape 三角帳篷 ➲ compare DOME TENT, FRAME TENT

ridi·cule /ˈrɪdɪkjuːl/ *noun, verb*
■ ***noun*** [U] unkind comments that make fun of sb/sth or make them look silly 嘲笑；奚落；譏笑 SYN **mockery**: *She is* ***an object of ridicule*** *in the tabloid newspapers.* 她是小報譏笑諷刺的對象。◇ *to* ***hold sb up to ridicule*** (= make fun of sb publicly) 公然取笑某人
■ ***verb*** ~ **sb/sth** to make sb/sth look silly by laughing at them or it in an unkind way 嘲笑；奚落；譏笑 SYN **make fun of**

ri·dicu·lous 🗝 /rɪˈdɪkjələs/ *adj.*
very silly or unreasonable 愚蠢的；荒謬的；荒唐的 SYN **absurd, ludicrous**: *I look ridiculous in this hat.* 我戴這頂帽子看上去很可笑。◇ *Don't be ridiculous! You can't pay £50 for a T-shirt!* 別犯傻了！你不會花 50 英鎊買一件 T 恤衫的！ ▸ **ri·dicu·lous·ly** *adv.*: *The meal was ridiculously expensive.* 這頓飯貴得離譜。 **ri·dicu·lous·ness** *noun* [U] IDM see SUBLIME *n.*

rid·ing 🗝 /ˈraɪdɪŋ/ *noun*
1 🗝 (*BrE* also **'horse riding**) (*NAmE* also **'horseback riding**) [U] the sport or activity of riding horses 騎馬: *I'm taking riding lessons.* 我在學習騎馬。◇ *riding boots* 馬靴 ◇ (*BrE*) *to* ***go riding*** 去騎馬 ◇ (*NAmE*) *to* ***go horseback riding*** 去騎馬 **2** **Riding** one of the three former parts of the English county of Yorkshire called the **East Riding**, the **North Riding** and the **West Riding** 區（英格蘭約克郡以前的東、西、北三個行政分區之一） ORIGIN From an Anglo-Saxon word meaning 'one third'. 源自盎格魯—撒克遜單詞，意為三分之一。

rife /raɪf/ *adj.* [not before noun] **1** if sth bad or unpleasant is **rife** in a place, it is very common there（壞事）盛行，普遍 SYN **widespread**: *It is a country where corruption is rife.* 這是個腐敗成風的國家。◇ *Rumours are rife that he is going to resign.* 到處都在傳，說他要辭職了。 **2** ~ (**with sth**) full of sth bad or unpleasant 充斥，充滿（壞事）: *Los Angeles is rife with gossip about the stars' private lives.* 洛杉磯盛傳明星私生活的流言蜚語。

riff /rɪf/ *noun* a short repeated pattern of notes in popular music or JAZZ（流行音樂或爵士樂的）重複段

rif·fle /ˈrɪfl/ *verb* [I, T] to turn over papers or the pages of a book quickly and without reading them all 迅速翻動（紙張或書頁） SYN **leaf**: ~ **through sth** *He was riffling through the papers on his desk.* 他很快地翻着他桌上的文件。◇ ~ **sth** *to riffle the pages of a book* 隨意翻動書頁

riff-raff /ˈrɪf ræf/ *noun* [U+sing./pl. v.] (*disapproving*) an insulting way of referring to people of low social class or people who are not considered socially acceptable 賤民；不三不四的下等人

rifle /ˈraɪfl/ *noun, verb*
■ ***noun*** a gun with a long BARREL which you hold to your shoulder to fire 步槍；來復槍
■ ***verb*** **1** [I, T] ~ (**through**) **sth** to search quickly through sth in order to find or steal sth 快速搜尋；匆忙翻找: *She rifled through her clothes for something suitable to wear.* 她急匆匆地在衣服堆裏找合適的衣服穿。 **2** [T] ~ **sth** to steal sth from somewhere 偷竊；盜取: *His wallet had been rifled.* 他的錢包被偷了。 **3** [T] ~ **sth + adv./prep.** to kick a ball very hard and straight in a game of football (SOCCER) 猛踢（足球）

rifle·man /ˈraɪflmən/ *noun* (*pl.* **-men** /-mən/) a soldier who carries a rifle（配備步槍的）步兵

'rifle range *noun* **1** [C] a place where people practise shooting with rifles 步槍射擊場 **2** [U] the distance that a bullet from a rifle will travel 步槍射程

rift /rɪft/ *noun* **1** a serious disagreement between people that stops their relationship from continuing 分裂；分歧；嚴重不和 SYN **breach, division**: *The rift within the party deepened.* 黨內的分歧加深了。◇ *Efforts to* ***heal the rift*** *between the two countries have failed.* 彌合兩國間分歧的各種努力都已失敗。 ➲ COLLOCATIONS at INTERNATIONAL **2** a large crack or opening in the ground, rocks or clouds 斷裂；裂縫；裂口

'rift valley *noun* a valley with steep sides formed when two parallel cracks develop in the earth's surface and the land between them sinks 地塹；裂谷

rig /rɪɡ/ *verb, noun*
■ ***verb*** (**-gg-**) [usually passive] **1** ~ **sth** to arrange or influence sth in a dishonest way in order to get the result that you want（以不正當的手段）操縱，控制 SYN **fix**: *He said the election had been rigged.* 他說選舉被人操縱了。◇ *to rig the market* (= to cause an artificial rise or fall in prices, in order to make a profit) 操縱市場 **2** ~ **sth** (**with sth**) to provide a ship or boat with ropes, sails, etc.; to fit the sails, etc. in position（給船隻）裝帆，提供索具 **3** ~ **sth** (**up**) (**with sth**) to fit equipment somewhere, sometimes secretly（秘密地）安裝，裝配: *The lights had been rigged (up) but not yet tested.* 燈已經裝好了，但還沒有經過測試。◇ *The car had been rigged with about 300 lbs of explosive.* 有人暗中在車上放了大約 300 磅炸藥。
PHR V **,rig sb/sth/yourself↔'out** (**in/with sth**) [often passive] (*old-fashioned*) to provide sb/sth with a particular kind of clothes or equipment 給…提供（服裝或設備）: *I was accepted for the job and rigged out in a uniform.* 我獲得錄用從事這份工作，並配發了制服。 **,rig sth↔'up** to make or to build sth quickly, using whatever materials are available（用現有的材料）匆匆做成，草草搭建: *We managed to rig up a shelter for the night.* 我們匆匆搭了個棚子過夜。
■ ***noun*** **1** (especially in compounds 尤用於構成複合詞) a large piece of equipment that is used for taking oil or gas from the ground or the bottom of the sea 鑽井設備；鑽塔: *an oil rig* 石油鑽塔 **2** the way that the MASTS and sails on a boat, etc. are arranged 帆裝（船桅和風帆等的安裝模式） **3** (*NAmE, informal*) a large lorry/truck 大卡車；大貨車 **4** equipment that is used for a special purpose 有專門用途的設備: *a CB radio rig* 民用波段無線電設備

rig·ging /ˈrɪɡɪŋ/ *noun* [U] **1** the ropes that support the MASTS and sails of a boat or ship（牽拉船桅和風帆的）繩索，索具 **2** the act of influencing sth in a dishonest way in order to get the result that you want 營私舞弊；操縱：*vote rigging* 操縱投票

Synonyms 同義詞辨析

right

correct

Both these words describe a belief, opinion, decision or method that is suitable or the best one for a particular situation. 以上兩詞均指看法、意見、決定或方法等恰當、合適。

right if sb is right to do or think sth, that is a good thing to do or think in that situation 指正確的、妥當的、恰當的：*You're right to be cautious.* 你謹慎是應當的。◇ *You made the right decision.* 你的決定是正確的。◇ *'It's not easy.' 'Yes, you're right.'* "這不容易。" "對，你說得沒錯。"

correct (of a method, belief, opinion or decision) right and suitable in a particular situation 指（方法、看法、意見或決定）正確的、恰當的、合適的：*What's the correct way to shut the machine down?* 這台機器應該怎麼關？◇ *I don't think she's correct to say he's incompetent.* 我認為她說他無能是不對的。

RIGHT OR CORRECT? 用 right 還是 correct？

Correct is more formal than **right** . It is more often used for methods and **right** is more often used for beliefs, opinions and decisions. * correct 較 right 正式，較常用以指方法，right 則較常用以指看法、意見和決定。

PATTERNS

- right/correct **about** sb/sth
- right/correct **to do** sth
- right/correct **in thinking/believing/saying** sth
- the right/correct **decision/judgement/conclusion**
- the right/correct **way/method/approach**
- **absolutely/quite** right/correct

right 🔑 /raɪt/ *adj., adv., noun, verb, exclamation*

■ ***adj.***

▸ **MORALLY GOOD** 正當 **1** 🔑 [not usually before noun] **~ (to do sth)** morally good or acceptable; correct according to law or a person's duty 正當；妥當：*You were quite right to criticize him.* 你批評他批評得很對。◇ *Is it ever right to kill?* 有沒有什麼情況下，殺人是對的？◇ *It seems **only right** to warn you of the risk.* 似乎應該警告你有風險。◇ *I hope we're doing **the right thing**.* 我希望我們這樣做是妥當的。**OPP** wrong

▸ **TRUE/CORRECT** 真實；正確 **2** 🔑 true or correct as a fact 正確的；真正的；真實的：*Did you get the answer right?* 你回答得正確嗎？◇ *'What's the **right time**?' '10.37.'* "現在的準確時間是幾點？" "10 點 37 分。" ◇ *'David, isn't it?' 'Yes, **that's right**.'* "是戴維嗎？" "對，沒錯。" ◇ (*informal*) *It was Monday you went to see Angie, right?* 你是星期一去看望安吉的，對不對？◇ *Let me **get this right*** (= understand correctly)—*you want us to do an extra ten hours' work for no extra pay?* 讓我先搞清楚這一點，你想讓我們加班十個小時而不給加班費，是不是？**OPP** wrong ➲ SYNONYMS at TRUE **3** 🔑 correct for a particular situation or thing, or for a particular person 適當的；正好的；恰當的：*Have you got the **right money*** (= the exact amount) *for the bus fare?* 你有數額剛好的零錢付公車車費嗎？◇ *Is this the right way to the beach?* 去海灘是走這條路嗎？◇ *You're not holding it **the right way up**.* 你把它拿倒了。◇ *Are you sure you've got that on **the right way round**?* 你肯定你那樣做是完全正確的嗎？◇ *Next time we'll **get it right**.* 下次我們就不會錯了。◇ *He's the right man for the job.* 他是這份工作的合適人選。◇ *I'm glad you split up. She wasn't right for you.* 我很高興你們分手了。她不適合你。◇ *I was waiting for the right moment to ask him.* 我在等待時機問他這件事。◇ *She knows all the **right people*** (= important people, for example those who can help her career). 她認識所有那些關鍵人物。◇ *His success was down to being **in the right place at the right time*** (= being able to take opportunities when they came). 他的成功之處就在於把握住了時機。**OPP** wrong **4** 🔑 [not before noun] correct in your opinion or judgement（意見或判斷）準確，確切，恰當：**~ (about sth)** *She was right about Tom having no money.* 她認為湯姆沒有錢，她的判斷是對的。◇ **~ (to do sth)** *You're right to be cautious.* 你保持謹慎是應當的。◇ *'It's not easy.' 'Yeah, **you're right**.'* "這不容易。" "對，你說得沒錯。" ◇ **~ (in doing sth)** *Am I **right in thinking** we've met before?* 我們以前見過面，我說得對嗎？**OPP** wrong

▸ **NORMAL** 正常 **5** 🔑 [not before noun] in a normal or good enough condition 正常；情況良好：*I don't feel quite right today* (= I feel ill/sick). 我今天感覺不太舒服。◇ *That sausage doesn't smell right.* 這香腸聞起來不對勁。◇ *Things aren't right between her parents.* 她父母的關係不太正常。◇ *If only I could have helped **put** matters **right**.* 要是我當時能幫着把錯誤糾正過來就好了。◇ *He's **not quite right in the head*** (= not mentally normal). 他精神不太正常。**OPP** wrong

▸ **NOT LEFT** 右面 **6** 🔑 [only before noun] of, on or towards the side of the body that is towards the east when a person faces north 右邊的：*my right eye* 我的右眼 ◇ *Keep on the right side of the road.* 靠馬路的右邊行走。◇ *Take a right turn at the intersection.* 在十字路口向右拐。➲ see also RIGHT-WING **OPP** left

▸ **COMPLETE** 完全 **7** [only before noun] (*BrE, informal*, especially *disapproving*) used to emphasize sth bad（強調壞事）真正的，完全的：*You made a right mess of that!* 你把這件事完全給弄糟了！◇ *I felt a right idiot.* 我覺得自己就像個十足的白痴。➲ see also ALL RIGHT

▸ **right·ness** *noun* [U]：*the rightness* (= justice) *of their cause* 他們正義的事業 ◇ *the rightness of his decision* 他的正確決定

IDM ˌ**give your right ˈarm for sth/to do sth** (*informal*) used to say that sb is willing to give up a lot in order to have or do sth that they really want 為…情願捨棄很多；不惜任何代價：*I'd have given my right arm to have been there with them.* 我就是放棄一切也會跟他們一起去那兒的。**(not) in your right ˈmind** (not) mentally normal 精神正常（或不正常）➲ SYNONYMS at MAD **(as) right as ˈrain** (*informal*) in excellent health or condition 十分健康；狀況奇佳 **right eˈnough** (*informal*) certainly; in a way that cannot be denied 當然；無疑；不可否認：*You heard me right enough* (= so don't pretend that you did not). 你肯定聽到我說了什麼。**right ˈon** (*informal*) used to express strong approval or encouragement（表示明確的贊同或鼓勵）完全正確 ➲ see also RIGHT-ON ˌ**right side ˈup** (*NAmE*) with the top part turned to the top; in the correct, normal position 正面朝上；位置正確；在正常位置：*I dropped my toast, but luckily it fell right side up.* 我把烤麪包掉在地上，但幸好它正面朝上。**OPP** upside down **ˈshe'll be right** (*AustralE, informal*) used to say that everything will be all right, even if there is a problem now 一切都會好的（即使現在有問題）ˌ**too ˈright** (*BrE, informal*) used to say that there is no doubt about sth 毫無疑問；一點不錯；對極啦：*'We need to stick together.' 'Too right!'* "我們得團結一致。" "對極啦！" ◇ *'I'll have to do it again.' 'Too right you will.'* "我得再做一次。" "你說得一點不錯。" ➲ more at BUTTON *n.*, FOOT *n.*, HEAD *n.*, HEART, IDEA, LEFT *adv.*, MIGHT *n.*, MR, NOTE *n.*, SIDE *n.*, TRACK *n.*

■ ***adv.***

▸ **EXACTLY** 正好 **1** 🔑 exactly; directly 正好；恰好；直接地：*Lee was standing **right behind** her.* 李就站在她身後。◇ *The wind was right in our faces.* 風迎面吹來。◇ *I'm **right behind you** on this one* (= I am supporting you). 在這件事情上，我完全支持你。◇ *The bus came right on time.* 公共汽車正好準時到達。

▸ **COMPLETELY** 完全 **2** 🔑 all the way; completely 一直；逕直；完全地：*The car spun right off the track.* 汽車完全開出了車道。◇ *I'm right out of ideas.* 我完全沒了主意。◇ *She kept right on swimming until she reached the other side.* 她一直游到對岸。

R

▸ **IMMEDIATELY** 立即 **3** 🔑 (*informal*) immediately; without delay 立即；馬上；毫不耽擱：*I'll be right back.* 我馬上就回來。◇ *I'll be right with you* (= I am coming very soon). 我這就過來。
▸ **CORRECTLY** 正確 **4** 🔑 correctly 正確地；確切地：*You guessed right.* 你猜着了。**OPP** wrong
▸ **SATISFACTORILY** 滿意 **5** 🔑 in the way that things should happen or are supposed to happen 順利；正常：*Nothing's going right for me today.* 今天沒有哪一件事讓我順心。**OPP** wrong
▸ **NOT LEFT** 右面 **6** 🔑 on or to the right side 在右邊；向右邊：*Turn right at the end of the street.* 在街的那頭往右拐。**OPP** left

IDM **ˌright and ˈleft** everywhere 到處；處處：*She owes money right and left.* 她到處欠債。**right aˈway/ˈoff** 🔑 immediately; without delay 立即；馬上；毫不耽擱：*I want it sent right away.* 馬上把它發出去。◇ *I told him right off what I thought of him.* 我直截了當地告訴了他我對他的看法。**ˌright, left and ˈcentre** = LEFT, RIGHT AND CENTRE at LEFT *adv.* **right ˈnow** **1** 🔑 at this moment 此刻；此時此刻：*He's not in the office right now.* 他現在不在辦公室。**2** 🔑 immediately 立即；馬上：*Do it right now!* 這件事馬上做！**right off the ˈbat** (*informal, especially NAmE*) immediately; without delay 立即；馬上；毫不耽擱：*We both liked each other right off the bat.* 我們倆一見如故。**see sb ˈright** (*NAmE* also **do sb ˈright**) (*informal*) to make sure that sb has all they need or want 確保（或負責）滿足某人的一切需求：*You needn't worry about money—I'll see you right.* 你不必擔心錢的問題，我會給你的。➲ more at ALLEY, HIT *v.*, SERVE *v.*, WORD *n.*

■ ***noun***

▸ **STH MORALLY GOOD** 正當的事 **1** 🔑 [U, C] what is morally good or correct 正當；公正；正義；正確：*She doesn't understand the difference between right and wrong.* 她不能明辨是非。◇ *You **did right** to tell me about it.* 你把這件事告訴我，做得很對。◇ *They both had some right on their side.* 他們雙方都有一定的道理。◇ *He wouldn't apologize. He knew he was **in the right*** (= had justice on his side). 他不肯道歉。他知道自己是有理的。◇ *It was difficult to establish **the rights and wrongs*** (= the true facts) *of the matter.* 很難確定這件事情的真相。**OPP** wrong
▸ **MORAL/LEGAL CLAIM** 正當 / 合法要求 **2** 🔑 [C, U] a moral or legal claim to have or get sth or to behave in a particular way 正當的要求；權利：**~ (to sth)** *Everyone has a right to a fair trial.* 每個人都有權獲得公正的審判。◇ **~ (to do sth)** *You have no right to stop me from going in there.* 你無權阻止我進去。◇ ***What gives you the right** to do that?* 你有什麼權利這樣做？◇ *She **had every right** to be angry.* 她完全有理由生氣。◇ *You're quite **within your rights** to ask for your money back.* 你完全有權要回你的錢。◇ ***By rights*** (= if justice were done) *half the money should be mine.* 按理說，應該有一半的錢歸我。◇ *There is no right of appeal against the decision.* 關於這項判決，沒有上訴權。◇ *Education is provided by the state **as of right*** (= everyone has a right to it). 受教育是國家賦予每一個人的權利。◇ *The property belongs to her **by right**.* 這份財產依法歸她所有。◇ *They had fought hard for **equal rights**.* 他們為了獲得平等權利已經進行了頑強的鬥爭。➲ see also ANIMAL RIGHTS, CIVIL RIGHTS, HUMAN RIGHT
▸ **FOR BOOK/MOVIE, ETC.** 書籍或電影等 **3** 🔑 **rights** [pl.] the authority to perform, publish, film, etc. a particular work, event, etc. 版權；發行權：*He sold the rights for $2 million.* 他以 200 萬元的價格出售了版權。◇ *all rights reserved* (= protected or kept for the owners of the book, film/movie, etc.) 版權所有
▸ **NOT LEFT SIDE** 右面 **4** 🔑 **the/sb's right** [sing.] the right side or direction 右邊；右方；右：*Take the first street **on the right**.* 走右手的第一條街。◇ *She seated me on her right.* 她讓我坐在她的右邊。**OPP** left **5** 🔑 [sing.] **the first, second, etc. ~** the first, second, etc. road on the right side 右邊的（第一條、第二條等）路：*Take the first right, then the second left.* 走右邊的第一條路，然後再走左邊的第二條路。**OPP** left **6** **a right** [sing.] a turn to the right 右拐；右轉彎：*to make a right* 向右轉彎 ◇ (*NAmE, informal*) *to hang a right* 右拐彎 **OPP** left

R

▸ **POLITICS** 政治 **7** 🔑 **the right, the Right** [sing.+sing./pl. v.] political groups that most strongly support the CAPITALIST system 右派組織（或政黨）➲ compare RIGHT WING (1)：*The Right in British politics is represented by the Conservative Party.* 英國政壇的右派是以保守黨為代表的。**OPP** left **8** 🔑 **the right** [sing.+sing./pl. v.] the part of a political party whose members are most conservative（政黨內的）右派，右翼：*He's on the right of the Labour Party.* 他是工黨內的右派成員。**OPP** left
▸ **IN BOXING** 拳擊 **9** [C] a blow that is made with your right hand 右手拳 **OPP** left

IDM **bang to ˈrights** (*BrE*) (*NAmE* **dead to ˈrights**) (*informal*) with definite proof of having committed a crime, so that you cannot claim to be innocent 證據確鑿；肯定無疑：*We've got you bang to rights handling stolen property.* 你在銷贓時被我們抓了個正着。**do ˈright by sb** (*old-fashioned*) to treat sb fairly 公平對待 **in your own ˈright** because of your personal qualifications or efforts, not because of your connection with sb else 憑自身的資格（或努力）：*She sings with a rock band, but she's also a jazz musician in her own right.* 她隨一支搖滾樂隊演唱，但她本身也是爵士樂樂師。**put/set sb/sth to ˈrights** to correct sb/sth; to put things in their right places or right order 糾正；改正；收拾；恢復秩序：*It took me ages to put things to rights after the workmen had left.* 工人們走後，我花了好長時間才收拾好。➲ more at WORLD, WRONG *n.*

■ ***verb***

▸ **RETURN TO POSITION** 回復位置 **1 ~ sb/sth/yourself** to return sb/sth/yourself to the normal, vertical position 使回到正常位置；把…扶正；使…直立：*They learnt to right a capsized canoe.* 他們學會了將傾覆的獨木舟翻過來。◇ *At last the plane **righted itself** and flew on.* 最後，飛機終於恢復了平穩，繼續飛行。
▸ **CORRECT** 改正 **2 ~ sth** to correct sth that is wrong or not in its normal state 改正；糾正；使恢復正常 **SYN** **put right**：*Righting the economy will demand major cuts in expenditure.* 復蘇經濟需要大量削減開支。

IDM **right a ˈwrong** to do sth to correct an unfair situation or sth bad that you have done 糾正錯誤；平反昭雪

■ ***exclamation*** (*BrE, informal*) **1** used to show that you accept a statement or an order（表示同意或遵從）是的，好的：*'You may find it hurts a little at first.' 'Right.'* "開始時，你會覺得有點疼。" "明白。" ◇ *'Barry's here.' 'Oh, right.'* "巴里在這兒。" "哦，太好了。" ◇ *'I'll have a whisky and soda.' '**Right you are**, sir.'* "我要一份威士忌加蘇打。" "馬上就送來，先生。" **2** used to get sb's attention to say that you are ready to do sth, or to tell them to do sth（引起注意，表示已做好準備或讓別人做某事）嗨，喂：*Right! Let's get going.* 行了！我們走吧。**3** used to check that sb agrees with you or has understood you（要確保對方同意或明白時說）對不：*So that's twenty of each sort, right?* 那麼，每一種都是二十個，對不對？◇ *And I didn't think any more of it, right, but Mum says I should see a doctor.* 我本來不再想這事了，知道嗎？可媽媽說我該看醫生。**4** (*ironic*) used to say that you do not believe sb or that you disagree with them（表示不相信或不同意）是嗎，好哇：*'I won't be late tonight.' '**Yeah, right**.'* "今天晚上我不會晚的。" "是麼，好哇。"

ˈright angle *noun* an angle of 90° 直角：*Place the table **at right angles/at a right angle** to the wall.* 將桌子跟牆垂直擺放。➲ **VISUAL VOCAB** page V71 ➲ compare ACUTE ANGLE, OBTUSE ANGLE, REFLEX ANGLE

ˈright-angled *adj.* having or consisting of a right angle 直角的；有直角的

ˌright-angled ˈtriangle (*especially BrE*) (*NAmE* usually **ˌright ˈtriangle**) *noun* a triangle with a right angle 直角三角形 ➲ **VISUAL VOCAB** page V71

ˌright ˈbrain *noun* [U, sing.] the right side of the human brain, that is thought to be used for creating new ideas and to be where emotions come from（人的）右腦（據信用於構思新思想和主管情感）➲ compare LEFT BRAIN

ˌright-ˈclick *verb* [T, I] **~ sth** | **~ (on sth)** to choose a particular function or item on a computer screen, etc., by pressing the button on a mouse that is on the right side 用鼠標右鍵點擊；右擊

Which Word? 詞語辨析

right / rightly

- **Right** and **rightly** can both be used as adverbs. In the sense 'correctly' or 'in the right way', **right** is the usual adverb. It is only used after verbs. * right 和 rightly 均可用作副詞。表示正確地、恰當地則通常用副詞 right；此詞只用於動詞之後：*He did it right.* 他做得對。◇ *Did I spell your name right?* 你的名字我拼得對不對？ **Rightly** cannot be used like this. In formal language **correctly** is used. 上述用法不能用 rightly，在正式用語中可用 correctly：*Is your name spelled correctly?* 你的名字拼正確了嗎？
- The usual meaning of **rightly** is 'for a good reason' and it comes before an adjective. * rightly 的通常意義為理所當然地，用於形容詞前：*They are rightly proud of their children.* 他們當然為他們的孩子而驕傲。It can be used to mean 'correctly' before a verb or in particular phrases. 該詞亦可表示正確地，用於動詞前或某些短語中：*As you rightly say, we have a serious problem.* 你說得對，我們有嚴重困難。In *NAmE* **rightly** is not at all common. 在美式英語中 rightly 一點也不常用。

right·eous /ˈraɪtʃəs/ *adj.* (*formal*) **1** morally right and good 公正的；正直的；正當的：*a righteous God* 公正的上帝 **2** that you think is morally acceptable or fair 正當的；公平合理的；正義的：***righteous anger/indignation, etc.*** 義憤等 ➲ see also SELF-RIGHTEOUS ▸ **right·eous·ly** *adv.* **right·eous·ness** *noun* [U]

ˌright ˈfield *noun* [sing.] (in BASEBALL 棒球) the part of the field to the right of the BATTER 右外場，右外野（擊球手右邊的場地）

right·ful /ˈraɪtfl/ *adj.* [only before noun] (*formal*) that is correct, right or legal 正確的；公正的；合法的 SYN **proper**：*The stolen car was returned to its **rightful** owner.* 被盜的汽車還給了其合法的主人。▸ **right·ful·ly** /-fəli/ *adv.*：*She was only claiming what was rightfully hers.* 她只要求得到理應屬於她的東西。

ˈright-hand *adj.* [only before noun] **1** on the right side of sth 右手的；右邊的；右面的：*on the right-hand side of the road* 在路的右邊 ◇ *the top right-hand corner of the screen* 屏幕的右上角 **2** intended for use by your right hand 右手的；供右手用的：*a right-hand glove* 右手的手套 OPP **left-hand**

ˌright-hand ˈdrive *adj.* (of a vehicle 車輛) with the driver's seat and STEERING WHEEL on the right side 右側駕駛的 OPP **left-hand drive**

ˌright-ˈhanded *adj.* **1** a person who is **right-handed** uses their right hand for writing, using tools, etc. 慣用右手的 **2** a **right-handed** tool is designed to be used with the right hand 供右手使用的 OPP **left-handed** ▸ **ˌright-ˈhanded** *adv.*

ˌright-ˈhander *noun* **1** a person who uses their right hand for writing, using tools, etc. 慣用右手的人 **2** a hit with the right hand 右手的一擊 OPP **left-hander**

ˌright-hand ˈman *noun* [sing.] a person who helps sb a lot and who they rely on, especially in an important job 左右手；得力助手：*the President's right-hand man* 總統的得力助手

ˌRight ˈHonourable *adj.* [only before noun] (*abbr.* **Rt Hon**) **1 the Right Honourable ...** a title of respect used when talking to or about a person of high social rank, especially a lord（對上層社會人士如貴族的尊稱）閣下 **2 the/my Right Honourable ...** the title of respect used by Members of Parliament in Britain when talking to or about a senior Member of Parliament during a debate（英國議會成員對資深成員的尊稱）閣下 ➲ compare HONOURABLE (6)

right·ist /ˈraɪtɪst/ *noun* a person who supports RIGHT-WING political parties and their ideas 右派人士；右翼分子 SYN **right-winger** OPP **leftist** ▸ **right·ist** *adj.*

right·ly 0⊸ /ˈraɪtli/ *adv.*
1 0⊸ for a good reason 正當地；理由充分地 SYN **justifiably**：*The school was rightly proud of the excellent exam results.* 學校為這次出色的考試成績感到驕傲，這是理所當然的。◇ *He was proud of his beautiful house, **and rightly so**.* 他為自己的漂亮房子感到驕傲，這是很自然的。◇ ***Quite rightly**, the environment is of great concern.* 當然，環境問題非常受關注。**2** 0⊸ in a correct or accurate way 正確地；恰當地；精確地 SYN **correctly**：***Rightly or wrongly**, many older people are afraid of violence in the streets.* 不管正不正當，反正許多年長者都害怕街頭暴力。◇ *As she rightly pointed out, the illness can affect adults as well as children.* 她說得對，這種病不僅影響兒童，也會影響成年人。◇ *I can't **rightly say** what happened.* 我說不準到底發生了什麼事。◇ ***I don't rightly know** where he's gone.* 我說不好他上哪兒去了。◇ ***If I remember rightly**, there's a train at six o'clock.* 如果我沒記錯的話，六點鐘有一趟火車。➲ note at RIGHT

ˌright-ˈminded (also **ˌright-ˈthinking**) *adj.* (of a person 人) having beliefs and opinions that most people approve of 有正義感的；正直的

right·most /ˈraɪtməʊst; *NAmE* -moʊst/ *adj.* [only before noun] furthest to the right 最右邊的；最右面的

righto /ˈraɪtəʊ; *NAmE* -oʊ/ (also **righty-ho**) *exclamation* (*old-fashioned*, *BrE*, *informal*) used to show that you accept a statement or an order 好；行；對

ˌright of aˈbode *noun* [U] official permission that allows a person to live in a particular country 居留權

ˌright-of-ˈcentre *adj.* = CENTRE-RIGHT

ˌright of ˈway *noun* (*pl.* **ˌrights of ˈway**) **1** [U] (*especially BrE*) legal permission to go onto or through another person's land（進入或穿越他人土地的）通行權：*Private property—no right of way.* 私有房產，禁止穿行。**2** [C] (*especially BrE*) a public path that goes through private land（穿越私有土地的）公用通道 **3** [U] the right to drive across or into a road before another vehicle（交通工具的）優先通行權：*I had right of way at the junction.* 我在這交叉路口有優先通行權。◇ *Whose right of way is it?* 這裏誰有優先通行權？

ˌright-ˈon *adj.* (*BrE*, *informal*, sometimes *disapproving*) having political opinions or being aware of social issues that are fashionable and LEFT-WING 政見入時的；左傾的：*right-on middle-class intellectuals* 左傾的中產階級知識分子

ˌRight ˈReverend *adj.* [only before noun] (*abbr.* **Rt Revd**) a title of respect used when talking about a BISHOP (= a senior priest)（尊稱主教）尊敬的，可敬的

ˈrights issue *noun* (*business* 商) an offer to buy shares in a company at a cheaper price to people who already own some shares in it 認股權發行，有購股權的證券發行（公司以優惠價格向現有股東發售新股）

right·size /ˈraɪtsaɪz/ *verb* [I, T] **~ (sth)** (*business* 商) to change the size of a company in order to reduce costs, especially by reducing the number of employees（通過裁員等）使公司規模適中，精簡公司的規模

ˌright-ˈthinking *adj.* = RIGHT-MINDED

ˌright ˈtriangle *noun* (*NAmE*) = RIGHT-ANGLED TRIANGLE

right·ward /ˈraɪtwəd; *NAmE* -wərd/ (also **right·wards** /ˈraɪtwədz; *NAmE* -wərdz/ especially in *BrE*) *adj.* **1** on or to the right 在右側的；向右的：*a rightward movement* 向右的移動 **2** towards more RIGHT-WING political ideas 右傾的：*a rightward shift in voting patterns* 選舉格局的右傾化轉變 ▸ **right·ward** (also **right·wards**) *adv.*

the ˌright ˈwing *noun* **1** [sing.+sing./pl. v.] the part of a political party whose members are least in favour of social change（政黨的）右翼：*He is on the right wing of the party.* 他屬於黨內的右翼。**2** [C, U] an attacking player or a position on the right side of the field in a sports game（體育比賽的）右邊鋒，右翼 OPP **left wing**

ˌright-ˈwing *adj.* strongly supporting the CAPITALIST system 右翼的；右派的：*right-wing policies* 右傾政策 OPP **left-wing**

ˌright-ˈwinger *noun* **1** a person on the right wing of a political party 右翼人士；右派成員：*She is a prominent*

R

Tory right-winger. 她是保守黨中赫赫有名的右派。**2** a person who plays on the right side of the field in a sports game（體育比賽的）右邊鋒 OPP **left-winger**

righty-ho /ˈraɪtihəʊ; *NAmE* -hoʊ/ *exclamation* (*old-fashioned, BrE, informal*) = RIGHTO

rigid AW /ˈrɪdʒɪd/ *adj.* **1** (often *disapproving*) (of rules, methods, etc. 規則、方法等) very strict and difficult to change 死板的；僵硬的 SYN **inflexible**：*The curriculum was too narrow and too rigid.* 課程設置過於狹窄和死板。◇ *His rigid adherence to the rules made him unpopular.* 他對規則的刻板堅持使得他不受歡迎。**2** (of a person 人) not willing to change their ideas or behaviour 固執的；僵化的；一成不變的 SYN **inflexible**：*rigid attitudes* 固執的態度 **3** (of an object or substance 物體或物質) stiff and difficult to move or bend 堅硬的；不彎曲的；僵直的：*a rigid support for the tent* 帳篷堅硬的支柱 ◇ *She sat upright, her body* ***rigid with fear.*** 她直挺挺地坐着，嚇得渾身發僵。◇ (*figurative*) *I was* ***bored rigid*** (= extremely bored). 我覺得無聊極了。▸ **ri·gid·ity** AW /rɪˈdʒɪdəti/ *noun* [U, C]：*the rigidity of the law on this issue* 法律在這個問題上的僵化處理 ◇ *the rigidity of the metal bar* 金屬柵欄的堅固性 **ri·gid·ly** AW *adv.*：*The speed limit must be rigidly enforced.* 必須嚴格執行限速規定。◇ *She stared rigidly ahead.* 她呆呆地盯着前方。

rig·mar·ole /ˈrɪɡmərəʊl; *NAmE* -roʊl/ *noun* [U, sing.] **1** a long and complicated process that is annoying and seems unnecessary（不必要的）冗長複雜的手續：*I couldn't face the whole rigmarole of getting a work permit again.* 我無法再次面對獲取工作許可證所需的各種冗長複雜的手續。**2** a long and complicated story 冗長曲折的故事

rigor mor·tis /ˌrɪɡə ˈmɔːtɪs; *NAmE* ˌrɪɡər ˈmɔːrtɪs/ *noun* [U] the process by which the body becomes stiff after death 屍僵；死後強直

rig·or·ous /ˈrɪɡərəs/ *adj.* **1** done carefully and with a lot of attention to detail 謹慎的；細緻的；徹底的 SYN **thorough**：*a rigorous analysis* 細緻的分析 **2** demanding that particular rules, processes, etc. are strictly followed 嚴格的；嚴厲的 SYN **strict**：*The work failed to meet their rigorous standards.* 工作沒有達到他們的嚴格標準。▸ **rig·or·ous·ly** *adv.*：*The country's press is rigorously controlled.* 這個國家的新聞出版事業受到嚴格控制。

rig·our (*especially US* **rigor**) /ˈrɪɡə(r)/ *noun* **1** [U] the fact of being careful and paying great attention to detail 謹慎；縝密；嚴謹：***academic/intellectual/scientific, etc. rigour*** 學術、思想、科學等方面的嚴謹 **2** [U] (*formal*) the fact of being strict or severe 嚴格；嚴厲 SYN **severity**：*This crime must be treated with the full rigour of the law.* 這一罪行必須嚴格依法審理。**3 the rigours of sth** [pl.] the difficulties and unpleasant conditions of sth 艱苦；嚴酷：*The plants were unable to withstand the rigours of a harsh winter.* 這些植物經受不住嚴冬的考驗。

ˈrig-out *noun* (*BrE, informal, often disapproving*) a set of clothes worn together 一套衣服；一身裝束：*Where are you going in that rig-out?* 你穿着那身打扮要去哪裏？

the Rig Veda /ˌrɪɡ ˈveɪdə; ˈviːdə/ *noun* [sing.] the oldest and most important of the Vedas (= Hindu holy texts)《梨俱吠陀》（印度教《吠陀》中最古老和最重要的一部）

rile /raɪl/ *verb* **~ sb | it riles sb that …** to annoy sb or make them angry 惹惱；激怒 SYN **anger**：*Nothing ever seemed to rile him.* 好像從來沒有什麼事讓他煩惱。

IDM **be/get (all) ˌriled ˈup** (*informal, especially NAmE*) to be or get very annoyed 十分生氣；惱火

Riley /ˈraɪli/ *noun* IDM see LIFE

rill /rɪl/ *noun* a shallow channel cut by water flowing over rock or soil 細溝

rim /rɪm/ *noun, verb*

■ ***noun*** **1** the edge of sth in the shape of a circle（圓形物體的）邊沿：*He looked at them over the rim of his glass.* 他從杯口的上方看着他們。◇ *The rims of her eyes were red with crying.* 她的眼眶都哭紅了。◇ *spectacles with gold rims* 金框眼鏡 ➲ picture at EDGE **2** the metal edge of a wheel onto which the tyre is fixed 輪輞；輪圈 ➲ VISUAL VOCAB page V51 **3 -rimmed** *adj.* having a particular type of rim 有…框（或邊）的：*gold-rimmed spectacles* 金框眼鏡 ◇ *red-rimmed eyes* (= for example, from crying) 眼眶紅紅的眼睛 ➲ see also HORN-RIMMED

■ ***verb*** (**-mm-**) [often passive] **~ sth** (*formal*) to form an edge around sth 形成…的邊沿；給…鑲邊

rime /raɪm/ *noun* [U] (*literary*) FROST 霧凇（顆粒狀的霜晶）

rim·less /ˈrɪmləs/ *adj.* [only before noun] (of glasses 眼鏡) having LENSES (= the transparent parts that you look through) that are not surrounded by frames 無框的

rind /raɪnd/ *noun* **1** [U] the thick outer skin of some types of fruit（某些水果的）厚皮，外殼：*lemon rind* 檸檬皮 ➲ compare PEEL *n.* (1), SKIN *n.* (4), ZEST (3) **2** [U, C] the thick outer skin of some foods such as BACON and some types of cheese（熏肉和某些乾酪等食物的）外皮

rings 戒指；環

diamond ring
鑽戒

key ring
鑰匙環

boxing ring
拳擊台

gas ring (*especially BrE*) **/ burner**
煤氣灶火圈

ring¹ /rɪŋ/ *noun, verb* ➲ see also RING²

■ ***noun***

▸ **JEWELLERY** 首飾 **1** [C] a piece of jewellery that you wear on your finger, consisting of a round band of gold, silver, etc., sometimes decorated with PRECIOUS STONES 戒指；指環：*a gold ring* 金戒指 ◇ *A diamond glittered on her* ***ring finger*** (= the finger next to the little finger, especially on the left hand). 一顆鑽石在她的無名指上閃閃發光。➲ VISUAL VOCAB page V65 ➲ see also ENGAGEMENT RING, SIGNET RING, WEDDING RING

▸ **CIRCLE** 圓圈 **2** [C] an object in the shape of a circle with a large hole in the middle 環狀物；圈形的東西：*a key ring* 鑰匙環 ◇ *curtain rings* 窗簾環 ◇ *onion rings* 洋葱圈 ➲ VISUAL VOCAB page V47 **3** [C] a round mark or shape 圓形標記；圓形：*She had dark rings around her eyes from lack of sleep.* 她因為缺覺，眼圈兒都黑了。◇ *The children sat on the floor in a ring.* 孩子們圍成一圈，坐在地板上。

▸ **FOR PERFORMANCE/COMPETITION** 表演；比賽 **4** [C] a confined area in which animals or people perform or compete, with seats around the outside for the audience 圓形表演場（或競技場）：*a boxing ring* 拳擊場 ◇ *a circus ring* 馬戲場 ➲ see also BULLRING

▸ **FOR COOKING** 烹飪 **5** [C] (*especially BrE*) a small flat place on a cooker/stove that is heated by gas or electricity and is used for cooking on 爐口；灶盤 SYN **burner**：*to turn off the gas ring* 關上煤氣灶

▸ **GROUP OF PEOPLE** 人群 **6** [C] a group of people who are working together, especially in secret or illegally（尤指秘密的或非法的）團夥，幫派，集團：*a spy ring* 間諜網 ◇ *a drugs ring* 販毒集團

IDM **run ˈrings around/round sb** (*informal*) to be much better at doing sth than sb else 做事遠比某人好；遙遙領先 ➲ more at HAT

■ ***verb*** (**ringed, ringed**)

▸ **SURROUND** 包圍 **1** [often passive] **~ sb/sth (with sth)** to surround sb/sth 包圍；環繞：*Thousands of demonstrators ringed the building.* 成千上萬的示威者包圍了大樓。

▸ **BIRD'S LEG** 鳥腿 **2 ~ sth** to put a metal ring around a bird's leg so that it can be easily identified in the future 給…戴上金屬環（以便將來辨認）

▸ **DRAW CIRCLE** 畫圓 **3 ~ sth** (*especially BrE*) to draw a circle around sth 繞⋯畫圓；把⋯圈起來 **SYN circle**：*Ring the correct answer in pencil.* 用鉛筆圈出正確答案。

ring² /rɪŋ/ *verb, noun* ➲ see also RING¹

■ *verb* (**rang** /ræŋ/, **rung** /rʌŋ/)

▸ **TELEPHONE** 電話 **1** (*BrE*) (also **call** *NAmE, BrE*) [T, I] to telephone sb/sth 給⋯打電話：**~ sb/sth up** *I'll ring you up later.* 我稍後再給你打電話。◇ *He rang up the police station.* 他給警察局打了電話。◇ **~ sb/sth** *When is the best time to ring New York?* 什麼時間給紐約打電話最好？◇ **~ (up)** *David rang up while you were out.* 你不在的時候戴維打電話來了。◇ *He said he was ringing from London.* 他說他是從倫敦打來的。◇ *I'm ringing about your advertisement in the paper.* 我打電話來問一下你們在報紙上登的廣告。◇ *She rang to say she'd be late.* 她打電話來說她要遲到。◇ **~ for sth** *Could you ring for a cab?* 你打電話叫輛出租車來好嗎？➲ note at PHONE **2** [I] (of a telephone 電話) to make a sound because sb is trying to telephone you 發出鈴聲：*Will you answer the telephone if it rings?* 電話鈴響時你接一下好嗎？

▸ **BELL** 鈴；鐘 **3** [T, I] if you **ring** a bell or if a bell **rings**, it produces a sound（使）發出鐘聲，響起鈴聲：**~ (sth)** *Someone was ringing the doorbell.* 有人在按門鈴。◇ *The church bells rang.* 教堂的鐘聲響了。◇ **~ for sb/sth** *Just ring for the nurse* (= attract the nurse's attention by ringing a bell) *if you need her.* 如果想找護士，按一下鈴就行了。

▸ **WITH SOUND** 聲響 **4** [I] **~ (with sth)** (*literary*) to be full of a sound; to fill a place with sound 回響；響徹 **SYN resound**：*The house rang with children's laughter.* 房子裏回響着孩子們的笑聲。◇ *Applause rang through the hall.* 掌聲響徹整個大廳。

▸ **WITH QUALITY** 特性 **5** [I] **~ (with sth)** to be full of a particular quality 充滿：*His words rang with pride.* 他的話充滿了驕傲。

▸ **OF EARS** 耳朵 **6** [I] to be uncomfortable and be unable to hear clearly, usually because you have heard a loud noise, etc. 嗡嗡作響：*The music was so loud it made my ears ring.* 音樂的聲音太大了，震得我的耳朵嗡嗡響。

IDM **ring a 'bell** (*informal*) to sound familiar to you, as though you have heard it before 聽起來耳熟：*His name rings a bell but I can't think where we met.* 他的名字聽着很熟，但我想不起我們在哪裏見過。 **ring the 'changes (with sth)** (*BrE*) to make changes to sth in order to have greater variety 使更多樣化；變換花樣：*Ring the changes with a new colour.* 用一種新的顏色來改變一下。 **ˌring in your 'ears/'head** to make you feel that you can still hear sth 在耳邊回響：*His warning was still ringing in my ears.* 他的警告依然在我耳邊回響。 **ˌring off the 'hook** (usually used in the progressive tenses 通常用於進行時) (*NAmE*) (of a telephone 電話) to ring many times 響聲不斷；鈴聲大作：*The phone has been ringing off the hook with offers of help.* 表示願意提供援助的電話接連不斷。 **ring 'true/'hollow/'false** to give the impression of being sincere/true or not sincere/true 給人以真實（或空洞、虛假）的印象：*It may seem a strange story but it rings true to me.* 這個故事也許顯得離奇，但我卻覺得很真實。➲ more at ALARM *n.*

PHR V **ˌring a'round** = RING ROUND **ˌring 'back | ˌring sb↔'back** (*BrE*) to telephone sb again, for example because they were not there when you called earlier, or to return a call they made to you（給某人）再打電話，回覆電話：*He isn't here now—could you ring back later?* 他現在不在，你過會兒再打電話來好嗎？◇ *I'll ask Simon to ring you back when he gets in.* 等西蒙來了，我讓他給你回電話。 **ˌring 'in** (*BrE*) to telephone a television or radio show, or the place where you work 給電視（或電台）節目打電話；給自己的工作單位打電話 **ˌring 'in sth** to ring bells to celebrate sth, especially the new year 鳴鐘歡慶（尤指新年） **ˌring 'off** (*BrE*) to put down the telephone because you have finished speaking 掛斷電話：*He rang off before I could explain.* 我還沒來得及解釋他就掛了。 **ˌring 'out** to be heard loudly and clearly 清晰可聞；發出清脆的響聲：*A number of shots rang out.* 這時聽見幾聲清脆的槍聲。 **ˌring 'round (sb/sth) | ˌring a'round (sb/sth)** (*BrE*) to telephone a number of people in order to organize sth or to get some information, etc. 電話通知，電話詢問（各人）：*I rang round all the travel agents in the area.* 我打電話詢問了那個地區所有的旅行社。 **ˌring 'through (to sb)** (*BrE*) to make a telephone call to sb, especially within the same building 打電話（給同一棟大樓內的人）：*Reception just rang through to say my visitor has arrived.* 接待處剛剛打電話來說我的客人到了。 **ˌring sth↔'up** to enter the cost of goods being bought in a shop/store on a CASH REGISTER by pressing the buttons; to make sales of a particular value 將（款額）輸入現金出納機；達到⋯銷售額：*She rang up all the items on the till.* 她將各項款額都記入了現金出納機。◇ *The company rang up sales of $166 million last year.* 公司去年的銷售額為 1.66 億元。

■ *noun*

▸ **OF BELL** 鈴；鐘 **1** [C] the sound that a bell makes; the act of ringing a bell 鈴聲；鐘聲；搖鈴；敲鐘：*There was a ring at the door.* 門鈴響了。◇ *He gave a couple of loud rings on the doorbell.* 他使勁地按了幾下門鈴。

▸ **SOUND** 聲響 **2** [sing.] a loud clear sound 清晰的響聲：*the ring of horse's hooves on the cobblestones* 馬蹄在鵝卵石上發出的清脆響聲

▸ **QUALITY** 特性 **3** [sing.] **~ (of sth)** a particular quality that words, sounds, etc. have（言語、聲音等的）特性：*His explanation **has a ring of truth** about it.* 他的解釋聽上去真實可信。◇ *Her protestation of innocence **had a hollow ring to it*** (= did not sound sincere). 她自稱無辜的辯白顯得空洞乏力。◇ *The story had a **familiar ring** to it* (= as if I had heard it before). 這個故事聽起來耳熟。

IDM **give sb a 'ring** (*BrE, informal*) to make a telephone call to sb 給某人打電話：*I'll give you a ring tomorrow.* 我明天給你打電話。➲ note at PHONE ➲ more at BRASS

ring-a-ring o' roses /ˌrɪŋ ə rɪŋ ə 'rəʊzɪz; *NAmE* 'roʊzɪz/ (*BrE*) (*NAmE* **ˌring around the 'rosy**) *noun* [U] a singing game played by children, in which the players hold hands and dance in a circle, falling down at the end of the song 玫瑰花環（歌謠遊戲，兒童手拉手圍成一圈跳舞，歌曲唱完時蹲下）

ring·back /'rɪŋbæk/ (also **Callback™**) *noun* [U, C] a telephone service that you can use if you call sb and their telephone is being used, so that your telephone will ring when the line is free; a call made using this service 回鈴聲（電話服務）；有回鈴音的電話

'ring bearer *noun* (*NAmE*) a person, usually a boy, who carries the rings for the BRIDE and GROOM at a wedding（婚禮上的）捧戒指男孩，捧戒指者

'ring binder *noun* a file for holding papers, in which metal rings go through the edges of the pages, holding them in place 活頁簿；活頁夾 ➲ VISUAL VOCAB page V69

'ring circuit (also **'ring main**) *noun* (*technical* 術語) an arrangement of wires which supply electricity to several different places in a room or building（房間或建築物內的）環形電路

ringed /rɪŋd/ *adj.* [only before noun] **1** having a ring or rings on 戴戒指的：*a ringed finger* 戴着戒指的手指 **2** (especially of an animal or bird 尤指獸或鳥) having a mark or marks like a ring on it 有環紋（或環斑）的：*a ringed plover* 胸部有帶狀紋的劍鴴

ringer /'rɪŋə(r)/ *noun* **1** = BELL-RINGER **2** (*NAmE*) a horse or person that takes part in a race illegally, for example by using a false name（以冒名頂替等手段）非法參賽的馬（或人） **IDM** see DEAD *adj.*

ring·ette /rɪŋ'et/ *noun* [U] a Canadian game similar to ICE HOCKEY, played with a straight stick and rubber ring, especially by women 冰圈運動，冰上爭圈（加拿大的一種類似冰球的運動，用直杆和橡皮圈，主要為女性參加）

'ring-fence *verb* (*BrE*) **1 ~ sth** (*finance* 財) to protect a particular sum of money by putting restrictions on it so that it can only be used for a particular purpose 限制（資金的）用途 **2 ~ sth** to protect sth by putting restrictions on it so that it can only be used by particular people or for a particular purpose 限制性地保護（以供專人專用）：*All employees can access the parts of the Intranet that are not ring-fenced.* 所有雇員都可進入內聯網中無使用權限制的部份。▸ **'ring fence** *noun*：*The*

R

government has promised to put a ring fence around funding for education. 政府已承諾資金保證用於教育。

'ring finger *noun* the finger next to the smallest one, especially on the left hand, on which a wedding ring is traditionally worn 無名指（尤指左手的，傳統上用以戴結婚戒指）➲ VISUAL VOCAB page V59

ring·ing /ˈrɪŋɪŋ/ *adj., noun*

■ ***adj.*** [only before noun] **1** (of a sound 聲響) loud and clear 響亮的；清晰的 **2** (of a statement, etc. 陳述等) powerful and made with a lot of force 有力的；強勁的：*a ringing endorsement of her leadership* 對她的領導的有力支持

■ ***noun*** [sing., U] an act or a sound of ringing 嗡嗡作響；嗡嗡聲：*There was an unpleasant ringing in my ears.* 我的耳朵裏有一種煩人的嗡嗡聲。

ring·lead·er /ˈrɪŋliːdə(r)/ *noun* (*disapproving*) a person who leads others in crime or in causing trouble 罪魁；頭目；元兇

ring·let /ˈrɪŋlət/ *noun* [usually pl.] a long curl of hair hanging down from sb's head 垂下的長鬈髮 ➲ VISUAL VOCAB page V60

'ring main *noun* (*technical* 術語) **1** an arrangement of cables that allows electricity to be supplied to a series of places from either of two directions（電路的）環形幹線 **2** = RING CIRCUIT **3** an arrangement of connected pipes that allows water, steam, etc. to enter and leave a system（管路的）環形主線

ring·mas·ter /ˈrɪŋmɑːstə(r); *NAmE* -mæs-/ *noun* a person in charge of a CIRCUS performance 馬戲表演領班（或指揮）

'ring pull (*BrE*) (*NAmE* **'pull tab**, **tab**) *noun* a small piece of metal with a ring attached which is pulled to open cans of food, drink, etc.（易拉罐等的）拉環；易拉環 ➲ VISUAL VOCAB page V33

'ring road (*BrE*) (*US* **'outer belt**) *noun* a road that is built around a city or town to reduce traffic in the centre 環路；環城路

ring·side /ˈrɪŋsaɪd/ *noun* [U] the area closest to the space in which a BOXING match or CIRCUS takes place（拳擊場或馬戲表演場等的）場邊，台邊區：*According to law, a doctor must be present at the ringside.* 按法律規定，場邊必須有一名醫生。◇ *a* ***ringside seat*** 靠近拳擊台的觀察席位

ring·tone /ˈrɪŋtəʊn; *NAmE* -toʊn/ *noun* the sound a telephone makes when sb is calling you. Ringtones are often short tunes, and the word is especially used to refer to the different sounds mobile phones/cell phones make when they ring.（尤指移動電話的）鈴聲

ring·toss /ˈrɪŋtɒs; *NAmE* -tɔːs; -tɑːs/ (*NAmE*) (*BrE* **hoopla**) *noun* [U] a game in which players try to throw rings over objects in order to win them as prizes 投環套物

ring·worm /ˈrɪŋwɜːm; *NAmE* -wɜːrm/ *noun* [U] an infectious skin disease that produces small round red areas 癬

rink /rɪŋk/ *noun* **1** = ICE RINK **2** = SKATING RINK (1)

rinky-dink /ˈrɪŋki dɪŋk/ *adj.* (*NAmE, informal*) of poor quality; cheap and/or old-fashioned 拙劣的；老舊廉價的：*a rinky-dink rhinestone necklace* 過時廉價的萊茵石項鏈 ◇ *a rinky-dink little town* 破破爛爛的小鎮子

rinse /rɪns/ *verb, noun*

■ ***verb*** **1 ~ sth** to wash sth with clean water only, not using soap（用清水）沖洗，洗涮：*Rinse the cooked pasta with boiling water.* 將煮過的意大利麪在沸水裏過一下。 **2 ~ sth** to remove the soap from sth with clean water after washing it 沖掉…的皂液；漂洗；清洗 ➲ SYNONYMS at CLEAN **3 ~ sth + adv./prep.** to remove dirt, etc. from sth by washing it with clean water（用清水）沖掉，洗刷：*She rinsed the mud from her hands.* 她沖洗掉手上的泥漿。◇ *I wanted to rinse the taste out of my mouth.* 我想漱漱口，去掉嘴裏的味道。

PHR V **,rinse sth↔'out** to make sth clean, especially a container, by washing it with water 沖洗，洗刷乾淨（容器等）：*Rinse the cup out before use.* 使用前將杯子沖洗一下。

■ ***noun*** **1** [C] an act of rinsing sth 漂洗；沖洗；洗刷：*I gave the glass a rinse.* 我把杯子沖洗了一下。◇ *Fabric conditioner is added during the final rinse.* 在最後一遍漂洗時加入織物柔順劑。 **2** [C, U] a liquid that you put on your hair when it is wet in order to change its colour 染髮劑：*a blue rinse* 藍色染髮劑 **3** [C, U] a liquid used for cleaning the mouth and teeth 漱口液

riot /ˈraɪət/ *noun, verb*

■ ***noun*** **1** [C] a situation in which a group of people behave in a violent way in a public place, often as a protest 暴亂；騷亂：*One prison guard was killed when a riot broke out in the jail.* 一位獄警在監獄騷亂中喪生。◇ ***food/race riots*** 爭搶食物的暴亂；種族騷亂 **2** [sing.] **~ of sth** (*formal*) a collection of a lot of different types of the same thing 豐富多彩；品種繁多：*The garden was a* ***riot of colour.*** 花園裏色彩繽紛。 **3 a riot** [sing.] (*old-fashioned, informal*) a person or an event that is very amusing and enjoyable 非常有趣的人（或事）

IDM **run 'riot 1** (of people 人) to behave in a way that is violent and/or not under control 撒野；恣意妄為 SYN **rampage**：*They let their kids run riot.* 他們聽任自己的孩子撒野。 **2** if your imagination, a feeling, etc. **runs riot**, you allow it to develop and continue without trying to control it（指想像、情感等）任意發揮，奔放 **3** (of plants 植物) to grow and spread quickly 生長繁茂；瘋長 ➲ more at READ *v.*

■ ***verb*** [I] (of a crowd of people 人群) to behave in a violent way in a public place, often as a protest 發生騷亂；鬧事 ▶ **riot·er** *noun*：*Rioters set fire to parked cars.* 暴徒放火焚燒停着的汽車。 **riot·ing** *noun* [U]：*Rioting broke out in the capital.* 首都爆發了騷亂事件。

'riot gear *noun* [U] the clothes and equipment used by the police when they are dealing with riots 防暴裝備

riot·ous /ˈraɪətəs/ *adj.* [usually before noun] **1** (*formal* or *law* 律) noisy and/or violent, especially in a public place 騷亂的；暴亂的：*riotous behaviour* 暴亂行為 ◇ *The organizers of the march were charged with assault and* ***riotous assembly.*** 遊行組織者被控侵犯人身及暴亂性非法集會。 **2** noisy, exciting and enjoyable in an uncontrolled way 狂歡的；縱情歡鬧的 SYN **uproarious**：*a riotous party* 狂歡聚會 ◇ *riotous laughter* 放縱的笑聲

riot·ous·ly /ˈraɪətəsli/ *adv.* extremely 極端；非常；極其：*riotously funny* 滑稽至極

'riot police *noun* [pl.] police who are trained to deal with people RIOTING 防暴警察

'riot shield (also **shield**) *noun* a piece of equipment made from strong plastic, used by the police to protect themselves from angry crowds 防暴盾牌

RIP (*BrE*) (also **R.I.P.** *US, BrE*) /ˌɑːr aɪ ˈpiː/ *abbr.* rest in peace (often written on graves) 安息（通常書於墓碑）

rip /rɪp/ *verb, noun*

■ ***verb*** **(-pp-) 1** [T, I] to tear sth or to become torn, often suddenly or violently（突然或猛烈地）撕破，裂開：**~ (sth)** *I ripped my jeans on the fence.* 我的牛仔褲在柵欄上劃破了。◇ *The flags had been ripped in two.* 旗幟都被撕成了兩半。◇ *I heard the tent rip.* 我聽到了帳篷撕裂的聲音。◇ **~ sth + adj.** *She* ***ripped the letter open.*** 她撕開那封信。 **2** [T] **~ sth + adv./prep.** to remove sth quickly or violently, often by pulling it 猛地扯開；突然拉開：*He ripped off his tie.* 他一把拽掉領帶。◇ *The carpet had been ripped from the stairs.* 地毯已經從樓梯上拖走了。 **3** [T] **~ sth** (*computing* 計) to copy sound or video files from a website or CD on to a computer（從網站或CD上）擷取（音頻或視頻文件） **4** (*computing* 計) = RASTERIZE

IDM **let 'rip (at sb)** (*informal*) to speak or do sth with great force, enthusiasm, etc. and without control 激動地說（或做）；忘乎所以地說（或做）：*When she gets angry with her boyfriend, she really lets rip at him.* 當她生男朋友氣的時候，她真的對他破口大罵。◇ *The group let rip with a single from their new album.* 樂隊充滿激情地表演了他們新唱片中的一首單曲。 **let 'rip | let sth 'rip** (*informal*) **1** to go or allow sth such as a car to go as fast as possible（使）全速前進：*Once on the open road, he let rip.* 一上空曠的公路，他就全速行駛。◇ *Come on Steve—let her rip.* 來吧，史蒂夫，全速前進吧。 **2** to do sth or to allow sth to happen as fast as possible 儘快做；使儘快發生：*This would cause inflation to let* *rip again.* 這又將導致急劇的通貨膨脹。 **rip sb/sth aˈpart/to ˈshreds/to ˈbits, etc.** to destroy sth; to criticize sb very strongly 摧毀；毀壞；猛烈抨擊 ➲ more at HEART, LIMB

PHR V **ˈrip at sth** to attack sth violently, usually by tearing or cutting it 猛烈撕扯；用力割 **ˌrip ˈinto sb (for/with sth)** to criticize sb and tell them that you are very angry with them 責備；斥責 **ˌrip ˈinto/ˈthrough sb/sth** to go very quickly and violently into or through sb/sth（快速而猛烈地）鑽入，穿透：*A bullet ripped into his shoulder.* 一顆子彈穿透了他的肩頭。 **ˌrip sb↔ˈoff** [usually passive] (*informal*) to cheat sb, by making them pay too much, by selling them sth of poor quality, etc. 敲詐；訛詐：*Tourists complain of being ripped off by local cab drivers.* 遊客抱怨被當地的出租車司機敲了竹槓。 ➲ related noun RIP-OFF (1) **ˌrip sth↔ˈoff** (*informal*) to steal sth 偷竊；盜取：*Thieves broke in and ripped off five computers.* 盜賊破門而入，偷走了五台電腦。 **ˌrip sth↔ˈup** to tear sth into small pieces 把某物撕碎：*He ripped up the letter and threw it in the fire.* 他把信撕碎，扔到火爐裏。

■ ***noun*** [usually sing.] **1** a long tear in cloth, paper, etc.（織物、紙張等）撕開的大口子 **2** = RIP CURRENT

ri·par·ian /raɪˈpeəriən; *NAmE* -ˈper-/ *adj.* [usually before noun] **1** (*technical* 術語) growing in, living in, or relating to areas of wet land near to a river or stream 生長（或棲息）在河邊濕地的；河邊的 **2** (*law* 律) on, near or relating to the bank of a river 堤岸（上）的；堤岸近處的

rip·cord /ˈrɪpkɔːd; *NAmE* -kɔːrd/ *noun* the string that you pull to open a PARACHUTE（降落傘的）開傘索

ˌrip ˈcurrent (also **rip**) *noun* a strong current of water that flows away from the coast 離岸流；裂流

ripe /raɪp/ *adj.* (**riper**, **rip·est**) **1** (of fruit or crops 水果或莊稼) fully grown and ready to be eaten 成熟的 **OPP** **unripe** **2** (of cheese or wine 乾酪或果酒) having a flavour that has fully developed 口味濃郁的；成熟的；醇美可口的 **SYN** **mature** **3** (of a smell 氣味) strong and unpleasant 強烈的；難聞的 **4 ~ (for sth)** ready or suitable for sth to happen 時機成熟的；適宜的：*This land is ripe for development.* 這片土地適宜開發。◇ *The conditions were ripe for social change.* 社會變革的時機已經成熟。◇ *Reforms were promised when **the time was ripe**.* 曾經作出承諾，時機一成熟就進行改革。 ▸ **ripe·ness** *noun* [U]

IDM **a/the ripe old age (of …)** an age that is considered to be very old （…的）高齡：*He lived to the ripe old age of 91.* 他活到了 91 歲的高齡。

ripen /ˈraɪpən/ *verb* [I, T] **~ (sth)** to become ripe; to make sth ripe（使）成熟

ˈrip-off *noun* (*informal*) **1** [usually sing.] something that is not worth what you pay for it 索價過高（或物非所值）的東西：*$70 for a T-shirt! What a rip-off!* * 70 塊錢買一件 T 恤衫！太不值了！ **2 ~ (of sth)** a copy of sth, especially one that is less expensive or not as good as the original thing 仿製品；冒牌貨：*The single is a rip-off of a 70s hit.* 這首單曲是 70 年代的一首熱門歌曲的翻版。

ri·poste /rɪˈpɒst; *NAmE* rɪˈpoʊst/ *noun* (*formal*) **1** a quick and clever reply, especially to criticism 機敏的回答；巧妙的反駁 **SYN** **retort**：*a witty riposte* 機智的回答 **2** a course of action that takes place in response to sth that has happened 反應；回應：*The US delivered an early riposte to the air attack.* 美國對空襲很快作出了反應。 ▸ **ri·poste** *verb* + **speech**

rip·per /ˈrɪpə(r)/ *noun* (*informal*) a person who is very good at SNOWBOARDING 滑雪板運動高手

rip·ping /ˈrɪpɪŋ/ *adj.* (*BrE, old-fashioned*) wonderful 極好的；美妙的

rip·ple /ˈrɪpl/ *noun, verb*

■ ***noun*** **1** a small wave on the surface of a liquid, especially water in a lake, etc. 波紋；細浪；漣漪：*The air was so still that there was hardly a ripple on the pond's surface.* 空氣靜止不動，池塘的水面上幾乎看不到波紋。 **2** a thing that looks or moves like a small wave（外觀或運動）如波紋的東西：*ripples of sand* 沙灘上的波紋 **3** [usually sing.] **~ of sth** a sound that gradually becomes louder and then quieter again 起伏的聲音：*a ripple of applause/laughter* 一陣陣的掌聲 / 笑聲 **4** [usually sing.] **~ of sth** a feeling that gradually spreads through a person or group of people 逐漸擴散的感覺：*A ripple of fear passed through him.* 一股恐懼感傳遍了他的全身。◇ *The announcement sent a ripple of excitement through the crowd.* 這件事一宣佈就在人群裏引起了一陣興奮。

■ ***verb*** **1** [I, T] to move or to make sth move in very small waves（使）如波浪般起伏：*The sea rippled and sparkled.* 大海波光粼粼。◇ *rippling muscles* 條條凸起的肌肉 ◇ **~ sth** *The wind rippled the wheat in the fields.* 田野上的麥浪在風中起伏。 **2** [I] + **adv./prep.** (of a feeling, etc. 感覺等) to spread through a person or a group of people like a wave 擴散；湧起：*A gasp rippled through the crowd.* 人群中傳出一片驚詫之聲。

ˈripple effect *noun* a situation in which an event or action has an effect on sth, which then has an effect on sth else 連鎖反應：*His resignation will have a ripple effect on the whole department.* 他的辭職將會在整個部門中引起連鎖反應。

ˈrip-roaring *adj.* [only before noun] (*informal*) **1** noisy, exciting and/or full of activity 喧鬧的；興奮的；狂歡的：*a rip-roaring celebration* 歡樂的慶典 **2 ~ drunk** extremely drunk 爛醉的 **3 ~ success** a great success 巨大的（成功）

Rip Van Winkle /ˌrɪp væn ˈwɪŋkl/ *noun* a person who is surprised to find how much the world has changed over a period of time 對世界變化之大感到驚訝的人；李伯 **ORIGIN** From the name of a character in a short story by the US writer Washington Irving. He sleeps for 20 years and wakes up to find that the world has completely changed. 源自美國作家華盛頓 • 歐文所著短篇小說中的人物瑞普 • 凡 • 温克爾，他沉睡 20 年後醒來，發現世間發生了天翻地覆的變化。

rise 🔑 /raɪz/ *noun, verb*

■ ***noun***

▸ **INCREASE** 增加 **1** 🔑 [C] an increase in an amount, a number or a level（數量或水平的）增加，提高：*The industry is feeling the effects of recent price rises.* 這一行業已經感覺到了最近提價的影響。◇ **~ in sth** *There has been a **sharp rise** in the number of people out of work.* 失業人數急劇增長。 ➲ LANGUAGE BANK at INCREASE

2 🔑 [C] (*BrE*) (*NAmE* **raise**) an increase in the money you are paid for the work you do 加薪；工資增長：*I'm going to ask for a rise.* 我打算要求加薪。◇ *He criticized the huge pay rises awarded to industry bosses.* 對於給企業老闆大幅度加薪，他提出了批評。

▸ **IN POWER/IMPORTANCE** 權力；重要性 **3** 🔑 [sing.] **~ (of sb/sth)** the act of becoming more important, successful, powerful, etc.（重要性、優勢、權力等的）增強：*the rise of fascism in Europe* 法西斯主義在歐洲的興起 ◇ *the **rise and fall** of the British Empire* 英帝國的興衰 ◇ *her meteoric **rise to power*** 她的迅速掌權

▸ **UPWARD MOVEMENT** 上升 **4** 🔑 [sing.] an upward movement 上升：*She watched the gentle **rise and fall** of his chest as he slept.* 她看着他睡着時微微起伏的胸膛。

▸ **SLOPING LAND** 斜坡 **5** [C] an area of land that slopes upwards 斜坡；小丘；小山 **SYN** **slope**：*The church was built at the top of a small rise.* 教堂建在一座小山頂上。 ➲ see also HIGH-RISE

IDM **get a rise out of sb** to make sb react in an angry way by saying sth that you know will annoy them, especially as a joke 惹惱；故意激怒 **give ˈrise to sth** (*formal*) to cause sth to happen or exist 使發生（或存在）：*The novel's success gave rise to a number of sequels.* 這部小說的成功帶來了一系列的續篇。

■ ***verb*** (**rose** /rəʊz; *NAmE* roʊz/, **risen** /ˈrɪzn/)

▸ **MOVE UPWARDS** 上升 **1** 🔑 [I] (+ **adv./prep.**) to come or go upwards; to reach a higher level or position 上升；攀升；提高；達到較高水平（或位置）：*Smoke was rising from the chimney.* 煙從煙囪裏升起。◇ *The river has risen (by) several metres.* 河水上升了好幾米。

▸ **GET UP** 起身 **2** 🔑 [I] (+ **adv./prep.**) (*formal*) to get up from a lying, sitting or KNEELING position 起牀；起立；站起來 **SYN** **get up**：*He was accustomed to rising (= getting out of bed) early.* 他習慣於早起。◇ *They rose from the*

R

table. 他們從餐桌旁站起身。◇ *She rose to her feet.* 她站起身來。➲ SYNONYMS at STAND

▸ **OF SUN/MOON** 太陽；月亮 **3** [I] when the sun, moon, etc. **rises**, it appears above the HORIZON 升起：*The sun rises in the east.* 太陽從東方升起。OPP **set**

▸ **END MEETING** 結束會議 **4** [I] (*formal*) (of a group of people 一群人) to end a meeting 休會；閉會；散會 SYN **adjourn**：*The House* (= members of the House of Commons) *rose at 10 p.m.* 下議院於晚上 10 點鐘散會。

▸ **INCREASE** 增加 **5** [I] to increase in amount or number（數量）增加，增長，提高：*rising fuel bills* 不斷增加的燃料費 ◇ *The price of gas rose.* 煤氣價格上漲了。◇ *Gas* ***rose in price.*** 煤氣漲價了。◇ *Unemployment rose (by) 3%.* 失業人數增長了 3%。◇ *Air pollution has risen above an acceptable level.* 空氣污染已經超標。➲ LANGUAGE BANK at INCREASE

▸ **BECOME POWERFUL/IMPORTANT** 變得強大／重要 **6** [I] **(+ adv./prep.)** to become more successful, important, powerful, etc. 變得更加成功（或重要、強大等）：*a rising young politician* 嶄露頭角的年輕政治家 ◇ *She* ***rose to power*** *in the 70s.* 她於 20 世紀 70 年代掌握了大權。◇ *He rose to the rank of general.* 他升至將級軍官。◇ *She* ***rose through the ranks*** *to become managing director.* 她從普通員工逐步晉升為總經理。

▸ **OF SOUND** 聲響 **7** [I] if a sound **rises**, it becomes louder and higher 提高；增強：*Her* ***voice rose*** *angrily.* 她氣得提高了嗓門。

▸ **OF WIND** 風 **8** [I] if the wind **rises**, it begins to blow more strongly 颳起來；颳得更猛 SYN **get up**

▸ **OF FEELING** 情感 **9** [I] (*formal*) if a feeling **rises** inside you, it begins and gets stronger 增強：*He felt anger rising inside him.* 他心裏直冒火。◇ *Her* ***spirits rose*** (= she felt happier) *at the news.* 聽到這個消息，她高興起來。

▸ **OF YOUR COLOUR** 臉色 **10** [I] (*formal*) if your colour **rises**, your face becomes pink or red with embarrassment 臉紅

▸ **OF HAIR** 毛髮 **11** [I] if hair **rises**, it stands vertical instead of lying flat 豎起；立起來：*The hair on the back of my neck rose when I heard the scream.* 聽到那尖叫聲，我不禁毛骨悚然。

▸ **FIGHT** 戰鬥 **12** [I] **~ (up) (against sb/sth)** (*formal*) to begin to fight against your ruler or government or against a foreign army 起義；反抗；奮起 SYN **rebel**：*The peasants rose in revolt.* 農民起來造反了。◇ *He called on the people to rise up against the invaders.* 他號召民眾起來反抗入侵者。➲ related noun UPRISING

▸ **BECOME VISIBLE** 變得可見 **13** [I] (*formal*) to be or become visible above the surroundings 聳立；矗立；高出：*Mountains rose in the distance.* 遠處山巒疊起。

▸ **OF LAND** 土地 **14** [I] if land **rises**, it slopes upwards 凸起；隆起：*The ground rose steeply all around.* 這塊地方四周都是陡坡。

▸ **OF BEGINNING OF RIVER** 河源 **15** [I] **+ adv./prep.** a river **rises** where it begins to flow 起源；發源：*The Thames rises in the Cotswold hills.* 泰晤士河起源於科茨沃爾德丘陵。

▸ **OF BREAD/CAKES** 麪包；蛋糕 **16** [I] when bread, cakes, etc. **rise**, they swell because of the action of YEAST or BAKING POWDER 發酵

▸ **OF DEAD PERSON** 死人 **17** [I] **~ (from sth)** to come to life again 復活；再生：*to rise from the dead* 復活 ◇ (*figurative*) *Can a new party* ***rise from the ashes*** *of the old one?* 在舊政黨的灰燼中會誕生出一個新的政黨嗎？

IDM **,rise and 'shine** (*old-fashioned*) usually used in orders to tell sb to get out of bed and be active（通常用來催促起牀）➲ more at GORGE *n.*, HACKLES, HEIGHT

PHR V **,rise a'bove sth** **1** to not be affected or limited by problems, insults, etc. 克服（障礙）；超越（限制）；戰勝（困難）：*She had the courage and determination to rise above her physical disability.* 她有戰勝自身殘疾的勇氣和決心。**2** to be wise enough or morally good enough not to do sth wrong or not to think the same as other people 不為…所動；超脫：*I try to rise above prejudice.* 我盡力擺脫偏見。**3** to be of a higher standard than other things of a similar kind 超群；出眾；突出：*His work rarely rises above the mediocre.* 他工作平平，很少有突出的表現。**'rise to sth** **1** to show that you are able to deal with an unexpected situation, problem, etc. 能夠處理，有能力處理（突發情況、問題等）：*Luckily, my mother* ***rose to the occasion.*** 幸好當時我母親挺身而出解決了問題。◇ *He was determined to* ***rise to the challenge.*** 他決心克服困難迎接挑戰。**2** to react when sb is deliberately trying to make you angry or get you interested in sth 上當；上鉤；進圈套：*I refuse to rise to that sort of comment.* 我拒絕對那樣的評論作出反應。◇ *As soon as I mentioned money he* ***rose to the bait.*** 我一提到錢，他就上鉤了。

Which Word? 詞語辨析

rise / raise

Verbs 動詞

- **Raise** is a verb that must have an object and **rise** is used without an object. When you **raise** something, you lift it to a higher position or increase it. 動詞 raise 後必須接賓語，而 rise 不接賓語。raise 表示舉起、提起、提升、增加：*He raised his head from the pillow.* 他從枕頭上抬起頭來。◇ *We were forced to raise the price.* 我們被迫提價。When people or things **rise**, they move from a lower to a higher position. 表示人或物從低處向高處上升用 rise：*She rose from the chair.* 她從椅子上站起來。◇ *The helicopter rose into the air.* 直升機升上了天空。**Rise** can also mean 'to increase in number or quantity'. * rise 亦表示數字上升或數量增加：*Costs are always rising.* 成本總是不斷地增加。

Nouns 名詞

- The noun **rise** means a movement upwards or an increase in an amount or quantity. 名詞 rise 表示上升、升起、（數量的）增加：*a rise in interest rates* 利率的上升 In *BrE* it can also be used to mean an increase in pay. 在英式英語中亦可指工資的增加：*Should I ask my boss for a rise?* 我應要求老闆增加工資嗎？In *NAmE* this is a **raise**. 在美式英語中此義用 raise 表示：*a three per cent pay raise* 百分之三的加薪 **Rise** can also mean the process of becoming more powerful or important. * rise 亦可表示地位提高：*his dramatic rise to power* 他的突然掌權

riser /ˈraɪzə(r)/ *noun* **1 early/late ~** a person who usually gets out of bed early/late in the morning（習慣於早或晚）起牀的人 **2** (*technical* 術語) the vertical part between two steps in a set of stairs 立板（樓梯踏步板的豎直部份）➲ picture at STAIRCASE ➲ compare TREAD *n.* (3)

ris·ible /ˈrɪzəbl/ *adj.* (*formal, disapproving*) deserving to be laughed at rather than taken seriously 可笑的；滑稽的 SYN **ludicrous, ridiculous**

ris·ing /ˈraɪzɪŋ/ *noun* a situation in which a group of people protest against, and try to get rid of, a government, a leader, etc. 起義；叛亂 SYN **revolt, uprising**

,rising 'damp *noun* [U] (*BrE*) a condition in which water comes up from the ground into the walls of a building, causing damage 從地下滲入牆壁的潮氣

risk /rɪsk/ *noun, verb*

■ *noun* **1** [C, U] the possibility of sth bad happening at some time in the future; a situation that could be dangerous or have a bad result 危險；風險：**~ (of sth/of doing sth)** *Smoking can increase the risk of developing heart disease.* 吸煙會增加得心臟病的危險。◇ *Patients should be made aware of the risks involved with this treatment.* 應該告訴病人這種治療所涉及的風險。◇ **~ (that …)** *There is still a risk that the whole deal will fall through.* 整樁買賣化為泡影的風險仍然存在。◇ **~ (to sb/sth)** *The chemicals* ***pose little risk*** (= are not dangerous) *to human health.* 這些化學物對人類健康沒有什麼危害。◇ *a* ***calculated risk*** (= one that you think is small compared with the possible benefits) 值得承擔的風險 ◇ *Any business venture contains an* ***element of risk.*** 任何商業投資都包含一定的風險因素。◇ *We could probably trust her with the information but it's just not*

R

worth the risk. 我們也許可以將這些資料託付給她，但實在不值得去承擔這樣的風險。 **2** [C] **~ (to sth)** a person or thing that is likely to cause problems or danger at some time in the future 危險人物；會帶來風險的事物：*The group was considered to be a risk to national security.* 這夥人被認為是威脅國家安全的危險分子。◇ *a major* ***health/fire risk*** 健康／火災的一大隱患 **3** [C] **a good/bad/poor ~** a person or business that a bank or an insurance company is willing/unwilling to lend money or sell insurance to because they are likely/unlikely to pay back the money etc.（風險很小／很大的）借款人，保險對象：*With five previous claims, he's now a bad insurance risk.* 由於已有了五次索賠要求，他現在是一位風險很大的受保人。

IDM **at 'risk (from/of sth)** in danger of sth unpleasant or harmful happening 有危險；冒風險：*As with all diseases, certain groups will be more at risk than others.* 所有的疾病都是如此，一些人比另一些人更容易受到威脅。◇ *If we go to war, innocent lives will be* ***put at risk.*** 如果我們發動戰爭，無辜的生命就會受到威脅。 **at the 'risk of doing sth** used to introduce sth that may sound stupid or may offend sb（用以引出可能聽上去愚蠢或冒犯人的話）冒着…的風險：*At the risk of showing my ignorance, how exactly does the Internet work?* 也許我難免顯得無知，可互聯網到底是怎麼運作的呢？ **at risk to yourself/sb/sth** with the possibility of harming yourself/sb/sth 冒傷及…的危險：*He dived in to save the dog at considerable risk to his own life.* 他冒着相當大的生命危險跳到水裏去救那隻狗。 **do sth at your ˌown 'risk** to do sth even though you have been warned about the possible dangers and will have to take responsibility for anything bad that happens 自擔風險；責任自負：*Persons swimming beyond this point do so at their own risk* (= on a notice). 游泳者越過此界限後果自負。◇ *Valuables are left at their owner's risk* (= on a notice). 貴重物品須看管，否則風險自負。 **run a 'risk (of sth/of doing sth)** to be in a situation in which sth bad could happen to you 冒風險；有…的危險：*People who are overweight run a risk of a heart attack or stroke.* 超重的人有犯心臟病和中風的危險。 **run the 'risk (of sth/of doing sth)** | **run 'risks** to be or put yourself in a situation in which sth bad could happen to you 冒…的危險；冒險（做某事）：*We don't want to run the risk of losing their business.* 我們不想冒險失去他們的生意。◇ *Investment is all about running risks.* 投資就是要冒風險。 **take a 'risk** | **take 'risks** to do sth even though you know that sth bad could happen as a result 冒險（做某事）：*That's a risk I'm not prepared to take.* 我不願意去冒這個險。◇ *You have no right to take risks with other people's lives.* 你沒有權利拿別人的生命去冒險。

■ ***verb*** **1** **~ sth** to put sth valuable or important in a dangerous situation, in which it could be lost or damaged 使…冒風險（或面臨危險）：*He risked his life to save her.* 他冒着生命危險去救她。◇ *She was risking her own and her children's health.* 她在使自己和子女的健康遭受威脅。◇ *He risked all his money on a game of cards.* 他冒險把自己所有的錢都押在了一場紙牌遊戲上。 **2** to do sth that may mean that you get into a situation which is unpleasant for you 冒…的風險（或危險）：**~ sth** *There was no choice. If they stayed there, they risked death.* 他們別無選擇。如果待在那兒，就面臨死亡。◇ **~ (sb/sth) doing sth** *They knew they risked being arrested.* 他們知道自己冒着被捕的危險。 **3** to do sth that you know is not really a good idea or may not succeed 冒險做；（明知結果而）大膽做：**~ sth** *He risked a glance at her furious face.* 他壯着膽子瞅了瞅她那張憤怒的臉。◇ *It was a difficult decision but we decided to* ***risk it.*** 這件事決心難下，但我們決定冒險一試。◇ **~ doing sth** *We've been advised not to risk travelling in these conditions.* 我們受到忠告，在這種條件下不要冒險出行。

IDM **risk ˌlife and 'limb** | **risk your 'neck** to risk being killed or injured in order to do sth 冒死；不惜受傷

'risk assessment *noun* [C, U] (*business* 商) the act of identifying possible risks, calculating how likely they are to happen and estimating what effects they might have, especially in the context of a company taking responsibility for the safety of its employees or members of the public 風險評估；（尤指公司中涉及員工或公眾安全的）危險性評估：*The employer has an obligation to carry out a risk assessment.* 雇主有義務對危險作出評估。

'risk-averse *adj.* not willing to do sth if it is possible that sth bad could happen as a result 不願冒風險的：*We live in a risk-averse culture.* 我們生活在沒有冒險精神的文化中。◇ *In business you cannot be innovative and risk-averse at the same time.* 經商不可能兼顧改革創新與風險規避。

'risk-taking *noun* [U] the practice of doing things that involve risks in order to achieve sth 冒險；承擔風險

risky /ˈrɪski/ *adj.* (**risk·ier**, **riski·est**) **HELP** You can also use **more risky** and **most risky**. 亦可用 more risky 和 most risky。) involving the possibility of sth bad happening 有危險（或風險）的 **SYN** **dangerous**：*Life as an aid worker can be a* ***risky business*** (= dangerous). 救援人員的工作會有危險。◇ *a risky investment* 有風險的投資 ◇ *It's far too risky to generalize from one set of results.* 僅根據一組結果進行概括是十分不可靠的。 ▸ **risk·ily** /-ɪli/ *adv.* **riski·ness** /-nəs/ *noun* [U]

ris·otto /rɪˈzɒtəʊ; *NAmE* rɪˈsɔːtoʊ; -ˈzɔː-/ *noun* (*pl.* **-os**) [C, U] an Italian dish of rice cooked with vegetables, meat, etc. 意大利肉汁燴飯

ris·qué /ˈrɪskeɪ; *NAmE* rɪˈskeɪ/ *adj.* a **risqué** performance, comment, joke, etc. is a little shocking, usually because it is about sex（表演、評論、笑話等）有傷風化的

ris·sole /ˈrɪsəʊl; *NAmE* -soʊl/ *noun* a small flat mass or ball of chopped meat that is fried. It is sometimes covered with BREADCRUMBS or, in the US, with PASTRY before it is cooked. 炸肉餅；炸肉丸

Rit·alin™ /ˈrɪtəlɪn/ *noun* a drug given to children who cannot keep quiet or still, to help them become calmer and concentrate better 立達寧，利他能（幫助多動兒童安靜下來並集中注意力的藥物）

rite /raɪt/ *noun* a ceremony performed by a particular group of people, often for religious purposes（宗教等的）儀式，典禮：*funeral rites* 喪葬儀式 ◇ *initiation rites* (= performed when a new member joins a secret society)（秘密團體的）入會儀式 ➲ COLLOCATIONS at RELIGION ➲ see also THE LAST RITES

ˌrite of 'passage *noun* a ceremony or an event that marks an important stage in sb's life（標誌人生重要階段的）通過儀式，重大事件

rit·ual /ˈrɪtʃuəl/ *noun, adj.*

■ ***noun*** [C, U] **1** a series of actions that are always performed in the same way, especially as part of a religious ceremony 程序；儀規；禮節；（尤指）宗教儀式：*religious rituals* 宗教儀式 ◇ *She objects to the ritual of organized religion.* 她反對有組織宗教的儀規。➲ COLLOCATIONS at RELIGION **2** something that is done regularly and always in the same way 習慣；老規矩：*Sunday lunch with the in-laws has become something of a ritual.* 星期天和姻親們共進午餐已經成了例行的公事。

■ ***adj.*** [only before noun] **1** done as part of a ritual or ceremony 儀式上的；慶典的：*ritual chanting* 禮儀上的聖詠演唱 **2** always done or said in the same way, especially when this is not sincere 習慣的；老套的；例行公事的：*ritual expressions of sympathy* 例行公事地表示同情 ▸ **ritu·al·ly** *adv.*：*The goat was ritually slaughtered.* 山羊按照儀式宰殺了。

ritu·al·is·tic /ˌrɪtʃuəˈlɪstɪk/ *adj.* [usually before noun] **1** connected with the rituals performed as part of a ceremony 儀式的：*a ritualistic act of worship* 崇拜儀式 **2** always done or said in the same way, especially when this is not sincere 老套的；例行公事的

ritu·al·ize (*BrE* also **-ise**) /ˈrɪtʃuəlaɪz/ *verb* [usually passive] **~ sth** (*formal*) to do sth in the same way or pattern every time 使儀式化；使程式化：*ritualized expressions of grief* 以例行的方式表達悲傷

ritzy /ˈrɪtsi/ *adj.* (*informal*) expensive and fashionable 昂貴時髦的；豪華的 **ORIGIN** From the **Ritz**, the name of several very comfortable and expensive hotels in

London and other cities. 源自里兹大酒店（the Ritz），該品牌的酒店以豪華著稱，見於倫敦等大城市。

rival 0⊶ /ˈraɪvl/ *noun, adj., verb*

■ **noun** 0⊶ **~ (to sb/sth) (for sth)** a person, company, or thing that competes with another in sport, business, etc. 競爭對手：*The two teams have always been rivals.* 這兩個隊一直是競爭對手。◇ *The Japanese are our biggest economic rivals.* 日本人是我們最大的經濟競爭對手。◇ *This latest design **has no rivals*** (= it is easily the best design available). 這種最新款式獨領風騷。▸ **rival** 0⊶ *adj.* [only before noun]：*a **rival bid/claim/offer*** 競標；對立的權利要求；競價 ◇ *fighting between rival groups* 對立團體間的爭鬥 ◇ *He was shot by a member of a rival gang.* 他被敵對團夥的一名成員開槍擊中。

■ **verb** (**-ll-**, *NAmE* also **-l-**) **~ sb/sth (for/in sth)** to be as good, impressive, etc. as sb/sth else 與…相匹敵；比得上 SYN **compare with**：*You will find scenery to rival anything you can see in the Alps.* 你看到的景色可與你在阿爾卑斯山所看到的景色相媲美。➲ see also UNRIVALLED

ri·val·ry /ˈraɪvlri/ *noun* [C, U] (*pl.* **-ries**) a state in which two people, companies, etc. are competing for the same thing 競爭；競賽；較量：**~ (with sb/sth) (for sth)** *a fierce rivalry for world supremacy* 奪取世界霸權的激烈競爭 ◇ **~ (between A and B) (for sth)** *There is a certain amount of friendly rivalry between the teams.* 兩隊間有某種程度上的友好較量。◇ *political rivalries* 政治對抗 ◇ *sibling rivalry* (= between brothers and sisters) 兄弟姐妹間的較勁

riven /ˈrɪvn/ *adj.* [not before noun] **~ (by/with sth)** (*formal*) **1** (of a group of people 一群人) divided because of disagreements, especially in a violent way 分裂；四分五裂：*a party riven by internal disputes* 由於內部分歧而四分五裂的政黨 **2** (of an object 物體) divided into two or more pieces 破裂；破碎

river 0⊶ /ˈrɪvə(r)/ *noun*

1 0⊶ (*abbr.* **R.**) a natural flow of water that continues in a long line across land to the sea/ocean 河；江：*the River Thames* 泰晤士河 ◇ *the Hudson River* 哈得孫河 ◇ *on the banks of the river* (= the ground at the side of a river) 在河岸上 ◇ *to travel **up/down river*** (= in the opposite direction to/in the same direction as the way in which the river is flowing) 逆流而上；順流而下 ◇ *the mouth of the river* (= where it enters the sea/ocean) 河口 ◇ *Can we swim **in the river**?* 我們可以下河游泳嗎？◇ *a boat on the river* 河上的一條船 ◇ *They have a house on the river* (= beside it). 他們在河邊有棟房子。➲ VISUAL VOCAB pages V3, V4, V5 **2 ~ (of sth)** a large amount of liquid that is flowing in a particular direction（液體）湧流：*Rivers of molten lava flowed down the mountain.* 大量的熔岩順着山坡流下來。IDM see SELL *v.*

river·bank /ˈrɪvəbæŋk; *NAmE* ˈrɪvər-/ *noun* the ground at the side of a river 河岸；河堤：*on the riverbank* 在河岸上 ➲ VISUAL VOCAB page V3

ˈriver bed *noun* the area of ground over which a river usually flows 河牀：*a dried-up river bed* 乾涸的河牀

ˈriver blindness *noun* [U] (*medical* 醫) a tropical skin disease caused by a PARASITE of certain flies that breed in rivers, which can also cause a person to become blind 河盲症，盤尾絲蟲病（熱帶皮膚病，由河中繁殖的蒼蠅寄生蟲引起，可導致失明）

river·front /ˈrɪvəfrʌnt; *NAmE* -vərf-/ *noun* (*especially NAmE*) an area of land next to a river with buildings, shops/stores, restaurants, etc. on it 濱河地區

river·ine /ˈrɪvəraɪn/ *adj.* [usually before noun] (*technical* 術語) on, near, or relating to a river or the banks of a river 河流（上）的；河流附近的；河岸（上）的

river·side /ˈrɪvəsaɪd; *NAmE* -vərs-/ *noun* [sing.] the ground along either side of a river 河畔；河岸：*a riverside path* 濱河小道 ◇ *a walk by the riverside* 河邊漫步

rivet /ˈrɪvɪt/ *noun, verb*

■ **noun** a metal pin that is used to fasten two pieces of leather, metal, etc. together 鉚釘

■ **verb** [usually passive] **1 ~ sb/sth** to hold sb's interest or attention so completely that they cannot look away or think of anything else 吸引住：*I was absolutely riveted by her story.* 我完全被她的故事吸引住了。◇ *My eyes **were riveted on** the figure lying in the road.* 我眼睛盯着躺在路上的人。**2 ~ sth** to fasten sth with rivets 鉚接；（用鉚釘）固定：*The steel plates were riveted together.* 鋼板被固定在一起。

IDM **be riveted to the spot/ground** to be so shocked or frightened that you cannot move 嚇呆了；呆若木雞

rivet·ing /ˈrɪvɪtɪŋ/ *adj.* (*approving*) so interesting or exciting that it holds your attention completely 吸引人的；引人入勝的 SYN **engrossing**

rivi·era /ˌrɪviˈeərə; *NAmE* -ˈerə/ *noun* (often **Riviera**) an area by the sea that is warm and popular for holidays, especially the Mediterranean coast of France 海濱度假勝地（尤指法國的地中海海濱）：*the French Riviera* 法國的里維埃拉地區

rivu·let /ˈrɪvjələt/ *noun* (*formal*) a very small river; a small stream of water or other liquid 小河；小溪；溪流；細流

RM /ˌɑːr ˈem/ *abbr.* (in Britain) Royal Marine（英國）皇家海軍陸戰隊 ➲ see also MARINE *n.*

RN /ˌɑːr ˈen/ *abbr.* **1** REGISTERED NURSE **2** (in Britain) Royal Navy（英國）皇家海軍

RNA /ˌɑːr en ˈeɪ/ *noun* [U] (*chemistry* 化) a chemical present in all living cells; like DNA it is a type of NUCLEIC ACID 核糖核酸

roach /rəʊtʃ; *NAmE* roʊtʃ/ *noun* **1** (*NAmE, informal*) = COCKROACH：*The apartments were infested with rats and roaches.* 公寓裏面到處都是老鼠和蟑螂。**2** (*pl.* **roach**) a small European FRESHWATER fish 擬鯉（見於歐洲的淡水小魚）**3** (*slang*) the end part of a cigarette containing MARIJUANA 大麻捲煙的煙蒂

road 0⊶ /rəʊd; *NAmE* roʊd/ *noun*

1 0⊶ a hard surface built for vehicles to travel on 路；道路；公路：*a **main/major/minor road*** 公路幹線；大/支路 ◇ *a **country/mountain road*** 鄉村道路；山路 ◇ *They live just **along/up/down the road*** (= further on the same road). 他們就住在這條路前面不遠的地方。◇ *The house is on a very busy road.* 房子位於一條交通非常繁忙的公路旁邊。◇ *He was walking **along the road** when he was attacked.* 他正在路邊散步，突然遭到襲擊。◇ *It takes about five hours **by road*** (= driving). 開車大約要花五個小時。◇ *It would be better to transport the goods by rail rather than **by road**.* 用鐵路運送這批貨物會比用公路好。◇ *Take the first road on the left and then follow the signs.* 走左邊的第一條路，然後循着路標走。◇ *We parked on a **side road**.* 我們把車停放在叉道上。◇ ***road accidents/safety/users*** 公路交通事故/安全；道路使用者 **2** 0⊶ **Road** (*abbr.* **Rd**) used in names of roads, especially in towns（用於道路名稱，尤指城鎮的）路：*35 York Road* 約克路 35 號 **3** the way to achieving sth 途徑；方法；路子：*to be **on the road to** recovery* 正在恢復之中 ◇ *We have discussed privatization, but we would prefer not to **go down that** particular **road**.* 我們已經討論了私有化問題，但不想採用這種方法。

IDM **ˈany road** (*NEngE*) = ANYWAY **(further) along/down the ˈroad** at some time in the future 今後；在將來：*There are certain to be more job losses further down the road.* 往後肯定會有更多人失業。**one for the ˈroad** (*informal*) a last alcoholic drink before you leave a party, etc. 告辭前喝的最後一杯酒 **on the ˈroad 1** travelling, especially for long distances or periods of time 在途中；（尤指）長途旅行中：*The band has been on the road for six months.* 那支樂隊巡迴演出已有六個月了。**2** (of a car 汽車) in good condition so that it can be legally driven（狀況良好）可行駛：*It will cost about £500 to get the car back on the road.* 要花大約 500 英鎊才能讓車子重新上路。**3** moving from place to place, and having no permanent home 居無定所；漂泊：*Life on the road can be very hard.* 流浪生活會非常艱辛。**the road to ˌhell is paved with good inˈtentions** (*saying*) it is not enough to intend to do good things; you must actually do them 黃泉路上徒有好意多；光說不練是不夠的 ➲ more at END *n.*, FURTHER *adv.*, HIT *v.*, RUBBER, SHOW *n.*

More About 補充説明

roads 路

Roads and streets 公路和街道

- In a town or city, **street** is the most general word for a road with houses and buildings on one or both sides. 在城鎮，street 為最普通的用語，指街道：*a street map of London* 倫敦街道圖 **Street** is not used for roads between towns, but streets in towns are often called **Road**. * street 不用以指城鎮間的道路，而城鎮裏的街道常稱作 Road：*Oxford Street* 牛津街 ◇ *Mile End Road* 邁爾恩德路 A **road map** of a country shows you the major routes between, around and through towns and cities. 一個國家的公路交通圖（road map）標有連接、環繞和穿越各城鎮的主要路線。
- Other words used in the names of streets include **Circle**, **Court**, **Crescent**, **Drive**, **Hill** and **Way**. **Avenue** suggests a wide street lined with trees. A **lane** is a narrow street between buildings or, in *BrE*, a narrow country road. 其他可用於街道名稱的詞有 Circle、Court、Crescent、Drive、Hill 和 Way。avenue 指寬闊的林蔭道，lane 指建築物間的小巷、胡同，或在英式英語中指鄉村小路。

The high street 市鎮商業大街

- **High street** is used in *BrE*, especially as a name, for the main street of a town, where most shops, banks, etc. are. * high street 用於英式英語，尤作商店、銀行等集中的市鎮商業大街名：*the record store in the High Street* 大街的唱片商店 ◇ *high street shops* 市鎮大街的商店 In *NAmE* **Main Street** is often used as a name for this street. 在美式英語中，此義常用 Main Street 表示。

Larger roads 較寬大的公路

- British and American English use different words for the roads that connect towns and cities. **Motorways**, (for example, the M57) in *BrE*, **freeways**, **highways** or **interstates**, (for example State Route 347, Interstate 94, the Long Island Expressway) in *NAmE*, are large divided roads built for long-distance traffic to avoid towns. 表示連接城鎮的公路時，英式英語和美式英語的用詞各異。motorway 用於英式英語（如 57 高速路），freeway、highway 或 interstate 用於美式英語（如 347 州道、94 州際公路、長島高速公路），它們均指城外分道行駛的長途高速公路。
- A **ring road** (*BrE*)/an **outer belt** (*NAmE*) is built around a city or town to reduce traffic in the centre. This can also be called a **beltway** in *NAmE*, especially when it refers to the road around Washington D.C. A **bypass** passes around a town or city rather than through the centre. * ring road（英式英語）/outer belt（美式英語）指為減少市中心的交通流量修建的環城公路。在美式英語中亦可叫做 beltway，不過該詞通常指華盛頓市的環城公路。bypass 指不穿越市中心，繞過城市的旁道。

road·block /ˈrəʊdblɒk; *NAmE* ˈroʊdblɑːk/ *noun* **1** a barrier put across the road by the police or army so that they can stop and search vehicles 路障 **2** (*NAmE*) something that stops a plan from going ahead 障礙

ˈroad fund licence (also **ˈtax disc**) *noun* (in Britain) a small circle of paper that is put on the window of a vehicle or on a motorcycle to show that the owner has paid the tax that allows them to use the vehicle on public roads （英國貼在機動車擋風玻璃上圓形的）路稅付訖證

ˈroad hog *noun* (*informal*, *disapproving*) a person who drives in a dangerous way without thinking about the safety of other road users 莽撞的司機

road·hold·ing /ˈrəʊdhəʊldɪŋ; *NAmE* ˈroʊdhoʊldɪŋ/ *noun* [U] the ability of a car to remain steady when it goes around a corner at a fast speed （汽車快速拐彎時的）穩定性能，抓地力

road·house /ˈrəʊdhaʊs; *NAmE* ˈroʊd-/ *noun* (*old-fashioned*, *NAmE*) a restaurant or bar on a main road in the country （郊外公路幹線上的）路邊旅館，路邊餐館

roadie /ˈrəʊdi; *NAmE* ˈroʊdi/ *noun* (*informal*) a person who works with a band of musicians on tour, and helps move and set up their equipment （樂隊巡迴演出時的）隨團雜務人員

road·kill /ˈrəʊdkɪl; *NAmE* ˈroʊd-/ *noun* **1** [U] an animal, or animals, that have been killed by a car on the road 路殺動物（在公路上被車撞死的動物） **2** [C, U] the killing of an animal by a car hitting it on the road 路殺（汽車在公路上撞死動物）

ˈroad map *noun* **1** a map that shows the roads of an area, especially one that is designed for a person who is driving a car （尤指為駕駛者設計的）公路交通圖 **2** a set of instructions or suggestions about how to do sth or find out about sth 指南

ˈroad movie *noun* a film/movie which is based on a journey made by the main character or characters （基於主角等旅行經歷的）公路電影，旅行電影

ˈroad pricing *noun* [U] the system of making drivers pay to use busy roads at certain times （繁忙路段的）道路收費制度

ˈroad rage *noun* [U] a situation in which a driver becomes extremely angry or violent with the driver of another car because of the way they are driving 公路暴怒（司機之間因駕駛問題而大動肝火）

road·run·ner /ˈrəʊdrʌnə(r); *NAmE* ˈroʊd-/ *noun* a N American bird of the CUCKOO family, that lives in desert areas and can run very fast 走鵑（杜鵑屬，見於北美）

ˈroad sense *noun* [U] the ability to behave in a safe way when driving, walking, etc. on roads 交通安全意識；道路安全意識

road·show /ˈrəʊdʃəʊ; *NAmE* ˈroʊdʃoʊ/ *noun* a travelling show arranged by a radio or television programme, or by a magazine, company or political party （電台、電視台、雜誌或公司組織的）巡迴演出，巡迴廣播，路演；（政黨的）巡迴宣傳

road·side /ˈrəʊdsaɪd; *NAmE* ˈroʊd-/ *noun* [sing.] the edge of the road 路邊；路旁：*We parked by the roadside.* 我們將車停放在路旁。◇ *a roadside cafe* 路邊咖啡店

ˈroad sign *noun* a sign near a road giving information or instructions to drivers 路標 ➲ **VISUAL VOCAB** page V3

road·ster /ˈrəʊdstə(r); *NAmE* ˈroʊd-/ *noun* (*old-fashioned*) a car with no roof and two seats 敞篷雙座小汽車

ˈroad tax *noun* [U] (in Britain) a tax that sb who owns a car must pay to drive on the roads （英國）公路稅

ˈroad test *noun* **1** a test to see how a vehicle functions or what condition it is in （車輛的）道路試驗 **2** (*NAmE*) = DRIVING TEST

ˈroad-test *verb* **~ sth** to test a vehicle to see how it functions or what condition it is in 使（車輛）經受道路試驗

ˈroad train *noun* (*especially AustralE*) a large lorry/truck pulling one or more TRAILERS 公路列車（掛一節或多節拖車的大貨車）

ˈroad trip *noun* (*informal*, *especially NAmE*) a trip made in a car over a long distance 開車長途旅行；公路旅行

road·way /ˈrəʊdweɪ; *NAmE* ˈroʊd-/ *noun* [C, U] a road or the part of a road used by vehicles 道路；車行道

road·works /ˈrəʊdwɜːks; *NAmE* ˈroʊdwɜːrks/ *noun* [pl.] (*BrE*) (*NAmE* **road·work** [U]) repairs that are being done to the road; an area where these repairs are being done 道路修補；修補中的路段

road·worthy /ˈrəʊdwɜːði; *NAmE* ˈroʊdwɜːrði/ *adj.* (of a vehicle 車輛) in a safe condition to drive 適合行駛的；可安全行駛的 ▶ **road·worthi·ness** *noun* [U]

roam /rəʊm; *NAmE* roʊm/ *verb* **1** [I, T] to walk or travel around an area without any definite aim or direction 徜徉；閒逛；漫步 **SYN** **wander**：(**+ adv./prep.**) *The sheep are allowed to roam freely on this land.* 綿羊可以

R

在這片地上自由走動。◇ **~ sth** *to roam the countryside/the streets, etc.* 在鄉間漫步、逛街等 **2** [I, T] (of the eyes or hands 眼睛或手) to move slowly over every part of sb/sth （緩慢地）掃遍，摸遍：**~ (over sth/sb)** *His gaze roamed over her.* 他聚精會神地上下打量她。◇ **~ sth/sb** *Her eyes roamed the room.* 她將房間打量了一遍。

roam·ing /ˈrəʊmɪŋ; *NAmE* ˈroʊ-/ *noun* [U] using a mobile/cell phone by connecting to a different company's network, for example when you are in a different country （移動電話的）漫遊：*international roaming charges* 國際漫遊費用

roan /rəʊn; *NAmE* roʊn/ *noun* an animal, especially a horse, that has hair of two colours mixed together 毛色斑雜的動物（尤指馬）：*a strawberry roan* (= with a mixture of brown and grey hair that looks pink) 一匹紅毛雜色馬 ▸ **roan** *adj.* [only before noun]

roar /rɔː(r)/ *verb, noun*

■ ***verb*** **1** [I] to make a very loud, deep sound 吼叫；咆哮：*We heard a lion roar.* 我們聽見了獅子的吼聲。◇ *The gun roared deafeningly.* 槍炮轟鳴聲震耳欲聾。◇ *The engine* ***roared to life*** (= started noisily). 發動機隆隆啟動。**2** [I, T] to shout sth very loudly 叫喊；大聲地說：*The crowd roared.* 人群一片喧譁。◇ **~ sth (out)** *The fans roared (out) their approval.* 崇拜者大聲叫好。◇ **+ speech** *'Stand back,' he roared.* "靠後站。"他吼道。**3** [I] to laugh very loudly 放聲大笑：*He looked so funny, we all roared.* 他看上去那麼滑稽，我們都哈哈大笑。◇ **~ with laughter** *It made them roar with laughter.* 這使他們大笑起來。**4** [I] **+ adv./prep.** (of a vehicle or its rider/driver 車輛或駕駛者) to move very fast, making a lot of noise 呼嘯而行；開得飛快：*She put her foot down and the car roared away.* 她踩下油門，車子呼嘯而去。**5** [I] (of a fire 火) to burn brightly with a lot of flames, heat and noise 熊熊燃燒 **IDM** see VICTORY *n.*

■ ***noun*** **1** a loud deep sound made by an animal, especially a LION, or by sb's voice 咆哮；吼叫：*His speech was greeted by a roar of applause.* 他的講話引來了雷鳴般的掌聲。◇ *roars of laughter* 放聲大笑 **2** a loud continuous noise made by the wind or sea, or by a machine （風或海的）呼嘯聲；（機器的）隆隆聲：*I could barely hear above the roar of traffic.* 除了車輛的轟鳴聲，我幾乎什麼也聽不見。

roar·ing /ˈrɔːrɪŋ/ *adj.* [only before noun] **1** making a continuous loud deep noise 咆哮的；呼嘯的；轟鳴的：*All we could hear was the sound of roaring water.* 我們只能聽到洶湧澎湃的濤聲。**2** (of a fire 火) burning with a lot of flames and heat 熊熊燃燒的

IDM **do a ˈroaring trade (in sth)** (*informal*) to sell a lot of sth very quickly 生意興隆；銷出大量（某物） **ˌroaring ˈdrunk** extremely drunk and noisy 耍酒瘋 **a ˌroaring sucˈcess** (*informal*) a very great success 巨大的成功

the ˌroaring ˈforties *noun* [pl.] an area of rough ocean between LATITUDES 40° and 50° south 咆哮西風帶（南緯 40 至 50 度之間盛行西風的海域）

the ˌroaring ˈtwenties *noun* [pl.] the years from 1920 to 1929, considered as a time when people were confident and cheerful 興旺的二十年代（指人們自信又快樂的 20 世紀 20 年代）

roast /rəʊst; *NAmE* roʊst/ *verb, noun, adj.*

■ ***verb*** **1** [T, I] **~ (sth)** to cook food, especially meat, without liquid in an oven or over a fire; to be cooked in this way 烘，烤，焙（肉等）：*to roast a chicken* 烤一隻雞 ◇ *the smell of roasting meat* 烤肉的香味 ➲ COLLOCATIONS at COOKING **2** [T, I] **~ (sth)** to cook nuts, BEANS, etc. in order to dry them and turn them brown; to be cooked in this way 烘烤，焙，炒（堅果、豆子等）：*roasted chestnuts* 炒栗子 **3** [T] **~ sb** (*informal or humorous*) to be very angry with sb; to criticize sb strongly （對某人）非常生氣，嚴厲批評 **4** [I, T] **~ (sth)** (*informal*) to become or to make sth become very hot in the sun or by a fire 曝曬；烘烤：*She could feel her skin beginning to roast.* 她感覺到皮膚開始曬得發燙了。

■ ***noun*** **1** (*BrE* also **joint**) a large piece of meat that is cooked whole in the oven 烤肉：*the Sunday roast* 星期日的烤肉 **2** (*NAmE*) (often in compounds 常構成複合詞) a party that takes place in sb's garden/yard at which food is cooked over an open fire 戶外燒烤野餐：*a hot dog roast* 熱狗燒烤野餐 **3** (*NAmE*) an event, especially a meal, at which people celebrate sb's life by telling funny stories about them 耍笑慶祝會（常為宴會，講述主角的滑稽事）

■ ***adj.*** [only before noun] cooked in an oven or over a fire 烤的；焙的：*roast chicken* 燒雞

roast·ing /ˈrəʊstɪŋ; *NAmE* ˈroʊ-/ *adj., noun*

■ ***adj.*** **1** [only before noun] used for roasting meat, vegetables, etc. 用於烤炙（或烘焙）的：*a roasting dish* 用於烘烤的盤子 **2** (also **ˌroasting ˈhot**) so hot that you feel uncomfortable 燥熱的；灼熱的：*a roasting hot day* 酷熱的一天

■ ***noun*** [U, sing.] (*slang*) an occasion when a woman has sex with more than one man （一女多男的）亂交

IDM **give sb/get a ˈroasting** to criticize sb or be criticized in an angry way 嚴厲批評；受到嚴厲批評

rob 0ꟷ /rɒb; *NAmE* rɑːb/ *verb* (**-bb-**)

~ sb/sth (of sth) to steal money or property from a person or place 搶劫；掠奪；盜取：*to* ***rob a bank*** 搶劫銀行 ◇ *The tomb had been robbed of its treasures.* 這座墳墓裏的財寶已被盜。➲ COLLOCATIONS at CRIME

IDM **ˌrob sb ˈblind** (*informal*) to cheat or trick sb so that they lose a lot of money 騙取某人大量錢財 **ˌrob the ˈcradle** (*NAmE, informal*) to have a sexual relationship with a much younger person 老牛吃嫩草，劫搖籃（指跟比自己年齡小很多的人發生性關係） **rob ˌPeter to pay ˈPaul** (*saying*) to borrow money from one person to pay back what you owe to another person; to take money from one thing to use for sth else 借新債還舊賬；拆東牆補西牆

PHR V **ˈrob sb/sth of sth** [often passive] to prevent sb having sth that they need or deserve 剝奪（某人所需或應得之物） **SYN** **deprive**：*A last-minute goal robbed the team of victory.* 最後一分鐘的進球奪去了這支球隊勝利的機會。◇ *He had been robbed of his dignity.* 他已失去了尊嚴。

rob·ber /ˈrɒbə(r); *NAmE* ˈrɑːb-/ *noun* a person who steals from a person or place, especially using violence or threats 強盜；盜賊；搶劫犯：*a bank robber* 銀行搶劫犯

rob·bery /ˈrɒbəri; *NAmE* ˈrɑːb-/ *noun* [U, C] (*pl.* **-ies**) the crime of stealing money or goods from a bank, shop/store, person, etc., especially using violence or threats 盜竊；搶劫；掠奪：*armed robbery* (= using a gun, knife, etc.) 持械搶劫 ◇ *There has been a spate of robberies in the area recently.* 最近這一地區接連發生了多起搶劫案。➲ COLLOCATIONS at CRIME ➲ compare BURGLARY, THEFT **IDM** see DAYLIGHT, HIGHWAY

robe /rəʊb; *NAmE* roʊb/ *noun, verb*

■ ***noun*** **1** a long loose outer piece of clothing, especially one worn as a sign of rank or office at a special ceremony 袍服，禮袍（常於典禮中穿着以顯示身分）：*coronation robes* 加冕禮袍 ◇ *cardinals in scarlet robes* 身披紅袍的樞機主教 **2** = BATHROBE

■ ***verb*** [usually passive] **~ sb/yourself (in sth)** (*formal*) to dress sb/yourself in long loose clothes or in the way mentioned （給某人）穿上禮袍：*a robed choir* 身着禮袍的唱詩班 ◇ *The priests were robed in black.* 各司祭都穿上了黑袍。

robin /ˈrɒbɪn; *NAmE* ˈrɑːb-/ *noun* **1** a small brown European bird with a red breast 歐亞鴝；歐洲知更鳥 **2** a grey American bird with a red breast, larger than a European robin 旅鶇，美洲知更鳥（毛灰色，胸部紅色，比歐亞鴝大）➲ see also ROUND ROBIN

ˌRobin ˈHood *noun* a person who takes or steals money from rich people and gives it to poor people 羅賓漢；劫富濟貧者 **ORIGIN** From the name of a character in traditional English stories who lived in a forest, robbing rich people and giving money to poor people. 源自英國民間傳說中劫富濟貧的綠林好漢羅賓漢。

robo·call /ˈrəʊbəʊkɔːl; *NAmE* ˈroʊboʊ-/ *noun* (*NAmE, informal, disapproving*) a phone call from a company that is trying to sell you sth, using an automatic DIALLING system to call your number and a recorded

R

message 機器人電話（自動撥號播放錄音信息的推銷電話）

robot /ˈrəʊbɒt; *NAmE* ˈroʊbɑːt/ *noun* **1** a machine that can perform a complicated series of tasks automatically 機器人；機械人：*These cars are built by robots.* 這些汽車是由機器人製造的。 **2** (especially in stories) a machine that is made to look like a human and that can do some things that a human can do（尤指故事中的）機器人，機械人 **3** (*SAfrE*) a TRAFFIC LIGHT 交通信號燈：*Turn left at the first robot.* 在第一個交通信號燈處向左拐。

ro·bot·ic /rəʊˈbɒtɪk; *NAmE* roʊˈbɑːtɪk/ *adj.* **1** connected with robots 機器人的：*a robotic arm* 機械手 **2** like a robot, making stiff movements, speaking without feeling or expression, etc. 像機器人的；呆板機械的

ro·bot·ics /rəʊˈbɒtɪks; *NAmE* roʊˈbɑːt-/ *noun* [U] the science of designing and operating ROBOTS 機器人科學（或技術）

ro·bust /rəʊˈbʌst; *NAmE* roʊ-/ *adj.* **1** strong and healthy 強健的；強壯的：*She was almost 90, but still very robust.* 她將近 90 歲了，但身體仍然十分強健。 **2** strong; able to survive being used a lot and not likely to break 結實的；耐用的；堅固的 SYN **sturdy**：*a robust piece of equipment* 經久耐用的設備 **3** (of a system or an organization 體制或機構) strong and not likely to fail or become weak 強勁的；富有活力的：*robust economic growth* 強勁的經濟增長 **4** strong and full of determination; showing that you are sure about what you are doing or saying 堅定的；信心十足的 SYN **vigorous**：*It was a typically robust performance by the Foreign Secretary.* 這是外交大臣典型的有信心的表現。 ▸ **ro·bust·ly** *adv.*：*The furniture was robustly constructed.* 傢具做得非常結實。◇ *They defended their policies robustly.* 他們堅定地捍衛自己的政策。 **ro·bust·ness** *noun* [U]

rock 🔑 /rɒk; *NAmE* rɑːk/ *noun, verb*

■ ***noun***

▸ **HARD MATERIAL** 硬物 **1** 🔑 [U, C] the hard solid material that forms part of the surface of the earth and some other planets 岩石：*They drilled through several layers of rock to reach the oil.* 他們鑽透了幾層岩石尋找石油。◇ *a cave with striking* ***rock formations*** (= shapes made naturally from rock) 有奇妙天然岩石造型的洞穴 ◇ *The tunnel was blasted out of solid rock.* 這條隧道是在實心岩石中炸出來的。◇ ***volcanic/igneous/sedimentary, etc. rocks*** 火山岩、火成岩、沉積岩等 **2** 🔑 [C] a mass of rock standing above the earth's surface or in the sea/ocean 石山；礁石：*the Rock of Gibraltar* 直布羅陀山 ◇ *The ship crashed into the infamous Sker Point rocks and broke into three pieces.* 這艘船撞上了惡名遠揚的斯戈爾尖岬暗礁群，斷為三截。 ➲ VISUAL VOCAB page V5 **3** 🔑 [C] a large single piece of rock 巨石塊；岩塊：*They clambered over the rocks at the foot of the cliff.* 他們吃力地爬過了絕壁腳下的巨石。◇ *The sign said 'Danger: falling rocks'.* 警示牌上寫着"危險：前有落石"。

▸ **STONE** 石頭 **4** 🔑 [C] (*NAmE*) a small stone 碎石；石子；小石塊：*Protesters pelted the soldiers with rocks.* 抗議者向士兵投擲石塊。

▸ **MUSIC** 音樂 **5** 🔑 (also **ˈrock music**) [U] a type of loud popular music, developed in the 1960s, with a strong beat played on electric GUITARS and drums 搖滾樂：*punk rock* 朋客搖滾樂 ◇ *a* ***rock band/star*** 搖滾樂隊／明星

▸ **SWEET/CANDY** 糖果 **6** (*BrE*) [U] a type of hard sweet/candy made in long sticks, often sold in places where people go on holiday/vacation by the sea/ocean 棒棒糖：*a stick of Brighton rock* 一支布賴頓棒棒糖

▸ **JEWEL** 寶石 **7** [C, usually pl.] (*NAmE, informal*) a PRECIOUS STONE, especially a diamond 寶石；（尤指）鑽石

▸ **PERSON** 人 **8** [C, usually sing.] a person who is emotionally strong and who you can rely on 可信賴的人；靠山：*He is my rock.* 他是我的主心骨。

IDM **(caught/stuck) between a ˌrock and a ˈhard place** in a situation where you have to choose between two things, both of which are unpleasant 進退兩難；左右為難 **get your ˈrocks off** (*slang*) **1** to have an ORGASM 達到性高潮 **2** to do sth that you really enjoy 做自己真正喜歡的事；享受 **on the ˈrocks** **1** a relationship or business that is **on the rocks** is having difficulties and is likely to fail soon（關係或生意）陷於困境，瀕臨崩潰：*Sue's marriage is on the rocks.* 蘇的婚姻觸礁。 **2** (of drinks 飲料) served with pieces of ice but no water 加冰塊（但不加水）的：*Scotch on the rocks* 加冰塊的蘇格蘭威士忌酒 ➲ more at STEADY *adj.*

■ ***verb***

▸ **MOVE GENTLY** 輕輕移動 **1** [I, T] to move gently backwards and forwards or from side to side; to make sb/sth move in this way（使）輕輕搖晃，緩緩擺動：(**+ adv./prep.**) *The boat* ***rocked from side to side*** *in the waves.* 小船在波浪中搖盪。◇ *She was* ***rocking backwards and forwards*** *in her seat.* 她在座位上前搖後晃。◇ **~ sb/sth (+ adv./prep.)** *He rocked the baby gently in his arms.* 他抱着孩子輕輕搖晃。

▸ **SHOCK** 驚嚇 **2** [T, often passive] **~ sb/sth** (rather *informal*) to shock sb/sth very much or make them afraid 驚嚇；使震驚；使害怕：*The country was rocked by a series of political scandals.* 一連串的政治醜聞震驚全國。◇ *The news rocked the world.* 這則消息震驚了全世界。

▸ **SHAKE** 搖動 **3** [I, T] to shake or to make sth shake violently（使）劇烈搖擺，猛烈晃動：*The house rocked when the bomb exploded.* 炸彈爆炸時，房子都晃動了。◇ **~ sth** *The town was rocked by an earthquake.* 小鎮受到地震的劇烈震動。◇ (*figurative*) *The scandal rocked the government* (= made the situation difficult for it). 醜聞使政府處境艱難。

▸ **DANCE** 舞蹈 **5** [I] (*old-fashioned*) to dance to rock music 隨搖滾樂跳舞；跳搖滾

▸ **BE GOOD** 好 **5 sth rocks** [I] (*slang*) used to say that sth is very good 很好；棒極了：*Her new movie rocks!* 她的新電影棒極了！

IDM **rock the ˈboat** (*informal*) to do sth that upsets a situation and causes problems 搗亂；惹麻煩：*She was told to keep her mouth shut and not rock the boat.* 有人叫她閉嘴，不要招惹是非。 ➲ more at FOUNDATION

rocka·billy /ˈrɒkəbɪli; *NAmE* ˈrɑːk-/ *noun* [U] a type of American music that combines ROCK AND ROLL and country music 鄉村搖滾樂（融合了搖滾樂和鄉村音樂的美國音樂）

ˌrock and ˈroll (also **ˌrock 'n' ˈroll**) *noun* [U] a type of music popular in the 1950s with a strong beat and simple tunes 搖滾樂

ˌrock ˈbottom *noun* [U] (*informal*) the lowest point or level that is possible 最低點；最低水平：*Prices hit rock bottom.* 價格降到了最低點。◇ *The marriage had reached rock bottom.* 婚姻已經走到了盡頭。 ▸ **ˌrock-ˈbottom** *adj.*：*rock-bottom prices* 最低價格

ˈrock cake *noun* (*BrE*) a small cake that has a hard rough surface and contains dried fruit 石頭蛋糕；乾果岩皮蛋糕

ˌrock ˈcandy *noun* [U] (*NAmE*) a type of hard sweet/candy made from sugar that is melted then allowed to form CRYSTALS 透明硬糖；冰糖

ˈrock climbing *noun* [U] the sport or activity of climbing steep rock surfaces 攀岩（運動）：*to go rock climbing* 去攀岩

ˈrock crystal *noun* [U] a pure clear form of QUARTZ (= a hard mineral) 無色水晶

rock·er /ˈrɒkə(r); *NAmE* ˈrɑːk-/ *noun* **1** one of the two curved pieces of wood on the bottom of a rocking chair（搖椅底部的）弧形搖桿 **2** (*especially NAmE*) = ROCKING CHAIR **3 Rocker** (*BrE*) a member of a group of young people in Britain, especially in the 1960s, who liked to wear leather jackets, ride motorcycles and listen to ROCK AND ROLL music 搖滾青年（尤指 20 世紀 60 年代的某些英國青年，喜歡穿皮夾克、騎摩托車、聽搖滾樂） ➲ compare MOD **4** a person who performs, dances to or enjoys rock music 搖滾樂表演者；跳搖滾舞的人；喜歡搖滾樂的人

IDM **be ˌoff your ˈrocker** (*informal*) to be crazy 發瘋；瘋狂

ˈrocker switch *noun* (*technical* 術語) a type of electrical switch often used, for example, for lights or electrical SOCKETS, where you press one end down to switch it on, and the other end down to switch it off again 翹板開關；搖桿開關

rock·ery /ˈrɒkəri; NAmE ˈrɑːk-/ *noun* (*pl.* **-ies**) (also **ˈrock garden**) a garden or part of a garden consisting of an arrangement of large stones with plants growing among them 假山花園；假山

rocket /ˈrɒkɪt; NAmE ˈrɑːkɪt/ *noun, verb*

■ ***noun*** **1** [C] a SPACECRAFT in the shape of a tube that is driven by a stream of gases let out behind it when fuel is burned inside 火箭： *a **space rocket*** 太空火箭 ◇ *The **rocket was launched** in 2007.* 這枚火箭發射於 2007 年。◇ *The idea **took off like a rocket*** (= it immediately became popular). 這種思想立即風靡一時。**2** [C] a MISSILE (= a weapon that travels through the air) that carries a bomb and is driven by a stream of burning gases 火箭武器；火箭（彈）： *a rocket attack* 火箭攻擊 **3** [C] a FIREWORK that goes high into the air and then explodes with coloured lights 焰火；煙花 **4** [U] (*BrE*) (*NAmE* **aru·gula**) a plant with long green leaves that have a strong flavour and are eaten raw in salads 大蒜芥；芝麻菜；紫花南芥

IDM **to give sb a ˈrocket | to get a ˈrocket** (*BrE, informal*) to speak angrily to sb because they have done sth wrong; to be spoken to angrily for this reason （受到）痛罵，斥責

■ ***verb*** **1** [I] (+ **adv./prep.**) to increase very quickly and suddenly 快速增長；猛增 **SYN** **shoot up**： *rocketing prices* 飛漲的價格 ◇ *Unemployment has rocketed up again.* 失業人數再次猛增。◇ *The total has rocketed from 376 to 532.* 總數從 376 猛增到 532。**2** [I] + **adv./prep.** to move very fast 迅速移動： *The car rocketed out of a side street.* 汽車從一條小路上嗖地一下開了出來。**3** to achieve or to make sb/sth achieve a successful position very quickly （使）迅速成功，迅速提高地位： [I, T] **~ (sb/sth) to sth** *The band **rocketed to stardom** with their first single.* 這支樂隊的第一首單曲使他們一舉成名。**4** [T] **~ sth** to attack a place with rockets 用火箭彈攻擊

ˈrocket-fuelled (*US* **ˈrocket-fueled**) *adj.* [only before noun] happening, moving or increasing very fast 急劇發生的；急速移動的；飛漲的： *There are already signs of rocket-fuelled growth.* 已經出現迅猛增長的跡象。

rock·et·ry /ˈrɒkɪtri; NAmE ˈrɑːk-/ *noun* [U] the area of science which deals with ROCKETS and with sending rockets into space; the use of rockets 火箭學；火箭技術

R

ˈrocket science *noun* [U]

IDM **it's not ˈrocket science** (*informal*) used to emphasize that sth is easy to do or understand 並非難事；不是很複雜 **SYN** **brain surgery**： *Go on, you can do it. It's not exactly rocket science, is it?* 繼續幹，你能做得到的。這並非難事，對嗎？

ˈrock face *noun* a vertical surface of rock, especially on a mountain （尤指山體的）岩石縱面，垂直岩石表面

rock·fall /ˈrɒkfɔːl; NAmE ˈrɑːk-/ *noun* the fact of rocks falling down; a pile of rocks that have fallen 岩崩；崩塌的岩石

ˈrock garden *noun* = ROCKERY

ˌrock-ˈhard *adj.* extremely hard or strong 極其堅硬的；極結實的

ˈrocking chair (also **rock·er** especially in *NAmE*) *noun* a chair with two curved pieces of wood under it that make it move backwards and forwards 搖椅 ➲ **VISUAL VOCAB** page V21

ˈrocking horse *noun* a wooden horse for children that can be made to ROCK backwards and forwards （兒童遊戲用的）木馬 ➲ **VISUAL VOCAB** page V37

ˈrock music *noun* = ROCK (5)

rock 'n' roll *noun* = ROCK AND ROLL

the Rock of Gibraltar /ˌrɒk əv dʒɪˈbrɔːltə(r); NAmE ˌrɑːk/ *noun* [sing.] a high CLIFF at the south-western edge of the Mediterranean Sea, near the town and port of Gibraltar. When people say that sth is like the Rock of Gibraltar, they mean it is very safe or solid. 直布羅陀巨岩（位於地中海西南端直布羅陀港城附近的一處懸崖，象徵十分安全或堅如磐石）： *When I invested my money with the company I was told it was as safe as the Rock of Gibraltar.* 我投資這家公司時，他們說它像直布羅陀巨岩一樣可靠。

ˈrock pool (*BrE*) (*NAmE* **ˈtide pool**) *noun* a small amount of water that collects between the rocks by the sea/ocean （海邊）岩石區潮水潭 ➲ **VISUAL VOCAB** page V5

ˈrock salt *noun* [U] a kind of salt that comes from the ground 岩鹽；石鹽

ˌrock ˈsolid *adj.* **1** that you can trust not to change or to disappear 穩固的；堅實的；可信賴的： *The support for the party was rock solid.* 這一政黨得到了堅定的支持。**2** extremely hard and not likely to break 堅硬的；不會碎的

rocky /ˈrɒki; NAmE ˈrɑːki/ *adj.* (**rock·ier**, **rocki·est**) **1** made of rock; full of rocks 岩石的；多岩石的： *a rocky coastline* 岩石嶙峋的海岸線 ◇ *rocky soil* 多石的土壤 **2** difficult and not certain to continue or to be successful 困難的；難以維持的；不穩定的： *a rocky marriage* 不穩定的婚姻

the ˌRocky Mountain ˈStates *noun* [pl.] the eight US states in the area of the Rocky Mountains 落基山脈諸州（位於美國落基山脈地區的八個州）

ro·coco /rəˈkəʊkəʊ; NAmE rəˈkoʊkoʊ/ (also **Rococo**) *adj.* used to describe a style of ARCHITECTURE, furniture, etc. that has a lot of decoration, especially in the shape of curls; used to describe a style of literature or music that has a lot of detail and decoration. The rococo style was popular in the 18th century. 洛可可式的，過分修飾的（用以描述裝飾精巧的建築、傢具等，以及描寫細膩入微的文學、音樂風格。洛可可風格盛行於 18 世紀）

rod /rɒd; NAmE rɑːd/ *noun* **1** (often used in compounds 常用於構成複合詞) a long straight piece of wood, metal or glass 杆；竿；棒 ➲ **VISUAL VOCAB** pages V21, V70 ➲ see also LIGHTNING ROD (1) **2** = FISHING ROD： *fishing with rod and line* 用魚竿釣魚 **3** (also **the rod**) (*old-fashioned*) a stick that is used for hitting people as a punishment （責打人用的）棍棒： *There used to be a saying: 'Spare the rod and spoil the child.'* 俗語說："孩子不打不成器。" **4** (*NAmE, slang*) a small gun 手槍

IDM **make a rod for your own ˈback** to do sth that will cause problems for you in the future 自找麻煩；自討苦吃 ➲ more at BEAT *v.*, RULE *v.*

rode *past tense of* RIDE

ro·dent /ˈrəʊdnt; NAmE ˈroʊ-/ *noun* any small animal that belongs to a group of animals with strong sharp front teeth. Mice, RATS and SQUIRRELS are all rodents. 齧齒動物 ➲ **VISUAL VOCAB** page V12

rodeo /ˈrəʊdiəʊ; rəʊˈdeɪəʊ; NAmE ˈroʊdioʊ; roʊˈdeɪoʊ/ *noun* (*pl.* **-os**) a public competition, especially in the US, in which people show their skill at riding wild horses and catching CATTLE with ropes （尤指美國的）牛仔競技比賽

roe /rəʊ; NAmE roʊ/ *noun* **1** [U, C] the mass of eggs inside a female fish (**hard roe**) or the SPERM of a male fish (**soft roe**), used as food 魚子： *cod's roe* 鱈魚子 **2** = ROE DEER

ˈroe deer *noun* (*pl.* **roe deer**) (also **roe**) a small European and Asian DEER 狍（一種產於歐亞的小鹿）

roent·gen·ium /ˌrɒntˈɡiːniəm; NAmE ˌrent-/ *noun* [U] (*symb.* **Rg**) a chemical element. Roentgenium is a RADIOACTIVE element that is produced artificially and has no known use. 錀（一種人工合成的放射性化學元素）

Roe v Wade /ˌrəʊ vɜːsəs ˈweɪd; NAmE ˌroʊ vɜːrsəs/ *noun* a legal case in the US Supreme Court that decided that ABORTION is allowed by the Constitution 羅訴韋德案（美國最高法院判決墮胎不違憲的案件）

roger /ˈrɒdʒə(r); NAmE ˈrɑːdʒ-/ *exclamation, verb*

■ ***exclamation*** people say **Roger!** in communication by radio to show that they have understood a message （用於無線電通訊，表示已聽懂信息）信息收到，明白

■ ***verb*** **~ sb** (*BrE, taboo, slang*) (of a man 男子) to have sex with sb 與某人性交

rogue /rəʊɡ; *NAmE* roʊɡ/ *noun, adj.*
■ ***noun*** **1** (*humorous*) a person who behaves badly, but in a harmless way 無賴；搗蛋鬼 **SYN scoundrel**：*He's a bit of a rogue, but very charming.* 他好搗蛋，但卻很討人喜歡。 **2** (*old-fashioned*) a man who is dishonest and immoral 騙子；惡棍；流氓 **SYN rascal**：*a* ***rogues' gallery*** (= a collection of pictures of criminals) 案犯相片集
■ ***adj.*** [only before noun] **1** (of an animal 動物) living apart from the main group, and possibly dangerous 離群的 **2** behaving in a different way from other similar people or things, often causing damage 行為失常的；暴戾的：*a rogue gene* 變異基因 ◇ *a rogue police officer* 暴戾的警官

roguish /ˈrəʊɡɪʃ; *NAmE* ˈroʊ-/ *adj.* (usually *approving*) (of a person 人) pleasant and amusing but looking as if they might do sth wrong 調皮搗蛋的；頑皮的：*a roguish smile* 頑皮的微笑 ▸ **roguish·ly** *adv.*

Ro·hyp·nol™ /rəʊˈhɪpnɒl; *NAmE* roʊˈhɪpnɑːl/ *noun* [U] a drug that makes you want to sleep, and which can make you unable to remember what happens for a period after you take it 洛喜普諾，羅眠樂（安眠藥，服後可致暫時失憶）

rois·ter·ing /ˈrɔɪstərɪŋ/ *adj.* (*old-fashioned*) having fun in a cheerful, noisy way 喧鬧作樂的

role 🔑 AW /rəʊl; *NAmE* roʊl/ *noun*
1 🔑 the function or position that sb has or is expected to have in an organization, in society or in a relationship 職能；地位；角色：*the role of the teacher in the classroom* 教師在課堂上的作用 ◇ *She refused to take on the traditional woman's role.* 她拒絕承擔傳統婦女的角色。◇ *In many marriages there has been a complete* ***role reversal*** (= change of roles) *with the man staying at home and the woman going out to work.* 許多夫妻徹底交換了角色，男人待在家裏而女人出外工作。 **2** 🔑 an actor's part in a play, film/movie, etc.（演員的）角色：*It is one of the greatest roles she has played.* 這是她所扮演過的最重要的角色之一。◇ *Who is in the* ***leading role*** (= the most important one)? 誰扮演主角？ ➲ COLLOCATIONS at CINEMA **3** 🔑 the degree to which sb/sth is involved in a situation or an activity and the effect that they have on it 影響程度；作用：*the role of diet in preventing disease* 飲食在預防疾病中的作用 ◇ *The media play a* ***major role*** *in influencing people's opinions.* 媒體在影響輿論方面發揮着重要作用。◇ *a* ***key/vital role*** 關鍵/至關重要的作用

ˈrole model *noun* a person that you admire and try to copy 楷模；行為榜樣

ˈrole-play *noun* a learning activity in which you behave in the way sb else would behave in a particular situation 角色扮演：*Role-play allows students to practise language in a safe situation.* 角色扮演可以使學生練習語言，說錯了也沒關係。 ▸ **ˈrole-play** *verb* [I, T] **~ (sth)**

ˈrole-playing game *noun* a game in which players pretend to be imaginary characters who take part in adventures, especially in situations from FANTASY literature 角色扮演遊戲（參加者假扮成幻想作品等中的虛構人物進行冒險）

rolls 捲

bread rolls
小圓麪包

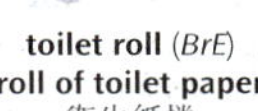
toilet roll (*BrE*)
roll of toilet paper
衞生紙捲

roll of tape
一捲膠帶

roll 🔑 /rəʊl; *NAmE* roʊl/ *noun, verb*
■ ***noun***
▸ **OF PAPER/CLOTH, ETC.** 紙、織物等 **1** 🔑 [C] **~ (of sth)** a long piece of paper, cloth, film, etc. that has been wrapped around itself or a tube several times so that it forms the shape of a tube 捲；捲軸：*a roll of film* 一捲膠捲 ◇ *Wallpaper is sold in rolls.* 壁紙論捲銷售。 ➲ VISUAL VOCAB page V33 ➲ see also TOILET ROLL
▸ **OF SWEETS/CANDY** 糖果 **2** 🔑 [C] **~ (of sth)** (*NAmE*) a paper tube wrapped around sweets/candy, etc. 一管：*a roll of mints* 一管薄荷糖 ➲ VISUAL VOCAB page V33
▸ **BREAD** 麪包 **3** 🔑 (also ˌ**bread ˈroll**) [C] a small LOAF of bread for one person 小麪包條；小圓麪包：*Soup and a roll: £3.50* 湯和麪包捲：3.50 英鎊 ◇ *a* ***chicken/cheese, etc. roll*** (= filled with chicken/cheese, etc.) 雞肉捲、奶酪捲等 ➲ compare BUN (2) ➲ see also SAUSAGE ROLL, SPRING ROLL, SWISS ROLL
▸ **OF BODY** 身體 **4** [sing.] an act of rolling the body over and over 翻滾；打滾：*The kittens were enjoying a roll in the sunshine.* 那些小貓在陽光下嬉戲打滾。 **5** [C] a physical exercise in which you roll your body on the ground, moving your back and legs over your head 滾翻；翻跟頭：*a* ***forward/backward roll*** 前/後滾翻
▸ **OF SHIP/PLANE** 船隻；飛機 **6** [U] the act of moving from side to side so that one side is higher than the other 搖晃；搖盪 ➲ compare PITCH *n.* (8)
▸ **OF FAT** 脂肪 **7** [C] an area of too much fat on your body, especially around your waist 脂肪堆積的部位，肥胖的部位（尤指腰部）：*Rolls of fat hung over his belt.* 一堆肥肉墜在他的腰帶上。
▸ **LIST OF NAMES** 名單 **8** [C] an official list of names 花名冊；名單：*the* ***electoral roll*** (= a list of all the people who can vote in an election) 選民名冊 ◇ *The chairman* ***called/took the roll*** (= called out the names on a list to check that everyone was present). 主席點了名。 ➲ see also PAYROLL (1)
▸ **SOUND** 聲音 **9** [C] **~ (of sth)** a deep continuous sound 隆隆聲；持續的轟鳴聲：*the distant roll of thunder* 遠處隆隆的雷聲 ◇ *a drum roll* 咚咚的鼓聲
▸ **OF DICE** 骰子 **10** [C] an act of rolling a DICE 擲骰子：*The order of play is decided by the roll of a dice.* 比賽順序是通過擲骰子決定的。
▸ **PHONETICS** 語音學 **11** = TRILL (3)
IDM **be on a ˈroll** (*informal*) to be experiencing a period of success at what you are doing 連連獲勝；連續交好運：*Don't stop me now—I'm on a roll!* 現在別阻止我，我正鴻運當頭呢！ **a ˌroll in the ˈhay** (*informal*) an act of having sex with sb 性交
■ ***verb***
▸ **TURN OVER** 翻轉 **1** 🔑 [I, T] to turn over and over and move in a particular direction; to make a round object do this（使）翻滾，滾動：**+ adv./prep.** *The ball rolled down the hill.* 球滾下了山。◇ *We watched the waves rolling onto the beach.* 我們望着波浪湧向海灘。◇ **~ sth + adv./prep.** *Delivery men were rolling barrels across the yard.* 送貨人正把桶滾到院子一邊。 **2** 🔑 [I, T] to turn over and over or round and round while remaining in the same place; to make sth do this（使）原地轉圈，原地打轉：(**+ adv./prep.**) *a dog rolling in the mud* 在泥漿裏打滾的狗 ◇ *Her eyes rolled.* 她那雙眼睛滴溜溜地轉動。◇ **~ sth (+ adv./prep.)** *She* ***rolled her eyes*** *upwards* (= to show surprise or disapproval). 她翻着白眼。◇ *He was rolling a pencil between his fingers.* 他用手指捻動着鉛筆。 **3** 🔑 [I, T] **~ (sb/sth) over (onto sth)** | **~ (sb/sth) (over) onto sth** to turn over to face a different direction; to make sb/sth do this（使）翻身，翻轉：**~ over (onto sth)** *She rolled over to let the sun brown her back.* 她翻了個身，讓太陽把她的背曬成古銅色。◇ **~ onto sth** *He rolled onto his back.* 他翻過身來仰面躺着。◇ **~ sb/sth (over) (onto sth)** *I rolled the baby over onto its stomach.* 我讓嬰兒翻過身去趴着。◇ *to* ***roll a dice/die*** (= in a game) 擲骰子 ◇ (*especially NAmE*) *She rolled her car in a 100 mph crash.* 她在時速 100 英里時翻了車。
▸ **MOVE (AS IF) ON WHEELS** 靠輪子滾動 **4** 🔑 [I, T] to move smoothly (on wheels or as if on wheels); to make sth do this（使）滾動，移動：(**+ adv./prep.**) *The car began to roll back down the hill.* 汽車開始倒着往山下滑。◇ *The traffic rolled slowly forwards.* 車流緩緩地向前挪動。◇ *Mist was rolling in from the sea.* 薄霧從海上湧來。◇ **~ sth (+ adv./prep.)** *He rolled the trolley across the room.* 他推着手推車穿過房間。
▸ **MAKE BALL/TUBE** 做成球/管 **5** 🔑 [T, I] **~ (sth) (up) (into sth)** to make sth/yourself into the shape of a ball or

tube 使…成球狀（或管狀）：*I rolled the string into a ball.* 我把線繩兒繞成了一個球。◇ *We rolled up the carpet.* 我們把地毯捲了起來。◇ *a rolled-up newspaper* 捲成捲的報紙 ◇ *I always* **roll my own** (= make my own cigarettes). 我總是自己捲煙抽。◇ *The hedgehog rolled up into a ball.* 刺猬團成了一個球。➲ compare UNROLL (1)

▸ **FOLD CLOTHING** 疊衣服 **6** [T] to fold the edge of a piece of clothing, etc. over and over on itself to make it shorter 把（衣服的邊）捲起來：**~ sth up** *Roll up your sleeves.* 把你的袖子挽起來。◇ **~ sth + adv./prep.** *She rolled her jeans to her knees.* 她把牛仔褲捲到了膝蓋處。➲ VISUAL VOCAB page V61

▸ **MAKE STH FLAT** 使平坦 **7** [T] **~ sth (out)** to make sth flat by pushing sth heavy over it 使平坦；壓平：*Roll the pastry on a floured surface.* 在撒了麪粉的板面上將油酥麪糰擀平。

▸ **WRAP UP** 包裹 **8** [T] **~ sb/sth/yourself (up) in sth** to wrap or cover sb/sth/yourself in sth（用某物）包裹，覆蓋：*Roll the meat in the breadcrumbs.* 用麪包屑將肉裹起來。◇ *He rolled himself up in the blanket.* 他把自己裹在毯子裏。

▸ **OF SHIP/PLANE/WALK** 船隻；飛機；行走 **9** [I, T] **~ (sth) (+ adv./prep.)** to move or make sth move from side to side（使）搖擺，搖晃：*He walked with a rolling gait.* 他搖搖晃晃地走着。◇ *The ship was rolling heavily to and fro.* 輪船劇烈地顛簸着。➲ compare PITCH *v.* (6)

▸ **MAKE SOUND** 發出聲音 **10** [I, T] to make a long continuous sound 發出持續的聲音：*rolling drums* 咚咚的鼓聲 ◇ *Thunder rolled.* 雷聲隆隆。◇ **~ sth** *to* **roll your r's** (= by letting your tongue VIBRATE with each 'r' sound) 發 r 的舌尖顫音

▸ **MACHINE** 機器 **11** [I, T] when a machine **rolls** or sb **rolls** it, it operates 啟動；開動：*They had to repeat the scene because the cameras weren't rolling.* 他們只好重新拍攝這個鏡頭，因為攝影機沒有啟動。◇ **~ sth** *Roll the cameras!* 開拍！

IDM **be 'rolling in money/it** (*informal*) to have a lot of money 非常富有；財源滾滾；腰纏萬貫 **let's 'roll** (*informal, especially NAmE*) used to suggest to a group of people that you should all start doing sth or going somewhere 咱們開始幹吧；咱們動身吧 **rolled into 'one** combined in one person or thing 融為一體；集於一身：*Banks are several businesses rolled into one.* 銀行集數種商業活動於一身。**ˌrolling in the 'aisles** (*informal*) laughing a lot 大笑；笑聲不斷：*She soon had us rolling in the aisles.* 她很快就讓我們笑個不停。**a rolling 'stone gathers no 'moss** (*saying*) a person who moves from place to place, job to job, etc. does not have a lot of money, possessions or friends but is free from responsibilities 滾石不生苔，頻遷不聚財 **'roll on ...!** (*BrE, informal*) used to say that you want sth to happen or arrive soon 趕快到來吧：*Roll on Friday!* 星期五快來吧！**roll up your 'sleeves** to prepare to work or fight 捋起袖子；準備動手；摩拳擦掌 **roll with the 'punches** to adapt yourself to a difficult situation 使自己適應艱苦環境 ➲ more at BALL *n.*, GRAVE[1] *n.*, HEAD *n.*, READY *adj.*, TONGUE *n.*

PHR V **ˌroll a'round** (*BrE* also **ˌroll a'bout**) to be laughing so much that you can hardly control yourself 大笑不止 **ˌroll sth↔'back** **1** to turn or force sth back or further away 擊退；使後退：*to roll back the frontiers of space* 拓展太空領域 **2** (*NAmE*) to reduce prices, etc. 降低，削減（價格等）：*to roll back inflation* 減低通貨膨脹 **ˌroll sth↔'down** **1** to open sth by turning a handle 搖開；旋開：*He rolled down his car window and started shouting at them.* 他搖下車窗，朝他們大聲喊起來。**2** to make a rolled piece of clothing, etc. hang or lie flat 展開，鋪開，攤開（捲狀物）：*to roll down your sleeves* 捋下袖子 **ˌroll 'in** (*informal*) **1** to arrive in great numbers or amounts 大量湧入；滾滾而來：*Offers of help are still rolling in.* 仍然不斷有人表示願意提供援助。**2** to arrive late at a place, without seeming worried or sorry 姍姍來遲：*Steve rolled in around lunchtime.* 到午飯時分，史蒂夫才慢吞吞地來了。**ˌroll sth↔'out** **1** to make sth flat by pushing sth over it 將…軋平：*Roll out the pastry.* 將油酥麪糰擀平。➲ VISUAL VOCAB page V28 **2** to officially make a new product available or start a new political CAMPAIGN 正式推出（新產品）；開展（新的政治運動）**SYN** **launch**：*The new model is to be rolled out in July.* 這種新型號將在七月份推出市場。➲ related noun ROLL-OUT **ˌroll 'over** (*informal*) to be easily defeated without even trying 不戰自敗；輕易認輸：*We can't expect them to just roll over for us.* 我們不能指望他們會乖乖地向我們認輸。**ˌroll sb↔'over** (*BrE, informal*) to defeat sb easily 輕易打敗某人：*They rolled us over in the replay.* 他們在重賽中輕而易舉地戰勝了我們。**ˌroll sth↔'over** (*technical* 術語) to allow money that sb owes to be paid back at a later date 將（債務）轉期；允許延期償還（欠款）：*The bank refused to roll over the debt.* 銀行拒不允許延期償還債款。➲ related noun ROLLOVER (1) **ˌroll 'up** (*informal*) to arrive 到達：*Bill finally rolled up two hours late.* 比爾最終遲到了兩個小時。◇ *Roll up! Roll up!* (= used to invite people who are passing to form an audience) 快來看哪！快來看哪！**ˌroll sth↔'up** to close sth by turning a handle（轉動把手）關閉：*She rolled up all the windows.* 她關上了所有的窗戶。

roll·back /ˈrəʊlbæk; *NAmE* ˈroʊl-/ *noun* [sing., U] (*especially NAmE*) **1** a reduction in a price or in pay, to a past level（價格或工資等的）下跌，回落 **2** the act of changing a situation, law, etc. back to what it was before（情形、法律等的）回復，恢復

'roll bar *noun* a metal bar over the top of a car without a roof, used to make the car stronger and to protect passengers if the car turns over（敞篷汽車頂部起加固和保護作用的）翻車防護杆，防滾保護杆

'roll-call *noun* [U, sing.] the reading of a list of names to a group of people to check who is there 點名：*Roll-call will be at 7 a.m.* 早晨 7 點鐘點名。◇ *The guest list reads like a roll-call of the nation's heroes.* 客人名單唸起來就像是在列數民族英雄。

ˌrolled 'gold *noun* [U] gold in the form of a thin layer that is rolled onto sth to cover it 軋製金箔；包金

ˌrolled 'oats *noun* [pl.] OATS that have had their shells removed before being crushed, used especially for making PORRIDGE 燕麥片（尤用以做麥片粥）

roll·er /ˈrəʊlə(r); *NAmE* ˈroʊ-/ *noun* **1** a piece of wood, metal or plastic, shaped like a tube, that rolls over and over and is used in machines, for example to make sth flat, or to move sth 滾筒；滾軸：*the heavy steel rollers under the conveyor belt* 傳送帶下沉重的鋼滾筒 **2** (often in compounds 常構成複合詞) a machine or piece of equipment with a part shaped like a tube so that it rolls backwards and forwards. It may be used for making sth flat, crushing or spreading sth. 碾軋機；碾子：*Flatten the surface of the grass with a roller.* 用碾軋機把草軋平。◇ *a paint roller* 塗料輥 ➲ VISUAL VOCAB page V20 ➲ see also STEAMROLLER *n.* **3** a piece of wood or metal, shaped like a tube, that is used for moving heavy objects 滾軸；滾柱：*We'll need to move the piano on rollers.* 我們需要用滾子來移動鋼琴。**4** a long, powerful wave in the sea/ocean 捲浪；巨浪：*Huge Atlantic rollers crashed onto the rocks.* 大西洋的巨浪沖擊着岩石。**5** a small plastic tube that hair is rolled around to give it curls 塑料髮捲 **SYN** **curler**：*heated rollers* 經過加熱的髮捲 ◇ *Her hair was* **in rollers**. 她的頭髮用髮捲捲着。➲ see also HIGH ROLLER

roller·ball /ˈrəʊləbɔːl; *NAmE* ˈroʊlərb-/ *noun* **1** a type of BALLPOINT pen 寶珠筆；圓珠筆 **2** = TRACKBALL

Roll·er·blade™ (*BrE*) (*NAmE* **Roller Blade™**) /ˈrəʊləbleɪd; *NAmE* ˈroʊlərb-/ *noun* = IN-LINE SKATE ➲ VISUAL VOCAB page V40 ▸ **Roll·er·blade** *verb* [I]

'roller blind *noun* a covering for a window made of a roll of cloth that is fixed at the top of the window and can be pulled up and down 捲軸窗簾 ➲ VISUAL VOCAB page V21

'roller coaster *noun* **1** a track at a FAIRGROUND that goes up and down very steep slopes and that people ride on in a small train for fun and excitement（遊樂場的）過山車，環滑車：*a roller-coaster ride* 乘坐過山車 **2** a situation that keeps changing very quickly 不斷變化的局勢：*The last few weeks have been a real roller coaster.* 過去的幾個星期，形勢真是變幻莫測。

'roller skate (also **skate**) *noun, verb*

- ***noun*** a type of boot with two pairs of small wheels attached to the bottom （四輪）旱冰鞋；滾軸溜冰鞋；輪式溜冰鞋： *a pair of roller skates* 一雙旱冰鞋
- ***verb*** [I] to move over a hard surface wearing roller skates 滑旱冰；溜旱冰；滾軸溜冰；輪式溜冰 ▸ **'roller skating** (also **skat·ing**) *noun* [U]

'roller towel *noun* a long roll of towel, usually in a public toilet/bathroom, part of which hangs down for you to dry your hands on （公廁等處套在滾筒上的）環狀擦手巾

rol·licking /'rɒlɪkɪŋ; *NAmE* 'rɑːl-/ *adj., noun*

- ***adj.*** [only before noun] cheerful and often noisy 嬉鬧的；喧鬧嬉戲的 **SYN** **exuberant**： *a rollicking comedy* 喧鬧的喜劇
- ***noun*** (*BrE, informal*) angry criticism for sth bad sb has done 指責；斥責： *He gave us both a rollicking.* 他把我們倆訓斥了一通。

roll·ing /'rəʊlɪŋ; *NAmE* 'roʊ-/ *adj.* [only before noun] **1** (of hills or countryside 丘陵或鄉村) having gentle slopes 起伏的 **2** done in regular stages or at regular intervals over a period of time 規則的；週而復始的： *a rolling programme of reform* 逐步推進的改革計劃

'rolling mill *noun* a machine or factory that produces flat sheets of metal 軋（鋼）機；軋（鋼）廠

'rolling pin *noun* a wooden or glass kitchen UTENSIL (= a tool) in the shape of a tube, used for rolling PASTRY flat 擀麪杖 ➲ **VISUAL VOCAB** pages V26, V28

'rolling stock *noun* [U] the engines, trains, etc. that are used on a railway/railroad （鐵路上運行的）全部車輛（包括機車、車廂等）

roll·mop /'rəʊlmɒp; *NAmE* 'roʊlmɑːp/ *noun* a piece of raw HERRING (= a type of fish) that is rolled up and preserved in VINEGAR, often sold in JARS 醋漬鯡魚肉糜捲（常瓶裝出售）

ˌroll of 'honour (*especially US* **'honor roll**) *noun* [usually sing.] a list of people who are being praised officially for sth they have done 榮譽名冊；光榮榜

'roll-on *adj.* [only before noun] spread or put on the body using a ball that moves around in the top of a bottle or container 滾抹式的；走珠式的： *a roll-on deodorant* 走珠除臭劑 ▸ **'roll-on** *noun*

ˌroll-ˌon ˌroll-'off *adj.* [usually before noun] (*abbr.* **'ro-ro**) (*BrE*) (of a ship 輪船) designed so that cars can be driven straight on and off 輪渡式的；汽車可直接上下的： *a roll-on roll-off car ferry* 汽車可直接上下的渡船

'roll-out *noun* an occasion when a company introduces or starts to use a new product 新產品發佈會；新產品的推出

roll·over /'rəʊləʊvə(r); *NAmE* 'roʊloʊvər/ *noun* **1** [U] (*technical* 術語) the act of allowing money that is owed to be paid at a later date 轉期；債項的延期償還 **2** [U, C] (*BrE*) a prize of money in a competition or LOTTERY in a particular week, that is added to the prize given in the following week if nobody wins it （比賽或彩票獎金的）累積，滾動增加： *a rollover jackpot* 滾動增加的累積獎金 **3** [U] (*especially NAmE*) the turning over of a vehicle during an accident 翻車；傾翻

Rolls-Royce™ /ˌrəʊlz 'rɔɪs; *NAmE* ˌroʊlz/ *noun* **1** (also *informal* **Rolls™**) a large, comfortable and expensive make of car made by a company in the UK 勞斯萊斯汽車（英國一種大型豪華轎車） **2 the ~ of sth** (*BrE*) something that is thought of as an example of the highest quality of a type of thing 最優質的品種；最優品： *This is the Rolls-Royce of canoes.* 這是獨木舟中的極品。

ˌroll-top 'desk *noun* a desk with a top that you roll back to open it 活動頂蓋寫字枱；捲蓋式辦公桌

'roll-up *noun* (*BrE, informal*) a cigarette that you make yourself with TOBACCO and special paper 手捲的紙煙

roly-poly /ˌrəʊli 'pəʊli; *NAmE* ˌroʊli 'poʊli/ *adj., noun*

- ***adj.*** [only before noun] (*informal*) (of people 人) short, round and fat 矮胖的；圓胖的 **SYN** **plump**
- ***noun*** (*pl.* **-ies**) (also **ˌroly-poly 'pudding**) [U, C] (*BrE*) a hot DESSERT (= a sweet dish) made from SUET PASTRY spread with jam and rolled up 果醬布丁捲（熱甜食）

ROM /rɒm; *NAmE* rɑːm/ *noun* [U] the abbreviation for 'read-only memory' (computer memory that contains instructions or data that cannot be changed or removed) 只讀存貯器（全寫為 read-only memory） ➲ compare CD-ROM

the Roma /'rəʊmə; *NAmE* 'roʊmə/ *noun* [pl.] the ROMANI people 羅姆人；吉卜賽人： *the Roma population of eastern Europe* 東歐的吉卜賽人口

ro·maine /rəʊ'meɪn; *NAmE* roʊ-/ (*NAmE*) (*BrE* **cos lettuce**) *noun* [C, U] a type of LETTUCE with long crisp leaves 直立萵苣；長葉生菜；蘿蔓萵苣

ro·maji /'rəʊmədʒi; *NAmE* 'roʊ-/ *noun* [U] (from *Japanese*) a system of writing Japanese that uses the ROMAN ALPHABET （拼寫日語的）羅馬字系統

Roman /'rəʊmən; *NAmE* 'roʊ-/ *adj., noun*

- ***adj.*** **1** connected with ancient Rome or the Roman Empire 古羅馬的；古羅馬帝國的： *a Roman road/temple/villa* 古羅馬的公路／廟宇／別墅 ◇ *Roman Britain* 古羅馬統治下的不列顛 **2** connected with the modern city of Rome 羅馬的；羅馬城的 **3** connected with the Roman Catholic Church 天主教的 **4 roman** **roman** type is ordinary printing type which does not lean forward 羅馬體的；西文白正體的： *Definitions in this dictionary are printed in roman type.* 這本詞典裏的釋義是用羅馬體印刷的。 ➲ compare ITALIC
- ***noun*** **1** [C] a member of the ancient Roman REPUBLIC or empire 古羅馬人 **2** [C] a person from the modern city of Rome （現代的）羅馬人，羅馬市民 **3 roman** [U] the ordinary style of printing that uses small letters that do not lean forward 羅馬體；西文白正體 ➲ compare ITALICS **IDM** see ROME

the ˌRoman 'alphabet *noun* [sing.] the alphabet that is used in English and in most western European languages 羅馬字母表

ˌRoman 'Catholic (also **Cath·olic**) *noun* (*abbr.* **RC**) a member of the part of the Christian Church that has the POPE as its leader 天主教徒 ▸ **ˌRoman 'Catholic** (also **Cath·olic**) *adj.* **ˌRoman Ca'tholicism** (also **Cath·oli·cism**) *noun* [U]

Ro·mance /rəʊ'mæns; 'rəʊmæns; *NAmE* 'roʊ-/ *adj.* [only before noun] **Romance** languages, such as French, Italian and Spanish, are languages that developed from Latin 羅曼語的（由拉丁語演變而成，如法語、意大利語、西班牙語等）

ro·mance /rəʊ'mæns; 'rəʊmæns; *NAmE* 'roʊ-/ *noun, verb*

- ***noun*** **1** [C] an exciting, usually short, relationship between two people who are in love with each other （通常指短暫的）浪漫史，愛情關係，風流韻事： *a holiday romance* 假日浪漫史 ◇ *They had a* ***whirlwind romance.*** 他們之間有過一段短暫的風流韻事。 **2** [U] love or the feeling of being in love 戀愛；愛情： *Spring is here and romance is in the air.* 春天來了，到處洋溢着愛情的氣息。 ◇ *How can you put the romance back into your marriage?* 怎樣才能使你的婚姻再次充滿綿綿愛意呢？ ➲ **COLLOCATIONS** at MARRIAGE **3** [U] a feeling of excitement and adventure, especially connected to a particular place or activity 傳奇色彩；浪漫氛圍： *the romance of travel* 旅行奇趣 **4** [C] a story about a love affair 愛情故事： *She's a compulsive reader of romances.* 她熱衷於閱讀愛情故事。 **5** [C] a story of excitement and adventure, often set in the past 傳奇故事： *medieval romances* 中世紀的傳奇故事
- ***verb*** **1** [I] to tell stories that are not true or to describe sth in a way that makes it seem more exciting or interesting than it really is 虛構（故事）；渲染 **2** [T] **~ sb** to have or to try to have a romantic relationship with sb 和（某人）談情說愛；追求（某人）

Ro·man·esque /ˌrəʊmə'nesk; *NAmE* ˌroʊ-/ *adj.* used to describe a style of ARCHITECTURE that was popular in western Europe from the 10th to the 12th centuries and that had round ARCHES, thick walls and tall PILLARS 羅馬式的，羅馬風格的（指 10 到 12 世紀盛行於西歐的一種建築風格，使用圓拱、厚牆、高柱子） ➲ see also NORMAN (1)

R

Rom·ani (also **Rom·any**) /ˈrɒməni; ˈrəʊm-; NAmE ˈrɑːm-; ˈroʊm-/ *noun* (*pl.* **-ies**) **1** [C] a member of a race of people, originally from Asia, who traditionally travel around and live in CARAVANS 羅姆人（原生活在亞洲的民族，以四處漂泊、住大篷車為傳統） ➲ see also ROMA, GYPSY (1) **2** [U] the language of Romani people 羅姆語 ▸ **Rom·ani** (also **Rom·any**) *adj.* [usually before noun]

ˌRoman ˈlaw *noun* the legal system of the ancient Romans, and the basis for CIVIL LAW in many countries 羅馬法（古羅馬法律，是很多國家制訂民法的依據）

ˌRoman ˈnose *noun* a nose that curves out at the top 高鼻梁

ˌRoman ˈnumeral *noun* one of the letters used by the ancient Romans to represent numbers and still used today, in some situations. In this system I = 1, V = 5, X = 10, L = 50, C = 100, D = 500, M = 1 000 and these letters are used in combinations to form other numbers. 羅馬數字：*Henry VIII* 亨利八世 ◇ *© BBC MMIX (2009)* * 2009 年英國廣播公司版權 ➲ picture at IDEOGRAM ➲ compare ARABIC NUMERAL

Romano- /rəˈmɑːnəʊ; NAmE -noʊ; roʊˈm-/ *combining form* (in nouns and adjectives 構成名詞和形容詞) Roman 羅馬（的）：*Romano-British pottery* 羅馬時代英國的陶器

ro·man·tic 0━ /rəʊˈmæntɪk; NAmE roʊ-/ *adj., noun*

■ ***adj.*** **1** 0━ connected or concerned with love or a sexual relationship 浪漫的；愛情的；情愛的：*a romantic candlelit dinner* 浪漫的燭光晚餐 ◇ *romantic stories/fiction/comedy* 言情故事／小說／喜劇 ◇ *I'm not interested in a romantic relationship.* 我對談情說愛不感興趣。 **2** 0━ (of people 人) showing feelings of love 多情的；表達愛情的：*Why don't you ever give me flowers? I wish you'd be more romantic.* 你為什麼從來不給我送花？我真希望你能浪漫一點。 **3** 0━ beautiful in a way that makes you think of love or feel strong emotions 浪漫的；富有情調的；美妙的：*romantic music* 富有情調的音樂 ◇ *romantic mountain scenery* 美妙的山區風光 **4** 0━ having an attitude to life where imagination and the emotions are especially important; not looking at situations in a realistic way 富於幻想而不切實際的：*a romantic view of life* 對於生活的不切實際的想法 ◇ *When I was younger, I had romantic ideas of becoming a writer.* 我年輕一些的時候幻想過要成為一名作家。 **5 Romantic** [usually before noun] used to describe literature, music or art, especially of the 19th century, that is concerned with strong feelings, imagination and a return to nature, rather than reason, order and INTELLECTUAL ideas 浪漫主義的，浪漫主義風格的（尤用以描述 19 世紀的文學、音樂或藝術，以情感強烈、想像和回歸自然為特徵）：*the Romantic movement* 浪漫主義運動 ◇ *Keats is one of the greatest Romantic poets.* 濟慈是最偉大的浪漫主義詩人之一。 ▸ **ro·man·tic·al·ly** /-kli/ *adv.*：*to be romantically involved with sb* 與某人墜入情網 ◇ *Their names have been linked romantically.* 他們的名字因戀愛關係而連在一起。 ◇ *He talked romantically of the past and his youth.* 他情深意切地談論着往昔和他的年少時光。

■ ***noun*** **1** a person who is emotional and has a lot of imagination, and who has ideas and hopes that may not be realistic 浪漫的人；耽於幻想的人：*an incurable romantic* 擺脫不了不切實際的幻想的人 ◇ *He was a romantic at heart and longed for adventure.* 他骨子裏是一位浪漫的人，渴望歷險。 **2 Romantic** a writer, a musician or an artist who writes, etc. in the style of Romanticism 浪漫主義作家（或音樂家、藝術家）

ro·man·ti·cism /rəʊˈmæntɪsɪzəm; NAmE roʊ-/ *noun* [U] **1** (also **Romanticism**) a style and movement in art, music and literature in the late 18th and early 19th century, in which strong feelings, imagination and a return to nature were more important than reason, order and INTELLECTUAL ideas 浪漫主義（18 世紀末 19 世紀初盛行於藝術、音樂及文學領域，以情感強烈、想像和回歸自然為特徵） ➲ compare REALISM (3) **2** the quality of seeing people, events and situations as more exciting and interesting than they really are 浪漫精神；浪漫的態度 **3** strong feelings of love; the fact of showing emotion, affection, etc. 強烈的愛情；情感的表達

ro·man·ti·cize (BrE also **-ise**) /rəʊˈmæntɪsaɪz; NAmE roʊ-/ *verb* [T, I] ~ (**sth**) to make sth seem more attractive or interesting than it really is 使浪漫化；使傳奇化；使更加富有吸引力：*romanticizing the past* 以傳奇的手法描述往事 ◇ *a romanticized picture of parenthood* 一幅理想化的為人父母的情景

Rome /rəʊm; NAmE roʊm/ *noun*

IDM **Rome wasn't built in a ˈday** (*saying*) used to say that a complicated task will take a long time and needs patience 羅馬不是一天建成的；複雜的工作不會一蹴而就 **when in ˈRome (do as the ˈRomans do)** (*saying*) used to say that when you are in a foreign country, or a situation you are not familiar with, you should behave in the way that the people around you behave 入鄉隨俗

romeo /ˈrəʊmiəʊ; NAmE ˈroʊmioʊ/ (also **Romeo**) *noun* (*pl.* **-os**) (often *humorous*) a young male lover or a man who has sex with a lot of women 年輕的男情人；風流放蕩的男子 ORIGIN From the name of the young hero of Shakespeare's play *Romeo and Juliet.* 源自莎士比亞戲劇《羅密歐與朱麗葉》中的年輕男主人公的名字。

romp /rɒmp; NAmE rɑːmp; rɔːmp/ *verb, noun*

■ ***verb*** [I] (+ **adv./prep.**) to play in a happy and noisy way 嬉戲喧鬧：*kids romping around in the snow* 在雪地裏嬉戲喧鬧的孩子

IDM **romp home/to victory** to easily win a race or competition 輕易地取勝：*Their horse romped home in the 2 o'clock race.* 他們的馬在兩點鐘的比賽中輕而易舉地獲得了勝利。 ◇ *The Dutch team romped to a 5–1 victory over Celtic.* 荷蘭隊以 5:1 輕鬆戰勝了凱爾特隊。

PHR V **ˌromp aˈway/aˈhead** (BrE, *informal*) to increase, make progress or win quickly and easily 快速增加；進步神速；輕易取勝 **ˌromp ˈthrough (sth)** (BrE, *informal*) to do sth easily and quickly 快速而輕易地做：*She romped through the exam questions.* 她很快就答完了試題。

■ ***noun*** (often used in newspapers 常用於報章) (*informal*) **1** [C] an enjoyable sexual experience that is not serious 風流韻事：*politicians involved in sex romps with call girls* 與電話應召女郎發生風流情事的政治人物 **2** [C] an amusing book, play or film/movie that is full of action or adventure 妙趣橫生的歷險故事書（或戲劇、電影） **3** [sing.] an easy victory in a sports competition （體育競賽中的）輕而易舉的勝利：*They won in a 5–1 romp.* 他們以 5:1 輕鬆取勝。

romp·ers /ˈrɒmpəz; NAmE ˈrɑːmpərz; ˈrɔːm-/ *noun* [pl.] (also **ˈromper suit** [C]) (*old-fashioned*) a piece of clothing worn by a baby, that covers the body and legs （幼兒的）連衫褲

ron·davel /rɒnˈdɑːvl; NAmE rɑːn-/ *noun* (*SAfrE*) a round HUT with a pointed roof that is usually made from THATCH (= dried grass) 圓形尖頂（茅）屋

rondo /ˈrɒndəʊ; NAmE ˈrɑːndoʊ/ *noun* (*pl.* **-os**) a piece of music in which the main tune is repeated several times, sometimes forming part of a longer piece 迴旋曲

roo /ruː/ *noun* (*informal*) = KANGAROO

rood screen /ˈruːd skriːn/ *noun* (*technical* 術語) a wooden or stone structure in some churches that divides the part near the ALTAR from the rest of the church（教堂內的）祭台屏風

roof 0━ /ruːf/ *noun, verb*

■ ***noun*** (*pl.* **roofs**) **1** 0━ the structure that covers or forms the top of a building or vehicle 頂部；屋頂；車頂：*a* ***flat/sloping roof*** 平頂；斜頂 ◇ *a* ***thatched/slate, etc. roof*** 茅草、石板瓦等屋頂 ◇ *The corner of the classroom was damp where the roof had leaked.* 教室漏雨的一角是濕的。 ◇ *Tim climbed on to the garage roof.* 蒂姆爬到車庫的房頂上。 ◇ *The roof of the car was not damaged in the accident.* 事故中，車頂沒有遭到損壞。 ➲ see also SUNROOF ➲ **VISUAL VOCAB** page V17 **2 -roofed** (in adjectives 構成形容詞) having the type of roof mentioned 有…頂的：*flat-roofed buildings* 平頂的大樓 **3** the top of an underground space such as a tunnel or CAVE 洞頂；隧道頂 **4 ~ of your mouth** the top of the inside of your mouth 口腔頂部；腭部

IDM go through the 'roof **1** (of prices, etc. 價格等) to rise or increase very quickly 飛漲；激增 **2** (also **hit the 'roof**) (*informal*) to become very angry 非常生氣；暴怒 **have a 'roof over your head** to have somewhere to live 有棲身之所 **under one 'roof | under the same 'roof** in the same building or house 在同一座建築中；同在一個屋簷下：*There are various stores and restaurants all under one roof.* 在同一棟大樓裏有各種商店和餐館。◇ *I don't think I can live under the same roof as you any longer.* 我覺得我再也不能和你生活在同一個屋簷下了。 **under your 'roof** in your home 在家裏：*I don't want her under my roof again.* 我再也不想讓她到我家來了。➲ more at HIT *v.*, RAISE *v.*

■ *verb* [often passive] to cover sth with a roof; to put a roof on a building 給…蓋頂；蓋上屋頂：**~ sth (in/over)** *The shopping centre is not roofed over.* 購物中心是露天的。◇ **~ sth with/in sth** *Their cottage was roofed with green slate.* 他們的小房子蓋的是綠瓦。

roof·er /ˈruːfə(r)/ *noun* a person whose job is to repair or build roofs 修理（或蓋）屋頂的工人

'roof garden *noun* a garden on the flat roof of a building 屋頂花園

roof·ing /ˈruːfɪŋ/ *noun* [U] **1** material used for making or covering roofs 蓋屋頂用的材料 **2** the process of building roofs 蓋屋頂

'roof rack (also **'luggage rack** especially in *NAmE*) *noun* a metal frame fixed to the roof of a car and used for carrying bags, cases and other large objects 車頂行李架 ➲ picture at RACK

roof·top /ˈruːftɒp; *NAmE* -tɑːp/ *noun* the outside part of the roof of a building 屋頂外部；外屋頂：*From the hill we looked out over the rooftops of Athens.* 我們從山上眺望雅典眾樓房的頂部。◇ *The prisoners staged a rooftop protest.* 囚犯在屋頂上舉行了抗議活動。

IDM ˌshout, etc. sth from the 'rooftops to talk about sth in a very public way 公開談論：*He was in love and wanted to shout it from the rooftops.* 他要大聲宣佈，他戀愛了。

rooi·bos /ˈrɔɪbɒs; *NAmE* -bɔːs/ *noun* [U] (*SAfrE*) a type of bush grown in South Africa whose leaves are dried and used to make tea （南非）洛依柏絲茶樹：*rooibos tea* 洛依柏絲香草茶

rook /rʊk/ *noun* **1** a large black bird of the CROW family. Rooks build their nests in groups at the tops of trees. 禿鼻烏鴉 **2** = CASTLE (2)

rook·ery /ˈrʊkəri/ *noun* (*pl.* **-ies**) a group of trees with rooks' nests in them 禿鼻烏鴉群棲林地

rookie /ˈrʊki/ *noun* (*informal*) **1** (*especially NAmE*) a person who has just started a job or an activity and has very little experience 新手；生手 **2** (*NAmE*) a member of a sports team in his or her first full year of playing that sport （第一年參加比賽的）新隊員

room 🔑 /ruːm; rʊm/ *noun, verb*

■ *noun*

▸ **IN BUILDING 建築物** **1** 🔑 [C] a part of a building that has its own walls, floor and ceiling and is usually used for a particular purpose 房間；室：*He walked out of the room and slammed the door.* 他走出房間，猛地關上了房門。◇ *They were in **the next room** and we could hear every word they said.* 他們在隔壁房間裏，我們可以聽到他們說的每一句話。◇ *a **dining/living/sitting room*** 飯廳；起居室 ◇ *They had to sit in the waiting room for an hour.* 他們不得不在候車室裏等了一個小時。◇ *I think Simon is in his room* (= bedroom). 我看西蒙就在他自己的房間裏。◇ *I don't want to watch television. I'll be in **the other room*** (= a different room). 我不想看電視。我到別的房間去吧。 **HELP** There are many compounds ending in **room**. You will find them at their place in the alphabet. 以 room 結尾的複合詞很多，可在各字母中的適當位置查到。

▸ **-ROOMED/-ROOM …室；…房間** **2** 🔑 (in adjectives 構成形容詞) having the number of rooms mentioned 有…室的；有…個房間的：*a three-roomed/three-room apartment* 三室的套房

▸ **IN HOTEL 旅館** **3** 🔑 [C] a bedroom in a hotel, etc. 客房：*a **double/single room*** 雙人／單人客房 ◇ *I'd like to book a room with a view of the lake.* 我想預訂一套可以看到湖面景色的客房。◇ *She lets out rooms to students.* 她把房間出租給學生。➲ COLLOCATIONS at TRAVEL

▸ **PLACE TO LIVE 居所** **4** **rooms** [pl.] (*old-fashioned, BrE*) a set of two or more rooms that you rent to live in（租用的）住所，寓所 **SYN** **lodgings**：*They lived in rooms in Kensington.* 他們住在肯辛頓的出租房間。

▸ **SPACE 空間** **5** 🔑 [U] empty space that can be used for a particular purpose 空間；餘地：**~ (for sb/sth)** *Is there enough room for me in the car?* 車上還有空間讓我坐嗎？◇ *There's room for one more at the table.* 這張桌子還有一個人的位置。◇ *Do you have room for a computer on your desk?* 你的寫字枱上還擺得下一台電腦嗎？◇ *Yes, there's **plenty of room**.* 是的，還很空呢。◇ *How can we **make room for** all the furniture?* 我們怎麼騰得出地方放這些傢具呢？◇ *I'll move the table—it **takes up too much room**.* 我要挪動一下這張桌子，它太佔地方了。◇ **~ (to do sth)** *Make sure you have plenty of room to sit comfortably.* 一定要找個寬敞地兒坐得舒服一點。➲ see also ELBOW ROOM, HEADROOM, HOUSEROOM, LEGROOM, STANDING ROOM

▸ **POSSIBILITY 可能性** **6** [U] **~ for sth** the possibility of sth existing or happening; the opportunity to do sth 可能性；機會：*He had to be certain. There could be **no room for doubt**.* 他必須確定無誤。不能有任何的猶疑。◇ *There's some **room for improvement** in your work* (= it is not as good as it could be). 你的工作還有改進的餘地。◇ *It is important to give children room to think for themselves.* 給孩子機會讓他們自己思考是很重要的。

▸ **PEOPLE 人** **7** [sing.] all the people in a room 房間裏所有的人：*The whole room burst into applause.* 屋裏的人發出一片掌聲。

IDM no room to swing a 'cat (*informal*) when sb says **there's no room to swing a cat**, they mean that a room is very small and that there is not enough space 沒有活動的餘地；連轉身都很難 ➲ more at ELEPHANT, MANOEUVRE *n.*, SMOKE *n.*

■ *verb* [I] **~ (with sb)** | **~ (together)** (*NAmE*) to rent a room somewhere; to share a rented room or flat/apartment with sb 租房；合住：*She and Nancy roomed together at college.* 她和南希在大學裏合住一處。

room·er /ˈruːmə(r); ˈrʊm-/ *noun* (*NAmE*) a person who rents a room in sb's house 租屋的房客

room·ful /ˈruːmfʊl; ˈrʊm-/ *noun* [sing.] a large number of people or things that are in a room 滿屋子（東西或人）：*He announced his resignation to a roomful of reporters.* 他向滿屋子的記者宣佈他辭職了。

roomie /ˈruːmi; ˈrʊmi/ *noun* (*NAmE, informal*) = ROOMMATE

'rooming house *noun* (*NAmE*) a building where rooms with furniture can be rented for living in（帶傢具的）出租公寓住房

room·mate /ˈruːmmeɪt; ˈrʊm-/ *noun* (also *informal* **roomie**) **1** a person that you share a room with, especially at a college or university（尤指大學裏的）室友，同住一室的人 **2** (both *NAmE*) (*BrE* **flat·mate**) a person who shares a flat/apartment with one or more others 合租公寓套間者；同公寓房客；樓友

'room service *noun* [U] a service provided in a hotel, by which guests can order food and drink to be brought to their rooms （旅館）客房送餐服務：*He ordered coffee from room service.* 他讓服務員送杯咖啡到他房裏。

'room temperature *noun* [U] the normal temperature inside a building 室溫；常溫：*Serve the wine **at room temperature**.* 這種葡萄酒宜室溫飲用。

roomy /ˈruːmi; ˈrʊmi/ *adj.* (**room·ier**, **roomi·est**) (*approving*) having a lot of space inside 寬敞的；寬大的 **SYN** **spacious**：*a surprisingly roomy car* 出奇寬敞的汽車 ▸ **roomi·ness** *noun* [U]

roost /ruːst/ *noun, verb*

■ *noun* a place where birds sleep （鳥類的）棲息處 **IDM** see RULE *v.*

■ *verb* [I] (of birds 鳥類) to rest or go to sleep somewhere 棲息 **IDM** see HOME *adv.*

R

roost·er /ˈruːstə(r)/ (*especially NAmE*) (*BrE also* **cock**) *noun* an adult male chicken 公雞；雄雞 ➲ compare HEN (1)

root 🔑 /ruːt/ *noun, verb*

■ ***noun***

▸ **OF PLANT** 植物 **1** 🔑 [C] the part of a plant that grows under the ground and absorbs water and minerals that it sends to the rest of the plant 根；根莖：*deep spreading roots* 扎得很深的根 ◇ *I pulled the plant up* ***by*** (= including) ***the roots.*** 我把這棵植物連根拔起。◇ *Tree roots can cause damage to buildings.* 樹根會給大樓造成損害。◇ ***root crops/vegetables*** (= plants whose roots you can eat, such as carrots) 根莖作物／蔬菜 ➲ COLLOCATIONS at LIFE ➲ VISUAL VOCAB pages V10, V11 ➲ see also GRASS ROOTS, TAPROOT

▸ **OF HAIR/TOOTH/NAIL** 頭髮；牙齒；指甲 **2** 🔑 [C] the part of a hair, tooth, nail or tongue that attaches it to the rest of the body 根；根部：*hair that is blonde at the ends and dark at the roots* 髮梢金黃而髮根黑的頭髮

▸ **MAIN CAUSE OF PROBLEM** 問題的主要原因 **3** 🔑 [C, usually sing.] the main cause of sth, such as a problem or difficult situation 根源；起因：*Money, or love of money, is said to be the root of all evil.* 有人說錢和愛錢是萬惡之源。◇ *We have to get to* ***the root of the problem.*** 我們必須找到問題的根源。◇ *What lies* ***at the root of*** *his troubles is a sense of insecurity.* 他的一切憂慮源於一種不安全感。◇ *What would you say was the* ***root cause*** *of the problem?* 你認為問題的起因是什麼？

▸ **ORIGIN** 起源 **4** 🔑 [C, usually pl.] the origin or basis of sth 起源；基礎；根基：*Flamenco has its roots in Arabic music.* 弗拉明科起源於阿拉伯音樂。

▸ **CONNECTION WITH PLACE** 與地方相關 **5** 🔑 **roots** [pl.] the feelings or connections that you have with a place because you have lived there or your family came from there 根（指與出生地或原籍相關聯的情感或聯繫）：*I'm proud of my Italian roots.* 我為我的意大利血統感到驕傲。◇ *After 20 years in America, I still feel my roots are in England.* 儘管在美國生活了 20 年，我還是覺得我的根在英國。

▸ **OF WORD** 單詞 **6** [C] (*linguistics* 語言) the part of a word that has the main meaning and that its other forms are based on; a word that other words are formed from 詞根：*'Walk' is the root of 'walks', 'walked', 'walking' and 'walker'.* * walk 是 walks、walked、walking 和 walker 的詞根。

▸ **MATHEMATICS** 數學 **7** [C] a quantity which, when multiplied by itself a particular number of times, produces another quantity 方根；根 ➲ see also CUBE ROOT, SQUARE ROOT

IDM **put down ˈroots** **1** (of a plant 植物) to develop roots 生根 **2** to settle and live in one place 定居：*After ten years travelling the world, she felt it was time to put down roots somewhere.* 遊歷世界十年之後，她覺得該是找個地方定居的時候了。 **ˌroot and ˈbranch** thoroughly and completely 完全徹底：*The government set out to destroy the organization root and branch.* 政府着手完全徹底地摧毀這個組織。◇ *root-and-branch reforms* 全面徹底的改革 **take ˈroot** **1** (of a plant 植物) to develop roots 生根 **2** (of an idea 思想) to become accepted widely 植根；深入人心：*Fortunately, militarism failed to take root in Europe as a whole.* 幸運的是，軍國主義沒有能夠深入整個歐洲。

■ ***verb***

▸ **OF PLANTS** 植物 **1** [I, T] **~ (sth)** to grow roots; to make or encourage a plant to grow roots（使）生根

▸ **SEARCH** 尋找 **2** [I] to search for sth by moving things or turning things over 翻尋 **SYN** **rummage**：**~ (about/around) for sth** *pigs rooting for food* 拱土覓食的豬 ◇ *Who's been rooting around in my desk?* 誰亂翻我的書桌了？◇ **~ (through sth) (for sth)** *'It must be here somewhere,' she said, rooting through the suitcase.* "它一定就在這裏的什麼地方。" 她一邊說一邊翻着衣箱。

▸ **SEX** 性 **3** [I, T] **~ (sb)** (*AustralE, NZE, taboo, slang*) to have sex with sb（與某人）性交

PHR V **ˈroot for sb** [no passive] (usually used in the progressive tenses 通常用於進行時) (*informal*) to support or encourage sb in a sports competition or when they are in a difficult situation（體育比賽或遭遇困難時）給…助威，給…加油：*We're rooting for the Bulls.* 我們為公牛隊加油。◇ *Good luck—I'm rooting for you!* 祝你好運，我支持你！ **ˌroot sth/sb↔ˈout** **1** to find the person or thing that is causing a problem and remove or get rid of them 找到並去除（禍根）；根除 **2** to find sb/sth after searching for a long time 終於發現（或找到） **ˌroot sb to ˈsth** to make sb unable to move because of fear, shock, etc. 使（因害怕、驚嚇等）呆住不動：*Embarrassment* ***rooted her to the spot.*** 她尷尬得呆住了。 **ˌroot sth↔ˈup** to dig or pull up a plant with its roots 連根挖起；連根拔起

ˈroot beer *noun* **1** [U] a sweet FIZZY drink (= with bubbles), that does not contain alcohol, made from GINGER and the roots of other plants. It is drunk especially in the US. 根汁汽水（用薑和其他植物的根製成，不含酒精，盛行於美國） **2** [C] a bottle, can or glass of root beer 一瓶（或聽、杯）根汁飲料

ˈroot-bound *adj.* = POT-BOUND

ˈroot canal *noun* the space inside the root of a tooth（牙）根管

ˈroot directory *noun* (*computing* 計) a file that contains all the other files in a program, system, etc. 根目錄

root·ed /ˈruːtɪd/ *adj.* **1** **~ in sth** developing from or being strongly influenced by sth 根源在於；由…產生：*His problems are deeply rooted in his childhood experiences.* 他的問題的禍根在於他童年的經歷。 **2** fixed in one place; not moving or changing 固定在某地的；穩固的；根深蒂固的：*She was rooted to her chair.* 她坐在椅子上一動不動。◇ *Their life is rooted in Chicago now.* 他們在芝加哥定居了。◇ *Racism is still deeply rooted in our society.* 種族主義在我們的社會中仍然根深蒂固。➲ see also DEEP-ROOTED **3** (*AustralE, slang*) extremely tired 疲憊不堪的；筋疲力盡的 **4** (*AustralE, slang*) too old or broken to use 老舊無用的；破得不能用的

IDM **rooted to the ˈspot** so frightened or shocked that you cannot move（驚嚇得）呆住不動

root·er /ˈruːtə(r)/ *noun* (*NAmE, informal*) a person who supports a particular team or player（運動隊或運動員的）支持者 **SYN** **supporter**

rootin'-tootin' /ˌruːtɪn ˈtuːtɪn/ *adj.* [only before noun] (*NAmE, informal*) enthusiastic, cheerful and lively 滿腔熱情的；熱情奔放的

root·less /ˈruːtləs/ *adj.* having nowhere that you really think of as home, or as the place where you belong 無根的；沒有歸宿的；漂泊的：*She had had a rootless childhood moving from town to town.* 她小時候居無定所，在各地流浪。 ▸ **root·less·ness** *noun* [U]

rootsy /ˈruːtsi/ *adj.* (*informal*) (of music 音樂) belonging to a particular tradition, and not changed from the original style 維持特定風格的；正統的

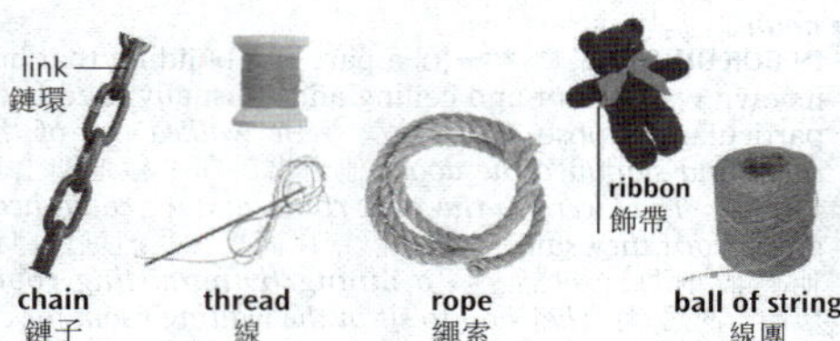

rope 🔑 /rəʊp; *NAmE* roʊp/ *noun, verb*

■ ***noun*** **1** 🔑 [C, U] very strong thick string made by twisting thinner strings, wires, etc. together 粗繩；線纜；繩索：*The rope broke and she fell 50 metres onto the rocks.* 繩索斷了，她從 50 米的高空摔到了岩石上。◇ *We tied his hands together with rope.* 我們用繩子把他的手綁在一起。◇ *The anchor was attached to a length of rope.* 鐵錨繫在一段纜繩上。◇ *Coils of rope lay on the quayside.* 碼頭上放着繞成一盤盤的繩子。➲ see also JUMP ROPE, SKIPPING ROPE, TOW ROPE **2** **the ropes** [pl.] the fence made of rope that is around the edge of the area where a BOXING or WRESTLING match takes place

R

（拳擊或摔跤場四周的）圍繩，圈繩 ➲ VISUAL VOCAB page V47 **3** [C] a number of similar things attached together by a string or thread 串在一起的相似的東西：*a rope of pearls* 一串珍珠

IDM **give sb enough 'rope** to allow sb freedom to do what they want, especially in the hope that they will make a mistake or look silly 放任自由，任其為所欲為（使其犯錯誤或出醜）：*The question was vague, giving the interviewee **enough rope to hang herself**.* 這個問題模棱兩可，讓參加面試的人胡亂發揮而自斃吧。 **on the 'ropes** (*informal*) very close to being defeated 瀕於失敗；即將失敗 **show sb/know/learn the 'ropes** (*informal*) to show sb/know/learn how a particular job should be done 向某人演示／知道／學會如何做某事 ➲ more at END *n.*, MONEY

■ *verb* **1** to tie one person or thing to another with a rope 用繩子捆（或綁、繫）：**~ A and B together** *The thieves had roped the guard's feet together.* 竊賊把門衛的雙腳捆在了一起。◇ **~ A to B** *I roped the goat to a post.* 我把山羊拴在一根柱子上。 **2 ~ sth** to tie sth with a rope so that it is held tightly and safely 用繩子繫牢；捆緊：*I closed and roped the trunk.* 我把箱子蓋上，用繩子捆結實。 **3 ~ sth** (*especially NAmE*) to catch an animal by throwing a circle of rope around it 用套索抓捕（動物）；套 **SYN** **lasso**

PHR V **,rope sb↔'in | ,rope sb 'into sth** [usually passive] (*informal*) to persuade sb to join in an activity or to help to do sth, even when they do not want to 勸說某人加入；說服某人幫忙：**~ to do sth** *Everyone was roped in to help with the show.* 每個人都被動員來為這次表演出力。◇ **~ doing sth** *Ben was roped into making coffee for the whole team.* 本給請來為全隊煮咖啡。 **,rope sth↔'off** to separate an area from another one, using ropes, to stop people from entering it 用繩子圍起（一片區域）：*Police roped off the street to investigate the accident.* 警察用繩子將街道圈起來調查事故。

,rope 'ladder *noun* a LADDER made of two long ropes connected by short pieces of wood or metal at regular intervals 繩梯

ropy (also **ropey**) /'rəʊpi; *NAmE* 'roʊpi/ *adj.* (*BrE, informal*) **1** not in good condition; of bad quality 狀況不佳的；質量差的；糟糕的：*We spent the night in a ropy old tent.* 我們在一個破舊的帳篷裏過了一夜。 **2** feeling slightly ill/sick 感覺不適的；生小病的

Roque·fort™ /'rɒkfɔː; *NAmE* 'roʊkfərt/ *noun* [U] a type of soft French cheese with blue marks and a strong flavour 羅克福爾乾酪（濃味的法國藍斑軟乾酪）

ro-ro /'rəʊ rəʊ; *NAmE* 'roʊ roʊ/ *abbr.* (*BrE*) ROLL-ON ROLL-OFF

Rorschach test /'rɔːʃɑːk test; *NAmE* 'rɔːrʃɑːk/ (also **'ink-blot test**) *noun* (*psychology* 心) a test in which people have to say what different shapes made by ink make them think of 羅夏測驗（測試者說出對各種墨跡的聯想）；羅夏克墨跡測驗

rort /rɔːt; *NAmE* rɔːrt/ *noun* (*AustralE, NZE, informal*) a dishonest thing that sb does 欺詐；不誠實行為：*a tax rort* 逃稅伎倆 ▸ **rort** [T, I]：**~ (sth)** *He was an expert at rorting the system* (= getting the best out of it for himself without actually doing anything illegal). 他善於鑽制度的空子。

ros·ary /'rəʊzəri; *NAmE* 'roʊ-/ *noun* (*pl.* **-ies**) **1** [C] a string of BEADS that are used by some Roman Catholics for counting prayers as they say them（天主教徒唸經時用的）數珠，唸珠 **2 the Rosary** [sing.] the set of prayers said by Roman Catholics while counting rosary BEADS（天主教徒唸的）玫瑰經

rose /rəʊz; *NAmE* roʊz/ *noun, adj.* ➲ see also RISE *v.*

■ *noun* **1** [C] a flower with a sweet smell that grows on a bush with THORNS (= sharp points) on its STEMS 玫瑰（花）；薔薇（花）：*a bunch of red roses* 一束紅玫瑰花 ◇ *a **rose bush/garden*** 玫瑰叢；玫瑰園 ◇ *a **climbing/rambling rose*** 攀緣的／蔓生的薔薇 ➲ VISUAL VOCAB page V11 **2** (also **,rose 'pink**) [U] a pink colour 粉紅色 **3** [C] a piece of metal or plastic with small holes in it that is attached to the end of a pipe or WATERING CAN so that the water comes out in a fine spray when you are watering plants（水管或噴壺的）蓮蓬式噴嘴 **4** = CEILING ROSE

IDM **be coming up 'roses** (*informal*) (of a situation 形勢) to be developing in a successful way 順利發展；蓬勃發展 **put 'roses in sb's cheeks** (*BrE, informal*) to make sb look healthy 使雙頰紅潤健康 **a ,rose by any other ,name would smell as 'sweet** (*saying*) what is important is what people or things are, not what they are called 玫瑰不叫玫瑰，依然芳香如故；名稱並不是重要的東西 ➲ more at BED *n.*, SMELL *v.*

■ *adj.* (also **,rose 'pink**) pink in colour 粉紅色的

rosé /'rəʊzeɪ; *NAmE* roʊ'zeɪ/ *noun* [U, C] (from *French*) a light pink wine 玫瑰紅葡萄酒；粉紅葡萄酒：*a bottle of rosé* 一瓶玫瑰紅葡萄酒 ◇ *an excellent rosé* 優質粉紅葡萄酒 ➲ compare RED WINE (1), WHITE WINE (1)

ros·eate /'rəʊziət; *NAmE* 'roʊ-/ *adj.* [usually before noun] (*literary* or *technical* 術語) pink in colour 粉紅色的；玫瑰色的

rose·bud /'rəʊzbʌd; *NAmE* 'roʊz-/ *noun* the flower of a ROSE before it is open 玫瑰花蕾

'rose-coloured (*especially US* **'rose-colored**) *adj.* **1** pink in colour 粉紅色的；玫瑰色的 **2** (also **'rose-tinted**) used to describe an idea or a way of looking at a situation as being better or more positive than it really is（描述對形勢的看法或觀點過於樂觀）：*a rose-tinted vision of the world* 對世界的理想化看法 ◇ *He tends to view the world **through rose-coloured spectacles**.* 他總是戴着玫瑰色的眼鏡看世界。

'rose hip *noun* = HIP *n.* (3)

rose·mary /'rəʊzməri; *NAmE* 'roʊzmeri/ *noun* [U] a bush with small narrow leaves that smell sweet and are used in cooking as a HERB 迷迭香（灌木，葉子窄小，氣味芬芳，可用於烹調）➲ VISUAL VOCAB page V32

Rosetta Stone /rəʊ'zetə; *NAmE* roʊ-/ *noun* [sing.] something, especially a discovery, that helps people to understand or find an explanation for a mystery or area of knowledge that not much was known about 有助於解釋神秘事物（或未知領域）的事物；有啟示作用的發現 **ORIGIN** From the name of an ancient stone with writing in three different languages on it that was found near Rosetta in Egypt in 1799. It has helped archaeologists to understand and translate many other ancient Egyptian texts. 源自 1799 年在埃及羅塞塔附近發現的刻有三種文字的古代羅塞塔石碑，考古學家由此解讀了很多其他古埃及文本。

R

ros·ette /rəʊ'zet; *NAmE* roʊ-/ *noun* **1** a round decoration made of RIBBON that is worn by supporters of a political party or sports team, or to show that sb has won a prize 玫瑰形飾物（用緞帶製成，政黨或運動隊的支持者所佩戴，亦作為獲獎的標誌）➲ picture at MEDAL **2** a thing that has the shape of a ROSE 玫瑰形的東西：*The leaves formed a dark green rosette.* 這些葉子聚在一起，像是一朵深綠色的玫瑰。

'rose water *noun* [U] a liquid with a sweet smell made from ROSES, used as a PERFUME or in cooking 玫瑰香水（用作香水或烹調用）

,rose 'window *noun* a decorative round window in a church, often with coloured glass (= STAINED GLASS) in it 圓花窗（常有彩色玻璃）

rose·wood /'rəʊzwʊd; *NAmE* 'roʊz-/ *noun* [U] the hard reddish-brown wood of a tropical tree, that has a pleasant smell and is used for making expensive furniture 黃檀木（產於熱帶，木質堅硬，氣味芳香，用於製作貴重傢具）

Rosh Hash·ana (also **Rosh Hash·anah**) /,rɒʃ hə'ʃɑːnə; *NAmE* ,rɑːʃ/ *noun* [U] the Jewish New Year festival, held in September 歲首節（猶太教曆新年，在九月份）

rosin /'rɒzɪn; *NAmE* 'rɑːzn/ *noun* [U] a substance that a player uses on the BOW of a musical instrument such as a VIOLIN so that it makes a better sound when it moves across the strings 松香 ▸ **rosin** *verb* **~ sth**

ros·ter /'rɒstə(r); *NAmE* 'rɑːs-; 'rɔːs-/ *noun, verb*

■ *noun* **1** a list of people's names and the jobs that they have to do at a particular time 值勤名單 **SYN** **rota**：

a duty roster 值勤表 **2** a list of the names of people who are available to do a job, play in a team, etc. 候選名單

■ ***verb* ~ sb (to do sth)** (*BrE*) to put sb's name on a roster 將（姓名）列入值勤名單： *The driver was rostered for Sunday.* 這名司機被安排在星期日值班。

ros·trum /ˈrɒstrəm; *NAmE* ˈrɑːs-; ˈrɔːs-/ *noun* (*pl.* **ros·trums** or **ros·tra** /-trə/) a small raised platform that a person stands on to make a speech, CONDUCT music, receive a prize, etc. 講壇；指揮台；領獎台

rosy /ˈrəʊzi; *NAmE* ˈroʊzi/ *adj.* (**rosi·er**, **rosi·est**) **1** pink and pleasant in appearance 粉紅色的；紅潤的： *She had rosy cheeks.* 她臉頰紅潤。 **2** likely to be good or successful 美好的；樂觀的 SYN **hopeful** : *The future is looking very rosy for our company.* 我們公司的前景一片光明。◇ *She* ***painted a rosy picture*** *of their life together in Italy* (= made it appear to be very good and perhaps better than it really was). 她把他們在意大利的共同生活描繪得非常美好。 IDM see GARDEN *n.*

rot /rɒt; *NAmE* rɑːt/ *verb, noun*

■ ***verb*** **(-tt-)** [I, T] to decay, or make sth decay, naturally and gradually （使）腐爛，腐敗變質 SYN **decompose** : *rotting leaves* 漸漸腐爛的葉子 ◇ **~ (away)** *The window frame had rotted away completely.* 窗框已經完全爛掉了。◇ (*figurative*) *prisoners thrown in jail and* ***left to rot*** 投入大牢後就無人過問的囚犯 ◇ **~ sth** *Too much sugar will rot your teeth.* 吃糖太多，就會出現蛀牙。 ➲ see also ROTTEN *adj.* (1)

■ ***noun*** [U] **1** the process or state of decaying and falling apart 腐爛；腐敗變質： *The wood must not get damp as rot can quickly result.* 木頭不能受潮，否則很快就會爛掉。 ➲ see also DRY ROT (1) **2 the rot** used to describe the fact that a situation is getting worse 形勢惡化： ***The rot set in*** *last year when they reorganized the department.* 去年他們重組這個部門時，衰敗就開始了。◇ *The team should manage to* ***stop the rot*** *if they play well this week.* 如果球隊本週比賽表現好，他們應該能夠阻止形勢的惡化。 **3** (*old-fashioned, BrE*) nonsense; silly things that sb says 廢話；胡說 SYN **rubbish** : *Don't talk such rot!* 別說這樣的廢話！

rota /ˈrəʊtə; *NAmE* ˈroʊtə/ *noun* (*BrE*) a list of jobs that need to be done and the people who will do them in turn 勤務輪值表 SYN **roster** : *Dave organized a cleaning rota.* 戴夫安排了打掃衛生輪值表。

ro·tary /ˈrəʊtəri; *NAmE* ˈroʊ-/ *adj., noun*

R

■ ***adj.*** [only before noun] **1** (of a movement 運動) moving in a circle around a central fixed point 旋轉的；繞軸轉動的： *rotary motion* 旋轉運動 **2** (of a machine or piece of equipment 機器或設備) having parts that move in this way 轉動的： *a rotary engine* 旋轉式發動機

■ ***noun*** (*pl.* **-ies**) (*NAmE*) = TRAFFIC CIRCLE

ˈRotary club *noun* a branch of an organization of business and professional people whose members meet for social reasons and to raise money for charity 扶輪（分）社（由商人和專業人士組成的社交與慈善組織分支）

ro·tate /rəʊˈteɪt; *NAmE* ˈroʊteɪt/ *verb* **1** [I, T] to move or turn around a central fixed point; to make sth do this （使）旋轉，轉動： *Stay well away from the helicopter when its blades start to rotate.* 直升機的螺旋槳開始轉動時，盡量離遠點兒。◇ **~ about/around sth** *winds rotating around the eye of a hurricane* 繞颶風風眼旋轉的風 ◇ **~ sth** *Rotate the wheel through 180 degrees.* 將方向盤轉動 180 度。 **2** [I, T] if a job **rotates**, or if people **rotate** a job, they regularly change the job or regularly change who does the job （工作）由…輪值；（人員）輪換，輪值： **(+ adv./prep.)** *The EU presidency rotates among the members.* 歐盟主席一職由其成員國輪流擔任。◇ *When I joined the company, I rotated around the different sections.* 我加入這個公司時，輪換過幾個不同的部門。◇ **~ sth** *We rotate the night shift so no one has to do it all the time.* 我們輪流值夜班，這樣就不會有人總是夜班了。 ▸ **ro·tat·ing** *adj.* [only before noun] : *rotating parts* 旋轉的部件 ◇ *a rotating presidency* 輪值主席之職

ro·ta·tion /rəʊˈteɪʃn; *NAmE* roʊ-/ *noun* **1** [U] the action of an object moving in a circle around a central fixed point 旋轉；轉動： *the daily rotation of the earth on its axis* 地球每天的自轉 **2** [C] one complete movement in a circle around a fixed point （旋轉的）一週，一圈： *This switch controls the number of rotations per minute.* 這個開關控制着每分鐘的轉數。 **3** [U, C] the act of regularly changing the thing that is being used in a particular situation, or of changing the person who does a particular job 輪換；交替；換班： ***crop rotation/the rotation of crops*** (= changing the crop that is grown on an area of land in order to protect the soil) 莊稼的輪作 ◇ *Wheat, maize and sugar beet are planted* ***in rotation.*** 小麥、玉米和甜菜是輪流種植的。◇ *The committee is chaired by all the members* ***in rotation.*** 委員會由所有成員輪流主持。 ▸ **ro·ta·tion·al** /-ʃənl/ *adj.* [only before noun]

Ro·ta·va·tor™ (also **Ro·to·va·tor™**) /ˈrəʊtəveɪtə(r); *NAmE* ˈroʊ-/ *noun* (*BrE*) a machine with blades that turn and break up soil 羅塔瓦多旋耕機

ROTC /ˈrɒtsi; *NAmE* ˈrɑːt-/ *abbr.* (*US*) Reserve Officers' Training Corps (an organization for students in the US who are training to be military officers while they are studying)（美國在校學生的）預備軍官訓練團

rote /rəʊt; *NAmE* roʊt/ *noun* [U] (often used as an adjective 常用作形容詞) the process of learning sth by repeating it until you remember it rather than by understanding the meaning of it 死記硬背： *to learn* ***by rote*** 死記硬背地學習 ◇ *rote learning* 死記硬背的學習

roti /ˈrəʊti; *NAmE* ˈroʊ-/ *noun* [U, C] **1** a type of S Asian bread that is cooked on a GRIDDLE （南亞）烙餅，烤餅 **2** (*IndE*) bread of any kind 麵包

ro·tis·serie /rəʊˈtɪsəri; *NAmE* roʊ-/ *noun* (from *French*) a piece of equipment for cooking meat that turns it around on a long straight piece of metal (called a SPIT) 電轉架烤肉爐

rotor /ˈrəʊtə(r); *NAmE* ˈroʊ-/ *noun* a part of a machine that turns around a central point （機器的）轉子，轉動部件： *rotor blades on a helicopter* 直升機的旋翼葉片 ➲ VISUAL VOCAB page V53

Ro·to·va·tor = ROTAVATOR

rot·ten /ˈrɒtn; *NAmE* ˈrɑːtn/ *adj., adv.*

■ ***adj.*** **1** (of food, wood, etc. 食物、樹木等) that has decayed and cannot be eaten or used 腐爛的；腐敗的；腐朽的： *the smell of rotten vegetables* 腐爛蔬菜的氣味 ◇ *The fruit is starting to* ***go rotten.*** 水果已經開始腐爛變質了。◇ *rotten floorboards* 腐朽的木地板 **2** [usually before noun] (*informal*) very bad 非常糟糕的；惡劣的 SYN **terrible** : *I've had a rotten day!* 我這一天倒霉透了！◇ *What rotten luck!* 真倒霉！◇ *She's a rotten singer.* 她是個蹩腳的歌手。 **3** [not usually before noun] (*informal*) dishonest 不誠實的；腐敗的： *The organization is* ***rotten to the core.*** 這個組織腐敗透頂。 **4** [not before noun] (*informal*) looking or feeling ill/sick 不舒服；不適： *She felt rotten.* 她感覺不舒服。 **5** [not before noun] (*informal*) feeling guilty about sth you have done 感到內疚（或慚愧）： *I feel rotten about leaving them behind.* 我丟下他們不管，感到很慚愧。 **6** [only before noun] (*informal*) used to emphasize that you are angry or upset about sth （強調非常生氣或沮喪）倒霉的，破爛的： *You can keep your rotten money!* 你就留着你的臭錢吧！ ▸ **rot·ten·ness** *noun* [U]

IDM **a rotten ˈapple** one bad person who has a bad effect on others in a group 帶來惡劣影響的人；害群之馬

■ ***adv.*** (*informal*) to a large degree; very much 很大程度上；非常： *She spoils the children rotten.* 她很溺愛孩子。◇ (*BrE*) *He fancies you (something) rotten.* 他非常迷戀你。

rot·ter /ˈrɒtə(r); *NAmE* ˈrɑːt-/ *noun* (*old-fashioned, BrE, informal*) a person who behaves badly towards other people 無賴；惡棍

Rott·weiler /ˈrɒtwaɪlə(r); -vaɪ-; *NAmE* ˈrɑːtwaɪ-; ˈrɔːtwaɪ-/ *noun* a large dog that can be very aggressive 羅特韋爾狗

ro·tund /rəʊˈtʌnd; *NAmE* roʊ-/ *adj.* (*formal* or *humorous*) having a fat round body 圓胖的；肥圓的 SYN **plump** : *the rotund figure of Mr Stevens* 史蒂文斯先生圓胖的體形 ▸ **ro·tund·ity** *noun* [U]

ro·tunda /rəʊˈtʌndə; *NAmE* roʊ-/ *noun* a round building or hall, especially one with a curved roof (= a DOME) 圓形建築，圓形大廳（尤指帶有圓頂的） ➲ VISUAL VOCAB page V14

rou·ble (*especially BrE*) (*NAmE* usually **ruble**) /ˈruːbl/ *noun* the unit of money in Russia 盧布（俄羅斯貨幣單位）

roué /ˈruːeɪ; *NAmE* ruːˈeɪ/ *noun* (*old-fashioned*) a man who drinks too much alcohol, uses illegal drugs, or is sexually immoral, especially a man who is fairly old（尤指上了年紀的）酒色之徒，癮君子

rouge /ruːʒ/ *noun* [U] (*old-fashioned*) a red powder used by women for giving colour to their cheeks 胭脂 ▸ **rouge** *verb* **~ sth**

rough 0‑ /rʌf/ *adj., noun, verb, adv.*

■ ***adj.*** (**rough·er, rough·est**)

▸ NOT SMOOTH 不平滑 **1** 0‑ having a surface that is not even or regular 粗糙的；不平滑的；高低不平的：*rough ground* 高低不平的地面 ◇ *The skin on her hands was hard and rough.* 她手上的皮膚粗糙而沒有彈性。◇ *Trim rough edges with a sharp knife.* 用鋒利的刀將參差不齊的邊切齊。OPP **smooth**

▸ NOT EXACT 不確切 **2** 0‑ not exact; not including all details 不確切的；粗略的；大致的 SYN **approximate**：*a **rough calculation/estimate** of the cost* 對成本的粗略計算／估計 ◇ *I've got a **rough idea** of where I want to go.* 我大致知道我想去哪裏了。◇ *There were about 20 people there, **at a rough guess**.* 那裏約計有 20 人。◇ *a rough draft of a speech* 講話草稿 ◇ *a rough sketch* 草圖

▸ VIOLENT 粗暴 **3** 0‑ not gentle or careful; violent 粗暴的；粗野的；猛烈的：*This watch is not designed for rough treatment.* 這塊手錶不可猛烈震動。◇ *They complained of rough handling by the guards.* 他們投訴警衛對他們動粗。◇ *rough kids* 粗野的小孩 ◇ *Don't try any **rough stuff** with me!* 別想對我撒野！ **4** 0‑ where there is a lot of violence or crime 犯罪盛行的；充斥暴力的；危險的：*the roughest neighbourhood in the city* 市內最危險的街區

▸ SEA 海洋 **5** 0‑ having large and dangerous waves 洶湧的；風浪很大的：*It was too rough to sail that night.* 那天夜裏風浪太大，無法行船。

▸ WEATHER 天氣 **6** wild and with storms 惡劣的；有暴風雨的

▸ DIFFICULT 困難 **7** 0‑ difficult and unpleasant 艱難的；討厭的；令人不快的 SYN **tough**：*He's had a really **rough time** recently* (= he's had a lot of problems). 他最近真是困難重重。◇ *We'll get someone in to do the rough work* (= the hard physical work). 我們會找個人來幹這重活。

▸ NOT WELL 不舒服 **8** (*BrE*) not feeling well 不舒服的；不適的：*You look rough—are you OK?* 你看上去不太舒服，你沒事吧？◇ *I had a rough night* (= I didn't sleep well). 我一夜沒睡好覺。

▸ PLAIN/BASIC 簡單；基本 **9** 0‑ simply made and not finished in every detail; plain or basic 粗糙的；不夠精細的；樸實簡單的：*rough wooden tables* 粗糙的木桌 ◇ *a rough track* 凹凸不平的小徑 ◇ (*BrE*) *rough paper for making notes on* 做筆記的草稿紙

▸ NOT SMOOTH 令人不舒服 **10** not smooth or pleasant to taste, listen to, etc. 味道差的；澀的；刺耳的；令人難受的：*a rough wine/voice* 口感極差的葡萄酒；刺耳的聲音 ▸ **rough·ness** *noun* [U] ➲ see also ROUGHLY (2)

IDM **a rough 'deal** the fact of being treated unfairly 不公平的待遇 **rough 'edges** small parts of sth or of a person's character that are not yet as good as they should be 瑕疵；美中不足之處：*The ballet still had some rough edges.* 這段芭蕾舞還有不足之處。◇ *He had a few rough edges knocked off at school.* 他在學校改掉了一些壞毛病。 **the ˌrough end of the 'pineapple** (*AustralE, informal*) a situation in which sb is treated badly or unfairly 受到不良（或不公平）對待的處境 ➲ more at RIDE *n.*

■ ***noun***

▸ IN GOLF 高爾夫球 **1 the rough** [sing.] the part of a GOLF COURSE where the grass is long, making it more difficult to hit the ball（高爾夫球場的）深草區 ➲ compare FAIRWAY

▸ DRAWING/DESIGN 繪畫；設計 **2** [C] (*technical* 術語) the first version of a drawing or design that has been done quickly and without much detail 草稿；草圖

▸ VIOLENT PERSON 暴徒 **3** [C] (*old-fashioned, informal*) a violent person 暴徒；粗野的人：*a gang of roughs* 一幫暴徒

IDM **in 'rough** (*especially BrE*) if you write or draw sth **in rough**, you make a first version of it, not worrying too much about mistakes or details 粗略地；大致上 **take the ˌrough with the 'smooth** to accept the unpleasant or difficult things that happen in life as well as the good things 好事壞事都接受；既能享樂也能吃苦 ➲ more at BIT

■ ***verb***

IDM **'rough it** (*informal*) to live in a way that is not very comfortable for a short time 暫時過艱苦的生活；渡過暫時的難關：*We can sleep on the beach. I don't mind roughing it for a night or two.* 我們可以睡在海灘上，我不介意吃一兩夜的苦。

PHR V **ˌrough sth↔'out** to draw or write sth without including all the details 畫…的草圖；草擬：*I've roughed out a few ideas.* 我已有幾個初步設想。 **ˌrough sb↔'up** (*informal*) to hurt sb by hitting or kicking them 毆打；施以暴力：*He claimed that guards had roughed him up in prison.* 他聲稱看守們在監獄裏毆打了他。

■ ***adv.*** using force or violence 粗魯地；粗野地：*Do they always play this rough?* 他們比賽總是這麼粗野嗎？

IDM **live/sleep 'rough** (*BrE*) to live or sleep outdoors, usually because you have no home and no money 風餐露宿（通常因為無家可歸或貧窮）：*young people sleeping rough on the streets* 露宿街頭的年輕人

rough·age /ˈrʌfɪdʒ/ *noun* [U] the part of food that helps to keep a person healthy by keeping the BOWELS working and moving other food quickly through the body 食物中的粗纖維 SYN **fibre**

ˌrough-and-'ready *adj.* [usually before noun] **1** simple and prepared quickly but good enough for a particular situation 簡單粗糙但可用的：*a rough-and-ready guide to the education system* 簡略的教育制度指南 **2** (of a person 人) not very polite, educated or fashionable 粗獷的；粗魯的；不拘小節的

ˌrough and 'tumble *noun* [U, sing.] **1 ~ (of sth)** a situation in which people compete with each other and are aggressive in order to get what they want 激烈的競爭；混戰：*the rough and tumble of politics* 政治上的混戰 **2** noisy and slightly violent behaviour when children or animals are playing together（兒童或動物一起嬉戲時的）吵鬧搗蛋行為

rough·cast /ˈrʌfkɑːst; *NAmE* -kæst/ *noun* [U] a type of PLASTER containing small stones that is used for covering the outside walls of buildings 粗灰泥 ▸ **rough-cast** *adj.*

'rough cut *noun* the first version of a film/movie, after the different scenes have been put together（影片的）初次剪輯版；毛片

'rough-cut *verb* **~ sth** to cut sth quickly, without paying attention to the exact size 粗切（或剪、割等）

ˌrough 'diamond (*BrE*) (*NAmE* **ˌdiamond in the 'rough**) *noun* a person who has many good qualities even though they do not seem to be very polite, educated, etc. 外粗內秀的人

rough·en /ˈrʌfn/ *verb* [I, T] to become rough; to make sth rough 變粗糙；使粗糙：*His voice roughened with every word.* 他說話的聲音越來越嘶啞。◇ **~ sth** *Cold weather roughens your skin.* 天氣寒冷，皮膚變得粗糙。

ˌrough-'hewn *adj.* [only before noun] **1** (of stone, wood, etc. 石頭、木材等) cut in a way that leaves it with a rough surface 被砍鑿得很粗糙的：*rough-hewn walls* 被弄得坑窪不平的牆壁 ◇ (*figurative*) *the rough-hewn features of his face* 他那飽經滄桑的臉 **2** (*formal*) (of a person or their behaviour 人或行為) not very polite or educated 粗魯的；粗野的

rough·house /ˈrʌfhaʊs; -haʊz/ *verb* [I, T] **~ (sb)** (*NAmE, informal*) to fight sb or play with sb roughly 打鬧；玩鬧：*Quit roughhousing, you two!* 你們兩個別打打鬧鬧了！

rough·ing /ˈrʌfɪŋ/ *noun* [U] (in ICE HOCKEY and AMERICAN FOOTBALL 冰上曲棍球和美式足球) an illegal use of force, for which a PENALTY may be given（可能受罰的）動作粗野，犯規衝撞

ˌrough ˈjustice *noun* [U] **1** punishment that does not seem fair 不太公平的懲罰： *It was rough justice that they lost in the closing seconds of the game.* 他們在比賽的最後幾秒鐘落敗，這不太公平。**2** treatment that is fair but not official or expected 算得上公平的待遇： *There was a certain amount of rough justice in his downfall.* 他的垮台也算是大致公平。

rough·ly 🔑 /ˈrʌfli/ *adv.*
1 🔑 approximately but not exactly 大約；大致；差不多： *Sales are up by roughly 10%.* 銷售額上升了大約10%。◇ *We live roughly halfway between here and the coast.* 我們住的地方大致在這裏和海濱中間。◇ *They all left at roughly the same time.* 他們都是大約同一時間離開的。◇ ***Roughly speaking**, we receive about fifty letters a week on the subject.* 關於這個問題，粗略地說，我們每週收到大約五十封來信。**2** 🔑 using force or not being careful and gentle 粗暴地；粗魯地： *He pushed her roughly out of the way.* 他粗暴地把她推到一邊。◇ *'What do you want?' she demanded roughly.* "你想怎麼樣？" 她粗聲粗氣地問道。**3** 🔑 in a way that does not leave a smooth surface 粗糙地；凹凸不平地： *roughly plastered walls* 灰泥抹得凹凸不平的牆壁

rough·neck /ˈrʌfnek/ *noun* (*informal*) **1** (*especially NAmE*) a man who is noisy, rude and aggressive 吵鬧而粗魯的人 **2** a man who works on an OIL RIG 石油鑽井工；油井工人

rough·shod /ˈrʌfʃɒd; *NAmE* -ʃɑːd/ *adv.*
IDM **ride, etc. ˈroughshod over sb** (*especially BrE*) (*US* usually **run ˈroughshod over sb**) to treat sb badly and not worry about their feelings（對某人）為所欲為，橫行霸道；任意踩躪

roul·ette /ruːˈlet/ *noun* [U] a gambling game in which a ball is dropped onto a moving wheel that has holes with numbers on it. Players bet on which hole the ball will be in when the wheel stops. 輪盤賭 ➲ see also RUSSIAN ROULETTE

round 🔑 /raʊnd/ *adj., adv., prep., noun, verb*
■ ***adj.*** (**round·er**, **round·est**) **1** 🔑 shaped like a circle or a ball 圓形的；環形的；球形的： *a round plate* 圓盤子 ◇ *These glasses suit people with round faces.* 這款眼鏡適合圓臉的人。◇ *The fruit are small and round.* 這種水果小而圓。◇ *Rugby isn't played with a round ball.* 橄欖球比賽用的不是圓球。◇ *the discovery that the world is round* 地球是圓的這一發現 ◇ *The child was watching it all with big round eyes* (= showing interest). 這孩子睜着又大又圓的眼睛看着這一切。◇ *a T-shirt with a round neck* 圓領 T 恤衫 ➲ see also ROUND-EYED, ROUND-TABLE **2** 🔑 having a curved shape 弧形的；圓弧的： *the round green hills of Donegal* 多尼戈爾那些圓圓的綠山岡 ◇ *round brackets* (= in writing) 圓括號 ◇ *She had a small mouth and round pink cheeks.* 她的嘴小小的，圓臉蛋紅紅的。**3** 🔑 [only before noun] a **round** figure or amount is one that is given as a whole number, usually one ending in 0 or 5 整數的；尾數是 0（或 5）的： *Make it a round figure—say forty dollars.* 湊個整數，就四十塊錢吧。◇ *Two thousand is a nice round number—put that down.* 兩千是個不錯的整數，記下吧。◇ *Well, **in round figures** (= not giving the exact figures) we've spent twenty thousand so far.* 嗯，說個約數吧，我們至今花了有兩萬了。▶ **round·ness** *noun* [U]: *His face had lost its boyish roundness.* 他的臉已不是小時候那副圓圓的娃娃臉了。

■ ***adv.*** (*especially BrE*) (*NAmE* usually **around**) For the special uses of **round** in phrasal verbs, look at the verb entries. For example, the meaning of **come round to sth** is given in the phrasal verb section of the entry for **come**. 關於 round 在短語動詞中的特殊用法，見有關動詞詞條。如 come round to sth 在詞條 come 的短語動詞部份。**1** 🔑 moving in a circle 旋轉；環繞；兜圈子： *Everybody joins hands and dances round.* 大家手拉着手，圍成一圈跳舞。◇ *How do you make the wheels go round?* 你是怎麼讓輪子轉起來的？◇ *The children were spinning **round and round**.* 孩子們一個勁地轉呀轉。◇ (*figurative*) *The thought kept going round and round in her head.* 這個想法一直縈繞在她的心頭。**2** 🔑 measuring or marking the edge or outside of sth 周長；周圍；繞一整圈： *a young tree measuring only 18 inches round* 周長只有 18 英寸的小樹 ◇ *They've built a high fence **all round** to keep intruders out.* 他們在周圍豎起了高高的籬笆，以防外人進入。**3** 🔑 on all sides of sb/sth 在周圍；圍繞： *A large crowd had gathered round to watch.* 一大群人聚在周圍觀看。**4** 🔑 at various places in an area 到處；四處： *People stood round waiting for something to happen.* 人們在各處站着，等待着發生什麼事情。**5** 🔑 in a circle or curve to face another way or the opposite way 調轉方向；轉過來： *He turned the car round and drove back again.* 他調轉車頭，又開了回來。◇ *She looked round at the sound of his voice.* 聽到他的聲音，她扭頭看了看。**6** 🔑 to the other side of sth 繞彎；迂迴；向另一側： *We walked round to the back of the house.* 我們繞到房子的後面。◇ *The road's blocked—you'll have to drive **the long way round**.* 這條路被堵了，你們得開車繞着走了。**7** 🔑 from one place, person, etc. to another 依次；挨個： *They've moved all the furniture round.* 他們把所有的傢具搬動了一遍。◇ *He went round interviewing people about local traditions.* 他到處找人訪談，瞭解當地的傳統。◇ *Pass the biscuits round.* 把餅乾傳給大家。◇ *Have we **enough cups to go round**?* 我們的杯子夠大家用嗎？**8** 🔑 (*informal*) to or at a particular place, especially where sb lives 到某地，在某地（尤指居住地）： *I'll be round in an hour.* 我過一個小時就到。◇ *We've invited the Frasers round this evening.* 我們已經邀請了弗雷澤一家今晚過來。➲ note at AROUND

IDM **ˌround aˈbout** **1** 🔑 approximately 大約： *We're leaving round about ten.* 我們十點鐘左右要離開。◇ *A new roof will cost round about £3 000.* 換新房頂大約要花 3 000 英鎊。**2** in the area near a place 在附近： *in Oxford and the villages round about* 在牛津及其附近的村莊 ➲ more at TIME *n.*

■ ***prep.*** (*especially BrE*) (*NAmE* usually **around**) **1** 🔑 in a circle 環繞；圍繞： *the first woman to sail round the world* 第一位環球航行的女性 ◇ *The earth moves round the sun.* 地球繞着太陽轉。**2** 🔑 on, to or from the other side of sth 繞過；在另一側： *Our house is round the next bend.* 前面一拐彎就是我們家。◇ *There she is, coming round the corner.* 她來了，繞過拐角過來了。◇ *There must be **a way round** the problem.* 這個問題一定有辦法解決。**3** 🔑 on all sides of sb/sth; surrounding sb/sth 在…周圍；包圍： *She put her arms round him.* 她張開雙臂摟住他。◇ *He had a scarf round his neck.* 他脖子上圍着圍巾。◇ *They were all sitting round the table.* 他們圍着桌子坐着。**4** 🔑 in or to many parts of sth 在…各處；到…各部份： *She looked all round the room.* 她將房間四下打量了一下。**5** to fit in with particular people, ideas, etc. 適應；圍繞（人、思想等）： *He has to organize his life round the kids.* 他不得不以孩子們為中心來安排自己的生活。➲ note at AROUND

IDM **ˌround ˈhere** 🔑 near where you are now or where you live 在附近： *There are no decent schools round here.* 附近沒有什麼像樣的學校。➲ more at MILLSTONE

■ ***noun***
▸ **STAGE IN PROCESS 進程** **1** a set of events which form part of a longer process 階段；輪次： *the next round of peace talks* 下一輪和談 ◇ *the final round of voting in the election* 選舉的最後一輪投票
▸ **IN SPORT 體育運動** **2** a stage in a sports competition 比賽階段；輪次；局；場： *the qualifying rounds of the National Championships* 全國錦標賽的資格賽 ◇ *Hewitt was knocked out of the tournament in the third round.* 休伊特在錦標賽的第三輪被淘汰出局。**3** a stage in a BOXING or WRESTLING match（拳擊或摔跤比賽的）回合： *The fight only lasted five rounds.* 比賽只持續了五個回合。**4** a complete game of GOLF; a complete way around the course in some other sports, such as SHOWJUMPING（高爾夫球、騎馬障礙賽等的）一輪比賽，一局： *We played a round of golf.* 我們打了一場高爾夫球。◇ *the first horse to jump a clear round* 乾淨利落地完成整套跳躍表演的第一匹馬
▸ **REGULAR ACTIVITIES/ROUTE 慣常的活動／路線** **5** a regular series of activities 一系列常規活動；慣常的活動： *the **daily round** of school life* 學校的日常生活 ◇ *Her life is one long round of parties and fun.* 她的生活就是沒完沒了的聚會娛樂。**6** a regular route that sb takes when delivering or collecting sth; a regular series of visits that sb makes（收發信函等的）固定路線；照例要出去

做的事情：*Dr Green was* **on** *her daily ward* **rounds.** 格林醫生在進行每日一次的巡查病房。◇ *(BrE) a postman on his delivery round* 正在投遞郵件的郵遞員 ➲ see also MILK ROUND (1), PAPER ROUND

▸ **DRINKS** 飲料 **7** a number of drinks bought by one person for all the others in a group（由一人給大家買的）一巡飲料：*a round of drinks* 一巡飲料 ◇ *It's my round* (= it is my turn to pay for the next set of drinks). 這一巡輪到我了。

▸ **BREAD** 麵包 **8** (*BrE*) a whole slice of bread; SANDWICHES made from two whole slices of bread 一整片麵包；（兩整片麵包做的）三明治：*Who's for another round of toast?* 誰還要烤麵包片？◇ *two rounds of beef sandwiches* 兩份牛肉三明治

▸ **CIRCLE** 圓 **9** a round object or piece of sth 圓形物體；圓塊：*Cut the pastry into rounds.* 將油酥麵糰分成一個個圓塊。

▸ **OF APPLAUSE/CHEERS** 掌聲；歡呼聲 **10 ~ of applause/cheers** a short period during which people show their approval of sb/sth by clapping, etc. 一陣：*There was a great round of applause when the dance ended.* 舞蹈結束的時候，爆發出了一陣熱烈的掌聲。

▸ **SHOT** 射擊 **11** a single shot from a gun; a bullet for one shot 一次射擊；一發子彈：*They fired several rounds at the crowd.* 他們朝人群開了幾槍。◇ *We only have three rounds of ammunition left.* 我們只剩下三發子彈了。

▸ **SONG** 歌曲 **12** (*music* 音) a song for two or more voices in which each sings the same tune but starts at a different time 輪唱曲

IDM **do/go the 'rounds (of sth)** **1** (*BrE*) (*NAmE* **make the 'rounds**) if news or a joke **does the rounds**, it is passed on quickly from one person to another 迅速傳開；迅速流傳 **2** (*BrE*) (also **make the 'rounds** *NAmE, BrE*) to go around from place to place, especially when looking for work or support for a political CAMPAIGN, etc. 到各處去，巡迴（找工作或尋求對政治運動的支持等） **in the 'round** **1** (of a work of art 藝術品) made so that it can be seen from all sides 圓雕的；可全方位觀看的；立體的：*an opportunity to see Canova's work in the round* 觀看卡諾瓦的圓雕藝術作品的機會 **2** (of a theatre or play 劇院或戲劇) with the people watching all around a central stage 舞台設在中央的

■ *verb* **1** [T] **~ sth** to go around a corner of a building, a bend in the road, etc. 繞行；繞過：*The boat rounded the tip of the island.* 小船繞過島的尖端。◇ *We rounded the bend at high speed.* 我們高速駛過這段彎路。 **2** [T, I] **~ (sth)** to make sth into a round shape; to form into a round shape（使）成圓形；變圓：*She rounded her lips and whistled.* 她撮起嘴唇吹口哨。◇ *His eyes rounded with horror.* 他嚇得兩眼圓睜。 **3** [T] **~ sth (up/down) (to sth)** to increase or decrease a number to the next highest or lowest whole number（將數字調高或調低）使成為整數；把（數字）四捨五入

PHR V **,round sth↔'off (with sth)** **1** (*NAmE* also **,round sth↔'out**) to finish an activity or complete sth in a good or suitable way 圓滿結束；圓滿完成：*She rounded off the tour with a concert at Carnegie Hall.* 她在卡內基大廳舉行一場音樂會，以此圓滿結束了她的巡迴演出。 **2** to take the sharp or rough edges off sth 去除…的稜角；使…的邊緣光滑：*You can round off the corners with sandpaper.* 你可以用砂紙把稜角打磨光滑。 **'round on sb** to suddenly speak angrily to sb and criticize or attack them 突然責罵（或指責）**SYN** **turn on**：*He rounded on journalists, calling them 'a pack of vultures'.* 他突然對記者大發雷霆，稱他們是一幫乘人之危的傢伙。 **,round sb/sth↔'up** **1** to find and gather together people, animals or things 將…聚攏起來；使聚集：*I rounded up a few friends for a party.* 我找了幾個朋友聚了聚。◇ *The cattle are rounded up in the evenings.* 到了晚上，牛都要圈起來。 **2** if police or soldiers **round up** a group of people, they find them and arrest or capture them 圍捕；圍剿 ➲ related noun ROUND-UP (2)

round·about /'raʊndəbaʊt/ *noun, adj.*

■ *noun* (*BrE*) **1** (*NAmE* **'traffic circle**, **ro·tary**) a place where two or more roads meet, forming a circle that all traffic must go around in the same direction（交通）環島：*At the roundabout, take the second exit.* 到環島後，走第二個出口。 ➲ see also MINI-ROUNDABOUT **2** (*NAmE* **'merry-go-round**) a round platform for children to play on in a park, etc. that is pushed round while the children are sitting on it（遊樂設施）旋轉平台 **3** (*BrE*) = MERRY-GO-ROUND (1) **IDM** see SWING *n.*

■ *adj.* [usually before noun] not done or said using the shortest, simplest or most direct way possible 迂迴的；間接的；兜圈子的：*It was a difficult and roundabout trip.* 這是一次艱難而曲折的旅行。◇ *He told us, in a very roundabout way, that he was thinking of leaving.* 他拐彎抹角地對我們說他想走了。

roundabout (*BrE*)
merry-go-round (*NAmE*)
旋轉平台

merry-go-round /
roundabout (*both BrE*)
carousel (*NAmE*)
旋轉木馬

'round bracket *noun* (*BrE*) = BRACKET *n.* (1)

round·ed 0-π /'raʊndɪd/ *adj.* [usually before noun] **1** 0-π having a round shape 圓形的：*a surface with rounded edges* 帶圓邊的面 ◇ *rounded shoulders* 曲背 **2** having a wide variety of qualities that combine to produce sth pleasant, complete and balanced 全面的；一應俱全的；完善的：*a smooth rounded taste* 舒爽醇厚的味道 ◇ *a fully rounded education* 非常全面的教育 **3** (*phonetics* 語音) (of a speech sound 語音) produced with the lips in a narrow round position 圓唇的 **OPP** **unrounded** ➲ see also WELL ROUNDED

roundel /'raʊndl/ *noun* (*technical* 術語) a round design that is used as a decoration or to identify an aircraft 圓形圖案（或標誌）；（飛機的）圓形識別標誌

round·ers /'raʊndəz; *NAmE* -ərz/ *noun* [U] a British game played especially in schools by two teams using a BAT and ball. Each player tries to hit the ball and then run around the four sides of a square before the other team can return the ball.（英國）圓場棒球 ➲ compare BASEBALL (1)

,round-'eyed *adj.* with eyes that are fully open because of surprise, fear, etc.（因為吃驚、害怕等）兩眼圓睜的

Round·head /'raʊndhed/ *noun* a person who supported Parliament against the King in the English Civil War (1642-49) 圓顱黨人（1642 年至 1649 年英格蘭內戰期間支持議會反對國王）➲ compare CAVALIER

round·house /'raʊndhaʊs/ *noun* a punch where the arm moves around in a wide curve 大弧度出拳；大掄拳

'roundhouse kick *noun* a move in KARATE and other MARTIAL ARTS, in which you turn on one foot as you make a high kick with the other（空手道等武術中的）迴旋踢，旋踢

round·ing /'raʊndɪŋ/ *noun* [U] (*phonetics* 語音) the fact of producing a speech sound with the lips in a rounded position 發圓唇音；圓唇

round·ly /'raʊndli/ *adv.* strongly or by a large number of people 有力地；廣泛地：*The report has been roundly criticized.* 這份報告受到了廣泛的批評。◇ *They were roundly defeated* (= they lost by a large number of points). 他們一敗塗地。

,round 'robin *noun* **1** (*sport* 體) a competition in which every player or team plays every other player or team 循環賽 **2** a letter that has been signed by a large number of people who wish to express their opinions about sth 聯名信（或意見書） **3** something that is made, written, etc. by several people who each add a part one after another 合作（或合寫等）的東西；接龍

R

創作：*a round robin story* 接龍故事 **4** a letter intended to be read by many people that is copied and sent to each one 大量複製傳閱的信件

ˌround-ˈshouldered *adj.* with shoulders that are bent forward or sloping downwards 曲背的；溜肩膀

rounds·man /ˈraʊndzmən/ *noun* (*pl.* **-men** /-mən/) **1** (*NAmE* **ˈroute man**) a person who delivers things to people in a particular area（特定區域的）送貨員 **2** (*NAmE*) the police officer in charge of a group of officers that is moving around an area（管區）巡警長 **3** (*AustralE*) a journalist who deals with a particular subject 專題記者

ˌround-ˈtable *adj.* [only before noun] (of discussions, meetings, etc. 討論、會議等) at which everyone is equal and has the same rights 圓桌的；參與者權利均等的：*round-table talks* 圓桌會談

ˌround-the-ˈclock (also **aˌround-the-ˈclock**) *adj.* [only before noun] lasting or happening all day and night 日夜不停的；持續一整天的：*round-the-clock nursing care* 全天的護理 ➲ see also AROUND/ROUND THE CLOCK at CLOCK *n.*

ˌround ˈtrip *noun* [C, U] a journey to a place and back again 來回旅行；往返旅程：*a 30-mile round trip to work* 上班往返 30 英里的路程 ◇ (*NAmE*) *It's 30 miles round trip to work.* 上班要走往返 30 英里的路程。 ▸ **ˌround-ˈtrip** *adj.*：(*NAmE*) *a round-trip ticket* 雙程票 ➲ see also RETURN TICKET

ˈround-up *noun* [usually sing.] **1** a summary of the most important points of a particular subject, especially the news（尤指新聞）概要，摘要：*We'll be back after the break with a round-up of today's other stories.* 休息之後我們會摘要報道今天其他的新聞。 **2** an act of bringing people or animals together in one place for a particular purpose 聚攏；驅集；聚集

round·worm /ˈraʊndwɜːm; *NAmE* -wɜːrm/ *noun* a small WORM that lives in the INTESTINES of pigs, humans and some other animals 蛔蟲；線蟲

rouse /raʊz/ *verb* **1** (*formal*) to wake sb up, especially when they are sleeping deeply 喚醒；使醒來：**～ sb from sleep/bed** *The telephone roused me from my sleep at 6 a.m.* 早晨 6 點鐘，電話鈴聲就把我從睡夢中吵醒了。 ◇ **～ sb** *Nicky roused her with a gentle nudge.* 尼基用胳膊肘輕輕地將她推醒。 **2** to make sb want to start doing sth when they were not active or interested in doing it 使活躍起來；使產生興趣：**～ sb/yourself (to sth)** *A lot of people were roused to action by the appeal.* 許多人響應號召行動起來。 ◇ **～ sb/yourself to do sth** *Richard couldn't rouse himself to say anything in reply.* 理查德沒有興趣回答。 **3 ～ sth** (*formal*) to make sb feel a particular emotion 激起（某種情感）：*to rouse sb's anger* 把某人惹火 ◇ *What* ***roused your suspicions*** (= what made you suspicious)? 你是怎麼起疑心的？ **4** [usually passive] **～ sb** to make sb angry, excited or full of emotion 激怒；使激動：*Chris is not easily roused.* 克里斯不容易激動。 ➲ see also AROUSE

rous·ing /ˈraʊzɪŋ/ *adj.* [usually before noun] **1** full of energy and enthusiasm 充滿活力（或激情）的：*a rousing cheer* 熱情的歡呼 ◇ *The team was given* ***a rousing reception*** *by the fans.* 球隊受到了球迷的熱烈歡迎。 **2** intended to make other people feel enthusiastic about sth 激勵的；激動人心的：*a rousing speech* 使人振奮的講話

roust /raʊst/ *verb* **～ sb (from sth)** (*NAmE*) to disturb sb or make them move from a place 打擾；擾亂；驅逐

roust·about /ˈraʊstəbaʊt/ *noun* (*especially NAmE*) a man with no special skills who does temporary work, for example on an OIL RIG or in a CIRCUS（油井或馬戲場等處的）雜工，非技術工 **SYN** **casual labourer**

rout /raʊt/ *noun, verb*

■ ***noun*** [sing.] a situation in which sb is defeated easily and completely in a battle or competition 潰敗；徹底失敗

IDM **put sb to ˈrout** (*literary*) to defeat sb easily and completely 徹底打敗；使潰敗

■ ***verb*** **～ sb** to defeat sb completely in a competition, a battle, etc. 徹底擊敗；使潰敗：*The Buffalo Bills routed the Atlanta Falcons 41–14.* 水牛城比爾隊以 41:14 大勝亞特蘭大獵鷹隊。

route 🔑 **AW** /ruːt; *NAmE* also raʊt/ *noun, verb*

■ ***noun*** **1** 🔑 a way that you follow to get from one place to another 路線；路途：*Which is the best route to take?* 哪一條是最佳路線？ ◇ *Motorists are advised to find an alternative route.* 建議駕駛者換一條路線。 ◇ *a coastal route* 沿海的路線 ◇ **～ (from A to B)** *the quickest route from Florence to Rome* 從佛羅倫薩到羅馬的最快捷的路線 ◇ *an* ***escape route*** 逃脫的路徑 ➲ see also EN ROUTE **2** 🔑 a fixed way along which a bus, train, etc. regularly travels or goods are regularly sent（公共汽車和列車等的）常規路線，固定線路：*The house is not on a* ***bus route.*** 這房子不在公交線上。 ◇ ***shipping routes*** 航運線路 ◇ ***a cycle route*** (= a path that is only for CYCLISTS) 自行車道 **3** 🔑 **～ (to sth)** a particular way of achieving sth 途徑；渠道：*the route to success* 成功之路 **4** 🔑 used before the number of a main road in the US（用於美國幹線公路號碼前）：*Route 66* * 66 號公路

■ ***verb*** (**rout·ing** or **route·ing**, **rout·ed**, **rout·ed**) **～ sb/sth (+ adv./prep.)** to send sb/sth by a particular route 按某路線發送：*Satellites route data all over the globe.* 衛星向全球各地傳遞信息。

Route 128 /ˌruːt ˌwʌn twentiˈeɪt/ *noun* (in the US) an area in Massachusetts where there are many companies connected with the computer and ELECTRONICS industries * 128 號公路高科技帶（位於美國馬薩諸塞州的計算機與電子工業區） **ORIGIN** From the name of an important road in the area. 源自該地區一條交通要道的名稱。

ˈroute man (*NAmE*) (*BrE* **rounds·man**) *noun* a person who delivers things to people in a particular area（特定區域的）送貨員

ˈroute march *noun* a long march for soldiers over a particular route, especially to improve their physical condition 長途行軍（尤其為鍛煉身體）；拉練

ˌRoute ˈOne *noun* [U] (*BrE*) (in football (SOCCER) 足球) kicking the ball a long way towards your opponent's end, used as a direct way of attacking, rather than passing the ball between players 長傳（直接）進攻

router¹ /ˈruːtə(r); *NAmE* also ˈraʊt-/ *noun* (*computing* 計) a device which sends data to the appropriate parts of a computer network 路由器（傳送信息的專用網絡的設備） ➲ **VISUAL VOCAB** page V66

router² /ˈraʊtə(r)/ *noun* an electric tool which cuts shallow lines in surfaces 槽刨

rou·tine 🔑 /ruːˈtiːn/ *noun, adj.*

■ ***noun*** **1** 🔑 [C, U] the normal order and way in which you regularly do things 常規；正常順序：*We are trying to get the baby into a routine for feeding and sleeping.* 我們試着讓嬰兒按時進食和睡覺。 ◇ *Make exercise a part of your* ***daily routine.*** 讓鍛煉成為你日常生活的一部份。 ◇ *We clean and repair the machines* ***as a matter of routine.*** 我們定期清洗和修理機器。 **2** 🔑 [U] (*disapproving*) a situation in which life is boring because things are always done in the same way 生活乏味；無聊：*She needed a* ***break from routine.*** 她需要擺脫一下刻板的生活。 **3** [C] a series of movements, jokes, etc. that are part of a performance（演出中的）一套動作，一系列笑話（等）：*a dance routine* 一套舞蹈動作 **4** [C] (*computing* 計) a list of instructions that enable a computer to perform a particular task 例行程序；例程

■ ***adj.*** [usually before noun] **1** 🔑 done or happening as a normal part of a particular job, situation or process 常規的；例行公事的；日常的：***routine enquiries/questions/tests*** 日常的詢問；常規審問／檢查 ◇ *The fault was discovered during a routine check.* 這個錯誤是在一次常規檢查中發現的。 **2** 🔑 not unusual or different in any way 平常的；正常的；毫不特別的：*He died of a heart attack during a routine operation.* 他在一次普通手術中死於心臟病。 **3** 🔑 (*disapproving*) ordinary and boring 乏味的；平淡的 **SYN** **dull, humdrum**：*a routine job* 平淡乏味的工作 ◇ *This type of work rapidly becomes routine.* 這種工作很快就變得乏味無聊。 ▸ **rou·tine·ly** *adv.*：*Visitors are routinely checked as they*

R

enter the building. 來訪者在進入大樓時都要接受例行檢查。

'routing number (*US*) (*BrE* **'sort code**) *noun* a number that is used to identify a particular bank（銀行）識別代碼

roux /ruː/ *noun* [C, U] (*pl.* **roux**) (from *French*) a mixture of fat and flour heated together until they form a solid mass, used for making sauces 油麪醬（用油和麪粉攪拌加熱而成濃稠湯料，用於製調味品）

rove /rəʊv; *NAmE* roʊv/ *verb* **1** [I, T] (*formal*) to travel from one place to another, often with no particular purpose 漫遊；漂泊；流浪 SYN **roam**：**+ adv./prep.** *A quarter of a million refugees roved around the country.* 這個國家有二十五萬難民流離失所。◇ **~ sth** *bands of thieves who roved the countryside* 在鄉村流竄的盜賊團夥 **2** [I] (**+ adv./prep.**) if sb's eyes **rove**, the person keeps looking in different directions（眼睛）轉來轉去，環視，打量

rover /'rəʊvə(r); *NAmE* 'roʊ-/ *noun* (*literary*) a person who likes to travel a lot rather than live in one place 漫遊者；流浪者

rov·ing /'rəʊvɪŋ; *NAmE* 'roʊ-/ *adj.* [usually before noun] travelling from one place to another and not staying anywhere permanently 流動的；漂泊的；漫遊的；巡迴的：*a roving reporter for ABC news* 美國廣播公司的流動新聞記者 ◇ *Patrick's roving lifestyle takes him between London and Los Angeles.* 帕特里克漂泊不定的生活方式使他在倫敦和洛杉磯之間奔波。

IDM **have a roving 'eye** (*old-fashioned*) to always be looking for the chance to have a new sexual relationship 總是找機會尋花問柳；眼神不安分

row[1] /rəʊ; *NAmE* roʊ/ *noun, verb* ➲ see also ROW[2]

■ *noun* **1** **~ (of sb/sth)** a number of people standing or sitting next to each other in a line; a number of objects arranged in a line 一排；一列；一行：*a row of trees* 一行樹木 ◇ *We sat* ***in a row*** *at the back of the room.* 我們在屋子的後面坐成一排。◇ *The vegetables were planted in neat rows.* 蔬菜種得整整齊齊。 **2** a line of seats in a cinema/movie theater, etc.（劇院、電影院等的）一排座位：*Let's sit in the back row.* 我們坐在最後一排吧。◇ *Our seats are five rows from the front.* 我們的座位在前面第五排。 **3** a complete line of STITCHES in knitting or CROCHET（編織中的）針行，一整行 ➲ VISUAL VOCAB page V41 **4 Row** used in the name of some roads（用於某些道路名稱）：*Manor Row* 莊園路 **5** [usually sing.] an act of ROWING a boat; the period of time spent doing this 划船（時間）：*We went for a row on the lake.* 我們去湖上划船了。➲ see also DEATH ROW, SKID ROW

IDM **in a 'row** **1** if sth happens several times **in a row**, it happens in exactly the same way each time, and nothing different happens in the time between 連續幾次地：*This is her third win in a row.* 這是她連續獲得的第三次勝利。 **2** if sth happens for several days, etc. **in a row**, it happens on each of those days 接連幾天（等）地：*Inflation has fallen for the third month in a row.* 通貨膨脹率連續第三個月在下降。➲ more at DUCK *n.*

■ *verb* **1** [I, T] to move a boat through water using OARS (= long wooden poles with flat ends) 划（船）：*We rowed around the island.* 我們繞着島划船。◇ **~ sth** *Grace rowed the boat out to sea again.* 格雷斯又划着船出海了。 **2** [T] **~ sb (+ adv./prep.)** to take sb somewhere in a boat with OARS 划船送（某人）：*The fisherman rowed us back to the shore.* 漁夫划船將我們送回到岸上。

row[2] /raʊ/ *noun, verb* ➲ see also ROW[1]

■ *noun* (*informal, especially BrE*) **1** [C] **~ (about/over sth)** a serious disagreement between people, organizations, etc. about sth 嚴重分歧；糾紛：*A row has broken out over education.* 在教育問題上出現了嚴重分歧。 **2** [C] a noisy argument between two or more people 吵架；爭吵 SYN **quarrel**：*She left him after a* ***blazing row.*** 大吵一場之後，她離他而去。◇ *family rows* 家庭裏的爭吵 ◇ *He* ***had a row with*** *his son.* 他跟兒子吵了一架。 **3** [sing.] a loud unpleasant noise 大的噪音 SYN **din, racket**：*Who's making that row?* 誰那麼吵？

■ *verb* [I] (*BrE, informal*) to have a noisy argument 吵架；大聲爭辯：*Mike and Sue are always rowing.* 邁克和蘇總是吵架。◇ **~ (with sb) (about sb/sth)** *She had rowed with her parents about her boyfriend.* 她和父母因為她的男朋友吵過架。

rowan /'rəʊən; 'raʊən; *NAmE* 'roʊən; 'raʊən/ (also **'rowan tree**, **,mountain 'ash**) *noun* a small tree that has red BERRIES in the autumn/fall 花楸（樹）；紅果花楸；歐洲花楸

row·boat /'rəʊbəʊt; *NAmE* 'roʊboʊt/ (*NAmE*) (*BrE* **'rowing boat**) *noun* a small open boat that you move using OARS 划艇 ➲ VISUAL VOCAB page V54

rowdy /'raʊdi/ *adj.* (**row·dier**, **row·di·est**) (of people 人) making a lot of noise or likely to cause trouble 吵鬧的；惹是生非的；搗亂的 SYN **disorderly**：*a rowdy crowd at the pub* 酒吧裏一群鬧哄哄的傢伙 ▸ **row·dily** *adv.* **row·di·ness** *noun* [U] **rowdy** *noun* (*pl.* **-ies**)：*rowdies and troublemakers* 吵鬧的人和惹麻煩的人

rowdy·ism /'raʊdiɪzəm/ *noun* [U] behaviour that is noisy and causes trouble 吵鬧行為；搗亂行為

rower /'rəʊə(r); *NAmE* 'roʊ-/ *noun* a person who ROWS a boat 划船者

row house /'rəʊ haʊs; *NAmE* 'roʊ/ (also **'town house**) (both *NAmE*) (*BrE* **,terraced 'house**) *noun* a house that is one of a row of houses that are joined together on each side 連排住宅 ➲ VISUAL VOCAB page V16

row·ing /'rəʊɪŋ; *NAmE* 'roʊɪŋ/ *noun* [U] the sport or activity of travelling in a boat using OARS 划船；划艇運動：*to go rowing* 去划船

'rowing boat (*BrE*) (*NAmE* **row·boat**) *noun* a small open boat that you move using OARS 划艇 ➲ VISUAL VOCAB page V54

'rowing machine *noun* a piece of sports equipment on which you make the same movements as sb who is ROWING a boat 划船練習架；（陸上）划艇機 ➲ VISUAL VOCAB page V42

row·lock /'rɒlək; 'rəʊlɒk; *NAmE* 'rɑːl-; 'roʊlɑːk/ (*BrE*) (*NAmE* **oar·lock**) *noun* a device fixed to the side of a boat for holding an OAR（小船邊緣的）槳架

royal /'rɔɪəl/ *adj., noun*

■ *adj.* [only before noun] **1** connected with or belonging to the king or queen of a country 國王的；女王的；皇家的；王室的：*the royal family* 王室 ◇ *the royal household* 王室 ➲ compare REGAL **2** (*abbr.* **R**) used in the names of organizations that serve or are supported by a king or queen（用於服務於國王或女王或受其贊助的組織名稱）：*the Royal Navy* 英國皇家海軍 ◇ *the Royal Society for the Protection of Birds* 皇家鳥類保護協會 **3** impressive; suitable for a king or queen 莊嚴的；盛大的；高貴的；適合國王（或女王）的 SYN **splendid**：*We were given a royal welcome.* 我們受到了盛大的歡迎。

■ *noun* [usually pl.] (*informal*) a member of a royal family 王室成員

the ,Royal A'cademy (also **the ,Royal Academy of 'Arts**) *noun* [sing.] a British organization whose members are famous artists. Its building in London contains an art school and space for exhibitions.（英國）皇家藝術院（成員為著名藝術家，在倫敦設有藝術學校和展廳）

the ,royal as'sent *noun* [sing.] (in Britain) the signature of an Act of Parliament by the king or queen so that it becomes law 御准（英國國王或女王對議會法案成為法例的批准）

,royal 'blue *adj.* deep bright blue 品藍的；寶藍的；藏藍的 ▸ **,royal 'blue** *noun* [U]

,Royal Com'mission *noun* **~ (on/into sth)** | **~ (to do sth)** (in Britain) a group of people who are officially chosen to examine a particular law or subject and suggest any changes or new laws that should be introduced（英國）皇家委員會

,Royal 'Highness *noun* **His/Her/Your Royal Highness** a title of respect used when talking to or about a member of the royal family（用作王室成員的尊稱）殿下：*Their Royal Highnesses, the Duke and Duchess of Kent* 肯特公爵和公爵夫人殿下

R

,royal 'icing *noun* [U] (*BrE*) a hard white covering for a fruit cake, made with sugar and the white part of eggs（水果蛋糕的）蛋白糖霜硬皮

roy·al·ist /'rɔɪəlɪst/ *noun* a person who believes that a country should have a king or queen 君主主義者；保皇主義者；保皇黨人 **SYN** **monarchist** ➲ compare REPUBLICAN *n.* (1) ▸ **roy·al·ist** *adj.*

,royal 'jelly *noun* [U] a substance that is produced by worker BEES and that is fed to a young queen bee 王漿；蜂王漿；蜂王乳：*health food products containing royal jelly* 含蜂王漿的保健食品

roy·al·ly /'rɔɪəli/ *adv.* (*old-fashioned*) very well; in a very impressive way or to a great degree 非常好地；以盛情；極度

the ,Royal 'Mail *noun* (in Britain) the service that collects and delivers letters（英國）郵政

,royal 'tennis *noun* [U] (*AustralE*) = REAL TENNIS

roy·alty /'rɔɪəlti/ *noun* (*pl.* **-ies**) **1** [U] one or more members of a royal family 王室成員：*The gala evening was attended by royalty and politicians.* 王室成員和政壇要人參加了這個晚會。◇ *We were treated like royalty.* 我們受到了君王般的禮遇。**2** [C, usually pl.] a sum of money that is paid to sb who has written a book, piece of music, etc. each time that it is sold or performed 版稅：*All royalties from the album will go to charity.* 這張音樂專輯的全部版稅收入將捐給慈善機構。◇ *She received £2 000* ***in royalties.*** 她得到了 2 000 英鎊的版稅。**3** [C, usually pl.] a sum of money that is paid by an oil or mining company to the owner of the land that they are working on 礦區土地使用費（由採礦或石油公司等付給土地所有人）

,royal 'warrant *noun* [usually sing.] a king's or queen's permission for a company to supply goods to them and to advertise this fact on the company's products, etc. 英廷供貨許可證，王室御用許可證（公司向英國王室供應貨物並可對此作產品廣告）

the ,royal '‘we’ *noun* [sing.] the use of ‘we’ instead of ‘I’ by a single person, as used traditionally by kings and queens in the past（舊時傳統上國王或女王的自稱，用 we 替代 I）

roz·zer /'rɒzə(r); *NAmE* 'rɑːz-/ *noun* (*old-fashioned*, *BrE*, *informal*) a police officer 警察

R

RP /,ɑː 'piː; *NAmE* ,ɑːr/ *noun* [U] the abbreviation for ‘received pronunciation’ (the standard form of British pronunciation, based on educated speech in southern England) 標準發音（全寫為 received pronunciation，基於英國南方受教育階層的發音）

RPI /,ɑː piː 'aɪ; *NAmE* ,ɑːr/ *abbr.* RETAIL PRICE INDEX 零售物價指數

rpm /,ɑː piː 'em; *NAmE* ,ɑːr/ *abbr.* revolutions per minute (a measurement of the speed of an engine or a record when it is playing) 每分鐘轉數

RRP /,ɑːr ɑː 'piː; *NAmE* ,ɑːr ɑːr/ *abbr.* recommended retail price 建議零售價格

RRSP /,ɑːr ɑːr es 'piː/ *abbr.* (*CanE*) registered retirement savings plan (a special type of savings plan in which you can save money without paying taxes on it until you stop working when you are older) 註冊退休儲蓄計劃（退休前免稅的儲蓄計劃）

RSA /,ɑːr es 'eɪ/ *abbr.* (in the UK) Royal Society of Arts（英國）皇家藝術學會

RSI /,ɑːr es 'aɪ/ *noun* [U] the abbreviation for ‘repetitive strain injury’ or ‘repetitive stress injury’ (pain and swelling, especially in the arms and hands, caused by performing the same movement many times in a job or an activity) 反複應力性損傷，重複性勞損（全寫為 repetitive strain injury 或 repetitive stress injury，由經常重複同一動作引起）

RSPCA /,ɑːr es piː siː 'eɪ/ *abbr.* (in the UK) Royal Society for the Prevention of Cruelty to Animals（英國）皇家防止虐待動物協會

RSS /,ɑːr es 'es/ *abbr.* (*computing* 計) Really Simple Syndication (a standard system for the distribution of information, especially news, from an Internet publisher to Internet users) 簡易信息聚合（標準互聯網信息傳送系統，尤用於傳送新聞）

RSVP (*BrE*) (also **R.S.V.P.** *US*, *BrE*) /,ɑːr es viː 'piː/ *abbr.* (written on invitations) please reply (from French ‘répondez s'il vous plaît’) 敬請賜覆（請柬用語，源自法語）

RTA /,ɑː tiː 'eɪ; *NAmE* ,ɑːr/ *abbr.* (*BrE*) road traffic accident 道路交通事故

RTF /,ɑː tiː 'ef; *NAmE* ,ɑːr/ *abbr.* (*computing* 計) rich text format (a type of file containing data that can be used with different programs or systems) * RTF 格式，普適文本格式（可為不同的程序或系統兼容）：*an RTF file* * RTF 文件

Rt Hon *abbr.* (*BrE*) (in writing 書寫形式) RIGHT HONOURABLE 閣下

Rt Revd (also **Rt. Rev.**) *abbr.* (*BrE*) (in writing 書寫形式) RIGHT REVEREND（尊稱主教）尊敬的，可敬的

rub 🔑 /rʌb/ *verb*, *noun*

■ *verb* (**-bb-**) **1** 🔑 [T, I] to move your hand, or sth such as a cloth, backwards and forwards over a surface while pressing firmly 擦；磨；搓：**~ sth** *She rubbed her chin thoughtfully.* 她若有所思地撫摩着下巴。◇ **~ sth/yourself with sth** *Rub the surface with sandpaper before painting.* 用砂紙打磨表面，然後再上油漆。◇ **~ sth/yourself against sth** *The cat rubbed itself against my legs.* 貓在我腿上蹭來蹭去。◇ **~ at sth** *I rubbed at the stain on the cloth.* 我擦了擦布上的污漬。◇ **~ against sth** *Animals had been rubbing against the trees.* 動物一直在這些樹上蹭來蹭去。◇ **~ sth/yourself + adj.** *Rub the surface smooth.* 將表面擦光。**2** 🔑 [T, I] to press two surfaces against each other and move them backwards and forwards; to be pressed together and move in this way（使）相互磨擦；搓：**~ sth (together)** *She rubbed her hands in delight.* 她高興得直搓手。◇ **~ (together)** *It sounded like two pieces of wood rubbing together.* 聽起來就像是兩塊木頭在一起磨擦。**3** 🔑 [I, T] (of a surface 表面) to move backwards and forwards many times against sth while pressing it, especially causing pain or damage 磨，摩擦（尤指引起疼痛或損害）：*The back of my shoe is rubbing.* 我的鞋後跟磨腳。◇ **~ on/against sth** *The wheel is rubbing on the mudguard.* 車輪蹭着擋泥板了。◇ **~ sth (+ adj.)** *The horse's neck was* ***rubbed raw*** (= until the skin came off) *where the rope had been.* 馬脖子上套過繮繩的地方皮都給磨掉了。**4** 🔑 [T] **~ sth + adv./prep.** to spread a liquid or other substance over a surface while pressing firmly 塗；抹；搽：*She rubbed the lotion into her skin.* 她把潤膚液揉搓進皮膚裏。

IDM **rub sb's 'nose in it** (*informal*) to keep reminding sb in an unkind way of their past mistakes 揭瘡疤；不斷惡意提起某人以往的過失 **rub 'salt into the wound** | **rub 'salt into sb's wounds** to make a difficult experience even more difficult for sb 在傷口上抹鹽；使雪上加霜 **rub 'shoulders with sb** (*NAmE* also **rub 'elbows with sb**) to meet and spend time with a famous person, socially or as part of your job 與某名人接觸（或交往）**rub sb up the wrong 'way** (*BrE*) (*NAmE* **rub sb the wrong 'way**) (*informal*) to make sb annoyed or angry, often without intending to, by doing or saying sth that offends them（無意中）惹人生氣，觸怒別人 ➲ more at TWO

PHR V **,rub a'long (with sb/together)** (*BrE*, *informal*) (of two people 兩個人) to live or work together in a friendly enough way 相處融洽；和諧共事 **,rub sb/oneself/sth↔'down** to rub the skin of a person, horse, etc. hard with sth to make it clean and dry 將（人、馬等）徹底擦乾 **,rub sth↔'down** to make sth smooth by rubbing it with a special material（用特別材料）將某物打磨光滑 **,rub it 'in** | **,rub sth 'in** [no passive] to keep reminding sb of sth they feel embarrassed about and want to forget 反複提及令人尷尬的事；觸及痛處：*I know I was stupid; you don't have to* ***rub it in.*** 我知道我當時很愚蠢，你不必老提這件事。**,rub 'off (on/onto sb)** (of personal qualities, behaviour, opinions, etc. 人的品質、行為、觀點等) to become part of a person's character as a result of that person spending time with sb who has those qualities, etc. 感染；傳給：*Her sense of fun has rubbed off on her children.* 她的幽默感已經傳給了她的孩子。**,rub sth↔'off (sth)** | **,rub 'off** to remove sth or to be removed by rubbing（被）擦掉，抹掉：*She rubbed off the dead skin.* 她擦掉了死皮。◇ *The gold colouring had begun to rub off.* 金黃色已經開始剝落了。◇ (*BrE*) *If you write on the blackboard, rub it off at the end of the lesson.* 如果你在黑板上寫字，下課時要擦掉。**,rub sb↔'out** (*NAmE, slang*) to murder sb 幹掉；做掉 **,rub sth↔'out** (*BrE*) (also **erase** *NAmE, BrE*) to remove the marks made by a pencil, etc., using a RUBBER/ERASER 用橡皮擦掉（字跡等）：*to rub out a mistake* 用橡皮擦掉錯處

■ **noun** **1** [C, usually sing.] an act of rubbing a surface 擦；抹；搓；揉：*She gave her knee a quick rub.* 她很快地揉了揉膝蓋。**2** **the rub** [sing.] (*formal* or *humorous*) a problem or difficulty 問題；困難：*The hotel is in the middle of nowhere and* ***there lies the rub****. We don't have a car.* 難就難在旅館很偏遠，我們又沒有汽車。

rub·ber 0–w /ˈrʌbə(r)/ *noun*

1 0–w [U] a strong substance that can be stretched and does not allow liquids to pass through it, used for making tyres, boots, etc. It is made from the liquid (= SAP) inside a tropical plant or is produced using chemicals. 橡膠：*a ball made of rubber* 皮球 ◇ *a rubber tree* 橡膠樹 ➲ see also FOAM RUBBER at FOAM *n.* (1), INDIA RUBBER **2** [C] (*BrE*) (also **eraser** *NAmE, BrE*) a small piece of rubber or a similar substance, used for removing pencil marks from paper; a piece of soft material used for removing CHALK marks from a BLACKBOARD 橡皮；黑板擦 ➲ VISUAL VOCAB page V69 **3** [C] (*old-fashioned, informal, especially NAmE*) = CONDOM **4** [C] (in some card games or sports) a competition consisting of a series of games or matches between the same teams or players（某些紙牌遊戲或體育運動中相同的對手或隊伍間）多輪決勝負的比賽

IDM **where the ,rubber meets the 'road** (*NAmE*) the point at which sth is tested and you really find out whether it is successful or true 接受考驗的時刻；檢驗成敗的時刻；檢驗真偽的時刻：*Here's where the rubber meets the road: will consumers actually buy the product?* 檢驗成敗的時刻到了：消費者真的會購買這種產品嗎？➲ more at BURN *v.* ► **rub·ber** *adj.* [usually before noun]：*a rubber ball* 皮球 ◇ *rubber gloves* 橡皮手套

,rubber 'band (*BrE* also **e,lastic 'band**) *noun* a thin round piece of rubber used for holding things together 橡皮圈；橡皮筋 ➲ VISUAL VOCAB page V69

,rubber 'boot (*NAmE*) (*BrE* **wel·ling·ton**, **,wellington 'boot**, *informal* **welly**) *noun* one of a pair of long rubber boots, usually reaching almost up to the knee, that you wear to stop your feet getting wet 及膝膠靴 ➲ VISUAL VOCAB page V64

,rubber 'bullet *noun* a bullet made of rubber intended to injure but not to kill people, used by the army or police to control violent crowds 橡皮子彈（防暴用）

,rubber 'dinghy (also **dinghy**) (*US* also **,rubber 'raft**) *noun* a small boat made of rubber that is filled with air, used especially for rescuing people from ships and planes 橡皮艇；橡皮筏

rub·ber·ized (*BrE* also **-ised**) /ˈrʌbəraɪzd/ *adj.* [only before noun] covered with rubber 橡膠包裹的；覆蓋橡膠的：*rubberized cloth* 膠布

rub·ber·neck /ˈrʌbənek; *NAmE* -bərn-/ *verb* [I] (*informal, especially NAmE*) to turn to look at sth while you are driving past it（駕車時）扭頭觀望 ► **rub·ber·neck·er** *noun*

'rubber plant *noun* a plant with thick shiny green leaves, often grown indoors 橡膠植物（葉厚且有光澤，常種於室內）

,rubber 'stamp *noun* **1** a small tool that you hold in your hand and use for printing the date, the name of an organization, etc. on a document 橡皮圖章 ➲ VISUAL VOCAB page V69 **2** (*disapproving*) a person or group that automatically gives approval to the actions or decisions of others 履行審批手續而沒有實權的人（或機構）；橡皮圖章：*Parliament is seen as a rubber stamp for decisions made elsewhere.* 議會被看作橡皮圖章，只會批准他人的決定。

,rubber-'stamp *verb* ~ **sth** (often *disapproving*) to give official approval to a law, plan, decision, etc., especially without considering it carefully（機械式）蓋公章；（未經慎重考慮而）正式通過

rub·bery /ˈrʌbəri/ *adj.* **1** looking or feeling like rubber 似橡膠的；有彈性的：*The eggs were overcooked and rubbery.* 雞蛋煮得太老了，像膠皮似的。**2** (of legs or knees 腿或膝蓋) feeling weak and unable to support your weight 虛弱的；軟弱無力的

rub·bing /ˈrʌbɪŋ/ *noun* a copy of writing or a design on a piece of stone or metal that is made by placing a piece of paper over it and rubbing with CHALK, a pencil, etc. 拓本 ➲ see also BRASS RUBBING

'rubbing alcohol (*NAmE*) (*BrE* **,surgical 'spirit**) *noun* [U] a clear liquid, consisting mainly of alcohol, used for cleaning wounds, etc. 醫用酒精；消毒用酒精

rub·bish 0–w /ˈrʌbɪʃ/ *noun, verb*

■ **noun** [U] **1** 0–w (*especially BrE*) things that you throw away because you no longer want or need them 垃圾；廢棄物：*a* ***rubbish bag/bin*** 垃圾袋；垃圾桶 ◇ *a* ***rubbish dump/heap/tip*** 垃圾場／堆／傾倒處 ◇ *The streets were littered with rubbish.* 街上到處都是垃圾。◇ ***garden/household rubbish*** 花園／生活垃圾 ➲ COLLOCATIONS at ENVIRONMENT ➲ see also GARBAGE (1), TRASH (1) **2** 0–w (*BrE, informal*) (also used as an adjective 也用作形容詞) something that you think is of poor quality 劣質的東西：*I thought the play was rubbish!* 我覺得這部戲很差！◇ *Do we have to listen to this rubbish music?* 我們一定要聽這樣差勁的音樂嗎？**3** 0–w (*BrE, informal*) comments, ideas, etc. that you think are stupid or wrong 廢話；瞎說 SYN **nonsense**：*Rubbish! You're not fat.* 瞎說！你並不胖。◇ *You're talking a load of rubbish.* 你說的是一大堆廢話。◇ *It's not rubbish—it's true!* 這不是瞎說，是真的！

■ **verb** (*BrE, informal*) (*NAmE* **trash**) ~ **sb/sth** to criticize sb/sth severely or treat them as though they are of no value 狠批；把…看得一文不值

British/American 英式/美式英語

rubbish / garbage / trash / refuse

- **Rubbish** is the usual word in *BrE* for the things that you throw away because you no longer want or need them. **Garbage** and **trash** are both used in *NAmE*. Inside the home, **garbage** tends to mean waste food and other wet material, while **trash** is paper, cardboard and dry material. 在英式英語中，rubbish 為常用詞，指垃圾、廢物。garbage 和 trash 均用於美式英語。生活垃圾中，garbage 多指廢棄的食物和其他濕物質，而 trash 則指廢棄的紙、硬紙板和乾物質。
- In *BrE*, you put your **rubbish** in a **dustbin** in the street to be collected by the **dustmen**. In *NAmE*, your **garbage** and **trash** goes in a **garbage/trash can** in the street and is collected by **garbage men/collectors**. 在英式英語中，垃圾為 rubbish，街上的垃圾桶為 dustbin，清除垃圾的工人叫 dustman。在美式英語中，垃圾為 garbage 和 trash，街上的垃圾桶為 garbage/trash can，清除垃圾的工人叫 garbage man/collector。
- **Refuse** is a formal word and is used in both *BrE* and *NAmE*. **Refuse collector** is the formal word for a dustman or garbage collector. * refuse 為正式用語，用於英式英語和美式英語均可。refuse collector 為 dustman 或 garbage collector 的正式說法。

rub·bishy /ˈrʌbɪʃi/ *adj.* (*BrE, informal*) of very poor quality 質量低劣的；非常差勁的 SYN **trashy**：*rubbishy old films* 質量很差的老電影

rub·ble /ˈrʌbl/ *noun* [U] broken stones or bricks from a building or wall that has been destroyed or damaged

R

碎石；碎磚：*The bomb* **reduced** *the houses* **to rubble**. 炸彈把那片房子炸成了一堆瓦礫。

'rub-down *noun* **1** the act of rubbing sb/sth with a cloth or special material, for example to make a person dry or to make sth dry, clean or smooth 擦拭；揩；抹；打磨；磨光：*You may need to give the floor a rub-down with glasspaper.* 你可能得用玻璃砂紙打磨一下地板。 **2** (*NAmE*) the act of rubbing and pressing a person's body with the hands to reduce pain in the muscles and joints 按摩 SYN **massage**

Rube Goldberg /ˌruːb ˈɡəʊldbɜːɡ; *NAmE* ˈɡoʊldbɜːrɡ/ (*NAmE*) (*BrE* **Heath Rob·in·son**) *adj.* [only before noun] (*humorous*) (of machines and devices 機器和裝置) having a very complicated design, especially when used to perform a very simple task; not practical 設計過於複雜的；不實用的

ru·bella /ruːˈbelə/ *noun* [U] (*medical* 醫) = GERMAN MEASLES

Ru·ben·esque /ˌruːbəˈnesk/ *adj.* (of a woman 女人) having a round body with large breasts and hips 體形豐滿的 ORIGIN From the name of the Flemish painter Peter Paul Rubens, who often painted women with large, fairly fat bodies. 源自佛蘭德畫家彼得•保羅•魯本斯的名字，他常畫高大豐滿的女人。

Ru·bi·con /ˈruːbɪkən; *NAmE* -kɑːn/ **the Rubicon** *noun* [sing.] the point at which a decision has been taken which can no longer be changed 無法退回的界限；界線：*Today we* **cross the Rubicon**. *There is no going back.* 今天我們要破釜沉舟，背水一戰了。ORIGIN From the **Rubicon**, a stream which formed the border between Italy and Gaul. When Julius Caesar broke the law by crossing it with his army in 49BC, it led inevitably to war. 源自意大利和高盧的界河魯比肯河（Rubicon）。公元前 49 年，凱撒違規帶兵越過魯比肯河，從而不可避免地引發了戰爭。

ru·bi·cund /ˈruːbɪkənd/ *adj.* (*literary*) (of a person's face 人的臉) having a healthy red colour 健康紅潤的 SYN **ruddy**

ru·bid·ium /rʊˈbɪdiəm/ *noun* [U] (*symb.* **Rb**) a chemical element. Rubidium is a rare soft silver-coloured metal that reacts strongly with water and burns when it is brought into contact with air. 銣

R

Rubik's Cube™ /ˈruːbɪks kjuːb/ *noun* a PUZZLE consisting of a plastic CUBE covered with coloured squares that you turn to make each side of the cube a different colour 魔方，魔術方塊（轉動大立方體上每一排的小立方體，使大立方體的每一面呈現同一顏色）

ruble *noun* (*especially NAmE*) = ROUBLE

ru·bric /ˈruːbrɪk/ *noun* (*formal*) a title or set of instructions written in a book, an exam paper, etc.（書本或試卷等上的）標題，提示，說明

ruby /ˈruːbi/ *noun* (*pl.* **-ies**) **1** [C] a dark red PRECIOUS STONE 紅寶石：*a ruby ring* 紅寶石戒指 **2** [U] a dark red colour 深紅色 ▸ **ruby** *adj.*：*ruby lips* 深紅色的嘴唇

ˌruby ˈwedding (*BrE*) (*US* **ˌruby anniˈversary**) (also **ˌruby ˈwedding anniversary** *US, BrE*) *noun* the 40th anniversary of a wedding 紅寶石婚（結婚 40 週年紀念）➲ compare DIAMOND WEDDING, GOLDEN WEDDING, SILVER WEDDING

ruched /ruːʃt/ *adj.* (of cloth, clothes, etc. 織物、衣服等) sewn so that they hang in folds 有褶邊的；有褶飾的：*ruched curtains* 帶褶邊的窗簾

ruck /rʌk/ *noun, verb*

▪ ***noun*** **1** [C] (in RUGBY 橄欖球) a group of players who gather round the ball when it is lying on the ground and push each other in order to get the ball 自由密集爭球 **2** [sing.] a group of people standing closely together or fighting 擁在一起的人群；混亂打鬥的人群 **3 the ruck** [sing.] (*disapproving*) ordinary people or events 普通人；尋常事：*She saw marriage to him as a way out of the ruck.* 她把同他結婚看作出人頭地的途徑。

▪ ***verb*** [I] (in RUGBY 橄欖球) to take part in a ruck (1) 進行自由密集爭球

PHR V **ˌruck ˈup** | **ˌruck sth↔ˈup** (of cloth 織物) to form untidy folds; to make sth do this（使）起皺褶：*Your dress is rucked up at the back.* 你的連衣裙後面起褶兒了。

ruck·sack /ˈrʌksæk/ (*BrE*) (also **back·pack** *NAmE, BrE*) *noun* a large bag, often supported on a light metal frame, carried on the back and used especially by people who go climbing or walking（尤指登山者或遠足者使用的）背包，旅行包 ➲ VISUAL VOCAB page V64

ruckus /ˈrʌkəs/ *noun* [sing.] (*informal, especially NAmE*) a situation in which there is a lot of noisy activity, confusion or argument 喧鬧；騷動；爭吵 SYN **commotion**

ruc·tions /ˈrʌkʃnz/ *noun* [pl.] (*especially BrE*) angry protests or arguments 憤怒的抗議；爭吵：*There'll be ructions if her father ever finds out.* 一旦讓她父親發現了，就會發生爭吵。

rud·der /ˈrʌdə(r)/ *noun* a piece of wood or metal at the back of a boat or an aircraft that is used for controlling its direction（船的）舵；（飛機的）方向舵 ➲ VISUAL VOCAB page V53

rud·der·less /ˈrʌdələs; *NAmE* -dərl-/ *adj.* (*formal*) with nobody in control; not knowing what to do 無人管理的；無指導的；漫無目的的

ruddy /ˈrʌdi/ *adj., adv.*

▪ ***adj.*** **1** (of a person's face 人的臉) looking red and healthy 紅潤健康的：*ruddy cheeks* 紅潤的面頰 ◇ *a ruddy complexion* 紅潤的臉色 **2** (*literary*) red in colour 紅色的：*a ruddy sky* 紅彤彤的天空 **3** [only before noun] (*BrE, informal*) a mild swear word that some people use to show that they are annoyed（表示生氣）討厭的，可惡的：*I can't get the ruddy car to start!* 我就是發動不了這破車！

▪ ***adv.*** (*BrE, informal*) a mild swear word used by some people to emphasize what they are saying, especially when they are annoyed（加強語氣，尤其生氣時）非常，該死：*There was a ruddy great hole in the ceiling.* 天花板上有一個要命的大洞。

rude 0-w /ruːd/ *adj.* (**ruder, rud·est**)

1 0-w having or showing a lack of respect for other people and their feelings 粗魯的；無禮的；粗野的 SYN **impolite**：*a rude comment* 粗魯的批評 ◇ **~ (to sb) (about sb/sth)** *The man was downright rude to us.* 這個傢伙對我們無禮至極。◇ *Why are you so rude to your mother?* 你為什麼對你的母親這麼沒禮貌？◇ *She was very rude about my driving.* 她對我的開車方法橫加指責。◇ **~ (to do sth)** *It's rude to speak when you're eating.* 吃東西的時候說話不禮貌。 **2** (*especially BrE*) (*NAmE* usually **crude**) connected with sex or the body in a way that people find offensive or embarrassing 猥褻的；下流的：*a rude gesture* 下流的手勢 ◇ *Someone made a rude noise.* 有人發出了淫猥的噪音。◇ *The joke is too rude to repeat.* 這個笑話太下流，不能重複了。 **3** [only before noun] (*formal*) sudden, unpleasant and unexpected 突然的；突如其來的；猛烈的：*Those expecting good news will get a rude shock.* 那些等着聽好消息的人會大吃一驚的。◇ *If the players think they can win this match easily, they are in for* **a rude awakening**. 如果選手們認為他們可以輕而易舉地贏這場比賽，他們會遭到當頭棒喝的。 **4** (*literary*) made in a simple, basic way 簡單的；粗糙的；原始的 SYN **primitive**：*rude shacks* 簡陋的小屋 ▸ **rude·ness** *noun* [U]：*She was critical to the point of rudeness.* 她挑剔得近乎無禮。

IDM **in rude ˈhealth** (*old-fashioned, BrE*) looking or feeling very healthy 非常健康；十分健壯

rude·ly 0-w /ˈruːdli/ *adv.*

1 0-w in a way that shows a lack of respect for other people and their feelings 粗魯地；無禮地：*They brushed rudely past us.* 他們粗暴無禮地與我們擦身而過。◇ *'What do you want?' she asked rudely.* "你要幹什麼？"她粗魯地問道。 **2** in a way that is sudden, unpleasant and unexpected 突然地；猛烈地；突如其來地：*I was rudely awakened by the phone ringing.* 我被突如其來的電話鈴聲吵醒了。

ru·di·men·tary /ˌruːdɪˈmentri/ *adj.* **1** (*formal*) dealing with only the most basic matters or ideas 基礎的；基本的 SYN **basic**：*They were given only rudimentary training in the job.* 他們僅僅受過基本的職業訓練。 **2** (*formal* or *technical* 術語) not highly or fully developed

未充分發展的；原始的 **SYN** **basic**： *Some dinosaurs had only rudimentary teeth.* 有些恐龍只有未充分長成的牙齒。

ru·di·ments /ˈruːdɪmənts/ *noun* [pl.] **the ~ (of sth)** (*formal*) the most basic or essential facts of a particular subject, skill, etc. 基礎；基本原理（或技能）**SYN** **basics**

rue /ruː/ *verb* (**rue·ing** or **ruing**, **rued**, **rued**) **~ sth** (*old-fashioned* or *formal*) to feel bad about sth that happened or sth that you did because it had bad results 對…感到懊惱；懊悔 **SYN** **regret**： *He* ***rued the day*** *they had bought such a large house.* 他懊悔他們買了這樣大的一所房子。

rue·ful /ˈruːfl/ *adj.* feeling or showing that you are sad or sorry 悲傷的；懊悔的；沮喪的： *a rueful smile* 慘然一笑 ▸ **rue·ful·ly** /ˈruːfəli/ *adv.*： *'So this is goodbye,' she said ruefully.* 她悲傷地說："那麼，這就是告別了。"

ruff /rʌf/ *noun* **1** a ring of coloured or marked feathers or fur around the neck of a bird or an animal 翎頜（鳥獸的環形彩色項毛）**2** a wide stiff white COLLAR with many folds in it, worn especially in the 16th and 17th centuries 飛邊（尤盛行於 16 和 17 世紀的白色輪狀皺領）

Synonyms 同義詞辨析

rude

cheeky • insolent • disrespectful • impolite • impertinent • discourteous

These are all words for people showing a lack of respect for other people. 以上各詞均指人粗魯、無禮。

rude having or showing a lack of respect for other people and their feelings 指粗魯的、無禮的、粗野的： *Why are you so rude to your mother?* 你為什麼對你的母親這麼沒禮貌？◇ *It's rude to speak when you're eating.* 吃東西時說話不禮貌。

cheeky (*BrE informal*) (especially of children) rude in an amusing or an annoying way（尤指小孩子）厚臉皮的、魯莽的、放肆的： *You cheeky monkey!* 你這厚臉皮的猴崽子！◇ *a cheeky grin* 厚顏無恥的齜牙一笑

insolent (*rather formal*) very rude, especially to sb who is older or more important（尤指對長者、重要人士）粗野的、無禮的、侮慢的 **NOTE** **Insolent** is used especially to talk about the behaviour of children towards adults. * insolent 尤用於形容孩子對成年人的行為。

disrespectful (*rather formal*) showing a lack of respect for sb/sth 指不尊敬、無禮、輕蔑： *Some people said he had been disrespectful to the President in his last speech.* 有些人說他在最近一次講話中對總統不尊重。

impolite (*rather formal*) not behaving in a pleasant way that follows the rules of society 指不禮貌、粗魯： *Some people think it is impolite to ask someone's age.* 有些人認為詢問別人的年齡是不禮貌的。**NOTE** **Impolite** is often used in the phrases *It seemed impolite* and *It would be impolite.* * impolite 常用於 it seemed impolite 和 it would be impolite 短語中。

impertinent (*rather formal*) not showing respect for sb who is older or more important 指（對長者或重要人士）粗魯無禮、不尊敬 **NOTE** **Impertinent** is often used by people such as parents and teachers when they are telling children that they are angry with them for being rude. * impertinent 常用於父母、老師等對孩子的粗魯行為表示氣憤： *Don't be impertinent!* 不要粗魯無禮！

discourteous (*formal*) having bad manners and not showing respect 指不禮貌、失禮、粗魯： *He didn't wish to appear discourteous.* 他不想顯得沒禮貌。

PATTERNS

- rude/cheeky/disrespectful/impolite/discourteous to sb
- rude/impolite/impertinent **to do sth**

ruf·fian /ˈrʌfiən/ *noun* (*old-fashioned*) a violent man, especially one who commits crimes 暴徒；惡棍 **SYN** **thug**

ruf·fle /ˈrʌfl/ *verb, noun*

■ ***verb*** **1** to disturb the smooth surface of sth, so that it is not even 弄皺；弄亂；使不平整： **~ sth** *She ruffled his hair affectionately.* 她情意綿綿地撥弄着他的頭髮。◇ **~ sth up** *The bird ruffled up its feathers.* 這隻鳥豎起了羽毛。**2** [often passive] **~ sb** to make sb annoyed, worried or upset 攪擾；激怒；使沮喪；使擔心 **SYN** **fluster**： *She was obviously ruffled by his question.* 她顯然被他的問題激怒了。◇ *He never* ***gets ruffled****, even under pressure.* 即使在壓力之下，他也從不感到沮喪。

IDM **ruffle sb's/a few ˈfeathers** (*informal*) to annoy or upset sb or a group of people 激怒；騷擾；使不安： *The senator's speech ruffled a few feathers in the business world.* 這位參議員的講話惹惱了一些商界人士。➲ more at SMOOTH *v.*

■ ***noun*** [usually pl.] a strip of cloth that is sewn in folds and is used to decorate a piece of clothing at the neck or wrists（領口、袖口等的）褶飾，花邊，荷葉邊 **SYN** **frill**

ruf·fled /ˈrʌfld/ *adj.* decorated with ruffles 有褶飾邊的 **SYN** **frilled**： *a ruffled blouse* 鑲着皺襇的女式襯衫

rug /rʌg/ *noun* **1** a piece of thick material like a small carpet that is used for covering or decorating part of a floor 小地毯；墊子： *a hearth rug* (= in front of a FIREPLACE) 壁爐前的小地毯 ➲ VISUAL VOCAB pages V21, V23 **2** (*BrE*) a piece of thick warm material, like a BLANKET, that is used for wrapping around your legs to keep warm（蓋腿的）厚毯子 **3** (*informal, especially NAmE*) = TOUPEE **IDM** see PULL *v.*, SWEEP *v.*

rugby /ˈrʌgbi/ (sometimes **Rugby**) (also ˌ**rugby ˈfoot·ball**) *noun* [U] a game played by two teams of 13 or 15 players, using an OVAL ball which may be kicked or carried. Teams try to put the ball over the other team's line. 橄欖球運動 ➲ VISUAL VOCAB page V44 **ORIGIN** Named after Rugby school, where the game was first played. 以第一次開展橄欖球運動的拉格比學校命名。

ˌ**Rugby ˈLeague** *noun* [U] a form of rugby, with 13 players in a team 聯盟橄欖球（每隊 13 人）

ˌ**Rugby ˈUnion** (also *informal* **rug·ger** especially in *BrE*) *noun* [U] a form of rugby, with 15 players in a team 聯合會橄欖球（每隊 15 人）

rug·ged /ˈrʌgɪd/ *adj.* **1** (of the landscape 地形) not level or smooth and having rocks rather than plants or trees 崎嶇的；凹凸不平的；多岩石的： *rugged cliffs* 岩石突兀的懸崖絕壁 ◇ *They admired the rugged beauty of the coastline.* 他們對海岸線上岩石密佈的美景讚歎不已。**2** [usually before noun] (*approving*) (of a man's face 男人的臉) having strong, attractive features 強健而富有魅力的；粗獷的 **3** [usually before noun] (of a person 人) determined to succeed in a difficult situation, even if this means using force or upsetting other people 堅強的；堅毅的： *a rugged individualist* 堅定的個人主義者 **4** (of equipment, clothing, etc. 設備、衣服等) strong and designed to be used in difficult conditions 結實的；耐用的： *A less rugged vehicle would never have made the trip.* 要不是這車結實，根本走不完這段路程。◇ *rugged outdoor clothing* 結實耐穿的戶外服裝 ▸ **rug·ged·ly** *adv.*： *ruggedly handsome* 粗獷英俊 **rug·ged·ness** *noun* [U]

rug·ger /ˈrʌgə(r)/ *noun* [U] (*informal, especially BrE*) = RUGBY UNION

ˈ**rugger-bugger** *noun* (*BrE, informal*) an enthusiastic player or supporter of RUGBY, especially one who is noisy and aggressive 粗野狂熱的橄欖球員（或球迷）

ˈ**rug rat** *noun* (*NAmE, informal*) a child 小孩

ruin 🔑 /ˈruːɪn/ *verb, noun*

■ ***verb*** **1** 🔑 **~ sth** to damage sth so badly that it loses all its value, pleasure, etc.; to spoil sth 毀壞；破壞；糟蹋 **SYN** **wreck**： *The bad weather ruined our trip.* 天氣惡劣，破壞了我們的旅行。◇ *That one mistake ruined his chances of getting the job.* 正是那個錯誤斷送了他得到那份工作的機會。◇ *My new shoes* ***got ruined*** *in the mud.*

R

我的新鞋被泥漿給糟蹋了。**2** 🔑 **~ sb/sth** to make sb/sth lose all their money, their position, etc. 使破產（或失去地位等）；毀滅：*If she loses the court case it will ruin her.* 如果敗訴，她就完了。◇ *The country was ruined by the war.* 這個國家因戰爭而遭到嚴重破壞。

■ **noun 1** 🔑 [U] the state or process of being destroyed or severely damaged 毀壞；破壞；毀滅：*A large number of churches* ***fell into ruin*** *after the revolution.* 革命過後，許多教堂都毀了。**2** 🔑 [U] the fact of having no money, of having lost your job, position, etc. 破產；一無所有；失去工作（或地位等）：*The divorce ultimately led to his ruin.* 離婚最終使得他一貧如洗。◇ *The bank stepped in to save the company from* ***financial ruin***. 銀行的介入使這家公司免於破產。**3** [sing.] something that causes a person, company, etc. to lose all their money, job, position, etc. 破產（或丟掉工作等）的根源；禍根 SYN **downfall**：*Gambling was his ruin.* 賭博毀了他。**4** 🔑 [C] (also **ruins** [pl.]) the parts of a building that remain after it has been destroyed or severely damaged 殘垣斷壁；廢墟：*The old mill is now little more than a ruin.* 老磨坊現在只剩下一點殘垣斷壁了。◇ *We visited the ruins of a Norman castle.* 我們參觀了一座諾曼式城堡的遺跡。◇ (*figurative*) *He was determined to build a new life out of the ruins of his career.* 他決心從事業失敗中爬起來，重新開始新的生活。

IDM **in 'ruins** destroyed or severely damaged 毀壞；嚴重受損；破敗不堪：*Years of fighting have left the area in ruins.* 經年的戰事已經使得這個地區滿目瘡痍。◇ *The scandal left his reputation in ruins.* 這件醜聞使他身敗名裂。➲ more at RACK *n.*

ruin·ation /ˌruːɪˈneɪʃn/ *noun* [U] (*formal*) the process of destroying sth/sb or being destroyed 毀滅；毀壞 SYN **destruction**：*Urban development has led to the ruination of vast areas of countryside.* 城市發展導致大片的鄉村遭到毀壞。

ru·ined 🔑 /ˈruːɪnd/ *adj.* [only before noun] (of a building, town, etc. 建築、城鎮等) destroyed or severely damaged so that only parts remain 毀壞的；嚴重受損的：*a ruined castle* 破爛不堪的城堡

ruin·ous /ˈruːɪnəs/ *adj.* (*formal*) **1** costing a lot of money and more than you can afford 耗資巨大的；無法承擔的：*ruinous legal fees* 巨額法律費用 **2** causing serious problems or damage 破壞性的；導致嚴重問題的；災難性的 SYN **devastating**：*The decision was to prove ruinous.* 後來證明這個決定造成了極大的損害。**3** (*formal*) (of a town, building, etc. 城鎮、建築等) destroyed or severely damaged 破敗的；嚴重受損的；已成廢墟的：*a ruinous chapel* 已成廢墟的小教堂 ◇ *The buildings were in a ruinous state.* 這些建築破爛不堪。▸ **ruin·ous·ly** *adv.*：*ruinously expensive* 貴得無法承受

R

rule 🔑 /ruːl/ *noun, verb*

■ **noun**

▸ **OF ACTIVITY/GAME** 活動；遊戲 **1** 🔑 [C] a statement of what may, must or must not be done in a particular situation or when playing a game 規則；規章；條例：*to* ***follow/obey/observe the rules*** 遵循／服從／遵守規則 ◇ *It's against all* ***rules and regulations***. 這違背了所有的規章制度。◇ *to* ***break a rule*** (= not follow it) 違反規定 ◇ *This explains the rules under which the library operates.* 這份材料說明了圖書館的運作方式。◇ *Without* ***unwritten rules*** *civilized life would be impossible.* 沒有不成文的規章，就不會有文明生活。➲ see also GROUND RULE (1)

▸ **ADVICE** 建議 **2** 🔑 [C] a statement of what you are advised to do in a particular situation 建議；應做之事：*There are no* ***hard and fast rules*** *for planning healthy meals.* 在安排健康飲食方面，沒有什麼硬性規定。◇ *The first rule is to make eye contact with your interviewer.* 首先是眼睛要直視面試主持人。➲ see also GOLDEN RULE

▸ **HABIT/NORMALLY TRUE** 習慣；常規 **3** [C, usually sing.] a habit; the normal state of things; what is true in most cases 習慣；常規；慣常的做法：*He makes it a rule never to borrow money.* 他的規矩是從不向人借錢。◇ *I go to bed early* ***as a rule***. 我一貫睡得早。◇ *Cold winters here are* ***the exception rather than the rule*** (= are rare). 在這裏，嚴寒的冬天並不多見。◇ ***As a general rule*** *vegetable oils are better for you than animal fats.* 一般來說，植物油比動物脂肪對人較有好處。

▸ **OF SYSTEM** 體系 **4** 🔑 [C] a statement of what is possible according to a particular system, for example the grammar of a language 定律；規則：*the rules of grammar* 語法規則

▸ **GOVERNMENT/CONTROL** 統治；控制 **5** 🔑 [U] the government of a country or control of a group of people by a particular person, group or system 統治；管理；支配；控制：***under Communist/civilian/military, etc. rule*** 在共產黨、文官、軍人等統治之下 ◇ ***majority rule*** (= government by the political party that most people have voted for) 獲選票多數的政黨組成政府的原則 ◇ *The 1972 act imposed* ***direct rule*** *from Westminster.* * 1972 年的法案強制實行了英國中央政府的直接統治。➲ see also HOME RULE

▸ **MEASURING TOOL** 測量工具 **6** [C] a measuring instrument with a straight edge 尺；直尺 ➲ see also SLIDE RULE

IDM **bend/stretch the 'rules** to change the rules to suit a particular person or situation 根據具體情況改變規則；通融 **play by sb's (own) 'rules** if sb **plays by their own rules** or makes other people **play by their rules**, they set the conditions for doing business or having a relationship 按某人定的規矩行事 **play by the 'rules** to deal fairly and honestly with people 按規則玩遊戲；處事公正誠實；循規蹈矩 **the rules of the 'game** the standards of behaviour that most people accept or that actually operate in a particular area of life or business 遊戲規則；大家共同遵守的行為標準 **the rule of 'law** the condition in which all members of society, including its rulers, accept the authority of the law 法治 **a rule of 'thumb** a practical method of doing or measuring sth, usually based on past experience rather than on exact measurement 實用的估算方法，經驗工作法（常依據經驗而非準確測量）**work to 'rule** to follow the rules of your job in a very strict way in order to cause delay, as a form of protest against your employer or your working conditions 按章工作 ➲ see also WORK-TO-RULE ➲ more at EXCEPTION

■ **verb**

▸ **GOVERN/CONTROL** 統治；控制 **1** 🔑 [T, I] to control and have authority over a country, a group of people, etc. 控制；統治；支配：**~ sth** *At that time John ruled England.* 當時是約翰統治着英格蘭。◇ (*figurative*) *Eighty million years ago, dinosaurs ruled the earth.* 八千萬年前，地球是恐龍的天下。◇ **~ (over sb/sth)** *Charles I ruled for eleven years.* 查理一世統治了十一年。◇ *She once ruled over a vast empire.* 她曾統治過一個幅員遼闊的帝國。◇ (*figurative*) *After the revolution, anarchy ruled.* 革命以後，無政府主義大行其道。**2** 🔑 [T, often passive] **~ sth** (often *disapproving*) to be the main thing that influences and controls sb/sth 支配；控制；操縱：*The pursuit of money ruled his life.* 對金錢的追求支配着他的生活。◇ *We live in a society where we are ruled by the clock.* 我們生活在一個人人都圍着時間轉的社會。

▸ **GIVE OFFICIAL DECISION** 作出正式決定 **3** [I, T] to give an official decision about sth 決定；裁定；判決 SYN **pronounce**：**~ (on sth)** *The court will rule on the legality of the action.* 法庭將裁定此舉是否合法。◇ **~ against/in favour of sb/sth** *The judge ruled against/in favour of the plaintiff.* 法官判原告敗訴／勝訴。◇ **~ sb/sth + adj.** *The deal may be ruled illegal.* 這筆交易可能會被判定為非法。◇ **~ sb/sth to be/have sth** *The deal was ruled to be illegal.* 這筆交易被判定為非法。◇ **~ that …** *The court ruled that the women were unfairly dismissed.* 法院裁定這些婦女是被不公平地開除的。◇ **it is ruled that …** *It was ruled that the women had been unfairly dismissed.* 已經裁定這些婦女被開除是不公平的。

▸ **DRAW STRAIGHT LINE** 畫直線 **4** [T] **~ sth** to draw a straight line using sth that has a firm straight edge 用直尺等畫（線）；畫（直線）：*Rule a line at the end of every piece of work.* 在每一篇作品的末尾畫一條直線。

IDM **rule the 'roost** (*informal*) to be the most powerful member of a group 當頭頭；充當首領；主宰 **rule (sb/sth) with a rod of 'iron** to control a person or a group of people very severely 殘酷統治；嚴厲控制 ➲ more at COURT *n.*, DIVIDE *v.*, HEART

PHR V **ˌrule 'off | ˌrule sth↔'off** to separate sth from the next section of writing by drawing a line underneath it 畫線隔開 **ˌrule sb/sth↔ˈout 1** 🔑 **~** (**as sth**) to state that sth is not possible or that sb/sth is not suitable 把…排除在外；認為…不適合 **SYN exclude**：*Police have not ruled out the possibility that the man was murdered.* 警方尚未排除那個男子是被謀殺的可能性。◇ *The proposed solution was ruled out as too expensive.* 建議的解決方案被認為花錢太多而遭否決。 **2** to prevent sb from doing sth; to prevent sth from happening 阻止；防止…發生：*His age effectively ruled him out as a possible candidate.* 他的年歲使他根本不可能成為候選人。 **ˌrule sb ˈout of sth** [usually passive] (in sport 體育運動) to state that a player, runner, etc. will not be able to take part in a sporting event; to prevent a player from taking part 聲明某人不能參賽；阻止某人參賽：*He has been ruled out of the match with a knee injury.* 他因膝傷已經無緣參加這場比賽。

ˈrule book *noun* (usually **the rule book**) the set of rules that must be followed in a particular job, organization or game 規則（或規章）手冊

ruled /ruːld/ *adj.* **ruled** paper has lines printed across it （紙張）有橫格的，有平行線的

ruler 🔑 /ˈruːlə(r)/ *noun*
1 🔑 a person who rules or governs 統治者；支配者 **2** 🔑 a straight strip of wood, plastic or metal, marked in centimetres or inches, used for measuring or for drawing straight lines 直尺 ➲ **VISUAL VOCAB** page V70

rul·ing /ˈruːlɪŋ/ *noun, adj.*
■ ***noun*** **~** (**on sth**) an official decision made by sb in a position of authority, especially a judge 裁決；裁定；判決：*The court will make its ruling on the case next week.* 法庭下週將對本案作出裁決。
■ ***adj.*** [only before noun] having control over a particular group, country, etc. 統治的；支配的；佔統治地位的：*the ruling party* 執政黨

rum /rʌm/ *noun, adj.*
■ ***noun*** **1** [U, C] a strong alcoholic drink made from the juice of SUGAR CANE 朗姆酒（一種用甘蔗汁釀製的烈性酒） **2** [C] a glass of rum 一杯朗姆酒
■ ***adj.*** [usually before noun] (*old-fashioned, BrE, informal*) strange 奇特的；古怪的 **SYN odd, peculiar**

rumba (also **rhumba**) /ˈrʌmbə/ *noun* a fast dance originally from Cuba; a piece of music for this dance 倫巴舞（源自古巴的一種快步舞）；倫巴舞曲

rum·ble /ˈrʌmbl/ *verb, noun*
■ ***verb*** **1** [I] to make a long deep sound or series of sounds 發出持續而低沉的聲音；發出隆隆聲：*The machine rumbled as it started up.* 機器轟鳴着發動起來。◇ *thunder rumbling in the distance* 遠處隆隆的雷聲 ◇ *I'm so hungry my* ***stomach's rumbling***. 我餓得肚子咕咕叫了。 **2** [I] **+ adv./prep.** to move slowly and heavily, making a rumbling sound 轟鳴着緩慢行進：*tanks rumbling through the streets* 隆隆地駛過街道的坦克 **3** [T] **~ sb** (*BrE, informal*) to discover the truth about sb or what they are trying to hide 發現…的真相；看穿（陰謀）：*They knew they had been rumbled.* 他們知道自己已經被識破了。 **4** [I] (*NAmE, informal*) (of a GANG of young people 一夥年輕人) to fight against another GANG 打群架
PHR V **ˌrumble ˈon** (*especially BrE*) (of an argument, a disagreement, etc. 爭論、分歧等) to continue slowly and steadily for a long time 緩慢而長久地持續；無休止地繼續下去：*Discussions rumble on over the siting of the new airport.* 關於新機場的選址問題，討論起來沒完沒了。
■ ***noun*** **1** [U, C] **~** (**of sth**) a long deep sound or series of sounds 持續而低沉的聲音；隆隆聲：*the rumble of thunder* 隆隆的雷聲 ◇ *Inside, the noise of the traffic was reduced to a distant rumble.* 進到屋裏，車輛的聲音減弱了，就像是遠處的隆隆聲。◇ (*figurative*) *Although an agreement has been reached, rumbles of resentment can still be heard.* 儘管已經達成了協議，但怨憤不滿之聲仍時有所聞。 **2** [C] (*NAmE, informal*) a fight in the street between two or more GANGS (= groups of young people) 打群架

ˈrumble strip *noun* (*informal*) a series of raised strips across a road or along its edge that make a loud noise when a vehicle drives over them in order to warn the driver to go slower or that he or she is too close to the edge of the road 齒紋震動帶（路面的隆起帶，車輛經過時發出很大響聲，提醒司機減速或不要太靠近路邊）

rum·bling /ˈrʌmblɪŋ/ *noun* **1** (also used as an adjective 也用作形容詞) a long deep sound or series of sounds 低沉而持續的聲音：*the rumblings of thunder* 隆隆的雷聲 ◇ *a rumbling noise* 轟隆轟隆的聲音 ◇ (*figurative*) *the rumblings of discontent* 嘖有煩言 **2** [usually pl.] things that people are saying that may not be true 傳言；傳聞；謠傳 **SYN rumour**：*There are rumblings that the election may have to be postponed.* 有傳言說選舉也許不得不延期。

rum·bus·tious /rʌmˈbʌstʃəs/ (*especially BrE*) (*NAmE* usually **ram·bunc·tious**) *adj.* [usually before noun] (*informal*) full of energy in a cheerful and noisy way 吵嚷的；喧鬧的 **SYN boisterous**

ru·min·ant /ˈruːmɪnənt/ *noun* (*technical* 術語) any animal that brings back food from its stomach and chews it again. Cows and sheep are both ruminants. 反芻動物 ▸ **ru·min·ant** *adj.*：*ruminant animals* 反芻動物

ru·min·ate /ˈruːmɪneɪt/ *verb* [I, T] **~** (**on/over/about sth**) | **+ speech** (*formal*) to think deeply about sth 沉思；認真思考 **SYN ponder** ▸ **ru·min·ation** /ˌruːmɪˈneɪʃn/ *noun* [C, U]

ru·mina·tive /ˈruːmɪnətɪv; *NAmE* -neɪtɪv/ *adj.* (*formal*) tending to think deeply and carefully about things 沉思的；冥思苦想的 **SYN pensive, thoughtful**：*in a ruminative mood* 陷於沉思 ▸ **ru·mina·tive·ly** *adv.*

rum·mage /ˈrʌmɪdʒ/ *verb, noun*
■ ***verb*** [I] **+ adv./prep.** to move things around carelessly while searching for sth 翻尋；亂翻；搜尋：*She was rummaging around in her bag for her keys.* 她在自己的包裏翻來翻去找鑰匙。◇ *I rummaged through the contents of the box until I found the book I wanted.* 我把箱子都翻遍了才找到我要的書。
■ ***noun*** [sing.] the act of looking for sth among a group of other objects in a way that makes them untidy 翻尋；翻箱倒櫃的尋找；搜尋：*Have a rummage around in the drawer and see if you can find a pen.* 翻翻抽屜，看能不能找到一支鋼筆。

ˈrummage sale (*especially NAmE*) (*BrE* also **ˈjumble sale**) *noun* a sale of old or used clothes, etc. to make money for a church, school or other organization 舊雜物義賣（為教堂、學校或其他機構籌款）

rummy /ˈrʌmi/ *noun* [U] a simple card game in which players try to collect particular combinations of cards 拉米紙牌遊戲（玩者要盡可能找出某種組合的牌）

ru·mour 🔑 (*especially US* **rumor**) /ˈruːmə(r)/ *noun, verb*
■ ***noun*** 🔑 [C, U] a piece of information, or a story, that people talk about, but that may not be true 謠言；傳聞：*to* ***start/spread a rumour*** 製造／散佈謠言 ◇ **~** (**of sth**) *There are widespread rumours of job losses.* 到處謠傳要裁員。◇ **~** (**about sth**) *Some malicious rumours are circulating about his past.* 有人別有用心地散佈謠言，說他過去如何如何。◇ **~** (**that …**) *I heard a rumour that they are getting married.* 我聽到傳聞，說他們要結婚了。◇ *Many of the stories are based on rumour.* 這些說法很多都是道聽途說。◇ ***Rumour has it*** (= people say) *that he was murdered.* 有傳言說他被殺害了。
■ ***verb*** **be rumoured** to be reported as a rumour and possibly not true 謠傳；傳說：**it is rumoured that …** ***It's widely rumoured that*** *she's getting promoted.* 到處都在傳要提拔她了。◇ **~ to be/have sth** *He was rumoured to be involved in the crime.* 有傳言說他捲入了這樁罪行。 ▸ **ru·moured** *adj.* [only before noun]：*He denied his father's rumoured love affair.* 他否認他父親被謠傳的風流韻事。

rumour-monger (*especially US* **ru·mor·mon·ger**) /ˈruːmə mʌŋɡə(r); *NAmE* ˈruːmər/ *noun* a person who spreads rumours 散佈謠言者

rump /rʌmp/ *noun* **1** [C] the round area of flesh at the top of the back legs of an animal that has four legs （獸類的）臀部 **2** [U] (also **ˌrump ˈsteak** [C, U]) a piece of good quality meat cut from the rump of a cow

R

後腿肉牛排 **3** [C, usually sing.] (*humorous*) the part of the body that you sit on （人的）屁股蛋子 **SYN backside** **4** [sing.] (*BrE*) the small or unimportant part of a group or an organization that remains when most of its members have left （團體或組織的）無足輕重的殘留部份

rum·ple /ˈrʌmpl/ *verb* **~ sth** to make sth untidy or not smooth and neat 弄皺；弄亂： *She rumpled his hair playfully.* 她頑皮地弄亂他的頭髮。◇ *The bed was rumpled where he had slept.* 牀上他睡過的地方有皺痕。

rum·pus /ˈrʌmpəs/ *noun* [usually sing.] (*informal*) a lot of noise that is made especially by people who are complaining about sth 喧鬧；吵吵嚷嚷 **SYN commotion**： *to cause a rumpus* 引起騷動

ˈ**rumpus room** *noun* (*NAmE, AustralE, NZE*) a room in a house for playing games in, sometimes in the BASEMENT 娛樂室（有時設在地下室）

rumpy pumpy /ˌrʌmpi ˈpʌmpi/ *noun* [U] (*BrE, informal, humorous*) the physical activity of sex 性行為

run /rʌn/ *verb, noun*

■ **verb** (**running**, **ran** /ræn/, **run**)

▸ **MOVE FAST ON FOOT** 奔跑 **1** [I] to move using your legs, going faster than when you walk 跑；奔跑： *Can you run as fast as Mike?* 你能和邁克跑得一樣快嗎？◇ *They turned and ran when they saw us coming.* 他們看見我們過來，轉身就跑。◇ *She* **came running** *to meet us.* 她跑着來迎接我們。◇ *The dogs ran off as soon as we appeared.* 我們一露面狗就跑了。 **HELP** In spoken English **run** can be used with **and** plus another verb, instead of with **to** and the infinitive, especially to tell somebody to hurry and do something. 在英語口語中，run 可以和 and 加另一個動詞連用，而不和 to 加動詞不定式連用，尤用於叫某人趕快去做某事： *Run and get your swimsuits, kids.* ◇ *I ran and knocked on the nearest door.* **2** [T] **~ sth** to travel a particular distance by running 跑（某段距離）： *Who was the first person to run a mile in under four minutes?* 是誰第一個用了不到四分鐘跑完一英里？ ➲ see also MILE (4) **3** [I] (sometimes **go running**) to run as a sport 跑步；做跑步運動： *She used to run when she was at college.* 她上大學的時候經常跑步。◇ *I often go running before work.* 我常常在上班前跑步。

▸ **RACE** 賽跑比賽 **4** [I, T] to take part in a race 參加賽跑： **~ (in sth)** *He will be running in the 100 metres tonight.* 今晚他將參加 100 米賽跑。◇ *There are only five horses running in the first race.* 只有五匹馬參加第一場比賽。◇ **~ sth** *to run the marathon* 參加馬拉松比賽◇ *Holmes ran a fine race to take the gold medal.* 霍姆斯賽跑表現不錯，獲得了金牌。 ➲ see also RUNNER (1) **5** [T, often passive] **~ sth** to make a race take place 開始（比賽）；使（比賽）開始： *The Derby will be run in spite of the bad weather.* 儘管天氣惡劣，德比馬賽仍將舉行。

▸ **HURRY** 趕緊 **6** [I] **+ adv./prep.** to hurry from one place to another 迅速趕往；匆忙跑（到另一處）： *I've spent the whole day running around after the kids.* 我整天都跟在孩子們後面跑來跑去。 ➲ see also RAT RUN

▸ **MANAGE** 管理 **7** [T] **~ sth** to be in charge of a business, etc. 管理；經營： *to run a hotel/store/language school* 經營一家旅店／商店／語言學校◇ *He has no idea how to run a business.* 他絲毫不懂企業管理。◇ *Stop trying to* **run my life** (= organize it) *for me.* 別老想操縱我的生活。◇ *The shareholders want more say in how the company is run.* 股東們想要在公司的經營管理上擁有更多的發言權。◇ *a badly run company* 經營不善的公司◇ *state-run industries* 國家經營的行業 ➲ see also RUNNING *n.* (2)

▸ **PROVIDE** 提供 **8** [T] **~ sth** to make a service, course of study, etc. available to people 提供，開設（服務、課程等） **SYN organize**： *The college runs summer courses for foreign students.* 這所大學為外國學生開設暑期課程。

▸ **VEHICLE/MACHINE** 車輛；機器 **9** [T] **~ sth** (*BrE*) to own and use a vehicle or machine 擁有並使用（車輛或機器等）： *I can't afford to run a car on my salary.* 我的工資養不起汽車。 **10** [I, T] to operate or function; to make sth do this （使）運轉，運行；操作： *Stan had the chainsaw running.* 斯坦開動了鏈鋸。◇ (*figurative*) *Her life had always run smoothly before.* 她以前的生活一直很穩定。◇ **~ on sth** *Our van runs on* (= uses) *diesel.* 我們的貨車用的是柴油。◇ **~ sth** *Could you run the engine for a moment?* 你來操作一會兒發動機好嗎？

▸ **BUSES/TRAINS** 公共汽車；火車 **11** [I] (**+ adv./prep.**) to travel on a particular route （按某路線）行駛： *Buses to Oxford run every half-hour.* 到牛津的汽車每半個小時發一趟。◇ *All the trains* **are running late** (= are leaving later than planned). 所有的列車都晚點了。 **12** [T] **~ sth** (**+ adv./prep.**) to make buses, trains, etc. travel on a particular route 使（按某一路線）行駛；使運行： *They run extra trains during the rush hour.* 他們在交通高峰時段加開了列車。

▸ **DRIVE SB** 開車送某人 **13** [T] **~ sb + adv./prep.** (*informal*) to drive sb to a place in a car 開車送： *Shall I run you home?* 我開車送你回家好嗎？

▸ **MOVE SOMEWHERE** 移往某處 **14** [I] **+ adv./prep.** to move, especially quickly, in a particular direction （向某處）快速移動： *The car ran off the road into a ditch.* 汽車猛地開出路面，掉進溝裏。◇ *A shiver ran down my spine.* 我猛然感到脊背發涼。◇ *The sledge ran smoothly over the frozen snow.* 雪橇在結了冰的雪地上平穩地滑行。◇ *The old tramlines are still there but now no trams run on them.* 昔日的電車軌道還在，現在卻沒有電車在上面運行了。 **15** [T] **~ sth + adv./prep.** to move sth in a particular direction 移動（某物）： *She ran her fingers nervously through her hair.* 她緊張地用手指撥弄頭髮。◇ *I* **ran my eyes over** *the page.* 我匆匆地看了看這一頁。

▸ **LEAD/STRETCH** 引導；伸展 **16** [I, T] to lead or stretch from one place to another; to make sth do this （使）導向；引導；（使）伸展，延伸： **+ adv./prep.** *He had a scar running down his left cheek.* 他左臉上豎着一道傷疤。◇ *The road runs parallel to the river.* 這條路和這條河是平行的。◇ **~ sth + adv./prep.** *We ran a cable from the lights to the stage.* 我們從電燈那裏拉了一條電纜通到舞台。

▸ **CONTINUE FOR TIME** 持續 **17** [I] **~ (for sth)** to continue for a particular period of time without stopping 持續；延續： *Her last musical ran for six months on Broadway.* 她最後的音樂劇在百老匯連續上演了六個月。◇ *This debate will* **run and run!** 這場辯論會沒完沒了地繼續下去！ **18** [I] **~ (for sth)** to operate or be valid for a particular period of time （在特定時間內）起作用，有效： *The permit runs for three months.* 許可證的有效期為三個月。◇ *The lease on my house only has a year left to run.* 我房子的租期只剩下一年了。

▸ **HAPPEN** 發生 **19** [I] (usually used in the progressive tenses 通常用於進行時) to happen at the time mentioned （在某時間）發生： **+ adv./prep.** *Programmes are* **running** *a few minutes* **behind schedule** *this evening.* 今晚播出的節目比預定的時間晚了幾分鐘。◇ *The murderer was given three life sentences, to run concurrently.* 這個殺人犯被判處三項無期徒刑，同時執行。

▸ **GUNS, DRUGS, ETC.** 槍支、毒品等 **20** [T] **~ sth** (**+ adv./prep.**) to bring or take sth into a country illegally and secretly 走私；非法攜運；秘密攜帶 **SYN smuggle** ➲ see also RUNNER (2)

▸ **OF STORY/ARGUMENT** 報道；論點 **21** [I, T] to have particular words, contents, etc. 包含（某種詞語、內容等）： *Their argument ran something like this ...* 他們的論點大致是這樣的…◇ **+ speech** *'Ten shot dead by gunmen,' ran the newspaper headline.* 報紙的標題為"槍手擊斃十人"。

▸ **LIQUID** 液體 **22** [I] **+ adv./prep.** to flow 流淌；流動： *The tears ran down her cheeks.* 淚水順着她的臉淌下來。◇ *Water was running all over the bathroom floor.* 浴室裏水流滿地。 **23** [T] to make liquid flow 使（液體）流動： **~ sth (into sth)** *She ran hot water into the bucket.* 她把熱水注入桶裏。◇ *to* **run the hot tap** (= to turn it so that water flows from it) 擰開熱水龍頭◇ **~ sth for sb** *I'll run a bath for you.* 我去給你放洗澡水。◇ **~ sb sth** *I'll run you a bath.* 我去給你放洗澡水。 **24** [I] to send out a liquid 輸出，放出（液體）： *Who left the tap running?* 誰沒關水龍頭？◇ *Your nose is running* (= MUCUS is flowing from it). 你流鼻涕了。◇ *The smoke makes my eyes run.* 煙熏得我直流眼淚。 **25** [I] (usually used in the progressive tenses 通常用於進行時) **~ with sth** to be

R

covered with a liquid 被（液體）覆蓋；流滿：*His face was running with sweat.* 他滿臉是汗。◇ *The bathroom floor was running with water.* 浴室的地面上全是水。

▸ **OF COLOUR 顏色 26** [I] if the colour **runs** in a piece of clothing when it gets wet, it dissolves and may come out of the clothing into other things 掉色；褪色

▸ **MELT 熔化 27** [I] (of a solid substance 固體) to melt 熔化：*The wax began to run.* 蠟開始熔化了。➲ see also RUNNY

▸ **BE/BECOME 是；成為 28** [I] **+ adj.** to become different in a particular way, especially a bad way 變成，成為，變得（尤指不利的變化）：*The river* **ran dry** (= stopped flowing) *during the drought.* 這條河在乾旱期間斷流了。◇ *Supplies are* **running low**. 物資供應漸趨不足。◇ *We've* **run short** *of milk.* 我們牛奶不夠了。◇ *You've got your rivals* **running scared**. 你已經使對手感到恐懼了。 **29** [I] **~ at sth** to be at or near a particular level 達到，接近（某程度）：*Inflation was running at 26%.* 通貨膨脹達到了 26%。

▸ **OF NEWSPAPER/MAGAZINE 報章雜誌 30** [T] **~ sth** to print and publish an item or a story 發表；刊登：*On advice from their lawyers they decided not to run the story.* 根據他們的律師的建議，他們決定不刊載這篇報道。

▸ **A TEST/CHECK 測試；檢驗 31** [T] **~ a test/check (on sth)** to do a test/check on sth（對…）進行（測試或檢驗）：*The doctors decided to run some more tests on the blood samples.* 醫生決定對血液樣本再進行一些化驗。

▸ **IN ELECTION 選舉 32** [I] to be a candidate in an election for a political position, especially in the US（尤指在美國）參加競選：*Bush ran a second time in 2004.* * 2004 年，布什第二次參選。◇ **~ for sb/sth** *to run for president* 競選總統 ◇ **~ in sth** *to run in the election* 參加競選 ➲ compare STAND *v.* (16)

▸ **OF TIGHTS/STOCKINGS 褲襪；長襪 33** [I] (*NAmE*) if TIGHTS or STOCKINGS **run**, a long thin hole appears in them 脫針；脫絲；抽絲 SYN **ladder**

IDM Most idioms containing **run** are at the entries for the nouns and adjectives in the idioms, for example **run riot** is at **riot**. 大多數含 run 的習語，都可在該等習語中的名詞及形容詞相關詞條找到，如 run riot 在詞條 riot 下。 **come 'running** to be pleased to do what sb wants 趕緊做某人喜歡的事；急於應某人的要求：*She knew she had only to call and he would come running.* 她知道只要打個電話，他就會高高興興地照辦。 **'run for it** (often used in orders 常用於命令) to run in order to escape from sb/sth 逃跑 **,up and 'running** working fully and correctly 全面而準確地運行：*It will be a lot easier when we have the database up and running.* 等我們把數據庫弄好以後，就省事多了。➲ more at CLOSE² *adv.*, HIT *v.*

PHR V **'run across sb/sth** to meet sb or find sth by chance 偶然遇見（或看到）

,run 'after sb (*informal*) to try to have a romantic or sexual relationship with sb 追求 SYN **pursue**：*He's always running after younger women.* 他老是追年輕女子。 **,run 'after sb/sth** to run to try to catch sb/sth 追逐；追趕 SYN **pursue**

,run a'long (*old-fashioned, informal*) used in orders to tell sb, especially a child, to go away（尤用以命令兒童）走開

,run a'round with sb (*NAmE* also **'run with sb**) (usually *disapproving*) to spend a lot of time with sb 與（某人）廝混；互相往來：*She's always running around with older men.* 她老是跟年紀較大的男人來往。

'run at sb [no passive] to run towards sb to attack or as if to attack them 向某人衝去：*He ran at me with a knife.* 他拿着刀朝我衝過來。

,run a'way (from sb/...) to leave sb/a place suddenly; to escape from sb/a place 突然離開；逃離：*He* **ran away from home** *at the age of thirteen.* 他十三歲時離家出走。◇ *Looking at all the accusing faces, she felt a sudden urge to run away.* 看着一張張臉上那責備的神情，她突然想趕快溜走。➲ related noun RUNAWAY **,run a'way from sth** to try to avoid sth because you are shy, lack confidence, etc. 避開；躲避；迴避：*You can't just run away from the situation.* 你不能就這麼迴避了事。

,run a'way with you if a feeling **runs away with you**, it gets out of your control 失去控制：*Her imagination tends to run away with her.* 她動輒想入非非。 **,run a'way/'off with sb** | **,run a'way/'off (together)** to leave home, your husband, wife, etc. in order to have a relationship with another person 與某人私奔：*She ran away with her boss.* 她與老闆私奔了。◇ *She and her boss ran away together.* 她和老闆一起私奔了。 **,run a'way with sth 1** to win sth clearly or easily 輕而易舉地贏得 **2** to believe sth that is not true 相信（不真實的東西）；誤以為：*I don't want you to* **run away with the impression** *that all I do is have meetings all day.* 我不想讓你誤以為我整天的工作就是開會。

,run back 'over sth to discuss or consider sth again 再次討論；重新考慮 SYN **review**：*I'll run back over the procedure once again.* 我將重新考慮這個程序。

,run sth 'by/'past sb (*informal*) to show sb sth or tell sb about an idea in order to see their reaction to it 給某人看，說給某人聽（以觀察其反應）

,run 'down 1 to lose power or stop working 耗盡能量；停止工作：*The battery has run down.* 電池沒電了。 **2** to gradually stop functioning or become smaller in size or number 逐漸失去作用；萎縮；衰減：*British manufacturing industry has been running down for years.* 英國的製造業多年來一直在萎縮。➲ related noun RUNDOWN (1) **,run sth↔'down 1** to make sth lose power or stop working 使耗盡能量；使停止工作：*If you leave your headlights on you'll soon run down the battery.* 如果你讓車頭燈一直亮着，很快就會把電池耗盡。 **2** to make sth gradually stop functioning or become smaller in size or number 使逐漸失去作用；使萎縮；使衰減：*The company is running down its sales force.* 公司正在削減銷售人員。➲ related noun RUNDOWN (1)

,run sb/sth↔'down 1 (of a vehicle or its driver 車輛或司機) to hit sb/sth and knock them/it to the ground 把…撞倒 **2** to criticize sb/sth in an unkind way 惡意批評；說…的壞話；貶低：*He's always running her down in front of other people.* 他總是在別人面前說她的壞話。 **3** to find sb/sth after a search（經過搜尋後）找到

,run sb↔'in (*old-fashioned, informal*) to arrest sb and take them to a police station 把某人扭送警察局 **,run sth↔'in** (*BrE*) (in the past) to prepare the engine of a new car for normal use by driving slowly and carefully（舊時）磨合運轉，磨合駕駛：(*figurative*) *Whatever system you choose, it must be run in properly.* 不管你選擇什麼樣的體系，都必須經過適當的磨合。

,run 'into sb (*informal*) to meet sb by chance 偶然遇見，碰到（某人）：*Guess who I ran into today!* 猜猜我今天碰見誰了！ **'run into sth 1** to enter an area of bad weather while travelling 途中遭遇（惡劣天氣）：*We ran into thick fog on the way home.* 在回家的路上，我們遇上了大霧。 **2** to experience difficulties, etc. 遇到（困難等）：*Be careful not to run into debt.* 小心不要背上債務。◇ *to* **run into danger/trouble/difficulties** 遭遇危險／麻煩／困難 **3** to reach a particular level or amount 達到（某種水平或數量）：*Her income runs into six figures* (= is more than £100 000, $100 000, etc.). 她的收入達到了六位數。 **'run into sb/sth** to crash into sb/sth 撞上：*The bus went out of control and ran into a line of people.* 公共汽車失控，撞上了一排人。 **'run sth into sb/sth** to make a vehicle crash into sb/sth 開（車）撞上：*He ran his car into a tree.* 他開車撞上了一棵樹。

,run 'off (*BrE*) (of a liquid 液體) to flow out of a container（從容器中）溢出，流出 **,run sth↔'off 1** to copy sth on a machine（用機器）複印，複製：*Could you run off twenty copies of the agenda?* 你給我複印二十份會議議程好嗎？ **2** to cause a race to be run 舉行，進行（賽跑等）：*The heats of the 200 metres will be run off tomorrow.* * 200 米預賽將在明天舉行。 **3** to make a liquid flow out of a container 使溢出；使流出 **,run 'off with sb** | **,run 'off (together)** = RUN AWAY WITH SB **,run 'off with sth** to steal sth and take it away 偷走：*The treasurer had run off with the club's funds.* 財務主管盜走了俱樂部的資金。

,run 'on to continue without stopping; to continue longer than is necessary or expected 持續；連續不斷；拖延：*The meeting will finish promptly—I don't want it to run on.* 會議必須按時結束，我不想拖延下去。 **'run on sth** [no passive] if your thoughts, a discussion, etc. **run on** a subject, you think or talk a lot about that subject 以…為主題（或中心）；圍繞

R

ˌrun ˈout 1 if a supply of sth **runs out**, it is used up or finished 用完；耗盡：*Time is running out for the trapped miners.* 被困礦工的時間不多了。 **2** if an agreement or a document **runs out**, it becomes no longer valid 過期；失效 SYN **expire** **ˌrun ˈout (of sth)** to use up or finish a supply of sth 用完，耗盡（供應品）：*We ran out of fuel.* 我們的燃料用光了。◇ *Could I have a cigarette? I seem to have run out.* 給我一支煙可以嗎？我的煙好像抽完了。 **ˌrun ˈout on sb** (*informal*) to leave sb that you live with, especially when they need your help 棄某人而去；拋棄某人 **ˌrun sb↔ˈout** [often passive] (in CRICKET 板球) to make a player stop BATTING by hitting the WICKET with the ball before the player has completed his or her run 將（正在跑的擊球員）截殺出局

ˌrun ˈover if a container or its contents **run over**, the contents come over the edge of the container 溢出 SYN **overflow** **ˌrun sb/sth↔ˈover** (of a vehicle or its driver 車輛或司機) to knock a person or an animal down and drive over their body or a part of it 撞倒並碾軋：*Two children were run over and killed.* 兩名兒童被軋死了。 **ˌrun ˈover sth** to read through or practise sth quickly 快速閱讀（或練習）：*She ran over her notes before giving the lecture.* 講課之前，她翻閱了一下自己的講稿。

ˌrun sth ˈpast sb = RUN STH BY/PAST SB：*Run that past me again.* 把那件事再說給我聽聽。

ˌrun sb↔ˈthrough (*literary*) to kill sb by sticking a knife, SWORD, etc. through them（用刀、劍等）刺死 **ˌrun ˈthrough sth 1** to discuss, repeat or read sth quickly 匆匆討論；快速閱讀；很快地重複：*He ran through the names on the list.* 他快速瀏覽了一下名單。◇ *Could we run through your proposals once again?* 我們再簡要討論一下你的建議，好嗎？ **2** [no passive] to pass quickly through sth 快速穿越；迅速傳遍：*An angry murmur ran through the crowd.* 憤怒的抱怨聲在人群中迅速蔓延。◇ *Thoughts of revenge kept running through his mind.* 報復的念頭不斷在他的腦子裏閃過。 **3** [no passive] to be present in every part of sth 遍佈：*A deep melancholy runs through her poetry.* 她的詩充滿了深深的感傷。 **4** to perform, act or practise sth 表演；扮演；排練：*Can we run through Scene 3 again, please?* 請大家再來排練一下第 3 場好嗎？ ➲ related noun RUN-THROUGH **5** to use up or spend money carelessly 揮霍：*She ran through the entire amount within two years.* 她不到兩年就把所有的錢揮霍光了。

ˈrun to sth 1 to be of a particular size or amount 達到，有（某一規模或數量）：*The book runs to nearly 800 pages.* 這本書有近 800 頁。 **2** (*especially BrE*) if you or your money will **not run to sth**, you do not have enough money for sth 有足夠…的錢；足夠…之用：*Our funds won't run to a trip abroad this year.* 今年我們沒有足夠的錢去國外旅行。

ˌrun sth↔ˈup 1 to allow a bill, debt, etc. to reach a large total 積欠（賬款、債務等）；累積 SYN **accumulate**：*How had he managed to run up so many debts?* 他怎麼欠了這麼多債？ **2** to make a piece of clothing quickly, especially by sewing 趕製（衣服，尤指縫紉）：*to run up a blouse* 趕製一件女式襯衫 **3** to raise sth, especially a flag 豎起，升起（旗幟等） **ˌrun ˈup against sth** to experience a difficulty 遭遇（困難）：*The government is running up against considerable opposition to its tax reforms.* 政府的稅務改革遇到了相當大的阻力。

ˈrun with sb = RUN AWAY/OFF WITH SB **ˈrun with sth** to accept or start to use a particular idea or method 採納（某種想法、方法等）：*OK, let's run with Jan's suggestion.* 好，咱們就照簡的建議辦吧。

■ ***noun***

▸ **ON FOOT 徒步 1** [C] an act of running; a period of time spent running or the distance that sb runs 跑；跑步；跑步的時間（或距離）：*I go for a run every morning.* 我每天早晨都去跑步。◇ *a five-mile run* 跑上五英里 ◇ *Catching sight of her he* ***broke into a run*** (= started running). 他一看見她就跑了起來。◇ *I decided* ***to make a run for it*** (= to escape by running). 我決定逃跑。◇ *She took the stairs* ***at a run.*** 她跑着上了樓梯。 ➲ see also FUN RUN

▸ **TRIP 旅程 2** [C] a trip by car, plane, boat, etc., especially a short one or one that is made regularly（尤指短程或定期，乘交通工具的）旅程，航程：*They took the car out for a run.* 他們開車出去兜風。 ➲ see also MILK RUN, RAT RUN, SCHOOL RUN

▸ **OF SUCCESS/FAILURE 成功；失敗 3** [C] a period of sth good or bad happening; a series of successes or failures 一段（幸運或倒霉的）時光；一系列（成功或失敗） SYN **spell**：*a run of good/bad luck* 一連串好運／厄運 ◇ *Liverpool lost to Leeds, ending an unbeaten run of 18 games.* 利物浦隊輸給了利茲隊，結束了連續 18 場不敗的紀錄。

▸ **OF PLAY/MOVIE 戲劇；電影 4** [C] a series of performances of a play or film/movie 連續上演（或放映）：*The show had a record-breaking run in the London theatre.* 這齣戲在倫敦劇院連續上演，打破了演出紀錄。

▸ **OF PRODUCT 產品 5** [C] the amount of a product that a company decides to make at one time 額定產量：*The first* ***print run*** *of 6 000 copies sold out.* 首印 6 000 冊已全部售空。

▸ **MONEY 錢 6** [C, usually sing.] **~ on the dollar, pound, etc.** a situation when many people sell dollars, etc. and the value of the money falls 拋售（美元、英鎊等） **7** [C, usually sing.] **~ on a bank** a situation when many people suddenly want to take their money out of a bank （到銀行）擠提，擠兌

▸ **SUDDEN DEMAND 急需 8** [C, usually sing.] **~ on sth** a situation when many people suddenly want to buy sth 爭購；搶購：*a run on the band's latest CD* 搶購這支樂隊最新的激光唱片

▸ **WAY THINGS HAPPEN 態勢 9** [sing.] **the ~ of sth** the way things usually happen; the way things seem to be happening on a particular occasion 態勢；狀況；趨勢；動向：*In* ***the normal run of things*** *the only exercise he gets is climbing in and out of taxis.* 正常情況下，他的唯一運動就是上下出租車。◇ (*BrE*) *Wise scored in the 15th minute* ***against the run of play*** (= although the other team had seemed more likely to score). 懷斯在比賽進行到 15 分鐘的時候出人意料地得分。

▸ **IN SPORTS 體育運動 10** [C] a sloping track used in SKIING and some other sports（滑雪或其他運動項目中的）坡道，滑道：*a ski/toboggan, etc. run* 滑雪道、雪橇滑道等 **11** [C] a point scored in the game of CRICKET or BASEBALL（板球或棒球中的）得分：*Our team won by four runs.* 我們隊以四分的優勢取勝。 ➲ see also HOME RUN

▸ **IN ELECTION 選舉 12** [sing.] (*NAmE*) an act of trying to get elected to public office 競選：*He made an unsuccessful run for governor in 2008.* * 2008 年他競選州長失敗。

▸ **FOR ANIMALS/BIRDS 畜；禽 13** [C] (often in compounds 常構成複合詞) a confined area in which animals or birds are kept as pets or on a farm 飼養場：*a chicken run* 養雞場

▸ **IN MUSIC 音樂 14** [C] a series of notes sung or played quickly up or down the SCALE （順着音階的）急奏，急唱

▸ **IN CARD GAMES 紙牌遊戲 15** [C] a series of cards held by one player 順子

▸ **IN TIGHTS/STOCKINGS 褲襪；長襪 16** [C] (*NAmE*) = LADDER *n.* (3)

▸ **ILLNESS 疾病 17 the runs** [pl.] (*informal*) = DIARRHOEA ➲ see also DRY RUN, DUMMY RUN, TRIAL RUN

IDM **the common, general, ordinary, usual run (of sth)** the average type of sth 普通類型：*He was very different from the general run of movie stars.* 他和一般的電影明星迥然不同。 **give sb/get/have the ˈrun of sth** to give sb/get/have permission to make full use of sth 允許某人充分使用；獲准充分使用：*Her dogs have the run of the house.* 她的狗可以在家裏自由活動。 **give sb a (good) run for their ˈmoney** to make sb try very hard, using all their skill and effort, in order to beat you in a game or competition 不讓…輕易取勝；與…進行激烈競爭 **on the ˈrun 1** trying to avoid being captured 躲避：*He's on the run from the police.* 他在躲避警方的追捕。 **2** (*informal*) continuously active and moving around 忙碌；不停地奔波：*I've been on the run all day and I'm exhausted.* 我忙了一整天，累極了。◇ *Here are some quick recipes for when you're eating on the run*

(= in a hurry). 這是一些供匆忙用餐時用的快餐食譜。 ➲ more at LONG *adj.*, SHORT *adj.*

run·about /ˈrʌnəbaʊt/ *noun* (*BrE, informal*) a small car, especially one used for short journeys（用於短途旅行的）小型汽車

run·around /ˈrʌnəraʊnd/ *noun*
IDM **give sb the ˈrunaround** (*informal*) to treat sb badly by not telling them the truth, or by not giving them the help or the information they need, and sending them somewhere else 隱瞞；搪塞；草草打發

run·away /ˈrʌnəweɪ/ *adj., noun*
■ ***adj.*** [only before noun] **1** (of a person 人) having left without telling anyone 逃跑的；出走的：*runaway children* 離家出走的兒童 **2** (of an animal or a vehicle 動物或車輛等) not under the control of its owner, rider or driver 失控的：*a runaway horse/car* 脫繮的馬；失控的汽車 **3** happening very easily or quickly, and not able to be controlled 輕易的；迅速的；難以控制的：*a runaway winner/victory* 輕易獲勝的人；輕而易舉的勝利 ◇ *the **runaway success** of her first play* 她第一齣戲的大獲成功 ◇ *runaway inflation* 來勢迅猛的通貨膨脹
■ ***noun*** a person who has suddenly left or escaped from sb/sth, especially a child who has left home without telling anyone 逃跑者，逃避者，離家出走者（尤指兒童）：*teenage runaways living on the streets* 流落街頭的離家出走的青少年

run·down /ˈrʌndaʊn/ *noun* [usually sing.] **1 ~ (in/of sth)** (*BrE*) a reduction in the amount, size or activity of sth, especially a business（尤指商業）削減，緊縮：*a rundown of transport services* 交通運輸的縮減 **2 ~ (on/of sth)** an explanation or a description of sth 解釋；描述：*I can give you a brief rundown on each of the applicants.* 我可以給你簡單介紹一下每名申請人的情況。

ˌrun-ˈdown *adj.* **1** (of a building or place 建築物或地方) in very bad condition; that has not been taken care of 破敗的；失修的 **SYN** **neglected**：*run-down inner-city areas* 破敗不堪的內城區 **2** (of a business, etc. 商業機構等) not as busy or as active as it used to be 衰敗的；不景氣的：*run-down transport services* 不景氣的交通運輸業 **3** [not before noun] (of a person 人) tired or slightly ill/sick, especially from working hard 疲憊；略感不適：*to be run-down* 疲憊不堪

rune /ruːn/ *noun* **1** one of the letters in an alphabet that people in northern Europe used in ancient times and cut into wood or stone 如尼字母（屬於北歐古文字體系）**2** a symbol that has a mysterious or magic meaning 神秘的記號；有魔力的符號 ▸ **runic** *adj.*：*runic inscriptions* 用古代北歐文字刻的碑文

rung /rʌŋ/ *noun* one of the bars that forms a step in a LADDER（梯子的）橫檔，梯級：*He put his foot on the bottom rung to keep the ladder steady.* 他用腳踩住最底下的橫檔穩住梯子。◇ (*figurative*) *to get a foot on the bottom rung of the career ladder* 從事業階梯的最低等級開始 ◇ *She was a few rungs above him on the social ladder.* 她的社會地位比他高了好幾等。 ➲ VISUAL VOCAB page V20 ➲ see also RING[2] *v.*

ˈrun-in *noun* **1 ~ (with sb)** (*informal*) an argument or a fight 爭論；爭吵；衝突：*The fiery player has had numerous run-ins with referees.* 這名脾氣暴躁的隊員曾和裁判員發生過無數次爭吵。**2 ~ (to sth)** (*BrE*) = RUN-UP (1)

run·nel /ˈrʌnl/ *noun* (*formal* or *literary*) a small stream or channel 小溪；小河；細流

run·ner /ˈrʌnə(r)/ *noun*
1 a person or an animal that runs, especially one taking part in a race 奔跑的人，奔跑的動物（尤指參加速度比賽者）：*a **long-distance/cross-country/marathon, etc. runner*** 長跑、越野賽跑、馬拉松等選手 ◇ *a list of runners* (= horses in a race) *and riders* 賽馬和騎手名單 ➲ see also FORERUNNER, FRONT RUNNER, ROADRUNNER **2** (especially in compounds 尤用於構成複合詞) a person who takes goods illegally into or out of a place 走私者；偷運者：*a drug runner* 毒品走私分子 ➲ see also GUNRUNNER **3** a strip of metal, plastic or wood that sth slides on or can move along on（金屬、塑料或木製的）條狀滑行裝置：*the runners of a sledge* 雪橇的滑板 **4** a plant STEM that grows along the ground and puts down roots to form a new plant 緣匐枝 **5** a long narrow piece of cloth or carpet on a piece of furniture or on the floor 長條飾布；長條地毯 **6** a person in a company or an organization whose job is to take messages, documents, etc. from one place to another 送信人；信差 **7** (*CanE*) a shoe that is used for running or doing other sport in 跑鞋；運動鞋
IDM **do a ˈrunner** (*BrE, informal*) to leave or run away from somewhere in a hurry, especially to avoid paying a bill or receiving a punishment 匆忙逃離；逃跑

ˌrunner ˈbean (also **ˌstring ˈbean**) *noun* (both *BrE*) a type of BEAN which is a long flat green POD growing on a climbing plant also called a runner bean. The pods are cut up, cooked and eaten as a vegetable. 紅花菜豆（植物）

ˌrunner-ˈup *noun* (*pl.* **runners-up**) a person or team that finishes second in a race or competition; a person or team that has not finished first but that wins a prize 第二名；亞軍；非冠軍的獲獎者：*Winner: Kay Hall. Runner-up: Chris Platts.* 冠軍：凱•霍爾。亞軍：克里斯•普拉茨。◇ *They finished runners-up behind Sweden.* 他們緊隨瑞典隊之後，獲得了第二名。◇ *The runners-up will all receive a £50 prize.* 沒有拿到冠軍的獲獎者都將得到 50 英鎊的獎金。

run·ning /ˈrʌnɪŋ/ *noun, adj.*
■ ***noun*** [U] **1** the action or sport of running 跑；跑步（運動）：*to **go running*** 去跑步 ◇ *running shoes* 跑鞋 **2** the activity of managing or operating sth 管理；操縱；操作：*the day-to-day running of a business* 企業的日常運營 ◇ *the **running costs** of a car* (= for example of fuel, repairs, insurance) 養車的費用 **3 -running** (in compounds 構成複合詞) the activity of bringing sth such as drugs, guns, etc. into a country secretly and illegally 走私；偷運：*drug-running* 毒品走私
IDM **in/out of the ˈrunning (for sth)** (*informal*) having some/no chance of succeeding or achieving sth 有（或沒有）成功的機會；能（或不能）獲得 **make the ˈrunning** (*BrE, informal*) to set the speed at which sth is done; to take the lead in doing sth 領跑；帶頭；做榜樣
■ ***adj.*** **1** used after a number and a noun such as 'year' 'day' or 'time', to say that sth has happened in the same way several times, without a change（置於數字和 year、day 或 time 等名詞後，表示同樣的事一再重複）連續：*She's won the championship three years running.* 她已連續三年獲得冠軍。◇ *It was the third day running that the train had been late.* 列車已經連續三天晚點了。◇ *No party has won an election four times running.* 沒有一個政黨在選舉中連續四次獲勝。 **2 running water** is water that is flowing somewhere or water that is supplied to a building and available to be used through taps/faucets（水）活的，流淌的，流動的：*I can hear the sound of running water.* 我聽到流水的聲音。◇ *a remote cottage without electricity or running water* 沒有電和自來水的偏僻村舍 **3** [only before noun] lasting a long time; continuous 持久的；連續不斷的 **SYN** **ongoing**：*For years he had fought a **running battle** with the authorities over the land.* 多年來，他為了那片土地同當局不斷抗爭。◇ *a running argument* 持久的爭論 ◇ *His old raincoat became a running joke* (= people kept laughing at it). 他那件舊雨衣一直被人取笑。 ➲ see also LONG-RUNNING **4 -running** (in compounds 構成複合詞) running or flowing in the way mentioned …地流動的：*a fast-running river* 湍急的河流
IDM **(go and) take a running ˈjump** (*old-fashioned, informal*) used to tell sb in a rude way to go away 滾開；走開 ➲ more at ORDER *n.*

ˈrunning back *noun* (in AMERICAN FOOTBALL 美式足球) an attacking player whose main job is to run forward carrying the ball（帶球進攻的）跑衛

ˌrunning ˈcommentary *noun* a continuous description of an event, especially a sporting event, that sb gives as it happens（尤指對賽事的）現場評述，實況報道：*to give a running commentary on the game* 現場報道比賽實況

ˈrunning dog *noun* **1** (*disapproving*) a person who follows a political system or set of beliefs without questioning them 走狗（盲目遵從政治體制或信仰的人） **2** a dog which has been bred to run, especially for racing or for pulling a SLEDGE across snow （尤指比賽或拉雪橇的）跑狗；拖橇犬

ˌrunning ˈhead *noun* (*technical* 術語) a title or word printed at the top of each page of a book （書的）頁首標題，眉題，天眉

ˈrunning mate *noun* [usually sing.] (*politics* 政) (in the US) a person who is chosen by the candidate in an election, especially that for president, to support them and to have the next highest political position if they win （美國）競選夥伴，（尤指）副總統候選人：*The presidential nominee was advised to choose a woman as a running mate.* 有人建議總統候選人找一位女性競選夥伴。

ˈrunning order *noun* [sing.] the order of the items in a television programme or a show; the order that members of a team will play in 播放順序；上場順序

ˌrunning reˈpairs *noun* [pl.] small things that you do to a piece of clothing, a vehicle, a machine, etc. to repair it or to keep it working 小修小補；修配

ˌrunning ˈsore *noun* a small area on the body that is infected and has liquid (called PUS) coming out of it 化膿處；膿瘡

ˈrunning time *noun* the amount of time that a film/movie, a journey, etc. lasts （電影）片長；（旅程等的）持續時間

ˌrunning ˈtotal *noun* the total number or amount of things, money, etc. that changes as you add each new item 流水式總計；流水賬總數

runny /ˈrʌni/ *adj.* (**run·nier**, **run·ni·est**) **1** (of your nose or eyes 鼻子或眼睛) producing a lot of liquid, for example when you have a cold 流鼻涕的；流眼淚的 **2** having more liquid than is usual; not solid 太稀的；水分過多的；軟的：*runny honey* 水分過多的蜂蜜 ◇ *Omelettes should be runny in the middle.* 煎蛋捲包餡應該是軟的。

ˈrun-off *noun* **1** [C] a second vote or competition that is held to find a winner because two people taking part in the first competition got the same result （對兩名得票相同者的）決勝投票；（比賽打平後的）附加賽 **2** [U, C] rain, water or other liquid that runs off land into streams and rivers （雨、水或其他液體的）地表徑流

ˌrun-of-the-ˈmill *adj.* (often *disapproving*) ordinary, with no special or interesting features 平凡的；普通的；乏味的

ˌrun-on ˈsentence *noun* two or more sentences or independent CLAUSES joined without the correct grammar 連寫句，串句（不按正確語法連接的兩個以上的句子或獨立從句）

ˈrun-out *noun* (in CRICKET 板球) a situation in which a player fails to complete a RUN before an opposing player hits the STUMPS with the ball, and so is OUT （擊球員的）被截殺出局

runt /rʌnt/ *noun* **1** the smallest, weakest animal of the young that are born from the same mother at the same time （一胎中）最弱小的動物：*the runt of the litter* 最弱小的幼崽 **2** (*informal, disapproving*) a rude way of referring to a small, weak or unimportant person 小矮個兒；小不點兒

ˈrun-through *noun* a practice for a performance of a play, show, etc. 排練；練習 SYN **rehearsal**

ˈrun-time *noun* [U, C] (*computing* 計) **1** the amount of time that a program takes to perform a task （程序所需的）運行時間 **2** the time when a program is performing a task （程序應用中的）運行時，運行時間

ˈrun-up *noun* (*BrE*) **1** (also *less frequent* **ˈrun-in**) **~ (to sth)** a period of time leading up to an important event; the preparation for this （重要事情的）前期；準備階段；準備：*an increase in spending in the run-up to Christmas* 聖誕節前花費的增加 ◇ *during the run-up to the election* 在選舉前的準備階段 **2** the act of running or the distance you run, to gain speed before you jump a long distance, throw a ball, etc. 助跑；助跑距離

run·way /ˈrʌnweɪ/ *noun* **1** a long narrow strip of ground with a hard surface that an aircraft takes off from and lands on 飛機跑道 ➲ COLLOCATIONS at TRAVEL **2** (*NAmE*) = CATWALK (1)

rupee /ruːˈpiː/ *noun* the unit of money in India, Pakistan and some other countries 盧比（印度、巴基斯坦等國的貨幣單位）

rup·ture /ˈrʌptʃə(r)/ *noun, verb*

■ **noun** [C, U] **1** (*medical* 醫) an injury in which sth inside the body breaks apart or bursts （體內組織等的）斷裂，破裂：*the rupture of a blood vessel* 血管破裂 **2** a situation when sth breaks or bursts 斷裂；爆裂：*ruptures of oil and water pipelines* 石油和輸水管道的爆裂 **3** (*informal*) a HERNIA of the ABDOMEN 疝氣：*I nearly gave myself a rupture lifting that pile of books.* 提那一大堆書差點兒讓我得了疝氣。 **4** (*formal*) the ending of agreement or of good relations between people, countries, etc. （關係的）破裂，決裂；絕交：*a rupture in relations between the two countries* 兩國關係的破裂 ◇ *Nothing could heal the rupture with his father.* 沒有什麼可以彌合他和父親之間的裂痕。

■ **verb** **1** [T, I] **~ (sth/yourself)** (*medical* 醫) to burst or break apart sth inside the body; to be broken or burst apart （使體內組織等）斷裂，裂開，破裂：*a ruptured appendix* 闌尾穿孔 ◇ *He ruptured himself* (= got a HERNIA) *trying to lift the piano.* 他試着搬動鋼琴，發了疝氣。 **2** [T, I] **~ (sth)** (*formal*) to make sth such as a container or a pipe break or burst; to be broken or burst （使容器或管道等）斷裂，破裂：*The impact ruptured both fuel tanks.* 衝撞使兩個燃料箱都爆裂了。 ◇ *A pipe ruptured, leaking water all over the house.* 一根水管斷裂，漏了滿屋子的水。 **3** [T] **~ sth** (*formal*) to make an agreement or good relations between people or countries end 使（友好關係）破裂；使絕交；毀掉（協議）：*the risk of rupturing North-South relations* 使南北關係破裂的危險

rural 0→ /ˈrʊərəl; *NAmE* ˈrʊrəl/ *adj.* [usually before noun] connected with or like the countryside 鄉村的；農村的；似農村的：*rural areas* 農村地區 ◇ *a rural economy* 農村經濟 ◇ *rural America* 美國鄉村 ◇ *a rural way of life* 鄉村的生活方式 ➲ compare URBAN (1)

ˌrural ˈdean *noun* = DEAN (2)

ˈrural route *noun* (*NAmE*) a route along which mail is delivered in rural areas 鄉村郵遞路線

Ruri·ta·nian /ˌrʊərɪˈteɪniən; *NAmE* ˌrʊrəˈt-/ *adj.* (especially of stories 尤指小說) full of romantic adventure 充滿浪漫冒險的；浪漫國的 ORIGIN From **Ruritania**, the name of an imaginary country in central Europe in stories by Anthony Hope. 源自安東尼 • 霍普所著小說中的虛構中歐國家魯里坦尼亞王國。

ruse /ruːz/ *noun* a way of doing sth or of getting sth by cheating sb 詭計；騙術 SYN **trick**

rush 0→ /rʌʃ/ *verb, noun*

■ **verb**

▸ **MOVE FAST** 快速移動 **1** 0→ [I, T] to move or to do sth with great speed, often too fast 迅速移動；急促：*We've got plenty of time; there's no need to rush.* 我們還有很多時間，用不着太急促。 ◇ *the sound of rushing water* 湍急的水聲 ◇ **+ adv./prep.** *Don't rush off, I haven't finished.* 別急着走哇，我還沒說完呢。 ◇ *I've been rushing around all day trying to get everything done.* 我一整天都四下忙活，想把所有的事都做完。 ◇ *People rushed to buy shares in the company.* 人們爭着搶購公司的股票。 ◇ **~ sth** *We had to rush our meal.* 我們只好匆匆忙忙地吃飯。

▸ **TAKE/SEND QUICKLY** 迅速帶走／送出 **2** 0→ [T] **~ sb/sth + adv./prep.** | **~ sb sth** to transport or send sb/sth somewhere with great speed 快速運輸；速送：*Ambulances rushed the injured to the hospital.* 救護車迅速將傷者送往醫院。 ◇ *Relief supplies were rushed in.* 救援物資很快就運來了。

▸ **DO STH TOO QUICKLY** 倉促行事 **3** 0→ [I, T] to do sth or to make sb do sth without thinking about it carefully （使）倉促行事，匆忙行事，做事草率：**~ into sth/into doing sth** *We don't want to rush into having a baby.* 我們不急着要孩子。 ◇ **~ sb** *Don't rush me. I need time to think about it.* 別催我，我需要時間考慮一下。 ◇ **~ sb** into sth/into doing sth *I'm not going to be rushed into anything.* 我不會受人催促草率地做任何事情。

▸ ATTACK 攻擊 **4** [T] **~ sb/sth** to try to attack or capture sb/sth suddenly 突襲；突擊抓捕：*A group of prisoners rushed an officer and managed to break out.* 一夥囚犯突然襲擊獄警，越獄了。◇ *Fans rushed the stage after the concert.* 音樂會結束後樂迷一下子湧向舞台。

▸ IN AMERICAN FOOTBALL 美式足球 **5** [T] **~ sb** (*NAmE*) to run into sb who has the ball 突襲，衝向（持球人）**6** [I] (*NAmE*) to move forward and gain ground by carrying the ball and not passing it 帶（球）奔跑；跑動帶（球）

▸ IN AMERICAN COLLEGES 美國大學 **7** [T] **~ sb** (*NAmE*) to give a lot of attention to sb, especially to a student because you want them to join your FRATERNITY or SORORITY（為物色、招募目的）特別關注，非常關心：*He is being rushed by Sigma Nu.* * Σ NU 聯誼會正在拉攏他。

IDM see FOOL *n.*, FOOT *n.*

PHR V **,rush sth↔'out** to produce sth very quickly 倉促生產；趕製：*The editors rushed out an item on the crash for the late news.* 編輯們趕着將墜機事件編入最新的新聞報道中。**,rush sth↔'through | ,rush sth 'through sth** to deal with official business very quickly by making the usual process shorter than usual 使快速通過；倉促處理：*to rush a bill through Parliament* 使議案在議會匆匆通過

■ ***noun***

▸ FAST MOVEMENT 迅速移動 **1** 🔑 [sing.] a sudden strong movement 猛烈移動；衝：*Shoppers **made a rush for** the exits.* 購物者衝向出口。◇ *She was trampled in the rush to get out.* 她在大夥兒往外衝的時候被人踩了。◇ *They listened to the rush of the sea below.* 他們聽着下面洶湧澎湃的海浪聲。◇ *The door blew open, letting in a rush of cold air.* 門被風颳開了，一股冷風吹了進來。◇ *He had a **rush of blood to the head** and punched the man.* 他一時衝動，揮拳打了那個男人。

▸ HURRY 匆忙 **2** 🔑 [sing., U] a situation in which you are in a hurry and need to do things quickly 匆忙；倉促：*I can't stop—I'm **in a rush**.* 我不能停下來，我忙着呢。◇ ***What's the rush?*** 幹嗎這麼急匆匆的？◇ *'I'll let you have the book back tomorrow.' '**There's no rush**.'* "我明天就把書還給你。" "不用着急。" ◇ *The words came out **in a rush**.* 那些話一股腦兒地倒出來。◇ *a **rush job*** (= one that has been done quickly) 倉促做完的活兒

▸ BUSY SITUATION 忙碌 **3** 🔑 [sing.] a situation in which people are very busy and there is a lot of activity 忙碌；繁忙：*The evening rush was just starting.* 繁忙的夜晚才剛開始。◇ *the Christmas rush* 聖誕節前的忙碌

▸ OF FEELING 感覺 **4** [sing.] **~ (of sth)** a sudden strong emotion or sign of strong emotion 迸發的情緒；情緒迸發：*a sudden **rush of excitement/fear/anger*** 突然感到的興奮／恐懼／憤怒 **5** [sing.] a sudden feeling of extreme pleasure or excitement 突如其來的極度愉悅（或興奮）：*Parachuting will give you the rush of a lifetime.* 跳傘給你一生難求的刺激感覺。◇ *Users of the drug report experiencing a rush that lasts several minutes.* 據報用這種藥的人有持續幾分鐘的亢奮感覺。

▸ SUDDEN DEMAND 急需 **6** [sing.] **~ (on/for sth)** a sudden large demand for goods, etc. 大量急需；爭購：*There's been a rush on umbrellas this week.* 本週出現了搶購雨傘的現象。➲ see also GOLD RUSH

▸ PLANT 植物 **7** [C, usually pl.] a tall plant like grass that grows near water. Its long thin STEMS can be dried and used for making BASKETS, the seats of chairs, etc. 燈芯草（乾燥後可用於編製籃子、坐墊等）：*rush matting* 燈芯草編的席子

▸ OF FILM/MOVIE 電影 **8 rushes** [pl.] (*technical* 術語) the first prints of a film/movie before they have been EDITED 樣片；毛片

▸ IN AMERICAN FOOTBALL 美式足球 **9** [C] an occasion when a player or players run towards a player on the other team who has the ball（向對方持球隊員的）突襲：*There was a rush on the quarterback.* 對方球員衝向四分衛。**10** [C] an occasion when a player runs forward with the ball 跑動帶球：*Johnson carried the ball an average of 6 yards per rush.* 約翰遜跑動帶球平均每次行進 6 碼。

▸ IN AMERICAN COLLEGES 美國大學 **11** [sing.] (*NAmE*) the time when parties are held for students who want to join a FRATERNITY or SORORITY 學生聯誼會納新活動（時間）：*rush week* 學生聯誼會納新活動週 ◇ *a rush party* 學生納新聯誼會 IDM see BUM *n.*

rushed /rʌʃt/ *adj.* done too quickly or made to do sth too quickly 倉促而就的；草率的 SYN **hurried**：*It was a rushed decision made at the end of the meeting.* 那是會議結束時匆忙作出的決定。◇ *Let's start work on it now so we're not too rushed at the end.* 我們現在就開始幹吧，免得最後太匆忙。IDM see FOOT *n.*

'rush hour *noun* [C, usually sing., U] the time, usually twice a day, when the roads are full of traffic and trains are crowded because people are travelling to or from work（上下班時的）交通高峰期：*the **morning/evening rush hour*** 早上的／傍晚的交通高峰期 ◇ *Don't travel **at rush hour/in the rush hour**.* 別在交通高峰期間乘車。◇ *rush-hour traffic* 交通高峰期的車流 ➲ COLLOCATIONS at DRIVING

rusk /rʌsk/ *noun* (*especially BrE*) a hard crisp biscuit for babies to eat（嬰兒食用的）脆餅乾

rus·set /'rʌsɪt/ *adj.* reddish-brown in colour 赤褐色的 ▸ **rus·set** *noun* [U]：*leaves of russet and gold* 赤褐色和金黃色的樹葉

Rus·sian /'rʌʃn/ *adj.*, *noun*

■ ***adj.*** from or connected with Russia 俄羅斯的

■ ***noun*** **1** [C] a person from Russia 俄羅斯人 **2** [U] the language of Russia 俄語

,Russian 'doll *noun* one of a set of hollow painted figures which fit inside each other 俄羅斯套娃

,Russian rou'lette *noun* [U] a dangerous game in which a person shoots at their own head with a gun that contains a bullet in only one of its chambers, so that the person does not know if the gun will fire or not 俄羅斯輪盤賭（危險遊戲，參加者用裝有一發子彈的轉輪手槍對準自己頭部射擊）：(*figurative*) *The airline was accused of playing Russian roulette with passenger safety.* 這家航空公司因無視乘客安全而受到指責。

Russo- /'rʌsəʊ; *NAmE* 'rʌsoʊ/ *combining form* (in nouns and adjectives 構成名詞和形容詞) Russian 俄羅斯的：*Russo-Japanese relations* 日俄關係

rust /rʌst/ *noun*, *verb*

■ ***noun*** [U] **1** a reddish-brown substance that is formed on some metals by the action of water and air 銹；鐵銹：*pipes covered with rust* 生了銹的管子 ◇ *rust spots* 銹斑 ◇ *a rust-coloured dress* 赤褐色連衣裙 ➲ see also RUSTY (1) **2** a plant disease that causes reddish-brown spots; the FUNGUS that causes this disease（植物的）銹病；銹菌

■ ***verb*** [I, T] if metal **rusts** or sth **rusts** it, it becomes covered with rust（使）生銹 SYN **corrode**：*old rusting farming implements* 生銹的舊農具 ◇ *Brass doesn't rust.* 黃銅不生銹。◇ **~ sth** *Water had got in and rusted the engine.* 發動機進水生銹了。▸ **rust·ed** *adj.*：*rusted iron* 生銹的鐵 ➲ see also RUSTY (1)

PHR V **,rust a'way** to be gradually destroyed by rust 銹壞

'rust belt *noun* (*especially US*) a region that used to have a lot of industry, but that has now decreased in importance and wealth, especially parts of the northern US where there were many factories that have now closed 銹帶（尤指美國北部衰敗或蕭條的工業區）

rus·tic /'rʌstɪk/ *adj.*, *noun*

■ ***adj.*** **1** (*approving*) typical of the country or of country people; simple 鄉村（人）的；鄉村（人）特色的；淳樸的：*an old cottage full of rustic charm* 充滿了鄉村魅力的舊農舍 **2** made very simply of rough wood 用粗糙木材做成的：*a rustic garden seat* 花園裏的粗木座椅 ◇ *a rustic fence* 用粗糙木材搭成的柵欄 ▸ **rus·ti·city** /rʌ'stɪsəti/ *noun* [U]

■ ***noun*** (*disapproving* or *humorous*) a person who lives in or comes from the country 鄉下人；鄉巴佬

rus·tle /'rʌsl/ *verb*, *noun*

■ ***verb*** **1** [I, T] **~ (sth)** if sth dry and light **rustles** or you **rustle it**, it makes a sound like paper, leaves, etc. moving or rubbing together（使）發出輕輕的摩擦聲，發出沙沙聲：*the sound of the trees rustling in the breeze*

R

樹木在微風中發出的沙沙聲 **2** [T] **~ sth** to steal farm animals 偷竊（牲口）

PHR V **,rustle sth↔'up (for sb)** (*informal*) to make or find sth quickly for sb and without planning 很快製作；迅速找到；倉促湊成： *I'm sure I can rustle you up a sandwich.* 我保證能馬上給你弄份三明治。◇ *She's trying to rustle up some funding for the project.* 她正設法儘快為這個項目籌集一些資金。

■ ***noun*** [sing.] a light dry sound like leaves or pieces of paper moving or rubbing against each other 輕輕的摩擦聲；沙沙聲： *There was a rustle of paper as people turned the pages.* 人們翻動書頁時發出沙沙的聲響。◇ *I heard a faint rustle in the bushes.* 我聽到樹叢裏發出一陣輕微的窸窣聲。

rust·ler /ˈrʌslə(r)/ *noun* a person who steals farm animals 盜竊牲口的人

rust·ling /ˈrʌslɪŋ/ *noun* **1** [U, C] the sound of light, dry things moving together 瑟瑟聲；沙沙聲： *the soft rustling of leaves* 樹葉柔和的沙沙聲 **2** [U] the act of stealing farm animals 偷竊牲口

rust·proof /ˈrʌstpruːf/ *adj.* **rustproof** metal has had a substance put on it so that it will not RUST 防銹的；經過防銹處理的

rusty /ˈrʌsti/ *adj.* (**rust·ier**, **rusti·est**) **1** covered with RUST 生銹的： *rusty metal* 生銹的金屬 ◇ *a rusty old car* 生了銹的舊汽車 **2** [not usually before noun] (*informal*) (of a sport, skill, etc. 體育運動、技能等) not as good as it used to be, because you have not been practising 荒疏；荒廢；退步： *My tennis is very rusty these days.* 最近我的網球荒疏了。◇ *I haven't played the piano for ages—I may be a little rusty.* 我很久沒有彈鋼琴，可能會有點生疏。
▸ **rusti·ness** *noun* [U]

rut /rʌt/ *noun* **1** [C] a deep track that a wheel makes in soft ground 車轍 **2** [C] a boring way of life that does not change 刻板乏味的生活： *I gave up my job because I felt I was **stuck in a rut**.* 我放棄了我的工作，因為我覺得那種生活呆板無聊。◇ *If you don't go out and meet new people, it's easy to **get into a rut**.* 如果你不出門結識新朋友，你的生活就容易變得刻板乏味。 **3** [U] (also **the rut**) the time of year when male animals, especially DEER, become sexually active （雄鹿等雄性動物的）發情期 ➲ see also RUTTED, RUTTING

ru·ta·baga /ˌruːtəˈbeɪɡə/ (*NAmE*) (*BrE* **swede**) (*ScotE* **tur·nip**) *noun* [C, U] a large round yellow root vegetable 蕪菁甘藍；大頭菜 ➲ VISUAL VOCAB page V31

ru·the·nium /ruːˈθiːniəm/ *noun* [U] (*symb.* **Ru**) a chemical element. Ruthenium is a hard silver-white metal that breaks easily and is found in PLATINUM ORES. 釕

ruth·er·ford·ium /ˌrʌðəˈfɔːdiəm; *NAmE* ˌrʌðərˈfɔːrd-/ *noun* [U] (*symb.* **Rf**) a chemical element. Rutherfordium is RADIOACTIVE and does not exist in nature but is produced artificially when atoms COLLIDE (= crash into each other). 鑪（放射性化學元素）

ruth·less /ˈruːθləs/ *adj.* (*disapproving*) (of people or their behaviour 人或其行為) hard and cruel; determined to get what you want and not caring if you hurt other people 殘酷無情的；殘忍的： *a ruthless dictator* 殘酷無情的獨裁者 ◇ *The way she behaved towards him was utterly ruthless.* 她對待他真是無情至極。◇ *He has a ruthless determination to succeed.* 他有不獲成功絕不罷休的堅定決心。 ▸ **ruth·less·ly** *adv.* **ruth·less·ness** *noun* [U]

rut·ted /ˈrʌtɪd/ *adj.* (of a road or path 道路或小徑) with deep tracks that have been made by wheels 有車轍的 ➲ see also RUT (1)

rut·ting /ˈrʌtɪŋ/ *adj.* (of male animals, especially DEER 雄性動物，尤指鹿) in a time of sexual activity 處於發情期的： *rutting deer* 處於發情期的鹿 ◇ *the rutting season* 交配季節 ➲ see also RUT (3)

RV /ˌɑː ˈviː; *NAmE* ˌɑːr/ (*NAmE*) (*BrE* **camp·er**, **'camper van**) (also **motor·home** *NAmE*, *BrE*) *noun* a large vehicle designed for people to live and sleep in when they are travelling (the abbreviation for 'recreational vehicle') 野營車，旅行房車（供旅行時居住，全寫為 recreational vehicle）

Rx /ˌɑːr ˈeks/ *noun* (*NAmE*) **1** the written abbreviation for a doctor's PRESCRIPTION 處方，藥方（prescription 的縮寫） **2** a solution to a problem 解決方法；辦法： *There's no Rx for unemployment.* 失業問題無法解決。

-ry ➲ -ERY

rye /raɪ/ *noun* [U] a plant that looks like BARLEY but that produces larger grain, grown as food for animals and for making flour and WHISKY; the grain of this plant 黑麥；黑麥粒： *rye bread* 黑麥麪包 ◇ *rye whisky* 黑麥威士忌酒 ➲ VISUAL VOCAB page V32

rye·grass /ˈraɪɡrɑːs; *NAmE* -ɡræs/ *noun* [U] a type of grass which is grown as food for animals 黑麥草（可作動物飼料）

R

Ss

S /es/ *noun, abbr., symbol*

■ ***noun*** (also **s**) [C, U] (*pl.* **Ss**, **S's**, **s's** /ˈesɪz/) the 19th letter of the English alphabet 英語字母表的第 19 個字母：*'Snow' begins with (an) S/'S'.* * snow 一詞以字母 s 開頭。➲ see also S-BEND

■ ***abbr.*** **1** (*pl.* **SS**) Saint 聖人；聖徒 **2** (especially for sizes of clothes) small（尤指服裝的尺碼）小號的；小型的 **3** (*NAmE* also **So.**) south; southern 南方（的）；南部（的）：*S Yorkshire* 約克郡南部 **4** SIEMENS 西門子（電導單位）➲ see also S AND H

■ ***symbol*** the symbol for ENTROPY 熵

-'s /s; z/ *suffix, short form*

■ ***suffix*** (added to nouns 加在名詞後) **1** belonging to（表示所屬關係）…的：*the woman's hat* 那個女人的帽子 ◇ *Peter's desk* 彼得的書桌 ◇ *children's clothes* 兒童服裝 **2** used to refer to sb's home or, in British English, a particular shop（指某人的家，英式英語亦指某商店等）…家，…店：*Shall we go to David's* (= David's house) *tonight?* 今晚我們去戴維家好嗎？◇ (*BrE*) *I'll call in at the chemist's on my way home* 我回家時順便要去藥店一趟。

■ ***short form*** (*informal*) **1** used after *he*, *she* or *it* and *where*, *what*, *who* or *how* to mean 'is' or 'has'（用於 he、she、it 和 where、what、who 以及 how 後，表示 is 或 has）：*She's still in the bath.* 她還在洗澡。◇ *What's he doing now?* 他現在幹什麼呢？◇ *It's time to go now.* 該走了。◇ *Who's taken my pen?* 誰拿走了我的筆？◇ *Where's he gone?* 他上哪兒去了？◇ *It's gone wrong again.* 它又出毛病了。**2** (used after *let* when making a suggestion that includes yourself and others 用於 let 後，建議自己和別人一起做某事) us 咱們；我們：*Let's go out for lunch.* 咱們出去吃午飯吧。

-s' *suffix* (forming the end of plural nouns 構成複數名詞的後綴) belonging to（表示所屬關係）…的：*the cats' tails* 這些貓的尾巴 ◇ *their wives' jobs* 他們妻子的工作

SA *abbr.* South Africa 南非

saag (also **sag**) /sæg; *BrE* also sɑːg/ *noun* [U] (*IndE*) = SPINACH

sab·bath /ˈsæbəθ/ (often **the Sabbath**) *noun* [sing.] (in Judaism and Christianity 猶太教和基督教) the holy day of the week that is used for resting and worshipping God. For Jews this day is Saturday and for Christians it is Sunday. 安息日（猶太教定為星期六，基督教定為星期日）：*to* ***keep/break the Sabbath*** (= to obey/not obey the religious rules for this day) 守 / 不守安息日

sab·bat·ic·al /səˈbætɪkl/ *noun* [C, U] a period of time when sb, especially a teacher at a university, is allowed to stop their normal work in order to study or travel（尤指供大學教師進行學術研究或旅遊的）公休假，休假：*to take a year's sabbatical* 享受一年的公休假 ◇ *a* ***sabbatical term/year*** 休假學期 / 學年 ◇ *He's* ***on sabbatical.*** 他正休假。

saber (*NAmE*) = SABRE

sable /ˈseɪbl/ *noun* **1** [C] a small animal from northern Asia with dark yellowish-brown fur 紫貂；黑貂 **2** [U] the skin and fur of the sable, used for making expensive coats and artists' brushes 貂皮，貂毛（可製作名貴大衣或畫筆）

sabo·tage /ˈsæbətɑːʒ/ *noun, verb*

■ ***noun*** [U] **1** the act of doing deliberate damage to equipment, transport, machines, etc. to prevent an enemy from using them, or to protest about sth（為防止敵人利用或表示抗議而對設備、交通等進行的）蓄意毀壞：*an act of* ***economic/military/industrial sabotage*** 經濟 / 軍事 / 工業破壞活動 ◇ *Police investigating the train derailment have not ruled out sabotage.* 警方調查火車出軌事件，沒有排除人為破壞的可能。**2** the act of deliberately spoiling sth in order to prevent it from being successful 故意妨礙；搗亂；刻意阻礙

■ ***verb*** **1 ~ sth** to damage or destroy sth deliberately to prevent an enemy from using it or to protest about sth 蓄意破壞，陰謀破壞（以防止敵方利用或表示抗議）：*The main electricity supply had been sabotaged by the rebels.* 叛亂者破壞了供電幹線。**2 ~ sth** to prevent sth from being successful or being achieved, especially deliberately 刻意阻礙；妨礙；搗亂：*Protesters failed to sabotage the peace talks.* 抗議者未能破壞和平談判。◇ *The rise in interest rates sabotaged any chance of the firm's recovery.* 由於利率的提高，公司的復蘇已無任何可能。

sabo·teur /ˌsæbəˈtɜː(r)/ *noun* a person who does deliberate damage to sth to prevent an enemy from using it, or to protest about sth（為防止敵方利用或為表示抗議的）蓄意破壞者，陰謀破壞者：*Saboteurs blew up a small section of the track.* 有人蓄意炸毀了一小段鐵路。◇ (*BrE*) ***hunt saboteurs*** (= people who try to stop people from hunting FOXES, etc.) 阻撓捕獵活動的人

sabre (*especially US* **saber**) /ˈseɪbə(r)/ *noun* **1** a heavy SWORD with a curved blade（彎刃）軍刀，馬刀 **2** a light SWORD with a thin blade used in the sport of FENCING（擊劍運動用的）佩劍，軍刀

ˈsabre-rattling (*especially US* **ˈsaber-rattling**) *noun* [U] the act of trying to frighten sb by threatening to use force 武力威脅；武力恫嚇

sabre·tooth (*BrE*) (*US* **saber·tooth**) /ˈseɪbətuːθ; *NAmE* -bərt-/ (*BrE* also **ˌsabre-toothed ˈtiger**) (*US* also **ˌsaber-toothed ˈtiger**) *noun* a large animal of the cat family with two very long curved upper teeth, that lived thousands of years ago and is now EXTINCT 劍齒虎（有一對劍形犬牙的大型貓科動物，已滅絕）

sac /sæk/ *noun* a part inside the body of a person, an animal or a plant, that is shaped like a bag, has thin skin around it, and contains liquid or air（人、動植物體內的）囊，液囊，氣囊

sac·charin /ˈsækərɪn/ *noun* [U] a sweet chemical substance used instead of sugar, especially by people who are trying to lose weight 糖精

sac·char·ine (also *less frequent* **sac·char·in**) /ˈsækəriːn; -rɪn/ *adj.* (*disapproving*) (of people or things 人或物) too emotional in a way that seems exaggerated 情感過分強烈而顯誇張的；故作多情的 **SYN** **sentimental**：*a saccharine smile* 甜蜜的笑容 ◇ *saccharine songs* 甜得發膩的歌

sacer·dotal /ˌsæsəˈdəʊtl; *NAmE* -sərˈdoʊtl/ *adj.* (*formal*) connected with a priest or priests 司祭的；司鐸的

sa·chet /ˈsæʃeɪ; *NAmE* sæˈʃeɪ/ *noun* **1** (*BrE*) (*NAmE* **packet**) a closed plastic or paper package that contains a very small amount of liquid or a powder（塑料或紙質）密封小袋：*a sachet of sauce/sugar/shampoo* 一小袋調味汁 / 糖 / 洗髮劑 ➲ VISUAL VOCAB page V33 **2** a small bag containing dried HERBS or flowers that you put with your clothes to make them smell pleasant（置於衣物中的）小香囊，小香袋

sack 🔑 /sæk/ *noun, verb*

■ ***noun*** **1** 🔑 [C] a large bag with no handles, made of strong rough material or strong paper or plastic, used for storing and carrying, for example flour, coal, etc. 麻布（或厚紙、塑料等）大袋 **2** 🔑 [C] (*NAmE*) a strong paper bag for carrying shopping（厚紙的）購物袋 **3** 🔑 [C] the contents of a sack 一滿袋；一大袋東西：*They got through a sack of potatoes.* 他們把一麻袋土豆吃完了。◇ (*NAmE*) *two sacks of groceries* 兩袋食品雜貨 **4** 🔑 **the sack** [sing.] (*BrE, informal*) being told by your employer that you can no longer continue working for a company, etc., usually because of sth that you have done wrong 開除；解雇；炒魷魚：*He* ***got the sack*** *for swearing.* 他因說髒話而被開除。◇ *Her work was so poor that she was* ***given the sack.*** 她工作幹得很差，被炒了魷魚。◇ *Four hundred workers face the sack.* 四百名工人面臨解雇的危險。**5 the sack** [sing.] (*informal, especially NAmE*) a bed 牀：*He caught them in the sack together.* 他撞見他們倆一起睡在牀上。**6** (usually **the sack**) [sing.] (*formal*) the act of stealing or destroying property in a captured town（在攻陷的城鎮中的）搶劫，劫掠：*the sack of Rome* 對羅馬城的洗劫 **IDM** see HIT *v.*

■ ***verb*** **1** 🔑 **~ sb** (*informal, especially BrE*) to dismiss sb from a job 解雇；炒魷魚 **SYN** **fire**：*She was sacked for*

S

refusing to work on Sundays. 她因拒絕在星期天上班被解雇了。➲ COLLOCATIONS at UNEMPLOYMENT **2 ~ sth** (of an army, etc., especially in the past) to destroy things and steal property in a town or building (尤指舊時軍隊等)破壞，劫掠：*Rome was sacked by the Goths in 410.* 羅馬在 410 年遭到哥特人的洗劫。 **3 ~ sb** (in AMERICAN FOOTBALL 美式足球) to knock down the QUARTERBACK 撞倒四分衛

PHR V **ˌsack ˈout** (*NAmE, informal*) to go to sleep or to bed 入睡；上牀睡覺

sack·but /ˈsækbʌt/ *noun* a type of TROMBONE used in the RENAISSANCE period 拉推號，古長號(文藝復興時期的長號)

sack·cloth /ˈsækklɒθ; *NAmE* -klɔːθ; -klɑːθ/ (also **sack·ing**) *noun* [U] a type of rough cloth made from JUTE, etc., used for making sacks 粗麻布；麻袋布

IDM **wear, put on, etc. ˌsackcloth and ˈashes** to behave in a way that shows that you are sorry for sth that you have done 懺悔；悔恨；後悔

sack·ful /ˈsækfʊl/ *noun* the amount contained in a SACK 一大袋(的量)：*two sackfuls of flour* 兩袋麪粉

sack·ing /ˈsækɪŋ/ *noun* **1** [C] an act of SACKING sb (= dismissing them from their job) 解雇 **2** [U] = SACKCLOTH

ˈsack race *noun* a race in which the competitors jump forward inside a sack 套袋賽跑，袋鼠跳(將雙腿套在袋中跳躍前進)

sac·ra·ment /ˈsækrəmənt/ *noun* (in Christianity 基督教) **1** [C] an important religious ceremony such as marriage, BAPTISM or COMMUNION 聖事，聖禮(如婚配、聖洗或聖餐等) **2 the sacrament** [sing.] the bread and wine that are eaten and drunk during the service of COMMUNION 聖餐(包括麪餅和葡萄酒) ▸ **sac·ra·men·tal** /ˌsækrəˈmentl/ *adj.* [usually before noun]：*sacramental wine* 聖餐中的葡萄酒

sac·red /ˈseɪkrɪd/ *adj.* **1** connected with God or a god; considered to be holy 上帝的；神的；神聖的：*a sacred image/shrine/temple* 聖像；聖地；聖殿 ◇ *sacred music* 聖樂 ◇ *Cows are sacred to Hindus.* 印度教徒認為牛是神聖的。 **2** very important and treated with great respect 受尊重的；受崇敬的 **SYN** **sacrosanct**：*Human life must always be sacred.* 人的生命在任何時候都必須得到尊重。◇ *For journalists* ***nothing is sacred*** (= they write about anything). 在記者眼裏，沒什麼是不可訴諸筆端的。 ▸ **sac·red·ness** *noun* [U] ➲ see also SANCTITY

S

ˌsacred ˈcow *noun* (*disapproving*) a custom, system, etc. that has existed for a long time and that many people think should not be questioned or criticized 不容置疑的習俗；批評不得的制度

sac·ri·fice /ˈsækrɪfaɪs/ *noun, verb*

■ ***noun*** **1** [C, U] the fact of giving up sth important or valuable to you in order to get or do sth that seems more important; sth that you give up in this way 犧牲；捨棄：*The makers of the product assured us that there had been no sacrifice of quality.* 這一產品的製造商向我們保證說他們沒有犧牲質量。◇ *Her parents* ***made sacrifices*** *so that she could have a good education.* 為了讓她受良好的教育，她的父母作了很多犧牲。◇ *to make the* ***final/supreme sacrifice*** (= to die for your country, to save a friend, etc.) 犧牲生命 **2** [C, U] **~ (to sb)** the act of offering sth to a god, especially an animal that has been killed in a special way; an animal, etc. that is offered in this way 祭獻；祭祀；祭獻的牲畜；祭品：*They offered sacrifices to the gods.* 他們向眾神獻上祭品。◇ *a human sacrifice* (= a person killed as a sacrifice) 用作祭品的人

■ ***verb*** **1** [T] to give up sth that is important or valuable to you in order to get or do sth that seems more important for yourself or for another person 犧牲；獻出：**~ sth for sb/sth** *She sacrificed everything for her children.* 她為子女犧牲了一切。◇ *The designers have sacrificed speed for fuel economy.* 設計者為節省燃料犧牲了速度。◇ **~ sth** *Would you sacrifice a football game to go out with a girl?* 你願意放棄一場足球賽，去跟一個女孩子約會嗎？ **2** [T, I] **~ (sb/sth)** to kill an animal or a person and offer it or them to a god, in order to please the god 以(人或動物)作祭獻

sac·ri·fi·cial /ˌsækrɪˈfɪʃl/ *adj.* [usually before noun] offered as a sacrifice 用於祭獻的：*a sacrificial lamb* 祭獻的羔羊

sac·ri·lege /ˈsækrəlɪdʒ/ *noun* [U, sing.] an act of treating a holy thing or place without respect (對聖物或聖地的)褻瀆；褻聖：(*figurative*) *It would be sacrilege to alter the composer's original markings.* 改動作曲家原有的記號是褻瀆行為。➲ COLLOCATIONS at RELIGION ▸ **sac·ri·le·gious** /ˌsækrəˈlɪdʒəs/ *adj.*

sac·ris·tan /ˈsækrɪstən/ *noun* a person whose job is to take care of the holy objects in a Christian church and to prepare the ALTAR for services (教堂的)聖器守司；管堂

sac·risty /ˈsækrɪsti/ *noun* (*pl.* **-ies**) a room in a church where a priest prepares for a service by putting on special clothes and where various objects used in worship are kept (教堂的)聖器室，祭衣間 **SYN** **vestry**

sacro·sanct /ˈsækrəʊsæŋkt; *NAmE* -kroʊ-/ *adj.* that is considered to be too important to change or question 神聖不容更改(或置疑)的 **SYN** **sacred**：*I'll work till late in the evening, but my weekends are sacrosanct.* 開夜車加班我願意，但週末休息沒商量。

sac·rum /ˈseɪkrəm; ˈsæk-/ *noun* (*pl.* **sacra** /-krə/ or **sac·rums**) (*anatomy* 解) a bone in the lower back, between the two hip bones of the PELVIS 骶骨

SAD /sæd/ *abbr.* SEASONAL AFFECTIVE DISORDER 季節性情感障礙

sad 🔑 /sæd/ *adj.* (**sad·der, sad·dest**)

▸ **UNHAPPY 不快樂** **1** 🔑 unhappy or showing unhappiness 悲哀的；難過的；顯得悲哀的：**~ (to do sth)** *We are very sad to hear that you are leaving.* 聽說你要走了，我們十分難過。◇ **~ (that …)** *I was sad that she had to go.* 知道她得走了，我心裏很難過。◇ **~ (about sth)** *I felt terribly sad about it.* 我對此深感遺憾。◇ *She looked sad and tired.* 她看上去又傷心又疲憊。◇ *He gave a slight, sad smile.* 他露出一絲苦笑。◇ *The divorce left him* ***sadder and wiser*** (= having learned from the unpleasant experience). 離婚使他吃了苦頭，但也學了乖。 **2** 🔑 that makes you feel unhappy 令人悲哀的；讓人難過的：*a sad story* 悲傷的故事 ◇ **~ (to do sth)** ***It was sad to*** *see them go.* 看着他們離去，真讓人難過。◇ **~ (that …)** ***It is sad that*** *so many of his paintings have been lost.* 他的畫作有很多已經失傳了，真可惜。◇ *We had some sad news yesterday.* 昨天我們聽到一些不幸的消息。◇ *He's a sad case—his wife died last year and he can't seem to manage without her.* 他是個不幸的人，去年妻子去世了。沒了妻子他好像就過不下去。◇ ***Sad to say*** (= unfortunately) *the house has now been demolished.* 可惜那座房子現在已經拆了。

▸ **UNACCEPTABLE 讓人無法接受** **3** 🔑 unacceptable; deserving blame or criticism 讓人無法接受的；該受責備(或批評)的 **SYN** **deplorable**：*a sad state of affairs* 糟糕的局面 ◇ ***It's a sad fact that*** *many of those killed were children.* 讓人難以接受的是遇難者中很多是孩子。

▸ **BORING 乏味** **4** (*informal*) boring or not fashionable 乏味的；過時的：*You sad old man.* 你這糟老頭子。◇ *You'd have to be sad to wear a shirt like that.* 你穿着那樣的襯衣會顯得老氣。

▸ **IN POOR CONDITION 狀況不佳** **5** in poor condition 狀況不佳的：*The salad consisted of a few leaves of sad-looking lettuce.* 色拉裏面拌了幾片生菜的殘葉。➲ see also SADLY, SADNESS

sad·den /ˈsædn/ *verb* [often passive] (*formal*) to make sb sad 使悲傷；使傷心；使難過：**~ sb** *We were deeply saddened by the news of her death.* 聽到她的死訊，我們深感悲傷。◇ **~ sb to do sth** *Fans were saddened to see the former champion play so badly.* 看到以前的冠軍表現如此差勁，球迷感到難過。◇ **it saddens sb that …** *It saddened her that people could be so cruel.* 人竟能如此殘忍，這讓她痛心。

sad·dle /ˈsædl/ *noun, verb*

■ ***noun*** **1** a leather seat for a rider on a horse 馬鞍：*She swung herself into the saddle.* 她一躍上馬。 **2** a seat on a bicycle or motorcycle (自行車或摩托車的)車座

➲ VISUAL VOCAB page V51 **3** a piece of meat from the back of an animal（動物的）脊肉

IDM **in the 'saddle** **1** in a position of authority and control 擔任領導職務；掌權；在位 **2** riding a horse 騎馬：*Three weeks after the accident he was back in the saddle.* 出事後三個星期，他就又騎上馬了。

■ *verb* **~ sth** to put a saddle on a horse 給（馬）上鞍

PHR V **,saddle 'up** | **,saddle sth↔'up** to put a saddle on a horse 給（馬）上鞍 **'saddle sb/yourself with sth** [often passive] to give sb/yourself an unpleasant responsibility, task, debt, etc. 使某人（或自己）肩負重擔：*I've been saddled with organizing the conference.* 我被派擔當組織會議的重任。◇ *The company was saddled with debts of £12 million.* 公司背着 1 200 萬英鎊的債務。

saddle·bag /'sædlbæg/ *noun* **1** one of a pair of bags put over the back of a horse 鞍囊；馬褡褳 **2** a bag attached to the back of a bicycle or motorcycle saddle（掛在自行車或摩托車後座上的）掛包

'saddle horse *noun* **1** a frame on which saddles are cleaned or stored 鞍具洗放架 **2** (*NAmE*) a horse which is used only for riding 騎用馬

sad·dler /'sædlə(r)/ *noun* a person whose job is making, repairing and selling SADDLES and other leather goods 鞍匠；馬具匠；馬具商

sad·dlery /'sædləri/ *noun* [U] SADDLES and leather goods for horses; the art of making these 馬具；馬具製作工藝

'saddle sore *adj.* feeling sore and stiff after riding a horse 騎馬後感覺胯疼腿僵的

'saddle stitch *noun* a STITCH of thread or piece of wire put through the fold of a magazine, etc. to hold it together 騎馬釘（用於雜誌等）

saddo /'sædəʊ; *NAmE* -doʊ/ *noun* (*pl.* **-os**) (*BrE, informal*) a person that you think is boring or not fashionable 乏味的人；老土：*a bunch of saddos who spend their lives playing computer games* 一群成天泡在電腦遊戲裏的無聊傢伙

sadhu /'sɑːduː/ *noun* (*pl.* **-us**) a Hindu holy man, especially one who lives away from people and society 娑度（印度教聖人，尤指離群索居的隱士）

Sadie Haw·kins Day /,seɪdi 'hɔːkɪnz deɪ/ *noun* (in the US) a day when there is a custom that women can invite men to a social event instead of waiting to be invited, especially to a **Sadie Hawkins Day** dance 賽迪・霍金斯節（美國節日，女士可主動邀請男士參加，尤指賽迪・霍金斯舞會）

sad·ism /'seɪdɪzəm/ *noun* [U] **1** enjoyment from watching or making sb suffer 施虐癖，施虐狂；虐待狂：*There's a streak of sadism in his nature.* 他本性中有幾分施虐傾向。 **2** a need to hurt sb in order to get sexual pleasure 性施虐狂 ➲ compare MASOCHISM (1)

sad·ist /'seɪdɪst/ *noun* a person who gets pleasure, especially sexual pleasure, from hurting other people 施虐狂者；（尤指）性施虐狂者 ▸ **sad·is·tic** /sə'dɪstɪk/ *adj.*：*He took sadistic pleasure in taunting the boy.* 嘲諷這孩子讓他感到施虐的快感。 **sad·is·tic·al·ly** /-kli/ *adv.*

sadly 🔑 /'sædli/ *adv.*
1 🔑 unfortunately 令人遺憾；不幸地：*Sadly, after eight years of marriage they had grown apart.* 不幸的是，結婚八年後，他們的感情日漸淡漠了。 **2** 🔑 in a sad way 悲傷地；傷心地：*She shook her head sadly.* 她難過地搖搖頭。 **3** 🔑 very much and in a way that makes you sad 極為；苦苦地：*She will be sadly missed.* 人們會很想她的。◇ *If you think I'm going to help you again, you're* ***sadly*** (= completely) ***mistaken.*** 你要是以為我還會再幫助你，那你就大錯特錯了。

sad·ness 🔑 /'sædnəs/ *noun*
1 🔑 [U, sing.] the feeling of being sad 悲傷；悲痛；難過：*memories tinged with sadness* 略帶悲傷的往事 ◇ *I felt a deep sadness.* 我感到深深的悲痛。 **2** [C, usually pl.] something which makes you sad 使人悲傷（或難過）的事：*our joys and sadnesses* 我們的歡樂和悲傷

sado·maso·chism /,seɪdəʊ'mæsəkɪzəm; *NAmE* -doʊ-/ *noun* [U] enjoyment from hurting sb and being hurt, especially during sexual activity 施虐受虐狂；（尤指）性施虐受虐狂 ▸ **sado·maso·chist** /,seɪdəʊ'mæsəkɪst; *NAmE* -doʊ-/ *noun* **sado·maso·chis·tic** /,seɪdəʊ,mæsə'kɪstɪk; *NAmE* -doʊ-/ *adj.*

sae /,es eɪ 'iː/ *noun* (*BrE*) the abbreviation for 'stamped addressed envelope' or 'self-addressed envelope' (an envelope on which you have written your name and address and usually put a stamp so that sb else can use it to send sth to you)（寫上姓名地址且通常貼有郵票的）回郵信封（全寫為 stamped addressed envelope 或 self-addressed envelope）：*Please enclose an sae for your test results.* 請附姓名地址郵資俱全的信封，以便通知化驗結果。➲ compare SASE

sa·fari /sə'fɑːri/ *noun* [U, C] **1** a trip to see or hunt wild animals, especially in east or southern Africa（尤指在非洲東部或南部的）觀賞（或捕獵）野獸的旅行；遊獵：*to* ***be/go on safari*** 去遊獵 **2** (*EAfrE*) a journey; a period of time spent travelling or when you are not at home or work 長途旅行；旅遊期間；外出期間：*I just got back from a month-long safari.* 我外出旅遊了一個月剛剛回來。◇ *It arrived while I was* ***on safari.*** 這是在我外出期間送達的。

sa'fari park *noun* a park in which wild animals move around freely and are watched by visitors from their cars 野生動物園

sa'fari suit *noun* a light-coloured suit worn by men in hot weather, especially one with pockets on the front of the jacket 獵裝（淺色男裝，天熱時穿，尤指前胸有衣袋的）

safe 🔑 /seɪf/ *adj., noun*
■ *adj.* (**safer, saf·est**)
▸ PROTECTED 受保護 **1** 🔑 [not before noun] protected from any danger or harm 處境（或情況）安全：*The children are quite safe here.* 孩子們在這裏十分安全。◇ *She didn't* ***feel safe*** *on her own.* 她一個人待着，覺得不安全。◇ *Will the car be safe parked in the road?* 車停在馬路上安全嗎？◇ **~ (from sb/sth)** *They aimed to make the country safe from terrorist attacks.* 他們力圖使國家免遭恐怖分子的襲擊。◇ *Your secret is safe with me* (= I will not tell anyone else). 你的秘密不會從我這兒傳出去。◇ *Here's your passport. Now* ***keep it safe.*** 這是你的護照。你可保管好了。 OPP **unsafe**
▸ WITHOUT PHYSICAL DANGER 對身體無害 **2** 🔑 not likely to lead to any physical harm or danger 不損害（或危害）健康的；安全的：**~ (for sb)** **(to do sth)** *Is the water here safe to drink?* 這兒的水能喝嗎？◇ *The street is not safe for children to play in.* 孩子在大街上玩不安全。◇ *It is one of the safest cars in the world.* 這是世界上最安全的車型之一。◇ *We watched the explosion* ***from a safe distance.*** 我們在安全距離之外觀看了爆破。◇ *Builders were called in to* ***make the building safe.*** 召來建築工加固這棟大樓。 OPP **unsafe**
▸ NOT HARMED/LOST 沒有受傷／丟失 **3** 🔑 not harmed, damaged, lost, etc. 未受傷害（或未遭損害、未丟失等）的：*We were glad she let us know she was safe.* 她告訴我們她平安無事，我們很高興。◇ *The missing child was found* ***safe and well.*** 走失的孩子平平安安地找回來了。◇ *They turned up* ***safe and sound.*** 他們安然無恙地出現了。◇ *A reward was offered for the animal's* ***safe return.*** 懸賞要求將動物安全送還。
▸ PLACE 地方 **4** 🔑 where sb/sth is not likely to be in danger or to be lost 無危險的；無丟失之虞的：*We all want to live in safer cities.* 我們都希望住在比較安全的城市裏。◇ *Keep your passport in a safe place.* 把護照放到保險的地方。 OPP **unsafe**
▸ WITHOUT RISK 無風險 **5** 🔑 not involving much or any risk; not likely to be wrong or to upset sb 風險小的；無風險的；不大會錯的；不致冒犯別人的：*a safe investment* 無風險的投資 ◇ *a safe subject for discussion* 沒有忌諱的討論題目 ◇ **~ (to do sth)** ***It's safe to assume*** *(that) there will always be a demand for new software.* 可以肯定地認為，人們對新的軟件一直有需求。◇ *It would be safer to take more money with you in case of emergency.* 多帶點錢保險些，以防急用。◇ (*disapproving*) *The show was well performed, but so safe and predictable.* 演出不錯，只是太四平八穩，缺少新意。

S

▸ PERSON 人 **6** [usually before noun] doing an activity in a careful way 謹慎的；小心的 SYN **careful**：*a safe driver* 謹慎的司機

▸ LAW 法律 **7** based on good evidence 有確鑿證據的：*a safe verdict* 確當的裁定 OPP **unsafe**

▸ APPROVING 贊同；滿意 **8** (*BrE, informal*) used by young people to show that they approve of sb/sth（年輕人用語，表示贊同）很好的，不錯的，令人滿意的：*I like him, he's safe.* 我喜歡他，他很不錯。◇ *That kid's safe.* 那小傢伙挺好的。 **9** (*BrE, informal*) used by young people as a way of accepting sth that is offered（年輕人用語，表示接受）可以：*'You want some?' 'Yeah, safe.'* "你要一些嗎？" "好的，行。" ➲ see also FAIL-SAFE

IDM **,better ,safe than 'sorry** (*saying*) used to say that it is wiser to be too careful than to act too quickly and do sth you may later wish you had not 寧可事先謹慎有餘，不要事後追悔莫及 **in safe 'hands | in the safe hands of sb** being taken care of well by sb 在可靠的人手裏；受到妥善照管：*I've left the kids in safe hands—with my parents.* 我把孩子託付給了靠得住的人，就是我父母。◇ *Their problem was in the safe hands of the experts.* 他們的問題交給行家處理了。 **on the 'safe side** being especially careful; taking no risks 謹慎為是；不冒險：*I took some extra cash just to be on the safe side.* 我多帶了一些現金，以防萬一。 **play (it) 'safe** to be careful; to avoid risks 謹慎行事；避免冒險 **(as) ,safe as 'houses** (*BrE*) very safe 非常安全 **safe in the knowledge that** confident because you know that sth is true or will happen 料定；確信：*She went out safe in the knowledge that she looked fabulous.* 她確信自己打扮得無可挑剔後才出門去。 **a safe pair of 'hands** (*especially BrE*) a person that you can trust to do a job well 靠得住的辦事人 ➲ more at BET *n.*

▪ **noun** a strong metal box or cupboard with a complicated lock, used for storing valuable things in, for example, money or jewellery 保險箱；保險櫃

,safe 'conduct (also **,safe 'passage**) *noun* [U, C] official protection from being attacked, arrested, etc. when passing through an area; a document that promises this 安全通行權；安全通行證；通行許可證：*The guerrillas were promised safe conduct out of the country.* 游擊隊員得到承諾，可以安全離開這個國家。

'safe deposit box (also **'safety deposit box**) *noun* a metal box for storing valuable things, usually kept in a special room at a bank（銀行的）保管箱；保險箱

safe·guard /ˈseɪfɡɑːd; *NAmE* -ɡɑːrd/ *verb, noun*

▪ **verb** [T, I] (*formal*) to protect sth/sb from loss, harm or damage; to keep sth/sb safe 保護；保障；捍衛：**~ sth** *to safeguard a person's interests* 維護某人的利益 ◇ *to safeguard jobs* 保住工作崗位 ◇ **~ sth/sb against/from sth** *The new card will safeguard the company against fraud.* 新卡將保護公司免遭詐騙。◇ **~ against sth** *The leaflet explains how to safeguard against dangers in the home.* 小冊子告訴人們在家裏如何防備各種危險。

▪ **noun ~ (against sth)** something that is designed to protect people from harm, risk or danger 安全設施；保護措施：*Stronger legal safeguards are needed to protect the consumer.* 需要有更有力的法律措施來保護消費者。

,safe 'haven *noun* a place where sb can go to be safe from danger or attack 安全的地方；避難所

'safe house *noun* a house used by people who are hiding, for example by criminals hiding from the police, or by people who are being protected by the police from other people who may wish to harm them（罪犯藏匿或警方保護人藏身等的）藏身處，安全屋

,safe 'keeping *noun* [U] **1** the fact of sth being in a safe place where it will not be lost or damaged 妥善保管；存放在安全處：*She had put her pocket **for safe keeping**.* 為安全起見，她把手錶放進了衣袋。 **2** the fact of sb/sth being taken care of by sb who can be trusted 安全照看；妥善照管：*The documents are **in the safe keeping** of our lawyers.* 那些文件由我們的律師妥善保管着。

safe·ly /ˈseɪfli/ *adv.*

1 without being harmed, damaged or lost 未受損傷（或損壞）；未丟失：*The plane landed safely.* 飛機安全降落。 **2** in a way that does not cause harm or that protects sb/sth from harm 安全地；無危害地：*The bomb has been safely disposed of.* 炸彈已安全處理。◇ *The money is safely locked in a drawer.* 錢鎖在抽屜裏，很穩當。 **3** without much possibility of being wrong 不大可能出錯地；有把握地：*We can **safely say** that he will accept the job.* 我們可以有把握地說，他會接受這份工作。 **4** without any possibility of the situation changing 安穩地；安定地：*I thought the kids were safely tucked up in bed.* 我以為孩子們好好地在牀上睡覺呢。 **5** without any problems being caused; with no risk 沒問題地；毫無風險地：*These recommendations can safely be ignored.* 這些推薦信大可不必理會。

'safe mode *noun* [U] (*computing* 計) a way of starting a computer that makes it easier to find a problem without the risk of losing data（計算機啟動的）安全模式

,safe 'passage *noun* [U, C] = SAFE CONDUCT

the 'safe period *noun* [sing.] the time just before and during a woman's PERIOD when she is unlikely to become pregnant（女性經期前或來經時不易懷孕的）安全期

'safe room *noun* = PANIC ROOM

,safe 'seat *noun* (*BrE*) a CONSTITUENCY where a particular political party has a lot of support and is unlikely to be defeated in an election（在選舉中）穩操勝券的選區

,safe 'sex *noun* [U] sexual activity in which people try to protect themselves from AIDS and other sexual diseases, for example by using a CONDOM 安全性交（採取針對艾滋病和其他性病的預防措施）

safety /ˈseɪfti/ *noun* (*pl.* **-ies**)

1 [U] the state of being safe and protected from danger or harm 安全；平安：*a place where children can play **in safety*** 可以讓兒童安全玩耍的地方 ◇ *The police are concerned for the safety of the 12-year-old boy who has been missing for three days.* 那個 12 歲的男孩失踪三天了，警方對他的安全感到擔憂。◇ *He was kept in custody **for his own safety**.* 拘押他是為了他本人的安全。 **2** [U] the state of not being dangerous 安全性；無危險：*I'm worried about the safety of the treatment.* 我擔心這種療法是否安全。◇ *safety standards* 安全標準 ◇ *a local campaign to improve **road safety*** 當地改善道路安全狀況的運動 ◇ *The airline has an excellent **safety record**.* 這家航空公司有極佳的安全紀錄。 **3** [U] a place where you are safe 安全處所：*I managed to swim **to safety**.* 我設法游到安全處。◇ *We watched the lions **from the safety of** the car.* 我們從車裏看獅子，很安全。◇ *They reached safety seconds before the building was engulfed in flames.* 他們到達安全地幾秒鐘之後，那房子就成了一片火海。 **4** [C] (*NAmE*) = SAFETY CATCH **5** [C] (*NAmE*) (in AMERICAN FOOTBALL) a defending player who plays in a position far away from the other team（美式足球）安全衞，防守隊員

IDM **,safety 'first** (*saying*) safety is the most important thing 安全第一 **there's ,safety in 'numbers** (*saying*) being in a group makes you safer and makes you feel more confident 人多保險

'safety belt *noun* = SEAT BELT

'safety catch (*especially BrE*) (*NAmE* usually **safety**) *noun* a device that stops a gun from being fired or a machine from working by accident（槍、炮等的）保險機，保險栓；（機器設備的）保險掣子

'safety curtain *noun* a curtain which can come down across the stage in a theatre, intended to stop a fire from spreading（劇場舞台的）防火簾，隔火帳，防火幕

'safety deposit box *noun* = SAFE DEPOSIT BOX

'safety glass *noun* [U] strong glass that does not break into sharp pieces 安全玻璃（受撞擊不會碎成尖銳碎片的高強度玻璃）

'safety island *noun* (*US*) = TRAFFIC ISLAND

'safety lamp *noun* a special lamp used by MINERS with a flame that does not cause underground gases to explode（礦工用的）安全燈；礦燈

'safety match *noun* a type of match that will light only if it is rubbed against a specially prepared rough surface, often on the side of its box 安全火柴

'safety measure *noun* something that you do in order to prevent sth bad or dangerous from happening 安全措施；預防措施

'safety net *noun* **1** an arrangement that helps to prevent disaster if sth goes wrong （防備不測的）保障措施；安全網：*a financial safety net* 金融"安全網" ◇ *people who have fallen through the safety net and ended up homeless on the streets* 未能享受保障措施終致流落街頭的人 **2** a net placed underneath ACROBATS, etc. to catch them if they fall （保護雜技演員等的）安全網

'safety pin *noun* a pin with a point bent back towards the head, that is covered when closed so that it cannot hurt you 安全別針 ➲ **VISUAL VOCAB** page V63

'safety razor *noun* a RAZOR with a cover over the blade to stop it from cutting the skin 安全剃刀；保險刀 ➲ compare CUT-THROAT RAZOR

'safety valve *noun* **1** a device that lets out steam or pressure in a machine when it becomes too great 安全閥 **2** a harmless way of letting out feelings of anger, excitement, etc. 疏導（情緒）的方法：*Exercise is a good safety valve for the tension that builds up at work.* 鍛煉身體是排解工作壓力的好辦法。

saf·flower /'sæflaʊə(r)/ *noun* [C, U] a plant with orange flowers, whose seeds produce an oil which is used in cooking 紅花（籽油可用於烹飪）

saf·fron /'sæfrən/ *noun* [U] **1** a bright yellow powder made from CROCUS flowers, used in cooking to give colour to food 藏紅花粉（用作烹飪時的染色調料） ➲ **VISUAL VOCAB** page V32 **2** a bright orange-yellow colour 橘黃色 ▸ **saf·fron** *adj.*：*Buddhist monks in saffron robes* 身穿黃袍的和尚

SAG /ˌes eɪ 'dʒiː/ *abbr.* SCREEN ACTORS GUILD

sag¹ /sæg/ *verb* (**-gg-**) **1** [I] to hang or bend down in the middle, especially because of weight or pressure（尤指由於承重或受壓）中間下垂，下凹：*a sagging roof* 凹陷的房頂 ◇ *The tent began to sag under the weight of the rain.* 雨水使得帳篷中間開始下墜。◇ *Your skin starts to sag as you get older.* 人老了，皮膚就會慢慢鬆弛。 **2** [I] to become weaker or fewer 減弱；減少：*Their share of the vote sagged badly at the last election.* 在上次選舉中他們的得票比率大幅下跌。 ▸ **sag** *noun* [U, C, usually sing.]：*Weight has caused the sag.* 承重導致下垂。 **IDM** see JAW *n.*

PHR V **ˌsag 'off | sag off sth** (*BrE, informal*) to stay away from school or work when you should be there, or leave before you should 逃學；曠課；曠工；早退：*We sagged off school and wrote the song.* 我們逃學寫了那首歌。

sag² /sɑːg/ *noun* = SAAG

saga /'sɑːgə/ *noun* **1** a long traditional story about adventures and brave acts, especially one from Norway or Iceland 薩迦（尤指古代挪威或冰島講述冒險經歷和英雄事跡的長篇故事） **2** a long story about events over a period of many years （講述許多年間發生的事情的）長篇故事，長篇小說：*a family saga* 家世小說 **3** a long series of events or adventures and/or a report about them 一連串的事件（或經歷）；一連串經歷的講述（或記述）：*The front page is devoted to the continuing saga of the hijack.* 頭版是對劫持事件的連續報道。◇ (*humorous*) *the saga of how I missed the plane* 有關我如何誤了飛機的一連串倒霉事兒

sa·ga·cious /sə'geɪʃəs/ *adj.* (*formal*) showing good judgement and understanding 精明練達的；洞察事理的 **SYN** wise ▸ **sa·ga·city** /sə'gæsəti/ *noun* [U]

sage /seɪdʒ/ *noun, adj.*

■ ***noun*** **1** [U] a plant with flat, light green leaves that have a strong smell and are used in cooking as a HERB 鼠尾草（可用作調料） ➲ **VISUAL VOCAB** page V32 **2** [C] (*formal*) a very wise person 哲人；智者；聖人

■ ***adj.*** (*literary*) wise, especially because you have a lot of experience 睿智的，賢明的（尤指因經驗豐富） ▸ **sage·ly** *adv.*：*She nodded sagely.* 她點點頭，一副洞悉一切的樣子。

sage·brush /'seɪdʒbrʌʃ/ *noun* [U] a plant with leaves that smell sweet that grows in dry regions in the western US; an area of ground covered with sagebrush 灌木蒿；灌木蒿叢

saggy /'sægi/ *adj.* (**sag·gier**, **sag·gi·est**) (*informal*) no longer firm; hanging or sinking down in a way that is not attractive 鬆垂的；鬆弛耷拉的；下陷的

Sa·git·tar·ius /ˌsædʒɪ'teəriəs; *NAmE* -'ter-/ *noun* **1** [U] the 9th sign of the ZODIAC, the ARCHER 黃道第九宮；人馬宮；人馬（星）座 **2** [sing.] a person born when the sun is in this sign, that is between 22 November and 20 December, approximately 屬人馬座的人（約出生於 11 月 22 日至 12 月 20 日） ▸ **Sa·git·tar·ian** *noun, adj.*

sago /'seɪgəʊ; *NAmE* -goʊ/ *noun* [U] hard white grains made from the soft inside of a type of PALM tree, often cooked with milk to make a DESSERT 西穀米，西米（由一種棕櫚莖髓製成的白色硬粒狀食物，常加牛奶製成甜點）：*sago pudding* 西米布丁

sa·guaro /sə'gwɑːrəʊ; *NAmE* -roʊ/ *noun* (*pl.* **-os**) a very large CACTUS that grows in the southern US and Mexico 薩瓜羅掌，巨山影掌（生長於美國南部和墨西哥的仙人掌）

sahib /sɑːb; 'sɑːɪb/ *noun* used in India, especially in the past, to address a European man, especially one with some social or official status （印度舊時對歐洲人的尊稱）先生，老爺

said /sed/ **1** *past tense, past part.* of SAY **2** *adj.* [only before noun] (*formal* or *law* 律) = AFOREMENTIONED：*the said company* 上述公司

sail 0-π /seɪl/ *verb, noun*

■ ***verb*** **1** 0-π [I, T] (of a boat or ship or the people on it 船或船上的人) to travel on water using sails or an engine （船）航行；（人）乘船航行：(**+ adv./prep.**) *to sail into harbour* 駛入海港 ◇ *The dinghy sailed smoothly across the lake.* 小艇平穩地駛過湖面。◇ *The ferry sails from Newhaven to Dieppe.* 渡船行駛於紐黑文和迪耶普之間。◇ *one of the first people to sail around the world* 最早進行環球航行的人之一 ◇ **~ sth** *to sail the Atlantic* 在大西洋上航行 **2** 0-π (also **go sailing**) [I, T] to control or travel on a boat with a sail, especially as a sport 駕駛（或乘坐）帆船航行（尤指作為體育運動）：*We spent the weekend sailing off the south coast.* 我們在南部海岸一帶駕帆船度過了週末。◇ *Do you* ***go sailing*** *often?* 你常去駕帆船玩嗎？◇ **~ sth** *She sails her own yacht.* 她駕駛自己的遊艇。 **3** [I] (of a boat or ship or the people in it 船隻或船上的人) to begin a journey on water 起航：*We sail at 2 p.m. tomorrow.* 我們明天下午兩點起航。◇ **~ for sth** *He sailed for the West Indies from Portsmouth.* 他從樸次茅斯起航，向西印度群島進發。 **4** [I] **+ adv./prep.** to move quickly and smoothly in a particular direction; (of people) to move in a confident manner 掠；飄；浮游；（人）昂首而行，氣宇軒昂地走：*clouds sailing across the sky* 飄過天空的雲彩 ◇ *The ball sailed over the goalie's head.* 球從守門員頭頂飛過。◇ *She sailed past, ignoring me completely.* 她翩然而過，看都不看我一眼。

IDM **sail close to the 'wind** to take a risk by doing sth that is dangerous or that may be illegal 冒大風險（幹危險或可能違法的事）

PHR V **ˌsail 'through (sth)** to pass an exam, a test, etc. without any difficulty 順利通過（考試等）

■ ***noun*** **1** 0-π [C, U] a sheet of strong cloth which the wind blows against to make a boat or ship travel through the water 帆：*As the boat moved down the river the wind began to fill the sails.* 船順河而下，風逐漸脹滿了帆。◇ *a ship* ***under sail*** (= using sails) 張帆行駛的船 ◇ *in the days of sail* (= when ships all used sails) 在帆船時代 ◇ *She moved away like a ship* ***in full sail*** (= with all its sails spread out). 她一陣風似的走了。 **2** 0-π [sing.] a trip in a boat or ship 乘船航行：*We went for a sail.* 我們乘船兜了一趟風。◇ *a two-hour sail across the bay* 橫渡海灣的兩小時航程 **3** [C] a set of boards attached to the arm of a WINDMILL （風車的）翼板

IDM **set 'sail (from/for ...)** (*formal*) to begin a trip by sea 起航；開航：*a liner setting sail from New York* 自紐約起航的郵輪 ◇ *We set sail (for France) at high tide.*

S

我們在漲潮時起航（前往法國）。➲ more at TRIM *v.*, WIND¹ *n.*

sail·board /ˈseɪlbɔːd; *NAmE* -bɔːrd/ (also **board**) *noun* = WINDSURFER (1) ▶ **sail·board·er** *noun* **sail·board·ing** *noun* [U]

sail·boat /ˈseɪlbəʊt; *NAmE* -boʊt/ (*NAmE*) (*BrE* **ˈsailing boat**) *noun* a boat with sails 帆船 ➲ VISUAL VOCAB page V54

sail·cloth /ˈseɪlklɒθ; *NAmE* -klɔːθ; -klɑːθ/ *noun* [U] a type of strong cloth used for making sails 厚篷帆布

sail·ing 0‑m /ˈseɪlɪŋ/ *noun*
1 0‑m [U] the sport or activity of travelling in a boat with sails 帆船運動；（乘帆船的）航行：*to go sailing* 去進行帆船運動 ◇ *a sailing club* 帆船俱樂部 **2** [C] one of the regular times that a ship leaves a port（從某港口開出的）航班：*There are six sailings a day.* 每天有六班船。
IDM see CLEAR *adj.*, PLAIN *adj.*

ˈsailing boat (*BrE*) (*NAmE* **sail·boat**) *noun* a boat with sails 帆船 ➲ VISUAL VOCAB page V54

ˈsailing ship *noun* a ship with sails（大型）帆船

sail·maker /ˈseɪlmeɪkə(r)/ *noun* a person whose job is to make or repair sails 製帆工；修帆工 ▶ **sail·mak·ing** *noun* [U]

sail·or 0‑m /ˈseɪlə(r)/ *noun*
1 0‑m a person who works on a ship as a member of the CREW 水手；海員 **2** 0‑m a person who sails a boat 駕船人
IDM **a good/bad ˈsailor** a person who rarely/often becomes sick at sea 很少 / 經常暈船的人

ˈsailor suit *noun* a suit for a child made in the style of an old-fashioned sailor's uniform（兒童的）水手裝

saint /seɪnt; *or, in British use before names*, snt/ *noun*
1 (*abbr.* **S**, **St**) a person that the Christian Church recognizes as being very holy, because of the way they have lived or died（因其生平或殉教事跡而獲基督教會追封的）聖人，聖徒：*St John* 聖約翰 ◇ *St Valentine's Day* 聖瓦倫廷節（情人節）◇ *The children were all named after saints.* 這些孩子都取了聖徒的名字。➲ see also PATRON SAINT, ST BERNARD **2** a very good, kind or patient person 聖人般的人（指特別善良、仁愛或有耐性的人）：*She's a saint to go on living with that man.* 能繼續和那個男人一起生活，她簡直是聖人。◇ *His behaviour would try **the patience of a saint**.* 他的行為就是再有修養的人也難以忍受。▶ **saint·hood** *noun* [U]

saint·ed /ˈseɪntɪd/ *adj.* [usually before noun] (*old-fashioned* or *humorous*) considered or officially stated to be a saint 被視為聖人的；被正式封為聖徒的：*And how is my sainted sister?* 我那大好人姐姐怎麼樣？

S

saint·ly /ˈseɪntli/ *adj.* like a SAINT; very holy and good 像聖人的；非常聖潔善良的：*to lead a saintly life* 過着聖潔的生活 ▶ **saint·li·ness** *noun* [U]

ˈsaint's day *noun* (in the Christian Church) a day of the year when a particular SAINT is remembered and on which, in some countries, people who are named after that SAINT have celebrations（基督教）聖人慶節

saith /seθ/ (*old use*) = SAYS

sake¹ /seɪk/ *noun* ➲ see also SAKE²
IDM **for Christ's, God's, goodness', heaven's, pity's, etc. ˈsake** used to emphasize that it is important to do sth or when you are annoyed about sth（強調重要或表示惱火）看在上帝分上，天哪，行行好吧，千萬：*Do be careful, for goodness' sake.* 千萬要小心。◇ *Oh, for heaven's sake!* 哎喲，天哪！◇ *For pity's sake, help me!* 行行好，幫幫我吧！HELP Some people find the use of **Christ**, **God** or **heaven** here offensive. 有人認為此處用 Christ、God 或 heaven 含冒犯意。**for sth's sake** because of the interest or value sth has, not because of the advantages it may bring 為某事本身的緣故；鑒於某事本身的價值：*I believe in education for its own sake.* 我相信教育本身就是有價值的。◇ *art for art's sake* 為藝術而藝術 **for the sake of sb/sth | for sb's/sth's sake** in order to help sb/sth or because you like sb/sth 為了某人（或某事）起見；因某人（或某事）的緣故：*They stayed together for the sake of the children.* 為了孩子，他們還待在一起。◇ *You can do it. Please, for my sake.* 這個你是能做的。求你了，就算為了我。◇ *I hope you're right, for all our sakes* (= because this is important for all of us). 我希望你沒事，這對我們大家都好。**for the sake of sth/of doing sth** in order to get or keep sth 為獲得（或保持）某物：*The translation sacrifices naturalness for the sake of accuracy.* 這篇譯文為求準確而不惜犧牲自然流暢。◇ *She gave up smoking for the sake of her health.* 為保持身體健康，她戒了煙。◇ *Don't get married **just for the sake of it**.* 不要為結婚而結婚。◇ *Let's suppose, **for the sake of argument*** (= in order to have a discussion), *that interest rates went up by 2%.* 為了便於討論，不妨設想利率提高了 2%。➲ more at OLD

sake² (also **saki**) /ˈsɑːki/ *noun* [U] a Japanese alcoholic drink made from rice 日本清酒 ➲ see also SAKE¹

sa·laam /səˈlɑːm/ *verb* [I, T] ~ (**sb**) (in some Eastern countries) to say hello to sb in a formal way by bending forward from the waist and putting your right hand on your FOREHEAD 行額手大禮（一些東方國家正式打招呼的方式，右手置額前鞠躬）▶ **sa·laam** *noun*

sal·acious /səˈleɪʃəs/ *adj.* (*formal*) (of stories, pictures, etc. 故事、圖片等) encouraging sexual desire or containing too much sexual detail 淫穢的；色情的 ▶ **sal·acious·ness** *noun* [U]

salad 0‑m /ˈsæləd/ *noun*
1 0‑m [U, C] a mixture of raw vegetables such as LETTUCE, tomato and CUCUMBER, usually served with other food as part of a meal（生吃的）蔬菜色拉，蔬菜沙拉：*All main courses come with salad or vegetables.* 所有主菜都配有色拉或蔬菜。◇ *Is cold meat and salad OK for lunch?* 午飯吃冷肉和色拉行嗎？◇ *a **side salad*** (= a small bowl of salad served with the main course of a meal) 配菜色拉（作為一道副菜）◇ *a **salad bowl*** (= a large bowl for serving salad in) 色拉碗 ➲ COLLOCATIONS at COOKING ➲ see also CAESAR SALAD, GREEN SALAD **2** 0‑m [C, U] (in compounds 構成複合詞) meat, fish, cheese, etc. served with salad（拌有肉、魚、奶酪等的）混合色拉，混合沙拉：*a chicken salad* 雞肉色拉 **3** 0‑m [U, C] (in compounds 構成複合詞) raw or cooked vegetables, etc. that are cut into small pieces, often mixed with MAYONNAISE and served cold with other food（或生或熟，多拌有蛋黃醬，與麵食、豆類等一起食用的）蔬菜色拉，蔬菜沙拉：*potato salad* 土豆色拉 ◇ *a pasta salad* 意大利粉色拉 ➲ see also FRUIT SALAD **4** [U] any green vegetable, especially LETTUCE, that is eaten raw in a salad 拌色拉的青菜（尤指生菜）：*salad plants* 色拉蔬菜
IDM **your ˈsalad days** (*old-fashioned*) the time when you are young and do not have much experience of life 年少不諳世事的歲月；涉世未深的青少年時代

ˈsalad cream *noun* [U] (*BrE*) a pale yellow sauce, similar to MAYONNAISE, sold in bottles and eaten on salads, in SANDWICHES, etc. 色拉醬；沙拉醬

ˈsalad dressing *noun* [U, C] = DRESSING (1)

sala·man·der /ˈsæləmændə(r)/ *noun* an animal like a LIZARD, with short legs and a long tail, that lives both on land and in water (= is an AMPHIBIAN) 蠑螈（兩棲動物，形似蜥蜴）➲ VISUAL VOCAB page V13

sa·lami /səˈlɑːmi/ *noun* [U, C] (*pl.* **sa·lamis**) a type of large spicy SAUSAGE served cold in thin slices 薩拉米香腸（味濃，多切片冷食）

saˈlami slicing *noun* [U] (*informal*) the act of removing sth gradually by small amounts at a time 逐漸的除去

sal·ar·ied /ˈsælərid/ *adj.* **1** (of a person 人) receiving a salary 領薪水的：*a salaried employee* 領薪水的雇員 **2** (of a job 工作) for which a salary is paid 付給薪水的：*a salaried position* 付給薪水的職位

sal·ary 0‑m /ˈsæləri/ *noun* (*pl.* **-ies**)
money that employees receive for doing their job, especially professional employees or people working in an office, usually paid every month 薪金，薪水（尤指按月發放的）：*an annual salary of $40 000* * 4 萬元的年薪 ◇ *a 9% salary increase* 加薪 9% ◇ *She's **on a salary of** £24 000.* 她的薪金是 24 000 英鎊。◇ (*BrE*) *He gets a **basic salary** plus commission.* 他領取基本薪金，外加佣金。◇ (*NAmE*) ***base salary*** 底薪 ➲ compare WAGE ➲ SYNONYMS at INCOME

sal·ary·man /'sælərimæn/ *noun* (*pl.* **-men** /-men/) (especially in Japan) a WHITE-COLLAR worker (= one who works in an office) （尤指日本的）白領階層人員，白領

sal·but·am·ol /sæl'bju:təmɒl; *NAmE* -mɔ:l; -mɑ:l/ *noun* [U] a drug that is used in the treatment of medical conditions such as ASTHMA 沙丁胺醇，舒喘寧（哮喘等用）

sale /seɪl/ *noun*
1 [U, C] an act or the process of selling sth 出售；銷售：*regulations governing the sale of alcoholic beverages* 含酒精飲料的銷售管理條例 ◇ *I haven't* ***made a sale*** *all week.* 整整一個星期我什麼也沒賣出去。◇ *She gets 10% commission on each sale.* 每筆生意她得 10% 的佣金。
2 **sales** [pl.] the number of items sold 銷售量：*Retail sales fell in November by 10%.* 十一月份零售額下降 10%。◇ *Export sales were up by 32% last year.* 去年出口銷售額增長了 32%。◇ *the* ***sales figures*** *for May* 五月份的銷售數字 ◇ *a* ***sales drive/campaign*** (= a special effort to sell more) 促銷活動 ⇨ COLLOCATIONS at BUSINESS
3 **sales** [U] (also **'sales department** [C]) the part of a company that deals with selling its products 銷售部：*a sales and marketing director* 市場銷售部經理 ◇ *She works in sales/in the sales department.* 她在銷售部工作。◇ *The Weldon Group has a 6 000 strong* ***sales force****.* 威爾登集團有 6 000 人的銷售隊伍。**4** [C] an occasion when a shop/store sells its goods at a lower price than usual 特價銷售；廉價出售；大減價：*The sale starts next week.* 特價促銷從下星期開始。◇ *the January sales* 元月大減價 ◇ *I bought a coat* ***in the sales****.* 我在大減價時買了一件外套。◇ *sale prices* 特價 **5** [C] an occasion when goods are sold, especially an AUCTION 銷售活動；（尤指）拍賣：*a contemporary art sale* 當代藝術品拍賣會 ⇨ see also CAR BOOT SALE, GARAGE SALE, JUMBLE SALE

IDM **for 'sale** available to be bought, especially from the owner 待售；供出售（尤指從物主手裏）：*I'm sorry, it's not for sale.* 抱歉，這個不賣。◇ *They've* ***put their house up for sale****.* 他們的房子現在出售。◇ *an increase in the number of stolen vehicles being* ***offered for sale*** 用於售賣的被盜車輛在數量上的增加 ◇ *a 'for sale' sign* "待售"標誌 **on 'sale** **1** available to be bought, especially in a shop/store （尤指在商店）出售，上市：*Tickets are on sale from the booking office.* 售票處正在售票。◇ *The new model* ***goes on sale*** *next month.* 新款下月上市。**2** (*especially NAmE, SAfrE*) being offered at a reduced price 折價銷售；減價出售：*All video equipment is on sale today and tomorrow.* 所有錄像設備今明兩天降價出售。**(on) ˌsale or re'turn** (*BrE*) (of goods 商品) supplied with the agreement that any item that is not sold can be sent back without having to be paid for 剩貨包退（任何售不出去的商品均可退給供貨商）

sale·able /'seɪləbl/ *adj.* good enough to be sold; that sb will want to buy 適銷的；有銷路的：*a saleable product* 適銷產品 ◇ *not in saleable condition* 不適合銷售 **OPP** **unsaleable**

ˌsale of 'work *noun* (*pl.* **ˌsales of 'work**) (*BrE*) a sale of things made by members of an organization, such as a church, often to make money for charity 自製物品義賣

sale·room /'seɪlru:m; -rʊm/ (*BrE*) (*NAmE* **sales·room**) *noun* a room where goods are sold at an AUCTION 拍賣場

'sales clerk (also **clerk**) (both *NAmE*) (*BrE* **'shop assistant**, **as·sist·ant**) *noun* a person whose job is to serve customers in a shop/store 店員；售貨員

sales·girl /'seɪlzgɜ:l; *NAmE* -gɜ:rl/ *noun* a girl or woman who works in a shop/store 女店員；女售貨員

sales·man /'seɪlzmən/, **sales·woman** /'seɪlzwʊmən/ *noun* (*pl.* **-men** /-mən/, **-women** /-wɪmɪn/) a man or woman whose job is to sell goods, for example, in a shop/store 售貨員；推銷員：*a car salesman* 汽車推銷員 ⇨ note at GENDER

sales·man·ship /'seɪlzmənʃɪp/ *noun* [U] skill in persuading people to buy things 推銷術；銷售技巧

sales·per·son /'seɪlzpɜ:sn; *NAmE* -pɜ:rsn/ *noun* (*pl.* **-people**) a person whose job is to sell goods, for example, in a shop/store 售貨員；推銷員

'sales representative (also *informal* **'sales rep**, **rep**) *noun* an employee of a company who travels around a particular area selling the company's goods to shops/stores, etc. 銷售代表

sales·room /'seɪlzru:m; -rʊm/ (*NAmE*) (*BrE* **sale·room**) *noun* a room where goods are sold at an AUCTION 拍賣場

'sales slip *noun* (*NAmE*) = RECEIPT (1)

'sales talk *noun* [U] talk that tries to persuade sb to buy sth 推銷商品的說辭

'sales tax *noun* [U, C] (in some countries) the part of the price you pay when you buy sth that goes to the government as tax 銷售稅（某些國家的稅種，由消費者負擔）

sales·woman *noun* ⇨ SALESMAN

sali·cyl·ic acid /ˌsælɪˌsɪlɪk 'æsɪd/ *noun* [U] a bitter chemical found in some plants, used in ASPIRIN (= a drug used for reducing pain and making your blood thinner) 水楊酸；鄰羥基苯甲酸

sa·li·ent /'seɪliənt/ *adj.* [only before noun] most important or noticeable 最重要的；顯著的；突出的：*She pointed out the* ***salient features*** *of the new design.* 她指出新設計的幾個顯著特徵。◇ *He summarized the* ***salient points****.* 他對要點作了歸納。

sa·line /'seɪlaɪn; *NAmE* -li:n/ *adj., noun*
■ ***adj.*** [usually before noun] (*technical* 術語) containing salt 鹽的；含鹽的；鹹的：*Wash the lenses in saline solution.* 用鹽溶液清洗鏡片。► **sal·in·ity** /sə'lɪnəti/ *noun* [U]：*to measure the salinity of the water* 測量水的鹹度
■ ***noun*** [U] (*technical* 術語) a mixture of salt in water 鹽水

Salis·bury steak /ˌsɔ:lzbri 'steɪk/ *noun* (*NAmE*) finely chopped beef mixed with egg and onions made into a flat, round shape and cooked under or over a strong heat 索爾茲伯里牛肉餅（用碎牛肉和蛋、洋葱調製，大火煎烤而成）

sal·iva /sə'laɪvə/ *noun* [U] the liquid that is produced in your mouth that helps you to swallow food 唾液

sal·iv·ary /sə'laɪvəri; 'sælɪvəri; *NAmE* 'sæləveri/ *adj.* (*technical* 術語) of or producing saliva 唾液的；產生唾液的

sali·vate /'sælɪveɪt/ *verb* [I] (*formal*) to produce more SALIVA in your mouth than usual, especially when you see or smell food （尤指看到或嗅到食物時）垂涎，流口水：(*figurative*) *He was salivating over the thought of the million dollars.* 想到那一百萬元，他垂涎欲滴。► **sali·va·tion** /ˌsælɪ'veɪʃn/ *noun* [U]

sal·low /'sæləʊ; *NAmE* -loʊ/ *adj., noun*
■ ***adj.*** (of a person's skin or face 人的皮膚或面色) having a slightly yellow colour that does not look healthy 灰黃的；蠟黃的 **SYN** **pasty**
■ ***noun*** a type of WILLOW tree that does not grow very tall 黃華柳

sally /'sæli/ *noun, verb*
■ ***noun*** (*pl.* **sal·lies**) **1** a remark that is intended to entertain or amuse sb 俏皮話 **SYN** **witticism** **2** a sudden attack by an enemy 出擊；突襲
■ ***verb*** (**sal·lies**, **sally·ing**, **sal·lied**, **sal·lied**)
PHR V **ˌsally 'forth/'out** (*old-fashioned* or *literary*) to leave a place in a determined or enthusiastic way 毅然出發；興沖沖地離開

sal·mon /'sæmən/ *noun* [C, U] (*pl.* **sal·mon**) a large fish with silver skin and pink flesh that is used for food. Salmon live in the sea but swim up rivers to lay their eggs. 鮭；大麻哈魚：*a whole salmon* 一整條鮭魚 ◇ *smoked salmon* 熏鮭魚 ◇ *wild and farmed salmon* 野生和人工養殖的鮭魚

sal·mon·ella /ˌsælmə'nelə/ *noun* [U] a type of bacteria that makes people sick if they eat infected food; an illness caused by this bacteria 沙門菌：*cases of salmonella poisoning* 沙門菌中毒病例 ◇ *an outbreak of salmonella* 沙門菌的爆發

ˌsalmon 'pink *adj.* orange-pink in colour, like the flesh of a salmon 鮭肉色的；橙紅色的 ► **ˌsalmon 'pink** *noun* [U]

salon /ˈsælɒn; *NAmE* səˈlɑːn; səˈlɔːn/ *noun* **1** a shop/store that gives customers hair or beauty treatment or that sells expensive clothes 美髮廳；美容廳；高級服裝店：*a beauty salon* 美容廳 ◇ *a hairdressing salon* 美髮廳 **2** (*old-fashioned*) a room in a large house used for entertaining guests（大宅中的）客廳，會客室 **3** (in the past) a regular meeting of writers, artists and other guests at the house of a famous or important person 沙龍（舊時作家、藝術家等在名流家中定期舉行的聚會）：*a literary salon* 文藝沙龍

sal·oon /səˈluːn/ *noun* **1** (also **saˈloon car**) (both *BrE*) (*NAmE* **sedan**) a car with four doors and a BOOT/TRUNK (= space at the back for carrying things) which is separated from the part where the driver and passengers sit 小轎車；（三廂）四門轎車：*a five-seater family saloon* 五座家庭式轎車 ➲ VISUAL VOCAB page V52 **2** (also **saˈloon bar**) (both *BrE*) = LOUNGE BAR **3** a bar where alcoholic drinks were sold in the western US and Canada in the past（舊時美國西部和加拿大的）酒吧，酒館 **4** a large comfortable room on a ship, used by the passengers to sit and relax in（客輪上的）交誼廳

sal·op·ettes /ˌsæləˈpets/ *noun* [pl.] a piece of clothing worn for SKIING or sailing, consisting of trousers/pants with a part that comes up over your shoulders（滑雪或帆船運動穿的）背帶褲，工裝褲

salsa /ˈsælsə; *NAmE* ˈsɑːlsə/ *noun* **1** [U] a type of Latin American dance music 薩爾薩舞曲（一種拉丁美洲舞曲）**2** [C, U] a dance performed to this music 薩爾薩舞 **3** [U] a sauce eaten with Mexican food 辛香番茄醬（常用於墨西哥食物）

sal·sify /ˈsælsəfi/ *noun* [U] (*BrE*) a plant with a long root that is cooked and eaten as a vegetable 蒜葉婆羅門參（可作蔬菜食用）

salt 0━ /sɔːlt; *BrE* also sɒlt; *NAmE* sɔːlt/ *noun*, *verb*, *adj*.

■ ***noun*** **1** 0━ [U] a white substance that is added to food to give it a better flavour or to preserve it. Salt is obtained from mines and is also found in sea water. It is sometimes called **common salt** to distinguish it from other chemical salts. 鹽；食鹽 SYN **sodium chloride**：*Pass the salt, please.* 請把鹽遞過來。◇ *a pinch of salt* (= a small amount of it) 一撮鹽 ◇ *Season with salt and pepper.* 放鹽和胡椒粉調味。◇ *sea salt* 海鹽 ➲ see also ROCK SALT **2** [C] (*chemistry* 化) a chemical formed from a metal and an acid 鹽（金屬和酸組成的化學物質）：*mineral salts* 礦鹽 ➲ see also EPSOM SALTS **3 salts** [pl.] a substance that looks or tastes like salt 形狀（或味道）像鹽的物質：*bath salts* (= used to give a pleasant smell to bath water)（放在洗澡水中使之芳香的）浴鹽 ➲ see also SMELLING SALTS

IDM **the salt of the ˈearth** a very good and honest person that you can always depend on 世上的鹽，地上的鹽（指善良而信實的人）➲ more at DOSE *n.*, PINCH *n.*, RUB *v.*, WORTH *adj.*

■ ***verb*** **1** [usually passive] **~ sth** to put salt on or in food 在（食物）中放鹽：*salted peanuts* 鹹花生米 ◇ *a pan of boiling salted water* 一鍋放了鹽的開水 **2 ~ sth (down)** to preserve food with salt 用鹽醃製（食物）：*salted fish* 鹹魚 **3 ~ sth** to put salt on roads to melt ice or snow 把鹽撒在路面上（以使冰雪融化）

PHR V **ˌsalt sth↔aˈway** to save sth for the future, secretly and usually dishonestly（通常指以欺瞞手段）秘密貯存：*She salted away the profits in foreign bank accounts.* 她把利潤偷偷存在外國的銀行賬戶上。

■ ***adj.*** [only before noun] containing, tasting of or preserved with salt 含鹽的；鹹的；用鹽醃製的：*salt water* 海水 ◇ *salt beef* 醃牛肉

ˌsalt-and-ˈpepper *adj.* = PEPPER-AND-SALT

salt·box /ˈsɔːltbɒks; *NAmE* -bɑːks; *BrE* also ˈsɒlt-/ *noun* (*NAmE*) a house that has two floors at the front and one floor at the back, with a roof that slopes down between the two floors（坡頂）鹽盒式房子

ˈsalt cellar *noun* **1** (*BrE*) (*NAmE* **ˈsalt shaker**) a small container for salt, usually with one hole in the top, that is used at the table（餐桌用）小鹽瓶 ➲ VISUAL VOCAB page V22 **2** (*NAmE*) a small open dish containing salt 鹽碟

ˈsalt flats *noun* [pl.] a flat area of land, covered with a layer of salt 鹽灘；鹽坪

salt·ine /sɔːlˈtiːn; sɒl-; *NAmE* sɔːl-/ (also **ˌsaltine ˈcracker**) *noun* (*NAmE*) a thin dry biscuit with salt on top of it 蘇打餅乾；鹽餅乾

sal·tire /ˈsæltaɪə(r); ˈsɔːl-/ (also **ˌsaltire ˈcross**) *noun* **1** a cross in the shape of an X, especially on a COAT OF ARMS or a flag * X 形十字；（尤指盾徽或旗子上的）X 形十字圖記 **2 the Saltire** the flag of Scotland, which is a white saltire on a blue background（藍底白斜十字的）蘇格蘭旗，蘇格蘭聖安德魯旗

ˈsalt marsh (also **ˈsalt meadow**) *noun* an area of open land near a coast that is regularly flooded by the sea 鹽沼，鹽生草澤（在海岸附近，常遭海水淹灌）

ˈsalt pan *noun* an area of low land where sea water has EVAPORATED to leave salt 鹽盤，淺鹽湖（低地因海水蒸發而形成）

salt·petre (*US* **salt·peter**) /ˌsɔːltˈpiːtə(r); *BrE* also ˌsɒlt-; *NAmE* ˌsɔːlt-/ *noun* [U] a white powder used for preserving food and making matches and GUNPOWDER 硝石；鉀硝；硝酸鉀

ˈsalt truck (*US*) (*BrE* **grit·ter**) *noun* a large vehicle used for putting salt, sand or GRIT on the roads in winter when there is ice on them 鋪沙機，撒鹽車，撒沙車（在冬天結冰的路面上使用）

ˈsalt water *noun* [U] sea water; water containing salt 海水；鹹水；鹽水 ▸ **ˈsalt·water** *adj.* [only before noun]：*saltwater fish* 鹹水魚 ➲ compare FRESHWATER

salty 0━ /ˈsɔːlti; *BrE* also ˈsɒlti; *NAmE* ˈsɔːlti/ *adj.* (**salt·ier**, **salti·est**)
1 0━ containing or tasting of salt 含鹽的；鹹的：*salty food* 鹹的食物 ◇ *salty sea air* 海邊帶鹹味的空氣 ➲ compare SWEET *adj.* (1) **2** (*old-fashioned*) (of language or humour 語言或幽默) amusing and sometimes slightly rude 有趣的；逗笑的；有趣而略嫌粗俗的 ▸ **salti·ness** *noun* [U]：*She could taste the saltiness of her tears.* 她嚐到了她眼淚的鹹味。

sa·lu·bri·ous /səˈluːbriəs/ *adj.* (*formal*) (of a place 地方) pleasant to live in; clean and healthy 環境宜人的；清潔而有益健康的 OPP **insalubrious**

salu·tary /ˈsæljətri; *NAmE* -teri/ *adj.* having a good effect on sb/sth, though often seeming unpleasant 有益的（儘管往往讓人不愉快）：*a **salutary lesson/experience/warning*** 有益的教訓／經歷／告誡 ◇ *The accident was a **salutary reminder** of the dangers of climbing.* 這次事故提醒人們注意登山的種種危險，倒也不無益處。

sa·lu·ta·tion /ˌsæljuˈteɪʃn/ *noun* **1** [C, U] (*formal*) something that you say to welcome or say hello to sb; the action of welcoming or saying hello to sb 招呼；致意；打招呼；致意的動作 **2** [C] (*technical* 術語) the words that are used in a letter to address the person you are writing to, for example 'Dear Sir'（信函中如 Dear Sir 之類的）稱呼語

sa·lute /səˈluːt/ *verb*, *noun*

■ ***verb*** **1** [I, T] to touch the side of your head with the fingers of your right hand to show respect, especially in the armed forces（尤指軍隊中）敬禮：*The sergeant stood to attention and saluted.* 中士立正敬禮。◇ **~ sb/sth** *to salute the flag/an officer* 向旗幟／長官敬禮 **2** [T] **~ sb/sth** (*formal*) to express respect and admiration for sb/sth 致敬；表示敬意 SYN **acknowledge**：*The players saluted the fans before leaving the field.* 球員在退場前向球迷致意。◇ *The president saluted the courage of those who had fought for their country.* 總統對那些為國戰鬥者的英勇精神表示敬意。

■ ***noun*** **1** [C] the action of raising your right hand to the side of your head as a sign of respect, especially between soldiers and officers（尤指士兵和軍官之間的）敬禮 **2** [C, U] a thing that you say or do to show your admiration or respect for sb/sth or to welcome sb 致敬；致意：*He raised his hat as a friendly salute.* 他舉帽友好致意。◇ *His first words were a salute to the people of South Africa.* 他開口首先向南非人民致敬。◇ *They all* *raised their glasses **in salute**.* 他們都舉杯致意。 **3** [C] an official occasion when guns are fired into the air to show respect for an important person 鳴禮炮；鳴炮致敬： *a 21-gun salute* 鳴炮 21 響的禮儀

sal·vage /ˈsælvɪdʒ/ *noun, verb*

▪ ***noun*** [U] **1** the act of saving things that have been, or are likely to be, damaged or lost, especially in a disaster or an accident（對財物等的）搶救： *the salvage of the wrecked tanker* 對失事油輪的搶救 ◇ *a **salvage company/operation/team*** 打撈公司；營救行動；搶救隊 **2** the things that are saved from a disaster or an accident 搶救出的財物： *an exhibition of the salvage from the wreck* 沉船打撈物品展覽

▪ ***verb*** **1** to save a badly damaged ship, etc. from being lost completely; to save parts or property from a damaged ship or from a fire, etc. 營救（失事船舶等）；搶救（失事船舶、火災等中的財物）： **~ sth** *The wreck was salvaged by a team from the RAF.* 失事船隻得到皇家空軍救援小組的救助。 ◇ *The house was built using salvaged materials.* 這棟房子是用回收的廢舊材料建成的。 ◇ **~ sth from sth** *We only managed to salvage two paintings from the fire.* 我們只從火災中搶救出兩幅畫。 **2 ~ sth** to manage to rescue sth from a difficult situation; to stop a bad situation from being a complete failure 挽救；挽回： *What can I do to salvage my reputation* (= get a good reputation again)? 我怎樣才能挽回我的名聲呢？ ◇ *He wondered what he could do to salvage the situation.* 他不知道怎樣才能挽救這個局面。 ◇ *United lost 5–2, salvaging a little pride with two late goals.* 聯隊以 2:5 失利，只靠後來兩次進球挽回了一點面子。

ˈsalvage yard *noun* (*NAmE*) a place where old machines, cars, etc. are broken up so that the metal can be sold or used again（廢舊機器、舊車等拆售的）廢品回收場

sal·va·tion /sælˈveɪʃn/ *noun* [U] **1** (in Christianity 基督教) the state of being saved from the power of evil 得救；救恩；救世： *to pray for the salvation of the world* 為世人得救而禱告 **2** a way of protecting sb from danger, disaster, loss, etc.（危險、災難、損失等的）避免方式，解救途徑：*Group therapy classes have been his salvation.* 他一直靠參加集體療法班來調節心理。

the Salˌvation ˈArmy *noun* [sing.] a Christian organization whose members wear military uniforms and work to help poor people（基督教的）救世軍

salve *noun, verb*

▪ ***noun*** /sælv; *NAmE* also sæv/ [U, C] a substance that you put on a wound or sore skin to help it heal or to protect it 藥膏；軟膏；油膏 ➲ see also LIPSALVE

▪ ***verb*** /sælv/ **~ your conscience** (*formal*) to do sth that makes you feel less guilty 使良心得到寬慰；減輕內疚感

sal·ver /ˈsælvə(r)/ *noun* a large plate, usually made of metal, on which drinks or food are served at a formal event 金屬托盤（正式場合用於上飲料或食物）

salvo /ˈsælvəʊ; *NAmE* -voʊ/ *noun* (*pl.* **-os** or **-oes**) the act of firing several guns or dropping several bombs, etc. at the same time; a sudden attack 齊射；齊投；奇襲： *The first salvo exploded a short distance away.* 第一批投下的炸彈在不遠處爆炸。 ◇ (*figurative*) *The newspaper article was **the opening salvo** in what proved to be a long battle.* 報上那篇文章是一場長期論戰的開篇第一炮。

sal vola·tile /ˌsæl vəˈlætəli/ *noun* [U] a type of SMELLING SALTS 碳酸銨（一種嗅鹽）

sal·war (also **shal·war**) /sʌlˈwɑː(r)/ *noun* light loose trousers/pants that are tight around the ankles, sometimes worn by S Asian women（南亞）女式收口寬鬆褲： *a salwar kameez* (= a salwar worn with a KAMEEZ) 寬鬆褲克米茲套裝

Sa·mar·itan /səˈmærɪtən/ *noun*

IDM **a ˌgood Saˈmaritan** a person who gives help and sympathy to people who need it 善良的撒瑪利亞人；善人；樂善好施者 **ORIGIN** From the Bible story of a person from Samaria who helps an injured man that nobody else will help. 源自《聖經》裏的故事，一個撒瑪利亞人向一個受傷但無人給予幫助的人伸出援助之手。

the Sa·mar·itans *noun* [pl.] a British charity that offers help to people who are very depressed and in danger of killing themselves, by providing a phone number that they can ring in order to talk to sb 撒瑪利亞會（英國慈善團體，為嚴重抑鬱和想自殺的人提供熱線電話談心服務）

sa·mar·ium /səˈmeəriəm; *NAmE* -ˈmer-/ *noun* [U] (*symb.* **Sm**) a chemical element. Samarium is a hard silver-white metal used in making strong MAGNETS. 釤

samba /ˈsæmbə/ *noun* a fast dance originally from Brazil; a piece of music for this dance 桑巴舞（源於巴西，節奏快）；桑巴舞曲

same 🔑 /seɪm/ *adj., pron., adv.*

▪ ***adj.*** **1** 🔑 exactly the one or ones referred to or mentioned; not different 同一的；相同的： *We have lived in the same house for twenty years.* 我們在同一座房子裏住了二十年了。 ◇ *Our children go to the **same** school **as** theirs.* 我們的孩子和他們的孩子上同一所學校。 ◇ *She's still the **same** fun-loving person **that** I knew at college.* 她仍愛耍愛鬧，還是上大學時的那副老樣子。 ◇ *This one works in **exactly the same** way as the other.* 這個跟那個運轉方法完全一樣。 ◇ *They both said **much the same** thing.* 他們兩人的話大致一樣。 ◇ *He used **the very same*** (= exactly the same) *words.* 他用了完全相同的字眼兒。 ◇ *I resigned last Friday and left that same day.* 我上星期五辭了職，當天就離開了。 **2** 🔑 exactly like the one or ones referred to or mentioned（與…）相同的，一模一樣的： *I bought the **same** car **as** yours* (= another car of that type). 我買了一輛車，和你那輛一模一樣。 ◇ *She was wearing the **same** dress **that** I had on.* 她穿的連衣裙和我穿的一樣。 ◇ *The same thing happened to me last week.* 上星期我也遇到了同樣的事。

IDM Most idioms containing **same** are at the entries for the nouns and verbs in the idioms, for example **be in the same boat** is at **boat**. 大多數含 same 的習語，都可在該等習語中的名詞及動詞相關詞條找到，如 be in the same boat 在詞條 boat 下。 **ˈsame old, ˈsame old** (*informal, especially NAmE*) used to say that a situation has not changed at all 老樣子；照舊不變： *'How's it going?' 'Oh, same old, same old.'* "情況怎麼樣？" "哦，還是老樣子。"

▪ ***pron.*** **1** 🔑 **the ~** (**as** …) the same thing or things（和…）同樣的事物，相同的事物： *I would do the same again.* 我願再做同樣的事。 ◇ *I think the same as you do about this.* 在這件事上，我的想法和你一樣。 ◇ *Just do the same as me* (= as I do). 跟着我做就行了。 ◇ *His latest movie is just **more of the same**—exotic locations, car chases and a final shoot-out.* 他的最新影片只不過是老一套，異國的場景、追車場面，以及最後的一場槍戰。 ◇ (*informal*) *'I'll have coffee.' 'Same for me, please* (= I will have one too).*'* "我喝咖啡。" "我也來一杯。" **2** 🔑 **the ~** (**as** …) having the same number, colour, size, quality, etc.（數目、顏色、大小、質量等）相同，一樣： *There are several brands and they're not all the same.* 有好幾個品牌，不一樣的。 ◇ *I'd like one the same as yours.* 我要一個和你一樣的。 **3 the same** (*BrE*) the same person 同一個人： *'Was that George on the phone?' 'The same* (= yes, it was George).*'* "是跟喬治通的電話嗎？" "正是。"

IDM **ˌall/ˌjust the ˈsame** 🔑 despite this 雖是這樣；儘管如此 **SYN** **nevertheless**： *He's not very reliable, but I like him just the same.* 他不太可靠，但我還是喜歡他。 ◇ *'Will you stay for lunch?' 'No, but thanks all the same.'* "留下來吃午飯，好嗎？" "不了，多謝。" ◇ *All the same, there's some truth in what she says.* 儘管如此，她說的還是有些道理的。 **be all the ˈsame to sb** to not be important to sb 對某人無關緊要（或無所謂）： *It's all the same to me whether we eat now or later.* 我們現在吃也行，過一會兒吃也行，我無所謂。 **ˌone and the ˈsame** the same person or thing 同一個人；同一事物： *It turns out that her aunt and my cousin are one and the same.* 原來她姑媽就是我表姐。 **(the) ˌsame aˈgain** 🔑 (*informal*) used to ask sb to serve you the same drink as before 同樣的（飲料）再來一份： *Same again, please!* 和剛才一樣的，請再來一份！ **ˌsame ˈhere** (*informal*) used to say that sth is also true of you 我也一樣；我也是： *'I can't wait to see it.' 'Same here.'* "我巴不得馬上看到它。" "我也一樣。" **(the) ˌsame to ˈyou** 🔑 (*informal*) used to answer a GREETING, an insult, etc.（回應問候、辱罵等）你也一樣： *'Happy Christmas!' 'And the same to you!'*

S

"聖誕快樂！""也祝您聖誕快樂！" ◇ *'Get lost!' 'Same to you!'* "滾！""你也滾！"

■ ***adv.*** (usually **the same**) in the same way 同樣：*We treat boys exactly* ***the same as*** *girls.* 男孩、女孩我們完全同等對待。◇ *(informal) He gave me five dollars,* ***same as usual.*** 和平時一樣，他給了我五塊錢。

same·ness /ˈseɪmnəs/ *noun* [U] the quality of being the same; a lack of variety 相同性；同一性；千篇一律；單調：*She grew tired of the sameness of the food.* 飯菜單調，她都吃膩了。

ˈsame-sex *adj.* [only before noun] **1** of the same sex 同性別的：*The child's same-sex parent acts as a role model.* 孩子的同性家長是孩子效仿的榜樣。**2** involving people of the same sex 涉及同性別的人的：*a same-sex relationship* 同性戀情

samey /ˈseɪmi/ *adj.* (*BrE, informal, disapproving*) not changing or different and therefore boring 千篇一律的；單調乏味的

sa·mosa /səˈməʊsə; *NAmE* -ˈmoʊ-/ *noun* a type of hot spicy S Asian food consisting of a triangle of thin crisp PASTRY filled with meat or vegetables and fried 薩莫薩三角炸餃（南亞食品）

samo·var /ˈsæməvɑː(r)/ *noun* a large container for heating water, used especially in Russia for making tea（尤指俄式）茶炊

samp /sæmp/ *noun* [U] (*SAfrE*) the inner parts of MAIZE/CORN seeds that are crushed roughly; a type of PORRIDGE that is made from this 玉米楂；玉米楂粥

sam·pan /ˈsæmpæn/ *noun* a small boat with a flat bottom used along the coast and rivers of China 舢板

sam·ple /ˈsɑːmpl; *NAmE* ˈsæmpl/ *noun, verb*

■ ***noun*** **1** a number of people or things taken from a larger group and used in tests to provide information about the group（抽查的）樣本，樣品：*The interviews were given to a* ***random sample*** *of students.* 隨機抽選出部份學生進行了採訪。◇ *The survey covers a* ***representative sample*** *of schools.* 調查覆蓋了一些有代表性的學校。◇ *a sample survey* 抽樣調查 **2** a small amount of a substance taken from a larger amount and tested in order to obtain information about the substance（化驗的）取樣，樣本，樣：*a blood sample* 血樣 ◇ *Samples of the water contained pesticide.* 水樣中含有殺蟲劑。➲ COLLOCATIONS at SCIENTIFIC **3** a small amount or example of sth that can be looked at or tried to see what it is like（作為標準或代表的）樣品，貨樣：*'I'd like to see a sample of your work,' said the manager.* "拿一件你做的貨樣給我看看。"經理說。◇ *a* ***free sample*** *of shampoo* 免費試用的洗髮劑 **4** (*technical* 術語) a piece of recorded music or sound that is used in a new piece of music（用於新樂曲中的）節錄樂曲，選錄樂曲（或聲音）

■ ***verb*** **1 ~ sth** to try a small amount of a particular food to see what it is like; to experience sth for a short time to see what it is like 嚐；品嚐；嘗試；體驗：*I sampled the delights of Greek cooking for the first time.* 我第一次體驗到希臘烹飪的樂趣。**2 ~ sb/sth** (*technical* 術語) to test, question, etc., part of sth or of a group of people in order to find out what the rest is like 抽樣檢驗；取樣；採樣：*12% of the children sampled said they prefer cats to dogs.* 在被抽樣調查的孩子中，12% 說他們喜歡貓勝過喜歡狗。**3 ~ sth** (*technical* 術語) to record part of a piece of music, or a sound, in order to use it in a new piece of music 節錄，選錄（一段音樂或聲音，用於新的樂曲中）

sam·pler /ˈsɑːmplə(r); *NAmE* ˈsæm-/ *noun* **1** a piece of cloth decorated with different STITCHES that people made in the past to show a person's skill at sewing（舊時的）刺繡樣本 **2** a collection that shows typical examples of sth, especially pieces of music（尤指樂曲的）集錦，薈萃

sam·pling /ˈsɑːmplɪŋ; *NAmE* ˈsæm-/ *noun* [U] **1** the process of taking a sample 抽樣；取樣：*statistical sampling* 統計抽樣 **2** (*technical* 術語) the process of copying and recording parts of a piece of music in an electronic form so that they can be used in a different piece of music（樂曲的）節錄，選錄

ˈsampling error *noun* (*statistics* 統計) a situation in which a set of results or figures does not show a true situation, because the group of people or things it was based on was not typical of a wider group 抽樣誤差（所抽樣本不具備代表性）

sam·urai /ˈsæmuraɪ/ *noun* (*pl.* **sam·urai**) (from *Japanese*) (in the past) a member of a powerful military class in Japan（舊時日本的）武士

sana·tor·ium /ˌsænəˈtɔːriəm/ (*NAmE* also **sani·tar·ium** /ˌsænəˈteəriəm; *NAmE* -ˈter-/) *noun* (*pl.* **-riums** or **-ria** /-riə/) a place like a hospital where patients who have a lasting illness or who are getting better after an illness are treated 療養院；休養所

sanc·tify /ˈsæŋktɪfaɪ/ *verb* (**sanc·ti·fies, sanc·ti·fied, sanc·ti·fy·ing, sanc·ti·fied**) [usually passive] (*formal*) **1 ~ sth** to make sth holy 使神聖化 **2 ~ sth** to make sth seem right or legal; to give official approval to sth 使正當化；使合法化；批准；認可：*This was a practice sanctified by tradition.* 這是一種合乎傳統的做法。▸ **sanc·ti·fi·ca·tion** /ˌsæŋktɪfɪˈkeɪʃn/ *noun* [U]

sanc·ti·mo·ni·ous /ˌsæŋktɪˈməʊniəs; *NAmE* -ˈmoʊ-/ *adj.* (*disapproving*) giving the impression that you feel you are better and more moral than other people 裝作聖潔的；偽善的；道貌岸然的 SYN **self-righteous** ▸ **sanc·ti·mo·ni·ous·ly** *adv.* **sanc·ti·mo·ni·ous·ness** *noun* [U]

sanc·tion /ˈsæŋkʃn/ *noun, verb*

■ ***noun*** **1** [C, usually pl.] **~ (against sb)** an official order that limits trade, contact, etc. with a particular country, in order to make it do sth, such as obeying international law 制裁：*Trade sanctions were imposed against any country that refused to sign the agreement.* 凡拒簽該協議的國家均受到貿易制裁。◇ *The economic sanctions have been lifted.* 經濟制裁業已取消。➲ COLLOCATIONS at INTERNATIONAL **2** [U] (*formal*) official permission or approval for an action or a change（正式）許可，批准 SYN **authorization**：*These changes will require the sanction of the court.* 這些變更須經法院認可。**3** [C] **~ (against sth)** a course of action that can be used, if necessary, to make people obey a law or behave in a particular way 制裁；約束；處罰 SYN **penalty**：*The ultimate sanction will be the closure of the restaurant.* 最嚴厲的處罰將是關閉這家餐館。

■ ***verb*** **1 ~ sth** (*formal*) to give permission for sth to take place 許可；准許；准予：*The government refused to sanction a further cut in interest rates.* 政府拒絕批准進一步降低利率。**2 ~ sb/sth** (*technical* 術語) to punish sb/sth; to impose a sanction (1) on sth 懲罰；實施制裁

sanc·tity /ˈsæŋktəti/ *noun* [U] **1 ~ (of sth)** the state of being very important and worth protecting 神聖不可侵犯：*the* ***sanctity of marriage*** 婚姻之神聖 **2** the state of being holy 神聖性；聖潔性：*a life of sanctity, like that of St Francis* 聖方濟各式的聖潔生活

sanc·tu·ary /ˈsæŋktʃuəri; *NAmE* -ueri/ *noun* (*pl.* **-ies**) **1** [C] an area where wild birds or animals are protected and encouraged to breed 鳥獸保護區；禁獵區 SYN **reserve**：*a* ***bird/wildlife sanctuary*** 鳥類 / 野生動物保護區 **2** [U] safety and protection, especially for people who are being chased or attacked 庇護；保護：*to take sanctuary in a place* 在某處避難 ◇ *The government offered sanctuary to 4 000 refugees.* 政府為 4 000 名難民提供了保護。◇ *She longed for the sanctuary of her own home.* 她渴望回到自己家中，不再擔驚受怕。**3** [C, usually sing.] a safe place, especially one where people who are being chased or attacked can stay and be protected 避難所；庇護所：*The church became a sanctuary for the refugees.* 教堂成為這些難民的庇護所。**4** [C] a holy building or the part of it that is considered the most holy 聖所；聖殿

sanc·tum /ˈsæŋktəm/ *noun* [usually sing.] (*formal*) **1** a private room where sb can go and not be disturbed（不受干擾的）私室，密室：*She once allowed me into her* ***inner sanctum.*** 有一次她讓我進入她的內室。**2** a holy place 聖所

sand /sænd/ *noun, verb*

■ ***noun*** **1** [U] a substance that consists of very small fine grains of rock. Sand is found on beaches, in

S

deserts, etc. 沙：*a grain of sand* 一粒沙子◇ *Concrete is a mixture of sand and cement.* 混凝土是沙和水泥的混合物。◇ *His hair was the colour of sand.* 他的頭髮呈沙褐色。◇ *The children were playing in the sand* (= for example, in a SANDPIT). 孩子們正在玩沙子。➲ VISUAL VOCAB pages V4, V5 **2** [U, C, usually pl.] a large area of sand on a beach 沙灘：*We went for a walk along the sand.* 我們去沙灘上散了散步。◇ *children playing on the sand* 在沙灘上玩耍的兒童◇ *miles of golden sands* 綿延數英里的金色沙灘 ➲ SYNONYMS at COAST ➲ see also SANDY (1) IDM see HEAD *n.*, SHIFT *v.*

■ ***verb*** **~ sth (down)** to make sth smooth by rubbing it with sandpaper or using a sander（用砂紙或打磨機）打磨

san·dal /ˈsændl/ *noun* a type of light open shoe that is worn in warm weather. The top part consists of leather bands that attach the SOLE to your foot. 涼鞋 ➲ VISUAL VOCAB page V64

san·dalled (*BrE*) (*US* **san·daled**) /ˈsændld/ *adj.* [only before noun] wearing sandals 穿涼鞋的：*sandalled feet* 穿着涼鞋的腳

san·dal·wood /ˈsændlwʊd/ *noun* [U] a type of oil with a sweet smell that is obtained from a hard tropical wood (also called sandalwood) and is used to make PERFUME 檀香油（提取自檀香木，用於製作香水）

sand·bag /ˈsændbæg/ *noun, verb*

■ ***noun*** a bag filled with sand used to build a wall as a protection against floods or explosions（用於防洪、防爆的）沙袋，沙包

■ ***verb*** **(-gg-) 1 ~ sth** to put sandbags in or around sth as protection against floods or explosions 在…堆沙袋；用沙袋封堵 **2 ~ sb** (*informal, especially NAmE*) to attack sb by criticizing them strongly; to treat sb badly 猛烈抨擊；粗暴對待

sand·bank /ˈsændbæŋk/ *noun* a raised area of sand in a river or the sea 沙洲；沙壩 ➲ VISUAL VOCAB pages V4, V5

sand·bar /ˈsændbɑː(r)/ *noun* a long mass of sand at the point where a river meets the sea that is formed by the movement of the water（河口的）沙洲

sand·blast /ˈsændblɑːst; *NAmE* -blæst/ *verb* [often passive] **~ sth** to clean, polish, decorate, etc. a surface by firing sand at it from a special machine 噴沙（用以清污、打磨或裝飾物體表面）

sand·box /ˈsændbɒks; *NAmE* -bɑːks/ (*NAmE*) (*BrE* **sand·pit**) *noun* an area in the ground or a shallow container, filled with sand for children to play in（供兒童玩的）沙坑 ➲ VISUAL VOCAB page V37

sand·cas·tle /ˈsændkɑːsl; *NAmE* -kæsl/ *noun* a pile of sand made to look like a castle, usually by a child on a beach（通常指兒童在沙灘上堆成的）沙堡

ˈsand dune *noun* = DUNE

sand·er /ˈsændə(r)/ *noun* an electric tool with a rough surface used for making wood smooth 打磨機

s and h (also **s & h**) *abbr.* (*NAmE*) shipping and handling 運輸與處理 ➲ compare P. AND P.

ˈsand iron *noun* (*BrE*) = SAND WEDGE

S & L /ˌes ənd ˈel/ *abbr.* SAVINGS AND LOAN ASSOCIATION

sand·lot /ˈsændlɒt; *NAmE* -lɑːt/ *adj.* [only before noun] (*NAmE*) (of a sport 體育運動) played for enjoyment rather than as a job for money 非職業的；業餘的

the sand·man /ˈsændmæn/ *noun* [sing.] an imaginary man who is said to help children get to sleep（傳說中使小孩入睡的）睡魔

ˈsand martin *noun* a bird like a small SWALLOW, that makes its nest in banks of sand 崖沙燕；灰沙燕

sand·paper /ˈsændpeɪpə(r)/ *noun, verb*

■ ***noun*** [U] strong paper with a rough surface covered with sand or a similar substance, used for rubbing surfaces in order to make them smooth 砂紙

■ ***verb*** (also **sand**) **~ sth (down)** to make sth smooth by rubbing it with sandpaper 用砂紙打磨

sand·piper /ˈsændpaɪpə(r)/ *noun* a small bird with long legs and a long beak that lives near rivers and lakes 鷸

sand·pit /ˈsændpɪt/ (*BrE*) (*NAmE* **sand·box**) *noun* an area in the ground or a shallow container, filled with sand for children to play in（供兒童玩的）沙坑 ➲ VISUAL VOCAB page V37

sand·shoe /ˈsændʃuː/ *noun* (*ScotE, AustralE, NZE*) a PLIMSOLL (= a type of light cloth sports shoe with a rubber SOLE) 膠底帆布鞋；體操鞋

sand·stone /ˈsændstəʊn; *NAmE* -stoʊn/ *noun* [U] a type of stone that is formed of grains of sand tightly pressed together, used in building 砂岩

sand·storm /ˈsændstɔːm; *NAmE* -stɔːrm/ *noun* a storm in a desert in which sand is blown into the air by strong winds 沙暴

ˈsand trap (also **trap**) *noun* (both *NAmE*) = BUNKER (3)

ˈsand wedge (*BrE* also **ˈsand iron**) *noun* a GOLF CLUB used for hitting the ball out of sand 沙坑杆，障礙球杆（將高爾夫球從沙坑中打出）

sand·wich /ˈsænwɪtʃ; -wɪdʒ/ *noun, verb*

■ ***noun* 1** (also *BrE, informal* **sar·nie**) two slices of bread, often spread with butter, with a layer of meat, cheese, etc. between them 夾心麵包片；三明治：*a cheese sandwich* 奶酪三明治◇ *a **sandwich bar*** (= a place that sells sandwiches) 三明治櫃枱 ➲ see also CLUB SANDWICH, OPEN SANDWICH **2** (*BrE*) (in compounds 構成複合詞) a SPONGE CAKE consisting of two layers with jam and/or cream between them 夾心蛋糕

■ ***verb***

PHR V **ˈsandwich sb/sth between sb/sth** [usually passive] to fit sth/sb into a very small space between two other things or people, or between two times 把…夾（或插）在…中間：*I was sandwiched between two fat men on the bus.* 在公共汽車上，我被兩個胖子擠在中間。**ˌsandwich A and B toˈgether (with sth)** to put sth between two things to join them（用…）結合，粘合：*Sandwich the cakes together with cream.* 用奶油把兩塊蛋糕粘在一起。

ˈsandwich board *noun* a pair of boards with advertisements on them that sb wears at the front and back of their body as they walk around in public 夾板廣告牌，三明治式廣告牌（掛在胸前和後背的一副廣告牌）

ˈsandwich course *noun* (*BrE*) a course of study which includes periods of study and periods of working in business or industry 工讀交替制課程（部份時間上課，部份時間實習）

sandy /ˈsændi/ *adj.* (**sand·ier**, **sand·iest**) **1** covered with or containing sand 鋪滿沙子的；含沙的：*a sandy beach* 沙灘◇ *sandy soil* 沙質土壤 **2** (of hair 頭髮) having a light colour, between yellow and red 沙褐色的；淺棕色的

S

sane /seɪn/ *adj.* (**saner**, **san·est**) **1** having a normal healthy mind; not mentally ill 精神健全的；神志正常的 SYN **of sound mind**：*No sane person would do that.* 沒有一個神志正常的人會做那樣的事。◇ *Being able to get out of the city at the weekend **keeps me sane**.* 要不是能出城過過週末，我簡直快懲瘋了。**2** sensible and reasonable 明智的；理智的；合乎情理的：*the sane way to solve the problem* 解決問題的明智方法 OPP **insane** ➲ see also SANITY ▶ **sane·ly** *adv.*

sang *past tense* of SING

sang·froid /sɒŋˈfrwɑː; *NAmE* sɑːŋ-/ *noun* [U] (from *French*) the ability to remain calm in a difficult or dangerous situation 鎮定；沉着

san·goma /sʌŋˈɡəʊmə; sʌŋˈɡɔːmə; *NAmE* -ˈɡoʊ-/ *noun* (*SAfrE*) a person who is believed to have magic powers that can be used, for example, to find out why sb is ill/sick or protect sb from being harmed 巫師

san·gria /sæŋˈɡriːə; sæŋˈɡriːə/ *noun* [U] (from *Spanish*) an alcoholic drink made of red wine mixed with fruit, and sometimes with LEMONADE or BRANDY added 桑格里亞酒（紅葡萄酒加水果和檸檬飲料或白蘭地調製而成）

san·guin·ary /ˈsæŋɡwɪnəri; *NAmE* -neri/ *adj.* (*formal*) involving or liking killing and blood（好）殺戮的；血腥的；嗜血成性的

san·guine /ˈsæŋɡwɪn/ *adj.* **~ (about sth)** (*formal*) cheerful and confident about the future 充滿信心的；

樂觀的 **SYN** **optimistic**： *They are less sanguine about the company's long-term prospects.* 他們對公司的遠景不那麼樂觀。◇ *He tends to **take a sanguine view** of the problems involved.* 他對涉及的問題持樂觀態度。
▸ **san·guine·ly** *adv.*

sani·tar·ium (*NAmE*) = SANATORIUM

sani·tary /ˈsænətri; *NAmE* -teri/ *adj.* **1** [only before noun] connected with keeping places clean and healthy to live in, especially by removing human waste 衞生的；環境衞生的；公共衞生的： *Overcrowding and **poor sanitary conditions** led to disease in the refugee camps.* 過度擁擠和惡劣的衞生狀況導致難民營中出現疾病。◇ *The hut had no cooking or sanitary facilities.* 這間茅屋裏沒有廚具和衞生設施。 **2** clean; not likely to cause health problems 清潔的；衞生的 **SYN** **hygienic**： *The new houses were more sanitary than the old ones had been.* 新房子比老房子衞生。 **OPP** **insanitary**

ˈsanitary towel (*BrE*) (*NAmE* **ˈsanitary napkin**) *noun* a thick piece of soft material that women wear outside their body to absorb the blood during their PERIOD 衞生巾；月經墊 ➲ compare TAMPON

sani·ta·tion /ˌsænɪˈteɪʃn/ *noun* [U] the equipment and systems that keep places clean, especially by removing human waste 衞生設備；衞生設施體系： *disease resulting from poor sanitation* 衞生條件差導致的疾病

sani·tize (*BrE* also **-ise**) /ˈsænɪtaɪz/ *verb* (*formal*) **1 ~ sth** (*disapproving*) to remove the parts of sth that could be considered unpleasant 去除…中使人不快的內容；淨化： *This sanitized account of his life does not mention his time in prison.* 這份生平記述對他的不光彩之處略而不表，沒有提及他在監獄的日子。 **2 ~ sth** to clean sth thoroughly using chemicals to remove bacteria（用化學製劑）消毒，使清潔 **SYN** **disinfect**

san·ity /ˈsænəti/ *noun* [U] **1** the state of having a normal healthy mind 精神健全；神志正常： *His behaviour was so strange that I began to doubt his sanity.* 他行為怪異，我有點懷疑他是否神智正常。◇ *to **keep/preserve your sanity*** 保持頭腦清醒 **2** the state of being sensible and reasonable 明智；理智；通情達理： *After a series of road accidents the police pleaded for sanity among drivers.* 在發生一系列交通事故之後，警方提請駕駛人要審慎駕車。 **OPP** **insanity** ➲ see also SANE

sank *past tense of* SINK

sans /sænz/ *prep.* (*literary* or *humorous*) without 無；沒有： *There were no potatoes so we had fish and chips sans the chips.* 那時沒有土豆，所以我們吃了不帶薯條的炸魚薯條。

S

San·skrit /ˈsænskrɪt/ *noun* [U] an ancient language of India belonging to the Indo-European family, in which the Hindu holy texts are written and on which many modern languages are based 梵語（古印度語，屬於印歐語系，用於印度教經文撰寫，也是很多現代語言的基礎）

sans serif (also **san·serif**) /ˌsæn ˈserɪf/ *noun* [U] (*technical* 術語) (in printing 印刷) a TYPEFACE in which the letters have no SERIF 無襯線字體

Santa Claus /ˈsæntə klɔːz/ (also **Santa**) (*BrE* also **ˌFather ˈChristmas**) *noun* an imaginary old man with red clothes and a long white beard. Parents tell small children that he brings them presents at Christmas. 聖誕老人

sap /sæp/ *noun, verb*

■ ***noun*** **1** [U] the liquid in a plant or tree that carries food to all its parts（植物體內運送養分的）液，汁： *Maple syrup is made from sap extracted from the sugar maple tree.* 槭糖漿是用糖槭樹中提取的樹液製成的。 **2** [C] (*informal, especially NAmE*) a stupid person that you can easily trick, or treat unfairly 笨蛋；易上當的人

■ ***verb*** (**-pp-**) to make sth/sb weaker; to destroy sth gradually 使虛弱；削弱；逐漸破壞： **~ sth** *The hot sun sapped our energy.* 火辣辣的太陽烤得我們虛軟無力。◇ **~ sb (of sth)** *Years of failure have sapped him of his confidence.* 連年失敗使他逐漸喪失了自信。

sapi·ent /ˈseɪpiənt/ *adj.* (*literary*) having great intelligence or knowledge 睿智的；博學的 ▸ **sapi·ence** /-əns/ *noun* [U] **sapi·ent·ly** *adv.*

sap·ling /ˈsæplɪŋ/ *noun* a young tree 幼樹

sapo·dilla /ˌsæpəˈdɪlə/ *noun* a large tropical American tree that produces a fruit that can be eaten and a substance used in CHEWING GUM 人心果（產於熱帶美洲，果實可食用，樹膠可製口香糖）

sap·per /ˈsæpə(r)/ *noun* (*BrE*) a soldier whose job is to build or repair roads, bridges, etc. 工兵；工程兵

sap·phic /ˈsæfɪk/ *adj.* (*formal*) relating to LESBIANS 女同性戀的 ▸ **sap·phism** /ˈsæfɪzəm/ *noun* [U]

sap·phire /ˈsæfaɪə(r)/ *noun* **1** [C, U] a clear, bright blue PRECIOUS STONE 藍寶石 **2** [U] a bright blue colour 寶藍色；天藍色 ▸ **sap·phire** *adj.*： *sapphire eyes* 寶藍色的眼睛

sappy /ˈsæpi/ *adj.* (**sap·pier**, **sap·piest**) **1** (*NAmE, informal*) = SOPPY **2** (of plants 植物) full of SAP (= liquid) 汁液豐富的

sap·wood /ˈsæpwʊd/ *noun* [U] the soft younger outer layers of the wood of a tree, inside the BARK 邊材，液材（處於樹皮和心材之間）➲ compare HEARTWOOD

Saran Wrap™ /səˈræn ræp/ *noun* [U] (*NAmE*) = PLASTIC WRAP

sar·casm /ˈsɑːkæzəm; *NAmE* ˈsɑːrk-/ *noun* [U] a way of using words that are the opposite of what you mean in order to be unpleasant to sb or to make fun of them 諷刺；嘲諷；挖苦： *'That will be useful,' she snapped with heavy sarcasm* (= she really thought it would not be useful at all). "還真有用咧。"她狠狠挖苦道。◇ *a **hint/touch/trace of sarcasm** in his voice* 他話語中的幾分嘲諷

sar·cas·tic /sɑːˈkæstɪk; *NAmE* sɑːrˈk-/ (also *BrE informal* **sarky**) *adj.* showing or expressing sarcasm 諷刺的；嘲諷的；挖苦的： *sarcastic comments* 冷嘲熱諷的話 ◇ *a sarcastic manner* 嘲諷的態度 ◇ *'There's no need to be sarcastic,' she said.* "不必挖苦人嘛。"她說。 ▸ **sar·cas·tic·al·ly** /-kli/ *adv.*

sar·coma /sɑːˈkəʊmə; *NAmE* sɑːrˈkoʊmə/ *noun* (*medical* 醫) a harmful (= MALIGNANT) lump (= a TUMOUR) that grows in certain parts of the body such as muscle or bone 肉瘤

sar·copha·gus /sɑːˈkɒfəgəs; *NAmE* sɑːrˈkɑːf-/ *noun* (*pl.* **sar·coph·agi** /sɑːˈkɒfəgaɪ; *NAmE* sɑːrˈkɑːf-/) a stone COFFIN (= box that a dead person is buried in), especially one that is decorated, used in ancient times（尤指古代有雕飾的）石棺

sar·dine /ˌsɑːˈdiːn; *NAmE* ˌsɑːrˈd-/ *noun* a small young sea fish (for example, a young PILCHARD) that is either eaten fresh or preserved in tins/cans 沙丁魚

IDM **(packed, crammed, etc.) like sarˈdines** (*informal*) pressed tightly together in a way that is uncomfortable or unpleasant 擁擠不堪；擠得水泄不通

sar·don·ic /sɑːˈdɒnɪk; *NAmE* sɑːrˈdɑːnɪk/ *adj.* (*disapproving*) showing that you think that you are better than other people and do not take them seriously 輕慢的；輕蔑的；嘲弄的 **SYN** **mocking**： *a sardonic smile* 訕笑 ▸ **sar·don·ic·al·ly** /-kli/ *adv.*

sarge /sɑːdʒ; *NAmE* sɑːrdʒ/ *noun* (*informal*) used to talk to or about a SERGEANT 中士；巡佐；警佐

sari /ˈsɑːri/ *noun* a long piece of cloth that is wrapped around the body and worn as the main piece of clothing by women in S Asia 莎麗（南亞婦女裹在身上的長巾）

sarin /ˈsɑːrɪn/ *noun* [U] a type of poisonous gas used in chemical weapons 沙林（用於化學武器的一種毒氣）

sarky /ˈsɑːki; *NAmE* ˈsɑːrki/ *adj.* (**sark·ier**, **sarki·est**) (*BrE, informal*) = SARCASTIC

sar·nie /ˈsɑːni; *NAmE* ˈsɑːrni/ *noun* (*BrE, informal*) = SANDWICH

sar·ong /səˈrɒŋ; *NAmE* -ˈrɔːŋ; -ˈrɑːŋ/ *noun* a long piece of cloth wrapped around the body from the waist or the chest, worn by Malaysian and Indonesian men and women 莎籠（馬來西亞人和印度尼西亞人裹在腰或胸以下的長條布，男女均穿）

sar·panch /ˈsɑːpʌntʃ; *NAmE* ˈsɑːrp-/ *noun* (in some S Asian countries) the head of a village or of a PANCHAYAT（一些南亞國家的）村長，村務委員長

SARS /sɑːz; *NAmE* sɑːrz/ *noun* [U] the abbreviation for 'severe acute respiratory syndrome' (an illness that is easily spread from person to person, which affects the lungs and can sometimes cause death) 嚴重急性呼吸道綜合症，嚴重急性呼吸道症候群（全寫為 severe acute respiratory syndrome，通稱非典型肺炎，是可致命的傳染病）: *No new SARS cases have been reported in the region.* 該區沒有新增非典型肺炎病例。

sar·sa·par·illa /ˌsɑːspəˈrɪlə; ˌsɑːsəpə-; *NAmE* ˌsɑːrs-/ *noun* **1** [U] a dried substance that is used to flavour drinks and medicines, obtained from a plant also called sarsaparilla 洋菝葜乾根（用於飲料和藥的調味）**2** [U, C] a drink made with sarsaparilla 洋菝葜根汁飲料；沙士飲料

sar·tor·ial /sɑːˈtɔːriəl; *NAmE* sɑːrˈt-/ *adj.* [only before noun] (*formal*) relating to clothes, especially men's clothes, and the way they are made or worn 服裝的；（尤指）男裝的；衣着的 ▸ **sar·tor·ial·ly** /-riəli/ *adv.*

SAS /ˌes eɪ ˈes/ *abbr.* Special Air Service (a group of highly trained soldiers in Britain who are used on very secret or difficult military operations) 特種空勤部隊，空軍特種部隊（英國一支用於秘密或艱巨軍事行動的部隊）

SASE *noun* (*NAmE*) the abbreviation used in writing for 'self-addressed stamped envelope' (an envelope on which you have written your name and address and put a stamp so that sb else can use it to send sth to you)（寫上姓名地址並貼有郵票的）回郵信封（書寫形式，全寫為 self-addressed stamped envelope）➲ compare SAE

sash /sæʃ/ *noun* **1** a long strip of cloth worn around the waist or over one shoulder, especially as part of a uniform（尤指制服的）腰帶，肩帶，飾帶 **2** either of a pair of windows, one above the other, that are opened and closed by sliding them up and down inside the frame（垂直推拉窗任何一扇的）窗扇

sashay /ˈsæʃeɪ; *NAmE* sæˈʃeɪ/ *verb* [I] **+ adv./prep.** to walk in a very confident but relaxed way, especially in order to be noticed 大搖大擺地走；神氣地走

ˈ**sash cord** *noun* a string or rope with a weight at one end attached to a sash window allowing it to stay open in any position（垂直推拉窗的）吊窗繩

sash·imi /ˈsæʃɪmi; *NAmE* sɑːˈshiːmi/ *noun* [U, C] (from *Japanese*) a Japanese dish consisting of slices of raw fish, served with sauce 生魚片（日本菜肴，蘸調味醬食用）

ˌ**sash ˈwindow** *noun* a window that consists of two separate parts, one above the other that you open by sliding one of the parts up or down 垂直推拉窗 ➲ VISUAL VOCAB page V17

Sas·quatch /ˈsæskwætʃ; -wɒtʃ; *NAmE* -wɑːtʃ/ *noun* = BIGFOOT

sass /sæs/ *noun, verb*

■ **noun** [U] (*informal, especially NAmE*) behaviour or talk that is rude and lacking respect 莽撞的行為；粗魯的話

■ **verb ~ sb** (*NAmE, informal*) to speak to sb in a rude way, without respect 對…粗魯地（或惡聲惡氣地）說話；對…出言不遜: *Don't sass your mother!* 跟你母親說話別大喊小叫的！

sas·sa·fras /ˈsæsəfræs/ *noun* a N American tree with pleasant-smelling leaves and BARK. Its leaves are sometimes used to make a type of tea. 檫樹，微白檫樹（產於北美，樹葉和樹皮味芳香，樹葉有時用來泡茶）

Sas·sen·ach /ˈsæsənæk; -næx/ *noun* (*ScotE, disapproving* or *humorous*) an English person 英格蘭人 ▸ **Sas·sen·ach** *adj.*

sassy /ˈsæsi/ *adj.* (**sas·sier**, **sas·si·est**) (*informal, especially NAmE*) **1** (*disapproving*) rude; showing a lack of respect 粗魯的；無禮的 **2** (*approving*) fashionable and confident 時髦且自信的: *his sassy, streetwise daughter* 他那又時髦又精通都市生存之道的女兒

SAT *noun* **1** **SAT™** /ˌes eɪ ˈtiː/ (in the US) the abbreviation for 'Scholastic Aptitude Test' (a test taken by HIGH SCHOOL students who want to go to a college or university)（美國）學業能力傾向測驗（全寫為 Scholastic Aptitude Test，美國的一種大學入學考試）: *to take the SAT* 參加學業能力傾向測驗 ◇ *I scored 1050 on the SAT.* 我在學業能力傾向測驗中得了 1 050 分。◇ *a SAT score* 學業能力傾向測驗成績 **2** /sæt/ (in Britain) the abbreviation for 'Standard Assessment Task' (now officially called NCT)（英國）標準課業測評考試（全寫為 Standard Assessment Task，現官方稱之為 NCT）

sat *past tense, past part.* of SIT

Satan /ˈseɪtn/ *noun* the DEVIL 撒旦；魔鬼

sa·tan·ic /səˈtænɪk; *NAmE* also seɪˈt-/ *adj.* **1** (often **Sa·tan·ic**) connected with the worship of the DEVIL 崇拜撒旦的: *satanic cults* 對撒旦的崇拜 **2** (*formal*) morally bad and evil 道德敗壞的；邪惡的 SYN **demonic** ▸ **sa·tan·ic·al·ly** /-kli/ *adv.*

sa·tan·ism /ˈseɪtənɪzəm/ *noun* [U] the worship of Satan 撒旦崇拜 ▸ **sa·tan·ist** /ˈseɪtənɪst/ *noun*

satay /ˈsæteɪ; *NAmE* ˈsɑː-/ *noun* [U, C] a SE Asian dish consisting of meat or fish cooked on sticks and served with a sauce made with PEANUTS 沙嗲烤肉，沙嗲烤魚（東南亞菜肴，蘸用花生做的醬食用）

satchel /ˈsætʃəl/ *noun* a bag with a long strap, that you hang over your shoulder or wear on your back, used especially for carrying school books 書包；肩背書包 ➲ VISUAL VOCAB page V70

sat·com (also **SATCOM**) /ˈsætkɒm; *NAmE* -kɑːm/ *noun* [U] satellite communications 衛星通信

sate /seɪt/ *verb* **~ sth** (*formal*) to satisfy a desire 滿足（慾望）

sated /ˈseɪtɪd/ *adj.* [not usually before noun] **~ (with sth)** (*formal*) having had so much of sth that you do not need any more 饜足；饜膩: *sated with pleasure* 倦於享樂

sat·el·lite /ˈsætəlaɪt/ *noun* **1** an electronic device that is sent into space and moves around the earth or another planet. It is used for communicating by radio, television, etc. and for providing information. 人造衛星: *a **weather/communications satellite*** 氣象 / 通信衛星 ◇ *The interview came live **by satellite** from Hollywood.* 採訪畫面是通過衛星從好萊塢現場傳來的。◇ ***satellite television/TV*** (= broadcast using a satellite) 衛星電視 ◇ *a **satellite broadcast/channel/picture*** 衛星廣播 / 頻道 / 照片 ➲ COLLOCATIONS at TELEVISION **2** a natural object that moves around a larger natural object in space 衛星: *The moon is a satellite of earth.* 月球是地球的衛星。 **3** town, a country or an organization that is controlled by and depends on another larger or more powerful one 衛星城；衛星國；外圍組織: *satellite states* 衛星國

ˈ**satellite dish** *noun* a piece of equipment that receives signals from a satellite, used to enable people to watch satellite television 衛星電視碟形天線

ˈ**satellite station** *noun* **1** a company that broadcasts television programmes using a satellite 衛星電視台 **2** a place where special equipment is used to follow the movements of satellites and receive information from them 衛星地面站

sati (also **sut·tee**) /ˈsʌtiː; sʌˈtiː/ *noun* **1** [U] the former practice in Hinduism of a wife burning herself with the body of her dead husband 薩底，寡婦自焚（舊時印度教習俗）**2** [C] a wife who did this 夫亡自焚殉夫的寡婦

sa·ti·ate /ˈseɪʃieɪt/ *verb* [usually passive] **~ sb/sth** (*formal*) to give sb so much of sth that they do not feel they want any more 滿足 ▸ **sa·ti·ation** /ˌseɪʃiˈeɪʃn/ *noun* [U]

sa·ti·ety /səˈtaɪəti/ *noun* [U] (*formal* or *technical* 術語) the state or feeling of being completely full of food, or of having had enough of sth 飽足；饜足；滿足

satin /ˈsætɪn; *NAmE* ˈsætn/ *noun, adj.*

■ **noun** [U] a type of cloth with a smooth shiny surface 緞子: *a white satin ribbon* 白色緞帶

■ **adj.** [only before noun] having the smooth shiny appearance of satin 緞子似的；平滑而有光澤的: *The paint has a satin finish.* 漆面像緞子一樣光滑。

sat·iny /ˈsætɪni; *NAmE* ˈsætni/ *adj.* looking or feeling like satin 緞子似的；光滑的: *her satiny skin* 她那綢緞般光滑的皮膚

S

sat·ire /ˈsætaɪə(r)/ *noun* [U, C] a way of criticizing a person, an idea or an institution in which you use humour to show their faults or weaknesses; a piece of writing that uses this type of criticism 諷刺；譏諷；諷刺作品：***political/social satire*** 政治 / 社會諷刺作品 ◇ *a work full of* ***savage/biting satire*** 一部充滿無情 / 辛辣諷刺的作品 ◇ *The novel is a stinging satire on American politics.* 這部小說是對美國政治的尖鋭諷刺。

sa·tir·ic·al /səˈtɪrɪkl/ (also *less frequent* **sa·tir·ic** /səˈtɪrɪk/) *adj.* using satire to criticize sb/sth 諷刺的；譏諷的：*a satirical magazine* 諷刺雜誌 ▸ **sa·tir·ic·al·ly** /-kli/ *adv.*

Synonyms 同義詞辨析

satisfaction

happiness • pride • contentment • fulfilment

These are all words for the good feeling that you have when you are happy or when you have achieved sth. 以上各詞均指幸福、欣慰、滿意的感覺和滿足的心情。

satisfaction the good feeling that you have when you have achieved sth or when sth that you wanted to happen does happen 指取得成就、達到願望時的滿足、滿意、欣慰：*He derived great satisfaction from knowing that his son was happy.* 得知兒子很幸福他深感欣慰。

happiness the good feeling that you have when you are happy 指幸福、快樂：*Money can't buy you happiness.* 金錢不能為你買到幸福。

pride a feeling of pleasure or satisfaction that you get when you or people who are connected with you have done sth well or own sth that other people admire 指自豪、驕傲、得意感：*The sight of her son graduating filled her with pride.* 兒子畢業的情景讓她充滿了自豪。

contentment (*rather formal*) a feeling of happiness or satisfaction with what you have 指對所擁有的一切感到滿意、滿足：*They found contentment in living a simple life.* 他們在簡樸的生活中得到滿足。

fulfilment a feeling of happiness or satisfaction with what you do or have done 指對所做的事感到滿意、滿足：*her search for personal fulfilment* 她對個人滿足的追求

SATISFACTION, HAPPINESS, CONTENTMENT OR FULFILMENT? 用 satisfaction、happiness、contentment 還是 fulfilment？

You can feel **satisfaction** at achieving almost anything, small or large; you feel **fulfilment** when you do sth useful and enjoyable with your life. **Happiness** is the feeling you have when things give you pleasure and can be quite a lively feeling; **contentment** is a quieter feeling that you get when you have learned to find pleasure in things. 取得成就（無論大小）時的滿足用 satisfaction；做了有益和令人愉快之事而感到滿意時用 fulfilment；某些事情給人帶來快樂或欣慰用 happiness；學會從事情中尋求快樂而得到恬靜的滿足則用 contentment。

PATTERNS

- satisfaction/happiness/pride/contentment/fulfilment **in** sth
- **real** satisfaction/happiness/pride/contentment/fulfilment
- **true** satisfaction/happiness/contentment/fulfilment
- **great** satisfaction/happiness/pride
- **quiet** satisfaction/pride/contentment
- to **feel** satisfaction/happiness/pride/contentment
- to **bring sb** satisfaction/happiness/pride/contentment/fulfilment
- to **find** satisfaction/happiness/contentment/fulfilment

S

sat·ir·ist /ˈsætərɪst/ *noun* a person who writes or uses SATIRE 諷刺作家；慣於諷刺的人

sat·ir·ize (*BrE* also **-ise**) /ˈsætəraɪz/ *verb* **~ sb/sth** to use SATIRE to show the faults in a person, an organization, a system, etc. 諷刺；譏諷

sat·is·fac·tion 0➝ /ˌsætɪsˈfækʃn/ *noun*

WORD FAMILY
satisfaction *noun* (≠ dissatisfaction)
satisfactory *adj.* (≠ unsatisfactory)
satisfy *verb*
satisfying *adj.* (≠ unsatisfying)
satisfied *adj.* (≠ dissatisfied) (≠ unsatisfied)

1 0➝ [U, C] the good feeling that you have when you have achieved sth or when sth that you wanted to happen does happen; sth that gives you this feeling 滿足；滿意；欣慰；令人滿意（或欣慰）的事：*to* ***gain/get/derive satisfaction*** *from sth* 從某事中得到滿足感 ◇ *a* ***look/smile of satisfaction*** 心滿意足的表情 / 笑容 ◇ *She looked back on her career* ***with*** *great* ***satisfaction***. 回顧自己的事業，她深感欣慰。◇ *He* ***had the satisfaction of*** *seeing his book become a best-seller.* 看到自己的作品成了暢銷書，他志得意滿。◇ *She didn't want to* ***give him the satisfaction of*** *seeing her cry.* 她不願當着他的面哭，讓他幸災樂禍。◇ *The company is trying to improve* ***customer satisfaction***. 公司力圖改進，讓顧客更加滿意。◇ *He was enjoying all the satisfactions of being a parent.* 他享受着做父親所能得到的一切樂趣。➲ see also DISSATISFACTION **2** [U] the act of FULFILLING a need or desire（需要或慾望的）滿足，達到：*the satisfaction of sexual desires* 性慾的滿足 ◇ *the satisfaction of your ambitions* 實現抱負 **3** [U] (*formal*) an acceptable way of dealing with a complaint, a debt, an injury, etc.（抗議、投訴等的）妥善處理；（債務的）清償；（傷害的）賠償：*I complained to the manager but I didn't get any satisfaction.* 我向經理投訴，但問題絲毫沒有得到解決。

IDM **to sb's satisˈfaction 1** if you do sth **to sb's satisfaction**, they are pleased with it 使某人滿意：*The affair was settled to the complete satisfaction of the client.* 問題解決了，顧客十分滿意。 **2** if you prove sth **to sb's satisfaction**, they believe or accept it 使某人確信（或信服）：*Can you demonstrate to our satisfaction that your story is true?* 你能不能證實一下，讓我們確信你說的是事實？

sat·is·fac·tory /ˌsætɪsˈfæktəri/ *adj.* good enough for a particular purpose 令人滿意的；夠好的；可以的 SYN **acceptable**：*a* ***satisfactory explanation/answer/solution/conclusion*** 令人滿意的解釋；站得住腳的回答；可行的解決辦法；足以服人的結論 ◇ *The work is satisfactory but not outstanding.* 工作做得可以，但不出色。◇ *The existing law is not* ***entirely/wholly satisfactory***. 現行法律並不十分完善。 OPP **unsatisfactory** ▸ **sat·is·fac·tor·ily** /-tərəli/ *adv.*：*Her disappearance has never been satisfactorily explained.* 她的失踪一直沒有得到令人信服的解釋。◇ *Our complaint was dealt with satisfactorily.* 我們的投訴得到了滿意的處理。

sat·is·fied 0➝ /ˈsætɪsfaɪd/ *adj.*

1 0➝ pleased because you have achieved sth or because sth that you wanted to happen has happened 滿意的；滿足的；欣慰的：*a satisfied smile* 滿意的微笑 ◇ *a satisfied customer* 滿意的顧客 ◇ **~ with sb/sth** *She's never satisfied with what she's got.* 她對自己的所得從不感到滿足。 OPP **dissatisfied** ➲ SYNONYMS at HAPPY **2** 0➝ **~ (that …)** | **~ (with sth)** believing or accepting that sth is true 確信的；信服的 SYN **convinced**：*I'm satisfied that they are telling the truth.* 我確信他們講的是真話。➲ compare UNSATISFIED

sat·isfy 0➝ /ˈsætɪsfaɪ/ *verb* (**sat·is·fies**, **sat·is·fy·ing**, **sat·is·fied**, **sat·is·fied**)

1 0➝ **~ sb** (not used in the progressive tenses 不用於進行時) to make sb pleased by doing or giving them what they want 使滿意；使滿足：*Nothing satisfies him—he's always complaining.* 什麼都難如他的意，他老在抱怨。◇ *The proposed plan will not satisfy everyone.* 擬議中的計劃不會讓所有人都滿意。 **2** 0➝ **~ sth** to provide what is wanted, needed or asked for 滿足（要求、需要等）：*The food wasn't enough to* ***satisfy his hunger***. 這食物不足以讓他解餓。◇ *to* ***satisfy sb's curiosity*** 滿足某人的好奇心 ◇ *The education system must* ***satisfy the needs*** *of* *all children.* 教育系統必須滿足所有兒童的需要。◇ *We cannot* ***satisfy demand*** *for the product.* 我們不能滿足對該產品的需求。◇ *She failed to satisfy all the requirements for entry to the college.* 她沒有達到進入那所學院的全部要求。 **3** 🗝 (not used in the progressive tenses 不用於進行時) (*formal*) to make sb certain sth is true or has been done 向…證實；使確信： **~ sb** *Her explanation did not satisfy the teacher.* 她的解釋沒有讓老師信服。◇ **~ sb of sth** *People need to be satisfied of the need for a new system.* 需要使人們明白建立一個新體系的必要性。◇ **~ sb/yourself (that)** ... *Once I had satisfied myself (that) it was the right decision, we went ahead.* 一旦我自己確信這個決定是正確的，我們便動手幹了起來。

sat·is·fy·ing 🗝 /ˈsætɪsfaɪɪŋ/ *adj.* giving pleasure because it provides sth you need or want 令人滿意（或滿足）的： *a satisfying meal* 可口的飯菜 ◇ *a satisfying experience* 令人滿意的經歷 ◇ ***It's satisfying to*** *play a game really well.* 打一場出色的比賽是一件愜意的事。 ▸ **sat·is·fy·ing·ly** *adv.*

Synonyms 同義詞辨析

satisfying

rewarding • pleasing • gratifying • fulfilling

These words all describe an experience, activity or fact that gives you pleasure because it provides sth you need or want. 以上各詞均形容經歷、活動或現實令人滿足或滿意。

satisfying that gives you pleasure because it provides sth you need or want 指令人滿意、滿足： *It's satisfying to play a game really well.* 一種遊戲玩得特別好是一樁愜意的事。

rewarding (of an experience or activity) that makes you happy because you think it is useful or important; worth doing 指（經歷或活動）有益的、有意義的、值得做的： *Nursing can be a very rewarding career.* 做護士可以是非常有意義的職業。

pleasing (*rather formal*) that gives you pleasure, especially to look at, hear or think about 尤指令看到、聽到、想到的人高興、滿意： *It was a simple but pleasing design.* 這是一項簡單但令人滿意的設計。

gratifying (*formal*) that gives you pleasure, especially because it makes you feel that you have done well 指令人高興，尤其對自己所做的事感到滿意： *It is gratifying to see such good results.* 看到這麼好的結果真令人欣慰。

fulfilling (of an experience or activity) that makes you happy, because it makes you feel your skills and talents are being used 指（經歷或活動）使人感到有意義、欣慰、滿足（因為自己的技能和才幹得以發揮）： *I'm finding the work much more fulfilling now.* 我現在覺得這工作有意義多了。

SATISFYING, REWARDING OR FULFILLING? 用 satisfying、rewarding **還是** fulfilling？

Almost any experience, important or very brief, can be **satisfying**. **Rewarding** and **fulfilling** are used more for longer, more serious activities, such as jobs or careers. **Satisfying** and **fulfilling** are more about your personal satisfaction or happiness; **rewarding** is more about your sense of doing sth important and being useful to others. 幾乎任何經歷（重要的或短暫的）均可用 satisfying。rewarding 和 fulfilling 多指較長或較重要的活動有意義，如工作或職業。satisfying 和 fulfilling 多指個人的滿足或幸福；rewarding 則多指做了重要的或對他人有益的事時得到的滿足感。

PATTERNS

- a satisfying/rewarding/gratifying/fulfilling **experience/feeling**
- (a) satisfying/rewarding/fulfilling **job/career/work**
- to **find sth** satisfying/rewarding/pleasing/gratifying

sat·nav (also **sat nav**) /ˈsætnæv/ *noun* [U, C] (*BrE*) the abbreviation for 'satellite navigation' (a computer system that uses information from SATELLITES to guide the driver of a vehicle) 衛星導航（全寫為 satellite navigation，利用接收到的衛星信息為駕車者導航的計算機系統）： *The drivers all have satnav in the van.* 司機都在貨車裏安裝了衛星導航。 ➲ **VISUAL VOCAB** page V52 ➲ compare GPS

sat·suma /sætˈsuːmə/ *noun* a type of small orange without seeds and with loose skin that comes off easily 薩摩蜜橘；無籽蜜橘

sat·ur·ate /ˈsætʃəreɪt/ *verb* **1 ~ sth** to make sth completely wet 使濕透；浸透 **SYN** **soak** ： *The continuous rain had saturated the soil.* 連綿不斷的雨把土地淋了個透。 **2** [often passive] **~ sth/sb (with/in sth)** to fill sth/sb completely with sth so that it is impossible or useless to add any more 使充滿；使飽和： *The company had saturated the market for personal organizers* (= so that no new buyers could be found). 那家公司的產品已使電子記事簿市場飽和。

sat·ur·ated /ˈsætʃəreɪtɪd/ *adj.* **1** [not usually before noun] completely wet 濕透；浸透 **SYN** **soaked** ➲ SYNONYMS at WET **2** [usually before noun] (*chemistry* 化) if a chemical SOLUTION (= a liquid with sth dissolved in it) is **saturated**, it contains the greatest possible amount of the substance that has been dissolved in it（溶液）飽和的： *a saturated solution of sodium chloride* 氯化鈉飽和溶液 **3** [usually before noun] (of colours 顏色) very strong 深的；濃的： *saturated reds* 深紅色

ˌsaturated ˈfat *noun* [C, U] a type of fat found, for example, in butter, fried food and many types of meat, which encourages the harmful development of CHOLESTEROL 飽和脂肪（存在於黃油、煎炸食品和很多肉類，能促使膽固醇增長，危害身體） ➲ see also MONOUNSATURATED FAT, POLYUNSATURATED FAT, TRANS-FATTY ACID, UNSATURATED FAT

sat·ur·ation /ˌsætʃəˈreɪʃn/ *noun* [U] **1** (often *figurative*) the state or process that happens when no more of sth can be accepted or added because there is already too much of it or too many of them 飽和；飽和狀態： *a business beset by price wars and* ***market saturation*** (= the fact that no new customers can be found) 一家受價格戰和市場飽和困擾的企業 ◇ ***saturation bombing*** *of the city* (= covering the whole city) 對那座城市的全面轟炸 ◇ *There was* ***saturation coverage*** (= so much that it was impossible to avoid it or add to it) *of the event by the media.* 媒體對這一事件做了連篇累牘的報道。 **2** (*chemistry* 化) the degree to which sth is absorbed in sth else, expressed as a PERCENTAGE of the greatest possible 飽和度

satuˈration point *noun* [U, sing.] **1** the stage at which no more of sth can be accepted or added because there is already too much of it or too many of them 飽和點；極限： *The market for computer games has reached saturation point.* 電腦遊戲市場已達到飽和。 **2** (*chemistry* 化) the stage at which no more of a substance can be absorbed into a liquid or VAPOUR 飽和點

Sat·ur·day 🗝 /ˈsætədeɪ; -di; *NAmE* -tərd-/ *noun* [C, U] (*abbr.* **Sat.**) the day of the week after Friday and before Sunday 星期六 **HELP** To see how **Saturday** is used, look at the examples at **Monday**. * Saturday 的用法見詞條 Monday 下的示例。 **ORIGIN** From the Old English for 'day of Saturn', translated from Latin *Saturni dies*. 源自古英語，原意為 day of Saturn（農神日），古英語則譯自拉丁文 Saturni dies。

Sat·urn /ˈsætɜːn; -tən; *NAmE* -tɜːrn/ *noun* a large planet in the SOLAR SYSTEM that has rings around it and is 6th in order of distance from the sun 土星

Sat·ur·na·lia /ˌsætəˈneɪliə; *NAmE* -tərˈn-/ *noun* [U] an ancient Roman festival that took place in December, around the time that Christmas now takes place 薩圖恩節，農神節（古羅馬十二月份的節日，在如今聖誕節左右）

S

sat·ur·na·lian /ˌsætəˈneɪliən; *NAmE* -tərˈn-/ *adj.* **1** relating to Saturnalia 薩圖恩節的；農神節的 **2** involving wild celebrations 狂歡的；熱烈歡慶的

sat·ur·nine /ˈsætənaɪn; *NAmE* -tərn-/ *adj.* (*literary*) (of a person or their face 人或面部表情) looking serious and threatening 嚴肅而令人畏懼的；陰沉的

satyr /ˈsætə(r); *NAmE* also ˈseɪtər/ *noun* (in ancient Greek stories) a god of the woods, with a man's face and body and a GOAT's legs and horns 薩堤爾（古希臘神話中半人半羊的森林之神）

sauce 🗝 /sɔːs/ *noun*
1 🗝 [C, U] a thick liquid that is eaten with food to add flavour to it 調味汁；醬：***tomato/cranberry/chilli, etc. sauce*** 番茄、越橘、辣椒等調味汁 ◇ *chicken in a white sauce* 白醬雞肉 ◇ *ice cream with a hot fudge sauce* 澆了熱巧克力醬的冰淇淋 ➲ see also SOY SAUCE, TARTARE SAUCE, WHITE SAUCE **2** [U] (*old-fashioned, BrE, informal*) talk or behaviour that is annoying or lacking in respect 討厭的話（或舉動）；無禮的話（或舉動）SYN **cheek**
IDM **what's ˌsauce for the ˈgoose is ˌsauce for the ˈgander** (*old-fashioned, saying*) what one person is allowed to do, another person must be allowed to do in a similar situation 適於此者亦應適於彼；應該一視同仁

ˈsauce boat *noun* a long low JUG used for serving or pouring sauce at a meal 船形醬汁盤

sauce·pan /ˈsɔːspən; *NAmE* -pæn/ (*especially BrE*) (*NAmE* usually **pot**) *noun* a deep round metal pot with a lid and one long handle or two short handles, used for cooking things over heat（帶蓋，有一長柄或兩耳的）深煮鍋 ➲ VISUAL VOCAB page V27

sau·cer /ˈsɔːsə(r)/ *noun* a small shallow round dish that a cup stands on; an object that is shaped like this 茶碟；茶托；碟狀物：*cups and saucers* 茶杯和茶碟 ➲ VISUAL VOCAB page V22 ➲ see also FLYING SAUCER

saucy /ˈsɔːsi/ *adj.* (**sau·cier**, **sau·ci·est**) rude or referring to sex in a way that is amusing but not offensive 粗魯的；粗俗的；不雅的；開色情玩笑的 SYN **cheeky**：*saucy jokes* 有味笑話 ◇ *a saucy smile* 無禮的一笑 ▸ **sau·cily** /-ɪli/ *adv.*

sauer·kraut /ˈsaʊəkraʊt; *NAmE* ˈsaʊərk-/ *noun* [U] (from *German*) CABBAGE (= a type of green vegetable) that is preserved in salt water and then cooked（酸）泡菜

sauna /ˈsɔːnə; ˈsaʊnə/ *noun* a period of time in which you sit or lie in a room (also called a sauna) which has been heated to a very high temperature. Some saunas involve the use of steam. 桑拿浴；蒸汽浴；三温暖：*a hotel with a swimming pool and sauna* 帶游泳池和桑拿浴室的旅館 ◇ *to* ***have/take a sauna*** 沐桑拿浴

saun·ter /ˈsɔːntə(r)/ *verb* [I] **+ adv./prep.** to walk in a slow relaxed way 悠閒地走；漫步；閒逛 SYN **stroll**：*He sauntered by, looking as if he had all the time in the world.* 他悠閒地走過，彷彿時間對他來說是無窮無盡的。 ▸ **saun·ter** *noun* [sing.]：*This part of the route should be an easy saunter.* 這段路想必好走。

saur·ian /ˈsɔːriən/ *adj., noun* (*biology* 生)
■ **adj.** relating to LIZARDS 蜥蜴的
■ **noun** a large REPTILE, especially a DINOSAUR 大型爬行動物（尤指恐龍）

saus·age /ˈsɒsɪdʒ; *NAmE* ˈsɔːs-/ *noun* [C, U] a mixture of finely chopped meat, fat, bread, etc. in a long tube of skin, cooked and eaten whole or served cold in thin slices 香腸；臘腸：***beef/pork sausages*** 牛肉／豬肉香腸 ◇ *200g of garlic sausage* * 200 克蒜味香腸 ➲ see also LIVER SAUSAGE
IDM **not a ˈsausage** (*old-fashioned, BrE, informal*) nothing at all 什麼都沒有

ˈsausage dog *noun* (*BrE, informal*) = DACHSHUND

ˈsausage meat *noun* [U] the mixture of finely chopped meat, fat, bread, etc. used for making sausages 香腸肉餡

ˌsausage ˈroll *noun* (*BrE*) a small tube of PASTRY filled with sausage meat and cooked 香腸捲（用油酥麪皮捲上香腸肉餡烤製而成）

ˈsausage tree *noun* a large African tree that produces large grey fruit that hang downwards and have a similar shape to a sausage 香腸樹，吊燈樹，臘腸樹（產於非洲，果實香腸狀）

sauté /ˈsəʊteɪ; *NAmE* soʊˈteɪ/ *verb* (**sauté·ing**, **sautéed**, **sautéed** or **sauté·ing**, **sautéd**, **sautéd**) **~ sth** to fry food quickly in a little hot fat 嫩煎；炒 ▸ **sauté** *adj.* [only before noun]：*sauté potatoes* 煎土豆

sav·age /ˈsævɪdʒ/ *adj., noun, verb*
■ **adj. 1** aggressive and violent; causing great harm 兇惡的；兇殘的；損害嚴重的 SYN **brutal**：*savage dogs* 惡狗 ◇ *She had been badly hurt in what police described as 'a savage attack'.* 她遭受襲擊而身受重傷，警方稱這是一次"野蠻的襲擊"。◇ *savage public spending cuts* 拚命削減公共開支 **2** involving very strong criticism 猛烈抨擊的：*The article was a savage attack on the government's record.* 文章對政府的業績進行了猛烈的抨擊。 **3** [only before noun] (*old-fashioned, taboo*) an offensive way of referring to groups of people or customs that are considered to be simple and not highly developed 蒙昧的；未開化的；野蠻的 SYN **primitive**：*a savage tribe* 野蠻部落 ▸ **sav·age·ly** *adv.*：*savagely attacked/criticized* 受到猛烈的攻擊／批評 ◇ *'No!' he snarled savagely.* "不！"他惡狠狠地嚷道。
■ **noun 1** (*old-fashioned, taboo*) an offensive word for sb who belongs to a people that is simple and not developed 野蠻人；未開化的人：*the development of the human race from primitive savages* 人類走出蒙昧的演進過程 **2** a cruel and violent person 兇狠殘暴的人：*He described the attack as the work of savages.* 他把這次襲擊稱為野蠻行徑。
■ **verb** [usually passive] **1 ~ sb** (of an animal 動物) to attack sb violently, causing serious injury 兇狠地攻擊（或傷害）；殘害：*She was* ***savaged to death*** *by a bear.* 她遭熊襲擊而喪命。 **2 ~ sb/sth** (*formal*) to criticize sb/sth severely 猛烈批評；激烈抨擊：*Her latest novel has been savaged by the critics.* 她最近的一部小說受到評論家的猛烈批評。

sav·agery /ˈsævɪdʒri/ *noun* [U] behaviour that is very cruel and violent 殘暴行為 SYN **violence**：*The police were shocked by the savagery of the attacks.* 警方對這些慘無人道的襲擊感到震驚。

sa·van·nah (also **sa·vanna**) /səˈvænə/ *noun* [C, U] a wide flat open area of land, especially in Africa, that is covered with grass but has few trees（尤指非洲的）稀樹草原 ➲ compare VELD

Synonyms 同義詞辨析

save

budget • economize • tighten your belt

These words all mean to spend less money. 以上各詞均含存錢、節儉之義。

save to keep money instead of spending it, often in order to buy a particular thing 常指為了買某物而攢錢、儲蓄：*I'm saving for a new car.* 我正攢錢想買輛新車。

budget to be careful about the amount of money you spend; to plan to spend an amount of money for a particular purpose 指謹慎花錢、把…編入預算：*If we budget carefully we'll be able to afford the trip.* 我們精打細算一點，就能夠負擔這次旅行。

economize to use less money, time, etc. than you normally use 指節省、節約、節儉

tighten your belt (*rather informal*) to spend less money because there is less available 指勒緊腰帶省吃儉用：*With the price increases, we are all having to tighten our belts.* 由於物價上漲，我們都只好勒緊褲腰帶了。

PATTERNS

- to save up/budget **for** sth
- to **have to** save/budget/economize/tighten our belts
- to **try to/manage to** save/budget/economize

sav·ant /ˈsævənt; *NAmE* sæˈvɑːnt/ *noun* (*formal*) **1** a person with great knowledge and ability 博學之士；學者；專家 **2** a person who is less intelligent than others but who has particular unusual abilities that other people do not have 獨通一行的人；獨開一竅的人

save 0ᐅ /seɪv/ *verb, noun, prep., conj.*

■ *verb*

▸ KEEP SAFE 使安全 **1** 0ᐅ [T] to keep sb/sth safe from death, harm, loss, etc. 救；救助；挽救；拯救：**~ sb/sth** *to* ***save sb's life*** 救某人的命 ◇ *Doctors were unable to save her.* 醫生未能把她救活。◇ *He's trying to save their marriage.* 他試圖挽救他們的婚姻。◇ *She needs to win the next two games to save the match.* 只有下面的兩場獲勝，她才能挽回敗局。◇ (*figurative*) *Thanks for doing that. You* ***saved my life*** (= helped me a lot). 謝謝你這麼做。你幫了我大忙。◇ **~ sb/sth (from sth)** *to save a rare species (from extinction)* 拯救珍稀物種（免於滅絕）◇ **~ sb/sth from doing sth** *She saved a little girl from falling into the water.* 她救下一個眼看要落入水中的小女孩。

▸ MONEY 錢 **2** 0ᐅ [I, T] to keep money instead of spending it, especially in order to buy a particular thing 儲蓄；攢錢：*I'm not very good at saving.* 我不大攢得住錢。◇ **~ (up) (for sth)** *I'm saving for a new bike.* 我正攢錢想買輛新自行車。◇ *We've been saving up to go to Australia.* 我們一直在攢錢，打算去澳大利亞。◇ **~ sth (up) (for sth)** *You should save a little each week.* 你應該每星期存一點錢。◇ *I've saved almost £100 so far.* 我至今已經攢了差不多 100 英鎊了。

▸ COLLECT STH 收集 **3** [T] **~ sth** to collect sth because you like it or for a special purpose 收集；收藏：*I've been saving theatre programmes for years.* 我收藏劇院的節目單已有多年了。◇ *If you save ten tokens you can get a T-shirt.* 積十張禮品券便可得到一件 T 恤衫。

▸ KEEP FOR FUTURE 留存 **4** 0ᐅ [T] to keep sth to use or enjoy in the future 保留；保存：**~ sth (for sth/sb)** *He's saving his strength for the last part of the race.* 他保存體力，以便在比賽的最後階段發力。◇ *We'll eat some now and save some for tomorrow.* 我們現在吃一些，留一些明天吃。◇ *Save some food for me.* 給我留點吃的。◇ **~ sb sth** *Save me some food.* 給我留點吃的。

▸ NOT WASTE 不浪費 **5** 0ᐅ [T, I] to avoid wasting sth or using more than necessary 節省；節約：**~ sth** *We'll take a cab to save time.* 我們坐出租車，好節省時間。◇ *Book early and save £50!* 及早訂票，可省 50 英鎊！◇ *We should try to save water.* 我們應設法節約用水。◇ **~ sth on sth** *The government is trying to save £1 million on defence.* 政府力圖在國防開支上節約 100 萬英鎊。◇ **~ sb sth (on sth)** *If we go this way it will save us two hours on the trip.* 如果走這條路，可以縮短兩小時的行程。◇ **~ on sth** *I save on fares by walking to work.* 我步行上班，可以省車錢。

▸ AVOID STH BAD 避免壞事 **6** 0ᐅ [T] to avoid doing sth difficult or unpleasant; to make sb able to avoid doing sth difficult or unpleasant 避免，免得（出現困難或不愉快的事）：**~ sb from doing sth** *The prize money saved her from having to find a job.* 她得到的獎金，使她免於去找工作。◇ **~ sth** *She did it herself to save argument.* 她自己去做了，以免發生爭論。◇ **~ sb sth** *Thanks for sending that letter for me—it saved me a trip.* 多謝你替我把那封信寄了，省得我跑一趟。◇ **~ doing sth** *He's grown a beard to save shaving.* 他留起了鬍子，省得再刮臉。◇ **~ sb doing sth** *If you phone for an appointment, it'll save you waiting.* 如果電話預約，你就免得等了。

▸ IN SPORT 體育運動 **7** 0ᐅ [T, I] **~ (sth)** (in football (SOCCER), etc. 足球等) to prevent an opponent's shot from going in the goal 救球（阻礙對方得分）：*to save a penalty* 撲出一個點球 ◇ *The goalie saved Johnson's long-range shot.* 守門員撲出了約翰遜的遠射。◇ (*BrE*) *The goalie saved brilliantly from Johnson's long-range shot.* 守門員漂亮地撲擋了約翰遜的遠射。

▸ COMPUTING 計算機技術 **8** 0ᐅ [T, I] **~ (sth)** to make a computer keep work, for example by putting it on a disk 保存；存盤：*Save data frequently.* 要不時把資料存盤。

IDM **not be able to do sth to ˌsave your ˈlife** (*informal*) to be completely unable to do sth 完全幹不了某事；死也做不了某事：*He can't interview people to save his life.* 要他的命，他也採訪不了人。 **save sb's ˈbacon/ˈneck** (*informal*) to rescue sb from a very difficult situation 解救某人擺脫困境 **save the ˈday/situˈation** to prevent failure or defeat, when this seems certain to happen 挽回敗局；扭轉局面：*Gerrard's late goal saved the day for Liverpool.* 傑拉德後來的進球為利物浦隊挽回了敗局。 **save (sb's) ˈface** to avoid or help sb avoid embarrassment（使）保全面子：*She was fired, but she saved face by telling everyone she'd resigned.* 明明是給解雇了，但她愛面子，逢人便說是她辭職了。 **save your ˈbreath** (*informal*) used to tell sb that it is not worth wasting time and effort saying sth because it will not change anything 免費口舌：*Save your breath—you'll never persuade her.* 不用白費口舌了，你永遠說服不了她。 **save your (own) ˈskin/ˈhide/ˈneck** to try to avoid death, punishment, etc., especially by leaving others in an extremely difficult situation（尤指不惜置他人於困境而）保全自己的性命，使自己免受懲罰：*To save his own skin, he lied and blamed the accident on his friend.* 為了自保，他竟然說謊，把事故的責任推到朋友身上。

■ *noun* (in football, etc. 足球等) an action by the GOALKEEPER that stops a goal being scored（守門員的）救球：*He made a spectacular save.* 他那撲救的動作令人歎為觀止。

■ *prep.* (also **save for**) (*old use* or *formal*) except sth 除了；除…外：*They knew nothing about her save her name.* 除名字外，他們對她一無所知。

■ *conj.* (*old use* or *formal*) except 除了：*They found out nothing more save that she had borne a child.* 他們只查明她生過一個孩子，其他情況一無所知。

Synonyms 同義詞辨析

save

rescue • bail out • redeem

These words all mean to prevent sb/sth from dying, losing sth, being harmed or embarrassed. 以上各詞均含拯救、挽救、營救之意。

save to prevent sb/sth from dying, being harmed or destroyed or losing sth 指救、救助、挽救、拯救：*Doctors were unable to save him.* 醫生未能把他救活。◇ *a campaign to save the panda from extinction* 一場拯救大熊貓免於滅絕的運動

rescue to save sb/sth from a dangerous or harmful situation 指營救、援救、搶救：*They were rescued by a passing cruise ship.* 他們被一艘經過的遊輪救起。

bail sb out to rescue sb/sth from a difficult situation, especially by providing money 尤指通過提供錢幫助某人脫離困境：*Don't expect me to bail you out if it all goes wrong.* 如果一切都搞砸了，就別指望我能解救你。

redeem (*formal, religion*) to save sb from the power of evil 指拯救、救贖：*He was a sinner, redeemed by the grace of God.* 他是一個罪人，承蒙上主的恩寵才獲得求贖。NOTE **Redeem** is also used in non-religious language in the phrase *redeem a situation*, which means to prevent a situation from being as bad as it might be. * redeem 亦用於非宗教語言中，如 redeem a situation 意為力挽狂瀾。

PATTERNS

- to save/rescue/redeem sb/sth **from** sth
- to save/rescue/redeem a **situation**
- to save/redeem **sinners/mankind**
- to rescue sb/bail sb out **financially**

saver /ˈseɪvə(r)/ *noun* **1** a person who saves money and puts it in a bank, etc. for future use 儲戶；存戶 **2** (often in compounds 常構成複合詞) something that helps you spend less money or use less of the thing mentioned 有助於節省的事物：*a* ***money/time saver*** 省錢／省時的事物 ➲ see also LIFESAVER

S

Savile Row /ˌsævl ˈrəʊ; *NAmE* ˈroʊ/ *noun* a street in London, England with many shops/stores that sell expensive clothes for men that are often specially made for each person 薩維爾街，裁縫街（英國倫敦的一條街道，聚集了售賣高檔訂製男裝的店鋪）：*He was wearing a Savile Row suit.* 他穿着在倫敦裁縫街訂製的西裝。

sav·ing /ˈseɪvɪŋ/ *noun* **1** [C] an amount of sth such as time or money that you do not need to use or spend 節省物；節省；節約：*Buy three and make a saving of 55p.* 買三件就能節省 55 便士。◇ *With the new boiler you can make big savings on fuel bills.* 用這種新鍋爐，能省一大筆燃料開銷。**2** **savings** [pl.] money that you have saved, especially in a bank, etc. 儲蓄金；存款：*He put all his savings into buying a boat.* 他用全部積蓄買了一條船。◇ *I opened a **savings account** at my local bank.* 我在本地銀行開了一個儲蓄賬戶。➲ COLLOCATIONS at FINANCE **3** **-saving** (in adjectives 構成形容詞) that prevents the waste of the thing mentioned or stops it from being necessary 節約的；節省…的：*energy-saving modifications* 節能改裝 ◇ *labour-saving devices* 節省人力的裝置 ◇ *space-saving fitted furniture* 節省空間的訂製的傢具 ➲ see also FACE-SAVING

ˌsaving ˈgrace *noun* [usually sing.] the one good quality that a person or thing has that prevents them or it from being completely bad 僅有的優點；唯一可取之處

ˌsavings and ˈloan association (*US*) (*BrE* **ˈbuilding society**) *noun* (*abbr.* **S&L**) an organization like a bank that lends money to people who want to buy a house. People also save money with a building society. 房屋互助協會（提供住房貸款及儲蓄服務）

sa·viour (*especially US* **sa·vior**) /ˈseɪvjə(r)/ *noun* **1** [usually sing.] a person who rescues sb/sth from a dangerous or difficult situation 救助者；拯救者；救星：*The new manager has been hailed as the saviour of the club.* 新任經理被譽為俱樂部的救星。**2** **the Saviour** [sing.] used in the Christian religion as another name for Jesus Christ 救主，救世主（耶穌基督）

savoir faire /ˌsævwɑː ˈfeə(r); *NAmE* ˌsævwɑːr ˈfer/ *noun* [U] (from *French*, *approving*) the ability to behave in the appropriate way in social situations（應付裕如的）社交能力；處世能力

sa·vory (*NAmE*) = SAVOURY

sa·vour (*especially US* **savor**) /ˈseɪvə(r)/ *verb, noun*

■ *verb* **1** ~ **sth** to enjoy the full taste or flavour of sth, especially by eating or drinking it slowly 品味；細品；享用 SYN **relish**：*He ate his meal slowly, savouring every mouthful.* 他慢慢地吃着，細細地品味每一口美食。**2** ~ **sth** to enjoy a feeling or an experience thoroughly 體會；體味；享受 SYN **relish**：*I wanted to savour every moment.* 我要細心品味，一刻也不錯過。

PHR V **ˈsavour of sth** [no passive] (*formal*) to seem to have an amount of sth, especially sth bad 意味着；有點…成分，帶有幾分…（尤指壞事）：*His recent comments savour of hypocrisy.* 他近來說的話有點虛偽。

■ *noun* [usually sing.] (*formal* or *literary*) a taste or smell, especially a pleasant one（尤指美好的）味道，氣味，滋味：(*figurative*) *For Emma, life had lost its savour.* 對埃瑪來說，生活已失去樂趣。

sa·voury (*especially US* **sa·vory**) /ˈseɪvəri/ *adj., noun*

■ *adj.* **1** having a taste that is salty not sweet 鹹味的；鹹口的：*savoury snacks* 鹹味點心 **2** having a pleasant taste or smell 好吃的；好聞的；香的；美味的：*a savoury smell from the kitchen* 從廚房裏傳來的香味 ➲ see also UNSAVOURY

■ *noun* [usually pl.] (*pl.* **-ies**) a small amount of a food with a salty taste, not a sweet one, often served at a party, etc.（在聚會等活動中常吃的）鹹味小吃

savoy /səˈvɔɪ/ (also **saˌvoy ˈcabbage**) *noun* [U, C] a type of CABBAGE with leaves that are not smooth 皺葉甘藍

savvy /ˈsævi/ *noun, adj.*

■ *noun* [U] (*informal*) practical knowledge or understanding of sth 實際知識；見識；瞭解：*political savvy* 政治見識

■ *adj.* (**sav·vier**, **sav·vi·est**) (*informal*, *especially NAmE*) having practical knowledge and understanding of sth; having COMMON SENSE 有見識的；懂實際知識的；通情達理的：*savvy shoppers* 精明的購物者

saw /sɔː/ *noun, verb* ➲ see also SEE *v.*

■ *noun* **1** (often in compounds 常構成複合詞) a tool that has a long blade with sharp points (called TEETH) along one of its edges. A saw is moved backwards and forwards by hand or driven by electricity and is used for cutting wood or metal. 鋸 ➲ see also CHAINSAW, CIRCULAR SAW, FRETSAW, HACKSAW, HANDSAW, JIGSAW (3) **2** (*old-fashioned*) a short phrase or sentence that states a general truth about life or gives advice 諺語；格言

■ *verb* (**sawed**, **sawn** /sɔːn/) (*NAmE* also **sawed**, **sawed**) **1** [I, T] to use a saw to cut sth 鋸：*The workmen sawed and hammered all day.* 工人又鋸又釘，幹了整整一天。◇ + **adv./prep.** *He accidentally sawed through a cable.* 他不小心鋸斷了電纜。◇ ~ **sth** (+ **adv./prep.**) *She sawed the plank in half.* 她把木板鋸成兩截。**2** [I, T] ~ (**away**) (**at sth**) | ~ **sth** to move sth backwards and forwards on sth as if using a saw 拉鋸似地來回移動（某物）：*She sawed away at her violin.* 她不停地拉着小提琴。◇ *He was sawing energetically at a loaf of bread.* 他正用力切着一條麪包。

PHR V **ˌsaw sth↔ˈdown** to cut sth and bring it to the ground using a saw 鋸倒：*The tree had to be sawn down.* 這棵樹只好鋸倒。**ˌsaw sth↔ˈoff** | **ˌsaw sth ˈoff sth** to remove sth by cutting it with a saw 鋸掉；鋸去：*We sawed the dead branches off the tree.* 我們鋸掉了樹上的枯枝。**ˌsaw sth↔ˈup (into sth)** to cut sth into pieces with a saw 把…鋸成（小塊或碎片）：*We sawed the wood up into logs.* 我們把木頭鋸成段段木材。

saw·dust /ˈsɔːdʌst/ *noun* [U] very small pieces of wood that fall as powder when wood is cut with a SAW 鋸末

saw·horse /ˈsɔːhɔːs; *NAmE* -hɔːrs/ *noun* a wooden frame that supports wood that is being cut with a SAW 鋸木架

sawm /səʊm; *NAmE* soʊm/ *noun* [U] the Muslim practice of not eating or drinking in the day during the ninth month of the Muslim year, called RAMADAN 齋戒（穆斯林曆九月裏的日間禁食）

saw·mill /ˈsɔːmɪl/ *noun* a factory in which wood is cut into boards using machinery 鋸木廠

ˌsawn-off ˈshotgun (*BrE*) (*NAmE* **ˌsawed-off ˈshotgun**) *noun* a SHOTGUN with part of its BARREL cut off 槍管鋸短的獵槍

sax /sæks/ *noun* (*informal*) = SAXOPHONE

Saxon /ˈsæksn/ *noun* a member of a race of people once living in NW Germany, some of whom settled in Britain in the 5th and 6th centuries 撒克遜人（早期居住在德國西北部，後其中一部份於 5、6 世紀定居在不列顛）➲ see also ANGLO-SAXON ▸ **Saxon** *adj.*：*Saxon churches/kings* 撒克遜教堂／國王

saxo·phone /ˈsæksəfəʊn; *NAmE* -foʊn/ (also *informal* **sax**) *noun* a metal musical instrument that you blow into, used especially in JAZZ 薩克斯管；薩克斯風 ➲ VISUAL VOCAB page V34

sax·opho·nist /sækˈsɒfənɪst; *NAmE* ˈsæksəfoʊnɪst/ *noun* a person who plays the saxophone 薩克斯管演奏者；薩克斯風演奏者

say /seɪ/ *verb, noun, exclamation*

■ *verb* (**says** /sez/, **said**, **said** /sed/)

▸ SPEAK 說 **1** [I, T] to speak or tell sb sth, using words 說；講；告訴：+ **speech** *'Hello!' she said.* "你好！"她說。◇ *'That was marvellous,' said Daniel.* "好極了。"丹尼爾說。HELP In stories the subject often comes after **said**, **says** or **say** when it follows the actual words spoken, unless it is a pronoun. 在故事、小說中用於直接引語後面時，往往先出 said、says 或 say，再出主語，除非主語是代詞。◇ ~ **sth** *Be quiet, I have something to say.* 安靜，我有話要說。◇ *I didn't believe a word she said.* 她說的話我一句都不信。◇ *That's a terrible **thing to say**.* 這話說不得。◇ *He knew that if he wasn't back by midnight, his parents would **have something to say about it*** (= be angry). 他知道，要是他半夜還不回去，父母就會不高興。◇ ~ **sth to sb** *She said nothing to me about it.* 她沒有跟我說過這件事。◇ ~ **to sb/yourself** + **speech** *I said to*

S

myself (= thought), *'That can't be right!'* 我心裏想："這不對呀！" ◇ **~ (that) …** *He said (that) his name was Sam.* 他說他叫薩姆。◇ **it is said that …** *It is said that she lived to be over 100.* 據說她活了 100 多歲。◇ **~ (what, how, etc. …)** *She finds it hard to say what she feels.* 她覺得心裏的感受難以言述。◇ *'That's impossible!' '**So you say** (= but I think you may be wrong).'* "這不可能！" "不見得。" ◇ *'Why can't I go out now?' 'Because I **say so**.'* "為什麼現在不讓我出去？" "因為我說了算。" ◇ *'What do you want it for?' '**I'd rather not say**.'* "你要這做什麼？" "我還是不說的好。" ◇ **~ to do sth** *He said to meet him here.* 他說來這兒跟他見面。◇ **sb/sth is said to be/have sth** *He is said to have been a brilliant scholar.* 據說他曾是個了不起的學者。

▸ **REPEAT WORDS** 複述 **2** **[T] ~ sth** to repeat words, phrases, etc. 唸；朗誦；背誦：*to say a prayer* 誦讀經文 ◇ *Try to say that line with more conviction.* 朗誦這一句時語氣要更加堅定。

▸ **EXPRESS OPINION** 表達見解 **3** [T, I] to express an opinion on sth 表達，表述（見解）：**~ sth** *Say what you like (= although you disagree) about her, she's a fine singer.* 隨你怎麼說，反正她唱歌唱得很好。◇ ***I'll say this for them**, they're a very efficient company.* 我要為他們說句公道話，他們公司的效率的確很高。◇ *Anna thinks I'm lazy—**what do you say*** (= what is your opinion)? 安娜覺得我懶，你說呢？◇ **~ (that) …** ***I can't say I blame** her for resigning* (= I think she was right). 她辭職，我不能說她不對。◇ ***I say*** (= suggest) *we go without them.* 依我說，我們自己去，不帶他們。◇ ***I wouldn't say** they were rich* (= in my opinion they are not rich). 要我說的話，他們並不富裕。◇ ***That's not to say** it's a bad movie* (= it is good but it is not without faults). 並不是說這部電影很糟糕。◇ **~ (what, how, etc. …)** ***It's hard to say** what caused the accident.* 很難說造成事故的原因是什麼。◇ *'When will it be finished?' '**I couldn't say*** (= I don't know).' "什麼時候能完？" "不好說。"

▸ **GIVE EXAMPLE** 舉例 **4** [T, no passive] to suggest or give sth as an example or a possibility 比方說；假設：**~ sth/sb** *You could learn the basics in, **let's say**, three months.* 比方說，三個月你就可以掌握基本知識。◇ *Let's take any writer, say* (= for example) *Dickens …* 我們隨便舉一個作家為例，比如說狄更斯⋯ ◇ **~ (that) …** *Say you lose your job: what would you do then?* 假設你把工作丟了，那你怎麼辦呢？

▸ **SHOW THOUGHTS/FEELINGS** 表明思想 / 感情 **5** [T] **~ sth (to sb)** to make thoughts, feelings, etc. clear to sb by using words, looks, movements, etc. 表明，顯示，表達（思想、感情）：*His angry glance **said it all**.* 他那憤憤的一瞥就道出了一切。◇ *That **says it all** really, doesn't it?* (= it shows clearly what is true) 這實際上就說明了一切，是不是？◇ *Just what is the artist trying to say in her work?* 這位藝術家究竟要在作品中表現什麼呢？

▸ **GIVE WRITTEN INFORMATION** 標示 **6** [T, no passive] (of sth that is written or can be seen 書面材料或可見的東西) to give particular information or instructions 提供信息；指示：**+ speech** *The notice said 'Keep Out'.* 告示上寫着"禁止入內"。◇ **~ sth** *The clock said three o'clock.* 時鐘顯示三點整。◇ **~ (that) …** *The instructions say (that) we should leave it to set for four hours.* 說明書上說我們應讓它凝結四小時。◇ **~ where, why, etc. …** *The book doesn't say where he was born.* 書上沒說他是在哪兒出生的。◇ **~ to do sth** *The guidebook says to turn left.* 旅遊指南上說應向左拐。

IDM **before you can say Jack 'Robinson** (*old-fashioned*) very quickly; in a very short time 轉瞬間；一剎那；說時遲，那時快 **,go without 'saying** to be very obvious or easy to predict 不用說；顯而易見：*Of course I'll help you. **That goes without saying**.* 我當然會幫你。這還用說嗎？ **have something, nothing, etc. to 'say for yourself** to be ready, unwilling, etc. to talk or give your views on sth 有話（或沒什麼等）要說：*She doesn't have much to say for herself* (= doesn't take part in conversation). 她沒多少要說的。◇ *He had plenty to say for himself* (= he had a lot of opinions and was willing to talk). 他有一肚子的話要說。◇ *Late again—what have you got to say for yourself* (= what is your excuse)? 又遲到了，這回你有什麼藉口呢？ **,having 'said that** (*informal*) used to introduce an opinion that makes what you have just said seem less strong（用以緩和語氣）雖然這麼說，話雖如此：*I sometimes get worried in this job. Having said that, I enjoy doing it, it's a challenge.* 我有時會為這份工作而感到憂慮。話雖如此，我還是滿喜歡幹的，因為這是一個挑戰。 **'I'll say!** (*old-fashioned, informal*) used for emphasis to say 'yes'（明確表示肯定）當然，我敢說，沒錯：*'Does she see him often?' 'I'll say! Nearly every day.'* "她常去找他嗎？" "沒錯！差不多天天去。" **I 'must say** (*informal*) used to emphasize an opinion（強調所發表的意見）：*Well, I must say, that's the funniest thing I've heard all week.* 嘿，聽我說，這是我整整一週聽到的最好笑的事情。 **,I 'say** (*old-fashioned, BrE, informal*) **1** used to express surprise, shock, etc.（表示驚奇、震驚等）：*I say! What a huge cake!* 乖乖！多大的一個蛋糕啊！ **2** used to attract sb's attention or introduce a new subject of conversation（用以引起注意或引出新的話題）：*I say, can you lend me five pounds?* 我說，你能借我五英鎊嗎？ **it says a 'lot, very 'little, etc. for sb/sth** (*informal*) it shows a good/bad quality that sb/sth has 說明某人（或某事物）很好（或不怎麼樣等）：*It says a lot for her that she never lost her temper.* 她從沒發過脾氣，這說明她很有涵養。◇ *It didn't say much for their efficiency that the order arrived a week late.* 訂貨晚到了一個星期，可見他們的效率難以恭維。 **I ,wouldn't say 'no (to sth)** (*informal*) used to say that you would like sth or to accept sth that is offered（表示想要或願意接受某物）：*I wouldn't say no to a pizza.* 我倒是想來塊比薩餅。◇ *'Tea, Brian?' 'I wouldn't say no.'* "要喝茶嗎，布賴恩？" "好哇。" **,least 'said ,soonest 'mended** (*BrE, saying*) a bad situation will pass or be forgotten most quickly if nothing more is said about it 只要沒人再說，事情就會過去 **the less/least said the 'better** the best thing to do is say as little as possible about sth 少說為妙 **,never say 'die** (*saying*) do not stop hoping 別泄氣；別氣餒；不言放棄 **not say boo to a 'goose** (*BrE*) (*NAmE* **not say boo to 'anyone**) to be very shy or gentle 非常膽怯；十分溫和：*He's so nervous he wouldn't say boo to a goose.* 他緊張得連大氣都不敢喘。 **'not to say** used to introduce a stronger way of describing sth（引出語氣更重的描述）即使不是⋯，雖不能說⋯：*a difficult, not to say impossible, task* 即便不是辦不到，也是難辦到的一項任務 **say 'cheese** used to ask sb to smile before you take their photograph（照相前請人微笑時說）"茄子" **say 'no (to sth)** to refuse an offer, a suggestion, etc. 拒絕；否定：*If you don't invest in this, you're saying no to a potential fortune.* 你如果不在這上面投資，那是存心不想發財。 **,say no 'more** (*informal*) used to say that you understand exactly what sb means or is trying to say, so it is unnecessary to say anything more 我早知道了；還用你說：*'They went to Paris together.' 'Say no more!'* "他們一起去了巴黎。" "我早知道了！" **,say your 'piece** to say exactly what you feel or think 說出心裏話 **say 'what?** (*NAmE, informal*) used to express surprise at what sb has just said（表示驚奇）你說什麼：*'He's getting married.' 'Say what?'* "他快結婚了。" "你說什麼？" **say 'when** used to ask sb to tell you when you should stop pouring a drink or serving food for them because they have enough（給飲料或食物時說）夠了請說一聲 **'that is to say** in other words 換句話說；也就是說：*three days from now, that is to say on Friday* 三天以後，也就是說星期五 **that's not 'saying much** used to say that sth is not very unusual or special 也沒什麼了不起；這說明不了什麼：*She's a better player than me, but that's not saying much* (= because I am a very bad player). 她比我高明，但那也沒什麼了不起（因為我很差）。 **that 'said** used to introduce an opinion that makes what you have just said seem less strong（用以緩和語氣）話雖如此 **there's no 'saying** used to say that it is impossible to predict what might happen 說不準；很難說：*There's no saying how he'll react.* 很難說他會有何種反應。 **there's something, not much, etc. to be said for sth/doing sth** there are/are not good reasons for doing sth, believing sth or agreeing with sth 有（或沒有太多等）理由去做（或相信、同意）某事 **to ,say the 'least** without exaggerating at all 毫不誇張地說：*I was surprised, to say the least.* 毫不誇張地說，我感到吃驚。 **to say 'nothing of sth**

S

used to introduce a further fact or thing in addition to those already mentioned 更不用說⋯；而且還 SYN **not to mention**： *It was too expensive, to say nothing of the time it wasted.* 這太貴了，更不用說它浪費的時間了。 **well 'said!** (*informal*) I agree completely 說得好；完全贊同： *'We must stand up for ourselves.' 'Well said, John.'* "我們必須自己起來保護自己。" "說得好，約翰。" **,what do/would you 'say (to sth/doing sth)** (*informal*) would you like sth/to do sth? 你同意⋯嗎；你看⋯好不好： *What do you say to eating out tonight?* 今晚到外邊吃飯，怎麼樣？ ◇ *Let's go away for a weekend. What do you say?* 我們出去過週末，你說好不好？ **what/whatever sb says, 'goes** (*informal*, often *humorous*) a particular person must be obeyed 凡是⋯說的，都得照辦；無論⋯說什麼，都能行得通： *Sarah wanted the kitchen painted green, and what she says, goes.* 薩拉想把廚房刷成綠色，而她說什麼，就得照辦。 **whatever you 'say** (*informal*) used to agree to sb's suggestion because you do not want to argue （因不想爭論而同意）由你，隨你 **when ,all is said and 'done** when everything is considered 說到底；畢竟；歸根到底： *I know you're upset, but when all's said and done it isn't exactly a disaster.* 我知道你挺沮喪的，但說到底，事情並沒什麼大不了的。 **who can 'say (...)?** used to say that nobody knows the answer to a question 誰知道（⋯）： *Who can say what will happen next year?* 誰能說得出明年會發生什麼事？ **who 'says (...)?** (*informal*) used to disagree with a statement or an opinion （表示不同意）誰說（⋯）： *Who says I can't do it?* 誰說我幹不了這個？ **who's to say (...)?** used to say that sth might happen or might have happened in a particular way, because nobody really knows （表示說不定某事會發生或本來會發生）誰說得準（⋯）： *Who's to say we would not have succeeded if we'd had more time?* 要是時間更充裕，沒準兒我們就已成功了，誰說得準呢？ **you can say 'that again** (*informal*) I agree with you completely 讓你說對了；一點沒錯；正是這樣： *'He's in a bad mood today.' 'You can say that again!'* "他今天情緒不好。" "讓你說對了！" **you can't say 'fairer (than 'that)** (*BrE, informal*) used to say that you think the offer you are making is reasonable or generous （出價時說）再公道不過了： *Look, I'll give you £100 for it. I can't say fairer than that.* 你看，我出 100 英鎊買它，這再公道不過了。 **you don't 'say!** (*informal*, often *ironic*) used to express surprise 我就知道；不會吧；不至於吧： *'They left without us.' 'You don't say!'* (= I'm not surprised) "他們撇下我們自個兒走了。" "真的嗎？" **you 'said it!** (*informal*) **1** (*BrE*) used to agree with sb when they say sth about themselves that you would not have been rude enough to say yourself （同意對方所作而礙於禮貌自己不便作出的評價）這話可是你說的： *'I know I'm not the world's greatest cook.' 'You said it!'* "我知道我的飯菜做得不是太好。" "這話可是你說的！" **2** (*NAmE*) used to agree with sb's suggestion （同意對方的提議）正合我心意 ➲ more at DARE *v.*, EASY *adv.*, ENOUGH *pron.*, GLAD, LET *v.*, MEAN *v.*, MIND *v.*, NEEDLESS, RECORD *n.*, SOON, SORRY *adj.*, SUFFICE, WORD *n.*

■ ***noun*** [sing., U] **~ (in sth)** the right to influence sth by giving your opinion before a decision is made 決定權；發言權： *We had no say in the decision to sell the company.* 在決定出售公司的問題上，我們沒有發言權。◇ *People want a greater say in local government.* 人們要求在當地的政務中有更大的發言權。◇ *The judge has the final say on the sentence.* 法官對判決有最後的決定權。

IDM **have your 'say** (*informal*) to have the opportunity to express yourself fully about sth 有機會充分發表意見： *She won't be happy until she's had her say.* 她要把話都說出來才舒暢。 ➲ see also SAY YOUR PIECE

■ ***exclamation*** (*NAmE, informal*) **1** used for showing surprise or pleasure （表示驚訝或興奮）嘿，嘖嘖： *Say, that's a nice haircut!* 嘖嘖，這個頭髮剪得很漂亮！ **2** used for attracting sb's attention or for making a suggestion or comment （提請別人注意、提出建議或作出評論）喂，我說： *Say, how about going to a movie tonight?* 我說，今晚去看場電影怎麼樣？

Which Word? 詞語辨析

say / tell

- **Say** never has a person as the object. You **say something** or **say something to somebody**. **Say** is often used when you are giving somebody's exact words. * say 從不以人作賓語，可說 say something 或 say something to somebody。say 常與直接引語連用： *'Sit down,' she said.* "坐下。" 她說。◇ *Anne said, 'I'm tired.'* 安妮說："我累了。" ◇ *Anne said (that) she was tired.* 安妮說她累了。◇ *What did he say to you?* 他對你說了些什麼？ You cannot use 'say about', but **say something about** is correct. 不能用 say about，但可說 say something about： *I want to say something /a few words /a little about my family.* 我想談談我的家庭。 **Say** can also be used with a clause when the person you are talking to is not mentioned. 沒有指明說話對象時，say 亦可與從句連用： *She didn't say what she intended to do.* 她沒說她想做什麼。
- **Tell** usually has a person as the object and often has two objects. * tell 常帶有兩個賓語，其中一個通常是人： *Have you told him the news yet?* 你告訴他這消息了嗎？ It is often used with 'that' clauses. 該詞常與 that 從句連用： *Anne told me (that) she was tired.* 安妮對我說她累了。 **Tell** is usually used when somebody is giving facts or information, often with *what, where*, etc. * tell 通常在某人告知事實或提供信息時使用，常與 what、where 等詞連用： *Can you tell me when the movie starts?* 你能告訴我電影什麼時候開演嗎？ (BUT 但： *Can you give me some information about the school?* 你能給我講講這所學校的情況嗎？) **Tell** is also used when you are giving somebody instructions. 發出指示時亦可用 tell： *The doctor told me to stay in bed.* 醫生要我臥牀休息。◇ *The doctor told me (that) I had to stay in bed.* 醫生對我說我必須臥牀休息。 OR 或： *The doctor said (that) I had to stay in bed.* 醫生說我必須臥牀休息。 NOT 不能說： ~~The doctor said me to stay in bed.~~

say·ing /'seɪɪŋ/ *noun* a well-known phrase or statement that expresses sth about life that most people believe is wise and true 諺語；格言；警句： *'Accidents will happen', as the saying goes.* 常言道："意外事，總難免。"

'say-so *noun* [sing.] (*informal*) permission that sb gives to do sth 許可；准許： *Nothing could be done without her say-so.* 未經她准許，什麼都不可以做。

IDM **on sb's 'say-so** based on a statement that sb makes without giving any proof 僅憑某人的空口白話；聽信某人不實之詞： *He hired and fired people on his partner's say-so.* 他雇誰辭誰全聽他的合夥人的一句話。

'S-bend *noun* a bend in a road or pipe that is shaped like an S （道路或管道的）S 形彎

scab /skæb/ *noun* **1** [C] a hard dry covering that forms over a wound as it heals 痂 **2** [U] a skin disease of animals （動物）疥癬 **3** [U] a disease of plants, especially apples and potatoes, that causes a rough surface （植物）瘡痂病，斑點病 **4** [C] (*informal, disapproving*) a worker who refuses to join a strike or takes the place of sb on strike 拒絕參加罷工的工人；頂替罷工者上班的工人；工賊 SYN **blackleg**

scab·bard /'skæbəd; *NAmE* -bərd/ *noun* a cover for a SWORD that is made of leather or metal （刀、劍的）鞘 SYN **sheath**

scab·by /'skæbi/ *adj.* covered in scabs 結痂的；有痂的

sca·bies /'skeɪbi:z/ *noun* [U] a skin disease that causes ITCHING and small red raised spots 疥瘡；疥蟎病

scab·rous /'skeɪbrəs; 'skæb-/ *adj.* **1** (*formal*) offensive or shocking in a sexual way 猥褻的；淫穢的；有傷風化的 SYN **indecent** **2** (*technical* 術語) having a rough surface 表面粗糙的 SYN **scaly**： *scabrous skin* 粗糙的皮膚

scads /skædz/ *noun* [pl.] **~ (of sth)** (*informal, especially NAmE*) large numbers or amounts of sth 大量；許多： *scads of $20 bills* 許多 20 元的鈔票

S

scaf·fold /ˈskæfəʊld; *NAmE* -foʊld/ *noun* **1** a platform used when EXECUTING criminals by cutting off their heads or hanging them from a rope 斷頭台；絞刑架 **2** a structure made of scaffolding, for workers to stand on when they are working on a building 腳手架；建築架；鷹架

scaf·fold·ing /ˈskæfəldɪŋ/ *noun* [U] poles and boards that are joined together to make a structure for workers to stand on when they are working high up on the outside wall of a building 腳手架（組）；鷹架

sca·lar /ˈskeɪlə(r)/ *adj.* (*mathematics* 數) (of a quantity 量) having size but no direction 純量的；標量的；無向量的 ➲ compare VECTOR ▸ **sca·lar** *noun*

scala·wag /ˈskæləwæg/ (*NAmE*) (*BrE* **scally·wag**) *noun* (*informal*) a person, especially a child, who behaves badly, but not in a serious way 調皮搗蛋的人，淘氣鬼（尤指兒童）**SYN** **scamp**

scald /skɔːld/ *verb, noun*
■ ***verb*** **~ sth/yourself** to burn yourself or part of your body with very hot liquid or steam 燙傷：*Be careful not to scald yourself with the steam.* 小心別讓蒸汽把你燙着。◇ (*figurative*) *Tears scalded her eyes.* 她熱淚盈眶。 ➲ **SYNONYMS** at BURN ➲ **COLLOCATIONS** at INJURY
■ ***noun*** an injury to the skin from very hot liquid or steam 燙傷

scald·ing /ˈskɔːldɪŋ/ *adj.* hot enough to SCALD 滾燙的；灼熱的：*scalding water* 滾燙的水 ◇ (*figurative*) *Scalding tears poured down her face.* 滾燙的淚水從她臉上撲簌簌地流下來。 ▸ **scald·ing** *adv.*：*scalding hot* 灼熱

scales 磅秤；比例；音階；鱗

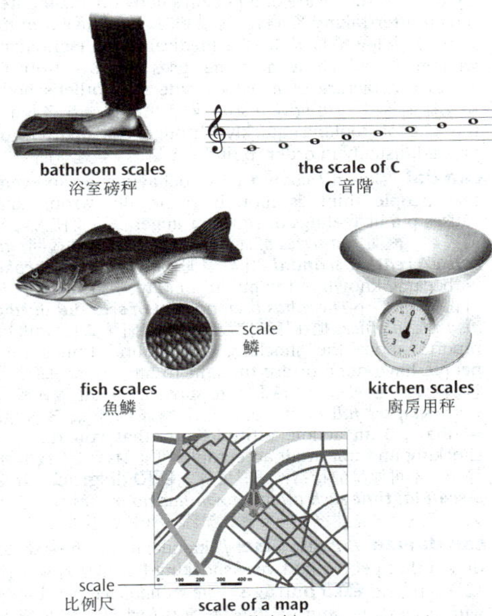

scale 🔑 /skeɪl/ *noun, verb*
■ ***noun***
▸ SIZE 規模 **1** 🔑 [sing., U] the size or extent of sth, especially when compared with sth else（尤指與其他事物相比較時的）規模，範圍，程度：*They entertain **on a large scale*** (= they hold expensive parties with a lot of guests). 他們大宴賓客。◇ *Here was corruption **on a grand scale**.* 這裏的腐敗現象曾十分嚴重。◇ *On a global scale, 77% of energy is created from fossil fuels.* 全球 77% 的能量產生自礦物燃料。◇ *to achieve **economies of scale** in production* (= to produce many items so the cost of producing each one is reduced) 實現規模生產 ◇ **~ of sth** *It was impossible to comprehend **the full scale** of the disaster.* 這場災難的深重程度當時還無法充分認識。◇ *It was not until morning that **the sheer scale** of the damage could be seen* (= how great it was). 直到早晨才看清了損害的嚴重程度。 ➲ see also FULL-SCALE, LARGE-SCALE, SMALL-SCALE
▸ RANGE OF LEVELS 等級 **2** 🔑 [C] a range of levels or numbers used for measuring sth 等級；級別：*a five-point pay scale* 五分制工資等級 ◇ *to evaluate performance on a scale from 1 to 10* 按 1 到 10 級來評估成績 ➲ see also RICHTER SCALE, SLIDING SCALE, TIME-SCALE **3** 🔑 [C, usually sing.] the set of all the different levels of sth, from the lowest to the highest 等級體系：***At the other end of the scale**, life is a constant struggle to get enough to eat.* 對於處在社會最底層的人來說，生活就是不斷地在溫飽線上掙扎求存。◇ *the social scale* 社會等級體系
▸ MARKS FOR MEASURING 衡量標度 **4** 🔑 [C] a series of marks at regular intervals on an instrument that is used for measuring 標度；刻度：*How much does it read on the scale?* 刻度顯示的是多少？
▸ WEIGHING INSTRUMENT 衡器 **5** 🔑 **scales** [pl.] (*NAmE* also **scale**) an instrument for weighing people or things 秤；磅秤；天平：***bathroom/kitchen/weighing scales*** 浴室磅秤；廚房用秤；秤 ◇ (*figurative*) *the **scales of justice*** (= represented as the two pans on a BALANCE (5)) 正義的天平 ➲ **VISUAL VOCAB** page V24
▸ OF MAP/DIAGRAM/MODEL 地圖；圖表；模型 **6** 🔑 [C] the relation between the actual size of sth and its size on a map, diagram or model that represents it 比例；比例尺：*a scale of 1:25 000* * 1:25 000 的比例 ◇ ***a scale model/drawing*** 按比例縮放的模型／圖畫 ◇ *Both plans are drawn to the same scale.* 兩張平面圖是按同一比例繪製的。◇ *Is this diagram **to scale*** (= are all its parts the same size and shape in relation to each other as they are in the thing represented)? 這張圖表是按比例畫的嗎？
▸ IN MUSIC 音樂 **7** [C] a series of musical notes moving upwards or downwards, with fixed intervals between each note, especially a series of eight starting on a particular note 音階：*the scale of C major* * C 大調音階 ◇ *to practise scales on the piano* 在鋼琴上練習音階 ➲ compare KEY *n.* (5), OCTAVE
▸ OF FISH/REPTILE 魚；爬行動物 **8** [C] any of the thin plates of hard material that cover the skin of many fish and REPTILES 鱗；鱗片
▸ IN WATER PIPES, ETC. 水管等 **9** (*BrE* also **fur**) [U] a hard greyish-white substance that is sometimes left inside water pipes and containers for heating water 水垢；水銹 ➲ see also LIMESCALE
▸ ON TEETH 牙齒 **10** [U] a hard substance that forms on teeth, especially when they are not cleaned regularly 牙垢；牙石 ➲ compare PLAQUE (2) **IDM** see TIP *v.*
■ ***verb***
▸ CLIMB 攀登 **1** **~ sth** (*formal*) to climb to the top of sth very high and steep 攀登；到達…頂點：*the first woman to scale Mount Everest* 第一位登上珠穆朗瑪峰的女性 ◇ (*figurative*) *He has **scaled the heights** of his profession.* 他登上了他事業的頂峰。
▸ FISH 魚 **2** **~ sth** to remove the small flat hard pieces of skin from a fish 去鱗
▸ TEETH 牙齒 **3** **~ sth** to remove TARTAR from the teeth by SCRAPING 刮除牙石：*The dentist scaled and polished my teeth.* 牙醫為我刮除牙石，拋光了牙齒。
▸ CHANGE SIZE 改變大小 **4** **~ sth** (**from sth**) (**to sth**) (*technical* 術語) to change the size of sth 改變…的大小：*Text can be scaled from 4 points to 108 points without any loss of quality.* 字體的大小可以從 4 點調到 108 點，但印刷質量絲毫不會降低。

PHR V **ˌscale sth↔ˈdown** (*NAmE* also **ˌscale sth↔ˈback**) to reduce the number, size or extent of sth 減少（數量）；縮小（規模或範圍）：*We are thinking of scaling down our training programmes next year.* 我們考慮在明年縮小培訓計劃。◇ *The IMF has scaled back its growth forecasts for the next decade.* 國際貨幣基金組織已經調低了它對未來十年的增長預測。 ➲ **SYNONYMS** at CUT **ˌscale sth↔ˈup** to increase the size or number of sth 增大，擴大（規模或數量）

sca·lene tri·angle /ˌskeɪliːn ˈtraɪæŋɡl/ *noun* (*geometry* 幾何) a triangle whose sides are all of different lengths 不等邊三角形；不規則三角形 ➲ VISUAL VOCAB page V71

scal·lion /ˈskæliən/ *noun* (*NAmE, IrishE*) = GREEN ONION, SPRING ONION

scal·lop /ˈskɒləp; *NAmE* ˈskæləp/ *noun, verb*

■ ***noun*** **1** a SHELLFISH that can be eaten, with two flat round shells that fit together 扇貝：*a scallop shell* 扇貝殼 **2** any one of a series of small curves cut on the edge of a piece of cloth, PASTRY, etc. for decoration（織物、糕點等的）扇形飾邊；荷葉邊

■ ***verb*** [usually passive] **~ sth** to decorate the edge of sth with small curves 給…加上扇形飾邊：*a scalloped edge* 扇形邊

scally /ˈskæli/ *noun* (*pl.* **-ies**) (*BrE, informal*) (used especially in Liverpool in NW England 尤用於英國西北部利物浦) a boy or young man who behaves badly or causes trouble 調皮搗蛋的男孩；行為不端（或滋事）的年輕男子

scally·wag /ˈskæliwæɡ/ (*BrE*) (*NAmE* **scala·wag**) *noun* (*informal*) a person, especially a child, who behaves badly, but not in a serious way 調皮搗蛋的人，淘氣鬼（尤指兒童）SYN **scamp**

scalp /skælp/ *noun, verb*

■ ***noun*** **1** the skin that covers the part of the head where the hair grows 頭皮 **2** (in the past) the skin and hair that was removed from the head of a dead enemy by some Native American peoples as a sign of victory（舊時美洲土著從被殺的敵人頭上剝下作為戰利品的）帶髮頭皮 **3** (*informal*) a symbol of the fact that sb has been defeated or punished（表示某人已被打敗或已受到懲罰的）標誌：*They have claimed some impressive scalps in their bid for the championship.* 他們宣稱已在奪取冠軍的征途上獲得顯著進展。

■ ***verb*** **1 ~ sb** to remove the skin and hair from the top of an enemy's head as a sign of victory（作為戰利品，從被殺的敵人頭上）剝下帶髮頭皮 **2** (*NAmE*) (*BrE* **tout**) **~ sth** to sell tickets for a popular event illegally, at a price that is higher than the official price, especially outside a theatre, STADIUM, etc.（尤指在劇院、體育場等外以高價）倒賣門票，賣黑市票

scal·pel /ˈskælpəl/ *noun* a small sharp knife used by doctors in medical operations 解剖刀；手術刀

scalp·er /ˈskælpə(r)/ (*NAmE*) (*BrE* **tout**, **ˈticket tout**) *noun* a person who buys tickets for concerts, sports events, etc. and then sells them to other people at a higher price（音樂會、體育比賽等以高價）倒賣門票者，票販子：*ticket scalpers* 票販子

scaly /ˈskeɪli/ *adj.* (**scali·er**, **scali·est**) (of skin 皮膚) covered with SCALES (8), or hard and dry, with small pieces that come off 有鱗屑的

ˌscaly ˈanteater *noun* = PANGOLIN

scam /skæm/ *noun* (*informal*) a clever and dishonest plan for making money 欺詐；詐財騙局 ➲ COLLOCATIONS at CRIME

scamp /skæmp/ *noun* (*old-fashioned*) a child who enjoys playing tricks and causing trouble 淘氣鬼；搗亂鬼 SYN **scallywag**

scam·per /ˈskæmpə(r)/ *verb* [I] **+ adv./prep.** (especially of children or small animals 尤指兒童或小動物) to move quickly with short light steps 歡快地奔走；蹦蹦跳跳

scampi /ˈskæmpi/ *noun* [U+sing./pl. v.] (*BrE*) large PRAWNS (= a type of sea creature) covered with BREADCRUMBS or BATTER and fried 炸大蝦：*scampi and chips* 炸大蝦和炸薯條

scan /skæn/ *verb, noun*

■ ***verb*** (**-nn-**) **1** [T] to look at every part of sth carefully, especially because you are looking for a particular thing or person 細看；察看；審視；端詳 SYN **scrutinize**：**~ sth for sth** *He scanned the horizon for any sign of land.* 他仔細眺望地平線，找尋陸地的踪影。◇ **~ sth** *She scanned his face anxiously.* 她急切地端詳着他的臉。 **2** [T, I] to look quickly but not very carefully at a document, etc. 粗略地讀；瀏覽；翻閱：**~ sth (for sth)** *I scanned the list quickly for my name.* 我很快瀏覽了一下名單，看有沒有我的名字。◇ **~ through sth (for sth)** *She scanned through the newspaper over breakfast.* 她邊吃早飯，邊瀏覽報紙。 **3** [T] **~ sth** to get an image of an object, a part of sb's body, etc. on a computer by passing X-RAYS, ULTRASOUND waves or ELECTROMAGNETIC waves over it in a special machine（X 射線、超聲波、電磁波等）掃描：*Their brains are scanned so that researchers can monitor the progress of the disease.* 研究人員對他們的大腦加以掃描，以監察病情的發展。 **4** [T] **~ sth** (of a light, RADAR, etc. 光束、雷達等) to pass across an area 掃描；掃掠：*Concealed video cameras scan every part of the compound.* 幾台暗藏的攝像機把院子裏的每一個角落都拍了進去。 **5** [I, T] **~ (sth)** (*computing* 計) (of a program 程序) to examine a computer program or document in order to look for a virus（為搜索病毒而）掃描（文件）：*This software is designed to scan all new files for viruses.* 這個軟件是為搜索所有新文件的病毒而設計。 **6** [T] **~ sth** (*computing* 計) to pass light over a picture or document using a SCANNER in order to copy it and put it in the memory of a computer（用掃描設備）掃描（圖像或文件）：*How do I scan a photo and attach it to an email?* 怎樣把照片掃描並以附件形式加在電子郵件裏呢？ **7** [I] (of poetry 詩歌) to have a regular rhythm according to fixed rules 符合韻律：*This line doesn't scan.* 這一行不合韻律。

PHR V **ˌscan sth ˈinto sth** | **ˌscan sth ˈin** (*computing* 計) to pass light over a picture or document using a SCANNER in order to copy it and put it in the memory of a computer 把…掃描進；掃描輸入：*Text and pictures can be scanned into the computer.* 文字和圖畫可以掃描進計算機。

■ ***noun*** **1** [C] a medical test in which a machine produces a picture of the inside of a person's body on a computer screen after taking X-RAYS 掃描檢查：*to have a brain scan* 做腦部掃描檢查 **2** [C] a medical test for pregnant women in which a machine uses ULTRASOUND to produce a picture of a baby inside its mother's body 胎兒掃描檢查：*to have a scan* 做胎兒掃描檢查 **3** [sing.] the act of looking quickly through sth written or printed, usually in order to find sth 瀏覽；快速查閱

scan·dal /ˈskændl/ *noun* **1** [C, U] behaviour or an event that people think is morally or legally wrong and causes public feelings of shock or anger 醜行；使人震驚的醜事；醜聞：*a series of sex scandals* 一系列性醜聞 ◇ *to* ***cause/create a scandal*** 引發醜聞 ◇ *The* ***scandal broke*** (= became known to the public) *in May.* 這樁醜聞是在五月份曝光的。◇ *There has been* ***no hint of scandal*** *during his time in office.* 他在任期間沒有任何醜聞。 **2** [U] talk or reports about the shocking or immoral things that people have done or are thought to have done 關於醜行的傳言（或報道）；醜聞：*to spread scandal* 散佈醜聞 ◇ *newspapers full of scandal* 充斥醜聞的報紙 **3** [sing.] **~ (that …)** an action, attitude, etc. that you think is shocking and not at all acceptable 可恥的行為（或態度等）；不可原諒的行為（或態度等）SYN **disgrace**：***It is a scandal that*** *such a large town has no orchestra.* 這麼大一座城市，竟然沒有一支管弦樂隊，真是說不過去。

scan·dal·ize (*BrE* also **-ise**) /ˈskændəlaɪz/ *verb* **~ sb** to do sth that people find very shocking（以出格行為）使震驚，使憤慨 SYN **outrage**：*She scandalized her family with her extravagant lifestyle.* 她奢侈的生活方式令家人側目。

scan·dal·mon·ger /ˈskændlmʌŋɡə(r)/ *noun* (*disapproving*) a person who spreads stories about the shocking or immoral things that other people have done 散佈醜聞者

scan·dal·ous /ˈskændələs/ *adj.* **1** shocking and unacceptable 可恥的；不可原諒的 SYN **disgraceful**：*a scandalous waste of money* 金錢的浪費觸目驚心 ◇ **it is scandalous that …** *It is scandalous that he has not been punished.* 他沒有受到懲罰，天理難容啊。 **2** [only before noun] containing talk about the shocking or immoral things that people have done or are thought to have done 講述醜聞的：*scandalous stories* 醜聞故事 ▸ **scan·dal·ous·ly** *adv.*：*scandalously low pay* 低得令人憤慨的工資

ˈscandal sheet *noun* (*disapproving*) a newspaper or magazine that is mainly concerned with shocking stories about the immoral behaviour and private lives of famous or important people 醜聞報，醜聞雜誌（報道名人或要人緋聞或私生活等）

Scan·di·navia /ˌskændɪˈneɪviə/ *noun* [U] a cultural region in NW Europe consisting of Norway, Sweden and Denmark and sometimes also Iceland, Finland and the Faroe Islands 斯堪的納維亞（歐洲西北部文化區，包括挪威、瑞典和丹麥，有時也包括冰島、芬蘭和法羅群島）▶ **Scan·di·navian** /ˌskændɪˈneɪviən/ *adj.*, *noun*

scan·dium /ˈskændiəm/ *noun* [U] (*symb.* **Sc**) a chemical element. Scandium is a silver-white metal found in various minerals. 鈧

scan·ner /ˈskænə(r)/ *noun* **1** a device for examining sth or recording sth using light, sound or X-RAYS 掃描儀；掃描器；掃描設備：*The identity cards are examined by an electronic scanner.* 用電子掃描器來檢驗身分證。**2** (*computing* 計) a device which copies pictures and documents so that they can be stored on a computer 掃描儀；掃描器：*a document scanner* 文件掃描儀 ➲ VISUAL VOCAB pages V66, V69 ➲ see also FLATBED SCANNER **3** a machine used by doctors to produce a picture of the inside of a person's body on a computer screen （醫用）掃描器：*a body scanner* 人體掃描器 **4** a piece of equipment for receiving and sending RADAR signals 掃掠天線；自動旋轉雷達天線

scan·sion /ˈskænʃn/ *noun* [U] (*technical* 術語) the rhythm of a line of poetry （詩行的）韻律

scant /skænt/ *adj.* [only before noun] hardly any; not very much and not as much as there should be 一丁點的；微小的；不足的；欠缺的：*I* ***paid scant attention to*** *what she was saying.* 我沒大注意她在說什麼。◇ *The firefighters went back into the house with* ***scant regard for*** *their own safety.* 消防員奮不顧身地返回那座房子。

scanty /ˈskænti/ *adj.* (**scant·ier**, **scanti·est**) **1** too little in amount for what is needed 不足的；欠缺的；太少的：*Details of his life are scanty.* 關於他的生平，詳細資料不多。**2** (of clothes 衣服) very small and not covering much of your body 小而暴露身體的：*a scanty bikini* 遮不住多少身體的比基尼泳裝 ▶ **scant·ily** *adv.*：*scantily dressed models* 衣着暴露的模特兒

-scape *combining form* (in nouns 構成名詞) a view or scene of …景（色）：*landscape* 風景 ◇ *seascape* 海景 ◇ *moonscape* 月景

scape·goat /ˈskeɪpɡəʊt; *NAmE* -ɡoʊt/ *noun* a person who is blamed for sth bad that sb else has done or for some failure 替罪羊；代人受過者 SYN **fall guy**：*She felt she had been made a scapegoat for her boss's incompetence.* 她覺得，本是老闆無能，但她卻成了替罪羊。▶ **scape·goat** *verb* **~ sb/sth**

scap·ula /ˈskæpjʊlə/ *noun* (*pl.* **scapu·lae** /-liː/ or **scapu·las**) (*anatomy* 解) the SHOULDER BLADE 肩胛（骨）➲ VISUAL VOCAB page V59

scar /skɑː(r)/ *noun*, *verb*

■ ***noun*** **1** a mark that is left on the skin after a wound has healed 傷疤；傷痕；瘢痕：*a scar on his cheek* 他臉上的傷疤 ◇ *Will the operation leave a scar?* 手術會不會留下疤痕？◇ *scar tissue* 瘢痕組織 **2** a permanent feeling of great sadness or mental pain that a person is left with after an unpleasant experience （精神上的）創傷；傷痕：*His years in prison have* ***left deep scars.*** 他在獄中的歲月給他留下了深深的創傷。**3** something unpleasant or ugly that spoils the appearance or public image of sth 有損外觀（或公共形象）的地方；污點；煞風景之處：*The town still bears the scars of war.* 城裏依舊可見戰爭的瘡痍。◇ *Racism has been a scar on the game.* 種族主義行為給這次比賽抹了黑。**4** an area of a hill or CLIFF where there is exposed rock and no grass （小山或懸崖上的）裸岩

■ ***verb*** (**-rr-**) [often passive] **1 ~ sb/sth** (of a wound, etc. 傷口等) to leave a mark on the skin after it has healed 在…上結疤；給…留下瘢痕：*His face was badly scarred.* 他的臉上留下了明顯的疤痕。**2 ~ sb** (of an unpleasant experience 不愉快的經歷) to leave sb with a feeling of sadness or mental pain 給…留下精神創傷：*The experience left her* ***scarred for life.*** 那段經歷給她留下終生的創傷。**3 ~ sth** to spoil the appearance of sth 損害…的外觀：*The hills are scarred by quarries.* 採石場破壞了這些山的景觀。◇ *battle-scarred buildings* 彈痕纍纍的建築物

scarab /ˈskærəb/ (also **ˈscarab beetle**) *noun* a large black BEETLE (= an insect with a hard shell); a design showing a scarab beetle 聖甲蟲；聖甲蟲雕飾物

scarce /skeəs; *NAmE* skers/ *adj.*, *adv.*

■ ***adj.*** (**scar·cer**, **scar·cest**) if sth is **scarce**, there is not enough of it and it is only available in small quantities 缺乏的；不足的；稀少的：***scarce resources*** 稀缺資源 ◇ *Details of the accident are scarce.* 事故的詳細情況瞭解不多。◇ *Food was becoming scarce.* 食物越來越緊缺。

IDM **ˌmake yourself ˈscarce** (*informal*) to leave somewhere and stay away for a time in order to avoid an unpleasant situation 躲開；迴避；溜走

■ ***adv.*** (*literary*) only just; almost not 勉強；剛；幾乎不；簡直不：*I can scarce remember him.* 我幾乎想不起他了。

scarce·ly /ˈskeəsli; *NAmE* ˈskers-/ *adv.* **1** only just; almost not 勉強；剛；幾乎不；簡直不：*I can scarcely believe it.* 我幾乎不敢相信。◇ *We scarcely ever meet.* 我們難得見一面。◇ *Scarcely a week goes by without some new scandal in the papers.* 報上幾乎週週都會登出新的醜聞。**2** used to say that sth happens immediately after sth else happens （表示接連發生）剛一…就：*He had scarcely put the phone down when the doorbell rang.* 他剛放下電話，門鈴就響了起來。◇ *Scarcely had the game started when it began to rain.* 比賽才開始就下起雨來了。**3** used to suggest that sth is not at all reasonable or likely 實在不應該；根本不可能：*It was scarcely an occasion for laughter.* 笑得實在不是時候。◇ *She could scarcely complain, could she?* 她壓根兒沒什麼好抱怨的，是不是？➲ note at HARDLY

scar·city /ˈskeəsəti; *NAmE* ˈskers-/ *noun* [U, C] (*pl.* **-ies**) if there is a **scarcity of** sth, there is not enough of it and it is difficult to obtain it 缺乏；不足；稀少 SYN **shortage**：*a time of scarcity* 物資短缺時期 ◇ *a scarcity of resources* 資源短缺

scare 0ᵕ /skeə(r); *NAmE* sker/ *verb*, *noun*

■ ***verb*** **1** 0ᵕ [T] to frighten sb 驚嚇；使害怕；使恐懼：**~ sb** *You scared me.* 你嚇了我一跳。◇ **it scares sb to do sth** *It scared me to think I was alone in the building.* 想到樓裏只有我一個人，怪害怕的。➲ SYNONYMS at FRIGHTEN **2** [I] to become frightened 受驚嚇；害怕；恐懼：*He doesn't scare easily.* 他不輕易害怕。➲ see also SCARY

IDM **scare the ˈshit out of sb** | **scare sb ˈshitless** (*taboo*, *slang*) to frighten sb very much 嚇得某人屁滾尿流 ➲ more at DAYLIGHTS, DEATH, LIFE

PHR V **ˌscare sb↔aˈway/ˈoff** 0ᵕ to make sb go away by frightening them 把…嚇跑：*They managed to scare the bears away.* 他們設法把熊嚇跑了。**ˈscare sb into doing sth** to frighten sb in order to make them do sth 威脅，恐嚇（某人做某事）：*Local businesses were scared into paying protection money.* 當地商家迫於威脅繳納了保護費。**ˌscare sb↔ˈoff** to make sb afraid of or nervous about doing sth, especially without intending to （尤指無意中）把人嚇倒，使人害怕，使恐懼：*Rising prices are scaring customers off.* 不斷上漲的價格把顧客紛紛嚇跑了。**ˌscare ˈup sth** (*NAmE*, *informal*) to find or make sth by using whatever is available （就現有材料）勉強湊合：*I'll see if I can scare up enough chairs for us all.* 我來看看能不能給大家湊夠椅子。

■ ***noun*** **1** 0ᵕ [C] (used especially in newspapers 尤用於報章) a situation in which a lot of people are anxious or frightened about sth 恐慌；恐懼：*a* ***bomb/health scare*** 炸彈／衛生恐慌 ◇ *recent scares about pesticides in food* 近來人們對含殺蟲劑食物的恐慌 ◇ *a* ***scare story*** (= a news report that spreads more anxiety or fear about sth than is necessary) 引起恐慌的報道 ◇ *to cause a major scare* 引起嚴重恐慌 ◇ ***scare tactics*** (= ways of persuading people to do sth by frightening them) 恐嚇戰術 **2** 0ᵕ [sing.] a sudden feeling of fear 驚嚇；驚恐：*You gave me a scare!* 你嚇了我一跳！◇ *We've had quite a scare.* 我們嚇得不輕。➲ see also SCARY

S

scare·crow /ˈskeəkrəʊ; NAmE ˈskerkroʊ/ *noun* a figure made to look like a person, that is dressed in old clothes and put in a field to frighten birds away 稻草人

scared /skeəd; NAmE skerd/ *adj.* frightened of sth or afraid that sth bad might happen 害怕；恐懼；畏懼；擔心：**~ (of doing sth)** *She is scared of going out alone.* 她不敢一個人外出。◇ **~ (of sb/sth)** *He's scared of heights.* 他有恐高症。◇ **~ (to do sth)** *People are scared to use the buses late at night.* 人們害怕在深夜乘坐公共汽車。◇ **~ (that ...)** *I'm scared (that) I'm going to fall.* 我擔心自己快掉下去了。◇ *The thieves got scared and ran away.* 小偷害怕了，就跑了。◇ *a scared look* 驚恐的表情 ◇ *I was **scared to death** (= very frightened).* 我嚇得要死。◇ *We were **scared stiff** (= very frightened).* 我們嚇得呆若木雞。➲ SYNONYMS at AFRAID **IDM** see SHADOW *n.*, WIT, WITLESS

scaredy-cat /ˈskeədi kæt; NAmE ˈskerdi/ (*US* also **ˈfraidy cat**) *noun* (*informal, disapproving*) a children's word for a person who is easily frightened（兒童用語）膽小鬼

scare·mon·ger /ˈskeəmʌŋgə(r); NAmE ˈskerm-/ *noun* (*disapproving*) a person who spreads stories deliberately to make people frightened or nervous 散佈恐怖消息的人；製造恐慌的人；危言聳聽的人 ▸ **scare·monger·ing** *noun* [U]

ˈscare quotes *noun* [pl.] QUOTATION MARKS that a writer puts around a word or phrase to show that it is used in an unusual way, usually one that the writer does not agree with 着重引號（表示引號內的詞或短語用法特別，通常為作者所不贊成）：*This pronouncement came from the organization's 'scientific' committee (the scare quotes are mine).* 這條聲明來自該機構的"科學"委員會（着重引號為本人所加）。

scarf /skɑːf; NAmE skɑːrf/ *noun, verb*

■ *noun* (*pl.* **scarves** /skɑːvz; NAmE skɑːrvz/ or *less frequent* **scarfs**) a piece of cloth that is worn around the neck, for example for warmth or decoration. Women also wear scarves over their shoulders or hair. 圍巾；披巾；頭巾：*a woollen/silk scarf* 羊毛／絲綢圍巾 ➲ VISUAL VOCAB page V65

■ *verb* (*NAmE*) (*BrE* **scoff**) [I, T] **~ (sth)** (*informal*) to eat a lot of sth quickly 貪婪地吃；狼吞虎嚥

scar·ify /ˈskærɪfaɪ; ˈskeə-; NAmE ˈsker-/ *verb* (**scari·fies, scari·fy·ing, scari·fied, scari·fied**) (*technical* 術語) **1 ~ sth** to break up an area of grass, etc. and remove pieces of material from it that are not wanted 翻鬆（草地等） **2 ~ sth** to make cuts in the surface of sth, especially skin 劃破（尤指皮膚）

S

scar·let /ˈskɑːlət; NAmE ˈskɑːrlət/ *adj.* bright red in colour 猩紅的；鮮紅的：*scarlet berries* 鮮紅的漿果 ◇ *She **went scarlet** with embarrassment.* 她窘得滿臉通紅。▸ **scar·let** *noun* [U]

ˌscarlet ˈfever *noun* [U] a serious infectious disease that causes fever and red marks on the skin 猩紅熱

ˌscarlet ˈwoman *noun* (*old-fashioned*) a woman who has sexual relationships with many different people 蕩婦

scarp /skɑːp; NAmE skɑːrp/ *noun* (*technical* 術語) a very steep slope 陡坡；懸崖

scar·per /ˈskɑːpə(r); NAmE ˈskɑːrp-/ *verb* [I] (*BrE, informal*) to run away; to leave 逃跑；溜號：*The police arrived, so we scarpered.* 警察來了，於是我們就溜走了。

Scart /skɑːt; NAmE skɑːrt/ (also **SCART**) *noun* a device with 21 pins, used to connect video equipment to, for example, a television * Scart 連接器；21 針音視頻信號連接器：*a Scart socket* * 21 針音視頻信號線插孔

scarves *pl.* of SCARF

scary /ˈskeəri; NAmE ˈskeri/ *adj.* (**scari·er, scari·est**) (*informal*) frightening 恐怖的；嚇人的：*It was a really scary moment.* 那一刻真是嚇人。◇ *a scary movie* 恐怖電影 ➲ see also SCARE *v.*

scat /skæt/ *noun* [U] a style of JAZZ singing in which the voice is made to sound like a musical instrument 擬聲唱法（模擬樂器的爵士樂歌唱方式）

scath·ing /ˈskeɪðɪŋ/ *adj.* criticizing sb or sth very severely 嚴厲批評的；無情抨擊的；尖刻地斥責的 **SYN** **withering**：*a **scathing attack** on the new management* 針對新的管理層的猛烈抨擊 ◇ **~ about sb/sth** *He was scathing about the government's performance.* 他尖銳地批評了政府的表現。▸ **scath·ing·ly** *adv.*：*'Oh, she's just a kid,' he said scathingly.* "咳，她還是個孩子呢。"他尖刻地挖苦道。

scato·logic·al /ˌskætəˈlɒdʒɪkl; NAmE -ˈlɑːdʒ-/ *adj.* (*formal*) connected with human waste from the body in an unpleasant way 與糞便有關的：*scatological humour* 下作的幽默

scat·ter /ˈskætə(r)/ *verb, noun*

■ *verb* **1** [T] to throw or drop things in different directions so that they cover an area of ground 撒；撒播：**~ sth** *They scattered his ashes at sea.* 他們把他的骨灰撒向大海。◇ **~ sth on/over/around sth** *Scatter the grass seed over the lawn.* 把草籽撒到草坪上。◇ **~ sth with sth** *Scatter the lawn with grass seed.* 在草坪上撒上草籽。 **2** [I, T] to move or to make people or animals move very quickly in different directions 散開；四散；使分散；驅散 **SYN** **disperse**：*At the first gunshot, the crowd scattered.* 槍聲一響，人群便逃散了。◇ **~ sb/sth** *The explosion scattered a flock of birds roosting in the trees.* 爆炸聲把棲息在樹叢中的鳥群驚散了。

■ *noun* [usually sing.] (also **scat·ter·ing** /ˈskætərɪŋ/ [sing.]) a small amount or number of things spread over an area 散落；三三兩兩；零零星星：*a scattering of houses* 稀稀落落的房屋

scat·ter·brain /ˈskætəbreɪn; NAmE -tərb-/ *noun* (*informal*) a person who is always losing or forgetting things and cannot think in an organized way 思想不集中的人；健忘的人 ▸ **scat·ter·brained** *adj.*

ˈscatter cushion (*BrE*) (*NAmE* **ˈthrow pillow**) *noun* a small CUSHION that can be placed on furniture, on the floor, etc. for decoration 散放的裝飾墊 ➲ VISUAL VOCAB page V21

ˈscatter diagram (also **scat·ter·gram** /ˈskætəgræm; NAmE -tərg-/) *noun* (*statistics* 統計) a diagram that shows the relationship between two VARIABLES by creating a pattern of dots（表示兩變量關係的）點聚圖，散佈圖

scat·tered /ˈskætəd; NAmE -tərd/ *adj.* spread far apart over a wide area or over a long period of time 分散的；零散的；疏落的：*a few scattered settlements* 幾個分散的村落 ◇ *sunshine with scattered showers* 晴，間有零星陣雨 ◇ *Her family are scattered around the world.* 她的家人散居在世界各地。

scatter·gun /ˈskætəgʌn; NAmE -tərg-/ (*BrE*) (*NAmE* **scatter·shot** /ˈskætəʃɒt; NAmE -tərʃɑːt/) *adj.* [only before noun] referring to a way of doing or dealing with sth by considering many different possibilities, people, etc. in a way that is not well organized（處事）雜亂無章的，亂無頭緒的，漫無邊際的：*The scattergun approach to marketing means that the campaign is not targeted at particular individuals.* 促銷運動採取漁翁撒網的方法，表示並非針對特定的人群。

scatty /ˈskæti/ *adj.* (**scat·tier, scat·ti·est**) (*BrE, informal*) tending to forget things and behave in a slightly silly way 健忘的；傻乎乎的

scav·enge /ˈskævɪndʒ/ *verb* **1** [T, I] (of a person, an animal or a bird 人、獸或鳥) to search through waste for things that can be used or eaten（從廢棄物中）覓食；撿破爛；拾荒：**~ sth (from sth)** *Much of their furniture was scavenged from other people's garbage.* 他們的傢具許多都是從別人扔掉的東西中撿來的。◇ **~ (through sth) (for sth)** *Dogs and foxes scavenged through the trash cans for something to eat.* 狗和狐狸從垃圾箱裏尋找食物。 **2** [T, I] (of animals or birds 獸或鳥) to eat dead animals that have been killed by another animal, by a car, etc. 吃（動物屍體）：**~ sth** *Crows scavenge carrion left on the roads.* 烏鴉吃棄在路上的腐肉。◇ **~ (on sth)** *Some fish scavenge on dead fish in the wild.* 在大自然中，有的魚以死魚為食。

scav·en·ger /ˈskævɪndʒə(r)/ *noun* an animal, a bird or a person that scavenges 食腐肉的獸（或鳥）；撿破爛的人；拾荒者

ˈ**scavenger hunt** *noun* a game in which players have to find various objects 撿拾遊戲（參加者必須找到各種物品）

SCE /ˌes siː ˈiː/ *abbr.* Scottish Certificate of Education (exams taken by Scottish school students at two different levels at the ages of 16 and 17-18) 蘇格蘭教育證書（考試）➲ see also HIGHER, STANDARD GRADE

scen·ario AW /səˈnɑːriəʊ; *NAmE* səˈnæriəʊ/ *noun* (*pl.* **-os**) **1** a description of how things might happen in the future 設想；方案；預測：*Let me suggest a* ***possible scenario.*** 我來設想一種可能出現的情況。◇ *The* ***worst-case scenario*** (= the worst possible thing that could happen) *would be for the factory to be closed down.* 最壞的情況可能是工廠關閉。◇ *a* ***nightmare scenario*** 最壞的可能 **2** a written outline of what happens in a film/movie or play（電影或戲劇的）劇情梗概 SYN **synopsis**

scene 0-w /siːn/ *noun*

▸ **PLACE** 地點 **1** 0-w [C, usually sing.] **~ (of sth)** the place where sth happens, especially sth unpleasant（尤指不愉快事件發生的）地點，現場：*the* ***scene of the accident/attack/crime*** 事故／襲擊／犯罪的現場 ◇ *Fire-fighters* ***were on the scene*** *immediately.* 消防隊立刻趕到現場。➲ SYNONYMS at PLACE

▸ **EVENT** 事件 **2** 0-w [C] **~ (of sth)** an event or a situation that you see, especially one of a particular type 事件；場面；情景：*The team's victory produced scenes of joy all over the country.* 球隊的勝利使舉國上下出現一派歡樂的場面。◇ *She witnessed some very distressing scenes.* 她目睹過一些令人非常痛苦的場面。

▸ **IN MOVIE/PLAY, ETC.** 電影、戲劇等 **3** 0-w [C] a part of a film/movie, play or book in which the action happens in one place or is of one particular type 場面；片段；鏡頭：*The movie opens with a scene in a New York apartment.* 電影開頭的一場戲發生在紐約一套公寓裏。◇ ***love/sex scenes*** 愛情戲；牀上戲 ◇ *I got very nervous before my big scene* (= the one where I have a very important part). 在演那場重頭戲之前，我非常緊張。**4** 0-w [C] one of the small sections that a play or an OPERA is divided into（戲劇或歌劇的）場：*Act I, Scene 2 of 'Macbeth'*《麥克佩斯》第 1 幕第 2 場

▸ **AREA OF ACTIVITY** 活動領域 **5 the scene, the … scene** [sing.] (*informal*) a particular area of activity or way of life and the people who are part of it 活動領域；界；壇；圈子：*After years at the top, she just vanished from the scene.* 她在圈內雄踞首位許多年，突然銷聲匿跡了。◇ *the* ***club/dance/music, etc. scene*** 俱樂部圈子、舞壇、音樂界等 ◇ *A newcomer has appeared on the* ***fashion scene.*** 時裝界出現了一位新人。

▸ **VIEW** 景象 **6** 0-w [C] a view that you see 景象；景色；風光：*a delightful rural scene* 賞心悅目的鄉村風光 ◇ *They went abroad for* ***a change of scene*** (= to see and experience new surroundings). 他們出國換換環境。➲ SYNONYMS at VIEW

▸ **PAINTING/PHOTOGRAPH** 繪畫；攝影 **7** 0-w [C] a painting, drawing, or photograph of a place and the things that are happening there 表現…景色的繪畫（或攝影）作品；以…風情為題材的繪畫（或攝影）作品：*an exhibition of Parisian street scenes* 巴黎街景繪畫作品展

▸ **ARGUMENT** 爭吵 **8** [C, usually sing.] a loud, angry argument, especially one that happens in public and is embarrassing（尤指當眾、有失體面的）爭吵，吵鬧：*She had* ***made a scene*** *in the middle of the party.* 她在聚會中間大鬧了一場。◇ *'Please leave,' he said. 'I don't want a scene.'* "請你走吧，" 他說，"我不想爭吵。"

IDM **behind the ˈscenes 1** in the part of a theatre, etc. that the public does not usually see 在後台；在幕後：*The students were able to go behind the scenes to see how programmes are made.* 學生可以跑到後台，去看看節目是怎麼製作出來的。**2** in a way that people in general are not aware of 秘密地；背地裏；在幕後：*A lot of negotiating has been going on behind the scenes.* 廣泛的談判一直在秘密進行。◇ *behind-the-scenes work* 幕後工作 **not sb's ˈscene** (*informal*) not the type of thing that sb likes or enjoys doing 不對某人的路子；不合某人的胃口 **set the ˈscene (for sth) 1** to create a situation in which sth can easily happen or develop 為…做好準備（或鋪平道路）：*His arrival set the scene for another argument.* 他這一來，又會引起一場爭論。**2** to give sb the information and details they need in order to understand what comes next（向…）介紹背景，事先介紹情況：*The first part of the programme was just setting the scene.* 節目的第一部份不過是介紹背景而已。

ˌ**scene-of-ˈcrime** *adj.* [only before noun] (*BrE*) relating to the part of the police service that examines the physical evidence of a crime that is present in the place where the crime was committed 犯罪現場的；作案現場的：*a scene-of-crime officer* 在作案現場取證的警察

scen·ery /ˈsiːnəri/ *noun* [U] **1** the natural features of an area, such as mountains, valleys, rivers and forests, when you are thinking about them being attractive to look at 風景；景色；風光：*The scenery is magnificent.* 景色壯麗。◇ *to enjoy the scenery* 欣賞風景 ➲ SYNONYMS at COUNTRY **2** the painted background that is used to represent natural features or buildings on a theatre stage 舞台佈景

scenic /ˈsiːnɪk/ *adj.* **1** [usually before noun] having beautiful natural scenery 風景優美的：*an area of scenic beauty* 風光秀麗的地區 ◇ *They took the* ***scenic route*** *back to the hotel.* 他們選了一條景色優美的路線回旅館。◇ *a scenic drive* 駕車欣賞沿路景色 **2** [only before noun] connected with scenery in a theatre 舞台佈景的：*scenic designs* 佈景設計 ▸ **scen·ic·al·ly** /-kli/ *adv.*：*scenically attractive areas* 景色迷人的地區

scent /sent/ *noun, verb*

■ ***noun*** **1** [U, C] the pleasant smell that sth has 香味：*The air was filled with the scent of wild flowers.* 空氣中瀰漫着野花的芬芳。◇ *These flowers have no scent.* 這些花不香。**2** [U, C, usually sing.] the smell that a person or an animal leaves behind and that other animals such as dogs can follow（人的）氣味，氣息；（動物留下的）臭跡，遺臭 SYN **trail**：*The dogs must have lost her scent.* 狗準是聞不到她的氣味了。**3** [U] (*especially BrE*) a liquid with a pleasant smell that you wear on your skin to make it smell nice 香水：*a bottle of scent* 一瓶香水 **4 ~ of sth** [sing.] the feeling that sth is present or is going to happen very soon 察覺；預感：*The scent of victory was in the air.* 勝利在望。

IDM **put/throw sb off the ˈscent** to do sth to stop sb from finding you or discovering sth 使失去線索；擺脫追踪者；使迷失尋找方向 **on the ˈscent (of sth)** close to discovering sth 已獲得線索；已掌握蛛絲馬跡

■ ***verb*** **1 ~ sth** to find sth by using the sense of smell 嗅出；聞到：*The dog scented a rabbit.* 狗嗅到了兔子的氣息。**2 ~ sth** to begin to feel that sth exists or is about to happen 覺察出；預感到 SYN **sense**：*The press could scent a scandal.* 記者覺察出有椿醜聞。◇ *By then, the team was scenting victory.* 到那時，隊員已經預感到即將獲勝了。**3** [often passive] **~ sth (with sth)** to give sth a particular, pleasant smell 使具有香味：*Roses scented the night air.* 夜空中瀰漫着玫瑰花香。

scent·ed /ˈsentɪd/ *adj.* having a strong pleasant smell 散發着濃香的；芬芳的

scent·less /ˈsentləs/ *adj.* without a smell 無氣味的

scep·ter (*NAmE*) = SCEPTRE

scep·tic (*BrE*) (*NAmE* **skep·tic**) /ˈskeptɪk/ *noun* a person who usually doubts that claims or statements are true, especially those that other people believe in 慣持懷疑態度的人；懷疑論者 ➲ see also EURO-SCEPTIC

scep·tical (*BrE*) (*NAmE* **skep·tical**) /ˈskeptɪkl/ *adj.* **~ (about/of sth)** having doubts that a claim or statement is true or that sth will happen 懷疑的：*I am sceptical about his chances of winning.* 我懷疑他取勝的可能性。◇ *The public remain sceptical of these claims.* 公眾對這些說法仍持懷疑態度。◇ *She looked highly sceptical.* 她一臉深表懷疑的神色。▸ **scep·tic·al·ly** (*BrE*) (*NAmE* **skep·tic·al·ly**) /-kli/ *adv.*

scep·ti·cism (*BrE*) (*NAmE* **skep·ti·cism**) /ˈskeptɪsɪzəm/ *noun* [U, sing.] an attitude of doubting that claims or statements are true or that sth will happen 懷疑態度；

S

懷疑主義：*Such claims should be regarded with a certain amount of scepticism.* 對這樣的說法，大可不必全信。

sceptre (*US* **scep·ter**) /ˈseptə(r)/ *noun* a decorated ROD carried by a king or queen at ceremonies as a symbol of their power（象徵王權的）節杖，權杖 ➲ compare MACE (1), ORB (2)

Schad·en·freude /ˈʃɑːdnfrɔɪdə/ *noun* [U] (from *German*) a feeling of pleasure at the bad things that happen to other people 幸災樂禍

sched·ule 🗝 AW /ˈʃedjuːl; *NAmE* ˈskedʒuːl/ *noun, verb*

■ ***noun*** **1** 🗝 [C, U] a plan that lists all the work that you have to do and when you must do each thing 工作計劃；日程安排：*I have a hectic schedule for the next few days.* 我今後幾天的日程緊得要命。◇ *We're working to a* ***tight schedule*** (= we have a lot of things to do in a short time). 我們的工作安排得很緊。◇ *Filming began* ***on schedule*** (= at the planned time). 拍攝如期開始。◇ *The new bridge has been finished two years* ***ahead of schedule.*** 新橋提前兩年落成。◇ *The tunnel project has already fallen* ***behind schedule.*** 隧道工程已經晚了工期。**2** 🗝 [C] (*NAmE*) = TIMETABLE *n.* (1)：*a train schedule* 列車時刻表 ◇ *Chinese will be on the school schedule from next year.* 從明年開始中文將排進學校的課程表。**3** [C] a list of the television and radio programmes that are on a particular channel and the times that they start（電視或廣播）節目表：*The channel's schedules are filled with old films and repeats.* 這個頻道安排的盡是老電影和重播節目。**4** [C] a written list of things, for example prices, rates or conditions（價格、收費或條款等的）一覽表，明細表，清單：*tax schedules* 稅率表 ➲ note at AGENDA

■ ***verb*** **1** 🗝 [usually passive] to arrange for sth to happen at a particular time 安排；為…安排時間；預定：**～ sth (for sth)** *The meeting is scheduled for Friday afternoon.* 會議安排在星期五下午。◇ *One of the scheduled events is a talk on alternative medicine.* 安排的活動中有一項是關於替代療法的演講。◇ *We'll be stopping here for longer than scheduled.* 我們在這裏停留的時間將比原定的久一點。◇ **～ sb/sth to do sth** *I'm scheduled to arrive in LA at 5 o'clock.* 我預計在 5 點鐘抵達洛杉磯。**2 ～ sth (as sth)** (*formal*) to include sth in an official list of things 列入，收進（正式目錄、清單等中）：*The substance has been scheduled as a poison.* 這種物質已被列為毒物。▸ **sched·uler** *noun*：*The President's schedulers allowed 90 minutes for TV interviews.* 為總統安排日程的官員留出了 90 分鐘的電視採訪時間。

ˌscheduled ˈcaste *noun* (in India) a CASTE (= division of society) that is listed in the Eighth Schedule of the Indian Constitution and recommended for special help in education and employment 列冊種姓（列在印度憲法第八表的社會階層，建議在教育和就業方面給予特別幫助）

ˈscheduled flight *noun* a plane service that leaves at a regular time each day or week（飛機）定期航班 ➲ compare CHARTER FLIGHT

ˌscheduled ˈtribe *noun* (in India) a TRIBE that is listed in the Eighth Schedule of the Indian Constitution and recommended for special help in education and employment 列冊部族（列在印度憲法第八表的部族，建議在教育和就業方面給予特別幫助）

schema /ˈskiːmə/ *noun* (*pl.* **sche·mas** or **sche·mata** /-mətə; skiːˈmɑːtə/) (*technical* 術語) an outline of a plan or theory（計劃或理論的）提要，綱要

sche·mat·ic AW /skiːˈmætɪk/ *adj.* **1** in the form of a diagram that shows the main features or relationships but not the details 略圖的；簡表的：*a schematic diagram* 略圖 **2** according to a fixed plan or pattern 嚴謹的；有章法的：*The play has a very schematic plot.* 這齣戲的劇情非常嚴謹。▸ **sche·mat·ic·al·ly** AW /-kli/ *adv.*：*The process is shown schematically in figure 3.* 流程見示意圖 3。

sche·ma·tize (*BrE* also **-ise**) /ˈskiːmətaɪz/ *verb* **～ sth** (*technical* 術語) to organize sth in a system 使系統化；使圖式化：*schematized data* 圖式化的資料

scheme 🗝 AW /skiːm/ *noun, verb*

■ ***noun*** **1** 🗝 (*BrE*) a plan or system for doing or organizing sth 計劃；方案；體系；體制：*a training scheme* 培訓方案 ◇ **～ (for doing sth)** *a local scheme for recycling newspapers* 當地的報紙回收計劃 ◇ **～ (to do sth)** *to* ***introduce/operate a scheme*** *to improve links between schools and industry* 引進／實施加強學校和業界之間聯繫的方案 ◇ *Under the new scheme only successful schools will be given extra funding.* 在新體制下，只有辦得好的學校才可獲得額外經費。➲ see also COLOUR SCHEME, PENSION SCHEME **2** 🗝 a plan for getting money or some other advantage for yourself, especially one that involves cheating other people 陰謀；詭計；計謀：*an elaborate scheme to avoid taxes* 周密的避稅方案

IDM **the/sb's ˈscheme of things** the way things seem to be organized; the way sb wants everything to be organized 格局；心中的安排：*My personal problems are not really important in the* ***overall scheme of things.*** 從全局來看，我個人的問題並非十分重要。◇ *I don't think marriage figures in his scheme of things.* 我想，婚姻在他的心目中是無足輕重的。

■ ***verb*** **1** [I, T] (*disapproving*) to make secret plans to do sth that will help yourself and possibly harm others 密謀；秘密策劃；圖謀 SYN **plot**：**～ (against sb)** *She seemed to feel that we were all scheming against her.* 她似乎覺得我們都在算計她。◇ **～ to do sth** *His colleagues, meanwhile, were busily scheming to get rid of him.* 與此同時，他的同事在加緊謀劃除掉他。◇ **～ sth** *Her enemies were scheming her downfall.* 她的敵人正密謀把她搞垮。**2** [T] **～ sth** (*SAfrE, informal*) to think or form an opinion about sth 想；認為：*What do you scheme?* 你認為怎麼樣？◇ *'Do you think he'll come?' 'I scheme so.'* "你認為他會來嗎？" "我想會來。"

schemer /ˈskiːmə(r)/ *noun* (*disapproving*) a person who plans secretly to do sth for their own advantage 搞陰謀的人；施詭計的人

schem·ing /ˈskiːmɪŋ/ *adj.* (*formal*) often planning secretly to do sth for your own advantage, especially by cheating other people 慣搞陰謀的；詭計多端的；狡詐的

the Schengen agreement /ˈʃeŋən əɡriːmənt/ *noun* an agreement between the countries of the European Union to remove controls at their borders so that, for example, people can move freely from one country to another without needing to show their passports 申根協議，申根公約，神根協議（取消歐盟國家之間邊境檢查的協議）

scherzo /ˈskeətsəʊ; *NAmE* ˈskertsoʊ/ *noun* (*pl.* **-os**) (from *Italian*) a short, lively piece of music, that is often part of a longer piece 諧謔曲

schil·ling /ˈʃɪlɪŋ/ *noun* the former unit of money in Austria (replaced in 2002 by the euro) 奧地利先令（2002 年為歐元所取代）

schism /ˈskɪzəm; ˈsɪzəm/ *noun* [C, U] (*formal*) strong disagreement within an organization, especially a religious one, that makes its members divide into separate groups 分裂；宗派活動；（尤指）教會分裂 ▸ **schis·mat·ic** /skɪzˈmætɪk; sɪzˈmætɪk/ *adj.*

schist /ʃɪst/ *noun* [U] a type of rock formed of layers of different minerals, that breaks naturally into thin flat pieces 片岩

schiz·oid /ˈskɪtsɔɪd/ *adj.* (*technical* 術語) similar to or suffering from schizophrenia 精神分裂般的；類精神分裂症的；（患）精神分裂症的：*schizoid tendencies* 精神分裂傾向

schizo·phre·nia /ˌskɪtsəˈfriːniə/ *noun* [U] a mental illness in which a person becomes unable to link thought, emotion and behaviour, leading to WITHDRAWAL from reality and personal relationships 精神分裂症

schizo·phren·ic /ˌskɪtsəˈfrenɪk/ *noun, adj.*

■ ***noun*** a person who suffers from schizophrenia 精神分裂症患者

■ ***adj.*** **1** suffering from schizophrenia 患精神分裂症的 **2** (*informal*) frequently changing your mind about sth or holding opinions about sth that seem to oppose each other 反覆無常的；自相矛盾的

schlep (also **schlepp**) /ʃlep/ *verb* (**-pp-**) (*informal, especially NAmE*) **1** [I] **+ adv./prep.** to go somewhere, especially if it is a slow, difficult journey, or you do not want to go（勞神耗時或不情願地）去，趕往 **2** [T] **~ sth (+ adv./prep.)** to carry or pull sth heavy 搬，抬，拖，拉（重物）：*I'm not schlepping these suitcases all over town.* 我可不想提着這幾個行李箱滿城跑。**ORIGIN** From Yiddish *shlepn*, 'to drag'. 源自意第緒語 shlepn，意為"拖"。▸ **schlep** (also **schlepp**) *noun* [sing.]

schlock /ʃlɒk; *NAmE* ʃlɑːk/ *noun* [U] (*NAmE, informal*) things that are cheap and of poor quality 低檔貨；便宜貨

schmaltz /ʃmɔːlts/ *noun* [U] (*informal, disapproving*) the quality of being too SENTIMENTAL 過分感傷 ▸ **schmaltzy** *adj.* (**schmaltz·ier**, **schmaltzi·est**)

schmo (also **shmo**) /ʃməʊ; *NAmE* ʃmoʊ/ *noun* (*pl.* **-oes**) (*NAmE, informal, disapproving*) a person who is stupid or foolish in an annoying way 笨蛋；傻瓜

schmooze /ʃmuːz/ *verb* [I, T] **~ (with) sb** (*informal, especially NAmE*) to talk in an informal and friendly way with sb, especially in order to gain an advantage by persuading people to like you and do what you want（尤指為利用某人而）閒談，閒聊 **SYN** **chat** ▸ **schmooz·er** *noun*

schmuck /ʃmʌk/ *noun* (*informal, disapproving, especially NAmE*) a stupid person 傻瓜；笨蛋；蠢貨：*He's such a schmuck!* 他真蠢！

schnapps /ʃnæps/ *noun* [U] (from *German*) a strong alcoholic drink made from grain（穀物釀製的）烈酒

schnau·zer /ˈʃnaʊzə(r)/ *noun* a dog with short rough hair which forms curls 髯狗；雪納瑞犬；史納沙犬

schnook /ʃnʊk/ *noun* (*NAmE, informal, disapproving*) a stupid or unimportant person 愚蠢的人；小人物

scholar /ˈskɒlə(r); *NAmE* ˈskɑːl-/ *noun* **1** a person who knows a lot about a particular subject because they have studied it in detail 學者：*a classical scholar* 研究拉丁文與希臘文的學者 ◇ *He was the most distinguished scholar in his field.* 他是這一領域成就最為卓著的學者。**2** a student who has been given a scholarship to study at a school, college or university 獎學金獲得者：*a Rhodes scholar* 羅得斯獎學金獲得者 **3** (*BrE, informal*) a clever person who works hard at school 聰穎勤奮的學生：*I was never much of a scholar.* 我從來不是那種用功的好學生。

schol·ar·ly /ˈskɒləli; *NAmE* ˈskɑːlərli/ *adj.* **1** (of a person 人) spending a lot of time studying and having a lot of knowledge about an academic subject 勤奮好學的；有學問的 **SYN** **academic** **2** connected with academic study 學術的；學術性的 **SYN** **academic**：*a scholarly journal* 學術期刊

schol·ar·ship /ˈskɒləʃɪp; *NAmE* ˈskɑːlərʃɪp/ *noun* **1** [C] an amount of money given to sb by an organization to help pay for their education 獎學金：*She **won a scholarship** to study at Stanford.* 她獲得了獎學金，得以在斯坦福大學求學。◇ *He went to drama school **on a scholarship**.* 他靠獎學金上了戲劇學校。**2** [U] the serious study of an academic subject and the knowledge and methods involved 學問；學術；學術研究 **SYN** **learning**：*a magnificent work of scholarship* 學術巨著

scho·las·tic /skəˈlæstɪk/ *adj.* [only before noun] (*formal*) **1** connected with schools and education 學校的；教育的；學業的：*scholastic achievements* 學業成績 **2** connected with scholasticism 經院哲學的

scho·las·ti·cism /skəˈlæstɪsɪzəm/ *noun* [U] a system of philosophy, based on religious principles and writing, that was taught in universities in the Middle Ages 經院哲學

school 🔑 /skuːl/ *noun, verb*

■ *noun*

▸ **WHERE CHILDREN LEARN** 兒童學習的處所 **1** 🔑 [C] a place where children go to be educated（中、小）學校：*My brother and I went to the same school.* 我和我哥哥上的是同一所學校。◇ (*formal*) *Which school do they attend?* 他們上的是哪一所學校？◇ *I'm going to the school today to talk to Kim's teacher.* 今天我要去學校和金的老師談一談。◇ *We need more money for roads, hospitals and schools.* 我們需要更多的資金來修公道、建醫院和辦學校。◇ *school buildings* 校舍 **2** 🔑 [U] (used without *the* or *a* 不與 the 和 a 連用) the process of learning in a school; the time during your life when you go to a school 上學；上學階段：(*BrE*) *to **start/leave school*** 入學；（受完義務教育）離開中學 ◇ (*NAmE*) *to **start/quit school*** 入學；（受完義務教育）離開中學 ◇ *Where did you go to school?* 你是在哪裏上學的？◇ (*BrE*) *All my kids are still **at school**.* 我的孩子還都在上學。◇ (*NAmE*) *All my kids are still **in school**.* 我的孩子還都在上學。◇ (*NAmE*) *to **teach school*** (= teach in a school) 教書 ◇ *The transition from school to work can be difficult.* 從在學校唸書到上班工作，這一轉變有時候可真不容易。➲ **COLLOCATIONS** at EDUCATION **3** 🔑 [U] (used without *the* or *a* 不與 the 和 a 連用) the time during the day when children are working in a school 上課（或上學）時間：*Shall I meet you after school today?* 今天放學後我去找你好嗎？◇ *School begins at 9.* * 9 點開始上課。◇ *The kids are **at/in school** until 3.30.* 孩子們到 3:30 才放學。◇ ***after-school** activities* 課後活動

▸ **STUDENTS AND TEACHERS** 師生 **4** 🔑 **the school** [sing.] all the children or students and the teachers in a school 學校全體師生：*I had to stand up in front of the whole school.* 我只得在全校師生面前站起來。

▸ **FOR PARTICULAR SKILL** 培養專門技能 **5** 🔑 [C] (often in compounds 常構成複合詞) a place where people go to learn a particular subject or skill 專業學校；專科學校：*a **drama/language/riding, etc. school*** 戲劇、語言、騎術等學校

▸ **COLLEGE/UNIVERSITY** 高等院校 **6** 🔑 [C, U] (*NAmE, informal*) a college or university; the time that you spend there 學院；大學；上大學時期：*famous schools like Yale and Harvard* 像耶魯和哈佛這樣的著名大學 ◇ *Where did you go to school?* 你是在哪裏上學的？➲ see also GRADUATE SCHOOL **7** 🔑 [C] a department of a college or university that teaches a particular subject（高等院校的）學院，系：*the **business/medical/law school*** 商學院；醫學院；法學院 ◇ *the School of Dentistry* 牙科系

▸ **OF WRITERS/ARTISTS** 作家；藝術家 **8** [C] a group of writers, artists, etc. whose style of work or opinions have been influenced by the same person or ideas 學派；流派：*the Dutch school of painting* 荷蘭畫派

▸ **OF FISH** 魚 **9** [C] a large number of fish or other sea animals, swimming together 群：*a school of dolphins* 一群海豚 ➲ compare SHOAL (1) **HELP** There are many compounds ending in **school**. You will find them at their place in the alphabet. 以 school 結尾的複合詞很多，可在各字母中的適當位置查到。

IDM **school(s) of ˈthought** a way of thinking that a number of people share 學派：*There are two schools of thought about how this illness should be treated.* 關於如何治療這種疾病，有兩派不同的意見。➲ more at OLD

■ *verb*

▸ **YOURSELF/ANIMAL** 自己；動物 **1** (*formal*) to train sb/yourself/an animal to do sth 訓練；使學會：**~ sb/sth/yourself (in sth)** *to school a horse* 馴馬 ◇ *She had schooled herself in patience.* 她磨練了自己的耐性。◇ **~ sb/sth/yourself to do sth** *I have schooled myself to remain calm under pressure.* 我練就一副在壓力之下保持鎮靜的本領。

▸ **CHILD** 兒童 **2 ~ sb** (*formal*) to educate a child 教育；培養：*She should be schooled with her peers.* 她應當與她的同齡人一起接受教育。

Grammar Point 語法説明

school

■ When a **school** is being referred to as an institution, you do not need to use *the*. * school 指機構時，不需用定冠詞 the：*When do the children finish school?* 孩子們什麼時候畢業？When you are talking about a particular building, *the* is used. 指校舍時要用定冠詞 the：*I'll meet you outside the school.* 我在學校外面等你。**Prison**, **jail**, **court**, and **church** work in the same way. * prison、jail、court 和 church 的用法相同：*Her husband spent three years in prison.* 她丈夫坐了三年牢。

➲ note at COLLEGE, HOSPITAL

S

British/American 英式/美式英語

at / in school

- In *BrE* somebody who is attending school is **at school**. 在英式英語中，at school 表示上學：*I was at school with her sister.* 我和她妹妹過去在同一個學校讀書。 In *NAmE* **in school** is used. 美式英語用 in school 表示：*I have a ten-year-old in school.* 我有個十歲的孩子在上學。 **In school** in *NAmE* can also mean 'attending a university'. 美式英語的 in school 亦可表示上大學。

ˈschool age *noun* [U] the age or period when a child normally attends school 學齡；學齡期：*children of school age* 學齡兒童 ◇ *school-age children* 學齡兒童

school·boy /ˈskuːlbɔɪ/ *noun* a boy who attends school（學校的）男生 ➲ SYNONYMS at STUDENT

school·child /ˈskuːltʃaɪld/ *noun* (*pl.* **school·chil·dren** /-tʃɪldrən/) (also *informal* **school·kid**) a child who attends school 學童；小學生 ➲ SYNONYMS at STUDENT

school·days /ˈskuːldeɪz/ *noun* [pl.] the period in your life when you go to school 學生時代：*She hadn't seen Laura since her schooldays.* 她自從離開學校就再沒見過勞拉。

ˈschool district *noun* (in the US) an area that contains several schools that are governed together 學區（美國制度，區內學校統一管轄）

ˈschool friend (also *less frequent* **school·mate**) *noun* (*especially BrE*) a friend who attends or attended the same school as you 學友；同窗；校友：*She met up with some of her old (= former) school friends.* 她與幾個老同學見面。

school·girl /ˈskuːlɡɜːl; *NAmE* -ɡɜːrl/ *noun* a girl who attends school（學校的）女生 ➲ SYNONYMS at STUDENT

school·house /ˈskuːlhaʊs/ *noun* **1** a school building, especially a small one in a village in the past（尤指舊時鄉村學校的）校舍 **2** a house for a teacher next to a small school（小型學校旁邊的）教師住房

schoolie /ˈskuːli/ *noun* (*AustralE*) a school student at the end of his or her time at school 即將畢業的中學生

ˈSchoolies Week (also **Schoolies**) *noun* [U] (in Australia) a time in November or December each year when Year 12 (final-year) school students celebrate leaving school by having a holiday/vacation in a town with a beach 中學畢業慶祝週（每年十一月或十二月澳大利亞 12 年級學生在海濱城鎮度假）

S

school·ing /ˈskuːlɪŋ/ *noun* [U] (*formal*) the education you receive at school 學校教育：*secondary schooling* 中等教育 ◇ *He had very little schooling.* 他沒上過幾天學。

school·kid /ˈskuːlkɪd/ *noun* (*informal*) = SCHOOLCHILD

ˌschool-ˈleaver *noun* (*BrE*) a person who has just left school, especially when they are looking for a job（尤指待業的）中學畢業生，離校生：*the problem of rising unemployment among school-leavers* 離校生失業人數不斷增長的問題

school·marm /ˈskuːlmɑːm; *NAmE* -mɑːrm/ *noun* (*disapproving, especially NAmE*) a woman who teaches in a school, especially one who is old-fashioned and strict（嚴厲）女教師 ▸ **school·marm·ish** *adj.*

school·mas·ter /ˈskuːlmɑːstə(r); *NAmE* -mæs-/, **school·mis·tress** /ˈskuːlmɪstrəs/ *noun* (*old-fashioned, especially BrE*) a teacher in a school, especially a private school（尤指私立中小學的）教師 ➲ compare MASTER *n.* (5)

school·mate /ˈskuːlmeɪt/ *noun* (*especially BrE*) = SCHOOL FRIEND

school·room /ˈskuːlruːm; -rʊm/ *noun* (*old-fashioned*) a classroom 教室

the ˈschool run *noun* [sing.] (*BrE*) the journey that parents make to take their children to school or to bring them home again（父母）接送學童上學（或放學）的行程

school·teach·er /ˈskuːltiːtʃə(r)/ *noun* a person whose job is teaching in a school（中小學）教師

school·work /ˈskuːlwɜːk; *NAmE* -wɜːrk/ *noun* [U] work that students do at school or for school 學校作業；課堂作業；課外作業：*She is struggling to keep up with her schoolwork.* 她在努力趕上課業。

school·yard /ˈskuːljɑːd; *NAmE* -jɑːrd/ *noun* (*NAmE*) an outdoor area of a school for children to play in 校園；（學校的）露天操場 ➲ compare PLAYGROUND (1)

schooner /ˈskuːnə(r)/ *noun* **1** a sailing ship with two or more MASTS (= posts that support the sails)（雙桅或多桅）縱帆船 **2** a tall glass for SHERRY or beer 雪利酒杯；大啤酒杯

schtick, **schtuck**, **schtum**, **schtup** = SHTICK, SHTOOK, SHTUM, SHTUP

schwa (also **shwa**) /ʃwɑː/ *noun* (*phonetics* 語音) a vowel sound in parts of words that are not stressed, for example the 'a' in *about* or the 'e' in *moment*; the PHONETIC symbol for this, /ə/ 非重讀央元音，混元音，輕母音（如 about 中的 a 或 moment 中的 e 所發的音）；音標符號 /ə/

sci·at·ic /saɪˈætɪk/ *adj.* [only before noun] (*anatomy* 解) of the hip or of the nerve which goes from the PELVIS to the THIGH (= the **sciatic nerve**) 坐骨的；坐骨神經的

sci·at·ica /saɪˈætɪkə/ *noun* [U] pain in the back, hip and outer side of the leg, caused by pressure on the sciatic nerve 坐骨神經痛

sci·ence 🔑 /ˈsaɪəns/ *noun*
1 🔑 [U] knowledge about the structure and behaviour of the natural and physical world, based on facts that you can prove, for example by experiments 科學；自然科學：*new developments in science and technology* 科學技術的新發展 ◇ *the advance of modern science* 現代科學的進展 ◇ *the laws of science* 科學定律 **2** 🔑 [U] the study of science 自然科學的學習與研究；理科：***science students/teachers/courses*** 理科學生／教師／課程 **3** 🔑 [U, C] a particular branch of science 自然科學學科：*to study one of the sciences* 攻讀一門自然科學 ➲ compare ART *n.* (6), HUMANITY (4) **4** [sing.] a system for organizing the knowledge about a particular subject, especially one concerned with aspects of human behaviour or society（尤指人文、社會）學科，學：*a science of international politics* 國際政治學 ➲ see also DOMESTIC SCIENCE, EARTH SCIENCE, LIFE SCIENCES, NATURAL SCIENCE, POLITICAL SCIENCE, ROCKET SCIENCE, SOCIAL SCIENCE **IDM** see BLIND *v.*

ˈscience fair *noun* (*NAmE*) a competition in which students at a school compete to present the best science project（學校的）科學競賽會，科學展覽

ˌscience ˈfiction (also *informal* **ˈsci-fi**) (*abbr.* **SF**) *noun* [U] a type of book, film/movie, etc. that is based on imagined scientific discoveries of the future, and often deals with space travel and life on other planets 科幻小說（或影片等）

ˈscience park *noun* an area where there are a lot of companies or organizations involved in scientific research and development 科技園區

sci·en·tif·ic 🔑 /ˌsaɪənˈtɪfɪk/ *adj.* [usually before noun]
1 🔑 involving science; connected with science 科學（上）的；關於科學的：*a scientific discovery* 科學發現 ◇ *scientific knowledge* 科學知識 ◇ *sites of scientific interest* 引起科學界關注的地方 **2** (of a way of doing sth or thinking 做事或思想的方法) careful and logical 細緻嚴謹的；科學的：*He took a very **scientific approach** to management.* 他採取了一種非常科學的管理方法。◇ *We need to be more scientific about this problem.* 在這個問題上我們需要更為嚴謹一些。**OPP** **unscientific** ➲ compare NON-SCIENTIFIC ▸ **sci·en·tif·ic·al·ly** /-kli/ *adv.*

sci·en·tism /ˈsaɪəntɪzəm/ *noun* [U] **1** a way of thinking or expressing ideas that is considered to be typical of scientists 科學思維；科學方法；科學態度 **2** complete belief in scientific methods, or in the truth of scientific knowledge 科學至上主義；唯科學主義

sci·en·tist 0→ /'saɪəntɪst/ *noun* a person who studies one or more of the NATURAL SCIENCES (= for example, physics, chemistry and biology) 科學家：*a research scientist* 從事研究的科學家 ◇ *nuclear scientists* 核科學家 ◇ *scientists and engineers* 科學家和工程師 ◇ *the cartoon figure of the mad scientist working in his laboratory* 瘋狂的科學家在實驗室工作的卡通形象 ➲ see also COMPUTER SCIENTIST, POLITICAL SCIENTIST, SOCIAL SCIENTIST

Sci·en·tol·ogy™ /ˌsaɪən'tɒlədʒi; *NAmE* -'tɑːl-/ *noun* [U] a religious system based on getting knowledge of yourself and spiritual FULFILMENT through courses of study and training 科學論派（宗教修行體系，倡導通過學習和訓練來獲得自我認識和精神上的圓滿）▸ **sci·en·tolo·gist** *noun*

sci-fi /'saɪ faɪ/ *noun* [U] (*informal*) = SCIENCE FICTION

scimi·tar /'sɪmɪtə(r)/ *noun* a short curved SWORD with one sharp edge, used especially in Eastern countries（多為東方人所用的）短彎刀

scin·tilla /sɪn'tɪlə/ *noun* [sing.] **~ (of sth)** (*formal*) (usually in negative sentences 通常用於否定句) a very small amount of sth 一星半點；毫厘：*There is not a scintilla of truth in what she says.* 她的話沒有半句可信。

scin·til·lat·ing /'sɪntɪleɪtɪŋ/ *adj.* very clever, amusing and interesting 才情洋溢的；妙趣橫生的：*a scintillating performance* 精彩的演出 ◇ *Statistics on unemployment levels hardly make for scintillating reading.* 失業統計數據讀來不大會有趣味。

scion /'saɪən/ *noun* **1** (*formal* or *literary*) a young member of a family, especially a famous or important one（尤指名門望族的）子弟 **2** (*technical* 術語) a piece of a plant, especially one cut to make a new plant 幼枝；（尤指）接穗

sci·rocco ➲ SIROCCO

ˈ**scissor kick** (also ˈ**scissors kick**) *noun* **1** (in swimming 游泳) a strong kick with the legs moving in opposite directions 剪步踢（剪式打腿動作） **2** (in football (SOCCER) 足球) an action of kicking the ball while jumping sideways in the air 側鉤

scis·sors 0→ /'sɪzəz; *NAmE* 'sɪzərz/ *noun* [pl.] a tool for cutting paper or cloth, that has two sharp blades with handles, joined together in the middle 剪刀：*a pair of scissors* 一把剪刀 ➲ **VISUAL VOCAB** pages V20, V26 ➲ see also NAIL SCISSORS ▸ **scis·sor** *adj.* [only before noun]：*The legs move in a scissor action.* 兩腿像剪刀似地運動。

sclera /'sklɪerə; *NAmE* 'sklɪrə/ (-rae /-riː/ or -ras /-rəz/) *noun* (*anatomy* 解) the white part of the eye 鞏膜 ➲ **VISUAL VOCAB** page V59

scler·osis /sklə'rəʊsɪs; *NAmE* -'roʊ-/ *noun* [U] (*medical* 醫) a condition in which soft TISSUE in the body becomes hard, in a way that is not normal 硬化；硬化症 ➲ see also MULTIPLE SCLEROSIS ▸ **scler·otic** /sklə'rɒtɪk; *NAmE* -'rɑːt-/ *adj.*

scoff /skɒf; *NAmE* skɔːf; skɑːf/ *verb* **1** [I, T] **~ (at sb/sth)** | **+ speech** to talk about sb/sth in a way that makes it clear that you think they are stupid or ridiculous 嘲笑；譏諷 **SYN** **mock**：*He scoffed at our amateurish attempts.* 他對我們不在行的嘗試嗤之以鼻。◇ *Don't scoff—she's absolutely right.* 別嘲笑她，她絕對正確。

Collocations 詞語搭配

Scientific research 科學研究

Theory 理論

- **formulate/advance** a theory/hypothesis 創立理論；提出假設
- **build/construct/create/develop** a simple/theoretical/mathematical model 創立一個簡單／理論／數學模型
- **develop/establish/provide/use** a theoretical/conceptual framework 創立／建立／提供／使用理論／概念框架
- **advance/argue/develop** the thesis that … 提出／論證／詳盡闡述…的論題
- **explore** an idea/a concept/a hypothesis 探討一個想法／概念／假設
- **make** a prediction/an inference 預測；推斷
- **base** a prediction/your calculations on sth 基於…做出預測／估算
- **investigate/evaluate/accept/challenge/reject** a theory/hypothesis/model 研究／評估／接受／質疑／拒絕接受一個理論／假設／模型

Experiment 實驗

- **design** an experiment/a questionnaire/a study/a test 設計一項實驗／問卷／研究／測試
- **do** research/an experiment/an analysis 做研究／實驗／分析
- **make** observations/measurements/calculations 觀察；測量；計算
- **carry out/conduct/perform** an experiment/a test/a longitudinal study/observations/clinical trials 進行實驗／測試／縱向研究／觀察／臨牀試驗
- **run** an experiment/a simulation/clinical trials 進行實驗／模擬／臨牀試驗
- **repeat** an experiment/a test/an analysis 重做實驗／測試／分析
- **replicate** a study/the results/the findings 做相同的研究；得出同樣的結果
- **observe/study/examine/investigate/assess** a pattern/a process/a behaviour/(*especially US*) a behavior 觀察／研究／審查／調查／評估一種模式／一個過程／一種行為
- **fund/support** the research/project/study 資助／支持一項研究／一個項目／一個專題研究
- **seek/provide/get/secure** funding for research 尋求／提供／得到／爭取到研究資金

Results 結果

- **collect/gather/extract** data/information 收集／提取數據／信息
- **yield** data/evidence/similar findings/the same results 得到數據／證據／類似調查結果／相同結果
- **analyse/examine** the data/soil samples/a specimen 分析／考查數據／土壤樣本／樣本
- **consider/compare/interpret** the results/findings 思考／比較／解釋結果／調查結果
- **fit** the data/model 與數據／模型相符合
- **confirm/support/verify** a prediction/a hypothesis/the results/the findings 證實／支持／核實預測／假設／結果／調查結果
- **prove** a conjecture/hypothesis/theorem 證明猜測／假設／定理
- **draw/make/reach** the same conclusions 得出同樣的結論
- **read/review** the records/literature 閱讀／評論記錄／文獻
- **describe/report** an experiment/a study 描述／報告一項實驗／研究
- **present/publish/summarize** the results/findings 提交／公佈／總結結果／調查結果
- **present/publish/read/review/cite** a paper in a scientific journal 向科學雜誌提交一篇論文；在科學雜誌發表一篇論文；閱讀／評論／引用科學雜誌上的一篇論文

S

2 (*BrE*) (*NAmE* **scarf**) [T] **~ (sth)** (*informal*) to eat a lot of sth quickly 貪婪地吃；狼吞虎嚥：*Who scoffed all the grapes?* 誰那麼貪嘴，把葡萄全吃光了？

scoff·law /ˈskɒflɔː; *NAmE* ˈskɔːf-; ˈskɑːf-/ *noun* (*NAmE, informal*) a person who often breaks the law but in a way that is not very serious 無視法律的人

scold /skəʊld; *NAmE* skoʊld/ *verb* [T, I] **~ sb (for sth/for doing sth)** | (**+ speech**) (*formal*) to speak angrily to sb, especially a child, because they have done sth wrong 訓斥，責罵（尤指孩子）**SYN** **rebuke**：*He scolded them for arriving late.* 他嫌他們遲到，訓了他們一通。▸ **scold·ing** *noun* [usually sing.]：*I got a **scolding** from my mother.* 我捱了我媽一陣數落。

scoli·osis /ˌskəʊliˈəʊsɪs; ˌskɒl-; *NAmE* ˌskoʊliˈoʊsɪs/ *noun* [U] (*medical* 醫) a condition in which the SPINE is curved in a way that is not normal 脊柱側凸；脊柱側彎

scone /skɒn; skəʊn; *NAmE* skɑːn; skoʊn/ *noun* a small round cake, sometimes with dried fruit in it and often eaten with butter, jam and cream spread on it 烤餅，司康餅（常抹黃油、果醬、奶油等，有時內夾乾果）

scoop /skuːp/ *noun, verb*

■ ***noun*** **1** [C] a tool like a large spoon with a deep bowl, used for picking up substances in powder form like flour, or for serving food like ice cream 勺；鏟子：*Use an ice-cream scoop.* 用冰淇淋勺。➲ **VISUAL VOCAB** page V26 **2** [C] the amount picked up by a scoop 一勺（的量）：*two scoops of mashed potato* 兩勺土豆泥 **3** [C] a piece of important or exciting news that is printed in one newspaper before other newspapers know about it 搶先報道的新聞；獨家新聞 **4 the scoop** [U] (*NAmE, informal*) the latest information about sb/sth, especially details that are not generally known（尤指詳情鮮為人知的）最新消息：*I got the inside scoop on his new girlfriend.* 我得知有關他新女友的最新內幕消息。

■ ***verb*** **1** to move or lift sth with a scoop or sth like a scoop 用勺兒舀；用鏟兒鏟：**~ sth (+ adv./prep.)** *She scooped ice cream into their bowls.* 她用勺把冰淇淋舀到他們的碗裏。◇ *First, scoop a hole in the soil.* 首先，在土裏挖一個坑。◇ *Scoop out the melon flesh.* 用勺把瓜瓤挖出來。◇ **~ sth up (+ adv./prep.)** *He quickly scooped the money up from the desk.* 他把桌上的錢一把抓起來。**2 ~ sb/sth (up) (+ adv./prep.)** to move or lift sb/sth with a quick continuous movement（敏捷地）抱起，拿起，撿起：*She scooped the child up in her arms.* 她一把抱起孩子。**3 ~ sb/sth** to publish a story before all the other newspapers, television companies, etc. 搶先報道：*The paper had inside information and scooped all its rivals.* 這家報紙獲得內部消息，搶在所有競爭對手之前發表了。**4 ~ sth** (*informal*) to win sth, especially a large sum of money or a prize 獲取，贏得（一大筆錢或豐厚的獎品）：*He scooped £10 000 on the lottery.* 他中彩得了1萬英鎊。

scooped /skuːpt/ (also **scoop**) *adj.* [only before noun] (of the neck of a woman's dress, etc. 連衣裙等的領子) cut low and round 低而圓的；深圓的：*a **scooped neck/neckline*** 深圓領；深領口

scoot /skuːt/ *verb* [I] (**+ adv./prep.**) (*informal*) to go or leave somewhere in a hurry 疾行；匆匆離去：*I'd better scoot or I'll be late.* 我得快走，要不我該遲到了。

scoot·er /ˈskuːtə(r)/ *noun* **1** (*BrE*) (also **ˈmotor scooter** *NAmE, BrE*) a light motorcycle, usually with small wheels and a curved metal cover at the front to protect the rider's legs 小型摩托車 ➲ **VISUAL VOCAB** page V51 **2** a child's vehicle with two small wheels attached to a narrow board with a vertical handle. The rider holds the handle, puts one foot on the board and pushes against the ground with the other.（兒童）滑板車

scope **AW** /skəʊp; *NAmE* skoʊp/ *noun, verb*

■ ***noun*** [U] **1** the opportunity or ability to do or achieve sth（做或實現某事的）機會，能力 **SYN** **potential**：**~ (for sth)** *There's still plenty of scope for improvement.* 還有很大的改進餘地。◇ *Her job offers very **little scope** for promotion.* 幹着那樣的工作，她幾乎沒有機會得到提拔。◇ **~ (for sb) (to do sth)** *The extra money will give us the scope to improve our facilities.* 有了這筆額外資金，我們就能把設備加以改進了。◇ *First try to do something that is **within your scope**.* 你先試着做一件自己力所能及的事。**2** the range of things that a subject, an organization, an activity, etc. deals with（題目、組織、活動等的）範圍：*Our powers are limited **in scope**.* 我們的權限不大。◇ *This subject lies **beyond the scope of** our investigation.* 這一問題超出了我們的調察範圍。◇ *These issues were **outside the scope** of the article.* 這些問題不屬本文論述範圍。**3 -scope** (in nouns 構成名詞) an instrument for looking through or watching sth with …鏡（觀察儀器）：*microscope* 顯微鏡 ◇ *telescope* 望遠鏡

■ ***verb*** **1 ~ sth** (*informal*) to look at or examine sth thoroughly 仔細看；徹底檢查：*His eyes scoped the room, trying to spot her in the crowd.* 他環顧房間四周，想在人群中找到她。**2 ~ sth (out)** (*especially NAmE*) to examine sth carefully before you start work on it so that you know the size of the task（開始某項工作前）瞭解，查清，探明：*The information helped us scope the project.* 這些信息幫助我們在開展工作前瞭解該項目的情況。

PHR V **ˌscope sth↔ˈout** to look at sth carefully in order to see what it is like 端詳；打量

scorch /skɔːtʃ; *NAmE* skɔːrtʃ/ *verb* **1** [T, I] **~ (sth)** | **~ sth + adj.** to burn and slightly damage a surface by making it too hot; to be slightly burned by heat（把…）燙壞，燒煳；烤焦（物體表面）：*I scorched my dress when I was ironing it.* 我把自己的連衣裙熨焦了。◇ *Don't stand so near the fire—your coat is scorching!* 別站得離火那麼近，你的外衣都快烤焦了！➲ **SYNONYMS** at BURN **2** [T, I] **~ (sth)** to become or to make sth become dry and brown, especially from the heat of the sun or from chemicals（使）枯黃，枯萎（尤指因曝曬或化學品的作用）：*scorched grass* 枯草 ◇ *The leaves will scorch if you water them in the sun.* 在太陽底下澆水，葉子會枯。**3** [I] **+ adv./prep.** (*BrE, informal*) to move very fast 疾馳；飛馳：*The car scorched off down the road.* 汽車沿公路飛馳而去。

scorched ˈearth policy *noun* (in a war) a policy of destroying anything in a particular area that may be useful to the enemy（戰爭中的）焦土政策

scorch·er /ˈskɔːtʃə(r); *NAmE* ˈskɔːrtʃ-/ *noun* (*informal*) **1** a very hot day 大熱天 **2** (*BrE*) (used mainly in newspapers 主要用於報章) a very good stroke, shot, etc. in a sport 精彩的擊球（或射門等）：*a scorcher of a free kick* 一記精準的任意球

scorch·ing /ˈskɔːtʃɪŋ; *NAmE* ˈskɔːrtʃ-/ *adj.* (*informal*) **1** very hot 酷熱的 **SYN** **baking** **2** (*especially BrE*) used to emphasize how strong, powerful, etc. sth is 猛烈的；激烈的；有力的：*a scorching critique of the government's economic policy* 對政府經濟政策的嚴厲批評

ˈscorch mark *noun* a mark made on a surface by burning 焦痕

score 0-ᴡ /skɔː(r)/ *noun, verb*

■ ***noun***

▸ **POINTS/GOALS, ETC.** 得分、進球等 **1** 0-ᴡ [C] the number of points, goals, etc. scored by each player or team in a game or competition（遊戲或比賽中的）得分，比分：*a **high/low score*** 高 / 低分 ◇ *What's the score now?* 現在比分是多少？◇ ***The final score** was 4–3.* 最終的比分是4:3。◇ *I'll **keep (the) score**.* 我來記分。**2** 0-ᴡ [C] (*especially NAmE*) the number of points sb gets for correct answers in a test（考試中的）分數，成績：*test scores* 考試分數 ◇ *an IQ score of 120* 智商120分 ◇ *a perfect score* 滿分

▸ **MUSIC** 音樂 **3** [C] a written or printed version of a piece of music showing what each instrument is to play or what each voice is to sing 總譜：*an orchestral score* 管弦樂總譜 ◇ *the score of Verdi's 'Requiem'* 威爾地《安魂曲》的總譜 **4** [C] the music written for a film/movie or play（電影或戲劇的）配樂：*an award for best original score* 最佳原創配樂獎

▸ **TWENTY** 二十 **5** [C] (*pl.* **score**) a set or group of 20 or approximately 20 * 20 個；約 20 個：*Several cabs and a score of cars were parked outside.* 外邊停着二十幾輛汽車和幾輛出租車。◇ *Doyle's success brought imitators **by the score*** (= very many). 多伊爾取得成功後，仿效者群起。◇ *the biblical age of three score years and ten* (= 70)《聖經》上所說的七十歲

▸ **MANY** 許多 **6 scores** [pl.] very many 大量；很多：*There were scores of boxes and crates, all waiting to be checked and loaded.* 大批的箱子和板條箱等着檢驗後裝運。

▸ **CUT** 刻痕 **7** [C] a cut in a surface, made with a sharp tool 刻痕；劃痕；傷痕

▸ **FACTS ABOUT SITUATION** 真實情況 **8 the score** [sing.] (*informal*) the real facts about the present situation 實情；真相：***What's the score?*** 情況怎麼樣？◇ *You don't have to lie to me. I **know the score**.* 你不必瞞我。我知道是怎麼回事。

IDM **on 'that/'this score** as far as that/this is concerned 就那個（或這個）來說；在那個（或這個）問題上：*You don't have to worry on that score.* 那件事你不必擔心。➲ more at EVEN *v.*, SETTLE *v.*

■ ***verb***

▸ **GIVE/GET POINTS/GOALS** 打分；得分 **1** [I, T] to win points, goals, etc. in a game or competition（在遊戲或比賽中）得分：*Fraser scored again in the second half.* 弗雷澤在下半場時再次得分。◇ **~ sth** *to score a goal/try/touchdown/victory* 射門得分；對方球門線後持球觸地得分；端區觸地得分；獲勝 **2** [I] to keep a record of the points, goals, etc. won in a game or competition（在遊戲或比賽中）記分：*Who's going to score?* 誰來記分呢？ **3** [T, I] to gain marks in a test or an exam（在考試中）得分：**~ sth** *She scored 98% in the French test.* 她法語考了 98 分。◇ **+ adv./prep.** *Girls usually score highly in language exams.* 在語言考試中，女生通常得高分。 **4** [T] **~ sth** to give sth/sb a particular number of points 評分；打分數：*The tests are scored by psychologists.* 測驗由心理學家評分。◇ *Score each criterion on a scale of 1 to 5.* 按 1 到 5 分給每一種標準打分。◇ *a scoring system* 評分體系 **5** [T] **~ sth** to be worth a particular number of points 分值是；得…分：*Each correct answer will score two points.* 每答對一題得兩分。

▸ **SUCCEED** 成功 **6** [T, I] to succeed; to have an advantage 獲得勝利；取得優勢：**~ (sth)** *The army continued to score successes in the south.* 軍隊在南方不斷取得勝利。◇ *She's scored again with her latest blockbuster.* 她的新作大獲成功，再次引起轟動。◇ **~ over sth** *Bicycles score over other forms of transport in towns.* 在城鎮，自行車比其他交通工具更勝一籌。

▸ **ARRANGE/WRITE MUSIC** 譜曲；作曲 **7** [T, usually passive] to arrange a piece of music for one or more musical instruments or for voices 編總譜（包括各種樂器及各聲部的樂譜）：**~ sth for sth** *The piece is scored for violin, viola and cello.* 這個樂譜是為小提琴、中提琴和大提琴演奏而編的。◇ **~ sth** *The director invited him to score the movie* (= write the music for it). 導演邀請他為電影配樂。

▸ **CUT** 刻痕 **8** [T] **~ sth** to make a cut or mark on a surface（在物體表面）劃下痕跡，刻出記號：*Score the card first with a knife.* 先用刀在卡片上劃出痕跡。

▸ **HAVE SEX** 發生性關係 **9** [I] **~ (with sb)** (*slang*) (especially of a man 尤指男人) to have sex with a new partner 和新伴侶發生性關係：*Did you score last night?* 你昨晚把她搞到手了嗎？

▸ **BUY DRUGS** 買毒品 **10** [T, I] **~ (sth)** (*slang*) to buy or get illegal drugs 買（或搞到）毒品

IDM **ˌscore a 'point/'points (off/against/over sb)** = SCORE OFF SB

PHR V **'score off sb** [no passive] (*especially BrE*) to show that you are better than sb, especially by making clever remarks, for example in an argument（尤指在辯論等活動中機靈地）駁倒，挫敗：*He was always trying to score off his teachers.* 他老和老師抬槓。 **ˌscore sth↔'out/'through** to draw a line or lines through sth 劃掉；刪去：*Her name had been scored out on the list.* 她的名字已從名單上劃掉了。

score·board /'skɔːbɔːd; *NAmE* 'skɔːrbɔːrd/ *noun* a large board on which the score in a game or competition is shown 記分牌

score·card /'skɔːkɑːd; *NAmE* 'skɔːrkɑːrd/ *noun* a card or piece of paper that people watching or playing a game can use to write the score on, or on which the score can be officially recorded 記分卡

'score draw *noun* (*BrE*) the result of a football (SOCCER) match in which both teams score the same number of goals（足球比賽中雙方入球數相等的）平局

score·less /'skɔːləs; *NAmE* 'skɔːrləs/ *adj.* (of a game 體育比賽) without either team getting any points, goals, etc. 雙方均未得分的；零比零的：*a scoreless draw* 零比零平局

score·line /'skɔːlaɪn; *NAmE* 'skɔːrl-/ *noun* (*BrE*) (used mainly in newspapers 主要用於報章) the final score or result in a game, competition, etc.（體育比賽的）最終比分，最終結果：*a 2–1 scoreline* 最終比分 2:1 ◇ *The team did not play as badly as the scoreline suggests.* 這支球隊的表現並不像最終比分所顯示的那樣糟糕。

scorer /'skɔːrə(r)/ *noun* **1** (in sports 體育運動) a player who scores points, goals, etc. 得分運動員；得分手：*United's **top scorer*** 聯隊的頭號得分手 **2** a person who keeps a record of the points, goals, etc. scored in a game or competition（在遊戲或比賽中的）記分人，記分員 **3 a high/low ~** a person who gets a high/low number of points in a test or exam（在測驗或考試中）得高分者，得低分者

'score sheet *noun* (*BrE*) a piece of paper on which the score of a game can be officially recorded（比賽中的）記分單

IDM **get your name on the 'score sheet** (*informal*) (used in newspapers 用於報章) to score a goal, etc. 有一球（或一分）記入名下

scorn /skɔːn; *NAmE* skɔːrn/ *noun, verb*

■ ***noun*** [U] a strong feeling that sb/sth is stupid or not good enough, usually shown by the way you speak 輕蔑；鄙視 **SYN** **contempt**：*Her fellow teachers **greeted** her proposal **with scorn**.* 別的老師對她的提議不屑一顧。◇ **~ for sb/sth** *They had nothing but scorn for his political views.* 他們對他的政治觀點只有鄙夷。

IDM **pour/heap 'scorn on sb/sth** to speak about sb/sth in a way that shows that you do not respect them or have a good opinion of them 嗤之以鼻；不屑一顧

■ ***verb*** **1 ~ sb/sth** to feel or show that you think sb/sth is stupid and you do not respect them or it 輕蔑；鄙視 **SYN** **dismiss**：*She scorned their views as old-fashioned.* 她對他們的觀點嗤之以鼻，認為陳腐過時。 **2** (*formal*) to refuse to have or do sth because you are too proud 不屑於（接受或做）；輕蔑地拒絕：**~ sth** *to scorn an invitation* 輕蔑地回絕邀請 ◇ **~ to do sth** *She would have scorned to stoop to such tactics.* 她就不會下作到使用那樣的伎倆。 **IDM** see HELL

scorn·ful /'skɔːnfl; *NAmE* 'skɔːrnfl/ *adj.* showing or feeling scorn 輕蔑的；鄙夷的 **SYN** **contemptuous**：*a scornful laugh* 輕蔑的冷笑 ◇ **~ of sth** *He was scornful of such 'female' activities as cooking.* 他看不起諸如做飯之類的"女人的"活兒。 ▸ **scorn·ful·ly** /-fəli/ *adv.*：*She laughed scornfully.* 她輕蔑地大笑。

Scor·pio /'skɔːpiəʊ; *NAmE* 'skɔːrpioʊ/ *noun* **1** [U] the 8th sign of the ZODIAC, the SCORPION 黃道第八宮；天蠍宮；天蠍（星）座 **2** [C] (*pl.* **-os**) a person born when the sun is in this sign, that is between 23 October and 21 November, approximately 屬天蠍座的人（約出生於 10 月 23 日至 11 月 21 日）

scor·pion /'skɔːpiən; *NAmE* 'skɔːrp-/ *noun* a small creature like an insect with eight legs, two front CLAWS (= curved and pointed arms) and a long tail that curves over its back and can give a poisonous sting. Scorpions live in hot countries. 蠍子 ➲ VISUAL VOCAB page V13

Scot /skɒt; *NAmE* skɑːt/ *noun* **1** a person from Scotland 蘇格蘭人 **2 the Scots** [pl.] the people of Scotland（統稱）蘇格蘭人 ➲ note at SCOTTISH

Scotch /skɒtʃ; *NAmE* skɑːtʃ/ *noun, adj.*

■ ***noun*** **1** [U] the type of WHISKY made in Scotland 蘇格蘭威士忌：*a bottle of Scotch* 一瓶蘇格蘭威士忌 **2** [C] a glass of Scotch 一杯蘇格蘭威士忌：*Do you want a Scotch?* 你要不要喝一杯蘇格蘭威士忌？

■ ***adj.*** of or connected with Scotland 蘇格蘭的 ➲ note at SCOTTISH

scotch /skɒtʃ; *NAmE* skɑːtʃ/ *verb* **~ sth** to stop sth from happening; to take action to end sth 阻止；挫敗；平息；終止：*Plans for a merger have been scotched.* 合併計劃停止實行。◇ *Rumours that he had fled the country*

S

were promptly scotched by his wife. 他的妻子立刻駁斥了他已逃到國外的謠言。

ˌScotch ˈbonnet *noun* a type of very hot CHILLI 蘇格蘭帽紅辣椒（極辣）

ˌScotch ˈbroth *noun* [U] (*BrE*) a thick soup containing vegetables and BARLEY (= a type of grain) 蘇格蘭濃湯（用蔬菜和大麥煮成）

ˌScotch ˈegg *noun* (*BrE*) a boiled egg covered with SAUSAGE MEAT and BREADCRUMBS, fried and eaten cold 蘇格蘭香腸蛋（雞蛋煮熟後外裹香腸肉和麪包屑，炸後作為冷餐食用）

ˈScotch tape™ (*NAmE*) (*BrE* **Sel·lo·tape™**, **ˈsticky tape**) *noun* [U] clear plastic tape that is sticky on one side, used for sticking things together 透明膠帶；賽勒塔普膠黏帶 ➲ VISUAL VOCAB page V69

ˌscot-ˈfree *adv.* (*informal*) without receiving the punishment you deserve 逃脫懲罰；逍遙法外：*They* **got off** *scot-free because of lack of evidence.* 由於證據不足，他們得以逍遙法外。 **ORIGIN** This idiom comes from the old English word 'scot' meaning 'tax'. People were scot-free if they didn't have to pay the tax. 本習語源自古英語 scot 一詞，意為賦稅。scot-free 表示無須納稅。

Scot·land Yard /ˌskɒtlənd ˈjɑːd; *NAmE* ˌskɑːtlənd ˈjɑːrd/ *noun* [U+sing./pl. v.] (in Britain) the main office of the London police, especially the department that deals with serious crimes in London 倫敦警察廳（尤指其刑偵處）；蘇格蘭場：*Scotland Yard's anti-terrorist squad* 倫敦警察廳反恐小組 ◊ *Scotland Yard has/have been called in.* 已向倫敦警察廳報了案。

Scots /skɒts; *NAmE* skɑːts/ *adj.*, *noun*

■ ***adj.*** of or connected with Scotland, and especially with the English language as spoken in Scotland or the Scots language 蘇格蘭的；（尤指）蘇格蘭英語的，蘇格蘭語的：*He spoke with a Scots accent.* 他說話帶蘇格蘭口音。◊ *She comes from an old Scots family.* 她出生於一個古老的蘇格蘭家族。

■ ***noun*** [U] a language spoken in Scotland, closely related to English but with many differences 蘇格蘭英語

Scot·tie /ˈskɒti; *NAmE* ˈskɑːti/ *noun* (*informal*) = SCOTTISH TERRIER

More About 補充說明

describing things from Scotland
描述來自蘇格蘭的事物

- The adjective **Scottish** is the most general word used to describe the people and things of Scotland, while **Scots** is only used to describe its people, its law and especially its language. 形容詞 Scottish 為含義最廣的用語，形容來自蘇格蘭的人和物。Scots 僅用於蘇格蘭人、蘇格蘭法律、尤其是蘇格蘭語：*Scottish dancing* 蘇格蘭舞蹈 ◊ *the Scottish parliament* 蘇格蘭議會 ◊ *a well-known Scots poet* 著名的蘇格蘭詩人 ◊ *a slight Scots accent* 輕微的蘇格蘭口音
- The adjective **Scotch** is now mainly used in fixed expressions such as *Scotch whisky* and *Scotch broth* and sounds old-fashioned or insulting if it is used in any other way. 形容詞 Scotch 現主要用於某些固定短語中，如 Scotch whisky（蘇格蘭威士忌）和 Scotch broth（蘇格蘭濃湯）。用於其他地方則顯得過時或帶有侮辱性。
- The noun **Scotch** means whisky, and the noun **Scots** refers to a language spoken in Scotland, closely related to English. A person who comes from Scotland is a **Scot**. 名詞 Scotch 指蘇格蘭威士忌，而名詞 Scots 指與英語密切相關的蘇格蘭語。蘇格蘭人用 Scot 表示：*The Scots won their match against England.* 蘇格蘭人在與英格蘭人的比賽中獲勝。

➲ note at BRITISH

Scot·tish /ˈskɒtɪʃ; *NAmE* ˈskɑːtɪʃ/ *adj.* of or connected with Scotland or its people 蘇格蘭的；蘇格蘭人的：*the Scottish Highlands* 蘇格蘭高地 ◊ *Scottish dancing* 蘇格蘭舞蹈

the ˌScottish ˈNational Party *noun* [sing.+sing./pl. v.] (*abbr.* **SNP**) a Scottish political party which wants Scotland to be an independent nation 蘇格蘭民族黨（主張蘇格蘭獨立）

the ˌScottish ˈParliament *noun* [sing.+sing./pl. v.] the parliament elected by the people of Scotland which has powers to make its own laws in areas such as education and health 蘇格蘭議會（由蘇格蘭人民選舉產生，有權制訂教育、健康等法規）

ˌScottish ˈterrier (also **Scot·tie**, *informal*) *noun* a small TERRIER (= type of dog) with rough hair and short legs 蘇格蘭㹴狗

scoun·drel /ˈskaʊndrəl/ *noun* (*old-fashioned*) a man who treats other people badly, especially by being dishonest or immoral 無賴；惡棍 **SYN** **rogue**

scour /ˈskaʊə(r)/ *verb* **1 ~ sth** (**for sb/sth**) to search a place or thing thoroughly in order to find sb/sth（徹底地）搜尋，搜查，翻找 **SYN** **comb**：*We scoured the area for somewhere to pitch our tent.* 我們四處查看，想找一個搭帳篷的地方。 **2 ~ sth** (**out**) to clean sth by rubbing its surface hard with rough material（用粗糙的物體）擦淨，擦亮：*I had to scour out the pans.* 我得把這些鍋擦乾淨。 **3 ~ sth** (**away/out**) | **~ sth** (**from/out of sth**) to make a passage, hole, or mark in the ground, rocks, etc. as the result of movement, especially over a long period 沖刷成；沖刷出：*The water had raced down the slope and scoured out the bed of a stream.* 水順着山坡流下來，沖刷出一條小河道。

scour·er /ˈskaʊərə(r)/ (also **ˈscouring pad**) *noun* a small ball of wire or stiff plastic used for cleaning pans（用以擦洗鍋的）金屬絲球，塑料絲球

scourge /skɜːdʒ; *NAmE* skɜːrdʒ/ *noun*, *verb*

■ ***noun*** **1** [usually sing.] **~ (of sb/sth)** (*formal*) a person or thing that causes trouble or suffering 禍害；禍根；災害：***the scourge of war/disease/poverty*** 戰爭／疾病／貧窮之苦 ◊ *Inflation was the scourge of the 1970s.* 通貨膨脹曾是 20 世紀 70 年代的禍患。 **2** a WHIP used to punish people in the past（舊時用作刑具的）鞭子

■ ***verb*** **1** [usually passive] **~ sb** (*literary*) to cause trouble or suffering to sb 折磨；使受苦難；使痛苦：*He lay awake, scourged by his conscience.* 他備受良心的折磨，不能入睡。 **2 ~ sb** (*old use*) to hit sb with a scourge 鞭打；鞭笞 **SYN** **whip**

Scouse /skaʊs/ *noun* (*BrE*, *informal*) **1** (also **Scouser** /ˈskaʊsə(r)/) [C] a person from Liverpool in NW England（英格蘭西北部的）利物浦人 **2** [U] a way of speaking, used by people from Liverpool 利物浦方言（或口音）
▸ **Scouse** *adj.*：*a Scouse accent* 利物浦口音

scout /skaʊt/ *noun*, *verb*

■ ***noun*** **1 the Scouts** [pl.] an organization (officially called the **Scout Association**) originally for boys, which trains young people in practical skills and does a lot of activities with them, for example camping 童子軍：*to join the Scouts* 參加童子軍 **2** (*BrE*) a boy or girl who is a member of the Scouts 童子軍成員：*Both my brothers were scouts.* 我的兩個哥哥都當過童子軍。◊ *a scout troop* 童子軍中隊 ➲ see also BOY SCOUT, GUIDE *n.* (6) ➲ compare BROWNIE **3** a person, an aircraft, etc. sent ahead to get information about the enemy's position, strength, etc. 偵察員；偵察機 **4** = TALENT SCOUT

■ ***verb*** **1** [T, I] to search an area or various areas in order to find or discover sth 偵察，搜尋（某處）：**~ sth** (**for sb/sth**) *They scouted the area for somewhere to stay the night.* 他們四處查看，想找個過夜的地方。◊ **~** (**around**) (**for sb/sth**) *The kids were scouting around for wood for the fire.* 孩子們正在四處尋找柴火。◊ *a military scouting party* 軍事偵察小分隊 **2** [I, T] **~** (**sb**) to look for sports players, actors, musicians, etc. who have special ability, so you can offer them work 物色（優秀運動員、演員、音樂家等）：*He scouts for Manchester United.* 他為曼徹斯特聯隊物色球員。

PHR V **ˌscout sth↔ˈout** to find out what an area is like or where sth is, by searching 搜索；偵察（地形）；勘察：*We went ahead to scout out the lie of the land.* 我們先一步出發，去偵察地形。

Scout·er /ˈskaʊtə(r)/ *noun* a person who is the leader of a group of scouts 童子軍隊長

scout·ing /ˈskaʊtɪŋ/ *noun* [U] the activities that boy and girl SCOUTS take part in; the Scout organization 童子軍活動；童子軍組織

scout·mas·ter /ˈskaʊtmɑːstə(r); *NAmE* -mæstər/ (also **ˈscout leader**) *noun* the adult in charge of a group of BOY SCOUTS 男童子軍團長（由成年人擔任）

scowl /skaʊl/ *verb, noun*

■ *verb* [I] ~ (**at sb/sth**) to look at sb/sth in an angry or annoyed way 怒視（某人或某物） SYN **glower**

■ *noun* an angry look or expression 怒容；不悅的神色： *He looked up at me with a scowl.* 他臉色陰沉，抬眼看了看我。

Scrab·ble™ /ˈskræbl/ *noun* [U] a board game in which players try to make words from letters printed on small plastic blocks and connect them to words that have already been placed on the board 拼字遊戲（用手中的字母組成新的單詞，並和枱面上已存在的單詞接上）

scrab·ble /ˈskræbl/ *verb* [I] ~ (**around/about**) (**for sth**) | + **adv./prep.** (*especially BrE*) to try to find or to do sth in a hurry or with difficulty, often by moving your hands or feet about quickly, without much control 忙亂地找；翻找；亂抓；亂動：*She scrabbled around in her bag for her glasses.* 她在包裏翻來翻去找眼鏡。◇ *He was scrabbling for a foothold on the steep slope.* 他在陡坡上掙扎着亂蹬，想找個能站穩腳的地方。◇ *a sound like rats scrabbling on the other side of the wall* 牆那面一種像老鼠亂抓的聲音

scrag·gly /ˈskræɡli/ *adj.* (*NAmE, informal*) thin and growing in a way that is not even 稀疏淩亂的；散亂的： *a scraggly beard* 稀稀拉拉的鬍子

scraggy /ˈskræɡi/ *adj.* (**scrag·gier**, **scrag·gi·est**) (*disapproving*) (of people or animals 人或動物) very thin and not looking healthy 骨瘦如柴的；面黃肌瘦的 SYN **scrawny**： *a scraggy old cat* 一隻瘦骨嶙峋的老貓

scram /skræm/ *verb* (**-mm-**) [I] (*old-fashioned, informal*) (usually used in orders 通常用於命令) to go away quickly 走開；滾： *Scram! I don't want you here.* 滾！不要待在我這兒。

scram·ble /ˈskræmbl/ *verb, noun*

■ *verb*

▸ **WALK/CLIMB** 行走；攀爬 **1** [I] + **adv./prep.** to move quickly, especially with difficulty, using your hands to help you （迅速而吃力地）爬，攀登 SYN **clamber**： *She managed to scramble over the wall.* 她手忙腳亂地翻過牆。◇ *He* ***scrambled to his feet*** *as we came in.* 我們進來時，他趕緊從地上爬起來。

▸ **PUSH/FIGHT** 推擠；爭搶 **2** [I] to push, fight or compete with others in order to get or to reach sth 爭搶；搶佔；爭奪： ~ **for sth** *The audience scrambled for the exits.* 觀眾競相朝出口擁去。◇ ~ **to do sth** *Shoppers were scrambling to get the best bargains.* 顧客爭先恐後地搶購最便宜的特價商品。

▸ **ACHIEVE STH WITH DIFFICULTY** 艱難地完成 **3** [T] to manage to achieve sth with difficulty, or in a hurry, without much control 艱難地（或倉促地）完成： ~ **sth** *Cork scrambled a 1–0 win over Monaghan.* 科克隊苦戰莫納亨隊，以 1:0 獲勝。◇ ~ **sth + adv./prep.** *Rooney managed to scramble the ball into the net.* 魯尼勉力把球送進了網窩。

▸ **EGGS** 蛋 **4** [T, usually passive] ~ **sth** to cook an egg by mixing the white and yellow parts together and heating them, sometimes with milk and butter 炒（蛋）： *scrambled eggs* 炒蛋

▸ **TELEPHONE/RADIO** 電話；無線電 **5** [T, often passive] ~ **sth** to change the way that a telephone or radio message sounds so that only people with special equipment can understand it 擾頻，倒頻（改變電話或無線電信號，聽眾只有通過專門設備才能收聽）： *scrambled satellite signals* 擾頻衞星信號

▸ **CONFUSE THOUGHTS** 擾亂思維 **6** [T] ~ **sth** to confuse sb's thoughts, ideas, etc. so that they have no order 擾亂（思維）： *Alcohol seemed to have scrambled his brain.* 酒精似乎擾亂了他的腦子。

▸ **AIRCRAFT** 飛機 **7** [T, I, usually passive] ~ (**sth**) to order that planes, etc. should take off immediately in an emergency; to take off immediately in an emergency 命令（飛機）緊急起飛；緊急起飛： *A helicopter was scrambled to help rescue three young climbers.* 直升機接到命令，緊急起飛前去營救三個登山的年輕人。◇ *They scrambled as soon as the call came through.* 命令剛一下達，他們便緊急起飛。

■ *noun*

▸ **DIFFICULT WALK/CLIMB** 艱難行走／攀爬 **1** [sing.] a difficult walk or climb over rough ground, especially one in which you have to use your hands （尤指需要手腳並用的）艱難行走，爬，攀登

▸ **PUSH/FIGHT** 推擠；爭搶 **2** [sing.] ~ (**for sth**) a situation in which people push, fight or compete with each other in order to get or do sth 爭搶；搶佔；爭奪 SYN **free-for-all**： *There was a mad scramble for the best seats.* 人們不顧一切地搶佔最好的座位。

▸ **MOTORCYCLE RACE** 摩托車比賽 **3** [C] a race for motorcycles over rough ground 摩托車越野賽

scram·bler /ˈskræmblə(r)/ *noun* a device that changes radio or telephone signals or messages so that they cannot be understood by other people 擾頻器；倒頻器

scram·bling /ˈskræmblɪŋ/ *noun* [U] (*BrE*) = MOTOCROSS

scrap /skræp/ *noun, verb*

■ *noun* **1** [C] a small piece of sth, especially paper, cloth, etc. 碎片，小塊（紙、織物等）： *She scribbled his phone number on a scrap of paper.* 她把他的電話號碼匆匆寫在一張小紙片上。◇ (*figurative*) *scraps of information* 零星消息 ◇ (*figurative*) *She was just a scrap of a thing* (= small and thin). 她是個不起眼的小東西。 **2** [sing.] (usually with a negative 通常與否定式連用) a small amount of sth 絲毫；一丁點 SYN **bit**： *It won't make a* ***scrap of difference.*** 這不會有絲毫的差別。◇ *There's not a scrap of evidence to support his claim.* 沒有絲毫證據支持他的說法。◇ *a barren landscape without a scrap of vegetation* 寸草不生的貧瘠地帶 **3** **scraps** [pl.] food left after a meal 殘羹剩飯： *Give the scraps to the dog.* 把剩菜餵狗吧。 **4** [U] things that are not wanted or cannot be used for their original purpose, but which have some value for the material they are made of 廢料；廢品： *We sold the car* ***for scrap*** (= so that any good parts can be used again). 我們把車當廢品賣了。◇ ***scrap metal*** 廢金屬 ◇ *a* ***scrap dealer*** (= a person who buys and sells scrap) 廢品商人 **5** [C] (*informal*) a short fight or disagreement 打架；爭吵 SYN **squabble**, **scuffle**： *He was always getting into scraps at school.* 他在學校老跟人打架。➲ see also SCRAPPY

■ *verb* (**-pp-**) **1** [T, often passive] ~ **sth** to cancel or get rid of sth that is no longer practical or useful 廢棄；取消；拋棄；報廢： *They had been forced to scrap plans for a new school building.* 他們已被迫撤銷了建築新校舍的計劃。◇ *The oldest of the aircraft were scrapped.* 最老的飛機報廢了。 **2** [I] (*informal*) to fight with sb 打架： *The bigger boys started scrapping.* 年齡較大的男孩打了起來。

scrap·book /ˈskræpbʊk/ *noun* a book with empty pages where you can stick pictures, newspaper articles, etc. 剪貼簿

scrape /skreɪp/ *verb, noun*

■ *verb*

▸ **REMOVE** 除去 **1** [T] to remove sth from a surface by moving sth sharp and hard like a knife across it 刮掉；削去： ~ **sth** (+ **adv./prep.**) *She scraped the mud off her boots.* 她刮掉了靴子上的泥。◇ ~ **sth + adj.** *The kids had scraped their plates clean.* 孩子們把自己的盤子擦得乾乾淨淨。

▸ **DAMAGE** 損壞 **2** [T] to rub sth by accident so that it gets damaged or hurt 擦壞；擦傷；刮壞；蹭破： ~ **sth** *She fell and scraped her knee.* 她摔了一跤，把膝蓋蹭破了。◇ ~ **sth + adv./prep.** *I scraped the side of my car on the wall.* 我車的一側被牆刮了。◇ *Sorry, I've scraped some paint off the car.* 抱歉，我把車刮掉了一塊漆。◇ *The wire had scraped the skin from her fingers.* 她的手指頭讓金屬絲刮掉了皮。

▸ **MAKE SOUND** 發出聲音 **3** [I, T] to make an unpleasant noise by rubbing against a hard surface; to make sth do this （使）發出刺耳的刮擦聲： (+ **adv./prep.**) *I could hear his pen scraping across the paper.* 我聽得見他的鋼

S

筆在紙上沙沙地響。◇ *We could hear her scraping away at the violin.* 我們聽得見她正一個勁兒吱吱呀呀地拉小提琴。◇ **~ sth (+ adv./prep.)** *Don't scrape your chairs on the floor.* 別把椅子在地板上蹭得嘎吱嘎吱響。

▸ **WIN WITH DIFFICULTY 艱難獲取 4** [T, I] **~ (sth)** to manage to win or to get sth with difficulty 艱難取得；勉強獲得：*The team scraped a narrow victory last year.* 這支隊去年險勝。◇ (*BrE*) *I just scraped a pass in the exam.* 我考試勉強及格。◇ *They* ***scraped a living*** *by playing music on the streets.* 他們在街頭演奏音樂，勉強維持生活。◇ *The government* ***scraped home*** (= just won) *by three votes.* 政府以三票的微弱優勢勉強過關。

▸ **MAKE HOLE IN GROUND 在地上挖坑 5** [T] **~ sth (out)** to make a hole or hollow place in the ground 挖坑；挖洞：*He found a suitable place, scraped a hole and buried the bag in it.* 他找了個合適的地方，挖個坑，把包埋了進去。

▸ **PULL HAIR BACK 朝後攏頭髮 6** [T] **~ your hair back** to pull your hair tightly back, away from your face 把頭髮攏在後面：*Her hair was scraped back from her face in a ponytail.* 她的頭髮攏在後面，紮成一個馬尾辮。

IDM **scrape (the bottom of) the 'barrel** (*disapproving*) to have to use whatever things or people you can get, because there is not much choice available （因別無選擇）將就，湊合 ➲ more at BOW[1] *v.*

PHR V **,scrape 'by (on sth)** to manage to live on the money you have, but with difficulty （靠…）勉強維持生計，餬口，艱難度日：*I can just scrape by on what my parents give me.* 我靠父母給的那點錢只能勉強度日。 **,scrape 'in | ,scrape 'into sth** to manage to get a job, a position, a place at college, etc., but with difficulty 勉強獲得（工作、職位、入學資格等）：*He scraped in with 180 votes.* 他以 180 票勉強當選。◇ *Our team just scraped into the semi-finals.* 我們這支隊勉強擠入半決賽。 **,scrape sth↔'out** to remove sth from inside sth else, using sth sharp or hard like a knife 挖出；掏出：*Scrape out the flesh of the melon with a spoon.* 用小勺挖出瓜瓤。 **,scrape 'through | ,scrape 'through sth** to succeed in doing sth with difficulty, especially in passing an exam 艱難完成；勉強通過（考試）：*I might scrape through the exam if I'm lucky.* 要是走運的話，我也許能勉強及格。 **,scrape sth↔to'gether/'up** to obtain or collect together sth, but with difficulty 勉強湊集；費力聚攏；艱難籌措：*We managed to scrape together eight volunteers.* 我們好不容易湊齊八名志願者。

■ ***noun***

▸ **ACTION/SOUND 動作；聲音 1** [sing.] the action or unpleasant sound of one thing rubbing roughly against another 刮；鏟；刮鏟聲；刮擦聲：*the scrape of iron on stone* 鐵摩擦石頭發出的嚓嚓聲

▸ **DAMAGE 損壞 2** [C] an injury or a mark caused by rubbing against sth rough 擦傷；擦痕：*She emerged from the overturned car with only a few scrapes and bruises.* 她從翻了的車裏鑽出來，只擦破一點皮，碰了幾塊瘀青。

▸ **DIFFICULT SITUATION 困境 3** [C] (*old-fashioned*) a difficult situation that you have caused yourself 自己造成的困境：*He was always getting into scrapes as a boy.* 他小時候老闖禍。

scraper /'skreɪpə(r)/ *noun* a tool used for scraping, for example for scraping mud from shoes or ice from a car 刮刀；刮削器；鏟子

scrap·heap /'skræphiːp/ *noun* a pile of things, especially of metal, that are no longer wanted or useful 廢物堆；（尤指）廢金屬堆

IDM **on the 'scrapheap** (*informal*) no longer wanted or considered useful 廢棄的；丟棄的

scra·pie /'skreɪpi/ *noun* [U] a serious disease that affects the NERVOUS SYSTEM of sheep 癢病（損傷羊的神經系統的嚴重疾病）

scrap·ing /'skreɪpɪŋ/ *noun* [usually pl.] a small amount of sth produced by scratching a surface 刮屑；削片

'scrap paper *noun* [U] loose pieces of paper used for writing notes on （散的）便條紙

scrappy /'skræpi/ *adj.* (**scrap·pier**, **scrap·pi·est**) **1** consisting of individual sections, events, etc. that are not organized into a whole 散亂的；不連貫的；支離破碎的 **SYN** **bitty**：*a scrappy essay* 一篇內容凌亂的文章 **2** (*especially BrE*) not tidy and often of poor quality 不整潔的；糟糕的：*The note was written on a scrappy bit of paper.* 便條寫在一片破紙上。➲ see also SCRAP *n.*

scrap·yard /'skræpjɑːd; *NAmE* -jɑːrd/ (*BrE*) (also **junk·yard** *NAmE*, *BrE*) *noun* a place where old cars, machines, etc. are collected, so that parts of them, or the metal they are made of, can be sold to be used again （堆放舊汽車、舊機器等的）廢品場

scratch 0-w /skrætʃ/ *verb, noun, adj.*

■ ***verb***

▸ **RUB WITH YOUR NAILS 用指甲撓 1** 0-w [T, I] to rub your skin with your nails, usually because it is ITCHING 撓，搔（癢處）：**~ sth/yourself** *John yawned and scratched his chin.* 約翰打個哈欠，撓撓下巴。◇ *The dog scratched itself behind the ear.* 狗用爪子撓撓耳後。◇ **~ (at sth)** *Try not to scratch.* 盡量別撓。◇ *She scratched at the insect bites on her arm.* 她撓了撓胳膊上蟲咬的包。

▸ **CUT SKIN 劃破皮膚 2** 0-w [T, I] to cut or damage your skin slightly with sth sharp 劃破，抓破，劃傷，抓傷（皮膚）：**~ (sb/sth/yourself)** *I'd scratched my leg and it was bleeding.* 我把腿抓出了血。◇ *Does the cat scratch?* 這隻貓抓人嗎？◇ **~ sb/sth/yourself on sth** *She scratched herself on a nail.* 她被釘子劃了一下。

▸ **DAMAGE SURFACE 損壞表面 3** 0-w [T] **~ sth** to damage the surface of sth, especially by accident, by making thin shallow marks on it（尤指意外地）擦破，劃損，刮壞：*Be careful not to scratch the furniture.* 小心別刮壞傢具。◇ *The car's paintwork is badly scratched.* 車的漆面劃損得很厲害。

▸ **MAKE/REMOVE MARK 造成／去除痕跡 4** 0-w [T] **~ sth + adv./prep.** to make or remove a mark, etc. on sth deliberately, by rubbing it with sth hard or sharp 刮出（或刮去）痕跡；劃下（或擦去）痕跡：*They scratched lines in the dirt to mark out a pitch.* 他們在泥地上劃出一個球場。◇ *We scratched some of the dirt away.* 我們刮掉了一些髒東西。◇ (*figurative*) *You can scratch my name off the list.* 你可以把我的名字從名單上勾掉。

▸ **MAKE SOUND 發出聲音 5** [I] (**+ adv./prep.**) to make an irritating noise by rubbing sth with sth sharp 刮（或擦、抓）出刺耳聲：*His pen scratched away on the paper.* 他的筆在紙上沙沙地響。

▸ **A LIVING 生計 6** [T] **~ a living** to make enough money to live on, but with difficulty 勉強維持生活

▸ **CANCEL 取消 7** [T, I] to decide that sth cannot happen or sb/sth cannot take part in sth, before it starts （未開始就）取消；撤銷；退出：**~ sb/sth** *to scratch a rocket launch* 取消火箭發射計劃 ◇ **~ sb/sth (from sth)** *The horse was scratched from the race because of injury.* 這匹馬因傷被取消了比賽資格。◇ **~ (from sth)** *She had scratched because of a knee injury.* 她因膝傷退出了比賽。

IDM **scratch your 'head (over sth)** to think hard in order to find an answer to sth 苦苦琢磨；苦思冥想；絞盡腦汁 **scratch the 'surface (of sth)** to deal with, understand, or find out about only a small part of a subject or problem 作膚淺的探討；淺嘗輒止；隔靴搔癢 **,you scratch 'my back and ,I'll scratch 'yours** (*saying*) used to say that if sb helps you, you will help them, even if this is unfair to others 禮尚往來；私相授受

PHR V **,scratch a'bout/a'round (for sth)** to search for sth, especially with difficulty （尤指艱難地）搜尋，查尋，查找 **,scratch sth↔'out** to remove a word, especially a name, from sth written, usually by putting a line through it 畫掉，勾掉，刪除（名字等）

■ ***noun***

▸ **MARK/CUT 劃痕；劃傷 1** 0-w [C] a mark, a cut or an injury made by scratching sb's skin or the surface of sth （皮膚或物體表面上的）劃痕，劃傷：*Her hands were covered in scratches from the brambles.* 她手上佈滿了荊棘劃的口子。◇ *a scratch on the paintwork* 漆面上的一道劃痕 ◇ *It's* ***only a scratch*** (= a very slight injury). 不過是輕微的劃傷。◇ *He escaped* ***without a scratch*** (= was not hurt at all). 他毫髮未損地逃了出去。

▸ **SOUND 聲音 2** [sing.] the unpleasant sound of sth sharp or rough being rubbed against a surface 刮（或擦、抓）的刺耳聲

▸ **WITH YOUR NAILS 用指甲 3** [sing.] the act of scratching a part of your body when it ITCHES 撓癢；搔癢：*Go on, have a good scratch!* 來吧，好好撓一撓！

IDM **from 'scratch** **1** without any previous preparation or knowledge 從頭開始；從零開始：*I learned German from scratch in six months.* 我從零學起，六個月學會了德語。 **2** from the very beginning, not using any of the work done earlier 從頭（做起）；從零開始：*They decided to dismantle the machine and start again from scratch.* 他們決定拆掉機器，從頭再來。 **up to 'scratch** as good as sth/sb should be 達到要求；合乎標準 SYN **satisfactory**：*His work simply isn't up to scratch.* 他的工作根本達不到要求。◇ *It'll take months to bring the band up to scratch.* 得幾個月工夫才能使樂隊像個樣子。

■ ***adj.*** (*BrE*) **1** put together in a hurry using whatever people or materials are available 倉促拼湊的：*a scratch team* 一支倉促組建的隊伍 **2** (especially in GOLF 尤指高爾夫球) with no HANDICAP 無讓步的；無讓杆的：*a scratch player* 參加無讓杆比賽的球手

'scratch card *noun* a card that you buy that has an area that you scratch off to find out if you have won some money or a prize 刮獎卡；刮刮卡

'scratch pad *noun* (*NAmE*) a small book of cheap paper for writing notes on 便箋簿

'scratch paper *noun* [U] (*NAmE*) cheap paper, or loose sheets of paper, for writing notes on 便條紙；草稿紙

scratchy /'skrætʃi/ *adj.* (**scratch·ier**, **scratchi·est**) **1** (of clothes or cloth 衣服或織物) rough and unpleasant to the touch 扎人的；粗糙刺激皮膚的 SYN **itchy** **2** (of a record, voice, etc. 錄音、聲音等) making a rough, unpleasant sound like sth being scratched across a surface 帶沙沙的雜音的：*a scratchy recording of Mario Lanza* 一盤有雜音的馬里奧•蘭扎演唱錄音帶 ◇ *a scratchy pen* 一支劃紙的鋼筆 **3** (of writing or drawings 字跡或圖畫) done without care 潦草的；粗製濫造的

scrawl /skrɔːl/ *verb, noun*

■ ***verb*** [T, I] to write sth in a careless untidy way, making it difficult to read 馬馬虎虎（或潦草）地寫 SYN **scribble**：**~ sth** (**across/in/on/over sth**) *I tried to read his directions, scrawled on a piece of paper.* 我盡量弄明白他草草寫在一片紙上的指示。◇ **~ across/in/on/over sth** *Someone had scrawled all over my notes.* 不知誰在我筆記上胡寫亂畫，弄得一塌糊塗。

■ ***noun*** a careless untidy way of writing; sth written in this way 不工整的字跡；潦草的筆跡；不工整的文字 SYN **scribble**：*Her signature was an illegible scrawl.* 她的簽名潦草難辨。◇ *I can't be expected to read this scrawl!* 這種潦潦草草的東西我能看懂嗎！◇ *The paper was covered in scrawls.* 滿篇潦潦草草。

scrawny /'skrɔːni/ *adj.* (**scrawn·ier**, **scrawni·est**) (*disapproving*) (of people or animals 人或動物) very thin in a way that is not attractive 乾瘦的；瘦巴巴的 SYN **scraggy**

scream 0-w /skriːm/ *verb, noun*

■ ***verb*** **1** 0-w [I, T] to give a loud, high cry, because you are hurt, frightened, excited, etc.（因傷痛、害怕、激動等）尖叫 SYN **shriek**：*He covered her mouth to stop her from screaming.* 他捂上她的嘴，不讓她叫出聲來。◇ **~ in/with sth** *The kids were screaming with excitement.* 孩子們興奮地喊叫着。◇ **~ out** (**in/with sth**) *People ran for the exits, screaming out in terror.* 人們驚恐萬狀，尖叫着奔向出口。◇ **~ yourself + adj.** *The baby was screaming itself hoarse.* 嬰兒哭得嗓子都啞了。 **2** 0-w [T, I] to shout sth in a loud, high voice because of fear, anger, etc.（向某人或為某事）高聲喊，大聲叫 SYN **yell**：**+ speech** *'Help!' she screamed.* "救命啊！" 她喊道。◇ **~** (**out**) (**for sth/sb**) *Someone was screaming for help.* 有人在喊救命。◇ **~ at sb** (**to do sth**) *He screamed at me to stop.* 他衝着我喊，要我停下來。◇ **~ sth** (**out**) (**at sb**) *She screamed abuse at him.* 她對他破口大罵。◇ **~** (**out**) **that …** *His sister screamed out that he was crazy.* 他姐姐大叫着說他昏了頭。 ➲ SYNONYMS at SHOUT **3** [I] to make a loud, high noise; to move fast, making this noise 發出大而尖的聲音；呼嘯而過 SYN **screech**：*Lights flashed and sirens screamed.* 燈光閃動，警報鳴叫。◇ **+ adv./prep.** *The powerboat screamed out to sea.* 汽艇呼嘯着出海了。

IDM **scream blue 'murder** (*BrE*) (*NAmE* **scream bloody 'murder**) to scream loudly and for a long time, especially in order to protest about sth 不停地叫嚷（尤指叫屈、鳴不平）

PHR V **,scream 'out** (**for sth**) to be in need of attention in a very noticeable way 亟須；亟待 SYN **call out**：*These books scream out to be included in a list of favourites.* 這幾本書亟須列入最受讀者喜愛的書目之中。

■ ***noun*** **1** 0-w [C] a loud high cry made by sb who is hurt, frightened, excited, etc.; a loud high noise 尖叫；尖銳刺耳的聲音：*She let out a scream of pain.* 她疼得大叫一聲。◇ *They ignored the baby's screams.* 他們對孩子的哭叫充耳不聞。◇ *He drove off with a scream of tyres.* 他駕車吱地一聲開走了。 **2** [sing.] (*old-fashioned, informal*) a person or thing that causes you to laugh 可笑的人（或物）：*He's a scream.* 他挺滑稽的。

scream·ing·ly /'skriːmɪŋli/ *adv.* extremely 極其；十足地：*It was screamingly obvious what we should do next.* 我們下一步該怎麼做，再清楚不過了。

scree /skriː/ *noun* [U, C] an area of small loose stones, especially on a mountain, which may slide when you walk on them 碎石坡；岩屑堆 ➲ VISUAL VOCAB pages V4, V5

screech /skriːtʃ/ *verb, noun*

■ ***verb*** **1** [I, T] to make a loud high unpleasant sound; to say sth using this sound 尖叫；發出尖銳刺耳的聲音；尖聲地說：*Monkeys were screeching in the trees.* 猴子在樹上吱吱地叫着。◇ *The wind screeched in his ears.* 風呼呼地從他耳邊吹過。◇ *screeching brakes* 尖銳的刹車聲 ◇ *He screeched with pain.* 他疼得叫起來。◇ **+ speech** *'No, don't!' she screeched.* "不，不行！" 她尖叫道。◇ **~** (**sth**) (**at sb**) *He screeched something at me.* 他衝我尖聲嚷了一句什麼。 **2** [I] (**+ adv./prep.**) (of a vehicle 車輛) to make a loud high unpleasant noise as it moves（行駛時）發出刺耳聲：*The car* ***screeched to a halt*** *outside the hospital.* 汽車嘎地在醫院外面停住。◇ *A police car screeched out of a side street.* 一輛警車哧的一聲從一條小巷裏駛了出來。

■ ***noun*** a loud high unpleasant cry or noise 刺耳的尖叫；尖銳刺耳的聲音：*a* ***screech of brakes/tyres*** 制動器／輪胎吱的一聲響 ◇ *She suddenly let out a screech.* 她猛地尖叫一聲。

screed /skriːd/ *noun* a long piece of writing, especially one that is not very interesting 冗長的文章；長篇大論

screen 0-w /skriːn/ *noun, verb*

■ ***noun***

▸ **OF TV/COMPUTER** 電視；計算機 **1** 0-w [C] the flat surface at the front of a television, computer, or other electronic device, on which you see pictures or information 屏幕；熒光屏：*a computer screen* 計算機屏幕 ◇ *a monitor with a 21 inch screen* * 21 英寸屏幕的顯示器 ◇ *They were staring at the television screen.* 當時他們正盯着電視屏幕。◇ *Move your cursor to the top of the screen.* 把你的光標移到屏幕頂端。◇ *the screen display* 屏幕顯示 ◇ *Can you do a printout of this screen for me* (= of all the information on it)? 你能幫我把這一屏幕打印出來嗎？ ➲ VISUAL VOCAB page V66 ➲ see also ON-SCREEN

▸ **FILMS/MOVIES/TV** 電影；電視 **2** 0-w [C] the large flat surface that films/movies or pictures are shown on 銀幕：*a* ***cinema/movie screen*** 電影銀幕 ◇ *an eight-screen cinema* 一家有八個放映廳的電影院 ◇ *The movie will be coming to your screens shortly.* 這部電影不久就會在你們那裏上映。 **3** 0-w (often **the screen**) [sing., U] films/movies or television in general（統稱）電影，電視：*He has adapted the play for the screen.* 他把那部劇改編成了電影劇本。◇ *Some actors never watch themselves* ***on screen***. 有的演員從來不看自己拍的戲。◇ *She was a star of* ***stage and screen*** (= plays and films/movies). 她是戲劇、電影兩棲明星。◇ *a screen actor* 電影演員 ➲ see also OFF-SCREEN, SILVER SCREEN, SMALL SCREEN **4** [C] the data or images shown on a computer screen（電腦屏幕上）一屏的內容；畫面：*Press the F1 key to display a help screen.* 按 F1 鍵顯示幫助畫面。

▸ **PIECE OF FURNITURE** 傢具 **5** 0-w [C] a vertical piece of furniture or equipment that is fixed or that can be moved to divide a room or to keep one area hidden or separate 隔板；屏風；幕；簾；帳：*The nurse put a screen around the bed.* 護士繞牀拉了一道簾子。 ➲ see also FIRE SCREEN

▸ **FOR HIDING/PROTECTING STH/SB 用以掩藏／保護** **6** [C] **~ (of sth)** something that prevents sb from seeing or being aware of sth, or that protects sb/sth 掩蔽物；掩護物；屏障；庇護：*We planted a screen of tall trees.* 我們種下一排大樹作為屏障。◇ (*figurative*) *All the research was conducted behind a screen of secrecy.* 整個研究始終是秘密進行的。➲ see also SMOKESCREEN, SUNSCREEN, WINDSCREEN

▸ **ON WINDOW/DOOR 窗／門上** **7** [C] (*especially NAmE*) a wire or plastic net that is held in a frame and fastened on a window, or a door, to let in air but keep out insects 紗窗；紗門：*screen doors* 紗門

▸ **IN CHURCH 教堂裏** **8** [C] a wood or stone structure in a church, that partly separates the main area from the ALTAR or CHOIR（攔在聖壇或唱詩班四周的木質或石砌）圍屏 **IDM** see RADAR

■ *verb*

▸ **HIDE STH/SB 遮蔽某物／某人** **1 ~ sth/sb (from sth/sb)** to hide or protect sth/sb by placing sth in front of or around them 掩藏；遮蔽；保護 **SYN** **shield**：*Dark glasses screened his eyes from the sun.* 他戴了一副墨鏡，保護眼睛不受陽光照射。

▸ **PROTECT SB 保護某人** **2 ~ sb from sb/sth** to protect sb from sth dangerous or unpleasant, especially to protect sb who has done sth illegal or dishonest 庇護；包庇；袒護 **SYN** **shield**

▸ **FOR DISEASE 檢查疾病** **3** [often passive] **~ sb (for sth)** to examine people in order to find out if they have a particular disease or illness 篩查；檢查：*Men over 55 should be regularly screened for prostate cancer.* * 55 歲以上的男性應定期做前列腺癌檢查。

▸ **CHECK 檢查** **4 ~ sb** (of a company, an organization, etc. 公司、組織等) to find out information about people who work or who want to work for you in order to make sure that they can be trusted 審查，調查（看是否可靠）：*Government employees may be screened by the security services.* 政府雇員可能要接受安全部門的審查。 **5 ~ sth** to check sth to see if it is suitable or if you want it 審查；篩選：*I use my voicemail to screen my phone calls.* 我用錄音信箱篩選打來的電話。

▸ **SHOW FILM/MOVIE/PROGRAMME 放映電影；播放節目** **6** [usually passive] **~ sth** to show a film/movie, etc. in a cinema/movie theater or on television 放映（電影）；播放（電視節目）：*a list of films to be screened as part of the festival* 作為節日活動部份內容擬放映的電影目錄 ➲ COLLOCATIONS at TELEVISION

PHR V **ˌscreen sth↔ˈoff** [often passive] to separate part of a room, etc. from the rest of it by putting a screen around it（用屏風等）隔開：*Beds can be screened off to give patients more privacy.* 可以把病牀隔開，以使病人少受干擾。 **ˌscreen sb↔ˈout** to decide not to allow sb to join an organization, enter a country, etc. because you think they may cause trouble 遴選後剔除某人；不准某人入境 **ˌscreen sth↔ˈout** to prevent sth harmful from entering or going through sth 遴選後剔除某物；遮擋某物穿透：*The ozone layer screens out dangerous rays from the sun.* 臭氧層能遮擋住來自太陽的有害射線。

ˈScreen Actors Guild *noun* (*abbr.* SAG) (in the US) an organization that protects the interests of actors in films and television（美國）影視演員協會

ˈscreen dump *noun* a copy of what is on a computer screen at a particular time; the act of printing this out（計算機）屏幕轉存，屏幕複製，屏幕打印，螢幕傾印

screener /ˈskriːnə(r)/ *noun* a person who checks people and their luggage at an airport（機場）安檢員

screen·ing /ˈskriːnɪŋ/ *noun* **1** [C] the act of showing a film/movie or television programme（電影的）放映；（電視節目的）播放：*This will be the movie's first screening in this country.* 這將是這部電影首次在這個國家上映。 **2** [U, C] the testing or examining of a large number of people or things for disease, faults, etc. 篩查：*breast cancer screening* 乳腺癌篩查

screen·play /ˈskriːnpleɪ/ *noun* the words that are written for a film/movie (= the SCRIPT), together with instructions for how it is to be acted and filmed 電影劇本 ➲ COLLOCATIONS at CINEMA

ˈscreen-print *verb* [T, I] **~ (sth)** to force ink or metal onto a surface through a screen of silk or artificial material to produce a picture 絲網壓印 ▸ **ˈscreen print** *noun*

ˈscreen saver *noun* a computer program that replaces a screen display on a computer with another, moving, display after a particular length of time, to stop the screen from being damaged 屏幕保護程序；螢幕保護程式

screen·shot /ˈskriːnʃɒt; *NAmE* -ʃɑːt/ *noun* (*computing* 計) an image of the display on a screen, used when showing how a program works 屏幕截圖，屏幕快照，螢幕快點（用於展示程序運行方式）

ˈscreen test *noun* a test to see if sb is suitable to appear in a film/movie（挑選電影演員時）試鏡頭

screen·writer /ˈskriːnraɪtə(r)/ *noun* a person who writes SCREENPLAYS 電影劇本作家 ➲ compare PLAYWRIGHT, SCRIPTWRITER

screw 🔑 /skruː/ *noun, verb*

■ *noun* **1** 🔑 [C] a thin pointed piece of metal like a nail with a raised SPIRAL line (called a THREAD) along it and a line or cross cut into its head. Screws are turned and pressed into wood, metal, etc. with a SCREWDRIVER in order to fasten two things together. 螺絲釘；螺絲：*One of the screws is loose.* 有一顆螺絲鬆了。◇ *Now tighten all the screws.* 現在把全部螺絲都擰緊。➲ COLLOCATIONS at DECORATE ➲ VISUAL VOCAB page V20 ➲ see also CORKSCREW *n.* **2** [C] an act of turning a screw（對螺絲的）旋擰 **3** [sing.] (*taboo, slang*) an act of having sex 性交 **4** [sing.] (*taboo, slang*) a partner in sex 性交對象：*a good screw* 好的性交對象 **5** [C] a PROPELLER on a ship, a boat or an aircraft 螺旋槳 **6** [C] (*BrE, slang*) a prison officer 監獄看守；獄警

IDM **have a ˈscrew loose** to be slightly strange in your behaviour 舉止略有異常；行為稍嫌古怪 **put the ˈscrews on (sb)** to force sb to do sth by frightening and threatening them 脅迫；威逼 ➲ more at TURN *n.*

■ *verb* **1** 🔑 [T] **~ sth + adv./prep.** to fasten one thing to another or make sth tight with a screw or screws 用螺絲固定（或擰牢）：*The bookcase is screwed to the wall.* 書架用螺絲固定在牆上了。◇ *You need to screw all the parts together.* 你得用螺絲把所有的零件固定在一起。◇ *Now screw down the lid.* 現在用螺絲將蓋子固定好。➲ compare UNSCREW **2** 🔑 [T] to twist sth around in order to fasten it in place 旋緊；擰緊：**~ sth + adv./prep.** *She screwed the cap back on the jar.* 她又把廣口瓶的蓋子擰上。◇ **~ sth + adj.** *Screw the bolt tight.* 把螺栓擰緊。➲ compare UNSCREW **3** 🔑 [I] **(+ adv./prep.)** to be attached by screwing 擰上去：*The bulb should just screw into the socket.* 把燈泡擰到燈口上就行。◇ *The lid simply screws on.* 這蓋子一擰就蓋好了。 **4** [T] to squeeze sth, especially a piece of paper, into a tight ball 把（紙等）揉成一團：**~ sth up (into sth)** *I screwed up the letter and threw it into the fire.* 我把那封信揉成一團，扔進了火裏。◇ **~ sth (up) into sth** *Screw the foil into a little ball.* 把箔紙揉成小團。➲ see also SCREWED-UP **5** [T] (*slang*) to cheat sb, especially by making them pay too much money for sth 詐騙（錢財等）：**~ sb** *We've been screwed.* 我們挨宰了。◇ **~ sb for sth** *How much did they screw you for* (= how much did you have to pay)? 他們坑了你多少錢？ **6** [I, T] **~ (sb)** (*taboo, slang*) to have sex with sb（和某人）性交

IDM **screw ˈhim, ˈyou, ˈthat, etc.** (*taboo, slang*) an offensive way of showing that you are annoyed or do not care about sb/sth 去他（或你）媽的；見他（或你、它）的鬼 **screw up your ˈcourage** to force yourself to be brave enough to do sth 鼓起勇氣：*I finally screwed up my courage and went to the dentist.* 我終於鼓起勇氣，去看了牙醫。➲ more at HEAD *n.*

PHR V **ˌscrew aˈround** (*taboo, slang*) to have sex with a lot of different people 亂搞；亂交 **ˌscrew sth ˈfrom/ˈout of sb** to force sb to give you sth 勒索；敲詐：*They screwed the money out of her by threats.* 他們威逼她交出了錢。 **ˌscrew ˈup** (*slang, especially NAmE*) to do sth badly or spoil sth 搞糟；攪亂；弄壞 **SYN** **mess up**：*You really screwed up there!* 你實在是搞了個一塌糊塗！

➲ related noun SCREW-UP **ˌscrew sb↔ˈup** (*slang*) to upset or confuse sb so much that they are not able to deal with problems in their life 使煩惱得不能正常生活；使神經不正常：*Her father's death really screwed her up.* 父親死後，她真是萬念俱灰。➲ see also SCREWED-UP **ˌscrew sth↔ˈup** **1** to fasten sth with screws 用螺絲固定：*to screw up a crate* 用螺絲釘把板條箱釘好 **2** (*BrE*) to fasten sth by turning it 擰牢；旋緊：*I screwed up the jar and put it back on the shelf.* 我把瓶子擰上蓋兒，放回擱架。**3** (*slang*) to do sth badly or spoil sth 搞糟；攪亂；弄壞：*Don't screw it up this time.* 這次可別搞砸了。➲ related noun SCREW-UP **ˌscrew your ˈeyes/ˈface↔up** to contract the muscles of your eyes or face because the light is too strong, you are in pain, etc.（因光線太強或疼痛等）瞇起眼睛，扭曲面部：*He took a sip of the medicine and screwed up his face.* 他喝了一小口藥後做了個怪相。

screw·ball /ˈskruːbɔːl/ *noun* (*informal, especially NAmE*) a strange or crazy person 怪人；狂人

screw·cap /ˈskruːkæp/ *noun* a top for a container, especially a wine bottle, that screws onto it（尤指酒瓶的）螺旋蓋，螺紋蓋 ▶ **screw·cap** *adj.* [only before noun]：*screwcap bottles/wine* 帶螺旋蓋的瓶子；螺旋蓋瓶裝葡萄酒

screw·driver /ˈskruːdraɪvə(r)/ *noun* **1** a tool with a narrow blade that is specially shaped at the end, used for turning screws 螺絲刀；改錐 ➲ **VISUAL VOCAB** page V20 **2** a COCKTAIL (= an alcoholic drink) made from VODKA and orange juice 伏特加橙汁雞尾酒；螺絲刀（雞尾酒）

ˌscrewed-ˈup *adj.* **1** (*informal*) upset and anxious, especially because of sth bad that has happened to you in the past（因以前有過不幸遭遇）焦慮而緊張的：*an extremely screwed-up kid* 一個十分神經質的孩子 **2** (*especially BrE*) twisted into a ball 揉起來的；搓成一團的：*a screwed-up tissue* 揉成一團的紙巾 **3** if your face or eyes are **screwed-up**, the muscles are tight, because you are worried, in pain, etc., or because the light is too bright（因擔憂、疼痛或光線太強等）面部扭曲，瞇起眼睛，皺着眉頭

ˈscrew-top (also **ˈscrew-topped**) *adj.* [only before noun] (of a container 容器) having a top or lid that screws onto it 有螺旋蓋的 ➲ **VISUAL VOCAB** page V33

ˈscrew-up *noun* (*pl.* **screw-ups**) (*slang*) an occasion when you do sth badly or spoil sth 搞糟；弄砸；出錯

screwy /ˈskruːi/ *adj.* (*informal*) strange or crazy 古怪的；荒誕的；瘋狂的

scrib·ble /ˈskrɪbl/ *verb, noun*

■ ***verb*** **1** [T, I] to write sth quickly and carelessly, especially because you do not have much time 草草記下，匆匆書寫（尤指因時間倉促）**SYN** **scrawl**：**~ sth** *He scribbled a note to his sister before leaving.* 臨行前，他給妹妹草草寫了一封短信。◇ **~ sth down** *She scribbled down her phone number and pushed it into his hand.* 她匆匆寫下自己的電話號碼，塞進他手裏。◇ **~ (away)** *Throughout the interview the journalists scribbled away furiously.* 在整個採訪過程中，記者忙不迭地記個不停。**2** [I] (**+ adv./prep.**) to draw marks that do not mean anything 胡寫；亂畫：*Someone had scribbled all over the table in crayon.* 不知誰用蠟筆胡寫亂畫，桌面上都塗滿了。

■ ***noun*** **1** [U, sing.] careless and untidy writing 潦草的文字 **SYN** **scrawl**：*How do you expect me to read this scribble?* 這種寫得歪歪扭扭的東西，讓我怎麼看？**2** [C, usually pl.] marks or pictures that seem to have no meaning 胡寫亂畫的東西 **SYN** **scrawl**：*The page was covered with a mass of scribbles.* 那頁紙上淨是胡寫亂畫的東西。

scrib·bler /ˈskrɪblə(r)/ *noun* **1** (*disapproving or humorous*) a journalist, author or other writer 耍筆桿子的 **2** (*CanE*) a book with plain paper for writing in, especially for children at school（尤指供在校兒童用的）練習本，習字本

scribe /skraɪb/ *noun* a person who made copies of written documents before printing was invented（印刷術發明之前的）抄寫員，抄書吏

scrim·mage /ˈskrɪmɪdʒ/ *noun* **1** a confused struggle or fight 混戰；群架；你爭我奪 **SYN** **scrum** **2** (in AMERICAN FOOTBALL 美式足球) a period of play that begins with the ball being placed on the ground 爭球 **3** (*NAmE*) a practice game of AMERICAN FOOTBALL, BASKETBALL, etc.（美式足球、籃球等的）隊內分組比賽，教學比賽

scrimp /skrɪmp/ *verb* [I] to spend very little money on the things that you need to live, especially so that you can save it to spend on sth else 省吃儉用，節衣縮食（尤指為了攢錢）：*They **scrimped and saved** to give the children a good education.* 他們省吃儉用，為的是攢錢讓孩子受到良好的教育。

scrip /skrɪp/ *noun* (*business* 商) an extra share in a business, given out instead of a DIVIDEND（股息的）臨時憑證；代價券

script /skrɪpt/ *noun, verb*

■ ***noun*** **1** [C] a written text of a play, film/movie, broadcast, talk, etc. 劇本；廣播（或講話等）稿：*That line isn't in the original script.* 原劇本中沒有那句台詞。**2** [U] writing done by hand 筆跡：*She admired his neat script.* 她欣賞他寫的一手好字。➲ see also MANUSCRIPT **3** [U, C] a set of letters in which a language is written（一種語言的）字母系統，字母表 **SYN** **alphabet**：*a document in Cyrillic script* 一份用西里爾字母書寫的文件 **4** [C] (*BrE*) a candidate's written answer or answers in an exam 筆試答卷 **5** [U, C] (*computing* 計) a series of instructions for a computer, carried out in a particular order, for example when a link in a website is clicked 腳本（程序）（計算機的一系列指令，按一定順序執行）：*The bug was caused by an error in the script.* 這個故障是由腳本程序出錯造成的。

■ ***verb*** [often passive] **~ sth** to write the script for a film/movie, play, etc. 為電影（或戲劇等）寫劇本

script·ed /ˈskrɪptɪd/ *adj.* read from a script 照書面稿唸的：*a scripted talk* 照稿子唸的講話 **OPP** **unscripted**

scrip·tor·ium /skrɪpˈtɔːriəm/ *noun* (*pl.* **scrip·tor·iums** or **scrip·toria** /-ˈtɔːriə/) (*old use*) a room for writing in, especially in a MONASTERY（尤指修道院的）繕寫室

scrip·ture /ˈskrɪptʃə(r)/ *noun* **1 Scripture** [U] (also **the Scriptures** [pl.]) the Bible《聖經》**2 scriptures** [pl.] the holy books of a particular religion（某宗教的）聖典，經文，經典：*Hindu scriptures* 印度教經文 ▶ **scrip·tural** /ˈskrɪptʃərəl/ *adj.*：*scriptural references*《聖經》引文

script·writer /ˈskrɪptraɪtə(r)/ *noun* a person who writes the words for films/movies, television and radio plays（電影、電視劇、廣播劇的）劇作家，編劇 ➲ compare PLAYWRIGHT, SCREENWRITER

scrof·ula /ˈskrɒfjʊlə; *NAmE* ˈskrɔːf-/ *noun* [U] (especially in the past) a disease in which the GLANDS swelled, probably a form of TUBERCULOSIS（尤指舊時）瘰癧（病毒導致腺體腫脹，一種結核病）

scroll /skrəʊl; *NAmE* skroʊl/ *noun, verb*

■ ***noun*** **1** a long roll of paper for writing on（供書寫的）長捲紙，卷軸 **2** a decoration cut in stone or wood with a curved shape like a roll of paper（石刻或木雕的）渦捲形裝飾

■ ***verb*** [I, T] (*computing* 計) to move text on a computer screen up or down so that you can read different parts of it 滾屏；滾動：**+ adv./prep.** *Use the arrow keys to scroll through the list of files.* 用箭頭鍵把文件目錄滾動一遍。◇ *Scroll down to the bottom of the document.* 向下滾動到文件末尾。◇ **~ sth** *Use the arrow keys to scroll the list of files.* 用箭頭鍵滾動文件目錄。

ˈscroll bar *noun* (*computing* 計) a strip at the edge of a computer screen that you use to scroll through a file with, using a mouse 滾動條 ➲ **VISUAL VOCAB** page V68

Scrooge /skruːdʒ/ *noun* [usually sing.] (*informal, disapproving*) a person who is very unwilling to spend money 吝嗇鬼；守財奴 **ORIGIN** From **Ebenezer Scrooge**, a character in Charles Dickens' *A Christmas Carol* who is extremely mean. 源自狄更斯小說《聖誕頌歌》中一個極其吝嗇的人物埃比尼澤•斯克魯奇（Ebenezer Scrooge）。

S

scrote /skrəʊt; *NAmE* skroʊt/ *noun* (*BrE, informal*) an insulting word for a man that you do not like or are angry with 混蛋（對男子的辱罵）

scro·tum /ˈskrəʊtəm; *NAmE* ˈskroʊ-/ *noun* (*pl.* **scro·tums** or **scrota** /ˈskrəʊtə; *NAmE* ˈskroʊ-/) the bag of skin that contains the TESTICLES in men and most male animals 陰囊

scrounge /skraʊndʒ/ *verb, noun*

■ ***verb*** [T, I] (*informal, disapproving*) to get sth from sb by asking them for it rather than by paying for it 白要；白拿 SYN **cadge**：**~ (sth) (off/from sb)** *He's always scrounging free meals off us.* 他老來我們家蹭飯吃。◇ **~ (for sth)** *What is she scrounging for this time?* 這次她又來要什麼？▸ **scroun·ger** *noun*：*a campaign against welfare scroungers* 抵制領福利金而不工作的懶人的運動

■ ***noun***

IDM **on the ˈscrounge** (*BrE, informal, disapproving*) trying to get sth by persuading sb to give it to you 討要；索要

scrub /skrʌb/ *verb, noun*

■ ***verb*** (**-bb-**) **1** [T, I] to clean sth by rubbing it hard, perhaps with a brush and usually with soap and water 擦洗；刷洗：**~ sth/yourself** *I found him in the kitchen, scrubbing the floor.* 我發現他在廚房擦地板。◇ **~ sth/yourself down** *She scrubbed the counters down with bleach.* 她用漂白劑把櫃枱擦洗乾淨。◇ **~ (at sth)** *The woman scrubbed at her face with a tissue.* 那女人用紙巾擦臉。◇ **~ sth/yourself + adj.** *Scrub the vegetables clean.* 把蔬菜刷洗乾淨。 **2** [T] **~ sth** (*informal*) to cancel sth that you have arranged to do 取消（原有安排）

PHR V **ˌscrub sth↔ˈoff | scrub sth off sth** to remove sth from the surface of an object by rubbing it hard with a brush, etc.（用刷子等）刷掉，擦掉：*This treatment involves scrubbing off the top layer of dead skin.* 這種治療需要把死皮的表層除去。 **ˌscrub sth↔ˈout** to clean the inside of sth by rubbing it hard with a brush and usually with soap and water（用刷子、肥皂等）把某物從裏到外擦洗乾淨 **ˌscrub ˈup** (of a doctor, nurse, etc. 醫生、護士等) to wash your hands and arms before performing a medical operation（手術前）擦洗手和臂

■ ***noun*** **1** [sing.] an act of scrubbing sth 擦洗；刷洗：*I've given the floor a good scrub.* 我把地板徹底擦洗了一遍。 **2** [U] small bushes and trees 灌木叢；矮樹叢：*The bird disappeared into the scrub.* 鳥消失在矮樹叢中。 **3** (also **scrub·land**) [U] an area of dry land covered with small bushes and trees 硬葉灌叢帶；低矮灌木叢林地 **4 scrubs** [pl.] (*technical* 術語) the special clothes worn by SURGEONS when they are doing medical operations 手術衣

scrub·ber /ˈskrʌbə(r)/ *noun* **1** (*BrE, informal*) an offensive word for a PROSTITUTE or for a woman who has sex with a lot of men 婊子；淫蕩女人 **2** a brush or other object that you use for cleaning things, for example pans（刷洗用的）刷子

ˈscrubbing brush (*BrE*) (*NAmE* **ˈscrub brush**) *noun* a stiff brush for cleaning floors and other surfaces（刷地板等的）硬毛刷，板刷

scrubby /ˈskrʌbi/ *adj.* **1** covered with small bushes and trees 長滿灌木和矮樹的；灌木叢生的：*a scrubby hillside* 灌木叢生的山坡 **2** (of trees 樹) small and not fully developed 低矮的；矮小的：*scrubby vegetation* 灌木植被

scrub·land /ˈskrʌblənd/ *noun* [U] = SCRUB (3)

ˈscrub nurse (*NAmE*) (*BrE* **ˈtheatre nurse**) *noun* a nurse with special training, who helps during operations 手術室護士

ˈscrub room *noun* a place in a hospital next to an operating room/theatre, where doctors and nurses get ready for operations（手術室隔壁的）刷手間，術前消毒室

scruff /skrʌf/ *noun* (*BrE, informal*) a dirty or untidy person 邋遢的人

IDM **by the scruff of the/sb's ˈneck** roughly holding the back of an animal's or person's neck 揪着動物（或人）的脖頸兒：*She grabbed him by the scruff of the neck and threw him out.* 她一把抓住他的脖子，將他扔了出去。

scruffy /ˈskrʌfi/ *adj.* (**scruff·ier**, **scruffi·est**) (*informal*) dirty or untidy 不整潔的；邋遢的 SYN **shabby**：*He looked a little scruffy.* 他看着有點邋遢。◇ *scruffy pair of jeans* 髒兮兮的牛仔褲 ▸ **scruff·ily** *adv.* **scruffi·ness** *noun* [U]

scrum /skrʌm/ *noun* **1** (also *formal* **scrum·mage**) a part of a RUGBY game when players from both sides link themselves together in a group, with their heads down, and push against the other side. The ball is then thrown between them and each side tries to get it.（橄欖球的）並列爭球 **2** the group of players who link themselves together in a scrum（橄欖球）並列爭球的全體前鋒 **3** (*especially BrE*) a crowd of people who are pushing each other 相互擁擠的人群：*There was a real scrum when the bus arrived.* 公共汽車到站時，人們一窩蜂都往上擠。

ˌscrum ˈhalf *noun* (in RUGBY 橄欖球) a player who puts the ball into the scrum 爭球前衛；傳鋒

scrum·mage /ˈskrʌmɪdʒ/ *noun, verb*

■ ***noun*** (*formal*) = SCRUM (1)

■ ***verb*** (also **ˌscrum ˈdown**) [I] (*sport* 體) to form a SCRUM during a game of RUGBY（橄欖球的）並列爭球

scrummy /ˈskrʌmi/ *adj.* (**scrum·mier**, **scrum·mi·est**) (*BrE, informal*) tasting very good 味道極好的；美味的 SYN **delicious**：*a scrummy cake* 非常可口的蛋糕

scrump·tious /ˈskrʌmpʃəs/ *adj.* (*informal*) tasting very good 美味的；非常好吃的 SYN **delicious**

scrumpy /ˈskrʌmpi/ *noun* [U] (*BrE*) a type of strong CIDER (= an alcoholic drink made from apples), made especially in the west of England（尤指產於英格蘭西部的）烈性蘋果酒

scrunch /skrʌntʃ/ *verb* **1** [I] to make a loud sound like the one that is made when you walk on GRAVEL (= small stones) 發咔嚓咔嚓聲；發出嘎吱聲 SYN **crunch**：*The snow scrunched underfoot.* 雪在腳下發出嘎吱嘎吱的聲音。 **2** [T] **~ sth (up)** to squeeze sth into a small round shape in your hands 把…揉成一團：*He scrunched up the note and threw it on the fire.* 他把便條揉成一團，扔進了火裏。 **3** [T] **~ sth (up)** to make sth become smaller 使蜷縮；使收縮：*The hedgehog scrunched itself up into a ball.* 刺猬蜷成一個圓球。 **4** [T] **~ sth** to create a HAIRSTYLE with loose curls by squeezing the hair with the hands（用手揉捏頭髮）做鬆鬈髮型 ▸ **scrunch** *noun* [sing.]：*the scrunch of tyres on the gravel* 輪胎碾在礫石上發出的咔嚓咔嚓聲

ˌscrunch-ˈdry *verb* **~ sth** to create a HAIRSTYLE with loose curls by drying the hair while squeezing it with your hand 用手擠乾（頭髮）以使鬆散鬈曲

scrunchy (also **scrunchie**) /ˈskrʌntʃi/ *noun* (*pl.* **-ies**) a RUBBER BAND covered in cloth used to fasten hair away from the face（包）布髮箍，布髮圈

scru·ple /ˈskruːpl/ *noun, verb*

■ ***noun*** [C, usually pl., U] a feeling that prevents you from doing sth that you think may be morally wrong（道德上的）顧忌，顧慮：*I overcame my moral scruples.* 我拋開了道德方面的顧慮。◇ *He* ***had no scruples about*** *spying on her.* 他肆無忌憚地暗中盯着她。◇ *She is totally* ***without scruple.*** 她完全無所顧忌。

■ ***verb*** [I] **not scruple to do sth** (*formal*) to be willing to do sth even if it might be wrong or immoral 無所顧忌地做；肆無忌憚地幹

scru·pu·lous /ˈskruːpjələs/ *adj.* **1** careful about paying attention to every detail 仔細的；細緻的；一絲不苟的 SYN **meticulous**：*You must be scrupulous about hygiene when you're preparing a baby's feed.* 給嬰兒準備食物時，對衞生絲毫馬虎不得。◇ *scrupulous attention to detail* 體察入微 **2 ~ (in sth/in doing sth)** careful to be honest and do what is right 審慎正直的；恪守道德規範的：*He was scrupulous in all his business dealings.* 他在所做的一切商業交易中都是清白的。 OPP **unscrupulous** ▸ **scru·pu·lous·ly** *adv.*：*Her house is scrupulously clean.* 她的家乾乾淨淨，纖塵不染。◇ *to be scrupulously honest* 極為誠實 **scru·pu·lous·ness** *noun* [U]

S

scru·tin·eer /ˌskruːtəˈnɪə(r); *NAmE* -ˈnɪr/ *noun* (*BrE*) a person who checks that an election or other vote is organized correctly and fairly 選舉（或其他投票）監督員；監票人

scru·tin·ize (*BrE* also **-ise**) /ˈskruːtənaɪz/ *verb* **~ sb/sth** to look at or examine sb/sth carefully 仔細查看；認真檢查；細緻審查：*She leaned forward to scrutinize their faces.* 她探身向前，端詳他們的面容。◇ *The statement was carefully scrutinized before publication.* 聲明在發表前經過仔細審閱。

scru·tiny /ˈskruːtəni/ *noun* [U] (*formal*) careful and thorough examination 仔細檢查；認真徹底的審查 **SYN inspection**：*Her argument doesn't really stand up to scrutiny.* 她的觀點經不起認真推敲。◇ *Foreign policy has* ***come under*** *close* ***scrutiny*** *recently.* 近來，政府的外交政策受到了認真徹底的審查。◇ *The documents should be available for* ***public scrutiny***. 這些文件須公諸於世，交由公眾審議。

scuba-diving /ˈskuːbə daɪvɪŋ/ (also **scuba**) *noun* [U] the sport or activity of swimming underwater using special breathing equipment consisting of a container of air which you carry on your back and a tube through which you breathe the air 戴水肺潛水：*to go scuba-diving* 進行戴水肺潛水 ➲ VISUAL VOCAB page V40

scud /skʌd/ *verb* (**-dd-**) [I] **+ adv./prep.** (*literary*) (of clouds 雲) to move quickly across the sky 飛掠；疾飛

scuff /skʌf/ *verb* **1 ~ sth (on sth)** to make a mark on the smooth surface of sth when you rub it against sth rough 磨損；磨壞：*I scuffed the heel of my shoe on the stonework.* 我的鞋跟被石板路面磨壞了。**2 ~ your feet, heels, etc.** to drag your feet along the ground as you walk 拖着腳走 ▸ **scuffed** *adj.*：*After only one day, his shoes were already scuffed and dirty.* 只一天，他的鞋就穿髒磨壞了。**scuff** (also **ˈscuff mark**) *noun*

scuf·fle /ˈskʌfl/ *noun, verb*

■ ***noun*** **~ (with sb)** | **~ (between A and B)** a short and not very violent fight or struggle（短暫而不太激烈的）肢體摩擦，衝突：***Scuffles broke out*** *between police and demonstrators.* 警察和示威者之間發生了衝突。➲ SYNONYMS at FIGHT

■ ***verb*** **1** [I] **~ (with sb)** (of two or more people 兩人或多人之間) to fight or struggle with each other for a short time, in a way that is not very serious（短暫而不嚴重地）扭打，衝突，爭鬥：*She scuffled with photographers as she left her hotel.* 在離開所住的旅館時，她和一些攝影記者發生了衝突。**2** [I] **+ adv./prep.** to move quickly making a quiet rubbing noise 窸窸窣窣地疾行：*Some animal was scuffling in the bushes.* 有隻動物在灌木叢中窸窸窣窣地穿行。

scuf·fling /ˈskʌflɪŋ/ *noun* [U] a low noise made by sth moving around（物體來回移動發出的）窸窸窣窣的響聲：*He could hear whispering and scuffling on the other side of the door.* 他聽見門那邊的低語聲和窸窸窣窣的走動聲。

scull /skʌl/ *noun, verb*

■ ***noun*** **1** [C, usually pl.] one of a pair of small OARS used by a single person ROWING a boat, one in each hand（單人雙槳船上的）短槳 **2 sculls** [pl.] a race between small light boats with pairs of sculls 雙槳賽艇比賽：***single/double sculls*** (= with one/two people in each boat) 單人／雙人雙槳賽艇比賽 **3** [C] a small light boat used in sculls races 雙槳賽艇

■ ***verb*** [I] to ROW a boat using sculls 用雙槳划船

scull·er /ˈskʌlə(r)/ *noun* a person who ROWS with sculls 划雙槳者；雙槳賽艇運動員

scull·ery /ˈskʌləri/ *noun* (*pl.* **-ies**) a small room next to the kitchen in an old house, originally used for washing dishes, etc. 洗滌室（老房子中設在廚房旁，洗滌餐具用）

scull·ing /ˈskʌlɪŋ/ *noun* [U] the sport of racing with SCULLS 雙槳賽艇比賽

sculpt /skʌlpt/ *verb* [usually passive] **1** to make figures or objects by CARVING or shaping wood, stone, CLAY, metal, etc. 雕刻；雕塑：**~ sth (in sth)** *a display of animals sculpted in ice* 冰雕動物展 ◇ **~ sth (from/out of sth)** *The figures were sculpted from single blocks of marble.* 這些雕像都是用整塊大理石雕成的。➲ COLLOCATIONS at ART **2 ~ sth** to give sth a particular shape 使具有某種形狀：*a coastline sculpted by the wind and sea* 在風和海水的作用下形成的海岸線

sculp·tor /ˈskʌlptə(r)/ *noun* a person who makes SCULPTURES 雕刻家；雕塑家

sculp·tress /ˈskʌlptrəs/ *noun* a woman who makes SCULPTURES 女雕刻家；女雕塑家 ➲ note at GENDER

sculp·ture /ˈskʌlptʃə(r)/ *noun* **1** [C, U] a work of art that is a solid figure or object made by CARVING or shaping wood, stone, CLAY, metal, etc. 雕像；雕塑品；雕刻品：*a marble sculpture of Venus* 維納斯的大理石雕像 ◇ *He collects modern sculpture.* 他收藏現代雕塑。➲ COLLOCATIONS at ART **2** [U] the art of making sculptures 雕刻術；雕塑術：*the techniques of sculpture in stone* 石雕技藝 ▸ **sculp·tural** /ˈskʌlptʃərəl/ *adj.*：*sculptural decoration* 雕飾

sculp·tured /ˈskʌlptʃəd; *NAmE* -tʃərd/ *adj.* [usually before noun] **1** (of figures or objects 人、物形象) CARVED or shaped from wood, stone, CLAY, metal, etc. 雕刻的；雕塑的 **2** (*approving*) (of part of the body 人體部位) having a clear and pleasing shape 線條清晰美觀的：*sculptured cheekbones* 像雕塑成的漂亮的顴骨

scum /skʌm/ *noun* **1** [U, sing.] a layer of bubbles or an unpleasant substance that forms on the surface of a liquid 浮沫；浮垢；浮渣：*Skim off any scum.* 撇淨浮沫。◇ *stinking water covered by a thick green scum* 蓋着厚厚一層綠色浮垢的臭水 **2** [U, pl.] (*informal*) an insulting word for people that you strongly disapprove of（罵人的話）渣滓，敗類：*Don't waste your sympathy on scum like that.* 對這樣的渣滓你沒必要同情。◇ *Drug dealers are* ***the scum of the earth*** (= the worst people there are). 毒品販子是社會渣滓。▸ **scummy** /ˈskʌmi/ *adj.*：*scummy water* 有浮垢的水 ◇ *scummy people dropping litter* 不講公德、亂丟雜物的人

scum·bag /ˈskʌmbæg/ *noun* (*slang, offensive*) an unpleasant person 討厭的人；卑鄙小人

scunge /skʌndʒ/ *noun* (*AustralE, NZE, informal*) **1** [U] dirt 污垢；塵土 **2** [C] an unpleasant person 討厭的人 **3** [C] a person who does not like to spend money 吝嗇鬼；摳門的人

scungy /ˈskʌndʒi/ *adj.* (**scun·gier**, **scun·gi·est**) (*AustralE, NZE, informal*) **1** dirty and unpleasant 骯髒的；污穢的 **2** not liking to spend money 吝嗇的；摳門的

scup·per /ˈskʌpə(r)/ *verb* **~ sth** (*BrE, informal*) to cause sb/sth to fail 使泡湯；使成泡影 **SYN foil**：*The residents' protests scuppered his plans for developing the land.* 居民的抗議使他開發這片土地的計劃泡了湯。

scur·ril·ous /ˈskʌrələs; *NAmE* ˈskɜːr-/ *adj.* (*formal*) very rude and insulting, and intended to damage sb's reputation 惡語誹謗的；用污言穢語謾罵的；辱罵的：*scurrilous rumours* 惡意中傷的謠言 ▸ **scur·ril·ous·ly** *adv.*

scurry /ˈskʌri; *NAmE* ˈskɜːri/ *verb* (**scur·ries**, **scurry·ing**, **scur·ried**, **scur·ried**) [I] **+ adv./prep.** to run with quick short steps 碎步疾跑 **SYN scuttle**：*She said goodbye and scurried back to work.* 她說聲再見，然後扭頭跑回去幹活了。◇ *Ants scurried around the pile of rotting food.* 螞蟻圍着那堆腐爛的食物跑來跑去。▸ **scurry** *noun* [sing.]

scurvy /ˈskɜːvi; *NAmE* ˈskɜːrvi/ *noun* [U] a disease caused by a lack of VITAMIN C from not eating enough fruit and vegetables 壞血病

scut·tle /ˈskʌtl/ *verb, noun*

■ ***verb*** **1** [I] **+ adv./prep.** to run with quick short steps 碎步疾跑 **SYN scurry**：*She scuttled off when she heard the sound of his voice.* 聽到他的說話聲，她趕緊跑開了。◇ *He held his breath as a rat scuttled past.* 見一隻老鼠跑過，他屏住了呼吸。**2** [T] **~ sth** to deliberately cause sth to fail（故意）破壞，阻止，阻撓 **SYN foil**：*Shareholders successfully scuttled the deal.* 股東成功地阻止了這樁交易。**3** [T] **~ sth** to sink a ship deliberately by making holes in the side or bottom of it 鑿沉（船）

■ ***noun*** = COAL SCUTTLE

S

scuttle·butt /ˈskʌtlbʌt/ *noun* [U] (*NAmE, slang*) stories about other people's private lives, that may be unkind or not true 流言蜚語；謠言 SYN **gossip**

scuzzy /ˈskʌzi/ *adj.* (**scuzz·ier**, **scuz·zi·est**) (*informal, especially NAmE*) dirty and unpleasant 骯髒討厭的；邋遢的

Scylla and Cha·ryb·dis /ˌsɪlə ənd kəˈrɪbdɪs; *NAmE* also tʃəˈr-/ *noun* used to refer to a situation in which an attempt to avoid one danger increases the risk from another danger 腹背受敵；進退兩難 ORIGIN From ancient Greek stories in which a female sea creature (called Scylla) tried to catch and eat sailors who passed between her cave and a whirlpool (called Charybdis). 源自古希臘神話，女海妖斯庫拉（Scylla）試圖抓住並吃掉從她的洞穴和卡律布狄斯漩渦（Charybdis）之間經過的水手。

scythe /saɪð/ *noun, verb*

- ***noun*** a tool with a long handle and a slightly curved blade, used for cutting long grass, etc. 長柄大鐮刀
- ***verb*** [T, I] **~ (sth)** to cut grass, etc. with a scythe 用長柄大鐮刀割：*the scent of newly scythed grass* 新割下的草散發的清香

SD card /ˌes ˈdiː kɑːd; *NAmE* kɑːrd/ *noun* the abbreviation for 'secure digital card' (= a type of MEMORY CARD, used with DIGITAL cameras, mobile/cell phones, music players, etc.) 閃存卡，SD 卡（全寫為 secure digital card，數字照相機、手機、音樂播放器等所使用的內存卡）

SDHC card /ˌes diː eɪtʃ ˈsiː kɑːd; *NAmE* kɑːrd/ *noun* the abbreviation for 'secure digital high capacity card' (= a type of MEMORY CARD, that can store more data than an SD card) 大容量閃存卡，大容量 SD 卡（全寫為 secure digital high capacity card，貯存容量超過 SD 卡）

the SDLP /ˌes diː el ˈpiː/ *abbr.* (in Northern Ireland) Social Democratic and Labour Party (a political party of the left that is supported mainly by Catholics) 社會民主工黨（北愛爾蘭主要由天主教徒支持的左翼政黨）

SE *abbr.* south-east; south-eastern 東南方（的）；東南部（的）：*SE Asia* 東南亞

sea 0- /siː/ *noun*

1 0- (often **the sea**) [U] (also *literary* **seas** [pl.]) (*especially BrE*) the salt water that covers most of the earth's surface and surrounds its continents and islands 海；海洋：*to travel* ***by sea*** 海上旅行 ◇ *a cottage* ***by the sea*** 海濱小屋 ◇ *The waste was dumped* ***in the sea.*** 廢物倒入海中。◇ *The wreck is lying at the bottom of the sea.* 沉船躺在海底。◇ *We left port and headed for* ***the open sea*** (= far away from land). 我們離開港口，向外海駛去。◇ *the cold seas of the Arctic* 北極地區寒冷的海洋 ◇ *a sea voyage* 海上航行 ◇ *a hotel room with sea view* 看得見大海的旅館客房 ➲ see also THE HIGH SEAS, OCEAN **2** 0- [C] (often **Sea**, especially as part of a name 常作 Sea，尤作名稱的一部份) a large area of salt water that is part of an ocean or surrounded by land 海：*the North Sea* 北海 ◇ *the Caspian Sea* 裏海 ➲ VISUAL VOCAB pages V4, V5 **3** 0- [C] (also **seas** [pl.]) the movement of the waves of the sea 海面情況；海浪狀況：*It was a calm sea.* 海上風平浪靜。◇ *The sea was very rough.* 海上風急浪高。**4** [sing.] **~ of sth** a large amount of sth that stretches over a wide area 大量；茫茫一片：*He looked down at the sea of smiling faces before him.* 他看着眼前這笑臉的海洋。

IDM **at ˈsea 1** 0- on the sea, especially in a ship, or in the sea 在海上（尤指乘船）；在海裏：*It happened on the second night at sea.* 事情發生在出海後的第二天夜裏。◇ *They were* ***lost at sea.*** 他們在海上迷失了方向。**2** confused and not knowing what to do 困惑；茫然；不知所措：*I'm* ***all at sea*** *with these new regulations.* 我全然不懂這些新的規章。**go to ˈsea** to become a sailor 去當水手；當海員 **out to ˈsea** far away from land where the sea is deepest 向（或在）外海：*She fell overboard and was swept out to sea.* 她從船上落入水中，被海浪沖向外海。**put (out) to ˈsea** to leave a port or HARBOUR by ship or boat 起航；出海 ➲ more at DEVIL, FISH *n.*

British/American 英式/美式英語

sea / ocean

- In *BrE*, the usual word for the mass of salt water that covers most of the earth's surface is the **sea**. In *NAmE*, the usual word is the **ocean**. 在英式英語中，覆蓋地球表面大部份地區的大片海水通常用 sea 表示。美式英語則通常用 ocean：*A swimmer drowned in the sea/ocean this morning.* 今天早上一名游泳者在海裏淹死了。
- The names of particular areas of seas, however, are fixed. 然而，特定的海洋名稱用 sea 或 ocean 是固定的：*the Mediterranean Sea* 地中海 ◇ *the Atlantic Ocean* 大西洋
- **Sea/ocean** are also used if you go to the coast on holiday/vacation. 到海濱度假亦可用 sea/ocean：*We're spending a week by the sea/at the ocean in June.* 我們六月份要在海濱度假一個星期。In *NAmE* it is also common to say 美式英語亦常說：*We're going to the beach for vacation.* 我們要去海濱度假。

➲ note at COAST

ˌsea ˈair *noun* [U] air near the sea/ocean, thought to be good for the health 海邊的空氣：*a breath of sea air* 呼吸一下海邊的空氣

ˈsea anemone *noun* a simple, brightly coloured sea creature that sticks onto rocks and looks like a flower 海葵

the sea·bed /ˈsiːbed/ *noun* [sing.] the floor of the sea/ocean 海底；海牀

sea·bird /ˈsiːbɜːd; *NAmE* -bɜːrd/ *noun* a bird that lives close to the sea, for example on CLIFFS or islands, and gets its food from it 海鳥 ➲ VISUAL VOCAB page V12

sea·board /ˈsiːbɔːd; *NAmE* -bɔːrd/ *noun* the part of a country that is along its coast 沿海地區；海濱：*Australia's eastern seaboard* 澳大利亞東部沿海地區

sea·borg·ium /siːˈbɔːɡiəm; *NAmE* -ˈbɔːrg-/ *noun* [U] (*symb.* **Sg**) a RADIOACTIVE chemical element. Seaborgium is produced when atoms COLLIDE (= crash into each other). 𨭎（放射性化學元素）

sea·borne /ˈsiːbɔːn; *NAmE* -bɔːrn/ *adj.* [only before noun] carried in ships 海運的：*a seaborne invasion* 海上入侵

ˌsea ˈbreeze *noun* a wind blowing from the sea/ocean towards the land（從海洋吹向陸地的）海風

ˈsea change *noun* [usually sing.] a strong and noticeable change in a situation 大轉變；巨變

ˌsea ˈcucumber *noun* an INVERTEBRATE animal that lives in the sea, with a thick body that is covered with lumps 海參

ˈsea dog *noun* (*informal*) a sailor who is old or who has a lot of experience 老水手；經驗豐富的水手

sea·farer /ˈsiːfeərə(r); *NAmE* -fer-/ *noun* (*old-fashioned* or *formal*) a sailor 水手；海員

sea·far·ing /ˈsiːfeərɪŋ; *NAmE* -fer-/ *adj.* [only before noun] connected with work or travel on the sea/ocean 海上勞作（或航行）的：*a seafaring nation* 航海民族 ▶ **sea·far·ing** *noun* [U]

ˈsea fish *noun* (*pl.* **sea fish**) a fish that lives in the sea, rather than in rivers or lakes 海魚

sea·food /ˈsiːfuːd/ *noun* [U] fish and sea creatures that can be eaten, especially SHELLFISH 海味，海鮮（尤指甲殼類）：*a seafood restaurant* 海鮮館 ◇ *a seafood cocktail* 海鮮冷盤

ˈsea fret *noun* = FRET *n.* (2)

sea·front /ˈsiːfrʌnt/ (often **the seafront**) *noun* [sing.] the part of a town facing the sea/ocean（城鎮的）濱海區，面海地區：*the grand houses along the seafront* 濱海區的豪宅

sea·going /ˈsiːɡəʊɪŋ; *NAmE* -ɡoʊ-/ *adj.* [only before noun] (of ships 船隻) built for crossing the sea/ocean 遠洋航行的

sea·grass /ˈsiːɡrɑːs; *NAmE* -ɡræs/ *noun* [U] a plant like grass that grows in or close to the sea 海草

ˌsea-ˈgreen *adj.* bluish-green in colour, like the sea（像海水似的）淡藍綠色的；海綠色的 ▸ **ˌsea ˈgreen** *noun* [U]

sea·gull /ˈsiːɡʌl/ *noun* = GULL：*a flock of seagulls* 一群海鷗

ˈsea horse *noun* a small sea fish that swims in a vertical position and has a head that looks like the head of a horse 海馬

seal /siːl/ *verb, noun*

■ ***verb***

▸ **CLOSE ENVELOPE** 封上信封 **1** ~ sth (up/down) to close an envelope, etc. by sticking the edges of the opening together 封上（信封）：*Make sure you've signed the cheque before sealing the envelope.* 一定要在支票上簽了名再封信封。◇ *a* ***sealed bid*** (= one that is kept in a sealed envelope and therefore remains secret until all other bids have been received) 密封（投）標

▸ **CLOSE CONTAINER** 密封容器 **2** [often passive] **~ sth** (**up**) (**with sth**) to close a container tightly or fill a crack, etc., especially so that air, liquid, etc. cannot get in or out 密封（容器）：*The organs are kept in sealed plastic bags.* 這些器官保存在密封塑料袋裏。

▸ **COVER SURFACE** 覆蓋表面 **3** [often passive] **~ sth** (**with sth**) to cover the surface of sth with a substance in order to protect it 封蓋…的表面：*The floors had been stripped and sealed with varnish.* 地板上東西挪空，塗上了清漆。

▸ **MAKE STH DEFINITE** 確定 **4 ~ sth** to make sth definite, so that it cannot be changed or argued about 確定；明確定下來；使成定局：*to seal a contract* 訂立合同 ◇ *They drank a glass of wine to seal their new friendship.* 他們乾了一杯，交成朋友。◇ *The discovery of new evidence* ***sealed his fate*** (= nothing could prevent what was going to happen to him). 新發現的證據決定了他的命運。

▸ **CLOSE BORDERS/EXITS** 關閉邊界／出口 **5 ~ sth** (of the police, army, etc. 警察、軍隊等) to prevent people from passing through a place 關閉；封閉；封鎖：*Troops have sealed the borders between the countries.* 軍隊已關閉了兩國邊界。**IDM** see LIP, SIGN *v.*

PHR V **ˌseal sth↔ˈin** to prevent sth that is contained in sth else from escaping 把…封閉在裏邊 **ˈseal sth in sth** to put sth in an envelope, container, etc. and seal it 把…封閉在…裏：*The body was sealed in a lead coffin.* 屍體安放在密閉的鉛棺中。**ˌseal sth↔ˈoff** (of the police, army 警察、軍隊) to prevent people from entering a particular area 封鎖；封閉

■ ***noun***

▸ **OFFICIAL MARK** 印章 **1** [C] an official design or mark, stamped on a document to show that it is genuine and carries the authority of a particular person or organization 印章；圖章；璽；印記：*The letter bore the president's seal.* 信上蓋有總統的印章。

▸ **MAKING STH DEFINITE** 確認 **2** [sing.] a thing that makes sth definite 表示確認的事物；保證；信物：*The project has been given the government's* ***seal of approval*** (= official approval). 項目已由政府正式批准。◇ *I looked upon the gift as a seal on our friendship.* 我把你的禮物看作我們之間友誼的見證。

▸ **ON CONTAINERS** 容器 **3** [C] a substance, strip of material, etc. used to fill a crack so that air, liquid, etc. cannot get in or out 密封墊（或帶等）：*a jar with a rubber seal in the lid* 蓋子上有密封墊的廣口瓶 ◇ *Only drink bottled water and check the seal isn't broken.* 只喝瓶裝水，並且要看封口開了沒有。

▸ **ON LETTERS/BOXES** 信件；盒子 **4** [C] a piece of WAX (= a soft substance produced by BEES), soft metal or paper that is placed across the opening of sth such as a letter or box and which has to be broken before the letter or box can be opened 封蠟；封鉛；封條；火漆：*He broke the wax seal and unrolled the paper.* 他揭去封蠟，把紙捲展開。**5** [C] a piece of metal, a ring, etc. with a design on it, used for stamping a WAX or metal seal 封蠟模（印）；封鉛模（印）

▸ **SEA ANIMAL** 海洋動物 **6** [C] a sea animal that eats fish and lives around coasts. There are many types of seal, some of which are hunted for their fur. 海豹：*a colony of seals* 一群海豹 ◇ *grey seals basking on the rocks* 在岩石上曬太陽的灰海豹

IDM **set the ˈseal on sth** (*formal*) to make sth definite or complete 使某事萬無一失；使某事圓滿：*Her election to the premiership set the seal on a remarkable political career.* 當選總理使她的政治生涯燦爛輝煌。**under ˈseal** (*formal*) (of a document 文件) in a sealed envelope that cannot be opened before a particular time 密封；加蓋印信

ˈsea lane *noun* an official route at sea that is regularly used by ships 海上航路；海上航線

seal·ant /ˈsiːlənt/ (also **seal·er**) *noun* [U, C] a substance that is put onto a surface to stop air, water, etc. from entering or escaping from it 密封劑；密封膠；防滲漏劑

ˈsea legs *noun* [pl.] the ability to walk easily on a moving ship and not to feel sick at sea 在顛簸的船上行走自如的本領；不暈船的本領：*It won't take you long to find your sea legs.* 不用多久你就會習慣船上生活。

seal·er /ˈsiːlə(r)/ *noun* **1** = SEALANT **2** a person who hunts SEALS 捕獵海豹者

ˈsea level *noun* [U] the average height of the sea/ocean, used as the basis for measuring the height of all places on land 海平面：*50 metres above sea level* 海拔 50 米

sea·lift /ˈsiːlɪft/ *noun* an operation to take people, soldiers, food, etc. to or from an area by ship, especially in an emergency（尤指緊急）海上運輸，海上補給 ▸ **sea·lift** *verb* ➲ compare AIRLIFT

seal·ing /ˈsiːlɪŋ/ *noun* [U] the activity of hunting SEALS 海豹捕獵

ˈsealing wax *noun* [U] a type of WAX that melts quickly when it is heated and becomes hard quickly when it cools, used in the past for SEALING letters, etc. 封蠟；火漆

ˈsea lion *noun* a large SEAL (= a sea animal with thick fur, that eats fish and lives around the coast) that lives by the Pacific Ocean 海獅

seal·skin /ˈsiːlskɪn/ *noun* [U] the skin and fur of some types of SEAL, used for making clothes 海豹皮（用作衣料）

seam /siːm/ *noun* **1** a line along which two edges of cloth, etc. are joined or sewn together（縫合兩塊布等的）線縫，接縫：*a shoulder seam* 衣服肩膀上的接縫 **2** a thin layer of coal or other material, between layers of rock under the ground 礦層；煤層：*They struck a* ***rich seam*** *of iron ore.* 他們開出一個富鐵礦層。◇ (*figurative*) *The book is a* ***rich seam of*** *information.* 這本書是一座豐富的知識寶庫。**3** a line where two edges meet, for example the edges of wooden boards（合在一起的兩塊木板等之間的）接縫，縫隙，裂縫

IDM **be bursting/bulging at the ˈseams** (*informal*) to be very full, especially of people 人滿為患；使幾乎脹破 **be falling/coming apart at the ˈseams** (*informal*) to be going very badly wrong and likely to stop functioning completely 接近崩潰；快要散架：*She was falling apart at the seams, spending most of her time in tears.* 她成天淚汪汪的，都快垮了。➲ more at FRAY *v.*

sea·man /ˈsiːmən/ *noun* (*pl.* **-men** /-mən/) a member of the navy or a sailor on a ship below the rank of an officer 水兵；水手；海員：*Seaman Bates*《水手貝茨》◇ *a merchant seaman* 商船船員 ➲ see also ABLE SEAMAN, ORDINARY SEAMAN

sea·man·ship /ˈsiːmənʃɪp/ *noun* [U] skill in sailing a boat or ship 航海術；船舶駕駛術

seamed /siːmd/ *adj.* **1** having a seam or seams 有（接）縫的：*seamed stockings* 有縫長襪 **2** (*literary*) covered with deep lines 佈滿皺紋的：*an old man with a brown seamed face* 棕色的臉上佈滿皺紋的老人

ˈsea mile *noun* = NAUTICAL MILE

seam·less /ˈsiːmləs/ *adj.* **1** without a SEAM 無（接）縫的：*a seamless garment* 無縫衣服 **2** with no spaces or pauses between one part and the next（兩部份之間）無空隙的，不停頓的：*a seamless flow of talk* 連貫流暢的談話 ▸ **seam·less·ly** *adv.*

seam·stress /ˈsiːmstrəs; ˈsem-/ *noun* (*old-fashioned*) a woman who can sew and make clothes or whose job is sewing and making clothes 會縫紉的女人；女裁縫

seamy /ˈsiːmi/ *adj.* (**seam·ier**, **seami·est**) unpleasant and immoral 污穢的；骯髒醜惡的 SYN **sordid**：*a seamy sex scandal* 齷齪的性醜聞 ◇ *the* **seamier side of** *life* 生活的陰暗面

se·ance /ˈseɪɒ̃s; *NAmE* ˈseɪɑːns/ *noun* a meeting at which people try to make contact with and talk to the spirits of dead people 降神會（設法和亡靈説話）

sea·plane /ˈsiːpleɪn/ (*NAmE* also **hydro·plane**) *noun* a plane that can take off from and land on water 水上飛機 ➲ VISUAL VOCAB page V53

sea·port /ˈsiːpɔːt; *NAmE* -pɔːrt/ *noun* a town with a HARBOUR used by large ships 海港城市：*the Baltic seaports* 波羅的海港口城市

ˈ**sea power** *noun* **1** [U] the ability to control the seas with a strong navy 海上力量；海軍實力 **2** [C] a country with a strong navy 海軍強國

sear /sɪə(r); *NAmE* sɪr/ *verb* **1** [T] **~ sth** to burn the surface of sth in a way that is sudden and powerful 燒灼；灼傷；烤焦；輕煎：*The heat of the sun seared their faces.* 烈日把他們的臉都曬傷了。◇ *Sear the meat first* (= cook the outside of it quickly at a high temperature) *to retain its juices.* 先把肉稍煎一下以保持肉汁。 **2** [I, T] (*formal*) to cause sb to feel sudden and great pain 使驟然感到劇痛：**+ adv./prep.** *The pain seared along her arm.* 她的胳膊一陣劇痛。◇ **~ sb** *Feelings of guilt seared him.* 他深感內疚。➲ see also SEARING

search 0━ /sɜːtʃ; *NAmE* sɜːrtʃ/ *noun, verb*

■ *noun* **1** 0━ **~ (for sb/sth)** an attempt to find sb/sth, especially by looking carefully for them/it 搜索；搜尋；搜查；查找：*a long search for the murder weapon* 長時間搜尋殺人兇器 ◇ *Detectives carried out a thorough search of the building.* 偵探對那棟大樓進行了徹底的搜查。◇ *She went into the kitchen* **in search of** (= looking for) *a drink.* 她進了廚房，想找點喝的。◇ *The search for a cure goes on.* 人們還在繼續探尋治療方法。◇ ***The search is on*** (= has begun) *for someone to fill the post.* 已在物色一個人來擔任這一職務。◇ *Eventually the search was called off.* 搜查最後被取消了。◇ *a* **search and rescue** *team* 搜救隊 **2** 0━ (*computing* 計) an act of looking for information in a computer DATABASE or network 搜索；檢索：*to do a search on the Internet* 在互聯網上進行搜索

■ *verb* **1** 0━ [I, T] to look carefully for sth/sb; to examine a particular place when looking for sb/sth 搜索；搜尋；搜查；查找：**~ (for sth/sb)** *She searched in vain for her passport.* 她翻找自己的護照，但沒找着。◇ *Police searched for clues in the area.* 警察在那一地帶查找線索。◇ **+ adv./prep.** *The customs officers searched through our bags.* 海關官員搜遍了我們的行李。◇ *I've* **searched high and low** *for those files.* 我為了找那些文件，四處都翻遍了。◇ **~ sth** *His house had clearly been searched and the book was missing.* 顯然有人來搜過他的房子，那本書不見了。◇ **~ sth for sth/sb** *Police searched the area for clues.* 警察在那一地帶查找線索。◇ *Firefighters searched the buildings for survivors.* 消防隊員在建築物中搜尋幸存者。◇ *searching the Web for interesting sites* 在網上尋找有趣的網站 **2** 0━ [T] (especially of the police 尤指警察) to examine sb's clothes, their pockets, etc. in order to find sth that they may be hiding 搜查；搜身：**~ sb** *Visitors are regularly searched as they enter the building.* 參觀者進入大樓時要接受例行的搜身檢查。◇ **~ sb for sth** *The youths were arrested and searched for anything that would incriminate them.* 警察逮捕了那些年輕人，並進行搜身，看能不能找到可以認定他們有罪的物證。➲ see also STRIP-SEARCH **3** 0━ [I] **~ (for sth)** to think carefully about sth, especially in order to find the answer to a problem 思索，細想（問題答案等）：*He searched desperately for something to say.* 他搜腸刮肚，想找點話說。➲ see also SOUL-SEARCHING

IDM ˌ**search ˈme** (*informal*) used to emphasize that you do not know the answer to sb's question（強調不知道答案）我怎麼知道：*'Why didn't she say anything?' 'Search me!'* "她怎麼一聲不吭？" "我怎麼知道！"

PHR V ˌ**search sth/sb↔ˈout** to look for sth/sb until you find them 找出；查到；搜尋到 SYN **track down**：*Fighter pilots searched out and attacked enemy aircraft.* 戰鬥機駕駛員發現敵機後便進行攻擊。

search·able /ˈsɜːtʃəbl; *NAmE* ˈsɜːrtʃ-/ *adj.* (of a computer DATABASE or network 計算機數據庫或網絡) having information organized in such a way that it can be searched for using a computer 可搜尋的；可檢索的：*a searchable database* 可檢索數據庫

ˈ**search engine** *noun* a computer program that searches the Internet for information, especially by looking for documents containing a particular word or group of words（計算機）搜索引擎

search·er /ˈsɜːtʃə(r); *NAmE* ˈsɜːrtʃ-/ *noun* **1** a person who is trying to find sth/sb 搜索者；查找者 **2** (*computing* 計) a program that helps you find information in a computer DATABASE or network; a search engine 檢索工具；搜索軟件；搜索引擎；搜尋器

search·ing /ˈsɜːtʃɪŋ; *NAmE* ˈsɜːrtʃ-/ *adj.* [usually before noun] (of a look, a question, etc. 眼神、問題等) trying to find out the truth about sth; thorough and serious 深挖細究的；認真徹底的：*a* ***searching investigation/analysis/examination*** 認真徹底的調查／分析／檢查 ◇ *He gave her a long* **searching look**. 他用探究的目光盯着她瞧。◇ *The police asked him some* **searching questions**. 警方問了他一些深入的問題。▶ **search·ing·ly** *adv.*

search·light /ˈsɜːtʃlaɪt; *NAmE* ˈsɜːrtʃ-/ *noun* a powerful lamp that can be turned in any direction, used, for example, for finding people or vehicles at night 探照燈

ˈ**search party** *noun* [C+sing./pl. v.] an organized group of people who are looking for a person or thing that is missing or lost 搜索隊

ˈ**search warrant** *noun* an official document that allows the police to search a building, for example to look for stolen property 搜查證；搜查令

sear·ing /ˈsɪərɪŋ; *NAmE* ˈsɪrɪŋ/ *adj.* [usually before noun] (*formal*) **1** so strong that it seems to burn you 灼人的；火辣辣的：*the searing heat of a tropical summer* 熱帶夏季灼人的熱浪 ◇ *searing pain* 火辣辣的疼痛 **2** (of words or speech 文字或話語) powerful and critical 猛烈批評的：*a searing attack on the government* 對政府的猛烈抨擊 ▶ **sear·ing·ly** *adv.* ➲ see also SEAR

sea·scape /ˈsiːskeɪp/ *noun* a picture or view of the sea 海景；海景畫 ➲ compare TOWNSCAPE

ˈ**sea shanty** *noun* (*BrE*) = SHANTY (2)

sea·shell /ˈsiːʃel/ *noun* the shell of a small creature that lives in the sea, often found empty when the creature has died 海貝殼

sea·shore /ˈsiːʃɔː(r)/ (usually **the seashore**) *noun* [usually sing.] the land along the edge of the sea or ocean, usually where there is sand and rocks 海岸；海濱 ➲ SYNONYMS at COAST ➲ VISUAL VOCAB pages V4, V5

sea·sick /ˈsiːsɪk/ *adj.* [not usually before noun] feeling ill/sick or wanting to VOMIT when you are travelling on a boat or ship 暈船：*to* ***be/feel/get seasick*** 暈船 ▶ ˈ**sea·sick·ness** *noun* [U]

sea·side /ˈsiːsaɪd/ (often **the seaside**) *noun* [sing.] (*especially BrE*) an area that is by the sea, especially one where people go for a day or a holiday/vacation（尤指人們遊玩、度假的）海邊，海濱：*a trip to the seaside* 去海濱旅行 ◇ *a day* ***at/by the seaside*** 海濱一日 ➲ SYNONYMS at COAST ▶ **sea·side** *adj.* [only before noun]：*a seaside resort* 海濱勝地 ◇ *a seaside vacation home* 海濱度假別墅

sea·son 0━ /ˈsiːzn/ *noun, verb*

■ *noun* **1** 0━ any of the four main periods of the year: spring, summer, autumn/fall and winter 季；季節：*the changing seasons* 四時更迭 **2 the dry/rainy/wet ~** a period of the year in tropical countries when it is either very dry or it rains a lot（熱帶地區的）旱／雨季 **3** 0━ a period of time during a year when a particular activity happens or is done（一年中開展某項活動的）季節，旺季：***the cricket/hunting/shooting, etc. season*** 板球賽季，狩獵季節等 ◇ *He scored his first goal of the season on Saturday.* 他在星期六的比賽中攻進了他在本賽季的第一個球。◇ *The female changes colour during the*

breeding season. 在繁殖季節，雌性改變身上的顏色。◇ *The hotels are always full during* ***the peak season*** (= when most people are on holiday/vacation). 在旺季，這些旅館總是客滿。◇ (*BrE*) *the* ***holiday season*** 度假旺季 ◇ (*NAmE*) *the* ***tourist season*** 旅遊旺季 ◇ (*NAmE*) *the* ***holiday season*** (= the time of Thanksgiving, Hanukkah, Christmas and New Year) 節假日（包括感恩節、猶太教修殿節、聖誕節和新年）◇ (*BrE*) *the* ***festive season*** (= Christmas and New Year) 聖誕節節期（即聖誕節和新年）➲ see also CLOSE SEASON, HIGH SEASON, LOW SEASON, OFF SEASON, THE SILLY SEASON **4** a period of time in which a play is shown in one place; a series of plays, films/movies or television programmes （一部戲劇在一地的）演出期，上演期；（一系列的戲劇、電影或電視節目的）會演，薈萃：*The play opens for a second season in London next week.* 下週，這部劇將在倫敦開始第二輪演出。◇ *a season of films by Alfred Hitchcock* 希區柯克電影作品展 **5** a period of time during one year when a particular style of clothes, hair, etc. is popular and fashionable （一年中時裝、髮型等的）流行期：*This season's look is soft and romantic.* 這段時間的流行風格是柔和、浪漫。

IDM **in 'season** **1** (of fruit or vegetables 水果、蔬菜) easily available and ready to eat because it is the right time of year for them 當令的；在旺季的 **2** (of a female animal 雌性動物) ready to reproduce 處於發情期 **SYN** **on heat** **out of 'season** **1** (of fruit or vegetables 水果、蔬菜) not easily available because it is not the right time of year for them 不合時令的；在淡季的 **2** at the times of year when few people go on holiday/vacation 度假淡季；旅遊淡季：*Hotels are cheaper out of season.* 在淡季，旅館要便宜些。 **season's 'greetings** used at Christmas to wish sb an enjoyable holiday 聖誕快樂（聖誕節祝賀語）

■ ***verb*** [T, I] **~ (sth)** (**with sth**) to add salt, pepper, etc. to food in order to give it more flavour 加調料調味；加作料：*Season the lamb with garlic.* 給羊肉加蒜調味。◇ *Add the mushrooms, and season to taste* (= add as much salt, pepper, etc. as you think is necessary). 加入蘑菇，並根據口味酌加調料。

sea·son·able /ˈsiːznəbl/ *adj.* usual or suitable for the time of year 當令的；應時的；合時令的：*seasonable temperatures* 合時令的氣溫 **OPP** **unseasonable**

sea·son·al /ˈsiːzənl/ *adj.* **1** happening or needed during a particular season; varying with the seasons 季節性的；隨季節變化的：*seasonal workers brought in to cope with the Christmas period* 為應付聖誕節期間的業務而招聘的臨時工 ◇ *seasonal variations in unemployment figures* 失業統計數字的季節性變化 **2** typical of or suitable for the time of year, especially Christmas 節令性的；適應節日需要的；（尤指）聖誕節的：*seasonal decorations* 聖誕節裝飾品 **OPP** **unseasonal** ▸ **sea·son·al·ly** /-nəli/ *adv.*：*seasonally adjusted unemployment figures* (= not including the changes that always happen in different seasons) 經季節因素調整的失業統計數字

ˌseasonal afˈfective disorder *noun* [U] (*abbr.* **SAD**) a medical condition in which a person feels sad and tired during late autumn/fall and winter when there is not much light from the sun 季節性情感障礙（秋冬兩季因白晝縮短而易發作的抑鬱症）

sea·son·al·ity /ˌsiːzəˈnæləti/ *noun* [U, sing.] (*technical* 術語) the fact of varying with the seasons 季節性：*a high degree of climatic seasonality* 明顯的季節性氣候變化

sea·soned /ˈsiːznd/ *adj.* **1** [usually before noun] (of a person 人) having a lot of experience of a particular activity 富有經驗的；老於此道的：*a* ***seasoned campaigner/performer/traveller, etc.*** 經驗豐富的社會運動家、表演者、旅行家等 **2** (of food 食物) with salt, pepper, etc. added to it 調好味的；加了作料的：*The sausage was very* ***highly seasoned***. 這香腸調味很濃。**3** (of wood 木料) made suitable for use by being left outside 風乾的，晾乾的（可加工使用）

sea·son·ing /ˈsiːzənɪŋ/ *noun* [U, C] a substance used to add flavour to food, especially salt and pepper 調味品；作料

ˈseason ticket *noun* a ticket that you can use many times within a particular period, for example on a regular train or bus journey, or for a series of games, and that costs less than paying separately each time 長期票（如火車通勤票、公交車月票、體育比賽套票等）：***an annual/a monthly/a weekly season ticket*** 年票；月票；週票 ◇ *a* ***season ticket holder*** 持長期票的人

seat 🔑 /siːt/ *noun, verb*

■ ***noun***

▸ **PLACE TO SIT** 可坐的地方 **1** 🔑 a place where you can sit, for example a chair 座位，坐處（如椅子等）：*She sat back in her seat.* 她坐在那裏，往後靠了靠。◇ *He put his shopping on the seat behind him.* 他把買的東西放在身後的座位上。◇ *Please* ***take a seat*** (= sit down). 請坐。◇ *Ladies and gentlemen, please* ***take your seats*** (= sit down). 各位來賓，請就座。◇ *a* ***window/corner seat*** (= one near a window/in a corner) 挨窗戶／角落裏的座位 ◇ *a* ***child seat*** (= for a child in a car) （汽車上的）幼兒座 ◇ *Would you prefer a* ***window seat*** *or an* ***aisle seat***? (= on a plane) 您想要靠窗的座位還是靠過道的座位？◇ *We used the branch of an old tree as a seat.* 我們坐在一棵老樹的樹杈上。◇ *We all filed back to our seats in silence.* 我們都默默無語，一個跟一個地回到座位上。➲ SYNONYMS at SIT ➲ VISUAL VOCAB page V52 ➲ see also BACK SEAT, BUCKET SEAT, HOT SEAT, LOVE SEAT, PASSENGER SEAT

▸ **-SEATER** …座位 **2** (in nouns and adjectives 構成名詞和形容詞) with the number of seats mentioned 有…座位的；有…座的：(*BrE*) *a ten-seater minibus* 十座小公共汽車 ◇ *an all-seater stadium* (= in which nobody is allowed to stand) 全坐席體育場

▸ **PART OF CHAIR** 椅子的一部份 **3** the part of a chair, etc. on which you actually sit （椅子等的）座部：*a steel chair with a plastic seat* 塑料座部的鋼架椅子

▸ **IN PLANE/TRAIN/THEATRE** 飛機；火車；劇院 **4** 🔑 a place where you pay to sit in a plane, train, theatre, etc. 座位：*to* ***book/reserve a seat*** (= for a concert, etc.) 預訂一個座位 ◇ *There are no seats left on that flight.* 那次航班沒座位了。

▸ **OFFICIAL POSITION** 職位 **5** 🔑 an official position as a member of a parliament, council, committee, etc. （議會、理事會、委員會等的）席位：*a seat on the city council/in Parliament/in Congress* 市政會／議會／國會席位 ◇ *to* ***win/lose a seat*** (= in an election) （在選舉中）贏得／失去一個席位 ◇ (*BrE*) *to* ***take your seat*** (= to begin your duties, especially in Parliament) （尤指在議會）就職 ◇ *The majority of seats on the board will be held by business representatives.* 理事會的多數席位將由工商界代表擔任。➲ see also SAFE SEAT

▸ **TOWN/CITY** 城鎮；市 **6 ~ of sth** (*formal*) a place where people are involved in a particular activity, especially a city that has a university or the offices of a government （尤指大學或政府機關）所在地；中心：*Washington is the* ***seat of government*** *of the US.* 華盛頓是美國政府所在地。◇ *a university town renowned as a* ***seat of learning*** 有學術重鎮之稱的大學城

▸ **COUNTRY HOUSE** 鄉村房舍 **7** (also **ˌcountry ˈseat**) (both *BrE*) a large house in the country, that belongs to a member of the upper class （上層社會人士的）鄉村宅第：*the family seat in Norfolk* 在諾福克的祖宅

▸ **PART OF BODY** 身體部位 **8** (especially *formal*) the part of the body on which a person sits 臀部 **SYN** **buttocks**

▸ **PART OF TROUSERS/PANTS** 褲子的一部份 **9** the part of a pair of trousers/pants that covers a person's seat （褲子的）後襠，臀部

IDM **(fly) by the seat of your 'pants** (*informal*) to act without careful thought and without a plan that you have made in advance, hoping that you will be lucky and be successful 臨時憑感覺碰運氣；憑經驗瞎碰 **SYN** **wing it** **be in the 'driving seat** (*BrE*) (*NAmE* **be in the 'driver's seat**) to be the person in control of a situation 擔任負責人；處於統領地位 ➲ more at BACK SEAT, BUM *n.*, EDGE *n.*

■ ***verb***

▸ **SIT DOWN** 坐下 **1 ~ sb/yourself** (*formal*) to give sb a place to sit; to sit down in a place 向…提供座位；（使）就座；坐；落座：*Please wait to be seated* (= in a restaurant, etc.). 請等候安排入座。◇ *Please* ***be seated*** (= sit down). 請就座。◇ *He seated himself behind the desk.* 他在書桌後面坐下。➲ SYNONYMS at SIT

S

▸ **OF BUILDING/VEHICLE 建築物；交通工具** **2** **~ sb** to have enough seats for a particular number of people 可坐…人；能容納…人：*The aircraft seats 200 passengers.* 這架飛機能坐 200 名乘客。

ˈseat belt (also **ˈsafety belt**) *noun* a belt that is attached to the seat in a car or a plane and that you fasten around yourself so that you are not thrown out of the seat if there is an accident（汽車或飛機上的）安全帶：*Fasten your seat belts.* 繫好安全帶。➲ COLLOCATIONS at DRIVING ➲ VISUAL VOCAB page V52

seat·ing /ˈsiːtɪŋ/ *noun* [U] places to sit; seats 可坐的地方；座位：*The theatre has seating for about 500 people.* 這家劇院可坐 500 人左右。◇ *The room had a* ***seating capacity*** *of over 200.* 這個房間能容 200 多人就座。◇ *the* ***seating arrangements*** *for the conference* 會議的座位安排

seat·mate /ˈsiːtmeɪt/ *noun* a person that you sit next to as you are travelling, especially on a plane（尤指飛機上的）鄰座乘客

ˈsea turtle *noun* (*NAmE*) = TURTLE (1)

ˈsea urchin (also **ur·chin**) *noun* a small sea creature with a round shell which is covered with SPIKES 海膽

ˌsea ˈwall *noun* a large strong wall built to stop the sea from flowing onto the land 海堤；防波堤

sea·ward /ˈsiːwəd; *NAmE* -wərd/ *adj.* towards the sea; in the direction of the sea 向海的；朝海的：*the seaward side of the coastal road* 海濱公路臨海的一側 ▸ **sea·ward** (also **sea·wards** /-wədz; *NAmE* -wərdz/) *adv.*：*Her gaze was fixed seawards.* 她凝望大海。

ˈsea water *noun* [U] water from the sea or ocean, that is salty 海水

sea·way /ˈsiːweɪ/ *noun* a passage from the sea through the land along which large ships can travel 海道（大型海輪可航行的通海河道）

sea·weed /ˈsiːwiːd/ *noun* [U, C] a plant that grows in the sea or ocean, or on rocks at the edge of the sea or ocean. There are many different types of seaweed, some of which are eaten as food. 海草；海藻

sea·worthy /ˈsiːwɜːði; *NAmE* -wɜːrði/ *adj.* (of a ship 船舶) in a suitable condition to sail 適宜航海的；能出海的 ▸ **sea·worthi·ness** *noun* [U]

se·ba·ceous /sɪˈbeɪʃəs/ *adj.* [usually before noun] (*biology* 生) producing a substance like oil in the body 分泌脂質的：*the sebaceous glands in the skin* 皮脂腺

S

seb·or·rhoea (*NAmE* **seb·or·rhea**) /ˌsebəˈrɪə; *NAmE* -ˈriːə/ *noun* [U] a medical condition of the skin in which an unusually large amount of SEBUM is produced by the SEBACEOUS GLANDS 皮脂溢；皮脂漏 ▸ **seb·or·rhoe·ic** (*NAmE* **seb·or·rhe·ic**) /ˌsebəˈriːɪk/ *adj.*

sebum /ˈsiːbəm/ *noun* [U] an oil-like substance produced by the SEBACEOUS GLANDS 皮脂

Sec. (*US* also **Secy.**) *abbr.* SECRETARY

sec /sek/ *noun* **a sec** [sing.] (*informal*) a very short time; a second 片刻；霎時：*Stay there. I'll be back* ***in a sec.*** 待着別走。我馬上回來。◇ *Hang on* (= wait) *a sec.* 稍等一下。

sec. *abbr.* second(s) 秒

SECAM /ˈsiːkæm/ *noun* [U] a television broadcasting system that is used in France and some other countries * SECAM 制式，賽康制式（法國和其他一些國家採用的電視播放系統）➲ compare NTSC, PAL

seca·teurs /ˌsekəˈtɜːz; *NAmE* -ˈtɜːrz/ *noun* [pl.] (*BrE*) a garden tool like a pair of strong scissors, used for cutting plant STEMS and small branches 整枝剪；修枝剪：*a pair of secateurs* 一把整枝剪

se·cede /sɪˈsiːd/ *verb* [I] **~ (from sth)** (*formal*) (of a state, country, etc. 州、邦、國家等) to officially leave an organization of states, countries, etc. and become independent 退出，脫離（組織等）：*The Republic of Panama seceded from Colombia in 1903.* 巴拿馬共和國於 1903 年脫離哥倫比亞。

se·ces·sion /sɪˈseʃn/ *noun* [U, C] **~ (from sth)** the fact of an area or group becoming independent from the country or larger group that it belongs to（地區或集團從所屬的國家或上級集團的）退出，脫離

se·ces·sion·ist /sɪˈseʃənɪst/ *adj.* [only before noun] supporting or connected with secession 贊成（或參與）脫離活動的；奉行分離主義的 ▸ **se·ces·sion·ist** *noun*：*a military campaign against the secessionists* 對分離主義者採取的軍事行動

se·clude /sɪˈkluːd/ *verb* **~ yourself/sb (from sb/sth)** (*formal*) to keep yourself/sb away from contact with other people（使）與…隔離，與…隔絕；（使）隱居，獨處

se·cluded /sɪˈkluːdɪd/ *adj.* **1** (of a place 地方) quiet and private; not used or disturbed by other people 僻靜的；清靜的；不受打擾的：*a* ***secluded garden/beach/spot, etc.*** 僻靜的花園、海灘、地點等 **2** without much contact with other people 隱居的；與世隔絕的 SYN **solitary**：*to lead a secluded life* 過隱居生活

se·clu·sion /sɪˈkluːʒn/ *noun* [U] the state of being private or of having little contact with other people 清靜；隱居；與世隔絕：*the seclusion and peace of the island* 島上的幽僻寧靜

sec·ond[1] 0→ /ˈsekənd/ *det., ordinal number, adv., noun, verb* ➲ see also SECOND[2]

■ ***det., ordinal number*** **1** 0→ happening or coming next after the first in a series of similar things or people; 2nd 第二（的）：*This is the second time it's happened.* 這已是第二次了。◇ *Italy scored a second goal just after half-time.* 下半場剛剛開始，意大利隊便射入第二個球。◇ *the second of June/June 2nd* 六月二日 ◇ *He was the second to arrive.* 他是第二個到的。◇ *We have one child and are expecting our second in July.* 我們有一個孩子，第二個預期在七月出生。 **2** 0→ next in order of importance, size, quality, etc. to one other person or thing（重要性、規模、質量等）居第二位的：*Osaka is Japan's* ***second-largest*** *city.* 大阪是日本的第二大城市。◇ *Birmingham, the UK's second city* 伯明翰，英國的第二大城市 ◇ *The spreadsheet application is* ***second only to*** *word processing in terms of popularity.* 就受歡迎程度而言，電子製表軟件僅次於文字處理軟件。◇ *As a dancer, he is* ***second to none*** (= nobody is a better dancer than he is). 他的舞技不亞於任何人。 **3** 0→ [only before noun] another; in addition to one that you already own or use 另外的；外加的：*They have a second home in Tuscany.* 他們在托斯卡納還有一個家。

■ ***adv.*** **1** 0→ after one other person or thing in order or importance 以第二名；以第二位：*She* ***came second*** *in the marathon.* 她在馬拉松比賽中獲得第二名。◇ *One of the smaller parties* ***came a close second*** (= nearly won). 其中一個較小的政黨差一點就獲勝了。◇ *I agreed to speak second.* 我同意第二個發言。◇ *He is a writer first and a scientist second.* 他首先是作家，然後才是科學家。◇ *I came* ***second*** ***(to) last*** (= the one before the last one) *in the race.* 我在賽跑中得了倒數第二。 **2** 0→ used to introduce the second of a list of points you want to make in a speech or piece of writing（用於列舉）第二，其次 SYN **secondly**：*She did it first because she wanted to, and second because I asked her to.* 她做那件事，首先是因為她自己想做，其次是因為我要她做。➲ LANGUAGE BANK at FIRST, PROCESS

■ ***noun*** **1** 0→ [C] (*symb.* ″) (*abbr.* **sec.**) a unit for measuring time. There are 60 seconds in one minute. 秒（時間單位）：*She can run 100 metres in just over 11 seconds.* 她跑 100 米只需 11 秒多一點。◇ ***For several seconds*** *he did not reply.* 一連幾秒鐘，他都沒有回答。◇ *The light flashes* ***every 5 seconds.*** 燈光每 5 秒鐘閃一次。◇ *The water flows at about 1.5 metres* ***per second.*** 水的流速約為每秒 1.5 米。 **2** 0→ [C] (also *informal* **sec**) a very short time 片刻；瞬間 SYN **moment**：*I'll be with you* ***in a second.*** 我馬上就去你那兒。◇ *They had finished* ***in/within seconds.*** 他們一下子就做完了。➲ see also SPLIT SECOND **3** [C] (*symb.* ″) a unit for measuring angles. There are 60 seconds in one minute. 秒（角度單位）：1° 6′ 10″ (= one degree, six minutes and ten seconds) * 1 度 6 分 10 秒 **4** **seconds** [pl.] (*informal*) a second amount of the same food that you have just eaten 再來的一份食物：*Seconds, anybody?* 有誰需要再

來一份嗎？ **5** [C, usually pl.] an item that is sold at a lower price than usual because it is not perfect 次貨；二等貨；等外品 **6** (also ˌ**second ˈgear**) [U] one of four or five positions of the gears in a vehicle （車輛的）二擋：*When it's icy, move off **in second**.* 路面有冰時，起步掛二擋。 **7** [C] a level of university degree at British universities. An **upper second** is a good degree and a **lower second** is average. 二級優等學位（英國大學學位等級，upper second 為二級上，較好 lower second 為二級下，一般）➲ compare FIRST *n.* (4), THIRD *n.* (2) **8** [C] a person whose role is to help and support sb else, for example in a BOXING match or in a formal DUEL in the past（拳擊比賽或舊時正式決鬥的）助手 **IDM** see JUST *adv.*, WAIT *v.*

■ *verb* **~ sth** to state officially at a meeting that you support another person's idea, suggestion, etc. so that it can be discussed and/or voted on 支持，贊成（主意、建議等）；附議：*Any proposal must be seconded by two other members of the committee.* 任何提案須有委員會其他兩名委員附議。◇ *(informal) 'Thank God that's finished.' 'I'll second that!'* (= I agree) "謝天謝地，總算幹完了。" "沒錯！" ➲ compare PROPOSE (4)

se·cond² /sɪˈkɒnd; *NAmE* -ˈkɑːnd/ *verb* [usually passive] **~ sb (from sth) (to sth)** *(especially BrE)* to send an employee to another department, office, etc. in order to do a different job for a short period of time 臨時調派；短期調任：*Each year two teachers are seconded to industry for six months.* 每年有兩名教師派到產業部門工作六個月。➲ see also SECOND¹ ▸ **se·cond·ment** *(BrE) noun* [U, C]：*They met while she was **on secondment** from the Foreign Office.* 兩人是在她從外交部調來短期任職時認識的。

sec·ond·ary 0➡ /ˈsekəndri; *NAmE* -deri/ *adj.* **1** 0➡ less important than sth else 次要的；從屬的；輔助的：*That is just a **secondary consideration**.* 那只不過是次要的考慮因素。◇ *Experience is what matters—age is **of secondary importance**.* 重要的是經驗，年齡是次要的。◇ **~ to sth** *Raising animals was only secondary to other forms of farming.* 與其他農業生產相對而言，動物飼養只是副業。 **2** 0➡ happening as a result of sth else 間接引發的；繼發性的；次生的：*a secondary infection* 繼發性感染 ◇ *a secondary effect* 間接結果 ◇ *a secondary colour* (= made from mixing two primary colours) 次色 **3** 0➡ [only before noun] connected with teaching children of 11-18 years 中等教育的；中學的：*secondary teachers* 中學教師 ◇ *the secondary curriculum* 中學課程 ➲ compare ELEMENTARY (1), PRIMARY *adj.* (3), TERTIARY ▸ **sec·ond·ar·ily** /ˈsekəndrəli; *NAmE* ˌsekənˈderəli/ *adv.*：*Their clothing is primarily functional and only secondarily decorative.* 他們的衣服首重實用，其次才講花式。

ˌ**secondary eduˈcation** *noun* [U] *(especially BrE)* education for children between the ages of 11 and 18 中等教育：*primary and secondary education* 中、小學教育

ˈ**secondary industry** *noun* [U, C] *(economics* 經) the section of industry that uses RAW MATERIALS to make goods 第二產業（用原材料生產商品的產業）➲ compare PRIMARY INDUSTRY, TERTIARY INDUSTRY

ˌ**secondary ˈmodern** *noun* (in Britain until the 1970s) a school for young people between the ages of 11 and 16 who did not go to a GRAMMAR SCHOOL 現代中等學校（20 世紀 70 年代以前英國一種中學，招收未考入文法學校的 11 至 16 歲學生）

ˌ**secondary ˈpicketing** *noun* [U] *(BrE)* the act of preventing workers who are not involved in a strike from supplying goods to the company where the strike is held 二級糾察封鎖（阻止未參加罷工的工人向公司供應貨物）

ˈ**secondary school** *noun* a school for young people between the ages of 11 and 16 or 18 中等學校；中學 ➲ compare PRIMARY SCHOOL, HIGH SCHOOL

ˈ**secondary source** *noun* a book or other source of information where the writer has taken the information from some other source and not collected it himself or herself 二手資料來源 ➲ compare PRIMARY SOURCE

ˌ**secondary ˈstress** *noun* [U, C] *(phonetics* 語音) the second strongest stress that is put on a syllable in a word or a phrase when it is spoken 次重音 ➲ compare PRIMARY STRESS

ˌ**second ˈbest** *adj.* **1** not as good as the best 次於最好的；第二好的：*The two teams seemed evenly matched but Arsenal **came off second best*** (= lost). 兩支球隊看似勢均力敵，但阿森納隊最後還是輸了。◇ *my second-best suit* 我的第二好的一套衣服 **2** not exactly what you want; not perfect 退而求其次的；將就的：*a second-best solution* 退而求其次的解決辦法 ▸ ˌ**second ˈbest** *noun* [U]：*Sometimes you have to **settle for*** (= be content with) ***second best**.* 有時候你只能退而求其次。

ˌ**second ˈchamber** *noun* *(especially BrE)* = UPPER HOUSE

ˌ**second ˈclass** *noun* [U] **1** a way of travelling on a train or ship that costs less and is less comfortable than FIRST CLASS. In Britain this is now usually called **standard class**.（火車的）二等車廂；（船的）二等艙 **2** (in Britain) the class of mail that costs less and takes longer to arrive than FIRST CLASS 第二類郵件（在英國投遞較第一類郵件慢，郵資也較低） **3** (in the US) the system of sending newspapers and magazines by mail 第二類郵件（美國報刊投遞類別） **4** [U, sing.] the second highest standard of degree given by a British university, often divided into upper second class and lower second class 二級優等學位（英國大學學位等級）

ˌ**second-ˈclass** *adj.* **1** *(disapproving)* (of a person 人) less important than other people 次要的；無足輕重的：*Older people should not be treated as **second-class citizens**.* 不應把老年人當二等公民對待。 **2** of a lower standard or quality than the best（質量、標準等）二流的，次等的：*a second-class education* 二流的教育 **3** [only before noun] connected with the less expensive way of travelling on a train, ship, etc.（車廂、船艙等）二等的：***second-class carriages/compartments/passengers*** 二等車廂／隔間／車廂乘客 **4** [only before noun] (in Britain) connected with letters, packages, etc. that you pay less to send and that are delivered less quickly 第二類的（英國郵件等級，投遞較第一類慢，郵資也較低）：***second-class letters/stamps*** 第二類信件；第二類郵件所貼的郵票 **5** (in the US) connected with the system of sending newspapers and magazines by mail 第二類的（美國郵件等級，用於投遞報刊） **6** [only before noun] used to describe a British university degree which is good but not of the highest class 二級優等的（英國大學學位）：*Applicants should have at least a second-class honours degree.* 申請者須有二級優等以上學位。 ▸ ˌ**second ˈclass** *adv.*：*to send a letter second class* 按第二類郵件投遞信件 ◇ *to travel second class* 乘二等艙

the ˌ**Second ˈComing** *noun* [sing.] a day in the future when Christians believe Jesus Christ will come back to earth 基督復臨（基督徒相信耶穌基督將再度降臨人間）

ˌ**second ˈcousin** *noun* a child of a cousin of your mother or father 父母表兄弟（或姐妹）的孩子；父母堂兄弟（或姐妹）的孩子

ˌ**second-deˈgree** *adj.* [only before noun] **1** **~ murder, assault, burglary, etc.** *(especially NAmE)* murder, etc. that is less serious than FIRST-DEGREE crimes 第二等級（謀殺、人身侵犯或入室盜竊等罪） **2** **~ burns** burns of the second most serious of three kinds, causing BLISTERS but no permanent marks 二度（燒傷）➲ compare FIRST-DEGREE, THIRD-DEGREE

sec·ond·er /ˈsekəndə(r)/ *noun* a person who SECONDS a proposal, etc. (= supports it so that it can be discussed) 附議者；贊成者 ➲ compare PROPOSER

ˌ**second-geneˈration** *adj.* **1** used to describe people who were born in the country they live in but whose parents came to live there from another country（移民後裔等）第二代的：*She was a second-generation Japanese-American.* 她是第二代日裔美國人。 **2** (of a product, technology, etc. 產品、技術等) at a more advanced stage of development than an earlier form 第二代的（更先進或改進了的）：*second-generation hand-held computers* 第二代掌上電腦

S

ˌsecond-ˈguess *verb* **1** [T] **~ sb/sth** to guess what sb will do before they do it 猜測；預言：*It was impossible to second-guess the decision of the jury.* 陪審團的決定不可能預測。**2** [T, I] **~ (sb/sth)** (*especially NAmE*) to criticize sb after a decision has been made; to criticize sth after it has happened 事後批評（或品評）；耍事後聰明

ˈsecond hand *noun* the hand on some watches and clocks that shows seconds（鐘錶的）秒針 ➲ picture at CLOCK

ˌsecond-ˈhand *adj.* **1** not new; owned by sb else before 舊的；用過的；二手的：*a second-hand bookshop* (= for selling second-hand books) 舊書店 ◇ (*especially BrE*) *second-hand cars* 二手車 **2** (often *disapproving*) (of news, information, etc. 消息、信息等) learned from other people, not from your own experience 間接得來的；二手的：*second-hand opinions* 來自他人的觀點 ▶ **ˌsecond-ˈhand** *adv.*：*I bought the camera second-hand.* 我買的這架照相機是二手貨。◇ *I only heard about it second-hand.* 我只是聽別人講的。➲ compare FIRST-HAND

ˌsecond ˈhome *noun* **1** [C] a house or flat/apartment that sb owns as well as their main home and uses, for example, for holidays/vacations 別業；第二寓所；別墅 **2** [sing.] a place where sb lives and which they know as well as, and like as much as, their home 第二故鄉；第二個家

ˌsecond in comˈmand *noun* a person who has the second highest rank in a group and takes charge when the leader is not there 副司令員；副指揮官

ˌsecond ˈlanguage *noun* a language that sb learns to speak well and that they use for work or at school, but that is not the language they learned first 第二語言：*ESL or English as a Second Language* * ESL —— 非母語英語

ˌsecond ˈlanguage acquisition *noun* [U] (*abbr.* **SLA**) (*linguistics* 語言) the learning of a second language 第二語言習得

ˌsecond lieuˈtenant *noun* an officer of lower rank in the army or the US AIR FORCE just below the rank of a LIEUTENANT 陸軍少尉；（美國）空軍少尉

ˌSecond ˈLife™ *noun* [U] (*abbr.* **SL**) a VIRTUAL WORLD on the Internet where people can communicate with each other, play games and pretend to live another life 第二人生（玩家可交流、玩遊戲和假裝過另一種生活的互聯網虛擬世界）

S

sec·ond·ly /ˈsekəndli/ *adv.* used to introduce the second of a list of points you want to make in a speech or piece of writing（用於列舉）第二，其次：*Firstly, it's expensive, and secondly, it's too slow.* 首先是價格貴，其次，速度太慢。

ˈsecond name *noun* (*especially BrE*) **1** a family name or surname 姓 **2** a second personal name 中間名：*His second name is Willem, after his grandfather.* 他的中間名是威廉，取自他祖父的名字。

ˌsecond ˈnature *noun* [U] **~ (to sb)** (**to do sth**) something that you do very easily and naturally, because it is part of your character or you have done it so many times 第二天性；習性

the ˌsecond ˈperson *noun* [sing.] (*grammar* 語法) the form of a pronoun or verb used when addressing sb 第二人稱：*In the phrase 'you are', the verb 'are' is in the second person and the word 'you' is a second-person pronoun.* 在短語 you are 中，動詞 are 是第二人稱形式，而單詞 you 是第二人稱代詞。➲ compare THE FIRST PERSON, THE THIRD PERSON

ˌsecond-ˈrate *adj.* not very good or impressive 二流的；平庸的；普通的 **SYN** **mediocre**：*a second-rate player* 平庸的運動員

ˌsecond ˈsight *noun* [U] the ability that some people seem to have to know or see what will happen in the future or what is happening in a different place 先見之明；預見力；千里眼

ˌsecond-ˈstring *adj.* [only before noun] (*especially NAmE*) (usually of a player in a sports team 通常指運動隊隊員) only used occasionally where sb/sth else is not available 替補的：*a second-string quarterback* 替補四分衛 ▶ **ˌsecond ˈstring** *noun*：*Wilson was a second string for New Zealand in last week's match.* 在上週的比賽中，威爾遜是新西蘭隊的替補隊員。

ˌsecond ˈwind *noun* [sing.] (*informal*) new energy that makes you able to continue with sth that had made you tired 恢復的精力；重振的精神；緩過勁來的狀況

the ˌSecond ˌWorld ˈWar (also **ˌWorld ˌWar ˈTwo**) *noun* [sing.] the second large international war, that was fought between 1939 and 1945 第二次世界大戰（發生於 1939 至 1945 年）

se·crecy /ˈsiːkrəsi/ *noun* [U] the fact of making sure that nothing is known about sth; the state of being secret 保密；秘密：*the need for absolute secrecy in this matter* 在這件事情上絕對保密的必要性 ◇ *Everyone involved was **sworn to secrecy**.* 所有相關人員均被要求宣誓保密。◇ *The whole affair is still **shrouded in secrecy**.* 整個事件依舊秘而不宣。

se·cret 0→ /ˈsiːkrət/ *adj., noun*

■ ***adj.*** **1** 0→ known about by only a few people; kept hidden from others 秘密的；保密的；外人不得而知的：***secret information/meetings/talks*** 秘密信息／會議／會談 ◇ **~ (from sb)** *He tried to **keep it secret** from his family.* 這件事他試圖瞞着家裏。◇ *Details of the proposals remain secret.* 提議的細節仍不得而知。◇ *a secret passage leading to the beach* 通往海灘的秘密通道 ➲ see also TOP SECRET **2** 0→ [only before noun] used to describe actions and behaviour that you do not tell other people about（指行為與習慣）暗中進行的，未公開的，隱秘的：*He's a secret drinker.* 他偷偷地喝酒。◇ *her secret fears* 她內心的擔憂 ◇ *a secret room* 秘室 **3** [not usually before noun] **~ (about sth)** (of a person or their behaviour 人或行為) liking to have secrets that other people do not know about; showing this 詭秘；神秘 **SYN** **secretive**：*They were so secret about everything.* 他們無論對什麼都那樣神秘兮兮的。◇ *Jessica caught a secret smile flitting between the two of them.* 傑西卡看見他們倆詭秘地相視一笑。▶ **se·cret·ly** 0→ *adv.*：*The police had secretly filmed the conversations.* 警察已秘密地把幾次談話拍攝下來。◇ *She was secretly pleased to see him.* 見到他，她心中竊喜。

■ ***noun*** **1** 0→ [C] something that is known about by only a few people and not told to others 秘密；機密：*Can you **keep a secret**?* 你能保守秘密嗎？◇ *The location of the ship is **a closely guarded secret**.* 那艘船的位置是高度機密。◇ *Shall we **let him in on*** (= tell him) ***the secret**?* 我們要不要把秘密透露給他？◇ *He **made no secret of** his ambition* (= he didn't try to hide it). 他並沒有掩飾自己的雄心壯志。◇ *She was dismissed for revealing trade secrets.* 她因泄露商業機密被解雇。◇ ***official/State secrets*** 官方／國家機密 **2** 0→ (usually **the secret**) [sing.] the best or only way to achieve sth; the way a particular person achieves sth 訣竅；秘訣：*Careful planning is the secret of success.* 仔細計劃是成功的訣竅。◇ *She still looks so young. What's her secret?* 她看上去依舊那麼年輕，她的保養秘訣是什麼呢？**3** [C, usually pl.] a thing that is not yet fully understood or that is difficult to understand 奧秘；奧妙：*the secrets of the universe* 宇宙的奧秘

IDM **in ˈsecret** 0→ without other people knowing about it 秘密地；暗中：*The meeting was held in secret.* 會議是秘密召開的。➲ more at GUILTY *adj.*, OPEN *adj.*

ˌsecret ˈagent (also **agent**) *noun* a person who is used by a government to find out secret information about other countries or governments 特工人員；特務；間諜 **SYN** **spy**

sec·re·tar·ial /ˌsekrəˈteəriəl; *NAmE* -ˈter-/ *adj.* involving or connected with the work of a secretary 秘書的；文秘工作的：*secretarial work* 文秘工作

sec·re·tar·iat /ˌsekrəˈteəriət; -iæt; *NAmE* -ˈter-/ *noun* the department of a large international or political organization which is responsible for running it, especially the office of a SECRETARY GENERAL（大型國際組織、政治組織的）秘書處，書記處

sec·re·tary 0-w /ˈsekrətri; *NAmE* -teri/ *noun* (*pl.* **-ies**) (*abbr.* **Sec.**)
1 0-w a person who works in an office, working for another person, dealing with letters and telephone calls, typing, keeping records, arranging meetings with people, etc. 秘書：*a **legal/medical secretary*** 法律／醫務秘書◇*Please contact my secretary to make an appointment.* 請和我的秘書聯繫，預約一個時間。➲ see also PRIVATE SECRETARY **2** 0-w an official of a club, society, etc. who deals with writing letters, keeping records, and making business arrangements（俱樂部、社團等的）幹事，文書：*the membership secretary* 組織幹事 **3** **Secretary** = SECRETARY OF STATE (1) ➲ see also HOME SECRETARY, PERMANENT UNDERSECRETARY **4** 0-w (*US*) the head of a government department, chosen by the President 部長；大臣：*Secretary of the Treasury* 財政部長 **5** 0-w (in Britain) an assistant of a government minister, an AMBASSADOR, etc.（英國的大臣、大使等的）助理 ➲ see also UNDERSECRETARY

ˌSecretary ˈGeneral *noun* the person who is in charge of the department that deals with the running of a large international or political organization（大型國際組織、政治組織的）秘書長，總幹事，總書記：*the former Secretary General of NATO* 北約前任秘書長

ˌSecretary of ˈState *noun* **1** (also **Sec·re·tary**) (in Britain) the head of an important government department（英國）大臣：*the Secretary of State for Education* 教育大臣◇*the Education Secretary* 教育大臣◇*the Foreign Secretary* 外交大臣 **2** (in the US) the head of the government department that deals with foreign affairs（美國）國務卿

se·crete /sɪˈkriːt/ *verb* **1** **~ sth** (of part of the body or a plant 身體或植物器官) to produce a liquid substance 分泌：*Insulin is secreted by the pancreas.* 胰島素是胰腺分泌的。**2** **~ sth (in sth)** (*formal*) to hide sth, especially sth small 隱藏，藏匿（小物件）：*The drugs were secreted in the lining of his case.* 毒品藏在他的皮箱內襯中。

se·cre·tion /sɪˈkriːʃn/ *noun* (*technical* 術語) **1** [U] the process by which liquid substances are produced by parts of the body or plants 分泌：*the secretion of bile by the liver* 肝臟分泌膽汁的過程 **2** [C, usually pl.] a liquid substance produced by parts of the body or plants 分泌物：*bodily secretions* 人體分泌物

se·cret·ive /ˈsiːkrətɪv/ *adj.* **~ (about sth)** tending or liking to hide your thoughts, feelings, ideas, etc. from other people（思想、情感等）不外露的；慣於掩藏自己的；有城府的：*He's very secretive about his work.* 他對自己的工作諱莫如深。▸ **se·cret·ive·ly** *adv.* **se·cret·ive·ness** *noun* [U]

ˌsecret poˈlice *noun* [sing.+sing./pl. v.] a police force that works secretly to make sure that citizens behave as their government wants 秘密警察

ˌsecret ˈservice *noun* [usually sing.] a government department that is responsible for protecting its government's military and political secrets and for finding out the secrets of other governments（政府的）特工部門，特務機關

sect /sekt/ *noun* (sometimes *disapproving*) a small group of people who belong to a particular religion but who have some beliefs or practices which separate them from the rest of the group 派別；宗派

sect·ar·ian /sekˈteəriən; *NAmE* -ˈter-/ *adj.* [usually before noun] (often *disapproving*) connected with the differences that exist between groups of people who have different religious views（宗教）教派的，派性的：***sectarian attacks/violence*** 教派攻擊／暴力活動◇*attempts to break down the **sectarian divide** in Northern Ireland* 旨在消除北愛爾蘭的宗教派系分歧的努力

sect·ar·ian·ism /sekˈteəriənɪzəm; *NAmE* -ˈter-/ *noun* [U] (often *disapproving*) strong support for one particular religious or political group, especially when this leads to violence between different groups 宗派主義

sec·tion 0-w AW /ˈsekʃn/ *noun, verb*

■ *noun*

▸ **PART/PIECE** 部份；部件 **1** 0-w [C] any of the parts into which sth is divided 部份；部門：*That section of the road is still closed.* 那段公路依舊封閉。◇*The library has a large biology section.* 這個圖書館有大量的生物學藏書。◇*the tail section of the plane* 飛機的尾部 **2** 0-w [C] a separate part of a structure from which the whole can be put together 部件；散件：*The shed comes in sections that you assemble yourself.* 棚房以散件出售，需要自己組裝。

▸ **OF DOCUMENT/BOOK** 文件；書籍 **3** 0-w [C] a separate part of a document, book, etc. 節；款；項；段；部份：*These issues will be discussed more fully in the next section.* 這些問題將在下一節中有更充分的討論。◇*the sports section of the newspaper* 報紙的體育欄

▸ **GROUP OF PEOPLE** 人的群體 **4** 0-w [C] a separate group within a larger group of people 階層；界；組：*an issue that will affect large sections of the population* 涉及人口中廣大階層的問題◇*the brass section of an orchestra* 管弦樂隊的銅管樂器組 ➲ see also RHYTHM SECTION

▸ **OF ORGANIZATION** 組織機構 **5** [C] a department in an organization, institution, etc. 部門；處；科；股；組 SYN **division**：*He's the director of the finance section.* 他是財務處處長。

▸ **DISTRICT** 地區 **6** [C] (*NAmE*) a district of a town, city or county 區；地區；地段：*the Dorchester section of Boston* 波士頓的多切斯特區

▸ **MEASUREMENT** 度量 **7** [C] (*NAmE*) a measure of land, equal to one square mile（土地單位）一平方英里

▸ **DIAGRAM** 圖 **8** [C] a drawing or diagram of sth as it would look if it were cut from top to bottom or from one side to the other 剖面圖；斷面圖：*The illustration shows a section through a leaf.* 圖中所示為葉的剖面。◇*The architect drew the house **in section**.* 建築師繪製了房子的剖面圖。➲ see also CROSS SECTION

▸ **MEDICAL** 醫療 **9** [C, U] (*medical* 醫) the act of cutting or separating sth in an operation 切開；切斷：*The surgeon performed a section (= made a cut) on the vein.* 外科醫生施行了靜脈切開手術。➲ see also CAESAREAN **10** [C] (*medical* 醫, *biology* 生) a very thin flat piece cut from body TISSUE to be looked at under a MICROSCOPE（供顯微鏡下觀察的）切片：*to examine a section from the kidney* 觀察腎臟切片

■ *verb*

▸ **MEDICAL/BIOLOGY** 醫療；生物學 **1** **~ sth** (*medical* 醫) to divide body TISSUE by cutting 切開；切斷 **2** **~ sth** (*biology* 生) to cut animal or plant TISSUE into thin slices in order to look at it under a MICROSCOPE 做（動物或植物組織的）切片

▸ **MENTAL PATIENT** 精神病人 **3** [often passive] **~ sb** (*BrE*) to officially order a mentally ill person to go and receive treatment in a PSYCHIATRIC hospital, using a law that can force them to stay there until they are successfully treated（依法令精神病人）強制入院治療

PHR V **ˌsection sth↔ˈoff** to separate an area from a larger one 隔出；劃出：*Parts of the town had been sectioned off.* 城市的部份地區被劃了出去。

sec·tion·al /ˈsekʃənl/ *adj.* [usually before noun] **1** connected with one particular group within a community or an organization（社團或組織中）某群體的，某階層的：*the sectional interests of managers and workers* 管理層和廣大工人的不同利益 **2** made of separate sections 組合式的：*a sectional building* 組合式建築 **3** connected with a CROSS SECTION of sth (= a surface or an image formed by cutting through sth from top to bottom) 剖面的；斷面的：*a sectional drawing* 剖面圖

ˌSection ˈEight *noun* (*NAmE*) **1** [U] (in the past) a part of US army law that dealt with dismissing a soldier who was considered not suitable 美國陸軍條例第八款（舊時據此開除被認為不適合當兵的軍人的軍籍）**2** [C] (*informal*) a soldier who has been dismissed from the US army because he is not mentally fit（由於心理不適而）遭開除軍籍的軍人

sec·tor 0-w AW /ˈsektə(r)/ *noun*
1 0-w a part of an area of activity, especially of a country's economy（尤指一國經濟的）部門，領域，行業：*the manufacturing sector* 製造業◇*service-sector jobs* (= in hotels, restaurants, etc.) 服務性行業的工作 ➲ COLLOCATIONS at ECONOMY ➲ see also THE PRIVATE

S

SECTOR, THE PUBLIC SECTOR **2** a part of a particular area, especially an area under military control（尤指軍事管制的）區域，地帶：*each sector of the war zone* 戰區的每個軍控地段 **3** (*geometry* 幾何) a part of a circle lying between two straight lines drawn from the centre to the edge 扇形 ➲ VISUAL VOCAB page V71

secu·lar /ˈsekjələ(r)/ *adj.* **1** not connected with spiritual or religious matters 現世的；世俗的；非宗教的：*secular music* 世俗音樂 ◇ *Ours is a secular society.* 我們的社會是個世俗社會。 **2** (of priests 司祭) living among ordinary people rather than in a religious community 教區的；在俗的

secu·lar·ism /ˈsekjələrɪzəm/ *noun* [U] (*technical* 術語) the belief that religion should not be involved in the organization of society, education, etc. 現世主義，世俗主義（認為社會結構和教育等應排除宗教的影響）▶ **secu·lar·ist** /-lərɪst/ *adj.* [usually before noun]

secu·lar·iza·tion (*BrE* also **-isa·tion**) /ˌsekjələraɪˈzeɪʃn; *NAmE* -rəˈz-/ *noun* [U] the process of removing the influence or power that religion has over sth 現世化；世俗化

secu·lar·ize (*BrE* also **-ise**) /ˈsekjələraɪz/ *verb* [often passive] **~ sth** to make sth SECULAR; to remove sth from the control or influence of religion 使現世化；使世俗化；使脫離宗教控制：*a secularized society* 世俗化社會

se·cure AW /sɪˈkjʊə(r); *NAmE* səˈkjʊr/ *adj.*, *verb*

■ ***adj.***

▸ HAPPY/CONFIDENT 滿足；自信 **1** feeling happy and confident about yourself or a particular situation 安心的；有把握的：*At last they were able to **feel secure** about the future.* 他們終於覺得不必為將來而擔憂了。◇ *She finished the match, **secure in the knowledge that** she was through to the next round.* 她打完比賽，知道自己已進入下一輪，心裏踏實了。OPP **insecure**

▸ CERTAIN/SAFE 可靠；保險 **2** likely to continue or be successful for a long time 可靠的；牢靠的；穩固的 SYN **safe**：*a **secure job/income*** 穩定的工作／收入 ◇ *It's not a very secure way to make a living.* 以此謀生終非長久之計。◇ *The future of the company looks secure.* 看來公司未來不會有問題。OPP **insecure** **3** **~ (against/from sth)** that cannot be affected or harmed by sth 安全的；穩妥的：*Information must be stored so that it is secure from accidental deletion.* 必須把資料保存起來，這樣才不至於無意中刪除。

▸ BUILDING/DOOR/ROOM 建築物；門；房間 **4** guarded and/or made stronger so that it is difficult for people to enter or leave 嚴密把守的；牢固的；堅固的：*Check that all windows and doors have been made as secure as possible.* 看看是不是所有的門窗都關緊了。◇ *a secure unit for child offenders* 少年犯拘留病房 OPP **insecure**

▸ FIRM 牢固 **5** not likely to move, fall down, etc. 牢固的；穩固的；堅固的 SYN **stable**：*The aerial doesn't look very secure to me.* 我看這天線不太牢固。◇ *It was difficult to maintain a secure foothold on the ice.* 在冰上不容易站穩腳。◇ (*figurative*) *Our relationship was now on a more secure footing.* 現在，我們的關係有一個更為穩固的基礎了。OPP **insecure** ▶ **se·cure·ly** AW *adv.*：*She locked the door securely behind her.* 她隨手把門鎖好。◇ *Make sure the ropes are securely fastened.* 務必把繩子拴牢。

■ ***verb*** (*formal*)

▸ GET STH 得到 **1** to obtain or achieve sth, especially when this means using a lot of effort（尤指經過努力）獲得，取得，實現：**~ sth** *to **secure a contract/deal*** 訂立合同；達成協議 ◇ *The team managed to secure a place in the finals.* 球隊拚得了決賽的一席之地。◇ *She secured 2 000 votes.* 她獲得 2 000 票。◇ **~ sth for sb/sth/yourself** *He secured a place for himself at law school.* 他在法學院取得了學籍。◇ **~ sb/sth/yourself sth** *He secured himself a place at law school.* 他取得了法學院的學籍。

▸ FASTEN FIRMLY 牢靠地固定 **2** **~ sth (to sth)** to attach or fasten sth firmly 拴牢；扣緊；關嚴：*She secured the rope firmly to the back of the car.* 她把繩子牢牢地拴在車後面。

▸ PROTECT FROM HARM 使不受危害 **3** to protect sth so that it is safe and difficult to attack or damage 保護；保衛；使安全：**~ sth against sth** *to secure a property against intruders* 保護房產以免外人闖入 ◇ **~ sth** *The windows were secured with locks and bars.* 窗戶已經插上栓，上了鎖，都關好了。◇ (*figurative*) *a savings plan that will secure your child's future* 為您孩子的未來提供保障的儲蓄計劃

▸ A LOAN 借貸 **4** **~ sth** to legally agree to give sb property or goods that are worth the same amount as the money that you have borrowed from them, if you are unable to pay the money back 抵押：*a loan secured on the house* 以房子作抵押的貸款

se·cur·ity AW /sɪˈkjʊərəti; *NAmE* səˈkjʊr-/ *noun* (*pl.* **-ies**)

▸ PROTECTION 保護 **1** [U] the activities involved in protecting a country, building or person against attack, danger, etc. 保護措施；安全工作：***national security*** (= the defence of a country) 國家安全 ◇ *airport security* 機場的安全措施 ◇ *They carried out **security checks** at the airport.* 他們在機場實行了安全檢查。◇ *The visit took place amidst **tight security*** (= the use of many police officers). 訪問是在戒備森嚴的情況下進行的。◇ *the **security forces/services*** (= the police, army, etc.) 安全部隊／機構 ◇ *a **high/maximum security prison*** (= for dangerous criminals) 高度／最高級戒備的監獄 ➲ COLLOCATIONS at INTERNATIONAL ➲ see also HIGH-SECURITY **2** [U+sing./pl. v.] the department of a large company or organization that deals with the protection of its buildings, equipment and staff 保衛部門；保安部門：*Security was/were called to the incident.* 保安人員被叫到事發現場。 **3** [U] protection against sth bad that might happen in the future 擔保；保證：*financial security* 財務擔保 ◇ ***Job security*** (= the guarantee that you will keep your job) *is a thing of the past.* 穩定的工作是過去的事了。

▸ FEELING HAPPY/SAFE 感覺愉快／安全 **4** [U] the state of feeling happy and safe from danger or worry 安全；平安：*the security of a loving family life* 安享天倫之樂 ◇ *She'd allowed herself to be lulled into **a false sense of security*** (= a feeling that she was safe when in fact she was in danger). 她不自覺地陷入了一種虛假的安全感之中。

▸ FOR A LOAN 貸款 **5** [U, C] a valuable item, such as a house, that you agree to give to sb if you are unable to pay back the money that you have borrowed from them 抵押品：*His home and business are being held **as security for** the loan.* 他是以房子和店鋪為抵押得到這筆貸款的。

▸ SHARES IN COMPANY 公司股份 **6** **securities** [pl.] (*finance* 財) documents proving that sb is the owner of shares, etc. in a particular company 證券 ➲ see also SOCIAL SECURITY

seˈcurity blanket *noun* **1** a BLANKET or other object that a child holds in order to feel safe（兒童藉以得到安全感的）安慰毯，安慰物 **2** something that provides protection against attack, danger, etc. 保護物；防護措施；安全保障：*A firewall provides an essential security blanket for your computer network.* 防火牆為計算機網絡提供了基本安全保障。 **3** (*BrE*) official orders or measures that prevent people from knowing about, seeing, etc. sth 保密令；保密措施：*The government has thrown a security blanket around the talks.* 政府明令禁止泄露談判內容。

the Seˈcurity Council (also **the ˌUN Seˈcurity Council**, **the ˌUnited Nations Seˈcurity Council**) *noun* [sing.] the part of the United Nations that tries to keep peace and order in the world, consisting of representatives of fifteen countries（聯合國）安全理事會

seˈcurity guard *noun* a person whose job is to guard money, valuables, a building, etc. 保安人員

seˈcurity risk *noun* a person who cannot be given secret information because they are a danger to a particular country, organization, etc., especially because of their political beliefs 危險分子（尤指危及國家、機構等安全的）

Seˈcurity Service *noun* a government organization that protects a country and its secrets from enemies 國家安全機構

Secy. *abbr.* (*US*) = SEC.

sedan /sɪ'dæn/ (*NAmE*) (*BrE* **sa·loon**, **sa'loon car**) *noun* a car with four doors and a BOOT/TRUNK (= space at the back for carrying things) which is separated from the part where the driver and passengers sit 小轎車；（三廂四門）轎車 ➲ VISUAL VOCAB page V52

se,dan 'chair *noun* a box containing a seat for one person, carried on poles by two people, used in the 17th and 18th centuries 轎子

sed·ate /sɪ'deɪt/ *adj., verb*

■ ***adj.*** [usually before noun] **1** slow, calm and relaxed 鎮定的；泰然的；不慌不忙的 SYN **unhurried**： *We followed the youngsters at a more sedate pace.* 我們跟在年輕人後面，步子稍慢一點。 **2** quiet, especially in a way that lacks excitement 寧靜的；不熱鬧的： *a sedate country town* 寧靜的鄉間小鎮 **3** (of a person 人) quiet and serious in a way that seems formal 莊重的；嚴肅的；不苟言笑的： *a sedate, sober man* 一個嚴肅審慎的人 ▶ **sed·ate·ly** *adv.*

■ ***verb*** [often passive] **~ sb/sth** to give sb drugs in order to make them calm and/or to make them sleep 給…服鎮靜劑 SYN **tranquillize**： *Most of the patients are heavily sedated.* 多數病人服了大劑量鎮靜藥。

sed·ation /sɪ'deɪʃn/ *noun* [U] the act of giving sb drugs in order to make them calm or to make them sleep; the state that results from this 藥物鎮靜；鎮靜狀態： *The victim's wife was last night being kept* ***under sedation*** *in the local hospital.* 昨晚，受害人的妻子在當地醫院用藥後處於鎮靜狀態。

seda·tive /'sedətɪv/ *noun* a drug that makes sb go to sleep or makes them feel calm and relaxed 鎮靜劑 SYN **tranquillizer** ▶ **seda·tive** *adj.* [usually before noun]： *the sedative effect of the drug* 這藥物的鎮靜效果

sed·en·tary /'sedntri; *NAmE* -teri/ *adj.* **1** (of work, activities, etc. 工作、活動等) in which you spend a lot of time sitting down 需要久坐的： *a* ***sedentary job/occupation/lifestyle*** 常久坐的工作 / 職業 / 生活方式 **2** (of people 人) spending a lot of time sitting down and not moving 慣於久坐不動的： *He became increasingly sedentary in later life.* 到晚年，他變得越來越不愛動了。 **3** (*technical* 術語) (of people or animals 人或動物) that stay and live in the same place or area 定居的；定棲的；不遷徙的：*Rhinos are largely sedentary animals.* 大致說來，犀牛是一種定棲動物。◇ *a sedentary population* 定居人口

Seder /'seɪdə(r)/ *noun* a Jewish CEREMONIAL service and dinner on the first night or first two nights of Passover 逾越節家宴（猶太教逾越節第一夜或第一第二兩夜舉行）

sedge /sedʒ/ *noun* [U] a plant like grass that grows in wet ground or near water 莎草；苔

sedi·ment /'sedɪmənt/ *noun* [U] **1** the solid material that settles at the bottom of a liquid 沉澱物 **2** (*geology* 地) sand, stones, mud, etc. carried by water or wind and left, for example, on the bottom of a lake, river, etc. 沉積物

sedi·ment·ary /,sedɪ'mentri/ *adj.* (*geology* 地) connected with or formed from the sand, stones, mud, etc. that settle at the bottom of lakes, etc. 沉積的；沉積形成的： *sedimentary rocks* 沉積岩

sedi·men·ta·tion /,sedɪmen'teɪʃn/ *noun* [U] (*geology* 地) the process of depositing sediment 沉積（過程）

se·di·tion /sɪ'dɪʃn/ *noun* [U] (*formal*) the use of words or actions that are intended to encourage people to oppose a government 煽動叛亂的言論（或行動） SYN **insurrection** ▶ **se·di·tious** /sɪ'dɪʃəs/ *adj.*： *seditious activity* 煽動叛亂的活動

se·duce /sɪ'dju:s; *NAmE* -'du:s/ *verb* **1 ~ sb** to persuade sb to have sex with you, especially sb who is younger or who has less experience than you 誘姦 **2 ~ sb** (**into sth/into doing sth**) to persuade sb to do sth that they would not usually agree to do by making it seem very attractive 誘騙；唆使 SYN **entice**： *The promise of huge profits seduced him into parting with his money.* 高額利潤的許諾誘使他把錢交了出來。

se·du·cer /sɪ'dju:sə(r); *NAmE* sɪ'du:sər/ *noun* a person who persuades sb to have sex with them 誘姦者

se·duc·tion /sɪ'dʌkʃn/ *noun* **1** [U, C] the act of persuading sb to have sex with you 誘姦： *Cleopatra's seduction of Caesar* 克里奧帕特拉對凱撒的引誘 **2** [C, usually pl., U] **~ (of sth)** the qualities or features of sth that make it seem attractive 誘惑力；魅力；吸引力 SYN **enticement**： *Who could resist the seductions of the tropical island?* 誰能不為這個熱帶海島的魅力而傾倒呢？

se·duc·tive /sɪ'dʌktɪv/ *adj.* **1** sexually attractive 誘人的；迷人的；有魅力的；性感的： *a seductive woman* 富有魅力的女人 ◇ *She used her most seductive voice.* 她運用了自己最有魅力的嗓音。 **2** attractive in a way that makes you want to have or do sth 有吸引力的；令人神往的 SYN **tempting**： *The idea of retiring to the south of France is highly seductive.* 退休後到法國南方去，這個主意令人心馳神往。 ▶ **se·duc·tive·ly** *adv.* **se·duc·tive·ness** *noun* [U]

se·duc·tress /sɪ'dʌktrəs/ *noun* a woman who persuades sb to have sex with her 勾引男人的女人

sedu·lous /'sedjuləs; *NAmE* 'sedʒələs/ *adj.* (*formal*) showing great care and effort in your work 勤勉的；孜孜不倦的；勤奮的 SYN **diligent** ▶ **sedu·lous·ly** *adv.*

see 🔑 /si:/ *verb, noun*

■ ***verb*** (**saw** /sɔ:/, **seen** /si:n/)

▸ **USE EYES** 用眼 **1** 🔑 [T, I] (not used in the progressive tenses 不用於進行時) to become aware of sb/sth by using your eyes 看見；見到；看出： **~ (sb/sth)** *She looked for him but couldn't see him in the crowd.* 她在人群裏找來找去，但沒看見他。◇ *The opera was the place to* ***see and be seen*** (= by other important or fashionable people). 歌劇院是個名流和時尚人士競顯丰采的地方。◇ **~ (that)** ... *He could see (that) she had been crying.* 他看得出她哭過。◇ **~ what, how, etc.** ... *Did you see what happened?* 你看見出什麼事了嗎？◇ **~ sb/sth + adj.** *I hate to see you unhappy.* 我不願見你不高興。◇ **~ sb/sth doing sth** *She was seen running away from the scene of the crime.* 有人看見她從犯罪現場跑開。◇ **~ sb/sth do sth** *I saw you put the key in your pocket.* 我見你把鑰匙放進了口袋裏。◇ **sb/sth is seen to do sth** *He was seen to enter the building about the time the crime was committed.* 有人看見他在案發時間前後進入那棟建築物。 **2** 🔑 [I] (not usually used in the progressive tenses 通常不用於進行時) to have or use the power of sight 看得見；看；有視力： *She will never see again* (= she has become blind). 她再也看不見東西了。◇ *On a clear day you* ***can see*** *for miles from here.* 在晴天，你從這兒能看出去很遠。◇ **~ to do sth** *It was getting dark and I* ***couldn't see*** *to read.* 天色黑下來，我看不成書了。

▸ **WATCH** 觀看 **3** 🔑 [T] (not usually used in the progressive tenses 通常不用於進行時) **~ sth** to watch a game, television programme, performance, etc. 觀看（比賽、電視節目、演出等）： *Did you see that programme on Brazil last night?* 昨晚你有沒有看那個介紹巴西的節目？◇ *In the evening we went to see a movie.* 晚上，我們去看了一場電影。◇ *Fifty thousand people saw the match.* 有五萬人觀看了那場比賽。 ➲ SYNONYMS at LOOK

▸ **LOOK UP INFORMATION** 檢索資料 **4** 🔑 [T] (used in orders 用於祈使句) **~ sth** to look at sth in order to find information 見；參見： *See page 158.* 參見第 158 頁。

▸ **MEET BY CHANCE** 偶然遇見 **5** 🔑 [T] **~ sb** (not usually used in the progressive tenses 通常不用於進行時) to be near and recognize sb; to meet sb by chance 遇見；碰到；邂逅： *Guess who I saw at the party last night!* 你猜猜，昨天我在晚會上碰見誰了！

▸ **VISIT** 拜訪 **6** 🔑 [T] **~ sb** to visit sb 拜訪；看望；探視： *Come and see us again soon.* 早點再來看我們。

▸ **HAVE MEETING** 會見 **7** 🔑 [T] **~ sb** (**about sth**) to have a meeting with sb 會見；會晤： *You ought to see a doctor about that cough.* 你得找個大夫看看你的咳嗽。◇ *What is it you want to see me about?* 你找我有什麼事？

▸ **SPEND TIME** 度過時間 **8** 🔑 [T] (often used in the progressive tenses 常用於進行時) **~ sb** to spend time with sb 與（某人）待在一起；交往： ***Are you seeing anyone*** (= having a romantic relationship with anyone)? 你是不是跟什麼人好上了？◇ *They've been* ***seeing a lot of each***

S

other (= spending a lot of time together) *recently.* 他們近來老泡在一起。

▸ **UNDERSTAND 理解 9** [I, T] (not usually used in the progressive tenses 通常不用於進行時) to understand sth 理解；明白；領會：*'It opens like this.' 'Oh, I see.'* "這樣就打開了。" "哦，我明白了。" ◇ **~ sth** *He didn't see the joke.* 他沒聽懂這則笑話。◇ *I don't think she* ***saw the point*** *of the story.* 我覺得她沒有領會故事的中心意思。◇ *I can see both sides of the argument.* 爭論雙方的觀點我都清楚。◇ *Make Lydia* ***see reason*** (= be sensible), *will you?* 你要讓莉迪婭明白道理好不好？◇ **~ (that)** … *Can't you see (that) he's taking advantage of you?* 他在利用你，難道你看不出來？◇ ***I don't see that it matters*** *what Josh thinks.* 喬希怎麼想有什麼要緊，我不明白。◇ **~ what, why, etc.** … *'It's broken.' 'Oh yes,* ***I see what you mean.***' "它破了。" "噢，我明白你的意思。" ◇ *'Can we go swimming?'* ***'I don't see why not*** (= yes, you can).' "我們可以去游泳嗎？" "可以呀。" ◇ **be seen to do sth** *The government not only has to do something, it must* ***be seen to be doing something*** (= people must be aware that it is doing sth). 政府不僅必須採取措施，而且必須讓人們知道它在採取措施。 ➲ SYNONYMS at UNDERSTAND

▸ **HAVE OPINION 認為 10** [T] **~ sth + adv./prep.** (not usually used in the progressive tenses 通常不用於進行時) to have an opinion of sth 認為；看待：*I see things differently now.* 現在，我看問題的方法不一樣了。◇ *Try to see things from her point of view.* 設法從她那個角度去看問題。◇ *Lack of money is the main problem,* ***as I see it*** (= in my opinion). 依我看，主要問題是缺錢。◇ ***The way I see it,*** *you have three main problems.* 我認為你有三個主要問題。 ➲ SYNONYMS at REGARD

▸ **IMAGINE 想像 11** [T] (not used in the progressive tenses 不用於進行時) to consider sth as a future possibility; to imagine sb/sth as sth 設想；想像：**~ sb/sth doing sth** *I can't see her changing her mind.* 我無法想像她會改變主意。◇ **~ sb/sth as sth** *His colleagues see him as a future director.* 他的同事認為他很可能是未來的負責人。 ➲ SYNONYMS at IMAGINE

▸ **FIND OUT 弄清 12** [I, T] (not usually used in the progressive tenses 通常不用於進行時) to find out sth by looking, asking or waiting （通過查看、打聽、等待）弄清，瞭解：*'Has the mail come yet?' 'I'll just go and see.'* "郵件來了沒有？" "我去看看。" ◇ *'Is he going to get better?' 'I don't know, we'll just have to* ***wait and see.***' "他會好起來嗎？" "不清楚，我們只能等着瞧了。" ◇ *We'll have a great time,* ***you'll see.*** 你瞧着吧，我們會很開心的。◇ **~ what, how, etc.** … *Go and see what the kids are doing, will you?* 你去看看孩子們在幹什麼好不好？◇ *We'll have to* ***see how it goes.*** 我們得看看情況怎麼樣。◇ **~ (that)** … *I see (that) interest rates are going up again.* 我知道利率又在提高了。◇ **it is seen that** … *It can be* ***seen that*** *certain groups are more at risk than others.* 看得出，有的組風險大，有的組風險小。 **13** [I, T] (not usually used in the progressive tenses 通常不用於進行時) to find out or decide sth by thinking or considering 考慮；定奪：*'Will you be able to help us?' 'I don't know, I'll have to see.'* "你能幫助我們嗎？" "不好說，我得考慮一下。" ◇ *'Can I go to the party?'* ***'We'll see*** (= I'll decide later).' "我能去參加聚會嗎？" "待會兒再看吧。" ◇ **~ what, whether, etc.** … ***I'll see what I can do*** *to help.* 我考慮考慮，看我能幫上什麼忙。

▸ **MAKE SURE 確保 14** [T] (not usually used in the progressive tenses 通常不用於進行時) **~ that** … to make sure that you do sth or that sth is done 確保；務必（做到）：*See that all the doors are locked before you leave.* 一定要把所有的門都鎖好了再走。

▸ **EXPERIENCE 經歷 15** [T] (not used in the progressive tenses 不用於進行時) **~ sth** to experience or suffer sth 經歷；遭受：*He has seen a great deal in his long life.* 他在漫長的一生中經歷了許多事情。◇ *I hope I never live to* ***see the day*** *when computers finally replace books.* 我可不願意活到那一天，看着計算機最終取代書籍。◇ *It didn't surprise her—she* ***had seen it all before.*** 她沒有大驚小怪，她以前全都見識過。

▸ **WITNESS EVENT 見證事件 16** [T] (not used in the progressive tenses 不用於進行時) **~ sth** to be the time when an event happens 為…發生的時間：*Next year sees the centenary of Mahler's death.* 明年是馬勒逝世一百周年。 **17** [T] (not used in the progressive tenses 不用於進行時) **~ sth** to be the place where an event happens 為…發生的地點 **SYN** **witness**：*This stadium has seen many thrilling football games.* 在這座體育場裏進行過許多激動人心的足球比賽。

▸ **HELP 幫助 18** [T] **~ sb + adv./prep.** to go with sb to help or protect them 送；護送：*I saw the old lady across* (= helped her cross) *the road.* 我護送老太太過馬路。◇ *May I see you home* (= go with you as far as your house)? 我可不可以送你回家？◇ *My secretary will* ***see you out*** (= show you the way out of the building). 我的秘書會把你送出去。

IDM Most idioms containing **see** are at the entries for the nouns and adjectives in the idioms, for example **not see the wood for the trees** is at **wood**. 大多數含 see 的習語，都可在該等習語中的名詞及形容詞相關詞條找到，如 not see the wood for the trees 在詞條 wood 下。 **for all (the world) to 'see** clearly visible; in a way that is clearly visible 明顯；顯而易見 **,let me 'see/let's see** (*informal*) used when you are thinking or trying to remember sth 讓我／咱們看看；讓我／咱們想一想：*Now let me see—how old is she now?* 讓我想一想，她現在多大了呢？ **see sth 'coming** to realize that there is going to be a problem before it happens 料到會有問題；意識到會出麻煩：*We should have seen it coming. There was no way he could keep going under all that pressure.* 我們本該料到的。承受着那麼大的壓力，他不可能堅持下去。 **,see for your'self** to find out or look at sth yourself in order to be sure that what sb is saying is true 親自看，親自瞭解（以核實）：*If you don't believe me, go and see for yourself!* 要是不信我說的，你自己去看看！ **see sb/sth for what they 'are/it 'is** to realize that sb/sth is not as good, pleasant, etc. as they/it seem 看清某人（或事物）的真實狀況（不是表面那樣） **seeing that** … (also *informal* **seeing as (how)** …) because of the fact that … 鑒於；由於；因為：*Seeing that he's been off sick all week he's unlikely to come.* 他請病假整整一週了，所以今天也不大可能來。 **'see you (a'round)** | **(I'll) be 'seeing you** | **,see you 'later** (*informal*) goodbye 再見：*I'd better be going now. See you!* 現在我可該走了。再見！ **you 'see** (*informal*) used when you are explaining sth （作解釋時說）你看，你知道，要知道：*You see, the thing is, we won't be finished before Friday.* 要知道，問題是星期五以前我們完不了事。

PHR V **'see about sth** to deal with sth 辦理；照料；料理；安排：*I must see about* (= prepare) *lunch.* 我得做午飯了。◇ *He says he won't help, does he? Well,* ***we'll soon see about that*** (= I will demand that he does help). 他說他不幫忙，是不是？好，我們這就去找他。◇ **~ doing sth** *I'll have to see about getting that roof repaired.* 我得找人把房頂修一修。 **'see sth in sb/sth** to find sb/sth attractive or interesting 看上；看中；覺得…有趣：***I don't know what she sees in him.*** 我不知道她看上他哪兒了。 **,see sb↔'off 1** to go to a station, an airport, etc. to say goodbye to sb who is starting a journey 為…送行；送別 **2** (*BrE*) to force sb to leave a place, for example by chasing them 趕走，驅逐（某人）：*The dogs saw them off in no time.* 幾條狗立刻把他們嚇走了。 **3** (*BrE*) to defeat sb in a game, fight, etc. （在遊戲、戰鬥等活動中）打敗，擊敗：*The home team saw off the challengers by 68 points to 47.* 主隊以 68:47 擊敗前來挑戰的客隊。 **,see sb↔'out** (not used in the progressive tenses 不用於進行時) (*BrE*) to last longer than the rest of sb's life 壽命比某人長；看着某人故去：*I've had this coat for years, and I'm sure it will see me out.* 這件外衣我穿了好多年，我敢說它能穿一輩子。 **,see sth↔'out** (not used in the progressive tenses 不用於進行時) (*BrE*) to reach the end or last until the end of sth 持續到…結束：*They had enough fuel to see the winter out.* 他們有足夠的燃料過冬。◇ *He saw out his career in Italy.* 他在意大利一直工作到退休。 **,see 'over sth** (*BrE*) to visit and look at a place carefully 察看（某處）：*We need to see over the house before we can make you an offer.* 我們需要好好看了房子以後才能給你開個價。 **,see 'through sb/sth** (not used in the progressive tenses 不用於進行時) to realize the truth about sb/sth 看透；識破：*We saw through him from the start.* 一開始我們就識破他了。◇ *I can see through your little game* (= I am

S

aware of the trick you are trying to play on me). 我看透了你的小把戲。 **ˌsee sth ˈthrough** (not usually used in the progressive tenses 通常不用於進行時) to not give up doing a task, project, etc. until it is finished 把（任務、工程等）進行到底；堅持完成： *She's determined to see the job through.* 她決心完成這項工作。 **ˌsee sb ˈthrough | ˌsee sb ˈthrough sth** (not used in the progressive tenses 不用於進行時) to give help or support to sb for a particular period of time 幫助（或支持）某人度過： *Her courage and good humour saw her through.* 她靠着頑強的勇氣和樂觀的性格挺了過來。◇ *I only have $20 to see me through the week.* 我只有 20 元來維持我這一週了。 **ˈsee to sth** to deal with sth 辦理；照管；料理： *Will you see to the arrangements for the next meeting?* 你來負責安排下次會議，好嗎？◇ *Don't worry—**I'll see to it**.* 別擔心，這事兒我來處理。◇ *We'll have to get that door seen to* (= repaired). 我們得找人把那扇門修一下。 **ˈsee to it that …** to make sure that … 確保；務使： *Can you see to it that the fax goes this afternoon?* 你保證今天下午就把傳真發出去，行嗎？

■ ***noun*** (*formal*) the district or office of a BISHOP or an ARCHBISHOP 主教（或大主教）教區；主教（或大主教）權限；牧座： *the Holy See* (= the office of the POPE)（羅馬）宗座

Synonyms 同義詞辨析

see

spot • catch • glimpse

These words all mean to become aware of sb/sth by using your eyes, especially suddenly or when it is not easy to see them/it. 以上各詞均含看見、見到、看出之意，尤指突然發現或注意到。

see to become aware of sb/sth by using your eyes 指看見、見到、看出： *She looked for him but couldn't see him in the crowd.* 她在人群裏找來找去，但沒看見他。◇ *He could see (that) she had been crying.* 他看得出她哭過。

spot to see or notice sb/sth, especially suddenly or when they are not easy to see or notice 指看見、看出，尤指突然發現或注意到： *I've just spotted a mistake on the front cover.* 我剛才在封面上發現了一處錯誤。

catch to see or notice sth for a moment, but not clearly or completely 指瞥見、察覺： *She **caught sight of** a car in the distance.* 她瞥見遠處有一輛車。◇ *He **caught a glimpse** of himself in the mirror.* 他看了一眼鏡子中的自己。

glimpse (*literary*) to see sb/sth for a moment, but not clearly or completely 指瞥見、看一眼： *He'd glimpsed her through the window as he passed.* 他路過時透過窗戶瞥見了她。

PATTERNS

- to see/spot **that/how/what/where/who …**
- to **suddenly** see/spot/catch/glimpse sb/sth

seed /siːd/ *noun, verb*

■ ***noun***

▸ **OF PLANTS/FRUIT 植物；果實** **1** [C, U] the small hard part produced by a plant, from which a new plant can grow 種子；籽： *a packet of wild flower seeds* 一包野花籽 ◇ *sesame seeds* 芝麻 ◇ ***Sow the seeds** outdoors in spring.* 春天把種子播在地裏。◇ *These vegetables can be **grown from seed**.* 這些蔬菜可以撒籽栽種。◇ ***seed potatoes*** (= used for planting) 留種的土豆 ➲ **COLLOCATIONS** at LIFE ➲ **VISUAL VOCAB** pages V10, V32 ➲ see also BIRDSEED **2** [C] (*NAmE*) = PIP *n.* (1) ➲ **VISUAL VOCAB** page V30

▸ **BEGINNING 起源** **3** [C, usually pl.] **~ (of sth)** the beginning of a feeling or a development which continues to grow 起源；起因；萌芽；開端： *the seeds of rebellion* 反叛的起因 ◇ *This **planted the seeds of** doubt in my mind.* 這件事在我心中播下了懷疑的種子。

▸ **IN TENNIS 網球** **4** [C] (especially in TENNIS 尤指網球) one of the best players in a competition. The seeds are given a position in a list to try and make sure that they do not play each other in the early parts of the competition. 種子選手： *The top seed won comfortably.* 頭號種子選手輕鬆獲勝。◇ *the number one seed* 一號種子選手

▸ **OF A MAN 男子** **5** [U] (*old-fashioned* or *humorous*) SEMEN 精液 **6** [U] (*literary*) all the people who are the children, grandchildren, etc. of one man（統稱某人的）子孫，後裔，後代

IDM **go/run to ˈseed** **1** (especially of a vegetable plant 尤指蔬菜) to produce flowers and seeds as well as leaves 花謝結籽 **2** to become much less attractive or good because of lack of attention 變得懶散頹廢（或意志消沉）；衰敗： *After his divorce, he let himself go to seed.* 離婚後，他自暴自棄。 ➲ more at SOW[1] *v.*

■ ***verb***

▸ **OF A PLANT 植物** **1** [I] to produce seeds 結籽 **2** [T] **~ itself** to produce other plants using its own seeds（種子）繁殖

▸ **AREA OF GROUND 土地** **3** [T, usually passive] **~ sth (with sth)** to plant seeds in an area of ground 在…播種： *a newly seeded lawn* 新撒了草籽的草坪

▸ **IN TENNIS 網球** **4** [T, usually passive] **~ sb** to make sb a seed in a competition 確定（某人）為種子選手： *He has been seeded 14th at Wimbledon next week.* 他被確定為下週温布爾登網球公開賽的第 14 號種子選手。

seed·bed /ˈsiːdbed/ *noun* **1** an area of soil which has been specially prepared for planting seeds in 苗牀 **2** [usually sing.] **~ (of/for sth)** a place or situation in which sth can develop（某事物發展的）有利環境；温牀

ˈseed cake *noun* [C, U] a cake containing CARAWAY seeds 籽香蛋糕；葛縷子籽糕餅

seed·corn /ˈsiːdkɔːn; *NAmE* -kɔːrn/ *noun* [U] **1** the grain that is kept for planting the next year's crops 糧種 **2** people or things that will be successful or useful in the future 有遠大前程的人（或事物）；日後有用的人（或事物）

seed·ed /ˈsiːdɪd/ *adj.* [usually before noun] **1** (especially of a TENNIS player 尤指網球運動員) given a number showing that they are one of the best players in a particular competition 確定為種子選手的： *a seeded player* 種子選手 **2** (of fruit 果實) with the seeds removed 去籽的；去核的： *seeded tomatoes* 去籽西紅柿

seed·less /ˈsiːdləs/ *adj.* [usually before noun] (of fruit 果實) having no seeds 無籽的；無核的： *seedless grapes* 無籽葡萄

seed·ling /ˈsiːdlɪŋ/ *noun* a young plant that has grown from a seed 秧苗；籽苗；幼苗 ➲ **VISUAL VOCAB** page V19

ˈseed money (also **ˈseed capital**) *noun* [U] money to start a new business, project, etc. 本錢；本金

ˈseed pearl *noun* a small PEARL 種珠（指定重量的小粒珍珠）

seeds·man /ˈsiːdzmən/ *noun* (*pl.* **-men** /-mən/) a person who grows and sells seeds 種農；種子商

seedy /ˈsiːdi/ *adj.* (**seed·ier**, **seedi·est**) (*disapproving*) dirty and unpleasant, possibly connected with immoral or illegal activities 骯髒的；污七八糟的；烏煙瘴氣的；下流的： *a seedy bar* 污七八糟的酒吧 ◇ *the seedy world of prostitution* 烏煙瘴氣的賣淫圈子 ◇ *a seedy-looking man* 一臉邪氣的男人 ▸ **seedi·ness** *noun* [U]

ˌSeeing ˈEye dog™ *noun* (*NAmE*) = GUIDE DOG

seek **AW** /siːk/ *verb* (**sought**, **sought** /sɔːt/) (*formal*) **1** [T, I] to look for sth/sb 尋找： **~ sth/sb** *Drivers are advised to seek alternative routes.* 請駕車者另尋其他路線。◇ **~ for sth/sb** (*BrE*) *They sought in vain for somewhere to shelter.* 他們怎麼也找不到一個藏身的地方。 **2** [T, I] **~ (sth)** to try to obtain or achieve sth 尋求；謀求；爭取： *to seek funding for a project* 為項目籌募資金 ◇ *Highly qualified secretary seeks employment.* (= in an advertisement) 優秀秘書求職（廣告用語）◇ *We are currently seeking new ways of expanding our membership.* 目前，我們正探索擴招會員的新途徑。 **3** [T] to ask sb for sth（向人）請求，尋求： **~ sth** *I think it's time we sought legal advice.* 我想我們現在該咨詢一下律師了。◇ **~ sth from sb** *She managed to calm him down and seek help from a neighbour.* 她設法使他平靜下來，

S

然後向一位鄰居求助。 **4** [I] **~ to do sth** to try to do sth 試圖；設法 SYN **attempt**：*They quickly sought to distance themselves from the protesters.* 他們迅速設法遠離抗議者。 **5 -seeking** (in adjectives and nouns 構成形容詞和名詞) looking for or trying to get the thing mentioned; the activity of doing this 尋求（或追求）…的；對…的尋求（或追求）：*attention-seeking behaviour* 為引起他人的注意而作出的行為 ◇ *Voluntary work can provide a framework for job-seeking.* 參與義務工作有助於奠定求職的基礎。 ➲ see also HEAT-SEEKING, SELF-SEEKING ➲ see also HIDE-AND-SEEK

IDM **seek your 'fortune** (*literary*) to try to find a way to become rich, especially by going to another place 外出尋找發財機會；外出闖蕩；闖世界

PHR V **,seek sb/sth 'out** to look for and find sb/sth, especially when this means using a lot of effort 挑選出；物色

seek·er /'siːkə(r)/ *noun* (often in compounds 常構成複合詞) a person who is trying to find or get the thing mentioned 尋找者；尋求者；追求者；謀求者：***an attention/a publicity seeker*** 故意引人注意的人；追求出名的人 ◇ *seekers after the truth* 追求真理的人 ➲ see also ASYLUM SEEKER, JOB SEEKER

seem 🔑 /siːm/ *linking verb*

1 🔑 **~ (to sb) (to be) sth** (not used in the progressive tenses 不用於進行時) to give the impression of being or doing sth（給人印象）好像，似乎，看來 SYN **appear**：**+ adj.** *You seem happy.* 你好像挺高興。◇ *Do whatever seems best to you.* 你覺得什麼最好，就做什麼。◇ **+ noun** *He seems a nice man.* 他看來是個好人。◇ **~ like sth** *It seemed like a good idea at the time.* 當時這主意好像不錯。◇ **~ (as though ...)** *It always seemed as though they would get married.* 他們一直彷彿是要結婚似的。◇ *'He'll be there, then?' '**So it seems** (= people say so).'*"這麼說，他要去那兒了？""似乎是這樣。"◇ **it seems that ...** *It seems that they know what they're doing.* 看來，他們知道自己在幹什麼。◇ **~ to do/be/have sth** *They seem to know what they're doing.* 看來，他們知道自己在幹什麼。 **2** 🔑 **~ to do/be/have sth** used to make what you say about your thoughts, feelings or actions less strong（用以緩和語氣）感到好像，覺得似乎：*I seem to have left my book at home.* 我大概是把書忘在家裏了。◇ *I can't seem to* (= I've tried, but I can't) *get started today.* 我怕是沒法在今天開始了。 **3** 🔑 **it seems | it would seem** used to suggest that sth is true when you are not certain or when you want to be polite（表示不確切或客氣）看來好像，似乎：**~ (that) ...** *It would seem that we all agree.* 我們大家似乎都同意。◇ **+ adj.** *It seems only reasonable to ask students to buy a dictionary.* 要學生買一本詞典似乎挺合情合理的。 ➲ LANGUAGE BANK at IMPERSONAL, OPINION, PERHAPS

S

seem·ing /'siːmɪŋ/ *adj.* [only before noun] (*formal*) appearing to be sth that may not be true 看似…（而實際未必）的；表面上的；貌似…的 SYN **apparent**：*a seeming impossibility* 表面看來不可能的事 ◇ *She handled the matter with seeming indifference.* 她看似漫不經心地處理了這件事。

seem·ing·ly /'siːmɪŋli/ *adv.* **1** in a way that appears to be true but may in fact not be 看似；貌似；表面上：*a seemingly stupid question* 看似愚蠢的問題 ◇ *a **seemingly endless** journey* 似乎永遠走不完的旅程 **2** (*formal*) according to what you have read or heard 據說；聽說；看來 SYN **apparently**：*Seemingly, he borrowed the money from the bank.* 據說，他從銀行貸出了那筆錢。

seem·ly /'siːmli/ *adj.* (*old-fashioned* or *formal*) appropriate for a particular social situation 合適的；得體的；合乎禮儀的 OPP **unseemly**

seen *past part.* of SEE

seep /siːp/ *verb* [I] **+ adv./prep.** (especially of liquids 尤指液體) to flow slowly and in small quantities through sth or into sth 滲；滲透 SYN **trickle**：*Blood was beginning to seep through the bandages.* 血開始從繃帶滲出來。◇ *Water seeped from a crack in the pipe.* 水從管道的一個裂縫中滲出。◇ (*figurative*) *Gradually the pain seeped away.* 疼痛漸漸消失了。

seep·age /'siːpɪdʒ/ *noun* [U, C, usually pl.] the process by which a liquid flows slowly and in small quantities through sth; the result of this process 滲；滲透；滲液：*Water gradually escapes by seepage through the ground.* 水逐漸從地上滲走了。◇ *oil seepages* 油滲

seer /sɪə(r); *NAmE* sɪr/ *noun* (*literary*) (especially in the past) a person who claims that they can see what is going to happen in the future（尤指舊時）預言家，先知 SYN **prophet**

seer·sucker /'sɪəsʌkə(r); *NAmE* 'sɪrs-/ *noun* [U] a type of light cotton cloth with a pattern of raised lines and squares on its surface 綯條紋薄織物；泡泡紗

'see-saw *noun, verb*

■ ***noun*** **1** (*NAmE* also **'teeter-totter**) [C] a piece of equipment for children to play on consisting of a long flat piece of wood that is supported in the middle. A child sits at each end and makes the see-saw move up and down. 蹺蹺板 **2** [sing.] a situation in which things keep changing from one state to another and back again 拉鋸局面（指來回往復，起伏不斷）

■ ***verb*** [I] **~ (from A to B)** to keep changing from one situation, opinion, emotion, etc. to another and back again（局勢、意見、感情等）搖擺不定，不斷反覆，交替：*Her emotions see-sawed from anger to fear.* 她一會兒氣，一會兒怕，情緒變來變去。◇ *Share prices see-sawed all day.* 整整一天，股票價格時漲時跌，不斷變化。

seethe /siːð/ *verb* [I] **1** to be extremely angry about sth but try not to show other people how angry you are 強壓怒火；生悶氣 SYN **fume**：*She seethed silently in the corner.* 她在角落裏默默地生悶氣。◇ **~ with sth** *He marched off, seething with frustration.* 他大為失望，氣呼呼地走開了。◇ **~ at sth** *Inwardly he was seething at this challenge to his authority.* 他在心裏因權威受到挑戰而悶悶不樂。 **2 ~ (with sth)** (*formal*) (of a place 地方) to be full of a lot of people or animals, especially when they are all moving around 充滿，遍佈，到處都是（人、動物）：*The resort is seething with tourists all year round.* 這處名勝一年四季遊人如鯽。◇ *He became caught up in a **seething mass** of arms and legs.* 他被捲進了摩肩接踵的人群。 **3** (*formal*) (of liquids 液體) to move around quickly and violently 翻滾；翻騰；洶動：*The grey ocean seethed beneath them.* 灰濛濛的大海在他們下面翻滾。

'see-through *adj.* (of cloth 織物) very thin so that you can see through it 薄至透明的；透視的：*a see-through blouse* 透明的女式襯衫

seg·ment *noun, verb*

■ ***noun*** /'segmənt/ **1** a part of sth that is separate from the other parts or can be considered separately 部份；份；片；段：*She cleaned a small segment of the painting.* 她擦乾淨了這幅畫的一小部份。◇ *Lines divided the area into segments.* 這一地區用線條分成了若干部份。 **2** one of the sections of an orange, a lemon, etc.（柑橘、檸檬等的）瓣 ➲ VISUAL VOCAB page V30 **3** (*geometry* 幾何) a part of a circle separated from the rest by a single line 弓形；圓缺 ➲ VISUAL VOCAB page V71 **4** (*phonetics* 語音) the smallest speech sound that a word can be divided into 音段

■ ***verb*** /seg'ment/ [often passive] **~ sth** (*technical* 術語) to divide sth into different parts 分割；劃分：*Market researchers often segment the population on the basis of age and social class.* 市場研究人員常常按年齡和社會階層劃分人口。◇ *The worm has a segmented body* (= with different sections joined together). 這條蟲子的身體是分節的。

seg·men·tal /seg'mentl/ *adj.* (*phonetics* 語音) relating to the individual sounds that make up speech, as opposed to PROSODIC features such as stress and INTONATION 音段的

seg·men·ta·tion /,segmen'teɪʃn/ *noun* [U, C, usually pl.] (*technical* 術語) the act of dividing sth into different parts; one of these parts 分割；劃分；分割成（或劃分成）的部份

seg·re·gate /'segrɪgeɪt/ *verb* (*formal*) **1 ~ sb (from sb)** to separate people of different races, religions or sexes and treat them in a different way 隔離並區別對待（不同種族、宗教或性別的人）：*a culture in which women* *are segregated from men* 婦女受到隔離歧視的文化 ◇ *a racially segregated community* 實行種族隔離的社會 ◇ *a segregated school* (= one for students of one race or religion only) 單一種族（或信仰）的學校 OPP **integrate** **2 ~ sth (from sth)** to keep one thing separate from another（使）分開，分離，隔離：*In all our restaurants, smoking and non-smoking areas are segregated from each other.* 在我們所有的餐館中，吸煙區和非吸煙區都是分開的。

seg·re·ga·tion /ˌseɡrɪˈɡeɪʃn/ *noun* [U] (*formal*) **1** the act or policy of separating people of different races, religions or sexes and treating them in a different way（對不同種族、宗教或性別的人所採取的）隔離並區別對待，隔離政策：***racial/religious segregation*** 種族 / 宗教隔離 ◇ *segregation by age and sex* 按照年齡和性別而實施的隔離 ➲ COLLOCATIONS at RACE **2** (*formal*) the act of separating people or things from a larger group 隔離（或分離）措施：*the segregation of smokers and non-smokers in restaurants* 把餐館中的吸煙者與非吸煙者分隔開的做法

seg·re·ga·tion·ist /ˌseɡrɪˈɡeɪʃənɪst/ *adj.* supporting the separation of people according to their sex, race or religion（性別、種族、宗教）隔離主義的：*segregationist policies* 隔離主義政策 ▶ **seg·re·ga·tion·ist** *noun*

segue /ˈseɡweɪ/ *verb* [I] **+ adv./prep.** to move smoothly from one song, subject, place, etc. to another（順利）轉到，接入（另一首歌、話題、地方等）：*a spiritual that segued into a singalong chorus* 一首轉為會眾集體跟唱的靈歌 ◇ *He then segued into a discussion of atheism.* 然後他轉入對無神論的論述。 ▶ **segue** *noun*

seine /seɪn/ (also **ˈseine net**) *noun* a type of fishing net which hangs down in the water and is pulled together at the ends to catch fish（捕魚用）圍網

seis·mic /ˈsaɪzmɪk/ *adj.* [only before noun] **1** connected with or caused by EARTHQUAKES 地震的；地震引起的：*seismic waves* 地震波 **2** having a very great effect; of very great size 影響深遠的；重大的：*a* ***seismic shift*** *in the political process* 政治進程中的劇變

seis·mo·graph /ˈsaɪzməɡrɑːf; *NAmE* -ɡræf/ *noun* an instrument that measures and records information about EARTHQUAKES 地震儀；測震儀

seis·mol·ogy /saɪzˈmɒlədʒi; *NAmE* -ˈmɑːl-/ *noun* [U] the scientific study of EARTHQUAKES 地震學 ▶ **seis·mo·logic·al** /ˌsaɪzməˈlɒdʒɪkl; *NAmE* -ˈlɑːdʒ-/ *adj.*：*the National Seismological Institute* 國家地震研究所 **seis·molo·gist** /-dʒɪst/ *noun*

seize /siːz/ *verb* **1** to take sb/sth in your hand suddenly and using force 抓住；捉住；奪 SYN **grab**：**~ sth from sb** *She tried to seize the gun from him.* 她試圖奪他的槍。◇ **~ sb/sth** *He seized her by the arm.* 他抓住她的胳膊。◇ *She* ***seized hold of*** *my hand.* 她抓住我的手。 **2 ~ sth (from sb)** to take control of a place or situation, often suddenly and violently（常指通過暴力突然）奪取，攻佔，控制：*They seized the airport in a surprise attack.* 他們突襲攻佔了機場。◇ *The army has* ***seized control of*** *the country.* 軍隊已經控制全國。◇ *He* ***seized power*** *in a military coup.* 他在軍事政變中奪取了政權。 **3 ~ sb** to arrest or capture sb 逮捕；捉拿；俘獲：*The men were seized as they left the building.* 這些人在離開那棟房子時被抓獲。 **4 ~ sth** to take illegal or stolen goods away from sb 起獲；沒收；扣押：*A large quantity of drugs was seized during the raid.* 在這次突擊行動中起獲了大量毒品。 **5 ~ a chance, an opportunity, the initiative, etc.** to be quick to make use of a chance, an opportunity, etc. 抓住，把握（機會、時機、主動等）SYN **grab**：*The party* ***seized*** *the* ***initiative with both hands*** (= quickly and with enthusiasm). 該黨迅速掌握主動。 **6 ~ sb** (of an emotion 情緒) to affect sb suddenly and deeply 突然侵襲；突然控制：*Panic seized her.* 她突然驚慌失措。◇ *He* ***was seized by*** *curiosity.* 他好奇心頓起。 **7** = SEIZE UP

PHR V **ˈseize on/upon sth** to suddenly show a lot of interest in sth, especially because you can use it to your advantage 突然大為關注，抓住（可利用的事物）SYN **pounce on/upon**：*The rumours were eagerly seized upon by the local press.* 當地報章迫不及待地對這些傳聞加以炒作。 **ˌseize ˈup** (*NAmE* also **seize**) **1** (of the parts of a machine 機器部件) to stop moving or working correctly 停止運轉；發生故障 **2** if a part of your body **seizes up**, you are unable to move it easily and it is often painful（身體）發僵

seiz·ure /ˈsiːʒə(r)/ *noun* **1** [U, C] **~ (of sth)** the use of legal authority to take sth from sb; an amount of sth that is taken in this way 起獲；沒收；充公；起獲的贓物；沒收的財產：*The court ordered the seizure of his assets.* 法庭下令沒收他的財產。◇ *the largest ever seizure of cocaine at a British port* 在英國口岸起獲的歷來數量最大的一批可卡因 **2** [U] **~ (of sth)** the act of using force to take control of a country, town, etc. 奪取；佔領；控制：*the army's seizure of power* 軍隊對政權的奪取 ◇ *the seizure of Burma by Japan in 1942* * 1942 年日軍對緬甸的佔領 **3** (*old-fashioned*) [C] a sudden attack of an illness, especially one that affects the brain（疾病，尤指腦病的）突然侵襲，發作

sel·dom /ˈseldəm/ *adv.* not often 不常；很少；難得 SYN **rarely**：*He had seldom seen a child with so much talent.* 有如此天賦的孩子他以往沒見過幾個。◇ *She* ***seldom, if ever,*** *goes to the theatre.* 她難得上劇院看場戲。◇ *They seldom watch television these days.* 這些日子他們很少看電視。◇ (*literary*) *Seldom had he seen such beauty.* 他以前很少見過這樣的美景。

se·lect 0-w AW /sɪˈlekt/ *verb, adj.*

■ *verb* **1** 0-w to choose sb/sth from a group of people or things, usually according to a system 選擇；挑選；選拔：**~ sb/sth for sth** *He hasn't been selected for the team.* 他未能入選該隊。◇ *All our hotels have been* ***carefully selected*** *for the excellent value they provide.* 我們的所有旅館都是精心挑選的，最為合算。◇ **~ sb/sth as sth** *She was selected as the parliamentary candidate for Bath.* 她被選為巴斯選區的議員候選人。◇ **~ sb/sth** *a* ***randomly selected*** *sample of 23 schools* 隨機抽選的 23 所學校作樣本 ◇ *selected poems of T.S. Eliot* * T • S • 艾略特詩選 ◇ *This model is available at selected stores only.* 這種款式只在特定商店有售。◇ **~ sb/sth to do sth** *Six theatre companies have been selected to take part in this year's festival.* 已選定六個劇團參加今年的戲劇節。◇ **~ what, which, etc. …** *Select what you want from the options available.* 從可選項中選擇你想要的。 ➲ SYNONYMS at CHOOSE **2 ~ sth** (*computing* 計) to mark sth on a computer screen; to choose sth, especially from a menu（在計算機屏幕上）選定；（從菜單中）選擇，選取：*Select the text you want to format by holding down the left button on your mouse.* 按住鼠標左鍵選取你想要格式化的文本。◇ *Select 'New Mail' from the 'Send' menu.* 從"發送"選單中選擇"新郵件"。

■ *adj.* **1** [only before noun] carefully chosen as the best out of a larger group of people or things 精選的；作為…精華的；優等的：*a select wine list* 精選葡萄酒目錄 ◇ *Only a* ***select few*** (= a small number of people) *have been invited to the wedding.* 婚禮只邀請了幾個至親好友參加。 **2** (of a society, club, place, etc. 社團、俱樂部、地方等) used by people who have a lot of money or a high social position 有錢、有社會地位的人使用的 SYN **exclusive**：*They live in a very select area.* 他們住在一個上層人士住宅區。◇ *a select club* 名流俱樂部

seˌlect comˈmittee *noun* (*BrE*) a small group of politicians or experts that have been chosen to examine a particular subject or problem 特別委員會（為研究某課題等而成立）

se·lect·ee /sɪˌlekˈtiː/ *noun* **1** a person who is chosen for sth 選中的人；人選 **2** (*NAmE*) a person who is chosen to do MILITARY SERVICE 選徵合格的士兵

se·lec·tion 0-w AW /sɪˈlekʃn/ *noun*

1 0-w [U] the process of choosing sb/sth from a group of people or things, usually according to a system 選擇；挑選；選拔：*The final team selection will be made tomorrow.* 明天將確定隊伍的最後人選。◇ *the* ***random selection*** *of numbers* 號碼的隨機抽取 ◇ *selection criteria* 挑選標準 ◇ *the selection process* 選拔過程 **2** 0-w [C] a number of people or things that have been chosen from a larger group 被挑選的人（或物）；被選中者；入選者：*A selection of readers' comments are published below.* 下面選登了部份讀者的意見。 ➲ SYNONYMS at

S

CHOICE **3** [C] a collection of things from which sth can be chosen 可供選擇的事物 SYN **choice, range**: *The showroom has a* ***wide selection*** *of kitchens.* 展廳裏有多種式樣的廚房可供選擇。➲ see also NATURAL SELECTION

se·lec·tion·al /sɪˈlekʃənl/ *adj.* (*linguistics* 語言) used to describe the process by which each word limits what kind of words can be used with it in normal language（正規語言中單詞對搭配詞）選擇的，限制的：*'Eat' has the selectional restriction that it must be followed by a kind of food, so 'I eat sky' is not possible.* * eat 一詞之後限跟某種食物，所以不可能說 I eat sky。

seˈlection committee *noun* a group of people who choose, for example, the members of a sports team（運動隊隊員等的）選拔委員會；遴選委員會

se·lect·ive AW /sɪˈlektɪv/ *adj.* **1** [usually before noun] affecting or concerned with only a small number of people or things from a larger group 選擇性的；有選擇的：*the selective breeding of cattle* 牛的選擇性培育 ◇ *selective strike action* 有選擇的罷工行動 **2 ~ (about/in sth)** tending to be careful about what or who you choose 認真挑選的；嚴格篩選的：*You will have to be selective about which information to include in the report.* 究竟要把哪些資料收入報告，你得仔細斟酌挑選。◇ *Their admissions policy is very selective.* 他們執行嚴格挑選的錄取政策。◇ *a selective school* (= one that chooses which children to admit, especially according to ability) 擇優錄取學生的學校 ▶ **se·lect·ive·ly** AW *adv.*: *The product will be selectively marketed in the US* (= only in some areas). 這種產品將有選擇地投放到美國某些地區的市場。**se·lect·iv·ity** /səˌlekˈtɪvəti/ *noun* [U]: *Schools are tending towards greater selectivity.* 學校對新生的選拔有趨嚴之勢。

seˌlective ˈservice *noun* [U] (*NAmE*) a system in which people have to spend a period of time in the armed forces by law 選徵兵役（法）

se·lect·or AW /sɪˈlektə(r)/ *noun* **1** (*BrE*) a person who chooses the members of a particular sports team（運動隊隊員的）選拔人 **2** a device in an engine, a piece of machinery, etc. that allows you to choose a particular function 選擇器；轉換器；換擋器

sel·en·ium /səˈliːniəm/ *noun* [U] (*symb.* **Se**) a chemical element. Selenium is a grey substance that is used in making electrical equipment and coloured glass. A lack of selenium in the human body can lead to illnesses such as DEPRESSION. 硒（化學元素，用於製造電氣設備和有色玻璃，人體缺此元素可致抑鬱等病）

S

self /self/ *noun* (*pl.* **selves** /selvz/)
1 [C, usually sing.] the type of person you are, especially the way you normally behave, look or feel（自己的）通常的行為方式，本來面目，慣常心態：*You'll soon be feeling* ***your old self*** *again* (= feeling well or happy again). 你很快就會恢復原樣的。◇ *He's not* ***his usual happy self*** *this morning.* 今天早上，他不像平素那樂呵呵的樣子。◇ *Only with a few people could she be* ***her real self*** (= show what she was really like rather than what she pretended to be). 只有和某幾個人在一起時，她才能表現出真實的自我。◇ *his* ***private/professional self*** (= how he behaves at home/work) 他在家裏／上班時的樣子 **2** [U] (also **the self** [sing.]) (*formal*) a person's personality or character that makes them different from other people 個性；自我：*Many people living in institutions have lost their sense of self* (= the feeling that they are individual people). 許多生活在福利院裏的人已經失去了個性意識。◇ *the inner self* (= a person's emotional and spiritual character) 內心的思想感情 ◇ *a lack of confidence in the self* 缺乏自信 **3** [U] (*formal*) your own advantage or pleasure rather than that of other people 個人利益；一己的享樂；私心：*She didn't do it for any reason of self.* 她那樣做決不是出於私心。**4** [C] used to refer to a person（指一個人）自己，本人：*You didn't hurt your little self, did you?* 小傢伙，你沒傷着自己吧？◇ *We look forward to seeing Mrs Brown and* ***your good self*** *this evening.* 我們期盼今晚能見到布朗夫人和您本人。IDM see FORMER

self- /self/ *combining form* (in nouns and adjectives 構成名詞和形容詞) of, to or by yourself or itself 自身的；對自身；由自身：*self-control* 自我控制 ◇ *self-addressed* 寫有自己姓名地址的 ◇ *self-taught* 自學的

ˌself-abˈsorbed *adj.* only concerned about or interested in yourself 只顧自己的；只關心自己的 ▶ **ˌself-abˈsorp·tion** *noun* [U]

ˌself-aˈbuse *noun* [U] **1** behaviour by which a person does harm to himself or herself 自我傷害；自殘；自虐 **2** (*old-fashioned*) = MASTURBATION at MASTURBATE

ˌself-ˈaccess *noun* [U] a method of learning in which students choose their materials and use them to study on their own 自主學習法（由學生自選材料並自學）：*a* ***self-access centre/library*** 自主學習中心／圖書館

ˌself-actual·iˈza·tion *noun* [U] the fact of using your skills and abilities and achieving as much as you can possibly achieve 自我實現（利用自身技能取得盡可能大的成就）SYN **self-realization**

ˌself-adˈdressed *adj.* if an envelope is **self-addressed**, sb has written their own address on it（信封）寫明回郵地址的

ˌself-adˈhesive *adj.* [usually before noun] covered on one side with a sticky substance so that it can be stuck to sth without the use of glue, etc. 自黏的：*self-adhesive tape* 自黏膠帶

ˌself-anˈalysis *noun* [U] the study of your own character and behaviour, especially your reasons for doing things 自我分析（對自身性格和行為的分析，尤指做事的動機）

ˌself-apˈpoint·ed *adj.* [usually before noun] (usually *disapproving*) giving yourself a particular title, job, etc., especially without the agreement of other people 自封的；自己任命的

ˌself-apˈprais·al *noun* [U, C] an act or the process of judging your own work or achievements 自我評估（或評價）

ˌself-asˈsembly *adj.* (*BrE*) (of furniture 傢具) bought in several parts that you have to put together yourself 自己組裝的：*cheap self-assembly kitchen units* 廉價的自己組裝的廚房設備 ▶ **ˌself-asˈsembly** *noun* [U]: *kitchen units for self-assembly* 需自己組裝的廚房設備

ˌself-asˈsert·ive *adj.* very confident and not afraid to express your opinions 非常自信的；有主見的 ▶ **ˌself-asˈsertion**, **ˌself-asˈsert·ive·ness** *noun* [U]

ˌself-asˈsess·ment *noun* [U] **1** the process of judging your own progress, achievements, etc. 自我評估（或評價）**2** (*BrE*) a system of paying tax in which you calculate yourself how much you should pay 自行估稅

ˌself-asˈsured *adj.* having a lot of confidence in yourself and your abilities 自信的；胸有成竹的 SYN **confident** ▶ **ˌself-asˈsurance** *noun* [U]

ˌself-aˈwareness *noun* [U] knowledge and understanding of your own character 自知；自明；自覺 ▶ **ˌself-aˈware** *adj.*

ˈself-build *noun* [U, C] (*BrE*) the building of homes by their owners; a home that is built in this way 自己建造住房；自己建造的住房：*self-build houses* 自建住宅

ˌself-ˈcatering *adj.* [usually before noun] (*BrE*) a **self-catering** holiday is one which provides you with accommodation and the equipment that is necessary to cook your own meals（度假方式）可自炊的，可下廚煮食的：*self-catering accommodation* 自炊式住宿 ▶ **ˌself-ˈcatering** *noun* [U]: (*BrE*) *All prices are based on a week's self-catering in shared accommodation.* 所有價格以自炊式合夥住宿一週來計算。

ˌself-ˈcentred (*especially US* **ˌself-ˈcentered**) *adj.* (*disapproving*) tending to think only about yourself and not thinking about the needs or feelings of other people 自我中心的；只考慮自己的 ▶ **ˌself-ˈcentred·ness** (*especially US* **ˌself-ˈcentered·ness**) *noun* [U]

ˌself-conˈfessed *adj.* [only before noun] admitting that you are a particular type of person or have a particular problem, especially a bad one 自己承認的；自己坦白的：*a self-confessed thief* 自首的竊賊

ˌself-ˈconfident *adj.* having confidence in yourself and your abilities 自信的 SYN **self-assured, confident**：*a self-confident child* 自信的孩子 ◇ *a self-confident manner* 自信的態度 ▶ **ˌself-ˈconfidence** *noun* [U]：*He has no self-confidence.* 他毫無自信。

ˌself-congratuˈlation *noun* [U] (*usually disapproving*) a way of behaving that shows that you think you have done sth very well and are pleased with yourself 沾沾自喜；自鳴得意 ▶ **ˌself-conˈgratulatory** *adj.*：*The winners gave themselves a self-congratulatory round of applause.* 這些獲勝者一齊鼓掌，慶賀自己的勝利。

ˌself-ˈconscious *adj.* **1 ~ (about sth)** nervous or embarrassed about your appearance or what other people think of you （因在意自己的外表或他人的看法）局促不安的，難為情的，不自然的：*He's always been self-conscious about being so short.* 他老為自己身材矮小而覺得難為情。 **2** (*often disapproving*) done in a way that shows you are aware of the effect that is being produced 刻意的；自己意識到的：*The humour of the play is self-conscious and contrived.* 這部劇的幽默是刻意而為的，而且牽強做作。 OPP **unselfconscious** ▶ **ˌself-ˈconsciously** *adv.*：*She was self-consciously aware of his stare.* 她意識到他在看她，感到不自在。 **ˌself-ˈconsciousness** *noun* [U]

ˌself-conˈtained *adj.* **1** not needing or depending on other people （指人）獨立的，自立的：*Her father was a quiet self-contained man.* 她父親生前是個好靜而獨立自主的人。 **2** able to operate or exist without outside help or influence （指事物）自給的，獨立的 SYN **independent**：*a self-contained community* 自給自足的社會 ◇ *Each chapter is self-contained and can be studied in isolation.* 每一章均自成一篇，可單獨學習。 **3** [usually before noun] (*BrE*) (of a flat/an apartment 公寓) having its own kitchen, bathroom and entrance 獨門獨戶的；設施齊全的：*self-contained accommodation* 獨門獨戶、設施齊全的住處

ˌself-contraˈdictory *adj.* containing two ideas or statements that cannot both be true 自相矛盾的 ▶ **ˌself-contraˈdiction** *noun* [U]

ˌself-conˈtrol *noun* [U] the ability to remain calm and not show your emotions even though you are feeling angry, excited, etc. 自制力；自我控制：*to lose/regain your* ***self-control*** 失去 / 恢復自制 ◇ *It took all his self-control not to shout at them.* 他強壓怒火，沒有衝他們叫嚷。 ▶ **ˌself-conˈtrolled** *adj.*

ˌself-corˈrecting *adj.* [usually before noun] that corrects or adjusts itself without outside help 自動糾正的；自動校正的；自動調節的：*The economic market is a self-correcting mechanism, that does not need regulation by government.* 經濟市場是一種自動調節的機制，不需要政府調控。

ˌself-ˈcriticism *noun* [U] the process of looking at and judging your own faults or weaknesses 自我批評（或批判） ▶ **ˌself-ˈcritical** *adj.*：*Don't be too self-critical.* 別太自責。

ˌself-deˈception *noun* [U] the act of making yourself believe sth that you know is not true 自我欺騙

ˌself-deˈfeating *adj.* causing more problems and difficulties instead of solving them; not achieving what you wanted to achieve but having an opposite effect 事與願違的；適得其反的；弄巧成拙的：*Paying children too much attention when they misbehave can be self-defeating.* 孩子有不良行為時，小題大做可能適得其反。

ˌself-deˈfence (*BrE*) (*NAmE* **ˌself-deˈfense**) *noun* [U] **1** something you say or do in order to protect yourself when you are being attacked, criticized, etc. 自衞；自我保護：*The man later told police that he was acting* ***in self-defence***. 事後那人告訴警察，他當時是出於自衞。 **2** the skill of being able to protect yourself from physical attack without using weapons 自衞術；防身術：*I'm taking classes in self-defence.* 我在上課學防身術。

ˌself-deˈlusion *noun* [U] the act of making yourself believe sth that you know is not true 自我欺騙

ˌself-deˈnial *noun* [U] the act of not having or doing the things you like, either because you do not have enough money, or for moral or religious reasons 克己；（宗教）棄絕自己 SYN **abstinence**

ˌself-ˈdeprecating *adj.* done in a way that makes your own achievements or abilities seem unimportant 自我貶低的；自謙的：*He gave a self-deprecating shrug.* 他自謙地聳聳肩。 ▶ **ˌself-depreˈcation** *noun* [U]

ˌself-deˈstruct *verb* [I] (especially of a machine, etc. 尤指機器等) to destroy itself, usually by exploding 自毀；自爆：*This tape will self-destruct in 30 seconds.* 這盤磁帶將在 30 秒後自毀。◇ (*figurative*) *In the last half-hour of the movie the plot rapidly self-destructs.* 在電影的最後半個小時裏，故事情節迅速了結。

ˌself-deˈstruction *noun* [U] the act of doing things to deliberately harm yourself 自毀 ▶ **ˌself-deˈstructive** *adj.*

ˌself-deˌtermiˈnation *noun* [U] (*formal*) **1** the right of a country or a region and its people to be independent and to choose their own government and political system （國家或地區及其人民的）自決權 SYN **independence** **2** the right or ability of a person to control their own FATE （個人）自主權，自主能力

ˌself-deˈvelopment *noun* [U] the process by which a person's character and abilities are developed （在性格、能力方面的）自我發展，自我提高：*Staff are encouraged to use the library for professional self-development.* 鼓勵員工利用圖書館提高自己的專業水平。

ˌself-ˈdiscipline *noun* [U] the ability to make yourself do sth, especially sth difficult or unpleasant 自律能力；自我約束能力：*It takes a lot of self-discipline to go jogging in winter.* 在冬天跑步是需要很大的自律力的。

ˌself-disˈcovery *noun* [U] the process of understanding more about yourself in order to make yourself happier 自我發現；尋找自我：*David left his boring job to go on* ***a journey of self-discovery***. 戴維辭掉了他那份無聊的工作，開始了尋找自我之旅。

ˌself-ˈdoubt *noun* [U, C] the feeling that you are not good enough 自我懷疑

ˌself-ˈdrive *adj.* [only before noun] (*BrE*) **1** a **self-drive** car is one that you hire and drive yourself 租車人自行駕駛的 **2** a **self-drive** holiday is one on which you use your own car or a car you hire to travel to the holiday area 自駕（遊）的

ˌself-ˈeducated *adj.* having learned things by reading books, etc. rather than at school or college 自我教育的；自學的；自修的

ˌself-efˈfacing *adj.* not wanting to attract attention to yourself or your abilities 謙遜的；不求聞達的 SYN **modest**：*He was a shy, self-effacing man.* 他是個靦腆謙遜的人。 ▶ **ˌself-efˈfacement** *noun* [U]

ˌself-emˈployed *adj.* working for yourself and not employed by a company, etc. 個體經營的；單幹的；自由職業的；自雇的：*a self-employed musician* 自己單幹的樂師 ◇ *retirement plans for the self-employed* (= people who are self-employed) 自由職業者退休計劃 ▶ **ˌself-emˈployment** *noun* [U]

ˌself-eˈsteem *noun* [U] a feeling of being happy with your own character and abilities 自尊（心） SYN **self-worth**：*to have* ***high/low self-esteem*** 自尊心強 / 弱 ◇ *You need to build your self-esteem.* 你需要樹立自尊心。

ˌself-ˈevident *adj.* obvious and needing no further proof or explanation 顯而易見的；不言而喻的；明擺着的：*The dangers of such action are self-evident.* 這樣的行動，其危險是明擺着的。◇ *a self-evident truth* 不證自明的真理 ▶ **ˌself-ˈevidently** *adv.*

ˌself-exˌamiˈnation *noun* [U] **1** the study of your own behaviour and beliefs to find out if they are right or wrong 自省；反省 **2** the act of checking your body for any signs of illness （對身體的）自我檢查

ˌself-exˈplanatory *adj.* easy to understand and not needing any more explanation 無須解釋的；明白易曉的；一目瞭然的

ˌself-exˈpression *noun* [U] the expression of your thoughts or feelings, especially through activities such as writing, painting, dancing, etc. 自我表現，自我表達（尤指通過寫作、繪畫、舞蹈等活動）: *You should encourage your child's attempts at self-expression.* 你應當鼓勵孩子嘗試表達自我。

ˌself-fulˈfil·ling *adj.* [usually before noun] a **self-fulfilling** PROPHECY is one that becomes true because people expect it to be true and behave in a way that will make it happen（預言等）自我應驗的，自我實現的: *If you expect to fail, you will fail. It's a* ***self-fulfilling prophecy.*** 你如果預期失敗，就會失敗。這是一種自我應驗的預測。

ˌself-fulˈfil·ment (*BrE*) (also **ˌself-fulˈfill·ment** *NAmE*) *noun* [U] the feeling of being happy and satisfied that you have everything you want or need 自我實現感；自我滿足感

ˌself-ˈgovern·ment *noun* [U] the government or control of a country or an organization by its own people or members, not by others 自治 ▸ **ˌself-ˈgovern·ing** *adj.*

ˌself-ˈharm *noun* [U] the practice of deliberately injuring yourself, for example by cutting yourself, as a result of having serious emotional or mental problems（故意）自我傷害（常由情感、精神問題所致）▸ **ˌself-ˈharm** *verb* [I]: *As a teenager I was self-harming regularly.* 我十幾歲時經常自殘。

ˌself-ˈhelp *noun* [U] the act of relying on your own efforts and abilities in order to solve your problems, rather than depending on other people for help 自助；自立；靠自己 ▸ **ˌself-ˈhelp** *adj.* [only before noun]: *a self-help discussion group for people suffering from depression* (= whose members help each other) 抑鬱症患者自助討論小組

ˌself-ˈimage *noun* the opinion or idea you have of yourself, especially of your appearance or abilities 自我形象；自我印象: *to have a* ***positive/negative self-image*** 有着正面的／負面的自我形象

ˌself-imˈport·ant *adj.* (*disapproving*) thinking that you are more important than other people 自大的；妄自尊大的；自負的 SYN **arrogant** ▸ **ˌself-imˈport·ance** *noun* [U] **ˌself-imˈport·ant·ly** *adv.*

ˌself-imˈposed *adj.* [usually before noun] a **self-imposed** task, duty, etc. is one that you force yourself to do rather than one that sb else forces you to do 自己強加的；自願負擔的；自己規定的

ˌself-imˈprove·ment *noun* [U] the process by which a person improves their knowledge, status, character, etc. by their own efforts（在知識、地位、性格等方面的）自我改進，自我提高

S

ˌself-inˈduced *adj.* (of illness, problems, etc. 疾病、問題等) caused by yourself 自己造成的: *self-induced vomiting* 自導嘔吐

ˌself-inˈdulgent *adj.* (*disapproving*) allowing yourself to have or do things that you like, especially when you do this too much or too often 放縱自己的；任性的 ▸ **ˌself-inˈdulgence** *noun* [U]

ˌself-inˈflict·ed *adj.* a **self-inflicted** injury, problem, etc. is one that you cause for yourself 加於自身的；自傷的: *a self-inflicted wound* 自傷

ˌself-ˈinterest *noun* [U] (*disapproving*) the fact of sb only considering their own interests and of not caring about things that would help other people 自私自利: *Not all of them were acting out of self-interest.* 他們當中，並非所有人的行動都是出於利己的目的。▸ **ˌself-ˈinterest·ed** *adj.*

self·ish /ˈselfɪʃ/ *adj.* caring only about yourself rather than about other people 自私的: *selfish behaviour* 自私的行為 ◇ *Do you think I'm being selfish by not letting her go?* 你覺得我不讓她走是自私嗎？◇ *What a selfish thing to do!* 這樣做，多麼自私！◇ *It was selfish of him to leave all the work to you.* 他把所有的工作都推給你，真是自私。OPP **unselfish, selfless** ▸ **self·ish·ly** *adv.*: *She looked forward, a little selfishly, to a weekend away from her family.* 她有點自私，就盼着能夠離家在外邊度個週末。**self·ish·ness** *noun* [U]

ˌself-ˈknowledge *noun* [U] an understanding of yourself 自我瞭解；自知之明

self·less /ˈselfləs/ *adj.* thinking more about the needs, happiness, etc. of other people than about your own 無私的: *a life of selfless service to the community* 無私服務於社會的一生 OPP **selfish** ▸ **self·less·ly** *adv.* **self·less·ness** *noun* [U]

ˌself-ˈlove *noun* [U] (*approving*) the feeling that your own happiness and wishes are important 自愛

ˌself-ˈmade *adj.* [usually before noun] having become rich and successful through your own hard work rather than having had money given to you 靠自己奮鬥成功的；白手起家的: *He was proud of the fact that he was a* ***self-made man.*** 他為自己白手起家而自豪。

ˌself-ˈmotivated *adj.* if a person is **self-motivated,** they are capable of hard work and effort without the need for encouragement 自我激勵的；自我勉勵的；主動的 ▸ **ˌself-motiˈva·tion** *noun* [U]

ˌself-mutiˈla·tion *noun* [U] the act of wounding yourself, especially when this is a sign of mental illness 自殘（尤指精神病徵候）

ˌself-oˈpinion·ated *adj.* (*disapproving*) believing that your own opinions are always right and refusing to listen to those of other people 剛愎自用的；固執己見的 SYN **opinionated**

ˌself-perˈpetu·at·ing *adj.* continuing without any outside influence 自我持續的；自我繼續的: *Revenge leads to a self-perpetuating cycle of violence.* 怨怨相報會導致永不休止的暴力。

ˌself-ˈpity *noun* [U] (often *disapproving*) a feeling of pity for yourself, especially because of sth unpleasant or unfair that has happened to you 自憐: *She's not someone who likes to* ***wallow in self-pity.*** 她不是那種喜歡自憐的人。▸ **ˌself-ˈpitying** *adj.*

ˌself-ˈportrait *noun* a painting, etc. that you do of yourself 自畫像

ˌself-posˈsessed *adj.* able to remain calm and confident in a difficult situation 沉着的；鎮定的；泰然自若的 ▸ **ˌself-posˈses·sion** *noun* [U]: *He soon recovered his usual self-possession.* 他很快恢復了平時沉着冷靜的樣子。

ˌself-preser·ˈva·tion *noun* [U] the fact of protecting yourself in a dangerous or difficult situation 自我保存；自我保護: *She was held back by some sense of self-preservation.* 一種自我保護意識使她沒有貿然行動。

ˌself-proˈclaimed *adj.* (often *disapproving*) giving yourself a particular title, job, etc. without the agreement or permission of other people 自稱的；自命的

ˌself-proˈmotion *noun* [U] (*disapproving*) the activity of making people notice you and your abilities, especially in a way that annoys other people 自我推銷；自我吹嘘: *The article was a piece of blatant self-promotion.* 這篇文章是露骨的自我吹捧。

ˌself-raising ˈflour (*US* **ˈbaking flour, ˌself-rising ˈflour**) *noun* [U] flour that contains BAKING POWDER 自發麵粉（含有發酵粉）➲ compare PLAIN FLOUR

ˌself-realiˈza·tion *noun* [U] the fact of using your skills and abilities and achieving as much as you can possibly achieve 自我實現（利用自身技能取得盡可能大的成就）SYN **self-actualization**

self-referen·tial /ˌself refəˈrenʃl/ *adj.* (*technical* 術語) (of a work of literature 文學作品) referring to the fact of actually being a work of literature, or to the author, or to other works that the author has written 自我指涉的，自指的（即指向同一文學作品，或涉及作者或作者的其他作品）

ˌself-reˈgard *noun* [U] a good opinion of yourself, which is considered bad if you have too little or too much 自尊；自我欣賞: *He suffers from a lack of self-regard.* 他缺乏自尊。▸ **ˌself-reˈgard·ing** *adj.*: *His biography is nothing but self-regarding nonsense.* 他的傳記只不過是自命不凡的一派胡言。

ˌself-ˈregulat·ing *adj.* something that is **self-regulating** controls itself 自控的；自動調節的: *a self-regulating economy* 自我調節的經濟 ▸ **ˌself-reguˈla·tion** *noun* [U]

ˌself-reˈliant *adj.* able to do or decide things by yourself, rather than depending on other people for help 自立的；自力更生的；自主的 **SYN independent** ▸ **ˌself-reˈliance** *noun* [U]

ˌself-reˈspect *noun* [U] a feeling of pride in yourself that what you do, say, etc. is right and good 自尊（心）

ˌself-reˈspect·ing *adj.* [only before noun] (especially in negative sentences 尤用於否定句) having pride in yourself because you believe that what you do is right and good 有自尊心的：*No self-respecting journalist would ever work for that newspaper.* 凡有自尊心的記者都不會為那家報紙工作。

ˌself-reˈstraint *noun* [U] the ability to stop yourself doing or saying sth that you want to because you know it is better not to 自我克制：*She* ***exercised*** *all her* ***self-restraint*** *and kept quiet.* 她好不容易才忍住沒說話。

ˌself-ˈrighteous *adj.* (*disapproving*) feeling or behaving as if what you say or do is always morally right, and other people are wrong 以正人君子自居的；自以為正直的 **SYN sanctimonious** ▸ **ˌself-ˈrighteous·ly** *adv.* **ˌself-ˈrighteous·ness** *noun* [U]

ˌself-rising ˈflour (also **ˈbaking flour**) (both *US*) (*BrE* **ˌself-raising ˈflour**) *noun* [U] flour that contains BAKING POWDER 自發麪粉（含有發酵粉） ➲ compare ALL-PURPOSE FLOUR

ˌself-ˈrule *noun* [U] the governing of a country or an area by its own people 自治

ˌself-ˈsacrifice *noun* [U] (*approving*) the act of not allowing yourself to have or do sth in order to help other people 自我犧牲：*the courage and self-sacrifice of those who fought in the war* 投身戰爭的人的勇氣和自我犧牲精神 ▸ **ˌself-ˈsacrifi·cing** *adj.*

self·same /ˈselfseɪm/ *adj.* [only before noun] **the, this, etc. selfsame …** used to emphasize that two people or things are the same（強調兩者完全相同）同一的 **SYN identical**：*Jane had been wondering that selfsame thing.* 簡一直在為同一件事納悶。

ˌself-ˈsatisfied *adj.* (*disapproving*) too pleased with yourself or your own achievements 自鳴得意的；沾沾自喜的 **SYN smug**：*He had a self-satisfied smirk on his face.* 他臉上掛着得意揚揚的笑容。 ▸ **ˌself-satisˈfac·tion** *noun* [U]：*a look of self-satisfaction* 沾沾自喜的神態

ˌself-ˈseeking *adj.* (*disapproving*) interested only in your own needs and interests rather than thinking about the needs of other people 追逐私利的 ▸ **ˌself-ˈseeking** *noun* [U]

ˌself-seˈlection *noun* [U] a situation in which people decide for themselves to do sth rather than being chosen to do it 自行決定；自我選擇 ▸ **ˌself-seˈlect·ing** *adj.*：*a self-selecting group* 自薦小組 **ˌself-seˈlected** *adj.*

ˌself-ˈservice *adj.* [usually before noun] a **self-service** shop/store, restaurant, etc. is one in which customers serve themselves and then pay for the goods 自我服務的；（商店）自選的；（餐廳）自助的 ▸ **ˌself-ˈservice** *noun* [U]：*The cafe provides quick self-service at low prices.* 那家小餐館提供價格低廉、方便快捷的自助餐。

ˌself-ˈserving *adj.* (*disapproving*) interested only in gaining an advantage for yourself 只為個人打算的；一心謀私利的

ˌself-ˈstarter *noun* (*approving*) a person who is able to work on their own and make their own decisions without needing anyone to tell them what to do 有主見的人；做事主動的人

ˌself-ˈstorage *noun* [U] a service that provides a place where you can store things and a key so that you can get them when you need them 自助寄存；自助貯物：*self-storage facilities/units* 自助寄存設備

ˌself-ˈstudy *noun* [U] the activity of learning about sth without a teacher to help you 自學；自修 ▸ **ˌself-ˈstudy** *adj.*：*self-study materials* 自學材料

ˌself-ˈstyled *adj.* [only before noun] (*disapproving*) using a name or title that you have given yourself, especially when you do not have the right to do it 自封的；自詡的

ˌself-sufˈficient *adj.* **~ (in sth)** able to do or produce everything that you need without the help of other people 自給自足的；自立的：*The country is totally self-sufficient in food production.* 在糧食生產上，這個國家完全做到了自給自足。 ▸ **ˌself-sufˈficiency** *noun* [U]

ˌself-supˈport·ing *adj.* having enough money to be able to operate without financial help from other people 資金自給的；經濟獨立的

ˌself-ˈtaught *adj.* having learned sth by reading books, etc., rather than by sb teaching you 自學的；自修的：*a self-taught artist* 自學成材的藝術家

ˌself-ˈwilled *adj.* (*disapproving*) determined to do what you want without caring about other people 任性的；固執的；倔強的 **SYN headstrong**

ˌself-ˈworth *noun* [U] a feeling of confidence in yourself that you are a good and useful person 自我價值感 **SYN self-esteem**

selkie /ˈselki/ (also **silkie**) *noun* (in Scottish stories 蘇格蘭傳說) an imaginary creature which sometimes looks like a human and sometimes looks like a SEAL 海豹人

sell 🔑 /sel/ *verb, noun*

■ *verb* (**sold, sold** /səʊld; *NAmE* soʊld/)

▸ **EXCHANGE FOR MONEY** 換取金錢 **1** 🔑 [T, I] to give sth to sb in exchange for money 出讓；轉讓：**~ sth (to sb) (for sth)** *I sold my car to James for £800.* 我把我的汽車轉讓給了詹姆斯，獲得 800 英鎊。◇ **~ sb sth (for sth)** *I sold James my car for £800.* 我以 800 英鎊把我的汽車賣給了詹姆斯。◇ **~ (sth) (at sth)** *They* ***sold*** *the business* ***at a profit/loss*** (= they gained/lost money when they sold it). 他們把公司讓出贏利／虧本讓出。◇ *We offered them a good price but they wouldn't sell.* 我們開了個好價錢，但他們不願賣。

▸ **OFFER FOR SALE** 出售 **2** 🔑 [T] **~ sth** to offer sth for people to buy 出售；售賣：*Most supermarkets sell a range of organic products.* 多數超級市場都經銷一系列有機產品。◇ *Do you sell stamps?* 你這兒賣郵票嗎？◇ *to sell insurance* 賣保險 ➲ compare CROSS-SELLING

▸ **BE BOUGHT** 售出；銷售 **3** 🔑 [T, I] to be bought by people in the way or in the numbers mentioned; to be offered at the price mentioned 銷售得…；賣出…；售價是…：**~ (sth)** *The magazine sells 300 000 copies a week.* 這本雜誌一週售出 30 萬冊。◇ *The book sold well and was reprinted many times.* 這本書銷路不錯，重印了好多次。◇ *The new design just didn't sell* (= nobody bought it). 新款式無人問津。◇ **~ for/at sth** *The pens sell for just 50p each.* 這些鋼筆每支只賣 50 便士。

▸ **PERSUADE** 推動；說服 **4** [I, T] to make people want to buy sth 促銷；推銷：*You may not like it but advertising sells.* 你也許不喜歡廣告，但它能促銷。◇ **~ sth** *It is quality not price that sells our products.* 我們的產品銷路好，靠的是質量，而不是價格。 **5** 🔑 [T] **~ sth/yourself (to sb)** to persuade sb that sth is a good idea, service, product, etc.; to persuade sb that you are the right person for a job, position, etc. 推薦；推銷；自薦；自我推銷：*Now we have to try and sell the idea to management.* 現在，我們必須設法說服管理層採納這個意見。◇ *You really have to sell yourself at a job interview.* 應聘面試的時候，你真得推銷你自己。

▸ **TAKE MONEY/REWARD** 收受錢財／報酬 **6** [T] **~ yourself (to sb)** (*disapproving*) to accept money or a reward from sb for doing sth that is against your principles 出賣自己；賣身 **SYN prostitute** ➲ see also SALE

IDM be ˈsold on sth (*informal*) to be very enthusiastic about sth 熱衷於；對…極感興趣 **sell your ˈbody** to have sex with sb in exchange for money 出賣肉體；賣淫 **sell sb down the ˈriver** (*informal*) to give poor or unfair treatment to sb you have promised to help 出賣（答應要幫助的人） **ORIGIN** From the custom of buying and selling slaves on the plantations on the Mississippi river in America. Slaves who caused trouble for their masters could be sold to plantation owners lower down the river, where conditions would be worse. 源自美國密西西比河沿岸種植園之間的奴隸買賣。惹麻煩的奴隸可能被主人賣到下游條件更為惡劣的種植園裏。 **sell sb/yourself ˈshort** to not value sb/yourself highly enough and show this by the way you treat or present them/yourself 低估，輕視，小瞧（某人或自己） **sell your**

S

'soul (to the devil) to do anything, even sth bad or dishonest, in return for money, success or power 出賣靈魂（或良心）➲ more at HOT *adj.*, PUP

PHR V **,sell sth↔'off** 1 to sell things cheaply because you want to get rid of them or because you need the money 甩賣；拋售；變賣 2 to sell all or part of an industry, a company or land 出售，賣掉（產業、公司或土地）：*The Church sold off the land for housing.* 教會賣掉了那塊地皮，用來蓋房子了。➲ related noun SELL-OFF **,sell sth↔'on** to sell to sb else sth that you have bought not long before（買進後不久）轉售，轉讓：*She managed the business for a year and then sold it on.* 這個企業她經營了一年，然後轉手賣給了別人。**,sell 'out | be ,sold 'out** (of tickets for a concert, sports game, etc. 音樂會、體育比賽等的票) to be all sold 售完：*The tickets sold out within hours.* 幾小時內票就賣光了。◇ *This week's performances are completely sold out.* 本週的演出門票全部售完。**,sell 'out (of sth) | be ,sold 'out (of sth)** to have sold all the available items, tickets, etc. 售空，賣光，賣罄（某種商品、門票等）；脫銷：*I'm sorry, we've sold out of bread.* 抱歉，我們的麪包賣完了。◇ *We are already sold out for what should be a fantastic game.* 想來這場比賽一定精彩，我們的門票已經賣光了。**,sell 'out (to sb/sth)** 1 (*disapproving*) to change or give up your beliefs or principles 背叛信念；背棄原則：*He's a talented screenwriter who has sold out to TV soap operas.* 他是個有才華的電影編劇，卻改行寫起電視肥皂劇來了。2 to sell your business or a part of your business 出售（財產、企業等）：*The company eventually sold out to a multinational media group.* 公司最終賣給了一個跨國傳媒集團。➲ related noun SELL-OUT **,sell 'up | ,sell sth↔'up** (*especially BrE*) to sell your home, possessions, business, etc., usually because you are leaving the country or retiring 賣光（家當、企業等）

■ ***noun*** [sing.] (*informal*) something that is not as good as it seemed to be 讓人失望的東西：*The band only played for about half an hour—it was a real sell.* 樂隊僅僅演奏了大約半個小時，真讓人失望。➲ see also HARD SELL

'sell-by date (*BrE*) (*US* **'pull date**) *noun* the date printed on food packages, etc. after which the food must not be sold（食品等的）最遲銷售日期，保質期：*This milk is past its sell-by date.* 這牛奶已經過了銷售期限。◇ (*figurative*) *These policies are way past their sell-by date.* 這些政策早成老皇曆了。

sell·er /ˈselə(r)/ *noun* 1 a person who sells sth 賣者；銷售者；賣方：*a flower seller* 賣花人 ◇ *The law is intended to protect both the buyer and the seller.* 這項法律旨在保護買賣雙方。➲ see also BOOKSELLER ➲ compare VENDOR 2 **a good, poor, etc. ~** a product that has been sold in the amounts or way mentioned（暢銷、滯銷等的）商品：*This particular model is one of our biggest sellers.* 這種型號是我們銷路最好的產品之一。➲ see also BEST-SELLER

IDM **a ,seller's 'market** a situation in which people selling sth have an advantage, because there is not a lot of a particular item for sale, and prices can be kept high 賣方市場

'selling point *noun* a feature of sth that makes people want to buy or use it 賣點（吸引顧客的產品特色）：*The price is obviously one of the main selling points.* 顯然，價格低是一大賣點。◇ *Sales departments try to identify a product's USP or 'unique selling point'.* 銷售部門試圖確定一種產品的"獨有賣點"。

'selling price *noun* the price at which sth is sold 銷售價 ➲ compare ASKING PRICE, COST PRICE

'sell-off *noun* 1 (*BrE*) the sale by the government of an industry or a service to individual people or private companies（國有企業的）出售 2 (*NAmE, business* 商) the sale of a large number of STOCKS and SHARES, after which their value usually falls（證券）拋售

Sel·lo·tape™ /ˈseləteɪp/ *noun* (also **'sticky tape**) (both *BrE*) (*NAmE* **'Scotch tape™**) [U] clear plastic tape that is sticky on one side, used for sticking things together 賽勒塔普膠黏帶；透明膠帶：*a roll of Sellotape* 一捲膠黏帶 ◇ *The envelope was stuck down with Sellotape.* 信封是用膠黏帶封口的。➲ VISUAL VOCAB page V69

sel·lo·tape /ˈseləteɪp/ *verb* **~ sth (to sth)** (*BrE*) to join or stick things together with Sellotape 用透明膠帶粘貼：*We found a note sellotaped to the front door.* 我們看見正門上有一張用透明膠帶貼的字條。

'sell-out *noun* [usually sing.] 1 a play, concert, etc. for which all the tickets have been sold 滿座的演出（或比賽等）：*Next week's final looks like being a sell-out.* 看來下週的決賽將是個滿場。◇ *a sell-out tour* 場場爆滿的巡迴演出 2 a situation in which sb is not loyal to a person or group who trusted them, by not doing sth that they promised to do, or by doing sth that they promised not to do 違反諾言；違背原則：*The workers see the deal as a union sell-out to management.* 工人認為這個協議是工會把他們出賣給了管理層。

seltzer /ˈseltsə(r)/ *noun* [U, C] FIZZY water (= with bubbles), usually containing minerals, used as a drink 塞爾茲（含汽）礦泉水

selv·edge (also **selv·age** especially in *NAmE*) /ˈselvɪdʒ/ *noun* an edge that is made on a piece of cloth, which stops the threads from coming apart (= stops it FRAYING)（布的）織邊；布邊

selves *pl.* of SELF

se·man·tic /sɪˈmæntɪk/ *adj.* [usually before noun] (*linguistics* 語言) connected with the meaning of words and sentences 語義的 ▸ **se·man·tic·al·ly** /-kli/ *adv.*：*semantically related words* 語義上相關聯的單詞

se,mantic 'field *noun* (*linguistics* 語言) a set of words with related meanings 語義場；語義域

se·man·tics /sɪˈmæntɪks/ *noun* [U] (*linguistics* 語言) 1 the study of the meanings of words and phrases 語義學 2 the meaning of words, phrases or systems（單詞、短語或其他符號系統的）含義

sema·phore /ˈseməfɔː(r)/ *noun, verb*

■ ***noun*** [U] a system for sending signals in which you hold your arms or two flags in particular positions to represent different letters of the alphabet 旗語

■ ***verb*** [I, T] **~ (sth) | ~ that ...** to send a message to sb by semaphore or a similar system of signals 打旗語；（用其他類似的信號系統）發信號

semb·lance /ˈsembləns/ *noun* [sing., U] **~ of sth** (*formal*) a situation in which sth seems to exist although this may not, in fact, be the case 表象；假象；外觀；外貌：*The ceasefire brought about a semblance of peace.* 停火協定帶來了表面的和平。◇ *Life at last returned to some semblance of normality.* 生活似乎終於恢復了正常。

semen /ˈsiːmən/ *noun* [U] the whitish liquid containing SPERM that is produced by the sex organs of men and male animals 精液

se·mes·ter /sɪˈmestə(r)/ *noun* one of the two periods that the school or college year is divided into 學期（一學年分兩個學期）：*the **spring/fall semester*** 春季 / 秋季學期 ➲ see also TERM *n.* (2) ➲ compare TRIMESTER (2)

semi /ˈsemi/ *noun* (*pl.* **semis**) 1 (*BrE, informal*) a SEMI-DETACHED house (= one that is joined to another house by one shared wall) 半獨立式住宅：*suburban semis* 郊區的半獨立式住宅 2 (*NAmE*) = SEMI-TRAILER 3 = SEMI-FINAL

semi- /ˈsemi/ *prefix* (in adjectives and nouns 構成形容詞和名詞) half; partly 半；部份：*semicircular* 半圓形的 ◇ *semi-final* 半決賽

,semi-'arid *adj.* (*technical* 術語) (of land or climate 土地或氣候) dry; with little rain 半乾旱的

,semi-auto'mat·ic *adj.* (of a gun 槍) able to load bullets automatically, and therefore very quickly, but not firing automatically 半自動的 ▸ **,semi-auto'mat·ic** *noun*

semi·breve /ˈsemibriːv/ (*BrE*) (*NAmE* **'whole note**) *noun* (*music* 音) a note that lasts as long as four CROTCHETS/QUARTER NOTES 全音符 ➲ picture at MUSIC

semi·circle /ˈsemisɜːkl; *NAmE* -sɜːrkl/ *noun* 1 (*geometry* 幾何) one half of a circle 半圓 ➲ VISUAL VOCAB page V71 2 the line that forms the edge of a semicircle 半圓弧線 3 a thing, or a group of people or things, shaped like a semicircle 半圓形：*a semicircle of chairs* 擺成半圓形的

椅子 ◇ *We sat in a semicircle round the fire.* 我們坐在爐火前，圍成一個半圓形。 ▸ **semi·cir·cu·lar** /ˌsemiˈsɜːkjələ(r); *NAmE* -ˈsɜːrk-/ *adj.*：*a semicircular driveway* 半圓形車道

semi·colon /ˌsemiˈkəʊlən; *NAmE* ˈsemikoʊ-/ *noun* the mark (;) used to separate the parts of a complicated sentence or items in a detailed list, showing a pause that is longer than a comma but shorter than a full stop/period 分號 ➲ compare COLON (1)

semi·con·duct·or /ˌsemikənˈdʌktə(r)/ *noun* (*technical* 術語) **1** a solid substance that CONDUCTS electricity in particular conditions, better than INSULATORS but not as well as CONDUCTORS 半導體 **2** a device containing a semiconductor used in ELECTRONICS 半導體裝置

ˌsemi-deˈtached *adj.* (of a house 住宅) joined to another house by a wall on one side that is shared 半獨立式的 ▸ **ˌsemi-deˈtached** *noun* (*BrE*) ➲ VISUAL VOCAB page V16 ➲ compare DETACHED (1) ➲ see also SEMI (1), TERRACED (1)

ˌsemi-ˈfinal (also **semi**) *noun* one of the two games or parts of a sports competition that are held to decide who will compete in the last part (the FINAL) 半決賽；準決賽：*He's through to the semi-final of the men's singles.* 他已進入男子單打半決賽。 ▸ **ˌsemi-ˈfinalist** *noun*：*They are semi-finalists for the fourth year in succession.* 這是他們連續第四年打入半決賽。

semi·metal /ˈsemimetl/ *noun* (*BrE*) = METALLOID

sem·inal /ˈsemɪnl/ *adj.* **1** (*formal*) very important and having a strong influence on later developments（對以後的發展）影響深遠的，有重大意義的：*a **seminal work/article/study*** 有巨大影響的著作／文章／研究 **2** [usually before noun] (*technical* 術語) of or containing SEMEN 精液的；含精液的：*seminal fluid* 精液

sem·inar /ˈsemɪnɑː(r)/ *noun* **1** a class at a university or college when a small group of students and a teacher discuss or study a particular topic（大學教師帶領學生作專題討論的）研討班：*Teaching is by lectures and seminars.* 教學形式為講座和研討班。◇ *a graduate seminar* 研究生研討班 ◇ *a seminar room* 研討室 ➲ COLLOCATIONS at EDUCATION **2** a meeting for discussion or training 研討會；培訓會：*a one-day management seminar* 為期一天的管理研討會

sem·in·ar·ian /ˌsemɪˈneəriən; *NAmE* -ˈner-/ *noun* a student in a seminary 神學院學生；修生

sem·in·ary /ˈsemɪnəri; *NAmE* -neri/ *noun* (*pl.* **-ies**) a college where priests, ministers or RABBIS are trained 神學院；修院

Sem·in·ole /ˈsemɪnəʊl; *NAmE* -oʊl/ *noun* (*pl.* **Sem·in·ole** or **Sem·in·oles**) a member of a Native American people, many of whom live in the US states of Oklahoma and Florida 塞米諾爾人（美洲土著，很多居於美國俄克拉何馬州和佛羅里達州）

semi·ot·ics /ˌsemiˈɒtɪks; *NAmE* -ˈɑːtɪks/ *noun* [U] the study of signs and symbols and of their meaning and use 符號學 ▸ **semi·ot·ic** *adj.*：*semiotic analysis* 符號分析

ˌsemi-ˈprecious *adj.* [usually before noun] (of a JEWEL 珠寶) less valuable than the most valuable types of JEWELS 次貴重的；半寶石的

ˌsemi-proˈfes·sion·al *adj.* **semi-professional** musicians or sports players are paid for what they do, but do not do it as their main job（音樂家或運動員）半職業的 ▸ **ˌsemi-proˈfes·sion· al** *noun*

semi·quaver /ˈsemikweɪvə(r)/ (*BrE*) (*NAmE* **ˌsixˈteenth note**) *noun* (*music* 音) a note that lasts half as long as a QUAVER/EIGHTH NOTE 十六分音符 ➲ picture at MUSIC

ˌsemi-ˈskilled *adj.* [usually before noun] (of workers 工人) having some special training or qualifications, but less than skilled people 半熟練的：*a semi-skilled machine operator* 半熟練機器操作員 ◇ *semi-skilled jobs* (= for people who have some special training) 半技術工作

ˌsemi-ˈskimmed *adj.* (*BrE*) (of milk 奶) that has had a lot of the fat removed 半脂的

Sem·ite /ˈsemaɪt/ *noun* a member of the peoples who speak Semitic languages, including Arabs and Jews 閃米特人（說閃米特語，包括阿拉伯人和猶太人）

Sem·it·ic /səˈmɪtɪk/ *adj.* **1** of or connected with the language group that includes Hebrew and Arabic 閃米特語族的，閃語的（包括希伯來語和阿拉伯語）**2** of or connected with the people who speak Semitic languages, especially Hebrew and Arabic 閃米特人（尤指操希伯來語和阿拉伯語的人）的；閃族的

semi·tone /ˈsemitəʊn; *NAmE* -toʊn/ (*BrE*) (*NAmE* **ˈhalf step**, **ˈhalf-tone**) *noun* (*music* 音) half a TONE on a musical SCALE, for example the INTERVAL between C and C♯ or between E and F 半音 ➲ compare STEP *n.* (10)

ˈsemi-trailer *noun* (*NAmE*) a TRAILER that has wheels at the back and is supported at the front by the vehicle that is pulling it 半掛車；半拖車

ˌsemi-ˈtropic·al *adj.* = SUBTROPICAL

semi·vowel /ˈsemivaʊəl/ *noun* (*phonetics* 語音) a speech sound that sounds like a vowel but functions as a consonant, for example /w/ and /j/ in the English words *wet* and *yet* 半元音

semo·lina /ˌseməˈliːnə/ *noun* [U] **1** large hard grains of WHEAT used when crushed for making PASTA and sweet dishes 麥糝，粗麪粉（用以製作意大利麪食和甜食）**2** a sweet dish made from semolina and milk, eaten for DESSERT in Britain and for breakfast in the US 粗麪粉布丁

sem·tex /ˈsemteks/ *noun* [U] a powerful EXPLOSIVE that is used for making bombs, often illegally 塞姆汀塑膠炸藥（常用於非法製造炸彈）

Sen. *abbr.* SENATOR 參議員：*Sen. John K Nordqvist* 約翰 • K • 諾德維斯參議員

sen·ate 0-w /ˈsenət/ *noun* (usually **the Senate**)
1 0-w [sing.] one of the two groups of elected politicians who make laws in some countries, for example in the US, Australia, Canada and France. The Senate is smaller than the other group but higher in rank. Many state parliaments in the US also have a Senate. 參議院（美國、澳大利亞、加拿大、法國等國家的兩個立法機構之一；美國許多州議會也設有參議院）：*a member of the Senate* 參議員 ◇ *a Senate committee* 參議院委員會 ➲ COLLOCATIONS at POLITICS ➲ compare CONGRESS (2), HOUSE OF REPRESENTATIVES **2** [C, usually sing., U] (in some countries) the group of people who control a university（某些國家的）大學理事會，大學評議會：*the senate of Loughborough University* 拉夫伯勒大學評議會 **3** [sing.] (in ancient Rome) the most important council of the government; the building where the council met（古羅馬的）元老院

sen·ator 0-w /ˈsenətə(r)/ *noun* (often **Senator**) (*abbr.* **Sen.**)
a member of a senate 參議員：*Senator McCarthy* 麥卡錫參議員 ◇ *She has served as a Democratic senator for North Carolina since 2009.* 自 2009 年以來，她一直是北卡羅來納州的民主黨參議員。 ▸ **sen·at·or·ial** /ˌsenəˈtɔːriəl/ *adj.* [only before noun]：*a senatorial candidate* 參議員候選人

send 0-w /send/ *verb* (**sent**, **sent** /sent/)
▸ **BY MAIL/RADIO** 通過郵政／無線電 **1** 0-w to make sth go or be taken to a place, especially by post/mail, email, radio, etc. 郵寄；發送：**~ sth** *to send a letter/package/cheque/fax/email* 寄信；寄包裹；寄支票；發傳真；發電子郵件 ◇ *She sent the letter by airmail.* 她寄的是航空信。◇ (*BrE*) *to send sth by post* 郵寄某物 ◇ (*NAmE*) *to send sth by mail* 郵寄某物 ◇ **~ sth to sb** *A radio signal was sent to the spacecraft.* 向宇宙飛船發出了無線電信號。◇ *The CD player was faulty so we sent it back to the manufacturers.* 那台激光唱片機有毛病，因此我們把它送回了廠家。◇ *Have you sent a postcard to your mother yet?* 你給你母親寄明信片了沒有？◇ **~ sb sth** *Have you sent your mother a postcard yet?* 你給你母親寄明信片了沒有？◇ *I'll send you a text message.* 我會給你發一條短信。
▸ **MESSAGE** 信息 **2** 0-w to tell sb sth by sending them a message 傳達；轉致；告知：**~ sth** *My parents **send their love**.* 我父母問您好。◇ **~ sth to sb** *What sort of message is that sending to young people?* 這給年輕人傳達的是什麼樣的信息呢？◇ **~ sb sth** *He sent me **word** to*

S

come. 他帶話要我來。◇ **~ sth (that)** ... *She sent word (that) she could not come.* 她帶信兒說她來不了。◇ **~ to do sth** (*formal*) *She sent to say that she was coming home.* 她託人捎話說她要回家了。

▸ **SB SOMEWHERE** 讓某人前往某處 **3** to tell sb to go somewhere or to do sth; to arrange for sb to go somewhere 派遣；打發；安排去：**~ sb** *Ed couldn't make it so they sent me instead.* 埃德去不了，所以他們就派我去了。◇ **~ sb + adv./prep.** *She sent the kids to bed early.* 她早早打發孩子們上牀睡覺。◇ *to send sb to prison/boarding school* 把某人關進監獄；安排某人上寄宿學校 ◇ **~ sb to do sth** *I've sent Tom to buy some milk.* 我叫湯姆去買牛奶了。

▸ **MAKE STH MOVE QUICKLY** 使某物快速移動 **4** to make sth/sb move quickly or suddenly 使快速（或猛然）移動：**~ sth/sb doing sth** *Every step he took sent the pain shooting up his leg.* 他每走一步，疼痛就順腿竄上來。◇ *The punch **sent him flying**.* 那一拳打得他整個人拋了出去。◇ **~ sth/sb + adv./prep.** *The report sent share prices down a further 8p.* 這份報告一公佈，股價又跌了8便士。

▸ **MAKE SB REACT** 使某人作出反應 **5** to make sb behave or react in a particular way 使作出（某種反應）；使表現出（某種行為）：**~ sb to sth** *Her music always sends me to sleep.* 她的音樂總使我進入夢鄉。◇ **~ sb into sth** *Her account of the visit sent us into fits of laughter.* 她講述參觀的經過，我們聽得一陣陣大笑。◇ **~ sb + adj.** *All the publicity nearly sent him crazy.* 成天生活在公眾的注意之下讓他差一點發瘋了。

IDM **send sb 'packing** (*informal*) to tell sb firmly or rudely to go away 叫某人捲鋪蓋；攆某人走 ➲ more at COVENTRY, LOVE *n.*, THING

PHR V **,send a'way (to sb) (for sth)** = SEND OFF (FOR STH) **,send sb↔'down** (*BrE*) **1** (*informal*) to send sb to prison 判（某人）入獄 **2** (*old-fashioned*) to order a student to leave a university because of bad behaviour 開除；勒令退學 **'send for sb** to ask or tell sb to come to you, especially in order to help you 請某人來（幫忙等）：*Send for a doctor, quickly!* 請個大夫來，快！ **'send for sth** to ask sb to bring or deliver sth to you 讓人帶來（或送來）某物：*His son found him and sent for help.* 他兒子找到了他，然後向人求救。◇ *She sent for the latest sales figures.* 她要求把最新的銷售統計數字給她送來。 **,send sb 'forth** (*old-fashioned* or *literary*) to send sb away from you to another place 派往；派遣 **,send 'forth sth** (*formal*) to produce a sound, signal, etc. so that other people can hear it, receive it, etc. 發出（聲音、信號等）：*He opened his mouth and sent forth a stream of noise.* 他張開嘴，發出一連串嗓音。 **,send sb↔'in** to order sb to go to a place to deal with a difficult situation 派某人去（應付困難局面）：*Troops were sent in to restore order.* 部隊被派去恢復秩序。 **,send sth↔'in** to send sth by post/mail to a place where it will be dealt with 寄去（處理）：*Have you sent in your application yet?* 你把申請書寄去了沒有？ **,send 'off (for sth)** | **,send a'way (to sb) (for sth)** to write to sb and ask them to send you sth by post/mail 郵購；函購；函索：*I've sent off for some books for my course.* 我已去函郵購一些上課用的書。 **,send sb↔'off** (*BrE*) (in a sports game 體育比賽) to order sb to leave the field because they have broken the rules of the game 罰某人下場：*Beckham was sent off for a foul in the second half.* 在下半場，貝克漢姆因犯規被罰下場。➲ related noun SENDING-OFF **,send sth↔'off** to send sth to a place by post/mail 寄出；發出：*I'm sending the files off to my boss tomorrow.* 明天我要把這些檔案給老闆寄去。 **,send sth↔'on 1** to send sth to a place so that it arrives before you get there 先期發運（或送達）：*We sent our furniture on by ship.* 我們提前把傢具水運過去了。 **2** to send a letter that has been sent to sb's old address to their new address 轉寄，轉投（信件）SYN **forward** **3** to send sth from one place/person to another 轉送；轉遞；轉達：*They arranged for the information to be sent on to us.* 他們託人把信息轉告我們。 **,send 'out for sth** to ask a restaurant or shop/store to deliver food to you at home or at work 請（某店）送來外賣食物：*Let's send out for a pizza.* 我們訂一份外送比薩餅吧。 **,send sth↔'out 1** to send sth to a lot of different people or places 分發；散發：*Have the invitations been sent out yet?* 請柬分發出去了沒有？ **2** to produce sth, such as light, a signal, sound, etc. 發出（光、信號、聲音等）SYN **emit** **,send sb/sth↔'up** (*informal*) to make people laugh at sb/sth by copying them/it in a funny way（通過滑稽模仿）取笑，諷刺，挖苦：*a TV programme that sends up politicians* 模仿取笑政治人物的電視節目 ➲ related noun SEND-UP **,send sb↔'up** (*US, informal*) to send sb to prison 判（某人）入獄

send·er /ˈsendə(r)/ *noun* a person who sends sth 發送人；郵寄人：*If undelivered, please return to sender.* 若無法投遞，請退還寄信人。

,sending-'off *noun* (*pl.* **sendings-off**) (*BrE*) (in football (SOCCER) 足球) a situation when a REFEREE tells a player to leave the field because they have broken the rules in a serious way（嚴重犯規）罰出場外

'send-off *noun* (*informal*) an occasion when people come together to say goodbye to sb who is leaving 送行；送別

'send-up *noun* (*informal*) an act of making sb/sth look silly by copying them in a funny way（為取笑的）滑稽模仿

Sen·eca /ˈsenəkə/ *noun* (*pl.* **Sen·eca** or **Sen·ecas**) a member of a Native American people, many of whom now live in the US states of New York and Ohio 塞內卡人（美洲土著，很多現居於美國紐約州和俄亥俄州）

sen·es·cence /sɪˈnesns/ *noun* [U] (*formal* or *technical* 術語) the process of becoming old and showing the effects of being old 衰老 ▸ **sen·es·cent** *adj.*

se·nile /ˈsiːnaɪl/ *adj.* behaving in a confused or strange way, and unable to remember things, because you are old 衰老的；年老糊塗的：*I think she's **going senile**.* 我想她是衰老了。➲ COLLOCATIONS at AGE ▸ **sen·il·ity** /səˈnɪləti/ *noun* [U]：*an old man on the verge of senility* 漸顯龍鍾之態的老年人

,senile de'mentia *noun* [U] a serious mental DISORDER in old people that causes loss of memory, loss of control of the body, etc. 老年性痴呆

se·nior /ˈsiːniə(r)/ *adj., noun*

■ *adj.*

▸ **OF HIGH RANK** 級別高 **1** **~ (to sb)** high in rank or status; higher in rank or status than others 級別（或地位）高的：*a **senior officer/manager/lecturer*** 高級軍官／經理／講師 ◇ *a **senior partner** in a law firm* 律師事務所的高級合夥人 ◇ *a **senior post/position*** 高級職位 ◇ *I have ten years' experience at senior management level.* 我有十年的高層管理經驗。◇ (*BrE*) *Junior nurses usually work alongside more senior nurses.* 初級護士通常和較高級的護士一起工作。◇ *He is senior to me.* 他的職位比我高。◇ *The meeting should be chaired by the most senior person present.* 會議應由在座的職位最高的人主持。OPP **junior**

▸ **IN SPORT** 體育運動 **2** [only before noun] for adults or people at a more advanced level 成人的；高級水平的：*to take part in senior competitions* 參加成人比賽 ◇ *He won the senior men's 400 metres.* 他獲得男子甲組400米冠軍。

▸ **FOR OLDER PEOPLE** 年長之人 **3** [only before noun] for SENIOR CITIZENS (= older people, especially those who have retired from work) 年紀大的；老年的；年老的：*Get one third off rail fares with a senior railcard.* 持有老年火車通行優惠卡可減免三分之一車費。◇ *senior discounts/concessions* 老年折扣／優惠

▸ **FATHER** 父親 **4 Senior** (*abbr.* **Snr**, **Sr**) used after the name of a man who has the same name as his son, to avoid confusion（父子同名時，加在父親的名字前）老 ➲ compare JUNIOR *adj* (3)

▸ **SCHOOL/COLLEGE** 中學；大學 **5** [only before noun] (*BrE*) (of a school or part of a school 學校或其分部) for children over the age of 11 or 13 中等的，中學的（招收11或13歲以上學生）**6** [only before noun] (*NAmE*) connected with the last year in HIGH SCHOOL or college（高中或大學）畢業年級的：*the senior prom* 畢業年級舞會

■ *noun*

▸ **OLDER PERSON** 較年長的人 **1** a person who is older than sb else 較…年長的人：*She was ten years his senior.* 她比他大十歲。◇ *My brother is my senior by two years.*

我哥哥比我大兩歲。 ➲ compare JUNIOR *n.* **2** (*especially NAmE*) = SENIOR CITIZEN
▸ **HIGHER RANK 較高級別 3** 🔑 a person who is higher in rank or status 級別（或地位）較高者；上級；上司： *She felt unappreciated both by her colleagues and her seniors.* 她覺得無論同事還是上司都不賞識她。
▸ **IN SPORT 體育運動 4** adults or people who have reached an advanced level 資深成人運動員；高水平運動員： *tennis coaching for juniors and seniors* 初、高級網球運動員訓練
▸ **IN SCHOOL/COLLEGE 中學／大學裏 5** (*BrE*) a child at a senior school; an older child in a school 中學生；高年級學生 **6** (in the US and some other countries) a student in the last year at a HIGH SCHOOL or college（美國等若干國家高中和大學的）畢業班學生： *high school seniors* 高中畢業班學生 ➲ compare SOPHOMORE

ˌsenior ˈcitizen (also **se·nior** especially in *NAmE*) *noun* an older person, especially sb who has retired from work. People often call sb a 'senior citizen' to avoid saying that they are old or using the word 'old-age pensioner'. 長者（委婉說法，尤指退休者）

ˌsenior ˈcommon room *noun* (*abbr.* **SCR**) (*BrE*) a room used for social activities by teaching staff in a college or university（大學的）教師聯誼活動室，教師交誼廳

ˌsenior ˈhigh school (also **ˌsenior ˈhigh**) *noun* (in the US) a school for young people between the ages of 14 and 18（美國）高中 ➲ compare JUNIOR HIGH SCHOOL

se·ni·or·ity /ˌsiːniˈɒrəti; *NAmE* -ˈɔːr-; -ˈɑːr-/ *noun* [U] **1** the fact of being older or of a higher rank than others 年長；級別高： *a position of seniority* 高級職位 **2** the rank that you have in a company because of the length of time you have worked there 資歷： *a lawyer with five years' seniority* 有五年從業經驗的律師 ◇ *Should promotion be based on merit or seniority?* 提拔一個人應當看業績，還是看資歷？

ˌsenior ˈmoment *noun* (*humorous*) an occasion when sb forgets sth, or does not think clearly (thought to be typical of what happens when people get older) 尊長表現（老年人失憶、忘事、糊塗的典型狀況）： *It was an important meeting and a bad time to **have a senior moment**.* 那是個重要會議，可不能犯糊塗給忘記了。

sen·sa·tion /senˈseɪʃn/ *noun* **1** [C] a feeling that you get when sth affects your body 感覺；知覺： ***a tingling/burning, etc. sensation*** 刺痛、燒灼等的感覺 ◇ *I had a sensation of falling, as if in a dream.* 我有一種墜落的感覺，像在夢中似的。 **2** [U] the ability to feel through your sense of touch 感覺能力；知覺能力 SYN **feeling**: *She seemed to have lost all sensation in her arms.* 她的兩條胳膊好像完全失去知覺了。 **3** [C, usually sing.] a general feeling or impression that is difficult to explain; an experience or a memory 直覺；莫名其妙的感覺；經歷；回憶： *He had the eerie sensation of being watched.* 他不安地感到有人在監視他。 ◇ *When I arrived, I had the sensation that she had been expecting me.* 我到那兒後，感覺到她一直在盼着我。 **4** [C, usually sing., U] very great surprise, excitement, or interest among a lot of people; the person or the thing that causes this surprise 轟動；譁然；引起轟動的人（或事物）： *News of his arrest **caused a sensation**.* 他被捕的消息引起了轟動。 ◇ *The band became a sensation overnight.* 一夜之間，這支樂隊名聲大振。

sen·sa·tion·al /senˈseɪʃənl/ *adj.* **1** causing great surprise, excitement, or interest 轟動的；引起譁然的 SYN **thrilling**: *The result was a sensational 4–1 victory.* 比賽結果是轟動性的，以 4:1 狂勝對手。 **2** (*disapproving*) (of a newspaper, etc. 報章等) trying to get your interest by presenting facts or events as worse or more shocking than they really are 譁眾取寵的；聳人聽聞的 **3** (*informal*) extremely good; wonderful 極好的；絕妙的 SYN **fantastic**: *You look sensational in that dress!* 你穿這件連衣裙漂亮極了！ ▸ **sen·sa·tion·al·ly** /-ʃənəli/ *adv.*: *They won sensationally against the top team.* 他們戰勝了那支頂級球隊，引起了轟動。 ◇ *The incident was sensationally reported in the press.* 報紙上對那一事件大肆渲染。 ◇ *He's sensationally good-looking!* 他長得太帥了！

sen·sa·tion·al·ism /senˈseɪʃənəlɪzəm/ *noun* [U] (*disapproving*) a way of getting people's interest by using shocking words or by presenting facts and events as worse or more shocking than they really are（指行文或報道）聳人聽聞，譁眾取寵 ▸ **sen·sa·tion·al·ist** /-ʃənəlɪst/ *adj.*: *sensationalist headlines* 聳人聽聞的標題

sen·sa·tion·al·ize (*BrE* also **-ise**) /senˈseɪʃənəlaɪz/ *verb* **~ sth** (*disapproving*) to exaggerate a story so that it seems more exciting or shocking than it really is 故作聳人聽聞地誇張；大肆渲染

sense 🔑 /sens/ *noun, verb*

■ ***noun***

▸ **SIGHT/HEARING, ETC. 視覺、聽覺等 1** 🔑 [C] one of the five powers (sight, hearing, smell, taste and touch) that your body uses to get information about the world around you 感覺官能（即視、聽、嗅、味、觸五覺）： *the five senses* 五種感覺官能 ◇ *Dogs have a keen* (= strong) ***sense of smell***. 狗的嗅覺很靈敏。 ◇ ***the sense organs*** (= eyes, ears, nose, etc.) 感覺器官 ◇ *I could hardly believe the evidence of my own senses* (= what I could see, hear, etc.). 我簡直不敢相信自己的感覺。 ◇ *The mixture of sights, smells and sounds around her made her senses reel.* 四周的物象、氣味和聲音紛至沓來，使她暈頭轉向。 ➲ see also SIXTH SENSE
▸ **FEELING 感覺 2** 🔑 [C] a feeling about sth important（對重大事情的）感覺，意識： *He felt an overwhelming sense of loss.* 他感到非常失落。 ◇ *a **strong sense of purpose/identity/duty, etc.*** 重大意義、很強的身分認同感、很強的責任感等 ◇ *Helmets can give cyclists a **false sense of security**.* 頭盔能給騎自行車的人一種虛假的安全感。 ◇ *I **had the sense that** he was worried about something.* 我感覺他有心事。
▸ **UNDERSTANDING/JUDGEMENT 理解；判斷 3** 🔑 [sing.] an understanding about sth; an ability to judge sth 理解力；判斷力： *One of the most important things in a partner is a **sense of humour*** (= the ability to find things funny or make people laugh). 作為一個生活伴侶，最重要的素質之一是幽默感。 ◇ *He has a very good **sense of direction*** (= finds the way to a place easily). 他的方向感很強。 ◇ *She has lost all sense of direction in her life.* 她完全喪失了生活的方向。 ◇ *Always try to keep a **sense of proportion*** (= of the relative importance of different things). 對事情隨時都要把握好孰輕孰重。 ◇ *a **sense of rhythm/timing*** 節奏感；時機感 ◇ *Alex doesn't have any **dress sense*** (= does not know which clothes look attractive). 亞歷克斯對服裝毫無鑒賞力。 ➲ see also ROAD SENSE **4** 🔑 [U] good understanding and judgement; knowledge of what is sensible or practical behaviour 見識；良好的判斷；清醒的認識： *You should **have the sense to** take advice when it is offered.* 你要知道好歹，別人給你忠告，就該接受。 ◇ ***There's no sense in*** (= it is not sensible) *worrying about it now.* 現在大可不必為那件事憂慮。 ◇ *Can't you **talk sense*** (= say sth sensible)? 你就不能說點正經的？ ◇ *There's a lot of sense in what Mary says.* 瑪麗說得很在理。 ➲ see also COMMON SENSE, GOOD SENSE
▸ **NORMAL STATE OF MIND 正常的精神狀態 5 senses** [pl.] a normal state of mind; the ability to think clearly 健全的心智；清醒的思維能力；理智： *If she threatens to leave, it should **bring him to his senses**.* 假如她威脅着要走，說不定他會清醒過來。 ◇ *He waited for Dora to **come to her senses** and return.* 他盼着多拉冷靜下來後回來。 ◇ (*old-fashioned*) *Are you **out of your senses**? You'll be killed!* 你瘋了嗎？你會丟了性命的！ ◇ (*old-fashioned*) *Why does she want to marry him? She must have **taken leave of her senses**.* 她怎麼會要嫁給他呢？她準是腦子有毛病了。
▸ **MEANING 意義 6** 🔑 [C] the meaning that a word or phrase has; a way of understanding sth 意義；含義；理解…的方式；看待…的角度： *The word 'love' is used in different senses by different people.* "愛"這個字不同的人用來表示不同的意思。 ◇ *education in its broadest sense* 最廣泛意義的教育 ◇ *He was a true friend, **in every sense of the word*** (= in every possible way). 無論從哪個角度講，他都是個真正的朋友。 ◇ ***In a sense*** (= in one way) *it doesn't matter any more.* 從某種意義上說，這事已無關緊要了。 ◇ ***In some senses*** (= in one or more ways) *the criticisms were justified.* 在一定意義上，那些批評意見是有道理的。 ◇ (*formal*) ***In no sense** can the issue be said to*

S

be resolved. 無論如何這個問題都不能說已經解決了。◇ There is a sense in which we are all to blame for the tragedy. 在某種意義上，對這個悲劇我們大家都有責任。
➲ note at SENSIBLE

IDM **knock/talk some 'sense into sb** to try and persuade sb to stop behaving in a stupid way, sometimes using rough or violent methods 開導某人別幹傻事；強使某人理智行事 **make 'sense 1** to have a meaning that you can easily understand 有道理；有意義；講得通：*This sentence doesn't make sense.* 這個句子不通。**2** to be a sensible thing to do 是明智的；合乎情理：*It makes sense to buy the most up-to-date version.* 買最新的版本是明智的。**3** to be easy to understand or explain 表述清楚；易於理解；道理明顯：*John wasn't making much sense on the phone.* 約翰在電話上說得不大清楚。◇ *Who would send me all these flowers? It makes no sense.* 誰會給我送這麼多花呢？真不可思議。**make 'sense of sth** to understand sth that is difficult or has no clear meaning 理解，弄懂（不易理解的事物）**see 'sense** to start to be sensible or reasonable 變得明智起來；開始明白事理 **a sense of oc'casion** a feeling or understanding that an event is important or special 隆重的（或特別的）氣氛：*Candles on the table gave the evening a sense of occasion.* 桌上點了一些蠟燭，使得那個晚上有一種特別的氣氛。➲ more at LEAVE *n.*

■ ***verb*** (not used in the progressive tenses 不用於進行時)

▸ **BECOME AWARE** 感覺 **1** to become aware of sth even though you cannot see it, hear it, etc. 感覺到；意識到；覺察出：**~ sth** *Sensing danger, they started to run.* 他們感到有危險，撒腿就跑。◇ **~ (that)** … *Lisa sensed that he did not believe her.* 莉薩意識到他不相信她。◇ *Thomas, she sensed, could convince anyone of anything.* 她覺得，托馬斯能說服任何人相信任何事。◇ **~ sb/sth doing sth** *He sensed someone moving around behind him.* 他感覺有人在他後面走動。◇ **~ sb/sth do sth** *He sensed something move in the bushes.* 他察覺到灌木叢中有什麼東西在動。◇ **~ how, what, etc.** … *She could sense how nervous he was.* 她能感覺到他有多緊張。

▸ **OF MACHINE** 機器 **2 ~ sth** to discover and record sth 檢測出：*equipment that senses the presence of toxic gases* 檢測有毒氣體的設備

sense·less /ˈsensləs/ *adj.* **1** (*disapproving*) having no meaning or purpose 無意義的；無目的的 **SYN** **pointless**：*senseless violence* 無謂的暴力 ◇ *His death was a senseless waste of life.* 他白浪費了性命，死得毫無意義。◇ *It's senseless to continue any further.* 再繼續下去毫無意義。**2** [not before noun] unconscious 失去知覺：*He was beaten senseless.* 他被打昏了。◇ *She drank herself senseless.* 她喝得不省人事。**3** not using good judgement 不明智的；愚蠢的：*The police blamed senseless drivers who went too fast.* 警察責怪莽撞司機開快車。▸ **sense·less·ly** *adv.*

S

sens·ibil·ity /ˌsensəˈbɪləti/ *noun* (*pl.* **-ies**) **1** [U, C] the ability to experience and understand deep feelings, especially in art and literature（尤指文藝方面的）感受能力，鑒賞力，敏感性：*a man of impeccable manners, charm and sensibility* 一個有魅力、懂感情、舉止無可挑剔的男人 ◇ *artistic sensibility* 藝術鑒賞力 **2 sensibilities** [pl.] a person's feelings, especially when the person is easily offended or influenced by sth（尤指易受傷害或影響的）感情：*The article offended her religious sensibilities.* 那篇文章傷害了她的宗教感情。

sens·ible /ˈsensəbl/ *adj.*

1 (of people and their behaviour 人及行為) able to make good judgements based on reason and experience rather than emotion; practical 明智的；理智的；合理的；切合實際的：*She's a sensible sort of person.* 她屬於那種通情達理的人。◇ *I think that's a very sensible idea.* 我看這個主意很妥當。◇ *Say something sensible.* 說點正經的。◇ *I think **the sensible thing** would be to take a taxi home.* 我想還是坐出租車回家比較好。**2** (of clothes, etc. 服裝等) useful rather than fashionable 樸素而實用的：*sensible shoes* 樸實而舒適的鞋 **3** (*formal* or *literary*) aware of sth 意識到；認識到：*I am sensible of the fact that mathematics is not a popular subject.* 我知道數學課不受歡迎。**OPP** for sense 3 **insensible**

HELP Use **silly** (sense 1) or **impractical** (senses 1 and 2) as the opposite for the other senses. 用 silly（第 1 義）或 impractical（第 1 及第 2 義）作為 sensible 義項 1 和 2 的反義詞。▸ **sens·ibly** /-əbli/ *adv.*：*to behave sensibly* 舉止得體 ◇ *He decided, very sensibly, not to drive when he was so tired.* 他很累，所以決定不開車，這是很明智的。◇ *She's always very sensibly dressed.* 她的着裝總是十分素雅得體。

Which Word? 詞語辨析

sensible / sensitive

Sensible and **sensitive** are connected with two different meanings of sense. * sensible 和 sensitive 與 sense 的兩個不同含義相聯繫。

- **Sensible** refers to your ability to make good judgements. * sensible 涉及判斷：*She gave me some very sensible advice.* 她給了我一些非常合理的建議。◇ *It wasn't very sensible to go out on your own so late at night.* 這麼晚一個人單獨外出是不太明智的。
- **Sensitive** refers to how easily you react to things and how much you are aware of things or other people. * sensitive 涉及反應和對人事物的感應：*a soap for sensitive skin* 敏感皮膚用的肥皂 ◇ *This movie may upset a sensitive child.* 這部影片可能使敏感的孩子感到難過。

sen·si·tive /ˈsensətɪv/ *adj.*

▸ **TO PEOPLE'S FEELINGS** 對他人的感情 **1** aware of and able to understand other people and their feelings 體貼的；體恤的；善解人意的：*a sensitive and caring man* 體貼的男人 ◇ **~ to sth** *She is very sensitive to other people's feelings.* 她很能體諒他人的感情。**OPP** **insensitive**

▸ **TO ART/MUSIC/LITERATURE** 對藝術／音樂／文學 **2** able to understand art, music and literature and to express yourself through them 感覺敏銳的；藝術感覺好的；有悟性的：*an actor's sensitive reading of the poem* 演員對那首詩富有表現力的朗誦 ◇ *a sensitive portrait* 栩栩如生的畫像

▸ **EASILY UPSET** 容易生氣 **3** easily offended or upset 易生氣的；易被惹惱的；神經過敏的：*You're far too sensitive.* 你也太敏感了。◇ **~ about sth** *He's very sensitive about his weight.* 他很忌諱別人說他胖。◇ **~ to sth** *She's very sensitive to criticism.* 她一聽批評就急。**OPP** **insensitive**

▸ **INFORMATION/SUBJECT** 信息；話題 **4** that you have to treat with great care because it may offend people or make them angry or embarrassed 須謹慎對待的；敏感的：*Health care is a politically sensitive issue.* 醫療衛生是一個政治敏感問題。

▸ **TO COLD/LIGHT/FOOD, ETC.** 對低溫、光、食物等 **5** reacting quickly or more than usual to sth 敏感的；過敏的：*sensitive areas of the body* 身體的敏感區 ◇ **~ to sth** *My teeth are very sensitive to cold food.* 我的牙齒對冷食過敏。**OPP** **insensitive**

▸ **TO SMALL CHANGES** 對細微變化 **6 ~ (to sth)** able to measure very small changes 靈敏的：*a sensitive instrument* 靈敏的儀器 ◇ (*figurative*) *The Stock Exchange is very sensitive to political change.* 證券市場對政局變化非常敏感。**OPP** **insensitive** ▸ **sen·si·tive·ly** *adv.*：*She handled the matter sensitively.* 她謹慎細緻地處理了那件事情。◇ *He writes sensitively.* 他文筆細膩。**IDM** see NERVE *n.*

sen·si·tiv·ity /ˌsensəˈtɪvəti/ *noun* (*pl.* **-ies**)

▸ **TO PEOPLE'S FEELINGS** 對他人的感情 **1** [U] **~ (to sth)** the ability to understand other people's feelings 體貼；體恤；體察：*sensitivity to the needs of children* 體察孩子們的需要 ◇ *She pointed out with tact and sensitivity exactly where he had gone wrong.* 她明確指出了他的錯誤所在，既委婉又體貼。

▸ **TO ART/MUSIC/LITERATURE** 對藝術／音樂／文學 **2** [U] the ability to understand art, music and literature and to express yourself through them 敏銳的感覺；悟性：*She played with great sensitivity.* 她的表演很有悟性。

▸ **BEING EASILY UPSET** 容易生氣 **3** [U, C, usually pl.] a tendency to be easily offended or upset by sth 容易生氣；易被惹惱；敏感：*He's a mixture of anger and sensitivity.* 他氣量小又太敏感。◇ *She was blind to the* *feelings and sensitivities of other people.* 她無視他人的情感和敏感之處。 OPP **insensitivity**

▸ **OF INFORMATION/SUBJECT** 信息；話題 **4** [U] the fact of needing to be treated very carefully because it may offend or upset people 敏感性：*Confidentiality is important because of the sensitivity of the information.* 這情報很敏感，務必保密。

▸ **TO FOOD/COLD/LIGHT, ETC.** 對食物、低温、光等 **5** [U, C, usually pl.] (*technical* 術語) the quality of reacting quickly or more than usual to sth 敏感性；過敏性：*food sensitivity* 食物過敏 ◇ *allergies and sensitivities* 過敏反應 ◇ *Some children develop a sensitivity to cow's milk.* 有的孩子對牛奶過敏。◇ *The eyes of some fish have a greater sensitivity to light than ours do.* 有些魚的眼睛比人類的眼睛對光更敏感。

▸ **TO SMALL CHANGES** 對細微變化 **6** [U] the ability to measure very small changes 靈敏度：*the sensitivity of the test* 測試的靈敏度

sen·si·tize (*BrE* also **-ise**) /ˈsensətaɪz/ *verb* [usually passive] **1 ~ sb/sth (to sth)** to make sb/sth more aware of sth, especially a problem or sth bad 使敏感（尤指對問題或不好的事）；使意識到：*People are becoming more sensitized to the dangers threatening the environment.* 人們越來越意識到危害環境的各種因素。 **2 ~ sb/sth (to sth)** (*technical* 術語) to make sb/sth sensitive to physical or chemical changes, or to a particular substance 使對…過敏 ▸ **sen·si·tiza·tion**, **-isa·tion** /ˌsensətaɪˈzeɪʃn; *NAmE* -təˈz-/ *noun* [U]

sen·sor /ˈsensə(r)/ *noun* a device that can react to light, heat, pressure, etc. in order to make a machine, etc. do sth or show sth （探測光、熱、壓力等的）傳感器，敏感元件，探測設備：*security lights with an infrared sensor* (= that come on when a person is near them) 帶紅外線傳感器的保安燈

sens·ory /ˈsensəri/ *adj.* [usually before noun] (*technical* 術語) connected with your physical senses 感覺的；感官的：*sensory organs* 感覺器官 ◇ *sensory deprivation* 感覺喪失

sens·ual /ˈsenʃuəl/ *adj.* **1** connected with your physical feelings; giving pleasure to your physical senses, especially sexual pleasure 感官的；肉慾的；愉悦感官的：*sensual pleasure* 感官之樂 **2** suggesting an interest in physical pleasure, especially sexual pleasure 喜歡感官享受的；耽於肉慾的：*sensual lips* 性感的嘴唇 ◇ *He was darkly sensual and mysterious.* 他耽於肉慾，而且讓人捉摸不透。 ▸ **sen·su·al·ity** /ˌsenʃuˈæləti/ *noun* [U]：*the sensuality of his poetry* 他的詩專注於感官享受 **sen·su·al·ly** /-ʃuəli/ *adv.*

sen·su·ous /ˈsenʃuəs/ *adj.* **1** giving pleasure to your senses 愉悦感官的：*sensuous music* 悦耳的音樂 ◇ *I'm drawn to the poetic, sensuous qualities of her paintings.* 我喜歡她的畫中那種充滿詩意、賞心悦目的特性。 **2** suggesting an interest in sexual pleasure 肉感的；性感的：*his full sensuous lips* 他的豐滿性感的嘴唇 ▸ **sen·su·ous·ly** *adv.* **sen·su·ous·ness** *noun* [U]

sent *past tense, past part.* of SEND

sen·tence 🔑 /ˈsentəns/ *noun, verb*

■ ***noun*** **1** 🔑 [C] (*grammar* 語法) a set of words expressing a statement, a question or an order, usually containing a subject and a verb. In written English sentences begin with a capital letter and end with a full stop/period (.), a question mark (?) or an exclamation mark/exclamation point (!). 句子 **2** 🔑 [C, U] the punishment given by a court 判決；宣判；判刑：***a jail/prison sentence*** 判處監禁 ◇ *a* ***light/heavy sentence*** 輕判；重判 ◇ *to be* ***under sentence of death*** 被判處死刑 ◇ *The judge* ***passed sentence*** (= said what the punishment would be). 法官宣佈了判決。◇ *The prisoner has* ***served*** (= completed) ***his sentence*** *and will be released tomorrow.* 犯人已服刑期滿，明天將獲釋。 ➲ **COLLOCATIONS** at JUSTICE ➲ see also DEATH SENTENCE, LIFE SENTENCE

■ ***verb*** [often passive] **~ sb (to sth)** | **~ sb to do sth** to say officially in court that sb is to receive a particular punishment 判決；宣判；判刑：*to be sentenced to death/life imprisonment/three years in prison* 被判死刑／終身監禁／三年徒刑

ˈ**sentence adverb** *noun* (*grammar* 語法) an adverb that expresses the speaker's attitude towards, or gives the subject of, the whole of the rest of the sentence 句副詞：*In 'Luckily, I didn't tell anyone' and 'Financially, we have a serious problem', 'luckily' and 'financially' are sentence adverbs.* 在句子 Luckily, I didn't tell anyone 和 Financially, we have a serious problem 中，luckily 和 financially 是句副詞。

sen·ten·cer /ˈsentənsə(r)/ *noun* (*formal*) a person who decides on the punishment for sb who is guilty of a crime 宣判人：*The judge was considered a tough sentencer.* 那位法官公認量刑嚴厲。

sen·ten·tious /senˈtenʃəs/ *adj.* (*formal, disapproving*) trying to sound important or intelligent, especially by expressing moral judgements 多格言警句的；（尤指）說教式的 ▸ **sen·ten·tious·ly** *adv.*

sen·tient /ˈsentiənt; ˈsenʃnt/ *adj.* [usually before noun] (*formal*) able to see or feel things through the senses 有感覺能力的；有知覺力的：*Man is a sentient being.* 人是有感覺的生物。

sen·ti·ment /ˈsentɪmənt/ *noun* **1** [C, U] (*formal*) a feeling or an opinion, especially one based on emotions（基於情感的）觀點，看法；情緒：*the spread of nationalist sentiments* 民族主義情緒的傳播 ◇ *This is a sentiment I wholeheartedly agree with.* 這種觀點我完全贊同。◇ *Public sentiment is against any change to the law.* 公眾的意見是反對對該法律作任何修改。 **2** [U] (sometimes *disapproving*) feelings of pity, romantic love, sadness, etc. which may be too strong or not appropriate（失之過度或不恰當的）傷感，柔情，哀傷：*There was no fatherly affection, no display of sentiment.* 沒有像父愛般的親昵，沒有顯得過於激動。◇ *There is no room for sentiment in business.* 在生意場上心腸不能軟。

sen·ti·men·tal /ˌsentɪˈmentl/ *adj.* **1** connected with your emotions, rather than reason 情感的（而非理性的）：*She kept the letters for sentimental reasons.* 她把那些信留作紀念。◇ *The ring wasn't worth very much but it had great* ***sentimental value****.* 那枚戒指值不了幾個錢，但卻極有情感價值。 **2** (often *disapproving*) producing emotions such as pity, romantic love or sadness, which may be too strong or not appropriate; feeling these emotions too much（失之過度或不恰當地）傷感的，充滿柔情的；多愁善感的：*a slushy, sentimental love story* 庸俗纏綿的言情小說 ◇ *He's not the sort of man who gets* ***sentimental about*** *old friendships.* 他不是那種為舊日的友情唏噓感傷的人。 OPP **unsentimental** ▸ **sen·ti·men·tal·ly** /-təli/ *adv.*

sen·ti·men·tal·ist /ˌsentɪˈmentəlɪst/ *noun* (sometimes *disapproving*) a person who is sentimental about things 好感傷者；多愁善感的人

sen·ti·men·tal·ity /ˌsentɪmenˈtæləti/ *noun* [U] (*disapproving*) the quality of being too sentimental 感傷情調；多愁善感

sen·ti·men·tal·ize (*BrE* also **-ise**) /ˌsentɪˈmentəlaɪz/ *verb* [T, I] **~ (sth)** (*disapproving*) to present sth in an emotional way, emphasizing its good aspects and not mentioning its bad aspects 帶着感情色彩描述好的方面：*Jackie was careful not to sentimentalize country life.* 傑基很注意，沒有過分渲染鄉村生活。

sen·ti·nel /ˈsentɪnl/ *noun* (*literary*) a soldier whose job is to guard sth 哨兵 SYN **sentry**：(*figurative*) *a tall round tower* ***standing sentinel*** *over the river* 一座高高的圓塔鎮守在河邊

sen·try /ˈsentri/ *noun* (*pl.* **-ies**) a soldier whose job is to guard sth 哨兵：*to be on sentry duty* 放哨

ˈ**sentry box** *noun* a small shelter for a sentry to stand in 崗亭；哨所

sepal /ˈsepl/ *noun* (*technical* 術語) a part of a flower, like a leaf, that lies under and supports the PETALS (= the delicate coloured parts that make up the head of the flower). Each flower has a ring of sepals called a CALYX. 萼片 ➲ **VISUAL VOCAB** page V11

sep·ar·able /ˈsepərəbl/ *adj.* **1 ~ (from sth)** that can be separated from sth, or considered separately 可分開的；可分隔的；可分離的：*The moral question is not entirely separable from the financial one.* 道德問題和財政問題不能截然分開。**2** (*grammar* 語法) (of a phrasal verb 短語動詞) that can be used with the object going either between the verb and the PARTICLE or after the particle 可分離的；可分開的；可分的：*The phrasal verb 'tear up' is separable because you can say 'She tore the letter up' or 'She tore up the letter'.* * tear up 是可以分開的短語動詞，因為既可以說 She tore the letter up，又可以說 She tore up the letter。**OPP** **inseparable** ▸ **sep·ar·abil·ity** /ˌseprəˈbɪləti/ *noun* [U]

sep·ar·ate *adj., verb*

> **WORD FAMILY**
> separate *adj.*
> separately *adv.*
> separable *adj.*
> (≠ inseparable)
> separate *verb*
> separated *adj.*
> separation *noun*

▪ ***adj.*** /ˈseprət/ **1 ~ (from sth/sb)** forming a unit by itself; not joined to sth else 單獨的；獨立的；分開的：*separate bedrooms* 獨立臥室 ◇ *Raw meat must be **kept separate** from cooked meat.* 生肉和熟肉必須分開存放。◇ *The school is housed in two separate buildings.* 學校設在兩棟獨立的樓房內。**2** [usually before noun] different; not connected 不同的；不相關的：*It happened on three separate occasions.* 這事在三個不同的場合發生過。◇ *For the past three years they have been leading totally separate lives.* 三年來，他們完全是各過各的生活。▸ **sep·ar·ate·ness** *noun* [U, sing.]：*Japan's long-standing sense of separateness and uniqueness* 日本那種由來已久的自成一體、孑然獨立的意識

IDM **go your separate ˈways 1** to end a relationship with sb 斷絕往來；分道揚鑣 **2** to go in a different direction from sb you have been travelling with 分路而行；分手 ➲ more at COVER *n.*

▪ ***verb*** /ˈsepəreɪt/ **1** [I, T] to divide into different parts or groups; to divide things into different parts or groups（使）分開，分離，分割；劃分：*Stir the sauce constantly so that it does not separate.* 不停地攪動醬汁，免得出現分層。◇ **~ sth** *Separate the eggs* (= separate the YOLK from the white). 把蛋黃和蛋清分開。◇ **~ sth from/and sth** *It is impossible to separate belief from emotion.* 信仰和感情是分不開的。◇ **~ sth into sth** *Make a list of points and separate them into 'desirable' and 'essential'.* 列出各點，把它們分成"渴望擁有的"和"絕對必要的"兩類。**2** [I, T] to move apart; to make people or things move apart（使）分離，分散：*South America and Africa separated 200 million years ago.* 南美洲和非洲於 2 億年前分離。◇ **~ from sth** *South America separated from Africa 200 million years ago.* * 2 億年前南美洲和非洲分離。◇ **~ into sth** *We separated into several different search parties.* 我們分成幾個搜索小組。◇ **~ sb/sth** *Police tried to separate the two men who were fighting.* 警察力圖把兩個打架的人分開。◇ *The war separated many families.* 這場戰爭使許多家庭離散。◇ **~ sb/sth from/and sb/sth** *Those suffering from infectious diseases were separated from the other patients.* 傳染病患者同其他病人隔離開來。**3** [T] to be between two people, areas, countries, etc. so that they are not touching or connected 隔開；阻隔：**~ sb/sth** *A thousand kilometres separates the two cities.* 兩座城市相隔一千公里。◇ **~ sb/sth from/and sb** *A high wall separated our back yard from the playing field.* 我們的後院和運動場之間隔着一堵高牆。**4** [I] to stop living together as a couple with your husband, wife or partner 分居：*They separated last year.* 他們於去年分居了。◇ **~ from sb** *He separated from his wife after 20 years of marriage.* 他和妻子在結婚 20 年後分居了。➲ COLLOCATIONS at MARRIAGE **5** [T] **~ sb/sth (from sb/sth)** to make sb/sth different in some way from sb/sth else 區分；區別 **SYN** **divide**：*Politics is the only thing that separates us* (= that we disagree about). 我們之間唯一的分歧是政治觀點。◇ *The judges found it impossible to separate the two contestants* (= they gave them equal scores). 裁判無法把兩位參賽者分出高下。◇ *Only four points separate the top three teams.* 領先的三隊只相差四分。**IDM** see MAN *n.*, SHEEP, WHEAT

PHR V **ˌseparate ˈout** | **ˌseparate sth↔ˈout** to divide into different parts; to divide sth into different parts 使某物分開；劃分：*to separate out different meanings* 區分出不同的意思

sep·ar·ated /ˈsepəreɪtɪd/ *adj.* no longer living with your husband, wife or partner（和某人）分居的：*Her parents are separated but not divorced.* 她父母分居但沒離婚。◇ **~ from sb** *He's been separated from his wife for a year.* 他和妻子分居一年了。➲ COLLOCATIONS at MARRIAGE

sep·ar·ate·ly /ˈseprətli/ *adv.* **~ (from sb/sth)** as a separate person or thing; not together 單獨地；分別地：*They were photographed separately and then as a group.* 他們先單獨照相，然後合影。◇ *Last year's figures are shown separately.* 去年的數字分別列出。

sep·ar·ates /ˈseprəts/ *noun* [pl.] individual pieces of clothing, for example skirts, jackets, and trousers/pants, that are designed to be worn together in different combinations（可與其他不同衣服搭配穿的）單件衣服

ˈseparate school *noun* (*CanE*) a public school for Catholic children in some parts of Canada（加拿大一些地區為天主教兒童設立的）教會學校

sep·ar·ation /ˌsepəˈreɪʃn/ *noun* **1** [U, sing.] the act of separating people or things; the state of being separate 分離；分開；分割；隔離：**~ (from sb/sth)** *the state's eventual separation from the federation* 那個州最終與聯邦的脫離 ◇ **~ (between A and B)** *the need for a clear separation between Church and State* 政教徹底分離的必要性 **2** [C] a period of time that people spend apart from each other 離別：*They were reunited after a separation of more than 20 years.* 他們離別 20 多年後重又聚首。**3** [C] a decision that a husband and wife make to live apart while they are still legally married 分居：*a legal separation* 合法分居 ➲ compare DIVORCE *n.* (1)

the ˌseparation of ˈpowers *noun* [sing.] the principle of the US Constitution that the political power of the government is divided between the President, Congress and the Supreme Court（美國憲法中行政、立法和司法的）三權分立制度 ➲ compare CHECKS AND BALANCES

sep·ar·at·ist /ˈseprətɪst/ *noun* a member of a group of people within a country who want to separate from the rest of the country and form their own government 分離主義者；獨立主義者：*Basque separatists* 巴斯克分裂主義者 ▸ **sep·ar·at·ism** /ˈseprətɪzəm/ *noun* [U] **sep·ar·at·ist** *adj.*：*a separatist movement* 分離主義運動

sep·ar·ator /ˈsepəreɪtə(r)/ *noun* a machine for separating things 分離器；分選機

Seph·ardi /seˈfɑːdi; *NAmE* -ˈfɑːrdi/ *noun* (*pl.* **Seph·ar·dim**) a Jew whose ANCESTORS came from Spain or N Africa 西班牙系猶太人（祖先居住在西班牙或北非）➲ compare ASHKENAZI ▸ **Seph·ar·dic** /-ɪk/ *adj.*

sepia /ˈsiːpiə/ *noun* [U] **1** a brown substance used in inks and paints and used in the past for printing photographs 烏賊墨顏料（或墨汁）**2** a reddish-brown colour 深褐色 ▸ **sepia** *adj.* [usually before noun]：***sepia ink/prints/photographs*** 深褐色墨水／印刷品／照片

sepoy /ˈsiːpɔɪ/ *noun* **1** in the past, an Indian soldier serving under a British or European officer（舊時英國或歐洲長官手下的）印度兵 **2** (*IndE*) a soldier or police officer of the lowest rank 士兵；警員

sep·sis /ˈsepsɪs/ *noun* [U] (*medical* 醫) an infection of part of the body in which PUS is produced 膿毒病；膿毒症

Sep·tem·ber /sepˈtembə(r)/ *noun* [U, C] (*abbr.* **Sept.**) the 9th month of the year, between August and October 九月 **HELP** To see how **September** is used, look at the examples at **April**. * September 的用法見詞條 April 下的示例。

sep·tet /sepˈtet/ *noun* **1** [C+sing./pl. v.] a group of seven musicians or singers 七重奏樂團；七重唱組合 **2** [C] a

S

piece of music for seven musicians or singers 七重奏（曲）；七重唱（曲）

sep·tic /ˈseptɪk/ *adj.* (of a wound or part of the body 傷口或身體部份) infected with harmful bacteria 感染病菌的；膿毒性的；腐敗性的：*a septic finger* 被感染的手指 ◇ *A dirty cut may go septic.* 傷口不乾淨容易受感染。

septi·cae·mia (*BrE*) (*NAmE* **septi·ce·mia**) /ˌseptɪˈsiːmiə/ *noun* [U] (*medical* 醫) infection of the blood by harmful bacteria 敗血病；敗血症 SYN **blood poisoning**

ˌseptic ˈtank *noun* a large container, usually underground, that holds human waste from toilets until the action of bacteria makes it liquid enough to be absorbed by the ground 化糞池

sep·tua·gen·ar·ian /ˌseptjuədʒəˈneəriən; *NAmE* -tʃuədʒəˈner-/ *noun* (*formal*) a person between 70 and 79 years old * 70 至 79 歲的人

sep·tum /ˈseptəm/ *noun* (*pl.* **septa** /ˈseptə/) (*anatomy* 解) a thin part that separates two hollow areas, for example the part of the nose between the NOSTRILS 人類隔膜；（動植物）隔片，隔壁

se·pul·chral /səˈpʌlkrəl/ *adj.* (*literary*) looking or sounding sad and serious; making you think of death 陰沉的；陰森森的；死一般的 SYN **funereal**：*He spoke in sepulchral tones.* 他說話語氣陰沉。

sep·ul·chre (*US* **sep·ul·cher**) /ˈseplkə(r)/ *noun* (*old use*) a place for a dead body, either cut in rock or built of stone（在岩石上鑿出或用石頭砌成的）墳墓，墓穴

se·quel /ˈsiːkwəl/ *noun* ~ (**to sth**) **1** a book, film/movie, play, etc. that continues the story of an earlier one（書、電影、戲劇等的）續篇，續集：*a sequel to the hit movie 'Madagascar'* 熱門影片《馬達加斯加》的續集 ➲ compare PREQUEL **2** [usually sing.] something that happens after an earlier event or as a result of an earlier event 後續的事；隨之而來的事；結果：*There was an interesting sequel to these events later in the year.* 這幾件事發生以後，當年就出現了一種有趣的結果。

se·quence AW /ˈsiːkwəns/ *noun, verb*

■ ***noun*** **1** [C] a set of events, actions, numbers, etc. which have a particular order and which lead to a particular result 一系列；一連串：*He described **the sequence of events** leading up to the robbery.* 他描述了搶劫案發生前的一系列有關情況。 **2** [C, U] the order that events, actions, etc. happen in or should happen in 順序；次序：*The tasks had to be performed in a particular sequence.* 這些任務必須按一定次序去執行。◇ *Number the pages **in sequence**.* 按順序標出頁碼。◇ *These pages are **out of sequence**.* 這幾頁排錯了次序。 **3** [C] a part of a film/movie that deals with one subject or topic or consists of one scene（電影中表現同一主題或場面的）一組鏡頭

■ ***verb*** **1** ~ **sth** (*technical* 術語) to arrange things into a sequence 按順序排列 **2** ~ **sth** (*biology* 生) to identify the order in which a set of GENES or parts of MOLECULES are arranged 測定（整套基因或分子成分的）序列：*The human genome has now been sequenced.* 人體基因組的序列現已測定。 ▸ **se·quen·cing** *noun* [U]：*a gene sequencing project* 基因測序項目

the ˌsequence of ˈtenses *noun* [sing.] (*grammar* 語法) the rules according to which the tense of a SUBORDINATE CLAUSE depends on the tense of a main clause, so that, for example, *'I think that you are wrong'* becomes *'I thought that you were wrong'* in the past tense 時態的呼應，時態的一致（從句的時態受主句時態的制約）

se·quen·cer /ˈsiːkwənsə(r)/ *noun* an electronic instrument for recording and storing sounds so that they can be played later as part of a piece of music 音序器；編曲機

se·quen·tial AW /sɪˈkwenʃl/ *adj.* (*formal*) following in order of time or place 按次序的；順序的；序列的：*sequential data processing* 順序數據處理 ▸ **se·quen·tial·ly** AW /-ʃəli/ *adv.*：*data stored sequentially on a computer* 順序存貯在計算機裏的數據

se·ques·ter /sɪˈkwestə(r)/ *verb* (*law* 律) **1** = SEQUESTRATE **2** ~ **sb** to keep a JURY together in a place, in order to prevent them from talking to other people about a court case, or learning about it in the newspapers, on television, etc. 隔離（避免陪審團與公眾接觸）

se·ques·tered /sɪˈkwestəd; *NAmE* -tərd/ *adj.* [usually before noun] (*literary*) (of a place 地方) quiet and far away from people 僻靜的；隱蔽的；與外界隔絕的

se·ques·trate /ˈsiːkwəstreɪt; sɪˈkwes-/ (also **se·ques·ter**) *verb* ~ **sth** (*law* 律) to take control of sb's property or ASSETS until a debt has been paid 扣押（債務人資產） ▸ **se·ques·tra·tion** /ˌsiːkwəˈstreɪʃn/ *noun* [U, C]

se·quin /ˈsiːkwɪn/ *noun* a small round shiny disc sewn onto clothing as decoration（裝飾衣服的）閃光小圓片 ▸ **se·quinned** (*NAmE* **se·quined**) /ˈsiːkwɪnd/ *adj.* [usually before noun]

se·quoia /sɪˈkwɔɪə/ *noun* a very tall N American tree, a type of redwood 紅杉

sera *pl.* of SERUM

ser·aph /ˈserəf/ *noun* (*pl.* **ser·aph·im** /-fɪm/ or **ser·aphs**) an ANGEL of the highest rank 撒拉弗，色辣芬（基督教中級別最高的天使）➲ compare CHERUB (1)

ser·aph·ic /səˈræfɪk/ *adj.* (*literary*) **1** as beautiful, pure, etc. as an angel 天使般美麗（或純潔等）的：***a seraphic child/nature*** 天使般可愛的孩子／純潔的本性 **2** extremely happy 無比快樂的：*a seraphic smile* 無比快樂的微笑

ser·en·ade /ˌserəˈneɪd/ *noun, verb*

■ ***noun*** **1** a song or tune played or sung at night by a lover outside the window of the woman he loves（男子在所愛慕的女子窗下歌唱或演奏的）小夜曲 **2** a gentle piece of music in several parts, usually for a small group of instruments（尤指供小型樂隊演奏的）小夜曲

■ ***verb*** ~ **sb** to sing or play music to sb (as done in the past by a man singing under her window to the woman he loved)（對所愛慕的女子）唱小夜曲，奏小夜曲

ser·en·dip·ity /ˌserənˈdɪpəti/ *noun* [U] the fact of sth interesting or pleasant happening by chance 巧事；機緣湊巧 ▸ **ser·en·dip·it·ous** /-ˈdɪpətəs/ *adj.*：*serendipitous discoveries* 偶然的幸運發現

se·rene /səˈriːn/ *adj.* calm and peaceful 平靜的；寧靜的；安詳的：*a lake, still and serene in the sunlight* 陽光下寧靜安謐的湖水 ▸ **se·rene·ly** *adv.*：*serenely beautiful* 寧靜而美麗 ◇ *She smiled serenely.* 她安詳地微笑。 **se·ren·ity** /səˈrenəti/ *noun* [U, sing.]：*The hotel offers a haven of peace and serenity away from the bustle of the city.* 那家旅館遠離鬧市，是一個幽靜安謐的好去處。

serf /sɜːf; *NAmE* sɜːrf/ *noun* (in the past) a person who was forced to live and work on land that belonged to a LANDOWNER whom they had to obey（舊時的）農奴

serf·dom /ˈsɜːfdəm; *NAmE* ˈsɜːrf-/ *noun* [U] the system under which crops were grown by serfs; the state of being a serf 農奴制；農奴身分：*the abolition of serfdom in Russia in 1861* * 1861 年農奴制在俄國的廢除

serge /sɜːdʒ; *NAmE* sɜːrdʒ/ *noun* [U] a type of strong cloth made of wool, used for making clothes 嗶嘰：*a blue serge suit* 一套藍色嗶嘰西服

ser·geant /ˈsɑːdʒənt; *NAmE* ˈsɑːrdʒ-/ *noun* (*abbr.* **Sergt**, **Sgt**) **1** a member of one of the middle ranks in the army and the AIR FORCE, below an officer 陸軍（或空軍）中士：*Sergeant Salter* 索爾特中士 ➲ see also FLIGHT SERGEANT, STAFF SERGEANT **2** (in Britain) a police officer just below the rank of an INSPECTOR（英國警察）巡佐 **3** (in the US) a police officer just below the rank of a LIEUTENANT or CAPTAIN（美國警察）警佐 ➲ see also SARGE

ˌsergeant ˈmajor *noun* (often used as a title 常用作頭銜) **1** a soldier of middle rank in the British army who is responsible for helping the officer who organizes the affairs of a particular REGIMENT (= a large group of soldiers) 准尉副官（英國陸軍中的團行政助理） **2** a soldier in the US army of the highest rank of NON-COMMISSIONED OFFICERS 軍士長（美國陸軍中最高級軍士）

S

ser·ial /ˈsɪəriəl; *NAmE* ˈsɪr-/ *noun, adj.*

■ ***noun*** a story on television or the radio, or in a magazine, that is broadcast or published in several separate parts 電視連續劇；廣播連續劇；雜誌連載小說

■ ***adj.*** **1** [usually before noun] (*technical* 術語) arranged in a series 順序排列的；排成系列的： *tasks carried out in the same serial order* 按同樣順序完成的任務 **2** [only before noun] doing the same thing in the same way several times 連續的；多次的： *a serial rapist* 一個連續作案的強姦犯 **3** [only before noun] (of a story, etc. 小說等) broadcast or published in several separate parts 以連續劇形式播出的；連載的： *a novel in serial form* 一部連載小說 ▸ **ser·ial·ly** /-iəli/ *adv.*

seri·al·ize (*BrE* also **-ise**) /ˈsɪəriəlaɪz; *NAmE* ˈsɪr-/ *verb* **~ sth** to publish or broadcast sth in parts as a serial 連載；連播： *The novel was serialized on TV in six parts.* 這部小說分六集在電視上播出。 ▸ **seri·al·iza·tion**, **-isa·tion** /ˌsɪəriəlaɪˈzeɪʃn; *NAmE* ˌsɪriələˈz-/ *noun* [C, U]： *a newspaper serialization of the book* 這部書在報上的連載

ˌserial ˈkiller *noun* a person who murders several people one after the other in a similar way 連環殺手

ˌserial moˈnogamy *noun* [U] the fact or custom of having more than one husband, wife or sexual partner in your life, but only one at a time 連續性單配偶生活，連續性一夫一妻制（指儘管一生多個配偶或性伴，但同一時間只有一個配偶或性伴）

ˈserial number *noun* a number put on a product, such as a camera, television, etc. in order to identify it 序列號；編號

ˈserial port *noun* (*computing* 計) a point on a computer where you connect a device such as a mouse that sends or receives data one BIT at a time 串行端口；序列埠

ser·ies 🔑 AW /ˈsɪəriːz; *NAmE* ˈsɪr-/ *noun* (*pl.* **ser·ies**)

1 🔑 [C, usually sing.] **~ of sth** several events or things of a similar kind that happen one after the other 一系列；連續；接連： *The incident sparked off a whole* ***series of events*** *that nobody had foreseen.* 那一事件引發出一連串誰都沒有料到的事。◇ *the latest in a series of articles on the nature of modern society* 論現代社會性質的一系列文章中最新的一篇 **2** 🔑 [C] a set of radio or television programmes that deal with the same subject or that have the same characters（廣播或電視上題材或角色相同的）系列節目 ➲ COLLOCATIONS at TELEVISION **3** [C] (*sport* 體) a set of sports games played between the same two teams（兩隊之間的）系列比賽： *the* ***World Series*** (= in BASEBALL) 世界系列美國職業棒球錦標賽 ◇ *England have lost the* ***Test series*** (= of CRICKET matches) *against India.* 英格蘭板球隊在同印度隊的系列比賽中落敗。 **4** [U, C] (*technical* 術語) an electrical CIRCUIT in which the current passes through all the parts in the correct order 串聯

serif /ˈserɪf/ *noun* a short line at the top or bottom of some styles of printed letters 襯線，截線（部份印刷體的西文字母頂端或底部的短線）： *a serif typeface* 襯線字體 ➲ compare SANS SERIF

ser·ious 🔑 /ˈsɪəriəs; *NAmE* ˈsɪr-/ *adj.*

▸ **BAD** 不好 **1** 🔑 bad or dangerous 不好的；嚴重的；有危險的： *a* ***serious illness/problem/offence*** 嚴重的疾病／問題／罪行 ◇ *to cause* ***serious injury/damage*** 導致重傷；造成嚴重破壞 ◇ *They pose a serious threat to security.* 他們對安全構成嚴重威脅。◇ *The consequences could be serious.* 後果可能是嚴重的。

▸ **NEEDING THOUGHT** 需思考 **2** 🔑 needing to be thought about carefully; not only for pleasure 需認真思考的；嚴肅的： *a serious article* 一篇嚴肅的文章 ◇ *a serious newspaper* 一份嚴肅的報紙 ◇ *It's time to give serious consideration to this matter.* 到了認真考慮這一問題的時候了。

▸ **IMPORTANT** 重要 **3** 🔑 that must be treated as important 重要的；須重視的： *We need to get down to the serious business of working out costs.* 我們該認真地把成本算出來了。◇ *The team is a serious contender for the title this year.* 該隊是今年不可輕視的奪標競爭對手。

▸ **NOT SILLY** 理智 **4** 🔑 thinking about things in a careful and sensible way; not silly 嚴肅的；穩重的： ***Be serious*** *for a moment; this is important.* 嚴肅點兒，這件事很重要。◇ *I'm afraid I'm not a very serious person.* 恐怕我不是一個非常嚴肅的人。

▸ **NOT JOKING** 不是開玩笑 **5** 🔑 sincere about sth; not joking or meant as a joke 當真的；認真的： *Believe me, I'm* ***deadly*** (= extremely) ***serious***. 相信我，我絕對是當真的。◇ *Don't laugh, it's a serious suggestion.* 別笑，這是一項嚴肅的建議。◇ **~ (about doing sth)** *Is she serious about wanting to sell the house?* 她真想把房子賣掉嗎？◇ **~ (about sb/sth)** *He's really serious about Penny and wants to get engaged.* 他對彭尼的確是認真的，他想跟她訂婚。◇ (*informal*) ***You can't be serious!*** (= you must be joking) 你一定是在開玩笑吧！◇ *You think I did it?* ***Be serious!*** (= what you suggest is ridiculous) 你認為這是我幹的？別傻了好不好！

▸ **LARGE AMOUNT** 大量 **6** (*informal*) used to emphasize that there is a large amount of sth（強調大量）： *You can earn serious money doing that.* 幹那個，你能掙一大筆錢。◇ *I'm ready to do some serious eating* (= I am very hungry). 我餓得很，得好好吃一頓。

Synonyms 同義詞辨析

serious

grave • earnest • solemn

These words all describe sb who thinks and behaves carefully and sensibly, but often without much joy or laughter. 以上各詞均形容人嚴肅、穩重、認真。

serious thinking about things in a careful and sensible way; not laughing about sth 指嚴肅的、穩重的、認真的： *He's not really a very serious person.* 他不是一個非常嚴肅的人。◇ ***Be serious*** *for a moment; this is important.* 嚴肅點兒，這件事很重要。

grave (*rather formal*) (of a person) serious in manner, as if sth sad, important, or worrying has just happened 指人嚴肅的、穩重的、認真的： *He looked very grave as he entered the room.* 他進屋時表情非常嚴肅。

earnest serious and sincere 指認真的、誠實的、真誠的： *The earnest young doctor answered all our questions.* 這個認真的年輕醫生回答了我們所有的問題。

solemn looking or sounding very serious, without smiling; done or said in a very serious and sincere way 指表情嚴肅的、冷峻的、莊嚴的、鄭重的： *Her expression grew solemn.* 她的表情顯得嚴肅起來。◇ *I made a* ***solemn promise*** *that I would return.* 我鄭重承諾過我會回來的。

PATTERNS

- a(n) serious/grave/earnest/solemn **expression/face**
- a serious/solemn **mood/atmosphere**

ser·ious·ly 🔑 /ˈsɪəriəsli; *NAmE* ˈsɪr-/ *adv.*

1 🔑 in a serious way 嚴重地；嚴肅地；認真地： *to be* ***seriously ill/injured*** 重病；重傷 ◇ *You're not seriously expecting me to believe that?* 你不是真的以為我會相信那樣的話吧？◇ *They are seriously concerned about security.* 他們非常關注安全問題。◇ *Smoking can seriously damage your health.* 吸煙會嚴重損害你的健康。 **2** 🔑 used at the beginning of a sentence to show a change from joking to being more serious（用於句首，表示轉為談正事）說正經的，說實在的： *Seriously though, it could be really dangerous.* 不過說實在的，這事說不好真的很危險。 **3** (*informal*) very; extremely 非常；極其： *They're seriously rich.* 他們極為富有。

IDM **take sb/sth ˈseriously** 🔑 to think that sb/sth is important and deserves your attention and respect 認真對待： *We take threats of this kind very seriously.* 我們對這類威脅非常重視。◇ *Why can't you ever take anything seriously?* 你怎麼對什麼都不當回事呢？

ser·ious·ness /ˈsɪəriəsnəs; *NAmE* ˈsɪr-/ *noun* [U, sing.] the state of being serious 嚴重；認真；嚴肅：*He spoke with a seriousness that was unusual in him.* 他說話時神情少有地認真。

IDM **in all 'seriousness** very seriously; not as a joke 非常嚴肅地；認認真真地；說實在的

ser·mon /ˈsɜːmən; *NAmE* ˈsɜːrmən/ *noun* **1** a talk on a moral or religious subject, usually given by a religious leader during a service 佈道；講道 ➲ SYNONYMS at SPEECH ➲ COLLOCATIONS at RELIGION **2** (*informal*, usually *disapproving*) moral advice that a person tries to give you in a long talk 冗長的說教

ser·mon·ize (*BrE* also **-ise**) /ˈsɜːmənaɪz; *NAmE* ˈsɜːrm-/ *verb* [I] (*disapproving*) to give moral advice, especially when it is boring or not wanted （尤指讓人厭煩地）說教，教訓 **SYN** **moralize**

sero·tonin /ˌserəˈtəʊnɪn; *NAmE* -ˈtoʊn-/ *noun* [U] a chemical in the brain that affects how messages are sent from the brain to the body, and also affects how a person feels 血清素，五羥色胺（神經遞質，亦影響情緒等）

ser·pent /ˈsɜːpənt; *NAmE* ˈsɜːrp-/ *noun* (*literary*) a snake, especially a large one 蛇；（尤指）大蛇

ser·pen·tine /ˈsɜːpəntaɪn; *NAmE* ˈsɜːrpəntiːn/ *adj.* (*literary*) bending and twisting like a snake 彎彎曲曲的；蜿蜒的；盤旋的；迂迴的 **SYN** **winding**：*the serpentine course of the river* 蜿蜒曲折的河道

ser·rated /səˈreɪtɪd/ *adj.* having a series of sharp points on the edge like a SAW 鋸齒狀的：*a knife with a* ***serrated edge*** 帶鋸齒刃的刀 ➲ VISUAL VOCAB page V26

ser·ra·tion /seˈreɪʃn/ *noun* a part on an edge or the blade of a knife that is sharp and pointed like a SAW 鋸齒邊；鋸齒刃

ser·ried /ˈserid/ *adj.* [usually before noun] (*literary*) standing or arranged closely together in rows or lines （行列）密排的，密集的，靠攏的：*serried ranks of soldiers* 密集排列的士兵

serum /ˈsɪərəm; *NAmE* ˈsɪrəm/ *noun* (*pl.* **sera** /-rə/ or **ser·ums**) **1** [U] (*biology* 生) the thin liquid that remains from blood when the rest has CLOTTED 血清 **2** [U, C] (*medical* 醫) serum taken from the blood of an animal and given to people to protect them from disease, poison, etc. 免疫血清：*snakebite serum* 抗蛇毒血清 **3** [U] any liquid like water in body TISSUE 漿液（體液的水樣部份）

ser·vant 🗝 /ˈsɜːvənt; *NAmE* ˈsɜːrv-/ *noun*
1 🗝 a person who works in another person's house, and cooks, cleans, etc. for them 僕人；用人：*a domestic servant* 家僕 ◇ *They treat their mother like a servant.* 他們像對待傭人一樣對待自己的母親。 **2** a person who works for a company or an organization （公司或機構的）雇員，職員：*a public servant* 公務員 ➲ see also CIVIL SERVANT **3** a person or thing that is controlled by sth 奴僕般受制（或獻身）於…的人；服務於…的事物：*He was willing to make himself a servant of his art.* 他甘願獻身於自己的藝術。 **IDM** see OBEDIENT

serve 🗝 /sɜːv; *NAmE* sɜːrv/ *verb, noun*

■ *verb*

▸ **FOOD/DRINK 食物；飲料** **1** 🗝 [T, I] to give sb food or drink, for example at a restaurant or during a meal （給某人）提供；端上：**~ (sth)** *Breakfast is served between 7 and 10 a.m.* 早餐供應時間從上午 7 點到 10 點。◇ *Pour the sauce over the pasta and serve immediately.* 把醬汁澆在意大利麪上就立刻上桌。◇ *Shall I serve?* 現在上菜好嗎？◇ **~ sth with sth** *Serve the lamb with new potatoes and green beans.* 羊肉要配新鮮土豆和青刀豆一起上。◇ **~ sth to sb** *They served a wonderful meal to more than fifty delegates.* 他們招待五十多位代表吃了一餐美味佳肴。◇ **~ sb with sth** *The delegates were served with a wonderful meal.* 代表們受到款待，吃了一餐美味佳肴。◇ **~ sb sth** *She served us a delicious lunch.* 她招待我們吃了一頓可口的午餐。◇ **~ sth + adj.** *The quiche can be served hot or cold.* 蛋奶餡餅熱吃也行，冷吃也行。 **2** [T] **~ sb/sth** (of an amount of food 食物的量) to be enough for sb/sth 夠…吃（或用）：*This dish will serve four hungry people.* 這盤菜夠四個飢餓的人吃。

▸ **CUSTOMERS 顧客** **3** 🗝 [T, I] **~ (sb)** (*especially BrE*) to help a customer or sell them sth in a shop/store 接待；服務：*Are you being served?* 有人接待您嗎？◇ *She was serving behind the counter.* 她在櫃枱服務。

▸ **BE USEFUL 有用** **4** 🗝 [T] **~ sth/sb** to be useful to sb in achieving or satisfying sth 對…有用；能滿足…的需要：*These experiments* ***serve*** *no useful* ***purpose.*** 這些實驗沒有任何實際意義。◇ *Most of their economic policies* ***serve the interests*** *of big business.* 他們的經濟政策多半符合大企業的利益。◇ *How can we best* ***serve the needs*** *of future generations?* 我們怎樣才最能滿足後代子孫的需要？◇ *His linguistic ability* ***served him well*** *in his chosen profession.* 他的語言能力對他所選擇的職業大有幫助。

▸ **PROVIDE STH 提供** **5** 🗝 [T] to provide an area or a group of people with a product or service （向一地或一群體）供應，提供：**~ sb/sth** *The centre will serve the whole community.* 這個中心將為整個社區提供服務。◇ **~ sb/sth with sth** *The town is well served with buses and major road links.* 這座城市乘坐公共汽車很方便，與幹線公路的聯接也很發達。

▸ **BE SUITABLE 適合** **6** [I] **~ (as sth)** to be suitable for a particular use, especially when nothing else is available 可用作，可當…使（尤指別無選擇時）：*The sofa will serve as a bed for a night or two.* 沙發可以當牀湊合一兩夜。

▸ **HAVE PARTICULAR RESULT 產生某種結果** **7** [I, T] to have a particular effect or result 產生…的效果（或結果）：**~ as sth** *The judge said the punishment would serve as a warning to others.* 法官說這種懲罰將對其他人起到殺一儆百的作用。◇ **~ to do sth** *The attack was unsuccessful and* ***served only to*** *alert the enemy.* 進攻未奏效，反而使敵人警覺起來。

▸ **WORK 工作** **8** 🗝 [I, T] to work or perform duties for a person, an organization, a country, etc. （為…）工作，服務，履行義務，盡職責：**~ (as sth)** *He served as a captain in the army.* 他曾是一名陸軍上尉。◇ **~ in/on/with sth** *She served in the medical corps.* 她在醫務部隊服過役。◇ **~ under/with sb** *He served under Edward Heath in the 1970s.* 他曾於 20 世紀 70 年代在愛德華・希思手下任職。◇ **~ sth** *I wanted to work somewhere where I could serve the community.* 我想找一個能夠為公眾服務的工作崗位。◇ **~ sb (as sth)** *He served the family faithfully for many years* (= as a servant). 他忠心耿耿，伺候這家人多年。 **9** [T, I] to spend a period of time in a particular job or training for a job 任期為；擔任（職務）時間達；培訓期為：**~ sth** *He served a one-year apprenticeship.* 他做了一年的學徒。◇ **~ as sth** *She was elected to serve as secretary of the local party.* 她當選為地方黨組織的書記。

▸ **TIME IN PRISON 監禁時間** **10** [T] **~ sth** to spend a period of time in prison 服（刑）：*prisoners serving life sentences* 服無期徒刑的囚犯 ◇ *She is serving two years for theft.* 她因盜竊罪正在服兩年徒刑。◇ *He has* ***served time*** (= been to prison) *before.* 他以前坐過牢。

▸ **OFFICIAL DOCUMENT 正式文件** **11** [T] (*law* 律) to give or send sb an official document, especially one that orders them to appear in court 把…送達；向（某人）送交：**~ sth (on sb)** *to serve a writ/summons on sb* 把令狀／傳票送達某人 ◇ **~ sb with sth** *to serve sb with a writ/summons* 向某人送交令狀／傳票

▸ **IN SPORT 體育運動** **12** [I, T] (in TENNIS, etc. 網球等) to start playing by throwing the ball into the air and hitting it 發（球）：*Who's serving?* 誰發球？◇ **~ sth** *She served an ace.* 她發球直接得分。

IDM **it serves sb 'right (for doing sth)** 🗝 used to say that sth that has happened to sb is their own fault and they deserve it 咎由自取；罪有應得：*Left you, did she? It serves you right for being so selfish.* 她離開了你，是嗎？那你活該，你太自私了。 **serve your/its 'turn** (*BrE*) to be useful for a particular purpose or period of time （在某方面或某期間）發揮作用，派上用場；足以滿足…的需要 **serve two 'masters** (usually used in negative sentences 通常用於否定句) to support two opposing parties, principles, etc. at the same time 侍奉二主（同時支持兩個敵對的黨派）；徘徊於兩種對立原則之間 ➲ more at FIRST *adv.*, MEMORY

PHR V **ˌserve sth↔'out** **1** to continue doing sth, especially working or staying in prison, for a fixed period of

S

time that has been set 幹至期滿；服滿刑期：*He has three more years in prison before he's served out his sentence.* 他要在監獄裏再待三年，才能服滿刑期。◇ (*BrE*) *They didn't want me to serve out my notice.* 他們想不等我幹到約定的離職時間就要我走。**2** (*BrE*) to share food or drink between a number of people 分發（食物或飲料）；（為眾人）分餐：*I went around the guests serving out drinks.* 我四處走動給客人斟飲料。**,serve sth↔'up** **1** to put food onto plates and give it to people 端上（食物）：*He served up a delicious meal.* 他端上一頓可口的飯菜。**2** to give, offer or provide sth 給出；提供：*She served up the usual excuse.* 她給出的藉口還是老一套。◇ *The teams served up some fantastic entertainment.* 這些隊獻上了精彩的表演。

■ ***noun*** (in TENNIS, etc. 網球等) the action of serving the ball to your opponent 發球

ser·ver /ˈsɜːvə(r); *NAmE* ˈsɜːrv-/ *noun* **1** (*computing* 計) a computer program that controls or supplies information to several computers connected in a network; the main computer on which this program is run 服務器；伺服器 ➲ COLLOCATIONS at EMAIL **2** (*sport* 體) a player who is serving, for example in TENNIS 發球者 **3** [usually pl.] a kitchen UTENSIL (= tool) used for putting food onto sb's plate 上菜用具（往各人盤子裏盛食物的叉、鏟、勺等）：*salad servers* 分色拉用的叉匙 ➲ VISUAL VOCAB page V22 **4** (*NAmE*) a person who serves food in a restaurant; a waiter or waitress （餐館給顧客上菜的）侍者 **5** a person who helps a priest during a church service （教堂做禮拜時的）助祭；輔祭

serv·ery /ˈsɜːvəri; *NAmE* ˈsɜːrv-/ *noun* (*pl.* **-ies**) (*BrE*) part of a restaurant where you collect your food to take back to your table 上菜處（顧客在餐館就餐時端取食物的地方）

ser·vice 0┳ /ˈsɜːvɪs; *NAmE* ˈsɜːrv-/ *noun, verb*

■ ***noun***

▸ **PROVIDING STH** 提供 **1** 0┳ [C] a system that provides sth that the public needs, organized by the government or a private company 公共服務系統；公共事業：*the* ***ambulance/bus/telephone, etc. service*** 救護車、公車、電話等服務系統◇ *The government aims to improve* ***public services****, especially education.* 政府致力於改善公共服務事業，尤其是教育。◇ ***Essential services*** (= the supply of water, gas, electricity) *will be maintained.* 生活必需的水、氣體燃料、電將維持供應。➲ see also EMERGENCY SERVICES, POSTAL SERVICE **2** 0┳ (also **Service**) [C] an organization or a company that provides sth for the public or does sth for the government 公共事業機構（或公司）：*the prison service* 監獄管理機構◇ *the BBC World Service* 英國廣播公司對外廣播 ➲ see also CIVIL SERVICE, DIPLOMATIC SERVICE, FIRE SERVICE, HEALTH SERVICE, INTERNAL REVENUE SERVICE, NATIONAL HEALTH SERVICE, SECRET SERVICE, SECURITY SERVICE, SOCIAL SERVICES **3** 0┳ [C, U] a business whose work involves doing sth for customers but not producing goods; the work that such a business does 服務性企業（或行業、業務）：*financial services* 金融公司◇ *the development of new* ***goods and services*** 新的商品和服務領域的開發◇ *Smith's Catering Services* (= a company) *offers the best value.* 史密斯餐飲公司提供最超值的餐飲服務。◇ *We guarantee (an) excellent service.* 我們保證提供優質服務。◇ *the* ***service sector*** (= the part of the economy involved in this type of business) 服務業◇ *a service industry* 服務性行業

▸ **IN HOTEL/SHOP/RESTAURANT** 旅館；商店；餐館 **4** 0┳ [U] the serving of customers in hotels, restaurants, and shops/stores （對顧客的）接待，服務：*The food was good but the service was very slow.* 飯菜不錯，但動作太慢。◇ *10% will be added to your bill for service.* 您付賬時要另加 10% 的服務費。◇ *Our main concern is to provide quality* ***customer service****.* 我們最關心的是為顧客提供優質服務。➲ COLLOCATIONS at RESTAURANT ➲ see also ROOM SERVICE, SELF-SERVICE

▸ **WORK FOR ORGANIZATION** 為機構工作 **5** 0┳ [U] **~ (to sth)** the work that sb does for an organization, etc., especially when it continues for a long time or is admired very much （尤指長期、受到敬重的）工作，效勞，服務：*She has just celebrated 25 years' service with the company.* 她剛慶祝了自己在公司任職 25 週年。◇ *The employees have good* ***conditions of service****.* 雇員有良好的工作條件。◇ *After retiring, she became involved in* ***voluntary service*** *in the local community.* 她在退休後投身於當地社區的志願服務工作。➲ see also JURY SERVICE at JURY DUTY

▸ **OF VEHICLE/MACHINE** 交通工具；機器 **6** [U] the use that you can get from a vehicle or machine; the state of being used 使用；使用狀況：*That computer gave us very good service.* 我們那台計算機很好用。◇ *The ship will be taken out of service within two years.* 那艘船將在兩年之內退役。**7** [C, U] an examination of a vehicle or machine followed by any work that is necessary to keep it operating well 檢修；維護；維修；保養：*a service engineer* 維修技師◇ (*BrE*) *I had taken the car in for a service.* 我把車送去檢修了。◇ (*NAmE*) *I had taken the car in for service.* 我把車送去檢修了。➲ see also AFTER-SALES SERVICE

▸ **SKILLS/HELP** 技藝；幫助 **8** [usually pl.] (*formal*) the particular skills or help that a person is able to offer （提供技術或幫助的）服務：**~ (of sb)** *You need the services of a good lawyer.* 你需要找一位好律師來幫助你。◇ **~ (as sb/sth)** *He offered his services as a driver.* 他說他願意開車。

▸ **ARMY/NAVY/AIR FORCE** 陸軍；海軍；空軍 **9** [C, usually pl., U] the army, the navy and the AIR FORCE; the work done by people in them 海陸空三軍；兵役：*Most of the boys went straight into* ***the services****.* 多數男生直接去服兵役了。◇ *He* ***saw service*** *in North Africa.* 他曾在北非服兵役。◇ *a service family* 軍人家庭 ➲ see also ACTIVE SERVICE, MILITARY SERVICE, NATIONAL SERVICE

▸ **RELIGIOUS CEREMONY** 宗教禮儀 **10** 0┳ [C] a religious ceremony 宗教禮儀；禮拜儀式：***morning/evening service*** 晨禱；晚禱◇ *to* ***hold/attend a service*** 舉行／參加禮拜◇ *a* ***funeral/marriage/memorial, etc. service*** 喪葬、結婚、追思等宗教儀式 ➲ COLLOCATIONS at RELIGION

▸ **BUS/TRAIN** 公共汽車；火車 **11** [C, usually sing.] a bus, train, etc. that goes regularly to a particular place at a particular time 班車；車次：*the cancellation of the 10.15 service to Glasgow* * 10 點 15 分開往格拉斯哥的車次取消

▸ **ON MOTORWAY** 高速公路 **12 services** [sing.+sing./pl. v.] (*BrE*) a place beside a MOTORWAY where you can stop for petrol, a meal, the toilets, etc. （可加油、用餐、上廁所等的）服務站：*motorway services* 高速公路服務站◇ *It's five miles to the next services.* 距下一個服務站還有五英里。➲ see also SERVICE AREA, SERVICE STATION

▸ **IN TENNIS** 網球 **13** [C] an act of hitting the ball in order to start playing; the way that you hit it 發球；發球方式 SYN **serve**：*It's your service* (= your turn to start playing). 該你發球了。◇ *Her service has improved.* 她的發球有了提高。

▸ **SET OF PLATES, ETC.** 整套餐具等 **14** [C] a complete set of plates, dishes, etc. that match each other 整套餐具：*a tea service* (= cups, SAUCERS, a TEAPOT and plates, for serving tea) 一套茶具 ➲ see also DINNER SERVICE

▸ **BEING SERVANT** 當僕人 **15** [U] (*old-fashioned*) the state or position of being a servant 僕人地位（或身分）：*to* ***be in/go into service*** (= to be/become a servant) 做／去當用人

▸ **OF OFFICIAL DOCUMENT** 正式文件 **16** [U] (*law* 律) the formal giving of an official document, etc. to sb 送達：*the service of a demand for payment* 繳款通知的送達

IDM **at the 'service of sb/sth | at sb's 'service** completely available for sb to use or to help sb 隨時可供使用（或可以幫助）：*Health care must be at the service of all who need it.* 醫療保健機構必須為所有需要者提供服務。◇ (*formal* or *humorous*) *If you need anything, I am* ***at your service****.* 您要是需要什麼，請儘管吩咐。**be of 'service (to sb)** (*formal*) to be useful or helpful （對某人）有用，有幫助：*Can I be of service to anyone?* 有誰需要我幫忙嗎？ **do sb a/no 'service** (*formal*) to do sth that is helpful/not helpful to sb 有助於（或無助於）某人：*She was doing herself no service by remaining silent.* 她老不吭氣，這對她自己沒好處。➲ more at PRESS *v.*

■ ***verb***

▸ **VEHICLE/MACHINE** 交通工具；機器 **1** [usually passive] **~ sth** to examine a vehicle or machine and repair it if necessary so that it continues to work correctly 檢修；維護；維修；保養：*We need to have the car serviced.* 我們得把車送去檢修一下了。

▸ PROVIDE STH 提供 **2 ~ sth/sb** to provide people with sth they need, such as shops/stores, or a transport system 提供服務 SYN **serve**：*Botley is well serviced by a regular bus route into Oxford.* 從博特利到牛津有一路公共汽車，按時發車，十分便利。◇ *This department services the international sales force* (= provides services for it). 這個部門向國際銷售人員提供服務。

▸ PAY INTEREST 支付利息 **3 ~ sth** (*technical* 術語) to pay interest on money that has been borrowed 支付（債務）利息：*The company can no longer **service its debts**.* 那家公司已無力支付債務利息。

ser·vice·able /ˈsɜːvɪsəbl; *NAmE* ˈsɜːrv-/ *adj.* suitable to be used 能用的：*The carpet is worn but still serviceable.* 地毯舊了，但還能用。

ˈservice area *noun* (*BrE*) a place on a MOTORWAY where you can stop and buy food, petrol, have a meal, go to the toilet, etc.（高速公路旁可停車用餐、加油、上廁所等的）服務站

ˈservice charge *noun* **1** an amount of money that is added to a bill, as an extra charge for a service（另加的）服務費：*That will be $50, plus a service charge of $2.50.* 您消費 50 元，另加 2.50 元的服務費。**2** (*BrE*) an amount of money that is added to a bill in a restaurant, for example 10% of the total, that goes to pay for the work of the staff（付給餐館侍者的）小費，服務費 **3** an amount of money that is paid to the owner of an apartment building for services such as putting out rubbish/garbage, cleaning the stairs, etc.（付給房東的）服務費，清潔費

ˈservice club *noun* (*NAmE*) an organization whose members do things to help their local community 社區服務俱樂部

ˈservice industry *noun* [U, C] (*economics* 經) = TERTIARY INDUSTRY

ser·vice·man /ˈsɜːvɪsmən; *NAmE* ˈsɜːrv-/, **ser·vice·woman** /ˈsɜːvɪswʊmən; *NAmE* ˈsɜːrv-/ *noun* (*pl.* **-men** /-mən/, **-women** /-wɪmɪn/) a man or woman who is a member of the armed forces（男、女）軍人 ➲ note at GENDER

ˈservice provider *noun* a business company that provides a service to customers, especially one that connects customers to the Internet 服務供應商（尤指互聯網服務供應商）：*an Internet service provider* 互聯網服務供應商

ˈservice road (*NAmE* also **ˈfrontage road**) *noun* a side road that runs parallel to a main road, that you use to reach houses, shops/stores, etc.（與主路平行的）輔路；（由大路通往房屋、商店等的）支路

ˈservice station *noun* **1** = GAS STATION, PETROL STATION **2** (*BrE*) an area and building beside a MOTORWAY where you can buy food and petrol, go to the toilet, etc.（高速公路旁可停車用餐、加油、上廁所等的）服務站：*a motorway service station* 高速公路服務站

ser·vicing /ˈsɜːvɪsɪŋ; *NAmE* ˈsɜːrv-/ *noun* [U] **1** the act of checking and repairing a vehicle, machine, etc. to keep it in good condition（車輛、機器等的）檢修，維修，保養，維護：*Like any other type of equipment it requires regular servicing.* 它和其他類型的設備一樣，也需要定期檢修。**2** (*finance* 財) the act of paying interest on money that has been borrowed（債務的）利息支付：*debt servicing* 債務利息的支付

ser·vi·ette /ˌsɜːviˈet; *NAmE* ˌsɜːrv-/ *noun* (*BrE*) a piece of cloth or paper used at meals for protecting your clothes and cleaning your lips and fingers 餐巾；餐巾紙 SYN **napkin**

ser·vile /ˈsɜːvaɪl; *NAmE* ˈsɜːrvl; -vaɪl/ *adj.* (*disapproving*) wanting too much to please sb and obey them 奴性的；逢迎的；恭順的 SYN **fawning** ▸ **ser·vil·ity** /sɜːˈvɪləti; *NAmE* sɜːrˈv-/ *noun* [U]

serv·ing /ˈsɜːvɪŋ; *NAmE* ˈsɜːrvɪŋ/ *noun* an amount of food for one person（供一個人吃的）一份食物：*This recipe will be enough for four servings.* 本食譜為四人量。

ser·vi·tor /ˈsɜːvɪtə(r); *NAmE* ˈsɜːrv-/ *noun* (*old use*) a male servant 男僕；男侍從

ser·vi·tude /ˈsɜːvɪtjuːd; *NAmE* ˈsɜːrvətuːd/ *noun* [U] (*formal*) the condition of being a SLAVE or being forced to obey another person 奴役（狀況）；任人差遣（的狀況）SYN **slavery**

servo /ˈsɜːvəʊ; *NAmE* ˈsɜːrvoʊ/ *noun* (*pl.* **-os**) (*technical* 術語) a part of a machine that controls a larger piece of machinery（機器的）伺服傳動裝置

ses·ame /ˈsesəmi/ *noun* [U] a tropical plant grown for its seeds and their oil, which are used in cooking 芝麻；脂麻：*sesame seeds* 芝麻粒兒 ➲ see also OPEN SESAME

ses·sion 0→ /ˈseʃn/ *noun*

1 0→ [C] a period of time that is spent doing a particular activity 一場；一節；一段時間：*a **photo/recording/training, etc. session*** 拍照、錄音、訓練等時段 ◇ *The course is made up of 12 two-hour sessions.* 這門課總共上 12 次，每次兩小時。➲ see also JAM SESSION **2** 0→ [C, U] a formal meeting or series of meetings of a court, parliament, etc.; a period of time when such meetings are held（法庭的）開庭，開庭期；（議會等的）會議，會期：*a session of the UN General Assembly* 一屆聯合國大會 ◇ *The court is now **in session**.* 法庭現在正在開庭。◇ *The committee met **in closed session*** (= with nobody else present). 委員會舉行了秘密會議。➲ see also QUARTER SESSIONS **3** [C] a school or university year 學年 **4** [C] an occasion when people meet to play music, especially Irish music, in a pub/bar（酒吧中）演奏會（尤指演奏愛爾蘭音樂）

ˈsession musician *noun* a musician who is hired to play on recordings but is not a permanent member of a band（樂隊為錄音而雇用的）臨時樂師

set 0→ /set/ *verb, noun, adj.*

■ *verb* (**set·ting, set, set**)

▸ PUT/START 放置；開始 **1** 0→ [T] **~ sth/sb + adv./prep.** to put sth/sb in a particular place or position 放；置；使處於：*She set a tray down on the table.* 她把托盤放到桌上。◇ *They ate everything that was set in front of them.* 他們把放在面前的東西都吃光了。◇ *The house is set* (= located) *in fifty acres of parkland.* 房子四周是五十英畝草地。 **2** 0→ [T] to cause sb/sth to be in a particular state; to start sth happening 使處於某種狀況；使開始：**~ sb/sth + adv./prep.** *Her manner immediately **set** everyone **at their ease**.* 她的態度立刻使大家感到輕鬆了。◇ *He pulled the lever and **set** the machine **in motion**.* 他扳動操縱桿，啟動了機器。◇ **~ sb/sth + adj.** *The hijackers **set** the hostages **free**.* 劫機者釋放了人質。◇ **~ sb/sth doing sth** *Her remarks set me thinking.* 她的話引起了我的深思。

▸ PLAY/BOOK/MOVIE 戲劇；書；電影 **3** 0→ [T, usually passive] **~ sth + adv./prep.** to place the action of a play, novel or film/movie in a particular place, time, etc. 把故事情節安排在；以…為…設置背景：*The novel is set in London in the 1960s.* 這部小説以 20 世紀 60 年代的倫敦為背景。

▸ CLOCK/MACHINE 鐘錶；機器 **4** 0→ [T] **~ sth (+ adv./prep.)** to prepare or arrange sth so that it is ready for use or in position 設置；調整好；安排就緒：*She set the camera on automatic.* 她把照相機調到自動狀態。◇ *I set my watch by* (= make it show the same time as) *the TV.* 我按電視對了手錶。◇ *Set the alarm for 7 o'clock.* 把鬧鐘設在 7 點。

▸ TABLE 餐桌 **5** 0→ [T] **~ a/the table** (**for sb/sth**) to arrange knives, forks, etc. on a table for a meal 擺放餐具：*Could you set the table for dinner?* 你把餐具擺好，準備開飯，好嗎？◇ *The table was set for six guests.* 桌上擺放了六位客人的餐具。

▸ JEWELLERY 珠寶 **6** [T, usually passive] to put a PRECIOUS STONE into a piece of jewellery 鑲嵌：**~ A in B** *She had the sapphire set in a gold ring.* 她請人把藍寶石鑲嵌到一枚金戒指上。◇ **~ B with A** *Her bracelet was set with emeralds.* 她的手鐲上鑲有綠寶石。

▸ ARRANGE 安排 **7** 0→ [T] **~ sth** to arrange or fix sth; to decide on sth 安排；確定；決定：*They haven't **set a date** for their wedding yet.* 他們還沒有確定婚期。◇ *The*

S

government has set strict limits on public spending this year. 今年，政府對公共開支規定了嚴格的限額。

▸ **EXAMPLE/STANDARD, ETC.** 榜樣、規範等 **8** 🔑 [T] **~ sth** to fix sth so that others copy it or try to achieve it 樹立；創立；開創：*This could* ***set a new fashion.*** 這或許會開創一種新時尚。◇ *They* ***set high standards*** *of customer service.* 他們制訂了嚴格的客戶服務標準。◇ *I am unwilling to* ***set a precedent.*** 我不想開先例。◇ *She* ***set a*** *new world* ***record*** *for the high jump.* 她創造了新的跳高世界紀錄。◇ *I rely on you to* ***set a good example.*** 我指望你來樹立一個好榜樣。

▸ **WORK/TASK** 工作；任務 **9** 🔑 [T] **~ sth (for sb) | ~ sb (to do sth)** to give sb a piece of work, a task, etc. 佈置；分配；指派：**~ sth** *Who will be setting* (= writing the questions for) *the French exam?* 誰出法語試題？◇ **~ sth for sth** *What books have been set* (= are to be studied) *for the English course?* 英語課指定了要用哪些書？◇ **~ sth for sb/yourself** *She's set a difficult task for herself.* 她給自己安排了一項艱巨任務。◇ **~ sb/yourself sth** *She's set herself a difficult task.* 她給自己安排了一項艱巨任務。◇ **~ sb/yourself to do sth** *I've set myself to finish the job by the end of the month.* 我要求自己在月底以前完成這項工作。

▸ **BECOME FIRM** 凝固 **10** 🔑 [I] to become firm or hard 凝固；凝結：*Leave the concrete to set for a few hours.* 讓混凝土凝固幾小時。◇ **+ adj.** *The glue had set hard.* 膠粘得很緊。

▸ **FACE** 臉 **11** [T, usually passive] **~ sth** to fix your face into a firm expression 使現出堅定的表情：*Her jaw was set in a determined manner.* 她下巴緊繃着，一副決不動搖的樣子。

▸ **HAIR** 頭髮 **12** [T] **~ sth** to arrange sb's hair while it is wet so that it dries in a particular style 固定髮型；做頭髮：*She had her hair washed and set.* 她去洗了頭，做了髮型。

▸ **BONE** 骨頭 **13** [T, I] **~ (sth)** to put a broken bone into a fixed position and hold it there, so that it will heal; to heal in this way 把（斷骨）復位；接（骨）：*The surgeon set her broken arm.* 醫生給她接上了手臂上的斷骨。

▸ **FOR PRINTING** 為印刷 **14** [T] **~ sth** (*technical* 術語) to use a machine or computer to arrange writing and images on pages in order to prepare a book, newspaper, etc. for printing 排版 ⊃ see also TYPESETTER

▸ **WORDS TO MUSIC** 為歌詞譜曲 **15** [T] **~ sth (to sth)** to write music to go with words 為…譜曲；給…配樂：*Schubert set many poems to music.* 舒伯特為許多詩歌譜了曲。

▸ **OF SUN/MOON** 太陽；月亮 **16** 🔑 [I] to go down below the HORIZON 落（下）：*We sat and watched the sun setting.* 我們坐着看太陽漸漸落下去。⊃ see also SUNSET *n.* (1) **OPP rise**

IDM Idioms containing **set** are at the entries for the nouns and adjectives in the idioms, for example **set the pace** is at **pace** *n.* 含 set 的習語，都可在該等習語中的名詞及形容詞相關詞條找到，如 set the pace 在詞條 pace 的名詞部份。

PHR V **ˈset about sb** (*BrE, old-fashioned, informal*) to attack sb 攻擊；抨擊 **ˈset about sth | ˌset about ˈdoing sth** [no passive] to start doing sth 開始做；着手做：*She set about the business of cleaning the house.* 她動手打掃起房子來。◇ *We need to set about finding a solution.* 我們得着手尋找一個解決辦法。

set sb aˈgainst sb to make sb oppose a friend, relative, etc. 使某人反對（朋友、親人等）：*She accused her husband of setting the children against her.* 她指責丈夫唆使孩子們跟她作對。 **set sth (off) against sth** **1** to judge sth by comparing good or positive qualities with bad or negative ones 權衡利弊（或優缺點）：*Set against the benefits of the new technology, there is also a strong possibility that jobs will be lost.* 權衡利弊，新技術的確有種種好處，但也很可能使一些人失去工作。**2** (*finance* 財) to record sth as a business cost as a way of reducing the amount of tax you must pay 把…按營業成本記賬以降低（稅額）：*to set capital costs off against tax* 把資金成本按營業成本記賬以減稅

ˌset sb/sth aˈpart (from sb/sth) to make sb/sth different from or better than others 使與眾不同；使突出；使優於…：*Her elegant style sets her apart from other journalists.* 她的高雅風格使她與其他記者截然不同。 **ˌset sth↔aˈpart (for sth)** [usually passive] to keep sth for a special use or purpose 留出，撥出（專用）：*Two rooms were set apart for use as libraries.* 留出兩個房間作為圖書室。

ˌset sth↔aˈside **1** to move sth to one side until you need it 把…放到一旁（或擱到一邊）**2** to save or keep money or time for a particular purpose 省出，留出（錢或時間）：*She tries to set aside some money every month.* 她每個月都盡量存點錢。**3** to not consider sth, because other things are more important 暫時不考慮（或放一放）**SYN disregard**：*Let's set aside my personal feelings for now.* 目前咱們就不要顧及我的個人感情了。**4** (*law* 律) to state that a decision made by a court is not legally valid 撤銷，駁回（法院的判決）；宣佈無效：*The verdict was set aside by the Appeal Court.* 上訴法庭駁回了那個裁決。

ˌset sth/sb↔ˈback to delay the progress of sth/sb by a particular time 使推遲；耽誤；使延誤：*The bad weather set back the building programme by several weeks.* 天氣惡劣，建築計劃延誤了幾個星期。⊃ related noun SETBACK **ˌset sb ˈback sth** [no passive] (*informal*) to cost sb a particular amount of money 使花費；使破費：*The repairs could set you back over £200.* 這次修理大概得花你 200 多英鎊。 **ˌset sth ˈback (from sth)** [usually passive] to place sth, especially a building, at a distance from sth 使（建築物等）與…拉開距離：*The house is set well back from the road.* 這座房子離公路挺遠。

ˌset sb↔ˈdown (*BrE*) (of a bus or train, or its driver 公共汽車、火車或司機) to stop and allow sb to get off 讓某人下車：*Passengers may be set down and picked up only at the official stops.* 乘客只有在正式車站方可上下車。 **ˌset sth↔ˈdown** **1** to write sth down on paper in order to record it 寫下；記下；登記 **2** to give sth as a rule, principle, etc. 制訂，規定（規則、原則等）：*The standards were set down by the governing body.* 這些標準是由管理機構制訂的。

ˌset ˈforth (*literary*) to start a journey 出發；動身；啟程 **ˌset sth↔ˈforth** (*formal*) to present sth or make it known 陳述；闡明 **SYN expound**：*The President set forth his views in a television broadcast.* 總統在電視講話中闡述了自己的觀點。

ˌset ˈin (of rain, bad weather, infection, etc. 雨、惡劣天氣、感染等) to begin and seem likely to continue 到來；開始：*The rain seemed to have set in for the day.* 這雨好像要下一天了。 **ˌset sth ˈin/ˈinto sth** [usually passive] to fasten sth into a flat surface so that it does not stick out from it 把…裝進…（或鑲入…中）：*a plaque set into the wall* 裝在牆上的飾板

ˌset ˈoff 🔑 to begin a journey 出發；動身；啟程：*We set off for London just after ten.* 剛過十點，我們就動身上倫敦去了。 **ˌset sth↔ˈoff** **1** 🔑 to make a bomb, etc. explode 使（炸彈等）爆炸：*A gang of boys were setting off fireworks in the street.* 一幫男孩子正在街上放煙火。**2** 🔑 to make an alarm start ringing 使（警報）響起；拉響（警報）：*Opening this door will set off the alarm.* 一開這道門，警鈴就會響。**3** to start a process or series of events 引發；激起：*Panic on the stock market set off a wave of selling.* 股市恐慌引發了一輪拋售潮。**4** to make sth more noticeable or attractive by being placed near it 襯托；使顯得更突出（或更漂亮）：*That blouse sets off the blue of her eyes.* 那件上衣襯托出了她的藍眼睛。 **ˌset sb ˈoff (doing sth)** to make sb start doing sth such as laughing, crying or talking 使某人笑（或哭、說等）起來

ˈset on/upon sb [usually passive] to attack sb suddenly 突然攻擊；襲擊：*I opened the gate, and was immediately set on by a large dog.* 我一開門，一條大狗就迎面撲來。

ˈset sb/sth on sb to make a person or an animal attack sb suddenly 使突然攻擊；使襲擊：*The farmer threatened to set his dogs on us.* 農場主威脅要放出狗來咬我們。

ˌset ˈout **1** 🔑 to leave a place and begin a journey 出發；動身；啟程：*They set out on the last stage of their journey.* 他們動身踏上最後一段行程。**2** to begin a job, task, etc. with a particular aim or goal（懷着目標）開始工作，展開任務：*She set out to break the world record.* 她一心努力要打破世界紀錄。◇ *They succeeded in what they set out to do.* 他們實現了既定的目標。 **ˌset sth↔**

'out **1** to arrange or display things 安排；擺放；陳列：*Her work is always very well set out.* 她總是把工作安排得很有條理。 **2** to present ideas, facts, etc. in an organized way, in speech or writing （有條理地）陳述，闡明：*He set out his objections to the plan.* 他陳述了他對這個計劃的反對意見。◇ *She set out the reasons for her resignation in a long letter.* 她寫了一封長信說明自己辭職的原因。

,set 'to (*old-fashioned, informal*) to begin doing sth in a busy or determined way 起勁地幹起來；毅然開始做

,set sb↔'up **1** to provide sb with the money that they need in order to do sth 資助，經濟上扶植（某人）：*A bank loan helped to set him up in business.* 他靠一筆銀行貸款做起了生意。 **2** (*informal*) to make sb healthier, stronger, more lively, etc. 使更健康（或強壯、活潑等）：*The break from work really set me up for the new year.* 放下工作稍事休息，的確使我更有精力在新的一年大幹一場了。 **3** (*informal*) to trick sb, especially by making them appear guilty of sth 誣陷，冤枉（某人）；栽贓：*He denied the charges, saying the police had set him up.* 他否認那些指控，說警察冤枉他了。➲ related noun SET-UP **,set sth↔'up** **1** 🔑 to build sth or put sth somewhere 建起；設立；設置：*The police set up roadblocks on routes out of the city.* 警察在城外的路上設置了路障。 **2** 🔑 to make a piece of equipment or a machine ready for use 安裝好，裝配好，調試好（設備或機器）：*She set up her stereo in her bedroom.* 她把立體聲音響裝了在卧室裏。 **3** 🔑 to arrange for sth to happen 安排；策劃：*I've set up a meeting for Friday.* 我已安排好在星期五開會。 **4** 🔑 to create sth or start it 創建；建立；開辦：*to set up a business* 開辦公司◇ *A fund will be set up for the dead men's families.* 將為死者家屬設立一項基金。 **5** to start a process or a series of events 引發；產生：*The slump on Wall Street set up a chain reaction in stock markets around the world.* 華爾街股價暴跌在全球股票市場上引起了連鎖反應。➲ related noun SET-UP

,set (yourself) 'up (as sb) to start running a business 立業；開始從事：*She took out a bank loan and set up on her own.* 她從銀行貸了一筆款，自己幹起來了。◇ *After leaving college, he set himself up as a freelance photographer.* 大學畢業後，他幹起了特約攝影師。

■ ***noun***

▸ **GROUP** 一組 **1** 🔑 [C] **~ (of sth)** a group of similar things that belong together in some way 一套，一副，一組（類似的東西）：*a set of six chairs* 六把成套的椅子◇ *a complete set of her novels* 一整套她的小說◇ *a set of false teeth* 一副假牙◇ *a new set of rules to learn* 要學的一套新規則◇ *You can borrow my keys—I have a spare set.* 你可以借用我的鑰匙，我還有一套。➲ see also TEA SET **2** 🔑 [C] a group of objects used together, for example for playing a game 一套，一副，一組（配套使用的東西）：*a chess set* 一副國際象棋 **3** [C+sing./pl. v.] (sometimes *disapproving*) a group of people who have similar interests and spend a lot of time together socially 一夥（或一幫、一群）人；階層；團夥：*the smart set* (= rich, fashionable people) 富裕時尚一族◇ *Dublin's literary set* 都柏林的文學圈子 ➲ see also JET SET

▸ **TV/RADIO** 電視機；收音機 **4** [C] a piece of equipment for receiving television or radio signals 電視機；收音機

▸ **FOR PLAY/MOVIE** 戲劇；電影 **5** [C] the SCENERY used for a play, film/movie, etc. 佈景：*We need volunteers to help build and paint the set.* 我們需要一些自願幫忙建造和粉刷佈景的人。 **6** [C, U] a place where a play is performed or part of a film/movie is filmed 舞台；攝影場：*The cast must all be on (the) set by 7 in the morning.* 全體演員必須在早上 7 點鐘到場。

▸ **IN SPORT** 體育運動 **7** [C] one section of a match in games such as TENNIS or VOLLEYBALL （網球、排球比賽等的）盤，局：*She won **in straight sets*** (= without losing a set). 她一盤未失，連連得勝。

▸ **MATHEMATICS** 數學 **8** [C] a group of things that have a shared quality 集；集合：*set theory* 集論

▸ **POP MUSIC** 流行音樂 **9** [C] a series of songs or pieces of music that a musician or group performs at a concert 一組歌曲（或樂曲）

▸ **CLASS** 班 **10** [C] (*BrE*) a group of school students with a similar ability in a particular subject （在某學科上能力相當的）一批學生：*She's in the top set for French.* 她的法語成績名列前茅。

▸ **OF FACE/BODY** 臉；身體 **11** [sing.] **~ of sth** the way in which sb's face or body is fixed in a particular expression, especially one showing determination （尤指堅定的）姿勢，姿態，神情：*She admired the firm set of his jaw.* 她喜歡他那副緊繃着下巴的剛毅神態。

▸ **HAIR** 頭髮 **12** [sing.] an act of arranging hair in a particular style while it is wet 頭髮的定型；做頭髮：*A **shampoo and set** costs £15.* 洗頭並做髮型共 15 英鎊。

▸ **BECOMING FIRM** 凝固 **13** [sing.] the state of becoming firm or solid 凝固；凝結

▸ **ANIMAL'S HOME** 獸穴 **14** [C] = SETT

▸ **PLANT** 植物 **15** [C] a young plant, SHOOT etc. for planting （供移植的）秧苗，插枝，球莖：*onion sets* 洋蔥苗

■ ***adj.***

▸ **IN POSITION** 處於某位置 **1** in a particular position 位於（或處於）…的：*a house set in 40 acres of parkland* 一所坐落在一片 40 英畝草地上的房子◇ *He had close-set eyes.* 他的兩眼靠得很近。

▸ **PLANNED** 安排好 **2** [usually before noun] planned or fixed 安排好的；確定的；固定的：*Each person was given set jobs to do.* 分配給每個人的工作都是預先確定好的。◇ *The school funds a set number of free places.* 學校資助固定數目的免費生。◇ *Mornings in our house always follow a set pattern.* 在我們家，每天早上的生活總是遵循一種固定的模式。➲ see also SET BOOK

▸ **OPINIONS/IDEAS** 意見；觀念 **3** not likely to change 固定的；頑固的；固執的：***set ideas/opinions/views** on how to teach* 不變的教學思想／主張／觀點◇ *As people get older, they get **set in their ways**.* 隨着年齡的增長，人就積習成性。

▸ **MEAL** 飯菜 **4** [only before noun] (of a meal in a restaurant 餐館的飯菜) having a fixed price and a limited choice of dishes 套餐的：*a **set dinner/lunch/meal*** 一份晚餐／午餐套餐；一份套餐◇ *Shall we have the **set menu**?* 我們吃套餐好嗎？

▸ **LIKELY/READY** 大概會；準備好 **5** likely to do sth; ready for sth or to do sth 有可能的；做好準備的：**~ for sth** *The team looks set for victory.* 看來這個隊能贏。◇ **~ to do sth** *Interest rates look set to rise again.* 看樣子利率又要提高了。◇ *Be set to leave by 10 o'clock.* 做好準備，最晚 10 點鐘走。➲ **LANGUAGE BANK** at EXPECT

▸ **FACE** 臉色 **6** [usually before noun] (of a person's expression 神情) fixed; not natural 呆板的；不自然的：*a set smile* 僵硬的笑容◇ *His face took on a set expression.* 他臉上現出凝滯的神態。

IDM **be (dead) set against sth/against doing sth** to be strongly opposed to sth 強烈反對（做）某事：*Why are you so dead set against the idea?* 你為什麼那樣死命地反對這個主意呢？ **be 'set on sth/on doing sth** to want to do or have sth very much; to be determined to do sth 一心想做；決心做；十分想得到 ➲ more at MARK *n.*

'set-aside *noun* [U] a system in which the government pays farmers not to use some of their land for growing crops; the land that the farmers are paid not to use 退耕補貼制度，退耕地（由政府補貼，鼓勵農民退耕部份耕地）

set·back /'setbæk/ *noun* a difficulty or problem that delays or prevents sth, or makes a situation worse 挫折；阻礙：*The team **suffered a** major **setback** when their best player was injured.* 最優秀的隊員受了傷，使得這支隊伍的實力大打折扣。◇ *The breakdown in talks represents a temporary setback in the peace process.* 談判破裂意味着和平進程暫時受阻。

,set 'book (also **,set 'text**) *noun* (both *BrE*) a book that students must study for a particular exam （考試）指定課本，指定用書

seth /seɪt/ *noun* (*IndE*) **1** a MERCHANT (= a person who sells goods in large quantities) or BANKER (= a person with an important job in a bank) 商人；銀行家 **2** a rich man 富人；有錢人 **3** a title added to a name to indicate high social status 塞斯（表示社會地位高的頭銜）

,set 'phrase *noun* a phrase that is always used in the same form 固定詞組；成語：*Don't worry about the grammar, just learn this as a set phrase.* 別管語法，只要把這個作為固定詞組來學習即可。

S

ˌset ˈpiece *noun* **1** a part of a play, film/movie, piece of music, etc. that has a well-known pattern or style, and is used to create a particular effect（戲劇、電影、音樂等中的）固定套路 **2** a move in a sports game that is well planned and practised（體育比賽的）攻防套路

ˌset ˈpoint *noun* (especially in TENNIS 尤指網球) a point that, if won by a player, will win them the SET *n.* (7) 盤點，盤末點（贏得整盤比賽的一分）

ˈset square (*BrE*) (*NAmE* **tri·angle**) *noun* an instrument for drawing straight lines and angles, made from a flat piece of plastic or metal in the shape of a triangle with one angle of 90° 三角板；三角尺 ➲ VISUAL VOCAB page V70

sett (also **set**) /set/ *noun* a hole in the ground where a BADGER lives 貛穴

set·tee /seˈtiː/ *noun* (*BrE*) a long comfortable seat with a back and arms, for two or more people to sit on 長沙發 **SYN** **sofa, couch**

set·ter /ˈsetə(r)/ *noun* **1** a large dog with long hair, sometimes used in hunting. There are several types of setter. 蹲伏獵狗，塞特種獵犬（體大毛長，有幾個品種） **2** (often in compounds 常構成複合詞) a person who sets sth 制訂者；規定者；安排者：*a quiz setter* 命題人 ➲ see also JET-SETTER, PACESETTER, TRENDSETTER

set·ting /ˈsetɪŋ/ *noun* **1** a set of surroundings; the place at which sth happens 環境；背景：***a rural/an ideal/a beautiful/an idyllic, etc. setting*** 鄉村、理想、優美、田園等的環境 ◊ *It was* ***the perfect setting*** *for a wonderful Christmas.* 環境氣氛無可挑剔，正是一個美好的聖誕節所需要的。➲ SYNONYMS at ENVIRONMENT **2** the place and time at which the action of a play, novel, etc. takes place（戲劇、小說等的）情節背景：*short stories with a contemporary setting* 以當代生活為背景的短篇小說 **3** a position at which the controls on a machine can be set, to set the speed, height, temperature, etc.（機器上調節速度、高度、溫度等的）擋，級，點：*The performance of the engine was tested at different settings.* 對引擎的性能在不同的擋上做了試驗。 **4** (*music* 音) music written to go with a poem, etc.（為詩等譜的）曲：*Schubert's setting of a poem by Goethe* 舒伯特為歌德的一首詩譜的曲 **5** a piece of metal in which a PRECIOUS STONE is fixed to form a piece of jewellery（鑲嵌寶石的）底座，底板，托板 **6** a complete set of equipment for eating with (knife, fork, spoon, glass, etc.) for one person, arranged on a table（擺在桌上供一人用的）一套餐具：*a place setting* 一個座位的整套餐具

S

set·tle 0**⊷** /ˈsetl/ *verb, noun*

■ *verb*

▸ **END ARGUMENT** 結束紛爭 **1** 0**⊷** [T, I] **~ (sth)** to put an end to an argument or a disagreement 結束（爭論、爭端等）；解決（分歧、糾紛等）：*to* ***settle a dispute/an argument/a matter*** 解決爭端 / 爭論 / 事情 ◊ *It's time you* ***settled your differences*** *with your father.* 現在你該解決同你父親之間的分歧了。◊ *There is pressure on the unions to settle.* 工會組織面臨消除紛爭的壓力。◊ *The company has agreed to* ***settle out of court*** (= come to an agreement without going to court). 那家公司同意庭外和解。

▸ **DECIDE/ARRANGE** 決定；安排 **2** 0**⊷** [T, often passive] to decide or arrange sth finally（最終）決定，確定，安排好：**~ sth** ***It's all settled****—we're leaving on the nine o'clock plane.* 一切都定下來了，我們乘九點的航班走。◊ *Bob will be there?* ***That settles it.*** *I'm not coming.* 鮑勃會去嗎？那好，我就不去了。◊ *He had to* ***settle his affairs*** *in Paris before he could return home.* 他得把他在巴黎的事情處理好才能回家。◊ **it is settled that …** *It's been settled that we leave on the nine o'clock plane.* 已經定好我們乘坐九點的航班離開。

▸ **CHOOSE PERMANENT HOME** 選擇永久住地 **3** 0**⊷** [I] **+ adv./prep.** to make a place your permanent home 定居：*She settled in Vienna after her father's death.* 父親死後，她就在維也納定居了。 **4** 0**⊷** [T, usually passive, I] **~ sth** | **+ adv./prep.** (of a group of people 一批人) to make your permanent home in a country or an area as COLONISTS 殖民；作為移民在殖民地定居：*This region was settled by the Dutch in the nineteenth century.* 荷蘭人於 19 世紀來到這一地區定居。

▸ **INTO COMFORTABLE POSITION/STATE** 進入舒適的位置 / 狀態 **5** [I, T] to make yourself or sb else comfortable in a new position 使處於舒適的位置：**~ (back) (+ adv./prep.)** *Ellie settled back in her seat.* 埃利舒適地靠着椅背坐下。◊ **~ sb/yourself (+ adv./prep.)** *He settled himself comfortably in his usual chair.* 他在自己慣常坐的椅子上舒舒服服地坐下來。◊ *I settled her on the sofa and put a blanket over her.* 我把她放在沙發上安頓好，給她蓋了一條毯子。 **6** [T] **~ sth + adv./prep.** to put sth carefully in a position so that it does not move 把…放好；安放：*She settled the blanket around her knees.* 她用毯子裹住膝蓋。 **7** [I, T] to become or make sb/sth become calm or relaxed（使）平靜下來，安靜下來，定下心來：*The baby wouldn't settle.* 嬰兒安靜不下來。◊ **~ sb/sth** *I took a pill to help settle my nerves.* 我吃了一片藥，好鎮定一下神經。◊ *This should settle your stomach.* 這樣你的胃應該就不難受了。

▸ **COME TO REST** 停留 **8** [I] **~ (on/over sth)** to fall from above and come to rest on sth; to stay for some time on sth 降落；停留：*Dust had settled on everything.* 到處落滿灰塵。◊ *Two birds settled on the fence.* 兩隻鳥落在籬笆上。◊ *I don't think the snow will settle* (= remain on the ground without melting). 我看這雪積不住。◊ *His gaze settled on her face.* 他的目光落在她臉上。

▸ **SINK DOWN** 沉降 **9** [I, T] **~ (sth)** to sink slowly down; to make sth do this（使）沉降，下陷，變得密實：*The contents of the package may have settled in transit.* 包裹裏的東西可能在運輸途中搖密實了。

▸ **PAY MONEY** 付錢 **10** [T, I] to pay the money that you owe 付清（欠款）；結算；結賬：**~ sth** *Please settle your bill before leaving the hotel.* 請您先結賬再離開旅館。◊ *The insurance company is refusing to settle her claim.* 保險公司拒付她提出的索賠款項。◊ **~ (up) (with sb)** *Let me settle with you for the meal.* 我來把飯費付給你。◊ *I'll pay now—we can settle up later.* 現在我來付賬，咱們以後再算。

IDM **settle a ˈscore/an acˈcount (with sb)** | **settle an old ˈscore** to hurt or punish sb who has harmed or cheated you in the past（和某人）算賬，清算舊賬；報復（某人）：*'Who would do such a thing?' 'Maybe someone with an old score to settle.'* "誰做得出這樣的事呢？""也許是結有宿怨的人吧。" ➲ more at DUST *n.*

PHR V **ˌsettle ˈdown** **1** 0**⊷** to get into a comfortable position, either sitting or lying 舒適地坐下（或躺下）：*I settled down with a book.* 我舒舒服服地坐下看書。 **2** 0**⊷** to start to have a quieter way of life, living in one place（在某地）定居下來，過安定的生活：*When are you going to get married and settle down?* 你打算什麼時候成家，安定下來？ ➲ COLLOCATIONS at AGE **ˌsettle ˈdown** | **ˌsettle sb↔ˈdown** 0**⊷** to become or make sb become calm, less excited, etc.（使某人）安靜下來，平靜下來：*It always takes the class a while to settle down at the start of the lesson.* 那個班一上課總得過一會兒才能安靜下來。 **settle (down) to sth** to begin to give your attention to sth 開始認真對待；定下心來做：*They finally settled down to a discussion of the main issues.* 他們終於開始討論一些主要問題了。◊ *He found it hard to settle to his work.* 他覺得定不下心來工作。 **ˈsettle for sth** to accept sth that is not exactly what you want but is the best that is available 勉強接受；將就：*In the end they had to settle for a draw.* 最後，他們只好接受平局的結果。◊ *I couldn't afford the house I really wanted, so I had to* ***settle for second best.*** 我真心想要的房子我買不起，所以只得退而求其次了。 **ˌsettle ˈin** | **ˌsettle ˈinto sth** to move into a new home, job, etc. and start to feel comfortable there 安頓下來；習慣於（新居）；適應（新工作）：*How are the kids settling into their new school?* 孩子們在新學校習慣了嗎？ **ˈsettle on sth** to choose or make a decision about sth after thinking about it 選定；決定：*Have you settled on a name for the baby yet?* 你給孩子起好名字沒有？ **ˈsettle sth on sb** (*law* 律) to formally arrange to give money or property to sb, especially in a WILL 轉讓（錢財）；（尤指在遺囑中）贈與

■ *noun* an old-fashioned piece of furniture with a long wooden seat and a high back and arms, often also with a box for storing things under the seat 高背長椅（老式木傢具，有扶手，座下多帶櫃）

set·tled /'setld/ *adj.* **1** not likely to change or move 不大可能變動的；穩定的：*settled weather* 持續不變的天氣 ◇ *a settled way of life* 安定的生活方式 **2** comfortable and happy with your home, job, way of life, etc. 舒適自在的；（對住所、工作、生活方式等）習慣的 OPP **unsettled**

settle·ment /'setlmənt/ *noun* **1** [C] an official agreement that ends an argument between two people or groups （解決紛爭的）協議：*to* ***negotiate a*** *peace* ***settlement*** 就和平協議進行談判 ◇ *The management and unions have* ***reached a settlement*** *over new working conditions.* 資方和工會已就新的工作條件達成協議。◇ *an* ***out-of-court settlement*** (= money that is paid to sb or an agreement that is made to stop sb going to court) 庭外和解 **2** [U] the action of reaching an agreement 解決；處理：*the settlement of a dispute* 爭端的解決 **3** [C] (*law* 律) the conditions, or a document stating the conditions, on which money or property is given to sb （關於錢財轉讓的）協議（書）：*a* ***divorce/marriage/property, etc. settlement*** 離婚、結婚、財產等協議 **4** [U] the action of paying back money that you owe （欠款的）支付，償付，結算：*the settlement of a debt* 債務的償還 ◇ *a cheque* ***in settlement*** *of a bill* 用於結賬的支票 **5** [C] a place where people have come to live and make their homes, especially where few or no people lived before （尤指拓荒安家的）定居點：*signs of an Iron Age settlement* 鐵器時代村落遺址 **6** [U] the process of people making their homes in a place 移民；殖民；開拓：*the settlement of the American West* 美國西部的開拓過程

'settlement house *noun* (*especially NAmE*) a public building in an area of a large city that has social problems, that provides social services such as advice and training to the people who live there 社區福利服務之家（為鄰里提供多方面服務）

set·tler /'setlə(r)/ *noun* a person who goes to live in a new country or region 移民；殖民者：*white settlers in Africa* 非洲的白人移民

ˌset-'to *noun* [sing.] (*informal, especially BrE*) a small fight or an argument 打架；爭吵

ˌset-ˌtop 'box *noun* a device that changes a DIGITAL television signal into a form which can be seen on an ordinary television 機頂盒（數字電視轉接裝置，把數字電視信號轉換成普通電視信號）

'set-up *noun* [usually sing.] (*informal*) **1** a way of organizing sth; a system 組織；機構；建制；體制：*I've only been here a couple of weeks and I don't really know the set-up.* 我剛來幾個星期，對這裏的組織情況不大瞭解。 **2** a situation in which sb tricks you or makes it seem as if you have done sth wrong 陷害；栽贓：*He didn't steal the goods. It was a set-up.* 那些商品不是他偷的，這是栽贓。

sevak /'seɪvæk/ *noun* (*IndE*) **1** a male servant 男僕；男傭 **2** a male SOCIAL WORKER 男社會福利工作者；男社工

seven 0-w /'sevn/ *number*
7 七 HELP There are examples of how to use numbers at the entry for **five**. 數詞用法示例見 five 條。

IDM **the seven-year 'itch** (*informal, humorous*) the desire for new sexual experience that is thought to be felt after seven years of marriage 七年之癢（婚後七年另覓新歡的慾望） ➲ more at SIX

the ˌseven 'seas *noun* [pl.] all of the earth's oceans 世界所有海洋

the ˌSeven 'Sisters *noun* [pl.] **1** the Pleiades, a group of seven stars 昴星團（的七顆亮星）；七姊妹星團 **2** a group of seven traditional women's (or formerly women's) universities in the eastern US with high academic standards and a high social status 七姐妹學院（美國東部學業標準高、有聲望的七所傳統女子學院）

seven·teen 0-w /ˌsevn'tiːn/ *number*
17 十七 ▸ **seven·teenth** /ˌsevn'tiːnθ/ *ordinal number, noun* HELP There are examples of how to use ordinal numbers at the entry for **fifth**. 序數詞用法示例見 fifth 條。

sev·enth 0-w /'sevnθ/ *ordinal number, noun*
■ ***ordinal number*** 7th 第七 HELP There are examples of how to use ordinal numbers at the entry for **fifth**. 序數詞用法示例見 fifth 條。

IDM **in seventh 'heaven** extremely happy 身處七重天；極樂；極為幸福：*Now that he's been promoted he's in seventh heaven.* 他得到擢升，簡直樂上天了。

■ ***noun*** each of seven equal parts of sth 七分之一

Seventh-Day Adventist /ˌsevnθ deɪ 'ædvəntɪst/ *noun* a member of a Christian religious group that believes that Christ will soon return to Earth 基督復臨安息日會信徒

sev·enty 0-w /'sevnti/
1 *number* 70 七十 **2** *noun* **the seventies** [pl.] numbers, years or temperatures from 70 to 79 七十幾；七十年代 ▸ **seven·ti·eth** /'sevntiəθ/ *ordinal number, noun* HELP There are examples of how to use ordinal numbers at the entry for **fifth**. 序數詞用法示例見 fifth 條。

IDM **in your 'seventies** between the ages of 70 and 79 * 70 多歲

sever /'sevə(r)/ *verb* (*formal*) **1** to cut sth into two pieces; to cut sth off sth 切開；割斷；切下；割下：**~ sth** *to sever a rope* 割斷繩子 ◇ *a severed artery* 切斷的動脈 ◇ **~ sth from sth** *His hand was severed from his arm.* 他的手從胳膊上截斷了。 **2 ~ sth** to completely end a relationship or all communication with sb 斷絕；中斷 SYN **break off**：*The two countries have* ***severed*** *all diplomatic* ***links***. 兩國斷絕了一切外交關係。

sev·eral 0-w /'sevrəl/ *det., pron., adj.*
■ ***det., pron.*** 0-w more than two but not very many 幾個；數個；一些：*Several letters arrived this morning.* 今天上午來了幾封信。◇ *He's written several books about India.* 他寫過幾本關於印度的書。◇ *Several more people than usual came to the meeting.* 到會的人比平時多了幾個。◇ *If you're looking for a photo of Alice you'll find several in here.* 你要是想找艾麗斯的照片的話，這兒有幾張。◇ *Several of the paintings were destroyed in the fire.* 那些畫有好幾幅被大火燒毀了。

■ ***adj.*** (*formal*) separate 各自的；分別的：*They said goodbye and went their* ***several ways***. 他們道別後，便各自走了。

sev·er·al·ly /'sevrəli/ *adv.* (*formal* or *law* 律) separately 各自；分別：*Tenants are* ***jointly and severally*** *liable for payment of the rent.* 租金由承租人共同且分別承擔。

sev·er·ance /'sevərəns/ *noun* [sing., U] (*formal*) **1** the act of ending a connection or relationship 斷絕；中斷：*the severance of diplomatic relations* 外交關係的斷絕 **2** the act of ending sb's work contract 解雇；辭退：*employees given notice of severance* 接到解聘通知的雇員 ◇ ***severance pay/terms*** 解雇金 / 條件

se·vere 0-w /sɪ'vɪə(r); *NAmE* -'vɪr/ *adj.* (**se·verer**, **se·ver·est**)
▸ VERY BAD 非常不好 **1** 0-w extremely bad or serious 極為惡劣的；十分嚴重的：*a severe handicap* 嚴重殘疾 ◇ *His injuries are severe.* 他的傷很重。◇ *severe weather conditions* 惡劣的天氣情況 ◇ *a severe winter* (= one during which the weather conditions are extremely bad) 嚴冬 ◇ *The party suffered severe losses during the last election.* 該黨在上次選舉中遭到慘敗。◇ *a severe shortage of qualified staff* 合格員工的嚴重短缺
▸ PUNISHMENT 懲罰 **2** 0-w **~ (on/with sb)** punishing sb in an extreme way when they break a particular set of rules 嚴厲的；重的 SYN **harsh**：*The courts are becoming more severe on young offenders.* 法庭對青少年犯罪者的處罰趨於嚴厲。◇ *a* ***severe punishment/sentence*** 重罰；重判
▸ NOT KIND 不和善 **3** 0-w not kind or sympathetic and showing disapproval of sb/sth 嚴厲的；苛刻的 SYN **stern**：*a severe expression* 冷厲的表情 ◇ *She was a severe woman who seldom smiled.* 她是個嚴肅的女人，臉上很少出現笑容。
▸ VERY DIFFICULT 非常困難 **4** extremely difficult and requiring a lot of skill or ability 艱難的；艱巨的；難度很大的 SYN **stiff**：*The marathon is a severe test of stamina.* 馬拉松賽跑是對耐力的嚴峻考驗。

S

▸ STYLE/APPEARANCE/CLOTHING 風格；外貌；衣着 **5** (*disapproving*) extremely plain and lacking any decoration 過於簡樸的： *Modern furniture is a little too severe for my taste.* 現代傢具有點過於簡樸，我不大喜歡。◇ *Her hair was short and severe.* 她的頭髮不長，也沒有花樣。 ▸ **se·vere·ly** 🗝 *adv.*： *severely disabled* 嚴重殘疾的 ◇ *areas severely affected by unemployment* 深受失業影響的地區 ◇ *Anyone breaking the law will be severely punished.* 違法者將受到嚴懲。◇ *a severely critical report* 一篇措辭嚴厲的批評報道 ◇ *Her hair was tied severely in a bun.* 她的頭髮簡單地盤成了一個髮髻。 **se·ver·ity** /sɪ'verəti/ *noun* [U]： *A prison sentence should match the severity of the crime.* 刑期長短要和罪行輕重一致。◇ *The chances of a full recovery will depend on the severity of her injuries.* 能否徹底康復取決於她受傷的嚴重程度。◇ *the severity of the problem* 問題的嚴重性 ◇ *He frowned with mock severity.* 他沉下臉來，裝出一副嚴厲的樣子。◇ *The elaborate facade contrasts strongly with the severity of the interior.* 精緻的門面同室內的簡樸形成強烈反差。

sev·ika /'seɪvɪkə/ *noun* (*IndE*) **1** a female servant 女僕；女傭 **2** a female SOCIAL WORKER 女社會福利工作者；女社工

Sev·ille orange /ˌsevɪl 'ɒrɪndʒ; *NAmE* 'ɔːr-; 'ɑːr-/ *noun* a type of bitter orange, used in making MARMALADE 酸橙（用於製酸果醬）

sew 🗝 /səʊ; *NAmE* soʊ/ *verb* (**sewed**, **sewn** /səʊn; *NAmE* soʊn/ or **sewed**)
1 🗝 [I, T] to use a needle and thread to make STITCHES in cloth 縫；做針線活： *My mother taught me how to sew.* 我母親教我做針線。◇ *to sew by hand/machine* 手工 / 機器縫製 ◇ **~ sth** *to sew a seam* 縫接縫 **2** 🗝 [T] to make, repair or attach sth using a needle and thread 縫製；縫補；縫上： **~ sth** *She sews all her own clothes.* 她所有的衣服都是自己縫的。◇ **~ sth on** *Can you sew a button on for me?* 你能給我釘個扣子嗎？◇ *Surgeons were able to sew the finger back on.* 外科醫生把斷指接上了。
PHR V **ˌsew sth↔'up** **1** to join or repair sth by sewing 縫合；縫補： *to sew up a seam* 縫上接縫 **2** [often passive] (*informal*) to arrange sth in an acceptable way 安排妥貼；辦好；使萬無一失： *It didn't take me long to sew up the deal.* 我沒費多大工夫就把那樁生意做成了。◇ *They think they* **have** *the election* **sewn up** (= they think they are definitely going to win). 他們認為這次選舉他們已萬無一失。

sew·age /'suːɪdʒ; *BrE* also 'sjuː-/ *noun* [U] used water and waste substances that are produced by human bodies, that are carried away from houses and factories through special pipes (= SEWERS)（下水道的）污水，污物： *a ban on the dumping of raw sewage* (= that has not been treated with chemicals) *at sea* 禁止把未經處理的污水排入海中 ◇ *sewage disposal* 污水處理 ➲ compare WASTEWATER

'sewage farm *noun* (*BrE*) = SEWAGE WORKS

'sewage plant (also **sewage 'treatment plant**) *noun* (*especially NAmE*) = SEWAGE WORKS

'sewage works (also **sewage 'treatment works**, **sewage dis'posal works**) *noun* [C+sing./pl. v.] (*BrE*) a place where chemicals are used to clean sewage so that it can then be allowed to go into rivers, etc. or used to make MANURE 污水處理廠

sewer /'suːə(r); *BrE* also 'sjuː-/ *noun* an underground pipe that is used to carry sewage away from houses, factories, etc. 污水管；下水道；陰溝

sew·er·age /'suːərɪdʒ; *BrE* also 'sjuː-/ *noun* [U] the system by which sewage is carried away from houses, factories, etc. and is cleaned and made safe by adding chemicals to it 排水系統；污水處理

'sewer grate *noun* (*US*) = GRATE (2)

sew·ing 🗝 /'səʊɪŋ; *NAmE* 'soʊ-/ *noun* [U]
1 🗝 the activity of making, repairing or decorating things made of cloth using a needle and thread 縫紉： *knitting and sewing* 編織和縫紉 ➲ VISUAL VOCAB page V41 **2** 🗝 something that is being sewn 縫製中的衣物： *a pile of sewing* 一堆針線活兒

'sewing machine *noun* a machine that is used for sewing things that are made of cloth 縫紉機 ➲ VISUAL VOCAB page V41

sewn *past part.* of SEW

sex 🗝 AW /seks/ *noun, verb*
■ *noun* **1** 🗝 [U, C] the state of being male or female 性別；性 SYN **gender**： *How can you tell what sex a fish is?* 你怎樣辨別一條魚的雌雄？◇ *a process that allows couples to choose the sex of their baby* 使夫婦能選擇嬰兒性別的程序 ◇ *Please indicate your sex and date of birth below.* 請在下面寫明你的性別和出生日期。◇ ***sex discrimination*** (= the act of treating men and women differently in an unfair way) 性別歧視 **2** 🗝 [C] either of the two groups that people, animals and plants are divided into according to their function of producing young 男性；女性；雄性；雌性： *a member of* **the opposite sex** 另一性別的人 ◇ ***single-sex** schools* 單一性別學校 ➲ see also FAIR SEX **3** 🗝 [U] physical activity between two people in which they touch each other's sexual organs, and which may include SEXUAL INTERCOURSE 性行為；性交；性活動： *It is illegal to* **have sex** *with a person under the age of 16.* 和 16 歲以下的未成年人發生性行為是違法的。◇ *gay sex* 同性戀性行為 ◇ *the* **sex act** 性行為 ◇ *a* **sex attack** 性攻擊 ◇ *a* **sex shop** (= one selling magazines, objects, etc. that are connected with sex) 性用品商店 ◇ ***sex education** in schools* 學校裏的性教育 ◇ *These drugs may affect your* **sex drive** (= your interest in sex and the ability to have it). 這些藥物可能影響你的性慾。 ➲ see also SAFE SEX, SEXUAL INTERCOURSE **4 -sexed** (in adjectives 構成形容詞) having the amount of sexual activity or desire mentioned 性行為…的；性慾…的： *a highly-sexed woman* 性慾旺盛的女人
■ *verb* **~ sth** (*technical* 術語) to examine an animal in order to find out whether it is male or female 辨識…的性別
PHR V **ˌsex sb↔'up** (*informal*) to make sb feel sexually excited 引起某人的性慾；勾引；挑逗 **ˌsex sth↔'up** (*informal*) to make sth seem more exciting and interesting 提高某事物的魅力；使更吸引人： *The profession is trying to sex up its image.* 這個行業正在設法使自身形象更加吸引人。

sexa·gen·ar·ian /ˌseksədʒə'neəriən; *NAmE* -'ner-/ *noun* a person between 60 and 69 years old * 60 到 69 歲的人；60 幾歲的人

'sex appeal *noun* [U] the quality of being attractive in a sexual way 性魅力；性感： *He exudes sex appeal.* 他渾身洋溢着性魅力。

'sex change *noun* [usually sing.] a medical operation in which parts of a person's body are changed so that they become like a person of the opposite sex 變性手術

'sex chromosome *noun* (*biology* 生) a CHROMOSOME that decides the sex of an animal or a plant 性染色體 ➲ see also X CHROMOSOME, Y CHROMOSOME

sex·ism AW /'seksɪzəm/ *noun* [U] the unfair treatment of people, especially women, because of their sex; the attitude that causes this（尤指對女性的）性別歧視，性別偏見： *legislation designed to combat sexism in the work place* 旨在抵制工作場所的性別歧視的法規 ◇ *a study of sexism in language* 對語言中存在的性別歧視的研究

sex·ist /'seksɪst/ *noun* (*disapproving*) a person who treats other people, especially women, unfairly because of their sex or who makes offensive remarks about them 性別歧視者 ▸ **sex·ist** *adj.*： *a sexist attitude* 性別歧視的態度 ◇ *sexist language* 有性別歧視的語言

sex·less /'seksləs/ *adj.* **1** that is neither male nor female, or does not seem to be either male or female 無性（別）的： *a sexless figure* 無性別特徵的體形 **2** in which there is no sexual desire or activity 性冷淡的；無性行為的

'sex life *noun* a person's sexual activities 性生活： *ways to improve your sex life* 改善性生活的辦法

'sex maniac *noun* a person who wants to have sex more often than is normal and who thinks about it all the time 性慾狂者

'sex object *noun* a person considered only for their sexual attraction and not for their character or their intelligence 性（交）對象

'sex offender *noun* a person who has been found guilty of illegal sexual acts 性犯罪者

sex·ology /sek'sɒlədʒi; *NAmE* -'sɑːl-/ *noun* [U] the scientific study of human sexual behaviour 性學 ▸ **sex·olo·gist** /-dʒɪst/ *noun*

sex·pot /'sekspɒt; *NAmE* -pɑːt/ *noun* (*informal*) a person who is thought to be sexually attractive 性感的人

'sex symbol *noun* a famous person who is thought by many people to be sexually attractive 性感偶像

sex·tant /'sekstənt/ *noun* an instrument for measuring angles and distances, used to calculate the exact position of a ship or an aircraft 六分儀（用以計算船舶或飛機的準確位置）

sex·tet /seks'tet/ *noun* **1** [C+sing./pl. v.] a group of six musicians or singers who play or sing together 六重奏樂團；六重唱組合 **2** [C] a piece of music for six musicians or singers 六重奏（曲）；六重唱（曲）

sex·ton /'sekstən/ *noun* a person whose job is to take care of a church and its surroundings, ring the church bell, etc.（負責看管教堂及其周邊設施、敲鐘等的）教堂司事

sex·tu·plet /'sekstʊplət; sek'stjuːplət; -'stʌp-/ *noun* one of six children born at the same time to the same mother 六胞胎之一

'sex typing *noun* [U] **1** (*psychology* 心) the process of putting people into categories according to what people consider to be typical of each sex 按性別特徵分類 **2** (*biology* 生) the process of finding out whether a person or other living thing is male or female, especially in difficult cases when special tests are necessary（尤指需要進行特別實驗的）性別分型

sex·ual 🔑 AW /'sekʃuəl/ *adj.*
1 🔑 [usually before noun] connected with the physical activity of sex 性行為的；性的：*sexual behaviour* 性行為 ◇ *They were not having a sexual relationship at the time.* 當時他們之間並沒有性關係。◇ *Her interest in him is purely sexual.* 她對他感興趣純粹是因為性的原因。◇ ***sexual orientation*** (= whether you are HETEROSEXUAL or HOMOSEXUAL) 性愛傾向（指異性戀或同性戀） **2** [only before noun] connected with the process of producing young 生殖的；有性繁殖的：*the **sexual organs*** (= the PENIS, VAGINA, etc.) 生殖器官 ◇ *sexual reproduction* 有性繁殖 **3** [usually before noun] connected with the state of being male or female 性別的；性的：*sexual characteristics* 性別特徵 ▸ **sex·ual·ly** 🔑 AW /'sekʃəli/ *adv.*：*sexually abused children* 受到性虐待的兒童 ◇ *She finds him sexually attractive.* 她覺得他富有性魅力。◇ *sexually explicit* 性方面露骨的 ◇ *Girls become sexually mature earlier than boys.* 女孩比男孩性成熟早。

,sexual 'harassment *noun* [U] comments about sex, physical contact, etc. usually happening at work, that a person finds annoying and offensive 性騷擾

,sexual 'intercourse (also **inter·course**) (also *formal* **co·itus**) *noun* [U] (*formal*) the physical activity of sex, usually describing the act of a man putting his PENIS inside a woman's VAGINA 性交；交媾

sexu·al·ity AW /,sekʃu'æləti/ *noun* [U] the feelings and activities connected with a person's sexual desires 性徵；性感覺；性慾；性行為：***male/female sexuality*** 男性／女性性行為 ◇ *He was confused about his sexuality.* 他對自己的性別感到困惑。

sex·ual·ize (*BrE* also **-ise**) /'sekʃuəlaɪz/ *verb* **~ sb/sth** to make sb/sth seem sexually attractive 使性感 ▸ **sex·ual·iza·tion, -isa·tion** /,sekʃuəlaɪ'zeɪʃn/ *noun* [U]

,sexually trans,mitted di'sease *noun* [C, U] (*abbr.* **STD**) any disease that is spread through sexual intercourse, such as SYPHILIS 性傳播疾病

'sex worker *noun* a polite way of referring to a PROSTITUTE 性工作者（以性行為換取金錢者的委婉說法）

sexy /'seksi/ *adj.* (**sex·ier**, **sexi·est**) **1** (of a person 人) sexually attractive 性感的：*the sexy lead singer* 性感的主唱 ◇ *She looked incredibly sexy in a black evening gown.* 她穿着黑色的晚禮服，顯得性感極了。 **2** sexually exciting 引起性慾的；性感的：*sexy underwear* 性感的內衣 ◇ *a sexy look* 撩人的眼神 **3** (of a person 人) sexually excited 性慾發作的；性興奮的：*The music and wine began to make him feel sexy.* 那音樂和酒逐漸使他性慾萌動。 **4** exciting and interesting 富有魅力的；迷人的；有吸引力的：*a sexy new range of software* 一系列很棒的新軟件 ◇ *Accountancy just isn't sexy.* 會計工作實在乏味。
▸ **sex·ily** *adv.* **sexi·ness** *noun* [U]

SF /,es 'ef/ *abbr.* SCIENCE FICTION 科幻小説（或影片等）

SFX /,es ef 'eks/ *abbr.* SPECIAL EFFECTS

SGML /,es dʒiː em 'el/ *abbr.* (*computing* 計) Standard Generalized Mark-up Language (a system used for marking text on a computer so that the text can be read on a different computer system or displayed in different forms) 標準通用置標語言

Sgt (*especially BrE*) (also **Sgt.** *NAmE, BrE*) *abbr.* SERGEANT 中士；巡佐；警佐：*Sgt Williams* 威廉斯中士

sh (also **shh**) /ʃ/ *exclamation* the way of writing the sound people make when they are telling sb to be quiet（用以讓別人安靜）嘘：*Sh! Keep your voice down!* 嘘！小聲點兒！

shabby /'ʃæbi/ *adj.* (**shab·bier**, **shab·bi·est**) **1** (of buildings, clothes, objects, etc. 建築物、衣服、物品等) in poor condition because they have been used a lot 破舊的；破敗的；破爛的 SYN **scruffy**：*She wore shabby old jeans and a T-shirt.* 她穿着一條破舊的牛仔褲和一件 T 恤衫。 **2** (of a person 人) badly dressed in clothes that have been worn a lot 衣着破舊的 SYN **scruffy**：*The old man was shabby and unkempt.* 老頭蓬頭垢面，衣衫襤褸。 **3** (of behaviour 行為) unfair or unreasonable 不公正的；不講理的 SYN **shoddy**：*She tried to make up for her shabby treatment of him.* 她先前待他不好，這時候想彌補一下。 ▸ **shab·bily** /'ʃæbɪli/ *adv.*：*shabbily dressed* 衣衫襤褸 ◇ *I think you were very shabbily treated.* 要我説，你真是受大委屈了。 **shab·bi·ness** *noun* [U]

shack /ʃæk/ *noun, verb*
■ ***noun*** a small building, usually made of wood or metal, that has not been built well 簡陋的小屋；棚屋
■ ***verb***
PHR V **,shack 'up with sb** | **be ,shacked 'up with sb** (*slang*) to start/be living with sb that you have a sexual relationship with, but that you are not married to 和（性伴侶）同居：*I hear he's shacked up with some woman.* 我聽説他跟一個女人同居了。

shackle /'ʃækl/ *verb* **1 ~ sb** to put shackles on sb 給（某人）戴鐐銬：*The hostage had been shackled to a radiator.* 當時人質被銬在暖氣片上。◇ *The prisoners were kept shackled during the trial.* 審判期間，犯人戴着鐐銬。 **2** [usually passive] **~ sb/sth** to prevent sb from behaving or speaking as they want 束縛；阻撓；成為…的羈絆

shackles /'ʃæklz/ *noun* [pl.] **1** two metal rings joined together by a chain and placed around a prisoner's wrists or ankles to prevent them from escaping or moving easily 鐐銬；手銬；腳鐐 **2 ~ (of sth)** (*formal*) a particular state, set of conditions or circumstances, etc. that prevent you from saying or doing what you want 枷鎖；桎梏；束縛：*a country struggling to free itself from the shackles of colonialism* 為擺脱殖民主義的枷鎖而鬥爭的國家

shade 🔑 /ʃeɪd/ *noun, verb*
■ ***noun***
▸ OUT OF SUN 背陰 **1** 🔑 [U] **~ (of sth)** an area that is dark and cool under or behind sth, for example a tree or building, because the sun's light does not get to it 陰涼處；背陰；（樹）陰：*We sat down **in the shade of** the wall.* 我們在牆根的背陰處坐下。◇ *The temperature can reach 40°C **in the shade**.* 背陰處溫度可達 40°C。◇ *The trees provide shade for the animals in the summer.* 夏天，這些樹為動物提供乘涼的地方。 ➲ see also SHADY
▸ ON LAMP, ETC. 燈等 **2** 🔑 [C] a thing that you use to prevent light from coming through or to make it less bright 燈罩：*I bought a new shade for the lamp.* 我給那

蓋燈買了一個新罩子。◇ *an eyeshade* 遮陽眼罩 ➲ see also LAMPSHADE, SUNSHADE

▸ **ON WINDOW** 窗戶 **3** [C] (also **ˈwindow shade**) (both *NAmE*) = BLIND *n.* (1) ➲ VISUAL VOCAB page V21

▸ **OF COLOUR** 色彩 **4** [C] **~ (of sth)** a particular form of a colour, that is, how dark or light it is 濃淡深淺；色度：*a* ***delicate/pale/rich/soft shade*** *of blue* 淡的／淺的／濃的／柔和的藍色 ➲ SYNONYMS at COLOUR

▸ **IN PICTURE** 繪畫 **5** [U] the dark areas in a picture, especially the use of these to produce variety 暗部；陰影部份：*The painting needs more* ***light and shade.*** 這幅畫明暗層次不夠。

▸ **OF OPINION/FEELING** 看法；感覺 **6** [C, usually pl.] **~ of sth** a different kind or level of opinion, feeling, etc. 差別；不同：*politicians of all shades of opinion* 持各種政見的政治人物 ◇ *The word has many shades of meaning.* 這個詞有很多層意思。

▸ **SLIGHTLY** 略微 **7 a shade** [sing.] a little; slightly 一點；略微 SYN **touch**：*He was feeling a shade disappointed.* 他略感失望。

▸ **FOR EYES** 眼睛 **8 shades** [pl.] (*informal*) = SUNGLASSES

▸ **GHOST** 鬼魂 **9** [C] (*literary*) the spirit of a dead person; a GHOST 陰魂；幽靈；鬼

IDM **put sb/sth in the ˈshade** to be much better or more impressive than sb/sth 使（某人或事物）黯然失色；使相形見絀：*I tried hard but her work put mine in the shade.* 我費了很大力氣，但她的成果讓我相形見絀。 **shades of sb/sth** (*informal*) used when you are referring to things that remind you of a particular person, thing or time （人物、事情、時間的）痕跡，影子，遺風：*short skirts and long boots—shades of the 1960s* 短裙和高筒靴——20 世紀 60 年代的餘韻

■ ***verb***

▸ **FROM DIRECT LIGHT** 直射光線 **1** to prevent direct light from reaching sth 給…遮擋（光線）：**~ sb/sth** *The courtyard was shaded by high trees.* 庭院蔭庇在大樹下。◇ **~ sb/sth from/against sth** *She shaded her eyes against the sun.* 她遮住眼睛避免陽光直射。

▸ **LAMP** 燈 **2** [usually passive] **~ sth** to provide a screen for a lamp, light, etc. to make it less bright 加燈罩：*a shaded lamp* 有罩的燈

▸ **PART OF PICTURE** 圖畫的部份 **3** to make a part of a drawing, etc. darker, for example with an area of colour or with pencil lines 把…塗暗；畫陰影：**~ sth** *What do the shaded areas on the map represent?* 地圖上顏色深的部份代表什麼？◇ **~ sth in** *I'm going to shade this part in.* 我要把這一部份畫得再暗一些。

▸ **JUST WIN** 險勝 **4 ~ sth** (*BrE, informal*) to just win a contest 險勝

PHR V **ˌshade ˈinto sth** to change gradually into sth else, so that you cannot tell where one thing ends and the other thing begins（界線模糊地）漸變：*The scarlet of the wings shades into pink at the tips.* 猩紅的翅膀到了翼端漸變淺紅。◇ *Distrust of foreigners can shade into racism.* 對外國人的不信任可能逐漸演變成種族主義。

Which Word? 詞語辨析

shade / shadow

- **Shade** [U] is an area or a part of a place that is protected from the heat of the sun and so is darker and cooler. * shade（不可數名詞）意為陰涼處：*Let's sit in the shade for a while.* 咱們在陰涼處坐一會兒吧。
- A **shadow** [C] is the dark shape made when a light shines on a person or an object. * shadow（可數名詞）意為影子：*As the sun went down we cast long shadows on the lawn.* 太陽落山時我們在草坪上留下長長的影子。
- **Shadow** [U] is an area of darkness in which it is difficult to distinguish things easily. * shadow（不可數名詞）意為陰影、背光處：*Her face was in deep shadow.* 她的臉在陰暗處。

shad·ing /ˈʃeɪdɪŋ/ *noun* **1** [U] the use of colour, pencil lines, etc. to give an impression of light and shade in a picture or to emphasize areas of a map, diagram, etc.（繪畫的）明暗法；（地圖、圖表等中）顏色濃淡強調某些部份的運用 **2 shadings** [pl.] slight differences that exist between different aspects of the same thing（同一事物不同層面之間的）細微差別

shadow /ˈʃædəʊ; *NAmE* -doʊ/ *noun, verb, adj.*

■ ***noun***

▸ **DARK SHAPE** 陰影 **1** [C] the dark shape that sb/sth's form makes on a surface, for example on the ground, when they are between the light and the surface 陰影；影子：*The children were having fun, chasing each other's shadows.* 孩子們追逐着彼此的影子，玩得很開心。◇ *The ship's sail* ***cast a shadow*** *on the water.* 船帆在水面上投下一片影子。◇ *The shadows lengthened as the sun went down.* 隨着太陽西下，影子越拉越長。◇ (*figurative*) *He didn't want to* ***cast a shadow on*** (= spoil) *their happiness.* 他不想給他們的幸福蒙上陰影。➲ picture at SHADE ➲ note at SHADE

▸ **DARKNESS** 黑暗 **2** [U] (also **shadows** [pl.]) DARKNESS in a place or on sth, especially so that you cannot easily see who or what is there 昏暗處；背光處；陰暗處：*His face was deep* ***in shadow,*** *turned away from her.* 他扭過頭去背着她，臉衝着暗處。◇ *I thought I saw a figure standing in the shadows.* 我好像看見陰暗處站着一個人。➲ note at SHADE

▸ **SMALL AMOUNT** 微量 **3** [sing.] **~ of sth** a very small amount of sth 少許；些微；一丁點 SYN **hint**：*A shadow of a smile touched his mouth.* 他嘴角透出一絲笑意。◇ *She knew* ***beyond a shadow of a doubt*** (= with no doubt at all) *that he was lying.* 她十分清楚他在說謊。

▸ **INFLUENCE** 影響 **4** [sing.] **~ of sb/sth** the strong (usually bad) influence of sb/sth（壞）影響：*The new leader wants to escape from the shadow of his predecessor.* 新任領導想要擺脱前任領導的影響。◇ *These people have been living for years* ***under the shadow*** *of fear.* 這些人多年來一直生活在恐懼的陰影中。

▸ **UNDER EYES** 眼睛下方 **5 shadows** [pl.] dark areas under sb's eyes, because they are tired, etc. 黑眼圈

▸ **SB THAT FOLLOWS SB** 跟隨的人 **6** [C] a person or an animal that follows sb else all the time 形影不離的人（或動物）

▸ **STH NOT REAL** 虛幻事物 **7** [C] a thing that is not real or possible to obtain 虛幻的事物；不可能得到的東西：*You can't spend all your life* ***chasing shadows.*** 你不能一輩子追求虛無縹緲的東西。➲ see also EYESHADOW, FIVE O'CLOCK SHADOW

IDM **be frightened/nervous/scared of your own ˈshadow** to be very easily frightened; to be very nervous 非常膽小（或十分緊張） **in/under the ˈshadow of** **1** very close to 在…近旁：*The new market is in the shadow of the City Hall.* 新建的市場緊挨着市政廳。 **2** when you say that sb is **in/under the shadow of** another person, you mean that they do not receive as much attention as that person 被（某人的光彩）所掩蓋 ➲ more at FORMER

■ ***verb***

▸ **FOLLOW AND WATCH** 跟蹤監視 **1 ~ sb** to follow and watch sb closely and often secretly 跟蹤；盯梢：*He was shadowed for a week by the secret police.* 他被秘密警察盯梢了一個星期。 **2 ~ sb** to be with sb who is doing a particular job, so that you can learn about it 跟隨…實地學習（或參觀）：*It is often helpful for teachers to*

S

shadow managers in industry. 教師跟隨業界的管理人員實地學習，常常會很有收穫。
▸ **COVER WITH SHADOW 投下陰影 3 ~ sth** to cover sth with a shadow 在…上投下（或覆蓋）陰影：*A wide-brimmed hat shadowed her face.* 一頂寬邊帽把她的臉罩在陰影中。◇ *The bay was shadowed by magnificent cliffs.* 巍峨的懸崖把海灣籠罩在陰影裏。➲ see also OVERSHADOW
■ ***adj.*** [only before noun] (*BrE, politics* 政) used to refer to senior politicians of the main opposition party who would become government ministers if their party won the next election 影子內閣的：*the shadow Chancellor* 影子內閣的財政大臣 ◇ *the shadow Cabinet* 影子內閣

'shadow-box *verb* [I] to BOX with an imaginary opponent, especially for physical exercise or in order to train （尤指訓練時與假想對手）做空拳攻防練習 ▸ **'shadow-boxing** *noun* [U]

shad·owy /ˈʃædəʊi; *NAmE* -doʊi/ *adj.* **1** dark and full of shadows 陰暗的；幽暗的；陰影中的；多陰的：*Someone was waiting in the shadowy doorway.* 有人守候在昏暗的門口。**2** [usually before noun] difficult to see because there is not much light 昏暗的；朦朧的；模糊的：***Shadowy figures*** *approached them out of the fog.* 從霧中模模糊糊出來幾個人影，向他們走去。**3** [usually before noun] that not much is known about 鮮為人知的；神秘莫測的：*the shadowy world of terrorism* 鮮為人知的恐怖主義世界

shady /ˈʃeɪdi/ *adj.* (**shadi·er**, **shadi·est**) **1** protected from direct light from the sun by trees, buildings, etc. 背陰的；陰涼的；多陰的：*a shady garden* 樹影婆娑的花園 ◇ *We went to find somewhere cool and shady to have a drink.* 我們去找了一個陰涼的地方去喝一杯。**2** (of a tree, etc. 樹等) providing shade from the sun 成蔭的 **3** [usually before noun] (*informal*) seeming to be dishonest or illegal 可疑的；鬼祟的；非法的：*a shady businessman/deal* 行為可疑的商人；一宗有問題的交易

shaft /ʃɑːft; *NAmE* ʃæft/ *noun, verb*
■ ***noun*** **1** (often in compounds 常構成複合詞) a long, narrow, usually vertical passage in a building or underground, used especially for a lift/elevator or as a way of allowing air in or out （電梯的）升降機井；通風井；豎井；井筒：*a **lift/elevator shaft*** 電梯井 ◇ *a mineshaft* 豎井 ◇ *a ventilation shaft* 通風井 **2** the long narrow part of an arrow, HAMMER, GOLF CLUB, etc. （箭、高爾夫球杆等的）杆；（錘等的）柄 **3** (often in compounds 常構成複合詞) a metal bar that joins parts of a machine or an engine together, enabling power and movement to be passed from one part to another （機器的）軸 ➲ see also CAMSHAFT, CRANKSHAFT **4** [usually pl.] either of the two poles at the front of a CARRIAGE or CART between which a horse is fastened in order to pull it （馬車的）轅 **5 ~ of light, sunlight, etc.** (*literary*) a narrow strip of light 一束，一道（光、陽光等）：*A shaft of moonlight fell on the lake.* 一束月光照在湖面上。◇ (*figurative*) *a shaft of inspiration* 一道靈光 **6 ~ of pain, fear, etc.** (*literary*) a sudden strong feeling of pain, etc. that travels through your body 一陣（疼痛、害怕等）：*Shafts of fear ran through her as she heard footsteps behind her.* 她聽見身後有腳步聲，感到一陣毛骨悚然。**7 ~ of sth** (*formal*) a clever remark that is intended to upset or annoy sb 譏諷；挖苦；尖酸的話：*a shaft of wit* 機智的調侃
IDM **give sb the 'shaft** (*NAmE, informal*) to treat sb unfairly 虧待，苛待（某人）
■ ***verb* ~ sb** (*informal*) to treat sb unfairly or cheat them 虧待；苛待；欺騙

shag /ʃæɡ/ *noun, verb, adj.*
■ ***noun*** **1** [U] a strong type of TOBACCO cut into long thin pieces 馬合煙（濃味粗煙絲）**2** [C] a large black bird with a long neck that lives near the sea 鸕鶿 **3** [C, usually sing.] (*BrE, taboo, slang*) an act of sex with sb 性交
■ ***verb*** (**-gg-**) [I, T] **~ (sb)** (*BrE, taboo, slang*) to have sex with sb 和…性交
■ ***adj.*** [only before noun] used to describe a carpet, etc., usually made of wool, that has long threads（地毯等）長絨的

shagged /ʃæɡd/ (also ˌ**shagged 'out**) *adj.* [not before noun] (*BrE, taboo, slang*) very tired 疲憊不堪；很累

shaggy /ˈʃæɡi/ *adj.* (**shag·gier**, **shag·gi·est**) **1** (of hair, fur, etc. 毛髮等) long and untidy 長而亂的；亂蓬蓬的：*a shaggy mane of hair* 一頭蓬亂的長髮 **2** having long untidy hair, fur, etc. 頭髮（或皮毛）蓬亂的：*a huge shaggy white dog* 皮毛亂蓬蓬的大白狗

ˌ**shaggy-'dog story** *noun* a very long joke with a silly or disappointing ending 冗長無趣的笑話

shah /ʃɑː/ *noun* the title of the kings of Iran in the past 沙（舊時伊朗國王的稱號）

shaikh = SHEIKH

shake 🔑 /ʃeɪk/ *verb, noun*
■ ***verb*** (**shook** /ʃʊk/, **shaken** /ˈʃeɪkən/)
▸ **OBJECT/BUILDING/PERSON 物品；建築物；人 1** 🔑 [I, T] to move or make sb/sth move with short quick movements from side to side or up and down 搖動；抖動；（使）顫動：*The whole house shakes when a train goes past.* 火車駛過時，整座房子都顫動起來。◇ **~ sb/sth** *Shake the bottle well before use.* 使用前搖勻瓶內物品。◇ *He shook her violently by the shoulders.* 他抓着她的肩膀使勁搖晃。◇ **~ sb/sth + adj.** *She **shook** her hair **loose**.* 她頭一搖，頭髮就散開了。**2** 🔑 [T] **~ sth + adv./prep.** to move sth in a particular direction by shaking 搖（出）；抖（掉）：*She bent down to shake a pebble out of her shoe.* 她彎下腰，把鞋裏的一粒石子抖出來。
▸ **YOUR HEAD 頭 3** 🔑 [T] **~ your head** to turn your head from side to side as a way of saying 'no' or to show sadness, disapproval, doubt, etc. 搖頭：*She shook her head in disbelief.* 她難以置信地搖搖頭。
▸ **HANDS 手 4** 🔑 [T] to take sb's hand and move it up and down as a way of saying hello or to show that you agree about sth （與某人）握手：**~ hands (with sb) (on sth)** *Do people in Italy shake hands when they meet?* 在意大利，人們見面時握手嗎？◇ *They shook hands on the deal* (= to show that they had reached an agreement). 他們達成了協議，相互握手祝賀。◇ **~ sb's hand** *He shook my hand warmly.* 他熱情地和我握手。◇ **~ sb by the hand** *Our host shook each of us warmly by the hand.* 主人熱情地和我們每個人握手。
▸ **YOUR FIST 拳頭 5** [T] **~ your fist (at sb)** to show that you are angry with sb; to threaten sb by shaking your FIST (= closed hand) 揮拳（威脅）
▸ **OF BODY 身體 6** 🔑 [I] **~ (with sth)** to make short quick movements that you cannot control, for example because you are cold or afraid 顫抖；發抖；戰慄；哆嗦 **SYN** **tremble**：*He was shaking with fear.* 他怕得發抖。◇ *I was **shaking like a leaf**.* 我像樹葉似的直哆嗦。◇ *Her hands had started to shake.* 她的手早已哆嗦起來。
▸ **OF VOICE 聲音 7** 🔑 [I] **~ (with sth)** (of sb's voice 嗓音) to sound unsteady, usually because you are nervous, upset or angry 顫抖
▸ **SHOCK SB 使震驚 8** 🔑 [T] (not used in the progressive tenses 不用於進行時) to shock or upset sb very much 使非常震驚；使十分不安：**~ sb** *He was badly shaken by the news of her death.* 聽到她的死訊，他大為震驚。◇ **~ sb up** *The accident really shook her up.* 這一事故使她非常震驚。
▸ **BELIEF/IDEA 信念；觀點 9** [T] **~ sth** to make a belief or an idea less certain 動搖：*The incident had **shaken her faith** in him.* 這件事動搖了她對他的信心。◇ *This announcement is bound to **shake the confidence** of the industry.* 這個聲明必將動搖這一行業的信心。
▸ **GET RID OF 去除 10** [T] to get rid of sth 去除；擺脫：**~ sth off** *I can't seem to shake off this cold.* 這場感冒我好像老好不了。◇ **~ sth** *He couldn't shake the feeling that there was something wrong.* 他總感覺有什麼地方不對頭。
IDM **shake in your 'shoes** (*informal*) to be very frightened or nervous 非常害怕（或緊張）；戰戰兢兢；心驚肉跳 **shake a 'leg** (*old-fashioned, informal*) used to tell sb to start to do sth or to hurry（用於催促）快點動手，行動快點 ➲ more at FOUNDATION
PHR V ˌ**shake 'down** (*informal*) to become familiar with a new situation and begin to work well in it 融入新環境；適應新工作 ˌ**shake sb/sth↔'down** (*NAmE, informal*) **1** to search a person or place in a very thorough way 徹底搜查（某人、某地）➲ related noun SHAKEDOWN **2** to threaten sb in order to get money from them

S

勒索；敲詐 **ˌshake sb↔ˈoff** to get away from sb who is chasing or following you 擺脫，甩掉（某人）**ˈshake on sth** to shake hands in order to show that sth has been agreed 握手確認（達成共識）：*They shook on the deal.* 他們達成了協議，相互握手祝賀。◇ *Let's **shake on it**.* 讓我們握手慶賀取得一致。**ˌshake sth↔ˈout** to open or spread sth by shaking, especially so that bits of dirt, dust, etc. come off it 抖開；將（某物）抖乾淨：*to shake out a duster* 把抹布抖乾淨 **ˌshake sb↔ˈup** to surprise sb and make them think about sth in a different way, become more active, etc. 震動；激勵；使震驚不安 **ˌshake sth↔ˈup** to make important changes in an organization, a profession, etc. in order to make it more efficient 徹底調整；重組（機構、行業等）➲ related noun SHAKE-UP

■ ***noun***

▸ **MOVEMENT 動作 1** 🔑 [C, usually sing.] an act of shaking sth/sb 搖動；抖動；顫動：*Give the bottle a good shake before opening.* 打開瓶子前，先使勁搖一搖。◇ *He dismissed the idea with a firm shake of his head* (= turning it from side to side to mean 'no'). 他堅定地搖了搖頭，否定了那個想法。◇ *She gave him a shake to wake him.* 她搖搖他，把他叫醒。➲ see also HANDSHAKE

▸ **OF BODY 身體 2 the shakes** [pl.] (*informal*) a physical condition in which you cannot stop your body from shaking because of fear, illness, or because you have drunk too much alcohol 顫抖；戰慄；哆嗦：*I always **get the shakes** before exams.* 考試前，我總是緊張得發抖。

▸ **DRINK 飲料 3** [C] = MILKSHAKE：*a strawberry shake* 一杯草莓奶昔

IDM **in two ˈshakes | in a couple of ˈshakes** (*informal*) very soon 立刻；馬上 ➲ more at FAIR *adj.*, GREAT *adj.*

shake·down /ˈʃeɪkdaʊn/ *noun* (*NAmE, informal*) **1** a situation in which sb tries to force sb else to give them money using violence, threats, etc. 勒索；敲詐 **2** a thorough search of sb/sth 徹底搜查：*a police shakedown of the area* 警方對這一地區的徹底搜查 **3** a test of a vehicle to see if there are any problems before it is used generally（交通工具的）試用，試航，試飛

shaken /ˈʃeɪkən/ (also **shaken ˈup**) *adj.* [not usually before noun] shocked, upset or frightened by sth 震驚；煩惱；恐懼

ˈshake-out *noun* [usually sing.] **1** a situation in which people lose their jobs and less successful companies are forced to close because of competition and difficult economic conditions 經濟衰退；經濟蕭條 **2** = SHAKE-UP

S

shaker /ˈʃeɪkə(r)/ *noun* **1** (often in compounds 常構成複合詞) a container that is used for shaking things 搖動器；混合器；（蓋上有孔的）作料瓶：*a salt shaker* 鹽瓶 ◇ *a cocktail shaker* 雞尾酒搖壺 ➲ **VISUAL VOCAB** page V22 **2 Shaker** a member of a religious group in the US who live in a community in a very simple way and do not marry or have partners 震顫派教徒（美國教派，教徒禁慾獨身，聚居一處，崇尚儉樸生活）**IDM** see MOVER

ˈshake-up (also **ˈshake-out**) *noun* **~ (in/of sth)** a situation in which a lot of changes are made to a company, an organization, etc. in order to improve the way in which it works（機構的）重大調整，重組：*a management shake-up* 管理層的大調整

shak·ing /ˈʃeɪkɪŋ/ *noun* [sing., U] the act of shaking sth/sb or the fact of being shaken 搖動；抖動；顫動

shaky /ˈʃeɪki/ *adj.* (**shaki·er**, **shaki·est**) **1** shaking and feeling weak because you are ill/sick, emotional or old 顫抖的；顫巍巍的 **SYN** **unsteady**：*Her voice sounded shaky on the phone.* 電話裏她的聲音聽着發顫。◇ *The old man was very shaky on his feet.* 老人站在那兒，顫巍巍的。**2** not firm or safe; not certain 不穩固的；不牢靠的；搖晃的；不確切的：*That ladder looks a little shaky.* 這梯子看來不大牢靠。◇ (*figurative*) *Her memories of the accident are a little shaky.* 那次事故她記不太清楚了。◇ (*figurative*) *The protesters are **on shaky ground*** (= it is not certain that their claims are valid). 抗議者未必站得住腳。**3** not seeming very successful; likely to fail 不大出色的；成問題的；可能失敗的 **SYN** **uncertain**：*Business is looking shaky at the moment.* 從目前看，業務舉步維艱。◇ *After a shaky start, they fought back to win 3–2.* 他們開局不順，但最終以 3:2 反敗為勝。▸ **shaki·ly** /-ɪli/ *adv.*：*'Get the doctor,' he whispered shakily.* "去請大夫。" 他顫聲低語說。

shale /ʃeɪl/ *noun* [U] a type of soft stone that splits easily into thin flat layers 頁岩 ▸ **shaly** *adj.*

shall 🔑 /ʃəl; *strong form* ʃæl/ *modal verb* (*negative* **shall not** *short form* **shan't** /ʃɑːnt; *NAmE* ʃænt/, *pt* **should** /ʃʊd/, *negative* **should not** *short form* **shouldn't** /ˈʃʊdnt/) (*especially BrE*)

1 🔑 (becoming *old-fashioned*) used with *I* and *we* for talking about or predicting the future（同 I 和 we 連用，表示將來）將要，將會：*This time next week I shall be in Scotland.* 下週這個時候我就在蘇格蘭了。◇ *We shan't be gone long.* 我們不會去很長時間的。◇ *I said that I should be pleased to help.* 我說過我樂意幫忙。**2** 🔑 used in questions with *I* and *we* for making offers or suggestions or asking advice（在疑問句中同 I 和 we 連用，表示提出或徵求意見）：*Shall I send you the book?* 我把書給你寄去，好不好？◇ *What shall we do this weekend?* 這個週末我們要做什麼呢？◇ *Let's look at it again, shall we?* 我們再看一遍，好不好？**3** (*old-fashioned* or *formal*) used to show that you are determined, or to give an order or instruction（表示決心、命令或指示）必須，一定，應該：*He is determined that you shall succeed.* 他決心使你成功。◇ *Candidates shall remain in their seats until all the papers have been collected.* 考生必須留在座位上，等所有試卷收好以後方可離去。➲ note at MODAL

Grammar Point 語法說明

shall / will

- In modern English the traditional difference between **shall** and **will** has almost disappeared, and **shall** is not used very much at all, especially in *NAmE*. **Shall** is now only used with *I* and *we*, and often sounds formal and old-fashioned. 在現代英語中，shall 和 will 的傳統區別幾乎不復存在。shall 基本上不怎麼用，尤其在美式英語中。shall 目前只與 I 和 we 連用，且聽起來常顯得正式並過時。People are more likely to say 人們更常會說：*I'll* (= I will) *be late.* 我要遲到了。and 和 *'You'll* (= you will) *apologize immediately.' 'No I won't!'* "你趕快賠個不是。" "不，我不！"
- In *BrE* **shall** is still used with *I* and *we* in questions or when you want to make a suggestion or an offer. 在英式英語中，shall 仍然與 I 和 we 連用，用於疑問句、提出建議或提供幫助：*What shall I wear to the party?* 我穿什麼衣服去參加聚會呢？◇ *Shall we order some coffee?* 我們要些咖啡好嗎？◇ *I'll drive, shall I?* 我來開車好嗎？

➲ note at SHOULD

shal·lot /ʃəˈlɒt; *NAmE* -ˈlɑːt/ *noun* a vegetable like a small onion with a very strong taste 青蔥；大蔥 ➲ **VISUAL VOCAB** page V31

shal·low 🔑 /ˈʃæləʊ; *NAmE* -loʊ/ *adj.* (**shal·low·er**, **shal·low·est**)

1 🔑 not having much distance between the top or surface and the bottom 淺的：*a shallow dish* 淺盤 ◇ *They were playing in **the shallow end*** (= of the swimming pool). 他們在游泳池的淺水區玩耍。◇ *These fish are found in shallow waters around the coast.* 這些魚生長在海邊淺水水域。**OPP** **deep** **2** (*disapproving*) (of a person, an idea, a comment, etc. 人、觀點、評論等) not showing serious thought, feelings, etc. about sth 膚淺的；淺薄的 **SYN** **superficial** **3** **shallow breathing** involves taking in only a small amount of air each time（呼吸）淺的，弱的 ▸ **shal·low·ly** *adv.*：*He was breathing shallowly.* 他呼吸短促。▸ **shal·low·ness** *noun* [U]

shal·lows /ˈʃæləʊz; *NAmE* -loʊz/ **the shallows** *noun* [pl.] a shallow place in a river or the sea（河海的）淺水處，淺灘

sha·lom /ʃəˈlɒm; *NAmE* -ˈloʊm/ *exclamation* a Hebrew word for 'hello' or 'goodbye' that means 'peace'（希伯來語，見面或告別時説）祝你平安

shalt /ʃælt/ *verb* **thou shalt** (*old use*) used to mean 'you shall', when talking to one person （意同 shall，用於第二人稱單數）

shal·war = SALWAR

sham /ʃæm/ *noun, adj., verb*
■ **noun** (*disapproving*) **1** [sing.] a situation, feeling, system, etc. that is not as good or true as it seems to be 假象；假情假義；偽善；偽裝：*The latest crime figures are a complete sham.* 最新的犯罪統計數字完全是捏造的。**2** [C, usually sing.] a person who pretends to be sth that they are not 假裝…的人；冒充者；假冒者 **3** [U] behaviour, feelings, words, etc. that are intended to make sb/sth seem to be better than they really are 虛假的行為（或感情、言語等）；偽善：*Their promises turned out to be full of sham and hypocrisy.* 他們的許諾到頭來全是空的、騙人的。
■ **adj.** [only before noun] (usually *disapproving*) not genuine but intended to seem real 虛假的；假裝的 **SYN** **false**：*a sham marriage* 假結婚
■ **verb** (**-mm-**) [I, T] **~ (sth)** | **+ adj.** to pretend sth 假裝；冒充：*Is he really sick or is he just shamming?* 他真病了，還是裝的？

shaman /ˈʃeɪmən; ˈʃɑːmən; ˈʃæmən/ *noun* a person in some religions and societies who is believed to be able to contact good and evil spirits and cure people of illnesses 薩滿（據信能和善惡神靈溝通，能治病的人）▸ **sha·man·ic** /ʃəˈmænɪk/ *adj.*

shama·teur /ˈʃæmətə(r); -tʃə(r)/ *noun* (*disapproving*) a person who makes money playing a sport but is officially an AMATEUR 冒牌業餘運動員（領取出場費）▸ **shama·teur·ism** /ˈʃæmətərɪzəm; -tʃər-/ *noun* [U]

shamba /ˈʃæmbə/ *noun* (*EAfrE*) a small farm or a field that is used for growing crops 小農場；農田

sham·ble /ˈʃæmbl/ *verb* [I] (**+ adv./prep.**) to walk in an awkward or lazy way, dragging your feet along the ground 拖着腳走；蹣跚

sham·bles /ˈʃæmblz/ *noun* [sing.] (*informal*) **1** a situation in which there is a lot of confusion 混亂局面；無序的場面；凌亂不堪；一片狼藉 **SYN** **mess**：*The press conference was a complete shambles.* 記者招待會一片混亂。◇ *What a shambles!* 好亂哪！◇ *The government is **in a shambles** over Europe.* 政府在歐洲問題上政策十分混亂。**2** a place which is dirty or untidy 骯髒（或凌亂）的地方 **SYN** **mess**：*The house was a shambles.* 那間屋子凌亂不堪。

sham·bol·ic /ʃæmˈbɒlɪk; *NAmE* -ˈbɑːl-/ *adj.* (*BrE, informal*) lacking order or organization 混亂的；沒有次序的；亂七八糟的 **SYN** **chaotic, disorganized**

shame 0-w /ʃeɪm/ *noun, verb, exclamation*
■ **noun** **1** 0-w [U] the feelings of sadness, embarrassment and GUILT that you have when you know that sth you have done is wrong or stupid 羞恥；羞愧；慚愧：*His face burned with shame.* 他的臉因羞愧而發燙。◇ *She hung her head in shame.* 她羞愧地低下了頭。◇ *He could not live with the shame of other people knowing the truth.* 別人知道了事情的真相，他羞得無地自容。◇ ***To my shame*** (= I feel shame that) *I refused to listen to her side of the story.* 使我感到慚愧的是，我拒絕聽她對事情的解釋。**2** [U] (*formal*) (only used in questions and negative sentences 僅用於疑問句和否定句) the ability to feel shame at sth you have done 羞恥心；羞愧感：*Have you no shame?* 你就不知道羞恥嗎？**3** 0-w **a shame** [sing.] used to say that sth is a cause for feeling sad or disappointed 令人惋惜的事；讓人遺憾的事 **SYN** **pity**：***What a shame*** *they couldn't come.* 他們不能來了，真是遺憾。◇ ***It's a shame about*** *Tim, isn't it?* 蒂姆的事讓人遺憾，你説是不是？◇ ***It's a shame that*** *she wasn't here to see it.* 她要是在這兒親眼看看，那該多好。◇ *It would be **a crying shame*** (= a great shame) *not to take them up on the offer.* 要是不接受他們的提議，將來後悔都來不及。**4** 0-w [U] the loss of respect that is caused when you do sth wrong or stupid 恥辱；丟臉：*There is **no shame in** wanting to be successful.* 有抱負不是什麼丟臉的事。◇ (*formal*) *She felt that her failure would **bring shame on** her family.* 她覺得她的失敗會使家人蒙羞。
IDM **put sb/sth to ˈshame** to be much better than sb/sth 大大勝過；使相形見絀；使自愧不如：*Their presentation put ours to shame.* 他們的演出使我們的相形見絀。**ˈshame on you, him, etc.** (*informal*) used to say that sb should feel ashamed for sth they have said or done （責備時説）真丟臉，真不害臊 ➲ more at NAME *v.*
■ **verb** **1 ~ sb** to make sb feel ashamed 使羞愧（或慚愧）：*His generosity shamed them all.* 他的大度使他們都感到羞愧。**2 ~ sb** (*formal*) to make sb feel that they have lost honour or respect 使蒙受恥辱；使丟臉：*You have shamed your family.* 你使你的家庭蒙受了恥辱。
PHR V **ˈshame sb into doing sth** to persuade sb to do sth by making them feel ashamed not to do it 使某人羞愧而不得不做（某事）：*She shamed her father into promising more help.* 她使父親感到過意不去，只好答應多給她些幫助。
■ **exclamation** (*SAfrE*) used to express sympathy, or to show that you like sb/sth （表示讚歎或喜愛）真可惜，太遺憾了，好極了，真棒：*Shame, she's so cute!* 哇，她簡直是太漂亮了！

shame·faced /ˌʃeɪmˈfeɪst/ *adj.* feeling or looking ashamed because you have done sth bad or stupid 面帶愧色的；羞慚的；慚愧的 **SYN** **sheepish**：*a shamefaced smile* 慚愧的笑容 ▸ **shame·faced·ly** /ˌʃeɪmˈfeɪstli; -ˈfeɪsɪdli/ *adv.*

shame·ful /ˈʃeɪmfl/ *adj.* that should make you feel ashamed 可恥的；丟臉的 **SYN** **disgraceful**：*shameful behaviour* 可恥的行為 ◇ *It was shameful the way she was treated.* 她竟然受到那樣的對待，太不像話了。▸ **shame·ful·ly** /-fəli/ *adv.*

shame·less /ˈʃeɪmləs/ *adj.* (*disapproving*) not feeling ashamed of sth you have done, although other people think you should 無恥的；沒廉恥的；不要臉的 **SYN** **unashamed** ▸ **shame·less·ly** *adv.* (usually *disapproving* but sometimes *approving*)：*The whole film is shamelessly romantic and glamorous.* 張揚的浪漫與華美貫穿整部電影。**shame·less·ness** *noun* [U]

sham·ing /ˈʃeɪmɪŋ/ *adj.* causing sb to feel ashamed 令人羞愧的：*a shaming defeat by a less experienced team* 令人羞愧地輸給一支經驗不如自己的隊伍

sham·my /ˈʃæmi/ *noun* (*pl.* **-ies**) (also ˌ**shammy ˈleather**) [U, C] (*informal*) = CHAMOIS (2)

sham·poo /ʃæmˈpuː/ *noun, verb*
■ **noun** (*pl.* **-os**) **1** [C, U] a liquid soap that is used for washing your hair; a similar liquid used for cleaning carpets, furniture covers or a car 洗髮劑；香波；（洗地毯、傢具罩套、汽車等的）洗滌劑：*a shampoo for greasy hair* 油性頭髮洗髮劑 ◇ *carpet shampoo* 地毯洗滌劑 **2** [C, usually sing.] an act of washing your hair using shampoo 用洗髮劑洗頭髮：*Rinse the hair thoroughly after each shampoo.* 每次用洗髮劑洗髮後都要徹底沖乾淨。◇ *a shampoo and set* (= an act of washing and styling sb's hair) 洗頭髮並做髮型
■ **verb** (**sham·pooed, sham·pooed**) **~ sth** to wash or clean hair, carpets, etc. with shampoo 用洗髮劑洗（頭髮）；用洗滌劑洗（地毯等）

sham·rock /ˈʃæmrɒk; *NAmE* -rɑːk/ *noun* a small plant with three leaves on each STEM. The shamrock is the national symbol of Ireland. 三葉草（愛爾蘭的國花）

shandy /ˈʃændi/ *noun* (*pl.* **-ies**) (*especially BrE*) **1** [U] a drink made by mixing beer with LEMONADE 香迪啤酒（摻檸檬汁的啤酒）**2** [C] a glass or can of shandy 一杯（或一罐）香迪啤酒：*Two shandies, please.* 請來兩杯香迪啤酒。

shang·hai /ˌʃæŋˈhaɪ/ *verb* (**shang·hai·ing** /-ˈhaɪɪŋ/, **shang·haied, shang·haied** /-ˈhaɪd/) **~ sb (into doing sth)** (*old-fashioned, informal*) to trick or force sb into doing sth that they do not really want to do 誆騙；強迫

Shangri-La /ˌʃæŋgri ˈlɑː/ *noun* [sing.] a place that is extremely beautiful and where everything seems perfect, especially a place far away from modern life 香格里拉；（遠離現代生活的）世外桃源 **ORIGIN** From

S

the name of an imaginary valley in Tibet in James Hilton's novel *Lost Horizon*, where people do not grow old. 源自詹姆斯•希爾頓的小說《失去的地平線》中虛構的西藏河谷香格里拉，那裏的人青春永駐。

shank /ʃæŋk/ *noun* **1** the straight narrow part between the two ends of a tool or an object 長柄；桿 **2** the part of an animal's or a person's leg between the knee and ankle（動物或人的）脛，小腿 **3** the top part of the leg of an animal, cooked and eaten（動物的）大腿肉：*braised lamb shanks* 燉羊腿

IDM **(on) Shanks's 'pony** (*BrE, informal*) walking, rather than travelling by car, bus, etc. 步行；徒步 SYN **on foot**

shan't /ʃɑːnt; *NAmE* ʃænt/ *short form* shall not 不會；不應該

shanty /ˈʃænti/ *noun* (*pl.* **-ies**) **1** a small house, built of pieces of wood, metal and cardboard, where very poor people live, especially on the edge of a big city 棚屋，簡陋小屋（常搭建於城市邊緣）**2** (also **'sea shanty**) (*US* **chanty, chantey**) a song that sailors traditionally used to sing while pulling ropes, etc. 水手號子（舊時水手邊拉繩索等邊唱的歌）

'shanty town *noun* an area in or near a town where poor people live in shanties 棚戶區，貧民窟（在城鎮中或近郊）

shape 🔑 /ʃeɪp/ *noun, verb*

■ **noun 1** 🔑 [C, U] the form of the outer edges or surfaces of sth; an example of sth that has a particular form 形狀；外形；樣子；呈…形狀的事物：*a rectangular shape* 長方形 ◇ *The pool was* **in the shape of** *a heart.* 游泳池呈心形。◇ *The island was originally circular* **in shape**. 這個島原先為圓形。◇ *Squares, circles and triangles are types of shape.* 正方形、圓形和三角形是形狀類別。◇ *Candles come in* **all shapes and sizes**. 有各種形狀和大小的蠟燭。◇ *You can recognize the fish by the shape of their fins.* 你可以根據鰭的形狀來辨認這種魚。◇ *This old T-shirt has completely lost its shape.* 這件舊T恤衫已經穿得完全走樣了。◇ (*figurative*) *The government provides money* **in the shape of** (= consisting of) *grants and student loans.* 政府以助學金和學生貸款的形式提供資助。➲ VISUAL VOCAB page V71 **2** 🔑 [C] a person or thing that is difficult to see clearly 模糊的影子 SYN **figure**：*Ghostly shapes moved around in the dark.* 有幾個鬼一樣的影子在黑暗中遊蕩。**3** 🔑 [U] the physical condition of sb/sth 狀況；情況：*What sort of shape was the car in after the accident?* 這車出過事故以後狀況如何？◇ *He's* **in good shape** *for a man of his age.* 作為那把年紀的人來說，他身體不錯。◇ *I like to* **keep in shape** (= keep fit). 我喜歡保持健康。**4** [U] the particular qualities or characteristics of sth 性質；特點：*Will new technology change the shape of broadcasting?* 新技術會改變廣播的方式嗎？

IDM **get (yourself) into 'shape** to take exercise, eat healthy food, etc. in order to become physically fit 強身健體 **get/knock/lick sb into 'shape** to train sb so that they do a particular job, task, etc. well 把某人培養成材（或訓練出來）**get/knock/lick sth into 'shape** to make sth more acceptable, organized or successful 把某事物整頓好；使某事物條理化（或更趨完善）：*I've got all the information together but it still needs knocking into shape.* 我把材料全都收集齊了，但還需要整理。**give 'shape to sth** (*formal*) to express or explain a particular idea, plan, etc. 表達，闡釋（觀點、計劃等）**in 'any (way,) shape or form** (*informal*) of any type 任何形式：*I don't approve of violence in any shape or form.* 我不贊成任何形式的暴力行為。**out of 'shape 1** not having the normal shape 變形的；走樣的：*The wheel had been twisted out of shape.* 輪子已經扭曲變形了。**2** (of a person 人) not in good physical condition 身體不好；不健康 **the ˌshape of ˌthings to 'come** the way things are likely to develop in the future 未來的狀況 **take 'shape** to develop and become more complete or organized 成形；有了模樣 ➲ more at BENT *adj.*

■ **verb 1** 🔑 [T] to make sth into a particular shape 使成為…形狀（或樣子）；塑造：**~ A into B** *Shape the dough into a ball.* 把和好的麪揉成一團。◇ **~ sth** *This tool is used for shaping wood.* 這個工具是用來加工木料的。**2** 🔑 [T] **~ sb/sth** to have an important influence on the way that sb/sth develops 決定…的形成；影響…的發展：*His ideas had been shaped by his experiences during the war.* 他的思想深受戰時經歷的影響。◇ *She had a leading role in shaping party policy.* 該黨奉行何種政策，她起着主導作用。**3** [I] **~ to do sth** to prepare to do sth, especially hit or kick sth 準備（做某動作）；擺好姿勢：*She was shaping to hit her second shot.* 她正準備再一次擊球。

IDM **'shape up or ship 'out** (*NAmE, informal*) used to tell sb that if they do not improve, work harder, etc. they will have to leave their job, position, etc. 不好好幹就捲鋪蓋：*He finally faced up to his drug problem when his band told him to shape up or ship out.* 樂隊警告他要麼好好幹，要麼走人，這使他終於正視自己的吸毒問題。

PHR V **ˌshape 'up 1** to develop in a particular way, especially in a good way 進展（順利）：*Our plans are shaping up nicely* (= showing signs that they will be successful). 我們的計劃進行得很好。**2** (*informal*) to improve your behaviour, work harder, etc. 改善（行為、工作等）：*If he doesn't shape up, he'll soon be out of a job.* 他要是不改好，很快就會丟飯碗的。

shaped 🔑 /ʃeɪpt/ *adj.* having the type of shape mentioned 具有（或呈）…形狀的：*a huge balloon* **shaped like** *a giant cow* 形似一頭巨牛的大氣球 ◇ *almond-shaped eyes* 杏眼 ◇ *an L-shaped room* * L 形房間 ➲ see also PEAR-SHAPED

shape·less /ˈʃeɪpləs/ *adj.* [usually before noun] (often *disapproving*) **1** not having any definite shape 無定形的；不成形的；樣子不好看的：*a shapeless sweater* 樣子難看的套頭衫 **2** lacking clear organization 結構混亂的；條理不清的 SYN **unstructured**：*a shapeless and incoherent story* 結構混亂、情節不連貫的故事 ► **shape·less·ly** *adv.* **shape·less·ness** *noun* [U]

shape·ly /ˈʃeɪpli/ *adj.* (especially of a woman's body 尤指女子體形) having an attractive curved shape 有曲線美的；勻稱的

shard /ʃɑːd; *NAmE* ʃɑːrd/ (also **sherd**) *noun* a piece of broken glass, metal, etc.（玻璃、金屬等的）碎片：*shards of glass* 玻璃碎片

share 🔑 /ʃeə(r); *NAmE* ʃer/ *verb, noun*

■ **verb**

► **USE AT THE SAME TIME** 同時使用 **1** 🔑 [T, I] **~ (sth) (with sb)** to have or use sth at the same time as sb else 共有；合用：*Sue shares a house with three other students.* 蘇和另外三個學生合住一所房子。◇ *There isn't an empty table. Would you mind sharing?* 沒有空桌子了。你願不願意和別人合坐？

► **DIVIDE BETWEEN PEOPLE** 分給若干人 **2** 🔑 [T] **~ sth (out) (among/between sb)** to divide sth between two or more people 分配；分攤：*We shared the pizza between the four of us.* 我們四個人把那份比薩餅分着吃了。➲ see also JOB-SHARING, POWER-SHARING

► **GIVE SOME OF YOURS** 把自己的分出一部份 **3** 🔑 [T, I] **~ (sth) (with sb)** to give some of what you have to sb else; to let sb use sth that is yours 分享；共享：*Eli shared his chocolate with the other kids.* 伊萊把他的巧克力和其他孩子一起分着吃了。◇ *The conference is a good place to share information and exchange ideas.* 研討會是互通信息、交流思想的好場所。◇ *John had no brothers or sisters and wasn't used to sharing.* 約翰沒有兄弟姐妹，所以不習慣和他人分享東西。

► **FEELINGS/IDEAS/PROBLEMS** 感情；想法；問題 **4** 🔑 [T, I] to have the same feelings, ideas, experiences, etc. as sb else 有同樣的感情（或想法、經歷等）：**~ sth** *They shared a common interest in botany.* 他們都對植物學感興趣。◇ *a view that is widely shared* 一種得到廣泛認同的觀點 ◇ *shared values* 共同的價值觀 ◇ **~ sth with sb** *People often share their political views with their parents.* 人常常跟自己的父母政治觀點一致。◇ **~ in sth** *I didn't really share in her love of animals.* 我並不像她那樣喜歡動物。**5** 🔑 [T, I] to tell other people about your ideas, experiences and feelings 把自己的想法（或經歷、感情）告訴別人：**~ sth** *Men often don't like to share their problems.* 男人往往不喜歡把自己的問題告訴他人。◇ *The two friends shared everything—they had no secrets.* 這一

S

對朋友無話不談，彼此之間毫無秘密。◇ **~ (sth with sb)** *Would you like to share your experience with the rest of the group?* 你願意把你的經驗與組裏其他人分享嗎？◇ *The group listens while one person shares* (= tells other people about their experiences, feelings, etc.). 一個人在談自己的情況時，小組的其他成員在旁聆聽。

▸ **BLAME/RESPONSIBILITY** 責任 **6** [I, T] to be equally involved in sth or responsible for sth 共同承擔；分擔：**~ in sth** *I try to get the kids to share in the housework.* 我努力讓孩子們分擔家務活兒。◇ **~ sth (with sb)** *Both drivers shared the blame for the accident.* 事故責任由兩個駕車人共同承擔。

IDM **share and share a'like** (*saying*) used to say that everyone should share things equally and in a fair way 平均分享；平均分擔 ➲ more at TROUBLE *n.*

■ ***noun***

▸ **PART/AMOUNT OF STH** 一部份；一定的量 **1** [C, usually sing.] **~ (of/in sth)** one part of sth that is divided between two or more people（在若干人之間分得的）一份：*How much was your share of the winnings?* 在贏的錢裏你那份有多少？◇ *Next year we hope to have a bigger share of the market.* 明年我們希望獲得更大的市場份額。◇ (*BrE*) *I'm looking for a* ***flat share*** (= a flat that is shared by two or more people who are not related). 我想找一套合租公寓。➲ see also MARKET SHARE, TIME-SHARE **2** [sing.] the part that sb has in a particular activity that involves several people（在多人參加的活動中所佔的）一份：*We all did our share.* 我們都盡力了。◇ **~ of sth** *Everyone must accept their share of the blame.* 每個人都必須承擔自己那份責任。**3** [sing.] **~ (of sth)** an amount of sth that is thought to be normal or acceptable for one person 正常的一份；可接受的一份：*I've had my share of luck in the past.* 以前，命運也不算虧待我。◇ *I've done my share of worrying for one day!* 就這一天而論，我操夠了心！

▸ **IN BUSINESS** 企業 **4** [C] **~ (in sth)** any of the units of equal value into which a company is divided and sold to raise money. People who own shares receive part of the company's profits. 股份：*shares in British Telecom* 英國電信公司的股份 ◇ *a fall in* ***share prices*** 股票價格的跌落 ➲ compare STOCK *n.* (4) ➲ see also ORDINARY SHARE

▸ **FARM EQUIPMENT** 農具 **5** [C] (*NAmE*) = PLOUGHSHARE

IDM see CAKE *n.*, FAIR *adj.*, LION, PIE

-share *combining form* **1** (in nouns) an arrangement to divide sth between two or more people, groups, etc.（構成名詞）分攤，分擔：*a job-share* (= a job that is done by two people who each work for part of the week) 工作分擔 ◇ (*BrE*) *a nanny share* (= an arrangement for sb to work for two families) 保母（兩家）共用 ➲ see also TIMESHARE **2** (in verbs) using an arrangement to divide sth between two or more people, groups, etc.（構成動詞）共用，合用：(*especially BrE*) *We encourage people to carshare to reduce congestion on the roads.* 我們鼓勵人們合夥用車以減少道路擁堵。◇ (*NAmE*) *to rideshare* 拼車

share·crop·per /ˈʃeəkrɒpə(r); *NAmE* ˈʃerkrɑːpər/ *noun* (*especially NAmE*) a farmer who gives part of his or her crop as rent to the owner of the land 佃農

share·hold·er /ˈʃeəhəʊldə(r); *NAmE* ˈʃerhoʊ-/ *noun* an owner of shares in a company or business 股東

share·hold·ing /ˈʃeəhəʊldɪŋ; *NAmE* ˈʃerhoʊ-/ *noun* the amount of a company or business that sb owns in the form of shares 持股；持股量

ˈshare index *noun* [usually sing.] a list that shows the current value of shares on the STOCK MARKET, based on the prices of shares of particular companies 股票價格指數

ˈshare option (*BrE*) (*NAmE* **ˈstock option**) *noun* a right given to employees to buy shares in their company at a fixed price 股票期權，認股期權（讓員工可按固定價格購買所屬公司的股票）

ˈshare-out *noun* [usually sing.] (*BrE*) an act of dividing sth between two or more people; the amount of sth that one person receives when it is divided 分配；分配額；份額

share·ware /ˈʃeəweə(r); *NAmE* ˈʃerwer/ *noun* [U] (*computing* 計) computer software (= programs, etc.) that is available free for a user to test, after which they must pay if they wish to continue using it 共享軟件，共享軟體（供買前試用）➲ compare FREEWARE

sha·ria (also **sha·riah**) /ʃəˈriːə/ *noun* [U] the system of religious laws that Muslims follow 伊斯蘭教教法

shark /ʃɑːk; *NAmE* ʃɑːrk/ *noun* **1** a large sea fish with very sharp teeth and a pointed FIN on its back. There are several types of shark, some of which can attack people swimming. 鯊魚 **2** (*informal, disapproving*) a person who is dishonest in business, especially sb who gives bad advice and gets people to pay too much for sth 坑矇拐騙的人；詐騙者 ➲ see also LOAN SHARK

sharp /ʃɑːp; *NAmE* ʃɑːrp/ *adj., adv., noun*

■ ***adj.*** (**sharp·er, sharp·est**)

▸ **EDGE/POINT** 鋒；尖 **1** having a fine edge or point, especially of sth that can cut or make a hole in sth 鋒利的；銳利的；尖的：*a sharp knife* 鋒利的刀 ◇ *sharp teeth* 鋒利的牙齒 **OPP** **blunt**

▸ **RISE/DROP/CHANGE** 升；降；變化 **2** [usually before noun] sudden and rapid, especially of a change in sth（變化）急劇的，驟然的：*a sharp drop in prices* 價格的驟降 ◇ *a sharp rise in crime* 犯罪率的急劇上升 ◇ *a sharp increase in unemployment* 失業人數的劇增 ◇ *He heard a* ***sharp intake of breath.*** 他聽到猛地倒吸一口氣的聲音。◇ *We need to give young criminals a* ***short, sharp shock*** (= a punishment that is very unpleasant for a short time). 對青少年罪犯我們需要給以短暫但嚴厲的懲處。

▸ **CLEAR/DEFINITE** 清楚；明確 **3** [usually before noun] clear and definite 清楚明確的；清晰的；鮮明的：*a sharp outline* 清晰的輪廓 ◇ *The photograph is not very sharp* (= there are no clear contrasts between areas of light and shade). 這張照片不是很清晰。◇ *She drew a* ***sharp distinction*** *between domestic and international politics.* 她將國內政治和國際政治截然分開。◇ *In* ***sharp contrast*** *to her mood, the clouds were breaking up to reveal a blue sky.* 烏雲漸漸散開，露出了藍天，這和她的情緒形成了鮮明的對照。◇ *The issue must be brought into sharper focus.* 必須使這個問題成為更清晰的焦點。

▸ **MIND/EYES** 頭腦；眼睛 **4** (of people or their minds, eyes, etc. 人或人的頭腦、眼睛等) quick to notice or understand things or to react 敏銳的；靈敏的；敏捷的：*to have sharp eyes* 有敏銳的眼睛 ◇ *a girl of sharp intelligence* 聰穎的女孩 ◇ *a sharp sense of humour* 很強的幽默感 ◇ *He kept a sharp lookout for any strangers.* 他警惕地守望着，不放過任何一個陌生人。◇ *It was very sharp of you to see that!* 你能看到這一點，很有洞察力！

▸ **CRITICAL** 批評性 **5** (of a person or what they say 人或言語) critical or severe 尖銳的；嚴厲的：*sharp criticism* 尖銳的批評 ◇ *Emma has a* ***sharp tongue*** (= she often speaks in an unpleasant or unkind way). 埃瑪說話尖刻。◇ **~ with sb** *He was very sharp with me when I was late.* 我遲到了，讓他狠狠訓了一通。

▸ **SOUNDS** 聲音 **6** [usually before noun] loud, sudden and often high in tone 突然而響亮的：*She read out the list in sharp, clipped tones.* 她清脆快速地宣讀了名單。◇ *There was a sharp knock on the door.* 敲門聲大作。

▸ **FEELING** 感覺 **7** (of a physical feeling or an emotion 感覺或感情) very strong and sudden, often like being cut or wounded（常指受傷似地）劇烈的，猛烈的 **SYN** **intense**：*He winced as a sharp pain shot through his leg.* 腿上一陣劇痛，疼得他齜牙咧嘴。◇ *Polly felt a sharp pang of jealousy.* 波利感到一陣強烈的嫉妒。

▸ **CURVES** 彎兒 **8** changing direction suddenly 急轉方向的：*a sharp bend in the road* 公路上的急轉彎 ◇ *a sharp turn to the left* 向左的急轉

▸ **FLAVOUR/SMELL** 味道；氣味 **9** strong and slightly bitter 強烈略苦的；辛辣的；刺鼻的：*The cheese has a distinctively sharp taste.* 這奶酪味道很衝。➲ **SYNONYMS** at BITTER

▸ **FROST/WIND** 霜；風 **10** used to describe a very cold or very severe FROST or wind 嚴寒的；凜冽的 ➲ see also RAZOR-SHARP

▸ **CLEVER AND DISHONEST** 狡詐 **11** (*disapproving*) (of a person or their way of doing business 人或做事方式) clever but possibly dishonest 狡猾的；詭詐的：*His lawyer's a* ***sharp operator.*** 他的律師是個老狐狸。◇ *The*

S

firm had to face some **sharp practice** from competing companies. 公司不得不面對競爭對手們的小動作。

▸ CLOTHES 衣服 **12** [usually before noun] (of clothes or the way sb dresses 衣服或衣着風格) fashionable and new 時髦的；入時的： *The consultants were a group of men in* **sharp suits**. 顧問都是些衣着入時的男人。◇ *Todd is a* **sharp dresser**. 托德衣着時髦。

▸ FACE/FEATURES 臉；相貌 **13** not full or round in shape 瘦削的；不豐滿的： *a man with a thin face and sharp features* (= a pointed nose and chin) 臉瘦而稜角分明的男人

▸ IN MUSIC 音樂 **14** used after the name of a note to mean a note a SEMITONE/HALF TONE higher （用於音符後，表示該音符）升半音的： *the Piano Sonata in C sharp minor* 升 C 小調鋼琴奏鳴曲 ➲ picture at MUSIC **OPP** flat ➲ compare NATURAL *adj.* (9) **15** above the correct PITCH (= how high or low a note sounds) 偏高音的：*That note sounded sharp.* 這個音聽着偏高。**OPP** flat

▸ **sharp·ness** *noun* [C, U]： *There was a sudden sharpness in her voice.* 她的嗓音突然抬高了。

IDM **look 'sharp** (*BrE, informal*) used in orders to tell sb to be quick or to hurry 趕快；趕緊： *You'd better look sharp or you'll be late.* 你得快點，不然就遲到了。 **not the sharpest knife in the 'drawer | not the sharpest tool in the 'box** (*informal, humorous*) not intelligent 不聰明；遲鈍： *He's not exactly the sharpest knife in the drawer, is he?* 他的腦子一點兒也不靈活，是不是？ **the 'sharp end (of sth)** (*BrE, informal*) the place or position of greatest difficulty or responsibility 最為困難（或責任極其重大）的地方（或職位）： *He started work at the sharp end of the business, as a salesman.* 他從這一行最為棘手的工作做起，當了推銷員。

■ *adv.*

▸ EXACTLY 準確地 **1** used after an expression for a time of day to mean 'exactly' （用於表時間的詞語後，表示準時）…整： *Please be here at seven o'clock sharp.* 請七點整到這裏。

▸ LEFT/RIGHT 左；右 **2** (*BrE*) **~ left/right** turning suddenly to the left or right 向左 / 向右急轉

▸ MUSIC 音樂 **3** (*comparative* **sharp·er**, *no superlative*) above the correct PITCH (= how high or low a note sounds) 偏高音地 **OPP** flat

■ *noun* **1** (*music* 音) a note played a SEMITONE/HALF TONE higher than the note that is named. The written symbol is (♯) 升半音： *It's a difficult piece to play, full of sharps and flats.* 這支樂曲不好演奏，到處是升半音、降半音。 **OPP** flat ➲ compare NATURAL *n.* (2) **2** **sharps** [pl.] (*medical* 醫) things with a sharp edge or point, such as needles and SYRINGES 銳利的東西（如針、注射器等）： *the safe disposal of sharps* 對有利刃或尖刺的東西的安全處置

S

sharp·en /ˈʃɑːpən; *NAmE* ˈʃɑːrpən/ *verb* **1** [T, I] **~ (sth)** to make sth sharper; to become sharper （使）變得鋒利，變得清晰： *This knife needs sharpening.* 這把刀需要磨了。◇ *The outline of the trees sharpened as it grew lighter.* 隨着天色轉亮，樹的輪廓變得清晰了。 **2** [I, T] **~ (sth)** if a sense or feeling **sharpens** or sth **sharpens** it, it becomes stronger and/or clearer（使感覺或感情）加強，加重，變得更明顯： *The sea air sharpened our appetites.* 海上的空氣增進了我們的食慾。 **3** [T] **~ sth** to make a disagreement between people, or an issue on which people disagree, clearer and more likely to produce a result 使尖銳；使明朗： *There is a need to sharpen the focus of the discussion.* 有必要使討論的焦點更加集中。 **4** [I, T] to become or make sth better, more skilful, more effective, etc. than before （使）提高，改善 **SYN** improve： **~ (up)** *He needs to sharpen up before the Olympic trials.* 在奧運會選拔賽之前，他需要進一步磨礪自己。◇ **~ sth (up)** *She's doing a course to sharpen her business skills.* 她正進修，以提高自己的業務技巧。 **5** [I, T] **~ (sth)** if your voice **sharpens** or sth **sharpens** it, it becomes high and loud in an unpleasant way （使聲音）變得尖銳，變得刺耳

sharp·en·er /ˈʃɑːpnə(r); *NAmE* ˈʃɑːrp-/ *noun* (usually in compounds 通常構成複合詞) a tool or machine that makes things sharp 磨具；削具： *a pencil sharpener* 捲筆刀 ◇ *a knife sharpener* 磨刀石 ➲ VISUAL VOCAB page V69

ˌ**sharp-'eyed** *adj.* able to see very well and quick to notice things 眼尖的；目光敏銳的 **SYN** observant： *A sharp-eyed reader spotted the mistake in yesterday's paper.* 一個眼尖的讀者發現了昨天報紙上的錯誤。

sharp·ish /ˈʃɑːpɪʃ; *NAmE* ˈʃɑːrpɪʃ/ *adv.* (*BrE, informal*) quickly; in a short time 迅速；不久；馬上

sharp·ly 🔑 /ˈʃɑːpli; *NAmE* ˈʃɑːrpli/ *adv.*

1 🔑 in a critical, rough or severe way 尖刻地；嚴厲地；猛烈地： *The report was sharply critical of the police.* 報道猛烈地抨擊了警方。◇ *'Is there a problem?' he asked sharply.* "有問題嗎？" 他厲聲喝問。 **2** 🔑 suddenly and by a large amount 急劇地；突然大幅度地： *Profits fell sharply following the takeover.* 接管後，利潤突然大幅度降低。◇ *The road fell sharply to the sea.* 公路陡然下坡，通向大海。 **3** 🔑 in a way that clearly shows the differences between two things 鮮明地；明顯地： *Their experiences contrast sharply with those of other children.* 他們的經歷和其他孩子的經歷形成鮮明的對比。 **4** 🔑 quickly and suddenly or loudly 迅疾而突然地；急促而大聲地： *She moved sharply across the room to block his exit.* 她疾步衝到門口，擋住他的去路。◇ *He rapped sharply on the window.* 他猛敲窗戶。 **5** 🔑 used to emphasize that sth has a sharp point or edge （用以強調物體尖銳或鋒利）： *sharply pointed* 尖尖的

sharp·shoot·er /ˈʃɑːpʃuːtə(r); *NAmE* ˈʃɑːrp-/ *noun* a person who is skilled at shooting a gun 神槍手；神射手

shat *past tense, past part.* of SHIT

shat·ter /ˈʃætə(r)/ *verb* **1** [I, T] to suddenly break into small pieces; to make sth suddenly break into small pieces （使）破碎，碎裂： **~ (into sth)** *He dropped the vase and it shattered into pieces on the floor.* 他失手把花瓶掉到地板上摔碎了。◇ *the sound of shattering glass* 玻璃破碎的聲音 ◇ **~ sth (into sth)** *The explosion shattered all the windows in the building.* 大樓所有的玻璃都在爆炸中震碎了。 **2** [T, I] to destroy sth completely, especially sb's feelings, hopes or beliefs; to be destroyed in this way （使感情、希望或信念等）粉碎，破滅；被粉碎；被破壞： **~ sth (into sth)** *Anna's self-confidence had been completely shattered.* 安娜的自信心徹底崩潰了。◇ *Her experience of divorce shattered her illusions about love.* 她的離婚經歷使她對愛情的幻想破滅了。◇ **~ (into sth)** *My whole world shattered into a million pieces.* 我的整個世界全塌了。 **3** [T] **~ sb** to make sb feel extremely shocked and upset 使極為驚愕難過；給予極大打擊： *The unexpected death of their son shattered them.* 兒子的意外死亡給他們帶來沉重的打擊。

shat·tered /ˈʃætəd; *NAmE* -tərd/ *adj.* **1** very shocked and upset 非常驚愕難過的；遭受極大打擊的： *The experience left her feeling absolutely shattered.* 她在這次經歷之後，感到徹底垮了。 **2** (*BrE, informal*) very tired 筋疲力盡的 **SYN** exhausted

shat·ter·ing /ˈʃætərɪŋ/ *adj.* **1** very shocking and upsetting 令人非常驚愕難過的；給人以極大打擊的： *a shattering experience* 令人痛苦不堪的經歷 ◇ *The news of his death came as a shattering blow.* 他的死訊讓人驚愕不已。 **2** very loud 非常響亮的 **SYN** deafening

▸ **shat·ter·ing·ly** *adv.*

'shatter-proof *adj.* designed not to SHATTER 防碎的；不碎的： *shatter-proof glass* 防碎玻璃

shauri /ˈʃaʊriː/ *noun* (*EAfrE*) something that needs to be discussed or decided; something that causes a problem 需要討論（或決定）的事；麻煩事；問題

shave 🔑 /ʃeɪv/ *verb, noun*

■ *verb* **1** 🔑 [I, T] to cut hair from the skin, especially the face, using a RAZOR 剃（鬚髮）；（尤指）刮臉： *Mike cut himself shaving.* 邁克刮鬍子時把臉劃破了。◇ **~ sb/sth/yourself** *The nurse washed and shaved him.* 護士給他洗了臉，刮了鬍子。◇ *a shaved head* 剃光的頭 ➲ VISUAL VOCAB page V60 ➲ see also SHAVEN **2** [T] **~ sth** to cut a small amount off a price, etc. （少量地）削減，調低，降價： *The firm had shaved profit margins.* 公司調低了利潤率。

PHR V ˌ**shave sth↔'off | ˌshave sth 'off sth** **1** to remove a beard or MOUSTACHE by shaving 剃掉，刮去（鬍鬚）： *Charles decided to shave off his beard.* 查爾斯決定刮掉鬍

子。 **2** to cut very thin pieces from the surface of wood, etc. 削掉；刨去；切掉： *I had to shave a few millimetres off the door to make it shut.* 我把門刨去了幾毫米才能關上。 **3** to reduce a number by a very small amount（微量地）減少，縮小： *He shaved a tenth of a second off the world record.* 他把世界紀錄縮短了十分之一秒。

■ ***noun*** an act of shaving 修面；刮臉；剃鬚： *I need a shave.* 我需要刮鬍子了。◇ *to have a shave* 刮臉 **IDM** see CLOSE² *adj.*

shaven /ˈʃeɪvn/ *adj.* with all the hair shaved off 剃光的；刮乾淨的： *a shaven head* 剃光的頭 ➲ see also CLEAN-SHAVEN ➲ compare UNSHAVEN ➲ **VISUAL VOCAB** page V60

shaver /ˈʃeɪvə(r)/ (also **eˌlectric ˈrazor**) *noun* an electric tool for shaving 電動剃鬚刀 ➲ **VISUAL VOCAB** page V24 ➲ compare RAZOR

ˈshaving cream, **ˈshaving foam** *noun* [U] special cream or FOAM for spreading over the face with a **shaving brush** before shaving 剃鬚膏；修面霜

shav·ings /ˈʃeɪvɪŋz/ *noun* [pl.] thin pieces cut from a piece of wood, etc. using a sharp tool, especially a PLANE（刨等削下的）削片；刨花

Sha·vu·oth /ʃəˈvuːəs; ʃɑːvʊˈɒt; *NAmE* ʃəˈvuːoʊt; -oʊθ/ (also **ˌFeast of ˈWeeks**, **Pente·cost**) *noun* [U] a Jewish festival that takes place 50 days after the second day of Passover 七七節，五旬節（猶太人節日，在逾越節次日之後第 50 天）

shawl /ʃɔːl/ *noun* a large piece of cloth worn by a woman around the shoulders or head, or wrapped around a baby（女用）披巾，披肩；襁褓

Shaw·nee /ˈʃɔːniː/ *noun* (*pl.* **Shaw·nee** or **Shaw·nees**) a member of a Native American people, many of whom now live in the US state of Oklahoma 肖尼人（美洲土著，很多現居於美國俄克拉何馬州）

she 🔑 /ʃi; *strong form* ʃiː/ *pron., noun*

■ ***pron.*** 🔑 (used as the subject of a verb 用作動詞的主語) a female person or animal that has already been mentioned or is easily identified 她；（指雌性動物）它： *'What does your sister do?' 'She's a dentist.'* "你姐姐做什麼工作？" "她是牙科醫生。" ◇ *Doesn't she* (= the woman we are looking at) *look like Sue?* 她看上去不是很像蘇嗎？ ➲ compare HER *pron.* ➲ note at GENDER

■ ***noun*** **1** [sing.] (*informal*) a female 女性；雌性： *What a sweet little dog. Is it a he or a she?* 多可愛的小狗啊！是公的，還是母的？ **2 she-** (in compound nouns 構成複合名詞) a female animal 雌性動物： *a she-wolf* 母狼

s/he *pron.* used in writing by some people when the subject of the verb could be either female (she) or male (he) 他／她（主語既可為女性又可為男性時可用於書面）： *If a student does not attend all the classes, s/he will not be allowed to take the exam.* 如果學生缺課，他／她就不能參加考試。

shea butter /ˈʃiː bʌtə(r); *BrE* also ˈʃiːə; *NAmE* also ˈʃeɪ/ *noun* [U] a type of fat obtained from the nuts of the **shea tree**, used in foods and COSMETICS 乳木果油（從乳果木的果實中提取的油脂，用於食品和化妝品）

sheaf /ʃiːf/ *noun* (*pl.* **sheaves** /ʃiːvz/) **1** a number of pieces of paper tied or held together 一疊，一沓，一紮（紙） **2** a bunch of WHEAT tied together after being cut（收割的）小麥捆

shear /ʃɪə(r); *NAmE* ʃɪr/ *verb* (**sheared**, **shorn** /ʃɔːn; *NAmE* ʃɔːrn/ or **sheared**) **1** [T] **~ sth** to cut the wool off a sheep 給（羊）剪（羊毛）： *It was time for the sheep to be shorn.* 是剪羊毛的時節了。◇ *sheep shearing* 剪羊毛 **2** [T] **~ sth** (*formal*) to cut off sb's hair 剪（頭髮）： *shorn hair* 剪得很短的頭髮 **3** [I, T] **~ (sth) (off)** (*technical* 術語) (especially of metal 尤指金屬) to break under pressure; to cut through sth and make it break 切斷；剪切；斷： *The bolts holding the wheel in place sheared off.* 固定這個輪子的幾個螺栓斷了。

PHR V **be ˈshorn of sth** (*literary*) to have sth important taken away from you 被剝奪；被褫奪： *Shorn of his power, the deposed king went into exile.* 權力被褫奪後，遭廢黜的國王流亡國外。

shears /ʃɪəz; *NAmE* ʃɪrz/ *noun* [pl.] a garden tool like a very large pair of scissors, used for cutting bushes and HEDGES 大剪刀（用來修剪灌木、樹籬等）： *a pair of garden shears* 一把園藝剪

shear·water /ˈʃɪəwɔːtə(r); *NAmE* ˈʃɪr-/ *noun* a bird with long wings that often flies low over the sea 剪水鸌，水薙鳥（常沿海浪波谷滑翔）

sheath /ʃiːθ/ *noun* (*pl.* **sheaths** /ʃiːðz/) **1** a cover that fits closely over the blade of a knife or other sharp weapon or tool（刀、劍等的）鞘；（工具的）套 ➲ picture at SWORD **2** any covering that fits closely over sth for protection 護套；護層；護皮： *the sheath around an electric cable* 電線護皮 **3** (*BrE*) = CONDOM (1) **4** a woman's dress that fits the body closely 緊身連衣裙

sheathe /ʃiːð/ *verb* **1 ~ sth** (*literary*) to put a knife or SWORD into a sheath 把（刀或劍）插入鞘中 **2** [usually passive] **~ sth (in/with sth)** to cover sth in a material, especially in order to protect it 給某物加護套（或護層、護皮）

ˈsheath knife *noun* a short knife with a SHEATH (= cover) 帶鞘的短刀；鞘刀

sheaves *pl.* of SHEAF

she·bang /ʃɪˈbæŋ/ *noun*

IDM **the whole sheˈbang** (*informal*) the whole thing; everything 整個事情；這一切

she·been /ʃɪˈbiːn/ *noun* (*informal*) (especially in Ireland, Scotland and South Africa) a place where alcoholic drinks are sold, usually illegally（尤指愛爾蘭、蘇格蘭和南非的）無執照酒館，非法售酒處

shed /ʃed/ *noun, verb*

■ ***noun*** (often in compounds 常構成複合詞) **1** a small simple building, usually built of wood or metal, used for keeping things in 簡易房，棚（用於貯藏物品）： *a bicycle shed* 自行車棚 ◇ (*BrE*) *a garden shed* 園藝工具棚 ➲ **VISUAL VOCAB** page V19 **2** (*BrE*) a large industrial building, used for working in or keeping equipment（工業上用於生產或存放設備的）廠房，工棚，庫房： *an engine shed* 發動機庫 **3** (*AustralE, NZE*) a building with open sides where the wool is cut off sheep (= they are SHEARED) or where cows are MILKED 剪羊毛棚；擠奶棚 ➲ see also COWSHED, POTTING SHED, WOODSHED

■ ***verb*** (**shed·ding**, **shed**, **shed**)

▸ **GET RID OF** 去除 **1 ~ sth** (often used in newspapers 常用於報章) to get rid of sth that is no longer wanted 去除；擺脫： *The factory is shedding a large number of jobs.* 這家工廠正大批裁員。◇ *a quick way to shed unwanted pounds* (= extra weight or fat on your body) 快速減肥的方法 ◇ *Museums have been trying hard to shed their stuffy image.* 博物館一直努力改變自己沉悶的形象。

▸ **DROP** 使落下 **2 ~ sth** (*formal*) to let sth fall; to drop sth 使落下；使掉下： *Luke shed his clothes onto the floor.* 盧克把衣服脫在地板上。◇ *A duck's feathers shed water immediately.* 鴨子的羽毛不沾水。 **3 ~ sth** (*BrE*) (of a vehicle 車輛) to lose or drop what it is carrying 掉落（貨物）：*The traffic jam was caused by a lorry **shedding its load**.* 交通堵塞是因為一輛卡車掉下了貨物。

▸ **SKIN/LEAVES** 皮；葉 **4 ~ sth** if an animal **sheds** its skin, or a plant **sheds** leaves, it loses them naturally 蛻；落

▸ **LIGHT** 光 **5 ~ sth (on/over sb/sth)** to send light over sth; to let light fall somewhere 散發出光；把光照到（或灑在）…上： *The candles shed a soft glow on her face.* 蠟燭在她的臉上映着一層柔光。

▸ **TEARS** 眼淚 **6 ~ tears** (*formal* or *literary*) to cry 哭；流淚： *She shed no tears when she heard he was dead.* 她聽到他的死訊時沒流一滴眼淚。

▸ **BLOOD** 血 **7 ~ blood** (*formal*) to kill or injure people, especially in a war（尤指在戰爭中）造成傷亡；使流血 ➲ see also BLOODSHED **IDM** see LIGHT *n.*

she'd /ʃiːd/ *short form* **1** she had **2** she would

ˈshe-devil *noun* a very cruel woman 狠毒的女人；女惡魔

shed·load /ˈʃedləʊd; *NAmE* -loʊd/ *noun* **~ (of sth)** (*BrE, informal*) a large amount of sth, especially money 大量（金錢等）；許多： *The project cost a shedload of money.* 這個項目花費了一大筆錢。◇ *This should save you shedloads.* 這應該可以幫你省下許多錢。

S

sheen /ʃiːn/ *noun* [sing., U] a soft smooth shiny quality 光澤；光輝；光彩 SYN **shine**：*hair with a healthy sheen* 閃着健康光澤的頭髮

sheep /ʃiːp/ *noun* (*pl.* **sheep**) an animal with a thick coat, kept on farms for its meat (called MUTTON or LAMB) or its wool 羊；綿羊：*a flock of sheep* 一群羊 ◇ *Sheep were grazing in the fields.* 羊在野地裏吃草。➲ compare EWE, LAMB, RAM *n.* (1) ➲ see also BLACK SHEEP
IDM **like 'sheep** (*disapproving*) if people behave **like sheep**, they all do what the others are doing, without thinking for themselves 盲從（不獨立思考） **sort out/separate the ˌsheep from the 'goats** to distinguish people who are good at sth, intelligent, etc. from those who are not 區分能手與常人；分清智者和庸人 ➲ more at COUNT *v.*, WELL *adv.*, WOLF *n.*

'sheep dip *noun* [U, C] a liquid which is used to kill insects, etc. in a sheep's coat; the container in which sheep are put to treat them with this 浴羊藥液（用以浸殺羊毛中的寄生蟲等）；（盛有藥液的）浴羊槽

sheep·dog /ˈʃiːpdɒɡ; *NAmE* -dɔːɡ; -dɑːɡ/ *noun* **1** a dog that is trained to help control sheep on a farm 牧羊犬 **2** (*BrE*) a dog of a breed that is often used for controlling sheep, especially a COLLIE 牧羊犬；柯利牧羊犬 ➲ see also OLD ENGLISH SHEEPDOG

sheep·fold /ˈʃiːpfəʊld; *NAmE* -foʊld/ *noun* an area in a field surrounded by a fence or wall where sheep are kept for safety 羊圈；羊欄

sheep·herd·er /ˈʃiːphɜːdə(r); *NAmE* -hɜːrd-/ *noun* (*NAmE*) = SHEPHERD

sheep·ish /ˈʃiːpɪʃ/ *adj.* looking or feeling embarrassed because you have done sth silly or wrong 窘迫的；難為情的；不好意思的 SYN **shamefaced**：*Mary gave her a sheepish grin.* 瑪麗難為情地衝她咧嘴一笑。▸ **sheep·ish·ly** *adv.*

sheep·skin /ˈʃiːpskɪn/ *noun* [U, C] the skin of a sheep with the wool still on it 帶毛綿羊皮：*a sheepskin coat/rug* 羊皮襖／毯

sheer /ʃɪə(r); *NAmE* ʃɪr/ *adj.*, *adv.*, *verb*
■ *adj.* **1** [only before noun] used to emphasize the size, degree or amount of sth（用來強調事物的大小、程度或數量）：*The area is under threat from the sheer number of tourists using it.* 這一地區由於遊客人數太多而面臨威脅。◇ *We were impressed by the sheer size of the cathedral.* 大教堂的宏大規模給我們留下了深刻的印象。**2** [only before noun] complete and not mixed with anything else 完全的；純粹的；十足的 SYN **utter**：*The concert was sheer delight.* 這場音樂會是一次十足的享受。◇ *I only agreed out of sheer desperation.* 我一時情急才同意的。**3** very steep 陡峭的：*sheer cliffs/slopes* 懸崖峭壁；陡坡 ◇ *Outside there was a sheer drop down to the sea below.* 外面是一道陡坡，直插大海。**4** (of cloth, etc. 織物等) thin, light and almost transparent 又薄又輕幾乎透明的：*sheer nylon* 透明尼龍
■ *adv.* straight up or down 垂直地；陡峭地：*The cliffs rise sheer from the beach.* 懸崖從海灘上拔地而起。◇ *The ground dropped sheer away at our feet.* 在我們腳下，地勢陡降。
■ *verb*
PHR V **ˌsheer a'way/'off (from sth)** to change direction suddenly, especially in order to avoid hitting sth 急轉，急拐（避開某物）：(*figurative*) *Her mind sheered away from images she did not wish to dwell on.* 她有意不去想那些她不願多想的事情。

sheet /ʃiːt/ *noun*
▸ ON BED 牀上 **1** a large piece of thin cloth used on a bed to lie on or lie under 牀單；被單：*Have you **changed the sheets*** (= put clean sheets on the bed)? 被單你換了嗎？◇ *He slid between the sheets and closed his eyes.* 他鑽進被子裏，閉上了眼睛。➲ VISUAL VOCAB page V23 ➲ see also DUST SHEET
▸ OF PAPER 紙 **2** a piece of paper for writing or printing on, etc. usually in a standard size 一張（通常指標準尺寸的紙）：*a **clean/blank sheet of paper*** (= with no writing on it) 一張白紙 ◇ *Pick up one of our free information sheets at reception.* 請在接待處拿一份我們的免費資料。
▸ FLAT THIN PIECE 片 **3** a flat thin piece of any material, normally square or RECTANGULAR 薄片，薄板（多指正方形或長方形的）：*a **sheet of glass/steel*** 一塊玻璃；一張鋼板 ◇ ***sheet metal*** (= metal that has been made into thin sheets) 金屬板 ◇ *Place the dough on a **baking sheet*** (= for cooking sth in an oven). 把麪糰放在烤板上。
▸ WIDE FLAT AREA 大片 **4** a wide flat area of sth, covering the surface of sth else 一大片（覆蓋物）：*The road was covered with a sheet of ice.* 路面結了一層冰。
▸ OF FIRE/WATER 火；水 **5** a large moving mass of fire or water 一大片，一大堆，一大攤（移動的火或水）：*a sheet of flame* 一片火海 ◇ *The rain was coming down **in sheets*** (= very heavily). 大雨傾盆而下。
▸ ON SAIL 帆上 **6** (*technical* 術語) a rope or chain fastened to the lower corner of a sail to hold it and to control the angle of the sail 帆腳索；拉帆繩 HELP There are other compounds ending **sheet**. You will find them at their place in the alphabet. 其他以 sheet 結尾的複合詞，可在各字母中的適當位置查到。IDM see CLEAN *adj.*

'sheet anchor *noun* a person or thing that you can depend on in a difficult situation（困難時的）靠山，指望，對策

sheet·ing /ˈʃiːtɪŋ/ *noun* [U] **1** metal, plastic, etc. made into flat thin pieces 薄片；壓片；薄膜：***metal/plastic/polythene sheeting*** 金屬薄片；塑料／聚乙烯薄膜 **2** cloth used for making sheets for beds 牀單布；被單布

ˌsheet 'lightning *noun* [U] LIGHTNING that appears as a broad area of light in the sky 片狀閃電 ➲ compare FORKED LIGHTNING

'sheet music *noun* [U] printed music as opposed to recorded music; printed music published on separate sheets of paper that are not fastened together to form a book 活頁樂譜（與錄音音樂相對）

sheikh /ʃeɪk; ʃiːk/ (also **shaikh** /ʃeɪk/) *noun* **1** an Arab prince or leader; the head of an Arab family, village, etc. 謝赫（阿拉伯的親王、酋長、首領、村長等）**2** a leader in a Muslim community or organization（伊斯蘭教）教長

sheikh·dom /ˈʃeɪkdəm; ˈʃiːk-/ *noun* an area of land ruled by a sheikh（阿拉伯）酋長統轄的領土，酋長國

sheila /ˈʃiːlə/ *noun* (*AustralE, NZE, slang*) a girl or young woman 小妞；少女；年輕女子

shekel /ˈʃekl/ *noun* **1** the unit of money in Israel 謝克爾（以色列貨幣單位） **2** an ancient silver coin used by the Jews 謝克爾（古代猶太人用的銀幣）

shel·duck /ˈʃeldʌk/ *noun* (*pl.* **shel·duck** or **shelducks**) a type of wild DUCK that lives on or near the coast 翹鼻麻鴨；花鳧

shelf /ʃelf/ *noun* (*pl.* **shelves** /ʃelvz/) **1** a flat board, made of wood, metal, glass, etc., fixed to the wall or forming part of a cupboard/closet, BOOKCASE, etc., for things to be placed on（固定在牆上的或櫥櫃、書架等的）架子，擱板：*I helped him put up some shelves in his bedroom.* 我幫他在卧室裏裝了幾個擱架。◇ *The book I wanted was on the top shelf.* 我想要的那本書在書架的最上層。◇ ***supermarket/library shelves*** 超市的貨架；圖書館的書架 ◇ *empty shelves* 空擱板 ➲ COLLOCATIONS at DECORATE, SHOPPING ➲ VISUAL VOCAB page V25 **2** (*geology* 地) a thing shaped like a shelf, especially a piece of rock sticking out from a CLIFF or from the edge of a mass of land under the sea（懸崖上或海底）突出的岩石；陸架；陸棚：*the continental shelf* 大陸架 ➲ see also SHELVE
IDM **on the 'shelf** (*informal*) **1** not wanted by anyone; not used（無用而）閒置的；擱置的 **2** (*old-fashioned*) (especially of women 尤指婦女) considered to be too old to get married 年齡大得嫁不出去的 **off the 'shelf** that can be bought immediately and does not have to be specially designed or ordered 現成有售的；不用訂製的：*I bought this package off the shelf.* 我買的這一盒是現貨。◇ *off-the-shelf software packages* 現成軟件包 ➲ compare OFF THE PEG at PEG *n.*

S

'shelf life *noun* [usually sing.] the length of time that food, etc. can be kept before it is too old to be sold（食品等的）貨架期，保存期

'shelf-stacker *noun* a person whose job is to fill shelves with goods to be sold, especially in a supermarket（尤指超市的）貨物上架員，上貨員

shell 🔑 /ʃel/ *noun, verb*

■ **noun** **1** 🔑 [C, U] the hard outer part of eggs, nuts, some seeds and some animals（蛋、堅果、某些種子和某些動物的）殼：*We collected shells on the beach.* 我們在海灘拾貝殼。◇ *snail shells* 蝸牛殼 ◇ *walnut shells* 核桃殼 ◇ *earrings made out of coconut shell* 用椰子殼做的耳墜 ➲ picture at SHELLFISH ➲ **VISUAL VOCAB** pages V13, V30, V32 ➲ see also EGGSHELL, NUTSHELL, SEASHELL, TORTOISESHELL **2** [C] any object that looks like the shell of a SNAIL or sea creature 殼狀物：*pasta shells* 貝殼形意大利麪 **3** [C] a metal case filled with EXPLOSIVE, to be fired from a large gun 炮彈 **4** (*NAmE*) = CARTRIDGE (1) **5** [C] the walls or outer structure of sth, for example, an empty building or ship after a fire or a bomb attack（房屋或船舶等的）骨架，框架，殼體：*The house was now a shell gutted by flames.* 房子燒得只剩個空骨架了。◇ (*figurative*) *My life has been an empty shell since he died.* 他死後，我的生活就成了一個徒有其表的空殼子。**6** [C] any structure that forms a hard outer frame（任何物體的）外殼，殼體：*the body shell of a car* 車身外殼 **7** [sing.] the outer layer of sb's personality; how they seem to be or feel（人的）表面性格，表面人格，表面感情，外表：*She had developed a shell of indifference.* 她養成一副冷漠的外表。

IDM **come out of your 'shell** to become less shy and more confident when talking to other people（和人交談時）放大膽子，不縮手縮腳 **to go, retreat, etc. into your 'shell** to become shyer and avoid talking to other people 變得羞怯（或內向、孤僻）

■ **verb** **1** [T, I] **~ (sth)** to fire shells at sth 炮擊：*They shelled the city all night.* 他們整夜炮轟那座城市。◇ *Just as they were leaving, the rebels started shelling.* 他們正要撤離，叛軍開始了炮擊。**2** [T] **~ sth** to remove the shell or covering from nuts, PEAS, etc. 給…去殼

PHR V **,shell 'out (for sth)** | **,shell sth↔'out (for sth)** (*informal*) to pay a lot of money for sth 付（一大筆錢）SYN **fork out**：*The band shelled out $100 000 for a mobile recording studio.* 樂隊花了 10 萬元購置一間移動錄音室。

she'll /ʃiːl/ *short form* she will

shel·lac /ʃəˈlæk; ˈʃelæk/ *noun, verb*

■ **noun** [U] a natural substance used in making varnish to protect surfaces and make them hard 蟲膠；紫（膠蟲）膠

■ **verb** (-ck-) **1 ~ sth** to cover sth with shellac 以蟲膠清漆覆蓋；用蟲膠清漆塗刷 **2** [usually passive] **~ sb** (*NAmE, informal*) to defeat sb very easily 輕易擊敗：*The Republicans got shellacked in the elections.* 共和黨在選舉中一敗塗地。

shell·fire /ˈʃelfaɪə(r)/ *noun* [U] attacks or explosions caused by SHELLS being fired from large guns 炮火；炮擊

shellfish 水生有殼動物

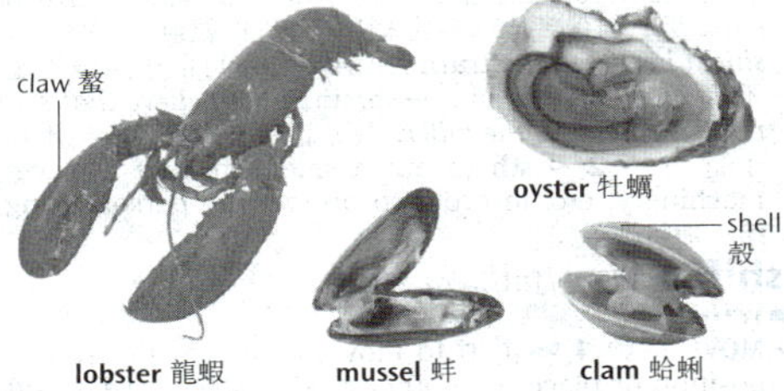

shell·fish /ˈʃelfɪʃ/ *noun* (*pl.* **shell·fish**) a creature with a shell, that lives in water, especially one of the types that can be eaten. OYSTERS and CRABS are both shellfish.（尤指可以吃的）水生有殼動物 ➲ compare CRUSTACEAN, MOLLUSC

'shell game *noun* (*NAmE*) **1** the **'shell game** a game in which three cups are moved around, and players must guess which is the one with a small object underneath 果殼猜測遊戲（移動三個杯子，參加者須猜測哪個杯子扣着小物體）**2** an act by an organization or a politician that tricks people in a clever way（機構或政客的）騙局，騙術

shell·ing /ˈʃelɪŋ/ *noun* [U] the firing of SHELLS from large guns 炮擊：*We suffered weeks of heavy shelling.* 我們遭受了幾星期的密集炮擊。

'shell shock *noun* [U] a mental illness that can affect soldiers who have been in battle for a long time 彈震症，戰鬥疲勞症（長時期作戰引起的精神疾患）

'shell-shocked *adj.* **1** shocked, confused or anxious because of a difficult situation, and unable to think or act normally（因困境而）嚇昏了頭的，糊塗得不知所措的，焦慮得無法應對的 **2** suffering from shell shock 患彈震症的

'shell suit *noun* (*BrE*) a loose pair of trousers/pants and matching jacket worn as informal clothes. Shell suits are made of a light, slightly shiny, material and are often brightly coloured. 休閒裝；休閒服 ➲ compare TRACKSUIT

shel·ter 🔑 /ˈʃeltə(r)/ *noun, verb*

■ **noun** **1** 🔑 [U] the fact of having a place to live or stay, considered as a basic human need 居所；住處：*Human beings need food, clothing and shelter.* 人類有衣、食、住的需求。**2** 🔑 [U] **~ (from sth)** protection from rain, danger or attack 遮蔽，庇護，避難（避雨、躲避危險或攻擊）：*to* ***take shelter*** *from the storm* 躲避暴風雨 ◇ *The fox was running for the shelter of the trees.* 狐狸朝樹叢跑，想要躲藏起來。◇ *People were desperately seeking shelter from the gunfire.* 人們拚命地找地方躲避炮火。**3** 🔑 [C] (often in compounds 常構成複合詞) a structure built to give protection, especially from the weather or from attack（尤指用以躲避風雨或攻擊的）遮蔽物，庇護處，避難處：*They built a rough shelter from old pieces of wood.* 他們用舊木條搭了一個簡陋的窩棚。◇ *an air-raid shelter* 防空洞 ➲ see also BUS SHELTER **4** [C] a building, usually owned by a charity, that provides a place to stay for people without a home, or protection for people or animals who have been badly treated（無家可歸者或受虐待者的）收容所，庇護所：*a night shelter for the homeless* 無家可歸者夜間收容所 ◇ *an animal shelter* 動物收容處 ➲ see also HOSTEL

■ **verb** **1** 🔑 [T] to give sb/sth a place where they are protected from the weather or from danger; to protect sb/sth 保護；掩蔽：**~ sb/sth from sb/sth** *Trees shelter the house from the wind.* 樹給房子擋住了風。◇ **~ sb/sth** *helping the poor and sheltering the homeless* 幫助貧窮者，庇護無家可歸者 ◇ *Perhaps I sheltered my daughter too much* (= protected her too much from unpleasant or difficult experiences). 也許我對女兒保護過度了。**2** 🔑 [I] **~ (from sth)** to stay in a place that protects you from the weather or from danger 躲避（風雨或危險）：*We sheltered from the rain in a doorway.* 我們在一處門廊裏避雨。

shel·tered /ˈʃeltəd; *NAmE* -tərd/ *adj.* **1** (of a place 地方) protected from bad weather 有遮蔽物（不受惡劣天氣侵襲）的：*a sheltered beach* 有天然屏障的海灘 **2** (sometimes *disapproving*) protected from the more unpleasant aspects or difficulties of life 受庇護的；受到保護的：*She had a very sheltered childhood.* 她有過一個備受呵護的童年。◇ *They both lead very sheltered lives.* 他們兩人都過着呵護備至的生活。**3** [only before noun] (*BrE*) (of houses, flats/apartments, etc. 房舍、公寓等) designed for people, especially old people, who can still live fairly independent lives, but with staff available to help them if necessary 為需要者（尤指老年人）提供照顧的：***sheltered accommodation/housing*** 福利院的住宿 ◇ *a* ***sheltered workshop*** *for the blind* 盲人福利工場

shelve /ʃelv/ *verb* **1** [T] **~ sth** to decide not to continue with a plan, either for a short time or permanently

擱置，停止（計劃）**SYN put on ice**：*The government has shelved the idea until at least next year.* 政府決定把這個想法先放一放，至少推遲到明年再說。**2** [T] **~ sth** to put books, etc. on a shelf 把…放在架子（或擱板）上 **3** [I] **(+ adv./prep.)** (of land 陸地) to slope downwards 傾斜；成斜坡：*The beach shelved gently down to the water.* 海灘緩緩地向下沒入水中。

shelves *pl.* of SHELF

shelv·ing /ˈʃelvɪŋ/ *noun* [U] shelves; material for making shelves 架子；擱板；做架子的材料：*wooden shelving* 木擱板

ˈshe-male *noun* (*informal*) a TRANSSEXUAL, especially one who works as a PROSTITUTE（尤指做妓女的）變性女子

she·nani·gans /ʃɪˈnænɪɡənz/ *noun* [pl.] (*informal*) secret or dishonest activities that people find interesting or amusing 詭計；惡作劇；耍手腕；鬼把戲

Sheng /ʃeŋ/ *noun* [U] (in Kenya) a simple form of language that includes words from English, Kiswahili and other African languages, used especially between young people in cities 盛語（肯尼亞的一種簡單的語言，包括英語、斯瓦希里語等非洲語言的詞彙，尤在城市青年之間使用）

shep·herd /ˈʃepəd; *NAmE* -ərd/ *noun, verb*

■ ***noun*** (*NAmE* also **sheep·herd·er**) a person whose job is to take care of sheep 牧羊人；羊倌

■ ***verb*** **~ sb + adv./prep.** to guide sb or a group of people somewhere, making sure they go where you want them to go 帶領；引；護送

shep·herd·ess /ˌʃepəˈdes; ˈʃepədəs; *NAmE* ˌʃepərˈdes; ˈʃepərdəs/ *noun* (*old-fashioned*) a woman who takes care of sheep 女牧羊人；牧羊女

ˌshepherd's ˈpie (also **ˌcottage ˈpie**) *noun* [C, U] (*especially BrE*) a dish of MINCED (= finely chopped) meat covered with a layer of MASHED potato 肉餡土豆泥餅；肉餡薯餅

sher·bet /ˈʃɜːbət; *NAmE* ˈʃɜːrbət/ *noun* **1** [U] (*BrE*) a powder that tastes of fruit and FIZZES when you put it in your mouth, eaten as a sweet/candy 果味汽水粉糖 **2** [C, U] (*NAmE*, becoming *old-fashioned*) = SORBET

sherd /ʃɜːd; *NAmE* ʃɜːrd/ *noun* = SHARD

sher·iff /ˈʃerɪf/ *noun* **1** (in the US) an elected officer responsible for keeping law and order in a county or town 縣治安官，城鎮治安官（美國民選地方官員）**2** (often **High Sheriff**) (in England and Wales) an officer representing the king or queen in counties, and some cities, who performs some legal duties and attends ceremonies 郡督（英格蘭和威爾士官員，為英王在各郡和部份城市的代表）**3** (in Scotland) a judge（蘇格蘭）法官 **4** (in Canada) an official who works in a court preparing court cases（加拿大法院準備訴訟案件的）執行員

S

ˈsheriff court *noun* a lower court in Scotland（蘇格蘭的）郡法院

Sher·lock /ˈʃɜːlɒk; *NAmE* ˈʃɜːrlɑːk/ (also **Sherlock Holmes** /həʊmz; *NAmE* hoʊmz/) *noun* (*informal*, sometimes *ironic*) a person who tries to find an explanation for a crime or sth mysterious or who shows that they understand sth quickly, especially sth that is not obvious（自命）福爾摩斯；（自命）有偵探頭腦的人：*Oh, well done, Sherlock. Did you figure that out all by yourself?* 喔，幹得好，大偵探。全是你自己推斷出來的嗎？ **ORIGIN** From Sherlock Holmes, a very clever detective in stories by Arthur Conan Doyle, published in the late 19th and early 20th centuries. 源自阿瑟·柯南·道爾於 19 世紀末 20 世紀初發表的一系列小說中一位十分機智的偵探夏洛克·福爾摩斯。

Sherpa /ˈʃɜːpə; *NAmE* ˈʃɜːrpə/ *noun* a member of a Himalayan people, who often guide people in the mountains, sometimes carrying their bags, etc. 夏爾巴人（居住在喜馬拉雅山脈的一個部族，常作山中嚮導或搬運工等）

sherry /ˈʃeri/ *noun* (*pl.* **-ies**) **1** [U, C] a strong yellow or brown wine, originally from southern Spain. It is often drunk before meals. 雪利酒（烈性葡萄酒，原產自西班牙南部）：***sweet/dry sherry*** 甜／無甜味的雪利酒 ◊ ***cream sherry*** (= a type of very sweet sherry) 濃甜雪利酒 ◊ *fine quality sherries* 優質雪利酒 ◊ ***a sherry glass*** (= a type of small narrow wine glass) 雪利酒杯（一種細小玻璃酒杯）**2** [C] a glass of sherry 一杯雪利酒：*I'll have a sherry.* 我要一杯雪利酒。

sher·wani /ʃɜːˈwɑːni; *NAmE* ʃɜːrˈw-/ *noun* a knee-length coat with buttons up to the neck, sometimes worn by men from S Asia（南亞男裝）高領及膝外套

she's *short form* **1** /ʃiːz; ʃiz/ she is **2** /ʃiːz/ she has

Shetland pony /ˌʃetlənd ˈpəʊni; *NAmE* ˈpoʊni/ *noun* a very small, strong horse with a rough coat 設得蘭矮種馬

shh = SH

Shia (also **Shi'a**) /ˈʃɪə/ *noun* (*pl.* **Shia** or **Shias**) **1** [U] one of the two main branches of the Islamic religion 什葉派（伊斯蘭教的兩大派別之一）➲ compare SUNNI (1) **2** [C] (also **Shi·ite**, **Shi'ite**) a member of the Shia branch of Islam 什葉派教徒

shi·atsu /ʃiˈætsuː/ *noun* [U] (from *Japanese*) = ACUPRESSURE

shib·bo·leth /ˈʃɪbəleθ/ *noun* (*formal*) **1** an old idea, principle or phrase that is no longer accepted by many people as important or appropriate to modern life 過時的觀點；陳舊的原則；陳詞濫調 **2** a custom, word, etc. that distinguishes one group of people from another 某群體特有的習慣（或用語等）**ORIGIN** From a Hebrew word meaning 'ear of corn'. In the Bible story, Jephthah, the leader of the Gileadites, was able to use it as a test to tell which were his own men, because others found the 'sh' sound difficult to pronounce. 源自希伯來語，意為"穀穗"。據《聖經》記載，基列人首領耶弗他能用這一詞語來分辨誰是自己人，因為異族人難以發準 sh 音。

shied *past tense, past part.* of SHY

shield /ʃiːld/ *noun, verb*

■ ***noun*** **1** a large piece of metal or leather carried by soldiers in the past to protect the body when fighting 盾（牌）**2** = RIOT SHIELD **3** a person or thing used to protect sb/sth, especially by forming a barrier 保護人；保護物；掩護物；屏障：*The gunman used the hostages as a* ***human shield***. 持槍歹徒用人質作人體盾牌。◊ *Water is not an effective shield against the sun's more harmful rays.* 水不能有效阻擋太陽中更有害的射線。◊ *She hid her true feelings behind a shield of cold indifference.* 她把自己的真實感情掩藏在一副冷漠的外表後面。**4** a plate or screen that protects a machine or the person using it from damage or injury（保護機器和操作者的）護罩，防護屏，擋板 **5** an object in the shape of a shield, given as a prize in a sports competition, etc. 盾形獎牌 ➲ picture at MEDAL **6** a drawing or model of a shield showing a COAT OF ARMS 盾形紋徽；盾形徽章 **7** (*NAmE*) a police officer's BADGE（警察的）盾形徽章

■ ***verb*** **1** to protect sb/sth from danger, harm or sth unpleasant 保護某人或某物（免遭危險、傷害或不快）：**~ sth against sth** *I shielded my eyes against the glare.* 我擋住眼睛以避開強光。◊ **~ sb/sth from sb/sth** *The ozone layer shields the earth from the sun's ultraviolet rays.* 臭氧層保護地球不受太陽紫外線的輻射。◊ *You can't shield her from the truth forever.* 你不可能永遠瞞着她，不讓她知道事實真相。◊ **~ sb/sth** *Police believe that somebody is shielding the killer.* 警方認為有人把殺人兇手窩藏了起來。**2 ~ sth** to put a shield around a piece of machinery, etc. in order to protect the person using it 給…加防護罩

shift 🔑 **AW** /ʃɪft/ *verb, noun*

■ ***verb***

▸ **MOVE** 移動 **1** 🔑 [I, T] to move, or move sth, from one position or place to another 轉移；挪動：*Lydia shifted uncomfortably in her chair.* 莉迪亞在椅子上不安地動來動去。◊ **~ (from …) (to …)** *The action of the novel shifts from Paris to London.* 小說情節從巴黎移到了倫敦。◊ **~ sth** *Could you help me shift some furniture?* 你能幫我挪幾件傢具嗎？◊ **~ sth (from …) (to …)** *He shifted his* *gaze from the child to her.* 他把目光從孩子身上移到她身上。◇ *She shifted her weight from one foot to the other.* 她把身體的重量從一隻腳換到另一隻腳上。 **2** [I, T] **~ (yourself)** (*BrE, informal*) to move quickly 趕快；快速移動 **SYN** **hurry**

▸ **SITUATION/OPINION/POLICY** 情況；意見；政策 **3** [I] (of a situation, an opinion, a policy etc. 情況、意見、政策等) to change from one state, position, etc. to another 改變；轉向： *Public attitudes towards marriage have shifted over the past 50 years.* * 50 年來，公眾對婚姻的態度已經改變。◇ **~ (from …) (to/towards/toward …)** *The balance of power shifted away from workers towards employers.* 強勢的一方從工人轉向雇主。 **4** [T] to change your opinion of or attitude towards sth, or change the way that you do sth 改變觀點（或態度、做事方式等）： **~ sth** *We need to shift the focus of this debate.* 我們需要轉換一下辯論的焦點。◇ **~ sth (from …) (to/towards/toward …)** *The new policy shifted the emphasis away from fighting inflation.* 新政策不再把重點放在抑制通貨膨脹上。

▸ **RESPONSIBILITY** 責任 **5** [T] **~ responsibility/blame (for sth) (onto sb)** to make sb else responsible for sth you should do or sth bad that you have done 推卸，轉嫁（責任）： *He tried to shift the blame for his mistakes onto his colleagues.* 他自己犯了錯誤，卻試圖把責任推給同事。

▸ **REMOVE MARK** 去除污跡 **6** [T] **~ sth** to remove sth such as a dirty mark 去除（污跡等） **SYN** **get rid of**： *a detergent that shifts even the most stubborn stains* 能去除極頑固的污漬的洗滌劑

▸ **SELL GOODS** 銷售商品 **7** [T] **~ sth** to sell goods, especially goods that are difficult to sell 銷售，出售（尤指銷路不好的商品）： *They cut prices drastically to try and shift stock.* 他們大幅度降價，試圖銷出存貨。

▸ **IN VEHICLE** 車輛 **8** [I] (*NAmE*) to change the gears when you are driving a vehicle 換（擋）： *to shift into second gear* 換成二擋

IDM **shift your 'ground** (usually *disapproving*) to change your opinion about a subject, especially during a discussion （尤指討論時）改變立場 **(the) ˌshifting 'sands (of sth)** used to describe a situation that changes so often that it is difficult to understand or deal with it 變幻莫測；變化無常

PHR V **ˌshift for your'self** (*BrE*) to do things without help from other people 獨立設法應付；獨立謀生；自立： *You're going to have to shift for yourself from now on.* 從今以後，你就得獨自謀生了。

■ ***noun***

▸ **CHANGE** 改變 **1** [C] **~ (in sth)** a change in position or direction 改變；轉移；轉換；變換： *a dramatic shift in public opinion* 公眾輿論的急劇變化 ◇ *a shift of emphasis* 重點的轉移 ➲ see also PARADIGM SHIFT

▸ **PERIOD OF WORK** 工作時間 **2** [C] a period of time worked by a group of workers who start work as another group finishes 班；輪班；輪班工作時間： *to be on the **day/night shift** at the factory* 在工廠上日班 / 夜班 ◇ *to work an eight-hour shift* 按每班八小時輪班工作 ◇ *working in shifts* 輪班工作 ◇ ***shift workers/work*** 輪班工作的工人；輪班作業 ➲ COLLOCATIONS at JOB ➲ see also SWING SHIFT **3** [C+sing./pl. v.] the workers who work a particular shift 輪班職工： *The night shift has/have just come off duty.* 上夜班的剛剛下班。

▸ **ON COMPUTER** 計算機 **4** [U] the system on a computer keyboard or TYPEWRITER that allows capital letters or a different set of characters to be typed; the key that operates this system （計算機鍵盤或打字機上的）轉換（鍵），換擋（鍵）： *a shift key* 轉換鍵 ◇ *Press shift + F11 to insert a new worksheet.* 按換擋鍵和 F11 插入一張新工作表。

▸ **CLOTHING** 服裝 **5** [C] a woman's simple straight dress 直筒式連衣裙 **6** [C] a simple straight piece of clothing worn by women in the past as underwear（舊時婦女穿的）直筒式內衣

shift·er /ˈʃɪftə(r)/ *noun* (*especially NAmE*) the GEARBOX of a vehicle or the set of gears on a bicycle （汽車的）變速箱，齒輪箱；（自行車的）傳動裝置

ˌshifting ˌculti'vation *noun* [U] (*technical* 術語) a way of farming in some tropical countries in which farmers use an area of land until it cannot be used for growing plants any more, then move to a new area of land （某些熱帶國家的）遷移農業，遷徙耕作，遊耕

shift·less /ˈʃɪftləs/ *adj.* (*disapproving*) lazy and having no ambition to succeed in life 沒志氣的；不思上進的；混日子的

shifty /ˈʃɪfti/ *adj.* (**shift·ier**, **shifti·est**) (*informal*) seeming to be dishonest; looking guilty about sth 看着不可靠的；賊眉鼠眼的；顯得心裏有鬼的 **SYN** **furtive**： *shifty eyes* 賊溜溜的眼睛 ◇ *to look shifty* 顯得賊頭賊腦的 ▸ **shift·ily** /-ɪli/ *adv.*

shii·take (also **shi·take**) /ʃɪˈtɑːki; ʃiː-/ (also **ˌshiitake 'mushroom**) *noun* (from *Japanese*) a type of Japanese or Chinese MUSHROOM 香菇；花菇；冬菇

Shi·ite (also **Shi'ite**) /ˈʃiːaɪt/ *noun* a member of the Shia branch of Islam （伊斯蘭教的）什葉派教徒 ➲ compare SUNNI (2) ▸ **Shi·ite** (also **Shi'ite**) *adj.* [usually before noun]

shil·ling /ˈʃɪlɪŋ/ *noun* **1** a British coin in use until 1971, worth 12 old pence. There were 20 shillings in one pound. 先令（英國 1971 年以前貨幣單位，一先令值 12 舊便士，20 先令合一英鎊） **2** the unit of money in Kenya, Uganda, Tanzania and Somalia 先令（肯尼亞、烏干達、坦桑尼亞和索馬里貨幣單位）

shilly-shally /ˈʃɪli ʃæli/ *verb* (**shilly-shallies**, **shilly-shally·ing**, **shilly-shallied**, **shilly-shallied**) [I] (*informal, disapproving*) to take a long time to do sth, especially to make a decision 猶豫；躊躇 **SYN** **dither**： *Stop shilly-shallying and make up your mind.* 別猶豫了，拿主意吧。

shim /ʃɪm/ *noun* (*NAmE*) a thin piece of wood, rubber, metal, etc. which is thicker at one end than the other, that you use to fill a space between two things that do not fit well together （木、橡膠、金屬等）楔子，墊片，填隙片

shim·mer /ˈʃɪmə(r)/ *verb, noun*

■ ***verb*** [I] to shine with a soft light that seems to move slightly 發出微弱的閃光；閃爍： *The sea was shimmering in the sunlight.* 陽光下海水波光閃爍。 ➲ SYNONYMS at SHINE

■ ***noun*** [U, sing.] a shining light that seems to move slightly 閃爍的光： *a shimmer of moonlight in the dark sky* 黑暗的夜空中忽明忽暗的月光

shimmy /ˈʃɪmi/ *verb* (**shim·mies**, **shimmy·ing**, **shim·mied**, **shim·mied**) [I] **+ adv./prep.** to dance or move in a way that involves shaking your hips and shoulders （抖動着肩膀和臀部）跳希米舞；一扭一擺地走

shin /ʃɪn/ *noun, verb*

■ ***noun*** the front part of the leg below the knee 脛；脛部 ➲ VISUAL VOCAB page V59

■ ***verb*** (**-nn-**) (*BrE*) (*NAmE* **shinny**)

PHR V **'shin/'shinny up/down sth** (*informal*) to climb up or down sth quickly, using your hands and legs 爬： *He shinned down the drainpipe and ran off.* 他順着排水管爬下去跑了。

'shin bone *noun* the front and larger bone of the two bones in the lower part of the leg between the knee and the ankle 脛骨 **SYN** **tibia** ➲ VISUAL VOCAB page V59

shin·dig /ˈʃɪndɪɡ/ *noun* (*informal*) a big noisy party 盛大而喧鬧的聚會；盛大舞會

shine /ʃaɪn/ *verb, noun*

■ ***verb*** (**shone**, **shone** /ʃɒn; *US* ʃoʊn/) **HELP** In sense 2 in *NAmE* **shined** can also be used for the past tense and past participle. In sense 3 **shined** is used for the past tense and past participle. 在美式英語中，作第 2 義時過去式和過去分詞也可用 shined，作第 3 義時過去式和過去分詞用 shined。 **1** [I] to produce or reflect light; to be bright 發光；反光；照耀： *The sun shone brightly in a cloudless sky.* 太陽在無雲的天空中明亮地照耀着。◇ *The dark polished wood shone like glass.* 拋光後的深色木料像玻璃一樣熠熠閃光。◇ (*figurative*) *Her eyes were shining with excitement.* 她興奮得兩眼放光。◇ *Excitement was shining in her eyes.* 她眼裏閃着興奮的光芒。 **2** (*NAmE* also **shined**, **shined**) [T] **~ sth (+ adv./prep.)** to aim or point the light of a lamp, etc. in a particular direction 把…照向；使…光投向： *He shone the flashlight around*

S

the cellar. 他用手電筒往地窖各處照了照。◇ (*figurative*) *Campaigners are shining a spotlight on the world's diminishing natural resources.* 從事這場運動的人要使公眾注意到世界上的自然資源日益減少。**3** (**shined**, **shined**) [T] **~ sth** to polish sth; to make sth smooth and bright 擦亮；擦光：*He shined shoes and sold newspapers to make money.* 他靠擦鞋、賣報掙錢。**4** [I] to be very good at sth 出色；出類拔萃：*He failed to shine academically but he was very good at sports.* 他學業不怎麼樣，但體育卻棒極了。◇ *She has set a* ***shining example*** *of loyal service over four decades.* 四十年間，她樹立了一個忠誠服務的光輝榜樣。➲ see also SHINY **IDM** see HAY, KNIGHT *n.*, RISE *v.*

PHR V **,shine 'through** (**sth**) (of a quality 某種品質) to be easy to see or notice 顯現出來；很明顯：*Her old professional skills shone through.* 她在行的專業技巧頓時顯現無遺。

■ ***noun*** [sing.] the bright quality that sth has when light is reflected on it 光亮；光澤：*a shampoo that gives your hair body and shine* 一種能使頭髮濃密發亮的洗髮劑

IDM **take a 'shine to sb/sth** (*informal*) to begin to like sb very much as soon as you see or meet them 一眼就看上；一見鍾情 **take the 'shine off sth** (*informal*) to make sth seem much less good than it did at first 使…黯然失色 ➲ more at RAIN *n.*

shiner /'ʃaɪnə(r)/ *noun* (*informal*) an area of dark skin that can form around sb's eye when they receive a blow to it（被打成的）青腫眼眶 **SYN** **black eye**

shin·gle /'ʃɪŋgl/ *noun* **1** [U] a mass of small smooth stones on a beach or at the side of a river（海濱或河邊的）卵石灘：*a shingle beach* 卵石海灘 ➲ **VISUAL VOCAB** pages V4, V5 **2** [C, U] a small flat piece of wood that is used to cover a wall or roof of a building 牆面板；木瓦；屋頂板 **3** [C] (*NAmE*) a board with a sign on it, in front of a doctor's or lawyer's office（診所或律師事務所掛的）招牌：*He* ***hung out his own shingle*** (= started a business as a doctor or lawyer). 他獨自掛牌開業了。

shin·gled /'ʃɪŋgld/ *adj.* (of a roof, building, etc. 房頂、建築物等) covered with shingles (2) 蓋木瓦的

shin·gles /'ʃɪŋglz/ *noun* [U] (*medical* 醫) a disease that affects the nerves and produces a band of painful spots on the skin 帶狀疱疹

shin·gly /'ʃɪŋgli/ *adj.* (of a beach 海灘) covered in shingle 遍佈卵石的

'shin guard (*BrE* also **'shin pad**) *noun* a piece of thick material that is used to protect the lower front part of the leg when playing sports 護脛，護腿板（體育運動時戴）

shinny /'ʃɪni/ *verb, noun*

■ ***verb*** (**shin·nies**, **shinny·ing**, **shin·nied**, **shin·nied**) (*NAmE*) (*BrE* **shin**)

PHR V **'shin/'shinny up/down sth** (*informal*) to climb up or down sth quickly, using your hands and legs 爬

■ ***noun*** (also **'shinny hockey**) [U] an informal form of ICE HOCKEY, played especially by children（尤指兒童玩的）簡化冰上曲棍球運動

'shin splints *noun* [pl.] sharp pain in the front parts of the lower legs caused by too much exercise, especially on a hard surface 外脛炎，脛骨骨膜炎（因運動過量引起的脛部疼痛）

Shinto /'ʃɪntəʊ; *NAmE* -toʊ/ (also **Shin·to·ism** /'ʃɪntəʊɪzəm; *NAmE* -toʊ-/) *noun* [U] a Japanese religion whose practices include the worship of ANCESTORS and a belief in nature spirits（日本）神道教

shinty /'ʃɪnti/ *noun* [U] a Scottish game similar to HOCKEY, played with curved sticks by teams of twelve players 簡化曲棍球（蘇格蘭運動，每隊 12 人）

shiny O━ /'ʃaɪni/ *adj.* (**shini·er**, **shini·est**) smooth and bright; reflecting the light 光亮的；鋥亮的；反光的；有光澤的：*shiny black hair* 有光澤的黑髮

IDM **shiny new** (*approving*) very new and attractive 新穎的；新奇的；新異的：*shiny new stuff/software* 新奇的玩意兒／軟件

Synonyms 同義詞辨析

shine

gleam • glow • sparkle • glisten • shimmer • glitter • twinkle • glint

These words all mean to produce or reflect light. 以上各詞均含發光、反光之意。

shine to produce or reflect light, especially brightly 指發光、反光、照耀：*The sun was shining and the sky was blue.* 陽光燦爛，天空一片蔚藍。

gleam to shine with a clear bright or pale light, especially a reflected light 指閃爍、隱約閃光、微光反射：*Moonlight gleamed on the water.* 月光照在水面上泛起粼粼波光。

glow (often of sth hot or warm) to produce a dull steady light 常指熱的物體發出微弱而穩定的光：*The end of his cigarette glowed red.* 他的煙頭發着微弱的紅光。

sparkle to shine brightly with small flashes of light 指閃爍、閃耀：*The diamonds sparkled in the light.* 鑽石在燈光下閃閃發亮。

glisten (of sth wet) to shine 指濕物閃光、閃亮：*The road glistened wet after the rain.* 雨後的道路潤澤閃亮。

shimmer to shine with a soft light that seems to shake slightly 指發出微弱的閃光、閃爍：*Everything seemed to shimmer in the heat.* 在高溫下所有的東西都好像在閃光。

glitter to shine brightly with small flashes of reflected light 指閃亮、閃耀：*The ceiling of the cathedral glittered with gold.* 大教堂的天花板金光閃閃。

SPARKLE OR GLITTER? 用 sparkle 還是 glitter？

There is very little difference in meaning between these two words. **Glitter** can sometimes suggest a lack of depth, but this is more frequent in the figurative use of **glitter** as a noun. 以上兩詞在意義上幾乎沒有差別。glitter 有時暗指缺乏深度，但這較常在 glitter 作名詞時作比喻義時用：*the superficial glitter of show business* 表面上光彩迷人的演藝業 **Sparkle** is also often used to talk about light reflected off a surface, but things that produce light can also sparkle. * sparkle 亦常用以指物體表面反光，但物體發出亮光也可用 sparkle：*Stars sparkled in the sky.* 星星在天空中閃爍。

twinkle to shine with a light that changes rapidly from bright to faint to bright again 指一明一暗地閃耀、閃爍：*Stars twinkled in the sky.* 星星在天空中閃爍。

glint to give small bright flashes of reflected light 指微微閃光、閃亮、反光：*The blade of the knife glinted in the darkness.* 刀刃在黑暗中亮了亮。

PATTERNS

- to shine/gleam/sparkle/glisten/shimmer/glitter/glint **on** sth
- to shine/gleam/glow/sparkle/glisten/shimmer/glitter/twinkle/glint **with** sth
- to shine/gleam/sparkle/glisten/shimmer/glitter/glint **in the sunlight**
- to shine/gleam/glisten/shimmer/glitter/glint **in the moonlight**
- the **stars** shine/sparkle/glitter/twinkle
- sb's **eyes** shine/gleam/glow/sparkle/glisten/glitter/twinkle/glint
- to shine/gleam/glow/glitter **brightly**
- to shine/gleam/glow/shimmer **softly**

ship O━ /ʃɪp/ *noun, verb*

■ ***noun*** O━ a large boat that carries people or goods by sea（大）船；艦：*There are two restaurants* ***on board ship.*** 船上有兩個餐廳。◇ *a* ***sailing/cargo/cruise ship*** 帆船；貨船；郵輪 ◇ *a* ***ship's captain/crew/company/cook*** 船長；船上的全體船員；船公司；船上廚師 ◇ *Raw materials and labour come* ***by ship,*** *rail or road.* 原料和工人經

水上、鐵路和公路運送而來。➲ COLLOCATIONS at TRAVEL ➲ VISUAL VOCAB page V54 ➲ see also AIRSHIP, FLAGSHIP, LIGHTSHIP **IDM** see JUMP *v.*, SINK *v.*, SPOIL *v.*, TIGHT *adj.*

■ *verb* (-pp-) **1** [T] **~ sb/sth + adv./prep.** to send or transport sb/sth by ship or by another means of transport 船運；運輸；運送：*The company ships its goods all over the world.* 公司把貨物運往世界各地。◇ *He was arrested and shipped back to the UK for trial.* 他被捕後被押解回英國接受審判。 **2** [I, T] to be available to be bought; to make sth available to be bought 上市；把…推向市場：*The software is due to ship next month.* 這個軟件定於下月上市。◇ **~ sth** *The company continues to ship more computer systems than its rivals.* 這家公司繼續比競爭對手推出更多的計算機系統。 **3** [T] **~ water** (of a boat, etc. 船等) to have water coming in over the sides 舷側進水 **IDM** see SHAPE *v.*

PHR V **ˌship sb↔ˈoff** (*disapproving*) to send sb to a place where they will stay 送走；遣送：*The children were shipped off to a boarding school at an early age.* 孩子們在幼年時就被送到了一所寄宿學校。

-ship *suffix* (in nouns 構成名詞) **1** the state or quality of 狀態；性質；品質：*ownership* 所有權 ◇ *friendship* 友誼 **2** the status or office of 地位；資格；職位：*citizenship* 公民資格 ◇ *professorship* 教授職位 **3** skill or ability as 技藝；技能：*musicianship* 音樂技藝 **4** the group of 集體：*membership* 全體成員

ship·board /ˈʃɪpbɔːd; *NAmE* -bɔːrd/ *adj.* [only before noun] happening on a ship 船上發生的：*shipboard romances* 船上戀情

ship·build·er /ˈʃɪpbɪldə(r)/ *noun* a person or company that builds ships 造船工人；造船公司 ▸ **ship·build·ing** *noun* [U]：*the shipbuilding industry* 造船工業

ship·load /ˈʃɪpləʊd; *NAmE* -loʊd/ *noun* as many goods or passengers as a ship can carry 船隻運載量

ship·mate /ˈʃɪpmeɪt/ *noun* sailors who are **shipmates** are sailing on the same ship as each other 同船船員

ship·ment /ˈʃɪpmənt/ *noun* **1** [U] the process of sending goods from one place to another 運輸；運送；裝運：*The goods are ready for shipment.* 貨物備妥待運。◇ *the illegal shipment of arms* 非法的軍火運輸 ◇ *shipment costs* 運費 **2** [C] a load of goods that are sent from one place to another 運輸的貨物：*arms shipments* 運送的幾批軍火 ◇ *a shipment of arms* 運送的一批軍火

ship·owner /ˈʃɪpəʊnə(r); *NAmE* -oʊn-/ *noun* a person or company that owns a ship or ships 船主；船東

ship·per /ˈʃɪpə(r)/ *noun* a person or company that arranges for goods to be sent from one place to another, especially by ship（船運貨物的）託運人，發貨人

ship·ping /ˈʃɪpɪŋ/ *noun* [U] **1** ships in general or considered as a group 船舶：*The canal is open to shipping.* 運河可以通航了。◇ *international* ***shipping lanes*** (= routes for ships) 國際海上航道 **2** the activity of carrying people or goods from one place to another by ship 航運；海運：*a shipping company* 船運公司 ◇ *She arranged for the shipping of her furniture to England.* 她正安排將傢具海運到英國。

ˈshipping forecast (*BrE*) (*US* **the ˈshipping news** [U]) *noun* a radio broadcast giving a report for ships on the weather conditions at sea 海上天氣預報

ˈship's chandler *noun* = CHANDLER

ship·shape /ˈʃɪpʃeɪp/ *adj.* [not usually before noun] clean and neat; in good condition and ready to use 整潔；井井有條；良好可用

ˌship-to-ˈshore *adj.* [only before noun] providing communication between people on a ship and people on land（指通訊）由船至岸的：*a ship-to-shore radio* 由船至岸無線電設備

ship·wreck /ˈʃɪprek/ *noun, verb*

■ *noun* **1** [U, C] the loss or destruction of a ship at sea because of a storm or because it hits rocks, etc. 船舶失事；海難：*They narrowly escaped shipwreck in a storm in the North Sea.* 他們在北海遇到風暴，船險些失事。 **2** [C] a ship that has been lost or destroyed at sea 失事的船；沉船：*The contents of shipwrecks belong to the state.* 一切沉船中的物品均屬國家所有。

■ *verb* **be shipwrecked** to be left somewhere after the ship that you have been sailing in has been lost or destroyed at sea 遭遇海難；船隻失事 ▸ **ship·wrecked** *adj.*：*a shipwrecked sailor* 遭遇海難的水手

ship·yard /ˈʃɪpjɑːd; *NAmE* -jɑːrd/ *noun* a place where ships are built or repaired 船塢；造船廠；修船廠：*shipyard workers* 船塢工人

shire /ˈʃaɪə(r); *or, in compounds,* -ʃə(r)/ *noun* (*BrE*) **1** [C] (*old use*) a county (now used in the names of some counties in Britain, for example *Hampshire*, *Yorkshire*) 郡（現在用於英國部份郡名，如 Hampshire、Yorkshire） **2** **the Shires** (also **the Shire Counties**) [pl.] counties in central England that are in country areas 英格蘭中部幾個郡

ˈshire horse *noun* a large powerful horse, used for pulling loads 中部大挽馬；夏爾馬

shirk /ʃɜːk; *NAmE* ʃɜːrk/ *verb* [I, T] to avoid doing sth you should do, especially because you are too lazy 逃避（工作）；躲懶：*Discipline in the company was strict and no one shirked.* 公司有嚴格的紀律，沒有人偷懶。◇ **~ from sth/doing sth** *A determined burglar will not shirk from breaking a window to gain entry.* 一個決計要下手的竊賊會不惜破窗而入。◇ **~ sth/doing sth** *She never shirked her responsibilities.* 她從不逃避自己的職責。 ▸ **shirk·er** *noun*

shirt 🔑 /ʃɜːt; *NAmE* ʃɜːrt/ *noun*

a piece of clothing (usually for men), worn on the upper part of the body, made of light cloth, with sleeves and usually with a COLLAR and buttons down the front（尤指男式的）襯衫：*to wear a shirt and tie* 穿襯衫，打領帶 ◇ *a short-sleeved shirt* 短袖襯衫 ◇ *a football shirt* 足球衫 ➲ VISUAL VOCAB page V63 ➲ see also NIGHTSHIRT, POLO SHIRT, STUFFED SHIRT, SWEATSHIRT, T-SHIRT

IDM **keep your ˈshirt on** (*informal*) used to tell sb not to get angry 別生氣；保持冷靜：*Keep your shirt on! It was only a joke.* 別生氣！開個玩笑而已。 **put your ˈshirt on sb/sth** (*BrE, informal*) to bet all your money on sb/sth 把所有的錢全押在…上 **the ˌshirt off sb's ˈback** anything that sb has, including the things they really need themselves, that sb else takes from them or they are willing to give（別人拿走或自願送掉的）全部家當

ˈshirt front *noun* the front part of a shirt, especially the stiff front part of a formal white shirt 襯衫的前襟（尤指禮服白襯衫前面硬挺的部分）

shirt·sleeve /ˈʃɜːtsliːv; *NAmE* ˈʃɜːrt-/ *noun* [usually pl.] a sleeve of a shirt 襯衫的袖子

IDM **in (your) ˈshirtsleeves** wearing a shirt without a jacket, etc. on top of it 只穿襯衫（未穿外衣）

ˈshirt tail *noun* the part of a shirt that is below the waist and is usually inside your trousers/pants 襯衫的下擺

shirty /ˈʃɜːti; *NAmE* ˈʃɜːrti/ *adj.* **~ (with sb)** (*BrE, informal*) angry or annoyed with sb about sth, and acting in a rude way 生氣；動怒；發脾氣

shish kebab /ˈʃɪʃ kɪbæb/ *noun* (*especially NAmE*) = KEBAB

S

shit /ʃɪt/ *exclamation, noun, verb, adj.*

■ *exclamation* (*taboo, slang*) a swear word that many people find offensive, used to show that you are angry or annoyed（表示氣憤或惱怒）：*Shit! I've lost my keys!* 他媽的！我把鑰匙丟了！ **HELP** Less offensive exclamations to use are **blast**, **darn it** (especially *NAmE*), **damn** or (*BrE*) **bother**. 冒犯程度比 shit 稍弱的有 blast、darn it（尤用於美式英語）、damn 或（英式英語）bother。

■ *noun* (*taboo, slang*) **1** [U] solid waste matter from the BOWELS 屎；糞便 **SYN** **excrement**：*a pile of dog shit on the path* 小路上的一堆狗屎 **HELP** A more polite way to express this example would be 'a pile of dog poo/poop'. 較有禮貌的說法是 a pile of dog poo/poop。 **2** [sing.] an act of emptying solid waste matter from the BOWELS 拉屎：*to have/take a shit* 拉屎 **3** [U] stupid remarks or writing; nonsense 胡扯；廢話；狗屁：*You're talking shit!* 你在瞎扯淡！◇ *She's so full of shit.*

她滿嘴廢話。➲ see also BULLSHIT *n.* **4** [C] (*disapproving*) an unpleasant person who treats other people badly 可鄙的人；討厭傢伙：*He's an arrogant little shit.* 他是個傲慢的卑鄙小人。 **5** [U] criticism or unfair treatment 責罵；欺侮：*I'm not going to take any shit from them.* 我可不受他們的氣。

IDM **beat, kick, etc. the 'shit out of sb** to attack sb violently so that you injure them 把某人打得屁滾尿流；揍扁 **in the 'shit | in ,deep 'shit** in trouble 遇到麻煩：*I'll be in the shit if I don't get this work finished today.* 要是今天不把這活兒做完，那我就慘了。 **like 'shit** really bad, ill/sick etc.; really badly 糟透；十分差勁：*I woke up feeling like shit.* 我醒來感覺很不舒服。◇ *We get treated like shit in this job.* 我們這個活兒真不是人幹的。 **no 'shit!** (often *ironic*) used to show that you are surprised, impressed, etc. or that you are pretending to be（表示或假裝驚訝等） **not give a 'shit (about sb/sth)** to not care at all about sb/sth 一點不在乎；毫不關心：*He doesn't give a shit about anybody else.* 別人他誰都不放在心上。 **shit 'happens** used to express the idea that we must accept that bad things often happen without reason 天有不測風雲；壞事難免會發生 **when the ,shit hits the 'fan** when sb in authority finds out about sth bad or wrong that sb has done 做了壞事（或錯事）被發現：*When the shit hits the fan, I don't want to be here.* 事情一旦敗露，我就不想待在這兒了。➲ more at BUG *v.*, CROCK, SCARE *v.*

■ ***verb*** (**shit·ting, shit, shit**) (*taboo, slang*) **HELP** **shat** /ʃæt/ and, in *BrE*, **shit·ted** are also used for the past tense and past participle. 過去時和過去分詞也用 shat，英式英語還用 shitted。 **1** [I, T] **~ (sth)** to empty solid waste matter from the BOWELS 拉屎 **HELP** A more polite way of expressing this is 'to go to the toilet/lavatory' (*BrE*), 'to go to the bathroom' (*NAmE*) or 'to go'. A more formal expression is 'to empty the bowels'. 較文雅的說法是 to go to the toilet/lavatory（英式英語）、to go to the bathroom（美式英語）或 to go。更正式的說法是 to empty the bowels。 **2** [T] **~ yourself** to empty solid waste matter from the BOWELS by accident 意外地拉屎 **3** [T] **~ yourself** to be very frightened 非常害怕

■ ***adj.*** (*taboo, slang, especially BrE*) very bad 非常糟糕：*You're shit and you know you are!* 你狗屁不是！知道吧，狗屁不是！◇ *They're a shit team.* 他們那支隊臭得很。

shi·take *noun* = SHIITAKE

shite /ʃaɪt/ *exclamation, noun* [U] (*BrE, taboo, slang*) another word for SHIT（shit 的變體）屎，糞便

'shit-faced *adj.* (*taboo, slang*) very drunk 喝得臉色煞白的；爛醉如泥的

S

shit·hole /'ʃɪthəʊl; *NAmE* -hoʊl/ *noun* (*taboo, slang*) a very dirty or unpleasant place 極其骯髒的地方；令人厭惡的地方

'shit-hot *adj.* (*taboo, slang*) extremely good at sth 十分精通的；駕輕就熟的：*a shit-hot lawyer* 精明的律師

shit·house /'ʃɪthaʊs/ *noun* (*taboo, slang*) a toilet/bathroom 廁所；衛生間

shit·less /'ʃɪtləs/ *adj.* (*taboo, slang*) **IDM** see SCARE *v.*

,shit-'scared *adj.* [not before noun] (*taboo, slang*) very frightened 嚇破膽；嚇得屁滾尿流

'shit stirrer *noun* (*BrE, taboo, slang*) a person who tries to make situations in which people disagree even worse 火上澆油的人；遇事生風的人 ▸ **'shit stirring** *noun* [U]

shitty /'ʃɪti/ *adj.* (*taboo, slang*) **1** unpleasant; very bad 令人厭惡的；非常糟糕的 **2** unfair or unkind 不公平的；不厚道的；卑劣的：*What a shitty way to treat a friend!* 這樣對待一個朋友，真做得出來！

shiver /'ʃɪvə(r)/ *verb, noun*

■ ***verb*** [I] (of a person 人) to shake slightly because you are cold, frightened, excited, etc. 顫抖，哆嗦（因寒冷、恐懼、激動等）：*Don't stand outside shivering—come inside and get warm!* 別站在外面凍得打哆嗦了，進來暖暖身子吧！◇ *He shivered at the thought of the cold, dark sea.* 那寒冷黑暗的大海，他想想都嚇得發抖。◇ **~ with sth** *to shiver with cold/excitement/pleasure, etc.* 冷得發抖、激動得發抖、高興得發抖等

■ ***noun*** **1** [C] a sudden shaking movement of your body because you are cold, frightened, excited, etc. 顫抖，哆嗦（因寒冷、恐懼、激動等）：*The sound of his voice* ***sent shivers down her spine.*** 一聽見他的說話聲，她就背上一陣陣發冷。◇ *He felt a cold shiver of fear run through him.* 他嚇得打了一個寒戰。 **2** **the shivers** [pl.] shaking movements of your body because of fear or a high temperature 寒戰，寒噤（因恐懼或發高燒）：*I don't like him. He* ***gives me the shivers.*** 我不喜歡他。一見他我就不寒而慄。◇ *Symptoms include headaches, vomiting and the shivers.* 症狀包括頭痛、嘔吐和打寒噤。

shiv·ery /'ʃɪvəri/ *adj.* shaking with cold, fear, illness, etc. 顫抖的，戰慄的，哆嗦的（因寒冷、恐懼、患病等）

shmo = SCHMO

shoal /ʃəʊl; *NAmE* ʃoʊl/ *noun* **1** a large number of fish swimming together as a group 魚群 ➲ compare SCHOOL *n.* (9) **2** a small hill of sand just below the surface of the sea 淺灘；水下沙洲

shock 🔑 /ʃɒk; *NAmE* ʃɑːk/ *noun, verb*

■ ***noun***

▸ **SURPRISE 震驚** **1** 🔑 [C, usually sing., U] a strong feeling of surprise as a result of sth happening, especially sth unpleasant; the event that causes this feeling 震驚；驚愕；令人震驚的事：*The news of my promotion* ***came as a shock.*** 我獲晉升的消息着實讓我一驚。◇ *He's still in* ***a state of shock.*** 他至今還驚魂未定。◇ *I got a terrible shock the other day.* 前兩天，可把我嚇壞了。◇ *She still hadn't got over the shock of seeing him again.* 竟然又見到了他，她到現在還驚愕不已。◇ (*informal*) *If you think the job will be easy,* ***you're in for a shock.*** 如果你以為這項工作容易，那你就會大吃一驚。◇ *Losing in the first round was* ***a shock to the system*** (= it was more of a shock because it was not expected). 首輪失利讓人大為震驚。◇ *The team suffered a shock defeat in the first round.* 球隊首戰失利，十分意外。➲ see also CULTURE SHOCK

▸ **MEDICAL 醫學上** **2** 🔑 [U] a serious medical condition, usually the result of injury in which a person has lost a lot of blood and they are extremely weak 休克：*She was taken to hospital* ***suffering from shock.*** 她因休克被送到醫院。◇ *He isn't seriously injured but he is* ***in*** (***a state of***) ***shock.*** 他傷得不重，但處於休克狀態。➲ see also SHELL SHOCK, TOXIC SHOCK SYNDROME

▸ **VIOLENT SHAKING 劇烈震動** **3** 🔑 [C, U] a violent shaking movement that is caused by an explosion, EARTHQUAKE, etc.（由爆炸、地震等引起的）劇烈震動，劇烈震盪：*The shock of the explosion could be felt up to six miles away.* 爆炸引起的劇烈震盪在六英里之外都能感覺到。◇ *The bumper absorbs shock on impact.* 遇到撞擊時保險槓能減輕震動。

▸ **FROM ELECTRICITY 電** **4** 🔑 [C] = ELECTRIC SHOCK：*Don't touch that wire or you'll* ***get a shock.*** 別碰那根電線，不然會觸電的。

▸ **OF HAIR 頭髮** **5** a thick mass of hair on a person's head 濃密的一堆（頭髮）

IDM **,shock 'horror** (*BrE, informal*, often *humorous*) used when you pretend to be shocked by sth that is not really very serious or surprising（假裝震驚時說）➲ see also SHOCK-HORROR

■ ***verb***

▸ **SURPRISE AND UPSET 震驚** **1** 🔑 [T] to surprise and upset sb 使震驚；使驚愕：**~ sb** *It shocks you when something like that happens.* 發生這樣的事情，使人覺得難以置信。◇ *We were all shocked at the news of his death.* 聽到他的死訊，我們都感到震驚。◇ **~ sb that …** *Neighbours were shocked that such an attack could happen in their area.* 竟有這樣的暴力行為發生在這一地區，鄰居們大為驚駭。◇ **~ sb to do sth** ***I was shocked to*** *hear that he had resigned.* 聽到他辭職的消息，我深感意外。

▸ **OFFEND/DISGUST 使氣憤／厭惡** **2** 🔑 [I, T] (of bad language, immoral behaviour, etc. 髒話、不道德行為等) to make sb feel offended or disgusted 使氣憤；使厭惡：*These movies deliberately set out to shock.* 這些電影存心讓人惡心。◇ **~ sb (to do sth)** *She enjoys shocking people by saying outrageous things.* 她喜歡故意說些不堪入耳的話讓人討厭。

▸ **shocked** 🔑 *adj.*：*For a few minutes we stood in* ***shocked silence.*** 一時間，我們站在那兒驚訝得說不出話來。

Synonyms 同義詞辨析

shock

appal • horrify • disgust • sicken • repel

These words all mean to surprise and upset sb very much. 以上各詞均含使人震驚、驚愕之意。

shock [often passive] to surprise sb, usually in a way that upsets them 指使震驚、使驚愕： *We were all shocked at the news of his death.* 聽到他的死訊，我們都感到震驚。

appal/appall to shock and upset sb very much 指使大為震驚、使驚駭： *The brutality of the crime has appalled the public.* 罪行之殘暴使公眾大為震驚。

horrify to make sb feel extremely shocked, upset or frightened 指使驚嚇、使驚恐、恐嚇： *The whole country was horrified by the killings.* 全國都對這些兇殺案感到大為震驚。

disgust to make sb feel shocked and almost ill because sth is so unpleasant 指使作嘔、使厭惡、使反感： *The level of violence in the movie really disgusted me.* 影片中的暴力程度實在讓我反感。

sicken (*BrE*) to make sb feel very shocked, angry and almost ill because sth is so unpleasant 指使大為震驚、使憤怒、使作嘔： *The public is becoming sickened by these images of violence and death.* 公眾看到這些充滿暴力和死亡的畫面大為震驚。

repel [often passive] (*rather formal*) to make sb feel rather disgusted 指使惡心、使厭惡： *I was repelled by the smell of drink on his breath.* 他滿口酒氣，讓我惡心。

PATTERNS

- shocked/appalled/horrified/disgusted **at** sb/sth
- to shock/appal/horrify/disgust sb **that** ...
- to shock/appal/horrify/disgust/sicken sb **to think/see/hear** ...
- **sb's behaviour** shocks/appals sb
- **violence/an idea** shocks/appals/horrifies/disgusts sb

'shock absorber *noun* a device that is fitted to each wheel of a vehicle in order to reduce the effects of travelling over rough ground, so that passengers can be more comfortable 減震器

shock·er /'ʃɒkə(r); *NAmE* 'ʃɑːk-/ *noun* (*informal*) **1** a film/movie, piece of news or person that shocks you 令人震驚的電影（或新聞、人） **2** something that is of very low quality 質量低劣的東西

'shock-headed (also **'shock-haired**) *adj.* (of people 人) having a lot of thick untidy hair 頭髮濃密蓬亂的

'shock-horror *adj.* intending to make people very shocked or very angry 意欲令人震驚（或憤怒）的；令人髮指的： *a shock-horror advertising campaign* 一次引起公憤的廣告活動 ➲ see also SHOCK *n.*

shock·ing 🔑 /'ʃɒkɪŋ; *NAmE* 'ʃɑːk-/ *adj.* **1** 🔑 that offends or upsets people; that is morally wrong 令人氣憤的；惹人憎惡的；不道德的： *shocking behaviour* 駭人聽聞的行為 ◇ *shocking news* 令人震驚的消息 ◇ *It is shocking that they involved children in the crime.* 令人髮指的是，他們教唆兒童參與犯罪活動。◇ *a shocking waste of money* 令人咋舌的揮霍行為 **2** (*informal, especially BrE*) very bad 非常糟糕的： *The house was left in a shocking state.* 那座房子破敗得不成樣子了。 ▸ **shock·ing·ly** *adv.* ： *a shockingly high mortality rate* 高得驚人的死亡率

,shocking 'pink *adj.* very bright pink in colour 豔粉紅色的 ▸ **,shocking 'pink** *noun* [U]

'shock jock *noun* (*informal, especially NAmE*) a DISC JOCKEY on a radio show who deliberately expresses opinions or uses language that many people find offensive 驚世駭俗的唱片節目主持人

shock·proof /'ʃɒkpruːf; *NAmE* 'ʃɑːk-/ *adj.* made so that it cannot be damaged if it is dropped or hit 防震的： *My watch is shockproof and waterproof.* 我的手錶防震防水。

'shock tactics *noun* [pl.] actions that are done to deliberately shock people in order to persuade them to do sth or to react in a particular way 震驚戰術，聳動視聽術（有意讓人震驚，以說服他人做某事或做出某種反應的策略）

'shock therapy (also **'shock treatment**) *noun* [U] a way of treating mental illness by giving ELECTRIC SHOCKS or a drug that has a similar effect 休克療法（通過電擊或有類似電擊作用的藥物來治療精神病）

'shock troops *noun* [pl.] soldiers who are specially trained to make sudden attacks on the enemy 突擊部隊

'shock wave *noun* **1** a movement of very high air pressure that is caused by an explosion, EARTHQUAKE, etc. （爆炸、地震等引起的）衝擊波 **2 shock waves** [pl.] feelings of shock that people experience when sth bad happens suddenly 震驚；震盪： *The murder sent shock waves through the whole community.* 兇殺案震驚了整個社區。

shod /ʃɒd; *NAmE* ʃɑːd/ *adj.* (*literary*) wearing shoes of the type mentioned 穿着…鞋的： *She turned on her elegantly shod heel.* 她突然轉身，邁開穿着雅致的皮鞋的雙腳離去了。 ➲ see also SHOE *v.* (shoeing, shod, shod)

shoddy /'ʃɒdi; *NAmE* 'ʃɑːdi/ *adj.* (**shod·dier**, **shod·di·est**) **1** (of goods, work, etc. 商品、工作等) made or done badly and with not enough care 做工粗糙的；粗製濫造的；劣質的 SYN **second-rate**： *shoddy goods* 劣質商品 ◇ *shoddy workmanship* 粗糙的做工 **2** dishonest or unfair 奸詐的；卑鄙的： *shoddy treatment* 不好的對待 ▸ **shod·dily** *adv.* **shod·di·ness** *noun* [U]

shoe 🔑 /ʃuː/ *noun, verb*

■ ***noun*** **1** 🔑 one of a pair of outer coverings for your feet, usually made of leather or plastic 鞋： *a pair of shoes* 一雙鞋 ◇ *He took his shoes and socks off.* 他脫掉鞋襪。◇ *What's your shoe size?* 你穿多大的鞋？◇ *a shoe brush* 鞋刷 ◇ *shoe polish* 鞋油 ➲ **VISUAL VOCAB** page V64 ➲ see also SNOWSHOE **2** = HORSESHOE

IDM **be in sb's shoes | put yourself in sb's shoes** to be in, or imagine that you are in, another person's situation, especially when it is an unpleasant or difficult one 處於某人的境地；設身處地： *I wouldn't like to be in your shoes when they find out about it.* 等他們弄清事情真相的時候，你的日子就很不好過了。 **if ,I were in 'your shoes** used to introduce a piece of advice you are giving to sb（引出建議）要是我處在你的境地，換了是你的話： *If I were in your shoes, I'd resign immediately.* 要是我處在你的地位，我就立刻辭職。 **if the shoe fits (, wear it)** (*NAmE*) (*BrE* **if the cap fits (, wear it)**) if you feel that a remark applies to you, you should accept it and take it as a warning or criticism 有則改之 **the shoe is on the other 'foot** (*NAmE*) (*BrE* **the boot is on the other 'foot**) used to say that a situation has changed so that sb now has power or authority over the person who used to have power or authority over them 情況正好相反；賓主易位 ➲ more at FILL *v.*, SHAKE *v.*, STEP *v.*

■ ***verb*** (**shoe·ing**, **shod**, **shod** /ʃɒd; *NAmE* ʃɑːd/) **~ sth** to put one or more HORSESHOES on a horse 給（馬）釘蹄鐵： *The horses were sent to the blacksmith to be shod.* 馬送到鐵匠那兒釘馬掌去了。

shoe·box /'ʃuːbɒks; *NAmE* -bɑːks/ *noun* **1** a box in which you take a pair of new shoes home from a shop 鞋盒 **2** (*disapproving*) a very small house with a square shape and no interesting features, especially one that is very similar to all the ones around it （尤指千篇一律的）小平房，鞋盒式住房

shoe·horn /'ʃuːhɔːn; *NAmE* -hɔːrn/ *noun, verb*

■ ***noun*** a curved piece of plastic or metal, used to help your heel slide into a shoe 鞋拔

■ ***verb*** **~ sth + adv./prep.** to succeed in putting sth into a small space or a place where it does not fit very easily 把…硬塞進： *They managed to shoehorn the material onto just one CD.* 他們設法把材料僅僅塞進一張光盤。

S

shoe·lace /ˈʃuːleɪs/ (also **lace**) (*NAmE* also **shoe·string**) *noun* a long thin piece of material like string that goes through the holes on a shoe and is used to fasten it 鞋帶：*a pair of shoelaces* 一副鞋帶 ◇ *to* **tie/untie** *your* **shoelaces** 繫／解鞋帶 ◇ *Your shoelace is undone.* 你的鞋帶鬆開了。 ➲ VISUAL VOCAB page V64

shoe·maker /ˈʃuːmeɪkə(r)/ *noun* a person whose job is making shoes and boots 鞋匠；製鞋工人 ➲ compare COBBLER (2) ▸ **shoe·mak·ing** *noun* [U]

shoe·shine /ˈʃuːʃaɪn/ *noun* [U] (*especially NAmE*) the activity of cleaning people's shoes for money 擦鞋（生意）：*a shoeshine stand on West 32nd Street* 西 32 街上的一家擦鞋攤

shoe·string /ˈʃuːstrɪŋ/ *noun, adj.*
■ **noun** (*NAmE*) = SHOELACE
IDM **on a ˈshoestring** (*informal*) using very little money 以極少的錢：*In the early years, the business was run on a shoestring.* 早年，這家店鋪是小本經營的。
■ **adj.** [only before noun] (*informal*) that uses very little money 用錢極少的：*The club exists on a shoestring budget.* 這家俱樂部靠一點小錢艱難度日。

ˌshoestring poˈtatoes *noun* [pl.] (*NAmE*) potatoes cut into long thin strips and fried in oil 炸薯條

ˈshoe tree *noun* an object shaped like a shoe that you put inside a shoe when you are not wearing it to help the shoe keep its shape 鞋楦

sho·gun /ˈʃəʊgən; *NAmE* ˈʃoʊ-/ *noun* (in the past) a Japanese military leader（舊時的）日本將軍

Shona /ˈʃəʊnə; *NAmE* ˈʃoʊ-/ *noun* [U] a language spoken by the Shona peoples of southern Africa, used in Zimbabwe and other parts of southern Africa 紹納語（非洲南部紹納人講的方言，用於津巴布韋等地區）

shone *past tense, past part.* of SHINE

shonky /ˈʃɒŋki; *NAmE* ˈʃɔːŋ-; ˈʃɑːŋ-/ *adj.* (**shonk·ier**, **shonki·est**) (*AustralE, NZE, informal*) not honest or legal 不誠實的；不合法的

shoo /ʃuː/ *verb, exclamation*
■ **verb** (**shoo·ing**, **shooed**, **shooed**) **~ sb/sth (+ adv./prep.)** to make sb/sth go away or to another place, especially by saying 'shoo' and waving your arms and hands（尤指發出噓聲並揮手）趕走，轟走：*He shooed the dog out of the kitchen.* 他噓噓地把狗趕出了廚房。
■ **exclamation** used to tell a child or an animal to go away（表示趕小孩或動物走的聲音）噓，去

S

shoo·fly pie /ˌʃuːflaɪ ˈpaɪ/ *noun* [C, U] (*NAmE*) an open PIE filled with brown sugar and TREACLE/MOLASSES 開口糖餡餅（用紅塘和糖漿填充）ORIGIN From the need to say *shoo!* to the flies that the sugar attracts. 用噓聲（shoo!）驅趕糖蜜招引的蒼蠅，故名。

ˈshoo-in *noun* **~ (for sth)** | **~ (to do sth)** (*NAmE, informal*) a person or team that will win easily 穩操勝券的人（或隊）

shook *past tense, past part.* of SHAKE

shoot 🔑 /ʃuːt/ *verb, noun, exclamation*
■ **verb** (**shot**, **shot** /ʃɒt; *NAmE* ʃɑːt/)
▸ WEAPON 武器 **1** 🔑 [I, T] to fire a gun or other weapon; to fire sth from a weapon 開（槍或其他武器）；射擊；發射：*Don't shoot—I surrender.* 別開槍，我投降。◇ **~ (sth) (at sb/sth)** *troops shooting at the enemy* 向敵人射擊的部隊 ◇ *The police rarely* **shoot to kill** (= try to kill the people they shoot at). 一般來説，警察開槍不是要打死人。◇ **~ sth (from sth)** *He shot an arrow from his bow.* 他張弓射了一箭。◇ *They shot the lock off* (= removed it by shooting). 他們開槍把鎖打掉。 ➲ COLLOCATIONS at WAR **2** 🔑 [T] to kill or wound a person or an animal with a bullet, etc. 射殺；射傷：**~ sb/sth/yourself** *A man was shot in the leg.* 一個人被射中腿部。◇ *He shot himself during a fit of depression.* 他一時心灰意冷，開槍自殺了。◇ *The guards were ordered to* **shoot on sight** *anyone trying to escape.* 衛兵接到命令，看見有誰企圖逃跑就立即開槍。◇ **~ sb/sth + adj.** *Three people were* **shot dead** *during the robbery.* 搶劫過程中有三人被開槍打死。**3** [T, I] **~ (sth)** (of a gun or other weapon 槍或其他武器) to fire bullets, etc. 發射（子彈等）：*This is just a toy gun—it doesn't shoot real bullets.* 這只是一支玩具槍，不能射真子彈。
▸ FOR SPORT 體育運動 **4** 🔑 [T, I] **~ (sth)** to hunt and kill birds and animals with a gun as a sport 打獵；狩獵；打（獵物）；獵殺：*to shoot pheasants* 打野雞 ◇ *They go* **shooting** *in Scotland.* 他們上蘇格蘭去打獵。
▸ MOVE QUICKLY 快速移動 **5** 🔑 [I, T] to move suddenly or quickly in one direction; to make sb/sth move in this way（使朝某方向）衝，奔，撲，射，飛馳：**+ adv./prep.** *A plane shot across the sky.* 飛機掠過天空。◇ *His hand shot out to grab her.* 他猛地伸出手去抓她。◇ *Flames were shooting up through the roof.* 火不斷從房頂竄上來。◇ (*figurative*) *The band's last single shot straight to number one in the charts.* 這支樂隊的最新單曲一推出便飆上排行榜的首位。◇ **~ sth + adv./prep.** *He shot out his hand to grab her.* 他猛地伸出手去抓她。
▸ OF PAIN 疼痛 **6** [I] to move suddenly and quickly and be very sharp 劇痛跳竄：*a shooting pain in the back* 背部的一陣劇痛 ◇ **+ adv./prep.** *The pain shot up her arm.* 疼痛順着她的胳膊竄了上來。
▸ DIRECT AT SB 朝向某人 **7** [T, no passive] to direct sth at sb suddenly or quickly 突然把…投向：**~ sth at sb** *Journalists were shooting questions at the candidates.* 記者紛紛向幾位候選人發問。◇ *She shot an angry glance at him.* 她很生氣，瞪了他一眼。◇ **~ sb sth** *She shot him an angry glance.* 她很生氣，瞪了他一眼。
▸ FILM/PHOTOGRAPH 電影；照片 **8** 🔑 [I, T] to make a film/movie or photograph of sth 拍攝；攝影：*Cameras ready? OK, shoot!* 攝影機準備好了嗎？好，開拍！◇ **~ sth (+ adv./prep.)** *Where was the movie shot?* 那部電影是在哪兒拍的？◇ *The movie was shot in black and white.* 那部電影以黑白片拍攝。
▸ IN SPORTS 體育運動 **9** [I, T] (in football (SOCCER), HOCKEY, etc. 足球、曲棍球等) to try to kick, hit or throw the ball into a goal or to score a point 射門；投籃：**~ (at sth)** *He should have shot instead of passing.* 他本該射門，不該傳球。◇ (*especially NAmE*) ◇ **~ sth** *After school we'd be on the driveway* **shooting baskets** (= playing BASKETBALL). 放學後，我們就在車行道上打籃球。**10** [T] **~ sth** (*informal*) (in GOLF 高爾夫球) to make a particular score in a complete ROUND or competition（在整場比賽中）擊出…杆：*She shot a 75 in the first round.* 她在第一場比賽中擊出 75 杆。
▸ PLAY GAME 玩遊戲 **11** [T] **~ sth** (*especially NAmE*) to play particular games 玩，打（某種遊戲）：*to shoot pool* 打普爾

IDM **be/get ˈshot of sb/sth** (*BrE, informal*) to get rid of sb/sth so you no longer have the problems they cause 擺脱；處理：*I'll be glad to get shot of this car.* 我很想賣掉這輛車。**have shot your ˈbolt** (*informal*) to have used all your power, money or supplies 竭盡全力；傾其所有 **be like shooting ˌfish in a ˈbarrel** (*informal*) used to emphasize how easy it is to do sth 易如反掌；探囊取物；手到擒來：*What do you mean you can't do it? It'll be like shooting fish in a barrel!* 你説幹不了是什麼意思？這不是小事一樁嘛！ **shoot the ˈbreeze/ˈbull** (*NAmE, informal*) to have a conversation in an informal way 聊天；閒聊 SYN **chat**：*We sat around in the bar, shooting the breeze.* 我們閒坐在酒吧裏聊天。**ˌshoot from the ˈhip** to react quickly without thinking carefully first 輕率應對；魯莽行事；倉促反應 **ˌshoot yourself in the ˈfoot** (*informal*) to do or say sth that will cause you a lot of trouble or harm, especially when you are trying to get an advantage for yourself 搬起石頭砸自己的腳 **ˌshoot it ˈout (with sb)** (*informal*) to fight against sb with guns, especially until one side is killed or defeated 開槍拚個你死我活；（和…）決一死戰：*The gang decided to shoot it out with the police.* 那夥匪徒決定開槍和警察死拚。➲ related noun SHOOT-OUT **shoot the ˈmessenger** to blame the person who gives the news that sth bad has happened, instead of the person who is really responsible 拿報信人出氣（而非責備問題的責任人）：*Don't shoot the messenger!* 別錯怪好人！ **ˌshoot your ˈmouth off (about sth)** (*informal*) **1** to talk with too much pride about sth 吹噓；大吹大擂 **2** to talk about sth that is private or secret 張揚；信口亂講（涉及隱私或秘密的事） **shoot the ˈrapids** to go in a boat over part of a river where the water flows very fast 急流划艇

PHR V **ˌshoot sb/sth↔ˈdown** **1** 🔑 to make sb/sth fall to the ground by shooting them/it 射倒；擊斃；擊落：*Several planes were shot down by enemy fire.* 幾架飛機被敵人的炮火擊落。 **2** to be very critical of sb's ideas, opinions, etc. 批駁，駁倒，徹底推翻（觀點、意見等）：*His latest theory has been* ***shot down in flames***. 他的最新理論被徹底推翻了。 **ˈshoot for sth** (*NAmE, informal*) to try to achieve or get sth, especially sth difficult 力爭達到；努力獲取：*We've been shooting for a pay raise for months.* 幾個月來，我們一直在爭取加薪。 **ˌshoot ˈoff** (*informal*) to leave very quickly 迅速離去 **SYN** **dash off**：*I had to shoot off at the end of the meeting.* 我不得不一散會就跑。 **ˌshoot sth ˈoff** (*NAmE*) to light FIREWORKS and make them go off 燃放（煙花） **SYN** **let off, set off** **ˌshoot ˈthrough** (*AustralE, NZE, informal*) to leave, especially in order to avoid sb/sth 離去；躲避：*I was only five when my Dad shot through.* 我父親出走時我才五歲。 **ˌshoot ˈup** **1** to grow very quickly 迅速長高：*Their kids have shot up since I last saw them.* 自我上次見了以後，他們家幾個孩子一下子長高了。 **2** to rise suddenly by a large amount 陡增；猛漲；迅速上升：*Ticket prices shot up last year.* 去年票價猛漲。➲ **LANGUAGE BANK** at INCREASE **3** (*slang*) to INJECT an illegal drug directly into your blood 注射（毒品） **ˌshoot sth↔ˈup** **1** to cause great damage to sth by shooting 開槍打壞；擊毀 **2** [no passive] (*slang*) to INJECT an illegal drug directly into your blood 注射（毒品）

■ ***noun***

▸ **PLANT** 植物 **1** the part that grows up from the ground when a plant starts to grow; a new part that grows on plants or trees 幼苗；嫩芽；新枝：*new green shoots* 綠色的新芽 ◇ *bamboo shoots* 竹筍 ➲ **VISUAL VOCAB** page V11

▸ **FILM/PHOTOGRAPHS** 電影；照片 **2** an occasion when sb takes professional photographs for a particular purpose or makes a film/movie 拍攝；攝影：*a fashion shoot* 時裝攝影 ➲ see also PHOTO SHOOT

▸ **FOR SPORT** 體育運動 **3** (*especially BrE*) an occasion when a group of people hunt and shoot animals or birds for sport; the land where this happens 狩獵；狩獵場

■ ***exclamation*** **1** (*NAmE*) used to show that you are annoyed when you do sth stupid or when sth goes wrong (to avoid saying 'shit') （做了蠢事或事情出了差錯感到懊惱，避免說 shit）：*Shoot! I've forgotten my book!* 倒霉！我忘了帶書！ **2** (*especially NAmE*) used to tell sb to say what they want to say （讓某人把話說出來）說吧，請講：*You want to tell me something? OK, shoot!* 你有話要告訴我？那好，說吧！

ˈshoot-ˈem-up *adj.* (*informal*) a **shoot-'em-up** computer game, etc. is one involving a lot of violence with guns （電腦遊戲等）充滿槍戰暴力的

shoot·er /ˈʃuːtə(r)/ *noun* **1** (especially in compounds 尤用於構成複合詞) a person or weapon that shoots 射手；射擊武器 ➲ see also PEA-SHOOTER, SHARPSHOOTER, SIX-SHOOTER, TROUBLESHOOTER **2** (*informal*) a gun 槍 **3** (*NAmE*) (used especially in news reports 尤用於新聞報道) a person who uses a gun to kill people （開槍殺人的）槍手，兇犯

shoot·ing 🔑 /ˈʃuːtɪŋ/ *noun*

1 🔑 [C] a situation in which a person is shot with a gun 槍擊；槍殺：*Terrorist groups claimed responsibility for the shootings and bomb attacks.* 恐怖主義組織聲稱對這幾起槍擊和爆炸事件負責。◇ *a serious shooting incident* 一起重大的槍擊事件 **2** [U] the sport of shooting animals and birds with guns 狩獵：*grouse shooting* 獵松雞 **3** 🔑 [U] the process of filming a film/movie （電影的）拍攝：*Shooting began early this year.* 拍攝於今年初開始。

ˈshooting gallery *noun* **1** a place where people shoot guns at objects for practice or to win prizes 射擊場；打靶場 **2** (*especially NAmE*) a place where people go to take drugs 吸毒場所；注射毒品場所

ˈshooting match *noun* an occasion when people or groups fight or attack each other 打架；鬥毆 **IDM** **the whole ˈshooting match** (*BrE, informal*) everything, or a situation which includes everything 所有東西；全部物品；整個

ˌshooting ˈstar (also **ˌfalling ˈstar**) *noun* a small METEOR (= a piece of rock in outer space) that travels very fast and burns with a bright light as it enters the earth's atmosphere 流星

ˈshooting stick *noun* a pointed stick that has a handle at the top which opens out to make a simple seat 摺疊座手杖（尖頭，上端的手柄可打開成為坐凳）

ˈshoot-out *noun* a fight that is fought with guns until one side is killed or defeated 你死我活的槍戰 ➲ see also PENALTY SHOOT-OUT

shop 🔑 /ʃɒp; *NAmE* ʃɑːp/ *noun, verb*

■ ***noun***

▸ **WHERE YOU BUY STH** 買東西的地方 **1** 🔑 [C] (*especially BrE*) a building or part of a building where you can buy goods or services 商店；店鋪：*a shoe shop* 鞋店 ◇ *There's a little gift shop around the corner.* 在街角附近有一家小禮品店。◇ (*BrE*) *a butcher's shop* 肉鋪 ◇ (*NAmE*) *a butcher shop* 肉鋪 ◇ (*BrE*) *I'm just going down* ***to the shops***. *Can I get you anything?* 我要上街去。你有要買的嗎？➲ **COLLOCATIONS** at SHOPPING ➲ **VISUAL VOCAB** pages V2, V3 ➲ see also BAKESHOP, BUCKET SHOP, COFFEE SHOP, CORNER SHOP, FACTORY SHOP

▸ **FOR MAKING/REPAIRING THINGS** 製造／修理東西 **2** (also **work·shop**) [C] (especially in compounds 尤用於構成複合詞) a place where things are made or repaired, especially part of a factory where a particular type of work is done 工廠；工場；作坊；（尤指）車間：*a repair shop* 修理廠 ◇ *a paint shop* (= where cars are painted) 噴漆車間 ➲ see also BODY SHOP

▸ **SHOPPING** 購物 **3** [sing.] (*BrE, informal*) an act of going shopping, especially for food and other items needed in the house 購物；採買：*I* ***do a*** *weekly* ***shop*** *at the supermarket.* 我一週上超市一次。

▸ **SCHOOL SUBJECT** 學校科目 **4** (also **ˈshop class**) [U] (both *NAmE*) = INDUSTRIAL ARTS

▸ **ROOM FOR TOOLS** 放工具的房間 **5** (also **work·shop**) [C] (*NAmE*) a room in a house where tools are kept for making repairs to the house, building things out of wood, etc. 工具貯藏室

IDM **all ˈover the shop** (*BrE, informal*) = ALL OVER THE PLACE at PLACE *n.* **ˌset up ˈshop** to start a business 開業；開張 ➲ more at BULL, HIT *v.*, MIND *v.*, SHUT *v.*, TALK *v.*

■ ***verb*** (-pp-)

▸ **BUY** 購買 **1** 🔑 [I] **~ (for sth)** to buy things in shops/stores 去商店買；在商店購物：*to shop for food* 去商店買食物 ◇ *He likes to shop at the local market.* 他喜歡到本地市場買東西。◇ *She was determined to go out and* ***shop till she dropped***. 她決定外出購物直到累得站不住才罷休。 **2** 🔑 **go shopping** [I] to spend time going to shops/stores and looking for things to buy 逛商店：*There should be plenty of time to go shopping before we leave New York.* 我們離開紐約前應該還有充足的時間去逛商店。◇ *'Where's Mum?' 'She went shopping.'* "媽媽呢？" "買東西去了。"

▸ **TELL POLICE ABOUT SB** 向警察告發 **3** [T] **~ sb (to sb)** (*BrE, informal*) to give information to sb, especially to the police, about sb who has committed a crime （向警察等）告發：*He didn't expect his own mother to shop him to the police.* 他沒想到自己的母親會向警方告發他。

PHR V **ˌshop aˈround (for sth)** to compare the quality or prices of goods or services that are offered by different shops/stores, companies, etc. so that you can choose the best 貨比三家而後買；比較選購：*Shop around for the best deal.* 要貨比三家，買最合算的。

shop·ahol·ic /ˌʃɒpəˈhɒlɪk; *NAmE* ˌʃɑːpəˈhɔːlɪk; -ˈhɑːl-/ *noun* (*informal*) a person who enjoys shopping very much and spends too much time or money doing it 購物狂 ▸ **shop·ahol·ic** *adj.*

ˈshop assistant (also **as·sist·ant**) (both *BrE*) (*NAmE* **ˈsales clerk, clerk**) *noun* a person whose job is to serve customers in a shop/store 店員；售貨員

ˈshop-bought (*BrE*) (*NAmE* **store-bought**) *adj.* [only before noun] bought from a shop/store and not made at

S

home 從商店買的（而非家裏做的）: *shop-bought cakes* 從商店買的糕點

shop·fit·ting /ˈʃɒpfɪtɪŋ; *NAmE* ˈʃɑːp-/ *noun* [U] the business of putting equipment and furniture into shops/stores 店鋪裝潢（業）▶ **shop·fit·ter** *noun*

shop ˈfloor *noun* [sing.] **1** the area in a factory where the goods are made by the workers（工廠的）生產區: *to work **on the shop floor*** 在生產區工作 **2** the workers in a factory, not the managers 工廠工人（非管理人員）

shop·front /ˈʃɒpfrʌnt; *NAmE* ˈʃɑːp-/ (*BrE*) (*NAmE* **store·front**) *noun* the outside of a shop/store that faces the street 商店門面；店面

shop·house /ˈʃɒphaʊs; *NAmE* ˈʃɑːp-/ *noun* (in SE Asia) a shop that opens onto the street and is used as the owner's home 店屋（東南亞兼作住房的門面房）

shop·keep·er /ˈʃɒpkiːpə(r); *NAmE* ˈʃɑːp-/ (also **store·keep·er** especially in *NAmE*) *noun* a person who owns or manages a shop/store, usually a small one（通常指小商店的）店主

shop·lift·ing /ˈʃɒplɪftɪŋ; *NAmE* ˈʃɑːp-/ *noun* [U] the crime of stealing goods from a shop/store by deliberately leaving without paying for them 冒充顧客在商店行竊（罪）➲ COLLOCATIONS at SHOPPING ▶ **shop·lift** *verb* [I, T] **~ (sth) shop·lift·er** *noun*: *Shoplifters will be prosecuted.* 在本店行竊者將被起訴。

shop·lot /ˈʃɒplɒt; *NAmE* ˈʃɑːplɑːt/ *noun* (*SEAsianE*) the amount of space that a shop/store fills 商店佔地面積

shop·per /ˈʃɒpə(r); *NAmE* ˈʃɑːp-/ *noun* a person who buys goods from shops/stores 購物者；（商店的）顧客: *The streets were full of Christmas shoppers.* 街上擠滿了為聖誕節採購的人。➲ see also MYSTERY SHOPPER, PERSONAL SHOPPER

shop·ping 0━ /ˈʃɒpɪŋ; *NAmE* ˈʃɑːp-/ *noun* [U] **1** 0━ the activity of going to shops/stores and buying things 購物: *to **go shopping*** 去購物 ◇ (*BrE*) *When shall I **do the shopping**?* 我什麼時候去買東西呢？◇ (*BrE*) *We **do our shopping** on Saturdays.* 我們星期六購物。◇ *a shopping basket* 購物籃 ◇ *a shopping trolley* 購物手推車 ◇ (*NAmE*) *a shopping cart* 購物手推車 ➲ see also WINDOW-SHOPPING **2** 0━ (*especially BrE*) the things that you have bought from shops/stores 從商店採買的東西: *to put the shopping in the car* 把買好的東西放進汽車

ˈshopping arcade *noun* = ARCADE (3)

ˈshopping bag *noun* **1** a large, strong bag made of cloth, plastic, etc. used for carrying your shopping 購物袋 ➲ VISUAL VOCAB page V33 **2** (*NAmE*) (*BrE* **ˈcarrier bag, car·rier**) a paper or plastic bag for carrying shopping（紙或塑料的）購物袋，手提袋

ˈshopping centre (*BrE*) (*NAmE* **ˈshopping center**) *noun* a group of shops/stores built together, sometimes under one roof 購物中心（集中一批商店，有時在同一建築物內）➲ VISUAL VOCAB pages V2, V3

ˈshopping list *noun* a list that you make of all the things that you need to buy when you go shopping 購物單；採購單: (*figurative*) *The union presented a shopping list of demands to the management.* 工會向資方提交了一份寫明各項要求的清單。

ˈshopping mall *noun* (*especially NAmE*) = MALL

ˈshop-soiled (*BrE*) (*NAmE* **shop·worn**) *adj.* (of goods 商品) dirty or not in perfect condition because they have been in a shop/store for a long time 在商店擺放舊了的: *a sale of shop-soiled goods at half price* 半價促銷商店陳貨

Collocations 詞語搭配

Shopping 購物

Shopping 購物

- **go/go out/be out** shopping 去／外出／在外購物
- **go to** (*especially BrE*) the shops/(*especially NAmE*) a store/(*especially NAmE*) the mall 去商店／商場
- **do** (*BrE*) the shopping/(*especially NAmE*) the grocery shopping/a bit of window-shopping 購物；逛街瀏覽一下櫥窗
- (*NAmE, informal*) **hit/hang out at** the mall 去逛商場；在商場閒逛
- **try on** clothes/shoes 試穿衣服／鞋
- **indulge in** some retail therapy 沉迷於購物療法（瘋狂購物以撫慰心靈）
- **go on** a spending spree 痛痛快快地花一通錢
- **cut/cut back on/reduce** your spending 減少花銷
- **be/get caught** shoplifting 在商店行竊被當場逮住
- **donate sth to/take sth to/find sth in** (*BrE*) a charity shop/(*NAmE*) a thrift store 把某物捐贈給／拿到慈善商店；在慈善商店發現某物
- **buy/sell/find sth at** (*BrE*) a car boot sale/(*BrE*) a jumble sale/a garage sale/(*NAmE*) a yard sale 在車尾箱甩賣／舊雜物義賣／車庫裏進行的舊物銷售／庭院拍賣會購買／出售／找到某物
- **find/get/pick up** a bargain 找到／買到便宜貨

At the shop/store 在商店

- **load/push/wheel** (*BrE*) a trolley/(*NAmE*) a cart 往手推車裏裝東西；推手推車
- **stand in/wait in** (*BrE*) the checkout queue/(*NAmE*) the checkout line 排隊付款
- (*NAmE*) **stand in line**/(*BrE*) **queue** at the checkout 在付款處排隊
- **bag** (*especially NAmE*) (your) groceries 把食品雜貨裝進袋子
- **pack (away)** (*especially BrE*) your shopping 將所購之物打包
- **stack/stock/restock** the shelves at a store (with sth)（把某物）放上／補齊放上商店的貨架
- **be (found) on/appear on** supermarket/shop/store shelves 在超市／商店有售
- **be in/have in/be out of/run out of** stock 有貨；脫銷
- **deal with/help/serve** customers 應付／幫助／服務顧客
- **run** a special promotion 搞特別促銷活動
- **be on** special offer 正在搞特價優惠

Buying goods 買商品

- **make/complete** a purchase 採購
- **buy/purchase sth** online/by mail order 網購；郵購
- **make/place/take** an order for sth 訂購某物
- **buy/order sth** in bulk/in advance 大批／提前購買／訂購某物
- **accept/take** credit cards 接受信用卡
- **pay** (in) cash/by (credit/debit) card/(*BrE*) with a gift voucher/(*NAmE*) with a gift certificate 用現金／（信用／借記）卡／禮券支付
- **enter** your PIN number 輸入你的個人密碼
- **ask for/get/obtain** a receipt 索要／拿到收據
- **return/exchange** an item/a product 退還／更換商品／產品
- **be entitled to/ask for/demand** a refund 有資格要求／要求退款
- **compare** prices 對比價格
- **offer (sb)/give (sb)/get/receive** a 30% discount 給（某人）／得到 30% 的折扣

ˌshop ˈsteward *noun* (*especially BrE*) a person who is elected by members of a TRADE/LABOR UNION in a factory or company to represent them in meetings with managers 工會談判代表

ˈshop talk *noun* [U] talk about your work or your business 有關工作（或公事）的談話

ˌshop ˈwindow (*BrE*) (*NAmE* **ˌstore ˈwindow**) (also **window**) *noun* the glass at the front of a shop/store and the area behind it where goods are shown to the public 商店櫥窗

shop·worn /ˈʃɒpwɔːn; *NAmE* ˈʃɑːpwɔːrn/ (*NAmE*) (*BrE* **ˈshop-soiled**) *adj.* (of goods 商品) dirty or not in perfect condition because they have been in a shop/store for a long time 在商店擺放舊了的：(*figurative*) *a shopworn argument* (= that is no longer new or useful) 陳舊的論點

shore /ʃɔː(r)/ *noun, verb*

■ ***noun*** **1** [C, U] the land along the edge of the sea or ocean, a lake or another large area of water （海洋、湖泊等大水域的）岸，濱：*a* ***rocky/sandy shore*** 岩 / 沙岸 ◇ *to swim from the boat* ***to the shore*** 下船游上岸 ◇ *a house* ***on the shores of*** *the lake* 湖畔的房子 ◇ *The ship was anchored* ***off shore.*** 船停泊在離岸不遠的地方。 **2 shores** [pl.] (especially *literary*) a country, especially one with a coast 國家（尤指瀕海國家）：*foreign shores* 外國 ◇ *What brings you to these shores?* 是什麼把你帶到這國家來的？

■ ***verb***

PHR V **ˌshore sth↔ˈup** **1** to support part of a building or other large structure by placing large pieces of wood or metal against or under it so that it does not fall down 用撐柱支撐 **2** to help to support sth that is weak or going to fail 支撐；穩住

shore·line /ˈʃɔːlaɪn; *NAmE* ˈʃɔːrl-/ *noun* [usually sing.] the edge of the sea, the ocean or a lake 海（或湖）濱線；海（或湖）岸線：*a rocky shoreline* 岩質海岸線 ◇ *The road follows the shoreline for a few miles.* 公路沿海岸線逶迤而行幾英里。

shorn *past part.* of SHEAR

short 0→ /ʃɔːt; *NAmE* ʃɔːrt/ *adj., adv., noun, verb*

■ ***adj.*** (**short·er**, **short·est**)

▸ LENGTH/DISTANCE 長度；距離 **1** 0→ measuring or covering a small length or distance, or a smaller length or distance than usual 短的：*He had short curly hair.* 他有一頭短鬈髮。◇ *a short walk* 短距離步行 ◇ *a short skirt* 短裙 OPP **long**

▸ HEIGHT 高度 **2** 0→ (of a person 人) small in height 個子矮的：*She was short and dumpy.* 她又矮又胖。OPP **tall**

▸ TIME 時間 **3** 0→ lasting or taking a small amount of time or less time than usual 短的；短期的；短暫的：*I'm going to France for a short break.* 我打算去法國度個短假。◇ *Which is the shortest day of the year?* 一年中哪一天最短？◇ *a short book* (= taking a short time to read, because it does not have many pages) 一本小書 ◇ *She has a very* ***short memory*** (= remembers only things that have happened recently). 她的記性很短暫。◇ (*informal*) ***Life's too short*** *to sit around moping.* 人生苦短，不能整天坐在那兒自尋煩悶。◇ *It was all over in a relatively* ***short space of time.*** 不一會兒工夫就完全結束了。OPP **long** **4** [only before noun] (of a period of time 一段時間) seeming to have passed very quickly 短短的：*Just two short years ago he was the best player in the country.* 短短兩年前，他還是全國最優秀的運動員。OPP **long**

▸ NOT ENOUGH 不足 **5** 0→ [not before noun] **~ (of sth)** not having enough of sth; lacking sth 不足；短缺：*I'm afraid I'm a little short* (= of money) *this month.* 這個月我恐怕手頭有點緊。◇ *She is not short of excuses when things go wrong.* 事情出了差錯，她老有藉口。 **6 ~ on sth** (*informal*) lacking or not having enough of a particular quality 缺乏，缺少（某種品質）：*He was a big strapping guy but short on brains.* 他五大三粗，但頭腦簡單。 **7** 0→ [not before noun] not easily available; not supplying as much as you need 緊俏；緊缺：*Money was short at that time.* 那時候，錢緊缺。 **8** [not before noun] **~ (of sth)** less than the number, amount or distance mentioned or needed 少於；缺少；未達到：*Her last throw was only three centimetres short of the world record.* 她的最後一擲距世界紀錄只差三厘米。◇ *The team was five players short.* 球隊還缺五名球員。◇ *She was just short of her 90th birthday when she died.* 她去世時就快過 90 歲生日了。

▸ OF BREATH 呼吸 **9 ~ of breath** having difficulty breathing, for example because of illness（呼吸）短促，困難；（氣）急

▸ NAME/WORD 名稱；單詞 **10 ~ for sth** being a shorter form of a name or word 簡略的；縮寫的：*Call me Jo—it's short for Joanna.* 叫我喬好了，這是喬安娜的簡稱。◇ *file transfer protocol or FTP* ***for short*** * file transfer protocol（文件傳輸協議）或簡稱 FTP

▸ RUDE 無禮 **11** [not before noun] **~ (with sb)** (of a person 人) speaking to sb using few words in a way that seems rude 簡單粗暴；簡慢無禮：*I'm sorry I was short with you earlier—I had other things on my mind.* 對不起，我剛才怠慢你了，我腦子裏在想別的事。

▸ VOWEL 元音 **12** (*phonetics* 語音) a **short** vowel is pronounced for a shorter time than other vowels 短音的：*Compare the short vowel in 'full' and the long vowel in 'fool'.* 比較 full 中的短元音和 fool 中的長元音。OPP **long** ➲ see also SHORTLY

▸ **short·ness** *noun* [U]：*She suffered from shortness of breath.* 她患有氣急的毛病。

IDM **a ˌbrick short of a ˈload, two ˌsandwiches short of a ˈpicnic, etc.** (*informal*) (of a person 人) stupid; not very intelligent 冒傻氣的；不大聰明的 **get the short end of the ˈstick** (*NAmE*) (*BrE* **ˌdraw the short ˈstraw**) to be the person in a group who is chosen or forced to perform an unpleasant duty or task 抽到倒霉籤；被派做苦差事 **give sb/sth/get short ˈshrift** to give sb/get little attention or sympathy 不重視（或同情）；不受重視（或同情） **have/be on a short ˈfuse** to have a tendency to get angry quickly and easily 動輒發火；性情暴躁；脾氣不好：*You may find your temper on a short fuse when confronting your teenager.* 對付十幾歲的半大孩子，你可能動不動就會生氣。 **in ˌshort ˈorder** quickly and without trouble 麻利；簡單省事 **in the ˈshort run** concerning the immediate future 從短期來看；眼下：*In the short run, unemployment may fall.* 從短期來看，失業率可能降低。 **in ˌshort supˈply** not existing in large enough quantities to satisfy demand 不充裕；短缺；緊缺：*Basic foodstuffs were in short supply.* 基本食物緊缺。◇ *Sunshine will be in short supply for the west coast.* 西海岸將不會有充足的陽光。 **little/nothing short of ˈsth** used when you are saying that sth is almost true, or is equal to sth 可以說是；無異於；近乎：*Last year's figures were little short of disastrous.* 去年的數字簡直是災難。◇ *The transformation has been nothing short of a miracle.* 這種變化堪稱奇跡。 **make short ˈwork of sth/sb** to defeat, deal with sth/sb quickly 乾淨利落地打敗（或處理）；三下五除二就打垮（或解決）：*Liverpool made short work of the opposition* (= in a football/SOCCER game). 利物浦隊乾淨利落地擊敗了對手。◇ *He made short work of his lunch* (= ate it quickly). 他三下兩下吃完午飯。 **ˌshort and ˈsweet** (*informal*) pleasant but not lasting a long time 短暫而美好；簡明扼要；緊湊：*We haven't much time so I'll keep it short and sweet.* 我們時間不多，我就長話短說吧。 ➲ more at DRAW *v.*, LIFE *n.*, LONG *adj.*, MEASURE *n.*, NOTICE *n.*, TERM *n.*, THICK *adj.*

■ ***adv.*** (**short·er**, **short·est**) **1** if you **go short of** or **run short of** sth, you do not have enough of it 缺少；不足：*I'd never let you go short of anything.* 我什麼都不會讓你缺的。◇ *Mothers regularly go short of food to ensure their children have enough.* 為了保證自己的孩子吃飽飯，做母親的經常忍飢捱餓。◇ *They had* ***run short of*** (= used most of their supply of) *fuel.* 他們燃料不夠用了。 **2** not as far as you need or expect 未達到；不及：*All too often you pitch the ball short.* 你投球老是距離不夠。 **3** before the time expected or arranged; before the natural time 中間（打斷）；過早地（終止）：*a career tragically* ***cut short*** *by illness* 因病不幸中斷的事業 ◇ *I'm afraid I'm going to have to* ***stop*** *you* ***short*** *there, as time is running out.* 時間快到了，恐怕我得就此打斷你了。

S

IDM **be caught 'short** (*BrE* also **be taken 'short**) **1** (*BrE, informal*) to suddenly feel an urgent need to go to the toilet/bathroom 突然感覺要上廁所；內急 **2** to be put at a disadvantage 被置於不利地位 **come 'short** (*SAfrE, informal*) to have an accident; to get into trouble 出事故；遇到麻煩 **fall 'short of sth** to fail to reach the standard that you expected or need 未達到；不符合：*The hotel fell far short of their expectations.* 旅館遠沒有他們預期的那麼好。 **short of (doing) sth** without sth; without doing sth; unless sth happens 沒有；如果不；除非：*Short of a miracle, we're certain to lose.* 除非發生奇跡，否則我們輸定了。◇ *Short of asking her to leave* (= and we don't want to do that) *there's not a lot we can do about the situation.* 要是不請她走，我們也就沒有多少辦法應付這種局面了。 **pull, bring, etc. sb up 'short** to make sb suddenly stop what they are doing 使某人突然停止：*I was brought up short by a terrible thought.* 一個可怕的念頭閃過，我一下子愣住了。 ➲ more at SELL *v.*, STOP *v.*

■ ***noun*** (*informal*) ➲ see also SHORTS **1** (*BrE*) a small strong alcoholic drink, for example of WHISKY 少量烈酒 **2** a short film/movie, especially one that is shown before the main film（尤指在正片前放映的）電影短片 **3** (*informal*) = SHORT CIRCUIT

IDM **in 'short** in a few words 總之；簡言之：*His novels belong to a great but vanished age. They are, in short, old-fashioned.* 他的小說屬於一個輝煌但已逝去的時代。一句話，已經過時了。 ➲ more at LONG *adj.*

■ ***verb*** [I, T] **~ (sth) (out)** (*informal*) = SHORT-CIRCUIT

short·age /ˈʃɔːtɪdʒ; *NAmE* ˈʃɔːrt-/ *noun* [C, U] a situation when there is not enough of the people or things that are needed 不足；缺少；短缺：***food/housing/water shortages*** 食物／住房／用水短缺 ◇ *a shortage of funds* 資金不足 ◇ ***There is no shortage of*** (= there are plenty of) *things to do in the town.* 城裏不愁找不到活兒幹。

ˈshort-arse (*BrE*) (*US* **ˈshort-ass**) *noun* (*slang, disapproving*) a person who is not very tall 矮子

ˌshort ˌback and ˈsides *noun* [sing.] (*BrE, old-fashioned*) a way of cutting a man's hair so that the hair is very short at the sides and the back of the head 蓋式髮型（腦後和兩側均剪得很短的男式髮型）

short·bread /ˈʃɔːtbred; *NAmE* ˈʃɔːrt-/ (*BrE* also **short·cake**) *noun* [U] a rich crisp biscuit/cookie made with flour, sugar and a lot of butter 黃油甜酥餅乾；牛油甜酥餅

short·cake /ˈʃɔːtkeɪk; *NAmE* ˈʃɔːrt-/ *noun* [U] **1** (*BrE*) = SHORTBREAD **2** a cake with a PASTRY base and cream and fruit on top 水果奶油酥餅：*strawberry shortcake* 草莓酥餅

S

ˌshort-ˈchange *verb* [often passive] **1 ~ sb** to give back less than the correct amount of money to sb who has paid for sth with more than the exact price 少找給（某人）零錢：*I think I've been short-changed at the bar.* 我覺得酒吧沒給我找夠零錢。 **2 ~ sb** to treat sb unfairly by not giving them what they have earned or deserve 虧待；剋扣

ˌshort ˈcircuit (also *informal* **short**) *noun* a failure in an electrical CIRCUIT, when electricity travels along the wrong route because of damaged wires or a fault in the connections between the wires 短路

ˌshort-ˈcircuit (also *informal* **short**) *verb* **1** [I, T] **~ (sth)** to have a short circuit; to make sth have a short circuit（使）短路：*The wires had short-circuited and burnt out.* 電線短路，燒壞了。 **2** [T] **~ sth** to succeed in doing sth more quickly than usual, without going through all the usual processes（做事）抄近路，走捷徑

short·com·ing /ˈʃɔːtkʌmɪŋ; *NAmE* ˈʃɔːrt-/ *noun* [usually pl.] a fault in sb's character, a plan, a system, etc. 缺點；短處 **SYN** **defect**

short·crust pastry /ˌʃɔːtkrʌst ˈpeɪstri; *NAmE* ˌʃɔːrt-/ *noun* [U] a type of PASTRY that CRUMBLES easily, used for making PIES, etc. 酥皮麪糰

ˌshort ˈcut (also **ˈshort cut**) *noun* **1** a quicker or shorter way of getting to a place 近路；捷徑：*You can **take a short cut** across the field.* 你可以抄近道從田裏穿過去。 **2** a way of doing sth that is quicker than the usual way（做某事的）快捷辦法，捷徑：*There are no short cuts to economic recovery.* 恢復經濟無捷徑可走。

short·en /ˈʃɔːtn; *NAmE* ˈʃɔːrtn/ *verb* [T, I] to make sth shorter; to become shorter（使）變短，縮短：**~ (sth)** *Injury problems could shorten his career.* 受傷的問題有可能縮短他的職業生涯。◇ *a shortened version of the game* 簡化了的比賽 ◇ *In November the temperatures drop and the days shorten.* 十一月氣溫下降，白天變短。◇ **~ sth to sth** *Her name's Katherine, generally shortened to Kay.* 她名叫凱瑟琳，通常簡稱凱。 **OPP** **lengthen**

short·en·ing /ˈʃɔːtnɪŋ; *NAmE* ˈʃɔːrt-/ *noun* [U] fat that is used for making PASTRY（製作油酥點心用的）起酥油

short·fall /ˈʃɔːtfɔːl; *NAmE* ˈʃɔːrt-/ *noun* **~ (in sth)** if there is a **shortfall in** sth, there is less of it than you need or expect 缺口；差額；虧空 **SYN** **deficit**

short·hair /ˈʃɔːtheə(r); *NAmE* ˈʃɔːrther/ *noun* a breed of cat with short hair 短毛貓 ➲ compare LONGHAIR

short·hand /ˈʃɔːthænd; *NAmE* ˈʃɔːrt-/ *noun* **1** (*NAmE* also **sten·og·raphy**) [U] a quick way of writing using special signs or abbreviations, used especially to record what sb is saying 速記（法）：*typing and shorthand* 打字和速記 ◇ *to take sth down **in shorthand*** 用速記記錄某事 ◇ *a shorthand typist* 速記打字員 **2** [U, C, usually sing.] **~ (for sth)** a shorter way of saying or referring to sth, which may not be as accurate as the more complicated way of saying it（對某事）簡略的表達方式

ˌshort-ˈhanded *adj.* [not usually before noun] not having as many workers or people who can help as you need 人手不足 **SYN** **short-staffed**

ˈshort-haul *adj.* [only before noun] that involves transporting people or goods over short distances, especially by plane（尤指空運）短途運輸的 **OPP** **long-haul**

short·horn /ˈʃɔːthɔːn; *NAmE* ˈʃɔːrthɔːrn/ *noun* a breed of cow with short horns 短角牛

shortie = SHORTY

short·list /ˈʃɔːtlɪst; *NAmE* ˈʃɔːrt-/ *noun, verb*

■ ***noun*** [usually sing.] a small number of candidates for a job, etc., who have been chosen from all the people who applied 入圍名單：*to draw up a shortlist* 擬就入圍名單 ◇ *a shortlist for a literary prize* 一項文學獎的入圍名單 ◇ *She is **on my shortlist** of great singers.* 她是我心目中的優秀歌唱家之一。

■ ***verb*** [usually passive] **~ sb/sth (for sth)** (*BrE*) to put sb/sth on a shortlist for a job, prize, etc. 把…列入入圍名單：*Candidates who are shortlisted for interview will be contacted by the end of the week.* 入圍參加面試的求職者將在週末以前得到通知。

ˌshort-ˈlived *adj.* lasting only for a short time 短暫的

short·ly 🔑 /ˈʃɔːtli; *NAmE* ˈʃɔːrt-/ *adv.* **1** 🔑 a short time; not long 不多時；不久：*She arrived shortly after us.* 我們剛到不多會兒她就到了。◇ *I saw him shortly before he died.* 在他去世前不久我還見過他一面。 **2** 🔑 soon 立刻；馬上：*I'll be ready shortly.* 我馬上就準備好了。 **3** in an angry and impatient way 沒好氣地；不耐煩地 **SYN** **sharply**

ˌshort-order ˈcook *noun* a person who works in a restaurant cooking food that can be prepared quickly 快餐廚師

ˌshort-ˈrange *adj.* [usually before noun] **1** (of weapons 武器) designed to travel only over short distances 短程的；近程的：*short-range missiles* 短程導彈 **2** (of plans, etc. 計劃等) connected with a short period of time in the future 短期的；近期的：*a short-range weather forecast* 短期天氣預報 ➲ compare LONG-RANGE

shorts /ʃɔːts; *NAmE* ʃɔːrts/ *noun* [pl.] **1** short trousers/pants that end above or at the knee 短褲：*a pair of tennis shorts* 一條網球短褲 ◇ *He was wearing a T-shirt and shorts.* 他穿着 T 恤衫和短褲。 ➲ **VISUAL VOCAB** page V63 **2** (*NAmE*) = BOXER SHORTS

ˌshort-ˈsighted *adj.* **1** (*especially BrE*) (*NAmE* usually **near·sighted**) able to see things clearly only if they are very close to you 近視的 **OPP** **long-sighted** **2** not thinking carefully about the possible effects of sth or what might happen in the future 目光短淺的；無遠見

的：*a short-sighted policy* 目光短淺的政策 ▸ **ˌshort ˈsight** (also **ˌshort-ˈsighted·ness**) *noun* [U]： *She suffered from short sight.* 她眼睛近視。◇ *Many people accused the government of short-sightedness.* 很多人譴責政府目光短淺。 **ˌshort-ˈsighted·ly** *adv.*

ˌshort-ˈstaffed *adj.* [not usually before noun] having fewer members of staff than you need or usually have 人員配備不足；人手短缺 **SYN** **short-handed** ➲ see also UNDERSTAFFED

ˌshort-ˈstay *adj.* [only before noun] (*BrE*) (of a place 地方) where you only stay for a short time 臨時停留的；暫住的： *a short-stay car park* 臨時停車場

ˌshort ˈstory *noun* a story, usually about imaginary characters and events, that is short enough to be read from beginning to end without stopping 短篇小説

ˌshort ˈtemper *noun* [sing.] a tendency to become angry very quickly and easily 暴躁脾氣 ▸ **ˌshort-ˈtempered** *adj.*

ˌshort-ˈterm *adj.* [usually before noun] lasting a short time; designed only for a short period of time in the future 短期的；近期的： *a short-term loan* 短期貸款◇ *to find work on a short-term contract* 找一份短期合同工作◇ *short-term plans* 近期計劃◇ *a short-term solution to the problem* 解決這個問題的短期措施◇ *His* ***short-term memory*** (= the ability to remember things that happened a short time ago) *is failing.* 他的短時記憶越來越差了。 ➲ compare LONG-TERM

ˌshort-ˈtermism *noun* [U] a way of thinking or planning that is concerned with the advantages or profits you could have now, rather than the effects in the future 只注重短期效益的思維方式

ˌshort ˈtime *noun* [U] (*BrE*) if workers are put on **short time**, they work for fewer hours than usual, because there is not enough work to do or not enough money to pay them 短工時；開工不足

ˌshort ˈwave *noun* [C, U] (*abbr.* **SW**) a radio wave that has a FREQUENCY between 3 and 30 MEGAHERTZ 短波 ➲ compare LONG WAVE, MEDIUM WAVE

shorty (also **shortie**) /ˈʃɔːti; *NAmE* ˈʃɔːrti/ *noun* (*pl.* **-ies**) (*informal*) a person who is shorter than average 矮子

Sho·shone /ʃəʊˈʃəʊni; *NAmE* ʃoʊˈʃoʊni/ *noun* (*pl.* **Sho·shone** or **Sho·shones**) a member of a Native American people many of whom now live in the US state of Wyoming 肖肖尼人（美洲土著，很多現居於美國懷俄明州）

shot 0⊷ /ʃɒt; *NAmE* ʃɑːt/ *noun, adj.* ➲ see also SHOOT, SHOT, SHOT *v.*

■ ***noun***

▸ **WITH GUN** 用槍炮 **1** 0⊷ [C] **~ (at sb/sth)** the act of firing a gun; the sound this makes 射擊；開槍（或炮）；槍（或炮）聲： *The man fired several shots from his pistol.* 那個男人用手槍開了幾槍。◇ *Someone* ***took a shot at*** *the car.* 有人朝轎車開槍。◇ *We heard some shots in the distance.* 我們聽見遠處有幾聲槍響。 ➲ see also GUNSHOT, POTSHOT **2** [C] **a good, bad, etc. ~** a person who shoots a gun in a particular way (well, badly, etc.) 優秀（或不高明等的）射手，槍手，炮手

▸ **BULLETS** 子彈 **3** (also **ˌlead ˈshot**) [U] a large number of small metal balls that you fire together from a SHOTGUN 鉛沙彈 ➲ see also BUCKSHOT **4** [C] (*pl.* **shot**) a large stone or metal ball that was shot from a CANNON or large gun in the past （舊時用大炮發射的石質或金屬的）彈丸

▸ **REMARK/ACTION** 言語；行動 **5** [C] a remark or an action that is usually one of a series, and is aimed against sb/sth that you are arguing or competing with（針對對手、多為一系列之一的）一席話，一擊： *This statement was* ***the opening shot*** *in the argument.* 這番話打響了爭論的第一炮。◇ *The supermarket* ***fired the first shot*** *in a price war today.* 今天，這家超市打響了價格戰的頭一炮。

▸ **ATTEMPT** 嘗試 **6** [C, usually sing.] **~ (at sth/at doing sth)** (*informal*) the act of trying to do or achieve sth 嘗試；努力： *The team are looking good for a shot at the title.* 看來這個隊力爭奪冠的勢頭不錯。◇ *I've never produced a play before but I'll* ***have a shot at*** *it.* 我從來沒有製作過一齣戲劇，不過我要嘗試一下。◇ *I'm willing to* ***give it a shot.*** 我願意試試。◇ *Just* ***give it your best shot*** (= try as hard as you can) *and you'll be fine.* 只要盡自己最大努力，你就會有好的結果。

▸ **IN SPORT** 體育運動 **7** 0⊷ [C] the action of hitting, kicking or throwing the ball in order to score a point or goal in a game 擊球；射門；投籃： *Taylor scored with a low shot into the corner of the net.* 泰勒一腳低射，把球射入網角。◇ *Good shot!* 好球！ **8** (often **the shot**) [sing.] the heavy ball that is used in the sports competition called THE SHOT-PUT 鉛球

▸ **PHOTOGRAPH** 照片 **9** [C] a photograph 照片： *I got some good shots of people at the party.* 我給參加聚會的人拍了幾張精彩的照片。 ➲ see also MUGSHOT, SNAPSHOT ➲ SYNONYMS at PHOTOGRAPH

▸ **SCENE IN FILM/MOVIE** 電影中的鏡頭 **10** [C] a scene in a film/movie that is filmed continuously by one camera（電影中的）鏡頭： *the opening shot of a character walking across a desert* 影片開頭呈現一個人穿越沙漠的鏡頭

▸ **DRUG** 藥物 **11** [C] (*informal, especially NAmE*) a small amount of a drug that is put into your body using a SYRINGE 注射 **SYN** **injection**： *a flu shot* (= to protect you against flu) 打預防流感的針◇ *a shot of morphine* 打一針嗎啡

▸ **DRINK** 飲料 **12** [C] (*informal*) a small amount of a drink, especially a strong alcoholic one 少量飲料；（尤指）少量烈酒： *a shot of whisky* 一點威士忌

▸ **OF SPACECRAFT** 航天器 **13** [C] an occasion when a SPACECRAFT is sent into space 發射： *The space shot was shown live on television.* 此次太空發射在電視上做了實況轉播。

▸ **HORSE/DOG IN RACE** 比賽中的馬 / 狗 **14** [sing.] (used with numbers 與數字連用) a horse, dog, etc. that has the particular chance of winning a race that is mentioned 有…獲勝可能的馬（或狗）： *The horse is a 10–1 shot.* 這匹馬的獲勝率為 10:1。 **HELP** You will find other compounds ending in **shot** at their place in the alphabet. 其他以 shot 結尾的複合詞可在各字母中的適當位置查到。

IDM **like a ˈshot** (*informal*) very quickly and without hesitating 立刻；飛快地；毫不猶豫： *If I had the chance to go there, I'd go like a shot.* 要是我有機會去那兒，我會毫不猶豫就去的。 **a shot across the/sb's ˈbows** something that you say or do as a warning to sb about what might happen if they do not change, etc.（若不改變就會有某種後果的）警告 **a shot in the ˈarm** something that gives sb/sth the help or encouragement they need 鼓舞的力量；令人振奮的事情；強心針 ➲ more at BIG *adj.*, CALL *v.*, DARK *n.*, LONG *adj.*, PARTING *adj.*

■ ***adj.*** **1 ~ (with sth)** (of cloth, hair, etc. 織物、毛髮等) having another colour showing through or mixed with the main colour 雜色的；閃色的： *shot silk* 閃色綢 **2** [not before noun] (*informal*) in a very bad condition; destroyed 破爛不堪；筋疲力盡；毀壞： *The brakes on this car are shot.* 這輛車上的剎車完全失靈了。◇ *I'm shot—I'm too old for this job.* 我一點力氣都沒有了，我這歲數幹不動這活兒了。◇ *After the accident his nerves were* ***shot to pieces.*** 經歷了那場事故，他的神經脆弱到了極點。

IDM **be/get ˈshot of sb/sth** (*BrE, informal*) to get rid of sb/sth so you no longer have the problems they cause 擺脱；解決；處理 **shot through with sth** containing a lot of a particular colour, quality or feature 佈滿，充滿，富有（某種顏色、品質或特徵）： *a voice shot through with emotion* 富有感情的聲音

shot·gun /ˈʃɒtɡʌn; *NAmE* ˈʃɑːt-/ *noun* a long gun that fires a lot of small metal bullets (called SHOT) and is used especially for shooting birds or animals 獵槍；散彈槍 ➲ see also SAWN-OFF SHOTGUN **IDM** see RIDE *v.*

ˌshotgun ˈwedding (also **ˌshotgun ˈmarriage**) *noun* (*old-fashioned, informal*) a wedding that has to take place quickly because the woman is pregnant（因女方懷孕而倉促舉行的）閃電式結婚

shot·making /ˈʃɒtmeɪkɪŋ; *NAmE* ˈʃɑːt-/ *noun* [U] (in GOLF, TENNIS, etc. 高爾夫球、網球等) a way of playing in which a player takes risks in order to win more points（冒險）準確擊球

S

Shoto·kan /ʃəʊ'təʊkæn; *NAmE* ʃoʊ'toʊ-/ *noun* [U] (from *Japanese*) a popular form of KARATE 松濤館(空手道的一個流派)

the 'shot-put *noun* [sing.] (also **'shot-putting**, **,putting the 'shot**) the event or sport of throwing a heavy metal ball (called a SHOT) as far as possible 推鉛球

Grammar Point 語法說明

should / ought / had better

- **Should** and **ought to** are both used to say that something is the best thing or the right thing to do, but **should** is much more common. * should 和 ought to 均用以表示應該做某事，不過 should 常用得多：*You should take the baby to the doctor's.* 你應該把這嬰兒帶去看看醫生。◇ *I ought to give up smoking.* 我應該戒煙。In questions, **should** is usually used instead of **ought to**. 在疑問句中，通常用 should 而不是 ought to：*Should we call the doctor?* 我們叫醫生來好嗎？
- **Had better** can also be used to say what is the best thing to do in a situation that is happening now. * had better 亦可用以表示在目前狀況下最好做某事：*We'd better hurry or we'll miss the train.* 我們最好快點，否則就趕不上火車了。
- You form the past by using **should have** or **ought to have**. 過去時用 should have 或 ought to have 構成：*She should have asked for some help.* 她本應該請求幫助的。◇ *You ought to have been more careful.* 你本應該更小心一點的。
- The forms **should not** or **shouldn't** (and **ought not to** or **oughtn't to**, which are rare in *NAmE* and formal in *BrE*) are used to say that something is a bad idea or the wrong thing to do. * should not 或 shouldn't(以及在美式英語中很少見，在英式英語中為正式用法的 ought not to 或 oughtn't to)表示不應該：*You shouldn't drive so fast.* 你不應該把車開得這麼快。
- The forms **should not have** or **shouldn't have** and, much less frequently, **ought not to have** or **oughtn't to have** are used to talk about the past. * should not have 或 shouldn't have 以及很少用的 ought not to have 或 oughtn't to have 均用於指過去：*I'm sorry, I shouldn't have lost my temper.* 對不起，我不該發脾氣。

S

should 0▬ /ʃəd; *strong form* ʃʊd/ *modal verb* (*negative* **should not**, *short form* **shouldn't** /'ʃʊdnt/)
1 0▬ used to show what is right, appropriate, etc., especially when criticizing sb's actions(尤用於糾正別人)應該，應當：*You shouldn't drink and drive.* 你不該酒後駕車。◇ *He should have been more careful.* 他應當更小心點兒才是。◇ *A present for me? You **shouldn't have**!* (= used to thank sb politely) 給我的禮物？您太客氣了！ **2** 0▬ used for giving or asking for advice(提出或徵詢建議)該，可以：*You should stop worrying about it.* 你該不要再為此事擔憂了。◇ *Should I call him and apologize?* 我是不是應該打電話向他道歉？◇ ***I should** wait a little longer, **if I were you**.* 假如我是你的話，我會再等一會兒。◇ (*ironic*) *'She doesn't think she'll get a job.' 'She should worry, with all her qualifications* (= she does not need to worry).' "她擔心找不到工作。" "她那麼好的條件，擔心什麼呀。" **3** 0▬ used to say that you expect sth is true or will happen(表示預期)應該會，可能：*We should arrive before dark.* 我們天黑以前應該能趕到。◇ *I should have finished the book by Friday.* 到星期五我應該能讀完那本書。◇ *The roads should be less crowded today.* 今天路上該不那麼擁擠了吧。 **4** 0▬ used to say that sth that was expected has not happened(表示與預期相反)本應，本當：*It should be snowing now, according to the weather forecast.* 按天氣預報，現在該下雪才是。◇ *The bus should have arrived ten minutes ago.* 公共汽車十分鐘以前就該到了。 **5** (*BrE, formal*) used after *I* or *we* instead of *would* for describing what you would do if sth else happened first(與 I 或 we 連用代替 would，表示虛擬結果)就將：*If I were asked to work on Sundays, I should resign.* 要是叫我星期天加班，我就辭職不幹了。 **6** (*formal*) used to refer to a possible event or situation(表示可能)假如，萬一：*If you should change your mind, do let me know.* 假如你改變主意的話，一定要告訴我。◇ *In case you should need any help, here's my number.* 萬一你需要幫助的話，這是我的電話號碼。◇ *Should anyone call* (= if anyone calls), *please tell them I'm busy.* 如果有人打電話來，請告訴他我正忙着。 **7** 0▬ used as the past form of *shall* when reporting what sb has said(在間接引語中用作 shall 的過去時)：*He asked me what time he should come.* (= His words were: 'What time shall I come?') 他問我他應該什麼時候來。◇ (*BrE, formal*) *I said* (*that*) *I should be glad to help.* 我說我樂意幫忙。 **8** 0▬ (*BrE*) used after *that* when sth is suggested or arranged(用於 that 引導的、表示建議或安排的從句中)：*She recommended that I should take some time off.* 她建議我應該休息一段時間。◇ *In order that training should be effective it must be planned systematically.* 為使培訓有成效，必須有系統的計劃。 **HELP** In both *NAmE* and *BrE* this idea can be expressed without 'should'. 在美式英語和英式英語中，表達這一意思均可省掉 should：*She recommended that I take some time off.* ◇ *In order that training be effective …* **9** used after *that* after many adjectives that describe feelings(用於許多表示感情的形容詞後的 that 從句中)：*I'm anxious that we should allow plenty of time.* 我殷切希望我們能留出充裕的時間。◇ *I find it astonishing that he should be so rude to you.* 他竟然對你這樣無禮，真叫我吃驚。 **10** (*BrE, formal*) used with *I* and *we* in polite requests(與 I 和 we 連用，表示客氣地請求)：*I should like to call my lawyer.* 我希望給我的律師打個電話。◇ *We should be grateful for your help.* 對您的幫助我會非常感激。 **11** 0▬ used with *I* and *we* to give opinions that you are not certain about(與 I 和 we 連用，表示沒有把握)：*I should imagine it will take about three hours.* 我想得用差不多三個小時吧。◇ *'Is this enough food for everyone?' '**I should think so**.'* "這些食物夠所有人吃嗎？" "我覺得夠了吧。" ◇ *'Will it matter?' '**I shouldn't think so**.'* "這有關係嗎？" "不會吧。" **12** used for expressing strong agreement(表示十分贊同)：*'I know it's expensive but it will last for years.' '**I should hope so too!**'* "我知道價錢貴，但能用好多年。" "我也是這麼想的！" ◇ *'Nobody will oppose it.' '**I should think not!**'* "誰也不會反對的。" "我想也是！" **13 why, how, who, what ~ sb/sth do** used to refuse sth or to show that you are annoyed at a request; used to express surprise about an event or a situation(表示拒絕、惱怒或驚奇)：*Why should I help him? He's never done anything for me.* 我幹嗎要幫他呢？他從來沒為我做過什麼。◇ *How should I know where you've left your bag?* 我怎麼知道你把包丟在哪兒了？◇ *I got on the bus and who should be sitting in front of me but Tony!* 我上了公共汽車，沒想到坐在我前面的竟然是托尼！ **14** used to tell sb that sth would amuse or surprise them if they saw or experienced it(表示假如對方看見或經歷某事物，一定會感興趣或吃驚)真該，真應當：*You should have seen her face when she found out!* 你真該看看她發現事情真相時臉上的表情！➲ note at MODAL

shoul·der 0▬ /'ʃəʊldə(r); *NAmE* 'ʃoʊ-/ *noun, verb*

■ *noun*

▸ **PART OF BODY 身體部位 1** 0▬ [C] either of the two parts of the body between the top of each arm and the neck 肩；肩膀；肩胛：*He slung the bag over his shoulder.* 他把包一甩，挎在肩上。◇ *She tapped him on the shoulder.* 她拍了拍他的肩膀。◇ *He looked back over his shoulder.* 他扭頭朝後看。◇ *She **shrugged her shoulders*** (= showing that she didn't know or care). 她聳了聳肩。◇ *an **off-the-shoulder** dress* 露肩連衣裙 ◇ *He carried the child on his shoulders.* 他把孩子扛在肩上。➲ COLLOCATIONS at PHYSICAL ➲ VISUAL VOCAB page V59

▸ **-SHOULDERED 肩膀… 2** (in adjectives 構成形容詞) having the type of shoulders mentioned …肩膀的：*broad-shouldered* 寬肩的 ➲ see also ROUND-SHOULDERED

▸ **CLOTHING 衣服 3** 0▬ [C] the part of a piece of clothing that covers the shoulder(衣服的)肩部：*a jacket with padded shoulders* 帶墊肩的夾克

▸ MEAT 肉 **4** [U, C] **~ (of sth)** meat from the top part of one of the front legs of an animal that has four legs 前腿連肩肉

▸ OF MOUNTAIN/BOTTLE, ETC. 山、瓶子等 **5** [C] **~ (of sth)** a part of sth, such as a bottle or mountain, that is shaped like a shoulder 山肩；瓶肩：*The village lay just around the shoulder of the hill.* 村子恰好坐落在山肩處。

▸ SIDE OF ROAD 公路邊 **6** [C] (*NAmE*) an area of ground at the side of a road where vehicles can stop in an emergency 路肩（公路兩側供車輛緊急停靠的地帶）：*No shoulder for next 5 miles.* 前方 5 英里之內沒有路肩。➲ see also HARD SHOULDER, SOFT SHOULDER

IDM **be looking over your 'shoulder** to be anxious and have the feeling that sb is going to do sth unpleasant or harmful to you 惴惴不安；小心提防 **on sb's shoulders** if blame, GUILT, etc. is **on sb's shoulders**, they must take responsibility for it 由某人承擔 **put your shoulder to the 'wheel** to start working very hard at a particular task 着手大幹起來；全力以赴 **a shoulder to 'cry on** used to describe a person who listens to your problems and gives you sympathy 傾訴的對象 **ˌshoulder to 'shoulder (with sb)** **1** physically close to sb 肩並肩地；緊挨着 **2** as one group that has the same aims, opinions, etc. 並肩；齊心協力 ➲ more at CHIP *n.*, COLD *adj.*, HEAD *n.*, OLD, RUB *v.*, STRAIGHT *adv.*

■ *verb*

▸ ACCEPT RESPONSIBILITY 承擔責任 **1** [T] **~ sth** to accept the responsibility for sth 承擔；擔負：*to* ***shoulder the responsibility/blame*** *for sth* 對某事承擔責任／過失 ◇ *women who shoulder the double burden of childcare and full-time work* 既撫養孩子又做全職工作，承擔着雙重負擔的婦女

▸ PUSH WITH SHOULDER 用肩推 **2** [T, I] to push forward with your shoulder in order to get somewhere 擠；闖：**~ your way + adv./prep.** *He shouldered his way through the crowd and went after her.* 他側身從人群中擠了過去，跟在她後面。◇ **+ adv./prep.** *She shouldered past a woman with a screaming baby.* 她從一個懷抱啼哭嬰兒的女人身邊擠了過去。 **3** [T] **~ sb/sth + adv./prep.** to push sb/sth out of your way with your shoulder （用肩膀）推開，頂開：*He shouldered the man aside.* 他一膀子把那男人撞到了一旁。

▸ CARRY ON SHOULDER 肩負 **4** [T] **~ sth** to carry sth on your shoulder 背；扛；挑；擔：*She shouldered her bag and set off home.* 她扛起包朝家走去。

'shoulder bag *noun* a bag, especially a HANDBAG, that is carried over the shoulder with a long narrow piece of leather, etc. （小）挎包 ➲ VISUAL VOCAB page V64

'shoulder blade *noun* either of the two large flat bones at the top of the back 肩胛骨 SYN **scapula** ➲ VISUAL VOCAB page V59

ˌshoulder-'high *adj.* as high as a person's shoulders 齊肩高的：*a shoulder-high wall* 一堵齊肩高的牆 ▸ **ˌshoulder-'high** *adv.*：*They carried him shoulder-high through the crowd.* 他們把他抬在肩頭，穿過人群。

Grammar Point 語法說明

should / would

- In modern English, the traditional difference between **should** and **would** in reported sentences, conditions, requests, etc. has disappeared and **should** is not used very much at all. In spoken English the short form **'d** is usually used. 在現代英語中，should 或 would 在間接引述中、在表示條件、請求等句子中的傳統區別已不復存在；should 基本上不怎麼用，在英語口語中常用簡約式 'd 表示：*I said I'd (I would) be late.* 我說我要遲到了。◇ *He'd (he would) have liked to have been an actor.* 他本來想當演員。◇ *I'd (I would) really prefer tea.* 我倒是更喜歡喝茶。
- The main use of **should** now is to tell somebody what they ought to do, to give advice, or to add emphasis. 現在 should 主要用於告訴某人應該做什麼、給予忠告或加強語氣：*We should really go and visit them soon.* 我們的確應該馬上去看看他們。◇ *You should have seen it!* 你應該看見的！

'shoulder-length *adj.* (especially of hair 尤指頭髮) long enough to reach your shoulders 齊肩的 ➲ VISUAL VOCAB page V60

'shoulder pad *noun* [usually pl.] **1** a small piece of thick cloth that is sewn into the shoulder of a dress, jacket, etc. to make a person's shoulders look bigger （衣服）墊肩 **2** a piece of hard plastic that people wear under their shirts to protect their shoulders when playing AMERICAN FOOTBALL, ICE HOCKEY, etc. （美式足球、冰球等運動衣內的）護肩 ➲ VISUAL VOCAB page V44

'shoulder strap *noun* **1** a strip of cloth on a dress or other piece of clothing that goes over your shoulder from the front to the back （衣服）肩帶 **2** a long strip of cloth, leather, etc. that is attached to a bag so that you can carry it over your shoulder （背包）肩帶

'shoulder surfing *noun* [U] (*informal*) the practice of watching a person who is getting money from a machine, filling out a form, etc., in order to find out their personal information 肩窺（窺視他人從提款機取款、填表等以瞭解其個人信息的做法）

shout 0-ᴡ /ʃaʊt/ *verb, noun*

■ *verb* **1** 0-ᴡ [I, T] to say sth in a loud voice; to speak loudly/angrily to sb 大聲說；叫；嚷；斥責；怒罵：*Stop shouting and listen!* 別嚷了，聽着！◇ **~ for sth** *I shouted for help but nobody came.* 我大聲呼救，但沒人來。◇ **~ at sb** *Then he started shouting and swearing at her.* 這時，他衝着她又叫又罵起來。◇ **~ at sb to do sth** *She shouted at him to shut the gate.* 她大聲吆喝他把大門關上。◇ **~ sth (at/to sb)** *to shout abuse/encouragement/orders* 高聲辱罵／鼓勵／命令 ◇ **~ that ...** *He shouted that he couldn't swim.* 他大叫他不會游泳。◇ **~ yourself + adj.** *She shouted herself hoarse, cheering on the team.* 她為運動隊加油，嗓子都喊啞了。◇ **+ speech** *'Run!' he shouted.* "跑！"他大喊一聲。 **2** 0-ᴡ [I] **~ (out)** to make a loud noise 呼叫；喊叫：*She shouted out in pain when she tried to move her leg.* 她想動動腿，結果疼得大叫起來。 **3** [I, T] (*AustralE, NZE*) to buy drinks or food for sb in a bar, restaurant, etc. （在酒吧、餐廳等）請人喝飲料（或吃東西）：*I'll shout—what are you drinking?* 我請客，你想喝什麼？◇ **~ (sb) sth** *Who's going to shout me a drink?* 誰要請我喝一杯？ ➲ SYNONYMS at next page

PHR V **ˌshout sb↔'down** to shout so that sb who is speaking cannot be heard 用喊叫聲蓋過某人的講話：*The speaker was shouted down by a group of protesters.* 一群抗議者大叫大嚷，蓋過了講話人的聲音。 **ˌshout sth↔'out** to say sth in a loud voice so that it can be clearly heard 大聲說出：*Don't shout out all the answers.* 別把所有的答案都大聲說出來。◇ **+ speech** *'I'm over here!' I shouted out.* "我在這邊！"我大聲喊道。

■ *noun* **1** 0-ᴡ a loud cry of anger, fear, excitement, etc. （憤怒、害怕、激動等的）呼喊，喊叫聲：*angry shouts* 憤怒的叫喊 ◇ *a shout of anger* 一聲怒吼 ◇ *I heard her warning shout too late.* 我聽到她的大聲警告，但已經太晚了。 **2** (*BrE, informal*) a person's turn to buy drinks 輪到某人請客（喝飲料）：*What are you drinking? It's my shout.* 你喝什麼？該我請客了。

IDM **be ˌin with a 'shout (of sth/of doing sth)** (*informal*) to have a good chance of winning sth or of achieving sth 成功在望 **give sb a 'shout** (*informal*) to tell sb sth 告訴某人：*Give me a shout when you're ready.* 準備好了告訴我一聲。

shout·ing /ˈʃaʊtɪŋ/ *noun* [U] loud cries from a number of people （多人的）叫喊，叫嚷：*Didn't you hear all the shouting?* 你難道沒有聽到那一片叫喊聲？

IDM **be all over bar the 'shouting** (*BrE*) (of an activity or a competition 活動或比賽) to be almost finished or decided, so that there is no doubt about the final result 基本大功告成；大局已定；勝負已分明 **within 'shouting distance** (*especially NAmE*) (*BrE* also **within 'spitting distance (of sth)**) (*informal*) very close 很近

'shouting match *noun* an argument or a disagreement when people shout loudly at each other 高聲的爭論

S

Synonyms 同義詞辨析

shout

yell • cry • scream • cheer • bellow • raise your voice

These words all mean to say sth in a very loud voice. 以上各詞均指大聲說出、叫嚷。

shout to say sth in a loud voice; to speak loudly and often angrily to sb 指大聲說、叫、嚷、斥責、怒罵： *Stop shouting and listen!* 別嚷了，注意聽！◇ *'Run!' he shouted.* "跑！"他大喊一聲。

yell to shout loudly, for example because you are angry, excited, frightened or in pain 指（因氣憤、激動、害怕或痛苦而）叫喊、大喊、吼叫： *She yelled at the boy to get down from the wall.* 她衝小孩大喊，讓他從牆上下來。

cry (*rather formal* or *literary*) to shout loudly 指喊叫、呼喊、呼叫： *She ran over to the window and cried for help.* 她跑到窗口呼喊救命。

scream to shout sth in a loud high voice because you are afraid, angry or excited 指（因害怕、氣憤或激動而）尖叫、大叫： *He screamed at me to stop.* 他衝着我大叫，要我停下來。

cheer (especially of a crowd of people) to shout loudly to show support or praise for sb, or to give them encouragement（尤指一群人）歡呼、喝彩、加油： *We all cheered as the team came onto the field.* 球隊入場時我們都歡呼起來。

bellow to shout in a loud deep voice, especially because you are angry 指大聲吼叫，尤指怒吼： *'Quiet!' the teacher bellowed.* "安靜！"老師大吼道。

raise your voice to speak loudly to sb, especially because you are angry（尤指因氣憤而）提高嗓門、大聲說話： *She never once raised her voice to us.* 她從未對我們提高嗓門說話。

PATTERNS

- to shout/yell/cry/raise your voice **to** sb
- to shout/yell/scream/bellow **at** sb
- to shout/yell/cry out/scream/bellow **in** pain/anguish/rage, etc.
- to shout/cry out/scream **for** joy/excitement/delight, etc.
- to shout/yell/cry out/scream **with** excitement/triumph, etc.
- to shout/yell/scream/bellow at sb **to do sth**
- to shout/yell/scream **abuse**
- to shout/yell/cry/scream **for help**

S

ˈshout-out *noun* (*informal, especially NAmE*) a public expression of thanks or welcome 公開道謝；當眾問候： *This is a shout-out to all our sponsors and advertisers.* 這是對我們所有贊助方和廣告商的公開致謝。

shouty /ˈʃaʊti/ *adj.* (*informal*) doing or involving a lot of shouting 大喊大叫的；吵吵嚷嚷的： *a shouty conversation on the stairs* 樓梯上的高聲談話

shove /ʃʌv/ *verb, noun*

■ *verb* **1** [I, T] to push sb/sth in a rough way 猛推；亂擠；推撞： *The crowd was **pushing and shoving** to get a better view.* 人們擠來擠去，想看得清楚點兒。◇ **+ adv./prep.** *The door wouldn't open no matter how hard she shoved.* 她怎麼使勁推，門都推不開。◇ **~ sb/sth (+ adv./prep.)** *He shoved her down the stairs.* 他把她推下樓梯。 **2** [T] **~ sth (+ adv./prep.)** (*informal*) to put sth somewhere roughly or carelessly 亂放；隨便放；胡亂丟；隨手扔： *She shoved the book into her bag and hurried off.* 她把書胡亂塞進包裏就急急忙忙走了。◇ *He came over and shoved a piece of paper into my hand.* 他走過來往我手裏塞了一張紙條。◇ *Shove your suitcase under the bed.* 把你的行李箱塞到牀底下吧。

IDM **ˈshove it** (*informal, especially NAmE*) used to say rudely that you will not accept or do sth（粗魯地表示不接受或不做某事）去他的，沒門兒，去他媽的： *'The boss wants that report now.' 'Yeah? Tell him he can shove it.'* "老闆現在要那份報告。" "是嗎？你告訴他沒門兒。"

PHR V **ˌshove ˈoff** (*BrE, informal*) used to tell sb rudely to go away 滾；滾開 **ˌshove ˈup** (*BrE, informal*) to move in order to make a space for sb to sit down beside you 挪出空位： *Shove up! Jan wants to sit down.* 挪一挪！簡要坐下來。

■ *noun* [usually sing.] a strong push 猛推： *You have to **give** the door **a shove** or it won't close.* 這門你得猛推一下，否則關不上。 IDM see PUSH *n.*

shovel /ˈʃʌvl/ *noun, verb*

■ *noun* **1** a tool with a long handle and a broad blade with curved edges, used for moving earth, snow, sand, etc. 鏟；鐵鏟： *workmen with picks and shovels* 手拿鎬鏟的工人 ◇ (*NAmE*) *The children took their **pails and shovels** to the beach.* 孩子們帶着桶和鏟子到海灘上去了。 ➲ VISUAL VOCAB page V19 ➲ compare SPADE (1) **2** the part of a large machine or vehicle that digs or moves earth（推土機、挖土機等的）鏟，鏟形部份

■ *verb* (**-ll-**, *US* **-l-**) **~ sth (+ adv./prep.)** to lift and move earth, stones, coal, etc. with a shovel 鏟；鏟起： *A gang of workmen were shovelling rubble onto a truck.* 一幫工人正用鐵鍬往卡車上裝碎石。◇ *They went out in freezing conditions to shovel snow.* 他們冒着嚴寒出去鏟雪。◇ (*NAmE*) *to **shovel the sidewalk/driveway*** (= to remove snow) 鏟除人行道 / 車行道上的積雪 ◇ (*figurative*) *He sat at the table, shovelling food into his mouth.* 他坐在桌前，一個勁地往嘴裏塞吃的。

shovel·ful /ˈʃʌvlfʊl/ *noun* the amount that a shovel can hold 一鏟（的量）

show 0-w /ʃəʊ; *NAmE* ʃoʊ/ *verb, noun*

■ *verb* (**showed**, **shown** /ʃəʊn; *NAmE* ʃoʊn/ or, rarely, 有時或作 **showed**)

▸ MAKE CLEAR 表明 **1** 0-w [T] to make sth clear; to prove sth 表明；證明： **~ (that) …** *The figures clearly show that her claims are false.* 這些數字清楚地表明，她的說法是錯誤的。◇ **~ sb that …** *Market research has shown us that people want quality, not just low prices.* 市場研究告訴我們，人們需要的是高質量，而不僅僅是低價格。◇ **~ sth** *a report showing the company's current situation* 表明公司當前狀況的一份報告 ◇ **~ sb/sth to be/have sth** *His new book shows him to be a first-rate storyteller.* 他的新著表明他講故事的本領是一流的。◇ **~ (sb) how, what, etc. …** *This shows how people are influenced by TV advertisements.* 這表明電視廣告對人們的影響。➲ LANGUAGE BANK at ILLUSTRATE

▸ LET SB SEE STH 給人看 **2** 0-w [T] to let sb see sth 給…看；出示；展示： **~ sth** *You have to show your ticket as you go in.* 進場必須出示門票。◇ **~ sth to sb** *If there's a letter from France please show it to me.* 如有法國來的信，請拿給我看看。◇ *Have you shown your work to anyone?* 你有沒有把你做的活兒給誰看過？◇ **~ sb sth** *Have you shown anyone your work?* 你有沒有給誰看過你做的活兒？

▸ TEACH 教 **3** 0-w [T] to help sb to do sth by letting them watch you do it or by explaining it（通過示範）教，解說；演示： **~ sth to sb** *She showed the technique to her students.* 她向學生演示了那個技巧。◇ **~ sb sth** *She showed her students the technique.* 她向學生演示了那個技巧。◇ *Can you show me how to do it?* 你能教我怎麼做嗎？

▸ POINT 指 **4** 0-w [T] **~ sb sth** to point to sth so that sb can see where or what it is 指給某人看；指出： *He showed me our location on the map.* 他在地圖上指出我們所處的方位。◇ **~ sb which, what, etc. …** *Show me which picture you drew.* 指給我看哪張畫是你畫的。

▸ GUIDE 引導 **5** 0-w [T] to lead or guide sb to a place 引；帶；領： **~ sb + adv./prep.** *The attendant showed us to our seats.* 服務員把我們帶到我們的座位。◇ *We were shown into the waiting room.* 我們被領進等候室。◇ **~ sb sth** *I'll go first and **show you the way**.* 我先走，給你帶路。➲ SYNONYMS at TAKE

▸ QUALITY/BEHAVIOUR/FEELING 品質；行為；感情 **6** 0-w [T] to make it clear that you have a particular quality 表現；體現： **~ sth** *to show great courage* 表現出極大的勇氣 ◇ **~ yourself + adj.** *She had shown herself unable to deal with money.* 她所做的事已表明她不善理財。◇ **~ yourself to be/have sth** *He has shown himself to be ready to make compromises.* 他表現出自己願意妥協。

◇ **~ that** … *He has shown that he is ready to make compromises.* 他表現出願意妥協。 **7** 🔑 [T] to behave in a particular way towards sb（對某人）表現出；對待；表示： **~ sth (for/to sb)** *They showed no respect for their parents.* 他們毫不尊敬自己的父母。◇ **~ sb sth** *They showed their parents no respect.* 他們毫不尊敬自己的父母。 **8** 🔑 [I, T] if a feeling or quality **shows**, or if you **show** it, people can see it 顯示出；流露出：*Fear showed in his eyes.* 他眼裏顯出了害怕的神色。◇ *She tried not to let her disappointment show.* 她極力掩飾自己的失望情緒。◇ *She's nearly forty now.* ***And it shows*** (= it's obvious). 她年近四十，一望便知。◇ **~ sth** *Her expression showed her disappointment.* 從她的表情可以看出她很失望。◇ *James began to* ***show signs of*** *impatience.* 詹姆斯開始顯得不耐煩。◇ **~ how, what, etc.** … *She tried not to show how disappointed she was.* 她極力掩飾她是多麼失望。

▸ **BE VISIBLE** 看得見 **9** 🔑 [I, T] if sth **shows**, people can see it. If sth **shows** a mark, dirt, etc., the mark can be seen. 露出；顯出： *She had a warm woollen hat and scarf on that left only her eyes and nose showing.* 她戴着保暖呢帽和圍巾，只露出了眼睛和鼻子。◇ **~ sth** *Their new white carpet showed every mark.* 他們新鋪的白地毯有一點髒都看得見。

▸ **INFORMATION** 信息 **10** 🔑 [T] (not usually used in the progressive tenses 通常不用於進行時) **~ sth** to give particular information, or a time or measurement 標示，表明（信息、時間、計量）： *The map shows the principal towns and rivers.* 這張地圖標出了主要城鎮和河流。◇ *The clock showed midnight.* 時鐘顯示已是午夜。◇ *The end-of-year accounts show a loss.* 年終賬面顯示出現了虧損。

▸ **OF PICTURE/PHOTOGRAPH** 圖畫；照片 **11** 🔑 [T] **~ sth** | **~ sb/sth (as sth)** | **~ sb/sth doing sth** to be of sb/sth; to represent sb/sth 描繪，描述，表現（為）： *She had objected to a photo showing her in a bikini.* 她曾反對給自己拍穿比基尼泳裝的照片。

▸ **FOR PUBLIC TO SEE** 讓公眾看 **12** 🔑 [I, T] to be or make sth available for the public to see 展覽；陳列；上映；演出： *The movie is now showing at all major movie theaters.* 這部影片目前正在各大影院上映。◇ **~ sth** *The movie is being shown now.* 這部影片目前正在上映。◇ *She plans to show her paintings early next year.* 她計劃明年初展出自己的繪畫作品。

▸ **PROVE** 證明 **13** [T, no passive] (*informal*) to prove that you can do sth or are sth 證明；表明： **~ sb (sth)** *They think I can't do it, but I'll show them!* 他們以為我做不了，我卻要做給他們看看！◇ **~ yourself to be/have sth** *He has shown himself to be a caring father.* 他已經證明了自己是個有愛心的父親。

▸ **ARRIVE** 到來 **14** [I] (*informal, especially NAmE*) to arrive where you have arranged to meet sb or do sth 如約趕到；出現；露面： *I waited an hour but he didn't show.* 我等了一個小時，可他一直沒露面。➲ see also SHOW UP

▸ **ANIMAL** 動物 **15** [T] **~ sth** to enter an animal in a competition 替（動物）報名參加比賽

IDM **it goes to 'show** used to say that sth proves sth 證明；表明： *It just goes to show what you can do when you really try.* 這就表明，一個人只要真下功夫，就能做成什麼事情。 **show sb the 'door** to ask sb to leave, because they are no longer welcome 要某人離開；下逐客令 **show your 'face** to appear among your friends or in public 露面；公開見人： *She stayed at home, afraid to show her face.* 她待在家裏，不敢露面。 **show your 'hand/'cards** (*BrE*) (*NAmE* **tip your 'hand**) to make your plans or intentions known 攤牌；讓對手摸着底細；公開自己的意圖 **show sb who's 'boss** to make it clear to sb that you have more power and authority than they have 讓某人知道誰說了算 **show the 'way** to do sth first so that other people can follow 示範 **show 'willing** (*BrE*) to show that you are ready to help, work hard, etc. if necessary 表示願意；有樂於…的意思 **(have) something, nothing, etc. to 'show for sth** (to have) something, nothing, etc. as a result of sth 在…方面有（或沒有等）成績；在…方面有（或沒有等）結果： *All those years of hard work, and nothing to show for it!* 苦幹這麼多年，卻毫無成績可言！➲ more at FLAG *n.*, PACE[1] *n.*, ROPE *n.*

PHR V **,show sb a'round/'round (sth)** 🔑 to be a guide for sb when they visit a place for the first time to show them what is interesting 領（某人）參觀；帶（某人）巡視： *We were shown around the school by one of the students.* 我們由一名學生領着參觀了學校。◇ *Has anyone shown you round yet?* 有沒有人帶你四處走走？ **,show 'off** 🔑 (*informal, disapproving*) to try to impress others by talking about your abilities, possessions, etc. 炫耀自己；賣弄自己： *He's just showing off because that girl he likes is here.* 他不過是在表現自己，因為他喜歡的那個姑娘在場。➲ related noun SHOW-OFF **,show sb/sth↔'off** 🔑 to show people sb/sth that you are proud of 炫耀；賣弄；顯示： *She wanted to show off her new husband at the party.* 她想在聚會上炫耀自己的新婚丈夫。◇ **~ how, what, etc.** … *He likes to show off how well he speaks French.* 他喜歡向人展示他法語講得有多好。 **,show sth↔'off** 🔑 (of clothing 服裝) to make sb look attractive, by showing their best features 使顯得漂亮；使奪目；襯托： *a dress that shows off her figure* 襯托出她優美身材的連衣裙 **,show 'through** | **,show 'through sth** to be able to be seen behind or under sth else（從某物）透出；（從某事）顯露： *The writing on the other side of the page shows through.* 寫在紙背面的字透了過來。◇ (*figurative*) *When he spoke, his bitterness showed through.* 他說話時流露出內心的辛酸。◇ *Veins showed through her pale skin.* 她蒼白的皮膚下一條條血管清晰可見。 **,show 'up** 🔑 (*informal*) to arrive where you have arranged to meet sb or do sth 如約趕到；出現；露面： *It was getting late when she finally showed up.* 天色已晚，她終於趕到了。 **,show 'up** | **,show sth↔'up** to become visible; to make sth become visible（使）看得見，變得明顯，顯現出來： *a broken bone showed up on the X-ray* 在 X 光照片上顯示出的一根斷骨 ◇ *The harsh light showed up the lines on her face.* 在耀眼的光線下，她臉上的皺紋清晰可見。 **,show sb↔'up** **1** (*BrE, informal*) to make sb feel embarrassed by behaving badly（因舉止不妥而）使人難堪，使人尷尬，使人丟臉： *He showed me up by snoring during the concert.* 他在音樂會上呼呼大睡，真給我丟臉。 **2** to make sb feel embarrassed by doing sth better than them（做得比別人好而）使人難堪，使人尷尬，使人丟臉

■ ***noun***

▸ **ENTERTAINMENT** 娛樂 **1** 🔑 [C] a theatre performance, especially one that includes singing and dancing 演出；歌舞表演： *to go to a show* 去看演出 ◇ *a one-woman/-man show* 女 / 男演員單人表演 ◇ *to put on/stage a show* 上演 / 演出節目 ◇ *She's the* ***star of the show!*** 她是這台演出的明星！➲ see also FLOOR SHOW, ROADSHOW **2** 🔑 [C] a programme on television or the radio（電視或廣播）節目： *to* ***host a show*** 主持節目 ◇ *a* ***TV/radio show*** 電視 / 廣播節目 ◇ *a* ***quiz show*** 知識問答節目 ➲ **COLLOCATIONS** at TELEVISION ➲ see also CHAT SHOW, GAME SHOW, ROADSHOW, TALK SHOW **3** [C] (*NAmE, informal*) a concert, especially of rock music（尤指搖滾）音樂會

▸ **OF COLLECTION OF THINGS** 收藏品 **4** 🔑 [C, U] an occasion when a collection of things are brought together for people to look at 展覽；展覽會： *an agricultural show* 農業展覽會 ◇ *The latest computers will be* ***on show*** *at the exhibition.* 最新型的計算機將在展覽會上展出。➲ see also FASHION SHOW, PEEP SHOW

▸ **OF FEELING** 感受 **5** [C] an action or a way of behaving that shows how you feel（體現內心感受的）動作，行為，樣子 **SYN** **display**： *a show of emotion* 激動的樣子 ◇ *a show of support* 表示支持 ◇ ***a show of force/strength*** *by the army* 軍隊顯示的武力 / 實力

▸ **INSINCERE ACT** 不真誠的行為 **6** [U, sing.] something that is done only to give a good impression, but is not sincere 裝出的樣子；虛假的外觀；假象：*He may seem charming, but it's all show!* 他看起來可能很有魅力，但那都是表面的！◇ *She pretends to be interested in opera, but it's only* ***for show***. 她做出一副對歌劇感興趣的樣子，但這不過是裝門面而已。◇ *He* ***made a great show of*** *affection, but I knew he didn't mean it.* 他大表愛慕之情，但我知道他不是真心的。

▸ **COLOURFUL SIGHT** 色彩繽紛的景象 **7** [C, U] a brightly coloured or pleasing sight 色彩繽紛的景象 **SYN** **display**： *a lovely show of spring flowers* 春天百花爭豔的美景

▸ **EVENT/SITUATION** 事情；場面 **8** [sing.] (*informal*) an event, a business or a situation where sth is being done or organized 事情；機構；場面： *She runs the whole show.*

整個這一攤兒都由她管。◇ *I won't interfere—it's your show.* 我不想插手，這歸你管。

▸ **GOOD/POOR SHOW** 好的 / 不好的表現 **9** [C, usually sing.] (*informal, especially BrE*) something that is done in a particular way 表现： *The team **put on a good show** in the competition.* 這支隊伍在比賽中有上佳表現。◇ *It's a poor show if he forgets your birthday.* 要是他忘了你的生日，那可太差勁了。

IDM **for 'show** intended to be seen but not used 供展覽的；裝門面的；中看不中用的： *These items are just for show—they're not for sale.* 這些物品僅供展覽，不作售賣。 **get the ˌshow on the 'road** (*informal*) to start an activity or a journey 開始；出發： *Let's get this show on the road!* 咱們這就開始吧！ **(jolly) good 'show!** (*old-fashioned, BrE, informal*) used to show you like sth or to say that sb has done sth well（喝彩）好，真棒 **a show of 'hands** a group of people each raising a hand to vote for or against sth 舉手表決 ➲ more at DOG *n.*, STEAL

ˌshow-and-'tell *noun* [U] an activity in which children have to bring sth to show their class and talk about it to them 展示和講述（學生自帶物品到課堂講述的活動）

show·boat /ˈʃəʊbəʊt; *NAmE* ˈʃoʊboʊt/ *verb, noun*

■ ***verb*** [I] (*informal*, often *disapproving*) to behave in a way that tries to show people how clever, skilful, etc. you are 賣弄；炫耀 ▸ **show·boat·ing** *noun* [U]

■ ***noun*** (*NAmE*) a boat on which musical shows are performed 演藝船

'show business (also *informal* **show·biz** /ˈʃəʊbɪz; *NAmE* ˈʃoʊ-/) *noun* [U] the business of providing public entertainment, for example in the theatre, in films/movies or in television 娛樂行業；娛樂界；演藝界： *to be in show business* 從事演藝工作 ◇ *show-business people/stars* 演藝界人士 / 明星 ◇ *That's showbiz!* 這就是娛樂界嘛！

show·case /ˈʃəʊkeɪs; *NAmE* ˈʃoʊ-/ *noun* **1** [usually sing.] **~ (for sb/sth)** an event that presents sb's abilities or the good qualities of sth in an attractive way 展示（本領、才華或優良品質）的場合： *The festival was a showcase for young musicians.* 音樂節是青年音樂家展現才華的場合。 **2** a box with a glass top or sides that is used for showing objects in a shop/store, museum, etc.（商店或博物館等的）玻璃櫃枱，玻璃陳列櫃 ▸ **show·case** *verb*： **~ sth** *Jack found a film role that showcased all his talents.* 傑克找到了充分展示他才華的電影角色。

show·down /ˈʃəʊdaʊn; *NAmE* ˈʃoʊ-/ *noun* [usually sing.] an argument, a fight or a test that will settle a disagreement that has lasted for a long time 決出勝負的較量；最後的決戰： *Management are facing a showdown with union members today.* 今天資方準備和工會成員攤牌。◇ *Fans gathered outside the stadium for the final showdown* (= the game that will decide the winner of the competition). 球迷聚集在體育場外等着看最後的決賽。

shower 🔑 /ˈʃaʊə(r)/ *noun, verb*

■ ***noun*** **1** 🔑 a piece of equipment producing a spray of water that you stand under to wash yourself; the small room or part of a room that contains a shower 淋浴器；淋浴間： *a hotel room with bath and shower* 配備有浴缸和淋浴器的旅館客房 ◇ *He's **in the shower**.* 他在淋浴間沖澡。◇ *a shower cubicle* 淋浴間 ➲ VISUAL VOCAB page V24 **2** 🔑 the act of washing yourself with a shower 淋浴： (*especially BrE*) *to **have a shower*** 洗淋浴 ◇ (*especially NAmE*) *to **take a shower*** 洗淋浴 ◇ *shower gel* 沐浴乳 **3** 🔑 a short period of rain or snow 陣雨；陣雪： *scattered showers* 零星小雨 ◇ *April showers* 四月的陣雨 ◇ *We were caught in a heavy shower.* 我們遇上一陣大雨。◇ *snow showers* 陣雪 ◇ *wintry showers* (= of snow) 寒冬的陣雪 **4** a large number of things that arrive or fall together 一大批；一陣；一連串： *a shower of leaves* 紛紛落下的葉子 ◇ *a shower of sparks from the fire* 火中迸發的一串火星 ◇ *a shower of kisses* 一陣親吻 **5** (*NAmE*) a party at which you give presents to a woman who is getting married or having a baby 送禮聚會（為即將結婚或分娩的婦女舉行）： ***a bridal/baby shower*** 為新娘 / 為準媽媽舉行的送禮聚會

■ ***verb*** **1** [I] to wash yourself under a shower（洗）淋浴： *She showered and dressed and went downstairs.* 她沖了澡，穿上衣服下樓去了。 **2** [I] **~ (down) on sb/sth | ~ down** to fall onto sb/sth, especially in a lot of small pieces 灑落；紛紛降落： *Volcanic ash showered down on the town after the eruption.* 火山噴發後，小城落了一層火山灰。 **3** [T] **~ sb with sth** to drop a lot of small things onto sb 拋灑；使紛紛降落： *The bride and groom were showered with rice as they left the church.* 新郎和新娘走出教堂時，人們朝他們拋灑大米。◇ *The roof collapsed, showering us with dust and debris.* 屋頂塌了下來，灰塵、碎片紛紛落在我們身上。 **4** [T] to give sb a lot of sth 大量地給： **~ sb with sth** *He showered her with gifts.* 他送給她許多禮物。◇ **~ sth on sb** *He showered gifts on her.* 他送給她許多禮物。

show·ery /ˈʃaʊəri/ *adj.* (of the weather 天氣) with frequent showers of rain 下陣雨的；多陣雨的： *a showery day* 陣雨天

show·girl /ˈʃəʊɡɜːl; *NAmE* ˈʃoʊɡɜːrl/ *noun* a female performer who sings and dances in a musical show 歌舞女演員

show·ground /ˈʃəʊɡraʊnd; *NAmE* ˈʃoʊ-/ *noun* a large outdoor area where FAIRS, farm shows, etc. take place（室外）展覽場地

'show house (also **'show home**) (both *BrE*) (*NAmE* **'model home**) *noun* a house in a group of new houses that has been painted and filled with furniture, so that people who might want to buy one of the houses can see what they will be like 樣品房，樣板間（供購買房子的顧客參觀）

show·ing /ˈʃəʊɪŋ; *NAmE* ˈʃoʊ-/ *noun* **1** an act of showing a film/movie 放映： *There are three showings a day.* 一天放映三場。 **2** [usually sing.] evidence of how well or how badly sb/sth is performing 表現： *the **strong/poor showing** of the Green Party in the election* 綠黨在這次選舉中的強勁 / 不佳表現 ◇ *On* (= judging by) *last week's showing, the team is unlikely to win today.* 從上星期的表現來看，這支隊伍今天不大可能獲勝。

show·jump·ing /ˈʃəʊdʒʌmpɪŋ; *NAmE* ˈʃoʊ-/ *noun* [U] the sport of riding a horse and jumping over a set of fences as quickly as possible（馬術項目）超越障礙比賽 ➲ VISUAL VOCAB page V46

show·man /ˈʃəʊmən; *NAmE* ˈʃoʊ-/ *noun* (*pl.* **-men** /-mən/) **1** a person who does things in an entertaining way and is good at getting people's attention 善於引起公眾注意的人；喜歡出風頭的人 **2** a person who organizes public entertainments, especially at FAIRGROUNDS（尤指露天遊樂場的）演出主持人，演出經理人

show·man·ship /ˈʃəʊmənʃɪp; *NAmE* ˈʃoʊ-/ *noun* [U] skill in doing things in an entertaining way and getting a lot of attention 主持演出的技巧；演藝才能；善於表演的技能

shown *past part.* of SHOW

'show-off *noun* (*informal, disapproving*) a person who tries to impress other people by showing how good he or she is at doing sth 愛炫耀的人；喜歡賣弄的人

show·piece /ˈʃəʊpiːs; *NAmE* ˈʃoʊ-/ *noun* an excellent example of sth that people are meant to see and admire（供展示用的）優質樣品

show·place /ˈʃəʊpleɪs; *NAmE* ˈʃoʊ-/ *noun* a place of great beauty, historical interest, etc. that is open to the public 風景名勝；古跡名勝；遊覽勝地

show·room /ˈʃəʊruːm; -rʊm; *NAmE* ˈʃoʊ-/ *noun* a large shop/store in which goods for sale, especially cars and electrical goods, are displayed 商品陳列室；展銷廳： *a car showroom* 汽車展銷廳

'show-stopper *noun* (*informal*) a performance that is very impressive and receives a lot of APPLAUSE from the audience 受到陣陣鼓掌喝彩的節目 ▸ **'show-stopping** *adj.* [only before noun]： *a show-stopping performance* 受到陣陣鼓掌喝彩的節目

show·time /ˈʃəʊtaɪm; *NAmE* ˈʃoʊ-/ *noun* [U] the time that a theatre performance will begin 開演時間： *It's five minutes to showtime and the theatre is packed.* 離演出開始還有五分鐘，劇場裏已座無虛席。◇ (*figurative, NAmE*) *Everybody ready? It's showtime!* 大家都準備好了嗎？演出馬上開始！

'show trial *noun* an unfair trial of sb in court, organized by a government for political reasons, not in order to find out the truth （出於政治目的）擺樣子的審判，走過場的審訊

showy /'ʃəʊi; *NAmE* 'ʃoʊi/ *adj.* (often *disapproving*) so brightly coloured, large or exaggerated that it attracts a lot of attention 豔麗的；花哨的 **SYN ostentatious**：*showy flowers* 豔麗的花朵 ▸ **show·ily** /-ɪli/ *adv.* **showi·ness** *noun* [U]

shrank *past tense of* SHRINK

shrap·nel /'ʃræpnəl/ *noun* [U] small pieces of metal that are thrown up and away from an exploding bomb 飛濺的彈片

shred /ʃred/ *verb, noun*

■ ***verb*** (**-dd-**) **~ sth** to cut or tear sth into small pieces 切碎；撕碎：*Serve the fish on a bed of shredded lettuce.* 先鋪一層碎生菜葉，再把魚放上，就可以上桌了。◇ *He was accused of shredding documents relating to the case* (= putting them in a SHREDDER). 他被指控把與案件有關的文件用碎紙機銷毀了。

■ ***noun*** **1** [usually pl.] a small thin piece that has been torn or cut from sth （撕或切的）細條，碎片 **SYN scrap**：*shreds of paper* 碎紙片 ◇ *His jacket had been* ***torn to shreds*** *by the barbed wire.* 他的夾克被鐵絲網掛得稀爛。**2** [usually sing.] **~ of sth** (used especially in negative sentences 尤用於否定句) a very small amount of sth 極少量；些許；一丁點：*There is* ***not a shred of evidence*** *to support his claim.* 沒有絲毫證據支持他的說法。

IDM **in 'shreds** **1** very badly damaged 損害嚴重 **SYN in tatters**：*Her nerves were in shreds.* 她的神經崩潰了。◇ *The country's economy is in shreds.* 國家經濟已是百孔千瘡。**2** torn in many places 破破爛爛的：*The document was in shreds on the floor.* 那在地上的文件被撕毀得破爛不堪。 **pick/pull/tear sb/sth to 'pieces/'shreds** (*informal*) to criticize sb, or their work or ideas, very severely 把某人（或其作品、觀點等）批駁得體無完膚

shred·der /'ʃredə(r)/ *noun* a machine that tears sth into small pieces, especially paper, so that nobody can read what was printed on it 切碎機；（尤指）碎紙機

shrew /ʃruː/ *noun* **1** a small animal like a mouse with a long nose 鼩鼱（形似鼠，吻長）**2** (*old-fashioned*) a bad-tempered unpleasant woman 潑婦；悍婦

shrewd /ʃruːd/ *adj.* (**shrewd·er**, **shrewd·est**) **1** clever at understanding and making judgements about a situation 精明的；敏鋭的；有眼光的；精於盤算的 **SYN astute**：*a shrewd businessman* 精明的商人 ◇ *She is a shrewd judge of character.* 她看人看得很準。**2** showing good judgement and likely to be right 判斷得準的；高明的：*a shrewd move* 高招 ◇ *I* ***have a shrewd idea*** *who the mystery caller was.* 這個神秘的來訪者是誰，我能猜個八九不離十。 ▸ **shrewd·ly** *adv.* **shrewd·ness** *noun* [U]

shrew·ish /'ʃruːɪʃ/ *adj.* (*old-fashioned*) (of women 女人) bad-tempered and always arguing 脾氣壞且愛爭吵的

Shri (also **Sri**) /ʃriː; sriː/ *noun* (*IndE*) **1** a title used before the names of gods or holy books, showing respect （用於頭銜或典籍前，表示尊敬）神，聖 **2** a title of respect for a man （對男子的尊稱）先生

shriek /ʃriːk/ *verb, noun*

■ ***verb*** **1** [I] to give a loud high shout, for example when you are excited, frightened or in pain 尖叫 **SYN scream**：**~ (in sth)** *She shrieked in fright.* 她嚇得尖叫起來。◇ **~ with sth** *The audience was shrieking with laughter.* 觀眾放聲大笑。◇ **~ at sb** (*figurative*) *The answer shrieked at her* (= was very obvious). 答案就明擺在她面前。 **2** [T] to say sth in a loud, high voice 尖聲說 **SYN scream**：**~ sth (at sb)** *She was shrieking abuse at them as they carried her off.* 他們把她抬走的時候，她衝着他們尖聲叫罵。◇ **+ speech** *'Look out!' he shrieked.* "小心！"他尖叫道。

■ ***noun*** a loud high shout, for example one that you make when you are excited, frightened or in pain 尖叫：*She let out a piercing shriek.* 她發出一聲刺耳的尖叫。◇ *a shriek of delight* 興奮的叫聲

shrift /ʃrɪft/ *noun* **IDM** see SHORT *adj.*

shrike /ʃraɪk/ *noun* a bird with a strong beak, that catches small birds and insects and sticks them on THORNS 伯勞（鳥，喙強有力，攫捉到小鳥和昆蟲後將其掛在荊棘上）

shrill /ʃrɪl/ *adj., verb*

■ ***adj.*** (**shrill·er**, **shrill·est**) **1** (of sounds or voices 聲音或嗓音) very high and loud, in an unpleasant way 刺耳的；尖聲的；尖厲的 **SYN piercing**：*a shrill voice* 刺耳的嗓音 **2** loud and determined but often unreasonable 鬧着非要…不可的；不依不饒的：*shrill demands/protests* 堅持要求；拚命反對 ▸ **shrilly** /'ʃrɪlli/ *adv.* **shrill·ness** *noun* [U]

■ ***verb*** **1** [I] to make an unpleasant high loud sound 發出刺耳的聲音；尖叫：*Behind him, the telephone shrilled.* 在他身後，電話鈴刺耳地響了起來。**2** [T] **+ speech** to say sth in a loud, high voice 尖聲說 **SYN shriek**：*'Wait for me!' she shrilled.* "等等我！"她尖聲叫道。

Shri·mati (also **Sri·mati**) /'ʃriːmʌti; 'sriː-/ *noun* (*IndE*) a title of respect or affection for a woman（對女子的敬稱或愛稱）女士，西里馬提

shrimp /ʃrɪmp/ *noun* (*pl.* **shrimps** or **shrimp**) **1** a small SHELLFISH that can be eaten, like a PRAWN but smaller. Shrimps turn pink when cooked. 蝦；小蝦 **2** (*NAmE*) = PRAWN：*grilled shrimp* 烤蝦

shrimp·ing /'ʃrɪmpɪŋ/ *noun* [U] the activity of catching shrimps 捕小蝦：*a shrimping net* 捕蝦網 ▸ **shrimp·er** *noun* (*especially NAmE*)：*shrimpers and fishermen in the Gulf of Mexico* 墨西哥灣捕魚蝦的漁民

shrine /ʃraɪn/ *noun* **1** a place where people come to worship because it is connected with a holy person or event 聖地；聖祠；神廟；神龕：**~ (to sb/sth)** *a shrine to the Virgin Mary* 敬奉聖母瑪利亞的朝聖地 ◇ **~ (of sb/sth)** *to visit the shrine of Mecca* 前往聖地麥加朝拜 **2 ~ (for sb)** | **~ (to sb/sth)** a place that people visit because it is connected with sb/sth that is important to them 具有重要意義的地方：*Wimbledon is a shrine for all lovers of tennis.* 溫布爾登是所有網球愛好者的聖地。

shrink /ʃrɪŋk/ *verb, noun*

■ ***verb*** (**shrank** /ʃræŋk/, **shrunk** /ʃrʌŋk/) or (**shrunk**, **shrunk**) **1** [I, T] **~ (sth)** to become smaller, especially when washed in water that is too hot; to make clothes, cloth, etc. smaller in this way （使）縮水，收縮，縮小，皺縮：*My sweater shrank in the wash.* 我的毛衣縮水了。**2** [I, T] to become or to make sth smaller in size or amount （使）縮小，收縮，減少：*The tumour had shrunk to the size of a pea.* 腫瘤已縮小到豌豆大小。◇ *The market for their products is shrinking.* 市場對他們產品的需求在減少。◇ **~ sth** *There was a movie called 'Honey, I Shrunk the Kids'.* 有部電影名叫《親愛的，我把孩子縮小了》。◇ *Television in a sense has shrunk the world.* 從某種意義上說電視把世界縮小了。 ➲ see also SHRUNKEN **3** [I] **+ adv./prep.** to move back or away from sth because you are frightened or shocked 退縮；畏縮 **SYN cower**：*He shrank back against the wall as he heard them approaching.* 聽見他們朝這邊來，他退到牆根。

IDM **a ˌshrinking 'violet** (*humorous*) a way of describing a very shy person （指羞怯的人）

PHR V **'shrink from sth** to be unwilling to do sth that is difficult or unpleasant 畏避，迴避（困難等）：*We made it clear to them that we would not shrink from confrontation.* 我們向他們清楚地表明，我們不會畏避交鋒。◇ **~ doing sth** *They did not shrink from doing what was right.* 只要做得對，他們就無所畏懼。

■ ***noun*** (*slang, humorous*) a PSYCHIATRIST or PSYCHOLOGIST 精神病學家；心理學家

shrink·age /'ʃrɪŋkɪdʒ/ *noun* [U] the process of becoming smaller in size; the amount by which sth becomes smaller 縮小；收縮；收縮量；收縮程度：*the shrinkage of heavy industry* 重工業的萎縮 ◇ *She bought a slightly larger size to allow for shrinkage.* 她買了一件尺碼稍大的以備縮水。

'shrink-wrapped *adj.* wrapped tightly in a thin plastic covering 用收縮塑料薄膜包裝的

shrivel /'ʃrɪvl/ *verb* (**-ll-**, *US* **-l-**) [I, T] to become or make sth dry and WRINKLED as a result of heat, cold or being

S

old （使）枯萎，乾枯，皺縮：**~ (up)** *The leaves on the plant had shrivelled up from lack of water.* 因為缺水，植物的葉子已經枯萎了。◇ **~ sth (up)** *The hot weather had shrivelled the grapes in every vineyard.* 天氣炎熱，各家葡萄園的葡萄都蔫了。▸ **shriv·elled** *adj.*：*a shrivelled old man* 一個乾巴老頭

shroom /ʃruːm; ʃrʊm/ (*informal, especially NAmE*) (also **magic mushroom** *BrE* or becoming *old-fashioned, NAmE*) *noun* a type of MUSHROOM that has an effect like some drugs and that may make people who eat it HALLUCINATE (= see things that are not there) 致幻蘑菇 ▸ **shroom** *verb* [I]：*Joe was shrooming last night and has a killer headache today.* 喬昨晚吃了致幻蘑菇，今天頭痛欲裂。

shroud /ʃraʊd/ *noun, verb*

■ ***noun*** **1** a piece of cloth that a dead person's body is wrapped in before it is buried 裹屍布；壽衣 **2 ~ of sth** (*literary*) a thing that covers, surrounds or hides sth 覆蓋物；遮蔽物：*The organization is cloaked in a shroud of secrecy.* 這個組織籠罩着一種詭秘的氣氛。◇ *a shroud of smoke* 一片煙霧

■ ***verb*** [usually passive] **1 ~ sth in sth** (of DARKNESS, clouds, cloth, etc. 黑暗、雲、織物等) to cover or hide sth 覆蓋；隱藏；遮蔽：*The city was shrouded in mist.* 城市籠罩在霧靄之中。**2 ~ sth in sth** to hide information or keep it secret and mysterious 隱瞞；保密：*His family background **is shrouded in mystery**.* 他的家庭背景蒙上了神秘的色彩。

'shroud-waving *noun* [U] (*BrE*) the practice of warning about the bad effect on medical care if more money is not provided by the government to pay for more doctors, hospitals, etc. 揮裹屍布示警（告誡政府不增加投入會對醫療保健產生嚴重影響）

Shrove Tuesday /ˌʃrəʊv ˈtjuːzdeɪ; -di; *NAmE* ˌʃroʊv ˈtuːz-/ *noun* [U, C] (in the Christian Church) the day before the beginning of Lent 懺悔日（基督教大齋期的前一天）➲ compare MARDI GRAS, PANCAKE DAY ➲ see also ASH WEDNESDAY

shrub /ʃrʌb/ *noun* a large plant that is smaller than a tree and that has several STEMS of wood coming from the ground 灌木 **SYN bush**

shrub·bery /ˈʃrʌbəri/ *noun* [C, U] (*pl.* **-ies**) an area planted with shrubs 灌木叢

shrubby /ˈʃrʌbi/ *adj.* (of plants 植物) like a SHRUB 像灌木的；灌木狀的

S

shrug /ʃrʌg/ *verb, noun*

■ ***verb*** (**-gg-**) [I, T, no passive] to raise your shoulders and then drop them to show that you do not know or care about sth 聳肩（表示不知道或不在乎）：*Sam shrugged and said nothing.* 薩姆聳聳肩膀，什麼也沒說。◇ **~ sth** *'I don't know,' Anna replied, shrugging her shoulders.* "我不知道。" 安娜聳聳肩膀，應了一句。

■ ***noun*** **1** [usually sing.] an act of raising your shoulders and then dropping them to show that you do not know or care about sth 聳肩（表示不知道或不在乎）：*Andy gave a shrug. 'It doesn't matter.'* 安迪聳聳肩："這沒關係。" **2** [C] a very short knitted piece of clothing that is open at the front and usually has sleeves made from the same piece as the back and front （女式）帶袖短披肩

PHR V **ˌshrug sth 'off/a'side** to treat sth as if it is not important 不把…當回事；對…滿不在乎；對…不予理睬 **SYN dismiss**：*Shrugging off her injury, she played on.* 她不管損傷，繼續進行比賽。◇ *He shrugged aside suggestions that he resign.* 對於要求他辭職的建議，他根本不予理會。**ˌshrug sb/sth 'off/a'way** to push sb/sth back or away with your shoulders 甩開；擺脫；抖落：*Kevin shrugged off his jacket.* 凱文肩膀一抖，脫掉了夾克。◇ *She shrugged him away angrily.* 她生氣地甩開他。

shrunk *past tense, past part.* of SHRINK

shrunk·en /ˈʃrʌŋkən/ *adj.* [usually before noun] that has become smaller (and less attractive) 皺縮的；乾枯的 **SYN wizened**：*a shrunken old woman* 乾癟老婦人

shtetl /ˈʃtetl/ *noun* a small Jewish town or village in eastern Europe in the past （東歐舊時的）猶太小鎮（或小村）

shtick (also **schtick**) /ʃtɪk/ *noun* [U, sing.] (*especially NAmE*) **1** a style of humour that is typical of a particular performer （獨特的）幽默風格；（某演員的）表演手法 **2** a particular ability that sb has 特長；擅長的本領

shtook (also **schtuck**) /ʃtʊk/ *noun* [U]

IDM **be in 'shtook** (*BrE, informal*) to be in serious trouble 遇到大麻煩；陷入嚴重困境

shtum (also **schtum**) /ʃtʊm/ *noun* [U]

IDM **keep/stay 'shtum** (*BrE, informal*) to not speak 保持沉默：*Police have appealed for witnesses, but it seems the locals are keeping shtum.* 警方已呼籲目擊者出來作證，但看來當地人都三緘其口。

shtup (also **schtup**) /ʃtʊp/ *verb* (**-pp-**) **~ sb** (*NAmE, slang*) to have sex with sb （與某人）發生性關係

shuck /ʃʌk/ *noun, verb*

■ ***noun*** (*NAmE*) the outer covering of a nut, plant, etc. or an OYSTER or a CLAM （堅果或牡蠣、蛤等的）殼；（植物的）莢；外皮

■ ***verb*** **~ sth** (*NAmE*) to remove the shell or covering of nuts, SHELLFISH, etc. 剝…的殼（或莢）；去…的外皮

shucks /ʃʌks/ *exclamation* (*old-fashioned, NAmE, informal*) used to express embarrassment or disappointment （表示窘迫或失望）

shud·der /ˈʃʌdə(r)/ *verb, noun*

■ ***verb*** **1** [I] to shake because you are cold or frightened, or because of a strong feeling （因寒冷、害怕或激動）發抖，打顫，戰慄：*Just thinking about the accident makes me shudder.* 只要一想起那場事故，我就發抖。◇ **~ with sth** *Alone in the car, she shuddered with fear.* 她一個人待在車裏，害怕得直哆嗦。◇ **~ at sth** ***I shuddered at the thought*** *of all the trouble I'd caused.* 一想到我闖的禍，就不寒而慄。◇ **~ to do sth** ***I shudder to think*** *how much this is all going to cost* (= I don't want to think about it because it is too unpleasant). 想想這一切得花多少錢，我就發怵。**2** [I] (of a vehicle, machine, etc. 交通工具、機器等) to shake very hard 強烈震動；劇烈抖動：*The bus shuddered to a halt.* 公共汽車劇烈地晃動着停了下來。

■ ***noun*** [usually sing.] **1** a shaking movement you make because you are cold, frightened or disgusted （因寒冷、害怕或反感等引起的）發抖，打顫，戰慄：*a shudder of fear* 害怕的顫抖 ◇ *She gave an involuntary shudder.* 她不由自主地抖了一下。**2** a strong shaking movement 強烈的震動；劇烈的抖動：*The elevator rose with a shudder.* 電梯猛震一下，升上去了。

shuf·fle /ˈʃʌfl/ *verb, noun*

■ ***verb*** **1** [I] **+ adv./prep.** to walk slowly without lifting your feet completely off the ground 拖着腳走：*He shuffled across the room to the window.* 他拖着腳走到房間那頭的窗戶跟前。◇ *The line shuffled forward a little.* 隊列往前挪了挪。**2** [T, I] **~ (sth)** to move from one foot to another; to move your feet in an awkward or embarrassed way （笨拙或尷尬地）把腳動來動去；坐立不安：*Jenny shuffled her feet and blushed with shame.* 珍妮來回倒換着腳，羞愧得臉紅了。**3** [T, I] **~ (sth)** to mix cards up in a PACK/DECK of PLAYING CARDS before playing a game 洗（牌）：*Shuffle the cards and deal out seven to each player.* 洗洗牌，然後給每人發七張。**4** [T] **~ sth** to move paper or things into different positions or a different order 把（紙張等）變換位置，打亂次序：*I shuffled the documents on my desk.* 我胡亂翻動桌上的文件。

■ ***noun*** [usually sing.] **1** a slow walk in which you take small steps and do not lift your feet completely off the ground 拖着腳走 **2** the act of mixing cards before a card game 洗牌：*Give the cards a good shuffle.* 把牌好好洗一洗。**3** a type of dancing in which you take small steps and do not lift your feet completely off the ground 曳步舞 **4** = RESHUFFLE

IDM **lose sb/sth in the 'shuffle** [usually passive] (*NAmE*) to not notice sb/sth or pay attention to sb/sth because of a confusing situation 在混亂中沒有注意到；忽略；遺失：*Middle children tend to get lost in the shuffle.* 排行居中的子女往往得不到充分的關注。**on 'shuffle** (of pieces of music stored on a music player, such as an MP3 player 播放器中的音樂) not in any special order 隨機播放： *I put the iPod on shuffle and hit play.* 我把iPod 設置成隨機播放，然後按播放鍵。

shuf·fle·board /ˈʃʌflbɔːd; *NAmE* -bɔːrd/ *noun* [U] a game in which players use long sticks to push discs towards spaces with numbers on a board 推移板遊戲（用推杆將圓盤推至推移板上的不同得分區）

shufti /ˈʃʊfti/ *noun* [sing.]
IDM **have a shufti (at sth)** (*BrE, informal*) to have a quick look at sth（對…）掃一眼；瞥

shun /ʃʌn/ *verb* (**-nn-**) **~ sb/sth** to avoid sb/sth 避開；迴避；避免： *She was shunned by her family when she remarried.* 她再婚後家裏人都躲着她。◇ *an actor who shuns publicity* 一個避免引起公眾注意的演員

shunt /ʃʌnt/ *verb, noun*
■ *verb* **1 ~ sth** to move a train or a coach/car of a train from one track to another 使（火車或火車車廂）轉軌 **2 ~ sb/sth + adv./prep.** (usually *disapproving*) to move sb/sth to a different place, especially a less important one 調往，轉至（次要的地方）： *John was shunted sideways to a job in sales.* 約翰被平級調動到銷售部門的一個崗位上。
■ *noun* **1** (*BrE, informal*) a road accident in which one vehicle crashes into the back of another 車輛追尾事故 **2** (*medical* 醫) a small tube put in your body in a medical operation to allow the blood or other FLUID to flow from one place to another 分流管

shush /ʃʊʃ/ *exclamation, verb*
■ *exclamation* used to tell sb to be quiet（叫別人安靜）噓
■ *verb* **~ sb** to tell sb to be quiet, especially by saying 'shush', or by putting your finger against your lips（尤指通過"噓"聲或把手指豎在嘴唇上）要某人安靜，噓： *Lyn shushed the children.* 林恩"噓"了一聲，讓孩子們安靜下來。

shut 🔑 /ʃʌt/ *verb, adj.*
■ *verb* (**shut·ting, shut, shut**) **1** 🔑 [T, I] **~ (sth)** to make sth close; to become closed 關閉；關上；合上： *Philip went into his room and shut the door behind him.* 菲利普進了自己的房間，隨手把門關上。◇ *I can't shut my suitcase—it's too full.* 我的手提箱合不上，裝得太滿了。◇ *She shut her eyes and fell asleep immediately.* 她閉上眼，立刻就睡着了。◇ *He shut his book and looked up.* 他合上書，抬起頭來。◇ *The window won't shut.* 這窗子關不上。◇ *The doors open and shut automatically.* 這些門都是自動開關的。 **2** 🔑 [I, T] **~ (sth)** (*BrE*) when a shop/store, restaurant, etc. **shuts** or when sb **shuts** it, it stops being open for business and you cannot go into it（使）停止營業，關門，打烊： *The bank shuts at 4.* 那家銀行 4 點鐘關門。➲ note at CLOSE[1]
IDM **shut your 'mouth/'face!** (*slang*) a rude way of telling sb to be quiet or stop talking（粗暴地要某人停止說話）住口，閉嘴 **shut up 'shop** (*BrE, informal*) to close a business permanently or to stop working for the day 停業；關張；倒閉；打烊 ➲ more at DOOR, EAR, EYE *n.*, MOUTH *n.*
PHR V **,shut sb/sth↔a'way** to put sb/sth in a place where other people cannot see or find them 把…藏起來；隔離；禁閉 **,shut yourself a'way** to go somewhere where you will be completely alone 獨自躲起來；隱藏 **,shut 'down** 🔑 (of a factory, shop/store, etc. or a machine 工廠、商店或機器等) to stop opening for business; to stop working 關張；停業；倒閉；關閉；停止運轉 ➲ related noun SHUTDOWN **,shut sth↔'down** 🔑 to stop a factory, shop/store, etc. from opening for business; to stop a machine from working（使）關張，停業，倒閉，關閉，停止運轉： *The computer system will be shut down over the weekend.* 計算機系統週末關閉。➲ related noun SHUTDOWN **,shut sb/yourself 'in (sth)** 🔑 to put sb in a room and keep them there; to go to a room and stay there 把某人（或自己）關在房間裏；把…關起來： *She shut the dog in the shed while she prepared the barbecue.* 她準備烤肉餐時把狗關起來。 **'shut sth in sth** to trap sth by closing a door, lid, etc. on it 把某物卡在…裏（或夾在…中）： *Sam shut his finger in the car door.* 薩姆給車門夾住了手指。 **,shut 'off** (of a machine, tool, etc. 機器、工具等) to stop working 關閉；關上；停止運轉： *The engines shut off automatically in an emergency.* 遇到緊急情況發動機便自動停止工作。 **,shut sth↔'off** **1** to stop a machine, tool, etc. from working 關閉機器（或工具等）；使機器（或工具等）停止運轉 **2** to stop a supply of gas, water, etc. from flowing or reaching a place 切斷煤氣（或水等）的供應；停止供應煤氣（或水等）： *A valve immediately shuts off the gas when the lid is closed.* 當蓋子合上時，立刻會有一個閥門切斷煤氣。 **,shut yourself 'off (from sth)** to avoid seeing people or having contact with anyone 躲開；不接觸： *Martin shut himself off from the world to write his book.* 馬丁不與外界接觸，專心寫他的書。 **,shut sb/sth 'off from sth** to separate sb/sth from sth 使與…隔離（或隔絕）： *Bosnia is shut off from the Adriatic by the mountains.* 波斯尼亞和亞得里亞海之間有群山相隔。 **,shut sb/sth↔'out (of sth)** **1** 🔑 to prevent sb/sth from entering a place 使…不能進入；擋住；遮住： *Mum, Ben keeps shutting me out of the bedroom!* 媽，本老不讓我進卧室！◇ *sunglasses that shut out 99% of the sun's harmful rays* 能遮擋 99% 的太陽有害射線的太陽鏡 **2** to not allow a person to share or be part of your thoughts; to stop yourself from having particular feelings 把某人排除在…外；不把…告訴某人；克制某種感情： *I wanted to shut John out of my life for ever.* 我想永遠不讓約翰走進我的生活。◇ *She learned to shut out her angry feelings.* 她學會了克制自己的憤怒。◇ *If you shut me out, how can I help you?* 如果你什麼也不告訴我，我怎麼幫你呢？ **,shut 'up** 🔑 (*informal*) to stop talking (often used as an order as a rude way of telling sb to stop talking)（常用來粗暴地讓某人停止說話）住口，閉嘴： *Just shut up and listen!* 住口，聽着！◇ *Will you tell Mike to shut up?* 你讓邁克閉嘴好不好？◇ *When they'd finally shut up, I started again.* 等他們最終住了嘴，我又重新開始講。 **,shut sb 'up** to make sb stop talking 使某人住口；讓某人閉嘴 **SYN** **silence**： *She kicked Anne under the table to shut her up.* 她在桌子底下踢了安妮一腳，讓她住嘴。 **,shut sth↔'up** to close a room, house, etc. 關上（房屋等） **,shut sb/sth 'up (in sth)** 🔑 to keep sb/sth in a place and prevent them from going anywhere 把…關（或藏）起來；把…關（或藏）在
■ *adj.* [not before noun] **1** 🔑 not open 關閉；合攏 **SYN** **closed**： *The door was shut.* 門關着。◇ *She slammed the door shut.* 她砰的一聲把門關上了。◇ *Keep your eyes shut.* 別睜開眼睛。 **2** 🔑 (*BrE*) not open for business 停業；關門 **SYN** **closed**： *Unfortunately the bank is shut now.* 不湊巧，銀行現在不營業。

shut·down /ˈʃʌtdaʊn/ *noun* the act of closing a factory or business or stopping a large machine from working, either temporarily or permanently 停業；停工；關閉；倒閉；停止運轉： *factory shutdowns* 工廠的倒閉 ◇ *the nuclear reactor's emergency shutdown procedures* 核反應堆的緊急關閉程序

'shut-eye *noun* [U] (*informal*) sleep 睡眠

'shut-in *noun* (*NAmE*) a person who cannot leave their home very easily because they are ill/sick or disabled 因病（或殘疾）外出困難的人；卧病在家的人

shut·out /ˈʃʌtaʊt/ *noun* (*NAmE*) a game in which one team prevents the other from scoring 完勝（比賽中不讓對手得分）

shut·ter /ˈʃʌtə(r)/ *noun* **1** [usually pl.] one of a pair of wooden or metal covers that can be closed over the outside of a window to keep out light or protect the windows from damage 活動護窗；百葉窗： *to open/close the shutters* 打開 / 關上護窗 ◇ (*BrE, figurative*) *More than 70 000 shopkeepers have been forced to **put up the shutters*** (= close down their businesses) *in the past year.* 去年，有 7 萬多家商店被迫關了門。➲ VISUAL VOCAB pages V17, V21 **2** the part of a camera that opens to allow light to pass through the LENS when you take a photograph（照相機的）快門
IDM **,bring/,put down the 'shutters** to stop letting sb know what your thoughts or feelings are; to stop letting yourself think about sth 掩藏自己的思想感情；鎖上心扉；不再想某件事

S

shut·ter·bug /ˈʃʌtəbʌg; *NAmE* ˈʃʌtər-/ *noun* (*NAmE*, *informal*) a person who likes to take a lot of photographs 攝影迷；攝影愛好者

shut·tered /ˈʃʌtəd; *NAmE* -tərd/ *adj.* with the shutters closed; with shutters fitted 關上（或裝有）護窗的

ˈshutter speed *noun* the length of time that a camera's SHUTTER remains open （照相機的）快門速度

shut·tle /ˈʃʌtl/ *noun, verb*

■ ***noun*** **1** a plane, bus or train that travels regularly between two places 來往於兩地之間的航班（或班車、火車）：*a shuttle service between London and Edinburgh* 往返於倫敦和愛丁堡之間的航班 **2** = SPACE SHUTTLE **3** a pointed tool used in making cloth to pull a thread backwards and forwards over the other threads that pass along the length of the cloth 梭；梭子 **4 the Shuttle** [sing.] a train service that takes cars and their passengers through the Channel Tunnel between England and France（英法之間英吉利海峽隧道的）穿梭火車

■ ***verb*** **1** [I] **~ (between A and B)** to travel between two places frequently 頻繁往來（於甲地和乙地之間）：*Her childhood was spent shuttling between her mother and father.* 她的童年是在父母之間穿梭往來中度過的。**2** [T] **~ sb (+ adv./prep.)** to carry people between two places that are close, making regular journeys between the two places（在較近的兩地之間定時）往返運送：*A bus shuttles passengers back and forth from the station to the terminal.* 一輛公共汽車在火車站和公共汽車終點站之間往返運送旅客。

shuttle·cock /ˈʃʌtlkɒk; *NAmE* -kɑːk/ (*NAmE* also **bird·ie**) *noun* the object that players hit backwards and forwards in the game of BADMINTON 羽毛球 ➲ VISUAL VOCAB page V45

ˌshuttle diˈplomacy *noun* [U] international talks in which people travel between two or more countries in order to talk to the different governments involved 穿梭外交

shwa *noun* = SCHWA

shy 🔑 /ʃaɪ/ *adj., verb*

■ ***adj.*** (**shyer**, **shy·est**) **1** 🔑 (of people 人) nervous or embarrassed about meeting and speaking to other people 羞怯的；靦腆的；怕生的 SYN **timid**：*a quiet, shy man* 靦腆、不大說話的人 ◇ *Don't be shy—come and say hello.* 別害羞，過來問個好。◇ *She was too shy to ask anyone for help.* 她太靦腆，不願向任何人求助。◇ *As a teenager I was* ***painfully shy***. 我十幾歲的時候靦腆得很。◇ *She's very shy with adults.* 她在大人面前很拘束。**2** 🔑 showing that sb is nervous or embarrassed about meeting and speaking to other people 顯得靦腆的；看着羞怯的：*a shy smile* 靦腆的微笑 **3** (of animals 動物) easily frightened and not willing to come near people 怕人的；易受驚的；膽小的：*The panda is a shy creature.* 熊貓是一種膽小的動物。**4** [not before noun] **~ of/about (doing) sth** afraid of doing sth or being involved in sth 害怕（做）；對（做）…心懷顧忌：*The band has never been shy of publicity.* 這支樂隊一向不憚招搖。◇ *He disliked her and had never been shy of saying so.* 他不喜歡她，而且從來不忌諱說出這種想法。**5** [not before noun] **~ (of sth)** (*informal, especially NAmE*) lacking the amount that is needed 欠缺；不足；未達到；不夠：*He died before Christmas, only a month shy of his 90th birthday.* 他在聖誕節前去世了，僅差一個月就滿 90 歲。◇ *We are still two players shy (of a full team).* 我們還缺兩名隊員（湊成一支隊）。**6 -shy** (in compounds 構成複合詞) avoiding or not liking the thing mentioned 躲避（或不喜歡）…的：*camera-shy* (= not liking to be photographed) 不愛照相 ◇ *He's always been work-shy.* 他總是躲避工作。▶ **shyly** *adv.* **shy·ness** *noun* [U] IDM see FIGHT *v.*, ONCE *adv.*

■ ***verb*** (**shies**, **shy·ing**, **shied**, **shied** /ʃaɪd/) [I] **~ (at sth)** (especially of a horse 尤指馬) to turn away with a sudden movement because it is afraid or surprised 被嚇退；被驚走：*My horse shied at the unfamiliar noise.* 這陌生的聲音把我的馬驚跑了。➲ see also COCONUT SHY

PHR V **ˌshy aˈway (from sth)** to avoid doing sth because you are nervous or frightened 畏避；迴避；躲避；避免做：*Hugh never shied away from his responsibilities.* 該自己承擔的責任，休從不迴避。◇ *The newspapers have shied away from investigating the story.* 各家報紙紛紛退避，不敢調查詳情。

shy·ster /ˈʃaɪstə(r)/ *noun* (*informal, especially NAmE*) a dishonest person, especially a lawyer 奸詐的律師；不擇手段的人；卑鄙小人

SI /ˌes ˈaɪ/ *abbr.* International System (used to describe units of measurement; from French 'Système International') 國際單位制（源自法語 Système International）：*SI units* 國際單位

Siamese cat /ˌsaɪəmiːz ˈkæt/ (also **Siam·ese**) *noun* a cat with short pale fur and a brown face, ears, tail and feet 暹羅貓

ˌSiamese ˈtwin *noun* = CONJOINED TWIN

sib /sɪb/ *noun* (*biology* 生) a brother or sister 胞親

sibi·lant /ˈsɪbɪlənt/ *adj., noun*

■ ***adj.*** (*formal* or *literary*) making an 's' or 'sh' sound 發嘶嘶聲的：*the sibilant sound of whispering* 竊竊私語聲

■ ***noun*** (*phonetics* 語音) a sibilant sound made in speech, such as /s/ and /z/ in the English words *sip* and *zip* 嘶音；噝擦音

sib·ling /ˈsɪblɪŋ/ *noun* (*formal* or *technical* 術語) a brother or sister 兄；弟；姐；妹：*squabbles between siblings* 兄弟姐妹間的口角 ◇ ***sibling rivalry*** (= competition between brothers and sisters) 兄弟姐妹間的競爭

sibyl /ˈsɪbl/ *noun* **1** in ancient times, a woman who was thought to be able to communicate messages from a god 西比爾，西比拉（傳說中能占卜未來的女子）**2** (*literary*) a woman who can predict the future 女預言家

sic /sɪk; siːk/ *adv., verb*

■ ***adv.*** (from *Latin*) written after a word that you have copied from somewhere, to show that you know that the word is wrongly spelled or wrong in some other way（註於引文後，表示原文存在拼寫等錯誤）原文如此：*In the letter to parents it said: 'The school is proud of it's [sic] record of excellence'.* 在致家長的信中寫道："The school is proud of it's（原文如此）record of excellence"。

■ ***verb*** (**-cc-**) **~ sb** (*NAmE, informal*) to attack sb 攻擊：*Sic him, Duke!* (= said to a dog) 杜克，咬他！（對狗說）

PHR V **ˈsic sth on sb** (*NAmE, informal*) to tell a dog to attack sb 放狗去咬某人

sick 🔑 /sɪk/ *adj., noun, verb*

■ ***adj.***

▸ **ILL** 患病 **1** 🔑 physically or mentally ill（身體或精神）生病的，有病的：*a sick child* 生病的孩子 ◇ *Her mother's very sick.* 她母親病得很厲害。◇ *Peter has* ***been off sick*** *(= away from work because he is ill) for two weeks.* 彼得因病兩週沒上班了。◇ *Emma has just* ***called in sick*** *(= telephoned to say she will not be coming to work because she is ill).* 埃瑪剛才打電話來請病假了。◇ *Britain's workers* ***went sick*** *(= did not go to work because they were ill) for a record number of days last year.* 去年英國工人的病假天數創下了紀錄。◇ (*NAmE*) *I can't afford to* ***get sick*** *(= become ill).* 我病不起。➲ COLLOCATIONS at ILL

▸ **WANTING TO VOMIT** 想嘔吐 **2** 🔑 [not usually before noun] (*especially BrE*) feeling that you want to VOMIT 想嘔吐；惡心：*Mum, I* ***feel sick***! 媽，我想吐！◇ *If you eat any more cake you'll* ***make yourself sick***. 你要是再吃蛋糕，就該吐了。◇ *a sick feeling in your stomach* 胃裏惡心的感覺

▸ **-SICK** 不適 **3** (in compounds 構成複合詞) feeling sick as a result of travelling on a ship, plane, etc. 暈船；暈機；暈車：*seasick* 暈船 ◇ *airsick* 暈機 ◇ *carsick* 暈車 ◇ *travel-sick* 旅行暈眩的

▸ **BORED** 厭倦 **4** 🔑 (*informal*) bored with or annoyed about sth that has been happening for a long time, and wanting it to stop（對…）厭倦的，厭煩的，厭惡的：**~ of sb/sth** *I'm sick of the way you've treated me.* 你對待我的那一套我都厭倦了。◇ *I'm* ***sick and tired of*** *your moaning.* 你的牢騷我都聽膩了。◇ *I'm* ***sick to death of*** *all of you!* 你們全都煩死人了！◇ **~ of doing sth** *We're sick of* *waiting around like this.* 這麼等來等去，我們感到很膩味。

▸ **CRUEL/STRANGE** 殘酷；古怪 **5** (*informal*) (especially of humour 尤指幽默) dealing with suffering, disease or death in a cruel way that some people think is offensive 令人毛骨悚然的；可怕的；殘酷的：*a sick joke* 令人毛骨悚然的笑話 ◇ *That's really sick.* 那真夠嚇人的。 **6** (*informal*) getting enjoyment from doing strange or cruel things 變態的；病態的：*a sick mind* 變態的心理 ◇ *People think I'm sick for having a rat as a pet.* 人們認為我養隻耗子當寵物是變態。◇ *We live in a sick society.* 我們生活在一個病態的社會裏。➲ see also HOMESICK, LOVESICK

IDM **be 'sick** (*BrE*) to bring food from your stomach back out through your mouth 嘔吐 **SYN** **vomit**：*I was sick three times in the night.* 夜裏我吐了三次。◇ *She had been* ***violently sick.*** 她一直吐得很厲害。 **be worried 'sick; be 'sick with worry** to be extremely worried 極度擔心；擔心得要命：*Where have you been? I've been worried sick about you.* 你上哪兒去了？把我急死了。 **fall 'sick** (also *old-fashioned* **take 'sick**) (*formal*) to become ill/sick 患病；生病 **make sb 'sick** to make sb angry or disgusted 使厭惡；使反感：*His hypocrisy makes me sick.* 他的虛偽讓我惡心。 **(as) sick as a 'dog** (*informal*) feeling very ill/sick; VOMITING a lot 病得很重；嘔吐得厲害 **(as) sick as a 'parrot** (*BrE, humorous*) very disappointed 大失所望 **sick at 'heart** (*formal*) very unhappy or disappointed 十分不快；非常失望 **sick to your 'stomach** **1** feeling very angry or worried 非常生氣；非常着急：*Nora turned sick to her stomach on hearing this news.* 聽了這個消息，諾拉變得憂心忡忡。 **2** (*NAmE*) feeling that you want to VOMIT 想嘔吐；惡心

■ ***noun***

▸ **VOMIT** 嘔吐 **1** [U] (*BrE, informal*) food that you bring back up from your stomach through your mouth 嘔吐物 **SYN** **vomit**

▸ **ILL PEOPLE** 病人 **2 the sick** [pl.] people who are ill/sick 病人：*All the sick and wounded were evacuated.* 所有傷病人員都給撤離了。

■ ***verb***

PHR V **,sick sth↔'up** (*BrE, informal*) to bring sth up from the stomach back out through your mouth 吐出 **SYN** **vomit**

'sick bag *noun* a paper bag on a boat or plane into which you can VOMIT（船或飛機上的）嘔吐用袋，衛生袋

sick·bay /'sɪkbeɪ/ *noun* a room or rooms, for example on a ship or in a school, with beds for people who are ill/sick（船上或學校等的）病室，保健室

sick·bed /'sɪkbed/ *noun* [sing.] the bed on which a person who is ill/sick is lying 病牀：*The President left his sickbed to attend the ceremony.* 總統帶病去出席那個儀式。

,sick 'building syndrome *noun* [U] a condition that affects people who work in large offices, making them feel tired and causing headaches, sore eyes and breathing problems, thought to be caused by, for example, the lack of fresh air or by chemicals in the air 病態建築綜合症，病態大樓症候群（辦公大樓中因新鮮空氣缺乏等原因而引起的疲倦、頭疼、眼睛疼痛、呼吸困難等症狀）

sick·en /'sɪkən/ *verb* (*BrE*) **1** [T] **~ sb** to make sb feel very shocked and angry 使大為震驚；使憤怒 **SYN** **disgust** **2** [I] to become ill/sick 患病；生病：(*old-fashioned*) *The baby sickened and died before his first birthday.* 嬰兒沒過週歲就病死了。◇ (*BrE*) *Faye hasn't eaten all day—she must* ***be sickening for something.*** 費伊一天沒吃飯了。她一定是哪兒不舒服了。

sick·en·ing /'sɪkənɪŋ/ *adj.* **1** making you feel disgusted or shocked 讓人厭惡的；令人作嘔的；令人震驚的 **SYN** **repulsive**：*the sickening stench of burnt flesh* 肉體燃燒所發出的令人作嘔的惡臭 **2** making you afraid that sb has been badly hurt or that sth has been broken 給人以不祥感覺的；讓人覺得不妙的：*Her head hit the ground with a sickening thud.* 她的頭撞在地上，那聲悶響讓人揪心。 **3** (*informal*) making you feel jealous or annoyed 令人忌妒的；讓人煩惱的：*'She's off to the Bahamas for a month.' 'How sickening!'*"她去巴哈馬群島了，要待一個月。""多讓人忌妒哇！" ▸ **sick·en·ing·ly** *adv.*

sickie /'sɪki/ *noun* (*BrE, informal*) a day when you say that you are ill/sick and cannot go to work when it is not really true 稱病缺勤；假病假：*to pull/throw/chuck a sickie* 裝病請假

sickle /'sɪkl/ *noun* a tool with a curved blade and a short handle, used for cutting grass, etc. 鐮刀 ➲ see also HAMMER AND SICKLE

'sick leave *noun* [U] permission to be away from work because of illness; the period of time spent away from work 病假：*to be on sick leave* 休病假

,sickle-cell a'naemia (also **'sickle-cell disease**) *noun* [U] a serious form of ANAEMIA (= a disease of the blood) that is found mostly in people of African family origins, and which is passed down from parents to children 鐮狀細胞貧血（多見於非裔的遺傳病）

sick·ly /'sɪkli/ *adj.* (**sick·lier**, **sick·li·est**) **1** often ill/sick 常生病的；多病的；愛鬧病的：*He was a sickly child.* 他是個愛鬧病的孩子。 **2** not looking healthy and strong 不健壯的；體弱的；有病容的 **SYN** **frail**：*She looked pale and sickly.* 她面色蒼白，病懨懨的。◇ *sickly plants* 長勢差的植物 **3** that makes you feel sick, especially because it is too sweet or full of false emotion（尤指太甜或充斥着虛情假義）令人生厭的，讓人惡心的：*a sickly sweet smell* 香得發膩的氣味 ◇ *She gave me a sickly smile.* 她朝我遞來一臉假笑。 **4** (of colours 顏色) unpleasant to look at 難看的；看着不舒服的：*a sickly green colour* 一種難看的綠色

sick·ness /'sɪknəs/ *noun* **1** [U] illness; bad health 疾病；不健康：*She's been off work because of sickness.* 她因病沒有上班。◇ *insurance against sickness and unemployment* 疾病和失業保險 ➲ **SYNONYMS** at ILLNESS **2** [U, C, usually sing.] a particular type of illness or disease …病；…症：***altitude/travel/radiation, etc. sickness*** 高原病、旅行眩暈、輻射病等 ➲ see also SLEEPING SICKNESS **3** [U] (*especially BrE*) the feeling that you are likely to VOMIT (= bring food back up from the stomach to the mouth); the fact of VOMITING 惡心；嘔吐 **SYN** **nausea**：*symptoms include sickness and diarrhoea* 症狀包括嘔吐和腹瀉 ◇ *The sickness passed off after a while.* 過了一會兒，就不覺得惡心了。➲ see also MORNING SICKNESS **4** [sing.] a feeling of great sadness, disappointment or disgust 悲傷；失望；厭惡；反感

'sickness benefit *noun* [U] (*BrE*) money paid by the government to people who are away from work because of illness 疾病補助金（由政府發放給因病不能上班的職工）➲ compare SICK PAY

sicko /'sɪkəʊ; *NAmE* -koʊ/ *noun* (*pl.* **-os**) (*informal, especially NAmE*) a person who gets enjoyment from doing strange and cruel things 從病態行為取樂的人；（精神）變態者：*child molesters and other sickos* 對兒童性騷擾者及其他變態狂

sick·out /'sɪkaʊt/ *noun* (*NAmE*) a strike in which all the workers at a company say they are sick and stay at home 集體稱病罷工

'sick pay *noun* [U] pay given to an employee who is away from work because of illness 病假工資 ➲ compare SICKNESS BENEFIT

sick·room /'sɪkru:m; -rʊm/ *noun* a room in which a person who is ill/sick is lying in bed 病房；病室

side /saɪd/ *noun, verb*

■ ***noun***

▸ **LEFT/RIGHT** 左；右 **1** [C, usually sing.] either of the two halves of a surface, an object or an area that is divided by an imaginary central line（由想像的中線分出的）一邊，一側：*They drive on the left-hand side of the road in Japan.* 在日本駕車靠左行。◇ *the right side of the brain* 腦的右半部 ◇ *satellite links to the other side of the world* 與世界的另一邊連線的衛星 ◇ *She was on the far side of the room.* 她在房間的那一邊。◇ *They crossed from one side of London to the other.* 他們從倫敦的這一頭到了另一頭。◇ *Keep on your side of the bed!* 你還是睡你那邊吧！ **2** [C, usually sing.] a position or an area to the left or right of sth（事物左方或右方的）一旁，一邊，一側：

S

*There is a large window **on either side of** the front door.* 前門兩側各有一個大窗戶。◇ *He crossed the bridge to **the other side** of the river.* 他過橋到了河對岸。◇ *people on both sides of the Atlantic* 大西洋兩岸的人 ◇ *She tilted her head **to one side**.* 她把頭歪到一邊。

▸ **NOT TOP OR BOTTOM 側面 3** [C] one of the flat surfaces of sth that is not the top or bottom, front or back 側面：*Write your name on the side of the box.* 把你的姓名寫在盒子的側面。◇ *There's a scratch on the side of my car.* 我的汽車側面有一道劃痕。◇ *The kitchen door is at the side of the house.* 廚房門開在房子的側面。◇ ***a side door/entrance/window*** 側門；側邊入口；側窗 ◇ *Now lay the jar on its side.* 現在把廣口瓶側着放倒。 **4** [C] the vertical or sloping surface around sth, but not the top or bottom of it 斜面；垂直面：*A path went up the side of the hill.* 沿着山坡往上有一條小路。◇ *Brush the sides of the tin with butter.* 在烤模的四周刷上黃油。 ➲ see also HILLSIDE, MOUNTAINSIDE

▸ **EDGE 邊緣 5** [C] a part or an area of sth near the edge and away from the middle 邊緣；邊：*She sat on the side of the bed.* 她坐在牀邊。◇ *A van was parked at the side of the road.* 路邊停着一輛載客麪包車。◇ *the south side of the lake* 湖的南側 ➲ see also BEDSIDE, FIRESIDE, RINGSIDE, RIVERSIDE, ROADSIDE, SEASIDE

▸ **OF BODY 身體 6** [C, usually sing.] either the right or left part of a person's body, from the ARMPIT (= where the arm joins the body) to the hip 側面；脅：*She has a pain down her right side.* 她身子右邊疼。◇ *He was lying on his side.* 他側臥着。

▸ **NEAR TO SB/STH 某人／某物的近旁 7** [sing.] a place or position very near to sb/sth 近旁；旁邊；身邊：*Keep close to my side.* 緊挨着我，別走開。◇ *Her husband stood at her side.* 她丈夫站在她身邊。

▸ **OF STH FLAT AND THIN 平而薄的東西 8** [C] either of two surfaces of sth flat and thin, such as paper or cloth 一面：*Write on one side of the paper only.* 只在紙的一面寫。◇ *Fry the steaks for two minutes on each side.* 牛排兩面各煎兩分鐘。

▸ **PAGE 頁 9** [C] the amount of writing needed to fill one side of a sheet of paper 一面紙的文字：*He told us not to write more than three sides.* 他告訴我們寫字不要超過三面紙。

▸ **MATHEMATICS 數學 10** [C] any of the flat surfaces of a solid object（立體的）面：*A cube has six sides.* 立方體有六面。 **11** [C] any of the lines that form a flat shape such as a square or triangle（平面圖形的）邊：*a shape with five sides* 五邊形 ◇ *The farm buildings form three sides of a square.* 這幾棟農舍構成一個正方形的三個邊。 ➲ VISUAL VOCAB page V71

S

▸ **-SIDED 有…面／邊 12** used in adjectives to state the number or type of sides（構成形容詞）有…面（或邊）的：*a six-sided object* 六面體 ◇ *a glass-sided container* 玻璃面的容器

▸ **IN WAR/ARGUMENT 戰爭；爭論 13** [C] one of the two or more people or groups taking part in an argument, war, etc. 一方；一派：*We have finally reached an agreement acceptable to all sides.* 我們最終達成一項各方都能接受的協議。◇ *At some point during the war he seems to have **changed sides**.* 戰爭期間，他好像在某個時候曾經轉投對方營壘。◇ *to be **on the winning/losing side*** 在獲勝／失敗一方 **14** [C] one of the opinions, attitudes or positions held by sb in an argument, a business arrangement, etc. 一方的意見（或態度、立場）：*We heard both **sides of the argument**.* 我們聽過了辯論雙方的意見。◇ *I just want you to hear **my side of the story** first.* 我只想要你先聽聽我的說法。◇ *Will you keep **your side of the bargain**?* 你那一方能不能遵守協議？

▸ **ASPECT 方面 15** [C] a particular aspect of sth, especially a situation or a person's character 方面：*These poems reveal her gentle side.* 這些詩顯示出她溫柔的一面。◇ *This is a side of Alan that I never knew existed.* 我以前從來不知道艾倫還有這樣的一面。◇ *It's good you can see **the funny side** of the situation.* 你能看到情況可笑的一面，這很好。◇ *I'll take care of that side of things.* 那方面的事情由我來處理。

▸ **FEELING THAT YOU ARE BETTER 優越感 16** [U] (*BrE, informal*) a feeling that you are better than other people 優越感；架子：*There was **no side** to him at all.* 他一點架子也沒有。

▸ **SPORTS TEAM 運動隊 17** [C] (*BrE*) a sports team 運動隊：*The French have a very strong side.* 法國隊非常強大。◇ *We were **on the winning/losing side**.* 我們支持獲勝／失利的一方。

▸ **OF FAMILY 親屬 18** [C] the part of your family that people belong to who are related either to your mother or to your father 母系；父系；血統：*a cousin on my father's side* (= a child of my father's brother or sister) 我父親那邊的表親

▸ **FOOD 食物 19** (*NAmE, informal*) = SIDE DISH：*Your dinner comes with a choice of two sides.* 您的正餐有兩道配菜可供選擇。

▸ **MEAT 肉 20** [C] **a ~ of beef/bacon, etc.** one of the two halves of an animal that has been killed for meat 一扇（牛肉／熏豬肉等）

▸ **TV CHANNEL 電視頻道 21** [C] (*old-fashioned, BrE, informal*) a television channel 電視頻道：*What's on the other side?* 另一個頻道上演什麼？

IDM **come down on 'one side of the fence or the 'other** to choose between two possible choices 二者擇其一；支持兩方中的一方 **from ˌside to 'side** moving to the left and then to the right and then back again 左右來回（搖擺）：*He shook his head slowly from side to side.* 他慢慢地搖了搖頭。◇ *The ship rolled from side to side.* 船左右搖晃。 **get on the right/wrong 'side of sb** to make sb pleased with you/annoyed with you 討得某人的歡心；惹得某人惱怒 **have sth on your 'side** to have sth as an advantage that will make it more likely that you will achieve sth 有…的優勢 **let the 'side down** (*especially BrE*) to fail to give your friends, family, etc. the help and support they expect, or to behave in a way that makes them disappointed 使自己人失望；未能幫助（或支持）自己的一方 **not leave sb's 'side** to stay with sb, especially in order to take care of them（尤指為了照顧）不離某人左右 **on/from all 'sides | on/from every 'side** in or from all directions; everywhere 從四面八方；到處：*We realized we were surrounded on all sides.* 我們意識到我們被四面包圍了。◇ *Disaster threatens on every side.* 災禍四伏。 **on the 'big, 'small, 'high, etc. side** (*informal*) slightly too big, small, high, etc. 稍偏大（或小、高等）：*These shoes are a little on the tight side.* 這雙鞋略有點緊。 **on the other side of the 'fence** in a situation that is different from the one that you are in 與自己所處情況不同的一面；事物的另一面 **on the ˌright/ˌwrong side of '40, '50, etc.** (*informal*) younger or older than 40, 50, etc. years of age 不到／已過 40 歲（或 50 歲等） **on the 'side** (*informal*) **1** in addition to your main job 作為副業；兼職；在正事之外：*a mechanic who buys and sells cars on the side* 兼做汽車買賣的機修工 **2** secretly or illegally 秘密地；偷偷摸摸地；非法地：*He's married but he has a girlfriend on the side.* 他有妻室，但暗地裏還有一個女友。 **3** (*especially NAmE*) (of food in a restaurant 餐館的食物) served at the same time as the main part of the meal, but on a separate plate 作為配菜 **on/to one 'side 1** out of your way 在（或到）一邊；在（或到）一旁：*I left my bags on one side.* 我把幾個包丟在一邊。 **2** to be dealt with later 擱置；暫不處理：*I put his complaint to one side until I had more time.* 我把他的投訴放到一邊，等時間充裕些再處理。◇ *Leaving that to one side for a moment, are there any other questions?* 把這個先放一放，還有沒有別的問題？ **be on sb's side** to support and agree with sb 站在某人一邊；和某人觀點一致：*I'm definitely on your side in this.* 在這個問題上，我毫不含糊地站在你這一邊。◇ *Whose side are you on anyway?* 你到底贊成誰的觀點呢？ **the other side of the 'coin** the aspect of a situation that is the opposite of or contrasts with the one you have been talking about 事情的另一面 **ˌside by 'side 1** close together and facing in the same direction 並排；並肩地：*There were two children ahead, walking side by side.* 前面有兩個孩子肩並肩走着。 **2** together, without any difficulties 並行不悖；相安無事：*We have been using both systems, side by side, for two years.* 兩年來，兩套系統我們一直同時使用，互不影響。◇ *The two communities exist happily side by side.* 兩個群體和睦共處，相安無事。 **take 'sides** to express support for sb in a disagreement 表示支持一方；表明立

場： *She didn't think it was wise to take sides in their argument.* 對於他們的辯論，她覺得向着誰都不明智。 **take/draw sb to one 'side** to speak to sb in private, especially in order to warn or tell them about sth 把某人拉到一邊（悄悄說話） **this side of …** before a particular time, event, age, etc. 在…之前： *They aren't likely to arrive this side of midnight.* 午夜之前他們不大可能趕到。 ➲ more at BED *n.*, BIT, BRIGHT *adj.*, CREDIT *n.*, DISTAFF, ERR, GRASS *n.*, KNOW *v.*, LAUGH *v.*, RIGHT *adj.*, SAFE *adj.*, SPLIT *v.*, THORN, TIME *n.*, TWO, WRONG *adj.*

■ *verb*

PHR V **'side with sb (against sb/sth)** to support one person or group in an argument against sb else 支持某人（反對…）；和某人站在一起（反對…）： *The kids always sided with their mother against me.* 孩子們總是和媽媽站在一邊，跟我唱對台戲。

side·bar /'saɪdbɑː(r)/ *noun* **1** a short article in a newspaper or magazine that is printed next to a main article, and gives extra information （報紙或雜誌的）花絮新聞 **2** a narrow area on the side of a computer screen or a WEB PAGE that is separate from the main part of the page （電腦屏幕或網頁的）側邊欄，邊註欄

side·board /'saɪdbɔːd; *NAmE* -bɔːrd/ (*NAmE* also **buf·fet**) *noun* **1** a piece of furniture in a DINING ROOM for putting food on before it is served, with drawers for storing knives, forks, etc. 餐具櫃 ➲ **VISUAL VOCAB** page V22 **2** = SIDEBURN

side·burn /'saɪdbɜːn; *NAmE* -bɜːrn/ (*BrE* also **side·board**) *noun* [usually pl.] hair that grows down the sides of a man's face in front of his ears （男子的）鬢角 ➲ **VISUAL VOCAB** page V60

side·car /'saɪdkɑː(r)/ *noun* a small vehicle attached to the side of a motorcycle in which a passenger can ride （摩托車的）跨斗，邊車

'side dish (*NAmE informal* **side**) *noun* a small amount of food, for example a salad, served with the main course of a meal （隨同主菜一起上的）配菜 SYN **side order**

'side effect *noun* [usually pl.] **1** an extra and usually bad effect that a drug has on you, as well as curing illness or pain （藥物的）副作用 **2** an unexpected result of a situation or course of action that happens as well as the result you were aiming for 意外的連帶後果

'side-foot *verb* **~ sth** to kick a ball with the inside part of your foot 用腳內側踢，側腳踢（球）

'side issue *noun* an issue that is less important than the main issue, and may take attention away from it 次要問題

side·kick /'saɪdkɪk/ *noun* (*informal*) a person who helps another more important or more intelligent person 助手；副手： *Batman and his young sidekick Robin* 蝙蝠俠和他的年輕助手羅賓

side·light /'saɪdlaɪt/ *noun* **1 ~ (on sb/sth)** a piece of information, usually given by accident or in connection with another subject, that helps you to understand sb/sth 意外線索；側面瞭解的情況；間接消息 **2** (*BrE*) either of a pair of small lights at the front of a vehicle （車輛前面的）側燈

side·line /'saɪdlaɪn/ *noun, verb*

■ *noun* **1** [C] an activity that you do as well as your main job in order to earn extra money 兼職；副業；兼營業務 **2 sidelines** [pl.] the lines along the two long sides of a sports field, TENNIS COURT, etc. that mark the outer edges; the area just outside these （球場等的）邊線，兩側場外區域： *The coach stood on the sidelines yelling instructions to the players.* 教練站在場外，大聲指揮運動員。

IDM **on/from the 'sidelines** watching sth but not actually involved in it 從旁觀者的角度；置身局外： *He was content to watch from the sidelines as his wife built up a successful business empire.* 他滿足於站在一旁，看妻子一步步地建立起一個成功的商業帝國。

■ *verb* [usually passive] **1 ~ sb** to prevent sb from playing in a team, especially because of an injury 使退出比賽，使下場（尤指由於受傷）： *The player has been sidelined by a knee injury.* 這名隊員因膝部受傷而下場。 **2 ~ sb** to prevent sb from having an important part in sth that other people are doing 把…排除在核心之外；使靠邊： *The vice-president is increasingly being sidelined.* 副總統被日益排擠到權力中心之外。

side·long /'saɪdlɒŋ; *NAmE* -lɔːŋ/ *adj.* [only before noun] (of a look 目光) out of the corner of your eye, especially in a way that is secret or disapproving 側眼偷看的；斜着眼看的；睨視的： *She cast **a sidelong glance** at Eric to see if he had noticed her blunder.* 她偷偷斜掃了埃里克一眼，看他有沒有留意到她的錯誤。 ▶ **side·long** *adv.*: *She looked sidelong at him.* 她斜眼看他。

,side-'on *adv.* (*BrE*) coming from the side rather than from the front or back 從側面；側向： *The car hit us side-on.* 那輛車從側面撞了我們。

'side order *noun* a small amount of food ordered in a restaurant to go with the main dish, but served separately （主菜之外）另點的配菜 SYN **side dish**: *a side order of fries* 另點的一份炸薯條

'side plate *noun* a small plate used for bread or other food that goes with a meal 麵包盤；小吃盤 ➲ **VISUAL VOCAB** page V22

sid·er·eal /saɪ'dɪəriəl; *NAmE* -'dɪr-/ *adj.* (*astronomy* 天) related to the stars that are far away, not the sun or planets 恒星的

'side road *noun* a smaller and less important road leading off a main road 支線；叉道；旁路

'side-saddle *adv.* if you ride a horse **side-saddle**, you ride with both your legs on the same side of the horse 在橫鞍上；側騎

'side salad *noun* a salad served with the main course of a meal 副菜色拉

side·show /'saɪdʃəʊ; *NAmE* -ʃoʊ/ *noun* **1** a separate small show or attraction at a FAIR or CIRCUS where you pay to see a performance or take part in a game （遊園會或馬戲中穿插的）小節目，雜耍 **2** an activity or event that is much less important than the main activity or event 次要活動；附帶事件

'side-splitting *adj.* (*informal*) extremely funny; making people laugh a lot 滑稽透頂的；令人捧腹的： *side-splitting anecdotes* 滑稽可笑的奇聞佚事 ▶ **'side-splittingly** *adv.*: *side-splittingly funny* 極其滑稽可笑的

side·step /'saɪdstep/ *verb* (**-pp-**) **1** [T] **~ sth** to avoid answering a question or dealing with a problem 迴避，規避（問題等）： *Did you notice how she neatly side-stepped the question?* 你有沒有注意到她多麼巧妙地迴避了那個問題？ **2** [T, I] **~ (sth)** to avoid sth, for example being hit, by stepping to one side 橫跨一步躲過；側移一步閃過： *He cleverly sidestepped the tackle.* 他巧妙地一晃，繞過阻截隊員。

'side street *noun* a less important street leading off a road in a town 小路；小街

side·swipe /'saɪdswaɪp/ *noun* **1** (*NAmE*) a hit from the side 擦邊撞擊；側撞；擦撞： *a sideswipe by a truck* 卡車的擦撞 **2 ~ (at sb/sth)** (*informal*) a critical comment made about sb/sth while you are talking about sb/sth completely different 藉機抨擊；借題發揮的批評： *It was a good speech, but he couldn't resist taking a sideswipe at his opponent.* 他的講話不錯，可他還是忍不住藉機把對手抨擊了一番。 ▶ **side·swipe** *verb* **~ sb/sth** (*NAmE*): *The bus sideswiped two parked cars.* 公共汽車擦邊撞上了兩輛停在那兒的汽車。

side·track /'saɪdtræk/ *verb* [usually passive] **~ sb (into doing sth)** to make sb start to talk about or do sth that is different from the main thing that they are supposed to be talking about or doing 使轉話題；使轉移目標 SYN **distract**: *I was supposed to be writing a letter but I'm afraid I **got sidetracked**.* 我本來應該在寫信，但後來恐怕是分心幹別的去了。

'side view *noun* a view of sth from the side 側景；側視圖；側面圖： *The picture shows a side view of the house.* 這張圖是房子的側面。

side·walk /'saɪdwɔːk/ (*NAmE*) (*BrE* **pave·ment**) *noun* a flat part at the side of a road for people to walk on （馬路邊的）人行道 ➲ **VISUAL VOCAB** page V3

S

ˈsidewalk artist (*NAmE*) (*BrE* **ˈpavement artist**) *noun* an artist who draws pictures in CHALK on the PAVEMENT/SIDEWALK, hoping to get money from people who pass 街頭畫家，馬路畫家（在人行道上用粉筆作畫討錢）

side·ward /ˈsaɪdwəd; *NAmE* -wərd/ *adj.* to, towards or from the side（向）一側的；（向）一邊的： *a sideward glance* 向旁邊看的一眼 ▸ **side·ward** (also **side·wards**) *adv.* : *He was blown sidewards by the wind.* 他被風吹到旁邊。

side·ways 0┳ /ˈsaɪdweɪz/ *adv.*
1 0┳ to, towards or from the side 往（或向、從）一側： *He looked sideways at her.* 他斜着眼看她。◇ *The truck skidded sideways across the road.* 卡車橫着滑到公路另一側。◇ *He has been moved sideways* (= moved to another job at the same level as before, not higher or lower). 他平級調動工作了。 **2** 0┳ with one side facing forwards 側着；側面朝前： *She sat sideways on the chair.* 她側坐在椅子上。 ▸ **side·ways** 0┳ *adj.* : *She slid him a sideways glance.* 她斜眼看了他一下。◇ *a sideways move* 側移
IDM see KNOCK *v.*

ˈside whiskers *noun* [pl.] hair growing on the sides of a man's face down to, but not on, the chin（男子的）絡腮鬍子，連鬢鬍子

side·wind·er /ˈsaɪdwaɪndə(r)/ *noun* a poisonous N American snake that moves sideways across the desert by throwing its body in an S shape 側進蛇，角響尾蛇（北美沙漠地帶毒蛇）

sid·ing /ˈsaɪdɪŋ/ *noun* **1** a short track beside a main railway/railroad line, where trains can stand when they are not being used（火車不用時停靠的）側線，岔線 **2** (*NAmE*) material used to cover and protect the outside walls of buildings 壁板；牆板；擋板

sidle /ˈsaɪdl/ *verb* [I] **+ adv./prep.** to walk somewhere in a shy or uncertain way as if you do not want to be noticed 猶猶豫豫地走；羞怯地走；悄悄地走： *She sidled up to me and whispered something in my ear.* 她悄悄走上前來，對我耳語了幾句。

SIDS /ˌes aɪ diː ˈes; sɪdz/ *noun* [U] the abbreviation for 'sudden infant death syndrome' (the sudden death while sleeping of a baby which appears to be healthy) 嬰兒猝死綜合症 **SYN** **cot death**

siege /siːdʒ/ *noun* **1** a military operation in which an army tries to capture a town by surrounding it and stopping the supply of food, etc. to the people inside（軍隊對城鎮的）圍困，包圍，圍攻，封鎖： *the siege of Troy* 特洛伊之圍 ◇ *The siege was finally lifted* (= ended) *after six months.* 六個月後封鎖最終解除了。◇ *The police placed the city centre under a virtual* ***state of siege*** (= it was hard to get in or out). 警方可說是已封鎖了市中心。 **2** a situation in which the police surround a building where people are living or hiding, in order to make them come out（警察對建築物的）包圍，封鎖 ➲ see also BESIEGE
IDM **under ˈsiege** **1** surrounded by an army or the police in a siege 被包圍；被圍困；被封鎖 **2** being criticized all the time or put under pressure by problems, questions, etc. 一再遭到批評的；受…困擾的 **lay ˈsiege to sth** **1** to begin a siege of a town, building, etc. 圍困，圍攻（城鎮、建築物等） **2** to surround a building, especially in order to speak to or question the person or people living or working there 包圍（某建築物，旨在和裏面的人對話或質詢）

ˈsiege mentality *noun* [sing., U] a feeling that you are surrounded by enemies and must protect yourself 受圍心態（感覺周圍都是敵人因而必須自衛）

sie·mens /ˈsiːmənz/ *noun* (*abbr.* **S**) (*physics* 物) the standard unit for measuring how well an object CONDUCTS electricity 西門子（電導單位）

si·enna /siˈenə/ *noun* [U] a type of dark yellow or red CLAY used for giving colour to paints, etc.（富鐵）黃土，褐土（用作顏料）

si·erra /siˈerə/ *noun* (especially in place names 尤用於地名) a long range of steep mountains with sharp points, especially in Spain and America（尤指西班牙和美洲的）鋸齒狀山脈： *the Sierra Nevada* 內華達山脈

si·esta /siˈestə/ *noun* a rest or sleep taken in the early afternoon, especially in hot countries（尤指在氣候炎熱的國家的）午睡，午休： *to* ***have/take a siesta*** 睡午覺 ➲ compare NAP *n.* (1)

sieve /sɪv/ *noun, verb*
■ ***noun*** a tool for separating solids from liquids or larger solids from smaller solids, made of a wire or plastic net attached to a ring. The liquid or small pieces pass through the net but the larger pieces do not. 濾器；篩子；笊籬；漏勺 ➲ VISUAL VOCAB page V26
IDM **have a memory/mind like a ˈsieve** (*informal*) to have a very bad memory; to forget things easily 記性差；健忘
■ ***verb*** **~ sth** to put sth through a sieve 篩；過篩；濾

sie·vert /ˈsiːvət; *NAmE* -vərt/ *noun* (*abbr.* **Sv**) (*physics* 物) a unit for measuring the effect of RADIATION 希沃特（輻射劑量當量單位）

sift /sɪft/ *verb* **1** [T] **~ sth** to put flour or some other fine substance through a SIEVE/SIFTER 篩（麪粉或顆粒較細的物質）： *Sift the flour into a bowl.* 把麪粉篩到碗裏。 **2** [T, I] to examine sth very carefully in order to decide what is important or useful or to find sth important 細查；詳審： **~ sth** *We will sift every scrap of evidence.* 我們將細查每一點證據。◇ **~ through sth** *Crash investigators have been sifting through the wreckage of the aircraft.* 調查墜機事件的專家一直在仔細檢查飛機殘骸。 **3** [T] **~ sth (out) from sth** to separate sth from a group of things 區分；挑選；精選： *She looked quickly through the papers, sifting out from the pile anything that looked interesting.* 她很快地翻了一下那摞文件，把所有看着有趣的東西都揀了出來。
PHR V **ˌsift sth↔ˈout** **1** to remove sth that you do not want from a substance by putting it through a SIEVE 篩除；篩去： *Put the flour through a sieve to sift out the lumps.* 把麪粉過篩，除去麪塊。 **2** to separate sth, usually sth you do not want, from a group of things 剔除；淘汰： *We need to sift out the applications that have no chance of succeeding.* 我們需要剔出那些成功無望的申請。

sift·er /ˈsɪftə(r)/ *noun* **1** (*NAmE*) a small SIEVE used for sifting flour（麪粉）篩子；羅 ➲ VISUAL VOCAB page V26 **2** a container with a lot of small holes in the top, used for shaking flour or sugar onto things 撒…瓶（蓋上有許多小孔，用於撒麪粉等粉狀物或糖）： *a sugar sifter* 撒糖瓶

sigh /saɪ/ *verb, noun*
■ ***verb*** **1** [I] to take and then let out a long deep breath that can be heard, to show that you are disappointed, sad, tired, etc. 歎氣；歎息： *He* ***sighed deeply*** *at the thought.* 想到這裏，他深深歎了口氣。◇ **~ with sth** *She* ***sighed with relief*** *that it was all over.* 事情總算全都過去了，她輕鬆地舒了一口氣。 **2** [T] **+ speech** to say sth with a sigh 歎着氣說；歎息道： *'Oh well, better luck next time,' she sighed.* "唉，就這樣了，但願下一次運氣好些。"她歎息道。 **3** [I] (*literary*) (especially of the wind 尤指風) to make a long sound like a sigh 悲鳴
■ ***noun*** an act or the sound of sighing 歎氣；歎息： *to* ***give/heave/let out a sigh*** 發出歎息 ◇ *a deep sigh* 深深的歎息 ◇ *'I'll wait,' he said with a sigh.* "我就等唄。"他歎口氣說。◇ *We all* ***breathed a sigh of relief*** *when it was over.* 事情過去後，我們大家都鬆了一口氣。

sight 0┳ /saɪt/ *noun, verb*
■ ***noun***
▸ **ABILITY TO SEE 視力** **1** 0┳ [U] the ability to see 視力；視覺 **SYN** **eyesight** : *to lose your sight* (= to become blind) 失明 ◇ *She has very good sight.* 她的視力很好。◇ *The disease has affected her sight.* 這種病影響了她的視力。◇ *He has very little sight in his right eye.* 他右眼視力極弱。
▸ **ACT OF SEEING 看見** **2** 0┳ [U] **~ of sb/sth** the act of seeing sb/sth 看見： *After ten days at sea, we had our first sight of land.* 我們在海上航行十天之後，首次看見陸地。◇ *I have been known to faint* ***at the sight of*** *blood.* 大家都知道，我看到血就會昏倒。◇ *The soldiers were given*

S

orders to shoot ***on sight*** (= as soon as they saw sb). 士兵得到命令，見人就射擊。◇ *She* ***caught sight*** *of a car in the distance.* 她看見遠處有一輛汽車。

▸ **HOW FAR YOU CAN SEE 視野 3** [U] the area or distance within which sb can see or sth can be seen 視力範圍；視野：*There was no one* ***in sight****.* 一個人也看不見。◇ *At last we* ***came in sight of*** *a few houses.* 最後，我們看到了幾座房屋。◇ *A bicycle came into sight on the main road.* 大路上出現了一輛自行車。◇ *The end is* ***in sight*** (= will happen soon). 結局已現端倪。◇ *Leave any valuables in your car* ***out of sight****.* 把貴重物品留在車裏，要放在看不見的地方。◇ *Keep* ***out of sight*** (= stay where you cannot be seen). 不要露面。◇ *She never lets her daughter* ***out of her sight*** (= always keeps her where she can see her). 她從來不讓女兒走出她的視線之外。◇ *Get out of my sight!* (= Go away!) 滾開！◇ *The boat disappeared* ***from sight****.* 那艘船從視野中消失了。◇ *The house was* ***hidden from sight*** *behind some trees.* 房子藏在樹林後面。◇ *He had placed himself directly in my* ***line of sight****.* 當時他恰好出現在我的視線中。

▸ **WHAT YOU CAN SEE 看見的事物 4** [C] a thing that you see or can see 看見（或看得見）的事物；景象；情景：*It's a spectacular sight as the flamingos lift into the air.* 一群紅鸛飛向空中，景象十分壯觀。◇ *The museum attempts to recreate* ***the sights and sounds of*** *wartime Britain.* 博物館試圖再現戰時英國的情景。◇ *He was a* ***sorry sight****, soaked to the skin and shivering.* 他渾身濕透，打着寒戰，一副悽慘的樣子。◇ *The bird is now a rare sight in this country.* 如今在這個國家，這種鳥已罕見了。➲ SYNONYMS at VIEW

▸ **INTERESTING PLACES 好玩的地方 5** **sights** [pl.] the interesting places, especially in a town or city, that are often visited by tourists 名勝；風景：*We're going to Paris for the weekend to* ***see the sights****.* 我們打算去巴黎過週末，參觀那裏的名勝。

▸ **RIDICULOUS/UNTIDY PERSON 可笑的／邋遢的人 6** **a sight** [sing.] (*informal, especially BrE*) a person or thing that looks ridiculous, untidy, unpleasant, etc. 滑稽可笑（或邋遢、髒亂、討厭）的人（或物）：*She looks a sight in that hat!* 她戴着那頂帽子，樣子夠滑稽的！

▸ **ON GUN/TELESCOPE 槍炮；望遠鏡 7** [C, usually pl.] a device that you look through to aim a gun, etc. or to look at sth through a TELESCOPE, etc. 瞄準具；觀測器：*He had the deer* ***in his sights*** *now.* 他現在瞄準了那頭鹿。◇ (*figurative*) *Even as a young actress, she always had Hollywood firmly in her sights* (= as her final goal). 她還是年輕演員的時候，就瞄準了好萊塢。

IDM **at first 'sight 1** when you first begin to consider sth 乍一看；初看時：*At first sight, it may look like a generous offer, but always read the small print.* 乍一看，對方給出的條件好像很優厚，但任何時候都不要小看那些小號字印刷的附加條款。 **2** when you see sb/sth for the first time 初次見到：*It was* ***love at first sight*** (= we fell in love the first time we saw each other). 我們一見鍾情。 **hate, be sick of, etc. the 'sight of sb/sth** (*informal*) to hate, etc. sb/sth very much 十分厭惡；討厭：*I can't stand the sight of him!* 我看見他就煩！ **in the sight of sb/in sb's sight** (*formal*) in sb's opinion 從某人的觀點來看；在某人看來：*We are all equal in the sight of God.* 在上帝眼裏我們都是平等的。 **lose 'sight of sb/sth 1** to become no longer able to see sb/sth 再也見不着：*They finally lost sight of land.* 他們終於看不見陸地了。 **2** to stop considering sth; to forget sth 忽略；忘記：*We must not lose sight of our original aim.* 我們決不能忘記我們最初的目標。 **ˌout of 'sight, ˌout of 'mind** (*saying*) used to say sb will quickly be forgotten when they are no longer with you 眼不見，心不想 **raise/lower your 'sights** to expect more/less from a situation 提高／降低要求；眼光變高／變低 **set your sights on sth/on doing sth** to decide that you want sth and to try very hard to get it 以…為奮鬥目標；決心做到：*She's set her sights on getting into Harvard.* 她決心要上哈佛大學。 **a (damn, etc.) sight better, etc. | a (damn, etc.) sight too good, etc.** (*informal*) very much better; much too good, etc. （好）得多；非常（好）：*She's done a darn sight better than I have.* 她幹得比我強多了。◇ *It's worth a damn sight more than I thought.* 它的價值比我原先想的高多了。 **a ˌsight for sore 'eyes** (*informal*) a person or thing that you are pleased to see; something that is very pleasant to look at 讓人見了很高興的人（或事物） **sight un'seen** if you buy sth **sight unseen**, you do not have an opportunity to see it before you buy it 在未見過的情況下；事先未經檢查 ➲ more at HEAVE *v.*, KNOW *v.*, NOWHERE, PRETTY *adj.*

■ ***verb*** **~ sth** (*formal*) to suddenly see sth, especially sth you have been looking for 看到，發現（期待的事物）：*After twelve days at sea, they sighted land.* 在海上航行十二天後他們發現了陸地。

Synonyms 同義詞辨析

sight

view • vision

These are all words for the area or distance that you can see from a particular position. 以上各詞均指視力範圍、視野。

sight the area or distance that you can see from a particular position 指視力範圍、視野：*He looked up the street, but there was no one in sight.* 他朝街上望去，一個人也沒看見。◇ *Leave any valuables in your car out of sight.* 把貴重物品留在車裏看不見的地方。

view (*rather formal*) the area or distance that you can see from a particular position 指視力範圍、視野：*The lake soon came into view.* 那湖很快便映入眼簾。

vision the area that you can see from a particular position 指視野：*The couple moved outside her field of vision* (= total area you can see from a particular position). 這對夫婦離開了她的視野。

SIGHT, VIEW OR VISION? 用 sight、view 還是 vision？

View is more literary than **sight** or **vision**. It is the only word for talking about how well you can see. * view 較 sight 和 vision 書面化，是其中唯一指視野清晰程度的詞：~~*I didn't have a good sight/vision of the stage.*~~ **Vision** must always be used with a possessive pronoun. * vision 總是與物主代詞連用：*my/his/her etc. (field of) vision* 我／他／她…的視野 It is not used with the prepositions *in, into* and *out of* that are very frequent with **sight** and **view**. * vision 不與介詞 in、into 和 out of 連用，但 sight 和 view 常與這些介詞連用：~~*There was nobody in vision.*~~ ◇ ~~*A tall figure came into vision.*~~

PATTERNS

- **in/out of** sight/view
- **in/within** sight/view **of** sth
- to **come into/disappear from** sight/view/sb's vision
- to **come in** sight/view **of** sb/sth
- to **block** sb's view/vision
- sb's **line of** sight/vision
- sb's **field of** view/vision

sight·ed /'saɪtɪd/ *adj.* **1** able to see; not blind 看得見的；有視力的：*the blind parents of sighted children* 有正常視力的孩子的盲人父母 **2** **-sighted** (in compounds 構成複合詞) able to see in the way mentioned 有…視力的；視力…的：*partially sighted* 有部份視力的◇ *short-sighted* 近視的◇ *long-sighted* 遠視的

sight·ing /'saɪtɪŋ/ *noun* an occasion when sb sees sb/sth, especially sth unusual or sth that lasts for only a short time 看見，目睹（不尋常或短暫出現的事物）：*a reported sighting of the Loch Ness monster* 據報道有人看見尼斯湖水怪

sight·less /'saɪtləs/ *adj.* (*literary*) unable to see 看不見的；盲的 **SYN** **blind**：*The statue stared down at them with sightless eyes.* 雕像用一雙盲眼俯視着他們。

'sight-line *noun* = LINE OF SIGHT

'sight-read *verb* [I, T] **~ (sth)** to play or sing written music when you see it for the first time, without practising it first 視奏，視唱（事先沒有練習，直接看着

S

樂譜演奏或演唱）▸ ˈ**sight-reader** *noun* ˈ**sight-reading** *noun* [U]

sight·see·ing /ˈsaɪtsiːɪŋ/ *noun* [U] the activity of visiting interesting buildings and places as a tourist 觀光；遊覽：*to go sightseeing* 去觀光 ◇ *Did you have a chance to do any sightseeing?* 你有沒有出去遊覽的機會？◇ *a sightseeing tour of the city* 遊覽那座城市 ➲ COLLOCATIONS at TRAVEL ▸ **sight·see** *verb* [I] (only used in the progressive tenses 僅用於進行時) **sight·seer** *noun* SYN **tourist**：*Oxford attracts large numbers of sightseers.* 牛津吸引着大量觀光客。

Synonyms 同義詞辨析

sign

indication • symptom • symbol • indicator • signal

These are all words for an event, action or fact that shows that sth exists, is happening or may happen in the future. 以上各詞均指跡象、徵兆、預兆。

sign an event, action or fact that shows that sth exists, is happening or may happen in the future 指跡象、徵兆、預兆：*Headaches may be a sign of stress.* 頭痛可能是緊張的跡象。

indication (*rather formal*) a remark or sign that shows that sth is happening or what sb is thinking or feeling 指標示、象徵：*They gave no **indication as to** how the work should be done.* 他們根本沒說明這項工作該怎樣做。

SIGN OR INDICATION? 用 sign 還是 indication？

An **indication** often comes in the form of sth that sb says; a **sign** is usually sth that happens or sth that sb does. * indication 常指通過某人的說話表明，sign 通常為發生的事或某人所做的事。

symptom a change in your body or mind that shows that you are not healthy; a sign that sth exists, especially sth bad 指症狀、徵候、徵兆：*Symptoms include a sore throat.* 症狀包括嗓子疼。◇ *The rise in inflation was just one symptom of the poor state of the economy.* 通脹上升不過是經濟不景氣的一個徵候。

symbol a person, object or event that represents a more general quality or situation 指象徵：*The dove is a universal symbol of peace.* 鴿子是和平的共同象徵。

indicator (*rather formal*) a sign that shows you what sth is like or how a situation is changing 指指示信號、標誌、跡象：*the economic indicators* 經濟指標

signal an event, action or fact that shows that sth exists, is happening or may happen in the future 指標誌、預示、信號：*Chest pains can be a warning signal of heart problems.* 胸部疼痛可能是心臟病的報警信號。

SIGN OR SIGNAL? 用 sign 還是 signal？

Signal is often used to talk about an event, action or fact that suggests to sb that they should do sth. **Sign** is not usually used in this way. * signal 常用以指應該採取行動的暗號、信號；sign 通常不用於此義：~~*Reducing prison sentences would send the wrong signs to criminals.*~~

PATTERNS

- a(n) sign/indication/symptom/symbol/indicator/signal **of** sth
- a(n) sign/indication/symptom/indicator/signal **that** …
- a **clear** sign/indication/symptom/symbol/indicator/signal
- an **obvious** sign/indication/symptom/symbol/indicator
- an **early** sign/indication/symptom/indicator/signal
- an **outward** sign/indication/symbol
- **to give** a(n) sign/indication/signal

S

sigma /ˈsɪɡmə/ *noun* the 18th letter of the Greek alphabet (Σ, σ) 希臘字母表的第 18 個字母

sign 🗝 /saɪn/ *noun, verb*

■ ***noun***

▸ SHOWING STH 顯示 **1** 🗝 [C, U] an event, an action, a fact, etc. that shows that sth exists, is happening or may happen in the future 跡象；徵兆；預兆 SYN **indication**：**~ (of sth/sb)** *Headaches may be a sign of stress.* 頭痛可能是緊張的跡象。◇ *There is no sign of John anywhere.* 哪兒都沒有約翰的影子。◇ *Call the police at the first sign of trouble.* 一有鬧事的苗頭就叫警察。◇ *There was no **sign of life** in the house* (= there seemed to be nobody there). 那座房子沒有一點住人的跡象。◇ *Her work is **showing some signs of** improvement.* 她的工作出現了一些改進的跡象。◇ **~ (of doing sth)** *The gloomy weather **shows no sign of** improving.* 陰沉的天氣沒有絲毫轉晴的跡象。◇ *The fact that he didn't say 'no' immediately is a **good sign**.* 他沒有馬上拒絕，這是好徵兆。◇ **~ (that …)** *If an interview is too easy, it's **a sure sign that** you haven't got the job.* 如果面試太簡單，那必定表示你沒得到那份工作。◇ *If I had noticed the **warning signs**, none of this would have happened.* 要是我當時注意到了那些警告信號，這種事就一樁也不會發生。

▸ FOR INFORMATION/WARNING 提供信息；用以提醒 **2** 🗝 [C] a piece of paper, wood or metal that has writing or a picture on it that gives you information, instructions, a warning, etc. 招牌；標牌；指示牌；標誌：*a **road/traffic sign*** 道路 / 交通標誌 ◇ *a **shop/pub sign*** 商店 / 酒吧招牌 ◇ *The sign on the wall said 'Now wash your hands'.* 牆上的牌子上寫着"請洗手"。◇ ***Follow the signs** for the city centre.* 照標牌的指示到市中心。

▸ MOVEMENT/SOUND 動作；聲音 **3** 🗝 [C] a movement or sound that you make to tell sb sth 示意的動作（或聲音）；手勢：*He **gave a** thumbs-up **sign**.* 他豎起了大拇指示意。◇ *She nodded as a sign for us to sit down.* 她點頭示意我們坐下。➲ see also V-SIGN

▸ SYMBOL 符號 **4** 🗝 [C] a mark used to represent sth, especially in mathematics 符號；記號：*a plus/minus sign* (+/−) 加號；減號 ◇ *a dollar/pound sign* ($/£) 元 / 英鎊的符號

▸ STAR SIGN 星座 **5** [C] (*informal*) = STAR SIGN：*What sign are you?* 你屬什麼星座？

IDM **a ˌsign of the ˈtimes** something that you feel shows what things are like now, especially how bad they are 時代特徵（含貶義）

■ ***verb***

▸ YOUR NAME 姓名 **1** 🗝 [I, T] to write your name on a document, letter, etc. to show that you have written it, that you agree with what it says, or that it is genuine 簽（名）；署（名）；簽字；簽署：*Sign here, please.* 請在這裏簽名。◇ **~ sth** *Sign your name here, please.* 請在這裏簽名。◇ *You haven't signed the letter.* 這封信您還沒有署名。◇ *to sign a cheque* 在支票上簽字 ◇ *The treaty was signed on 24 March.* 條約是 3 月 24 日簽訂的。◇ *The player was signing autographs for a group of fans.* 這名隊員正在為一群球迷簽名。◇ **~ yourself + noun** *He signed himself 'Jimmy'.* 他署名"吉米"。

▸ CONTRACT 合同 **2** [T, I] to arrange for sb, for example a sports player or musician, to sign a contract agreeing to work for your company; to sign a contract agreeing to work for a company 和…簽約（達成雇聘關係）：**~ sb** *United have just signed a new goalie.* 聯隊最近和一名新守門員簽約。◇ **~ for sth** *He signed for United yesterday.* 昨天他和聯隊簽了約。◇ **~ with sth** *The band signed with Virgin Records.* 樂隊同維京唱片公司簽了約。

▸ MAKE MOVEMENT/SOUND 做出動作；發出聲音 **3** [I, T] **~ (to/for sb) (to do sth)** | **~ that** … to make a request or tell sb to do sth by using a sign, especially a hand movement 示意；打手勢 SYN **signal**：*The hotel manager signed to the porter to pick up my case.* 旅館經理示意行李員替我拿箱子。

▸ FOR DEAF PERSON 對聾人 **4** [I, T] to use sign language to communicate with sb 打手語：*She learnt to sign to help her deaf child.* 為幫助她耳聾的孩子，她學會了手語。◇ **~ sth** *An increasing number of plays are now being signed.* 現在越來越多的戲劇配上了手語。

▸ **sign·er** *noun*：*the signers of the petition* 在請願書上簽名的人 ◇ *signers communicating information to deaf people* 向聾人傳遞信息的手語譯員

IDM **ˌsigned and ˈsealed | ˌsigned, ˌsealed and deˈlivered** definite, because all the legal documents have been signed 簽名蓋章完畢的；鐵定的；成定局的 **sign on the dotted ˈline** (*informal*) to sign a document to show that you have agreed to buy sth or do sth 在簽字處簽上姓名（表示同意）；簽名同意：*Just sign on the dotted line and the car is yours.* 只要在虛線上簽名，這車就歸你了。➲ more at PLEDGE *n.*

PHR V **ˌsign sth↔aˈway** to lose your rights or property by signing a document 簽字放棄，簽字讓與（權利或財產）**ˈsign for sth** to sign a document to show that you have received sth 簽收 **ˌsign ˈin/ˈout | ˌsign sb↔ˈin/ˈout** to write your/sb's name when you arrive at or leave an office, a club, etc. 簽到；簽退；替某人簽到 / 簽退：*All visitors must sign in on arrival.* 來客均須簽到。◇ *You must sign guests out when they leave the club.* 客人離開俱樂部時，你必須為他們簽退。**ˌsign ˈoff 1** (*BrE*) to end a letter 結束寫信 **SYN** **finish**：*She signed off with 'Yours, Janet'.* 她在信末寫上"你的珍妮特"。**2** to end a broadcast by saying goodbye or playing a piece of music（以說再見或播放音樂的形式）結束廣播 **ˌsign sth↔ˈoff** to give your formal approval to sth, by signing your name 簽字認可；簽名贊同 **ˌsign ˈoff on sth** (*NAmE, informal*) to express your approval of sth formally and definitely 批准：*The President hasn't signed off on this report.* 這份報告總統沒有批准。**ˌsign ˈon** (*BrE, informal*) to sign a form stating that you are an unemployed person so that you can receive payment from the government 辦理失業登記（以領取失業救濟金）**ˌsign ˈon/ˈup | ˌsign sb↔ˈon/ˈup** to sign a form or contract which says that you agree to do a job or become a soldier; to persuade sb to sign a form or contract like this（使）簽約受雇（或入伍）**SYN** **enlist**：*He signed on for five years in the army.* 他簽了在部隊服役五年的合同。◇ *The company has signed up three top models for the fashion show.* 為時裝表演，公司簽約聘了三名頂尖模特兒。**ˌsign sth↔ˈover (to sb)** to give your rights or property to sb else by signing a document 簽字轉讓（權利或財產）：*She has signed the house over to her daughter.* 她簽署了轉讓手續，把房子過到女兒名下。**ˌsign ˈup (for sth)** to arrange to do a course of study by adding your name to the list of people doing it 報名（參加課程）**ˌsign ˈup to sth 1** (*BrE*) to commit yourself to a project or course of action, especially one that you have agreed with a group of other people, countries or organizations 簽署同意；簽訂：*How many countries have signed up to the Kyoto protocol on climate change?* 有多少個國家簽訂了關於氣候變化的《京都議定書》？**2 ~ to do sth** to agree to take part in sth 同意參與：*We have about 100 people signed up to help so far.* 到目前為止我們有大約 100 人同意提供幫助。

sign·age /ˈsaɪnɪdʒ/ *noun* [U] (*technical* 術語) signs, especially ones that give instructions or directions to the public（統稱）標誌，標識，標記

sig·nal 🔑 /ˈsɪɡnəl/ *noun, verb, adj.*

■ ***noun*** **1** 🔑 a movement or sound that you make to give sb information, instructions, a warning, etc. 信號；暗號 **SYN** **sign**：*a **danger/warning/distress, etc. signal*** 危險、警告、遇難等信號 ◇ *At an agreed signal they left the room.* 收到約定的信號後，他們離開了房間。◇ *The siren was a signal for everyone to leave the building.* 警報器一響，就是要所有人離開大樓。◇ *When I **give the signal**, run!* 我一發信號，你就跑！◇ (*NAmE*) *All I get is a **busy signal** when I dial his number* (= his phone is being used). 我什麼時候撥他的電話聽到的都是忙音。◇ ***hand signals*** (= movements that CYCLISTS and drivers make with their hands to tell other people that they are going to stop, turn, etc.) 騎車人和駕車人的示意手勢 ➲ see also TURN SIGNAL **2** 🔑 an event, an action, a fact, etc. that shows that sth exists or is likely to happen 標誌；預示；信號 **SYN** **indication**：*The rise in inflation is a **clear signal** that the government's policies are not working.* 通貨膨脹率的上升清楚地表明，政府的政策不起作用。◇ *Chest pains can be a **warning signal** of heart problems.* 胸部疼痛可能是心臟病的警告信號。◇ *Reducing prison sentences would **send the wrong signals** to criminals.* 減刑會向犯罪分子發出錯誤的信息。➲ SYNONYMS at SIGN **3** 🔑 a piece of equipment that uses different coloured lights to tell drivers to go slower, stop, etc., used especially on railways/railroads and roads（尤指鐵路和公路上的）指示燈，信號燈，紅綠燈：*traffic signals* 交通信號燈 ◇ *a stop signal* 停車信號 **4** 🔑 a series of electrical waves that carry sounds, pictures or messages, for example to a radio, television or mobile/cell phone（傳輸聲音、圖像或其他信息的電波）信號：*TV signals* 電視信號 ◇ *a high-frequency signal* 高頻信號 ◇ *a radar signal* 雷達信號 ◇ *to **detect/pick up signals*** 探測 / 收到信號 ◇ *to **emit a signal*** 發射信號 ◇ *I couldn't **get a signal** on my cell phone.* 我的手機接收不到信號了。

■ ***verb*** (**-ll-**, *US* **-l-**) **1** 🔑 [I, T] to make a movement or sound to give sb a message, an order, etc. 發信號；發暗號；示意：*Don't fire until I signal.* 等我發出信號後再開槍。◇ *Did you signal before you turned right?* 右轉彎前你示意了嗎？◇ **~ (to sb) (for sth)** *He signalled to the waiter for the bill.* 他示意服務員結賬。◇ **~ to/for sb to do sth** *He signalled to us to join him.* 他示意要我們去他那兒。◇ **~ sb to do sth** *She signalled him to follow.* 她示意他跟她走。◇ **~ sth** *The referee signalled a foul.* 裁判鳴哨示意犯規。◇ **~ (that)** ... *She signalled (that) it was time to leave.* 她示意該走了。◇ **~ which, what, etc.** ... *You must signal which way you are going to turn.* 你要朝哪個方向轉，必須發出信號。**2** [T] **~ sth** to be a sign that sth exists or is likely to happen 標誌；表明；預示 **SYN** **indicate**：*This announcement signalled a clear change of policy.* 這個聲明顯示政策有明顯的改變。◇ *The scandal surely signals the end of his political career.* 毫無疑問，這樁醜聞預示他的政治生涯就此結束。**3** [T] to do sth to make your feelings or opinions known 表達；表示；顯示：**~ sth** *He signalled his discontent by refusing to vote.* 他拒絕投票以示不滿。◇ **~ (that)** ... *She has signalled (that) she is willing to stand as a candidate.* 她表示願意作為候選人參加競選。

■ ***adj.*** [only before noun] (*formal*) important and noticeable 重大的；顯要的：*a signal honour* 極大的榮譽 ▸ **sig·nal·ly** /-nəli/ *adv.*：*They have signally failed to keep their election promises.* 他們顯然沒有履行自己的競選承諾。

ˈsignal box *noun* (*BrE*) a building beside a railway/railroad from which rail signals are operated（鐵路上的）信號房

sig·nal·ler (*US* also **sig·nal·er**) /ˈsɪɡnələ(r)/ *noun* = SIGNALMAN

sig·nal·man /ˈsɪɡnəlmən/ *noun* (*pl.* **-men** /-mən/) (also **sig·nal·ler**) (*BrE*) **1** a person whose job is operating signals on a railway（鐵路上的）信號員，信號工 **2** a person trained to give and receive signals in the army or navy（軍隊的）信號兵，通信兵

ˌsignal-to-ˈnoise ratio *noun* **1** (*technical* 術語) the strength of an electronic signal that you want to receive, compared to the strength of the signals that you do not want 信號噪聲比；信噪比 **2** a measure of how much useful information you receive, compared to information which is not useful 訊息對雜訊比；訊雜比

sig·na·tory /ˈsɪɡnətri; *NAmE* -tɔːri/ *noun* (*pl.* **-ies**) **~ (to/of sth)** (*formal*) a person, a country or an organization that has signed an official agreement（協議的）簽署者，簽署方，簽署國：*a signatory of the Declaration of Independence* 《獨立宣言》的簽署者 ◇ *Many countries are signatories to/of the Berne Convention.* 很多國家都是《伯爾尼公約》的簽署國。

sig·na·ture 🔑 /ˈsɪɡnətʃə(r)/ *noun*

1 🔑 [C] your name as you usually write it, for example at the end of a letter 簽名；署名：*Someone had forged her signature on the cheque.* 有人在支票上偽造了她的簽名。◇ *They collected 10 000 signatures for their petition.* 他們在請願書上徵集了 1 萬人的簽名。◇ *He was attacked for having **put his signature to** the deal.* 他因在協議上簽了字而受到攻擊。**2** [U] (*formal*) the act of signing sth 簽名；署名；簽字；簽署：*Two copies of the contract will be sent to you for signature.* 合同一式兩份，將送交您簽署。**3** [C, usually sing.] a particular quality that makes sth different from other similar things and makes it easy to recognize 明顯特徵；鮮明特色；識別標誌：*Bright colours are his signature.* 他總愛用亮麗的

S

色彩。➲ see also DIGITAL SIGNATURE, KEY SIGNATURE, TIME SIGNATURE

'signature tune *noun* (*BrE*) a short tune played at the beginning and end of a particular television or radio programme, or one that is connected with a particular performer（電視、廣播節目的或某主持人主持節目時播放的）信號曲，開始曲，結束曲 ➲ compare THEME MUSIC

sign·board /'saɪnbɔːd; *NAmE* -bɔːrd/ *noun* a piece of wood that has some information on it, such as a name, and is displayed outside a shop/store, hotel, etc.（商店、旅館等的）招牌，告示牌，廣告牌

sig·net ring /'sɪgnət rɪŋ/ *noun* a ring with a design cut into it, that you wear on your finger 圖章戒指 ➲ **VISUAL VOCAB** page V65

sig·nifi·cance AW /sɪg'nɪfɪkəns/ *noun* [U, C] **1** the importance of sth, especially when this has an effect on what happens in the future（尤指對將來有影響的）重要性，意義：*a decision of major political significance* 具有重大政治意義的決定 ◇ *The new drug has great significance for the treatment of the disease.* 這種新藥對於這種病的治療有重大的意義。◇ *They discussed the **statistical significance** of the results.* 他們討論了這些結果在統計學上的意義。 **2** the meaning of sth 意思；含義：*She couldn't grasp the full significance of what he had said.* 她未能充分領會他那番話的意思。◇ *Do these symbols have any particular significance?* 這些符號有什麼特別的含義嗎？➲ compare INSIGNIFICANCE

sig·nifi·cant 0-w AW /sɪg'nɪfɪkənt/ *adj.*
1 0-w large or important enough to have an effect or to be noticed 有重大意義的；顯著的：*a highly significant discovery* 有重大意義的發現 ◇ *The results of the experiment are not **statistically significant**.* 從統計學的觀點看，實驗結果意義不明顯。◇ *There are no significant differences between the two groups of students.* 這兩組學生沒有明顯差別。◇ *Your work has shown a significant improvement.* 你的工作有了顯著改進。◇ ***It is significant that** girls generally do better in examinations than boys.* 很明顯，女生的考試成績一般比男生的好。➲ compare INSIGNIFICANT **2** 0-w having a particular meaning 有某種意義的：*It is significant that he changed his will only days before his death.* 他在臨終前幾天修改遺囑，這很能說明問題。 **3** [usually before noun] having a special or secret meaning that is not understood by everyone 別有含義的；意味深長的 SYN **meaningful**：*a significant **look/smile*** 意味深長的眼神／微笑

S

sig·nifi·cant·ly 0-w AW /sɪg'nɪfɪkəntli/ *adv.*
1 0-w in a way that is large or important enough to have an effect on sth or to be noticed 有重大意義地；顯著地；明顯地：*The two sets of figures are not significantly different.* 這兩組數字沒有明顯的差別。◇ *Profits have increased significantly over the past few years.* 幾年來，利潤大幅度提高了。 **2** 0-w in a way that has a particular meaning 有某種意義：*Significantly, he did not deny that there might be an election.* 值得注意的是，他沒有否認可能舉行選舉。 **3** in a way that has a special or secret meaning 別有含義地；意味深長地：*She paused significantly before she answered.* 她在回答之前意味深長地停頓了一下。

sig,nificant 'other *noun* (*often humorous*) your husband, wife, partner or sb that you have a special relationship with 有特殊關係的那一位（如配偶、情人、戀人）

sig·ni·fi·ca·tion /,sɪgnɪfɪ'keɪʃn/ *noun* (*formal* or *linguistics* 語言) [U, C] the exact meaning of sth, especially a word or phrase（尤指詞或短語的）含義，意思，意義

sig·ni·fied /'sɪgnɪfaɪd/ *noun* (*linguistics* 語言) the meaning expressed by a LINGUISTIC sign, rather than its form 所指（語言符號的意義）➲ compare SIGNIFIER

sig·ni·fier /'sɪgnɪfaɪə(r)/ *noun* (*linguistics* 語言) the form of a LINGUISTIC sign, for example its sound or its printed form, rather than the meaning it expresses 能指（語言符號的形式）➲ compare SIGNIFIED

sig·nify AW /'sɪgnɪfaɪ/ *verb* (**sig·ni·fies**, **sig·ni·fy·ing**, **sig·ni·fied**, **sig·ni·fied**) (*formal*) **1** [T] to be a sign of sth 表示；說明；預示 SYN **mean**：**~ sth** *This decision signified a radical change in their policies.* 這個決定表明了他們的政策發生了根本的變化。◇ **~ that …** *This mark signifies that the products conform to an approved standard.* 這個標誌說明這些產品符合指定的標準。◇ *The white belt signifies that he's an absolute beginner.* 白腰帶表示他完全是個新手。 **2** [T] to do sth to make your feelings, intentions, etc. known 表達，表示，顯示（感情、意願等）：**~ sth** *She signified her approval with a smile.* 她笑了笑表示贊同。◇ **~ that …** *He nodded to signify that he agreed.* 他點頭表示同意。 **3** [I] (usually used in questions or negative sentences 通常用於疑問句或否定句) to be important or to matter 具有重要性；要緊：*His presence no longer signified.* 他在不在場已不重要。

sign·ing /'saɪnɪŋ/ *noun* **1** [U] the act of writing your name at the end of an official document to show that you accept it 簽署；簽字：*the signing of the Treaty of Rome*《羅馬條約》的簽署 **2** [C] (*BrE*) a person who has just signed a contract to join a particular sports team or record or film company（運動隊、唱片公司或電影公司的）簽約受聘者，簽約受雇者 **3** [U] the act of making an official contract that arranges for sb to join a sports team or a record or film company 簽約聘用，簽約雇用（安排某人加入運動隊、唱片公司或電影公司） **4** [U] the act of using sign language 手勢語的使用：*the use of signing in classrooms* 手勢語在課堂上的使用

'sign language *noun* [U, C] a system of communicating with people who cannot hear, by using hand movements rather than spoken words 手勢語

sign·post /'saɪnpəʊst; *NAmE* -poʊst/ *noun, verb*
■ ***noun*** a sign at the side of a road giving information about the direction and distance of places 路標：*Follow the signposts to the superstore.* 跟着路標走就能到超市。◇ (*figurative*) *The chapter headings are useful signposts to the content of the book.* 看章節標題有助於瞭解書的內容。➲ **VISUAL VOCAB** page V3
■ ***verb*** (*BrE*) **1** [usually passive] **~ sth** to mark a road, place, etc. with signposts 設置路標：*The route is well signposted.* 這條路線路標設置完善。 **2 ~ sth** to show clearly the way that an argument, a speech, etc. will develop 介紹（論證、講話等的）要點：*You need to signpost for the reader the various points you are going to make.* 你需要向讀者介紹你將闡述的各個論點。 ▸ **sign·post·ing** *noun* [U]

sign·writer /'saɪnraɪtə(r)/ (also **'sign painter**) *noun* a person who paints signs and advertisements for shops/stores and businesses 畫招牌者；畫廣告者 ▸ **'sign-writing** *noun* [U]

Sikh /siːk/ *noun* a member of a religion (called **Sikhism**) that developed in Punjab in the late 15th century and is based on a belief that there is only one God 錫克教教徒（錫克教在 15 世紀晚期產生於旁遮普地區，相信一神論） ▸ **Sikh** *adj.*

sil·age /'saɪlɪdʒ/ *noun* [U] grass or other green crops that are stored without being dried and are used to feed farm animals in winter 青貯飼料

si·lence 0-w /'saɪləns/ *noun, verb, exclamation*
■ ***noun*** **1** 0-w [U] a complete lack of noise or sound 寂靜；無聲 SYN **quiet**：*Their footsteps echoed in the silence.* 他們的腳步聲在一片寂靜中迴盪着。◇ *A scream broke the silence of the night.* 一聲尖叫劃破了寂靜的夜晚。◇ *I need **absolute silence** when I'm working.* 我工作時需要絕對的安靜。 **2** 0-w [C, U] a situation when nobody is speaking 沉默；緘默；默不作聲：*an **embarrassed/awkward silence*** 難堪／尷尬的沉默 ◇ *a moment's stunned silence* 一時驚愕得說不出話來 ◇ *I got used to his long silences.* 我已習慣了他半天不說話的樣子。◇ *They finished their meal **in total silence**.* 他們默不作聲地吃完飯。◇ *She lapsed into silence again.* 她又沉默下來。◇ *There was a **deafening silence*** (= one that is very noticeable). 四下裏靜得刺耳。◇ *a two-minute silence in honour of those who had died* 為死去的人默哀兩分鐘 **3** [U, sing.] a situation in which sb refuses to talk about sth or to answer questions 緘默；緘口不談；拒絕回答：*She **broke her***

public **silence** *in a TV interview.* 她接受了一次電視採訪，就此結束了她不在公開場合說話的狀態。◇ **~ (on sth)** *The company's silence on the subject has been taken as an admission of guilt.* 在外界看來，公司在這個問題上保持沉默便是承認有罪。◇ *the* **right to silence** (= the legal right not to say anything when you are arrested) 沉默權 ◇ *There is* **a conspiracy of silence** *about what is happening* (= everyone has agreed not to discuss it). 對於發生的事情，大家一致保持緘默。 **4** [U] a situation in which people do not communicate with each other by letter or telephone 互相不通音信的情形；無書信或電話聯繫： *The phone call came after months of silence.* 幾個月沒有音信之後，打來了一個電話。

IDM **,silence is 'golden** (*saying*) it is often best not to say anything 沉默是金 ➲ more at HEAVY *adj.*, PREGNANT

■ ***verb*** **1 ~ sb/sth** to make sb/sth stop speaking or making a noise 使安靜；使不說話： *She silenced him with a glare.* 她瞪了他一眼，他就不作聲了。◇ *Our bombs silenced the enemy's guns* (= they destroyed them). 我們的轟炸把敵人的炮火打啞了。 **2 ~ sb/sth** to make sb stop expressing opinions that are opposed to yours 壓制，使不再發表（反對意見）： *All protest had been silenced.* 一切反對的聲音都被壓了下去。◇ *Her recent achievements have silenced her critics.* 她近來取得的成果讓那些批評她的人無話可說了。

■ ***exclamation*** (*formal*) used to tell people to be quiet（用以讓人們安靜）安靜，靜下來： *Silence in court!* 在法庭內要保持肅靜！

si·len·cer /'saɪlənsə(r)/ *noun* **1** (*BrE*) (*NAmE* **muf·fler**) a device that is fixed to the EXHAUST of a vehicle in order to reduce the amount of noise that the engine makes （發動機的）消音器 ➲ **VISUAL VOCAB** page V51 **2** a device that is fixed to the end of a gun in order to reduce the amount of noise that it makes when it is fired （槍支的）消音器

si·lent 🔑 /'saɪlənt/ *adj.*

1 🔑 (of a person 人) not speaking 不說話的；沉默的： *to* **remain/stay/keep silent** 保持沉默 ◇ *They huddled together in silent groups.* 他們一群群地圍在一起，默不作聲。◇ *As the curtain rose, the audience* **fell silent**. 幕啟時，觀眾安靜下來。◇ *He gave me* **the silent treatment** (= did not speak to me because he was angry). 他對我不予理睬。 **2** 🔑 [only before noun] (especially of a man 尤指男人) not talking very much 很少說話的；不愛說話的；少言寡語的 **SYN** **quiet**： *He's the* **strong silent** *type.* 他是那種強悍而沉默寡言的人。 **3** 🔑 where there is little or no sound; making little or no sound 無聲的；安靜的；不喧鬧的 **SYN** **quiet**： *At last the traffic* **fell silent**. 車輛的喧囂終於消逝了。◇ *The streets were silent and deserted.* 大街小巷闃無一人。 **4** 🔑 [only before noun] not expressed with words or sound 不用言語表達的；無聲的： *a* **silent prayer/protest** 默禱；無聲的抗議 ◇ *They nodded in* **silent agreement**. 他們默默地點頭表示同意。 **5 ~ (on/about sth)** not giving information about sth; refusing to speak about sth 不提供情況的；未談及的；拒絕講的： *The report is strangely silent on this issue.* 很奇怪，報告對這個問題避而不談。◇ *the* **right to remain silent** (= the legal right not to say anything when you are arrested) 沉默權 **6** [only before noun] (of old films/movies 過去的電影) with pictures but no sound 無聲的；無聲電影的： *a* **silent film/movie** 無聲電影 ◇ *stars of the* **silent screen** 無聲電影時代的明星 **7** (of a letter in a word 單詞中的字母) written but not pronounced 不發音的： *The 'b' in 'lamb' is silent.* * lamb 中的 b 不發音。

si·lent·ly /'saɪləntli/ *adv.* **1** without speaking 默默地；不說話地： *They marched silently through the streets.* 隊伍無聲地穿過街道。 **2** without making any or much sound 悄悄地；靜靜地 **SYN** **quietly**： *She crept silently out of the room.* 她悄悄溜出房間。 **3** without using words or sounds to express sth 無聲地；默默地；不用言語表達地： *She prayed silently.* 她默默地禱告。◇ *He silently agreed with much of what she had said.* 對於她所講的，有很多他暗自贊同。

IDM **sit/stand ,silently 'by** to do or say nothing to help sb or deal with a difficult situation 袖手旁觀；坐視

the ,silent ma'jority *noun* [usually sing.] the large number of people in a country who think the same as each other, but do not express their views publicly 沉默的大多數（不公開表達自己意見的廣大民眾）

,silent 'partner (*NAmE*) (*BrE* **,sleeping 'partner**) *noun* a person who has put money into a business company but who is not actually involved in running it 隱名合夥人，隱名股東（在企業中有股份但不參與經營）

sil·hou·ette /,sɪlu'et/ *noun, verb*

■ ***noun*** **1** [C, U] the dark outline or shape of a person or an object that you see against a light background（淺色背景襯托出的）暗色輪廓： *the silhouette of chimneys and towers* 煙囱和塔樓的輪廓 ◇ *The mountains stood out* **in silhouette**. 群山的輪廓襯托了出來。 **2** [C] the shape of a person's body or of an object （人的）體形；（事物的）形狀： *The dress is fitted to give you a flattering silhouette.* 穿這件連衣裙，你顯得更有身段了。 **3** [C] a picture that shows sb/sth as a black shape against a light background, especially one that shows the side view of a person's face 剪影；（尤指人臉的）側影

■ ***verb*** [usually passive] **~ sb/sth** (**against sth**) to make sth appear as a silhouette 使呈現暗色輪廓： *A figure stood in the doorway, silhouetted against the light.* 門口站着一個人，屋裏的亮光映襯出他的輪廓。

sil·ica /'sɪlɪkə/ *noun* [U] (*symb.* **SiO_2**) a chemical containing silicon found in sand and in rocks such as QUARTZ, used in making glass and CEMENT 二氧化硅；二氧化矽

'silica gel *noun* [U] a substance made from silica in the form of grains, which keeps things dry by absorbing water 硅膠，矽膠（顆粒狀乾燥劑）

sili·cate /'sɪlɪkeɪt/ *noun* [C, U] **1** (*chemistry* 化) any COMPOUND containing SILICON and OXYGEN 硅酸鹽；矽酸鹽： *aluminium silicate* 硅酸鋁 **2** a mineral that contains silica. There are many different silicates and they form a large part of the earth's CRUST. 硅酸鹽礦物；矽酸鹽礦物

sil·icon /'sɪlɪkən/ *noun* [U] (*symb.* **Si**) a chemical element. Silicon exists as a grey solid or as a brown powder and is found in rocks and sand. It is used in making glass and TRANSISTORS. 硅；矽

,silicon 'chip *noun* a very small piece of silicon used to carry a complicated electronic CIRCUIT 硅片；矽晶片

sili·cone /'sɪlɪkəʊn; *NAmE* -koʊn/ *noun* [U] a chemical containing silicon. There are several different types of silicone, used to make paint, artificial rubber, VARNISH, etc. 硅酮；聚硅氧烷；矽酮： *a silicone breast implant* 硅酮隆胸植入物

,Silicon 'Valley *noun* [U] the area in California where there are many companies connected with the computer and ELECTRONICS industries, sometimes used to refer to any area where there are a lot of computer companies 硅谷，矽谷（美國加利福尼亞州一處計算機和電子公司聚集地，有時用以指任何計算機公司聚集地）

sili·cosis /,sɪlɪ'kəʊsɪs; *NAmE* -'koʊ-/ *noun* [U] (*medical* 醫) a serious lung disease caused by breathing in dust containing SILICA 硅肺，矽肺，硅沉着病，矽肺病（長期吸入二氧化硅造成的肺部疾病）

silk 🔑 /sɪlk/ *noun*

1 🔑 [U] fine soft thread produced by SILKWORMS （蠶）絲 **2** 🔑 [U] a type of fine smooth cloth made from silk thread 絲織物；絲綢： *a silk blouse* 女式絲綢襯衫 ◇ *silk stockings* 長筒絲襪 ◇ *made of pure silk* 純絲做的 ◇ *Her skin was* **as smooth as silk**. 她的皮膚像絲綢一樣光滑。 ➲ see also WATERED SILK **3** [U] silk thread used for sewing （用於縫紉的）絲線 **4 silks** [pl.] clothes made of silk, especially the coloured shirts worn by people riding horses in a race (= JOCKEYS) 絲綢衣服（尤指騎師在賽馬時穿的彩色賽馬衫） **5** [C] (*BrE, law* 律) a type of lawyer who represents the government (= a KING's/QUEEN's COUNSEL) 王室律師；王室法律顧問： *to take silk* (= to become this type of lawyer) 擔任王室律師

IDM **make a silk ,purse out of a sow's 'ear** to succeed in making sth good out of material that does not seem very good at all 用劣材製精品；化腐朽為神奇

S

silk·en /ˈsɪlkən/ *adj.* (*literary*) **1** [usually before noun] soft, smooth and shiny like silk 絲綢一樣的；柔軟光潔的：*silken hair* 柔軟光滑的頭髮 **2** [usually before noun] smooth and gentle 柔和的；溫和的；輕柔的：*her silken voice* 她那柔和的嗓音 **3** [only before noun] made of silk 絲製的；絲質的；絲綢的：*silken ribbons* 絲帶

silkie /ˈsɪlki/ *noun* = SELKIE

ˈsilk screen *noun* **1** [U] a method of printing in which ink is forced through a design cut in a piece of fine cloth 絲網印刷；絹印：*silk-screen prints* 絲網印刷的圖案 **2** [C] a picture, etc. produced by this method 絲網印刷畫；絲網印花；絹印畫：*Warhol's silk screen of Marilyn Monroe* 沃霍爾所作的瑪麗蓮 • 夢露絲網印刷畫 ▸ **ˈsilk-screen** *verb* **~ sth**

silk·worm /ˈsɪlkwɜːm; *NAmE* -wɜːrm/ *noun* a CATERPILLAR (= a small creature like a WORM with legs) that produces silk thread 蠶

silky /ˈsɪlki/ *adj.* (**silk·ier**, **silki·est**) **1** soft, smooth and shiny like silk 絲綢一樣的；柔軟光潔的：*silky fur* 像絲綢一樣的毛皮 **2** [usually before noun] smooth and gentle 柔和的；溫和的；輕柔的：*He spoke in a silky tone.* 他說話柔聲細語的。 **3** made of silk or cloth that looks like silk 絲（或像絲的織物）製的；絲綢（或像絲綢的織物）的：*a silky dress* 絲質連衣裙 ▸ **silk·ily** *adv.*：*'How have I changed?' he asked silkily.* "我變得怎麼樣了？" 他柔聲問道。**silki·ness** *noun* [U] **silky** *adv.*：*The leaves are grey and silky smooth.* 葉子呈灰色，平整光潔。

sill /sɪl/ *noun* **1** = WINDOWSILL **2** a piece of metal that forms part of the frame of a vehicle below the doors（車體的）門檻

silly 0➡ /ˈsɪli/ *adj., noun*

■ ***adj.*** (**sil·lier**, **sil·li·est**) **1** 0➡ showing a lack of thought, understanding or judgement 愚蠢的；不明事理的；沒頭腦的；傻的 SYN **foolish**：*a silly idea* 愚蠢的想法 ◇ *That was **a silly thing to do!*** 那事做得蠢！◇ *Her work is full of silly mistakes.* 她滿篇都是愚蠢的錯誤。◇ *'I can walk home.' 'Don't be silly—it's much too far!'* "我可以走回家去。" "別犯傻了，遠得很哪！" ◇ *You silly boy!* 你這傻小子！ **2** 0➡ stupid or embarrassing, especially in a way that is more typical of a child than an adult（尤指像小孩一樣）可笑的，荒唐的，冒傻氣的 SYN **ridiculous**：*a silly sense of humour* 無聊的幽默感 ◇ *a silly game* 無聊的遊戲 ◇ *I **feel silly** in these clothes.* 穿上這些衣服，我覺得很可笑。◇ *She had a silly grin on her face.* 她一臉憨笑。◇ (*especially BrE*) *I got it for a silly price* (= very cheap). 我買它差不多沒花錢。 **3** 0➡ not practical or serious 不實用的；鬧着玩的：*We had to wear these silly little hats.* 我們不得不戴這些傻裏傻氣的小帽子。◇ *Why worry about a silly thing like that?* 幹嘛為那種無謂的事發愁啊？ ▸ **sil·li·ness** *noun* [U]

IDM **ˌdrink, ˌlaugh, ˌshout, etc. yourself ˈsilly** (*informal*) to drink, laugh, shout, etc. so much that you cannot behave in a sensible way 喝（或笑、叫等）得傻裏傻氣的 **play ˈsilly buggers** (*BrE, informal*) to behave in a stupid and annoying way 胡鬧；頑皮；做怪樣子 ➲ more at GAME *n.*

■ ***noun*** (*BrE* also **ˌsilly ˈbilly**) [sing.] (*informal*) often used when speaking to children to say that they are not behaving in a sensible way（常用於向孩子指出其愚蠢行為）傻孩子，淘氣鬼：*No, silly, those aren't your shoes!* 不對，傻孩子，那不是你的鞋！

the ˈsilly season *noun* [sing.] (*BrE*) the time, usually in the summer, when newspapers are full of unimportant stories because there is little serious news 無聊季節（通常為夏季，因沒有重大新聞，報上充斥着無聊內容）

silo /ˈsaɪləʊ; *NAmE* -loʊ/ *noun* (*pl.* **-os**) **1** a tall tower on a farm used for storing grain, etc. 筒倉 ➲ VISUAL VOCAB pages V2, V3 **2** an underground place where nuclear weapons or dangerous substances are kept（核武器的）發射井；（危險物品的）地下貯藏庫 **3** an underground place where SILAGE is made and stored 青貯窖

silt /sɪlt/ *noun, verb*

■ ***noun*** [U] sand, mud, etc. that is carried by flowing water and is left at the mouth of a river or in a HARBOUR（沉積在河口或港口的）泥沙，淤泥，粉沙 ▸ **silty** *adj.*：*silty soils* 粉砂土

■ ***verb***

PHR V **ˌsilt sth↔ˈup** | **ˌsilt ˈup** to block sth with silt; to become blocked with silt（使）淤塞：*Sand has silted up the river delta.* 泥沙把這條河的三角洲淤塞了。◇ *The harbour has now silted up.* 港口現已淤塞。

sil·ver 0➡ /ˈsɪlvə(r)/ *noun, adj., verb*

■ ***noun*** **1** 0➡ [U] (*symb.* **Ag**) a chemical element. Silver is a greyish-white PRECIOUS METAL used for making coins, jewellery, decorative objects, etc. 銀：*a silver chain* 銀鏈 ◇ *made of **solid silver*** 純銀製造 ◇ *a silver mine* 銀礦 **2** [U] coins that are made of silver or a metal that looks like silver 銀幣（銀或似銀金屬製成的硬幣）：*I need £2 in silver for the parking meter.* 我需要在停車收費器裏投 2 英鎊銀幣。 **3** 0➡ [U] dishes, decorative objects, etc. that are made of silver 銀器：*They've had to sell the family silver to pay the bills.* 他們不得不賣掉家傳的銀器去支付賬單。 **4** 0➡ [U] a shiny greyish-white colour 銀色；銀白色；銀灰色 ➲ see also SILVERY **5** [U, C] = SILVER MEDAL：*She won silver in last year's championships.* 她在去年的錦標賽上獲得銀牌。◇ *The team won two silvers and a bronze.* 這個運動隊獲得兩枚銀牌和一枚銅牌。

IDM **on a silver ˈplatter** if you are given sth **on a silver platter**, you do not have to do much to get it 無須費勁；唾手可得：*These rich kids expect to have it all handed to them on a silver platter.* 這些富家子弟指望一切都有人拱手送上。 ➲ more at BORN *v.*, CLOUD *n.*, CROSS *v.*

■ ***adj.*** 0➡ shiny greyish-white in colour 銀色的；銀白色的；銀灰色的：*a silver car* 銀灰色汽車 ◇ *silver hair* 銀髮 ➲ see also SILVERY

■ ***verb*** **1** [usually passive] **~ sth** to cover the surface of sth with a thin layer of silver or sth that looks like silver 給…鍍（或包）銀；給…鍍（或包）似銀的物質 **2 ~ sth** (especially *literary*) to make sth become bright like silver 使具有銀色光澤；使變成銀色：*Moonlight was silvering the countryside.* 月光下的鄉村泛着銀光。

ˌsilver anniˈversary *noun* (*especially US*) **1** (also **ˌsilver ˈwedding anniversary** *BrE, NAmE*) (*BrE* **ˌsilver ˈwedding**) the 25th anniversary of a wedding 銀婚（結婚 25 週年紀念） **2** (*BrE* **ˌsilver ˈjubilee**) the 25th anniversary of an important event; a celebration of sth that began 25 years ago * 25 週年；25 週年紀念

silver·back /ˈsɪlvəbæk; *NAmE* -vərb-/ *noun* a male adult GORILLA with white or silver hair across its back 銀背大猩猩（背部有白色或銀白色毛的雄性成年大猩猩）

ˌsilver ˈband *noun* (*BrE*) a BRASS BAND which uses silver-coloured instruments 銀樂隊（使用銀色樂器的銅管樂隊）

ˌsilver ˈbirch *noun* [C, U] a tree with smooth, very pale grey or white BARK and thin branches, that grows in northern countries 歐洲樺；銀樺

sil·ver·fish /ˈsɪlvəfɪʃ; *NAmE* -vərf-/ *noun* (*pl.* **sil·ver·fish**) a small silver insect without wings that lives in houses and that can cause damage to materials such as cloth and paper 蠹魚，衣魚（蛀食織物、紙張等的小蟲）

ˌsilver ˈfoil *noun* [U] (*BrE*) = FOIL *n.* (1)

ˌsilver ˈjubilee (*BrE*) (*US* **ˌsilver anniˈversary**) *noun* [usually sing.] the 25th anniversary of an important event; a celebration of sth that began 25 years ago * 25 週年；25 週年紀念：*the silver jubilee of the Queen's accession* 女王登基 25 週年大慶 ◇ *The college celebrated its silver jubilee last year.* 這所學院去年舉行了建院 25 週年慶祝活動。 ➲ compare DIAMOND JUBILEE, GOLDEN JUBILEE

ˌsilver ˈmedal *noun* [C] (also **sil·ver** [U, C]) a MEDAL that is given to the person or the team that wins the second prize in a race or competition 銀質獎章；銀牌：*an Olympic silver medal winner* 獲奧運會銀牌的運動員 ➲ compare BRONZE MEDAL, GOLD MEDAL ▸ **ˌsilver ˈmedallist** (*BrE*) (*NAmE* **ˌsilver ˈmedalist**) *noun*：*He's an Olympic silver medallist.* 他是奧運會銀牌得主。

ˌsilver ˈpaper *noun* [U] (*BrE*) very thin, shiny sheets of ALUMINIUM/ALUMINUM that are used for wrapping chocolate, etc.（包巧克力等的）錫紙

S

ˌsilver ˈplate *noun* [U] metal that is covered with a thin layer of silver; objects that are made of this metal 鍍（或包）銀金屬；鍍（或包）銀金屬器皿 ▸ **ˌsilver-ˈplated** *adj.*

the ˌsilver ˈscreen *noun* [sing.] (*old-fashioned*) the film/movie industry 電影業

ˌsilver ˈservice *noun* [U] a style of serving food at formal meals in which the person serving uses a silver fork and spoon 銀級服務（正式用餐時侍者用銀叉和銀勺上菜）

sil·ver·smith /ˈsɪlvəsmɪθ; *NAmE* -vərs-/ *noun* a person who makes, repairs or sells articles made of silver 銀匠；銀器商

ˌsilver ˈsurfer *noun* (*informal*) an old person who spends a lot of time using the Internet 銀髮網民（指經常上互聯網的老年人）

sil·ver·tail /ˈsɪlvəteɪl; *NAmE* ˈsɪlvər-/ *noun* (*AustralE, informal*) a famous or socially important person 名人；要人；有社會地位的人

ˌsilver ˈtongue *noun* (*formal*) great skill at persuading people to do or to believe what you say 口才；辯才 ▸ **ˌsilver-ˈtongued** *adj.*

sil·ver·ware /ˈsɪlvəweə(r); *NAmE* -vərwer/ *noun* [U] **1** objects that are made of or covered with silver, especially knives, forks, dishes, etc. that are used for eating and serving food 銀器，鍍銀器皿（尤指餐具）：*a piece of silverware* 一件銀器 **2** (also **flat·ware**) (both *NAmE*) (also **cut·lery** especially in *BrE*) knives, forks and spoons, used for eating and serving food 餐具（刀、叉和匙） **3** (*BrE, informal*) a silver cup that you win in a sports competition（體育比賽中的）銀杯 SYN **trophy**

ˌsilver ˈwedding (*BrE*) (*US* **ˌsilver anniˈversary**) (also **ˌsilver ˈwedding anniversary** *US, BrE*) *noun* the 25th anniversary of a wedding 銀婚（結婚 25 週年紀念）：*They celebrated their silver wedding in May.* 他們於五月份慶祝了銀婚紀念日。➲ compare DIAMOND WEDDING, GOLDEN WEDDING, RUBY WEDDING

sil·very /ˈsɪlvəri/ *adj.* [usually before noun] **1** shiny like silver; having the colour of silver 閃着銀光的；銀色的：*silvery light* 銀光 ◇ *a silvery grey colour* 銀灰色 **2** (*literary*) (especially of a voice 尤指嗓音) having a pleasant musical sound 銀鈴般的；悅耳的

sim /sɪm/ *noun* (*informal*) a computer or video game that SIMULATES (= artificially creates the feeling of experiencing) an activity such as flying an aircraft or playing a sport 模擬電腦（或電子）遊戲

ˈSIM card *noun* the abbreviation for 'subscriber identification module' (a plastic card inside a mobile/cell phone that stores information to identify the phone and the person using it) 用戶識別模塊卡，SIM 卡（全寫為 subscriber identification module，移動電話內存貯的識別手機和用戶信息的塑料卡）➲ COLLOCATIONS at PHONE

sim·ian /ˈsɪmiən/ *adj.* (*technical* 術語) like a MONKEY or an ape; connected with monkeys or apes 像猿（或猴）的；猿（或猴）的

simi·lar 🔑 AW /ˈsɪmələ(r)/ *adj.* like sb/sth but not exactly the same 相像的；相仿的；類似的：*We have very similar interests.* 我們興趣相仿。◇ **~ (to sb/sth)** *My teaching style is similar to that of most other teachers.* 我的教學風格和多數教師相似。◇ **~ (in sth)** *The two houses are similar in size.* 兩座房子大小差不多。◇ *The brothers look very similar.* 弟兄幾個長得很像。◇ *All our patients have broadly similar problems.* 我們所有的病人問題大致相似。OPP **different, dissimilar**

simi·lar·ity AW /ˌsɪməˈlærəti/ *noun* (*pl.* **-ies**) **1** [U, sing.] the state of being like sb/sth but not exactly the same 相像性；相仿性；類似性 SYN **resemblance**：**~ (between A and B)** *The report highlights the similarity between the two groups.* 這份報告強調兩組之間的相似性。◇ **~ (to sb/sth)** *She bears a **striking similarity** to her mother.* 她跟她母親十分相像。◇ **~ (in sth)** *There is some similarity in the way they sing.* 他們的演唱風格有點像。◇ *They are both doctors but that is where the similarity ends.* 兩人都是醫生，但他們的相似之處僅此而已。**2** [C] a feature that things or people have that makes them like each other 相像處；相似點；類似的地方 SYN **resemblance**：*a study of the similarities and differences between the two countries* 對這兩個國家的異同點的研究 ◇ **~ in/of sth** *similarities in/of style* 風格上的相似之處 ◇ **~ to/with sb/sth** *The karate bout has many similarities to a boxing match.* 空手道比賽和拳擊比賽有許多類似的地方。OPP **difference, dissimilarity**

simi·lar·ly 🔑 AW /ˈsɪmələli; *NAmE* -lərli/ *adv.* **1** 🔑 in almost the same way 相似地；類似地；差不多地：*Husband and wife were similarly successful in their chosen careers.* 夫婦倆在各自所選擇的事業上都很成功。**2** 🔑 used to say that two facts, actions, statements, etc. are like each other 同樣；也：*The United States won most of the track and field events. Similarly, in swimming, the top three places went to Americans.* 美國隊贏得了田徑比賽大多數項目的勝利。同樣，在游泳方面，美國人也囊括了前三名。

Language Bank 用語庫

similarly

Making comparisons 進行比較

- This chart **provides a comparison of** the ways that teenage boys and girls in the UK spend their free time. 這個圖表對英國十幾歲的男生和女生打發空閒時間的方式進行了對比。
- In many cases, the results for boys and girls are virtually **the same/identical**. 在許多情況下，對男女生的調查結果實際上是相同的。
- In many cases, the results for boys are virtually **the same as/identical to** the results for girls. 在許多情況下，對男生的調查結果實際上和對女生的調查結果是相同的。
- **Both** boys **and** girls spend the bulk of their free time with friends. 男生和女生的大部份空閒時間都和朋友一起度過。
- Most of the boys do more than two hours of sport a week, **as do** many of the girls. 大多數男生每週會做兩個多小時的運動，這和許多女生是一樣的。
- **Like** many of the girls, most of the boys spend a large part of their free time using the Internet. 像許多女孩子一樣，大多數男孩子也把大量空閒時間花在上網。
- The girls particularly enjoy using social networking websites. **Similarly**, nearly all the boys said they spent at least two to three hours a week on these sites. 女生們特別喜歡上社交網站。同樣，幾乎所有男生都說他們每週在這些網站上花的時間至少有兩到三個小時。

➲ Language Banks at CONTRAST, ILLUSTRATE, PROPORTION, SURPRISING

sim·ile /ˈsɪməli/ *noun* [C, U] (*technical* 術語) a word or phrase that compares sth to sth else, using the words *like* or *as*, for example *a face like a mask* or *as white as snow*; the use of such words and phrases 明喻；明喻的運用 ➲ compare METAPHOR

si·mili·tude /sɪˈmɪlɪtjuːd; *NAmE* -tuːd/ *noun* [U] (*formal*) **~ (between A and B)** | **~ (to sb/sth)** the state of being similar to sth 相似；類似；相仿：*the similitude between humans and gorillas* 人類和大猩猩的相像

sim·mer /ˈsɪmə(r)/ *verb, noun*

▪ *verb* **1** [T, I] **~ (sth)** to cook sth by keeping it almost at boiling point; to be cooked in this way 用文火燉；煨：*Simmer the sauce gently for 10 minutes.* 把調味汁用文火燉 10 分鐘。◇ *Leave the soup to simmer.* 讓湯煨着。➲ COLLOCATIONS at COOKING **2** [I] **~ (with sth)** to be filled with a strong feeling, especially anger, which you have difficulty controlling 充滿（難以控制的感情，尤指憤怒）SYN **seethe**：*She was still simmering with resentment.* 她依舊憋着一肚子的怨恨。◇ *Anger simmered*

S

inside him. 他心裏鬱結着怒火。 **3** [I] (of an argument, a disagreement, etc. 爭論、分歧等) to develop for a period of time without any real anger or violence being shown 即將爆發；醞釀： *This argument has been simmering for months.* 這場爭論已醞釀了幾個月了。

PHR V **,simmer 'down** (*informal*) to become calm after a period of anger or excitement 平息下來；平靜下來： *I left him alone until he simmered down.* 等他平靜下來之後我才去找他。

■ **noun** [sing.] the state when sth is almost boiling 即將沸騰狀態；文火燉；小火煨： *Bring the sauce to a simmer and cook for 5 minutes.* 改用文火，把調味汁燉 5 分鐘。

sim·nel cake /ˈsɪmnəl keɪk/ *noun* [C, U] a type of cake made with dried fruit, traditionally eaten in Britain at Easter（英國人在復活節吃的）果脯蛋糕

Simon says /ˌsaɪmən ˈsez/ *noun* [U] a children's game in which players should only do what a person says if he/she says 'Simon says ... ' at the beginning of the instruction 得令遊戲（兒童遊戲，有人在發指令開始時說"西蒙說"，參加者才能照做）

sim·pat·ico /sɪmˈpætɪkəʊ; *NAmE* -koʊ/ *adj.* (*informal*, from *Spanish*) **1** (of a person 人) pleasant; easy to like 和善的；討人喜歡的 **2** (of a person 人) with similar interests and ideas to yours 志趣相投的 SYN **compatible**

sim·per /ˈsɪmpə(r)/ *verb* [I, T] to smile in a silly and annoying way 矯揉造作地笑；扭捏作態地笑： *a silly simpering girl* 扭捏作態、嘻嘻傻笑的女孩子 ◊ **+ speech** *'You're such a darling,' she simpered.* "你可真討人喜歡。"她賣弄風情地笑着說。 ▶ **sim·per** *noun* [sing.] **sim·per·ing·ly** /ˈsɪmpərɪŋli/ *adv.*

sim·ple 0‑w /ˈsɪmpl/ *adj.* (**sim·pler, sim·plest**) HELP You can also use **more simple** and **most simple**. 亦可用 more simple 和 most simple。

▸ EASY 容易 **1** 0‑w not complicated; easy to understand or do 易於理解的；易做的；簡單的 SYN **easy**： *a simple solution* 簡單的解決辦法 ◊ *The answer is really quite simple.* 實際上答案相當簡單。◊ *This machine is very simple to use.* 這台機器操作非常簡單。◊ *We lost because we played badly. It's* **as simple as that**. 我們輸了是因為我們打得不好。原因就這麼簡單。◊ *Give the necessary information but* **keep it simple**. 說說基本情況，簡單一點。

▸ BASIC/PLAIN 基本；樸素 **2** 0‑w basic or plain without anything extra or unnecessary 樸素的；簡樸的；不加裝飾的： *simple but elegant clothes* 素雅的衣服 ◊ *We had a simple meal of soup and bread.* 我們喝湯，吃麵包，湊合了一頓。◊ *The accommodation is simple but spacious.* 住處簡樸但寬敞。 OPP **fancy**

▸ FOR EMPHASIS 強調 **3** used before a noun to emphasize that it is exactly that and nothing else（用在名詞前表示強調）純粹的，完全的，不折不扣的： *Nobody wanted to believe the simple truth.* 誰也不願意相信這明顯的事實。◊ *It was a matter of simple survival.* 這完全是能不能生存的問題。◊ *It's nothing to worry about—just a simple headache.* 不用擔心，只是有點兒頭痛。◊ *I had to do it* **for the simple reason that** (= because) *I couldn't trust anyone else.* 我之所以這麼做，純粹是因為我信不過任何人。 ➲ SYNONYMS at PLAIN

▸ WITH FEW PARTS 少部位 **4** 0‑w [usually before noun] consisting of only a few parts; not complicated in structure 部位少的；結構簡單的： *simple forms of life, for example amoebas* 如變形蟲之類的簡單生命形式 ◊ *a simple machine* 結構簡單的機器 ◊ (*grammar* 語法) *a* **simple sentence** (= one with only one verb) 簡單句

▸ ORDINARY 普通 **5** 0‑w [only before noun] (of a person 人) ordinary; not special 普通的；一般的；平凡的： *I'm a simple country girl.* 我是一個普普通通的鄉村姑娘。

▸ NOT INTELLIGENT 智力低下 **6** [not usually before noun] (of a person 人) not very intelligent; not mentally normal 智力低下；遲鈍；笨： *He's not mad—just a little simple.* 他不是瘋，只是智力稍低。

▸ GRAMMAR 語法 **7** used to describe the present or past tense of a verb that is formed without using an auxiliary verb, as in *She loves him* (= the simple present tense) or *He arrived late* (= the simple past tense)（無須用助動詞構成的動詞時態）簡單的，一般的 ➲ see also SIMPLY IDM see PURE

,simple 'fracture *noun* an injury when a bone in your body is broken but does not come through the skin 單純骨折；無創骨折 ➲ compare COMPOUND FRACTURE

,simple 'interest *noun* [U] (*finance* 財) interest that is paid only on the original amount of money that you invested, and not on any interest that it has earned 單利 ➲ compare COMPOUND INTEREST

,simple-'minded *adj.* (*disapproving*) not intelligent; not able to understand how complicated things are 智力低下的；愚蠢的；頭腦簡單的： *a simple-minded person* 頭腦簡單的人 ◊ *a simple-minded approach* 笨方法

simple·ton /ˈsɪmpltən/ *noun* (*old-fashioned*) a person who is not very intelligent and can be tricked easily 傻瓜；易上當受騙的人

sim·plex /ˈsɪmpleks/ *noun* (*linguistics* 語言) a simple word that is not made of other words 簡單詞；單純詞 ➲ compare COMPOUND *n.* (3)

sim·pli·city /sɪmˈplɪsəti/ *noun* (*pl.* **-ies**) **1** [U] the quality of being easy to understand or use 簡單（性）；容易（性）： *the relative simplicity of the new PC* 新型個人電腦的相對簡易 ◊ ***For the sake of simplicity****, let's divide the discussion into two parts.* 為了方便起見，我們把討論分成兩部份。 **2** [U] (*approving*) the quality of being natural and plain 質樸；淳樸： *the simplicity of the architecture* 建築風格的質樸 ◊ *the simplicity of country living* 鄉村生活的淳樸 **3** [C, usually pl.] an aspect of sth that is easy, natural or plain 簡單（或質樸、樸素）之處： *the simplicities of our old way of life* 我們過去的生活方式的種種淳樸之處

IDM **be sim,plicity it'self** to be very easy or plain 非常簡單；非常樸素

sim·pli·fi·ca·tion /ˌsɪmplɪfɪˈkeɪʃn/ *noun* **1** [U, sing.] the process of making sth easier to do or understand 簡化： *Complaints have led to (a) simplification of the rules.* 因為人們的抱怨，規則簡化了。 **2** [C] the thing that results when you make a problem, statement, system, etc. easier to understand or do 簡化的事物： *A number of simplifications have been made to the taxation system.* 稅收制度已經歷過多次簡化。 ➲ compare OVERSIMPLIFICATION at OVERSIMPLIFY

sim·plify /ˈsɪmplɪfaɪ/ *verb* (**sim·pli·fies, sim·pli·fy·ing, sim·pli·fied, sim·pli·fied**) **~ sth** to make sth easier to do or understand 使簡化；使簡易： *The application forms have now been simplified.* 申請表格現已簡化了。◊ *I hope his appointment will* **simplify matters**. 我希望他任命以後事情會好辦一些。◊ *a simplified version of the story for young children* 供小朋友閱讀的故事簡寫本

sim·plis·tic /sɪmˈplɪstɪk/ *adj.* (*disapproving*) making a problem, situation, etc. seem less difficult or complicated than it really is（把問題、局面等）過分簡單化的 ▶ **sim·plis·tic·al·ly** /-kli/ *adv.*

sim·ply 0‑w /ˈsɪmpli/ *adv.*

1 0‑w used to emphasize how easy or basic sth is（強調簡單）僅僅，只，不過 SYN **just**： *Simply add hot water and stir.* 只需加上熱水攪動就行。◊ *The runway is simply a strip of grass.* 所謂跑道不過是一長條草地而已。◊ *Fame is often* **simply a matter of** *being in the right place at the right time.* 成名常常是身在其位，恰逢其時，僅此而已。◊ *You can enjoy all the water sports, or simply lie on the beach.* 你可以進行所有的水上運動，或只是躺在沙灘上。 **2** used to emphasize a statement（強調某說法）確實，簡直 SYN **absolutely**： *You simply must see the play.* 那齣戲你真得看看。◊ *The view is simply wonderful!* 景色美極了！◊ *That is simply not true!* 那根本不是真的！◊ *I haven't seen her for simply ages.* 我真是好久沒見她了。 **3** 0‑w in a way that is easy to understand 簡單地： *The book explains grammar simply and clearly.* 這本書對語法解釋得簡明扼要。◊ *Anyway,* **to put it simply**, *we still owe them £2 000.* 反正簡單地說，我們還欠他們 2 000 英鎊。 **4** 0‑w in a way that is natural and plain 簡樸地；樸素地： *The rooms are simply furnished.* 房間都陳設簡樸。◊ *They live simply* (= they do not spend much money). 他們生活簡樸。 **5** used to introduce a summary or an explanation of sth that you have just said or done（引出概括或解釋）不過，只是： *I don't want to be rude,*

S

it's simply that we have to be careful who we give this information to. 我不是有意無禮，只不過這份資料給誰我們必須很慎重。

sim·sim /ˈsɪmsɪm/ *noun* [U] an E African word for SESAME (= a type of plant whose seeds and their oil are used in cooking)（東非用語）芝麻

simu·lac·rum /ˌsɪmjuˈleɪkrəm/ *noun* (*pl.* **simu·lacra** /-krə/) (*formal*) something that looks like sb/sth else or that is made to look like sb/sth else 假象；模擬物；幻影 **SYN** copy

simu·late **AW** /ˈsɪmjuleɪt/ *verb* **1 ~ sth** to pretend that you have a particular feeling 假裝；冒充；裝作 **SYN** **feign**：*I tried to simulate surprise at the news.* 聽到這個消息後，我竭力裝出一副吃驚的樣子。 **2 ~ sth** to create particular conditions that exist in real life using computers, models, etc., usually for study or training purposes（用計算機或模型等）模擬：*Computer software can be used to simulate conditions on the seabed.* 計算機軟件可用於模擬海底狀況。 **3 ~ sth** to be made to look like sth else 模仿；冒充：*a gas heater that simulates a coal fire* 模仿煤爐的煤氣暖爐

simu·lated **AW** /ˈsɪmjuleɪtɪd/ *adj.* [only before noun] not real, but made to look, feel, etc. like the real thing 假裝的；仿造的；模擬的：*simulated leather* 人造革 ◇ *'How wonderful!' she said with simulated enthusiasm.* "多棒啊！" 她裝出一副興致勃勃的樣子說道。◇ *The experiments were carried out under simulated examination conditions.* 試驗是在模擬的情況下進行的。

simu·la·tion **AW** /ˌsɪmjuˈleɪʃn/ *noun* **1** [C, U] a situation in which a particular set of conditions is created artificially in order to study or experience sth that could exist in reality 模擬；仿真：*a computer simulation of how the planet functions* 行星活動方式的計算機模擬圖像 ◇ *a simulation model* 仿真模型 **2** [U] the act of pretending that sth is real when it is not 假裝；冒充：*the simulation of genuine concern* 假裝真誠關心

simu·la·tor /ˈsɪmjuleɪtə(r)/ *noun* a piece of equipment that artificially creates a particular set of conditions in order to train sb to deal with a situation that they may experience in reality 模擬裝置：*a flight simulator* 飛行模擬器

sim·ul·cast /ˈsɪmlkɑːst; *NAmE* also ˈsaɪm-/ *verb* (**sim·ul·cast**, **sim·ul·cast**) **~ sth** to broadcast sth on radio and television at the same time or on both AM and FM radio（電台和電視）聯播；（電台的調幅台和調頻台）聯播 ▶ **sim·ul·cast** *noun*

sim·ul·tan·eous /ˌsɪmlˈteɪniəs; *NAmE* ˌsaɪml-/ *adj.* happening or done at the same time as sth else 同時發生（或進行）的；同步的：*There were several simultaneous attacks by the rebels.* 反叛者同時發動了幾起攻擊。◇ ***simultaneous translation/interpreting*** 同聲傳譯 ▶ **sim·ul·tan·eity** /ˌsɪmltəˈneɪəti; *NAmE* ˌsaɪmltəˈniːəti/ *noun* [U] **sim·ul·tan·eous·ly** *adv.*：*The game will be broadcast simultaneously on TV and radio.* 比賽將同時在電視和電台轉播。➲ LANGUAGE BANK at PROCESS

ˌsimulˌtaneous eˈquations *noun* [pl.] (*mathematics* 數) EQUATIONS involving two or more unknown quantities that have the same values in each equation 聯立方程

SIN /ˌes aɪ ˈen/ *abbr.* (*CanE*) SOCIAL INSURANCE NUMBER

sin /sɪn/ *noun, verb, abbr.*

■ ***noun*** **1** [C] an offence against God or against a religious or moral law 罪，罪惡，罪過（對神的冒犯或對宗教戒律、道德規範的違犯）：*to commit a sin* 犯罪 ◇ *Confess your sins to God and he will forgive you.* 向上帝懺悔，上帝就會寬恕你。◇ *The Bible says that stealing is a sin.* 《聖經》上說偷盜有罪。➲ COLLOCATIONS at RELIGION ➲ see also MORTAL SIN, ORIGINAL SIN **2** [U] the act of breaking a religious or moral law 罪行，犯罪（違犯宗教戒律、道德規範的行為）：*a life of sin* 罪過的一生 **3** [C, usually sing.] (*informal*) an action that people strongly disapprove of 過錯；過失；惡行：*It's a sin to waste taxpayers' money like that.* 這樣揮霍納稅人的錢太不應該。➲ see also SINFUL, SINNER

IDM **be/do sth for your sins** (*informal, humorous, especially BrE*) used to say that sth that sb does is like a punishment（表示所做的事無異於懲罰）自作自受，活該：*She works with us in Accounts, for her sins!* 她跟我們一樣也在賬務室做事，活該如此！ **(as) miserable/ugly as ˈsin** (*informal*) used to emphasize that sb is very unhappy or ugly 可憐得 / 難看得要命 ➲ more at MULTITUDE, LIVE[1]

■ ***verb*** (**-nn-**) [I] to break a religious or moral law 犯戒律；犯過失：*Forgive me, Lord, for I have sinned.* 主啊，寬恕我吧，我犯了罪。◇ **~ against sb/sth** *He was **more sinned against than sinning*** (= although he did wrong, other people treated him even worse). 他過錯無多而報應太重。

■ ***abbr.*** (*mathematics* 數) SINE 正弦

ˈsin bin *noun* (*informal*) (in some sports, for example ICE HOCKEY 冰球等體育運動) a place away from the playing area where the REFEREE sends a player who has broken the rules 被罰下場的球員座位；受罰席

since 🗝 /sɪns/ *prep., conj., adv.*

■ ***prep.*** **1** 🗝 (used with the present perfect or past perfect tense 與現在完成時或過去完成時連用) from a time in the past until a later past time, or until now 自…以後；從…以來：*She's been off work since Tuesday.* 星期二以來她一直沒上班。◇ *We've lived here since 2006.* 從 2006 年開始我們便住在這裏。◇ *I haven't eaten since breakfast.* 早飯以後我還沒吃過東西呢。◇ *He's been working in a bank since leaving school.* 他中學畢業以後一直在一家銀行工作。◇ *Since the party she had only spoken to him once.* 那次聚會以後，她只和他說過一次話。◇ *'They've split up.' '**Since when?**'* "他們分手了。" "什麼時候的事兒？" ◇ *That was years ago. I've changed jobs **since then**.* 那是多年以前的事了。自那以來我已經換過幾個工作了。 **HELP** Use **for**, not **since**, with a period of time. 指一段時間用 for，不用 since：*I've been learning English for five years.* ◇ ~~*I've been learning English since five years.*~~ **2 ~ when?** used when you are showing that you are angry about sth（表示氣憤）何曾，什麼時候：*Since when did he ever listen to me?* 他什麼時候聽過我的話？

■ ***conj.*** **1** 🗝 (used with the present perfect, past perfect or simple present tense in the main clause 與用現在完成時、過去完成時或一般現在時的主句連用) from an event in the past until a later past event, or until now 從…以後；自…以來：*Cath hasn't phoned since she went to Berlin.* 卡思自從去了柏林還沒有打來過電話。◇ *It was the first time I'd had visitors since I'd moved to London.* 那是我搬到倫敦以後第一次有人來看我。◇ *It's twenty years since I've seen her.* 我已經二十年沒見她了。◇ *How long is it since we last went to the theatre?* 我們多久沒去看戲了？◇ *She had been worrying **ever since** the letter arrived.* 自從接到那封信後她就一直焦慮不安。 **2** 🗝 because; as 因為；由於；既然：*We thought that, since we were in the area, we'd stop by and see them.* 我們想，既然到了這個地方，就該順便去看看他們。

■ ***adv.*** (used with the present perfect or past perfect tense 與現在完成時或過去完成時連用) **1** 🗝 from a time in the past until a later past time, or until now 自…以後；從…以來：*He left home two weeks ago and we haven't heard from him since.* 他兩週前離家外出，我們至今還沒有他的音信。◇ *The original building has **long since*** (= long before now) *been demolished.* 原來的建築老早就拆了。 **2** 🗝 at a time after a particular time in the past 此後；後來：*We were divorced two years ago and she has since remarried.* 我們兩年前離了婚，之後她又再婚了。

sin·cere 🗝 /sɪnˈsɪə(r); *NAmE* -ˈsɪr/ *adj.* (*superlative* **sin·cerest**, no *comparative*)

1 🗝 (of feelings, beliefs or behaviour 感情、信念或行為) showing what you really think or feel 真誠的；誠摯的；誠懇的 **SYN** **genuine**：*a sincere attempt to resolve the problem* 解決這一問題的認真嘗試 ◇ *sincere regret* 真誠的悔恨 ◇ *Please accept our sincere thanks.* 請接受我們誠摯的謝意。◇ *a sincere apology* 誠懇的道歉 **2** 🗝 (of a person 人) saying only what you really think or feel 誠實的；坦率的 **SYN** **honest**：*He seemed sincere enough when he said he wanted to help.* 他表示願意幫忙，樣子很真誠。◇ **~ in sth** *She is never completely sincere in what she says about people.* 她談論別人，一向不盡坦誠。 **OPP** **insincere** ▶ **sin·cer·ity** /sɪnˈserəti/ *noun* [U]：*She spoke with total sincerity.* 她講的是由衷之言。◇ *I can say*

S

in all sincerity that I knew nothing of these plans. 我可以十分坦誠地說，這些計劃我一無所知。

sin·cere·ly 0‑ /sɪnˈsɪəli; NAmE -ˈsɪrli/ *adv.* in a way that shows what you really feel or think about sb/sth 真誠地；誠實地： *I sincerely believe that this is the right decision.* 我真心實意地相信這個決定是正確的。◇ *'I won't let you down.' 'I sincerely hope not.'* "我不會讓你失望的。" "但願如此。"
IDM **Yours sincerely** 0‑ (*BrE*) (*NAmE* **Sincerely (yours)**) (*formal*) used at the end of a formal letter before you sign your name, when you have addressed sb by their name（正式信函署名前的套語，只用於以收信人姓氏相稱呼的信函）➲ WRITING TUTOR page WT24

Sindhi /ˈsɪndi/ *noun* [U] a language spoken in Sind in Pakistan and in western India 信德語（通行於巴基斯坦信德省和印度西部）

sine /saɪn/ *noun* (*abbr.* **sin**) (*mathematics* 數) the RATIO of the length of the side opposite one of the angles in a RIGHT-ANGLED triangle that are less than 90° to the length of the longest side 正弦 ➲ compare COSINE, TANGENT

sine·cure /ˈsɪnɪkjʊə(r); ˈsaɪn-; NAmE -kjʊr/ *noun* (*formal*) a job that you are paid for even though it involves little or no work 閒職；掛名職位

sine die /ˌsaɪni ˈdaɪiː; ˌsmeɪ ˈdiːeɪ/ *adv.* (from *Latin*, *formal*, *law* 律) without a future date being arranged 無限期地： *The case was adjourned sine die.* 此案無限期延遲審理。

sine qua non /ˌsmeɪ kwɑː ˈnəʊn; NAmE ˈnoʊn/ *noun* [sing.] **~ (of/for sth)** (from *Latin*, *formal*) something that is essential before you can achieve sth else 必要條件

sinew /ˈsɪnjuː/ *noun* **1** [C, U] a strong band of TISSUE in the body that joins a muscle to a bone 肌腱 **2** [usually pl.] (*literary*) a source of strength or power 力量的來源；關鍵環節；要害之處 IDM see STRAIN *v.*

sinewy /ˈsɪnjuːi/ *adj.* (of a person or an animal 人或動物) having a thin body and strong muscles 肌肉發達的；矯健的；強健的 SYN **wiry**

sin·ful /ˈsɪnfl/ *adj.* (*formal*) morally wrong or evil 不道德的；邪惡的 SYN **immoral**： *sinful thoughts* 邪惡的想法 ◇ *It is sinful to lie.* 說謊是不道德的。◇ (*informal*) *It's sinful to waste good food!* 浪費好好的食物是有罪的！ ▸ **sin·ful·ly** /-fəli/ *adv.* **sin·ful·ness** *noun* [U]

sing 0‑ /sɪŋ/ *verb* (**sang** /sæŋ/, **sung** /sʌŋ/)
1 0‑ [I, T] to make musical sounds with your voice in the form of a song or tune 唱（歌）；演唱： *She usually sings in the shower.* 她常常邊沖澡邊唱歌。◇ *I just can't sing in tune!* 我一唱就走調！◇ **~ to sb** *He was singing softly to the baby.* 他對寶寶輕聲哼着歌。◇ **~ sth to sb** *Will you sing a song to us?* 你給我們唱支歌好嗎？◇ **~ sb sth** *Will you sing us a song?* 你給我們唱支歌好嗎？◇ **~ sth** *Now I'd like to sing a song by the Beatles.* 現在我來唱一首披頭士樂隊的歌。◇ **~ sb to sleep** *She sang the* ***baby to sleep*** (= sang until the baby went to sleep). 她哼着歌把寶寶哄睡了。➲ COLLOCATIONS at MUSIC **2** 0‑ [I] (of birds 鳥) to make high musical sounds 鳴；啼；啼囀： *The birds were singing outside my window.* 鳥兒在我窗外啼囀。 **3** [I] (+ adv./prep.) to make a high ringing sound like a whistle 嗚嗚作響；發嗖嗖聲： *Bullets sang past my ears.* 子彈嗖嗖地從我耳邊飛過。 ▸ **sing** *noun* [sing.]： *Let's have a sing.* 我們唱支歌吧。
IDM **sing a different 'tune** to change your opinion about sb/sth or your attitude towards sb/sth 改變觀點（或態度）；改弦易轍 **sing from the same 'hymn/'song sheet** (*BrE*, *informal*) to show that you are in agreement with each other by saying the same things in public 唱同一調子（在公開場合口徑一致）➲ more at FAT *adj.*
PHR V **ˌsing aˈlong (with sb/sth)** | **ˌsing aˈlong (to sth)** to sing together with sb who is already singing or while a record, radio, or musical instrument is playing 隨着（某人、唱片等）唱： *Do sing along if you know the words.* 要是知道歌詞，你就跟着唱吧。➲ related noun SINGALONG **'sing of sth** (*old-fashioned* or *formal*) to mention sth in a song or a poem, especially to praise it（用詩歌）講述，歌頌，讚美 **ˌsing 'out** to sing or say sth clearly and loudly 叫出；唱出： *A voice suddenly sang out above the rest.* 在一片嘈雜聲中突然傳出一個人的聲音。 **ˌsing 'up** (*BrE*) (*NAmE* **ˌsing 'out**) to sing more loudly 更大聲地唱；放開嗓門唱： *Sing up, let's hear you.* 大聲唱，我們聽不見。

sing·along /ˈsɪŋəlɒŋ; NAmE -lɔːŋ; -lɑːŋ/ (*BrE* also **'sing-song**) *noun* an informal occasion at which people sing songs together 眾人自娛歌唱會

singe /sɪndʒ/ *verb* (**singe·ing**, **singed**, **singed**) [T, I] **~ (sth)** to burn the surface of sth slightly, usually by mistake; to be burnt in this way（尤指不小心）烤焦，燙煳： *He singed his hair as he tried to light his cigarette.* 他點煙時把頭髮給燎了。◇ *the smell of singeing fur* 毛皮燒焦的氣味 ➲ SYNONYMS at BURN

sing·er 0‑ /ˈsɪŋə(r)/ *noun* a person who sings, or whose job is singing, especially in public 唱歌的人；歌唱家；歌手： *She's a wonderful singer.* 她唱歌唱得非常好。◇ *an opera singer* 歌劇演員

sing·ing 0‑ /ˈsɪŋɪŋ/ *noun* [U] the activity of making musical sounds with your voice 唱歌；歌唱： *the beautiful singing of birds* 鳥兒動聽的歌唱 ◇ *choral singing* 合唱 ◇ *There was singing and dancing all night.* 通宵唱歌跳舞。◇ *a singing teacher* 聲樂教師 ◇ *She has a beautiful singing voice.* 她有一副唱歌的好嗓子。

sin·gle 0‑ /ˈsɪŋgl/ *adj.*, *noun*, *verb*
■ ***adj.***
▸ **ONE** 一個 **1** 0‑ [only before noun] only one 僅有一個的；單一的；單個的： *He sent her a single red rose.* 他送給她一枝紅玫瑰。◇ *a* ***single-sex school*** (= for boys only or for girls only) 男子（或女子）學校 ◇ *All these jobs can now be done by one single machine.* 所有這些工作現在只用一台機器就可以完成。◇ *I couldn't understand a single word she said!* 她講的東西我一個字都聽不懂！◇ *the European* ***single currency****, the euro* 歐洲單一貨幣歐元 ◇ (*BrE*) *a* ***single honours*** *degree* (= for which you study only one subject) 單科榮譽學位
▸ **FOR EMPHASIS** 強調 **2** 0‑ [only before noun] used to emphasize that you are referring to one particular person or thing on its own（特指某人或事物）： *Unemployment is the single most important factor in the growing crime rates.* 失業是犯罪率日益上升最重要的一個因素。◇ *We eat rice* ***every single day****.* 我們天天吃米飯。
▸ **NOT MARRIED** 未婚 **3** 0‑ (of a person 人) not married or having a romantic relationship with sb 單身的；未婚的；無伴侶的： *The apartments are ideal for single people living alone.* 這些公寓供單身者獨自居住最為理想。◇ *Are you still single?* 你還是單身嗎？➲ see also SINGLE PARENT
▸ **FOR ONE PERSON** 供一個人使用 **4** 0‑ [only before noun] intended to be used by only one person 單人的： *a* ***single bed/room*** 單人牀 / 房間 ➲ VISUAL VOCAB page V23 ➲ compare DOUBLE *adj.* (3)
▸ **TICKET** 票 **5** [only before noun] (*BrE*) (also **one-way** *NAmE*, *BrE*) a **single** ticket, etc. can be used for travelling to a place but not back again 單程的： *a single ticket* 單程票 ◇ *How much is the single fare to Glasgow?* 去格拉斯哥的單程票多少錢？➲ compare RETURN *n.* (7) IDM see FILE *n.*, GLANCE *n.*
■ ***noun***
▸ **TICKET** 票 **1** [C] (*BrE*) a ticket that allows you to travel to a place but not back again 單程票： *How much is a single to York?* 去約克的單程票多少錢？➲ compare RETURN *n.* (7)
▸ **MUSIC** 音樂 **2** [C] a piece of recorded music, usually popular music, that consists of one song; a CD that a single is recorded on 單曲（常指流行音樂）；單曲激光唱片： *The band releases its new single next week.* 這支樂隊將於下週發行新的單曲唱片。➲ compare ALBUM (2)
▸ **ROOM** 房間 **3** 0‑ [C] a room in a hotel, etc. for one person（旅館等的）單人房間 ➲ compare DOUBLE *n.* (5)
▸ **MONEY** 錢 **4** [C] (*NAmE*) a bill/note that is worth one dollar 一元紙幣 ➲ compare DOUBLE *n.* (5)
▸ **UNMARRIED PEOPLE** 未婚者 **5** **singles** [pl.] people who are not married and do not have a romantic relationship with sb else 單身者；無伴侶者： *They organize*

parties for singles. 他們為單身者組織聚會。◇ *a **singles bar/club*** 單身酒吧／俱樂部

▸ IN SPORT 體育運動 **6 singles** [U+sing./pl. v.] (especially in TENNIS 尤指網球) a game when only one player plays against one other; a series of two or more of these games 單打（比賽）：*the women's singles champion* 女子單打冠軍 ◇ *the first round of the men's singles* 男子單打第一輪 ◇ *a singles match* 單打比賽 ◇ *She's won three singles titles this year.* 她今年獲得三個單打冠軍。➲ compare DOUBLES *n.* (6) **7** [C] (in CRICKET 板球) a hit from which a player scores one RUN (= point) 一分打 **8** [C] (in BASEBALL 棒球) a hit that only allows the player to run to FIRST BASE 一壘打

■ ***verb***

PHR V **ˌsingle sb/sth↔ˈout (for sth/as sb/sth)** to choose sb/sth from a group for special attention 單獨挑出：*She was singled out for criticism.* 把她單挑出來進行批評。◇ *He was singled out as the outstanding performer of the games.* 他被評選為這次運動會表現最出色的運動員。

ˌsingle ˈbed (*NAmE* also **ˌtwin ˈbed**) *noun* a bed big enough for one person 單人牀 ➲ **VISUAL VOCAB** page V23

ˌsingle-ˈbreast·ed *adj.* (of a jacket or coat 上衣) having only one row of buttons that fasten in the middle 單排扣的 ➲ compare DOUBLE-BREASTED

ˌsingle ˈcombat *noun* [U] fighting between two people, usually with weapons 一對一的搏鬥（通常用武器）

ˌsingle ˈcream *noun* [U] (*BrE*) thin cream which is used in cooking and for pouring over food 稀奶油 ➲ compare DOUBLE CREAM

ˌsingle-ˈdecker *noun* a bus with only one level 單層公共汽車 ➲ **VISUAL VOCAB** page V57 ➲ compare DOUBLE-DECKER (1)

ˌsingle ˈfigures *noun* [pl.] a number that is less than ten 個位數；一位數：*Inflation is down to single figures.* 通貨膨脹率降到一位數了。◇ *The number of people who fail each year is now **in single figures**.* 每年考試不及格的學生現在不足十人。

ˌsingle-ˈhanded *adv.* on your own with nobody helping you 獨自；單槍匹馬地；獨立 **SYN** **alone**：*to sail around the world single-handed* 單人環球航行 ▸ **ˌsingle-ˈhanded** *adj.*：*a single-handed voyage* 單人航行 **ˌsingle-ˈhanded·ly** *adv.*

ˌsingle ˈmarket *noun* [usually sing.] (*economics* 經) a group of countries that have few or no restrictions on the movement of goods, money and people between the members of the group 單一市場（由若干國家構成，成員國之間對於相互間的商品交易、貨幣流通及人員往來極少或沒有限制）

ˌsingle-ˈminded *adj.* only thinking about one particular aim or goal because you are determined to achieve sth 一心一意的；專心致志的：*the single-minded pursuit of power* 一心追逐權力 ◇ *She is very single-minded about her career.* 她一心專注於自己的事業。▸ **ˌsingle-ˈminded·ly** *adv.* **ˌsingle-ˈminded·ness** *noun* [U]

single·ness /ˈsɪŋɡlnəs/ *noun* [U] **1 ~ of purpose** the ability to think about one particular aim or goal because you are determined to succeed （目標）專一 **2** the state of not being married or having a partner 單身；單身生活

ˌsingle ˈparent *noun* a person who takes care of their child or children without a husband, wife or partner 單親：*a single-parent family* 單親家庭

sing·let /ˈsɪŋɡlət/ *noun* (*BrE*) a piece of clothing without sleeves, worn under or instead of a shirt; a similar piece of clothing worn by runners, etc. 背心；無袖汗衫；運動背心 ➲ compare VEST

single·ton /ˈsɪŋɡltən/ *noun* **1** a single item of the kind that you are talking about （所提及的）單項物，單個的人 **2** a person who is not married or in a romantic relationship 單身男子（或女子） **3** a person or an animal that is not a twin, etc. （非孿生的）單生兒，單生幼畜

ˌsingle transˌferable ˈvote *noun* [sing.] (*politics* 政) a system for electing representatives in which a person's vote can be given to their second or third choice if their first choice is defeated, or if their first choice wins with more votes than they need 單一可轉移投票制，單記可讓渡投票制（所選的第一位候選人失敗或所得票數已經超過必要數額，選票可轉給所選的第二或第三候選人）

ˌsingle-ˈuse *adj.* [only before noun] made to be used once only 供一次使用的：*disposable single-use cameras* 一次性相機

sin·gly /ˈsɪŋɡli/ *adv.* alone; one at a time 單個地；單獨地；一個一個地 **SYN** **individually**：*The stamps are available singly or in books of ten.* 郵票有單枚的，也有十枚一冊的。◇ *Guests arrived singly or in groups.* 客人有單個來的，也有三三兩兩一起到的。

ˈsing-song *noun, adj.*

■ ***noun*** **1** [C] (*BrE*) = SINGALONG **2** [sing.] a way of speaking in which a person's voice keeps rising and falling 聲音起伏的說話腔調

■ ***adj.*** [only before noun] a **sing-song** voice keeps rising and falling 說話音調起伏的

sin·gu·lar /ˈsɪŋɡjələ(r)/ *noun, adj.*

■ ***noun*** [sing.] (*grammar* 語法) a form of a noun or verb that refers to one person or thing 單數；單數形式：*The singular of 'bacteria' is 'bacterium'.* * bacteria 的單數形式是 bacterium。◇ *The verb should be **in the singular**.* 這個動詞應當用單數形式。➲ compare PLURAL

■ ***adj.*** **1** (*grammar* 語法) connected with or having the singular form 單數的；單數形式的：*a **singular noun/verb/ending*** 單數名詞／動詞／詞尾 **2** (*formal*) very great or obvious 非凡的；突出的；顯著的 **SYN** **outstanding**：*landscape of singular beauty* 無比優美的風景 **3** (*literary*) unusual; strange 奇特的；奇怪的；異常的 **SYN** **eccentric**：*a singular style of dress* 奇特的衣服

sin·gu·lar·ity /ˌsɪŋɡjuˈlærəti/ *noun* [U] (*formal*) the quality of sth that makes it unusual or strange 奇特；奇怪；異常

sin·gu·lar·ly /ˈsɪŋɡjələli; *NAmE* -lərli/ *adv.* (*formal*) very; in an unusual way 非常；特別；異常地：*singularly beautiful* 特別漂亮 ◇ *He chose a singularly inappropriate moment to make his request.* 他選在一個極其不恰當的時刻提出要求。

Sin·hal·ese /ˌsɪnhəˈliːz; ˌsɪnə-/ *noun* (*pl.* **Sin·hal·ese**) **1** [C] a member of a race of people living in Sri Lanka 僧伽羅人（居住在斯里蘭卡） **2** [U] the language of the Sinhalese 僧伽羅語 ▸ **Sin·hal·ese** *adj.*

sin·is·ter /ˈsɪnɪstə(r)/ *adj.* seeming evil or dangerous; making you think sth bad will happen 邪惡的；險惡的；不祥的；有凶兆的：*There was something cold and sinister about him.* 他給人一種冷酷陰險的感覺。◇ *There is another, more sinister, possibility.* 還有另一種更糟糕的可能。

sink 0‑ /sɪŋk/ *verb, noun, adj.*

■ ***verb*** (**sank** /sæŋk/, **sunk** /sʌŋk/ or *less frequent* **sunk**, **sunk**)

▸ IN WATER/MUD, ETC. 在水／泥等裏 **1** 0‑ [I] to go down below the surface or towards the bottom of a liquid or soft substance 下沉；下陷；沉沒：*The ship sank to the bottom of the sea.* 船沉入海底。◇ *We're sinking!* 我們正在下沉！◇ *The wheels started to sink into the mud.* 車輪漸漸陷進泥裏。◇ *to **sink like a stone*** 立即沉沒

▸ BOAT 船隻 **2** 0‑ [T] **~ sth** to damage a boat or ship so that it goes below the surface of the sea, etc. 使下沉；使沉沒：*a battleship sunk by a torpedo* 被魚雷擊沉的戰列艦

▸ FALL/SIT DOWN 倒下；坐下 **3** [I] **+ adv./prep.** (of a person 人) to move downwards, especially by falling or sitting down 倒下；坐下 **SYN** **collapse**：*I sank into an armchair.* 我坐到扶手椅上。◇ *She **sank back** into her seat, exhausted.* 她筋疲力盡，又坐回椅子上。◇ *The old man had **sunk to his knees**.* 老頭跪在了地上。

▸ MOVE DOWNWARDS 下降 **4** 0‑ [I] (of an object 物體) to move slowly downwards 下沉；下陷；沉降：*The sun was sinking in the west.* 太陽西下。◇ *The foundations of the building are starting to sink.* 樓房的地基開始下陷。

▸ BECOME WEAKER 減弱 **5** [I] to decrease in amount, volume, strength, etc. 降低；減少；減弱：*The pound*

S

has sunk to its lowest recorded level against the dollar. 英鎊對美元的比價降到了有記錄以來最低水平。◇ *He is clearly sinking fast* (= getting weaker quickly and will soon die). 很明顯，他的身體在急劇衰弱。

▸ **OF VOICE** 聲音 **6** [I] to become quieter 變低；變小 **SYN** **fade**：*Her voice sank to a whisper.* 她的聲音變成了耳語。

▸ **DIG IN GROUND** 在地上挖掘 **7** [T] **~ sth** to make a deep hole in the ground 挖，掘（深坑、深洞）**SYN** **drill**：*to sink a well/shaft/mine* 掘水井 / 豎井 / 礦井 **8** [T] **~ sth (+ adv./prep.)** to place sth in the ground by digging 埋入；打下：*to sink a post into the ground* 在地上埋入一根杆子 ➲ see also SUNKEN

▸ **PREVENT SUCCESS** 使不成功 **9** [T] **~ sth/sb** (*informal*) to prevent sb or sb's plans from succeeding 使失敗；使受挫；阻撓：*I think I've just sunk my chances of getting the job.* 我想，都是我自己不好，葬送了得到那份工作的機會。◇ *If the car breaks down, we'll* ***be sunk*** (= have serious problems). 要是車壞了，咱們可就慘了。

▸ **BALL** 球 **10** [T] **~ sth** to hit a ball into a hole in GOLF or SNOOKER（高爾夫球）擊球入洞；（斯諾克）擊球入袋：*He sank a 12-foot putt to win the match.* 他以一記 12 英尺的輕擊入洞贏了比賽。

▸ **ALCOHOL** 酒 **11** [T] **~ sth** (*BrE, informal*) to drink sth quickly, especially a large amount of alcohol 猛喝；灌

IDM **be 'sunk in sth** to be in a state of unhappiness or deep thought 陷入不快（或沉思）中：*She just sat there, sunk in thought.* 她只一味地坐在那兒，陷入了沉思。 **(like rats) deserting/leaving a sinking 'ship** (*humorous, disapproving*) used to talk about people who leave an organization, a company, etc. that is having difficulties, without caring about the people who are left（比喻只顧自己而離開處於困境中的機構等）（像）逃離沉船（的老鼠） **sink your 'differences** to agree to forget about your disagreements 摒棄分歧；擱置歧見 **a/that 'sinking feeling** (*informal*) an unpleasant feeling that you get when you realize that sth bad has happened or is going to happen 不祥的感覺；沮喪之情 **,sink or 'swim** to be in a situation where you will either succeed by your own efforts or fail completely 不自救，必沉淪；自己努力，以求生存：*The new students were just left to sink or swim.* 學校完全讓新生自生自滅。 **,sink so 'low | sink to sth** to have such low moral standards that you do sth very bad 墮落到這種地步；沉淪到某種程度：*Stealing from your friends? How could you sink so low?* 偷到你的朋友頭上了？你怎麼能墮落到這種地步呢？◇ *I can't believe that anyone would sink to such depths.* 我無法相信竟然有人能墮落到這種程度。➲ more at HEART

PHR V **,sink 'in | ,sink 'into sth** **1** (of words, an event, etc. 話語、事情等) to be fully understood or realized 被完全理解；被充分意識到：*He paused to allow his words to sink in.* 他停了一下，好讓人充分領會他的意思。◇ *The full scale of the disaster has yet to sink in.* 人們還沒有完全意識到這場災難的嚴重程度。 **2** (of liquids 液體) to go down into another substance through the surface 滲透；滲入：*The rain sank into the dry ground.* 雨水滲進了乾地裏。 **'sink into sth** to go gradually into a less active, happy or pleasant state 漸漸進入（沉寂、不快等的）狀態：*She sank into a deep sleep.* 她沉沉地睡去。◇ *He sank deeper into depression.* 他越來越消沉。 **,sink 'into sth | ,sink sth 'into sth** to go, or to make sth sharp go, deep into sth solid（把某物）插入：*The dog sank its teeth into my leg* (= bit it). 狗狠咬了我的腿。◇ *I felt her nails sink into my wrist.* 我感覺她的指甲掐進了我的手腕裏。 **,sink sth 'into sth** to spend a lot of money on a business or an activity, for example in order to make money from it in the future 把資金投入企業（或活動）：*We sank all our savings into the venture.* 我們把所有的積蓄都投進了這一創投項目。

■ ***noun*** **1** a large open container in a kitchen that has taps/faucets to supply water and that you use for washing dishes in（廚房裏的）洗滌池，洗碗槽：*Don't just leave your dirty plates in the sink!* 別把髒盤子往洗碗槽裏一放就不管了！◇ *I felt chained to the kitchen sink* (= I had to spend all my time doing jobs in the house). 我覺得就像拴在了灶台上一樣。➲ picture at PLUG ➲ VISUAL VOCAB page V25 **2** (*especially NAmE*) = WASH-BASIN **IDM** see KITCHEN

■ ***adj.*** [only before noun] (*BrE*) located in a poor area where social conditions are bad 位於社會條件差的貧窮地區的；貧民窟的：*the misery of life in* ***sink estates*** 貧民窟裏的悲慘生活 ◇ *a* ***sink school*** 貧困地區的學校

sink·er /ˈsɪŋkə(r)/ *noun* a weight that is attached to a FISHING LINE or net to keep it under the water（釣絲或漁網上的）鉛錘，墜子 **IDM** see HOOK *n.*

sink·hole /ˈsɪŋkhəʊl; *NAmE* -hoʊl/ (also **'swallow hole**) *noun* (*geology* 地) a large hole in the ground that a river flows into, created over a long period of time by water that has fallen as rain 落水洞（在地面下，雨水長期滲落形成）

sin·ner /ˈsɪnə(r)/ *noun* (*formal*) a person who has committed a SIN or SINS (= broken God's law) 罪人

Sinn Fein /ˌʃɪn ˈfeɪn/ *noun* [U+sing./pl. v.] an Irish political party that wants Northern Ireland and the Republic of Ireland to become one country 新芬黨（愛爾蘭政黨，主張北愛爾蘭和愛爾蘭共和國統一）

Sino- /ˈsaɪnəʊ; *NAmE* -noʊ/ *combining form* (in nouns and adjectives 構成名詞和形容詞) Chinese 中國的；中國人（的）：*Sino-Japanese relations* 中日關係

sinu·ous /ˈsɪnjuəs/ *adj.* (*literary*) turning while moving, in an elegant way; having many curves 彎曲有致的；蜿蜒的：*a sinuous movement* 婀娜多姿的動作 ◇ *the sinuous grace of a cat* 貓的靈活優美 ◇ *the sinuous course of the river* 彎彎曲曲的河道 ▸ **sinu·ous·ly** *adv.*

si·nus /ˈsaɪnəs/ *noun* any of the hollow spaces in the bones of the head that are connected to the inside of the nose 竇；竇道：*blocked sinuses* 竇性傳導阻滯

si·nus·itis /ˌsaɪnəˈsaɪtɪs/ *noun* [U] the painful swelling of the sinuses（鼻）竇炎

-sion ➲ -ION

Sioux /suː/ *noun* (*pl.* **Sioux**) a member of a Native American people many of whom live in the US states of North and South Dakota 蘇人（美洲土著，很多居於美國北達科他州和南達科他州）

sip /sɪp/ *verb, noun*

■ ***verb*** **(-pp-)** [I, T] to drink sth, taking a very small amount each time 小口喝；抿：**~ (at sth)** *She sat there, sipping at her tea.* 她坐在那兒抿着茶。◇ **~ sth** *He slowly sipped his wine.* 他慢酌淺飲。

■ ***noun*** a very small amount of a drink that you take into your mouth 一小口（飲料）：*to* ***have/take a sip*** *of water* 喝一小口水

si·phon (also **sy·phon**) /ˈsaɪfn/ *noun, verb*

■ ***noun*** a tube that is used to move liquid from one container to another lower container 虹吸管

■ ***verb*** **1 ~ sth (+ adv./prep.)** to move a liquid from one container to another, using a siphon 用虹吸管吸（或抽）：*I siphoned the gasoline out of the car into a can.* 我用虹吸管把汽車裏的汽油抽到桶裏。◇ *The waste liquid needs to be siphoned off.* 需要把廢液抽走。 **2 ~ sth (+ adv./prep.)** (*informal*) to remove money from one place and move it to another, especially dishonestly or illegally（尤指私自或非法）抽走，轉移（錢）**SYN** **divert**：*She has been accused of* ***siphoning off*** *thousands of pounds from the company into her own bank account.* 她被指控把公司的幾千英鎊轉移到了自己的賬戶裏。

sippy cup /ˈsɪpi kʌp/ *noun* (*NAmE, informal*) a cup with a lid that has holes in it so that a baby can suck liquid from it（幼兒用）鴨嘴杯

sir 🔑 /sɜː(r); sə(r)/ *noun*

1 🔑 used as a polite way of addressing a man whose name you do not know, for example in a shop/store or restaurant, or to show respect（對不認識的男性的尊稱）先生：*Good morning, sir. Can I help you?* 早上好，先生。您要點什麼？◇ *Are you ready to order, sir?* 先生，可以點菜了嗎？◇ *'Report to me tomorrow, corporal!' 'Yes, sir!'* "下士，明天來向我報告！" "是，長官！" ◇ *'Thank you very much.' 'You're welcome, sir. Have a nice day.'* "多謝。" "不客氣，先生。祝您愉快。" ➲ compare MA'AM (1) ➲ see also MADAM (1) **2** 🔑 **Dear Sir/Sirs** used at the beginning of a formal business letter when you do not know the name of the man or people that you are dealing with（正式信函中對不知其名的男性收信人的稱呼）先生，閣下：*Dear Sir/Sirs* 親愛的先生／諸位先生 ◇ *Dear Sir or Madam* 親愛的先生或女士 **3** **Sir** a title that is used before the first name of a man who has received one of the highest British honours (= a KNIGHT), or before the first name of a BARONET（貴族頭銜，用於爵士或准男爵的名字或姓名前面）爵士：*Sir Paul McCartney* 保羅 • 麥卡特尼爵士 ◇ *Thank you, Sir Paul.* 謝謝，保羅爵士。➲ compare LADY (6) **4** (*BrE*) used as a form of address by children in school to a male teacher（中小學生對男教師的稱呼）先生，老師：*Please, sir, can I open a window?* 老師，請允許我打開一扇窗戶好嗎？➲ compare MISS *n.* (4)

IDM **ˌno ˈsir! | ˌno siˈree!** (*informal, especially NAmE*) certainly not 決不：*We will never allow that to happen! No sir!* 我們決不能允許那樣的事情發生！決不能！ **ˌyes ˈsir! | ˌyes siˈree!** (*informal, especially NAmE*) used to emphasize that sth is true（強調所言不虛）的確：*That's a fine car you have. Yes sir!* 你這輛車真好。的確好！

sire /ˈsaɪə(r)/ *noun, verb*

■ **noun** **1** (*technical* 術語) the male parent of an animal, especially a horse 雄性種獸；（尤指）公種馬 ➲ compare DAM *n.* (2) **2** (*old use*) a word that people used when they addressed a king（舊時對國王的稱呼）陛下

■ **verb** **1 ~ sth** to be the male parent of an animal, especially a horse（種馬等雄性動物）生殖，繁殖 **2 ~ sth** (*old-fashioned* or *humorous*) to become the father of a child 成為父親

siree (also **sir·ree**) /səˈriː/ *exclamation* (*NAmE, informal*) used for emphasis, especially after 'yes' or 'no'（加強語氣，尤在 yes 或 no 之後）：*He's not going to do it, no siree.* 他不會幹這事的，絕對不會。

siren /ˈsaɪrən/ *noun* **1** a device that makes a long loud sound as a signal or warning 汽笛；警報器：*an air-raid siren* 空襲警報器 ◇ *A police car raced past with its siren wailing.* 一輛警車鳴着警報器飛馳而過。 **2** (in ancient Greek stories) any of a group of sea creatures that were part woman and part bird, or part woman and part fish, whose beautiful singing made sailors sail towards them into rocks or dangerous waters 塞壬（古希臘神話中半人半鳥或半人半魚的女海妖，以美妙歌聲誘使航海者駛向礁石或進入危險水域） **3** a woman who is very attractive or beautiful but also dangerous 妖冶而危險的女人；性感妖女 **4 ~ voices/song/call** (*literary*) the TEMPTATION to do sth that seems very attractive but that will have bad results 危險的誘惑：*The government must resist the siren voices calling for tax cuts.* 政府萬萬不可聽信那些鼓吹減稅的動聽言辭。

sir·loin /ˈsɜːlɔɪn; *NAmE* ˈsɜːrl-/ (also **ˌsirloin ˈsteak**) *noun* [U, C] good quality beef that is cut from a cow's back 牛裏脊肉；牛上腰肉

si·rocco (also **sci·rocco**) /sɪˈrɒkəʊ; *NAmE* sɪˈrɑːkoʊ/ *noun* (*pl.* **-os**) a hot wind that blows from Africa into southern Europe 西洛哥風（從非洲吹到歐洲南部的熱風）

sis /sɪs/ *noun* (*informal*) sister (used when you are speaking to her)（用於直接稱呼）姐姐，妹妹

sisal /ˈsaɪsl/ *noun* [U] strong FIBRES made from the leaves of a tropical plant also called sisal, used for making rope, floor coverings, etc. 西沙爾麻，劍麻（用同名熱帶植物製成的纖維，用於製繩、織地毯等）

sissy (*BrE* also **cissy**) /ˈsɪsi/ *noun* (*pl.* **-ies**) (*informal, disapproving*) a boy that other men or boys laugh at because they think he is weak or frightened, or only interested in the sort of things girls like 柔弱（或怯懦）的男孩；女孩子氣的男孩 **SYN** **wimp** ▸ **sissy** *adj.*

sis·ter /ˈsɪstə(r)/ *noun*

1 a girl or woman who has the same mother and father as another person 姐；妹：*She's my sister.* 她是我姐姐。◇ *an* **older/younger sister** 姐姐；妹妹 ◇ (*informal*) *a* **big/little/kid sister** 大姐；小妹；年幼的妹妹 ◇ *We're sisters.* 我們是姐妹。◇ *Do you have any* **brothers or sisters**? 你有兄弟姐妹嗎？◇ *My best friend has been like a sister to me* (= very close). 我最要好的一個朋友待我親如姐妹。➲ see also HALF-SISTER, STEPSISTER **2** used for talking to or about other members of a women's organization or other women who have the same ideas, purpose, etc. as yourself（稱志同道合者）姐妹：*They supported their sisters in the dispute.* 在爭論中，她們支持自己的姐妹。 **3** **Sister** (*BrE*) a senior female nurse who is in charge of a hospital WARD 護士長 ➲ see also CHARGE NURSE **4** **Sister** a female member of a religious group, especially a NUN 女教友；（尤指）修女：*Sister Mary* 修女瑪麗 ◇ *the Sisters of Charity* 仁愛修女會 **5** (in the US) a member of a SORORITY (= a club for a group of female students at a college or university)（美國大學）女生聯誼會會員 **6** (*NAmE, informal*) used by black people as a form of address for a black woman（黑人的互相稱謂）大姐 **7** (usually used as an adjective 通常用作形容詞) a thing that belongs to the same type or group as sth else 同類型的；同一批的；如同姐妹的：*our sister company in Italy* 我們在意大利的姊妹公司 ◇ *a sister ship* 同一類型的船

sis·ter·hood /ˈsɪstəhʊd; *NAmE* -tərh-/ *noun* **1** [U] the close loyal relationship between women who share ideas and aims（志同道合者之間的）姐妹情誼 **2** [C+sing./pl. v.] a group of women who live in a community together, especially a religious one 婦女團體；修女會

ˈsister-in-law *noun* (*pl.* **sisters-in-law**) the sister of your husband or wife; your brother's wife; the wife of your husband or wife's brother 大（或小）姨子；大（或小）姑子；嫂子；弟媳；妯娌；丈夫（或妻子）的嫂子（或弟媳）➲ compare BROTHER-IN-LAW

sis·ter·ly /ˈsɪstəli; *NAmE* -tərli/ *adj.* typical of or like a sister 姐妹的；姐妹般的：*She gave him a sisterly kiss.* 她像姐姐一樣親了他一下。

Sisy·phean /ˌsɪsɪˈfiːən/ *adj.* (of a task 任務) impossible to complete 不可能完成的；永無休止的 **ORIGIN** From the Greek myth in which **Sisyphus** was punished for the bad things he had done in his life with the never-ending task of rolling a large stone to the top of a hill, from which it always rolled down again. 源自希臘神話，西緒福斯（Sisyphus）因前生罪惡受懲罰，無休止地將一塊巨石滾到山頂，而巨石總是一再滾落。

Grammar Point 語法說明

sit

■ You can use *on*, *in* and *at* with **sit**. You **sit on** a chair, a step, the edge of the table, etc. You **sit in** an armchair. If you are **sitting at** a table, desk, etc. you are sitting in a chair close to it, usually so that you can eat a meal, do some work, etc. * sit 可與 on、in 和 at 連用：坐在椅子上、台階上、桌子邊上等用 sit on；坐在扶手椅上用 sit in；坐在桌子、書桌等旁吃飯、工作等用 sit at。

S

sit /sɪt/ *verb* (**sit·ting**, **sat**, **sat** /sæt/)

▸ **ON CHAIR, ETC.** 在椅子等上面 **1** [I] to rest your weight on your bottom with your back vertical, for example on/in a chair 坐：*She sat and stared at the letter in front of her.* 她坐在那兒，凝視着面前的那封信。◇ **+ adv./prep.** *May I sit here?* 我可以坐在這兒嗎？◇ *Just sit still!* 坐着別動！◇ *He went and sat beside her.* 他走過去坐在她身邊。◇ *She was sitting at her desk.* 她坐在書桌前。◇ **~ doing sth** *We sat talking for hours.* 我們坐着談了好幾個小時。➲ see also SIT DOWN **2** [T] **~ sb + adv./prep.** to put sb in a sitting position 使坐；使就座：*He lifted the child and sat her on the wall.* 他抱起孩子，讓她坐在牆頭上。

▸ **OF THINGS** 事物 **3** [I] to be in a particular place 處在；坐落在；被放在：**+ adv./prep.** *A large bus was sitting outside.* 外面停着一輛大巴士。◇ *The pot was sitting in a pool of water.* 罐子已放在水裏。◇ *The jacket sat beautifully on her shoulders* (= fitted well). 那件夾克穿在她身上很合身。◇ **+ adj.** *The box sat unopened on the shelf.* 盒子擱在架子上，沒有打開。

▸ **HAVE OFFICIAL POSITION** 擔任職務 **4** [I] to have an official position as sth or as a member of sth（在…中）任職；任（…的）代表；擔任：**~ as sth** *He was sitting as a* *temporary judge.* 由他擔任臨時法官。◇ *They both sat as MPs in the House of Commons.* 他們兩人都曾是下議院議員。◇ **~ in/on sth** *She sat on a number of committees.* 她在幾個委員會裏任職。◇ **~ for sth** *For years he sat for Henley* (= was the MP for that CONSTITUENCY). 他多年擔任代表亨利選區的議會議員。

▸ **OF PARLIAMENT, ETC.** 議會等 **5** [I] (of a parliament, committee, court of law, etc. 議會、委員會、法庭等) to meet in order to do official business 開會；開庭： *Parliament sits for less than six months of the year.* 議會一年的開會時間不足六個月。

▸ **EXAM** 考試 **6** [T, I] (rather *formal*) to do an exam 參加考試；應試： (*BrE*) **~ sth** *Candidates will sit the examinations in June.* 考生將在六月參加考試。◇ *Most of the students sit at least 5 GCSEs.* 大多數學生至少參加 5 門普通中等教育證書考試。◇ (*especially NAmE*) ◇ **~ for sth** *He was about to sit for his entrance exam.* 當時他正要參加入學考試。

▸ **OF BIRD** 鳥 **7** [I] (+ **adv./prep.**) to rest on a branch, etc. or to stay on a nest to keep the eggs warm 停落；棲；孵（卵）

▸ **OF DOG** 狗 **8** [I] to sit on its bottom with its front legs straight 蹲；坐： *Rover! Sit!* 羅弗！蹲下！

▸ **TAKE CARE OF CHILDREN** 照看小孩 **9** [I] **~ (for sb)** = BABYSIT： *Who's sitting for you?* 誰給你看着孩子呢？
➲ see also HOUSE-SIT

IDM **be ˌsitting ˈpretty** (*informal*) to be in a good situation, especially when others are not（尤指在他人處境不好時）處境好 **sit at sb's ˈfeet** to admire sb very much, especially a teacher or sb from whom you try to learn 崇拜；拜倒在某人腳下 **sit comfortably, easily, well, etc. (with sth)** to seem right, natural, suitable, etc. in a particular place or situation（在某位置或某場合）顯得合適，顯得自然，如魚得水： *His views did not sit comfortably with the management line.* 他的意見和管理部門的方針不大吻合。 **sit in ˈjudgement (on/over/upon sb)** to decide whether sb's behaviour is right or wrong, especially when you have no right to do this 褒貶（某人）；（對某人）妄加評判： *How dare you sit in judgement on me?* 你怎麼敢對我妄加評論？ **sit on the ˈfence** to avoid becoming involved in deciding or influencing sth 騎牆；持觀望態度： *He tends to sit on the fence at meetings.* 開會時他往往持觀望態度。 **ˌsit ˈtight 1** to stay where you are rather than moving away or changing position 待着不動；守在原地： *We sat tight and waited to be rescued.* 我們守在原地，等待救援。 **2** to stay in the same situation, without changing your mind or taking any action 靜觀事態變化；不輕舉妄動： *Shareholders are being advised to sit tight until the crisis passes.* 股東們得到的忠告是，靜待危機過去。
➲ more at BOLT *adv.*, LAUREL, SILENTLY

PHR V **ˌsit aˈbout/aˈround** (often *disapproving*) to spend time doing nothing very useful 無所事事地消磨時間；閒坐： *I'm far too busy to sit around here.* 我忙得不可開交，沒空在這兒閒坐。◇ **~ doing sth** *He just sits around watching TV.* 他只會閒坐着看電視。 **ˌsit ˈback 1** to sit on sth, usually a chair, in a relaxed position 舒舒服服地坐好： *He sat back in his chair and started to read.* 他安穩地坐在椅子上，讀起書來。 **2** to relax, especially by not getting too involved in or anxious about sth 袖手旁觀（尤指不積極參與或不掛念某事）： *She's not the kind of person who can sit back and let others do all the work.* 她不是那種自己歇着，什麼活兒都讓別人幹的人。 **ˌsit ˈby** to take no action to stop sth bad or wrong from happening 坐視不管；無動於衷： *We cannot just sit by and watch this tragedy happen.* 我們不能坐視這樣的悲劇發生。 **ˌsit ˈdown | ˌsit yourself ˈdown** 🔑 to move from a standing position to a sitting position 坐下；就座： *Please sit down.* 請坐。◇ *He sat down on the bed.* 他在牀邊坐下。◇ *They sat down to consider the problem.* 他們坐下來考慮這一問題。◇ *Come in and sit yourselves down.* 都進來坐下。 **ˌsit ˈdown and do sth** to give sth time and attention in order to try to solve a problem or achieve sth 坐下來認真做某事： *This is something that we should sit down and discuss as a team.* 這件事我們應當坐下來一起認真討論一下。 **ˈsit for sb/sth** [no passive] to be a model for an artist or a photographer 為…做模特： *to sit for your portrait* 擺好姿勢讓畫家畫肖像 ◇ *She sat for Augustus John.* 她為奧古斯塔斯•約翰當過模特。 **ˌsit ˈin for sb** to do sb's job or perform their duties while they are away, sick, etc. 頂班；代某人履行職責 **SYN** **stand in for** **ˌsit ˈin on sth** to attend a meeting, class, etc. in order to listen to or learn from it rather than to take an active part 列席（會議）；旁聽（課） **ˈsit on sth** (*informal*) to have received a letter, report, etc. from sb and then not replied or taken any action concerning it 拖延；積壓；擱置： *They have been sitting on my application for a month now.* 他們壓着我的申請不辦有一個月了。 **ˌsit sth↔ˈout 1** to stay in a place and wait for sth unpleasant or boring to finish 耐心等到結束；熬到結束： *We sat out the storm in a cafe.* 我們坐在一家咖啡館裏，一直等到暴風雨過去。 **2** to not take part in a dance, game or other activity 坐在一旁（不參加跳舞、遊戲等活動） **ˈsit through sth** to stay until the end of a performance, speech, meeting, etc. that you think is boring or too long 坐到（表演、演講、會議等）結束： *We had to sit through nearly two hours of speeches.* 我們不得不耐着性子聽完將近兩個小時的講話。 **ˌsit ˈup 1** to be or move yourself into a sitting position, rather than lying down or leaning back 坐起來；坐直： *Sit up straight—don't slouch.* 坐直了，別無精打采的。 **2** to not go to bed until later than usual 熬夜；遲睡： *We sat up half the night, talking.* 我們談到了半夜才睡。 **ˌsit ˈup (and do sth)** (*informal*) to start to pay careful attention to what is happening, being said, etc. 關注起來；警覺起來： *The proposal had made his clients **sit up and take notice**.* 這項建議引起了他的主顧們的關注。 **ˌsit sb ˈup** to move sb into a sitting position after they have been lying down 使坐起來

Synonyms 同義詞辨析

sit

sit down • be seated • take a seat • perch

These words all mean to rest your weight on your bottom with your back upright, for example on a chair. 以上各詞均含坐下之意。

sit to rest your weight on your bottom with your back upright, for example on a chair 指坐： *May I sit here?* 我可以坐在這兒嗎？◇ *Sit still, will you!* 坐着別動！ **NOTE** **Sit** is usually used with an adverb or prepositional phrase to show where or how sb sits, but sometimes another phrase or clause is used to show what sb does while they are sitting. * sit 通常與副詞或介詞短語連用，表示坐的地方或方式，但有時也與另一短語或從句連用，表明坐着時在做某事： *We sat talking for hours.* 我們坐着談了好幾個小時。

sit down/ sit yourself down to move from a standing position to a sitting position 指坐下、就座： *Please sit down.* 請坐。◇ *Come in and sit yourselves down.* 都進來坐下。

be seated (*formal*) to be sitting 指坐着： *She was seated at the head of the table.* 她坐在桌子的上座。 **NOTE** **Be seated** is often used as a formal way of inviting sb to sit down. * be seated 常為請人就座的正式表達方式： *Please be seated.* 請就座。

take a seat to sit down 指坐下、就座 **NOTE** **Take a seat** is used especially as a polite way of inviting sb to sit down. * take a seat 尤作請人就座的禮貌用語： *Please take a seat.* 請坐。

perch (*rather informal*) to sit on sth, especially on the edge of sth 指坐在…上，尤指坐在…邊沿： *She perched herself on the edge of the bed.* 她坐在牀沿上。 **NOTE** **Perch** is always used with an adverb or prepositional phrase to show where sb is perching. * perch 總是與副詞或介詞短語連用表示坐的地方。

PATTERNS

- to sit/sit down/be seated/take a seat/perch **on** sth
- to sit/sit down/be seated/take a seat **in** sth

S

sitar /sɪˈtɑː(r); ˈsɪtɑː(r)/ *noun* a musical instrument from S Asia like a GUITAR, with a long neck and two sets of metal strings 西塔爾（源自南亞形似吉他的弦樂器） ➲ VISUAL VOCAB page V36

sit·com /ˈsɪtkɒm; *NAmE* -kɑːm/ (also *formal* **ˌsituation ˈcomedy**) *noun* [C, U] a regular programme on television that shows the same characters in different amusing situations 情景喜劇

ˈsit-down *noun* [sing.] (*BrE, informal*) a rest while sitting in a chair 坐下休息：*I need a cup of tea and a sit-down.* 我需要坐下來，喝杯茶，休息一下。▸ **ˈsit-down** *adj.* [only before noun]：*a sit-down protest* (= in which people sit down to block a road or the entrance to a building until people listen to their demands) 靜坐抗議 ◇ *a sit-down meal for 50 wedding guests* (= served to people sitting at tables) 為 50 位參加婚禮的客人擺坐式的宴席

site 0⁻ⁿ AW /saɪt/ *noun, verb*

■ *noun* **1** 0⁻ⁿ a place where a building, town, etc. was, is or will be located（建築物、城鎮等的）地點，位置，建築工地：*the site of a sixteenth century abbey* 一座十六世紀的修道院的舊址 ◇ *to work on a* ***building/construction site*** 在建築工地工作 ◇ *A site has been chosen for the new school.* 已為新學校選了校址。◇ *All the materials are* ***on site*** *so that work can start immediately.* 所有材料都已運抵工地，可以立即開工。➲ SYNONYMS at PLACE **2** 0⁻ⁿ a place where sth has happened or that is used for sth 現場；發生地；場所：*the site of the battle* 戰場 ◇ *an archaeological site* 考古現場 ◇ *a* ***camping/caravan site*** 營地；旅行拖車停車點 **3** 0⁻ⁿ (*computing* 計) a place on the Internet where a company, an organization, a university, etc. puts information 網站；站點 ➲ COLLOCATIONS at EMAIL ➲ see also MIRROR SITE, WEBSITE

■ *verb* [often passive] **~ sth + adv./prep.** to build or place sth in a particular position 使坐落在；為…選址：*There was a meeting to discuss the siting of the new school.* 已開會討論了新學校的選址。◇ *The castle is magnificently sited high up on a cliff.* 城堡坐落在高高的懸崖，十分壯觀。

ˈsit-in *noun* a protest in which a group of workers, students, etc. refuse to leave their factory, college, etc. until people listen to their demands（建築物內的）靜坐罷工，靜坐示威：*to* ***hold/stage a sit-in*** 舉行靜坐示威

sit·ter /ˈsɪtə(r)/ *noun* **1** a person who sits or stands somewhere so that sb can paint a picture of them or photograph them 擺姿勢讓人畫像（或拍照）的人 **2** (*especially NAmE*) = BABYSITTER **3** (*BrE, informal*) (in football (SOCCER) 足球) an easy chance to score a goal 得分良機

sit·ting /ˈsɪtɪŋ/ *noun* **1** a period of time during which a court or a parliament deals with its business（法院或議會的）開會，會議，開庭（期間） **2** a time when a meal is served in a hotel, etc. to a number of people at the same time（旅館等分段安排客人用餐的）一輪，一次：*A hundred people can be served* ***at one sitting*** (= at the same time). 可同時供一百人就餐。**3** a period of time that a person spends sitting and doing an activity 一次（坐着活動的時間）：*I read the book* ***in one sitting.*** 我坐下來一口氣就把那本書看完了。**4** a period of time when sb sits or stands to have their picture painted or be photographed（擺姿勢讓人畫像或拍照的）一次（時間）

ˌsitting ˈduck (also **ˌsitting ˈtarget**) *noun* a person or thing that is easy to attack 易受攻擊者；易被擊中的目標

ˈsitting room *noun* (*BrE*) = LIVING ROOM

ˌsitting ˈtenant *noun* (*BrE*) a person who is living in a rented house or flat and who has the legal right to stay there（房屋或公寓有合法權利的）現有房客，現租戶

situ ➲ IN SITU

situ·ate /ˈsɪtʃueɪt/ *verb* (*formal*) **1 ~ sth + adv./prep.** to build or place sth in a particular position 使位於；使坐落於 **2 ~ sth + adv./prep.** to consider how an idea, event, etc. is related to other things that influence your view of it 將…置於；使聯繫：*Let me try and situate the events in their historical context.* 我盡量把這些事件與其歷史背景聯繫起來。

situ·ated /ˈsɪtʃueɪtɪd/ *adj.* [not before noun] (*formal*) **1** in a particular place or position 位於；坐落在：*My bedroom was situated on the top floor of the house.* 我的卧室在房子的頂層。◇ *The hotel is* ***beautifully situated*** *in a quiet spot near the river.* 旅館環境優美，坐落在河邊一個僻靜的地方。◇ *All the best theatres and restaurants are situated within a few minutes' walk of each other.* 所有最好的劇院和飯店相隔只有幾分鐘的路。**2** (of a person, an organization, etc. 人、組織等) in a particular situation or in particular circumstances 處於…狀況；處境…：*Small businesses are well situated to benefit from the single market.* 小企業所處的形勢有利於從單一市場中受益。

situ·ation 0⁻ⁿ /ˌsɪtʃuˈeɪʃn/ *noun*

1 0⁻ⁿ all the circumstances and things that are happening at a particular time and in a particular place 情況；狀況；形勢；局面：*to be* ***in a difficult situation*** 處境困難 ◇ *You could get into* ***a situation where*** *you have to decide immediately.* 你可能遇上一種情況，使你不得不立刻作出決定。◇ *We have all been in similar embarrassing situations.* 我們都遇到過類似的尷尬局面。◇ *the present* ***economic/financial/political, etc. situation*** 目前的經濟、財政、政治等形勢 ◇ *He could see no way out of the situation.* 他找不到擺脱困境的出路。◇ *In your situation, I would look for another job.* 假如我是你的話，我會另找工作。◇ *What we have here is a crisis situation.* 我們在這裏所面臨的是一個危急局面。◇ *I'm in a* ***no-win situation*** (= whatever I do will be bad for me). 我處在一種注定要失敗的境地。**2** (*formal*) the kind of area or surroundings that a building or town has（建築物或城鎮的）地理位置，環境特點：*The town is in a delightful situation in a wide green valley.* 小城坐落在一個寬闊而草木蒼翠的河谷中，環境宜人。**3** (*old-fashioned* or *formal*) a job 職業；工作崗位：***Situations Vacant*** (= the title of the section in a newspaper where jobs are advertised) 招聘（報章中的招聘廣告欄） ➲ SYNONYMS at next page
IDM see SAVE *v.* ▸ **situ·ation·al** /ˌsɪtʃuˈeɪʃənl/ *adj.*

ˌsituation ˈcomedy *noun* [C, U] (*formal*) = SITCOM

ˈsit-up (also **crunch**) *noun* an exercise for making your stomach muscles strong, in which you lie on your back on the floor and raise the top part of your body to a sitting position 仰卧起坐 ➲ VISUAL VOCAB page V42

six 0⁻ⁿ /sɪks/ *number*

6 六 HELP There are examples of how to use numbers at the entry for **five**. 數詞用法示例見 five 條。

IDM **at ˌsixes and ˈsevens** (*informal*) in confusion; not well organized 亂七八糟；淩亂 **be ˌsix feet ˈunder** (*informal*) to be dead and in a grave 入土；在九泉之下 **hit/knock sb for ˈsix** (*BrE*) to affect sb very deeply 極大地影響某人 **it's six of ˌone and half a dozen of the ˈother** (*saying*) used to say that there is not much real difference between two possible choices 半斤八兩；不相上下

the ˌSix ˈCounties *noun* [pl.] a way of referring to Northern Ireland, used especially by people who want the whole of Ireland to be one country 北愛爾蘭六郡（尤指希望愛爾蘭統一的人對北愛爾蘭的一種提法）

ˌsix-ˈfigure *adj.* [only before noun] used to describe a number that is 100 000 or more 六位數的：*a six-figure salary* 六位數的薪金

six·fold /ˈsɪksfəʊld; *NAmE* -foʊld/ *adj., adv.* ➲ -FOLD

ˈsix-gun *noun* = SIX-SHOOTER

the ˌSix ˈNations *noun* [sing.] a RUGBY competition between England, France, Ireland, Italy, Scotland and Wales（英格蘭、法國、愛爾蘭、意大利、蘇格蘭、威爾士之間的）橄欖球六國聯賽

ˈsix-pack *noun* **1** a set of six bottles or cans sold together, especially of beer（尤指啤酒）六瓶裝，六罐裝 **2** (*informal*) stomach muscles that are very strong and that you can see clearly across sb's stomach 塊塊隆起的腹肌；六塊腹肌

six·pence /ˈsɪkspəns/ *noun* a British coin in use until 1971, worth six old pence 六便士硬幣（英國 1971 年以前使用）

'six-shooter (also **'six-gun**) *noun* (*especially NAmE*) a small gun that holds six bullets 六發左輪手槍

six·teen /ˌsɪksˈtiːn/ *number* 16 十六 ▸ **six·teenth** /ˌsɪksˈtiːnθ/ *ordinal number, noun* HELP There are examples of how to use ordinal numbers at the entry for **fifth**. 序數詞用法示例見 fifth 條。

ˌsix'teenth note (*NAmE*) (*BrE* **semi·quaver**) *noun* (*music* 音) a note that lasts half as long as a QUAVER/EIGHTH NOTE 十六分音符 ➲ picture at MUSIC

sixth /sɪksθ/ *ordinal number, noun*
■ ***ordinal number*** 6th 第六 HELP There are examples of how to use ordinal numbers at the entry for **fifth**. 序數詞用法示例見 fifth 條。
■ ***noun*** each of six equal parts of sth 六分之一

'sixth form *noun* [usually sing.] (*BrE*) the two final years at school for students between the ages of 16 and 18 who are preparing to take A LEVELS (= advanced level exams) 第六學級（英國中等學校的最後兩年，學生年齡在 16 至 18 歲之間，準備參加高級證書考試）：*Sue is in the sixth form now.* 蘇正在讀中學最後兩年。

ˌsixth-form 'college *noun* (in Britain) a school for students over the age of 16 （英國）第六學級學院

'sixth-former *noun* (*BrE*) a student who is in the sixth form at school 第六學級學生

ˌsixth 'sense *noun* [sing.] a special ability to know sth without using any of the five senses that include sight, touch, etc. 第六感覺；直覺：*My sixth sense told me to stay here and wait.* 直覺告訴我應該待在這兒等着。

sixty /ˈsɪksti/
1 *number* 60 六十 **2** *noun* **the sixties** [pl.] numbers, years or temperatures from 60 to 69 六十幾；六十年代 ▸ **six·ti·eth** /ˈsɪkstiəθ/ *ordinal number, noun* HELP There are examples of how to use ordinal numbers at the entry for **fifth**. 序數詞用法示例見 fifth 條。

IDM **in your 'sixties** between the ages of 60 and 69 *60 多歲

the ˌsixty-four ˌthousand ˌdollar 'question *noun* (*informal*) the thing that people most want to know, or that is most important 最想知道（或最重要）的事情；關鍵問題 ORIGIN From the name of a US television show which gave prizes of money to people who answered questions correctly. The correct answer to the last question was worth $64 000. 源自美國有獎競答電視節目名稱，答對最後一題的獎金為 64 000 元。

size /saɪz/ *noun, verb*
■ ***noun***
▸ HOW LARGE/SMALL 大小 **1** [U, C] how large or small a person or thing is 大小：*an area **the size of*** (= the same size as) *Wales* 一個面積相當於威爾士的地區 ◇ *They complained about the size of their gas bill.* 他們抱怨煤氣費用太高。◇ *Dogs come **in all shapes and sizes**.* 狗有大有小，模樣也各不相同。◇ *The facilities are excellent for a town that size.* 對於如此規模的一個城鎮來說，其市政設施堪稱一流。◇ *The kitchen is **a good size*** (= not small). 這廚房夠大的。◇ *It's similar **in size** to a tomato.* 大小和西紅柿差不多。 **2** [U] the large amount or extent of sth 大量；大規模：*You should have seen the size of their house!* 你真該看看他們的房子有多大！◇ *We were shocked at the size of his debts.* 他欠債之多讓我們震驚。
▸ OF CLOTHES/SHOES/GOODS 服裝；鞋；商品 **3** [C, U] one of a number of standard measurements in which clothes, shoes and other goods are made and sold 尺碼；號：*The jacket was the wrong size.* 這件夾克尺碼不對。◇ *It's not my size.* 這個號我不能穿。◇ *They didn't have the jacket **in my size**.* 那款夾克沒有我穿的尺碼。◇ *She's a size 12 in clothes.* 她穿 12 號的衣服。◇ *The hats are made in three sizes: small, medium and large.* 這些帽子分小、中、大三個尺碼。◇ *I need a bigger/smaller size.* 我需要一件尺碼稍大／稍小的。◇ *What size do you take?* 你穿多大號的？◇ *She takes (a) size 5 in shoes.* 她穿 5 號鞋。◇ *Do you have these shoes in (a) size 5?* 這款鞋有 5 號的嗎？◇ *Try this one **for size*** (= to see if it is the

Synonyms 同義詞辨析

situation

circumstances • position • conditions • things • the case • state of affairs

These are all words for the conditions and facts that are connected with and affect the way things are. 以上各詞均指情況、狀況。

situation all the things that are happening at a particular time and in a particular place 指情況、狀況、形勢、局面：*the present economic situation* 目前的經濟形勢

circumstances the facts that are connected with and affect a situation, an event or an action; the conditions of a person's life, especially the money they have 指條件、環境、狀況、境況、（尤指）經濟狀況：*The ship sank in mysterious circumstances.* 那艘船神秘地沉沒了。

position the situation that sb is in, especially when it affects what they can and cannot do 指處境、地位、狀況：*She felt she was in a position of power.* 她覺得她自己有權力。

conditions the circumstances in which people live, work or do things; the physical situation that affects how sth happens 指居住、工作或做事情的環境、境況、條件，影響某事發生的物質環境、狀態、條件：*We were forced to work outside in freezing conditions.* 我們被迫在戶外冰凍的環境下工作。

CIRCUMSTANCES OR CONDITIONS? 用 circumstances 還是 conditions？

Circumstances refers to sb's financial situation; **conditions** are things such as the quality and amount of food or shelter they have. The **circumstances** that affect an event are the facts surrounding it; the **conditions** that affect it are usually physical ones, such as the weather. * circumstances 指人的經濟狀況；conditions 指人的食宿狀況。circumstances 指影響某事的周邊環境；conditions 通常指影響某事的物質環境，如天氣。

things (*rather informal*) the general situation, as it affects sb 指形勢、局面、情況、事態：*Hi, Jane! How are things?* 喂，簡，近來怎麼樣？◇ *Think things over before you decide.* 先把情況考慮周全再作決定。

the case the true situation 指實情、事實：*If that is the case* (= if the situation described is true), *we need more staff.* 如果真是那樣，我們就需要更多的員工了。

state of affairs a situation 指事態、情況、形勢：*How did this unhappy state of affairs come about?* 這種不幸的情況是怎麼發生的呢？

SITUATION OR STATE OF AFFAIRS? 用 situation 還是 state of affairs？

State of affairs is mostly used with *this*. It is also used with adjectives describing how good or bad a situation is, such as *happy*, *sorry*, *shocking*, *sad* and *unhappy*, as well as those relating to time, such as *present* and *current*. **Situation** is much more frequent and is used in a wider variety of contexts. * state of affairs 多與 this 連用，亦與表示形勢好壞的形容詞（如 happy、sorry、shocking、sad 和 unhappy）以及與時間有關的形容詞（如 present 和 current）連用。situation 常用得多，且用於更廣泛的語境中。

PATTERNS

- **in** (a) particular situation/circumstances/position/state of affairs
- the/sb's **economic/financial/social** situation/circumstances/position/conditions
- (a/an) **happy/unhappy** situation/circumstances/position/state of affairs
- to **look at/review** the situation/circumstances/conditions/things

S

correct size). 試試這件，看尺碼合適不合適。◇ *The glass can be* ***cut to size*** (= cut to the exact measurements) *for you.* 玻璃可以切割成你要的尺寸。 **HELP** To ask about the size of something, you usually say *How big?*. You use *What size?* to ask about something that is produced in fixed measurements. 問某物的大小，通常說 How big?。What size? 則用來詢問有幾種固定尺寸的製成品。

▸ **-SIZED/-SIZE** …大小 **4** (in adjectives 構成形容詞) having the size mentioned …大小的；…規模的： *a medium-sized house* 中等大小的房子 ◇ *Cut it into bite-size pieces.* 把它切成能一口吃下去的小塊。 ➲ see also KING-SIZE, MAN-SIZED, PINT-SIZED, QUEEN-SIZE

▸ **STICKY SUBSTANCE** 膠料 **5** [U] a sticky substance that is used for making material stiff or for preparing walls for WALLPAPER （使織物等堅挺的）膠料，漿料；（貼壁紙用的）塗料

IDM **cut sb down to 'size** to show sb that they are not as important as they think they are 使某人有自知之明；讓某人知道自己是誰 **that's about the 'size of it** (*informal*) that's how the situation seems to be 情況大致就是這樣： *'So they won't pay up?' 'That's about the size of it.'* "這麼說他們不願意打算還清欠款？" "基本是這樣。"

■ ***verb***

▸ **GIVE SIZE** 定大小 **1** [usually passive] **~ sth** to mark the size of sth; to give a size to sth 標定…的大小；確定…的尺寸： *The screws are sized in millimetres.* 這些螺絲是用毫米標定大小的。

▸ **CHANGE SIZE** 改變大小 **2** [usually passive] **~ sth** to change the size of sth 改變…的大小： *The fonts can be sized according to what effect you want.* 可根據你想要的效果改變字號。

▸ **MAKE STICKY** 使膠黏 **3 ~ sth** to cover sth with a sticky substance called SIZE 上膠料；上漿；上塗料

PHR V **,size sb/sth↔'up** (*informal*) to form a judgement or an opinion about sb/sth 估量；判斷 **SYN** **sum up**： *She knew that he was looking at her, sizing her up.* 她知道他在盯着她看，打量她。◇ *He sized up the situation very quickly.* 他很快對形勢作出了判斷。

size·able (also **siz·able**) /'saɪzəbl/ *adj.* fairly large 相當大的 **SYN** **considerable**： *The town has a sizeable Sikh population.* 城裏有為數眾多的錫克教教徒。

,size 'zero *noun* [U, C] (in the US) the smallest size for women's clothes, used to describe women who are extremely thin 零號（在美國指女服的最小號，用以描述極瘦女子）： *size zero models and celebrities* 瘦極了的模特兒和名人 ◇ *She is a size zero.* 她瘦得不能再瘦。

siz·zle /'sɪzl/ *verb* [I] to make the sound of food frying in hot oil 發出（油煎食物的）嘶嘶聲： *sizzling sausages* 煎得嘶嘶作響的香腸 ▸ **siz·zle** *noun* [sing.]

siz·zling /'sɪzlɪŋ/ *adj.* **1** very hot 酷熱的： *sizzling summer temperatures* 夏日灼人的高溫 **2** very exciting 熱烈的；激情迸發的： *a sizzling love affair* 熱烈的風流韻事

sjam·bok /'ʃæmbɒk; *NAmE* -bɑːk/ *noun* (*SAfrE*) a long, stiff WHIP made of leather 粗長皮鞭

ska /skɑː/ *noun* [U] a type of fast popular music with strong rhythms, developed in Jamaica in the 1960s and that developed into REGGAE 斯卡（20 世紀 60 年代興起於牙買加的一種節奏強而快的流行音樂，後來發展成雷蓋音樂）

skank /skæŋk/ *noun* (*informal, especially NAmE*) an unpleasant person 缺德的人；討厭鬼

skanky /'skæŋki/ *adj.* (*informal, especially NAmE*) very unpleasant 令人反感的；令人討厭的

skate /skeɪt/ *verb, noun*

■ ***verb*** **1** [I, T] to move on skates (usually referring to ICE SKATING, if no other information is given) （通常指）滑冰，溜冰： *Can you skate?* 你會滑冰嗎？◇ *It was so cold that we were able to* ***go skating*** *on the lake.* 天氣極冷，我們能到湖上去滑冰了。◇ **~ sth** *He skated an exciting programme at the American Championships.* 他在美國錦標賽上滑出一組扣人心弦的動作。 **2** [I] to ride on a SKATEBOARD 滑（滑板） **IDM** see THIN *adj.*

PHR V **,skate 'over sth** to avoid talking about or considering a difficult subject 迴避；避免涉及： *He politely skated over the issue.* 他禮貌地避開了那個問題。

■ ***noun*** **1** = ICE SKATE, ROLLER SKATE： *a pair of skates* 一雙冰鞋 ➲ VISUAL VOCAB page V44 **2** (*pl.* **skate** or **skates**) a large flat sea fish that can be eaten 鰩（扁體魚，可食用）

IDM **get/put your 'skates on** (*BrE, informal*) used to tell sb to hurry 趕緊；趕快： *Get your skates on or you'll miss the bus.* 快點，要不你就趕不上公共汽車了。

skate·board /'skeɪtbɔːd; *NAmE* -bɔːrd/ *noun* a short narrow board with small wheels at each end, which you stand on and ride as a sport 滑板： *a* ***skateboard park/ramp*** 滑板場 / 坡道 ▸ **skate·board** *verb* [I] **skate·board·er** *noun* **skate·board·ing** *noun* [U]： *a skateboarding magazine* 滑板運動雜誌 ➲ VISUAL VOCAB page V40

skate·park /'skeɪtpɑːk; *NAmE* -pɑːrk/ *noun* an area built for people to use SKATEBOARDS, with slopes, curves, etc. 滑板運動場（有斜坡、曲面等）

skater /'skeɪtə(r)/ *noun* **1** a person who skates for pleasure or as a sport 滑冰者；溜冰者；滑冰運動員： *a* ***figure/speed skater*** 花樣滑冰 / 速滑運動員 ➲ see also ICE SKATER **2** = SKATEBOARDER： *Extreme skaters perform jumps, spins, flips, etc.* 極限滑板運動員能做跳躍、旋轉、空翻等動作。

'skate shoe (*especially NAmE*) (also **Heely™** especially in *BrE*) *noun* a sports shoe that has one or more wheels underneath it 暴走鞋；飛行鞋；滑輪運動鞋

skat·ing /'skeɪtɪŋ/ *noun* [U] **1** (also **'ice skating**) the sport or activity of moving on ice on SKATES 滑冰；溜冰： *to go skating* 去滑冰 ➲ see also FIGURE-SKATING, SPEED SKATING **2** = ROLLER SKATING **IDM** see THIN *adj.*

'skating rink (also **rink**) *noun* **1** = ICE RINK ➲ VISUAL VOCAB page V40 **2** an area or a building where you can ROLLER SKATE 旱冰場；旱冰館；輪式溜冰場

ske·dad·dle /skɪ'dædl/ *verb* [I] (*informal, humorous*) to move away or leave a place quickly, especially in order to avoid sb 匆忙離去，溜走（尤指為了躲避某人）

skeet·er /'skiːtə(r)/ *noun* (*NAmE, informal, humorous*) = MOSQUITO

skeet shooting /'skiːt ʃuːtɪŋ/ (*NAmE*) (*BrE* **,clay 'pigeon shooting**) *noun* a sport in which a disc of baked clay (called a **clay pigeon**) is thrown into the air for people to shoot at 泥鴿飛靶射擊運動

skein /skeɪn/ *noun* a long piece of wool, thread, or YARN that is loosely tied together 一束，一綹（毛線、線或紗）

skel·etal /'skelətl/ *adj.* **1** (*technical* 術語) connected with the skeleton of a person or an animal 骨骼的 **2** looking like a skeleton 骨瘦如柴的： *skeletal figures dressed in rags* 衣衫襤褸、骨瘦如柴的人 **3** that exists only in a basic form, as an outline 梗概的；提綱性的；提要性的；輪廓的： *He has written only a skeletal plot for the book so far.* 那本書他目前只寫了一個情節梗概。

skel·eton /'skelɪtn/ *noun* **1** [C] the structure of bones that supports the body of a person or an animal; a model of this structure 骨骼；骨架；骨骼標本： *The human skeleton consists of 206 bones.* 人的骨骼由 206 塊骨頭組成。◇ *a dinosaur skeleton* 恐龍骨架 ➲ VISUAL VOCAB page V59 **2** [C] (*informal*) a very thin person or animal 骨瘦如柴的人（或動物） **3** [C, usually sing.] the main structure that supports a building, etc. （建築物等的）骨架，框架 **SYN** **framework**： *Only the concrete skeleton of the factory remained.* 廠房只剩下混凝土骨架了。 **4** [C, usually sing.] the basic outline of a plan, piece of writing, etc. to which more details can be added later 梗概；提綱；提要；輪廓： *Examples were used to flesh out the skeleton of the argument.* 通過例證使乾巴巴的論點充實起來。 **5** [C] **~ staff, crew, etc.** the smallest number of people, etc. that you need to do sth （維持運轉所需的）最少人員，基幹人員： *There will only be a skeleton staff on duty over the holiday.* 假期將只留必需的少數職員值班。◇ *We managed to operate a skeleton bus service during the strike.* 罷工期間，我們設法保持最起碼的公共汽車營運。 **6** [C] (*sport* 體) a type of SLEDGE/

SLED (= a vehicle for sliding over ice) for racing, used by one person lying on their front with their feet pointing backwards（一種單人比賽用的）俯式冰橇 **7** [U] the sport or event of racing down a special track of ice on a skeleton 俯式冰橇運動：*Canada won gold and silver in the skeleton.* 加拿大選手在俯式冰橇項目中包攬金銀牌。

IDM **a skeleton in the 'cupboard** (*BrE*) (also **a skeleton in the 'closet** *NAmE, BrE*) (*informal*) something shocking, embarrassing, etc. that has happened to you or your family in the past that you want to keep secret 隱衷；不可外揚的家醜

'skeleton key *noun* a key that will open several different locks 萬能鑰匙

skelm /skelm/ *noun* (*SAfrE*) a person that you believe is a criminal or that you do not trust 地痞；流氓；無賴；不可信任的人

skep·tic (*NAmE*) (*BrE* **scep·tic**) /ˈskeptɪk/ *noun* a person who usually doubts that claims or statements are true, especially those that other people believe in 慣持懷疑態度的人；懷疑論者

skep·tical (*NAmE*) (*BrE* **scep·tical**) /ˈskeptɪkl/ *adj.* **~ (about/of sth)** having doubts that a claim or statement is true or that sth will happen 懷疑的：*I am skeptical about his chances of winning.* 我懷疑他獲勝的可能性。◇ *The public remain skeptical of these claims.* 公眾對這些說法仍持懷疑態度。◇ *She looked highly skeptical.* 她一臉深表懷疑的神色。▶ **skep·tic·al·ly** (*NAmE*) (*BrE* **scep·tic·al·ly**) /-kli/ *adv.*

skep·ti·cism (*NAmE*) (*BrE* **scep·ti·cism**) /ˈskeptɪsɪzəm/ *noun* [U, sing.] an attitude of doubting that claims or statements are true or that sth will happen 懷疑態度；懷疑主義：*Such claims should be regarded with a certain amount of skepticism.* 對這樣的說法，大可不必全信。

sketch /sketʃ/ *noun, verb*

■ ***noun*** **1** a simple picture that is drawn quickly and does not have many details 素描；速寫；草圖：*The artist is making sketches for his next painting.* 畫家正為他的下一幅作品畫素描。◇ *She drew a* ***sketch map*** *of the area to show us the way.* 她畫了一幅這個地區的略圖，用來給我們指路。➲ **SYNONYMS** at PICTURE ➲ **COLLOCATIONS** at ART **2** a short funny scene on television, in the theatre, etc. 幽默短劇；小品：*The drama group did a sketch about a couple buying a new car.* 劇社上演了一齣夫妻二人買新車的短劇。 **3** a short report or story that gives only basic details about sth 簡報；速寫；概述：*a biographical sketch of the Prime Minister* 首相生平簡介

■ ***verb*** **1** [T, I] **~ (sb/sth)** to make a quick drawing of sb/sth 畫素描；畫速寫：*He quickly sketched the view from the window.* 他很快勾勒出了窗外的風景。**2** [T] **~ sth (out)** to give a general description of sth, giving only the basic facts 概述；簡述 SYN **outline**：*She sketched out her plan for tackling the problem.* 她簡要敘述了解決問題的計劃。

PHR V **,sketch sth↔'in** to give more information or details about sth 補充說明；給…補充細節

sketch·book /ˈsketʃbʊk/ (also **'sketch pad**) *noun* a book of sheets of paper for drawing on 素描簿；速寫冊；寫生本

sketchy /ˈsketʃi/ *adj.* (**sketch·ier**, **sketch·iest**) not complete or detailed and therefore not very useful 粗略的；概略的；不完備的 SYN **rough**：*He gave us a very sketchy account of his visit.* 他跟我們非常粗略地講了他參觀的情況。◇ *sketchy notes* 簡略的筆記 ▶ **sketch·ily** *adv.* **sketchi·ness** *noun* [U]

skew /skjuː/ *verb* **1** [T] **~ sth** to change or influence sth with the result that it is not accurate, fair, normal, etc. 歪曲；曲解；使不公允；影響…的準確性：*to skew the statistics* 影響統計數字的準確性 **2** [I] **+ adv./prep.** (*BrE*) to move or lie at an angle, especially in a position that is not normal 偏離；歪斜：*The ball skewed off at a right angle.* 球呈直角偏離彈了出去。

skew·bald /ˈskjuːbɔːld/ *adj.* (of a horse 馬) with areas on it of white and another colour, usually not black 白花斑的（通常不帶黑色）➲ compare PIEBALD ▶ **skew·bald** *noun*：*He was riding a skewbald.* 他騎着一匹白花斑馬。

skewed /skjuːd/ *adj.* **1** (of information 信息) not accurate or correct 歪曲的；有偏頗的；不準確的 SYN **distorted**：*skewed statistics* 不準確的統計 **2 ~ (towards sb/sth)** directed towards a particular group, place, etc. in a way that may not be accurate or fair 偏向（或偏重）…的：*The book is heavily skewed towards American readers.* 這本書嚴重傾向於美國讀者。 **3** not straight or level 偏的；斜的；歪的：*The car had ended up skewed across the road.* 汽車最終斜着停在公路上。➲ see also ASKEW

skew·er /ˈskjuːə(r)/ *noun, verb*

■ ***noun*** a long thin pointed piece of metal or wood that is pushed through pieces of meat, vegetables, etc. to hold them together while they are cooking, or used to test whether sth is completely cooked（烹飪用）扦子，串肉扦

■ ***verb*** **~ sth** to push a skewer or other thin pointed object through sth 用扦子串住

,skew-'whiff *adj.* (*BrE, informal*) not straight 偏的；斜的；歪的

ski /skiː/ *noun, adj., verb*

■ ***noun*** (*pl.* **skis**) **1** one of a pair of long narrow pieces of wood, metal or plastic that you attach to boots so that you can move smoothly over snow 滑雪板：*a pair of skis* 一副滑雪板 ➲ **VISUAL VOCAB** pages V48, V53 **2** = WATERSKI

■ ***adj.*** [only before noun] connected with the sport of skiing 滑雪的：*ski boots* 滑雪靴 ◇ *the ski slopes* 滑雪坡

■ ***verb*** (**ski·ing**, **skied**, **skied**) **1** [I] **(+ adv./prep.)** to move over snow on skis, especially as a sport 滑雪（運動） **2 go skiing** [I] to spend time skiing for pleasure 滑雪（作為娛樂）：*We went skiing in France in March.* 三月份我們去法國滑雪了。➲ see also SKIING, WATERSKI

skid /skɪd/ *verb, noun*

■ ***verb*** (**-dd-**) [I] (usually of a vehicle 通常指車輛) to slide sideways or forwards in an uncontrolled way 側滑；打滑；滑行：*The car skidded on the ice and went straight into the wall.* 汽車在冰上打滑，逕直撞到了牆上。◇ *The taxi* ***skidded to a halt*** *just in time.* 出租車滑行了一段路後，及時停了下來。◇ *Her foot skidded on the wet floor and she fell heavily.* 她的腳在濕地板上一滑，重重地摔了一跤。

■ ***noun*** **1** the movement of a vehicle when it suddenly slides sideways in an uncontrolled way 側滑；打滑；突然向一側滑行：*The motorbike* ***went into a skid.*** 摩托車朝一側滑了出去。◇ *The* ***skid marks*** *on the road showed how fast the car had been travelling.* 公路上留下的滑行痕跡說明這輛車當時開得有多快。 **2** a part that is underneath some aircraft, beside the wheels, and is used for landing（飛機的）起落橇，滑橇：*the skids of a helicopter* 直升機的起落橇 ➲ **VISUAL VOCAB** page V53

IDM **put the 'skids under sb/sth** (*informal*) to stop sb/sth from being successful or making progress 使失敗；使走下坡路 **be on the 'skids** (*informal*) to be in a bad situation that will get worse 逐漸衰落；走下坡路

skid·pan /ˈskɪdpæn/ *noun* an area with a surface that is especially prepared so that drivers can practise controlling skids（供駕車者練習控制車輛打滑的）轉向試驗場

,skid 'row *noun* [U] (*informal, especially NAmE*) used to describe the poorest part of a town, the sort of place where people who have no home or job and who drink too much alcohol live（城市中流浪、失業、酗酒的人聚居的）貧民區：*to be on skid row* 住在貧民區

skier /ˈskiːə(r)/ *noun* a person who skis 滑雪者

skies *pl.* of SKY

skiff /skɪf/ *noun* a small light boat for ROWING or sailing, usually for one person（通常指單人的）小划艇，小帆船

skif·fle /ˈskɪfl/ *noun* a type of music popular in the 1950s, that was a mixture of JAZZ and FOLK MUSIC 即興搖滾樂（流行於 20 世紀 50 年代，結合了爵士樂和民間音樂）

S

ski·ing /ˈskiːɪŋ/ *noun* [U] the sport or activity of moving over snow on skis 滑雪（運動）：*to go skiing* 去滑雪 ◇ *downhill/cross-country skiing* 速降／越野滑雪 ◇ *a skiing holiday/instructor/lesson/vacation* 滑雪假日／教練／課／假期

ski·joring /ˈskiːdʒɔːrɪŋ; ˌskiːˈdʒɔːr-/ *noun* [U] the activity of being pulled over snow or ice on skis, by a horse or dog 乘馬（或狗）拉雪橇

ˈski jump *noun* a very steep artificial slope that ends suddenly and that is covered with snow. People ski down the slope, jump off the end and see how far they can travel through the air before landing. 跳台滑雪 ▸ **ˈski jumper** *noun* **ˈski jumping** *noun* [U]：*Is ski jumping an Olympic sport?* 跳台滑雪是奧運會項目嗎？◇ *the Swiss ski-jumping team* 瑞士跳台滑雪隊

skil·ful 0-w (*especially US* **skill·ful**) /ˈskɪlfl/ *adj.*
1 0-w (of a person 人) good at doing sth, especially sth that needs a particular ability or special training 技術好的；功夫深的；熟練的 SYN **accomplished**：*a skilful player/performer/teacher* 技術好的運動員；功夫深的表演者；會教學的老師 **2** 0-w made or done very well 製作精良的；處理巧妙的 SYN **professional**：*Thanks to her skilful handling of the affair, the problem was averted.* 多虧她對事情處理得巧妙，才避免了麻煩。▸ **skil·ful·ly** 0-w /-fəli/ *adv.*

ˈski lift *noun* a machine for taking SKIERS up a slope so that they can then ski down（運送滑雪者上坡的）上山吊椅

skill 0-w /skɪl/ *noun*
1 0-w [U] the ability to do sth well 技巧；技藝：*The job requires skill and an eye for detail.* 這項工作需要技巧和敏銳的眼光。◇ **~ in/at sth/doing sth** *What made him remarkable as a photographer was his skill in capturing the moment.* 他捕捉瞬間畫面的能力使他成為一名不同凡響的攝影師。 **2** 0-w [C] a particular ability or type of ability 技術；技能：*We need people with practical skills like carpentry.* 我們需要有木工等實用技術的人。◇ *management skills* 管理技巧

skilled 0-w /skɪld/ *adj.*
1 0-w having enough ability, experience and knowledge to be able to do sth well 有技能的；熟練的：*a skilled engineer/negotiator/craftsman* 高明的工程師；老練的談判者；技術熟練的工匠 ◇ *a shortage of **skilled labour*** (= people who have had training in a skill) 缺乏技術工人 ◇ **~ in/at sth/doing sth** *She is **highly skilled** at dealing with difficult customers.* 應付難纏的顧客她很有一手。 **2** 0-w (of a job 工作) needing special abilities or training 需要專門技術的 SYN **expert**：*Furniture-making is very skilled work.* 做傢具是技術性很強的活兒。OPP **unskilled**

skil·let /ˈskɪlɪt/ *noun* (*NAmE*) = FRYING PAN

skill·ful (*NAmE*) = SKILFUL

ˈskill set *noun* a person's range of skills or abilities（某人）一應技能綜合

skim /skɪm/ *verb* (**-mm-**) **1** [T] to remove fat, cream, etc. from the surface of a liquid 撇去（液體上的油脂或乳脂等）：**~ sth off/from sth** *Skim the scum off the jam and let it cool.* 撇去果醬上的浮沫，讓它冷卻。◇ **~ sth** *Skim the jam and let it cool.* 撇去果醬上的浮沫，讓它冷卻。 **2** [I, T, no passive] to move quickly and lightly over a surface, not touching it or only touching it occasionally; to make sth do this（使）掠過，擦過，滑過：**~ along/over, etc. sth** *We watched the birds skimming over the lake.* 我們看着鳥兒貼着湖面飛過。◇ **~ sth** *The speedboat took off, skimming the waves.* 快艇擦着波浪飛馳而去。◇ (*figurative*) *This report has barely **skimmed the surface** of the subject.* 報告對這個問題談得很膚淺。◇ **~ sth across, over, etc. sth** (*BrE*) *Small boys were skimming stones across the water.* 幾個小男孩用石塊打水漂。➲ see also SKIP *v.* (7) **3** [I, T] to read sth quickly in order to find a particular point or the main points 瀏覽；略讀：**~ through/over sth** *He skimmed through the article trying to find his name.* 他瀏覽文章找自己的名字。◇ **~ sth** *I always skim the financial section of the newspaper.* 我總要瀏覽一下報紙上的金融版。 **4** [T] **~ sth (from sth)** (*informal*) to steal small amounts of money frequently over a period of time 慣偷（小數額的錢） **5** [I, T] **~ (sth)** to illegally copy electronic information from a credit card in order to use it without the owner's permission 盜用（信用卡電子信息）
PHR V **ˌskim sth/sb↔ˈoff** to take for yourself the best part of sth, often in an unfair way（常指不公平地）攫取（最好的部份）；撈取（精華部份）

ˌskimmed ˈmilk (*BrE*) (also **ˌskim ˈmilk** *NAmE, BrE*) *noun* [U] milk that contains less fat than normal because the cream has been removed from it 脫脂奶

skimp /skɪmp/ *verb* [I] **~ (on sth)** to try to spend less time, money, etc. on sth than is really needed 節省，吝惜（時間、錢等）：*Older people should not skimp on food or heating.* 老人吃飯和取暖不應吝惜。

skimpy /ˈskɪmpi/ *adj.* (**skimp·ier**, **skimpi·est**) **1** (of clothes 衣服) very small and not covering much of your body 小而暴露的：*a skimpy dress* 短而暴露的連衣裙 **2** (*disapproving*) not large enough in amount or size（數量或大小）不足的，不夠的：*a skimpy meal* 吃不飽的一頓飯 ◇ *They provided only skimpy details.* 他們提供的細節不充分。

skin 0-w /skɪn/ *noun, verb*
■ ***noun***
▸ **ON BODY** 身體 **1** 0-w [U, C] the layer of TISSUE that covers the body 皮；皮膚：*to have **dark/fair/olive, etc. skin*** 皮膚黝黑、白皙、淺褐色等 ◇ *The snake sheds its skin once a year.* 蛇一年蛻一次皮。◇ *cosmetics for sensitive skins* 過敏性皮膚適用的化妝品 ◇ *skin cancer* 皮膚癌 ➲ COLLOCATIONS at PHYSICAL ➲ see also FORESKIN, REDSKIN
▸ **-SKINNED** 有…皮膚 **2** (in adjectives 構成形容詞) having the type of skin mentioned …皮膚的：*dark-skinned* 深色皮膚的 ◇ *fair-skinned* 白皙皮膚的 ➲ see also THICK-SKINNED, THIN-SKINNED
▸ **OF DEAD ANIMAL** 死獸 **3** 0-w [C, U] (often in compounds 常構成複合詞) the skin of a dead animal with or without its fur, used for making leather, etc.（獸）皮；毛皮；皮張：*The skins are removed and laid out to dry.* 皮剝下來，攤開晾乾。◇ *a tiger skin rug* 虎皮毯
▸ **OF FRUIT/VEGETABLES** 水果；蔬菜 **4** 0-w [C, U] the outer layer of some fruits and vegetables（某些果實和蔬菜的）皮，殼：*Remove the skins by soaking the tomatoes in hot water.* 把西紅柿放在熱水裏燙一下去皮。➲ VISUAL VOCAB page V30 ➲ see also BANANA SKIN ➲ compare PEEL *n.* (1), RIND (1), ZEST (3)
▸ **OF SAUSAGE** 香腸 **5** [C, U] the thin outer layer of a SAUSAGE 外皮；腸衣：*Prick the skins before grilling.* 烤前先在腸衣上扎孔。
▸ **ON LIQUIDS** 液體 **6** [C, U] the thin layer that forms on the surface of some liquids, especially when they become cold（尤指冷卻時形成的）薄層，皮：*A skin had formed on the top of the milk.* 奶上結了一層奶皮。
▸ **OUTSIDE LAYER** 外殼 **7** [C] a layer that covers the outside of sth 外殼；外層：*the outer skin of the earth* 地殼 ◇ *the metal skin of the aircraft* 飛機的金屬外殼 **8** [C] a special cover for any small electronic device that you can carry with you so that you can listen to music（便攜式電子音樂播放器的）護套，保護殼：*You can create your own custom skin for your iPod.* 你可以為你的 iPod 製作個性化護套。
▸ **IN A COMPUTER PROGRAM** 計算機程序 **9** [C] (*computing* 計) the INTERFACE of a computer program (= the way a computer program presents information on screen), that the user can change to suit their particular preferences 電腦程式的用戶界面（可按個人喜好變換）
IDM **by the ˌskin of your ˈteeth** (*informal*) if you do sth **by the skin of your teeth**, you only just manage to do it 剛好；勉強 **get under sb's ˈskin** (*informal*) to annoy sb 惹某人生氣（或惱火）：*Don't let him get under your skin.* 別讓他惹你生氣。 **have got sb under your ˈskin** (*informal*) to be extremely attracted to sb 極其迷戀；被某人深深打動 **it's no skin off ˈmy, ˈyour, ˈhis, etc. nose** (*informal*) used to say that sb is not upset or annoyed about sth because it does not affect them in a bad way（指某人沒有受到不良影響）這不關某人的事，這跟某人沒關係 **make your ˈskin crawl** to make you

feel afraid or full of disgust 使人毛骨悚然；讓人起雞皮疙瘩 **(nothing but/all/only) skin and 'bone** (*informal*) extremely thin in a way that is not attractive or healthy 瘦得皮包骨；瘦骨嶙峋 ➲ more at JUMP *v.*, SAVE *v.*, THICK *adj.*, THIN *adj.*

■ *verb* (-nn-)

‣ **ANIMAL/FRUIT/VEGETABLE** 動物；水果；蔬菜 **1 ~ sth** to take the skin off an animal, a fruit or a vegetable 剝皮；扒皮；削皮：*You'll need four ripe tomatoes, skinned and chopped.* 需要四個熟了的西紅柿，去皮切碎。

‣ **PART OF BODY** 身體部位 **2 ~ sth** to rub the skin off part of your body by accident 擦破（身體某部位的）皮膚：*He skinned his knees climbing down the tree.* 他從樹上爬下來時把膝蓋蹭破了。**IDM** see EYE *n.*, WAY *n.*

PHR V **,skin 'up** (*BrE, informal*) to make a cigarette containing MARIJUANA 用大麻做紙煙

skin·care /'skɪnkeə(r); *NAmE* -ker/ *noun* [U] the use of creams and special products to look after your skin 皮膚護理；護膚

,skin-'deep *adj.* [not usually before noun] (of a feeling or an attitude 感情或態度) not as important or strongly felt as it appears to be 不深刻；膚淺 **SYN** **superficial**

IDM see BEAUTY

'skin-diving *noun* [U] the sport or activity of swimming underwater with simple breathing equipment but without a special suit for protection 自由潛水（只用簡單呼吸設備）：*to go skin-diving* 去自由潛泳 ▸ **'skin-diver** *noun*

skin·flint /'skɪnflɪnt/ *noun* (*informal, disapproving*) a person who does not like spending money 吝嗇鬼；鐵公雞 **SYN** **miser**

skin·ful /'skɪnfʊl/ *noun* [usually sing.] (*BrE, slang*) a large quantity of alcohol to drink, enough to make you very drunk 足以喝醉的量

'skin graft *noun* a medical operation in which healthy skin is taken from one part of sb's body and placed over another part to replace skin that has been burned or damaged; a piece of skin that is moved in this way 植皮；皮膚移植；皮移植片

skin·head /'skɪnhed/ *noun* a young person with very short hair, especially one who is violent, aggressive and RACIST 光頭仔（尤指暴虐、好鬥的青年種族主義者）

skink /skɪŋk/ *noun* a LIZARD with short legs or with no legs 石龍子（蜥蜴，肢體不發達或完全退化）

skinny /'skɪni/ *adj.*, *noun*

S

■ *adj.* (**skin·nier**, **skin·ni·est**) **1** (*informal*, usually *disapproving*) very thin, especially in a way that you find unpleasant or ugly 極瘦的；乾瘦的；皮包骨的：*skinny legs* 乾瘦的腿 **2** (of clothes 衣服) designed to fit closely to the body 緊身的：*a skinny sweater* 緊身套頭衫 **3** (*NAmE, informal*) low in fat 低脂肪的：*a skinny latte* 低脂肪的熱奶沫咖啡

■ *noun* [U] **the ~ (on sb/sth)** (*NAmE, informal*) information about sb/sth, especially details that are not generally known（不公開的）信息；內幕消息：*This book gives you the skinny on Hollywood.* 這本書披露了好萊塢的內幕。

'skinny-dipping *noun* [U] (*informal*) swimming without any clothes on 裸泳

skint /skɪnt/ *adj.* [not usually before noun] (*BrE, informal*) having no money 沒錢；不名一文

skin·tight /'skɪn'taɪt/ *adj.* (of clothes 衣服) fitting very closely to the body 緊身的

skip /skɪp/ *verb*, *noun*

■ *verb* (-pp-)

‣ **MOVE WITH JUMPS** 蹦蹦跳跳地走 **1** [I] (+ **adv./prep.**) to move forwards lightly and quickly making a little jump with each step 蹦蹦跳跳地走：*She skipped happily along beside me.* 她連蹦帶跳，高高興興地跟着我走。

‣ **JUMP OVER ROPE** 跳繩 **2** [I] (*BrE*) (*NAmE* **,jump 'rope**, **,skip 'rope**) [T] to jump over a rope which is held at both ends by yourself or by two other people and is passed again and again over your head and under your feet 跳繩：*The girls were skipping in the playground.* 姑娘們在操場上跳繩。◇ *She likes to skip rope as a warm-up.* 她喜歡以跳繩來熱身。

‣ **NOT DO STH** 不做某事 **3** [T] **~ sth** to not do sth that you usually do or should do 不做（應做的事等）；不參加：*I often skip breakfast altogether.* 我常常乾脆不吃早飯。◇ (*especially NAmE*) *She decided to* **skip class** *that afternoon.* 她決定那天下午逃課。 **4** [T, I] to leave out sth that would normally be the next thing that you would do, read, etc. 跳過（正常的步驟等）；略過；漏過：**~ sth** *You can skip the next chapter if you have covered the topic in class.* 下一章，你要是在課堂上已經講到了，就可以跳過。◇ **~ over sth** *I skipped over the last part of the book.* 那本書的最後一部份我略過沒讀。◇ **~ to sth** *I suggest we skip to the last item on the agenda.* 我建議我們跳到議程的最後一項。

‣ **CHANGE QUICKLY** 快速轉換 **5** [I] **+ adv./prep.** to move from one place to another or from one subject to another very quickly 快速轉移；驟然轉換（話題）：*She kept skipping from one topic of conversation to another.* 她一再轉換談話的話題。

‣ **LEAVE SECRETLY** 秘密離去 **6** [T] **~ sth** to leave a place secretly or suddenly 悄悄溜走；突然離開：*The bombers skipped the country shortly after the blast.* 爆炸後不久，放置炸彈的人就逃離了這個國家。

‣ **STONES** 石塊 **7** (*BrE* also **skim**) [T] **~ sth (across, over, etc. sth)** to make a flat stone jump across the surface of water 打水漂：*The boys were skipping stones across the pond.* 那幾個男孩子用石塊往水塘裏打水漂。

IDM **'skip it** (*informal*) used to tell sb rudely that you do not want to talk about sth or repeat what you have said（粗暴地表示不想談論或重複說）別提這事兒，不說這個了：*'What were you saying?' 'Oh, skip it!'* "你剛才說什麼來着？" "噢，不提了！"

PHR V **,skip 'off/'out** to leave secretly or suddenly 溜走；突然離去 **,skip 'out on sb** (*NAmE*) to leave sb, especially when they need you（尤指不顧某人而）離開，溜走

■ *noun*

‣ **MOVEMENT** 動作 **1** a skipping movement 蹦跳：*She gave a skip and a jump and was off down the street.* 她一蹦一跳就順着馬路跑了。

‣ **CONTAINER FOR WASTE** 廢料箱 **2** (*BrE*) (*NAmE* **Dumpster™**) a large open container for putting old bricks, rubbish/garbage, etc. in. The skip is then loaded on a lorry/truck and taken away. 廢料桶（裝工地廢料、垃圾等，由卡車拖走）

,ski pants *noun* [pl.] **1** trousers/pants worn for skiing 滑雪褲 **2** narrow trousers/pants made from a type of cloth that stretches and with a part that goes under the foot 健美褲；踩腳褲

'ski-plane *noun* a plane with two parts like skis fixed to the bottom so that it can land on snow or ice 滑橇起落架飛機；雪上飛機 ➲ **VISUAL VOCAB** page V53

'ski pole (*BrE* also **'ski stick**) *noun* a stick used to push yourself forward while skiing 滑雪杖；滑雪杆

skip·per /'skɪpə(r)/ *noun*, *verb*

■ *noun* **1** the captain of a small ship or fishing boat（小船或漁船的）船長 **2** (*informal, especially BrE*) the captain of a sports team（運動隊的）隊長

■ *verb* **~ sth** to be the captain of a boat, sports team, etc. 當船長（或運動隊隊長等）：*to skipper a yacht* 當帆船船長 ◇ (*especially BrE*) *He skippered the team to victory.* 他率領隊伍取得了勝利。

'skipping rope (*BrE*) (*NAmE* **'jump rope**) *noun* a piece of rope, usually with a handle at each end, that you hold, turn over your head and then jump over, for fun or to keep fit 跳繩 ➲ **VISUAL VOCAB** page V37

skir·mish /'skɜːmɪʃ; *NAmE* 'skɜːrmɪʃ/ *noun*, *verb*

■ *noun* **1** a short fight between small groups of soldiers, etc., especially one that is not planned 小規模戰鬥；小衝突；（尤指）遭遇戰 **2** a short argument, especially between political opponents（尤指政治上對立雙方的）小爭執，小爭論

■ *verb* [I] to take part in a short fight or argument 發生小規模戰鬥（或衝突、爭執） ▸ **skir·mish·er** *noun* **skir·mish·ing** *noun* [U]：*There are reports of skirmishing* along the border. 有報道稱在邊界一帶發生了小規模衝突。

skirt 🔑 /skɜːt; *NAmE* skɜːrt/ *noun, verb*

■ ***noun*** **1** 🔑 [C] a piece of clothing for a woman or girl that hangs from the waist 女裙：*a* ***long/short/straight/pleated, etc. skirt*** 長裙、短裙、直筒裙、百褶裙等 ➲ VISUAL VOCAB page V61 **2** [C] (also **skirts** [pl.]) the part of a dress, coat, etc. that hangs below the waist（連衣裙、外衣等的）下襬 **3** [C] an outer covering or part used to protect the base of a vehicle or machine（車輛或機器基座的）擋板，裙板：*the rubber skirt around the bottom of a hovercraft* 氣墊船底部四周的橡膠圍裙 ➲ VISUAL VOCAB page V54

■ ***verb*** **1** [T, I] to be or go around the edge of sth 環繞…的四周；位於…的邊緣；沿…的邊緣走：**~ sth** *They followed the road that skirted the lake.* 他們順着湖邊公路走。◇ **~ around/round sth** *I skirted around the field and crossed the bridge.* 我沿着田邊走，又繞過了那座橋。**2** [T, I] to avoid talking about a subject, especially because it is difficult or embarrassing 繞開，迴避（話題）：**~ sth** *He carefully skirted the issue of where they would live.* 他小心地避開了他們將住在何處這個問題。◇ **~ around/round sth** *She tactfully skirted around the subject of money.* 她巧妙地避口不提錢的事。

ˈskirting board (also **skirt·ing**) (both *BrE*) (*NAmE* **base·board**) *noun* [C, U] a narrow piece of wood that is fixed along the bottom of the walls in a house 踢腳板；壁腳板

ˈski run (also **run**) *noun* a track that is marked on a slope that you ski down 滑雪道；滑雪坡

skit /skɪt/ *noun* **~** (**on sth**) a short piece of humorous writing or a performance that makes fun of sb/sth by copying them 幽默短文，滑稽短劇，幽默諷刺小品（常用模仿手法）：*a skit on daytime TV programmes* 戲評日間電視節目的幽默短文

ˈski tow *noun* **1** a machine which pulls you up the mountain on your skis（運送滑雪者上坡的）電纜車，上山吊椅 **2** a rope which pulls you when you are WATERSKIING（水橇運動的）拖繩

skit·ter /ˈskɪtə(r)/ *verb* [I] **+ adv./prep.** to run or move very quickly and lightly 輕捷地跑；輕快地動

skit·tish /ˈskɪtɪʃ/ *adj.* **1** (of horses 馬) easily excited or frightened and therefore difficult to control 易驚而難以駕馭的 **2** (of people 人) not very serious and with ideas and feelings that keep changing 輕浮的；易變的；反覆無常的 **3** (*especially NAmE, business* 商) likely to change suddenly 說變就變的；變幻莫測的：*skittish financial markets* 變幻莫測的金融市場 ▸ **skit·tish·ly** *adv.* **skit·tish·ness** *noun* [U]

skit·tle /ˈskɪtl/ *noun* **1** [C] (in Britain) a wooden or plastic object used in the game of skittles（英國滾球撞柱遊戲的）木柱，塑料柱 **2** **skittles** [U] (in Britain) a game in which players roll a ball at nine skittles and try to knock over as many of them as possible（英國）滾球撞柱遊戲 ➲ compare TENPIN BOWLING

skive /skaɪv/ *verb* [I, T] (*BrE, informal*) to avoid work or school by staying away or leaving early 躲避（工作）；逃（學）SYN **bunk off**：*'Where's Tom?' 'Skiving as usual.'* "湯姆去哪了？" "和往常一樣，溜了。" ◇ **~ off** *She always skives off early on Fridays.* 每到星期五，她總是早早就溜了。◇ **~ sth** *I skived the last lecture.* 最後一節課我溜了。▸ **skiver** *noun*

skivvy /ˈskɪvi/ *noun, verb*

■ ***noun*** (*pl.* **-ies**) **1** [C] (*BrE, informal*) a servant, usually female, who does all the dirty or boring jobs in a house 僕人，傭人（通常指幹粗活、髒活的女傭）：*He treats his wife like a skivvy.* 他待妻子就跟對奴僕似的。**2** **skiv·vies** [pl.] (*NAmE, informal*) underwear, especially men's underwear（尤指男式）內衣

■ ***verb*** (**skiv·vies, skivvy·ing, skiv·vied, skiv·vied**) [I] (*BrE, informal*) to do dirty or boring jobs 幹粗活；幹髒活；做用人

skolly /ˈskɒli; *NAmE* ˈskɑːli/ *noun* (*pl.* **-ies**) (*SAfrE, informal*) a young person who commits crimes or behaves badly 惡少；小流氓

skua /ˈskjuːə/ *noun* a large brownish bird that lives near the sea. It eats fish, which it sometimes takes from other birds. 賊鷗（褐色掠食性海鳥）

skul·dug·gery (also **skull·dug·gery**) /skʌlˈdʌɡəri/ *noun* [U] (*old-fashioned* or *humorous*) dishonest behaviour or activities 陰謀詭計；花招；欺騙

skulk /skʌlk/ *verb* [I] **+ adv./prep.** (*disapproving*) to hide or move around secretly, especially when you are planning sth bad 潛伏；偷偷摸摸地走動；鬼鬼祟祟地活動：*There was someone skulking behind the bushes.* 有人藏在灌木後面。

skull /skʌl/ *noun* **1** the bone structure that forms the head and surrounds and protects the brain 顱骨；頭（蓋）骨 SYN **cranium**：*a fractured skull* 破裂的顱骨 ➲ VISUAL VOCAB page V59 **2** (*informal*) the head or the brain 腦袋；腦子；腦瓜：*Her skull was crammed with too many thoughts.* 她腦瓜子裏想法太多。◇ (*informal*) *When will he* ***get it into his thick skull*** *that I never want to see him again!* 那笨頭笨腦的傢伙什麼時候才能明白我再也不想見他了！

ˌskull and ˈcrossbones *noun* [sing.] a picture of a human skull above two crossed bones, used in the past on the flags of PIRATE ships, and now used as a warning on containers with dangerous substances inside 骷髏旗，骷髏畫（舊時畫在海盜旗上，現在作為警示印在危險物品的容器上）

skull·cap /ˈskʌlkæp/ *noun* a small round cap worn on top of the head, especially by male Jews and Catholic BISHOPS, CARDINALS, etc.（多為猶太男子所戴的）無簷小圓帽，無簷便帽；（天主教主教、樞機主教等所戴的）主教帽 ➲ see also YARMULKE

skull·dug·gery = SKULDUGGERY

skunk /skʌŋk/ (*NAmE* also **pole·cat**) *noun* **1** [C] a small black and white N American animal that can produce a strong unpleasant smell to defend itself when it is attacked 北美臭鼬 **2** [U] (*slang*) = SKUNKWEED IDM see DRUNK *adj.*

skunk·weed /ˈskʌŋkwiːd/ (also *slang* **skunk**) *noun* [U] a strong type of CANNABIS 強效大麻

skunk·works /ˈskʌŋkwɜːks; *NAmE* -wɜːrks/ *noun* (*pl.* **skunk·works**) (*NAmE, informal*) a small laboratory or department of a large company used for doing new scientific research or developing new products（大公司從事科研和新產品開發的）實驗室，科研部門，研發部門

sky 🔑 /skaɪ/ *noun, verb*

■ ***noun*** 🔑 [C, U] (*pl.* **skies**) the space above the earth that you can see when you look up, where clouds and the sun, moon and stars appear 天；天空 HELP You usually say **the sky**. When **sky** is used with an adjective, use **a … sky**. You can also use the plural form **skies**, especially when you are thinking about the great extent of the sky. 通常說 the sky。與形容詞連用時說 a ... sky。也可以用複數形式 skies，尤其指天空遼闊無邊：*What's that in the sky?* 天上那個東西是什麼？◇ *The sky suddenly went dark and it started to rain.* 天空驟然轉暗，隨即下起雨來。◇ *the night sky* 夜空 ◇ *a cloudless sky* 無雲的天空 ◇ *cloudless skies* 無雲的天空 ◇ *a land of blue skies and sunshine* 一個藍天麗日的國度 ◇ *The skies above London were ablaze with a spectacular firework display.* 倫敦上空煙火綻放，景象壯觀。➲ COLLOCATIONS at WEATHER

IDM **the sky's the ˈlimit** (*informal*) there is no limit to what sb can achieve, earn, do, etc. 無窮盡；什麼都可能；不可限量：*With a talent like his, the sky's the limit.* 以他的稟賦，前途不可限量。➲ more at GREAT *adj.*, PIE, PRAISE *v.*

■ ***verb*** (**skies, sky·ing, skied, skied**) **~ sth** to hit a ball very high into the air 把（球）擊向高空：*She skied her tee shot.* 她開球那一杆打了一個高空球。

ˌsky-ˈblue *adj.* bright blue in colour, like the sky on a clear day 天藍色的；蔚藍色的 ▸ **ˌsky ˈblue** *noun* [U]

sky·box /ˈskaɪbɒks; *NAmE* -bɑːks/ *noun* (*NAmE*) an area of expensive seats, separated from other areas, high up in a sports ground（體育場的）貴賓看台

S

sky·cap /ˈskaɪkæp/ *noun* (*NAmE*) a person whose job is to carry people's bags at an airport 機場行李工

sky·div·ing /ˈskaɪdaɪvɪŋ/ *noun* [U] a sport in which you jump from a plane and fall for as long as you safely can before opening your PARACHUTE 延緩張傘跳傘運動；特技跳傘運動： *to go skydiving* 進行特技跳傘 ➲ VISUAL VOCAB page V50 ▸ **sky·diver** *noun*

ˌsky-ˈhigh *adj.* very high; too high 極高的；太高的： *His confidence is still sky-high.* 他依舊信心十足。◊ *sky-high interest rates* 極高的利率 ▸ **ˌsky-ˈhigh** *adv.*： *After the election, prices went sky-high.* 選舉後，物價飛漲。

sky·lark /ˈskaɪlɑːk; *NAmE* -lɑːrk/ *noun* a small bird that sings while it flies high up in the sky 雲雀

sky·light /ˈskaɪlaɪt/ *noun* a small window in a roof（房頂的）天窗 ➲ VISUAL VOCAB page V17

sky·line /ˈskaɪlaɪn/ *noun* the outline of buildings, trees, hills, etc. seen against the sky（建築物、樹、山等在天空映襯下的）輪廓線： *the New York skyline* 紐約的空中輪廓線

ˈsky marshal *noun* = AIR MARSHAL (2)

Skype™ /skaɪp/ *noun* [U] a telephone and/or video-chatting system that works by direct communication between users' computers on the Internet, without the need for a central SERVER * Skype 網絡通話系統 ➲ compare VoIP

Skype·cast /ˈskaɪpkɑːst; *NAmE* -kæst/ *noun* a public telephone call on Skype in which many people take part in a discussion, that may be recorded and made available on the Internet * Skype 網絡電話會議；多方視訊通話 ▸ **Skype·cast·ing** /ˈskaɪpkɑːstɪŋ; *NAmE* -kæst-/ *noun* [U]： *A Skypecasting session can include up to 100 people.* 一次 Skype 網絡電話會議最多可讓 100 人參加。

sky·rocket /ˈskaɪrɒkɪt; *NAmE* -rɑːk-/ *verb* [I] (of prices, etc. 價格等) to rise quickly to a very high level 飛漲；猛漲

sky·scraper /ˈskaɪskreɪpə(r)/ *noun* a very tall building in a city 摩天大樓 ➲ VISUAL VOCAB pages V2, V3, V15

ˈsky surfing *noun* [U] the sport of jumping from a plane and travelling through the air on a board before landing with a PARACHUTE 空中滑板運動；空中滑翔

sky·wards /ˈskaɪwədz; *NAmE* -wərdz/ (also **sky·ward**) *adv.* towards the sky; up into the sky 向天空；朝天空： *She pointed skywards.* 她指向天空。◊ *The rocket soared skywards.* 火箭呼嘯着朝天上飛去。

S

SLA /ˌes el ˈeɪ/ *abbr.* (*linguistics* 語言) SECOND LANGUAGE ACQUISITION

slab /slæb/ *noun* **1** a thick flat piece of stone, wood or other hard material（石、木等堅硬物質的）厚板： *a **slab of marble/concrete*** 大理石板；混凝土板 ◊ *The road was paved with smooth **stone slabs**.* 道路用平整的石板鋪成。◊ ***paving slabs*** 鋪路石板 ◊ *a dead body **on the slab*** (= on a table in a MORTUARY) 停屍桌上的屍體 **2** a thick, flat slice or piece of sth 厚片；厚塊： *a slab of chocolate* 一大塊巧克力 ◊ *slabs of meat* 切成厚片的肉

slack /slæk/ *adj.*, *noun*, *verb*

■ ***adj.*** (**slack·er**, **slack·est**) **1** not stretched tight 不緊的；鬆弛的 SYN **loose**： *She was staring into space, her mouth slack.* 她雙唇微張，失神地望着前方。◊ *The rope suddenly went slack.* 繩子突然鬆了。◊ *slack muscles* 鬆弛的肌肉 **2** (of business 生意) not having many customers or sales; not busy 蕭條的；冷清的；清淡的： *a slack period* 蕭條期 **3** (*disapproving*) not putting enough care, attention or energy into sth and so not doing it well enough 懈怠的；不用心的；敷衍了事的；吊兒郎當的： *He's been very slack in his work lately.* 近來他工作很不認真。◊ *Discipline in the classroom is very slack.* 班裏紀律十分鬆懈。 ▸ **slack·ly** *adv.*： *Her arms hung slackly by her sides.* 她的雙手無力地垂放在身體的兩側。 **slack·ness** *noun* [U]

■ ***noun*** [U] ➲ see also SLACKS **1** the part of a rope, etc. that is hanging loosely（繩索的）鬆弛部份： *There's too much slack in the tow rope.* 拖纜太鬆。 **2** people, money or space that should be used more fully in an organization（組織中人員、資金或地方的）富餘部份，閒置部份： *There's very little slack in the budget.* 預算中沒有多少剩餘款項。 **3** very small pieces of coal 煤屑；煤末

IDM **cut sb some ˈslack** (*informal*) to be less critical of sb or less strict with them 不過於挑剔某人；對某人寬容些： *Hey, cut him some slack! He's doing his best!* 哎，別對他那麼吹毛求疵！他已經盡全力了！ **take up the ˈslack 1** to improve the way money or people are used in an organization 提高（資金或人員使用的）效率 **2** to pull on a rope, etc. until it is tight 收緊鬆弛的繩索

■ ***verb*** [I] to work less hard than you usually do or should do 懈怠；怠惰；偷懶

PHR V **ˌslack ˈoff (on sth)** to do sth more slowly or with less energy than before 鬆懈；放鬆；懈怠

slack·en /ˈslækən/ *verb* **1** [I, T] to gradually become, or to make sth become, slower, less active, etc.（使）放慢，減緩，蕭條 SYN **relax**： **~ (off)** *We've been really busy, but things are starting to slacken off now.* 近來我們的確很忙，不過現在情況開始有所緩解了。◊ **~ sth** *She slackened her pace a little* (= walked a little more slowly). 她略微放慢腳步。 **2** [I, T] to become, or to make sth become, less tight（使）變得鬆弛 SYN **loosen**： *His grip slackened and she pulled away from him.* 他抓得不那麼緊了，她順勢掙脫開來。◊ **~ sth** *He slackened the ropes slightly.* 他把繩子稍稍放鬆一些。

slack·er /ˈslækə(r)/ *noun* (*informal*, *disapproving*) a person who is lazy and avoids work 偷懶的人；怠惰的人

slacks /slæks/ *noun* [pl.] (*old-fashioned* or *NAmE*, *formal*) trousers/pants for men or women, that are not part of a suit 便褲；寬鬆的長褲： *a pair of slacks* 一條便褲

slag /slæg/ *noun*, *verb*

■ ***noun*** **1** [U] the waste material that remains after metal has been removed from rock 礦渣；熔渣；爐渣 **2** [C] (*BrE*, *slang*) an offensive word for a woman, used to suggest that she has a lot of sexual partners 蕩婦；破鞋

■ ***verb*** (**-gg-**)

PHR V **ˌslag sb↔ˈoff** (*BrE*, *slang*) to say cruel or critical things about sb 臭罵；貶損；辱罵： *I hate the way he's always slagging off his colleagues.* 他老損他的同事，我看不慣。

ˈslag heap *noun* (*BrE*) a large pile of slag from a mine 礦渣堆；熔渣堆

slain *past part.* of SLAY

slake /sleɪk/ *verb* (*literary*) **1 ~ your thirst** to drink so that you no longer feel thirsty 緩和（口渴）；解（渴） SYN **quench 2 ~ sth** to satisfy a desire 滿足（慾望）

sla·lom /ˈslɑːləm/ *noun* a race for people on SKIS or in CANOES along a winding course marked by poles（滑雪）迴轉賽；（獨木舟）障礙賽

slam /slæm/ *verb*, *noun*

■ ***verb*** (**-mm-**) **1** [I, T] to shut, or to make sth shut, with a lot of force, making a loud noise（使…）砰地關上 SYN **bang**： *I heard the door slam behind him.* 我聽見他砰地把身後的門關上。◊ **+ adj.** *A window slammed shut in the wind.* 風吹得一扇窗戶咣地關上了。◊ **~ sth** *He stormed out of the house, slamming the door as he left.* 他怒氣沖沖地從房子裏出來，把門砰地關上。◊ **~ sth + adj.** *She slammed the lid shut.* 她砰的一聲蓋上蓋子。◊ **+ adv./prep.** *She slammed out of the room* (= went out and slammed the door behind her). 她隨手砰的一聲關上門出去了。 **2** [T] **~ sth + adv./prep.** to put, push or throw sth into a particular place or position with a lot of force 用力一放；使勁一推；猛勁一摔： *She slammed down the phone angrily.* 她氣呼呼地啪的一聲掛上電話。◊ *He slammed on the brakes* (= stopped the car very suddenly). 他猛地剎住汽車。 **3** [T] **~ sb/sth** (used especially in newspapers 尤用於報章) to criticize sb/sth very strongly 猛烈抨擊 IDM see DOOR

PHR V **ˌslam ˈinto/aˈgainst sb/sth | ˌslam sth ˈinto/aˈgainst sb/sth** to crash into sth with a lot of force; to make sth crash into sth with a lot of force（使）重重地撞上 ➲ SYNONYMS at CRASH

■ ***noun*** [usually sing.] an act of slamming sth; the noise of sth being slammed 猛關（或推、摔、撞等）；猛摔（或撞）的聲音： *She gave the door a good hard slam.* 她使勁一推，門砰的一聲關上了。➲ see also GRAND SLAM

ˈslam dunk *noun* **1** (in BASKETBALL 籃球) the act of jumping up and putting the ball through the net with a lot of force 強力灌籃；扣籃 **2** (*NAmE, informal*) something that is certain to be successful 必定成功的事；穩操勝券的事：*Politically, this issue is a slam dunk for the party.* 在政治上，這一課題是這個黨的一張勝券。

ˈslam-dunk *verb* **～ sth** (in BASKETBALL 籃球) to jump up and put the ball through the net with a lot of force 扣籃

slam·mer /ˈslæmə(r)/ *noun* **1 the slammer** [sing.] (*slang*) prison 監獄 **2** [C] (also **teˌquila ˈslammer**) an alcoholic drink made by mixing TEQUILA and LEMONADE, which is drunk quickly after covering the glass and hitting it on the table to make the drink fill with bubbles 龍舌蘭雞尾酒（加檸檬汽水等）

slan·der /ˈslɑːndə(r); *NAmE* ˈslæn-/ *noun, verb*

■ ***noun*** [C, U] a false spoken statement intended to damage the good opinion people have of sb; the legal offence of making this kind of statement 口頭誹謗；口頭誹謗罪：*a vicious slander on the company's good name* 對那家公司良好聲譽的惡意誹謗 ◇ *He's suing them for slander.* 他控告他們口頭誹謗。➲ compare LIBEL ▸ **slan·der·ous** /-dərəs/ *adj.*：*a slanderous remark* 誹謗性話語

■ ***verb*** **～ sb/sth** to make a false spoken statement about sb that is intended to damage the good opinion that people have of them 口頭誹謗；詆譭；中傷：*He angrily accused the investigators of slandering both him and his family.* 他氣憤地指責調查者詆譭他和他的家人。➲ compare LIBEL

slang /slæŋ/ *noun* [U] very informal words and expressions that are more common in spoken language, especially used by a particular group of people, for example, children, criminals, soldiers, etc. 俚語：*teenage slang* 青少年俚語 ◇ *a* ***slang word/expression/term*** 俚語 ➲ see also RHYMING SLANG

ˈslanging match *noun* (*BrE, informal*) an angry argument in which people insult each other 互相謾罵

slangy /ˈslæŋi/ *adj.* (**slang·ier**, **slangi·est**) containing a lot of slang 充滿俚語的：*a slangy style* 大量使用俚語的文體

slant /slɑːnt; *NAmE* slænt/ *verb, noun*

■ ***verb*** **1** [I, T] to slope or to make sth slope in a particular direction or at a particular angle（使）傾斜，歪斜：**+ adv./prep.** (*literary*) *The sun slanted through the window.* 太陽斜照進窗戶。◇ **～ sth + adv./prep.** *Slant your skis a little more to the left.* 把滑雪板略微向左斜一點。**2** [T] **～ sth (+ adv./prep.)** (sometimes *disapproving*) to present information based on a particular way of thinking, especially in an unfair way 有傾向性地陳述；有偏向地報道：*The findings of the report had been slanted in favour of the manufacturers.* 報告中的調查結果偏袒製造商。

■ ***noun*** **1** a sloping position 傾斜；歪斜；斜線；斜面：*The sofa faced the fire* ***at a slant.*** 沙發斜對着壁爐。◇ *Cut the flower stems* ***on the slant.*** 把花莖斜着切斷。**2 ～ (on sth/sb)** a way of thinking about sth, especially one that shows support for a particular opinion or side in a disagreement（有傾向性的）觀點，態度：*She put a* ***new slant*** *on the play.* 她對那齣戲提出了一種新的見解。

slant·ed /ˈslɑːntɪd; *NAmE* ˈslæntɪd/ *adj.* **1** sloping in one direction 傾斜的；歪斜的：*She had slanted brown eyes.* 她有一雙棕色的丹鳳眼。**2 ～ (towards sb/sth)** tending to be in favour of one person or thing in a way that may be unfair to others 有傾向性的；有偏向性的：*a biased and slanted view of events* 對事件有失公正、帶傾向性的觀點

slant·ing /ˈslɑːntɪŋ; *NAmE* ˈslæntɪŋ/ *adj.* not straight or level; sloping 不直的；不平的；斜的；歪的：*slanting eyes/handwriting/rain* 斜眼；歪斜的字跡；斜落的雨

slap /slæp/ *verb, noun, adv.*

■ ***verb*** (**-pp-**) **1** [T] **～ sb/sth (+ adv./prep.)** to hit sb/sth with the flat part of your hand（用手掌）打，拍，摑 SYN **smack**：*She slapped his face hard.* 她狠狠給了他一個耳光。◇ *She slapped him hard across the face.* 她狠狠給了他一個耳光。◇ *'Congratulations!' he said, slapping me on the back.* "祝賀你！"他拍着我的背説。**2** [T] **～ sth + adv./prep.** to put sth on a surface in a quick, careless and often noisy way, especially because you are angry（尤指生氣地）啪的一聲放下，隨意扔放：*He slapped the newspaper down on the desk.* 他啪的一聲把報紙摔在桌上。◇ *She slapped a $10 bill into my hand.* 她啪地把一張 10 元鈔票放在我手裏。**3** [I] **+ adv./prep.** to hit against sth with the noise of sb being slapped 啪地擊打（或撞上）：*The water slapped against the side of the boat.* 水拍擊船舷。➲ see also HAPPY SLAPPING

PHR V **ˌslap sb aˈbout/aˈround** (*informal*) to hit sb regularly or often 常常打，動輒毆打（某人）：*Her ex-husband used to slap her around.* 她的前夫過去動不動就打她。**ˌslap sb/sth↔ˈdown** (*informal*) to criticize sb in an unfair way, often in public, so that they feel embarrassed or less confident 訓斥；申斥；公開指責 **ˈslap sth on sb/sth** (*informal*) to order, especially in a sudden or an unfair way, that sth must happen or sb must do sth 強制實行；強迫某人做：*The company slapped a ban on using email on the staff.* 公司對員工使用電子郵件發出禁令。**ˌslap sth ˈon sth** (*informal*) to increase the price of sth suddenly 忽然提價：*They've slapped 50p on the price of a pack of cigarettes.* 他們把一包香煙的價格一下子提高了 50 便士。**ˌslap sth ˈon sth | ˌslap sth↔ˈon** to spread sth on a surface in a quick, careless way（在…上）胡亂塗抹，隨意塗抹：*Just slap some paint on the walls and it'll look fine.* 在牆上隨便刷點漆，就看着漂亮了。◇ *I'd better slap some make-up on before I go out.* 我出門以前最好是簡單化化妝。

■ ***noun*** **1** [C] the action of hitting sb/sth with the flat part of your hand（用手掌）打，拍，摑：*She gave him a slap across the face.* 她打了他一個耳光。◇ *He gave me a hearty slap on the back.* 他熱情地在我背上拍了一下。**2** [sing.] the noise made by hitting sb/sth with the flat part of your hand; a similar noise made by sth else 拍打聲；類似拍打的聲音：*the gentle slap of water against the shore* 水輕輕的拍岸聲 **3** [U] (*BrE, informal*) = MAKE-UP (1)

IDM **slap and ˈtickle** (*old-fashioned, BrE, informal*) enthusiastic kissing and CUDDLING between lovers（情人之間的）擁抱親吻 **a slap in the ˈface** an action that seems to be intended as a deliberate insult to sb 一記耳光；侮辱；打擊 **a slap on the ˈwrist** (*informal*) a warning or mild punishment 警告；輕微的懲罰

■ ***adv.*** (also **ˌslap ˈbang**) (*informal*) **1** straight, and with great force 猛然；逕直：*Storming out of her room, she went slap into Luke.* 她怒氣沖沖地衝出房間，迎面和盧克撞了個滿懷。**2** exactly 恰好；正好：*Their apartment is slap bang in the middle of town.* 他們住的公寓恰巧在全城的中心。

slap·dash /ˈslæpdæʃ/ *adj.* done, or doing sth, too quickly and carelessly 倉促馬虎的；毛躁的；潦草的：*She has a very slapdash approach to keeping accounts.* 她記賬十分潦草馬虎。◇ *a slapdash piece of writing* 一篇粗製濫造的文章

ˌslap-ˈhappy *adj.* (*informal*) **1** cheerful, but careless about things that should be taken seriously 嘻嘻哈哈的；什麼都不放在心上的；大大咧咧的：*a slap-happy approach to life* 大大咧咧的生活態度 **2** (*especially NAmE*) = PUNCH-DRUNK

slap·head /ˈslæphed/ *noun* (*BrE, informal*) an unkind way of referring to a man with little or no hair on his head 稀髮佬；禿子

slap·per /ˈslæpə(r)/ *noun* (*BrE, slang*) an offensive word for a woman, used to suggest that she has a lot of sexual partners 蕩婦；淫婦

slap·stick /ˈslæpstɪk/ *noun* [U] the type of humour that is based on simple actions, for example people hitting each other, falling down, etc. 打鬧劇；粗俗滑稽劇

ˈslap-up *adj.* [only before noun] (*BrE, informal*) (of a meal 飯菜) large and very good 豐盛高檔的

slash /slæʃ/ *verb, noun*

■ ***verb*** **1 ～ sth** to make a long cut with a sharp object, especially in a violent way（用利器）砍，劈 SYN **slit**：*Someone had slashed the tyres on my car.* 有人把我的汽車輪胎割破了。◇ *She tried to kill herself by slashing her wrists.* 她試圖割腕自殺。◇ *We had to* ***slash our way*** *through the undergrowth with sticks.* 我們揮舞着木棍一

S

路劈砍，才在密林裏開出一條路，穿了過去。**2** [often passive] **~ sth** (*informal*) (often used in newspapers 常用於報章) to reduce sth by a large amount 大幅度削減；大大降低：*to slash costs/prices/fares, etc.* 大幅度降低成本、價格、車費等 ◇ *The workforce has been slashed by half.* 職工人數裁減了一半。➲ SYNONYMS at CUT

PHR V **'slash at sb/sth (with sth)** to attack sb violently with a knife, etc.（用刀等）猛砍，砍擊

■ *noun* **1** [C] a sharp movement made with a knife, etc. in order to cut sb/sth（用刀等的）砍，劈 **2** [C] a long narrow wound or cut（長而窄的）傷口，切口，砍痕：*a slash across his right cheek* 他右臉上的一道刀傷 ◇ (*figurative*) *Her mouth was a slash of red lipstick.* 她的嘴就是口紅抹出的一道縫。**3** [C] (*BrE* also **ob·lique**) the symbol (/) used to show alternatives, as in *lunch and/or dinner* and *4/5 people* and to write FRACTIONS, as in ¾ 斜槓；斜線號 ➲ see also BACKSLASH, FORWARD SLASH **4 a slash** [sing.] (*BrE, slang*) an act of URINATING 撒尿：*He's just nipped out to have a slash.* 他剛才急急忙忙跑出去撒了一泡尿。

,slash-and-'burn *adj.* **1** relating to a method of farming in which existing plants, crops, etc. are cut down and burned before new seeds are planted 刀耕火種的；燒墾的：*slash-and-burn agriculture* 刀耕火種農業 **2** aggressive and causing a lot of harm or damage 好鬥的；殘忍的

slash·er /ˈslæʃə(r)/ (also **'slasher film**, **'slasher movie**) *noun* a frightening film/movie, in which an unknown person kills a lot of people 殺人狂電影

slat /slæt/ *noun* **1** one of a series of thin flat pieces of wood, metal or plastic, used in furniture, fences, etc.（傢具、柵欄等上的）板條，窄條，横檔 ➲ VISUAL VOCAB page V21 **2** (*technical* 術語) a part of the wing of an aircraft, on the front of the wing, that can be moved up or down to control upward or downward movement 前缘縫翼（機翼前緣的一部份，可使其上下移動來控制飛機的升降）➲ VISUAL VOCAB page V53

slate /sleɪt/ *noun, verb*

■ *noun* **1** [U] a type of dark grey stone that splits easily into thin flat layers 板岩；石板：*a slate quarry* 板岩採石場 ◇ *The sea was the colour of slate.* 大海的顏色像石板。**2** [C] a small thin piece of slate, used for covering roofs（蓋房頂的）石板瓦：*A loose slate had fallen from the roof.* 一塊鬆動的石板瓦從房頂上掉了下來。**3** [C] (*NAmE*) a list of the candidates in an election（選舉中的）候選人名單：*a slate of candidates* 候選人名單 ◇ *the Democratic slate* 民主黨候選人名單 **4** [C] a small sheet of slate in a wooden frame, used in the past in schools for children to write on（舊時學生用以寫字的）石板 **IDM** see CLEAN *adj.*, WIPE *v.*

■ *verb* **1 ~ sb/sth (for sth)** (*BrE*) to criticize sb/sth, especially in a newspaper（尤指在報紙上）批評，抨擊：*to slate a book/play/writer* 批評一部書／一齣戲／一位作家 **2** [usually passive] to plan that sth will happen at a particular time in the future 預定；計劃；安排：**~ sth for sth** *The houses were first slated for demolition five years ago.* 這些房子在五年前就確定要拆除了。◇ **~ sth to do sth** *The new store is slated to open in spring.* 新商店預計春天開業。**3** [usually passive] (*informal, especially NAmE*) to suggest or choose sb for a job, position, etc. 推舉；選定：**~ sb for sth** *I was told that I was being slated for promotion.* 我聽説，我被定為提升的人選。◇ **~ sb to do sth** *He is slated to play the lead in the new musical.* 他獲選在新的音樂劇中擔任主角。

slated /ˈsleɪtɪd/ *adj.* covered with pieces of SLATE 蓋石板瓦的：*a slated roof* 石板瓦房頂

,slate-'grey *adj.* bluish-grey in colour, like slate 石板灰的；藍灰色的

slather /ˈslæðə(r)/ *verb*

PHR V **'slather sth on sth** | **'slather with/in sth** | **,slather sth↔'on** to cover sth with a thick layer of a substance（在…上）厚厚塗抹：*hot dogs slathered with mustard* 抹了厚厚一層芥末的熱狗

slat·ted /ˈslætɪd/ *adj.* [usually before noun] made of slats (= thin pieces of wood) 用板條做的：*slatted blinds* 百葉窗

slat·tern /ˈslætən; *NAmE* -tərn/ *noun* (*old-fashioned*) a dirty untidy woman 邋遢的女人 ▸ **slat·tern·ly** *adj.*：*a slatternly girl* 邋裏邋遢的女孩子

slaty (also **slatey**) /ˈsleɪti/ *adj.* **1** having a dark grey colour 深灰色的；石板色的：*a slaty sky* 灰暗的天空 **2** containing SLATE; like SLATE 含板岩的；石板似的：*slaty rock* 板岩

slaugh·ter /ˈslɔːtə(r)/ *noun, verb*

■ *noun* [U] **1** the killing of animals for their meat 屠宰；宰殺：*cows taken for slaughter* 待宰奶牛 **2** the cruel killing of large numbers of people at one time, especially in a war（尤指戰爭中的）屠殺，殺戮 **SYN** **massacre**：*the wholesale slaughter of innocent people* 對無辜民眾的大規模殺戮 **IDM** see LAMB *n.*

■ *verb* **1 ~ sth** to kill an animal, usually for its meat 屠宰；宰殺 **SYN** **butcher** **2 ~ sb/sth** to kill a large number of people or animals violently 屠殺；殺戮 **SYN** **massacre**：*Men, women and children were slaughtered and villages destroyed.* 村莊被毀，男人、女人和兒童慘遭殺戮。**3 ~ sb/sth** (*informal*) to defeat sb/sth by a large number of points in a sports game, competition, etc.（在體育比賽等競賽中）大比分擊敗，使慘敗：*We were slaughtered 10–1 by the home team.* 我們以 1:10 慘敗給主隊。

slaugh·ter·house /ˈslɔːtəhaʊs; *NAmE* -tərh-/ *noun* (*BrE* also **ab·at·toir**) a building where animals are killed for food 屠宰場

Slav /slɑːv/ *noun* a member of any of the races of people of central and eastern Europe who speak Slavic languages 斯拉夫人

slave /sleɪv/ *noun, verb*

■ *noun* **1** a person who is owned by another person and is forced to work for them 奴隸：*She treated her daughter like a slave.* 她對待女兒像對待奴隸一樣。**2** a person who is so strongly influenced by sth that they cannot live without it, or cannot make their own decisions 完全受（某事物）控制的人；完全依賴（某事物）的人：**~ of sth** *We are slaves of the motor car.* 我們離不了汽車。◇ **~ to sth** *Sue's a slave to fashion.* 蘇是個拚命趕時髦的人。**3** (*technical* 術語) a device that is directly controlled by another one 從動裝置

■ *verb* [I] **~ (away) (at sth)** to work very hard 苦幹；辛勤地工作：*I've been slaving away all day trying to get this work finished.* 我整天苦幹，想把這項工作趕完。◇ *I haven't got time to spend hours* **slaving over a hot stove** (= doing a lot of cooking). 我沒時間老圍着灶台轉。

'slave-driver *noun* (*disapproving*) a person who makes people work extremely hard 殘酷的監工；逼迫他人拚命幹活兒的人 **SYN** **tyrant**

,slave 'labour (*especially US* **,slave 'labor**) *noun* [U] **1** work that is done by slaves; the slaves who do the work 奴隸勞動；幹苦役的奴隸：*Huge palaces were built by slave labour.* 宏偉的宮殿是奴隸建成的。**2** (*informal*) work that is very hard and very badly paid 繁重而報酬很低的工作：*I left because the job was just slave labour.* 我之所以離開是因為那工作簡直是奴隸幹的。

slaver¹ /ˈslævə(r)/ *verb* [I] (usually of an animal 通常指動物) to let SALIVA (= the liquid produced in the mouth) run out of the mouth, especially when hungry or excited（尤指因飢餓或興奮）流口水，垂涎：*slavering dogs* 淌着口水的狗

slaver² /ˈsleɪvə(r)/ *noun* **1** (in the past) a person who bought and sold SLAVES（舊時）奴隸販子 **2** a ship that was used in the past for carrying SLAVES（舊時）販運奴隸的船

slav·ery /ˈsleɪvəri/ *noun* [U] **1** the state of being a SLAVE 奴隸身分：*to* **be sold into slavery** 被賣為奴 **2** the practice of having SLAVES 奴隸制；蓄奴：*the abolition of slavery* 奴隸制的廢除 **OPP** **freedom**

'slave trade *noun* [sing.] the buying and selling of people as SLAVES, especially in the 17th–19th centuries（尤指 17–19 世紀的）奴隸買賣

Slav·ic /ˈslɑːvɪk/ (also **Slav·on·ic**) *adj.* of or connected with Slavs or their languages, which include Russian, Polish, Czech and a number of other languages 斯拉夫人的；斯拉夫語的

slav·ish /ˈsleɪvɪʃ/ *adj.* (*disapproving*) following or copying sb/sth exactly without having any original thought at all 無獨創性的；盲從的；照搬的：*a slavish adherence to the rules* 墨守成規 ▸ **slav·ish·ly** *adv.*

Sla·von·ic /sləˈvɒnɪk; *NAmE* -ˈvɑːn-/ *adj.* = SLAVIC

slay /sleɪ/ *verb* (**slew** /sluː/, **slain** /sleɪn/) **1** ~ **sb/sth** (*old-fashioned* or *literary*) to kill sb/sth in a war or a fight（在戰爭或搏鬥中）殺，殺死：*St George slew the dragon.* 聖喬治殺死了那條龍。**2** ~ **sb** (*especially NAmE*) (used especially in newspapers 尤用於報章) to murder sb 殺害；殘害；謀殺：*Two passengers were slain by the hijackers.* 兩名乘客遭劫機者殺害。**3** ~ **sb** (*old-fashioned, informal, especially NAmE*) to have a strong effect on sb, especially to make them laugh（尤指藉着使人發笑而）深深影響，迷住：*Those old movies still slay me!* 那些老影片依舊讓我着迷！ ▸ **slay·ing** *noun*：(*especially NAmE*) *the drug-related slayings of five people* 那宗和毒品有關的五人被殺的案子

sleaze /sliːz/ *noun* **1** [U] dishonest or illegal behaviour, especially by politicians or business people（尤指政客或商人的）舞弊，欺詐，違法行為：*allegations of sleaze* 關於舞弊的指控 ◇ *The candidate was seriously damaged by the sleaze factor.* 那位候選人的形象因醜聞而受到嚴重損害。**2** [U] behaviour or conditions that are unpleasant and not socially acceptable, especially because sex is involved（尤指涉及性行為的）污穢，骯髒，烏煙瘴氣：*the sleaze of a town that was once a naval base* 一度是海軍基地的小城裏那烏煙瘴氣的社會氛圍 **3** [C] (also **sleaze·bag** /ˈsliːzbæɡ/, **sleaze·ball** /ˈsliːzbɔːl/ especially in *NAmE*) a dishonest or immoral person 奸徒；卑鄙的人；下流坯

sleazy /ˈsliːzi/ *adj.* (**sleaz·ier**, **sleazi·est**) (*informal*) **1** (of a place 地方) dirty, unpleasant and not socially acceptable, especially because sex is involved（尤指涉及性行為的）骯髒的，污穢的，烏煙瘴氣的，藏污納垢的 SYN **disreputable**：*a sleazy bar* 烏煙瘴氣的酒吧 **2** (of people 人) immoral and unpleasant 不正派的；道德敗壞的；墮落的；卑鄙的：*a sleazy reporter* 不正派的記者 ▸ **sleazi·ness** *noun* [U]

sled /sled/ *noun, verb* (-**dd**-) (*especially NAmE*) = SLEDGE ▸ **sled·ding** /ˈsledɪŋ/ *noun* [U]

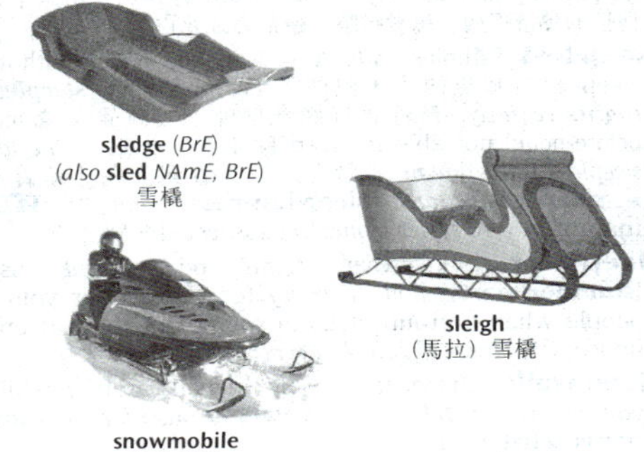

sledge (*BrE*) (*also* **sled** *NAmE, BrE*) 雪橇

sleigh（馬拉）雪橇

snowmobile 機動雪橇

sledge /sledʒ/ (*BrE*) (also **sled** *NAmE, BrE*) *noun, verb*

■ *noun* a vehicle for travelling over snow and ice, with long narrow strips of wood or metal instead of wheels. Larger sledges are pulled by horses or dogs and smaller ones are used for going down hills as a sport or for pleasure. 雪橇 ⊃ compare SLEIGH, TOBOGGAN

■ *verb* [I] to ride on a sledge/sled 乘雪橇：*We were hoping we could* **go sledging**. 我們本來希望能去乘雪橇。

sledge·ham·mer /ˈsledʒhæmə(r)/ *noun* a large heavy hammer with a long handle（有長柄的）大錘

IDM **use a ˌsledgehammer to crack a ˈnut** to use more force than is necessary 掄着大錘砸核桃；殺雞用牛刀

sledg·ing /ˈsledʒɪŋ/ *noun* [U] **1** (*BrE*) (*NAmE* **sledding**) the activity of riding on a sledge 滑雪橇：*to go sledging* 去滑雪橇 **2** (in CRICKET) insults to players in the opposing team in order to destroy their concentration（板球運動中為分散對手注意力的）辱罵 ⊃ compare TRASH TALK

sleek /sliːk/ *adj., verb*

■ *adj.* (**sleek·er**, **sleek·est**) **1** (*approving*) smooth and shiny 光滑的；光亮的 SYN **glossy**：*sleek black hair* 烏黑油亮的頭髮 ◇ *the sleek dark head of a seal* 黑乎乎、油光光的海豹腦袋 **2** (*approving*) having an elegant smooth shape 線條流暢的；造型優美的：*a sleek yacht* 造型優美的遊艇 ◇ *the* **sleek lines** *of the new car* 新車流暢的線條 **3** (*often disapproving*) (of a person 人) looking rich, and dressed in elegant and expensive clothes 闊氣的；衣冠楚楚的；時髦的：*a sleek and ambitious politician* 衣冠楚楚、野心勃勃的政客 ▸ **sleek·ly** *adv.* **sleek·ness** *noun* [U]

■ *verb* ~ **sth** (**back/down**) to make sth, especially hair, smooth and shiny 使（頭髮等）發油光；使平整光亮：*His glossy hair was sleeked back over his ears.* 他那油亮的頭髮平平整整地梳向耳後。

Synonyms 同義詞辨析

sleep

doze • nap • snooze

These words all mean to rest with your eyes closed and your mind and body not active. 以上各詞均含睡覺、入睡之意。

sleep to rest with your eyes shut and your mind and body not active 指睡、睡覺、入睡：*Did you sleep well?* 你睡得好嗎？◇ *I couldn't sleep last night.* 我昨天晚上睡不着。NOTE It is more usual to say that sb is **asleep** than that they are **sleeping**; but if you use an adverb to say how they are sleeping, use **sleeping**. 表示在睡覺，asleep 較 sleeping 常用，但如果用副詞表示睡的狀態就用 sleeping：*'What's Ashley doing?' 'Sh! She's asleep.'* "阿什利在幹什麼？" "噓，她在睡覺。" ◇ *The baby was sleeping peacefully.* 嬰兒睡得很安穩。◇ ~~*The baby was asleep peacefully.*~~

doze to sleep lightly, waking up easily, often when you are not in bed 指打瞌睡、打盹兒，通常不是躺在牀上：*He was dozing in front of the TV.* 他在電視機前打瞌睡。

nap to sleep for a short time, especially during the day 尤指日間的小睡、打盹

snooze (*informal*) to sleep lightly for a short time, especially during the day and usually not in bed 尤指日間的小睡、打盹，通常不是躺在牀上：*My brother was snoozing on the sofa.* 我弟弟正在沙發上打盹。

PATTERNS

- to sleep/doze **lightly/fitfully**
- to doze/snooze **gently**

sleep 0-π /sliːp/ *verb, noun*

■ *verb* (**slept**, **slept** /slept/) **1** 0-π [I] (+ **adv./prep.**) to rest with your eyes closed and your mind and body not active 睡；睡覺；入睡：*to* **sleep well/deeply/soundly/badly** 睡得好；沉睡；酣睡；睡得不好 ◇ *I couldn't sleep because of the noise.* 嘈雜聲吵得我睡不着。◇ *I had to sleep on the sofa.* 我只得睡在沙發上。◇ *He slept solidly for ten hours.* 他整整睡了十個小時。◇ *I slept at my sister's house last night* (= stayed the night there). 昨晚我住在妹妹家了。◇ *We both slept right through* (= were not woken up by) *the storm.* 我們兩人睡得很沉，渾然不知有暴風雨。◇ *She only sleeps for four hours a night.* 她每天晚上只睡四個小時。◇ *We sometimes* **sleep late** *at*

S

the weekends (= until late in the morning). 週末我們有時候睡懶覺。◇ *I put the sleeping baby down gently.* 我把睡着的寶寶輕輕放下。◇ *What are our* ***sleeping arrangements*** *here* (= where shall we sleep)? 我們在這兒睡覺是怎麼安排的？ **HELP** It is more common to say that somebody **is asleep** than to say that somebody **is sleeping. Sleep** can only be used in the passive with a preposition such as **in** or **on**. * somebody is asleep 比 somebody is sleeping 更常見。sleep 只有和 in 或 on 等介詞連用時才可以用被動語態：*It was clear her bed hadn't been slept in.* **2** [T, no passive] **~ sb** to have enough beds for a particular number of people 可供…人睡覺；可供…人住宿：*The apartment sleeps six.* 這套公寓能睡六個人。◇ *The hotel sleeps 120 guests.* 這家旅館可供 120 位客人住宿。

IDM **let sleeping dogs 'lie** (*saying*) to avoid mentioning a subject or sth that happened in the past, in order to avoid any problems or arguments 過去的事就不要再提了；不要沒事找事 **sleep like a 'log/'baby** (*informal*) to sleep very well 沉睡；酣睡 **sleep 'tight** (*informal*) used especially to children before they go to bed to say that you hope they sleep well（尤用以打發孩子睡覺）睡個好覺：*Goodnight, sleep tight!* 晚安，睡個好覺！➲ more at ROUGH *adv.*, WINK *n.*

PHR V **,sleep a'round** (*informal, disapproving*) to have sex with a lot of different people 到處跟人睡覺；亂搞男女關係 **,sleep 'in** to sleep until after the time you usually get up in the morning 遲起；睡過頭；睡懶覺 **,sleep sth↔'off** to get better after sth, especially drinking too much alcohol, by sleeping 靠睡覺來消除；睡一覺熬過酒勁：*Let's leave him to* ***sleep it off.*** 咱們讓他睡吧，一覺醒來就沒事了。 **'sleep on sth** (*informal*) to delay making a decision about sth until the next day, so that you have time to think about it 把…留待第二天決定；把…拖延到第二天再說：*Could I sleep on it and let you know tomorrow?* 能不能讓我晚上考慮考慮，明天答覆你？ **,sleep 'over** to stay the night at sb else's home 在別人家裏過夜：*It's very late now—why don't you sleep over?* 現在已經很晚了，為什麼不就睡這兒呢？◇ *Can I sleep over at my friend's house?* 我能不能在我朋友家過夜？➲ related noun SLEEPOVER **'sleep together | 'sleep with sb** (*informal*) to have sex with sb, especially sb you are not married to 和某人（尤指非配偶）發生性關係：*I know he's going out with her, but I don't think they're sleeping together.* 我知道他跟她在談戀愛，不過我想他們還不至於上牀吧。◇ *Everyone knows she sleeps with the boss.* 人人知道她跟老闆睡覺。

■ *noun* **1** 🗝 [U] the natural state of rest in which your eyes are closed, your body is not active, and your mind is not conscious 睡覺；睡眠：*I need to* ***get some sleep.*** 我得睡一會兒。◇ *I didn't* ***get much sleep*** *last night.* 昨晚我沒睡好。◇ *Can you give me something to help me* ***get to sleep*** (= start sleeping)? 你能不能給我點能讓我入睡的東西？◇ ***Go to sleep***—*it's late.* 快睡吧，不早了。◇ *He cried out* ***in his sleep.*** 他在睡夢中大叫。◇ *Anxiety can be caused by* ***lack of sleep.*** 睡眠不足可能導致焦慮。◇ *His talk nearly* ***sent me to sleep*** (= it was boring). 他的講話差點讓我睡着了。◇ *Try to go* ***back to sleep.*** 再繼續睡吧。**2** 🗝 [sing.] a period of sleep 睡眠時間；一覺：*Did you have a good sleep?* 睡得好嗎？◇ *Ros fell into a deep sleep.* 羅斯睡着了，睡得很沉。◇ *I'll feel better after a* ***good night's sleep*** (= a night when I sleep well). 好好睡一晚，我就會覺得好些了。 **3** [U] (*informal*) the substance that sometimes forms in the corners of your eyes after you have been sleeping 眼屎

IDM **be able to do sth in your 'sleep** (*informal*) to be able to do sth very easily because you have done it many times before 閉着眼睛也能做 **,go to 'sleep** (*informal*) if part of your body **goes to sleep**, you lose the sense of feeling in it, usually because it has been in the same position for too long（身體某部位）麻木，發麻 **not lose 'sleep/lose no 'sleep over sth** to not worry much about sth 不大為某事操心：*It's not worth losing sleep over.* 那件事不值得焦慮。 **put sb to 'sleep** (*informal*) to make sb unconscious before an operation by using drugs (called an ANAESTHETIC)（用藥物）麻醉 **put sth to 'sleep** to kill a sick or injured animal by giving it drugs so that it dies without pain. People say 'put to sleep' to avoid saying 'kill'.（用藥物）使長眠，無痛苦地殺死（生病或受傷的動物）➲ more at WINK *n.*

sleep·er /ˈsliːpə(r)/ *noun* **1** (used with an adjective 與形容詞連用) a person who sleeps in a particular way 睡得…的人：*a* ***heavy/light/sound sleeper*** 睡得很沉／輕／香的人 **2** a person who is asleep 睡覺者；睡眠者：*Only the snores of the sleepers broke the silence of the house.* 只有睡覺的人發出的鼾聲打破了屋內的寂靜。**3** a night train with beds for passengers on it 卧鋪列車：*the London–Edinburgh sleeper* 倫敦到愛丁堡的卧鋪列車 **4** = SLEEPING CAR **5** (*BrE*) (*NAmE* **tie**) one of the heavy pieces of wood or concrete on which the rails on a railway/railroad track are laid（鐵路）枕木，軌枕 ➲ VISUAL VOCAB page V58 **6** (*informal, especially NAmE*) a film/movie, play or book that for a long time is not very successful and then is suddenly a success（出人意外地成功的）冷門電影（或戲劇、著作等） **7** (also **,sleeper 'agent**) a SPY who is sent to live in a country as a normal citizen and is not used until much later 休眠間諜（暫時不從事間諜活動） **8** (*BrE*) a ring or piece of metal that you wear in an ear that has been PIERCED (= had a hole made in it) to keep the hole from closing（為保持耳環孔不閉合而戴的）耳環，耳釘

'sleeping bag *noun* a thick warm bag that you use for sleeping in, for example when you are camping 睡袋 ➲ VISUAL VOCAB page V23

,Sleeping 'Beauty *noun* used to refer to sb who has been asleep for a long time 睡了很長時間的人：*OK, Sleeping Beauty, time to get up.* 好啦，睡美人，該起牀了。 **ORIGIN** From the European fairy tale about a beautiful girl who sleeps for a hundred years and is woken up when a prince kisses her. 源自歐洲童話，沉睡百年的美麗少女被王子的親吻喚醒。

'sleeping car (also **sleep·er**) *noun* a coach/car on a train with beds for people to sleep in 卧鋪車廂

,sleeping 'partner (*BrE*) (*NAmE* **,silent 'partner**) *noun* a person who has put money into a business company but who is not actually involved in running it 隱名合夥人，隱名股東（在企業中有股份但不參與經營）

'sleeping pill (*BrE* also **'sleeping tablet**) *noun* a pill containing a drug that helps you to sleep 安眠藥

,sleeping po'liceman *noun* (*BrE, informal*) = SPEED HUMP

'sleeping sickness *noun* [U] a tropical disease carried by the TSETSE FLY that causes a feeling of wanting to go to sleep and usually causes death 昏睡病（由采采蠅傳播的熱帶疾病，患者嗜睡，通常導致死亡）

sleep·less /ˈsliːpləs/ *adj.* **1** [only before noun] without sleep 沒有睡覺的；不眠的：*I've had a few* ***sleepless nights*** *recently.* 最近我有好幾個晚上沒睡覺。 **2** [not before noun] not able to sleep 睡不着；失眠：*She lay sleepless until dawn.* 她躺在那兒，直到天亮才睡着。▶ **sleep·less·ly** *adv.* **sleep·less·ness** *noun* [U] **SYN** **insomnia**：*to suffer from sleeplessness* 受失眠之苦

sleep·over /ˈsliːpəʊvə(r); *NAmE* -oʊ-/ (*NAmE* also **'slumber party**) *noun* a party for children or young people when a group of them spend the night at one house（兒童或年輕人在某人家玩樂並過夜的）聚會

sleep·walk /ˈsliːpwɔːk/ *verb* [I] to walk around while you are asleep 夢遊 ▶ **sleep·walk·er** (also *formal* **som·nam·bu·list**) *noun*

sleepy /ˈsliːpi/ *adj.* (**sleep·ier**, **sleepi·est**) **1** needing sleep; ready to go to sleep 睏倦的；瞌睡的 **SYN** **drowsy**：*a sleepy child* 打瞌睡的孩子◇ *He had begun to feel sleepy.* 他已覺得睏了。◇ *The heat and the wine made her sleepy.* 周圍暖洋洋的，又喝了酒，她感覺昏昏欲睡。 **2** (of places 地方) quiet and where nothing much happens 安靜的；冷清的；不熱鬧的：*a sleepy little town* 寧靜的小城 ▶ **sleep·ily** /-ɪli/ *adv.*：*She yawned sleepily.* 她睏得打着哈欠。 **sleepi·ness** *noun* [U]

sleepy·head /ˈsliːpihed/ *noun* (*informal*) a way of addressing sb who is not completely awake（稱呼沒睡醒的人）懶鬼，瞌睡蟲：*Come on sleepyhead—time to get up.* 快點吧，懶鬼，該起牀了。

sleet /sliːt/ *noun, verb*
■ ***noun*** [U] a mixture of rain and snow 雨夾雪
■ ***verb*** [I] when **it is sleeting**, a mixture of rain and snow is falling from the sky 下雨夾雪

sleeve 🔑 /sliːv/ *noun*
1 🔑 a part of a piece of clothing that covers all or part of your arm 袖子： *a dress with* ***short/long sleeves*** 短袖／長袖連衣裙 ◇ *Dan* ***rolled up his sleeves*** *and washed his hands.* 丹挽起袖子洗了洗手。 ➲ VISUAL VOCAB pages V61, V63 ➲ see also SHIRTSLEEVE **2 -sleeved** (in adjectives 構成形容詞) having sleeves of the type mentioned 有…袖子的： *a short-sleeved shirt* 短袖襯衫 ➲ VISUAL VOCAB page V63 **3** (also **jacket** especially in *NAmE*) a stiff paper or cardboard envelope for a record 唱片套： *a colourful sleeve design* 色彩斑斕的唱片套設計 **4** a tube that covers a part of a machine to protect it （機器的）套筒，套管 ▸ **sleeve·less** *adj.*： *a sleeveless dress* 無袖連衣裙 ➲ VISUAL VOCAB page V61
IDM **have/keep sth up your 'sleeve** to keep a plan or an idea secret until you need to use it 有錦囊妙計；胸中自有主張 ➲ more at ACE *n.*, CARD *n.*, LAUGH *v.*, ROLL *v.*, TRICK *n.*, WEAR *v.*

'sleeve note *noun* (*BrE*) = LINER NOTE

sleigh /sleɪ/ *noun* a SLEDGE (= a vehicle that slides over snow), especially one pulled by horses （尤指馬拉的）雪橇： *a sleigh ride* 乘雪橇 ➲ picture at SLEDGE

sleight of hand /ˌslaɪt əv ˈhænd/ *noun* [U] **1** (also *formal* **le·ger·de·main**) skilful movements of your hand that other people cannot see （隱蔽的）敏捷手法，靈巧手法： *The trick is done simply by sleight of hand.* 變這個戲法全憑手法敏捷。 **2** the fact of tricking people in a clever way 把戲；花招：*Last year's profits were more the result of financial sleight of hand than genuine growth.* 去年的贏利更多是因為財務手法，而不是真正的增長。

slen·der /ˈslendə(r)/ *adj.* (**slen·derer**, **slen·derest**)
HELP You can also use **more slender** and **most slender**. 亦可用 more slender 和 most slender。 **1** (*approving*) (of people or their bodies 人或人體) thin in an attractive or elegant way 苗條的；纖細的 SYN **slim**： *her slender figure* 她苗條的身材 ◇ *long, slender fingers* 修長纖細的手指 **2** thin or narrow 細的；窄的： *a glass with a slender stem* 高腳酒杯 **3** small in amount or size and hardly enough 微薄的；不足的： *to win by a* ***slender margin/majority*** 以微弱優勢／多數獲勝 ◇ *people of* ***slender means*** (= with little money) 窮人 ◇ *Australia held a slender 1–0 lead at half-time.* 澳大利亞隊在上半場終時以 1:0 的微弱優勢領先。 ▸ **slen·der·ness** *noun* [U]

slept *past tense, past part.* of SLEEP

sleuth /sluːθ/ *noun* (*old-fashioned* or *humorous*) a person who investigates crimes 偵探 SYN **detective**： *an amateur sleuth* 業餘偵探

sleuth·ing /ˈsluːθɪŋ/ *noun* [U] the act of investigating a crime or mysterious event 偵查，調查（犯罪案件或神秘事件）： *to do some private sleuthing* 進行私人偵查

slew /sluː/ *verb, noun* ➲ see also SLAY *v.*
■ ***verb*** [I, T] (especially of a vehicle 尤指車輛) to turn or slide suddenly in another direction; to make a vehicle do this （使）突然轉向，急轉： **+ adv./prep.** *The car skidded and slewed sideways.* 汽車打滑，向一側偏去。◇ **~ sth + adv./prep.** *He slewed the motorbike over as they hit the freeway.* 他們衝到高速公路時，他趕緊把摩托車調轉方向。
■ ***noun*** [sing.] **~ of sth** (*informal, especially NAmE*) a large number or amount of sth 大量；許多

slice 🔑 /slaɪs/ *noun, verb*
■ ***noun*** **1** 🔑 a thin flat piece of food that has been cut off a larger piece （切下的食物）薄片，片： *a slice of bread* 一片麵包 ◇ *Cut the meat into thin slices.* 把肉切成薄片。 **2** (*informal*) a part or share of sth 部份；份額： *Our firm is well placed to grab a large slice of the market.* 我們公司處境有利，足以獲得巨大的市場份額。 **3** a kitchen UTENSIL (= tool) that you use to lift and serve pieces of food 鍋鏟；（餐桌用）小鏟：*a fish slice* 煎魚鏟 ➲ VISUAL VOCAB page V26 **4** (*sport* 體) (in GOLF, TENNIS, etc. 高爾夫球、網球等) a stroke that makes the ball spin to one side rather than going straight ahead 削球；側旋球；斜切打
IDM **a ˌslice of ˈlife** a film/movie, play or book that gives a very realistic view of ordinary life 反映現實生活的電影（或戲劇、書） ➲ more at ACTION, CAKE *n.*, PIE
■ ***verb*** **1** 🔑 [T] **~ sth (up)** to cut sth into slices 把…切成（薄）片： *to slice (up) onions* 把洋蔥切成片 ◇ *Slice the cucumber thinly.* 把黃瓜切成薄薄的片。◇ *a sliced loaf* 切片麵包 ➲ COLLOCATIONS at COOKING ➲ VISUAL VOCAB page V28 ➲ see also SALAMI SLICING **2** 🔑 [I] to cut sth easily with or as if with a sharp blade 切；割；劃： **+ adv./prep.** *He accidentally* ***sliced through*** *his finger.* 他不小心把指頭割破了。◇ *A piece of glass sliced into his shoulder.* 一塊玻璃劃破他的肩膀。◇ (*figurative*) *Her speech sliced through all the confusion surrounding the situation.* 她一席話把整個事態的一切紛擾剖析得清清楚楚。◇ **~ sth (+ adj.)** *The knife sliced his jacket.* 那把刀劃破了他的上衣。◇ *He sliced the fruit open.* 他把水果切開了。◇ (*figurative*) *The ship sliced the water.* 船破浪前進。 **3** [T] **~ sth** (*sport* 體) to hit a ball so that it spins and does not move in the expected direction 削（球）；斜切打： *He managed to slice a shot over the net.* 他設法把球斜切過網。 **4** [T] **~ sth** (in GOLF 高爾夫球) to hit the ball so that it flies away in a curve, when you do not mean to （無意中）打出弧線球 **5** [T] **~ sth** (*NAmE, informal*) to reduce sth by a large amount 大幅度削減；大量降低： *The new tax has sliced annual bonuses by 30 percent.* 由於徵收新稅，年度紅利減少了 30%。
IDM **ˌslice and ˈdice (sth)** (*computing* 計) to divide information into small parts in order to study it more closely or to see it in different ways 切割，分割（信息）： *The software lets you slice and dice the data and display it in different formats.* 這軟件使你能夠對數據進行切割，以不同的格式顯示出來。 ➲ more at WAY *n.*
PHR V **ˌslice sth↔ˈoff/aˈway** | **ˌslice sth ˈoff sth** to cut sth from a larger piece 切下；割下： *Slice a piece off.* 切下一片。◇ (*figurative*) *He sliced two seconds off the world record.* 他把世界紀錄縮短了兩秒。

ˌsliced ˈbread *noun* [U] bread that is sold already cut into slices 切片麵包： *a loaf of sliced bread* 一條切片麵包
IDM **the best thing since sliced ˈbread** (*informal*) if you say that sth is **the best thing since sliced bread**, you think it is extremely good, interesting, etc. 極好（或極有意思等）的事物

slick /slɪk/ *adj., noun, verb*
■ ***adj.*** (**slick·er**, **slick·est**) **1** (sometimes *disapproving*) done or made in a way that is clever and efficient but often does not seem to be sincere or lacks important ideas 華而不實的；虛有其表的；取巧的： *a slick advertising campaign* 華而不實的廣告攻勢 ◇ *a slick performance* 表面熱鬧但內容貧乏的演出 **2** (sometimes *disapproving*) speaking very easily and smoothly but in a way that does not seem sincere 花言巧語的；能說會道的；油滑的 SYN **glib**： *slick TV presenters* 伶牙俐齒的電視節目主持人 ◇ *a slick salesman* 花言巧語的推銷員 **3** done quickly and smoothly 嫻熟的；靈巧的；流暢的 SYN **skilful**： *The crowd enjoyed the team's slick passing.* 觀眾欣賞了這支球隊嫻熟的傳接配合。◇ *a slick gear change* 靈巧的換擋 **4** smooth and difficult to hold or move on 滑的；滑溜溜的 SYN **slippery**： *The roads were slick with rain.* 下雨路滑。 ▸ **slick·ly** *adv.*： *The magazine is slickly produced.* 這份雜誌辦得華而不實。 **slick·ness** *noun* [U]
■ ***noun*** **1** (also **ˈoil slick**) an area of oil that is floating on the surface of the sea （海上）浮油，浮油膜 **2** a small area of sth wet and shiny 一小片濕而亮的地方： *a slick of sweat* 涔涔的汗水
■ ***verb*** [usually passive] **~ sth + adv./prep.** to make hair very flat and smooth by putting oil, water, etc. on it 使（頭髮）平整光溜： *His hair was* ***slicked back/down*** *with gel.* 他的頭髮用了髮膠，朝後／朝下梳得平平整整的。

slick·er /ˈslɪkə(r)/ *noun* (*NAmE*) a long loose coat that keeps you dry in the rain （長而寬鬆的）雨衣 ➲ see also CITY SLICKER

slide 🔑 /slaɪd/ *verb, noun*
■ ***verb*** (**slid**, **slid** /slɪd/)
▸ **MOVE SMOOTHLY/QUIETLY** 滑行；悄悄地移動 **1** 🔑 [I, T] to move easily over a smooth or wet surface; to make sth

move in this way（使）滑行，滑動：(**+ adv./prep.**) *We slid down the grassy slope.* 我們從草坡上滑了下來。◇ *The drawers slide in and out easily.* 這幾個抽屜好推好拉。◇ **~ sth + adv./prep.** *She slid her hand along the rail.* 她把手搭在欄杆上滑動着。◇ **~ (sth) + adj.** *The automatic doors slid open.* 自動門慢慢開了。 **2** [I, T] to move quickly and quietly, for example in order not to be noticed; to make sth move in this way（使）快捷而悄聲地移動 SYN **slip**：**+ adv./prep.** *He slid into bed.* 他不聲不響地鑽進被子。◇ *She slid out while no one was looking.* 她趁着沒人看見溜了出去。◇ **~ sth + adv./prep.** *The man slid the money quickly into his pocket.* 那人很快把錢塞進自己的口袋。

▸ BECOME LOWER/WORSE 降低；衰落 **3** [I] **~ (from …) (to …)** to become gradually lower or of less value 逐漸降低；貶值：*Shares slid to a 10-year low.* 股價跌到了 10 年來的最低點。 **4** [I] **~ (down/into/towards sth)** to move gradually into a worse situation 衰落（成）；逐漸陷入；逐漸衰退（到）：*The industry has slid into decline.* 這個行業已成衰退之勢。◇ *They were sliding towards bankruptcy.* 他們正逐漸瀕臨破產。◇ *He got depressed and began to **let things slide*** (= failed to give things the attention they needed). 他意氣消沉，得過且過。

■ ***noun***

▸ BECOMING LOWER/WORSE 降低；衰落 **1** [C, usually sing.] a change to a lower or worse condition 降低；跌落；衰落：*a downward slide in the price of oil* 石油價格的下跌 ◇ *the team's slide down the table* 球隊排名的下降 ◇ *talks to prevent **a slide into** civil war* 旨在避免陷入內戰的談判 ◇ *The economy is **on the slide*** (= getting worse). 經濟日益衰退。

▸ ON ICE 在冰上 **2** [sing.] a long, smooth movement on ice or a smooth surface（在冰上或光滑表面上的）滑行，滑動 SYN **skid**：*Her car went into a slide.* 她的車打起滑來。

▸ FOR CHILDREN 兒童 **3** [C] a structure with a steep slope that children use for sliding down 滑梯：*to go down the slide* 溜滑梯 ➲ VISUAL VOCAB page V37

▸ FALL OF ROCK 山岩崩塌 **4** [C] a sudden fall of a large amount of rock or earth down a hill 山崩；岩崩；土崩；崩塌 SYN **landslide**：*I was afraid of starting a slide of loose stones.* 我當時擔心會引起鬆散石塊崩塌。

▸ PHOTOGRAPH 照片 **5** [C] a small piece of film held in a frame that can be shown on a screen when you shine a light through it 幻燈片 SYN **transparency**：*a talk with colour slides* 借助彩色幻燈片的講話

▸ COMPUTERS 計算機 **6** [C] one page of an electronic presentation, that may contain text and images, that is usually viewed on a computer screen or projected onto a larger screen 幻燈片：*I'm still working on the slides for my presentation.* 我還在準備演示用的幻燈片。

▸ FOR MICROSCOPE 顯微鏡 **7** [C] a small piece of glass that sth is placed on so that it can be looked at under a MICROSCOPE 載物玻璃片 ➲ VISUAL VOCAB page V70

▸ PART OF MUSICAL INSTRUMENT 樂器部件 **8** [C] a part of a musical instrument or other device that slides backwards and forwards（樂器上的）拉管，滑管，滑動裝置 ➲ VISUAL VOCAB page V34

▸ FOR HAIR 頭髮 **9** [C] (*BrE*) = HAIRSLIDE

'slide projector *noun* a piece of equipment for displaying SLIDES (= small pieces of film held in frames) on a screen 幻燈機 ➲ compare DATA PROJECTOR, OVERHEAD PROJECTOR

sli·der /ˈslaɪdə(r)/ *noun* **1** a device for controlling sth such as the volume of a radio, which you slide up and down or from side to side（控制收音機音量等的）滑桿，滑動器 **2** (*computing* 計) an ICON that you can slide up and down or from side to side with the mouse 滾動條滑塊 **3** a FRESHWATER, TURTLE from N America 紅腹彩龜（北美淡水龜）

'slide rule *noun* a long narrow instrument like a ruler, with a middle part that slides backwards and forwards, used for calculating numbers 計算尺；滑尺

'slide show (also **slide·show**) *noun* **1** a number of slides (= small pieces of film held in frames) shown to an audience using a SLIDE PROJECTOR, often during a lecture（常指講演中的）幻燈片放映 **2** (*computing* 計) a piece of software that shows a number of images on a computer screen in a particular order 幻燈片放映軟件；幻燈片放映軟體：*a slideshow presentation* 幻燈片演示

ˌsliding ˈdoor *noun* a door that slides across an opening rather than swinging away from it 滑門；推拉門

ˌsliding ˈscale *noun* a system in which the rate at which sth is paid varies according to particular conditions 浮動費率制（根據情況上下浮動費率的交納制度）：*Fees are calculated **on a sliding scale** according to income* (= richer people pay more). 按浮動費率制根據收入高低計算收費。

slight 0‑ /slaɪt/ *adj., noun, verb*

■ ***adj.*** (**slight·er**, **slight·est**) **1** 0‑ very small in degree 輕微的；略微的：*a slight increase/change/delay/difference* 略微的增長／變化／拖延／差異 ◇ *I woke up with a slight headache.* 我醒來時有點頭痛。◇ *The damage was slight.* 損失很小。◇ *She takes offence at the slightest thing* (= is very easily offended). 她動輒生氣。◇ *There was **not the slightest** hint of trouble.* 當時看不出絲毫會出現麻煩的跡象。 **2** small and thin in size 細小的；纖細的；瘦小的：*a slight woman* 瘦小的女子 **3** (*formal*) not deserving serious attention 無須重視的；不足道的：*This is a very slight novel.* 這是一部頗不足道的小說。

IDM **not in the ˈslightest** not at all 一點也不；毫不；根本沒有：*He didn't seem to mind in the slightest.* 他好像一點都不在乎。

■ ***noun* ~ (on sb/sth)** an act or a remark that criticizes sth or offends sb 侮慢；冷落；輕視 SYN **insult**：*Nick took her comment as a slight on his abilities as a manager.* 尼克覺得，她的話是藐視他當經理的能力。

■ ***verb*** [usually passive] **~ sb** to treat sb rudely or without respect 侮慢；冷落；輕視 SYN **insult**：*She felt **slighted** because she hadn't been invited.* 她沒有受到邀請，覺得受了冷落。▸ **slight·ing** *adj.* [only before noun]：*slighting remarks* 不敬的話語

slight·ly 0‑ /ˈslaɪtli/ *adv.*

1 0‑ a little 略微；稍微：*a slightly different version* 略有不同的說法 ◇ *We took a slightly more direct route.* 我們選擇了一條略近的路線。◇ *I knew her slightly.* 我對她略知一二。◇ *'Are you worried?' 'Only slightly.'* "你擔心嗎？" "稍微有點。" **2** a **slightly built** person is small and thin 身材瘦小的

slim /slɪm/ *adj., verb, noun*

■ ***adj.*** (**slim·mer**, **slim·mest**) **1** (*approving*) (of a person 人) thin, in a way that is attractive 苗條的；纖細的：*a slim figure/body/waist* 苗條的體形／身材；纖細的腰肢 ◇ *She was tall and slim.* 她是個瘦高個兒。◇ *How do you manage to stay so slim?* 你是怎樣把身材保持得這麼苗條的？◇ (*figurative*) *Many companies are a lot slimmer than they used to be* (= have fewer workers). 許多公司的員工比過去少多了。 **2** thinner than usual 單薄的：*a **slim volume** of poetry* 一本薄薄的詩集 **3** not as big as you would like or expect 微薄的；不足的；少的；小的 SYN **small**：*a **slim chance** of success* 成功的可能性不大 ◇ *The party was returned to power with a **slim majority**.* 該黨以微弱多數重新上台。➲ see also SLIMMER, SLIMMING ▸ **slim·ness** *noun* [U]

■ ***verb*** (**-mm-**) [I] (*BrE*) (usually used in the progressive tenses 通常用於進行時) to try to become thinner, for example by eating less（靠節食等）變苗條，減肥 SYN **diet**：*You can still eat breakfast when you are slimming.* 你減肥也可以吃早飯嘛！➲ COLLOCATIONS at DIET

PHR V **ˌslim ˈdown** to become thinner, for example as a result of eating less（靠節食等）變苗條，減肥 **ˌslim ˈdown** | **ˌslim sth↔ˈdown** to make a company or an organization smaller, by reducing the number of jobs in it; to be made smaller in this way 精簡（機構）；裁減（人員）；減少（崗位）：*They're restructuring and slimming down the workforce.* 他們正對職工加以重組和裁減。◇ *The industry may have to slim down even further.* 這個行業可能還得進一步壓縮。◇ *the new, slimmed-down company* 精簡人員後的新公司 ➲ see also SLIMMING

■ ***noun*** [U] an African word for AIDS（非洲用語）艾滋病

S

slime /slaɪm/ *noun* [U] any unpleasant thick liquid substance 污濁的泥漿；黏液：*The pond was full of mud and green slime.* 池子裏滿是淤泥和綠色的污水。➲ see also SLIMY

slime·ball /ˈslaɪmbɔːl/ (also **slime·bag** /ˈslaɪmbæg/) *noun* (*informal*) an unpleasant or disgusting person 令人反感的人；卑劣的人

slim·line /ˈslɪmlaɪn/ *adj.* [only before noun] **1** smaller or thinner in design than usual 式樣小巧的；薄型的：*a slimline phone* 小巧的電話 **2** (*BrE*) (of a drink 飲料) containing very little sugar 低糖的：*slimline tonic water* 低糖奎寧水

slim·mer /ˈslɪmə(r)/ *noun* (*BrE*) a person who is trying to lose weight 減肥者；減輕體重者：*a calorie-controlled diet for slimmers* 控制熱量的減肥食譜 ➲ see also SLIM

slim·ming /ˈslɪmɪŋ/ *noun* [U] (*BrE*) the practice of trying to lose weight 減肥；減輕體重：*a slimming club* 減肥俱樂部 ➲ see also SLIM

slimy /ˈslaɪmi/ *adj.* (**slimi·er**, **slimi·est**) **1** like or covered with SLIME 似泥漿的；粘有黏液的：*thick slimy mud* 黏稠的污泥 ◇ *The walls were black, cold and slimy.* 牆又黑又冷，上面滿是黏濕的污跡。 **2** (*informal, disapproving*) (of a person or their manner 人或態度) polite and extremely friendly in a way that is not sincere or honest 諂媚的；討好的；假惺惺的

sling /slɪŋ/ *verb, noun*

■ **verb** (**slung**, **slung** /slʌŋ/) **1** (*informal, especially BrE*) to throw sth somewhere in a careless way（隨便地）扔，丟 SYN **chuck**：**~ sth + adv./prep.** *Don't just sling your clothes on the floor.* 不要把衣服往地板上一扔就不管了。◇ **~ sb sth** *Sling me an apple, will you?* 扔個蘋果給我，好嗎？ ➲ see also MUD-SLINGING **2** [often passive] **~ sth + adv./prep.** to put sth somewhere where it hangs loosely 掛；吊：*Her bag was slung over her shoulder.* 她將包挎在肩上。◇ *We slung a hammock between two trees.* 我們在兩棵樹之間掛了一個吊牀。 **3** [often passive] **~ sb + adv./prep.** (*informal*) to put sb somewhere by force; to make sb leave somewhere 遣送；押往；攆走；驅逐：*They were slung out of the club for fighting.* 他們因打架被趕出了俱樂部。

IDM **sling your 'hook** (*BrE, informal*) (used especially in orders 尤用於命令) to go away 走開；滾蛋

PHR V **ˌsling 'off at sb** (*AustralE, NZE, informal*) to laugh at sb in an unkind way 嘲笑；譏笑

■ **noun** **1** a band of cloth that is tied around a person's neck and used to support a broken or injured arm（懸吊受傷手臂的）懸帶，吊腕帶：*He had his arm **in a sling**.* 他用懸帶吊着胳膊。 **2** a device consisting of a band, ropes, etc. for holding and lifting heavy objects（懸掛或起吊重物的）吊索，吊鏈，吊帶：*The engine was lifted in a sling of steel rope.* 引擎用鋼絲吊索吊了起來。 **3** a device like a bag for carrying a baby on your back or in front of you（用以背嬰兒的）吊兜 **4** (in the past) a simple weapon made from a band of leather, etc., used for throwing stones 投石器（舊時武器）SYN **catapult**

sling·back /ˈslɪŋbæk/ *noun* a woman's shoe that is open at the back with a narrow piece of leather, etc. around the heel 露跟女鞋（後幫為窄帶）➲ VISUAL VOCAB page V64

sling·shot /ˈslɪŋʃɒt; *NAmE* -ʃɑːt/ (*NAmE*) (*BrE* **cata·pult**) *noun* a stick shaped like a Y with a rubber band attached to it, used by children for shooting stones 彈弓 ➲ picture at CATAPULT

slink /slɪŋk/ *verb* (**slunk**, **slunk** /slʌŋk/) [I] **+ adv./prep.** to move somewhere very quietly and slowly, especially because you are ashamed or do not want to be seen 偷偷摸摸地走；躲躲閃閃地走；溜 SYN **creep**：*John was trying to slink into the house by the back door.* 約翰想從後門溜進房子裏。◇ *The dog howled and slunk away.* 那狗淒厲地叫着並退走了。

slinky /ˈslɪŋki/ *adj.* (**slink·ier**, **slinki·est**) **1** (of a woman's clothes 女式服裝) fitting closely to the body in a sexually attractive way 緊身而性感的；身體線條畢現的 **2** (of movement or sound 動作或聲音) smooth and slow, often in a way that is sexually attractive 裊娜的；婀娜多姿的；柔媚的；柔美的

slip /slɪp/ *verb, noun*

■ **verb** (**-pp-**)

▸ SLIDE/FALL 滑；倒 **1** [I] **~ (over)** to slide a short distance by accident so that you fall or nearly fall 滑倒；滑跤：*She slipped over on the ice and broke her leg.* 她在冰上滑倒把腿摔斷了。◇ *As I ran up the stairs, my foot slipped and I fell.* 我跑上樓梯時失腳摔倒了。

▸ OUT OF POSITION 脱離位置 **2** [I] (**+ adv./prep.**) to slide out of position or out of your hand 滑落；滑離；脱落：*His hat had slipped over one eye.* 他的帽子滑下來遮住了一隻眼睛。◇ *The fish slipped out of my hand.* 魚從我手裏溜掉了。◇ *The child **slipped from his grasp** and ran off.* 他一把沒抓牢，讓那孩子跑掉了。◇ (*figurative*) *She was careful not to let her control slip.* 她小心翼翼，不讓自己失控。

▸ GO/PUT QUICKLY 快速地走／放置 **3** [I] **+ adv./prep.** to go somewhere quickly and quietly, especially without being noticed 悄悄疾行；溜 SYN **creep**：*She slipped out of the house before the others were awake.* 她趁別人還沒醒，溜出了房子。◇ *The ship slipped into the harbour at night.* 船在夜間悄然進港。◇ (*figurative*) *She knew that time was slipping away.* 她知道時間在飛逝。 **4** [T] to put sth somewhere quickly, quietly or secretly 迅速放置；悄悄塞；偷偷放：**~ sth + adv./prep.** *Anna slipped her hand into his.* 安娜悄悄把手伸過去，讓他握住。◇ *I managed to slip a few jokes into my speech.* 我設法在講話中穿插了幾個笑話。◇ *I managed to **slip in** a few jokes.* 我設法穿插了幾個笑話。◇ **~ sth to sb** *They'd slipped some money to the guards.* 他們悄悄塞給衞兵一些錢。◇ **~ sb sth** *They'd slipped the guards some money.* 他們悄悄塞給衞兵一些錢。

▸ BECOME WORSE 變差 **5** [I] to fall to a lower level; to become worse 下降；退步；變差：*His popularity has slipped recently.* 近來他已不如過去那樣受歡迎。◇ *That's three times she's beaten me—I **must be slipping!*** 她已經贏了我三回了，我一定是退步了！

▸ INTO DIFFICULT SITUATION 陷入困境 **6** [I] **+ adv./prep.** to pass into a particular state or situation, especially a difficult or unpleasant one 陷入，進入（困難或不愉快的處境）：*He began to **slip into** debt.* 他開始欠債了。◇ *The patient had **slipped into** a coma.* 病人陷入昏迷狀態。◇ *We seem to have slipped behind schedule.* 我們好像已經趕不上日程安排了。

▸ CLOTHES ON/OFF 穿／脱衣服 **7** [I, T] to put clothes on or to take them off quickly and easily（迅速且容易地）穿上，脱下：**+ adv./prep.** *to **slip into/out of a dress*** 麻利地穿上／脱掉連衣裙 ◇ **~ sth + adv./prep.** *to **slip your shoes on/off*** 蹬上／脱了鞋 ◇ *He slipped a coat over his sweatshirt.* 他將一件外衣披在長袖套衫上。

▸ GET FREE 擺脱 **8** [T] to get free; to make sth/sb/yourself free from sth 擺脱；掙脱；鬆開；放走：**~ sth** *The ship had slipped its moorings in the night.* 那艘船在夜間漂離了停泊處。◇ **~ (sth) + adj.** *The animal had **slipped free** and escaped.* 那頭動物掙脱逃跑了。

IDM **let 'slip sth** to give sb information that is supposed to be secret 泄露；無意中說出：*I happened to **let it slip** that he had given me £1 000 for the car.* 我一不小心說出了他花 1 000 英鎊買走我那輛車的事。◇ *She tried not to let slip what she knew.* 她盡量不把她所知道的事泄露出去。 **let sth 'slip (through your fingers)** to miss or fail to use an opportunity 錯過（機會）；失去（機會）：*Don't let the chance to work abroad slip through your fingers.* 這個出國工作的機會你可不要錯過。 **slip your 'mind** if sth **slips your mind**, you forget it or forget to do it 被遺忘 **ˌslip one 'over on sb** (*informal*) to trick sb 欺騙；愚弄 **slip through the 'net** when sb/sth **slips through the net**, an organization or a system fails to find them and deal with them 漏網；被漏掉：*We tried to contact all former students, but one or two slipped through the net.* 我們試圖同所有的校友取得聯繫，但有一兩個未能找到。➲ more at GEAR *n.*, TONGUE *n.*

PHR V **ˌslip a'way** to stop existing; to disappear or die 消失；消亡；死去：*Their support gradually slipped away.* 他們逐漸失去支持。 **ˌslip 'out** when sth **slips out**, you say it without really intending to 無意中說出（或泄露）：*I'm sorry I said that. It just slipped out.* 抱歉，

S

我說了這樣的話。這不過是無意中說出口的。**,slip 'up** (*informal*) to make a careless mistake 疏忽；不小心出差錯：*We can't afford to slip up.* 我們疏忽不得。➲ related noun SLIP-UP

■ ***noun***

▸ **SMALL MISTAKE 差錯** **1** a small mistake, usually made by being careless or not paying attention 差錯；疏漏；紕漏：*He recited the whole poem without making a single slip.* 他一字不差地背誦了全詩。➲ see also FREUDIAN SLIP ➲ **SYNONYMS** at MISTAKE

▸ **PIECE OF PAPER 紙** **2** a small piece of paper, especially one for writing on or with sth printed on it 紙條；便條；小紙片：*I wrote it down on a slip of paper.* 我把它記在一張紙條上。◇ *a betting slip* 賭注單 ➲ see also PAYSLIP

▸ **ACT OF SLIPPING 滑跤** **3** an act of slipping 滑跤；滑倒；失腳：*One slip and you could fall to your death.* 一失腳，你就會摔死。

▸ **CLOTHING 衣服** **4** a piece of women's underwear like a thin dress or skirt, worn under a dress 襯裙

▸ **IN CRICKET 板球** **5** a player who stands behind and to one side of the BATSMAN and tries to catch the ball; the position on the field where this player stands（擊球員後側的）守場員；守場員所站的位置

IDM **give sb the 'slip** (*informal*) to escape or get away from sb who is following or chasing you 擺脫某人的追蹤；甩掉某人的跟踪 **a 'slip of a boy, girl, etc.** (*old-fashioned*) a small or thin, usually young, person 小男孩（或女孩等）；瘦男孩（或女孩等） **a slip of the 'pen/'tongue** a small mistake in sth that you write or say 筆誤；口誤：*Did I call you Richard? Sorry, Robert, just a slip of the tongue.* 我剛才是不是叫你理查德了？對不起，羅伯特，我是一時口誤。 **there's ,many a 'slip 'twixt ,cup and 'lip** (*saying*) nothing is completely certain until it really happens because things can easily go wrong 到嘴的鴨子也會飛走（指沒有十拿九穩的事）

'slip case *noun* a stiff cover that a book or other object fits into（書等的）硬套，盒

'slip cover (*NAmE*) (*BrE* **,loose 'cover**) *noun* a cover for a chair, etc. that you can take off, for example to wash it（椅子等的）活套，活罩

'slip knot *noun* a knot that can slide easily along the rope, etc. on which it is tied, in order to make the LOOP or rope tighter or looser 活結；滑結

'slip-on *noun* a shoe that you can slide your feet into without having to tie LACES 無帶（或無扣）便鞋：*a pair of slip-ons* 一雙無帶便鞋 ◇ *slip-on shoes* 無帶便鞋

S

slip·page /'slɪpɪdʒ/ *noun* [U, C, usually sing.] **1** failure to achieve an aim or complete a task by a particular date 延誤；逾期 **2** a slight or gradual fall in the amount, value, etc. of sth（微弱或逐漸的）下降，降低，貶值

,slipped 'disc *noun* a painful condition caused when one of the discs between the bones of the SPINE in a person's back moves out of place 椎間盤突出；滑出椎間盤

slip·per /'slɪpə(r)/ *noun* a loose soft shoe that you wear in the house 室內便鞋；拖鞋：*a pair of slippers* 一雙拖鞋 ➲ **VISUAL VOCAB** page V64 ➲ see also CARPET SLIPPER

slip·pered /'slɪpəd; *NAmE* -pərd/ *adj.* wearing slippers 穿拖鞋的；穿便鞋的：*slippered feet* 穿着拖鞋的雙腳

slip·pery /'slɪpəri/ *adj.* **1** (also *informal* **slippy**) difficult to hold or to stand or move on, because it is smooth, wet or polished 滑的；滑得抓不住（或站不穩、難以行走）的：*slippery like a fish* 滑得像條魚似的 ◇ *In places the path can be wet and slippery.* 這條小徑有些路段又濕又滑。◇ *His hand was slippery with sweat.* 他的手汗津津的。 **2** (*informal*) (of a person 人) that you cannot trust 油滑的；滑頭滑腦的；靠不住的：*Don't believe what he says—he's a slippery customer.* 他說什麼你可別信，他是個滑頭的傢伙。 **3** (*informal*) (of a situation, subject, problem, etc. 情況、課題、問題等) difficult to deal with and that you have to think about carefully 難以應對的；棘手的：*Freedom is a slippery concept* (= because its meaning changes according to your point of view). 自由是一個難以明確的概念。

IDM **the/a slippery 'slope** a course of action that is difficult to stop once it has begun, and can lead to serious problems or disaster 使人滑向深淵的斜坡；危險的境地

slippy /'slɪpi/ *adj.* (**slip·pier**, **slip·piest**) (*informal*) = SLIPPERY

'slip road (*BrE*) (*NAmE* **ramp**) *noun* a road used for driving onto or off a major road such as a MOTORWAY or INTERSTATE（進出高速公路等的）支路，匝道 ➲ compare ACCESS ROAD

slip·shod /'slɪpʃɒd; *NAmE* -ʃɑːd/ *adj.* done without care; doing things without care 馬虎的；敷衍了事的 **SYN** **careless**

slip·stream /'slɪpstriːm/ *noun* [sing.] the stream of air behind a vehicle that is moving very fast（高速行駛的交通工具後面的）滑流，低壓氣穴

'slip-up *noun* (*informal*) a careless mistake 疏漏；差錯

slip·way /'slɪpweɪ/ *noun* a sloping track leading down to water, on which ships are built or pulled up out of the water for repairs, or from which they are launched（造船或修船的）船台，滑台，滑道

slit /slɪt/ *noun, verb*

■ ***noun*** a long narrow cut or opening 狹長的切口；長而窄的口子；狹縫；裂縫：*a long skirt with a slit up the side* 側開衩的長裙 ◇ *His eyes narrowed into slits.* 他的眼睛瞇成兩道縫。

■ ***verb*** (**slit·ting**, **slit**, **slit**) to make a long narrow cut or opening in sth 在…上開狹長口子；切開；劃破：**~ sth** *Slit the roll with a sharp knife.* 用快刀把麪包切開。◇ *The child's throat had been slit.* 那孩子的喉嚨被人割破了。◇ *Her skirt was slit at both sides* (= designed with an opening at the bottom on each side). 她的裙子兩邊都開了衩。◇ **~ sth + adj.** *He slit open the envelope and took out the letter.* 他拆開信封，抽出信來。

'slit-eyed *adj.* having narrow eyes (often used in an offensive way to refer to people from E Asia) 細長眼的（常用以描述東亞人，含冒犯意）

slither /'slɪðə(r)/ *verb* **1** [I] **+ adv./prep.** to move somewhere in a smooth, controlled way, often close to the ground 滑行；蛇行；爬行 **SYN** **glide**：*The snake slithered away as we approached.* 我們一走近，蛇就爬走了。 **2 + adv./prep.** to move somewhere without much control, for example because the ground is steep or wet（因地面陡峭或濕滑等）跌跌撞撞地溜行，踉踉蹌蹌地走 **SYN** **slide**：*We slithered down the slope to the road.* 我們跌跌撞撞地從坡上滑到了公路上。◇ *They were slithering around on the ice.* 他們在冰上踉踉蹌蹌地滑行。

slith·ery /'slɪðəri/ *adj.* difficult to hold or stand on because it is wet or smooth; moving in a slithering way 滑溜溜的；滑行的；跌跌撞撞地滑行的

slitty-eyed /,slɪti 'aɪd/ *adj.* (*offensive*) having narrow eyes (often used in an offensive way to refer to people from E Asia) 細長眼的（常用以描述東亞人，含冒犯意）

sliver /'slɪvə(r)/ *noun* a small or thin piece of sth that is cut or broken off from a larger piece（切下或碎裂的）小塊，薄片：*slivers of glass* 玻璃碎片 ◇ (*figurative*) *A sliver of light showed under the door.* 門底下現出一絲亮光。

Sloane /sləʊn; *NAmE* sloʊn/ *noun* (*BrE, informal*, often *disapproving*) a young person, especially a woman, from a rich upper-class background, especially one who lives in a fashionable area of London（尤指住在倫敦時髦地區的）闊小姐，富家子弟

slob /slɒb; *NAmE* slɑːb/ *noun, verb*

■ ***noun*** (*informal, disapproving*) a person who is lazy and dirty or untidy 懶惰而邋遢的人：*Get out of bed, you fat slob!* 起牀吧，你這個胖懶蟲！

■ ***verb*** (**-bb-**)

PHR V **,slob a'round/'out** (*BrE, informal*) to spend time being lazy and doing nothing 遊手好閒；無所事事

slob·ber /'slɒbə(r); *NAmE* 'slɑːb-/ *verb* [I] to let SALIVA come out of your mouth 流涎；流口水 **SYN** **dribble**

PHR V **'slobber over sb/sth** (*informal, disapproving*) to show how much you like or want sb/sth without any pride or control 對…垂涎欲滴；毫不掩飾地表示喜愛

sloe /sləʊ; *NAmE* sloʊ/ *noun* a bitter wild fruit like a small PLUM that grows on a bush called a BLACKTHORN 黑刺李（果）

ˌsloe ˈeyes *noun* [pl.] attractive, dark eyes, usually ones that are long and thin（通常指細長的）迷人黑眼睛 ▶ **ˌsloe-ˈeyed** *adj.*

ˌsloe ˈgin *noun* [U] a strong alcoholic drink made by leaving sloes in GIN so that the gin has the flavour and the colour of the sloes 黑刺李杜松子酒

slog /slɒg; *NAmE* slɑːg/ *verb, noun*

■ *verb* (-gg-) (*informal*) **1** [I, T] to work hard and steadily at sth, especially sth that takes a long time and is boring or difficult 埋頭苦幹；堅持不懈地做：**~ (away) (at sth)** *He's been slogging away at that piece of music for weeks.* 他苦練那段樂曲已有好幾個星期了。◇ **~ (through sth)** *The teacher made us slog through long lists of vocabulary.* 老師讓我們下苦功記住一些長長的詞彙表。◇ **~ your way through sth** *She slogged her way through four piles of ironing.* 她辛辛苦苦一連熨了四堆衣服。**2** [I, T] to walk or travel somewhere steadily, with great effort or difficulty 頑強地走；奮力前行；艱難行進：**+ adv./prep.** *I've been slogging around the streets of London all day.* 整整一天，我一直在倫敦街頭走來走去。◇ **~ your way through sth** *He started to slog his way through the undergrowth.* 他踏上了穿越林莽的艱難征程。**3** [T, I] **~ (sth) (+ adv./prep.)** to hit a ball very hard but often without skill 猛擊，笨拙地猛擊（球）

IDM **ˌslog it ˈout** (*BrE, informal*) to fight or compete in order to prove who is the strongest, the best, etc. 決出勝負；決一雌雄 ➲ more at GUT *n.*

■ *noun* [U, C, usually sing.] a period of hard work or effort 一段時間的艱苦工作（或努力）：*Writing the book took ten months of hard slog.* 這本書是苦熬十個月寫出來的。◇ *It was a long slog to the top of the mountain.* 到山頂的路漫長而艱難。

slo·gan /ˈsləʊgən; *NAmE* ˈsloʊ-/ (also *NAmE, informal* **ˈtag line**) *noun* a word or phrase that is easy to remember, used for example by a political party or in advertising to attract people's attention or to suggest an idea quickly 標語；口號：*an* ***advertising slogan*** 廣告口號 ◇ *a* ***campaign slogan*** 競選口號 ◇ *The crowd began chanting anti-government* ***slogans***. 人群開始反複高呼反政府口號。

slo·gan·eer·ing /ˌsləʊgəˈnɪərɪŋ; *NAmE* ˌsloʊgəˈnɪrɪŋ/ *noun* [U] (*disapproving*) the use of slogans in advertisements, by politicians, etc. 標語口號的使用

slo-mo /ˈsləʊ məʊ; *NAmE* ˈsloʊ moʊ/ *noun* [U] (*informal*) = SLOW MOTION

sloop /sluːp/ *noun* a small sailing ship with one MAST (= a post to support the sails) 單桅帆船

slop /slɒp; *NAmE* slɑːp/ *verb, noun*

■ *verb* (-pp-) **1** [I] **+ adv./prep.** (of a liquid 液體) to move around in a container, often so that some liquid comes out over the edge 晃盪；（常指）溢出，濺出：*Water was slopping around in the bottom of the boat.* 船底有水在晃盪。◇ *As he put the glass down the beer slopped over onto the table.* 他放下杯子時，啤酒撒到了桌子上。**2** [T] **~ sth (+ adv./prep.)** to make liquid or food come out of a container in an untidy way 倒出；使潑出；使濺灑 SYN **spill**：*He got out of the bath, slopping water over the sides.* 他從浴缸裏出來，水也跟着漫出來。◇ *She slopped some beans onto a plate.* 她往盤子裏倒了一些豆子。

PHR V **ˌslop aˈbout/aˈround** (*BrE, informal*) **1** to spend time relaxing or being lazy 休息；放鬆；偷懶：*He used to slop around all day in his pyjamas.* 以前，他時常整天穿着睡衣閒逛。**2** to move around in water, mud. etc.（在水、泥等裏）趟來趟去，走動 **ˌslop ˈout** (*BrE*) when prisoners **slop out**, they empty the containers that they use as toilets（囚犯）倒便桶

■ *noun* [U] (also **slops** [pl.]) **1** waste food, sometimes fed to animals 泔水；（倒掉的）剩飯菜 **2** liquid or partly liquid waste, for example URINE or dirty water from baths 污水；髒水：*a slop bucket* 污水桶

slope 🔑 /sləʊp; *NAmE* sloʊp/ *noun, verb*

■ *noun* **1** 🔑 [C] a surface or piece of land that slopes (= is higher at one end than the other) 斜坡；坡地 SYN **incline**：*a grassy slope* 長滿草的斜坡 ◇ *The town is built* ***on a slope***. 這座城建在斜坡上。**2** 🔑 [C, usually pl.] an area of land that is part of a mountain or hill 山坡：*the eastern slopes of the Andes* 安第斯山脈東坡 ◇ *ski slopes* 滑雪斜坡 ◇ *He spends all winter* ***on the slopes*** (= SKIING). 整個冬天他都在山坡上滑雪。➲ VISUAL VOCAB pages V4, V5 **3** 🔑 [sing., U] the amount by which sth slopes 斜度；坡度：*a* ***gentle/steep slope*** 緩坡；陡坡 ◇ *a slope of 45 degrees* * 45 度的坡度 ◇ *the angle of slope* 傾角 IDM see SLIPPERY

■ *verb* **1** 🔑 [I] (+ adv./prep.) (of a horizontal surface 水平面) to be at an angle so that it is higher at one end than the other 傾斜；有坡度：*The garden slopes away towards the river.* 花園向河邊傾斜下去。◇ *sloping shoulders* 斜肩 **2** 🔑 [I] (+ adv./prep.) (of sth vertical 垂直物) to be at an angle rather than being straight or vertical 傾斜：*His handwriting slopes backwards.* 他寫的字向後斜。◇ *It was a very old house with sloping walls.* 這房子已經很舊，牆都歪了。**3** [I] **+ adv./prep.** (*BrE, informal*) to go somewhere quietly, especially in order to avoid sth/sb 悄悄地走；潛行；溜 SYN **slink**：*They got bored waiting for him and* ***sloped off***. 他們等他等得不耐煩，就悄悄走了。

sloppy /ˈslɒpi; *NAmE* ˈslɑːpi/ *adj.* (**slop·pier**, **slop·pi·est**) **1** that shows a lack of care, thought or effort 馬虎的；凌亂的；草率的：*sloppy thinking* 不認真的思考 ◇ *Your work is sloppy.* 你的工作做得不認真。◇ *a sloppy worker* 幹活馬虎的人 **2** (of clothes 衣服) loose and without much shape 肥大而難看的 SYN **baggy**：*a sloppy T-shirt* 寬大鬆垮的 T 恤衫 **3** (*informal, especially BrE*) romantic in a silly or embarrassing way 庸俗傷感的：*a sloppy love story* 庸俗傷感的愛情故事 **4** containing too much liquid 太稀的：*Don't make the mixture too sloppy.* 別調得太稀。◇ (*informal*) *She gave him a big sloppy kiss.* 她張開濕乎乎的嘴唇狠狠地親了他一口。▶ **slop·pily** /-ɪli/ *adv.*：*a sloppily run department* 管理鬆懈的部門 **slop·pi·ness** *noun* [U]：*There is no excuse for sloppiness in your work.* 你在工作中敷衍了事，這無論如何說不過去。

sloppy joe /ˌslɒpi ˈdʒəʊ; *NAmE* ˌslɑːpi ˈdʒoʊ/ *noun* (*NAmE*) finely chopped meat served in a spicy tomato sauce inside a BUN (= bread roll)（塗在麵包捲裏的）茄汁肉末醬

slosh /slɒʃ; *NAmE* slɑːʃ/ *verb* (*informal*) **1** [I] **+ adv./prep.** (of liquid 液體) to move around making a lot of noise or coming out over the edge of sth 嘩啦嘩啦地晃盪；撒出；濺出：*The water was sloshing around under our feet.* 水在我們腳下嘩啦嘩啦地流動。◇ *Some of the paint sloshed out of the can.* 桶裏撒出了一些油漆。**2** [T] **~ sth + adv./prep.** to make liquid move in a noisy way; to use liquid carelessly 使（液體）嘩啦嘩啦地搖盪；攪動（液體）；連倒帶撒：*The children were sloshing water everywhere.* 孩子們把水撒得四處都是。◇ *She sloshed coffee into the mugs.* 她嘩嘩地把咖啡倒進杯子裏。**3** [I] **+ adv./prep.** to walk noisily in water or mud（在水或泥裏）撲哧撲哧地走：*We all sloshed around in the puddles.* 我們都噗噗地踩着一攤攤的積水。

PHR V **ˌslosh aˈbout/aˈround** (*BrE, informal*) (especially of money 尤指錢) to be available or present in large quantities 可大量獲得；大量存在

sloshed /slɒʃt; *NAmE* slɑːʃt/ *adj.* (*informal*) drunk 喝醉的

slot /slɒt; *NAmE* slɑːt/ *noun, verb*

■ *noun* **1** a long narrow opening, into which you put or fit sth（投放或插入東西的）窄縫，扁口：*to put some coins in the slot* 往投幣口中塞幾個硬幣 **2** a position, a time or an opportunity for sb/sth, for example in a list, a programme of events or a series of broadcasts（名單、日程安排或廣播節目表中的）位置，時間，機會：*He has a regular slot on the late-night programme.* 他在深夜節目中有一檔固定欄目。◇ *Their album has occupied the Number One slot for the past six weeks.* 他們的唱片在最近六週佔據排行榜首位。◇ *the airport's take-off and landing slots* 機場的起飛降落時間表

■ *verb* (-tt-) [T, I] to put sth into a space that is available or designed for it; to fit into such a space 投放；插入；（被）塞進；（被）裝入：**~ sth + adv./prep.** *He slotted*

S

a cassette into the VCR. 他把錄像帶插入錄像機中。◇ The bed comes in sections which can be quickly **slotted together**. 這種牀以散件出售，可以快速組裝起來。◇ **+ adv./prep.** The dishwasher slots neatly between the cupboards. 洗碗機剛好可以放在兩個碗櫥之間。**IDM** see PLACE *n.*

PHR V **ˌslot sb/sth↔ˈin** to manage to find a position, time or an opportunity for sb/sth 為…安排時間（或提供機會）；安置：*I can slot you in between 3 and 4.* 我可以把你插到第 3 和第 4 之間。◇ *We slotted in some extra lessons before the exam.* 我們在考試前加了幾節課。

sloth /sləʊθ; *NAmE* sloʊθ/ *noun* **1** [C] a S American animal that lives in trees and moves very slowly 樹懶（南美洲熱帶動物，行動緩慢）**2** [U] (*formal*) the bad habit of being lazy and unwilling to work 懶散；怠惰

sloth·ful /ˈsləʊθfl; *NAmE* ˈsloʊθfl/ *adj.* (*formal*) lazy 懶散的；怠惰的

ˈslot machine *noun* **1** (*BrE*) a machine with an opening for coins, used for selling things such as cigarettes and bars of chocolate 投幣自動售貨機 **2** (*especially NAmE*) (also **ˌone-armed ˈbandit** *NAmE, BrE*) (*BrE* also **ˈfruit machine**) a gambling machine that you put coins into and that gives money back if particular pictures appear together on the screen 吃角子老虎賭博機；老虎機

slot·ted /ˈslɒtɪd; *NAmE* ˈslɑːt-/ *adj.* [usually before noun] (*technical* 術語) **1** having a SLOT or SLOTS in it 有窄縫的；帶扁口的；開槽的 **2** (of a screw 螺絲釘) having a SLOT in it rather than a cross shape 槽頭的，一字形槽口的（非十字形的）➲ compare PHILLIPS

ˌslotted ˈspoon *noun* a large spoon with holes in it 大漏勺；笊籬

slouch /slaʊtʃ/ *verb, noun*

■ ***verb*** [I] (**+ adv./prep.**) to stand, sit or move in a lazy way, often with your shoulders and head bent forward 沒精打采地站（或坐、走）；低頭垂肩地站（或坐、走）：*Sit up straight. Don't slouch.* 挺起胸坐直，別歪歪斜斜的。

■ ***noun*** [usually sing.] a way of standing or sitting in which your shoulders are not straight, so that you look tired or lazy 沒精打采地站（或坐）的姿態

IDM **be no ˈslouch** (*informal*) to be very good at sth or quick to do sth 擅長於；幹得麻利：*She's no slouch on the guitar.* 她是彈吉他的好手。

slouchy /ˈslaʊtʃi/ *adj.* (**slouch·ier**, **slouchi·est**) **1** (*disapproving*) holding your body in a lazy way, often with your shoulders and head bent forward 懶散的；垂肩弓背的；佝僂的：*his slouchy posture* 他那懶散疲沓的姿勢 **2** (*approving*) (of clothes 衣服) without a firm outline; not stiff 鬆沓沓的；軟搭搭的：*The slouchy suede boots look great with slim pants.* 這雙軟幫絨面革靴子配緊身褲看上去很棒。

slough¹ /slʌf/ *verb* to lose a layer of dead skin, etc. 蛻（皮）；使脱落：**~ sth** *a snake sloughing its skin* 正在蛻皮的蛇 ◇ **~ sth off** *Slough off dead skin cells by using a facial scrub.* 用臉部磨砂膏去除皮膚死皮。

PHR V **ˌslough sth↔ˈoff** (*formal*) to get rid of sth that you no longer want 摒棄；拋棄；擺脱：*Responsibilities are not sloughed off so easily.* 責任不是那麼容易推卸的。

slough² /slaʊ; *NAmE* sluː/ *noun* (*literary*) **1** [sing.] **~ of misery, despair, etc.** a state of sadness with no hope 苦難的深淵；絕望的境地 **2** [C] a very soft wet area of land 泥沼；泥淖；沼澤

the Slough of Des·pond /ˌslaʊ əv dɪˈspɒnd; *NAmE* dɪˈspɑːnd/ *noun* [sing.] a mental state in which a person feels no hope and is very afraid 絕望的深淵；極度沮喪：*He was sinking into the Slough of Despond.* 他那時正陷入極度沮喪的狀態。**ORIGIN** From the name of a place that Christian, the main character, must travel through in John Bunyan's *The Pilgrim's Progress*. 源自約翰・班揚所著《天路歷程》中的主人公克里斯琴（英文意為基督徒）必須途經的地方"絕望之沼"。

slov·en·ly /ˈslʌvnli/ *adj.* careless, untidy or dirty in appearance or habits 邋遢的；衣冠不整的；凌亂的；馬虎的：*He grew lazy and slovenly in his habits.* 他養成了懶散邋遢的習慣。▶ **slov·en·li·ness** *noun* [U]

Which Word? 詞語辨析

slow / slowly

■ **Slowly** is the usual adverb from the adjective **slow**. **Slow** is sometimes used as an adverb in informal language, on road signs, etc. It can also be used to form compounds. * slowly 是常用副詞，源自形容詞 slow。有時，slow 作為非正式用語或在路標等中也用作副詞，亦可用以構成複合詞：*Slow. Major road ahead.* 慢行。前方幹道。◇ *a slow-acting drug* 藥效慢的藥 ◇ ~~*They walk very slow.*~~ In the comparative both **slower** and **more slowly** are used. 比較級作 slower 和 more slowly 均可：*Can you speak slower/more slowly?* 你說慢點行嗎？

slow 0→ /sləʊ; *NAmE* sloʊ/ *adj., adv., verb*

■ ***adj.*** (**slow·er**, **slow·est**)

▸ **NOT FAST 速度低** **1** 0→ not moving, acting or done quickly; taking a long time; not fast 緩慢的；遲緩的；耗時的；慢的：*a slow driver* 開車慢的人 ◇ *Progress was slower than expected.* 進展比預計的緩慢。◇ *The country is experiencing slow but steady economic growth.* 國家經濟正在緩慢但穩步地增長。◇ *Collecting data is a **painfully slow** process.* 收集材料的過程慢得讓人難受。◇ *a slow, lingering death* 緩慢而拖延時日的死亡 ◇ *Oh you're so slow; come on, hurry up!* 哎喲，你可真慢；加把勁，快點！◇ *The slow movement opens with a cello solo.* 慢樂章開頭是一段大提琴獨奏。◇ *She gave a slow smile.* 她慢慢地笑了笑。**2** 0→ not going or allowing you to go at a fast speed 慢速的；低速的：*I missed the fast train and had to get the slow one* (= the one that stops at all the stations). 我誤了快車，只得坐慢車。

▸ **WITH DELAY 拖延** **3** 0→ hesitating to do sth or not doing sth immediately 遲遲不…；不樂意；慢吞吞的：**~ to do sth** *She wasn't slow to realize what was going on.* 她很快意識到出了什麼事。◇ **~ in doing sth** *His poetry was slow in achieving recognition.* 他的詩遲遲得不到賞識。◇ **~ doing sth** *They were very slow paying me.* 他們遲遲不付錢給我。

▸ **NOT CLEVER 不聰明** **4** 0→ not quick to learn; finding things hard to understand 遲鈍的；笨的；理解力差的：*He's the slowest in the class.* 他是班裏最遲鈍的。

▸ **NOT BUSY 不忙碌** **5** not very busy; containing little action 不忙碌的；清淡的；冷清的 **SYN** **sluggish**：*Sales are slow* (= not many goods are being sold). 銷售不旺。

▸ **WATCH/CLOCK 錶；鐘** **6** [not before noun] showing a time earlier than the correct time 慢：*My watch is five minutes slow* (= it shows 1.45 when it is 1.50). 我的手錶慢五分鐘。

▸ **IN PHOTOGRAPHY 攝影** **7** **slow** film is not very sensitive to light（膠片）曝光慢的

▶ **slow·ness** *noun* [U]：*There was impatience over the slowness of reform.* 人們對改革的緩慢進程缺乏耐心。

IDM **do a slow ˈburn** (*NAmE, informal*) to slowly get angry 慢慢生起氣來 ➲ more at MARK *n.*, UPTAKE

■ ***adv.*** (**slow·er**, **slow·est**) (used especially in the comparative and superlative forms, or in compounds 尤用於比較級、最高級形式或構成複合詞) at a slow speed 慢速地；緩慢地 **SYN** **slowly**：*Could you go a little slower?* 你能走慢點嗎？◇ *slow-drying paint* 慢乾漆 ◇ *slow-moving traffic* 緩慢行進的車輛 ◇ (*NAmE*) *Drive slow!* 慢駛！

IDM **go ˈslow (on sth)** to show less enthusiasm for achieving sth（對某事）熱情減退：*The government is going slow on tax reforms.* 政府對於稅務改革漸漸失去了熱情。➲ see also GO-SLOW

■ ***verb*** [I, T] to go or to make sth/sb go at a slower speed or be less active（使）放慢速度，減緩，鬆勁：*Economic growth has slowed a little.* 經濟增長稍有減緩。◇ *The bus **slowed to a halt**.* 公共汽車減速停了下來。◇ **~ down/up** *The car slowed down as it approached the junction.* 汽車在駛近交叉路口時放慢了速度。◇ *The game slowed up little in the second half.* 比賽節奏在下半場幾乎沒有減慢。◇ *You must slow down* (= work less hard) *or you'll make yourself ill.* 你得鬆鬆勁，不然會累病的。

◇ **~ sth/sb down/up** *The ice on the roads was slowing us down.* 公路上有冰，減緩了我們的速度。◇ **~ sth/sb** *We hope to slow the spread of the disease.* 我們希望能夠減緩疾病的傳播速度。➲ see also SLOWDOWN

slow·coach /ˈsləʊkəʊtʃ; *NAmE* ˈsloʊkoʊtʃ/ (*BrE*) (*NAmE* **ˈslow·poke**) *noun* (*informal*) a person who moves, acts or works too slowly 動作遲緩的人

ˈslow cooker *noun* an electric pot used for cooking meat and vegetables slowly in liquid 電燜燒鍋；電燉鍋

slow·down /ˈsləʊdaʊn; *NAmE* ˈsloʊ-/ *noun* **1** a reduction in speed or activity 減速；減緩：*a slowdown in economic growth* 經濟增長的減緩 **2** (*NAmE*) (*BrE* **ˌgo-ˈslow**) a protest that workers make by doing their work more slowly than usual 怠工 ➲ compare WORK-TO-RULE

ˌslow ˈfood *noun* [U] traditional food and ways of producing, cooking and eating it 慢餐，慢食（指傳統食品及其生產、烹飪和食用）➲ compare FAST FOOD

ˈslow lane *noun* [sing.] the part of a major road such as a MOTORWAY or INTERSTATE where vehicles drive slowest 慢車道

IDM **in the ˈslow lane** not making progress as fast as other people, countries, companies, etc. 在慢車道上；被甩在後面；落後

slow·ly 0-π /ˈsləʊli; *NAmE* ˈsloʊli/ *adv.*
at a slow speed; not quickly 慢速地；緩慢地；遲緩地：*to move slowly* 慢慢移動 ◇ *Please could you speak more slowly?* 請您說慢一點好不好？◇ *The boat chugged slowly along.* 船突突地緩慢前進。◇ *He found that life moved slowly in the countryside.* 他發現鄉村的生活節奏慢。◇ *Don't rush into a decision.* ***Take it slowly.*** 不要急於做決定。慢慢來。◇ *Slowly things began to improve.* 慢慢地，情況開始好轉了。➲ note at SLOW

IDM **ˌslowly but ˈsurely** making slow but definite progress 緩慢但扎實地；穩扎穩打地：*We'll get there slowly but surely.* 我們雖慢，但準能趕到那兒。

ˌslow ˈmotion *noun* [U] (in a film/movie or on television 電影或電視) the method of showing action at a much slower speed than it happened in real life 慢動作：*Some scenes were filmed* ***in slow motion.*** 幾組鏡頭被拍成了慢動作。◇ *a slow-motion replay* 慢動作重放

slow·poke /ˈsləʊpəʊk; *NAmE* ˈsloʊpoʊk/ (*NAmE*) (*BrE* **slow·coach**) *noun* (*informal*) a person who moves, acts or works too slowly 動作遲緩的人

ˈslow-witted *adj.* not able to think quickly; slow to learn or understand things 腦子反應慢的；頭腦遲鈍的 OPP **quick-witted**

ˈslow-worm (also **blind·worm**) *noun* a small European REPTILE with no legs, like a snake 慢缺肢蜥，盲蛇蜥（生活在歐洲的無腿爬行動物）

SLR /ˌes el ˈɑː(r)/ *abbr.* single-lens reflex (used to describe a camera in which there is only one LENS which both forms the image on the film and provides the image in the VIEWFINDER)（照相機）單鏡頭反光式，單反

slub /slʌb/ *noun* a lump or thick place in wool or thread（毛線或線的）粗節，糙粒 ▸ **slubbed** /slʌbd/ *adj.*

sludge /slʌdʒ/ *noun* [U] **1** thick, soft, wet mud or a substance that looks like it 爛泥；淤泥；爛泥狀沉積物 SYN **slime**：*There was some sludge at the bottom of the tank.* 油箱底有油泥。**2** industrial or human waste that has been treated 工業淤渣；工業礦泥；生活污物：*industrial sludge* 工業淤渣 ◇ *the use of sewage sludge as a fertilizer on farm land* 把下水道污泥用作農田肥料的做法

slug /slʌg/ *noun, verb*
■ ***noun*** **1** a small soft creature, like a SNAIL without a shell, that moves very slowly and often eats garden plants 緩步蟲；蛞蝓 ➲ VISUAL VOCAB page V13 **2** (*informal*) a small amount of a strong alcoholic drink 少量，一小杯（烈性酒）：*He took another slug of whisky.* 他又喝了一點威士忌。**3** (*informal, especially NAmE*) a bullet 子彈 **4** (*NAmE, informal*) a piece of metal shaped like a coin used to get things from machines, etc., sometimes illegally 硬幣形金屬片，假硬幣（有時用以從自動售貨機中騙取東西）
■ ***verb*** (**-gg-**) **1 ~ sb** (*informal*) to hit sb hard, especially with your closed hand 用力打；狠揍 **2 ~ sth** (in BASEBALL 棒球) to hit the ball hard 猛擊（球）

IDM **ˌslug it ˈout** to fight or compete until it is clear who has won 決出勝負；一決雌雄

slug·fest /ˈslʌgfest/ *noun* (*informal, especially NAmE*) an angry argument in which people insult each other 爭吵；對罵：*The battle between the two Democrats is turning into a nasty little slugfest.* 兩個民主黨人之間的鬥爭正演化成一場令人厭惡的謾罵。

slug·gard /ˈslʌgəd; *NAmE* -gərd/ *noun* (*formal*) a slow, lazy person 懶惰的人；懶散的人 ▸ **slug·gard·ly** *adj.*

slug·ger /ˈslʌgə(r)/ *noun* (*NAmE, informal*) **1** (in BASEBALL 棒球) a player who hits the ball, especially one who hits it very hard and for long distances 擊球手；（尤指）擊球強手；強打；強棒 **2** (*approving*) used when speaking to or about sb, especially a young boy, who tries really hard at sth, and that you feel affection for 猛人（尤指男孩）：*Hang in there, slugger. You can do it!* 堅持，拚命三郎。你行的！

slug·gish /ˈslʌgɪʃ/ *adj.* moving, reacting or working more slowly than normal and in a way that seems lazy 緩慢的；遲緩的；懶洋洋的：*sluggish traffic* 緩緩移動的車流 ◇ *a sluggish economy* 經濟停滯 ◇ *the sluggish black waters of the canal* 運河裏緩慢流動的黑乎乎的河水 ◇ *He felt very heavy and sluggish after the meal.* 飯後他感覺身子很沉，不想動。▸ **slug·gish·ly** *adv.* **slug·gish·ness** *noun* [U]

sluice /sluːs/ *noun, verb*
■ ***noun*** (also **ˈsluice gate**) a sliding gate or other device for controlling the flow of water out of or into a CANAL, etc. 水閘；閘門
■ ***verb*** **1** [T] **~ sth (down/out)** | **~ sth (with sth)** to wash sth with a stream of water 沖洗：*The ship's crew was sluicing down the deck.* 船員們正在沖洗甲板。**2** [I] **+ adv./prep.** (of water 水) to flow somewhere in large quantities（大量地）流，瀉

slum /slʌm/ *noun, verb*
■ ***noun*** an area of a city that is very poor and where the houses are dirty and in bad condition 貧民窟；棚屋區：*a slum area* 貧民區 ◇ ***city/urban slums*** 城市貧民窟 ◇ *She was brought up in the slums of Leeds.* 她是在利茲的貧民區長大的。
■ ***verb*** (**-mm-**) [I] (usually **be slumming**) (*informal*) to spend time in places or conditions that are much worse than those you are used to 過苦日子；過簡樸生活：*There are plenty of ways you can cut costs on your trip without slumming.* 在旅行中，有許多辦法既可以減少開銷又不至於讓自己過得太苦。

IDM **ˈslum it** (often *humorous*) to accept conditions that are worse than those you are used to 將就着過簡樸生活；過窮日子：*Several businessmen had to slum it in economy class.* 幾個商人只好將就着坐在經濟艙裏。

slum·ber /ˈslʌmbə(r)/ *noun, verb*
■ ***noun*** [U, C, usually pl.] (*literary*) sleep; a time when sb is asleep 睡眠：*She fell into a deep and peaceful slumber.* 她睡着了，睡得又沉又香。
■ ***verb*** [I] (*literary*) to sleep 睡；睡眠

ˈslumber party *noun* (*NAmE*) = SLEEPOVER

slum·lord /ˈslʌmlɔːd; *NAmE* -lɔːrd/ *noun* (*NAmE, informal*) a person who owns houses or flats/apartments in a poor area and who charges very high rent for them even though they are in bad condition（收取高額租金的）貧民窟房東

slump /slʌmp/ *verb, noun*
■ ***verb*** **1** [I] to fall in price, value, number, etc., suddenly and by a large amount（價格、價值、數量等）驟降，猛跌，銳減 SYN **drop**：*Sales have slumped this year.* 今年銷售量銳減。◇ **~ by sth** *Profits slumped by over 50%.* 利潤突降 50% 以上。◇ **~ (from sth) (to sth)** *The paper's circulation has slumped to 90 000.* 此報紙的發行量驟減至 9 萬份。**2** [I] **+ adv./prep.** to sit or fall down heavily 重重地坐下（或倒下）：*The old man slumped down in his chair.* 老先生一屁股跌坐到椅子上。◇ *She slumped to her knees.* 她撲通一聲跪倒在地。
■ ***noun*** **1 ~ (in sth)** a sudden fall in sales, prices, the value of sth, etc.（銷售量、價格、價值等的）驟降，

S

猛跌，鋭減 SYN **decline**：*a slump in profits* 利潤鋭減 **2** a period when a country's economy or a business is doing very badly 蕭條期；衰退：*the slump of the 1930s* * 20 世紀 30 年代的大蕭條 ◇ *The toy industry is in a slump.* 玩具業現在不景氣。➲ compare BOOM *n.* (1)

slumped /slʌmpt/ *adj.* [not usually before noun] **~ (against/over sth)** sitting with your body leaning forward, for example because you are asleep or unconscious（因睡着或昏迷等）彎着身子坐，伏：*The driver was slumped exhausted over the wheel.* 司機伏在方向盤上，疲憊不堪。

slung *past tense, past part.* of SLING

slunk *past tense, past part.* of SLINK

slur /slɜː(r)/ *verb, noun*

■ ***verb*** (**-rr-**) **1 ~ sth | + speech** to pronounce words in a way that is not clear so that they run into each other, usually because you are drunk or tired 含混不清地說話（通常因醉酒或疲勞）：*She had drunk too much and her speech was slurred.* 她喝得太多了，話都說不利索了。**2 ~ sth** (*music* 音) to play or sing a group of two or more musical notes so that each one runs smoothly into the next 連奏；連唱 **3 ~ sb/sth** to harm sb's reputation by making unfair or false statements about them 誹謗；詆譭；污辱

■ ***noun*** **1 ~ (on sb/sth)** an unfair remark about sb/sth that may damage other people's opinion of them 誹謗；詆譭；污辱 SYN **insult**：*She had dared to **cast a slur** on his character.* 她竟敢對他的人品加以詆譭。◇ (*especially NAmE*) *The crowd started throwing bottles and shouting **racial slurs**.* 人群開始扔瓶子，並高聲地進行種族污辱。**2** (*music* 音) a curved sign used to show that two or more notes are to be played smoothly and without a break 連奏線；連唱線

slurp /slɜːp; *NAmE* slɜːrp/ *verb* (*informal*) **1** [T, I] to make a loud noise while you are drinking sth（喝東西時）發出嘖嘖的聲音：**~ sth** *He was slurping his tea.* 他正咂着嘴喝茶。◇ **~ (from sth)** *She slurped noisily from her cup.* 她端着杯子，嘖嘖作響地喝着。**2** [I] to make a noise like this 嘖嘖地響：*The water slurped in the tank.* 水在箱裏嘶嘶地響。▸ **slurp** *noun* [usually sing.]：*She took a slurp from her mug.* 她嘖地從杯子裏喝了一口。

slurry /ˈslʌri; *NAmE* ˈslɜːri/ *noun* [U] a thick liquid consisting of water mixed with animal waste, CLAY, coal dust or CEMENT（由水和動物糞便、土、煤末或水泥混合而成的）泥漿，稀泥

S

slush /slʌʃ/ *noun* [U] **1** partly melted snow that is usually dirty 融雪；雪泥：*In the city the clean white snow had turned to grey slush.* 在城市裏，潔白的雪已化為灰色的雪泥。**2** (*informal, disapproving*) stories, films/movies or feelings that are considered to be silly and without value because they are too emotional and romantic 矯揉造作的言情小說（或電影）；庸俗的言情 ▸ **slushy** *adj.*：*slushy pavements* 雪泥覆蓋的人行道 ◇ *slushy romantic fiction* 矯揉造作的言情小說

ˈslush fund *noun* (*disapproving*) a sum of money kept for illegal purposes, especially in politics（尤指用於政治目的的）非法基金

slut /slʌt/ *noun* (*disapproving, offensive*) **1** a woman who has many sexual partners 蕩婦；淫婦 **2** a woman who is very untidy or lazy 邋遢女人；懶婆娘 ▸ **slut·tish** *adj.*

sly /slaɪ/ *adj.* **1** (*disapproving*) acting or done in a secret or dishonest way, often intending to trick people 詭詐的；狡詐的 SYN **cunning**：*a sly political move* 詭詐的政治手段 ◇ (*humorous*) *You sly old devil! How long have you known?* 你這個老滑頭！你知道有多久了？**2** [usually before noun] suggesting that you know sth secret that other people do not know 詭秘的（表示自己知道別人不知道的秘密）SYN **knowing**：*a **sly smile/grin/look/glance, etc.*** 詭秘的微笑、咧嘴一笑、神色、一瞥等 ▸ **slyly** *adv.*：*He glanced at her slyly.* 他詭秘地朝她瞥了一眼。**sly·ness** *noun* [U]

IDM **on the ˈsly** secretly; not wanting other people to discover what you are doing 秘密地；偷偷地；背地裏：*He has to visit them on the sly.* 他只得偷偷地去看望他們。

smack /smæk/ *verb, noun, adv.*

■ ***verb*** **1** [T] **~ sb/sth** (*especially BrE*) to hit sb with your open hand, especially as a punishment 用巴掌打；摑：*I think it's wrong to smack children.* 我覺得打孩子不對。➲ compare SPANK **2** [T] **~ sth + adv./prep.** to put sth somewhere with a lot of force so that it makes a loud noise 啪的一聲使勁放（或扔、甩等）SYN **bang**：*She smacked her hand down on to the table.* 她啪地一拍桌子。◇ *He smacked a fist into the palm of his hand.* 他用拳頭啪地猛擊一下手掌。**3** [I] **+ adv./prep.** to hit against sth with a lot of force 使勁碰（或撞）SYN **crash**：*Two players accidentally smacked into each other.* 兩名運動員不巧撞在了一起。IDM see LIP

PHR V **ˈsmack of sth** to seem to contain or involve a particular unpleasant quality 有…味道；帶有…意味：*Her behaviour smacks of hypocrisy.* 她的行為有點虛偽。◇ *Today's announcement smacks of a government cover-up.* 今天的聲明頗有政府想掩蓋事實的味道。**ˌsmack sb↔ˈup** (*BrE, informal*) to hit sb hard with your hand, many times（多次）用手狠打，猛摑

■ ***noun*** **1** [C] (*especially BrE*) a sharp hit given with your open hand, especially to a child as a punishment 打巴掌，摑（尤指對小孩的懲戒）：*You'll get a smack on your backside if you're not careful.* 要是不小心，就打你的屁股。**2** [C] (*informal*) a hard hit given with a closed hand（打的）一拳 SYN **punch**：*a smack on the jaw* 在下巴上打了一拳 **3** [C, usually sing.] a short loud sound 啪的一聲；砰的一聲：*She closed the ledger with a smack.* 她啪的一聲合上了賬簿。**4** [C] (*informal*) a loud kiss 出聲的吻；響吻：*a **smack on the lips/cheek*** 在嘴上/臉上響亮地親一下 **5** [U] (*slang*) the drug HEROIN 海洛因；白麵兒：*smack addicts* 吸白粉成癮的人 **6** [C] (*BrE*) a small fishing boat 小漁船

■ ***adv.*** (*informal*) **1** (*NAmE* also **ˈsmack-dab**) exactly or directly in a place 恰好；直接；不偏不倚地：*It landed **smack in the middle** of the carpet.* 它正好落在地毯中央。**2** with sudden, violent force, often making a loud noise 猛地；猛然作聲地：*The car drove smack into a brick wall.* 汽車嗵地一聲撞上了磚牆。

smack·er /ˈsmækə(r)/ *noun* **1** (*informal*) a loud kiss 出聲的吻；響吻 **2** (*slang*) a British pound or US dollar * 1 英鎊；1 美元

smack·ing /ˈsmækɪŋ/ *noun* [sing., U] (*especially BrE*) an act of hitting sb, especially a child, several times with your open hand, as a punishment（打）一個巴掌；（用巴掌）一頓揍：*He gave both of the children a good smacking.* 他把兩個孩子都狠揍了一頓。◇ *We don't approve of smacking.* 我們不贊成打孩子。

small 🔑 /smɔːl/ *adj., adv., noun*

■ ***adj.*** (**small·er**, **small·est**)

▸ **NOT LARGE** 小 **1** 🔑 not large in size, number, degree, amount, etc.（尺寸、數量、程度等）小的：*a small house/town/car/man* 小房子；小鎮；小型汽車；小個子男人 ◇ *A much smaller number of students passed than I had expected.* 通過考試的學生比我預計的少得多。◇ *They're having a relatively small wedding.* 他們的婚禮不準備大辦。◇ *That dress is too small for you.* 那件連衣裙你穿太小。◇ *'I don't agree,' he said in a small (= quiet) voice.* "我不同意。" 他小聲說。**2** 🔑 (*abbr.* **S**) used to describe one size in a range of sizes of clothes, food, products used in the house, etc.（服裝、食品、家庭用品等）小號的，小型的：*small, medium, large* 小號、中號、大號 ◇ *This is too big—have you got a small one?* 這個太大了，有沒有小的？**3** 🔑 not as big as sth else of the same kind（同類事物中）小的：*the small intestine* 小腸

▸ **YOUNG** 年幼 **4** 🔑 young 年幼的；幼小的：*They have three small children.* 他們有三個年幼的孩子。◇ *We travelled around a lot when I was small.* 我小的時候，我們時常四處旅行。◇ *As a small boy he had spent most of his time with his grandparents.* 他幼年時多半時間是跟爺爺奶奶在一起。

▸ **NOT IMPORTANT** 不重要 **5** 🔑 slight; not important 些微的；不重要的：*I made only a few small changes to the report.* 我對報告只做了幾處小改動。◇ *She noticed several small errors in his work.* 她注意到他作業中有幾處小錯。

◇ *Everything had been planned down to the smallest detail.* 一切都已做了細緻入微的安排。◇ *It was* ***no small*** *achievement getting her to agree to the deal.* 能讓她同意那筆交易可是個不小的成就。

▸ BUSINESS 企業 **6** 🔑 [usually before noun] not doing business on a very large scale 小規模的： *a small farmer* 小農場主 ◇ *The government is planning to give more help to small businesses.* 政府正計劃給予小企業更多幫助。

▸ LETTERS 字母 **7** [usually before noun] not written or printed as capitals 小寫的： *Should I write 'god'* ***with a small*** *'g' or a capital?* * god 裏面的字母 g，我該寫成小寫還是大寫？◇ *She's a socialist* ***with a small*** *'s'* (= she has socialist ideas but is not a member of a socialist party). 她信仰社會主義，但不是社會黨人。

▸ NOT MUCH 少 **8** [only before noun] (used with uncountable nouns 與不可數名詞連用) little; not much 極少的；不多的： *The government has small cause for optimism.* 幾乎沒有什麼可以使政府感到樂觀的。◇ *They have small hope of succeeding.* 他們成功的希望不大。 ▸ **small·ness** *noun* [U]

IDM **be grateful/thankful for small 'mercies** to be happy that a situation that is bad is not as bad as it could have been 為情況不太壞而慶幸： *Well, at least you weren't hurt. I suppose we should be grateful for small mercies.* 嗨，至少你沒受傷。我想這就該讓我們知足了。 **it's a ˌsmall 'world** (*saying*) used to express your surprise when you meet sb you know in an unexpected place, or when you are talking to sb and find out that you both know the same person （意外遇見某人或發現對方也認識某人時表示驚訝）世界真小 **look/feel 'small** to look or feel stupid, weak, ashamed, etc. 顯得（或感覺）矮人一截；愧不如人 ➲ more at BIG *adj.*, GREAT *adj.*, HOUR, STILL *adj.*, SWEAT *v.*, WAY *n.*, WONDER *n.*

■ *adv.* (**small·er**, **small·est**) **1** into small pieces 成為小塊： *Chop the cabbage up small.* 把捲心菜剁碎。 **2** in a small size 小小地： *You can fit it all in if you write very small.* 你字寫小點，就可以全部填進去。

■ *noun* **1 the ~ of the/sb's back** [sing.] the lower part of the back where it curves in 後腰 ➲ VISUAL VOCAB page V59 **2 smalls** [pl.] (*old-fashioned, BrE, informal*) small items of clothing, especially underwear 小件衣服（尤指內衣）

'small ads *noun* [pl.] (*BrE, informal*) = CLASSIFIED ADVERTISEMENTS

'small arms *noun* [pl.] small light weapons that you can carry in your hands 輕武器

ˌsmall 'beer (*BrE*) (*NAmE* **ˌsmall po'tatoes**) *noun* [U] (*informal*) a person or thing that has no great importance or value, especially when compared with sb/sth else （相比較之下）無足輕重的人（或事物）

'small-bore *adj.* **1** a **small-bore** gun is narrow inside （槍）小口徑的 **2** (*informal, especially NAmE*) not important 無足輕重的；微不足道的： *small-bore issues* 無關緊要的問題

ˌsmall 'capitals (also **ˌsmall 'caps**) *noun* [pl.] (*technical* 術語) capital letters which are the same height as LOWER-CASE letters 小大寫字母（與小寫字母同等高度的大寫字母）

ˌsmall 'change *noun* [U] **1** coins of low value 小面值硬幣；零錢： *Have you got any small change for the phone?* 你有沒有打電話的零錢？ **2** something that is of little value when compared with sth else （相比較之下）沒有什麼價值的東西

ˌsmall 'claims court *noun* a local court which deals with cases involving small amounts of money 小額索賠地方法院

ˌsmall 'fortune *noun* [usually sing.] (*informal*) a lot of money 一大筆錢： *That holiday cost me a small fortune.* 那次度假花了我一大筆錢。

'small fry *noun* [U+sing./pl. v.] (*informal*) people or things that are considered unimportant compared to sb/sth else （相比較之下）不重要的人（或事物）： *That's small fry to her.* 對她來說，那不值一提。◇ *People like us are small fry to such a large business.* 對於這樣一家大公司來說，我們這樣的人不過是小魚小蝦。

small·hold·er /ˈsmɔːlhəʊldə(r); *NAmE* -hoʊ-/ *noun* (*BrE*) a person who owns or rents a small piece of land for farming 小農場主；小農業經營者

small·hold·ing /ˈsmɔːlhəʊldɪŋ; *NAmE* -hoʊ-/ *noun* a small piece of land used for farming 一小塊耕地

small·ish /ˈsmɔːlɪʃ/ *adj.* fairly small 相當小的；頗小的： *a smallish town* 相當小的城鎮

ˌsmall-'minded *adj.* (*disapproving*) having fixed opinions and ways of doing things and not willing to change them or consider other people's opinions or feelings; interested in small problems and details and not in things which are really important 狹隘的；固執己見的；心胸狹窄的；目光短淺的 **SYN** **intolerant**, **petty** ▸ **ˌsmall-'minded·ness** *noun* [U]

ˌsmall po'tatoes (*NAmE*) (*BrE* **ˌsmall 'beer**) *noun* [U] (*informal*) a person or thing that has no great importance or value, especially when compared with sb/sth else （尤指相比較之下）無足輕重的人（或事物）

small·pox /ˈsmɔːlpɒks; *NAmE* -pɑːks/ *noun* [U] a serious infectious disease (now extremely rare) that causes fever, leaves permanent marks on the skin and often causes death 天花

the ˌsmall 'print (*BrE*) (*NAmE* **the ˌfine 'print**) *noun* [U] the important details of an agreement or a legal document that are usually printed in small type and are therefore easy to miss （協議或法律文件中易於被忽略但重要的）小號字印刷的附加條款： *Read all the small print before signing.* 把小號字印刷的附加條款全部看過以後再簽字。

ˌsmall-'scale *adj.* **1** (of an organization, activity, etc. 組織、活動等) not large in size or extent; limited in what it does 小型的；小範圍的；小規模的： *small-scale farming* 小規模農業 ◇ *a small-scale study of couples in second marriages* 對再婚夫婦的小範圍研究 **2** (of maps, drawings, etc. 地圖、圖樣等) drawn to a small scale so that not many details are shown 按小比例繪製的；小比例尺的 **OPP** **large-scale**

the ˌsmall 'screen *noun* [sing.] television (when contrasted with cinema) 電視（與電影相對而言）： *This will be the film's first showing on the small screen.* 這將是這部電影首次在電視上播放。◇ *his first small-screen role* 他的第一個電視劇角色

'small talk *noun* [U] polite conversation about ordinary or unimportant subjects, especially at social occasions 寒暄；閒談；聊天

'small-time *adj.* [only before noun] (*informal, disapproving*) (often of criminals 常指罪犯) not very important or successful 不太重要的；不高明的 **SYN** **petty**： *a small-time crook* 手段不高明的騙子 ➲ compare BIG TIME

'small-town *adj.* [only before noun] **1** (*disapproving*) not showing much interest in new ideas or what is happening outside your own environment 鄉鎮氣的；保守狹隘的；落後閉塞的 **SYN** **narrow-minded**： *small-town values* 保守狹隘的價值觀 **2** connected with a small town 小城鎮的： *small-town America* (= people who live in small towns in America) 美國的小城鎮人口

smarmy /ˈsmɑːmi; *NAmE* ˈsmɑːrmi/ *adj.* (**smarm·ier**, **smarmi·est**) (*informal, disapproving*) too polite in a way that is not sincere 過分殷勤的；諂媚的 **SYN** **smooth**： *a smarmy salesman* 逢迎討好的推銷員

smart 🔑 /smɑːt; *NAmE* smɑːrt/ *adj.*, *verb*

■ *adj.* (**smart·er**, **smart·est**)

▸ CLEAN/NEAT 整潔 **1** 🔑 (*especially BrE*) (of people 人) looking clean and neat; well dressed in fashionable and/or formal clothes 衣冠楚楚的；衣着講究的： *You look very smart in that suit.* 你穿上這套衣服顯得很精神。 **2** 🔑 (*especially BrE*) (of clothes, etc. 衣服等) clean, neat and looking new and attractive 整潔而漂亮的；光鮮的： *They were wearing their smartest clothes.* 他們都穿了最講究的衣服。

▸ INTELLIGENT 聰明 **3** 🔑 (*especially NAmE*) intelligent 聰明的；機敏的；精明的： *She's smarter than her brother.* 她比她哥哥聰明。◇ *That was a* ***smart*** *career* ***move.*** 那是

S

個人事業發展上的一着妙棋。◇ *OK, I admit it was not the smartest thing I ever did* (= it was a stupid thing to do). 好吧，我承認那件事我辦得很不漂亮。➲ SYNONYMS at INTELLIGENT

▸ **FASHIONABLE** 時髦 **4** (*especially BrE*) connected with fashionable rich people 時髦人物的；高檔的：*smart restaurants* 高檔餐館 ◇ *She mixes with **the smart set**.* 她跟那幫時髦人物交往。

▸ **QUICK** 快速 **5** (of a movement, etc. 動作等) quick and usually done with force 快速的；敏捷的；迅速而有力的 SYN **brisk**：*He was struck with a smart crack on the head.* 他頭上突然被猛擊了一下。◇ *We set off at a smart pace.* 我們快步出發了。

▸ **COMPUTER-CONTROLLED** 計算機控制 **6** (of a device, especially of a weapon/bomb 尤指武器、炸彈等裝置) controlled by a computer, so that it appears to act in an intelligent way 智能的：*smart bombs* 精靈炸彈 ◇ *This smart washing machine will dispense an optimal amount of water for the load.* 這台智能洗衣機會根據衣物多少適當安排進水量。

▸ **smart·ly** *adv.*：(*especially BrE*) *smartly dressed* 衣着光鮮 ◇ *He ran off pretty smartly* (= quickly and suddenly). 他一下子跑掉了。**smart·ness** *noun* [U]

■ *verb* **1** [I] **~ (from sth)** to feel a sharp stinging pain in a part of your body 感到劇烈刺痛：*His eyes were smarting from the smoke.* 他給煙熏得兩眼生疼。**2** [I] **~ (from/over sth)** to feel upset about a criticism, failure, etc.（因批評、失敗等）難過，煩惱：*They are still smarting from the 4–0 defeat last week.* 他們仍為上星期 0:4 慘敗而難過。➲ see also SMARTS

smart alec (*BrE*) (*NAmE* **smart aleck**) /ˈsmɑːt ælɪk; *NAmE* ˈsmɑːrt/ (also **ˈsmarty-pants**) (*BrE* also **ˈsmart-arse**) (*NAmE* also **ˈsmart-ass**) *noun* (*informal, disapproving*) a person who thinks they are very clever and likes to show people this in an annoying way 自詡聰明的人；好逞能的人

ˈsmart bomb *noun* a weapon controlled by an electronic device that is intended to cause damage to the target while avoiding damage to other people, buildings, etc. that are in the area（直中目標不傷其他的）智能炸彈；制導炸彈

ˈsmart card *noun* a small plastic card on which information is stored in electronic form 智能卡；靈通卡；高級磁卡 ➲ see also CHIP CARD

smart·en /ˈsmɑːtn; *NAmE* ˈsmɑːrtn/ *verb*

PHR V **ˌsmarten sb/sth↔ˈup** | **ˌsmarten (yourself) ˈup** (*especially BrE*) to make yourself, another person or a place look neater or more attractive（使）整潔起來，變得光鮮亮麗：*The hotel has been smartened up by the new owners.* 新主人把旅館修葺一新。

smart·ish /ˈsmɑːtɪʃ; *NAmE* ˈsmɑːrt-/ *adj., adv.* (*informal, especially BrE*) quick; quickly 很快的（地）；迅速的（地）：*We set off at a smartish pace.* 我們快步出發了。◇ *You'd better move smartish.* 你最好快一些。

the ˈsmart money *noun* [U] **1** money that is invested or bet by people who have expert knowledge 行家的投資（或賭注）；明智的投資（或賭注）：*It seems the smart money is no longer in insurance* (= is no longer being invested in insurance companies). 似乎專業投資不再投向保險業。◇ *The smart money is on him for the best actor award.* 內行認為他將獲最佳演員獎。**2** people who have expert knowledge of sth 有專業知識的人；知情者；行家：*The smart money says that he's likely to withdraw from the leadership campaign.* 據知情者說，他很可能退出領導人競選。

smart·phone /ˈsmɑːtfəʊn; *NAmE* ˈsmɑːrtfoʊn/ *noun* a mobile phone/cell phone that also has some of the functions of a computer（兼有某些計算機功能的）智能手機，智慧型手機

smarts /smɑːts; *NAmE* smɑːrts/ *noun* [U] (*NAmE, informal*) intelligence 智慧；聰明才智：*She made it to the top on her smarts.* 她靠自己的聰明才智獲得成功。

ˈsmarty-pants *noun* = SMART ALEC

smash 🔑 /smæʃ/ *verb, noun*

■ *verb*

▸ **BREAK** 打碎 **1** 🔑 [T, I] **~ (sth)** to break sth, or to be broken, violently and noisily into many pieces（嘩啦一聲）打碎，打破，破碎：*Several windows had been smashed.* 幾扇窗戶劈里啪啦打碎了。◇ *He smashed the radio to pieces.* 他啪的一聲把收音機摔得稀巴爛。◇ *The glass bowl smashed into a thousand pieces.* 玻璃碗咣的一聲摔了個粉碎。

▸ **HIT VERY HARD** 猛烈撞擊 **2** 🔑 [I, T] to move with a lot of force against sth solid; to make sth do this（使）猛烈撞擊，猛烈碰撞：**+ adv./prep.** *the sound of waves smashing against the rocks* 浪濤猛烈撞擊礁石的聲音 ◇ *The car smashed into a tree.* 汽車猛地撞到了樹上。◇ **~ sth + adv./prep.** *Mark smashed his fist down on the desk.* 馬克狠狠地把拳頭砸在桌上。➲ SYNONYMS at CRASH **3** 🔑 [T, I] to hit sth very hard and break it, in order to get through it（用力）撞開，擊穿，闖過：**~ sth + adv./prep.** *They had to smash holes in the ice.* 他們只好奮力在冰上鑿洞。◇ *The elephant smashed its way through the trees.* 大象橫衝直撞，闖過樹叢。◇ **~ sth + adj.** *We had to smash the door open.* 我們只得用力把門撞開。◇ **+ adv./prep.** *They had smashed through a glass door to get in.* 他們砸破一道玻璃門進去了。**4** [T] **~ sth/sb (+ adv./prep.)** to hit sth/sb very hard 猛擊 SYN **slam**：*He smashed the ball into the goal.* 他一記勁射，球進了。

▸ **DESTROY/DEFEAT** 搗毀；打敗 **5** [T] **~ sth/sb** to destroy, defeat or put an end to sth/sb 搗毀；打敗；粉碎；使結束：*Police say they have smashed a major drugs ring.* 警方說他們摧毀了一個大販毒集團。◇ *She has smashed the world record* (= broken it by a large amount). 她大破世界紀錄。

▸ **CRASH VEHICLE** 撞車 **6** [T] **~ sth (up)** to crash a vehicle 撞毀（車輛）：*He's smashed (up) his new car.* 他把自己的新車撞毀了。➲ SYNONYMS at CRASH

▸ **IN TENNIS, ETC.** 網球等 **7** [T] **~ sth** to hit a high ball downwards and very hard over the net 打高壓球；扣球

PHR V **ˌsmash sth↔ˈdown** to make sth fall down by hitting it hard and breaking it（用力）擊倒，打翻：*The police had to smash the door down.* 警察不得不破門而入。**ˌsmash sth↔ˈin** to make a hole in sth by hitting it with a lot of force（用力）打破，撞壞：*Vandals had smashed the door in.* 破壞分子把門撞破了。◇ (*informal*) *I wanted to **smash his face in*** (= hit him hard in the face). 當時我真想把他的臉打癟。**ˌsmash sth↔ˈup** to destroy sth deliberately（蓄意）搗毀，破壞：*Youths had broken into the bar and smashed the place up.* 一群年輕人闖進酒吧，把裏面砸了個亂七八糟。

■ *noun*

▸ **ACT OF BREAKING** 破碎；打碎 **1** 🔑 [sing.] an act of breaking sth noisily into pieces; the sound this makes 破碎；打碎；破碎（或打碎）的嘩啦聲：*The cup hit the floor with a smash.* 杯子掉到地上嘩啦一聲摔碎了。

▸ **VEHICLE CRASH** 撞車 **2** [C] (*BrE*) an accident in which a vehicle hits another vehicle 撞車：*a car smash* 撞車事故

▸ **IN TENNIS, ETC.** 網球等 **3** [C] a way of hitting the ball downwards and very hard 高壓球；扣球

▸ **SONG/MOVIE/PLAY** 歌曲；電影；戲劇 **4** (also **ˌsmash ˈhit**) [C] a song, film/movie or play that is very popular 十分走紅的歌曲（或電影、戲劇）：*her latest chart smash* 她的最新一首十分走紅的上榜歌曲

ˌsmash-and-ˈgrab *adj.* [only before noun] (*BrE*) relating to the act of stealing from a shop/store by breaking a window and taking the goods you can see or reach easily 砸櫥窗搶劫的：*a smash-and-grab raid* 砸櫥窗搶劫

smashed /smæʃt/ *adj.* [not before noun] (*slang*) very drunk 大醉

smash·er /ˈsmæʃə(r)/ *noun* (*old-fashioned, BrE, informal*) a very good or attractive person or thing 很好的人；很漂亮的人；十分討人喜歡的人（或事物）

smash·ing /ˈsmæʃɪŋ/ *adj.* (*old-fashioned, BrE, informal*) very good or enjoyable 非常好的；十分愉快的 SYN **great**：*We had a smashing time.* 我們過得非常愉快。

ˈsmash-up *noun* (*informal*) a crash in which vehicles are very badly damaged 嚴重撞車事故

smat·ter·ing /ˈsmætərɪŋ/ *noun* [sing.] **~ (of sth)** a small amount of sth, especially knowledge of a language

（尤指對語言）略知，淺知：*He only has a smattering of French.* 他只懂一點法語。

smear /smɪə(r); *NAmE* smɪr/ *verb, noun*

■ *verb* **1** [T] to spread an OILY or soft substance over a surface in a rough or careless way（用油性或稀軟物質）胡亂塗抹 **SYN** **daub**：**~ sth on/over sth** *The children had smeared mud on the walls.* 那幾個孩子往牆上抹了泥巴。◇ **~ sth with sth** *The children had smeared the walls with mud.* 那幾個孩子往牆上抹了泥巴。 **2** [T] **~ sth** to make sth dirty or GREASY 弄髒；弄上油污：*His glasses were smeared.* 他的眼鏡髒了。◇ *smeared windows* 髒了的窗戶 **3** [T] **~ sb/sth** to damage sb's reputation by saying unpleasant things about them that are not true 誹謗；詆譭 **SYN** **slander**：*The story was an attempt to smear the party leader.* 這篇報道是企圖玷污該黨領袖的聲譽。 **4** [T, I] **~ (sth)** to rub writing, a drawing, etc. so that it is no longer clear; to become not clear in this way 把（字跡、圖畫等）蹭得模糊不清；變得模糊不清 **SYN** **smudge**：*The last few words of the letter were smeared.* 信的最後幾個字蹭得看不清了。

■ *noun* **1** an OILY or dirty mark 污跡；污漬；污點：*a smear of jam* 果醬漬 ➲ SYNONYMS at MARK **2** a story that is not true about sb that is intended to damage their reputation, especially in politics（尤指政治上的）抹黑，醜化：*He was a victim of a* ***smear campaign****.* 他受到對方的譭謗攻擊。 **3** (*BrE*) = SMEAR TEST

ˈsmear test (also **smear**, **ˌcervical ˈsmear**) (all *BrE*) (*NAmE* **ˈPap smear**) *noun* a medical test in which a very small amount of TISSUE from a woman's CERVIX is removed and examined for cancer cells 塗片試驗（從婦女子宮頸取少許組織，以檢查是否有癌細胞）

smell 🔑 /smel/ *verb, noun*

■ *verb* (**smelled**, **smelled**) (*BrE* also **smelt**, **smelt** /smelt/)
1 🔑 [I] to have a particular smell 有（或發出）…氣味：**+ adj.** *The room smelt damp.* 屋子裏有潮氣。◇ *Dinner smells good.* 飯菜聞起來很香啊。◇ *a bunch of sweet-smelling flowers* 一束散發着馨香的花 ◇ **~ of sth** *His breath smelt of garlic.* 他嘴裏有蒜味。◇ **~ like sth** *What does the perfume smell like?* 這種香水聞起來像什麼？ **2** 🔑 [T, no passive] (not used in the progressive tenses; often with *can* or *could* 不用於進行時；常與 can 或 could 連用) to notice or recognize a particular smell 聞到，嗅到（氣味）：**~ sth** *He said he could smell gas when he entered the room.* 他一進屋就說聞到了煤氣味。◇ *The dog had smelt a rabbit.* 狗嗅到了兔子的氣味。◇ *I could smell alcohol on his breath.* 我聞到他呼吸氣中有酒味。◇ **~ sth doing sth** *Can you smell something burning?* 你有沒有聞到什麼東西燒焦了？◇ **~ (that)** … *I could smell that something was burning.* 我聞得到有什麼東西燒焦了。 **3** [I] (not used in the progressive tenses; often with *can* or *could* 不用於進行時，常與 can 或 could 連用) to be able to notice and recognize smells 能聞到氣味；能嗅到氣味：*I can't smell because I've got a bad cold.* 我患了重感冒聞不到氣味。 **4** 🔑 [T] **~ sth** (not usually used in the passive 通常不用於被動語態) to put your nose near sth and breathe in so that you can discover or identify its smell 聞，嗅（氣味） **SYN** **sniff**：*Smell this and tell me what you think it is.* 你聞一下這個，然後告訴我是什麼。◇ *I bent down to smell the flowers.* 我彎下腰聞花香。 **5** 🔑 [I] (not used in the progressive tenses 不用於進行時) to have an unpleasant smell 有難聞的氣味；散發着臭氣：*The drains smell.* 下水道散發着臭氣。◇ ***It smells*** *in here.* 這兒有一股難聞的氣味。◇ *He hadn't washed for days and was beginning to smell.* 他好久沒洗澡了，身上都有味兒了。 **6** [T, no passive] **~ sth** to feel that sth exists or is going to happen 覺察出；感覺到：*He smelt danger.* 他意識到了危險。◇ *I can smell trouble.* 我感覺會有麻煩。

IDM **come up/out of sth smelling of ˈroses** (*informal*) to still have a good reputation, even though you have been involved in sth that might have given people a bad opinion of you 雖捲入…而好名聲依舊；事後於名譽無損 **ˌsmell a ˈrat** (*informal*) to suspect that sth is wrong about a situation 懷疑事情不妙；感覺情況不對 ➲ more at ROSE *n.*, WAKE *v.*

PHR V **ˌsmell sb/sth↔ˈout 1** to be aware of fear, danger, trouble, etc. in a situation 覺察到，意識到（壞事、危險、麻煩等）：*He could always smell out fear.* 別人有什麼恐懼，他總能覺察到。 **2** to find sth by smelling 嗅出；聞出：*dogs trained to smell out drugs* 受過訓練的緝毒犬

■ *noun* **1** 🔑 [C, U] the quality of sth that people and animals sense through their noses 氣味：*a* ***faint/strong smell*** *of garlic* 淡淡的／濃重的蒜味 ◇ *a* ***sweet/fresh/musty smell*** 香甜的／新鮮的／發霉的氣味 ◇ *There was a smell of burning in the air.* 空氣中有一股燒東西的焦煳味。◇ *The smells from the kitchen filled the room.* 滿屋子都是從廚房飄來的氣味。 **2** 🔑 [sing.] an unpleasant smell 難聞的氣味；臭味：*What's that smell?* 這是一股什麼臭味？◇ *Yuk! What a smell!* 哎喲！多難聞的氣味！ **3** 🔑 [U] the ability to sense things with the nose 嗅覺：*Dogs have a very good* ***sense of smell****.* 狗的嗅覺非常靈敏。◇ *Taste and smell are closely connected.* 味覺和嗅覺有密切的聯繫。 **4** [C] the act of smelling sth 嗅；聞 **SYN** **sniff**：*He took one smell of the liquid and his eyes began to water.* 他聞了一下那種液體，就流起淚來了。

IDM see SWEET *adj.*

Vocabulary Building 詞彙擴充

Smells 氣味

Describing smells 描述氣味

These adjectives describe pleasant smells 下列形容詞描述令人愉悅的氣味：

- **scented** candles 香燭
- **aromatic** oils 芳香油
- **fragrant** perfume 芬芳的香水
- **sweet-smelling** flowers 芳香撲鼻的花

To describe unpleasant smells you can use 描述令人不快的氣味可以說：

- **smelly** cheese 有難聞氣味的奶酪
- **stinking** fish 發臭的魚
- **musty** old books 發霉的舊書
- **acrid** smoke 嗆人的煙

Types of smell 各種氣味

Pleasant smells 令人愉悅的氣味：

- the rich **aroma** of fresh coffee 新鮮咖啡醇厚的香味
- a herb with a delicate **fragrance** 散發淡雅香氣的芳草
- a rose's sweet **perfume** 玫瑰的芳香
- the **scent** of wild flowers 野花的芬芳

Unpleasant smells 難聞的氣味：

- nasty household **odours** 家裏難聞的氣味
- the **stench** of rotting meat 腐肉的惡臭
- the **stink** of stale sweat 汗臭味
- the **reek** of beer and tobacco 啤酒和煙草的強烈臭味

ˈsmelling salts *noun* [pl.] a chemical with a very strong smell, kept in a small bottle, used especially in the past for putting under the nose of a person who has become unconscious 嗅鹽（有刺鼻的氣味，舊時用作蘇醒劑）

smelly /ˈsmeli/ *adj.* (**smell·ier**, **smelli·est**) (*informal*) having an unpleasant smell 有難聞氣味的；有臭味的：*smelly feet* 臭腳

smelt /smelt/ *verb* **~ sth** to heat and melt ORE (= rock that contains metal) in order to obtain the metal it contains 熔煉；提煉（金屬）：*a method of smelting iron* 一種煉鐵方法 ➲ see also SMELL *v.*

smelt·er /ˈsmeltə(r)/ *noun* a piece of equipment for smelting metal 熔爐

smidgen (also **smidg·eon**, **smid·gin**) /ˈsmɪdʒən/ *noun* [sing.] **~ (of sth)** (*informal*) a small piece or amount of sth 少量；一點點：*'Sugar?' 'Just a smidgen.'* "放糖嗎？" "只放一點。"

S

smile 🔑 /smaɪl/ *verb, noun*
■ *verb* **1** 🔑 [I] to make a smile appear on your face 微笑；笑：*to* **smile** *sweetly/faintly/broadly, etc.* 嫣然一笑、淡然一笑、咧嘴一笑等 ◇ *He smiled with relief.* 他寬慰地笑了。◇ *He never seems to smile.* 他好像從來都不笑。◇ **~ at sb/sth** *She smiled at him and he* **smiled back**. 她衝他笑笑，他也衝她笑笑。◇ *I had to smile at* (= was amused by) *his optimism.* 對他的樂觀態度，我只好一笑置之。**2** [T] to say or express sth with a smile 微笑着說；微笑地表示：**~ sth** *She smiled her thanks.* 她笑了笑表示感謝。◇ **+ speech** *'Perfect,' he smiled.* "好極了。" 他微笑着說。**3** [T, no passive] **~ sth** to give a smile of a particular type 現出（某種）笑容：*to smile a small smile* 微微一笑 ◇ *She smiled a smile of dry amusement.* 她心裏覺得很滑稽，但只是含蓄地微微一笑。**IDM** see EAR
PHR V ˈ**smile on sb/sth** (*formal*) if luck, etc. **smiles on** you, you are lucky or successful 有利於；垂青；帶來好運
■ *noun* 🔑 the expression that you have on your face when you are happy, amused, etc. in which the corners of your mouth turn upwards 微笑；笑容：*'Oh, hello,' he said,* **with a smile**. "嗨，你好。" 他微笑着說。◇ *She* **gave a** *wry* **smile**. 她苦笑一下。◇ *He had a big smile on his face.* 他笑容滿面。◇ *I'm going to* **wipe that smile off your face** (= make you stop thinking this is funny). 我會讓你笑不出來的。
IDM **all ˈsmiles** looking very happy, especially soon after you have been looking worried or sad （尤指愁眉苦臉或悲傷之後）一臉笑意，喜滋滋的：*Twelve hours later she was all smiles again.* 十二小時之後，她又喜笑顏開了。

smiley /ˈsmaɪli/ *noun* **1** a simple picture of a smiling face that is drawn as a circle with two eyes and a curved mouth 笑臉圖（用 ☺ 表示）**2** a simple picture or series of keyboard symbols :-) that represents a smiling face. The symbols are used, for example, in email or text messages to show that the person sending the message is pleased or joking. 微笑符（例如用 :-) 表示）

smil·ing·ly /ˈsmaɪlɪŋli/ *adv.* with a smile or smiles 微笑着

smirk /smɜːk; *NAmE* smɜːrk/ *verb* [I] to smile in a silly or unpleasant way that shows that you are pleased with yourself, know sth that other people do not know, etc. 自鳴得意地笑；傻笑：*It was hard not to smirk.* 讓人忍俊不禁。◇ *He smirked unpleasantly when we told him the bad news.* 我們把壞消息告訴他時，他臉上現出一絲奸笑。▸ **smirk** *noun*：*She had a self-satisfied smirk on her face.* 她滿臉揚揚得意的樣子。

smite /smaɪt/ *verb* (**smote** /sməʊt; *NAmE* smoʊt/, **smit·ten** /ˈsmɪtn/) (*old use* or *literary*) **1 ~ sb/sth** to hit sb/sth hard; to attack or punish sb 重打；猛擊；攻擊；懲罰 **2 ~ sb** to have a great effect on sb, especially an unpleasant or serious one 使深感（不安、不快等）；深深影響 ➲ see also SMITTEN

smith /smɪθ/ *noun* = BLACKSMITH ➲ see also GOLDSMITH, GUNSMITH, LOCKSMITH, SILVERSMITH

smith·er·eens /ˌsmɪðəˈriːnz/ *noun* [pl.]
IDM **smash, blow, etc. sth to smitheˈreens** (*informal*) to destroy sth completely by breaking it into small pieces 把某物砸（或打等）得粉碎

smithy /ˈsmɪði; *NAmE* -θi/ *noun* (*pl.* **-ies**) a place where a BLACKSMITH works 鐵匠鋪

smit·ten /ˈsmɪtn/ *adj.* [not usually before noun] **1 ~ (with/by sb/sth)** (especially *humorous*) suddenly feeling that you are in love with sb 突然愛上；一下子愛上：*From the moment they met, he was completely smitten by her.* 從一見面的那一刻起，他就完全被她迷住了。**2 ~ with/by sth** severely affected by a feeling, disease, etc. 痛感；備受…的煎熬 ➲ see also SMITE

smock /smɒk; *NAmE* smɑːk/ *noun* **1** a loose comfortable piece of clothing like a long shirt, worn especially by women （多為女性穿的）寬鬆式襯衫 **2** a long loose piece of clothing worn over other clothes to protect them from dirt, etc. 罩衣；工作服：*an artist's smock* 畫家的罩衫

smock·ing /ˈsmɒkɪŋ; *NAmE* ˈsmɑːk-/ *noun* [U] decoration on clothing consisting of very small tight folds which are sewn together （衣服的）褶襉，縮褶

smog /smɒɡ; *NAmE* smɑːɡ/ *noun* [U, C] a form of air pollution that is or looks like a mixture of smoke and FOG, especially in cities 煙霧（煙與霧混合的空氣污染物，尤見於城市）：*attempts to reduce smog caused by traffic fumes* 旨在降低車輛尾氣造成的煙霧的措施 ➲ **VISUAL VOCAB** page V6 ▸ **smoggy** *adj.*

smoke 🔑 /sməʊk; *NAmE* smoʊk/ *noun, verb*
■ *noun* **1** 🔑 [U] the grey, white or black gas that is produced by sth burning 煙：*cigarette smoke* 香煙產生的煙 ◇ *Clouds of thick black smoke billowed from the car's exhaust.* 從汽車排氣管冒出一股股黑色濃煙。**2** 🔑 [C, usually sing.] (*informal*) an act of smoking a cigarette 吸煙；抽煙：*Are you coming outside for a smoke?* 你是不是出來抽支煙？
IDM **go up in ˈsmoke** **1** to be completely burnt 被燒燬；被燒光：*The whole house went up in smoke.* 整座房子被燒燬了。**2** if your plans, hopes, etc. **go up in smoke**, they fail completely 告吹；成泡影；破滅 **(there is) no smoke without ˈfire** (*BrE*) (*NAmE* **where there's smoke, there's ˈfire**) (*saying*) if sth bad is being said about sb/sth, it usually has some truth in it 無火不生煙；無風不起浪 **a smoke-filled ˈroom** (*disapproving*) a decision that people describe as being made in **a smoke-filled room** is made by a small group of people at a private meeting, rather than in an open and DEMOCRATIC way （少數人密謀決策的）密室 ➲ more at BLOW *v.*
■ *verb* **1** 🔑 [T, I] **~ (sth)** to suck smoke from a cigarette, pipe, etc. into your mouth and let it out again 吸（煙）；抽（煙）：*He was smoking a large cigar.* 他正抽着一支大雪茄。◇ *How many cigarettes do you smoke a day?* 你一天抽幾支香煙？◇ *Do you mind if I smoke?* 我抽煙你介意嗎？**2** 🔑 [I] to use cigarettes, etc. in this way as a habit （習慣性）吸煙，抽煙：*Do you smoke?* 你抽煙嗎？◇ *She smokes heavily.* 她的煙癮大。➲ see also CHAIN-SMOKE **3** 🔑 [I] to produce smoke 冒煙：*smoking factory chimneys* 冒着煙的工廠煙囱 ◇ *the smoking remains of burnt-out cars* 燒燬的車輛還在冒煙的殘骸 **4** 🔑 [T, usually passive] **~ sth** to preserve meat or fish by hanging it in smoke from wood fires to give it a special taste 熏製（肉或魚）：*smoked salmon* 熏鮭魚
PHR V ˌ**smoke sb/sth↔ˈout** **1** to force sb/sth to come out of a place by filling it with smoke 用煙熏出來：*to smoke out wasps from a nest* 把黃蜂從窩裏熏出來 **2** to take action to discover where sb is hiding or to make a secret publicly known 查清（某人藏匿處）；揭露（秘密）：*The police are determined to smoke out the leaders of the gang.* 警方決心查出犯罪團夥頭目的藏匿處。

ˈ**smoke alarm** (also ˈ**smoke detector**) *noun* a device that makes a loud noise if smoke is in the air to warn you of a fire 煙霧報警器（用於預防火災）

ˈ**smoke bomb** *noun* a bomb that produces clouds of smoke when it explodes 發煙彈；煙幕彈

ˌ**smoked ˈglass** *noun* [U] glass that has been deliberately made dark by smoke （通過煙熏處理的）煙色玻璃

ˈ**smoke-free** *adj.* free from cigarette smoke; where smoking is not allowed 無人吸煙的；禁止吸煙的：*a smoke-free working environment* 無煙工作環境

smoke·less /ˈsməʊkləs; *NAmE* ˈsmoʊk-/ *adj.* [usually before noun] **1** able to burn without producing smoke （燃燒時）不產生煙的，無煙的：*smokeless fuels* 無煙燃料 **2** free from smoke 不冒煙的；無煙的：*a smokeless zone* (= where smoke from factories or houses is not allowed) 無煙區（禁止工廠或家庭使用有煙燃料的地區）

smoker /ˈsməʊkə(r); *NAmE* ˈsmoʊk-/ *noun* a person who smokes TOBACCO regularly 吸煙者：*a* **heavy smoker** (= sb who smokes a lot) 煙癮大的人 ◇ *a* **smoker's cough** 吸煙過多引起的咳嗽 ◇ *a* **cigarette/cigar/pipe smoker** 抽香煙／雪茄／煙斗的人 **OPP** **non-smoker**

smoke·screen /ˈsməʊkskriːn; *NAmE* ˈsmoʊk-/ *noun* **1** something that you do or say in order to hide what

S

you are really doing or intending 煙幕（用以掩蓋真相的言行）；障眼法 **2** a cloud of smoke used to hide soldiers, ships, etc. during a battle（戰鬥中用以掩蔽士兵、艦船等的）煙幕

'smoke shop *noun* (*NAmE*) a shop/store selling cigarettes, TOBACCO, etc. 煙草商店；煙行

'smoke signal *noun* [usually pl.] **1** a signal that is sent to sb who is far away, using smoke 煙霧信號 **2** a sign of what sb is thinking or doing（思想或行動的）標記，跡象

smoke·stack /'sməʊkstæk; *NAmE* 'smoʊk-/ *noun* (*especially NAmE*) **1** a tall CHIMNEY that takes away smoke from factories（工廠的）大煙囱 **2** (*BrE* also **fun·nel**) a metal CHIMNEY, for example on a ship or an engine, through which smoke comes out（輪船或火車頭上的）金屬煙囱

Smokey the Bear /ˌsməʊki ðə 'beə(r); *NAmE* ˌsmoʊki ðə 'ber/ *noun* **1** the symbol used by the US Forest Service on signs and advertising about preventing forest fires 防火護林熊（美國林業局用於森林防火標誌和廣告的標記）**2** (also ˌ**Smokey 'Bear**, **'Smokey**) (*informal*) (in the US) a member of the police force that is responsible for the highway（美國）高速公路巡邏警

smok·ing 🔑 /'sməʊkɪŋ; *NAmE* 'smoʊk-/ *noun* [U] the activity or habit of smoking cigarettes, etc. 吸煙；抽煙：*No Smoking* (= for example, on a notice) 禁止吸煙 ◇ *Would you like smoking or non-smoking?* (= for example, in a restaurant) 你喜歡在吸煙區還是非吸煙區？◇ *He's trying to* ***give up smoking***. 他正設法戒煙。 ➲ compare NON-SMOKING

ˌ**smoking 'gun** *noun* [sing.] (*informal*) something that seems to prove that sb has done sth wrong or illegal 犯錯（或犯法的）證據：*This memo could be the smoking gun that investigators have been looking for.* 這份備忘錄可能是調查人員一直在尋找的證據。

'smoking jacket *noun* a man's comfortable jacket worn in the past, often made of VELVET 吸煙服（舊時男人穿的寬鬆便服，多用絲絨做成）

smoko /'sməʊkəʊ; *NAmE* 'smoʊkoʊ/ *noun* (*pl.* **-os**) (*AustralE, NZE, informal*) a rest from work, for example to smoke a cigarette（抽煙等）工間休息

smoky /'sməʊki; *NAmE* 'smoʊki/ *adj.* (**smoki·er**, **smoki·est**) **1** full of smoke 煙霧瀰漫的：*a smoky atmosphere* 煙霧瀰漫的空氣 ◇ *a smoky pub* 煙霧騰騰的酒吧 **2** producing a lot of smoke 多煙的；冒出大量煙的：*a smoky fire* 冒着濃煙的火 **3** tasting or smelling like smoke 有煙熏味的：*a smoky flavour* 煙熏味 **4** having the colour or appearance of smoke 煙灰色的；似煙的：*smoky blue glass* 灰藍色玻璃 OPP **clear**

smol·der (*NAmE*) = SMOULDER

smooch /smuːtʃ/ *verb* [I] (*informal*) to kiss and hold sb closely, especially when you are dancing slowly（尤指慢舞時）接吻擁抱

smoodge /smuːdʒ/ *verb* [I] **~ (to sb)** (*AustralE, NZE, informal*) to behave in a friendly way towards sb because you want them to give you sth or do sth for you（和某人）套近乎；討好 ▸ **smoodge** *noun* [U]：*What's wrong with a bit of smoodge between friends?* 朋友之間互相恭維一下有什麼不妥？

smooth 🔑 /smuːð/ *adj.*, *verb*

■ *adj.* (**smooth·er**, **smooth·est**)

▸ FLAT/EVEN 平整；平滑 **1** 🔑 completely flat and even, without any lumps, holes or rough areas 平整的；平坦的；平滑的；光滑的：*a lotion to make your skin feel soft and smooth* 能使皮膚柔軟光滑的護膚液 ◇ *The water was as smooth as glass.* 水平如鏡。◇ *a paint that gives a smooth, silky finish* 使表面如絲般光滑的油漆 ◇ *Over the years, the stone steps had worn smooth.* 日久天長，石階已經磨得光溜溜的。OPP **rough**

▸ WITHOUT LUMPS 無結塊 **2** 🔑 (of a liquid mixture 液體混合物) without any lumps 無結塊的；混合均勻的：*Mix the flour with the milk to form a smooth paste.* 把麪粉和牛奶和成均勻的麪糊。

▸ WITHOUT PROBLEMS 順利 **3** 🔑 happening or continuing without any problems 順利的；平穩的：*They are introducing new measures to ensure the smooth running of the business.* 他們正採取新措施，以確保公司平穩運轉。◇ *They could not ensure a smooth transfer of political power.* 他們無法保證政權的順利交接。

▸ MOVEMENT 運動 **4** 🔑 even and regular, without sudden stops and starts 平穩的；連續而流暢的：*The car's improved suspension gives you a smoother ride.* 汽車懸架經過改進，乘坐起來更平穩。◇ *The plane made a smooth landing.* 飛機平穩降落。◇ *She swung herself over the gate in one smooth movement.* 她從柵欄門上一躍而過。

▸ MAN 人 **5** (often *disapproving*) (of people, especially men, and their behaviour 人（尤指男人）及行為) very polite and pleasant, but in a way that is often not very sincere 圓通的；八面玲瓏的 SYN **smarmy**：*I don't like him. He's far too smooth for me.* 我不喜歡他。他太圓滑。◇ *He's something of a* ***smooth operator***. 可以說，他是一個八面玲瓏的滑頭。

▸ DRINK/TASTE 飲料；味道 **6** pleasant and not bitter 醇和的；香醇的：*This coffee has a smooth, rich taste.* 這種咖啡味道醇厚。

▸ VOICE/MUSIC 噪音；音樂 **7** nice to hear, and without any rough or unpleasant sounds 悅耳的；圓潤的

▸ **smooth·ness** *noun* [U]：*the smoothness of her skin* 她的皮膚細膩光滑 ◇ *They admired the smoothness and efficiency with which the business was run.* 他們欽佩這家公司協調高效的管理方式。IDM see ROUGH *n.*

■ *verb* **1** to make sth smooth 使平整；使平坦；使平滑；使光滑：**~ sth (back/down/out)** *He smoothed his hair back.* 他朝後捋了捋頭髮。◇ *She was smoothing out the creases in her skirt.* 她正設法弄平裙子上的皺褶。◇ **~ sth + adj.** *He took the letter and smoothed it flat on the table.* 他接過信，在桌上展平。 **2 ~ sth on/into/over sth** to put a layer of a soft substance over a surface（將軟物質）均勻塗抹於：*Smooth the icing over the top of the cake.* 在蛋糕頂上均勻地鋪一層糖霜。

IDM **smooth the 'path/'way** to make it easier for sb/sth to develop or make progress 鋪平道路：*These negotiations are intended to smooth the path to a peace treaty.* 這些談判目的在於為簽訂和平條約鋪平道路。 **smooth (sb's) ruffled 'feathers** to make sb feel less angry or offended 使息怒；勸解

PHR V ˌ**smooth sth↔a'way/'out** to make problems or difficulties disappear 消除（問題）；克服（困難） ˌ**smooth sth↔'over** to make problems or difficulties seem less important or serious, especially by talking to people 緩和；調解；斡旋：*She spoke to both sides in the dispute in an attempt to smooth things over.* 她和爭執雙方談話，試圖進行調解。

smoothie /'smuːði/ *noun* **1** (*informal*) a man who dresses well and talks very politely and confidently but who is often not honest or sincere 體面而圓通的男人；八面玲瓏的男人 **2** a drink made of fruit or fruit juice mixed with milk or ice cream 水果奶昔，思慕雪（水果或果汁加牛奶或冰淇淋攪拌而成）

smooth·ly 🔑 /'smuːðli/ *adv.*

1 🔑 in an even way, without suddenly stopping and starting again 平穩地；連續而流暢地：*Traffic is now flowing smoothly again.* 現在，交通又暢通了。◇ *The engine was running smoothly.* 發動機在平穩運轉。 **2** 🔑 without problems or difficulties 順利地：*The interview* ***went smoothly***. 面談進展順利。 **3** in a calm or confident way 平靜地；自信地：*'Would you like to come this way?' he said smoothly.* "你上這邊來好嗎？" 他平靜地說。 **4** 🔑 in a way that produces a smooth surface or mixture 平整地；平滑地；均勻地：*The colours blend smoothly together.* 這些顏色可以均勻地配在一起。

ˌ**smooth 'muscle** *noun* [U] (*anatomy* 解) the type of muscle found in the organs inside the body, that is not under conscious control 平滑肌；不隨意肌

ˌ**smooth-'talking** *adj.* (usually *disapproving*) talking very politely and confidently, especially to persuade sb to do sth, but in a way that may not be honest or sincere 花言巧語的；巧舌如簧的

s'more /smɔː(r)/ *noun* (*NAmE*) a cooked MARSHMALLOW eaten with chocolate between two GRAHAM CRACKERS (= a type of cookie) that is traditionally cooked over a

S

fire when camping 棉花糖巧克力夾心餅（用兩塊全麥餅乾夾棉花軟糖和巧克力製作而成）

smor·gas·bord /ˈsmɔːɡəsbɔːd; *NAmE* ˈsmɔːrɡəsbɔːrd/ *noun* [U, sing.] (from *Swedish*) a meal at which you serve yourself from a large range of hot and cold dishes 自助餐

smote *past tense of* SMITE

smother /ˈsmʌðə(r)/ *verb* **1 ~ sb (with sth)** to kill sb by covering their face so that they cannot breathe 使窒息而死；悶死 **SYN suffocate**：*He smothered the baby with a pillow.* 他用枕頭把嬰兒悶死了。 **2 ~ sth/sb with/in sth** to cover sth/sb thickly or with too much of sth（用某物）厚厚地覆蓋：*a rich dessert smothered in cream* 塗了厚厚一層奶油的多脂甜點 ◇ *She smothered him with kisses.* 她劈頭蓋腦給他一通狂吻。 **3 ~ sth** to prevent sth from developing or being expressed 抑制；扼殺；忍住 **SYN stifle**：***to smother a yawn/giggle/grin*** 把哈欠忍了回去；憋住不笑出聲來；剛想張嘴笑又收了回去 ◇ *The voices of the opposition were effectively smothered.* 反對黨的聲音被有效地壓制了下去。 **4 ~ sb** to give sb too much love or protection so that they feel restricted（因溺愛等）使…覺得壓抑：*Her husband was very loving, but she felt smothered.* 丈夫對她百般寵愛，但這讓她覺得不自在。 **5 ~ sth** to make a fire stop burning by covering it with sth 把（火）悶熄：*He tried to smother the flames with a blanket.* 他試圖用毯子把火撲滅。

smoul·der (*especially US* **smol·der**) /ˈsməʊldə(r); *NAmE* ˈsmoʊ-/ *verb* **1** [I] to burn slowly without a flame（無明火地）陰燃，悶燃：*The bonfire was still smouldering the next day.* 到了第二天，篝火還在悶燃。◇ *a smouldering cigarette* 慢慢燃燒的香煙 ◇ (*figurative*) *The feud smouldered on for years.* 這場冤仇積結了多年。 **2** [I] (*formal*) to be filled with a strong emotion that you do not fully express（感情）鬱積，壓在心頭 **SYN burn**：**~ (with sth)** *His eyes smouldered with anger.* 他眼裏冒着強壓的怒火。◇ **~ (in sth)** *Anger smouldered in his eyes.* 強壓的怒火在他眼裏燃燒。

SMS /ˌes em ˈes/ *noun, verb*

■ ***noun*** **1** [U] the abbreviation for 'short message service' (a system for sending short written messages from one mobile/cell phone to another)（手機的）短信服務（全寫為 short message service） **2** [C] a message sent by SMS（手機）短信，短消息，簡訊 **SYN text, text message**：*I'm trying to send an SMS.* 我正想發短信。 ➲ COLLOCATIONS at PHONE ➲ compare EMS

■ ***verb*** [T, I] **~ (sb)** to send a message to sb by SMS（用手機）發短信，發簡訊 **SYN text, text message**：*He SMSed me every day.* 以往他每天給我發短信。◇ *If you have any comments, just email or SMS.* 假如你有任何意見，可發電子郵件或短信。◇ *She spends her time chatting and SMSing.* 她通過聊天和發短信消磨時間。

smudge /smʌdʒ/ *noun, verb*

■ ***noun*** a dirty mark with no clear shape（模糊的）污跡，污痕 **SYN smear**：*a smudge of lipstick on a cup* 留在杯子上的口紅印

■ ***verb*** **1** [T, I] **~ (sth)** to touch or rub sth, especially wet ink or paint, so that it is no longer clear; to become not clear in this way 把…擦模糊（或弄得看不清楚）；變模糊：*He had smudged his signature with his sleeve.* 他用袖子把自己的簽字擦得看不清了。◇ *Tears had smudged her mascara.* 她的睫毛膏被淚水弄糊了。◇ *Her lipstick had smudged.* 她的口紅糊了。 **2** [T] **~ sth** to make a dirty mark on a surface 弄髒；留下污跡 **SYN smear**：*The mirror was smudged with fingerprints.* 鏡子上有髒手印。

smudgy /ˈsmʌdʒi/ *adj.* **1** with dirty marks on 有髒痕的；有污跡的 **2** (of a picture, writing, etc. 圖畫、字跡等) with edges that are not clear 模糊不清的 **SYN blurred**

smug /smʌɡ/ *adj.* (*disapproving*) looking or feeling too pleased about sth you have done or achieved 沾沾自喜的；自鳴得意的 **SYN complacent**：***a smug expression/smile/face, etc.*** 沾沾自喜的表情、笑容、面容等 ◇ *What are you looking so smug about?* 你怎麼這樣一副神氣活現的樣子？ ► **smug·ly** *adv.* **smug·ness** *noun* [U]

smug·gle /ˈsmʌɡl/ *verb* **~ sth/sb (+ adv./prep.)** to take, send or bring goods or people secretly and illegally into or out of a country, etc. 走私；私運；偷運：*They were caught smuggling diamonds into the country.* 他們走私鑽石入境時被發現了。◇ *He managed to smuggle a gun into the prison.* 他設法把一支槍偷偷送進了監獄。◇ *smuggled drugs* 走私的毒品 ➲ COLLOCATIONS at CRIME

smug·gler /ˈsmʌɡlə(r)/ *noun* a person who takes goods into or out of a country illegally 走私者

smug·gling /ˈsmʌɡlɪŋ/ *noun* [U] the crime of taking, sending or bringing goods secretly and illegally into or out of a country 走私（罪）：*drug smuggling* 毒品走私

smut /smʌt/ *noun* **1** [U] (*informal*) stories, pictures or comments about sex that deal with it in a way that some people find offensive 淫穢小說（或圖片、言語） **2** [U, C] dirt, ASH, etc. that causes a black mark on sth; a black mark made by this（黑色）污物，灰垢，污跡，污點

smutty /ˈsmʌti/ *adj.* [usually before noun] (*informal*) (of stories, pictures and comments 小說、圖片和言語) dealing with sex in a way that some people find offensive 淫穢的；下流的；猥褻的：*smutty jokes* 下流笑話

snack /snæk/ *noun, verb*

■ ***noun*** **1** (*informal*) a small meal or amount of food, usually eaten in a hurry 點心；小吃；快餐：*a mid-morning snack* 上午吃的點心 ◇ *I only have time for a snack at lunchtime.* 中午，我的時間只夠吃點心。◇ *Do you serve bar snacks?* 你這兒賣不賣快餐？◇ *a snack lunch* 快餐午飯 **2** (*AustralE, informal*) a thing that is easy to do 易辦到的事；"小菜一碟"：*It'll be a snack.* 這不過是小事一樁。

■ ***verb*** [I] **~ on sth** to eat snacks between or instead of main meals 吃點心（或快餐、小吃）：*It's healthier to snack on fruit rather than chocolate.* 作為點心，水果比巧克力更有益於健康。

ˈsnack bar *noun* a place where you can buy a small quick meal, such as a SANDWICH 快餐櫃枱；快餐部；小吃部；點心鋪

snaf·fle /ˈsnæfl/ *verb* **~ sth** (*BrE, informal*) to take sth quickly for yourself, especially before anyone else has had the time or opportunity（尤指搶先）攫取，偷竊

snafu /snæˈfuː/ *noun* [sing.] (*NAmE, informal*) a situation in which nothing happens as planned（一切均未按計劃發生的）混亂局面：*It was another bureaucratic snafu.* 又讓官僚主義搞成了一團糟。

snag /snæɡ/ *noun, verb*

■ ***noun*** **1** (*informal*) a problem or difficulty, especially one that is small, hidden or unexpected（尤指潛在的、意外的、不嚴重的）問題，困難，障礙，麻煩 **SYN difficulty**：*There is just one small snag—where is the money coming from?* 只有一個小問題：錢從哪兒來？◇ *Let me know if you run into any snags.* 要是遇到什麼麻煩就告訴我。 **2** an object or a part of an object that is rough or sharp and may cut sth 突出物；尖齒；尖角；尖刺 **3** (*AustralE, NZE, informal*) a SAUSAGE 香腸

■ ***verb*** (**-gg-**) **1** [T, I] to catch or tear sth on sth rough or sharp; to become caught or torn in this way（在帶尖的東西上）鈎住，掛破，被鈎住，被掛破：**~ sth on/in sth** *I snagged my sweater on the wire fence.* 我的毛衣被鐵絲網鈎住了。◇ **~ sth** *The fence snagged my sweater.* 柵欄把我的毛衣掛住了。◇ **~ (on/in sth)** *The nets snagged on some rocks.* 漁網纏在礁石上了。 **2** [T] **~ sth (from sb)** (*NAmE, informal*) to succeed in getting sth quickly, often before other people 抓住；搶先獲得：*I snagged a ride from Joe.* 我截住喬的車搭了一段路。

snag·gle /ˈsnæɡl/ *noun, verb*

■ ***noun*** an untidy or confused collection of things 繁雜（或混亂）的事物：*a snaggle of restrictions* 雜亂無章的種種限制

■ ***verb*** [I] to become twisted, untidy or confused 纏結在一起；變凌亂；變混亂：*My hair snaggles when I wash it.* 我的頭髮一洗就打結。

ˈsnaggle-tooth *noun* (*informal*) a tooth which sticks out or is a strange shape 齙牙；歪牙 ► **ˈsnaggle-toothed** *adj.*

S

snail /sneɪl/ *noun* a small soft creature with a hard round shell on its back, that moves very slowly and often eats garden plants. Some types of snail can be eaten. 蝸牛 ➲ **VISUAL VOCAB** page V13

IDM **at a 'snail's pace** very slowly 非常緩慢

'snail mail *noun* [U] (*informal, humorous*) used especially by people who use email to describe the system of sending letters by ordinary mail 蝸牛郵件（電郵使用者用以指普通郵寄）

snake /sneɪk/ *noun, verb*

■ ***noun*** a REPTILE with a very long thin body and no legs. There are many types of snake, some of which are poisonous. 蛇：*a snake coiled up in the grass* 一條蛇盤在草叢裏 ◇ *Venomous snakes spit and hiss when they are cornered.* 毒蛇在無法逃脱時會發出憤怒的呼呼嘶嘶的聲音。

IDM **a ˌsnake (in the 'grass)** (*disapproving*) a person who pretends to be your friend but who cannot be trusted 陰險的人；潛伏的敵人；虛假的人

■ ***verb*** [I, T] to move like a snake, in long twisting curves; to go in a particular direction in long twisting curves 曲折前行；蛇行；蜿蜒伸展 **SYN** **meander**：**+ adv./prep.** *The road snaked away into the distance.* 公路蜿蜒伸向遠方。◇ **~ its way + adv./prep.** *The procession snaked its way through narrow streets.* 隊伍沿着狹窄的街道曲折穿行。

snake·bite /'sneɪkbaɪt/ *noun* [C, U] **1** a wound that you get when a poisonous snake bites you 毒蛇咬傷 **2** an alcoholic drink made of equal parts of beer and CIDER 蘋果雞尾酒（啤酒加蘋果酒各半調製而成）

Snake·board™ /'sneɪkbɔːd; *NAmE* -bɔːrd/ *noun* ➲ STREETBOARD

'snake charmer *noun* an entertainer who seems to be able to control snakes and make them move by playing music to them 耍蛇人；弄蛇人

'snake eyes *noun* [pl.] (*informal*) a result in a game when you throw two dice and both show one dot 蛇眼（擲出的兩枚骰子均為一點）

'snake oil *noun* [U] (*informal, especially NAmE*) something, for example medicine, that sb tries to sell you, but that is not effective or useful 推銷者的所謂"萬應靈藥"；毫無用處（或效果）的推銷品：*a snake-oil salesman* 劣質品推銷員

snake·pit /'sneɪkpɪt/ *noun* **1** a hole in the ground in which snakes are kept 蛇洞；蛇坑 **2** a place which is extremely unpleasant or dangerous 蛇窩（令人反感或極其危險的地方）

ˌsnakes and 'ladders (*BrE*) *noun* [U] a children's game played on a special board with pictures of snakes and LADDERS on it. Players move their pieces up the ladders to go forward and down the snakes to go back. 蛇梯棋（棋子走梯子圖案前進，順着蛇後退）➲ see also CHUTES AND LADDERS ➲ **VISUAL VOCAB** page V38

snake·skin /'sneɪkskɪn/ *noun* [U] the skin of a snake, used for making expensive shoes, bags, etc. 蛇皮（用於製作名貴的鞋、包等）

snaky /'sneɪki/ *adj.* (*AustralE, NZE, informal*) angry 生氣的；發怒的：*What are you snaky about?* 你為啥發火？

snap /snæp/ *verb, noun, adj., exclamation*

■ ***verb*** (-pp-)

▸ **BREAK** 斷開 **1** [T, I] to break sth suddenly with a sharp noise; to be broken in this way（使咔嚓）斷裂，綳斷：**~ sth** *The wind had snapped the tree in two.* 風把樹咔嚓一聲颳斷了。◇ **~ sth off** (**sth**) *He snapped a twig off a bush.* 他啪地從灌木上折下一小枝。◇ **~** (**off**) *Suddenly, the rope snapped.* 突然，繩子啪地綳斷了。◇ *The branch she was standing on must have snapped off.* 她當時踩的樹枝一定是突然折斷了。

▸ **OPEN/CLOSE/MOVE INTO POSITION** 打開；關上；進入適當位置 **2** [I, T] to move, or to move sth, into a particular position quickly, especially with a sudden sharp noise（使啪地）打開，關上，移到某位置：**+ adj.** *The lid snapped shut.* 蓋子啪地合上了。◇ *His eyes snapped open.* 他兩眼唰地睜開了。◇ **+ adv./prep.** *He snapped to attention and saluted.* 他啪一下立正敬禮。◇ **~ sth + adj.** *She snapped the bag shut.* 她啪的一聲把包合上了。

▸ **SPEAK IMPATIENTLY** 不耐煩地説 **3** [T, I] to speak or say sth in an impatient, usually angry, voice 厲聲説；怒氣沖沖地説；不耐煩地説：**+ speech** *'Don't just stand there,' she snapped.* "別光站在那兒。"她生氣地説。◇ **~** (**at sb**) *I was tempted to snap back angrily at him.* 我真想沒好氣地頂他幾句。◇ **~ sth** *He snapped a reply.* 他氣沖沖地回了一句。

▸ **OF ANIMAL** 動物 **4** [I] **~** (**at sb/sth**) to try to bite sb/sth 咬 **SYN** **nip**：*The dogs snarled and snapped at our heels.* 幾條狗邊叫邊向着我們的腳後跟咬來。

▸ **TAKE PHOTOGRAPH** 拍照 **5** [T, I] (*informal*) to take a photograph 拍照；攝影：**~ sth** *A passing tourist snapped the incident.* 一個過路的遊客把這件事拍了下來。◇ **~** (**away**) *She seemed oblivious to the crowds of photographers snapping away.* 成群的攝影者不停地拍照，她好像渾然不覺。

▸ **LOSE CONTROL** 失去控制 **6** [I] to suddenly be unable to control your feelings any longer because the situation has become too difficult 突然失去自制力；一下子無法自持：*My patience finally snapped.* 我終於忍不住了。◇ *When he said that, something snapped inside her.* 聽他説到這裏，她內心的感情一下子翻騰起來。◇ *And that did it. I snapped.* 就這一下，我再也承受不住了。

▸ **FASTEN CLOTHING** 扣衣服 **7** [I, T] **~** (**sth**) (*NAmE*) to fasten a piece of clothing with a snap 用子母扣扣，用摁扣扣（衣服）

IDM **snap your 'fingers** to make a sharp noise by moving your second or third finger quickly against your thumb, to attract sb's attention, or to mark the beat of music, for example 打榧子，彈指頭（捻拇指作響）**ˌsnap 'out of it/sth | ˌsnap sb 'out of it/sth** [no passive] (*informal*) to make an effort to stop feeling unhappy or depressed; to help sb to stop feeling unhappy（使）拋掉不愉快情緒，擺脱鬱悶心境：*You've been depressed for weeks. It's time you snapped out of it.* 你情緒低落好幾週了。現在該振作起來了。**ˌsnap 'to it** (*informal*) used, especially in orders, to tell sb to start working harder or more quickly（尤用於催促）加把勁，趕快 ➲ more at HEAD *n.*

PHR V **ˌsnap sth↔'out** to say sth in a sharp unpleasant way 厲聲説出：*The sergeant snapped out an order.* 中士厲聲下達命令。**ˌsnap sth↔'up** (*informal*) to buy or obtain sth quickly because it is cheap or you want it very much 搶購；搶先弄到手：*All the best bargains were snapped up within hours.* 所有最划得來的便宜貨幾小時之內就被搶購一空了。◇ (*figurative*) *She's been snapped up by Hollywood to star in two major movies.* 好萊塢搶先邀請她在兩部大片中擔當主角。

■ ***noun***

▸ **SHARP NOISE** 尖厲的聲音 **1** [C] a sudden sharp noise, especially one made by sth closing or breaking（尤指關上或斷裂的聲音）啪嗒聲，咔嚓聲：*She closed her purse with a snap.* 她啪嗒一聲合上了錢包。◇ *the snap of a twig* 小樹枝折斷的咔嚓聲

▸ **PHOTOGRAPH** 照片 **2** (also **snap·shot**) [C] a photograph, especially one taken quickly（尤指搶拍的）照片：*holiday snaps* 假日拍的照片

▸ **CARD GAME** 撲克牌遊戲 **3** **Snap** [U] a card game in which players take turns to put cards down and try to be the first to call out 'snap' when two similar cards are put down together "對兒"牌遊戲（遊戲者輪流下牌，出現相同的牌時要搶先喊"對兒"）

▸ **FASTENER** 扣子 **4** (*NAmE*) (*BrE* **'press stud**, **pop·per**) a type of button used for fastening clothes, consisting of two metal or plastic sections that can be pressed together 摁扣；子母扣 ➲ **VISUAL VOCAB** page V63 ➲ see also BRANDY SNAP, COLD SNAP

IDM **be a 'snap** (*NAmE, informal*) to be very easy to do 十分容易（做）：*This job's a snap.* 這活兒不過是小菜一碟。

■ ***adj.*** [only before noun] made or done quickly and without careful thought or preparation 匆忙的；倉促的：*It was a **snap decision**.* 那是個倉促的決定。◇ *They held a **snap election**.* 他們臨時舉行了選舉。

■ ***exclamation*** **1** you say **snap!** in the card game called 'Snap' when two cards that are the same are put down（在"對兒"牌遊戲中出現同樣的牌時喊的）對兒

S

2 (*BrE, informal*) people say **snap!** to show that they are surprised when two things are the same（對於兩件相同事物表示驚訝）真巧：*Snap! I've just bought that CD too!* 真是巧了！我也剛買了那張光盤！

snap·dragon /ˈsnæpdræɡən/ *noun* a small garden plant with red, white, yellow or pink flowers that open and shut like a mouth when squeezed 齧龍花，金魚草（庭園植物，花的口部呈唇形，裂片閉合）

snap·per /ˈsnæpə(r)/ *noun* **1** [C, U] a fish that lives in warm seas and is used for food 鯛魚（食用魚，盛產於熱帶海域）**2** [C] (*informal, BrE*) a photographer, especially one who takes pictures of famous people for newspapers and magazines（尤指為報章雜誌拍攝名人照片的）攝影者

snappy /ˈsnæpi/ *adj.* (**snap·pier**, **snap·pi·est**) **1** (of a remark, title, etc. 言語、標題等) clever or amusing and short 精練的；簡潔的：*a snappy slogan* 精練的口號 ◇ *a snappy answer* 簡潔的回答 **2** [usually before noun] (*informal*) attractive and fashionable 漂亮入時的：*a snappy outfit* 漂亮的套裝 ◇ *She's a* ***snappy dresser***. 她衣着入時。**3** (of people or their behaviour 人或其行為) tending to speak to people in a bad-tempered, impatient way 煩躁的；沒好氣的 **4** lively; quick 活潑的；敏捷的：*a snappy tune* 活潑的曲調 ▸ **snap·pily** *adv.*：*He summarized the speech snappily.* 他對講話做了精練的摘要。◇ *snappily dressed* 衣着入時的 ◇ *'What?' she asked snappily.* "什麼？" 她不耐煩地問。**snap·pi·ness** *noun* [U]

IDM **ˌmake it ˈsnappy** (*informal*) used to tell sb to do sth quickly or to hurry（用於催促）趕緊，快點

snap·shot /ˈsnæpʃɒt; *NAmE* -ʃɑːt/ *noun* **1** = SNAP *n.* (2)：*snapshots of the children* 孩子們的照片 ➲ **SYNONYMS** at PHOTOGRAPH **2** [usually sing.] a short description or a small amount of information that gives you an idea of what sth is like 簡介；簡要說明

snare /sneə(r); *NAmE* sner/ *noun, verb*

■ ***noun*** **1** a device used for catching small animals and birds, especially one that holds their leg so that they cannot escape（捕鳥、獸的）陷阱，羅網，套子 **SYN** **trap** **2** (*formal*) a situation which seems attractive but is unpleasant and difficult to escape from 陷阱；圈套；騙局 **3** the metal strings that are stretched across the bottom of a snare drum（綳在小鼓下鼓皮的）響弦

■ ***verb*** **~ sth/sb** to catch sth, especially an animal, in a snare 設陷阱（或羅網、套子）捕捉 **SYN** **trap**：*to snare a rabbit* 套兔子 ◇ (*figurative*) *Her one thought was to snare a rich husband.* 她一心要攀住一個有錢的丈夫。◇ (*figurative*) *He found himself snared in a web of intrigue.* 他發現自己中了圈套。

ˈsnare drum *noun* a small drum with metal strings across one side that make a continuous sound when the drum is hit 小鼓（一面綳有金屬響弦）➲ VISUAL VOCAB page V35

snarf /snɑːf; *NAmE* snɑːrf/ *verb* **~ sth** (*informal, especially NAmE*) to eat or drink sth very quickly or in a way that people think is GREEDY 很快地吃（或喝）；貪婪地吃（或喝）：*The kids snarfed up all the cookies.* 孩子們一頓狼吞虎嚥，把曲奇餅全吃光了。

snarky /ˈsnɑːki; *NAmE* ˈsnɑːrki/ *adj.* (*NAmE, informal*) criticizing sb in an unkind way 尖銳批評的；諷刺挖苦的：*a snarky remark* 尖刻的指責

snarl /snɑːl; *NAmE* snɑːrl/ *verb, noun*

■ ***verb*** **1** [I] **~ (at sb/sth)** (of dogs, etc. 狗等) to show the teeth and make a deep angry noise in the throat 齜牙低吼：*The dog snarled at us.* 狗朝我們低聲吼叫。**2** [T] to speak in an angry or bad-tempered way 咆哮着說；不耐煩地說：**+ speech (at sb)** *'Get out of here!' he snarled.* "滾開！" 他吼道。◇ **~ sth (at sb)** *She snarled abuse at anyone who happened to walk past.* 誰碰巧走過，她就衝誰叫罵。

PHR V **ˌsnarl ˈup | ˌsnarl sth↔ˈup** **1** to involve sb/sth in a situation that stops their movement or progress; to become involved in a situation like this 阻塞；妨礙（某事物）：*The accident snarled up the traffic all day.* 這次事故使交通堵塞了整整一天。**2** to become caught or twisted; to make sth do this（使）纏結：*The sheets kept getting snarled up.* 牀單老纏到一起。➲ related noun SNARL-UP

■ ***noun*** **1** [usually sing.] a deep sound that an animal makes when it is angry and shows its teeth（動物的）齜牙低吼：*The dog bared its teeth in a snarl.* 那條狗齜着牙低聲吼叫。**2** [usually sing.] an act of speaking in an angry or bad-tempered way; the sound you make when you are angry, in pain, etc. 憤怒叫嚷（聲）；咆哮（聲）；疼痛叫聲：*a snarl of hate* 充滿仇恨的吼聲 **3** = SNARL-UP：*rush-hour traffic snarls* 高峰時間的交通阻塞 **4** (*informal*) something that has become twisted in an untidy way 纏結物；蓬亂的事物：*She used conditioner to remove the snarls from her hair.* 她用護髮劑梳順了頭髮。

ˈsnarl-up (also **snarl**) *noun* (*BrE, informal*) a situation in which traffic is unable to move 交通阻塞 **SYN** **jam**

snatch /snætʃ/ *verb, noun*

■ ***verb*** **1** [T, I] to take sth quickly and often rudely or roughly 一把抓起；一下奪過 **SYN** **grab**：**~ sth (+ adv./prep.)** *She managed to snatch the gun from his hand.* 她設法從他手裏奪過了槍。◇ *Gordon snatched up his jacket and left the room.* 戈登一把抓起上衣，出了房間。◇ **(+ adv./prep.)** *Hey, you kids! Don't all snatch!* 嗨，孩子們！別搶啊！**2** [T] **~ sb/sth (from sb/sth)** to take sb/sth away from a person or place, especially by force; to steal sth 奪去；搶走；偷竊 **SYN** **steal**：*The raiders snatched $100 from the cash register.* 劫匪從現金出納機裏搶走了 100 元。◇ *The baby was snatched from its parents' car.* 嬰兒是從父母的車上被搶走的。**3** [T] **~ sth** to take or get sth quickly, especially because you do not have much time 抓緊時間做；乘機獲得：*I managed to snatch an hour's sleep.* 我偷空兒睡了一小時的覺。◇ *The team snatched a dramatic victory in the last minute of the game.* 該隊在比賽的最後一分鐘戲劇性地獲勝。

PHR V **ˈsnatch at sth** **1** to try to take hold of sth with your hands 伸手抓；試圖奪：*He snatched at the steering wheel but I pushed him away.* 他伸手來抓方向盤，但我把他推開了。**2** to take an opportunity to do sth 抓住機會：*We snatched at every moment we could be together.* 一有時間，我們就待在一起。

■ ***noun*** **1** a very small part of a conversation or some music that you hear（聽到的）隻言片語，音樂片段 **SYN** **snippet**：*a snatch of music* 音樂片段 ◇ *I only caught snatches of the conversation.* 我只聽到談話的一些片段。**2** an act of moving your hand very quickly to take or steal sth 抓；奪；搶奪；偷竊：*a bag snatch* 手提包搶奪 ◇ *to* ***make a snatch*** *at sth* 搶奪某物 **3** (*taboo, slang*) an offensive word for a woman's outer sex organs（女性的）陰部

IDM **in ˈsnatches** for short periods rather than continuously 斷斷續續地：*Sleep came to him in brief snatches.* 他時睡時醒。

snatch·er /ˈsnætʃə(r)/ *noun* (often in compounds 常構成複合詞) a person who takes sth quickly with their hand and steals it 搶劫者：*a purse snatcher* 搶錢包的賊

ˈsnatch squad *noun* [C+sing./pl. v.] a group of police officers or soldiers whose job is to remove people from a crowd who are considered to be causing trouble（驅逐領頭鬧事者的）搜捕隊，鎮暴部隊

snazzy /ˈsnæzi/ *adj.* (**snaz·zier**, **snaz·zi·est**) (*informal*) (of clothes, cars, etc. 服裝、汽車等) fashionable, bright and modern, and attracting your attention 漂亮而時髦的；吸引人的 **SYN** **jazzy, smart**：*a snazzy tie* 漂亮的領帶

sneak /sniːk/ *verb, noun, adj.*

■ ***verb*** **HELP** The usual past form is **sneaked**, but **snuck** is now very common in informal speech in *NAmE* and some people use it in *BrE* too. However, many people think that it is not correct and it should not be used in formal writing. 過去式通常為 sneaked，但在美式英語非正式的口語中，現在普遍用 snuck，在英式英語中也有人用 snuck。不過，許多人認為這不正確，不應在正式書面語中使用。**1** [I] **+ adv./prep.** to go somewhere secretly, trying to avoid being seen 偷偷地走；溜 **SYN** **creep**：*I sneaked up the stairs.* 我躡手躡腳地上了樓。**2** [T] to do sth or take sb/sth somewhere secretly, often without permission 偷偷地做；偷帶；偷拿：**~ sth** *We sneaked a* *look at her diary.* 我們偷偷看了一眼她的日記。◇ **~ sth to sb** *I managed to sneak a note to him.* 我設法偷偷給他遞了張條子。◇ **~ sb sth** *I managed to sneak him a note.* 我設法偷偷給他遞了張條子。 **3** [T] **~ sth** (*informal*) to secretly take sth small or unimportant 偷走（不重要的或小的東西） SYN **pinch**: *I sneaked a cake when they were out of the room.* 趁他們不在屋裏，我偷偷拿了一塊蛋糕。 **4** [I] **~ (on sb) (to sb)** (*old-fashioned, BrE, disapproving*) to tell an adult that another child has done sth wrong, especially in order to cause trouble（兒童向成人）打小報告，告狀 SYN **snitch**: *Did you sneak on me to the teacher?* 你有沒有向老師告我的狀？

PHR V **,sneak 'up (on sb/sth)** to move towards sb very quietly so that they do not see or hear you until you reach them 偷偷走近： *He sneaked up on his sister and shouted 'Boo!'.* 他偷偷溜到妹妹身邊，然後大喊一聲"嘿！"

■ ***noun*** (*old-fashioned, BrE, disapproving*) a person, especially a child, who tells sb about sth wrong that another person has done 打小報告的人，告狀者（尤指兒童） SYN **snitch**

■ ***adj.*** [only before noun] done without any warning 突然的；出其不意的： *a sneak attack* 偷襲

sneak·er /'sni:kə(r)/ (*NAmE*) (*BrE* **train·er**, **'training shoe**) *noun* [usually pl.] a shoe that you wear for sports or as informal clothing 運動鞋；便鞋： *He wore old jeans and a pair of sneakers.* 他穿一條舊牛仔褲，腳蹬運動鞋。 ➲ VISUAL VOCAB page V64

sneak·ing /'sni:kɪŋ/ *adj.* [only before noun] if you have a **sneaking** feeling for sb or about sth, you do not want to admit it to other people, because you feel embarrassed, or you are not sure that this feeling is right（指不願公開的感覺）暗中的，私下的： *She had always had a sneaking affection for him.* 以前她一直暗暗傾心於他。◇ *I have a sneaking suspicion that she knows more than she's telling us.* 我私下懷疑，她還知道一些情況，不想告訴我們。

,sneak 'preview *noun* an opportunity to see sth before it is officially shown to the public（公開放映前的）預映，試映

'sneak thief *noun* a person who steals things without using force or breaking doors or windows（偷而不搶的）小偷

sneaky /'sni:ki/ *adj.* (**sneak·ier**, **sneaki·est**) (*informal*) behaving in a secret and sometimes dishonest or unpleasant way 悄悄的；偷偷摸摸的；鬼鬼祟祟的 SYN **crafty**: *That was a sneaky trick!* 這種把戲可不夠光明正大！ ▸ **sneak·ily** /-ɪli/ *adv.*

sneer /snɪə(r); *NAmE* snɪr/ *verb, noun*

■ ***verb*** [I, T] to show that you have no respect for sb by the expression on your face or by the way you speak 嘲笑；譏諷；嗤笑 SYN **mock**: **~ (at sb/sth)** *He sneered at people who liked pop music.* 他嘲笑喜歡流行音樂的人。◇ *a sneering comment* 譏諷的話 ◇ **+ speech** *'You? A writer?' she sneered.* "你？是作家？"她不屑地説。 ▸ **sneer·ing·ly** /'snɪərɪŋli; *NAmE* 'snɪr-/ *adv.*

■ ***noun*** [usually sing.] an unpleasant look, smile or comment that shows you do not respect sb/sth 嘲笑；譏諷： *A faint sneer of satisfaction crossed her face.* 她的臉上掠過一絲得意的冷笑。

sneeze /sni:z/ *verb, noun*

■ ***verb*** [I] to have air come suddenly and noisily out through your nose and mouth in a way that you cannot control, for example because you have a cold 打噴嚏： *I've been sneezing all morning.* 我一上午直打噴嚏。

IDM **not to be 'sneezed at** (*informal*) good enough to be accepted or considered seriously 值得認真對待；不可輕視： *In those days, $20 was not a sum to be sneezed at.* 那時候，20 元可不能不當回事。

■ ***noun*** the act of sneezing or the noise you make when you sneeze 噴嚏；噴嚏聲： *coughs and sneezes* 咳嗽和噴嚏 ◇ *She gave a violent sneeze.* 她打了個大噴嚏。

snicker /'snɪkə(r)/ *verb* (*especially NAmE*) (*BrE* also **snig·ger**) [I] **~ (at sb/sth)** to laugh in a quiet unpleasant way, especially at sth rude or at sb's problems or mistakes 竊笑；暗笑 SYN **titter** ▸ **snicker** *noun*

snide /snaɪd/ *adj.* (*informal*) criticizing sb/sth in an unkind and indirect way 諷刺的；挖苦的： ***snide comments/remarks*** 挖苦的議論／話語 ▸ **snide·ly** *adv.*

sniff /snɪf/ *verb, noun*

■ ***verb*** **1** [I] to breathe air in through your nose in a way that makes a sound, especially when you are crying, have a cold, etc. 抽鼻子（尤指哭泣、患感冒等時出聲地用鼻子吸氣）： *We all had colds and couldn't stop sniffing and sneezing.* 我們都感冒了，一個勁地抽鼻子，打噴嚏。 **2** [T, I] to breathe air in through the nose in order to discover or enjoy the smell of sth（吸着氣）嗅，聞 SYN **smell**: **~ sth** *sniffing the fresh morning air* 吸着早晨的新鮮空氣 ◇ *to sniff glue* 吸膠毒 ◇ **~ (at sth)** *The dog sniffed at my shoes.* 那條狗嗅我的鞋。 ➲ see also GLUE-SNIFFING **3** [T, I] **+ speech** | **~ (sth)** to say sth in a complaining or disapproving way 抱怨；不以為然地説： *'It's hardly what I'd call elegant,' she sniffed.* "要我説，這很難稱得上雅致。"她不以為然地説。

IDM **not to be 'sniffed at** (*informal*) good enough to be accepted or considered seriously 值得認真對待；不可輕視： *In those days, $20 was not a sum to be sniffed at.* 那時候，20 元不能不當回事。

PHR V **,sniff a'round/'round** (*informal*) to try to find out information about sb/sth, especially secret information 探查，打探，訪查（秘密信息）： *We don't want journalists sniffing around.* 我們不需要四處打探的記者。 **'sniff around/round sb** [no passive] (*especially BrE*) to try to get sb as a lover, employee, etc. 追求，尋求聘用（某人）： *Hollywood agents have been sniffing around him.* 一些好萊塢的經紀人一直追着想簽下他。 **'sniff at sth** to show no interest in or respect for sth 對…嗤之以鼻（或不屑一顧） **,sniff sb/sth↔'out** **1** to discover or find sb/sth by using your sense of smell 嗅出： *The dogs are trained to sniff out drugs.* 這些狗是經過訓練的嗅毒犬。 **2** (*informal*) to discover or find sb/sth by looking 看出；覺察出： *Journalists are good at sniffing out a scandal.* 做記者的善於發現醜聞。

■ ***noun*** **1** [C] an act or the sound of sniffing 吸氣（聲）；抽鼻子（聲）；嗅；聞： *She took a deep sniff of the perfume.* 她使勁聞了聞香水。◇ *My mother gave a sniff of disapproval.* 我母親哼了一聲，表示不同意。◇ *His sobs soon turned to sniffs.* 不多時，他的嗚咽變成了啜泣。 **2** [sing.] **~ of sth** an idea of what sth is like or that sth is going to happen 感覺；察覺： *The sniff of power went to his head.* 權力在握的感覺使他得意忘形。◇ *They make threats but back down at the first sniff of trouble.* 他們起先氣勢洶洶，但一看情形不妙立刻軟了下來。 **3** [sing.] **~ of sth** a small chance of sth 微小的可能性： *She didn't get even a sniff at a medal.* 她根本不可能拿到獎牌。

IDM **have a (good) ,sniff a'round** to examine a place carefully 仔細檢查（某處）

'sniffer dog *noun* (*informal, especially BrE*) a dog that is trained to find drugs or EXPLOSIVES by smell（訓練來嗅查毒品或炸藥的）嗅探犬

snif·fle /'snɪfl/ *verb, noun*

■ ***verb*** [I, T] (**+ speech**) to sniff or keep sniffing, especially because you are crying or have a cold（尤指因哭泣或患感冒）抽鼻子

■ ***noun*** an act or the sound of sniffling 抽鼻子（聲）： *After a while, her sniffles died away.* 過了一會兒，她抽鼻子的聲音逐漸平息了。

IDM **get, have, etc. the 'sniffles** (*informal*) to get, have, etc. a slight cold 患輕感冒

sniffy /'snɪfi/ *adj.* **~ (about sth)** (*informal*) not approving of sth/sb because you think they are not good enough for you（對…）輕視，不屑一顧

snif·ter /'snɪftə(r)/ *noun* **1** (*especially NAmE*) a large glass used for drinking BRANDY 白蘭地酒杯 **2** (*old-fashioned, BrE, informal*) a small amount of a strong alcoholic drink 少量烈酒

snig·ger /'snɪgə(r)/ *verb, noun*

■ ***verb*** (*BrE*) (also **snicker** *NAmE, BrE*) [I, T] **~ (at sb/sth)** | **+ speech** to laugh in a quiet unpleasant way, especially at sth rude or at sb's problems or mistakes 竊笑；暗笑

SYN **titter**：*What are you sniggering at?* 你偷偷笑什麼呢？

■ ***noun*** (*BrE*) (also **snicker** *NAmE, BrE*) a quiet unpleasant laugh, especially at sth rude or at sb's problems or mistakes 竊笑；暗笑 **SYN** **titter**

snip /snɪp/ *verb, noun*

■ ***verb*** (**-pp-**) [T, I] to cut sth with scissors using short quick strokes（用剪刀快速）剪，剪斷，剪開：**~ sth** *Snip a tiny hole in the paper.* 在紙上剪一個小孔。◇ **~ (at/through sth)** *She snipped at the loose threads hanging down.* 她把垂下來的線頭剪掉。

PHR V ˌ**snip sth**↔ˈ**off** to remove sth by cutting it with scissors in short quick strokes（快速）剪去，剪掉

■ ***noun*** **1** [C] an act of cutting sth with scissors; the sound that this makes 剪；剪東西的咔嚓聲：*Make a series of small snips along the edge of the fabric.* 順着布邊細碎地剪。◇ *Snip, snip, went the scissors.* 剪刀咔嚓咔嚓地剪着。 **2 snips** [pl.] a tool like large scissors, used for cutting metal（剪金屬用的）平頭剪 **3 a snip** [sing.] (*BrE, informal*) a thing that is cheap and good value 價廉物美的東西；便宜貨 **SYN** **bargain**：*It's a snip at only £25.* 這個只賣 25 英鎊，真是便宜。

snipe /snaɪp/ *verb, noun*

■ ***verb*** **1** [I] **~ (at sb/sth)** to shoot at sb from a hiding place, usually from a distance 狙擊；打冷槍：*Gunmen continued to snipe at people leaving their homes to find food.* 槍手不斷伏擊外出找尋食物的人。 **2** [I] **~ (at sb/sth)** to criticize sb in an unpleasant way 冷言冷語地指摘；抨擊 ▸ **snip·ing** *noun* [U]：*Aid workers remain in the area despite continuous sniping.* 儘管冷槍不斷，但救援人員仍然留在這一地區。

■ ***noun*** (*pl.* **snipe**) a bird with a long straight beak that lives on wet ground 沙錐（喙長直，生活在潮濕地區）

sniper /ˈsnaɪpə(r)/ *noun* a person who shoots at sb from a hidden position 狙擊手

snip·pet /ˈsnɪpɪt/ *noun* **1** a small piece of information or news 一小條（消息）；一則（新聞）：*Have you got any interesting snippets for me?* 你有沒有什麼有趣的消息告訴我？◇ *a snippet of information* 一點消息 **2** a short piece of a conversation, piece of music, etc. 一小段（談話、音樂等）**SYN** **snatch, extract**

snippy /ˈsnɪpi/ *adj.* (*NAmE, informal*) rude; not showing respect 粗野無禮的；盛氣凌人的

snit /snɪt/ *noun*

IDM **be in a ˈsnit** (*NAmE*) to be bad-tempered and refuse to speak to anybody for a time because you are angry about sth 氣惱；生悶氣

S

snitch /snɪtʃ/ *verb* [I] **~ (on sb) (to sb)** (*informal, disapproving*) to tell a parent, teacher, etc. about sth wrong that another child has done（向家長、教師等）告發，告密，告狀 **SYN** **sneak**：*Johnnie snitched on me to his mom.* 約翰尼在他媽媽那兒告了我的狀。▸ **snitch** *noun*：*You little snitch! I'll never tell you anything again!* 你這傢伙就愛告密！以後我什麼話都不跟你說了！

snivel /ˈsnɪvl/ *verb* (**-ll-**, *US* **-l-**) [I] to cry and complain in a way that people think is annoying（令人討厭地）哭訴 **SYN** **whine**

sniv·el·ling (*especially US* **sniv·el·ing**) /ˈsnɪvlɪŋ/ *adj.* [only before noun] (*disapproving*) tending to cry or complain a lot in a way that annoys people 哭哭啼啼的；愛哭訴的：*a snivelling little brat* 愛哭鬧的小淘氣

snob /snɒb; *NAmE* snɑːb/ *noun* (*disapproving*) **1** a person who admires people in the higher social classes too much and has no respect for people in the lower social classes 勢利小人；諂上欺下的人：*She's such a snob!* 她就是那麼一個勢利的人！ **2** a person who thinks they are much better than other people because they are intelligent or like things that many people do not like 自以為優越的人；自命高雅的人：*an* ***intellectual snob*** 自命知識淵博的人◇ *a* ***food/wine, etc. snob*** 自命精於品味美食、葡萄酒等的人◇ *There is a* ***snob value*** *in driving the latest model.* 開最新款式的車能滿足一種庸俗的虛榮心。

snob·bery /ˈsnɒbəri; *NAmE* ˈsnɑːb-/ *noun* [U] (*disapproving*) the attitudes and behaviour of people who are snobs 勢利態度（或行為）；自以為優越的態度（或行為）：*intellectual snobbery* 智力上的自我優越感 ➲ see also INVERTED SNOBBERY

snob·bish /ˈsnɒbɪʃ; *NAmE* ˈsnɑːb-/ (also *informal* **snobby** /ˈsnɒbi; *NAmE* ˈsnɑːbi/) *adj.* (*disapproving*) thinking that having a high social class is very important; feeling that you are better than other people because you are more intelligent or like things that many people do not like 勢利的；自命不凡的 ▸ **snob·bish·ness** *noun* [U]

snog /snɒg; *NAmE* snɑːg/ *verb* (**-gg-**) [I, T] (*BrE, informal*) (of two people 兩個人) to kiss each other, especially for a long time（尤指長時間地）接吻：*They were snogging on the sofa.* 他們正在沙發上接吻。◇ **~ sb** *I caught him snogging my friend.* 我撞見他正在吻我的朋友。 ▸ **snog** *noun* [sing.]

snood /snuːd/ *noun* a net or bag worn over the hair at the back of a woman's head for decoration（女用）束髮網

snook /snuːk/ *noun* **IDM** see COCK *v.*

snook·er /ˈsnuːkə(r)/ *noun, verb*

■ ***noun*** **1** [U] a game for two people played on a long table covered with green cloth. Players use CUES (= long sticks) to hit a white ball against other balls (15 red and 6 of other colours) in order to get the coloured balls into pockets at the edge of the table, in a particular set order. 斯諾克（供兩人打的落袋枱球，打球人用球杆打白色母球，按一定順序撞 15 個紅球和 6 個其他顏色的球入袋）：*to* ***play snooker*** 打斯諾克◇ ***a game of snooker*** 斯諾克比賽◇ ***a snooker hall/player/table, etc.*** 斯諾克廳、斯諾克運動員、斯諾克球桌等 ➲ compare BILLIARDS, POOL *n.* (6) **2** [C] a position in snooker in which one player has made it very difficult for the opponent to play a shot within the rules（斯諾克比賽中的）障礙球

■ ***verb*** [usually passive] **1 ~ sb** (in the game of snooker 斯諾克比賽) to have your opponent in a snooker (2) 設障礙球 **2 ~ sb/sth** (*BrE, informal*) to make it impossible for sb to do sth, especially sth they want to do 阻撓；使落空：*Any plans I'd had for the weekend were by now well and truly snookered.* 我原先設想的各項週末計劃，這時候就徹底落空了。 **3 ~ sb** (*NAmE, informal*) to cheat or trick sb 欺騙；使上當

snoop /snuːp/ *verb, noun*

■ ***verb*** [I] (*informal, disapproving*) to find out private things about sb, especially by looking secretly around a place 窺探；打探；探聽：**~ (around/round sth)** *Someone's been snooping around my apartment.* 有個人一直在我住所周圍窺探。◇ **~ (on sb)** *journalists snooping on politicians* 跟踪政治人物的記者

■ ***noun*** **1** (also **snoop·er**) a person who looks around a place secretly to find out private things about sb 窺探者；打探他人私事的人 **2** [sing.] a secret look around a place 窺探：*He had a snoop around her office.* 他在她的辦公室周圍窺探一番。

snoot /snuːt/ *noun* (*NAmE, informal*) **1** a person's nose（人的）鼻子 **2** (*disapproving*) a person who treats other people as if they are not as good or as important as them 鼻子朝天的人（瞧不起別人）；勢利眼

snooty /ˈsnuːti/ (also *informal* **snotty**) *adj.* (**snoot·ier**, **snooti·est**) (*disapproving*) treating people as if they are not as good or as important as you 傲慢的；目中無人的 **SYN** **snobbish** ▸ **snoot·ily** *adv.* **snooti·ness** *noun* [U]

snooze /snuːz/ *verb* [I] (*informal*) to have a short light sleep, especially during the day and usually not in bed（尤指在白天）小睡，打盹：*My brother was snoozing on the sofa.* 我弟弟正在沙發上打盹。➲ SYNONYMS at SLEEP ▸ **snooze** *noun* [sing.]：*I often have a snooze after lunch.* 我常在午飯後睡個小覺。

ˈ**snooze button** *noun* a button on a CLOCK RADIO which you press when you wake up, so that you can sleep a little longer and be woken up again after a short time（收音機鬧鐘的）小睡催醒按鈕

snore /snɔː(r)/ *verb, noun*

■ ***verb*** [I] to breathe noisily through your nose and mouth while you are asleep 打鼾；打呼嚕：*I could hear Paul* *snoring in the next room.* 我聽得見保羅在隔壁房間裏打呼嚕。 ▶ **snorer** *noun* **snor·ing** *noun* [U]： *loud snoring* 響亮的鼾聲

■ ***noun*** noisy breathing while you are asleep 打呼嚕（聲）；打鼾（聲）： *She lay awake listening to his snores.* 她沒睡着，躺在那兒聽他打呼嚕。

snor·kel /ˈsnɔːkl; *NAmE* ˈsnɔːrkl/ *noun* a tube that you can breathe air through when you are swimming under the surface of the water （浮潛用的）呼吸管 ➲ VISUAL VOCAB page V40 ▶ **snor·kel** *verb* (-ll-, *especially US* -l-) [I]

snor·kel·ling (*especially US* **snor·kel·ing**) /ˈsnɔːkəlɪŋ; *NAmE* ˈsnɔːrk-/ *noun* [U] the sport or activity of swimming underwater with a snorkel 帶呼吸管潛水；浮潛： *to go snorkelling* 去浮潛 ➲ VISUAL VOCAB page V40

snort /snɔːt; *NAmE* snɔːrt/ *verb, noun*

■ ***verb*** **1** [I, T] to make a loud sound by breathing air out noisily through your nose, especially to show that you are angry or amused （表示氣憤或被逗樂）噴鼻息，哼： *The horse snorted and tossed its head.* 馬打了個響鼻兒，晃晃腦袋。◇ **~ with sth** *to snort with laughter* 撲哧一聲笑了◇ **~ in sth** *She snorted in disgust.* 她厭惡地哼了一聲。◇ **+ speech** *'You!' he snorted contemptuously.* "你！"他輕蔑地哼了一聲。 **2** [T] **~ sth** to take drugs by breathing them in through the nose 用鼻子吸（毒品）： *to snort cocaine* 吸可卡因

■ ***noun*** **1** a loud sound that you make by breathing air out noisily through your nose, especially to show that you are angry or amused （尤指表示氣憤或被逗樂的）噴鼻息，哼： *to* **give a snort** 哼了一聲◇ *a snort of disgust* 厭惡的哼聲◇ *I could hear the snort and stamp of a horse.* 我能聽見馬打響鼻兒、跺蹄子的聲音。 **2** a small amount of a drug that is breathed in through the nose; an act of taking a drug in this way （用鼻子吸入的）毒品；用鼻子吸毒： *to take a snort of cocaine* 吸一下可卡因

snot /snɒt; *NAmE* snɑːt/ *noun* [U] (*informal*) a word that some people find offensive, used to describe the liquid substance (= MUCUS) that is produced in the nose 鼻涕（有人認為是粗俗用語）

snotty /ˈsnɒti; *NAmE* ˈsnɑːti/ *adj.* (**snot·tier**, **snot·ti·est**) (also **ˌsnotty-ˈnosed**) (*informal*) **1** = SNOOTY **2** full of or covered in snot 流鼻涕的；滿是鼻涕的： *a snotty nose* 流着鼻涕的鼻子◇ *snotty kids* 淌着鼻涕的小孩

snout /snaʊt/ *noun* **1** the long nose and area around the mouth of some types of animal, such as a pig （豬等動物的）口鼻部，吻 ➲ VISUAL VOCAB page V12 ➲ compare MUZZLE **2** (*informal, humorous*) a person's nose （人的）鼻子 **3** a part of sth that sticks out at the front 吻狀突出物： *the snout of a pistol* 手槍槍管

snow 0➜ /snəʊ; *NAmE* snoʊ/ *noun, verb*

■ ***noun*** **1** 0➜ [U] small soft white pieces (called FLAKES) of frozen water that fall from the sky in cold weather; this substance when it is lying on the ground 雪；雪花；積雪： ***Snow was falling*** *heavily.* 正下着大雪。◇ *We had snow in May this year.* 今年五月我們這兒下了雪。◇ *The snow was beginning to melt.* 積雪開始融化了。◇ *Children were playing in the snow.* 孩子們正在雪地裏玩。◇ *20 cm of snow were expected today.* 原來預計今天下 20 厘米厚的雪。◇ *The snow didn't settle* (= stay on the ground). 雪沒積起來。◇ *Her skin was* ***as white as snow***. 她的皮膚雪白。 ➲ COLLOCATIONS at WEATHER ➲ VISUAL VOCAB pages V4, V5 **2 snows** [pl.] (*literary*) an amount of snow that falls in one particular place or at one particular time （某地或某時的）降雪量；一場雪： *the first snows of winter* 冬天的頭幾場雪◇ *the snows of Everest* 珠穆朗瑪峰的積雪

IDM **as clean, pure, etc. as the driven ˈsnow** extremely clean, pure, etc. 冰清玉潔；純潔無瑕

■ ***verb*** **1** 0➜ [I] when **it snows**, snow falls from the sky 下雪： *It's been snowing heavily all day.* 大雪下了一整天。 **2** [T] **~ sb** (*NAmE, informal*) to impress sb a lot by the things you say, especially if these are not true or not sincere （用花言巧語）矇，唬： *He really snowed me with all his talk of buying a Porsche.* 他嘴上老說要買一輛保時捷，還真把我唬住了。

IDM **be snowed ˈin/ˈup** to be unable to leave a place because of heavy snow 被雪困住 **be snowed ˈunder (with sth)** to have more things, especially work, than you feel able to deal with （事情太多而）應接不暇，忙得不可開交： *I'd love to come but I'm completely snowed under at the moment.* 我很想來，但眼下實在是忙得沒工夫。 **be snowed ˈup** (especially of a road 尤指道路) to be blocked with snow 被雪封住

snow·ball /ˈsnəʊbɔːl; *NAmE* ˈsnoʊ-/ *noun, verb*

■ ***noun*** **1** [C] a ball that you make out of snow to throw at sb/sth in a game 雪球： *a snowball fight* 雪仗 **2** [sing.] (often used as an adjective 常用作形容詞) a situation that develops more and more quickly as it continues 滾雪球般發展的情形： *All this publicity has had a* ***snowball effect*** *on the sales of their latest album.* 這些宣傳對他們最新唱片的銷售產生了一種滾雪球效應。 **3** [C] a drink that is a mixture of LEMONADE and a LIQUEUR (= a strong sweet alcoholic drink) made with eggs 雪球雞尾酒（含白蘭地蛋酒和檸檬汽水）

IDM **not have a ˌsnowball's chance in ˈhell** (*informal*) to have no chance at all 根本不可能；毫無機會

■ ***verb*** [I] if a problem, a plan, an activity, etc. **snowballs**, it quickly becomes much bigger, more serious, more important, etc. 滾雪球般迅速增大（或趨於嚴重、變得重要等）

the ˈSnow Belt *noun* [sing.] (*informal*) the northern and north-eastern states of the US where the winters are very cold 霜凍地帶（美國北部和東北部各州）

snow·bird /ˈsnəʊbɜːd; *NAmE* ˈsnoʊbɜːrd/ *noun* (*NAmE, informal*) a person who spends the winter in a warmer climate, especially an old person from the north of the US, or from Canada, who spends the winter in the south 到溫暖地帶過冬的人；（尤指美國北方或加拿大到南方過冬的）候鳥老人

ˈsnow-blind *adj.* unable to see because of the light reflected from a large area of snow 雪盲的 ▶ **ˈsnow-blindness** *noun* [U]

snow·blow·er /ˈsnəʊbləʊə(r); *NAmE* ˈsnoʊbloʊər/ *noun* a machine that removes snow from roads or paths by blowing it to one side 吹雪機

snow·board /ˈsnəʊbɔːd; *NAmE* ˈsnoʊbɔːrd/ *noun* a long wide board that a person stands on to move over snow in the sport of snowboarding 滑雪板

snow·board·ing /ˈsnəʊbɔːdɪŋ; *NAmE* ˈsnoʊbɔːrd-/ *noun* [U] the sport of moving over snow on a snowboard 滑雪板運動： *to go snowboarding* 去進行滑雪板運動◇ *Snowboarding is now an Olympic sport.* 滑雪板運動現在是奧運會比賽項目。 ▶ **snow·board·er** *noun*

snow·bound /ˈsnəʊbaʊnd; *NAmE* ˈsnoʊ-/ *adj.* **1** (of a person or vehicle 人或車輛) trapped in a particular place and unable to move because a lot of snow has fallen 被雪困住的 **2** (of a road or building 道路或建築物) that you cannot use or reach because a lot of snow has fallen 被雪封住的

ˈsnow cannon (*BrE*) (also **ˈsnow gun** *US, BrE*) *noun* a machine which makes artificial snow and blows it onto SKI slopes 造雪機，噴雪炮（給滑雪道人工噴雪）

ˈsnow-capped *adj.* (*literary*) (of mountains and hills 山) covered with snow on top 頂部被雪覆蓋的

ˈsnow chains *noun* [pl.] chains that are put on the wheels of a car so that it can drive over snow 雪地防滑鏈（汽車在雪地上行駛時用）

ˈsnow-covered (also *literary* **ˈsnow-clad**) *adj.* [usually before noun] covered with snow 被雪覆蓋的： *snow-covered fields* 白雪覆蓋的田野

snow·drift /ˈsnəʊdrɪft; *NAmE* ˈsnoʊ-/ *noun* a deep pile of snow that has been blown together by the wind （風吹成的）雪堆

snow·drop /ˈsnəʊdrɒp; *NAmE* ˈsnoʊdrɑːp/ *noun* a small white flower that appears in early spring 雪花蓮（早春開白花）

snow·fall /ˈsnəʊfɔːl; *NAmE* ˈsnoʊ-/ *noun* [C, U] an occasion when snow falls; the amount of snow that falls in a particular place in a period of time 下雪；降雪（量）： *a* ***heavy/light snowfall*** 大雪；小雪◇ *an area of low snowfall* 降雪量少的地區◇ *What is the average*

S

annual snowfall for this state? 這個國家的年平均降雪量是多少？

snow·field /ˈsnəʊfiːld; *NAmE* ˈsnoʊ-/ *noun* a large area that is always covered with snow, for example in the mountains 雪原（終年積雪的地區）

snow·flake /ˈsnəʊfleɪk; *NAmE* ˈsnoʊ-/ *noun* a small soft piece of frozen water that falls from the sky as snow 雪花；雪片

ˈsnow gun (*BrE* also **ˈsnow cannon**) *noun* a machine which makes artificial snow and blows it onto SKI slopes 造雪機，噴雪炮（給滑雪道人工噴雪）

ˈsnow job *noun* (*NAmE, informal*) an attempt to trick sb or to persuade them to support sth by telling them things that are not true, or by praising them too much 花言巧語的勸說；誘騙

the snow·line /ˈsnəʊlaɪn; *NAmE* ˈsnoʊ-/ *noun* [sing.] the level on mountains above which snow never melts completely 雪線 ➲ VISUAL VOCAB pages V4, V5

snow·man /ˈsnəʊmæn; *NAmE* ˈsnoʊ-/ *noun* (*pl.* **-men** /-men/) a figure like a man that people, especially children, make out of snow for fun（用雪堆成的）雪人

snow·mobile /ˈsnəʊməbiːl; *NAmE* ˈsnoʊmoʊ-/ (also **ski-mobile**) *noun* a vehicle that can move over snow and ice easily 機動雪橇；雪地機動車 ➲ picture at SLEDGE

ˈsnow pea (*NAmE*) (*BrE* **mange·tout**) *noun* [usually pl.] a type of very small PEA that grows in long, flat green PODS that are cooked and eaten whole 豌豆

snow·plough (*NAmE* **snow·plow**) /ˈsnəʊplaʊ; *NAmE* ˈsnoʊ-/ *noun, verb*

■ *noun* a vehicle or machine for cleaning snow from roads or railways 雪犁，掃雪機（用以清除公路或鐵路上的積雪）

■ *verb* [I] to bring the two points of your SKIS together, in order to go slower or stop（滑雪時）犁式制動，犁式滑降

snow·shoe /ˈsnəʊʃuː; *NAmE* ˈsnoʊ-/ *noun* one of a pair of flat frames that you attach to the bottom of your shoes so that you can walk on deep snow without sinking in 雪鞋（平面框式結構，可固定在鞋上，在深雪中行走時穿）

snow·slide /ˈsnəʊslaɪd; *NAmE* ˈsnoʊ-/ *noun* (*NAmE*) = AVALANCHE

snow·storm /ˈsnəʊstɔːm; *NAmE* ˈsnoʊstɔːrm/ *noun* a very heavy fall of snow, usually with a strong wind 雪暴；暴風雪

S

ˌsnow-ˈwhite *adj.* pure white in colour 雪白的：*snow-white sheets* 雪白的牀單

snowy /ˈsnəʊi; *NAmE* ˈsnoʊi/ *adj.* (**snow·ier**, **snowi·est**) **1** [usually before noun] covered with snow 被雪覆蓋的：*snowy fields* 白雪覆蓋的田野 **2** (of a period of time 一段時間) when a lot of snow falls 下雪多的：*a snowy weekend* 大雪紛飛的週末 **3** (*literary*) very white, like new snow 雪白的：*snowy hair* 白髮

SNP /ˌes en ˈpiː/ *abbr.* SCOTTISH NATIONAL PARTY 蘇格蘭民族黨

Snr *abbr.* = SR

snub /snʌb/ *verb, noun, adj.*

■ *verb* (**-bb-**) **1 ~ sb** to insult sb, especially by ignoring them when you meet 冷落；怠慢 SYN **cold-shoulder**：*I tried to be friendly, but she snubbed me completely.* 我盡量和氣，但她根本不答理我。 **2 ~ sth** to refuse to attend or accept sth, for example as a protest 拒不出席；拒不接受；抵制 SYN **boycott**：*All the country's leading players snubbed the tournament.* 全國的頂尖運動員都抵制那次比賽。

■ *noun* **~ (to sb)** an action or a comment that is deliberately rude in order to show sb that you do not like or respect them 冷落；怠慢的言辭（或行為）SYN **insult**：*Her refusal to attend the dinner is being seen as a deliberate snub to the President.* 在人們看來，她拒不出席宴會是有意讓總統難堪。

■ *adj.* [only before noun] (of a nose 鼻子) short, flat and turned up at the end 短平而上翹的 ► **ˌsnub-ˈnosed** *adj.*：*a snub-nosed child* 鼻子短平且上翹的孩子 ◇ *a snub-nosed revolver* (= with a short BARREL) 短管左輪手槍

snuck *past tense, past part.* of SNEAK

snuff /snʌf/ *verb, noun*

■ *verb* **1** [T] **~ sth (out)** to stop a small flame from burning, especially by pressing it between your fingers or covering it with sth 掐滅，悶熄，熄滅（小火苗）SYN **extinguish** **2** [I, T] **~ (sth)** (of an animal 動物) to smell sth by breathing in noisily through the nose 出聲地嗅：*The dogs were snuffing gently at my feet.* 幾隻狗輕輕地嗅着我的腳。

IDM **ˈsnuff it** (*BrE, slang, humorous*) to die 死

PHR V **ˌsnuff sth↔ˈout** to stop or destroy sth completely 扼殺；消滅：*An innocent child's life has been snuffed out by this senseless shooting.* 這胡亂一槍就要了一個無辜孩子的命。

■ *noun* [U] TOBACCO in the form of a powder that people take by breathing it into their noses 鼻煙

IDM **ˌup to ˈsnuff** (*NAmE*) (*BrE* **ˌup to the ˈmark**) as good as it/they should be 達到要求；符合標準 SYN **up to scratch**

snuff·box /ˈsnʌfbɒks; *NAmE* -bɑːks/ *noun* a small, usually decorated, box for holding snuff 鼻煙盒

snuf·fle /ˈsnʌfl/ *verb, noun*

■ *verb* **1** [I, T] (**+ speech**) to breathe noisily because you have a cold or you are crying（因感冒或哭泣）鼻子呼哧出聲，抽鼻子 SYN **sniff**：*I could hear the child snuffling in her sleep.* 我聽見這女孩睡着了還在抽鼻子。 **2** [I] **~ (about/around)** if an animal **snuffles**, it breathes noisily through its nose, especially while it is smelling sth 哧哧地嗅

■ *noun* (also *less frequent* **snuf·fling**) an act or the sound of snuffling 抽鼻子（聲）；嗅；嗅東西時發出的呼哧聲：*The silence was broken only by the snuffles of the dogs.* 除了不時聽見狗喘氣的聲音，四下裏一片寂靜。◇ *His breath came in snuffles.* 他呼哧呼哧地呼吸着。

IDM **get, have, etc. the ˈsnuffles** (*informal*) to get/have a cold 患感冒

ˈsnuff movie *noun* a film/movie that shows a real murder, intended as entertainment 謀殺實況影片

snug /snʌg/ *adj., noun*

■ *adj.* **1** warm, comfortable and protected, especially from the cold 温暖舒適的；保暖的 SYN **cosy**：*a snug little house* 温暖舒適的小房子 ◇ *I spent the afternoon snug and warm in bed.* 我在牀上躺了一下午，又暖和又舒服。 **2** fitting sb/sth closely 貼身的；緊身的；嚴密的；嚴實的：*The elastic at the waist gives a nice snug fit.* 腰間的鬆緊帶使衣服正好緊緊貼在身上。 ► **snug·ly** *adv.*：*I left the children tucked up snugly in bed.* 我給孩子們掖好被子，讓他們睡得暖和。◇ *The lid should fit snugly.* 蓋子要蓋緊。 **snug·ness** *noun* [U]

■ *noun* (*BrE*) a small comfortable room in a pub, with seats for only a few people（酒吧裏的）包間，雅座

snug·gle /ˈsnʌgl/ *verb* [I, T] to get into, or to put sb/sth into, a warm comfortable position, especially close to sb（使）依偎，緊貼，蜷伏：**+ adv./prep.** *The child* ***snuggled up to*** *her mother.* 女孩依偎着她母親。◇ *He* ***snuggled down*** *under the bedclothes.* 他躺下以後蓋上被子，很舒服。◇ *She snuggled closer.* 她把身子蜷得更緊些。◇ **~ sth + adv./prep.** *He snuggled his head onto her shoulder.* 他把頭倚在她肩上。

So. *abbr.* (*NAmE*) south; southern 南方（的）；南部（的）

so 0→ /səʊ; *NAmE* soʊ/ *adv., conj., noun*

■ *adv.* **1** 0→ to such a great degree（表示程度）這麼，這樣，那麼，那樣，如此：*Don't look so angry.* 別那樣怒氣沖沖的。◇ *There's no need to worry so.* 沒必要這樣着急。◇ **~ … (that) …** *She spoke so quietly (that) I could hardly hear her.* 她說話輕得我幾乎聽不見。◇ **~ … as to do sth** *I'm not so stupid as to believe that.* 我還不至於傻得連那樣的話都相信。◇ (*formal, especially BrE*) ***Would you be so kind as to*** *lock the door when you leave?* 請您離開時把門鎖上好嗎？ **2** 0→ very; extremely 很；極：*I'm so glad to see you.* 見到你真高興。◇ *We have so much to do.* 我們有很多事要做。◇ *Their attitude is* ***so very*** *English.* 他們的態度是十足的英國人的態度。◇ *The article was* ***just so much*** (= nothing but) *nonsense.* 那篇文章純

粹是胡說八道。◇ (*BrE*) *He sat there* **ever so** *quietly.* 他靜悄悄地坐在那兒。◇ (*BrE*) *I do love it so.* 我實在是太喜歡它了。 **3** 🔑 **not ~ … (as …)** (used in comparisons 用於比較) not to the same degree 不如…（這麼…）；不像…（那樣…）：*I haven't enjoyed myself so much for a long time.* 我好長時間沒有這麼快活了。◇ *It wasn't so good as last time.* 這次不如上次好。◇ *It's not so easy as you'd think.* 不像你想的那麼容易。◇ *He was not so quick a learner as his brother.* 他學東西不像他哥哥那麼快。◇ *It's* **not so much** *a hobby* **as** *a career* (= more like a career than a hobby). 這與其說是愛好，不如說是職業。◇ (*disapproving*) *Off she went* **without so much as** (= without even) *a 'goodbye'.* 她連聲"再見"都沒說就走了。 **4** used to show the size, amount or number of sth（表示大小或數量）這麼，那麼：*The fish was about so big* (= said when using your hands to show the size). 那條魚差不多有這麼長。◇ *There are* **only so many** (= only a limited number of) *hours in a day.* 一天不過這麼幾個小時。 **5** 🔑 used to refer back to sth that has already been mentioned（指剛說過的事物）這樣，如此：*'Is he coming?' '***I hope so.***'* "他來嗎？" "我希望他來。" ◇ *'Did they mind?' '***I don't think so.***'* "他們有沒有介意？" "我想沒有。" ◇ *If she notices, she never* **says so.** 就算她留意到，她也從來不說。◇ *I might be away next week.* **If so,** *I won't be able to see you.* 下星期我可能外出。要是那樣，我就見不到你了。◇ *We are very busy—***so much so that** *we won't be able to take time off this year.* 我們很忙，忙得今年都沒時間休假了。◇ *Programs are expensive, and* **even more so** *if you have to keep altering them.* 買軟件很貴，要是老得更換，那就更貴了。◇ *I hear that you're a writer—***is that so** (= is that true)*?* 聽說你是作家，是嗎？◇ *He thinks I dislike him but that just isn't so.* 他以為我討厭他，其實不是那麼回事。◇ *George is going to help me, or* **so he says** (= that is what he says). 喬治會幫我，他是這麼說的。◇ *They asked me to call them and I* **did so** (= I called). 他們要我叫他們，於是我就叫了。 **6** 🔑 also 也：*Times have changed and* **so have I.** 時代變了，我也變了。◇ *'I prefer the first version.' '***So do we.***'* "我喜歡第一稿。" "我們也是。"

HELP You cannot use **so** with negative verbs. Use **neither** or **either**. * so 不與動詞的否定式連用。否定中用 neither 或 either：*'I'm not hungry.' '***Neither am I/I'm not*** *very hungry* ***either.***'* "我不餓。" "我也不太餓。"

7 used to agree that sth is true, especially when you are surprised（尤指感到驚訝時表示同意）的確如此：*'You were there, too.' '***So I was***—I'd forgotten.'* "當時你也在那兒。" "是啊，我給忘了。" ◇ *'There's another one.' '***So there is.***'* "還有一個。" "可不是嗎。" **8** (*informal*) used, often with a negative, before adjectives and noun phrases to emphasize sth that you are saying（常與否定詞連用，置於形容詞和名詞短語前以加強語氣）：*He is* **so not** *the right person for you.* 他這個人絕對不適合你。◇ *That is* **so not** *cool.* 那實在不怎麼樣。 **9** (*informal*) used, especially by children, to say that what sb says is not the case and the opposite is true（兒童常用以反駁對方）偏偏，就：*'You're not telling the truth, are you?' 'I am, so!'* "你說的不是實話，對不對？" "就是實話，就是！" **10** used when you are showing sb how to do sth or telling them how sth happened（演示或描述事由）這樣：*Stand with your arms out, so.* 兩臂伸開站着，像這樣。◇ (*literary*) **So it was that** *he finally returned home.* 就這樣，他終於回到了家。

IDM **and 'so forth | and 'so on (and 'so forth)** 🔑 used at the end of a list to show that it continues in the same way（表示列舉未盡）等等，諸如此類：*We discussed everything—when to go, what to see and so on.* 我們什麼都商量過了，什麼時候走、看什麼等等。 **… or so** 🔑 used after a number, an amount, etc. to show that it is not exact（用於數目、數量等後）…左右，…上下：*There were twenty or so* (= about twenty) *people there.* 那兒有差不多二十個人。◇ *We stayed for an hour or so.* 我們待了一個小時左右。 **so as to do sth** with the intention of doing sth 為了做某事；以便做某事：*We went early so as to get good seats.* 為了佔到好座位，我們早早就去了。 **so 'be it** (*formal*) used to show that you accept sth and will not try to change it or cannot change it（表示完全接受）就那樣好了：*If he doesn't want to be involved, then so be it.* 要是他不想參與，那就隨他的便好了。 **ˌso much for 'sth** **1** used to show that you have finished talking about sth（表示就某事講完了）關於…就講這麼多，…到此為止：*So much for the situation in Germany. Now we turn our attention to France.* 德國的形勢就講到這裏。現在我們來看看法國的情況。 **2** (*informal*) used to suggest that sth has not been successful or useful（表示行不通或沒用）作罷好了，快別提了：*So much for that idea!* 快別提那個主意了！ **so … that** (*formal*) in such a way that 這樣…為的是；如此…以至：*The programme has been so organized that none of the talks overlap.* 日程做了精心安排，以使每一講都沒有重複內容。 **(all) the 'more so because …** used to give an important extra reason why sth is true（表示另外的重要原因）尤其因為：*His achievement is remarkable; all the more so because he had no help at all.* 他的成就非同一般，而由於他沒有得到過任何幫助，更顯不凡。

■ ***conj.*** **1** 🔑 used to show the reason for sth（表示因果關係）因此，所以：*It was still painful so I went to see a doctor.* 那地方還疼，因此我去看了醫生。 **2** 🔑 **~ (that …)** used to show the result of sth（引出結果）因此，所以：*Nothing more was heard from him so that we began to wonder if he was dead.* 此後再沒收到他的消息，於是我們開始懷疑他是不是死了。 **3** 🔑 **~ (that …)** used to show the purpose of sth（表示目的）為了，以便：*But I gave you a map so you wouldn't get lost!* 但我怕你迷路，給過你一張地圖！◇ *She worked hard so that everything would be ready in time.* 她努力工作，為的是及時做好各項準備。 **4** 🔑 used to introduce the next part of a story（引出下文）：*So after shouting and screaming for an hour she walked out in tears.* 就這樣，又嚷又叫了一個小時後，她流着淚走了出來。 **5** 🔑 (*informal*) used to show that you think sth is not important, especially after sb has criticized you for it（認為某事無關緊要，尤用於反駁他人的指責時）：*So I had a couple of drinks on the way home. What's wrong with that?* 我不過是在回家的路上喝了兩杯。這怎麼啦？◇ *'You've been smoking again.' 'So?'* "你近來又抽煙了。" "抽又怎麼啦？" **6** 🔑 (*informal*) used to introduce a comment or a question（引出評論或問題）：*So, let's see. What do we need to take?* 那麼，大家想想，我們需要帶什麼？◇ *So, what have you been doing today?* 那你今天都幹什麼了？ **7** (*informal*) used when you are making a final statement（引出結束語）：*So, that's it for today.* 好，今天就講到這裏。 **8** (*informal*) used in questions to refer to sth that has just been said（在問句中代指剛談論的事）：*So there's nothing we can do about it?* 這麼說，我們一點辦法都沒有了？◇ *'I've just got back from a trip to Rome.' 'So, how was it?'* "我去了一趟羅馬，剛回來。" "是嗎？怎麼樣？" **9** used when stating that two events, situations, etc. are similar（指出兩種情況等相類似）：**Just as** *large companies are having to cut back,* **so** *small businesses are being forced to close.* 大公司不得不緊縮，小企業則被迫關閉。

IDM **so 'what?** (*informal*) used to show that you think sth is not important, especially after sb has criticized you for it（認為某事無關緊要，尤用於反駁他人的指責時）：*'He's fifteen years younger than you!' 'So what?'* "他比你小十五歲呢！" "那又怎麼啦？" ◇ *So what if nobody else agrees with me?* 就算沒有一個人贊成我的意見，那又怎麼樣？

■ ***noun*** = SOH

soak /səʊk; *NAmE* soʊk/ *verb, noun*

■ ***verb*** **1** [T, I] to put sth in liquid for a time so that it becomes completely wet; to become completely wet in this way 浸泡；浸濕；浸透；濕透：**~ sth (in sth)** *I usually soak the beans overnight.* 我通常把豆子泡一夜。◇ *If you soak the tablecloth before you wash it, the stains should come out.* 先把桌布浸一浸再洗，污跡就能去掉。◇ **~ (in sth)** *Leave the apricots* **to soak** *for 20 minutes.* 把杏子浸泡 20 分鐘。◇ *I'm going to go and soak in the bath.* 我要去泡個澡。 **2** [T] **~ sb/sth** to make sb/sth completely wet 使濕透；把…浸濕 **SYN** **drench**：*A sudden shower of rain soaked the spectators.* 突如其來的一陣雨把觀眾淋了個透。 **3** [T] **~ sb** (*informal*) to obtain a lot of money from sb by making them pay very high taxes or prices 向（某人）敲竹槓；宰（某人）；向（某

S

人）徵收重稅：*He was accused of soaking his clients.* 他被指控向客戶敲竹槓。

PHR V **'soak into/through sth** | **soak 'in** (of a liquid 液體) to enter or pass through sth 滲入；滲透：*Blood had soaked through the bandage.* 血透過繃帶滲了出來。**,soak sth↔'off/'out** to remove sth by leaving it in water 把…泡掉 **,soak sth↔'up** **1** to take in or absorb liquid 吸收，吸掉（液體）：*Use a cloth to soak up some of the excess water.* 用布把多餘的水吸去。**2** to absorb sth into your senses, your body or your mind（通過感官、身心）吸取，攝取：*We were just sitting soaking up the atmosphere.* 我們就坐在那兒感受着那裏的氣氛。

■ **noun** (also **soak·ing**) [sing.] **1** an act of leaving sth in a liquid for a period of time; an act of making sb/sth wet 浸泡；浸漬；濕透：*Give the shirt a good soak before you wash it.* 把襯衫好好泡一泡再洗。**2** (*informal*) a period of time spent in a bath 洗澡；泡澡

soaked /səʊkt; *NAmE* soʊkt/ *adj.* **1** [not usually before noun] **~ (with sth)** very wet 濕透 SYN **drenched**：*He woke up soaked with sweat.* 他醒了，渾身大汗淋漓。◇ *You're* ***soaked through!*** (= completely wet) 你都濕透了！◇ *They were* ***soaked to the skin.*** 他們渾身濕透。◇ *You'll* ***get soaked*** *if you go out in this rain.* 冒這樣的雨出去，你會成落湯雞的。◇ *Your clothes are soaked!* 你的衣服全都濕透了！➲ SYNONYMS at WET **2 -soaked** used with nouns to form adjectives describing sth that is made completely wet with the thing mentioned（和名詞組成形容詞）浸透了…的，被…浸濕的：*a blood-soaked cloth* 一塊浸透了鮮血的布 ◇ *rain-soaked clothing* 雨水淋透的衣服

soak·ing /ˈsəʊkɪŋ; *NAmE* ˈsoʊ-/ (also **,soaking 'wet**) *adj.* completely wet 濕透的；濕淋淋的 SYN **sopping**：*That coat is soaking—take it off.* 那上衣濕透了，脫下來吧。◇ *We arrived home soaking wet.* 我們回到家時，渾身濕淋淋的。

so-and-so /ˈsəʊ ən səʊ; *NAmE* ˈsoʊ ən soʊ/ *noun* (*pl.* **so-and-sos**) (*informal*) **1** [usually sing.] used to refer to a person, thing, etc. when you do not know their name or when you are talking in a general way（指叫不上名字的人、物，或泛指）某某人（或事物）：*What would you say to Mrs So-and-so who has called to complain about a noisy neighbour?* 要是哪位太太嫌鄰居太吵鬧，打電話投訴，你怎麼跟她說？**2** an annoying or unpleasant person. People sometimes say **so-and-so** to avoid using an offensive word. 惱人的傢伙；討厭鬼：*He's an ungrateful so-and-so.* 他是個忘恩負義的傢伙。

S

soap 0-w /səʊp; *NAmE* soʊp/ *noun, verb*

■ **noun** **1** 0-w [U, C] a substance that you use with water for washing your body 肥皂：*soap and water* 肥皂和水 ◇ *a* ***bar/piece of soap*** 一條／一塊肥皂 ◇ *soap bubbles* 肥皂泡 **2** [C] (*informal*) = SOAP OPERA：*soaps on TV* 電視上播出的肥皂劇 ◇ *She's a US soap star.* 她是美國肥皂劇明星。

■ **verb** **~ yourself/sb/sth** to rub yourself/sb/sth with soap 抹肥皂；用肥皂擦洗 ➲ see also SOFT-SOAP

soap·box /ˈsəʊpbɒks; *NAmE* ˈsoʊpbɑːks/ *noun* a small temporary platform that sb stands on to make a speech in a public place, usually outdoors（多指戶外的）臨時演講台

IDM **get/be on your 'soapbox** (*informal*) to express the strong opinions that you have about a particular subject 發表激烈的意見

'soap flakes *noun* [pl.] very small thin pieces of soap that are sold in boxes, used for washing clothes by hand 肥皂片（手洗衣物用）

'soap opera (also *informal* **soap**) *noun* [C, U] a story about the lives and problems of a group of people which is broadcast every day or several times a week on television or radio 肥皂劇 ➲ COLLOCATIONS at TELEVISION

'soap powder *noun* [U, C] (*BrE*) a powder made from soap and other substances that you use for washing your clothes, especially in a machine 洗衣粉；肥皂粉

soap·stone /ˈsəʊpstəʊn; *NAmE* ˈsoʊpstoʊn/ *noun* [U] a type of soft stone that feels like soap, used in making decorative objects 皂石（質軟，用作裝飾材料）

soap·suds /ˈsəʊpsʌdz; *NAmE* ˈsoʊp-/ *noun* [pl.] = SUDS

soapy /ˈsəʊpi; *NAmE* ˈsoʊpi/ *adj.* [usually before noun] **1** full of soap; covered with soap 滿是肥皂的；塗滿肥皂的 **2** tasting or feeling like soap 有肥皂味的；摸着像肥皂的

soar /sɔː(r)/ *verb* **1** [I] if the value, amount or level of sth **soars**, it rises very quickly 急升；猛增 SYN **rocket**：***soaring costs/prices/temperatures*** 猛增的成本；飛漲的物價；驟升的溫度 ◇ *Unemployment has soared to 18%.* 失業率猛升到了 18%。**2** [I] **~ (up) (into sth)** to rise quickly and smoothly up into the air 升空；升騰：*The rocket soared (up) into the air.* 火箭升空。◇ (*figurative*) *Her spirits soared* (= she became very happy and excited). 她情緒高漲。**3** [I] to fly very high in the air or remain high in the air 高飛；翱翔：*an eagle soaring high above the cliffs* 在山崖上空高高翱翔的鷹 **4** [I] to be very high or tall 高聳；聳立：*soaring mountains* 屹立的群山 ◇ *The building soared above us.* 在我們眼前，那座大樓巍然高聳。**5** [I] when music **soars**, it becomes higher or louder（音樂）升高，增強：*soaring strings* 激昂的弦樂

soar·away /ˈsɔːrəweɪ/ *adj.* [only before noun] (*BrE*) (especially of success 尤指成功) very great; growing very quickly 巨大的；迅速獲得的

SOB /ˌes əʊ ˈbiː; *NAmE* ˌes oʊ ˈbiː/ *noun* (*slang, especially NAmE*) = SON OF A BITCH

sob /sɒb; *NAmE* sɑːb/ *verb, noun*

■ **verb** **(-bb-)** **1** [I] to cry noisily, taking sudden, sharp breaths 抽噎；啜泣；嗚咽：*I heard a child sobbing loudly.* 我聽見有個孩子在嗚嗚地哭。◇ *He started to sob uncontrollably.* 他不由自主地抽噎起來。**2** [T] to say sth while you are crying 哭訴；泣訴；抽噎着說：**+ speech** *'I hate him,' she sobbed.* "我恨他。" 她抽噎着說。◇ **~ sth (out)** *He sobbed out his troubles.* 他哭着述說了自己的煩惱。

IDM **sob your 'heart out** to cry noisily for a long time because you are very sad 悲切地哭泣；很傷心地哭泣

■ **noun** an act or the sound of sobbing 抽噎（聲）；啜泣（聲）；嗚咽（聲）：*He gave a deep sob.* 他發出一聲低沉的抽噎聲。◇ *Her body was racked* (= shaken) *with sobs.* 她哭得身子一抽一抽的。

sober /ˈsəʊbə(r); *NAmE* ˈsoʊ-/ *adj., verb*

■ **adj.** **1** [not usually before noun] not drunk (= not affected by alcohol) 未醉：*I promised him that I'd stay sober tonight.* 我答應過他，今晚我不會喝醉。◇ *He was* ***as sober as a judge*** (= completely sober). 他一點沒醉。**2** (of people and their behaviour 人及其行為) serious and sensible 持重的；冷靜的：*a sober assessment of the situation* 對形勢的冷靜估計 ◇ *He is honest, sober and hard-working.* 他誠實、穩重、勤奮。◇ ***On sober reflection*** (= after some serious thought), *I don't think I really need a car after all.* 冷靜地想了想以後，我覺得我其實並不需要車。**3** (of colours or clothes 顏色或服裝) plain and not bright 素淨的；淡素的：*a sober grey suit* 一套素淨的灰西裝 ▶ **sober·ly** *adv.* IDM see STONE COLD

■ **verb** [T, I] **~ (sb)** to make sb behave or think in a more serious and sensible way; to become more serious and sensible（使）變得持重，變得冷靜：*The bad news sobered us for a while.* 壞消息使我們冷靜了一會兒。◇ *He suddenly sobered.* 他突然嚴肅起來。

PHR V **,sober 'up** | **,sober sb 'up** to become or to make sb no longer drunk（使）醒酒：*Stay here with us until you've sobered up.* 你就待在我們這兒，等酒醒了再走。

sober·ing /ˈsəʊbərɪŋ; *NAmE* ˈsoʊ-/ *adj.* making you feel serious and think carefully 令人警醒的；使人冷靜的：*a* ***sobering effect/experience/thought, etc.*** 令人警醒的效果、經歷、思想等 ◇ ***It is sobering*** *to realize that this is not a new problem.* 意識到這並不是新問題，就會使人冷靜下來。

so·bri·ety /səˈbraɪəti/ *noun* [U] (*formal*) **1** the state of being sober (= not being drunk) 未醉 OPP **insobriety** **2** the fact of being sensible and serious 持重；冷靜

so·bri·quet /ˈsəʊbrɪkeɪ; *NAmE* ˈsoʊ-/ (also **sou·bri·quet**) *noun* (*formal*) an informal name or title that you give sb/sth 綽號；外號 SYN **nickname**

ˈ**sob story** *noun* (*informal, disapproving*) a story that sb tells you just to make you feel sorry for them, especially one that does not have that effect or is not true（目的在於引起同情或憐憫的）傷感故事

Soc. *abbr.* (in writing) SOCIETY（書寫形式）協會，學會：*Royal Geographical Soc.* 皇家地理學會

soca /ˈsəʊkə; *NAmE* ˈsoʊ-/ *noun* [U] a type of dance music, originally from the Caribbean, which mixes SOUL and CALYPSO 索卡樂，靈卡樂（源於加勒比海的舞曲，融合了靈樂和卡利普索民歌）

ˌ**so-ˈcalled** AW *adj.* **1** [only before noun] used to show that you do not think that the word or phrase that is being used to describe sb/sth is appropriate（表示不認同）所謂的：*the opinion of a so-called 'expert'* 一個所謂的"專家"的意見 ◇ *How have these so-called improvements helped the local community?* 這些所謂的進步對當地社會有什麼幫助呢？ **2** [usually before noun] used to introduce the word that people usually use to describe sth（引出約定俗成的稱謂）人稱…的，號稱…的：*artists from the so-called 'School of London'* 號稱"倫敦派"的一群藝術家

soc·cer /ˈsɒkə(r); *NAmE* ˈsɑːk-/ (*BrE* also **foot·ball**) (also *BrE formal* **Asˌsociation ˈfootball**) (also *BrE informal* **footy, footie**) *noun* [U] a game played by two teams of 11 players, using a round ball which players kick up and down the playing field. Teams try to kick the ball into the other team's goal. 足球運動：*soccer players* 足球運動員 ◇ *a **soccer pitch/team/match*** 足球場／隊／比賽 ➲ VISUAL VOCAB page V44

ˈ**soccer mom** *noun* (*NAmE, informal*) a mother who spends a lot of time taking her children to activities such as sports and music lessons, used as a way of referring to a typical mother from the MIDDLE CLASSES 足球媽媽（花許多時間帶孩子參加體育活動、音樂課等的母親，尤指典型的中產階級母親）

so·ci·able /ˈsəʊʃəbl; *NAmE* ˈsoʊ-/ (also *less frequent* **so·cial**) *adj.* (of people 人) enjoying spending time with other people 好交際的；合群的；友好的 SYN **gregarious**：*She's a sociable child who'll talk to anyone.* 她是個合群的孩子，跟誰都有話說。◇ *I'm not feeling very sociable this evening.* 今晚我不大想跟人應酬。◇ *We had a very sociable weekend* (= we did a lot of things with other people). 我們大夥過了一個十分熱鬧的週末。➲ compare ANTISOCIAL OPP **unsociable** ▸ **so·ci·abil·ity** /ˌsəʊʃəˈbɪləti; *NAmE* ˌsoʊ-/ *noun* [U]

so·cial 0‑w /ˈsəʊʃl; *NAmE* ˈsoʊʃl/ *adj., noun*

■ *adj.*

▸ CONNECTED WITH SOCIETY 社會 **1** 0‑w [only before noun] connected with society and the way it is organized 社會的：*social issues/problems/reforms* 社會議題／問題／改革 ◇ *a call for social and economic change* 進行社會和經濟變革的要求 **2** 0‑w [only before noun] connected with your position in society 社會上的；社會地位的：***social class/background*** 社會階層／背景 ◇ *social advancement* (= improving your position in society) 社會地位的提高

▸ ACTIVITIES WITH OTHERS 社交活動 **3** 0‑w [only before noun] connected with activities in which people meet each other for pleasure 社交的；交際的；聯誼的：*a busy **social life*** 繁忙的社交生活 ◇ *Team sports help to develop a child's **social skills*** (= the ability to talk easily to other people and do things in a group). 集體體育運動有助於培養孩子的交際能力。◇ *Social events and training days are arranged for all the staff.* 所有員工都獲安排聯誼活動和培訓。◇ *Join a social club to make new friends.* 加入一個社交俱樂部，好交一些新朋友。

▸ ANIMALS 動物 **4** [only before noun] (*technical* 術語) living naturally in groups, rather than alone 群居的

▸ FRIENDLY 友好 **5** = SOCIABLE

▸ **so·cial·ly** 0‑w /-ʃəli/ *adv.*：*The reforms will bring benefits, socially and politically.* 這些改革措施在社會領域和政治領域均會帶來益處。◇ *This type of behaviour is no longer socially acceptable.* 這種行為已不為社會所接受。◇ *a socially disadvantaged family* (= one that is poor and from a low social class) 社會地位低下的家庭 ◇ *We meet at work, but never socially.* 我們上班常見面，但在社交場合從未碰見過。◇ *Carnivores are usually socially complex mammals.* 在哺乳動物中，食肉動物通常有着複雜的社會關係。

■ *noun* **1** [C] (*old-fashioned*) a party that is organized by a group or club 聯誼會；聯歡會 **2 the social** [U] (*BrE, informal*) = SOCIAL SECURITY：*We're living on the social now.* 我們現在靠社會保障金維持生活。

ˌ**social ˈbookmarking** *noun* [U] (*computing* 計) a way of BOOKMARKING (= storing and labelling) the addresses of pages on the Internet, using a special service that enables you to make them available to other Internet users 社交書籤，網路書籤，網摘（可將收藏的網址在互聯網上與人分享）

ˌ**social ˈclimber** *noun* (*disapproving*) a person who tries to improve their position in society by becoming friendly with people who belong to a higher social class 攀附權貴藉以擠入上流社會的人；趨炎附勢向上爬的人

ˌ**social ˈconscience** *noun* [sing., U] the state of being aware of the problems that affect a lot of people in society, such as being poor or having no home, and wanting to do sth to help these people 社會良知；社會責任感

ˌ**social ˈcontract** (also ˌ**social ˈcompact**) *noun* [sing.] an agreement among citizens to behave in a way that benefits everybody 社會契約，民約（以公益約束行為）

ˌ**social deˈmocracy** *noun* [U, C] a political system that combines the principles of SOCIALISM with the greater personal freedom of DEMOCRACY; a country that has this political system of government 社會民主主義；社會民主主義國家 ▸ ˌ**social ˈdemocrat** *noun* ˌ**social demoˈcratic** *adj.* [only before noun]

ˌ**social engiˈneering** *noun* [U] the attempt to change society and to deal with social problems according to particular political beliefs, for example by changing the law 社會工程（根據政治信念改造社會）

ˈ**social fund** *noun* [usually sing.] a sum of money that can be used to help people who have financial, family or other social problems 社會基金（向困難者提供資助）

ˌ**social ˈhousing** *noun* [U] (in Britain) houses or flats/apartments that are provided by a local council or another organization for people to buy or rent at a low price 社會福利住房（由英國的地方政府或其他機構提供的低價或低租金住房）

ˌ**Social Inˈsurance number** *noun* (*abbr.* **SIN**) a number that the Canadian government uses to identify you, and that you use when you fill out official forms, apply for a job, etc.（加拿大政府用於識別身分等的）社會保險號碼

so·cial·ism /ˈsəʊʃəlɪzəm; *NAmE* ˈsoʊ-/ *noun* [U] a set of political and economic theories based on the belief that everyone has an equal right to a share of a country's wealth and that the government should own and control the main industries 社會主義 ➲ compare CAPITALISM, COMMUNISM, SOCIAL DEMOCRACY

so·cial·ist /ˈsəʊʃəlɪst; *NAmE* ˈsoʊ-/ *noun* a person who believes in or supports socialism; a member of a political party that believes in socialism 社會主義者；社會黨黨員 ▸ **so·cial·ist** *adj.* [usually before noun]：*a socialist country* 社會主義國家 ◇ *socialist beliefs* 社會主義信仰 ◇ *the ruling Socialist Party* 執政的社會黨

so·cial·is·tic /ˌsəʊʃəˈlɪstɪk; *NAmE* ˌsoʊ-/ *adj.* [usually before noun] (often *disapproving*) having some of the features of socialism 有社會主義傾向的；有一定社會主義特點的

ˌ**socialist ˈrealism** *noun* [U] a theory that was put into practice in some COMMUNIST countries, especially in the Soviet Union under Stalin, that art, music and literature should be used to show people the principles of a SOCIALIST society and encourage them to support it 社會主義現實主義（尤指斯大林領導時期的蘇聯等一些共產黨國家實踐的理論，即藝術、音樂和文學應要表現和支持社會主義）

S

so·cial·ite /ˈsəʊʃəlaɪt; *NAmE* ˈsoʊ-/ *noun* (sometimes *disapproving*) a person who goes to a lot of fashionable parties and is often written about in the newspapers, etc. 上流社會名人；社交名流

so·cial·iza·tion (*BrE* also **-isa·tion**) /ˌsəʊʃəlaɪˈzeɪʃn; *NAmE* ˌsoʊʃələˈz-/ *noun* [U] (*formal*) the process by which sb, especially a child, learns to behave in a way that is acceptable in their society 適應社會的過程；社會化

so·cial·ize (*BrE* also **-ise**) /ˈsəʊʃəlaɪz; *NAmE* ˈsoʊ-/ *verb* **1** [I] **~ (with sb)** to meet and spend time with people in a friendly way, in order to enjoy yourself （和他人）交往，交際 **SYN** **mix**: *I enjoy socializing with the other students.* 我喜歡和同學來往。◇ *Maybe you should socialize more.* 也許你應該多和人交往。 **2** [T, often passive] **~ sb (to do sth)** (*formal*) to teach people to behave in ways that are acceptable to their society 使適應社會：*The family has the important function of socializing children.* 家庭有教孩子適應社會的重要作用。 **3** [T, usually passive] **~ sth** to organize sth according to the principles of SOCIALISM 使社會主義化；按社會主義原則行事

ˌsocialized ˈmedicine *noun* [U] (*US*) medical and hospital care provided by the government for everyone by paying for it with public money 公費醫療制度

ˌsocial ˈnetworking *noun* [U] communication with people who share your interests using a website or other service on the Internet 網絡社交；社交網絡活動：*a social networking site* 社交網站 ➲ COLLOCATIONS at EMAIL

ˌsocial psyˈchology *noun* [U] the study of people's behaviour, attitudes, etc. in society 社會心理學 ▸ **ˌsocial psyˈchologist** *noun*

ˌsocial ˈscience *noun* **1** [U] (also **ˌsocial ˈstudies**) the study of people in society 社會科學 **2** [C] a particular subject connected with the study of people in society, for example geography, ECONOMICS or SOCIOLOGY 社會科學學科

ˌsocial ˈscientist *noun* a person who studies social science 社會科學家

ˌsocial ˈsecretary *noun* the person who organizes social activities for an organization or for another person 社交秘書（負責為機構或個人組織社交活動）

ˌsocial seˈcurity *noun* [U] **1** (*BrE*) (also **wel·fare** *NAmE*, *BrE*) money that the government pays regularly to people who are poor, unemployed, sick, etc. 社會保障金（政府定期向貧窮、失業、患病等人發放）：*to live on social security* 靠社會保障金生活 ◇ *social security payments* 社會保障金支付款項 **2 Social Security** (in the US) a system in which people pay money regularly to the government when they are working and receive payments from the government when they are unable to work, especially when they are sick or too old to work （美國）社會保障制度 ➲ compare NATIONAL INSURANCE

ˌSocial Seˈcurity number *noun* (*abbr.* **SSN**) (in the US) an official identity number that everyone is given when they are born 社會安全號碼（美國人出生時得到的正式身分號碼）

ˌsocial ˈservices *noun* [pl.] a system that is organized by the local government to help people who have financial or family problems; the department or the people who provide this help 社會福利制度（由當地政府組織，向困難者提供幫助的制度）；社會福利部門；社會福利工作人員：*a leaflet on the range of social services available* 宣傳現有社會福利範圍的傳單 ◇ *the local social services department* 當地的社會福利部門

ˌsocial ˈstudies *noun* [pl.] = SOCIAL SCIENCE (1)

ˈsocial work *noun* [U] paid work that involves giving help and advice to people living in the community who have financial or family problems 社會福利工作

ˈsocial worker *noun* a person whose job is social work 社會福利工作者

so·ci·etal /səˈsaɪətl/ *adj.* [only before noun] (*technical* 術語) connected with society and the way it is organized 社會的；關於社會的

so·ci·ety 0‑ /səˈsaɪəti/ *noun* (*pl.* **-ies**) **1** 0‑ [U] people in general, living together in communities 社會（以群體形式生活在一起的人的總稱）：*policies that will benefit society as a whole* 將有利於整個社會的政策 ◇ *Racism exists at all levels of society.* 種族主義存在於社會各階層。◇ *They carried out research into the roles of men and women in today's society* 他們就男人和女人在當今社會中所扮演的角色展開研究。 **2** 0‑ [C, U] a particular community of people who share the same customs, laws, etc. 社會（共同遵守一定的習俗、法律等的特定群體）：*modern industrial societies* 現代工業社會 ◇ *demand created by a consumer society* 消費型社會所產生的需求 ◇ *Can Britain ever be a classless society?* 英國能否有朝一日成為一個無階級社會？◇ *They were discussing the problems of Western society.* 當時他們正在討論西方社會的問題。 **3** 0‑ [C] (*abbr.* **Soc.**) (especially in names 尤用於名稱) a group of people who join together for a particular purpose 社團；協會；學會：*a member of the drama society* 劇社成員 ◇ *the American Society of Newspaper Editors* 美國報紙主編協會 ➲ see also BUILDING SOCIETY, FRIENDLY SOCIETY **4** [U] the group of people in a country who are fashionable, rich and powerful 上流社會：*Their daughter married into **high society**.* 他們的女兒嫁到了上層社會。◇ *a society wedding* 上層社會的婚禮 **5** [U] (*formal*) the state of being with other people 相伴；交往 **SYN** **company**: *He was a solitary man who avoided the society of others.* 他是個孤僻的人，不願和人交往。

socio- /ˈsəʊsiəʊ; *NAmE* ˈsoʊsioʊ/ *combining form* (in nouns, adjectives and adverbs 構成名詞、形容詞和副詞) connected with society or the study of society 社會的；社會學的：*socio-economic* 社會與經濟的 ◇ *sociolinguistics* 社會語言學

so·cio·cul·tural /ˌsəʊsiəʊˈkʌltʃərəl; *NAmE* ˌsoʊsioʊ-/ *adj.* relating to society and culture 社會與文化的

ˌsocio-ˌecoˈnomic *adj.* relating to society and economics 社會與經濟的；社經的：*people from different socio-economic backgrounds* 有不同社會與經濟背景的人

socio·lect /ˈsəʊsiəʊlekt; *NAmE* ˈsoʊsioʊ-/ *noun* (*linguistics* 語言) a variety of a language that the members of a particular social class or social group speak 社會方言（某社會階層或群體使用的一種語言變體）

socio·lin·guis·tics /ˌsəʊsiəʊlɪŋˈɡwɪstɪks; *NAmE* ˌsoʊsioʊ-/ *noun* [U] the study of the way language is affected by differences in social class, region, sex, etc. 社會語言學 ▸ **socio·lin·guis·tic** /ˌsəʊsiəʊlɪŋˈɡwɪstɪk; *NAmE* ˌsoʊsioʊ-/ *adj.*

soci·olo·gist /ˌsəʊsiˈɒlədʒɪst; *NAmE* ˌsoʊsiˈɑːl-/ *noun* a person who studies sociology 社會學家

soci·ology /ˌsəʊsiˈɒlədʒi; *NAmE* ˌsoʊsiˈɑːl-/ *noun* [U] the scientific study of the nature and development of society and social behaviour 社會學 ▸ **socio·logic·al** /ˌsəʊsiəˈlɒdʒɪkl; *NAmE* ˌsoʊsiəˈlɑːdʒ-/ *adj.*: *sociological theories* 社會學理論 **socio·logic·al·ly** /-kli/ *adv.*

socio·path /ˈsəʊsiəʊpæθ; *NAmE* ˈsoʊsioʊ-/ *noun* a person who has a mental illness and who behaves in an aggressive or dangerous way towards other people （因心理障礙而有攻擊或傷害他人行為的）反社會者

socio·politic·al /ˌsəʊsiəʊpəˈlɪtɪkl; *NAmE* ˌsoʊsioʊ-/ *adj.* relating to society and politics 社會與政治的

sock 0‑ /sɒk; *NAmE* sɑːk/ *noun, verb*

■ *noun* **1** 0‑ a piece of clothing that is worn over the foot, ankle and lower part of the leg, especially inside a shoe 短襪：*a pair of socks* 一雙短襪 **2** (*informal*) a strong blow, especially with the FIST （尤指用拳頭）猛擊，重擊：*He gave him a sock on the jaw.* 他朝他的下巴猛擊了一拳。

IDM **blow/knock sb's ˈsocks off** (*informal*) to surprise or impress sb very much 使某人萬分驚愕；給某人留下深刻印象 **put a ˈsock in it** (*old-fashioned, BrE, informal*) used to tell sb to stop talking or making a noise （讓某人安靜）住嘴，別出聲 ➲ more at PULL *v.*

■ *verb* **~ sb** (*informal*) to hit sb hard 猛擊；狠打：*She got angry and socked him in the mouth.* 她生氣了，朝他嘴巴

S

一拳揮過去。◇ (*figurative*) *The banks are socking customers with higher charges.* 銀行提高手續費，損害了客戶的利益。

IDM **'sock it to sb** (*informal* or *humorous*) to do sth or tell sb sth in a strong and effective way 直截了當地做某事；強硬地對某人説某事：*Go in there and sock it to 'em!* 你進去，直截了當地告訴他們！

PHR V **,sock sth↔a'way** (*NAmE*) to save money 儲存（錢）；積攢（錢）

socket /'sɒkɪt; *NAmE* 'sɑːkɪt/ *noun* **1** (also **'power point**) (both *BrE*) (*NAmE* **out·let**, **re·cep·tacle**) a device in a wall that you put a plug into in order to connect electrical equipment to the power supply of a building（電源）插座：*a wall socket* 牆壁插座 ➲ picture at PLUG **2** a device on a piece of electrical equipment that you can fix a plug, a light BULB, etc. into （電器上的）插口，插孔，管座：*an aerial socket on the television* 電視機上的天線插孔 **3** a curved hollow space in the surface of sth that another part fits into or moves around in 托座；孔穴；窩；槽；臼：*His eyes bulged in their sockets.* 他的兩眼從眼窩裏鼓出來。

sod /sɒd; *NAmE* sɑːd/ *noun, verb*

■ ***noun*** **1** (*BrE, taboo, slang*) used to refer to a person, especially a man, that you are annoyed with or think is unpleasant （指討厭的人，尤指男人）討厭鬼：*You stupid sod!* 你這個討厭的蠢貨！ **2** (*BrE, taboo, slang*) used with an adjective to refer to a person, especially a man （與形容詞連用，指人，尤指男人）傢伙：*The poor old sod got the sack yesterday.* 那位可憐的老兄昨天給解雇了。◇ *You lucky sod!* 你小子好福氣呀！ **HELP** You can use words like **man**, **boy**, **devil** or **thing** instead. 也可用 man、boy、devil 或 thing 等詞代替。 **3** (*BrE, taboo, slang*) a thing that is difficult or causes problems 難辦的事；惹麻煩的事：*It was a real sod of a job.* 這活兒真是棘手。 **4** [usually sing.] (*formal* or *literary*) a layer of earth with grass growing on it; a piece of this that has been removed 長草的土層；（移植的）草皮：*under the sod* (= in your grave) 入土

■ ***verb*** (**-dd-**) **~ sth** (*BrE, taboo, slang*) (only used in orders 僅用於命令) a swear word that many people find offensive, used when sb is annoyed about sth or to show that they do not care about sth （表示煩惱或不在乎）去他媽的：*Sod this car! It's always breaking down.* 這輛車他媽的老出毛病。◇ *Oh, sod it! I'm not doing any more.* 哼，去他媽的！我不幹了。 **IDM** see LARK *n.*

PHR V **,sod 'off** (*BrE, taboo, slang*) (usually used in orders 通常用於命令) to go away 滾；滾蛋：*Sod off, the pair of you!* 你們倆，都給我滾！

soda /'səʊdə; *NAmE* 'soʊdə/ *noun* **1** [U, C] = SODA WATER：*a Scotch and soda* 一杯加汽水的蘇格蘭威士忌 **2** (also *old-fashioned* **'soda pop**) (both *NAmE*) [U, C] a sweet FIZZY drink (= a drink with bubbles) made with soda water, fruit flavour and sometimes ice cream 蘇打汽水（加果味，有時加入冰淇淋）：*He had an ice-cream soda.* 他喝了一杯冰淇淋果味汽水。 **3** [U] a chemical substance in common use that is a COMPOUND of SODIUM 蘇打；純鹼；無水碳酸鈉：***baking/washing soda*** 小蘇打；洗滌鹼 ➲ see also CAUSTIC SODA, SODIUM BICARBONATE, SODIUM CARBONATE

'soda bread *noun* [U] bread that rises because of SODIUM BICARBONATE that is added instead of YEAST (popular in Ireland) 蘇打麪包（愛爾蘭人常吃）

'soda fountain *noun* (*NAmE*) **1** (*BrE* **'soda siphon**) a bottle containing soda water or another drink, with a device that you press to pour the drink and put bubbles into it （壓杆式）蘇打水瓶，汽水瓶 **2** (*old-fashioned*) a type of bar where you can buy sodas to drink, ICE CREAMS, etc. 冷飲櫃枱；冷飲部

,sod 'all *noun* [U] (*BrE, taboo, slang*) a phrase that some people find offensive, used to mean 'none at all' or 'nothing at all' 他媽的一個也沒有

'soda pop *noun* (*old-fashioned*) = SODA (2)

'soda siphon (*BrE*) (*NAmE* **'soda fountain**) *noun* a bottle containing soda water or another drink, with a device that you press to pour the drink and put bubbles into it （壓桿式）蘇打水瓶，汽水瓶

'soda water (also **soda**) *noun* **1** [U] FIZZY water (= water with bubbles) used as a drink on its own or to mix with alcoholic drinks or fruit juice (originally made with SODIUM BICARBONATE) 汽水；蘇打水 **2** [C] a glass of soda water 一杯汽水

sod·den /'sɒdn; *NAmE* 'sɑːdn/ *adj.* **1** extremely wet 濕透的；濕漉漉的 **SYN** **soaked**：*sodden grass* 濕漉漉的草 **2 -sodden** extremely wet with the thing mentioned 被…濕透的；浸透…的；飽含…的：*a rain-sodden jacket* 雨水淋透的夾克

sod·ding /'sɒdɪŋ; *NAmE* 'sɑːd-/ *adj.* [only before noun] (*BrE, taboo, slang*) a swear word that many people find offensive, used to emphasize a comment or an angry statement （用以加強語氣）：*I couldn't understand a sodding thing!* 我他媽的一點兒都搞不懂！

so·dium /'səʊdiəm; *NAmE* 'soʊ-/ *noun* [U] (*symb.* **Na**) a chemical element. Sodium is a soft silver-white metal that is found naturally only in COMPOUNDS, such as salt. 鈉

,sodium bi'carbonate (also **bi,carbonate of 'soda**, **'baking soda**) (also *informal* **bi·carb**) *noun* [U] (*symb.* **$NaHCO_3$**) a chemical in the form of a white powder that dissolves and is used in baking to make cakes, etc. rise and become light, and in making FIZZY drinks and some medicines 碳酸氫鈉；小蘇打

sodium carbonate /,səʊdiəm 'kɑːbənət; *NAmE* ,soʊdiəm 'kɑːrbənət/ (also **'washing soda**) *noun* [U] (*symb.* **Na_2CO_3**) a chemical in the form of white CRYSTALS or powder that dissolves and is used in making glass, soap and paper, and for making water soft 碳酸鈉

,sodium 'chloride *noun* [U] (*symb.* **NaCl**) common salt (a chemical made up of SODIUM and CHLORINE) 氯化鈉；食鹽

Sodom and Gom·or·rah /,sɒdəm ən gə'mɒrə; *NAmE* ,sɑːdəm ən gə'mɔːrə/ *noun* a place that is full of people behaving in a sexually immoral way 淫蕩的地方；罪惡之城：*The village had a reputation as a latter-day Sodom and Gomorrah.* 這個村子曾經被稱為現代版的邪惡之城。 **ORIGIN** From the names of two cities in the Bible which were destroyed by God to punish the people for their sexually immoral behaviour. 源自《聖經》中兩座城所多瑪和蛾摩拉的名稱，上帝為懲罰市民的淫蕩行為而將其毀滅。

sod·om·ite /'sɒdəmaɪt; *NAmE* 'sɑːd-/ *noun* (*old-fashioned, formal*) a person who practises sodomy 雞姦者

sod·om·ize (*BrE* also **-ise**) /'sɒdəmaɪz; *NAmE* 'sɑːd-/ *verb* **~ sb** (*disapproving*) to have ANAL sex with sb 雞姦

sod·omy /'sɒdəmi; *NAmE* 'sɑːd-/ *noun* [U] a sexual act in which a man puts his PENIS in sb's, especially another man's, ANUS 雞姦

,Sod's 'Law *noun* [U] (*BrE, humorous*) the tendency for things to happen in just the way that you do not want, and in a way that is not useful 事與願違的傾向，造物弄人法則（指發生的事情常和人的願望恰恰相反）：*We always play better when we are not being recorded—but that's Sod's Law, isn't it?* 我們總是不錄音的時候演奏得好些，真是應了那句老話，越該做好的時候越做不好，是不是？◇ *It was Sod's Law—the only day he could manage was the day I couldn't miss work.* 真是天不遂人願，他只有那天抽得出時間，偏偏我上班離不開。

sofa /'səʊfə; *NAmE* 'soʊfə/ *noun* a long comfortable seat with a back and arms, for two or more people to sit on 長沙發 **SYN** **settee, couch** ➲ **VISUAL VOCAB** page V21

'sofa bed *noun* a sofa that can be folded out to form a bed （可打開變成牀的）兩用沙發，沙發牀 ➲ **VISUAL VOCAB** page V23

soft 0-w /sɒft; *NAmE* sɔːft/ *adj.* (**soft·er**, **soft·est**)

▸ **NOT HARD** 不硬 **1** 0-w changing shape easily when pressed; not stiff or firm 軟的；柔軟的：*soft margarine* 軟人造黃油 ◇ *soft feather pillows* 柔軟的羽毛枕頭 ◇ *The grass was soft and springy.* 草柔軟而有彈性。 **2** 0-w less hard than average 硬度較低的；較軟的：*soft rocks such*

S

as limestone 諸如石灰岩之類的軟岩石 ◇ *soft cheeses* 軟奶酪 **OPP hard**

▸ **NOT ROUGH** 不粗糙 **3** smooth and pleasant to touch 柔滑的；細滑的；細膩的：*soft skin* 柔滑的皮膚 **OPP rough**

▸ **WITHOUT ANGLES/EDGES** 無稜角 **4** not having sharp angles or hard edges 無稜角的；輪廓不鮮明的；線條柔和的：*This season's fashions focus on warm tones and soft lines.* 本季時裝主要流行暖色調和柔和線條。◇ *The moon's pale light cast soft shadows.* 淡淡的月光投下柔和的暗影。

▸ **LIGHT/COLOURS** 光線；色彩 **5** [usually before noun] not too bright, in a way that is pleasant and relaxing to the eyes 柔和的；悅目的：*a soft pink* 柔和的粉紅色 ◇ *the soft glow of candlelight* 柔和的燭光 **OPP harsh**

▸ **RAIN/WIND** 風雨 **6** not strong or violent 不強烈的；小的；和緩的 **SYN light**：*A soft breeze rustled the trees.* 微風吹拂，樹葉颯颯作響。

▸ **SOUNDS** 聲音 **7** not loud, and usually pleasant and gentle 輕的；輕柔的；柔和悅耳的 **SYN quiet**：*soft background music* 輕柔的背景音樂 ◇ *a soft voice* 柔和悅耳的嗓音

▸ **SYMPATHETIC** 同情 **8** kind and sympathetic; easily affected by other people's suffering 有同情心的；仁厚的；心腸軟的：*Julia's soft heart was touched by his grief.* 朱莉婭心腸軟，見他悲傷動了惻隱之心。**OPP hard**

▸ **NOT STRICT** 不嚴厲 **9** (usually *disapproving*) not strict or severe; not strict or severe enough 不（夠）嚴厲的；態度偏軟的；（對…）心慈手軟的 **SYN lenient**：**~ (on sb/sth)** *The government is not becoming soft on crime.* 政府對犯罪行為並非日漸手軟。◇ **~ (with sb)** *If you're too soft with these kids they'll never respect you.* 你要是太遷就這些孩子，他們永遠不會尊敬你。**OPP tough**

▸ **CRAZY** 失去理智 **10** (*informal, disapproving*) stupid or crazy 愚蠢的；沒頭腦的；腦子發昏的：*He must be going soft in the head.* 他準是腦子出毛病了。

▸ **NOT BRAVE/TOUGH ENOUGH** 不夠勇敢／頑強 **11** (*informal, disapproving*) not brave enough; wanting to be safe and comfortable 畏首畏尾的；不夠潑辣的；但求安穩的：*Stay in a hotel? Don't be so soft. I want to camp out under the stars.* 住旅館？別那麼貪圖安逸了。我想頂着星星在野外過夜。

▸ **TOO EASY** 太容易 **12** (*disapproving*) not involving much work; too easy and comfortable 輕鬆的；安逸的：*They had got too used to the soft life at home.* 他們實在是過慣了家裏的安逸生活。**OPP hard**

▸ **WATER** 水 **13** not containing mineral salts and therefore good for washing 軟性的（無礦鹽因而適用於洗滌）：*You won't need much soap—the water here is very soft.* 你不必多用肥皂，這兒的水很軟。**OPP hard**

▸ **CONSONANTS** 輔音 **14** (*phonetics* 語音) not sounding hard, for example 'c' in 'city' and 'g' in 'general' 發軟音的（如 city 中 c 字母和 general 中 g 字母的發音）**OPP hard**

▸ **soft·ness** *noun* [U, sing.]：*the softness of her skin* 她皮膚的柔滑 ◇ *the softness of the water* 水的軟性 ➲ see also SOFTLY

IDM have a soft 'spot for sb/sth (*informal*) to like sb/sth 喜歡某人（或某物）：*She's always had a soft spot for you.* 她一直喜歡你。➲ more at OPTION, TOUCH *n.*

soft·ball /ˈsɒftbɔːl; *NAmE* ˈsɔːft-/ *noun* **1** [U] a game similar to BASEBALL but played on a smaller field with a larger, softer ball 壘球運動 **2** [C] the ball used in softball 壘球

ˌsoft-ˈboiled *adj.* (of eggs 蛋) boiled for a short time so that the YOLK is still soft or liquid 煮得嫩的 ➲ compare HARD-BOILED (1)

ˌsoft ˈcentre *noun* (*BrE*) **1** [usually pl.] a chocolate with a soft mixture inside 軟夾心巧克力 **2** if sb has a **soft centre**, they are not really as severe as they seem（表面嚴厲）心腸軟 ▸ **ˌsoft-ˈcentered** *adj.*

ˈsoft-core *adj.* [usually before noun] showing or describing sexual activity without being too detailed or shocking 軟性色情的；（性描寫等）隱晦的，含蓄的 ➲ compare HARD-CORE (2)

ˌsoft ˈdrink *noun* a cold drink that does not contain alcohol 軟飲料（不含酒精）➲ compare HARD *adj.* (11)

ˌsoft ˈdrug *noun* an illegal drug, such as CANNABIS, that some people take for pleasure, that is not considered very harmful or likely to cause ADDICTION 軟毒品（危害不很大或不易成癮，如大麻）➲ compare HARD DRUG

soft·en /ˈsɒfn; *NAmE* ˈsɔːfn/ *verb* **1** [I, T] to become, or to make sth softer（使）變軟，軟化：*Fry the onions until they soften.* 把洋蔥炒軟。◇ **~ sth** *a lotion to soften the skin* 潤膚露 ◇ *Linseed oil will soften stiff leather.* 亞麻籽油可軟化僵硬的皮革。**2** [I, T] **~ (sth)** to become or to make sth less bright, rough or strong（使）柔和，和緩：*Trees soften the outline of the house.* 樹木使房子的輪廓顯得柔和。**3** [I, T] to become or to make sb/sth more sympathetic and less severe or critical（使）態度緩和，變溫和，變寬厚：*She felt herself softening towards him.* 她感覺自己對他逐漸溫和起來。◇ *His face softened as he looked at his son.* 他看着兒子，緊繃的面孔鬆弛下來。◇ **~ sb/sth** *She softened her tone a little.* 她稍稍緩和了一下語氣。**4** [T] **~ sth** to reduce the force or the unpleasant effects of sth 減輕；減緩；削弱 **SYN cushion**：*Airbags are designed to soften the impact of a car crash.* 氣囊用來減輕汽車碰撞的衝擊力。**IDM** see BLOW *n.*

PHR V ˌsoften sb↔ˈup (*informal*) **1** to try to persuade sb to do sth for you by being very nice to them before you ask them 打動；誘導；拉攏：*Potential customers are softened up with free gifts before the sales talk.* 談生意之前，先送給潛在的客戶一些贈品，以聯絡感情。**2** to make an enemy weaker and easier to attack 削弱，瓦解（敵人力量）

soft·en·er /ˈsɒfnə(r); *NAmE* ˈsɔːf-/ *noun* **1** [C] a device that is used with chemicals to make hard water soft（硬水）軟化器：*a water softener* 硬水軟化器 **2** [U, C] a substance that you add when washing clothes to make them feel soft（衣物的）柔順劑

ˌsoft ˈerror *noun* (*computing* 計) an error or fault that makes a program or OPERATING SYSTEM stop working, but that can often be corrected by switching the computer off then on again 軟差錯（可通過關機重啟糾正）

ˌsoft ˈfocus *noun* [U] a method of producing a photograph so that the edges of the image are not clear, in order to make it look more romantic and attractive 軟聚焦（攝影技巧）

ˌsoft ˈfruit *noun* [C, U] small fruits without large seeds or hard skin, such as STRAWBERRIES or CURRANTS 無核小果（如草莓或醋栗）➲ **VISUAL VOCAB** page V30

ˌsoft ˈfurnishings *noun* [pl.] (*BrE*) CUSHIONS, curtains and other things made from cloth that are found in a house 室內織物陳設（如靠墊、窗簾等）

ˈsoft goods *noun* [pl.] **1** things that are made of cloth, such as clothes and curtains 紡織品，布製品（如服裝、窗簾等）**2** (*business* 商) any type of cloth 布料 **SYN textiles**

ˌsoft-ˈhearted *adj.* kind, sympathetic and emotional 有同情心的；心腸軟的；熱心腸的 **SYN kind-hearted** **OPP hard-hearted**

softie (also **softy**) /ˈsɒfti; *NAmE* ˈsɔːfti/ *noun* (*pl.* **-ies**) (*informal*) a kind, sympathetic or emotional person 有同情心的人；心腸軟的人；熱心腸的人：*There's no need to be afraid of him—he's a big softie.* 沒必要害怕他，他心特好。

soft·ly /ˈsɒftli; *NAmE* ˈsɔːftli/ *adv.* in a soft way 輕輕地；輕柔地；溫和地；柔和地：*She closed the door softly behind her.* 她隨手輕輕關上門。◇ *'I missed you,' he said softly.* "我想你了。"他柔聲說道。◇ *The room was softly lit by a lamp.* 屋裏點着一盞燈，光線很柔和。◇ *a softly tailored suit* 一套裁剪線條很柔和的西裝

ˌsoftly-ˈsoftly *adj.* (*BrE, informal*) (of a way of doing sth 做事方式) careful and patient, with no sudden actions 細緻耐心的：*The police used a* ***softly-softly approach*** *with him.* 警方對他採取了耐心細緻的方法。

ˌsoftly-ˈspoken *adj.* = SOFT-SPOKEN

ˈsoft pedal *noun* (*music* 音) a PEDAL on a piano that is pressed to make the sound quieter（鋼琴的）弱音踏板

ˌsoft-ˈpedal *verb* (-ll-, *US* also -l-) [T, I] **~ (on) sth** (*informal*) to treat sth as less serious or important than it really is 低調處理；降低…的調門；對…輕描淡寫： *Television has been accused of soft-pedalling bad news.* 有人指責電視對壞消息輕描淡寫。

ˌsoft ˈporn *noun* [U] films/movies, books, pictures, etc. that show or describe sexual activity in a way that is sexually exciting but not in a very detailed or violent way 軟色情作品（指非赤裸裸描寫性行為的電影、書籍、圖畫等） ➲ compare HARD PORN

ˌsoft ˈsell *noun* [sing.] a method of selling that involves persuading sb to buy sth rather than using pressure or aggressive methods 軟推銷；勸誘推銷 ➲ compare HARD SELL

ˈsoft-shoe *noun, verb*

■ ***noun*** [U] a type of dance like TAP, performed with soft shoes which do not make a noise 軟鞋踢踏舞： *a soft-shoe shuffle* 軟鞋曳步舞

■ ***verb*** **1** [I] to perform a soft-shoe dance 跳軟鞋踢踏舞 **2** [I] **+ adv./prep.** to move somewhere very quietly, without attracting attention 躡手躡腳地走；悄悄地移動

ˌsoft ˈshoulder *noun* (*NAmE*) a strip of ground with a soft surface at the edge of a road （公路邊未鋪砌的）軟質路肩 ➲ compare VERGE

ˌsoft-ˈsoap *verb* **~ sb** (*informal*) to say nice things to sb in order to persuade them to do sth（為讓某人做某事）說好聽的，奉承，灌迷魂湯；勸誘 ▸ **ˌsoft ˈsoap** *noun* [U]

ˌsoft-ˈspoken (also *less frequent* **ˌsoftly-ˈspoken**) *adj.* having a gentle and quiet voice 低聲細氣的

ˌsoft ˈtarget *noun* a person or thing that it is very easy to attack 易受攻擊的人（或事物）；軟目標

ˌsoft ˈtissue *noun* [U, C] (*anatomy* 解) the parts of the body that are not bone, for example the skin and muscles（皮膚、肌肉等）軟組織

ˈsoft top *noun* a type of car that has a soft roof that can be folded down or removed; the roof of such a car 軟頂篷汽車；（汽車的）軟頂篷 ➲ see also CONVERTIBLE

ˌsoft ˈtoy (*BrE*) (also **ˌstuffed ˈanimal** *NAmE, BrE*) *noun* a toy in the shape of an animal, made of cloth and filled with a soft substance（動物造型的）軟體玩具，布絨玩具 ➲ **VISUAL VOCAB** page V37

soft·ware 0-w /ˈsɒftweə(r); *NAmE* ˈsɔːftwer/ *noun* [U] the programs, etc. used to operate a computer 軟件；軟體： ***application/system software*** 應用／系統軟件 ◇ ***design/educational/music-sharing, etc. software*** 設計、教育、音樂共享等軟件 ◇ *to* ***install/run*** *a piece of* ***software*** 安裝／運行一個軟件 ◇ *Will the* ***software run*** *on my machine?* 這個軟件在我的機器上能用嗎？ ➲ compare HARDWARE (1)

ˈsoftware engineer *noun* a person who writes computer programs 軟件工程師；軟體工程師

ˈsoftware package *noun* (*computing* 計) = PACKAGE *n.* (4)

soft·wood /ˈsɒftwʊd; *NAmE* ˈsɔːft-/ *noun* [U, C] wood from trees such as PINE, that is cheap to produce and can be cut easily 軟質木，軟木（如松木） ➲ compare HARDWOOD

softy = SOFTIE

soggy /ˈsɒɡi; *NAmE* ˈsɑːɡi/ *adj.* (**sog·gier**, **sog·gi·est**) wet and soft, usually in a way that is unpleasant 濕而軟的；潮濕的；受潮的： *We squelched over the soggy ground.* 我們咕唧咕唧地走過泥濘的土地。 ◇ *soggy bread* 受潮的麵包

soh (also **so**) /səʊ; *NAmE* soʊ/ (also **sol**) *noun* (*music* 音) the fifth note of a MAJOR SCALE 大調音階的第 5 音

soi-disant /ˌswɑː diːˈzɒ̃; *NAmE* -ˈzɑ̃ː/ *adj.* [only before noun] (from *French*) used to show sb's description of himself/herself, usually when you do not agree with it 自詡的；自稱的；自命的： *a soi-disant novelist* 自封的小說家

soi·gnée /ˈswɑːnjeɪ; *NAmE* swɑːnˈjeɪ/ *adj.* (from *French*, *formal*) (of a woman 女性) elegant; carefully and neatly dressed 優雅的；衣着講究的；穿戴整潔的

soil 0-w /sɔɪl/ *noun, verb*

■ ***noun*** [U, C] **1** 0-w the top layer of the earth in which plants, trees, etc. grow 土壤： ***poor/dry/acid/sandy/fertile, etc. soil*** 貧瘠、乾旱、酸性、沙質、肥沃等的土壤 ◇ *the study of rocks and soils* 對岩石和土壤的研究 ◇ *soil erosion* 土壤侵蝕 **2** (*literary*) a country; an area of land 國土；領土；土地： *It was the first time I had set foot on African soil.* 那是我第一次踏足非洲大地。

■ ***verb*** [often passive] **~ sth** (*formal*) to make sth dirty 弄髒： *soiled linen* 髒了的日用織品 ◇ (*figurative*) *I don't want you* ***soiling your hands*** *with this sort of work* (= doing sth unpleasant or wrong). 我不希望你幹這種事，免得髒了你的手。 ➲ see also SHOP-SOILED

Synonyms 同義詞辨析

soil

mud • dust • clay • land • earth • dirt • ground

These are all words for the top layer of the earth in which plants grow. 以上各詞均指土壤。

soil the top layer of the earth in which plants grow 指土壤： *Plant the seedlings in damp soil.* 把幼苗種在濕潤的土壤裏。

mud wet soil that is soft and sticky 指泥、淤泥、泥漿： *The car wheels got stuck in the mud.* 汽車輪子陷到泥裏去了。

dust a fine powder that consists of very small pieces of rock, earth, etc. 指沙石、沙土、塵土： *A cloud of dust rose as the truck set off.* 卡車起動時揚起一片灰塵。

clay a type of heavy sticky soil that becomes hard when it is baked and is used to make things such as pots and bricks 指黏土、陶土： *The tiles are made of clay.* 這些磚是用陶土製成的。

land an area of ground, especially of a particular type 尤指某種類型的地帶、土地： *an area of rich, fertile land* 富饒肥沃的地域

earth the substance that plants grow in 指土、泥、泥土 **NOTE** **Earth** is often used about the soil found in gardens or used for gardening. * earth 常用以指花園裏或種花用的泥土： *She put some earth into the pot.* 她在花盆裏放了一些泥土。

dirt (*especially NAmE*) soil, especially loose soil 指泥土，尤指鬆土、散土： *Pack the dirt firmly around the plants.* 將植物周圍的土培實。

ground an area of soil 指土地： *The car got stuck in the muddy ground.* 汽車陷到泥地裏了。 ◇ *They drove across miles of rough, stony ground.* 他們駛過數英里崎嶇不平、多石的土地。 **NOTE** **Ground** is not used for loose soil. * ground 不用以指鬆土、散土： ~~*a handful of dry ground*~~

PATTERNS

- **good/rich** soil/land/earth
- **fertile/infertile** soil/land/ground
- to **dig** the soil/mud/clay/land/earth/ground
- to **cultivate** the soil/land/ground

ˈsoil science *noun* [U] the study of soil, for example the study of its structure or characteristics 土壤學（研究土壤結構或特性等）

soirée /ˈswɑːreɪ; *NAmE* swɑːˈreɪ/ *noun* (from *French*, *formal*) a formal party in the evening, especially at sb's home（尤指在家裏舉行的）社交晚會

so·journ /ˈsɒdʒən; *NAmE* ˈsoʊdʒɜːrn/ *noun* (*literary*) a temporary stay in a place away from your home 逗留；暫住；旅居 ▸ **so·journ** *verb* [I] **+ adv./prep.**

sol /sɒl; *NAmE* soʊl/ *noun* = SOH

sol·ace /ˈsɒləs; *NAmE* ˈsɑːləs/ *noun* [U, sing.] (*formal*) a feeling of emotional comfort when you are sad or

S

disappointed; a person or thing that makes you feel better or happier when you are sad or disappointed 安慰；慰藉；給以安慰的人（或事物） SYN **comfort**: *He sought solace in the whisky bottle.* 他借酒澆愁。◇ *She turned to Rob for solace.* 她到羅布那兒尋求慰藉。◇ *His grandchildren were a solace in his old age.* 他晚年從孫兒們身上得到安慰。 ▸ **so·lace** *verb*: **~ sb** (*literary*) *She smiled, as though solaced by the memory.* 她笑了，彷彿在往事的回憶中得到了安慰。

solar /ˈsəʊlə(r); *NAmE* ˈsoʊ-/ *adj.* [only before noun] **1** of or connected with the sun 太陽的：*solar radiation* 太陽輻射 ◇ *the solar cycle* 太陽活動週 **2** using the sun's energy 太陽能的：***solar power/heating*** 太陽能；太陽能加熱 ➲ COLLOCATIONS at ENVIRONMENT ➲ VISUAL VOCAB page V8

ˌsolar ˈcell *noun* a device that converts light and heat energy from the sun into electricity 太陽能電池

ˈsolar cooker *noun* (*IndE*) a container for cooking food that uses heat from the sun 太陽能鍋

sol·ar·ium /səˈleəriəm; *NAmE* -ˈler-/ *noun* a room whose walls are mainly made of glass, or which has special lamps, where people go to get a SUNTAN (= make their skin go brown) using light from the sun or artificial light 日光浴室；日光室

ˌsolar ˈpanel *noun* a piece of equipment on a roof that uses light and heat energy from the sun to produce hot water and electricity 太陽能電池板 ➲ VISUAL VOCAB page V8

solar plexus /ˌsəʊlə ˈpleksəs; *NAmE* ˌsoʊlər/ *noun* [sing.] **1** (*anatomy* 解) a system of nerves at the base of the stomach 腹腔神經叢 **2** (*informal*) the part of the body at the top of the stomach, below the RIBS 心口：*a painful punch in the solar plexus* 胸口上捱的很疼的一拳

ˈsolar system *noun* **1 the solar system** [sing.] the sun and all the planets that move around it 太陽系 **2** [C] any group of planets that all move around the same star 類太陽系

ˌsolar ˈyear *noun* the time it takes the earth to go around the sun once, approximately 365¼ days 太陽年

sold *past tense, past part.* of SELL

sol·der /ˈsəʊldə(r); ˈsɒldə(r); *NAmE* ˈsɑːdər/ *noun, verb*
■ ***noun*** [U] a mixture of metals that is heated and melted and then used to join metals, wires, etc. together 焊料；焊錫
■ ***verb*** **~ sth (to/onto sth)** | **~ (A and B together)** to join pieces of metal or wire with solder 焊接；焊合

S

ˈsoldering iron *noun* a tool that is heated and used for joining metals and wires by soldering them 烙鐵

sol·dier 🔑 /ˈsəʊldʒə(r); *NAmE* ˈsoʊl-/ *noun, verb*
■ ***noun*** 🔑 a member of an army, especially one who is not an officer 軍人；（尤指）士兵：*soldiers in uniform* 穿軍裝的士兵 ◇ *soldiers on duty* 值勤的士兵 ➲ see also FOOT SOLDIER (1)
■ ***verb***
PHR V **ˌsoldier ˈon** to continue with what you are doing or trying to do, especially when this is difficult or unpleasant 堅持；硬挺着

sol·dier·ing /ˈsəʊldʒərɪŋ; *NAmE* ˈsoʊl-/ *noun* [U] the life or activity of being a soldier 軍旅生活；行伍生涯；當兵

sol·dier·ly /ˈsəʊldʒəli; *NAmE* ˈsoʊldʒərli/ *adj.* typical of a good soldier 有軍人氣質的；英武的

ˌsoldier of ˈfortune *noun* a person who fights for any country or person who will pay them 雇傭兵 SYN **mercenary**

sol·diery /ˈsəʊldʒəri; *NAmE* ˈsoʊl-/ *noun* [U+sing./pl. v.] (*old-fashioned*) a group of soldiers, especially of a particular kind （尤指某種類型的）軍隊，隊伍

ˌsold ˈout *adj.* **1** if a concert, match, etc. is **sold out**, there are no more tickets available for it（音樂會、比賽等）票已售完的，滿場的，滿座的 **2** if a shop/store is **sold out** of a product, it has no more of it left to sell（商品）銷售一空的

sole AW /səʊl; *NAmE* soʊl/ *adj., noun, verb*
■ ***adj.*** [only before noun] **1** only; single 僅有的；唯一的：*the **sole surviving** member of the family* 那一家唯一在世的成員 ◇ *My **sole reason** for coming here was to see you.* 我到這兒唯一的原因就是來看你。◇ *This is the sole means of access to the building.* 這是這棟建築物唯一的入口。**2** belonging to one person or group; not shared 獨佔的；專有的；全權處理的：*She has **sole responsibility** for the project.* 那個項目由她一人負責。◇ *the **sole owner*** 擁有全部產權的物主
■ ***noun*** **1** [C] the bottom surface of the foot 腳掌；腳底（板）：*The hot sand burned the **soles of their feet**.* 灼熱的沙地使他們的腳掌感到火辣辣的。➲ VISUAL VOCAB page V59 **2** [C] the bottom part of a shoe or sock, not including the heel 鞋底；襪底：*leather soles* 皮的鞋底 ➲ VISUAL VOCAB page V64 ➲ compare HEEL *n.* (3) **3 -soled** (in adjectives 構成形容詞) having the type of soles mentioned 有…底的：*rubber-soled shoes* 膠底鞋 **4** [U, C] (*pl.* **sole**) a flat sea fish that is used for food 鰨（可食用比目魚）
■ ***verb*** [usually passive] **~ sth** to repair a shoe by replacing the sole 給（鞋）換底

sol·ecism /ˈsɒlɪsɪzəm; *NAmE* ˈsɑːl-/ *noun* (*formal*) **1** a mistake in the use of language in speech or writing 語言錯誤；語病 **2** an example of bad manners or unacceptable behaviour 失禮；粗俗的舉止（或話語）

sole·ly AW /ˈsəʊlli; *NAmE* ˈsoʊlli/ *adv.* only; not involving sb/sth else 僅；只；唯；單獨地：*She was motivated solely by self-interest.* 她所追求的完全是私利。◇ *Selection is based solely on merit.* 選拔唯賢。◇ *He became solely responsible for the firm.* 他成了公司唯一的負責人。

sol·emn /ˈsɒləm; *NAmE* ˈsɑːləm/ *adj.* **1** (of a person) not happy or smiling 冷峻的；表情嚴肅的 SYN **serious**: *Her face grew solemn.* 她的臉顯得嚴肅起來。◇ *a solemn expression* 冷峻的表情 OPP **cheerful 2** done, said, etc. in a very serious and sincere way 莊嚴的；嚴正的；鄭重的：***a solemn oath/undertaking/vow, etc.*** 莊嚴的誓言、鄭重的承諾、嚴肅的誓約等 **3** (of a religious ceremony or formal occasion 宗教儀式或正式場合) performed in a serious way 莊嚴的；隆重的：*a solemn ritual* 隆重的儀式 ▸ **sol·emn·ly** *adv.*: *He nodded solemnly.* 他鄭重地點了點頭。◇ *She solemnly promised not to say a word to anyone about it.* 她鄭重承諾不向任何人透露一個字。◇ *The choir walked solemnly past.* 唱詩班莊嚴地走過。

so·lem·nity /səˈlemnəti/ *noun* **1** [U] the quality of being solemn 莊嚴；莊重；嚴肅；鄭重：*He was smiling, but his eyes retained a look of solemnity.* 他臉上掛着笑容，但眼神依舊嚴肅。◇ *He was buried with great pomp and solemnity.* 他的葬禮盛大而隆重。**2 solemnities** [pl.] (*formal*) formal things that people do at a serious event or occasion （重大場合的）禮儀，儀式：*to observe the solemnities of the occasion* 遵守這一場合的禮儀

sol·em·nize (*BrE* also **-ise**) /ˈsɒləmnaɪz; *NAmE* ˈsɑːl-/ *verb* **~ sth** (*formal*) to perform a religious ceremony, especially a marriage 舉行（宗教儀式，尤指婚禮）

so·len·oid /ˈsɒlənɔɪd; ˈsəʊl-; *NAmE* ˈsoʊl-; ˈsɑːl-/ *noun* (*physics* 物) a piece of wire, wound into circles, which acts as a MAGNET when carrying an electric current 螺線管（通電時產生磁場）

ˌsol-ˈfa *noun* (also **ˌtonic ˌsol-ˈfa**) (*music* 音) a system of naming the notes of the SCALE, used in teaching singing （歌唱教學的）首調唱名法

so·licit /səˈlɪsɪt/ *verb* **1** [T, I] (*formal*) to ask sb for sth, such as support, money or information; to try to get sth or persuade sb to do sth 索求，請求…給予（援助、錢或信息）；徵求；籌集：**~ sth (from sb)** *They were planning to solicit funds from a number of organizations.* 他們正計劃向一些機構募集資金。◇ **~ sb (for sth)** *Historians and critics are solicited for their opinions.* 向歷史學家和批評家徵求了意見。◇ **~ (for sth)** *to solicit for money* 籌款 ◇ **~ sb to do sth** *Volunteers are being solicited to assist with the project.* 正在徵求志願者來協助該項目。**2** [I, T] **~ (sb)** (of a PROSTITUTE 妓女) to offer to have sex with people in return for money 招徠（嫖客）；拉（客）：*Prostitutes solicited openly in the streets.* 妓女公然在街上拉客。◇ *the crime of soliciting* 拉客賣淫罪 ▸ **so·lici·ta·tion**

/səˌlɪsɪˈteɪʃn/ *noun* [U, C] (*especially NAmE*) ： *the solicitation of money for election funds* 競選資金籌集活動

so·lici·tor /səˈlɪsɪtə(r)/ *noun* **1** (*BrE*) a lawyer who prepares legal documents, for example for the sale of land or buildings, advises people on legal matters, and can speak for them in some courts of law 事務律師；訴狀律師（代擬法律文書、提供法律咨詢等的一般辯護律師）➲ note at LAWYER **2** (*NAmE*) a person whose job is to visit or telephone people and try to sell them sth 推銷員 **3** (*NAmE*) the most senior legal officer of a city, town or government department（城鎮或政府部門負責法律事務的）法務官

Soˌlicitor ˈGeneral *noun* (*pl.* **Solicitors General**) a senior legal officer in Britain or the US, next in rank below the ATTORNEY GENERAL（英國）副檢察長；（美國）司法部副部長

so·lici·tous /səˈlɪsɪtəs/ *adj.* (*formal*) being very concerned for sb and wanting to make sure that they are comfortable, well or happy 操心的；關懷的；關切的 **SYN** **attentive** ▸ **so·lici·tous·ly** *adv.* (*formal*)

so·lici·tude /səˈlɪsɪtjuːd; *NAmE* -tuːd/ *noun* [U] **~ (for sb/sth)** (*formal*) anxious care for sb's comfort, health or happiness 牽掛；關懷；關切： *I was touched by his solicitude for the boy.* 他對孩子的關懷讓我感動。

solid 🔑 /ˈsɒlɪd; *NAmE* ˈsɑːl-/ *adj., noun*

■ ***adj.***

▸ **NOT LIQUID/GAS 非液體／氣體** **1** 🔑 hard or firm; not in the form of a liquid or gas 固體的；堅硬的： *The planet Jupiter may have no solid surface at all.* 木星表面可能根本就不是固體的。◇ *The boat bumped against a solid object.* 船撞到了硬物。◇ *She had refused all solid food.* 所有的固體食物她都不肯吃。◇ *It was so cold that the stream had **frozen solid**.* 天氣很冷，小河凍得結成冰了。◇ *The boiler uses **solid fuel**.* 這個鍋爐燒固體燃料。

▸ **WITHOUT HOLES OR SPACES 無空隙** **2** 🔑 having no holes or spaces inside; not hollow 無空隙的；非中空的；實心的： *They were drilling through solid rock.* 他們正在把實心岩鑽通。◇ *The stores are **packed solid*** (= very full and crowded) *at this time of year.* 每年一到這個時候，商店總是擠得水泄不通。

▸ **STRONG 結實** **3** 🔑 strong and made well 結實的；堅固的；牢固的： *These chains seem fairly solid.* 這些鏈子看着挺結實。

▸ **RELIABLE 可靠** **4** 🔑 that you can rely on; having a strong basis 可靠的；可信賴的；堅實的： *As yet, they have no solid evidence.* 他們至今沒有任何可靠的證據。◇ *This provided a solid foundation for their marriage.* 這為他們的婚姻提供了堅實的基礎。◇ *The Irish team were **solid as a rock** in defence.* 愛爾蘭隊的防守堅如磐石。

▸ **GOOD BUT NOT SPECIAL 不錯** **5** definitely good and steady but perhaps not excellent or special 相當不錯（但談不上出色或獨特）的： *2008 was a year of solid achievement.* * 2008 年是成績卓著的一年。◇ *He's a solid player.* 他是個相當不錯的運動員。

▸ **MATERIAL 材料** **6** 🔑 [only before noun] made completely of the material mentioned (that is, the material is not only on the surface) 純質的；純…的；全…的： *a solid gold bracelet* 純金手鐲

▸ **PERIOD OF TIME 一段時間** **7** (*informal*) without a pause; continuous 連續的；不間斷的；整整的： *The essay represents a solid week's work.* 這篇文章是用整整一星期寫出來的。◇ *It rained for two hours solid this afternoon.* 今天下午連着下了兩個小時的雨。

▸ **COLOUR 色彩** **8** of the colour mentioned and no other colour 純色的；單色的： *One cat is black and white, the other solid black.* 一隻貓是黑白花色的，另一隻貓是純黑色的。

▸ **SHAPE 形狀** **9** (*geometry* 幾何) a shape that is **solid** has length, width and height and is not flat 立體的；立方的： *A cube is a solid figure.* 立方體是一種立體圖形。 ➲ **VISUAL VOCAB** page V71

▸ **IN AGREEMENT 一致** **10** in complete agreement; agreed on by everyone 一致的；意見統一的： *The strike was solid, supported by all the members.* 這次罷工是統一行動，得到所有成員的支持。➲ see also ROCK SOLID

■ ***noun***

▸ **NOT LIQUID/GAS 非液體／氣體** **1** 🔑 a substance or an object that is solid, not a liquid or a gas 固體： *liquids and solids* 液體與固體 ◇ *The baby is not yet on solids* (= eating solid food). 嬰兒還不能吃固體食物。

▸ **SHAPE 形狀** **2** (*geometry* 幾何) a shape which has length, width and height, such as a CUBE 立體圖形

soli·dar·ity /ˌsɒlɪˈdærəti; *NAmE* ˌsɑːl-/ *noun* [U] support by one person or group of people for another because they share feelings, opinions, aims, etc. 團結；齊心協力；同心同德；相互支持： *community solidarity* 社區團結 ◇ **~ with sb** *to **express/show solidarity** with sb* 表示／表明支持某人 ◇ *Demonstrations were held as **a gesture of solidarity** with the hunger strikers.* 人們舉行示威遊行，以表示對絕食抗議者的支持。

so·lid·ify /səˈlɪdɪfaɪ/ *verb* (**so·lidi·fies**, **so·lidi·fy·ing**, **so·lidi·fied**, **so·lidi·fied**) **1** [I, T] **~ (into sth)** | **~ (sth)** to become solid; to make sth solid（使）凝固，變硬，變得結實： *The mixture will solidify into toffee.* 這種混合物凝固後就成了太妃糖。◇ *solidified lava* 固結熔岩 **2** [I, T] (*formal*) (of ideas, etc. 觀念等) to become or to make sth become more definite and less likely to change（使）變得堅定，變得穩固，鞏固： **~ (into sth)** *Vague objections to the system solidified into firm opposition.* 先前對這一制度不大明朗的反對演變成了堅決的抵制。◇ **~ sth** *They solidified their position as Britain's top band.* 他們鞏固了自己作為英國頂尖樂隊的地位。▸ **so·lidi·fi·ca·tion** /səˌlɪdɪfɪˈkeɪʃn/ *noun* [U]

so·lid·ity /səˈlɪdəti/ *noun* [U] the quality or state of being solid 固態；堅固性；可靠性： *the strength and solidity of Romanesque architecture* 羅馬式建築堅固結實的特性 ◇ *Her writings have extraordinary depth and solidity.* 她寫的東西立意極深，內容特別充實。◇ *the solidity of his support for his staff* 他對自己的工作班子的有力支持

sol·id·ly /ˈsɒlɪdli; *NAmE* ˈsɑːl-/ *adv.* **1** in a firm and strong way 堅固地；結實地；牢固地： *a large, solidly-built house* 建造得堅固的大房子 ◇ *He stood solidly in my path.* 他把我的路擋得死死的。 **2** continuously; without stopping 連續地；不間斷地；整整地： *It rained solidly for three hours.* 雨下了整整三個小時。 **3** agreeing with or supporting sb/sth completely 一致地；完全支持： *The state is solidly Republican.* 這個州是共和黨的天下。

ˌsolid-ˈstate *adj.* (*technical* 術語) using or containing solid SEMICONDUCTORS 固態半導體的；固體的： *a solid-state radio* 固態半導體收音機

so·lilo·quy /səˈlɪləkwi/ *noun* [C, U] (*pl.* **-ies**) a speech in a play in which a character, who is alone on the stage, speaks his or her thoughts; the act of speaking thoughts in this way 獨白（的台詞）；獨白 **SYN** **monologue**： *Hamlet's famous soliloquy, 'To be or not to be …'* 哈姆雷特那段“生存還是毀滅…”的著名獨白 ◇ *the playwright's use of soliloquy* 這位劇作家對於獨白的運用 ▸ **so·lilo·quize, -ise** /səˈlɪləkwaɪz/ *verb* [I]

sol·ip·sism /ˈsɒlɪpsɪzəm; *NAmE* ˈsɑːl-/ *noun* [U] (*philosophy* 哲) the theory that only the SELF exists or can be known 唯我論 ▸ **sol·ip·sis·tic** /ˌsɒlɪpˈsɪstɪk; *NAmE* ˌsɑːl-/ *adj.*

soli·taire /ˌsɒlɪˈteə(r); *NAmE* ˈsɑːləter/ *noun* **1** [U] (*BrE*) a game for one person in which you remove pieces from their places on a special board after moving other pieces over them. The aim is to finish with only one piece left on the board. 單人跳棋 **2** (*NAmE*) (*BrE* **pa·tience**) [U] a card game for only one player 單人紙牌遊戲 **3** [C] a single PRECIOUS STONE; a piece of jewellery with a single precious stone in it 獨粒寶石；獨粒寶石首飾

soli·tary /ˈsɒlətri; *NAmE* ˈsɑːləteri/ *adj., noun*

■ ***adj.*** **1** [usually before noun] done alone; without other people 獨自的；單獨的： *She enjoys long solitary walks.* 她喜歡獨自長距離散步。◇ *He led a solitary life.* 他過着獨居生活。 **2** (of a person or an animal 人或動物) enjoying being alone; frequently spending time alone 喜歡（或慣於）獨處的： *He was a solitary child.* 他是一個孤僻的孩子。◇ *Tigers are solitary animals.* 虎是獨居動物。 **3** (of a person, thing or place 人、物或處所) alone, with no other people or things around 單個的；孤單的；孤零零的 **SYN** **single**： *a solitary farm* 孤然孑立的農場 ◇ *A solitary light burned dimly in the hall.* 大廳裏點着

S

一盞孤燈，發出昏暗的光。 **4** [usually before noun] (especially in negative sentences and questions 尤用於否定句和疑問句) only one 唯一的；僅有的 SYN **single**：*There was not a solitary shred of evidence* (= none at all). 一丁點證據都沒有。 ▸ **soli·tari·ness** *noun* [U]

■ ***noun*** (*pl.* **-ies**) **1** [U] (*informal*) = SOLITARY CONFINEMENT **2** [C] (*formal*) a person who chooses to live alone 獨居者；隱士

,solitary con'finement (also *informal* **soli·tary**) *noun* [U] a punishment in which a prisoner is kept alone in a separate cell 單獨監禁；單獨禁閉：*to be in solitary confinement* 被單獨監禁

soli·tude /'sɒlɪtjuːd; *NAmE* 'sɑːlətuːd/ *noun* [U] the state of being alone, especially when you find this pleasant 獨處；獨居 SYN **privacy**：*She longed for peace and solitude.* 她渴望安寧，渴望獨享清靜。

solo /'səʊləʊ; *NAmE* 'soʊloʊ/ *adj., noun*

■ ***adj.*** [only before noun] **1** done by one person alone, without anyone helping them 獨自的；單獨的：*his first solo flight* 他的首次單飛 ◇ *a solo effort* 一人之力 **2** connected with or played as a musical solo 獨唱的；獨奏的：*a solo artist* (= for example a singer who sings on their own, not as part of a group) 獨唱歌手 ◇ *a piece for solo violin* 小提琴獨奏曲 ▸ **solo** *adv.*：*She wanted to fly solo across the Atlantic.* 她想獨自一人駕機飛越大西洋。◇ *After three years with the band he decided to* ***go solo.*** 在樂隊裏待了三年之後，他決定單飛。

■ ***noun*** (*pl.* **-os**) **1** a piece of music, dance or entertainment performed by only one person 獨唱；獨奏；獨舞；單人表演：*a guitar solo* 吉他獨奏 ➲ compare DUET **2** a flight in which the pilot flies alone without an INSTRUCTOR (= teacher) 單飛

solo·ist /'səʊləʊɪst; *NAmE* 'soʊloʊ-/ *noun* a person who plays an instrument or performs alone 獨奏者；獨唱者；單獨表演者

Solo·mon /'sɒləmən; *NAmE* 'sɑːl-/ *noun* used to talk about a very wise person 智者；聰明人：*In this job you need to exhibit the wisdom of Solomon.* 做這份工作需要表現出所羅門王一樣的才智。 ORIGIN From Solomon in the Bible, a king of Israel who was famous for being wise. 源自《聖經》中以智慧著稱的以色列王所羅門。

sol·stice /'sɒlstɪs; *NAmE* 'sɑːlstəs/ *noun* either of the two times of the year at which the sun reaches its highest or lowest point in the sky at midday, marked by the longest and shortest days 至（點）；（夏或冬）至：*the* ***summer/winter solstice*** 夏至；冬至 ➲ VISUAL VOCAB page V72

S

sol·uble /'sɒljəbl; *NAmE* 'sɑːl-/ *adj.* **1 ~ (in sth)** that can be dissolved in a liquid 可溶的：*soluble aspirin* 可溶性阿司匹林 ◇ *Glucose is soluble in water.* 葡萄糖可溶於水。 **2** (*formal*) (of a problem 問題) that can be solved 可解決的；可解的 OPP **insoluble** ▸ **solu·bil·ity** /,sɒlju'bɪləti; *NAmE* ,sɑːl-/ *noun* [U]

so·lu·tion 🔑 /sə'luːʃn/ *noun*

1 🔑 [C] **~ (to sth)** a way of solving a problem or dealing with a difficult situation 解決辦法；處理手段 SYN **answer**：*Attempts to* ***find a solution*** *have failed.* 試圖找到解決辦法的種種努力全都失敗了。◇ *There's no simple solution to this problem.* 這個問題沒有簡單的解決辦法。 ◇ *Do you have a better solution?* 你有更好的解決辦法嗎？ **2** 🔑 [C] **~ (to sth)** an answer to a PUZZLE or to a problem in mathematics 答案；解；謎底：*The solution to last week's quiz is on page 81.* 上星期測驗的答案在第81頁。 **3** 🔑 [C, U] a liquid in which sth is dissolved 溶液：*an alkaline solution* 鹼溶液 ◇ *saline solution* 鹽溶液 **4** [U] the process of dissolving a solid or gas in a liquid 溶解（過程）：*the solution of glucose in water* 葡萄糖在水中的溶解

solve 🔑 /sɒlv; *NAmE* sɑːlv; sɔːlv/ *verb*

1 🔑 **~ sth** to find a way of dealing with a problem or difficult situation 解決；處理：*Attempts are being made to solve the problem of waste disposal.* 正在想辦法解決廢物處理的問題。 **2** 🔑 **~ sth** to find the correct answer or explanation for sth 解答；破解：*to solve an equation/ a puzzle/a riddle* 解方程；解難題；解謎 ◇ *to solve a crime/mystery* 破案；解開奧秘

solv·ency /'sɒlvənsi; *NAmE* 'sɑːl-/ *noun* [U] the state of not being in debt (= not owing money) 無債務；不負債

solv·ent /'sɒlvənt; *NAmE* 'sɑːl-/ *noun, adj.*

■ ***noun*** [U, C] a substance, especially a liquid, that can dissolve another substance 溶劑；溶媒

■ ***adj.*** **1** [not usually before noun] having enough money to pay your debts; not in debt 有償付能力；無債務 OPP **insolvent** **2** (*technical* 術語) able to dissolve another substance, or be dissolved in another substance 有溶解力的；可溶解的：*Lead is more solvent in acidic water.* 鉛在酸性水中更易溶解。

'solvent abuse *noun* [U] the practice of breathing in gases from glue or similar substances in order to produce a state of excitement 溶媒濫用，揮發性溶劑使用（如嗅膠毒以產生興奮感） ➲ see also GLUE-SNIFFING

solv·er /'sɒlvə(r); *NAmE* 'sɑːl-; 'sɔːl-/ *noun* a person who finds an answer to a problem or a difficult situation （問題的）解決者；（困難局面的）處理者：*She's a good* ***problem solver.*** 她是解決問題的高手。

sombre (*BrE*) (*US* **som·ber**) /'sɒmbə(r); *NAmE* 'sɑːm-/ *adj.* **1** dark in colour; dull 昏暗的；陰沉的；暗淡的 SYN **drab**：*dressed in sombre shades of grey and black* 穿着灰色和黑色的暗色調衣服 **2** sad and serious 陰鬱的；沮喪的 SYN **melancholy**：*Paul was in a* ***sombre mood.*** 保羅當時心情憂鬱。◇ *The year ended on a sombre note.* 那一年在沉悶的氣氛中結束了。 ▸ **sombre·ly** (*BrE*) (*US* **som·berly**) *adv.* **sombre·ness** (*BrE*) (*US* **som·berness**) *noun* [U]

som·brero /sɒm'breərəʊ; *NAmE* sɑːm'breroʊ/ *noun* (*pl.* **-os**) a Mexican hat for men that is tall with a very wide BRIM, turned up at the edges 墨西哥闊邊帽 ➲ VISUAL VOCAB page V65

some 🔑 *det., pron., adv.*

■ ***det.*** /səm; *strong form* sʌm/ **1** 🔑 used with uncountable nouns or plural countable nouns to mean 'an amount of' or 'a number of', when the amount or number is not given（與不可數名詞或複數可數名詞連用）一些，若干：*There's still some wine in the bottle.* 瓶子裏還有些葡萄酒。◇ *Have some more vegetables.* 再吃點蔬菜吧。 HELP In negative sentences and questions **any** is usually used instead of 'some'. 在否定句和疑問句中，通常用 any，而不用 some：*I don't want any more vegetables.* ◇ *Is there any wine left?* However, **some** is used in questions that expect a positive reply. 但在預料會得到肯定回答的疑問句中仍用 some：*Would you like some milk in your coffee?* ◇ *Didn't you borrow some books of mine?* **2** 🔑 /sʌm/ used to refer to certain members of a group or certain types of a thing, but not all of them（指群體中的某些成員或事物的某些類型）某些，部份，有的：*Some people find this more difficult than others.* 這件事有人覺得難，有人覺得不難。◇ *I like some modern music* (= but not all of it). 我喜歡某些現代音樂。 **3** 🔑 /sʌm/ a large number or amount of sth 好些；不少的；相當多的：*It was with some surprise that I heard the news.* 聽到這個消息我吃驚不小。◇ *We've known each other for some years now.* 我們倆認識有些年頭了。◇ *We're going to be working together for* ***some time*** (= a long time). 我們要在一起工作相當一段時間。 **4** 🔑 /sʌm/ a small amount or number of sth 少量的；不多的：*There is some hope that things will improve.* 情況好轉還是有希望的。 **5** 🔑 used with singular nouns to refer to a person, place, thing or time that is not known or not identified（與單數名詞連用，表示未知或未確指的人、地、事物或時間）某個：*There must be some mistake.* 一定是出了什麼差錯。◇ *He's in* ***some kind of*** *trouble.* 他遇到了什麼麻煩。◇ *She won a competition in* ***some*** *newspaper* ***or other.*** 她在某報舉辦的競賽中得了獎。◇ *I'll see you again some time, I'm sure.* 我敢肯定，什麼時候我們還會再見面的。 **6** /sʌm/ (*informal*, sometimes *ironic*) used to express a positive or negative opinion about sb/sth（表達褒貶意見時用）真可謂，算不上：*That was some party!* 那才叫晚會！◇ *Some expert you are! You know even less than me.* 你也算專家！你還不如我呢。

■ ***pron.*** /sʌm/ **~ (of sb/sth)** **1** 🔑 used to refer to an amount of sth or a number of people or things when the amount or number is not given（數量不確切時用）有些人，有些事物：*Some disapprove of the idea.* 有些人不贊成這個主意。◇ *You'll find some in the drawer.* 你會在抽屜裏找到一些。◇ *Here are some of our suggestions.* 這是我們的一些建議。**HELP** In negative sentences and questions **any** is usually used instead of 'some'. 在否定句和疑問句中，通常用 any，而不用 some：*I don't want any.* ◇ *Do you have any of the larger ones?* However, **some** is used in questions that expect a positive reply. 但在預料會得到肯定回答的疑問句中仍用 some：*Would you like some?* ◇ *Weren't you looking for some of those?* **2** a part of the whole number or amount being considered 部份；有的；有些；若干：*All these students are good, but some work harder than others.* 這些學生全都不錯，但有的很用功，有的沒那麼用功。◇ *Some of the music was weird.* 這音樂有些地方有點怪。

IDM **... and 'then some** (*informal*) and a lot more than that 遠不止這些；此外還有不少：*We got our money's worth and then some.* 我們不僅得了按價錢應得的，而且還饒上了不少。

■ ***adv.*** /sʌm/ **1** used before numbers to mean 'approximately'（用於數詞前，意同 approximately）大約，差不多：*Some thirty people attended the funeral.* 大約有三十人參加了葬禮。**2** (*NAmE, informal*) to some degree 稍微；有點：*He needs feeding up some.* 他需要多吃些東西補一補。◇ *'Are you finding the work any easier?' 'Some.'* "你是不是覺得工作順手一些了？" "是順手一些了。"

-some *suffix* **1** (in adjectives 構成形容詞) producing; likely to 引起（或易於）…的：*fearsome* 可怕的 ◇ *quarrelsome* 愛爭吵的 **2** (in nouns 構成名詞) a group of the number mentioned …人（或…個）一組：*a foursome* 四人組合

some·body /ˈsʌmbədi/ *pron.*
= SOMEONE：*Somebody should have told me.* 應該有人告訴我才是。◇ *She thinks she's really somebody in that car.* 她以為，坐上那輛車，她就真成個人物了。**OPP** nobody

'some day (also **someday**) *adv.* at some time in the future 總有一天；有朝一日；將來：*Some day he'll be famous.* 總有一天他會成名的。

some·how /ˈsʌmhaʊ/ *adv.*
1 (also *NAmE informal* **some·way, some·ways**) in a way that is not known or certain 以某種方式（或方法）：*We must stop him from seeing her somehow.* 不管怎麼着，我們都不能讓他見到她。◇ ***Somehow or other*** *I must get a new job.* 我必須想方設法找份新工作。**2** for a reason that you do not know or understand 由於某種未知的原因；不知為什麼；不知怎麼地：*Somehow, I don't feel I can trust him.* 不知為什麼，我覺得不能信任他。◇ *She looked different somehow.* 不知怎麼地，她看上去變了。

some·one /ˈsʌmwʌn/ (also **some·body**) *pron.*
1 a person who is not known or mentioned by name 某人：*There's someone at the door.* 門口有個人。◇ *Someone's left their bag behind.* 有人把包落下了。◇ *It's time for someone new* (= a new person) *to take over.* 現在該換個新人來幹了。◇ *It couldn't have been me—it must have been* ***someone else*** (= a different person). 那不可能是我，準是別人。◇ *Should we call a doctor or someone?* 我們要不要請個大夫什麼的？**HELP** The difference between **someone** and **anyone** is the same as the difference between **some** and **any**. Look at the notes there. * someone 和 anyone 的區別與 some 和 any 的區別相同。參看該兩詞條下的註解。**2** an important person 重要人物：*He was a small-time lawyer keen to* ***be someone***. 他是個沒有什麼名堂卻總想出人頭地的律師。➲ compare NOBODY

some·place /ˈsʌmpleɪs/ *adv., pron.* (*NAmE*) = SOMEWHERE：*It has to go someplace.* 它一定是擱在什麼地方了。◇ *Can't you do that* ***someplace else***? 那件事你就不能換個地方幹嗎？◇ *We need to find* ***someplace to*** *live.* 我們需要找個住的地方。

som·er·sault /ˈsʌməsɔːlt; *NAmE* -mərs-/ *noun, verb*
■ ***noun*** a movement in which sb turns over completely, with their feet over their head, on the ground or in the air 翻滾；空翻；筋斗：*to* ***do/turn a somersault*** 做翻滾動作 ◇ *He turned back somersaults.* 他做了幾個後空翻。◇ (*figurative*) *Her heart did a complete somersault when she saw him.* 她一見到他，心裏咯噔了一下。
■ ***verb*** [I] (+ **adv./prep.**) to turn over completely in the air 做翻滾；做空翻：*The car hit the kerb and somersaulted into the air.* 汽車撞到馬路牙子上，騰空翻了出去。

some·thing /ˈsʌmθɪŋ/ *pron., adv.*
■ ***pron.*** **1** a thing that is not known or mentioned by name 某事；某物：*We stopped for something to eat.* 我們停下來吃點東西。◇ *Give me* ***something to do***. 給我點活兒幹吧。◇ *There's something wrong with the TV.* 電視出毛病了。◇ ***There's something about*** *this place that frightens me.* 這個地方有點兒讓我害怕。◇ *Don't just stand there.* ***Do something!*** 別在那兒乾站着，做點什麼吧！◇ *His name is Alan something* (= I don't know his other name). 他的名字叫艾倫什麼的。◇ *She's a professor of* ***something or other*** (= I'm not sure what) *at Leeds.* 她是利茲大學某個學科的教授。◇ *He's* ***something in*** (= has a job connected with) *television.* 他是搞電視的。◇ *The car hit a tree* ***or something***. 汽車撞上了樹或別的什麼東西。◇ *I could just eat* ***a little something***. 我只能吃一點點東西。**HELP** The difference between **something** and **anything** is the same as the difference between **some** and **any**. Look at the notes there. * something 和 anything 的區別與 some 和 any 的區別相同。參看該兩詞條下的註解。**2** (*informal*) a thing that is thought to be important or worth taking notice of 想來重要（或值得注意）的事物：*There's* ***something in*** (= some truth or some fact or opinion worth considering in) *what he says.* 他的話不無道理。◇ *It's* ***quite something*** (= a thing that you should feel happy about) *to have a job at all these days.* 如今能有份工作就該知足了。◇ *'We should finish by tomorrow.'* ***'That's something*** (= a good thing), *anyway.'* "我們明天應該就能結束了。" "那也好哇。" **3** (*informal*) used to show that a description or an amount, etc. is not exact（表示不確切的描述或數量）大致，左右：*She called at* ***something after*** *ten o'clock.* 她十點多鐘來過電話。◇ *a new comedy aimed at* ***thirty-somethings*** (= people between thirty and forty years old) 一部以三十幾歲的人為主要觀眾的新喜劇 ◇ *It tastes* ***something like*** *melon.* 這吃起來有點像甜瓜。◇ *They pay six pounds an hour.* ***Something like that.*** 他們按每小時六英鎊付費，大致如此。◇ *She found herself* ***something of a*** (= to some degree a) *celebrity.* 她發現自己差不多成名人了。◇ *The programme's* ***something to do with*** (= in some way about) *the environment.* 這是一個環境類節目。◇ *He gave her a wry look,* ***something between*** *amusement and regret.* 他用頗耐玩味的目光看她一眼，說不清是開心，還是悵惋。

IDM **'make something of yourself** to be successful in life 有所成就；獲得成功 **something 'else 1** a different thing; another thing 另外一件事；別的東西：*He said something else that I thought was interesting.* 他講的另外一件事我覺得挺有意思的。**2** (*informal*) a person, a thing or an event that is much better than others of a similar type 出色的人（或事物）：*I've seen some fine players, but she's something else.* 優秀運動員我見過不少，但她出類拔萃。

■ ***adv.*** (*non-standard*) used with an adjective to emphasize a statement（與形容詞連用）很，非常：*She was swearing something terrible.* 她罵得很難聽。

some·time /ˈsʌmtaɪm/ *adv., adj.*
■ ***adv.*** (also **'some time**) at a time that you do not know exactly or has not yet been decided 在某時（不確切或尚未決定）：*I saw him sometime last summer.* 我去年夏天什麼時候見過他。◇ *We must get together sometime.* 我們一定要找個時間聚一下。
■ ***adj.*** [only before noun] (*formal*) **1** used to refer to what sb used to be（指某人曾經是…）從前的，一度的：*Thomas Atkins, sometime vicar of this parish* 本教區先前的牧師托馬斯•阿特金斯 **2** (*NAmE*) used to refer to what sb does occasionally（指某人做某事）偶爾的：*a sometime contributor to this magazine* 一位偶爾給本刊投稿的作者

some·times /ˈsʌmtaɪmz/ *adv.*
occasionally rather than all of the time 有時；間或：*Sometimes I go by car.* 有時我坐車去。◇ *He sometimes*

S

writes to me. 他偶爾給我寫封信。◇ *I like to be on my own sometimes.* 有時候我喜歡一個人待着。

some·way /'sʌmweɪ/ (also **someways**) *adv.* (*NAmE, informal*) = SOMEHOW (1)

some·what AW /'sʌmwɒt; *NAmE* -wʌt/ *adv.* to some degree 有點；有幾分；稍微 SYN **rather**: *I was somewhat surprised to see him.* 見到他我頗感詫異。◇ *The situation has changed somewhat since we last met.* 自我們上次見面以來情況有些變化。◇ *What happened to them remains* **somewhat of** *a mystery.* 他們到底出了什麼事，到現在仍可以說是個謎。

some·where /'sʌmweə(r); *NAmE* -wer/ (*NAmE* also **some·place**) *adv.* in, at or to a place that you do not know or do not mention by name 在某處；到某處：*I've seen him somewhere before.* 我以前在哪兒見過他。◇ *Can we go somewhere warm?* 我們能不能去個暖和的地方？◇ *I've already looked there—it must be* **somewhere else**. 我已經去那兒看過了，肯定是在別處。◇ *He went to school in York* **or somewhere** (= I'm not sure where). 他是在約克還是什麼地方上的學。◇ *They live* **somewhere or other** *in France.* 他們住在法國的一個什麼地方。HELP The difference between **somewhere** and **anywhere** is the same as the difference between **some** and **any**. Look at the notes there. * somewhere 和 anywhere 的區別與 some 和 any 的區別相同。參看該兩詞條下的註解。▸ **some·where** (*NAmE* also **some·place**) *pron.*: *We need to find* **somewhere to** (= a place to) *live.* 我們需要找個住處。◇ *I know somewhere we can go.* 我知道有個地方我們可以去。
IDM **'get somewhere** (*informal*) to make progress in what you are doing 有進展 **somewhere around, between, etc. sth** approximately the number or amount mentioned 大約…；…左右：*It cost somewhere around two thousand dollars.* 買下來要花大約兩千元。

som·mer /'sɒmə; *NAmE* 'sɑːmə/ *adv.* (*SAfrE, informal*) just; simply 只是；僅僅：*He sommer hit me without saying anything.* 他只是打了我，什麼也沒說。

som·nam·bu·list /sɒm'næmbjəlɪst; *NAmE* sɑːm-/ *noun* (*formal*) = SLEEPWALKER ▸ **som·nam·bu·lism** /-lɪzəm/ *noun* [U]

som·no·lent /'sɒmnələnt; *NAmE* 'sɑːm-/ *adj.* (*formal*) **1** almost asleep 瞌睡的；睏倦的；睡意矇矓的：*a somnolent cat* 打瞌睡的貓 ◇ (*figurative*) *a somnolent town* 安謐的小城 **2** making you feel tired 催眠的；使人昏昏欲睡的：*a somnolent Sunday afternoon* 使人昏昏欲睡的星期天下午 ▸ **som·no·lence** *noun* [U]

S

son /sʌn/ *noun* **1** [C] a person's male child 兒子：*We have two sons and a daughter.* 我們有兩個兒子，一個女兒。◇ *They have three grown-up sons.* 他們有三個成年的兒子。◇ *He's the son of an Oxford professor.* 他是牛津大學一位教授的兒子。◇ *Maine & Sons, Grocers* (= the name of a company on a sign) 梅因父子雜貨店 ➲ COLLOCATIONS at CHILD **2** [sing.] (*informal*) a friendly form of address that is used by an older man to a young man or boy（年長者對年輕男子或男孩的愛稱）孩子：*Well, son, how can I help you?* 那麼，孩子，我能為你做點什麼呢？ **3** [C] (*literary*) a man who belongs to a particular place or country, etc.（某個地方、國家等的）男性成員，子孫：*one of France's most famous sons* 法國最著名的人士之一 **4 my son** (*formal*) used by a priest to address a boy or man（司鐸對男子或男孩的稱呼）孩子 **5 the Son** [sing.] Jesus Christ as the second member of the TRINITY 聖子（耶穌基督）：*the Father, the Son and the Holy Spirit* 聖父、聖子和聖靈 IDM see FATHER *n.*, FAVOURITE *adj.*, PRODIGAL

sonar /'səʊnɑː(r); *NAmE* 'soʊ-/ *noun* [U] equipment or a system for finding objects underwater using sound waves 聲納（利用聲波探測水下物體的裝置或系統）➲ compare RADAR

son·ata /sə'nɑːtə/ *noun* a piece of music for one instrument or for one instrument and a piano, usually divided into three or four parts 奏鳴曲

son et lu·mi·ère /ˌsɒn eɪ 'luːmjeə(r); *NAmE* ˌsɔːn eɪ luːm'jer/ *noun* [U] (from *French*) a performance held at night at a famous place that tells its history with special lights and sound 聲光表演（在名勝地點舉行，借助聲光效果，介紹該地掌故）

song /sɒŋ; *NAmE* sɔːŋ/ *noun* **1** [C] a short piece of music with words that you sing 歌；歌曲：*a* ***folk/love/pop, etc. song*** 民歌、情歌、流行歌曲等 ◇ *We sang a song together.* 我們一起唱了一首歌。➲ COLLOCATIONS at MUSIC ➲ see also SWANSONG **2** [U] songs in general; music for singing（統稱）歌曲；歌唱；聲樂：*The story is told through song and dance.* 故事是通過歌舞的形式來表現的。◇ *Suddenly he* ***burst into song*** (= started to sing). 突然間，他放聲唱了起來。➲ see also PLAINSONG **3** [U, C] the musical sounds that birds make（鳥的）鳴囀，啼囀：*the song of the blackbird* 黑鸝的鳴囀
IDM **for a 'song** (*informal*) very cheaply; at a low price 非常便宜；以低價 **a song and 'dance (about sth) 1** (*BrE, informal, disapproving*) if you make a **song and dance** about sth, you complain or talk about it too much when this is not necessary 小題大做的抱怨；無謂的吵鬧；胡攪蠻纏 **2** [C] (*NAmE, informal*) a long explanation about sth, or excuse for sth 冗長的解釋；絮叨的託辭 **on 'song** (*informal*) working or performing well 性能良好；運轉順暢 ➲ more at SING

song·bird /'sɒŋbɜːd; *NAmE* 'sɔːŋbɜːrd/ *noun* a bird that has a musical call, for example a BLACKBIRD or THRUSH 鳴禽

song·book /'sɒŋbʊk; *NAmE* 'sɔːŋ-/ *noun* a book containing the music and words of different songs 歌曲集；歌本

song·smith /'sɒŋsmɪθ; *NAmE* 'sɔːŋ-/ *noun* (*informal*) a person who writes popular songs 寫流行曲的人

song·ster /'sɒŋstə(r); *NAmE* 'sɔːŋ-/ *noun* (*old-fashioned*) **1** a word sometimes used in newspapers to mean 'singer'（報章上有時用以表示 singer）歌手，歌唱家 **2** a SONGBIRD 鳴禽

song·stress /'sɒŋstrəs; *NAmE* 'sɔːŋ-/ *noun* a word sometimes used in newspapers to mean 'a woman singer'（報章上有時用以表示 woman singer）女歌手，女歌唱家

song·writer /'sɒŋraɪtə(r); *NAmE* 'sɔːŋ-/ *noun* a person who writes the words and usually also the music for songs 歌詞作者；歌曲的詞曲作者：***singer-songwriter*** *Paul Simon* 歌手兼詞曲作者保羅•西蒙

song·writ·ing /'sɒŋraɪtɪŋ; *NAmE* 'sɔːŋ-/ *noun* [U] the process of writing songs 歌曲創作

sonic /'sɒnɪk; *NAmE* 'sɑːnɪk/ *adj.* (*technical* 術語) connected with sound or the speed of sound 聲音的；聲速的：*sonic waves* 聲波

ˌsonic 'boom *noun* the EXPLOSIVE sound that is made when an aircraft travels faster than the speed of sound 音爆，聲震（飛機超聲速飛行時發出的巨大聲響）

'son-in-law *noun* (*pl.* **'sons-in-law**) the husband of your daughter 女婿 ➲ compare DAUGHTER-IN-LAW

son·net /'sɒnɪt; *NAmE* 'sɑːnɪt/ *noun* a poem that has 14 lines, each containing 10 syllables, and a fixed pattern of RHYME 十四行詩；商籟體：*Shakespeare's sonnets* 莎士比亞的十四行詩

sonny /'sʌni/ *noun* [sing.] (*old-fashioned*) a word used by an older person to address a young man or boy（年長者對年輕男子或男孩的稱呼）孩子

ˌson of a 'bitch *noun* (*pl.* **sons of bitches**) (also **SOB** especially in *NAmE*) (*taboo, slang*) an offensive word for a person that you think is bad or very unpleasant 狗娘養的；王八蛋；渾蛋：*I'll kill that son of a bitch when I get my hands on him!* 我要是逮住那個王八蛋，非要了他的狗命不可！

ˌson of a 'gun *noun* (*NAmE, informal*) **1** a person or thing that you are annoyed with 龜孫子；破爛貨：*My car's at the shop—the son of a gun broke down again.* 我的車在修理廠呢，這破玩意兒又壞了。 **2** used to express the fact that you are surprised or annoyed（表示驚訝或氣惱）好傢伙，他媽的：*Well, son of a gun—and I thought the old guy couldn't dance!* 嘿，好傢伙，我還

以為那老傢伙不會跳舞呢！ **3** (*old-fashioned*) used by a man to address or talk about a male friend that he admires and likes（男性稱呼或談論所欽佩或喜歡的男性朋友）哥們兒：*Frank, you old son of a gun—I haven't seen you for months.* 弗蘭克，老哥們兒，好幾個月沒見你了。

so·nor·ous /ˈsɒnərəs; *NAmE* ˈsɑːn-/ *adj.* (*formal*) having a pleasant full deep sound 雄渾的；渾厚的：*a sonorous voice* 渾厚的嗓音 ▶ **so·nor·ity** /səˈnɒrəti; *NAmE* -ˈnɔːr-/ *noun* [U, C]：*the rich sonority of the bass* 男低音飽滿渾厚的音色 **so·nor·ous·ly** *adv.*

sook /suːk; sʊk/ *noun* (*informal, AustralE, NZE, CanE*) **1** a person who is not brave 膽小鬼；懦夫 SYN **coward, crybaby** **2** a young cow that has been fed from a bottle, not by its mother 用奶瓶餵養的小牛

soon /suːn/ *adv.* (**soon·er, soon·est**)
1 in a short time from now; a short time after sth else has happened 很快；馬上；不久：*We'll be home soon./We'll soon be home.* 我們很快就要到家了。◇ *She sold the house* ***soon after*** *her husband died.* 丈夫去世後不久，她就把房子賣了。◇ *I soon realized the mistake.* 我很快意識到犯了錯誤。◇ *It soon became clear that the programme was a failure.* 沒多久便清楚地看出，這個節目不受歡迎。◇ (*informal*) ***See you soon!*** 再見！ **2** early; quickly 早；快：***How soon*** *can you get here?* 你多快能趕到這兒？◇ *We'll deliver the goods* ***as soon as*** *we can.* 我們將儘快交貨。◇ *Please send it* ***as soon as possible.*** 請儘快把它寄出去。◇ *Next Monday is* ***the soonest*** *we can deliver.* 我們交貨最早要到下星期一。◇ *They arrived home sooner than expected.* 他們很快就到家了，比預料的要早。◇ ***The sooner*** *we set off,* ***the sooner*** *we will arrive.* 我們越早出發就越早到達。◇ *The note said, 'Call Bill soonest'* (= as soon as possible). 紙條上寫着："儘快給比爾打電話"。◇ ***All too soon*** *the party was over.* 轉眼之間，聚會就結束了。➲ see also ASAP

IDM **no sooner said than ˈdone** used to say that sth was, or will be, done immediately 說幹就幹 **no sooner … than …** used to say that sth happens immediately after sth else 一…就；剛…就：*No sooner had she said it than she burst into tears.* 她剛一說完，淚水便奪眶而出。➲ note at HARDLY **the ˌsooner the ˈbetter** very soon; as soon as possible 儘早；越快越好：*'When shall I tell him?' 'The sooner the better.'* "我什麼時候告訴他呢？" "越快越好。" **ˌsooner or ˈlater** at some time in the future, even if you are not sure exactly when 遲早；早晚有一天：*Sooner or later you will have to make a decision.* 你早晚得拿個主意。 **ˌsooner rather than ˈlater** after a short time rather than after a long time 趁早不趁晚；及早：*We urged them to sort out the problem sooner rather than later.* 我們敦促他們及早解決那個問題。 **I, etc. would sooner do sth (than sth else)** to prefer to do sth (than do sth else) 寧願做某事（而不願做另一件事）：*She'd sooner share a house with other students than live at home with her parents.* 她寧可和其他學生合住，也不願跟父母住在家裏。➲ more at ANY TIME, JUST *adv.*, SAY *v.*

soot /sʊt/ *noun* [U] black powder that is produced when wood, coal, etc. is burnt 煤煙子；油煙 ➲ see also SOOTY

soothe /suːð/ *verb* **1 ~ sb** to make sb who is anxious, upset, etc. feel calmer 安慰；撫慰；勸慰 SYN **calm**：*The music soothed her for a while.* 音樂讓她稍微安靜了一會兒。 **2 ~ sth** to make a TENSE or painful part of your body feel more comfortable 減輕，緩解，緩和（身體某部位的緊張或疼痛） SYN **relieve**：*This should soothe the pain.* 這個應該能緩解疼痛。◇ *Take a warm bath to soothe tense, tired muscles.* 洗個熱水澡，讓緊張疲勞的肌肉放鬆一下。 ▶ **sooth·ing** *adj.*：*a soothing voice/lotion* 讓人感到安慰的嗓音；鎮痛液 **sooth·ing·ly** *adv.*：*'There's no need to worry,' he said soothingly.* "不必擔憂。" 他寬慰道。

PHR V **ˈsoothe sth↔aˈway** to remove a pain or an unpleasant feeling 解除；消除；消釋

sooth·er /ˈsuːðə(r)/ *noun* (*CanE*) a specially shaped rubber or plastic object for a baby to suck 橡皮奶頭；塑料奶頭；奶嘴 SYN **dummy**

sooth·say·er /ˈsuːθseɪə(r)/ *noun* (*old use*) a person who is believed to be able to tell what will happen in the future 占卜者；預言者

sooty /ˈsʊti/ *adj.* **1** covered with SOOT 沾滿煤煙子的 **2** of the colour of SOOT 煤煙子一樣黑的；炭黑色的

sop /sɒp; *NAmE* sɑːp/ *noun* [usually sing.] **~ (to sb/sth)** a small, not very important, thing that is offered to sb who is angry or disappointed in order to make them feel better（為緩和某人憤怒或失望情緒而贈與的）小東西

soph·ist /ˈsɒfɪst; *NAmE* ˈsɑːf-/ *noun* **1** a teacher of philosophy in ancient Greece, especially one with an attitude of doubting that statements are true（古希臘的）哲學教師；（尤指懷質疑態度的）哲人，智者 **2** a person who uses clever but wrong arguments 詭辯者；詭辯家

so·phis·ti·cate /səˈfɪstɪkeɪt/ *noun* (*formal*) a sophisticated person 世故的人；見多識廣的人

so·phis·ti·cated /səˈfɪstɪkeɪtɪd/ *adj.* **1** having a lot of experience of the world and knowing about fashion, culture and other things that people think are socially important 見多識廣的；老練的；見過世面的：*the sophisticated pleasures of city life* 城市生活中五花八門的享樂 ◇ *Mark is a smart and sophisticated young man.* 馬克是一個聰明老成的年輕人。➲ compare NAIVE (2) **2** (of a machine, system, etc. 機器、體系等) clever and complicated in the way that it works or is presented 複雜巧妙的；先進的；精密的：*highly sophisticated computer systems* 十分先進的計算機系統 ◇ *Medical techniques are becoming more sophisticated all the time.* 醫療技術日益複雜精妙。 **3** (of a person 人) able to understand difficult or complicated ideas 水平高的；在行的：*a sophisticated audience* 有鑒賞力的觀眾 OPP **unsophisticated**

so·phis·ti·ca·tion /səˌfɪstɪˈkeɪʃn/ *noun* [U] the quality of being sophisticated 世故；複雜巧妙；高水平

soph·is·try /ˈsɒfɪstri; *NAmE* ˈsɑːf-/ *noun* (*pl.* **-ies**) (*formal*) **1** [U] the use of clever arguments to persuade people that sth is true when it is really false 詭辯術 **2** [C] a reason or an explanation that tries to show that sth is true when it is really false 詭辯

sopho·more /ˈsɒfəmɔː(r); *NAmE* ˈsɑːf-/ *noun* (*US*) **1** a student in the second year of a course of study at a college or university（大學）二年級學生 **2** a HIGH SCHOOL student in the 10th grade（高中）二年級學生 ➲ compare FRESHMAN (1), JUNIOR *n.* (4), SENIOR *n.* (6)

sop·or·if·ic /ˌsɒpəˈrɪfɪk; *NAmE* ˌsɑːp-/ *adj.* (*formal*) making you want to go to sleep 催眠的；讓人瞌睡的：*the soporific effect of the sun* 太陽讓人昏昏欲睡的作用

sop·ping /ˈsɒpɪŋ; *NAmE* ˈsɑːp-/ (also **ˌsopping ˈwet**) *adj.* (*informal*) very wet 濕透的 SYN **soaking**

soppy /ˈsɒpi; *NAmE* ˈsɑːpi/ (*especially BrE*) (**sop·pier, sop·pi·est**) (*NAmE* usually **sappy**) *adj.* (*informal*) silly and SENTIMENTAL; full of unnecessary emotion 一味情意纏綿的；感情過於豐富的；多愁善感的：*soppy love songs* 纏綿的情歌

sop·rano /səˈprɑːnəʊ; *NAmE* səˈprɑːnoʊ; -ˈpræn-/ *noun, adj.*
■ ***noun*** (*pl.* **-os** /-nəʊz; *NAmE* -noʊz/) a singing voice with the highest range for a woman or boy; a singer with a soprano voice 女高音；童聲高音；女高音歌手；童聲高音歌手 ➲ compare ALTO *n.* (1), MEZZO-SOPRANO, TREBLE *n.* (2)
■ ***adj.*** [only before noun] (of a musical instrument 樂器) with the highest range of notes in its group 高音的：*a soprano saxophone* 高音薩克斯管 ➲ compare ALTO *adj.*, BASS[1] *adj.*, TENOR *adj.*

soˌprano reˈcorder (*NAmE*) (*BrE* **ˌdescant reˈcorder**) *noun* (*music* 音) the most common size of RECORDER (= a musical instrument in the shape of a pipe that you blow into), with a high range of notes 高音直笛

sor·bet /ˈsɔːbeɪ; *NAmE* ˈsɔːrbət/ (*BrE* also **ˈwater ice**) *noun* [C, U] a sweet frozen food made from sugar, water and fruit juice, often eaten as a DESSERT 雪糕；冰糕

sor·cer·er /ˈsɔːsərə(r); *NAmE* ˈsɔːrs-/ *noun* (in stories) a man with magic powers, who is helped by evil spirits（故事中的）術士，男巫，巫師

S

sor·cer·ess /ˈsɔːsərəs; *NAmE* ˈsɔːrs-/ *noun* (in stories) a woman with magic powers, who is helped by evil spirits（故事中的）女術士，女巫，巫婆

sor·cery /ˈsɔːsəri; *NAmE* ˈsɔːrs-/ *noun* [U] magic that uses evil spirits 法道；巫術 SYN **black magic**

sor·did /ˈsɔːdɪd; *NAmE* ˈsɔːrdɪd/ *adj.* **1** immoral or dishonest 卑鄙的；醜惡的；無恥的：*It was a shock to discover the truth about his sordid past.* 他以往的醜行被發現時，人們感到震驚。◇ *I didn't want to hear the* ***sordid details*** *of their relationship.* 我不想聽他們之間的那些齷齪細節。 **2** very dirty and unpleasant 骯髒的；污穢的 SYN **squalid**：*people living in sordid conditions* 生活環境骯髒不堪的人

sore 🗝 /sɔː(r)/ *adj., noun*

■ ***adj.*** **1** 🗝 if a part of your body is **sore**, it is painful, and often red, especially because of infection or because a muscle has been used too much（發炎）疼痛的；痠痛的：*to have a sore throat* 嗓子疼 ◇ *His feet were sore after the walk.* 他走路把腳都走疼了。◇ *My stomach is still sore* (= painful) *after the operation.* 手術後，我的胃還在疼。➲ SYNONYMS at PAINFUL **2** [not before noun] **~ (at sb/about sth)** (*informal, especially NAmE*) upset and angry, especially because you have been treated unfairly 氣惱；憤慨；憤憤不平 SYN **annoyed** ▸ **sore·ness** *noun* [U]：*an ointment to reduce soreness and swelling* 止痛消腫軟膏

IDM **a ˌsore ˈpoint** a subject that makes you feel angry or upset when it is mentioned 心病；疼處；傷心事：*It's a sore point with Sue's parents that the children have not been baptized yet.* 孩子們至今未受洗禮，這是蘇的父母的一件傷心事。 **stand/stick out like a sore ˈthumb** to be very noticeable in an unpleasant way 招眼；扎眼 ➲ more at BEAR *n.*, SIGHT *n.*

■ ***noun*** a painful, often red, place on your body where there is a wound or an infection 痛處；傷處；瘡 SYN **wound**：*open sores* 開放性潰瘍 ➲ see also BEDSORE, CANKER SORE, COLD SORE

sore·ly /ˈsɔːli; *NAmE* ˈsɔːrli/ *adv.* seriously; very much 嚴重地；非常：*I was* ***sorely tempted*** *to complain, but I didn't.* 我極想發牢騷，但還是沒開口。◇ *If you don't come to the reunion you'll be* ***sorely missed****.* 你要是不來參加團聚，大家會非常想念你的。

sor·ghum /ˈsɔːgəm; *NAmE* ˈsɔːrgəm/ *noun* [U] very small grain grown as food in tropical countries; the plant that produces this grain 高粱；高粱米

sor·or·ity /səˈrɒrəti; *NAmE* -ˈrɔːr-; -ˈrɑːr-/ *noun* (*pl.* **-ies**) (*NAmE*) a club for a group of women students at an American college or university（美國大學裏的）女生聯誼會 ➲ compare FRATERNITY (2)

sor·rel /ˈsɒrəl; *NAmE* ˈsɔːr-/ *noun* [U] a plant with leaves that taste bitter and are used in salads or in making soup or sauces 酸模（葉子味苦，可用於做色拉、湯或醬汁）

sor·row /ˈsɒrəʊ; *NAmE* ˈsɑːroʊ/ *noun, verb*

■ ***noun*** **1** [U] **~ (at/for/over sth)** (rather *formal*) a feeling of great sadness because sth very bad has happened 悲傷；悲痛；悲哀 SYN **grief**：*He expressed his sorrow at the news of her death.* 聽到她的死訊，他表示哀傷。◇ *They said that the decision was made* ***more in sorrow than in anger****.* 他們說作出這個決定，與其說是出於氣憤，不如說是出於悲傷。 **2** [C] a very sad event or situation 傷心事；悲傷事；不幸：*the joys and sorrows of childhood* 童年的歡樂和悲傷

■ ***verb*** [I] (*literary*) to feel or express great sadness 感到（或表示）悲傷：*the sorrowing relatives* 悲傷的親屬

sor·row·ful /ˈsɒrəʊfl; *NAmE* ˈsɑːroʊ-/ *adj.* (*literary*) very sad 悲傷的；悲痛的；悲哀的：*her sorrowful eyes* 她那悲傷的眼睛 ▸ **sor·row·ful·ly** /-fəli/ *adv.*

sorry 🗝 /ˈsɒri; *NAmE* ˈsɑːri; ˈsɔːri/ *adj., exclamation*

■ ***adj.*** (**sor·rier, sor·ri·est**) HELP You can also use **more sorry** and **most sorry**. 亦可用 more sorry 和 most sorry。 **1** 🗝 [not before noun] feeling sad and sympathetic 難過；惋惜；同情：**~ (that)** ... *I'm sorry that your husband lost his job.* 你丈夫把工作丟了，我很惋惜。◇ **~ (to see, hear, etc.)** *We're sorry to hear that your father's in hospital again.* 聽說你父親又住院了，我們心裏都不好受。◇ **~ (about sth)** *No one is sorrier than I am about what happened.* 發生了這樣的事，我比誰都難過。 **2** 🗝 [not before noun] feeling sad and ashamed about sth that has been done 歉疚；慚愧；過意不去：**~ (about sth)** *We're very sorry about the damage to your car.* 損壞了你的車，我們真是過意不去。◇ **~ (for sth/doing sth)** *He says he's really sorry for taking the car without asking.* 他沒打招呼就用了車，他說他為此感到非常抱歉。◇ **~ (that)** ... *She was sorry that she'd lost her temper.* 她為自己發了脾氣而感到愧疚。◇ *If you* ***say you're sorry*** *we'll forgive you.* 你要是道歉，我們就原諒你。 **3** 🗝 [not before noun] feeling disappointed about sth and wishing you had done sth different or had not done sth 後悔；遺憾；不忍：**~ (that)** ... *She was sorry that she'd lost contact with Mary.* 她懊悔跟瑪麗失去了聯繫。◇ *You'll be sorry if I catch you!* 要是讓我抓着，你會後悔的！◇ **~ to do sth** *I was genuinely sorry to be leaving college.* 大學畢業時，我打心底裏捨不得離去。 **4** [only before noun] very sad or bad, especially making you feel pity or disapproval 悲慘的；破敗的；可憐的：*The business is in a* ***sorry state****.* 公司境況真是糟糕。◇ *They were a* ***sorry sight*** *when they eventually got off the boat.* 他們最終從船上下來，一副慘兮兮的樣子。

IDM **be/feel sorry for sb** 🗝 to feel pity or sympathy for sb 憐憫；同情：*He decided to help Jan as he felt sorry for her.* 他同情簡的遭遇，決定幫助她。 **feel sorry for yourself** (*informal, disapproving*) to feel unhappy; to pity yourself 感覺不幸；自我憐憫：*Stop feeling sorry for yourself and think about other people for a change.* 別老覺得自己委屈了，也替別人想一想吧。 **I'm sorry 1** 🗝 used when you are apologizing for sth（道歉時用）很抱歉，請原諒：*I'm sorry, I forgot.* 對不起，我忘了。◇ *Oh, I'm sorry. Have I taken the one you wanted?* 喲，對不起。我是不是拿了你想要的那個？◇ *I'm sorry. I can't make it tomorrow.* 很抱歉。我明天不行。 **2** 🗝 used for disagreeing with sb or politely saying 'no'（表示不同意或委婉地拒絕）對不起：*I'm sorry, I don't agree.* 對不起，我不同意。◇ *I'm sorry, I'd rather you didn't go.* 恕我直言，我看你還是不去為好。 **3** 🗝 used for introducing bad news（引出壞消息）很遺憾：*I'm sorry to have to tell you you've failed.* 我只能遺憾地告訴你，你不及格。 **I'm ˈsorry to say** used for saying that sth is disappointing（表示某事令人失望）我遺憾地說：*He didn't accept the job, I'm sorry to say.* 我很遺憾，他不接受那項工作。 ➲ more at SAFE *adj.*

■ ***exclamation*** **1** 🗝 used when you are APOLOGIZING for sth（道歉時用）很抱歉，請原諒：*Sorry I'm late!* 對不起，我來晚了！◇ *Did I stand on your foot? Sorry!* 我是不是踩你腳了？抱歉！◇ *Sorry to bother you, but could I speak to you for a moment?* 不好意思打攪你，我能不能跟你說幾句話？◇ *Sorry, we don't allow dogs in the house.* 對不起，我們是不讓狗進屋的。◇ *He didn't even* ***say sorry****.* 他連句道歉的話也沒有說。 **2** 🗝 (*especially BrE*) used for asking sb to repeat sth that you have not heard clearly（請某人重複你沒聽清楚的話）你說什麼，請再說一遍：*Sorry? Could you repeat the question?* 你說什麼？能不能把你的問題再說一遍？ **3** 🗝 used for correcting yourself when you have said sth wrong（糾正自己說錯的話）不對，應該是：*Take the first turning, sorry, the third turning on the right.* 到第一個，不，到第三個路口往右拐。

sort 🗝 /sɔːt; *NAmE* sɔːrt/ *noun, verb*

■ ***noun*** **1** 🗝 [C] a group or type of people or things that are similar in a particular way 種類；類別；品種 SYN **kind**：*'What* ***sort of*** *music do you like?' 'Oh,* ***all sorts****.'* "你喜歡哪一類音樂？" "噢，哪一類都喜歡。" ◇ ***This sort of*** *problem is quite common./****These sorts of*** *problems are quite common.* 這類問題相當普遍。/ 這幾類問題相當普遍。◇ *He's the sort of person who only cares about money.* 他這種人一心只想着錢。◇ *For dessert there's a fruit pie* ***of some sort*** (= you are not sure what kind). 甜點是一種水果派。◇ *Most people went on training courses* ***of one sort or another*** (= of various types) *last year.* 多數人去年都上過這樣那樣的培訓班。◇ (*informal*) *There were snacks—peanuts, olives,* ***that sort of thing****.* 有各種小吃，花生米、橄欖什麼的。◇ (*informal*) *There are* ***all sorts of*** *activities* (= many different ones) *for kids at the campsite.* 在營地有為孩子們組織的各種各樣的活動。◇ (*informal*) ***What sort of** price did you want to pay?* (= approximately how much) 你想出什麼樣的價？◇ (*informal*) ***What sort of** time do you call this?* (= I'm very angry that you have come so late.) 你看看這都什麼時候了？ ➲ note at KIND **2** [C, usually sing.] (*informal, especially BrE*) a particular type of person 某一種（或某一類）人：*My brother would never cheat on his wife; he's not that sort.* 我哥哥永遠不會背着妻子在外面拈花惹草，他不是那種人。 **3** (*computing* 計) [sing.] the process of putting data in a particular order 分類；排序：*to do a sort* 進行分類

IDM **it takes all sorts (to make a world)** (*saying*) used to say that you think sb's behaviour is very strange or unusual but that everyone is different and likes different things（認為某人行為怪誕或不尋常時說）世界之大無奇不有，林子大了什麼鳥都有 **of 'sorts** (*informal*) used when you are saying that sth is not a good example of a particular type of thing（表示某事物不夠好）勉強算的，湊合的：*He offered us an apology of sorts.* 他給我們勉強道了個歉。 **out of 'sorts** (*especially BrE*) ill/sick or upset 身體不適；心情煩惱：*She was tired and out of sorts by the time she arrived home.* 她回到家裏，又累又煩。 **sort of** (*informal*) **1** 🔑 to some extent but in a way that you cannot easily describe 有幾分；有那麼一點：*She sort of pretends that she doesn't really care.* 她擺出一副並不真正在乎的樣子。◇ *'Do you understand?' 'Sort of.'* "你懂了嗎？" "有點懂了。" **2** 🔑 (also **sort of like**) (*BrE, informal*) used when you cannot think of a good word to use to describe sth, or what to say next（想不出恰當的詞或不知下面該怎麼說時用）可以說，可說是：*We're sort of doing it the wrong way.* 我們的方法好像有點不對頭。 **a sort of sth** 🔑 (*informal*) used for describing sth in a not very exact way（表示不十分準確）近似於某物，有點像是某物：*I had a sort of feeling that he wouldn't come.* 我隱約覺得他不會來。◇ *They're a sort of greenish-blue colour.* 它們的顏色近乎帶淡綠的藍色。 ➲ more at KIND *n.*

■ *verb* **1** 🔑 to arrange things in groups or in a particular order according to their type, etc.; to separate things of one type from others 整理；把…分類：**~ sth** *sorting the mail* 分理信件 ◇ **~ sth into sth** *The computer sorts the words into alphabetical order.* 計算機按字母順序排列這些單詞。◇ *Rubbish can easily be separated and sorted into plastics, glass and paper.* 垃圾很容易分開，可歸入塑料、玻璃和紙三類。◇ **~ sth from sth** *Women and children sorted the ore from the rock.* 婦女和孩子把礦石從岩石中分揀出來。 ➲ see also SORT OUT **2** 🔑 [often passive] **~ sth** (*informal, especially BrE*) to deal with a problem successfully or organize sth/sb properly 妥善處理；安排妥當：*I'm really busy—can you sort it?* 我真的很忙，你能處理一下嗎？ ➲ compare SORTED **IDM** see MAN *n.*, SHEEP, WHEAT

PHR V **,sort itself 'out** (of a problem 問題) to stop being a problem without anyone having to take action 自行化解：*It will all sort itself out in the end.* 問題最後都會自行解決。 **,sort sth↔'out 1** 🔑 (*informal*) to organize the contents of sth; to tidy sth 理順；整理：*The cupboards need sorting out.* 櫃櫥該整理一下了。 **2** to organize sth successfully 把…安排好：*If you're going to the bus station, can you sort out the tickets for tomorrow?* 你要去汽車站的話，能不能把明天的車票買好？ **,sort sth↔'out (from sth)** to separate sth from a larger group（從…中）區分出來，辨別出來：*Could you sort out the toys that can be thrown away?* 你把可以扔掉的玩具挑出來，好嗎？ ➲ related noun SORT-OUT **,sort sth/sb/yourself 'out** 🔑 (*especially BrE*) to deal with sb's/your own problems successfully 妥善處理某人（或自己）的問題：*If you can wait a moment, I'll sort it all out for you.* 要是你能等一會兒，我就可以把什麼都給你弄好。◇ *You load up the car and I'll sort the kids out.* 你裝車，我把孩子們安頓好。 **,sort sb↔'out** (*informal*) to deal with sb who is causing trouble, etc. especially by punishing or attacking them 整治，懲罰，收拾（某人）：*Wait till I get my hands on him—I'll soon sort him out!* 等他落到我手裏，我很快會收拾他！ **'sort through sth (for sth)** to look through a number of things, either in order to find sth or to put them in order 翻查；歸整：*I sorted through my paperwork.* 我把文件紙張都歸整好了。◇ *She sorted through her suitcase for something to wear.* 她翻遍行李箱找件衣服穿。

'sort code (*BrE*) (*US* **'routing number**) *noun* a number that is used to identify a particular bank 銀行代碼

sorted /'sɔːtɪd; *NAmE* 'sɔːrt-/ *adj.* [not before noun] (*BrE, informal*) completed, solved or organized 完成的；已解決的；整理好的：*Don't worry. We'll soon have this sorted.* 別擔心，我們馬上把這弄好。◇ *It's our problem. We'll **get it sorted**.* 這是我們的問題，我們來處理。◇ *It's all sorted.* 全都弄好了。◇ *It's time you **got yourself sorted**.* 現在你該把自己的事好好安排一下了。 ➲ compare SORT *v.* (2)

sor·tie /'sɔːti; *NAmE* 'sɔːrti/ *noun* **1** a flight that is made by an aircraft during military operations; an attack made by soldiers（在軍事行動中飛機的）出動架次；（軍隊的）出擊 **SYN** **raid** **2** a short trip away from your home or the place where you are（短暫）外出，出門 **SYN** **foray** **3 ~ into sth** an effort that you make to do or join sth new 嘗試參與；一試身手 **SYN** **foray**：*His first sortie into politics was unsuccessful.* 他初涉政壇並不成功。

'sorting office *noun* (*BrE*) a place where mail is sorted before being delivered 郵件分揀室

'sort-out *noun* (*BrE, informal*) an act of arranging or organizing the contents of sth in a tidy or neat way and removing things you do not want 整理；清理

SOS /,es əʊ 'es; *NAmE* oʊ/ *noun* [sing.] **1** a signal or message that a ship or plane sends when it needs urgent help（船舶或飛機發出的）緊急呼救信號：*to send an SOS* 發出緊急呼救信號 ◇ *an SOS message* 緊急呼救信號 **2** an urgent request for help 緊急求助的請求：*We've received an SOS from the area asking for food parcels.* 我們收到來自那一地區的緊急求援信息，他們急需食物包。 ➲ see also MAYDAY

sosa·tie /sə'sɑːti/ *noun* (*SAfrE*) small pieces of meat or vegetables that are cooked on a stick, usually over an open fire 烤肉串；烤蔬菜串 **SYN** **kebab**

,so-'so *adj.* (*informal*) not particularly good or bad; average 一般的；普通的；中等的；不好也不差的：*'How are you feeling today?' 'So-so.'* "你今天感覺怎麼樣？" "還可以。" ▶ **,so-'so** *adv.*：*I only did so-so in the exam.* 我在考試中考得一般。

sotto voce /,sɒtəʊ 'vəʊtʃi; *NAmE* ,sɑːtoʊ 'voʊ-/ *adv.* (from *Italian, formal*) in a quiet voice so that not everyone can hear 小聲地；輕聲地 ▶ **sotto voce** *adj.*

sou /suː/ *noun* [sing.] (*old-fashioned, BrE, informal*) if you do not have a **sou**, you have no money at all 一點錢；一文錢

sou·bri·quet /'suːbrɪkeɪ/ *noun* = SOBRIQUET

souf·flé /'suːfleɪ; *NAmE* suː'fleɪ/ *noun* [C, U] a dish made from egg whites, milk and flour mixed together to make it light, flavoured with cheese, fruit, etc. and baked until it rises 蛋奶酥；舒芙蕾：*a cheese soufflé* 奶酪蛋奶酥

sough /saʊ; sʌf/ *verb* [I] (*literary*) (especially of the wind 尤指風) to make a soft whistling sound 作沙沙聲；作颯颯聲

sought **AW** *past tense, past part.* of SEEK

'sought after *adj.* wanted by many people, because it is of very good quality or difficult to get or to find 爭相獲得的；吃香的；廣受歡迎的：*This design is the most sought after.* 這款設計最受歡迎。◇ *a much sought-after actress* 非常走紅的女演員

souk /suːk/ *noun* a market in an Arab country（阿拉伯國家的）露天市場

soul 🔑 /səʊl; *NAmE* soʊl/ *noun*

▸ SPIRIT OF PERSON 人的靈魂 **1** 🔑 [C] the spiritual part of a person, believed to exist after death 靈魂：*He believed his immortal soul was in peril.* 他認為他不死的靈魂有墮入地獄的危險。◇ *The howling wind sounded like the wailing of lost souls* (= the spirits of dead people who are not in heaven). 怒吼的風如同墮入地獄的靈魂在哀聲慟哭。 ➲ COLLOCATIONS at RELIGION

S

▸ **INNER CHARACTER** 內在個性 **2** 🔑 [C] a person's inner character, containing their true thoughts and feelings 心性；內心；心靈：*There was a feeling of restlessness deep in her soul.* 她內心深處感到焦躁不安。
▸ **SPIRITUAL/MORAL/ARTISTIC QUALITIES** 精神／道德／藝術品質 **3** 🔑 [sing.] the spiritual and moral qualities of humans in general（人類整體的）精神狀況，道德品質 SYN **psyche**：*the dark side of the human soul* 人類精神世界中陰暗的一面 **4** [U, C] strong and good human feeling, especially that gives a work of art its quality or enables sb to recognize and enjoy that quality 真摯情感；高尚情操；氣魄：*It was a very polished performance, but it lacked soul.* 這場演出技藝很精湛，但缺少真摯的情感。 **5** [sing.] **the ~ of sth** a perfect example of a good quality 典範；化身：*He is the soul of discretion.* 他是謹慎的典範。
▸ **PERSON** 人 **6** [C] (becoming *old-fashioned*) a person of a particular type 某種人：*She's lost all her money, poor soul.* 可憐的人，她的錢全沒了。◇ *You're a brave soul.* 你真勇敢。 **7** [C] (especially in negative sentences 尤用於否定句) a person 人：*There wasn't a soul in sight* (= nobody was in sight). 連個人影都不見。◇ *Don't tell a soul* (= do not tell anyone). 誰也別告訴。◇ (*literary*) *a village of 300 souls* (= with 300 people living there) 一個 300 人的村子
▸ **MUSIC** 音樂 **8** (also **'soul music**) [U] a type of music that expresses strong emotions, made popular by African American musicians 靈樂，靈歌，靈魂音樂（感情強烈，源於非洲裔美國人的音樂）：*a soul singer* 靈樂歌手
IDM **good for the 'soul** (*humorous*) good for you, even if it seems unpleasant 其實有好處：*'Want a ride?' 'No thanks. Walking is good for the soul.'* "搭車嗎？""不，謝謝。步行有步行的好處。" ➲ more at BARE *v.*, BODY, GOD, HEART, LIFE, SELL *v.*

'soul-destroy·ing *adj.* (of a job or task 工作或任務) very dull and boring, because it has to be repeated many times or because there will never be any improvement 非常枯燥的；十分單調的；消磨精神的

'soul food *noun* [U] the type of food that was traditionally eaten by black people in the southern US 美國南方黑人的傳統食物

soul·ful /'səʊlfl; *NAmE* 'soʊlfl/ *adj.* expressing deep feelings, especially feelings of sadness or love 深情的；（尤指）悽婉的，脈脈含情的：*soulful eyes* 深情的眼睛 ◇ *a soulful song* 一首悽婉的歌 ▸ **soul·ful·ly** /-fəli/ *adv.* **soul·ful·ness** *noun* [U]

S

soul·less /'səʊlləs; *NAmE* 'soʊl-/ *adj.* **1** (of things and places 事物或處所) lacking any attractive or interesting qualities that make people feel happy 沒有生氣的；呆板的；乏味的 SYN **depressing**：*They live in soulless concrete blocks.* 他們住在了無生氣的混凝土樓房裏。 **2** (of a person 人) lacking the ability to feel emotions 不懂感情的；淡漠的

soul·mate /'səʊlmeɪt; *NAmE* 'soʊlmeɪt/ *noun* a person that you have a special friendship with because you understand each other's feelings and interests 知心朋友；知己

'soul music *noun* [U] = SOUL (8)

'soul-searching *noun* [U] the careful examination of your thoughts and feelings, for example in order to reach the correct decision or solution to sth 反省；內省

sound 🔑 /saʊnd/ *noun, verb, adj., adv.*
■ **noun**
▸ **STH YOU HEAR** 聲音 **1** 🔑 [C] something that you can hear 聲音；響聲 SYN **noise**：*a* **high/low sound** 高的／低的聲音 ◇ *a* **clicking/buzzing/scratching, etc. sound** 咔嗒、嗡嗡、嚓嚓等的聲音 ◇ *the different sounds and smells of the forest* 森林裏的各種聲音、各種氣息 ◇ *She heard the sound of footsteps outside.* 她聽見外面有腳步聲。◇ *He crept into the house trying not to* **make a sound**. 他躡手躡腳地溜進房子裏，盡量不弄出一點聲響。 **2** 🔑 [U] continuous rapid movements (called VIBRATIONS) that travel through air or water and can be heard when they reach a person's or an animal's ear 聲；聲響：*Sound travels more slowly than light.* 聲比光傳播得慢。➲ note at NOISE
▸ **FROM TELEVISION/RADIO** 電視；收音機 **3** 🔑 [U] what you can hear coming from a television, radio, etc., or as part of a film/movie 聲音；音響：*Could you* **turn the sound up/down**? 你能把音量調大／調小一些嗎？◇ *The* **sound quality** *of the tapes was excellent.* 磁帶的音響效果極佳。
▸ **OF MUSICIANS** 音樂家 **4** [C, U] the effect that is produced by the music of a particular singer or group of musicians 嗓音；音樂風格：*I like their sound.* 我喜歡他們的音樂風格。
▸ **IMPRESSION** 印象 **5** [sing.] **the ~ of sth** the idea or impression that you get of sb/sth from what sb says or what you read 印象；感覺：*They had a wonderful time* **by the sound of it**. 聽起來他們好像過得很愉快。◇ **From the sound of things** *you were lucky to find him.* 看起來你能找到他真是幸運。◇ *They're consulting a lawyer? I* **don't like the sound of that**. 他們正向一位律師咨詢？這消息不大好哇。
▸ **WATER** 水域 **6** [C] (often in place names 常用於地名) a narrow passage of water that joins two larger areas of water 海峽；海灣 SYN **strait**
IDM **like, etc. the sound of your own 'voice** (*disapproving*) to like talking a lot or too much, usually without wanting to listen to other people 愛囉嗦；喜歡說個沒完 **within (the) sound of sth** (*BrE*) near enough to be able to hear sth 在聽得見…的範圍內：*a house within sound of the sea* 聽得見海浪聲的房子
■ **verb** (not usually used in the progressive tenses 通常不用於進行時)
▸ **GIVE IMPRESSION** 給以印象 **1** 🔑 *linking verb* to give a particular impression when heard or read about 聽起來好像；讓人聽着好像：**+ adj.** *His voice sounded strange on the phone.* 他的聲音在電話裏聽着挺怪的。◇ *She didn't sound surprised when I told her the news.* 我把消息告訴她時，她好像並不感到驚訝。◇ *His explanation sounds reasonable to me.* 他的解釋我聽着有道理。◇ *Leo* **made it sound** *so easy. But it wasn't.* 利奧把這事說得好像挺簡單，其實不是那麼回事。◇ **+ noun** *She sounds just the person we need for the job.* 看來她正是我們要找的幹這份工作的人。◇ **~ like sb/sth** *You sounded just like your father when you said that.* 你說這話，聽着跟你父親一模一樣。◇ **~ as if/as though ...** *I hope I don't sound as if/as though I'm criticizing you.* 我希望不要聽起來好像我在批評你。
HELP In spoken English people often use **like** instead of **as if** or **as though**, especially in *NAmE*, but this is not considered correct in written *BrE*. 英語口語中，尤其是美式英語，常用 like 代替 as if 或 as though；書面英式英語中，此用法被視為不正確。
▸ **-SOUNDING** 聽起來… **2** (in adjectives 構成形容詞) giving the impression of having a particular sound 聽起來…的：*an Italian-sounding name* 聽着像意大利人的名字 ◇ *fine-sounding words* 聽上去華而不實的話語
▸ **PRODUCE SOUND** 發出聲音 **3** [I, T] to produce a sound; to make sth such as a musical instrument produce a sound（使）發出聲音，響：*The bell sounded for the end of the class.* 下課鈴響了。◇ (*BrE*) **~ sth** *Passing motorists sounded their horns in support.* 開車路過的人揿響喇叭表示支持。
▸ **GIVE WARNING/SIGNAL** 發出警報／信號 **4** 🔑 [T] **~ sth** to give a signal such as a warning by making a sound 鳴警報；拉響警報；發出警報：*When I saw the smoke, I tried to* **sound the alarm**. 看到煙後，我就設法發出警報。◇ (*figurative*) *Scientists have* **sounded a note of caution** *on the technique.* 科學家已告誡人類慎重對待這項技術。◇ *Leaving him out of the team may* **sound the death knell** *for our chances of winning* (= signal the end of our chances). 不讓他參加比賽，也許就意味着我們全無獲勝的可能了。
▸ **PRONOUNCE** 發音 **5** [T] **~ sth** (*technical* 術語) to pronounce sth 發（音）：*You don't sound the 'b' in the word 'comb'.* 說 comb 時字母 b 不發音。
▸ **MEASURE DEPTH** 測量深度 **6** [T, I] **~ (sth)** (*technical* 術語) to measure the depth of the sea or a lake by using a line with a weight attached, or an electronic instrument 測（海或湖的）深度
IDM **(it) ˌsounds like a plan to 'me** (*especially NAmE*) used to agree to a suggestion that you think is good（這）聽起來真是不錯 ➲ more at NOTE *n.*, SUSPICIOUSLY

PHR V **,sound 'off (about sth)** (*informal, disapproving*) to express your opinions loudly or in an aggressive way 高談闊論；夸夸其談 **,sound sb↔'out (about/on sth)** | **,sound sth↔'out** to try to find out from sb what they think about sth, often in an indirect way 試探某人（對某事）的看法；探口風：*I wanted to sound him out about a job.* 我想就一項工作探探他的口風。◇ *They decided to sound out her interest in the project.* 他們決定試探一下她對那個項目的興趣。

■ ***adj.*** (**sound·er**, **sound·est**)

▸ **RELIABLE** 可靠 **1** sensible; that you can rely on and that will probably give good results 明智的；合理的；正確的；可靠的：*a person of sound judgement* 判斷力強的人 ◇ *He gave me some very sound advice.* 他給了我一些非常合理的忠告。◇ *This gives the design team a sound basis for their work.* 這為設計組開展工作提供了堅實的基礎。◇ *The proposal makes sound commercial sense.* 這項建議從營利的角度看是完全合情合理的。◇ *Their policies are environmentally sound.* 他們的政策對環境沒有不利的影響。**OPP** unsound

▸ **THOROUGH** 透徹 **2** [only before noun] good and thorough 透徹的；完備的；全面的：*a sound knowledge/understanding of sth* 對某事透徹的瞭解 / 理解 ◇ *He has **a sound grasp of** the issues.* 他對這些問題掌握得很全面。

▸ **NOT DAMAGED/HURT** 無損傷；未受傷 **3** in good condition; not damaged, hurt, etc. 完好的；健康的；無損傷的；未受傷的：*We arrived home **safe and sound**.* 我們安然無恙地到了家。◇ *to be **of sound mind*** (= not mentally ill) 神志健全 ◇ *The house needs attention but the roof is sound.* 房子需要修葺，不過屋頂還完好無損。**OPP** unsound

▸ **SLEEP** 睡眠 **4** [usually before noun] deep and peaceful 酣暢的；香甜的：*to have a sound night's sleep* 一夜酣睡 ◇ *to be a **sound sleeper*** 睡得很沉的人

▸ **GOOD, BUT NOT EXCELLENT** 良好 **5** good and accurate, but not excellent 不錯的；實實在在的：*a sound piece of writing* 一篇不錯的文章 ◇ *a sound tennis player* 頗具實力的網球運動員

▸ **PHYSICAL PUNISHMENT** 體罰 **6** severe 嚴厲的；重的：*to give sb a sound beating* 痛打某人一頓

▸ **sound·ness** *noun* [U]：*soundness of judgement* 判斷力強 ◇ *financial soundness* 良好的財政狀況 ◇ *the soundness of the building's foundations* 建築物地基的堅固 ➲ see also SOUNDLY

IDM **(as) sound as a 'bell** (*informal*) in perfect condition 狀況極佳；十分健康

■ ***adv.*** **~ asleep** very deeply asleep 酣（睡）；（睡得）沉

sound·alike /'saʊndəlaɪk/ *noun* a person who sounds very similar to sb who is famous 聲音很像名人的人

the 'sound barrier *noun* [sing.] the point at which an aircraft's speed is the same as the speed of sound, causing reduced control, a very loud noise (called a SONIC BOOM) and various other effects 音障；聲障：*to break the sound barrier* (= to travel faster than the speed of sound) 突破音障（即超過音速運行）

'sound bite *noun* a short phrase or sentence taken from a longer speech, especially a speech made by a politician, that is considered to be particularly effective or appropriate（來自政治家講話等的）摘引精句，名言

'sound card *noun* (*computing* 計) a device that can be put into a computer to allow the use of sound with MULTIMEDIA software 聲卡；音效卡

sound·check /'saʊndtʃek/ *noun* a process of checking that the equipment used for recording music, or for playing music at a concert, is working correctly and producing sound of a good quality（對錄音或音響設備的）校音

'sound effect *noun* [usually pl.] a sound that is made artificially, for example the sound of the wind or a battle, and used in a film/movie, play, computer game, etc. to make it more realistic 音響效果

'sound engineer *noun* a person who works in a recording or broadcasting studio and whose job is to control the levels and balance of sound 音響師

sound·ing /'saʊndɪŋ/ *noun* **1** **soundings** [pl.] careful questions that are asked in order to find out people's opinions about sth 意見調查；徵詢意見：*They will **take soundings** among party members.* 他們將在黨員中間徵詢意見。◇ *What do your soundings show?* 你的調查結果如何？ **2** [C] a measurement that is made to find out how deep water is 水深測量：*They **took soundings** along the canal.* 他們沿運河測量了水深。

'sounding board *noun* a person or group of people that you discuss your ideas with before you make them known or reach a decision 決策咨詢人（或班子）

sound·less /'saʊndləs/ *adj.* without making any sound; silent 無聲的；寂靜的：*Her lips parted in a soundless scream.* 她張開嘴想喊，但喊不出聲來。▸ **sound·less·ly** *adv.*

sound·ly /'saʊndli/ *adv.* **1** if you sleep **soundly**, you sleep very well and very deeply 酣（睡）；（睡得）沉 **2** in a way that is sensible or can be relied on 明智地；可靠地：*a soundly based conclusion* 有充分依據的結論 **3** completely and thoroughly 完全徹底地：*The team was soundly defeated.* 這支隊一敗塗地。 **4** strongly; firmly 堅固地；牢固地：*These houses are soundly built.* 這些房子蓋得結實。 **5** very well, but not in an excellent way 不錯地；很好但並非優異地：*He played soundly.* 他在比賽中表現還不錯。 **6** (of physical punishment 體罰) severely 嚴厲地：*He was soundly beaten by his mother.* 他被母親狠揍了一頓。

sound·proof /'saʊndpruːf/ (also **sound·proofed**) *adj.* made so that sound cannot pass through it or into it 隔音的：*a soundproof room* 隔音室 ▸ **sound·proof** *verb* **~ sth**

'sound stage *noun* a platform or a special area where sound can be recorded, for example for a film/movie（電影製作等的）錄音平台，錄音場

'sound system *noun* equipment for playing recorded or live music and for making it louder 音響系統

sound·track /'saʊndtræk/ *noun* **1** all the music, speech and sounds that are recorded for a film/movie（電影的）聲跡，聲帶：*The soundtrack of 'Casablanca' took weeks to edit.* 《卡薩布蘭卡》的聲帶花了好幾個星期才剪輯好。 **2** some of the music, and sometimes some speech, from a film/movie or musical that is released on CD, the Internet, etc. for people to buy 電影（或音樂劇）原聲音樂（或配音、對白）：*I've just bought the soundtrack of the latest Miyazaki movie.* 我剛買了宮崎駿最新電影的原聲唱片。➲ COLLOCATIONS at CINEMA

'sound wave *noun* a VIBRATION in the air, in water, etc. that we hear as sound 聲波

soup 0-π /suːp/ *noun, verb*

■ ***noun*** 0-π [U, C] a liquid food made by boiling meat, vegetables, etc. in water, often eaten as the first course of a meal 湯；羹：*a bowl of soup* 一碗湯 ◇ *chicken soup* 雞湯 ◇ (*BrE*) ***tinned/packet soups*** 罐裝 / 袋裝湯 ◇ (*NAmE*) ***canned/packaged soups*** 罐裝 / 袋裝湯 ◇ ***a soup spoon/plate*** 湯匙；湯盤 ➲ VISUAL VOCAB page V22

IDM **from ,soup to 'nuts** (*NAmE, informal*) from beginning to end 從頭到尾；完全；全部：*She told me the whole story from soup to nuts.* 她把事情的來龍去脈都告訴了我。 **in the 'soup** (*informal*) in trouble 遇到麻煩：*We're all in the soup now.* 我們這下遇到麻煩了。

■ ***verb***

PHR V **,soup sth↔'up** (*informal*) to make changes to sth such as a car or computer, so that it is more powerful or exciting than before 通過改裝（汽車、計算機等）增強功能

soup·çon /'suːpsɒn; *NAmE* '-sɑːn/ *noun* [sing.] (from *French*, sometimes *humorous*) a very small amount 微量；一丁點

'soup kitchen *noun* a place where people who have no money can get soup and other food free 施食處（為窮人免費提供食物）

soupy /'suːpi/ *adj.* **1** similar to soup 湯似的；羹一般的：*a soupy stew* 像湯一樣的燉菜 **2** (of the air 空氣) very damp and unpleasant 潮濕難忍的；陰濕的 **3** (*informal*) emotional in a way that is exaggerated and embarrassing 過於傷感的；太多愁善感的

S

sour 0-π /ˈsaʊə(r)/ *adj., verb*

■ **adj.** **1** 0-π having a taste like that of a lemon or of fruit that is not ready to eat 酸的；有酸味的： *sour apples* 酸蘋果 ◇ *a sour flavour* 酸味 OPP **sweet** ➲ see also SWEET-AND-SOUR ➲ SYNONYMS at BITTER **2** 0-π (especially of milk 尤指牛奶) having an unpleasant taste or smell because it is not fresh 酸腐的；餿的： *to* ***turn/go sour*** 餿了 ➲ SYNONYMS at BITTER **3** (of people 人) not cheerful; bad-tempered and unpleasant 陰鬱的；悶悶不樂的；沒好氣的： *a sour and disillusioned woman* 心灰意冷、幻想破滅的女人 ◇ *a sour face* 陰鬱的臉色 ◇ *The meeting ended on a* ***sour note*** *with several people walking out.* 幾個人退席，會議不歡而散。 ▸ **sour·ly** *adv.*： *'Who asked you?' he said sourly.* "誰問你了？" 他沒好氣地說。 **sour·ness** *noun* [U]

IDM **go/turn 'sour** to stop being pleasant or working properly 變壞；惡化；出毛病： *Their relationship soon went sour.* 他們的關係很快有了嫌隙。 **sour 'grapes** (*saying*) used to show that you think sb is jealous and is pretending that sth is not important （表示某人表面貶低某事物，實則是嫉妒）酸葡萄： *He said he didn't want the job anyway, but that's just sour grapes.* 他說他其實並不想幹這份工作，這不過是吃不着葡萄就說葡萄酸而已。

■ **verb** **1** [I, T] (of relationships, attitudes, people, etc. 關係、態度、人等) to change so that they become less pleasant or friendly than before; to make sth do this （使）變壞，惡化： *The atmosphere at the house soured.* 屋子裏的氣氛不對了。 ◇ **~ sth** *The disagreement over trade tariffs has soured relations between the two countries.* 貿易關稅上的分歧導致兩國關係惡化。 **2** [I, T] **~ (sth)** if milk **sours** or if sth **sours** it, it becomes sour and has an unpleasant taste or smell （牛奶等）變味，酸腐；使變酸腐

source 0-π AW /sɔːs; *NAmE* sɔːrs/ *noun, verb*

■ **noun** **1** 0-π a place, person or thing that you get sth from 來源；出處： *renewable* ***energy sources*** 可再生能源 ◇ *Your local library will be a useful* ***source of*** *information.* 你們當地的圖書館將是很好的資料來源。 ◇ *What is their main source of income?* 他們的主要收入來源是什麼？ **2** 0-π [usually pl.] a person, book or document that provides information, especially for study, a piece of written work or news 信息來源；原始資料： *He refused to name his sources.* 他拒絕說出消息的來源。 ◇ *Government sources indicated yesterday that cuts may have to be made.* 政府方面昨天透露，削減可能勢在必行。 ◇ *source material* 原始資料 ◇ *Historians use a wide range of* ***primary and secondary sources*** *for their research.* 歷史學家在研究中使用大量的原始資料和二手資料。 **3** 0-π a person or thing that causes sth, especially a problem 起源；根源；原因： *a source of violence* 暴力的根源 ◇ *a source of confusion* 困惑的緣由 **4** the place where a river or stream starts 源頭；發源地： *the source of the Nile* 尼羅河的發源地 ➲ VISUAL VOCAB pages V4, V5

IDM **at 'source** at the place or the point that sth comes from or begins 在源頭；從一開始： *Is your salary taxed at source* (= by your employer)? 你領的是稅後工資嗎？

■ **verb** [often passive] **~ sth (from …)** (*business* 商) to get sth from a particular place （從…）獲得： *We source all the meat sold in our stores from British farms.* 我們商店裏賣的肉均從英國農場購進。 ➲ see also OUTSOURCE

source·book /ˈsɔːsbʊk; *NAmE* ˈsɔːrs-/ *noun* a collection of texts on a particular subject, used especially as an introduction to the subject （有關某專題的）原始資料集，緒論資料集

'source code *noun* [U] (*computing* 計) a computer program written in text form that must be translated into MACHINE CODE before it can run on a computer 源（代）碼；原始碼

ˌsour 'cream (*BrE* also **ˌsoured 'cream**) *noun* [U] cream that has been made sour by adding bacteria to it, used in cooking 酸奶油（烹飪用）

sour·dough /ˈsaʊədəʊ; *NAmE* ˈsaʊərdoʊ/ *noun* [U] DOUGH (= a mixture of flour, fat and water) that is left to FERMENT so that it has a sour taste, used for making bread; bread made with this DOUGH 酸麪糰；發麪麪包

'sour-faced *adj.* [usually before noun] (of a person 人) having a bad-tempered or unpleasant expression 臉色陰沉的；顯得不高興的

sour·puss /ˈsaʊəpʊs; *NAmE* ˈsaʊərpʊs/ *noun* (*informal*) a person who is not cheerful or pleasant 陰鬱的人；整天繃着臉的人；性情乖戾的人

sousa·phone /ˈsuːzəfəʊn; *NAmE* -foʊn/ *noun* a BRASS instrument like a TUBA, used in marching bands in the US 蘇薩大號，蘇沙低音號（美國行進樂隊用）

souse /saʊs/ *verb* **~ sth/sb** [usually passive] to SOAK sth/sb completely in a liquid 把…浸透；使濕透；醃

soused /saʊst/ *adj.* **1** [only before noun] (of fish 魚) preserved in salt water and VINEGAR 醃製的： *soused herring* 醃鯡魚 **2** (*old-fashioned, informal*) drunk 喝醉的

south 0-π /saʊθ/ *noun, adj., adv.*

■ **noun** [U, sing.] (*abbr.* **S**, **So.**) **1** 0-π (usually **the south**) the direction that is on your right when you watch the sun rise; one of the four main points of the COMPASS 南；南方： *Which way is south?* 哪邊是南？ ◇ *warmer weather coming from the south* 受南方的影響而漸暖的天氣 ◇ *He lives* ***to the south of*** (= further south than) *the city.* 他住在城外南邊。 ➲ picture at COMPASS ➲ compare EAST, NORTH, WEST **2** 0-π **the south**, **the South** the southern part of a country, a region or the world 南方；南部： *birds flying to the south for the winter* 飛往南方過冬的鳥 ◇ *They bought a villa in the South of France.* 他們在法國南部買了一座別墅。 ◇ *Houses are less expensive in the North than in the South* (= of England). 英格蘭北方的房子比南方便宜。 **3** **the South** the southern states of the US 美國南方各州；美國南方 ➲ see also DEEP SOUTH **4** **the South** the poorer countries in the southern half of the world （南半球的）發展中國家

■ **adj.** (*abbr.* **S**, **So.**) [only before noun] **1** 0-π in or towards the south 南方的；向南的；南部的： *South Wales* 南威爾士 ◇ *They live on the south coast.* 他們住在南海岸。 **2** 0-π a **south wind** blows from the south 南風的；南方吹來的 ➲ compare SOUTHERLY

■ **adv.** **1** 0-π towards the south 向南；朝南： *This room faces south.* 這間房朝南。 **2** **~ of sth** nearer to the south than sth …以南；在…之南： *They live ten miles south of Bristol.* 他們居住在布里斯托爾以南 10 英里的地方。 **3** **~ of sth** (*informal, NAmE* or *finance* 財) less or lower than sth 少於；低於： *The drug is achieving revenues just south of $1 billion per quarter.* 藥品每個季度的收益僅略低於 10 億。 OPP **north**

IDM **down 'south** (*informal*) to or in the south, especially of England （尤指英格蘭）往南方，在南方： *They've gone to live down south.* 他們到南方去住了。

ˌSouth Aˈmerica *noun* [U] the continent which is to the south of Central America and N America 南美洲 ➲ compare LATIN AMERICA

south·bound /ˈsaʊθbaʊnd/ *adj.* travelling or leading towards the south 南行的；向南的： *southbound traffic* 南行的車輛 ◇ *the southbound carriageway of the motorway* 高速公路的南向車行道

the ˌSouth-'East *noun* (*BrE*) the south-eastern part of England which is the richest part of the country and has the highest population 英格蘭東南部（英國最富有、人口最多的地區）

ˌsouth-'east *noun* (usually **the south-east**) [sing.] (*abbr.* **SE**) the direction or region at an equal distance between south and east 東南；東南方；東南地區 ➲ picture at COMPASS ▸ **ˌsouth-'east** *adv., adj.*

ˌsouth-'easter·ly *adj.* **1** [only before noun] in or towards the south-east 東南方的；向東南的；東南部的 **2** [usually before noun] (of winds 風) blowing from the south-east 從東南吹來的

ˌsouth-'eastern *adj.* [only before noun] (*abbr.* **SE**) connected with the south-east 東南的；東南方向的

ˌsouth-'eastwards (also **ˌsouth-'eastward**) *adv.* towards the south-east 向東南；朝東南 ▸ **ˌsouth-'eastward** *adj.*

south·er·ly /ˈsʌðəli; *NAmE* -ərli/ *adj., noun*

■ **adj.** **1** [only before noun] in or towards the south 南方的；向南的；南部的： *travelling in a southerly direction* 朝南行進 **2** [usually before noun] (of winds 風) blowing

S

from the south 從南方吹來的：*a warm southerly breeze* 從南邊吹來的和煦微風 ➲ compare SOUTH

■ ***noun*** (*pl.* **-ies**) a wind that blows from the south 南風

south·ern /ˈsʌðən; *NAmE* -ərn/ (also **Southern**) *adj.* (*abbr.* **S**) [usually before noun] located in the south or facing south; connected with or typical of the south part of the world or a region 南方的；向南的；南部的：*the southern slopes of the mountains* 山的南坡 ◇ *southern Spain* 西班牙南部 ◇ *a southern accent* 南方口音

ˌsouthern ˈbelle *noun* (*old-fashioned, NAmE*) a young attractive woman from the southern US （美國）南方美女

the ˌSouthern ˈCone *noun* [sing.] the region of S America which consists of Brazil, Paraguay, Uruguay, Argentina and Chile 南錐地區（南美洲的巴西、巴拉圭、烏拉圭、阿根廷和智利）

the ˌSouthern ˈCross *noun* [sing.] a group of stars in the shape of a cross that can be seen from the southern HEMISPHERE 南十字（星）座

south·ern·er /ˈsʌðənə(r); *NAmE* -ərn-/ *noun* a person who comes from or lives in the southern part of a country 南方人

the ˌSouthern ˈLights *noun* [pl.] (also **aur·ora aus·tra·lis**) bands of coloured light that are sometimes seen in the sky at night in the most southern countries of the world 南極光

south·ern·most /ˈsʌðənməʊst; *NAmE* -ərnmoʊst/ *adj.* [usually before noun] furthest south 最南的；最南端的；最南部的：*the southernmost part of the island* 島的最南端

south·paw /ˈsaʊθpɔː/ *noun* (*informal, especially NAmE*) a person who prefers to use their left hand rather than their right, especially in a sport such as BOXING （尤指拳擊等運動中）慣用左手的人，左撇子

the ˌSouth ˈPole *noun* [sing.] the point of the earth that is furthest south 南極 ➲ VISUAL VOCAB page V72

ˌsouth-south-ˈeast *noun* [sing.] (*abbr.* **SSE**) the direction at an equal distance between south and south-east 南東南；南東南方；南南東 ▸ **ˌsouth-south-ˈeast** *adv.*

ˌsouth-south-ˈwest *noun* [sing.] (*abbr.* **SSW**) the direction at an equal distance between south and south-west 南西南；南西南方；南南西 ▸ **ˌsouth-south-ˈwest** *adv.*

south·wards /ˈsaʊθwədz; *NAmE* -wərdz/ (also **south·ward**) *adv.* towards the south 向南；朝南：*to turn southwards* 轉向南 ▸ **south·ward** *adj.*：*in a southward direction* 向南

ˌsouth-ˈwest *noun* (usually **the south-west**) [sing.] (*abbr.* **SW**) the direction or region at an equal distance between south and west 西南；西南方；西南地區 ➲ picture at COMPASS ▸ **ˌsouth-ˈwest** *adv., adj.*

ˌsouth-ˈwester·ly *adj.* **1** [only before noun] in or towards the south-west 西南方的；向西南的；西南部的 **2** [usually before noun] (of winds 風) blowing from the south-west 從西南吹來的

ˌsouth-ˈwestern *adj.* [only before noun] (*abbr.* **SW**) connected with the south-west 西南的；西南方向的

ˌsouth-ˈwestwards (also **ˌsouth-ˈwestward**) *adv.* towards the south-west 向西南；朝西南 ▸ **ˌsouth-ˈwestward** *adj.*

sou·venir /ˌsuːvəˈnɪə(r); *NAmE* -ˈnɪr; ˈsuːvənɪr/ *noun* a thing that you buy and/or keep to remind yourself of a place, an occasion or a holiday/vacation; something that you bring back for other people when you have been on holiday/vacation 紀念物；紀念品；（度假或外遊買回來送人的）禮物 SYN **memento**：*I bought the ring as a **souvenir of** Greece.* 我買了一枚戒指，留作對希臘的紀念。◇ *a **souvenir shop*** 紀念品商店 ➲ COLLOCATIONS at TRAVEL

souv·la·ki /suːˈvlæki/ *noun* [U, C] a Greek dish consisting of pieces of meat cooked on sticks 希臘肉串

sou'·wester /ˌsaʊˈwestə(r)/ *noun* **1** a hat made of shiny material that keeps out the rain, with a long wide piece at the back to protect the neck 防雨帽（後沿寬長可護頸）➲ VISUAL VOCAB page V65 **2** a strong wind or storm coming from the south-west 西南強風；西南風暴

sov·er·eign /ˈsɒvrɪn; *NAmE* ˈsɑːvrən/ *noun, adj.*

■ ***noun*** **1** (*formal*) a king or queen 君主；元首 **2** an old British gold coin worth one pound 金鎊（舊時英國金幣，面值一英鎊）

■ ***adj.*** (*formal*) **1** [only before noun] (of a country or state 國家) free to govern itself; completely independent 有主權的；完全獨立的 SYN **autonomous** **2** having complete power or the greatest power in the country 掌握全部權力的；有至高無上的權力的：*a sovereign ruler* 最高統治者

sov·er·eign·ty /ˈsɒvrənti; *NAmE* ˈsɑːv-/ *noun* [U] (*formal*) **1 ~ (over sth)** complete power to govern a country 主權；最高統治權；最高權威：*The country claimed sovereignty over the island.* 那個國家聲稱對該島擁有主權。◇ *the sovereignty of Parliament* 議會的最高權威 ◇ (*figurative*) *the idea of consumer sovereignty* 消費者至上的觀念 **2** the state of being a country with freedom to govern itself 獨立自主：*The declaration proclaimed the **full sovereignty** of the republic.* 這份宣言宣告這個共和國完全獨立自主。➲ COLLOCATIONS at INTERNATIONAL

So·viet /ˈsəʊviət; ˈsɒv-; *NAmE* ˈsoʊviet; ˈsɑːv-/ *adj.* [usually before noun] connected with the former USSR 蘇聯的

so·viet /ˈsəʊviət; ˈsɒv-; *NAmE* ˈsoʊviet; ˈsɑːv-/ *noun* **1** [C] an elected local, district or national council in the former USSR 蘇維埃（前蘇聯的各級代表會議）**2 the Soviets** [pl.] (*especially NAmE*) the people of the former USSR 蘇聯人

sow[1] /səʊ; *NAmE* soʊ/ *verb* ➲ see also SOW[2] (**sowed, sown** /səʊn; *NAmE* soʊn/ or **sowed, sowed**) **1** [T, I] to plant or spread seeds in or on the ground 播種；種：**~ (sth)** *Sow the seeds in rows.* 一壟一壟地播種。◇ *Water well after sowing.* 播種後要澆足水。◇ **~ sth with sth** *The fields around had been sown with wheat.* 近處的地裏種上了小麥。➲ COLLOCATIONS at FARMING **2** [T] **~ sth (in sth)** to introduce or spread feelings or ideas, especially ones that cause trouble 灌輸；激起；散佈；煽動：*to sow doubt in sb's mind* 使某人心懷疑慮 ◇ *to sow confusion* 製造混亂

IDM **sow the seeds of sth** to start the process that leads to a particular situation or result 成為…的肇端；播下…的種子 **sow (your) wild ˈoats** (of young men 青年男子) to go through a period of wild behaviour while young, especially having a lot of romantic or sexual relationships 過放蕩不羈的生活 ➲ more at REAP

sow[2] /saʊ/ *noun* a female pig 母豬 ➲ compare BOAR, HOG *n.* ➲ see also SOW[1] IDM see SILK

sower /ˈsəʊə(r); *NAmE* ˈsoʊ-/ *noun* a person or machine that puts seeds in the ground 播種者；播種機

soya /ˈsɔɪə/ (*BrE*) (*NAmE* **soy**) *noun* [U] the plant on which soya beans grow; the food obtained from soya beans 大豆（作物）；大豆食物：*a soya crop* 大豆作物 ◇ *soya flour* 大豆粉

ˈsoya bean (*BrE*) (*NAmE* **soy·bean** /ˈsɔɪbiːn/) *noun* a type of BEAN, originally from SE Asia, that is used instead of meat or animal PROTEIN in some types of food 大豆

ˈsoya milk *noun* [U] a liquid made from soya beans, used instead of milk 豆奶；豆漿

soy sauce /ˌsɔɪ ˈsɔːs/ (also **ˌsoya ˈsauce**) *noun* [U] a thin dark brown sauce that is made from soya beans and has a salty taste, used in Chinese and Japanese cooking 醬油

soz·zled /ˈsɒzld; *NAmE* ˈsɑːzld/ *adj.* (*BrE, slang*) very drunk 大醉的；爛醉的

spa /spɑː/ *noun* **1** a place where water with minerals in it, which is considered to be good for your health, comes up naturally out of the ground; the name given to a town that has such a place and where there are, or were, places where people could drink the water 礦泉療養地；礦泉城：*Leamington Spa* 利明頓礦泉城 ◇ *a spa town* 有礦泉的城鎮 ◇ *spa waters* 礦泉水 **2** a place where people can relax and improve their health, with, for example, a swimming pool 休閒健身中心：*a superb*

S

***health spa** which includes sauna, Turkish bath and fitness rooms* 內設桑拿浴室、蒸汽浴室和健身房的第一流的休閒健身中心 **3** (*especially NAmE*) = JACUZZI

space /speɪs/ *noun, verb*

■ ***noun***

▸ **EMPTY AREA 空間 1** [U] an amount of an area or of a place that is empty or that is available for use（可利用的）空地，空間 **SYN room**：***floor/office/shelf, etc. space*** 樓面面積、辦公室裏的空間、擱架上的空當等 ◇ *We must make good use of the available space.* 我們必須充分利用現有空間。◇ *That desk **takes up** too much **space**.* 那張桌子佔的地方太大。◇ *There is very little **storage space** in the department.* 這個部門存放東西的地方很小。◇ *Can we **make space** for an extra chair?* 我們能不能騰個空再放一把椅子？◇ *How much **disk space** will it take up?* (= on a computer) 這會佔用多少磁盤空間？ **2** [C] an area or a place that is empty 空；空隙；空子；空當：*a large/small/narrow/wide space* 大／小／窄／寬的空當 ◇ *a space two metres by three metres* 長三米寬兩米的空間 ◇ *a **parking space*** 停車的空地 ◇ *crowded together in a confined space* 一起擠在狹小的空間 ◇ *I'll clear a space for your books.* 我來騰出一塊地方好放你的書。◇ *Put it in the space between the table and the wall.* 桌子和牆中間有個空，把它放那兒去。 **3** [U] the quality of being large and empty, allowing you to move freely 寬敞；空曠；開闊 **SYN spaciousness**：*The room has been furnished and decorated to give a feeling of space.* 經過裝潢和佈置之後，這個房間給人一種寬敞的感覺。 **4** [C, U] a large area of land that has no buildings on it（無建築物的）大片空地，開闊地：*the **wide open spaces** of the Canadian prairies* 加拿大一片片廣袤的草原 ◇ *It's a city with fine buildings and plenty of **open space**.* 這座城市既有漂亮的建築又有開闊的空地。 ➲ SYNONYMS at LAND

▸ **OUTSIDE EARTH'S ATMOSPHERE 地球大氣以外 5** (also **ˌouter ˈspace**) [U] the area outside the earth's atmosphere where all the other planets and stars are 外層空間；太空：*the first woman in space* 第一位進入太空的女性 ◇ *the possibility of visitors from **outer space*** 出現外層空間來客的可能性 ◇ *a space flight/mission* 太空飛行；太空飛行任務

▸ **PERIOD OF TIME 一段時間 6** [C, usually sing.] a period of time 一段時間；期間：*Forty-four people died **in the space of** five days.* 五天裏死了四十四個人。◇ *They had achieved a lot **in a short space of time**.* 他們在短時間內取得了很大的成績。◇ *Leave a space of two weeks between appointments.* 每次約見要間隔兩個星期。

▸ **IN WRITING/PRINTING 書寫；印刷 7** [U, C] the part of a line, page or document that is empty 空白；空行；空格：*Don't waste space by leaving a wide margin.* 頁邊不要留太寬浪費版面。◇ *There was not enough space to print all the letters we received.* 版面有限，無法悉數刊載我們收到的所有來信。◇ *Leave a space after the comma.* 逗號後面要留一個空格。

▸ **FREEDOM 自由 8** [U] the freedom and the time to think or do what you want to 自我支配的自由；屬於自己的空間：*She was upset and **needed space**.* 她心境不佳，需要一片自己的天地。◇ *You have to **give** teenagers plenty **of space**.* 必須給青少年充足的自由空間。 ➲ see also BREATHING SPACE

▸ **WHERE THINGS EXIST/MOVE 空間 9** [U] the whole area in which all things exist and move 空間：*It is quite possible that space and time are finite.* 很有可能空間和時間是有限的。

IDM **look/stare/gaze into ˈspace** to look straight in front of you without looking at a particular thing, usually because you are thinking about sth 若有所思地望着前方；出神地凝視前方 ➲ more at WASTE *n.*, WATCH *v.*

■ ***verb*** [often passive] **~ sth (+ adv./prep.)** to arrange things so that they have regular spaces between them 以一定間隔排列：***evenly spaced** plants* 間隔均勻的秧苗 ◇ *a row of **closely spaced** dots* 一行排列緊密的小點 ◇ *Space the posts about a metre apart.* 這些杆子之間要間隔一米左右。

PHR V **ˌspace ˈout** (*informal, especially NAmE*) to take no notice of what is happening around you, especially as a result of taking drugs 精神恍惚，神志迷糊（常因吸毒） ➲ see also SPACED OUT **ˌspace sth↔ˈout** to arrange things with a wide space between them 使拉開間距；使隔開：*The houses are spaced out in this area of town.* 在城市的這一地區，房屋坐落稀疏。

ˈspace-age *adj.* [usually before noun] (*informal*) (especially of design or technology 尤指樣式或技術) very modern and advanced 太空時代的；非常先進的：*a space-age kitchen* 太空時代的廚房

ˈspace bar *noun* a bar on the keyboard of a computer or TYPEWRITER that you press to make spaces between words（計算機或打字機的）空格鍵 ➲ VISUAL VOCAB page V66

ˈspace cadet *noun* (*slang*) a person who behaves strangely and often forgets things, as though he or she is using drugs 行為異常的人；精神恍惚的人

space·craft /ˈspeɪskrɑːft; *NAmE* -kræft/ *noun* (*pl.* **space·craft**) a vehicle that travels in space 航天器；宇宙飛船；太空船

ˌspaced ˈout (also **spacey**) *adj.* (*informal*) not completely conscious of what is happening around you, often because of taking drugs 精神恍惚的，神志迷糊的（常指因吸食毒品）

ˈspace heater *noun* (*NAmE*) an electric device for heating a room 小型取暖器

space·man /ˈspeɪsmæn/ *noun* (*pl.* **-men** /-men/) **1** (*informal*) a man who travels into space; an ASTRONAUT 宇航員；航天員；太空人 **2** (in stories) a creature that visits the earth from another planet（小說中的）外星人 **SYN alien** ➲ see also SPACEWOMAN

ˈspace probe *noun* = PROBE *n.* (2)

the ˈspace race *noun* competition between the US and the Soviet Union in the 1950s and 60s to be the first to explore space 太空競賽（20 世紀 50 和 60 年代美國和蘇聯之間為取得宇宙探索領先地位而進行的競爭）

space·ship /ˈspeɪsʃɪp/ *noun* a vehicle that travels in space, carrying people 宇宙飛船；太空船

ˈspace shuttle (also **shuttle**) *noun* a SPACECRAFT designed to be used, for example, for travelling between the earth and a space station 航天飛機；太空梭

ˈspace station *noun* a large structure that is sent into space and remains above the earth as a base for people working and travelling in space 太空站；航天站；宇宙空間站

space·suit /ˈspeɪssuːt; *BrE* also -sjuːt/ *noun* a special suit that covers the whole body and has a supply of air, allowing sb to survive and move around in space 航天服；宇航服；太空衣

ˈspace-time *noun* [U] (*physics* 物) the universe considered as a CONTINUUM with four measurements—length, width, depth and time—inside which any event or physical object is located 時空（一體）

space·walk /ˈspeɪswɔːk/ *noun* a period of time that an ASTRONAUT spends in space outside a SPACECRAFT 太空行走（宇航員在宇宙飛船外的活動）

space·woman /ˈspeɪswʊmən/ *noun* (*pl.* **-women** /-wɪmɪn/) a woman who travels into space 女宇航員；女太空人

spacey /ˈspeɪsi/ *adj.* = SPACED OUT

spa·cial = SPATIAL

spa·cing /ˈspeɪsɪŋ/ *noun* [U] **1** the amount of space that is left between things, especially between the words or lines printed on a page（空間）間隔；（尤指）字距，行距：***single/double spacing*** (= with one or two lines left between lines of type) 單倍／雙倍行距 **2** the amount of time that is left between things happening（時間）間隔

spa·cious /ˈspeɪʃəs/ *adj.* (*approving*) (of a room or building 房間或建築物) large and with plenty of space for people to move around in 寬敞的 **SYN roomy** ▸ **spa·cious·ly** *adv.* **spa·cious·ness** *noun* [U]：*White walls can give a feeling of spaciousness.* 白牆能給人一種寬敞的感覺。

spade /speɪd/ *noun* **1** [C] a garden tool with a broad metal blade and a long handle, used for digging 鍬；鏟：*Turn the soil over with a spade.* 用鍬把地翻一遍。◇

S

(*BrE*) *The children took their* ***buckets and spades*** *to the beach.* 孩子們帶上自己的桶和鏟子到海灘去了。➲ VISUAL VOCAB page V19 ➲ compare SHOVEL **2 spades** [pl., U] one of the four sets of cards (called SUITS) in a PACK/DECK of cards. The cards have a black design shaped like pointed leaves with short STEMS（紙牌中的）黑桃：*the five/queen/ace of spades* 黑桃五／王后／A ➲ VISUAL VOCAB page V37 **3** [C] a card from the set of spades 黑桃牌：*You must play a spade if you have one.* 你如果有黑桃牌，就必須打出來。**4** [C] (*taboo, slang*) an offensive word for a black person 黑人；黑鬼

IDM **in 'spades** (*informal*) in large amounts or to a great degree 大量；非常：*He'd got his revenge now, and in spades.* 現在他報了仇，毫不留情地報了仇。➲ more at CALL *v.*

spade·work /ˈspeɪdwɜːk; *NAmE* -wɜːrk/ *noun* [U] the hard work that has to be done in order to prepare for sth 艱苦的前期準備工作

spa·ghetti /spəˈgeti/ *noun* [U] PASTA in the shape of long thin pieces that look like string when they are cooked 意大利細麵條

spa·ghetti bol·ognese (also **spa·ghetti bol·ognaise**) /spəˌgeti ˌbɒləˈneɪz; *NAmE* ˌboʊlənˈjeɪz/ *noun* [U, C] a dish of spaghetti with a sauce of meat, tomatoes, etc. 意大利波倫亞麵條（用肉醬、番茄醬等做澆頭）

spa,ghetti 'western *noun* a film/movie about COWBOYS, made in Europe by Italian companies（意大利公司在歐洲製作的）意大利式西部片

spake /speɪk/ (*old use*) *past tense* of SPEAK

spam /spæm/ *noun* [U] **1 Spam™** finely chopped cooked meat that has been pressed together in a container, usually sold in cans and served cold in slices（斯帕姆）午餐肉 **2** (*informal*) advertising material sent by email to people who have not asked for it 濫發的電郵；垃圾電郵 ➲ COLLOCATIONS at EMAIL ➲ compare JUNK MAIL, SPIM

spam·ming /ˈspæmɪŋ/ *noun* [U] (*informal*) the practice of sending mail, especially advertising material, through the Internet to a large number of people who have not asked for it 大量發出垃圾電郵（尤指濫發電郵廣告）▸ **spam·mer** /ˈspæmə(r)/ *noun*

span /spæn/ *noun, verb, adj.*

■ *noun* **1** the length of time that sth lasts or is able to continue 持續時間：*I worked with him over a span of six years.* 我和他共事達六年之久。◇ *The project must be completed within a specific* ***time span***. 這項工程必須在規定期限內完成。◇ *Small children have a short* ***attention span***. 幼兒注意力持續時間短。➲ see also LIFESPAN **2 ~ (of sth)** a range or variety of sth 範圍；包括的種類：*Managers have a* ***wide span of*** *control.* 經理的職權範圍很大。◇ *These forests cover a broad span of latitudes.* 這些森林綿延在多個緯度上。**3** the part of a bridge or an ARCH between one vertical support and another（橋或拱的）墩距，跨距，跨度：*The bridge crosses the river in a single span.* 河上的橋為單跨橋。**4** the width of sth from one side to the other 寬度；翼展：*The kite has a span of 1.5 metres.* 風箏寬 1.5 米。➲ see also WINGSPAN

■ *verb* (**-nn-**) **1 ~ sth** to last all through a period of time or to cover the whole of it 持續；貫穿：*His acting career spanned 55 years.* 他的演藝生涯長達 55 年。◇ *Family photos spanning five generations were stolen.* 一家五代人的照片失竊了。**2 ~ sth** to include a large area or a lot of things 包括（廣大地區）；涵蓋（多項內容）：*The operation, which spanned nine countries, resulted in 200 arrests.* 這次行動涉及九個國家，逮捕了 200 人。**3 ~ sth** to stretch right across sth, from one side to the other 橫跨；跨越 SYN **cross**：*a series of bridges spanning the river* 架在河上的一系列橋梁

■ *adj.* IDM see SPICK

span·dex /ˈspændeks/ *noun* = LYCRA

span·gle /ˈspæŋgl/ *verb, noun*

■ *verb* [usually passive] **~ sth (with sth)** to cover or to decorate sth with small pieces of sth shiny 用閃光片佈滿（或裝飾）➲ see also STAR-SPANGLED BANNER

■ *noun* a small piece of shiny metal or plastic used to decorate clothes（裝飾服裝的）閃光金屬片，閃光塑料片 SYN **sequin**

Spang·lish /ˈspæŋglɪʃ/ *noun* [U] (*informal*) language which is a mixture of Spanish and English, especially a type of Spanish that includes many English words 西英混合語（尤指包含很多英語詞的西班牙語）

span·iel /ˈspænjəl/ *noun* a dog with large soft ears that hang down. There are several types of spaniel. 獚，西班牙獵狗（大耳下垂，品種甚多）

Span·ish /ˈspænɪʃ/ *adj., noun*

■ *adj.* from or connected with Spain 西班牙的

■ *noun* [U] the language of Spain, Mexico and most countries in Central and S America 西班牙語（通用於西班牙、墨西哥以及中、南美洲多數國家）

,Spanish 'fly *noun* (*pl.* **,Spanish 'flies**) **1** [C] a bright green insect that has a strong smell and produces a harmful substance 西班牙綠菁 **2** [U] a poisonous mixture made from the crushed bodies of these insects, that is said to give people a strong desire to have sex 西班牙綠菁混合劑（有毒性，據信可催情）

the ,Spanish Inqui'sition *noun* [sing.] **1** the organization set up by the Roman Catholic Church in Spain in the 15th century to punish people who opposed its beliefs, known for its cruel and severe methods 西班牙宗教法庭（15 世紀設立於西班牙的羅馬天主教會組織，因殘酷迫害異教而知名）**2** (often *humorous*) used to say that you do not like the fact that sb is questioning you a lot about sth（表示不滿）逼問，追問：*What is this? The Spanish Inquisition?* 這是怎麼回事？嚴刑逼供嗎？

,Spanish 'moss *noun* [U] a tropical American plant that has long thin grey leaves and that grows over trees 鐵蘭；西班牙蘚

spank /spæŋk/ *verb* **~ sb/sth** to hit sb, especially a child, several times on their bottom as a punishment 打（小孩的）屁股 ➲ compare SMACK *v.* (1) ▸ **spank** *noun*

spank·ing /ˈspæŋkɪŋ/ *noun, adv., adj.*

■ *noun* [C, U] a series of hits on the bottom, given to sb, especially a child, as a punishment 打屁股（尤指打小孩）：*to give sb a spanking* 打某人屁股 ◇ *I don't agree with spanking.* 我不贊成打屁股。

■ *adv.* (*informal*) when you say that sth is **spanking** new, etc. you are emphasizing that it is very new, etc. 非常；十足

■ *adj.* [only before noun] (*informal*) very fast, good or impressive 飛快的；了不起的；令人讚歎的：*The horse set off* ***at a spanking pace***. 那匹馬一溜煙飛奔而去。

span·ner /ˈspænə(r)/ (*BrE*) (also **wrench** *NAmE, BrE*) *noun* a metal tool with a specially shaped end for holding and turning NUTS and BOLTS (= small metal rings and pins that hold things together) 扳手；扳子；扳鉗 ➲ VISUAL VOCAB page V20 ➲ compare ADJUSTABLE SPANNER

IDM **(throw) a 'spanner in the works** (*BrE*) (*NAmE* **(throw) a ('monkey) 'wrench in the works**) (to cause) a delay or problem with sth that sb is planning or doing 干擾；出難題；從中搗亂

spar /spɑː(r)/ *verb, noun*

■ *verb* (**-rr-**) **1** [I] **~ (with sb)** to make the movements used in BOXING, either in training or to test the speed of your opponent's reaction 練習拳擊；虛晃一拳 **2** [I] **~ (with sb)** to argue with sb, usually in a friendly way（多指在友好氣氛中）辯論，爭論

■ *noun* **1** a strong pole used to support the sails, etc. on a ship（船上用作桅杆等的）圓材 **2** a structure that supports the wing of an aircraft（飛機的）翼梁

spare 0-w /speə(r); *NAmE* sper/ *adj., verb, noun*

■ *adj.*

▸ NOT USED/NEEDED 用不着 **1** 0-w [usually before noun] that is not being used or is not needed at the present time 不用的；閒置的：*We've got a spare bedroom, if you'd like to stay.* 要是願意你就住下，我們空着一間卧室。◇ *I'm afraid I haven't got any* ***spare cash***. 恐怕我手頭沒有多餘的現金。◇ *Are there any tickets* ***going spare*** (= are there any available, not being used by sb else)? 有多餘的票嗎？

S

▸ **EXTRA** 外加 **2** 0⊸ [only before noun] kept in case you need to replace the one you usually use; extra 備用的；外加的：*a spare key/tyre* 備用鑰匙 / 輪胎 ◇ *Take some spare clothes in case you get wet.* 多帶幾件衣服，以備身上弄濕了好穿。

▸ **TIME** 時間 **3** 0⊸ available to do what you want with rather than work 空閒的；空餘的：*He's studying music in his* ***spare time.*** 他在空閒時間學音樂。◇ *I haven't had a spare moment this morning.* 我一上午一會兒也沒閒着。

▸ **PERSON** 人 **4** thin, and usually quite tall 瘦的；瘦高的

IDM **go 'spare** (*BrE, informal*) to become very angry or upset 氣急敗壞；焦慮萬分

■ ***verb***

▸ **TIME/MONEY/ROOM/THOUGHT, ETC.** 時間、錢、房間、心思等 **1** to make sth such as time or money available to sb or for sth, especially when it requires an effort for you to do this 抽出；撥出；留出；勻出：**~ sth/sb** *I'd love to have a break, but I can't spare the time just now.* 我是想休息一下，可眼下找不出時間。◇ *Could you spare one of your staff to help us out?* 你能不能從你手下抽一個人過來幫幫我們？◇ **~ sth/sb for sb/sth** *We can only spare one room for you.* 我們只能給你騰出一個房間。◇ *You should* ***spare a thought for*** (= think about) *the person who cleans up after you.* 你應該為隨後打掃的人着想啊。◇ **~ sb sth** *Surely you can spare me a few minutes?* 你應該能為我空出幾分鐘時間吧？

▸ **SAVE SB PAIN/TROUBLE** 免得痛苦 / 麻煩 **2** to save sb/yourself from having to go through an unpleasant experience 省得；免去：**~ sb/yourself sth** *He wanted to spare his mother any anxiety.* 他不想讓母親有絲毫的擔憂。◇ *Please* ***spare me*** (= do not tell me) ***the*** *gruesome* ***details.*** 那些讓人毛骨悚然的細節就請你不要講了。◇ *You could have spared yourself an unnecessary trip by phoning in advance.* 你要是先打個電話就用不着跑這一趟了。◇ **~ sb/yourself from sth** *She was spared from the ordeal of appearing in court.* 她無須出庭受折磨了。

▸ **NOT HARM/DAMAGE** 不傷害 / 損壞 **3** [usually passive] **~ sb/sth** (**from sth**) (*formal*) to allow sb/sth to escape harm, damage or death, especially when others do not escape it 饒恕；赦免；放過；使逃脱：**~ sb/sth** (**from sth**) *They killed the men but spared the children.* 他們殺死了大人，但放過了孩子。◇ *During the bombing only one house was spared* (= was not hit by a bomb). 在轟炸中，只有一座房子幸免。◇ **~ sb/sth sth** *Hong Kong was spared a direct hit, but the storm still brought heavy rains and powerful winds.* 香港雖然未遭正面吹襲，但風暴還是帶來了大雨和強風。

▸ **NO EFFORT/ EXPENSE, ETC.** 盡力、破費等 **4 ~ no effort, expense, etc.** to do everything possible to achieve sth or to do sth well without trying to limit the time or money involved 不吝惜（時間、金錢）：*He spared no effort to make her happy again.* 為使她重新快樂起來，他想盡了辦法。◇ ***No expense was spared*** *in furnishing the new office.* 裝潢新辦公室不惜工本。

▸ **WORK HARD** 努力工作 **5 not ~ yourself** to work as hard as possible 不遺餘力

IDM **spare sb's 'blushes** (*BrE*) to save sb from an embarrassing situation 不讓某人難堪；免得某人丟面子 **spare sb's 'feelings** to be careful not to do or say anything that might upset sb 不惹某人難受；避免觸及某人的痛處 **to 'spare** if you have time, money, etc. **to spare**, you have more than you need 多餘；富餘：*I've got absolutely no money to spare this month.* 我這個月一點兒富餘錢都沒有。◇ *We arrived at the airport with five minutes to spare.* 我們趕到機場時還剩五分鐘。

■ ***noun*** **1** 0⊸ an extra thing that you keep in case you need to replace the one you usually use (used especially about a tyre of a car) 備用品；備用輪胎：*to get the spare out of the boot/trunk* 從汽車行李箱中取出備用輪胎 ◇ *I've lost my key and I haven't got a spare.* 我把鑰匙丟了，還沒有備用的。**2 spares** [pl.] (*especially BrE*) = SPARE PARTS：*It can be difficult to get spares for some older makes of car.* 有些舊型號汽車可能不好買配件。

ˌspare 'part *noun* [usually pl.] a new part that you buy to replace an old or broken part of a car, machine, etc. 備件；配件；零件

ˌspare 'rib *noun* a RIB of PORK (= meat from a pig) with most of the meat cut off 豬排骨：*barbecued spare ribs* 烤排骨

ˌspare 'tyre (*BrE*) (*NAmE* **ˌspare 'tire**) *noun* **1** an extra wheel for a car 備用輪胎 **2** (*humorous*) a large roll of fat around sb's waist 肥胖的腰

spar·ing /ˈspeərɪŋ; *NAmE* ˈsper-/ *adj.* careful to use or give only a little of sth 慎用的；儉省的；吝惜的：*Doctors now advise only* ***sparing use of*** *such creams.* 現在大夫建議，這種乳霜要慎用。◇ **~ with sth** *He was always sparing with his praise.* 他從不輕易說讚揚話。▸ **spar·ing·ly** *adv.*：*Use the cream very sparingly.* 這種乳霜要盡可能少用。

spark /spɑːk; *NAmE* spɑːrk/ *noun, verb*

■ ***noun*** **1** [C] a very small burning piece of material that is produced by sth that is burning or by hitting two hard substances together 火花；火星：*A shower of sparks flew up the chimney.* 煙囱裏飛出無數火星。**2** [C] a small flash of light produced by an electric current 電火花：*sparks from a faulty light switch* 漏電的電燈開關發出的火花 ◇ *A spark ignites the fuel in a car engine.* 汽車發動機中的燃料由火花點燃。**3** [C, usually sing.] **~ of sth** a small amount of a particular quality or feeling（指品質或感情）一星，絲毫，一丁點 **SYN** **glimmer**：*a spark of hope* 一線希望 **4** [U, sing.] a special quality of energy, intelligence or enthusiasm that makes sb very clever, amusing, etc. 生氣；活力；才華；熱情：*As a writer he seemed to lack creative spark.* 作為作家，他似乎缺少創作激情。**5** [C] an action or event that causes sth important to develop, especially trouble or violence 誘因；導火線：*the sparks of revolution* 革命的導火線 **6** [C, usually pl.] feelings of anger or excitement between people 憤怒的情感；激烈的情緒：***Sparks flew*** *at the meeting* (= there was a lot of argument). 會上爭論激烈，火星四濺。**IDM** see BRIGHT *adj.*

■ ***verb*** **1** [T] to cause sth to start or develop, especially suddenly 引發；觸發：**~ sth** *The proposal would spark a storm of protest around the country.* 這一提案將引發全國性的抗議浪潮。◇ *Winds brought down power lines, sparking a fire.* 大風颳斷電線，引起了火災。◇ **~ sth off** *The riots were sparked off by the arrest of a local leader.* 騷亂是因逮捕一名當地領導人而觸發的。**2** [I] to produce small flashes of fire or electricity 冒火花；飛火星；產生電火花：*a sparking, crackling fire* 劈啪直響、火星飛迸的火 ◇ (*figurative*) *The game suddenly sparked to life.* 比賽突然變得激烈起來。

PHR V **ˌspark 'up sth** (*BrE*) to begin a conversation, an argument, a friendship, etc., often suddenly 激起，突然引發（交談、爭論、友誼等）：*I tried to spark up a conversation with her.* 我設法跟她攀談起來。

spar·kle /ˈspɑːkl; *NAmE* ˈspɑːrkl/ *verb, noun*

■ ***verb*** **1** [I] **~** (**with sth**) to shine brightly with small flashes of light 閃爍；閃耀：*sparkling eyes* 炯炯有神的眼睛 ◇ *Her jewellery sparkled in the candlelight.* 燭光下，她的首飾光彩熠熠。➲ note at SHINE **2** [I] **~** (**with sth**) to be full of life, enthusiasm or humour 生氣勃勃；熱情奔放；神采飛揚：*He always sparkles at parties.* 在各種聚會上，他總是光芒四射。

■ ***noun*** [C, U] **1** a series of flashes of light produced by light hitting a shiny surface 閃爍（或閃耀）的光：*the sparkle of glass* 玻璃閃耀的亮光 ◇ (*figurative*) *There was a sparkle of excitement in her eyes.* 她眼裏閃耀着激動的光芒。**2** the quality of being lively and original 生動新穎；亮點：*The performance lacked sparkle.* 這場演出缺少亮點。

spark·ler /ˈspɑːklə(r); *NAmE* ˈspɑːrk-/ *noun* a type of small FIREWORK that you hold in your hand and light. It burns with many bright SPARKS. 煙花棒

spark·ling /ˈspɑːklɪŋ; *NAmE* ˈspɑːrk-/ *adj.* **1** (also *less frequent, informal* **sparkly** /ˈspɑːkli; *NAmE* ˈspɑːrkli/) shining and flashing with light 閃爍的；閃耀的：*the calm and sparkling waters of the lake* 平靜的波光粼粼的湖水 ◇ *sparkling blue eyes* 亮晶晶的藍眼睛 **2** (of drinks 飲料) containing bubbles of gas 起泡的 **SYN** **fizzy**：*a sparkling wine* 汽酒 ◇ *sparkling mineral water* 有汽礦泉水

3 interesting and amusing 妙趣橫生的：*a sparkling conversation/personality* 妙趣橫生的談話；風趣的人 **4** excellent; of very good quality 出色的；上乘的 SYN **brilliant**：*The champion was **in sparkling form**.* 奪冠者狀態極佳。

'spark plug (also **plug**) (*BrE* also **'sparking plug**) *noun* a part in a car engine that produces a SPARK (= a flash of electricity) which makes the fuel burn and starts the engine 火花塞

sparky /'spɑːki; *NAmE* 'spɑːrki/ *adj.* (*BrE, informal*) full of life; interesting and amusing 生氣勃勃的；充滿活力的；有意思的：*a sparky personality* 活潑的性格

'sparring partner *noun* **1** a person that you regularly have friendly arguments or discussions with 切磋問題的對手 **2** (in BOXING 拳擊運動) a person that a BOXER regularly practises with 陪練員

spar·row /'spærəʊ; *NAmE* -roʊ/ *noun* a small brown and grey bird, common in many parts of the world 麻雀

spar·row·hawk /'spærəʊhɔːk; *NAmE* -roʊ-/ *noun* a small BIRD OF PREY (= a bird that kills other creatures for food) of the HAWK family 雀鷹

sparse /spɑːs; *NAmE* spɑːrs/ *adj.* (*comparative* **sparser**, no *superlative*) only present in small amounts or numbers and often spread over a large area 稀少的；稀疏的；零落的：*the sparse population of the islands* 那些島上零星的人口 ◇ *Vegetation becomes sparse higher up the mountains.* 山上越高的地方植物越稀少。◇ *The information available on the subject is sparse.* 這個題目資料匱乏。▸ **sparse·ly** *adv.*：*a **sparsely populated** area* 人口稀少的地區 **sparse·ness** *noun* [U]

spar·tan /'spɑːtn; *NAmE* 'spɑːrtn/ *adj.* (of conditions 生活條件) simple or severe; lacking anything that makes life easier or more pleasant 斯巴達式的；簡樸的；清苦的 ORIGIN From **Sparta**, a powerful city in ancient Greece, where the people were not interested in comfort or luxury. 源自斯巴達（Sparta），古希臘的強大城邦。斯巴達人不追求舒適奢華。OPP **luxurious**

spasm /'spæzəm/ *noun* **1** [C, U] a sudden and often painful contracting of a muscle, which you cannot control 痙攣；抽搐：*a muscle spasm* 肌肉痙攣 ◇ *The injection sent his leg **into spasm**.* 一針打下去，他的腿就痙攣了。 **2** [C] **~ (of sth)** a sudden strong feeling or reaction that lasts for a short time（感情或反應）一陣陣發作，陣發：*a **spasm of** anxiety/anger/coughing/pain, etc.* 突然一陣焦慮、憤怒、咳嗽、疼痛等

spas·mod·ic /spæz'mɒdɪk; *NAmE* -'mɑːd-/ *adj.* **1** happening suddenly for short periods of time; not regular or continuous 一陣陣的；陣發性的；斷斷續續的：*There was spasmodic fighting in the area yesterday.* 昨天，那一地區發生過零星的戰鬥。 **2** (*technical* 術語) caused by your muscles becoming tight in a way that you cannot control 痙攣（性）的：*spasmodic movements* 痙攣性動作 ▸ **spas·mod·ic·al·ly** /-kli/ *adv.*

spas·tic /'spæstɪk/ *adj.* **1** (*medical* 醫 or *old-fashioned*) having or caused by CEREBRAL PALSY, an illness which makes it difficult for sb to control their muscles and movements. Using this word is now often considered offensive 患痙攣性麻痺症的，痙攣性麻痺症引起的（此詞現常被認為有冒犯意）：*spastic children* 痙攣性麻痺症患兒 ◇ *spastic reactions* 痙攣性麻痺症反應 **2** (*informal*) an offensive word, sometimes used by children to mean 'stupid'（有時兒童用以罵人愚蠢）笨拙的，無能的 ▸ **spas·tic** *noun*

spat /spæt/ *noun* **1** (*informal*) a short argument or disagreement about sth unimportant 小爭吵；小彆扭；口角 **2** [usually pl.] a cloth covering for the ankle that was worn in the past by men over the shoe and fastened with buttons at the side（舊時男子用的）鞋罩 ➲ see also SPIT *v.* (spitting, spat, spat)

spate /speɪt/ *noun* [usually sing.] **~ of sth** a large number of things, which are usually unpleasant, that happen suddenly within a short period of time 一連串，接二連三（通常指不愉快的事物）：*The bombing was the latest in a spate of terrorist attacks.* 這次炸彈爆炸事件是一連串恐怖主義襲擊中最近的一起。

IDM **in (full) 'spate** (*especially BrE*) (of a river 河流) containing more water and flowing more strongly than usual 暴漲；發洪水：*After heavy rain, the river was in spate.* 大雨過後，河水暴漲。◇ (*figurative*) *Celia was **in full spate*** (= completely involved in talking and not likely to stop or able to be interrupted). 西莉亞口若懸河，滔滔不絕。

spa·tial (also **spa·cial**) /'speɪʃl/ *adj.* (*formal* or *technical* 術語) relating to space and the position, size, shape, etc. of things in it 空間的：*changes taking place in the spatial distribution of the population* 人口的地域分佈所發生的變化 ◇ *the development of a child's spatial awareness* (= the ability to judge the positions and sizes of objects) 孩子空間意識的形成 ▸ **spa·tial·ly** /-ʃəli/ *adv.*

spat·ter /'spætə(r)/ *verb, noun*

■ *verb* **1** [T] to cover sb/sth with drops of liquid, dirt, etc., especially by accident 濺；灑 SYN **splash**：**~ sb/sth** *blood-spattered walls* 血染的牆壁 ◇ **~ sb/sth with sth** *As the bus passed, it spattered us with mud.* 公共汽車開過時濺了我們一身泥。◇ **~ sth on/over sb/sth** *Oil was spattered on the floor.* 地板上落滿了油點。 **2** [I] **+ adv./prep.** (of liquid 液體) to fall on a surface in drops, often noisily 灑落；滴滴答答地落下：*We heard the rain spattering on the roof.* 我們聽見雨點劈里啪啦地打在房頂上。

■ *noun* (also **spat·ter·ing**) [sing.] **~ (of sth)** a number of drops of a liquid or small amounts of sth that hit a surface; the noise this makes 灑；濺；滴答聲；飛濺聲：*a spatter of rain against the window* 雨點打在窗戶上的劈啪聲 ◇ *a spattering of blood* 點點血跡 ◇ (*figurative*) *a spatter of applause* 稀稀落落的掌聲

spat·ula /'spætʃələ/ *noun* **1** a tool with a broad flat blade used for mixing and spreading things, especially in cooking and painting（烹飪、油漆等活動中用以調拌或塗敷的）鏟，刮勺，抹刀，刮刀 ➲ VISUAL VOCAB pages V26, V27, V70 **2** (*especially NAmE*) (*BrE* usually **'fish slice**) a kitchen UTENSIL that has a broad flat blade with narrow holes in it, attached to a long handle, used for turning and lifting food when cooking 鍋鏟（鏟面有細長孔）➲ VISUAL VOCAB page V26 **3** (*BrE*) (*NAmE* **'tongue depressor**) a thin flat instrument that doctors use for pressing the tongue down when they are examining sb's throat 壓舌板

spawn /spɔːn/ *verb, noun*

■ *verb* **1** [I, T] **~ (sth)** (of fish, FROGS, etc. 魚、蛙等) to lay eggs 產卵 **2** [T] **~ sth** (often *disapproving*) to cause sth to develop or be produced 引發；引起；導致；造成：*The band's album spawned a string of hit singles.* 這支樂隊的專輯繁衍出一連串走紅的單曲唱片。

■ *noun* [U] a soft substance containing the eggs of fish, FROGS etc.（魚、蛙等的）卵 ➲ see also FROGSPAWN

spay /speɪ/ *verb* **~ sth** (*technical* 術語) to remove the OVARIES of a female animal, to prevent it from breeding 切除雌獸的卵巢；劁（雌獸）：*Have you had your cat spayed?* 你的母貓劁了沒有？

spaza /'spɑːzə/ *noun* (*SAfrE*) a small shop/store that sb operates from their home, selling food, drinks, cigarettes, etc. to local people, especially in a TOWNSHIP（尤指黑人城鎮的）家庭雜貨店，街頭小店

speak /spiːk/ *verb* (**spoke** /spəʊk; *NAmE* spoʊk/, **spoken** /'spəʊkən; *NAmE* 'spoʊ-/)

WORD FAMILY
speak *verb*
speaker *noun*
speech *noun*
spoken *adj.* (≠ unspoken)

▸ HAVE CONVERSATION 交談 **1** [I] to talk to sb about sth; to have a conversation with sb 談；談話；交談：**~ (to sb) (about sth/sb)** *I've spoken to the manager about it.* 那件事我已經和經理談過了。◇ *The President refused to speak to the waiting journalists.* 總統拒絕同等候的記者講話。◇ *'Can I speak to Susan?' 'Speaking.'* (= at the beginning of a telephone conversation) "請讓蘇珊接電話好嗎？" "我就是。" ◇ *'Do you know him?' 'Not to speak to.'* (= only by sight) "你認識他嗎？" "沒說過話。" ◇ *I saw her in the street but we didn't speak.* 我在街上看見她了，但我們沒有談話。◇ (*especially NAmE*) **~ (with sb) (about sth/sb)** *Can I speak with you for a minute?* 我能跟你談一會兒嗎？➲ SYNONYMS at TALK

S

▸ **USE VOICE 說話 2** 🔑 [I] to use your voice to say sth 說話；講話：*He can't speak because of a throat infection.* 他嗓子發炎不能說話。◇ *Please speak more slowly.* 請講慢點。◇ *Without speaking, she stood up and went out.* 她沒有說話，站起身來走了出去。◇ *He speaks with a strange accent.* 他說話的口音很特別。◇ *She has a beautiful speaking voice.* 她說話的音色很美。

▸ **MENTION/DESCRIBE 提起；講述 3** 🔑 [I] **~ of/about sth/sb** to mention or describe sth/sb 提起；講述：*She still speaks about him with great affection.* 說起他來她依舊一往情深。◇ *Witnesses spoke of a great ball of flame.* 目擊者都談到有個大火球。◇ *Speaking of travelling,* (= referring back to a subject just mentioned) *are you going anywhere exciting this year?* 說到旅遊，你今年要去什麼好玩的地方嗎？ ➲ note at MENTION

▸ **A LANGUAGE 語言 4** 🔑 [T] (not used in the progressive tenses 不用於進行時) **~ sth** to be able to use a particular language 會說，會講（某種語言）：*to speak several languages* 會講幾種語言 ◇ *to speak a little Urdu* 會說一點烏爾都語 ◇ *Do you speak English?* 你會說英語嗎？ **5** 🔑 [T, I] to use a particular language to express yourself 用（某種語言）說話：**~ sth** *What language is it they're speaking?* 他們講的是什麼語？◇ **~ in sth** *Would you prefer it if we spoke in German?* 我們用德語講好嗎？

▸ **-SPEAKING 講…語 6** (in adjectives 構成形容詞) speaking the language mentioned 講…語的：*French-speaking Canada* 加拿大法語區 ◇ *non-English-speaking students* 不會講英語的學生

▸ **MAKE SPEECH 發表講話 7** 🔑 [I] (**+ adv./prep.**) to make a speech to an audience 發言；演說；演講：*to speak in public* 公開演講 ◇ *to speak on the radio* 在電台上講話 ◇ *to speak at a conference* 在會上發言 ◇ *Professor Wilson was invited to speak about the results of his research.* 威爾遜教授獲邀就自己的研究成果發言。◇ *She* ***spoke in favour of*** *the new tax.* 她發表演說，支持新稅。◇ *He has a number of* ***speaking engagements*** *this week.* 他這個星期安排了幾次演講。

▸ **SAY/STATE 說；講述 8** [T] **~ sth** to say or state sth 說；講述：*She was clearly* ***speaking the truth.*** 她講的顯然是實情。◇ *He spoke the final words of the play.* 劇中最後的台詞是他說的。

IDM **be on 'speaking terms (with sb)** | **be 'speaking (to sb)** to be willing to be polite or friendly towards sb, especially after an argument（與某人）和好如初，和睦相處：*She's not been on speaking terms with her uncle for years.* 多年來她跟她叔叔一直不說話。◇ *Are they speaking to each other again yet?* 他們倆和好了沒有？ **'generally, 'broadly, 'roughly, 'relatively, etc. speaking** used to show that what you are saying is true in a general, etc. way 總的、一般、粗略、相對等說來：*Generally speaking, the more you pay, the more you get.* 一般來說，花錢多，買的東西就多。◇ *There are, broadly speaking, two ways of doing this.* 大致說來，做這件事有兩種方法。◇ *Personally speaking, I've always preferred Italian food.* 就我個人來講，我總是偏愛意大利菜。 ➲ LANGUAGE BANK at GENERALLY **no .../nothing to 'speak of** such a small amount that it is not worth mentioning 不值一提；微不足道：*They've got no friends to speak of.* 他們沒一個像樣的朋友。◇ *She's saved a little money but nothing to speak of.* 她攢了一點錢，不過數目不值一提。 **,so to 'speak** used to emphasize that you are expressing sth in an unusual or amusing way 可以說；可謂：*They were all very similar. All cut from the same cloth, so to speak.* 他們都十分相像。可以說就跟一塊布上剪下來似的。 **speak for it'self/them'selves** to be so easy to see and understand that you do not need to say anything else about it/them 不言而喻；有目共睹：*Her success speaks for itself.* 她的成功有目共睹。 **speak for my'self/her'self/him'self, etc.** to express what you think or want yourself, rather than sb else doing it for you 自己說（而非讓別人替自己說）：*I'm quite capable of speaking for myself, thank you!* 我自己會說，謝謝了！ **speak for your'self** (*informal*) used to tell sb that a general statement they have just made is not true of you（告訴某人不要以為自己的概括性意見適用於大家）只說你自己，那是你：*'We didn't play very well.' 'Speak for yourself!'* (= I think that I played well.) "我們打得不太好。" "是說你自己吧！" **speaking as sth** used to say that you are the type of person mentioned and are expressing your opinion from that point of view（表示從某種角度看問題）作為…來說：*Speaking as a parent, I'm very concerned about standards in education.* 作為家長，我十分關注教育的水平。 **speak your 'mind** to say exactly what you think, in a very direct way 說心裏話；說實在的；坦率地說 **,speak out of 'turn** to say sth when you should not, for example because it is not the right time or you are not the right person to say it 說話不合時宜（或不合身分） **speak 'volumes (about/for sth/sb)** to tell you a lot about sth/sb, without the need for words 充分說明；清楚表明 **speak 'well/'ill of sb** (*formal*) to say good or bad things about sb 稱讚（或貶損）某人；說某人的好話（或壞話） ➲ more at ACTION *n.*, DEVIL, FACT, ILL *adv.*, LANGUAGE, MANNER, STRICTLY, TURN *n.*

PHR V **'speak for sb** to state the views or wishes of a person or a group; to act as a representative for sb 代（或代表）某人講話 **'speak of sth** (*formal*) to be evidence that sth exists or is present 表明；說明：*Everything here speaks of perfect good taste.* 這裏的一切都體現出極為高雅的情趣。 **,speak 'out (against sth)** 🔑 to state your opinions publicly, especially in opposition to sth and in a way that takes courage 挺身（反對某事物）；公開站出來（反對） ➲ see also OUTSPOKEN **'speak to sb (about sth)** (*informal*) to talk to sb in a serious way about sth wrong they have done, to try to stop them doing it again（為某事）數說某人 **,speak 'up** 🔑 usually used in orders to tell sb to speak more loudly 大聲點說：*Please speak up—we can't hear you at the back.* 請大聲點講，我們在後面聽不見。 **,speak 'up (for sb/sth)** 🔑 to say what you think clearly and freely, especially in order to support or defend sb/sth 明確表態；（尤指為…）說好話，辯護

-speak /spiːk/ *combining form* (in nouns 構成名詞) (*informal*, often *disapproving*) the language used by a particular group of people, especially when it is difficult for other people to understand or they find it annoying（尤指令他人費解或厭煩的）圈中行話，用語：*management-speak* 管理層用語 ◇ *Visitors to websites don't want to read marketing-speak.* 網頁瀏覽者不想看推銷語言。

speak·easy /ˈspiːkiːzi/ *noun* (*pl.* **-ies**) a place in the US where people could buy alcohol illegally, at the time in the 1920s and 1930s when it was illegal to make or sell alcohol（美國 20 世紀 20、30 年代禁酒期間）非法經營的酒店

speak·er 🔑 /ˈspiːkə(r)/ *noun*
1 🔑 a person who gives a talk or makes a speech 發言者；演講者：*He was a* ***guest speaker*** *at the conference.* 他是會議的特邀演講人。◇ *She was a brilliant* ***public speaker.*** 她很擅長在公開場合演講。 **2** 🔑 a person who is or was speaking 說話者：*I looked around to see who the speaker was.* 我四下環顧看說話的是誰。 **3** 🔑 a person who speaks a particular language 講（某種語言）的人：*Chinese speakers* 講漢語的人 ◇ *a* ***native speaker*** *of English* 以英語為母語的人 **4** (**the**) **Speaker** the title of the person whose job is to control the discussions in a parliament（議會的）議長：*the Speaker of the House of Commons/Representatives* 英國下議院 / 美國眾議院議長 **5** 🔑 the part of a radio, computer or piece of musical equipment that the sound comes out of 揚聲器；喇叭 ➲ VISUAL VOCAB page V21 ➲ see also LOUDSPEAKER

speak·er·phone /ˈspiːkəfəʊn; *NAmE* -ərfoʊn/ *noun* a telephone that can be used without being held, because it contains a MICROPHONE and a LOUDSPEAKER 揚聲電話（內置麥克風和揚聲器，使用時無須拿起聽筒）

spear /spɪə(r); *NAmE* spɪr/ *noun, verb*
■ ***noun*** **1** a weapon with a long wooden handle and a sharp metal point used for fighting, hunting and fishing in the past 矛；標槍 ➲ picture at SWORD **2** the long pointed STEM of some plants（某些植物的）嫩枝，幼芽 ➲ VISUAL VOCAB page V31
■ ***verb*** **~ sth/sb** to throw or push a spear or other pointed object through sth/sb 用矛刺；用尖物刺穿：*They were standing in the river spearing fish.* 他們站在河裏叉魚。

S

◇ *She speared an olive with her fork.* 她用叉子叉了一個橄欖。

spear·head /ˈspɪəhed; *NAmE* ˈspɪrhed/ *noun, verb*

■ ***noun*** [usually sing.] a person or group that begins an activity or leads an attack against sb/sth 先鋒；前鋒；先頭部隊

■ ***verb*** **~ sth** to begin an activity or lead an attack against sb/sth 做…的先鋒；帶頭做；領先突擊：*He is **spearheading a campaign** for a new stadium in the town.* 他正發起一項運動，呼籲在城裏新建一座體育場。

spear·mint /ˈspɪəmɪnt; *NAmE* ˈspɪrm-/ *noun* [U] a type of MINT used especially in making sweets/candy and TOOTHPASTE 留蘭香；綠薄荷：*spearmint chewing gum* 留蘭香口香糖 ➲ compare PEPPERMINT (1)

spec /spek/ *noun, verb*

■ ***noun*** (*BrE*) a detailed description of sth, especially the design and materials needed to produce sth 規格：*We want the machine manufactured to our own spec.* 我們要求這台機器按我們自己的規格來製造。➲ see also SPECIFICATION, SPECS (2)

IDM **on ˈspec** (*BrE, informal*) when you do sth **on spec**, you are trying to achieve sth without organizing it in advance, but hoping you will be lucky 碰運氣

■ ***verb*** (**-cc-**) **~ sth** (*BrE*) to design and make sth to a particular standard 按特定標準設計並製造：*The camera is well specced at the price.* 就價錢來說，這台照相機的配置很不錯。

speccy = SPECKY

spe·cial /ˈspeʃl/ *adj., noun*

■ ***adj.*** **1** [usually before noun] not ordinary or usual; different from what is normal 特殊的；特別的；不尋常的；不一般的 **SYN** **exceptional**：*The school will only allow this in special circumstances.* 學校只有在特殊情況下才會同意這種事。◇ *Some of the officials have special privileges.* 有些官員享受特權。◇ *There is **something special** about this place.* 這個地方有幾分特別。**2** more important than others; deserving or getting more attention than usual 重要的；格外看重的；特別關照的：*What are your special interests?* 你有哪些主要的愛好？◇ *She's a very special friend.* 她是我特別要好的朋友。◇ *Our special guest on next week's show will be ...* 我們下週節目的特邀嘉賓是…◇ *Don't lose it—it's special.* 別丟了，這可不是一般東西。**3** organized or intended for a particular purpose 特設的；有專門目的的；起專門作用的：*a special event* 特設活動 ◇ *These teachers need special training.* 這些教師需要專門的培訓。**4** used by or intended for one particular person or group of people 專用的；專門針對…的；特有的：*She has a special way of smiling.* 她微笑的樣子有些特別。◇ *He sent a special message to the men.* 他給那些人專門去了一封信。**5** [only before noun] better or more than usual 更好的；格外的：*As an only child she got special attention.* 她是個獨生女，所以備受關愛。◇ *Please take special care of it.* 請對它多加關照。➲ compare ESPECIAL

■ ***noun*** **1** something that is not usually available but is provided for a particular purpose or on one occasion 特別活動（或節目等）；特製產品：*an election-night special on television* 選舉之夜電視特別節目 ◇ *The menu changes regularly and there are daily specials to choose from.* 菜譜定期更換，而且每天都有特色菜供選擇。**2** (*informal, especially NAmE*) a price for a particular product in a shop/store or restaurant that is lower than usual 特價：*There's a special on coffee this week.* 本週咖啡特價。

IDM **on ˈspecial** (*especially NAmE*) on sale at a lower price for a short period of time （短期）特價：*The chocolates were on special at my local store.* 我家附近商店的巧克力在做特價。

ˈspecial agent *noun* a DETECTIVE who works for the FEDERAL government in the US, for example for the FBI 特工；特務

ˈSpecial Branch *noun* [U+sing./pl. v.] (also **the Special Branch** [sing.+sing./pl. v.]) the department of the British police force that deals with the defence of the country against political crimes and TERRORISM （英國警察部門的）政治保安處

Synonyms 同義詞辨析

speaker

communicator • gossip • talker

These are all words for a person who talks or who is talking, especially in a particular way. 以上各詞均指說話者，尤指以某種方式說話的人。

speaker a person who is or was speaking; a person who speaks a particular language 指發言者、講某種語言的人：*I looked around to see who the speaker was.* 我四下環顧看說話的是誰。◇ *a fluent Arabic speaker* 阿拉伯語講得流利的人

communicator (*rather formal*) a person who is able to describe their ideas and feelings clearly to others 指交際者、交流者：*The ideal candidate will be an effective communicator.* 理想的候選人定要是善於溝通的人。

gossip (*disapproving*) a person who enjoys talking about other people's private lives 指喜歡傳播流言蜚語的人、愛說長道短（或說三道四）的人：*Myra is a dear, but she's also a terrible gossip.* 邁拉是很可愛，但也是個討厭的長舌婦。

talker a person who talks in a particular way or who talks a lot 指以某種方式說話的人、愛說話的人：*He's a very persuasive talker.* 他是一個說話很有說服力的人。◇ *She's a (great) talker* (= she talks a lot). 她很健談。

SPEAKER OR TALKER? 用 speaker 還是 talker？

Talker is used when you are talking about how much sb talks or how well they talk. It is not used for the person who is or was talking. * talker 用以指說話多或少，或者話說得如何的人，不用以指正在或曾經在說話的人：~~*I looked round to see who the talker was.*~~ You can say that sb is *a good/persuasive speaker* but that means that they are good at making speeches. If you mean that they speak well in conversation, use **talker**. * good/persuasive speaker 指的是擅長演講的人。如果指健談或能言善辯的人就用 talker。

PATTERNS

- a **good/great** speaker/communicator/talker
- an **effective/excellent** speaker/communicator

ˌspecial ˈconstable *noun* (in Britain) a person who is not a professional police officer but who is trained to help the police force, especially during an emergency 臨時警察，糾察（英國在非常時期協助警察維持治安）

ˌspecial deˈlivery *noun* [U] a service that delivers a letter, etc. faster than normal （信件等的）特快專遞

ˌspecial deˈvelopment area (also **ˌspecial ˈarea**) *noun* an area of the UK for which special laws exist in order to help the economy to develop （英國）經濟發展特區，經濟開發區

ˌspecial eduˈcation *noun* [U] the education of children who have physical or learning problems 特殊教育（為有身體障礙或學習障礙的兒童而設）

ˌspecial efˈfects (also **SFX**) *noun* [pl.] unusual or exciting pieces of action in films/movies or television programmes, that are created by computers or clever photography to show things that do not normally exist or happen （電影或電視節目的）特技效果

ˌspecial ˈinterest group (also **ˌspecial ˈinterest**) *noun* (*especially NAmE*) a group of people who work together to achieve sth that they are particularly interested in, especially by putting pressure on the government, etc. （尤指對政府施壓的）特別利益集團

spe·cial·ism /ˈspeʃəlɪzəm/ *noun* **1** [C] an area of study or work that sb SPECIALIZES in 專業；專長：*a business degree with a specialism in computing* 專修計算機技術的商業學位 ◇ *Dr Crane's specialism is tropical diseases.* 克萊

S

恩博士的研究領域是熱帶病。 **2** [U] the fact of SPECIALIZING in a particular subject 專業化

spe·cial·ist /ˈspeʃəlɪst/ *noun*
1 a person who is an expert in a particular area of work or study 專家： *a specialist in Japanese history* 日本史專家 **2** a doctor who has SPECIALIZED in a particular area of medicine 專科醫生： *a cancer specialist* 癌症專科醫生 ➲ compare GENERALIST ▸ **spe·cial·ist** *adj.* [only before noun]： *specialist magazines* 專業雜誌 ◇ *You need some specialist advice.* 你需要咨詢專業人士。

spe·ci·al·ity /ˌspeʃiˈæləti/ (*BrE*) (also **spe·cial·ty** *NAmE, BrE*) *noun* (*pl.* **-ies**) **1** a type of food or product that a restaurant or place is famous for because it is so good 特產；特色菜： *Seafood is a speciality on the island.* 海味是島上的特產。◇ *local specialities* 土特產 **2** an area of work or study that sb gives most of their attention to and knows a lot about; sth that sb is good at 專業；專長： *My speciality is international tax law.* 我的專業是國際稅法。

spe·cial·ize (*BrE* also **-ise**) /ˈspeʃəlaɪz/ *verb* [I] **~ (in sth)** to become an expert in a particular area of work, study or business; to spend more time on one area of work, etc. than on others 專門研究（或從事）；專攻： *Many students prefer not to specialize too soon.* 很多學生不願過早地確定專業。◇ *He specialized in criminal law.* 他專攻刑法。◇ *The shop specializes in hand-made chocolates.* 這家商店專營手工製作的巧克力。 ▸ **spe·cial·iza·tion, -isa·tion** /ˌspeʃəlaɪˈzeɪʃn; *NAmE* -ləˈz-/ *noun* [U, C]

spe·cial·ized (*BrE* also **-ised**) /ˈspeʃəlaɪzd/ *adj.* designed or developed for a particular purpose or area of knowledge 專用的；專業的；專門的： *specialized equipment* 專用設備 ◇ *specialized skills* 專門技能

ˌspecial ˈlicence *noun* (*BrE*) a licence allowing two people to get married at a time or place that is not usually allowed 結婚特別許可（批准在通常不允許的時間或地點結婚）

spe·cial·ly /ˈspeʃəli/ *adv.*
1 for a particular purpose, person, etc. 專門地；特意： *The ring was specially made for her.* 這枚戒指是為她訂做的。◇ *a specially designed diet plan* 專門制訂的飲食方案 ◇ *We came specially to see you.* 我們特意來看你。 **2** (*informal*) more than usual or more than other things 格外；特別；尤其： *It will be hard to work today—specially when it's so warm and sunny outside.* 今天無心工作，尤其是外面這樣風和日麗。◇ *I hate homework. Specially history.* 我討厭家庭作業，特別是歷史。 ➲ note at ESPECIALLY

S

ˌspecial ˈneeds *noun* [pl.] (*especially BrE*) needs that a person has because of mental or physical problems（智力或身體障礙者的）特殊需要： *She teaches children with special needs.* 她教的是有特殊需要的兒童。

ˌspecial ˈoffer *noun* [C, U] a product that is sold at less than its usual price, especially in order to persuade people to buy it; the act of offering goods in this way 特價商品；特價銷售： *Shop around for special offers.* 去四處轉轉，看有沒有特價商品。◇ *a special offer on perfume* 香水特價銷售 ◇ *French wine is* ***on special offer*** *this week.* 法國葡萄酒本週特價銷售。

ˌspecial ˈpleading *noun* [U] trying to persuade sb about sth by mentioning only the arguments that support your opinion and ignoring the arguments that do not support it（只談有利於自己觀點的論據的）詭辯

ˌspecial ˈschool *noun* a school for children who have physical or learning problems 特殊學校（為有身體障礙或學習障礙的兒童設立）

spe·cialty /ˈspeʃəlti/ *noun* (*pl.* **-ies**) (*especially NAmE* or *medical* 醫) = SPECIALITY： *regional specialties* 地方特產 ◇ *specialty stores* 特產商店 ◇ *Her specialty is taxation law.* 她的專長是稅法。◇ *Doctors training for General Practice must complete programmes in a number of specialties, including Paediatrics.* 接受全科培訓的醫生必須修完包括兒科學在內的多門專業課程。

spe·cies /ˈspiːʃiːz/ *noun* (*pl.* **spe·cies**) a group into which animals, plants, etc. that are able to breed with each other and produce healthy young are divided, smaller than a GENUS and identified by a Latin name 種，物種（分類上小於屬）： *a rare species of beetle* 一種稀有甲蟲 ◇ *There are many species of dog(s).* 狗有許多種。◇ *a conservation area for* ***endangered species*** 瀕危物種保護區

the ˈspecies barrier *noun* [sing.] the natural system which is thought to prevent diseases spreading from one type of animal or plant to another（防止疾病在物種之間傳播的）物種屏障，種群屏障

spe·cies·ism /ˈspiːʃiːzɪzəm/ *noun* [U] (*disapproving*) the belief that humans are more important than animals, which causes people to treat animals badly 物種歧視（認為人類比動物重要，因此虐待動物） ▸ **spe·cies·ist** *adj., noun*

spe·cif·ic AW /spəˈsɪfɪk/ *adj.*
1 detailed and exact 明確的；具體的 SYN **precise**： *I gave you specific instructions.* 我給過你明確的指示。◇ *'I'd like your help tomorrow.' 'Can you* ***be more specific*** *(= tell me exactly what you want)?'* "我想讓你明天來幫幫我。" "你能不能說得具體些？" **2** [usually before noun] connected with one particular thing only 特定的 SYN **particular**： *children's television programmes aimed at a specific age group* 針對特定年齡段的少兒電視節目 ◇ *The money was collected for a specific purpose.* 這筆錢是為一個特定用途而收的。◇ *children with specific learning difficulties* (= in one area only) 某一方面有學習困難的兒童 **3 ~ to sth** (*formal*) existing only in one place or limited to one thing 特有的；獨特的 SYN **peculiar**： *a belief that is specific to this part of Africa* 非洲這一地區特有的一種觀念

spe·cif·ic·al·ly AW /spəˈsɪfɪkli/ *adv.*
1 in a detailed and exact way 明確地；具體地： *I specifically told you not to go near the water!* 我明確告訴過你不要靠近水邊！ **2** connected with or intended for one particular thing only 特意；專門地： *liquid vitamins specifically designed for children* 專為兒童設計的維生素水劑 ◇ *a magazine aimed specifically at working women* 專門面向職業婦女的雜誌 **3** used when you want to add more detailed and exact information 具體來說；確切地說： *The newspaper, or more specifically, the editor, was taken to court for publishing the photographs.* 那家報紙，更確切地說是那家報紙的編輯，因刊登那些照片而遭起訴。

speci·fi·ca·tion AW /ˌspesɪfɪˈkeɪʃn/ *noun* [C, U] a detailed description of how sth is, or should be, designed or made 規格；規範；明細單；說明書： *the technical specifications of the new model* (= of car) 新型號的技術規格 ◇ *The house has been built exactly* ***to our specifications.*** 房子完全是按照我們的工程設計書建造的。◇ *The office was furnished* ***to a high specification.*** 辦公室是按高規格裝潢的。

speˌcific ˈgravity *noun* [U] = RELATIVE DENSITY

speci·fi·city AW /ˌspesɪˈfɪsəti/ *noun* [U] (*formal*) the quality of being specific 明確性；具體性；獨特性

spe·cif·ics AW /spəˈsɪfɪks/ *noun* [pl.] the details of a subject that you need to think about or discuss 詳情；細節： *Okay, that's the broad plan—let's get down to the specifics.* 好，這是總的計劃。下面來談談具體細節。

spe·cify AW /ˈspesɪfaɪ/ *verb* (**speci·fies, speci·fy·ing, speci·fied, speci·fied**) to state sth, especially by giving an exact measurement, time, exact instructions, etc. 具體說明；明確規定；詳述；詳列： **~ sth** *Remember to specify your size when ordering clothes.* 訂購服裝時記着要詳細說明你要的號碼。◇ **~ who, what, etc. …** *The contract clearly specifies who can operate the machinery.* 合同明確規定誰可以操作機器。◇ **~ that …** *The regulations specify that calculators may not be used in the examination.* 考試規則明確規定考試時不得使用計算器。 ▸ **spe·ci·fi·able** AW /ˈspesɪfaɪəbl/ *adj.*

speci·men /ˈspesɪmən/ *noun* **1** a small amount of sth that shows what the rest of it is like 樣品；樣本；標本 SYN **sample**： *Astronauts have brought back specimens of rock from the moon.* 宇航員從月球帶回了岩石標本。 ➲ COLLOCATIONS at SCIENTIFIC **2** a single example of sth, especially an animal or a plant（尤指動植物的）單一實例：*The aquarium has some interesting specimens of unusual tropical fish.* 水族館裏有一些罕見的熱帶魚，很有意思。◇ (*humorous*) *They were fine specimens of British youth!* 他們堪稱英國青年的優秀代表！ ➲ SYNONYMS at EXAMPLE **3** a small quantity of blood, URINE, etc. that is taken from sb and tested by a doctor（化驗的）抽樣，血樣，尿樣：*to **provide/take a specimen*** 提供／採血樣

spe·cious /ˈspiːʃəs/ *adj.* (*formal*) seeming right or true but actually wrong or false 似是而非的；貌似有理的 SYN **misleading**：*a specious argument* 似是而非的論點

speck /spek/ *noun* a very small spot; a small piece of dirt, etc. 小點；污點：*The ship was now just a speck in the distance.* 此時，那艘船不過是遠處的一個小點。◇ *specks of dust* 塵埃 ➲ SYNONYMS at MARK

speckle /ˈspekl/ *noun* [usually pl.] a small coloured mark or spot on a background of a different colour 斑點；色斑

speck·led /ˈspekld/ *adj.* covered with small marks or spots 佈滿斑點的；有色斑的 SYN **flecked**

specky (also **speccy**) /ˈspeki/ *adj.* (*BrE, offensive*) wearing glasses 戴眼鏡的；四隻眼的

specs /speks/ *noun* [pl.] **1** (*informal, especially BrE*) = GLASSES：*I need a new pair of specs.* 我需要一副新眼鏡。 **2** (*NAmE*) ➲ SPEC

spec·tacle /ˈspektəkl/ *noun* **1** **spectacles** [pl.] (*formal*) = GLASSES：*a pair of spectacles* 一副眼鏡 ◇ *a spectacle case* (= to put your glasses in) 眼鏡盒 **2** [C, U] a performance or an event that is very impressive and exciting to look at 精彩的表演；壯觀的場面：*The carnival parade was a magnificent spectacle.* 狂歡節遊行場面熱烈，蔚為大觀。 **3** [C] a sight or view that is very impressive to look at 壯觀的景象：*The sunset was a stunning spectacle.* 夕陽西斜，異常壯觀。 **4** [sing.] an unusual or surprising sight or situation that attracts a lot of attention 奇特的現象；出人意外的情況：*I remember the sad spectacle of her standing in her wedding dress, covered in mud.* 我記得她穿着婚紗、滿身泥污站在那兒的悽慘樣。

IDM **make a ˈspectacle of yourself** to draw attention to yourself by behaving or dressing in a ridiculous way in public 出洋相；出醜

spec·tacu·lar /spekˈtækjələ(r)/ *adj., noun*

■ ***adj.*** very impressive 壯觀的；壯麗的；令人驚歎的 SYN **breathtaking**：*spectacular scenery* 壯麗的景色 ◇ *Messi scored a spectacular goal.* 梅西攻進了一個精彩入球。◇ *It was a spectacular achievement on their part.* 這是他們取得的一項了不起的成就。 ▸ **spec·tacu·lar·ly** *adv.*：*It has been a spectacularly successful year.* 這是成績輝煌的一年。

■ ***noun*** an impressive show or performance 壯觀的場面；精彩的表演：*a Christmas TV spectacular* 精彩的聖誕節電視節目

spec·tate /spekˈteɪt/ *verb* [I] to watch sth, especially a sports event 觀看（體育比賽等）

spec·ta·tor /spekˈteɪtə(r); *NAmE* ˈspekteɪtər/ *noun* a person who is watching an event, especially a sports event（尤指體育比賽的）觀看者，觀眾

specˈtator sport *noun* a sport that many people watch; a sport that is interesting to watch 群眾愛看的體育運動

spec·tra *pl.* of SPECTRUM

spec·tral /ˈspektrəl/ *adj.* **1** (*literary*) like a GHOST; connected with a ghost 鬼一般的；幽靈似的；鬼的；幽靈的 **2** (*technical* 術語) connected with a SPECTRUM 譜的；光譜的：*spectral bands* 光譜帶

spectre (*US* **spec·ter**) /ˈspektə(r)/ *noun* **1** ~ (**of sth**) something unpleasant that people are afraid might happen in the future 恐懼；恐慌；憂慮：*The country is haunted by the spectre of civil war.* 內戰彷彿一觸即發，舉國上下一片恐慌。◇ *These weeks of drought have once again **raised the spectre** of widespread famine.* 幾星期來的乾旱再次引起了群眾對大饑荒的恐慌。 **2** (*literary*) a GHOST 鬼；幽靈：*Was he a spectre returning to haunt her?* 是不是他的幽靈回來找她了？

spec·trom·eter /spekˈtrɒmɪtə(r); *NAmE* -ˈtrɑːm-/ *noun* (*technical* 術語) a piece of equipment for measuring the WAVELENGTHS of SPECTRA 分光計

spec·tro·scope /ˈspektrəskəʊp; *NAmE* -skoʊp/ *noun* (*technical* 術語) a piece of equipment for forming and looking at SPECTRA 分光鏡 ▸ **spec·tro·scop·ic** /ˌspektrəˈskɒpɪk; *NAmE* -ˈskɑːp-/ *adj.*：*spectroscopic analysis* 光譜分析

spec·tros·copy /spekˈtrɒskəpi; *NAmE* -ˈtrɑːs-/ *noun* [U] (*chemistry* 化, *physics* 物) the study of forming and looking at SPECTRA using spectrometers, spectroscopes, etc. 光譜學

spec·trum /ˈspektrəm/ *noun* (*pl.* **spec·tra** /ˈspektrə/) **1** a band of coloured lights in order of their WAVELENGTHS, as seen in a RAINBOW and into which light may be separated 光譜：*A spectrum is formed by a ray of light passing through a prism.* 一束光通過棱鏡就會形成光譜。◇ *Red and violet are at opposite ends of the spectrum.* 紅色和紫色位於光譜的兩端。 **2** a range of sound waves or several other types of wave 聲譜；波譜；頻譜：*the **electromagnetic/radio/sound spectrum*** 電磁波譜；射頻頻譜；聲譜 **3** [usually sing.] a complete or wide range of related qualities, ideas, etc. 範圍；各層次；系列；幅度：*a broad spectrum of interests* 廣泛的興趣範圍 ◇ *We shall hear views from across the political spectrum.* 我們要聽取各個政治派別的看法。

specu·late /ˈspekjuleɪt/ *verb* **1** [I, T] to form an opinion about sth without knowing all the details or facts 推測；猜測；推斷：~ (**about/on/as to sth**) *We all speculated about the reasons for her resignation.* 我們大家都推測過她辭職的原因。◇ ~ **why, how, etc.** … *It is useless to speculate why he did it.* 對他為什麼這麼做妄加猜測毫無用處。◇ ~ **that** … *We can speculate that the stone circles were used in some sort of pagan ceremony.* 我們可以推測，這些石頭排成的圓圈是用於某種異教崇拜儀式的。 **2** [I] ~ (**in/on sth**) to buy goods, property, shares, etc., hoping to make a profit when you sell them, but with the risk of losing money 投機；做投機買賣：*He likes to speculate on the stock market.* 他喜歡炒股。

specu·la·tion /ˌspekjuˈleɪʃn/ *noun* **1** [U, C] the act of forming opinions about what has happened or what might happen without knowing all the facts 推測；猜測；推斷：~ (**that** …) *There was widespread speculation that she was going to resign.* 人們紛紛推測她將辭職。◇ *His private life is the subject of much speculation.* 他的私生活引起諸多猜測。◇ ~ (**about/over sth**) *Today's announcement ends months of speculation about the company's future.* 今天的聲明使得幾個月來關於公司未來的種種猜測就此煙消雲散。◇ *She dismissed the newspaper reports as **pure speculation**.* 她說報紙上的報道毫無根據，純屬臆斷。◇ *Our speculations proved right.* 事實證明，我們的推斷是對的。 **2** [U, C] ~ (**in sth**) the activity of buying and selling goods or shares in a company in the hope of making a profit, but with the risk of losing money 投機買賣；炒股

specu·la·tive /ˈspekjələtɪv; *NAmE* also ˈspekjəleɪtɪv/ *adj.* **1** based on guessing or on opinions that have been formed without knowing all the facts 推測的；猜測的；推斷的 **2** showing that you are trying to guess sth 揣摩的；忖度的；試探的：*She cast a speculative look at Kate.* 她帶着疑問的眼神看了凱特一眼。 **3** (of business activity 商業活動) done in the hope of making a profit but involving the risk of losing money 投機性的；風險性的 ▸ **specu·la·tive·ly** *adv.*

specu·la·tor /ˈspekjuleɪtə(r)/ *noun* a person who buys and sells goods or shares in a company in the hope of making a profit 投機商；投機倒把者：*property speculators* 房地產投機商

specu·lum /ˈspekjələm/ *noun* (*medical* 醫) a metal instrument that is used to make a hole or tube in the body wider so it can be examined 窺器；擴張器

sped *past tense, past part.* of SPEED

S

speech 0-m /spiːtʃ/ *noun*
1 0-m [C] **~ (on/about sth)** a formal talk that a person gives to an audience 演說；講話；發言： *to give/make/deliver a speech on human rights* 就人權問題發表演講 ◇ *He made the announcement* ***in a speech*** *on television.* 他在一次電視講話中發表了這一聲明。◇ *Several people made speeches at the wedding.* 有幾個人在婚禮上講了話。 **2** 0-m [U] the ability to speak 說話的能力： *I seemed to have lost the* ***power of speech.*** 我好像話都說不出來了。◇ *a speech defect* 言語能力缺陷 ◇ ***freedom of speech*** (= the right to say openly what you think) 言論自由 **3** 0-m [U] the way in which a particular person speaks 說話方式： *Her speech was slurred—she was clearly drunk.* 她說話含混不清，她顯然是喝醉了。 **4** 0-m [U] the language used when speaking 口語： *This expression is used mainly in speech, not in writing.* 這種表達主要用於口語，而不是書面語。◇ *speech sounds* 語音 **5** [C] a group of lines that an actor speaks in a play in the theatre （戲劇中的）台詞： *She has the longest speech in the play.* 在這部劇中，她的台詞最長。 ➲ see also FIGURE OF SPEECH

Synonyms 同義詞辨析

speech

lecture • address • talk • sermon

These are all words for a talk given to an audience.
以上各詞均指講話、發言。

speech a formal talk given to an audience 指演說、講話、發言： *Several people made speeches at the wedding.* 有幾個人在婚禮上講了話。

lecture a talk given to a group of people to tell them about a particular subject, often as part of a university or college course 通常指大學裏的講座、講課、演講： *a lecture on the Roman army* 關於羅馬軍隊的講座 ◇ *a course/series of lectures* 講座課程；系列講座

address a formal speech given to an audience 指演說、演講： *a televised presidential address* 總統的電視演講

SPEECH OR ADDRESS? 用 speech 還是 address？

A **speech** can be given on a public or private occasion; an **address** is always public. * speech 指公開或私下場合的講話均可，而 address 總是指公開的演講：
~~*He gave an address at the wedding.*~~

talk a fairly informal session in which sb tells a group of people about a subject 指相當不正式的報告、演講： *She gave an interesting talk on her visit to China.* 她做了個關於她在中國訪問的有趣報告。

sermon a talk on a moral or religious subject, usually given by a religious leader during a service 指佈道、講道： *to preach a sermon* 佈道

PATTERNS

- a **long/short** speech/lecture/address/talk/sermon
- a **keynote** speech/lecture/address
- to **write/prepare/give/deliver/hear** a(n) speech/lecture/address/talk/sermon
- to **attend/go to** a lecture/talk

ˈspeech act *noun* (*linguistics* 語言) something that sb says, considered as an action, for example 'I forgive you' 言語行為（如 I forgive you）

ˈspeech bubble *noun* a circle around the words that sb says in a CARTOON 話泡泡（漫畫中圈出人物所說的話的圓圈）

ˈspeech community *noun* all the people who speak a particular language or variety of a language （講某語言或語言變體的）言語社區，語言社群： *the Kodava speech community in India* 印度的果達古語社區 ◇ *speech communities such as high school students or hip hop fans* 中學生或嘻哈音樂迷之類的言語社區

ˈspeech day *noun* an event held once a year in some British schools at which there are speeches and prizes （英國部份學校一年一度的）授獎演講日

speechi·fy·ing /ˈspiːtʃɪfaɪɪŋ/ *noun* [U] (*informal, disapproving*) the act of making speeches in a very formal way, trying to sound important 煞有介事的講話；裝腔作勢的演講

speech·less /ˈspiːtʃləs/ *adj.* not able to speak, especially because you are extremely angry or surprised （尤指氣得或驚訝得）說不出話的： *Laura was speechless with rage.* 勞拉氣得說不出話來。 ▸ **speech·less·ly** *adv.* **speech·less·ness** *noun* [U]

ˈspeech marks *noun* [pl.] = QUOTATION MARKS

ˈspeech recognition (also **ˈvoice recognition**) *noun* [U] technology that allows a computer to understand spoken words （計算機）語音識別

ˈspeech synthesis *noun* [U] the production of speech from written language by a computer （計算機）語音合成，言語合成

ˌspeech ˈtherapy *noun* [U] special treatment to help people who have problems in speaking clearly, for example in pronouncing particular sounds 言語治療；言語矯治 ▸ **ˌspeech ˈtherapist** *noun*

ˈspeech-writer *noun* a person whose job is to write speeches for a politician or public figure 演說稿撰寫員

speed 0-m /spiːd/ *noun, verb*
■ ***noun***
▸ **RATE OF MOVEMENT/ACTION** 運動／行動速率 **1** 0-m [C, U] the rate at which sb/sth moves or travels （運動的）速度，速率： *He reduced speed and turned sharp left.* 他減慢速度，向左急轉。◇ *The train began to* ***pick up speed*** (= go faster). 火車開始加速。◇ *The car was* ***gathering speed.*** 汽車逐漸加速。◇ *a* ***speed*** *of 50 mph/80 kph* 每小時 50 英里／80 公里的速度 ◇ *at* ***high/low/full/top speed*** 以高／低／全／最高速 ◇ *at* ***breakneck speed*** (= fast in a way that is dangerous) 以不要命的速度 ◇ *travelling at* ***the speed of light/sound*** 以光速／音速行進 ➲ see also AIRSPEED, GROUND SPEED **2** 0-m [C, U] the rate at which sth happens or is done （發生或進行的）速度；進度： *the processing speed of the computer* 計算機的處理速度 ◇ *This course is designed so that students can progress at their own speed.* 這門課的設計思路是讓學生自己掌握進度。◇ *We aim to increase the speed of delivery* (= how quickly goods are sent). 我們力爭加快送貨速度。 **3** 0-m [U] the quality of being quick or rapid 快；迅速： *The accident was due to excessive speed.* 事故的原因在於速度過快。◇ *She was overtaken by the* ***speed of events*** (= things happened more quickly than she expected). 事態發展迅速為她始料所不及。◇ (*formal*) *A car flashed past them* ***at speed*** (= fast). 一輛汽車從他們身邊疾馳而過。
▸ **IN PHOTOGRAPHY** 攝影 **4** [C] a measurement of how sensitive film for cameras, etc. is to light 感光度 **5** [C] the time taken by a camera SHUTTER to open and close 快門速度： *shutter speeds* 快門速度
▸ **ON BICYCLE/CAR** 自行車；汽車 **6** [C] (especially in compounds 尤用於構成複合詞) a gear on a bicycle, in a car, etc. 排擋；速： *a four-speed gearbox* 有四擋的變速箱 ◇ *a ten-speed mountain bike* 十速山地自行車
▸ **DRUG** 毒品 **7** [U] (*informal*) an illegal AMPHETAMINE drug that is taken to give feelings of excitement and energy 苯丙胺，安非他明（一種興奮劑）

IDM **full speed/steam aˈhead** with as much speed or energy as possible 全速（或全力）向前 **up to ˈspeed (on sth)** **1** (of a person, company, etc. 人、公司等) performing at an expected rate or level （在某事上）達到應有的速度，達標： *the cost of* ***bringing*** *the chosen schools* ***up to speed*** 使選定的學校達標所需的費用 **2** (of a person 人) having the most recent and accurate information or knowledge 瞭解最新情況；跟上形勢： *Are you up to speed yet on the latest developments?* 你瞭解最新的進展情況嗎？ ➲ more at HASTE, TURN *n.*

■ ***verb*** (**speed·ed**, **speed·ed**) **HELP** In senses 1 and 2 **sped** is also used for the past tense and past participle. 作第 1 及第 2 義時，過去時和過去分詞也用 sped。

S

▸ **MOVE/HAPPEN QUICKLY** 快速運動／發生 **1** [I] + **adv./prep.** (*formal*) to move along quickly 快速前行：*He sped away on his bike.* 他飛快地騎着車走了。 **2** [T] **~ sb/sth + adv./prep.** (*formal*) to take sb/sth somewhere very quickly, especially in a vehicle 快速運送：*The cab speeded them into the centre of the city.* 出租汽車載着他們迅速駛往市中心。 **3** [T] **~ sth** (*formal*) to make sth happen more quickly 加速；促進：*The drugs will speed her recovery.* 這些藥會加速她的康復。

▸ **DRIVE TOO FAST** 超速駕駛 **4** [I] (usually used in the progressive tenses 通常用於進行時) to drive faster than the speed that is legally allowed 超速駕駛；超速行駛：*The police caught him speeding.* 警察發現他超速行駛。

PHR V **ˌspeed ˈup** | **ˌspeed sth↔ˈup** 0-w to move or happen faster; to make sth move or happen faster（使）加速：*The train soon speeded up.* 火車很快加速了。◇ *Can you try and* **speed things up** *a bit?* 你能不能設法加快一點事情的進度？

speed·boat /ˈspiːdbəʊt; *NAmE* -boʊt/ *noun* a boat with a motor that can travel very fast 快艇 ➲ VISUAL VOCAB page V54

ˈspeed breaker *noun* (*IndE*) a SPEED HUMP（設在路上的）減速路脊

ˈspeed camera *noun* (*BrE*) a machine which takes pictures of vehicles that are being driven too fast. The pictures are then used as evidence so that the drivers can be punished.（拍攝超速車輛的）超速監控攝像機 ➲ COLLOCATIONS at DRIVING

ˈspeed dating *noun* [U] meeting people at an event organized for single people who want to begin a romantic relationship, where you are allowed to spend only a few minutes talking to one person before you have to move on to meet the next person 快速相親，閃電約會（為單身者安排的約會方式，每人只限與一人交談幾分鐘即轉往下一人）

ˈspeed hump (*especially BrE*) (*NAmE* usually **ˈspeed bump**) (also *BrE informal* **ˌsleeping poˈliceman**) *noun* a raised area across a road that is put there to make traffic go slower（設在路上的）減速路脊

speed·ing /ˈspiːdɪŋ/ *noun* [U] the traffic offence of driving faster than the legal limit 超速駕駛；超速行駛 ➲ COLLOCATIONS at DRIVING

ˈspeed limit *noun* the highest speed at which you can legally drive on a particular road（道路的）最高車速限制：*You should always keep to the speed limit.* 任何時候你都不得超過最高速度限制。◇ *to* ***break/exceed the speed limit*** 不遵守／超過限定速度 ◇ *The road has a 30 mph speed limit.* 這條公路限定時速 30 英里。➲ COLLOCATIONS at DRIVING

speedo /ˈspiːdəʊ; *NAmE* -doʊ/ *noun* (*pl.* **-os**) **1** (*BrE, informal*) = SPEEDOMETER **2** **Speedo™** [usually pl.] a SWIMMING COSTUME, especially a style of tight TRUNKS for men and boys（尤指）男式緊身游泳褲；游泳衣：*a pair of Speedos* 一條緊身游泳褲

speed·om·eter /spiːˈdɒmɪtə(r); *NAmE* -ˈdɑːm-/ (also *informal* **speedo**) *noun* an instrument in a vehicle which shows how fast the vehicle is going（車輛的）速度計 ➲ VISUAL VOCAB page V52

ˈspeed-read *verb* [I, T] **~ (sth)** to read sth very quickly, paying attention to the general meaning of sentences and phrases rather than to every word 快速閱讀，速讀（注意大意）▸ **ˈspeed-reading** *noun* [U]

ˈspeed skating *noun* [U] the sport of SKATING on ice as fast as possible 速度滑冰 ➲ compare FIGURE-SKATING

speed·ster /ˈspiːdstə(r)/ *noun* (*informal*) **1** a person who drives a vehicle very fast 快速駕駛者；飆車者 **2** a machine or vehicle that works well at high speeds 高速運轉的機器；快速行駛的車輛

ˈspeed trap (*BrE* also **ˈradar trap**) *noun* a place on a road where police use special equipment to catch drivers who are going too fast 汽車超速監視區

speed·way /ˈspiːdweɪ/ *noun* **1** [U] (*BrE*) the sport of racing motorcycles on a special track（摩托車）賽車運動 **2** [C] (*NAmE*) a special track for racing cars or motorcycles on（汽車或摩托車的）賽車跑道

speed·well /ˈspiːdwel/ *noun* [U, C] a small wild plant with bright blue or pinkish-white flowers 婆婆納（開鮮豔藍色或粉白色花的野生植物）

speedy /ˈspiːdi/ *adj.* (**speed·ier**, **speedi·est**) **1** happening or done quickly or without delay 迅速的；儘快的 **SYN** **rapid**：*We wish you* ***a speedy recovery*** (= from an illness or injury). 我們祝願你早日康復。◇ *a speedy reply* 即時的答覆 **2** moving or working very quickly 快速的；高速的：*speedy computers* 高速計算機 ➲ SYNONYMS at FAST ▸ **speed·ily** *adv.*：*All enquiries will be dealt with as speedily as possible.* 所有詢問都將從速處理。

spele·olo·gist /ˌspiːliˈɒlədʒɪst; *NAmE* -ˈɑːlə-/ *noun* a scientist who studies CAVES or a person who goes into caves as a sport 洞穴學家；洞穴探險家 ➲ compare CAVER, POTHOLER, SPELUNKER ▸ **spele·ology** /ˌspiːliˈɒlədʒi; *NAmE* -ˈɑːlə-/ *noun* [U]

spell 0-w /spel/ *verb, noun*

■ *verb* (**spelt**, **spelt** /spelt/ or **spelled**, **spelled**) **1** 0-w [T] **~ sth** to say or write the letters of a word in the correct order 用字母拼；拼寫：*How do you spell your surname?* 你的姓怎麼拼？◇ *I thought her name was Catherine, but it's Kathryn spelt with a 'K'.* 我原以為她叫 Catherine，其實是 Kathryn，以 K 開頭。 **2** 0-w [I, T] to form words correctly from individual letters 拼出，會拼（單詞）：*I've never been able to spell.* 我一直不會拼寫。◇ **~ sth + adj.** *You've spelt my name wrong.* 你把我的名字拼錯了。➲ see also MISSPELL **3** 0-w [T] **~ sth** (of letters of a word 構成單詞的字母) to form words when they are put together in a particular order 拼作；拼成：*C—A—T spells 'cat'.* * C—A—T 拼作 cat。 **4** [T] **~ sth (for sb/sth)** to have sth, usually sth bad, as a result; to mean sth, usually sth bad 招致，意味着（通常指壞事）：*The crop failure spelt disaster for many farmers.* 對許多農民來說，莊稼歉收就意味着災難。 **5** [T] **~ sb** (*NAmE, informal*) to replace for a short time sb who is doing a particular activity so that they can rest（短時間）替換，頂替：*Carter will be here in an hour to spell you.* 卡特一小時後過來替換你。

PHR V **ˌspell sth↔ˈout** **1** to explain sth in a simple, clear way 解釋明白；講清楚：*You know what I mean—I'm sure I don't need to spell it out.* 你明白我的意思，肯定不需要我解釋了。◇ **~ why, what, etc.** ... *Let me spell out why we need more money.* 我來說說清楚，我們為什麼還需要錢。 **2** to say or write the letters of a word in the right order 用字母拼；拼寫：*Could you spell that name out again?* 你能不能把那個名字再拼一次？

■ *noun* **1** 0-w [C] a short period of time during which sth lasts（持續的）一段時間：*a spell of warm weather* 一段天氣溫暖的日子 ◇ *a* ***cold/hot/wet/bright, etc. spell*** 一段寒冷、炎熱、多雨、晴朗等的日子 ◇ *There will be rain at first, with* ***sunny spells*** *later.* 開始會有雨，雨後間晴。◇ *She went to the doctor complaining of* ***dizzy spells***. 她去找醫生看病，說自己一陣一陣地頭昏。 **2** [C] a period of time doing sth or working somewhere（幹某事或在某處工作的）一段時間：*She had a spell as a singer before becoming an actress.* 在當演員以前她唱過一陣子歌。◇ *I spent a* ***brief spell*** *on the Washington Post.* 我曾在《華盛頓郵報》工作過一小段時間。 **3** [C] words that are thought to have magic power or to make a piece of magic work; a piece of magic that happens when sb says these magic words 咒語；符咒；魔法：*a* ***magic spell*** 魔咒 ◇ *a book of spells* 咒語集 ◇ *The wizard recited a spell.* 巫師唸了一道咒語。◇ *to* ***cast/put a spell on sb*** 對某人施魔法 ◇ *to* ***be under a spell*** (= affected by magic) 中了魔法 **4** [sing.] a quality that a person or thing has that makes them so attractive or interesting that they have a strong influence on you 魅力；魔力 **SYN** **charm**：*I completely* ***fell under her spell***. 我完全給她迷住了。**IDM** see WEAVE *v.*

spell·bind·ing /ˈspelbaɪndɪŋ/ *adj.* holding your attention completely 讓人着魔的；迷人的 **SYN** **enthralling**：*a spellbinding performance* 使人入迷的演出

spell·bound /ˈspelbaʊnd/ *adj.* [not usually before noun] with your attention completely held by what you are listening to or watching 入迷；出神；着魔：*a storyteller*

S

who can hold audiences spellbound 講故事能讓聽眾如痴如醉的人

spell·check /ˈspeltʃek/ *verb* **~ sth** to use a computer program to check your writing to see if your spelling is correct（用計算機程序）檢查拼寫 ▸ **spell·check** *noun* = SPELLCHECKER

spell·checker /ˈspeltʃekə(r)/ *noun* a computer program that checks your writing to see if your spelling is correct（計算機中的）拼寫檢查程序

spell·er /ˈspelə(r)/ *noun* if sb is a **good/bad speller**, they find it easy/difficult to spell words correctly 拼寫能力強（或差）的人

spell·ing 🔑 /ˈspelɪŋ/ *noun*
1 🔑 [U] the act of forming words correctly from individual letters; the ability to do this 拼寫；拼寫能力：*a **spelling mistake*** 拼寫錯誤 ◇ *the differences between British and American spelling* 英式英語和美式英語在拼寫方面的區別 ◇ *My spelling is terrible.* 我的拼寫很糟糕。
2 🔑 [C] the way that a particular word is written 拼法：*a list of difficult spellings* 難拼單詞表

ˈspelling bee *noun* a competition in which people have to spell words 拼字比賽

spelt *past tense, past part.* of SPELL

spe·lunk·ing /spɪˈlʌŋkɪŋ/ (*NAmE*) (*BrE* **cav·ing**, **pot·hol·ing**) *noun* [U] the sport or activity of going into CAVES under the ground 洞穴探察；洞穴探險 ➲ VISUAL VOCAB page V40 ▸ **spe·lunk·er** /spɪˈlʌŋkə(r)/ *noun* (*NAmE*) (*BrE* **caver**, **pot·holer**)

spend 🔑 /spend/ *verb, noun*
■ *verb* (**spent**, **spent** /spent/) **1** 🔑 [T, I] to give money to pay for goods, services, etc. 用，花（錢）：**~ sth** *I've spent all my money already.* 我已經把我的錢全都花完了。◇ **~ sth on sth/on doing sth** *She spent £100 on a new dress.* 她花 100 英鎊買了一條新連衣裙。◇ **~ (sth doing sth)** *The company has spent thousands of pounds updating their computer systems.* 公司花了幾千英鎊更新計算機系統。◇ *I just can't seem to stop spending.* 我似乎就是沒法不花錢。 **2** 🔑 [T] to use time for a particular purpose; to pass time 花（時間）；度過：**~ sth + adv./prep.** *We spent the weekend in Paris.* 我們在巴黎度過了週末。◇ *How do you spend your spare time?* 你在空閒時間幹什麼？◇ **~ sth on sth** *How long did you spend on your homework?* 你做家庭作業用了多長時間？◇ **~ sth doing sth** *I spend too much time watching television.* 我看電視花的時間太多。◇ **~ sth in doing sth** *Most of her life was spent in caring for others.* 她大半輩子的時間都用來照顧別人了。 **3** 🔑 [T, often passive] to use energy, effort, etc., especially until it has all been used 花費，消耗，用盡（精力等）：**~ sth on sth** *She spends too much effort on things that don't matter.* 她在一些無關緊要的事情上花費精力太多。◇ **~ itself** *The storm had finally spent itself.* 暴風雨終於停歇了。➲ see also SPENT
IDM **spend the ˈnight with sb 1** to stay with sb for a night 在某人家裏住一夜：*My daughter's spending the night with a friend.* 我女兒要在一個朋友那裏過夜。 **2** (also **spend the ˈnight together**) to stay with sb for a night and have sex with them 和某人一起過夜並發生性關係 **spend a ˈpenny** (*old-fashioned, BrE*) people say 'spend a penny' to avoid saying 'use the toilet'（委婉說法，與 use the toilet 同義）解手，方便
■ *noun* [sing.] (*informal*) the amount of money spent for a particular purpose or over a particular length of time（為某目的或某段時間內的）花銷，花費，開銷

spend·er /ˈspendə(r)/ *noun* a person who spends money in the particular way mentioned 花錢…的人：*a big spender* (= who spends a lot of money) 花錢大手大腳的人

spend·ing /ˈspendɪŋ/ *noun* [U] the amount of money that is spent by a government or an organization（政府或其他機構的）開支，支出，花銷：*to increase **public spending*** 增加公共開支 ➲ SYNONYMS at COST

ˈspending money *noun* [U] money that you can spend on personal things for pleasure or entertainment 零花錢；零用錢

spend·thrift /ˈspendθrɪft/ *noun* (*disapproving*) a person who spends too much money or who wastes money 花錢無度的人；揮霍者 ▸ **spend·thrift** *adj.* [usually before noun]

spent /spent/ *adj.* **1** [usually before noun] that has been used, so that it cannot be used again 用過已廢的；失效的：*spent matches* 用過的火柴 **2** (*formal*) very tired 筋疲力盡的 SYN **exhausted**：*After the gruelling test, he felt totally spent.* 緊張的考試過後，他感覺筋疲力盡了。
IDM **a ˌspent ˈforce** a person or group that no longer has any power or influence 威勢不再的人（或集團）；不再有影響力的人（或集團）➲ see also SPEND *v.*

sperm /spɜːm; *NAmE* spɜːrm/ *noun* (*pl.* **sperm** or **sperms**) **1** [C] a cell that is produced by the sex organs of a male and that can combine with a female egg to produce young 精子：*He has a low **sperm count*** (= very few live male cells). 他的精液精子計數低。 **2** [U] the liquid that is produced by the male sex organs that contains these cells 精液 SYN **semen** ➲ COLLOCATIONS at LIFE

sperm·ato·zoon /ˌspɜːmətəˈzəʊən; *NAmE* ˌspɜːrmətəˈzoʊən/ *noun* (*pl.* **sperm·ato·zoa** /-ˈzəʊə; *NAmE* -ˈzoʊə/) (*biology* 生) a sperm 精子

ˈsperm bank *noun* a place where sperm is kept and then used to help women become pregnant artificially 精子庫（保存精子以便幫助女子進行人工受孕）

spermi·cide /ˈspɜːmɪsaɪd; *NAmE* ˈspɜːrm-/ *noun* [U, C] a substance that kills sperm, used during sex to prevent the woman from becoming pregnant 殺精子劑 ▸ **spermi·cidal** /ˌspɜːmɪˈsaɪdl; *NAmE* ˌspɜːrm-/ *adj.* [only before noun]

ˈsperm whale *noun* a large WHALE that is hunted for its oil and fat 抹香鯨 ➲ VISUAL VOCAB page V12

spew /spjuː/ *verb* **1** [I, T] to flow out quickly, or to make sth flow out quickly, in large amounts（使）噴出，湧出：**+ adv./prep.** *Flames spewed from the aircraft's engine.* 飛機發動機噴出火焰。◇ **~ sth + adv./prep.** *Massive chimneys were spewing out smoke.* 一座座高大的煙囱冒着煙。 **2** [I, T] (*BrE, informal*) to VOMIT (= bring food from the stomach back out through the mouth) 嘔吐：**~ (up)** *He spewed up on the pavement.* 他在人行道上吐了。◇ **~ sth (up)** *She spewed up the entire meal.* 她把吃的飯全吐出來了。

SPF /ˌes piː ˈef/ *abbr.* sun protection factor (a number that tells you how much protection a particular cream or liquid gives you from the harmful effects of the sun)（護膚霜等的）防曬指數，防曬係數

sphag·num /ˈsfægnəm/ (also **ˈSphagnum moss**) *noun* [U] a type of MOSS that grows in wet areas, used especially for planting plants in pots, making FERTILIZER, etc. 泥炭蘚（尤用於盆種花草、積肥等）

sphere AW /sfɪə(r); *NAmE* sfɪr/ *noun* **1** (*geometry* 幾何) a solid figure that is completely round, with every point on its surface at an equal distance from the centre 球；球體；球形 ➲ VISUAL VOCAB page V71 **2** any object that is completely round, for example a ball 圓球；球狀物 **3** an area of activity, influence or interest; a particular section of society 範圍；領域；階層；界 SYN **domain**：*the political sphere* 政界 ◇ *This area was formerly within the **sphere of influence** of the US.* 這一地區先前屬於美國的勢力範圍。◇ *He and I moved in totally different social spheres.* 我和他進入了完全不同的社會圈子。 **4 -sphere** (in nouns 構成名詞) a region that surrounds a planet, especially the earth（包圍地球等的大氣的）層：*ionosphere* 電離層 ◇ *atmosphere* 大氣層

spher·ic·al AW /ˈsferɪkl; *NAmE* also ˈsfɪr-/ *adj.* shaped like a sphere 球形的；球狀的 SYN **round** ▸ **spher·ic·al·ly** AW /-kli/ *adv.*

spher·oid /ˈsfɪərɔɪd; *NAmE* ˈsfɪr-/ *noun* (*technical* 術語) a solid object that is approximately the same shape as a sphere 球（狀）體；扁球體；橢球體

sphinc·ter /ˈsfɪŋktə(r)/ *noun* (*anatomy* 解) a ring of muscle that surrounds an opening in the body and can contract to close it 括約肌：*the anal sphincter* 肛門括約肌

sphinx /sfɪŋks/ *noun* (often **the Sphinx**) an ancient Egyptian stone statue of a creature with a human head

S

and the body of a LION lying down. In ancient Greek stories the Sphinx spoke in RIDDLES. 斯芬克斯，獅身人面像（古埃及石像；在希臘神話中，斯芬克斯說話慣用謎語）

spic /spɪk/ *noun* (*taboo, slang, especially NAmE*) a very offensive word for a person from a country where Spanish is spoken, for example a Mexican or Puerto Rican 西班牙語區的人（如墨西哥人或波多黎各人，有強烈冒犯意）

IDM **,spic and 'span** = SPICK AND SPAN at SPICK

spice /spaɪs/ *noun, verb*

■ ***noun*** **1** [C, U] one of the various types of powder or seed that come from plants and are used in cooking. Spices have a strong taste and smell （調味）香料：*common spices such as ginger and cinnamon* 薑和肉桂等常見香料 ◇ *a spice jar* 香料瓶 ➲ VISUAL VOCAB page V32 **2** [U] extra interest or excitement 額外的趣味（或刺激等）：*We need an exciting trip to add some spice to our lives.* 我們需要一次新奇的旅行來調劑一下生活。

IDM see VARIETY

■ ***verb*** **1** **~ sth (up)** (**with sth**) to add spice to food in order to give it more flavour 在…中加香料 **2** **~ sth (up)** (**with sth**) to add interest or excitement to sth 給…增添趣味；使…變得刺激：*He exaggerated the details to spice up the story.* 他添油加醋，使故事更有趣味。

spick /spɪk/ *adj.*

IDM **,spick and 'span** (also **,spic and 'span**) [not usually before noun] neat and clean 整潔乾淨；清清爽爽：*Their house is always spick and span.* 他們家總是收拾得清清爽爽。

spicy /'spaɪsi/ *adj.* (**spici·er**, **spici·est**)

1 (of food 食物) having a strong taste because spices have been used to flavour it 加有香料的；用香料調味的 SYN **hot** **2** (*informal*) (of a story, piece of news, etc. 故事、新聞等) exciting and slightly shocking 刺激的；粗俗的 ▸ **spici·ness** *noun* [U]

spider /'spaɪdə(r)/ *noun*

a small creature with eight thin legs. Many spiders spin webs (= nets of thin threads) to catch insects for food. 蜘蛛 ➲ VISUAL VOCAB page V13

'spider monkey *noun* a S American MONKEY with very long arms and legs and a long PREHENSILE tail 蜘蛛猴（棲於南美洲，四肢長，並有長捲尾）➲ VISUAL VOCAB page V12

'spider's web (*especially BrE*) (also **'spider web** especially in *NAmE*) (also **web**) *noun* a fine net of threads made by a spider to catch insects 蜘蛛網：(*figurative*) *to be caught in a spider's web of confusion* 陷入混亂不堪的局面 ➲ see also COBWEB

spi·dery /'spaɪdəri/ *adj.* long and thin, like the legs of a spider （像蜘蛛腿一樣）細長的：*spidery fingers* 修長的手指 ◇ *spidery writing* (= consisting of thin lines that are not very clear) 細長而不易辨認的筆畫

spied *past tense, past part.* of SPY

spiel /ʃpiːl; spiːl/ *noun* (*informal, usually disapproving*) a long speech that sb has used many times, that is intended to persuade you to believe sth or buy sth 油嘴滑舌的游說；一長串招徠生意的套話

spies /spaɪz/ *noun pl.* of SPY

spiff /spɪf/ *verb*

PHR V **,spiff 'up** | **,spiff sb/sth↔'up** (*NAmE, informal*) to make yourself/sb/sth look neat and attractive 把…收拾得整齊漂亮；打扮；裝扮

spif·fing /'spɪfɪŋ/ *adj.* (*BrE, old-fashioned, informal*) extremely good or pleasant 極好的；很棒的 SYN **excellent**

spiffy /'spɪfi/ *adj.* (*NAmE, informal*) attractive and fashionable 漂亮而時髦的

spigot /'spɪgət/ *noun* **1** (*technical* 術語) a device in a tap/faucet that controls the flow of liquid from a container （龍頭中的）塞，栓 **2** (*US*) any tap/faucet, especially one outdoors （尤指戶外的）龍頭

spike /spaɪk/ *noun, verb*

■ ***noun*** **1** [C] a thin object with a sharp point, especially a pointed piece of metal, wood, etc. 尖狀物；尖頭；尖刺：*a row of iron spikes on a wall* 牆頭的一排尖鐵 ◇ *Her hair stood up in spikes.* 她的頭髮一縷一縷地翹着。➲ see also SPIKE HEEL **2** [C, usually pl.] a metal point attached to the SOLE of a sports shoe to prevent you from slipping while running （防滑）鞋釘 ➲ compare CLEAT (2), (3) **3** **spikes** [pl.] shoes fitted with these metal spikes, used for running （賽跑用的）釘鞋：*a pair of spikes* 一雙釘鞋 **4** [C] a long pointed group of flowers that grow together on a single STEM 穗；穗狀花序 **5** [C, usually sing.] (*informal, especially NAmE*) a sudden large increase in sth 猛增；急升：*a spike in oil prices* 油價的急劇上漲

■ ***verb*** **1** [T] **~ sb/sth** (**on sth**) to push a sharp piece of metal, wood, etc. into sb/sth; to injure sth on a sharp point 用尖物刺入（或扎破）SYN **stab** **2** [T] **~ sth** (**with sth**) to add alcohol, poison or a drug to sb's drink or food without them knowing 在…中偷偷摻入（烈酒、毒藥或毒品）：*He gave her a drink spiked with tranquillizers.* 他給了她一杯偷偷放了鎮靜劑的飲料。◇ (*figurative*) *Her words were spiked with malice.* 她的話暗含惡意。**3** [T] **~ sth** to reject sth that a person has written or said; to prevent sth from happening or being made public 拒絕發表；阻止…傳播；阻撓：*The article was spiked for fear of legal action against the newspaper.* 因擔心被提起訴訟，報社未發表那篇文章。**4** [I] **~ (to sth)** (*especially NAmE*) to rise quickly and reach a high value 迅速升值；急劇增值：*The US dollar spiked to a three-month high.* 美元猛然升值到三個月來的最高價。

IDM **spike sb's 'guns** (*BrE*) to spoil the plans of an opponent 打亂對手的計劃

spiked /spaɪkt/ *adj.* with one or more spikes 有尖刺的；帶釘的：*spiked running shoes* 帶釘的跑鞋 ◇ *short spiked hair* 刺猬頭

,spike 'heel *noun* a very thin high heel on a woman's shoe; a shoe with such a heel （女式鞋的）細高跟；細高跟鞋 SYN **stiletto**

spiky /'spaɪki/ *adj.* **1** having sharp points 有尖刺的：*spiky plants, such as cacti* 帶刺的植物，如仙人掌 **2** (of hair 頭髮) sticking straight up from the head 刺猬式的 ➲ VISUAL VOCAB page V60 **3** (*BrE*) (of people 人) easily annoyed or offended 動輒生氣的；氣量小的 ▸ **spiki·ness** *noun* [U]

spill /spɪl/ *verb, noun*

■ ***verb*** (**spilled**, **spilled**) (*BrE* also **spilt**, **spilt** /spɪlt/) **1** [I, T] (especially of liquid 尤指液體) to flow over the edge of a container by accident; to make liquid do this （使）灑出，潑出，溢出：*Water had spilled out of the bucket onto the floor.* 桶裏的水灑出來了，灑了一地。◇ **~ sth** *He startled her and made her spill her drink.* 她讓他嚇了一跳，把飲料弄灑了。◇ *Thousands of gallons of crude oil were spilled into the ocean.* 成千上萬加侖的原油泄漏，流進了海洋。**2** [I] **+ adv./prep.** (of people 人) to come out of a place in large numbers and spread out 湧出；蜂擁而出：*The doors opened and people spilled into the street.* 門開了，人們湧上街道。◇ (*figurative*) *Light spilled from the windows.* 燈光從窗口照射出來。

IDM **spill the 'beans** (*informal*) to tell sb sth that should be kept secret or private 泄露秘密；說漏嘴 **spill (sb's) 'blood** (*formal* or *literary*) to kill or wound people 使流血；傷害；殺死 **spill your 'guts (to sb)** (*NAmE, informal*) to tell sb everything you know or feel about sth, because you are upset （向某人）傾訴心裏話 ➲ more at CRY *v.*

PHR V **,spill sth↔'out** | **,spill 'out** to tell sb all about a problem etc. very quickly; to come out quickly 傾訴；湧出：*Has she been spilling out her troubles to you again?* 她是不是又向你訴苦了？◇ *When he started to speak, the words just spilled out.* 他一開口就滔滔不絕。**,spill 'over (into sth)** **1** to fill a container and go over the edge 溢出；漫出：*She filled the glass so full that the water spilled over.* 她往杯子裏倒水倒得太滿，都溢出來了。◇ (*figurative*) *Her emotions suddenly spilled over.* 她突然就控制不住自己的感情了。**2** to start in one area and then affect other areas 波及：*Unrest has spilt over into areas outside the city.* 騷亂已經波及城市的周邊地區。➲ related noun OVERSPILL, SPILLOVER

■ ***noun*** **1** (also *formal* **spill·age**) [C, U] an act of letting a liquid come or fall out of a container; the amount

S

of liquid that comes or falls out 灑出（量）；潑出（量）；溢出（量）；泄漏（量）：*Many seabirds died as a result of the oil spill.* 許多海鳥死於這次石油泄漏。◇ *I wiped up the coffee spills on the table.* 我把灑在桌上的咖啡擦掉。 **2** [C] a long match, or a thin piece of twisted paper, used for lighting fires, oil lamps, etc.（點火用的）長梗火柴，紙捻 **3** [C, usually sing.] a fall, especially from a bicycle or a boat （尤指從自行車或船上）摔下，跌落：*to take a spill* （騎車）摔一跤 **IDM** see THRILL *n.*

spill·age /ˈspɪlɪdʒ/ *noun* [U, C] (*formal*) = SPILL：*Put the bottle in a plastic bag in case of spillage.* 把瓶子裝在塑料袋裏，以免灑得到處都是。

spilli·kins /ˈspɪlɪkɪnz/ (*BrE*) (*NAmE* **jack·straw**) *noun* [U] a game in which you remove a small stick from a pile, without moving any of the other sticks 挑棒遊戲（挑出一堆小棒中的一根而不觸動其他的小棒）

spill·over /ˈspɪləʊvə(r); *NAmE* -oʊ-/ *noun* [C, U] **1** something that is too large or too much for the place where it starts, and spreads to other places 容納不下的部份；溢出部份：*A second room was needed for the spillover of staff and reporters.* 還需要一個房間給沒有安置的員工和記者。 **2** the results or the effects of sth that have spread to other situations or places 影響

spill·way /ˈspɪlweɪ/ *noun* (*technical* 術語) a passage for the extra water from a DAM (= a wall across a river that holds water back) 溢洪道

spim /spɪm/ *noun* [U] (*informal*) advertising sent as messages on the Internet to people who have not asked for it （互聯網）即時通信垃圾廣告 ➲ compare SPAM **ORIGIN** From the letters for *SPam via Instant Messaging.* 源自 SPam via Instant Messaging 的縮寫。

spin 🔑 /spɪn/ *verb, noun*

■ *verb* (**spin·ning**, **spun**, **spun** /spʌn/)

▸ **TURN ROUND QUICKLY 快速旋轉** **1** 🔑 [I, T] to turn round and round quickly; to make sth do this （使）快速旋轉：(**+ adv./prep.**) *The plane was spinning out of control.* 飛機失去控制，不停地旋轉。◇ *a spinning ice skater* 做旋轉動作的溜冰者 ◇ *My head is spinning* (= I feel as if my head is going around and I can't balance). 我覺得天旋地轉。◇ **~ (round/around)** *The dancers spun round and round.* 舞者不停地旋轉。◇ **~ sth (round/around)** *to spin a ball/coin/wheel* 轉動球／硬幣／輪子 **2** 🔑 [I, T] **~ (sb) round/around | + adv./prep.** to turn round quickly once; to make sb do this （使）急轉身，猛轉回頭，急轉彎：*He spun around to face her.* 他猛地回過身來，面對着她。

▸ **MAKE THREAD 紡線** **3** [I, T] to make thread from wool, cotton, silk, etc. by twisting it 紡（線）；紡（紗）：*She sat by the window spinning.* 她坐在窗前紡線。◇ **~ sth** *to spin and knit wool* 紡毛線織毛活 ◇ **~ A into B** *spinning silk into thread* 把蠶絲紡成線 ◇ **~ B from A** *spinning thread from silk* 用蠶絲紡線

▸ **OF SPIDER/SILKWORM 蜘蛛；蠶** **4** [T] **~ sth** to produce thread from its body to make a web or COCOON 吐（絲）；作（繭）；結（網）：*a spider spinning a web* 結網的蜘蛛

▸ **DRIVE/TRAVEL QUICKLY 高速駕駛／行進** **5** [I] **+ adv./prep.** to drive or travel quickly 駕車飛馳；疾馳：*They went spinning along the roads on their bikes.* 他們騎自行車沿公路疾馳。

▸ **DRY CLOTHES 甩乾衣服** **6** [T] **~ sth** to remove the water from clothes that have just been washed, in a SPIN DRYER （用旋轉式脫水機）甩乾衣服

▸ **PRESENT INFORMATION 陳述** **7** [T] **~ sth (as sth)** to present information or a situation in a particular way, especially one that makes you or your ideas seem good 有傾向性地陳述；（尤指）以有利於自己的口吻描述：*An aide was already spinning the senator's defeat as 'almost as good as an outright win'.* 一名助手已經開始將那位參議員的失敗描述成"幾乎是大獲全勝"。

IDM **spin (sb) a 'yarn, 'tale, etc.** to try to make sb believe a long story that is not true 杜撰故事，編造故事（以讓人信以為真）➲ more at HEEL *n.*

PHR V **,spin 'off (from sth) | ,spin sth↔'off (from sth)** to happen or to produce sth as a new or unexpected result of sth that already exists 脫胎（於某事物）；（從某事物）派生，衍生；隨之而產生：*products spinning off from favourite books* 從一些暢銷書衍生出的產品 ➲ related noun SPIN-OFF **,spin sth↔'off** (*business* 商) (*especially NAmE*) to form a new company from parts of an existing one 從…脫離出來（組建新公司）：*The transportation operation will be spun off into a separate company.* 運輸部門將脫離出來組建為一家獨立公司。 **,spin sth↔'out** to make sth last as long as possible 拉長；拖長

■ *noun*

▸ **FAST TURNING MOVEMENT 高速旋轉** **1** [C, U] a very fast turning movement 高速旋轉：*the earth's spin* 地球的自轉 ◇ *the spin of a wheel* 輪子的轉動 ◇ *Give the washing a short spin.* 把洗過的衣服稍稍甩一下。 **2** [C, usually sing.] if an aircraft goes into a **spin**, it falls and turns round rapidly （飛機的）旋衝，螺旋

▸ **IN CAR 乘汽車** **3** [C] (*informal*, becoming *old-fashioned*) a short ride in a car for pleasure 兜風：*Let's* **go for a spin**. 咱們兜風去吧。

▸ **IN TENNIS/CRICKET 網球；板球** **4** [U] the way you make a ball turn very fast when you throw it or hit it 旋轉：*She puts a lot of spin on the ball.* 她打出的球旋轉得很厲害。◇ *a* **spin bowler** (= in CRICKET, a BOWLER who uses spin) 投旋轉球的板球投球手 ➲ see also TOPSPIN

▸ **ON INFORMATION 陳述** **5** [sing., U] (*informal*) a way of presenting information or a situation in a particular way, especially one that makes you or your ideas seem good （尤指有利於自己的）導向性陳述：*Politicians put their own spin on the economic situation.* 政治人物對經濟形勢各執一詞。

IDM **in a (flat) 'spin** very confused, worried or excited 暈頭轉向；急得團團轉；十分激動：*Her resignation put her colleagues in a spin.* 她的辭職令同事們摸不着頭腦。

spina bif·ida /ˌspaɪnə ˈbɪfɪdə/ *noun* [U] a medical condition in which some bones in the SPINE have not developed normally at birth, often causing PARALYSIS (= loss of control or feeling) in the legs 脊柱裂（先天性椎骨背側閉合不全）

spin·ach /ˈspɪnɪtʃ; -ɪdʒ/ *noun* [U] a vegetable with large dark green leaves that are cooked or eaten in salads 菠菜

spinal /ˈspaɪnl/ *adj.* [usually before noun] (*technical* 術語) connected with the SPINE (= the long bone in the back) 脊的；脊柱的；脊髓的：*spinal injuries* 脊椎損傷

,spinal 'column *noun* the SPINE 脊柱

,spinal 'cord *noun* the mass of nerves inside the SPINE that connects all parts of the body to the brain 脊髓 ➲ VISUAL VOCAB page V59

'spinal tap (*NAmE*) (*BrE* **,lumbar 'puncture**) *noun* the removal of liquid from the lower part of the SPINE with a hollow needle 腰椎穿刺（放液）

spin·dle /ˈspɪndl/ *noun* **1** a long straight part that turns in a machine, or that another part of the machine turns around 軸；心軸；指軸 **2** a thin pointed piece of wood used for spinning wool into thread by hand （手紡用的）繞線杆，紡錘

spindly /ˈspɪndli/ *adj.* (*informal*, often *disapproving*) very long and thin and not strong 長而纖弱的；細長而瘦弱的：*spindly legs* 細長的腿

'spin doctor *noun* (*informal*) a person whose job is to present information to the public about a politician, an organization, etc. in the way that seems most positive （政治人物、組織等的）輿論導向專家

,spin 'dryer (also **,spin 'drier**) *noun* (*BrE*) a machine that partly dries clothes that you have washed by turning them round and round very fast to remove the water 旋轉式脫水機；甩乾機 ➲ compare TUMBLE DRYER ▸ **,spin-'dry** *verb* **~ sth**

spine /spaɪn/ *noun* **1** the row of small bones that are connected together down the middle of the back 脊柱；脊椎 **SYN** **backbone** ➲ VISUAL VOCAB page V59 **2** any of the sharp pointed parts like needles on some plants and animals （植物的）刺；（動物的）刺毛：*Porcupines use their spines to protect themselves.* 豪豬用身上的刺毛來自衛。 ➲ see also SPINY **3** the narrow part of the cover of a book that the pages are joined to 書脊

'spine-chilling *adj.* (of a book, film/movie, etc. 書、電影等) frightening in an exciting way 令人毛骨悚然的 ▸ **'spine-chiller** *noun*

spine·less /'spaɪnləs/ *adj.* **1** (*disapproving*) (of people 人) weak and easily frightened 沒有骨氣的；怯懦的 **2** (of animals 動物) having no SPINE (= the long bone in the back) 無脊椎的；無脊柱的 **3** (of animals or plants 動物或植物) having no SPINES (= sharp parts like needles) 無刺的

spi·net /spɪ'net; *NAmE* 'spɪnət/ *noun* **1** a kind of HARPSICHORD (= an early type of musical instrument), played like a piano 斯皮耐琴（小型撥弦鍵琴） **2 ~ piano/organ** (*US*) a small piano/electronic organ 小型鋼琴／電子琴

'spine-tingling *adj.* (of an event, a piece of music, etc. 活動、樂曲等) enjoyable because it is very exciting or frightening 令人欣快的；緊張刺激的；驚險的

spin·naker /'spɪnəkə(r)/ *noun* a large extra sail on a racing YACHT that you use when the wind is coming from behind （賽艇的）大三角帆（順風時用） ➲ VISUAL VOCAB page V56

spin·ner /'spɪnə(r)/ *noun* **1** (in CRICKET 板球) a BOWLER who uses SPIN (4) when throwing the ball 投旋轉球的投球手 **2** a person who spins thread 紡線者；紡紗工 **3** a device that spins around, used on a fishing line to attract fish （釣魚用的）旋式誘餌

spin·ney /'spɪni/ *noun* (*BrE*) a small area of trees 小樹林 SYN copse

spin·ning /'spɪnɪŋ/ *noun* [U] **1** the art or the process of twisting wool, etc. to make thread 紡線（手藝）；紡紗（手藝） **2 Spinning™** a type of exercise performed on an EXERCISE BIKE, usually in a class （通常在健身班上做的）騎健身車練習

'spinning wheel *noun* a simple machine that people used in their homes in the past for twisting wool, etc. It has a large wheel operated with the foot. 紡車（舊時的簡易紡紗機，有一大輪，用腳操縱）

'spin-off *noun* **~ (from/of sth) 1** an unexpected but useful result of an activity that is designed to produce sth else （意外但有用的）副產品，派生物： *commercial spin-offs from medical research* 醫學研究引出的有商業價值的副產品 **2** a book, a film/movie, a television programme, or an object that is based on a book, film/movie or television series that has been very successful （根據成功的書、電影或電視劇製作的）派生作品，搭車產品： *The TV comedy series is a spin-off of the original movie.* 這部電視喜劇連續劇是電影原作的副產品。◇ *spin-off merchandise from the latest Disney movie* 根據最新的迪斯尼影片開發的商品

spin·ster /'spɪnstə(r)/ *noun* (*old-fashioned*, often *disapproving*) a woman who is not married, especially an older woman who is not likely to marry 老處女；老姑娘 HELP This word should not now be used to mean simply a woman who is not married. 如今，不可用這個詞泛指未婚女子。 ➲ compare BACHELOR (1) ▸ **spin·ster·hood** /-hʊd/ *noun* [U]： *For most women, marriage used to bring a higher status than spinsterhood.* 從前，就多數婦女而言，結婚的比獨身的更有地位。

spiny /'spaɪni/ *adj.* (of animals or plants 動物或植物) having sharp points like needles 有刺毛的；帶刺的；多刺的 ➲ see also SPINE (2)

,spiny 'anteater *noun* = ECHIDNA

spiral /'spaɪrəl/ *noun, adj., verb*

■ ***noun* 1** a shape or design, consisting of a continuous curved line that winds around a central point, with each curve further away from the centre 螺旋形；螺旋式： *The birds circled in a slow spiral above the house.* 鳥兒在房子上空緩緩盤旋。 **2** a continuous harmful increase or decrease in sth, that gradually gets faster and faster 逐漸加速上升（或下降）： *the destructive spiral of violence in the inner cities* 內城區日益嚴重的暴力行為 ◇ *measures to control the inflationary spiral* 控制日益惡化的通貨膨脹的措施 ◇ *the **upward/downward spiral** of sales* 日漸上升／下降的銷售額

■ ***adj.*** moving in a continuous curve that winds around a central point 螺旋形的；螺旋式的： *A snail's shell is spiral in form.* 蝸牛殼呈螺旋形。 ▸ **spir·al·ly** *adv.*

■ ***verb*** (**-ll-**, *NAmE* usually **-l-**) **1** [I] (**+ adv./prep.**) to move in continuous circles, going upwards or downwards 螺旋式上升（或下降）；盤旋上升（或下降）： *The plane spiralled down to the ground.* 飛機盤旋降落。 **2** [I] to increase rapidly 急劇增長： *the spiralling cost of health care* 急劇上漲的醫療費用 ◇ **+ adv./prep.** *Prices are spiralling out of control.* 物價飛漲，失去控制。

PHR V **,spiral 'down/'downward** to decrease rapidly 急劇減少

,spiral-'bound *adj.* (of a book 書) held together by wire which is wound through holes along one edge 螺旋裝訂的

,spiral 'staircase *noun* a set of stairs that curve upwards around a central post 螺旋式樓梯

spir·ant /'spaɪərənt/ (*NAmE*) (*BrE* **frica·tive**) *noun, adj.* (*phonetics* 語音) a speech sound made by forcing breath out through a narrow space in the mouth with the lips, teeth or tongue in a particular position, for example /f/ and /ʃ/ in *fee* and *she* 摩擦音；擦音 ▸ **spir·ant** (*NAmE*) (*BrE* **frica·tive**) *adj.* ➲ compare PLOSIVE

spire /'spaɪə(r)/ *noun* a tall pointed structure on the top of a building, especially a church （教堂等頂部的）尖塔，尖頂

spirit 🔑 /'spɪrɪt/ *noun, verb*

■ ***noun***

▸ **MIND/FEELINGS/CHARACTER** 思想；感情；性格 **1** 🔑 [U, C] the part of a person that includes their mind, feelings and character rather than their body 精神；心靈： *the power of the human spirit to overcome difficulties* 人類克服困難的精神力量 **2** 🔑 **spirits** [pl.] a person's feelings or state of mind 情緒；心境： *to be in **high/low spirits*** 情緒高漲／低落 ◇ *You must try and **keep your spirits up*** (= stay cheerful). 你必須設法保持高昂的情緒。◇ *My **spirits sank** at the prospect of starting all over again.* 想到一切都得從頭再來，我的情緒一下子低落了。 **3** [C] (always with an adjective 總是與形容詞連用) a person of the type mentioned （某種類型的）人： *a brave spirit* 勇敢的人 ◇ ***kindred spirits*** (= people who like the same things as you) 志趣相投的人 ➲ see also FREE SPIRIT

▸ **COURAGE/DETERMINATION** 勇氣；決心 **4** 🔑 [U] courage, determination or energy 勇氣；志氣；意志；活力： *Show a little **fighting spirit**.* 要表現出一點鬥志。◇ *Although the team lost, they played with tremendous spirit.* 儘管輸了，但隊員表現得極為勇猛。◇ *They took away his freedom and broke his spirit.* 他們奪去了他的自由，摧垮了他的意志。

▸ **LOYAL FEELINGS** 忠心 **5** 🔑 [U, sing.] loyal feelings towards a group, team or society （對團體、隊伍、社會的）忠心： *There's not much **community spirit** around here.* 這裏集體精神比較薄弱。 ➲ see also TEAM SPIRIT

▸ **ATTITUDE** 態度 **6** [sing.] a state of mind or mood; an attitude 心態；態度： *We approached the situation in the wrong spirit.* 我們以前對待局勢的心態不對。◇ *'OK, I'll try'. '**That's the spirit**'* (= the right attitude).' "好吧，我來試試。" "這就對了。" ◇ *The party went well because everyone **entered into the spirit of things**.* 晚會很成功，因為每個人都很投入。 ➲ see also PARTY SPIRIT

▸ **TYPICAL QUALITY** 根本屬性 **7** [sing.] the typical or most important quality or mood of sth 本質；精髓；基本精神：*The exhibition captures the **spirit of the age/times**.* 這個展覽會抓住了時代精神。

▸ **REAL MEANING** 真實意義 **8** [U] the real or intended meaning or purpose of sth 真實意義；實質： *Obey the spirit, not the letter* (= the narrow meaning of the words) *of the law.* 要依照法律的精神實質，而不是字面意思。

▸ **SOUL** 靈魂 **9** 🔑 [C] the soul thought of as separate from the body and believed to live on after death; a GHOST 靈魂；鬼魂；幽靈： *He is dead, but his spirit lives on.* 他死了，但他的靈魂將永存。◇ *It was believed that people could be possessed by evil spirits.* 從前，人們相信人有可能被惡鬼纏身。 ➲ see also THE HOLY SPIRIT

▸ **IMAGINARY CREATURE** 想像中的生靈 **10** [C] (*old-fashioned*) an imaginary creature with magic powers, for example, a FAIRY or an ELF 仙子；小精靈；小妖精

S

▸ **ALCOHOL** 酒精 **11** 🔑 [C, usually pl.] (*especially BrE*) a strong alcoholic drink 烈酒：*I don't drink whisky or brandy or any other spirits.* 我不喝威士忌和白蘭地，也不喝其他烈性酒。 **12** [U] a special type of alcohol used in industry or medicine 工業酒精；醫用酒精 ➲ see also METHYLATED SPIRIT, SURGICAL SPIRIT, WHITE SPIRIT

IDM **in 'spirit** in your thoughts 在心裏；在精神上：*I shall be with you in spirit* (= thinking about you though not with you physically). 我的心將和你在一起。 **the ˌspirit is 'willing (but the ˌflesh is 'weak)** (*humorous, saying*) you intend to do good things but you are too lazy, weak or busy to actually do them 心靈固然願意，肉體卻軟弱；心有餘而力不足；力不從心 **as/when/if the ˌspirit 'moves you** as/when/if you feel like it 要是願意的話：*I'll go for a run this evening, if the spirit moves me.* 今晚要是有興致的話，我要去跑步。 ➲ more at FIGHT *v.*, RAISE *v.*

■ ***verb* ~ sth + adv./prep.** to take sb/sth away in a quick, secret or mysterious way 偷偷帶走；讓人不可思議地弄走：*After the concert, the band was **spirited away** before their fans could get near them.* 音樂會結束後，樂隊沒等歌迷靠近就神秘地消失了。

spir·it·ed /ˈspɪrɪtɪd/ *adj.* [usually before noun] full of energy, determination or courage 精神飽滿的；堅定的；勇猛的：*a spirited young woman* 充滿朝氣的年輕女子 ◊ *a spirited discussion* 熱烈的討論 ◊ *She put up a spirited defence in the final game.* 她在最後一場比賽中進行了頑強的防守。 ➲ compare DISPIRITED ➲ see also HIGH-SPIRITED, PUBLIC-SPIRITED ▸ **spir·it·ed·ly** *adv.*

spir·it·less /ˈspɪrɪtləs/ *adj.* (*formal*) without energy, enthusiasm or determination 沒有生氣的；無精打采的；淡漠的；沉悶的

ˈspirit level (also **level**) *noun* a glass tube partly filled with liquid, with a bubble of air inside. Spirit levels are used to test whether a surface is level, by the position of the bubble. （氣泡）水準儀 ➲ **VISUAL VOCAB** page V20

spir·it·ual 🔑 /ˈspɪrɪtʃuəl/ *adj., noun*

■ ***adj.*** [usually before noun] **1** 🔑 connected with the human spirit, rather than the body or physical things 精神的；心靈的：*a spiritual experience* 心靈體驗 ◊ *spiritual development* 精神上的發展 ◊ *a lack of spiritual values in the modern world* 現代世界精神價值的缺失 ◊ *We're concerned about your **spiritual welfare**.* 我們擔心你的心理健康。 **OPP** **material 2** 🔑 connected with religion 宗教的：*a spiritual leader* 宗教領袖 ➲ compare TEMPORAL (1) ▸ **spir·itu·al·ly** /-tʃuəli/ *adv.*：*a spiritually uplifting book* 陶冶性情的書

IDM **your ˌspiritual 'home** the place where you are happiest, especially a country where you feel you belong more than in your own country because you share the ideas and attitudes of the people who live there 在精神上認同的某個地方；精神家園

■ ***noun*** (also **ˌNegro 'spiritual**) a religious song of the type originally sung by black SLAVES in America 靈歌（宗教歌曲，最初為美國黑人奴隸所唱）

spir·itu·al·ism /ˈspɪrɪtʃuəlɪzəm/ *noun* [U] the belief that people who have died can send messages to living people, usually through a MEDIUM (= a person who has special powers) 招魂說，招魂術（認為亡靈可通過巫師或以其他方式向活人傳達信息）

spir·itu·al·ist /ˈspɪrɪtʃuəlɪst/ *noun* a person who believes that people who have died can send messages to living people 信奉招魂說的人

spir·itu·al·ity /ˌspɪrɪtʃuˈæləti/ *noun* [U] the quality of being concerned with religion or the human spirit 精神性

spir·itu·al·ized (*BrE* also **-ised**) /ˈspɪrɪtʃuəlaɪzd/ *adj.* (*formal*) raised to a spiritual level 達至精神層次的；精神化的：*She tends to have intense, spiritualized friendships.* 她交朋友往往熱情而且注重精神層面。

spit /spɪt/ *verb, noun*

■ ***verb*** (**spit·ting**, **spat**, **spat** /spæt/) **HELP** **Spit** is also sometimes used for the past tense and past participle, especially in *NAmE*. 過去時和過去分詞有時也用 spit，尤其在美式英語中。

▸ **FROM MOUTH** 從嘴裏 **1** [T] to force liquid, food, etc. out of your mouth 吐，唾（唾沫、食物等）：**~ sth (out)** *She took a mouthful of food and then suddenly spat it out.* 她吃了一口食物，突然又吐了出來。◊ **~ sth (from sth)** *He was spitting blood from a badly cut lip.* 他嘴唇傷得不輕，正不停地唾血。 **2** [I] to force SALIVA (= the liquid that is produced in the mouth) out of your mouth, often as a sign of anger or lack of respect 啐唾沫（常表示憤怒或鄙視）：*He coughed and spat.* 他咳嗽一聲，吐了口痰。◊ **~ at/on/in sb/sth** *The prisoners were spat on by their guards.* 監獄看守朝犯人身上吐唾沫。◊ *She spat in his face and went out.* 她朝他臉上啐了一口，然後走了出去。

▸ **SAY STH ANGRILY** 憤怒地說 **3** [T] to say sth in an angry or aggressive way 怒斥：**+ speech** *'You liar!' she spat.* "你撒謊！"她怒叱道。◊ **~ sth (at sb)** *He was dragged out of the court, spitting abuse at the judge and jury.* 他被拖出法庭，嘴裏還不停地罵着法官和陪審團。

▸ **OF AN ANIMAL** 動物 **4** [I] to make a short angry sound（發怒時）發呼嚕呼嚕聲：*Snakes spit and hiss when they are cornered.* 蛇陷入絕境時會發出嘶嘶呼呼的聲音。

▸ **OF STH COOKING/BURNING** 烹煮／燃燒的東西 **5** [I] to make a noise and throw out fat, SPARKS, etc. 嗞嗞地冒油；劈啪作響；爆出火花：*sausages spitting in the frying pan* 在煎鍋裏嗞嗞冒油的香腸 ◊ *The logs on the fire crackled and spat.* 火中的木頭劈啪作響，爆出火花。

▸ **RAIN** 雨 **6** [I] (*informal*) (only used in the progressive tenses 僅用於進行時) when **it is spitting**, it is raining lightly 下小雨

IDM **ˌspit it 'out** (*informal*) usually used in orders to tell sb to say sth when they seem frightened or unwilling to speak 有話就講；有什麼儘管說出來：*If you've got something to say, spit it out!* 有什麼話，你儘管說出來！ **spit 'venom/'blood** to show that you are very angry; to speak in an angry way 怒氣沖天；咬牙切齒 **within 'spitting distance (of sth)** (*BrE*) (also **within 'shouting distance** *NAmE, BrE*) (*informal*) very close 很近

PHR V **ˌspit 'up** (*NAmE, informal*) (especially of a baby 尤指嬰兒) to VOMIT (= bring food from the stomach back out through the mouth) 嘔吐

■ ***noun***

▸ **IN/FROM MOUTH**（從）嘴裏 **1** [U] the liquid that is produced in your mouth 唾液；唾沫 **SYN** **saliva** **2** [C, usually sing.] the act of spitting liquid or food out of your mouth 啐唾沫；吐痰；吐食物

▸ **PIECE OF LAND** 一塊陸地 **3** [C] a long thin piece of land that sticks out into the sea/ocean, a lake, etc. 岬；沙嘴 ➲ **VISUAL VOCAB** pages V4, V5

▸ **FOR COOKING MEAT** 烤肉 **4** [C] a long thin straight piece of metal that you put through meat to hold and turn it while you cook it over a fire 烤肉扦

IDM **ˌspit and 'polish** (*informal*) thorough cleaning and polishing of sth 徹底的擦洗

spite 🔑 /spaɪt/ *noun, verb*

■ ***noun*** [U] a feeling of wanting to hurt or upset sb 惡意；怨恨 **SYN** **malice**：*I'm sure he only said it **out of spite**.* 我相信他只是為了泄憤才那麼說的。

IDM **in 'spite of sth** 🔑 if you say that sb did sth **in spite of** a fact, you mean it is surprising that that fact did not prevent them from doing it 不管；儘管 **SYN** **despite**：*In spite of his age, he still leads an active life.* 儘管年事已高，他依舊過着一種忙碌的生活。◊ *They went swimming in spite of all the danger signs.* 他們無視所有那些危險水域告示牌，還是去游泳了。◊ *English became the official language for business **in spite of the fact that** the population was largely Chinese.* 雖然當地居民主要是中國人，英語卻成了商業上正式使用的語言。 ➲ **LANGUAGE BANK** at HOWEVER **in 'spite of yourself** if you do sth **in spite of yourself**, you do it although you did not intend or expect to 不由自主地：*He fell asleep, in spite of himself.* 他還是不由自主地睡着了。

■ ***verb*** (only used in the infinitive with *to* 僅用於帶 to 的不定式中) **~ sb** to deliberately annoy or upset sb 故意使煩惱；存心使苦惱：*They're playing the music so loud just to spite us.* 他們把音樂放得這麼響就是存心要攪擾我們。 **IDM** see NOSE *n.*

S

spite·ful /ˈspaɪtfl/ *adj.* behaving in an unkind way in order to hurt or upset sb 惡意的；居心不良的；故意使人苦惱的 **SYN** **malicious** ▶ **spite·ful·ly** /-fəli/ *adv.* : *'I don't need you,' she said spitefully.* "我不需要你。" 她故意氣他地說。 **spite·ful·ness** *noun* [U]

spit-roast /ˈspɪt rəʊst; *NAmE* roʊst/ *verb* **~ sth** to cook meat on a SPIT *n.* (4) 用烤肉扦烤（肉）

ˌspitting ˈimage *noun*
IDM **be the spitting image of sb** to look exactly like sb else 和某人長得一模一樣： *She's the spitting image of her mother.* 她長得酷似她的母親。

spit·tle /ˈspɪtl/ *noun* [U] (*old-fashioned*) the liquid that forms in the mouth 唾沫；口水 **SYN** **saliva, spit**

spit·toon /spɪˈtuːn/ *noun* a container, used especially in the past, for people to SPIT into 痰盂

spiv /spɪv/ *noun* (*old-fashioned, BrE, slang, disapproving*) a man who makes his money by being dishonest in business, especially one who dresses in a way that makes people believe he is rich and successful 衣冠楚楚的奸商

splash /splæʃ/ *verb, noun*
■ *verb* **1** [I] **+ adv./prep.** (of liquid 液體) to fall noisily onto a surface 潑灑；嘩啦嘩啦地濺；劈里啪啦地落： *Water splashed onto the floor.* 水嘩的一聲潑灑在地板上。◇ *Rain splashed against the windows.* 雨點啪啦啪啦地打在窗戶上。 **2** [T] to make sb/sth wet by making water, mud, etc. fall on them/it 把（水、泥等）潑在…上，濺在…上；朝…上潑（或濺）： **~ sth on/onto/over sb/sth** *He splashed cold water on his face.* 他把冷水往臉上潑。◇ **~ sb/sth with sth** *He splashed his face with cold water.* 他朝臉上潑冷水。◇ *My clothes were splashed with mud.* 我衣服上濺滿了泥。◇ **~ sb/sth** *Stop splashing me!* 別濺我了！ **3** [I] (**+ adv./prep.**) to move through water making drops fly everywhere （在水中）濺着水花行走，拍打着水游： *The kids were splashing through the puddles.* 孩子們嘩啦嘩啦地濺着水花從水坑裏蹚過。◇ *People were having fun in the pool, swimming or just splashing around.* 人們在游泳池裏或者游泳，或者只是拍打戲水，開心地玩着。 **4** [T] **~ sth with sth** [usually passive] to decorate sth with areas of bright colour, not in a regular pattern 用（潑灑色斑）裝飾： *The walls were splashed with patches of blue and purple.* 牆壁上隨意潑成了大塊的藍色和紫色。
PHR V **ˈsplash sth across/over sth** to put a photograph, news story, etc. in a place where it will be easily noticed 把（照片、新聞報道等）安排在顯著位置；在突出位置刊載 **ˌsplash ˈdown** (of a SPACECRAFT 航天器) to land in the sea or ocean 濺落（在海洋裏） ➲ related noun SPLASHDOWN **ˌsplash ˈout (on sth)** | **ˌsplash sth↔ˈout (on/for sth)** (*BrE, informal*) to spend a lot of money on sth 花大筆的錢（買某物等）： *We're going to splash out and buy a new car.* 我們打算揮霍一下，買輛新車。◇ *He splashed out hundreds of pounds on designer clothes.* 他花了幾百英鎊買名牌服裝。
■ *noun* **1** [C] the sound of sth hitting liquid or of liquid hitting sth 落水聲；濺潑聲： *We heard the splash when she fell into the pool.* 她掉進游泳池時我們聽見撲通的一聲。 **2** [C] a small amount of liquid that falls onto sth; the mark that this makes 濺上的液體；濺灑後留下的污漬： *splashes of water on the floor* 灑在地板上的一攤攤水 ◇ *dark splashes of mud on her skirt* 濺在她裙子上的黑泥點 **3** [C] a small area of bright colour or light that contrasts with the colours around it 色塊；光斑： *These flowers will give a splash of colour throughout the summer.* 這些花會給整個夏天增添一片亮麗的色彩。 **4** [sing.] (*BrE, informal*) a small amount of liquid that you add to a drink 摻入飲料的少量液體： *coffee with just a splash of milk* 只加了少量牛奶的咖啡 ➲ compare DASH *n.* (3) **5** [sing.] an article in a newspaper, etc. that is intended to attract a lot of attention （報章等旨在招徠讀者的）重點文章
IDM **make, cause, etc. a ˈsplash** (*informal*) to do sth in a way that attracts a lot of attention or causes a lot of excitement 引起廣泛關注；引起轟動

splash·back /ˈsplæʃbæk/ *noun* (*BrE*) a surface behind a sink or cooker/stove which protects the wall from liquids （洗滌槽或鍋灶後壁的）防濺擋板 ➲ VISUAL VOCAB page V25

splash·down /ˈsplæʃdaʊn/ *noun* [C, U] a landing of a SPACECRAFT in the sea/ocean 濺落（指航天器墜入海洋）

splashy /ˈsplæʃi/ *adj.* (**splash·ier**, **splashi·est**) (*especially NAmE*) bright and very easy to notice 鮮明醒目的；華麗而招搖的；張大聲勢的

splat /splæt/ *noun* [sing.] (*informal*) the sound made by sth wet hitting a surface with force （濕物落在平面上的）啪嗒聲： *The tomato hit the wall with a splat.* 西紅柿啪的一聲打在牆上。 ▶ **splat** *adv.* : *The omelette fell splat onto the floor.* 煎蛋餅吧唧一下掉到了地上。

splat·ter /ˈsplætə(r)/ *verb* **1** [I] (**+ adv./prep.**) (of large drops of liquid 大滴的液體) to fall or hit sth noisily 啪嗒啪嗒地落下（或擊打）： *Heavy rain splattered on the roof.* 大雨劈里啪啦地打在屋頂上。 **2** [T, I] to drop or throw water, paint, mud, etc. on sb/sth; to make sb/sth wet or dirty by landing on them in large drops 把（水等）潑灑在…上；淋濕；濺污： **~ sb/sth (+ adv./prep.)** *The walls were splattered with blood.* 牆上血跡斑斑。◇ **+ adv./prep.** *Coffee had splattered across the front of his shirt.* 他的襯衣前襟上灑了一大片咖啡。

splay /spleɪ/ *verb* [T, I] **~ (sth) (out)** to make fingers, legs, etc. become further apart from each other or spread out; to be spread out wide apart 使（手指、腿等）叉開，分開，張開，展開： *She lay on the bed, her arms and legs splayed out.* 她四肢攤開躺在牀上。◇ *His long fingers splayed across her back.* 他把長長的手指叉開貼在她背上。

ˌsplay-ˈfoot *noun* a broad flat foot which turns away from the other foot 八字腳；外翻足 ▶ **ˌsplay-ˈfooted** *adj.*

spleen /spliːn/ *noun* **1** [C] a small organ near the stomach that controls the quality of the blood cells 脾： *a ruptured spleen* 破裂的脾 ➲ VISUAL VOCAB page V59 **2** [U] (*literary*) anger 憤怒；怒氣： *He vented his spleen* (= shouted in an angry way) *on the assembled crowd.* 他把怒氣撒在了聚集的人群身上。 ➲ see also SPLENETIC

splen·did /ˈsplendɪd/ *adj., exclamation*
■ *adj.* (*especially BrE*) **1** (*old-fashioned*) excellent; very good 極佳的；非常好的 **SYN** **great** : *What a splendid idea!* 這主意妙極了！◇ *We've all had a splendid time.* 我們大家都玩得很開心。 **2** very impressive; very beautiful 壯麗的；雄偉的；豪華的；華麗的： *splendid scenery* 壯麗的風景 ◇ *The hotel stands* ***in splendid isolation,*** *surrounded by moorland.* 那旅館巋然獨立，周圍是一片荒原。 ▶ **splen·did·ly** *adv.* : *You all played splendidly.* 你們都表現得很出色。
■ *exclamation* (*old-fashioned, especially BrE*) used to show that you approve of sth, or are pleased （表示讚許或滿意）好極了，痛快： *You're both coming? Splendid!* 你們倆都要來？太好了！

splen·dif·er·ous /splenˈdɪfərəs/ *adj.* (*informal, humorous*) extremely good or pleasant 極好的；美妙的

splen·dour (*especially US* **splen·dor**) /ˈsplendə(r)/ *noun* **1** [U] grand and impressive beauty 壯麗；雄偉；豪華；華麗 **SYN** **grandeur** : *a view of Rheims Cathedral, in all its splendour* 盡顯其宏偉壯觀的蘭斯大教堂 ◇ *The palace has been restored to its former splendour.* 宮殿經過修葺，重現出昔日的富麗堂皇。 **2** **splendours** [pl.] the beautiful and impressive features or qualities of sth, especially a place （尤指某地的）壯麗景色，恢弘氣勢： *the splendours of Rome* (= its fine buildings, etc.) 羅馬的壯麗景色

splen·et·ic /spləˈnetɪk/ *adj.* (*formal*) often bad-tempered and angry 脾氣壞的；常發怒的

splice /splaɪs/ *verb, noun*
■ *verb* **1 ~ sth (together)** to join the ends of two pieces of rope by twisting them together 絞接，捻接（兩段繩子） **2 ~ sth (together)** to join the ends of two pieces of film, tape, etc. by sticking them together 膠接，粘接（膠片、磁帶等）
IDM **get ˈspliced** (*old-fashioned, BrE, informal*) to get married 結婚

S

■ ***noun*** the place where two pieces of film, tape, rope, etc. have been joined 膠接處；粘接處；絞接處

spli·cer /ˈsplaɪsə(r)/ *noun* a person or machine that joins pieces of tape, cable, etc. together （磁帶等的）膠接者；接片機；（電纜等的）絞接器

spliff /splɪf/ *noun* (*BrE, slang*) a cigarette containing CANNABIS 大麻煙捲

splint /splɪnt/ *noun* a long piece of wood or metal that is tied to a broken arm or leg to keep it still and in the right position（固定斷肢的）夾板

splin·ter /ˈsplɪntə(r)/ *noun, verb*

■ ***noun*** a small thin sharp piece of wood, metal, glass, etc. that has broken off a larger piece （木頭、金屬、玻璃等的）尖碎片，尖細條 SYN **shard**

■ ***verb*** **1** [I, T] (of wood, glass, stone, etc. 木頭、玻璃、石頭等) to break, or to make sth break, into small, thin sharp pieces （使）裂成碎片 SYN **shatter**：*The mirror cracked but did not splinter.* 鏡子裂了，但沒碎。◇ **~ sth** *The impact splintered the wood.* 木頭被撞成了碎片。 **2** [I] (of a group of people 團體) to divide into smaller groups that are no longer connected; to separate from a larger group 分裂；分離出來：*The party began to splinter.* 那個黨開始分裂。◇ **~ (off) (from sth)** *Several firms have splintered off from the original company.* 從原公司分離出好幾個企業。

ˈsplinter group *noun* a small group of people that has separated from a larger one, especially in politics（尤指政黨的）小派別

split 🔑 /splɪt/ *verb, noun*

■ ***verb*** (**split·ting, split, split**)

▸ **DIVIDE 分開** **1** 🔑 [T, I] **~ (sth)** to divide, or to make a group of people divide, into smaller groups that have very different opinions 分裂，使分裂（成不同的派別）：*a debate that has* ***split*** *the country* ***down the middle*** 使全國分成兩大派的一場爭論 ◇ *The committee split over government subsidies.* 在政府補貼的問題上，委員會出現了相互對立的意見。 **2** 🔑 [T, I] to divide, or to make sth divide, into two or more parts 分開，使分開（成為幾個部份）：**~ sth (into sth)** *She split the class into groups of four.* 她按四人一組把全班分成若干小組。◇ **~ (into sth)** *The results split neatly into two groups.* 結果清晰地分成兩類。 ➲ see also SPLIT UP **3** 🔑 [T] to divide sth into two or more parts and share it between different people, activities, etc. 分擔；分攤；分享：**~ sth (with sb)** *She split the money she won with her brother.* 她把得到的錢與弟弟分了。◇ **~ sth between sb/sth** *His time is split between the London and Paris offices.* 他一半時間在倫敦的辦事處，一半時間在巴黎的辦事處。 ➲ see also SPLIT UP

▸ **TEAR 撕裂** **4** 🔑 [I, T] to tear, or to make sth tear, along a straight line （使）撕裂：*Her dress had split along the seam.* 她的連衣裙順着接縫裂開了。◇ **~ (sth) open** *The cushion split open and sent feathers everywhere.* 墊子撕破了，羽毛掉得到處都是。◇ **~ sth** *Don't tell me you've split another pair of pants!* 你不會又把一條褲子撐破了吧！

▸ **CUT 割傷** **5** [T] to cut sb's skin and make it BLEED 劃破；割破；碰破：**~ sth open** *She split her head open on the cupboard door.* 她碰到碗櫥門上把頭碰破了。◇ **~ sth** *How did you split your lip?* 你怎麼把嘴唇劃破了？

▸ **END RELATIONSHIP 斷絕關係** **6** [I] (*informal*) to leave sb and stop having a relationship with them （和某人）斷絕關係，分手；離開（某人）：**~ (with sb)** *The singer split with his wife last June.* 那歌手去年六月和妻子分手了。◇ **~ (from sb)** *She intends to split from the band at the end of the tour.* 她打算在巡迴演出結束後離開樂隊。 ➲ see also SPLIT UP

▸ **LEAVE 離開** **7** [I] (*old-fashioned, informal*) to leave a place quickly （迅速）離開，走：*Let's split!* 咱們快走吧！

IDM **split the ˈdifference** (when discussing a price, etc.) to agree on an amount that is at an equal distance between the two amounts that have been suggested （講價等）各讓一步，折衷 **split ˈhairs** to pay too much attention in an argument to differences that are very small and not important 在細節上過分糾纏 **split an inˈfinitive** to place an adverb between 'to' and the infinitive of a verb, for example to say 'to strongly deny a rumour'. Some people consider this to be bad English style. 使用分裂不定式（在 to 和不定式之間插入副詞，如 to strongly deny a rumour，有人認為這種用法有語病） **split your ˈsides (laughing/with laughter)** to laugh a lot at sb/sth 笑破肚皮；笑彎腰 **split the ˈticket** (*US, politics* 政) to vote for candidates from more than one party 投兩黨或兩黨以上候選人的票 ➲ more at MIDDLE *n.*

PHR V **ˌsplit aˈway/ˈoff (from sth)** | **ˌsplit sth↔aˈway/ˈoff (from sth)** to separate from, or to separate sth from, a larger object or group （使）脫離，分裂出去，分離：*A rebel faction has split away from the main group.* 一幫反叛者從核心組織中分裂了出去。◇ *The storm split a branch off from the main trunk.* 暴風雨把一根樹枝從樹幹上颳了下來。 **ˈsplit on sb (to sb)** (*BrE, informal*) to tell sb in authority about sth wrong, dishonest, etc. that sb else has done （向…）告發，揭發：*Don't worry—he won't split on us.* 別擔心，他不會出賣我們的。 **ˌsplit ˈup (with sb)** 🔑 to stop having a relationship with sb （和某人）斷絕關係，分手：*My parents split up last year.* 我父母去年離婚了。◇ *She's split up with her boyfriend.* 她和男朋友分手了。 **ˌsplit sb ˈup** to make two people stop having a relationship with each other 使斷絕關係；拆散：*My friend is doing her best to split us up.* 我的朋友竭力想拆散我們。 **ˌsplit sb ˈup** | **ˌsplit ˈup** 🔑 to divide a group of people into smaller parts; to become divided up in this way （把…）分成小組，化整為零：*We were split up into groups to discuss the question.* 我們分組討論了那個問題。◇ *Let's split up now and meet again at lunchtime.* 我們現在先分開，午飯時再集合。 **ˌsplit sth↔ˈup** 🔑 to divide sth into smaller parts 劃分；分解：*The day was split up into 6 one-hour sessions.* 一天的活動分作 6 個時段，每個時段一小時。

■ ***noun***

▸ **DISAGREEMENT 分歧** **1** 🔑 [C] (*informal*) a disagreement that divides a group of people or makes sb separate from sb else 分歧；分裂；分離：**~ (within sth)** *a damaging split within the party leadership* 黨的領導層內部不利的分歧現象 ◇ **~ (with sb/sth)** *the years following his bitter split with his wife* 他和妻子痛苦離婚後的那些年 ◇ **~ (between A and B)** *There have been reports of a split between the Prime Minister and the Cabinet.* 有報道說首相和內閣之間存在分歧。

▸ **DIVISION 劃分** **2** 🔑 [sing.] a division between two or more things; one of the parts that sth is divided into 劃分；分別；份額：*He demanded a 50–50 split in the profits.* 他要求利潤對半分成。

▸ **TEAR/HOLE 裂縫；裂口** **3** 🔑 [C] a long crack or hole made when sth tears 裂縫；裂口：*There's a big split in the tent.* 帳篷上撕了一個大口子。

▸ **BANANA DISH 香蕉甜食** **4** [C] a sweet dish made from fruit, especially a BANANA cut in two along its length, with cream, ice cream, etc. on top 香蕉船，水果船（將香蕉等縱切成條狀作底，上覆奶油或冰淇淋等）：*a banana split* 香蕉船

▸ **BODY POSITION 身體姿勢** **5 the splits** [pl.] (*US* also **split** [sing.]) a position in which you stretch your legs flat across the floor in opposite directions with the rest of your body vertical 劈叉：*a gymnast* ***doing the splits*** 做劈叉的體操運動員

ˌsplit ˈend *noun* a hair on your head that has divided into parts at the end because it is dry or in poor condition 分叉的髮梢

ˌsplit inˈfinitive *noun* (*grammar* 語法) the form of the verb with 'to', with an adverb placed between 'to' and the verb, as in *She seems to really like it*. Some people consider this to be bad English style. 分裂不定式（在 to 和不定式動詞之間插入副詞，如 She seems to really like it，有人認為這種用法有語病）

ˌsplit-ˈlevel *adj.* (of a room, floor, etc. 房間、地板等) having parts at different levels 錯層式的

ˌsplit ˈpea *noun* [usually pl.] a type of dried PEA, split into halves 乾豌豆瓣

ˌsplit-persoˈnality disorder *noun* = MULTIPLE-PERSONALITY DISORDER

ˌsplit ˈscreen *noun* a way of displaying two or more pictures or pieces of information at the same time on a television, cinema or computer screen 分畫面，分屏（在電視、電影或計算機屏幕上同時顯示兩個或兩個以上的畫面或文件）▶ ˌ**split-ˈscreen** *adj.* [only before noun]: *a movie with several split-screen sequences* 一部有幾個分畫面鏡頭的電影

ˌ**split ˈsecond** *noun* a very short moment of time 瞬間；刹那：*Their eyes met* ***for a split second.*** 在一刹那間，他們的目光交匯在了一起。

ˌ**split-ˈsecond** *adj.* [only before noun] done very quickly or very accurately 一瞬間作出的；做得非常精確的：*She had to make a split-second decision.* 她必須在瞬間作出決定。◇ *The success of the raid depended on* ***split-second timing.*** 襲擊的成功取決於分秒不差的時間安排。

ˌ**split ˈshift** *noun* two separate periods of time that you spend working in a single day, with several hours between them 間隔班（工作時間分成間隔幾小時的兩段輪班）：*I work split shifts in a busy restaurant.* 我在一家繁忙的餐館上間隔班。

splits·ville /ˈsplɪtsvɪl/ *noun* [sing.] (*NAmE, slang*) the end of a relationship 散夥；分手；離異：*Within three months of the honeymoon, it was splitsville for Ron and Mimi.* 羅恩和米米蜜月之後不到三個月就散夥了。

ˌ**split ˈticket** *noun* (in elections in the US) a vote in which sb votes for candidates from two different parties（在美國的各級選舉中）投兩黨候選人的選票 ▶ ˌ**split-ˈticket** *adj.*: *a split-ticket vote* 投兩黨候選人的選票

split·ting /ˈsplɪtɪŋ/ *adj.* [only before noun] if you have a **splitting headache**, you have a very bad pain in your head（頭痛）欲裂的

splodge /splɒdʒ; *NAmE* splɑːdʒ/ (*BrE*) (also **splotch** /splɒtʃ; *NAmE* splɑːtʃ/*NAmE, BrE*) *noun* a large mark or spot of ink, paint, mud, etc.; a small area of colour or light 一塊污漬；一片污跡；色塊；光斑

splosh /splɒʃ; *NAmE* splɑːʃ/ *verb, noun* (*BrE, informal*)

■ *verb* [I] + **adv./prep.** to move through water, making soft sounds（在水裏）啪嗒啪嗒地移動，濺潑着前行：*Children were sploshing about in the pool.* 孩子們在游泳池裏嘩嘩地游來游去。

■ *noun* **1** the soft sound of sth moving through or falling into water 濺潑聲；嘩啦聲 **2** a small amount of liquid that moves through the air 濺起的少量液體

splurge /splɜːdʒ; *NAmE* splɜːrdʒ/ *noun, verb*

■ *noun* [usually sing.] (*informal*) an act of spending a lot of money on sth that you do not really need 亂花錢；糟蹋錢；揮霍

■ *verb* [T, I] ~ (**sth**) (**on sth**) (*informal*) to spend a lot of money on sth that you do not really need 亂花（錢）；糟蹋（錢）；揮霍

splut·ter /ˈsplʌtə(r)/ *verb, noun*

■ *verb* **1** [T, I] to speak quickly and with difficulty, making soft SPITTING sounds, because you are angry or embarrassed 氣急敗壞地說；慌張地說 SYN **sputter**: + **speech** (**out**) *'But, but ... you can't!' she spluttered.* "可是，可是…你不能啊！"她急促而慌亂地說。◇ ~ (**with sth**) *Her father spluttered with indignation.* 她父親氣得說話都語無倫次了。**2** [I] to make a series of short EXPLOSIVE sounds 發噗噗聲；發劈啪聲 SYN **sputter**: *The firework spluttered and went out.* 花炮劈里啪啦地噴完後滅了。◇ *She fled from the blaze,* ***coughing and spluttering.*** 她從大火中逃出來，一邊咳嗽，一邊噗噗地吐氣。

■ *noun* a short EXPLOSIVE sound 噗的一聲；啪的一聲：*The car started with a loud splutter.* 汽車突的一聲發動了。

spoil 0‑w /spɔɪl/ *verb, noun*

■ *verb* (**spoiled**, **spoiled** /spɔɪld/) (*BrE* also **spoilt**, **spoilt** /spɔɪlt/) **1** 0‑w [T] ~ **sth** to change sth good into sth bad, unpleasant, useless, etc. 破壞；搞壞；糟蹋；毀掉 SYN **ruin**: *Our camping trip was spoilt by bad weather.* 天氣不好，破壞了我們的露營旅行。◇ *Don't let him spoil your evening.* 別讓他搞得你一晚上不開心。◇ *The tall buildings have spoiled the view.* 那些高樓大廈破壞了這一帶的景致。◇ *Don't eat too many nuts—you'll* ***spoil your appetite*** (= will no longer be hungry at the proper time to eat). 別吃太多堅果，會影響你的食慾。◇ (*BrE*) *spoiled ballot papers* (= not valid because not correctly marked) 廢選票 **2** 0‑w [T] ~ **sb** to give a child everything that they ask for and not enough discipline in a way that has a bad effect on their character and behaviour 溺愛；嬌慣；寵壞 SYN **overindulge**: *She spoils those kids of hers.* 她那幾個孩子給她寵壞了。**3** [T] ~ **sb/yourself** to make sb/yourself happy by doing sth special 善待；格外關照：*Why not spoil yourself with a weekend in a top hotel?* 為什麼不到頂級飯店度個週末，讓自己享受享受呢？◇ *He really spoiled me on my birthday.* 我生日那天他真讓我受寵若驚。**4** [I] (of food 食物) to become bad so that it can no longer be eaten 變壞；變質；腐敗 SYN **go off**

IDM **be ˈspoiling for a fight** to want to fight with sb very much 按捺不住想打架 **spoil the ˌship for a haʼp'orth/haʼpennyworth of ˈtar** (*saying*) to spoil sth good because you did not spend enough money or time on a small but essential part of it 因小失大 ➲ more at COOK *n.*

■ *noun* **1 the spoils** [pl.] (*formal* or *literary*) goods taken from a place by thieves or by an army that has won a battle or war 贓物；戰利品；掠奪物 **2 spoils** [pl.] the profits or advantages that sb gets from being successful 成功所帶來的好處；權力地位的連帶利益：*the spoils of high office* 身居高位的連帶利益 **3** [U] (*technical* 術語) waste material that is brought up when a hole is dug, etc.（開掘等時挖出的）棄土，廢石方

spoil·age /ˈspɔɪlɪdʒ/ *noun* [U] (*technical* 術語) the decay of food which means that it can no longer be used（食物的）變質，腐敗

spoil·er /ˈspɔɪlə(r)/ *noun* **1** a part of an aircraft's wing that can be raised in order to interrupt the flow of air over it and so slow the aircraft's speed（機翼的）擾流片，阻流板 **2** a raised part on a fast car that prevents it from being lifted off the road when travelling very fast（汽車的）氣流偏導器 **3** (*especially NAmE*) a candidate for a political office who is unlikely to win but who may get enough votes to prevent one of the main candidates from winning 選舉中的攪局者（無望獲勝但所得選票可能使某主要候選人無法當選）**4** a person or thing that intends or is intended to stop sb/sth being successful 阻礙…成功的人（或事物）；搞砸…的人（或事物）**5** information that you are given about what is going to happen in a film/movie, television series etc. before it is shown to the public（在電影、電視連續劇等公映前提供的）劇情介紹 **6** a newspaper story, book, etc. that is produced very quickly in order to take attention away from one produced by a COMPETITOR that appears at the same time（為競爭而迅速發表的）抵消影響的報道（或書籍等）

spoil·sport /ˈspɔɪlspɔːt; *NAmE* -spɔːrt/ *noun* (*informal*) a person who spoils other people's enjoyment, for example by not taking part in an activity or by trying to stop other people from doing it 掃興的人：*Don't be such a spoilsport!* 別讓人掃興！

the ˈspoils system *noun* [sing.] the arrangement in US politics which allows the President to give government jobs to supporters after winning an election（美國當選總統把官職分給支持者的）政黨分肥制，賜職制

spoilt /spɔɪlt/ (*BrE*) (also **spoiled** /spɔɪld/*NAmE, BrE*) *adj.* (of a child 孩子) rude and badly behaved because they are given everything they ask for and not enough discipline 寵壞的；嬌慣壞的：*a spoiled brat* 嬌慣壞的淘氣鬼 ◇ *He's* ***spoilt rotten*** (= a lot). 他給慣得一點樣子都沒有了。

IDM **be spoilt for ˈchoice** (*BrE*) to have such a lot of things to choose from that it is very difficult to make a decision（東西多得）挑花眼

spoke /spəʊk; *NAmE* spoʊk/ *noun* one of the thin bars or long straight pieces of metal that connect the centre of a wheel to its outer edge, for example on a bicycle 輻條；輪輻 ➲ VISUAL VOCAB page V51

IDM **put a ˈspoke in sb's wheel** (*BrE*) to prevent sb from putting their plans into operation 破壞某人的計劃；阻撓某人實行計劃 ➲ see also SPEAK *v.* (spoke, spoken)

S

spoken 0‑ /'spəʊkən; *NAmE* 'spoʊ-/ *adj.* **1** 0‑ involving speaking rather than writing; expressed in speech rather than in writing 口語的；口頭的；以口頭形式表達的： *spoken English* 英語口語 ◇ *spoken commands* 口頭指令 **2** (following an adverb 用於副詞後) speaking in the way mentioned 說話…的： *a quietly spoken man* 說話斯文的男人 ➲ see also OUTSPOKEN

Synonyms 同義詞辨析

spoken

oral • vocal

These words all describe producing language using the voice, rather than writing. 以上各詞均指口頭的、用口語的。

spoken (of language) produced using the voice; said rather than written 指口語的、口頭的： *an exam in spoken English* 英語口語考試

oral [usually before noun] spoken rather than written 指口頭的、口述的： *There will be a test of both oral and written French.* 將有一次法語口試和筆試。

SPOKEN OR ORAL? 用 spoken 還是 oral？

Both of these words can be used to refer to language skills and the communication of information. 上述兩詞均可用於語言技巧和信息交流： *spoken/oral French* 法語口語 ◇ *a spoken/oral presentation* 口頭報告

In these cases **oral** is slightly more technical than **spoken**. **Oral** but not **spoken** can also be used with words such as *tradition*, *culture* and *legends* to talk about the way in which people pass stories down from one generation to the next, and in legal contexts followed by words such as *evidence* and *hearing*. 在上述例子中，oral 較 spoken 專業一些，oral 亦可與 tradition、culture 和 legends 等詞連用，指通過口頭世代相傳的；spoken 則不能這樣用。在法律語境中，oral 後可接 evidence 和 hearing 等詞，spoken 則不能。

vocal [usually before noun] connected with the voice 指嗓音的、發音的： *vocal music* 聲樂 ◇ *the vocal organs* (= the tongue, lips, etc.) 發聲器官 NOTE **Vocal** is used to talk about the ability to produce sounds using the voice, and is often used in musical contexts when referring to singing. * vocal 關乎發音的能力，常用於音樂語境中，指歌唱。

PATTERNS

- spoken/oral **French/English/Japanese, etc.**
- spoken/oral **language skills**

S

'spoken for *adj.* [not before noun] already claimed or being kept for sb 已經有人要；留給某人： *I'm afraid you can't sit there—those seats are spoken for.* 恐怕您不能坐那兒，那些座位有人預訂了。◇ (*old-fashioned*) *Liza is already spoken for* (= she is already married or has a partner). 莉莎已名花有主了。

the ˌspoken 'word *noun* [sing.] language expressed in speech, rather than being written or sung 口頭說的話

spokes·man /'spəʊksmən; *NAmE* 'spoʊ-/, **spokes·woman** /'spəʊkswʊmən; *NAmE* 'spoʊ-/ *noun* (*pl.* **-men** /-mən/, **-women** /-wɪmɪn/) a person who speaks on behalf of a group or an organization 發言人： *a police spokesman* 警方發言人 ◇ **~ for sb/sth** *A spokeswoman for the government denied the rumours.* 一位政府女發言人否認了那些傳言。➲ note at GENDER

spokes·per·son /'spəʊkspɜːsn; *NAmE* 'spoʊkspɜːrsn/ *noun* (*pl.* **-persons** or **-people**) **~ (for sb/sth)** a person who speaks on behalf of a group or an organization 發言人

spon·dee /'spɒndiː; *NAmE* 'spɑːn-/ *noun* (*technical* 術語) a unit of sound in poetry consisting of two strong or long syllables （詩歌的）揚揚格

sponge /spʌndʒ/ *noun, verb*

■ ***noun*** **1** [C] a piece of artificial or natural material that is soft and light and full of holes and can hold water easily, used for washing or cleaning （或天然或人造、擦洗物品用的）海綿塊： (*figurative*) *His mind was like a sponge, ready to absorb anything.* 他的腦子跟海綿似的，什麼都能吸收。➲ VISUAL VOCAB pages V24, V60 **2** [U] artificial sponge used for filling furniture, CUSHIONS, etc. （用以填充傢具、墊子等的）人造海綿 **3** [C] a simple sea creature with a light body full of holes, from which natural sponge is obtained 海綿動物 **4** [C, U] (*BrE*) = SPONGE CAKE： *a chocolate sponge* 巧克力海綿蛋糕

■ ***verb*** **1** [T] **~ sb/yourself/sth (down)** to wash sb/yourself/sth with a wet cloth or SPONGE 用濕布（或海綿）擦；揩拭 SYN **wipe**： *She sponged his hot face.* 她用濕毛巾擦了擦他那滾燙的臉。◇ *Take your jacket off and I'll sponge it down with water.* 把你的夾克脫下來，我要用海綿蘸上水把它擦一擦。 **2** [T] **~ sth + adv./prep.** to remove sth using a wet cloth or SPONGE 用濕布（或海綿）擦掉；揩去 SYN **wash**： *We tried to sponge the blood off my shirt.* 我們試着把我襯衫上的血跡擦掉。 **3** [I] **~ (off/on sb)** (*informal, disapproving*) to get money, food, etc. regularly from other people without doing anything for them or offering to pay 白要；白吃；揩油；蹭（飯等） SYN **scrounge**： *He spent his life sponging off his relatives.* 他靠向親戚們蹭吃蹭喝過了一輩子。

'sponge bag (also **'toilet bag**, **wash·bag**) (all *BrE*) (*NAmE* **'toiletry bag**) *noun* a small bag for holding your soap, TOOTHBRUSH, etc. when you are travelling 盥洗用品袋 ➲ VISUAL VOCAB page V24

'sponge bath *noun* (*NAmE*) an act of washing the whole of sb's body when they cannot get out of bed because they are sick, injured or old （為臥牀不起者所作的）擦身浴，擦澡

'sponge cake (also **sponge**) *noun* [C, U] (*BrE*) a light cake made from eggs, sugar and flour, with or without fat 海綿蛋糕；鬆蛋糕

ˌsponge 'pudding *noun* [U, C] (*BrE*) a hot DESSERT (= a sweet dish) like a sponge cake that usually has jam or fruit on top 海綿布丁；鬆軟布丁

spon·ger /'spʌndʒə(r)/ *noun* (*informal*) a person who gets money, food, etc. from other people without doing anything for them or offering to pay 吃白食的人；揩油者

spongi·form /'spʌndʒɪfɔːm; *NAmE* -fɔːrm/ *adj.* (*technical* 術語) having or relating to a structure with holes in it like a SPONGE 海綿狀（組織）的 ➲ see also BSE

spongy /'spʌndʒi/ *adj.* soft and able to absorb water easily like a SPONGE 海綿似的；柔軟吸水的 SYN **springy**： *spongy moss* 海綿似的苔蘚 ◇ *The ground was soft and spongy.* 土地鬆軟，像海綿似的。◇ *The bread had a spongy texture.* 那種麪包很鬆軟。▸ **spon·gi·ness** *noun* [U]

spon·sor /'spɒnsə(r); *NAmE* 'spɑːn-/ *noun, verb*

■ ***noun*** **1** a person or company that pays for a radio or television programme, or for a concert or sporting event, usually in return for advertising （廣播電視節目、音樂會或運動會的）贊助者，贊助商： *The race organizers are trying to attract sponsors.* 比賽的組織者在想方設法吸引贊助者。 **2** a person who agrees to give sb money for a charity if that person succeeds in completing a particular activity 為慈善活動捐資的人；義賽（或義演等）捐款者： *I'm collecting sponsors for next week's charity run.* 我正在為下星期的募款賽跑徵集捐款者。 **3** a person or company that supports sb by paying for their training or education （培訓或教育的）資助者 **4** a person who introduces and supports a proposal for a new law, etc. （法案等的）倡議者，發起人，倡導者： *the sponsor of the new immigration bill* 新移民法案的倡議者 **5** a person who agrees to be officially responsible for another person 保人；保證人 **6** a person who presents a child for Christian BAPTISM or CONFIRMATION 代父（或母）；教父（或母）；（洗禮、堅信禮等的）引領人 SYN **godparent**

■ ***verb*** **1 ~ sth** (of a company, etc. 公司等) to pay the costs of a particular event, programme, etc. as a way of advertising 贊助（活動、節目等）: *sports events sponsored by the tobacco industry* 由煙草業贊助的體育賽事 **2 ~ sth** to arrange for sth official to take place 主辦；舉辦；促成: *The US is sponsoring negotiations between the two sides.* 美國正在安排雙方的談判。 **3 ~ sb (for sth/to do sth)** to agree to give sb money for a charity if they complete a particular task 為慈善活動捐資；為義賽捐款: *Will you sponsor me for a charity walk I'm doing?* 我正在參加競走義賽，請您捐款好嗎？◇ *a sponsored swim* 有贊助的游泳活動 **4 ~ sb (through sth)** to support sb by paying for their training or education 資助（某人的培訓或教育）: *She found a company to sponsor her through college.* 她找到一家願資助她讀完大學的公司。 **5 ~ sth** to introduce a proposal for a new law, etc. 倡議，提交（法案等）: *The bill was sponsored by a Labour MP.* 這項議案是一位工黨議員提交的。

spon·sor·ship /ˈspɒnsəʃɪp; NAmE ˈspɑːnsərʃɪp/ *noun* **1** [U, C] financial support from a sponsor 資助；贊助款: *a $50 million sponsorship deal* * 5 000 萬元的贊助協議 ◇ *The project needs to raise £8 million in sponsorship.* 這個項目需要籌集 800 萬英鎊的資助。◇ *We need to find sponsorships for the expedition.* 我們需要為這次探險找到贊助。 **2** [U] the act of sponsoring sb/sth or being sponsored 資助；主辦；倡議: *the senator's sponsorship of the job training legislation* 那位參議員對制訂職業培訓法規的倡議

spon·tan·eity /ˌspɒntəˈneɪəti; NAmE ˌspɑːn-/ *noun* [U] the quality of being spontaneous 自發性；自然

spon·tan·eous /spɒnˈteɪniəs; NAmE spɑːn-/ *adj.* **1** not planned but done because you suddenly want to do it 自發的；非籌劃安排的: *a spontaneous offer of help* 主動提出幫助 ◇ *The audience burst into spontaneous applause.* 觀眾自發地鼓起掌來。 **2** often doing things without planning to, because you suddenly want to do them 常心血來潮的 **3** (*technical* 術語) happening naturally, without being made to happen 自發的；自然的；自身造成的: *spontaneous remission of the disease* 疾病的自然緩解 **4** done naturally, without being forced or practised 自然的；非勉強的；無雕飾的: *a tape recording of spontaneous speech* 一段自然講話的磁帶錄音 ◇ *a wonderfully spontaneous performance of the piece* 對那支樂曲極其淳樸自然的演奏 ▸ **spon·tan·eous·ly** *adv.*: *We spontaneously started to dance.* 我們情不自禁地跳起舞來。◇ *The bleeding often stops spontaneously.* 這種出血常常會自己停止。

sponˌtaneous comˈbustion *noun* [U] the burning of a mineral or vegetable substance caused by chemical changes inside it and not by fire or heat from outside 自燃

spoof /spuːf/ *noun, verb*

■ ***noun*** (*informal*) a humorous copy of a film/movie, television programme, etc. that exaggerates its main features（對電影、電視節目等的）滑稽模仿: *It's a spoof on horror movies.* 這是對恐怖片的滑稽模仿。

■ ***verb*** **1 ~ sth** to copy a film/movie, television programme, etc. in an amusing way by exaggerating its main features 滑稽地模仿（電影、電視節目等）: *It is a movie that spoofs other movies.* 這是一部誇張地模仿其他電影的影片。 **2 ~ sth** to send an email that appears to come from sb else's email address（冒充他人電郵地址）發送電郵；發送仿真電郵；電郵欺騙: *Someone has been spoofing my address.* 有人一直在冒充我的電郵地址發送電郵。 ▸ **spoof·ing** *noun* [U]

spook /spuːk/ *noun, verb*

■ ***noun*** (*informal*) **1** a GHOST 鬼: *a castle haunted by spooks* 鬧鬼的城堡 **2** (*especially NAmE*) a SPY 間諜；特工: *a CIA spook* 中央情報局特工

■ ***verb*** [T, usually passive, I] **~ (sb/sth)** (*informal, especially NAmE*) to frighten a person or an animal; to become frightened 嚇；驚嚇；受驚: *We were spooked by the strange noises and lights.* 那奇怪的聲音和亮光把我們嚇壞了。◇ *The horse spooked at the siren.* 警報器一響，馬受驚了。

spooky /ˈspuːki/ *adj.* (**spook·ier**, **spooki·est**) **HELP** You can also use **more spooky** and **most spooky**. 亦可用 more spooky 和 most spooky。 (*informal*) strange and frightening 怪異嚇人的；陰森可怖的 **SYN** **creepy**: *a spooky old house* 陰森森的老房子 ◇ *I was just thinking about her when she phoned. Spooky!* 我正在想她，她就來電話了。你說怪不怪！

spool /spuːl/ *noun, verb*

■ ***noun*** (*especially NAmE*) = REEL *n.* (1): *a spool of thread* 一軸線 ➲ **VISUAL VOCAB** page V41

■ ***verb*** **1** [T] **~ sth + adv./prep.** to wind sth onto or off a spool 把…繞到線軸上（或從線軸上繞下來） **2** [T, I] **~ (sth)** (*computing* 計) to move data and store it for a short time, for example on a disk, especially before it is printed 假脫機（輸出或輸入）

spoon 🔑 /spuːn/ *noun, verb*

■ ***noun*** **1** 🔑 a tool that has a handle with a shallow bowl at the end, used for stirring, serving and eating food 勺；匙；調羹: *a soup spoon* 湯匙 ◇ *a wooden spoon* 木勺 ➲ **VISUAL VOCAB** page V22 ➲ see also DESSERTSPOON, GREASY SPOON, TABLESPOON, TEASPOON (1) **2** = SPOONFUL **IDM** see BORN

■ ***verb*** **~ sth + adv./prep.** to lift and move food with a spoon 用勺舀: *She spooned the sauce over the chicken pieces.* 她用勺把沙司澆到雞塊上。

spoon·bill /ˈspuːnbɪl/ *noun* a large bird with long legs, a long neck and a beak that is wide and flat at the end 琵鷺

spoon·er·ism /ˈspuːnərɪzəm/ *noun* a mistake in which you change around the first sounds of two words by mistake when saying them, often with a humorous result, for example *well-boiled icicle* for *well-oiled bicycle* 首音誤置（說話時誤把兩個單詞的首音掉換，常造成滑稽效果） **ORIGIN** Named after **W.A. Spooner** (1844–1930), the head of New College, Oxford, who was said to have made many mistakes like this when he spoke. 名稱源自斯普納（W.A. Spooner, 1844–1930）。斯普納曾任牛津大學新學院院長，據說他在講話中出現過許多首音誤置。

ˈspoon-feed *verb* **1** (*disapproving*) to teach people sth in a way that gives them too much help and does not make them think for themselves 填鴨式灌輸；滿堂灌: **~ sb (with sth)** *The students here do not expect to be spoon-fed.* 這兒的學生不希望教師滿堂灌。◇ **~ sth to sb** *They had information spoon-fed to them.* 他們的知識是以滿堂灌的方式傳授給他們的。 **2 ~ sb** to feed sb, especially a baby, with a spoon 用勺餵（嬰兒）

spoon·ful /ˈspuːnfʊl/ (also **spoon**) *noun* the amount that a spoon can hold 一勺（的量）: *two spoonfuls of sugar* 兩勺糖

spoor /spʊə(r); NAmE spʊr/ *noun* [sing.] a track or smell that a wild animal leaves as it travels（野獸走過留下的）足跡，嗅跡

spor·ad·ic /spəˈrædɪk/ *adj.* happening only occasionally or at intervals that are not regular 偶爾發生的；間或出現的；陣發性的；斷斷續續的 **SYN** **intermittent**: ***sporadic fighting/gunfire/violence, etc.*** 零星的戰鬥、一陣一陣的炮火、間或發生的暴力事件等 ◇ *sporadic outbreaks of the disease* 那種疾病的偶爾爆發 ▸ **spor·ad·ic·al·ly** /-kli/ *adv.*: *She attended lectures only sporadically.* 她只是偶爾聽聽課。◇ *Fighting continued sporadically for two months.* 戰鬥斷斷續續地進行了兩個月。

spore /spɔː(r)/ *noun* (*biology* 生) one of the very small cells that are produced by some plants and that develop into new plants 孢子: *Ferns, mosses and fungi spread by means of spores.* 蕨類植物、苔蘚和真菌通過孢子傳播蔓生。 ➲ **COLLOCATIONS** at LIFE

spor·ran /ˈspɒrən; NAmE ˈspɑː-/ *noun* a flat bag, usually made of leather or fur, that is worn by men in front of the KILT as part of the Scottish national dress 毛皮袋（蘇格蘭男子民族服裝的一部份，繫在褶襇短裙前）

sport 🔑 /spɔːt; NAmE spɔːrt/ *noun, verb*

■ ***noun*** **1** 🔑 [U] (*BrE*) (*NAmE* **sports** [pl.]) activity that you do for pleasure and that needs physical effort or skill, usually done in a special area and according to fixed rules 體育運動: *There are excellent facilities for sport and recreation.* 有完善的體育娛樂設施。◇ *I'm not interested in sport.* 我對體育運動不感興趣。◇ *the use of drugs in sport* 毒品在體育運動中的使用 **2** 🔑 [C] a particular form of sport（某項）體育運動: *What's your favourite* *sport?* 你最喜歡哪一項體育運動？◇ ***team/water sports*** 集體項目／水上運動 ◇ *a sports club* 體育運動俱樂部 ➲ VISUAL VOCAB pages V43–V48 ➲ see also BLOOD SPORT, FIELD SPORTS, SPECTATOR SPORT, WINTER SPORTS **3** [C] (*AustralE, NZE, informal*) used as a friendly way of addressing sb, especially a man（用作友好稱呼，尤指對男子）朋友，老兄，哥們兒：*Good on you, sport!* 老兄，你真行！ **4** [U] (*formal*) enjoyment or fun 樂趣；消遣；玩笑；逗樂：*The comments were only made **in sport**.* 那些話只不過是開個玩笑。◇ *to **make sport of*** (= to joke about) ***sb/sth*** 開某人／某事的玩笑 **5** [C] (*biology* 生) a plant or an animal that is different in a noticeable way from its usual type 突變；芽變；變種

IDM **be a (good) 'sport** (*informal*) to be generous, cheerful and pleasant, especially in a difficult situation（尤指在困境中）開朗大度，講交情：*She's a good sport.* 她很講交情。◇ *Go on, be a sport* (= used when asking sb to help you). 來來來，別不夠朋友。

■ *verb* **1** [T] **~ sth** to have or wear sth in a proud way 得意地穿戴；誇示；故意顯示 SYN **wear**：*to sport a beard* 故意蓄着大鬍子 ◇ *She was sporting a T-shirt with the company's logo on it.* 她穿了一件帶有公司徽標的 T 恤衫，很是炫耀。 **2** [I] **+ adv./prep.** (*literary*) to play in a happy and lively way 開心活潑地玩；嬉戲

sport·ing /ˈspɔːtɪŋ; *NAmE* ˈspɔːrtɪŋ/ *adj.* **1** [only before noun] connected with sports 體育運動的：*a major sporting event* 一項重要的體育賽事 ◇ *a range of sporting activities* 一系列體育活動 ◇ *His main sporting interests are golf and tennis.* 他在體育方面主要愛好高爾夫球和網球。◇ (*NAmE*) *a store selling sporting goods* 經營體育用品的商店 **2** (*especially BrE*) fair and generous in your treatment of other people, especially in a game or sport 風格高的；有良好體育風尚的 OPP for sense 2 **unsporting** ▸ **sport·ing·ly** *adv.*：*He sportingly agreed to play the point again.* 他風格高，同意那一分重打。

IDM **a ˌsporting 'chance** a reasonable chance of success 比較有成功希望的機會

'sports car (*US* also **'sport car**) *noun* a low fast car, often with a roof that can be folded back 跑車（車身低，頂篷多可摺疊）➲ VISUAL VOCAB page V52

sports·cast /ˈspɔːtskɑːst; *NAmE* ˈspɔːrtskæst/ *noun* (*NAmE*) a television or radio broadcast of sports news or a sports event（電視台或廣播電台的）體育節目

sports·cast·er /ˈspɔːtskɑːstə(r); *NAmE* ˈspɔːrtskæstər/ *noun* (*NAmE*) a person who introduces and presents a sportscast（電視台或廣播電台的）體育節目廣播員，體育比賽解說員

'sports centre *noun* (*BrE*) a building where the public can go to play many different kinds of sports, swim, etc. 體育中心（可進行多種體育活動）

'sports day (*BrE*) (*NAmE* **'field day**) *noun* a special day at school when there are no classes and children compete in sports events（學校的）運動會

'sports jacket (*NAmE* also **'sport jacket**) *noun* a man's jacket for informal occasions, sometimes made of TWEED 男式便服外套；粗花呢夾克

sports·man /ˈspɔːtsmən; *NAmE* ˈspɔːrts-/, **sports·woman** /ˈspɔːtswʊmən; *NAmE* ˈspɔːrts-/ *noun* (*pl.* **-men** /-mən/, **-women** /-wɪmɪn/) (*especially BrE*) a person who plays a lot of sport, especially as a professional 運動員；體育運動愛好者；（尤指）職業運動者 SYN **athlete**：*a keen sportswoman* 喜愛體育運動的女子 ◇ *He is one of this country's top professional sportsmen.* 他是本國的頂級職業運動員之一。➲ note at GENDER

sports·man·like /ˈspɔːtsmənlaɪk; *NAmE* ˈspɔːrts-/ *adj.* behaving in a fair, generous and polite way, especially when playing a sport or game 有運動員風範的，有體育精神的（多指體育比賽中光明磊落、有氣度）：*a sportsmanlike attitude* 光明磊落、互相敬重謙讓的態度

sports·man·ship /ˈspɔːtsmənʃɪp; *NAmE* ˈspɔːrts-/ *noun* [U] fair, generous and polite behaviour, especially when playing a sport or game 運動員風範，體育精神（多指體育比賽中光明磊落、有氣度）

sports·per·son /ˈspɔːtspɜːsn; *NAmE* ˈspɔːrtspɜːrsn/ *noun* (*pl.* **-per·sons** or **-people**) (*especially BrE*) a person who takes part in sport, especially sb who is very good at it 運動員；體育運動愛好者；（尤指）擅長體育運動者 SYN **athlete**

'sports shirt (*NAmE* also **'sport shirt**) *noun* a man's shirt for informal occasions 男式運動衫

sports·wear /ˈspɔːtsweə(r); *NAmE* ˈspɔːrtswer/ *noun* [U] **1** (*especially BrE*) clothes that are worn for playing sports, or in informal situations 運動服裝 **2** (*especially NAmE*) clothes that are worn in informal situations 便裝

ˌsport u'tility vehicle *noun* (*abbr.* **SUV**) (*especially NAmE*) a type of large car, often with FOUR-WHEEL DRIVE and made originally for travelling over rough ground 運動型多功能車（四輪驅動、可在崎嶇路段行駛）

sporty /ˈspɔːti; *NAmE* ˈspɔːrti/ *adj.* (**sport·ier**, **sporti·est**) (*informal*) **1** (*especially BrE*) liking or good at sport 愛好（或擅長）體育運動的：*I'm not very sporty.* 我不擅長體育運動。 **2** (of clothes 衣服) bright, attractive and informal; looking suitable for wearing for sports 漂亮帥氣的；適合運動時穿着的：*a sporty cotton top* 漂亮帥氣的棉布上衣 **3** (of cars 汽車) fast and elegant 車形優美速度快的：*a sporty Mercedes* 一輛又快又靚的奔馳汽車

spot 0➔ /spɒt; *NAmE* spɑːt/ *noun, verb, adj.*

■ ***noun***

▸ **SMALL MARK** 斑點；點 **1** 0➔ a small round area that has a different colour or feels different from the surface it is on 斑點：*Which has spots, the leopard or the tiger?* 有斑點的是豹還是虎？◇ *The male bird has a red spot on its beak.* 雄鳥喙上有一個紅點。◇ (*BrE*) *She was wearing a black skirt with white spots.* 她穿着一條黑底白點的裙子。➲ see also BEAUTY SPOT, SUNSPOT ➲ SYNONYMS at PATCH **2** 0➔ a small dirty mark on sth 污跡；污漬；髒點：*His jacket was covered with spots of mud.* 他的上衣滿是泥點。◇ *rust spots* 銹斑 ➲ SYNONYMS at MARK **3** 0➔ [usually pl.] a small mark or lump on a person's skin, sometimes with a yellow head to it（皮膚上的）丘疹，疱疹，粉刺；膿疱：*The baby's whole body was covered in small red spots.* 當時這孩子渾身佈滿小紅疙瘩。◇ (*BrE*) *teenagers worried about their spots* 為長粉刺而煩惱的青少年 ➲ compare PIMPLE, RASH *n.* (1), ZIT

▸ **PLACE** 地點 **4** 0➔ a particular area or place 地點；場所；處所：*a **quiet/secluded/lonely, etc. spot*** 寧靜、僻靜、寂靜等的地方 ◇ *He showed me **the exact spot** where he had asked her to marry him.* 他把他當時向她求婚的確切地點指給我看。◇ *She stood **rooted to the spot** with fear* (= unable to move). 她嚇得呆若木雞地站在那裏。◇ *a tourist spot* 旅遊景點 ➲ see also BLACK SPOT, BLIND SPOT, HOT SPOT, NIGHTSPOT, TROUBLE SPOT ➲ SYNONYMS at PLACE

▸ **SMALL AMOUNT** 少量 **5** [usually sing.] **~ of sth** (*BrE, informal*) a small amount of sth 少量；一點 SYN **bit**：*He's in a spot of trouble.* 他遇到一點麻煩。 **6** [usually pl.] **~ (of sth)** a small amount of a liquid 幾滴，少許（液體）：*I felt a few spots of rain.* 我感覺飄來幾滴雨。

▸ **PART OF SHOW** 一段節目 **7** a part of a television, radio, club or theatre show that is given to a particular entertainer or type of entertainment（電視、廣播中或俱樂部、劇院演出中）某演員的固定節目，某類節目的固定欄目：*a **guest/solo spot*** 嘉賓／獨唱節目

▸ **IN COMPETITION** 競賽 **8** a position in a competition or an event 排名位置：*two teams battling for top spot* 爭奪冠軍地位的兩個隊

▸ **LIGHT** 燈光 **9** (*informal*) = SPOTLIGHT

IDM **in a (tight) 'spot** (*informal*) in a difficult situation 處於困境 **on the 'spot 1** immediately 當場；當下：*He answered the question on the spot.* 他當場就回答了那個問題。◇ *an on-the-spot parking fine* 當場繳納的違章停車罰款 **2** at the actual place where sth is happening 在現場：*An ambulance was on the spot within minutes.* 幾分鐘之內，一輛救護車便趕到現場。◇ *an on-the-spot report* 現場報道 **3** (*NAmE* also **in 'place**) in one exact place, without moving in any direction 在原地：*Running on the spot is good exercise.* 原地跑步是一種很好的鍛煉。 **put sb on the 'spot** to make sb feel awkward or embarrassed by asking them a difficult question（提出難題）使某人尷尬，使某人為難：*The interviewer's questions really put him on the spot.* 採訪者的問題的確使他

尷尬。➲ more at BRIGHT *adj.*, GLUE *v.*, HIT *v.*, KNOCK *v.*, LEOPARD, RIVET *v.*, SOFT, TIGHT *adj.*

■ ***verb*** (-tt-) **1** (not used in the progressive tenses 不用於進行時) to see or notice a person or thing, especially suddenly or when it is not easy to do so 看見；看出；注意到；發現：**~ sb/sth** *I finally spotted my friend in the crowd.* 我終於在人群中看見了我的朋友。◇ *I've just spotted a mistake on the front cover.* 我剛才在封面上發現了一處錯誤。◇ *Can you spot the difference between these two pictures?* 你能不能看出這兩幅畫有什麼不同？◇ **~ sb/sth doing sth** *Neighbours spotted smoke coming out of the house.* 鄰居們發現有煙從這所房子裏冒出來。◇ **~ that …** *No one spotted that the gun was a fake.* 沒有人留意到那是一支假槍。◇ **~ what, where, etc. …** *I soon spotted what the mistake was.* 我很快就看出錯誤所在了。➲ see also SPOTTER ➲ **SYNONYMS** at SEE **2 ~ sb/sth** (*NAmE, sport* 體) to give your opponent or the other team an advantage（對比賽對手）讓分，讓子，讓步：*We spotted the opposing team two goals.* 我們讓對手兩個球。

IDM **be spotted with sth** to be covered with small round marks of sth 滿是…斑點：*His shirt was spotted with oil.* 他的襯衣上滿是油點。

■ ***adj.*** [only before noun] (*business* 商) connected with a system of trading where goods are delivered and paid for immediately after sale 現貨交易的；立即支付的：*spot prices* 現貨價格

ˌspot ˈcheck *noun* a check that is made suddenly and without warning on a few things or people chosen from a group to see that everything is as it should be 抽查；抽樣檢查：*to carry out random spot checks on vehicles* 對車輛進行抽檢

ˈspot kick *noun* (*BrE*) = PENALTY KICK

spot·less /ˈspɒtləs; *NAmE* ˈspɑːt-/ *adj.* perfectly clean 極清潔的；非常潔淨的 **SYN** **immaculate**：*a spotless white shirt* 潔白的襯衣 ◇ *She keeps the house spotless.* 她把家裏收拾得一塵不染。◇ (*figurative*) *He has a spotless record so far.* 他的操行記錄至今無任何污點。▶ **spot·less·ly** *adv.*：*spotlessly clean* 潔淨得一塵不染

spot·light /ˈspɒtlaɪt; *NAmE* ˈspɑːt-/ *noun, verb*

■ ***noun*** **1** (also *informal* **spot**) [C] a light with a single, very bright BEAM that can be directed at a particular place or person 聚光燈：*The room was lit by spotlights.* 房間被聚光燈照亮。➲ **VISUAL VOCAB** page V21 **2 the spotlight** [U] the area of light that is made by a spotlight 聚光燈照亮的地方；聚光燈照明圈：*She stood alone on stage in the spotlight.* 她獨自站在舞台的聚光燈下。**3 the spotlight** [U] attention from newspapers, television and the public 媒體和公眾的注意：*Unemployment is once again **in the spotlight**.* 失業問題再次受到人們的關注。◇ *The issue will come **under the spotlight** when parliament reassembles.* 等議會重開的時候，這個問題將成為焦點。◇ *The report has **turned the spotlight on** the startling rise in street crime.* 報道使人們將關注的目光投向街頭犯罪激增的問題。

■ ***verb*** (**spot·lit**, **spot·lit** /-lɪt/) **HELP** Especially in sense 2, **spotlighted** is also used for the past tense and past participle. 第 2 義的過去時和過去分詞也可用 spotlighted。**1 ~ sth** to shine a spotlight on sb/sth 用聚光燈照：*a spotlit stage* 聚光燈照亮的舞台 **2 ~ sth** to give special attention to a problem, situation, etc. so that people notice it 特別關注，突出報道（以使公眾注意）**SYN** **highlight**：*The programme spotlights financial problems in the health service.* 節目突出報道了公共醫療服務的財政問題。

ˌspot ˈon *adj.* [not before noun] (*BrE, informal*) exactly right 完全正確；對極了：*His assessment of the situation was spot on.* 他對形勢的判斷完全準確。

spot·ted /ˈspɒtɪd; *NAmE* ˈspɑːt-/ (also **spotty**) *adj.* **1** (of cloth, etc. 織物等) having a regular pattern of round dots on it 有花點的：*a black and white spotted dress* 黑白點相間的連衣裙 **2** having marks on it, sometimes in a pattern 有斑點的：*a leopard's spotted coat* 豹的花斑皮毛

ˌspotted ˈdick *noun* [U] (*BrE*) a hot DESSERT (= a sweet dish) like a SPONGE CAKE with dried fruit in it 葡萄乾布丁

spot·ter /ˈspɒtə(r); *NAmE* ˈspɑːt-/ *noun* **1** (especially in compounds 尤用於構成複合詞) a person who looks for a particular type of thing or person, as a hobby or job 探子（愛好或專門搜尋物品或人才）：*a talent spotter* (= sb who visits clubs and theatres looking for new performers) 星探 ➲ see also TRAINSPOTTER **2** (also **ˈspotter plane**) a plane used for finding out what an enemy is doing 偵察機

spotty /ˈspɒti; *NAmE* ˈspɑːti/ *adj.* **1** (*BrE*, usually *disapproving*) (of a person 人) having a lot of spots on the skin 多丘疹的；多粉刺的 **SYN** **pimply**：*a spotty adolescent* 滿臉粉刺的少年 ◇ *a spotty face* 佈滿丘疹的臉 **2** (*NAmE*) = PATCHY (2) **3** = SPOTTED：*a spotty dress* 帶圓點的連衣裙

spouse /spaʊs; spaʊz/ *noun* (*formal* or *law* 律) a husband or wife 配偶 ▶ **spou·sal** /ˈspaʊzl; ˈspaʊsl/ *adj.* [only before noun]：(*formal*) *spousal consent* 配偶的同意 ◇ *spousal abuse* 虐待配偶

spout /spaʊt/ *noun, verb*

■ ***noun*** **1** a pipe or tube on a container, that you can pour liquid out through（容器的）嘴：*the spout of a teapot* 茶壺嘴 ➲ **VISUAL VOCAB** page V25 **2** a stream of liquid coming out of somewhere with great force（噴出的）水柱，液體柱 **SYN** **fountain**

IDM **be/go up the ˈspout** (*BrE, slang*) to be/go wrong; to be spoilt or not working 弄錯；搞糟；出問題；有毛病：*Well, that's my holiday plans gone up the spout!* 唉，我的休假計劃全泡湯了！

■ ***verb*** **1** [T, I] to send out sth, especially a liquid, in a stream with great force; to come out of sth in this way 噴出；噴射 **SYN** **pour**：**~ sth (from sth)** *The wound was still spouting blood.* 傷口還在噴血。◇ **~ from/out of sth** *Clear water spouted from the fountains.* 清澈的水從噴泉中噴射出來。**2** [I] (of a WHALE 鯨) to send out a stream of water from a hole in its head 噴水 **3** [I, T] (*informal, disapproving*) to speak a lot about sth; to repeat sth in a boring or annoying way 滔滔不絕地說；喋喋不休地說：**~ (off/on) (about sth)** *He's always spouting off about being a vegetarian.* 他老把自己吃素掛在嘴邊。◇ *What are you spouting on about now?* 你這會兒又在嘮叨什麼呢？◇ **~ sth** *He could spout poetry for hours.* 他聊起詩來一聊就是半天。◇ *She could do nothing but spout insults.* 她只會沒完沒了地罵人。

sprain /spreɪn/ *verb* **~ sth** to injure a joint in your body, especially your wrist or ankle, by suddenly twisting it 扭傷（關節）：*I stumbled and sprained my ankle.* 我摔了一跤，把腳脖子扭了。➲ **COLLOCATIONS** at INJURY ➲ **SYNONYMS** at INJURE ▶ **sprain** *noun*：*a bad ankle sprain* 踝關節嚴重扭傷

sprang *past tense* of SPRING

sprat /spræt/ *noun* a very small European sea fish that is used for food 黍鯡，西鯡（海生，棲於歐洲，可食）

sprawl /sprɔːl/ *verb, noun*

■ ***verb*** **1** [I] (**+ adv./prep.**) to sit or lie with your arms and legs spread out in a relaxed or awkward way 伸開四肢坐（或躺）：*He was sprawling in an armchair in front of the TV.* 他伸開手腳坐在電視機前的一張扶手椅上。◇ *Something hit her and **sent her sprawling** to the ground.* 不知什麼東西擊中了她，把她打趴在地上。◇ *I tripped and **went sprawling**.* 我絆了一下，摔了個四腳朝天。**2** [I] **+ adv./prep.** to spread in an untidy way; to cover a large area 蔓延；雜亂無序地拓展：*The town sprawled along the side of the lake.* 小鎮順着湖的邊緣擴展。

■ ***noun*** **1** [C, usually sing., U] a large area covered with buildings that spreads from the city into the countryside in an ugly way（城市）雜亂無序拓展的地區：*attempts to control the fast-growing **urban sprawl*** 為控制城市過快過亂的拓展所作的努力 **2** [C, usually sing.] an act of spreading to cover a large area in an untidy way; sth that spreads like this 隨意擴展；蔓延；蔓延物

sprawled /sprɔːld/ *adj.* sitting or lying with your arms and legs spread out in a lazy or awkward way 四肢攤開懶散地坐（或躺）着的：*He was lying sprawled in an*

S

armchair, watching TV. 他四肢伸開正懶散地靠在扶手椅上看電視。

sprawl·ing /ˈsprɔːlɪŋ/ *adj.* [only before noun] spreading in an untidy way 蔓延的；雜亂無序伸展的：*a modern sprawling town* 一座雜亂無序拓展的現代城鎮

spray /spreɪ/ *noun, verb*

■ **noun** **1** [U, C] very small drops of a liquid that are sent through the air, for example by the wind 浪花；水花；飛沫：*sea spray* 海上的浪花 ◇ *A cloud of fine spray came up from the waterfall.* 飛瀑濺起一片水霧。◇ *(figurative) a spray of machine-gun bullets* 一陣雨點般的機槍掃射 **2** [U, C] (especially in compounds 尤用於構成複合詞) a substance that is forced out of a container such as an AEROSOL, in very small drops 噴劑；噴霧的液體：*a can of insect spray* (= used to kill insects) 一罐噴霧殺蟲劑 ◇ *body spray* 噴霧香水 ➲ **VISUAL VOCAB** page V33 ➲ see also HAIRSPRAY **3** [C] a device or container, for example an AEROSOL, that you use to apply liquid in fine drops 噴霧器：*a throat spray* 潤喉劑噴筒 **4** [C] an act of applying liquid to sth in very small drops 噴霧；液體的噴灑：*I gave the plants a quick spray.* 我給這些花草略微噴了噴水。**5** [C] a small branch of a tree or plant, with its leaves and flowers or BERRIES, that you use for decoration（用作裝飾的）小樹枝，小花枝 **SYN** **sprig** **6** [C] an attractive arrangement of flowers or jewellery, that you wear（戴在身上的）一簇花，枝狀飾物：*a spray of orchids* 一簇蘭花

■ **verb** **1** [T, I] to cover sb/sth with very small drops of a liquid that are forced out of a container or sent through the air 噴；噴灑；向…噴灑：**~ (sth) (on/onto/over sb/sth)** *Spray the conditioner onto your wet hair.* 往你的濕頭髮上噴些護髮素。◇ *Champagne sprayed everywhere.* 香檳酒噴得到處都是。◇ **~ sb/sth (with sth)** *The crops are regularly sprayed with pesticide.* 莊稼定期噴灑殺蟲劑。◇ **~ sth + adj.** *She's had the car sprayed blue.* 她讓人把汽車噴成了藍色。 **2** [T, I] to cover sb/sth with a lot of small things with a lot of force 向…掃射（或拋灑）；往…上撒：**~ sb/sth with sth** *The gunman sprayed the building with bullets.* 持槍歹徒向那座房子掃射。◇ **+ adv./prep.** *Pieces of glass sprayed all over the room.* 房間裏滿地都是玻璃碎片。 **3** [I] (especially of a male cat 尤指雄貓) to leave small amounts of URINE to mark its own area 撒尿（以示領地佔有）

ˈspray can *noun* a small metal container that has paint in it under pressure and that you use to spray paint onto sth 噴霧罐；噴漆罐

spray·er /ˈspreɪə(r)/ *noun* a piece of equipment used for spraying liquid, especially paint or a substance used to kill insects that damage crops 噴漆器；噴霧器；噴槍：*a paint/crop sprayer* 噴漆器；農用噴霧器

S

ˈspray gun *noun* a device for spraying paint onto a surface, that works by air pressure 噴槍

ˈspray-on *adj.* [only before noun] (*especially BrE*) that you can spray onto sth/sb from a special container 噴霧式的；噴塗式的：*a spray-on water repellent for shoes* 噴塗式皮鞋防水劑

ˈspray paint *noun* [U] paint that is kept in a container under pressure and that you can spray onto sth 噴漆 ▸ **ˈspray-paint** *verb* **~ A (with B) | ~ B (on A)**

spread /spred/ *verb, noun*

■ **verb** (**spread, spread**)

▸ **OPEN/ARRANGE** 展開；鋪開 **1** [T] **~ sth (out) (on/over sth)** to open sth that has been folded so that it covers a larger area than before 展開；打開：*to spread a cloth on a table* 在桌上鋪桌布 ◇ *Sue spread the map out on the floor.* 蘇在地板上攤開地圖。◇ *The bird spread its wings.* 鳥展開翅膀。 **2** [T] **~ sth (out) (on/over sth)** to arrange objects so that they cover a large area and can be seen easily 攤開；使散開：*Papers had been spread out on the desk.* 各種報紙攤在書桌上。

▸ **ARMS/LEGS** 雙臂；雙腿 **3** [T] **~ sth (out)** to move your arms, legs, fingers, etc. far apart from each other 張開；伸開：*She spread her arms and the child ran towards her.* 她張開雙臂，孩子向她跑來。

▸ **AMONG PEOPLE** 在人們中間 **4** [I, T] to affect or make sth affect, be known by, or used by more and more people 傳播；散佈；（使）流傳：**(+ adv./prep.)** *The disease spreads easily.* 這種疾病容易傳播。◇ *Within weeks, his confidence had spread throughout the team.* 短短幾個星期，他的信心感染了全體隊員。◇ *Use of computers **spread rapidly** during that period.* 在那個時期，計算機的應用迅速普及開來。◇ **~ sth** *to **spread rumours/lies** about sb* 散佈關於某人的謠言／謊言 ◇ *The disease is spread by mosquitoes.* 這種疾病通過蚊子傳播。

▸ **COVER LARGE AREA** 覆蓋大面積 **5** [I, T] to cover, or to make sth cover, a larger and larger area（使）蔓延，擴散，散開：**(+ adv./prep.)** *The fire rapidly spread to adjoining buildings.* 大火迅速蔓延到了鄰近的建築物。◇ *Water began to spread across the floor.* 水開始漫過地板。◇ *A smile spread slowly across her face.* 微笑慢慢在她臉上綻開。◇ **~ sth** *Using too much water could spread the stain.* 用水太多可能使污跡擴散。 **6** [T] **~ sb/sth** to cause sb/sth to be in a number of different places 使分散；使分佈：*Seeds and pollen are spread by the wind.* 種子和花粉是隨風傳播的。◇ *We have 10 000 members spread all over the country.* 我們有 1 萬名成員分佈在全國各地。 **7** [I] **~ (out) + adv./prep.** to cover a large area 延伸；伸展；擴張：*The valley spread out beneath us.* 山谷在我們下方延伸。

▸ **SOFT LAYER** 稀軟的層面 **8** [T, I] to put a layer of a substance onto the surface of sth; to be able to be put onto a surface 塗；敷：**~ (A on/over B)** *to spread butter on pieces of toast* 在烤麪包片上抹黃油 ◇ **~ (B with A)** *pieces of toast spread with butter* 抹了黃油的烤麪包片 ◇ *If the paint is too thick, it will not spread evenly.* 油漆如果太稠就塗不均勻。

▸ **DIVIDE/SHARE** 劃分；分攤 **9** [T] to separate sth into parts and divide them between different times or different people 分（若干次）進行；由（若干人）分擔：**~ sth** *Why not pay monthly and spread the cost of your car insurance?* 你為什麼不把汽車保險費按月分期支付呢？◇ **~ sth (out) (over sth)** *A series of five interviews will be spread over two days.* 一共五次面談，分兩天進行。◇ **~ sth between sb/sth** *We attempted to spread the workload between the departments.* 我們試圖把工作分攤給各部門。

IDM **spread like ˈwildfire** (of news, etc. 消息等) to become known by more and more people very quickly 像野火般蔓延；迅速傳開 **spread your ˈnet** to consider a wide range of possibilities or cover a large area, especially to try to find sb/sth 考慮到多種可能；大面積地排查；撒開網（尋找）：*They have spread their net far and wide in the search for a new team coach.* 他們撒開網四處物色新的球隊教練。 **spread your ˈwings** to become more independent and confident and try new activities, etc. 展翅高飛（更自信地嘗試新事物） **spread the ˈword** to tell people about sth 散佈消息 **spread yourself too ˈthin** to try to do so many different things at the same time that you do not do any of them well 樣樣都抓哪樣都抓不好

PHR V **ˌspread ˈout | ˌspread yourself ˈout** **1** to stretch your body or arrange your things over a large area 伸展身體；攤開東西：*There's more room to spread out in first class.* 頭等艙寬敞些，伸得開腿。◇ *Do you have to spread yourself out all over the sofa?* 你就非得躺下，把整個大沙發全佔了才行嗎？ **2** to separate from other people in a group, to cover a larger area 散開：*The searchers spread out to cover the area faster.* 搜索人員分散開來，好更快地搜索這一地區。

■ **noun**

▸ **INCREASE** 擴大 **1** [U] an increase in the amount or number of sth that there is, or in the area that is affected by sth 傳播；散佈；擴展；蔓延：*to prevent the spread of disease* 防止疾病的傳播 ◇ *to encourage the spread of information* 促進信息的傳播 ◇ *the spread of a city into the surrounding areas* 城市向周邊地區的擴展 ➲ see also MIDDLE-AGE SPREAD

▸ **RANGE/VARIETY** 廣泛；多樣 **2** [C, usually sing.] a range or variety of people or things 廣泛；多樣：*a **broad spread** of opinions* 各種各樣的意見

▸ **ON BREAD** 麪包 **3** [C, U] a soft food that you put on bread 抹在麪包上的東西：*Use a low-fat spread instead of* butter. 不要抹黃油，抹點低脂肪的東西吧。◇ *cheese spread* 奶酪醬

▸ **AREA COVERED** 所佔區域 **4** [C, usually sing.] **~ (of sth)** the area that sth exists in or happens in 涉及區域；活動範圍：*The company has a good geographical spread of hotels in this country.* 該公司在這個國家開設的飯店地理分佈相當廣。 **5** [C, usually sing.] **~ (of sth)** how wide sth is or the area that sth covers 寬度；面積；翼展：*The bird's wings have a spread of nearly a metre.* 這隻鳥翼展近一米。

▸ **IN NEWSPAPER/MAGAZINE** 報刊 **6** [C] an article or advertisement in a newspaper or magazine, especially one that covers two opposite pages（尤指橫貫兩版的）文章，廣告：*The story continued with **a double-page spread** on the inside pages.* 這篇報道在報紙的內頁有橫貫兩版的後續部份。➲ see also CENTRE SPREAD

▸ **MEAL** 餐食 **7** [C] (*informal*) a large meal, especially one that is prepared for a special occasion 豐盛的餐食：*They had laid on a huge spread for the party.* 他們為聚會安排了豐盛的食物。

▸ **OF LAND/WATER** 陸地；水域 **8** [C, usually sing.] **~ (of sth)** (*NAmE*) an area of land or water 區域；一大片：*a vast spread of water* 浩瀚的水域 ◇ *They have a huge spread in California* (= a large farm or RANCH). 他們在加利福尼亞擁有大片的土地。

▸ **FINANCE** 金融 **9** [U] the difference between two rates or prices（兩種價格或比率的）差額，差幅

▸ **ON BED** 牀 **10** [C] (*NAmE*) = BEDSPREAD

ˌspread ˈbetting *noun* [U] a type of betting on a sports event in which you bet money on whether you think the predicted number of goals, points, etc. is too high or too low. The amount of money you win or lose depends on the extent to which you are right or wrong. 差額投注，差價賭博（判斷得分、點數等預測數目過高還是過低的體育博彩，輸贏款額依判斷的準確程度而定）▸ **ˌspread ˈbet** *noun*

spread·eagled /ˌspredˈiːɡld/ (*BrE*) (*NAmE* **spread·eagle**) *adj.* [not usually before noun] in a position with your arms and legs spread out 四肢攤開 ▸ **spread·eagle** /ˌspredˈiːɡl/ *verb* **~ sb**

spread·er /ˈspredə(r)/ *noun* a device or machine that spreads things 塗抹用具；塗抹器；散佈機：*a muck spreader* 糞肥散佈機

spread·sheet /ˈspredʃiːt/ *noun* a computer program that is used, for example, when doing financial or project planning. You enter data in rows and columns and the program calculates costs, etc. from it.（計算機）電子表格程序

Sprech·ge·sang /ˈʃprexɡəzæŋ/ *noun* [U] (from *German, music* 音) a style of singing which is between speaking and singing 朗誦唱（介乎說話和歌唱之間的唱法）

spree /spriː/ *noun* **1** a short period of time that you spend doing one particular activity that you enjoy, but often too much of it（常指過分）玩樂，作樂；縱樂：*a **shopping/spending spree*** 瘋狂購物；大肆花錢 ◇ *He's out **on a spree**.* 他到外面瀟灑去了。 **2** (used especially in newspapers 尤用於報章) a period of activity, especially criminal activity 一陣，一通（犯罪活動）：*to go on a killing spree* 一陣殺戮

sprig /sprɪɡ/ *noun* a small STEM with leaves on it from a plant or bush, used in cooking or as a decoration（烹飪或裝飾用）帶葉小枝：*a sprig of parsley/holly/heather* 一小枝歐芹／冬青／帚石楠

spring 彈簧

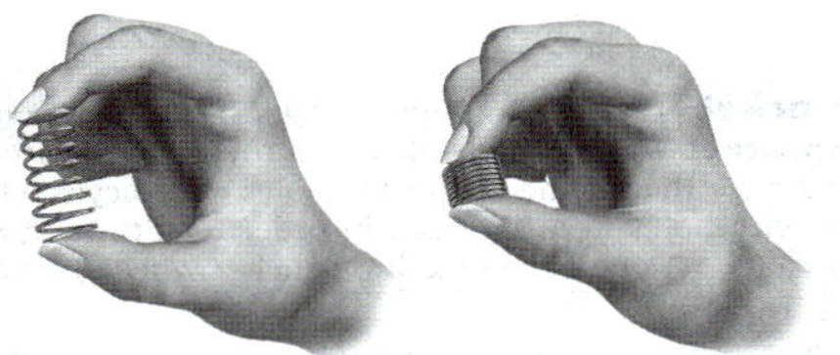

spright·ly /ˈspraɪtli/ (also *less frequent* **spry**) *adj.* (especially of older people 尤指年長者) full of life and energy 精力充沛的；精神矍鑠的 SYN **lively**：*a sprightly 80-year-old* 精神矍鑠的 80 歲老人 ▸ **spright·li·ness** *noun* [U]

spring 0ᵽ /sprɪŋ/ *noun, verb*

■ ***noun***

▸ **SEASON** 季節 **1** 0ᵽ [U, C] the season between winter and summer when plants begin to grow 春天；春季：*flowers that bloom **in spring/in the spring*** 春天開的花 ◇ *He was born in the spring of 1944.* 他生於 1944 年春。◇ *There's a feeling of spring in the air today.* 今天可以感到一點春天的氣息。◇ *spring flowers* 春天的花

▸ **TWISTED WIRE** 彈簧 **2** 0ᵽ [C] a twisted piece of metal that can be pushed, pressed or pulled but which always returns to its original shape or position afterwards 彈簧；發條：*bed springs* 牀墊彈簧 **3** [U] the ability of a spring to return to its original position 彈性；彈力：*The mattress has lost its spring.* 那個牀墊失去彈性了。

▸ **WATER** 水 **4** 0ᵽ [C] a place where water comes naturally to the surface from under the ground 泉：*a mountain spring* 山泉 ◇ *spring water* 泉水

▸ **CHEERFUL QUALITY** 活力 **5** [U, sing.] a cheerful, lively quality 活力；朝氣：*She walked along **with a spring in her step**.* 她邁着輕快的步伐向前走去。

▸ **SUDDEN JUMP** 跳躍 **6** [C] a quick sudden jump upwards or forwards 跳；躍：*With a spring, the cat leapt on to the table.* 貓一躍跳上桌子。 IDM see JOY

■ ***verb*** (**sprang** /spræŋ/, **sprung** /sprʌŋ/) (*NAmE* also **sprung, sprung**)

▸ **JUMP/MOVE SUDDENLY** 跳躍 **1** 0ᵽ [I] (**+ adv./prep.**) (of a person or an animal 人或動物) to move suddenly and with one quick movement in a particular direction 跳；躍；蹦 SYN **leap**：*He turned off the alarm and sprang out of bed.* 他止住鬧鐘，從牀上跳了下來。◇ *Everyone **sprang to their feet*** (= stood up suddenly) *when the principal walked in.* 校長進來時，所有的人都立刻站了起來。◇ *The cat crouched ready to spring.* 那貓躬起背準備跳。◇ (*figurative*) *to **spring to sb's defence/assistance*** (= to quickly defend or help sb) 連忙站出來保護／幫助某人 **2** 0ᵽ [I] (of an object 物體) to move suddenly and violently 突然猛烈地移動：**+ adv./prep.** *The branch sprang back and hit him in the face.* 樹枝彈回來打在他臉上。◇ **+ adj.** *She turned the key and the lid sprang open.* 她一擰鑰匙，蓋子啪地打開了。

▸ **SURPRISE** 使吃驚 **3** [T] to do sth, ask sth or say sth that sb is not expecting 突如其來地做；冷不防地問；突然說：**~ sth** *She sprang a surprise by winning the tournament.* 這次比賽她獲得冠軍，爆了個大冷門。◇ **~ sth on sb** *I'm sorry to **spring it on you**, but I've been offered another job.* 我很抱歉這樣突然告訴您，我另有工作了。

▸ **APPEAR SUDDENLY** 突然出現 **4** [I] **+ adv./prep.** to appear or come somewhere suddenly 突然出現（或來到）：*Tears sprang to her eyes.* 她眼裏一下子湧出了淚水。

▸ **FREE PRISONER** 救出被拘禁者 **5** [T] **~ sb** (*informal*) to help a prisoner to escape 幫助…逃跑（或越獄）；營救：*Plans to spring the hostages have failed.* 營救人質的計劃失敗了。

IDM **ˌspring into ˈaction** | **ˌspring into/to ˈlife** (of a person, machine, etc. 人、機器等) to suddenly start working or doing sth 突然工作（或行動）起來：*'Let's go!' he said, springing into action.* 他突然行動起來，說道："咱們走！" ◇ *The town springs into life* (= becomes busy) *during the carnival.* 狂歡節期間，全城突然熱鬧起來。 **spring a ˈleak** (of a boat or container 船舶或容器) to develop a hole through which water or another liquid can pass 出現裂縫；開裂漏水 **spring a ˈtrap** **1** to make a trap for catching animals close suddenly 使捕獸器突然合上 **2** to try to trick sb into doing or saying sth; to succeed in this 設套誘使某人做（或說）➲ more at HOPE *n.*, MIND *n.*

PHR V **ˈspring for sth** (*NAmE, informal*) to pay for sth for sb else（替別人）付…的賬：*I'll spring for the drinks tonight.* 今晚的飲料我來付賬。 **ˈspring from sth** (*formal*) to be caused by sth; to start from sth 由某事物造成；起源於（或來自）某事物：*The idea for the novel sprang*

S

from a trip to India. 寫這部小說的想法源於一次去印度的旅行。ˈ**spring from …** (*informal*) to appear suddenly and unexpectedly from a particular place 突如其來地從（某處）出現：*Where on earth did you spring from?* 你究竟是從哪兒冒出來的？ˌ**spring ˈup** to appear or develop quickly and/or suddenly 迅速出現；突然興起

spring·board /ˈsprɪŋbɔːd; *NAmE* -bɔːrd/ *noun* **1** a strong board that you jump on and use to help you jump high in DIVING and GYMNASTICS（跳水或體操中的）跳板 **2 ~ (for/to sth)** something that helps you start an activity, especially by giving you ideas（有助於開展某事的）基礎，出發點：*The document provided a springboard for a lot of useful discussion.* 這份文件引發出許多有益的討論。▸ **spring·board** *verb* [I, T]：**~ (sth) (into sth)** *The company expects that this strategic move would allow it to springboard into the US market.* 公司希望這次戰略行動會成為公司進入美國市場的跳板。

spring·bok /ˈsprɪŋbɒk; *NAmE* -bɑːk/ *noun* **1** [C] a small ANTELOPE from southern Africa that can jump high into the air 跳羚（產於非洲南部，個頭兒小，能跳得很高） **2 Springboks** [pl.] the name of the South African national RUGBY team 跳羚隊（南非國家橄欖球隊）

ˌ**spring ˈchicken** *noun*
IDM **be no ˌspring ˈchicken** (*humorous*) to be no longer young 老大不小；不再年輕

ˌ**spring-ˈclean** *verb* [T, I] **~ (sth)** to clean a house, room, etc. thoroughly, including the parts you do not usually clean 徹底打掃（房屋等）：*Fran decided to spring-clean the apartment.* 弗朗決定把房間徹底打掃一下。▸ ˌ**spring ˈclean** *noun* [sing.]：(*BrE*) *The place needed a good spring clean before we could move in.* 那地方得來個大掃除，然後我們才能搬進去。

ˌ**spring ˈgreens** *noun* [pl.] leaves of young CABBAGE plants of certain types 嫩捲心菜葉

ˌ**spring-ˈloaded** *adj.* containing a metal spring that presses one part against another 彈簧承載的；彈頂的

ˌ**spring ˈonion** (*BrE*) (*NAmE* ˌ**green ˈonion**, **scal·lion**) *noun* a type of small onion with a long green STEM and leaves. Spring onions are often eaten raw in salads. 大蔥 ➲ VISUAL VOCAB page V31

ˌ**spring ˈroll** (*especially BrE*) *noun* a type of Chinese food consisting of a tube of thin PASTRY, filled with vegetables and/or meat and fried until it is crisp 春捲 ➲ see also EGG ROLL

ˌ**spring ˈtide** *noun* a TIDE in which there is a very great rise and fall of the sea, and which happens near the new moon and the full moon each month 朔望大潮（在每個月的新月和滿月期間發生）

spring·time /ˈsprɪŋtaɪm/ *noun* [U] the season of spring 春季；春天；春令：*a visit to Holland* ***in springtime/in the springtime*** 春季遊覽荷蘭

springy /ˈsprɪŋi/ (**spring·ier**, **springi·est**) *adj.* **1** returning quickly to the original shape after being pushed, pulled, stretched, etc. 有彈性（或彈力）的：*We walked across the springy grass.* 我們走過鬆軟的草地。**2** full of energy and confidence 矯健的；有活力的：*She's 73, but hasn't lost that youthful, springy step.* 她 73 歲了，但走起路來依舊矯健輕捷。

sprin·kle /ˈsprɪŋkl/ *verb, noun*

■ ***verb*** **1** [T] to shake small pieces of sth or drops of a liquid on sth 撒；灑；把…撒（或灑）在…上：**~ A on/onto/over B** *Sprinkle chocolate on top of the cake.* 給蛋糕灑上巧克力。◇ *She sprinkled sugar over the strawberries.* 她在草莓上撒了點糖。◇ **~ B with A** *She sprinkled the strawberries with sugar.* 她在草莓上撒了點糖。 **2** [T, usually passive] **~ sth with sth** to include a few of sth in sth else 使某物包含少量的另一物；用…點綴 **SYN** **strew**：*His poems are sprinkled with quotations from ancient Greek.* 他的詩歌不時穿插有古希臘引文。 **3** [I] (*NAmE*) **if it sprinkles**, it rains lightly 下小雨 **SYN** **drizzle**：*It's only sprinkling. We can still go out.* 雨不大，我們還可以出去。

■ ***noun*** [sing.] **1** = SPRINKLING：*Add a sprinkle of cheese and serve.* 再撒點奶酪，然後端上桌。 **2** (*especially NAmE*) light rain 小雨：*We've only had a few sprinkles (of rain) recently.* 近來我們這裏只下過幾場小雨。

sprink·ler /ˈsprɪŋklə(r)/ *noun* **1** a device with holes in that is used to spray water in drops on plants, soil or grass 灑水器；噴灑器 ➲ VISUAL VOCAB page V19 **2** a device inside a building which automatically sprays out water if there is a rise in temperature because of a fire（建築物內的）消防噴淋，自動噴水滅火裝置

sprin·kles /ˈsprɪŋklz/ (*NAmE*) (*BrE* ˌ**hundreds and ˈthousands**) *noun* [pl.] extremely small pieces of coloured sugar, used to decorate cakes, etc.（裝飾糕點等用的）着色珠子糖，糖屑

sprink·ling /ˈsprɪŋklɪŋ/ (also **sprin·kle**) *noun* a small amount of a substance that is dropped somewhere, or a number of things or people that are spread or included somewhere 少量（落、撒或包含的某種物質）；少數（分散在或包括在某處的人）：*Add a sprinkling of pepper.* 加一點胡椒粉。◇ *Most were men, but there was also a sprinkling of young women.* 多數是男人，不過也有為數不多的年輕婦女。

sprint /sprɪnt/ *verb, noun*

■ ***verb*** [I, T] to run or swim a short distance very fast 短距離快速奔跑（或游泳）：**+ adv./prep.** *He sprinted for the line.* 他向終點線衝去。◇ *Three runners sprinted past.* 三名運動員飛跑了過去。◇ *She jumped out of the car and sprinted for the front door.* 她跳下車，朝前門跑去。◇ **~ sth** *I sprinted the last few metres.* 我全速跑完最後幾米。

■ ***noun*** **1** a race in which the people taking part run, swim, etc. very fast over a short distance 短跑比賽；短距離速度競賽：*a 100-metre sprint* * 100 米短跑 ◇ *the world sprint champion* 短跑世界冠軍 ➲ VISUAL VOCAB page V47 **2** [usually sing.] a short period of running, swimming, etc. very fast 短距離快速奔跑（或游泳等）；衝刺：*a sprint for the line* 向終點線的衝刺 ◇ *a sprint for the bus* 衝向公共汽車 ◇ *She won in a sprint finish.* 她在最後的衝刺中取得勝利。▸ **sprint·er** *noun*

sprite /spraɪt/ *noun* (in stories) a small creature with magic powers, especially one that likes playing tricks（傳說中的）小仙子，小精靈，小妖精

spritz /sprɪts/ *verb* **~ sth** (*especially NAmE*) to spray very small drops of liquid on sth quickly 噴：*Lightly spritz your hair with water.* 往你頭髮上輕輕噴點水。▸ **spritz** *noun*

spritz·er /ˈsprɪtsə(r)/ *noun* a drink made with wine (usually white) mixed with either SODA WATER or SPARKLING mineral water (= with bubbles in it) 汽酒：*a white wine spritzer* 一杯白葡萄汽酒

sprocket wheel 鏈輪

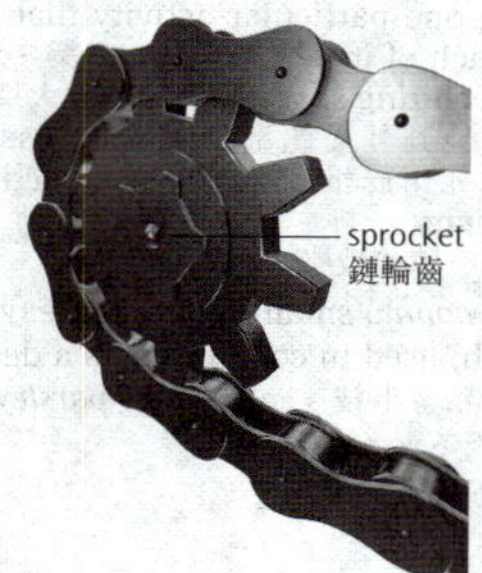

sprocket /ˈsprɒkɪt; *NAmE* ˈsprɑːkɪt/ *noun* **1** (also ˈ**sprocket wheel**) a wheel with a row of teeth around the edge that connect with the holes of a bicycle chain or with holes in a film, etc. in order to turn it 鏈輪；輸片齒輪 **2** one of the teeth on such a wheel 鏈輪齒；鏈齒

sprog /sprɒg; *NAmE* sprɑːg/ *noun* (*BrE*, *informal*, *humorous*) a child or baby 小孩；嬰兒

sprout /spraʊt/ *verb, noun*
■ ***verb*** **1** [I] (of plants or seeds 植物或種子) to produce new leaves or BUDS; to start to grow 發芽；抽芽；抽條；生長：*new leaves sprouting from the trees* 樹上長出的新葉 ◇ *The seeds will sprout in a few days.* 這些種子幾天後就會發芽。 **2** [I, T] to appear; to develop sth, especially in large numbers 出現；（使）湧現出：*Hundreds of mushrooms had sprouted up overnight.* 一夜之間長出來好幾百朵蘑菇。◇ **~ sth** *The town has sprouted shopping malls, discos and nightclubs in recent years.* 最近幾年，城裏湧現出不少購物中心、迪斯科舞廳和夜總會。 **3** [T, I] to start to grow sth; to start to grow on sb/sth 長出（某物）；（某物）長出：**~ sth** *Tim has sprouted a beard since we last saw him.* 我們上次見到蒂姆以後，蒂姆長出了鬍子。◇ **~ from sth** *Hair sprouted from his chest.* 他胸前長出了毛。
■ ***noun*** **1** = BRUSSELS SPROUT **2** a new part growing on a plant 苗；新芽；嫩枝

spruce /spruːs/ *noun, verb, adj.*
■ ***noun*** **1** [C, U] an EVERGREEN forest tree with leaves like needles 雲杉 **2** [U] the soft wood of the spruce, used, for example, in making paper 雲杉木
■ ***verb***
PHR V **ˌspruce ˈup | ˌspruce sb/sth/yourself↔ˈup** to make sb/sth/yourself clean and neat 打扮；把…收拾整潔：*She spruced up for the interview.* 她為參加面試打扮了一番。◇ *The city is sprucing up its museums and galleries.* 這座城市正在美化自己的博物館和美術館。
■ ***adj.*** (of people or places 人或處所) neat and clean in appearance 整潔的

spruit /spreɪt/ *noun* (*SAfrE*) a stream, sometimes one that only flows when there has been a lot of rain（只在雨季有水的）小河道，小溪

sprung /sprʌŋ/ *adj.* fitted with metal springs 裝有彈簧的；彈簧支撐的：*a sprung mattress* 彈簧牀墊 ➲ see also SPRING, SPRANG, SPRUNG *v.*

spry /spraɪ/ *adj.* = SPRIGHTLY

spud /spʌd/ *noun* (*especially BrE, informal*) a potato 土豆

spume /spjuːm/ *noun* [U] (*literary*) the mass of white bubbles that forms in waves when the sea is rough（海浪的）泡沫 **SYN** **foam**

spun *past part.* of SPIN

spunk /spʌŋk/ *noun* **1** [U] (*informal*) courage; determination 勇氣；膽量；決心 **2** [U] (*BrE, taboo, slang*) = SEMEN **3** [C] (*informal, AustralE, informal*) a sexually attractive person 性感的人

spunky /ˈspʌŋki/ *adj.* (*informal*) **1** brave and determined; full of enthusiasm 勇敢堅定的；勁頭十足的：*She is bright, tough and spunky.* 她聰明、頑強而且幹勁十足。 **2** (*AustralE, informal*) sexually attractive 性感的：*a top babe with a spunky boyfriend* 有個性感男友的絕色女子

spur /spɜː(r)/ *noun, verb*
■ ***noun*** **1** a sharp pointed object that riders sometimes wear on the heels of their boots and use to encourage their horse to go faster 馬刺；靴刺 **2** [usually sing.] **~ (to sth)** a fact or an event that makes you want to do sth better or more quickly 鞭策；激勵；刺激；鼓舞 **SYN** **motivation**：*His speech was a powerful spur to action.* 他的講話很有鼓動力。 **3** an area of high ground that sticks out from a mountain or hill 山嘴；尖坡；支脈 **4** a road or a railway/railroad track that leads from the main road or line（公路或鐵路的）支線，岔線
IDM **on the ˌspur of the ˈmoment** suddenly, without planning in advance 一時衝動之下；心血來潮：*I phoned him up on the spur of the moment.* 我一時心動，給他打了電話。◇ *a spur-of-the-moment decision* 心血來潮的決定 **win/earn your ˈspurs** (*formal*) to achieve fame or success 獲得名望；取得成功
■ ***verb*** (**-rr-**) **1** to encourage sb to do sth or to encourage them to try harder to achieve sth 鞭策；激勵；刺激；鼓舞：**~ sb/sth (on) to sth/to do sth** *Her difficult childhood spurred her on to succeed.* 她艱辛的童年激勵她取得成功。◇ **~ sb/sth into sth** *I was spurred into action by the letter.* 那封信激勵我行動起來。◇ **~ sb/sth (on)** *The band has been spurred on by the success of their last single.* 最近一張單曲唱片的成功使樂隊受到鼓舞。 **2 ~ sth** to make sth happen faster or sooner 促進，加速，刺激（某事發生）：*The agreement is essential to spurring economic growth around the world.* 這項協議對於促進世界經濟的增長是至關重要的。 **3 ~ sth** to encourage a horse to go faster, especially by pushing the spurs on your boots into its side 策（馬）前進；（尤指用馬刺）策（馬）加速

spuri·ous /ˈspjʊəriəs; *NAmE* ˈspjʊr-/ *adj.* **1** false, although seeming to be genuine 虛假的；偽造的：*He had managed to create the entirely spurious impression that the company was thriving.* 他設法製造出一種徹頭徹尾的假象，讓人誤以為公司一派興旺。 **2** based on false ideas or ways of thinking 建立在錯誤的觀念（或思想方法）之上的；謬誤的：*a spurious argument* 謬誤的論據
▸ **spuri·ous·ly** *adv.*

spurn /spɜːn; *NAmE* spɜːrn/ *verb* **~ sb/sth** to reject or refuse sb/sth, especially in a proud way（尤指傲慢地）拒絕 **SYN** **shun**：*Eve spurned Mark's invitation.* 伊夫一口回絕了馬克的邀請。◇ *a spurned lover* 遭到輕蔑拒絕的痴心愛慕者

spurt /spɜːt; *NAmE* spɜːrt/ *verb, noun*
■ ***verb*** **1** [I, T] (of liquid or flames 液體或火焰) to burst or pour out suddenly; to produce sudden, powerful streams of liquid or flames 噴出；冒出：**~ (from sth)** *Blood was spurting from her nose.* 血從她鼻子裏汩汩流出來。◇ **~ out (of/from sth)** *Red and yellow flames spurted out of the fire.* 爐火吐出紅色黃色的火焰。◇ **~ sth** *Her nose was spurting blood.* 她鼻子汩汩冒着血。◇ **~ sth + adv./prep.** *The volcano spurted clouds of steam and ash high into the air.* 火山把團團熱氣和灰塵噴向高空。 **2** [I] **+ adv./prep.** to increase your speed for a short time to get somewhere faster（短暫地）加速前進；衝刺：*She spurted past me to get to the line first.* 她衝刺超過我，率先抵達終點線。
■ ***noun*** **1** an amount of liquid or flames that comes out of somewhere with great force 湧出的液體；噴出的火舌：*a great spurt of blood* 一大股急速噴出的血 **2** a sudden increase in speed, effort, activity or emotion for a short period of time（速度、幹勁、活動或感情的）短時間激增，迸發：*You'd better **put on a spurt** (= hurry up) if you want to finish that work today.* 你要是想今天完成那項工作，最好狠加一把勁。◇ *Babies get very hungry during growth spurts.* 嬰兒在猛長期會很餓。◇ *a sudden spurt of anger* 突然發作的怒火
IDM **in ˈspurts** in short periods of great activity, powerful movement, etc., rather than in a steady, continuous way 一陣陣地；一股股地：*The water came out of the tap in spurts.* 水急速地從水龍頭裏噴出來。

sput·nik /ˈspʌtnɪk; ˈspʊt-/ *noun* (from *Russian*) a SATELLITE of the type that was put into space by the Soviet Union（蘇聯）人造地球衛星，人造衛星

sput·ter /ˈspʌtə(r)/ *verb* **1** [I] if an engine, a lamp or a fire **sputters**, it makes a series of short EXPLOSIVE sounds（引擎、燈或火）發劈啪聲 **SYN** **splutter**：*sputtering fireworks* 劈啪作響的煙火 **2** [T] **+ speech | ~ sth** to speak quickly and with difficulty, making soft SPITTING sounds, because you are angry or shocked 氣急敗壞地說；急促而語無倫次地說 **SYN** **splutter**：*'W-What?' sputtered Anna.* "什…什麼？"安娜氣急敗壞地說。

spu·tum /ˈspjuːtəm/ *noun* [U] (*medical* 醫) liquid from the throat or lungs, especially when it is coughed up because of disease（尤指因疾病而咳出的）痰：*blood in the sputum* 痰中的血絲

spy /spaɪ/ *noun, verb*
■ ***noun*** (*pl.* **spies**) a person who tries to get secret information about another country, organization or person, especially sb who is employed by a government or the police 間諜；密探：*He was denounced as a foreign spy.* 有人告發他是外國間諜。◇ *a police spy* 警方密探 ◇ *a **spy plane/satellite*** (= used to watch the activities of the enemy) 間諜飛機／衛星 ◇ *Video spy cameras are being used in public places.* 隱蔽的攝像機在監視着公共場所。
■ ***verb*** (**spies**, **spy·ing**, **spied**, **spied**) **1** [I] to collect secret information about another country, organization or person 從事間諜活動；搜集情報：*He spied for his*

S

government for more than ten years. 他做過十多年的政府間諜。 **2** [T] **~ sb/sth** (*literary* or *formal*) to suddenly see or notice sb/sth 突然看見；發現： *In the distance we spied the Pacific for the first time.* 在遠處，我們突然第一次看到了太平洋。

IDM **ˌspy out the ˈland** to collect information before deciding what to do （事先）摸清情況，窺察虛實

PHR V **ˈspy on sb/sth** to watch sb/sth secretly 暗中監視，窺探（某人或事物）： *Have you been spying on me?* 你是不是一直在暗中監視我？ **ˌspy sth↔ˈout** to get information about sth 查明，瞭解清楚（某事）

spy·glass /ˈspaɪɡlɑːs; *NAmE* -ɡlæs/ *noun* a small TELESCOPE 小型望遠鏡

spy·hole /ˈspaɪhəʊl; *NAmE* -hoʊl/ *noun* a small hole in a door that you can look through to see who is on the other side before opening the door （門上的）觀察孔，貓眼兒

spy·mas·ter /ˈspaɪmɑːstə(r); *NAmE* -mæs-/ *noun* a person who controls a group of spies 間諜組織的首腦；間諜頭子

Sq. *abbr.* (used in written addresses) SQUARE （書寫地址時用）廣場： *6 Hanover Sq.* 漢諾威廣場 6 號

sq (also **sq.** especially in *NAmE*) *abbr.* (in measurements) square 平方（用於度量）： *10 sq cm* * 10 平方厘米

squab·ble /ˈskwɒbl; *NAmE* ˈskwɑːbl/ *verb* [I] **~ (with sb) (about/over sth)** to argue noisily about sth that is not very important（為小事）爭吵，發生口角 **SYN** **bicker**： *My sisters were squabbling over what to watch on TV.* 我的姐妹正為看哪個電視節目爭吵。 ▸ **squab·ble** *noun*： *family squabbles* 家庭內部的爭吵 ◇ *There were endless squabbles over who should sit where.* 為誰該坐哪兒吵個沒完沒了。

squad /skwɒd; *NAmE* skwɑːd/ *noun* [C+sing./pl. v.] **1** a section of a police force that deals with a particular type of crime （對付某類犯罪活動的）警察隊伍： *the* ***drugs/fraud, etc. squad*** 緝毒隊、反欺詐小組等 ➲ see also FLYING SQUAD **2** (in sport 體育運動) a group of players, runners, etc. from which a team is chosen for a particular game or match 運動（代表）隊： *the* ***Olympic/national squad*** 奧林匹克代表隊；國家隊 ◇ *They still have not named their squad for the World Cup qualifier.* 他們尚未確定參加世界杯預選賽的運動員名單。 **3** a small group of soldiers working or being trained together （軍隊的）班 ➲ see also FIRING SQUAD **4** a group of people who have a particular task （特殊任務）小組，隊 ➲ see also DEATH SQUAD, HIT SQUAD

ˈsquad car *noun* a police car 警車

squad·die /ˈskwɒdi; *NAmE* ˈskwɑːdi/ *noun* (*BrE, slang*) a new soldier; a soldier of low rank 新兵蛋子；列兵

squad·ron /ˈskwɒdrən; *NAmE* ˈskwɑːd-/ *noun* [C+sing./pl. v.] a group of military aircraft or ships forming a section of a military force （空軍或海軍的）中隊： ***a bomber/fighter squadron*** 轟炸機 / 戰鬥機中隊

ˈsquadron leader *noun* an officer of high rank in the British AIR FORCE （英國的）空軍中隊長，空軍少校

squalid /ˈskwɒlɪd; *NAmE* ˈskwɑːlɪd/ *adj.* (*disapproving*) **1** (of places and living conditions 處所及生活環境) very dirty and unpleasant 骯髒的；邋遢的 **SYN** **filthy**： *squalid housing* 骯髒的房屋 ◇ *squalid, overcrowded refugee camps* 骯髒而擁擠的難民營 **2** (of situations or activities 情況或活動) involving low moral standards or dishonest behaviour 道德敗壞的；醜惡的；卑鄙的 **SYN** **sordid**： *It was a squalid affair involving prostitutes and drugs.* 那是一樁涉及賣淫與毒品的醜事。

squall /skwɔːl/ *noun, verb*

■ ***noun*** a sudden strong and violent wind, often during rain or snow storms 颮（常指暴風雨或暴風雪中突起的狂風）

■ ***verb*** [I] (usually used in the progressive tenses 通常用於進行時) (*disapproving*) to cry very loudly and noisily 大聲啼哭；號哭： *squalling kids* 大聲啼哭的孩子

squally /ˈskwɔːli/ *adj.* (of weather 天氣) involving sudden, violent and strong winds 有狂風的；颳颮的： *squally showers* 狂風陣雨

squalor /ˈskwɒlə(r); *NAmE* ˈskwɑːl-/ *noun* [U] dirty and unpleasant conditions 骯髒；邋遢： *the poverty and squalor of the slums* 貧民窟的貧窮和骯髒 ◇ *He had lost his job and was living* ***in squalor***. 他丟了工作，過得很糟糕。

squan·der /ˈskwɒndə(r); *NAmE* ˈskwɑːn-/ *verb* **~ sth (on sb/sth)** to waste money, time, etc. in a stupid or careless way 浪費，揮霍（金錢、時間等）： *He squandered all his money on gambling.* 他把自己所有的錢都糟蹋在賭博上了。

square 🔑 /skweə(r); *NAmE* skwer/ *adj., noun, verb, adv.*

■ ***adj.***

▸ **SHAPE 形狀** **1** 🔑 (*geometry* 幾何) having four straight equal sides and four angles of 90°正方形的；四方形的： *a square room* 正方形的房間 ➲ **VISUAL VOCAB** page V71 **2** 🔑 forming an angle of 90° exactly or approximately 成直角的；方的： *The book had rounded, not square, corners.* 這本書是圓角的，而不是方角的。◇ *square shoulders* 寬而挺的肩膀 ◇ *He had a firm, square jaw.* 他的下巴方正而堅定。

▸ **MEASUREMENT 量度** **3** 🔑 used after a unit of measurement to say that sth measures the same amount on each of four sides（用於表示長度的單位後，表示某物四個邊等長）…見方的： *a carpet four metres square* 四米見方的地毯 **4** 🔑 (*abbr.* **sq**) used after a number to give a measurement of area （用於數字後表示面積）平方： *an area of 36 square metres* * 36 平方米的面積

▸ **BROAD/SOLID 寬闊；結實** **5** used to describe sth that is broad or that looks solid in shape 寬闊的；結實的；厚實的： *a man of* ***square build*** 體格魁梧的男子 ➲ see also FOUR-SQUARE

▸ **LEVEL/PARALLEL 相齊；平行** **6** [not before noun] **~ (with sth)** level with or parallel to sth （和某物）相齊，平行： *tables arranged square with the wall* 順着牆壁擺放的一些桌子

▸ **WITH MONEY 錢** **7** (*informal*) if two people are **square**, neither of them owes money to the other 彼此無欠賬的；兩清的；結清賬的： *Here's the £10 I owe you—now we're square.* 這是我欠你的 10 英鎊，這下我們兩清了。

▸ **IN SPORT 體育運動** **8 ~ (with sb)** if two teams are **square**, they have the same number of points 打平的；平局的： *The teams were* ***all square*** *at half-time.* 兩隊上半場打成平局。

▸ **FAIR/HONEST 公平；誠實** **9** fair or honest, especially in business matters （尤指在生意上）公平的，公正的，誠實的： ***a square deal*** 公平交易 ◇ *Are you being square with me?* 你對我是以誠相待嗎？

▸ **IN AGREEMENT 一致** **10 ~ with sth** in agreement with sth （和某事物）相一致的，相吻合的： *That isn't quite square with what you said yesterday.* 那跟你昨天所講的不大吻合。

▸ **BORING 乏味** **11** (*informal, disapproving*) (of a person 人) considered to be boring, for example because they are old-fashioned or work too hard at school 乏味的；古板的；太循規蹈矩的

IDM **a square ˈmeal** a good, satisfying meal 一頓豐盛的飯： *He looks as though he hasn't had a square meal for weeks.* 看他那樣子，就好像幾個星期沒吃過一頓像樣的飯了。 **a square ˈpeg (in a round ˈhole)** (*BrE, informal*) a person who does not feel happy or comfortable in a particular situation, or who is not suitable for it 用非所長者；方枘圓鑿

■ ***noun***

▸ **SHAPE 形狀** **1** 🔑 [C] a shape with four straight sides of equal length and four angles of 90°; a piece of sth that has this shape 正方形；四方形；正方形物： *First break the chocolate into squares.* 先把巧克力掰成方塊。◇ *The floor was tiled in squares of grey and white marble.* 地上鋪的是灰白兩色的大理石方磚。 ➲ see also SET SQUARE, T-SQUARE

▸ **IN TOWN 城鎮** **2** 🔑 [C] an open area in a town, usually with four sides, surrounded by buildings （通常為方形的）廣場： *The hotel is just off the* ***main square***. 旅館就在主廣場附近。◇ *the* ***market/town/village square***

集市 / 鎮 / 村廣場 **3 Square** [sing.] (*abbr.* **Sq.**) (used in addresses 用於地址)：*They live at 95 Russell Square.* 他們住在拉塞爾廣場 95 號。

▸ **MATHEMATICS** 數學 **4** [C] the number obtained when you multiply a number by itself 平方；二次冪：*The square of 7 is 49.* * 7 的平方是 49。

▸ **BORING PERSON** 乏味的人 **5** [C] (*informal, disapproving*) a person who is considered to be boring, for example because they are old-fashioned or because they work too hard at school 乏味的人；古板的人；老古董；書呆子

IDM **back to square 'one** a return to the situation you were in at the beginning of a project, task, etc., because you have made no real progress（因無進展）回到起點，從頭再來：*If this suggestion isn't accepted, we'll be back to square one.* 如果這個建議得不到採納，我們就得從頭再來了。

■ ***verb***

▸ **SHAPE** 使成形 **1** to make sth have straight edges and corners 使成正方形；使成四方形：**~ sth** *It was like trying to **square a circle**. That is, it was impossible.* 這就好比要把圓的變成方的。也就是說，是不可能的。◇ **~ sth off** *The boat is rounded at the front but squared off at the back.* 這條船船頭是圓的，船尾則是方的。

▸ **MATHEMATICS** 數學 **2** [usually passive] **~ sth** to multiply a number by itself 使成平方；使成二次冪：*Three squared is written 3^2.* * 3 的平方寫作 3^2。◇ *Four squared equals 16.* * 4 的平方等於 16。

▸ **SHOULDERS** 肩膀 **3 ~ yourself/your shoulders** to make your back and shoulders straight to show you are ready or determined to do sth 挺直身子；挺起胸膛：*Bruno squared himself to face the waiting journalists.* 布魯諾挺起胸膛面對等候的記者。

▸ **IN SPORT** 體育運動 **4 ~ sth** (*especially BrE*) to make the number of points you have scored in a game or competition equal to those of your opponents（使）打成平局，打平：*His goal squared the game 1–1.* 他進了一球，使比賽打成 1:1 平。

▸ **PAY MONEY** 付錢 **5 ~ sb** (*informal*) to pay money to sb in order to get their help 賄賂；收買；買通：*They must have squared the mayor before they got their plan underway.* 一定是買通了市長，他們的計劃才得以實施。

PHR V **ˌsquare sth↔a'way** [usually passive] (*NAmE*) to put sth in order; to finish sth completely 歸整；辦妥；了結

ˌsquare 'off (against sb) (*NAmE*) to fight or prepare to fight sb（和某人）打鬥；擺好架勢（和某人）打鬥

ˌsquare 'up (to sb/sth) **1** to face a difficult situation and deal with it in a determined way 勇敢地面對；毅然面對 **2** to face sb as if you are going to fight them 氣勢洶洶地面對（某人）；擺好與（某人）打鬥的架勢

ˌsquare 'up (with sb) to pay money that you owe（向某人）付清欠款；（與某人）結清賬：*Can I leave you to square up with the waiter?* 我先走，你來和服務員結賬好不好？

'square sth with sth | **'square with sth** to make two ideas, facts or situations agree or combine well with each other; to agree or be CONSISTENT with another idea, fact or situation（使）與…一致，與…相符：*The interests of farmers need to be squared with those of consumers.* 農場主的利益需要同消費者的利益相一致。◇ *How can you **square this with your conscience**?* 做這樣的事你怎麼能問心無愧呢？◇ *Your theory does not square with the facts.* 你的理論與事實不符。

'square sth with sb to ask permission or check with sb that they approve of what you want to do 就…徵得…同意（或認可）：*I think I'll be able to come, but I'll square it with my parents first.* 我想我能來，不過我要先徵得我父母的同意。

■ ***adv.*** (only used *after* the verb 僅用於動詞後) directly; not at an angle 正對着地；逕直地 **SYN** **squarely**：*I looked her square in the face.* 我直視着她的臉。

IDM see FAIR *adv.*

'square-bashing *noun* [U] (*BrE, informal*) training for soldiers, which involves marching and holding weapons in different positions（士兵的）隊列訓練

ˌsquare 'bracket (*BrE*) (*NAmE* **bracket**) *noun* [usually pl.] either of a pair of marks, [ ], placed at the beginning and end of extra information in a text, especially comments made by an editor 方括號

squared /skweəd; *NAmE* skwerd/ *adj.* marked with squares; divided into squares 有正方形標記的；分成正方形形狀的：*squared paper* 方格紙

'square dance *noun* **1** a traditional dance from the US in which groups of four couples dance together, starting the dance by facing each other in a square 方形舞，方塊舞（美國傳統舞蹈，每組四對男女面對面圍成方形起舞）**2** a social event at which people dance square dances 方形舞會

square·head /'skweəhed; *NAmE* 'skwer-/ *noun* (*informal, especially NAmE*) **1** a person who is stupid or not able to do sth 笨蛋；無能的人 **2** an offensive word for a person from Germany, Holland or Scandinavia; a person whose family originally came from there 北歐佬（含冒犯意，指德國、荷蘭或斯堪的納維亞人）；北歐裔人

'square knot *noun* (*NAmE*) = REEF KNOT

square·ly /'skweəli; *NAmE* 'skwerli/ *adv.* (usually used *after* the verb 通常用於動詞後) **1** directly; not at an angle or to one side 正對着地；逕直地；不偏不倚地：*She looked at me squarely in the eye.* 她直直地看着我的眼睛。◇ *He stood squarely in front of them, blocking the entrance.* 他就對着他們站在那裏，擋住入口。◇ (*figurative*) *We must meet the challenge squarely* (= not try to avoid it). 我們必須正面迎接這一挑戰。**2** directly or exactly; without confusion 直接了當；明確無誤；毫不含糊地：*The responsibility for the crisis rests squarely on the government.* 這一危機的責任全在政府。**IDM** see FAIRLY

the ˌSquare 'Mile *noun* [sing.] (*BrE, informal*) a name used for the City of London, where there are many banks and financial businesses 倫敦市（銀行和金融業的聚集地）

ˌsquare 'root *noun* (*mathematics* 數) a number which when multiplied by itself produces a particular number 平方根：*The square root of 64 ($\sqrt{64}$) is 8 ($8 \times 8 = 64$).* * 64 的平方根是 8。➲ compare CUBE ROOT

squar·ish /'skweərɪʃ; *NAmE* 'skwer-/ *adj.* almost square in shape 近似方形的；略呈方形的

squash /skwɒʃ; *NAmE* skwɑːʃ; skwɔːʃ/ *verb, noun*

■ ***verb*** **1** [T] to press sth so that it becomes soft, damaged or flat, or changes shape 壓軟（或擠軟、壓壞、壓扁等）；把…壓（或擠）變形：**~ sth/sb** *The tomatoes at the bottom of the bag had been squashed.* 袋底的西紅柿給壓爛了。◇ **~ sth against sth** *He squashed his nose against the window.* 他趴在窗戶上，把鼻子都擠扁了。◇ **~ sth + adj.** *Squash your cans flat before recycling.* 把飲料罐壓扁了再送去回收。➲ picture at SQUEEZE **2** [I, T] to push sb/sth or yourself into a space that is too small（使）擠進；塞入：**+ adv./prep.** *We all squashed into the back of the car.* 我們都擠到了汽車後部。◇ **~ sb/sth + adv./prep.** *How many people are they going to try and squash into this bus?* 他們打算把多少人塞進這輛公共汽車？◇ *She was squashed between the door and the table.* 她被擠在門和桌子中間。**3** [T] **~ sth** to stop sth from continuing; to destroy sth because it is a problem for you 打斷；制止；去除；粉碎 **SYN** **quash**：*to squash a plan/an idea/a revolt* 使計劃落空；否定想法；鎮壓反叛◇ *If parents don't answer children's questions, their natural curiosity will be squashed.* 如果父母不回答孩子的問題，就會挫傷他們好奇的天性。◇ *The statement was an attempt to squash the rumours.* 這份聲明旨在闢謠。

PHR V **ˌsquash 'up (against sb/sth)** | **ˌsquash sb/sth↔'up (against sb/sth)** to move so close to sb/sth else that it is uncomfortable（使）擠在一起：*We squashed up to make room for Sue.* 我們擠了擠，給蘇騰出個地方。◇ *I was squashed up against the wall.* 我被擠得緊貼牆壁。

■ ***noun*** **1** (also *formal* **'squash rackets**) [U] a game for two players, played in a COURT surrounded by four walls, using RACKETS and a small rubber ball（軟式）牆網球；壁球：*a **squash court*** 壁球場◇ *to **play squash*** 打壁球 ➲ **VISUAL VOCAB** page V45 **2** [U, C] (*BrE*) a drink made with fruit juice, sugar and water 果汁飲料：*a glass of **orange/lemon squash*** 一杯橙汁 / 檸檬汁◇ *Two orange squashes, please.* 請來兩杯橙汁。**3** [C, U] (*pl.* **squash**, *BrE* also **squashes**) a type of vegetable that

S

grows on the ground. **Winter squash** have hard skin and orange flesh. **Summer squash** have soft yellow or green skin and white flesh. 南瓜小果（主要種類為筍瓜 winter squash 和西葫蘆 summer squash）➲ VISUAL VOCAB page V31 **4** [sing.] (*informal*) if sth is a **squash**, there is hardly enough room for everything or everyone to fit into a small space 擁擠的環境（或處所）：*It's a real squash with six of us in the car.* 我們六個人坐在這輛車上，可真夠擠的。

squashy /ˈskwɒʃi; *NAmE* ˈskwɑːʃi; ˈskwɔːʃi/ *adj.* soft and easy to crush or squeeze 軟而易壓壞（或壓扁）的

squat /skwɒt; *NAmE* skwɑːt/ *verb, noun, adj.*
■ *verb* (-tt-) **1** [I] **~ (down)** to sit on your heels with your knees bent up close to your body 蹲坐；蹲 **2** [I, T] **~ (sth)** to live in a building or on land which is not yours, without the owner's permission 偷住，擅自佔用（房子或地方）：*They ended up squatting in the empty houses on Oxford Road.* 他們落得在牛津路偷住空房的境地。
■ *noun* **1** (*especially BrE*) a building that people are living in without permission and without paying rent 偷住的房子：*to live in a squat* 擅自住在他人空着的房子裏 **2** a squatting position of the body 蹲坐；蹲 **3** = SQUAT THRUST
■ *adj.* short and wide or fat, in a way that is not attractive 矮而寬的；矮胖的：*a squat tower* 矮而粗的塔 ◇ *a squat muscular man with a shaven head* 剃光頭的矮壯男人

squat·ter /ˈskwɒtə(r); *NAmE* ˈskwɑːt-/ *noun* a person who is living in a building or on land without permission and without paying rent 擅自佔用他人房子（或土地）的人

ˈ**squat thrust** (also **squat**) *noun* an exercise in which you start with your hands on the floor and your knees bent, and then quickly move both legs backwards and forwards together 俯撐下蹲促腿，俯撐腿屈伸（雙手撐地下蹲後雙腿同時前後跳動）

squaw /skwɔː/ *noun* (*old use*) a word for a Native American woman that is now often considered offensive 美洲印第安女人（常含冒犯意）

squawk /skwɔːk/ *verb* **1** [I] (of birds 鳥) to make a loud sharp sound 發出刺耳的尖叫聲：*The parrot squawked and flew away.* 鸚鵡尖聲叫了叫飛走了。**2** [T, I] **(+ speech)** to speak or make a noise in a loud, sharp voice because you are angry, surprised, etc. 尖聲高叫；怒聲叫嚷；吃驚地尖聲說話：*'You did what?!' she squawked.* "你幹了什麼？！"她驚叫道。▸ **squawk** *noun*：*The bird gave a startled squawk.* 鳥發出嘎嘎的驚叫聲。◇ *a squawk of protest* 大聲的抗議

squeak /skwiːk/ *verb, noun*
■ *verb* **1** [I] to make a short high sound that is not very loud 短促而尖厲地叫；吱吱叫；嘎吱作響：*My new shoes squeak.* 我的新皮鞋走路嘎吱嘎吱響。◇ *The mouse ran away, squeaking with fear.* 那隻老鼠嚇得尖叫着溜了。◇ *One wheel makes a horrible squeaking noise.* 一個車輪發出討厭的吱吱聲。**2** [T, I] **(+ speech)** to speak in a very high voice, especially when you are nervous or excited（尤指緊張或激動時）尖聲說話：*'Let go of me!' he squeaked nervously.* "放開我！"他緊張地尖叫道。**3** [I] **+ adv./prep.** to only just manage to win sth, pass a test, etc. 勉強通過；僥幸成功；險勝：*We squeaked into the final with a goal in the last minute.* 我們靠最後一分鐘的入球僥幸進入決賽。
■ *noun* a short, high cry or sound, that is not usually very loud 短促而尖厲的叫聲；吱吱聲；尖叫聲 ➲ see also BUBBLE AND SQUEAK

squeak·er /ˈskwiːkə(r)/ *noun* (*informal, especially NAmE*) a competition or election won by only a small amount or likely to be won by only a small amount（很可能）以微弱優勢贏得的比賽（或選舉）；險勝的比賽（或選舉）

squeaky /ˈskwiːki/ *adj.* making a short, high sound; squeaking 發短促尖叫聲的；吱吱叫的；嘎吱作響的：*squeaky floorboards* 嘎吱作響的地板 ◇ *a high squeaky voice* 又高又尖的嗓子

ˌ**squeaky ˈclean** *adj.* (*informal*) **1** completely clean, and therefore attractive 非常乾淨的：*squeaky clean hair* 光潔的頭髮 **2** morally correct in every way; that cannot be criticized 品行完美的；一塵不染的；無可挑剔的

squeal /skwiːl/ *verb, noun*
■ *verb* **1** [I] to make a long, high sound 尖聲長叫；發出長而尖的聲音：*The pigs were squealing.* 豬尖叫着。◇ *The car squealed to a halt.* 汽車嘎的一聲停了下來。◇ *Children were running around squealing with excitement.* 孩子們跑來跑去，興奮地尖叫着。**2** [T, I] **(+ speech)** to speak in a very high voice, especially when you are excited or nervous（尤指激動或緊張時）尖聲說，高聲嚷着說：*'Don't!' she squealed.* "不要！"她尖叫道。**3** [I] **~ (on sb)** (*informal, disapproving*) to give information, especially to the police, about sth illegal that sb has done 告密；告發
■ *noun* a long high cry or sound 拖長的尖叫聲；長而尖的聲音：*a squeal of pain* 疼痛的尖叫 ◇ *a squeal of delight* 快樂的尖叫 ◇ *He stopped with a squeal of brakes.* 他嘎的一聲把車剎住了。

squeam·ish /ˈskwiːmɪʃ/ *adj.* **1** easily upset, or made to feel sick by unpleasant sights or situations, especially when the sight of blood is involved 易心煩意亂的；易惡心的；神經脆弱的 **2** not wanting to do sth that might be considered dishonest or immoral 誠實謹慎的；正派的 **3 the squeamish** *noun* [pl.] people who are squeamish 易心煩意亂的人；神經脆弱的人：*This movie is not for the squeamish.* 這部電影不是給神經脆弱的人看的。
▸ **squeam·ish·ness** *noun* [U]

squee·gee /ˈskwiːdʒiː/ *noun* **1** a tool with a rubber edge and a handle, used for removing water from smooth surfaces such as windows 橡皮刮水刷 ➲ VISUAL VOCAB page V20 **2** (also ˈ**squeegee mop**) a tool for washing floors, that has a long handle with two thick pieces of soft material at the end, which may be squeezed together using a piece of machinery attached to the handle 膠棉拖把 ➲ VISUAL VOCAB page V20

ˈ**squeegee merchant** *noun* (*BrE, informal*) a person who cleans the front windows of cars that have stopped in traffic and then asks the driver to pay them money, even if the driver did not want them to do it 要賴擦車仔（停車時不待車主允許便去擦擋風玻璃然後伸手要錢）

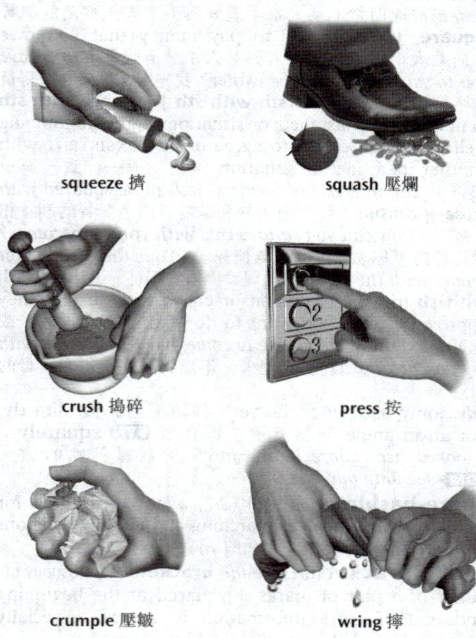

S

squeeze 🔑 /skwiːz/ *verb, noun*

■ ***verb***

▸ **PRESS WITH FINGERS** 用手指擠壓 **1** 🔑 [T, I] **~ (sth)** to press sth firmly, especially with your fingers 擠壓；捏：*to squeeze a tube of toothpaste* 擠牙膏 ◇ *to squeeze the trigger of a gun* (= to fire it) 扣動槍的扳機 ◇ *He squeezed her hand and smiled at her.* 他捏了捏她的手，衝她笑笑。◇ *Just take hold of the tube and squeeze.* 拿住軟管擠就行了。

▸ **GET LIQUID OUT** 擠出液體 **2** 🔑 [T] to get liquid out of sth by pressing or twisting it hard （從某物中）榨出，擠出，擰出：**~ sth out of/from sth** *to squeeze the juice from a lemon* 把一個檸檬的汁擠出來 ◇ (*figurative*) *She felt as if every drop of emotion had been squeezed from her.* 她覺得自己的激情似乎已經榨盡了。◇ **~ sth (out)** *He took off his wet clothes and squeezed the water out.* 他脱下濕衣服，擰乾了水。◇ *freshly squeezed orange juice* 現榨的橙汁 ◇ **~ sth + adj.** *Soak the cloth in warm water and then squeeze it dry.* 把衣服在温水裏泡一下，然後把它擰乾。

▸ **INTO/THROUGH SMALL SPACE** 進入／通過狹小的空間 **3** [T, I] to force sb/sth/yourself into or through a small space （使）擠入；擠過；塞入：**~ sb/sth into, through, etc. sth** *We managed to squeeze six people into the car.* 我們在那輛車上擠進了六個人。◇ (*figurative*) *We managed to squeeze a lot into a week* (= we did a lot of different things). 我們把很多事擠在一個星期裏做完了。◇ **~ into, through, etc. sth** *to squeeze into a tight dress/a parking space* 勉強穿上一件窄連衣裙；把車勉強開進一個停車位 ◇ *to squeeze through a gap in the hedge* 從籬笆上的豁口擠過去 ◇ **~ through, in, past, etc.** *If you move forward a little, I can squeeze past.* 你朝前挪一挪，我就可以擠過去了。

▸ **THREATEN** 威脅 **4** [T] **~ sb (for sth)** (*informal*) to get sth by putting pressure on sb, threatening them, etc. 向…勒索（或榨取）；逼迫…給：*He's squeezing me for £500.* 他逼我拿出 500 英鎊。

▸ **LIMIT MONEY** 限制金額 **5** [T] **~ sb/sth** to strictly limit or reduce the amount of money that sb/sth has or can use 嚴格限制，削減，緊縮（資金）：*High interest rates have squeezed the industry hard.* 高利率使這個行業舉步維艱。

IDM ˌ**squeeze sb ˈdry** to get as much money, information, etc. out of sb as you can 榨取某人所擁有的一切；榨乾某人的錢財；逼某人講出所知道的一切

PHR V ˌ**squeeze sb/sth↔ˈin** to give time to sb/sth, although you are very busy 擠出時間見某人（或做某事）：*If you come this afternoon the doctor will try to squeeze you in.* 你要是今天下午來，大夫可以擠時間給你看看。ˌ**squeeze sb/sth↔ˈout (of sth)** to prevent sb/sth from continuing to do sth or be in business 擠垮；把…擠出（某行業等）：*Supermarkets are squeezing out small shops.* 超市正擠垮小商店。ˌ**squeeze sth ˈout of/ˈfrom sb** to get sth by putting pressure on sb, threatening them, etc. 向…勒索（或榨取）；逼迫…給：*to squeeze a confession from a suspect* 逼迫嫌疑犯招供 ˌ**squeeze ˈup (against sb/sth)** | ˌ**squeeze sb↔ˈup (against sb/sth)** to move close to sb/sth so that you are pressed against them/it （使）擠緊：*There'll be enough room if we all squeeze up a little.* 大家稍稍擠一擠，地方就夠了。◇ *I sat squeezed up against the wall.* 我被擠得緊貼着牆坐着。

■ ***noun***

▸ **PRESSING WITH FINGERS** 用手指擠壓 **1** 🔑 [C, usually sing.] an act of pressing sth, usually with your hands 擠壓；捏：*He gave my hand a little squeeze.* 他輕輕捏了捏我的手。◇ *Give the tube another squeeze.* 把軟管再擠一下。

▸ **OF LIQUID** 液體 **2** 🔑 [C] a small amount of liquid that is produced by pressing sth 榨出的液體；小量擠出的汁：*a squeeze of lemon juice* 擠出的一點檸檬汁

▸ **IN SMALL SPACE** 在狹小空間裏 **3** [sing.] a situation where it is almost impossible for a number of people or things to fit into a small or restricted space 擠；塞：*It was **a tight squeeze** but we finally got everything into the case.* 箱子塞得很緊，不過我們最終還是把所有東西都裝進去了。◇ *Seven people in the car was a bit of a squeeze.* 那輛車坐了七個人是有點擠。

▸ **REDUCTION IN MONEY** 錢的減少 **4** [C, usually sing.] a reduction in the amount of money, jobs, etc. available; a difficult situation caused by this （可獲得的錢、工作崗位等的）減少，削減；拮据；經濟困難：*a **squeeze on** profits* 利潤的減少 ◇ *We're really **feeling the squeeze** since I lost my job.* 自從我丟了工作後，我們的確感覺到手頭拮据。◇ *a **credit squeeze*** 信貸緊縮

▸ **BOYFRIEND/GIRLFRIEND** 男／女朋友 **5** [sing.] (*informal, especially NAmE*) a boyfriend or girlfriend 男朋友；女朋友：*Who's his **main squeeze**?* 他最要好的女朋友是誰？

IDM **put the ˈsqueeze on sb (to do sth)** (*informal*) to put pressure on sb to act in a particular way; to make a situation difficult for sb 逼迫某人（做某事）；使某人處境困難

ˈ**squeeze box** *noun* (*informal*) an ACCORDION or a CONCERTINA （六角）手風琴

squelch /skweltʃ/ *verb* **1** [I] (**+ adv./prep.**) to make a wet sucking sound 發吧唧聲，發撲哧聲（如走在泥濘中似的）：*The mud squelched as I walked through it.* 我撲哧撲哧地穿過泥濘。◇ *Her wet shoes squelched at every step.* 她的鞋裏進了水，走一步吧唧一聲。◇ *We squelched across the muddy field.* 我們撲哧撲哧地穿過泥濘的田地。**2** [T] **~ sth** (*NAmE*) to stop sth from growing, increasing or developing 制止；壓制；遏制；限制 **SYN** **squash**：*to squelch a rumour/strike/fire* 制止謠言；鎮壓罷工；控制火勢的蔓延 ▸ **squelch** *noun* [usually sing.]：*He pulled his foot out of the mud with a squelch.* 他撲哧一聲從爛泥裏拔出腳來。**squelchy** *adj.*：*squelchy ground* 踩上去撲哧撲哧響的濕地

squib /skwɪb/ *noun* a small FIREWORK 小爆竹 **IDM** see DAMP *adj.*

squid /skwɪd/ *noun* [C, U] (*pl.* **squid** or **squids**) a sea creature that has a long soft body, eight arms and two TENTACLES (= long thin parts like arms) around its mouth, and that is sometimes used for food 槍烏賊；魷魚

squidgy /ˈskwɪdʒi/ *adj.* (*informal, especially BrE*) soft and wet, and easily SQUASHED 濕軟易擠壓的

squiffy /ˈskwɪfi/ *adj.* (*BrE, informal*) slightly drunk 微醉的

squig·gle /ˈskwɪɡl/ *noun* a line, for example in sb's HANDWRITING, that is drawn or written in a careless way with twists and curls in it （寫或畫的）彎彎曲曲的線條；潦草的筆跡：*Are these dots and squiggles supposed to be your signature?* 這一堆點點畫畫就是你的簽名嗎？▸ **squig·gly** /ˈskwɪɡli/ *adj.*

squil·lion /ˈskwɪljən/ *noun* (*informal*, often *humorous*) a very large number 無數；萬千：*a squillion-dollar budget* 天文數字的預算

squint /skwɪnt/ *verb, noun*

■ ***verb*** **1** [I, T] to look at sth with your eyes partly shut in order to keep out bright light or to see better 瞇着眼睛看：*to squint into the sun* 瞇起眼睛看太陽 ◇ *She was squinting through the keyhole.* 她瞇着眼從鎖眼往裏看。◇ *He squinted at the letter in his hand.* 他瞇着眼看手裏的信。◇ **~ sth** *When he squinted his eyes, he could just make out a house in the distance.* 他瞇着眼睛，只能隱約看見遠處有一所房子。**2** [I] (*BrE*) (of an eye 眼睛) to look in a different direction from the other eye 斜視：*His left eye squints a little.* 他左眼有點斜視。**3** [I] to have eyes that look in different directions （人）患斜視

■ ***noun*** **1** [C, usually sing.] a condition of the eye muscles which causes each eye to look in a different direction 斜視：*He was born with a squint.* 他生下來就斜視。**2** [sing.] (*BrE, informal*) a short look 瞥；瞟：***Have a squint** at this.* 你看看這個。

squire /ˈskwaɪə(r)/ *noun* **1** (also **Squire**) (in the past in England) a man of high social status who owned most of the land in a particular country area （舊時英格蘭的）鄉紳，大地主 **2** **Squire** (*BrE, informal* or *humorous*) used by a man as a friendly way of addressing another man （男子對另一男子的友好稱呼）先生：*What can I get you, Squire?* 您要點什麼，先生？**3** (in the past) a young man who was an assistant to a KNIGHT before becoming a knight himself （舊時騎士的）扈從

squire·archy /ˈskwaɪərɑːki; *NAmE* -ɑːrki/ *noun* [C+sing./pl. v.] (in the past in England) the people of high social

S

status who owned large areas of land, considered as a social or political group（英格蘭舊時的）地主階層，鄉紳階層

squirm /skwɜːm; *NAmE* skwɜːrm/ *verb* **1** [I] to move around a lot making small twisting movements, because you are nervous, uncomfortable, etc.（因緊張、不舒服等）動來動去，來回扭動，坐卧不寧 SYN **wriggle**：(+ **adv./prep.**) *The children were squirming restlessly in their seats.* 孩子們在位子上心神不定地動來動去。◇ **+ adj.** *Someone grabbed him but he managed to squirm free.* 有人抓住他，但他設法掙脫了。**2** [I] to feel great embarrassment or shame 十分尷尬；羞愧難當；無地自容：*It made him squirm to think how badly he'd messed up the interview.* 一想到自己把面試搞得有多糟，他就覺得無地自容。

squir·rel /ˈskwɪrəl; *NAmE* ˈskwɜːrəl/ *noun, verb*

■ **noun** a small animal with a long thick tail and red, grey or black fur. Squirrels eat nuts and live in trees. 松鼠 ➲ VISUAL VOCAB page V12 ➲ see also GROUND SQUIRREL

■ **verb** (**-ll-**, *especially US* **-l-**)

PHR V **ˌsquirrel sth↔aˈway** to hide or store sth so that it can be used later 儲藏；貯存：*She had money squirrelled away in various bank accounts.* 她把錢儲存在幾個不同的銀行賬戶上。

squir·rel·ly /ˈskwɪrəli; *NAmE* ˈskwɜːrəli/ *adj.* (*NAmE, informal*) **1** unable to keep still or be quiet 無法保持安靜的；靜不下來的：*squirrelly kids* 鬧哄哄的一些孩子 **2** crazy 瘋狂的；發瘋的

squirt /skwɜːt; *NAmE* skwɜːrt/ *verb, noun*

■ **verb** **1** [T, I] to force liquid, gas, etc. in a thin fast stream through a narrow opening; to be forced out of a narrow opening in this way（使）噴射；噴 SYN **spurt**：**~ sth** (**+ adv./prep.**) *The snake can squirt poison from a distance of a metre.* 這種蛇能把毒液噴射到一米遠處。◇ *I desperately squirted water on the flames.* 我拚命朝火上噴水。◇ (**+ adv./prep.**) *When I cut the lemon, juice squirted in my eye.* 我切檸檬時，檸檬汁濺到了我眼睛裏。**2** [T] to hit sb/sth with a stream of water, gas, etc.（用…）向…噴射 SYN **spray**：**~ sb/sth** (**with sth**) *The children were squirting each other with water from the hose.* 孩子們用軟水管相互噴水。◇ **~ sth** (**at sb**) *He squirted a water pistol at me* (= made the water come out of it). 他用玩具水槍朝我噴水。

■ **noun** **1** a thin, fast stream of liquid that comes out of a small opening 噴射出的一股液體 SYN **spray**：*a squirt of perfume* 噴出的一股香水 **2** (*informal, disapproving*) a word used to refer to a short, young or unimportant person that you do not like or that you find annoying 妄自尊大的年輕人；不知天高地厚的人

S

ˈsquirt gun *noun* (*NAmE*) = WATER PISTOL

squish /skwɪʃ/ *verb* (*informal*) **1** [I, T] **~** (**sth**) if sth soft **squishes** or **is squished**, it is crushed out of shape when it is pressed（被）壓壞，擠壞 **2** [I] to make a soft wet sucking sound 發吧唧聲；發吱嘎聲

squishy /ˈskwɪʃi/ *adj.* (*informal*) soft and wet 濕軟的；黏乎乎的

squit /skwɪt/ *noun* (*BrE*) **1** (*offensive*) a small or unimportant person 小人物；無名小卒；無足輕重的人 **2 the squits** (also **the squit·ters** /ˈskwɪtəz; *NAmE* -tərz/) [pl.] (*informal*) = DIARRHOEA

Sr (also **Snr**) (both *BrE*) (also **Sr.** *NAmE, BrE*) *abbr.* SENIOR 老；大 ➲ compare JR

Sri, **Srimati** = SHRI, SHRIMATI

SS *abbr.* **1** SAINTS：*SS Philip and James* 聖腓力和聖雅各 **2** /ˌes ˈes/ STEAMSHIP 汽船；輪船：*the SS Titanic* 泰坦尼克號輪船

SSN /ˌes es ˈen/ *abbr.* SOCIAL SECURITY NUMBER

St *abbr.* **1** (also **st**) (both *BrE*) (also **St.**, **st.** *NAmE, BrE*) (used in written addresses) Street（書寫地址時用）街，路：*Fleet St* 弗利特街（或譯艦隊街）**2 St.** (*NAmE*) State 州 **3** (also **St.** especially in *NAmE*) SAINT

st (*BrE*) (also **st.** *NAmE, BrE*) *abbr.* STONE (a British measurement of weight) 英石（英國重量單位）：*9st 2lb* * 9 英石 2 磅

stab /stæb/ *verb, noun*

■ **verb** (**-bb-**) **1** [T] **~ sb** to push a sharp, pointed object, especially a knife, into sb, killing or injuring them（用刀等銳器）刺，戳，捅：*He was stabbed to death in a racist attack.* 他遭到種族主義者的襲擊，被刺死了。◇ *She stabbed him in the arm with a screwdriver.* 她用螺絲刀在他胳膊上戳了一下。**2** [T, I] to make a short, aggressive or violent movement with a finger or pointed object（用手指或尖物）戳，捅，刺 SYN **jab, prod**：**~ sth** (**at/into/through sth**) *He stabbed his finger angrily at my chest.* 他氣呼呼地用指頭戳我的胸口。◇ **~ sb/sth** (**with sth**) *She stabbed the air with her fork.* 她用叉子在空中比畫。◇ **~ at/into/through sth** (*figurative*) *The pain stabbed at his chest.* 他胸部疼得像刀扎似的。

IDM **stab sb in the ˈback** to do or say sth that harms sb who trusts you 在某人背後捅刀子；陷害（或中傷）信任你的人 SYN **betray**

■ **noun** **1** an act of stabbing or trying to stab sb/sth; a wound caused by stabbing 刺；戳；捅；刺（或戳、捅）的傷口：*He received several stabs in the chest.* 他胸部被刺了幾刀。◇ *She died of a single* **stab wound** *to the heart.* 她因心臟被刺中一刀而身亡。**2** a sudden sharp pain or unpleasant feeling 突然一陣劇痛（或難受的感覺）：*She felt a sudden* **stab of pain** *in the chest.* 她胸部突然感到一陣劇痛。◇ ***a stab of guilt/fear/pity/jealousy, etc.*** 一陣內疚、恐懼、憐憫、嫉妒等 **3** [usually sing.] (*informal*) an attempt to do sth 嘗試；企圖：**~** (**at sth**) *He found the test difficult but nevertheless* ***made a good stab at it.*** 儘管他覺得試題很難，但還是盡力去做了。◇ **~** (**at doing sth**) *Countless people* ***have had a stab at*** *solving the riddle.* 無數人試圖解開這個謎。

IDM **a ˌstab in the ˈback** (*informal*) an act that harms sb, done by a person they thought was a friend 背後捅刀子；對信任你的人的陷害（或中傷）➲ more at DARK *n.*

stab·bing /ˈstæbɪŋ/ *noun, adj.*

■ **noun** an occasion when a person is stabbed with a knife or other pointed object 持刀（或其他利器）傷人事件：*a fatal stabbing* 持刀傷人致死事件

■ **adj.** [usually before noun] (of pain 疼痛) very sharp, sudden and strong 突然而劇烈的；刀刺似的

sta·bil·ity AW /stəˈbɪləti/ *noun* [U] the quality or state of being steady and not changing or being disturbed in any way (= the quality of being stable) 穩定（性）；穩固（性）：***political/economic/social stability*** 政治／經濟／社會穩定 ◇ *the stability of the dollar on the world's money markets* 美元在世界貨幣市場上的穩定性 ◇ *Being back with their family should provide emotional stability for the children.* 回到家人身邊會使兒童的情緒穩定下來。OPP **instability**

sta·bil·ize (*BrE* also **-ise**) AW /ˈsteɪbəlaɪz/ *verb* [I, T] to become or to make sth become firm, steady and unlikely to change; to make sth stable（使）穩定，穩固：*The patient's condition stabilized.* 患者的病情穩定下來。◇ **~ sth** *government measures to stabilize prices* 政府穩定物價的措施 ◇ *Doctors stabilized the patient's condition.* 大夫們使患者的病情穩定下來。➲ compare DESTABILIZE ▸ **sta·bil·iza·tion**, **-isa·tion** AW /ˌsteɪbəlaɪˈzeɪʃn; *NAmE* -ləˈz-/ *noun* [U]：*economic stabilization* 穩定經濟的工作

sta·bil·izer (*BrE* also **-iser**) /ˈsteɪbəlaɪzə(r)/ *noun* **1** a device that keeps sth steady, especially one that stops an aircraft or a ship from rolling to one side 穩定裝置；（飛機的）安定面；（船舶的）減搖裝置 **2 stabil·izers** [pl.] (*BrE*) (*NAmE* **ˈtraining wheels**) small wheels that are fitted at each side of the back wheel on a child's bicycle to stop it from falling over（兒童自行車後輪兩側的）穩定輪 ➲ VISUAL VOCAB page V51 **3** (*technical* 術語) a chemical that is sometimes added to food or paint to stop the various substances in it from becoming separate 穩定劑

stable ⚷ AW /ˈsteɪbl/ *adj., noun, verb*

> **WORD FAMILY**
> **stable** *adj.* (≠ unstable)
> **stability** *noun* (≠ instability)
> **stabilize** *verb*

■ **adj.** **1** ⚷ firmly fixed; not likely to move, change or fail 穩定的；穩固的；牢固

的 SYN **steady**： *stable prices* 穩定的價格 ◇ *a stable relationship* 穩定的關係 ◇ *This ladder doesn't seem very stable.* 這架梯子好像不太穩。◇ *The patient's condition is stable* (= it is not getting worse). 患者病情穩定。 **2** (of a person 人) calm and reasonable; not easily upset 穩重的；沉穩的；持重的 SYN **balanced**： *Mentally, she is not very stable.* 她的心理狀態不十分穩定。 **3** (*technical* 術語) (of a substance 物質) staying in the same chemical or ATOMIC state（化學狀態或原子狀態）穩定的： *chemically stable* 化學狀態穩定的 OPP **unstable** ▸ **sta·bly** /ˈsteɪbli/ *adv.*

■ *noun* **1** [C] a building in which horses are kept 馬廄 ➲ VISUAL VOCAB pages V2, V3 **2** (*BrE* also **stables**) [C+sing./pl. v.] an organization that keeps horses for a particular purpose（養馬作特定用途的）養馬場；馬房： (*BrE*) *a* ***riding/racing stables*** 騎用 / 賽馬養馬場 ◇ *His stables are near Oxford.* 他的養馬場在牛津附近。 **3** [C] a group of RACEHORSES owned or trained by the same person 統稱某人擁有（或訓練）的賽馬： *There have been just three winners from his stable this season.* 這個賽季他的馬只有三匹獲勝。 **4** [sing.] a group of people who work or trained in the same place; a group of products made by the same company（在同一地方工作或訓練的）一批人；（同一公司生產的）系列產品： *actors from the same stable* 同一劇團的演員 ◇ *the latest printer from the Epson stable* 愛普生系列最新款式打印機

■ *verb* ~ **sth** to put or keep a horse in a stable 使（馬）入廐；把（馬）拴在馬廐： *Where do you stable your pony?* 你的矮種馬養在哪兒？

ˈstable boy, **ˈstable girl** (*BrE* also **ˈstable lad**) *noun* a person who works in a stable 飼養馬的人；馬倌；馬夫

ˈstable companion *noun* = STABLEMATE

ˌstable ˈdoor (*BrE*) (*NAmE* **ˌDutch ˈdoor**) *noun* a door which is divided into two parts so that the top part can be left open while the bottom part is kept shut 馬廐式兩截門（上下兩部份可分別開關）

IDM **close, lock, etc. the stable door after the horse has ˈbolted** (*BrE*) (*US* **close, etc. the barn door after the horse has eˈscaped**) to try to prevent or avoid loss or damage when it is already too late to do so 馬跑了才去關廐門；賊走關門，為時已晚

stable·man /ˈsteɪblmæn/ *noun* (*pl.* **-men** /-men/) a person who works in a stable 飼養馬的人；馬倌；馬夫

stable·mate /ˈsteɪblmeɪt/ *noun* **1** a horse, especially a racing horse, from the same stable as another horse 同一馬廐的馬（尤指賽馬） **2** (also **ˈstable companion**) a person or product from the same organization as another person or product 同機構的人（或產品）；同事；同夥： *the 'Daily Mirror' newspaper and its Scottish stablemate the 'Daily Record'* 《每日鏡報》及其蘇格蘭姊妹報《每日紀事報》

stab·ling /ˈsteɪblɪŋ/ *noun* [U] buildings or space where horses can be kept 飼養馬的場所

stac·cato /stəˈkɑːtəʊ; *NAmE* -toʊ/ *adj.* **1** (*music* 音) with each note played separately in order to produce short, sharp sounds 斷音的；斷奏的： *staccato sounds* 斷音曲調 OPP **legato** **2** with short, sharp sounds 發不連貫爆發性聲音的；短促刺耳的： *a peculiar staccato voice* 特有的不連貫而且刺耳的嗓音 ◇ *staccato bursts of gunfire* 一陣陣劈里啪啦的槍炮聲 ▸ **stac·cato** *adv.*

stack /stæk/ *noun, verb*

■ *noun* **1** [C] a pile of sth, usually neatly arranged（通常指碼放整齊的）一疊，一摞，一堆： *a stack of books* 一摞書 ◇ *a stack hi-fi system* (= where a radio, CD player, etc. are arranged on top of each other) 一套高保真組合音響 ➲ see also HAYSTACK **2** [C] ~ (**of sth**) (*informal, especially BrE*) a large number or amount of sth; a lot of sth 大量；許多；一大堆： *stacks of money* 許多錢 ◇ *There's a stack of unopened mail waiting for you at the house.* 家裏有一大堆信等你拆呢。◇ *I've got stacks of work to do.* 我有一大堆活兒要做。 **3** [C] a tall CHIMNEY, especially on a factory（尤指工廠的）大煙囱 ➲ see also CHIMNEY STACK (2), SMOKESTACK (1) **4** **the stacks** [pl.] the part of a library, sometimes not open to the public, where books that are not often needed are stored（圖書館中貯藏使用頻率較低的書的）書庫 **5** [C] (*computing* 計) a way of storing information in a computer in which the most recently stored item is the first to be RETRIEVED (= found or got back) 存貯棧 **6** [C] (*geology* 地) a tall thin part of a CLIFF that has been separated from the land and stands on its own in the sea 海蝕柱 IDM see BLOW *v.*

■ *verb* **1** [T, I] ~ (**sth**) (**up**) to arrange objects neatly in a pile; to be arranged in this way（使）放成整齊的一疊（或一摞、一堆）： *to stack boxes* 把箱子摞起來 ◇ *logs stacked up against a wall* 靠牆碼放着的木頭 ◇ *Do these chairs stack?* 這些椅子能摞起來嗎？◇ *stacking chairs* 可摞在一起的椅子 **2** [T] ~ **sth** (**with sth**) to fill sth with piles of things 使成疊（或成摞、成堆）地放在…；使碼放在…： *They were busy stacking the shelves with goods.* 他們正忙着擺貨物上架呢。 **3** [I, T] ~ (**sth**) (**up**) if aircraft **stack** (**up**) or **are stacked** (**up**) over an airport, there are several flying around waiting for their turn to land（令飛機）分層盤旋等待着陸

IDM **ˈstack it** (*informal*) to fall over or off sth, especially in a way that makes you look silly and makes other people laugh（笨拙地）跌倒： *I tried a spin on the ice and stacked it.* 我試圖在冰面上旋轉，結果笨拙地跌倒了。

PHR V **ˌstack ˈup** **1** to keep increasing in quantity until there is a large pile, a long line, etc. 積聚成一大堆（或一長排等）： *Cars quickly stacked up behind the bus.* 公共汽車後面的汽車很快排成了長龍。 **2** (used especially in questions or in negatives 尤用於疑問句或否定句) to compare with sb/sth else; to be as good as sb/sth else（與其他人或事物）相比；比得上 SYN **measure up**： *Let's try him in the job and see how he stacks up.* 咱們讓他幹這活兒試試，看看他比別人幹得怎麼樣。◇ ~ **against sb/sth** *A mobile home simply doesn't stack up against a traditional house.* 活動房屋怎麼也比不上傳統的房屋。 **3** (used especially in negatives 尤用於否定句) to seem reasonable; to make sense 看來合理；講得通；合乎情理： *That can't be right. It just doesn't stack up.* 那不可能是對的，簡直不合情理。

stacked /stækt/ *adj.* [not usually before noun] if a surface is **stacked with** objects, there are large numbers or piles of them on it 放有大量…；放有成疊（或成摞、成堆）…： *a table stacked with glasses* 擺滿了玻璃杯的桌子

IDM **the cards/odds are stacked aˈgainst you** you are unlikely to succeed because the conditions are not good for you 形勢對你不利 **the cards/odds are stacked in your ˈfavour** you are likely to succeed because the conditions are good and you have an advantage 形勢對你有利

sta·dium /ˈsteɪdiəm/ *noun* (*pl.* **sta·diums** or **sta·dia** /ˈsteɪdiə/) a large sports ground surrounded by rows of seats and usually other buildings 體育場；運動場： *a* ***football/sports stadium*** 足球場；運動場 ◇ *an* ***all-seater stadium*** 全坐席體育場

staff /stɑːf; *NAmE* stæf/ *noun, verb*

■ *noun* **1** [C, usually sing., U] all the workers employed in an organization considered as a group 全體職工（或雇員）： *medical staff* 全體醫務人員 ◇ (*BrE*) *teaching staff* 全體教師 ◇ (*BrE*) *We have 20 part-time* ***members of staff.*** 我們有 20 名兼職員工。◇ (*NAmE*) ***staff members*** 職工 ◇ ***staff development/training*** 員工培訓 ◇ *a* ***staff restaurant/meeting*** 職工食堂 / 大會 ◇ (*especially BrE*) *a lawyer* ***on the staff*** *of the Worldwide Fund for Nature* 任職於世界自然基金會的律師 ➲ COLLOCATIONS at JOB ➲ see also GROUND STAFF **2** [sing.] (*NAmE*) the people who work at a school, college or university, but who do not teach students（大、中、小學的）管理人員，行政人員： *students, faculty and staff* 學生和教職人員 **3** [C+sing./pl. v.] a group of senior army officers who help a commanding officer（軍隊的）全體參謀人員： *a staff officer* 參謀 ➲ see also CHIEF OF STAFF, GENERAL STAFF **4** [C] (*old-fashioned* or *formal*) a long stick used as a support when walking or climbing, as a weapon, or as a symbol of authority 拐杖；棍棒；權杖 **5** (*especially NAmE*) (*BrE* also **stave**) [C] (*music* 音) a set of five lines on which music is written 五線譜 ➲ picture at MUSIC

IDM **the ˌstaff of ˈlife** (*literary*) a basic food, especially bread 主食；（尤指）麵包

S

■ *verb* [T, usually passive] **~ sth** to work in an institution, a company, etc.; to provide people to work there 在…工作；任職於；為…配備職員： *The advice centre is staffed entirely by volunteers.* 在咨詢中心工作的全部是志願者。◇ *The charity provided money to staff and equip two hospitals.* 這個慈善機構提供資金裝備了兩家醫院並配備了人員。◇ *a fully staffed department* 人員配備齊全的部門 ➲ see also OVERSTAFFED, SHORT-STAFFED, UNDERSTAFFED ▸ **staf·fing** *noun* [U]： *staffing levels* 人員配備情況

Grammar Point 語法說明

staff

- In *BrE* **staff** (sense 1) can be singular 在英式英語中，staff（第 1 義）可作單數： *a staff of ten* (= a group of ten people) 職工十人 or plural 亦可作複數： *I have ten staff working for me.* 我手下有十名職員。 If it is the subject of a verb, this verb is plural. 該詞如果作動詞的主語，動詞用複數： *The staff in this shop are very helpful.* 這家店的員工非常樂意幫忙。
- In *NAmE* **staff** (senses 1 and 2) can only be singular. 在美式英語中，staff（第 1 及第 2 義）只能作單數： *a staff of ten* (but not ~~*ten staff*~~) 職工十人（但不作 ten staff）◇ *The staff in this shop are very helpful.* 這家店的員工非常樂意幫忙。
- The plural form **staffs** is less frequent but is used in both *BrE* and *NAmE* to refer to more than one group of people. 複數形式 staffs 較少用，但在英式英語和美式英語中均指兩批或以上的職員： *the senator and his staff* (*singular*) 參議員及他的工作人員（單數）◇ *senators and their staffs* (*plural*) 參議員及他們各自的工作人員（複數）

staff·er /ˈstɑːfə(r); *NAmE* ˈstæf-/ *noun* (*NAmE*) a member of staff in a big organization 大機構的職員

ˈ**staff nurse** *noun* (in Britain) a qualified hospital nurse（英國）醫院護士

ˈ**staff officer** *noun* a military officer who helps an officer of very high rank or who works at a military HEADQUARTERS or a government department 參謀

staff·room /ˈstɑːfruːm; -rʊm; *NAmE* ˈstæf-/ *noun* (*BrE*) a room in a school where teachers can go when they are not teaching 教師室；教員室

S

ˈ**staff sergeant** *noun* a member of the army or the US AIR FORCE just above the rank of a SERGEANT 陸軍上士；（美國）空軍中士： *Staff Sergeant Bob Woods* 陸軍上士鮑勃・伍茲

stag /stæg/ *noun* a male DEER 雄鹿 ➲ compare BUCK *n.* (2), DOE, HART

IDM **go ˈstag** (*NAmE, old-fashioned, informal*) (of a man 男子) to go to a party without a partner 不帶女伴參加聚會

ˈ**stag beetle** *noun* a large insect with a mouth that has parts like the horns of an animal 鍬甲；鹿角甲蟲

stage 0⊶ /steɪdʒ/ *noun, verb*

■ *noun*

▸ **PERIOD/STATE 時期；狀態** **1** 0⊶ [C] a period or state that sth/sb passes through while developing or making progress（發展或進展的）時期，階段，狀態： *This technology is still in its* ***early stages.*** 這項技術還處於其早期開發狀態。◇ *The children are at different stages of development.* 這些孩子處於不同的成長階段。◇ *The product is at the design stage.* 產品處於設計階段。◇ *People tend to work hard* ***at this stage*** *of life.* 人在這個人生階段往往發奮努力。◇ ***At one stage*** *it looked as though they would win.* 有一段時間，他們好像大有獲勝的希望。◇ *Don't worry about the baby not wanting to leave you—it's* ***a stage they go through.*** 寶寶不肯離開你別擔心，他們總要經過這個階段。

▸ **PART OF PROCESS 程序** **2** 0⊶ [C] a separate part that a process, etc. is divided into 段；步；步驟 **SYN** **phase**： *We did the first stage of the trip by train.* 旅行的第一段我們乘的是火車。◇ *The police are building up a picture of the incident* ***stage by stage.*** 警方正逐步摸清那次事件的經過。◇ *The pay increase will be introduced* ***in stages*** (= not all at once). 加薪將分步進行。◇ *We can take the argument one stage further.* 我們可以把辯論更深入一步。➲ LANGUAGE BANK at PROCESS

▸ **THEATRE 劇場** **3** 0⊶ [C] a raised area, usually in a theatre, etc. where actors, dancers, etc. perform（多指劇場中的）舞台： *The audience threw flowers onto the stage.* 觀眾把鮮花拋向舞台。◇ *There were more than 50 people* ***on stage*** *in one scene.* 有一場戲中舞台上的人有 50 多個。◇ *They marched* ***off stage*** *to the sound of trumpets.* 在號角聲中，他們闊步退下舞台。➲ see also BACKSTAGE, OFFSTAGE, ONSTAGE **4** 0⊶ (often **the stage**) [sing.] the theatre and the world of acting as a form of entertainment 戲劇；戲劇表演；戲劇界： *His parents didn't want him to* ***go on the stage*** (= to be an actor). 他父母不想讓他當演員。◇ *She was a popular star of* ***stage and screen*** (= theatre and cinema/movies). 她是觀眾喜愛的舞台銀幕兩棲明星。

▸ **IN POLITICS 政界** **5** [sing.] an area of activity where important things happen, especially in politics（政治等活動的）領域；（政治）舞台： *She was forced to the centre of* ***the political stage.*** 她被推到了政治舞台的中心。◇ *Germany is playing a leading role on* ***the international stage.*** 德國在國際政治舞台上扮演着主導角色。➲ see also CENTRE STAGE

▸ **CARRIAGE 馬車** **6** [C] (*old-fashioned, informal*) = STAGECOACH ➲ see also LANDING STAGE

IDM **set the ˈstage for sth** to make it possible for sth to happen; to make sth likely to happen 使某事成為可能；為某事鋪平道路

■ *verb* **1 ~ sth** to organize and present a play or an event for people to see 上演；舉辦；舉行： *to stage a ceremony/an event/an exhibition* 舉行儀式／活動／展覽 ◇ *The local theatre group is staging a production of 'Hamlet'.* 當地劇團在上演《哈姆雷特》。◇ *Birmingham has bid to stage the next national athletics championships.* 伯明翰申辦下屆全國田徑錦標賽。 **2 ~ sth** to organize and take part in action that needs careful planning, especially as a public protest 組織；籌劃： *to* ***stage a strike/demonstration/march/protest*** 組織罷工／示威／遊行／抗議活動 **3 ~ sth** to make sth happen 使發生；使出現： *The dollar* ***staged a recovery*** *earlier today.* 今天早些時候，美元出現回升。◇ *After five years in retirement, he* ***staged a comeback*** *to international tennis.* 退役五年之後，他又復出國際網壇。

stage·coach /ˈsteɪdʒkəʊtʃ; *NAmE* -koʊtʃ/ *noun* a large CARRIAGE pulled by horses, that was used in the past to carry passengers, and often mail, along a regular route（舊時的）驛站馬車，公共馬車

stage·craft /ˈsteɪdʒkrɑːft; *NAmE* -kræft/ *noun* [U] skill in presenting plays in a theatre 舞台表演技巧；劇場表演藝術

ˈ**stage direction** *noun* a note in the text of a play telling actors when to come on to or leave the stage, what actions to perform, etc. 舞台指示（劇本中關於演員上下場、表演動作等的說明）

ˌ**stage ˈdoor** *noun* the entrance at the back of a theatre used by actors, staff, etc. 劇場後門（供演職人員進出）

ˈ**stage fright** *noun* [U] nervous feelings felt by performers before they appear in front of an audience 怯場（演員出場前的緊張不安）

stage·hand /ˈsteɪdʒhænd/ *noun* a person whose job is to help move SCENERY, etc. in a theatre, to prepare the stage for the next play or the next part of a play 舞台工作人員（負責移動佈景、準備道具等）

ˌ**stage ˈleft** *adv.* on the left side of a stage in a theatre, as seen by an actor facing the audience（演員面對觀眾時的）舞台左側

ˌ**stage-ˈmanage** *verb* **1 ~ sth** to act as stage manager for a performance in a theatre 擔任舞台監督 **2 ~ sth** to arrange and carefully plan an event that the public will see, especially in order to give a particular impression 精心安排，周密策劃（公共活動）

ˌ**stage ˈmanager** *noun* the person who is responsible for the stage, lights, SCENERY, etc. during the performance of a play in a theatre 舞台監督

ˈ**stage name** *noun* a name that an actor uses instead of his or her real name（演員的）藝名

ˌ**stage ˈright** *adv.* on the right side of a stage in a theatre, as seen by an actor facing the audience（演員面對觀眾時的）舞台右側

ˈ**stage-struck** *adj.* enjoying the theatre a lot and wishing very much to become an actor 醉心舞台渴望當演員的

ˌ**stage ˈwhisper** *noun* **1** words that are spoken quietly by an actor to the audience and that the other people on stage are not supposed to hear 低聲旁白（演員避開台上其他角色説給觀眾聽的） **2** words that are spoken quietly by sb but that they in fact want everyone to hear 故意讓所有人聽見的悄悄話：*'I knew this would happen,' she said in a stage whisper.* "我早知道會出這樣的事。"她輕聲說給所有人聽。

stagey = STAGY

stag·fla·tion /stægˈfleɪʃn/ *noun* [U] an economic situation where there is high INFLATION (= prices rising continuously) but no increase in the jobs that are available or in business activity 滯脹（高通脹與低就業率或經濟低迷並存）

stag·ger /ˈstægə(r)/ *verb* **1** [I, T] to walk with weak unsteady steps, as if you are about to fall 搖搖晃晃地走；蹣跚；踉蹌 SYN **totter**：(+ **adv./prep.**) *The injured woman staggered to her feet.* 受傷的女人搖搖晃晃地站起身來。◇ *He staggered home, drunk.* 他喝醉酒，踉蹌着回了家。◇ *We seem to stagger from one crisis to the next.* 我們彷彿在接連不斷的危機中舉步維艱。◇ (*figurative*) *The company is* **staggering under the weight** *of a £10m debt.* 公司在 1 000 萬英鎊債務的重壓下步履艱難。◇ **~ sth** *I managed to stagger the last few steps.* 我好不容易跌跌撞撞走了這最後幾步。 **2** [T] to shock or surprise sb very much 使震驚；使大吃一驚 SYN **amaze**：**~ sb** *Her remarks staggered me.* 她的話讓我震驚。◇ **it staggers sb that …** *It staggers me that the government is doing nothing about it.* 政府對此竟然袖手旁觀，我覺得不可思議。 **3** [T] **~ sth** to arrange for events that would normally happen at the same time to start or happen at different times 使交錯；使錯開：*There were so many runners that they had to stagger the start.* 參加賽跑的選手很多，他們不得不把起跑的時間錯開。▶ **stag·ger** *noun*：*to walk with a stagger* 蹣跚着走

stag·gered /ˈstægəd; *NAmE* -gərd/ *adj.* **1** [not before noun] **~ (at/by sth)** | **~ (to hear, learn, see, etc.)** very surprised and shocked at sth you are told or at sth that happens 震驚；大吃一驚 SYN **amazed**：*I was staggered at the amount of money the ring cost.* 那戒指那麼貴，我非常吃驚。 **2** arranged in such a way that not everything happens at the same time 交錯的；錯開的：*staggered working hours* (= people start and finish at different times) 互相交錯的工作時間

stag·ger·ing /ˈstægərɪŋ/ *adj.* (rather *informal*) so great, shocking or surprising that it is difficult to believe 令人難以相信的 SYN **astounding** ▶ **stag·ger·ing·ly** *adv.*：*staggeringly beautiful/expensive* 漂亮／昂貴得令人難以置信

sta·ging /ˈsteɪdʒɪŋ/ *noun* **1** [C, U] the way in which a play is produced and presented on stage 演出形式；演出風格：*a modern staging of 'King Lear'* 以現代風格演出的《李爾王》 **2** [U] a temporary platform used for standing or working on 臨時工作台（或工作架）

ˈ**staging post** *noun* a place where people, planes, ships, etc. regularly stop during a long journey 中途站（或機場、停靠碼頭）

stag·nant /ˈstægnənt/ *adj.* **1** **stagnant** water or air is not moving and therefore smells unpleasant（水或空氣）不流動而污濁的 **2** not developing, growing or changing 停滯的；不發展的；無變化的 SYN **static**：*a stagnant economy* 停滯的經濟

stag·nate /stægˈneɪt; *NAmE* ˈstægneɪt/ *verb* **1** [I] to stop developing or making progress 停滯；不發展；不進步：*Profits have stagnated.* 利潤原地踏步。◇ *I feel I'm stagnating in this job.* 我覺得，幹這份工作我沒有長進。 **2** [I] to be or become stagnant 因不流動而變得污濁：*The water in the pond was stagnating.* 池塘裏的水逐漸變成了死水。▶ **stag·na·tion** /stægˈneɪʃn/ *noun* [U]：*a period of economic stagnation* 經濟停滯時期

ˈ**stag night** *noun* [usually sing.] **1** (*BrE*) the night before a man's wedding, often spent with his male friends 男子婚前夜（常與男性朋友一同度過） **2** (also ˈ**stag party**) (both *BrE*) (*NAmE* ˈ**bachelor party**) a party that a man has with his male friends just before he gets married, often the night before 男子婚前派對（只招待男性朋友） ➲ compare HEN PARTY

stagy (also **stagey**) /ˈsteɪdʒi/ *adj.* not natural, as if it is being acted by sb in a play 不自然的；做作的；演戲似的

staid /steɪd/ *adj.* (**staid·er**, **staid·est**) not amusing or interesting; boring and old-fashioned 沒意思的；古板的；一本正經的

stain /steɪn/ *verb*, *noun*

■ ***verb*** **1** [T, I] to leave a mark that is difficult to remove on sth; to be marked in this way （被）玷污；留下污漬：**~ (sth) (with sth)** *I hope it doesn't stain the carpet.* 希望它別把地毯弄髒。◇ *This carpet stains easily.* 這塊地毯不耐髒。◇ **~ sth + adj.** *The juice from the berries stained their fingers red.* 漿果汁把他們的手指染成了紅色。 **2** [T] to change the colour of sth using a coloured liquid 給…染色（或着色）：**~ sth** *to stain wood* 給木料上色 ◇ *Stain the specimen before looking at it under the microscope.* 先把標本染色，再放到顯微鏡下觀察。◇ **~ sth + adj.** *They stained the floors dark brown.* 他們把地板塗成了深棕色。 **3** [T] **~ sth** (*formal*) to damage the opinion that people have of sth 玷污，敗壞（名聲）：*The events had stained the city's reputation unfairly.* 這些事件使該市背上了不應有的惡名。

■ ***noun*** **1** [C] a dirty mark on sth, that is difficult to remove 污點；污漬：***a blood/a coffee/an ink, etc. stain*** 血跡、咖啡漬、墨痕等 ◇ ***stubborn stains*** (= that are very difficult to remove) 頑固的污漬 ◇ *How can I get this stain out?* 我怎麼才能把這點污漬除去？◇ *The carpet has been treated so that it is* ***stain-resistant*** (= it does not stain easily). 這地毯已經過處理，不易掛污。➲ SYNONYMS at MARK **2** [U, C] a liquid used for changing the colour of wood or cloth 染色劑；着色劑 **3** [sing.] **a ~ on sth** (*formal*) something that damages a person's reputation, so that people think badly of them（名聲上的）污點

stained /steɪnd/ *adj.* (often in compounds 常構成複合詞) covered with stains or marked with a stain 滿是污痕的；沾有污漬的：*My dress was stained.* 我的連衣裙弄上了污漬。◇ *paint-stained jeans* 沾滿油漆的牛仔褲 ➲ SYNONYMS at DIRTY

ˌ**stained ˈglass** *noun* [U] pieces of coloured glass that are put together to make windows, especially in churches 彩色玻璃

stain·less steel /ˌsteɪnləs ˈstiːl/ *noun* [U] a type of steel that does not RUST (= change colour) 不銹鋼

stair 0➡ /steə(r); *NAmE* ster/ *noun*

1 0➡ **stairs** [pl.] a set of steps built between two floors inside a building 樓梯：*We had to carry the piano up three* ***flights of stairs***. 我們不得不抬着鋼琴上了三段樓梯。◇ *The children ran* ***up/down the stairs***. 孩子們跑上／跑下樓去。◇ ***at the bottom/top of the stairs*** 在樓梯下端／頂端 ◇ *He remembered passing her* ***on the stairs***. 他記得在樓梯上與她擦肩而過。➲ see also DOWNSTAIRS, UPSTAIRS **2** 0➡ [C] one of the steps in a set of stairs 梯級：*How many stairs are there up to the second floor?* 上到第三層一共有多少磴樓梯？➲ picture at STAIRCASE **3** [sing.] (*literary*) = STAIRCASE：*The house had a panelled hall and a fine oak stair.* 房子的門廳裝有鑲板牆裙，樓梯是用高級櫟木建造的。▶ **stair** *adj.* [only before noun]：*the stair carpet* 樓梯地毯

IDM **below ˈstairs** (*old-fashioned*, *BrE*) in the part of a house where the servants lived in the past（舊時）在僕人住的地方

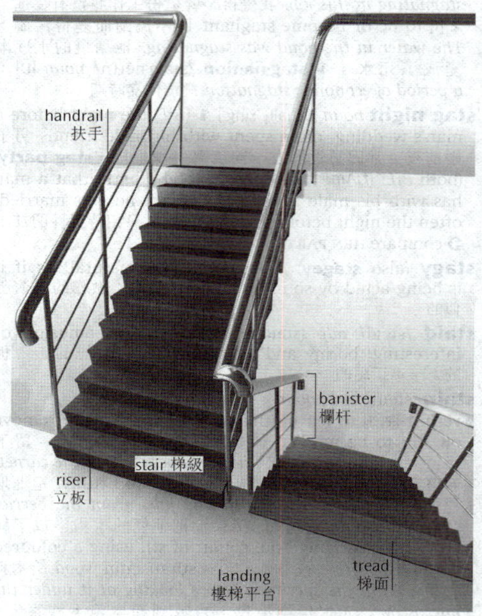

stair·case /ˈsteəkeɪs; *NAmE* ˈsterk-/ *noun* a set of stairs inside a building including the posts and rails (= BANISTERS) that are fixed at the side （建築物內的）樓梯：*a marble/stone/wooden staircase* 大理石／石／木樓梯 ➲ see also SPIRAL STAIRCASE

stair·lift /ˈsteəlɪft; *NAmE* ˈsterl-/ *noun* a piece of equipment in the form of a seat that sb can sit on to be moved up and down stairs, used by people who find it difficult to walk up and down stairs without help 座椅式升降器（供無法步行上下樓的人使用）

stair·way /ˈsteəweɪ; *NAmE* ˈsterweɪ/ *noun* a set of stairs inside or outside a building （建築物內或外的）樓梯，階梯

stair·well /ˈsteəwel; *NAmE* ˈsterwel/ *noun* [usually sing.] the space in a building in which the stairs are built 樓梯井（建築物內樓梯佔用的空間）

S

stake /steɪk/ *noun, verb*

■ ***noun*** **1** [C] a wooden or metal post that is pointed at one end and pushed into the ground in order to support sth, mark a particular place, etc. 樁；標樁；籬笆樁 ➲ **VISUAL VOCAB** page V19 **2 the stake** [sing.] a wooden post that sb could be tied to in former times before being burnt to death (= killed by fire) as a punishment 火刑柱：*Joan of Arc was* ***burnt at the stake.*** 聖女貞德被處以火刑。 **3** [C] money that sb invests in a company 股本；股份：*a 20% stake in the business* 那家公司 20% 的股份 **4** [sing.] **~ in sth** an important part or share in a business, plan, etc. that is important to you and that you want to be successful （在公司、計劃等中的）重大利益，重大利害關係：*She has a personal stake in the success of the play.* 這齣戲成功與否對她個人有重大利害關係。◇ *Many young people no longer feel they have a stake in society.* 很多年輕人不再覺得他們與社會休戚相關。 **5** [C] something that you risk losing, especially money, when you try to predict the result of a race, game, etc., or when you are involved in an activity that can succeed or fail 賭注：*How much was the stake* (= how much did you bet)? 下了多少注？◇ *They were playing cards for* ***high stakes*** (= a lot of money). 他們當時正在打撲克，賭注很高。 **6 stakes** [pl.] the money that is paid to the winners in horse racing 賽馬獎金 **7 stakes** [U] used in the names of some horse races （用於某些賽馬賽事的名稱）…賽

IDM **at ˈstake** that can be won or lost, depending on the success of a particular action 成敗難料；得失都可能；有風險：*We cannot afford to take risks when people's lives are at stake.* 在人命交關的事情上，不容我們有閃失。◇ *The prize at stake is a place in the final.* 這次如果獲勝，便能進入決賽。 **go to the ˈstake over/for sth** to be prepared to do anything in order to defend your opinions or beliefs 為堅持自己的觀點（或信仰）甘冒一切危險；為維護自己的觀點（或信仰）不惜赴湯蹈火 **in the … stakes** used to say how much of a particular quality a person has, as if they were in a competition in which some people are more successful than others （評論一個人的某種品質高或低）要是比…的話，論…：*John doesn't do too well in the personality stakes.* 論人格魅力，約翰很一般。 ➲ more at UP *v.*

■ ***verb*** **1 ~ sth (on sth)** to risk money or sth important on the result of sth （就某事）以…打賭，拿…冒險 **SYN** **bet**：*He staked £25 on the favourite* (= for example, in horse racing). 他在那匹眾人看好的馬上押了 25 英鎊。◇ *She staked her political career on tax reform, and lost.* 她把自己的政治前程押在稅制改革上，結果賭輸了。◇ *That's him over there—I'd* ***stake my life on it*** (= I am completely confident). 就是那邊那個人，我敢拿腦袋打賭。 **2 ~ sth (up)** to support sth with a stake (1) 用樁支撐：*to stake newly planted trees* 用木樁支撐新植的樹

IDM **stake (out) a/your ˈclaim (to/for/on sth)** to say or show publicly that you think sth should be yours 公開宣佈自己（對某物）的擁有權；向公眾表示某物應屬於自己：*Adams staked his claim for a place in the Olympic team with his easy win yesterday.* 亞當斯昨天輕鬆獲勝，這無異於告訴人們奧運代表隊中應有他的位置。

PHR V **ˌstake sth↔ˈout 1** to clearly mark the limits of sth that you claim is yours 清楚地界定自認為屬於自己的東西 **2** to state your opinion, position, etc. on sth very clearly 明確闡述自己的看法（或立場等）：*The President staked out his position on the issue.* 總統明確闡述了他在這個問題上的立場。 **3** to watch a place secretly, especially for signs of illegal activity 監視：*Detectives had been staking out the house for several weeks.* 偵探們已對這所房子監視了幾個星期。 ➲ related noun STAKE-OUT

stake·hold·er /ˈsteɪkhəʊldə(r); *NAmE* -hoʊ-/ *noun* **1** a person or company that is involved in a particular organization, project, system, etc., especially because they have invested money in it （某組織、工程、體系等的）參與人，參與方；有權益關係者：*The government has said it wants to create a* ***stakeholder economy*** *in which all members of society feel that they have an interest in its success.* 政府表示希望建立一種人人參與的經濟模式，讓社會全體成員覺得其繁榮將給每個人帶來利益。 **2** a person who holds all the bets placed on a game or race and who pays the money to the winner 賭金保管人

ˈstake-out *noun* a situation in which police watch a building secretly to find evidence of illegal activities 警察監視

stal·ac·tite /ˈstæləktaɪt; *NAmE* stəˈlæktaɪt/ *noun* a long pointed piece of rock hanging down from the roof of a CAVE (= a hollow place underground), formed over a long period of time as water containing LIME runs off the roof 鐘乳石（向下懸垂）

stal·ag·mite /ˈstæləgmaɪt; *NAmE* stəˈlæg-/ *noun* a piece of rock pointing upwards from the floor of a CAVE (= a hollow place underground), that is formed over a long period of time from drops of water containing LIME that fall from the roof 石筍（向上生長）

stale /steɪl/ *adj.* **1** (of food, especially bread and cake 食物，尤指麵包和糕點) no longer fresh and therefore unpleasant to eat 不新鮮的 **2** (of air, smoke, etc. 空氣、煙等) no longer fresh; smelling unpleasant 不新鮮的；（空氣）污濁的；（煙味）難聞的：*stale cigarette smoke* 難聞的煙味兒 ◇ *stale sweat* 汗臭味 **3** something that is **stale** has been said or done too many times before and is no longer interesting or exciting 陳腐的；沒有新意的；老掉牙的：*stale jokes* 老掉牙的笑話 ◇ *Their marriage* ***had gone stale.*** 他們的婚姻已了無熱情。 **4** a person who is **stale** has done the same thing for too long and so is unable to do it well or produce any new ideas （因持續做某事時間太長）厭倦的，膩煩的：*After*

ten years in the job, she felt stale and needed a change. 在那個崗位幹了十年之後，她覺得膩了，需要換換工作。
▶ **stale·ness** *noun* [U]

stale·mate /ˈsteɪlmeɪt/ *noun* **1** [U, C, usually sing.] a disagreement or a situation in a competition in which neither side is able to win or make any progress（辯論或競賽中出現的）僵局，僵持局面 SYN **impasse**：*The talks ended in (a) stalemate.* 談判陷入僵局，無果而終。 **2** [U, sing.] (in CHESS 國際象棋) a situation in which a player cannot successfully move any of their pieces and the game ends without a winner 僵局；和棋 ➲ compare CHECKMATE (1)

Sta·lin·ism /ˈstɑːlɪnɪzəm/ *noun* [U] the policies and beliefs of Stalin, especially that the Communist party should be the only party and that the central government should control the whole political and economic system 斯大林主義（尤指共產黨一黨制及中央政府掌控政治經濟）▶ **Sta·lin·ist** *adj., noun*

stalk /stɔːk/ *noun, verb*
■ *noun* **1** a thin STEM that supports a leaf, flower or fruit and joins it to another part of the plant or tree; the main STEM of a plant（葉）柄；（花）梗；（果實的）柄；（植物的）莖，稈：*flowers on long stalks* 長莖上的花 ◇ *celery stalks* 芹菜莖 ◇ *He ate the apple, stalk and all.* 他把那個蘋果吃了個乾淨，連梗都沒剩下。➲ VISUAL VOCAB pages V11, V30 **2** a long thin structure that supports sth, especially an organ in some animals, and joins it on to another part 柄；（動物的）肉柄，肉莖：*Crabs have eyes on stalks.* 螃蟹的眼睛長在肉柄上。
■ *verb* **1** [T, I] ~ (**sth/sb**) to move slowly and quietly towards an animal or a person, in order to kill, catch or harm it or them 偷偷接近，潛近（獵物或人）：*The lion was stalking a zebra.* 獅子偷偷接近斑馬。◇ *He stalked his victim as she walked home, before attacking and robbing her.* 她步行回家時，他偷偷地接近然後下手襲擊，並且搶劫了她。 **2** [T] ~ **sb** to illegally follow and watch sb over a long period of time, in a way that is annoying or frightening（非法）跟踪，盯梢：*She claimed that he had been stalking her over a period of three years.* 她聲稱，三年來他一直在盯她的梢。 **3** [I] + **adv./prep.** to walk in an angry or proud way 怒沖沖地走；趾高氣揚地走：*He stalked off without a word.* 他一言未發，怒沖沖地走了。 **4** [T, I] ~ (**sth**) to move through a place in an unpleasant or threatening way 令人厭惡地穿過；威脅地通過：*The gunmen stalked the building, looking for victims.* 這些持槍歹徒兇神惡煞地打樓裏走過，尋找襲擊的目標。◇ (*figurative*) *Fear stalks the streets of the city at night.* 夜間，這座城市的大街小巷籠罩着恐怖氣氛。

stalk·er /ˈstɔːkə(r)/ *noun* **1** a person who follows and watches another person over a long period of time in a way that is annoying or frightening 跟踪者；盯梢者 **2** a person who follows an animal quietly and slowly, especially in order to kill or capture it 悄悄接近獵物的獵人

stalk·ing /ˈstɔːkɪŋ/ *noun* [U] the crime of following and watching sb over a long period of time in a way that is annoying or frightening 跟踪罪

ˈstalking horse *noun* [sing.] **1** a person or thing that is used to hide the real purpose of a particular course of action 用以掩人耳目的人（或物）；用以掩蔽的事物 **2** a politician who competes against the leader of their party in order to see how much support the leader has; a stronger candidate can then compete against the leader more seriously（為試探對手支持率而推出的）掩護性候選人

stall /stɔːl/ *noun, verb*
■ *noun* **1** [C] a table or small shop with an open front that people sell things from, especially at a market 貨攤，攤位，售貨亭（尤指集市上的）SYN **stand**：*a market stall* 集市上的貨攤 ➲ VISUAL VOCAB page V3 ➲ see also BOOKSTALL **2** [C] a section inside a farm building that is large enough for one animal to be kept in 牲畜棚；馬廄；牛棚 **3** [C] (*especially NAmE*) a small area in a room, surrounded by glass, walls, etc., that contains a shower or toilet（房間內的）小隔間，淋浴室，洗手間 **4 the stalls** (also **the ˈorchestra stalls**) (both *BrE*) [pl.] (*NAmE* **the orchestra** [sing.]) the seats that are nearest to the stage in a theatre（劇場的）正廳前排座位：*the front row of the stalls* 正廳第一排 **5** [C, usually pl.] the seats at the front of a church where the CHOIR (= singers) and priests sit（教堂內）唱詩班和牧師的座位 **6** [C, usually sing.] a situation in which a vehicle's engine suddenly stops because it is not getting enough power（車輛發動機的）熄火；（車輛的）拋錨 **7** [C, usually sing.] a situation in which an aircraft loses speed and goes steeply downwards（飛機的）失速
■ *verb* **1** [I, T] (of a vehicle or an engine 車輛或發動機) to stop suddenly because of a lack of power or speed; to make a vehicle or engine do this（使）熄火，拋錨：*The car stalled and refused to start again.* 汽車熄火打不着了。◇ ~ **sth** *I stalled the car three times during my driving test.* 我考駕照時車子熄了三次火。 **2** [I] ~ (**on/over sth**) to try to avoid doing sth or answering a question so that you have more time 故意拖延（以贏得時間）：*They are still stalling on the deal.* 他們仍在拖時間，而不急於達成協議。◇ *'What do you mean?' she asked, **stalling for time**.* "你這是什麼意思？" 她問，故意拖延着時間。 **3** [T] ~ **sb** to make sb wait so that you have more time to do sth 拖住（以贏得時間做某事）：*See if you can stall her while I finish searching her office.* 你看能不能拖住她，我好把她的辦公室搜查完。 **4** [T, I] ~ (**sth**) to stop sth from happening until a later date; to stop making progress 暫緩；擱置；停頓：*attempts to revive the stalled peace plan* 旨在重新啟動擱置了的和平計劃的努力 ◇ *Discussions have once again stalled.* 討論再次停頓下來。

stall·hold·er /ˈstɔːlhəʊldə(r); *NAmE* -hoʊ-/ *noun* (*BrE*) a person who sells things from a stall in a market, etc. 攤販；貨攤主

stal·lion /ˈstæliən/ *noun* a fully grown male horse, especially one that is used for breeding 牡馬；（尤指）種馬 ➲ compare COLT (1), GELDING, MARE

stal·wart /ˈstɔːlwət; *NAmE* -wərt/ *noun, adj.*
■ *noun* ~ (**of sth**) a loyal supporter who does a lot of work for an organization, especially a political party（政黨等組織的）忠誠擁護者，堅定分子
■ *adj.* [usually before noun] **1** loyal and able to be relied on, even in a difficult situation 忠誠的；忠實的 SYN **faithful**：*stalwart supporters* 忠實的擁護者 **2** (*formal*) physically strong 健壯的；強壯的

sta·men /ˈsteɪmən/ *noun* (*technical* 術語) a small thin male part in the middle of a flower that produces POLLEN and is made up of a STALK supporting an ANTHER. The centre of each flower usually has several stamens. 雄蕊 ➲ VISUAL VOCAB page V11

stam·ina /ˈstæmɪnə/ *noun* [U] the physical or mental strength that enables you to do sth difficult for long periods of time 耐力；耐性；持久力：*It takes a lot of stamina to run a marathon.* 跑馬拉松需要很大的耐力。 ➲ COLLOCATIONS at DIET

stam·mer /ˈstæmə(r)/ *verb, noun*
■ *verb* [I, T] to speak with difficulty, repeating sounds or words and often stopping, before saying things correctly 口吃；結結巴巴地說 SYN **stutter**：*Many children stammer but grow out of it.* 很多小孩口吃，但長大後就改過來了。◇ + **speech** *'W-w-what?' he stammered.* "什…什…什麼？" 他結巴着說。◇ ~ **sth** (**out**) *She was barely able to stammer out a description of her attacker.* 她只能勉強結結巴巴地說一說襲擊她的人是什麼模樣。
▶ **stam·mer·er** *noun*
■ *noun* [sing.] a problem that sb has in speaking in which they repeat sounds or words or often pause before saying things correctly 口吃；結巴

stamp 0‑ /stæmp/ *noun, verb*
■ *noun*
▸ ON LETTER/PACKAGE 信函；包裹 **1** 0‑ (also *formal* **ˈpostage stamp**) [C] a small piece of paper with a design on it that you buy and stick on an envelope or a package before you post it 郵票：*a 28p stamp* 一張 28 便士的郵票 ◇ *Could I have three first-class stamps, please?* 請給我拿三張第一類郵件的郵票。◇ *He has been collecting stamps since he was eight.* 他從八歲開始集郵。◇ *a stamp album* 集郵冊 ➲ VISUAL VOCAB page V41

S

▸ **PRINTING TOOL** 印章 **2** 🔑 [C] a tool for printing the date or a design or mark onto a surface 印；章；戳：*a date stamp* 日期戳 ➲ see also RUBBER STAMP
▸ **PRINTED DESIGN/WORDS** 印記 **3** 🔑 [C] a design or words made by stamping sth onto a surface 印記；戳記：*The passports, with the visa stamps, were waiting at the embassy.* 那些護照都加蓋了簽證章，在大使館等待領取。◇ (*figurative*) *The project has the government's* ***stamp of approval****.* 工程已獲得政府批准。
▸ **PROOF OF PAYMENT** 付款證明 **4** [C] a small piece of paper with a design on it, stuck on a document to show that a particular amount of money has been paid 印花：*a TV licence stamp* 電視收視許可證印花
▸ **CHARACTER/QUALITY** 特徵；特性 **5** [sing.] **~ (of sth)** (*formal*) the mark or sign of a particular quality or person 特徵；痕跡；烙印：*All his work* ***bears the stamp*** *of authority.* 他的一切工作都具有權威性。 **6** [sing.] (*formal*) a kind or class, especially of people 類型，種類（尤指人）：*men of a different stamp* 另一類人
▸ **OF FOOT** 腳 **7** [sing.] an act or sound of stamping the foot 跺腳（聲）；踩踏（聲）：*The stamp of hoofs alerted Isabel.* 馬蹄聲引起了伊莎貝爾的警覺。
■ ***verb***
▸ **FOOT** 腳 **1** 🔑 [T, I] **~ (sth)** to put your foot down heavily and noisily on the ground 跺（腳）；重踩；重踏：*I tried* ***stamping my feet*** *to keep warm.* 我跺了一陣腳想暖和暖和。◇ *Sam* ***stamped his foot*** *in anger.* 薩姆氣得直跺腳。◇ *The audience were stamping and cheering.* 觀眾又是跺腳，又是歡呼。
▸ **WALK** 走 **2** [I] **+ adv./prep.** to walk with loud heavy steps 邁着重重的步伐走 SYN **stomp**：*She turned and stamped out of the room.* 她扭身咚咚地走出了房間。
▸ **PRINT DESIGN/WORDS** 蓋印／章 **3** 🔑 [T, often passive] to print letters, words, a design, etc. onto sth using a special tool 在…上蓋（字樣或圖案等）；把（字樣或圖案等）蓋在…上：**~ A (with B)** *The box was stamped with the maker's name.* 盒子上蓋有製作者的印章。◇ *Wait here to have your passport stamped.* 請在這裏等候給護照蓋章。◇ **~ B on A** *I'll stamp the company name on your cheque.* 我來給你的支票蓋上公司的章。◇ *The maker's name was stamped in gold on the box.* 盒子上蓋有製作者的金字印章。➲ see also RUBBER-STAMP, STAMP STH ON STH at STAMP *v.*
▸ **SHOW FEELING/QUALITY** 顯露感情／性質 **4** [T, usually passive] to make a feeling show clearly on sb's face, in their actions, etc. 顯示出（感情）：**~ A with B** *Their faces were stamped with hostility.* 他們的神情充滿敵意。◇ **~ B over, across, etc. A** *The crime had revenge stamped all over it.* 從各方面看這次犯罪都是復仇行為。 **5** [T] **~ sb as sth** to show that sb has a particular quality 表明（某人）是…：*Her success has stamped her as one of the country's top riders.* 她的成績表明她是全國最出色的騎手之一。
▸ **ON LETTER/PACKAGE** 信函；包裹 **6** [T, usually passive] **~ sth** to stick a stamp on a letter or package 在…上貼郵票
▸ **CUT OUT OBJECT** 衝壓 **7** [T] **~ sth (out) (of/from sth)** to cut and shape an object from a piece of metal or plastic using a special machine or tool 衝壓
PHR V **'stamp on sth** **1** to put your foot down with force on sth 用力踩：*The child stamped on the spider.* 小孩踩了那隻蜘蛛一腳。 **2** to stop sth from happening or stop sb from doing sth, especially by using force or authority 壓制；鎮壓：*All attempts at modernization were stamped on by senior officials.* 旨在實現現代化的努力統統受到高級官員的壓制。 **'stamp sth on sth** to make sth have an important effect or influence on sth 在…上打上…印記；把…銘刻在…中：*She stamped her own interpretation on the role.* 她給那個角色注入了自己的詮釋。 **,stamp sth↔'out** **1** to get rid of sth that is bad, unpleasant or dangerous, especially by using force or a lot of effort（尤指通過武力或不懈努力）消除，消滅，鎮壓 SYN **eliminate**：*to stamp out racism* 消滅種族主義 **2** to put out a fire by bringing your foot down heavily on it 踩滅（火）

'stamp collecting *noun* [U] the hobby of collecting stamps from different countries 集郵 ➲ VISUAL VOCAB page V41 ▸ **'stamp collector** *noun*

'stamp duty *noun* [U] a tax in Britain on some legal documents 印花稅

,stamped addressed 'envelope *noun* (*abbr.* **SAE**) (*BrE*) an envelope on which you have written your name and address and put a stamp so that sb else can use it to send sth to you（寫上姓名地址且通常貼有郵票的）回郵信封：*Please enclose a stamped addressed envelope to get your test results.* 請附姓名地址郵資俱全的信封，以便把化驗結果寄給你。

stam·pede /stæm'piːd/ *noun, verb*
■ ***noun*** [C, usually sing.] **1** a situation in which a group of people or large animals such as horses suddenly start running in the same direction, especially because they are frightened or excited（人群的）奔逃，蜂擁；（獸群的）驚跑，狂奔：*A stampede broke out when the doors opened.* 門一開，人們蜂擁而出。 **2** a situation in which a lot of people are trying to do or achieve the same thing at the same time 熱潮；風尚；風氣：*Falling interest rates has led to a stampede to buy property.* 不斷下降的利率引發了一場購房熱。
■ ***verb*** **1** [I, T] **~ (sth)** (of large animals or people 獸群或人群) to run in a stampede; to make animals do this（使）狂奔，湧向：*a herd of stampeding elephants* 一群狂奔的大象 ◇ *A huge bunch of kids came stampeding down the corridor.* 一大群孩子順着走廊湧了過來。 **2** [T, usually passive] **~ sb (into sth/into doing sth)** to make sb rush into doing sth without giving them time to think about it 使倉促行事：*I refuse to be stampeded into making any hasty decisions.* 我不願倉促行事，草率作決定。

'stamping ground (*NAmE* also **'stomping ground**) *noun* (*informal*) a place that sb likes and where they often go（某人）愛去的地方 SYN **haunt**

stance /stæns; *BrE* also stɑːns/ *noun* **1 ~ (on sth)** the opinions that sb has about sth and expresses publicly（公開表明的）觀點，態度，立場 SYN **position**：*What is the newspaper's stance on the war?* 那家報紙對這場戰爭持什麼立場？ **2** the way in which sb stands, especially when playing a sport（尤指體育運動中的）站立姿勢

stanch /stɔːntʃ; stæntʃ/ *verb* (*especially NAmE*) = STAUNCH

stan·chion /'stæntʃən; 'stɑːn-/ *noun* (*formal*) a vertical pole used to support sth（用以支撐的）杆，支柱

stand 🔑 /stænd/ *verb, noun*
■ ***verb*** (**stood**, **stood** /stʊd/)
▸ **ON FEET/BE VERTICAL** 站立；直立 **1** 🔑 [I] to be on your feet; to be in a vertical position 站立；立；直立：*She was too weak to stand.* 她虛弱得站都站不住。◇ *a bird standing on one leg* 單腿獨立的鳥 ◇ ***Don't just stand there***—*do something!* 別光站着，幹點什麼！◇ *I was standing only a few feet away.* 當時我就站在幾英尺遠的地方。◇ *We all* ***stood around*** *in the corridor waiting.* 我們分散站在過道裏等着。◇ ***to stand on your head/hands*** (= to be upside down, balancing on your head/hands) 用頭／用手倒立 ◇ *After the earthquake, only a few houses were* ***left standing****.* 地震後只剩幾座房子沒倒。◇ **+ adj.** ***Stand still*** *while I take your photo.* 我給你照相，站着別動。 **2** 🔑 [I] to get up onto your feet from another position 站起來；起立：*Everyone stood when the President came in.* 總統進來時大家都起立。◇ **~ up** *We stood up in order to get a better view.* 我們站起身來以便看得更清楚。
▸ **PUT UPRIGHT** 使直立 **3** [T] **~ sth/sb + adv./prep.** to put sth/sb in a vertical position somewhere 使直立；豎放；使站立：*Stand the ladder up against the wall.* 把梯子靠牆立好。◇ *I stood the little girl on a chair so that she could see.* 我讓小女孩站到椅子上，好讓她看得見。
▸ **BE IN PLACE/CONDITION** 位置；狀態 **4** 🔑 [I] **+ adv./prep.** to be in a particular place 位於（某處）：*The castle stands on the site of an ancient battlefield.* 那座城堡坐落在一片古戰場上。◇ *An old oak tree once stood here.* 以前這兒長着一棵老橡樹。 **5** [I] **(+ adj.)** to be in a particular condition or situation 處於（某種狀態或情形）：*The house* ***stood empty*** *for a long time.* 那所房子空了好長一

S

段時間。◇ *'You're wrong about the date—it was 1988.' 'I **stand corrected** (= accept that I was wrong).'* "你把日期搞錯了，是 1988 年。" "你說得對，是我搞錯了。" ◇ *You never **know where you stand with** her—one minute she's friendly, the next she'll hardly speak to you.* 你從來拿不準你和她的關係如何，她一會兒跟你親熱，一會兒連話也不大跟你說。◇ ***As things stand**, there is little chance of a quick settlement of the dispute.* 照目前的形勢，儘快解決爭端的可能微乎其微。

▸ **BE AT HEIGHT/LEVEL** 高度；水平 **6** [I] **+ noun** (not used in the progressive tenses 不用於進行時) to be a particular height 高度為；高達：*The tower stands 30 metres high.* 塔高 30 米。**7** [I] **~ at sth** to be at a particular level, amount, height, etc. 達特定水平（或數量、高度等）：*Interest rates stand at 3%.* 利率為 3%。◇ *The world record then stood at 6.59 metres.* 當時的世界紀錄是 6.59 米。

▸ **OF CAR/TRAIN, ETC.** 汽車、火車等 **8** [I] **+ adv./prep.** to be in a particular place, especially while waiting to go somewhere 停；停靠：*The train standing at platform 3 is for London, Victoria.* 停在第 3 站台的火車開往倫敦維多利亞站。

▸ **OF LIQUID/MIXTURE** 液體；混合物 **9** [I] to remain still, without moving or being moved 停滯；不流動；放着不動：*Mix the batter and let it stand for twenty minutes.* 攪好麵糊以後，放上二十分鐘。◇ *standing pools of rainwater* 雨水窪

▸ **OFFER/DECISION** 提議；決定 **10** [I] if an offer, a decision, etc. made earlier **stands**, it is still valid 保持有效；維持不變：*My offer still stands.* 我的出價仍然算數。◇ *The world record stood for 20 years.* 那項世界紀錄 20 年未被打破。

▸ **BE LIKELY TO DO STH** 很可能 **11** [I] **~ to do sth** to be in a situation where you are likely to do sth 很可能做某事：*You stand to make a lot from this deal.* 你很可能會從這筆生意中大賺一筆。

▸ **HAVE OPINION** 觀點 **12** [I] **~ (on sth)** to have a particular attitude or opinion about sth or towards sb （對某事）持某種態度，有某一觀點，採取某種立場：***Where do you stand** on private education?* 你對民辦教育持什麼觀點？

▸ **DISLIKE** 不喜歡 **13** 🔑 [T, no passive] (not used in the progressive tenses 不用於進行時) used especially in negative sentences and questions to emphasize that you do not like sb/sth（尤用於否定句和疑問句，強調不喜歡）容忍，忍受 **SYN** **bear**：**~ sb/sth** *I **can't stand** his brother.* 他弟弟讓我受不了。◇ *I can't stand the sight of blood.* 一看見血我就難受。◇ *I **can't stand it** when you do that.* 你那麼做，我受不了。◇ **~ doing sth** *She couldn't stand being kept waiting.* 叫她等着，她會受不了。◇ **~ sb/sth doing sth** *I can't stand people interrupting all the time.* 我不能容忍老有人打岔。◇ *How do you stand him being here all the time?* 他老在這兒，你怎麼受得了呢？ ➔ **SYNONYMS** at HATE

▸ **SURVIVE TREATMENT** 承受 **14** 🔑 [T] **~ sth** used especially with *can/could* to say that sb/sth can survive sth or can TOLERATE sth without being hurt or damaged（尤與 can 或 could 連用）經受，承受，經得起：*His heart won't stand the strain much longer.* 他的心臟對這種壓力承受不了多久。◇ *Modern plastics can stand very high and very low temperatures.* 新型塑料能承受很高和很低的溫度。

▸ **BUY DRINK/MEAL** 買飲料／餐點 **15** [T, no passive] to buy a drink or meal for sb 花錢請（某人喝飲料或吃飯）；買…請客：**~ sth** *He stood drinks all round.* 他請客，讓大家喝了飲料。◇ **~ sb sth** *She was kind enough to stand us a meal.* 她真好，請我們吃了飯。

▸ **IN ELECTION** 選舉 **16** 🔑 (*especially BrE*) (*NAmE* usually **run**) [I] **~ (for/as sth)** to be a candidate in an election 做候選人；參選：*He **stood for parliament*** (= tried to get elected as an MP). 他競選過議會議員。◇ *She stood unsuccessfully as a candidate in the local elections.* 她參加過地方選舉，但未能當選。

IDM Idioms containing **stand** are at the entries for the nouns and adjectives in the idioms, for example **stand on ceremony** is at **ceremony**. 含 stand 的習語，都可在該等習語中的名詞及形容詞相關詞條找到，如 stand on ceremony 在詞條 ceremony 下。

PHR V **,stand a'side 1** to move to one side 站到一邊；讓開：*She stood aside to let us pass.* 她站到一邊讓我們過。**2** to not get involved in sth 不參與；不介入；置身事外：*Don't stand aside and let others do all the work.* 不要袖手旁觀，工作都讓別人去做。**3** to stop doing a job so sb else can do it 退居一旁；讓位予他人；靠邊

,stand 'back (from sth) 1 🔑 to move back from a place 往後站；退後：*The police ordered the crowd to stand back.* 警察命令人群往後退。**2** to be located away from sth 位於離…有一段距離的地方：*The house stands back from the road.* 房子離公路有一段距離。**3** 🔑 to think about a situation as if you are not involved in it 置身事外（來考慮）：*It's time to stand back and look at your career so far.* 現在你該從旁觀者的角度來審視一下自己迄今的職業生涯了。

Synonyms 同義詞辨析

stand

get up • stand up • rise • get to your feet • be on your feet

These words all mean to be in an upright position with your weight on your feet, or to put yourself in this position. 以上各詞均含站立、直立、站起來之意。

stand to be in an upright position with your weight on your feet 指站立、直立：*She was too weak to stand.* 她虛弱得站都站不住。◇ ***Stand still** when I'm talking to you!* 我跟你說話，站着別動！**NOTE** *Stand* is usually used with an adverb or prepositional phrase to show where or how sb stands, but sometimes another phrase or clause is used to show what sb does while they are standing. * stand 通常與副詞或介詞短語連用，表示站的地方或方式，但有時也與另一短語或從句連用，表明站着時在做某事：*We stood talking for a few minutes.* 我們站着談了幾分鐘。◇ *He stood and looked out to sea.* 他站着向大海望去。

get up to get into a standing position from a sitting, kneeling or lying position 指從坐、跪或躺的姿勢站起來：*Please don't get up!* 請不要站起來！

stand up to be in a standing position; to stand after sitting 指站立、起立：*Stand up straight!* 立正！◇ *Everyone would stand up when the teacher entered the classroom.* 老師走進教室時大家都會起立。

STAND, GET UP OR STAND UP? 用 stand、get up 還是 stand up？

Stand usually means 'to be in a standing position' but can also mean 'to get into a standing position'. **Stand up** can be used with either of these meanings, but its use is more restricted: it is used especially when sb tells sb or a group of people to stand. **Get up** is the most frequent way of saying 'get into a standing position', and this can be from a sitting, kneeling or lying position; if you **stand up**, this is nearly always after sitting, especially on a chair. If you want to tell sb politely that they do not need to move from their chair, use **get up**. * stand 通常含站立、直立之義，但亦含站起來、起來之義。stand up 用於上述兩種意思均可，但其用法較受限制，主要用於指讓某人或一群人站起來。get up 是表達從坐着、跪着或躺着的姿勢站起來最常用的表達法；stand up 則幾乎總是指從坐着的姿勢，尤指從椅子上站起來。如果想禮貌地告訴某人不必從椅子上起來，用 get up：~~*Please don't stand up!*~~

rise (*formal*) to get into a standing position from a sitting, kneeling or lying position 指從坐、跪或躺的姿勢站起來：*Would you all rise, please, to welcome our visiting speaker.* 請大家起立，歡迎我們的客座演講者。

get to your feet to stand up after sitting, kneeling or lying 指坐、跪或躺後站起來：*I helped her to get to her feet.* 我扶着她讓她站起來。

be on your feet to be standing up 指站着：*I've been on my feet all day.* 我已經站了一整天。

S

ˌ**stand beˈtween sb/sth and sth** to prevent sb from getting or achieving sth 阻礙（某人獲得某物）：*Only one game stood between him and victory.* 只要再贏一場比賽他就能勝出。

ˌ**stand ˈby 1** to be present while sth bad is happening but not do anything to stop it 袖手旁觀；無動於衷：*How can you stand by and see him accused of something he didn't do?* 你怎麼能眼睜睜看着他遭人誣陷而袖手旁觀呢？ ➲ related noun BYSTANDER **2** to be ready for action 做好隨時行動的準備；做好準備：*The troops are standing by.* 部隊隨時待命出動。 ➲ related noun STANDBY ˈ**stand by sb** to help sb or be friends with them, even in difficult situations 支持；幫助；忠於：*her famous song, 'Stand by your man'* 她的著名歌曲《忠於你的男人》 ˈ**stand by sth** to still believe or agree with sth you said, decided or agreed earlier 仍然遵守諾言（或協議等）：*She still stands by every word she said.* 她依舊恪守她說過的每一句話。

ˌ**stand ˈdown 1 ~ (as sth)** to leave a job or position 離職；退職；下台：*He stood down to make way for someone younger.* 他退下來好為年輕人讓路。 **2** (of a witness 證人) to leave the WITNESS BOX/STAND in court after giving evidence 退出證人席

ˈ**stand for sth** [no passive] **1** (not used in the progressive tenses 不用於進行時) to be an abbreviation or symbol of sth（指縮寫或符號）是…意思，代表：*'The book's by T.C. Smith.' 'What does the 'T.C.' stand for?'* "這部書是 T.C. Smith 寫的。" "T.C. 是哪兩個字的縮寫？" **2** to support sth 支持；主張：*I hated the organization and all it stood for* (= the ideas that it supported). 我厭惡那個組織，也厭惡它的一切主張。 **3** **not stand for sth** to not let sb do sth or sth happen 容忍；忍受：*I'm not standing for it any longer.* 這種事我再也不能容忍了。

ˌ**stand ˈin (for sb)** to take sb's place 代替，頂替（某人） SYN **deputize**：*My assistant will stand in for me while I'm away.* 我不在期間，由我的助手頂替。 ➲ related noun STAND-IN

ˌ**stand ˈout (as sth)** to be much better or more important than sb/sth 出色；傑出；更為重要：*Four points stand out as being more important than the rest.* 有四點比其餘各點更為重要。 ➲ see also OUTSTANDING

ˌ**stand ˈout (from/against sth)** to be easily seen; to be noticeable 顯眼；突出：*The lettering stood out well against the dark background.* 那種字體在深色背景下十分醒目。◇ *She's the sort of person who* ***stands out in a crowd.*** 她是那種在人群中很顯眼的人。

ˌ**stand ˈover sb** be near sb and watch them 監督；監視：*I don't like you standing over me while I'm cooking.* 我不喜歡做飯時你在一旁盯着我。

S

ˌ**stand ˈup** to be on your feet 站起；站立；起立：*There were no seats left so I had to stand up.* 沒有座位了，所以我只好站着。◇ *You'll look taller if you* ***stand up straight.*** 站直身子，你會顯得高些。 ˌ**stand sb ˈup** (*informal*) to deliberately not meet sb you have arranged to meet, especially sb you are having a romantic relationship with（尤指戀人）故意失約使某人空等：*I've been stood up!* 人家讓我空等一場！ ˌ**stand ˈup for sb/sth** to support or defend sb/sth 支持；維護：*Always stand up for your friends.* 任何時候都要支持自己的朋友。◇ *You must stand up for your rights.* 你必須維護自己的權利。◇ *She had learnt to stand up for herself.* 她學會了自我保護。 ˌ**stand ˈup (to sth)** to remain valid even when tested, examined closely, etc. 經得起（檢驗、審查等）：*His argument simply doesn't stand up to close scrutiny.* 他的論點完全經不起仔細推敲。◇ *I'm afraid this document will never stand up in a court of law.* 恐怕這份文件在法庭上是根本站不住的。 ˌ**stand ˈup to sb** to resist sb; to not accept bad treatment from sb without complaining 抵抗；勇敢反對；不甘忍受某人的欺負（或不公平對待）：*It was brave of her to stand up to those bullies.* 她不向那幾個壞蛋屈服，真是勇敢。 ˌ**stand ˈup to sth** (of materials, products, etc. 材料、產品等) to remain in good condition despite rough treatment 能承受，經受得住，耐（…） SYN **withstand**：*The carpet is designed to stand up to a lot of wear and tear.* 這種地毯設計得十分耐用。

■ ***noun***

▸ **OPINION** 觀點 **1** [usually sing.] **~ (on sth)** an attitude towards sth or an opinion that you make clear to people 態度；立場；觀點：*to take a firm stand on sth* 在某事上採取堅定的立場 ◇ *He was criticized for his tough stand on immigration.* 他因在移民問題上立場強硬受到批評。

▸ **DEFENCE** 保衛 **2** [usually sing.] a strong effort to defend yourself or your opinion about sth 保衛；捍衛；維護；抵抗：*We must* ***make a stand against*** *further job losses.* 我們必須採取措施，防止進一步裁員。◇ *the rebels' desperate last stand* 反叛者最後的瘋狂抵抗

▸ **FOR SHOWING/HOLDING STH** 展示；擺放 **3** a table or a vertical structure that goods are sold from, especially in the street or at a market 貨攤；售貨亭 SYN **stall**：*a hamburger/newspaper stand* 漢堡包售賣亭；報攤 ➲ see also NEWS-STAND **4** (*especially BrE*) a table or a vertical structure where things are displayed or advertised, for example at an exhibition（展示或推介物品的）桌，台，攤位：*a* ***display/an exhibition/a trade stand*** 展位；展銷台 **5** (often in compounds 常構成複合詞) a piece of equipment or furniture that you use for holding a particular type of thing 架；座：*a* ***bicycle/microphone/cake, etc. stand*** 自行車停靠架、麥克風架、蛋糕座等 ➲ VISUAL VOCAB pages V51, V70 ➲ see also HATSTAND, MUSIC STAND, NIGHTSTAND, WASHSTAND

▸ **AT SPORTS GROUND** 體育場 **6** a large sloping structure at a STADIUM with rows where people sit or stand to watch the game 看台 ➲ see also GRANDSTAND

▸ **IN COURT** 法庭 **7** [usually sing.] = WITNESS BOX：*He* ***took the stand*** *as the first witness.* 他第一個出庭作證。

▸ **IN CRICKET** 板球 **8** [usually sing.] the period of time in which two people who are BATTING (= hitting the ball) play together and score points 兩個擊球員同時在場上並跑動得分的階段；雙人配對：*Clinch and Harris shared an* ***opening stand*** *of 69.* 克林奇和哈里斯兩位擊球員，比賽一開始時搭檔，共得 69 分。

▸ **FOR BAND/ORCHESTRA, ETC.** 樂隊、交響樂隊等 **9** a raised platform for a band, an ORCHESTRA, a speaker, etc.（用於演出或演講等的）舞台，高台，台 ➲ see also BANDSTAND

▸ **FOR TAXIS/BUSES, ETC.** 出租車、公共汽車等 **10** a place where taxis, buses, etc. park while they are waiting for passengers 停車處；站 ➲ compare TAXI RANK

▸ **OF PLANTS/TREES** 植物；樹 **11 ~ (of sth)** (*technical* 術語) a group of plants or trees of one kind 林分：*a stand of pines* 松樹叢

▸ **OF LAND** 土地 **12** (*SAfrE*) a piece of land that you can buy and use for building a house, etc. on（建房等用的）地皮，地塊：*A developer bought the land and divided it into stands.* 開發商買下這塊土地將其分為多塊建築用地。 ➲ see also HANDSTAND, ONE-NIGHT STAND IDM see FIRM *adj.*

ˈ**stand-alone** *adj.* [usually before noun] (especially of a computer 尤指計算機) able to be operated on its own without being connected to a larger system 獨立的

stand·ard /ˈstændəd; *NAmE* -dərd/ *noun, adj.*

■ ***noun***

▸ **LEVEL OF QUALITY** 品質標準 **1** [C, U] **~ (of sth)** a level of quality, especially one that people think is acceptable（品質的）標準，水平，規格，規範：*a fall in academic standards* 學術水準的下降 ◇ *We aim to maintain* ***high standards*** *of customer care.* 我們的宗旨是始終以高標準為顧客服務。◇ *The standard of this year's applications is very low.* 今年的申請標準很低。◇ *He failed to* ***reach the required standard,*** *and did not qualify for the race.* 他未能達到所要求的標準，因而不具備參賽資格。◇ *Her work is not* ***up to standard*** (= of a good enough standard). 她的工作不合格。◇ *Who* ***sets the standard*** *for water quality?* 水質標準由誰來制訂？◇ *A number of Britain's beaches fail to* ***meet*** *European* ***standards*** *on cleanliness.* 英國有幾處海灘不符合歐洲的清潔標準。◇ *In the shanty towns there are very poor* ***living standards.*** 棚戶區的生活水平很低。 ➲ see also STANDARD OF LIVING, SUBSTANDARD **2** [C, usually pl.] a level of quality that is normal or acceptable for a particular person or in a particular situation 正常的水平；應達到的標準：*You'd better* ***lower your standards*** *if you want to find somewhere cheap to live.* 要想找個便宜的地方住，你最好降低

要求。◇ *It was a simple meal by Eddie's standards.* 在埃迪看來，那不過是一頓便飯。◇ *The equipment is slow and heavy* ***by modern standards.*** 按現代標準，那台設備又慢又笨重。

▸ LEVEL OF BEHAVIOUR 行為標準 **3** **standards** [pl.] a level of behaviour that sb considers to be morally acceptable 行為標準；道德水準：*a man of high moral standards* 道德水準高的人 ◇ *Standards aren't what they used to be.* 現在的行為標準和過去不一樣了。➲ see also DOUBLE STANDARD

▸ UNIT OF MEASUREMENT 度量衡標準 **4** [C] a unit of measurement that is officially used; an official rule used when producing sth 法定度量衡標準；法定含量；技術規範；產品規格：*a reduction in the weight standard of silver coins* 銀幣法定重量標準的降低 ◇ *industry standards* 工業標準 ➲ see also GOLD STANDARD

▸ FLAG 旗幟 **5** [C] a flag that is used during official ceremonies, especially one connected with a particular military group 儀式上使用的旗幟；（尤指）軍旗

▸ SONG 歌曲 **6** [C] a song that has been recorded by many different singers （很多歌手錄製過的）歌曲

■ ***adj.***

▸ AVERAGE/NORMAL 普通；正常 **1** average or normal rather than having special or unusual features 普通的；正常的；通常的；標準的：*A standard letter was sent to all candidates.* 給所有求職者均寄去了一封標準函。◇ *Televisions are a standard feature in most hotel rooms.* 電視機是多數旅館房間裏的標準設施。◇ *the standard rate of tax* (= paid by everyone) 標準稅率 ◇ *It is* ***standard practice*** *to search visitors as they enter the building.* 對進入這棟建築物的來訪者進行搜查是例行做法。◇ *All vehicles come with a CD player* ***as standard.*** 所有汽車售出時通常都配有 CD 播放機。

▸ SIZE/MEASUREMENT 尺寸；量度 **2** [usually before noun] following a particular standard set, for example, by an industry （符合）標準的；按一定規格製作的：*standard sizes of clothes* 服裝的標準尺寸

▸ BOOK/WRITER 著作；作者 **3** [only before noun] read by most people who are studying a particular subject 權威性的

▸ LANGUAGE 語言 **4** [usually before noun] (of spelling, pronunciation, grammar, etc. 拼寫、讀音、語法等) believed to be correct and used by most people 標準的；規範的：*Standard English* 規範的英語 ➲ compare NON-STANDARD (1), SUBSTANDARD

ˈstandard-bearer *noun* a leader in a political group or campaign 旗手；領袖

ˌstandard deˈduction *noun* [usually sing.] (*US*) a fixed amount of money that you can earn free of tax 工資免稅標準；工資免稅額

ˌstandard deviˈation *noun* (*mathematics* 數) the amount by which measurements in a set vary from the average for the set 標準偏離；標準差

ˌstandard ˈerror *noun* (*statistics* 統計) a method of measuring how accurate an estimate is （衡量估計準確性的）標準誤差

ˈStandard Grade *noun* (in Scotland 蘇格蘭) an exam in a particular subject at a lower level than HIGHERS. Standard Grades are usually taken in a number of different subjects at the age of 16. 標準級別考試（學生通常在 16 歲時參加）

stand·ard·ize (*BrE* also **-ise**) /ˈstændədaɪz; *NAmE* -dərd-/ *verb* **~ sth** to make objects or activities of the same type have the same features or qualities; to make sth standard 使標準化；使符合標準（或規格）：*a standardized contract/design/test* 標準化合同／設計／考試 ▸ **stand·ard·iza·tion**, **-isa·tion** /ˌstændədaɪˈzeɪʃn; *NAmE* -dərdəˈz-/ *noun* [U]：*the standardization of components* 部件的標準化

ˈstandard lamp (*BrE*) (also **ˈfloor lamp** *NAmE*, *BrE*) *noun* a tall lamp that stands on the floor 落地燈 ➲ VISUAL VOCAB page V21

ˌstandard of ˈliving *noun* (*pl.* **ˌstandards of ˈliving**) the amount of money and level of comfort that a particular person or group has 生活水平

ˈstandard time *noun* [U] the official time of a country or an area 標準時

stand·by /ˈstændbaɪ/ *noun, adj.*

■ ***noun*** (*pl.* **stand·bys**) a person or thing that can always be used if needed, for example if sb/sth else is not available or if there is an emergency 後備人員；備用物品：*I always keep a pizza in the freezer as a standby.* 我總會在冰箱裏放一個比薩餅應急。◇ *a standby electricity generator* 備用發電機

IDM **on ˈstandby** **1** ready to do sth immediately if needed or asked 隨時可以投入行動；處於待命狀態；招之即來：*The emergency services were* ***put on standby*** *after a bomb warning.* 接到炸彈警報後，各緊急救助部門進入待命狀態。 **2** ready to travel or go somewhere if a ticket or sth that is needed suddenly becomes available 候補座位（如臨時有票或具備其他必要條件便可立即出發的）：*He was* ***put on standby*** *for the flight to New York.* 這班飛往紐約的班機，他候補待位。

■ ***adj.*** [only before noun] a **standby** ticket for a flight, concert, etc. cannot be bought in advance and is only available a very short time before the plane leaves or the performance starts （機票、音樂會門票等）最後時刻出售的

ˈstand-down *noun* [U, C] a period when people, especially soldiers, relax after a period of duty or danger 停工休息期；（尤指士兵的）休整期

stand·ee /stænˈdiː/ *noun* (*NAmE*, *ScotE*) a person who is standing, for example in a bus or at a concert 站立者；站立乘客；站票觀眾

ˈstand-in *noun* **1** a person who does sb's job for a short time when they are not available 代替者 **2** a person who replaces an actor in some scenes in a film/movie, especially dangerous ones （尤指影視中做危險動作的）替身演員

stand·ing /ˈstændɪŋ/ *adj., noun*

■ ***adj.*** [only before noun] **1** existing or arranged permanently, not formed or made for a particular situation 長期存在的；永久性的；常設的：*a* ***standing army*** 常備軍 ◇ (*BrE*) *a* ***standing charge*** (= an amount of money that you pay in order to use a service, such as gas or water) 長期支付的開銷 ◇ *a* ***standing committee*** 常務委員會 ◇ *It's a* ***standing joke*** (= something that a group of people regularly laugh at). 那是一個活笑柄。◇ *We have a* ***standing invitation*** *to visit them anytime.* 他們邀請我們隨時去他們家做客。 **2** done from a position in which you are standing rather than sitting or running 站着進行的：*a* ***standing jump/start*** 立定跳遠；站立式起跑 ◇ *The speaker got a* ***standing ovation*** (= people stood up to clap after the speech). 演講者贏得了聽眾的起立鼓掌。➲ see also FREE-STANDING

■ ***noun*** **1** [U] the position or reputation of sb/sth within a group of people or in an organization 地位；級別；身分；名聲 SYN **status**：*the* ***high/low standing*** *of politicians with the public* 在公眾中聲望高／低的政治人物 ◇ *The contract has no legal standing.* 那份合同在法律上沒有約束力。 **2** [U] the period of time that sth has existed 持續時間：*a friendship of many years' standing* 多年的友情 ➲ see also LONG-STANDING **3** **standings** [pl.] a list of people, teams, etc. showing their positions in a sports competition （運動員或運動隊比賽成績的）排名，名次

ˌstanding ˈorder *noun* [C, U] an instruction that you give to your bank to pay sb a fixed amount of money from your account on the same day each week/month, etc. （客戶給銀行的）定期付款指令，按期付款委託書 ➲ compare BANKER'S ORDER, DIRECT DEBIT

ˈstanding room *noun* [U] space for people to stand in, especially in a theatre, sports ground, etc. （尤指劇場、體育場等）站立的空間：*standing room for 12 000 supporters* 可供 12 000 名支持者站立的地方 ◇ *It was* ***standing room only*** *at the concert* (= all the seats were sold). 音樂會只剩站票了。

ˈstanding stone *noun* a tall vertical stone that was shaped and put up by PREHISTORIC people in western Europe （西歐）史前巨石柱

S

ˈstand-off *noun* **~ (between A and B)** a situation in which no agreement can be reached（雙方）僵持局面 **SYN** **deadlock**

ˌstand-off ˈhalf (also **ˌfly ˈhalf**) *noun* (in RUGBY 橄欖球) a player who plays behind the SCRUM HALF 並列爭球前衛；並列傳鋒

stand-offish /ˌstænd ˈɒfɪʃ; *NAmE* -ˈɔːf-; -ˈɑːf-/ *adj.* (*informal*) not friendly towards other people 冷淡的；冷漠的；不友好的 **SYN** **aloof**

stand·out /ˈstændaʊt/ *noun* (*NAmE, informal*) a person or thing that is very noticeable because they are or it is better, more impressive, etc. than others in a group 突出的人（或事物）▸ **stand·out** *adj.* [only before noun]：*the standout track on this album* 這張專輯裏最突出的那首歌

stand·pipe /ˈstændpaɪp/ *noun* a pipe that is connected to a public water supply and used to provide water outside a building 豎管（用於在戶外公共場所供水）

stand·point /ˈstændpɔɪnt/ *noun* [usually sing.] an opinion or a way of thinking about ideas or situations 立場；觀點 **SYN** **perspective**：*a **political/theoretical, etc. standpoint*** 政治、理論等觀點 ◇ *He is writing **from the standpoint** of someone who knows what life is like in prison.* 他從一個瞭解監獄生活的人的立場寫作。

St Andrew's Day /ˌsnt ˈændruːz deɪ; *NAmE* ˌseɪnt/ *noun* 30 November, a Christian festival of the national SAINT of Scotland 聖安德烈節（11 月 30 日，紀念蘇格蘭主保聖人的基督教節日）

stand·still /ˈstændstɪl/ *noun* [sing.] a situation in which all activity or movement has stopped 停止；停頓；停滯 **SYN** **halt**：*The security alert **brought** the airport **to a standstill**.* 安全警戒使機場陷入停頓狀態。◇ *Traffic in the northbound lane is **at a complete standstill**.* 北行車道的交通完全堵塞。

ˌstand-ˈto *noun* [U] the state of being ready to fight or attack 作好戰鬥準備

ˈstand-up *adj., noun*

■ ***adj.*** [only before noun] **1** **stand-up** comedy consists of one person standing in front of an audience and telling jokes（喜劇節目）單人表演的，單口的 **2** (*especially BrE*) a **stand-up** argument, fight, etc. is one in which people shout loudly at each other or are violent towards each other（爭論、打鬥等）激烈的 **3** worn, used, etc. in a vertical position 直立的；挺立的：*a stand-up collar* 立領

■ ***noun*** **1** [U] stand-up comedy 獨角喜劇；單口相聲：*When did you start doing stand-up?* 你什麼時候開始表演獨白喜劇的？ **2** [C] a person who performs stand-up comedy 獨白喜劇演員；單口相聲演員：*She started out as a stand-up.* 她出道時是個獨角喜劇演員。

stank *past tense of* STINK

Stan·ley knife™ /ˈstænli naɪf/ *noun* (*BrE*) a very sharp knife with a blade in the shape of a triangle that can be replaced 斯坦利刀（刀刃鋒利，呈三角形，可更換）

stanza /ˈstænzə/ *noun* (*technical* 術語) a group of lines in a repeated pattern that form a unit in some types of poem（詩的）節，段 **SYN** **verse**

staphylo·coc·cus /ˌstæfɪləˈkɒkəs; *NAmE* -ˈkɑːk-/ *noun* (*medical* 醫) a type of bacteria that can cause infections in some parts of the body such as the skin and eyes 葡萄球菌（可感染皮膚和眼睛等身體部位）

staple /ˈsteɪpl/ *adj., noun, verb*

■ ***adj.*** [only before noun] forming a basic, large or important part of sth 主要的；基本的；重要的：*The staple crop is rice.* 主要農作物為水稻。◇ *Jeans are a staple part of everyone's wardrobe.* 在每個人的衣櫥裏，牛仔褲是必不可少的。

■ ***noun*** **1** a small piece of wire that is used in a device called a STAPLER and is pushed through pieces of paper and bent over at the ends in order to fasten the pieces of paper together 訂書釘 ➲ **VISUAL VOCAB** page V69 **2** a small piece of metal in the shape of a U that is hit into wooden surfaces using a HAMMER, used especially for holding electrical wires in place * U 形釘；U 形電線卡 **3** a basic type of food that is used a lot 基本食物；主食：*Aid workers helped distribute corn, milk and other staples.* 救助人員協助分發穀物、牛奶及其他必需的食物。 **4** something that is produced by a country and is important for its economy（某國的）主要產品，支柱產品：*Rubber became the staple of the Malayan economy.* 橡膠成了馬來亞經濟的支柱產品。 **5 ~ (of sth)** a large or important part of sth 主要部份；重要內容：*Royal gossip is a staple of the tabloid press.* 圍繞王室成員的蜚短流長是小報的主要內容。

■ ***verb*** **~ sth + adv./prep.** to attach one thing to another using a staple or staples 用訂書釘裝訂：*Staple the invoice to the receipt.* 把發票訂到收據上。◇ *Staple the invoice and the receipt together.* 把發票和收據訂在一起。

ˌstaple ˈdiet *noun* [U, C] **~ (of sth)** **1** the food that a person or an animal normally eats（某人或動物的）主要食物：*a staple diet of meat and potatoes* 以肉和土豆作為主要食物 ◇ *Bamboo is the panda's staple diet.* 大熊貓的基本食物是竹子。 **2** something that is used a lot 家常便飯；主要內容；慣用手段：*Sex and violence seem to be the staple diet of television drama.* 性和暴力好像是電視劇離不開的內容。

ˈstaple gun *noun* a device for fixing paper to walls, etc. using STAPLES 釘槍，打釘器（用以把紙釘到牆上等）

stapler /ˈsteɪplə(r)/ *noun* a small device used for putting staples into paper, etc. 訂書機 ➲ **VISUAL VOCAB** page V69

ˈstaple remover *noun* a small device used for removing staples from paper, etc.（訂書釘）起釘器，拔釘器 ➲ **VISUAL VOCAB** page V69

star 🔑 /stɑː(r)/ *noun, verb*

■ ***noun***

▸ **IN SKY** 天空 **1** 🔑 [C] a large ball of burning gas in space that we see as a point of light in the sky at night 恒星；星：*There was a big moon and hundreds of stars were shining overhead.* 頭頂是一輪明月和成百上千顆閃爍的星星。◇ *Sirius is the brightest star in the sky.* 天狼星是天空中最亮的一顆星。◇ *We camped out **under the stars**.* 我們露天宿營。➲ see also FALLING STAR, LODESTAR, POLE STAR, SHOOTING STAR, STARRY

▸ **SHAPE** 形狀 **2** 🔑 [C] an object, a decoration, a mark, etc., usually with five or six points, whose shape represents a star 星狀物；星形飾物；星號：*a horse with a white star on its forehead* 前額有一塊星形白斑的馬 ◇ *a sheriff's star* 行政司法長官的星徽 ◇ *I've put a star by the names of the girls in the class.* 我在班裏女生名字旁都畫了一個星號。◇ *a four-star general* 四星上將

▸ **MARK OF QUALITY** 質量標誌 **3** 🔑 [C, usually sing.] a mark that represents a star and tells you how good sth is, especially a hotel or restaurant（尤指旅館或餐館的）星級：***three-/four-/five-star** hotels* 三星級 / 四星級 / 五星級飯店 ◇ *What star rating does this restaurant have?* 這家餐館是幾星級的？

▸ **PERFORMER** 表演者 **4** 🔑 [C] a famous and excellent singer, performer, sports player, etc. 歌唱（或表演）明星；體壇高手；才華出眾者：***pop/rock/Hollywood, etc. stars*** 流行音樂歌星、搖滾歌星、好萊塢影星等 ◇ *a **football/tennis, etc. star*** 足球、網球等明星 ◇ *He's so good—I'm sure he'll be a big star.* 他太棒了，我相信他會成為大明星的。◇ *She acts well but she hasn't got **star quality**.* 她演得不錯，但缺少成為一個明星的素質。◇ *The best models receive **star treatment**.* 最優秀的模特兒會受到明星級的待遇。➲ see also ALL-STAR, FILM STAR, MEGASTAR, MOVIE STAR, SUPERSTAR **5** 🔑 [C] a person who has the main part, or one of the main parts, in a film/movie, play, etc.（電影、戲劇等的）主角，主演：*She was the star of many popular television series.* 她在許多觀眾喜愛的電視連續劇中擔任過主角。◇ *The **star of the show** was a young Italian singer.* 那台節目的主角是位年輕的意大利歌唱家。◇ *the **star role/part*** 主角 ➲ see also STAR TURN

▸ **BEST OF GROUP** 最優秀者 **6** [C] (often used before another noun 常用於另一名詞前) a person or thing that is the best of a group 最優秀（或出色、成功）者：*a star student* 最優秀的學生 ◇ *Paula is the star of the class.* 葆拉是班裏的尖子。◇ *He was the **star performer** at the championships.* 他是那屆錦標賽上的最佳運動員。◇ *The **star prize** is a weekend for two in Paris.* 特等獎是二

人巴黎週末遊。◇ *The monkey was* **the star attraction** (= the best or most popular act) *at the show.* 那隻猴子是節目中最矚目的明星。

▸ **HELPFUL PERSON 提供幫助的人** **7** [C, usually sing.] (*informal*) used to show that you feel very grateful for sth that sb has done or that you think they are wonderful（表示萬分感激或讚歎）: *Thanks! You're a star!* 多謝多謝！你真是個大好人！

▸ **INFLUENCE ON SB'S FUTURE 對某人將來的影響** **8** **stars** [pl.] a description of what sb thinks is going to happen to sb in the future, based on the position of the stars and planets when they were born 星象（根據人出生時天體的位置而描述的命運）**SYN** **horoscope**: *Do you read your stars in the paper?* 你讀不讀報上的星座運程，看自己的運氣如何？

IDM **see 'stars** (*informal*) to see flashes of light in front of your eyes, usually because you have been hit on the head（因撞擊頭部等）兩眼直冒金星 **'stars in your eyes** if sb has **stars in their eyes**, they have dreams of becoming famous, especially as an entertainer 成名的夢想；（尤指成為藝人的）明星夢 ➲ more at REACH *v.*, THANK

■ ***verb*** (-rr-)

▸ **PERFORM IN MOVIE/PLAY 在電影／戲劇中扮演角色** **1** 🔑 [I] **~ (with/opposite sb) (in sth)** to have one of the main parts in a film/movie, play, etc. 主演；擔任主角: *She starred opposite Cary Grant in 'Bringing up Baby'.* 她和加利•格蘭特在《育嬰奇譚》中聯袂出演男女主角。◇ *No one has yet been chosen for the* ***starring role*** (= the main part). 主演還沒選定。➲ COLLOCATIONS at CINEMA **2** 🔑 [T, no passive] **~ sb** if a film/movie, play, etc. **stars** sb, that person has one of the main parts 使主演；由…擔任主角: *a movie starring Meryl Streep and Pierce Brosnan* 由梅麗爾•斯特里普和皮爾斯•布魯斯南主演的電影 ◇ *The studio wants to star her in a sequel to last year's hit.* 製片廠為去年一部大獲成功的影片籌拍續集，想聘她擔任主角。➲ see also CO-STAR

▸ **MARK WITH SYMBOL 標記號** **3** [T, usually passive] **~ sth** to put a symbol shaped like a star (= an ASTERISK) next to a word, etc. in order to make people notice it 給…標星號: *Treat all the sections that have been starred as priority.* 要優先處理所有標星號的部份。

,star 'anise *noun* [U, C] a small fruit in the shape of a star, used in cooking as a spice 八角茴香 ➲ **VISUAL VOCAB** page V32

star·board /'stɑːbəd; *NAmE* 'stɑːrbərd/ *noun* [U] the side of a ship or an aircraft that is on the right when you are facing forward（船舶或飛機的）右舷，右側 ➲ compare PORT *n.* (5)

star·burst /'stɑːbɜːst; *NAmE* 'stɑːrbɜːrst/ *noun* a bright light in the shape of a star, or a shape that looks like a star exploding 星狀亮光；星爆般的形狀

starch /stɑːtʃ; *NAmE* stɑːrtʃ/ *noun, verb*

■ ***noun*** **1** [U, C] a white CARBOHYDRATE food substance found in potatoes, flour, rice, etc.; food containing this 澱粉；含澱粉的食物: *There's too much starch in your diet.* 你的日常飲食中澱粉含量太高。◇ *You need to cut down on starches.* 你得少吃些含澱粉的東西。 **2** [U] starch prepared in powder form or as a spray and used for making clothes, sheets, etc. stiff（漿衣服、牀單等用的）澱粉漿

■ ***verb*** [usually passive] **~ sth** to make clothes, sheets, etc. stiff using starch 把（衣服、牀單等）漿一漿: *a starched white shirt* 漿過的白襯衫

starchy /'stɑːtʃi; *NAmE* 'stɑːrtʃi/ *adj.* **1** (of food 食物) containing a lot of starch 富含澱粉的 **2** (*informal, disapproving*) (of a person or their behaviour 人或行為) very formal; not friendly or relaxed 拘束的；古板的；拘泥的

'star-crossed *adj.* (*literary*) not able to be happy because of bad luck or FATE 命運乖蹇的；不幸的: *Shakespeare's star-crossed lovers, Romeo and Juliet* 羅密歐和朱麗葉這一對莎士比亞筆下命運多舛的戀人

star·dom /'stɑːdəm; *NAmE* 'stɑːrdəm/ *noun* [U] the state of being famous as an actor, a singer, etc. 明星的地位（或身分）: *The group is being* ***tipped for stardom*** (= people say they will be famous). 這支樂隊被譽為明日之星。◇ *She* ***shot to stardom*** *in a Broadway musical.* 她在一部百老匯音樂劇中一炮而紅。

star·dust /'stɑːdʌst; *NAmE* 'stɑːrd-/ *noun* [U] **1** a magic quality that some famous people with a great natural ability seem to have（天賦很高的名人似乎擁有的）魔力 **2** (*astronomy* 天) stars that are very far from the earth and appear like bright dust in the sky at night 星塵（遠離地球的恆星，在夜空中看似明亮塵埃）

stare 🔑 /steə(r); *NAmE* ster/ *verb, noun*

■ ***verb*** 🔑 [I] **~ (at sb/sth)** to look at sb/sth for a long time 盯着看；凝視；注視: *I screamed and everyone stared.* 我尖叫一聲，眾人都盯着我看。◇ *I stared blankly at the paper in front of me.* 我茫然地看着面前那張紙。◇ *He sat* ***staring into space*** (= looking at nothing). 他坐在那兒凝視着前方。◇ *She looked at them with dark staring eyes.* 她那雙深邃的眼睛專注地看着他們。

IDM **be staring sb in the 'face** **1** to be obvious or easy to see 明擺着；顯而易見: *The answer was staring us in the face.* 答案明擺在我們面前。 **2** to be certain to happen 必定發生: *Defeat was staring them in the face.* 他們必遭失敗。 **be staring sth in the 'face** to be unable to avoid sth 不可避免: *They were staring defeat in the face.* 對他們來說，失敗不可避免。

PHR V **,stare sb 'out** (*BrE*) (also **,stare sb 'down** *NAmE, BrE*) to look into sb's eyes for a long time until they feel embarrassed and are forced to look away 盯得某人轉移目光（或慌了神）

■ ***noun*** 🔑 an act of looking at sb/sth for a long time, especially in a way that is unfriendly or that shows surprise（尤指不友好或吃驚的）盯，凝視，注視: *She gave him a blank stare.* 她面無表情地看了他一眼。➲ SYNONYMS at LOOK

Synonyms 同義詞辨析

stare

gaze • peer • glare

These words all mean to look at sb/sth for a long time.
以上各詞均含盯着看、凝視、注視之意。

stare to look at sb/sth for a long time, especially with surprise or fear, or because you are thinking 尤指吃驚、害怕或深思地盯着看、凝視、注視: *I screamed and everyone stared.* 我尖叫一聲，眾人都盯着我看。

gaze (*rather formal*) to look steadily at sb/sth for a long time, especially with surprise or love, or because you are thinking 尤指吃驚、愛戀或深思地凝視、注視、盯着: *We all gazed at Marco in amazement.* 我們都驚異地注視着馬可。

peer to look closely or carefully at sth, especially when you cannot see it clearly 尤指看不清楚時仔細看、端詳

glare to look angrily at sb/sth for a long time 指怒目而視: *I looked at her and she glared stonily back.* 我看了她一眼，她便冷冷地回瞪着我。

PATTERNS

- to stare/gaze/peer/glare **at** sb/sth
- to stare/gaze/peer/glare **suspiciously**
- to stare/gaze/peer **anxiously/intently**
- to stare/gaze/glare **wildly/fiercely**

star·fish /'stɑːfɪʃ; *NAmE* 'stɑːrfɪʃ/ *noun* (*pl.* **star·fish**) a flat sea creature in the shape of a star with five arms 海星

star·fruit /'stɑːfruːt; *NAmE* 'stɑːrf-/ *noun* (*pl.* **star·fruit**) a green or yellow tropical fruit with a shape like a star 五斂子；楊桃 ➲ **VISUAL VOCAB** page V30

star·gazer /'stɑːgeɪzə(r); *NAmE* 'stɑːrg-/ *noun* (*informal*) a person who studies ASTROLOGY or ASTRONOMY 占星術士；天文學家 ▸ **star·gaz·ing** *noun* [U]

stark /stɑːk; *NAmE* stɑːrk/ *adj., adv.*

■ ***adj.*** (**stark·er**, **stark·est**) **1** (often *disapproving*) looking severe and without any colour or decoration 了無修飾的；荒涼的；粗陋的: *I think white would be too*

S

stark for the bedroom. 我覺得卧室裏用白色未免太素了。◇ *The hills stood stark against the winter sky.* 在冬日的天空下，小山了無生氣。 **2** unpleasant; real, and impossible to avoid 嚴酷的；赤裸裸的；真實而無法迴避的 **SYN bleak**： *The author paints a stark picture of life in a prison camp.* 作者描繪出一幅冷酷而真實的戰俘營生活畫面。◇ *a stark choice* 殘酷的抉擇 ◇ *The remains of the building stand as a stark reminder of the fire.* 房子的斷壁殘垣是那場大火無情的見證。◇ *He now faces the* ***stark reality*** *of life in prison.* 他現在要面對獄中生活的嚴酷現實了。 ➲ SYNONYMS at PLAIN **3** very different to sth in a way that is easy to see （指區別）明顯的，鮮明的 **SYN clear**： *stark differences* 鮮明的區別 ◇ *Social divisions in the city are stark.* 城市裏各社會階層有明確的分野。◇ *The good weather was* ***in stark contrast to*** *the storms of previous weeks.* 這時的好天氣和前幾個星期的暴風雨形成鮮明的對比。 **4** [only before noun] complete and total 完全的；十足的 **SYN utter**： *The children watched in stark terror.* 孩子們極端恐懼地看着。 ▸ **stark·ly** *adv.*： *The interior is starkly simple.* 室內粗陋簡樸。◇ *The lighthouse stood out starkly against the dark sky.* 在黑暗的天空映襯下，燈塔巍然兀立。◇ *We are starkly aware of the risks.* 我們完全清楚所面臨的種種風險。 **stark·ness** *noun* [U]

■ *adv.* **~ naked** completely naked 一絲不掛；赤裸 **IDM** see RAVING

stark·ers /ˈstɑːkəz; *NAmE* ˈstɑːrkərz/ *adj.* [not before noun] (*BrE, informal*) not wearing any clothes 一絲不掛；赤裸 **SYN naked**

star·less /ˈstɑːləs; *NAmE* ˈstɑːrləs/ *adj.* with no stars in the sky 沒有星星的： *a starless night* 沒有星星的夜晚

star·let /ˈstɑːlət; *NAmE* ˈstɑːrlət/ *noun* a young woman actor who plays small parts and hopes to become famous 尚未成名的年輕女演員

star·light /ˈstɑːlaɪt; *NAmE* ˈstɑːrl-/ *noun* [U] light from the stars 星光： *We walked home by starlight.* 我們藉着星光走回家。

star·ling /ˈstɑːlɪŋ; *NAmE* ˈstɑːrlɪŋ/ *noun* a common bird with dark shiny feathers and a noisy call 椋鳥

star·lit /ˈstɑːlɪt; *NAmE* ˈstɑːrlɪt/ *adj.* with light from the stars 星光照耀的： *a starlit night* 星光照耀的夜晚

ˈstar network *noun* (*computing* 計) a network in which computers are connected to a central unit, rather than to each other 星狀網（通過中央主機聯接）

S

ˌStar of ˈDavid *noun* (*pl.* **Stars of David**) a star with six points that is used as a symbol of Judaism and the state of Israel 大衞之星，六角星（猶太教和以色列的標誌）

starry /ˈstɑːri/ *adj.* [usually before noun] **1** (of the sky 天空) full of stars 佈滿星星的： *a beautiful starry night* 繁星滿天的美麗夜晚 **2** looking like a star 像星星的： *starry flowers* 像星星似的花朵 **3** (of eyes 眼睛) shining like stars 閃閃發光的；明亮的

ˌstarry-ˈeyed *adj.* (*informal*) full of emotion, hopes or dreams about sb/sth in a way that is not realistic 天真的；空想的

the ˌStars and ˈStripes *noun* [sing.] the national flag of the US 星條旗（美國國旗）

star·ship /ˈstɑːʃɪp; *NAmE* ˈstɑːrʃ-/ *noun* (in SCIENCE FICTION 科幻小說) a large SPACECRAFT in which people or other creatures travel through space 星際飛船；星艦

ˈstar sign (also *informal* **sign**) *noun* one of the twelve signs of the ZODIAC 星座（黃道十二宮之一）： *'What's your star sign?' 'Aquarius.'* "你屬什麼星座？" "水瓶座。"

the ˌStar-ˌSpangled ˈBanner *noun* [sing.] the national ANTHEM (= song) of the US 星條旗之歌（美國國歌）

ˈstar-struck *adj.* very impressed by famous people such as actors, football players, etc. 崇拜明星的；追星族的

ˈstar-studded *adj.* including many famous performers 明星薈萃的： *a star-studded cast* 明星薈萃的演出陣容

Synonyms 同義詞辨析

start

begin • start off • kick off • commence • open

These words are all used to talk about things happening from the beginning, or people doing the first part of sth. 以上各詞均用以指事情開始發生或開始做某事。

start to begin to happen or exist; to begin in a particular way or from a particular point 指開始發生或存在、以…開始、以…為起點： *When does the class start?* 什麼時候上課？

begin to start to happen or exist; to start in a particular way or from a particular point; to start speaking 指開始發生或存在、以…開始、以…為起點、開始講話： *When does the concert begin?* 音樂會什麼時候開始？

START OR BEGIN? 用 start 還是 begin？

There is not much difference in meaning between these words. **Start** is more frequent in spoken English and in business contexts; **begin** is more frequent in written English and is often used when you are describing a series of events. 上述兩詞在意義上無多大差別，start 較常用於英語口語和商業語境中，begin 較常用於英語書面語中，描述一系列事情： *The story begins on the island of Corfu.* 故事從科孚島開始。 **Start** is not used to mean 'begin speaking'. * start 不用以指開始講話： ~~*'Ladies and gentlemen,' he started.*~~

start off (*rather informal*) to start happening or doing sth; to start by doing or being sth 指進行或開展起來、首先進行、一開始是： *The discussion started off mildly enough.* 討論頗為溫和地開展起來。

kick off (*informal*) to start an event or activity, especially in a particular way; (of an event, activity, etc.) to start, especially in a particular way 尤指以…開始（活動）、（活動）以…開始： *Tom will kick off with a few comments.* 湯姆講話時要先發表幾點意見。◇ *The festival kicks off on Monday, September 13.* 節期從 9 月 13 日星期一開始。

commence (*formal*) to start happening 指開始發生： *The meeting is scheduled to commence at noon.* 會議定於午間召開。

open to start an event or activity in a particular way; (of an event, film/movie or book) to start, especially in a particular way 指以…開始（活動）、（活動、電影或書）以…開頭／開篇： *The story opens with a murder.* 故事以一宗謀殺案作序幕。

PATTERNS

- to start/begin/start off/kick off/commence/open **with** sth
- to start/begin/start off/kick off/commence/open **by** doing sth
- to start/begin/start off/commence **as** sth
- a **campaign/season/meeting** starts/begins/starts off/kicks off/commences/opens
- a **film/movie/book** starts/begins/starts off/opens

start 0‑ /stɑːt; *NAmE* stɑːrt/ *verb, noun*

■ *verb*

▸ **DOING STH 做事** **1** 0‑ [T, I] to begin doing or using sth 開始，着手，動手（做或使用）： **~ sth** *I start work at nine.* 我每天九點開始工作。◇ *He's just started a new job.* 他剛剛着手一項新工作。◇ *I only started* (= began to read) *this book yesterday.* 我昨天才開始看這本書。◇ *We need to start* (= begin using) *a new jar of coffee.* 我們得新開一罐咖啡了。◇ *The kids start school next week.* 孩子們下星期開學。◇ **~ to do sth** *It started to rain.* 下起雨來了。◇ *Mistakes were starting to creep in.* 不知不覺間，開始出錯了。◇ **~ doing sth** *She started laughing.* 她笑了起來。◇ **~ (on sth)** *It's a long story. Where shall I start?* 說來話長。我該從哪兒說起呢？◇ *It's time you started on your homework.* 你該做功課了。◇ *Can you start* (= a new job) *on Monday?* 你可以星期一就來上班嗎？◇ **~ by**

doing sth *Let's start by reviewing what we did last week.* 我們開始先來複習一下上星期學的內容。◇ **+ adj.** *The best professional musicians* ***start young.*** 卓有成就的音樂家很早就接觸音樂。➲ note at BEGIN

▸ **HAPPENING** 發生 **2** [I, T] to start happening; to make sth start happening（使）發生，開始進行：*When does the class start?* 什麼時候上課？◇ *Have you any idea where the rumour started?* 你知不知道謠言是從哪兒傳出來的？◇ **~ sth** *Who started the fire?* 誰放的火？◇ *Do you start the day with a good breakfast?* 你早晨起來會先好好吃一頓早飯嗎？◇ *You're always trying to start an argument.* 你總是想挑起爭論。◇ **~ sb/sth doing sth** *The news started me thinking.* 那條消息讓我思考起來。

▸ **MACHINE/VEHICLE** 機器；車輛 **3** [T, I] **~ (sth)** when you **start** a machine or a vehicle or it **starts**, it begins to operate 開動；發動；啟動：*Start the engines!* 發動引擎！◇ *I can't get the car started.* 這輛車我發動不起來。◇ *The car won't start.* 這輛車發動不起來。

▸ **EXISTING** 存在 **4** [I, T] to begin to exist; to make sth begin to exist（使）出現；發起；創辦；開辦：**~ (up)** *There are a lot of small businesses starting up in that area.* 小型企業在那一地區大量湧現。◇ **~ sth (up)** *They decided to start a catering business.* 他們決定開辦一家宴會承辦公司。

▸ **JOURNEY** 旅行 **5** [I] **~ (out)** to begin a journey; to leave 出發；動身；起程 SYN **set off, set out**：*What time are we starting tomorrow?* 我們明天什麼時候出發？

▸ **GOING/WALKING** 走 **6** [I] **+ adv./prep.** to begin to move in a particular direction 起身走向；向…而去：*I started after her* (= began to follow her) *to tell her the news.* 我起身朝她追去，好把消息告訴她。◇ *He started for the door, but I blocked his way.* 他向門口走去，但我擋住了他的去路。

▸ **IN PARTICULAR WAY/FROM PLACE/LEVEL** 方式；地方；層次 **7** [I, T] to begin, or to begin sth such as a career, in a particular way that changed later 以…起步（或起家）；起初是：**~ as sth** *She started as a secretary but ended up running the department.* 她起初只是一個秘書，但最後掌管起了整個部門。◇ **~ out/off (as sth)** *The company started out with 30 employees.* 公司創業之初只有 30 名員工。◇ **~ sth (as sth)** *He* ***started life*** *as a teacher before turning to journalism.* 他剛工作時當過教師，後來改行搞起了新聞。**8** [I] **+ adv./prep.** to begin from a particular place, amount or situation（從…）開始；（由…）起：*The trail starts just outside the town.* 小徑從剛出城的地方開始。◇ *Hotel prices start at €50 a night for a double room.* 旅館的雙人房間一宿 50 歐元起價。◇ *The evening started badly when the speaker failed to turn up.* 那天晚上的活動一開始挺糟糕，因為演講者沒有來。

▸ **MOVE SUDDENLY** 突然一動 **9** [I] to move suddenly and quickly because you are surprised or afraid 突然一驚 SYN **jump**：*The sudden noise made her start.* 突如其來的聲音嚇了她一跳。

IDM **ˌdon't (you) 'start** (*informal*) used to tell sb not to complain or be critical（制止某人抱怨或挑剔）別抱怨，別挑剔：*Don't start! I told you I'd be late.* 別抱怨啦！我跟你說過我要遲到的。**get 'started** to begin doing sth（使）開始；着手；動手：*It's nearly ten o'clock. Let's get started.* 快十點了，咱們開始吧。**you, he, she, etc. 'started it** (*informal*) you, he, she, etc. began a fight or an argument 是你（或他、她等）挑起來的：*'Stop fighting, you two!' 'He started it!'* "你們倆，別打了！" "是他先動手的！" **'start something** (*informal*) to cause trouble 製造麻煩；惹是生非 **to 'start with 1** used when you are giving the first and most important reason for sth（給出首要理由）首先，第一：*To start with it's much too expensive ...* 首先是太貴… **2** at the beginning 起初；開始時：*The club had only six members to start with.* 這家俱樂部起初僅有六名會員。◇ *I'll have melon to start with.* 我要先吃甜瓜。◇ *She wasn't keen on the idea to start with.* 她一開始並不喜歡這個主意。➲ more at ALARM *n.*, BALL *n.*, FOOT *n.*

PHR V **ˌstart 'back** to begin to return somewhere 動身（或起程）返回 **ˌstart 'off 1** to begin to move 開始活動；動身：*The horse started off at a steady trot.* 馬穩步小跑起來。**2** to begin happening; to begin doing sth 進行（或開展）起來：*The discussion started off mildly enough.* 討論頗為溫和地開展起來。**3** to begin by doing or being sth 首先進行；一開始是：*Let's start off with some gentle exercises.* 我們先來做點強度低的運動。◇ *We started off by introducing ourselves.* 我們一開始先自我介紹。◇ **+ adj.** *The leaves start off green but turn red later.* 樹葉起先是綠色，到後來會變紅。◇ **~ doing sth** *I started off working quite hard, but it didn't last.* 我一開始非常勤奮，但沒有堅持下去。**ˌstart sb 'off (on sth) 1** [no passive] to make sb begin doing sth 使開始（做某事）：*What started her off on that crazy idea?* 她怎麼會有那樣古怪的念頭呢？◇ *Don't say anything to her—you'll start her off again* (= make her get angry). 什麼也別跟她說，不然你又要惹她生氣了。◇ **~ doing sth** *Kevin started us all off laughing.* 凱文把我們大家都逗笑了。**2** to help sb begin doing sth 幫助某人開始（某事）：*My mother started me off on the piano when I was three.* 三歲時我母親就讓我開始練鋼琴了。◇ **~ doing sth** *His father started him off farming.* 他父親指點他做農活兒。**'start on sb** [no passive] to attack sb physically or with words（使用暴力或言語）向某人發起攻擊 **ˌstart 'on at sb (about sth)** | **ˌstart 'on (at sb) about sth** (*informal*) to begin to complain about sth or criticize sb 開始責備（某人）；開始抱怨（某事）：*She started on at me again about getting some new clothes.* 她又數落起我來，纏着要買幾件新衣服。◇ *Don't start on about him not having a job.* 你不要埋怨他沒工作。**ˌstart 'out 1** to begin to do sth, especially in business or work 開始從事，着手（某工作）；從業：*to start out in business* 做起生意來 ◇ *She started out on her legal career in 2001.* 她於 2001 年開始從事法律工作。**2** to have a particular intention when you begin sth 最初想要；起先打算：**~ to do sth** *I started out to write a short story, but it soon developed into a novel.* 我起先打算寫一篇短篇小說，但很快就寫成了長篇小說。**ˌstart 'over** (*especially NAmE*) to begin again 重新開始：*She wasn't happy with our work and made us start over.* 她對我們幹的活兒不滿意，要我們返工。**ˌstart 'up** | **ˌstart sth↔'up** to begin working, happening, etc.; to make sth do this（使）啟動，發動，開始：*I heard his car start up.* 我聽見他的汽車發動了。◇ *Start up the engines!* 發動引擎！➲ see also START-UP

■ ***noun***

▸ **BEGINNING** 開始 **1** [C, usually sing.] the point at which sth begins 開頭；開端：*a perfect start to the day* 那一天的美好開端 ◇ *Things didn't look too hopeful at the start of the year.* 在年初，情況顯得並不十分樂觀。◇ *The meeting* ***got off to a good/bad start*** (= started well/badly). 會議有一個良好的 / 糟糕的開端。◇ *The trip was a disaster* ***from start to finish.*** 那次旅行從頭到尾糟糕透頂。◇ *We've had problems* ***(right) from the start.*** 我們從（一）開始就遇到了困難。◇ (*informal*) *This could be the start of something big.* 這或許是要有大事的苗頭。**2** [sing.] the act or process of beginning sth 開始：*I'll paint the ceiling if you* ***make a start on*** *the walls.* 你要是動手刷牆，我就刷天花板吧。◇ *I want to make an early start in the morning.* 我想早上早點出發。◇ *She's moving abroad to make a* ***fresh start*** (= to begin a new life). 她要移居國外，開始新的生活。➲ see also FALSE START, KICK-START

▸ **OPPORTUNITY** 機會 **3** [C, usually sing.] the opportunity that you are given to begin sth in a successful way 起始優勢；良好的基礎條件：*They worked hard to give their children a good* ***start in life.*** 他們力爭為孩子們奠定一個良好的基礎。◇ *The job gave him his start in journalism.* 那份工作是他加入新聞界的開始。

▸ **IN RACE** 比賽 **4 the start** [sing.] the place where a race begins 起點：*The runners lined up at the start.* 賽跑運動員在起跑線上一字排開。**5** [C, usually sing.] an amount of time or distance that sb has as an advantage over other people at the beginning of a race 起跑的提前量（時間或距離）：*She went into the second round with a five-minute start on the rest of the cyclists.* 她進入了第二輪比賽，並取得其他自行車選手提前五分鐘出發的優勢。◇ *I gave the younger children a start.* 我讓年幼的孩子提前起跑。➲ see also HEAD START **6** [C, usually pl.] (*sport* 體) a race or competition that sb has taken part in（參加的）比賽：*She has been beaten only once in six starts.* 她參加了六次比賽，只敗過一次。

▸ SUDDEN MOVEMENT 突然一動 **7** [C, usually sing.] an act of moving your body quickly and suddenly because you are surprised, afraid, etc. 突然一驚：*She woke from the dream* ***with a start.*** 她猛地一驚，從夢中醒來。◇ *You gave me quite a start!* 你嚇了我一大跳！

IDM **for a 'start** (*informal*) used to emphasize the first of a list of reasons, opinions, etc.（強調一系列理由、意見等的第一條）首先：*I'm not working there—for a start, it's too far to travel.* 我不去那邊幹活兒。首先，路太遠，去不了。➲ more at FIT *n.*, FLYING START

start·er /'stɑːtə(r); *NAmE* 'stɑːrt-/ *noun* **1** (*especially BrE*) (*NAmE* usually **ap·pe·tiz·er**) a small amount of food that is served before the main course of a meal（主菜之前的）開胃小吃，開胃品 ➲ COLLOCATIONS at RESTAURANT ➲ compare HORS D'OEUVRE **2** a person, horse, car, etc. that is in a race at the beginning 參賽人；參賽的馬（或汽車等）：*Only 8 of the 28 starters completed the course.* * 28 名參賽者中，只有 8 人完成了全程。➲ compare NON-STARTER **3** a person who gives the signal for a race to start（賽跑等的）發令員 **4** a device used for starting the engine of a vehicle（發動機的）啟動裝置，啟動器 **5** a person who begins doing a particular activity in the way mentioned 起步（或啟動）…的人：*He was a* ***late starter*** *in the theatre* (= older than most people when they start). 他從事戲劇表演起步較晚。◇ *a* ***slow starter*** 做事起步慢的人 ➲ see also SELF-STARTER **6** (often used as an adjective 常用作形容詞) something that is intended to be used by sb who is starting to do sth 在起步階段使用的；啟動時用的：*a* ***starter home*** (= a small home for sb who is buying property for the first time) 供初次購房者購買的房屋 ◇ *a* ***starter kit/pack*** 入門工具包

IDM **for 'starters** (*informal*) used to emphasize the first of a list of reasons, opinions, etc., or to say what happens first（強調一系列理由、意見等的第一條或表示首先發生的事）首先，作為開頭 **under ˌstarter's 'orders** (of a runner, rider, etc. 賽跑運動員、騎手等) waiting for a signal to start a race 等待發令員發令

'starting blocks (also **the blocks**) *noun* [pl.] the two blocks on the ground that runners push their feet against at the beginning of a race 起跑器 ➲ VISUAL VOCAB page V47

'starting gate *noun* a barrier that is raised to let horses or dogs start running in a race（賽馬或賽狗等比賽用的）起跑門

'starting pistol *noun* a gun used for signalling the start of a race（速度競賽）發令槍

S

'starting point *noun* **1 ~ (for sth)** a thing, an idea or a set of facts that can be used to begin a discussion or process（討論或過程的）起點，基礎：*The article served as a useful starting point for our discussion.* 這篇文章成了我們展開討論的良好起點。**2** the place where you begin a journey（旅行的）起點，出發點

'starting price *noun* the final ODDS that are given for a horse or dog just before a race begins（賽馬或賽狗的）臨賽賠率

star·tle /'stɑːtl; *NAmE* 'stɑːrtl/ *verb* to surprise sb suddenly in a way that slightly shocks or frightens them 使驚嚇；使嚇一跳；使大吃一驚：**~ sb/sth** *I didn't mean to startle you.* 我不是存心要嚇唬你。◇ *The explosion startled the horse.* 爆炸聲使馬受了驚。◇ *I was startled by her question.* 她的問題讓我大吃一驚。◇ **it startles sb to do sth** *It startled me to find her sitting in my office.* 我一進辦公室，發現她坐在裏面，把我嚇了一跳。➲ SYNONYMS at SURPRISE ▸ **star·tled** /'stɑːtld; *NAmE* 'stɑːrtld/ *adj.*：*She looked at him with startled eyes.* 她用吃驚的目光看着他。◇ *He looked startled.* 他顯得很驚訝。◇ *She jumped back like a startled rabbit.* 她像受驚的兔子似的跳了回去。

start·ling /'stɑːtlɪŋ; *NAmE* 'stɑːrt-/ *adj.* **1** extremely unusual and surprising 驚人的；讓人震驚的：*a startling discovery* 驚人的發現 **2** (of a colour 顏色) extremely bright 極鮮亮的：*startling blue eyes* 藍盈盈的眼睛 ▸ **start·ling·ly** *adv.*

'start-up *adj.*, *noun*

■ ***adj.*** [only before noun] connected with starting a new business or project（新企業或工程）開辦階段的，啟動時期的：*start-up costs* 啟動經費

■ ***noun*** a company that is just beginning to operate, especially an Internet company 剛成立的公司，新企業（尤指互聯網公司）

ˌstar 'turn *noun* [usually sing.] the main performer or entertainer in a show（節目的）主要演員，主要環節

star·va·tion /stɑː'veɪʃn; *NAmE* stɑːr'v-/ *noun* [U] the state of suffering and death caused by having no food 飢餓；捱餓；餓死：*to* ***die of/from starvation*** 餓死 ◇ *Millions will* ***face starvation*** *next year as a result of the drought.* 由於發生旱災，明年將有數百萬人面臨飢餓的威脅。◇ *a* ***starvation diet*** (= one in which you do not have much to eat) 不足果腹的食物 ◇ *They were on* ***starvation wages*** (= extremely low wages). 他們掙的工資不夠維持基本生活。

starve /stɑːv; *NAmE* stɑːrv/ *verb* **1** [I, T] to suffer or die because you do not have enough food to eat; to make sb suffer or die in this way（使）捱餓，餓死：*The animals were left to starve to death.* 那些動物只能等着餓死。◇ *pictures of starving children* 展示飢餓兒童的圖片 ◇ *The new job doesn't pay as much but we won't starve!* 新工作的工資沒有過去多，不過我們不至於捱餓！◇ **~ sb/yourself** *She's starving herself to try to lose weight.* 她試圖通過節食來減肥。**2 -starved** (in adjectives 構成形容詞) not having sth that you need 缺乏…的；急需…的：*supply-starved rebels* 補給匱乏的反叛者 ➲ see also CASH-STARVED

IDM **be 'starving (for sth)** (also **be 'starved** especially in *NAmE*) (*informal*) to feel very hungry 餓得很：*When's the food coming? I'm starving!* 食物什麼時候上來？我快餓死了！

PHR V **ˌstarve sb into 'sth/into 'doing sth** to force sb to do sth by not allowing them to get any food or money 斷絕食物（或資金）來源以迫使某人做某事 **ˌstarve sb/sth of 'sth** (*NAmE* also **ˌstarve sb/sth for 'sth**) [usually passive] to not give sth that is needed 使某人（或事物）得不到所需要的：*I felt starved of intelligent conversation.* 讓我感到痛苦的是無法與有識之士交談。◇ *The department has been starved of resources.* 這個部門一直缺少資源。**ˌstarve sb↔'out (of sth)** to force sb to leave a particular building or area by not allowing them to get any food 以斷絕食物來源迫使某人出來

stash /stæʃ/ *verb*, *noun*

■ ***verb*** **~ sth + adv./prep.** (*informal*) to store sth in a safe or secret place 存放；貯藏；隱藏：*She has a fortune* ***stashed away*** *in various bank accounts.* 她有一大筆錢存在幾個不同的銀行賬戶下。

■ ***noun*** [usually sing.] (*informal*) an amount of sth that is kept secretly 一批貯藏物：*a stash of money* 一筆存款

sta·sis /'steɪsɪs/ *noun* [U, C] (*pl.* **sta·ses** /-siːz/) (*formal*) a situation in which there is no change or development 停滯；靜止

stat /stæt/ *noun* (*NAmE*, *informal*) = STATISTIC (3)

state 0‐ᵚ /steɪt/ *noun*, *adj.*, *verb*

■ ***noun***

▸ CONDITION OF SB/STH 狀態 **1** 0‐ᵚ [C] the mental, emotional or physical condition that a person or thing is in 狀態；狀況；情況：*a confused* ***state of mind*** 思緒紛亂 ◇ *He was in a state of permanent depression.* 他一直處於消沉狀態。◇ *anxieties about the state of the country's economy* 對於國家經濟狀況的擔憂 ◇ *The building is in a bad* ***state of repair*** (= needs to be repaired). 那座房子年久失修。◇ *She was in a* ***state of shock.*** 她震驚不已。◇ (*BrE, informal*) *Look at the state of you! You can't go out looking like that.* 看看你這副樣子！你可不能就這麼出去。◇ *You're* ***not in a fit state*** *to drive.* 你現在的狀態不宜開車。➲ SYNONYMS at CONDITION

▸ COUNTRY 國家 **2** 0‐ᵚ (also **State**) [C] a country considered as an organized political community controlled by one government 國家：*the Baltic States* 波羅的海諸國 ◇ *European Union member states* 歐盟成員國 ➲ see also CITY STATE, NATION STATE, POLICE STATE, WELFARE STATE ➲ note at COUNTRY

▸ **PART OF COUNTRY** 國家的一部份 **3** (also **State**) [C] (*abbr.* **St.**) an organized political community forming part of a country 州；邦：*the states of Victoria and Western Australia* 維多利亞和西澳大利亞兩州 ◇ *the southern states of the US* 美國南方各州

▸ **GOVERNMENT** 政府 **4** (also **the State**) [U, sing.] the government of a country 政府：***matters/affairs of state*** 國家大事 ◇ *people who are financially dependent on the state* 依靠國家救濟的人 ◇ *a state-owned company* 國營公司 ◇ *They wish to limit the power of the State.* 他們希望限制政府權力。

▸ **OFFICIAL CEREMONY** 正式禮儀 **5** [U] the formal ceremonies connected with high levels of government or with kings and queens（適用於國家元首或政府首腦的）正式禮儀，隆重儀式：*The president was driven **in state** through the streets.* 總統乘車隆重地從街上穿過。

▸ **THE US** 美國 **6 the States** [pl.] (*informal*) the United States of America 美國：*I've never been to the States.* 我從未去過美國。

IDM **be in/get into a 'state** (*informal, especially BrE*) **1** to be/become excited or anxious 興奮；緊張；焦慮：*She was in a real state about her exams.* 她對考試感到很緊張。 **2** to be dirty or untidy 邋遢；凌亂；不整潔：*What a state this place is in!* 這地方真夠亂的！ **in a state of 'grace** (in the Roman Catholic Church) having been forgiven by God for the wrong or evil things you have done（羅馬天主教指靈魂上沒有大罪的狀態）受天主眷愛，蒙受恩寵 **a state of af'fairs** a situation 事態；情況；形勢：*This state of affairs can no longer be ignored.* 再不能無視這種情況了。 ➲ SYNONYMS at SITUATION **the state of 'play 1** the stage that has been reached in a process, etc. which has not yet been completed 進展情況；發展階段：*What is the current state of play in the peace talks?* 和平談判目前進展得怎麼樣？ **2** (*especially BrE*) the score in a sports match, especially in CRICKET（板球等比賽的）比分

■ ***adj.*** (also **State**) [only before noun]

▸ **GOVERNMENT** 政府 **1** provided or controlled by the government of a country 國家提供（或控制）的：*state education* 公辦教育 ◇ *families dependent on state benefits* (= in Britain, money given by the government to people who are poor) 靠政府救濟金生活的家庭 ◇ *state secrets* (= information that could be harmful to a country if it were discovered by an enemy) 國家機密

▸ **OFFICIAL** 官方 **2** connected with the leader of a country attending an official ceremony 國事禮儀（或規格）的：*The Queen is on a state visit to Moscow.* 女王正對莫斯科進行國事訪問。◇ *the state opening of Parliament* 隆重的議會開幕式 ◇ *the state apartments* (= used for official ceremonies) 國事活動廳

▸ **PART OF COUNTRY** 國家的一部份 **3** connected with a particular state of a country, especially in the US 州的；邦的：*a **state prison/hospital/university, etc.*** 州監獄、州立醫院、州立大學等 ◇ ***state police/troopers*** 州警察 ◇ *a state tax* 州稅

■ ***verb*** **1** to formally write or say sth, especially in a careful and clear way 陳述；說明；聲明：**~ sth** *He has already stated his intention to run for election.* 他已聲明打算參加競選。◇ *The facts are clearly stated in the report.* 報道對事實真相作了清楚的說明。◇ *There is no need to **state the obvious*** (= to say sth that everyone already knows). 顯而易見的事實就不必陳述了。◇ **~ how, what, etc. …** *State clearly how many tickets you require.* 說清楚你需要多少張票。◇ **~ that …** *He stated categorically that he knew nothing about the deal.* 他明確表示對協議的事一無所知。◇ **it is stated that …** *It was stated that standards at the hospital were dropping.* 據稱，那家醫院的醫療水準在不斷下降。◇ **sth is stated to be/have sth** *The contract was stated to be invalid.* 那份合同宣佈作廢。 ➲ SYNONYMS at DECLARE **2** [usually passive] **~ sth** to fix or announce the details of sth, especially on a written document 規定；公佈：*This is not one of their stated aims.* 在他們宣佈的目標裏沒有這一條。◇ *You must arrive at the time stated.* 你必須在規定時間到達。◇ *Do not exceed the stated dose* (= of medicine). 不要超過規定的劑量。

state·craft /'steɪtkrɑːft; *NAmE* -kræft/ *noun* [U] skill in managing state and political affairs 治國才能；政務才能

the 'State Department *noun* the US government department of foreign affairs（美國）國務院

state·hood /'steɪthʊd/ *noun* [U] **1** the fact of being an independent country and of having the rights and powers of a country 獨立國家地位 **2** the condition of being one of the states within a country such as the US or Australia 州（或邦）的地位：*West Virginia was granted statehood in 1863.* 西弗吉尼亞於 1863 年獲准成為一個州。

'state house *noun* [usually sing.] (in the US) a building in which a state LEGISLATURE (= parliament) meets（美國）州議會大廈

state·less /'steɪtləs/ *adj.* not officially a citizen of any country 無國籍的 ▸ **state·less·ness** *noun* [U]

state·let /'steɪtlət/ *noun* a small state, especially one that is formed when a larger state breaks up（尤指大國分裂後形成的）小國

,state 'line *noun* the line between two states in the US（美國）州界，州界線：*the Nevada-California state line* 內華達和加利福尼亞兩州州界

state·ly /'steɪtli/ *adj.* **1** impressive in size, appearance or manner 宏大的；壯觀的；氣宇不凡的；儀態高貴的 **SYN** **majestic**：*an avenue of stately chestnut trees* 兩邊有雄偉高大栗樹的林蔭道 ◇ *a tall, stately woman* 儀態高貴的高個子女人 **2** slow, formal and elegant 緩慢莊嚴的；優雅從容的：*a stately dance* 緩慢優雅的舞蹈 ◇ *The procession made its stately progress through the streets of the city.* 遊行隊伍緩慢而莊嚴地穿過城市的街道。 ▸ **state·li·ness** *noun* [U]

,stately 'home *noun* (*BrE*) a large, impressive house of historical interest, especially one that the public may visit（具歷史價值，尤指可供人參觀的）豪華大宅 ➲ VISUAL VOCAB page V15

state·ment /'steɪtmənt/ *noun, verb*

■ ***noun*** **1** [C] something that you say or write that gives information or an opinion 說明；說法；表白；表態：*Are the following statements true or false?* 下面的說法對不對？◇ *Your statement is misleading.* 你的表述令人誤解。◇ *Is that a statement or a question?* 這是在表態呢，還是提出問題呢？◇ *The play makes a strong political statement.* 這齣戲表明一種鮮明的政治立場。 ➲ see also FASHION STATEMENT **2** [C] **~ (on/about sth)** a formal or official account of facts or opinions 聲明；陳述；報告 **SYN** **declaration**：***a formal/ a public/a written/an official statement*** 正式／公開／書面／官方聲明 ◇ *A government spokesperson **made a statement** to the press.* 政府發言人向新聞界發表了一份聲明。◇ *The prime minister is expected to **issue a statement** on the policy change this afternoon.* 人們預計首相將在今天下午就政策的改變發表聲明。◇ *The police asked me to **make a statement*** (= a written account of facts concerning a crime, used in court if legal action follows). 警方要求我寫一份供述。 **3** [C] a printed record of money paid, received, etc. 結算單；清單；報表：*The directors are responsible for preparing the company's financial statements.* 幾位董事負責填寫公司的財務報表。◇ *My bank sends me monthly statements.* 銀行按月給我寄來結算單。 ➲ see also BANK STATEMENT **4** [C] (in England and Wales 英格蘭和威爾士) an official report on a child's special needs made by a local education authority（地方教育主管部門針對兒童的特殊需要做出的）評估報告：*a statement of special educational needs* 特殊教育需要評估報告 **5** [U] (*formal*) the act of stating or expressing sth in words（文字）陳述，表述 **SYN** **expression**：*When writing instructions, clarity of statement is the most important thing.* 編寫操作說明時，表述清晰明白至為重要。

IDM **,make a 'statement** to express or reveal an opinion or characteristic in a very clear way, although often without words 表明（意見或個性，但通常不是用語言）：*The cleaning staff extended their strike mainly to make a statement about how determined they were.* 清潔工人延長了罷工時間，主要目的是表明他們的決心。◇ *The way you dress makes a statement about you.* 你的衣着表明了你的性格。

S

■ *verb* [often passive] **~ sb** (in England and Wales 英格蘭和威爾士) to officially decide and report that a child has special needs for his or her education 對兒童進行特殊教育評估認定：*statemented children* 評估認定須接受特殊教育的學童

Synonyms 同義詞辨析

statement

comment • announcement • remark • declaration • observation

These are all words for sth that you say or write, especially sth that gives information or an opinion. 以上各詞均指口頭或書面的說明、宣佈。

statement something that you say or write that gives information or an opinion, often in a formal way 通常指正式的說明、聲明、陳述、報告：*A government spokesperson made a statement to the press.* 政府發言人向新聞界發表了一份聲明。

comment something that you say or write that gives an opinion on sth or is a response to a question about a particular situation 指議論、評論、意見：*She made helpful comments on my work.* 她對我的工作提出了有益的意見。

announcement a spoken or written statement that informs people about sth 指公告、佈告、通告：*the announcement of a peace agreement* 和平協議公告

remark something that you say or write that gives an opinion or thought about sb/sth 指談論、言論、評述：*He made a number of rude remarks about the food.* 他對這食物作了許多無禮的評論。

declaration (*rather formal*) an official or formal statement, especially one that states an intention, belief or feeling, or that gives information 指官方或正式的公告、宣告、宣言、聲明：*the declaration of war* 宣戰

observation (*rather formal*) a comment, especially one based on sth you have seen, heard or read 尤指根據所見、所聞、所讀而作的評論：*He began by making a few general observations about the report.* 開頭他先對這個報告作了幾點概括性的評論。

COMMENT, REMARK OR OBSERVATION? 用 comment、remark 還是 observation？

A **comment** can be official or private. A **remark** can be made in public or private but is always unofficial and the speaker may not have considered it carefully. An **observation** is unofficial but is usually more considered than a remark. * comment 既可是官方的也可是私下的；remark 既可是公開的也可是私下的，但總是非官方的，說話者可能未經深思熟慮；observation 是非官方的，但通常較 remark 多幾分考慮。

PATTERNS

- a(n) statement/comment/announcement/remark/declaration/observation **about** sth
- a(n) statement/comment/observation **on** sth
- a(n) **public/official** statement/comment/announcement/declaration
- to **make** a(n) statement/comment/announcement/remark/declaration/observation
- to **issue** a(n) statement/announcement/declaration

S

ˌstate of ˈsiege *noun* a situation in which the government limits people's freedom to enter or leave a city, town or building 戒嚴（或封鎖）狀態

ˌstate of the ˈart *adj.* using the most modern or advanced techniques or methods; as good as it can be at the present time 應用最先進技術（或方法）的；最先進的：*The system was state of the art.* 這一系統是當時最先進的。◇ *a state-of-the-art system* 目前最先進的系統

the ˌState of the ˈUnion Address *noun* [sing.] (in the US) a speech about the achievements and plans of the government that the President gives to Congress once a year 國情咨文（美國總統就政府業績和規劃在國會所作的年度講話）

state·room /ˈsteɪtruːm; -rʊm/ *noun* **1** a private room on a large ship（輪船上的）特等客艙 **2** a room used by important government members, members of a royal family, etc. on formal occasions（政府要員或王室成員等使用的）會客廳，議事廳，國事活動廳

ˌstate's atˈtorney *noun* (*US*) a lawyer who represents a state in a court（美國）州檢察官

ˈstate school *noun* **1** (*BrE*) (*NAmE* **ˈpublic school**) a school that is paid for by the government and provides free education 公立學校 ➲ compare PRIVATE SCHOOL, PUBLIC SCHOOL (2) **2** (*NAmE*) = STATE UNIVERSITY

ˌstate's ˈevidence *noun* [U] (*US, law* 律) if a criminal **turns state's evidence**, he or she gives evidence against the people who committed a crime with him or her 同案犯證據；知情人的證據

state·side /ˈsteɪtsaɪd/ *adj., adv.* (*US, informal*) connected with the US; in or towards the US (used when the person speaking is not in the US)（用以在境外指美國）美國的（地），在美國的（地），去美國的（地）：*When are you next planning a trip stateside?* 你計劃下一次什麼時候去美國？

states·man /ˈsteɪtsmən/ *noun* (*pl.* **-men** /-mən/) a wise, experienced and respected political leader 政治家：*the party's* **elder statesman** 該黨元老

states·man·like /ˈsteɪtsmənlaɪk/ *adj.* having or showing the qualities and abilities of a statesman 具有政治家風範的；像政治家的：*He was commended for his statesmanlike handling of the crisis.* 他處理那場危機時，因表現出政治家的才幹而受到稱讚。

states·man·ship /ˈsteɪtsmənʃɪp/ *noun* [U] skill in managing state affairs 政治才能；治國才幹

states·per·son /ˈsteɪtspɜːsn; *NAmE* -pɜːrsn/ *noun* (*pl.* **-people**) a wise, experienced and respected political leader 政治家

ˌstates' ˈrights *noun* [pl.] (in the US 美國) the rights of each state in relation to the national government, such as the right to make some laws and to have its own police force 州權（相對於國家政府的權力，如制訂某些法律和擁有自己的警察）

ˌstate ˈtrooper (also **troop·er**) *noun* (*NAmE*) (in the US 美國) a member of a State police force 州警察

ˈstate university (also **ˈstate school**) *noun* (both *NAmE*) a university that is managed by a state of the US（美國）州立大學

state·wide /ˈsteɪtwaɪd/ *adj., adv.* happening or existing in all parts of a state of the US（美國）全州性的（地），在全州範圍內的（地）：*a statewide election* 州選舉 ◇ *She won 10% of the vote statewide.* 她贏得全州 10% 的選票。

static /ˈstætɪk/ *adj., noun*

■ *adj.* **1** not moving, changing or developing 靜止的；靜態的；停滯的：*Prices on the stock market, which have been static, are now rising again.* 股市價格一直停滯不動，現在又在上漲了。◇ *a static population level* 穩定的人口水平 **2** (*physics* 物) (of a force 力) acting as a weight but not producing movement 靜力的：*static pressure* 靜壓 OPP **dynamic**

■ *noun* [U] **1** noise or other effects that disturb radio or television signals and are caused by particular conditions in the atmosphere 天電（干擾） **2** (also **ˌstatic elecˈtricity**) electricity that gathers on or in an object which is not a CONDUCTOR of electricity 靜電：*My hair gets full of static when I brush it.* 我梳頭時頭髮就有好多靜電。 **3 statics** the science that deals with the forces that balance each other to keep objects in a state of rest 靜力學 ➲ compare DYNAMIC *n.* (2) **4** (*NAmE, informal*) angry or critical comments or behaviour 抨擊；指責；憤慨

sta·tin /ˈstætɪn/ *noun* a drug that people take to lower the level of CHOLESTEROL (= a substance in the body that can cause heart disease) in their blood. There are several types of statin. 膽固醇合成酶抑制劑；他汀

sta·tion 0-π /ˈsteɪʃn/ *noun, verb*

■ ***noun***

▸ **FOR TRAINS/BUSES** 火車；公共汽車 **1** 0-π a place where trains stop so that passengers can get on and off; the buildings connected with this 火車站：*I get off at the next station.* 我在下一站下車。◇ *the main station* 中心車站 ◇ *Penn Station* 賓州車站 ◇ *a* ***train station*** 火車站 ◇ (*BrE* also) *a* ***railway station*** 火車站 ◇ (*BrE*) ***a tube/an underground station*** 地鐵站 ◇ (*NAmE*) *a* ***subway station*** 地鐵站 **2** 0-π (usually in compounds 通常構成複合詞) a place where buses stop; the buildings connected with this 公共汽車站；長途汽車站：*a* ***bus/coach station*** 公共汽車 / 長途汽車站 **HELP** In Britain, the word **station** on its own usually refers to the train station. 在英國，station 單獨使用時通常指火車站：*Can you tell me the way to the station?* In the US it is usual to say which station you are talking about. 在美國，station 通常指明是什麼車站：*the train station* ◇ *the Greyhound Bus station*

▸ **FOR WORK/SERVICE** 工作；服務 **3** 0-π (usually in compounds 通常構成複合詞) a place or building where a service is organized and provided or a special type of work is done 站；所；局：*a police station* 警察局 ◇ (*BrE*) *a* ***petrol station*** 加油站 ◇ (*NAmE*) *a* ***gas station*** 加油站 ◇ *an agricultural research station* 農業研究所 ◇ *a pollution monitoring station* 污染監測站 ➲ compare SPACE STATION

▸ **RADIO/TV COMPANY** 廣播 / 電視公司 **4** 0-π (often in compounds 常構成複合詞) a radio or television company and the programmes it broadcasts 電台；電視台：*a local* ***radio/TV station*** 地方廣播電台 / 電視台 ◇ *He tuned to another station.* 他換了一個台。

▸ **SOCIAL POSITION** 社會地位 **5** (*old-fashioned* or *formal*) your social position 社會地位；身分：*She was definitely getting ideas* ***above her station.*** 她明顯是抱有超出自己身分的想法。

▸ **POSITION** 位置 **6** a place where sb has to wait and watch or be ready to do work if needed 須堅守的位置；崗位；戰位：*You are not to leave your station without permission.* 未經允許，不得離開崗位。➲ see also DOCKING STATION

▸ **LARGE FARM** 大農場 **7** (usually in compounds 通常構成複合詞) a large sheep or CATTLE farm in Australia or New Zealand（澳大利亞或新西蘭放養牛或羊的）大型牧場

▸ **FOR ARMY/NAVY** 陸軍；海軍 **8** a small base for the army or navy; the people living in it 軍事基地；駐軍：*a naval station* 海軍基地 ➲ see also ACTION STATIONS
IDM see PANIC *n.*

■ ***verb***

▸ **ARMED FORCES** 武裝部隊 **1** [often passive] **~ sb + adv./prep.** to send sb, especially from one of the armed forces, to work in a place for a period of time 派駐；使駐紮：*troops stationed abroad* 駐紮在國外的部隊

▸ **GO TO POSITION** 前往 **2 ~ sb/yourself + adv./prep.** (*formal*) to go somewhere and stand or sit there, especially to wait for sth; to send sb somewhere to do this 到某處站（或坐）；把…安置到（某處）：*She stationed herself at the window to await his return.* 她待在窗前等他回來。

ˈstation agent (*US*) (*BrE* **sta·tion·mas·ter**) *noun* a person in charge of a train station（火車站）站長

sta·tion·ary /ˈsteɪʃənri; *NAmE* -neri/ *adj.* **1** not moving; not intended to be moved 不動的；靜止的；固定的；不可移動的：*I remained stationary.* 我待着沒動。◇ *The car collided with a stationary vehicle.* 小汽車撞到一輛停着的車上。◇ *a stationary exercise bike* 固定式健身自行車 **OPP** **mobile** **2** not changing in condition or quantity 不變的；穩定的 **SYN** **static**：*a stationary population* 穩定的人口

sta·tion·er /ˈsteɪʃənə(r)/ *noun* (*especially BrE*) **1** a person who owns or manages a shop selling stationery 文具商 **2 stationer's** (*pl.* **stationers**) a shop that sells stationery 文具店：*Is there a stationer's near here?* 這附近有沒有文具店？

sta·tion·ery /ˈsteɪʃənri; *NAmE* -neri/ *noun* [U] **1** materials for writing and for using in an office, for example paper, pens and envelopes 文具 ➲ **VISUAL VOCAB** page V69 **2** special paper for writing letters on 信紙；信箋

ˈstation house *noun* (*NAmE*) = POLICE STATION

sta·tion·mas·ter /ˈsteɪʃnmɑːstə(r); *NAmE* -mæs-/ (*BrE*) (*US* **ˈstation agent**) *noun* a person in charge of a train station（火車站）站長

ˈstation wagon (*NAmE*) (*BrE* **eˈstate car**, **estate**) *noun* a car with a lot of space behind the back seats and a door at the back for loading large items 旅行轎車；客貨兩用車 ➲ **VISUAL VOCAB** page V52

stat·ism /ˈsteɪtɪzəm/ *noun* [U] a political system in which the central government controls social and economic affairs 中央集權制 ▸ **stat·ist** *adj.*, *noun*

stat·is·tic **AW** /stəˈtɪstɪk/ *noun* **1** **statistics** (also *informal* **stats**) [pl.] a collection of information shown in numbers 統計數字；統計資料：***crime/unemployment, etc. statistics*** 犯罪、失業等統計資料 ◇ *According to official statistics the disease killed over 500 people.* 根據官方的統計數字，500 多人死於這種疾病。◇ ***Statistics show*** *that far more people are able to ride a bicycle than can drive a car.* 統計資料表明，會騎自行車的人比會開汽車的人多得多。◇ *These statistics are misleading.* 這些統計資料會引起誤解。➲ see also VITAL STATISTICS **2** **statistics** (also *informal* **stats**) [U] the science of collecting and analysing statistics 統計學：*There is a compulsory course in statistics.* 有一門統計學的必修課。**3** (*NAmE, informal* **stat**) [C] a piece of information shown in numbers（一項）統計數據：*An important statistic is that 94 per cent of crime relates to property.* 一個重要數據是 94% 的犯罪同財產有關。◇ *I felt I was no longer being treated as a person but as a statistic.* 我感覺我不再被看作人，而被看作一個統計數字了。▸ **stat·is·tic·al** **AW** /stəˈtɪstɪkl/ *adj.*：*statistical analysis* 統計分析 **stat·is·tic·al·ly** **AW** /-kli/ *adv.*：*The difference between the two samples was not* ***statistically significant.*** 在統計學的意義上，這兩個樣品沒有顯著的差異。

stat·is·ti·cian **AW** /ˌstætɪˈstɪʃn/ *noun* a person who studies or works with statistics 統計學家；統計員

sta·tive /ˈsteɪtɪv/ *adj.* (*linguistics* 語言) (of verbs 動詞) describing a state rather than an action. **Stative** verbs (for example *be, seem, understand, like, own*) are not usually used in the progressive tenses. 表示狀態的 ➲ compare DYNAMIC *adj.* (4)

stats /stæts/ *noun* (*informal*) = STATISTICS (1), (2)

ˈstat sheet *noun* (*NAmE*) a piece of paper or a document which gives details of sth in the form of numbers, especially of a team's or a player's performance 數據單，數據文件，統計表（以數字形式提供某事的細節，尤用於運動隊或運動員表現）

statu·ary /ˈstætʃuəri; *NAmE* -eri/ *noun* [U] (*formal*) statues 雕塑；雕像；塑像：*a collection of marble statuary* 一批大理石雕像

statue 0-π /ˈstætʃuː/ *noun* a figure of a person or an animal in stone, metal, etc., usually the same size as in real life or larger 雕塑，雕像，塑像（大小通常等於或大於真人或實物）➲ **COLLOCATIONS** at ART ➲ **VISUAL VOCAB** pages V2, V3

the ˌStatue of ˈLiberty *noun* a statue at the entrance of New York HARBOUR, which represents a female figure carrying a book of laws in one hand and a TORCH in the other and is a symbol of welcome to people coming to live in the US（美國紐約港的）自由女神像

statu·esque /ˌstætʃuˈesk/ *adj.* (*formal*) (usually of a woman 通常指女性) tall and beautiful in an impressive way; like a statue 又高又美的；雕塑般的 **SYN** **imposing**

statu·ette /ˌstætʃuˈet/ *noun* a small statue 小雕像；小塑像

stat·ure /ˈstætʃə(r)/ *noun* [U] (*formal*) **1** the importance and respect that a person has because of their ability and achievements 聲望；名望：*an actress of considerable stature* 頗有名望的女演員 ◇ *The orchestra has grown in stature.* 這支管弦樂隊的聲望有所提高。**2** a person's

S

height 身高；個子：*a woman of short stature* 身材矮小的女人 ◇ *He is small in stature.* 他個頭小。

sta·tus **AW** /ˈsteɪtəs; *NAmE* also ˈstætəs/ *noun* [usually sing.]
1 [U, C] the legal position of a person, group or country 法律地位（或身分）：*They were granted refugee status.* 他們獲得了難民身分。◇ *The party was denied legal status.* 那個黨沒有獲得合法地位。 **2** [U, C, usually sing.] the social or professional position of sb/sth in relation to others 地位；身分；職位：*low status jobs* 地位低下的工作 ◇ *to have a high social status* 擁有很高的社會地位 ◇ *Women are only asking to be given equal status with men.* 婦女只是要求得到和男人平等的地位。◇ *She achieved celebrity status overnight.* 她一夜之間成為名流。 **3** [U] high rank or social position 高級職位；社會上層地位：*The job brings with it status and a high income.* 擔任這一職務既有顯貴的地位又有豐厚的收入。 **4** [U, C, usually sing.] the level of importance that is given to sth 重視（或崇尚）程度：*the high status accorded to science in our culture* 我們的文化對科學的高度崇尚 **5** [U] the situation at a particular time during a process （進展的）狀況，情形：*What is the current status of our application for funds?* 我們申請資金目前的狀況如何？

ˈstatus bar *noun* (*computing* 計) an area that you see along the bottom of your computer screen that gives you information about the program that you are using or the document that you are working on （電腦屏幕底部顯示程序或文件信息的）狀態條，狀態列

status quo /ˌsteɪtəs ˈkwəʊ; *NAmE* ˈkwoʊ/ *noun* [sing.] (*from Latin*) the situation as it is now, or as it was before a recent change 現狀；原來的狀況：*to* ***defend/restore the status quo*** 維持現狀；恢復原來的狀況 ◇ *conservatives who want to* ***maintain the status quo*** 想維持現狀的保守派

ˈstatus symbol *noun* a possession that people think shows their high social status and wealth 社會地位與財富的象徵：*Exotic pets are the latest status symbol.* 養珍禽異獸是表現社會地位的最時髦方式。

stat·ute /ˈstætʃuːt/ *noun* **1** a law that is passed by a parliament, council, etc. and formally written down 成文法；法令；法規：*Penalties are laid down* ***in the statute.*** 法規中有關於懲罰措施的規定。◇ *Corporal punishment was banned* ***by statute*** *in 1987.* * 1987 年通過的法令明文禁止體罰。 **2** a formal rule of an organization or institution 章程；條例；規程：***Under the statutes*** *of the university they had no power to dismiss him.* 按大學的規章制度，校方無權開除他。

ˈstatute book *noun* a collection of all the laws made by a government 法典；法令全書；法規彙編：*It's not yet* ***on the statute book*** (= it has not yet become law). 這項內容還未成為正式法規。

ˈstatute law *noun* [U] all the written laws of a parliament, etc. as a group 成文法 ➲ compare CASE LAW, COMMON LAW

ˌstatute of limiˈtations *noun* (*law* 律) the legal limit on the period of time within which action can be taken on a crime or other legal question 時效；訴訟時效法規；追訴權時效法

statu·tory /ˈstætʃətri; *NAmE* -tɔːri/ *adj.* [usually before noun] fixed by law; that must be done by law 法定的；依法必須執行的：*The authority failed to carry out its statutory duties.* 主管部門未履行自己的法定職責。◇ *When you buy foods you have certain statutory rights.* 在購買食物時，你有一定的法定權利。 ▸ **statu·tor·ily** *adv.*

ˌstatutory ˈholiday *noun* (*CanE*) a public holiday that is fixed by law 法定假日

ˌstatutory ˈinstrument *noun* (*law* 律) a law or other rule which has legal status 有法律地位的規章（或規定）；有效立法

ˌstatutory ofˈfence (*BrE*) (*NAmE* **ˌstatutory ofˈfense**) *noun* (*law* 律) a crime that is described by law and can be punished by a court 法定罪行

ˌstatutory ˈrape *noun* [U] (*NAmE, law* 律) the crime of having sex with sb who is not legally old enough 法定強姦罪（與未成年少女發生性行為）

staunch /stɔːntʃ/ *adj., verb*
■ *adj.* (*superlative* **staunch·est**, no *comparative*) strong and loyal in your opinions and attitude 忠實的；堅定的 **SYN** **faithful**：*a staunch supporter of the monarchy* 堅定地擁護君主制的人 ◇ *one of the president's staunchest allies* 總統最忠實的盟友之一 ◇ *a staunch Catholic* 篤信天主教的教徒 ▸ **staunch·ly** *adv.*：*She staunchly defended the new policy.* 她堅定地維護新政策。◇ *The family was staunchly Protestant.* 那一家人是忠實的新教徒。 **staunch·ness** *noun* [U]
■ *verb* (also **stanch** especially in *NAmE*) **~ sth** (*formal*) to stop the flow of sth, especially blood 止住（血等的）流出

stave /steɪv/ *noun, verb*
■ *noun* **1** a strong stick or pole 棍；棒；桶板；木柱：*fence staves* 籬笆樁 **2** (*BrE*) (also **staff** *NAmE, BrE*) (*music* 音) a set of five lines on which music is written 五線譜 ➲ picture at MUSIC
■ *verb* (**staved, staved** or **stove, stove** /stəʊv; *NAmE* stoʊv/)
PHR V **ˌstave sth↔ˈin** to break or damage sth by pushing it or hitting it from the outside 使向內塌陷；壓凹；撞破：*The side of the boat was staved in when it hit the rocks.* 船觸礁把船舷撞扁了。 **ˌstave sth↔ˈoff** (**staved, staved**) to prevent sth bad from affecting you for a period of time; to delay sth 暫時擋住（壞事）；延緩，推遲（某事物）：*to stave off hunger* 暫時解餓

stay /steɪ/ *verb, noun*
■ *verb* **1** [I] to continue to be in a particular place for a period of time without moving away 停留；待：*to stay in bed* 待在牀上 ◇ *'Do you want a drink?' 'No, thanks, I can't stay.'* "你要不要喝一杯？""不，謝謝，我不能久待。" ◇ *Stay there and don't move!* 待在那兒別動！◇ *We ended up staying for lunch.* 我們最終還是留了下來吃午飯。◇ *She* ***stayed at home*** (= did not go out to work) *while the children were young.* 孩子們小的時候，她沒出去上班。◇ *I'm* ***staying late*** *at the office tonight.* 今晚我要在辦公室待到很晚。◇ *My hat won't stay on!* 我的帽子怎麼都戴不住！◇ *Can you* ***stay behind*** *after the others have gone and help me clear up?* 你能不能等別人走後留下來幫我收拾收拾？◇ *We stayed to see what would happen.* 我們留下來看會發生什麼事。◇ **~ doing sth** *They stayed talking until well into the night.* 他們待在那兒一直談到深夜。 **HELP** In spoken English **stay** can be used with **and** plus another verb, instead of with **to** and the infinitive, to show purpose or to tell somebody what to do. 英語口語中，stay 後面可接 and 加另一個動詞，而不用 to 加不定式，以表示目的或要某人做某事：*I'll stay and help you.* 我留下來幫你吧。◇ *Can you stay and keep an eye on the baby?* 你可以留下來照看嬰兒嗎？ **2** [I] to continue to be in a particular state or situation 保持；繼續是 **SYN** **remain**：**+ adj.** *He never stays angry for long.* 他生氣時間從來不會長。◇ *I can't stay awake any longer.* 我睏得再也熬不住了。◇ *The store stays open until late on Thursdays.* 這商店每星期四都會開到很晚。◇ **+ adv./prep.** *I don't know why they stay together* (= remain married or in a relationship). 我不知道他們為什麼還在一起。◇ *Inflation stayed below 4% last month.* 上月的通貨膨脹率保持在 4% 以下。◇ **+ noun** *We promised to stay friends for ever.* 我們約定永遠做朋友。 **3** [I] to live in a place temporarily as a guest or visitor 暫住；逗留：*We found out we were staying in the same hotel.* 我們發現大家住在同一家旅館裏。◇ *My sister's coming to stay next week.* 下星期我妹妹要來住幾天。◇ *He's staying with friends this weekend.* 這個週末他要和幾個朋友一起過。◇ *I stayed three nights at my cousin's house.* 我在我表兄家住了三夜。 **HELP** In Indian, Scottish and South African English **stay** can mean 'to live in a place permanently'. 在印度、蘇格蘭和南非英語中，stay 可以指定居：*Where do you stay* (= where do you live)?

IDM **be here to ˈstay | have come to ˈstay** to be accepted or used by most people and therefore a permanent part of our lives 為多數人所接受；得到普遍認可：*It looks like televised trials are here to stay.* 看來電視直播審判成了一種風氣。 **stay!** used to tell a dog not to move（命令狗隻）別動 **stay the 'course** to continue doing sth until it has finished or been completed, even though it is difficult 堅持到底：*Very few of the trainees have stayed the course.* 極少受訓者堅持到底。 **stay your 'hand** (*old-fashioned* or *literary*) to stop yourself from doing sth; to prevent you from doing sth 住手；不做（某事） **stay the 'night** (*especially BrE*) to sleep at sb's house for one night（在某人家）過夜：*You can always stay the night at our house.* 你什麼時候來都可以在我們家過夜。 **stay 'put** (*informal*) if sb/sth **stays put**, they continue to be in the place where they are or where they have been put 待在原地；留在原處 ➲ more at CLEAR *adv.*, LOOSE *adj.*

PHR V **,stay a'round** (*informal*) to not leave somewhere 待着不走；不離開：*I'll stay around in case you need me.* 我就待在這兒，也許你用得着我。 **,stay a'way (from sb/sth)** 🔑 to not go near a particular person or place 離開，不接近（某人）；不去（某處）：*I want you to stay away from my daughter.* 我要你離我女兒遠遠的。 **,stay 'in** to not go out or to remain indoors 不外出；待在室內：*I feel like staying in tonight.* 今晚我想待在家裏。 **,stay 'on** to continue studying, working, etc. somewhere for longer than expected or after other people have left 留下來繼續（學習、工作等） **,stay 'out** 1 to continue to be outdoors or away from your house at night 待在戶外；不在家；（晚上）不回家 2 (of workers 工人) to continue to be on strike 繼續罷工 **,stay 'out of sth** 1 🔑 to not become involved in sth that does not concern you 不介入；不干預 2 🔑 to avoid sth 避開；遠離：*to stay out of trouble* 避免惹麻煩 **,stay 'over** to sleep at sb's house for one night（在某人家）過夜 **,stay 'up** to go to bed later than usual 深夜不睡；熬夜：*You've got school tomorrow. I don't want you **staying up late**.* 你明天要上學，我不想你熬夜。

■ **noun** 1 🔑 a period of staying; a visit 停留；逗留（時間）；做客：*I enjoyed my stay in Prague.* 我在布拉格逗留期間過得很開心。◇ *an overnight stay* 留下過夜 2 a rope or wire that supports a ship's MAST, a pole, etc.（船桅的）支索；（杆子等的）牽索，撐條 ➲ see also MAINSTAY

IDM **a ,stay of exe'cution** (*law* 律) a delay in following the order of a court 緩期執行：*to grant a stay of execution* 准予緩期執行

'stay-at-home *noun, adj.*

■ **noun** (*informal*, often *disapproving*) a person who rarely goes out or does anything exciting 不愛出門的人；戀家的人

■ **adj.** a **stay-at-home** mother or father is one who stays at home to take care of their children instead of going out to work 全職照顧家庭的

stay·cation /,steɪ'keɪʃn/ *noun* a holiday/vacation that you spend at or near your home 居家假；宅假；不出城度假

stay·er /'steɪə(r)/ *noun* (*BrE*) a person or an animal, especially a horse, with the ability to keep going in a tiring race or competition 有持久力的人；有耐力的動物（尤指賽馬）

'staying power *noun* [U] the ability to continue doing sth difficult or tiring until it is finished 持久力；耐力 **SYN** **stamina**

St Bernard /,snt 'bɜːnəd; *NAmE* ,seɪnt bɜːr'nɑːrd/ *noun* a large strong dog, originally from Switzerland, where it was trained to help find people who were lost in the snow 聖貝爾納德狗，瑞士救護犬（訓練來搜尋雪地失踪者）

St Chris·to·pher /,snt 'krɪstəfə; *NAmE* ,seɪnt 'krɪstəfər/ *noun* a small MEDAL with a picture of St Christopher (the PATRON SAINT of travellers) on it, that some people wear or carry with them when they go on a journey because they believe it will protect them from danger 聖克里斯托弗像章（旅行者為求平安而佩戴或攜帶的旅行主保像章）

STD /,es tiː 'diː/ *noun* 1 the abbreviation for 'sexually transmitted disease' (a disease that is passed from one person to another during sexual activity) 性傳播疾病（全寫為 sexually transmitted disease） 2 (*BrE*) the abbreviation for 'subscriber trunk dialling' (a system of making direct telephone calls over long distances) 用戶

中繼撥號，用戶長途撥號制（全寫為 subscriber trunk dialling）

St David's Day /,snt 'deɪvɪdz deɪ; *NAmE* ,seɪnt/ *noun* 1 March, a Christian festival of the national SAINT of Wales, when many Welsh people wear a DAFFODIL 聖大衛節（3 月 1 日，紀念威爾士主保聖人的基督教節日，很多威爾士人佩戴黃水仙）

stead /sted/ *noun*

IDM **in sb's/sth's 'stead** (*formal*) instead of sb/sth 代替某人（或某物）：*Foxton was dismissed and John Smith was appointed in his stead.* 福克斯頓被解職，受命接替他的是約翰 • 史密斯。 **stand sb in good 'stead** to be useful or helpful to sb when needed（需要時）對某人有用，對某人有利：*Your languages will stand you in good stead when it comes to finding a job.* 你懂得幾種語言，找工作時就會顯出優勢。

stead·fast /'stedfɑːst; *NAmE* -fæst/ *adj.* (*literary*, *approving*) not changing in your attitudes or aims 堅定的；不動搖的 **SYN** **firm**：*steadfast loyalty* 忠貞不渝 ◇ **~ in sth** *He remained steadfast in his determination to bring the killers to justice.* 他要將殺人兇手繩之以法的決心一直沒有動搖。 ▸ **stead·fast·ly** *adv.* **stead·fast·ness** *noun* [U]

steady 🔑 /'stedi/ *adj., verb, adv., exclamation*

■ **adj.** (**stead·ier**, **steadi·est**) 1 🔑 developing, growing, etc. gradually and in an even and regular way（發展、增長等）穩步的，持續的，勻速的 **SYN** **constant**：*five years of steady economic growth* 經濟持續五年的發展 ◇ *a steady decline in numbers* 數量逐漸下降 ◇ *We are making slow but steady progress.* 我們雖然緩慢但是在穩步前進。◇ *The castle receives a **steady stream** of visitors.* 前來參觀城堡的遊客流量保持穩定。 2 🔑 not changing and not interrupted 穩定的；恆定的 **SYN** **regular**：*His breathing was steady.* 他呼吸平穩。◇ *a **steady job/income*** 穩定的工作／收入 ◇ *She drove at a steady 50 mph.* 她以每小時 50 英里的穩定速度駕駛。◇ *They set off at a steady pace.* 他們以不緊不慢的速度出發了。◇ *a **steady boyfriend/girlfriend*** (= with whom you have a serious relationship or one that has lasted a long time) 關係穩定的男朋友／女朋友 ◇ *to have a steady relationship* 有穩定的關係 3 🔑 firmly fixed, supported or balanced; not shaking or likely to fall down 穩的；平穩的；穩固的：*He held the boat steady as she got in.* 他把船穩住，讓她上了船。◇ *I met his steady gaze.* 我迎向他凝視的目光。◇ *Such fine work requires a good eye and **a steady hand**.* 做這樣精細的工作，眼要尖，手要穩。 **OPP** **unsteady** 4 (of a person 人) sensible; who can be relied on 沉穩的；可靠的 ▸ **steadi·ly** 🔑 *adv.*：*The company's exports have been increasing steadily.* 公司的出口量一直穩步增長。◇ *The situation got steadily worse.* 情況逐漸惡化。◇ *He looked at her steadily.* 他凝視着她。◇ *The rain fell steadily.* 雨不緊不慢地下着。 **steadi·ness** *noun* [U]

IDM **(as) steady as a 'rock** extremely steady and calm; that you can rely on 十分可靠；穩如泰山；安如磐石 ➲ more at READY *adj.*

■ **verb** (**stead·ies**, **steady·ing**, **stead·ied**, **stead·ied**) 1 [T, I] **~ (yourself/sb/sth)** to stop yourself/sb/sth from moving, shaking or falling; to stop moving, shaking or falling 使穩；使平穩；穩住：*She steadied herself against the wall.* 她靠牆站穩。◇ *The lift rocked slightly, steadied, and the doors opened.* 電梯微微一晃又穩了下來，接着門開了。 2 [I] to stop changing and become regular again 恢復平穩；穩定下來：*Her heartbeat steadied.* 她的心跳平穩下來。◇ **~ against sth** *The pound steadied against the dollar.* 英鎊對美元的匯率穩定下來。 3 [T] **~ sb/sth** to make sb/sth calm 使平靜；使冷靜；使鎮定：*He took a few deep breaths to **steady his nerves**.* 他深深地吸了幾口氣，讓自己平靜下來。

■ **adv.** in a way that is steady and does not change or shake 穩定地；持續地；穩固地：*In trading today the dollar **held steady** against the yen.* 在今天的交易中，美元對日元的匯率保持穩定。

IDM **go 'steady (with sb)** (*old-fashioned*, *informal*) to have a romantic or sexual relationship with sb, in

S

which you see the other person regularly（和情侶）關係穩定

■ ***exclamation*** (*informal*) **1 ~ on** (becoming *old-fashioned*) used to tell sb to be careful about what they are saying or doing, for example because it is extreme or not appropriate（要求對方注意言行）哎，注意點：*Steady on! You can't say things like that about somebody you've never met.* 注意點！你從沒見過的人，不要那樣議論人家。 **2** used to tell sb to be careful（提醒對方小心）注意，當心，小心：*Steady! Don't fall off.* 小心！別摔下來。

steak /steɪk/ *noun* **1** (also *less frequent* **beef·steak**) [U, C] a thick slice of good quality beef 牛排：***fillet/rump/sirloin steak*** 裹脊／後腿肉／腰肉牛排◇*How would you like your steak done?* 您要求您的牛排做到幾成熟？◇*a* ***steak knife*** (= one with a special blade for eating steak with) 牛排餐刀 ➲ VISUAL VOCAB page V22 **2** [U, C] a thick slice of any type of meat 肉排；肉塊：*pork steak* 豬排◇*a gammon steak* 一厚片火腿 **3** [U] (often in compounds 常構成複合詞) beef that is not of the best quality, often sold in small pieces and used in PIES, STEWS, etc. 碎牛肉（不是最佳部位，常剁碎出售，可以燉或做餡等）：***braising/stewing steak*** 適合於燉的牛肉塊◇*a steak and kidney pie* 牛肉腰子餡餅 **4** [C] a large thick piece of fish 魚排；魚塊：*a cod steak* 鱈魚排

steak·house /ˈsteɪkhaʊs/ *noun* a restaurant that serves mainly steak 牛排餐館

steak tar·tare /ˌsteɪk tɑːˈtɑː(r); *NAmE* tɑːrˈtɑːr; ˈtɑːrtər/ *noun* [U, C] (from *French*) a dish made with raw chopped beef and raw eggs 韃靼牛排（用切碎的生牛肉加生雞蛋等）

steal 0‑ᵘ /stiːl/ *verb, noun*

■ ***verb*** (**stole** /stəʊl/; *NAmE* stoʊl/, **stolen** /ˈstəʊlən; *NAmE* ˈstoʊ-/) **1** 0‑ᵘ [I, T] to take sth from a person, shop/store, etc. without permission and without intending to return it or pay for it 偷；竊取：**~ (from sb/sth)** *We found out he'd been stealing from us for years.* 我們發現他從我們家偷東西已經好多年了。◇**~ sth (from sb/sth)** *My wallet was stolen.* 我的錢包給人偷了。◇*I* ***had*** *my wallet* ***stolen***. 我的錢包給人偷了。◇*Thieves stole jewellery worth over £10 000.* 竊賊偷走了價值 1 萬多英鎊的珠寶。◇*It's a crime to handle stolen goods.* 經銷贓物是犯法的。◇(*figurative*) *to steal sb's ideas* 剽竊某人的觀點 ➲ COLLOCATIONS at CRIME **2** [I] **+ adv./prep.** to move secretly and quietly so that other people do not notice you 偷偷地（或悄悄地）移動 SYN **creep**：*She stole out of the room so as not to wake the baby.* 她生怕驚醒嬰兒，躡手躡腳地從房間裏出來。◇(*figurative*) *A chill stole over her body.* 她突然感到渾身發冷。 **3** [T] **~ sth** (in BASEBALL 棒球) to run to the next BASE before another player from your team hits the ball, so that you are closer to scoring 偷（壘）：*He tried to steal second base but was out.* 他試圖偷二壘但被判出局。

IDM **steal a ˈglance/ˈlook (at sb/sth)** to look at sb/sth quickly so that nobody sees you doing it 偷偷看⋯一眼 **steal sb's ˈheart** (*literary*) to make sb fall in love with you 博得某人的歡心 **steal a ˈkiss (from sb)** (*literary*) to kiss sb suddenly or secretly 突然吻一下；偷吻 **steal a ˈmarch (on sb)** [no passive] to gain an advantage over sb by doing sth before them 搶先（某人）一步；搶得先機 **steal the ˈshow** [no passive] to attract more attention and praise than other people in a particular situation 吸引更多的注意；搶風頭：*As always, the children stole the show.* 和往常一樣，最引人注意的是孩子們。 **steal sb's ˈthunder** to get the attention, success, etc. that sb else was expecting, usually by saying or doing what they had intended to say or do 搶了某人的風頭（或功勞）；搶先講（或做）

■ ***noun*** (*NAmE*) (in BASEBALL 棒球) the act of running to another BASE while the PITCHER is throwing the ball 偷壘

IDM **be a ˈsteal** (*informal, especially NAmE*) to be for sale at an unexpectedly low price 以極低價出售；很便宜：*This suit is a steal at $80.* 這套西服只賣 80 元，跟白給差不多了。

stealth /stelθ/ *noun, adj.*

■ ***noun*** [U] the fact of doing sth in a quiet or secret way 偷偷摸摸；不聲張的活動；秘密行動：*The government was accused of trying to introduce the tax* ***by stealth***. 有人指責政府想不事聲張地開徵這種稅。◇*Lions rely on stealth when hunting.* 獅子捕食全憑偷襲。

■ ***adj.*** [only before noun] (of an aircraft 飛機) designed in a way that makes it difficult to be discovered by RADAR 隱形的：*a stealth bomber* 隱形轟炸機

ˈstealth tax *noun* (*BrE, disapproving*) a new tax that is collected in a way that is not very obvious, so people are less aware that they are paying it 隱性稅

stealthy /ˈstelθi/ *adj.* doing things quietly or secretly; done quietly or secretly 偷偷摸摸的；不聲張的；秘密的：*a stealthy animal* 行動詭秘的動物◇*a stealthy movement* 隱蔽的移動 ▸ **stealth·ily** /-ɪli/ *adv.*

steam 0‑ᵘ /stiːm/ *noun, verb*

■ ***noun*** [U] **1** 0‑ᵘ the hot gas that water changes into when it boils 水蒸氣；蒸汽：*Steam rose from the boiling kettle.* 壺裏的水開了，冒着蒸汽。 **2** 0‑ᵘ the power that is produced from steam under pressure, used to operate engines, machines, etc. 蒸汽動力：*the introduction of steam in the 18th century* * 18 世紀蒸汽動力的引進◇*steam power* 蒸汽動力◇*the steam age* 蒸汽時代◇*a* ***steam train/engine*** 蒸汽火車／機 **3** very small drops of water that form in the air or on cold surfaces when warm air suddenly cools 水汽 SYN **condensation**：*She wiped the steam from her glasses.* 她擦去眼鏡上的水汽。

IDM **full speed/steam aˈhead** with as much speed or energy as possible 全速前進；全力 **ˌget up/ˌpick up ˈsteam 1** (*informal*) to become gradually more powerful, active, etc. 聲勢逐漸強大；漸成氣候；慢慢活躍起來：*His election campaign is beginning to get up steam.* 他的競選活動逐漸形成聲勢。 **2** (of a vehicle 車輛) to increase speed gradually 逐漸提速 **ˌlet off ˈsteam** (*informal*) to get rid of your energy, anger or strong emotions by doing sth active or noisy 釋放精力；發泄怨氣；宣泄感情 **ˌrun out of ˈsteam** (*informal*) to lose energy and enthusiasm and stop doing sth, or do it less well 筋疲力盡；喪失熱情 **get, etc. somewhere under your own ˈsteam** (*informal*) to go somewhere without help from other people 靠自己的力量去某處

■ ***verb*** **1** [I] to send out steam 蒸發；散發蒸汽；冒水汽：*a mug of steaming hot coffee* 一大杯熱氣騰騰的咖啡 **2** [T, I] **~ (sth)** to place food over boiling water so that it cooks in the steam; to be cooked in this way 蒸（食物）：*steamed fish* 蒸魚 ➲ COLLOCATIONS at COOKING ➲ VISUAL VOCAB page V27 **3** [I] **+ adv./prep.** (of a boat, ship, etc. 船舶等) to move using the power produced by steam 依靠蒸汽動力行駛：*The boat steamed across the lake.* 汽船從湖上駛過。 **4** [I] **+ adv./prep.** (especially of a person 尤指人) to go somewhere very quickly 快速行走；疾行：*He spotted her steaming down the corridor towards him.* 他看見她沿着走廊向他疾步走來。◇(*figurative*) *The company is steaming ahead with its investment programme.* 公司正全力以赴實施自己的投資方案。

IDM **be/get (all) steamed ˈup (about/over sth)** (*BrE*) (*NAmE* **be ˈsteamed (about sth)**) (*informal*) to be/become very angry or excited about sth（變得）非常氣憤，非常激動

PHR V **ˌsteam sth↔ˈoff | ˌsteam sth ˈoff sth** to remove one piece of paper from another using steam to make the glue that is holding them together softer 用蒸汽使（紙張等）脫離（或分開） **ˌsteam sth↔ˈopen** to open an envelope using steam to make the glue softer 用蒸汽脫膠開啟（信封） **ˌsteam ˈup | ˌsteam sth↔ˈup** to become, or to make sth become, covered with steam（使）蒙上水汽：*As he walked in, his glasses steamed up.* 他進去的時候，眼鏡上起了一層霧。

steam·boat /ˈstiːmbəʊt; *NAmE* -boʊt/ *noun* a boat driven by steam, used especially in the past on rivers and along coasts 汽船；輪船

steam·er /ˈstiːmə(r)/ *noun* **1** a boat or ship driven by steam 汽船；輪船 ➲ see also PADDLE STEAMER **2** a metal container with small holes in it, that is placed over a pan of boiling water in order to cook food in the steam 蒸鍋；蒸籠 ➲ VISUAL VOCAB page V27

steam·ing /ˈstiːmɪŋ/ *adj., noun*
■ *adj.* **1** (*BrE, informal*) very angry 非常憤怒的 **2** (also ˌ**steaming** ˈ**hot**) very hot 非常熱的
■ *noun* [U] (*informal*) a crime in which a group of thieves move quickly through a crowded public place, stealing things as they go 結夥沿路偷竊

steam·roll·er /ˈstiːmrəʊlə(r); *NAmE* -roʊ-/ *noun, verb*
■ *noun* a large slow vehicle with a ROLLER, used for making roads flat 蒸汽壓路機
■ *verb* (*NAmE* usually ˈ**steam roll**) [T, I] **~ (sb/sth) (+ adv./prep.)** to defeat sb or force them to do sth, using your power or authority （憑藉力量或權威）打敗，壓服，迫使： *The team steamrollered their way to victory.* 這支隊以不可阻擋之勢獲得勝利。◇ *She knew that she'd let herself be steamrollered.* 她知道自己會屈服於對方的威勢。

steam·ship /ˈstiːmʃɪp/ *noun* (*abbr.* **SS**) a ship driven by steam 汽船；輪船

ˈ**steam shovel** *noun* (*especially NAmE*) a large machine for digging, that originally worked by steam （蒸汽）挖土機，挖掘機

steamy /ˈstiːmi/ *adj.* (**steam·ier**, **steami·est**) **1** full of steam; covered with steam 充滿蒸汽的；蒙着水汽的： *a steamy bathroom* 水汽瀰漫的浴室 ◇ *steamy windows* 蒙着一層水汽的窗戶 ◇ *the steamy heat of Tokyo* 東京的潮濕悶熱 **2** (*informal*) sexually exciting 色情的 SYN **erotic**

steed /stiːd/ *noun* (*literary* or *humorous*) a horse to ride on 坐騎

steel 🔑 /stiːl/ *noun, verb*
■ *noun* **1** 🔑 [U] a strong hard metal that is made of a mixture of iron and CARBON 鋼： *the iron and steel industry* 鋼鐵工業 ◇ *The frame is made of steel.* 這個架子是鋼製的。◇ *The bridge is reinforced with huge steel girders.* 這座橋用巨大的鋼梁加固了。➲ see also STAINLESS STEEL **2** 🔑 [U] the industry that produces steel 鋼鐵工業： *Steel used to be important in South Wales.* 以前鋼鐵工業在南威爾士很重要。◇ *steel workers* 煉鋼工人 ◇ *a steel town* 一座鋼鐵城 **3** [C] a long thin straight piece of steel with a rough surface, used for rubbing knives on to make them sharp 鋼製磨刀棒 ➲ VISUAL VOCAB page V26 **4** [U] (*old use* or *literary*) weapons that are used for fighting 兵器： *the clash of steel* 刀劍交擊的哐噹聲
IDM **of** ˈ**steel** having a quality like steel, especially a strong, cold or hard quality 鋼鐵般堅強（或冷漠、堅硬）的： *She felt a hand of steel* (= a strong, firm hand) *on her arm.* 她感覺一隻有力的手抓住了她的胳膊。◇ *You need a cool head and* ***nerves of steel*** (= great courage). 你需要有冷靜的頭腦、非常的魄力。◇ *There was a hint of steel in his voice* (= he sounded cold and firm). 他的語調顯得冷靜而堅決。
■ *verb* to prepare yourself to deal with sth unpleasant 準備對付；下決心應付： **~ yourself (for/against sth)** *As she waited, she steeled herself for disappointment.* 她等着的時候，就冷了心不指望了。◇ **~ yourself to do sth** *He steeled himself to tell them the truth.* 他硬下心來把實情告訴了他們。

ˌ**steel** ˈ**band** *noun* a group of musicians who play music on drums that are made from empty metal oil containers. Steel bands originally came from the West Indies. 鋼鼓樂隊（敲擊用空油桶製成的鼓，源自西印度群島）

ˌ**steel** ˈ**drum** (also ˌ**steel** ˈ**pan**) *noun* a musical instrument used in West Indian music, made from a metal oil container which is hit in different places with two sticks to produce different notes 鋼鼓（用金屬油桶製成的西印度樂器，用兩根鼓棒敲擊各處發出各種音調） ➲ VISUAL VOCAB page V35

ˌ**steel** ˈ**wool** (*BrE* also ˌ**wire** ˈ**wool**) *noun* [U] a mass of fine steel threads that you use for cleaning pots and pans, making surfaces smooth, etc. 鋼絲球（用以擦洗或磨光）

steel·work·er /ˈstiːlwɜːkə(r); *NAmE* -wɜːrk-/ *noun* a person who works in a place where steel is made 煉鋼工人

steel·works /ˈstiːlwɜːks; *NAmE* -wɜːrks/ *noun* (*pl.* **steel·works**) [C+sing./pl. v.] a factory where steel is made 煉鋼廠

steely /ˈstiːli/ *adj.* **1** (of a person's character or behaviour 人的性格或行為) strong, hard and unfriendly 強硬的；冷冰冰的： *a cold, steely voice* 冷冰冰的腔調 ◇ *a look of steely determination* 一副下定決心、不可動搖的神態 **2** like steel in colour （色澤）似鋼的： *steely blue eyes* 灰藍色的眼睛 ▸ **steeli·ness** *noun* [U]

steep 🔑 /stiːp/ *adj., verb*
■ *adj.* (**steep·er**, **steep·est**) **1** 🔑 (of a slope, hill, etc. 斜坡、山等) rising or falling quickly, not gradually 陡的；陡峭的： *a* ***steep hill/slope/bank*** 陡峭的山；陡坡／岸 ◇ *a* ***steep climb/descent/drop*** 陡直的爬升／下降／下落 ◇ *a steep flight of stairs* 一段很陡的樓梯 ◇ *The path grew steeper as we climbed higher.* 我們越往上爬路就越陡。**2** 🔑 [usually before noun] (of a rise or fall in an amount 數量的上升或下降) sudden and very big 突然的；急劇的；大起大落的 SYN **sharp**： *a steep decline in the birth rate* 出生率的驟降 ◇ *a steep rise in unemployment* 失業率的暴升 **3** (*informal*) (of a price or demand 價格或要求) too much; unreasonable 過高的；過分的；不合理的 SYN **expensive**： *£2 for a cup of coffee seems a little steep to me.* 一杯咖啡 2 英鎊在我看來有點貴得離譜。▸ **steep·ly** 🔑 *adv.*： *a steeply sloping roof* 大坡度房頂 ◇ *The path climbed steeply upwards.* 上去的路很陡。◇ *Prices rose steeply.* 物價猛漲。**steep·ness** *noun* [U]
■ *verb*
IDM **be** ˈ**steeped in sth** (*formal*) to have a lot of a particular quality 深深浸淫；飽含（某品質）： *a city steeped in history* 歷史古城
PHR V ˈ**steep sth in sth** to put food in a liquid and leave it for some time so that it becomes soft and flavoured by the liquid 在（液體）中浸泡（食物） ˈ**steep yourself in sth** (*formal*) to spend a lot of time thinking or learning about sth 沉浸於；潛心於： *They spent a month steeping themselves in Chinese culture.* 他們花了一個月時間潛心鑽研中國文化。

steep·en /ˈstiːpən/ *verb* [I, T] **~ (sth)** to become or to make sth become steeper （使）變陡： *After a mile, the slope steepened.* 過了一英里後，山坡變陡了。

steeple /ˈstiːpl/ *noun* a tall pointed tower on the roof of a church, often with a SPIRE on it （教堂的）尖塔

steeple·chase /ˈstiːpltʃeɪs/ (also **chase**) *noun* **1** a long race in which horses have to jump over fences, water, etc. 越野障礙賽馬 ➲ compare FLAT RACING **2** a long race in which people run and jump over gates and water, etc. around a track 障礙賽跑

steeple·chaser /ˈstiːpltʃeɪsə(r)/ *noun* a horse or a person that takes part in steeplechases 參加越野障礙賽馬的馬；障礙賽跑選手

steeple·jack /ˈstiːpldʒæk/ *noun* a person whose job is painting or repairing towers, tall CHIMNEYS, etc. 高空作業工人（粉刷或修理高塔、大煙囪等）

steer 🔑 /stɪə(r); *NAmE* stɪr/ *verb, noun*
■ *verb* **1** 🔑 [T, I] **~ (sth /sb) (+ adv./prep.)** to control the direction in which a boat, car, etc. moves 駕駛（船、汽車等）；掌方向盤： *He steered the boat into the harbour.* 他把船開進港。◇ (*figurative*) *He took her arm and steered her towards the door.* 他抓住她的胳膊，把她帶往門口。◇ *You row and I'll steer.* 你划槳，我來掌舵。**2** 🔑 [T, I] **~ (sth) (+ adv./prep.)** (of a boat, car, etc. 船、汽車等) to move in a particular direction 行駛： *The ship steered a course between the islands.* 船在島嶼之間穿行。◇ *The ship steered into port.* 船駛進港口。**3** [T] **~ sth + adv./prep.** to take control of a situation and influence the way in which it develops 操縱；控制；引導： *He managed to steer the conversation away from his divorce.* 他設法避開他離婚這話題。◇ *She steered the team to victory.* 她率領全隊取得勝利。◇ *The skill is in steering a middle course between the two extremes.* 本領就在於避開這兩個極端，走中間路線。IDM see CLEAR *adv.*
■ *noun* **1** [sing.] (*BrE*) a piece of advice or information that helps you do sth or avoid a problem 建議；勸告；忠告： *Can anyone give me a steer on this?* 有人能就這一點給我個建議嗎？**2** [C] a BULL (= a male cow) that has been CASTRATED (= had part of its sex organs

S

removed), kept for its meat 閹公牛；肉用公牛 ➲ compare BULLOCK, OX (1)

steer·age /ˈstɪərɪdʒ; *NAmE* ˈstɪr-/ *noun* [U] (in the past) the part of a ship where passengers with the cheapest tickets used to travel（舊時客輪的）統艙，大艙

steer·ing /ˈstɪərɪŋ; *NAmE* ˈstɪr-/ *noun* [U] the machinery in a vehicle that you use to control the direction it goes in（車輛等的）轉向裝置 ➲ see also POWER STEERING

ˈsteering column *noun* the part of a car or other vehicle that the STEERING WHEEL is fitted on（汽車等的）轉向柱

ˈsteering committee (also **ˈsteering group**) *noun* a group of people that a government or an organization chooses to direct an activity and to decide how it will be done 指導委員會；程序委員會

ˈsteering wheel *noun* the wheel that the driver turns to control the direction that a vehicle goes in 方向盤；舵輪 ➲ VISUAL VOCAB page V52

stego·saur /ˈstegəsɔː(r)/ (also **stego·saurus** /ˌstegəˈsɔːrəs/) *noun* a DINOSAUR with a small head, four legs and two rows of SPIKES along its back 劍龍（背部有三角形骨板的恐龍）

stein /staɪn/ *noun* (from *German*) a large decorated cup for drinking beer, usually made of EARTHENWARE and often with a lid 飾花大啤酒杯（多為陶質，常帶蓋）

stel·lar /ˈstelə(r)/ *adj.* [usually before noun] **1** (*technical* 術語) connected with the stars 星的；恒星的 ➲ compare INTERSTELLAR **2** (*informal*) excellent 優秀的；精彩的；傑出的：*a stellar performance* 精彩的演出

stem /stem/ *noun, verb*

■ ***noun*** **1** the main long thin part of a plant above the ground from which the leaves or flowers grow; a smaller part that grows from this and supports flowers or leaves（花草的）莖；（花或葉的）梗，柄 ➲ VISUAL VOCAB page V11 **2** the long thin part of a wine glass between the bowl and the base（高腳酒杯的）腳 ➲ VISUAL VOCAB page V22 **3** the thin tube of a TOBACCO pipe 煙斗柄 **4 -stemmed** (in adjectives 構成形容詞) having one or more stems of the type mentioned 有…莖（或梗）的：*a long-stemmed rose* 一枝長莖玫瑰 **5** (*grammar* 語法) the main part of a word that stays the same when endings are added to it 詞幹；語幹：*'Writ' is the stem of the forms 'writes', 'writing' and 'written'.* * writ 是 writes、writing 和 written 三個詞的詞幹。

IDM **from ˌstem to ˈstern** all the way from the front of a ship to the back 從船頭到船尾

■ ***verb*** (-mm-) **~ sth** to stop sth that is flowing from spreading or increasing 阻止；封堵；遏止：*The cut was bandaged to stem the bleeding.* 傷口已包紮止血。◇ *They discussed ways of **stemming the flow** of smuggled drugs.* 他們討論了遏制走私毒品流通的辦法。◇ *The government had failed to **stem the tide** of factory closures.* 政府沒有控制住工廠的倒閉潮。

PHR V **ˈstem from sth** (not used in the progressive tenses 不用於進行時) to be the result of sth 是…的結果；起源於；根源是 ➲ LANGUAGE BANK at BECAUSE

ˈstem cell *noun* a basic type of cell which can divide and develop into cells with particular functions. All the different kinds of cells in the human body develop from stem cells. 幹細胞

stem·ware /ˈstemweə(r); *NAmE* -wer/ *noun* [U] (*technical* 術語) glasses and glass bowls that have a STEM 有腳玻璃器皿

stench /stentʃ/ *noun* [sing.] a strong, very unpleasant smell 臭氣；惡臭 SYN **reek**：*an overpowering stench of rotting fish* 腐爛的魚臭氣熏天 ◇ (*figurative*) *The stench of treachery hung in the air.* 到處都是可恥的叛變的氣息。

sten·cil /ˈstensl/ *noun, verb*

■ ***noun*** a thin piece of metal, plastic or card with a design cut out of it, that you put onto a surface and paint over so that the design is left on the surface; the pattern or design that is produced in this way（印文字或圖案用的）模板；（用模板印的）文字，圖案

■ ***verb*** (-ll-, *NAmE* also -l-) [T, I] **~ (sth)** to make letters or a design on sth using a stencil 用模板印（文字或圖案）

steno /ˈstenəʊ; *NAmE* -noʊ/ *noun* (*pl.* -os) (*NAmE, informal*) **1** [C] = STENOGRAPHER **2** [U] = STENOGRAPHY

sten·og·raph·er /stəˈnɒɡrəfə(r); *NAmE* -ˈnɑːɡ-/ (also *informal* **steno**) *noun* (*especially NAmE*) a person whose job is to write down what sb else says, using a quick system of signs or abbreviations 速記員

sten·og·raphy /stəˈnɒɡrəfi; *NAmE* -ˈnɑːɡ-/ (also *informal* **steno**) *noun* [U] (*NAmE*) = SHORTHAND (1)

stent /stent/ *noun* (*medical* 醫) a small support that is put inside a BLOOD VESSEL tube in the body, for example in order to stop sth blocking it（防止栓塞等而植入的）血管支架

sten·tor·ian /stenˈtɔːriən/ *adj.* (*formal*) (of a voice 嗓音) loud and powerful 洪亮的

step 0-w /step/ *noun, verb*

■ ***noun***

▸ MOVEMENT/SOUND 動作；聲音 **1** 0-w [C] the act of lifting your foot and putting it down in order to walk or move somewhere; the sound this makes 邁步；腳步聲：*a baby's first steps* 嬰兒學步 ◇ *He **took a step** towards the door.* 他朝門口邁了一步。◇ *We heard steps outside.* 我們聽見外面有腳步聲。➲ see also FOOTSTEP, GOOSE-STEP

▸ WAY OF WALKING 步履 **2** [C, usually sing.] the way that sb walks 步伐；步態：*He walked with a quick light step.* 他邁着輕快的步子走着。

▸ DISTANCE 距離 **3** 0-w [C] the distance that you cover when you take a step 一步（的距離）：*It's only a few steps further.* 再走幾步就到了。◇ *He turned around and **retraced his steps*** (= went back the way he had come). 他轉身原路往回走。◇ *She moved a step closer to me.* 她朝我靠近一步。◇ *The hotel is only a short step from the beach.* 旅館離海灘只有幾步路。

▸ IN SERIES/PROCESS 系列；過程 **4** 0-w [C] one of a series of things that you do in order to achieve sth 步驟；措施：*This was a first step towards a united Europe.* 這是向建立統一歐洲的目標邁出的第一步。◇ *It's a **big step** giving up your job and moving halfway across the world.* 你放棄工作搬到地球的另一端，可真不簡單。◇ *We are **taking steps** to prevent pollution.* 我們正在採取措施防止污染。◇ *This won't solve the problem but it's **a step in the right direction**.* 這雖不能解決問題，卻是朝正確方向邁出的一步。◇ *The new drug is a major **step forward** in the treatment of the disease.* 發現這種新藥是治療這一疾病的重大進展。➲ SYNONYMS at ACTION **5** 0-w [C] one of a series of things that sb does or that happen, which forms part of a process 步；階段 SYN **stage**：*Having completed the first stage, you can move on to step 2.* 第一階段完成後，你就可以接着進行第二步了。◇ *I'd like to take this idea **a step further**.* 我想把這一思想深化一步。◇ *This was a big **step up*** (= to a better position) *in his career.* 這是他在事業上向前邁出的一大步。◇ *I'll explain it to you **step by step**.* 我來一步一步地給你解釋。◇ *a **step-by-step** guide to building your own home* 自建房舍的分步驟指導手冊

▸ STAIR 台階 **6** 0-w [C] a surface that you put your foot on in order to walk to a higher or lower level, especially one of a series 台階；梯級：*She was sitting on the bottom step of the staircase.* 她正坐在最下面一級樓梯上。◇ *We walked down some stone steps to the beach.* 我們走下幾級石階，來到海灘上。◇ *A short **flight of steps** led up to the door.* 上幾磴台階就到了門口。➲ VISUAL VOCAB pages V17, V20 ➲ see also DOORSTEP (1)

▸ IN DANCE 舞蹈 **7** [C, usually pl.] a series of movements that you make with your feet and which form a dance 舞步 ➲ see also QUICKSTEP

▸ EXERCISE 健身運動 **8** [U] (often in compounds 常構成複合詞) a type of exercise that you do by stepping on and off a raised piece of equipment 踏板操：*step aerobics* 有氧踏板操 ◇ *a step class* 踏板操訓練班

▸ LADDER 梯子 **9 steps** [pl.] (*BrE*) a STEPLADDER 摺梯；梯子：*a pair of steps* 一架摺梯 ◇ *We need the steps to get into the attic.* 我們得踩着梯子才能爬到閣樓上去。

▸ IN MUSIC 音樂 **10** [C] (*NAmE*) the interval between two notes that are next to each other in a SCALE 音級；度 ➲ compare TONE (7), SEMITONE

IDM **break ˈstep** to change the way you are walking so that you do not walk in the same rhythm as the people

S

you are walking or marching with 走亂步伐 **fall into 'step (beside/with sb)** to change the way you are walking so that you start walking in the same rhythm as the person you are walking with （和某人）合上步伐，步調一致起來：*He caught her up and fell into step beside her.* 他趕上她，跟着她的步子往前走。**in/out of 'step (with sb/sth)** **1** putting your feet on the ground in the right/wrong way, according to the rhythm of the music or the people you are moving with （和某人）步伐一致（或不一致）；（和音樂）合拍（或不合拍）**2** having ideas that are the same as or different from other people's （和某人）想法一致（或不一致）：*She was out of step with her colleagues.* 她和同事們想法不一樣。**mind/watch your 'step** **1** to walk carefully 走路小心 **2** to behave in a careful and sensible way 言行小心謹慎 **one step ˌforward, two steps 'back** (*saying*) used to say that every time you make progress, sth bad happens that means that the situation is worse than before 進一步，退兩步 **a/one step a'head (of sb/sth)** when you are **one step ahead** of sb/sth, you manage to avoid them or to achieve sth more quickly than they do 避開（某人或某事物）；領先（某人或某事物）一步 **a/one step at a 'time** when you do sth **one step at a time** you do it slowly and gradually 一步一步；逐步；按部就班

■ ***verb*** (-pp-) [I] **+ adv./prep.** to lift your foot and move it in a particular direction or put it on or in sth; to move a short distance 邁步；踩；踏；行走：*to step onto/off a bus* 上／下公共汽車 ◇ *I stepped forward when my name was called out.* 我聽見叫我名字時向前邁了一步。◇ *She stepped aside to let them pass.* 她閃到一邊讓他們過去。◇ *We stepped carefully over the broken glass.* 我們小心翼翼地從碎玻璃上走了過去。◇ *I turned around quickly and stepped on his toes.* 我一個急轉身，踩到了他的腳上。◇ (*figurative*) *Going into the hotel is like stepping back in time.* 走進這家旅館就像是回到了過去。

IDM **step into the 'breach** to do sb's job or work when they are suddenly or unexpectedly unable to do it 臨時頂替某人工作；臨時頂缺 **step into sb's 'shoes** to continue a job or the work that sb else has started 接替某人的工作 **'step on it** (*informal*) used especially in orders to tell sb to drive faster （尤用以要求加速駕駛）開快點，趕快 **step on sb's 'toes** (*NAmE, informal*) = TREAD ON SB'S TOES at TREAD **step out of 'line | be/get out of 'line** to behave badly or break the rules 表現不好；不守規矩；越軌；出格 **step up to the 'plate** (*especially NAmE*) to do what is necessary in order to benefit from an opportunity or deal with a crisis 開始行動，採取措施（以抓住機會或應對危機）：*It's important for world leaders to step up to the plate and honor their commitments on global warming.* 對世界領導人來說，重要的是開始行動，兌現他們在全球變暖問題上的承諾。

PHR V **ˌstep a'side/'down** to leave an important job or position and let sb else take your place 讓位；退位 **ˌstep 'back (from sth)** to think about a situation calmly, as if you are not involved in it yourself 跳出（某事物的）圈子看問題：*We are learning to step back from ourselves and identify our strengths and weaknesses.* 我們正努力學會走出自我的樊籬，認清我們自身的優點和缺點。**ˌstep 'forward** to offer to help sb or give information 主動站出來（幫忙或提供信息）；自告奮勇 **ˌstep 'in** to help sb in a disagreement or difficult situation 居間調停；居中斡旋；施以援手：*A local businessman stepped in with a large donation for the school.* 當地一位商人出面捐了一筆巨款給學校。◇ *The team coach was forced to step in to stop the two athletes from coming to blows.* 運動隊教練不得不介入，才使兩個運動員沒有動起手來。**ˌstep 'out** (*especially NAmE*) to go out 出去：*I'm just going to step out for a few minutes.* 我就出去一小會兒。**ˌstep 'up** to come forward 走上前去：*She stepped up to receive her prize.* 她走上前去領獎。**ˌstep sth↔'up** to increase the amount, speed, etc. of sth 增加，提高（數量、速度等）：*He has stepped up his training to prepare for the race.* 他為準備那場賽跑加強了訓練。

step- /step-/ *combining form* (in nouns 構成名詞) related as a result of one parent marrying again （因父母再婚而構成的親緣關係）繼…：*stepmother* 繼母

step·brother /ˈstepbrʌðə(r)/ *noun* the son from an earlier marriage of your STEPMOTHER or STEPFATHER 繼兄，繼弟（繼母與其前夫或繼父與其前妻所生的兒子）➲ compare HALF-BROTHER

'step change *noun* [usually sing.] (*BrE*) a big change or improvement in sth 巨大變化；顯著進步（或改善）：*His speech called for a step change in attitudes to the environment in the 21st century.* 他的演講呼籲在 21 世紀徹底改變對待環境的態度。

step·child /ˈsteptʃaɪld/ *noun* (*pl.* **step·chil·dren** /-tʃɪldrən/) a child of your husband or wife by an earlier marriage 繼子；繼女

step·daugh·ter /ˈstepdɔːtə(r)/ *noun* a daughter that your husband or wife has from an earlier marriage to another person 繼女

step·fam·ily /ˈstepfæməli/ *noun* (*pl.* **-ies**) the family that is formed when sb marries a person who already has children 有繼子女的家庭；有繼父（或繼母）的家庭

step·father /ˈstepfɑːðə(r)/ *noun* the man who is married to your mother but who is not your real father 繼父

Step·ford wife /ˌstepfəd ˈwaɪf; *NAmE* -fərd/ *noun* a woman who does not behave or think in an independent way, always following the accepted rules of society and obeying her husband without thinking 斯特福德式妻子（缺乏獨立性、只知遵守社會既定準則和順從丈夫）：*She's gradually turning into a Stepford wife.* 她正逐漸變成一味順從丈夫的妻子。**ORIGIN** From the title of the book and film/movie *The Stepford Wives*, in which a group of women who behave in this way are in fact robots. 源自小說和同名電影《斯特福德的妻子們》，影片中的女人實為機器人。

step·lad·der /ˈsteplædə(r)/ *noun* a short LADDER that is made of two parts, one with steps, that are joined together at the top, so that it can stand on its own or be folded flat for carrying or storing 摺梯；梯子 ➲ **VISUAL VOCAB** page V20

step·mother /ˈstepmʌðə(r)/ *noun* the woman who is married to your father but who is not your real mother 繼母

step·ney /ˈstepni/ *noun* (*IndE*) a spare wheel for a car （汽車）備用輪胎

'step-parent *noun* a stepmother or stepfather 繼母；繼父

steppe /step/ *noun* [C, usually pl., U] a large area of land with grass but few trees, especially in SE Europe and Siberia （尤指東南歐及西伯利亞樹少的）大草原，乾草原：*the vast Russian steppes* 遼闊的俄羅斯大草原

'stepping stone *noun* **1** one of a line of flat stones that you step on in order to cross a stream or river （小溪、小河中的）踏腳石 **2** something that allows you to make progress or begin to achieve sth 進身之階；墊腳石；敲門磚：*a stepping stone to a more lucrative career* 涉足更賺錢的行業的敲門磚

step·sis·ter /ˈstepsɪstə(r)/ *noun* the daughter from an earlier marriage of your STEPMOTHER or STEPFATHER 繼姐，繼妹（繼母與其前夫或繼父與其前妻所生的女兒）➲ compare HALF-SISTER

step·son /ˈstepsʌn/ *noun* a son that your husband or wife has from an earlier marriage to another person 繼子

step·wise /ˈstepwaɪz/ *adj.* **1** in a series of steps, rather than continuously 逐步的；逐漸的 **2** (*music* 音) (of a MELODY 旋律) moving in a way that uses only the notes that are next to each other in a SCALE （按音階）級進的

-ster *suffix* (in nouns 構成名詞) a person who is connected with or has the quality of 與…有關的人；有…品質的人：*gangster* 犯罪團夥成員 ◇ *youngster* 年輕人

stereo /ˈsteriəʊ; *NAmE* -oʊ/ *noun* (*pl.* **-os**) **1** (also **'stereo system**) [C] a machine that plays CDs, etc., sometimes with a radio, that has two separate SPEAKERS so that you hear different sounds from each 立體聲音響系統：*a car/personal stereo* 車用／個人立體聲音響 ◇ *Let's put some music on the stereo.* 我們在立體聲音響上放點

音樂吧。**2** [U] the system for playing recorded music, speech, etc. in which the sound is directed through two channels 立體聲音響（系統）: *to broadcast **in stereo*** 用立體聲廣播 ➲ compare MONO (1) ▶ **stereo** (also *formal* **stereo·phon·ic** /ˌsteriəˈfɒnɪk; *NAmE* -ˈfɑːnɪk/) *adj.* [only before noun]: *stereo sound* 立體聲 ➲ compare QUADRAPHONIC

stereo·scop·ic /ˌsteriəˈskɒpɪk; *NAmE* -ˈskɑːpɪk/ *adj.* **1** (*technical* 術語) able to see objects with length, width and depth, as humans do 有立體視覺的: *stereoscopic vision* 立體視覺 **2** (of a picture, photograph, etc. 圖畫、照片等) that is made so that you see the objects in it with length, width, and depth when you use a special machine 有立體效果的 SYN **three-D**

stereo·type /ˈsteriətaɪp/ *noun, verb*

■ ***noun*** a fixed idea or image that many people have of a particular type of person or thing, but which is often not true in reality 模式化觀念（或形象）；老一套；刻板印象: ***cultural/gender/racial stereotypes*** 有關文化的／性別的／種族的舊框框 ◇ *He doesn't conform to the usual stereotype of the businessman with a dark suit and briefcase.* 他不同於人們一般印象中穿黑色西裝、提公文包的商人形象。➲ COLLOCATIONS at RACE ▶ **stereo·typ·ical** /ˌsteriəˈtɪpɪkl/ *adj.*: *the stereotypical image of feminine behaviour* 關於女性行為舉止的模式化觀念 **stereo·typ·ical·ly** /-kli/ *adv.*

■ ***verb*** [often passive] to form a fixed idea about a person or thing which may not really be true 對⋯形成模式化（或類型化）的看法: **~ sb** *Children from certain backgrounds tend to be stereotyped by their teachers.* 教師往往模式化地根據學生的某些背景把他們歸類。◇ **~ sb as sth** *Why are professors stereotyped as absent-minded?* 為什麼在人們心目中教授就一定健忘呢？▶ **stereo·typed** *adj.*: *a play full of stereotyped characters* 充斥着模式化人物的戲劇 **stereo·typ·ing** *noun* [U]: *sexual stereotyping* 性別的模式化

ster·ile /ˈsteraɪl; *NAmE* ˈsterəl/ *adj.* **1** (of humans or animals 人或動物) not able to produce children or young animals 不能生育的；不育的 SYN **infertile** ➲ compare FERTILE (2) **2** completely clean and free from bacteria 無菌的；消過毒的: *sterile bandages* 消毒繃帶 ◇ *sterile water* 消過毒的水 **3** (of a discussion, an argument, etc. 討論、爭論等) not producing any useful result 無結果的；沒有實際價值的 SYN **fruitless**: *a sterile debate* 沒有結果的辯論 **4** lacking individual personality, imagination or new ideas 刻板的；無個性的；缺乏新意的: *The room felt cold and sterile.* 那房間讓人覺得陰冷而沒有生氣。◇ *He felt creatively and emotionally sterile.* 他感覺自己既缺乏創意又沒有充沛的感情。**5** (of land 土地) not good enough to produce crops 貧瘠的 ▶ **ster·il·ity** /stəˈrɪləti/ *noun* [U]: *The disease can cause sterility in men and women.* 這種疾病可能導致男女不育。◇ *the meaningless sterility of statistics* 統計數字的枯燥無味 ◇ *She contemplated the sterility of her existence.* 她思量着自己空虛無聊的生活。

ster·il·ize (*BrE* also **-ise**) /ˈsterəlaɪz/ *verb* **1** [often passive] **~ sth** to kill the bacteria in or on sth 滅菌；消毒: *to sterilize surgical instruments* 給外科手術器械消毒 ◇ *sterilized milk/water* 消過毒的牛奶／水 **2** [usually passive] **~ sb/sth** to make a person or an animal unable to have babies, especially by removing or blocking their sex organs 使絕育 ▶ **ster·il·iza·tion, -isa·tion** /ˌsterəlaɪˈzeɪʃn; *NAmE* -ləˈz-/ *noun* [U, C]

ster·il·izer (*BrE* also **-iser**) /ˈsterəlaɪzə(r)/ *noun* a machine or piece of equipment that you use to make objects or substances completely clean and free from bacteria 消毒器；滅菌器

ster·ling /ˈstɜːlɪŋ; *NAmE* ˈstɜːrlɪŋ/ *noun, adj.*

■ ***noun*** [U] the money system of Britain, based on the pound 英鎊（英國貨幣）: *the value of sterling* 英鎊的價值 ◇ *You can be paid in pounds sterling or American dollars.* 可以付你英鎊，也可以付你美元。

■ ***adj.*** [usually before noun] (*formal*) of excellent quality 優秀的；傑出的: *He has done **sterling work** on the finance committee.* 他在財務委員會工作優異。

ˌsterling ˈsilver *noun* [U] silver of a particular standard of PURITY 標準純銀（達到規定的純度）

stern /stɜːn; *NAmE* stɜːrn/ *adj., noun*

■ ***adj.*** (**stern·er**, **stern·est**) **1** serious and often disapproving; expecting sb to obey you 嚴厲的；苛刻的；要求別人服從的 SYN **strict**: *a **stern face/expression/look*** 嚴厲的面容／表情／目光 ◇ *a **stern warning*** 嚴厲的警告 ◇ *Her voice was stern.* 她聲調嚴厲。◇ *The police are planning sterner measures to combat crime.* 警方正制訂更嚴厲的措施打擊犯罪活動。**2** serious and difficult 嚴峻的；難對付的: *We face stern opposition.* 我們遇到激烈的反對。▶ **stern·ly** *adv.* **stern·ness** *noun* [U]

IDM **be made of sterner ˈstuff** to have a stronger character and to be more determined in dealing with problems than other people 性格十分堅強；有很大的毅力

■ ***noun*** the back end of a ship or boat 船尾 ➲ VISUAL VOCAB page V54 ➲ compare BOW[1] *n.*, POOP (1) IDM see STEM *n.*

ster·num /ˈstɜːnəm; *NAmE* ˈstɜːrnəm/ *noun* (*pl.* **ster·nums** or **sterna** /-nə/) (*anatomy* 解) the BREASTBONE 胸骨 ➲ VISUAL VOCAB page V59

ster·oid /ˈsterɔɪd; *BrE* also ˈstɪər-; *NAmE* also ˈstɪr-/ *noun* a chemical substance produced naturally in the body. There are several different steroids and they can be used to treat various diseases and are also sometimes used illegally by people playing sports to improve their performance. 類固醇；甾族化合物

stetho·scope /ˈsteθəskəʊp; *NAmE* -skoʊp/ *noun* an instrument that a doctor uses to listen to sb's heart and breathing 聽診器

stet·son (*BrE*) (*NAmE* **Stetson™**) /ˈstetsn/ *noun* a tall hat with a wide BRIM, worn especially by American COWBOYS 斯特森高頂寬邊帽；牛仔帽

steve·dore /ˈstiːvədɔː(r)/ *noun* a person whose job is moving goods on and off ships 碼頭工人；碼頭裝卸工 ➲ see also DOCKER

stew /stjuː; *NAmE* stuː/ *noun, verb*

■ ***noun*** [U, C] a dish of meat and vegetables cooked slowly in liquid in a container that has a lid 燉的菜，煨的菜（有肉和蔬菜）: *beef stew and dumplings* 牛肉燉丸子 ◇ *I'm making a stew for lunch.* 我燉個菜中午吃。

IDM **get (yourself)/be in a ˈstew (about/over sth)** (*informal*) to become/feel very anxious or upset about sth（為某事）坐立不安，心煩意亂

■ ***verb*** **1** [T, I] **~ (sth)** to cook sth slowly, or allow sth to cook slowly, in liquid in a closed dish 燉；煨: *stewed apples* 燉蘋果 ◇ *The meat needs to stew for two hours.* 這肉得燉兩小時。➲ see also STEWED **2** [I] (**+ adv./prep.**) to think or worry about sth 思考；擔憂: *I've been stewing over the problem for a while.* 這個問題我已經考慮了一會兒。◇ *Leave him to stew.* 讓他自個兒想想。

IDM **let sb stew in their own ˈjuice** (*informal*) to leave sb to worry and suffer the unpleasant effects of their own actions 讓某人自作自受

stew·ard /ˈstjuːəd; *NAmE* ˈstuːərd/ *noun* **1** a man whose job is to take care of passengers on a ship, an aircraft or a train and who brings them meals, etc.（輪船、飛機或火車上的）乘務員，服務員 **2** a person who helps to organize a large public event, for example a race, public meeting, etc.（比賽、集會等大型公眾活動的）統籌人 SYN **marshal** **3** a person whose job is to arrange for the supply of food to a college, club, etc.（大學、俱樂部等的）伙食管理員 ➲ see also SHOP STEWARD **4** a person employed to manage another person's property, especially a large house or land（私人家中的）管家

stew·ard·ess /ˌstjuːəˈdes; ˈstjuːə-; *NAmE* ˈstuːərdəs/ *noun* **1** (*old-fashioned*) a female FLIGHT ATTENDANT（飛機上的）女乘務員；空中小姐 **2** a woman whose job is to take care of the passengers on a ship or train（輪船或火車上的）女乘務員，女服務員 ➲ note at GENDER

stew·ard·ship /ˈstjuːədʃɪp; *NAmE* ˈstuːərdʃɪp/ *noun* [U] (*formal*) the act of taking care of or managing sth, for example property, an organization, money or valuable objects 管理；看管；組織工作: *The organization certainly prospered under his stewardship.* 不可否認，這個組織在他的管理下興旺了起來。

stewed /stjuːd; *NAmE* stuːd/ *adj.* (of tea 茶) tasting too strong and bitter because it has been left in the pot too long（因久泡）太釅的，泡苦了的

St George's Day /ˌsnt ˈdʒɔːdʒɪz deɪ; *NAmE* ˌseɪnt ˈdʒɔːrdʒɪz/ *noun* 23 April, the day of the national SAINT of England 聖喬治節（4 月 23 日，紀念英格蘭主保聖人的節日）

STI /ˌes tiː ˈaɪ/ *noun* the abbreviation for 'sexually transmitted infection' (an infection that is passed from one person to another during sexual activity) 性傳播感染，性行為造成的感染（全寫為 sexually transmitted infection）

sticks 棒狀物

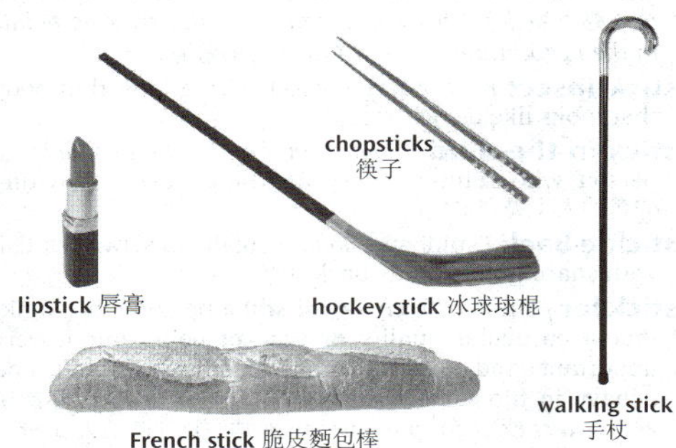

stick 🔑 /stɪk/ *verb, noun*

■ *verb* (**stuck, stuck** /stʌk/)

▸ **PUSH STH IN** 推入 **1** 🔑 [T, I] to push sth, usually a sharp object, into sth; to be pushed into sth 將…刺入（或插入）；刺；戳；插入：**~ sth + adv./prep.** *The nurse stuck the needle into my arm.* 護士把針扎進我的胳膊。◇ *Don't stick your fingers through the bars of the cage.* 不要把指頭伸進籠子裏。◇ **+ adv./prep.** *I found a nail sticking in the tyre.* 我發現輪胎上扎了一根釘子。

▸ **ATTACH** 粘貼 **2** 🔑 [T, I] to fix sth to sth else, usually with a sticky substance; to become fixed to sth in this way 粘貼；粘住：**~ sth + adv./prep.** *He stuck a stamp on the envelope.* 他把一張郵票貼到信封上。◇ *We used glue to stick the broken pieces together.* 我們用膠水把碎片粘到一起。◇ *I stuck the photos into an album.* 我把照片貼到相冊上。◇ **+ adv./prep.** *Her wet clothes were sticking to her body.* 濕衣服貼在她身上。◇ *The glue's useless—the pieces just won't stick.* 這種膠水不行，這幾片東西根本粘不住。

▸ **PUT** 放置 **3** 🔑 [T] **~ sth + adv./prep.** (*informal*) to put sth in a place, especially quickly or carelessly（尤指迅速或隨手）放置：*Stick your bags down there.* 把你們的包擱到那兒吧。◇ *He stuck his hands in his pockets and strolled off.* 他把兩手揣在口袋裏溜達着走了。◇ *Can you stick this on the noticeboard?* 你能不能把這個貼到佈告牌上？◇ *Peter stuck his head around the door and said, 'Coffee, anyone?'* 彼得從門後伸進頭來問："咖啡，哪位要？" ◇ (*informal*) *Stick 'em up!* (= put your hands above your head—I have a gun!) 舉起手來！ **4** [T] **sb can stick sth** (*informal*) used to say in a rude and angry way that you are not interested in what sb has, offers, does, etc.（無禮或生氣地表示）對…不感興趣：*I got sick of my boss's moaning and told him he could stick the job.* 我煩透了老闆的牢騷，便跟他說那活兒他自己幹吧，我才不稀罕。

▸ **BECOME FIXED** 卡住 **5** 🔑 [I] **~ (in sth)** to become fixed in one position and impossible to move（在某物中）卡住，陷住，動不了 **SYN** **jam**：*The key has stuck in the lock.* 鑰匙卡在鎖裏了。◇ *This drawer keeps sticking.* 這個抽屜老卡住。

▸ **DIFFICULT SITUATION** 困境 **6** [T] (*BrE, informal*) (usually used in negative sentences and questions 通常用於否定句和疑問句) to accept a difficult or unpleasant situation or person 容忍；忍受 **SYN** **stand**：**~ sth/sb** *I don't know how you stick that job.* 我不知道那活兒你怎麼受得了。◇ *The problem is, my mother can't stick my boyfriend.* 問題是，我母親不能接受我男朋友。◇ **~ doing sth** *John can't stick living with his parents.* 約翰受不了和父母住在一起。

▸ **BECOME ACCEPTED** 被接受 **7** [I] to become accepted 被接受；被證明成立：*The police couldn't* ***make the charges stick*** (= show them to be true). 警方無法證明那些指控成立。◇ *His friends called him Bart and* ***the name has stuck*** (= has become the name that everyone calls him). 朋友們稱他巴特，這名字就叫開了。

▸ **IN CARD GAMES** 紙牌遊戲 **8** [I] to not take any more cards 不再要牌 ➲ see also STUCK *adj.*

IDM **stick in your ˈmind** (of a memory, an image, etc. 往事、形象等) to be remembered for a long time 經久不忘；銘記在心：*One of his paintings in particular sticks in my mind.* 他有一幅畫我記得特別清楚。 **stick in your ˈthroat/ˈcraw** (*informal*) **1** (of words 話語) to be difficult or impossible to say 難以啟齒；說不出口 **2** (of a situation 情況) to be difficult or impossible to accept; to make you angry 難以接受；無法接受；令人氣憤 **stick your ˈneck out** (*informal*) to do or say sth when there is a risk that you may be wrong 做不保險的事；說不保險的話；冒險 **stick to your ˈguns** (*informal*) to refuse to change your mind about sth even when other people are trying to persuade you that you are wrong 不聽別人勸告；堅持己見；一意孤行 ➲ more at BOOT *n.*, FINGER *n.*, KNIFE *n.*, MILE, MUD, NOSE *n.*, OAR, SORE *adj.*, TELL

PHR V **ˌstick aˈround** (*informal*) to stay in a place, waiting for sth to happen or for sb to arrive 不走開；待在原地：*Stick around; we'll need you to help us later.* 別走開，過一會兒我們還需要你幫忙呢。 **ˈstick at sth** to continue to work in a serious and determined way to achieve sth 堅持不懈地做（某事）；持之以恆；鍥而不捨：*If you want to play an instrument well, you've got to* ***stick at it.*** 要想練好一種樂器，你必須持之以恆。

ˈstick by sb [no passive] to be loyal to a person and support them, especially in a difficult situation 堅持忠於；不離棄（某人） **ˈstick by sth** [no passive] to do what you promised or planned to do 信守，遵守，貫徹（承諾、計劃等）：*They stuck by their decision.* 他們決心已下，矢志不渝。 **ˌstick sth↔ˈdown** (*informal*) to write sth somewhere 寫下；記下：*I think I'll stick my name down on the list.* 我想我還是把名字寫到名單上吧。 **ˌstick ˈout** to be noticeable or easily seen 醒目；顯眼；引人注目 **SYN** **stand out**：*They wrote the notice in big red letters so that it would stick out.* 他們用紅色大字寫出通知，這樣會顯眼一些。 **ˌstick ˈout (of sth)** | **ˌstick sth↔ˈout (of sth)** 🔑 to be further out than sth else or come through a hole; to push sth further out than sth else or through a hole（使從某物中）伸出，探出，突出：*His ears stick out.* 他長着一對招風耳。◇ *She stuck her tongue out at me.* 她衝我吐了吐舌頭。◇ *Don't stick your arm out of the car window.* 不要把胳膊伸出車窗。 **ˌstick it/sth ˈout** (*informal*) to continue doing sth to the end, even when it is difficult or boring 堅持到底；忍受下去：*She didn't like the course but she* ***stuck it out*** *to get the certificate.* 她並不喜歡這門課，但為了拿證書還是耐着性子學完了。 **ˌstick ˈout for sth** (*informal*) to refuse to give up until you get what you need or want 堅持要求；不得到…不罷休：*They are sticking out for a higher pay rise.* 他們堅持要求更大幅度地提高工資。 **ˈstick to sth 1** 🔑 to continue doing sth despite difficulties 堅持（做某事，不怕困難）：*She finds it impossible to stick to a diet.* 飲食老受限制，她覺得受不了。**2** 🔑 to continue doing or using sth and not want to change it 堅持；維持；固守；堅持保留：*He promised to help us and he* ***stuck to his word*** (= he did as he had promised). 他答應過幫助我們，他沒有失信。◇ *'Shall we meet on Friday this week?' 'No, let's stick to Saturday.'* "這個星期我們星期五見面怎麼樣？" "不，還是照舊在星期六吧。" ◇ *She stuck to her story.* 她堅持自己所說的。 **ˌstick toˈgether** (*informal*) (of people 人) to stay together and support each other 團結在一起 **ˌstick ˈup** 🔑 to point upwards or be above a surface 豎立；向上突出：*The branch was sticking up out of the water.* 樹枝從水下伸了出來。 **ˌstick ˈup for sb/yourself/sth** [no passive] (*informal*) to support or defend sb/yourself/sth 支持，

S

捍衛（某人、自己、某事物）：*Stick up for what you believe.* 你相信什麼，就要捍衛它。◇ *She taught her children to stick up for themselves at school.* 她教育子女在學校要勇於自衛。◇ *Don't worry—I'll stick up for you.* 別擔心，有我呢。**'stick with sb/sth** [no passive] (*informal*) **1** to stay close to sb so that they can help you 緊跟，不離開（某人，以便得到幫助）**2** to continue with sth or continue doing sth 持續；堅持：*They decided to stick with their original plan.* 他們決定繼續執行原來的計劃。

■ ***noun***

▸ **FROM TREE** 樹木 **1** 🔑 [C] a thin piece of wood that has fallen or been broken from a tree 枝條；枯枝；柴火棍兒：*We collected dry sticks to start a fire.* 我們撿了些枯枝生起火來。◇ *The boys were throwing sticks and stones at the dog.* 男孩子們朝那條狗扔枝條扔石頭。◇ *Her arms and legs were like sticks* (= very thin). 她胳膊和腿瘦得跟柴火棍兒似的。

▸ **FOR WALKING** 走路 **2** 🔑 [C] (*especially BrE*) = WALKING STICK：*The old lady leant on her stick as she talked.* 老太太說話時拄着拐棍。➲ see also SHOOTING STICK, WHITE STICK

▸ **IN SPORT** 體育運動 **3** [C] a long thin object that is used in some sports to hit or control the ball 球棍：*a hockey stick* 曲棍球球棍 ➲ **VISUAL VOCAB** page V44

▸ **LONG THIN PIECE** 條狀物 **4** 🔑 [C] (often in compounds 常構成複合詞) a long thin piece of sth 條狀物；棍狀物：*a stick of dynamite* 一根炸藥棒 ◇ *carrot sticks* 胡蘿蔔條 ◇ (*NAmE*) *a stick of butter* 一條黃油 ➲ **VISUAL VOCAB** page V33 ➲ see also FRENCH STICK **5** [C] (often in compounds 常構成複合詞) a thin piece of wood or plastic that you use for a particular purpose（木料或塑料製成的有特定用途的）棍，條，籤：*pieces of pineapple on sticks* 一串串插在小棍上的菠蘿塊 ➲ see also CHOPSTICK, COCKTAIL STICK, DRUMSTICK, MATCHSTICK, YARDSTICK

▸ **OF GLUE, ETC.** 膠水等 **6** [C] a quantity of a substance, such as solid glue, that is sold in a small container with round ends and straight sides, and can be pushed further out of the container as it is used 一管，一支（膠棒等）➲ see also LIPSTICK

▸ **IN PLANE/VEHICLE** 飛機；車輛 **7** [C] (*informal, especially NAmE*) the control stick of a plane （飛機的）操縱桿，駕駛桿 ➲ see also JOYSTICK (2) **8** [C] (*informal, especially NAmE*) a handle used to change the gears of a vehicle （車輛的）變速桿，換擋桿 ➲ see also GEAR LEVER, STICK SHIFT

▸ **FOR ORCHESTRA** 管弦樂隊 **9** [C] a BATON, used by the person who CONDUCTS an ORCHESTRA 指揮棒

▸ **CRITICISM** 批評 **10** [U] (*BrE, informal*) criticism or severe words 批評；指責：*The referee* **got a lot of stick** *from the home fans.* 裁判飽受主隊球迷的指責。

▸ **COUNTRY AREAS** 鄉村地區 **11 the sticks** [pl.] (*informal*, usually *disapproving*) country areas, a long way from cities 邊遠鄉村地區：*We live* **out in the sticks**. 我們住在偏遠的鄉村。

▸ **PERSON** 人 **12** [C] (*old-fashioned, BrE, informal*) a person 人；傢伙：*He's not such a bad* **old stick**. 他老兄人不算壞。**HELP** There are many other compounds ending in **stick**. You will find them at their place in the alphabet. 以 stick 結尾的複合詞還有很多，可在各字母中的適當位置查到。**IDM** see BEAT *v.*, BIG *adj.*, CARROT, CLEFT *adj.*, SHORT *adj.*, UP *v.*, WRONG *adj.*

sticka·bil·ity /ˌstɪkəˈbɪləti/ *noun* [U] (*informal*) **1** (*NAmE* also **stick-to-itiveness**) the ability to keep doing sth, even if it is sometimes boring 持之以恒的能力；忍耐力 **SYN** **persistence**, **tenacity**：*The long list of jobs on her CV suggests a lack of stickability.* 她簡歷上的那一長串工作說明她缺乏忍耐力。**2** (of a website 網站) the ability to keep visitors interested for more than a short time（使訪客長期感興趣的）吸引力

stick·ball /ˈstɪkbɔːl/ *noun* an informal game similar to BASEBALL, played with a stick and a rubber ball 棍球（用棍擊橡膠球，類似於棒球的非正式運動）

stick·er /ˈstɪkə(r)/ *noun* a sticky label with a picture or message on it, that you stick onto sth 粘貼標籤；貼紙：*bumper stickers* (= on cars) 汽車保險槓粘貼標籤 ◇ *a sticker album* (= to collect stickers in) 粘貼標籤收集冊 ➲ SYNONYMS at LABEL

'sticker price *noun* (*NAmE*) the price that is marked on sth, especially a car（尤指汽車的）標價

'sticker shock *noun* [U] (*NAmE*) the unpleasant feeling that people experience when they find that sth is much more expensive than they expected 價格震驚（發現價格比想像的要高得多）

'stick figure (*NAmE*) (*BrE* **'matchstick figure**) *noun* a picture of a person drawn only with thin lines for the arms and legs, a circle for the head, etc. 人物線條畫；簡筆人物畫

'sticking plaster *noun* (*BrE*) = PLASTER (3)

'sticking point *noun* something that people do not agree on and that prevents progress in a discussion 分歧點；癥結：*This was one of the major sticking points in the negotiations.* 這是談判中主要的難點之一。

'stick insect *noun* a large insect with a long thin body that looks like a stick 竹節蟲

'stick-in-the-mud *noun* (*informal, disapproving*) a person who refuses to try anything new or exciting 守舊的人；墨守成規的人

stickle·back /ˈstɪklbæk/ *noun* a small FRESHWATER fish with sharp points on its back 刺魚

stick·ler /ˈstɪklə(r)/ *noun* **~ (for sth)** a person who thinks that a particular quality or type of behaviour is very important and expects other people to think and behave in the same way 非常看重（某品質或行為）的人：*a stickler for punctuality* 非常注重守時的人

'stick-on *adj.* [only before noun] (of an object 物品) with glue on one side so that it sticks to sth 一面帶黏膠的：*stick-on labels* 背膠標籤

stick·pin /ˈstɪkpɪn/ *noun* (*NAmE*) a decorative pin that is worn on a tie to keep it in place, or as a piece of jewellery（領帶的）裝飾別針

'stick shift *noun* (*NAmE, informal*) **1** (*NAmE* also **'gear shift**) (*BrE* **'gear lever**, **'gear·stick**) a handle used to change the gears of a vehicle 變速桿；換擋桿 **2** a vehicle that has a stick shift 手動變速車 ➲ compare AUTOMATIC *n.* (2)

stick-to-itiveness /ˌstɪk ˈtuː ɪtəvnəs/ *noun* [U] (*NAmE, informal*) = STICKABILITY (1)

'stick-up *noun* (*informal, especially NAmE*) = HOLD-UP (2)：*This is a stick-up!* 這是持槍搶劫！

sticky 🔑 /ˈstɪki/ *adj.*, *noun*

■ ***adj.*** (**stick·ier**, **sticki·est**) **1** 🔑 made of or covered in a substance that sticks to things that touch it 黏（性）的：*sticky fingers covered in jam* 粘滿果醬的黏乎乎的手指 ◇ *Stir in the milk to make a soft but not sticky dough.* 把牛奶攪進去，和成軟而不黏的麪糰。**2** 🔑 (of paper, labels, etc. 紙、標籤等) with glue on one side so that you can stick it to a surface 一面帶黏膠的 **3** (*informal*) (of the weather 天氣) hot and damp 悶熱的 **4** (*informal*) (of a person 人) feeling hot and uncomfortable 感到熱得難受的 **SYN** **sweaty** **5** (*informal*) difficult or unpleasant 難辦的；棘手的；讓人為難的：*a sticky situation* 棘手的局面 **6** (*computing* 計) (of a website 網站) so interesting and well organized that the people who visit it stay there for a long time 吸引人長時間訪問的；富有吸引力的 ▸ **stick·ily** /-ɪli/ *adv.* **sticki·ness** *noun* [U] **IDM** **have sticky 'fingers** (*informal*) to be likely to steal sth 好偷東西的；有順手牽羊的毛病 **a ˌsticky 'wicket** (*BrE, informal*) a difficult situation 困難的處境 ➲ more at END *n.*

■ ***noun*** (*pl.* **-ies**) (also **'sticky note**) a small piece of sticky paper that you use for writing a note on, and that can be easily removed 告事貼 ➲ compare POST-IT

sticky·beak /ˈstɪkibiːk/ *noun* (*AustralE, NZE, informal*) a person who tries to find out information about other people's private lives in a way that is annoying or rude 愛打聽的人；好探聽隱私的人；包打聽 ▸ **sticky·beak** *verb* [I]：*I don't mean to stickybeak, but when is he going to leave?* 我不是要多管閒事，但是他什麼時候要離開呢？

'sticky tape *noun* [U] (*BrE*) = SELLOTAPE

stiff 0-π /stɪf/ *adj., adv., noun, verb*
■ ***adj.*** (**stiff·er**, **stiff·est**)
▸ **DIFFICULT TO BEND/MOVE** 不易彎曲 / 活動 **1** 0-π firm and difficult to bend or move 不易彎曲（或活動）的；硬的；挺的：*stiff cardboard* 硬紙板 ◇ *a stiff brush* 硬刷子 ◇ *The windows were stiff and she couldn't get them open.* 窗戶緊，她開不了。
▸ **MUSCLES** 肌肉 **2** 0-π when a person is **stiff**, their muscles hurt when they move them 僵硬的；一動就疼的：*I'm really stiff after that bike ride yesterday.* 昨天騎了那趟自行車，我覺得渾身痠痛。◇ *I've got a **stiff neck**.* 我脖子發僵。
▸ **MIXTURE** 混合物 **3** 0-π thick and almost solid; difficult to stir 稠的；難攪動的：*Whisk the egg whites until stiff.* 把蛋清打成稠的。
▸ **DIFFICULT/SEVERE** 困難；嚴厲 **4** more difficult or severe than usual 困難的；艱難的；嚴厲的；激烈的：*It was a **stiff climb** to the top of the hill.* 費了好大勁才爬到山頂。◇ *The company faces **stiff competition** from its rivals.* 公司遇到對手的激烈競爭。◇ *The new proposals have met with **stiff opposition**.* 新提案遭到強烈的反對。◇ *There are **stiff fines** for breaking the rules.* 違反規則要受重罰。◇ *a **stiff breeze/wind*** (= one that blows strongly) 強風
▸ **NOT FRIENDLY** 不友好 **5** (of a person or their behaviour 人或其行為) not friendly or relaxed 不友好的；生硬的：*The speech he made to welcome them was stiff and formal.* 他那番歡迎他們的話講得生硬刻板。
▸ **PRICE** 價格 **6** (*informal*) costing a lot or too much 高昂的；過高的：*There's a stiff $30 entrance fee to the exhibition.* 展覽會的入場費高達 30 元。
▸ **ALCOHOLIC DRINK** 酒 **7** [only before noun] strong; containing a lot of alcohol 烈性的；酒精度數高的：*a stiff whisky* 烈性威士忌
▸ **stiff·ly** 0-π *adv.* **stiff·ness** *noun* [U]：*pain and stiffness in her legs* 她兩腿又疼又僵的感覺
IDM **(keep) a stiff upper ˈlip** to keep calm and hide your feelings when you are in pain or in a difficult situation（面對痛苦或困境）不動聲色，沉着而不外露
■ ***adv.*** **1** (*informal*) very much; to an extreme degree 非常；極其：*be **bored/scared/worried stiff*** 非常厭煩 / 害怕 / 擔心 **2 frozen ~** (of wet material 含水的東西) very cold and hard because the water has become ice（凍）僵；（凍）硬：*The clothes on the washing line were frozen stiff.* 掛在晾衣繩上的衣服凍硬了。◇ *I came home from the game frozen stiff* (= very cold). 我看完比賽回到家裏，都快凍僵了。
■ ***noun*** (*slang*) the body of a dead person 死屍
■ ***verb*** **~ sb** (*NAmE, informal*) to cheat sb or not pay them what you owe them, especially by not leaving any money as a tip 詐騙；不還錢；（尤指）不給小費

ˌstiff-ˈarm *verb* (*NAmE*) = STRAIGHT-ARM

stiff·en /ˈstɪfn/ *verb* **1** [I, T] to make yourself or part of your body firm, straight and still, especially because you are angry or frightened（尤指因氣憤或害怕，使渾身或身體的一部份）變僵硬，變僵直，繃緊：**~ (with sth)** *She stiffened with fear.* 她嚇呆了。◇ **~ sth (with sth)** *I stiffened my back and faced him.* 我挺直了腰桿面對着他。 **2** [I, T] (of part of the body 身體的一部份) to become, or to make sth become, difficult to bend or move（使）難以彎曲，難以活動，發僵：**~ (up)** *My muscles had stiffened up after the climb.* 爬上去以後我兩腿都發僵了。◇ **~ sth** *stiffened muscles* 發僵的肌肉 **3** [T, I] **~ (sth)** to make an attitude or idea stronger or more powerful; to become stronger （使）變強硬，變堅定 **SYN** **strengthen**：*The threat of punishment has only **stiffened their resolve*** (= made them even more determined to do sth). 懲罰的威脅益發堅定了他們的決心。 **4** [T] **~ sth (with sth)** to make sth, such as cloth, firm and unable to bend 使硬挺

ˌstiff-ˈnecked *adj.* proud and refusing to change 固執的；倔強的；犟的

stiffy /ˈstɪfi/ *noun* (*pl.* **-ies**) (*taboo, slang*) an ERECTION (1) of a man's PENIS（陰莖的）勃起

stifle /ˈstaɪfl/ *verb* **1** [T] **~ sth** to prevent sth from happening; to prevent a feeling from being expressed 壓制；扼殺；阻止；抑制 **SYN** **suppress**：*She managed to stifle a yawn.* 她忍住了哈欠。◇ *They hope the new rules will not stifle creativity.* 他們希望新規則不會壓制創意。◇ *The government failed to stifle the unrest.* 政府沒有制止住動亂。 **2** [I, T] to feel unable to breathe, or to make sb unable to breathe, because it is too hot and/or there is no fresh air （使）窒息，無法自如地呼吸，感覺窒悶 **SYN** **suffocate**：*I felt I was stifling in the airless room.* 在那間悶氣的房間裏我感覺都快憋死了。◇ **~ sb** *Most of the victims were stifled by the fumes.* 多數受害者是因煙霧窒息而死的。 ▸ **stif·ling** /ˈstaɪflɪŋ/ *adj.*：*a stifling room* 悶得讓人透不過氣來的房間 ◇ ***'It's stifling** in here—can we open a window?'* "這裏悶得人難受，我們能不能開一扇窗戶？" ◇ *At 25, she found family life stifling.* 她 25 歲時感到家庭生活令人窒息。 **stif·ling·ly** *adv.*：*The room was stiflingly hot.* 房間裏熱得人喘不上氣來。

stigma /ˈstɪgmə/ *noun* **1** [U, C, usually sing.] feelings of disapproval that people have about particular illnesses or ways of behaving 恥辱；羞恥：*the social stigma of alcoholism* 酗酒在社會上的惡名 ◇ *There is no longer any stigma attached to being divorced.* 離婚不再是什麼丟臉的事。 **2** [C] (*biology* 生) the part in the middle of a flower where POLLEN is received（花的）柱頭 ➲ **VISUAL VOCAB** page V11

stig·mata /ˈstɪgmətə; stɪgˈmɑːtə/ *noun* [pl.] marks that look like the wounds made by nails on the body of Jesus Christ, believed by some Christians to have appeared as holy marks on the bodies of some SAINTS 聖傷，聖痕（據信出現在某些聖徒身上，與耶穌身上釘子留下的傷痕相似）

stig·ma·tize (*BrE* also **-ise**) /ˈstɪgmətaɪz/ *verb* [usually passive] **~ sb/sth** (*formal*) to treat sb in a way that makes them feel that they are very bad or unimportant 使感到羞恥；侮蔑 ▸ **stig·ma·tiza·tion**, **-isa·tion** /ˌstɪgmətaɪˈzeɪʃn; *NAmE* -təˈz-/ *noun* [U]

stile 梯磴

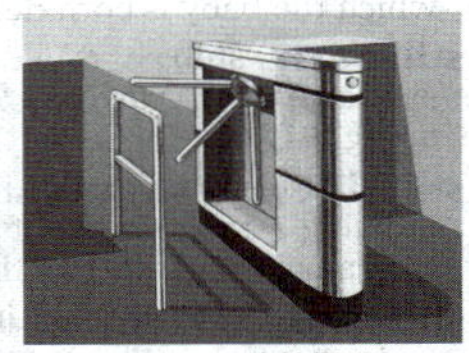
turnstile 旋轉柵門

stile /staɪl/ *noun* a set of steps that help people climb over a fence or gate in a field, etc.（供人翻越田地等的圍欄、柵欄門等的）台階，梯磴 ➲ **VISUAL VOCAB** page V3

stil·etto /stɪˈletəʊ; *NAmE* -toʊ/ *noun* (*pl.* **-os** or **-oes**) **1** (also **ˌstiletto ˈheel**) (*especially BrE*) a woman's shoe with a very high narrow heel; the heel on such a shoe 細高跟女鞋；（女鞋的）細高跟 **SYN** **spike heel** ➲ **VISUAL VOCAB** page V64 **2** a small knife with a narrow pointed blade 短劍；匕首

still 0-π /stɪl/ *adv., adj., noun, verb*
■ ***adv.*** **1** 0-π continuing until a particular point in time and not finishing 還；還是；仍然；依舊：*I wrote to them last month and I'm still waiting for a reply.* 我上個月給他們寫了信，到現在還在等回音。◇ *Mum, I'm still hungry!* 媽，我還餓！◇ *Do you still live at the same address?* 你還住在原地址嗎？◇ *There's still time to change your mind.* 你還有時間改變主意。◇ *It was, and still is, my favourite movie.* 那部影片以前是我最喜歡的，現在仍然是。 **2** 0-π despite what has just been said（雖然…）還是；但；不過：*We searched everywhere but we still couldn't find it.* 我們四處找，但還是沒找到。◇ *The weather was cold and wet. Still, we had a great time.* 天氣又冷又潮，不過我們仍舊玩得很開心。 **3** used for making a comparison stronger（加強比較級）還要，更：*The next day was warmer still.* 第二天更暖和了。◇ *If you can manage to get two tickets that's better still.* 要是你能設法弄到兩張票，那就更好了。 **4 ~ more/another** even more 還有（更多）：*There was still*

S

more bad news to come. 隨後還傳來了其他的壞消息。
IDM see LESS *adv.*

■ ***adj.*** **1** not moving; calm and quiet 靜止的；平靜的；安靜的；寂靜的：*still water* 平靜的水面 ◇ ***Keep still*** *while I brush your hair.* 我給你梳頭時你不要動。◇ *The kids found it hard to* ***stay still.*** 孩子們覺得待着不動很難做到。◇ *Can't you* ***sit still?*** 你就不能老老實實坐一會兒嗎？◇ *We stayed in a village where* ***time has stood still*** (= life has not changed for many years). 我們待在一個時間似乎凝滯了的村子裏。 **2** with no wind 無風的：*a still summer's day* 無風的夏日 ◇ *the still night air* 夜間寧靜的空氣 **3** (*BrE*) (of a drink 飲料) not containing bubbles of gas; not FIZZY 不含碳酸氣的；不起泡的：*still mineral water* 無汽礦泉水

IDM **the still of the 'night** (*literary*) the time during the night when it is quiet and calm 萬籟俱寂的夜晚；夜闌人靜 **a/the still small 'voice** (*literary*) the voice of God or your CONSCIENCE, that tells you to do what is morally right（來自上主）輕微細弱的聲音；良心的呼喚 **still waters run 'deep** (*saying*) a person who seems to be quiet or shy may surprise you by knowing a lot or having deep feelings 靜水流深；木訥寡言者也許胸藏丘壑

■ ***noun*** **1** a photograph of a scene from a film/movie or video（電影或錄像的）定格畫面；劇照：*a publicity still from his new movie* 他的新電影的廣告劇照 **2** a piece of equipment that is used for making strong alcoholic drinks（製酒的）蒸餾器：*a whisky still* 威士忌蒸餾器 ➲ see also DISTIL (2)

■ ***verb*** [I, T] (*literary*) to become calm and quiet; to make sth calm and quiet（使）靜止，平靜，安靜：*The wind stilled.* 風停了。◇ **~ sb/sth** *She spoke quietly to still the frightened child.* 她輕聲安慰受到驚嚇的孩子。◇ (*figurative*) *to still sb's doubts/fears* 消除某人的疑慮／恐懼

still·birth /ˈstɪlbɜːθ; *NAmE* -bɜːrθ/ *noun* [C, U] a birth in which the baby is born dead 死產

still·born /ˈstɪlbɔːn; *NAmE* -bɔːrn/ *adj.* **1** born dead 死產的：*a stillborn baby* 死產兒 **2** not successful; not developing 失敗的；夭折的

ˌstill ˈlife *noun* [U, C] (*pl.* **still lifes**) the art of painting or drawing arrangements of objects such as flowers, fruit, etc.; a painting, etc. like this 靜物畫技法；靜物畫

still·ness /ˈstɪlnəs/ *noun* [U] the quality of being quiet and not moving 靜止；安靜；寧靜：*The sound of footsteps on the path broke the stillness.* 小路上的腳步聲打破了寧靜。

S

stilt /stɪlt/ *noun* [usually pl.] **1** one of a set of posts that support a building so that it is high above the ground or water（支撐建築物高出地面或水面的）樁子，支柱 **2** one of two long pieces of wood that have a step on the side that you can stand on, so that you can walk above the ground 高蹺：*a circus performer* ***on stilts*** 馬戲團裏踩高蹺的演員

stilt·ed /ˈstɪltɪd/ *adj.* (*disapproving*) (of a way of speaking or writing 言談或寫作) not natural or relaxed; too formal 生硬的；不自然的：*We made stilted conversation for a few moments.* 我們不自然地客套了幾句。▸ **stilt·ed·ly** *adv.*

Stil·ton™ /ˈstɪltən/ *noun* [U, C] a type of English cheese with blue lines of MOULD running through it and a strong flavour 斯蒂爾頓乾酪（一種英國奶酪，有藍色黴紋，味濃）

stimu·lant /ˈstɪmjələnt/ *noun* (*formal*) **1** a drug or substance that makes you feel more awake and gives you more energy 興奮劑：*Coffee and tea are mild stimulants.* 咖啡和茶是輕度興奮劑。 **2 ~ (to sth)** an event or activity that encourages more activity 有激勵作用的事物

stimu·late /ˈstɪmjuleɪt/ *verb* **1 ~ sth** to make sth develop or become more active; to encourage sth 促進；激發；激勵：*The exhibition has stimulated interest in her work.* 展覽增進了人們對她作品的興趣。◇ *The article can be used to stimulate discussion among students.* 這篇文章可用來活躍學生的討論。 **2** to make sb interested and excited about sth 刺激；使興奮：**~ sb** *Parents should give children books that stimulate them.* 父母應給孩子能啟發他們的書。◇ *Both men and women are stimulated by erotic photos* (= sexually). 色情照片對男女都有刺激作用。◇ **~ sb to do sth** *The conference stimulated him to study the subject in more depth.* 這次會議促使他更深入地研究那個課題。 **3 ~ sth** (*technical* 術語) to make a part of the body function 促進（身體某部份）的功能：*The women were given fertility drugs to stimulate the ovaries.* 那些婦女得到了促進卵巢功能的生育藥。 ▸ **stimu·la·tion** /ˌstɪmjuˈleɪʃn/ *noun* [U]：*sensory/intellectual/sexual/visual/physical stimulation* 感官／智力／性／視覺／身體刺激

stimu·lat·ing /ˈstɪmjuleɪtɪŋ/ *adj.* **1** full of interesting or exciting ideas; making people feel enthusiastic 趣味盎然的；激勵人的；振奮人心的 SYN **inspiring**：*a stimulating discussion* 饒有趣味的討論 ◇ *a stimulating teacher* 能夠引發興趣的老師 ➲ SYNONYMS at INTERESTING **2** making you feel more active and healthy 增加活力的；增進健康的：*shower gel containing plant extracts that have a stimulating effect on the skin* 含有對皮膚有益的植物精華的沐浴凝膠

stimu·lus /ˈstɪmjələs/ *noun* (*pl.* **stim·uli** /-laɪ/) **~ (to/for sth)** | **~ (to do sth)** **1** [usually sing.] something that helps sb/sth to develop better or more quickly 促進因素；激勵因素；刺激物：*Books provide children with ideas and a stimulus for play.* 書不僅給孩子們提供想法，而且使他們玩得更有意思。◇ *The new tax laws should act as a stimulus to exports.* 新稅法應該能促進出口。 **2** something that produces a reaction in a human, an animal or a plant（使生物產生反應的）刺激，刺激物：***sensory/verbal/visual*** *stimuli* 感官／言語／視覺刺激 ◇ *The animals were conditioned to respond to* ***auditory stimuli*** (= sounds). 經過訓練，那些動物對聲音形成了條件反射。

sting /stɪŋ/ *verb, noun*

■ ***verb*** (**stung**, **stung** /stʌŋ/) **1** [T, I] **~ (sb/sth)** (of an insect or plant 昆蟲或植物) to touch your skin or make a very small hole in it so that you feel a sharp pain 刺；蜇；叮：*I was stung on the arm by a wasp.* 我的胳膊給黃蜂蜇了一下。◇ *Be careful of the nettles—they sting!* 小心給蕁麻扎着，蕁麻有刺！ **2** [I, T] to feel, or to make sb feel, a sharp pain in a part of their body（使）感覺刺痛，感覺灼痛：*I put some antiseptic on the cut and it stung for a moment.* 我在割破的地方抹了點抗菌劑，一時間十分刺痛。◇ *My eyes were stinging from the smoke.* 煙熏得我眼睛疼。◇ **~ sth** *Tears stung her eyes.* 她流淚流得眼睛疼。➲ SYNONYMS at HURT **3** [T] to make sb feel angry or upset 激怒；使不安：**~ sb** *He was stung by their criticism.* 他們的批評使他心煩意亂。◇ *They launched a stinging attack on the government.* 他們對政府進行了猛烈的抨擊。◇ **~ sb to/into sth** *Their cruel remarks stung her into action.* 他們傷人的話激怒了她，使她採取了行動。◇ **~ sb into doing sth** *He was stung into answering in his defence.* 他被激怒了，不得不作出回應為自己辯護。 **4** [T, often passive] **~ sb (for sth)** (*informal*) to charge sb more money than they expected; to charge sb who did not expect to pay 對（某人）敲竹槓；敲詐；欺詐：*I got stung for a £100 meal.* 我捱宰了，一頓飯吃了 100 英鎊。

PHR V **'sting sb for sth** (*BrE, informal*) to borrow money from sb 向某人借錢

■ ***noun*** **1** (*NAmE* also **sting·er**) [C] the sharp pointed part of an insect or creature that can go into the skin leaving a small, painful and sometimes poisonous wound（昆蟲的）螫針，刺；（植物的）刺，刺毛：*the sting of a bee* 蜜蜂的螫針 ◇ *The scorpion has a sting in its tail.* 蠍子尾巴上有螫針。➲ VISUAL VOCAB page V13 **2** [C] a wound that is made when an insect, a creature or a plant stings you 刺傷；蜇傷；叮傷：*A wasp or bee sting is painful but not necessarily serious.* 被黃蜂或蜜蜂蜇一下疼是疼，但未必礙事。 **3** [C, U] any sharp pain in your body or mind（身體或心靈的）劇痛，痛苦：*the sting of salt in a wound* 傷口上撒鹽引起的劇痛 ◇ *He smiled at her, trying to* ***take the sting out of*** *his words* (= trying to make the situation less painful or difficult). 他衝她微微一笑，想使他的話不至於刺痛她。 **4** [C] a clever secret plan by the police to catch criminals（警察為抓捕罪犯而設的）圈套：*a sting operation* *to catch heroin dealers in Detroit* 在底特律設圈套抓捕海洛因販子的行動 **5** [C] (*especially NAmE*) a clever plan by criminals to cheat people out of a lot of money（罪犯詐騙錢財的）騙局，詭計

IDM **a ˌsting in the ˈtail** (*informal*) an unpleasant feature that comes at the end of a story, an event, etc. and spoils it 煞風景的結局

ˈstinging nettle *noun* = NETTLE

sting·ray /ˈstɪŋreɪ/ *noun* a large wide flat sea fish that has a long tail with a sharp sting in it that can cause serious wounds 刺魟（大型扁寬海魚，尾部有尖刺）

stingy /ˈstɪndʒi/ *adj.* (**stin·gier**, **stin·gi·est**) (*informal*) not given or giving willingly; not generous, especially with money 小氣的；吝嗇的 **SYN** **mean**：*You're stingy!* (= not willing to spend money) 你真小氣！◇ *Don't be so stingy with the cream!* 別那麼捨不得放奶油！ ▸ **stingi·ness** *noun* [U]

stink /stɪŋk/ *verb, noun*

■ *verb* (**stank** /stæŋk/, **stunk** /stʌŋk/) or (**stunk**, **stunk**) (*informal*) **1** [I] **~ (of sth)** to have a strong, unpleasant smell 有臭味；有難聞的氣味 **SYN** **reek**：*Her breath stank of garlic.* 她嘴裏有股大蒜味。◇ ***It stinks** of smoke in here.* 這兒有股煙味。 **2** [I] **~ (of sth)** to seem very bad, unpleasant or dishonest 讓人覺得很糟糕；令人厭惡；似乎有不正當行為：*The whole business stank of corruption.* 這件事從頭到尾都有腐敗嫌疑。◇ *'What do you think of the idea?' 'I think **it stinks**.'* "你覺得這個主意怎麼樣？" "我覺得是個餿主意。"

PHR V **ˌstink sth↔ˈout** to fill a place with a strong, unpleasant smell 使充滿臭味（或難聞氣味）

■ *noun* (*informal*) **1** [C, usually sing.] a very unpleasant smell 惡臭；難聞氣味 **SYN** **reek**：*the stink of sweat and urine* 難聞的汗味尿味 **2** [sing.] a lot of trouble and anger about sth 吵鬧；爭吵：*The whole business caused quite a stink.* 整件事引起了軒然大波。◇ *We'll **kick up a stink*** (= complain a lot and cause trouble) *if they try to close the school down.* 假如他們想關閉這所學校，我們就要大鬧一場。

ˈstink bomb *noun* a container that produces a very bad smell when it is broken. Stink bombs are used for playing tricks on people. 臭彈（破碎時發出惡臭，用於惡作劇）

stink·er /ˈstɪŋkə(r)/ *noun* (*informal*) a person or thing that is very unpleasant or difficult 討厭的人；棘手的事

stink·ing /ˈstɪŋkɪŋ/ *adj., adv.*

■ *adj.* **1** having a very strong, unpleasant smell 臭的；發惡臭的；十分難聞的：*I was pushed into a filthy, stinking room.* 我被推進一間又髒又臭的屋子裏。 **2** [only before noun] (*informal, especially BrE*) very bad or unpleasant 很糟糕的；令人討厭的：*I've got a stinking cold.* 我得了這該死的感冒。 **3** [only before noun] (*BrE, informal*) showing a lot of anger 憤怒不已的；氣急敗壞的：*I wrote them a stinking letter to complain.* 我給他們去信氣憤地抱怨了一通。

■ *adv.* (*informal*, usually *disapproving*) extremely 極其；非常：*They must be **stinking rich**.* 他們一定富得流油。

stinky /ˈstɪŋki/ *adj.* (**stink·ier**, **stink·iest**) (*informal*) **1** having an extremely bad smell 發惡臭的；十分難聞的 **2** extremely unpleasant or bad 令人厭惡的；糟糕透頂的

stint /stɪnt/ *noun, verb*

■ *noun* **~ (as sth)** a period of time that you spend working somewhere or doing a particular activity 從事某項工作（或活動）的時間：*He **did a stint** abroad early in his career.* 他剛參加工作時在國外幹過一段時間。◇ *a two-year stint in the Navy* 在海軍服役兩年

■ *verb* [I, T] (usually used in negative sentences 通常用於否定句) to provide or use only a small amount of sth 節省；吝惜：**~ (on sth)** *She never stints on the food at her parties.* 她舉辦聚會吃的東西從不小氣。◇ **~ yourself** *We don't need to stint ourselves—have some more!* 我們沒必要節省，多吃點！ ➲ see also UNSTINTING

sti·pend /ˈstaɪpend/ *noun* (*formal*) an amount of money that is paid regularly to sb, especially a priest, as wages or money to live on（尤指神職人員的）生活津貼，薪俸；獻儀：*a monthly stipend* 月俸 ◇ (*especially NAmE*) *a summer internship with a small stipend* 薪水微薄的暑期實習

sti·pen·diary /staɪˈpendiəri; *NAmE* -dieri/ *noun* (*pl.* **-ies**) (also **stiˌpendiary ˈmagistrate**) (in Britain) a MAGISTRATE who is paid for his or her work（英國）受薪治安法官

stip·ple /ˈstɪpl/ *verb* [often passive] **~ sth** (*technical* 術語) to paint or draw sth using small dots or marks 點畫；點彩畫出 ▸ **stip·pling** /ˈstɪplɪŋ/ *noun* [U]

stipu·late /ˈstɪpjuleɪt/ *verb* (*formal*) to state clearly and firmly that sth must be done, or how it must be done 規定；明確要求 **SYN** **specify**：**~ sth** *A delivery date is stipulated in the contract.* 合同中規定了交貨日期。◇ **~ that …** *The job advertisement stipulates that the applicant must have three years' experience.* 招聘廣告明確要求應聘者必須有三年工作經驗。◇ **~ what, how, etc. …** *The policy stipulates what form of consent is required.* 保險單規定了哪一種是所需的同意形式。 ▸ **stipu·la·tion** /ˌstɪpjuˈleɪʃn/ *noun* [C, U]：*The only stipulation is that the topic you choose must be related to your studies.* 唯一的要求是所選的題目必須與你的研究科目有關。

stir 0➔ /stɜː(r)/ *verb, noun*

■ *verb* (**-rr-**)

▸ MIX 使混合 **1** 0➔ [T] to move a liquid or substance around, using a spoon or sth similar, in order to mix it thoroughly 攪動；攪和；攪拌：**~ sth** *She stirred her tea.* 她攪了攪茶。◇ **~ sth into sth** *The vegetables are stirred into the rice while it is hot.* 趁米飯熱時把蔬菜拌進去。◇ **~ sth in** *Stir in the milk until the sauce thickens.* 把牛奶攪進去，直到醬汁變稠為止。 ➲ SYNONYMS at MIX ➲ COLLOCATIONS at COOKING

▸ MOVE 移動 **2** [I, T] to move, or to make sth move, slightly（使）微動：*She heard the baby stir in the next room.* 她聽見嬰兒在隔壁有動靜。◇ **~ sth/sb** *A slight breeze was stirring the branches.* 微風吹動着樹枝。◇ *A noise stirred me from sleep.* 響聲把我從睡夢中驚醒。 **3** [I, T] to move, or to make sb move, in order to do sth（使）行動，活動：*You haven't stirred from that chair all evening!* 你坐在那把椅子上一晚上沒動了！◇ **~ yourself/sb** *Come on, stir yourself. You're late!* 快，快走吧。你要遲到了！◇ *Their complaints have finally stirred him into action.* 他們的抱怨最終促使他採取了行動。

▸ FEELINGS 感覺 **4** [T] **~ sb (to sth)** to make sb excited or make them feel sth strongly 打動；激發：*a book that really stirs the imagination* 很能激發人的想像力的書 ◇ *She was stirred by his sad story.* 他那悲慘的故事打動了她。 **5** [I] (of a feeling or a mood 感情或情緒) to begin to be felt 開始感到；逐漸產生；萌動；被喚起：*A feeling of guilt began to stir in her.* 她心裏漸漸生出了內疚感。

▸ CAUSE TROUBLE 引起麻煩 **6** [T, I] **~ (it)** (*BrE, informal, disapproving*) to try to cause trouble 撥弄是非：*You're just stirring it!* 你這不是搬弄是非嗎！ ➲ see also STIRRER

IDM **stir the ˈblood** to make sb excited 使人興奮；激起熱情 **stir your ˈstumps** (*old-fashioned, BrE, informal*) to begin to move; to hurry 起身走；趕快

PHR V **ˌstir sb↔ˈup** to encourage sb to do sth; to make sb feel they must do sth 激勵；鼓動 **ˌstir sth↔ˈup** **1** to make people feel strong emotions 激起（感情）：*to stir up hatred* 激起仇恨 **2** to try to cause arguments or problems 挑起，煽動（爭執或事端）：*to stir up a debate* 挑起爭論 ◇ *Whenever he's around, he always manages to **stir up trouble**.* 什麼時候只要有他在，他就總要挑起點事來。◇ *We've got enough problems without you trying to **stir things up**.* 我們麻煩事兒已經夠多的了，你就別再挑撥是非了。 **3** to make sth move around in water or air（水或空氣中）攪起；吹起：*The wind stirred up a lot of dust.* 風吹起大量塵土。

■ *noun* **1** [sing.] excitement, anger or shock that is felt by a number of people（一些人感到的）激動，憤怒，震動 **SYN** **commotion**：*Her resignation **caused quite a stir**.* 她的辭職引起很大震動。 **2** [C, usually sing.] the action of stirring sth 攪動；攪和；攪拌：*Could you give the rice a stir?* 你把米飯攪一攪好嗎？

ˈstir-crazy *adj.* (*informal, especially NAmE*) showing signs of mental illness because of being kept in prison（因遭囚禁而）精神失常的

S

ˈstir-fry *verb, noun* (*pl.* **-ies**)

■ ***verb*** **~ sth** to cook thin strips of vegetables or meat quickly by stirring them in very hot oil 翻炒；炒；煸：*stir-fried chicken* 油爆雞 ➲ COLLOCATIONS at COOKING ➲ VISUAL VOCAB page V27

■ ***noun*** a hot dish made by stir-frying small pieces of meat, fish and/or vegetables 炒菜

stir·rer /ˈstɜːrə(r)/ *noun* (*BrE, informal, disapproving*) a person who likes causing trouble, especially between other people, by spreading secrets 喜歡製造事端的人；（尤指）好撥弄是非者

stir·ring /ˈstɜːrɪŋ/ *noun, adj.*

■ ***noun*** **~ (of sth)** the beginning of a feeling, an idea or a development（感情、想法或發展的）開始，出現，萌動，醞釀：*She felt a stirring of anger.* 她感覺自己忍不住要生氣了。

■ ***adj.*** [usually before noun] causing strong feelings; exciting 令人激情澎湃的；激動人心的：*a stirring performance* 動人的表演 ◇ *stirring memories* 令人心潮澎湃的回憶

stir·rup /ˈstɪrəp/ *noun* one of the metal rings that hang down on each side of a horse's SADDLE, used to support the rider's foot 馬鐙

ˈstirrup pants *noun* [pl.] women's tight trousers/pants with a narrow strip of cloth at the bottom of each leg that fits under the foot（女式）健美踏腳褲

stitch /stɪtʃ/ *noun, verb*

■ ***noun*** **1** [C] one of the small lines of thread that you can see on a piece of cloth after it has been sewn; the action that produces this（縫紉的）一針，針腳；縫：*Try to keep the stitches small and straight.* 針腳要盡量縫得小而直。➲ VISUAL VOCAB page V41 **2** [C] one of the small circles of wool that you make around the needle when you are knitting（編織的）一針：*to* ***drop a stitch*** (= to lose one that you have made) 漏一針 **3** [C, U] (especially in compounds 尤用於構成複合詞) a particular style of sewing or knitting that you use to make the pattern you want 縫法；針法；編織法：*chain stitch* 鏈式線步 **4** [C] a short piece of thread, etc. that doctors use to sew the edges of a wound together（縫合傷口的）縫線：*The cut needed eight stitches.* 這道傷口需要縫八針。➲ COLLOCATIONS at INJURY **5** [C, usually sing.] a sudden pain in the side of your body, usually caused by running or laughing 肋部突然的疼痛（多由奔跑或笑引起）；岔氣：*Can we slow down? I've got a stitch.* 我們慢一點好不好？我岔氣了。

IDM **in ˈstitches** (*informal*) laughing a lot 大笑不止；笑破肚皮：*The play* ***had us in stitches***. 那齣戲讓我們笑得前仰後合。 **not have a stitch ˈon | not be wearing a ˈstitch** (*informal*) to be naked 一絲不掛；赤裸 **a stitch in ˈtime (saves ˈnine)** (*saying*) it is better to deal with sth immediately because if you wait it may become worse or more difficult and cause extra work 及時縫一針能省九針；小洞及時補，免遭大洞苦

■ ***verb*** **1 ~ sth (+ adv./prep.)** to use a needle and thread to repair, join, or decorate pieces of cloth 縫；縫補 **SYN** **sew**：*Her wedding dress was stitched by hand.* 她的婚紗是手工縫製的。◇ (*figurative*) *An agreement was hastily stitched together* (= made very quickly). 倉促達成了一項協議。 **2 ~ sth (up)** to sew the edges of a wound together 縫合（傷口）：*The cut will need to be stitched.* 這傷口需要縫合。

PHR V **ˌstitch sb↔ˈup** (*BrE, informal*) to cheat sb or put them in a position where they seem guilty of sth they have not done 算計某人；誣陷某人 **ˌstitch sth↔ˈup** **1** to use a needle and thread to join things together 縫合 **2** (*BrE, informal*) to arrange or complete sth 辦妥；做成：*to stitch up a deal* 做成一筆交易 ◇ *They think they have the US market stitched up.* 他們覺得美國市場已是萬無一失。

stitch·ing /ˈstɪtʃɪŋ/ *noun* [U] a row of stitches（一行）針腳

ˈstitch-up *noun* (*BrE, informal*) a situation in which sb deliberately cheats you or causes you to be wrongly blamed for sth 故意欺騙；誣陷

St John's Wort /snt ˌdʒɒnz ˈwɜːt; *NAmE* seɪnt ˌdʒɑːnz ˈwɜːrt/ *noun* [U, C] a HERB with yellow flowers, used in medicines 金絲桃，聖約翰草（可入藥）

stoat /stəʊt; *NAmE* stoʊt/ *noun* a small wild animal with a long body and brown fur that, in northern areas, turns white in winter. The white fur is called ERMINE. 掃雪；短尾鼬；波拿巴特鼬

stock 0-w /stɒk; *NAmE* stɑːk/ *noun, verb, adj.*

■ ***noun***

› SUPPLY 供應 **1** 0-w [U, C] a supply of goods that is available for sale in a shop/store（商店的）現貨，存貨，庫存：*We have a fast turnover of stock.* 我們的貨物週轉快。◇ *That particular model is not currently* ***in stock***. 那種型號目前沒貨。◇ *I'm afraid we're temporarily* ***out of stock***. 很遺憾，我們暫時脱銷了。◇ *We don't carry a large stock of pine furniture.* 松木傢具我們備貨不多。 ➲ COLLOCATIONS at SHOPPING **2** 0-w [C, U] **~ (of sth)** a supply of sth that is available for use 儲備物；備用物；供應物：*She's built up a good stock of teaching materials over the years.* 這些年來她積累了大量教學資料。◇ *Food stocks are running low.* 貯存的食物快吃完了。◇ *a country's* ***housing stock*** (= all the houses available for living in) 一個國家的住房保有量

› FINANCE 金融 **3** [U] the value of the shares in a company that have been sold 股本；資本 **4** [C, usually pl.] a share that sb has bought in a company or business 股份；股票：*stock prices* 股票價格 ◇ (*NAmE*) *to invest in* ***stocks and bonds*** 投資股票與債券 ➲ compare SHARE *n.* (4) **5** [U, C] (*BrE*) money that is lent to a government at a fixed rate of interest; an official document that gives details of this 公債；公債券：*government stock* 政府債券 ◇ *to invest in* ***stocks and shares*** 投資債券與股票

› FARM ANIMALS 家畜 **6** [U] farm animals, such as cows and sheep, that are kept for their meat, wool, etc. 家畜；牲畜：*breeding stock* 種畜 ➲ see also LIVESTOCK

› FAMILY/ANCESTORS 家族；祖先 **7** [U] **of farming, noble, French, etc. ~** having the type of family or ANCESTORS mentioned 家族；世系；出身 **SYN** **descent**

› FOOD 食物 **8** [U, C] a liquid made by cooking bones, meat, etc. in water, used for making soups and sauces 高湯；原湯：*vegetable stock* 菜湯

› FOR PUNISHMENT 刑具 **9 stocks** [pl.] a wooden structure with holes for the feet, used in the past to lock criminals in as a form of punishment, especially in a public place 足枷 ➲ compare PILLORY

› RESPECT 尊敬 **10** [U] (*formal*) the degree to which sb is respected or liked by other people 名聲；聲望；評價：*Their* ***stock is high/low***. 他們的聲望高／低。

› OF GUN 槍 **11** [C] the part of a gun that you hold against your shoulder when firing it 槍托

› PLANT 植物 **12** [U, C] a garden plant with brightly coloured flowers with a sweet smell 紫羅蘭

› THEATRE 戲劇 **13** [C] (*NAmE*) = STOCK COMPANY (2) ➲ see also LAUGHING STOCK, ROLLING STOCK

IDM **on the ˈstocks** in the process of being made, built or prepared 在製作（或建造、準備）中：*Our new model is already on the stocks and will be available in the spring.* 我們已着手生產新的款式，明年春天就可以上市。 **put ˈstock in sth** (*especially NAmE*) to have a particular amount of belief in sth（在某種程度上）相信，信任：*She no longer puts much stock in their claims.* 她再不太過相信他們的斷言了。 **take ˈstock (of sth)** to stop and think carefully about the way in which a particular situation is developing in order to decide what to do next（對某情況）加以總結，作出評估，進行反思 ➲ more at LOCK *n.* ➲ see also STOCKTAKING

■ ***verb*** **1 ~ sth** (of a shop/store 商店) to keep a supply of a particular type of goods to sell 存貨：*Do you stock green tea?* 你們的庫存有綠茶嗎？ **2** [often passive] **~ sth (with sth)** to fill sth with food, books, etc. 貯備，貯存（食物、書籍等）：*The pond was well stocked with fish.* 池塘裏養了許多魚。◇ *a well-stocked library* 藏書豐富的圖書館

PHR V **ˌstock sth↔ˈup** to fill sth with goods, food, etc. 在…中備足貨品（或食物等）：*We need to stock up the freezer.* 我們需要在冰櫃裏存滿東西。 **ˌstock ˈup (on/with sth)** to buy a lot of sth so that you can use it later 貯備，備足（某物）：*We ought to stock up on film before our trip.* 我們應該在旅行前備足膠捲。

■ ***adj.*** [only before noun] **1** (*disapproving*) a **stock** excuse, answer, etc. is one that is often used because it is easy and convenient, but that is not very original 老一套的；陳腐的：*'No comment,' was the actor's stock response.* "無可奉告。"那位演員回答什麼問題都是這一句老話。**2** usually available for sale in a shop/store（商店裏）常備的，通常有的 SYN **standard**：*stock sizes* 常備尺碼

stock·ade /stɒˈkeɪd; *NAmE* stɑːˈk-/ *noun* a line or wall of strong wooden posts built to defend a place（防禦用的）柵欄，圍樁

stock·broker /ˈstɒkbrəʊkə(r); *NAmE* ˈstɑːkbroʊ-/ (also **broker**) *noun* a person or an organization that buys and sells shares for other people 股票經紀人；股票經紀商

ˈ**stockbroker belt** *noun* [sing.] (*BrE*) an area outside a large city, where many rich people live（大城市外圍的）富人住宅帶

stock·brok·ing /ˈstɒkbrəʊkɪŋ; *NAmE* ˈstɑːkbroʊ-/ *noun* [U] the work of a stockbroker 證券（或股票）經紀業務

ˈ**stock car** *noun* an ordinary car that has been made stronger for use in stock-car racing（經加固用以參加普通型汽車賽的）改裝賽車

ˈ**stock-car racing** *noun* [U] (*BrE*) (*NAmE* ˌ**demolition** ˈ**derby**) a type of race in which the competing cars are allowed to hit each other 普通汽車賽（參賽車輛可以相互碰撞）

ˈ**stock company** *noun* (*NAmE*) **1** a company owned by people who have shares in it 股份公司 **2** (also **stock**) a theatre company that does several different plays in a season; a REPERTORY company 保留劇目輪演劇團

ˈ**stock cube** *noun* a solid CUBE made from the dried juices of meat or vegetables, sold in packs and used for making soups, sauces, etc. 固體湯料；湯塊

ˈ**stock exchange** *noun* [usually sing.] a place where shares in companies are bought and sold; all of the business activity involved in doing this 證券交易（所）；股票交易（所）：*the London Stock Exchange* 倫敦證券交易所 ◇ *to lose money on the stock exchange* 在股票交易中賠錢

stock·fish /ˈstɒkfɪʃ; *NAmE* ˈstɑːk-/ *noun* **1** [U] COD or similar fish that is dried without salt 淡鱈魚乾；淡魚乾 **2** [C] (*pl.* **stock·fish** or **stock·fishes**) (*SAfrE*) a large sea fish that is used for food 無鬚鱈（可食用）；好望角無鬚鱈

stock·hold·er /ˈstɒkhəʊldə(r); *NAmE* ˈstɑːkhoʊ-/ *noun* (*especially NAmE*) a person who owns STOCKS and shares in a business 股票持有人；股東

stock·inet (also **stock·in·ette**) /ˌstɒkɪˈnet; *NAmE* ˌstɑːk-/ *noun* [U] a type of soft cloth that stretches easily and is used for making bandages 彈性針織布料；鬆緊織物

stock·ing /ˈstɒkɪŋ; *NAmE* ˈstɑːk-/ *noun* **1** either of a pair of thin pieces of clothing that fit closely over a woman's legs and feet 長筒女襪：*a pair of silk stockings* 一雙長筒絲襪 ➲ compare TIGHTS (1) ➲ see also BODY STOCKING **2** = CHRISTMAS STOCKING

IDM **in your** ˌ**stocking(ed)** ˈ**feet** wearing socks or stockings but not shoes 只穿襪不穿鞋

ˈ**stocking filler** (*BrE*) (*NAmE* ˈ**stocking stuffer**) *noun* a small present that is put in a CHRISTMAS STOCKING 聖誕襪小禮物

ˌ**stock-in-ˈtrade** *noun* [U] a person's **stock-in-trade** is sth that they do, say or use very often or too often 慣做的事（或說的話、用的東西）：*Famous people and their private lives are the stock-in-trade of the popular newspapers.* 名人和名人的私生活是通俗報紙慣有的內容。

stock·ist /ˈstɒkɪst; *NAmE* ˈstɑːk-/ *noun* (*BrE*) a shop/store or company that sells a particular product or type of goods（某種產品或某類貨品的）專營商店 SYN **retailer**

stock·job·ber /ˈstɒkdʒɒbə(r); *NAmE* ˈstɑːkdʒɑːb-/ *noun* = JOBBER

stock·man /ˈstɒkmən; *NAmE* ˈstɑːk-/ *noun* (*pl.* **-men** /-mən/) **1** a man whose job is to take care of farm animals 畜牧工；飼養員 **2** (*NAmE*) a man who owns farm animals 牧場主 **3** (*NAmE*) a man who is in charge of the goods in a WAREHOUSE, etc. 倉庫管理員

ˈ**stock market** (also **market**) *noun* the business of buying and selling shares in companies and the place where this happens; a STOCK EXCHANGE 證券交易（所）；股票交易（所）；股市：*to make money on the stock market* 在股票市場上賺錢 ◇ *a stock market crash* (= when prices of shares fall suddenly and people lose money) 股票市場的暴跌 ➲ COLLOCATIONS at ECONOMY

ˈ**stock option** (*NAmE*) (*BrE* ˈ**share option**) *noun* a right given to employees to buy shares in their company at a fixed price 股票期權（員工按固定價格購買所屬公司股票的權利）

stock·pile /ˈstɒkpaɪl; *NAmE* ˈstɑːk-/ *noun, verb*

■ ***noun*** a large supply of sth that is kept to be used in the future if necessary 囤聚的物資：*the world's stockpile of nuclear weapons* 全世界的核武器儲備

■ ***verb* ~ sth** to collect and keep a large supply of sth 儲備大量（物資）

stock·pot /ˈstɒkpɒt; *NAmE* ˈstɑːkpɑːt/ *noun* a pot in which meat, fish, vegetables, or bones are cooked to make STOCK 湯鍋

stock·room /ˈstɒkruːm; -rʊm; *NAmE* ˈstɑːk-/ *noun* a room for storing things in a shop/store, an office, etc. 倉庫；貯藏室

ˌ**stock-ˈstill** *adv.* without moving at all 靜止地；一動不動地：*We stood stock-still watching the animals.* 我們一動不動地站着觀看那些動物。

stock·tak·ing /ˈstɒkteɪkɪŋ; *NAmE* ˈstɑːk-/ *noun* [U] **1** (*especially BrE*) the process of making a list of all the goods in a shop/store or business 盤點；清點存貨；盤貨 ➲ compare INVENTORY *n.* (2) **2** the process of thinking carefully about your own situation or position（自我）總結，評估，反思

stocky /ˈstɒki; *NAmE* ˈstɑːki/ *adj.* (**stock·ier**, **stocki·est**) (of a person 人) short, with a strong, solid body 矮壯的；敦實的 SYN **thickset** ▸ **stock·ily** *adv.*

stock·yard /ˈstɒkjɑːd; *NAmE* ˈstɑːkjɑːrd/ *noun* a place where farm animals are kept for a short time before they are sold at a market 牲畜欄，牲畜圍場（用以安置牲畜，準備運往市場）

stodge /stɒdʒ; *NAmE* stɑːdʒ/ *noun* [U] (*BrE, informal, usually disapproving*) heavy food that makes you feel very full 吃下去感覺撐的食物；易飽的食物

stodgy /ˈstɒdʒi; *NAmE* ˈstɑːdʒi/ *adj.* (*informal, especially BrE*) **1** (of food 食物) heavy and making you feel very full 吃下去感覺撐的；易飽的 **2** serious and boring; not exciting 滯澀的；古板的；枯燥無味的

stoep /stuːp; stʊp/ *noun* (*SAfrE*) a raised area outside the door of a house, with a roof over it, where you can sit and relax, eat meals, etc. 屋前遊廊；門廊

stogy (also **stogie**) /ˈstəʊgi; *NAmE* ˈstoʊgi/ *noun* (*pl.* **-ies**) (*NAmE*) a cheap cigar 廉價雪茄

stoic /ˈstəʊɪk; *NAmE* ˈstoʊɪk/ *noun* (*formal*) a person who is able to suffer pain or trouble without complaining or showing what they are feeling 斯多葛派人（對痛苦或困難能默默承受或泰然處之）▸ **stoic** (also **sto·ic·al** /-kl/) *adj.*：*her stoic endurance* 她默默承受一切的堅忍性格 ◇ *his stoical acceptance of death* 他坦然面對死亡的態度 **sto·ic·al·ly** /-kli/ *adv.* ORIGIN From the **Stoics**, a group of ancient Greek philosophers, who believed that wise people should not allow themselves to be affected by painful or pleasant experiences. 源自斯多葛派（Stoics），古希臘哲學流派，認為智者不應為苦樂所動。

sto·icism /ˈstəʊɪsɪzəm; *NAmE* ˈstoʊ-/ *noun* [U] (*formal*) the fact of not complaining or showing what you are feeling when you are suffering 對痛苦的默默承受或泰然處之；堅忍：*She endured her long illness with stoicism.* 她默默忍受長期的病痛。

stoke /stəʊk; *NAmE* stoʊk/ *verb* **1 ~ sth (up) (with sth)** to add fuel to a fire, etc. 給…添加（燃料）：*to stoke up a fire with more coal* 往火裏再添一些煤 ◇ *to stoke a furnace* 給爐子添煤 **2 ~ sth (up)** to make people feel sth more strongly 煽動；激起：*to stoke up envy* 激起妒忌 **3 ~ sth**

S

(**up**) to make sth increase or develop more quickly 促使…的增加；刺激…的發展；加劇：*They were accused of stoking the crisis.* 他們被指控對這次危機起了推波助瀾的作用。

PHR V **,stoke 'up (on/with sth)** (*informal*) to eat or drink a lot of sth, especially so that you do not feel hungry later 吃飽；吃好；喝足：*Stoke up for the day on a good breakfast.* 早飯要吃得飽飽的，整整一天呢。

stoked /stəʊkt; *NAmE* stoʊkt/ *adj.* (*NAmE, informal*) excited and pleased about sth 興奮的；滿足的：*I'm really stoked that they chose me for the team.* 他們選我加入這個隊，我興奮極了。

stoker /'stəʊkə(r); *NAmE* 'stoʊ-/ *noun* a person whose job is to add coal or other fuel to a fire, etc., especially on a ship or a steam train（尤指輪船或蒸汽機車上的）司爐

stok·vel /'stɒkfel; *NAmE* 'stɑːk-/ *noun* (*SAfrE*) a group of people who agree to pay regular amounts of money and take turns to receive all or part of what is collected 集資互助組（成員定期繳納款項並輪流領取全部或部份集資款）

stole /stəʊl; *NAmE* stoʊl/ *noun* a piece of clothing consisting of a wide band of cloth or fur, worn by a woman around the shoulders; a similar piece of clothing worn by a priest 女用披肩；（司祭佩戴的）聖帶 ➲ see also STEAL *v.* (stole, stolen)

stolid /'stɒlɪd; *NAmE* 'stɑːl-/ *adj.* (usually *disapproving*) not showing much emotion or interest; remaining always the same and not reacting or changing 不動感情的；不關心的；淡漠的；無動於衷的 ▸ **stol·id·ly** *adv.* **stol·id·ity** /stə'lɪdəti/ *noun* [U]

stoma /'stəʊmə; *NAmE* 'stoʊ-/ *noun* (*pl.* **stomas** or **sto·mata** /'stəʊmətə/) **1** (*biology* 生) a tiny PORE (= hole) in the outer layer of a plant's leaf or STEM 氣孔（植物葉或莖表皮的小孔）**2** (*biology* 生) a small opening like a mouth, in some animals（某些動物的）氣門，呼吸孔 **3** (*medical* 醫) an artificial opening made in an organ of the body , especially in the COLON or TRACHEA（尤指結腸或氣管上的）造口

stom·ach 0━ /'stʌmək/ *noun, verb*

■ ***noun*** 0━ the organ inside the body where food goes when you swallow it; the front part of the body below the chest 胃；腹部：*stomach pains* 肚子疼 ◇ *an upset stomach* 胃部不適 ◇ (*BrE* also) *a stomach upset* 胃部不適 ◇ *It's not a good idea to drink* (= alcohol) ***on an empty stomach*** (= without having eaten anything). 空腹不宜喝酒。◇ *You shouldn't exercise* ***on a full stomach.*** 你不應該吃飽了就運動。◇ *The attacker kicked him in the stomach.* 襲擊者一腳踢在他肚子上。◇ *Lie on your stomach with your arms by your side.* 手臂放在兩側趴下。➲ COLLOCATIONS at PHYSICAL ➲ VISUAL VOCAB page V59 ➲ see also TUMMY

IDM **have no 'stomach for sth 1** to not want to eat sth 不想吃…；對…沒有胃口：*She had no stomach for the leftover stew.* 她不想吃剩下的燉菜。**2** to not have the desire or courage to do sth 沒有做某事的慾望（或勇氣）：*They had no stomach for a fight.* 他們不想打架。 **turn your 'stomach** to make you feel upset, sick or disgusted 讓某人反感（或惡心、厭惡）：*Pictures of the burnt corpses turned my stomach.* 那些燒焦的屍體的照片讓我直惡心。➲ more at BUTTERFLY, EYE *n.*, FEEL *v.*, PIT *n.*, PUMP *v.*, STRONG

■ ***verb*** (especially in negative sentences or questions 尤用於否定句或疑問句) **1 ~ sth** to approve of sth and be able to enjoy it; to enjoy being with a person 欣賞；欣然接受；喜歡和…相處：*I* ***can't stomach*** *violent films.* 我不喜歡暴力片。◇ *I find him very* ***hard to stomach.*** 我覺得很難和他相處。 **2 ~ sth** to be able to eat sth without feeling ill/sick 能吃；吃得下：*She* ***couldn't stomach*** *any breakfast.* 她早上什麼都吃不下。

'stomach ache *noun* [C, U] pain in or near your stomach 胃痛；腹痛

'stomach pump *noun* a machine with a tube that doctors use to remove poisonous substances from sb's stomach through their mouth 洗胃泵；胃唧筒

stomp /stɒmp; *NAmE* stɑːmp; stɔːmp/ *verb* [I] **+ adv./prep.** (*informal*) to walk, dance, or move with heavy steps 邁着重重的步子走（或跳舞、移動）：*She stomped angrily out of the office.* 她怒氣沖沖，重步走出辦公室。

stompie /'stɒmpi; *NAmE* 'stɑːm-/ *noun* (*SAfrE, informal*) a cigarette that has been partly smoked; the end of a cigarette that is thrown away after it has been smoked（已經吸過的）半截煙；煙蒂

'stomping ground *noun* (*NAmE, informal*) = STAMPING GROUND

stone 0━ /stəʊn; *NAmE* stoʊn/ *noun, verb*

■ ***noun***

▸ **HARD SUBSTANCE** 硬物質 **1** 0━ [U] (often used before nouns or in compounds 常用於名詞前或構成複合詞) a hard solid mineral substance that is found in the ground, often used for building 石頭；石料；岩石：*Most of the houses are built of stone.* 這些房子多數是用石頭建造的。◇ *stone walls* 石牆 ◇ *a stone floor* 石地板 ◇ *a flight of stone steps* 一段石台階 ➲ see also DRYSTONE WALL, LIMESTONE, SANDSTONE, SOAPSTONE **2** 0━ [C] (*especially BrE*) a small piece of rock of any shape 石塊；石子：*a pile of stones* 一堆石塊 ◇ *Some children were throwing stones into the lake.* 幾個孩子正朝湖裏扔石頭。➲ see also HAILSTONE, PHILOSOPHER'S STONE **3** 0━ [C] (usually in compounds 通常構成複合詞) a piece of stone shaped for a particular purpose 加工成某形狀為某用途的石塊：*These words are carved on the stone beside his grave.* 在他的墓碑上刻着這樣的話。➲ see also CORNERSTONE (1), FOUNDATION STONE, GRAVESTONE, HEADSTONE, LODESTONE, MILLSTONE, PAVING STONE, STEPPING STONE (1), TOMBSTONE

▸ **JEWEL** 寶石 **4** [C] = PRECIOUS STONE

▸ **IN FRUIT** 水果 **5** [C] (*especially BrE*) (*NAmE* usually **pit**) a hard shell containing the nut or seed in the middle of some types of fruit 果核：***cherry/peach stones*** 櫻桃核；桃核 ➲ VISUAL VOCAB page V30

▸ **IN BODY** 體內 **6** [C] (often in compounds 常構成複合詞) a small piece of hard material that can form in the BLADDER OR KIDNEY and cause pain（膀胱或腎臟中的）結石：*kidney stones* 腎結石 ➲ see also GALLSTONE

▸ **MEASUREMENT OF WEIGHT** 重量單位 **7** [C] (*pl.* **stone**) (*abbr.* **st**) (in Britain) a unit for measuring weight, equal to 6.35 kg or 14 pounds 英石（英國重量單位，相當於 6.35 千克或 14 磅）：*He weighs over 15 stone.* 他體重超過 15 英石。◇ *She's trying to lose a stone.* 她試圖減去一英石的體重。

IDM **carved/set in 'stone** (of a decision, plan, etc. 決定、計劃等) unable to be changed 不可改變：*People should remember that our proposals aren't set in stone.* 人們應該記住我們的建議不是一成不變的。 **leave no stone un'turned** to try every possible course of action in order to find or achieve sth 千方百計；想盡辦法 **a 'stone's throw** a very short distance away 很近的距離；不遠處：*We live just a stone's throw from here.* 我們就住在附近。◇ *The hotel is within a stone's throw of the beach.* 旅館離海灘很近。➲ more at BLOOD *n.*, HEART, KILL *v.*, PEOPLE *n.*, ROLL *v.*

■ ***verb***

▸ **THROW STONES** 扔石塊 **1** [usually passive] **~ sb/sth** to throw stones at sb/sth 向…扔石塊；用石頭砸：*Shops were looted and vehicles stoned.* 商店遭哄搶，車輛被砸壞。◇ *to be* ***stoned to death*** (= as a punishment) 用石頭砸死（一種刑罰）

▸ **FRUIT** 水果 **2** (*BrE*) (also **pit** *NAmE, BrE*) **~ sth** to remove the stone from the inside of a fruit 去掉果核：*stoned black olives* 去核黑橄欖

IDM **,stone the 'crows | ,stone 'me** (*old-fashioned, BrE*) used to express surprise, shock, anger, etc.（表示驚奇、震驚、氣憤等）哎呀

the 'Stone Age *noun* [sing.] the very early period of human history when tools and weapons were made of stone 石器時代：(*figurative*) *My dad's taste in music is from the Stone Age* (= very old-fashioned). 我老爸的音樂品味都老得掉渣了。▸ **'stone-age** *adj.* [only before noun]：(*figurative*) *stone-age* (= very out-of-date) *computers* 原始計算機

,stone 'circle *noun* a circle of large tall vertical stones from PREHISTORIC times, thought to have been used for religious or other ceremonies 史前環狀巨石陣（據信為禮制建築）

ˌstone ˈcold *adj.* completely cold, when it should be warm or hot 冰涼的；涼透的：*The soup was stone cold.* 湯全涼了。

IDM **ˌstone-cold ˈsober** having drunk no alcohol at all 滴酒未沾；完全清醒

stoned /stəʊnd; *NAmE* stoʊnd/ *adj.* [not usually before noun] (*informal*) not behaving or thinking normally because of the effects of a drug such as MARIJUANA or alcohol（在毒品或酒精作用下）暈暈乎乎，飄飄然

ˌstone ˈdead *adj.* (*BrE*) completely dead or completely destroyed 完全死了的；完全毀壞的

ˌstone ˈdeaf *adj.* completely unable to hear 完全聾的；失聰的

stone·ground /ˈstəʊngraʊnd; *NAmE* ˈstoʊn-/ *adj.* (of flour for bread, etc. 製作麵包等的麵粉) made by being crushed between heavy stones 石磨研磨的

stone·mason /ˈstəʊnmeɪsn; *NAmE* ˈstoʊn-/ *noun* a person whose job is cutting and preparing stone for buildings 石工；石匠

stone·wall /ˌstəʊnˈwɔːl; *NAmE* ˈstoʊn-/ *verb* [T, I] **~ (sb/sth)** (especially in politics) to delay a discussion or decision by refusing to answer questions or by talking a lot 防守擋擊（政治上指通過沉默或冗長發言等手段阻礙議事或拖延決議）

stone·ware /ˈstəʊnweə(r); *NAmE* ˈstoʊnwer/ *noun* [U] pots, dishes, etc. made from CLAY that contains a small amount of the hard stone called FLINT 炻器；粗陶器；缸瓦器

stone·washed /ˈstəʊnwɒʃt; *NAmE* ˈstoʊnwɔːʃt; -wɑːʃt/ *adj.* (of jeans, etc. 牛仔褲等) washed in a special way so that the cloth loses some colour and looks older 石磨水洗的

stone·work /ˈstəʊnwɜːk; *NAmE* ˈstoʊnwɜːrk/ *noun* [U] the parts of a building that are made of stone（建築物的）石造部份

stoni·ly /ˈstəʊnɪli; *NAmE* ˈstoʊn-/ *adv.* in a way that shows a lack of feeling or sympathy 冷漠地；無情地；鐵石心腸地：*She stared stonily at him for a minute.* 她冷冷地盯着他看了片刻。

stonk·er /ˈstɒŋkə(r); *NAmE* ˈstɑːŋk-; ˈstɔːŋk-/ *noun* (*BrE, informal*) an extremely large or impressive thing 特大型；令人印象深刻的事物

stonk·ing /ˈstɒŋkɪŋ; *NAmE* ˈstɑːŋk-; ˈstɔːŋk-/ *adj.* [usually before noun] (*BrE, informal*) extremely large or impressive 龐大的；絕妙的；出色的

stony /ˈstəʊni; *NAmE* ˈstoʊni/ *adj.* (**stoni·er**, **stoni·est**) **1** having a lot of stones on it or in it 多石的；石頭的：*stony soil* 多石的土壤 **2** showing a lack of feeling or sympathy 冷漠的；無情的；鐵石心腸的 SYN **cold**：*They listened to him in stony silence.* 他們冷漠地靜靜聽他講。

IDM **fall on stony ˈground** to fail to produce the result or the effect that you hope for; to have little success 未產生預期的結果（或效果）；沒有開花結果 **stony ˈbroke** = FLAT BROKE at FLAT *adv.*

ˌstony-ˈfaced *adj.* not showing any friendly feelings 冷淡的；冷漠的

stood *past tense, past part.* of STAND

stooge /stuːdʒ/ *noun* **1** (*informal*, usually *disapproving*) a person who is used by sb to do things that are unpleasant or dishonest 受人驅使的人；奴才；走狗 **2** a performer in a show whose role is to appear silly so that the other performers can make jokes about him or her（供其他演員作弄打趣的）丑角

stool /stuːl/ *noun* **1** (often in compounds 常構成複合詞) a seat with legs but with nothing to support your back or arms 凳子：*a bar stool* 酒吧高凳 ◇ *a piano stool* 鋼琴凳 ➲ VISUAL VOCAB pages V23, V25, V36 **2** (*medical* 醫) a piece of solid waste from your body 大便；糞便 IDM see TWO

ˈstool pigeon *noun* (*informal*) a person, especially a criminal, who helps the police to catch another criminal, for example by spending time with them and getting secret information（向警察提供情報的）線人，內線 SYN **informer**

stoop /stuːp/ *verb, noun*

■ ***verb*** **1** [I] **~ (down)** to bend your body forwards and downwards 俯身；彎腰：*She stooped down to pick up the child.* 她俯身抱起孩子。◇ *The doorway was so low that he had to stoop.* 門廊很矮，他低下頭才過去。**2** [I] to stand or walk with your head and shoulders bent forwards（站立或行走時）弓背：*He tends to stoop because he's so tall.* 他個子太高了，所以時常弓着背。

IDM **stoop so ˈlow (as to do sth)** (*formal*) to drop your moral standards far enough to do sth bad or unpleasant 卑鄙（或墮落）到…地步：*She was unwilling to believe anyone would stoop so low as to steal a ring from a dead woman's finger.* 她無法相信真有人會齷齪到這種地步，竟然從一個死去的女人手指上偷戒指。

PHR V **ˈstoop to sth** to drop your moral standards to do sth bad or unpleasant 卑鄙（或墮落）到做某事：*You surely don't think I'd stoop to that!* 你不會認為我會下作到那種地步吧！◇ **~ doing sth** *I didn't think he'd stoop to cheating.* 我覺得他總不至於作弊吧。

■ ***noun*** **1** [sing.] if sb has a **stoop**, their shoulders are always bent forward 曲背；駝背 **2** [C] (*NAmE*) a raised area outside the door of a house with steps leading up to it 門廊

stooped /stuːpt/ *adj.* **1** standing or walking with your head and shoulders bent forwards 弓背站立（或行走）的 **2 stooped shoulders** are bent forwards 曲背的

stop 0-w /stɒp; *NAmE* stɑːp/ *verb, noun*

■ ***verb*** (**-pp-**)

▸ **NOT MOVE 不動** **1** 0-w [I, T] to no longer move; to make sb/sth no longer move（使）停止，停下：*The car stopped at the traffic lights.* 汽車在交通信號燈前停了下來。◇ *We stopped for the night in Port Augusta.* 我們中途在奧古斯塔港停留過夜。◇ **~ sb/sth** *He was stopped by the police for speeding.* 他因超速行駛被警察截住了。

▸ **NOT CONTINUE 不繼續** **2** 0-w [I, T] to no longer continue to do sth; to make sb/sth no longer do sth（使）中斷，停止：**~ (doing sth)** *That phone never stops ringing!* 那個電話沒有不響的時候！◇ *Please stop crying and tell me what's wrong.* 快別哭了，告訴我出了什麼事。◇ *She criticizes everyone and the trouble is, she* ***doesn't know when to stop.*** 她誰都批評；而且，問題是她批評起來就沒個完。◇ *Can't you just stop?* 你就不能停一停嗎？◇ **~ sb/sth** *Stop me* (= make me stop talking) *if I'm boring you.* 你要是覺得我煩就打斷我。◇ ***Stop it!*** *You're hurting me.* 住手！你把我弄疼了。◇ **~ what ...** *Mike immediately stopped what he was doing.* 邁克立刻停下手頭的事情。

HELP Notice the difference between **stop doing sth** and **stop to do sth**. *We stopped taking pictures means 'We were no longer taking pictures.'; We stopped to take pictures means 'We stopped what we were doing so that we could start taking pictures.'* 注意 stop doing sth 和 stop to do sth 之間的區別：We stopped taking pictures 意思是我們不再照相了；而 We stopped to take pictures 意思則是我們停下正在做的事而去照相。

▸ **END 結束** **3** 0-w [I, T] to end or finish; to make sth end or finish（使）結束，終止：*When is this fighting going to stop?* 這場戰鬥要打到什麼時候？◇ *The bus service stops at midnight.* 公共汽車午夜停止服務。◇ **~ doing sth** *Has it stopped raining yet?* 雨停了沒有？◇ **~ sth** *Doctors couldn't stop the bleeding.* 醫生止不住血。◇ *The referee was forced to stop the game because of heavy snow.* 由於下大雪，裁判被迫終止了比賽。

▸ **PREVENT 阻止** **4** 0-w [T] to prevent sb from doing sth; to prevent sth from happening 阻止；阻礙；阻攔；防止：**~ sb/sth** *I want to go and you can't stop me.* 我要走，你攔不住我。◇ *We need more laws to stop pollution.* 我們需要制訂更多法律來防止污染。◇ ***There's no stopping us now*** (= nothing can prevent us from achieving what we want to achieve). 現在什麼都無法阻擋我們了。◇ **~ sb/sth from doing sth** *There's nothing to stop you from accepting the offer.* 你儘可以接受那個提議。◇ *You can't stop people from saying what they think.* 人們怎麼想就會怎麼說，你阻止不了。◇ (*BrE* also) **~ sb/sth doing**

S

sth *You can't stop people saying what they think.* 人們怎麼想就會怎麼說，你阻止不了。

▸ **FOR SHORT TIME** 短時間 [I] **5** to end an activity for a short time in order to do sth 暫停，暫時中斷（以便做某事）: **~ for sth** *I'm hungry. Let's stop for lunch.* 我餓了。我們停下來吃午飯吧。◇ **~ to do sth** *We stopped to admire the scenery.* 我們中途停下來欣賞一下風景。◇ *People just don't* ***stop to think*** *about the consequences.* 人們做事情就是不肯停下來想想後果。**HELP** In spoken English, **stop** can be used with **and** plus another verb, instead of with **to** and the infinitive, to show purpose. 在英語口語中，stop 可以與 and 及另一動詞連用，而不用帶 to 的不定式表示目的：*He stopped and bought some flowers.* ◇ *Let's stop and look at the map.*

▸ **NOT FUNCTION** 不工作 **6** [I, T] to no longer work or function; to make sth no longer work or function（使）停止工作，停止運轉：*Why has the engine stopped?* 發動機怎麼停了？◇ *I felt as if my heart had stopped.* 我覺得我的心好像都不跳了。◇ **~ sth** *I stopped the tape and pressed rewind.* 我停了磁帶，按下倒回鍵。

▸ **STAY** 逗留 **7** [I] (*BrE, informal*) to stay somewhere for a short time, especially at sb's house 逗留，待，留下（做某事）：*I'm not stopping. I just came to give you this message.* 我不待了。我就是來告訴你這件事。◇ **~ for sth** *Can you stop for tea?* 你能留下來喝茶嗎？

▸ **MONEY** 錢 **8** [T] to prevent money from being paid 止付；停付；扣除：**~ sth** *to* ***stop a cheque*** (= tell the bank not to pay it) 通知銀行止付支票 ◇ **~ sth from sth** (*BrE*) *Dad threatened to stop £1 a week from our pocket money if we didn't clean our rooms.* 父親威脅說，我們要是不把自己的房間收拾乾淨，他就每星期扣我們 1 英鎊的零花錢。

▸ **CLOSE HOLE** 堵塞洞孔 **9** [T] **~ sth (up) (with sth)** to block, fill or close a hole, an opening, etc. 堵塞；塞住；阻塞：*Stop up the other end of the tube, will you?* 你把管子的另一頭堵上好不好？◇ *I stopped my ears but still heard her cry out.* 我捂上耳朵，但還能聽見她大聲喊叫。

IDM **stop at 'nothing** to be willing to do anything to get what you want, even if it is dishonest or wrong 不擇手段 **ˌstop the 'clock** to stop measuring time in a game or an activity that has a time limit（在計時比賽或活動中）停錶 **ˌstop 'short | ˌstop sb 'short** to suddenly stop, or make sb suddenly stop, doing sth（使）突然停住：*He stopped short when he heard his name.* 聽見有人喊他的名字，他突然停住了。**stop short of sth/of doing sth** to be unwilling to do sth because it may involve a risk, but to nearly do it 差一點兒沒做某事；險些做出某事：*She stopped short of calling the president a liar.* 她差一點兒沒指責總統說謊。➲ more at BUCK *n.*, TRACK *n.*

PHR V **ˌstop 'by (sth)** to make a short visit somewhere 過去坐坐；順路造訪：*I'll stop by this evening for a chat.* 今晚我想過去聊聊。◇ *Could you stop by the store on the way home for some bread?* 回家時你能不能順路進那家店裏買點麵包？**ˌstop 'in** (*BrE, informal*) to stay at home rather than go out 待在家裏（不外出）**ˌstop 'off (at/in ...)** to make a short visit somewhere during a trip in order to do sth 中途停留（在某處）：*We stopped off at a hotel for the night.* 我們中途停下來在一家旅館住了一宿。**ˌstop 'out** (*BrE, informal*) to stay out late at night 夜裏很晚不回家 **ˌstop 'over (at/in ...)** to stay somewhere for a short time during a long journey（長途旅行在某處）中途停留：*I wanted to stop over in India on the way to Australia.* 在去澳大利亞的途中我想在印度稍作停留。➲ related noun STOPOVER **ˌstop 'up** (*BrE, informal*) to stay up late 熬夜；遲睡

■ ***noun***

▸ **ACT OF STOPPING** 停止；阻止 **1** an act of stopping or stopping sth; the state of being stopped 停止；終止；停留；阻止：*The trip included an overnight stop in Brussels.* 這次旅行需要在布魯塞爾停留過夜。◇ *She* ***brought*** *the car* ***to a stop****.* 她停住汽車。◇ *Work has temporarily* ***come to a stop*** *while the funding is reviewed.* 資金審查期間工作暫停。◇ *It is time to* ***put a stop to*** *the violence.* 現在是終止暴行的時候了。◇ *Babies do not grow at a steady rate but* ***in stops and starts****.* 嬰兒成長的速度並非一成不變，而是長長停停，停停長長。➲ see also NON-STOP *adj., adv.*, WHISTLE-STOP *adj.*

▸ **OF BUS/TRAIN** 公共汽車；火車 **2** a place where a bus or train stops regularly for passengers to get on or off 車站：*I get off at the next stop.* 我在下一站下車。◇ *Is this your stop?* 你在這一站下車嗎？➲ see also BUS STOP, PIT STOP, REQUEST STOP

▸ **PUNCTUATION** 標點符號 **3** (*BrE*) = FULL STOP

▸ **MUSIC** 音樂 **4** a row of pipes on an organ that produce the different sounds（管風琴的）音管 **5** a handle on an organ that the player pushes in or pulls out to control the sound produced by the pipes（管風琴的）音栓

▸ **PHONETICS** 語音學 **6** a speech sound made by stopping the flow of air coming out of the mouth and then suddenly releasing it, for example /p, k, t/ 塞音 **SYN** **plosive** ➲ see also GLOTTAL STOP **IDM** see FULL STOP *n.*, PULL *v.*

stop·cock /ˈstɒpkɒk; *NAmE* ˈstɑːpkɑːk/ (also **cock**) *noun* a tap that controls the flow of liquid or gas through a pipe（調節管道流量的）旋塞，活栓

stop·gap /ˈstɒpɡæp; *NAmE* ˈstɑːp-/ *noun* something that you use or do for a short time while you are looking for sth better 權宜之計；臨時替代的東西：*The arrangement was only intended as a stopgap.* 這種安排不過是權宜之計而已。◇ *a stopgap measure* 臨時措施

ˌstop-'go (*especially BrE*) (*especially NAmE* **ˌstop-and-'go**) *adj.* [usually before noun] (*disapproving*) **1** starting and then stopping 走走停停的：*stop-go driving in heavy traffic* 在交通繁忙的道路上走走停停的行駛 **2** used to describe the policy of first restricting and then encouraging economic activity and growth（形容經濟政策）先緊縮後刺激的：*the damaging stop-go economic cycle* 經濟上緊縮後刺激、刺激後緊縮的破壞性的循環

'stop light *noun* [C] **1** (*BrE*) a red TRAFFIC LIGHT 停車燈；紅燈 **2** (also **stop·lights** [pl.]) (*NAmE*) = TRAFFIC LIGHT **3** (*NAmE*) = BRAKE LIGHT

stop·over /ˈstɒpəʊvə(r); *NAmE* ˈstɑːpoʊ-/ (*NAmE* also **lay·over**) *noun* a short stay somewhere between two parts of a journey 中途停留：*We had a two-day stopover in Fiji on the way to Australia.* 我們去澳大利亞時中途在斐濟停留了兩天。➲ COLLOCATIONS at TRAVEL

stop·page /ˈstɒpɪdʒ; *NAmE* ˈstɑːp-/ *noun* **1** [C] a situation in which people stop working as part of a protest or strike 停工；罷工 **2** [C] (*sport* 體) an interruption in the game for a particular reason 中斷比賽：*Play resumed quickly after the stoppage.* 比賽中斷後不久又繼續進行。◇ ***stoppage time*** (= added on at the end of the game if there have been stoppages) 比賽補時時間 **3** [C] a situation in which sth does not move forward or is blocked 堵塞；阻塞：*a stoppage of blood to the heart* 通往心臟血液的阻塞 **4** **stoppages** [pl.] (*old-fashioned, BrE, formal*) an amount of money that an employer takes from people's wages for tax and other payments（工資中用於納稅等的）扣除款

stop·per /ˈstɒpə(r); *NAmE* ˈstɑːp-/ (*NAmE* also **plug**) *noun* an object that fits into the top of a bottle to close it 瓶塞 ➲ VISUAL VOCAB page V70 ▸ **stop·per** *verb* **~ sth**

'stopping train *noun* (*BrE*) a train that stops at a lot of stations between main stations（鐵路的）慢車

ˌstop 'press *noun* [U] late news that is added to a newspaper after printing has begun（報紙開印後臨時插入的）最新消息

'stop street *noun* (*SAfrE*) a place where one road joins or crosses another at which there is a sign indicating that vehicles must stop before continuing 停車交叉路口

stop·watch /ˈstɒpwɒtʃ; *NAmE* ˈstɑːpwɑːtʃ/ *noun* a watch that you can stop and start by pressing buttons, in order to time a race, etc. accurately（賽跑等記時用的）秒錶，跑錶，碼錶

stor·age /ˈstɔːrɪdʒ/ *noun* [U] **1** the process of keeping sth in a particular place until it is needed; the space where things can be kept 貯存，貯藏（空間）：*tables that fold flat for storage* 便於存放的摺疊桌 ◇ *There's a lot of storage space in the loft.* 閣樓上有很大的存貯空間。◇ *food storage facilities* 食物貯存設施 ◇ *We need more storage now.* 現在我們需要更多的貯存場所。➲ see also

COLD STORAGE **2** (*computing* 計) the process of keeping information, etc. on a computer; the way it is kept 存貯（方式）: *the storage and retrieval of information* 信息的存貯與檢索 ◇ *data storage* 數據存貯 **3** the process of paying to keep furniture, etc. in a special building until you want it 保管；存放: *When we moved we had to put our furniture* ***in storage*** *for a while.* 搬家時我們不得不把傢具送出去存放一陣子。

'storage battery (*NAmE*) (*BrE* **ac·cu·mu·la·tor**) *noun* a large battery that you can fill with electrical power (= that you can RECHARGE) 蓄電池

'storage heater *noun* (*BrE*) an electric HEATER that stores heat when electricity is cheaper, for example at night 蓄熱電暖器

store /stɔː(r)/ *noun, verb*

■ ***noun*** **1** [C] a large shop that sells many different types of goods （大型）百貨商店: *a big department store* 大型百貨商店 ➲ see also CHAIN STORE, VARIETY STORE **2** [C] (*NAmE*) a shop, large or small 商店；店鋪: *a health food store* 保健食品商店 ◇ *a liquor store* 出售酒類的商店 ➲ **COLLOCATIONS** at SHOPPING ➲ **VISUAL VOCAB** pages V2, V3 ➲ see also CONSIGNMENT STORE, CONVENIENCE STORE, GENERAL STORE, PACKAGE STORE **3** [C] a quantity or supply of sth that you have and use 貯存物；備用物: *her secret store of chocolate* 她私下存放的巧克力 ◇ *a vast store of knowledge* 豐富的知識 **4** [pl.] **stores** goods of a particular kind or for a particular purpose （某類或作某用途的）商品，物品: *medical stores* 醫療用品 **5** [C] (often **stores**) a place where goods of a particular kind are kept 倉庫；貯藏所: *a grain store* 糧倉 ◇ *weapons stores* 武器庫

IDM **in store (for sb)** waiting to happen to sb 即將發生（在某人身上）；等待着（某人）: *We don't know what life* ***holds in store*** *for us.* 我們不知道等待我們的將是什麼樣的生活。◇ *If she had known what* ***lay in store*** *for her, she would never have agreed to go.* 要是她事先知道會有什麼遭遇的話，她是決不會同意去的。◇ *They think it'll be easy but they have a* ***surprise in store***. 他們以為事情容易，到時候他們會吃驚的。 **set/put (great, etc.) 'store by sth** to consider sth to be important （十分）看重，重視（某事物）: *She sets great store by her appearance.* 她十分看重自己的外貌。◇ *It is unwise to put too much store by these statistics.* 過分重視這些統計數字是不明智的。 ➲ more at HIT *v.*, MIND *v.*

■ ***verb*** **1** **~ sth (away/up)** to put sth somewhere and keep it there to use later 貯存；貯藏；保存: *animals storing up food for the winter* 貯存食物過冬的動物 ◇ *He hoped the electronic equipment was safely stored away.* 他希望那些電子設備得到妥善保存。 **2** **~ sth** to keep information or facts in a computer or in your brain （在計算機裏）存貯；記憶: *Thousands of pieces of data are stored in a computer's memory.* 在計算機的存貯器中存有成千上萬條數據。

PHR V **,store sth↔'up** to not express strong feelings or deal with problems when you have them, especially when this causes problems later （把強烈的感情或問題）鬱積，憋在心裏: *She had stored up all her anger and eventually snapped.* 她所有的憤怒鬱積在一起，終於爆發了。◇ *By ignoring your feelings you are only* ***storing up trouble*** *for yourself.* 你迴避自己的感受，將來會有麻煩的。

'store-bought (*NAmE*) (*BrE* **'shop-bought**) *adj.* [only before noun] bought from a shop/store and not made at home 從商店買的（而非家裏做的）: *store-bought cookies* 在商店裏買的餅乾

'store-brand (*US*) (*BrE* **,own-'brand**, **,own-'label**) *adj.* used to describe goods that are marked with the name of the shop/store in which they are sold rather than with the name of the company that produced them 店家商標的，自有品牌的（指產品以商店自定的品牌出售）

'store card *noun* a card that a particular shop/store provides for regular customers so that they can use it to buy goods that they will pay for later （商店發給老顧客的）賒賬卡 ➲ compare CREDIT CARD

'store detective *noun* a person employed by a large shop/store to watch customers and make sure they do not steal goods 商店專抓行竊者的雇員

store·front /'stɔːfrʌnt; *NAmE* 'stɔːrf-/ *noun* (*NAmE*) **1** (*BrE* **shop·front**) the outside of a shop/store that faces the street 商店門面；店面 **2** a room at the front of a shop/store 店面；鋪面；鋪面房: *They run their business from a small storefront.* 他們在一間狹小的鋪面房中做生意。◇ *a storefront office* 設在店面房中的辦公室 **3** a place on the Internet where you can buy goods and services 網上店鋪；虛擬店面: *Welcome to our* ***online storefront***. 歡迎到我們的網上店鋪。

store·house /'stɔːhaʊs; *NAmE* 'stɔːrh-/ *noun* **1** a building where things are stored 倉庫；貨棧 **SYN** **warehouse** **2 ~ of information, knowledge, etc.** a place or thing that has or contains a lot of information （信息或知識等的）寶庫

store·keep·er /'stɔːkiːpə(r); *NAmE* 'stɔːrk-/ *noun* (*especially NAmE*) = SHOPKEEPER

store·room /'stɔːruːm; -rʊm/ *noun* a room used for storing things 貯藏室

'store window (*NAmE*) (*BrE* **,shop 'window**) (also **window**) *noun* the glass at the front of a shop/store and the area behind it where goods are shown to the public 商店櫥窗

storey (*especially BrE*) (*especially US* **story**) /'stɔːri/ *noun* (*pl.* **stor·eys**, *NAmE* **stor·ies**) **1** a level of a building; a floor 樓層: *the* ***upper/lower storey*** *of the house* 房子的上面／下面一層 ◇ *a* ***single-storey/two-storey*** *building* 單層建築物；兩層樓房 ➲ see also MULTI-STOREY CAR PARK ➲ **VISUAL VOCAB** page V16 **2** **-storeyed** (*BrE*) (*NAmE* **-storied**) (in adjectives 構成形容詞) (of a building 樓房) having the number of levels mentioned 有…層的: *a four-storeyed building* 四層樓房

Which Word? **詞語辨析**

storey / floor

- You use **storey** (*BrE*)/ **story** (*NAmE*) mainly when you are talking about the number of levels a building has. * storey（英式英語）/story（美式英語）主要用以指建築物的樓層數目: *a five-storey house* 一棟五層樓的房屋 ◇ *The office building is five storeys high.* 辦公大樓有五層樓高。
- **Floor** is used mainly to talk about which particular level in the building someone lives on, goes to, etc. * floor 主要指居住或前往等的某樓層: *His office is on the fifth floor.* 他的辦公室在五樓。

➲ note at FLOOR

stor·ied /'stɔːrid/ *adj.* (*NAmE*) **1** [only before noun] mentioned in stories; famous; well known 廣為流傳的；有名的；眾所周知的: *the rock star's storied career* 那位搖滾歌星盡人皆知的演唱生涯 **2** **-storied** = -STOREYED at STOREY *n.* (2)

stork /stɔːk; *NAmE* stɔːrk/ *noun* a large black and white bird with a long beak and neck and long legs, that lives near water but often builds its nest on the top of a high building. There is a tradition that says that it is storks that bring people their new babies. 鸛（有送子的寓意）

storm /stɔːm; *NAmE* stɔːrm/ *noun, verb*

■ ***noun*** **1** very bad weather with strong winds and rain, and often THUNDER and LIGHTNING 暴風雨: ***fierce/heavy/violent storms*** 狂風暴雨 ◇ *A few minutes later* ***the storm broke*** (= began). 不一會兒暴風雨降臨了。◇ *I think we're* ***in for a storm*** (= going to have one). 我覺得我們躲不過一場暴風雨了。◇ *storm damage* 暴風雨造成的損害 ➲ note at RAIN ➲ **COLLOCATIONS** at WEATHER **2** (in compounds 構成複合詞) very bad weather of the type mentioned 和風暴有關的惡劣天氣: *a* ***thunderstorm/snowstorm/sandstorm*** 雷暴；暴風雪；沙暴 ➲ see also ELECTRICAL STORM, RAINSTORM **3** **~ (of sth)** a situation in which a lot of people suddenly express very strong feelings about sth （群情迸發的）浪潮: *a storm of protest* 抗議的浪潮 ◇ *A political*

S

storm is brewing over the Prime Minister's comments. 首相的評論即將醞釀出一場政治風暴。 **4 ~ of sth** a sudden loud noise that is caused by emotion or excitement（因激動或興奮而爆發出的）暴風雨般的聲音，轟鳴 **SYN** **roar**: *a storm of applause* 如雷掌聲 ➲ see also BRAINSTORM

IDM **a storm in a 'teacup** (*BrE*) (*NAmE* **a tempest in a 'teapot**) a lot of anger or worry about sth that is not important 大驚小怪，小題大做，茶杯裏的風暴（小事引起的大風波） **take sth/sb by 'storm 1** to be extremely successful very quickly in a particular place or among particular people 在某處大獲成功；使觀眾等傾動: *The play took London by storm.* 這部劇很快就風靡倫敦。 **2** to attack a place suddenly and capture it 突襲攻佔某處 ➲ more at CALM *n.*, PORT *n.*

■ *verb* **1** [T, I] to suddenly attack a place 突襲；攻佔: **~ sth** *Police stormed the building and captured the gunman.* 警察突襲那棟樓房，抓獲了持槍歹徒。◇ **~ into sth** *Soldiers stormed into the city at dawn.* 士兵在拂曉時分攻進城裏。 **2** [I] **+ adv./prep.** to go somewhere quickly and in an angry, noisy way 氣呼呼地疾走；闖；衝: *She stormed into my office waving a newspaper.* 她揮舞着一張報紙怒氣沖沖地闖進我的辦公室。◇ *He burst into tears and stormed off.* 他突然大哭起來，氣呼呼地跑了。 **3** [T] **+ speech** to say sth in a loud angry way 怒吼；大發雷霆: *'Don't you know who I am?' she stormed.* "你不知道我是誰嗎？" 她怒喝道。

'storm cloud *noun* [usually pl.] a dark cloud that you see when bad weather is coming 暴風雲: (*figurative*) *The storm clouds of revolution were gathering.* 烏雲滾滾，山雨欲來，革命即將爆發。

'storm door *noun* an extra door that is fitted to the outside door of a house, etc. to give protection from bad weather（用來防風、擋雨、禦寒的）外重門

storm·ing /'stɔːmɪŋ; *NAmE* 'stɔːrm-/ *adj.* [only before noun] (*BrE*) (of a performance 表現) very impressive; done with a lot of energy 出色的；精力充沛的；勁頭十足的: *Arsenal scored three late goals in a storming finish.* 阿森納隊後來以三個進球轟轟烈烈地完成了比賽。

'storm-tossed *adj.* [only before noun] (*literary*) affected or damaged by storms 在暴風雨中飄搖的；遭暴風雨損壞的

'storm trooper *noun* a soldier who is specially trained for violent attacks, especially one in Nazi Germany in the 1930s and 1940s（尤指納粹德國的）衝鋒隊員；突擊隊員

S

'storm water *noun* [U] water covering the ground in large quantities because of heavy rain 暴雨積水；潦水

'storm window *noun* an extra window that is fitted to a window of a house to give protection from bad weather 風雨防護窗，防風窗（防惡劣天氣的外重窗）

stormy /'stɔːmi; *NAmE* 'stɔːrmi/ *adj.* (**storm·ier, stormi·est**) **1** with strong winds and heavy rain or snow 有暴風雨（或暴風雪）的: *a dark and stormy night* 黑暗的暴風雨之夜 ◇ *stormy weather* 狂風暴雨的天氣 ◇ *stormy seas* (= with big waves) 波濤洶湧的大海 **2** full of strong feelings and angry arguments 群情激憤的；激烈爭吵的: *a stormy debate* 唇槍舌劍的辯論 ◇ *a stormy relationship* 衝突不斷的關係

story 0-w /'stɔːri/ *noun* (*pl.* **-ies**)

1 0-w **~ (about/of sth/sb)** a description of events and people that the writer or speaker has invented in order to entertain people（虛構的）故事；小說: ***adventure/detective/love, etc. stories*** 歷險、偵探、愛情等小說 ◇ *a story about time travel* 一部關於穿越時間旅行的小說 ◇ *Shall I **tell you a story**?* 我給你講個故事好嗎？◇ *He **read** the children **a story**.* 他給孩子們讀了一則故事。◇ *a **bedtime story*** 臨睡前給小孩講的故事 ➲ COLLOCATIONS at LITERATURE ➲ see also FAIRY STORY at FAIRY TALE, GHOST STORY, SHORT STORY **2** 0-w **~ (about/of sth/sb)** an account, often spoken, of what happened to sb or of how sth happened（真實情況的）敘述，描述: *It was many years before **the full story** was made public.* 許多年之後，事情的全貌才公之於眾。◇ *The police didn't believe her story.* 警方不相信她對事情的描述。◇ *We must stick to our story about the accident.* 對事故的說法我們必須一口咬定，再不改口。◇ *I can't decide until I've heard **both sides of the story**.* 雙方的說法都聽了以後我才能作決定。◇ *It's a story of courage.* 這件事真體現了勇氣。◇ *Many years later I returned to Africa but **that's another story*** (= I am not going to talk about it now). 多年以後我又重返非洲，不過這是後話了。 ➲ see also COCK AND BULL STORY, HARD-LUCK STORY, LIFE STORY, SHAGGY-DOG STORY, SOB STORY, SUCCESS STORY, TALL STORY ➲ SYNONYMS at REPORT **3** 0-w an account of past events or of how sth has developed 對往事的敘述: *He told us the story of his life.* 他對我們講述了他的生活經歷。◇ *the story of the Beatles* 披頭士樂隊的傳奇故事 ◇ *the story of the building of the bridge* 這座橋的建築始末 **4** 0-w a report in a newspaper, magazine or news broadcast 新聞報道: *a front-page story* 頭版報道 ◇ *Now for a summary of tonight's main news stories.* 現在是今晚主要新聞綜述。 ➲ see also COVER STORY, LEAD STORY **5** 0-w (also **story·line**) the series of events in a book, film/movie, play, etc.（書籍、電影、戲劇等的）情節 **SYN** **plot**: *Her novels always have the same basic story.* 她的小說基本情節都一樣。 **6** (*informal*) something that sb says which is not true 謊言；假話: *She knew the child had been **telling stories** again.* 她知道這孩子又在說謊了。 **7** (*NAmE*) = STOREY

IDM **the story goes (that) ...** | **so the story goes** used to describe sth that people are saying although it may not be correct 據說；傳聞；謠傳: *She never saw him again—or so the story goes.* 從此她再沒有見過他，或者據說如此。 **that's the ˌstory of my 'life** (*informal*) when you say **that's the story of my life** about an unfortunate experience you have had, you mean you have had many similar experiences 我就是這個命（表示一生中有很多類似的不幸經歷） ➲ more at LIKELY *adj.*, LONG *adj.*, OLD, PITCH *v.*, TELL

story·board /'stɔːribɔːd; *NAmE* -bɔːrd/ *noun* a series of drawings or pictures that show the outline of the story of a film/movie, etc.（電影等的）劇情梗概系列圖片 ▸ **story·board** *verb* **~ sth** **storyboarding** *noun* [U]: *the storyboarding process* 分鏡頭腳本設計

story·book /'stɔːribʊk/ *noun* a book of stories for children 兒童故事書；童話書: *a picture in a storybook* 故事書中的插圖 ◇ *storybook characters* 童話中的人物 ◇ *storybook adventures* (= like the ones in stories for children) 故事書裏那種神奇的歷險

story·line /'stɔːrilaɪn/ *noun* the basic story in a novel, play, film/movie, etc.（小說、戲劇、電影等的）故事情節，本事 **SYN** **plot**

story·tell·er /'stɔːritelə(r)/ *noun* a person who tells or writes stories 講故事的人；故事（或小說）作者 ▸ **story·tell·ing** *noun* [U]

stoup /stuːp/ *noun* (*technical* 術語) a stone container for holy water in a church（教堂的）聖水鉢

stout /staʊt/ *adj.*, *noun*

■ *adj.* (**stout·er, stout·est**) **1** (of a person 人) rather fat 肥胖的；肥壯的 **SYN** **plump** **2** [usually before noun] strong and thick 粗壯結實的；厚實牢固的: *a stout pair of shoes* 一雙厚實耐穿的鞋 **3** [usually before noun] (*formal*) brave and determined 頑強的；堅毅的；不屈不撓的: *He put up a stout defence in court.* 他在法庭上進行了頑強的辯護。 ▸ **stout·ly** *adv.*: *He was tall and stoutly built.* 他長得五大三粗的。◇ *'I disagree,' said Polly stoutly.* "我不同意。" 波利拒不妥協地說。 **stout·ness** *noun* [U]

■ *noun* [U, C] strong dark beer made with MALT or BARLEY 烈性黑啤酒

ˌstout-'hearted *adj.* (*old-fashioned*, *literary*) brave and determined 勇敢堅毅的

stove 0-w /stəʊv; *NAmE* stoʊv/ *noun*

1 0-w a piece of equipment that can burn various fuels and is used for heating rooms（用於取暖的）爐子，火爐: *a **gas/wood-burning stove*** 燒煤氣／木柴的火爐 **2** 0-w (*especially NAmE*) (*BrE* also **cook·er**) (*NAmE* also **range**) a large piece of equipment for cooking food, containing an oven and gas or electric rings on top（帶烤箱、燃氣爐或電爐的）廚房灶具，爐具: *She put a pan of water on the stove.* 她在灶上放了一鍋水。◇ (*NAmE*, *BrE*) *Most people don't want to spend hours **slaving over***

a hot stove (= cooking). 人們大都不願意老圍着灶台轉。
➲ see also STAVE, STOVE, STOVE *v.*

stove·top /ˈstəʊvtɒp; *NAmE* ˈstoʊvtɑːp/ *noun* (*NAmE*) (*BrE* **hob**) the top part of a cooker where food is cooked in pans; a similar surface that is built into a kitchen unit and is separate from the oven 爐盤；爐頭：*stovetop cooking* 使用爐盤烹飪 ➲ **VISUAL VOCAB** page V25

stow /stəʊ; *NAmE* stoʊ/ *verb* **~ sth (away) (in sth)** to put sth in a safe place 妥善放置；把…收好：*She found a seat, stowed her backpack and sat down.* 她找到一個座位，把背包放好，坐了下來。

PHR V **ˌstow aˈway** to hide in a ship, plane, etc. in order to travel secretly 無票偷乘（船、飛機等）➲ related noun STOWAWAY

stow·age /ˈstəʊɪdʒ; *NAmE* ˈstoʊ-/ *noun* [U] space provided for stowing things away, in a boat or a plane （船或飛機上）存放物品處

stow·away /ˈstəʊəweɪ; *NAmE* ˈstoʊ-/ *noun* a person who hides in a ship or plane before it leaves, in order to travel without paying or being seen 偷乘船（或飛機）者

St Pat·rick's Day /ˌsnt ˈpætrɪks deɪ; *NAmE* ˌseɪnt/ *noun* 17 March, a Christian festival of the national SAINT of Ireland, when many Irish people wear a SHAMROCK 聖帕特里克節（3 月 17 日，紀念愛爾蘭主保聖人的基督教節日，很多愛爾蘭人佩戴三葉草）

strad·dle /ˈstrædl/ *verb* **1 ~ sth/sb** to sit or stand with one of your legs on either side of sb/sth 騎；跨坐；分腿站立：*He swung his leg over the motorcycle, straddling it easily.* 他一騙腿輕而易舉地騎上摩托車。 **2 ~ sth** to cross, or exist on both sides of, a river, a road or an area of land 跨過，橫跨（河流、道路或一片土地）：*The mountains straddle the French-Swiss border.* 這座山脈橫跨法國和瑞士邊界。 **3 ~ sth** to exist within, or include, different periods of time, activities or groups of people 橫跨，同屬（不同時期、活動或群體）；兩棲於（不同活動）：*a writer who straddles two cultures* 橫貫兩種文化的作家

strafe /strɑːf; *NAmE* streɪf/ *verb* **~ sth** to attack a place with bullets or bombs from an aircraft flying low 低空掃射（或轟炸）

strag·gle /ˈstræɡl/ *verb* **1** [I] **(+ adv./prep.)** to grow, spread or move in an untidy way in different directions 蔓生；雜亂地蔓延；散佈：*The town straggled to an end and the fields began.* 城邊上橫七豎八的建築不再蔓延，田野展現出來。 **2** [I] **(+ adv./prep.)** to move slowly behind a group of people that you are with so that you become separated from them 掉隊；落在後面：*On the way the kids straggled behind us.* 在路上，那幾個孩子落在了我們後面。

strag·gler /ˈstræɡlə(r)/ *noun* [usually pl.] a person or an animal that is among the last or the slowest in a group to do sth, for example, to finish a race or leave a place 掉隊者；落在最後的人（或動物）

strag·gly /ˈstræɡli/ *adj.* growing or hanging in a way that does not look tidy or attractive 蔓生的；雜亂地蔓延的：*a thin woman with grey, straggly hair* 灰髮蓬亂的瘦女人

straight 🔑 /streɪt/ *adv., adj., noun*

■ *adv.* (**straight·er, straight·est**)

▸ **NOT IN CURVE** 不彎曲 **1** 🔑 not in a curve or at an angle; in a straight line 筆直地；平正地；成直線：*Keep* ***straight on*** *for two miles.* 一直向前走兩英里。◇ *Can you stretch your arms out straighter?* 你能把胳膊伸得再直一些嗎？◇ *He was too tired to walk straight.* 他累得走都走不直了。◇ *I can't shoot straight* (= accurately). 我射不準。◇ *She looked me straight in the eye.* 她直眼看着我。

▸ **IMMEDIATELY** 立刻 **2** 🔑 by a direct route; immediately 直接；逕直；立即：*Come straight home after school.* 放學後直接回家來。◇ *I was so tired I went straight to bed.* 我太累，逕直上牀睡了。◇ *She went straight from college to a top job.* 她大學一畢業就幹上了一份優越的工作。◇ *I'm going to the library* ***straight after*** *the class.* 我一下課就馬上去圖書館。◇ *I'll come* ***straight to the point***—*your work isn't good enough.* 我開門見山地說吧，你的工作做得不夠好。

▸ **IN LEVEL/CORRECT POSITION** 處於平正 / 合適的位置 **3** 🔑 in or into a level or vertical position; in or into the correct position 正；直；平正地：*Sit up straight!* 直起腰來！◇ *She pulled her hat straight.* 她把帽子拉正了。

▸ **HONESTLY** 如實 **4** honestly and directly 坦率地；直截了當地：*I told him straight that I didn't like him.* 我坦率地告訴他說我不喜歡他。◇ *Are you* ***playing straight*** *with me?* 你沒跟我耍花招吧？

▸ **WITHOUT INTERRUPTION** 不間斷 **5** continuously without interruption 連續不斷地；一連：*They had been working for 16 hours straight.* 他們已經一連工作了 16 個小時。

IDM **go ˈstraight** (*informal*) to stop being a criminal and live an honest life 改邪歸正；重新做人 **play it ˈstraight** to be honest and not try to trick sb 誠實無欺；公平正直 **ˌstraight aˈway** 🔑 immediately; without delay 立即；馬上 **SYN** **at once**：*I'll do it straight away.* 這件事我馬上就做。 **ˌstraight from the ˈshoulder** if you say sth **straight from the shoulder**, you are being very honest and direct, even if what you are saying is critical 坦誠；直言不諱 **ˌstraight ˈoff/ˈout** (*informal*) without hesitating 毫不猶豫；直率：*She asked him straight off what he thought about it all.* 她率直地問他對這一切有什麼想法。 **ˌstraight ˈup** (*BrE, informal*) used to ask if what sb has said is true or to emphasize that what you have said is true （詢問或強調所說的話的真實性）真的，確實：*I saw it—straight up!* 我親眼看見了，真的！
➲ more at HIT *v.*, HORSE *n.*, THINK *v.*

■ *adj.* (**straight·er, straight·est**)

▸ **WITHOUT CURVES** 不彎曲 **1** 🔑 without a bend or curve; going in one direction only 直的：*a straight line* 直線 ◇ *a straight road* 筆直的公路 ◇ *long straight hair* (= without curls) 又長又直的頭髮 ◇ *a boat sailing* ***in a straight line*** 直線航行的船 ◇ *straight-backed chairs* 直背椅

▸ **CLOTHING** 服裝 **2** 🔑 not fitting close to the body and not curving away from the body 直筒型（非緊身）的：*a straight skirt* 直筒裙

▸ **AIM/BLOW** 瞄準；打擊 **3** going directly to the correct place 準的；正中目標的：*a straight punch to the face* 不偏不倚打在臉上的一拳

▸ **IN LEVEL/CORRECT POSITION** 處於平正 / 合適的位置 **4** 🔑 positioned in the correct way; level, vertical or parallel to sth 平正的；正的；直的；與…平行的：*Is my tie straight?* 我的領帶正不正？

▸ **CLEAN/NEAT** 整潔 **5** [not usually before noun] clean and neat, with everything in the correct place 整潔；整齊；井井有條：*It took hours to get the house straight.* 用了好半天才把房子收拾出來。

▸ **HONEST** 坦誠 **6** honest and direct 坦誠的；直率的：*a straight answer to a straight question* 問得直率，答得坦誠 ◇ *I don't think you're being straight with me.* 我覺得你沒有跟我坦誠相見。◇ *It's time for some* ***straight talking.*** 現在該開誠佈公地談談了。➲ **SYNONYMS** at HONEST

▸ **CHOICE** 選擇 **7** [only before noun] simple; involving only two clear choices 簡單明瞭的；非此即彼的：*It was a* ***straight choice*** *between taking the job and staying out of work.* 要麼接受這份工作，要麼繼續失業，此外別無其他選擇。◇ (*BrE*) *The election was a* ***straight fight*** *between the two main parties.* 那次選舉是兩大黨直接交鋒。

▸ **ACTOR/PLAY** 演員；戲劇 **8** [only before noun] (of an actor or a play 演員或戲劇) not connected with comedy or musical theatre, but with serious theatre 嚴肅的，正統的（與喜劇、音樂劇無關）

▸ **WITHOUT INTERRUPTION** 不間斷 **9** [only before noun] one after another in a series, without interruption 連續的；不間斷的 **SYN** **consecutive**：*The team has had five straight wins.* 這支隊已連贏五場比賽了。

▸ **ALCOHOLIC DRINK** 酒精飲料 **10** (*NAmE*) (*BrE* **neat**) not mixed with water or anything else 純的；不摻水（或其他東西）的

▸ **NORMAL/BORING** 規矩；無趣 **11** (*informal*) you can use **straight** to describe a person who is normal and ordinary, but who you consider dull and boring 規矩老實的；本分無趣的；正統的

▸ **SEX** 性 **12** (*informal*) HETEROSEXUAL 異性戀的 **OPP** **gay**
▸ **straight·ness** *noun* [U]

IDM **get sth ˈstraight** to make a situation clear; to make sure that you or sb else understands the situation 明確某事；把某事弄清楚：*Let's get this straight—you*

S

really had no idea where he was? 我們把這個明確一下，你當時真的不知道他在哪兒？ **put/set sb 'straight (about/on sth)** to correct sb's mistake; to make sure that sb knows the correct facts when they have had the wrong idea or impression 糾正某人；指出某人的錯誤；使某人瞭解真相 **(earn/get) straight 'A's** (*especially NAmE*) (to get) the best marks/grades in all your classes（成績）全優：*a straight A student* 全優生 **the ˌstraight and 'narrow** (*informal*) the honest and morally acceptable way of living 誠實正當的生活；正路：*His wife is trying to keep him on the straight and narrow.* 他妻子想方設法讓他要誠實正派。 **a straight 'face** if you keep a **straight face**, you do not laugh or smile, although you find sth funny 繃着的臉；忍着不笑的臉 ➲ see also STRAIGHT-FACED ➲ more at RAMROD, RECORD *n.*

■ **noun**

▸ **SEX** 性 **1** (*informal*) a person who has sexual relationships with people of the opposite sex, rather than the same sex 異性戀者：*gays and straights* 同性戀者和異性戀者

▸ **OF ROAD/TRACK** 公路；跑道 **2** (*NAmE* also **straight·away**) a straight part of a RACETRACK or road 直道部份；直道 ➲ see also THE HOME STRAIGHT

ˌstraight-'arm (also **ˌstiff-'arm**) (both *NAmE*) (*BrE* **ˌhand sb↔'off**) *verb* **~ sb** (in sport 體育運動) to push away a player who is trying to stop you, with your arm straight 伸直手臂擋開（對手）

ˌstraight 'arrow *noun* (*NAmE, informal*) a person who is very honest or who never does anything exciting or different 老實巴交的人；循規蹈矩的人

straight·away /ˌstreɪtəˈweɪ/ *adv., noun*

■ **adv.** ➲ STRAIGHT *adv.* (2)

■ **noun** (*NAmE*) = STRAIGHT *n.* (2)

'straight edge *noun* a strip of wood, metal or plastic with a straight edge used for drawing accurate straight lines, or checking them（用以畫或測定直線的）直尺，標尺，規板

straight·en /ˈstreɪtn/ *verb* **1** [T, I] to become straight; to make sth straight（使）變直，變正：**~ sth (out)** *I straightened my tie and walked in.* 我把領帶拉正，走了進去。◇ **~ (out)** *The road bends here then straightens out.* 公路在這兒拐彎，然後就直了。 **2** [T, I] to make your body straight and vertical 挺直，端正（身體）：**~ sth** *He stood up and straightened his shoulders.* 他站起身，挺起肩膀。◇ **~ sth/yourself up** *I straightened myself up to answer the question.* 我直起身來回答問題。◇ **~ (up)** *Straighten up slowly, then repeat the exercise ten times.* 慢慢挺直身體，然後把這個動作重複十次。

PHR V **ˌstraighten sb↔'out** to help sb to deal with problems or understand a confused situation 幫人解決問題；為人解除困惑 **ˌstraighten sth↔'out** to deal with a confused situation by organizing things that are causing problems 清理；整頓：*I need time to straighten out my finances.* 我需要時間清理一下我的財務。 **ˌstraighten sth↔'up** to make sth neat and tidy 整理；收拾整齊

ˌstraight-'faced *adj.* without laughing or smiling, even though you may be amused 繃着臉的；忍住不笑的

straight·for·ward **AW** /ˌstreɪtˈfɔːwəd; *NAmE* -ˈfɔːrwərd/ *adj.* **1** easy to do or to understand; not complicated 簡單的；易懂的；不複雜的 **SYN** easy：*a straightforward process* 簡單的過程 ◇ *It's quite straightforward to get here.* 來這兒相當容易。 **2** (of a person or their behaviour 人或行為) honest and open; not trying to trick sb or hide sth 坦誠的；坦率的；率直的 ▸ **straight·for·ward·ly** *adv.*：*Let me put it more straightforwardly.* 我來把它說得更直截了當一些。 **straight·for·ward·ness** *noun* [U]

straight·jacket *noun* = STRAITJACKET

ˌstraight-'laced *adj.* = STRAIT-LACED

'straight man *noun* a person in a show whose role is to provide the main entertainer with opportunities to make jokes（表演中）捧哏的配角

ˌstraight 'ticket *noun* (in elections in the US) a vote in which sb chooses all the candidates from the same party 清一色選票（美國選舉中支持同一政黨全部候選人的選票）➲ compare SPLIT TICKET ▸ **ˌstraight-'ticket** *adj.*：*straight-ticket voting* 選同一政黨全部候選人的投票

strain 0̶ /streɪn/ *noun, verb*

■ **noun**

▸ **WORRY/ANXIETY** 擔憂；焦慮 **1** 0̶ [U, C] pressure on sb/sth because they have too much to do or manage, or sth very difficult to deal with; the problems, worry or anxiety that this produces 壓力；重負；重壓之下出現的問題（或擔憂等）：*Their marriage is* **under great strain** *at the moment.* 眼下他們的婚姻關係非常緊張。◇ *These repayments are* **putting a strain on** *our finances.* 償還這些債務對我們的財務狀況形成了壓力。◇ *Relax, and let us* **take the strain** (= do things for you). 你歇一下，我們來頂一會兒。◇ *The transport service cannot cope with the strain of so many additional passengers.* 運輸部門無法應對臨時增加這麼多乘客所帶來的緊張局面。◇ *You will learn to cope with the* **stresses and strains** *of public life.* 你要學會怎樣應付公眾人物生活的緊張和辛勞。◇ *I found it a strain having to concentrate for so long.* 我覺得這麼長時間全神貫注挺累的。 ➲ **SYNONYMS** at PRESSURE

▸ **PHYSICAL PRESSURE** 物理壓力 **2** 0̶ [U, C] the pressure that is put on sth when a physical force stretches, pushes, or pulls it 壓力；拉力；張力；應力：*The rope broke* **under the strain**. 繩子給拉斷了。◇ *You should try not to place too much strain on muscles and joints.* 你要盡量不讓肌肉和關節太吃力。◇ *The ground here cannot* **take the strain** *of a large building.* 這塊地承受不住大型建築的壓力。◇ *The cable has a 140kg* **breaking strain** (= it will break when it is stretched or pulled by a force greater than this). 這種纜索的斷裂應變力為 140 公斤。

▸ **INJURY** 損傷 **3** [C, U] an injury to a part of your body, such as a muscle, that is caused by using it too much or by twisting it 勞損；拉傷；扭傷：*a calf/groin/leg strain* 腿肚子／腹股溝／腿部拉傷 ◇ *muscle strain* 肌肉勞損

▸ **TYPE OF PLANT/ANIMAL/DISEASE** 動植物／疾病種類 **4** [C] a particular type of plant or animal, or of a disease caused by bacteria, etc.（動、植物的）系，品系，品種；（疾病的）類型：*a new strain of mosquitoes resistant to the poison* 對這種毒藥有抗藥性的新品種蚊子 ◇ *This is only one of the many strains of the disease.* 這種病有許多類型，這只是其中之一。

▸ **IN SB'S CHARACTER** 性格 **5** [C, usually sing.] a particular tendency in the character of a person or group, or a quality in their manner 個性特點；性格傾向；稟性 **SYN** **streak**：*He had a definite strain of snobbery in him.* 他這個人明顯有一股勢利小人的氣味。

▸ **OF MUSIC** 音樂 **6** [C, usually pl.] (*formal*) the sound of music being played or sung 樂曲；曲調；旋律：*She could hear the strains of Mozart through the window.* 她聽見從窗戶飄出的莫扎特的旋律。

■ **verb**

▸ **INJURE** 損傷 **1** [T] **~ sth/yourself** to injure yourself or part of your body by making it work too hard 損傷；拉傷；扭傷：*to strain a muscle* 拉傷肌肉 ➲ **SYNONYMS** at INJURE ➲ **COLLOCATIONS** at INJURY

▸ **MAKE EFFORT** 盡力 **2** [T, I] to make an effort to do sth, using all your mental or physical strength 盡力；竭力；使勁：**~ sth to do sth** *I* **strained my ears** (= listened very hard) *to catch what they were saying.* 我豎起耳朵去聽他們在說些什麼。◇ **~ sth** *Necks were strained for a glimpse of the stranger.* 大家伸長了脖子想看一看這個陌生人。◇ **~ to do sth** *People were straining to see what was going on.* 人們翹首企足看發生了什麼事。◇ **~ (sth) (for sth)** *He burst to the surface, straining for air.* 他衝出水面，使勁吸氣。◇ *Bend gently to the left without straining.* 輕輕向左彎，不要用力。

▸ **STRETCH TO LIMIT** 使達到極限 **3** [T] **~ sth** to try to make sth do more than it is able to do 過度使用；使不堪承受：*The sudden influx of visitors is straining hotels in the town to the limit.* 遊客突然湧入，城裏的旅館全都爆滿。◇ *His constant complaints were straining our patience.* 他沒完沒了的抱怨讓我們忍無可忍。◇ *The dispute has strained relations between the two countries* (= made them difficult). 這場爭端使兩國關係緊張起來。

▸ **PUSH/PULL HARD** 用力推／拉 **4** [I] **+ adv./prep.** to push hard against sth; to pull hard on sth 用力推（或拉）；

S

拉緊：*She strained against the ropes that held her.* 她使勁掙了掙拴着她的繩子。◇ *The dogs were* ***straining at the leash****, eager to get to the park.* 幾條狗用力拽着皮帶，急於要去公園。

▸ SEPARATE SOLID FROM LIQUID 過濾 **5** [T] to pour food, etc. through sth with very small holes in it, for example a SIEVE, in order to separate the solid part from the liquid part 濾；過濾：**~ sth** *Use a colander to strain the vegetables.* 把蔬菜放在漏筐裏控控水。◇ **~ sth off** *Strain off any excess liquid.* 濾掉多餘的液體。

IDM **strain at the 'leash** (*informal*) to want to do sth very much 急於；迫不及待：*Like all youngsters, he's straining at the leash to leave home.* 跟所有年輕人一樣，他也急於離家生活。 **strain every 'nerve/'sinew (to do sth)** (*formal*) to try as hard as you can to do sth 竭盡全力（做某事）➲ more at CREAK *v.*

strained /streɪnd/ *adj.* **1** showing the effects of worry or pressure 神色不寧的；緊張的；憔悴的 SYN **tense**：*Her face looked strained and weary.* 她的臉色顯得憔悴疲憊。◇ *He spoke in a low, strained voice.* 他焦慮地低聲說話。 **2** (of a situation 狀況) not relaxed or friendly 緊張的；不友好的 SYN **tense**：*There was a strained atmosphere throughout the meeting.* 會議自始至終氣氛緊張。◇ *Relations between the two families are strained.* 兩家關係緊張。 **3** not natural; produced by a deliberate effort 不自然的；做作的；勉強的 SYN **forced**：*She gave a strained laugh.* 她勉強笑了一下。

strain·er /'streɪnə(r)/ *noun* a kitchen UTENSIL (= a tool) with a lot of small holes in it, used for separating solids from liquids 濾器；濾盆；濾網：*a tea-strainer* 濾茶器

strait /streɪt/ *noun* **1** (also **straits**) [pl.] (especially in the names of places 尤用於地名) a narrow passage of water that connects two seas or large areas of water 海峽；（聯結兩大水域的）水道：*the Strait(s) of Gibraltar* 直布羅陀海峽 **2 straits** [pl.] a very difficult situation especially because of lack of money （尤指經濟拮据引起的）困境，境況窘迫：*The factory is* ***in dire straits****.* 工廠岌岌可危。◇ *She found herself in desperate financial straits.* 她發覺自己經濟狀況極為窘迫。

strait·ened /'streɪtnd/ *adj.* [only before noun] (*formal*) without enough money or as much money as there was before 經濟拮据的；窮困的；經濟狀況惡化的：*The family of eight was living* ***in straitened circumstances****.* 八口之家日子過得很拮据。

strait·jacket (also **straight·jacket**) /'streɪtdʒækɪt/ *noun* **1** a piece of clothing like a jacket with long arms which are tied to prevent the person wearing it from behaving violently. Straitjackets are sometimes used to control people who are mentally ill. 約束衣，緊身衣（有時用以束縛精神病患者） **2** (*disapproving*) a thing that stops sth from growing or developing 束縛；桎梏；約束：*the straitjacket of taxation* 納稅的束縛

strait-laced (also **straight-laced**) /ˌstreɪt 'leɪst/ *adj.* (*disapproving*) having strict or old-fashioned ideas about people's moral behaviour （在道德行為上）拘謹保守的，古板的

strand /strænd/ *noun, verb*

■ ***noun*** **1** a single thin piece of thread, wire, hair, etc. （線、繩、金屬線、毛髮等的）股，縷：*a strand of wool* 一股羊毛◇ *a few strands of dark hair* 幾綹黑髮◇ *She wore a single strand of pearls around her neck.* 她脖子上戴着單串珍珠。 **2** one of the different parts of an idea, a plan, a story, etc. （觀點、計劃、故事等的）部份，方面：*We heard every strand of political opinion.* 各派的政治觀點我們都聽到了。◇ *The author draws the different strands of the plot together in the final chapter.* 作者在最後一章把不同的情節線索歸攏到了一起。 **3** (*literary* or *IrishE*) the land along the edge of the sea or ocean, or of a lake or river （海洋、湖或河的）岸，濱

■ ***verb*** [usually passive] **1 ~ sb** to leave sb in a place from which they have no way of leaving 使滯留：*The strike left hundreds of tourists stranded at the airport.* 這場罷工使成百上千的遊客滯留在機場。 **2 ~ sth** to make a boat, fish, WHALE, etc. be left on land and unable to return to the water 使擱淺：*The ship was stranded on a sandbank.* 船在沙洲上擱淺了。

strange 0▬ /streɪndʒ/ *adj.* (**stran·ger, stran·gest**)
1 0▬ unusual or surprising, especially in a way that is difficult to understand 奇怪的；奇特的；異常的：*A strange thing happened this morning.* 今天上午發生了一件怪事。◇ *She was looking at me in a very strange way.* 她用十分異樣的目光看着我。◇ **~ (that)** … *It's strange (that) we haven't heard from him.* 奇怪，我們一直沒有他的消息。◇ **~ (how …)** *It's strange how childhood impressions linger.* 童年的印象經久不忘，真是不可思議。◇ ***That's strange****—the front door's open.* 真奇怪，正門開着。◇ *I'm looking forward to the exam,* ***strange as it may seem****.* 別人可能感到奇怪，我在盼望這場考試。◇ *There was* ***something strange*** *about her eyes.* 她的眼睛有些異常。◇ ***Strange to say****, I don't really enjoy television.* 說來奇怪，我不大喜歡看電視。 **2** 0▬ not familiar because you have not been there before or met the person before 陌生的；不熟悉的：*a strange city* 陌生的城市◇ *to wake up in a strange bed* 在陌生的牀上醒來◇ *Never accept lifts from strange men.* 千萬別搭陌生男人的車。◇ **~ to sb** *At first the place was strange to me.* 起先我對這個地方不熟悉。 ▸ **strange·ness** *noun* [U]

IDM **feel 'strange** 0▬ to not feel comfortable in a situation; to have an unpleasant physical feeling 感覺不自在；感覺不舒服：*She felt strange sitting at her father's desk.* 坐在父親的書桌前，她感覺不自在。◇ *It was terribly hot and I started to feel strange.* 酷熱難當，我逐漸感到不舒服。 ➲ more at TRUTH

strange·ly 0▬ /'streɪndʒli/ *adv.*
in an unusual or surprising way 異常地；奇怪地；不可思議地：*She's been acting very strangely lately.* 近來她舉止十分反常。◇ *The house was strangely quiet.* 房子裏靜得出奇。◇ *strangely shaped rocks* 奇形怪狀的岩石◇ ***Strangely enough****, I don't feel at all nervous.* 真奇怪，我一點也不緊張。

strang·er 0▬ /'streɪndʒə(r)/ *noun*
1 0▬ a person that you do not know 陌生人：*There was a* ***complete stranger*** *sitting at my desk.* 我書桌前坐着一個從未見過的陌生人。◇ *They got on well together although they were* ***total strangers****.* 儘管以前素未謀面，但他們相處融洽。◇ *We've told our daughter not to speak to strangers.* 我們告訴女兒不要和陌生人講話。◇ **~ to sb** *She remained a stranger to me.* 我一直未能瞭解她。 **2** 0▬ a person who is in a place that they have not been in before 外地人；新來者：*Sorry, I don't know where the bank is. I'm a stranger here myself.* 對不起，我不知道銀行在哪兒。我不是本地人。◇ **~ to** … *He must have been a stranger to the town.* 他當時一定是剛到這個鎮子。

IDM **be no/a 'stranger to sth** (*formal*) to be familiar/not familiar with sth because you have/have not experienced it many times before 熟悉（或不熟悉）某事；習慣（或不習慣）某事：*He is no stranger to controversy.* 他對爭論見得多了。

stran·gle /'stræŋɡl/ *verb* **1 ~ sb** to kill sb by squeezing or pressing on their throat and neck 扼死；勒死；掐死：*to strangle sb to death* 把某人掐死◇ *He strangled her with her own scarf.* 他用她自己的圍巾把她勒死了。 **2 ~ sth** to prevent sth from growing or developing 抑制；壓制；扼殺：*The current monetary policy is strangling the economy.* 現行貨幣政策抑制了經濟的發展。

stran·gled /'stræŋɡld/ *adj.* (of a cry, sb's voice, etc. 哭聲、說話聲等) not clear because it stops before it has completely finished 哽塞的；哽咽的；頓住的：*There was a strangled cry from the other room.* 隔壁傳來一聲哽咽。

strangle·hold /'stræŋɡlhəʊld; *NAmE* -hoʊld/ *noun* [sing.]
1 a strong hold around sb's neck that makes it difficult for them to breathe 掐脖子；卡脖子 **2 ~ (on sth)** complete control over sth that makes it impossible for it to grow or develop well 壓制；束縛：*The company now had a stranglehold on the market.* 這家公司現在壟斷了市場。

stran·gler /'stræŋɡlə(r)/ *noun* a person who kills sb by squeezing their throat tightly 扼（或勒、掐）死人者

S

stran·gu·lated /ˈstræŋɡjuleɪtɪd/ *adj.* **1** (*medical* 醫) (of a part of the body 身體一部份) squeezed so tightly that blood etc. cannot pass through it 絞窄性的 **2** (*formal*) (of a voice 聲音) sounding as though the throat is tightly squeezed, usually because of fear or worry 嗓子被扼住似的，哽塞的（通常由於恐懼或擔憂）：*He gave a strangulated squawk.* 他像嗓子被勒住似的嘎叫了一聲。

stran·gu·la·tion /ˌstræŋɡjuˈleɪʃn/ *noun* [U] **1** the act of killing sb by squeezing their throat tightly; the state of being killed in this way 扼死；勒死；掐死：*to die of slow strangulation* 被緩慢勒死 **2** (*disapproving*) the act of preventing sth from growing or developing 抑制；壓制；扼殺：*the strangulation of the human spirit* 對人的精神壓制

strap /stræp/ *noun, verb*

■ ***noun*** a strip of leather, cloth or other material that is used to fasten sth, keep sth in place, carry sth or hold onto sth 帶子：*the shoulder straps of her dress* 她連衣裙上的肩帶 ◇ *a watch with a leather strap* 皮錶帶的手錶 ➲ **VISUAL VOCAB** pages V51, V64

■ ***verb*** (**-pp-**) **1 ~ sth + adv./prep.** to fasten sb/sth in place using a strap or straps 用帶子繫（或捆、紮、扣）好：*He strapped the knife to his leg.* 他把刀綁到腿上。◇ *Everything had to be strapped down to stop it from sliding around.* 所有東西必須綁定，免得來回滑動。◇ *Are you strapped in* (= wearing a seat belt in a car, plane, etc.)? 您繫好安全帶了嗎？ **2 ~ sth (up)** to wrap strips of material around a wound or an injured part of the body 包紮；給…打繃帶 **SYN** **bandage**：*I have to keep my leg strapped up for six weeks.* 我的腿必須打六星期繃帶。

strap·less /ˈstræpləs/ *adj.* (especially of a dress or BRA 尤指連衣裙或胸罩) without straps 無肩帶的；無吊帶的

strapped /stræpt/ *adj.* **~ (for cash, funds, etc.)** (*informal*) having little or not enough money 缺錢的；手頭緊的

strap·ping /ˈstræpɪŋ/ *adj.* [only before noun] (*informal*) (of people 人) big, tall and strong 魁梧的；高大健壯的：*a strapping lad* 身材魁梧的小伙子

strappy /ˈstræpi/ *adj.* (**strap·pier**, **strap·pi·est**) (*informal*) (of shoes or clothes 鞋或衣服) having straps 有帶子的：*white strappy sandals* 白色條帶涼鞋

strata *pl.* of STRATUM

strata·gem /ˈstrætədʒəm/ *noun* (*formal*) a trick or plan that you use to gain an advantage or to trick an opponent（為爭鬥或為迷惑對手的）計策，計謀

stra·tegic **AW** /strəˈtiːdʒɪk/ (also *less frequent* **stra·tegic·al** /-dʒɪkl/) *adj.* [usually before noun] **1** done as part of a plan that is meant to achieve a particular purpose or to gain an advantage 根據全局而安排的；戰略性的：*strategic planning* 全局性規劃 ◇ *a strategic decision to sell off part of the business* 賣掉企業一部份的戰略決策 ◇ *Cameras were set up at strategic points* (= in places where they would be most effective) *along the route.* 在沿途一些最佳位置架設了攝像機。 **2** connected with getting an advantage in a war or other military situation 戰略性的；戰略上的：*Malta was of vital strategic importance during the war.* 在那次戰爭中，馬耳他的戰略意義至為關鍵。 **3** (of weapons, especially nuclear weapons 武器，尤指核武器) intended to be fired at an enemy's country rather than used in a battle 戰略性的 ➲ compare TACTICAL (3) ▸ **stra·tegic·al·ly** **AW** /-kli/ *adv.*：*a strategically placed microphone* 安放在最佳位置的麥克風 ◇ *a strategically important target* 有重大戰略意義的目標

strat·egist **AW** /ˈstrætədʒɪst/ *noun* a person who is skilled at planning things, especially military activities 戰略家；善於籌劃部署的人

strat·egy 🔑 **AW** /ˈstrætədʒi/ *noun* (*pl.* **-ies**) **1** 🔑 [C] a plan that is intended to achieve a particular purpose 策略；計策；行動計劃：*the government's economic strategy* 政府的經濟策略 ◇ **~ for doing sth** *to develop a strategy for dealing with unemployment* 制訂解決失業問題的對策 ◇ **~ to do sth** *It's all part of an overall strategy to gain promotion.* 這都不過是一個爭取提拔的完整計劃的一部份。 **2** 🔑 [U] the process of planning sth or putting a plan into operation in a skilful way 策劃；規劃；部署；統籌安排：*marketing strategy* 營銷策劃 **3** 🔑 [U, C] the skill of planning the movements of armies in a battle or war; an example of doing this 戰略；戰略部署：*military strategy* 軍事戰略 ◇ *defence strategies* 防禦部署 ➲ **COLLOCATIONS** at WAR ➲ compare TACTIC

strati·fi·ca·tion /ˌstrætɪfɪˈkeɪʃn/ *noun* [U] (*technical* 術語) the division of sth into different layers or groups 分層；成層：*social stratification* 社會階層化

strat·ify /ˈstrætɪfaɪ/ *verb* (**strati·fies**, **strati·fy·ing**, **strati·fied**, **strati·fied**) [usually passive] **~ sth** (*formal* or *technical* 術語) to arrange sth in layers or STRATA（使）分層，成層：*a highly stratified society* 高度分化的社會 ◇ *stratified rock* 成層岩

strato·sphere /ˈstrætəsfɪə(r); *NAmE* -sfɪr/ *noun* **the stratosphere** [sing.] the layer of the earth's atmosphere between about 10 and 50 kilometres above the surface of the earth 平流層；同溫層 ➲ compare IONOSPHERE ▸ **strato·spher·ic** /ˌstrætəˈsferɪk; *NAmE* also -ˈsfɪr-/ *adj.*：*stratospheric clouds* 平流層雲

IDM **in/into the ˈstratosphere** at or to an extremely high level 在（或到）極高水平：*The technology boom sent share prices into the stratosphere.* 科技熱潮使得股價飆升到極高的水平。

stra·tum /ˈstrɑːtəm; *NAmE* ˈstreɪtəm/ *noun* (*pl.* **strata** /-tə/) **1** (*geology* 地) a layer or set of layers of rock, earth, etc. 層；岩層；地層 **2** (*formal*) a class in a society 階層：*people from all social strata* 來自不同社會階層的人

stra·tus /ˈstreɪtəs; ˈstrɑːtəs/ *noun* [U] (*technical* 術語) a type of cloud that forms a continuous grey sheet covering the sky 層雲

stra·vaig (also **stra·vage**) /strəˈveɪɡ/ *verb* [I] (**+ adv./prep.**) (*IrishE, ScotE*) to walk around without an aim 遊蕩；徘徊；漫步

straw /strɔː/ *noun* **1** [U] STEMS of WHEAT or other grain plants that have been cut and dried. Straw is used for making MATS, hats, etc., for packing things to protect them, and as food for animals or for them to sleep on.（收割後乾燥的）禾稈，麥稈，稻草：*a mattress filled with straw* 稻草填充的墊子 ◇ *a straw hat* 草帽 ➲ compare HAY (1) **2** [C] a single STEM or piece of straw 一根禾稈（或麥稈、稻草）：*He was leaning over the gate chewing on a straw.* 他嘴裏嚼着一根麥稈，靠到柵門上。 **3** (also **ˈdrinking straw**) a thin tube of plastic or paper that you suck a drink through（喝飲料用的）吸管 ➲ **VISUAL VOCAB** page V33

IDM **clutch/grasp at ˈstraws** to try all possible means to find a solution or some hope in a difficult or unpleasant situation, even though this seems very unlikely（在危難中）抓救命稻草，不放過任何微小的機會 **the last/final ˈstraw** | **the ˌstraw that breaks the camel's ˈback** the last in a series of bad events, etc. that makes it impossible for you to accept a situation any longer 壓垮駱駝的最後一根稻草；終於使人不堪忍受的最後一件事（或因素等） **a straw in the ˈwind** (*BrE*) a small sign of what might happen in the future（預示發生某事的）跡象，苗頭，徵兆 ➲ more at BRICK *n.*, DRAW *v.*

straw·berry /ˈstrɔːbəri; *NAmE* -beri/ *noun* (*pl.* **-ies**) a soft red fruit with very small yellow seeds on the surface, that grows on a low plant 草莓：*strawberries and cream* 奶油草莓 ◇ *strawberry plants* 草莓植株 ➲ **VISUAL VOCAB** page V30

ˌstrawberry ˈblonde (also **ˌstrawberry ˈblond**) *adj.* (of hair 頭髮) a light reddish-yellow colour 草莓紅色的；淺紅黃色的

ˌstraw ˈpoll (*NAmE* also **ˌstraw ˈvote**) *noun* an occasion when a number of people are asked in an informal way to give their opinion about sth or to say how they are likely to vote in an election（選舉前的）非正式民意測驗

stray /streɪ/ *verb, adj., noun*

■ ***verb*** **1** [I] (**+ adv./prep.**) to move away from the place where you should be, without intending to 迷路；偏離；走失：*He strayed into the path of an oncoming car.*

S

他偏到了一輛迎面駛來的汽車的行車路線上。◇ *Her eyes kept straying over to the clock on the wall.* 她的目光不時瞟向牆上的鐘。 **2** [I] (**+ adv./prep.**) to begin to think about or discuss a different subject from the one you should be thinking about or discussing 偏離正題；走神；離題： *My mind kept straying back to our last talk together.* 我老走神，一再回想起我們上次在一起交談的情景。◇ *We seem to be straying from the main theme of the debate.* 我們似乎是偏離了辯論的主題。 **3** [I] (of a person who is married or in a relationship 已婚者或有固定關係者) to have a sexual relationship with sb who is not your usual partner 有外遇；在別處拈花惹草

■ ***adj.*** [only before noun] **1** (of animals normally kept as pets 常指寵物) away from home and lost; having no home 走失的；無主的： *stray dogs* 走失的狗 **2** separated from other things or people of the same kind 零星的；孤立的；離群的；走散的： *A civilian was killed by a **stray bullet**.* 一個平民被流彈打死。◇ *a few stray hairs* 幾根散亂的頭髮

■ ***noun*** **1** an animal that has got lost or separated from its owner or that has no owner 走失的寵物（或家畜）；無主的寵物（或家畜） ➲ see also WAIF **2** a person or thing that is not in the right place or is separated from others of the same kind 離群者；走散者；不在原位置的東西

streak /striːk/ *noun, verb*

■ ***noun*** **1** a long thin mark or line that is a different colour from the surface it is on 條紋；條痕： *streaks of grey in her hair* 她頭上的綹綹白髮 ◇ *dirty streaks on the window* 窗戶上的道道污痕 ➲ **SYNONYMS** at MARK **2** a part of a person's character, especially an unpleasant part（尤指不好的）性格特徵： *a ruthless/vicious/mean streak* 冷酷／邪惡／卑鄙的性格 ◇ *a streak of cruelty* 幾分殘忍 **3** a series of successes or failures, especially in a sport or in gambling（尤指體育比賽或賭博中）順的時候，背的時候，運氣，手氣： *a streak of good luck* 運氣好的一段時間 ◇ *to hit* (= have) *a **winning streak*** 碰上順的時候 ◇ *to be on a **winning/losing streak*** 趕上順的／背的時候 ◇ *a **lucky/unlucky streak*** 運氣好／不好的階段

■ ***verb*** **1** [T] to mark or cover sth with streaks 在…上畫條紋（或留下條痕）；使佈滿條紋（或條痕）： **~ sth** *Tears streaked her face.* 她臉上是道道淚痕。◇ *She's had her hair streaked* (= had special chemicals put on her hair so that it has attractive coloured lines in it). 她把頭髮做了條染。◇ **~ sth with sth** *His face was streaked with mud.* 他臉上滿是一條條的污泥。 **2** [I] **+ adv./prep.** to move very fast in a particular direction 飛奔；疾馳 **SYN** **speed**： *A car pulled out and streaked off down the road.* 一輛汽車駛出後沿着公路疾馳而去。 **3** [I] (**+ adv./prep.**) (*informal*) to run through a public place with no clothes on as a way of getting attention 裸奔

streak·er /ˈstriːkə(r)/ *noun* a person who runs through a public place with no clothes on as a way of getting attention 裸奔者

streaky /ˈstriːki/ *adj.* marked with lines of a different colour 有條紋（或條痕）的： *streaky blonde hair* 染成的一綹一綹的金髮 ◇ *The wallpaper was streaky with grease.* 壁紙上道道油漬。◇ (*BrE*) *streaky bacon* (= with layers of fat in it) 五花鹹肉

stream 🗝 /striːm/ *noun, verb*

■ ***noun*** **1** 🗝 a small narrow river 小河；溪： *mountain streams* 山澗 ➲ **VISUAL VOCAB** pages V2, V3 ➲ see also DOWNSTREAM, UPSTREAM, THE GULF STREAM **2** 🗝 **~** (**of sth**) a continuous flow of liquid or gas 流；（液）流；（氣）流： *A stream of blood flowed from the wound.* 一股鮮血從傷口流出來。 ➲ see also BLOODSTREAM **3** 🗝 **~** (**of sth/sb**) a continuous flow of people or vehicles（人）流；（車）流： *I've had a **steady stream** of visitors.* 我不斷有客人。◇ *Cars filed past in an endless stream.* 汽車川流不息，魚貫而過。 **4** 🗝 **~ of sth** a large number of things that happen one after the other 一連串，接二連三，源源不斷（的事情）： *a **constant stream** of enquiries* 接連不斷的詢問 ◇ *The agency provided me with a **steady stream** of work.* 這介紹所讓我不斷有活幹。 **5** (*especially BrE*) a group of students of the same age and level of ability in some schools（將同齡學生按能力編在一起的）班，組： *She was put into the fast stream.* 她被分在快班。

IDM **be/come on 'stream** to be in operation or available 投產；投入使用： *The new computer system comes on stream next month.* 新的計算機系統下月投入使用。

■ ***verb*** **1** [I, T] (of liquid or gas 液體或氣體) to move or pour out in a continuous flow; to produce a continuous flow of liquid or gas 流；流動；流出： (**+ adv./prep.**) *Tears streamed down his face.* 淚水順着他的臉往下流。◇ *a streaming cold* (= with a lot of liquid coming from the nose) 流鼻涕的感冒 ◇ **~ with sth** *Her head was streaming with blood.* 她頭上流着血。◇ **~ from sth** *Blood was streaming from her head.* 血從她頭上流出來。◇ *Black smoke streamed from the exhaust.* 排氣管裏冒出黑煙。◇ **~ sth** *The exhaust streamed black smoke.* 排氣管裏冒出黑煙。 **2** (of people or things 人或東西) [I] **+ adv./prep.** to move somewhere in large numbers, one after the other 魚貫而行；一個接一個地移動： *People streamed across the bridge.* 橋上行人川流不息。 **3** [I] to move freely, especially in the wind or water 飄動；飄揚： *Her scarf streamed behind her.* 她的圍巾在身後飄動。 **4** (*especially BrE*) (*NAmE* usually **track**) [T, usually passive] **~ sb** (in schools 學校) to put school students into groups according to their ability 按能力分班（或分組）： *Pupils are streamed for French and Maths.* 學生按能力分成法語組和數學組。 **5** [T] **~ sth** (*computing* 計) to play video or sound on a computer by receiving it as a continuous stream, from the Internet for example, rather than needing to wait until the whole of the material has been DOWNLOADED 用流式傳輸，流播（無須待整個文件下載到計算機便可播放互聯網上的視頻或音頻文件）

stream·er /ˈstriːmə(r)/ *noun* **1** a long narrow piece of coloured paper, used to decorate a place for a party or other celebration 裝飾彩紙條 **2** a long narrow piece of cloth or other material 條幅；橫幅

stream·ing /ˈstriːmɪŋ/ *noun* [U] (*especially BrE*) = BANDING： *Streaming within comprehensive schools is common practice.* 綜合中學常把學生按能力分班。

stream·line /ˈstriːmlaɪn/ *verb* [usually passive] **1 ~ sth** to give sth a smooth even shape so that it can move quickly and easily through air or water 使成流線型： *The cars all have a new streamlined design.* 這些汽車都是流線型新款。 **2 ~ sth** to make a system, an organization, etc. work better, especially in a way that saves money 使（系統、機構等）效率更高；（尤指）使增產節約： *The production process is to be streamlined.* 生產流程還需改進。

ˌstream of 'consciousness *noun* [U] a continuous flow of ideas, thoughts, and feelings, as they are experienced by a person; a style of writing that expresses this without using the usual methods of description and conversation 意識流；意識流創作手法

street 🗝 /striːt/ *noun, adj.*

■ ***noun*** 🗝 **1** [C] (*abbr.* **St**, **st**) a public road in a city or town that has houses and buildings on one side or both sides 大街；街道： *The bank is just across the street.* 銀行就在街對過。◇ *to walk **along/down/up the street*** 沿着街道走 ◇ *the town's narrow cobbled streets* 鎮上狹窄的卵石街道 ◇ *92nd Street* 第 92 大街 ◇ *10 Downing Street* 唐寧街 10 號 ◇ *He is used to being recognized **in the street**.* 街上常有人認出他來，他習以為常了。◇ *a **street map/plan** of York* 約克街道地圖／平面圖 ◇ ***street theatre/musicians*** 街頭戲劇／樂手 ◇ *My office is **at street level*** (= on the ground floor). 我的辦公室在一樓。◇ *It's not safe to **walk the streets** at night.* 夜間在街上走不安全。 ➲ note at ROAD ➲ see also BACKSTREET *n.*, HIGH STREET, SIDE STREET **2** [sing.] the ideas and opinions of ordinary people, especially people who live in cities, which are considered important（尤指城市裏）街頭民意： *The feeling I get from the street is that we have a good chance of winning this election.* 我從街頭民意調查感覺到我們很有機會贏得這場選舉。◇ *The **word on the street** is that it's not going to happen.* 民眾普遍認為此事不會發生。

IDM **(out) on the 'streets/'street** (*informal*) without a home; outside, not in a house or other building 無家可歸；流落街頭；在外面大街上： *the problems of young people living on the streets* 年輕人流落街頭的種種問題

◇ *If it had been left to me I would have put him out on the street long ago.* 換了我，早就把他趕出家門了。 **on/walking the 'streets** working as a PROSTITUTE 做妓女；靠賣淫為生 **'streets ahead (of sb/sth)** (*BrE, informal*) much better or more advanced than sb/sth else（比某人或事物）好得多，先進得多：*a country that is streets ahead in the control of environmental pollution* 一個在整治環境污染方面遠遠走在前面的國家 **the streets are ˌpaved with 'gold** (*saying*) used to say that it seems easy to make money in a place（表示在某地掙錢容易）遍地都是黃金 **(right) up your 'street** (*especially BrE*) (*NAmE* usually **(right) up your 'alley**) (*informal*) very suitable for you because it is sth that you know a lot about or are very interested in（正）適合你；（正）和你對口：*This job seems right up your street.* 這工作看來對你正合適。➲ more at EASY *adj.*, HIT *v.*, MAN *n.*

■ ***adj.*** [only before noun] informal and based on the daily life of ordinary people in cities 街頭的：*street sports such as skateboarding and skating* 街頭運動，如滑板和溜冰 ◇ *street newspapers sold by the homeless* 無家可歸者賣的街頭報紙 ◇ *street culture/dance/law* 街頭文化；街舞；街頭法規

street·board /'striːtbɔːd; *NAmE* -bɔːrd/ (also **Snake-board™**) *noun* two small boards joined with a short pole and with wheels on, which you stand on and ride as a sport 街頭蛇行滑板（用短橫杆連接兩塊腳踏板構成，下有輪子）▸ **street·board·ing** (also **snake·board·ing**) *noun* [U]

street·car /'striːtkɑː(r)/ (also **trol·ley**) (both *US*) (*BrE* **tram**, **tram·car**) *noun* a vehicle driven by electricity, that runs on rails along the streets of a town and carries passengers 有軌電車 ➲ VISUAL VOCAB page V58

'street cred (also **cred**) (*informal*) (also *less frequent* **'street credibility**) *noun* [U] a way of behaving and dressing that is acceptable to young people, especially those who live in cities and have experienced the problems of real life 街頭信譽，街頭形象（青年人推崇的行為方式和着裝風格，尤指城市青年）：*Those clothes do nothing for your street cred.* 穿那些衣服你可一點也不時髦。

ˌstreet 'furniture *noun* [U] (*technical* 術語) equipment such as road signs, street lights, etc. placed at the side of a road 街道設施（如路標、路燈等）

'street light (*BrE* also **'street lamp**) *noun* a light at the top of a tall post in the street 路燈；街燈 ➲ compare LAMP POST ➲ VISUAL VOCAB pages V2, V3

'street people *noun* (*especially NAmE*) people who have no home and who live outside in a town（城市）無家可歸者 SYN **the homeless**

'street-smart *adj.* (*NAmE*) = STREETWISE ➲ compare BOOK-SMART

'street smarts *noun* [pl.] (*NAmE, informal*) the knowledge and experience that is needed to deal with the difficulties and dangers of life in a big city 都市生活訣竅，都市人的精明，街頭智慧（應對大都市生活的困難和危險所需的知識和經驗）

ˌstreet 'theatre (*BrE*) (*NAmE* **ˌstreet 'theater**) *noun* [U] plays or other performances that are done in the street 街頭戲劇；街頭演出

'street value *noun* [usually sing.] a price for which sth that is illegal or has been obtained illegally can be sold（非法物品的）黑市價值：*drugs with a street value of over £1 million* 黑市價值超過 100 萬英鎊的毒品

street·walk·er /'striːtwɔːkə(r)/ *noun* (*old-fashioned*) a PROSTITUTE who looks for customers on the streets 街頭拉客的妓女

street·wise /'striːtwaɪz/ (*NAmE* also **'street-smart**) *adj.* (*informal*) having the knowledge and experience that is needed to deal with the difficulties and dangers of life in a big city 適應都市生活的；有都市人的精明勁兒的

strength 0‑w /streŋθ/ *noun*

▸ **BEING PHYSICALLY STRONG** 強壯；牢固 **1** 0‑w [U, sing.] the quality of being physically strong 體力；力氣；力量：*He pushed against the rock with all his strength.* 他用全力推那塊石頭。◇ *It may take a few weeks for you to build up your strength again.* 可能需要幾個星期你才能恢復體力。◇ *He had a physical strength that matched his outward appearance.* 他的體力與外形相稱。◇ **~ to do sth** *She didn't have the strength to walk any further.* 她再也走不動了。 **2** 0‑w [U] the ability that sth has to resist force or hold heavy weights without breaking or being damaged 強度：*the strength of a rope* 繩子的強度 ➲ see also INDUSTRIAL-STRENGTH

▸ **BEING BRAVE** 勇敢 **3** 0‑w [U, sing.] the quality of being brave and determined in a difficult situation 毅力；堅強決心；意志力量：*During this ordeal he was able to draw strength from his faith.* 在這次磨難中，他得以從自己的信仰中吸取力量。◇ *She has a remarkable **inner strength**.* 她有非凡的意志力量。◇ *You have shown great **strength of character**.* 你表現得很有毅力。

▸ **POWER/INFLUENCE** 實力；勢力 **4** 0‑w [U] the power and influence that sb/sth has 實力：*Political power depends upon economic strength.* 政治權力取決於經濟實力。◇ *Their superior military strength gives them a huge advantage.* 他們軍事實力較強，佔有巨大優勢。◇ *to negotiate from **a position of strength*** 以實力地位談判 ◇ *The rally was intended to be **a show of strength** by the socialists.* 社會主義者組織這次集會意在顯示力量。

▸ **OF OPINION/FEELING** 意見；感情 **5** 0‑w [U] how strong or deeply felt an opinion or a feeling is 強烈程度；深度：*the strength of public opinion* 公眾輿論的強烈程度 ◇ *This view has recently gathered strength* (= become stronger or more widely held). 這種觀點近來已為更多人接受了。◇ *I was surprised by the strength of her feelings.* 她感情之強烈讓我吃驚。

▸ **ADVANTAGE** 優勢 **6** 0‑w [C] a quality or an ability that a person or thing has that gives them an advantage 優勢；優點；長處：*The ability to keep calm is one of her many strengths.* 能夠保持冷靜是她的多項長處之一。◇ *the **strengths and weaknesses** of an argument* 一個論點的有力之處與薄弱之處

▸ **OF NATURAL FORCE** 自然力 **7** 0‑w [U] how strong a natural force is 強度；力度：*the strength of the sun* 太陽的強度 ◇ *wind strength* 風力 ◇ *the strength and direction of the tide* 潮水的流速與方向

▸ **OF FLAVOUR** 味道 **8** [U, C] how strong a particular flavour or substance is 濃度；濃淡程度：*Add more curry powder depending on the strength required.* 按所要求的口味輕重再加點咖喱粉。◇ *a range of beers with different strengths* (= with different amounts of alcohol in them) 各種不同度數的啤酒

▸ **OF CURRENCY** 貨幣 **9** [U] how strong a country's CURRENCY (= unit of money) is in relation to other countries' CURRENCIES 強弱（程度）：*the strength of the dollar* 美元的強弱

▸ **NUMBER IN GROUP** 群體人數多寡 **10** [U] the number of people in a group, a team or an organization 人數多寡；人力：*The strength of the workforce is about to be doubled from 3 000 to 6 000.* 職工人數將翻一番，由 3 000 人增加為 6 000 人。◇ *The team will be back **at full strength*** (= with all the best players) *for the next match.* 這支隊在下場比賽將恢復最佳的陣容。◇ *The protesters turned out **in strength*** (= in large numbers). 抗議者大量聚集。◇ *These cuts have left the local police force **under strength*** (= with fewer members than it needs). 這幾次裁減造成地方警力不足。

IDM **go from ˌstrength to 'strength** to become more and more successful 越來越興旺發達；不斷取得成功：*Since her appointment the department has gone from strength to strength.* 自她上任以來，這個部門越來越興旺了。 **on the strength of sth** because sb has been influenced or persuaded by sth 憑藉（或根據）某事物；在某事物的影響下：*I got the job on the strength of your recommendation.* 由於您的推薦，我得到了那份工作。➲ more at TOWER *n.*

strength·en /'streŋθn/ *verb* [I, T] to become stronger; to make sb/sth stronger 加強；增強；鞏固：*Her position in the party has strengthened in recent weeks.* 最近幾個星期以來，她在黨內的地位有所增強。◇ *Yesterday the*

S

pound strengthened against the dollar. 昨天，英鎊對美元的匯率上升了。◇ *The wind had strengthened overnight.* 夜裏，風更大了。◇ **~ sb/sth** *Repairs are necessary to strengthen the bridge.* 這座橋需要加固。◇ *The exercises are designed to strengthen your stomach muscles.* 這些活動目的在於增強你的腹部肌肉。◇ *The move is clearly intended to strengthen the President's position as head of state.* 這一舉措顯然意在加強總統作為國家元首的地位。◇ *The new manager has strengthened the side by bringing in several younger players.* 新經理通過引進幾名年輕隊員加強了隊伍的實力。◇ *Their attitude only strengthened his resolve to fight on.* 他們採取的態度反而使他堅定了繼續戰鬥的決心。◇ *The new evidence will strengthen their case.* 新的證據將使他們的論據更為充分。 **OPP** **weaken**

strenu·ous /ˈstrenjuəs/ *adj.* **1** needing great effort and energy 費力的；繁重的；艱苦的 **SYN** **arduous**： *a strenuous climb* 艱難的攀登 ◇ *Avoid* ***strenuous exercise*** *immediately after a meal.* 剛吃完飯避免劇烈運動。◇ *How about a stroll in the park?* ***Nothing too strenuous.*** 在公園裏散散步怎麼樣？不會太累的。 **2** showing great energy and determination 勁頭十足的；奮力的；頑強的： *The ship went down although* ***strenuous efforts*** *were made to save it.* 儘管人們為營救這條船作了很大的努力，它還是沉了。 ▸ **strenu·ous·ly** *adv.*： *He still works out strenuously every morning.* 他仍然每天早晨努力鍛煉。◇ *The government* ***strenuously denies*** *the allegations.* 政府堅稱那些說法不是事實。

strep throat /ˌstrep ˈθrəʊt; *NAmE* ˈθroʊt/ *noun* (*NAmE, informal*) an infection of the throat 膿毒性咽喉炎

strepto·coc·cus /ˌstreptəˈkɒkəs; *NAmE* -ˈkɑːkəs/ *noun* (*pl.* **streptococci** /ˌstreptəˈkɒkaɪ; *NAmE* -ˈkɑːkaɪ/) (*medical* 醫) a type of bacteria, some types of which can cause serious infections and illnesses 鏈球菌

stress 🔑 **AW** /stres/ *noun, verb*

■ ***noun***

▸ **MENTAL PRESSURE** 精神壓力 **1** 🔑 [U, C] pressure or worry caused by the problems in sb's life 精神壓力；心理負擔；緊張： *Things can easily go wrong when people are* ***under stress.*** 人在壓力之下，辦事情就容易出差錯。◇ *to suffer from stress* 有精神壓力 ◇ *coping with stress* 應對壓力 ◇ *She failed to withstand the* ***stresses and strains*** *of public life.* 她承受不了作為一個公眾人物的生活壓力和緊張。◇ ***stress-related*** *illnesses* 與精神壓力有關的疾病 ◇ ***emotional/mental stress*** 情感／精神壓力 ◇ *Stress is often a factor in the development of long-term sickness.* 心理壓力常常是形成長期病的一個因素。◇ ***stress management*** (= dealing with stress) 對於壓力的應對 ➲ SYNONYMS at PRESSURE ➲ COLLOCATIONS at DIET

▸ **PHYSICAL PRESSURE** 物理壓力 **2** 🔑 [U, C] **~ (on sth)** pressure put on sth that can damage it or make it lose its shape 壓力；應力： *When you have an injury you start putting stress on other parts of your body.* 一旦受傷，你便會讓身體其他部位受力。◇ *a* ***stress fracture*** *of the foot* (= one caused by such pressure) 足部應力性骨折

▸ **EMPHASIS** 強調 **3** [U] **~ (on sth)** special importance given to sth 強調；重要性： *She* ***lays*** *great* ***stress on*** *punctuality.* 她十分注重守時。◇ *I think the company places too much stress on cost and not enough on quality.* 我認為公司對成本強調有餘，而對質量重視不足。

▸ **ON WORD/SYLLABLE** 單詞；音節 **4** 🔑 [U, C] (*phonetics* 語音) an extra force used when pronouncing a particular word or syllable 重音；重讀： *We worked on pronunciation, stress and intonation.* 我們學習了語音、重讀和語調。◇ ***primary/secondary stress*** 主重音；次重音 ◇ *In 'strategic' the stress falls on the second syllable.* * strategic 一詞的重音在第二音節。 ➲ compare INTONATION (1)

▸ **IN MUSIC** 音樂 **5** [U, C] extra force used when making a particular sound in music 加強（音）

▸ **ILLNESS** 疾病 **6** [U] illness caused by difficult physical conditions 環境惡劣引起的疾病： *Those most vulnerable to heat stress are the elderly.* 上了年紀的人最容易因受熱而生病。

■ ***verb***

▸ **EMPHASIZE** 強調 **1** 🔑 [T] to emphasize a fact, an idea, etc. 強調；着重： **~ sth** *He stressed the importance of a good education.* 他強調了接受良好教育的重要性。◇ **~ that ...** *I must stress that everything I've told you is strictly confidential.* 我必須強調，我告訴你的一切都要嚴加保密。◇ **+ speech** *'There is,' Johnson stressed, 'no real alternative.'* 約翰遜強調說："別無真正能夠替代的辦法。" ◇ **it is stressed that ...** *It must be stressed that this disease is very rare.* 必須着重指出，這種病非常罕見。◇ **~ how, what, etc. ...** *I cannot stress too much how important this is.* 這事的重要性我不用再三強調。

▸ **WORD/SYLLABLE** 單詞；音節 **2** 🔑 [T] **~ sth** to give extra force to a word or syllable when saying it 重讀；用重音讀： *You stress the first syllable in 'happiness'.* * happiness 一詞重讀第一個音節。 **3** 🔑 [I, T] to become or make sb become too anxious or tired to be able to relax（使）焦慮不安，疲憊不堪： **~ out** *I try not to stress out when things go wrong.* 出問題時，我盡量不緊張。◇ **~ sb (out)** *Driving in cities really stresses me (out).* 在城市裏開車讓我真的很緊張。

Synonyms 同義詞辨析

stress

emphasize

These words both mean to give extra force to a syllable, word or phrase when you are saying it. 以上兩詞均含重讀（音節、單詞或短語）之意。

stress to give extra force to a word or syllable when saying it 指重讀、用重音讀（單詞或音節）： *You stress the first syllable in 'happiness'.* * happiness 一詞重讀第一個音節。

emphasize to give extra force to a word or phrase when saying it, especially to show that it is important 指重讀、強調（詞或短語）、加強語氣： *'Let nothing ... nothing,' he emphasized the word, 'tempt you.'* 他強調說："要抵制一切…一切的誘惑。"

stressed 🔑 **AW** /strest/ *adj.*

1 🔑 (also *informal* ˌ**stressed** ˈ**out**) [not before noun] too anxious and tired to be able to relax 焦慮不安；心力交瘁 **2** (of a syllable 音節) pronounced with emphasis 重讀的 **OPP** **unstressed** **3** [only before noun] (*technical* 術語) that has had a lot of physical pressure put on it 受壓的；受應力的： *stressed metal* 受壓金屬

stress·ful **AW** /ˈstresfl/ *adj.* causing a lot of anxiety and worry 壓力重的；緊張的： *a stressful job* 造成沉重壓力的工作 ◇ *It was a stressful time for all of us.* 對我們所有人來說，那是一段艱難的時期。

ˈ**stress mark** *noun* a mark used to show where the stress is placed on a particular word or syllable 重音符號 ➲ see also PRIMARY STRESS, SECONDARY STRESS

ˈ**stress-timed** *adj.* (*phonetics* 語音) (of a language 語言) having a regular rhythm of PRIMARY STRESSES. English is considered to be a stress-timed language. 重音節拍的（如英語） ➲ compare SYLLABLE-TIMED

stretch 🔑 /stretʃ/ *verb, noun*

■ ***verb***

▸ **MAKE BIGGER/LOOSER** 使變大／變鬆 **1** 🔑 [T, I] **~ (sth)** to make sth longer, wider or looser, for example by pulling it; to become longer, etc. in this way 拉長；拽寬；撐大；抻鬆： *Is there any way of stretching shoes?* 有什麼辦法能把鞋撐大嗎？◇ *This sweater has stretched.* 這件毛衣給撐得變形了。 **2** 🔑 [I] (of cloth 織物) to become bigger or longer when you pull it and return to its original shape when you stop 有彈性（或彈力）： *The jeans stretch to provide a perfect fit.* 這條牛仔褲有彈性，可以完全貼身。

▸ **PULL TIGHT** 拉緊 **3** 🔑 [T] to pull sth so that it is smooth and tight 拉緊；拉直；繃緊： **~ sth** *Stretch the fabric tightly over the frame.* 把布在架子上繃緊。◇ **~ sth + adj.** *Make sure that the rope is stretched tight.* 務必要把繩子拉緊。

▸ **YOUR BODY** 身體 **4** 🔑 [I, T] to put your arms or legs out straight and contract your muscles 伸展；舒展： *He stretched and yawned lazily.* 他伸了伸懶腰，打了個哈

S

欠。◇ **~ sth** *The exercises are designed to stretch and tone your leg muscles.* 這些活動目的在於伸展和增強你的腿部肌肉。

▸ **REACH WITH ARM 伸手夠着 5** [I, T] to put out an arm or a leg in order to reach sth 伸出，伸長（胳膊、腿）：**+ adv./prep.** *She stretched across the table for the butter.* 她伸手到桌子那頭去拿黃油。◇ **~ sth + adv./prep.** *I stretched out a hand and picked up the book.* 我伸出一隻手，把書撿起來。

▸ **OVER AREA 覆蓋地域 6** [I] **+ adv./prep.** to spread over an area of land 延伸；綿延 **SYN extend**：*Fields and hills stretched out as far as we could see.* 放眼望去，田野山丘綿延不絕。

▸ **OVER TIME 時間 7** [I] **+ adv./prep.** to continue over a period of time 延續：*The town's history stretches back to before 1500.* 該鎮的歷史可以上溯到公元 1500 年以前。◇ *The talks look set to stretch into a second week.* 看來談判十有八九要延續到下個星期了。

▸ **MONEY/SUPPLIES/TIME 錢；物資；時間 8** [I] **~ (to sth)** (used in negative sentences and questions about an amount of money 用於否定句和疑問句，指一筆錢) to be enough to buy or pay for sth 足夠買（或支付）：*I need a new car, but my savings won't stretch to it.* 我需要一輛新車，但我的積蓄不夠。 **9** [T] **~ sb/sth** to make use of a lot of your money, supplies, time, etc.（大量地）使用，消耗：*The influx of refugees has* ***stretched*** *the country's resources* ***to the limit.*** 難民的大量湧入把這個國家的資源消耗殆盡。◇ *We can't take on any more work—we're fully stretched as it is.* 我們不能再接受其他工作了，現在我們已經滿負荷了。

▸ **SB'S SKILL/INTELLIGENCE 技能；智力 10** [T] **~ sb/sth** to make use of all sb's skill, intelligence, etc. 使竭盡所能；使全力以赴；使發揮出全部本領：*I need a job that will stretch me.* 我需要一份能讓我充分發揮才智的工作。

▸ **TRUTH/BELIEF 實情；信條 11** [T] **~ sth** to use sth in a way that would not normally be considered fair, acceptable, etc. 濫用；隨意歪曲：*He admitted that he had maybe* ***stretched the truth*** *a little* (= not been completely honest). 他承認可能有點言過其實了。◇ *The play's plot* ***stretches*** *credulity* ***to the limit.*** 這齣戲的劇情簡直就是胡編濫造。

IDM **stretch your 'legs** (*informal*) to go for a short walk after sitting for some time（久坐之後）散散步，活動活動腿腳：*It was good to get out of the car and stretch our legs.* 我們下了車活動活動腿腳，真不錯。 **stretch a 'point** to allow or do sth that is not usually acceptable, especially because of a particular situation 破例；通融 ➲ more at RULE *n.*

PHR V **,stretch 'out | ,stretch yourself 'out** to lie down, usually in order to relax or sleep 躺下（通常為休息或睡覺）：*He stretched himself out on the sofa and fell asleep.* 他在沙發上躺下睡着了。

■ ***noun***

▸ **AREA OF LAND/WATER 土地；水域 1** [C] **~ (of sth)** an area of land or water, especially a long one 一片；一泓；一段：*an unspoilt stretch of coastline* 一段未破壞原貌的海岸線 ◇ *a particularly dangerous stretch of road* 特別危險的路段 ◇ *You rarely see boats on this stretch of the river.* 這一河段船隻罕見。

▸ **PERIOD OF TIME 一段時間 2** [C] a continuous period of time（連續的）一段時間 **SYN spell**：*They worked in four-hour stretches.* 他們工作四小時一班。◇ *She used to read for hours* ***at a stretch*** (= without stopping). 她以前看書常常連看幾小時。 **3** [C, usually sing.] (*informal*) a period of time that sb spends in prison 服刑期：*He did a ten-year stretch for fraud.* 他因欺詐罪服刑十年。

▸ **OF BODY 身體 4** [C, U] an act of stretching out your arms or legs or your body and contracting the muscles; the state of being stretched 伸展；舒展：*We got out of the car and* ***had a*** *good* ***stretch.*** 我們下車好好舒展了一下身體。◇ *Only do these more difficult stretches when you are warmed up.* 要做了準備活動以後再做這些較難的伸展運動。◇ *Stay in this position and feel the stretch in your legs.* 保持這個姿勢，體會腿部繃緊的感覺。

▸ **OF FABRIC 織物 5** [U] the ability to be made longer or wider without breaking or tearing 彈性；伸縮性：*You need a material with plenty of stretch in it.* 你需要一種彈性很大的布料。◇ *stretch jeans* 彈力牛仔褲

▸ **ON RACETRACK 跑道 6** [C, usually sing.] a straight part at the end of a racing track（終點）直道 **SYN straight**：*the* ***finishing/home stretch*** 終點直道 ◇ (*figurative*) *The campaign has entered its final stretch.* 競選已進入最後衝刺階段。

IDM **at full 'stretch** using as much energy as possible, or the greatest possible amount of supplies 竭盡全力；以最大財力物力：*Fire crews have been operating at full stretch.* 各消防隊一直在全力以赴。 **not by any stretch of the imagination | by no stretch of the imagination** used to say strongly that sth is not true, even if you try to imagine or believe it 任憑怎麼想也不；再怎麼說也不：*She could not, by any stretch of the imagination, be called beautiful.* 再怎麼說，她也稱不上漂亮。

stretch·er /ˈstretʃə(r)/ *noun, verb*

■ ***noun*** a long piece of strong cloth with a pole on each side, used for carrying sb who is sick or injured and who cannot walk 擔架：*He was carried off on a stretcher.* 他被人用擔架抬走了。◇ *stretcher cases* (= people too badly injured to be able to walk) 必需用擔架抬的傷員

■ ***verb*** **~ sb + adv./prep.** [usually passive] to carry sb somewhere on a stretcher 用擔架抬：*He was stretchered off the pitch with a broken leg.* 他腿骨折了，從球場上抬了下去。

'stretcher-bearer *noun* a person who helps to carry a stretcher, especially in a war or when there is a very serious accident 抬擔架者

,stretch 'limo *noun* (also *formal* **,stretch limou'sine**) a very large car that has been made longer so that it can have extra seats 超長豪華轎車

'stretch marks *noun* [pl.] the marks that are left on a person's skin after it has been stretched, particularly after a woman has been pregnant（尤指女性生育後的）妊娠紋

stretchy /ˈstretʃi/ *adj.* (**stretch·ier**, **stretchi·est**) that can easily be made longer or wider without tearing or breaking 有彈性的：*stretchy fabric* 有彈性的織物

strew /struː/ *verb* (**strewed**, **strewed** or **strewed**, **strewn** /struːn/) **1** [usually passive] to cover a surface with things 把…佈滿（或散佈在）；在…上佈滿（或散播）**SYN scatter**：**~ A on, over, across, etc. B** *Clothes were strewn across the floor.* 衣服扔得滿地都是。◇ **~ B with A** *The floor was strewn with clothes.* 滿地都是衣服。◇ (*figurative*) *The way ahead is strewn with difficulties.* 前面的道路佈滿艱難險阻。 **2 ~ sth** to be spread or lying over a surface 佈滿；撒滿；散播在…上：*Leaves strewed the path.* 樹葉落滿小徑。

strewth /struːθ/ *exclamation* (*old-fashioned, BrE, slang*) used to express surprise, anger, etc.（表示驚奇、憤怒等）喲，哎呀，天哪

stri·ation /straɪˈeɪʃn/ *noun* [usually pl.] (*technical* 術語) a striped pattern on sth, especially on a muscle（尤指肌肉上的）條紋

stricken /ˈstrɪkən/ *adj.* (*formal*) **1** seriously affected by an unpleasant feeling or disease or by a difficult situation 受煎熬的；患病的；遭受挫折的：*She raised her stricken face and begged for help.* 她仰起苦悶的臉，乞求幫助。◇ *We went to the aid of the stricken boat.* 我們前去救助那艘失事的船。◇ **~ with/by sth** *Whole villages were stricken with the disease.* 整村整村的人染上了這種病。◇ *He was stricken by a heart attack on his fiftieth birthday.* 他在五十歲生日那天心臟病發作。 **2** (in compounds 構成複合詞) seriously affected by the thing mentioned 遭受…的；受…之困的：*poverty-stricken families* 貧困家庭 ➲ see also GRIEF-STRICKEN, HORROR-STRICKEN at HORROR-STRUCK, PANIC-STRICKEN

strict /strɪkt/ *adj.* (**strict·er**, **strict·est**)

1 that must be obeyed exactly 嚴格的（指必須恪守）：***strict rules/regulations/discipline*** 嚴格的規則／規章制度／紀律 ◇ *She left* ***strict instructions*** *that she was not to be disturbed.* 她嚴格指示務必不要打擾她。◇ *He told me* ***in the strictest confidence*** (= on the understanding that I would tell nobody else). 他相信我絕對口緊，便告訴了我。◇ *She's on a very strict diet.* 她正嚴格節食。 **2** demanding that rules, especially rules

S

about behaviour, should be obeyed 要求嚴格的；嚴厲的：*a **strict teacher/parent/disciplinarian*** 嚴格的教師 / 父（或母）親 / 執行紀律者 ◇ *She's very strict about things like homework.* 她對作業之類的事要求非常嚴格。◇ *They were always very strict with their children.* 他們對子女一向十分嚴格。 **3** obeying the rules of a particular religion, belief, etc. exactly 恪守教規（或信條等）的：*a strict Muslim* 恪守教規的穆斯林 ◇ *a strict vegetarian* 純粹的素食者 **4** [usually before noun] very exact and clearly defined 嚴密的；嚴謹的；精確的：*It wasn't illegal **in the strict sense** (**of the word**).* 嚴格說來，這不算違法。
▸ **strict·ness** *noun* [U]

strict·ly /ˈstrɪktli/ *adv.*
1 with a lot of control and rules that must be obeyed 嚴格地：*She was brought up very strictly.* 她從小家教很嚴。◇ *The industry is strictly regulated.* 這個行業有嚴格的管理。 **2** used to emphasize that sth happens or must happen in all circumstances（強調在一切情況都是如此）絕對地，無論如何 SYN **absolutely**：*Smoking is strictly forbidden.* 嚴禁吸煙。◇ *My letter is, of course, strictly private and confidential.* 當然，我的信純屬私人信件，務須保密。 **3** in all details; exactly 完全地；確切地：*This is not strictly true.* 這不完全正確。 **4** used to emphasize that sth only applies to one particular person, thing or situation（強調只適用於某人、物或情況）只，僅限於 SYN **purely**：*We'll look at the problem from a strictly legal point of view.* 我們將只從法律的角度來看待這個問題。◇ *I know we're friends, but this is strictly business.* 我知道我們是朋友，但這事完全是公務。
IDM **ˈstrictly speaking** if you are using words or rules in their exact or correct sense 嚴格說來：*Strictly speaking, the book is not a novel, but a short story.* 嚴格說來，這部小說不能算長篇，而是短篇。

stric·ture /ˈstrɪktʃə(r)/ *noun* (*formal*) **1** [usually pl.] **~ (on sb/sth)** a severe criticism, especially of sb's behaviour 指摘；非難 **2 ~ (against/on sth)** a rule or situation that restricts your behaviour 限制；約束；束縛 SYN **restriction**：*strictures against civil servants expressing political opinions* 對於公務員發表政治見解的禁令

stride /straɪd/ *verb, noun*
■ ***verb*** (*pt* **strode** /strəʊd; *NAmE* stroʊd/) [I] (not used in the perfect tenses 不用於完成時) **+ adv./prep.** to walk with long steps in a particular direction 大步走；闊步行走：*We strode across the snowy fields.* 我們大步流星地穿過雪封的曠野。◇ *She came striding along to meet me.* 她大步走上前來迎接我。
■ ***noun*** **1** one long step; the distance covered by a step 大步；一步（的距離）SYN **pace**：*He crossed the room in two strides.* 他兩大步跨到屋子另一頭。◇ *I was gaining on the other runners **with every stride**.* 我正一步步趕上其他運動員。 **2** your way of walking or running 步態；步伐：*his familiar purposeful stride* 他那熟悉而堅定的步伐 ◇ *She did not slow her stride until she was face to face with us.* 她沒有放慢腳步，逕直走到我們面前。 **3** an improvement in the way sth is developing 進展；進步；發展：*We're **making great strides** in the search for a cure.* 在探索治療辦法方面，我們正不斷取得重大進展。 **4 strides** [pl.] (*AustralE, informal*) trousers/pants 褲子
IDM **get into your ˈstride** (*BrE*) (*NAmE* **hit (your) ˈstride**) to begin to do sth with confidence and at a good speed after a slow, uncertain start 進入狀態；開始順利地做某事 **put sb off their ˈstride** to make sb take their attention off what they are doing and stop doing it so well 使分心；拖某人後腿 **(match sb) ˌstride for ˈstride** to keep doing sth as well as sb else, even though they keep making it harder for you 盡量不落後（於某人）**take sth in your ˈstride** (*BrE*) (*NAmE* **take sth in ˈstride**) to accept and deal with sth difficult without letting it worry you too much 從容處理；泰然處之 **without breaking ˈstride** (*especially NAmE*) without stopping what you are doing 步調不變；陣腳不亂

stri·dent /ˈstraɪdnt/ *adj.* **1** having a loud, rough and unpleasant sound 刺耳的：*a strident voice* 刺耳的嗓音 ◇ *strident music* 刺耳的音樂 **2** aggressive and determined 強硬的；咄咄逼人的：*He is a strident advocate of nuclear power.* 他是發展核能的堅定擁護者。◇ *strident criticism* 猛烈的抨擊 ▸ **stri·dency** /ˈstraɪdənsi/ *noun* [U] **stri·dent·ly** *adv.*

strife /straɪf/ *noun* **1** [U] (*formal* or *literary*) angry or violent disagreement between two people or groups of people 衝突；爭鬥；傾軋 SYN **conflict**：*civil strife* 內亂 ◇ *The country was torn apart by strife.* 這個國家被內部紛爭搞得四分五裂。 **2** (*AustralE, NZE*) trouble or difficulty of any kind 麻煩；糾紛；困難

strike /straɪk/ *verb, noun*
■ ***verb*** (**struck, struck** /strʌk/)
▸ **HIT SB/STH 擊打；碰撞 1** [T] **~ sb/sth** (*formal*) to hit sb/sth hard or with force 撞；碰；撞擊；碰撞：*The ship struck a rock.* 船觸礁了。◇ *The child ran into the road and was struck by a car.* 孩子跑到公路上給車撞了。◇ *The tree was **struck by lightning**.* 樹遭到雷擊。◇ *He fell, striking his head on the edge of the table.* 他摔倒了，頭碰在桌棱上。◇ *The stone struck her on the forehead.* 那塊石頭擊中她的額頭。➲ SYNONYMS at HIT **2** [T] **~ sb/sth** (**sth**) (*formal*) to hit sb/sth with your hand or a weapon 打；擊：*She struck him in the face.* 她摑了他一記耳光。◇ *He struck the table with his fist.* 他用拳頭打桌子。◇ *Who struck the first blow* (= started the fight)*?* 是誰先動手的？
▸ **KICK/HIT BALL 踢 / 擊球 3** [T] **~ sth** (*formal*) to hit or kick a ball, etc. 擊打，踢（球等）：*He walked up to the penalty spot and struck the ball firmly into the back of the net.* 他走到罰球點，穩穩地把球踢入網內。
▸ **ATTACK 攻擊 4** [I] to attack sb/sth, especially suddenly 突擊；攻擊：*The lion crouched ready to strike.* 獅子蹲身準備襲擊。◇ *Police fear that the killer may strike again.* 警方擔心殺人犯可能再次下手。
▸ **OF DISASTER/DISEASE 災難；疾病 5** [I, T] to happen suddenly and have a harmful or damaging effect on sb/sth 侵襲；爆發：*Two days later tragedy struck.* 兩天後悲劇發生了。◇ **~ sb/sth** *The area was struck by an outbreak of cholera.* 那一地區爆發了霍亂。
▸ **THOUGHT/IDEA/IMPRESSION 想法；念頭；印象 6** [T] (not used in the progressive tenses 不用於進行時) (of a thought or an idea 想法或念頭) to come into sb's mind suddenly 突然想到；一下子想起；猛地意識到：**~ sb** *An awful thought has just struck me.* 剛才我腦子裏突然閃過一個可怕的念頭。◇ *I was struck by her resemblance to my aunt.* 我猛然發現她長得跟我姑姑很像。◇ **it strikes sb how, what, etc. …** *It suddenly struck me how we could improve the situation.* 我一下子明白我們如何能改善局面了。 **7** [T] to give sb a particular impression 給（某人）以…印象；讓（某人）覺得：**~ sb (as sth)** *His reaction struck me as odd.* 他的反應令我詫異。◇ *How does the idea strike you?* 你覺得這個主意怎麼樣？◇ *She strikes me as a very efficient person.* 在我眼裏，她是個很幹練的人。◇ **it strikes sb that …** *It strikes me that nobody is really in favour of the changes.* 我覺得沒人真正贊成這些變動。
▸ **OF LIGHT 光 8** [T] **~ sth** to fall on a surface 照在…上；照射：*The windows sparkled as the sun struck the glass.* 陽光照得玻璃窗熠熠閃光。
▸ **DUMB/DEAF/BLIND 啞；聾；瞎 9** [T] **~ sb + adj.** [usually passive] to put sb suddenly into a particular state 頓時使處於某狀態：*to be struck dumb/deaf/blind* 一時什麼也說不出 / 聽不見 / 看不見
▸ **OF WORKERS 工人 10** [I] **~ (for sth)** to refuse to work, because of a disagreement over pay or conditions 罷工：*The union has voted to strike for a pay increase of 6%.* 工會投票決定罷工，要求加薪 6%。◇ *Striking workers picketed the factory.* 罷工的工人在工廠附近設置了糾察隊。
▸ **MATCH 火柴 11** [T, I] **~ (sth)** to rub sth such as a match against a surface so that it produces a flame; to produce a flame when rubbed against a rough surface 擦，劃（火柴）；擊出（火星）：*to strike a match on a wall* 在牆上擦火柴 ◇ *The sword struck sparks off the stone floor.* 劍砍在石地上，火星飛濺。◇ *The matches were damp and he couldn't make them strike.* 火柴受潮了，他劃不着。
▸ **OF CLOCK 鐘 12** [I, T] to show the time by making a ringing noise, etc. 敲；鳴；報時 SYN **chime**：*Did you hear the clock strike?* 你聽見鐘響了嗎？◇ **~ sth** *The clock has just struck three.* 時鐘剛剛敲過三點。

S

▸ **MAKE SOUND 發出聲音 13** [T] **~ sth** to produce a musical note, sound, etc. by pressing a key or hitting sth 彈奏；奏響；發出（聲音）：*to strike a chord on the piano* 在鋼琴上奏出和弦

▸ **GOLD/OIL, ETC. 金、石油等 14** [T] **~ sth** to discover gold, oil, etc. by digging or DRILLING 開採出；鑽探到：*They had struck oil!* 他們開採出了石油！

▸ **GO WITH PURPOSE 有目的地走 15** [I] **~ (off/out)** to go somewhere with great energy or purpose 行進；加勁走：*We left the road and struck off across the fields.* 我們下了公路，穿過曠野往前走。

IDM **be ˈstruck by/on/with sb/sth** (*informal*) to be impressed or interested by sb/sth; to like sb/sth very much 被某人（或某物）打動；迷戀某人（或某物）：*I was struck by her youth and enthusiasm.* 她年輕熱情，把我迷住了。◇ *We're not very struck on that new restaurant.* 我們不大看得上那家新餐館。 **strike a ˈbalance (between A and B)** to manage to find a way of being fair to two opposing things; to find an acceptable position which is between two things（在對立二者之間）找到折衷辦法；平衡（對立的雙方） **strike a ˈbargain/ˈdeal** to make an agreement with sb in which both sides have an advantage 達成（對雙方都有利的）協議 **strike a blow for/against/at sth** to do sth in support of/against a belief, principle, etc. 維護（或損害）某種信念或原則等：*He felt that they had struck a blow for democracy.* 他感覺他們維護了民主制度。 **strike fear, etc. into sb/sb's heart** (*formal*) to make sb be afraid, etc. 使某人感到恐懼等 **strike ˈgold** to find or do sth that brings you a lot of success or money 打開成功（或財富）之門；踏上通往成功（或財富）之路：*He has struck gold with his latest novel.* 他憑藉最新的一部小說叩開了成功之門。 **strike it ˈrich** (*informal*) to get a lot of money, especially suddenly or unexpectedly 暴富；（意外）發大財 **strike (it) ˈlucky** (*informal*) to have good luck 交好運 **strike a ˈpose/an ˈattitude** to hold your body in a particular way to create a particular impression 擺出某種姿態 **strike while the iron is ˈhot** (*saying*) to make use of an opportunity immediately 趁熱打鐵 **ORIGIN** This expression refers to a blacksmith making a shoe for a horse. He has to strike/hammer the iron while it is hot enough to bend into the shape of the shoe. 原意是指打馬掌的鐵匠必須趁熱打鐵才能將其彎成馬蹄形。 **within ˈstriking distance (of sth)** near enough to be reached or attacked easily; near enough to reach or attack sth easily 近在咫尺；在攻擊距離之內：*The beach is within striking distance.* 海灘近在咫尺。◇ *The cat was now within striking distance of the duck.* 此時，貓就在可攻擊鴨子的距離內。➲ more at CHORD, HARD *adj.*, HOME *adv.*, LIGHTNING *n.*, NOTE *n.*, PAY DIRT

PHR V **ˈstrike at sb/sth** **1** to try to hit sb/sth, especially with a weapon 朝…打去：*He struck at me repeatedly with a stick.* 他拿着棍子一再朝我打過來。 **2** to cause damage or have a serious effect on sb/sth 損害；有損於；嚴重影響到：*to strike at the root of the problem* 從根源入手解決問題 ◇ *criticisms that* ***strike at the heart of*** *the party's policies* 直指該黨政策之要害的批評意見 **ˌstrike ˈback (at/against sb)** to try to harm sb in return for an attack or injury you have received 反擊；回擊 **ˌstrike sb ˈdown** [usually passive] **1** (of a disease, etc. 疾病等) to make sb unable to lead an active life; to make sb seriously ill; to kill sb 摧垮；使病倒；使喪命：*He was struck down by cancer at the age of thirty.* 他三十歲那年被癌症奪去了性命。 **2** to hit sb very hard, so that they fall to the ground 擊倒，撞倒（某人） **ˌstrike sth ↔ˈdown** (*especially NAmE*) to decide that a law is illegal and should not apply 取消，撤銷（法規）：*The Supreme Court struck down a Texas state law.* 最高法院撤銷了得克薩斯州的一條法律。 **ˌstrike sth↔ˈoff** to remove sth with a sharp blow; to cut sth off 打掉；砍掉；砍下：*He struck off the rotten branches with an axe.* 他用斧子把枯樹枝砍掉。 **ˌstrike sb/sth ˈoff (sth)** (also **ˌstrike sb/sth ˈfrom sth**) to remove sb/sth's name from sth, such as the list of members of a professional group 把某人（或某事物）除名：*Strike her name off the list.* 把她的名字從名單上刪掉。◇ *The doctor was struck off* (= not allowed to continue to work as a doctor) *for incompetence.* 那名醫生因不稱職而遭取消了執業資格。 **ˌstrike ˈout 1** to start being independent 獨立出去；自立謀生：*I knew it was time I struck out on my own.* 我知道我該獨立謀生了。 **2** (*NAmE, informal*) to fail or be unsuccessful 失敗；砸鍋：*The movie struck out and didn't win a single Oscar.* 那部影片砸鍋了，奧斯卡獎一項都沒得着。 **ˌstrike ˈout (at sb/sth) 1** to aim a sudden violent blow at sb/sth 揮拳猛擊；猛打：*He lost his temper and struck out wildly.* 他發了脾氣，大打出手。 **2** to criticize sb/sth, especially in a public speech or in a book or newspaper（尤指公開）抨擊：*In a recent article she strikes out at her critics.* 她最近寫了一篇文章，對批評她的人予以駁斥。 **ˌstrike ˈout | ˌstrike sb↔ˈout** (in BASEBALL 棒球) to fail to hit the ball three times and therefore not be allowed to continue hitting; to make sb do this（使）三擊不中出局 ➲ related noun STRIKEOUT **ˌstrike sth↔ˈout/ˈthrough** to remove sth by drawing a line through it 畫掉；刪去 **SYN** **cross out**：*The editor struck out the whole paragraph.* 編輯把整段全部刪去了。 **ˌstrike ˈout (for/towards sth)** to move in a determined way (towards sth)（奮力朝某處）去；趕往（某處）：*He struck out* (= started swimming) *towards the shore.* 他朝岸邊游去。 **ˌstrike ˈup (with sth) | ˌstrike ˈup sth** (of a band, an ORCHESTRA, etc. 樂隊等) to begin to play a piece of music 開始演奏：*The orchestra struck up and the curtain rose.* 管弦樂隊奏起音樂，幕啟。◇ *The band struck up a waltz.* 樂隊奏起一支華爾茲舞曲。 **ˌstrike ˈup sth (with sb)** to begin a friendship, a relationship, a conversation, etc.（和某人）建立友誼，開始來往，交談起來：*He would often strike up conversations with complete strangers.* 他愛和完全不相識的人攀談。

■ ***noun***

▸ **OF WORKERS 工人 1** 🔑 a period of time when an organized group of employees of a company stops working because of a disagreement over pay or conditions 罷工；罷課；罷市：*the train drivers' strike* 火車司機罷工 ◇ *a strike by teachers* 教師舉行的罷課 ◇ *an* ***unofficial/a one-day strike*** 未得到批准的／為期一天的罷工 ◇ *Air traffic controllers are threatening to* ***come out on/go on strike****.* 空中交通管制員威脅要舉行罷工。◇ *Half the workforce are now* (***out***) ***on strike****.* 現在有半數職工罷工。◇ *The train drivers have voted to* ***take strike action****.* 火車司機投票表決採取罷工行動。◇ *The student union has called for a* ***rent strike*** (= a refusal to pay rent as a protest). 學生會呼籲拒繳房租。➲ see also GENERAL STRIKE, HUNGER STRIKE

▸ **ATTACK 攻擊 2** 🔑 a military attack, especially by aircraft dropping bombs 軍事進攻；襲擊；（尤指）空襲：*an* ***air strike*** 空襲 ◇ *They decided to launch a* ***pre-emptive strike****.* 他們決定先發制人的攻擊。

▸ **HITTING/KICKING 擊；踢 3** [usually sing.] an act of hitting or kicking sth/sb 擊；打；踢：*His spectacular strike in the second half made the score 2–0.* 他在下半場令人歎為觀止的一腳射門把比分改寫為 2:0。➲ see also BIRD STRIKE, LIGHTNING STRIKE

▸ **IN BASEBALL 棒球 4** an unsuccessful attempt to hit the ball 擊球未中；擊

▸ **IN BOWLING 保齡球 5** a situation in TENPIN BOWLING when a player knocks down all the pins with the first ball 全中（第一球撞倒全部十柱球）

▸ **DISCOVERY OF OIL 石油的發現 6** [usually sing.] a sudden discovery of sth valuable, especially oil（珍貴東西的）意外發現；（尤指石油的）發現

▸ **BAD THING/ACTION 壞事；不利的行動 7** (*NAmE*) **~ (against sb/sth)** a bad thing or action that damages sb/sth's reputation（有損聲譽的）不利因素，打擊：*The amount of fuel that this car uses is a big strike against it.* 耗油量大是這輛車的一大缺點。

IDM **ˌthree strikes and you're ˈout | the ˌthree ˈstrikes rule** used to describe a law which says that people who commit three crimes will automatically go to prison 三振出局法（三次犯罪即入獄的法律） **ORIGIN** From baseball, in which a batter who misses the ball three times is out. 源自棒球，擊球手三次擊球不中即出局。

'strike-bound *adj.* unable to operate because employees have stopped working as a protest 因罷工而停頓的：*a strike-bound airport* 因罷工而陷於癱瘓的機場

'strike-breaker *noun* a person who continues to work while other employees are on strike; a person who is employed to replace people who are on strike 破壞罷工者；頂替罷工者工作的人 ➲ compare BLACKLEG ▶ **'strike-breaking** *noun* [U]

'strike force *noun* [C+sing./pl. v.] a military or police force that is ready to act quickly when necessary 突擊部隊；警察快速行動部隊

strike·out /'straɪkaʊt/ *noun* (in BASEBALL 棒球) a situation in which the player who is supposed to be hitting the ball has to stop because he or she has tried to hit the ball three times and failed （三擊不中）出局

striker /'straɪkə(r)/ *noun* **1** a worker who has stopped working because of a disagreement over pay or conditions 罷工者；罷課者；罷市者 **2** (in football (SOCCER) 足球) a player whose main job is to attack and try to score goals 前鋒

'strike rate *noun* [usually sing.] (*sport* 體) the number of times a player is successful in relation to the number of times they try to score or win 進球率；得分率

'strike zone *noun* (in BASEBALL 棒球) the area between a BATTER's upper arms and their knees, to which the ball must be PITCHED 好球區，好球帶（指擊球手大臂和膝部之間的部位，投球必須投中此區）

strik·ing 0➡ /'straɪkɪŋ/ *adj.*
1 0➡ interesting and unusual enough to attract attention 引人注目的；異乎尋常的；顯著的 SYN **marked**：*a striking feature* 顯著的特徵 ◇ *She bears* ***a striking resemblance*** *to her older sister.* 她酷似她姐姐。◇ ***In striking contrast to*** *their brothers, the girls were both intelligent and charming.* 姑娘們既聰明伶俐，又嫵媚動人，跟她們的兄弟形成鮮明的對照。➲ LANGUAGE BANK at SURPRISING **2** 0➡ very attractive, often in an unusual way 嫵媚動人的；標致的；俊秀的 SYN **stunning**：*striking good looks* 姣好的面容 ▶ **strik·ing·ly** *adv.*：*The two polls produced strikingly different results.* 兩次投票產生的結果截然不同。◇ *She is strikingly beautiful.* 她美麗動人。

Strim·mer™ /'strɪmə(r)/ *noun* (*BrE*) an electric garden tool held in the hands and used for cutting grass that is difficult to cut with a larger machine 草坪修剪器 ➲ VISUAL VOCAB page V19

Strine /'straɪn/ (also **strine**) *noun* (*informal*) **1** [U] Australian English, especially when spoken in an informal way and with a strong accent 斯確拉因（澳大利亞英語，尤指地方口音重的英語）**2** [C] an Australian 澳大利亞人 ▶ **Strine** *adj.*：*a Strine accent* 澳大利亞口音

string 0➡ /strɪŋ/ *noun, verb, adj.*
■ ***noun***
▸ FOR TYING/FASTENING 捆 / 繫用 **1** 0➡ [U, C] material made of several threads twisted together, used for tying things together; a piece of string used to fasten or pull sth or keep sth in place 細繩；線；帶子：*a* ***piece/length of string*** 一根 / 一段細繩 ◇ *He wrapped the package in brown paper and tied it with string.* 他用棕色包裝紙把包裹包好，又用細繩捆上。◇ *The key is hanging on a string by the door.* 鑰匙拴在門邊的帶子上。➲ picture at ROPE ➲ see also DRAWSTRING, G-STRING, THE PURSE STRINGS
▸ THINGS JOINED 串接物 **2** 0➡ [C] a set or series of things that are joined together, for example on a string 一串：*a string of pearls* 一串珍珠 ◇ *The molecules join together to form long strings.* 分子連接在一起形成長串。➲ VISUAL VOCAB page V65
▸ SERIES 系列 **3** [C] a series of things or people that come closely one after another 一系列；一連串；一批：*a string of hits* 接二連三的成功 ◇ *He owns a string of racing stables.* 他有好多個賽馬訓練場。
▸ COMPUTING 計算機技術 **4** [C] a series of characters (= letters, numbers, etc.) 字符串；信息串
▸ MUSICAL INSTRUMENTS 樂器 **5** [C] a tightly stretched piece of wire, NYLON, or CATGUT on a musical instrument, that produces a musical note when the instrument is played 弦 ➲ VISUAL VOCAB pages V34, V36 **6 the strings** [pl.] the group of musical instruments in an ORCHESTRA that have strings, for example VIOLINS; the people who play them （管弦樂團的）弦樂器，弦樂器組：*The opening theme is taken up by the strings.* 開始的主旋律由弦樂繼續發展。➲ VISUAL VOCAB page V34 ➲ compare BRASS (2), PERCUSSION (1), WOODWIND
▸ ON TENNIS RACKET 網球拍 **7** [C] any of the tightly stretched pieces of NYLON, etc. in a RACKET, used for hitting balls in TENNIS and some other games 弦
▸ CONDITIONS 條件 **8 strings** [pl.] special conditions or restrictions 特定條件（或限制）：*Major loans like these always come with strings.* 諸如此類的大宗貸款總有一些附帶條件。◇ *It's a business proposition, pure and simple.* ***No strings attached.*** 這只是個業務建議，僅此而已。沒有任何附帶條件。
IDM **have another string/more strings to your bow** (*BrE*) to have more than one skill or plan that you can use if you need to 還另有一手；有兩手準備 ➲ more at APRON, LONG *adj.*, PULL *v.*
■ ***verb*** (**strung, strung** /strʌŋ/)
▸ HANG DECORATION 懸掛裝飾物 **1** to hang or tie sth in place, especially as decoration 懸掛；繫；紮：**~ sth + adv./prep.** *We strung paper lanterns up in the trees.* 我們把紙燈籠掛在樹上。◇ **~ A on, along, in, etc. B** *Flags were strung out along the route.* 沿途懸掛着旗子。◇ **~ B with A** *The route was strung with flags.* 沿途懸掛着旗子。
▸ JOIN THINGS 串接東西 **2 ~ sth + adv./prep.** to put a series of small objects on string, etc.; to join things together with string, etc. 用線（或細繩等）串，把…連在一起 SYN **thread**：*She had strung the shells on a silver chain.* 她把貝殼串在一條銀鏈子上。◇ (*figurative*) *carbon atoms strung together to form giant molecules* 連在一起構成巨分子的碳原子
▸ RACKET/MUSICAL INSTRUMENT 球拍；樂器 **3 ~ sth** to put a string or strings on a RACKET or musical instrument 給…裝弦 ➲ see also HIGHLY STRUNG
PHR V **,string sb a'long** (*informal*) to allow sb to believe sth that is not true, for example that you love them, intend to help them, etc. 哄；愚弄：*She has no intention of giving you a divorce; she's just stringing you along.* 她無意跟你離婚，不過是騙着你玩的。**,string a'long (with sb)** (*BrE, informal*) to go somewhere with sb, especially because you have nothing else to do 跟隨；伴隨 **,string sth↔'out** to make sth last longer than expected or necessary 延長；拖長時間：*They seem determined to string the talks out for an indefinite period.* 他們好像一心要把談判無限期地拖下去。➲ see also STRUNG OUT **,string sth↔to'gether** to combine words or phrases to form sentences 把（單詞或短語）聯成句子：*I can barely string two words together in Japanese.* 我那點日語只能勉強把兩個單詞拼湊在一起。**,string sb↔'up** (*informal*) to kill sb by hanging them, especially illegally （尤指非法地）吊死某人
■ ***adj.*** [only before noun]
▸ MUSICAL INSTRUMENT 樂器 **1** consisting of musical instruments that have strings; connected with these musical instruments 由弦樂器組成的；弦樂器的：*a string quartet* 弦樂四重奏 ◇ *a string player* 弦樂器演奏者
▸ MADE OF STRING 用線製成 **2** made of string or sth like string 線織的；線的：*a* ***string bag/vest*** 網兜；網眼背心

,string 'bass *noun* a word for a DOUBLE BASS, used especially by JAZZ musicians 低音提琴（尤為爵士樂樂師用語）

,string 'bean *noun* **1** (*BrE*) = RUNNER BEAN **2** (*NAmE*) = GREEN BEAN

,stringed 'instrument *noun* any musical instrument with strings that you play with your fingers or with a BOW 弦樂器 ➲ VISUAL VOCAB page V34

strin·gent /'strɪndʒənt/ *adj.* (*formal*) **1** (of a law, rule, regulation, etc. 法律、規則、規章等) very strict and that must be obeyed 嚴格的；嚴厲的：*stringent air quality regulations* 嚴格的空氣質量管理條例 **2** (of financial conditions 財政狀況) difficult and very strictly controlled because there is not much money 緊縮的；短缺的；銀根緊的：*the government's stringent economic policies*

S

政府緊縮銀根的經濟政策 ▸ **strin·gency** /-nsi/ *noun* [U]：*a period of financial stringency* 財政緊縮時期 **strin·gent·ly** *adv.*：*The rules are stringently enforced.* 這些條例得到嚴格執行。

string·er /ˈstrɪŋə(r)/ *noun* a journalist who is not on the regular staff of a newspaper, but who often supplies stories for it 特約記者

ˌstring ˈvest *noun* (*especially BrE*) a man's VEST made from a type of cloth with a regular pattern of large holes（男式）網眼背心

stringy /ˈstrɪŋi/ *adj.* (*disapproving*) **1** (of hair 頭髮) long and thin and looking as if it has not been washed 細長而乾枯的；細長而稀疏的 **2** (of food 食物) containing long thin pieces like string and difficult to chew 多筋的；纖維多而不嫩的；柴的：*tough, stringy meat* 又老筋又多的肉 **3** (of a person or part of their body 人或人體的一部份) thin so that you can see the muscles 瘦得露出筋的：*a stringy neck* 瘦得青筋畢露的脖子

strip 0→ /strɪp/ *verb, noun*

■ **verb** (-pp-)

▸ **TAKE OFF CLOTHES** 脫衣 **1** 0→ [I, T] to take off all or most of your clothes or another person's clothes 脫光衣服；脫掉大部份衣服；扒光…的衣服 **SYN** **undress**：*I stripped and washed myself all over.* 我脫掉衣服，把全身洗了洗。◇ **~ down to sth** *She stripped down to her underwear.* 她把衣服脫得只剩下了內衣。◇ **~ (sth) off** *We stripped off and ran down to the water.* 我們脫掉衣服，跑進水裏。◇ **~ sb (to sth)** *He stood there* ***stripped to the waist*** (= he had no clothes on the upper part of his body). 他脫光了上衣站在那裏。◇ **~ sb + adj.** *He was* ***stripped naked*** *and left in a cell.* 他被扒得一絲不掛，丟在一間牢房裏。 **2** [I] to take off your clothes as a form of entertainment; to perform a STRIPTEASE 進行脫衣表演；表演脫衣舞

▸ **REMOVE LAYER** 除去一層 **3** 0→ [T] to remove a layer from sth, especially so that it is completely exposed 除去，剝去（一層）；（尤指）剝光：**~ sth (off)** *Strip off all the existing paint.* 把現有的油漆全部刮掉。◇ *After the guests had gone, I stripped all the beds* (= removed all the sheets in order to wash them). 客人走後，我把鋪的牀單全都撤了下來。◇ **~ A off/from B** *Deer had stripped all the bark off the tree.* 鹿把樹皮全都啃光了。◇ **~ B of A** *Deer had stripped the tree of its bark.* 鹿啃掉了樹皮。

▸ **REMOVE EVERYTHING** 拿走所有東西 **4** [T] to remove all the things from a place and leave it empty 從（某處）拿走所有東西；使（某處）空無一物：**~ sth (out)** *We had to strip out all the old wiring and start again.* 我們不得不將原有的線路全部拆除，從頭再來。◇ **~ sth + adj.** *Thieves had stripped the house bare.* 竊賊把房子劫掠一空。

▸ **MACHINE** 機器 **5** [T] **~ sth (down)** to separate a machine, etc. into parts so that they can be cleaned or repaired 拆卸；拆開 **SYN** **dismantle**：*They taught us how to strip down a car engine and put it back together again.* 他們教我們拆卸、安裝汽車引擎。

▸ **PUNISHMENT** 懲罰 **6** [T] **~ sb of sth** to take away property or honours from sb, as a punishment 剝奪；褫奪：*He was disgraced and stripped of his title.* 他名譽掃地，被取消了頭銜。

PHR V **ˌstrip sth↔aˈway** **1** to remove a layer from sth 剝去；剝下；揭去：*First, you need to strip away all the old plaster.* 首先，你得把原來的灰泥全部刮掉。 **2** to remove anything that is not true or necessary 揭去，揭穿，清除（虛假或不必要的東西）：*The movie aims to strip away the lies surrounding Kennedy's life.* 這部電影旨在揭穿有關肯尼迪生平的種種謊言。

■ **noun**

▸ **LONG, NARROW PIECE** 條狀物 **1** 0→ a long narrow piece of paper, metal, cloth, etc.（紙、金屬、織物等）條，帶：*a strip of material* 一塊布條 ◇ *Cut the meat into strips.* 把肉切成條。➲ see also RUMBLE STRIP **2** 0→ a long narrow area of land, sea, etc.（陸地、海域等）狹長地帶；帶狀水域：*the Gaza Strip* 加沙地帶 ◇ *The islands are separated by a narrow strip of water.* 兩個島之間一衣帶水。➲ see also AIRSTRIP, LANDING STRIP

▸ **OF SPORTS TEAM** 運動隊 **3** [usually sing.] (*BrE*) (*NAmE* **uniform**) the uniform that is worn by the members of a sports team when they are playing 隊服：*Juventus in their famous black and white strip* 身穿他們聞名遐邇的黑白條隊服的尤文圖斯隊 ◇ *the team's* ***away strip*** (= that they use when playing games away from home) 球隊的客場隊服 ➲ VISUAL VOCAB page V44

▸ **TAKING CLOTHES OFF** 脫衣 **4** [usually sing.] an act of taking your clothes off, especially in a sexually exciting way and in front of an audience 脫衣舞：*to do a strip* 表演脫衣舞 ◇ *a strip show* 脫衣舞表演 ➲ see also STRIPTEASE

▸ **STREET** 街道 **5** (*NAmE*) a street that has many shops, stores, restaurants, etc. along it 商業街：*Sunset Strip* 森塞特商業街

▸ **PICTURE STORY** 連環畫 **6** (*NAmE*) = COMIC STRIP **IDM** see TEAR[1] *v.*

ˌstrip carˈtoon (also **cartoon**) *noun* (*BrE*) = COMIC STRIP

ˈstrip club (also **ˈstrip joint** especially in *NAmE*) *noun* a club where people go to watch performers take their clothes off in a sexually exciting way 脫衣舞夜總會

stripe 0→ /straɪp/ *noun*

1 0→ a long narrow line of colour, that is a different colour from the areas next to it 條紋；線條：*a zebra's black and white stripes* 斑馬的黑白條紋 ◇ *a white tablecloth with red stripes* 白地紅條的桌布 ➲ see also PINSTRIPE, THE STARS AND STRIPES **2** a narrow piece of cloth, often in the shape of a V, that is worn on the uniform of a soldier or police officer to show their rank（軍裝或警服上表示等級的）條，槓 **3** (*especially NAmE*) a type, category or opinion 種類；類型；觀點：*politicians* ***of every stripe*** 形形色色的政界人士 ◇ *commentators* ***of all political stripes*** 持各種政治觀點的評論員 ◇ *She's an educator* ***of a very different*** *stripe.* 她完全是另外一種類型的教育家。

striped 0→ /straɪpt/ (also *BrE, informal* **stripy**) *adj.* marked with a pattern of stripes 有條紋的：*a striped shirt* 條紋襯衫 ◇ *a blue and white striped jacket* 藍白條上衣 ➲ VISUAL VOCAB page V61

ˈstrip light *noun* a light consisting of a long glass tube that is used especially in offices, kitchens, etc. 長條狀燈 ▸ **ˈstrip lighting** *noun* [U]

strip·ling /ˈstrɪplɪŋ/ *noun* (*old-fashioned* or *humorous*) a young man who is older than a boy but who does not seem to be a real man yet 年輕男子；小伙子

ˈstrip mall *noun* (*NAmE*) a line of shops/stores and restaurants beside a main road（公路旁邊的）購物飲食街，商店街

ˈstrip mining *noun* [U] (*NAmE*) a type of mining in which coal is taken out of the ground near the surface 露天開採；露天剝採 ➲ see also OPENCAST

ˌstripped-ˈdown *adj.* [usually before noun] **1** keeping only the most basic or essential features, with everything else removed 只保留最基本特徵的；精簡的；簡約的：*a stripped-down version of the song* 這首歌的簡約版 **2** (of a machine or vehicle 機器或車輛) taken to pieces, with all the parts removed 拆卸的；拆開的

strip·per /ˈstrɪpə(r)/ *noun* **1** [C] a performer who takes his or her clothes off in a sexually exciting way in front of an audience 脫衣舞演員：*a male stripper* 脫衣舞男演員 **2** [U, C] (especially in compounds 尤用於構成複合詞) a substance or tool that is used for removing paint, etc. from sth 剝離劑；脫漆劑；剝離器：*paint stripper* 脫漆劑

ˈstrip search *noun* an act of searching a person for illegal drugs, weapons, etc., for example at an airport or in a prison, after they have been made to take off all their clothes（對懷疑非法攜帶毒品、武器等的人進行的）光身搜查 ▸ **ˈstrip-search** *verb* **~ sb**

strip·tease /ˈstrɪptiːz/ *noun* [C, U] a form of entertainment, for example in a bar or club, when a performer removes his or her clothes in a sexually exciting way, usually to music, in front of an audience 脫衣舞

stripy (also **stripey**) /ˈstraɪpi/ *adj.* (*BrE, informal*) = STRIPED：*a stripy jumper* 條紋套頭毛衣

strive /straɪv/ *verb* (**strove** /strəʊv; *NAmE* stroʊv/, **striven** /ˈstrɪvn/ or *less frequent* **strived**, **strived**) [I] (*formal*) to

S

try very hard to achieve sth 努力；奮鬥；力爭；力求：~ (**for sth**) *We encourage all members to strive for the highest standards.* 我們鼓勵所有成員為達到最高標準而努力。◇ ~ (**against sth**) *striving against corruption* 與腐敗現象作鬥爭 ◇ ~ **to do sth** *Newspaper editors all strive to be first with a story.* 報紙編輯都力爭率先報道。 ▸ **striv·ing** *noun* [U, sing.]: *our striving for perfection* 我們爭取完善的努力

strobe /strəʊb; *NAmE* stroʊb/ (also **'strobe light**) *noun* a bright light that flashes rapidly on and off, used especially at DISCOS 頻閃閃光燈（尤用於迪斯科舞廳）

strob·ing /'strəʊbɪŋ; *NAmE* 'stroʊb-/ *noun* [U] (*technical* 術語) the effect, sometimes seen in the lines and stripes in a television picture, of sudden movements or flashing 頻閃，殘影（有時出現於電視圖像條紋中的突然抖動或閃光）

strode *past tense of* STRIDE

stroke 🔑 /strəʊk; *NAmE* stroʊk/ *noun, verb*

■ ***noun***

▸ **HITTING MOVEMENT** 擊打動作 **1** 🔑 an act of hitting a ball, for example with a BAT or RACKET 擊球（動作）：*What a beautiful stroke!* 擊球動作多漂亮呀！◇ *He won by two strokes* (= in GOLF, by taking two fewer strokes than his opponent). 他以少於對手兩杆的成績獲勝。 **2** a single movement of the arm when hitting sb/sth（打、擊等的）一下，一擊：*His punishment was six strokes of the cane.* 給他的懲罰是捱六教鞭。

▸ **IN SWIMMING/ROWING** 游泳；划船 **3** any of a series of repeated movements in swimming or ROWING 划水動作；划槳動作：*She took a few more strokes to reach the bank.* 她又划幾下，游到了岸邊。 ➲ **VISUAL VOCAB** page V45 **4** (often in compounds 常構成複合詞) a style of swimming 游泳姿勢：*Butterfly is the only stroke I can't do.* 只有蝶泳我不會。 ➲ see also BACKSTROKE, BREASTSTROKE **5** the person who sets the speed at which everyone in a boat ROWS（指揮船上其他槳手的）尾槳手

▸ **GENTLE TOUCH** 撫摩 **6** [usually sing.] (*especially BrE*) an act of moving your hand gently over a surface, usually several times 輕撫；撫摩：*He gave the cat a stroke.* 他撫摩了一下貓。

▸ **OF PEN/BRUSH** 筆；刷子 **7** a mark made by moving a pen, brush, etc. once across a surface 一筆；一畫；筆畫：*to paint with fine brush strokes* 一小刷一小刷地刷漆 ◇ ***At the stroke of a pen*** (= by signing sth) *they removed thousands of people from the welfare system.* 他們大筆一揮，就把成千上萬的人排除在福利制度之外。

▸ **ACTION** 行動 **8** ~ (**of sth**) a single successful action or event（成功的）舉動；（高明的）舉措；（巧妙的）辦法；（成功的）事情：*Your idea was a* ***stroke of genius.*** 你的主意很高明。◇ *It was a* ***stroke of luck*** *that I found you here.* 我在這兒看見你純屬巧遇。◇ *It was a* ***bold stroke*** *to reveal the identity of the murderer on the first page.* 在頭版上披露謀殺犯的身分，這是一個大膽的舉措。◇ *She* ***never does a stroke*** (***of work***) (= never does any work). 她一向什麼活兒都不幹。 ➲ see also MASTERSTROKE

▸ **OF CLOCK** 鐘 **9** each of the sounds made by a clock or bell giving the hours 鐘聲；鳴；敲：*At the first stroke it will be 9 o'clock exactly.* 等到鐘敲第一下時就是 9 點整。◇ ***on the stroke of*** *three* (= at 3 o'clock exactly) 三點整

▸ **ILLNESS** 疾病 **10** a sudden serious illness when a blood VESSEL (= tube) in the brain bursts or is blocked, which can cause death or the loss of the ability to move or to speak clearly 中風：*to* ***have/suffer a stroke*** 患中風 ◇ *The stroke left him partly paralysed.* 他因中風身體局部癱瘓了。

IDM **at a (single) 'stroke | at one 'stroke** with a single immediate action 一下子；一舉：*They threatened to cancel the whole project at a stroke.* 他們威脅要一下子砍掉整個項目。 **put sb off their 'stroke** (*BrE*) to make sb make a mistake or hesitate in what they are doing 擾亂某人；使某人亂了方寸

■ ***verb***

▸ **TOUCH GENTLY** 輕撫 **1** 🔑 ~ **sth** (*especially BrE*) to move your hand gently and slowly over an animal's fur or hair 輕撫，撫摩（動物的毛皮）：*He's a beautiful dog. Can I stroke him?* 這隻狗真漂亮，我可以摸一摸嗎？ ➲ see also PET *v.* (1) **2** 🔑 ~ **sth/sb** to move your hand gently over a surface, sb's hair, etc. 輕撫，撫摩（物體表面或頭髮等）：*He stroked her hair affectionately.* 他深情地撫摩着她的頭髮。

▸ **MOVE STH GENTLY** 輕挪 **3** ~ **sth + adv./prep.** to move sth somewhere with a gentle movement 輕挪；輕觸；輕拭：*She stroked away his tears.* 她輕輕拭去他的眼淚。◇ *He stroked the ball between the posts.* 他輕輕一觸，把球踢進門柱之間。

▸ **BE NICE TO SB** 待某人好 **4** ~ **sb** (*informal, especially NAmE*) to be very nice to sb, especially to get them to do what you want 待（某人）非常好；（尤指）順着（某人）以便為自己辦事

'stroke play (also **'medal play**) *noun* [U] a way of playing GOLF in which your score depends on the number of times you hit the ball in the whole game, rather than on the number of holes that you win（高爾夫球）比杆賽 ➲ compare MATCH PLAY

stroll /strəʊl; *NAmE* stroʊl/ *verb, noun*

■ ***verb*** [I] (+ **adv./prep.**) to walk somewhere in a slow relaxed way 散步；遛達；閒逛：*People were strolling along the beach.* 人們在海灘漫步。

■ ***noun*** a slow relaxed walk 散步；遛達；閒逛：*We went for a stroll in the park.* 我們去公園散了散步。

stroll·er /'strəʊlə(r); *NAmE* 'stroʊ-/ *noun* **1** a person who is enjoying a slow relaxed walk 散步者；閒逛者 **2** (*NAmE*) (*BrE* **buggy, push·chair**) a small folding seat on wheels in which a small child sits and is pushed along（摺疊式）嬰兒車，童車 ➲ picture at PUSHCHAIR

strong 🔑 /strɒŋ; *NAmE* strɔːŋ/ *adj.* (**strong·er** /-gə(r)/, **strong·est** /-gɪst/)

> **WORD FAMILY**
> strong *adj.*
> strongly *adv.*
> strength *noun*
> strengthen *verb*

▸ **HAVING PHYSICAL POWER** 有體力 **1** 🔑 (of people, animals, etc. 人、動物等) having a lot of physical power so that you can lift heavy weights, do hard physical work, etc. 強壯的；強健的：*strong muscles* 強健的肌肉 ◇ *She wasn't a strong swimmer* (= she could not swim well). 她游泳不大行。◇ *He's strong enough to lift a car!* 他力氣大得能抬起一輛汽車！ **2** 🔑 (of a natural or physical force 自然力或物理力) having great power 強的；強勁的：*Stay indoors in the middle of the day, when the sun is strongest.* 中午陽光最強的時候待在室內。◇ *a* ***strong wind/current*** 強風/流 ◇ *a strong magnet* 強磁鐵 **3** 🔑 having a powerful effect on the body or mind（對身、心影響）強烈的，深刻的：*a strong drug* 強效藥物

▸ **HAVING POWER OVER PEOPLE** 有影響力 **4** 🔑 having a lot of power or influence 有權勢的；有影響的；有實力的：*a* ***strong leader/government*** 重權在握的領導人；強有力的政府 **5** **the strong** [pl.] people who are rich or powerful 有錢人；有勢者；強勢群體

▸ **HARD TO RESIST/DEFEAT/ATTACK** 難以抵抗/擊敗/攻擊 **6** 🔑 very powerful and difficult for people to fight against or defeat 強的；強大的；厲害的：*a strong team* 強隊 ◇ (*figurative*) *The temptation to tell her everything was very strong.* 非常想把一切全都告訴她。 **7** 🔑 (of an argument, evidence, etc. 論點、證據等) difficult to attack or criticize 難以辯駁的；確鑿的：*There is strong evidence of a link between exercise and a healthy heart.* 有充分的證據證明鍛煉有益於心臟健康。◇ *You have a strong case for getting your job back.* 你有充分的理由要求恢復你的工作。

▸ **OPINION/BELIEF/FEELING** 觀點；信念；感情 **8** [only before noun] (of a person 人) holding an opinion or a belief very firmly and seriously 堅決的；堅定的；不動搖的；始終不渝的 **SYN** **firm**：*a* ***strong supporter/opponent*** *of the government* 堅決擁護/反對政府的人 **9** 🔑 (of an opinion, a belief or a feeling 觀點、信念或感情) very powerful 堅定的；強烈的；深厚的：*strong support for the government* 對政府的堅決擁護 ◇ *People have strong feelings about this issue.* 人們對這個問題反應強烈。

▸ **NOT EASILY BROKEN** 不易破碎 **10** 🔑 (of objects 物體) not easily broken or damaged; made well 堅固的；結實的：*a strong chair* 結實的椅子

S

▸ **NOT EASILY UPSET 不脆弱 11** not easily upset or frightened; not easily influenced by other people 堅強的；不易受驚嚇的；有主見的：*You need strong nerves to ride a bike in London.* 在倫敦騎自行車，你可得有膽量。◇ *It's difficult, I know. But be strong!* 我知道這不容易。不過要堅強！◇ *a strong personality* 堅強的個性 ➲ see also HEADSTRONG, STRONG-MINDED, STRONG-WILLED

▸ **LIKELY TO SUCCEED 有望成功 12** likely to succeed or happen 有望成功的；可能性大的：*a strong candidate for the job* 有望獲得這份工作的人選 ◇ *You're **in a strong position** to negotiate a deal.* 你們很有希望通過談判達成協議。◇ *There's **a strong possibility** that we'll lose the game.* 我們很有可能會輸掉比賽。

▸ **GOOD AT STH 擅長 13** good at sth 擅長的；突出的：*The play has a very strong cast.* 這部劇演員陣容強大。◇ *Mathematics was never my **strong point*** (= I was never very good at it). 數學從來不是我的強項。

▸ **NUMBER 數目 14** great in number 大量的；眾多的：*There was a strong police presence at the demonstration.* 示威現場出現了大批警察。 **15** used after numbers to show the size of a group （用於數字後，表示某集體的規模）多達…的，計有…的：*a 5 000-strong crowd* 多達 5 000 人的群眾 ◇ *The crowd was 5 000 strong.* 聚集的人群有 5 000 人。

▸ **HEALTHY 健康 16** (of a person 人) not easily affected by disease; healthy 健康的；強壯的；身體好的：*Are you feeling stronger now after your rest?* 休息過後，你是不是感覺好些了？➲ SYNONYMS at WELL

▸ **FIRMLY ESTABLISHED 穩固 17** firmly established; difficult to destroy 穩固的；牢固的：*a strong marriage* 鞏固的婚姻 ◇ *The college has strong links with local industry.* 這所學院同當地產業界有牢固的聯繫。

▸ **BUSINESS 商業 18** (of prices, an economy, etc. 價格、經濟等) having a value that is high or increasing 堅挺的；行情看漲的；呈強勢的：*strong share prices* 行情看漲的股票價格 ◇ *The euro is getting stronger against the dollar.* 歐元對美元呈強勢走向。 **19** (of a business or an industry 企業或某行業) in a safe financial position 經營狀況良好的；景氣的：*Their catering business remained strong despite the recession.* 儘管出現經濟衰退，他們的酒席承辦生意仍然景氣。

▸ **EASY TO SEE/HEAR/FEEL/SMELL 易於看／聽／感覺／嗅到 20** easy to see, hear, feel or smell; very great or INTENSE 醒目的；響亮的；明顯感覺得到的；濃烈的；強烈的：*a strong smell* 濃烈的氣味 ◇ *a strong feeling of nausea* 強烈的惡心感覺 ◇ *a strong voice* (= loud) 洪亮的嗓音 ◇ *strong colours* 濃重的色彩 ◇ *a face with strong features* (= large and noticeable) 輪廓分明的面孔 ◇ *She spoke with a strong Australian accent.* 她說話帶有濃重的澳大利亞口音。◇ *He was under strong pressure to resign.* 他承受着要辭職的巨大壓力。

S

▸ **FOOD 食物 21** having a lot of flavour 味重的：*strong cheese* 味重的奶酪

▸ **DRINKS 飲料 22** containing a lot of a substance 濃的；釅的：*strong black coffee* 不加牛奶的濃咖啡

▸ **WORDS 言辭 23** (of words or language 言辭或言語) having a lot of force, often causing offence to people 強硬的；冒犯的：*The movie has been criticized for **strong language*** (= swearing). 這部電影因有髒話而受到批評。

▸ **GRAMMAR 語法 24** [usually before noun] (of a verb 動詞) forming the past tense and past participle by changing a vowel, not by adding a regular ending, for example *sing, sang* 強變化的（通過改變元音而不是加規則的詞尾來構成動詞過去時和過去分詞，如 sing、sang）

▸ **PHONETICS 語音學 25** [usually before noun] used to describe the way some words are pronounced when they have stress. For example, the strong form of *and* is /ænd/. 強讀式的，重讀的（某些詞重讀時的讀音，如 and 的強式讀音為 /ænd/）OPP **weak**

▸ **strong·ly** *adv.*: *a strongly built boat* 一艘建得結實的船 ◇ *a light shining strongly* 一盞發着強光的燈 ◇ *a strongly worded protest* 措辭強硬的抗議 ◇ *He was strongly opposed to the idea.* 他堅決反對那個主意。◇ *This is an issue I feel strongly about* (= I have firm opinions about). 這個問題我堅持自己的看法。◇ *The room smelt strongly of polish.* 那個房間裏散發着濃濃的上光劑的氣味。

IDM **be a bit 'strong** (*BrE, informal*) used to say that you think what sb has said is unfair or too critical（認為某人的話有失公允或過於苛刻時說）有點言重了 **be 'strong on sth 1** to be good at sth 擅長某事：*I'm not very strong on dates* (= I can't remember the dates of important events). 我不大記得住日期。 **2** to have a lot of sth 某事物有很多；強於某一方面：*The report was strong on criticism, but short on practical suggestions.* 這份報告批評的話說得多，但可行的建議提得少。 **be sb's 'strong suit** to be a subject that sb knows a lot about 為某人所長：*I'm afraid geography is not my strong suit.* 恐怕地理不是我的強項。 **come on 'strong** (*informal*) to make your feelings clear in an aggressive way, especially your sexual feelings towards sb 言行過分；（尤指）露骨地調情 **going 'strong** (*informal*) to continue to be healthy, active or successful 保持健康；活躍依舊；興盛不衰：*My grandmother is 90 and still going strong.* 我奶奶 90 歲了，還挺硬朗。 **ˌhave a ˌstrong 'stomach** to be able to see or do unpleasant things without feeling sick or upset 能忍受令人惡心的事 ➲ more at CARD *n.*

'strong-arm *adj.* [only before noun] (*disapproving*) using threats or violence in order to make people do what you want 橫施淫威的；以暴力強制的：*to use **strong-arm tactics** against your political opponents* 用強制手段對付政敵

strong·box /'strɒŋbɒks; *NAmE* 'strɔːŋbɑːks/ *noun* a strong, usually metal, box for keeping valuable things in 保險箱；保險櫃

ˌstrong 'force *noun* (*physics* 物) one of the four FUNDAMENTAL FORCES in the universe, which holds the parts of the NUCLEUS of an atom together 強力（宇宙四種基本力之一，將原子核各部份結合在一起）➲ see also ELECTROMAGNETISM, GRAVITY (1), WEAK FORCE

strong·hold /'strɒŋhəʊld; *NAmE* 'strɔːŋhoʊld/ *noun* **1** an area in which there is a lot of support for a particular belief or group of people, especially a political party 有廣泛支持的地方；勢力強大的地方：*a Republican stronghold/a stronghold of Republicanism* 共和黨勢力強大的地區 **2** a castle or a place that is strongly built and difficult to attack 堡壘；要塞；據點 **3** an area where there are a large number of a particular type of animal（某種動物的）主要棲息地：*This valley is one of the last strongholds of the Siberian tiger.* 這條山谷是西伯利亞虎最後的幾個主要棲息地之一。

strong·man /'strɒŋmæn; *NAmE* 'strɔːŋ-/ *noun* (*pl.* **-men** /-men/) **1** a leader who uses threats or violence to rule a country 鐵腕人物；獨裁者 **2** a physically very strong man, especially sb who performs in a CIRCUS（尤指馬戲團裏的）大力士

ˌstrong-'minded *adj.* having strong opinions that are not easily influenced by what other people think or say 有主見的；堅持己見的 SYN **determined**

strong·room /'strɒŋruːm; -rʊm; *NAmE* 'strɔːŋ-/ *noun* a room, for example in a bank, with thick walls and a strong solid door, where valuable items are kept（銀行等的）保險庫

ˌstrong 'safety *noun* (in AMERICAN FOOTBALL 美式足球) a defending player who plays opposite the attacking team's strongest side 強衞（針對攻方攻勢最強的一邊進行防守）

ˌstrong-'willed *adj.* determined to do what you want to do, even if other people advise you not to 意志堅強的；堅持己見的

stron·tium /'strɒntiəm; 'strɒnʃ-; *NAmE* 'strɑːnʃ-; 'strɑːnt-/ *noun* [U] (*symb.* **Sr**) a chemical element. Strontium is a soft silver-white metal. 鍶

strop /strɒp; *NAmE* strɑːp/ *noun* [sing.] (*BrE, informal*) a very bad mood when you are annoyed about sth 惱怒；懊惱：*Don't **get in a strop**—I'm only a few minutes late.* 別生氣，我不過晚了幾分鐘。

strophe /'strəʊfi; *NAmE* 'stroʊfi/ *noun* (*technical* 術語) a group of lines forming a section of a poem 詩節 ➲ compare STANZA ▸ **stroph·ic** /'strəʊfɪk; *NAmE* 'stroʊf-/ *adj.*

Synonyms 同義詞辨析

structure

framework • form • composition • construction • fabric

These are all words for the way the different parts of sth combine together or the way that sth has been made. 以上各詞均指事物各個不同部份的組合、構造。

structure the way in which the parts of sth are connected together or arranged; a particular arrangement of parts 指結構、構造： *the structure of the building/human body* 建築物／人體結構 ◇ *the social structure of society* 社會的社會結構 ◇ *the grammatical structures of a language* 一種語言的語法結構 ◇ *a salary structure* 工資結構

framework a set of beliefs, ideas or rules that forms the basis of a system or society 指構成某個體系或社會基礎的信仰、觀點、準則： *The report provides a framework for further research.* 報告提供了進一步研究的原則。

form [U] the arrangement of parts in a whole, especially in a work of art of piece of writing（尤指藝術作品或文章的）結構、形式：*As a photographer, shape and form were more important to him than colour.* 作為攝影師，形狀和結構對他來説比顏色更重要。

composition [U] *(rather formal)* the different parts or people that combine to form sth; the way in which they combine 指不同部份或人的構成、組合方式： *recent changes in the composition of the workforce* 勞動力組合最近的變化

construction [U] the way that sth has been built or made 指建造或構造的方式： *ships of steel construction* 鋼結構船

fabric *(rather formal)* the basic structure of a society or an organization that enables it to function successfully 指社會、機構等的基本結構： *This is a trend which threatens **the very fabric of society**.* 這趨勢威脅社會的基本結構。

PATTERNS

- the **basic** structure/framework/form/composition/construction/fabric of sth
- a **simple/complex** structure/framework/form
- the **economic/political/social** structure/framework/composition/fabric of sth
- the **chemical/genetic** structure/composition of sth

stroppy /ˈstrɒpi; *NAmE* ˈstrɑːpi/ *adj.* (*BrE, informal*) (**strop·pier**, **strop·pi·est**) (of a person 人) easily annoyed and difficult to deal with 動輒生氣的；性情暴躁的；易怒難處的： *Don't **get stroppy** with me—it isn't my fault!* 別衝我生氣，這不是我的錯！

strove *past tense* of STRIVE

struck *past tense, past part.* of STRIKE

struc·tural AW /ˈstrʌktʃərəl/ *adj.* [usually before noun] connected with the way in which sth is built or organized 結構（或構造）上的：*Storms have caused structural damage to hundreds of homes.* 幾場暴風雨使幾百間住房的結構受損。◇ *structural changes in society* 社會結構的變化 ▸ **struc·tur·al·ly** AW /-ərəli/ *adv.* : *The building is structurally sound.* 這座房子結構完好。◇ *The languages are structurally different.* 這些語言在結構上有差別。

ˌstructural engiˈneer *noun* a person whose job is to plan large buildings, bridges, etc. 結構工程師（設計大型建築、橋梁等）

struc·tur·al·ism /ˈstrʌktʃərəlɪzəm/ *noun* [U] (in literature, language and social science 文學、語言及社會科學) a theory that considers any text as a structure whose various parts only have meaning when they are considered in relation to each other 結構主義（認為任何一篇文字為一結構體系，其各個部份只有在相互關係中才有意義） ➲ compare DECONSTRUCTION ▸ **struc·tur·al·ist** /-rəlɪst/ *noun, adj.* : *a structuralist approach* 結構主義方法

ˌstructural linˈguistics *noun* [U] the part of LINGUISTICS that deals with language as a system of related structures 結構主義語言學（把語言作為相關聯的結構體系）

struc·ture 0➔ AW /ˈstrʌktʃə(r)/ *noun, verb*

■ ***noun*** **1** 0➔ [U, C] the way in which the parts of sth are connected together, arranged or organized; a particular arrangement of parts 結構；構造： *the structure of the building* 這座建築物的結構 ◇ *changes in the social and economic structure of society* 一個社會在社會結構和經濟結構上的變化 ◇ *the grammatical structures of a language* 一種語言的語法結構 ◇ *a salary structure* 工資結構 **2** 0➔ [C] a thing that is made of several parts, especially a building 結構體；（尤指）建築物： *a stone/brick/wooden structure* 石／磚／木結構建築物 ➲ SYNONYMS at BUILDING **3** 0➔ [U, C] the state of being well organized or planned with all the parts linked together; a careful plan 精心組織；周密安排；體系： *Your essay needs (a) structure.* 你這篇文章組織不好。

■ ***verb*** [usually passive] to arrange or organize sth into a system or pattern 使形成體系；系統安排；精心組織： **~ sth** *How well does the teacher structure the lessons?* 老師對課程組織安排得如何？◇ *Make use of the toys in structured group activities.* 在精心安排的分組活動中運用這些玩具。◇ **~ sth around sth** *The exhibition is structured around the themes of work and leisure.* 展覽是圍繞工作與休閒的主題來佈置的。

stru·del /ˈstruːdl/ *noun* [U, C] (from *German*) a cake made from pieces of fruit, especially apple, rolled in thin PASTRY and baked 果餡捲（餅）

strug·gle 0➔ /ˈstrʌɡl/ *verb, noun*

■ ***verb*** **1** 0➔ [I] to try very hard to do sth when it is difficult or when there are a lot of problems 奮鬥；努力；爭取： **~ (for sth)** *a country struggling for independence* 為獨立而奮鬥的國家 ◇ *Shona **struggled for breath**.* 肖納艱難地喘着氣。◇ *life as a struggling artist* (= one who is very poor) 藝術家拮据的生活 ◇ **~ to do sth** *They struggled just to pay their bills.* 他們辛苦所得僅敷日用。 **2** 0➔ [I] **+ adv./prep.** to move somewhere or do sth with difficulty 艱難地行進；吃力地進行： *I struggled up the hill with the heavy bags.* 我背着幾個沉重的包吃力地爬上山去。◇ *Paul struggled out of his wheelchair.* 保羅掙扎着下了輪椅。 **3** 0➔ [I] to fight against sb/sth in order to prevent a bad situation or result 鬥爭；抗爭： **~ (against sb/sth)** *He struggled against cancer for two years.* 他同癌症抗爭了兩年。◇ **~ (with sb/sth)** *Lisa struggled with her conscience before talking to the police.* 莉薩經過一番良心上的鬥爭，終於對警方說了。 **4** 0➔ [I] to fight sb or try to get away from them 搏鬥；扭打；掙扎脫身： *I struggled and screamed for help.* 我掙扎着，高聲呼救。◇ **~ together** *Ben and Jack struggled together on the grass.* 本和傑克在草地上扭打起來。◇ **~ with sb** *James was hit in the mouth as he struggled with the raiders.* 詹姆斯在同幾個劫匪搏鬥時嘴上捱了打。◇ **+ adj.** *How did she manage to **struggle free**?* 她是怎麼逃脫的？ **5** [I] **~ (with sb) (for sth)** to compete or argue with sb, especially in order to get sth 爭奪；辯論： *rival leaders struggling for power* 互相對立的領導人爭奪權力

PHR V **ˌstruggle aˈlong/ˈon** to continue despite problems 在困難中堅持；勉力維持

■ ***noun*** **1** 0➔ [C] a hard fight in which people try to obtain or achieve sth, especially sth that sb else does not want them to have 鬥爭；奮鬥；努力： *a **power/leadership struggle*** 爭奪權力；領導權的鬥爭 ◇ **~ (with sb) (for/against sth)** *a struggle for independence* 為獨立的鬥爭 ◇ **~ (with sb) (to do sth)** *He is engaged in a bitter struggle with his rival to get control of the company.* 為取得對公司的控制權，他正同對手進行一場激烈的鬥爭。◇ **~ (between A and B)** *the struggle between good and evil* 善惡之爭 ◇ *She will not give up her children without a struggle.* 她不會輕易放棄自己的孩子。 ➲ SYNONYMS at CAMPAIGN **2** 0➔ [C] a physical fight between two people or groups of people, especially when one of them is trying to escape, or to get sth from the other 搏鬥；扭打；（尤指）搶奪，掙扎脱身：*There were no signs of a struggle at the murder scene.* 兇殺現場沒有搏鬥痕跡。➲ SYNONYMS at FIGHT **3** 0┳ [sing.] **~ (to do sth)** something that is difficult for you to do or achieve 難事 SYN **effort**：*It was a real struggle to be ready on time.* 要按時做好準備確非易事。

strum /strʌm/ *verb* (**-mm-**) [I, T] **~ (on) sth** to play a GUITAR or similar instrument by moving your fingers up and down across the strings 彈奏（吉他等樂器）：*As she sang she strummed on a guitar.* 她邊唱邊彈吉他。

strum·pet /ˈstrʌmpɪt/ *noun* (*old use, disapproving*) a PROSTITUTE, or a woman who looks and behaves like one 妓女；婊子；淫婦

strung *past tense, past part.* of STRING

ˌstrung ˈout *adj.* [not before noun] **1** spread out in a line 一條線地伸展開來：*a group of riders strung out along the beach* 沿海灘散開的一隊騎手 **2 ~ (on sth)** (*slang*) strongly affected by an illegal drug such as HEROIN（吸毒後）神志恍惚

ˌstrung ˈup *adj.* [not before noun] (*BrE, informal*) very nervous, worried or excited 十分緊張；非常焦慮；異常興奮

strut /strʌt/ *verb, noun*

■ ***verb*** (**-tt-**) [I] to walk proudly with your head up and chest out to show that you think you are important 趾高氣揚地走；高視闊步：*The players strutted and posed for the cameras.* 運動員昂首闊步，擺好姿勢讓記者拍照。

IDM **ˌstrut your ˈstuff** (*informal*) to proudly show your ability, especially at dancing or performing（尤指在跳舞或表演時）賣弄自己那一套，露一手

■ ***noun*** **1** a long thin piece of wood or metal used to support or make part of a vehicle or building stronger 支柱；撐杆；支杆；支撐 **2** [sing.] (*disapproving*) an act of walking in a proud and confident way 趾高氣揚的步態；高視闊步的樣子

strych·nine /ˈstrɪkniːn/ *noun* [U] a poisonous substance used in very small amounts as a medicine 士的寧；馬錢子鹼

St Swithin's Day /ˌsnt ˈswɪðɪnz deɪ; *NAmE* ˌseɪnt/ *noun* 15 July, a Christian festival. In Britain it is said that if it rains on this day it will rain for the next forty days. 聖斯威辛瞻禮日（7 月 15 日，基督教節日，在英國據說如該日下雨則將持續下雨四十天）

stub /stʌb/ *noun, verb*

■ ***noun*** **1** a short piece of a cigarette, pencil, etc. that is left when the rest of it has been used（煙、鉛筆等的）殘餘部份，殘端 **2** the small part of a ticket, cheque, etc. that you keep as a record when you have given the main part to sb 存根；票根 ➲ picture at MONEY

■ ***verb*** (**-bb-**) **~ your toe (against/on sth)** to hurt your toe by accident by hitting it against sth hard 腳趾不小心踢到…上

PHR V **ˌstub sth↔ˈout** to stop a cigarette, etc. from burning by pressing the end against sth hard 把（香煙等）弄滅

stub·ble /ˈstʌbl/ *noun* [U] **1** the lower short stiff part of the STEMS of crops such as WHEAT that are left in the ground after the top part has been cut and collected（作物收割後留在地裏的）茬 **2** the short stiff hairs that grow on a man's face when he has not shaved recently 鬍子茬 ➲ VISUAL VOCAB page V60 ▸ **stub·bly** /ˈstʌbli/ *adj.*

stub·born /ˈstʌbən; *NAmE* -bərn/ *adj.* **1** (often *disapproving*) determined not to change your opinion or attitude 固執的；執拗的；頑固的；倔強的 SYN **obstinate**：*He was too stubborn to admit that he was wrong.* 他死不認錯。◇ *She can be* ***as stubborn as a mule***. 她可以倔得像頭騾子。◇ *stubborn pride* 死要面子 ◇ *a stubborn resistance to change* 頑固抵制變革 ◇ *a stubborn refusal to listen* 硬是不聽 **2** difficult to get rid of or deal with 難以去除（或對付）的 SYN **persistent**：***a stubborn cough/stain*** 久治不癒的咳嗽；頑漬 ◇ *a stubborn problem* 難題 ▸ **stub·born·ly** *adv.*：*She stubbornly refused to pay.* 她怎麼都不肯付錢。◇ *Unemployment remains stubbornly high.* 失業率居高不下。 **stub·born·ness** *noun* [U]

stubby /ˈstʌbi/ *adj., noun*

■ ***adj.*** [usually before noun] short and thick 短而粗的；矮壯的：*stubby fingers* 又短又粗的指頭

■ ***noun*** (*pl.* **-ies**) (*AustralE, NZE*) **1** [C] (*informal*) a small fat bottle of beer usually holding 0.375 litres 矮啤酒瓶（容量通常為 0.375 升） **2 Stubbies™** [pl.] a pair of short trousers/pants for men 男式短褲

stucco /ˈstʌkəʊ; *NAmE* -koʊ/ *noun* [U] a type of PLASTER that is used for covering ceilings and the outside walls of buildings（塗牆壁或天花板用的）粉飾灰泥 ▸ **stuc·coed** *adj.*：*a stuccoed wall* 拉毛粉飾的牆

stuck /stʌk/ *adj.* [not before noun] ➲ see also STICK *v.* **1** unable to move or to be moved 動不了；無法移動；卡住；陷住：*The wheels were stuck in the mud.* 車輪陷到了泥裏。◇ *This drawer keeps* ***getting stuck***. 這個抽屜動不動就卡住。◇ *She got the key stuck in the lock.* 她把鑰匙卡在鎖裏了。◇ *I can't get out—I'm stuck.* 我出不去，我被卡住了。 **2** in an unpleasant situation or place that you cannot escape from 陷（入）；困（於）：*We were stuck in traffic for over an hour.* 我們堵車堵了一個多小時。◇ *I hate being stuck at home all day.* 我討厭整天困在家裏出不去。 **3 ~ (on sth)** unable to answer or understand sth 被難住；答不上來；卡殼：*I got stuck on the first question.* 頭一個問題我就答不上來。◇ *I'll help you if you're stuck.* 你要是難住了，我來幫你。 **4 ~ (for sth)** not knowing what to do in a particular situation 不知所措；（為某事）犯愁：*If you're stuck for something to do tonight, come out with us.* 你要是正愁今晚沒事做，就跟我們一塊兒出去吧。◇ *I've never known him to be stuck for words before.* 我從不知道他也會有詞窮句蹇的時候。 **5 ~ with sb/sth** (*informal*) unable to get rid of sb/sth that you do not want 擺脱不了；甩不掉：*I was stuck with him for the whole journey.* 一路上我一直沒能擺脱他。

IDM **ˌget stuck ˈin | ˌget stuck ˈinto sth** (*BrE, informal*) to start doing sth in an enthusiastic way, especially to start eating 起勁地幹起某事；（尤指）大吃起來 ➲ more at GROOVE, ROCK *n.*, TIME WARP

ˌstuck-ˈup *adj.* (*informal, disapproving*) thinking that you are more important than other people and behaving in an unfriendly way towards them 自命不凡的；趾高氣揚的 SYN **snobbish**

stud /stʌd/ *noun* **1** [C] a small piece of jewellery with a part that is pushed through a hole in your ear, nose, etc. 釘狀首飾；耳釘；鼻釘：*diamond studs* 鑽石耳釘 ➲ VISUAL VOCAB page V65 **2** [C] a small round piece of metal that is attached to the surface of sth, especially for decoration（尤指裝飾用的）飾釘，嵌釘：*a leather jacket with studs on the back* 後背有飾釘的皮夾克 **3** [C, usually pl.] (*BrE*) one of several small metal or plastic objects that are fixed to the bottom part of a FOOTBALL BOOT or running shoe（足球鞋或跑鞋上的）鞋釘 ➲ compare CLEAT (3) **4** [C] a small metal object used in the past for fastening a COLLAR onto a shirt 領扣 ➲ see also PRESS STUD **5** [C, U] an animal, especially a horse, that is kept for breeding; a place where animals, especially horses, are kept for breeding 種公畜；種馬；種畜場；種馬場：*a stud farm* 種馬場 ◇ *The horse was retired from racing and* ***put out to stud*** (= kept for breeding). 那匹賽馬被淘汰下來，留作種馬。 **6** [C] (*informal*) a man who has many sexual partners and who is thought to be sexually attractive 亂搞關係的男人；風流男子

stud·ded /ˈstʌdɪd/ *adj.* **1** decorated with small raised pieces of metal 用飾釘裝飾的：*a studded leather belt* 飾釘裝飾的皮帶 **2 ~ with sth** having a lot of sth on or in it 佈滿（或有很多）…的：*The sky was clear and studded with stars.* 天空晴朗，繁星點點。◇ *an essay studded with quotations* 旁徵博引的文章 ➲ see also STAR-STUDDED ▸ **stud** *verb* (**-dd-**)：**~ sth** *Stars studded the sky.* 繁星滿天。

stu·dent 0┳ /ˈstjuːdnt; *NAmE* ˈstuː-/ *noun*

1 0┳ a person who is studying at a university or college 大學生；研究生：*a* ***medical/science, etc. student*** 醫科、理科等學生 ◇ *a* ***graduate/postgraduate/research student*** 研究生 ◇ *an* ***overseas student*** 留學生 ◇ *a* ***student teacher/nurse*** 實習教師／護士 ◇ *a* ***student grant/loan***

(= money that is given/lent to students to pay for their studies) 助學金；學生貸款 ◇ ***student fees*** (= to pay for the cost of teaching) 學費 ◇ *She's a student at Sussex University.* 她是薛塞克斯大學的學生。➲ see also MATURE STUDENT **2** 🔑 a person who is studying at a school, especially a SECONDARY SCHOOL 學生；（尤指）中學生：*a 15-year-old high school student* * 15 歲的中學生 ➲ compare PUPIL (1) ➲ see also A STUDENT **3 ~ of sth** (*formal*) a person who is very interested in a particular subject 研究者；學者：*a keen student of human nature* 熱衷於探究人性的人

Synonyms 同義詞辨析

student

pupil • schoolboy/schoolchild/schoolgirl

These are all words for a child that attends school. 以上各詞均指學生。

student a person who is studying in a school, especially an older child 指在校學習的學生，尤指較大的學生：*Students are required to be in school by 8.30.* 學生須在 8:30 以前到校。◇ *Any high school student could tell you the answer.* 隨便一個高中生都可以告訴你答案。

pupil (*BrE*) a person who is being taught, especially a child in a school 指學生，尤指小學生：*The school has over 850 pupils.* 這所小學有 850 多名學生。
NOTE **Pupil** is used only in British English and is starting to become old-fashioned. **Student** is often preferred, especially by teachers and other people involved in education, and especially when talking about older children. * pupil 只用於英式英語，並已開始過時。現在較常用 student，尤其是教師和教育工作者，多指較大的學生。

schoolboy / schoolgirl / schoolchild a boy, girl or child who attends school 指學校的男生、女生、學童、小學生：*Since she was a schoolgirl she had dreamed of going on the stage.* 自從上學以來她就一直夢想着成為演員。NOTE These words emphasize the age of the children or this period in their lives; they are less often used to talk about teaching and learning. 以上各詞均強調童年或學齡時期，較少用於教與學：~~*an able schoolboy/schoolgirl/schoolchild*~~

PATTERNS

- a(n) **good/bright/able/brilliant/star/outstanding** student/pupil
- a **naughty** schoolboy/schoolgirl/schoolchild
- a **disruptive** student/pupil
- a(n) **ex-/former** student/pupil
- a **school** student/pupil
- to **teach** students/pupils/schoolboys/schoolgirls/schoolchildren

stu·dent·ship /ˈstjuːdəntʃɪp; *NAmE* ˈstuː-/ *noun* (*BrE*) one of a small number of places that a university gives to students who wish to continue studying or to do research after they have finished their degree; an amount of money that is given to a student who wins one of these places 學位後研修生資格（學生獲得學位後在大學繼續學習研究）；學位後研修生獎學金

ˌstudents' ˈunion (also **ˌstudent ˈunion**) *noun* **1** a building where students at a university or college can go to meet socially （大學或學院的）學生活動中心 **2** (*BrE*) an association of students at a particular university or college, concerned with students' rights, living conditions, etc. （大學或學院）學生會

ˌstudent ˈteaching (*US*) (*BrE* **ˈteaching practice**) *noun* [U] the part of a course for people who are training to become teachers which involves teaching classes of students 教學實習

stud·ied /ˈstʌdid/ *adj.* [only before noun] (*formal*) deliberate and carefully planned 刻意的；精心安排的：*She introduced herself with studied casualness.* 她故作輕鬆地做了自我介紹。

More About 補充說明

students

- A **student** is a person who is studying at a school, college, university, etc. * student 指在校學習的學生。
- An **undergraduate** is a student who is studying for their first degree at a university or college. * undergraduate 指大學裏攻讀學士學位的學生。
- In *BrE*, a **graduate** is a person who has completed a first degree at a university or college. In *NAmE* **graduate** is usually used with another noun and can also apply to a person who has finished high school. 在英式英語中，graduate 指大學本科畢業生。在美式英語中，graduate 通常與另一名詞連用，亦可指中學畢業生：*a high school graduate* 中學畢業生 ◇ *a graduate student* 研究生
- A **postgraduate** is a person who has finished a first degree and is doing advanced study or research. This is the usual term in *BrE*, but it is formal in *NAmE* and **graduate student** is usually used instead. * postgraduate 指研究生，在英式英語中為常用詞，在美式英語中則為正式用語，通常用 graduate student 取代。

stu·dio 🔑 /ˈstjuːdiəʊ; *NAmE* ˈstuːdioʊ/ *noun* (*pl.* **-os**) **1** 🔑 a room where radio or television programmes are recorded and broadcast from, or where music is recorded （廣播、電視的）錄音室，錄像室，演播室，製作室；（音樂）錄音棚：*a **television studio*** 電視演播室 ◇ *a **studio audience*** (= one in a studio, that can be seen or heard as a programme is broadcast) 演播室現場的觀眾（或聽眾）◇ *a **recording studio*** 錄音棚 **2** 🔑 a place where films/movies are made or produced 電影攝影棚 **3** 🔑 a company that makes films/movies 電影公司；電影製片廠：*She works for a major Hollywood studio.* 她為好萊塢一家大電影公司工作。◇ *a studio executive* 電影公司經理 **4** 🔑 a room where an artist works （藝術家的）工作室：*a sculptor's studio* 雕塑家的工作室 **5** a place where dancing is taught or where dancers practise （舞蹈）練功房：*a dance studio* 舞蹈練功房 **6** (*BrE* also **ˈstudio flat**) (*NAmE* also **ˈstudio apartment**) a small flat/apartment with one main room for living and sleeping in and usually a kitchen and bathroom 單間公寓（一個房間兼作起居室和臥室，通常帶廚房和盥洗室）

stu·di·ous /ˈstjuːdiəs; *NAmE* ˈstuː-/ *adj.* spending a lot of time studying or reading 勤奮的；好學的；用功的 SYN **scholarly**：*a studious young man* 勤奮的小伙子

stu·di·ous·ly /ˈstjuːdiəsli; *NAmE* ˈstuː-/ *adv.* in a way that is carefully planned and deliberate 刻意地；成心：*He studiously avoided answering the question.* 他刻意不去回答那個問題。

stud·muf·fin /ˈstʌdmʌfɪn/ *noun* (*informal, especially NAmE*) a man who is considered sexually attractive 性感的男人

study 🔑 /ˈstʌdi/ *noun, verb*

■ ***noun*** (*pl.* **-ies**)

▸ **ACTIVITY OF LEARNING 學習 1** 🔑 [U] the activity of learning or gaining knowledge, either from books or by examining things in the world 學習；研究：*a room set aside for **private study*** 單留出來的書房 ◇ ***academic/literary/scientific, etc. study*** 學術、文學、科學等研究 ◇ *It is important to develop good **study skills**.* 培養良好的學習方法很重要。◇ *Physiology is the study of how living things work.* 生理學是研究生物機能的學科。**2** 🔑 **studies** [pl.] (*formal*) a particular person's learning activities, for example at a college or university 功課；課業；學業：*to continue your studies* 繼續學業

▸ **ACADEMIC SUBJECT 學科 3** 🔑 **studies** [U+sing./pl. v.] used in the names of some academic subjects （用於某些學科名稱）：*business/media/American studies* 商學；傳媒學；美國研究

S

▸ **DETAILED EXAMINATION** 仔細檢查 **4** [U] the act of considering or examining sth in detail 細緻考慮；仔細檢查；審視：*These proposals deserve careful study.* 這些建議值得認真研究。 **5** [C] a piece of research that examines a subject or question in detail（專題）研究，調查：*to **make/carry out/conduct a study*** 進行 / 開展 / 從事一項研究 ◇ ***This study shows/confirms/suggests** that …* 這研究證明 / 證實 / 顯示… ◇ *a detailed study of how animals adapt to their environment* 關於動物如何適應環境的深入研究 ➲ **COLLOCATIONS** at SCIENTIFIC ➲ see also CASE STUDY

▸ **ROOM** 房間 **6** [C] a room, especially in sb's home, used for reading and writing 書房

▸ **ART** 繪畫 **7** [C] a drawing or painting of sth, especially one done for practice or before doing a larger picture 習作；試作；試畫：*a study of Chartres Cathedral* 沙特爾大教堂試畫 ◇ *a nude study* 裸體畫習作

▸ **MUSIC** 音樂 **8** (*BrE*) (also **étude** *NAmE, BrE*) [C] a piece of music designed to give a player practice in technical skills 練習曲

▸ **PERFECT EXAMPLE** 典型 **9** [sing.] **~ (in sth)** (*formal*) a perfect example of sth 典型；範例：*His face was a study in concentration.* 他臉上完全是一副全神貫注的表情。 **IDM** see BROWN *adj.*

■ ***verb*** (**stud·ies**, **study·ing**, **stud·ied**, **stud·ied**)

▸ **LEARN** 學習 **1** [T, I] **~ (for sth)** to spend time learning about a subject by reading, going to college, etc. 學習；攻讀：**~ (sth)** *How long have you been studying English?* 你學英語多久了？ ◇ *Don't disturb Jane, she's studying for her exams.* 不要打擾簡，她正在溫習功課，準備考試呢。 ◇ **~ (sth) at …** *My brother studied at the Royal College of Art.* 我哥哥曾就學於皇家美術學院。 ◇ **~ (sth) under …** *a composer who studied under Nadia Boulanger* (= was taught by Nadia Boulanger) 曾師從納迪亞 • 布朗熱的作曲家 ◇ **~ to do/be sth** *Nina is studying to be an architect.* 尼娜在學建築。 ➲ **COLLOCATIONS** at EDUCATION

▸ **EXAMINE CAREFULLY** 認真檢查 **2** [T] **~ sth** to watch, or look at sb/sth carefully in order to find out sth 審視；端詳；細看：*Scientists are studying photographs of the planet for signs of life.* 科學家仔細察看行星照片，看有無生命跡象。 ◇ *He studied her face thoughtfully.* 他一邊端詳她的臉，一邊沉思。 ◇ *Fran was studying the menu.* 弗蘭在仔細地看菜單。 **3** [T] to examine sth carefully in order to understand it 研究；調查：**~ sth** *We will study the report carefully before making a decision.* 我們將認真研究這份報告，然後再作決定。 ◇ **~ how, what, etc. …** *The group will study how the region coped with the loss of thousands of jobs.* 該小組將考察這一地區是如何應對減少幾千個工作崗位的局面的。 ➲ **SYNONYMS** at EXAMINE

ˈstudy bedroom *noun* (*BrE*) a student's room containing a bed and a desk（學生宿舍的）書房兼寢室

ˈstudy hall *noun* [U] (*NAmE*) a period of time during the school day when students study quietly on their own, usually with a teacher present 自習課

stuff /stʌf/ *noun, verb*

■ ***noun*** [U] **1** (*informal*, sometimes *disapproving*) used to refer to a substance, material, group of objects, etc. when you do not know the name, when the name is not important or when it is obvious what you are talking about（事物名稱不詳、無關緊要或所指事物明顯時用）東西，物品，玩意兒：*What's all that sticky stuff on the carpet?* 地毯上那黏乎乎的都是什麼玩意兒？ ◇ *The chairs were covered in some sort of plastic stuff.* 椅子都包了一種塑料膜。 ◇ *This wine is good stuff.* 這酒不錯。 ◇ (*disapproving*) *I don't know how you can eat that stuff!* 我不明白你怎麼能吃那種東西！ ◇ *They sell stationery **and stuff** (**like that**).* 他們出售文具之類的東西。 ◇ *Where's all my stuff* (= my possessions)? 我那些東西都哪兒去了？ ◇ (*disapproving*) *Could you move all that stuff off the table?* 請你把桌上那些玩意兒全都拿走好不好？ ➲ see also FOODSTUFF ➲ **SYNONYMS** at THING **2** (*informal*) used to refer in a general way to things that people do, say, think, etc.（泛指）活兒，話，念頭，東西：*I've got loads of stuff to do today.* 我今天有好多事兒要做。 ◇ *I like reading **and stuff**.* 我喜歡看書什麼的。 ◇ *The band did some **great stuff** on their first album.* 這支樂隊首張專輯有幾支很棒的曲子。 ◇ *This is all **good stuff**. Well done!* 這一切都不錯。幹得漂亮！ ◇ *What's all this 'Mrs Smith' stuff? Call me Anna.* 哪來的什麼"史密斯夫人"那一套？叫我安娜就好了。 ◇ *I don't believe in **all that stuff** about ghosts.* 我不信什麼鬼呀魂呀的。 **3 ~ (of sth)** (*formal* or *literary*) the most important feature of sth; something that sth else is based on or is made from 基本特徵；特質；根本；基礎；原料：*The trip was magical; the stuff of which dreams are made.* 那次旅行很奇妙，宛如夢境。 ◇ *Parades and marches were **the very stuff of** politics in the region.* 遊行示威是那一地區政治活動的基本內容。 ◇ *Let's see what stuff you're made of* (= what sort of person you are). 我們來看看你是怎樣一個人。 ➲ see also HOT STUFF

IDM **do your ˈstuff** (*informal*) to do what you are good at or what you have been trained to do 施展自己的本事；露一手：*Some members of the team are just not doing their stuff* (= doing as well as they should). 隊中幾名成員壓根兒沒有使出自己的本事。 ◇ (*figurative*) *The medicine has clearly done its stuff.* 這藥顯然起作用了。 **not give a ˈstuff** (*BrE, slang*) to not care at all about sth 一點不在乎 **ˌstuff and ˈnonsense** *exclamation* (*old-fashioned, informal*) used to describe sth that is stupid or not true 廢話；胡說八道 ➲ more at KID *n.*, KNOW *v.*, STERN *adj.*, STRUT *v.*, SWEAT *v.*

■ ***verb*** **1** to fill a space or container tightly with sth 填滿；裝滿；塞滿；灌滿：**~ A with B** *She had 500 envelopes to stuff with leaflets.* 她得在 500 個信封裏裝上傳單。 ◇ **~ B in, into, under, etc. A** *She had 500 leaflets to stuff into envelopes.* 她得把 500 份傳單裝進信封裏。 ◇ **~ sth** *The fridge is stuffed to bursting.* 冰箱滿得都快撐破了。 ◇ **~ sth + adj.** *All the drawers **were stuffed full of** letters and papers.* 所有抽屜裏都放滿了信函文件。 **2 ~ sth + adv./prep.** to push sth quickly and carelessly into a small space 把…塞進（或填進） **SYN** **shove**: *She stuffed the money under a cushion.* 她把錢塞到軟墊底下。 ◇ *His hands were stuffed in his pockets.* 他兩手插在口袋裏。 **3 ~ sth** to fill a vegetable, chicken, etc. with another type of food 在（蔬菜、雞等）裏填入（另外一種食物）；給…裝餡：*Are you going to stuff the turkey?* 你打算給火雞加填料嗎？ ◇ *stuffed peppers* 釀柿子椒 **4** (*informal*) to eat a lot of food or too much food; to give sb a lot or too much to eat（使）吃撐，吃足，吃得過飽：**~ sb/yourself** *He sat at the table stuffing himself.* 他坐在桌前大吃大嚼。 ◇ **~ sb/yourself with sth** *Don't stuff the kids with chocolate before their dinner.* 正餐前不要給孩子一個勁地吃巧克力。 ◇ **~ your face** *We stuffed our faces at the party.* 我們在聚會時都吃撐了。 **5** [usually passive] **~ sth** to fill the dead body of an animal with material and preserve it, so that it keeps its original shape and appearance 製作（動物）標本：*They had had their pet dog stuffed.* 他們請人把他們的寵物狗製成了標本。

IDM **get ˈstuffed** (*BrE, informal*) used to tell sb in a rude and angry way to go away, or that you do not want sth 滾開；不稀罕 **ˈstuff it** (*informal*) used to show that you have changed your mind about sth or do not care about sth（表示改變了主意或不在乎）管它呢，去它的：*I didn't want a part in the play, then I thought—stuff it—why not?* 我本來沒想在劇中扮演角色，然後又一想，管它呢！幹嗎不演？ **you, etc. can stuff sth** (*informal*) used to tell sb in a rude and angry way that you do not want sth（粗暴或氣憤地拒絕）還是收起你的寶貝吧：*I told them they could stuff their job.* 我告訴他們說我不稀罕他們的工作。

stuffed /stʌft/ *adj.* [not before noun] (*informal*) having eaten so much that you cannot eat anything else 飽 **SYN** **full**

ˌstuffed ˈanimal *noun* **1** (*especially NAmE*) (*BrE* also **ˌsoft ˈtoy**) a toy in the shape of an animal, made of cloth and filled with a soft substance 填充玩具動物；（動物造型的）布絨玩具 ➲ **VISUAL VOCAB** page V37 **2** a dead animal that has been STUFFED 動物標本：*stuffed animals in glass cases* 玻璃櫃裏的動物標本

ˌstuffed ˈshirt *noun* (*informal, disapproving*) a person who is very serious, formal or old-fashioned 一本正經的人；古板的人；保守的人

ˌstuffed ˈup *adj.* if you are **stuffed up**, your nose is blocked and you are not able to breathe easily 鼻子不通氣的；鼻塞的

stuff·ing /ˈstʌfɪŋ/ *noun* [U] **1** (*NAmE* also **dress·ing**) a mixture of finely chopped food, such as bread, onions and HERBS, placed inside a chicken, etc. before it is cooked to give it flavour（烹飪前塞入雞等膛內的）填料 **2** soft material used to fill CUSHIONS, toys, etc.（墊子、玩具等的）填充物 SYN **filling** IDM see KNOCK *v.*

stuffy /ˈstʌfi/ *adj.* (**stuff·ier**, **stuffi·est**) **1** (of a building, room, etc. 建築物、房間等) warm in an unpleasant way and without enough fresh air 悶熱的；悶人的；通風不暢的：*a stuffy room* 悶熱的房間 ◇ *It gets very hot and stuffy in here in summer.* 這裏夏天很熱很悶。**2** (*informal, disapproving*) very serious, formal, boring or old-fashioned 一本正經的；古板的；無聊的；保守的：*a stuffy, formal family* 一本正經而又古板的一家人 ◇ *plain, stuffy clothes* 樸素刻板的衣服 **3** (*especially NAmE*) if you have a **stuffy** nose, your nose is blocked because you have a cold （鼻子）不通的，堵住的；鼻塞的 ▸ **stuffi·ness** *noun* [U]

stul·ti·fy·ing /ˈstʌltɪfaɪɪŋ/ *adj.* (*formal*) making you feel very bored and unable to think of new ideas 乏味得使人呆滯的；使人思維遲鈍的：*the stultifying effects of work that never varies* 一成不變的工作造成的使人呆滯的後果 ▸ **stul·tify** *verb* (**stul·ti·fies**, **stul·ti·fy·ing**, **stul·ti·fied**, **stul·ti·fied**) **~ sb** **stul·ti·fy·ing·ly** *adv.*

stum·ble /ˈstʌmbl/ *verb* **1** [I] to hit your foot against sth while you are walking or running and almost fall 絆腳 SYN **trip**：*The child stumbled and fell.* 孩子絆了一下，摔倒了。◇ **~ over/on sth** *I stumbled over a rock.* 我在石頭上絆了一下。**2** [I] **+ adv./prep.** to walk or move in an unsteady way 跌跌撞撞地走；蹣跚而行：*We were stumbling around in the dark looking for a candle.* 黑暗中，我們東跌西撞地找蠟燭。**3** [I] **~ (over/through sth)** to make a mistake or mistakes and stop while you are speaking, reading to sb or playing music （不順暢地）說，讀，演奏：*In her nervousness she stumbled over her words.* 她因緊張說話結結巴巴的。◇ *I stumbled through the piano piece with difficulty.* 我斷斷續續地好不容易彈完了那支鋼琴曲。▸ **stum·ble** *noun*

PHR V **ˈstumble across/on/upon sth/sb** to discover sth/sb unexpectedly 意外發現；偶然遇見：*Police have stumbled across a huge drugs ring.* 警方無意中發現一個龐大的販毒集團。**ˈstumble into sth** to become involved in sth by chance 無意間涉足某事：*I stumbled into acting when I left college.* 我離開大學後無意間進了演藝界。

ˈstumbling block *noun* **~ (to sth)** | **~ (to doing sth)** something that causes problems and prevents you from achieving your aim 障礙物；絆腳石 SYN **obstacle**

stump /stʌmp/ *noun, verb*

■ ***noun*** **1** [C] the bottom part of a tree left in the ground after the rest has fallen or been cut down 樹墩；樹樁 **2** [C] the end of sth or the part that is left after the main part has been cut, broken off or worn away 殘餘部份；殘根；殘段：*the stump of a pencil* 鉛筆頭 **3** [C] the short part of sb's leg or arm that is left after the rest has been cut off 殘肢 **4** [C, usually pl.] (in CRICKET 板球) one of the set of three vertical wooden sticks (called **the stumps**) that form the WICKET （三柱門的）柱 **5 the stump** [sing.] (*informal, especially NAmE*) the fact of a politician before an election going to different places and trying to get people's support by making speeches （政治人物在選舉前的）巡迴演說：*The senator gave his standard stump speech.* 那位參議員舉行了一次公式化的競選巡迴演說。◇ *politicians **on the stump*** 作巡迴演說的政治人物 IDM see STIR *v.*

■ ***verb*** **1** [T, usually passive] **~ sb** (*informal*) to ask sb a question that is too difficult for them to answer or give them a problem that they cannot solve 把…難住；難倒 SYN **baffle**：*I'm stumped. I don't know how they got here before us.* 我搞不懂了。我不知道他們怎麼比我們來得還早。◇ *Kate was **stumped for words*** (= unable to answer). 凱特張口結舌。**2** [I] **+ adv./prep.** to walk in a noisy, heavy way, especially because you are angry or upset （尤指憤怒或煩惱時）腳步重重地走 SYN **stomp**：*He stumped off, muttering under his breath.* 他嘴裏嘟噥着，腳步重重地走了。**3** [I, T] **+ adv./prep.** | **~ sth** (*NAmE*) to travel around making political speeches, especially before an election （尤指在選舉前）作巡迴演說：*He stumped around the country trying to build up support.* 他在全國各地巡迴演講，爭取更多的支持。**4** [T] **~ sb** (in CRICKET 板球) to put a BATSMAN out of the game by touching the stumps with the ball when he or she is out of the area in which the ball can be hit （以球觸三柱門）使（擊球手）出局

PHR V **ˌstump ˈup (for sth)** | **ˌstump ˈup sth (for sth)** (*BrE, informal*) to pay money for sth （為…）付錢，掏腰包 SYN **cough up**：*We were asked to stump up for the repairs.* 人家要我們出修理費。◇ *Who is going to stump up the extra money?* 額外的錢誰來出？

stumpy /ˈstʌmpi/ *adj.* (*disapproving*) short and thick 短而粗的 SYN **stubby**：*stumpy fingers* 又短又粗的手指 ◇ *a stumpy tail* 短而粗的尾巴

stun /stʌn/ *verb* (**-nn-**) **1 ~ sb/sth** to make a person or an animal unconscious for a short time, especially by hitting them on the head 使昏迷；（尤指）打昏 SYN **knock out**：*The fall stunned me for a moment.* 那一下摔得我昏迷了片刻。◇ *The animals are stunned before slaughter.* 屠宰前要先把動物擊昏。**2 ~ sb** to surprise or shock sb so much that they cannot think clearly or speak 使震驚（或驚愕、目瞪口呆）SYN **astound** ➲ SYNONYMS at SURPRISE **3 ~ sb** to impress sb very much 給（某人）以深刻印象；使深深感動 SYN **amaze**：*They were stunned by the view from the summit.* 在峰頂看到的景色使他們驚歎不已。▸ **stunned** *adj.*：*She was too stunned to speak.* 她驚愕得說不出話來。◇ *There was a **stunned silence** when I told them the news.* 我把消息講了後，他們驚愕得啞然一片。

stung *past tense, past part.* of STING

ˈstun grenade *noun* a small bomb that shocks people so that they cannot do anything, without seriously injuring them 眩暈彈，震撼手榴彈（使人無法動彈但不會造成重創）

ˈstun gun *noun* a weapon that makes a person or an animal unconscious or unable to move for a short time, usually by giving them a small electric shock 眩暈槍（一種使人或動物短時失去知覺或無法動彈的武器）

stunk *past part.* of STINK

stun·ner /ˈstʌnə(r)/ *noun* (*informal*) **1** a person (especially a woman) or a thing that is very attractive or exciting to look at 魅力十足的女子（或人）；絕妙的事物 **2** something, such as a piece of news, that is very surprising or shocking 令人震驚的事情（如新聞等）

stun·ning /ˈstʌnɪŋ/ *adj.* (rather *informal*) **1** extremely attractive or impressive 極有魅力的；絕妙的；給人以深刻印象的 SYN **beautiful**：*You look absolutely stunning!* 你看上去漂亮極了！◇ *a stunning view of the lake* 無比優美的湖光水色 **2** extremely surprising or shocking 令人驚奇萬分的；令人震驚的：*He suffered a stunning defeat in the election.* 他在選舉中慘敗。▸ **stun·ning·ly** *adv.*：*stunningly beautiful* 極為美麗 ◇ *a stunningly simple idea* 一個簡單得出奇的主意

stunt /stʌnt/ *noun, verb*

■ ***noun*** **1** a dangerous and difficult action that sb does to entertain people, especially as part of a film/movie （尤指電影中的）特技表演：*He did all his own stunts.* 所有特技都是他自己演的。◇ *a stunt pilot* 特技飛行員 ➲ COLLOCATIONS at CINEMA **2** (sometimes *disapproving*) something that is done in order to attract people's attention 意在引人注意的花招；噱頭：*a publicity stunt* 宣傳噱頭 **3** (*informal*) a stupid or dangerous act 愚蠢行為；危險舉動：*I've had enough of her childish stunts.* 她那些幼稚的愚蠢行為我受夠了。◇ *Don't you ever **pull a stunt** like that again!* 你再別那樣逞能了！

■ ***verb*** **~ sb/sth** to prevent sb/sth from growing or developing as much as they/it should 阻礙生長；妨礙發展；遏制：*The constant winds had stunted the growth of plants and bushes.* 老是颳風，花草、灌木長不大。◇ *His illness had not stunted his creativity.* 疾病沒有扼殺他的創意。

S

stunt·ed /ˈstʌntɪd/ *adj.* that has not been able to grow or develop as much as it should 發育不足的；生長不良的；未能充分發展的：*stunted trees* 沒能長大的樹 ◇ *the stunted lives of children deprived of education* 未受教育的孩子所過的局限生活

stunt·man /ˈstʌntmæn/, **stunt·woman** /ˈstʌntwʊmən/ *noun* (*pl.* **-men** /-men/, **-women** /-wɪmɪn/) a person whose job is to do dangerous things in place of an actor in a film/movie, etc.; a person who does dangerous things in order to entertain people（電影等中的）特技替身演員；特技表演者

stu·pefy /ˈstjuːpɪfaɪ; *NAmE* ˈstuː-/ *verb* (**stu·pe·fies**, **stu·pe·fy·ing**, **stu·pe·fied**, **stu·pe·fied**) [often passive] **~ sb** to surprise or shock sb; to make sb unable to think clearly 使驚訝（或驚呆、思維不清、神志不清）：*He was stupefied by the amount they had spent.* 得知他們花了那麼多錢，他都驚呆了。◇ *She was stupefied with cold.* 她給凍迷糊了。▸ **stu·pe·fac·tion** /ˌstjuːpɪˈfækʃn; *NAmE* ˌstuː-/ *noun* [U]

stu·pe·fy·ing /ˈstjuːpɪfaɪɪŋ; *NAmE* ˈstuː-/ *adj.* **1** making you unable to think clearly 使人思維不清的；令人神志不清的：*stupefying boredom* 膩煩得讓人發傻 **2** very surprising or shocking 駭人的；令人震驚的 ▸ **stu·pe·fy·ing·ly** *adv.*：*The party was stupefyingly dull.* 這次聚會無聊透了。

stu·pen·dous /stjuːˈpendəs; *NAmE* stuː-/ *adj.* extremely large or impressive, especially greater or better than you expect 極大的；令人驚歎的；了不起的 **SYN** **staggering**：*stupendous achievements* 極大的成就 ◇ *stupendous costs* 驚人的花銷 ▸ **stu·pen·dous·ly** *adv.*

stu·pid 🔑 /ˈstjuːpɪd; *NAmE* ˈstuː-/ *adj.*, *noun*

■ ***adj.*** (**stu·pider**, **stu·pidest**) **HELP** **More stupid** and **most stupid** are also common. * more stupid 和 most stupid 也常用。**1** 🔑 showing a lack of thought or good judgement 欠考慮的；糊塗的 **SYN** **foolish**, **silly**：*a stupid mistake* 愚蠢的錯誤 ◇ *It was a pretty stupid thing to do.* 做那樣的事實在愚蠢。◇ *I was* ***stupid enough*** *to believe him.* 我可真夠糊塗的，竟然相信他的話。◇ ***It was stupid of you*** *to get involved.* 你捲進去了，真是愚蠢。**2** 🔑 (*disapproving*) (of a person 人) slow to learn or understand things; not clever or intelligent 笨的；傻的；腦子不好使的：*He'll manage—he isn't stupid.* 他可以的，他不笨。◇ *Forgetting my notes made me* ***look stupid.*** 我忘了帶筆記，弄得自己像個傻瓜。**3** [only before noun] (*informal*) used to emphasize that you are annoyed with sb/sth（用以加強語氣）討厭的，惱人的：*I can't get the stupid thing open!* 這破玩意兒我怎麼也打不開！◇ *Get your stupid feet off the chair!* 把你的臭腳從椅子上挪開！▸ **stu·pid·ly** *adv.*：*I stupidly agreed to lend him the money.* 我真傻，竟然同意借給他錢了。◇ *Todd stared stupidly at the screen.* 托德呆呆地盯着屏幕。

■ ***noun*** [sing.] (*informal*) if you call sb **stupid**, you are telling them, usually in a joking way, that you think they are not being very intelligent 傻子，笨蛋（常用於開玩笑）：*Yes, stupid, it's you I'm talking to!* 對，傻子，我在跟你說話呢！

stu·pid·ity /stjuːˈpɪdəti; *NAmE* stuː-/ *noun* (*pl.* **-ies**) **1** [U, C, usually pl.] behaviour that shows a lack of thought or good judgement 愚蠢行為；糊塗：*I couldn't believe my own stupidity.* 我幹的蠢事我自己都不能相信。◇ *the errors and stupidities of youth* 年輕時犯的錯誤和做的蠢事 **2** [U] the state or quality of being slow to learn and not clever or intelligent 愚蠢；笨

stu·por /ˈstjuːpə(r); *NAmE* ˈstuː-/ *noun* [sing., U] a state in which you are unable to think, hear, etc. clearly, especially because you have drunk too much alcohol, taken drugs or had a shock（尤指由於醉酒、吸毒或震驚而出現的）神志不清，恍惚，麻痺狀態：*He drank himself into a stupor.* 他喝得爛醉。◇ *a drunken stupor* 酩酊大醉

sturdy /ˈstɜːdi; *NAmE* ˈstɜːrdi/ *adj.* (**stur·dier**, **stur·di·est**) **1** (of an object 物品) strong and not easily damaged 結實的；堅固的 **SYN** **robust**：*a sturdy pair of boots* 一雙結實的靴子 ◇ *a sturdy table* 結實的桌子 **2** (of people and animals, or their bodies 人、動物或身體) physically strong and healthy 強壯的；健壯的：*a man of sturdy build* 體格健壯的男人 ◇ *sturdy legs* 強壯有力的腿 ◇ *a sturdy breed of cattle* 一種體格強壯的牛 **3** not easily influenced or changed by other people 堅決的；堅定的；頑強的 **SYN** **firm**, **determined**：*The village has always maintained a sturdy independence.* 這個村子始終頑強地保持着獨立。▸ **stur·dily** /-ɪli/ *adv.*：*The boat was sturdily made.* 這艘船造得結實。◇ *a sturdily built young man* 體格健壯的年輕男子 ◇ *a sturdily independent community* 頑強地保持獨立的社區 **stur·di·ness** *noun* [U]

stur·geon /ˈstɜːdʒən; *NAmE* ˈstɜːrdʒən/ *noun* [C, U] (*pl.* **stur·geon** or **stur·geons**) a large sea and FRESHWATER fish that lives in northern regions. Sturgeon are used for food and the eggs (called CAVIAR) are also eaten. 鱘

stut·ter /ˈstʌtə(r)/ *verb*, *noun*

■ ***verb*** **1** [T, I] to have difficulty speaking because you cannot stop yourself from repeating the first sound of some words several times 口吃；結結巴巴地說 **SYN** **stammer**：**+ speech** *'W-w-what?' he stuttered.* "什…什…什麼？"他結結巴巴地說。◇ **~ (sth)** *I managed to stutter a reply.* 我結結巴巴，好不容易應了一句。**2** [I] (of a vehicle or an engine 車輛或發動機) to move or start with difficulty, making short sharp noises or movements 突突地吃力行駛（或艱難啟動、艱難運轉）：*The car stuttered along in first gear.* 汽車掛了一擋，突突地緩緩前進。

■ ***noun*** [sing.] a speech problem in which a person finds it difficult to say the first sound of a word and repeats it several times 口吃；結巴：*He had a terrible stutter.* 他患嚴重口吃。

St ˈValentine's Day /ˌsnt ˈvæləntaɪnz deɪ; *NAmE* ˌseɪnt/ *noun* the day (14 February), when people send a card to the person that they love, often without signing their name on it 聖瓦倫廷節，情人節（2 月 14 日，人們常以匿名形式送情人卡）

sty /staɪ/ *noun* **1** (*pl.* **sties**) = PIGSTY **2** (also **stye**) (*pl.* **sties** or **styes**) an infection of the EYELID (= the skin above or below the eye) which makes it red and sore 麥粒腫；瞼腺炎

Sty·gian /ˈstɪdʒiən/ *adj.* [usually before noun] (*literary*) very dark, and therefore frightening 黑黝黝的；陰森森的：*Stygian gloom* 陰森幽暗 **ORIGIN** From the **Styx**, the river in the underworld which the souls of the dead had to cross in Greek myth. 源自 Styx 一詞，即希臘神話中死人的靈魂必須渡過的冥河。

style 🔑 **AW** /staɪl/ *noun*, *verb*

■ ***noun***

▸ **WAY STH IS DONE** 做事方式 **1** 🔑 [C, U] **~ (of sth)** the particular way in which sth is done 方式；作風：*a style of management* 管理方式 ◇ *a management style* 管理方式 ◇ *furniture to suit your style of living* 適合你的生活方式的傢具 ◇ *a study of different teaching styles* 對不同教學方式的研究 ◇ ***I like your style*** (= I like the way you do things). 我喜歡你做事的方式。◇ *Caution was* ***not her style*** (= not the way she usually behaved). 她不是那種謹小慎微的人。◇ *I'm surprised he rides a motorbike—I'd have thought big cars were* ***more his style*** (= what suited him). 沒想到他騎的是摩托車。我還以為他喜歡大轎車呢。➲ see also LIFESTYLE

▸ **DESIGN OF CLOTHES/HAIR** 服式；髮型 **2** 🔑 [C] a particular design of sth, especially clothes 樣式；款式：*We stock a wide variety of styles and sizes.* 我們有各種款式各種尺碼的貨品。◇ *Have you thought about having your hair in a shorter style?* 你有沒有想過剪個短髮型？➲ COLLOCATIONS at FASHION ➲ see also HAIRSTYLE **3** 🔑 [U] the quality of being fashionable in the clothes that you wear（指服裝）時新，時髦，流行式樣：*style-conscious teenagers* 講究時髦的青少年 ◇ *Short skirts are back* ***in style*** (= fashionable). 短裙子又流行起來了。

▸ **BEING ELEGANT** 格調優雅 **4** 🔑 [U] the quality of being elegant and made to a high standard 優雅格調；精緻性；品位；風度；氣派：*The hotel has been redecorated but it's lost a lot of its style.* 旅館已重新裝修，但昔日的優雅格調所剩無幾。◇ *She does everything with style and grace.* 她凡事都做得優雅得體。

▸ **OF BOOK/PAINTING/BUILDING** 書；畫；建築物 **5** 🔑 [C, U] the features of a book, painting, building, etc. that make it typical of a particular author, artist, historical

S

period, etc. 風格；體：*a style of architecture* 建築風格◇ *a fine example of Gothic style* 哥特風格的佳例◇ *a parody written* ***in the style of*** *Molière* 一部模仿莫里哀風格的滑稽喜劇

▸ **USE OF LANGUAGE** 語言運用 **6** [U, C] the correct use of language 語言規範；好的文風：*It's not considered good style to start a sentence with 'but'.* 人們認為，一句話用 but 開頭不是好的文風。◇ *Please follow* ***house style*** (= the rules of spelling, etc. used by a particular publishing company). 請遵循本社的行文格式。

▸ **-STYLE** …樣式 **7** (in adjectives 構成形容詞) having the type of style mentioned …式的；…風格的：*Italian-style gardens* 意大利風格的花園◇ *a buffet-style breakfast* 自助式早餐 ➲ see also OLD-STYLE

▸ **IN A PLANT** 植物 **8** (*biology* 生) the long thin part of a flower that carries the STIGMA 花柱 ➲ **VISUAL VOCAB** page V11

IDM **in (great, grand, etc.) style** in an impressive way 氣派；隆重；氣勢非凡：*She always celebrates her birthday in style.* 她的生日總是過得很排場。◇ *He won the championship in great style.* 他贏得了冠軍，盡顯大將風度。➲ more at CRAMP *v.*

■ *verb*

▸ **CLOTHES/HAIR, ETC.** 服裝、頭髮等 **1 ~ sth** to design, make or shape sth in a particular way 把…設計（或縫製、做）成某種式樣：*an elegantly styled jacket* 式樣高雅的上衣◇ *He'd had his hair styled at an expensive salon.* 他去一家豪華美容廳做了頭髮。

▸ **GIVE NAME/TITLE** 稱呼 **2 ~ sb/sth/yourself + noun** (*formal*) to give sb/sth/yourself a particular name or title 稱呼；命名；稱：*He styled himself Major Carter.* 他自稱卡特少校。

PHR V **'style sth/yourself on sth/sb** to copy the style, manner or appearance of sb/sth 模仿…的風格（或舉止、外觀）**SYN** **model**：*a coffee bar styled on a Parisian cafe* 仿照巴黎一家咖啡館而設計的咖啡館◇ *He styled himself on Elvis Presley.* 他模仿埃爾維斯 • 普雷斯利唱歌。

'style sheet *noun* (*computing* 計) a file which is used for creating documents in a particular style 樣式表，格式頁（用以創建文檔）

sty·li *pl.* of STYLUS

styl·ing **AW** /ˈstaɪlɪŋ/ *noun* [U] **1** the act of cutting and/or shaping hair in a particular style （髮型的）修剪，造型：*styling gel* 定型髮膠 **2** the way in which sth is designed 式樣；款式：*The car has been criticized for its outdated body styling.* 這種轎車因其過時的車身式樣而受到批評。

styl·ish **AW** /ˈstaɪlɪʃ/ *adj.* (*approving*) fashionable; elegant and attractive 時髦的；新潮的；高雅的；雅致的 **SYN** **classy**：*his stylish wife* 他那時髦的妻子◇ *a stylish restaurant* 雅致的餐館◇ *It was a stylish performance by both artists.* 這是兩位藝術家演出的一場高雅節目。▸ **styl·ish·ly** *adv.* **styl·ish·ness** *noun* [U]

styl·ist /ˈstaɪlɪst/ *noun* **1** a person whose job is cutting and shaping people's hair 髮型師 **2** a writer who takes great care to write or say sth in an elegant or unusual way 語言風格優美（或獨特）的人；文體家 **3** a person whose job is to create or design a particular style or image for a product, a person, an advertisement, etc. （產品、人、廣告等的）造型設計師，形象設計師 **4** a person who designs fashionable clothes 時裝設計師 **5** (in sport or music 體育運動或音樂) a person who performs with style 表現得有格調的人

styl·is·tic /staɪˈlɪstɪk/ *adj.* [only before noun] connected with the style an artist uses in a particular piece of art, writing or music 風格上的；文體上的：*stylistic analysis* 風格分析◇ *stylistic features* 風格特點 ▸ **styl·is·tic·al·ly** /-kli/ *adv.*

styl·is·tics /staɪˈlɪstɪks/ *noun* [U] the study of style and the methods used in written language 文體學；風格學

styl·ized (*BrE* also **-ised**) **AW** /ˈstaɪlaɪzd/ *adj.* drawn, written, etc. in a way that is not natural or realistic （繪畫、寫作等手法）非寫實的：*a stylized drawing of a house* 用非寫實手法畫的一座房子◇ *the highly stylized form of acting in Japanese theatre* 日本戲劇中高度非寫實的表演形式 ▸ **styl·iza·tion, -isa·tion** /ˌstaɪlaɪˈzeɪʃn; *NAmE* -ləˈz-/ *noun* [U]

Stylo·phone™ /ˈstaɪləfəʊn; *NAmE* -foʊn/ *noun* a small electronic musical instrument played by touching its keyboard with a STYLUS 斯笛洛風電子琴（用觸筆彈奏）

sty·lus /ˈstaɪləs/ *noun* (*pl.* **sty·luses** or **sty·li** /ˈstaɪlaɪ/) **1** a device on a RECORD PLAYER that looks like a small needle and is placed on the record in order to play it （唱機的）唱針 **2** (*computing* 計) a special pen used to write text or draw an image on a special computer screen 觸控筆（用以在電腦屏幕上書寫、畫畫等）➲ **VISUAL VOCAB** page V66

sty·mie /ˈstaɪmi/ *verb* (**sty·mie·ing** or **sty·my·ing**, **sty·mied**, **sty·mied**) **~ sb/sth** (*informal*) to prevent sb from doing sth that they have planned or want to do; to prevent sth from happening 阻撓；阻礙；阻止；妨礙 **SYN** **foil**

styp·tic /ˈstɪptɪk/ *adj.* (*medical* 醫) able to stop the loss of blood from a wound 能止血的：*I use a styptic pencil on shaving cuts.* 我用止血筆處理刮鬍子割破的傷口。

Styro·foam™ /ˈstaɪrəfəʊm; *NAmE* -foʊm/ *noun* [U] (*especially NAmE*) = POLYSTYRENE：*Styrofoam cups* 舒泰龍泡沫塑料杯

sua·sive /ˈsweɪsɪv/ *adj.* (*linguistics* 語言) (of verbs 動詞) having a meaning that includes the idea of persuading 表勸説的；説服的 ▸ **sua·sion** /ˈsweɪʒn/ *noun* [U]

suave /swɑːv/ *adj.* (especially of a man 尤指男子) confident, elegant and polite, sometimes in a way that does not seem sincere 精明練達的；圓滑的 ▸ **suave·ly** *adv.*

sub /sʌb/ *noun, verb*

■ *noun* (*informal*) **1** = SUBMARINE **2** a substitute who replaces another player in a team 替補隊員：*He came on as sub.* 他作為替補上場。 **3** (*BrE*) a SUBSCRIPTION (= money that you pay regularly when you are a member of a club, etc.) （向俱樂部等定期交納的）會員費 **4** (*BrE*) a SUBEDITOR 助理編輯；審校人 **5** (*NAmE, informal*) a SUBSTITUTE TEACHER 代課教師

■ *verb* **1** [T] **~ sb** to replace a sports player with another player during a game （在比賽中）替換（隊員）**SYN** **substitute**：*He was subbed after just five minutes because of a knee injury.* 他僅上場了五分鐘便因膝部受傷被替換下場。 **2** [I] **~ (for sb)** to do sb else's job for them for a short time 暫代（某人）工作；替班 **SYN** **substitute** **3** [T] **~ sth for sth** to use sth instead of sth else, especially instead of the thing you would normally use 代用；替代（尤指通常使用的東西）**SYN** **substitute**：*For a lower-calorie version of the recipe, try subbing milk for cream.* 要降低這道菜的熱量，可用牛奶代替奶油。 **4** [T] **~ sb sth** (*BrE, informal*) to lend sb money for a short time 短期借（款）給：*Could you sub me £50 till next week?* 借我 50 英鎊，下星期還你，可以嗎？

sub- /sʌb/ *prefix* **1** (in nouns and adjectives 構成名詞和形容詞) below; less than 在…以下；少於；低於；亞於；次於：*sub-zero temperatures* 零度以下氣溫◇ *a subtropical* (= almost tropical) *climate* 亞熱帶氣候◇ *substandard* 低於標準的 **2** (in nouns and adjectives 構成名詞和形容詞) under 在…下面（或底下）：*subway* 地下鐵路◇ *submarine* 潛艇 **3** (in verbs and nouns 構成動詞和名詞) a smaller part of sth 分支；分部；分：*subdivide* 再劃分◇ *subset* 子集

sub·al·tern /ˈsʌbltən; *NAmE* səˈbɔːltərn/ *noun* any officer in the British army who is lower in rank than a captain （英國）陸軍中尉

ˌsub-ˈaqua *adj.* [only before noun] (*BrE*) connected with sports that are done underwater 水下運動的：*sub-aqua diving* 潛水◇ *sub-aqua equipment* 潛水設備

sub·atom·ic /ˌsʌbəˈtɒmɪk; *NAmE* -ˈtɑːm-/ *adj.* [usually before noun] (*physics* 物) smaller than, or found in, an atom 亞原子的；比原子小的；原子內的：*subatomic particles* 亞原子粒子

sub·clause /ˈsʌbklɔːz/ *noun* (*law* 律) one of the parts of a clause (= section) in a legal document （法律文件的）下設條款，次條款，子條款

sub·com·mit·tee /ˈsʌbkəmɪti/ *noun* [C+sing./pl. v.] a smaller committee formed from a main committee in

S

order to study a particular subject in more detail（委員會內的）小組委員會

sub·com·pact /ˈsʌbkəmpækt/ *noun* (*NAmE*) a small car, smaller than a COMPACT 超小型汽車

sub·con·scious /ˌsʌbˈkɒnʃəs; *NAmE* -ˈkɑːn-/ *adj.*, *noun*

■ ***adj.*** [usually before noun] connected with feelings that influence your behaviour even though you are not aware of them 下意識的；潛意識的：*subconscious desires* 下意識的慾望 ◇ *the subconscious mind* 潛意識 ➲ compare CONSCIOUS (3), UNCONSCIOUS (2) ▸ **sub·con·scious·ly** *adv.*：*Subconsciously, she was looking for the father she had never known.* 她在下意識地尋找自己從未見過的父親。

■ ***noun*** **the/your subconscious** [sing.] the part of your mind that contains feelings that you are not aware of 下意識；潛意識 ➲ compare THE UNCONSCIOUS

sub·con·tin·ent /ˌsʌbˈkɒntɪnənt; *NAmE* -ˈkɑːn-/ *noun* [usually sing.] a large land mass that forms part of a continent, especially the part of Asia that includes India, Pakistan and Bangladesh 次大陸（尤指包括印度、巴基斯坦和孟加拉國在內的南亞次大陸）：*the Indian subcontinent* 印度次大陸

sub·con·tract *verb*, *noun*

■ ***verb*** /ˌsʌbkənˈtrækt; *NAmE* ˌsʌbˈkɑːntrækt/ to pay a person or company to do some of the work that you have been given a contract to do 分包；轉包：**～ sth (to sb/sth)** *We subcontracted the work to a small engineering firm.* 我們把工作轉包給了一家小型工程公司。◇ **～ sb/sth (to do sth)** *We subcontracted a small engineering firm to do the work.* 我們轉包給了一家小型工程公司去幹那項工作。▸ **sub·con·tract·ing** *noun* [U]

■ ***noun*** /ˌsʌbˈkɒntrækt; *NAmE* -kɑːn-/ a contract to do part of the work that has been given to another person or company 分包合同；轉包合同

sub·con·tract·or /ˌsʌbkənˈtræktə(r); *NAmE* sʌbˈkɑːntræk-/ *noun* a person or company that does part of the work given to another person or company 分包商；分包人

sub·cul·ture /ˈsʌbkʌltʃə(r)/ *noun* (sometimes *disapproving*) the behaviour and beliefs of a particular group of people in society that are different from those of most people（某群體特有的）亞文化行為觀念，次文化：*the* ***criminal/drug/youth, etc. subculture*** 犯罪、吸毒、青少年群體等的亞文化

sub·cuta·ne·ous /ˌsʌbkjuˈteɪmiəs/ *adj.* [usually before noun] (*technical* 術語) under the skin 皮下的：*a subcutaneous injection* 皮下注射 ▸ **sub·cuta·ne·ous·ly** *adv.*

S

sub·dir·ec·tory /ˈsʌbdərektəri; -dɪ-; -daɪ-/ *noun* (*pl.* **-ies**) (*computing* 計) a DIRECTORY (= list of files or programs) which is inside another directory 子目錄

sub·div·ide /ˈsʌbdɪvaɪd; ˌsʌbdɪˈvaɪd/ *verb* [T, often passive, I] **～ (sth) (into sth)** to divide sth into smaller parts; to be divided into smaller parts（被）再分割，再分

sub·div·ision *noun* **1** /ˌsʌbdɪˈvɪʒn/ [U] the act of dividing a part of sth into smaller parts 再分割；再分；細分 **2** /ˈsʌbdɪvɪʒn/ [C] one of the smaller parts into which a part of sth has been divided 進一步分成的部份；分支；分部：*a police subdivision* (= the area covered by one particular police force) 警察部門下屬的管轄分區 ◇ *subdivisions within the Hindu caste system* 印度教種姓制度內的不同等級 **3** /ˈsʌbdɪvɪʒn/ [C] (*NAmE*) an area of land that has been divided up for building houses on（分割成小塊的）建房土地

sub·due /səbˈdjuː; *NAmE* -ˈduː/ *verb* (rather *formal*) **1 ～ sb/sth** to bring sb/sth under control, especially by using force 制伏；征服；控制 SYN **defeat**：*Troops were called in to subdue the rebels.* 軍隊被調來鎮壓反叛者。**2 ～ sth** to calm or control your feelings 抑制，壓制，克制（感情）SYN **suppress**：*Julia had to subdue an urge to stroke his hair.* 朱莉婭得克制住自己，不去撫摩他的頭髮。

sub·dued /səbˈdjuːd; *NAmE* -ˈduːd/ *adj.* **1** (of a person 人) unusually quiet, and possibly unhappy 悶悶不樂的；抑鬱的；默不作聲的：*He seemed a bit subdued to me.* 我覺得他當時有點悶悶不樂。◇ *She was in a subdued mood.* 她心情抑鬱。◇ *The reception was a subdued affair.* 招待會開得冷冷清清的。**2** (of light or colours 光線或色彩) not very bright 柔和的：*subdued lighting* 柔和的燈光 **3** (of sounds 聲音) not very loud 壓低的；小聲的：*a subdued conversation* 小聲的談話 **4** (of business activity 商業活動) not very busy; with not much activity 不活躍的；低迷的；蕭條的：*a period of subdued trading* 貿易蕭條時期

sub·edi·tor /ˌsʌbˈedɪtə(r)/ (also *informal* **sub**) *noun* (*BrE*) a person whose job is to check and make changes to the text of a newspaper or magazine before it is printed 助理編輯；審校人 ▸ **sub·edit** *verb* [I, T] **～ (sth)**

sub·group /ˈsʌbgruːp/ *noun* a smaller group made up of members of a larger group 小組；（團體中的）部份

sub·head·ing /ˌsʌbˈhedɪŋ/ *noun* a title given to any of the sections into which a longer piece of writing has been divided 小標題；子標題

sub·human /ˌsʌbˈhjuːmən/ *adj.* (*disapproving*) not working or behaving like a normal human; not fit for humans 非人的；不齒於人類的；不適合人類的：*subhuman behaviour* 不齒於人類的行為 ◇ *They were living in subhuman conditions.* 他們生活在非人的條件下。➲ compare INHUMAN, SUPERHUMAN

sub·ject 🔑 *noun*, *adj.*, *verb*

■ ***noun*** /ˈsʌbdʒɪkt; -dʒekt/

▸ **OF CONVERSATION/BOOK** 談話；書籍 **1** 🔑 a thing or person that is being discussed, described or dealt with 主題；題目；話題；題材；問題：*an unpleasant* ***subject of conversation*** 不愉快的話題 ◇ *books on many different subjects* 題材廣泛的各種書籍 ◇ *a magazine article* ***on the subject of*** *space travel* 一篇談航天旅行的雜誌文章 ◇ *I have nothing more to say on the subject.* 關於這個問題，我再沒有要說的了。◇ *I wish you'd* ***change the subject*** (= talk about sth else). 我希望你換個話題。◇ *How did we* ***get onto the subject of*** *marriage?* 我們怎麼談到婚姻問題上了？◇ *We seem to have* ***got off the subject*** *we're meant to be discussing.* 我們似乎偏離了應當討論的題目。◇ *Nelson Mandela is the subject of a new biography.* 納爾遜•曼德拉是一本新傳記的傳主。◇ *Climate change is still very much a* ***subject for debate****.* 氣候變化仍然是人們時常爭論的話題。

▸ **AT SCHOOL/COLLEGE** 學校 **2** 🔑 an area of knowledge studied in a school, college, etc. 學科；科目；課程：*Biology is my favourite subject.* 生物是我最喜歡的學科。

▸ **OF PICTURE/PHOTOGRAPH** 繪畫；攝影 **3** a person or thing that is the main feature of a picture or photograph, or that a work of art is based on 表現對象；繪畫（或拍攝）題材：*Focus the camera on the subject.* 把相機的焦距調到被拍對象上。◇ *Classical landscapes were a popular subject with many 18th century painters.* 古典風景畫是 18 世紀許多畫家所喜歡用的題材。

▸ **OF EXPERIMENT** 實驗 **4** a person or thing being used to study sth, especially in an experiment 接受試驗者；實驗對象：*We need male subjects between the ages of 18 and 25 for the experiment.* 我們需要 18 至 25 歲之間的男性來接受試驗。

▸ **GRAMMAR** 語法 **5** a noun, noun phrase or pronoun representing the person or thing that performs the action of the verb (*I* in *I sat down.*), about which sth is stated (*the house* in *the house is very old*) or, in a passive sentence, that is affected by the action of the verb (*the tree* in *the tree was blown down in the storm*) 主語；主詞 ➲ compare OBJECT *n.* (4), PREDICATE *n.*

▸ **OF COUNTRY** 國家 **6** a person who has the right to belong to a particular country, especially one with a king or queen（尤指君主制國家的）國民，臣民：*a British subject* 英國國民

■ ***adj.*** /ˈsʌbdʒekt; -dʒɪkt/ (*formal*) **1 ～ to sth** likely to be affected by sth, especially sth bad 可能受…影響的；易遭受…的：*Flights are subject to delay because of the fog.* 由於有霧，航班可能延誤。**2 ～ to sth** depending on sth in order to be completed or agreed 取決於；視…而定：*The article is ready to publish, subject to your approval.* 那篇文章準備好了，可以發表，就等你批准了。◇ *All the holidays on offer are subject to availability.* 所有特價度假產品售完即止。**3 ～ to sth/sb** under the authority of sth/sb 受…支配；服從於：*All nuclear installations are* *subject to international safeguards.* 一切核設施均須執行國際防護措施。 **4** [only before noun] controlled by the government of another country 受異族統治的；臣服的： *subject peoples* 被他國統治的民族

■ ***verb*** /səbˈdʒekt/ **~ sth** (**to sth**) (*formal*) to bring a country or group of people under your control, especially by using force 使臣服；使順從；（尤指）壓服： *The Roman Empire subjected most of Europe to its rule.* 羅馬帝國把歐洲多數地區置於自己的統治之下。 ▸ **sub·jec·tion** /səbˈdʒekʃn/ *noun* [U]

PHR V **subˈject sb/sth to sth** [often passive] to make sb/sth experience, suffer or be affected by sth, usually sth unpleasant 使經受；使遭受： *to be subjected to ridicule* 受到嘲笑 ◇ *The city was subjected to heavy bombing.* 那座城市遭受猛烈轟炸。◇ *The defence lawyers claimed that the prisoners had been subjected to cruel and degrading treatment.* 辯護律師聲稱囚犯遭到了殘暴和侮辱性的對待。

sub·ject·ive /səbˈdʒektɪv/ *adj.* **1** based on your own ideas or opinions rather than facts and therefore sometimes unfair 主觀的（非客觀的）： *a highly subjective point of view* 非常主觀的看法 ◇ *Everyone's opinion is bound to be subjective.* 每個人的意見都必定是主觀的。 **2** (of ideas, feelings or experiences 思想、感情或經歷) existing in sb's mind rather than in the real world 主觀的（非現實世界的） **3** [only before noun] (*grammar* 語法) the **subjective** case is the one which is used for the subject of a sentence 主語的；主格的 **OPP** **objective** ▸ **sub·ject·ive·ly** *adv.* ： *People who are less subjectively involved are better judges.* 主觀因素介入愈少，愈能作出恰當的判斷。◇ *subjectively perceived changes* 主觀感受到的變化 **sub·ject·iv·ity** /ˌsʌbdʒekˈtɪvəti/ *noun* [U] ： *There is an element of subjectivity in her criticism.* 她的批評有主觀因素。

sub·ject·iv·ism /səbˈdʒektɪvɪzəm/ *noun* [U] (*philosophy* 哲) the theory that all knowledge and moral values are subjective rather than based on truth that actually exists in the real world 主觀主義；主觀論

ˈsubject matter *noun* [U] the ideas or information contained in a book, speech, painting, etc.（著作、講話、繪畫等的）主題，題材，主要內容： *The artist was revolutionary in both subject matter and technique.* 這位畫家在內容和手法兩方面都有重大創新。◇ *She's searching for subject matter for her new book.* 她要寫一部新書，正尋找題材。

sub ju·dice /ˌsʌb ˈdʒuːdəsi; -seɪ; -keɪ/ *adj.* [not usually before noun] (from *Latin*, *law* 律) if a legal case is **sub judice**, it is still being discussed in court and it is therefore illegal for anyone to talk about it in newspapers, etc. 在審理中，尚未裁決（任何人公諸報端等均屬違法）

sub·ju·gate /ˈsʌbdʒugeɪt/ *verb* [usually passive] **~ sb/sth** (*formal*) to defeat sb/sth; to gain control over sb/sth 征服；制伏；使屈服；使服從： *a subjugated race* 被征服的民族 ◇ *Her personal ambitions had been subjugated to* (= considered less important than) *the needs of her family.* 她個人的雄心壯志讓位給了家庭的需要。 ▸ **sub·ju·ga·tion** /ˌsʌbdʒuˈgeɪʃn/ *noun* [U] ： (*formal*) *the subjugation of Ireland by England* 英格蘭對愛爾蘭的征服

sub·junct·ive /səbˈdʒʌŋktɪv/ *noun* (*grammar* 語法) the form (or MOOD) of a verb that expresses wishes, possibility or UNCERTAINTY; a verb in this form 虛擬式；虛擬語氣： *The verb is in the subjunctive.* 這個動詞是虛擬語氣。◇ *In 'I wish I were taller', 'were' is a subjunctive.* 在 I wish I were taller 中，were 是虛擬式。 ▸ **sub·junct·ive** *adj.* ： *the subjunctive mood* 虛擬語氣

sub·let /ˌsʌbˈlet/ *verb* (**sub·let·ting**, **sub·let**, **sub·let**) [T, I] **~ (sth)** (**to sb**) to rent to sb else all or part of a property that you rent from the owner 轉租，分租（租來的物業） ➲ COLLOCATIONS at HOUSE

ˌsub lieuˈtenant *noun* an officer in the British navy just below the rank of LIEUTENANT（英國）海軍中尉

sub·lim·ate /ˈsʌblɪmeɪt/ *verb* **~ sth** (*psychology* 心) to direct your energy, especially sexual energy, to socially acceptable activities such as work, exercise, art, etc. 升華，使高尚化（把性慾衝動等轉移到工作、鍛煉、藝術等社會可接受的活動中） **SYN** **channel** ▸ **sub·lim·ation** /ˌsʌblɪˈmeɪʃn/ *noun* [U]

sub·lime /səˈblaɪm/ *adj., noun*

■ ***adj.*** **1** of very high quality and causing great admiration 崇高的；壯麗的；宏偉的；令人讚歎的： *sublime beauty* 令人讚歎的美 ◇ *a sublime combination of flavours* 搭配巧妙的幾種味道 **2** (*formal*, often *disapproving*) (of a person's behaviour or attitudes 人的行為或態度) extreme, especially in a way that shows they are not aware of what they are doing or are not concerned about what happens because of it 極端的；極端而盲目的；一味的： *the sublime confidence of youth* 年輕人目空一切的自信 ▸ **sub·lime·ly** *adv.* ： *sublimely beautiful* 美得令人讚歎 ◇ *She was sublimely unaware of the trouble she had caused.* 她壓根兒沒察覺自己鬧出了亂子。 **sub·lim·ity** /səˈblɪməti/ *noun* [U]

■ ***noun*** **the sublime** [sing.] something that is sublime 崇高的事物；壯麗的景象；絕妙的東西： *He transforms the most ordinary subject into the sublime.* 經他一點化，極普通的題材也能變得令人叫絕。

IDM **from the sublime to the riˈdiculous** used to describe a situation in which sth serious, important or of high quality is followed by sth silly, unimportant or of poor quality 從高超到荒謬；從高妙到低俗

sub·lim·inal /ˌsʌbˈlɪmɪnl/ *adj.* affecting your mind even though you are not aware of it 下意識的；潛意識的： *subliminal advertising* 隱性廣告 ▸ **sub·lim·in·al·ly** *adv.*

ˌsub-maˈchine gun *noun* a light MACHINE GUN that you can hold in your hands to fire 衝鋒槍；輕型自動（或半自動）槍

sub·mar·ine /ˌsʌbməˈriːn; ˈsʌbməriːn/ *noun, adj.*

■ ***noun*** (also *informal* **sub**) **1** a ship that can travel underwater 潛艇： *a nuclear submarine* 核潛艇 ◇ *a submarine base* 潛艇基地 **2** (also **ˌsubmarine ˈsandwich**, **hero**) (all *NAmE*) a long bread roll split open along its length and filled with various types of food 潛艇三明治，長捲三明治（用長捲麪包縱向切開，內夾各種食物）

■ ***adj.*** [only before noun] (*technical* 術語) existing or located under the sea 水下的；海底的： *submarine plant life* 海底植物 ◇ *submarine cables* 海底電纜

sub·mar·iner /sʌbˈmærɪnə(r); *NAmE* also ˌsʌbməˈriːnər/ *noun* a sailor who works on a submarine 潛艇水兵

sub·merge /səbˈmɜːdʒ; *NAmE* -ˈmɜːrdʒ/ *verb* **1** [I, T] to go under the surface of water or liquid; to put sth or make sth go under the surface of water or liquid（使）潛入水中，沒入水中，浸沒，淹沒： *The submarine had had time to submerge before the warship could approach.* 潛水艇沒等軍艦靠近就及時潛入水下了。◇ **~ sth** *The fields had been submerged by floodwater.* 農田被洪水淹沒了。 **2** [T] **~ sth** to hide ideas, feelings, opinions, etc. completely 湮沒，湮滅，掩蓋（思想、感情等）： *Doubts that had been submerged in her mind suddenly resurfaced.* 她心裏早已湮滅的疑團突然又浮現出來。 ▸ **sub·merged** *adj.* ： *Her submerged car was discovered in the river by police divers.* 她被河水淹沒的汽車給警方的潛水員找到了。 **sub·mer·sion** /səbˈmɜːʃn; *NAmE* -ˈmɜːrʒn/ *noun* [U]

sub·mers·ible /səbˈmɜːsəbl; *NAmE* -ˈmɜːrs-/ *adj., noun*

■ ***adj.*** (*NAmE* also **sub·merg·ible** /səbˈmɜːdʒəbl; *NAmE* -ˈmɜːrdʒ-/) that can be used underwater 水下使用的： *a submersible camera* 水下攝影機

■ ***noun*** a SUBMARINE (= a ship that can travel underwater) that goes underwater for short periods 可潛船；潛水器

sub·mis·sion **AW** /səbˈmɪʃn/ *noun* **1** [U] the act of accepting that sb has defeated you and that you must obey them 屈服；投降；歸順 **SYN** **surrender** ： *a gesture of submission* 投降的手勢 ◇ *to* ***beat/force/starve sb into submission*** 打得／強迫／餓得某人屈服 **2** [U, C] the act of giving a document, proposal, etc. to sb in authority so that they can study or consider it; the document, etc. that you give 提交；呈遞；提交（或呈遞）的文件、建議等： *When is the final date for the submission of proposals?* 呈交提案的最後日期是什麼時候？ ◇ *They prepared a report for submission to the council.* 他們準備了一份報告要提交給理事會。◇ *All parties will have the opportunity to* ***make submissions***

relating to this case. 各方均有機會提交與此案有關的陳述。 **3** [C] (*law* 律) a statement that is made to a judge in court（向法官提出的）看法，意見

sub·mis·sive /səbˈmɪsɪv/ *adj.* too willing to accept sb else's authority and willing to obey them without questioning anything they want you to do 唯命是從的；順從的；馴服的；聽話的：*He expected his daughters to be meek and submissive.* 他期望女兒都溫順聽話。◇ *She followed him like a submissive child.* 她對他百依百順，像個聽話的孩子。**OPP** **assertive** ▸ **sub·mis·sive·ly** *adv.*: *'You're right and I was wrong,' he said submissively.* "你說得對，是我錯了。"他恭順地說。 **sub·mis·sive·ness** *noun* [U]

sub·mit **AW** /səbˈmɪt/ *verb* (**-tt-**) **1** [T] **~ sth (to sb/sth)** to give a document, proposal, etc. to sb in authority so that they can study or consider it 提交，呈遞（文件、建議等）：*to* ***submit an application/a claim/a complaint*** 呈遞申請書 / 書面要求；提交控訴書◇ *Completed projects must be submitted by 10 March.* 完成的方案必須在 3 月 10 日前提交。 **2** [I, T] (*formal*) to accept the authority, control or greater strength of sb/sth; to agree to sth because of this 順從；屈服；投降；不得已接受 **SYN** **give in to sb/sth, yield**：**~ (to sb/sth)** *She refused to submit to threats.* 面對威脅，她拒不低頭。◇ **~ yourself (to sb/sth)** *He submitted himself to a search by the guards.* 他不情願地讓衛兵搜查。 **3** [T] **~ that ...** (*law* 律 or *formal*) to say or suggest sth 表示；認為；主張；建議：*Counsel for the defence submitted that the evidence was inadmissible.* 被告律師認為這一證據不可採納。

sub·nor·mal /ˌsʌbˈnɔːml; *NAmE* -ˈnɔːrml/ *adj.* **1** (*technical* 術語) lower than normal 低於正常的；正常值以下的；偏低的：*subnormal temperatures* 偏低的氣溫 **2** (sometimes *offensive*) having less than the normal level of intelligence 低能的；弱智的：*educationally subnormal children* 學習能力低下的兒童

sub·note·book /ˌsʌbˈnəʊtbʊk; *NAmE* -ˈnoʊt-/ (also **sub·note** /ˈsʌbnəʊt; *NAmE* -noʊt/, **ˈmini-note**) *noun* a small LAPTOP computer 小型筆記本電腦；小筆電 ➲ compare NETBOOK, NOTEBOOK (3)

sub·or·din·ate **AW** *adj., noun, verb*

■ ***adj.*** /səˈbɔːdɪnət; *NAmE* -ˈbɔːrd-/ **1 ~ (to sb)** having less power or authority than sb else in a group or an organization 隸屬的；從屬的；下級的：*In many societies women are subordinate to men.* 在許多社會中，婦女都從屬於男人。 **2 ~ (to sth)** less important than sth else 次要的 **SYN** **secondary**：*All other issues are subordinate to this one.* 所有其他問題都沒有這一問題重要。

■ ***noun*** /səˈbɔːdɪnət; *NAmE* -ˈbɔːrd-/ a person who has a position with less authority and power than sb else in an organization 下級；部屬 **SYN** **inferior**：*the relationship between subordinates and superiors* 上下級關係

■ ***verb*** /səˈbɔːdɪneɪt; *NAmE* -ˈbɔːrd-/ **~ sb/sth (to sb/sth)** to treat sb/sth as less important than sb/sth else 把…置於次要地位；使從屬於：*Safety considerations were subordinated to commercial interests.* 商業利益置於安全考慮之上。 ▸ **sub·or·din·ation** **AW** /səˌbɔːdɪˈneɪʃn; *NAmE* -ˌbɔːrd-/ *noun* [U]

suˌbordinate ˈclause (also **deˌpendent ˈclause**) *noun* (*grammar* 語法) a group of words that is not a sentence but adds information to the main part of a sentence, for example *when it rang* in *She answered the phone when it rang.* 從句；從屬分句；從屬子句 ➲ compare COORDINATE CLAUSE, MAIN CLAUSE

suˌbordinating conˈjunction *noun* (*grammar* 語法) a word that begins a subordinate clause, for example 'although' or 'because' 從屬連詞；主從連詞；從屬連接詞 ➲ compare COORDINATING CONJUNCTION

sub·orn /səˈbɔːn; *NAmE* səˈbɔːrn/ *verb* **~ sb** (*law* 律) to pay or persuade sb to do sth illegal, especially to tell lies in court 收買，買通（使作偽證等）；唆使（他人犯法）：*to suborn a witness* 收買證人

sub·par /ˌsʌbˈpɑː(r)/ *adj.* (*especially NAmE*) below a level of quality that is usual or expected 不到一般（或預期）水平的；低於標準的：*a subpar performance* 低水平的演出

sub·plot /ˈsʌbplɒt; *NAmE* -plɑːt/ *noun* a series of events in a play, novel, etc. that is separate from but linked to the main story（戲劇、小說等的）次要情節，從屬情節

sub·poena /səˈpiːnə/ *noun, verb*

■ ***noun*** (*law* 律) a written order to attend court as a witness to give evidence（傳喚證人出庭的）傳票

■ ***verb*** **~ sb (to do sth)** (*law* 律) to order sb to attend court and give evidence as a witness 以傳票傳喚（證人出庭）：*The court subpoenaed her to appear as a witness.* 法庭傳喚她出庭作證。➲ COLLOCATIONS at JUSTICE

ˌsub-ˈpost office *noun* (*BrE*) a small local post office（本地的）小郵局

sub·prime /ˌsʌbˈpraɪm/ *adj.* (*finance* 財) connected with the practice of lending money to people who may not be able to pay the money back, because they have a bad CREDIT RATING 次級的，次貸的（指貸款給信用差、可能無力還款的人）：*subprime mortgages/loans/lending* 次級按揭 / 貸款 / 放款◇ *subprime lenders/borrowers* 次級放款人 / 借款人

sub·rou·tine /ˈsʌbruːtiːn/ (also **sub·pro·gram** /ˈsʌbprəʊɡræm; *NAmE* -proʊ-/) *noun* (*computing* 計) a set of instructions which repeatedly perform a task within a program 子例程，子程序，子程式（程序中反複執行某任務的一系列指令）

sub-Saharan /ˌsʌb səˈhɑːrən/ *adj.* [only before noun] from or relating to areas in Africa that are south of the Sahara Desert 撒哈拉沙漠以南（非洲地區）的：*sub-Saharan Africa* 非洲撒哈拉沙漠以南的地區

sub·scribe /səbˈskraɪb/ *verb* **1** [I] **~ (to sth)** to pay an amount of money regularly in order to receive or use sth 定期訂購（或訂閱等）：*Which journals does the library subscribe to?* 圖書館訂有哪些報刊？◇ *We subscribe to several sports channels* (= on TV). 我們付費收看好幾個體育頻道。◇ *He subscribed to a newsgroup* (= on the Internet). 他成了一個網上新聞組的用戶。 **2** [I] **~ (to sth)** to pay money regularly to be a member of an organization or to support a charity 定期交納（會員費）；定期（向慈善機構）捐款；定期捐助：*He subscribes regularly to Amnesty International.* 他定期向大赦國際捐款。 **3** [I] **~ (for sth)** (*finance* 財) to apply to buy shares in a company 認購（股份）➲ see also OVERSUBSCRIBED **4** [T, usually passive] **~ sth** to apply to take part in an activity, use a service, etc. 申請；預訂；報名：*The tour of Edinburgh is fully subscribed.* 去愛丁堡旅遊的名額已經滿了。

PHR V **subˈscribe to sth** (*formal*) to agree with or support an opinion, a theory, etc. 同意；贊成 **SYN** **believe in sth**：*The authorities no longer subscribe to the view that disabled people are unsuitable as teachers.* 當局不再支持殘疾人不適宜做教師的觀點。

sub·scriber /səbˈskraɪbə(r)/ *noun* **1** a person who pays money, usually once a year, to receive regular copies of a magazine or newspaper（報刊的）訂閱人，訂購者，訂戶 **2** (*BrE*) a person who gives money regularly to help the work of an organization such as a charity（慈善機關等的）定期捐款者，定期捐助者 **3** a person who pays to receive a service 消費者；用戶：*subscribers to cable television* 有線電視用戶

sub·scrip·tion /səbˈskrɪpʃn/ *noun* [C, U] **1** an amount of money you pay, usually once a year, to receive regular copies of a newspaper or magazine, etc.; the act of paying this money（報刊等的）訂閱費，訂購款，訂閱，訂購：*an annual subscription* 一年期訂閱◇ **~ (to/for sth)** *to* ***take out a subscription*** *to 'Newsweek'* 訂閱《新聞週刊》◇ *to* ***cancel/renew a subscription*** 退訂；續訂◇ *Copies are available by subscription.* 此刊物供訂購。 **2** (*BrE*) a sum of money that you pay regularly to a charity, or to be a member of a club or to receive a service; the act of paying this money（向慈善機構的）定期捐款；（俱樂部的）會員費；（服務的）用戶費；會員費（或服務費）的交納 **SYN** **donation**：*a monthly subscription to Oxfam* 每月給樂施會的捐款 **3** the act of people paying money for sth to be done 集體資助；集體捐助：*A statue in his memory was erected by* ***public***

subscription. 由公眾捐資建起一座紀念他的雕像。 ➲ SYNONYMS at PAYMENT

sub'scription concert *noun* (*BrE*) any of the concerts in a series for which the tickets are sold in advance 聯票音樂會（預售系列音樂會中的一場）

sub·sec·tion /'sʌbsekʃn/ *noun* a part of a section, especially of a legal document 分部；分段；（尤指法律文件的）分款，分項

sub·se·quent AW /'sʌbsɪkwənt/ *adj.* (*formal*) happening or coming after sth else 隨後；後來；之後；接後 OPP **previous**：*subsequent generations* 後代 ◇ *Subsequent events confirmed our doubts.* 後來發生的事證實了我們的疑慮。◇ *Developments on this issue will be dealt with in a subsequent report.* 這個問題的發展將在以後的報道中予以說明。

sub·se·quent·ly AW /'sʌbsɪkwəntli/ *adv.* (*formal*) afterwards; later; after sth else has happened 隨後；後來；之後；接着：*The original interview notes were subsequently lost.* 採訪記錄原稿後來丟失了。◇ *Subsequently, new guidelines were issued to all employees.* 隨後，新的準則發給了所有雇員。

'subsequent to *prep.* (*formal*) after; following 在…之後；繼…之後：*There have been further developments subsequent to our meeting.* 在我們的會議之後又有新發展。

sub·ser·vi·ent /səb'sɜːviənt; *NAmE* -'sɜːrv-/ *adj.* **1 ~ (to sb/sth)** (*disapproving*) too willing to obey other people 恭順的；馴服的；諂媚的；卑躬屈膝的：*The press was accused of being subservient to the government.* 有人指責新聞界一味迎合政府的旨意。 **2 ~ (to sth)** (*formal*) less important than sth else 次要；從屬於：*The needs of individuals were subservient to those of the group as a whole.* 個人的需要服從於整個集體的需要。 ▸ **sub·ser·vi·ence** /-əns/ *noun* [U]

sub·set /'sʌbset/ *noun* (*technical* 術語) a smaller group of people or things formed from the members of a larger group 分組；小組；子集

sub·side /səb'saɪd/ *verb* **1** [I] to become calmer or quieter 趨於平靜；平息；減弱；消退：*She waited nervously for his anger to subside.* 她提心吊膽地等他的怒氣平息下來。◇ *I took an aspirin and the pain gradually subsided.* 我服了一片阿司匹林，疼痛逐漸緩解了。 **2** [I] (of water 水) to go back to a normal level 回落；減退：*The flood waters gradually subsided.* 洪水緩緩回落。 **3** [I] (of land or a building 地面或建築物) to sink to a lower level; to sink lower into the ground 下沉；沉降；下陷：*Weak foundations caused the house to subside.* 由於地基不實，房子出現下陷。

sub·sid·ence /səb'saɪdns; 'sʌbsɪdns/ *noun* [U] the process by which an area of land sinks to a lower level than normal, or by which a building sinks into the ground（地面或建築物的）下沉，沉降，下陷

sub·sidi·ar·ity /səbˌsɪdi'ærəti; ˌsʌbsɪdi-; *NAmE* -'erəti/ *noun* [U] the principle that a central authority should not be very powerful, and should only control things which cannot be controlled by local organizations 輔助原則，輔從原則（中央權力機關應只控制地方上無法操控的事務）

sub·sid·iary AW /səb'sɪdiəri; *NAmE* -dieri/ *adj.*, *noun*

▪ *adj.* **1 ~ (to sth)** connected with sth but less important than it 輔助的；附帶的；次要的 SYN **additional**：*subsidiary information* 輔助資料 ◇ *a subsidiary matter* 附帶問題 ◇ (*BrE*) *I'm taking History as a* ***subsidiary subject*** (= one that is not studied in as great depth as a main subject). 我把歷史課作為輔修科目。 **2** (of a business company 公司) owned or controlled by another company 附屬的；隸屬的

▪ *noun* (*pl.* **-ies**) a business company that is owned or controlled by another larger company 附屬公司；子公司

sub·sid·ize (*BrE* also **-ise**) AW /'sʌbsɪdaɪz/ *verb* **~ sb/sth** to give money to sb or an organization to help pay for sth; to give a subsidy 資助；補助；給…發津貼 SYN **fund**：*The housing projects are subsidized by the government.* 這些住房項目得到政府的補貼。◇ *She's not prepared to subsidize his gambling any longer.* 她再不願意拿錢供他去賭博了。 ▸ **sub·sid·iza·tion, -isa·tion** /ˌsʌbsɪdaɪ'zeɪʃn; *NAmE* -də'z-/ *noun* [U]

sub·sidy AW /'sʌbsədi/ *noun* (*pl.* **-ies**) [C, U] money that is paid by a government or an organization to reduce the costs of services or of producing goods so that their prices can be kept low 補貼；補助金；津貼：*agricultural subsidies* 農業補貼 ◇ *to reduce the level of subsidy* 降低補貼金額 ➲ COLLOCATIONS at FARMING

sub·sist /səb'sɪst/ *verb* **1** [I] **~ (on sth)** to manage to stay alive, especially with limited food or money（尤指靠有限的食物或錢）維持生活，度日：*Old people often subsist on very small incomes.* 老人往往靠十分微薄的收入艱難度日。 **2** [I] (*formal*) to exist; to be valid 存在；有效：*The terms of the contract subsist.* 合同條款有效。

sub·sist·ence /səb'sɪstəns/ *noun* [U] the state of having just enough money or food to stay alive 勉強維持生活：*Many families are living below the level of subsistence.* 許多家庭難以度日。◇ *to live below (the)* ***subsistence level*** 生活在基本生活水平線以下 ◇ *They had no visible means of subsistence.* 他們生計無着。◇ ***subsistence agriculture/farming*** (= growing enough only to live on, not to sell) 收成僅夠自身口糧的自給農業 ◇ ***subsistence crops*** 生存作物 ◇ *He worked a 16-hour day for a* ***subsistence wage*** (= enough money to buy only basic items). 他一天工作 16 個小時，工資才夠勉強維持生計。

sub·soil /'sʌbsɔɪl/ *noun* [U] the layer of soil between the surface of the ground and the hard rock underneath it 底土；心土 ➲ compare TOPSOIL

sub·son·ic /ˌsʌb'sɒnɪk; *NAmE* -'sɑːn-/ *adj.* less than the speed of sound; flying at less than the speed of sound 亞音速的；亞音速飛行的 ➲ compare SUPERSONIC

sub·stance 0-w /'sʌbstəns/ *noun*

1 0-w [C] a type of solid, liquid or gas that has particular qualities 物質；物品；東西：*a* ***chemical/radioactive, etc. substance*** 化學、放射性等物質 ◇ ***banned/illegal substances*** (= drugs) 禁用／非法物品 ◇ *a sticky substance* 一種黏糊糊的東西 **2** [U] the quality of being based on facts or the truth 事實基礎；根據：*It was malicious gossip, completely* ***without substance***. 這是惡意造謠，完全沒有事實根據。◇ *The commission's report* ***gives substance to*** *these allegations.* 委員會的報告為這些說法提供了事實根據。◇ *There is some substance in what he says.* 他的話是有一定根據的。 **3** [U] the most important or main part of sth 主旨；要點；實質；基本內容：*Love and guilt form* ***the substance of*** *his new book.* 他的新書主要講愛情與罪孽。◇ *I agreed with what she said* ***in substance***, *though not with every detail.* 對於她所說的，雖然不是每個細節我都同意，但基本內容卻是贊同的。 **4** [U] (*formal*) importance 重要性 SYN **significance**：*matters* ***of substance*** 重大問題 ◇ *Nothing of any substance was achieved in the meeting.* 會議沒有取得任何實質性成果。

IDM **a man/woman of 'substance** (*formal*) a rich and powerful man or woman 有錢有勢的男人／女人

sub·standard /ˌsʌb'stændəd; *NAmE* -ərd/ *adj.* not as good as normal; not acceptable 不達標的；不合格的 SYN **inferior**：*substandard goods* 次貨

sub·stan·tial 0-w /səb'stænʃl/ *adj.*

1 0-w large in amount, value or importance 大量的；價值巨大的；重大的 SYN **considerable**：*substantial sums of money* 大筆大筆的錢 ◇ *a substantial change* 重大變化 ◇ *Substantial numbers of people support the reforms.* 相當多的人支持這些改革措施。◇ *He ate a substantial breakfast.* 他吃了一頓豐盛的早餐。 **2** 0-w [usually before noun] (*formal*) large and solid; strongly built 大而堅固的；結實的；牢固的：*a substantial house* 結實的房子

sub·stan·tial·ly 0-w /səb'stænʃəli/ *adv.*

1 0-w very much; a lot 非常；大大地 SYN **considerably**：*The costs have increased substantially.* 成本大大提高了。◇ *The plane was substantially damaged in the crash.* 失事飛機損壞嚴重。 **2** (*formal*) mainly; in most details, even if not completely 基本上；大體上；總的來說：*What she says is substantially true.* 她的話大體符合事實。

sub·stan·ti·ate /səb'stænʃieɪt/ *verb* **~ sth** (*formal*) to provide information or evidence to prove that sth is

S

true 證實；證明： *The results of the tests substantiated his claims.* 這些檢驗的結果證實了他的說法。 ▸ **sub·stan·ti·ation** /səbˌstænʃiˈeɪʃn/ *noun* [U]

sub·stan·tive /səbˈstæntɪv; ˈsʌbstəntɪv/ *adj., noun*

■ ***adj.*** (*formal*) dealing with real, important or serious matters 實質性的；本質上的；重大的；嚴肅認真的： *substantive issues* 實質性問題 ◇ *The report concluded that no substantive changes were necessary.* 報告的結論是，無須作任何重大變更。

■ ***noun*** (*old-fashioned, grammar* 語法) a noun 名詞

sub·sta·tion /ˈsʌbsteɪʃn/ *noun* a place where the strength of electric power from a POWER STATION is reduced before it is passed on to homes and businesses 變電站；變電所

sub·sti·tute 0‑ᵚ **AW** /ˈsʌbstɪtjuːt; *NAmE* -tuːt/ *noun, verb*

■ ***noun*** **1** 0‑ᵚ a person or thing that you use or have instead of the one you normally use or have 代替者；代替物；代用品： *a meat substitute* 肉食替代品 ◇ *a substitute family* 收養家庭 ◇ **~ for sb/sth** *Paul's father only saw him as a substitute for his dead brother.* 保羅的父親只是把保羅當作他死去的哥哥來看待。◇ *The course teaches you the theory but* ***there's no substitute for*** *practical experience.* 這門課教的是理論，但沒有任何東西能代替實踐經驗。◇ *The local bus service was a* ***poor substitute for*** *their car.* 他們坐當地的公交車，這比坐自己的汽車可差遠了。 **2** 0‑ᵚ (also *informal* **sub**) a player who replaces another player in a sports game 替補（運動員）： *He was brought on as (a) substitute after half-time.* 他作為替補隊員在下半場上場。

■ ***verb*** 0‑ᵚ [I, T] to take the place of sb/sth else; to use sb/sth instead of sb/sth else（以…）代替；取代： **~ for sb/sth** *Nothing can substitute for the advice your doctor is able to give you.* 大夫所能給你的忠告是無可替代的。◇ **~ A for B** *Margarine can be substituted for butter in this recipe.* 做這道菜可以用人造黃油代替黃油。◇ **~ B with/by A** *Butter can be substituted with margarine in this recipe.* 做這道菜可以用人造黃油代替黃油。◇ **~ sb/sth** *Beckham was substituted in the second half after a knee injury* (= somebody else played instead of Beckham in the second half). 下半場貝克漢姆膝蓋受傷被換下。 **HELP** When **for**, **with** or **by** are not used, as in the last example, it can be difficult to tell whether the person or thing mentioned is being used, or has been replaced by somebody or something else. The context will usually make this clear. 像最後一個例句這種情況，由於 for、with 或 by 均不出現，可能難以斷定所說的人或事物是在使用的，還是被取代的，通常上下文能使意思明瞭。 ▸ **sub·sti·tu·tion** **AW** /ˌsʌbstɪˈtjuːʃn; *NAmE* -ˈtuː-/ *noun* [U, C]： *the substitution of low-fat spreads for butter* 用低脂的麪包抹醬代替黃油 ◇ *Two substitutions were made during the game.* 比賽中換了兩次人。

ˌsubstitute ˈteacher (also *informal* **sub**) (both *NAmE*) (*BrE* **supˈply teacher**) *noun* a teacher employed to do the work of another teacher who is away because of illness, etc. 代課教師

sub·strate /ˈsʌbstreɪt/ *noun* (*technical* 術語) a substance or layer which is under sth or on which sth happens, for example the surface on which a living thing grows and feeds 底層；基底；基層

sub·stra·tum /ˈsʌbstrɑːtəm; *NAmE* ˈsʌbstreɪtəm/ *noun* (*pl.* **sub·strata** /ˈsʌbstrɑːtə; *NAmE* ˈsʌbstreɪtə/) (*technical* 術語) a layer of sth, especially rock or soil, that is below another layer（尤指岩石或土壤的）下層，底層

sub·struc·ture /ˈsʌbstrʌktʃə(r)/ *noun* a base or structure that is below another structure and that supports it 基礎；下部結構；下層建築： *a substructure of timber piles* 木樁下部結構 ◇ (*figurative*) *the substructure of national culture* 民族文化的基礎 ➲ compare SUPERSTRUCTURE (1)

sub·sume /səbˈsjuːm; *NAmE* -ˈsuːm/ *verb* [usually passive] **~ sth + adv./prep.** (*formal*) to include sth in a particular group and not consider it separately 將…歸入（或納入）： *All these different ideas can be subsumed under just two broad categories.* 所有這些不同的想法可歸為兩大類。

sub·tend /səbˈtend/ *verb* **~ sth** (*geometry* 幾何) (of a line or CHORD 直線或弦) to be opposite to an ARC or angle 對向（弧或角）

sub·ter·fuge /ˈsʌbtəfjuːdʒ; *NAmE* -tərf-/ *noun* [U, C] (*formal*) a secret, usually dishonest, way of behaving（欺騙性）秘密手段；詭計

sub·ter·ra·nean /ˌsʌbtəˈreɪniən/ *adj.* [usually before noun] (*formal*) under the ground 地下的： *a subterranean cave* 地下洞穴

sub·text /ˈsʌbtekst/ *noun* a hidden meaning or reason for doing sth 字面背後的意思；潛台詞；潛在原因

sub·title /ˈsʌbtaɪtl/ *noun, verb*

■ ***noun*** **1** [usually pl.] words that translate what is said in a film/movie into a different language and appear on the screen at the bottom. Subtitles are also used, especially on television, to help deaf people (= people who cannot hear well).（電影或電視上的）字幕： *a Polish film with English subtitles* 附有英語字幕的波蘭影片 ◇ *Is the movie dubbed or are there subtitles?* 這部電影是配音的還是帶字幕的？ **2** a second title of a book that appears after the main title and gives more information 副標題；小標題

■ ***verb*** [usually passive] to give a subtitle or subtitles to a book, film/movie, etc. 給…加副標題；給（電影等）加字幕： **~ sth** *a Spanish film subtitled in English* 一部加了英語字幕的西班牙影片 ◇ **~ sth + noun** *The book is subtitled 'New language for new times'.* 這部書的副標題是"新時代的新語言"。 ➲ compare DUB (3)

sub·tle /ˈsʌtl/ *adj.* (**sub·tler**, **sub·tlest**) **HELP** **More subtle** is also common. * more subtle 也常用。 **1** (*often approving*) not very noticeable or obvious 不易察覺的；不明顯的；微妙的： ***subtle colours/flavours/smells, etc.*** 淡淡的色彩、味道、氣味等 ◇ *There are* ***subtle differences*** *between the two versions.* 兩個版本之間有一些細微的差異。◇ *She's been dropping subtle hints about what she'd like as a present.* 她不斷隱隱暗示喜歡什麼樣的禮物。 **2** (of a person or their behaviour 人或其行為) behaving in a clever way, and using indirect methods, in order to achieve sth 機智的；機巧的；狡猾的： *I decided to try a more subtle approach.* 我決定智取。 **3** organized in a clever way 巧妙的： *a subtle plan* 巧妙的計劃 ◇ *a subtle use of lighting in the play* 燈光在劇中的巧妙運用 **4** good at noticing and understanding things 敏鋭的；頭腦靈活的： *The job required a subtle mind.* 那項工作需要一個頭腦敏鋭的人去做。 ▸ **subtly** /ˈsʌtli/ *adv.*： *Her version of events is subtly different from what actually happened.* 她對事件的描述跟實際發生的情況有些微妙的出入。◇ *Not very subtly, he raised the subject of money.* 他沒有拐彎抹角，直接提出了錢的問題。

subtle·ty /ˈsʌtlti/ *noun* (*pl.* **-ies**) **1** [U] the quality of being subtle 細微；微妙；狡猾；巧妙；敏鋭： *It's a thrilling movie even though it lacks subtlety.* 這部電影雖説不算精巧，但還是扣人心弦的。 **2** [C, usually pl.] the small but important details or aspects of sth 細小但重要的地方；微妙之處： *the subtleties of language* 語言的微妙之處

sub·total /ˈsʌbtəʊtl; *NAmE* -toʊtl/ *noun* the total of a set of numbers which is then added to other totals to give a final number 部份和；小計

sub·tract /səbˈtrækt/ *verb* [T, I] **~ (sth) (from sth)** to take a number or an amount away from another number or amount 減；減去 **SYN** **take away** : *6 subtracted from 9 is 3.* * 9 減 6 等於 3。 **OPP** **add** ▸ **sub·trac·tion** /səbˈtrækʃn/ *noun* [U, C] ➲ compare ADDITION (1)

sub·trop·ic·al /ˌsʌbˈtrɒpɪkl; *NAmE* -ˈtrɑːp-/ (also **ˌsemi-ˈtropical**) *adj.* in or connected with regions that are near tropical parts of the world 亞熱帶的；副熱帶的

the sub·trop·ics /ˌsʌbˈtrɒpɪks; *NAmE* -ˈtrɑːp-/ *noun* [pl.] the regions of the earth which are near the TROPICS 亞熱帶；副熱帶

sub·urb /ˈsʌbɜːb; *NAmE* -ɜːrb/ *noun* (also *NAmE informal* **the burbs**) an area where people live that is outside the centre of a city 郊區；城外： *a suburb of London* 倫敦郊區 ◇ *a London suburb* 倫敦郊區 ◇ *They live* ***in the suburbs.*** 他們住在城外。 ➲ COLLOCATIONS at TOWN

sub·ur·ban /səˈbɜːbən; *NAmE* -ˈbɜːrb-/ *adj.* **1** in or connected with a suburb 郊區的；城外的：*suburban areas* 郊區地帶 ◇ *a suburban street* 郊區街道 ◇ *life in suburban London* 倫敦郊區的生活 **2** (*disapproving*) boring and ordinary 平淡乏味的；呆板的：*a suburban lifestyle* 平淡乏味的生活方式

sub·ur·ban·ite /səˈbɜːbənaɪt; *NAmE* -ˈbɜːrb-/ *noun* (often *disapproving*) a person who lives in the SUBURBS of a city 郊區居民

sub·ur·bia /səˈbɜːbiə; *NAmE* -ˈbɜːrb-/ *noun* [U] (often *disapproving*) the SUBURBS and the way of life, attitudes, etc. of the people who live there 郊區及其居民的生活方式（或態度等）

sub·ven·tion /səbˈvenʃn/ *noun* (*formal*) an amount of money that is given by a government, etc. to help an organization（政府等給予某機構的）資助金，補助金；撥款

sub·ver·sive /səbˈvɜːsɪv; *NAmE* -ˈvɜːrs-/ *adj.* trying or likely to destroy or damage a government or political system by attacking it secretly or indirectly 顛覆性的；暗中起破壞作用的 SYN **seditious** ▸ **sub·ver·sive** *noun*：*He was a known political subversive.* 他是一個有名的政治顛覆分子。 **sub·ver·sive·ly** *adv.* **sub·ver·sive·ness** *noun* [U]

sub·vert /səbˈvɜːt; *NAmE* -ˈvɜːrt/ *verb* (*formal*) **1** [T, I] **~ (sth)** to try to destroy the authority of a political, religious, etc. system by attacking it secretly or indirectly 顛覆；暗中破壞 SYN **undermine 2** [T] **~ sth** to try to destroy a person's belief in sth or sb 使背叛；使變節；策反 SYN **undermine** ▸ **sub·ver·sion** /səbˈvɜːʃn; *NAmE* -ˈvɜːrʒn/ *noun* [U]

sub·way /ˈsʌbweɪ/ *noun* **1** (*NAmE*) an underground railway/railroad system in a city 地下鐵道；地鐵交通：*the New York subway* 紐約地鐵 ◇ *a **subway station/train*** 地鐵站 / 列車 ◇ *a downtown subway stop* 鬧市區的地鐵站 ◇ *to **ride/take the subway*** 乘地鐵 ➲ note at UNDERGROUND ➲ **VISUAL VOCAB** page V58 **2** (*BrE*) a path that goes under a road, etc. which people can use to cross to the other side（穿越馬路等的）地下人行道 SYN **underpass**

sub·woof·er /ˈsʌbwʊfə(r)/ *noun* (*technical* 術語) a part of a LOUDSPEAKER that produces very low sounds（擴音器的）低音音箱

sub-ˈzero *adj.* [usually before noun] (of temperatures 氣溫) below zero 零下的；零度以下的

suc·ceed 🔑 /səkˈsiːd/ *verb*
1 🔑 [I] to achieve sth that you have been trying to do or get; to have the result or effect that was intended 達到目的；實現目標；辦到；做成：*Our plan succeeded.* 我們的計劃成功了。◇ **~ in doing sth** *He succeeded in getting a place at art school.* 他被美術學校錄取了。◇ *I tried to discuss it with her but **only succeeded** in making her angry* (= I failed and did the opposite of what I intended). 我本想跟她商量，結果卻把她惹火了。➲ see also SUCCESS **2** 🔑 [I] to be successful in your job, earning money, power, respect, etc. 成功；有成就；有作為：*You will have to work hard if you are to succeed.* 要想有所作為，你必須苦幹。◇ **~ in sth** *She doesn't have the ruthlessness required to succeed in business.* 要在生意場上幹出一番名堂，她缺乏必要的冷酷心腸。◇ **~ as sth** *He had hoped to succeed as a violinist.* 他曾希望做一名有成就的小提琴家。➲ see also SUCCESS **3** [T] **~ sb/sth** to come next after sb/sth and take their/its place or position 接替；繼任；隨後出現 SYN **follow**：*Who succeeded Kennedy as President?* 接替肯尼迪任總統的是誰？◇ *Their early success was succeeded by a period of miserable failure.* 他們起初獲得成功，但隨後有一段慘痛的失敗時期。◇ *Strands of DNA are reproduced through **succeeding generations**.* * DNA（脫氧核糖核酸）鏈通過後代得到複製。➲ see also SUCCESSION **4** [I] **~ (to sth)** to gain the right to a title, property, etc. when sb dies 繼承：*She succeeded to the throne* (= became queen) *in 1558.* 她於 1558 年繼承王位。➲ see also SUCCESSION

IDM **nothing succeeds like sucˈcess** (*saying*) when you are successful in one area of your life, it often leads to success in other areas 一事成，百事順

suc·cess 🔑 /səkˈses/ *noun*
1 🔑 [U] the fact that you have achieved sth that you want and have been trying to do or get; the fact of becoming rich or famous or of getting a high social position 成功；勝利；發財；成名：*What's the secret of your success?* 你成功的秘訣是什麼？◇ **~ (in doing sth)** *I didn't **have much success in** finding a job.* 我找工作沒什麼結果。◇ **~ (in sth)** *They didn't have much success in life.* 他們一生沒取得多大成就。◇ *Confidence is **the key to success**.* 信心是成功的關鍵。◇ *economic success* 經濟上的成功 ◇ *Their plan will probably **meet with little success**.* 他們的計劃大概難有所成。◇ *She was surprised by the book's success* (= that it had sold a lot of copies). 那本書獲得成功出乎她的意料。 **2** 🔑 [C] a person or thing that has achieved a good result and been successful 成功的人（或事物）：*The party was a big success.* 這次聚會非常成功。◇ *He's proud of his daughter's successes.* 他為女兒的種種成就感到自豪。◇ *She wasn't a success as a teacher.* 她教書沒教出什麼名堂。◇ *He was determined to **make a success** of the business.* 他決心把這門生意做紅火。 OPP **failure** IDM see ROARING, SUCCEED, SWEET *adj.*

suc·cess·ful 🔑 /səkˈsesfl/ *adj.*
1 🔑 achieving your aims or what was intended 達到目的的；有成效的：**~ (in sth/in doing sth)** *They were successful in winning the contract.* 他們終於爭取到了那份合同。◇ **~ (at sth/at doing sth)** *I wasn't very successful at keeping the news secret.* 我沒能把這條消息嚴格保密。◇ *We congratulated them on the successful completion of the project.* 我們祝賀他們項目順利竣工。 **2** 🔑 having become popular and/or made a lot of money 獲得成功的；有成就的：*The play was very successful on Broadway.* 那部劇在百老匯大獲成功。◇ *a successful actor* 走紅的演員 ◇ *The company has had another successful year.* 公司又度過了一個興旺發達之年。 OPP **unsuccessful** ▸ **suc·cess·ful·ly** 🔑 /-fəli/ *adv.*

Synonyms 同義詞辨析

successful

profitable • commercial • lucrative • economic

These words all describe sb/sth that is making or is likely to make money. 以上各詞均指賺錢的、贏利的、有利可圖的。

successful making a lot of money, especially by being popular 指賺錢的、成功的：*The play was very successful on Broadway.* 那齣劇在百老匯大獲成功。◇ *The company has had another successful year.* 公司又度過了一個興旺發達之年。

profitable making a profit 指有利潤的、贏利的：*a highly profitable business* 一家贏利很高的企業

commercial [only before noun] making or intended to make a profit 指營利的、以獲利為目的的：*The movie was not a commercial success* (= made no profit). 這部電影票房收入不佳。

lucrative (of business or work) producing or paying a large amount of money; making a large profit 指生意或工作賺大錢的、獲利多的：*They do a lot of business in lucrative overseas markets.* 他們在利潤豐厚的海外市場上生意很多。

economic (often used in negative sentences) (of a process, business or activity) producing enough profit to continue（常用於否定句中）指（工序、業務或活動）有利可圖的、可賺錢的、合算的：*Small local shops stop being economic when a supermarket opens up nearby.* 附近有超市開業的話，當地的小商店就沒有利潤可賺了。

PATTERNS

- a successful/profitable/lucrative **business**
- a successful/profitable/lucrative **year**
- a(n) commercial/economic **success**

S

suc·ces·sion AW /sək'seʃn/ *noun* **1** [C, usually sing.] a number of people or things that follow each other in time or order 一連串；一系列；連續的人（或事物） SYN **series**：*a succession of visitors* 絡繹不絕的來訪者 ◇ *He's been hit by a succession of injuries since he joined the team.* 自入隊以來他一再受傷。◇ *She has won the award for the third year **in succession**.* 這是她連續第三年獲得此獎。◇ *They had three children **in quick succession**.* 短短幾年間，他們接連生了三個孩子。◇ *The gunman fired three times **in rapid succession**.* 歹徒連開三槍。 **2** [U] the regular pattern of one thing following another thing 交替；更迭：*the succession of the seasons* 四季的更迭 **3** [U] the act of taking over an official position or title; the right to take over an official position or title, especially to become the king or queen of a country 繼承；繼任；（尤指王位的）繼承權：*He became chairman **in succession to** Bernard Allen.* 他接替伯納德•艾倫任主席。◇ *She's third **in order of succession** to the throne.* 她在王位繼承人順位中排第三。➲ see also SUCCEED (3), (4)

suc'cession planning *noun* [U] (*business* 商) the process of training and preparing employees in a company or an organization so that there will always be sb to replace a senior manager who leaves（公司或機構的）繼任規劃，接班人培訓規劃

suc·ces·sive AW /sək'sesɪv/ *adj.* [only before noun] following immediately one after the other 連續的；接連的；相繼的 SYN **consecutive**：*This was their fourth successive win.* 這是他們連續第四次獲勝。◇ *Successive governments have tried to tackle the problem.* 歷屆政府都試圖解決這個問題。 ▸ **suc·ces·sively** AW *adv.*：*This concept has been applied successively to painting, architecture and sculpture.* 這一概念相繼應用於繪畫、建築和雕塑中。

suc·ces·sor AW /sək'sesə(r)/ *noun* **~ (to sb/sth)** a person or thing that comes after sb/sth else and takes their/its place 接替者；繼任者；接替的事物；後繼的事物：*Who's the likely successor to him as party leader?* 誰較可能接替他擔任黨的領袖？◇ *Their latest release is a **worthy successor** to their popular debut album.* 繼首張唱片大受歡迎之後，他們最新推出的專輯再獲成功。➲ compare PREDECESSOR

suc'cess story *noun* a person or thing that is very successful 獲得巨大成功的人（或事物）

suc·cinct /sək'sɪŋkt/ *adj.* (*approving*) expressed clearly and in a few words 簡明的；言簡意賅的 SYN **concise**：*Keep your answers as succinct as possible.* 你們的答案要盡可能簡潔明瞭。◇ *a succinct explanation* 簡明的解釋 ▸ **suc·cinct·ly** *adv.*：*You put that very succinctly.* 你說得十分簡明扼要。 **suc·cinct·ness** *noun* [U]

S

suc·co·tash /'sʌkətæʃ/ *noun* [U] (*US*) a dish of CORN (MAIZE) and BEANS cooked together 煮玉米菜豆；沙可達玉米粥

Suc·coth /sʊ'kəʊt; 'sʌkəθ; *NAmE* 'su:koʊt; su:'koʊt/ (also **ˌFeast of 'Tabernacles**) *noun* [U] a Jewish festival that takes place in the autumn/fall, during which shelters are made using natural materials 帳棚節，住棚節（秋季的猶太節日，期間會用天然材料搭建帳棚）

suc·cour (*US* **suc·cor**) /'sʌkə(r)/ *noun, verb*

■ ***noun*** [U] (*literary*) help that you give to sb who is suffering or having problems 救助；救援；幫助

■ ***verb* ~ sb** (*literary*) to help sb who is suffering or having problems 救助；救援；幫助

suc·cu·bus /'sʌkjʊbəs/ *noun* (*pl.* **suc·cu·bi** /-baɪ/) (*literary*) a female evil spirit, supposed to have sex with a sleeping man（傳說與睡眠中的男子交媾的）女妖精 ➲ compare INCUBUS (2)

suc·cu·lent /'sʌkjələnt/ *adj., noun*

■ ***adj.* 1** (*approving*) (of fruit, vegetables and meat 水果、蔬菜和肉) containing a lot of juice and tasting good 汁多味美的 SYN **juicy**：*a succulent pear/steak* 汁多味美的梨；鮮美多汁的牛排 **2** (*technical* 術語) (of plants 植物) having leaves and STEMS that are thick and contain a lot of water 肉質的；多汁的 ▸ **suc·cu·lence** /-əns/ *noun* [U]

■ ***noun*** (*technical* 術語) any plant with leaves and STEMS that are thick and contain a lot of water, for example a CACTUS 肉質植物

suc·cumb /sə'kʌm/ *verb* [I] to not be able to fight an attack, an illness, a TEMPTATION, etc. 屈服；屈從；抵擋不住（攻擊、疾病、誘惑等）：*The town succumbed after a short siege.* 該城被圍困不久即告失守。◇ **~ to sth** *His career was cut short when he succumbed to cancer.* 他的事業隨着他死於癌症而中斷。◇ *He finally succumbed to Lucy's charms and agreed to her request.* 他最終為露西的魅力所傾倒，答應了她的請求。

such 🔑 /sʌtʃ/ *det., pron.*

1 🔑 of the type already mentioned（指上文）這樣的，那樣的，類似的：*They had been invited to a Hindu wedding and were not sure what happened on such occasions.* 有人邀請他們去參加一個印度教徒的婚禮，但他們不清楚這樣的慶典會是怎樣一種場面。◇ *He said he didn't have time or made **some such** excuse.* 他說他沒時間或別的諸如此類的藉口。◇ *She longed to find somebody who understood her problems, and in him she thought she had found such a person.* 她渴望找一個理解她困難的人，覺得他就是這樣一個人。◇ *We were second-class citizens and they treated us **as such**.* 我們是二等公民，他們也就這樣對待我們。◇ *Accountants were boring. Such (= that) was her opinion before meeting Ian!* 做會計的個個乏味，在認識伊恩以前她一直是這樣想的！ **2** 🔑 of the type that you are just going to mention（指後文）這樣的，那樣的，下述一類的：***There is no such thing** as a free lunch.* 世上沒有免費午餐之類的好事兒。◇ *Such advice as he was given (= it was not very much) has proved almost worthless.* 他所得到的那點建議結果證明幾乎完全沒用。◇ *The knot was fastened **in such a way** that it was impossible to undo.* 那個結繫死了，沒法解開。◇ *The damage was such that it would cost thousands to repair.* 損壞嚴重，要修好就得花幾千塊錢。 **3** 🔑 **~ (is, was, etc.) sth that ...** used to emphasize the great degree of sth（強調程度）這樣，非常，如此程度：*This issue was of such importance that we could not afford to ignore it.* 這個問題十分重要，我們疏忽不得。◇ *Why are you in such a hurry?* 你幹嗎這麼急匆匆的？◇ (*informal*) *It's such a beautiful day!* 天氣多麼好哇！◇ (*formal*) *Such is the elegance of this typeface that it is still a favourite of designers.* 這種字體很優美，至今仍深受設計人員喜歡。

IDM **... and such** and similar things or people 諸如此類的事物（或人）：*The centre offers activities like canoeing and sailing and such.* 這個中心開展划艇、帆船之類的活動。 **as 'such** 🔑 as the word is usually understood; in the exact sense of the word 從字面意義看；嚴格說來：*The new job is not a promotion as such, but it has good prospects.* 擔任這一新的職務算不上是真正的提職，不過有美好的前途。◇ *'Well, did they offer it to you?' 'No, not as such, but they said I had a good chance.'*"那麼，他們把它給你了？""不，不完全是那樣，可是他們說我很有希望。" **such as 1** 🔑 for example 例如；…等：*Wild flowers such as primroses are becoming rare.* 報春花之類的野花越來越稀罕了。◇ *'There are loads of things to do.' 'Such as?' (= give me an example)*"該做的事有一大堆。""比如呢？" **2** 🔑 of a kind that; like 像…這樣；像…那種；諸如…之類：*Opportunities such as this did not come every day.* 這樣的機會不是天天都有的。➲ LANGUAGE BANK at E.G. **ˌsuch as it 'is/they 'are** used to say that there is not much of sth or that it is of poor quality（數量不多或質量不好時說）雖說不多，儘管不好：*The food, such as it was, was served at nine o'clock.* 那飯雖說是粗茶淡飯，卻到九點鐘才端上來。

'such-and-such *pron., det.* (*informal*) used for referring to sth without saying exactly what it is（指沒有明確說出的事物）某：*Always say at the start of an application that you're applying for such-and-such a job because ...* 寫求職信務須一開頭就說明你申請某職務，因為…

such·like /'sʌtʃlaɪk/ *pron.* things of the type mentioned 諸如此類的事物：*You can buy brushes, paint, varnish and suchlike there.* 你在那兒能買到刷子、油漆、清漆之類的東西。 ▸ **such·like** *det.*：*food, drink, clothing and suchlike provisions* 食物、飲料、服裝以及其他諸如此類的日用品

suck /sʌk/ *verb, noun*

■ *verb* **1** [T] **~ sth (+ adv./prep.)** to take liquid, air, etc. into your mouth by using the muscles of your lips 吮吸；吸；咂；啜：*to suck the juice from an orange* 吸橙子的汁 ◇ *She was noisily sucking up milk through a straw.* 她正用吸管咕嘟咕嘟地喝牛奶。 **2** [I, T] to keep sth in your mouth and pull on it with your lips and tongue 含在嘴裏吸食：**~ at/on sth** *The baby sucked at its mother's breast.* 嬰兒在吮吸母親的奶。◇ *She sucked on a mint.* 她嘴裏咂着一顆薄荷糖。◇ **~ sth** *She sucked a mint.* 她嘴裏咂着一顆薄荷糖。◇ *Stop sucking your thumb!* 別吮手指頭！ **3** [T] to take liquid, air, etc. out of sth 抽吸；抽取：**~ sth + adv./prep.** *The pump sucks air out through the valve.* 氣泵通過閥門把空氣抽出去。◇ **~ sth + adj.** *Greenfly can literally suck a plant dry.* 蚜蟲的確能把一株植物吸乾。 **4** [T] **~ sb/sth + adv./prep.** to pull sb/sth with great force in a particular direction（以巨大的力量）吸，吸引，使捲入：*The canoe was sucked down into the whirlpool.* 划艇被捲進了漩渦。 **5 sth sucks** [I] (*slang*) used to say that sth is very bad（表示厭惡）臭，惡心：*Their new CD sucks.* 他們新出的唱片難聽死了。 ➲ compare ROCK *v.* (5)

IDM **ˌsuck it and ˈsee** (*BrE, informal*) used to say that the only way to know if sth is suitable is to try it 試試看 **ˌsuck it ˈup** (*NAmE, informal*) to accept sth bad and deal with it well, controlling your emotions 逆來順受；忍氣吞聲 ➲ more at DRY *adj.*, TEACH

PHR V **ˌsuck sb ˈin** | **ˌsuck sb ˈinto sth** [usually passive] to involve sb in an activity or a situation, especially one they do not want to be involved in 把某人捲入（某事） **ˌsuck ˈup (to sb)** (*informal, disapproving*) to try to please sb in authority by praising them too much, helping them, etc., in order to gain some advantage for yourself 奉承；巴結

■ *noun* [usually sing.] an act of sucking 吸；吮；啜；咂

suck·er /ˈsʌkə(r)/ *noun, verb*

■ *noun* **1** (*informal*) a person who is easily tricked or persuaded to do sth 容易上當受騙的人；沒有主見的人 **2 ~ for sb/sth** (*informal*) a person who cannot resist sb/sth or likes sb/sth very much 不由得對…入迷的人；酷愛…的人：*I've always been a sucker for men with green eyes.* 我一向對綠眼睛男人着迷。 **3** a special organ on the body of some animals that enables them to stick to a surface（動物的）吸盤 ➲ VISUAL VOCAB page V13 **4** a disc shaped like a cup, usually made of rubber or plastic, that sticks to a surface when you press it against it（橡膠或塑料等製成的）吸盤 **5** a part of a tree or bush that grows from the roots rather than from the main STEM or the branches and can form a new tree or bush 吸根 **6** (*NAmE, slang*) used to refer in a general way to a person or thing, especially for emphasis（泛指人或物，尤表示強調）傢伙，東西，玩意兒：*The pilot said, 'I don't know how I got the sucker down safely.'* 機師說：“我不知道是怎麼把這玩意兒安全降落下來的。” **7** (*NAmE, informal*) = LOLLIPOP

■ *verb*

PHR V **ˌsucker sb ˈinto sth/into doing sth** (*NAmE, informal*) to persuade sb to do sth that they do not really want to do, especially by using their lack of knowledge or experience（尤指利用他人無知）欺騙，使上當：*I was suckered into helping.* 我受騙幫忙去了。

ˈsucker punch *noun* a blow that the person who receives it is not expecting 突如其來的一拳；毫無防備的一擊 ▸ **ˈsucker punch** *verb* **~ sb**

suckle /ˈsʌkl/ *verb* **1** [T] **~ sb/sth** (of a woman or female animal 婦女或雌獸) to feed a baby or young animal with milk from the breast or UDDER 給…餵奶；給…哺乳：*a cow suckling her calves* 給小牛吃奶的母牛 ◇ (*old-fashioned*) *a mother suckling a baby* 給嬰兒哺乳的母親 **2** [I] (of a baby or young animal 嬰兒或幼獸) to drink milk from its mother's breast or UDDER 吸奶；吃奶

suck·ling /ˈsʌklɪŋ/ *noun* (*old-fashioned*) a baby or young animal that is still drinking milk from its mother 乳兒；乳獸 IDM see MOUTH *n.*

ˈsuck·ling pig *noun* [U, C] a young pig still taking milk from its mother, that is cooked and eaten（烤）乳豬

su·crose /ˈsuːkrəʊz; -krəʊs; *NAmE* -kroʊs; -kroʊz/ *noun* [U] (*chemistry* 化) the form of sugar that is obtained from SUGAR CANE and SUGAR BEET 蔗糖

suc·tion /ˈsʌkʃn/ *noun* [U] the process of removing air or liquid from a space or container so that sth else can be sucked into it or so that two surfaces can stick together 吸；抽吸；吸出：*Vacuum cleaners work by suction.* 真空吸塵器靠抽吸除塵。◇ *a* **suction pump/pad** 抽吸泵；吸力墊 ▸ **suc·tion** *verb* **~ sth** (*technical* 術語)

sud·den /ˈsʌdn/ *adj.* happening or done quickly and unexpectedly 突然的；忽然的；驟然的：*a sudden change* 驟變 ◇ *Don't make any sudden movements.* 不要突然地做任何動作。◇ *His death was very sudden.* 他死得很突然。◇ *It was only decided yesterday. It's all been very sudden.* 這是昨天才決定的，一切都非常突然。 ▸ **sud·den·ness** *noun* [U]

IDM **ˌall of a ˈsudden** quickly and unexpectedly 突然；猛地：*All of a sudden someone grabbed me around the neck.* 猛不防有人抓住了我的脖子。

ˌsudden ˈdeath *noun* [U] a way of deciding the winner of a game when the scores are equal at the end. The players or teams continue playing and the game ends as soon as one of them gains the lead. 突然死亡法（比賽出現平局時在加時賽中先得分者即為勝方）：*a sudden-death play-off in golf* 高爾夫球突然死亡法加賽

sud·den·ly /ˈsʌdənli/ *adv.* quickly and unexpectedly 突然；忽然；猛地；驟然：*'Listen!' said Doyle suddenly.* “你聽！”多伊爾突然說。◇ *I suddenly realized what I had to do.* 我突然明白該怎麼做了。◇ *It all happened so suddenly.* 一切都來得那麼突然。

su·doku /ˌsuˈdəʊkuː; -ˈdɒk-; *NAmE* -ˈdoʊk-; -ˈdɑːk-/ *noun* [C, U] a number puzzle with nine squares, each containing nine smaller squares, in which you have to put the numbers one to nine so that a number appears only once in each of the nine squares and in each row of nine across and down the puzzle 數獨遊戲（九個大方格中各有九個小方格，要求在空格中填數字一到九，且縱、橫排各不重複）：*He passes the time doing sudokus.* 他做數獨遊戲打發時間。 ➲ VISUAL VOCAB page V39

suds /sʌdz/ (also **soap·suds**) *noun* **1** [pl.] a mass of very small bubbles that forms on top of water that has soap in it 肥皂泡沫 SYN **lather**：*She was up to her elbows in suds.* 她肘部以下都是肥皂沫子。 **2** [U] (*old-fashioned, NAmE, informal*) beer 啤酒

sue /suː; *BrE* also sjuː/ *verb* **1** [T, I] **~ (sb) (for sth)** to make a claim against sb in court about sth that they have said or done to harm you 控告；提起訴訟：*to sue sb for breach of contract* 控告某人違反合同 ◇ *to sue sb for $10 million* (= in order to get money from sb) 控告某人要求得到 1 000 萬元 ◇ *to sue sb for damages* 起訴某人要求賠償損失 ◇ *They threatened to sue if the work was not completed.* 他們威脅說，如果不完成工作，就要提起訴訟。 **2** [I] **~ for sth** (*formal*) to formally ask for sth, especially in court（尤指在法庭上）提出請求：*to sue for divorce* 起訴要求離婚 ◇ *The rebels were forced to sue for peace.* 反叛者被迫求和。

suede /sweɪd/ *noun* [U] soft leather with a surface like VELVET on one side, used especially for making clothes and shoes 絨面革；仿麂皮：*a suede jacket* 絨面革夾克

suet /ˈsuːɪt; *BrE* also ˈsjuːɪt/ *noun* [U] hard fat from around the KIDNEYS of cows, sheep, etc., used in cooking（牛、羊等腎周圍的）板油：*suet pudding* (= one made using suet) 脂油布丁

suf·fer /ˈsʌfə(r)/ *verb*

1 [I] to be badly affected by a disease, pain, sadness, a lack of sth, etc.（因疾病、痛苦、悲傷等）受苦，受難，受折磨：*I hate to see animals suffering.* 我不忍心看動物受苦。◇ **~ from sth** *He suffers from asthma.* 他患有哮喘。◇ *road accident victims suffering from shock* 交通事故中受到驚嚇的受害者 ◇ *Many companies are suffering from a shortage of skilled staff.* 許多公司苦於缺乏熟練員工。◇ **~ for sth** *He made a rash decision and now he is suffering for it.* 他當初草率決定，現在吃苦頭了。 **2** [T]

S

~ sth to experience sth unpleasant, such as injury, defeat or loss 遭受；蒙受： *He suffered a massive heart attack.* 他的心臟病發作很嚴重。◇ *The party suffered a humiliating defeat in the general election.* 該黨在大選中慘敗。◇ *The company suffered huge losses in the last financial year.* 公司在上一財政年度出現巨額虧損。 **3** [I] to become worse 變差；變糟： *His school work is suffering because of family problems.* 由於家庭問題，他的學業日漸退步。

IDM **not suffer fools 'gladly** to have very little patience with people that you think are stupid 不願遷就笨人；不能容忍愚蠢者

suf·fer·ance /ˈsʌfərəns/ *noun* [U]

IDM **on 'sufferance** if you do sth **on sufferance**, sb allows you to do it although they do not really want you to 經勉強同意；由於（某人的）寬容： *He's only staying here on sufferance.* 他是經人勉強同意待在這兒的。

suf·fer·er /ˈsʌfərə(r)/ *noun* a person who suffers, especially sb who is suffering from a disease 患病者；受苦者；受難者： *cancer sufferers* 癌症患者 ◇ *She received many letters of support from fellow sufferers.* 許多和她有共同遭遇的人給她來信，表示支持。

suf·fer·ing /ˈsʌfərɪŋ/ *noun*

1 [U] physical or mental pain 疼痛；痛苦；折磨；苦難： *Death finally brought an end to her suffering.* 死亡終於結束了她的痛苦。◇ *This war has caused widespread human suffering.* 這場戰爭給許許多多的人帶來了苦難。 **2 sufferings** [pl.] feelings of pain and unhappiness 痛苦；苦惱： *The hospice aims to ease the sufferings of the dying.* 善終關懷醫院旨在減輕臨終者的痛苦。

suf·fice /səˈfaɪs/ *verb* [I] *(formal)* (not used in the progressive tenses 不用於進行時) to be enough for sb/sth 足夠；足以： *Generally a brief note or a phone call will suffice.* 通常寫個便條或打個電話就足夠了。◇ **~ to do sth** *One example will suffice to illustrate the point.* 舉一個例子就足以說明這一點。

IDM **suffice (it) to say (that)** ... used to suggest that although you could say more, what you do say will be enough to explain what you mean 無須多說；只需說…就夠了

suf·fi·ciency AW /səˈfɪʃnsi/ *noun* [sing.] **~ (of sth)** *(formal)* an amount of sth that is enough for a particular purpose 足量；充足

suf·fi·cient AW /səˈfɪʃnt/ *adj.*

enough for a particular purpose; as much as you need 足夠的；充足的： *Allow sufficient time to get there.* 留出充足的時間好趕過去。◇ **~ to do sth** *These reasons are not sufficient to justify the ban.* 這些理由不足以證明實施禁令有理。◇ **~ for sth/sb** *Is £100 sufficient for your expenses?* * 100 英鎊夠你花銷嗎？ OPP **insufficient** ➲ see also SELF-SUFFICIENT ▸ **suf·fi·cient·ly** AW *adv.*： *The following day she felt sufficiently well to go to work.* 第二天，她感覺好轉，完全可以去上班了。

suf·fix /ˈsʌfɪks/ *noun (grammar* 語法) a letter or group of letters added to the end of a word to make another word, such as *-ly* in *quickly* or *-ness* in *sadness* 後綴，詞尾（加在詞尾，用以構成新詞，如 quickly 中的 -ly 或 sadness 中的 -ness） ➲ compare AFFIX *n.*, PREFIX *n.* (1)

suf·fo·cate /ˈsʌfəkeɪt/ *verb* **1** [I, T] to die because there is no air to breathe; to kill sb by not letting them breathe air（使）窒息而死；（把…）悶死： *Many dogs have suffocated in hot cars.* 許多狗在熱烘烘的汽車裏給悶死了。◇ **~ sb/sth** *The couple were suffocated by fumes from a faulty gas fire.* 由於劣質煤氣取暖器漏氣，這對夫婦窒息而死。◇ *He put the pillow over her face and suffocated her.* 他用枕頭捂住她的臉，把她憋死了。◇ *(figurative) She felt suffocated by all the rules and regulations.* 她受不了所有那些條條框框的束縛。 **2** [I] **be suffocating** if **it is suffocating**, it is very hot and there is little fresh air 讓人感覺悶熱；憋氣： *Can I open a window? It's suffocating in here!* 我可以打開窗戶嗎？這裏面都快把人悶死了！ ▸ **suf·fo·ca·tion** /ˌsʌfəˈkeɪʃn/ *noun* [U]： *to die of suffocation* 窒息而死

suf·fo·cat·ing /ˈsʌfəkeɪtɪŋ/ *adj.* **1** making it difficult to breathe normally 令人呼吸困難的；悶的；使人窒息的 SYN **stifling**： *The afternoon heat was suffocating.* 下午熱得讓人透不過氣來。 **2** restricting what sb/sth can do 起扼制作用的；壓制的；束縛性的： *Some marriages can sometimes feel suffocating.* 有些婚姻有時候讓人覺得受到束縛。

suf·fra·gan /ˈsʌfrəgən/ (also **suffragan 'bishop**) *noun* a BISHOP who is an assistant to a bishop of a particular DIOCESE 教區隸屬主教

suf·frage /ˈsʌfrɪdʒ/ *noun* [U] the right to vote in political elections 選舉權；投票權： *universal suffrage* (= the right of all adults to vote) 普選權 ◇ *women's suffrage* 婦女的選舉權

suf·fra·gette /ˌsʌfrəˈdʒet/ *noun* a member of a group of women who, in Britain and the US in the early part of the 20th century, worked to get the right for women to vote in political elections（20 世紀初葉英國和美國的）婦女爭取選舉權團體的成員

suf·fuse /səˈfjuːz/ *verb* [often passive] **~ sb/sth (with sth)** *(literary)* (especially of a colour, light or feeling 尤指顏色、光線或感情) to spread all over or through sb/sth 佈滿；瀰漫於；充滿： *Her face was suffused with colour.* 她滿臉通紅。◇ *Colour suffused her face.* 她滿臉通紅。

Sufi /ˈsuːfi/ *noun* a member of a Muslim group who try to become united with God through prayer and MEDITATION and by living a very simple, strict life 蘇非派信徒（伊斯蘭教一宗派成員，主張通過虔修默禱，生活簡樸禁慾達到人主合一） ▸ **Suf·ism** *noun* [U]

su·fur·ia /suːˈfuːriə/ *noun (EAfrE)* a metal pot used for cooking 金屬鍋；鐵罐鍋

sugar /ˈʃʊgə(r)/ *noun, verb, exclamation*

■ ***noun*** **1** [U] a sweet substance, often in the form of white or brown CRYSTALS, made from the juices of various plants, used in cooking or to make tea, coffee, etc. sweeter 食糖： *a* ***sugar plantation/refinery/bowl*** 甘蔗園；煉糖廠；糖罐 ◇ *This juice contains* ***no added sugar***. 這種果汁沒有加糖。◇ *Do you* ***take sugar*** (= have it in your tea, coffee, etc.)? 您放糖嗎？ ➲ see also BROWN SUGAR, CANE SUGAR, CASTER SUGAR, GRANULATED SUGAR, ICING SUGAR **2** [C] the amount of sugar that a small spoon can hold or that is contained in a small CUBE, added to tea, coffee, etc. 一匙糖；一塊方糖： *How many sugars do you take in coffee?* 您在咖啡裏放幾塊方糖？ **3** [C, usually pl.] *(technical* 術語) any of various sweet substances that are found naturally in plants, fruit, etc.（植物、水果等所含的）糖： *fruit sugars* 果糖 ◇ *a person's* ***blood sugar*** *level* (= the amount of GLUCOSEin their blood) 人的血糖含量 **4** [U] *(informal, especially NAmE)* a way of addressing sb that you like or love（愛稱）寶貝兒，親愛的： *See you later, sugar.* 回頭見，親愛的。

■ ***verb*** **~ sth** to add sugar to sth; to cover sth in sugar 在…中加糖；在…上撒糖；給…裹上糖衣 IDM see PILL *n.*

■ ***exclamation*** used to show that you are annoyed when you do sth stupid or when sth goes wrong (to avoid saying 'shit')（做了蠢事或出現差錯時表示懊惱，用作 shit 的委婉語）哎呀，真是的： *Oh sugar! I've forgotten my book!* 哎呀！我忘記帶書了！

'sugar beet *noun* [U] a plant with a large round root, from which sugar is made 甜菜

'sugar cane *noun* [U] a tall tropical plant with thick STEMS from which sugar is made 甘蔗

'sugar-coat *verb* **~ sth** to do sth that makes an unpleasant situation seem less unpleasant 美化，粉飾（不愉快的情況）

,sugar-'coated *adj.* **1** covered with sugar 裹有糖的；包糖衣的 **2** *(disapproving)* made to seem attractive, in a way that tricks people 巧加粉飾的；使表面吸引的： *a sugar-coated promise* 甜言蜜語的許諾

'sugar cube *(especially NAmE)* (*BrE* also **'sugar lump**) *noun* a small CUBE of sugar, used in cups of tea or coffee 方糖

'sugar daddy *noun (informal)* a rich older man who gives presents and money to a much younger woman, usually in return for sex 甜爹（對年輕女子慷慨大方的闊老色迷）

sug·ar·ing /ˈʃʊɡərɪŋ/ *noun* [U] **1** a way of removing hair from your skin using a mixture of sugar and water 糖水脫毛法 **2** the process of boiling juice from a MAPLE tree until it becomes sugar 槭糖熬製

ˈsugar lump (also *informal* **lump**) (both *BrE*) (also **ˈsugar cube** *NAmE*, *BrE*) *noun* a small CUBE of sugar, used in cups of tea or coffee 方糖

sugar·plum /ˈʃʊɡəplʌm; *NAmE* -ɡərp-/ *noun* (*especially NAmE*) a small round sweet/candy 小圓糖果；糖豆

ˈsugar snap (also **ˌsugar snap ˈpea**, **ˈsugar pea**) *noun* a type of PEA which is eaten while still in its POD（連莢食用）甜豌豆

sug·ary /ˈʃʊɡəri/ *adj.* **1** containing sugar; tasting of sugar 含糖的；甜的：*sugary snacks* 甜點心 **2** (*disapproving*) seeming too full of emotion in a way that is not sincere（態度等）甜膩膩的，媚人的；甜言蜜語的 SYN **sentimental**：*a sugary smile* 媚笑 ◇ *sugary pop songs* 甜膩膩的流行歌曲

sug·gest 0-ㄇ /səˈdʒest; *NAmE* also səɡˈdʒ-/ *verb* **1** 0-ㄇ to put forward an idea or a plan for other people to think about 建議；提議 SYN **propose**：**~ sth (to sb)** *May I suggest a white wine with this dish, Sir?* 先生，吃這道菜，我給您推薦一種白葡萄酒，好嗎？◇ **~ itself (to sb)** *A solution immediately suggested itself to me* (= I immediately thought of a solution). 我馬上想到了一個解決辦法。◇ **~ (that) ...** *I suggest (that) we go out to eat.* 我提議我們出去吃吧。◇ **~ doing sth** *I suggested going in my car.* 我提議坐我的車去。◇ **it is suggested that ...** *It has been suggested that bright children take their exams early.* 有人提議天資好的孩子提前考試。◇ (*BrE* also) *It has been suggested that bright children should take their exams early.* 有人提議天資好的孩子提前考試。➲ LANGUAGE BANK at ARGUE **2** 0-ㄇ to tell sb about a suitable person, thing, method, etc. for a particular job or purpose 推薦；舉薦 SYN **recommend**：**~ sb/sth for sth** *Who would you suggest for the job?* 要你說，誰適合做這個工作？◇ **~ sb/sth as sth** *She suggested Paris as a good place for the conference.* 她推薦說，巴黎是舉行這次會議的理想地點。◇ **~ sb/sth** *Can you suggest a good dictionary?* 你能推薦一本好詞典嗎？ HELP You cannot 'suggest somebody something'. 不能說 suggest somebody something：~~*Can you suggest me a good dictionary?*~~ ◇ **~ how, what, etc. ...** *Can you suggest how I might contact him?* 我怎麼才能聯繫上他，你能出個主意嗎？ **3** 0-ㄇ to put an idea into sb's mind; to make sb think that sth is true 使想到；使認為；表明 SYN **indicate**：**~ (that) ...** *All the evidence suggests (that) he stole the money.* 所有證據都表明是他偷了錢。◇ **~ sth** *The symptoms suggest a minor heart attack.* 症狀顯示這是輕微心臟病發作。◇ **~ sth to sb** *What do these results suggest to you?* 照你看，這些結果說明什麼呢？ **4** to state sth indirectly 暗示；言下之意是說 SYN **imply**：**~ (that) ...** *Are you suggesting (that) I'm lazy?* 你言下之意是說我懶？◇ **~ sth** *I would never suggest such a thing.* 我根本不會有這樣的意思。

sug·gest·ible /səˈdʒestəbl; *NAmE* also səɡˈdʒ-/ *adj.* easily influenced by other people 易受他人影響的：*He was young and highly suggestible.* 當時他年輕，很容易聽信他人。

sug·ges·tion 0-ㄇ /səˈdʒestʃən; *NAmE* also səɡˈdʒ-/ *noun* **1** 0-ㄇ [C] an idea or a plan that you mention for sb else to think about 建議；提議：*Can I* ***make a suggestion****?* 我提個建議好嗎？◇ *Do you* ***have any suggestions****?* 你有什麼建議嗎？◇ **~ (for/about/on sth)** *I'd like to hear your suggestions for ways of raising money.* 關於籌集資金的辦法，我想聽聽你的意見。◇ *Are there any suggestions about how best to tackle the problem?* 這個問題最好怎樣解決，大家有沒有什麼建議？◇ *We welcome any comments and suggestions on these proposals.* 對於這些方案的任何評論和建議，我們一概歡迎。◇ **~ (that ...)** *He agreed with my suggestion that we should change the date.* 他同意我提出的更改日期的建議。◇ *We are* ***open to suggestions*** (= willing to listen to ideas from other people). 我們願意聽取大家的建議。◇ *We need to get it there by four. Any suggestions?* 我們需要在四點以前把東西送過去。大家有什麼辦法嗎？ **2** 0-ㄇ [U, C, usually sing.] a reason to think that sth, especially sth bad, is true 使人作（尤其是不好的事情的）推測的理由 SYN **hint**：**~ of sth** *A spokesman dismissed any suggestion of a boardroom rift.* 發言人的話打消了人們關於董事會不和的所有推測。◇ **~ that ...** *There was no suggestion that he was doing anything illegal.* 說他在從事非法活動無任何根據。 **3** [C, usually sing.] a slight amount or sign of sth 微量；些微；跡象 SYN **trace**：*She looked at me with just a suggestion of a smile.* 她看着我，臉上帶着一絲笑意。 **4** [U] putting an idea into people's minds by connecting it with other ideas 暗示；聯想：*Most advertisements work through suggestion.* 多數廣告都是通過暗示而發揮作用。◇ *the power of suggestion* 暗示力

IDM **at/on sb's sugˈgestion** because sb suggested it 根據某人的建議；在某人的提議下：*At his suggestion, I bought the more expensive printer.* 在他的建議下，我買了那部比較貴的打印機。

sug·gest·ive /səˈdʒestɪv; *NAmE* also səɡˈdʒ-/ *adj.* **1** **~ (of sth)** reminding you of sth or making you think about sth 使人想起…的；引起聯想的：*music that is suggestive of warm summer days* 使人想起溫暖夏日的音樂 **2** making people think about sex 性暗示的；性挑逗的：*suggestive jokes* 黃色笑話 ▶ **sug·gest·ive·ly** *adv.*：*He leered suggestively.* 他色迷迷地斜瞟一眼。

sui·cidal /ˌsuːɪˈsaɪdl; *BrE* also ˌsjuːɪ-/ *adj.* **1** people who are **suicidal** feel that they want to kill themselves 想自殺的；有自殺傾向的：*On bad days I even felt suicidal.* 趕上不順的日子，我都覺得不想活了。◇ *suicidal tendencies* 自殺傾向 **2** very dangerous and likely to lead to death; likely to cause very serious problems or disaster 自殺性的；有致命危險的；毀滅性的；災難性的：*a suicidal leap into the swollen river* 不顧死活地跳進上漲的河水 ◇ ***It would be suicidal*** *to risk going out in this weather.* 在這種天氣冒險出去，真是不要命了。◇ *The new economic policies could prove suicidal for the party.* 新經濟政策可能給該黨帶來災難性的後果。 ▶ **sui·cid·al·ly** /-dəli/ *adv.*：*suicidally depressed* 沮喪消沉得想自殺

sui·cide /ˈsuːɪsaɪd; *BrE* also ˈsjuːɪ-/ *noun* **1** [U, C] the act of killing yourself deliberately 自殺：*to* ***commit suicide*** 自殺 ◇ *an* ***attempted suicide*** (= one in which the person survives) 自殺未遂 ◇ *a* ***suicide letter/note*** (= written before sb tries to commit suicide) 絕命書 ◇ *a* ***suicide bomber*** (= who expects to die while trying to kill other people with a bomb) 自殺式爆炸者 ➲ see also ASSISTED SUICIDE **2** [U] a course of action that is likely to ruin your career, position in society, etc. 自殺性行為；自毀；自取滅亡的行為：*It would have been political suicide for him to challenge the allegations in court.* 假如當時他在法庭上質疑那些指控，那無異於自毀政治前程。 **3** [C] (*formal*) a person who commits suicide 自殺者

ˈsuicide pact *noun* an agreement between two or more people to kill themselves at the same time（集體）自殺協議

sui generis /ˌsuːi ˈdʒenərɪs; ˌsuːaɪ; ˈɡenərɪs/ *adj.* (from Latin, *formal*) different from all other people or things 獨特的；特有的 SYN **unique**

suit 0-ㄇ /suːt; *BrE* also sjuːt/ *noun, verb*

■ *noun* **1** 0-ㄇ a set of clothes made of the same cloth, including a jacket and trousers/pants or a skirt 西服；西裝；套裝：*a business suit* 公務裝 ◇ *a pinstripe suit* 一套細條紋西裝 ◇ *a* ***two-/three-piece suit*** (= of two/three pieces of clothing) 一套兩件／三件式西裝 ➲ VISUAL VOCAB page V61 ➲ see also DINNER SUIT, JUMPSUIT, LEISURE SUIT, LOUNGE SUIT, SAILOR SUIT, SHELL SUIT, SWEATSUIT, TRACKSUIT, TROUSER SUIT **2** 0-ㄇ a set of clothing worn for a particular activity（從事特定活動時穿的）成套服裝：*a diving suit* 潛水服 ◇ *a suit of armour* 一套盔甲 ➲ see also BOILER SUIT, SPACESUIT, SWIMSUIT, WETSUIT **3** any of the four sets that form a PACK/DECK of cards（撲克牌中）所有同花色的牌：*The suits are called hearts, clubs, diamonds and spades.* 撲克牌的四種花色分別叫紅桃、梅花、方塊和黑桃。 ➲ VISUAL VOCAB page V37 **4** = LAWSUIT：*to file/bring a suit against sb*

S

控告某人◇ *a divorce suit* 離婚訴訟 ➲ see also PATERNITY SUIT **5** [usually pl.] (*informal*) a person with an important job as a manager in a company or organization, especially one thought of as being mainly concerned with financial matters or as having a lot of influence （具影響力的）高級行政人員（尤指財務方面的） **IDM** see BIRTHDAY, FOLLOW, STRONG

■ **verb** [no passive] (not used in the progressive tenses 不用於進行時) **1** 🔑 to be convenient or useful for sb 對（某人）方便；滿足（某人）需要；合（某人）心意： **~ sb/sth** *Choose a computer to suit your particular needs.* 選一台適合你個人需要的電腦。◇ *If we met at 2, would that suit you?* 我們兩點鐘見面，你方便嗎？◇ *If you want to go by bus, that* ***suits me fine.*** 要是你想坐公共汽車走，那對我也合適。◇ *He can be very helpful, but only when it suits him.* 有時候他非常肯幫忙，不過那得合他心意。◇ **it suits sb to do sth** *It suits me to start work at a later time.* 對我來說，最好晚一點再開始工作。 **2** 🔑 **~ sb** (especially of clothes, colours, etc. 尤指服裝、顏色等) to make you look attractive 相配；合身： *Blue suits you. You should wear it more often.* 你適合穿藍色，你該多穿藍色衣服。◇ *I don't think this coat really suits me.* 我覺得這件大衣不大適合我穿。 **3 ~ sb/sth** (*especially BrE*) (usually used in negative sentences 通常用於否定句) to be right or good for sb/sth 適合；適宜；有利於： *This hot weather doesn't suit me.* 天這麼熱，我真受不了。

IDM **suit your/sb's book** (*BrE, informal*) to be convenient or useful for you/sb 對某人方便（或有用） **suit sb ˌdown to the ˈground** (*BrE, informal*) to be very convenient or acceptable for sb 對某人非常方便；很合某人心意： *This job suits me down to the ground.* 這份工作我非常滿意。 **ˌsuit yourˈself** (*informal*) **1** to do exactly what you would like 隨自己的意願： *I choose my assignments to suit myself.* 我根據自己的喜好選任務。**2** usually used in orders to tell sb to do what they want, even though it annoys you （表示聽憑對方的意願）自便，隨便： *'I think I'll stay in this evening.' 'Suit yourself!'* "今晚我就不出去了。" "隨你的便！"

PHR V **ˈsuit sth to sth/sb** to make sth appropriate for sth/sb 使適合（或適應）某事物（或人）： *He can suit his conversation to whoever he's with.* 無論跟誰說話，他都能說到一塊兒。

suit·able 🔑 /ˈsuːtəbl; *BrE* also ˈsjuː-/ *adj.* right or appropriate for a particular purpose or occasion 合適的；適宜的；適當的；適用的： *a suitable candidate* 合適的人選◇ **~ for sth/sb** *This programme is not suitable for children.* 這個節目兒童不宜。◇ *a suitable place for a picnic* 適合野餐的地方◇ **~ to do sth** *I don't have anything suitable to wear for the party.* 我沒有適合在聚會上穿的衣服。◇ *Would now be a suitable moment to discuss my report?* 現在討論我的報告合適不合適？ **OPP** **unsuitable** ▶ **suit·abil·ity** /ˌsuːtəˈbɪləti; *BrE* also ˌsjuː-/ *noun* [U]： *There is no doubt about her suitability for the job.* 毫無疑問，她適合做這個工作。

suit·ably /ˈsuːtəbli; *BrE* also ˈsjuː-/ *adv.* **1** in a way that is right or appropriate for a particular purpose or occasion 合適地；適宜地；適當地： *I am not really suitably dressed for a party.* 我穿這樣的衣服參加聚會並不十分得體。◇ *suitably qualified candidates* 十分符合條件的人選 **2** showing the feelings, etc. that you would expect in a particular situation 如你所料地；自然： *He was suitably impressed when I told him I'd won.* 我告訴他我贏了，他當然覺得我真行。

suit·case 🔑 /ˈsuːtkeɪs; *BrE* also ˈsjuː-/ (also **case**) *noun* a case with flat sides and a handle, used for carrying clothes, etc. when you are travelling （旅行用的）行李箱，手提箱： *to* ***pack/unpack a suitcase*** 把東西裝進手提箱；取出手提箱裏的東西 ➲ VISUAL VOCAB page V64

suite /swiːt/ *noun* **1** a set of rooms, especially in a hotel （尤指旅館的）一套房間，套房： *a* ***hotel/private/honeymoon suite*** 旅館 / 私人 / 蜜月套房◇ *a* ***suite of rooms/offices*** 一套房間；辦公套房 ➲ see also EN SUITE **2** a set of matching pieces of furniture 一套傢具： *a* ***bathroom/bedroom suite*** 一套衞生間 / 卧室傢具◇ (*BrE*) *a* ***three-piece suite*** *with two armchairs and a sofa* 由兩張單人沙發和一張長沙發組成的三件套傢具 **3** a piece of music made up of three or more related parts, for example pieces from an OPERA 組曲（由三個或更多相關部份組成）： *Stravinsky's Firebird Suite* 斯特拉文斯基的組曲《火鳥》 **4** (*computing* 計) a set of related computer programs 套；套裝軟件： *a suite of software development tools* 一套軟件開發工具

suit·ed 🔑 /ˈsuːtɪd; *BrE* also ˈsjuː-/ *adj.* [not before noun] **1** 🔑 right or appropriate for sb/sth 合適；適宜；適當： **~ (to sb/sth)** *She was* ***ideally suited*** *to the part of Eva Peron.* 她演愛娃 • 庇隆這個角色再合適不過了。◇ *This diet is suited to anyone who wants to lose weight fast.* 這食譜適合每一個希望迅速減肥的人。◇ **~ (for sb/sth)** *He is not really suited for a teaching career.* 他不大適合做教師。 **OPP** **unsuited** **2** 🔑 if two people are **suited** or **well suited**, they are likely to make a good couple 般配的： *Jo and I are very well suited.* 我跟喬非常合得來。◇ *They were not suited to one another.* 他們倆彼此不配。 **OPP** **unsuited** **3** wearing a suit, or a suit of the type mentioned 穿西裝的；穿…套裝的： *sober-suited city businessmen* 城市裏那些穿着素淨的生意人

suit·ing /ˈsuːtɪŋ; *BrE* also ˈsjuːtɪŋ/ *noun* [U] cloth made especially of wool, used for making suits 西服毛料： *men's suiting* 男西裝毛料

suitor /ˈsuːtə(r); *BrE* also ˈsjuː-/ *noun* **1** (*old-fashioned*) a man who wants to marry a particular woman 求婚者 **2** (*business* 商) a company that wants to buy another company 有意收購另一公司的公司

su·kuma wiki /sʊˌkuːmə ˈwiːkiː/ *noun* [U] (*EAfrE*) a vegetable with dark green leaves that are cooked; KALE 羽衣甘藍（菜）： *a meal of ugali and sukuma wiki* 蒸玉米粉糰加羽衣甘藍菜的一餐

sul·fate, **sul·fide**, **sul·fur**, **sul·fur·ic acid** (*US*) = SULPHATE, SULPHIDE, SULPHUR, SULPHURIC ACID

sulk /sʌlk/ *verb, noun*

■ **verb** [I] (*disapproving*) to look angry and refuse to speak or smile because you want people to know that you are upset about sth 面有慍色；生悶氣： *He went off to sulk in his room.* 他回到自己的房間，生起悶氣來。

■ **noun** (*BrE* also **the sulks** [pl.]) a period of not speaking and being bad-tempered because you are angry about sth 慍怒；生悶氣： *Jo was* ***in a sulk*** *upstairs.* 喬在樓上生悶氣。◇ *to have the sulks* 滿臉不高興

sulky /ˈsʌlki/ *adj.* (*disapproving*) bad-tempered or not speaking because you are angry about sth 面有慍色的；生悶氣的： *Sarah had looked sulky all morning.* 薩拉一上午都不高興地板着臉。◇ *a sulky child* 悶悶不樂的孩子 ▶ **sulk·ily** /-ɪli/ *adv.* **sulki·ness** *noun* [U]

sul·len /ˈsʌlən/ *adj.* (*disapproving*) **1** bad-tempered and not speaking, either on a particular occasion or because it is part of your character 面有慍色的；悶悶不樂的；鬱鬱寡歡的： *Bob looked pale and sullen.* 鮑勃臉色蒼白，悶悶不樂。◇ *She gave him a sullen glare.* 她滿臉不高興地瞪了他一眼。◇ *sullen teenagers* 面色陰鬱的青少年 **2** (*literary*) (of the sky or weather 天空或天氣) dark and unpleasant 陰沉的 ▶ **sul·len·ly** *adv.* **sul·len·ness** *noun* [U]

sully /ˈsʌli/ *verb* (**sul·lies**, **sully·ing**, **sul·lied**, **sul·lied**) (*formal* or *literary*) **1 ~ sth** to spoil or reduce the value of sth 敗壞；有損於 **2 ~ sth** to make sth dirty 弄髒；玷污

sul·phate (*BrE*) (*US* **sul·fate**) /ˈsʌlfeɪt/ *noun* [C, U] (*chemistry* 化) a COMPOUND of SULPHURIC ACID and a chemical element 硫酸鹽： *copper sulphate* 硫酸銅

sul·phide (*BrE*) (*US* **sul·fide**) /ˈsʌlfaɪd/ *noun* [C, U] (*chemistry* 化) a COMPOUND of sulphur and another chemical element 硫化物

sul·phur (*BrE*) (*US* **sul·fur**) /ˈsʌlfə(r)/ *noun* [U] (*symb.* **S**) a chemical element. Sulphur is a pale yellow substance that produces a strong unpleasant smell when it burns and is used in medicine and industry. 硫；硫磺

HELP The spelling **sulfur** has been adopted by the International Union of Pure and Applied Chemistry and by the Royal Society of Chemistry in the UK. However, **sulphur** still remains the usual spelling in British, Irish, South African and Indian English. Both spellings are used in Canadian, Australian and New Zealand English. * sulfur 這一拼寫已為國際理論化學與應用化學聯合

S

會和英國皇家化學學會採用。不過，在英國、愛爾蘭、南非和印度的英語中常見的拼寫仍然是 sulphur。在加拿大、澳大利亞和新西蘭的英語中，兩種拼寫均可使用。
▸ **sul·phur·ous** (*BrE*) (*US* **sul·fur·ous**) /ˈsʌlfərəs/ *adj.* : *sulphurous fumes* 燃燒硫磺產生的煙霧

ˌsulphur diˈoxide (*BrE*) (*US* **ˌsulfur diˈoxide**) *noun* [U] (*symb.* **SO_2**) a poisonous gas with a strong smell, that is used in industry and causes air pollution 二氧化硫

sul·phur·ic acid (*BrE*) (*US* **sul·fur·ic acid**) /sʌlˌfjʊərɪk ˈæsɪd; *NAmE* -ˌfjʊr-/ *noun* [U] (*symb.* **H_2SO_4**) a strong clear acid 硫酸

sul·tan /ˈsʌltən/ *noun* the title given to Muslim rulers in some countries 蘇丹（某些穆斯林國家統治者的稱號）: *the Sultan of Brunei* 文萊蘇丹

sul·tana /sʌlˈtɑːnə; *NAmE* -ˈtænə/ *noun* **1** (*BrE*) (*NAmE* **ˌgolden ˈraisin**) a small dried GRAPE without seeds, used in cakes, etc. 無核小葡萄乾（用於糕點等） **2** the wife, mother, sister or daughter of a sultan 蘇丹女眷（指后妃、王太后、姊妹或女兒）

sul·tan·ate /ˈsʌltəneɪt/ *noun* **1** the rank or position of a SULTAN 蘇丹的職位 **2** an area of land that is ruled over by a SULTAN 蘇丹統治的領土: *the Sultanate of Oman* 阿曼蘇丹國 **3** the period of time during which sb is a SULTAN 蘇丹的統治時期

sul·try /ˈsʌltri/ *adj.* (**sul·trier**, **sul·tri·est**) **1** (of the weather or air 天氣或空氣) very hot and uncomfortable 悶熱的 SYN **muggy**: *a sultry summer afternoon* 夏天一個悶熱的下午 **2** (*formal*) (of a woman or her appearance 女子或其外表) sexually attractive; seeming to have strong sexual feelings 姿色迷人的；風情萬種的；性感的 SYN **sexy**: *a sultry smile* 迷人的微笑 ◇ *a sultry singer* 嗓音撩人的歌手 ▸ **sul·tri·ness** *noun* [U]

sum 0- AW /sʌm/ *noun, verb*
■ ***noun*** **1** 0- [C] **~ (of sth)** an amount of money 金額；款項: *You will be fined the sum of £200.* 你將被罰款 200 英鎊。◇ *a large sum of money* 一大筆錢 ◇ *a six-figure sum* 一筆六位數的款項 ➲ see also LUMP SUM **2** 0- [C, usually sing.] **~ (of sth)** the number you get when you add two or more numbers together 和；總和；總數: *The sum of 7 and 12 is 19.* * 7 加 12 的和是 19。 **3** (also **ˌsum ˈtotal**) [sing.] **the ~ of sth** all of sth, especially when you think that it is not very much 全部，一切（尤指數量不大）: *This is the sum of my achievements so far.* 這就是我目前的全部成就。 **4** [C] a simple problem that involves calculating numbers 算術；（數字的）簡單計算: *to* ***do a sum*** *in your head* 做心算 ◇ *I was good at sums at school.* 我當學生時擅長算術。◇ *If I've got my sums right, I should be able to afford the rent.* 要是我算對了的話，我應該負擔得起這筆租金。
IDM **be greater/more than the ˌsum of its ˈparts** to be better or more effective as a group than you would think just by looking at the individual members of the group 個體相加不如集體的力量大 **in ˈsum** (*formal*) used to introduce a short statement of the main points of a discussion, speech, etc. 總之；總而言之
■ ***verb*** (**-mm-**)
PHR V **ˌsum ˈup | ˌsum sth↔ˈup** **1** 0- to state the main points of sth in a short and clear form 總結；概括 SYN **summarize**: ***To sum up****, there are three main ways of tackling the problem ...* 概括起來說，這一問題主要有三種解決辦法… ◇ **~ what ...** *Can I just sum up what we've agreed so far?* 我可否就我們目前已經達成的共識作個概括？ ➲ LANGUAGE BANK at CONCLUSION **2** (of a judge 法官) to give a summary of the main facts and arguments in a legal case, near the end of a trial（審理結束前）作概述 ➲ related noun SUMMING-UP **ˌsum sb/sth↔ˈup** **1** to describe or show the most typical characteristics of sb/sth, especially in a few words 簡而言之: *Totally lazy—that just about sums him up.* 懶到家了，這大體上就是他的真實寫照。 **2** to form or express an opinion of sb/sth 估量，判斷（某人或事物） SYN **size up**: *She quickly summed up the situation and took control.* 她很快就看出是怎麼回事，並控制住局面。 ➲ related noun SUMMING-UP

summa cum laude /ˌsʊmə ˌkʊm ˈlɔːdi; ˈlaʊdeɪ/ *adv., adj.* (from *Latin*) (in the US 美國) at the highest level of achievement that students can reach when they finish their studies at college 以優異成績（三等優異成績的第一等）: *He graduated summa cum laude from Harvard.* 他以最優等成績從哈佛大學畢業。 ➲ compare CUM LAUDE, MAGNA CUM LAUDE

sum·mar·ize (*BrE* also **-ise**) AW /ˈsʌməraɪz/ *verb* [T, I] **~ (sth)** to give a summary of sth (= a statement of the main points) 總結；概括；概述: *The results of the research are summarized at the end of the chapter.* 在這一章末尾對研究結果作了總結。 ➲ LANGUAGE BANK at CONCLUSION

sum·mary 0- AW /ˈsʌməri/ *noun, adj.*
■ ***noun*** 0- (*pl.* **-ies**) a short statement that gives only the main points of sth, not the details 總結；概括；概要: *The following is a summary of our conclusions.* 現將我們的幾點結論綜述如下。◇ *a news summary* 新聞綜述 ◇ *a two-page summary of a government report* 一份兩頁的政府報告摘要 ◇ ***In summary****, this was a disappointing performance.* 總的來說，這場演出令人失望。 ➲ WRITING TUTOR page WT14
■ ***adj.*** [only before noun] **1** (*formal*) giving only the main points of sth, not the details 總結性的；概括的；概要的: *a summary financial statement* 財務彙總報表 ◇ *I made a summary report for the records.* 我對記錄內容做了扼要報告。 **2** (sometimes *disapproving*) done immediately, without paying attention to the normal process that should be followed 從速從簡的；即決的；草草的: ***summary justice/execution*** 即決裁判；草草處決 ◇ *a summary judgement* 草草判決 ▸ **sum·mar·ily** /ˈsʌmərəli; *NAmE* səˈmerəli/ *adv.*: *to be summarily dismissed/executed* 被草草開除／處決

sum·mat /ˈsʌmət; ˈsəmət/ *noun* (*NEngE, non-standard*) a way of writing a spoken form of 'something'（something 的一種書寫形式）

sum·ma·tion AW /sʌˈmeɪʃn/ *noun* **1** [usually sing.] (*formal*) a summary of what has been done or said 總結；概括: *What he said was a fair summation of the discussion.* 他這番話對討論作了恰當的總結。 **2** (*formal*) a collection of different parts that forms a complete account or impression of sb/sth 彙總物；綜合體: *The exhibition presents a summation of the artist's career.* 展覽全面體現了這位畫家的藝術生涯。 **3** (*NAmE, law* 律) a final speech that a lawyer makes near the end of a trial in court, after all the evidence has been given（判決前的）法庭辯論總結

sum·mer 0- /ˈsʌmə(r)/ *noun* [U, C] the warmest season of the year, coming between spring and autumn/fall 夏天；夏季: *We're going away* ***in the summer****.* 夏天我們要外出。◇ *It's very hot here* ***in summer****.* 這裏夏天很熱。◇ *in the summer of 2009* 在 2009 年夏季 ◇ *late/early summer* 夏末；初夏 ◇ *this/next/last summer* 今年／下一個／上一個夏天 ◇ *a cool/hot/wet summer* 涼爽的／炎熱的／多雨的夏天 ◇ *It is now* ***high summer*** (= the hottest part of summer). 正值盛夏。◇ *a summer's day* 夏日 ◇ *a summer dress* 夏天穿的連衣裙 ◇ *the* ***summer holidays/vacation*** 暑假 ◇ *two summers ago* 兩年前 ➲ see also INDIAN SUMMER IDM see SWALLOW *n.*

ˈsummer camp *noun* [C, U] (in the US) a place where children go during the summer and take part in sports and other activities 夏令營

ˈsummer house *noun* **1** a small building in a garden/yard for sitting in in good weather（花園或院子裏的）涼亭 **2** (also **ˈsummer home**) (*NAmE*) a house that sb lives in only during the summer 避暑別墅

ˌsummer ˈpudding *noun* [C, U] (*BrE*) a cold DESSERT (= a sweet dish) made from BERRIES surrounded by slices of bread that have absorbed their juice 夏令布丁（麵包片圍在漿果四周浸透果汁的冷盤甜食）

ˈsummer school *noun* [C, U] courses that are held in the summer at a university or college or, in the US, at a school 暑期班（一般在大學開設，美國中小學也有）

ˌsummer ˈstock *noun* [U] (*NAmE*) the production of special plays and other entertainment in areas where people are on holiday/vacation（度假勝地的）夏季特別娛樂表演，夏令劇目

S

ˌsummer student *noun* (*CanE*) a student, especially a university student, who is working at a job for the summer 暑期工（夏季打工的學生，尤指大學生）

ˈsummer time (*BrE*) (*NAmE* **ˈdaylight saving time**) *noun* [U] the period during which in some countries the clocks are put forward one hour, so that it is light for an extra hour in the evening 夏令時（有些國家實行夏時制，將時鐘撥快一小時，以節約照明能源）

sum·mer·time /ˈsʌmətaɪm; *NAmE* -mərt-/ *noun* [U] the season of summer 夏季；夏天；夏令：*It's beautiful here in (the) summertime.* 這裏夏天很美。

sum·mery /ˈsʌməri/ *adj.* typical of or suitable for the summer 夏季的；夏季特有的；適合夏季的：*summery weather* 夏日的天氣 ◇ *a light summery dress* 夏天穿的薄連衣裙 OPP **wintry**

ˌsumming-ˈup *noun* (*pl.* **summings-up**) **1** a speech that the judge makes near the end of a trial in court, in which he or she reminds the JURY about the evidence and the most important points in the case before the JURY makes its decision（審理結束前法官向陪審團作的）證據概述 **2** an occasion when sb states the main points of an argument, etc. 總結；概括

sum·mit /ˈsʌmɪt/ *noun* **1** the highest point of sth, especially the top of a mountain 最高點；頂點；山頂：*We reached the summit at noon.* 中午時分我們抵達峰頂。◇ *This path leads to the summit.* 這條路通往山頂。◇ (*figurative*) *the summit of his career* 他事業的頂峰 ➲ VISUAL VOCAB pages V4, V5 **2** an official meeting or series of meetings between the leaders of two or more governments at which they discuss important matters（政府間的）首腦會議；峰會：*a summit in Moscow* 在莫斯科舉行的首腦會議 ◇ *a summit conference* 峰會 ➲ COLLOCATIONS at INTERNATIONAL

sum·mon /ˈsʌmən/ *verb* **1 ~ sb (to do sth)** (*formal*) to order sb to appear in court 傳喚，傳訊（出庭）SYN **summons**：*He was summoned to appear before the magistrates.* 他被傳喚在地方法院出庭。 **2 ~ sb (to sth) | ~ sb to do sth** (*formal*) to order sb to come to you 召喚：*In May 1688 he was urgently summoned to London.* * 1688 年 5 月，他被緊急召往倫敦。◇ *She summoned the waiter.* 她召喚服務員過來。 **3 ~ sth** (*formal*) to arrange an official meeting 召集，召開（會議）SYN **convene**：*to summon a meeting* 召集會議 **4 ~ sth** (*formal*) to call for or try to obtain sth 籲求；請求；爭取：*to* ***summon assistance/help/reinforcements*** 請求援助／幫助／增援 **5 ~ sth (up)** to make an effort to produce a particular quality in yourself, especially when you find it difficult 鼓起；振作；使出 SYN **muster**：*She was trying to summon up the courage to leave him.* 當時她試圖鼓起勇氣離開他。◇ *I couldn't even summon the energy to get out of bed.* 我甚至連下牀的力氣都沒有。
PHR V **ˌsummon sth↔ˈup** to make a feeling, an idea, a memory, etc. come into your mind 喚起；使想起 SYN **evoke**：*The book summoned up memories of my childhood.* 這本書喚起我童年的記憶。

sum·mons /ˈsʌmənz/ *noun, verb*
■ ***noun*** (*pl.* **sum·monses** /-zɪz/) **1** (*NAmE* also **cit·ation**) an order to appear in court（法院的）傳喚，傳票：*to issue a summons against sb* 向某人發出傳票 ◇ *The police have been unable to* ***serve a summons on*** *him.* 警方一直無法把傳票送達他本人。◇ *She received a summons to appear in court the following week.* 她收到一張傳票，讓她下週出庭。 **2** an order to come and see sb 召喚；召見令：*to obey a royal summons* 聽從國王的召喚
■ ***verb*** to order sb to appear in court 傳（某人）出庭；傳喚 SYN **summon**：**~ sb (for sth)** *She was summonsed for speeding.* 她因超速行車被傳訊。◇ **~ sb to do sth** *He was summonsed to appear in court.* 他被傳喚出庭。

sumo /ˈsuːməʊ; *NAmE* -moʊ/ (also **ˌsumo ˈwrestling**) *noun* [U] a Japanese style of WRESTLING, in which the people taking part are extremely large 相撲：*a sumo wrestler* 相撲運動員

sump /sʌmp/ *noun* **1** a hole or hollow area in which liquid waste collects 集水坑；污水坑 **2** (*NAmE* also **ˈoil pan**) the place under an engine that holds the engine oil（發動機下面的）集油槽，油底殼

sump·tu·ous /ˈsʌmptʃuəs/ *adj.* (*formal*) very expensive and looking very impressive 華貴的；豪華的；奢華的：*a sumptuous meal* 盛宴 ◇ *We dined in sumptuous surroundings.* 我們在富麗堂皇的環境中用餐。▸ **sump·tu·ous·ly** *adv.* **sump·tu·ous·ness** *noun* [U]

ˌsum ˈtotal *noun* [sing.] (sometimes *disapproving*) the whole of sth; everything 全部；一切；總共：*A photo, a book of poems and a gold ring—this was the sum total of his possessions.* 一張照片、一本詩集和一枚金戒指，這就是他的全部家當。

sun 🔑 /sʌn/ *noun, verb*
■ ***noun*** **1** 🔑 **the sun, the Sun** [sing.] the star that shines in the sky during the day and gives the earth heat and light 太陽；日：*the sun's rays* 太陽的光線 ◇ *the* ***rising/setting sun*** 初升的／西下的太陽 ◇ ***The sun was shining*** *and birds were singing.* 陽光照耀，鳥兒啼囀。◇ *The sun was just setting.* 太陽剛往下落。➲ COLLOCATIONS at WEATHER **2** 🔑 (usually **the sun**) [sing., U] the light and heat from the sun 太陽的光和熱；陽光；日光 SYN **sunshine**：*the warmth of the afternoon sun* 下午溫暖的陽光 ◇ *This room gets the sun in the mornings.* 這間屋子上午可以曬着太陽。◇ *We sat* ***in the sun***. 我們坐在陽光下。◇ *The sun was blazing hot.* 陽光灼熱逼人。◇ *Too much sun ages the skin.* 曬太陽過多會使皮膚衰老。◇ *We did our best to keep* ***out of the sun***. 我們盡量避開陽光照射。◇ *They've booked a holiday* ***in the sun*** (= in a place where it is warm and the sun shines a lot). 他們已經預訂好了去陽光充足的地方度假。◇ *Her face had obviously* ***caught the sun*** (= become red or brown) *on holiday.* 她的臉明顯地在假期曬黑了。◇ *I was driving westwards and I* ***had the sun in my eyes*** (= the sun was shining in my eyes). 我驅車向西行駛，陽光直晃眼。➲ see also SUNNY (1) **3** [C] (*technical* 術語) any star around which planets move 恒星
IDM **under the ˈsun** used to emphasize that you are talking about a very large number of things（強調事物數量很大）天下，世上，全世界：*We talked about everything under the sun.* 天南地北，我們無所不談。 **with the ˈsun** when the sun rises or sets 日出時；日落時：*I get up with the sun.* 我日出即起。➲ more at HAY, PLACE *n.*
■ ***verb*** (**-nn-**) **~ yourself** to sit or lie in a place where the sun is shining on you 曬太陽：*We lay sunning ourselves on the deck.* 我們躺在甲板上曬太陽。

ˈsun-baked *adj.* **1** made hard and dry by the heat of the sun 曬得乾硬的：*sun-baked earth* 被太陽烤乾的土地 **2** receiving a lot of light and heat from the sun 太陽曝曬的；烈日下的：*sun-baked beaches* 太陽曝曬的海灘

sun·bathe /ˈsʌnbeɪð/ *verb* [I] to sit or lie in the sun, especially in order to go brown (get a SUNTAN) 沐日光浴；曬太陽 ➲ note at BATH

sun·beam /ˈsʌnbiːm/ *noun* a stream of light from the sun（一束）陽光

sun·bed /ˈsʌnbed/ *noun* a bed for lying on under a SUNLAMP 太陽燈日光浴牀 ➲ compare SUNLOUNGER

the Sun·belt /ˈsʌnbelt/ *noun* [sing.] the southern and south-western parts of the US that are warm for most of the year 陽光地帶（美國南部和西南部地區，全年大部份時間氣候溫暖）

sun·block /ˈsʌnblɒk; *NAmE* -blɑːk/ *noun* [U, C] a cream that you put on your skin to protect it completely from the harmful effects of the sun 防曬霜；防曬油

sun·burn /ˈsʌnbɜːn; *NAmE* -bɜːrn/ *noun* [U] the condition of having painful red skin because you have spent too much time in the sun 曬斑；曬傷 ➲ compare SUNTAN

sun·burned /ˈsʌnbɜːnd; *NAmE* -bɜːrnd/ (also **sun·burnt** /ˈsʌnbɜːnt; *NAmE* -bɜːrnt/) *adj.* **1** suffering from sunburn 曬傷的：*Her shoulders were badly sunburned.* 她的肩膀嚴重曬傷了。 **2** (*BrE*) (of a person or of skin 人或皮膚) having an attractive brown colour from being in the sun 曬得黝黑而好看的 SYN **tanned**：*She looked fit and sunburned.* 她看上去挺健康，曬得一身古銅色。

sun·burst /ˈsʌnbɜːst; *NAmE* -bɜːrst/ *noun* an occasion when the sun appears from behind the clouds and sends out bright streams of light 雲開日出；陽光突現

S

sun·cream /ˈsʌnkriːm/ *noun* [U, C] (*especially BrE*) cream that you put on your skin to protect it from the harmful effects of the sun 防曬霜；防曬乳

sun·dae /ˈsʌndeɪ; -di/ *noun* a cold DESSERT (= a sweet dish) of ice cream covered with a sweet sauce, nuts, pieces of fruit, etc., usually served in a tall glass 聖代冰淇淋（加甜汁、果仁、水果粒等）

Sun·day /ˈsʌndeɪ; -di/ *noun* (*abbr.* **Sun.**)
1 [C, U] the day of the week after Saturday and before Monday, thought of as either the first or the last day of the week 星期日；星期天 **HELP** To see how **Sunday** is used, look at the examples at **Monday**. * Sunday 的用法見詞條 Monday 下的示例。**ORIGIN** From the Old English for 'day of the sun', translated from Latin *dies solis*. 源自古英語，原意為 day of the sun（太陽日），古英語則譯自拉丁文 dies solis。 **2** [C, usually pl.] (*BrE, informal*) a newspaper published on a Sunday 每逢星期日出版的報紙；星期日報
IDM **your ˌSunday ˈbest** (*informal, humorous*) your best clothes 自己最好的衣服 ➲ more at MONTH

ˈSunday school *noun* [C, U] a class that is organized by a church or SYNAGOGUE where children can go for a short time on Sundays to learn about the Christian or Jewish religion 主日學校（基督教堂或猶太教堂在星期日為兒童提供宗教教育）

ˈsun deck *noun* the part of a ship where passengers can sit to enjoy the sun, or a similar area beside a restaurant or swimming pool （輪船的）日光甲板；（餐館或游泳池旁邊的）日光平台，曬台

sun·der /ˈsʌndə(r)/ *verb* **~ sth/sb (from sth/sb)** (*formal* or *literary*) to split or break sth/sb apart, especially by force （尤指強制地）分開，使分離，割裂 ➲ see also ASUNDER

sundial 日晷

sun·dial /ˈsʌndaɪəl/ *noun* a device used outdoors, especially in the past, for telling the time when the sun is shining. A pointed piece of metal throws a shadow on a flat surface that is marked with the hours like a clock, and the shadow moves around as the sun moves across the sky. 日規；日晷

sun·down /ˈsʌndaʊn/ *noun* [U] (*especially NAmE*) the time when the sun goes down and night begins 日落時分 **SYN** **sunset**

sun·down·er /ˈsʌndaʊnə(r)/ *noun* (*BrE, informal*) an alcoholic drink, drunk around the time when the sun goes down 夕暮酒（夕陽西下時喝）

ˈsun-drenched *adj.* [only before noun] (*approving*) having a lot of hot sun 充滿陽光的；陽光充足的：*sun-drenched Mediterranean beaches* 陽光充沛的地中海海灘

sun·dress /ˈsʌndres/ *noun* a dress that does not cover the arms, neck or shoulders, worn in hot weather 太陽裙，背心裙（領口低，無袖）

ˈsun-dried *adj.* [only before noun] (especially of food 尤指食物) dried naturally by the heat of the sun 曬乾的：*sun-dried tomatoes* 曬乾的西紅柿

sun·dries /ˈsʌndriz/ *noun* [pl.] various items, especially small ones, that are not important enough to be named separately 雜物；雜項物品

sun·dry /ˈsʌndri/ *adj.* [only before noun] (*formal*) various; not important enough to be named separately 雜項的：*a watch, a diary and sundry other items* 一塊手錶、一本日記和其他一些零碎的東西
IDM **ˌall and ˈsundry** (*informal*) everyone, not just a few special people 所有人；各色人等：*She was known to all and sundry as Bella.* 人人都叫她貝拉。◇ *The club is open to all and sundry.* 這個俱樂部什麼人都可以加入。

sun·flower /ˈsʌnflaʊə(r)/ *noun* a very tall plant with large yellow flowers, grown in gardens or for its seeds and their oil that are used in cooking 向日葵；葵花：*sunflower oil* 葵花籽油 ➲ VISUAL VOCAB page V11

sung *past part.* of SING

sun·glasses /ˈsʌnglɑːsɪz; *NAmE* -glæs-/ (also *informal* **shades**) *noun* [pl.] a pair of glasses with dark glass in them that you wear to protect your eyes from bright light from the sun 太陽鏡；墨鏡：*a pair of sunglasses* 一副太陽鏡 ➲ see also DARK GLASSES

ˈsun hat *noun* a hat worn to protect the head and neck from the sun 闊邊遮陽帽 ➲ VISUAL VOCAB page V65

sunk *past part.* of SINK

sunk·en /ˈsʌŋkən/ *adj.* **1** [only before noun] that has fallen to the bottom of the sea or the ocean, or of a lake or river 沉沒的；沉入水底的 **SYN** **submerged**：*a sunken ship* 沉船 ◇ *sunken treasure* 沉在水底的財寶 **2** (of eyes or cheeks 眼睛或面頰) hollow and deep as a result of disease, getting old, or not having enough food 凹陷的，深陷的（尤因疾病、年老或飢餓） **3** [only before noun] at a lower level than the area around 低於周圍平面的；低窪處的：*a sunken garden* 低地花園

ˈsun-kissed *adj.* [usually before noun] made warm or brown by the sun 曬暖的；曬黑的：*sun-kissed bodies on the beach* 沙灘上曬得黝黑的身體

sun·lamp /ˈsʌnlæmp/ *noun* a lamp that produces ULTRAVIOLET light that has the same effect as the sun and can turn the skin brown 太陽燈（能發出紫外線，與日照有相同效果）

sun·less /ˈsʌnləs/ *adj.* without any sun; receiving no light from the sun 無陽光的；陽光照不到的 **SYN** **gloomy**：*a sunless day* 無陽光的一天 **OPP** **sunny**

sun·light /ˈsʌnlaɪt/ *noun* [U] the light from the sun 陽光；日光：*a **ray/pool of sunlight*** 一束／一片陽光 ◇ ***shafts of bright sunlight*** 一道道明亮的陽光 ◇ *The morning sunlight flooded into the room.* 早晨的陽光瀉入房間。

sun·lit /ˈsʌnlɪt/ *adj.* [usually before noun] receiving light from the sun 陽光照耀的：*sunlit streets* 陽光照耀的街道

ˈsun lounge (*BrE*) (also **sun·room** *NAmE, BrE*) *noun* a room with large windows, and often a glass roof, that lets in a lot of light 日光室，陽光間（帶大窗戶，常有玻璃屋頂）

sun·loun·ger /ˈsʌnlaʊndʒə(r)/ *noun* (*BrE*) a chair with a long seat that supports your legs, used for sitting or lying on in the sun 日光浴椅；日光浴牀 ➲ compare LOUNGER, SUNBED ➲ VISUAL VOCAB page V19

Sunni /ˈsʊni; ˈsʌni/ *noun* (*pl.* **Sunni** or **Sun·nis**) **1** [U] one of the two main branches of the Islamic religion 遜尼派（伊斯蘭教兩大主要派別之一） ➲ compare SHIA **2** [C] a member of the Sunni branch of Islam 遜尼派教徒 ➲ compare SHIITE ▸ **Sun·nite** /ˈsʊnaɪt; ˈsʌn-/ *adj.* [usually before noun]

sun·nies /ˈsʌniz/ [pl.] *noun* (*AustralE, NZE, informal*) SUNGLASSES 太陽鏡；墨鏡

sunny /ˈsʌni/ *adj.* (**sun·nier**, **sun·ni·est**) **1** with a lot of bright light from the sun 陽光充足的：*a sunny day* 陽光明媚的日子 ◇ *sunny weather* 豔陽高照的天氣 ◇ *The outlook for the weekend is hot and sunny.* 預計本週末天氣晴朗炎熱。◇ *a sunny garden* 充滿陽光的花園 ◇ *Italy was at its sunniest.* 當時意大利正值陽光最充沛的時節。 **2** cheerful and happy 歡樂的；快樂的：*a sunny disposition* 開朗的性情

ˈsunny side *noun* the side of sth that receives most light from the sun 曬着太陽的一邊；向陽面：(*figurative*) *the sunny side of life* (= the more cheerful aspects of life) 人生的光明面
IDM **ˌsunny side ˈup** (*NAmE*) (of an egg 蛋) fried on one side only 只煎一面的

sun·rise /ˈsʌnraɪz/ *noun* **1** [U] the time when the sun first appears in the sky in the morning 日出 **SYN** **dawn**：*We got up at sunrise.* 我們在日出時起牀。

S

2 [C, usually sing.] the colours in the part of the sky where the sun first appears in the morning 朝霞： *the pinks and yellows of the sunrise* 一道道粉紅和金黃的朝霞

'sunrise industry *noun* a new industry, especially one connected with ELECTRONICS or computers, that is successful and growing 朝陽產業；（尤指與電子或計算機相關的）新興產業 ➲ compare SUNSET INDUSTRY

sun·roof /'sʌnruːf/ *noun* (*pl.* **-roofs**) a part of the roof of a car that you can open to let air and light in （汽車車頂可開啟的）活動頂板，天窗

sun·room /'sʌnruːm; -rʊm/ (*especially NAmE*) (*BrE* also **'sun lounge**) *noun* a room with large windows, and often a glass roof, that lets in a lot of light 日光室，陽光間（帶大窗戶，常有玻璃屋頂）

sun·screen /'sʌnskriːn/ *noun* [C, U] a cream or liquid that you put on your skin to protect it from the harmful effects of the sun 防曬霜；防曬油： *a high factor* (= strong) *sunscreen* 防曬係數高的防曬霜

sun·set /'sʌnset/ *noun, adj., verb*

■ ***noun*** **1** [U] the time when the sun goes down and night begins 日落；傍晚： *Every evening* ***at sunset*** *the flag was lowered.* 每天傍晚日落時都要降旗。 **2** [C] the colours in the part of the sky where the sun slowly goes down in the evening 晚霞： *a spectacular sunset* 絢爛的晚霞 **3** [C] a fixed period of time after which a law or the effect of a law will end （法律的）自動廢止期，效力消滅期： *There is a five-year sunset on the new tax.* 新稅種的有效施行期限為五年。

■ ***adj.*** [only before noun] **1** used to describe a colour that is like one of the colours in a sunset 霞紅色的；淺橘紅色的： *sunset yellow* 日落黃 **2** used to describe sth that is near its end, or that happens at the end of sth 衰落的；最後期的： *This is his sunset tour after fifty years as a singer.* 這是他五十年歌手生涯結束前最後一次巡迴演出。 **3** (of a law or the effect of a law 法律或法律效力) designed to end or to end sth after a fixed period of time 定期廢止的： *a two-year sunset clause in the new law* 新法律中的一條實施期限為兩年的"日落條款"

■ ***verb*** (**-tt-**) [I, T] **~ (sth)** (of a law or the effect of a law 法律或法律效力) to end or to end sth after a fixed period of time （使）定期屆滿廢止： *The tax relief will sunset after a year.* 稅款減免將在一年後廢止。

'sunset industry *noun* an old industry that has started to become less successful 夕陽產業；夕陽工業 ➲ compare SUNRISE INDUSTRY

S

'sunset provision (also **'sunset clause**) *noun* (*law* 律) part of a law, rule or agreement that states that it will no longer apply from a particular date 日落條款（法律、規定或協議中說明自某日期起即行廢止的條款）

sun·shade /'sʌnʃeɪd/ *noun* **1** a light umbrella or other object such as an AWNING, that is used to protect people from hot sun 遮陽傘；遮陽篷： *a child's buggy fitted with a sunshade* 裝有陽傘的嬰兒車 ➲ VISUAL VOCAB page V19 ➲ compare PARASOL **2 sunshades** [pl.] a pair of dark glasses that you wear to protect your eyes from bright light from the sun, especially ones that fix on to your ordinary glasses （尤指加在普通眼鏡上的）太陽鏡，墨鏡

sun·shine /'sʌnʃaɪn/ *noun* [U] **1** the light and heat of the sun 陽光；日光： *the warm spring sunshine* 春天和煦的陽光 ➲ COLLOCATIONS at WEATHER **2** (*informal*) happiness 歡樂；幸福： *She brought sunshine into our dull lives.* 她給我們乏味的生活帶來了歡樂。 **3** (*BrE, informal*) used for addressing sb in a friendly, or sometimes a rude way （友好地稱呼某人，有時顯得不禮貌）朋友，老兄： *Hello, sunshine!* 你好啊，老兄！◇ *Look, sunshine, who do you think you're talking to?* 喂，哥們兒，知道你在跟誰說話嗎？ IDM see RAY

'sunshine law *noun* (*US*) a law that forces government organizations to make certain types of information available to the public 公開法，陽光法案（要求政府機構公開某些類型的信息）

sun·spot /'sʌnspɒt; *NAmE* -spɑːt/ *noun* a dark area that sometimes appears on the sun's surface （太陽）黑子

sun·stroke /'sʌnstrəʊk; *NAmE* -stroʊk/ *noun* [U] an illness with fever, weakness, headache, etc. caused by too much direct sun, especially on the head 日射熱；中暑

sun·tan /'sʌntæn/ *noun* [usually sing.] = TAN *n.* (2)： *Where have you been to get that suntan?* 你上哪兒去了，曬得黑黑的？ ➲ compare SUNBURN ▶ **sun·tan** *adj.* [only before noun]： *suntan oil* 防曬油 **sun·tanned** *adj.* = TANNED： *a suntanned face* 曬得黝黑的臉龐

sun·trap /'sʌntræp/ *noun* a place that is sheltered from the wind and gets a lot of sun 避風向陽處

sun·up /'sʌnʌp/ *noun* [U] (*especially NAmE*) the time when the sun rises and day begins 日出

'sun-worship·per *noun* (*informal*) a person who enjoys lying in the sun very much 迷戀日光浴的人

sup /sʌp/ *verb* (**-pp-**) [I, T] **~ (sth)** (*NEngE* or *old-fashioned*) to drink sth, especially in small amounts （小口地）喝；呷；啜 ▶ **sup** *noun*

super /'suːpə(r); *BrE* also 'sjuː-/ *adj., adv., noun*

■ ***adj.*** (*informal*, becoming *old-fashioned*) extremely good 頂好的；超級的；頂呱呱的： *a super meal* 一頓美餐 ◇ *We had a super time in Italy.* 我們在意大利過得十分愜意。◇ *She was super* (= very kind) *when I was having problems.* 我遇到問題的時候，她待我好極了。

■ ***adv.*** (*informal*) especially; particularly 特別；格外： *He's been super understanding.* 他特別體諒人。

■ ***noun*** **1** (*BrE, informal*) a SUPERINTENDENT in the police （英國的）警官；（美國的）警長 **2** (*NAmE*) a SUPERINTENDENT of a building （大樓的）管理人

super- /'suːpə(r); *BrE* also 'sjuː-/ *combining form* **1** (in adjectives, adverbs and nouns 構成形容詞、副詞和名詞) extremely; more or better than normal 極；超；超級： *super-rich* 極富有的 ◇ *superhuman* 超出常人的 ◇ *superglue* 強力膠 **2** (in nouns and verbs 構成名詞和動詞) above; over 上；上方： *superstructure* 上層建築 ◇ *superimpose* 使疊加

super·abun·dance /ˌsuːpərə'bʌndəns; *BrE* also ˌsjuː-/ *noun* [sing., U] (*formal*) much more than enough of sth 過多；過剩 ▶ **super·abun·dant** *adj.*

super·annu·ated /ˌsuːpər'ænjueɪtɪd; *BrE* also ˌsjuː-/ *adj.* [usually before noun] (*formal* or *humorous*) (of people or things 人或東西) too old for work or to be used for their original purpose 年老不能工作的；陳舊不中用的；過時的： *superannuated rock stars* 過氣搖滾歌星

super·annu·ation /ˌsuːpərˌænju'eɪʃn; *BrE* also ˌsjuː-/ *noun* [U] (*especially BrE*) a pension that you get, usually from your employer, when you stop working when you are old and that you pay for while you are working; the money that you pay for this （通常由原雇主發的）退休金，養老金

su·perb /suː'pɜːb; sjuː-; *NAmE* suː'pɜːrb/ *adj.* excellent; of very good quality 極佳的；卓越的；質量極高的： *a superb player* 一名傑出的運動員 ◇ *The car's in superb condition.* 這輛車車況極好。◇ *His performance was absolutely superb.* 他的表演精彩絕倫。◇ *You look superb.* 你看上去棒極了。 ➲ SYNONYMS at EXCELLENT ▶ **su·perb·ly** *adv.*： *a superbly illustrated book* 一部配有精美插圖的書 ◇ *She plays superbly.* 她演奏得好極了。

the 'Super Bowl™ *noun* an AMERICAN FOOTBALL game played every year to decide the winner of the National Football League （美國）超級杯美式足球賽

super·bug /'suːpəbʌg; 'sjuː-; *NAmE* 'suːpərb-/ *noun* a type of bacteria that cannot easily be killed by ANTIBIOTICS 超級細菌（抗生素不能輕易殺死） ➲ see also MRSA

super·cen·ter (*US*) (*BrE* **super·centre**) /'suːpəsentə(r); 'sjuː-; *NAmE* 'suːpər-/ *noun* (*especially US*) a very large shop/store, especially a grocery store that also sells lots of other goods 超大購物中心（尤指食品雜貨超市）

super·charged /'suːpətʃɑːdʒd; 'sjuː-; *NAmE* 'suːpərtʃɑːrdʒd/ *adj.* **1** (of an engine 發動機) powerful because it is supplied with air or fuel at a pressure that is higher than normal （用增壓器）增壓的，提高功率的 **2** (*informal*) stronger, more powerful or more effective than usual 異常強烈的；格外強勁的；特別有效的： *supercharged words, like 'terrorism' or 'fascism'* 諸如 terrorism

或 fascism 等語義格外強烈的詞 ▸ **super·charg·er** *noun*：*VW's supercharger for its 16-valve engine* 大眾汽車 16 閥發動機專用增壓器

super·cili·ous /ˌsuːpəˈsɪliəs; ˌsjuː-; *NAmE* ˌsuːpərˈs-/ *adj.* (*disapproving*) behaving towards other people as if you think you are better than they are 傲慢的；高傲的 **SYN** **superior** ▸ **super·cili·ous·ly** *adv.* **super·cili·ous·ness** *noun* [U]

super·com·puter /ˈsuːpəkəmpjuːtə(r); ˈsjuː-; *NAmE* ˈsuːpərk-/ *noun* a powerful computer with a large amount of memory and a very fast CENTRAL PROCESSING UNIT 超級計算機

super·con·duct·iv·ity /ˌsuːpəˌkɒndʌkˈtɪvəti; ˌsjuː-; *NAmE* ˌsuːpərˌkɑːn-/ *noun* [U] (*physics* 物) the property (= characteristic) of some substances at very low temperatures to let electricity flow with no RESISTANCE 超導（電）性

super·con·duct·or /ˈsuːpəkəndʌktə(r); ˈsjuː-; *NAmE* ˈsuːpərk-/ *noun* (*physics* 物) a substance that has SUPERCONDUCTIVITY 超導體

super·con·tin·ent /ˈsuːpəkɒntɪnənt; ˈsjuː-; *NAmE* ˈsuːpərkɑːn-/ *noun* (*geology* 地) any of the very large areas of land, for example Gondwana or Laurasia, that existed millions of years ago 超大陸（存在於幾百萬年之前，如岡瓦納古陸或勞亞古陸）

super-duper /ˌsuːpə ˈduːpə(r); ˌsjuː-; *NAmE* ˌsuːpər/ *adj.* (*old-fashioned, informal*) excellent 極好的；特好的

super·ego /ˌsuːpərˈiːgəʊ; ˌsjuː-; *NAmE* ˌsuːpərˈiːgoʊ/ *noun* [usually sing.] (*pl.* **-os**) (*psychology* 心) the part of the mind that makes you aware of right and wrong and makes you feel guilty if you do wrong 超我 ➲ compare EGO (2), ID

super·fi·cial /ˌsuːpəˈfɪʃl; ˌsjuː-; *NAmE* ˌsuːpərˈf-/ *adj.* **1** (*often disapproving*) not studying or looking at sth thoroughly; seeing only what is obvious 粗略的；膚淺的；粗枝大葉的；淺薄的：*a superficial analysis* 粗略的分析 ◇ *The book shows only a superficial understanding of the historical context.* 這部書表現出對歷史背景膚淺的理解。 **2** appearing to be true, real or important until you look at it more carefully 表面的；外面的；外表的：*superficial differences/similarities* 表面的相異／相似之處 ◇ *When you first meet her, she gives a superficial impression of warmth and friendliness.* 初次見面時，她總給人以熱情親切的表面印象。 **3** (of a wound or damage 傷口或損壞) only affecting the surface and therefore not serious 表層的；表皮的：*a superficial injury* 皮外傷 ◇ *superficial burns* 表面燒傷 **4** (*disapproving*) not concerned with anything serious or important and lacking any depth of understanding or feeling 淺薄的；膚淺的 **SYN** **shallow**：*a superficial friendship* 淺薄的交情 ◇ *The guests engaged in superficial chatter.* 客人閒聊起來。◇ *She's so superficial!* 她太膚淺了！ **5** (*technical* 術語) of or on the surface of sth 表面的；淺表的：*superficial veins* 淺靜脈 ◇ *a superficial deposit of acidic soils* 沉積在表層的酸性土壤 ▸ **super·fici·al·ity** /ˌsuːpəˌfɪʃiˈæləti; ˌsjuː-; *NAmE* ˌsuːpərˌf-/ *noun* [U] **super·fi·cial·ly** /-ʃəli/ *adv.*

super·fine /ˈsuːpəfaɪn; ˈsjuː-; *NAmE* ˈsuːpərf-/ *adj.* (*technical* 術語) **1** extremely light or thin; made of extremely small pieces 極輕的；極細的：*superfine fibres* 微細的纖維 ◇ *superfine powder* 超細粉末 **2** of extremely good quality 質量極高的；特級的：*superfine cloth* 特級布料

su·per·flu·ous /suːˈpɜːfluəs; sjuː-; *NAmE* suːˈpɜːrf-/ *adj.* (*formal*) more than you need or want 過剩的；過多的；多餘的 **SYN** **unnecessary**：*She gave him a look that made words superfluous.* 她看了他一眼，這已表明一切，無須多言了。 ▸ **su·per·flu·ity** /ˌsuːpəˈfluːəti; ˌsjuː-; *NAmE* ˌsuːpərˈf-/ *noun* [U, sing.] (*formal*) **su·per·flu·ous·ly** *adv.*

super·food *noun* /ˈsuːpəfuːd; ˈsjuː-; *NAmE* ˈsuːpər-/ a type of food that some people think is very good for you and helps to prevent disease 超級食品（一些人認為有益健康且可防病的食品）：*the health benefits of so-called superfoods* 所謂的超級食品對健康的益處

super·glue /ˈsuːpəgluː; ˈsjuː-; *NAmE* ˈsuːpərg-/ *noun* [U] a very strong glue that sticks very quickly and is used in small quantities for repairing things 強力膠

super·grass /ˈsuːpəgrɑːs; ˈsjuː-; *NAmE* ˈsuːpərgræs/ *noun* (*BrE, informal*) a criminal who informs the police about the activities of a large number of other criminals, usually in order to get a less severe punishment（為求得寬大處理）向警方告密的罪犯 ➲ compare GRASS *n.* (5)

super·group /ˈsuːpəgruːp; ˈsjuː-; *NAmE* ˈsuːpərg-/ *noun* a very successful and very famous band that plays rock music, especially one whose members have already become famous in other bands（尤指成員已在其他樂隊出名的）超級搖滾樂隊

super·heated /ˌsuːpəˈhiːtɪd; ˌsjuː-; *NAmE* ˌsuːpərh-/ *adj.* (*physics* 物) **1** (of a liquid 液體) that has been heated under pressure above its boiling point without becoming a gas 過熱的（加壓加熱至超過沸點而未變成氣體） **2** (of a gas 氣體) that has been heated above its temperature of SATURATION (= below which it becomes a liquid) 過熱的（加熱至超過飽和點）

super·heavy·weight /ˌsuːpəˈheviweɪt; ˌsjuː-; *NAmE* ˌsuːpərˈh-/ *noun* a BOXER of the heaviest class, weighing 91 kilograms or more 超重量級拳擊手（體重為 91 公斤或以上）

super·hero /ˈsuːpəhɪərəʊ; ˈsjuː-; *NAmE* ˈsuːpərhɪroʊ; -hiːroʊ/ *noun* (*pl.* **-oes**) a character in a story, film/movie, etc. who has unusual strength or power and uses it to help people; a real person who has done sth unusually brave to help sb（小說、電影等中的）超級英雄；傑出的英雄人物 **OPP** **supervillain**

super·high·way /ˌsuːpəˈhaɪweɪ; ˌsjuː-; *NAmE* ˌsuːpərˈh-/ *noun* **1** (*NAmE, old-fashioned*) = INTERSTATE *n.* **2** = INFORMATION SUPERHIGHWAY

super·human /ˌsuːpəˈhjuːmən; ˌsjuː-; *NAmE* ˌsuːpərˈh-/ *adj.* having much greater power, knowledge, etc. than is normal 超出常人的；非凡的 **SYN** **heroic**：*superhuman strength* 非凡的力量 ◇ *It took an almost **superhuman effort** to contain his anger.* 他以超常的克制力強壓住怒火。 ➲ compare SUBHUMAN

super·im·pose /ˌsuːpərɪmˈpəʊz; ˌsjuː-; *NAmE* ˌsuːpərɪmˈpoʊz/ *verb* **1 ~ sth (on/onto sth)** to put one image on top of another so that the two can be seen combined 使（圖像甲）疊映在（圖像乙）上：*A diagram of the new road layout was superimposed on a map of the city.* 新公路的規劃示意圖被疊映在該城市的地圖上。 **2 ~ sth (on/onto sth)** to add some of the qualities of one system or pattern to another one in order to produce sth that combines the qualities of both 使重疊；使疊加；使附加於：*She has tried to superimpose her own attitudes onto this ancient story.* 她嘗試過把自己的看法加入這個古老的故事裏。 ▸ **super·im·pos·ition** /ˌsuːpərˌɪmpəˈzɪʃn; *BrE* also ˌsjuː-/ *noun* [U]

super·in·tend /ˌsuːpərɪnˈtend; *BrE* also ˌsjuː-/ *verb* **~ sth** (*formal*) to be in charge of sth and make sure that everything is working, being done, etc. as it should be 主管；監督；監管 **SYN** **supervise** ▸ **super·in·tend·ence** /-əns/ *noun* [U]

super·in·tend·ent /ˌsuːpərɪnˈtendənt; *BrE* also ˌsjuː-/ *noun* **1** a person who has a lot of authority and manages and controls an activity, a place, a group of workers, etc. 主管人；負責人；監管人；監督人：*a park superintendent* 公園負責人 ◇ *the superintendent of schools in Dallas* 達拉斯教育局長 **2** (*abbr.* **Supt**) (in Britain 英國) a police officer just above the rank of CHIEF INSPECTOR 中級警官，警司（官階僅高於巡長）：*Superintendent Livesey* 利夫西警官 **3** (*abbr.* **Supt.**) (in the US 美國) the head of a police department 警察局長，警長 **4** (*NAmE*) a person whose job is to be in charge of a building and make small repairs, etc. to it（大樓的）管理人

su·per·ior 🔑 /suːˈpɪəriə(r); sjuː-; *NAmE* suːˈpɪr-/ *adj.*, *noun*

■ ***adj.*** **1** 🔑 **~ (to sb/sth)** better in quality than sb/sth else; greater than sb/sth else（在品質上）更好的；佔優勢的；更勝一籌的：***vastly superior*** 強得多 ◇ *superior intelligence* 更強的智力 ◇ *This model is technically superior to its competitors.* 這一款式在技術上超過了與之競爭的產品。◇ *Liverpool were clearly the superior team.* 利物浦

S

隊明顯更勝一籌。◇ *The enemy won because of their superior numbers* (= there were more of them). 敵人由於在人數上佔優而取勝。 **OPP** **inferior** **2** ⊶ **~ (to sb)** higher in rank, importance or position（在級別、重要性或職位上）更高的：*my superior officer* 我的上級軍官 ◇ *superior status* 更高的地位 ◇ *a superior court of law* 上級法院 **OPP** **inferior** **3** (*disapproving*) showing by your behaviour that you think you are better than others 有優越感的；高傲的 **SYN** **arrogant**：*a superior manner* 神氣活現的態度 ◇ *He always looks so superior.* 他總是顯得那麼有優越感。 **4** (used especially in advertisements 尤用於廣告) of very good quality; better than other similar things 質量卓越的；出類拔萃的；超群的：*superior apartments* 高級公寓套房

■ ***noun*** **1** a person of higher rank, status or position 級別（或地位、職位）更高的人；上級；上司：*your social superiors* 社會地位比自己高的人 ◇ *He's my* ***immediate superior*** (= the person directly above me). 他是我的頂頭上司。◇ *I'm going to complain to your superiors.* 我要去找你的上級投訴。 **OPP** **inferior** **2** used in titles for the head of a religious community（用作宗教團體領導的頭銜）：*Mother Superior* 修女會院長

su·per·ior·ity /suːˌpɪəriˈɒrəti; sjuː-; *NAmE* suːˌpɪriˈɔːr-; -ˈɑːr-/ *noun* [U] **1 ~ (in sth) | ~ (to/over sth/sb)** the state or quality of being better, more skilful, more powerful, greater, etc. than others 優越（性）；優勢：*the superiority of this operating system* 這款操作系統的優越性 ◇ *to have* ***naval/air superiority*** (= more ships/planes than the enemy) 有海上／空中優勢 **2** behaviour that shows that you think you are better than other people 優越感；神氣活現的樣子；盛氣凌人的行為：*an air of superiority* 神氣活現的樣子 **OPP** **inferiority**

su,peri'ority complex *noun* a feeling that you are better or more important than other people, often as a way of hiding your feelings of failure 自大情結，優越感（常為掩飾失敗感）

su·per·la·tive /suˈpɜːlətɪv; sjuː-; *NAmE* suːˈpɜːrl-/ *adj.*, *noun*

■ ***adj.*** **1** excellent 極佳的；卓越的；最優秀的 **SYN** **first-rate**：*a superlative performance* 精彩絕倫的演出 **2** (*grammar* 語法) relating to adjectives or adverbs that express the highest degree of sth, for example *best*, *worst*, *slowest* and *most difficult*（形容詞或副詞）最高級的 ➲ compare COMPARATIVE *adj.* (3) ▶ **su·per·la·tive·ly** *adv.*

■ ***noun*** (*grammar* 語法) the form of an adjective or adverb that expresses the highest degree of sth（形容詞或副詞的）最高級：*It's hard to find enough superlatives to describe this book.* 用再多的盛讚之辭也難以描述這本書。 ➲ compare COMPARATIVE *n.*

S

super·man /ˈsuːpəmæn; ˈsjuː-; *NAmE* ˈsuːpərm-/ *noun* (*pl.* **-men** /-men/) a man who is unusually strong or intelligent or who can do sth extremely well 有非凡才能的人；超人 ➲ compare SUPERWOMAN

super·mar·ket ⊶ /ˈsuːpəmɑːkɪt; ˈsjuː-; *NAmE* ˈsuːpərmɑːrkət/ (*NAmE* also **'grocery store**) *noun* a large shop/store that sells food, drinks and goods used in the home. People choose what they want from the shelves and pay for it as they leave. 超級市場；超市

super·max /ˈsuːpəmæks; ˈsjuː-; *NAmE* ˈsuːpər-/ *noun* (*especially NAmE*) a maximum security prison, intended for very dangerous prisoners 頂級監獄（防備極為森嚴、為極危險的犯人設立的監獄）

super·model /ˈsuːpəmɒdl; ˈsjuː-; *NAmE* ˈsuːpərmɑːdl/ *noun* a very famous and highly paid fashion model 超級名模

super·nat·ural /ˌsuːpəˈnætʃrəl; ˌsjuː-; *NAmE* ˌsuːpərˈn-/ *adj.* **1** that cannot be explained by the laws of science and that seems to involve gods or magic 超自然的；神奇的；神靈魔怪的 **SYN** **paranormal**：*supernatural powers* 超自然力量 ◇ *supernatural strength* 神奇的力量 ➲ compare NATURAL *adj.* (1) **2** **the supernatural** *noun* [sing.] events, forces or powers that cannot be explained by the laws of science and that seem to involve gods or magic 超自然物；超自然力量；神怪奇異的事 **SYN** **the paranormal**：*a belief in the supernatural* 對超自然力量的相信 ▶ **super·nat·ur·al·ly** /-ˈnætʃrəli/ *adv.*

super·nova /ˌsuːpəˈnəʊvə; ˌsjuː-; *NAmE* ˌsuːpərˈnoʊvə/ *noun* (*pl.* **super·novae** /-viː/ or **super·novas**) (*astronomy* 天) a star that suddenly becomes much brighter because it is exploding 超新星 ➲ compare NOVA

super·numer·ary /ˌsuːpəˈnjuːmərəri; ˌsjuː-; *NAmE* ˌsuːpərˈnuːməreri/ *adj.* (*formal*) more than you normally need; extra 多餘的；過剩的；額外的

super·ordin·ate /ˌsuːpərˈɔːdɪnət; ˌsjuː-; *NAmE* -ˈɔːrd-/ (also **hyper·nym**) *noun* (*linguistics* 語言) a word with a general meaning that includes the meanings of other particular words, for example 'fruit' is the superordinate of 'apple', 'orange', etc. 上義詞，上位詞（如 fruit 是 apple、orange 等的上義詞） ➲ compare HYPONYM ▶ **super·ordin·ate** *adj.* ➲ compare SUBORDINATE *adj.*

super·pose /ˌsuːpəˈpəʊz; ˌsjuː-; *NAmE* ˌsuːpərˈpoʊz/ *verb* **~ sth** to put sth on or above sth else 把…放在上面；疊放：*They had superposed a picture of his head onto someone else's body.* 他們把他的頭像貼在別人的身體上。 ▶ **super·pos·ition** *noun* /-pəˈzɪʃn/

super·power /ˈsuːpəpaʊə(r); ˈsjuː-; *NAmE* ˈsuːpərp-/ *noun* one of the countries in the world that has very great military or economic power and a lot of influence, for example the US 超級大國

super·script /ˈsuːpəskrɪpt; ˈsjuː-; *NAmE* ˈsuːpərs-/ *adj.* (*technical* 術語) written or printed above the normal line of writing or printing 寫（或印）在正常字符上方的；標在上面（或上角）的 ▶ **super·script** *noun* [U]

super·sede /ˌsuːpəˈsiːd; ˌsjuː-; *NAmE* ˌsuːpərˈs-/ *verb* **~ sth/sb** [often passive] to take the place of sth/sb that is considered to be old-fashioned or no longer the best available 取代，替代（已非最佳選擇或已過時的事物）：*The theory has been superseded by more recent research.* 這一理論已為新近的研究所取代。

super·size /ˈsuːpəsaɪz; ˈsjuː-; *NAmE* ˈsuːpər-/ *adj.*, *verb*

■ ***adj.*** (also **super·sized**) bigger than normal 超大的：*supersize portions of fries* 超大份炸薯條 ◇ *supersized clothing* 超大碼衣服

■ ***verb*** [T, I] **~ (sb/sth)** to make sb/sth bigger; to become bigger（使）變大，更大；（使）膨脹：*We are being supersized into obesity* (= made very fat) *by the fast food industry.* 我們正被快餐業催肥。◇ *TV ads encourage kids to supersize.* 電視廣告促使孩子變得越來越胖。

super·sonic /ˌsuːpəˈsɒnɪk; ˌsjuː-; *NAmE* ˌsuːpərˈsɑːnɪk/ *adj.* faster than the speed of sound 超音速的；超聲速的：*a supersonic aircraft* 超音速飛機 ◇ *supersonic flight* 超聲速飛行 ➲ compare SUBSONIC

super·star /ˈsuːpəstɑː(r); ˈsjuː-; *NAmE* ˈsuːpərs-/ *noun* a very famous performer, for example an actor, a singer or a sports player 超級明星

super·state /ˈsuːpəsteɪt; ˈsjuː-; *NAmE* ˈsuːpərs-/ *noun* a very powerful state, especially one that is formed by several nations joining or working together 超級強國；（尤指由幾個國家組成或進行合作的）超國家，政治共同體：*the European superstate* 歐洲超國家

super·sti·tion /ˌsuːpəˈstɪʃn; ˌsjuː-; *NAmE* ˌsuːpərˈs-/ *noun* [U, C] (often *disapproving*) the belief that particular events happen in a way that cannot be explained by reason or science; the belief that particular events bring good or bad luck 迷信；迷信觀念（或思想）：*According to superstition, breaking a mirror brings bad luck.* 按照迷信的說法，摔碎鏡子會帶來噩運。

super·sti·tious /ˌsuːpəˈstɪʃəs; ˌsjuː-; *NAmE* ˌsuːpərˈs-/ *adj.* believing in superstitions 迷信的；有迷信觀念的：*superstitious beliefs* 迷信觀念 ◇ *I'm superstitious about the number 13.* 我相信 13 這個數字不吉利。 ▶ **super·sti·tious·ly** *adv.*

super·store /ˈsuːpəstɔː(r); ˈsjuː-; *NAmE* ˈsuːpərs-/ *noun* a very large supermarket or a large shop/store that sells a wide variety of one type of goods 大型超市；大型商場：*a computer superstore* 計算機商城

super·struc·ture /ˈsuːpəstrʌktʃə(r); ˈsjuː-; *NAmE* ˈsuːpərs-/ *noun* **1** a structure that is built on top of sth, for example the upper parts of a ship or the part of a building above the ground（船舶的）上層結構；（建築物的）上部結構 ➲ compare SUBSTRUCTURE **2** (*formal*) the systems and beliefs in a society that have developed from more simple ones（社會的）上層建築

super·tank·er /ˈsuːpətæŋkə(r); ˈsjuː-; *NAmE* ˈsuːpərt-/ *noun* a very large ship for carrying oil, etc. 超級油輪

ˌSuper ˈTuesday *noun* [sing.] (*informal*) a day on which several US states hold PRIMARY elections 超級星期二（美國幾個州的初選日）

super·vene /ˌsuːpəˈviːn; ˌsjuː-; *NAmE* ˌsuːpərˈv-/ *verb* [I] (*formal*) to happen, especially unexpectedly, and have a powerful effect on the existing situation（尤指意外）發生並帶來重大影響

super·vil·lain /ˈsuːpəvɪlən; ˈsjuː; *NAmE* ˈsuːpər-/ *noun* a very bad character in a story, especially one with magical powers（小說中的）超級惡棍，超級惡魔，超級反派 OPP **superhero**

super·vise /ˈsuːpəvaɪz; ˈsjuː-; *NAmE* ˈsuːpərv-/ *verb* [T, I] to be in charge of sb/sth and make sure that everything is done correctly, safely, etc. 監督；管理；指導；主管：**~ (sb/sth)** *to supervise building work* 監理建築工程 ◇ **~ sb doing sth** *She supervised the children playing near the pool.* 她照料着在水池附近玩的幾個孩子。▶ **super·vi·sion** /ˌsuːpəˈvɪʒn; ˌsjuː-; *NAmE* ˌsuːpərˈv-/ *noun* [U, C]：*Very young children should not be left to play without supervision.* 不能讓幼兒在沒人照看的情況下獨自玩耍。◇ *The drug should only be used **under medical supervision**.* 這種藥須遵醫囑方可使用。◇ *I have weekly supervisions* (= meetings with a TUTOR or SUPERVISOR). 我每週同導師見一次面。

ˌsuperˈvision order *noun* (*law* 律) in the UK, an order made by a court which says that the local government or a PROBATION OFFICER must be responsible for a child, help them and check that they behave well 監管令（英國法院要求地方政府或緩刑監視官對少年進行監督）

super·visor /ˈsuːpəvaɪzə(r); ˈsjuː-; *NAmE* ˈsuːpərv-/ *noun* a person who supervises sb/sth 監督人；指導者；主管人：*I have a meeting with my supervisor about my research topic.* 我要就研究課題同導師見一次面。▶ **super·vis·ory** /ˌsuːpəˈvaɪzəri; ˌsjuː-; *NAmE* ˌsuːpərˈv-/ *adj.*：*She has a supervisory role on the project.* 她負責這個項目的監督工作。

super·woman /ˈsuːpəwʊmən; ˈsjuː-; *NAmE* ˈsuːpərw-/ *noun* (*pl.* **-women** /-wɪmɪn/) a woman who is unusually strong or intelligent or who can do sth extremely well, especially a woman who has a successful career and also takes care of her home and family 有非凡才能的女子；超級女人（尤指事業和家庭都成功的）➲ compare SUPERMAN

su·pine /ˈsuːpaɪn; *BrE* also ˈsjuː-/ *adj.* (*formal*) **1** lying flat on your back 仰卧的；平躺着的：*a supine position* 仰卧姿勢 ➲ compare PRONE (3) **2** (*disapproving*) not willing to act or disagree with sb because you are lazy or morally weak 得過且過的；苟安的；軟弱的 ▶ **su·pine·ly** *adv.*

sup·per /ˈsʌpə(r)/ *noun* [U, C] the last meal of the day, either a main meal, usually smaller and less formal than dinner, or a SNACK eaten before you go to bed 晚飯；晚餐；夜宵：*I'll do my homework after supper.* 晚飯後我要做家庭作業。◇ *What's for supper?* 晚飯吃什麼？◇ *We'll have an early supper tonight.* 今天我們要早點吃晚飯。➲ note at MEAL ➲ compare TEA (5)

sup·plant /səˈplɑːnt; *NAmE* -ˈplænt/ *verb* **~ sb/sth** (*formal*) to take the place of sb/sth (especially sb/sth older or less modern) 取代，替代（尤指年老者或落後於時代的事物）SYN **replace**

sup·ple /ˈsʌpl/ *adj.* **1** able to bend and move parts of your body easily into different positions（身體）柔軟的，靈活的；柔韌性好的：*her slim, supple body* 她苗條靈活的身體 ◇ *These exercises will help to keep you supple.* 這些鍛煉項目有助於你保持身體的柔韌性。**2** soft and able to bend easily without cracking 易彎曲的；柔韌的：*Moisturizing cream helps to keep your skin soft and supple.* 保濕霜有助於保持皮膚柔軟有彈性。▶ **supple·ness** *noun* [U]

sup·ple·ment AW *noun, verb*

■ *noun* /ˈsʌplɪmənt/ **1** a thing that is added to sth else to improve or complete it 增補（物）；補充（物）；添加物：***vitamin/dietary supplements*** (= VITAMINS and other foods eaten in addition to what you usually eat) 補充的維生素；補充飲食 ◇ **~ to sth** *Industrial sponsorship is a supplement to government funding.* 工業界的贊助是對政府撥款的補充。**2** an extra separate section, often in the form of a magazine, that is sold with a newspaper（報紙的）增刊：*the Sunday **colour supplements*** 星期日彩色增刊 **3 ~ (to sth)** a book or a section at the end of a book that gives extra information or deals with a special subject（書籍的）補編，補遺，附錄：*the supplement to the Oxford English Dictionary*《牛津英語詞典》補編 **4** (*BrE*) an amount of money that you pay for an extra service or item, especially in addition to the basic cost of a holiday/vacation 額外費用，附加費（尤指度假服務的）SYN **surcharge**：*There is a £10 supplement for a single room.* 住單間另付 10 英鎊。◇ *Safety deposit boxes are available **at a supplement**.* 有貴重物品保管箱可供使用，費用另計。

■ *verb* /ˈsʌplɪment/ to add sth to sth in order to improve it or make it more complete 增補；補充：**~ sth with sth** *a diet supplemented with vitamin pills* 搭配有維生素片的飲食 ◇ **~ sth** *He supplements his income by giving private lessons.* 他當家庭教師以補充收入。▶ **sup·ple·men·ta·tion** /ˌsʌplɪmenˈteɪʃn/ *noun* [U]

sup·ple·men·tary AW /ˌsʌplɪˈmentri/ (*especially BrE*) (*NAmE* usually **sup·ple·men·tal** /ˌsʌplɪˈmentl/) *adj.* provided in addition to sth else in order to improve or complete it 增補性的；補充性的；額外的；外加的 SYN **additional**：*supplementary information* 補充信息

suppleˌmentary ˈangle *noun* (*mathematics* 數) either of two angles which together make 180° 補角 ➲ compare COMPLEMENTARY ANGLE

sup·ple·tion /səˈpliːʃn/ *noun* [U] (*linguistics* 語言) the use of a word as a particular form of a verb when the word is not related to the main form of the verb, for example 'went' as the past tense of 'go' 不規則詞形屈折，異幹互補（如 went 作為 go 的過去時）▶ **sup·ple·tive** /səˈpliːtɪv/ *adj.*

sup·pli·cant /ˈsʌplɪkənt/ (also **sup·pli·ant** /ˈsʌpliənt/) *noun* (*formal*) a person who asks for sth in a HUMBLE way, especially from God or a powerful person（尤指向神靈或有權勢者）懇求者，哀求者，祈求者

sup·pli·ca·tion /ˌsʌplɪˈkeɪʃn/ *noun* [U, C] (*formal*) the act of asking for sth with a very HUMBLE request or prayer 懇求；哀求；祈求：*She knelt in supplication.* 她跪地禱求。

sup·plier /səˈplaɪə(r)/ *noun* a person or company that supplies goods 供應者；供貨商；供貨方：*a leading supplier of computers in the UK* 英國一家主要電腦供應商

sup·ply 🔑 /səˈplaɪ/ *noun, verb*

■ *noun* **1** 🔑 [C] an amount of sth that is provided or available to be used 供應量；供給量；儲備：*The water supply is unsafe.* 供水不穩定。◇ *Supplies of food are almost exhausted.* 貯存的食物快吃完了。◇ *We cannot guarantee adequate supplies of raw materials.* 我們不能保證提供充足的原料。◇ *Books were **in short supply*** (= there were not enough of them). 書籍供應短缺。**2** 🔑 **supplies** [pl.] the things such as food, medicines, fuel, etc. that are needed by a group of people, for example an army or EXPEDITION（軍隊或探險隊等的）補給，補給品：*Our supplies were running out.* 我們的補給快用完了。◇ *a transport plane carrying food and **medical supplies** for refugees* 一架為難民運送食物和醫療用品的運輸機 **3** 🔑 [U] the act of supplying sth 供應；供給；提供；補給：*The UN has agreed to allow the supply of emergency aid.* 聯合國已同意允許提供緊急援助。◇ *A stroke can disrupt the supply of oxygen to the brain.* 中風可導致大腦供氧中斷。◇ *The electricity supply* (= the system supplying electricity) *had been cut off.* 電力供應被切斷了。

■ *verb* 🔑 (**sup·plies**, **sup·ply·ing**, **sup·plied**, **sup·plied**) to provide sb/sth with sth that they need or want,

S

especially in large quantities（尤指大量）供應，供給，提供：**~ sth to sb/sth** *Foreign governments supplied arms to the rebels.* 一些外國政府向反叛者提供武器。◇ **~ sb/sth with sth** *Foreign governments supplied the rebels with arms.* 一些外國政府向反叛者提供武器。◇ **~ sb/sth** *Local schools supply many of the volunteers.* 許多志願者來自當地學校。◇ *foods supplying our daily vitamin needs* 為我們提供日常所需維生素的食物

sup,ply and de'mand *noun* [U] (*economics* 經) the relationship between the amount of goods or services that are available and the amount that people want to buy, especially when this controls prices 供求關係

sup'ply chain *noun* [usually sing.] (*business* 商) the series of processes involved in the production and supply of goods, from when they are first made, grown, etc. until they are bought or used 供應鏈

sup'ply line *noun* a route along which food, equipment, etc. is transported to an army during a war（戰爭中軍隊的）補給線

sup'ply-side *adj.* [only before noun] (*economics* 經) connected with the policy of reducing taxes in order to encourage economic growth 供應學派的（主張減稅以刺激經濟）

sup'ply teacher (*BrE*) (*NAmE* **'substitute teacher**) *noun* a teacher employed to do the work of another teacher who is away because of illness, etc. 代課教師

sup·port 🔑 /sə'pɔːt; *NAmE* sə'pɔːrt/ *verb, noun*

■ *verb*

▸ **ENCOURAGE/GIVE HELP** 鼓勵；支持 **1** 🔑 to help or encourage sb/sth by saying or showing that you agree with them/it 支持；擁護；鼓勵 SYN **back**：**~ sb/sth** *to support a proposal* 支持一項提議 ◇ *These measures are **strongly supported** by environmental groups.* 這些措施得到環境保護組織的大力支持。◇ *If you raise it at the meeting, I'll support you.* 如果你在會上提出這個問題，我將支持你。◇ **~ sb/sth in sth** *The government supported the unions in their demand for a minimum wage.* 政府支持這些工會組織提出的確定最低工資的要求。 **2** 🔑 **~ sb** to give or be ready to give help to sb if they need it 幫助；援助：*an organization that supports people with AIDS* 一個向艾滋病患者提供援助的組織 ◇ *The company will support customers in Europe* (= solve their problems with a product). 這家公司將向歐洲客戶提供技術支持。

▸ **PROVIDE MONEY, ETC.** 提供資金等 **3** 🔑 **~ sth** to help or encourage sth to be successful by giving it money 資助；贊助 SYN **sponsor**：*Several major companies are supporting the project.* 幾家大公司正在對這一項目提供資助。 **4** 🔑 **~ sb/sth/yourself** to provide everything necessary, especially money, so that sb/sth can live or exist 養活；贍養；扶養；維持：*Mark has two children to support from his first marriage.* 馬克得扶養他第一次婚姻生的兩個孩子。◇ *He turned to crime to support his drug habit.* 他為維持吸毒的惡習而走上犯罪的道路。◇ *The atmosphere of Mars could not support life.* 生命無法在火星的大氣環境下生存。

▸ **HOLD IN POSITION** 支撐 **5** 🔑 **~ sb/sth** to hold sb/sth in position; to prevent sb/sth from falling 支撐；支承；支護：*a platform supported by concrete pillars* 混凝土支柱支撐的平台 ◇ *Support the baby's head when you hold it.* 你抱嬰兒時要把頭扶好。

▸ **HELP PROVE STH** 證實 **6** 🔑 **~ sth** to help to show that sth is true 證實；提供依據 SYN **corroborate**：*The witness's story was not supported by the evidence.* 目擊者的描述與證據不符。 ➲ LANGUAGE BANK at EVIDENCE

▸ **SPORTS TEAM** 運動隊 **7** 🔑 **~ sth** (*BrE*) to like a particular sports team, watch their games, etc. 支持；喜愛：*Which team do you support?* 你喜歡哪個隊？

▸ **POP/ROCK CONCERT** 流行／搖滾音樂會 **8 ~ sb/sth** (of a band or singer 樂隊或歌手) to perform in a pop or rock concert before the main performer（在流行或搖滾音樂會上）當助演，熱場：*They were supported by a local Liverpool band.* 利物浦當地的一支樂隊為他們作助興演出。

▸ **COMPUTER** 計算機 **9 ~ sth** (of a computer or computer system 計算機或計算機系統) to allow a particular program, language or device to be used with it 支持；支援：*This digital audio player supports multiple formats.* 這台數字音頻播放器支持多種格式。

■ *noun*

▸ **ENCOURAGEMENT/MONEY** 鼓勵；資金 **1** 🔑 [U] **~ (for sth)** encouragement and help that you give to sb/sth because you approve of them and want them to be successful 支持；擁護；鼓勵；資助：*There is strong public support for the change.* 公眾大力支持這一變革。◇ *Can I rely on your support* (= will you vote for me) *in the election?* 我能指望你投我的票嗎？◇ *Only a few people spoke **in support of** the proposal.* 只有幾個人表示支持這一提議。◇ *Local businesses have provided **financial support**.* 當地企業提供了財政資助。◇ *She has no visible means of support* (= no work, income etc.). 她沒有明確的生計來源。

▸ **HELP** 幫助 **2** 🔑 [U] sympathy and help that you give to sb who is in a difficult or unhappy situation 幫助；救助；援助：*Her family and friends have given her lots of support.* 家人和朋友給了她許多幫助。 ➲ see also MORAL SUPPORT

▸ **HOLDING IN POSITION** 支撐 **3** 🔑 [C] a thing that holds sth and prevents it from falling 支撐物；支承；支柱；支座：*The supports under the bridge were starting to bend.* 橋下的支柱開始彎曲。◇ (*figurative*) *When my father died, Jim was a real support.* 我父親死後，吉姆成了真正的頂梁柱。 **4** 🔑 [U] the act of holding sth firmly in position or preventing it from falling 支撐；支承；支護：*I wrapped a bandage around my ankle to give it some support.* 我在腳踝上纏上繃帶，好把它固定住。◇ *She held on to his arm for support.* 她抓着他的胳膊，好站穩。 **5** 🔑 [C] something you wear to hold an injured or weak part of your body firmly in position（身體部位的）支持器，托：*a **knee/back support*** 護膝；護背

▸ **PROOF** 證據 **6** 🔑 [U] evidence that helps to show that sth is true or correct 證據；依據：*The statistics offer further support for our theory.* 這些統計數字為我們的理論提供了進一步的依據。

▸ **POP/ROCK CONCERT** 流行／搖滾音樂會 **7** [U] a band or singer who performs in a pop or rock concert before the main performer 助演嘉賓：*The support (act) has yet to be confirmed.* 助演尚未確定。

▸ **TECHNICAL HELP** 技術幫助 **8** [U] technical help that a company gives to customers using their computers or other products（公司向客戶提供的）技術支援：*We offer free **technical support**.* 我們免費提供技術支援。

sup·port·er 🔑 /sə'pɔːtə(r); *NAmE* -'pɔːrt-/ *noun* **1** 🔑 a person who supports a political party, an idea, etc. 支持者；擁護者：*a **strong/loyal/staunch supporter*** 積極的／忠實的／堅定的支持者 ◇ *Labour supporters* 工黨的支持者 **2** 🔑 (*BrE*) a person who supports a particular sports team（運動隊的）支持者 SYN **fan**：*I'm an Arsenal supporter.* 我是阿森納隊的球迷。 ➲ see also ATHLETIC SUPPORTER

sup'port group *noun* a group of people who meet to help each other with a particular problem 互助小組：*a support group for single parents* 單身父母互助小組

sup·port·ing /sə'pɔːtɪŋ; *NAmE* -'pɔːrt-/ *adj.* [only before noun] **1** a **supporting** actor in a play or film/movie has an important part but not the leading one（演員、角色）次要的；配角的：*The movie featured Robert Lindsay in a **supporting role**.* 羅伯特·林賽在這部影片中擔任配角。 **2** (*formal*) helping to show that sth is true 能確證的：*There was a wealth of supporting evidence.* 有大量證據。 **3** carrying the weight of sth 支承的；支撐的；承重的：*a supporting wall* 承重牆

sup·port·ive /sə'pɔːtɪv; *NAmE* -'pɔːrt-/ *adj.* giving help, encouragement or sympathy to sb 給予幫助的；支持的；鼓勵的；同情的：*a supportive family* 理解支持自己的家人 ◇ *She was very supportive during my father's illness.* 在我父親生病期間，她給了很多幫助。

sup·pose 🔑 /sə'pəʊz; *NAmE* sə'poʊz/ *verb* **1** 🔑 [I, T] to think or believe that sth is true or possible (based on the knowledge that you have)（根據所知）認為，推斷，料想：*Getting a visa isn't as simple as you might suppose.* 辦簽證不像你想的那麼容易。◇ *Prices will go up, **I suppose**.* 我覺得物價將會上漲。◇ **~ sb/sth to be/have sth** (*formal*) *This combination of qualities is*

S

generally supposed to be extremely rare. 一般認為，同時具有這樣一些品質極為罕見。◇ **~ sb/sth (to be/have) sth** | **~ sb/sth + adj.** (*formal*) *She had supposed him (to be) very rich.* 她原以為他很有錢。◇ **~ sb/sth + noun** (*formal*) *I had supposed his wife a younger woman.* 我原以為他妻子要更年輕。◇ **~ (that)** ... *I don't suppose for a minute that he'll agree* (= I'm sure that he won't). 我認為他決不會同意。◇ ***Why do you suppose** he resigned?* 你憑什麼推斷他辭職了呢？◇ ***There is no reason to suppose** she's lying.* 認為她在說謊完全沒道理。◇ *I suppose you think it's funny, do you?* (= showing anger). 你好像覺得這很好笑，是不是？ **HELP** 'That' is nearly always left out, especially in speech. * that 一般都省去，在口語中尤其如此。 **2** 🔑 [T] to pretend that sth is true; to imagine what would happen if sth were true 假定；假設；設想： **~ (that)** ... *Suppose flights are fully booked on that day—which other day could we go?* 假定那天的航班都訂滿了，我們還可以在哪天走呢？◇ *Let us suppose, for example, that you are married with two children.* 比方說，我們假設你成家了，還有兩個孩子。◇ **~ sth** (*formal*) *The theory supposes the existence of life on other planets.* 這個理論假定其他行星存在生命。◇ **~ sb/sth (to be/have) sth** | **~ sb/sth + adj./noun** (*formal*) *Suppose him (to be) dead—what then?* 假設他死了，那怎麼辦？ **3** 🔑 [I, T] used to make a statement, request or suggestion less direct or less strong（婉轉表達）我看，要我說，要不： *I could take you in the car, **I suppose*** (= but I don't really want to). 要不你坐我的車。◇ *'Can I borrow the car?' 'I **suppose so**'* (= Yes, but I'm not happy about it).' "我能借這輛車嗎？" "應該可以吧。" ◇ **~ (that)** ... ***I don't suppose** (that) I could have a look at your newspaper, could I?* 我能不能看看您的報紙？◇ *Suppose we take a later train?* 要不我們坐晚一點的火車？

IDM **be supposed to do/be sth** **1** 🔑 to be expected or required to do/be sth according to a rule, a custom, an arrangement, etc.（按規定、習慣、安排等）應當，應，該，須： *You're supposed to buy a ticket, but not many people do.* 按說應當買票，不過買的人不多。◇ *I thought we were supposed to be paid today.* 我以為我們今天會領到薪水呢。◇ *The engine doesn't sound like it's supposed to.* 發動機聽起來不對勁。◇ *You were supposed to be here an hour ago!* 你本該在一小時以前就到這兒！◇ *How was I supposed to know you were waiting for me?* 我哪知道你在等我？◇ *'Yes and no.' '**What is that supposed to mean?**'* (= showing that you are annoyed) "是但又不是。" "這算什麼意思呢？" **2** 🔑 to be generally believed or expected to be/do sth 一般認為，人們普遍覺得會： *I haven't seen it myself, but it's supposed to be a great movie.* 這部電影我沒看過，不過人們普遍認為很不錯。 **not be supposed to do sth** 🔑 to not be allowed to do sth 不准；不應當；不得： *You're not supposed to walk on the grass.* 不准踐踏草地。

sup·posed /səˈpəʊzd; *NAmE* səˈpoʊzd/ *adj.* [only before noun] used to show that you think that a claim, statement or way of describing sb/sth is not true or correct, although it is generally believed to be 誤以為的；誤信的；所謂的 **SYN** **alleged**： *This is the opinion of the supposed experts.* 這是所謂專家的看法。◇ *When did this supposed accident happen?* 這場所謂的事故發生在什麼時候？

sup·posed·ly /səˈpəʊzɪdli; *NAmE* -ˈpoʊ-/ *adv.* according to what is generally thought or believed but not known for certain 據信；據傳；據說 **SYN** **allegedly**： *The novel is supposedly based on a true story.* 據說這部小說是以一個真實的故事為依據的。

sup·pos·ing /səˈpəʊzɪŋ; *NAmE* -ˈpoʊ-/ *conj.* **~ (that)** used to ask sb to pretend that sth is true or to imagine that sth will happen 假定；假設；設想： *Supposing (that) you are wrong, what will you do then?* 假設你錯了，那你會怎麼辦？◇ *But supposing he sees us?* 可他要是看見我們呢？

sup·pos·ition /ˌsʌpəˈzɪʃn/ *noun* (*formal*) **1** [C] **~ (that ...)** an idea that you think is true although you may not be able to prove it 推測的想法；推斷的結論 **SYN** **assumption**： *The police are working on the supposition that he was murdered.* 警方正根據他被謀殺的假定展開調查。 **2** [U] the act of believing or claiming that sth is true even though it cannot be proved 推測；推斷： *The report is based entirely on supposition.* 這篇報道完全建立在推測的基礎上。

sup·posi·tory /səˈpɒzətri; *NAmE* səˈpɑːzətɔːri/ *noun* (*pl.* **-ies**) a small piece of solid medicine that is placed in the RECTUM or VAGINA and left to dissolve gradually 栓劑

sup·press /səˈpres/ *verb* **1** **~ sth** (usually *disapproving*) (of a government, ruler, etc. 政府、統治者等) to put an end, often by force, to a group or an activity that is believed to threaten authority 鎮壓；（武力）平定；壓制 **SYN** **quash**： *The rebellion was brutally suppressed.* 叛亂遭到了殘酷的鎮壓。 **2** **~ sth** (usually *disapproving*) to prevent sth from being published or made known 禁止（發表）；查禁；封鎖： *The police were accused of suppressing vital evidence.* 警方被指隱瞞關鍵證據。 **3** **~ sth** to prevent yourself from having or expressing a feeling or an emotion 抑制；控制；忍住： *to suppress a smile* 忍住沒笑 ◇ *She was unable to suppress her anger.* 她按捺不住怒火。 **4** **~ sth** to prevent sth from growing, developing or continuing 壓制；阻止；抑制： *drugs that suppress the appetite* 抑制食慾的藥

sup·pres·sant /səˈpresnt/ *noun* a drug that is used to prevent one of the body's functions from working normally（對人體功能的）遏抑劑： *an appetite suppressant* 食慾遏抑劑

sup·pres·sion /səˈpreʃn/ *noun* [U] the act of SUPPRESSING sth 鎮壓；壓制；抑制： *the suppression of a rebellion* 對叛亂的鎮壓 ◇ *the suppression of emotion* 對感情的抑制

sup·pres·sor /səˈpresə(r)/ *noun* a thing or person that SUPPRESSES sb/sth 鎮壓者；壓制者；查禁者；抑制物： *the body's pain suppressors* 疼痛抑制基因

sup·pur·ate /ˈsʌpjureɪt/ *verb* [I] (*formal*) (of a cut, wound, etc. 傷口等) to produce a thick yellow liquid (called PUS) because of infection 化膿 ▶ **sup·pur·ation** /ˌsʌpjuˈreɪʃn/ *noun* [U]

supra·nation·al /ˌsuːprəˈnæʃnəl; *BrE* also ˌsjuː-/ *adj.* (*formal*) involving more than one country 超國家的（指涉及不止一個國家）

supra·seg·men·tal /ˌsuːprəsegˈmentl; *BrE* also ˌsjuː-/ *adj.* (*phonetics* 語音) relating to features of speech such as stress and INTONATION as opposed to individual speech sounds 超音段的（與單個語音相對的重音和音調等語音特徵）

su·prema·cist /suːˈpreməsɪst; *BrE* also sjuː-/ *noun* a person who believes that their own race is better than others and should be in power 種族優越論者： *a white supremacist* 白人至上主義者

su·prem·acy /suːˈpreməsi; *BrE* also sjuː-/ *noun* [U] a position in which you have more power, authority or status than anyone else 至高無上；最大權力；最高權威；最高地位： *the battle for supremacy in the region* 爭奪地區霸權的較量 ◇ *the dangerous notion of white supremacy* (= that white races are better than others and should control them) 危險的白人至上觀念 ◇ **~ over sb/sth** *The company has established total supremacy over its rivals.* 公司奠定了超越競爭對手的絕對優勢。

su·preme /suːˈpriːm; *BrE* also sjuː-/ *adj.* [usually before noun] **1** highest in rank or position（級別或地位）最高的，至高無上的： *the Supreme Commander of the armed forces* 武裝部隊的最高統帥 ◇ *the supreme champion* 絕對冠軍 ◇ *It is an event in which she **reigns supreme**.* 這個比賽項目她所向無敵。 **2** very great or the greatest in degree（程度）很大的，最大的： *to make the **supreme sacrifice*** (= die for what you believe in) 作出最大犧牲（為信仰犧牲生命）◇ *a supreme effort* 最大的努力 ◇ *She smiled with supreme confidence.* 她充滿自信地微微一笑。

the Suˌpreme ˈBeing *noun* [sing.] (*formal*) God 上帝；無上的天主

the Suˌpreme ˈCourt (also **ˌHigh ˈCourt**) *noun* [sing.] the highest court in a country or state 最高法院；州最高法院

Synonyms 同義詞辨析

sure

confident • convinced • certain • positive • clear

These words all describe sb who knows without doubt that sth is true or will happen. 以上各詞均指確信、肯定、有把握。

sure [not before noun] without any doubt that you are right, that sth is true, that you will get sth or that sth will happen 指確信、肯定、有把握、必定：*'Is that John over there?' 'I'm not sure.'* “那邊那個人是約翰嗎？”“我說不準。” ◇ *Are you sure about that?* 這事你肯定嗎？◇ *England must win this game to be sure of qualifying.* 英格蘭隊必須拿下這場比賽才能確保獲得資格。 NOTE **Sure** is often used in negative statements and questions, because there is some doubt or anxiety over the matter. If there is no doubt, people often say *quite sure*. * sure 常用於否定句和疑問句，表示有所懷疑或擔憂。毫無疑問時常用 quite sure： *I'm quite sure (that) I left my bag here* (= I have no doubt about it). 我肯定是把包丟在這兒了。

confident completely sure that sth will happen in the way that you want or expect 指肯定、確信、有把握： *I'm quite confident that you'll get the job.* 我肯定你能得到那份工作。◇ *The team feels confident of winning.* 這個隊覺得有把握取勝。 NOTE **Confident** is a stronger and more definite word than **sure** and is more often used in positive statements, when you feel no anxiety. * confident 較 sure 語氣強，而且更肯定，在無所擔憂的情況下較常用於肯定句中。

convinced [not before noun] completely sure that sth is true or right, especially because the evidence seems to prove it or sb else has persuaded you to believe it 指堅信、深信、確信，尤指有證據證明或經說服： *I'm convinced that she's innocent.* 我堅信她是清白無辜的。

certain [not usually before noun] sure that you are right or that sth is true 指確信、肯定、無疑： *Are you absolutely certain about this?* 你對這事絕對確信無疑嗎？

SURE OR CERTAIN? 用 sure 還是 certain？

Like **sure**, **certain** is often used in negative statements and questions. It is slightly more formal than **sure**; **sure** is more frequent, especially in spoken English. * certain 與 sure 一樣，常用於否定句和疑問句中，但比 sure 稍正式些。sure 較常用，尤其是在英語口語中。

positive [not before noun] (*rather informal*) completely sure that sth is true 指有絕對把握、確信、肯定： *She was positive that he'd been there.* 她確信他曾在場。◇ *'Are you sure?' 'Positive.'* “你敢肯定嗎？”“絕對肯定。”

clear (often used in negative statements and questions) having no doubt or confusion about sth（常用於否定句與疑問句中）指無疑的、清楚的、明白的： *My memory isn't really clear on that point.* 那一點我記不太清楚了。

PATTERNS

- sure/confident/convinced/certain/positive/clear **about** sth
- sure/confident/convinced/certain **of** sth
- sure/confident/convinced/certain/positive/clear **that** ...
- sure/certain/clear **who/what/how**, etc.
- to **feel** sure/confident/convinced/certain/positive
- **quite/absolutely/completely/fairly/pretty** sure/confident/convinced/certain/positive/clear
- **not altogether** sure/confident/convinced/certain/clear

S

su·preme·ly /suːˈpriːmli; *BrE* also sjuː-/ *adv.* extremely 極其；極為： *supremely confident* 信心十足 ◇ *They managed it all supremely well.* 這件事他們幹得極其出色。

su·premo /suːˈpriːməʊ; sjuː-; *NAmE* suːˈpriːmoʊ/ *noun* (*pl.* **-os**) (*BrE, informal*) a person who has the most power or authority in a particular business or activity（企業或活動的）最高領導人，總管，總指揮： *the Microsoft supremo, Bill Gates* 微軟總裁比爾•蓋茨

Supt (also **Supt.** especially in *NAmE*) *abbr.* (in the police force) SUPERINTENDENT（英國）警司；（美國）警長： *Chief Supt Pauline Clark* 波林•克拉克總警司

sura (also **surah**) /ˈsʊərə; *NAmE* ˈsʊrə/ *noun* a chapter or section of the Koran（《古蘭經》的）章

sur·charge /ˈsɜːtʃɑːdʒ; *NAmE* ˈsɜːrtʃɑːrdʒ/ *noun, verb*

■ *noun* **~ (on sth)** an extra amount of money that you must pay in addition to the usual price 額外費用；附加費；增收費 SYN **supplement**

■ *verb* **~ sb (sth)** to make sb pay a surcharge 向（某人）收取額外費用： *We were surcharged £50 for travelling on a Friday.* 因為在星期五旅行，我們多付了 50 英鎊。

sur·coat /ˈsɜːkəʊt; *NAmE* ˈsɜːrkoʊt/ *noun* a piece of clothing without sleeves, worn in the past over a suit of ARMOUR 蘇爾外套（舊時的無袖鎧甲罩衣）

sure 0→ /ʃʊə(r); ʃɔː(r); *NAmE* ʃʊr/ *adj., adv.*

■ *adj.* (**surer, sur·est**) HELP You can also use **more sure** and **most sure**, especially in sense 1. 亦可用 more sure 和 most sure，尤用於第 1 義。 **1** 0→ [not before noun] confident that you know sth or that you are right 確信；確知；肯定；有把握 SYN **certain**： *'Is that John over there?' '**I'm not sure**'.* “那邊那個人是約翰嗎？”“我說不準。” ◇ *You don't sound very sure.* 聽你這口氣，你自己也不大肯定。◇ **~ (that)** ... *I'm pretty sure (that) he'll agree.* 他會同意的，對此我有相當的把握。◇ *Are you sure you don't mind?* 你確實不在意？◇ **~ of sth** *I hope you are sure of your facts.* 我希望你能肯定你說的都是事實。◇ **~ about sth** *Are you sure about that?* 這事你肯定嗎？◇ **~ how, whether, etc.** ... *Ask me if you're **not sure how** to do it.* 你要是拿不準怎麼幹，就問我。◇ *I'm **not sure whether** I should tell you this.* 我拿不準該不該把這事告訴你。 OPP **unsure** **2** 0→ [not before noun] certain that you will receive sth or that sth will happen 一定，必定，無疑（將會得到或發生）： **~ of sth** *You're always sure of a warm welcome there.* 到了那裏你肯定會受到熱烈歡迎。◇ **~ of doing sth** *England must win this game to be sure of qualifying for the World Cup.* 英格蘭隊必須拿下這場比賽才能確保獲得世界杯的參賽資格。 **3** 0→ **~ to do sth** certain to do sth or to happen 一定，必定，無疑（會做或會發生）： *The exhibition is sure to be popular.* 這一展覽肯定受歡迎。◇ *It's sure to rain.* 一準會下雨。 ➲ SYNONYMS at CERTAIN **4** [usually before noun] that can be trusted or relied on 不容置疑的；確切的；可靠的；保險的： *It's a **sure sign** of economic recovery.* 這是經濟復蘇的確切跡象。◇ *There's only one sure way to do it.* 做這件事只有一個保險的辦法。◇ *He is a **sure bet** for the presidential nominations* (= certain to succeed). 他是總統候選人提名的鐵定人選。 ➲ SYNONYMS at CERTAIN **5** [usually before noun] steady and confident 沉着自信的；胸有成竹的： *We admired her sure touch at the keyboard.* 我們欣賞她沉着自信的彈奏風格。

IDM **be sure to do sth** used to tell sb to do sth 一定要，務必（去做某事）： *Be sure to give your family my regards.* 務必代我向你的家人問好。 HELP In spoken English **and** plus another verb can be used instead of **to** and the infinitive. 英語口語中，可用 and 加動詞代替帶 to 的不定式： *Be sure and call me tomorrow.* **for ˈsure** 0→ (*informal*) without doubt 無疑；肯定： *No one knows for sure what happened.* 沒有人確切地知道發生了什麼事。◇ *I think he'll be back on Monday, but I can't say for sure.* 我想他星期一會回來，不過我不敢肯定。◇ ***One thing is for sure**—it's not going to be easy.* 有一點可以肯定，事情不會很容易。◇ (*NAmE*) *'Will you be there?' 'For sure.'* “你去嗎？”“肯定去。” **make ˈsure (of sth/that ...)** **1** 0→ to do sth in order to be certain that sth else happens 確保；設法保證： *Make sure (that) no one finds out about this.* 絕對不要讓任何人發現這件事。◇ *They scored another goal and made sure of victory.* 他們又進了一個球，這就贏定了。◇ *Our staff will do their* best to make sure you enjoy your visit. 我們的人員會竭盡全力使您到訪愉快。**2** 🔑 to check that sth is true or has been done 查明，核實，弄清（某事屬實或已做）：*She looked around to make sure that she was alone.* 她往四下裏看看，是不是只有她一個人。◇ *I think the door's locked, but I'll just go and make sure.* 我覺得門已經鎖上了，不過我還是去看看好放心。**'sure of yourself** (sometimes *disapproving*) very confident 自信；自以為是：*She seems very sure of herself.* 她好像十分自信。**,sure 'thing** (*informal, especially NAmE*) used to say 'yes' to a suggestion or request（答應建議或要求）當然，一定：*'Are you coming?' 'Sure thing.'* "你來嗎？" "當然。" **to be 'sure** (*formal*) used to admit that sth is true（承認屬實）誠然，固然，無可否認：*He is intelligent, to be sure, but he's also very lazy.* 他固然聰明，但也很懶。

■ **adv.** (*informal, especially NAmE*) **1** 🔑 used to say 'yes' to sb（表示同意）當然：*'Will you open the wine?' 'Sure, where is it?'* "你把葡萄酒打開好嗎？" "沒問題，酒在哪兒？" ◇ *Did it hurt? Sure it hurt.* 疼不疼？當然疼了。**2** used to emphasize sth that you are saying（加強語氣）確實，的確：*Boy, it sure is hot.* 嗬，這天兒可真熱。◇ *'Amazing view'. 'Sure is.'* "景色真美。" "沒錯。" ◇ *That song* ***sure as hell*** *sounds familiar.* 這首歌確實耳熟。◇ *He sure looked unhappy.* 他的確顯得不高興。**3** used to reply to sb who has just thanked you for sth（回答他人的感謝）不用客氣，應該的：*'Thanks for the ride.' 'Sure—anytime.'* "謝謝你載我過來。" "不用客氣，隨時願意效勞。"

IDM **(as) sure as eggs is 'eggs** (*old-fashioned, BrE, informal*) used to say that sth is definitely true 千真萬確；的的確確 **,sure e'nough** used to say that sth happened as expected（表示不出所料）果真，果然：*I said he'd forget, and sure enough he did.* 我說他會忘記，他果然就忘了。

'sure-fire *adj.* [only before noun] (*informal*) certain to be successful or to happen as you expect 必定成功的；肯定會發生的：*a sure-fire success* 定能獲得的成功

,sure-'footed (also **foot·sure**) *adj.* **1** not likely to fall when walking or climbing on rough ground 腳步穩的；不會摔倒的 **2** confident and unlikely to make mistakes, especially in difficult situations 沉着的；穩健的

Which Word? 詞語辨析

surely / certainly

- You use **surely**, especially in *BrE*, to show that you are almost certain about what you are saying and you want other people to agree with you. * surely 表示對所說的話幾乎肯定無疑，並希望別人同意自己的看法，尤用於英式英語：*Surely this can't be right?* 這不可能是對的吧？**Surely** in negative sentences shows that something surprises you and you do not want to believe it. 在否定句中，surely 表示某事使人感到吃驚而不願相信：*You're surely not thinking of going, are you?* 你不是想走吧？
- **Certainly** usually means 'without doubt' or 'definitely', and is used to show that you strongly believe something or to emphasize that something is really true. * certainly 常指無疑地，確定地，用以表示堅信某事或強調某事屬實：*I'll certainly remember this trip!* 我絕不會忘記這次旅行！In informal *NAmE* this would be 非正式的美式英語說法為：*I'll sure remember this trip!* 我絕不會忘記這次旅行！
- Compare 比較：*The meal was certainly too expensive* (= there is no doubt about it). 這頓飯的確太貴了（毫無疑問）。and 和 *The meal was surely too expensive?* (= that is my opinion. Don't you agree?) 這頓飯不是太貴了嗎？（我這樣認為，你不同意嗎？）
- In formal language only, **surely** can be used to mean 'without doubt'. 只有在正式用語中，surely 才表示無疑：*This will surely end in disaster.* 這無疑將以災難告終。

➲ note at COURSE, SURE

sure·ly 🔑 /ˈʃʊəli; ˈʃɔːli; *NAmE* ˈʃʊrli/ *adv.* **1** 🔑 used to show that you are almost certain of what you are saying and want other people to agree with you（對自己的話很有把握，希望他人同意）想必：*Surely we should do something about it?* 我們總得想個辦法吧？◇ *It's surely only a matter of time before he is found, isn't it?* 找到他只是個時間問題，對不對？**2** 🔑 used with a negative to show that sth surprises you and you do not want to believe it（用於否定句，表示難以置信）：*Surely you don't think I was responsible for this?* 你一定不會以為出了這事是我的責任吧？◇ *'They're getting married.' '* ***Surely not!*** *'* "他們要結婚了。" "不會吧！" ◇ *They won't go, surely?* 他們不會真的要走吧？**3** (*formal*) without doubt; certainly 無疑；必定：*He knew that if help did not arrive soon they would surely die.* 他知道，如果救援沒能及早來到，他們必死無疑。**4** (*old-fashioned, NAmE, informal*) used to say 'yes' to sb or to agree to sth（表示肯定或同意）當然 **IDM** see SLOWLY

sure·ness /ˈʃʊənəs; ˈʃɔːn-; *NAmE* ˈʃʊrn-/ *noun* [U] the quality of being confident and steady; not hesitating or doubting 沉着自信；胸有成竹；有把握；確信不疑：*an artist's sureness of touch* 畫家胸有成竹的筆觸 ◇ *her sureness that she had done the right thing* 她確信自己做得對

surety /ˈʃʊərəti; ˈʃɔːr-; *NAmE* ˈʃʊr-/ *noun* [C, U] (*pl.* **-ies**) (*law* 律) **1** money given as a promise that you will pay a debt, appear in court, etc. 保證金：*She was granted bail with a surety of $500.* 她交了 500 元保證金，獲得保釋。**2** a person who accepts responsibility if sb else does not pay a debt, appear in court, etc. 保證人；擔保人：*to act as surety for sb* 為某人做擔保人

surf /sɜːf; *NAmE* sɜːrf/ *noun, verb*

■ ***noun*** [U] large waves in the sea or ocean, and the white FOAM that they produce as they fall on the beach, on rocks, etc. 激浪；拍岸浪花：*the sound of surf breaking on the beach* 激浪拍岸的聲音 ◇ *Sydney, surf capital of the world* (= where the sport of surfing is very popular) 世界衝浪之都悉尼

■ ***verb*** **1** (often **go surfing**) [I, T] **~ (sth)** to take part in the sport of riding on waves on a SURFBOARD 進行衝浪運動；衝浪 **2** [T] **~ the Net/Internet** to use the Internet（互聯網上）衝浪，漫遊，瀏覽：*I was surfing the Net looking for information on Indian music.* 我正上網查找關於印度音樂的資料。

sur·face 🔑 /ˈsɜːfɪs; *NAmE* ˈsɜːrfɪs/ *noun, verb*

■ ***noun*** **1** 🔑 [C] the outside or top layer of sth 表面；表層；面：*an uneven road surface* 凹凸不平的路面 ◇ *We'll need a flat surface to play the game on.* 我們得有個平面才能玩這個遊戲。◇ *Teeth have a hard surface layer called enamel.* 牙齒有一層叫做釉質的堅硬表層。◇ *a broad leaf with a large* ***surface area*** 表面積很大的闊葉 **2** 🔑 [C, usually sing.] the top layer of an area of water or land 水面；地面；液面：*the earth's surface* 地球表面 ◇ *These plants float on the surface of the water.* 這些植物漂浮在水面上。**3** 🔑 [C] the flat upper part of a piece of furniture, that is used for working on（傢具的）頂面，操作枱：*a work surface* 操作枱 ◇ *She's cleaned all the kitchen surfaces.* 她把廚房的所有枱面全都收拾乾淨了。**4** [sing.] the outer appearance of a person, thing or situation; the qualities that you see or notice, that are not hidden 表面；外表；外觀：*Rage bubbled just below the surface of his mind.* 怒火在他心中燃燒，隨時可能迸發。

IDM **on the 'surface** when not thought about deeply or thoroughly; when not looked at carefully 表面上；從外表看；乍一看：*It seems like a good idea on the surface but there are sure to be problems.* 這主意乍一看不錯，但肯定存在問題。◇ *On the surface, he appeared unchanged.* 看外表他好像沒變。➲ more at SCRATCH *v.*

■ ***verb*** **1** [I] to come up to the surface of water 升到水面；浮出水面 **SYN** **emerge**：*The ducks dived and surfaced again several metres away.* 鴨子潛入水中，然後在幾米開外鑽出水面。**2** [I] to suddenly appear or become obvious after having been hidden for a while（隱藏或被掩蓋一段時間後）露面，重新出現，顯露，披露

S

SYN emerge：*Doubts began to surface.* 質疑聲開始出現。◇ *She surfaced again years later in London.* 多年後她又出現在倫敦。 **3** [I] (*informal*) to wake up or get up after being asleep 醒來；起牀：*He finally surfaced around noon.* 他終於在中午時分醒來。 **4** [T] **~ sth** to put a surface on a road, path, etc. 鋪設（路面等）

'surface mail *noun* [U] letters, etc. carried by road, rail or sea, not by air 水陸路郵件；平寄郵件

'surface structure *noun* (*grammar* 語法) the structure of a well-formed sentence in a language, rather than its UNDERLYING form 表層結構 ➲ compare DEEP STRUCTURE

,surface 'tension *noun* [U] (*technical* 術語) the property (= characteristic) of liquids by which they form a layer at their surface, and which makes sure that this surface covers as small an area as possible 表面張力

,surface-to-'air *adj.* [only before noun] (especially of MISSILES 尤指導彈) fired from the ground or from ships and aimed at aircraft 地對空的；艦對空的

,surface-to-'surface *adj.* [only before noun] (especially of MISSILES 尤指導彈) fired from the ground or from ships and aimed at another point on the ground or a ship 地（或艦）對地（或艦）的

sur·fac·tant /sɜːˈfæktənt; *NAmE* sɜːrˈf-/ *noun* [C, U] **1** (*technical* 術語) a substance that reduces the SURFACE TENSION of a liquid, often forming bubbles in the liquid 表面活性劑（減少液體表面張力，常形成氣泡） **2** (*medical* 醫) a substance that keeps the lungs working well to prevent breathing problems 肺表面活性物質（維持肺部良好工作、防止呼吸困難）

surf·board /ˈsɜːfbɔːd; *NAmE* ˈsɜːrfbɔːrd/ (also **board**) *noun* a long narrow board used for SURFING 衝浪板

sur·feit /ˈsɜːfɪt; *NAmE* ˈsɜːrfɪt/ *noun* [usually sing.] **~ (of sth)** (*formal*) an amount that is too large 過量 **SYN excess**

surf·er /ˈsɜːfə(r); *NAmE* ˈsɜːrfər/ *noun* **1** a person who goes SURFING 進行衝浪運動的人 **2** (also **'Net surfer**) (*informal*) a person who spends a lot of time using the Internet（互聯網上）衝浪者，漫遊者；網迷 ➲ see also SILVER SURFER

surfie /ˈsɜːfi; *NAmE* ˈsɜːrfi/ *noun* (*AustralE, NZE, informal*) a person who is enthusiastic about SURFING, especially a young man 衝浪迷（尤指男青年）

surf·ing /ˈsɜːfɪŋ; *NAmE* ˈsɜːrf-/ *noun* [U] **1** the sport of riding on waves while standing on a narrow board called a SURFBOARD 衝浪運動：*to go surfing* 去衝浪 ➲ **VISUAL VOCAB** page V50 **2** the activity of looking at different things on the Internet in order to find sth interesting, or of changing between TV channels in order to find an interesting programme（互聯網上）衝浪，漫遊，瀏覽；來回轉換電視頻道（以尋找有趣節目）

S

'surf lifesaver *noun* (*AustralE, NZE*) = LIFEGUARD

,surf 'n' 'turf *noun* [U] (*NAmE*) SEAFOOD and STEAK served together as a meal 海鮮牛排餐

surge /sɜːdʒ; *NAmE* sɜːrdʒ/ *verb, noun*

■ *verb* **1** [I] **+ adv./prep.** to move quickly and with force in a particular direction 湧；洶湧；湧動：*The gates opened and the crowd surged forward.* 大門打開了，人群向前湧去。◇ *Flood waters surged into their homes.* 洪水湧進了他們的房子。 **2** [I] **(+ adv./prep.)** to fill sb with a strong feeling 使強烈地感到 **SYN sweep**：*Relief surged through her.* 她頓覺寬慰。 **3** [I] (of prices, profits, etc. 物價、利潤等) to suddenly increase in value 急劇上升；飛漲；激增：*Share prices surged.* 股價猛漲。➲ related noun UPSURGE **4** [I] (of the flow of electrical power 電流) to increase suddenly 急衝；電湧

■ *noun* **1 ~ (of sth)** a sudden increase of a strong feeling（強烈感情的）突發 **SYN rush**：*She felt a sudden surge of anger.* 她突然感覺怒火中燒。◇ *a surge of excitement* 一陣興奮 ➲ see also UPSURGE **2** a sudden increase in the amount or number of sth; a large amount of sth（數量的）急劇上升，激增；大量；一大批：**~ (in sth)** *a surge in consumer spending* 消費開支的激增 ◇ *We are having trouble keeping up with the recent surge in demand.* 對於近來出現的需求猛增，我們難以應對。◇ **~ (of sth)** *After an initial surge of interest, there has been little call for our services.* 過了開始的一陣新鮮勁後，對我們服務的需求就變得很小。➲ see also UPSURGE **3 ~ (of sth)** a sudden, strong forward or upward movement 奔湧向前；突然的向上運動：*a tidal surge* 漲潮 **4** a sudden increase in the flow of electrical power through a system 電流急衝；電湧：*An electrical surge damaged the computer's disk drive.* 電流急衝損壞了計算機的磁盤驅動器。

sur·geon /ˈsɜːdʒən; *NAmE* ˈsɜːrdʒən/ *noun* a doctor who is trained to perform surgery (= medical operations that involve cutting open a person's body) 外科醫生：*a **brain/heart, etc. surgeon*** 腦外科、心臟外科等醫生 ➲ compare PHYSICIAN

,Surgeon 'General *noun* (*pl.* **Surgeons General**) (in the US) the head of a public health service or of a medical service in the armed forces（美國）衞生局局長，軍醫處長：*Surgeon General's warning: cigarette smoking causes cancer* 衞生局局長警告大家：吸煙致癌

sur·gery /ˈsɜːdʒəri; *NAmE* ˈsɜːrdʒ-/ *noun* (*pl.* **-ies**) **1** [U] medical treatment of injuries or diseases that involves cutting open a person's body and often removing or replacing some parts; the branch of medicine connected with this treatment 外科手術；外科學：***major/minor surgery*** 大手術；小手術 ◇ *to **undergo** heart **surgery*** 接受心臟手術 ◇ *He will require surgery on his left knee.* 他的左膝需要做手術。**HELP** In American English the countable form can be used. 美式英語可用可數形式：*She had three surgeries over ten days.* ➲ **COLLOCATIONS** at ILL ➲ see also OPEN-HEART SURGERY, PLASTIC SURGERY **2** [U, C] (*BrE*) the time during which a doctor, dentist or VET is available to see patients 應診時間：***morning/afternoon/evening surgery*** 上午／下午／晚間應診時間 ◇ *surgery hours* 應診時間 ◇ *Is there a surgery this evening?* 今晚有沒有醫生應診？ **3** [C] (*BrE*) (*NAmE* **office**) a place where a doctor, dentist or VET sees patients 診室；門診處：*a **doctor's/dentist's surgery*** 醫生的／牙醫的診室 **4** [C] (*BrE*) a time when people can meet their Member of Parliament to ask questions and get help（議員的）接待時間：*a constituency surgery* 接待選區選民時間

sur·gi·cal /ˈsɜːdʒɪkl; *NAmE* ˈsɜːrdʒ-/ *adj.* [only before noun] used in or connected with surgery 外科的；外科手術的：*surgical procedures* 手術程序 ◇ *a surgical ward* (= for patients having operations) 外科手術病房 ► **sur·gi·cal·ly** /-kli/ *adv.*：*The lumps will need to be surgically removed.* 這些腫塊需手術切除。

,surgical 'spirit (*BrE*) (*NAmE* **'rubbing alcohol**) *noun* [U] a clear liquid, consisting mainly of alcohol, used for cleaning wounds, etc. 醫用酒精；消毒用酒精

surly /ˈsɜːli; *NAmE* ˈsɜːrli/ *adj.* (**sur·lier**, **sur·li·est**) bad-tempered and rude 脾氣壞的；乖戾的；態度粗暴的：*a surly youth* 脾氣暴躁的年輕人 ► **sur·li·ness** *noun* [U]

sur·mise *verb, noun*

■ *verb* /səˈmaɪz; *NAmE* sərˈm-/ [T, I] **~ (sth)** | **~ (that) …** | **~ what, where, etc. …** | **+ speech** (*formal*) to guess or suppose sth using the evidence you have, without definitely knowing 推測；猜測 **SYN conjecture**：*From the looks on their faces, I surmised that they had had an argument.* 看他們的臉色，我猜想他們之間發生了爭執。

■ *noun* /ˈsɜːmaɪz; *NAmE* ˈsɜːrm-/ [U, C, usually sing.] (*formal*) a guess based on some facts that you know already 推測；猜測：*This is pure surmise on my part.* 這純粹是我的猜測。

sur·mount /səˈmaʊnt; *NAmE* sərˈm-/ *verb* (*formal*) **1 ~ sth** to deal successfully with a difficulty 克服；解決 **SYN overcome**：*She was well aware of the difficulties that had to be surmounted.* 她很清楚必須克服哪些困難。 **2** [usually passive] **~ sth** to be placed on top of sth 處於（某物）上面；置於（某物）頂端：*a high column surmounted by a statue* 頂端立着一尊雕像的高大柱子

sur·name 🔑 /ˈsɜːneɪm; *NAmE* ˈsɜːrn-/ *noun* (*especially BrE*) a name shared by all the members of a family (written last in English names) 姓 ➲ compare FAMILY NAME, LAST NAME

sur·pass /səˈpɑːs; *NAmE* sərˈpæs/ *verb* [T, I] ~ (**sb/sth/yourself**) (*formal*) to do or be better than sb/sth 超過；勝過；優於：*He hopes one day to surpass the world record.* 他希望有一天能刷新世界紀錄。◇ *Its success has* ***surpassed all expectations.*** 它所取得的成功遠遠超出了預期。◇ *Her cooking was always good, but this time she had* ***surpassed herself*** (= done better than her own high standards). 她的廚藝向來不錯，但這一次她更是勝過以往。◇ *scenery of surpassing beauty* 無比優美的景色

sur·plice /ˈsɜːpləs; *NAmE* ˈsɜːrp-/ *noun* a loose white piece of clothing with wide sleeves worn by priests and singers in the CHOIR during church services（教士和唱詩班穿的）白色罩衣

sur·plus /ˈsɜːpləs; *NAmE* ˈsɜːrp-/ *noun, adj.*

■ ***noun*** [C, U] **1** an amount that is extra or more than you need 過剩；剩餘；過剩量；剩餘額：*food surpluses* 過剩的食物 ◇ *Wheat was* ***in surplus*** *that year.* 那一年小麥過剩。 **2** the amount by which the amount of money received is greater than the amount of money spent 盈餘；順差：*a trade surplus of £400 million* * 4 億英鎊的貿易盈餘 ◇ *The balance of payments was* ***in surplus*** *last year* (= the value of exports was greater than the value of imports). 去年國際收支有盈餘。➲ **COLLOCATIONS** at INTERNATIONAL ➲ compare DEFICIT (1)

■ ***adj.*** more than is needed or used 過剩的；剩餘的；多餘的：*surplus cash* 剩餘的現金 ◇ *Surplus grain is being sold for export.* 過剩的穀物正銷往國外。◇ ~ **to sth** *These items are* ***surplus to requirements*** (= not needed). 這幾項不需要。

sur·prise 🔑 /səˈpraɪz; *NAmE* sərˈp-/ *noun, verb*

■ ***noun*** **1** 🔑 [C] an event, a piece of news, etc. that is unexpected or that happens suddenly 意想不到（或突然）的事；令人驚奇的事（或消息等）：*What a nice surprise!* 真是讓人驚喜！◇ *a surprise attack* 突然襲擊 ◇ *There are few surprises in this year's budget.* 今年的預算案沒有多少出人意料的地方。◇ *I have a surprise for you!* 我要告訴你一件你意想不到的事！◇ *It* ***comes as no surprise*** *to learn that they broke their promises.* 得知他們食言並不讓人覺得意外。◇ *Her letter* ***came as a*** *complete* ***surprise.*** 萬萬沒想到會收到她的信。◇ *There are lots of* ***surprises in store for*** *visitors to the gallery.* 參觀畫展的人將會發現許多令他們驚奇的東西。◇ *Visitors to the gallery are* ***in for a few surprises.*** 參觀畫展的人將會見到一些令他們驚奇的東西。 **2** 🔑 [U, C] a feeling caused by sth happening suddenly or unexpectedly 驚奇；驚訝；意外：*a look of surprise* 驚訝的表情 ◇ *She looked up* ***in surprise.*** 她驚訝地抬起頭。◇ ~ (**at sth**) *He gasped* ***with surprise*** *at her strength.* 發現她有這麼大的力氣，他大吃一驚。◇ ~ (**at seeing, hearing, etc.**) *They couldn't conceal their surprise at seeing us together.* 看見我們在一起，他們表現出掩飾不住的詫異。◇ ***I got a surprise*** *when I saw the bill.* 一看賬單我吃了一驚。◇ ***Much to my surprise,*** *I passed.* 壓根兒沒想到，我及格了。◇ ***To everyone's surprise,*** *the plan succeeded.* 出乎所有人的意料，那個計劃竟然取得了成功。◇ *Imagine our surprise when he walked into the room!* 你想像一下，他走進房間時，我們多麼驚奇！ **3** [U] the use of methods that cause feelings of surprise 出人意表的做事方式；出奇制勝的策略：*A successful campaign should have* ***an element of surprise.*** 成功的宣傳活動需有出奇制勝之處。

IDM **surˌprise, surˈprise** (*informal*) **1** (*ironic, often disapproving*) used to show that sth is not a surprise to you, as you could easily have predicted that it would happen or be true（認為不足為怪時說）這有什麼好奇怪的：*One of the candidates was the manager's niece, and surprise, surprise, she got the job.* 求職者中有一個是經理的姪女，結果她被錄用了。這有什麼奇怪的呢。 **2** used when giving sb a surprise（讓某人感到意外時說）想不到吧：*Surprise, surprise! Look who's here!* 想不到吧！看看這是誰！ **take sb/sth by surˈprise** to attack or capture sb/sth unexpectedly or without warning 突襲；出其不意地抓獲：*The police took the burglars by surprise.* 警方出其不意地逮捕了入室竊賊。 **take sb by surˈprise** to happen unexpectedly so that sb is slightly shocked; to surprise sb 使某人驚詫；出乎某人意料：*His frankness took her by surprise.* 她沒料到他竟如此坦率。

■ ***verb*** **1** 🔑 to make sb feel surprised 使驚奇；使詫異；使感到意外：~ **sb** *It wouldn't surprise me if they got married soon.* 即使他們很快就結婚，我也不會感到意外。◇ ~ **sb how, what, etc.** … *It's always surprised me how popular he is.* 他怎麼那麼受歡迎，我百思不得其解。◇ **it surprises sb that** … *It surprises me that you've never sung professionally.* 想不到你從來沒搞過專業演唱。◇ **it surprises sb to do sth** *Would it surprise you to know that I'm thinking of leaving?* 如果我告訴你我打算離開這裏，你覺得意外嗎？ **2** ~ **sb** to attack, discover, etc., sb suddenly and unexpectedly 出其不意地攻擊；使措手不及；無意中發現：*The army attacked at night to surprise the rebels.* 軍隊在夜間發起攻擊，把叛亂者打了個措手不及。◇ *We arrived home early and surprised a burglar trying to break in.* 我們回家早，無意中發現一個竊賊正要入室行竊。

Synonyms 同義詞辨析

surprise

startle • amaze • stun • astonish • take sb aback • astound

These words all mean to make sb feel surprised.
以上各詞均含使驚奇、使詫異之意。

surprise to give sb the feeling that you get when sth happens that you do not expect or do not understand, or sth that you do expect does not happen; to make sb feel surprised 指使驚奇、使詫異、使感到意外：*The outcome didn't surprise me at all.* 這一結果完全在我的意料之中。

startle to surprise sb suddenly in a way that slightly shocks or frightens them 指驚嚇、使嚇一跳、使大吃一驚：*Sorry, I didn't mean to startle you.* 對不起，我不是存心要嚇唬你。◇ *The explosion startled the horse.* 爆炸聲使馬受了驚。

amaze to surprise sb very much 指使驚奇、使驚愕、使驚詫：*Just the huge size of the place amazed her.* 僅僅地方之大就使她十分驚奇。

stun (*rather informal*) (often in newspapers) to surprise or shock sb so much that they cannot think clearly or speak（常用於報章）指使震驚、使驚愕、使目瞪口呆

astonish to surprise sb very much 指使十分驚訝、使大為驚奇：*The news astonished everyone.* 這消息使大家十分驚訝。

AMAZE OR ASTONISH? 用 amaze 還是 astonish？

These two words have the same meaning and in most cases you can use either. If you are talking about sth that both surprises you and makes you feel ashamed, use **astonish**. 上述兩詞意思相同，多數情況下可通用。如果指某事既使人驚愕又使人羞愧則用 astonish：*He was astonished by his own stupidity.* 他對自己的愚蠢感到十分震驚。

take sb aback [usually passive] (especially of sth negative) to surprise or shock sb（尤指不好的事）使大吃一驚、使震驚：*We were rather taken aback by her hostile reaction.* 她敵視的反應使我們大吃一驚。

astound to surprise or shock sb very much 指使震驚、使大驚：*His arrogance astounded her.* 他的傲慢使她震驚。

PATTERNS

- **It** surprises sb/startles sb/amazes sb/stuns sb/astonishes sb/takes sb aback/astounds sb
- to surprise/startle/amaze/stun/astonish/astound sb **that** …
- to surprise/amaze sb **what/how** …
- to surprise/startle/amaze/stun/astonish/astound sb **to know/find/learn/see/hear** …
- to be surprised/startled/stunned **into** (doing) sth

S

sur·prised /sə'praɪzd; NAmE sər'p-/ adj. feeling or showing surprise 驚奇的；驚訝的；覺得奇怪的；感覺意外的： *a surprised look* 驚訝的神色 ◇ *She looked surprised when I told her.* 我告訴她時她顯得很驚訝。◇ **~ (at/by sb/sth)** *I was surprised at how quickly she agreed.* 我沒想到她這麼快就同意了。◇ *I'm surprised at you, behaving like that in front of the kids.* 我真想不到，當着孩子們的面你竟做出這種舉動。◇ **~ (to see, hear, etc.)** *They were surprised to find that he'd already left.* 他們驚奇地發現他已經走了。◇ **~ (that ...)** *You shouldn't be surprised (that) he didn't come.* 他沒來，你不必感到意外。◇ ***Don't be surprised if*** *I pretend not to recognise you.* 要是我假裝不認識你，你別覺得奇怪。◇ *'Will she cancel the party?' '**I wouldn't be surprised.**'* "她會取消這次聚會嗎？" "即使取消我也不感到奇怪。" ➲ compare UNSURPRISED

sur·pris·ing /sə'praɪzɪŋ; NAmE sər'p-/ adj. causing surprise 令人吃驚的；使人驚奇的；出人意料的；奇怪的： *It's not surprising (that) they lost.* 他們吃了敗仗，不奇怪。◇ *We had a surprising amount in common.* 我們共同之處出奇地多。◇ *It's surprising what people will do for money.* 人為了錢什麼幹不出來，想想真令人愕然。 ▸ **sur·pris·ing·ly** adv.： *She looked surprisingly well.* 她看上去身體出奇地好。◇ *Surprisingly, he agreed straight away.* 真想不到，他馬上同意了。◇ ***Not surprisingly*** *on such a hot day, the beach was crowded.* 在這樣的大熱天，海灘上人頭攢動是不足為奇的。

Language Bank 用語庫

surprising

Highlighting interesting data 強調有趣的數據

- **What is surprising** about these results **is** that boys are more likely to be left-handed than girls. 這些結果令人吃驚的是男生比女生更可能是左撇子。
- **Surprisingly**, boys are more likely to be left-handed than girls. 令人吃驚的是男生比女生更可能是左撇子。
- **Interestingly**, even when both parents are left-handed, there is still only a 26% chance of their children being left-handed. 有趣的是即使父母都是左撇子，他們的孩子也只有 26% 的機率是左撇子。
- **One of the most interesting** findings is that only 2% of the left-handers surveyed have two left-handed parents. 研究結果其中最有趣一點是在受調查的左撇子中只有 2% 的人父母都是左撇子。
- **It is interesting to note that** people are more likely to be left-handed if their mother is left-handed than if their father is. 有趣的是，左撇子母親比左撇子父親的孩子更可能成為左撇子。
- **The most striking** feature of these results **is** that left-handed mothers are more likely to have left-handed children. 這些結果中最引人注目的一點是左撇子母親更可能生左撇子孩子。

➲ Language Banks at CONTRAST, EMPHASIS, ILLUSTRATE, SIMILARLY

sur·real /sə'riːəl/ (also *less frequent* **sur·real·is·tic**) adj. very strange; more like a dream than reality, with ideas and images mixed together in a strange way 離奇的；怪誕的；夢幻般的；超現實的

sur·real·ism /sə'riːəlɪzəm/ noun [U] a 20th century style and movement in art and literature in which images and events that are not connected are put together in a strange or impossible way, like a dream, to try to express what is happening deep in the mind 超現實主義，超現實主義派（20 世紀文藝流派，以離奇怪誕的方式把無關聯的形象和事情串連在一起） ▸ **sur·real·ist** adj. [usually before noun]： *a surrealist painter/painting* 超現實主義畫家／繪畫 **sur·real·ist** noun： *the surrealist Salvador Dali* 超現實主義畫家薩爾瓦多•達利

sur·real·is·tic /səˌriːə'lɪstɪk/ adj. **1** = SURREAL **2** connected with surrealism 超現實主義的： *a surrealistic painting* 超現實主義繪畫

sur·ren·der /sə'rendə(r)/ verb, noun
■ **verb 1** [I, T] to admit that you have been defeated and want to stop fighting; to allow yourself to be caught, taken prisoner, etc. 投降 SYN **give in**： **~ (to sb)** *The rebel soldiers were forced to surrender.* 叛軍被迫投降。◇ **~ yourself (to sb)** *The hijackers eventually surrendered themselves to the police.* 劫機者最終向警方投降。 **2** (*formal*) to give up sth/sb when you are forced to（被迫）放棄，交出 SYN **relinquish**： **~ sth/sb to sb** *He agreed to surrender all claims to the property.* 他同意放棄對那筆財產的一切權利要求。◇ *They surrendered their guns to the police.* 他們向警察交出了槍。◇ **~ sth/sb** *The defendant was released to await trial but had to surrender her passport.* 被告被釋放候審，但須交出護照。
PHR V **sur'render to sth | sur'render yourself to sth** (*formal*) to stop trying to prevent yourself from having a feeling, habit, etc. and allow it to control what you do 聽任（感情、習慣等）擺佈（或發展）： *He finally surrendered to his craving for drugs.* 他最終克制不住，吸起毒來。
■ **noun** [U, sing.] **1 ~ (to sb/sth)** an act of admitting that you have been defeated and want to stop fighting 投降： *They demanded (an)* ***unconditional surrender***. 他們要求無條件投降。 ➲ COLLOCATIONS at WAR **2** the fact of allowing yourself to be controlled by sth 屈服；屈從： *They accused the government of a surrender to business interests.* 他們指責政府唯商界利益是從。 **3 ~ of sth (to sb)** an act of giving sth to sb else even though you do not want to, especially after a battle, etc.（尤指在戰爭等過後）放棄，交出： *They insisted on the immediate surrender of all weapons.* 他們堅持要求立即交出全部武器。

sur'render value noun the amount of money that you get if you end a life insurance policy before its official end date（在到期之前終止人壽保險單所得的）解約退還金，退保價值

sur·rep·ti·tious /ˌsʌrəp'tɪʃəs; NAmE ˌsɜːr-/ adj. done secretly or quickly, in the hope that other people will not notice 秘密的；趁人不注意趕緊進行的 SYN **furtive**： *She sneaked a surreptitious glance at her watch.* 她偷偷看了一眼手錶。 ▸ **sur·rep·ti·tious·ly** adv.

sur·ro·gacy /'sʌrəgəsi; NAmE 'sɜːr-/ noun [U] the practice of giving birth to a baby for another woman who is unable to have babies herself 代孕

sur·ro·gate /'sʌrəgət; NAmE 'sɜːr-/ adj. (*formal*) used to describe a person or thing that takes the place of, or is used instead of, sb/sth else 替代的；代用的： *She saw him as a sort of surrogate father.* 在她心目中，他彷彿是能替代父親角色的人。 ▸ **sur·ro·gate** noun

surrogate 'mother noun a woman who gives birth to a baby for another woman who is unable to have babies herself 代孕母親

sur·round /sə'raʊnd/ verb, noun
■ **verb 1** to be all around sth/sb 圍繞；環繞： **~ sth/sb** *Tall trees surround the lake.* 環湖都是大樹。◇ *the membranes surrounding the brain* 腦膜 ◇ *As a child I was surrounded by love and kindness.* 幼年時我備受關愛。◇ **~ sth/sb with sth** *The lake is surrounded with/by trees.* 湖邊樹木環繞。 **2** to move into position all around sb/sth, especially so as to prevent them from escaping; to move sb/sth into position in this way 包圍；圍住： **~ sb/sth** *Police surrounded the building.* 警方包圍了那棟房子。◇ **~ sb/sth with sth** *They've surrounded the building with police.* 他們跟警察一起包圍了那棟房子。 **3 ~ sth/sb** to be closely connected with sth/sb 與…緊密相關；圍繞： *publicity surrounding the divorce* 媒體圍繞這樁離婚事件的報道 **4 ~ yourself with sb/sth** to choose to have particular people or things near you all the time 喜歡結交（某類人）；喜歡身邊總有（某類東西）： *I like to surround myself with beautiful things.* 我喜歡身邊老有漂亮的東西。
■ **noun** a border or an area around the edge of sth, especially one that is decorated（物品的）邊，飾邊；周圍 ➲ VISUAL VOCAB page V21

S

sur·round·ing 0▬ /səˈraʊndɪŋ/ *adj.* [only before noun] that is near or around sth 周圍的；附近的：*Oxford and the surrounding area* 牛津及其周圍地區

sur·round·ings 0▬ /səˈraʊndɪŋz/ *noun* [pl.] everything that is around or near sb/sth 環境 SYN **environment**：*to work in pleasant surroundings* 在愉快的環境中工作 ◇ *The buildings have been designed to blend in with their surroundings.* 這些建築物設計巧妙，與周圍環境渾然一體。 ➲ SYNONYMS at ENVIRONMENT

surˈround sound *noun* [U] a system for reproducing sound using several SPEAKERS (= the pieces of equipment that the sound comes out of) placed around the person listening in order to produce a more realistic sound 環繞音響系統；環繞立體聲系統

sur·tax /ˈsɜːtæks; *NAmE* ˈsɜːrt-/ *noun* [U] a tax charged at a higher rate than the normal rate, on income above a particular level（對超過一定金額的收入徵收的）附加稅

Sur·titles™ /ˈsɜːtaɪtlz; *NAmE* ˈsɜːrt-/ *noun* [pl.] words that translate what is being sung in an OPERA, or spoken in a play in the theatre, into a different language and appear on a screen above or beside the stage 台詞譯文字幕（打在歌劇院或戲院舞台上方或側面）

sur·veil·lance /sɜːˈveɪləns; *NAmE* sɜːrˈv-/ *noun* [U] the act of carefully watching a person suspected of a crime or a place where a crime may be committed（對犯罪嫌疑人或可能發生犯罪的地方的）監視 SYN **observation**：*The police are keeping the suspects* ***under constant surveillance.*** 警方正對嫌疑人實施不間斷監視。◇ ***surveillance cameras/equipment*** 監視攝像機 / 設備

sur·vey 0▬ AW *noun, verb*

■ *noun* /ˈsɜːveɪ; *NAmE* ˈsɜːrveɪ/ **1** 0▬ an investigation of the opinions, behaviour, etc. of a particular group of people, which is usually done by asking them questions 民意調查；民意測驗：*A recent survey showed 75% of those questioned were in favour of the plan.* 最近的民意調查顯示，有 75% 的調查對象支持這項計劃。◇ *The* ***survey revealed*** *that …* 民意測驗顯示…◇ *to* ***conduct/carry out a survey*** 進行一項民意調查 **2** 0▬ the act of examining and recording the measurements, features, etc. of an area of land in order to make a map or plan of it 測量；勘測；測繪：*an aerial survey* (= made by taking photographs from an aircraft) 航空測量 ◇ *a geological survey* 地質勘察 **3** (*BrE*) an examination of the condition of a house, etc., usually done for sb who is thinking of buying it（尤指為欲購房者所做的）房屋鑒定 **4** a general study, view or description of sth 總體研究；全面評述；概述：*a comprehensive survey of modern music* 現代音樂概述

■ *verb* /səˈveɪ; *NAmE* sərˈveɪ/ **1** 0▬ **~ sth** to look carefully at the whole of sth, especially in order to get a general impression of it 查看；審視；審察 SYN **inspect**：*The next morning we surveyed the damage caused by the fire.* 次日清早我們查看了火災的破壞情況。◇ *He surveyed himself in the mirror before going out.* 出門前他對着鏡子把自己審視了一番。 **2 ~ sth** to study and give a general description of sth 總體研究；全面評述；概述：*This chapter briefly surveys the current state of European politics.* 本章對歐洲政治的現狀作了簡略概述。 **3 ~ sth** to measure and record the features of an area of land, for example in order to make a map or in preparation for building 測量；勘測；測繪 **4 ~ sth** (*BrE*) to examine a building to make sure it is in good condition（對建築物的）鑒定，檢查 **5** 0▬ **~ sb/sth** to investigate the opinions or behaviour of a group of people by asking them a series of questions（對…）做民意調查，進行民意測驗 SYN **interview**：*We surveyed 500 smokers and found that over three quarters would like to give up.* 我們對 500 名吸煙者進行了調查，發現有超過四分之三的人願意戒煙。

ˈsurvey course *noun* (*NAmE*) a college course that gives an introduction to a subject for people who are thinking about studying it further（大學的）概論課程，概況課程

sur·vey·or /səˈveɪə(r); *NAmE* sərˈv-/ *noun* **1** a person whose job is to examine and record the details of a piece of land（土地）測量員，勘測員 **2** (*BrE*) (*NAmE* **in·spect·or**) a person whose job is to examine a building to make sure it is in good condition, usually done for sb who is thinking of buying it（建築物）鑒定人 **3** (*BrE*) an official whose job is to check that sth is accurate, of good quality, etc. 檢驗員；檢驗官：*the surveyor of public works* 市政工程檢驗官 ➲ see also QUANTITY SURVEYOR

sur·viv·able /səˈvaɪvəbl; *NAmE* sərˈv-/ *adj.* (of an accident or experience 事故或經歷) able to be survived 可幸免於難的；可幸存的：*a survivable air crash* 沒有釀成死亡的飛機失事

sur·vival AW /səˈvaɪvl; *NAmE* sərˈv-/ *noun* **1** [U] the state of continuing to live or exist, often despite difficulty or danger 生存；存活；幸存：*the* ***struggle/battle/fight for survival*** 為生存而鬥爭 / 戰鬥 / 拚搏 ◇ *His only* ***chance of survival*** *was a heart transplant.* 只有進行心臟移植，他才有望活下去。◇ *Exporting is necessary for our economic survival.* 必須有出口，才能維持我們的經濟。 **2** [C] **~ (from sth)** something that has continued to exist from an earlier time 殘存物；幸存事物 SYN **relic**：*The ceremony is a survival from pre-Christian times.* 這種儀式是從公元前遺留下來的。

IDM **the surˌvival of the ˈfittest** the principle that only the people or things that are best adapted to their surroundings will continue to exist 適者生存

sur·vival·ist /səˈvaɪvəlɪst; *NAmE* sərˈv-/ *noun* a person who prepares for a dangerous or unpleasant situation such as a war by learning how to survive outdoors, practising how to use weapons, storing food, etc. 求生訓練學員，戶外生存受訓者（為防備險惡狀況而學習戶外求生技能） ▶ **sur·vival·ism** /səˈvaɪvəlɪzəm; *NAmE* sərˈv-/ *noun* [U]

surˈvival kit *noun* a set of emergency equipment, including food, medical supplies and tools 救生包（裝有食物、醫療用品和工具）

sur·vive 0▬ AW /səˈvaɪv; *NAmE* sərˈv-/ *verb*

1 0▬ [I] to continue to live or exist 生存；存活；繼續存在：*She was the last surviving member of the family.* 她是這家人中僅存的一員。◇ *Of the six people injured in the crash, only two survived.* 因這次撞車事故受傷的六人中，只有兩人活了下來。◇ (*humorous*) *'How are you these days?' 'Oh, surviving.'* "你近來好嗎？" "唔，湊合過吧。" ◇ *Don't worry, it's only a scratch—you'll survive.* 別擔心，只不過是劃傷，你沒事的。◇ **~ from sth** *Some strange customs have survived from earlier times.* 有些奇怪的風俗是從早年留存下來的。◇ **~ on sth** *I can't survive on £40 a week* (= it is not enough for my basic needs). 一星期 40 英鎊，我無法維持生活。◇ **~ as sth** *He survived as party leader until his second election defeat.* 直至第二次參選失敗他才不再擔任黨的領導人。 **2** 0▬ [T] to continue to live or exist despite a dangerous event or time 幸存；幸免於難；渡過難關：**~ sth** *The company managed to survive the crisis.* 公司設法渡過了危機。◇ *Many birds didn't survive the severe winter.* 很多鳥死於這次嚴冬。◇ **~ sth + adj.** *Few buildings survived the war intact.* 戰爭之後沒幾座完好的建築了。 **3** [T] **~ sb/sth** to live or exist longer than sb/sth 比…活（或存在）的時間長 SYN **outlive**：*She survived her husband by ten years.* 丈夫死後她又活了十年。

sur·vivor AW /səˈvaɪvə(r); *NAmE* sərˈv-/ *noun* a person who continues to live, especially despite being nearly killed or experiencing great danger or difficulty 幸存者；生還者；挺過困難者：*the* ***sole/only survivor*** *of the massacre* 那場大屠殺的唯一幸存者 ◇ *The plane crashed in an area of dense jungle. There were no survivors.* 飛機墜落在一個叢林茂密的地區。無人生還。◇ *There are only a few survivors from the original team* (= members who remain in it while others have been replaced). 最初的隊員只剩下幾名了。◇ *She'll cope. She's one of life's great survivors* (= sb who deals very well with difficult situations). 她能挺過去。生活中什麼樣的困難她都能對付。

sus = SUSS

sus·cep·ti·bil·ity /səˌseptəˈbɪləti/ *noun* (*pl.* **-ies**) **1** [U, sing.] **~ (to sth)** the state of being very likely to be influenced, harmed or affected by sth 易受影響（或傷害等）的特性；敏感性；過敏性：*susceptibility to disease* 易患病

S

的體質 **2 susceptibilities** [pl.] a person's feelings which are likely to be easily hurt 感情脆弱處 SYN **sensibilities**：*It was all carried out without any consideration for the susceptibilities of the bereaved family.* 這樣做全然沒有考慮到死者家人的感受。

sus·cep·tible /sə'septəbl/ *adj.* **1** [not usually before noun] **~ (to sb/sth)** very likely to be influenced, harmed or affected by sb/sth 易受影響（或傷害等）；敏感；過敏：*He's highly susceptible to flattery.* 他愛聽恭維話。◇ *Some of these plants are more susceptible to frost damage than others.* 這些植物中有一些較其他的易受霜凍危害。◇ *Salt intake may lead to raised blood pressure in susceptible adults.* 鹽的攝入可能導致易病的成年人血壓升高。**2** easily influenced by feelings and emotions 好動感情的；感情豐富的；善感的 SYN **impressionable**：*She was both charming and susceptible.* 她迷人而多情。**3 ~ (of sth)** (*formal*) allowing sth; capable of sth 容許…的；可能…的；可以…的：*Is this situation not susceptible of improvement by legislation?* 這種狀況有沒有可能通過立法加以改善？

sushi /'su:ʃi/ *noun* [U] a Japanese dish of small cakes of cold cooked rice, flavoured with VINEGAR and served with raw fish, etc. on top 壽司（日本食物，小糕餅狀冷米飯配生魚片等）：*a sushi bar* 壽司店

sus·pect 0⊶ *verb, noun, adj.*

> **WORD FAMILY**
> suspect *verb*
> suspected *adj.*
> suspicion *noun*
> suspicious *adj.*
> suspiciously *adv.*
> suspect *noun, adj.*

■ ***verb*** /sə'spekt/ (not used in the progressive tenses 不用於進行時) **1** 0⊶ [T, I] to have an idea that sth is probably true or likely to happen, especially sth bad, but without having definite proof 疑有，覺得（尤指壞事可能屬實或發生）：**~ (sth)** *If you suspect a gas leak, do not strike a match or even turn on an electric light.* 假如你懷疑有煤氣泄漏，不要劃火柴，甚至連電燈都不要開。◇ *Suspecting nothing, he walked right into the trap.* 他毫無覺察，逕直走入陷阱。◇ *As I had suspected all along, he was not a real policeman.* 他並不是真的警察，我一直就覺得不像。◇ **~ (that) …** *I began to suspect (that) they were trying to get rid of me.* 我開始覺察出，他們試圖擺脫掉我。◇ **it is suspected that …** *It was suspected that the drugs had been brought into the country by boat.* 有人懷疑毒品是用船運入該國的。◇ **~ sb/sth to be/have sth** *She suspected him to be an impostor.* 她懷疑他是個冒名行騙者。**2** 0⊶ [T] to have an idea that sb is guilty of sth, without having definite proof 懷疑（某人有罪）：**~ sb/sth of sth** *He resigned after being suspected of theft.* 他被懷疑偷竊，隨後就辭職了。◇ **~ sb/sth of doing sth** *The drug is suspected of causing over 200 deaths.* 人們懷疑這種藥物造成 200 多人死亡。◇ **~ sb/sth** *Whom do the police suspect?* 警方懷疑誰？**3** [T] **~ sth** to be suspicious about sth; to not trust sth 懷疑；感覺有問題；不信任：*I suspected her motives in offering to help.* 她主動要幫忙，我懷疑她的動機。▶ **sus·pected** *adj.*：*a suspected broken arm* 懷疑骨折的胳膊 ◇ *suspected tax evasion* 逃稅嫌疑 ◇ *suspected terrorists* 被懷疑從事恐怖主義活動的人

■ ***noun*** 0⊶ /'sʌspekt/ a person who is suspected of a crime or of having done sth wrong 嫌疑犯；嫌疑分子；可疑對象：*a murder suspect* 殺人嫌疑犯 ◇ *He is the **prime suspect** in the case.* 他是這個案子的首要嫌疑人。

■ ***adj.*** /'sʌspekt/ **1** that may be false and that cannot be relied on 不可信的；靠不住的 SYN **questionable**：*Some of the evidence they produced was highly suspect.* 他們出示的證據中有些相當成問題。**2** that you suspect to be dangerous or illegal 可疑的；可能有危險的；有違法嫌疑的 SYN **suspicious**：*a suspect package* (= one that may contain drugs, a bomb, etc.) 可疑包裹

sus·pend AW /sə'spend/ *verb* **1 ~ sth/sb (from sth) (by/on sth)** (*formal*) to hang sth from sth else 懸；掛；吊：*A lamp was suspended from the ceiling.* 一盞吊燈懸在天花板上。◇ *Her body was found suspended by a rope.* 人們發現她的屍體吊在繩子上。**2 ~ sth** to officially stop sth for a time; to prevent sth from being active, used, etc. for a time 暫停；中止；使暫停發揮作用（或使用等）：*Production has been suspended while safety checks are carried out.* 在進行安全檢查期間生產暫停。◇ *The constitution was suspended as the fighting grew worse.* 鑒於戰鬥趨於激烈，憲法暫停實施。◇ *In the theatre we willingly **suspend disbelief*** (= temporarily believe that the characters, etc. are real). 在劇院看戲時，我們自願對一切暫不置疑。**3 ~ sth** to officially delay sth; to arrange for sth to happen later than planned 延緩；暫緩；推遲：*The introduction of the new system has been suspended until next year.* 新制度推遲到明年再行實施。◇ *to suspend judgement* (= delay forming or expressing an opinion) 暫不判斷 **4** [usually passive] **~ sb (from sth)** to officially prevent sb from doing their job, going to school, etc. for a time 使暫時停職（或停學等）：*The police officer was suspended while the complaint was investigated.* 投訴調查期間，這名警員被暫停職務。**5 be suspended in sth** (*technical* 術語) to float in liquid or air without moving 懸浮 ➲ see also SUSPENSION

su,spended ani'mation *noun* [U] **1** the state of being alive but not conscious or active 不省人事；假死 **2** a feeling that you cannot do anything because you are waiting for sth to happen 蟄伏狀態

su,spended 'sentence *noun* a punishment given to a criminal in court which means that they will only go to prison if they commit another crime within a particular period of time 緩刑

sus·pend·er /sə'spendə(r)/ *noun* **1** [C, usually pl.] (*BrE*) (*NAmE* **gar·ter**) a short circle of ELASTIC for holding up a sock or STOCKING 吊襪帶 **2 suspenders** (*NAmE*) (*BrE* **braces**) [pl.] long narrow pieces of cloth, leather, etc. for holding trousers/pants up. They are fastened to the top of the trousers/pants at the front and back and passed over the shoulders. 吊褲帶；背帶 ➲ VISUAL VOCAB page V61

su'spender belt *noun* (*BrE*) (*NAmE* **'garter belt**) a piece of women's underwear like a belt, worn around the waist, used for holding STOCKINGS up（女用）吊襪腰帶

sus·pense /sə'spens/ *noun* [U] a feeling of worry or excitement that you have when you feel that sth is going to happen, sb is going to tell you some news, etc.（對即將發生的事等的）擔心；焦慮；興奮；懸念：*a tale of mystery and suspense* 一個神秘莫測、充滿懸念的故事 ◇ *Don't **keep us in suspense**. Tell us what happened!* 別讓我們心老懸着了，告訴我們出了什麼事！◇ *I couldn't bear the suspense a moment longer.* 這樣提心吊膽，我一刻也受不了了。

sus·pen·sion AW /sə'spenʃn/ *noun* **1** [U, C] the act of officially removing sb from their job, school, team, etc. for a period of time, usually as a punishment 暫令停職（或停學、停賽等）：*suspension from school* 暫被停學 ◇ *The two players are appealing against their suspensions.* 這兩名運動員請求取消對他們的停賽處罰。**2** [U, sing.] the act of delaying sth for a period of time, until a decision has been taken 暫緩；推遲；延期：*These events have led to the suspension of talks.* 這些事件導致談判延期。**3** [U, C] the system by which a vehicle is supported on its wheels and which makes it more comfortable to ride in when the road surface is not even（車輛減震用的）懸架 **4** [C, U] (*technical* 術語) a liquid with very small pieces of solid matter floating in it; the state of such a liquid 懸浮液；懸浮 ➲ see also SUSPEND

su'spension bridge *noun* a bridge that hangs from steel cables that are supported by towers at each end 懸索橋；吊橋 ➲ VISUAL VOCAB page V14

sus·pi·cion 0⊶ /sə'spɪʃn/ *noun*

1 0⊶ [U, C] a feeling that sb has done sth wrong, illegal or dishonest, even though you have no proof 懷疑；嫌疑：*They drove away slowly to avoid arousing suspicion.* 他們緩緩駕車離去，以免引起懷疑。◇ *He was arrested **on suspicion of** murder.* 他因涉嫌謀殺而被捕。◇ **~ (that …)** *I have **a sneaking suspicion** that she's not telling the truth.* 我暗自懷疑她沒講實話。➲ see also SUSPECT **2** 0⊶ [C] **~ (that …)** a feeling or belief that sth is true, even though you have no proof 感覺；看法：*I have a horrible suspicion that we've come to the wrong station.*

我感覺不妙，我們可能去錯車站了。 **3** 🔑 [U, C] the feeling that you cannot trust sb/sth 猜疑；懷疑；不放心： *Their offer was greeted with some suspicion.* 他們的主動熱情遭到一些猜疑。 **4** [sing.] **~ of sth** (*formal*) a small amount of sth 少許；一點兒 **SYN** **hint**： *His mouth quivered in the suspicion of a smile.* 他嘴唇微微一顫，露出一絲笑意。

IDM **above/beyond su'spicion** too good, honest, etc. to have done sth wrong, illegal or dishonest 無可置疑： *Nobody who was near the scene of the crime is above suspicion.* 犯罪現場附近的任何人都不能排除嫌疑。 **under su'spicion (of sth)** suspected of doing sth wrong, illegal or dishonest 有嫌疑；涉嫌： *The whole family is currently under suspicion of her murder.* 目前這一家人都涉嫌謀殺她。◇ *A number of doctors* ***came under suspicion*** *of unethical behaviour.* 一些醫生涉嫌有不道德行為。 ➲ more at FINGER *n.*

sus·pi·cious 🔑 /sə'spɪʃəs/ *adj.*

1 🔑 **~ (of/about sb/sth)** feeling that sb has done sth wrong, illegal or dishonest, without having any proof 感覺可疑的；懷疑的： *They became suspicious of his behaviour and contacted the police.* 他們開始覺得他行為可疑，便報了警。◇ *a suspicious look* 懷疑的神情 ◇ *You have a very* ***suspicious mind*** (= you always think that people are behaving in an illegal or dishonest way). 你疑心很重。 **2** 🔑 making you feel that sth is wrong, illegal or dishonest 令人懷疑的；可疑的： *Didn't you notice anything suspicious in his behaviour?* 你難道沒有注意到他行為有可疑之處？◇ *She died in* ***suspicious circumstances.*** 她死得蹊蹺。◇ *Police are not treating the fire as suspicious.* 警方認為這場火災沒有可疑之處。◇ *It was all very suspicious.* 這一切十分可疑。 **3** 🔑 **~ (of sb/sth)** not willing or able to trust sb/sth 不信任的；持懷疑態度的 **SYN** **sceptical**： *I was suspicious of his motives.* 我懷疑他的動機。◇ *Many were suspicious of reform.* 很多人對改革持懷疑態度。 ➲ see also SUSPECT

sus·pi·cious·ly /sə'spɪʃəsli/ *adv.* **1** in a way that shows you think sb has done sth wrong, illegal or dishonest 懷疑地；有疑心地： *The man looked at her suspiciously.* 那個男人以狐疑的目光看着她。 **2** in a way that makes people think sth wrong, illegal or dishonest is happening 令人懷疑地；形跡（或神色等）可疑地： *Let me know if you see anyone acting suspiciously.* 如發現有人形跡可疑，你就告訴我。 **3** in a way that shows you think there may be sth wrong with sth 以懷疑的態度；不信任地： *She eyed the fish on her plate suspiciously.* 她不放心地看着自己盤子裏的魚。

IDM **look/sound suspiciously like sth** (often *humorous*) to be very similar to sth 看／聽上去與某事物相像得令人起疑： *Their latest single sounds suspiciously like the last one.* 他們的最新單曲唱片聽着和前一張很像。

suss (also **sus**) /sʌs/ *verb* [T, I] **~ (sb/sth) (out)** | **~ that ...** | **~ how, what, etc. ...** (*BrE, informal*) to realize sth; to understand the important things about sb/sth 意識到；認識到；發現： *I think I've* ***got him sussed*** (= now I understand him). 我想我已瞭解他了。◇ *If you want to succeed in business you have to suss out the competition.* 要想在生意場上立足，你必須真正明白競爭是怎麼回事。◇ *He cheated on her for years, but she never sussed.* 他有外遇多年了，但她從來沒有察覺。

sussed /sʌst/ *adj.* (*BrE, informal*) knowing what you need to know about the situations and people around you, so that you are not easily tricked and are able to take care of yourself 有（處世）經驗而不易上當的；門檻精的

sus·tain **AW** /sə'steɪn/ *verb* **1** **~ sb/sth** to provide enough of what sb/sth needs in order to live or exist 維持（生命、生存）： *Which planets can sustain life?* 哪些行星可以維持生命的存在？◇ *The love and support of his family sustained him during his time in prison.* 家人的關愛和支持幫助他度過了獄中的歲月。 **2** **~ sth** to make sth continue for some time without becoming less 使保持；使穩定持續 **SYN** **maintain**： *a period of sustained economic growth* 經濟持續增長的時期 ◇ *a sustained attack* 持續的攻擊 ◇ *She managed to sustain everyone's interest until the end of her speech.* 她使每個人興趣盎然，一直聽她把話講完。 **3** **~ sth** (*formal*) to experience sth bad 遭受；蒙受；經受 **SYN** **suffer**： *to sustain damage/an injury/a defeat* 遭受損失；受傷；遭到失敗 ◇ *The company* ***sustained losses*** *of millions of dollars.* 公司遭受了數以百萬元計的巨大損失。 **4** **~ sth** to provide evidence to support an opinion, a theory, etc. 證明；證實 **SYN** **uphold**： *The evidence is not detailed enough to sustain his argument.* 這一證據過於籠統，不足以證明他的論點。 **5** **~ sth** (*formal*) to support a weight without breaking or falling 支撐；承受住 **SYN** **bear**： *The ice will not sustain your weight.* 這冰承受不了你的體重。 **6** **~ sth** (*law* 律) to decide that a claim, etc. is valid 認可；確認；准許；支持 **SYN** **uphold**： *The court sustained his claim that the contract was illegal.* 法庭支持他的觀點，認定該合同不合法。◇ ***Objection sustained!*** (= said by a judge when a lawyer makes an OBJECTION in court) 反對成立！

sus·tain·able **AW** /sə'steɪnəbl/ *adj.* **1** involving the use of natural products and energy in a way that does not harm the environment（對自然資源和能源的利用）不破壞生態平衡的，合理利用的： *sustainable forest management* 合理的森林管理 ◇ *an environmentally sustainable society* 保持生態環境平衡的社會 **2** that can continue or be continued for a long time 可持續的： *sustainable economic growth* 經濟的可持續增長 **OPP** **unsustainable** ▸ **sus·tain·abil·ity** **AW** /səˌsteɪnə'bɪləti/ *noun* [U] **sus·tain·ably** /-bli/ *adv.*

sus·ten·ance **AW** /'sʌstənəns/ *noun* [U] (*formal*) **1** the food and drink that people, animals and plants need to live and stay healthy 食物；營養；養料： *There's not much sustenance in a bowl of soup.* 一碗湯沒多少營養。◇ (*figurative*) *Arguing would only give further sustenance to his allegations.* 越是爭論，他越會覺得自己那些說法有道理。 **2** **~ (of sth)** the process of making sth continue to exist 維持；保持： *Elections are essential for the sustenance of parliamentary democracy.* 選舉制度是維持議會民主所必不可少的。

sutra /'suːtrə/ *noun* **1** a rule or statement in Sanskrit literature, or a set of rules（梵文的）箴言，格言，經 **2** a Buddhist or Jainist holy text（佛教或耆那教的）修多羅，經

sut·tee = SATI

su·ture /'suːtʃə(r)/ *noun, verb*

■ ***noun*** (*medical* 醫) a STITCH or stitches made when sewing up a wound, especially after an operation（傷口的）縫合，縫線

■ ***verb*** **~ sth** (*medical* 醫) to sew up a wound 縫合（傷口）

SUV /ˌes juː 'viː/ *abbr.* SPORT UTILITY VEHICLE

su·zer·ainty /'suːzəreɪnti; -rənti/ *noun* [U] (*formal*) the right of a country to rule over another country 宗主權

Sv *abbr.* SIEVERT

svelte /svelt; sfelt/ *adj.* (*approving*) (of a person, especially a woman 人，尤指女子) thin and attractive 苗條的；身材修長的

Sven·gali /sven'gɑːli/ *noun* a person who has the power to control another person's mind, make them do bad things, etc. 能控制他人思想的人；能使人幹壞事（或唯命是從）的人 **ORIGIN** From the name of a character in George du Maurier's novel *Trilby.* 源自喬治・杜・莫里哀的小說《軟氈帽》中的人物斯文加利。

SW *abbr.* **1** (*especially BrE*) SHORT WAVE 短波： *SW and LW radio* 短波及長波無線電設備 **2** south-west; south-western 西南方（的）；西南部（的）： *SW Australia* 澳大利亞西南部

swab /swɒb; *NAmE* swɑːb/ *noun, verb*

■ ***noun*** **1** a piece of soft material used by a doctor, nurse, etc. for cleaning wounds or taking a sample from sb's body for testing （醫用的）拭子，藥籤 **2** an act of taking a sample from sb's body, with a swab 用拭子對（人體）化驗標本的採集： *to take a throat swab* 用棉籤從咽部採集化驗樣品

■ ***verb*** (**-bb-**) **1** **~ sth** to clean or remove liquid from a wound, etc., using a swab 用拭子擦拭 **2** **~ sth (down)** to clean or wash a floor, surface, etc. using water and a cloth, etc. 擦洗，擦拭（地板等）

S

swad·dle /ˈswɒdl; *NAmE* ˈswɑːdl/ *verb* **~ sb/sth** (*old-fashioned*) to wrap sb/sth, especially a baby, tightly in clothes or a piece of cloth（用衣服或布）緊裹，包裹（尤指嬰兒）

ˈswaddling clothes *noun* [pl.] strips of cloth used in the past for wrapping a baby tightly 包裹嬰兒的布；襁褓

swag /swæg/ *noun* **1** [U] (*old-fashioned, informal*) goods that have been stolen 被盜貨品；贓物 **SYN loot 2** [C, usually pl.] cloth that is hung in large curved folds as decoration, especially above a window（掛於窗戶等上方的）裝飾性布幔（或帷幕） **3** (*AustralE, NZE*) a pack of things tied or wrapped together and carried by a traveller（旅行者攜帶的）包裹；行囊 **4** [C, usually pl.] a bunch of flowers or fruit that is CARVED onto walls, etc. as decoration 垂花飾（雕刻裝飾，形狀為串起來的花、果等）

swag·ger /ˈswægə(r)/ *verb, noun*
- ■ ***verb*** [I] (+ **adv./prep.**) (usually *disapproving*) to walk in an extremely proud and confident way 神氣十足地走；大搖大擺地走 **SYN strut**
- ■ ***noun*** [sing.] (*disapproving*) a way of walking or behaving that seems too confident 神氣十足；大搖大擺

swag·man /ˈswægmæn/ *noun* (*pl.* **-men** /-men/) (*AustralE, NZE, old use*) a man who travels around looking for work, carrying his possessions wrapped in a cloth 背着行囊四處找工作的人

Swa·hili /swəˈhiːli; swɑːˈh-/ (also **Ki·swa·hili**) *noun* [U] a language widely used in E Africa, especially between people who speak different first languages 斯瓦希里語（通行於東非，尤作第二語言）

swain /sweɪn/ *noun* (*old use* or *humorous*) a young man who is in love 情郎

swal·low 🔑 /ˈswɒləʊ; *NAmE* ˈswɑːloʊ/ *verb, noun*
- ■ ***verb***
- ▸ **FOOD/DRINK** 食物；飲料 **1** 🔑 [T, I] to make food, drink, etc. go down your throat into your stomach 吞下；嚥下：**~ (sth)** *Always chew food well before swallowing it.* 什麼食物都要先嚼碎再吞嚥。◇ *I had a sore throat and it hurt to swallow.* 當時我嗓子疼，嚥東西就疼。◇ **~ sth + adj.** *The pills should be swallowed whole.* 這些藥要吞服。
- ▸ **MOVE THROAT MUSCLES** 做吞嚥動作 **2** 🔑 [I] to move the muscles of your throat as if you were swallowing sth, especially because you are nervous（由於緊張等）做吞嚥動作：*She **swallowed hard** and told him the bad news.* 她硬下心把壞消息告訴了他。
- ▸ **COMPLETELY COVER** 完全覆蓋 **3** [T, often passive] to take sb/sth in or completely cover it so that they cannot be seen or no longer exist separately 吞沒；淹沒；侵吞：**~ sb/sth** *I watched her walk down the road until she was swallowed by the darkness.* 我看着她沿公路越走越遠，直至消失在黑暗中。◇ **~ sb/sth up** *Large areas of countryside have been swallowed up by towns.* 大片大片的鄉村地區被城鎮吞噬。
- ▸ **USE UP MONEY** 用盡錢 **4** [T] **~ sb/sth (up)** to use up sth completely, especially an amount of money 用盡，耗盡，花光（錢等）：*Most of my salary gets swallowed (up) by the rent and bills.* 我的工資大多支付房租和各種日常費用了。
- ▸ **BELIEVE** 相信 **5** [T] to accept that sth is true; to believe sth 相信；信以為真：**~ sth** *I found her excuse very **hard to swallow**.* 我覺得她的理由很難讓人相信。◇ **~ sth + adj.** *He told her a pack of lies, but she **swallowed it whole**.* 他對她講了一堆假話，可她全都信以為真。
- ▸ **FEELINGS** 感情 **6** [T] **~ sth** to hide your feelings 不流露；掩飾；抑制：*to swallow your doubts* 不流露懷疑 ◇ *You're going to have to **swallow your pride** and ask for your job back.* 你得放下架子，去求人家給你恢復原職。
- ▸ **ACCEPT INSULTS** 忍受侮辱 **7** [T] **~ sth** to accept insults, criticisms, etc. without complaining or protesting 默默忍受（侮辱、批評等）：*I was surprised that he just sat there and swallowed all their remarks.* 讓我吃驚的是他就坐在那兒默默地任憑他們評論。**IDM** see BITTER *adj.*
- ■ ***noun***
- ▸ **BIRD** 鳥 **1** a small bird with long pointed wings and a tail with two points, that spends the winter in Africa but flies to northern countries for the summer 燕
- ▸ **OF FOOD/DRINK** 食物；飲料 **2** an act of swallowing; an amount of food or drink that is swallowed at one time 嚥；吞；一次吞嚥的量；一口

IDM **one ˌswallow doesn't make a ˈsummer** (*saying*) you must not take too seriously a small sign that sth is happening or will happen in the future, because the situation could change 別略有好事就以為佳時已到；好事可能純屬偶然；一燕不成夏（不能單憑微小的跡象而下定論）

ˈswallow dive (*BrE*) (*NAmE* **ˈswan dive**) *noun* a DIVE performed with your arms stretched out sideways until you are close to the water 燕式跳水（接近水面前保持雙臂向兩側張開）

ˈswallow hole *noun* = SINKHOLE

swam *past tense* of SWIM

swami /ˈswɑːmi/ *noun* (also used as a title 亦用作稱號) a Hindu religious teacher 印度教宗教教師：*Swami Vivekanand* 維韋卡南達導師（法號辨喜）

swamp /swɒmp; *NAmE* swɑːmp/ *noun, verb*
- ■ ***noun*** [C, U] an area of ground that is very wet or covered with water and in which plants, trees, etc. are growing 沼澤（地） **SYN marsh**：*tropical swamps* 熱帶沼澤 ▸ **swampy** *adj.*：*swampy ground* 沼澤地
- ■ ***verb*** [often passive] **1** to make sb have more of sth than they can deal with 使不堪承受；使疲於應對；使應接不暇 **SYN inundate**：**~ sb/sth with sth** *The department was swamped with job applications.* 面對紛至沓來的求職申請，這個部門疲於應對。◇ **~ sb/sth** *In summer visitors swamp the island.* 夏天，這個島上遊客熙熙攘攘，人滿為患。**2 ~ sth** to fill or cover sth with a lot of water 淹；淹沒 **SYN engulf**：*The little boat was swamped by the waves.* 小船被大浪淹沒了。

ˈswamp fever *noun* [U] **1** a serious disease that affects horses 沼澤熱；馬傳染性貧血 **2** (*old-fashioned*) = MALARIA 瘧疾

swamp·land /ˈswɒmplænd; *NAmE* ˈswɑːmp-/ *noun* [U, pl.] a large area of SWAMP 沼澤地

swan /swɒn; *NAmE* swɑːn/ *noun, verb*
- ■ ***noun*** a large bird that is usually white and has a long thin neck. Swans live on or near water. 天鵝
- ■ ***verb*** (**-nn-**) [I] + **adv./prep.** (*BrE, informal, disapproving*) to go around enjoying yourself in a way that annoys other people or makes them jealous 悠遊；悠然閒逛：*They've gone swanning off to Paris for the weekend.* 他們週末到巴黎瀟灑去了。

ˈswan dive (*NAmE*) (*BrE* **ˈswallow dive**) *noun* a DIVE performed with your arms stretched out sideways until you are close to the water 燕式跳水（接近水面前保持雙臂向兩側張開）

swank /swæŋk/ *verb* [I] (*old-fashioned, BrE, informal, disapproving*) to behave in way that is too proud or confident 炫耀；賣弄

swanky /ˈswæŋki/ (**swank·ier**, **swanki·est**) (*especially BrE*) (also **swank** especially in *NAmE*) *adj.* (*informal, approving*) fashionable and expensive in a way that is intended to impress people 擺闊的；時髦且豪華的：*a swanky new hotel* 時髦豪華的新旅館

swan·song /ˈswɒnsɒŋ; *NAmE* ˈswɑːnsɔːŋ/ *noun* [sing.] the last piece of work produced by an artist, a musician, etc. or the last performance by an actor, ATHLETE, etc.（藝術家、音樂家等）最後的作品；（演員的）告別演出；（運動員的）告別比賽

swap (also **swop**) /swɒp; *NAmE* swɑːp/ *verb, noun*
- ■ ***verb*** (**-pp-**) **1** [I, T] to give sth to sb and receive sth in exchange 交換（東西）：**~ (sth) (with sb)** *I've finished this magazine. Can I swap with you?* 這本雜誌我看完了，能跟你交換一下嗎？◇ **~ sth for sth** *I swapped my red scarf for her blue one.* 我用我的紅圍巾換了她的藍圍巾。◇ **~ sth** *Can we **swap places**? I can't see the screen.* 咱倆交換一下座位好不好？我看不見銀幕。◇ *We spent the evening in the pub **swapping stories** (= telling each other stories) about our travels.* 我們一晚上坐在酒吧裏

S

講述各自的旅途經歷。◇ **~ sb sth for sth** *I swapped him my CD for his posters.* 我拿我的光盤換了他的海報。 **2** [I] **~ (over)** to start doing sb else's job, etc. while they do yours 交換（工作）: *I'll drive there and then we'll swap over on the way back.* 去的時候我開車，回來的時候咱倆再倒換過來。 **3** [T] (*especially BrE*) to replace one person or thing with another 用…替換；把…換成；掉換：**~ sb/sth (for sb/sth)** *I think I'll swap this sweater for one in another colour.* 我想把這件毛衣換成其他顏色的。◇ **~ sb/sth (over)** *I'm going to swap you over. Mike will go first and Jon will go second.* 我打算把你倆掉換一下。邁克先去，喬恩後去。 **IDM** see PLACE *n.*

■ ***noun*** **1** [usually sing.] an act of exchanging one thing or person for another 交換；掉換：*Let's* ***do a swap****. You work Friday night and I'll do Saturday.* 咱倆調個班吧。你星期五晚間上，我星期六上。 **2** a thing or person that has been exchanged for another 交換物；被掉換者：*Most of my football stickers are swaps.* 我的足球粘貼標籤多數都是跟別人換來的。

'swap meet *noun* (*especially NAmE*) an occasion at which people buy and sell or exchange items that interest them 物品交流會；收藏品交流會：*a swap meet for collectors of Star Trek memorabilia* 《星際迷航》紀念品收藏者交流會

sward /swɔːd; *NAmE* swɔːrd/ *noun* [C, U] (*literary*) an area of grass 草地；草皮

swarm /swɔːm; *NAmE* swɔːrm/ *noun, verb*

■ ***noun*** **~ (of sth)** **1** a large group of insects, especially BEES, moving together in the same direction 一大群（蜜蜂等昆蟲）：*a* ***swarm of bees/locusts/flies*** 一大群蜜蜂／蝗蟲／蒼蠅 **2** a large group of people, especially when they are all moving quickly in the same direction 一大群，一大批（向同方向移動的人） **SYN** **horde**

■ ***verb*** **1** [I] **+ adv./prep.** (often *disapproving*) (of people, animals, etc. 人、動物等) to move around in a large group 成群地來回移動：*Tourists were swarming all over the island.* 島上到處是旅遊者熙來攘往。 **2** (of BEES and other flying insects 蜜蜂或其他飛行昆蟲) to move around together in a large group, looking for a place to live 成群地飛來飛去

PHR V **'swarm with sb/sth** to be full of people or things 到處是人（或物）；擠滿：*The capital city is swarming with police.* 首都到處是警察。

swar·thy /'swɔːði; *NAmE* 'swɔːrði/ *adj.* (especially of a person or their face 尤指人或人臉) having dark skin 深膚色的；皮膚黝黑的

swash /swɒʃ; *NAmE* swɔːʃ; swɑːʃ/ *noun* [sing.] (*technical* 術語) the flow of water up the beach after a wave has BROKEN（浪頭拍岸後的）沖激，濺潑，掃浪

swash·buck·ling /'swɒʃbʌklɪŋ; *NAmE* 'swɔːʃ-; 'swɑːʃ-/ *adj.* [only before noun] (especially of films/movies 尤指電影) set in the past and full of action, adventure, fighting with SWORDS, etc. 表現古代驚險打鬥的；有傳奇歷險情節的：*a swashbuckling tale of adventure on the high seas* 公海上的傳奇歷險故事 ◇ *the swashbuckling hero of Hollywood epics* 好萊塢史詩片中的傳奇英雄

swas·tika /'swɒstɪkə; *NAmE* 'swɑːs-/ *noun* an ancient symbol in the form of a cross with its ends bent at an angle of 90°, used in the 20th century as the symbol of the German Nazi party 萬字符（四臂順同一旋轉方向折成直角的正十字形，20 世紀時德國納粹黨以之為黨徽）

swat /swɒt; *NAmE* swɑːt/ *verb* (**-tt-**) **~ sth** to hit sth, especially an insect, using your hand or a flat object 拍，打（昆蟲等） ▶ **swat** *noun*

swatch /swɒtʃ; *NAmE* swɑːtʃ/ *noun* a small piece of cloth used to show people what a larger piece would look or feel like（織物的小塊）樣品；布樣

swathe /sweɪð/ *noun, verb*

■ ***noun*** (also **swath** /swɒθ; *NAmE* swɑːθ/) (*formal*) **1** a long strip of land, especially one on which the plants or crops have been cut（尤指割了莊稼的）一長條田地：*The combine had cut a swathe around the edge of the field.* 聯合收割機把莊稼繞田邊割了一長條。◇ *Development has affected vast swathes of our countryside.* 開發影響了鄉村廣大地區。 **2** a large strip or area of sth 一長條；一長片：*The mountains rose above a swathe of thick cloud.* 群峰聳立在雲海之上。

IDM **cut a 'swathe through sth** (of a person, fire, etc. 人、火等) to pass through a particular area destroying a large part of it 把（某地的一大片）夷為平地；使…大部份遭受破壞

■ ***verb*** [usually passive] **~ sb/sth (in sth)** (*formal*) to wrap or cover sb/sth in sth 包；裹；覆蓋：*He was lying on the hospital bed, swathed in bandages.* 他裹着繃帶，躺在醫院的病牀上。

'SWAT team *noun* (*especially US*) a group of police officers who are especially trained to deal with violent situations. SWAT stands for 'Special Weapons and Tactics'. 特警隊（SWAT 全寫為 Special Weapons and Tactics）

sway /sweɪ/ *verb, noun*

■ ***verb*** **1** [I, T] to move slowly from side to side; to move sth in this way（使）搖擺，搖動：**(+ adv./prep.)** *The branches were swaying in the wind.* 樹枝在風中搖曳。◇ *Vicky swayed and fell.* 維基搖晃着倒下了。◇ **~ sth (+ adv./prep.)** *They danced rhythmically, swaying their hips to the music.* 他們伴着音樂扭動屁股，有節奏地跳舞。 **2** [T, often passive] **~ sb** to persuade sb to believe sth or do sth 說服；使相信；使動搖 **SYN** **influence**：*He's easily swayed.* 他很容易動搖。◇ *She wasn't swayed by his good looks or his clever talk.* 他相貌不凡，談吐風趣，但她不為其所動。

■ ***noun*** [U] **1** a movement from side to side 搖擺；擺動 **2** (*literary*) power or influence over sb 統治；勢力；支配；控制；影響：*Rebel forces* ***hold sway*** *over much of the island.* 該島很大一部份控制在叛軍手裏。◇ *He was quick to exploit those who fell* ***under his sway****.* 他毫不猶豫地利用受他控制的那些人。

swear 🔑 /sweə(r); *NAmE* swer/ *verb* (**swore** /swɔː(r)/, **sworn** /swɔːn; *NAmE* swɔːrn/)

1 🔑 [I] to use rude or offensive language, usually because you are angry 咒罵；詛咒；說髒話：*She fell over and swore loudly.* 她摔倒了，大罵了一聲。◇ **~ at sb/sth** *Why did you let him swear at you like that?* 你怎麼讓他那樣辱罵你呢？ **2** 🔑 [T, no passive] to make a serious promise to do sth 鄭重承諾；發誓要；表示決心要 **SYN** **vow**：**~ sth** *He swore revenge on the man who had killed his father.* 他發誓要向那個殺死他父親的人報仇。◇ **~ (that) …** *I swear (that) I'll never leave you.* 我保證決不離開你。 **HELP** 'That' is usually left out, especially in speech. * that 常省略，在口語中尤其如此。◇ **~ to do sth** *She made him swear not to tell anyone.* 她要他發誓不告訴任何人。 **3** 🔑 [T] to promise that you are telling the truth 賭咒發誓地說；肯定地說：**~ (that) …** *She swore (that) she'd never seen him before.* 她明確表示自己以前從未見過他。◇ ***I could have sworn*** (= I am sure) *I heard the phone ring.* 我敢肯定我聽見電話鈴響了。◇ **~ to sb/on sth (that) …** ***I swear to God*** *I had nothing to do with it.* 我可以對天發誓，這跟我一點關係也沒有。 **4** 🔑 [I, T] to make a public or official promise, especially in court（尤指在法庭上）發誓，鄭重承諾：**~ (on sth)** *Witnesses were required to swear on the Bible.* 證人須手按《聖經》宣誓。◇ **~ that …** *Are you willing to stand up in court and swear that you don't recognize him?* 你願出庭起誓說你不認識他嗎？◇ **~ to do sth** *Remember, you have sworn to tell the truth.* 別忘記，你宣過誓要講實話。◇ **~ sth** *Barons had to swear an oath of allegiance to the king.* 男爵須宣誓效忠國王。 **5** [T] **~ sb to secrecy/silence** to make sb promise not to tell sth to anyone 使起誓（保密）：*Everyone was sworn to secrecy about what had happened.* 關於已發生的事，每個人都依照要求起誓不外傳。 ➲ see also SWORN *adj.*

IDM **swear 'blind** (*informal*) to say that sth is definitely true 一口咬定 **swear like a 'trooper** (*old-fashioned, BrE*) to often use very rude or offensive language 滿口髒話；動不動就破口大罵

PHR V **'swear by sb/sth** **1** to name sb/sth to show that you are making a serious promise 以…名義發誓；對…發誓：*I swear by almighty God that I will tell the truth.* 我向全能的上帝起誓，我以下所說句句屬實。 **2** (not used in the progressive tenses 不用於進行時) to be certain that sth is good or useful 極信賴；對…推崇備至：*She swears by meditation as a way of relieving stress.* 她深信冥想有助於緩解壓力。 **ˌswear sb↔ˈin | ˌswear sb ˈinto sth** [often passive] to make sb promise to do a job correctly, to be loyal to an organization, a country, etc. 使某人宣誓就職；使某人宣誓忠於某組織（或國家等）：*He was sworn in as president.* 他宣誓就任總統。◇ *The new prime minister was sworn into office.* 新首相宣誓就職。 ➲ related noun SWEARING-IN **ˌswear ˈoff sth** (*informal*) to promise that you will not do or use sth again 保證不再做某事（或用某物）；發誓放棄…：*I decided to swear off burgers forever.* 我決心永遠不再吃漢堡包。 **ˈswear to sth** (*informal*) to say that sth is definitely true 一口咬定：*I think I put the keys back in the drawer, but I couldn't swear to it* (= I'm not completely sure). 我想我把鑰匙放回抽屜裏了，不過我不敢肯定。

swear·ing 0-π /ˈsweərɪŋ; *NAmE* ˈswerɪŋ/ *noun* [U] rude or offensive language 詛咒語；罵人的話；髒話：*I was shocked at the swearing.* 我聽到這髒話很震驚。

ˌswearing-ˈin *noun* [U, sing.] the act of publicly asking sb to promise to be loyal and perform their duties well when they start a new job, etc. 宣誓就職：*the swearing-in of the new President* 新總統的宣誓就職

ˈswear word *noun* a rude or offensive word, used, for example, to express anger（表示氣憤等的）詛咒語，罵人的話，髒話 SYN **expletive**

sweat 0-π /swet/ *noun, verb*

■ ***noun***

▸ LIQUID ON SKIN 汗水 **1** 0-π [U] drops of liquid that appear on the surface of your skin when you are hot, ill/sick or afraid 汗 SYN **perspiration**：*beads of sweat* 汗珠 ◇ *She wiped the sweat from her face.* 她擦去臉上的汗水。◇ *By the end of the match, the sweat was pouring off him.* 到比賽結束時，他已經大汗淋漓了。 ➲ see also SWEATY **2** 0-π [usually sing.] the state of being covered with sweat 出汗；流汗；一身汗：*I woke up in a sweat.* 我醒來時渾身是汗。◇ *She completed the routine without even* ***working up a sweat.*** 她完成了一套常規動作，連一滴汗都沒出。◇ *He* ***breaks out in a sweat*** *just at the thought of flying.* 他一想到飛行，就渾身冒汗。◇ *He started having night sweats.* 他開始夜間盜汗。 ➲ see also COLD SWEAT

▸ HARD WORK 繁重的工作 **3** [U] hard work or effort 繁重的工作；艱苦的勞動；累活兒；艱苦努力：(*informal*) *Growing your own vegetables sounds like a lot of sweat.* 自己種菜吃，這恐怕很累吧。◇ (*literary*) *She achieved success by* ***the sweat of her brow*** (= by working very hard). 她靠吃苦流汗獲得了成功。

S

▸ CLOTHES 衣服 **4 sweats** [pl.] (*informal, especially NAmE*) a SWEATSUIT or SWEATPANTS 運動服；運動褲：*I hung around the house all day in my sweats.* 我穿着運動服在家裏晃蕩了一整天。

IDM **be/get in a ˈsweat (about sth)** to be/become anxious or frightened about sth（為某事）擔心，焦慮，害怕 **break ˈsweat** (*BrE*) (*NAmE* **break a ˈsweat**) (*informal*) to use a lot of physical effort 花大力氣；苦幹：*He hardly needed to break sweat to reach the final.* 他幾乎不費勁兒就取得了決賽權。 **no ˈsweat** (*informal*) used to tell sb that sth is not difficult or a problem when they thank you or ask you to do sth（回答致謝或請求）沒什麼，小事一樁：*'Thanks for everything.' 'Hey, no sweat!'* "謝謝你幫了這麼多忙。" "嘿，沒什麼！" ➲ more at BLOOD *n.*

■ ***verb***

▸ PRODUCE LIQUID ON SKIN/SURFACE 出汗；滲出液體 **1** 0-π [I, T] when you **sweat**, drops of liquid appear on the surface of your skin, for example when you are hot, ill/sick or afraid 出汗；流汗 SYN **perspire**：*to sweat heavily* 汗流浹背 ◇ **~ sth** *He was* ***sweating buckets*** (= a lot). 他大汗淋漓。 **2** [I] if sth **sweats**, the liquid that is contained in it appears on its surface（物體表面）滲出水分，結水珠：*The cheese was beginning to sweat.* 奶酪開始出水了。

▸ WORK HARD 努力工作 **3** [I] **~ (over sth)** to work hard at sth 艱苦努力；辛苦地幹：*Are you still sweating over that report?* 你還在為那篇報道傷腦筋嗎？

▸ WORRY 擔心 **4** [I] (*informal*) to worry or feel anxious about sth 擔心；焦慮；不安：*They really made me sweat during the interview.* 面試過程中，他們的確使我忐忑不安。

▸ HEAT FOOD 烹調 **5** [T, I] **~ (sth)** (*BrE*) if you **sweat** meat or vegetables or let them **sweat**, you heat them slowly with a little fat in a pan that is covered with a lid 燜

IDM **don't ˈsweat it** (*NAmE, informal*) used to tell sb to stop worrying about sth 別擔心；別發愁 **don't sweat the ˈsmall stuff** (*NAmE, informal*) used to tell sb not to worry about small details or unimportant things 不要為雞毛蒜皮的事傷腦筋 **sweat ˈblood** (*informal*) to work very hard 苦幹；賣命地工作 ➲ more at GUT *n.*

PHR V **ˌsweat sth↔ˈoff** to lose weight by doing a lot of hard exercise to make yourself sweat 通過排汗減輕體重 **ˌsweat it ˈout** (*informal*) to be waiting for sth difficult or unpleasant to end, and be feeling anxious about it 熬過；焦急地等待到最後

sweat·band /ˈswetbænd/ *noun* a band of cloth worn around the head or wrist, for absorbing sweat（紮在頭上或手腕上的）吸汗帶

ˌsweated ˈlabour *noun* [U] (*BrE*) hard work that is done for low wages in poor conditions; the people who do this work 血汗活兒（勞動條件惡劣、工資低廉）；血汗勞工

sweat·er 0-π /ˈswetə(r)/ *noun* a knitted piece of clothing made of wool or cotton for the upper part of the body, with long sleeves. In British English the word is used to describe a piece of clothing with no buttons. In American English a sweater can have buttons and be like a jacket. 毛衣，線衣（英式英語指套頭無扣的；美式英語可指開襟有扣的） ➲ VISUAL VOCAB page V63

sweat·pants /ˈswetpænts/ (also *informal* **sweats**) *noun* [pl.] (*especially NAmE*) loose warm trousers/pants, usually made of thick cotton and worn for relaxing or playing sports in（厚長）運動褲

sweat·shirt /ˈswetʃɜːt; *NAmE* -ʃɜːrt/ *noun* a piece of clothing for the upper part of the body, with long sleeves, usually made of thick cotton and often worn for sports（長袖）運動衫

sweat·shop /ˈswetʃɒp; *NAmE* -ʃɑːp/ *noun* (*disapproving*) a place where people work for low wages in poor conditions 血汗工廠，血汗工場（工資低廉、勞動條件惡劣）

sweat·suit /ˈswetsuːt; *BrE* also -sjuːt/ *noun* (also *informal* **sweats** [pl.]) (both *NAmE*) a sweatshirt and SWEATPANTS worn together, for relaxing or playing sports in（長袖）運動服

sweaty /ˈsweti/ *adj.* (**sweat·ier**, **sweati·est**) **1** covered or damp with sweat 滿是汗的；汗津津的；汗水濕透的：*sweaty feet* 汗濕的腳 ◇ *He felt all hot and sweaty.* 他感覺全身發熱，滿身是汗。 **2** [only before noun] making you become hot and covered with sweat 熱得讓人出汗的：*It was sweaty work, under the hot sun.* 在火辣辣的太陽下幹這活兒，讓人汗流浹背。

swede /swiːd/ (*BrE*) (*NAmE* **ru·ta·baga**) (*ScotE* **tur·nip**) *noun* [C, U] a large round yellow root vegetable 大頭菜 ➲ VISUAL VOCAB page V31

sweep 0-π /swiːp/ *verb, noun*

■ ***verb*** (**swept**, **swept** /swept/)

▸ WITH BRUSH OR HAND 用刷子或手 **1** 0-π [T, I] to clean a room, surface, etc. using a BROOM (= a type of brush on a long handle) 掃；打掃；清掃：**~ (sth)** *to sweep the floor* 清掃地板 ◇ **~ sth + adj.** *The showroom had been emptied and swept clean.* 陳列室已經清理出來，打掃乾淨了。 **2** 0-π [T] **~ sth + adv./prep.** to remove sth from a surface using a brush, your hand, etc. 掃去；清除：*She swept the crumbs into the wastebasket.* 她把麪包屑掃進廢紙簍裏。◇ *He swept the leaves up into a pile.* 他把樹葉掃成一堆。

▸ MOVE QUICKLY/WITH FORCE 快速／猛烈移動 **3** [T] **~ sb/sth + adv./prep.** to move or push sb/sth suddenly and with a lot of force（迅猛地）推送，吹走，沖走，帶走：*The little boat was swept out to sea.* 小船被吹到大海去了。◇ *She let herself be swept along by the crowd.* 她任由自己被人流挾裹着前行。 **4** [I, T] (of weather, fire, etc. 風、

雨、雪、火等) to move suddenly and/or with force over an area or in a particular direction 猛烈吹過；掠過；席捲；橫掃：**+ adv./prep.** *Rain swept in through the broken windows.* 雨水從破窗戶打進屋內。◇ **~ sth** *Strong winds regularly sweep the islands.* 這些島上經常颳大風。

▸ **OF A PERSON 人 5** [I] **+ adv./prep.** to move quickly and/or smoothly, especially in a way that impresses or is intended to impress other people 步態輕盈地走；大模大樣地走：*Without another word she swept out of the room.* 她再沒說話，大模大樣地走出房間。◇ (*figurative*) *He swept into the lead with an almost perfect performance.* 他以幾近完美的表現跨入領先位置。 **6** [T] **~ sth + adv./prep.** to move sth, especially your hand or arm, quickly and smoothly in a particular direction 揮動，舞動（手、臂等）：*He rushed to greet her, sweeping his arms wide.* 他張開雙臂舞動着，衝過去迎接她。

▸ **OF FEELINGS 感受 7** [I] **+ adv./prep.** to suddenly affect sb strongly 突然襲來：*A wave of tiredness swept over her.* 她感到渾身疲憊。◇ *Memories came sweeping back.* 往事倏地又浮現在腦海中。

▸ **OF IDEAS/FASHIONS 思想；時尚 8** [I, T] to spread quickly 迅速傳播：**+ adv./prep.** *Rumours of his resignation swept through the company.* 他辭職的傳言在全公司傳播開了。◇ **~ sth** *the latest craze sweeping America* 風靡美國的最新時尚

▸ **LOOK/MOVE OVER AREA 掃視；掠過 9** [I, T] to move over an area, especially in order to look for sth 掃視；掠過；搜索：**+ adv./prep.** *His eyes swept around the room.* 他把房間掃視了一遍。◇ **~ sth** *Searchlights swept the sky.* 探照燈在空中掃來掃去。

▸ **TOUCH SURFACE 輕觸表面 10** [T] **~ sth** to move, or move sth, over a surface, touching it lightly（使）輕輕掠過，輕輕擦過：*Her dress swept the ground as she walked.* 她行走時衣裙拖在地上。

▸ **HAIR 頭髮 11** [T] **~ sth + adv./prep.** to brush, COMB, etc. your hair in a particular direction 梳；刷；掠：*Her hair was swept back from her face.* 她的頭髮是從前邊往後梳的。

▸ **OF LANDSCAPE 地貌 12** [I] **+ adv./prep.** to form a long smooth curve 蜿蜒；呈緩坡延伸：*The hotel gardens sweep down to the beach.* 旅館的花園呈緩坡一直延伸到海灘。

▸ **IN SPORT 體育運動 13** [T] **~ sth** (*NAmE*) to win all the games in a series of games against another team or all the parts of a contest（在系列比賽中）獲得全部勝利，囊括各項冠軍：*The Blue Jays have a chance to sweep the series.* 藍鳥隊有機會橫掃系列賽。◇ *New Jersey swept Detroit last season.* 在上個賽季，新澤西隊全勝底特律隊。

IDM **sweep the 'board** to win all the prizes, etc. in a competition（在比賽中）囊括所有獎項 **,sweep sb off their 'feet** to make sb fall suddenly and deeply in love with you 使某人立刻迷上自己；使某人對自己一見傾心 **sweep (sb) to 'power** to win an election by a large number of votes; to make sb win an election with a large number of votes（使某人）以壓倒性優勢在選舉中獲勝 **sweep to 'victory** to win a contest easily 輕易贏得（競賽）：*Obama swept to victory in 2008.* 奧巴馬在 2008 年輕鬆取勝。 **sweep sth under the 'carpet** (*US* also **sweep sth under the 'rug**) to try to stop people from finding out about sth wrong, illegal, embarrassing, etc. that has happened or that you have done 掩蓋某事

PHR V **,sweep sb a'long/a'way** [usually passive] to make sb very interested or involved in sth, especially in a way that makes them forget everything else 使某人醉心；驅使某人專注：*They were swept along by the force of their emotions.* 他們受感情的威力所驅使。 **,sweep sth↔a'side** to ignore sth completely 對…置之不理；不理會；全然無視：*All their advice was swept aside.* 他們所有的忠告全被當成了耳邊風。 **,sweep sth↔a'way** to get rid of sth completely 消滅；徹底消除；完全打消：*Any doubts had long since been swept away.* 一切懷疑早已完全消除。 **,sweep sth↔'out** to remove all the dust, dirt, etc. from a room or building using a brush 打掃乾淨，清掃乾淨（房間等） **,sweep sb↔'up** to lift sb up with a sudden smooth movement 一把抱起某人：*He swept her up into his arms.* 他一把將她抱進懷裏。

■ ***noun***

▸ **WITH BRUSH 用刷子 1** [C, usually sing.] an act of cleaning a room, surface, etc. using a BROOM 掃；打掃；清掃：*Give the room a good sweep.* 把房間好好打掃一下。

▸ **CURVING MOVEMENT 揮動 2** [C] a smooth curving movement 揮動；掠：*He indicated the door with a sweep of his arm.* 他一揮胳膊指向門。

▸ **LANDSCAPE 地貌 3** [C, usually sing.] a long, often curved, piece of road, river, coast, etc.（道路、河流、海岸等）一長段，綿延彎曲的地帶，呈緩坡狀的地帶：*the broad sweep of white cliffs around the bay* 環繞海灣的一片白色懸崖

▸ **RANGE 範圍 4** [U] the range of an idea, a piece of writing, etc. that considers many different things 廣泛性；廣博的範圍；廣度：*Her book covers the long sweep of the country's history.* 她的著作涵蓋了該國漫長的歷史。

▸ **MOVEMENT/SEARCH OVER AREA 巡行；搜索 5** [C] a movement over an area, for example in order to search for sth or attack sth 巡行；搜索；掃蕩：*The rescue helicopter made another sweep over the bay.* 救援直升機在海灣上空又搜索了一遍。

▸ **CHIMNEY 煙囱 6** [C] = CHIMNEY SWEEP

▸ **GAMBLING 賭博 7** [C] (*NAmE* also **sweeps**) (*informal*) = SWEEPSTAKE

▸ **IN SPORT 體育運動 8** [C] (*NAmE*) a series of games that a team wins against another team; the fact of winning all the parts of a contest（兩支球隊對賽其中一方）全勝的一系列比賽；囊括冠軍：*a World Series sweep* 在世界系列賽中囊括冠軍

▸ **TELEVISION 電視 9** **the sweeps** [pl.] (*NAmE*) a time when television companies examine their programmes to find out which ones are the most popular, especially in order to calculate advertising rates 節目調查時間（電視台為查明節目受歡迎度，尤為計算廣告費） **IDM** see CLEAN *adj.*

sweep·er /ˈswiːpə(r)/ *noun* **1** a person whose job is to sweep sth 打掃者；清掃者；清潔工：*a road sweeper* 馬路清潔工 **2** a thing that sweeps sth 清掃器；清潔器：*a carpet sweeper* 地毯清潔器 ➲ see also MINESWEEPER **3** (*BrE*) (in football (SOCCER) 足球) a player who plays behind the other defending players in order to try and stop anyone who passes them 自由中衛

sweep·ing /ˈswiːpɪŋ/ *adj.* **1** [usually before noun] having an important effect on a large part of sth 影響廣泛的；大範圍的；根本性的：***sweeping reforms/changes*** 全面改革；徹底變化 ◇ *Security forces were given sweeping powers to search homes.* 安全部隊獲授予入戶搜查的絕對權力。 **2** [usually before noun] (*disapproving*) too general and failing to think about or understand particular examples（過分）籠統的；一概而論的：***a sweeping generalization/statement*** 籠統的概括；一概而論的說法 **3 ~ victory** a victory by a large number of votes, etc.（在投票等中的）大勝，全勝 **4** [only before noun] forming a curved shape 弧線的；彎曲的：*a sweeping gesture* (= with your hand or arm) 揮動的動作 ◇ *a sweeping staircase* 弧形樓梯

sweep·stake /ˈswiːpsteɪk/ (*NAmE* also **sweep·stakes**) *noun* a type of betting in which the winner gets all the money bet by everyone else 賭金全贏制

sweet 0→ /swiːt/ *adj., noun*

■ ***adj.*** (**sweet·er, sweet·est**)

▸ **FOOD/DRINK 食物；飲料 1** 0→ containing, or tasting as if it contains, a lot of sugar 含糖的；甜的：*a cup of hot sweet tea* 一杯加糖熱茶 ◇ *sweet food* 甜食 ◇ *I had a craving for something sweet.* 我饞甜的東西。◇ *This wine is too sweet for me.* 這種葡萄酒對我來說太甜了。 ➲ compare BITTER (4), SALTY (1) **OPP** **sour**

▸ **SMELL 氣味 2** 0→ having a pleasant smell 香的；芳香的；芬芳的 **SYN** **fragrant**：*a sweet-smelling rose* 芬芳的玫瑰 ◇ *The air was sweet with incense.* 空氣中瀰漫着燃香的香氣。

▸ **SOUND 聲音 3** having a pleasant sound 悅耳的；好聽的：*a sweet voice* 甜潤的嗓音

S

▸ **PURE 純淨 4** pleasant and not containing any harmful substances 純淨的；清新的；新鮮的：*the sweet air of a mountain village* 山村的清新空氣

▸ **SATISFYING 令人滿意 5** making you feel happy and/or satisfied 令人愉快的；愜意的；舒暢的：*Goodnight.* ***Sweet dreams.*** 晚安。祝你做個甜蜜的夢。◊ *I can't tell you how sweet this victory is.* 取得這場勝利，別提多麼痛快了。

▸ **ATTRACTIVE 惹人喜愛 6** (*especially BrE*) (especially of children or small things 尤指兒童或小物品) attractive 惹人喜愛的；可愛的 **SYN cute**：*His sister's a sweet young thing.* 他妹妹是個討人喜歡的小傢伙。◊ *You look sweet in this photograph.* 你這張照片照得很可愛。◊ *We stayed in a sweet little hotel on the seafront.* 我們住在海濱一家小巧玲瓏的旅館裏。

▸ **KIND 善良 7** having or showing a kind character 善良的；好心的；和藹的；溫柔的：*She gave him her sweetest smile.* 她向他投以極溫柔的一笑。◊ ***It was sweet of them to offer to help.*** 他們主動幫忙，真是好心人。

▸ **GOOD 好 8 Sweet!** (*NAmE, informal*) used to show that you approve of sth（表示讚許）好啊，太棒了：*Free tickets? Sweet!* 免費贈票？太棒了！

IDM be 'sweet on sb (*old-fashioned, informal*) to like sb very much in a romantic way 熱戀某人 **have a sweet 'tooth** (*informal*) to like food that contains a lot of sugar 愛吃甜食 **in your ˌown sweet 'time/'way** how and when you want to, even though this might annoy other people 任憑自己的意願：*He always does the work, but in his own sweet time.* 工作他總是在做，但只在自己高興的時候做。 **keep sb 'sweet** (*informal*) to say or do pleasant things in order to keep sb in a good mood so that they will agree to do sth for you 討好某人；哄着某人 **she's 'sweet** (*AustralE, NZE, informal*) everything is all right 一切都好 **sweet F'A | sweet Fanny 'Adams** (*BrE, informal*) nothing at all. People say 'sweet FA' to avoid saying 'fuck all'. 一點都沒有，什麼都沒有（委婉說法，與 fuck all 同義） **sweet 'nothings** romantic words 情話：*to whisper sweet nothings in sb's ear* 向某人低訴喁喁情話 **the sweet smell of suc'cess** (*informal*) the pleasant feeling of being successful 成功的喜悅；成功的美妙滋味 ➲ more at HOME *n.*, ROSE *n.*, SHORT *adj.*

■ ***noun***

▸ **FOOD 食物 1** 🔑 [C] (*BrE*) a small piece of sweet food, usually made with sugar and/or chocolate and eaten between meals 糖果 **SYN candy**：*a packet of boiled sweets* 一袋硬糖 ◊ *a sweet shop* 糖果店 **2** [C, U] (*BrE*) a sweet dish eaten at the end of a meal（餐後的）甜食，甜點 **SYN afters, dessert, pudding**：*I haven't made a sweet today.* 我今天沒做甜點。◊ *Would you like some more sweet?* 你想再吃點甜食嗎？

▸ **PERSON 人 3** [U] (*old-fashioned*) a way of addressing sb that you like or love（稱呼親愛的人）親愛的，寶貝兒：*Don't you worry, my sweet.* 你可別擔心，寶貝兒。

ˌsweet-and-'sour *adj.* [only before noun] (of food 食物) cooked in a sauce that contains sugar and VINEGAR or lemon 甜酸的；糖醋的：*Chinese sweet-and-sour pork* 中式糖醋豬肉

sweet·bread /'swiːtbred/ *noun* [usually pl.] the THYMUS (= an organ in the neck) or the PANCREAS (= an organ near the stomach) of a young cow or sheep, eaten as food（食用的小牛或羊的）胸腺，胰臟

sweet·corn /'swiːtkɔːn; *NAmE* -kɔːrn/ (*BrE*) (*NAmE* **corn**) *noun* [U] the yellow seeds of a type of MAIZE (CORN) plant, also called sweetcorn, which grow on thick STEMS and are cooked and eaten as a vegetable（甜）玉米粒：*tinned sweetcorn* 甜玉米粒罐頭 ➲ **VISUAL VOCAB** page V31 ➲ see also CORN ON THE COB

sweet·en /'swiːtn/ *verb* **1 ~ sth** to make food or drinks taste sweeter by adding sugar, etc. 使變甜；加糖於 **2 ~ sb (up)** (*informal*) to try to make sb more willing to help you, agree to sth, etc. by giving them money, praising them, etc. 討好；拉攏；哄；收買；恭維 **3 ~ sth** to make sth more pleasant or acceptable 使令人愉快；使更合心意；改善；緩和 **IDM** see PILL *n.*

sweet·en·er /'swiːtnə(r)/ *noun* **1** [U, C] a substance used to make food or drink taste sweeter, used instead of sugar 甜味劑：*artificial sweetener(s)* 人造甜味劑 ➲ **COLLOCATIONS** at DIET **2** [C] (*informal*) something that is given to sb in order to persuade them to do sth, especially when this is done in a secret or dishonest way 用以拉攏人的錢物；賄賂

sweet·heart /'swiːthɑːt; *NAmE* -hɑːrt/ *noun* **1** [sing.] (*informal*) used to address sb in a way that shows affection（用作稱呼語）親愛的，寶貝兒：*Do you want a drink, sweetheart?* 想喝一杯嗎，親愛的？**2** [C] (*becoming old-fashioned*) a person with whom sb is having a romantic relationship 戀人；愛人；心上人：*They were childhood sweethearts.* 他們倆是青梅竹馬。

sweetie /'swiːti/ *noun* (*informal*) **1** [C] (*BrE*) a child's word for a sweet/a piece of candy（兒童語）糖果 **2** [C] a person who is kind and easy to like 招人喜歡的人；可愛的人：*He's a real sweetie.* 他的確招人喜歡。**3** [sing.] used to address sb in a way that shows affection（用作稱呼語）親愛的

sweet·ish /'swiːtɪʃ/ *adj.* fairly sweet 有點甜的；帶甜味的

sweet·ly /'swiːtli/ *adv.* **1** in a pleasant way 令人愉快地；可愛地：*She smiled sweetly at him.* 她朝他嫣然一笑。**2** in a way that smells sweet 氣味芬芳地：*a sweetly scented flower* 氣味芬芳的花 **3** in a way that is without difficulties or problems 順利地；順順當當地：*Everything went sweetly and according to plan.* 一切按計劃順利進行。◊ *He headed the ball sweetly into the back of the net.* 他把球穩穩地頂入網窩。

sweet·meat /'swiːtmiːt/ *noun* (*old use*) a sweet/candy; any food preserved in sugar 糖果；甜食；蜜餞；果脯

sweet·ness /'swiːtnəs/ *noun* [U] **1** the quality of being pleasant 令人愉快；討人喜歡：*a smile of great sweetness* 十分甜蜜的微笑 **2** the quality of tasting or smelling sweet 甜；芬芳：*The air was filled with the sweetness of mimosa.* 空氣中彌漫着含羞草的芬芳。

IDM be (all) ˌsweetness and 'light 1 (of a person 人) to be pleasant, friendly and polite 和藹可親；溫文爾雅 **2** (of a situation 情況) to be enjoyable and easy to deal with 簡單而有趣

ˌsweet 'pea *noun* a climbing garden plant with pale flowers that have a sweet smell 香豌豆 ➲ **VISUAL VOCAB** page V11

ˌsweet 'pepper (*BrE* also **pep·per**) (*NAmE* also **'bell pepper**) *noun* a hollow fruit, usually red, green or yellow, eaten as a vegetable either raw or cooked 甜椒；柿子椒；燈籠椒 ➲ **VISUAL VOCAB** page V31

ˌsweet po'tato *noun* [C, U] a root vegetable that looks like a red potato, but that is yellow inside and tastes sweet 紅薯；甘薯 ➲ **VISUAL VOCAB** page V31

'sweet spot *noun* **1** the area on a BAT which hits the ball in the most effective way（球拍或球棒的）最佳擊球點，甜區 **2** a location or combination of characteristics that produces the best results 最有效點；所有特點的完美組合：*This series aims to hit a sweet spot between romantic comedy and thriller.* 這連續劇旨在達到浪漫喜劇和驚悚片的完美結合。

'sweet-talk *verb* **~ sb (into sth/into doing sth)** (*disapproving*) to try to persuade sb to do sth by praising them and telling them things they like to hear 對…甜言蜜語；給…灌迷魂湯：*I can't believe you let him sweet-talk you into working for him!* 我無法相信，他幾句好話就哄得你為他效力！▸ **'sweet talk** *noun* [U]

sweet Wil·liam /ˌswiːt 'wɪljəm/ *noun* a garden plant with groups of red, pink, or white flowers that smell sweet 美國石竹，鬚苞石竹（花園植物，開紅色、粉紅或白色芳香花簇）

swell 🔑 /swel/ *verb, noun, adj.*

■ ***verb*** (**swelled** /sweld/, **swol·len** /'swəʊlən; *NAmE* 'swoʊ-/ or **swelled, swelled**) **1** 🔑 [I] **~ (up)** to become bigger or rounder 膨脹；腫脹：*Her arm was beginning to swell up where the bee had stung her.* 她胳膊給蜜蜂蜇了，腫了起來。**2** [I, T] to curve out or make sth curve out（使）凸出，鼓出：**~ (out)** *The sails swelled (out) in the wind.* 船帆鼓滿了風。◊ **~ sth (out)** *The wind swelled (out) the sails.* 風鼓起了帆。**3** [T, I] to increase or make sth increase in number or size （使）增加，增大，擴大：**~ sth (to sth)** *Last year's profits were swelled by a fall in production costs.* 去年因生產成本下降，利潤有所增加。◇ *We are looking for more volunteers to* ***swell the ranks*** (= increase the number) *of those already helping.* 我們期盼有更多的志願者加入，以壯大目前已在提供幫助的隊伍。◇ **~ (to sth)** *Membership has swelled to over 20 000.* 成員增加到 2 萬餘人。**OPP** **shrink** **4** [I] (of a sound 聲音) to become louder 變得更響亮；增強：*The cheering swelled through the hall.* 歡呼聲越來越大，響徹大廳。**5** [I] **~ (with sth)** to be filled with a strong emotion 充滿（激情）：*to swell with pride* 滿腔豪情 ➲ see also SWOLLEN *adj.*

■ ***noun*** **1** [C, usually sing.] the movement of the sea when it rises and falls without the waves breaking 海浪的湧動；湧浪：*The boat was caught in a heavy* (= strong) *swell.* 船遇上了大浪湧。**2** [sing.] (*formal*) the curved shape of sth, especially a part of the body（尤指身體部位）凸起的形狀，鼓出處，隆起處：*the firm swell of her breasts* 她挺拔的乳峰 **3** [sing.] a situation in which sth increases in size, number, strength, etc. 增加；增大；擴大；增強：*a growing swell of support* 越來越多的支持◇ *a swell of pride* 自豪感的增強 ➲ see also GROUNDSWELL **4** [sing.] (of music or noise 樂音或噪聲) a gradual increase in the volume of sth 逐漸增強 **SYN** **crescendo** **5** (*old-fashioned, informal*) an important or fashionable person 重要人士；時髦人物

■ ***adj.*** (*old-fashioned, NAmE, informal*) very good, enjoyable, etc. 很愉快的；極有趣的：*We had a swell time.* 我們過得開心極了。

swell·ing 0‑ᵂ /ˈswelɪŋ/ *noun*
1 0‑ᵂ [U] the condition of being larger or rounder than normal (= of being SWOLLEN) 膨脹；腫脹：*Use ice to reduce the swelling.* 用冰敷消腫。**2** 0‑ᵂ [C] a place on your body that has become larger or rounder than normal as the result of an illness or injury 腫脹處；浮腫處：*The fall left her with a painful swelling above her eye.* 她摔了一跤，眼睛上方起了一個包，挺疼的。

swel·ter /ˈsweltə(r)/ *verb* [I] to be very hot in a way that makes you feel uncomfortable 熱得難受：*Passengers sweltered in temperatures of over 90°F.* 在超過 90 華氏度的高温下，乘客熱得要命。▸ **swel·ter·ing** *adj.* **SYN** **stifling**：*sweltering heat* 酷熱難耐的高温 **swel·ter·ing·ly** *adv.*：*swelteringly hot* 酷熱

swept *past tense, past part.* of SWEEP

ˌswept-ˈback *adj.* [only before noun] **1** (of hair 頭髮) pulled back from your face 往後梳的；往後紮的 **2** (of an aircraft wing 機翼) pointing backwards 後掠的；後彎的

ˈswept-up *adj.* = UPSWEPT

swerve /swɜːv; *NAmE* swɜːrv/ *verb* [I] (especially of a vehicle 尤指車輛等) to change direction suddenly, especially in order to avoid hitting sb/sth 突然轉向；急轉彎：*She swerved sharply to avoid a cyclist.* 她猛地急轉彎，以避開一個騎自行車的人。◇ *The bus suddenly swerved into his path.* 公共汽車突然拐到了他走的路上。◇ *The ball swerved into the net.* 球在空中劃了一條弧線，進了球門。▸ **swerve** *noun*

swift /swɪft/ *adj., noun*
■ ***adj.*** (**swift·er**, **swift·est**) **1** happening or done quickly and immediately; doing sth quickly 迅即發生的；馬上做出的；迅速的：*swift action* 迅速的行動◇ *a swift decision* 迅即作出的決定◇ **~ to do sth** *The White House was swift to deny the rumours.* 白宮立刻對這些傳言予以否認。**2** moving very quickly; able to move very quickly 速度快的；敏捷的；矯健的：*a swift current* 湍急的水流 ◇ *a swift runner* 跑得飛快的人 ➲ SYNONYMS at FAST ▸ **swift·ly** *adv.*：*She moved swiftly to the rescue.* 她迅速趕來營救。**swift·ness** *noun* [U, sing.]
■ ***noun*** a small bird with long narrow wings, similar to a SWALLOW 雨燕

swig /swɪɡ/ *verb* (**-gg-**) **~ sth** (*informal*) to take a quick drink of sth, especially alcohol 大口喝（酒等）：*They sat around swigging beer from bottles.* 他們閒坐着，對着瓶子大口地喝啤酒。▸ **swig** *noun*：*She took a swig of wine.* 她喝了一大口葡萄酒。

swill /swɪl/ *verb, noun*
■ ***verb*** **1** [T] **~ sth (out/down)** (*especially BrE*) to clean sth by pouring large amounts of water in, on or through it 沖洗；灌洗；涮 **SYN** **rinse**：*She swilled the glasses with clean water.* 她用清水涮了杯子。**2** [T] **~ sth (down)** (*informal*) to drink sth quickly and/or in large quantities 大口喝；痛飲 **3** [T, I] to move, or to make a liquid move, in a particular direction or around a particular place（使）晃盪，搖動，流動：**~ sth + adv./prep.** *He swilled the juice around in his glass.* 他搖了搖杯子裏的果汁。◇ **+ adv./prep.** *Water swilled around in the bottom of the boat.* 船底上的水來回晃盪。
■ ***noun*** **1** (also **pig·swill**) [U] a mixture of waste food and water that is given to pigs to eat（給豬吃的）泔腳，剩飯菜，餿水 **2** [U] (*informal*) drink or food that is unpleasant or of a poor quality 不好喝的飲料；難吃的食物；劣質飲料（或食物）**3** [C, usually sing.] (*informal*) a large amount of a drink that you take into your mouth 一大口飲料：*He had a quick swill of wine.* 他猛地灌下一大口葡萄酒。

swim 0‑ᵂ /swɪm/ *verb, noun*
■ ***verb*** (**swim·ming**, **swam** /swæm/, **swum** /swʌm/) **1** 0‑ᵂ [I, T] (of a person 人) to move through water in a horizontal position using the arms and legs 游水；游泳：*I can't swim.* 我不會游泳。◇ *The boys swam across the lake.* 男孩子們游到了湖對岸。◇ *They spent the day swimming and sunbathing.* 他們整整一天都在游泳和曬太陽。◇ **~ sth** *Can you swim backstroke yet?* 你會仰泳了嗎？◇ *How long will it take her to swim the Channel?* 她游過英吉利海峽得用多長時間？➲ note at BATH **2** 0‑ᵂ [I] **go swimming** to spend time swimming for pleasure 游泳（作為娛樂）：*I go swimming twice a week.* 我每星期游泳兩次。**3** 0‑ᵂ [I] (**+ adv./prep.**) (of a fish, etc. 魚等) to move through or across water 游；游動：*A shoal of fish swam past.* 一群魚游了過去。◇ *Ducks were swimming around on the river.* 鴨子在河面上游來游去。**4** [I] (usually **be swimming**) to be covered with a lot of liquid 浸；泡；灑滿；充溢着：**~ (in sth)** *The main course was swimming in oil.* 主菜油汪汪的。◇ **~ (with sth)** *Her eyes were swimming with tears.* 她兩眼噙滿淚水。**5** [I] (of objects, etc. 物體等) to seem to be moving around, especially when you are ill/sick or drunk 彷彿在旋轉，似在晃動（尤指生病或酒醉時的感覺）：*The pages swam before her eyes.* 書頁彷彿在她眼前晃動。**6** [I] to feel confused and/or as if everything is spinning around 眩暈；感覺天旋地轉：*His head swam and he swayed dizzily.* 他感覺天旋地轉，搖晃起來。**IDM** see SINK *v.*
■ ***noun*** **1** [sing.] a period of time during which you swim 游泳：*Let's* ***go for a swim.*** 我們去游個泳吧。**2** (*especially NAmE*) (in compounds) related to or used for swimming（構成複合詞）與游泳有關的，游泳時用的：*a swim meet* (= a swimming competition between teams) 游泳比賽◇ *swim trunks* 游泳褲
IDM **in the ˈswim (of things)** (*informal*) involved in things that are happening in society or in a particular situation 積極參與社會生活（或某活動）；合潮流

swim·mer /ˈswɪmə(r)/ *noun* a person who can swim; a person who is swimming 會游泳者；游泳者：*a* ***good/strong swimmer*** 水性好的人；擅長游泳的人◇ *They watched the swimmers splashing through the water.* 他們看着游泳的人撲通撲通濺着水花游過去。◇ *a shallow pool for* ***non-swimmers*** 供不會游泳的人用的淺水池

swim·ming 0‑ᵂ /ˈswɪmɪŋ/ *noun* [U]
the sport or activity of swimming 游泳；游泳運動：*Swimming is a good form of exercise.* 游泳是很好的鍛煉方式。➲ VISUAL VOCAB page V45

ˈswimming bath *noun* [usually pl.] (*old-fashioned, BrE*) a public swimming pool inside a building 室內游泳池

ˈswimming cap (also **ˈswimming hat**) (both *BrE*) (also **ˈbathing cap** *NAmE, BrE*) *noun* a soft rubber or plastic cap that fits closely over your head to keep your hair dry while you are swimming 游泳帽

ˈswimming costume *noun* (*BrE*) = SWIMSUIT

swim·ming·ly /ˈswɪmɪŋli/ *adv.* (*informal*) without any problems or difficulties 順利地；順順當當地： *We hope everything will* **go swimmingly**. 我們希望一切進展順利。

ˈswimming pool (also **pool**) *noun* **1** an area of water that has been created for people to swim in 游泳池： *an* **indoor/outdoor swimming pool** 室內／室外游泳池 ◇ *a* **heated swimming pool** 溫水游泳池 ◇ *an* **open-air swimming pool** 露天游泳池 **2** the building that contains a public swimming pool 游泳場；游泳館： *She trained five times a week at her local swimming pool.* 她每星期在當地的游泳池訓練五次。

ˈswimming trunks (also **trunks**) (*NAmE* also **ˈswim trunks**) *noun* [pl.] a piece of clothing covering the lower part of the body and sometimes the top part of the legs, worn by men and boys for swimming（男式）游泳褲： *a pair of swimming trunks* 一條游泳褲 ➲ picture at TRUNK

swim·suit /ˈswɪmsuːt; *BrE* also -sjuːt/ *noun* (*BrE* also **ˈswimming costume**) (also **ˈbathing suit** *NAmE* or *old-fashioned*) a piece of clothing worn for swimming, especially the type worn by women and girls（尤指女式）游泳衣

swim·wear /ˈswɪmweə(r); *NAmE* -wer/ *noun* [U] clothing that you wear for swimming 游泳衣；泳裝

swin·dle /ˈswɪndl/ *verb, noun*

■ ***verb*** to cheat sb in order to get sth, especially money, from them 詐騙；騙取： **~ sb** (**out of sth**) *They swindled him out of hundreds of dollars.* 他們詐騙了他好幾百元。◇ **~ sth** (**out of sb**) *They swindled hundreds of dollars out of him.* 他們詐騙了他好幾百元。 ▸ **swind·ler** /ˈswɪndlə(r)/ *noun* SYN **con man**

■ ***noun*** [usually sing.] a situation in which sb uses dishonest or illegal methods in order to get money from a company, another person, etc. 詐騙；騙取 SYN **con**： *an insurance swindle* 保險詐騙案

swine /swaɪn/ *noun* (*pl.* **swines** or **swine**) **1** [C] (*informal*) an unpleasant person 討厭的人： *He's an arrogant little swine!* 他是個傲慢的小討厭鬼！ **2** [C] (*BrE, informal*) a difficult or unpleasant thing or task 令人不愉快的事物；難處理的東西： *The car can be a swine to start.* 這輛車有時很難發動。 **3 swine** [pl.] (*old use* or *technical* 術語) pigs 豬： *a herd of swine* 一群豬 ◇ ***swine fever*** (= a disease of pigs) 豬瘟 IDM see PEARL

ˈswine flu *noun* [U] **1** a serious illness that affects pigs 豬流感 **2** a serious illness spread between humans, that is GENETICALLY similar to swine flu in pigs, that in some cases causes death（人類感染的）豬流感（基因與豬流感相似，可引致死亡）

swine·herd /ˈswaɪnhɜːd; *NAmE* -hɜːrd/ *noun* (*old use*) a person whose job is to take care of pigs 養豬的人；豬倌

swing /swɪŋ/ *verb, noun*

■ ***verb*** (**swung, swung** /swʌŋ/)

▸ **HANG AND MOVE** 擺動 **1** [I, T] to move backwards or forwards or from side to side while hanging from a fixed point; to make sth do this（使）擺動，搖擺，搖盪： *His arms swung as he walked.* 他邊走邊擺着雙臂。◇ *As he pushed her, she swung higher and higher* (= while sitting on a swing). 隨着他推她，她在鞦韆上越盪越高。◇ **~ from sth** *A set of keys swung from her belt.* 她腰帶上掛着的一串鑰匙擺來擺去。◇ **~ sth** *He sat on the stool, swinging his legs.* 他坐在凳子上晃動着兩條腿。 **2** [I, T] to move from one place to another by holding sth that is fixed and pulling yourself along, up, etc. 縱身躍向；盪向；懸吊到： **+ adv./prep.** *The gunshot sent monkeys swinging away through the trees.* 槍聲一響，猴子紛紛在樹叢中飛躍盪走。◇ **~ yourself + adv./prep.** *He swung himself out of the car.* 他縱身跳下車。

▸ **MOVE IN CURVE** 弧線運動 **3** [I, T] to move or make sth move with a wide curved movement（使）弧線運動，轉彎，轉動： **+ adv./prep.** *A line of cars swung out of the palace gates.* 一隊汽車拐出了宮門。◇ **~ sth + adv./prep.** *He swung his legs over the side of the bed.* 他把兩腿移過來放下牀。◇ **+ adj.** *The door swung open.* 門開了。◇ **~ sth + adj.** *She swung the door open.* 她把門推開。

▸ **TURN QUICKLY** 迅速轉向 **4** [I, T] to turn or change direction suddenly; to make sth do this（使）突然轉向，突然轉身： **+ adv./prep.** *The bus swung sharply to the left.* 公共汽車猛地拐向左邊。◇ **~ sth + adv./prep.** *He swung the camera around to face the opposite direction.* 他猛地將照相機轉了個方向對着反面。

▸ **TRY TO HIT** 試圖擊中 **5** [I, T] to try to hit sb/sth（揮動某物）朝…打去： **~ at sb/sth** *She swung at me with the iron bar.* 她揮着鐵棍朝我打來。◇ **~ sth** (**at sb/sth**) *He swung another punch in my direction.* 他朝着我這邊又揮了一拳。

▸ **CHANGE OPINION/MOOD** 改變意見／情緒 **6** [I, T] to change or make sb/sth change from one opinion, mood, etc. to another（使）改變（意見、情緒等）： **~** (**from A**) (**to B**) *The state has swung from Republican to Democrat.* 這個州原先支持共和黨，現在倒向了民主黨。◇ **~** (**between A and B**) *His emotions swung between fear and curiosity.* 他時而害怕，時而好奇。◇ *The game could swing either way* (= either side could win it). 這場比賽勝負未卜。◇ **~ sb/sth** (**to sth**) *I managed to swing them round to my point of view.* 我設法使他們轉而接受了我的觀點。

▸ **DO/GET STH** 做；獲得 **7** [T] (*informal*) to succeed in getting or achieving sth, sometimes in a slightly dishonest way（有時略微不正當地）獲得，搞到，辦成： **~ sth** *We're trying to* ***swing it*** *so that we can travel on the same flight.* 我們正在想法子，好坐上同一個航班。◇ **~ sb sth** *Is there any chance of you swinging us a couple of tickets?* 你有沒有可能幫我們弄幾張票？

▸ **OF MUSIC** 音樂 **8** [I] to have a strong rhythm 有強勁的節奏；節奏感強

▸ **OF PARTY** 聚會 **9** [I] (*informal*) if a party, etc. **is swinging**, there are a lot of people there having a good time 熱鬧；令人開心

IDM **swing the ˈbalance** = TIP THE BALANCE/SCALES at TIP *v.* **swing both ˈways** (*informal*) to be BISEXUAL (= sexually attracted to both men and women) 雙性戀；既喜歡異性也喜歡同性 **ˌswing for the ˈfences** (*NAmE*) to really try to achieve sth great, even when it is not reasonable to expect to be so successful 全力一搏；迎難而上： *entrepreneurs who think big and swing for the fences* 志向高遠、迎難而上的企業家 **ˌswing into ˈaction** to start doing sth quickly and with a lot of energy 立即行動起來；馬上大幹起來 **ˌswing the ˈlead** (*old-fashioned, BrE, informal*) (usually used in the progressive tenses 通常用於進行時) to pretend to be ill/sick when in fact you are not, especially to avoid work 裝病偷懶： *I don't think there's anything wrong with her—she's just swinging the lead.* 我認為她沒有什麼病，只不過是在裝病偷懶而已。 ORIGIN The lead was a weight at the bottom of a line that sailors used to measure how deep water was when the ship was near land. 'Swinging the lead' was thought to be an easy task, and came to mean avoiding hard work. * lead 是船靠近陸地時水手測量水深用的水鉈。swinging the lead 被認為是件輕鬆的工作，逐漸變成"逃避幹重活"的意思。 ➲ more at ROOM *n.*

PHR V **ˌswing ˈby** | **ˈswing by sth** (*NAmE, informal*) to visit a place or person for a short time 進某處一會兒；短暫拜訪；看望某人一下 SYN **drop by**： *I'll swing by your house on the way home from work.* 下班回家路過時我會到你家一下。

■ ***noun***

▸ **MOVEMENT** 運動 **1** [C] a swinging movement or rhythm 擺動；揮動；轉動；強勁節奏： *He took a wild swing at the ball.* 他對準球猛地揮拍一擊。◇ *the swing of her hips* 她臀部的扭動

▸ **OF OPINION/MOOD** 意見；情緒 **2** [C] a change from one opinion or situation to another; the amount by which sth changes 改變；改變的程度： *He is liable to abrupt* ***mood swings*** (= for example from being very happy to being very sad). 他的情緒容易大起大落。◇ *Voting showed a 10% swing to Labour.* 投票顯示 10% 的人轉而支持工黨。

▸ **HANGING SEAT** 鞦韆 **3** [C] a seat for swinging on, hung from above on ropes or chains 鞦韆： *The kids were playing on the swings.* 孩子們在盪鞦韆。 ➲ VISUAL VOCAB page V37

▸ **IN GOLF** 高爾夫球 **4** [sing.] the swinging movement you make with your arms and body when you hit the ball in the game of GOLF 揮杆動作： *I need to work on my swing.* 我需要改進揮杆動作。

▸ MUSIC 音樂 **5** [U] a type of JAZZ with a smooth rhythm, played especially by big dance bands in the 1930s 搖擺樂（流行於 20 世紀 30 年代）

▸ JOURNEY 行程 **6** [sing.] (*NAmE*) a quick journey, especially one made by a politician, in which sb visits several different places in a short time（尤指從政者在多處逗留的）短期快速行程： *a three-day campaign swing through California* 為期三天的加利福尼亞州巡迴競選旅程

IDM **get in/into the 'swing (of sth)** (*informal*) to get used to an activity or a situation and become fully involved in it 熟悉（某種情況）；融入（某種活動或環境之中） **go with a 'swing** (*BrE*) **1** (of a party or an activity 聚會或活動) to be lively and enjoyable 熱鬧有趣；氣氛熱烈 **2** (of music 音樂) to have a strong rhythm 有強勁的節奏 **in full 'swing** having reached a very lively level 在熱烈進行中；處於興盛階段： *When we arrived the party was already in full swing.* 我們趕到時，聚會已進入高潮。 **,swings and 'roundabouts** (*BrE, informal*) used to say that there are advantages and disadvantages whatever decision you make（表示無論如何決定都有利有弊）有得必有失： *If you earn more, you pay more in tax, so it's all swings and roundabouts.* 賺的越多，繳的稅也越多，所以有得必有失。

,swing 'bridge *noun* (*BrE*) a bridge that can be moved to one side to allow tall ships to pass 平旋橋；平轉橋

,swing 'door (*BrE*) (*NAmE* **,swinging 'door**) *noun* a door that you can open in either direction and that closes itself when you stop holding it open 雙開式彈簧門

swinge·ing /'swɪndʒɪŋ/ *adj.* [usually before noun] (*BrE*) **1** large and likely to cause people problems, especially financial problems 巨額的；嚴重的；巨大的： *swingeing cuts in benefits* 補助金的大量削減 ◇ *swingeing tax increases* 徵稅大幅提高 **2** extremely critical of sb/sth 尖銳的；猛烈的： *a swingeing attack on government policy* 猛烈抨擊政府的政策

swing·er /'swɪŋə(r)/ *noun* (*old-fashioned, informal*) **1** a person who is fashionable and has an active social life 時髦活躍的人物 **2** a person who has sex with many different people 性開放者；濫交者

swing·ing /'swɪŋɪŋ/ *adj.* [usually before noun] (*old-fashioned, informal*) lively and fashionable 活躍而時髦的

,swinging 'door (*NAmE*) (*BrE* **,swing 'door**) *noun* a door that you can open in either direction and that closes itself when you stop holding it open 雙開式彈簧門

'swing set *noun* a frame for children to play on including one or more SWINGS and often a SLIDE 鞦韆組合架（常帶滑梯）

'swing shift *noun* (*NAmE, informal*) the SHIFT (= period of time worked each day) from 3 or 4 o'clock in the afternoon until 11 or 12 at night; the workers who work this SHIFT 中班（從下午 3、4 點至夜裏 11、12 點）；中班人員

,swing 'state *noun* (*politics* 政) (in an election for president in the US) a state where none of the candidates can be certain of getting the most support 搖擺州（指美國總統大選中無一候選人有把握獲勝的州）

,swing 'vote *noun* [C, sing.] (*NAmE*) the votes of people who do not always vote for the same political party and have not decided which party to vote for in an election 搖擺選票（指無一貫明確黨派立場的選民舉棋不定的選票）

,swing 'voter (*NAmE*) (*BrE* **,floating 'voter**) *noun* a person who does not always vote for the same political party and who has not decided which party to vote for in an election 游離選民（不確定投哪一政黨的票）

,swing-'wing *adj.* [only before noun] used to describe an aircraft wing that can be moved forward for landing, etc. and backward for rapid flight （飛機）可變後掠翼的

swipe /swaɪp/ *verb, noun*

■ *verb* **1** [I, T] **~ (at) sb/sth** to hit or try to hit sb/sth with your hand or an object by swinging your arm 揮拳打；揚起巴掌打；揮起（物體）擊打： *He swiped at the ball and missed.* 他揮棒擊球但沒擊中。 **2** [T] **~ sth** (*informal*) to steal sth 偷竊 SYN **pinch** **3** [T] **~ sth** to pass a plastic card, such as a credit card, through a special machine that is able to read the information that is stored on it 刷（磁卡）

■ *noun* **~ (at sb/sth)** (*informal*) **1** an act of hitting or trying to hit sb/sth by swinging your arm or sth that you are holding 掄打；揮擊： *She **took a swipe at** him with her umbrella.* 她掄起雨傘朝他打去。 **2** an act of criticizing sb/sth 批評；抨擊： *He used the interview to **take a swipe at his critics**.* 他利用這次採訪對批評他的人予以回擊。

'swipe card (also **'key card** especially in *NAmE*) *noun* a special plastic card with information recorded on it which can be read by an electronic device 磁卡；集成電路卡： *Access to the building is by swipe card only.* 這棟樓用磁卡才能進去。

swirl /swɜːl; *NAmE* swɜːrl/ *verb, noun*

■ *verb* [I, T] to move around quickly in a circle; to make sth do this （使）打旋，旋動，起漩渦： **(+ adv./prep.)** *The water swirled down the drain.* 水打着漩流進了下水道。◇ *A long skirt swirled around her ankles.* 她的長裙在腳踝旁邊擺動。◇ *swirling mists* 繚繞的薄霧 ◇ **~ sth (+ adv./prep.)** *He took a mouthful of water and swirled it around his mouth.* 他含了一口水，在嘴裏轉來轉去。

■ *noun* **1** the movement of sth that twists and turns in different directions and at different speeds 打旋；旋動；漩渦 **2** a pattern or an object that twists in circles 螺旋形；漩渦狀（物體）

swish /swɪʃ/ *verb, noun, adj.*

■ *verb* [I, T] to move quickly through the air in a way that makes a soft sound; to make sth do this 唰地（或嗖地、呼地等）揮動；（使）快速空中移動： **(+ adv./prep.)** *A large car swished past them and turned into the embassy gates.* 一輛大型轎車嗖地從他們身邊駛過，拐進了大使館的大門。◇ *The pony's tail swished.* 小馬唰唰地甩着尾巴。◇ **~ sth (+ adv./prep.)** *The pony swished its tail.* 小馬唰唰地甩着尾巴。◇ *She swished her racket aggressively through the air.* 她咄咄逼人地把球拍揮舞得呼呼作響。

■ *noun* [sing.] the movement or soft sound made by sth moving quickly, especially through the air 快速的空中移動（或揮動、擺動等）；（快速空中揮動等的）唰唰聲，嗖嗖聲，呼呼聲

■ *adj.* (*BrE, informal*) looking expensive and fashionable 華貴入時的；豪華的 SYN **smart**： *a swish restaurant* 豪華餐館

Swiss /swɪs/ *adj., noun* (*pl.* **Swiss**)

■ *adj.* from or connected with Switzerland 瑞士的

■ *noun* a person from Switzerland 瑞士人

,Swiss 'Army knife™ *noun* a small knife with several different blades and tools such as scissors, that fold into the handle 瑞士軍刀（多功能小摺疊刀）

'Swiss ball™ *noun* = EXERCISE BALL

,Swiss 'chard *noun* [U] = CHARD

,Swiss 'cheese *noun* [U, C] any hard cheese with holes in it 瑞士乾酪（中間有孔）

,Swiss 'roll (*BrE*) (*NAmE* **'jelly roll**) *noun* a thin flat cake that is spread with jam, etc. and rolled up 捲筒蛋糕（夾有果醬等）

switch 🔑 /swɪtʃ/ *noun, verb*

■ *noun* **1** 🔑 a small device that you press or move up and down in order to turn a light or piece of electrical equipment on and off （電路的）開關，閘，轉換器： *a light switch* 電燈開關 ◇ *an on-off switch* 通斷開關 ◇ *That was in the days before electricity was available **at the flick of a switch**.* 那是在過去，還沒有到開關一響就有電的時代。◇ *Which switch do I press to turn it off?* 我按哪個開關就能把它關了？◇ *to throw a switch* (= to move a large switch) 扳動開關 **2** a change from one thing to another, especially when this is sudden and complete （尤指突然徹底的）改變，轉變： **~ (in/of sth)** *a switch of priorities* 輕重緩急的改變 ◇ **~ (from A to B)** *She made the*

S

switch from full-time to part-time work when her first child was born. 第一個孩子出生後她就從全職工作改為兼職工作。◇ *a policy switch* 政策的轉變 **3** (*NAmE*) the POINTS on a railway/railroad line（鐵路的）轉轍器，道岔 **4** a thin stick that bends easily（細軟）枝條；鞭子：*a riding switch* 馬鞭

■ *verb* **1** [I, T] to change or make sth change from one thing to another（使）改變，轉變，突變：**~ (over) (from sth) (to sth)** *We're in the process of switching over to a new system of invoicing.* 我們正在轉用新的發票制度。◇ **~ between A and B** *Press these two keys to switch between documents on screen.* 按這兩個鍵就可以在屏幕上的文件之間切換。◇ **~ sth (over) (from sth) (to sth)** *When did you switch jobs?* 你什麼時候調動工作的？ **2** [T] to exchange one thing for another 交換；掉換；轉換；對調 SYN **swap**：**~ sth** *The dates of the last two exams have been switched.* 最後兩門考試的日期掉換了。◇ **~ sth over/around/round** *I see you've switched the furniture around* (= changed its position). 我看出來你把傢具重擺了。◇ **~ sth with sth** *Do you think she'll notice if I switch my glass with hers?* 要是把我的杯子跟她的換了，你認為她看得出來嗎？ **3** [I, T] to do sb else's job for a short time or work during different hours so that they can do your job or work during your usual hours 調班；臨時掉換工作時間 SYN **swap**：**~ (with sb)** *I can't work next weekend—will you switch with me?* 下個週末我不能上班，咱倆調個班好不好？◇ **~ sth (with sb)** *Have you been able to switch your shift with anyone?* 你找着能跟你調班的人了嗎？◇ **~ (sth) (over/around/round)** *Can we switch our shifts around?* 我們可以換個班嗎？

PHR V **,switch 'off** (*informal*) to stop thinking about sth or paying attention to sth 不再想着；不再注意；失去興趣：*When I hear the word 'football' I switch off* (= because I am not interested in it). 我聽見"足球"兩個字就膩味。◇ *The only time he really switches off* (= stops thinking about work, etc.) *is when we're on vacation.* 只有在我們外出度假的時候，他才真正無牽無掛。 **,switch 'off/'on | ,switch sth↔'off/'on** to turn a light, machine, etc. off/on by pressing a button or switch 關/開（電燈、機器等）：*Please switch the lights off as you leave.* 你離開的時候請把燈關了。◇ *How do you switch this thing on?* 這東西怎麼開？ **,switch 'over | ,switch sth↔'over** (*BrE*) to change stations on a radio or television 換台；換頻道

switch·back /ˈswɪtʃbæk/ *noun* **1** a road or railway/railroad track that has many sharp bends as it goes up a steep hill, or one that rises and falls steeply many times（公路或鐵路坡道上的）之字形路線；（公路或鐵路的）不斷起伏的路線 **2** (*NAmE*) a 180 degree bend in a road that is going up a steep hill（陡坡路上的）急轉彎，180 度的轉彎 **3** (*old-fashioned, BrE*) = ROLLER COASTER

switch·blade /ˈswɪtʃbleɪd/ (*especially NAmE*) (*BrE* also **'flick knife**) *noun* a knife with a blade inside the handle that jumps out quickly when a button is pressed 彈簧刀

switch·board /ˈswɪtʃbɔːd; *NAmE* -bɔːrd/ *noun* the central part of a telephone system used by a company, etc., where telephone calls are answered and PUT THROUGH (= connected) to the appropriate person or department; the people who work this equipment（電話的）交換機，交換台，總機：*a switchboard operator* 交換台接線員 ◇ *Call the switchboard and ask for extension 410.* 你先打電話到總機，然後要求轉分機 410。◇ *Hundreds of fans jammed the switchboard for over an hour.* 在一個多小時裏，好幾百個崇拜者打去電話，交換台應接不暇。

,switched 'on *adj.* **1 ~ (to sth)** aware of new things that are happening 對新事物有認識的；懂時髦的：*We're trying to get people switched on to the benefits of healthy eating.* 我們正努力讓大家意識到健康飲食的好處。◇ *an organization for switched-on young people* 一個新潮年輕人組織 **2** made to feel interested and excited 激起興趣的；興致勃發的；為之振奮的：*People get really switched on by this music.* 這首樂曲確實令人激情勃發。

'switch-hitter *noun* (in BASEBALL 棒球) a player who can hit with the BAT on either side of their body 能左右開弓的擊球手

switch·over /ˈswɪtʃəʊvə(r); *NAmE* -oʊ-/ *noun* a change from one system, method, policy, etc. to another（制度、方法、政策等的）轉變，轉換：*the switchover from analogue to digital TV* 從模擬到數字電視的轉變

swivel /ˈswɪvl/ *noun, verb*

■ *noun* (often used as an adjective 常用作形容詞) a device used to connect two parts of an object together, allowing one part to turn around without moving the other 轉節；轉環；旋軸；旋轉接頭：*a swivel chair* (= one on which the seat turns around without moving the base) 轉椅 ⇨ VISUAL VOCAB page V69

■ *verb* (**-ll-**, *US* **-l-**) **1** [T, I] **~ (sth) (+ adv./prep.)** to turn or make sth turn around a fixed central point（使）旋轉，轉動 SYN **spin**：*She swivelled the chair around to face them.* 她把椅子轉過來朝着他們。 **2** [I, T] **~ (sth) (+ adv./prep.)** to turn or move your body, eyes or head around quickly to face another direction 轉身；轉動（身體、眼睛或頭）SYN **swing**：*He swivelled around to look at her.* 他轉過身來看着她。

swizz (also **swiz**) /swɪz/ *noun* [usually sing.] (*BrE, informal*) something unfair or disappointing 騙局；令人失望的事：*What a swizz!* 真令人失望！

swiz·zle stick /ˈswɪzl stɪk/ *noun* a stick used to remove the bubbles from SPARKLING drinks such as CHAMPAGNE（消除香檳酒等起泡飲料泡沫的）攪棒

swol·len /ˈswəʊlən; *NAmE* ˈswoʊlən/ *adj.*
1 (of a part of the body 身體的一部份) larger than normal, especially as a result of a disease or an injury 腫脹的；腫起來的：*swollen glands* 腫脹的腺體 ◇ *Her eyes were red and swollen from crying.* 她哭得兩眼又紅又腫。 **2** (of a river 河流) containing more water than normal 漲水的；上漲的 ⇨ see also SWELL *v.*

swoon /swuːn/ *verb* **1** [I] **~ (over sb)** to feel very excited, emotional, etc. about sb that you think is sexually attractive, so that you almost become unconscious 痴迷；對（某人）神魂顛倒：*He's used to having women swooning over him.* 他對有女人痴迷於他司空見慣了。 **2** [I] (*old-fashioned*) to become unconscious 昏厥；昏倒 SYN **faint** ▶ **swoon** *noun* [sing.] (*old-fashioned*)：*to go into a swoon* 昏厥

swoop /swuːp/ *verb, noun*

■ *verb* **1** [I] **(+ adv./prep.)** (of a bird or plane 鳥或飛機) to fly quickly and suddenly downwards, especially in order to attack sb/sth（尤指為了襲擊）向下猛衝，俯衝 SYN **dive**：*The aircraft swooped down over the buildings.* 飛機俯衝到那些建築物上方。 **2** [I] **~ (on sb/sth)** (especially of police or soldiers 尤指警察或士兵) to visit or attack sb/sth suddenly and without warning 突然襲擊；突擊搜查；突然行動

■ *noun* **1** an act of moving suddenly and quickly through the air in a downward direction, as a bird does（鳥等的）向下猛衝，俯衝 SYN **dive 2 ~ (on sth/sb)** an act of arriving somewhere or attacking sth/sb in a way that is sudden and unexpected 突然襲擊；突擊搜查；突然行動 SYN **raid**：*Large quantities of drugs were found during a police swoop on the star's New York home.* 警方對這個明星在紐約的住所進行突擊搜查，發現了大量毒品。 IDM see FELL *adj.*

swoosh /swuːʃ/ *verb* [I] **+ adv./prep.** to move quickly through the air in a way that makes a sound 嗖嗖地迅速移動：*Cars and trucks swooshed past.* 汽車和卡車嗖嗖地疾駛而過。 ▶ **swoosh** *noun* [sing.]

swop = SWAP

sword /sɔːd; *NAmE* sɔːrd/ *noun* a weapon with a long metal blade and a handle 劍；刀：*to* ***draw/sheathe a sword*** (= to take it out/put it into its cover) 拔劍；把劍插入鞘

IDM **put sb to the 'sword** (*old-fashioned* or *literary*) to kill sb with a sword 用劍刺死某人 **a/the sword of 'Damocles** (*literary*) a bad or unpleasant thing that might happen to you at any time and that makes you feel worried or frightened 達摩克利斯劍（喻指令人憂慮或畏懼的、隨時可能降臨的災禍）ORIGIN From the legend in which **Damocles** had to sit at a meal at the court of Dionysius with a sword hanging by a single hair above his head. He had praised Dionysius' happiness, and Dionysius wanted him to understand how quickly happiness can be lost. 源自達摩克利斯 (Damocles) 在利劍下用餐的傳説。達摩克利斯曾讚美狄奧尼西奧斯所享受的幸福，後者請他在宮中飲宴，命人將一把利劍用一根頭髮懸掛於他頭頂，以此讓他明白幸福易逝。 **turn swords into 'ploughshares** (*literary*) to stop fighting and return to peaceful activities 鑄劍為犁；化干戈為玉帛；偃武修文 ➲ more at CROSS *v.*, DOUBLE-EDGED, PEN *n.*

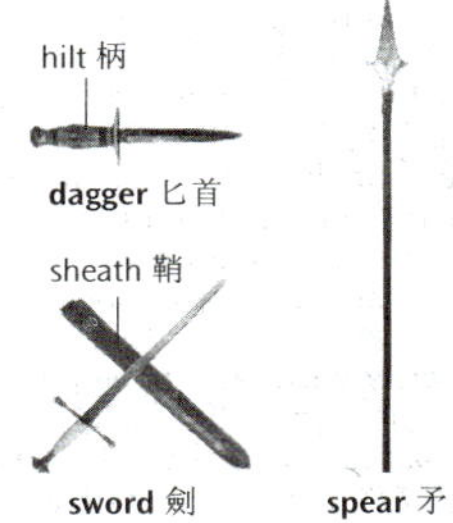

'sword dance *noun* a Scottish dance in which people dance between and over SWORDS that are placed on the ground 劍舞（蘇格蘭舞蹈，在置於地上的刀劍間穿行）

sword·fish /'sɔːdfɪʃ; *NAmE* 'sɔːrd-/ *noun* [C, U] (*pl.* **sword·fish**) a large sea fish with a very long thin pointed upper JAW 箭魚；劍魚

sword·play /'sɔːdpleɪ; *NAmE* 'sɔːrd-/ *noun* [U] **1** the sport or skill of FENCING 擊劍；劍術 **2** clever and amusing comments and replies that are made quickly 機智的巧辯 SYN repartee

swords·man /'sɔːdzmən; *NAmE* 'sɔːrdz-/ *noun* (*pl.* **-men** /-mən/) (usually used with an adjective) a person who fights with a SWORD（通常與形容詞連用）劍客，劍手：*a fine swordsman* 劍術高超的劍客

swords·man·ship /'sɔːdzmənʃɪp; *NAmE* 'sɔːrdz-/ *noun* [U] skill in fighting with a SWORD 劍術

swore *past tense* of SWEAR

sworn /swɔːn; *NAmE* swɔːrn/ *adj.* [only before noun] **1** made after you have promised to tell the truth, especially in court（尤指在法庭上）宣過誓的，宣誓證明的：*a sworn statement* 宣誓證詞 **2 ~ enemies** people, countries, etc. that have a strong hatred for each other 不共戴天的仇敵 ➲ see also SWEAR *v.*

swot /swɒt; *NAmE* swɑːt/ *noun, verb*

■ ***noun*** (*BrE*) (*US* **grind**) (*informal, disapproving*) a person who spends too much time studying 只知一味用功學習的人；書呆子

■ ***verb*** (**-tt-**) [I] **~** (**for sth**) (*BrE, informal*) to study very hard, especially in order to prepare for an exam（尤指為準備考試）刻苦學習，用功

PHR V **,swot sth↔'up | ,swot 'up on sth** (*BrE, informal*) to study a particular subject very hard, especially in order to prepare for an exam（尤指為準備考試）刻苦學習（某門課程）：*Make sure you swot up on the company before the interview.* 面試前一定要用心掌握公司的情況。

'SWOT analysis *noun* a study done by an organization in order to find its strengths and weaknesses, and what problems or opportunities it should deal with. SWOT is formed from the initial letters of 'strengths', 'weaknesses', 'opportunities' and 'threats'. * SWOT 分析，強弱利弊分析（為 strengths、weaknesses、opportunities 和 threats 的首字母，機構對自身實力與弱點以及應處理的問題或應利用機遇的分析）

swum *past part.* of SWIM

swung *past tense, past part.* of SWING

syb·ar·it·ic /ˌsɪbə'rɪtɪk/ *adj.* [usually before noun] (*formal*) connected with a desire for pleasure 貪圖享樂的；驕奢淫逸的：*his sybaritic lifestyle* 他驕奢淫逸的生活方式

syca·more /'sɪkəmɔː(r)/ *noun* **1** [C, U] (*especially BrE*) a European tree of the MAPLE family, with leaves that have five points and seeds shaped like a pair of wings 西卡莫；西卡莫槭；假挪威槭 ➲ VISUAL VOCAB page V10 **2** [C] (*especially NAmE*) an American PLANE TREE（美國）懸鈴木 **3** [U] the valuable hard wood of the European sycamore 西卡莫木材

syco·phant /'sɪkəfænt/ *noun* (*formal, disapproving*) a person who praises important or powerful people too much and in a way that is not sincere, especially in order to get sth from them 阿諛奉承的人；諂媚者；拍馬者 ▸ **syco·phancy** /'sɪkəfənsi/ *noun* [U] **syco·phan·tic** /ˌsɪkə'fæntɪk/ *adj.*：*a sycophantic review* 獻媚奉承的評論

syl·lab·ary /'sɪləbəri; *NAmE* -beri/ *noun* (*pl.* **-ies**) (*technical* 術語) a set of written characters representing syllables and used as an alphabet in some languages 音節文字；音節表

syl·lab·ic /sɪ'læbɪk/ *adj.* (*phonetics* 語音) **1** based on syllables 音節的；分音節的：*syllabic stress* 音節重音 **2** (of a consonant 輔音) forming a whole syllable, for example /l/ in *settle* 成音節的

syl·lable /'sɪləbl/ *noun* any of the units into which a word is divided, containing a vowel sound and usually one or more consonants 音節：*a word with two syllables* 雙音節單詞 ◇ *a two-syllable word* 雙音節單詞 ◇ *'Potato' is stressed on the second syllable.* * potato 一詞的重音在第二個音節上。IDM see WORD *n.*

'syllable-timed *adj.* (*phonetics* 語音) (of a language 語言) having a regular rhythm of syllables 有規則音節節拍的；音節定速的 ➲ compare STRESS-TIMED

syl·la·bub /'sɪləbʌb/ *noun* [C, U] (*BrE*) a cold DESSERT (= a sweet dish) made from cream that has been mixed very quickly with sugar, wine, fruit juice, etc. to make it thick 乳酒凍（用奶油加糖、葡萄酒、果汁等拌製）

syl·la·bus /'sɪləbəs/ *noun* (*pl.* **syl·la·buses** or *less frequent* **syl·labi** /'sɪləbaɪ/) a list of the topics, books, etc. that students should study in a particular subject at school or college 教學大綱 ➲ COLLOCATIONS at EDUCATION ➲ compare CURRICULUM

syl·lo·gism /'sɪlədʒɪzəm/ *noun* (*technical* 術語) a way of arguing in which two statements are used to prove that a third statement is true, for example: 'All humans must die; I am a human; therefore I must die.' 三段論（由兩個前提得出結論的推理方法，如"凡人必有一死；我是人；所以我必有一死。"）▸ **syl·lo·gist·ic** /ˌsɪlə'dʒɪstɪk/ *adj.* [only before noun]

sylph /sɪlf/ *noun* **1** an imaginary spirit 氣精；氣仙 **2** a girl or woman who is thin and attractive 苗條女子

sylph·like /'sɪlflaɪk/ *adj.* (of a woman or girl 女人或少女) thin in an attractive way 體態輕盈柔美的；苗條的

syl·van /'sɪlvən/ *adj.* (*literary*) connected with forests and trees 森林的；樹木的

sym·bi·osis /ˌsɪmbaɪ'əʊsɪs; *NAmE* -'oʊsɪs/ *noun* [U, C] (*pl.* **sym·bi·oses** /-'əʊsiːz; *NAmE* -'oʊsiːz/) **1** (*biology* 生) the relationship between two different living creatures that live close together and depend on each other in particular ways, each getting particular benefits from the other 共生（關係）**2** a relationship between people, companies, etc. that is to the advantage of both 合作關係；互惠互利的關係 ▸ **sym·bi·ot·ic** /-'ɒtɪk; *NAmE* -'ɑːtɪk/ *adj.*：*a symbiotic relationship* 一種互惠互利的關係 **sym·bi·ot·ic·al·ly** /ˌsɪmbaɪ'ɒtɪkli; *NAmE* -'ɑːtɪk-/ *adv.*

sym·bol 🔑 AW /'sɪmbl/ *noun*
1 🔑 **~** (**of sth**) a person, an object, an event, etc. that represents a more general quality or situation 象徵：*White has always been a symbol of purity in Western cultures.* 在西方文化中，白色一向象徵純潔。◇ *Mandela became a symbol of the anti-apartheid struggle.* 曼德拉成為反種族隔離鬥爭的象徵。➲ SYNONYMS at SIGN
2 🔑 **~** (**for sth**) a sign, number, letter, etc. that has a fixed meaning, especially in science, mathematics and music 符號；代號；記號：*What is the chemical symbol for copper?* 銅的化學符號是什麼？◇ *A list of symbols used*

on the map is given in the index. 這份地圖所使用的符號全部列在索引中。 ➲ see also SEX SYMBOL, STATUS SYMBOL

sym·bol·ic AW /sɪm'bɒlɪk; *NAmE* -'bɑːlɪk/ *adj.* **~ (of sth)** containing symbols, or being used as a symbol 使用象徵的；作為象徵的；象徵性的：*The dove is symbolic of peace.* 鴿子是和平的象徵。◇ *The Channel Tunnel has enormous symbolic significance for a united Europe.* 英吉利海峽隧道對於建立一個統一的歐洲具有重大的象徵意義。◇ *The new regulations are largely symbolic* (= they will not have any real effect). 新的制度基本上是象徵性的。▸ **sym·bol·ic·al·ly** AW /sɪm'bɒlɪkli; *NAmE* -'bɑːlɪk-/ *adv.*：*a symbolically significant gesture* 有象徵意義的舉動

sym·bol·ism AW /'sɪmbəlɪzəm/ *noun* [U] the use of symbols to represent ideas, especially in art and literature（尤指文藝中的）象徵主義，象徵手法 ➲ COLLOCATIONS at LITERATURE ▸ **sym·bol·ist** /'sɪmbəlɪst/ *adj.*, *noun*：*the symbolist poet Rimbaud* 象徵主義詩人蘭波

sym·bol·ize (*BrE* also **-ise**) AW /'sɪmbəlaɪz/ *verb* **~ sth** to be a symbol of sth 象徵；是…的象徵；代表 SYN **represent**：*The use of light and dark symbolizes good and evil.* 用光明與黑暗來象徵善與惡。◇ *He came to symbolize his country's struggle for independence.* 他逐漸成為祖國為爭取獨立而鬥爭的象徵。

sym·met·rical /sɪ'metrɪkl/ (also **sym·met·ric** /sɪ'metrɪk/) *adj.* (of a body, a design, an object, etc. 身體、圖案、物體等) having two halves, parts or sides that are the same in size and shape 對稱的：*a symmetrical pattern* 對稱的圖案 OPP **asymmetric** ▸ **sym·met·ric·al·ly** /-kli/ *adv.*

sym·metry /'sɪmətri/ *noun* [U] **1** the exact match in size and shape between two halves, parts or sides of sth 對稱：*the perfect symmetry of the garden design* 花園圖案的完全對稱 ➲ picture at AXIS **2** the quality of being very similar or equal 相似；相仿；相等：*the increasing symmetry between men's and women's jobs* 男女職業的日漸趨同

sym·pa·thet·ic 0-π /ˌsɪmpə'θetɪk/ *adj.*
1 0-π **~ (to/towards sb)** kind to sb who is hurt or sad; showing that you understand and care about their problems 同情的；有同情心的；表示同情的：*a sympathetic listener* 體恤別人的聽者 ◇ *I did not feel at all sympathetic towards Kate.* 我對凱特一點也不同情。◇ *I'm here if you need a* **sympathetic ear** (= sb to talk to about your problems). 要是你想訴訴苦，那就跟我說吧。**2** 0-π **~ (to/towards sb/sth)** showing that you approve of sb/sth or that you share their views and are willing to support them 贊同的；支持的：*to be sympathetic to the party's aims* 贊同該黨的目標 ◇ *Russian newspapers are largely sympathetic to the president.* 俄羅斯報章大都支持總統。**3** (of a person 人) easy to like 讓人喜歡的；招人喜愛的：*a* **sympathetic character** *in a novel* 小說中一個討人喜歡的人物 ◇ *I don't find her a very sympathetic person.* 我覺得她並不十分招人喜歡。HELP This meaning is not very common and you should use **likeable** or **pleasant** instead. 這個詞義不大常用，可用 likeable 或 pleasant 代替。OPP **unsympathetic** ▸ **sym·pa·thet·ic·al·ly** *adv.*：*to smile at sb sympathetically* 向某人微笑表示贊同 ◇ *We hope this application will be treated sympathetically* (= it will be approved). 我們希望這份申請能得到批准。

sym·pa·thize (*BrE* also **-ise**) /'sɪmpəθaɪz/ *verb* **1** [I, T] **~ (with sb/sth)** | **+ speech** to feel sorry for sb; to show that you understand and feel sorry about sb's problems 同情：*I find it very hard to sympathize with him.* 我覺得很難去同情他。**2** [I] **~ with sb/sth** to support sb/sth 贊同；支持：*He has never really sympathized with the aims of Animal Rights activists.* 他從來沒有真正贊同過動物權利保護者的目標。

sym·pa·thizer (*BrE* also **-iser**) /'sɪmpəθaɪzə(r)/ *noun* a person who supports or approves of sb/sth, especially a political cause or party 贊同者；支持者：*communist sympathizers* 共產主義的擁護者

sym·pathy 0-π /'sɪmpəθi/ *noun* (*pl.* **-ies**)
1 0-π [U, C, usually pl.] the feeling of being sorry for sb; showing that you understand and care about sb's problems 同情：*to* **express/feel sympathy** *for sb* 向某人表示體恤；對某人感到同情 ◇ ***I have no sympathy for*** *Jan, it's all her own fault.* 我不同情簡，那都是她自己的錯。◇ *I wish he'd show me a little more sympathy.* 我多希望他能再體諒我一點。◇ ***Our*** *heartfelt* ***sympathy goes out*** *to the victims of the war.* 我們對戰爭的受害者表示由衷的同情。◇ (*formal*) *May we* **offer our** *deepest* **sympathies** *on the death of your wife.* 我們謹對尊夫人去世表示最深切的慰唁。**2** 0-π [U, C, usually pl.] the act of showing support for or approval of an idea, a cause, an organization, etc. 贊同；支持：*The seamen went on strike* **in sympathy with** (= to show their support for) *the dockers.* 海員舉行罷工，以表示對碼頭工人的支持。◇ *Her sympathies lie with the anti-abortion lobby.* 她支持反墮胎的團體。**3** [U] friendship and understanding between people who have similar opinions or interests 意氣相投；志同道合：*There was no personal sympathy between them.* 他們個人之間全無相投之處。

IDM **in 'sympathy with sth** happening because sth else has happened 因…而出現；相應發生：*Share prices slipped in sympathy with the German market.* 受德國市場影響，股票價格出現下跌。**out of 'sympathy with sb/sth** not agreeing with or not wanting to support sb/sth 不贊成，不支持（某人或事物）

sym·phony /'sɪmfəni/ *noun* (*pl.* **-ies**) a long complicated piece of music for a large ORCHESTRA, in three or four main parts (called MOVEMENTS) 交響樂；交響曲：*Beethoven's Fifth Symphony* 貝多芬的第五交響曲 ➲ COLLOCATIONS at MUSIC ▸ **sym·phon·ic** /sɪm'fɒnɪk; *NAmE* -'fɑːn-/ *adj.*：*Mozart's symphonic works* 莫扎特的交響樂作品

'symphony orchestra *noun* a large ORCHESTRA that plays CLASSICAL music 交響樂團：*the Boston Symphony Orchestra* 波士頓交響樂團

sym·po·sium /sɪm'pəʊziəm; *NAmE* -'poʊ-/ *noun* (*pl.* **sym·po·sia** /-ziə/ or **sym·po·siums**) **~ (on sth)** a meeting at which experts have discussions about a particular subject; a small conference 專題討論會；研討會；小型討論會

symp·tom /'sɪmptəm/ *noun* **1** a change in your body or mind that shows that you are not healthy 症狀：*flu symptoms* 流感症狀 ◇ *Look out for symptoms of depression.* 留心看有無抑鬱症狀。◇ *Symptoms include a headache and sore throat.* 症狀包括頭痛和咽喉疼痛。**2** a sign that sth exists, especially sth bad 徵候；徵兆 SYN **indication**：*The rise in inflation was just one symptom of the poor state of the economy.* 通脹上升不過是經濟不景氣的一個徵候。➲ SYNONYMS at SIGN

symp·tom·at·ic /ˌsɪmptə'mætɪk/ *adj.* being a sign of an illness or a problem 作為症狀的；（有）症狀的；作為徵候的：*a symptomatic infection* 有症狀感染 ◇ **~ of sth** *These disagreements are symptomatic of the tensions within the party.* 出現意見分歧表明該黨內部的關係緊張。

symp·tom·ize /'sɪmptəmaɪz/ *verb* **~ sth** (*US*) to be a sign or SYMPTOM of sth 是…的症狀（或徵候）

syn·aes·the·sia (also **syn·es·the·sia**) /ˌsɪnəs'θiːziə; *NAmE* -'θiːʒə/ *noun* [U] (*biology* 生) the fact of experiencing some things in a different way from most other people, for example experiencing colours as sounds or shapes as tastes, or feeling sth in one part of the body when a different part is STIMULATED 聯覺，伴生感覺（對一種感官的刺激作用觸發另一種感官知覺）

syna·gogue /'sɪnəgɒg; *NAmE* -gɑːg/ *noun* a building where Jews meet for religious worship and teaching 猶太會堂；猶太教堂

syn·apse /'saɪnæps; 'sɪn-/ *noun* (*biology* 生) a connection between two nerve cells（神經元的）突觸 ▸ **syn·ap·tic** /saɪ'næptɪk; sɪ'n-/ *adj.*：*the synaptic membranes* 突觸膜

sync (also **synch**) /sɪŋk/ *noun* [U] (*informal*)

IDM **in 'sync 1** moving or working at exactly the same time and speed as sb/sth else 同步：*The soundtrack is* **not in sync** *with the picture.* 聲跡與畫面不同步。**2** in agreement with sb/sth; working well with sb/sth

S

一致；協調：*His opinions were in sync with those of his colleagues.* 他的看法和同事的一致。**out of 'sync** **1** not moving or working at exactly the same time and speed as sb/sth else 不同步 **2** not in agreement with sb/sth; not working well with sb/sth 不一致；不協調 ➲ see also LIP-SYNC, SYNCHRONIZATION at SYNCHRONIZE

syn·chron·ic /sɪŋˈkrɒnɪk; *NAmE* -ˈkrɑːn-/ *adj.* (*linguistics* 語言) relating to a language as it is at a particular point in time （語言）共時的 ➲ compare DIACHRONIC

syn·chron·icity /ˌsɪŋkrəˈnɪsəti/ *noun* [U] (*technical* 術語) the fact of two or more things happening at exactly the same time 同步性；同時發生

syn·chron·ize (*BrE* also **-ise**) /ˈsɪŋkrənaɪz/ *verb* [I, T] to happen at the same time or to move at the same speed as sth; to make sth do this （使）同步，在時間上一致，同速進行：**~ (with sth)** *The sound track did not synchronize with the action.* 聲跡與動作不同步。◇ **~ sth (with sth)** *Let's synchronize our watches* (= make them show exactly the same time). 咱們對一下錶吧。▸ **syn·chron·iza·tion, -isa·tion** /ˌsɪŋkrənaɪˈzeɪʃn; *NAmE* -nəˈz-/ (also *informal* **sync**) *noun* [U]

ˌsynchronized ˈswimming (*BrE* also **-ised**) *noun* [U] a sport in which groups of SWIMMERS move in patterns in the water to music 花樣游泳（組員伴着音樂同步進行）

syn·chron·ous /ˈsɪŋkrənəs/ *adj.* (*technical* 術語) happening or existing at the same time 同時發生（或存在）的；同步的；共時的

syn·cline /ˈsɪŋklaɪn/ *noun* (*geology* 地) an area of ground where layers of rock in the earth's surface have been folded into a curve that is lower in the middle than at the ends 向斜層 ➲ compare ANTICLINE

syn·co·pated /ˈsɪŋkəpeɪtɪd/ *adj.* (*music* 音) in **syncopated** rhythm the strong beats are made weak and the weak beats are made strong 切分的，切分音樂的（節拍強弱倒置）▸ **syn·co·pa·tion** /ˌsɪŋkəˈpeɪʃn/ *noun* [U]

syn·cope /ˈsɪŋkəpi/ *noun* [U] (*phonetics* 語音) the dropping of a sound or sounds in the middle of a word when it is spoken, for example the pronunciation of *library* as /ˈlaɪbri/ 詞中語音省略（如將 library 發成 /ˈlaɪbri/）

syn·cre·tism /ˈsɪŋkrətɪzəm/ *noun* [U] **1** (*technical* 術語) the mixing of different religions, philosophies or ideas （不同宗教、哲學或思想的）融合 **2** (*linguistics* 語言) the mixing of different forms of the same word during the development of a language （語言發展過程中詞的）屈折形式融合，輯合

syn·dic·al·ism /ˈsɪndɪkəlɪzəm/ *noun* [U] the belief that factories, businesses, etc. should be owned and managed by all the people who work in them 工團主義，工聯主義（認為企業應由全體員工共同擁有及管理）

syn·dic·al·ist /ˈsɪndɪkəlɪst/ *noun* a person who believes in syndicalism 工團主義者；工聯主義者 ▸ **syn·dic·al·ist** *adj.*

syn·di·cate *noun*, *verb*

▪ ***noun*** /ˈsɪndɪkət/ a group of people or companies who work together and help each other in order to achieve a particular aim 辛迪加；企業聯合組織；財團；私人聯合會

▪ ***verb*** /ˈsɪndɪkeɪt/ [usually passive] **~ sth** to sell an article, a photograph, a television programme, etc. to several different newspapers, etc. 把（文章、圖片、電視節目等）出售給多個媒體：*His column is syndicated throughout the world.* 他的專欄文章在世界各地的報刊發表。▸ **syn·di·ca·tion** /ˌsɪndɪˈkeɪʃn/ *noun* [U]

syn·drome /ˈsɪndrəʊm; *NAmE* -droʊm/ *noun* **1** a set of physical conditions that show you have a particular disease or medical problem 綜合症；綜合症狀：*PMS or premenstrual syndrome* 月經前綜合症 ◇ *This syndrome is associated with frequent coughing.* 這種綜合症與經常咳嗽有關。➲ see also AIDS, DOWN'S SYNDROME, ECONOMY CLASS SYNDROME, SICK BUILDING SYNDROME, TOURETTE'S SYNDROME **2** a set of opinions or a way of behaving that is typical of a particular type of person, attitude or social problem 典型意見；典型表現：*With teenagers, be prepared for the 'Me, me, me!' syndrome* (= they think of themselves first). 跟青少年在一起，對他們那種凡事只想到"我、我、我！"的典型心理不要大驚小怪。

syn·ec·doche /sɪˈnekdəki/ *noun* [U, C] (*technical* 術語) a word or phrase in which a part of sth is used to represent a whole, or a whole is used to represent a part of sth. For example, in 'Australia lost by two goals', *Australia* is used to represent the Australian team. 舉偶法，提喻法（用局部代表整體或用整體代表局部的修辭手段）

syn·ergy /ˈsɪnədʒi; *NAmE* -ərdʒi/ *noun* [U, C] (*pl.* **-ies**) (*technical* 術語) the extra energy, power, success, etc. that is achieved by two or more people or companies working together, instead of on their own 協同作用，協同增效作用（人或公司共同協作所產生的效果優於各自單獨行動的效果）▸ **syn·er·gis·tic** /ˌsɪnəˈdʒɪstɪk; *NAmE* ˌsɪnər-/ *adj.* **syn·er·gis·tic·al·ly** /-kli/ *adv.*

synod /ˈsɪnəd; *BrE* also -nɒd/ *noun* an official meeting of Church members to discuss religious matters and make important decisions 教會會議

syno·nym /ˈsɪnənɪm/ *noun* a word or expression that has the same or nearly the same meaning as another in the same language 同義詞：*'Big' and 'large' are synonyms.* * big 和 large 是同義詞。➲ compare ANTONYM

syn·onym·ous /sɪˈnɒnɪməs; *NAmE* -ˈnɑːn-/ *adj.* **1** (of words or expressions 詞語) having the same, or nearly the same, meaning 同義的 **2 ~ (with sth)** so closely connected with sth that the two things appear to be the same 等同於…的：*Wealth is not necessarily synonymous with happiness.* 財富未必等同於幸福。▸ **syn·onym·ous·ly** *adv.*

syn·onymy /sɪˈnɒnɪmi; *NAmE* -ˈnɑːn-/ *noun* [U] the fact of two or more words or expressions having the same meaning 同義；同義關係

syn·op·sis /sɪˈnɒpsɪs; *NAmE* -ˈnɑːp-/ *noun* (*pl.* **syn·op·ses** /-siːz/) a summary of a piece of writing, a play, etc. （著作、劇本等的）大綱，提要，概要，梗概 ▸ **syn·op·tic** /sɪˈnɒptɪk; *NAmE* -ˈnɑːp-/ *adj.* (*formal*)

syn·ovial /saɪˈnəʊviəl; sɪˈn-; *NAmE* sɪˈnoʊ-/ *adj.* (*biology* 生) (of a joint 關節) having a MEMBRANE (= a piece of very thin skin) containing liquid between the bones, which allows the joint to move freely （含）滑膜的

syn·tac·tic /sɪnˈtæktɪk/ *adj.* (*linguistics* 語言) connected with SYNTAX 句法的 ▸ **syn·tac·tic·al·ly** /-kli/ *adv.*：*to be syntactically correct* 在句法上正確

syn·tagm /ˈsɪntæm/ *noun* (also **syn·tagma** /ˌsɪnˈtægmə/) (*linguistics* 語言) a unit of language consisting of sets of PHONEMES, words, or phrases that are arranged in order （語言）組合體 ▸ **syn·tag·mat·ic** /ˌsɪntægˈmætɪk/ *adj.*

syn·tax /ˈsɪntæks/ *noun* [U] **1** (*linguistics* 語言) the way that words and phrases are put together to form sentences in a language; the rules of grammar for this 句法；句法規則 ➲ compare MORPHOLOGY (2) **2** (*computing* 計) the rules that state how words and phrases must be used in a computer language 句法；語構

synth /sɪnθ/ *noun* (*informal*) = SYNTHESIZER

syn·the·sis /ˈsɪnθəsɪs/ *noun* (*pl.* **syn·the·ses** /-siːz/) **1** [U, C] **~ (of sth)** the act of combining separate ideas, beliefs, styles, etc.; a mixture or combination of ideas, beliefs, styles, etc. 綜合；結合；綜合體：*the synthesis of art with everyday life* 藝術與日常生活的結合 ◇ *a synthesis of traditional and modern values* 傳統價值觀和現代價值觀的綜合體 **2** [U] (*technical* 術語) the natural chemical production of a substance in animals and plants （物質在動植物體內的）合成：*protein synthesis* 蛋白質的合成 **3** [U] (*technical* 術語) the artificial production of a substance that is present naturally in animals and plants （人工的）合成：*the synthesis of penicillin* 青黴素的合成 **4** [U] (*technical* 術語) the production of sounds, music or speech by electronic means （用電子手段對聲音、音樂或語音的）合成：*speech synthesis* 語音合成

S

syn·the·size (*BrE* also **-ise**) /ˈsɪnθəsaɪz/ *verb* **1** **~ sth** (*technical* 術語) to produce a substance by means of chemical or BIOLOGICAL processes（通過化學手段或生物過程）合成 **2** **~ sth** to produce sounds, music or speech using electronic equipment （音響）合成 **3** **~ sth** to combine separate ideas, beliefs, styles, etc. 綜合

syn·the·sizer (*BrE* also **-iser**) /ˈsɪnθəsaɪzə(r)/ (also *informal* **synth**) *noun* an electronic machine for producing different sounds. Synthesizers are used as musical instruments, especially for copying the sounds of other instruments, and for copying speech sounds. 音響合成器： *a speech synthesizer* 語音合成器 ➲ compare KEYBOARD *n.* (3)

syn·thet·ic /sɪnˈθetɪk/ *adj., noun*

■ ***adj.*** **1** artificial; made by combining chemical substances rather than being produced naturally by plants or animals 人造的；（人工）合成的 **SYN** **man-made**： *synthetic drugs/fabrics* 合成藥物 / 織物 ➲ SYNONYMS at ARTIFICIAL **2** (also **ag·glu·tin·ative**) (*linguistics* 語言) (of languages 語言) using changes to the ends of words rather than separate words to show the functions of words in a sentence 綜合（型）的 ➲ compare ANALYTIC (1) ▸ **syn·thet·ic·al·ly** /-kli/ *adv.*

■ ***noun*** an artificial substance or material 合成物；合成纖維（織物）；合成劑： *cotton fabrics and synthetics* 棉織物與合成織物

syph·ilis /ˈsɪfɪlɪs/ *noun* [U] a disease that gets worse over a period of time, spreading from the sexual organs to the skin, bones, muscles and brain. It is caught by having sex with an infected person. 梅毒 ▸ **syph·il·it·ic** /ˌsɪfɪˈlɪtɪk/ *adj.*

sy·phon = SIPHON

syr·inge /sɪˈrɪndʒ/ *noun, verb*

■ ***noun*** **1** (also **hypo·der·mic**, **ˌhypodermic syˈringe**) a plastic or glass tube with a long hollow needle that is used for putting drugs, etc. into a person's body or for taking a small amount of blood from a person（皮下）注射器 **2** a plastic or glass tube with a rubber part at the end, used for sucking up liquid and then pushing it out 吸管；唧筒 ➲ VISUAL VOCAB page V70

■ ***verb*** **~ sth** to clean sb's ear by spraying liquid into it with a SYRINGE 用注射器清洗（耳朵）： *I had my ears syringed.* 我的耳朵已用注射器清洗乾淨。

syrup /ˈsɪrəp/ *noun* [U] **1** a sweet liquid made from sugar and water, often used in cans of fruit 糖水（罐頭水果常用）： *pears in syrup* 糖水梨 **2** any thick sweet liquid made with sugar, used especially as a sauce 糖漿 ➲ see also CORN SYRUP, GOLDEN SYRUP, MAPLE SYRUP

syr·upy /ˈsɪrəpi/ *adj.* **1** thick and sticky like syrup; containing syrup 糖漿般黏稠的；含糖漿的 **2** (*disapproving*) extremely emotional and romantic and therefore unpleasant; too SENTIMENTAL 纏綿的；過分多情的： *a syrupy romantic novel* 一部纏綿的言情小說

sys·tem 🔑 /ˈsɪstəm/ *noun*

1 🔑 [C] an organized set of ideas or theories or a particular way of doing sth （思想或理論）體系；方法；制度；體制： *the British educational system* 英國的教育制度 ◇ **~ for doing sth** *a new system for assessing personal tax bills* 新的個人稅額估定辦法 ◇ **~ of sth** *a system of government* 政體 ➲ see also BINARY, METRIC SYSTEM **2** 🔑 [C] a group of things, pieces of equipment, etc. that are connected or work together 系統： *a transport system* 運輸系統 ◇ *heating systems* 供熱系統 ◇ *a stereo system* 立體聲音響系統 ◇ *a security system* 保安系統 ➲ see also ECOSYSTEM, EXPERT SYSTEM, OPERATING SYSTEM, PUBLIC ADDRESS SYSTEM, SOLAR SYSTEM **3** 🔑 [C] a human or an animal body, or a part of it, when it is being thought of as the organs and processes that make it function 身體；（器官）系統： *You have to wait until the drugs have passed out of your system.* 你必須等到藥物排出體外。◇ *the male reproductive system* 男性生殖系統 ➲ see also CENTRAL NERVOUS SYSTEM, DIGESTIVE SYSTEM, IMMUNE SYSTEM **4** **the system** [sing.] (*informal*, usually *disapproving*) the rules or people that control a country or an organization, especially when they seem to be unfair because you cannot change them（尤指不公正的統治或管理）制度，體系，集團： *You can't* ***beat the system*** (= you must accept it). 你鬥不過現行的體制。◇ *young people rebelling against the system* 反抗現行體制的年輕人

IDM **get sth out of your ˈsystem** (*informal*) to do sth so that you no longer feel a very strong emotion or have a strong desire 宣泄，排解，消解（強烈的感情或慾望）： *I was very angry with him, but now I feel I've got it out of my system.* 我當時很生他的氣，不過現在我感覺氣已經消了。

sys·tem·at·ic /ˌsɪstəˈmætɪk/ *adj.* done according to a system or plan, in a thorough, efficient or determined way 成體系的；系統的；有條理的；有計劃有步驟的： *a* ***systematic approach to*** *solving the problem* 系統地解決問題的辦法 ◇ *a systematic attempt to destroy the organization* 力圖摧毀那個組織的有計劃有步驟的行動 ◇ *The prisoner was subjected to systematic torture.* 犯人受到蓄意折磨。 **OPP** **unsystematic** ▸ **sys·tem·at·ic·al·ly** /-kli/ *adv.*： *The search was carried out systematically.* 搜查已按照部署執行。

sys·tem·atize (*BrE* also **-ise**) /ˈsɪstəmətaɪz/ *verb* **~ sth** (*formal*) to arrange sth according to a system 使系統化；使成體系；使條理化 **SYN** **organize** ▸ **sys·tem·atiza·tion**, **-isa·tion** /ˌsɪstəmətaɪˈzeɪʃn; *NAmE* -təˈz-/ *noun* [U]

sys·tem·ic /sɪˈstemɪk; sɪˈstiːmɪk/ *adj.* (*technical* 術語) **1** affecting or connected with the whole of sth, especially the human body 涉及全系統的；系統的；影響全身的；全身的 **2** **systemic** chemicals or drugs that are used to treat diseases in plants or animals enter the body of the plant or animal and spread to all parts of it（農藥等）內吸的： *systemic weedkillers* 內吸除草劑 ▸ **sys·tem·ic·al·ly** *adv.*

ˈsystem operator (also **ˈsystems operator**) *noun* (*computing* 計) a person who manages a computer system or electronic communication service 計算機系統（或電訊服務）管理員；系統操作員

ˈsystems analyst *noun* a person whose job is to analyse the needs of a business company or an organization and then design processes for working efficiently using computer programs 系統分析員 ▸ **ˈsystems analysis** *noun* [U]

ˈsystem unit *noun* (*computing* 計) the main part of a computer, separate from the keyboard and monitor, that contains the unit that controls all the other parts of the system 系統單元，系統部件（獨立於鍵盤和顯示器、包含中央處理器的電腦主體部份）

sys·tole /ˈsɪstəli/ *noun* (*medical* 醫) the part of the heart's rhythm when the heart PUMPS blood 心縮期 ▸ **sys·tol·ic** /ˌsɪsˈtɒlɪk; *NAmE* -ˈtɑːl-/ *adj.*

S

Tt

T (also **t**) /tiː/ *noun* [C, U] (*pl.* **Ts, T's, t's** /tiːz/) the 20th letter of the English alphabet 英語字母表的第 20 個字母：*'Tin' begins with (a) T/'T'.* * tin 一詞以字母 t 開頭。➲ see also T-BONE STEAK, T-JUNCTION, T-SHIRT, T-SQUARE

IDM **to a 'T/'tee** (*informal*) used to say that sth is exactly right for sb, succeeds in doing sth in exactly the right way, etc.（用以表示完全合適）恰好，絲毫不差：*Her new job suits her to a T.* 她的新工作對她再合適不過了。◇ *The novel captures the feeling of the pre-war period to a T.* 這部小說對戰前時期的情懷把握得恰到好處。➲ more at DOT *v.*

TA /ˌtiː ˈeɪ/ *abbr.* **1** (*BrE*) TERRITORIAL ARMY（英國）本土防衛義勇軍；國防義勇軍 **2** (*NAmE*) TEACHING ASSISTANT

ta /tɑː/ *exclamation* (*BrE, slang*) thank you 謝謝

taa·rab /ˈtɑːrʌb/ *noun* [U] a type of music that is popular in E Africa, especially along the coast, and that is influenced by Arabian and Indian music 塔拉勃樂（受阿拉伯和印度音樂影響的東非流行樂，尤盛行於沿海地區）

tab /tæb/ *noun, verb*

■ *noun* **1** a small piece of paper, cloth, metal, etc. that sticks out from the edge of sth, and that is used to give information about it, or to hold it, fasten it, etc. 標籤；籤條；突耳；凸舌：*Insert tab A into slot 1* (= for example to make a model, box, etc.). 將凸舌 A 插入 1 號孔（如製作模型、盒子等）。 **2** = TAB STOP **3** (*NAmE*) = PULL TAB **4** a bill for goods you receive but pay for later, especially for food or drinks in a restaurant or bar; the price or cost of sth（待付的）賬單，賬款；（尤指）餐飲賬單；費用：*a bar tab* 酒吧賬單 ◇ *Can I put it on my tab?* 我可以記賬嗎？◇ *The tab for the meeting could be $3 000.* 這次會議的費用可能是 3 000 元。 **5** (*informal*) a small solid piece of an illegal drug 藥片，藥丸（指毒品）：*a tab of Ecstasy* 一粒迷幻藥片 **6** = TABLATURE：*guitar tabs* 吉他奏法樂譜

IDM **keep (close) tabs on sb/sth** (*informal*) to watch sb/sth carefully in order to know what is happening so that you can control a particular situation 監視；密切注視：*It's not always possible to keep tabs on everyone's movements.* 監視每個人的行動並不總是能辦得到的。➲ more at PICK *v.*

■ *verb* (**-bb-**) **1 ~ sb (as) sth** (*especially NAmE*) to say that sb is suitable for a particular job or role or describe them in a particular way 說（某人）適合於（某工作或角色）；把（某人）視為⋯：*He has been tabbed by many people as a future champion.* 許多人都說他是未來的冠軍。 **2 ~ sth** to use the TAB KEY when you are using a keyboard 使用製表鍵

tab·ard /ˈtæbəd; -bɑːd; *NAmE* -bərd; -bɑːrd/ *noun* a simple piece of clothing consisting of back and front sections without sleeves, and a hole for the head 褡伯坎肩，搭肩衫（由前後兩片組成，無領無袖）

Tab·asco™ /təˈbæskəʊ; *NAmE* -koʊ/ *noun* [U] a red spicy sauce made from PEPPERS 塔巴斯科辣椒醬

tab·bou·leh /təˈbuːleɪ; *BrE* also ˈtæbuːleɪ/ *noun* [U] an Arab dish consisting of crushed WHEAT with chopped tomatoes, onions and HERBS 塔博勒色拉，麥粒番茄色拉（阿拉伯菜，用碎麥粒和切碎的番茄、洋蔥和香草調製而成）

tabby /ˈtæbi/ *noun* (*pl.* **-ies**) (also **'tabby cat**) a cat with brown or grey fur marked with dark lines or spots 斑貓（毛皮灰色或褐色，帶有深色斑條或斑點）

tab·er·nacle /ˈtæbənækl; *NAmE* -bərn-/ *noun* **1** [C] a place of worship for some groups of Christians（某些基督教派的）禮拜堂，會堂：*a Mormon tabernacle* 摩門教教堂 **2** **the tabernacle** [sing.] a small place of worship that could be moved, used by the Jews in ancient times when they were travelling in the desert 會幕，帳棚神幕（古代猶太人在沙漠旅途中用作聖所）

'tab key (also **tab**, *formal* **tabu·la·tor**) *noun* a button on a keyboard that you use to move to a certain fixed position in a line of a document that you are typing（鍵盤上的）跳格鍵，製表鍵，Tab 鍵

tabla /ˈtæblə; ˈtʌb-/ *noun* a pair of small drums played with the hands and used in S Asian music, usually to accompany other instruments 塔布拉雙鼓（用於南亞音樂中的成對小手鼓，通常作為伴奏樂器）

tab·lat·ure /ˈtæblətʃə(r)/ (also **tab**) *noun* [U, C] a way of representing musical notes on paper by showing the position of the fingers on a musical instrument rather than the actual notes; an example of this 奏法記譜法（根據演奏者的手指位置記譜）；奏法樂譜；古記譜法：*The book contains lyrics and guitar tablatures for over 100 songs.* 這本書有 100 多首歌的歌詞和吉他奏法譜。

table 🔑 /ˈteɪbl/ *noun, verb*

■ *noun*

▸ **FURNITURE 傢具** **1** 🔑 a piece of furniture that consists of a flat top supported by legs 桌子；枱子；几：*a kitchen table* 廚房用桌 ◇ *A table for two, please* (= in a restaurant). 請安排兩人一桌的位子。◇ *I'd like to **book a table** for tonight* (= in a restaurant). 我想為今天晚上預訂一個桌位。◇ *to **set the table*** (= to put the plates, knives, etc. on it for a meal) 擺餐具 ◇ (*BrE* also) *to **lay the table*** 擺餐具 ◇ *to **clear the table*** (= take away the dirty plates, etc. at the end of a meal)（餐後）清理餐桌 ◇ *He questioned her next morning over the breakfast table* (= during breakfast). 第二天早上，他一邊吃着早餐一邊查問她。◇ (*BrE, formal*) *Children must learn to behave **at table**.* 小孩必須學會吃飯時的規矩。◇ *a **billiard/snooker/pool table*** 枱球／斯諾克／普爾球枱 ➲ VISUAL VOCAB page V40 **HELP** There are many compounds ending in **table**. You will find them at their place in the alphabet. 以 table 結尾的複合詞很多，可在各字母中的適當位置查到。

▸ **PEOPLE 人** **2** the people sitting at a table for a meal or to play cards, etc.（就餐或玩牌等的）一桌人：*He kept the whole table entertained with his jokes.* 他笑話不斷，把全桌人逗得直樂。➲ see also ROUND-TABLE

▸ **LIST OF FACTS/NUMBERS 細目／數字表** **3** 🔑 a list of facts or numbers arranged in a special order, usually in rows and columns 表；一覽表：*a **table of contents*** (= a list of the main points or information in a book, usually at the front of the book) 目錄 ◇ *Table 2 shows how prices and earnings have increased over the past 20 years.* 表 2 顯示了過去 20 年來價格和收入的增長情況。➲ see also PERIODIC TABLE

▸ **IN SPORT 體育運動** **4** a list of sports teams, countries, schools, etc. that shows their position in a competition, etc.（競賽等的）名次表，排名榜，積分表：*If Arsenal win this game they'll go to the top of the table.* 阿森納隊如果贏得這場比賽，就會登上積分榜首。◇ *school performance league tables* 校級聯賽積分表

▸ **MATHEMATICS 數學** **5** = MULTIPLICATION TABLE：*Do you know your six times table?* 你會背六的乘法口訣嗎？➲ see also TURNTABLE, WATER TABLE

IDM **ˌbring sth to the 'party/'table** to contribute sth useful to a discussion, project, etc. 為（討論、項目等）作出貢獻：*What Hislop brought to the table was real commitment and energy.* 希斯洛普作出的貢獻是他全身心的投入和幹勁。 **on the 'table** **1** (*BrE*) (of a plan, suggestion, etc. 計劃、建議等) offered to people so that they can consider or discuss it 提供考慮；提交討論：*Management have put several new proposals on the table.* 管理部門已將幾項新的建議提交討論。 **2** (*especially NAmE*) (of a plan, suggestion, etc. 計劃、建議等) not going to be discussed or considered until a future date 擱置 **turn the 'tables (on sb)** to change a situation so that you are now in a stronger position than the person who used to be in a stronger position than you 扭轉形勢；轉變局面；轉弱為強 ➲ more at CARD *n.*, DRINK *v.*, WAIT *v.*

■ *verb* **1 ~ sth** (*BrE*) to present sth formally for discussion（正式）提出，把⋯列入議事日程：*They have tabled a motion for debate at the next Party Conference.* 他們已經提出一項動議，在下次黨的會議上進行辯論。 **2 ~ sth** (*NAmE*) to leave an idea, a proposal, etc. to be discussed at a later date（將主意、建議等）擱置：*They voted to table the proposal until the following meeting.* 他們投票決定把這項建議留到下次會議討論。

T

tab·leau /'tæbləʊ; *NAmE* -loʊ/ *noun* (*pl.* **tab·leaux** /-ləʊ; -ləʊz; *NAmE* -loʊ; -loʊz/) **1** a scene showing, for example, events and people from history, that is presented by a group of actors who do not move or speak 舞台造型；靜態畫面：*The procession included a tableau of the Battle of Hastings.* 遊行隊伍中包括黑斯廷斯戰役的人物造型。◇ (*figurative*) *She stood at the door observing the peaceful domestic tableau around the fire.* 她站在門口，看着爐火周圍闔家祥和的景象。 **2** a work of art, especially a set of statues, showing a group of people, animals, etc. 群像（尤指雕塑）

table·cloth /'teɪblklɒθ; *NAmE* -klɔːθ; -klɑːθ/ *noun* a cloth that you use for covering a table, especially when you have a meal（尤指餐桌的）桌布，枱布 ➲ VISUAL VOCAB page V22

'**table dancing** *noun* [U] sexually exciting dancing which is performed close to a customer's table in a bar or club 桌邊舞（酒吧或夜總會中的性感舞蹈）

table d'hôte /ˌtɑːbl 'dəʊt; *NAmE* 'doʊt/ *adj.* a **table d'hôte** meal in a restaurant costs a fixed price and there are only a limited number of dishes to choose from 定餐的；套餐的：*the table d'hôte menu* 定餐菜單 ▸ **table d'hôte** *noun* [U]：*The restaurant offers both table d'hôte and à la carte.* 這家餐館不僅供應定餐，還可以點菜。

'**table football** (*BrE*) (*NAmE* **foosball**) *noun* [U] an indoor game for two people or teams, played by moving rows of small models of football (SOCCER) players in order to move a ball on a board that has marks like a football (SOCCER) field 桌上足球；足球機

'**table lamp** *noun* a small lamp that you can put on a table, etc. 枱燈；桌燈 ➲ VISUAL VOCAB page V21

table·land /'teɪbllænd/ *noun* a large area of high flat land 台地；高原 SYN **plateau**

'**table linen** *noun* [U] the cloths that you use during a meal, for example TABLECLOTHS and NAPKINS 餐桌用布（如桌布、餐巾等）

'**table manners** *noun* [pl.] the behaviour that is considered correct while you are having a meal at a table with other people 餐桌規矩；進餐禮節

'**table mat** *noun* (*BrE*) a small piece of wood or cloth that you put under a hot dish or plate to protect the surface of the table 餐具墊；隔熱桌墊 ➲ VISUAL VOCAB page V22

'**table napkin** *noun* = NAPKIN (1)

table·spoon /'teɪblspuːn/ *noun* **1** a large spoon, used especially for serving food 餐匙，湯匙（尤用於分食物）➲ VISUAL VOCAB page V22 **2** (also **table·spoon·ful** /-fʊl/) (*abbr.* **tbsp**) the amount a tablespoon can hold 一餐匙，一湯匙（的量）：*Add two tablespoons of water.* 加兩湯匙的水。

T

tab·let 0-π /'tæblət/ *noun*
1 0-π (*especially BrE*) a small round solid piece of medicine that you swallow 藥片；片劑 SYN **pill**：*vitamin tablets* 維生素片 ◇ *Take two tablets with water before meals.* 每次兩片，飯前用水沖服。**2** an amount of another substance in a small round solid piece 丸：*water purification tablets* 淨水丸 **3** a flat piece of stone that has words written on it, especially one that has been fixed to a wall in memory of an important person or event（固定於牆上作紀念的）牌，碑，匾 SYN **plaque**：(*figurative*) *We can be very flexible—our entry requirements are not set in* ***tablets of stone*** (= they can be changed). 我們可以非常靈活，加入條件並非鐵板釘釘。 **4** = TABLET PC **5 ~ of soap** (*old-fashioned, formal*) a piece of soap 一塊肥皂 **6** (*NAmE*) a number of pieces of paper for writing or drawing on, that are fastened together at one edge 便箋本；拍紙簿

'**table tennis** (also *informal* '**ping-pong** both *BrE*) (*NAmE* '**Ping-Pong™**) *noun* [U] a game played like TENNIS with BATS and a small plastic ball on a table with a net across it 乒乓球運動 ➲ VISUAL VOCAB page V45

table·top /'teɪbltɒp; *NAmE* -tɑːp/ *noun* the top or the surface of a table 桌面；枱面 ▸ **table·top** *adj.* [only before noun]：*a tabletop machine* (= that can be used on a table) 枱式機器 ◇ (*BrE*) *a tabletop sale* (= where goods for sale are displayed on tables) 枱面商品展銷

ˌ**Tablet P'C™** (also **tab·let**) *noun* a small computer that is easy to carry, with a large touch screen and sometimes without a physical keyboard 平板電腦（大觸摸屏小型便攜式電腦，有時不帶有形鍵盤）

table·ware /'teɪblweə(r); *NAmE* -wer/ *noun* [U] the word used in shops/stores, etc. for items that you use for meals, such as plates, glasses, knives and forks（商店用語）餐具

'**table wine** *noun* [U, C] a fairly cheap wine, suitable for drinking with meals 佐餐葡萄酒

tab·loid /'tæblɔɪd/ *noun* **1** a newspaper with small pages (usually half the size of those in larger papers) 小報（版面通常比大報小一半）➲ compare BERLINER, BROADSHEET **2** (sometimes *disapproving*) a newspaper of this size with short articles and a lot of pictures and stories about famous people, often thought of as less serious than other newspapers 通俗小報（文短圖多，內容多為名人佚事，常被視為不太嚴肅）：*The story made the front page in all the tabloids.* 這件事成了所有小報的頭版新聞。 ➲ compare QUALITY NEWSPAPER ➲ see also RED-TOP ▸ **tab·loid** *adj.* [only before noun]：*a serious paper in a new tabloid format* 一份以小報形式重新編排的嚴肅報紙 ◇ *tabloid journalists* 小報記者 ◇ *a tabloid newspaper* 通俗小報 ◇ *the tabloid press* 通俗小報界

taboo /tə'buː/ *noun* (*pl.* **ta·boos**) **~ (against/on sth)** **1** a cultural or religious custom that does not allow people to do, use or talk about a particular thing as people find it offensive or embarrassing（文化或宗教習俗方面的）禁忌，忌諱，戒律：*an incest taboo* 亂倫禁忌 ◇ *a taboo on working on a Sunday* 禁止星期日工作的習俗 ◇ *to* ***break/violate a taboo*** 觸犯禁忌 ◇ *Death is one of the great taboos in our culture.* 在我們的文化中，"死亡"是一大忌。 **2** a general agreement not to do sth or talk about sth 禁止；避諱：*The subject is still a taboo in our family.* 這個話題在我們家裏仍然諱莫如深。 ▸ **taboo** *adj.*：*in the days when sex was a* ***taboo subject*** 在談性色變的時代

ta'boo word *noun* a word that many people consider offensive or shocking, for example because it refers to sex, the body or people's race 禁忌詞

tabor /'teɪbə(r)/ *noun* a musical instrument like a small drum, used in the past 塔波鼓

'**tab stop** (also **tab**) *noun* a fixed position in a line of a document that you are typing that shows where a piece of text or a column of figures, etc. will begin（打字）首行固定鍵位

tabu·lar /'tæbjələ(r)/ *adj.* [usually before noun] presented or arranged in a TABLE (= in rows and columns) 表格式的；列成表的；製成表的：*tabular data* 列成表的數據 ◇ *The results are presented* ***in tabular form.*** 結果以表格形式列出。

tab·ula rasa /ˌtæbjʊlə 'rɑːzə/ *noun* (*pl.* **tab·ulae rasae** /ˌtæbjʊliː 'rɑːziː/) (from *Latin, formal*) **1** a situation in which there are no fixed ideas about how sth should develop 白板（指對未來發展沒有既定的想法） **2** the human mind as it is at birth, with no ideas or thoughts in it 空白（指人出生時沒有思想和觀點的純淨頭腦）；白紙般的思想

tabu·late /'tæbjuleɪt/ *verb* **~ sth** to arrange facts or figures in columns or lists so that they can be read easily 列成表格；列表顯示 ▸ **tabu·la·tion** /ˌtæbju'leɪʃn/ *noun* [U, C]

tabu·la·tor /'tæbjuleɪtə(r)/ *noun* = TAB KEY

tacho·graph /'tækəgrɑːf; *NAmE* -græf/ *noun* a device that is used in vehicles such as large lorries/trucks and some types of buses to measure their speed, how far they have travelled and when the driver has stopped to rest（機動車的）測速計，里程表

tach·om·eter /tæ'kɒmɪtə(r); *NAmE* -'kɑːm-/ *noun* a device that measures the rate that sth turns and is used to measure the speed of an engine in a vehicle 轉速計，轉速表（車輛發動機用）

tacit /ˈtæsɪt/ *adj.* [usually before noun] that is suggested indirectly or understood, rather than said in words 心照不宣的；不言而喻的；默示的：***tacit approval/support/knowledge*** 默許；暗中支持；只可意會的認識 ◇ *By* ***tacit agreement****, the subject was never mentioned again.* 根據達成的默契，這個話題從未再提起過。 ▸ **tacit·ly** *adv.*

taci·turn /ˈtæsɪtɜːn; *NAmE* -tɜːrn/ *adj.* (*formal*) tending not to say very much, in a way that seems unfriendly 不苟言笑的；沉默寡言的；緘默不語的 ▸ **taci·turn·ity** /ˌtæsɪˈtɜːnəti; *NAmE* -ˈtɜːrn-/ *noun* [U]

tack /tæk/ *noun, verb*

■ ***noun*** **1** [U, sing.] the way in which you deal with a particular situation; the direction of your words or thoughts 方針；方法；思路：*a complete* ***change of tack*** 方法的完全改變 ◇ *It was a brave decision to* ***change tack*** *in the middle of the project.* 在項目進行過程當中改變方針是個大膽的決定。◇ *When threats failed, she decided to* ***try/take a different tack****.* 威脅不成，她便決定變換策略。◇ *His thoughts wandered off* ***on another tack****.* 他離開了原來的思路。 **2** [C, U] (*technical* 術語) the direction that a boat with sails takes as it sails at an angle to the wind in order to fill its sails （帆船的）搶風調向，搶風行駛：*They were sailing on (a)* ***port/starboard tack*** (= with the wind coming from the left/right side). 他們正在左／右舷搶風行使。 **3** [C] a small nail with a sharp point and a flat head, used especially for fixing a carpet to the floor （尤指把地毯釘在地板上的）平頭釘，大頭釘：*a carpet tack* 地毯釘 ➲ compare NAIL *n.* (2) **4** [C] (*NAmE*) = THUMBTACK ➲ **VISUAL VOCAB** page V69 ➲ see also BLU-TACK **5** [C] a long loose STITCH used for holding pieces of cloth together temporarily, before you sew them finally 粗線腳縫；假縫 **6** [U] (*technical* 術語) the equipment that you need for riding a horse, such as a SADDLE and BRIDLE 鞍轡；馬具 **IDM** see BRASS

■ ***verb*** **1** [T] **~ sth + adv./prep.** to fasten sth in place with a tack or tacks （用平頭釘）釘住 **SYN** **nail**：*The carpet was tacked to the floor.* 地毯是用平頭釘釘在地板上的。 **2** [T] **~ sth** (**+ adv./prep.**) to fasten pieces of cloth together temporarily with long loose STITCHES before sewing them finally 綳；用粗線腳縫 **3** [I] (*technical* 術語) to change the direction of a sailing boat so that the wind blows onto the sails from the opposite side; to do this several times in order to travel in the direction that the wind is coming from 搶風行駛；換搶；作之字形航行

PHR V **ˌtack sth↔ˈon** | **ˌtack sth ˈonto sth** (*informal*) to add sth to sth that already exists, especially in a careless way （尤指漫不經心地）附加，增補，添加：*The poems were tacked on at the end of the book.* 這幾首詩給附在書的末尾。

tackie (also **tak·kie**) /ˈtæki/ *noun* (*SAfrE*) **1** a shoe with a rubber SOLE (= the part underneath), worn when dressing informally or for taking part in sports 膠底便鞋；運動鞋 ➲ compare TRAINER **2** (*informal*) a tyre on a car, etc. 輪胎

tackle 0➝ /ˈtækl/ *verb, noun*

■ ***verb*** **1** 0➝ [T] **~ sth** to make a determined effort to deal with a difficult problem or situation 應付，處理，解決（難題或局面）：*The government is determined to tackle inflation.* 政府決心解決通貨膨脹問題。 **2** 0➝ [T] **~ sb** (**about sth**) to speak to sb about a problem or difficult situation 與某人交涉；向某人提起（問題或困難情況） **SYN** **confront**：*I tackled him about the money he owed me.* 我就他欠我錢的事與他進行了交涉。 **3** [T, I] **~** (**sb**) (in football (SOCCER), HOCKEY, etc. 足球、曲棍球等) to try and take the ball from an opponent 搶球；搶斷；搶截；鏟斷：*He was tackled just outside the penalty area.* 他就在罰球區外讓對方把球搶斷。 **4** [I, T] **~** (**sb**) (in RUGBY or AMERICAN FOOTBALL 橄欖球或美式足球) to make an opponent fall to the ground in order to stop them running 擒抱摔倒；阻截 **5** [T] **~ sb** to deal with sb who is violent or threatening you 抓獲；擒獲；給以顏色：*He tackled a masked intruder at his home.* 他在家裏抓住了一個私自闖入的蒙面人。

■ ***noun*** **1** [C] an act of trying to take the ball from an opponent in football (SOCCER), etc.; an act of knocking an opponent to the ground in RUGBY or AMERICAN FOOTBALL （足球等）搶斷球，阻截鏟球；（橄欖球或美式足球）擒抱摔倒，阻截 ➲ **VISUAL VOCAB** page V44 **2** [C] (*NAmE*) (in AMERICAN FOOTBALL 美式足球) a player whose job is to stop opponents by knocking them to the ground 阻截隊員 **3** [U] the equipment used to do a particular sport or activity, especially fishing 用具；體育器材；（尤指）漁具 ➲ see also BLOCK AND TACKLE **4** [U] (*BrE, slang*) a man's sexual organs 雞巴；陽具

tack·ler /ˈtæklə(r)/ *noun* (*BrE*) a player who tries to TACKLE an opponent in some sports （某些體育運動的）阻截隊員

tacky /ˈtæki/ *adj.* (**tack·ier, tacki·est**) **1** (*informal*) cheap, badly made and/or lacking in taste 低劣的；蹩腳的；俗氣的；乏味的：*tacky souvenirs* 蹩腳的紀念品 ◇ *The movie had a really tacky ending.* 這部電影的結尾真差勁。 **2** (of paint, glue, etc. 油漆、膠水等) not dry and therefore slightly sticky 未乾透的；發黏的 ▸ **tacki·ness** *noun* [U]

taco /ˈtækəʊ; *NAmE* ˈtɑːkoʊ/ *noun* (*pl.* **-os**) (from *Spanish*) a type of Mexican food consisting of a crisp fried PANCAKE that is folded over and filled with meat, BEANS, etc. 墨西哥煎玉米粉捲（以肉、豆等作餡）

tact /tækt/ *noun* [U] the ability to deal with difficult or embarrassing situations carefully and without doing or saying anything that will annoy or upset other people （處事、言談等的）老練，圓通，得體，乖巧 **SYN** **sensitivity**：*Settling the dispute required great tact and diplomacy.* 解決這個爭端需要十分老練和嫻熟的外交手腕。◇ *She is not exactly known for her tact.* 她並不以策略見稱。

tact·ful /ˈtæktfl/ *adj.* careful not to say or do anything that will annoy or upset other people 圓通的；得體的；不得罪人的 **SYN** **diplomatic**：*That wasn't a very tactful thing to say!* 說這種話可不太得體！◇ *I tried to find a tactful way of telling her the truth.* 我設法找一個妥善的辦法，把實情告訴她。 **OPP** **tactless** ▸ **tact·ful·ly** /-fəli/ *adv.*：*a tactfully worded reply* 措辭得體的答覆 ◇ *I tactfully suggested he should see a doctor.* 我婉轉地建議他去看醫生。

tac·tic /ˈtæktɪk/ *noun* **1** [C, usually pl.] the particular method you use to achieve sth 策略；手段；招數：*They tried all kinds of tactics to get us to go.* 他們施盡所有的招數想讓我們離開。◇ *This was just the latest in a series of* ***delaying tactics****.* 這只是一系列拖延戰術中的一個新花招。◇ *The manager discussed tactics with his team.* 經理和他手下的一班人討論了策略問題。◇ *Confrontation is not always the best tactic.* 對抗並非總是上策。◇ *It's time to try a change of tactic.* 現在是改弦易轍的時候了。 **2** **tactics** [pl.] the art of moving soldiers and military equipment around during a battle or war in order to use them in the most effective way 戰術；兵法 ➲ compare STRATEGY

tac·tic·al /ˈtæktɪkl/ *adj.* **1** [usually before noun] connected with the particular method you use to achieve sth 戰術上的；策略上的 **SYN** **strategic**：*tactical planning* 對策謀劃 ◇ *to have a tactical advantage* 擁有戰術上的優勢 ◇ *Telling your boss you were looking for a new job was a* ***tactical error*** (= it was the wrong thing to do at that time). 你把正在另找工作的事告訴了老闆，是個策略上的錯誤。 **2** [usually before noun] carefully planned in order to achieve a particular aim 有謀略的；手段高明的；善於謀劃的 **SYN** **strategic**：*a tactical decision* 高明的決策 ➲ see also TACTICAL VOTING **3** [only before noun] (especially of weapons 尤指武器) used or having an effect over short distances or for a short time 戰術的；短程的：***tactical weapons/missiles*** 戰術武器／導彈 ➲ compare STRATEGIC (3) **4** [only before noun] connected with military tactics 作戰的：*He was given tactical command of the operation.* 他被授以這次軍事行動的作戰指揮權。 ▸ **tac·tic·al·ly** /-kli/ *adv.*：*At the time, it was tactically the right thing to do.* 當時這樣做在策略上是正確的。◇ *The enemy was tactically superior.* 敵人擁有戰術上的優勢。

ˌtactical ˈvoting *noun* [U] (*BrE*) the act of voting for a particular person or political party, not because you support them, but in order to prevent sb else from being elected（並非真心支持而是為防止他人當選的）戰術投票，策略性投票

tac·ti·cian /tæk'tɪʃn/ *noun* a person who is very clever at planning the best way to achieve sth 有策略的人；手段高明的人

tact·ile /'tæktaɪl; *NAmE* -tl/ *adj.* [usually before noun] connected with the sense of touch; using your sense of touch 觸覺的；有觸覺的；能觸知的：*tactile stimuli* 觸覺刺激 ◇ *visual and tactile communication* 視覺和觸覺交流 ◇ *tactile fabric* (= pleasant to touch) 手感好的織物 ◇ *tactile maps* (= that you can touch and feel) 觸摸地圖 ◇ *He's a very tactile man* (= he enjoys touching people). 他這個人非常愛撫摸他人。

tact·less /'tæktləs/ *adj.* saying or doing things that are likely to annoy or to upset other people 言行不得體的；得罪人的；不圓通的；沒策略的 SYN **insensitive**：*a tactless remark* 不得體的話 ◇ *It was tactless of you to comment on his hair!* 你竟對他的頭髮說三道四，真是缺心眼！ OPP **tactful** ▸ **tact·less·ly** *adv.* **tact·less·ness** *noun* [U]

tad /tæd/ *noun* **a tad** [sing.] (*informal*) a very small amount 少量；一點兒：*Could you turn the sound down just a tad?* 你把音量調低一點兒好嗎？ ▸ **a tad** *adv.* *It's a tad too expensive for me.* 這對我來說稍微貴了一點兒。

tad·pole /'tædpəʊl; *NAmE* -poʊl/ (*NAmE* also **polli·wog**) *noun* a small creature with a large head and a small tail, that lives in water and is the young form of a FROG or TOAD 蝌蚪 ➲ VISUAL VOCAB page V13

tae kwon do /ˌtaɪ ˌkwɒn 'dəʊ; *NAmE* ˌkwɑːn 'doʊ/ *noun* [U] a Korean system of fighting without weapons, similar to KARATE 跆拳道

taf·feta /'tæfɪtə/ *noun* [U] a type of stiff shiny cloth made from silk or a similar material, used especially for making dresses 塔夫綢

Taffy /'tæfi/ *noun* (*pl.* **-ies**) (also **Taff** /tæf/) (*BrE, informal*, often *offensive*) a person from Wales 威爾士人

taffy /'tæfi/ *noun* (*pl.* **-ies**) [U, C] (*NAmE*) a type of soft sweet/candy made of brown sugar boiled until it is very thick and given different shapes and colours 太妃糖；乳脂糖

tag /tæg/ *noun, verb*

■ ***noun*** **1** [C] (often in compounds 常構成複合詞) a small piece of paper, cloth, plastic, etc. attached to sth to identify it or give information about it 標籤；標牌：*He put name tags on all his shirts.* 他給自己所有的襯衣都縫上了標有姓名的籤條。◇ *a gift tag* (= tied to a present) 禮品籤 ◇ *The police use electronic tags to monitor the whereabouts of young offenders on probation.* 警方利用電子跟踪器監視緩刑期間的青年罪犯。➲ SYNONYMS at LABEL ➲ see also PRICE TAG **2** [C, usually sing.] a name or phrase that is used to describe a person or thing in some way 稱呼；諢名：*They are finally ready to drop the tag 'the new Beatles'.* 他們終於準備放棄"新披頭士樂隊"這一稱謂。◇ *The 'lucky' tag stuck for years.* "幸運兒"這個諢名叫了好多年。 **3** [C] (*linguistics* 語言) a word or phrase that is added to a sentence for emphasis, for example *I do* in *Yes, I do* 附加語（為加強語氣，如 Yes, I do 一句中的 I do）➲ see also QUESTION TAG **4** [C] (*computing* 計) a set of letters or symbols that are put before and after a piece of text or data in order to identify it or show that it is to be treated in a particular way 標記；標籤；標識符 **5** [C] a short QUOTATION or saying in a foreign language（外國語的）語錄，引語，格言，諺語：*the Latin tag 'Si vis pacem, para bellum.'* (= if you want peace, prepare for war) 拉丁語格言："欲要和平，輒需備戰。" **6** (*BrE* also **tig**) [U] a children's game in which one child chases the others and tries to touch one of them 捉人（兒童遊戲） **7** [C] a symbol or name used by a GRAFFITI writer and painted in a public place（在公共場所塗鴉者用的）符號，名字

■ ***verb*** (**-gg-**) **1 ~ sth/sb** to fasten a tag onto sth/sb 給…加上標籤：*Each animal was tagged with a number for identification.* 每隻動物都繫上了標有號碼的小牌，以便辨認。➲ see also ELECTRONIC TAGGING **2 ~ sb/sth as sth** to give sb/sth a name that describes what they are or do 把…稱作；給…起諢名 SYN **label**：*The country no longer wanted to be tagged as a Third World nation.* 這個國家不願意再被稱為第三世界國家。 **3 ~ sth** (*computing* 計) to add a set of letters or symbols to a piece of text or data in order to identify it or show that it is to be treated in a particular way 加標識符（或標記、標籤）

PHR V **ˌtag aˈlong (behind/with sb)** to go somewhere with sb, especially when you have not been asked or invited 跟隨，尾隨（尤指未經同意或邀請） **ˌtag sth↔ˈon | ˌtag sth ˈonto sth** to add sth to the end of sth that already exists, especially in a careless way（尤指漫不經心地）給…加上，附加：*An apology was tagged onto the end of the letter.* 信的結尾順便附了一句抱歉的話。

Taga·log /tə'gɑːlɒg; *NAmE* -lɔːg/ *noun* [U] the national language spoken in the Philippine islands 他加祿語（通行於菲律賓群島）

ta·gine (also **ta·jine**) /tə'ʒiːn; tə'dʒiːn/ *noun* **1** [C, U] a hot dish made with meat and vegetables, cooked with liquid and spices in a closed container 塔吉鍋燉菜（燜燉加調料的肉菜） **2** [C] a container made of CLAY, with a pointed lid, for cooking and serving tagine, originally used in North Africa 塔吉鍋（陶製、尖蓋、用於烹飪和上菜，源於北非）

taglia·telle /ˌtæljə'teli; *NAmE* ˌtɑːl-/ *noun* [U] (from *Italian*) PASTA in the shape of long flat strips 意大利扁麪條

'tag line *noun* (*NAmE, informal*) **1** = PUNCHLINE **2** = SLOGAN

'tag question *noun* (*grammar* 語法) = QUESTION TAG

'tag team *noun* **1** a team of two WRESTLERS who take turns to fight in the same match（摔跤比賽中輪流出賽的）車輪戰兩人組 **2** (*informal, especially NAmE*) two people working or performing together 兩人組；雙人組合：*The show used a tag team of interviewers.* 節目採用了兩人搭檔提問訪談。

ta·hini /tɑː'hiːni; tə'h-/ (also **ta·hina** /tɑː'hiːnə; tə'h-/) *noun* [U] a thick mixture made with crushed SESAME seeds, eaten in the Middle East（中東）芝麻醬

t'ai chi ch'uan /ˌtaɪ tʃiː 'tʃwɑːn/ (also **ˌt'ai 'chi**) *noun* [U] (from *Chinese*) a Chinese system of exercises consisting of sets of very slow controlled movements 太極拳

taiga /'taɪgə/ *noun* [sing., U] forest that grows in wet ground in far northern regions of the earth 泰加林（北方濕地的針葉林）；北方森林：*the Siberian taiga* 西伯利亞針葉林

tail 0‑ᵂ /teɪl/ *noun, verb*

■ ***noun***

▸ OF BIRD/ANIMAL/FISH 鳥獸；魚 **1** 0‑ᵂ [C] the part that sticks out and can be moved at the back of the body of a bird, an animal or a fish 尾；尾巴：*The dog ran up, wagging its tail.* 那條狗搖着尾巴跑上前去。◇ *The male has beautiful tail feathers.* 雄鳥有美麗的尾羽。➲ VISUAL VOCAB page V12 ➲ see also PONYTAIL

▸ -TAILED 有…尾巴 **2** (in adjectives 構成形容詞) having the type of tail mentioned 有…尾巴的：*a white-tailed eagle* 白尾雕

▸ OF PLANE/SPACECRAFT 飛機；宇宙飛船 **3** 0‑ᵂ [C] the back part of a plane, SPACECRAFT, etc. 尾部；後部：*the tail wing* 尾翼 ➲ VISUAL VOCAB page V53

▸ BACK/END OF STH 後部；末尾 **4** [C] **~ (of sth)** a part of sth that sticks out at the back like a tail 尾狀後部；尾狀物：*the tail of a kite* 風箏的尾墜 **5** [C] **~ (of sth)** the last part of sth that is moving away from you（離去事物的）末尾部份：*the tail of the procession* 遊行隊伍的末尾 ➲ see also TAIL END

▸ JACKET 上衣 **6 tails** [pl.] (also **tail·coat** [C]) a long jacket divided at the back below the waist into two pieces that become narrower at the bottom, worn by men at very formal events 燕尾服；男式晚禮服：*The men all wore top hat and tails.* 男士都頭戴高頂禮帽，身穿晚禮服。➲ see also COAT-TAILS, SHIRT TAIL ➲ compare DINNER JACKET, MORNING COAT

▸ SIDE OF COIN 硬幣的面 **7 tails** [U] the side of a coin that does not have a picture of the head of a person on it, used as one choice when a coin is TOSSED to decide sth 硬幣反面，硬幣文面（沒有頭像的一面）➲ compare HEAD *n.* (7)

▸ PERSON WHO FOLLOWS SB 跟蹤者 **8** [C] (*informal*) a person who is sent to follow sb secretly and find out information about where that person goes, what they do, etc. 盯梢人；暗探：*The police have* ***put a tail on him.*** 警方已派人對他進行盯梢。

▸ **tail·less** *adj.*：*Manx cats are tailless.* 馬恩島貓沒有尾巴。

IDM **on sb's 'tail** (*informal*) following behind sb very closely, especially in a car（尤指開車）盯梢，尾隨 **the tail (is) wagging the 'dog** used to describe a situation in which the most important aspect is being influenced and controlled by sb/sth that is not as important（用以描述次要部份影響和支配主要部份）主次顛倒，喧賓奪主，大權旁落 **turn 'tail** to run away from a fight or dangerous situation（危急時刻）轉身逃跑，逃逸，臨陣脫逃 **with your tail between your 'legs** (*informal*) feeling ashamed or unhappy because you have been defeated or punished 無地自容；垂頭喪氣；灰溜溜 ➲ more at BRIGHT-EYED, CHASE *v.*, HEAD *n.*, NOSE *n.*, STING *n.*

■ ***verb*** **~ sb** to follow sb closely, especially in order to watch where they go and what they do 跟蹤；尾隨；盯梢 SYN **shadow**：*A private detective had been tailing them for several weeks.* 私人偵探幾個星期來一直在跟踪他們。IDM see TOP *v.*

PHR V **,tail a'way/'off** (*especially BrE*) to become smaller or weaker 變得越來越小（或弱）；逐漸消失：*The number of tourists tails off in October.* 十月份遊客人數越來越少。◇ *'But why ... ?' Her voice tailed away.* "但是為什麼…？" 她的聲音細了下去。**,tail 'back** (of traffic 車輛) to form a tailback 排成長隊

tail·back /'teɪlbæk/ *noun* **1** [C] (*BrE*) a long line of traffic that is moving slowly or not moving at all, because sth is blocking the road（車輛因受阻而排成的）長隊，長蛇陣 **2** [C, U] = HALFBACK (2), (3)

tail·board /'teɪlbɔːd; *NAmE* -bɔːrd/ *noun* = TAILGATE *n.* (1)

tail·bone /'teɪlbəʊn; *NAmE* -boʊn/ *noun* the small bone at the bottom of the SPINE 尾骨；尾椎 SYN **coccyx** ➲ VISUAL VOCAB page V59

tail·coat /'teɪlkəʊt; *NAmE* -koʊt/ *noun* a long jacket divided at the back below the waist into two pieces that become narrower at the bottom, worn by men at formal events 燕尾服；男子晚禮服 SYN **tails**

,tail 'end *noun* [sing.] the very last part of sth 末尾；末端；尾端；結尾部份：*the tail end of the queue* 隊尾

tail·gate /'teɪlɡeɪt/ *noun, verb*

■ ***noun*** **1** (also **tail·board**) a door at the back of a lorry/truck that opens downwards and that you can open or remove when you are loading or unloading the vehicle（卡車的）後攔板，後擋板 **2** the door that opens upwards at the back of a car that has three or five doors (called a HATCHBACK)（三門或五門轎車的）尾門，艙蓋式後背門

■ ***verb*** **1** [I, T] **~ (sb/sth)** (*informal, especially NAmE*) to drive too closely behind another vehicle 緊跟（另一車輛）行駛 **2** [I] (*NAmE*) to eat food and drinks outdoors, served from the tailgate of a car 旅行野餐（打開轎車艙蓋式後背門就餐）

'tail light *noun* a red light at the back of a car, bicycle or train（車輛的）尾燈，後燈 ➲ VISUAL VOCAB page V52

tailor /'teɪlə(r)/ *noun, verb*

■ ***noun*** a person whose job is to make men's clothes, especially sb who makes suits, etc. for individual customers（尤指為顧客個別訂製男裝的）裁縫

■ ***verb*** to make or adapt sth for a particular purpose, a particular person, etc. 專門製作；訂做：**~ sth to/for sb/sth** *Special programmes of study are tailored to the needs of specific groups.* 為滿足特定群體的需要，特製了專門的課程。◇ **~ sth to do sth** *Most travel agents are prepared to tailor travel arrangements to meet individual requirements.* 為了滿足個別人士需要，大多數旅行社都願意作出專門的旅遊安排。

tailored /'teɪləd; *NAmE* -lərd/ *adj.* **1** (of clothes 衣服) made to fit well or closely 訂做的；合身的：*a tailored jacket* 訂做的夾克衫 **2** made for a particular person or purpose 特製的；專門的 SYN **tailor-made**

tailor·ing /'teɪlərɪŋ/ *noun* [U] **1** the style or the way in which a suit, jacket, etc. is made 裁剪式樣；裁縫手藝：*Clever tailoring can flatter your figure.* 巧妙的裁剪可以使你的身材顯得優美。**2** the job of making men's clothes（男裝）裁縫業，成衣活

,tailor-'made *adj.* **1 ~ (for sb/sth)** | **~ (to sth/to do sth)** made for a particular person or purpose, and therefore very suitable 特製的；專門設置的；非常合適的：*a tailor-made course of study* 專門設置的課程 ◇ *a trip tailor-made just for you* 專門為你安排的旅行 ◇ *She seems tailor-made for the job* (= perfectly suited for it). 她似乎生來就是為了專門做這項工作的。**2** (of clothes 衣服) made by a TAILOR for a particular person 訂做的 SYN **bespoke**：*a tailor-made suit* 訂做的西服

tail·piece /'teɪlpiːs/ *noun* **1 ~ (to sth)** a part that you add to the end of a piece of writing to make it longer or complete（文章結尾的）附加部份，續補部份 **2** (*music* 音) a piece of wood that the lower ends of the strings of some musical instruments are attached to（弦樂器的）繫弦板

tail·pipe /'teɪlpaɪp/ *noun* (*especially NAmE*) = EXHAUST *n.* (2)

tail·plane /'teɪlpleɪn/ *noun* a small horizontal wing at the back of an aircraft（飛機的）橫尾翼，水平尾翼 ➲ VISUAL VOCAB page V53

tail·spin /'teɪlspɪn/ *noun* [sing.] **1** a situation in which a pilot loses control of an aircraft and it spins as it falls quickly towards the ground, with the back making larger circles than the front（飛機的）尾旋，尾螺旋 **2** a situation that suddenly becomes much worse and is not under control 惡化的局勢；慌亂；混亂；失控：*Following the announcement, share prices went into a tailspin.* 公告宣佈後，股市一片混亂。

tail·wind /'teɪlwɪnd/ *noun* a wind that blows from behind a moving vehicle, a runner, etc. 順風 ➲ compare HEADWIND

taint /teɪnt/ *verb, noun*

■ ***verb*** [often passive] **~ sth (with sth)** (*formal*) to damage or spoil the quality of sth or the opinion that people have of sb/sth 使腐壞；污染；玷污，敗壞（名聲）：*The administration was tainted with scandal.* 醜聞使得政府聲名狼藉。▸ **taint·ed** *adj.*：*tainted drinking water* 污染的飲用水

■ ***noun*** [usually sing.] the effect of sth bad or unpleasant that spoils the quality of sb/sth 腐壞；污染；玷污：*to be free from the taint of corruption* 不受腐敗影響

tai·pan /'taɪpæn/ *noun* (from *Chinese*) **1** a foreign person who is in charge of a business in China 大班（舊時對中國洋行老闆的稱呼）**2** an extremely poisonous Australian snake 太潘蛇（產於澳大利亞，毒性劇烈）

ta·jine = TAGINE

take 0→ /teɪk/ *verb, noun*

■ ***verb*** (**took** /tʊk/, **taken** /'teɪkən/)

▸ CARRY/LEAD 攜帶；帶領 **1** 0→ [T] to carry or move sth from one place to another 攜帶；拿走；取走；運走：**~ sth (with you)** *I forgot to take my bag with me when I got off the bus.* 我下公共汽車時忘了拿包。◇ **~ sth to sb/sth** *Take this to the bank for me, would you?* 請替我把這送到銀行去好嗎？◇ *Shall I take a gift to my host family?* 我要不要給主人家帶件禮物呢？◇ **~ sb sth** *Shall I take my host family a gift?* 我要不要給主人家帶件禮物呢？**2** 0→ [T] to go with sb from one place to another, especially to guide or lead them 帶去；引領：**~ sb** *It's too far to walk—I'll take you by car.* 步行路太遠，我開車送你去。◇ **~ sb to sth** *A boy took us to our room.* 服務員帶我們到房間。◇ **~ sb doing sth** *I'm taking the kids swimming later.* 我待會兒帶孩子們去游泳。◇ **~ sb to do sth** *The boys were taken to see their grandparents most weekends.* 大多數週末都有人帶這些男孩去看望爺爺奶奶。**3** 0→ [T] **~ sb/sth + adv./prep.** to make sb/sth go

T

from one level, situation, etc. to another 使達到，把…推向，把…帶到（另一個層次、層面等）：*Her energy and talent took her to the top of her profession.* 她憑着充沛的精力和天賦的才能達到了事業的頂峰。◇ *The new loan takes the total debt to $100 000.* 加上這筆新貸款，負債總額達到 10 萬元。◇ *I'd like to take my argument a stage further.* 我想把我的論點進行進一步的發揮。◇ *He believes he has the skills to take the club forward.* 他相信他有能力使俱樂部繼續發展。◇ *We'll take the matter forward at our next meeting* (= discuss it further). 我們將在下一次會議上進一步討論這個問題。

▸ **REACH AND HOLD** 伸手取 **4** 🔑 [T] **~ sb/sth** to put your hands or arms around sb/sth and hold them/it; to reach for sb/sth and hold them/it 拿；抱；握；取；接：*I passed him the rope and he took it.* 我把繩子遞給他，他接了過去。◇ *Free newspapers: please take one.* 報紙免費，請取一份。◇ *Can you take* (= hold) *the baby for a moment?* 你能先抱一下孩子嗎？◇ *He took her hand/took her by the hand* (= held her hand, for example to lead her somewhere). 他拉着她的手。◇ *She took the child in her arms and kissed him.* 她把孩子摟在懷裏親吻他。

▸ **REMOVE** 移開 **5** 🔑 [T] **~ sth/sb + adv./prep.** to remove sth/sb from a place or a person 拿開；取出；挪開：*Will you take your books off the table?* 把你的書從桌子上拿走好嗎？◇ *The sign must be taken down.* 這個指示牌一定要摘下來。◇ *He took some keys out of his pocket.* 他從口袋裏取出幾把鑰匙。◇ *My name had been taken off the list.* 我的名字從名單上畫掉了。◇ *She was playing with a knife, so I took it away from her.* 她在玩一把刀子，於是我把刀子從她手裏奪了過來。◇ (*informal*) *She was playing with a knife, so I took it off her.* 她在玩一把刀子，於是我把刀子從她手裏奪了過來。◇ (*figurative*) *The new sports centre will* **take the pressure off** *the old one.* 新的體育運動中心將減輕老體育運動中心的壓力。 **6** 🔑 [T] **~ sth** to remove sth without permission or by mistake 擅自拿走；偷走；誤拿：*Someone has taken my scarf.* 有人把我的圍巾拿走了。◇ *Did the burglars take anything valuable?* 入室竊賊偷走了貴重的東西沒有？◇ (*figurative*) *The storms* **took the lives** *of 50 people.* 這場暴風雨奪走了 50 人的生命。**7** 🔑 [T] to get sth from a particular source 從…中取出；取材於：**~ sth from sth** *The scientists are taking water samples from the river.* 科學家正從河中採水樣。◇ *The machine takes its name from its inventor.* 這機器是根據發明者的姓名命名的。◇ **~ sth out of sth** *Part of her article is taken straight* (= copied) *out of my book.* 她的文章有一部份是從我的書中抄來的。

▸ **CAPTURE** 捕獲 **8** 🔑 [T] to capture a place or person; to get control of sth 奪取；攻佔；抓獲；控制：**~ sth (from sb)** *The rebels succeeded in taking the town.* 反叛者攻佔了那個城鎮。◇ *The state has* **taken control of** *the company.* 政府已經接管了這家公司。◇ **~ sb + noun** *The rebels took him prisoner.* 反叛者把他俘虜了。◇ *He was* **taken prisoner** *by the rebels.* 他被反叛者俘虜了。

▸ **CHOOSE/BUY** 選擇；購買 **9** 🔑 [T] **~ sth** to choose, buy or rent sth 選中；買下；租用：*I'll take the grey jacket.* 我要那件灰色夾克衫。◇ *We took a room at the hotel for two nights.* 我們在旅館開了個房間，住了兩夜。 **10** [T] **~ sth** (*formal*) to buy a newspaper or magazine regularly 經常購買（某報紙或期刊）：*We take the 'Express'.* 我們訂閱的是《快報》。

▸ **EAT/DRINK** 食用；飲用 **11** 🔑 [T] **~ sth** to eat, drink, etc. sth 吃；喝；服（藥）：*Do you take sugar in your coffee?* 你的咖啡裏要放糖嗎？◇ *The doctor has given me some medicine to take for my cough.* 醫生已給我開了治咳嗽的藥吃。◇ *He started taking drugs* (= illegal drugs) *at college.* 他上大學時就開始吸毒。

▸ **MATHEMATICS** 數學 **12** [T] **~ A (away) from B | B ~ away A | ~ A away** (not used in the progressive tenses 不用於進行時) to reduce one number by the value of another 減去 SYN **subtract**：*Take 5 from 12 and you're left with 7.* * 12 減 5，剩 7。◇ (*informal*) *80 take away 5 is 75.* * 80 減去 5 等於 75。

▸ **WRITE DOWN** 寫下 **13** 🔑 [T] **~ sth** to find out and record sth; to write sth down 記錄；摘錄；記下：*The police officer took my name and address.* 警察記下了我的姓名和地址。◇ *Did you* **take notes** *in the class?* 你在課堂上做了筆記嗎？

Synonyms 同義詞辨析

take

lead • escort • drive • show • walk • guide • usher • direct

These words all mean to go with sb from one place to another. 以上各詞均含帶去、引領之義。

take to go with sb from one place to another, for example in order to show them sth or to show them the way to a place 指帶去、帶路、引領：*It's too far to walk—I'll take you by car.* 步行路太遠，我開車送你去。

lead to go with or go in front of sb in order to show them the way or to make them go in the right direction 指帶路、領路、引領：*Firefighters led the survivors to safety.* 消防隊員把幸存者帶到了安全的地方。

escort to go with sb in order to protect or guard them or to show them the way 指護衞、護送：*The president arrived, escorted by twelve bodyguards.* 總統在十二名保鏢的護送下到達。

drive to take sb somewhere in a car, taxi, etc 指駕車送（人）：*My mother drove us to the airport.* 我母親開車把我們送到了機場。

show to take sb to a particular place, in the right direction, or along the correct route 指引領、帶領：*The attendant showed us to our seats.* 服務員把我們帶到我們的座位。

walk to go somewhere with sb on foot, especially in order to make sure that they get there safely; to take an animal, especially a dog, for a walk or make an animal walk somewhere 指陪伴或護送（人）走、牽着或趕着（動物）走、遛（狗）：*He always walked her home.* 他經常護送她走回家。◇ *Have you walked the dog yet today?* 你今天遛狗了嗎？

guide to show sb the way to a place, often by going with them; to show sb a place that you know well 指給某人領路（或導遊）、指引：*She guided us through the busy streets.* 她帶領我們穿過了繁忙的街道。◇ *We were guided around the museums.* 我們被領着參觀了博物館。

usher (*rather formal*) to politely take or show sb where they should go, especially within a building 指把…引往、引導、引領，尤指在建築物內：*She ushered her guests to their seats.* 她把客人引領到座位上。

direct (*rather formal*) to tell or show sb how to get somewhere or where to go 指給某人指路、為某人領路：*A young woman directed them to the station.* 一名年輕女子給他們指了去車站的路。

PATTERNS

- to take/lead/escort/drive/show/walk/guide/usher/direct sb **to/out of/into** sth
- to take/lead/escort/drive/show/walk/guide sb **around/round**
- to take/lead/escort/drive/walk sb **home**
- to take/lead/escort/guide sb **to safety**
- to lead/show **the way**

▸ **PHOTOGRAPH** 拍照 **14** 🔑 [T] **~ sth** to photograph sb/sth 拍照；照相；攝影：*to* **take a photograph/picture/snapshot** *of sb/sth* 給（某人／某物）照相／拍照／拍快照◇ *to* **have your picture/photo taken** 讓人給你拍照

▸ **MEASUREMENT** 計量 **15** 🔑 [T] **~ sth** to test or measure sth 量取；測定：*to take sb's temperature* 給某人量體溫 ◇ *I need to have my blood pressure taken.* 我需要量一下血壓。

▸ **SEAT** 座位 **16** 🔑 [T] **~ sth** to sit down in or use a chair, etc. 就（座）；佔據（座位）：*Are these seats taken?* 這些座位有人嗎？◇ *Come in;* **take a seat**. 進來，坐下。 ➲ SYNONYMS at SIT

▸ **GIVE EXAMPLE** 舉例 **17** [T] **~ sb/sth** used to introduce sb/sth as an example 以…為例；將…作為例證：*Lots of couples have problems in the first year of marriage. Take*

Ann and Paul. 在婚後頭一年裏，許多夫婦都出現一些問題。安和保羅就是個例子。

▸ **ACCEPT/RECEIVE** 接受；收到 **18** [T] (not usually used in the progressive tenses or in the passive 通常不用於進行時或被動語態) **~ sth** to accept or receive sth 接受；收到：*If they offer me the job, I'll take it.* 如果他們給我這份工作，我就接受。◇ *She was accused of taking bribes.* 她被控受賄。◇ *Does the hotel take credit cards?* 這家旅館接受信用卡付款嗎？◇ *I'll take the call in my office.* 我要在辦公室裏接這個電話。◇ *Why should I* ***take the blame*** *for somebody else's mistakes?* 我為什麼要代人受過呢？◇ *If you* ***take my advice*** *you'll have nothing more to do with him.* 你要是聽我的勸告，就不要再和他有什麼瓜葛。◇ *Will you take $10 for the book* (= will you sell it for $10)? 這本書 10 塊錢你賣嗎？◇ *The store took* (= sold goods worth) *$100 000 last week.* 這家商店上星期的營業額為 10 萬元。 **19** [T] (not usually used in the progressive tenses 通常不用於進行時) **~ sb** to accept sb as a customer, patient, etc. 接納；接待（顧客、患者等）：*The school doesn't take boys* (= only has girls). 這所學校不收男生。◇ *The dentist can't take any new patients.* 這位牙科醫生接待不了新患者了。 **20** [T] (not usually used in the progressive tenses 通常不用於進行時) **~ sth** to experience or be affected by sth 遭受；經受；承受：*The school took the full force of the explosion.* 這所學校在爆炸中毀壞最嚴重。◇ *Can the ropes* ***take the strain*** (= not break)? 這些繩子能承受住這一張力嗎？◇ *The team took a terrible beating.* 這個隊遭到慘敗。 **21** [T, no passive] **~ sth** (not usually used in the progressive tenses 通常不用於進行時) to be able to bear sth 忍受；容忍；承受：*She can't* ***take criticism.*** 她受不了批評。◇ *I don't think I can take much more of this heat.* 我覺得再也忍受不了這種高溫了。◇ *I find his attitude a little* ***hard to take.*** 我覺得他的態度有點兒令人難以接受。 **22** [T] **~ sth/sb + adv./prep.** to react to sth/sb in a particular way（以某種方式）對待，處理：*He took the criticism surprisingly well.* 他對待這一批評的態度竟意外的好。◇ *These threats are not to be taken lightly.* 這些威脅可不能等閒視之。◇ *I wish you'd take me seriously.* 我希望你認真對待我的話。◇ *She took it in the spirit in which it was intended.* 她根據其精神實質來認識此事。

▸ **CONSIDER** 考慮 **23** [T] (not used in the progressive tenses 不用於進行時) to understand or consider sth in a particular way 領會；理解；考慮：**~ sth (as sth)** *She took what he said as a compliment.* 她把他說的看作是稱譽。◇ *How am I supposed to take that remark?* 我應該怎麼理解那話的意思？◇ *Taken overall, the project was a success.* 總的看來，這個項目是成功的。◇ **~ sth to do sth** *What did you take his comments to mean?* 你認為他的意見是什麼意思？ **24** [T] (not used in the progressive tenses 不用於進行時) to consider sb/sth to be sb/sth, especially when you are wrong（尤指錯誤地）以為，把…看作；誤認為：**~ sb/sth for sb/sth** *Even the experts took the painting for a genuine Van Gogh.* 連行家都誤以為這幅畫是凡 • 高的真跡。◇ *Of course I didn't do it!* ***What do you take me for*** (= what sort of person do you think I am)? 那當然不是我幹的！你把我當成什麼人啦？◇ **~ sb/sth to be sb/sth** *I took the man with him to be his father.* 我誤以為和他在一起的那個男人是他父親。

▸ **HAVE FEELING/OPINION** 有感情／看法 **25** [T] (not usually used in the progressive tenses 通常不用於進行時) **~ sth** to have a particular feeling, opinion or attitude 產生（感情）；持有（看法）；採取（態度）：*My parents always* ***took an interest*** *in my hobbies.* 我父母總是關心重視我的愛好。◇ *Don't* ***take offence*** (= be offended) *at what I said.* 我講的話你別見怪。◇ *I* ***took a dislike*** *to him.* 我對他產生了反感。◇ *He takes the view that children are responsible for their own actions.* 他的觀點是孩子應對自己的行為負責。

▸ **ACTION** 行動 **26** [T] **~ sth** to use a particular course of action in order to deal with or achieve sth 採取（措施）；採用（方法）：*The government is* ***taking action*** *to combat drug abuse.* 政府正在採取措施，打擊濫用藥物。◇ *We need to take a different approach to the problem.* 我們應該採用另一種方法來解決這一問題。 **27** [T] **~ sth** used with nouns to say that sb is doing sth, performing an action, etc.（與名詞連用，表示舉動、動作等）：*to take a step/walk/stroll* 邁步；散步；遛達 ◇ *to take a bath/shower/wash* 洗澡；淋浴；洗一洗 ◇ *to take a look/glance* 看一看；瞥一眼 ◇ *to take a bite/drink/sip* 咬／喝／呷一口 ◇ *to take a deep breath* 深吸一口氣 ◇ *to take a break/rest* 暫歇一下；休息一下 ◇ (BrE) *No decision will be taken on the matter until next week.* 到下星期才會對這一問題作出決定。

▸ **FORM/POSITION** 形式；位置 **28** [T] **~ sth** to have a particular form, position or state 採用（形式）；就任（職位）；出現（狀況）：*Our next class will take the form of a debate.* 我們下一堂課將採用辯論的形式。◇ *The new President takes office in January.* 新總統將於一月份就職。

▸ **TIME** 時間 **29** [T, no passive, I] to need or require a particular amount of time 需要…時間；費時：**~ sth** *The journey to the airport takes about half an hour.* 到機場大約需要半小時。◇ **~ sth to do sth** ***It takes*** *about half an hour to get to the airport.* 到機場大概需要半小時。◇ *That cut is taking a long time to heal.* 那傷口需要很長時間才能癒合。◇ **~ sb sth (to do sth)** *It took her three hours to repair her bike.* 她花了三個小時修理自行車。◇ *It'll take her time to recover from the illness.* 她康復需要時間。◇ **~ sth for sb to do sth** *It'll* ***take time*** (= take a long time) *for her to recover from the illness.* 她的病需要很長時間才能痊癒。◇ **+ adv.** *I need a shower—I* ***won't take long.*** 我要沖個澡，用不了多長時間。➲ note at LAST[1]

▸ **NEED** 需要 **30** [T, no passive] to need or require sth in order to happen or be done 需要；要求：**~ sb/sth to do sth** *It only takes one careless driver to cause an accident.* 只要有一個粗心大意的駕駛者便會發生車禍。◇ *It doesn't take much to make her angry.* 她動輒就發脾氣。 **~ sth** (informal) *He didn't take much persuading* (= he was easily persuaded). 不用費多少口舌就能說服他。 **31** [T, no passive] (not used in the progressive tenses 不用於進行時) **~ sth** (of machines, etc. 機器等) to use sth in order to work 使用；用：*All new cars take unleaded petrol.* 所有的新汽車都使用無鉛汽油。

▸ **SIZE OF SHOES/CLOTHES** 鞋／衣服的尺碼 **32** [T, no passive] (not used in the progressive tenses 不用於進行時) **~ sth** to wear a particular size in shoes or clothes 穿用（…尺碼的鞋或衣服）：*What size shoes do you take?* 你穿多大號的鞋？

▸ **HOLD/CONTAIN** 裝得下；包含 **33** [T, no passive] (not used in the progressive tenses 不用於進行時) **~ sth/sb** to have enough space for sth/sb; to be able to hold or contain a particular quantity 容納；裝；盛：*The bus can take 60 passengers.* 這輛公共汽車可載 60 名乘客。◇ *The tank takes 50 litres.* 這罐能容 50 升。

▸ **TEACH/LEAD** 講授；帶領 **34** [T] **~ sb (for sth)** | **~ sth** to be the teacher or leader in a class or a religious service 授（課）；主持（宗教禮儀）：*The head teacher usually takes us for French.* 校長通常給我們上法語課。

▸ **STUDY** 學習 **35** [T] **~ sth** to study a subject at school, college, etc. 學習，讀，修（課程）：*She is planning to take a computer course.* 她打算修一門計算機課。◇ *How many subjects are you taking this year?* 你今年修多少門課？

▸ **EXAM** 考試 **36** [T] **~ sth** to do an exam or a test 參加（考試或測驗）：*When did you take your driving test?* 你什麼時候參加了駕駛執照考試？

▸ **TRANSPORT/ROAD** 交通工具；道路 **37** [T] **~ sth** to use a form of transport, a road, a path, etc. to go to a place 乘坐，搭乘（交通工具）；取（道）；走（路線）：*to* ***take the bus/plane/train*** 乘公共汽車／飛機／火車 ◇ *to take a cab* 乘出租汽車 ◇ *Take the second road on the right.* 第二個路口向右拐。◇ *It's more interesting to take the coast road.* 走海濱公路更有意思。

▸ **GO OVER/AROUND** 越過；繞路走 **38** [T] **~ sth (+ adv./prep.)** to go over or around sth 跨過；跳過；繞過：*The horse took the first fence well.* 那匹馬輕快地躍過了第一道柵欄。◇ *He takes bends much too fast.* 他拐彎時車開得太快。

▸ **IN SPORTS** 體育運動 **39** [T] **~ sth** (of a player in a sports game 體育比賽中的運動員) to kick or throw the ball from a fixed or agreed position 踢；擲：*to take a* ***penalty/free kick/corner*** 主罰點球／任意球；開角球

▸ **VOTE/SURVEY** 投票；調查 **40** [T] **~ sth** to use a particular method to find out people's opinions 付諸（表決）；舉

T

行（投票）；進行（調查）：*to take a vote/poll/survey* 付諸表決；進行民意測驗 / 調查

‣ BE SUCCESSFUL 成功 **41** [I] to be successful; to work 成功；起作用；行得通：*The skin graft failed to take.* 表皮移植未能成功。

‣ GRAMMAR 語法 **42** [T] (not used in the progressive tenses 不用於進行時) **~ sth** (of verbs, nouns, etc. 動詞、名詞等) to have or require sth when used in a sentence or other structure（用於句子或其他結構中時）有，需要：*The verb 'rely' takes the preposition 'on'.* 動詞 rely 需要和介詞 on 連用。

IDM Most idioms containing **take** are at the entries for the nouns and adjectives in the idioms, for example **take the biscuit** is at **biscuit**. 大多數含 take 的習語，都可在該等習語中的名詞及形容詞相關詞條找到，如 take the biscuit 在詞條 biscuit 下。 **I, you, etc. can't take sb 'anywhere** (*informal*, often *humorous*) used to say that you cannot trust sb to behave well in public（用以表示不相信某人會在公共場合行為得體）到哪兒都拿不出去 **have (got) what it 'takes** (*informal*) to have the qualities, ability, etc. needed to be successful 具備（成功）所需要的一切條件（或素質、能力等） **take sth as it 'comes | take sb as they 'come** to accept sth/sb without wishing it/them to be different or without thinking about it/them very much in advance 安於現狀；順其自然：*She takes life as it comes.* 她對待生活的態度是順其自然。 **'take it (that ...)** to suppose; to assume 假定；假設；設想；以為：*I take it you won't be coming to the party?* 我想你不會來參加聚會吧？ **take it from 'me (that ...)** (*informal*) used to emphasize that what you are going to say is the truth 我敢擔保；我說的肯定沒錯：*Take it from me—he'll be a millionaire before he's 30.* 不信你等着瞧，他到不了 30 歲就會成為百萬富翁。 **take it on/upon yourself to do sth** to decide to do sth without asking permission or advice 擅自作主；自作主張 **sb can take it or 'leave it 1** used to say that you do not care if sb accepts or rejects your offer 要就要，不要就拉倒；取捨請便 **2** used to say that sb does not have a strong opinion about sth 可有可無；無所謂；無偏好：*Dancing? I can take it or leave it.* 跳舞？我跳不跳都行。 **take it/a lot 'out of sb** (*informal*) to make sb physically or mentally tired 使精疲力竭；使心力交瘁：*Taking care of small children really takes it out of you.* 照看小孩確實會使你精疲力竭。 **take some/a lot of 'doing** (*informal*) to need a lot of effort or time; to be very difficult to do 費力；費時；難辦；難做 **,take 'that!** (*informal*) used as an exclamation when you are hitting sb or attacking them in some other way（打人時說）看打，接招

PHR V **,take sb a'back** [usually passive] to shock or surprise sb very much 使…震驚；使…大吃一驚

,take 'after sb [no passive] **1** (not used in the progressive tenses 不用於進行時) to look or behave like an older member of your family, especially your mother or father（外貌或行為）像（父或母）：*Your daughter doesn't take after you at all.* 你女兒長得一點兒都不像你。 **2** (*NAmE, informal*) to follow sb quickly 追趕；跟蹤：*I was afraid that if I started running the man would take after me.* 我害怕如果我跑起來，那人會追來。

,take a'gainst sb/sth [no passive] (*old-fashioned, BrE*) to start not liking sb/sth for no clear reason（說不清原因地）開始不喜歡

,take sb/sth↔a'part (*informal*) **1** to defeat sb easily in a game or competition（運動或比賽）輕易打敗，把…打得一敗塗地 **2** to criticize sb/sth severely 嚴厲抨擊

,take sth↔a'part to separate a machine or piece of equipment into the different parts that it is made of 拆卸，拆散，拆開（機器等） SYN **dismantle**

,take sth↔a'way 1 ⊶ to make a feeling, pain, etc. disappear 解除，消除（感情、痛苦等）：*I was given some pills to take away the pain.* 給我開了一些止痛藥片。 **2** ⊶ (*BrE*) (*NAmE* **,take sth↔'out**) to buy cooked food at a restaurant and carry it away to eat, for example at home（從餐館買飯菜等）帶回食用；買外賣食物：*Two burgers to take away, please.* 請來兩份漢堡包，帶走。 ➲ related noun TAKEAWAY, TAKEOUT **,take a'way from sth** [no passive] to make the effort or value of sth seem less 減少；減弱；貶低 SYN **detract from**：*I don't want to take away from his achievements, but he couldn't have done it without my help.* 我不想貶低他的成就，但是如果沒有我的幫助，他是做不成的。

,take sb↔'back to allow sb, such as your husband, wife or partner, to come home after they have left because of a problem 允許（因不合而離去的配偶等）回家；與…重歸於好 **,take sb 'back (to ...)** to make sb remember sth 使回想起：*The smell of the sea took him back to his childhood.* 大海的氣味使他回想起孩提時代。

,take sth↔'back 1 ⊶ if you **take** sth **back** to a shop/store, or a shop/store **takes** sth **back**, you return sth that you have bought there, for example because it is the wrong size or does not work 退回；同意收回（退貨） **2** to admit that sth you said was wrong or that you should not have said it 收回，撤回（說過的話）：*OK, I take it all back!* 好吧，我把我說過的話統統收回。

,take sth↔'down 1 ⊶ to remove a structure, especially by separating it into pieces 拆掉；拆除；拆卸：*to take down a tent* 拆掉帳篷 **2** to pull down a piece of clothing worn below the waist without completely removing it 往下拽，拉低（下身衣服）：*to take down your trousers/pants* 把褲子 / 內褲往下拽一拽 **3** ⊶ to write sth down 寫下；記錄：*Reporters took down every word of his speech.* 記者把他講的每一句話都記錄了下來。

,take sb↔'in 1 ⊶ to allow sb to stay in your home 留宿；收留：*to take in lodgers* 收房客 ◇ *He was homeless, so we took him in.* 他無家可歸，我們便收留了他。 **2** ⊶ [often passive] to make sb believe sth that is not true 欺騙；矇騙 SYN **deceive**：*Don't be taken in by his charm—he's ruthless.* 不要被他那迷人的風度所蒙蔽，其實他冷酷無情。 ➲ SYNONYMS at CHEAT **,take sth↔'in 1** ⊶ to absorb sth into the body, for example by breathing or swallowing 吸入，吞入（體內）：*Fish take in oxygen through their gills.* 魚用鰓吸取氧氣。 ➲ related noun INTAKE **2** to make a piece of clothing narrower or tighter 改小，改瘦（衣服） OPP **let out** **3** [no passive] to include or cover sth 包括；包含：*The tour takes in six European capitals.* 這次旅遊包括六個歐洲國家的首都。 **4** [no passive] to go to see or visit sth such as a film/movie 去看，觀看（電影等）：*I generally take in a show when I'm in New York.* 我每次去紐約通常總會看一場演出。 **5** ⊶ to take notice of sth with your eyes 注意到；看到：*He took in every detail of her appearance.* 他仔仔細細打量了她一番。 **6** ⊶ to understand or remember sth that you hear or read 理解；領會；記住：*Halfway through the chapter I realized I hadn't taken anything in.* 這一章我讀到一半才意識到我根本沒有看懂。

,take 'off ⊶ **1** ⊶ (of an aircraft, etc. 飛機等) to leave the ground and begin to fly 起飛：*The plane took off an hour late.* 飛機起飛晚了一個小時。 ➲ related noun TAKE-OFF OPP **land** **2** (*informal*) to leave a place, especially in a hurry 匆匆離去；急忙離開：*When he saw me coming he took off in the opposite direction.* 他見我走過來便趕快轉身走了。 **3** (of an idea, a product, etc. 觀念、產品等) to become successful or popular very quickly or suddenly 突然大受歡迎；迅速流行：*The new magazine has really taken off.* 這份新雜誌真是大受歡迎。 **,take sb↔'off 1** to copy sb's voice, actions or manner in an amusing way（以詼諧的方式）模仿，學某人的樣子 SYN **impersonate** **2** (in sports, entertainment, etc. 體育運動、娛樂等) to make sb stop playing, acting, etc. and leave the field or the stage 換下；中止；取消：*He was taken off after twenty minutes.* 二十分鐘後，他被替換下場。 **,take sth↔'off 1** ⊶ to remove sth, especially a piece of clothing from your/sb's body 脫下（衣服）；摘掉：*to take off your coat* 脫掉大衣 ◇ *He took off my wet boots and made me sit by the fire.* 他脫掉我濕漉漉的靴子，讓我在火爐旁坐下。 OPP **put on** **2** ⊶ to have a period of time as a break from work 休假；休息：*I've decided to take a few days off next week.* 我已決定下星期休息幾天。 **3** [often passive] to stop a public service, television programme, performances of a show, etc. 取消；停演：*The show was taken off because of poor audience figures.* 該劇目因不賣座而停演了。 **4** to remove some of sb's hair, part of sb's body, etc. 剪掉（頭髮）；截去，切除（人體部位）：*The hairdresser asked me how much she should take off.* 理髮

師問我頭髮剪多少。◇ *The explosion nearly took his arm off.* 他的胳膊差點兒被炸掉。 **ˌtake yourself/sb ˈoff (to …)** (*informal*) to leave a place; to make sb leave a place（使）離去，走掉；帶走 **ˌtake sb ˈoff sth** [often passive] to remove sb from sth such as a job, position, piece of equipment, etc. 調離，解除（工作、職務等）；撤掉，拆除（器械）： *The officer leading the investigation has been taken off the case.* 主持調查此案的警員已被撤下。◇ *After three days she was taken off the ventilator.* 三天之後給她摘掉了呼吸器。 **ˌtake sth ˈoff sth 1** to remove an amount of money or a number of marks, points, etc. in order to reduce the total 扣除，減去（款額、分數等）： *The manager took $10 off the bill.* 經理從賬單上劃掉 10 元。◇ *That experience took ten years off my life* (= made me feel ten years older). 那段經歷使我老了十年。 **2** [often passive] to stop sth from being sold 停止銷售： *The slimming pills were taken off the market.* 市場上已停止銷售這種減肥藥片。

ˌtake sb↔ˈon 1 ⊶ (*especially BrE*) to employ sb 聘用；雇用： *to take on new staff* 雇用新員工 ◇ *She was taken on as a trainee.* 她受聘當實習生。 **2** [no passive] to play against sb in a game or contest; to fight against sb（運動或比賽）同某人較量；反抗；與某人戰鬥： *to take somebody on at tennis* 與某人比賽打網球 ◇ *The rebels took on the entire Roman army.* 反叛者與整個羅馬軍隊戰鬥。 **ˌtake sth↔ˈon** [no passive] to begin to have a particular quality, appearance, etc. 呈現，具有（特徵、外觀等）： *The chameleon can take on the colours of its background.* 變色龍可以變成周圍環境的顏色。◇ *His voice took on a more serious tone.* 他說話的語氣變得嚴肅起來。 **ˌtake sth/sb↔ˈon 1** to decide to do sth; to agree to be responsible for sth/sb 決定做；同意負責；承擔（責任）： *I can't take on any extra work.* 我不能承擔任何額外工作。◇ *We're not taking on any new clients at present.* 目前我們不接收新客戶。 **2** (of a bus, plane or ship 公共汽車、飛機或船隻) to allow sb/sth to enter 接納（乘客）；裝載： *The bus stopped to take on more passengers.* 公共汽車停下讓其他乘客上車。◇ *The ship took on more fuel at Freetown.* 輪船在弗里敦停靠加燃料。

ˌtake sb↔ˈout to go to a restaurant, theatre, club, etc. with sb you have invited 帶某人出去（到餐館、劇院、俱樂部等） **ˌtake sb/sth↔ˈout** (*informal*) to kill sb or destroy sth 殺死；毀滅： *They took out two enemy bombers.* 他們摧毀了敵人的兩架轟炸機。 **ˌtake sth↔ˈout 1** to remove sth from inside sb's body, especially a part of it 切除，摘除（人體內的一部份）： *How many teeth did the dentist take out?* 牙科醫生拔了幾顆牙？ **2** to obtain an official document or service 獲得，領到（正式文件或服務）： *to take out an insurance policy/a mortgage/a loan* 領到保險單／按揭貸款；獲得貸款 ◇ *to take out an ad in a newspaper* 在報紙上刊登廣告 **3** (*NAmE*) (*BrE* **ˌtake sth↔aˈway**) to buy cooked food at a restaurant and carry it away to eat, for example at home（從餐館買飯菜等）帶回食用；買外賣食物 ➲ related noun TAKEAWAY, TAKEOUT **ˌtake sth↔ˈout (against sb)** to start legal action against sb by means of an official document 發出（傳票）： *The police have taken out a summons against the driver of the car.* 警方已向這輛汽車的駕駛人發出傳票。 **ˌtake sth↔ˈout (of sth)** to obtain money by removing it from your bank account（從銀行賬戶中）提取（款） **ˌtake sth ˈout of sth** to remove an amount of money from a larger amount, especially as a payment 扣除；減去；抽出： *The fine will be taken out of your wages.* 罰款將從你的工資中扣除。 **ˌtake it/sth ˈout on sb** to behave in an unpleasant way towards sb because you feel angry, disappointed, etc., although it is not their fault 向…發泄；拿…撒氣： *OK, so you had a bad day. Don't take it out on me.* 好，這麼說你今天遇上了很多倒霉事。可也別拿我當出氣筒。◇ *She tended to take her frustrations out on her family.* 她心裏不痛快總是在家裏人身上發泄。

ˌtake sb ˈout of himself/ herself to make sb forget their worries and become less concerned with their own thoughts and situation 使擺脫苦惱；為某人消愁

ˌtake ˈover (from sth) to become bigger or more important than sth else; to replace sth 佔上風；取而代之： *Try not to let negative thoughts take over.* 盡量別受消極的想法左右。◇ *It has been suggested that mammals took over from dinosaurs 65 million years ago.* 有人提出哺乳動物是在 6 500 萬年前取代恐龍的。 **ˌtake ˈover (from sb) | ˌtake sth↔ˈover (from sb) 1** ⊶ to begin to have control of or responsibility for sth, especially in place of sb else 接替；接任；接管；接手 **2** ⊶ to gain control of a political party, a country, etc. 控制，接管（政黨、國家等）： *The army is threatening to take over if civil unrest continues.* 軍方揚言如果內亂繼續就實行軍管。 **ˌtake sth↔ˈover** ⊶ to gain control of a business, a company, etc., especially by buying shares 接收，接管（企業、公司等，尤指通過購買股份）： *CBS Records was taken over by Sony.* 哥倫比亞廣播公司的唱片公司已被索尼公司收購。 ➲ related noun TAKEOVER

ˌtake sb ˈthrough sth to help sb learn or become familiar with sth, for example by talking about each part in turn 幫助某人深入瞭解；給某人解說： *The director took us through the play scene by scene.* 導演一幕一幕地給我們說戲。

ˈtake to sth [no passive] **1** to go away to a place, especially to escape from danger（尤指為逃避危險）逃往，躲到： *The rebels took to the hills.* 反叛者躲進山裏。 **2** to begin to do sth as a habit 開始沉湎於；養成…習慣： **~ doing sth** *I've taken to waking up very early.* 我已形成習慣，醒得很早。 **3** to develop an ability for sth 培養…的能力： *She took to tennis as if she'd been playing all her life.* 她網球打得很好，好像一生都在從事這項運動似的。 **ˈtake to sb/sth** [no passive] to start liking sb/sth 開始喜歡；對…產生好感： *I took to my new boss immediately.* 我立刻對新老闆產生了好感。◇ *He hasn't taken to his new school.* 他對新學校還沒有產生興趣。

ˌtake ˈup to continue, especially starting after sb/sth else has finished 繼續；接下去： *The band's new album takes up where their last one left off.* 這個樂隊的新唱片集是接上一集的樂曲錄製的。 **ˌtake ˈup sth** ⊶ to fill or use an amount of space or time 佔用（時間）；佔據（空間）： *The table takes up too much room.* 這張桌子太佔地方。◇ *I won't take up any more of your time.* 我不再佔用你的時間了。 **ˌtake sth↔ˈup 1** to make sth such as a piece of clothing shorter 將（衣服等）改短： *This skirt needs taking up.* 這條裙子需要改短。 OPP **let down** **2** ⊶ to learn or start to do sth, especially for pleasure（尤指為消遣）學着做，開始做： *They've taken up golf.* 他們學起打高爾夫球來了。◇ *She has taken up* (= started to learn to play) *the oboe.* 她學起吹雙簧管來了。 **3** to start or begin sth such as a job 開始從事： *He takes up his duties next week.* 他下週就要開始履行職責。 **4** to join in singing or saying sth 加入（一起唱或說）： *to take up the chorus* 加入合唱 ◇ *Their protests were later taken up by other groups.* 其他小組後來也加入了他們抗議的行列。 **5** to continue sth that sb else has not finished, or that has not been mentioned for some time 繼續（他人未完成的事）；接着講（以前提過的事）： *She took up the story where Tim had left off.* 她接着講蒂姆未講完的故事。◇ *I'd like to take up the point you raised earlier.* 我想繼續談一談你早些時候提出的問題。 **6** to move into a particular position 進入，佔據（位置）： *I took up my position by the door.* 我把住了門口。 **7** to accept sth that is offered or available 接受（建議或能得到的東西）： *to take up a challenge* 接受挑戰 ◇ *She took up his offer of a drink.* 他請她喝一杯，她接受了。 **ˌtake ˈup with sb** (*informal*) to begin to be friendly with sb, especially sb with a bad reputation 開始結交（尤指名聲不好的人） **ˌtake sb ˈup on sth 1** to question sb about sth, because you do not agree with them 質問；查問： *I must take you up on that point.* 那個問題我一定要找你問個明白。 **2** (*informal*) to accept an offer, a bet, etc. from sb 接受（提議、打賭等）： *Thanks for the invitation—we'll take you up on it some time.* 謝謝你的盛情邀請，改日我們一定奉陪。 **ˌtake sth ˈup with sb** to speak or write to sb about sth that they may be able to deal with or help you with 向…提出；與…交涉： *They decided to take the matter up with their MP.* 他們決定向本地區議員反映這一問題。 **be ˌtaken ˈup with sth/sb** to be giving all your time and energy to sth/sb 致力於；專心於；對…一心一意

be ˈtaken with sb/sth to find sb/sth attractive or interesting 被…吸引；迷上；對…感興趣： *We were all very*

T

taken with his girlfriend. 我們都覺得他的女朋友非常討人喜歡。◇ *I think he's quite taken with the idea.* 我認為他對這個想法十分感興趣。

■ ***noun* 1** a scene or part of a film/movie that is filmed at one time without stopping the camera（不停機一次連續拍攝的）場景，鏡頭：*We managed to get it right in just two takes.* 我們僅拍攝了兩個鏡頭就把這部份戲拍好了。 **2** [usually sing.] (*informal*) an amount of money that sb receives, especially the money that is earned by a business during a particular period of time 收入額；進項 **SYN** **takings**：*How much is my share of the take?* 我的那一份收入是多少？ **3 ~ on sth** (*informal*) the particular opinion or idea that sb has about sth 看法；意見：*What's his take on the plan?* 他對這項計劃有什麼意見？◇ *a new take on the Romeo and Juliet story* (= a way of presenting it) 對《羅密歐與朱麗葉》故事的重新演繹 ➲ see also DOUBLE TAKE

IDM **be on the 'take** (*informal*) to accept money from sb for helping them in a dishonest or illegal way 受賄；貪贓枉法

take·away /ˈteɪkəweɪ/ (*BrE*) (*NAmE* **'take·out**) (also **'carry-out** *US, ScotE*) *noun* **1** a restaurant that cooks and sells food that you take away and eat somewhere else 外賣餐館 **2** a meal that you buy at this type of restaurant 外賣的飯菜；外賣食物：*Let's have a takeaway tonight.* 咱們今晚吃一頓外賣的飯菜吧。

take·down /ˈteɪkdaʊn/ *noun* **1** a move in which a WRESTLER quickly gets his/her opponent down to the floor from a standing position （摔跤中的）摔倒 **2** (*informal*) an arrest or unexpected visit by the police （警方的）抓捕行動，臨檢，突檢

'take-home pay *noun* [U] the amount of money that you earn after you have paid tax, etc. （扣除稅項等之後的）實得工資

'take-off *noun* **1** [U, C] the moment at which an aircraft leaves the ground and starts to fly （飛機的）起飛：*The plane is ready for take-off.* 飛機準備隨時起飛。◇ *take-off speed* 起飛速度 ◇ (*figurative*) *The local economy is poised for take-off.* 當地的經濟蓄勢待發。**OPP** **landing** **2** [C, U] the moment when your feet leave the ground when you jump 起跳 **3** [C] if you do a **take-off** of sb, you copy the way they speak or behave, in a humorous way to entertain people （對他人言行的）滑稽模仿

take·over /ˈteɪkəʊvə(r); *NAmE* -oʊ-/ *noun* [C, U] **1** an act of taking control of a company by buying most of its shares 收購；接收；接管：*a **takeover bid** for the company* 收購這家公司的出價 ➲ COLLOCATIONS at BUSINESS **2** an act of taking control of a country, an area or a political organization by force （對國家、地區、政治組織等的）強行接管，控制

taker /ˈteɪkə(r)/ *noun* **1** [usually pl.] a person who is willing to accept sth that is being offered 接受者；收受人：*They won't find many takers for the house at that price.* 以這樣的要價，他們不會為房子找到多少承讓人的。 **2** (often in compounds 常構成複合詞) a person who takes sth 接受者：*drug takers* 吸毒者 ◇ *It is better to be a giver than a taker.* 施比受有福。

'take-up *noun* [U, sing.] the rate at which people accept sth that is offered or made available to them （福利等的）領受率：*a low take-up of government benefits* 政府救濟金的低領取率

tak·ings /ˈteɪkɪŋz/ *noun* [pl.] (*BrE*) the amount of money that a shop/store, theatre, etc. receives from selling goods or tickets over a particular period of time （某一時期的）進賬，票房收入：*The box office takings are up on last week.* 票房收入較上星期有所增長。

tak·kie = TACKIE

tala /ˈtɑːlə/ *noun* a traditional pattern of rhythm in CLASSICAL Indian music 塔拉（古印度音樂的傳統節拍組合）

tal·cum pow·der /ˈtælkəm paʊdə(r)/ (also *informal* **talc** /tælk/) *noun* [U] a fine soft powder, usually with a pleasant smell, that you put on your skin to make it feel smooth and dry 滑石粉；爽身粉；撲粉

tale /teɪl/ *noun* **1** a story created using the imagination, especially one that is full of action and adventure （尤指充滿驚險的）故事；歷險記：*Dickens' 'A Tale of Two Cities'* 狄更斯的《雙城記》◇ ***a fairy/moral/romantic, etc. tale*** 童話、寓言、愛情故事等 ➲ see also FOLK TALE **2** an exciting spoken description of an event, which may not be completely true （精彩但不一定完全真實的）講述，敘述：*I love listening to his tales of life at sea.* 我喜歡聽他講述他的海上生活。◇ *I've heard tales of people seeing ghosts in that house.* 我聽說有人在那棟房子裏見到過鬼。◇ *The team's **tale of woe** continued on Saturday* (= they lost another match). 上星期六這支隊又遭敗績。◇ *Her experiences provide a **cautionary tale*** (= a warning) *for us all.* 她的經歷成了我們大家的前車之鑒。➲ see also TELLTALE **IDM** see OLD, TELL

tal·ent /ˈtælənt/ *noun* **1** [C, U] a natural ability to do sth well 天才；天資；天賦：*to **have** great artistic **talent*** 很有藝術天賦 ◇ *a man **of many talents*** 多才多藝的男子 ◇ **~ (for sth/for doing sth)** *She showed considerable talent for getting what she wanted.* 她很有天資，能夠達成自己的目標。◇ *a **talent competition/contest/show*** (= in which people perform, to show how well they can sing, dance, etc.) 新秀選拔賽／大獎賽／演出 **2** [U, C] people or a person with a natural ability to do sth well 有才能的人；人才；天才：*There is **a wealth of** young **talent** in British theatre.* 英國戲劇界年青一代人才輩出。◇ *He is a great talent.* 他是個了不起的人才。 **3** [U] (*BrE, slang*) people who are sexually attractive （統稱）性感的人：*He likes to spend his time chatting up the local talent.* 他喜歡把時間花在和當地的妞兒搭訕上。

tal·ent·ed /ˈtæləntɪd/ *adj.* having a natural ability to do sth well 有才能的；天才的；有才幹的：*a talented player* 天才運動員

'talent scout (also **scout**, **'talent spotter**) *noun* a person whose job is to find people who are good at singing, acting, sport, etc. in order to give them work （歌唱、戲劇、體育運動等的）人才發掘者，新秀發現者，星探

tal·is·man /ˈtælɪzmən/ *noun* an object that is thought to have magic powers and to bring good luck 護身符；驅邪物

talk 0-ᴡ /tɔːk/ *verb, noun*

■ ***verb***

▸ **SPEAK TO SB** 與人說話 **1** 0-ᴡ [I, T] to say things; to speak in order to give information or to express feelings, ideas, etc. 說話；講話；談話：*Stop talking and listen!* 別說話，注意聽！◇ *We talked on the phone for over an hour.* 我們在電話裏談了一個多小時。◇ **~ (to/with sb) (about sb/sth)** *Who were you talking to just now?* 你剛才在跟誰說話？◇ *We looked around the school and talked with the principal.* 我們參觀了那所學校，並跟校長進行了交談。◇ *Ann and Joe **aren't talking** to each other right now* (= they refuse to speak to each other because they have argued). 安和喬兩人現在互不理睬。◇ *When they get together, all they talk about is football.* 他們在一起時，談論的都是足球。◇ ***What are you talking about?*** (= used when you are surprised, annoyed and/or worried by sth that sb has just said) 你在胡說什麼？（對他人所言感到驚奇，不悅或擔憂時用）◇ ***I don't know what you're talking about*** (= used to say that you did not do sth that sb has accused you of). 我不知道你在說什麼（表示自己沒有做對方指責的事）。◇ **~ of sth** *Mary is talking of looking for another job.* 瑪麗說起要另找一份工作。◇ **~ yourself + adj.** *We **talked ourselves hoarse**, catching up on all the news.* 我們互訴近況，把嗓子都說啞了。

▸ **DISCUSS** 討論 **2** 0-ᴡ [I, T] to discuss sth, usually sth serious or important 討論，談論，商談，洽談（通常指重大的事）：*This situation can't go on. We need to talk.* 這種情況不能再繼續下去了。我們需要談一談。◇ *The two sides in the dispute say they are ready to talk.* 爭執雙方說他們願意商談。◇ **~ (to/with sb) (about sth)** *Talk to your doctor if you're still worried.* 如果你仍然不放心，就找醫生談一談。◇ **~ sth** *to talk business* 談公事

▸ **SAY WORDS** 說話 **3** 0-ᴡ [I, T] to say words in a language （用某種語言）講，說：*The baby is just starting to talk.* 這嬰兒剛開始咿呀學語。◇ **~ in sth** *We couldn't understand them because they were talking in Chinese.* 我們聽

不懂他們在講些什麼，因為他們說的是中國話。◇ **~ sth** *Are they talking Swedish or Danish?* 他們說的是瑞典語還是丹麥語？

▸ **SENSE/NONSENSE 有／無理** **4** [T] **~ sth** to say things that are/are not sensible 說，講（有理、無理的話）: *She talks a lot of sense.* 她講得很在理。◇ (*BrE*) *You're talking rubbish!* 你胡說八道！◇ *See if you can **talk some sense into him*** (= persuade him to be sensible). 看你能否給他講通道理。

▸ **FOR EMPHASIS 加強語氣** **5** [T] **be talking sth** (*informal*) used to emphasize an amount of money, how serious sth is, etc.（用以強調款額、情況嚴重程度等）講的是，指的是： *We're talking £500 for three hours' work.* 咱們講的可是工作三個小時酬金 500 英鎊。

▸ **ABOUT PRIVATE LIFE 私生活** **6** [I] to talk about a person's private life 說閒話；講人壞話；嚼舌頭 **SYN** **gossip**: *Don't phone me at work— **people will talk**.* 別在上班時給我打電話，人家會說閒話的。

▸ **GIVE INFORMATION 提供信息** **7** [I] to give information to sb, especially unwillingly 供出消息；供認；招認： *The police questioned him but he refused to talk.* 警察審問他，但他拒不招供。

IDM **look who's 'talking | 'you can/can't talk | you're a 'fine one to talk** (*informal*) used to tell sb that they should not criticize sb else for sth because they do the same things too（用以表示自己同樣不對時不要批評別人）還有臉說別人： *'George is so careless with money.' 'Look who's talking!'* "喬治真是亂花錢。" "虧你還有臉說別人！" **now you're 'talking** (*informal*) used when you like what sb has suggested very much（表示贊同對方的話）你這算說對了，你所言正合我意 **'talk about ...** (*informal*) used to emphasize sth（用以強調）這才叫，真是…不得了： *Talk about mean! She didn't even buy me a card.* 這才叫吝嗇呢！她連張賀卡都沒給我買。 **talk 'dirty** (*informal*) to talk to sb about sex in order to make them sexually excited 說下流話 **talk a good 'game** (*NAmE*) to talk in a way that sounds convincing, but may not be sincere 說得好聽；說得天花亂墜 **talk the hind leg off a 'donkey** (*informal*) to talk too much, especially about boring or unimportant things 嘮叨個沒完沒了；喋喋不休 **talking of sb/sth** (*informal, especially BrE*) used when you are going to say more about a subject that has already been mentioned（繼續談論時用）提起，說起，談及，至於： *Talking of Sue, I met her new boyfriend last week.* 談到蘇，上星期我遇到了她的新男友。 **talk 'shop** (usually *disapproving*) to talk about your work with the people you work with, especially when you are also with other people who are not connected with or interested in it 說行話；三句話不離本行（尤指當着外行的面） **,talk the 'talk** (*informal*, sometimes *disapproving*) to be able to talk in a confident way that makes people think you are good at what you do 說得頭頭是道： *You can talk the talk, but can you walk the walk?* (= can you act in a way that matches your words?) 你說得頭頭是道，可你能做到嗎？ **talk through your 'hat** (*old-fashioned, informal*) to say silly things while you are talking about a subject you do not understand 胡說；信口開河；瞎扯 **talk 'tough (on sth)** (*informal, especially NAmE*) to tell people very strongly what you want 強硬地說；強烈地要求 **talk 'turkey** (*informal, especially NAmE*) to talk about sth seriously 鄭重其事地談；嚴肅認真地談 **talk your way out of sth/of doing sth** to make excuses and give reasons for not doing sth; to manage to get yourself out of a difficult situation 靠能言善辯開脫；以話解圍： *I managed to talk my way out of having to give a speech.* 我好說歹說總算逃脫了發言差事。 **'you can/can't talk** (*informal*) = LOOK WHO'S TALKING **you're a 'fine one to talk** (*informal*) = LOOK WHO'S TALKING ➲ more at DEVIL, KNOW *v.*, LANGUAGE, MONEY, SENSE *n.*, TURN *n.*

PHR V **,talk a'round/'round sth** to talk about sth in a general way without dealing with the most important parts of it 拐彎抹角地說；不着邊際地說 **'talk at sb** to speak to sb without listening to what they say in reply（不理會對方反應）對某人大發議論，滔滔不絕地對某人說 **,talk 'back (to sb)** to answer sb rudely, especially sb in authority（尤指對掌權者）回嘴，頂嘴 ➲ related noun BACK TALK **,talk sb/sth↔'down** to help a pilot of a plane to land by giving instructions from the ground 引導（飛行員）着陸；引降 **,talk sth↔'down** to make sth seem less important or successful than it really is 貶低；貶抑： *You shouldn't talk down your own achievements.* 你不該貶低自己的成績。 **,talk 'down to sb** to speak to sb as if they were less important or intelligent than you 以高人一等的口氣說話 **,talk sb 'into/'out of sth** to persuade sb to do/not to do sth 說服某人做／不

Synonyms 同義詞辨析

talk

discuss • speak • communicate • debate • consult

These words all mean to share news, information, ideas or feelings with another person or other people, especially by talking with them. 以上各詞均含交流、交談之意。

talk to speak in order to give information, express feelings or share ideas 指說話、講話、談話： *We talked on the phone for over an hour.* 我們在電話裏談了一個多小時。

discuss (*rather formal*) to talk and share ideas on a subject or problem with other people, especially in order to decide sth 指談論、討論、商量： *Have you discussed the problem with anyone?* 你與誰商量過這個問題嗎？ **NOTE** You cannot say 'discuss about sth'. 不能說 discuss about sth： ~~*I'm not prepared to discuss about this on the phone.*~~

speak to talk to sb about sth; to have a conversation with sb 指談話、交談： *I've spoken to the manager about it.* 那件事我已經和經理談過了。◇ *'Can I speak to Susan?' 'Speaking.'* (= at the beginning of a telephone conversation) "請問蘇珊在嗎？" "我就是。"（電話中交談）

TALK OR SPEAK? 用 talk 還是 speak？

Speak can suggest a more formal level of communication than **talk**. You **speak** to sb about sth to try to achieve a particular goal or to tell them to do sth. You **talk** to sb in order to be friendly or to ask their advice. 與 talk 比較，speak 所指的交談可能更正式。與某人交談試圖達到某一目的或讓對方做某事用 speak，為表示友好或詢問建議用 talk： *Have you talked to your parents about the problems you're having?* 你同你父母談過你所面臨的問題嗎？◇ *I've spoken to Ed about it and he's promised not to let it happen again.* 我已經同埃德談過了，他答應不讓這種事情再次發生。

communicate (*rather formal*) to exchange information or ideas with sb 指與某人交流信息或意見： *We only communicate by email.* 我們只通過電子郵件進行交流。◇ *Dolphins use sound to communicate with each other.* 海豚用聲音相互溝通。 **NOTE** **Communicate** is often used when the speaker wants to draw attention to the means of communication used. 說話者要讓人注意交流的方式時常用 communicate。

debate to discuss sth, especially formally, before making a decision or finding a solution（尤指正式）討論、辯論： *Politicians will be debating the bill later this week.* 政界將在本週晚些時候討論這項議案。

consult (*rather formal*) to discuss sth with sb in order to get their permission for sth, or to help you make a decision 指（與某人）商議、商量（以得到許可或幫助決策）： *You shouldn't have done it without consulting me.* 你不該不和我商量就做了這件事。

PATTERNS

- to talk/discuss sth/speak/communicate/debate/consult **with** sb
- to talk/speak **to** sb
- to talk/speak to sb/consult sb **about** sth
- to talk/speak **of** sth

T

做某事：*I didn't want to move abroad but Bill talked me into it.* 我本不想移居國外，但是比爾把我給說服了。◇ **~ doing sth** *She tried to talk him out of leaving.* 她極力勸他不要離去。**ˌtalk sth↔ˈout** to discuss sth thoroughly in order to make a decision, solve a problem, etc. 把…談透；協商作出（決定）；協商解決（問題）**ˌtalk sth↔ˈover (with sb)** to discuss sth thoroughly, especially in order to reach an agreement or make a decision 詳細討論，詳談（以達成協議或作出決定）：*You'll find it helpful to talk things over with a friend.* 把情況和朋友詳細聊一聊，你會覺得大有幫助。**ˌtalk sb ˈround (to sth)** (*BrE*) to persuade sb to accept sth or agree to sth 說服；勸說某人同意：*We finally managed to talk them round to our way of thinking.* 我們最後總算說服他們接受我們的想法。**ˌtalk sb ˈthrough sth** to explain to sb how sth works so that they can do it or understand it 給某人解說：*Can you talk me through the various investment options?* 你能給我詳述可以選擇的各種投資方法嗎？**ˌtalk sth ↔ˈthrough** to discuss sth thoroughly until you are sure you understand it 把某事談透 **ˌtalk sb/sth ˈup** to describe sb/sth in a way that makes them sound better than they really are 過分誇獎；吹捧

■ ***noun***

▸ **CONVERSATION** 交談 **1** 🔑 [C] **~ (with sb) (about sth)** a conversation or discussion 交談；談話；討論；商討：*I had a long **talk** with my boss about my career prospects.* 我和老闆就我的事業前景進行了一次長談。◇ *I had to have a heart-to-heart talk with her.* 我得推心置腹地和她談一談。➲ SYNONYMS at DISCUSSION

▸ **FORMAL DISCUSSIONS** 正式討論 **2** 🔑 **talks** [pl.] formal discussions between governments or organizations（政府或組織之間正式的）洽談，會談，談判：***arms/pay/peace, etc. talks*** 軍備、工資、和平等談判 ◇ *to **hold talks*** 舉行會談 ◇ **~ (between A and B) (on/over sth)** *Talks between management and workers **broke down** over the issue of holiday pay.* 勞資雙方就假日工資的談判破裂了。◇ *A further **round of talks** will be needed if the dispute is to be resolved.* 要解決糾紛，還需再舉行一輪談判。

▸ **SPEECH** 講話 **3** 🔑 [C] **~ (on sth)** a speech or lecture on a particular subject（專題）報告，演講：*She **gave a talk** on her visit to China.* 她作了一次訪華報告。➲ SYNONYMS at SPEECH

▸ **WORDS WITHOUT ACTIONS** 空話 **4** [U] (*informal*) words that are spoken, but without the necessary facts or actions to support them 空話；空談：*It's just talk. He'd never carry out his threats.* 這只不過是說說而已。他絕不會把他的恫嚇付諸行動。◇ *Don't pay any attention to her—she's **all talk**.* 別聽她的，她光說空話。

▸ **STORIES/RUMOURS** 傳聞；謠言 **5** [U] **~ (of sth/of doing sth)** | **~ (that …)** stories that suggest a particular thing might happen in the future 傳言；謠言；流言蜚語；揣測：*There was talk in Washington of sending in troops.* 華盛頓有派兵的謠傳。◇ *She dismissed the stories of her resignation as newspaper talk.* 她不理會有關她辭職的報道，認為那不過是報紙的謠言。

▸ **TOPIC/WAY OF SPEAKING** 話題；說話方式 **6** [U] (often in compounds 常構成複合詞) a topic of conversation or a way of speaking 話題；說話方式：*business talk* 商務談話 ◇ *She said it was just **girl talk** that a man wouldn't understand.* 她說這是女生話題，男人是聽不懂的。◇ *The book teaches you how to understand Spanish **street talk*** (= slang). 這本書教你如何理解西班牙俚語。◇ *It was tough talk, coming from a man who had begun the year in a hospital bed.* 這話出自年初住進醫院的一位男子之口，語氣很強硬。➲ see also SMALL TALK, SWEET TALK, TRASH TALK

IDM **the talk of sth** the person or thing that everyone is talking about in a particular place（某地人人談論的）話題，談論中心：*Overnight, she became **the talk of the town*** (= very famous). 一夜之間，她成了街頭巷尾談論的話題。➲ more at FIGHT *v.*

talka·tive /ˈtɔːkətɪv/ *adj.* liking to talk a lot 愛多說話的；多嘴的；饒舌的；健談的：*He's not very talkative, is he?* 他的話不多，是吧？◇ *She was in a talkative mood.* 她滔滔不絕，話興正濃。

talk·back /ˈtɔːkbæk/ *noun* [U] (*technical* 術語) a system that allows people working in a recording or broadcasting studio to talk to each other without their voices being recorded or heard on the radio（錄音或播音室的）內部聯絡系統，內部對講系統

talk·er /ˈtɔːkə(r)/ *noun* a person who talks in a particular way or who talks a lot 說話…的人；愛說話的人：*a brilliant talker* 能言善辯的人 ◇ *She's a (great) talker* (= she talks a lot). 她很健談。◇ *He's more a talker than a doer* (= he talks instead of doing things). 他說得多做得少。➲ SYNONYMS at SPEAKER IDM see FAST *adj.*

talkie /ˈtɔːki/ *noun* [usually pl.] (*old-fashioned, especially NAmE*) a film/movie that has sounds and not just pictures 有聲電影 ➲ see also WALKIE-TALKIE

ˌtalking ˈdrum *noun* a type of drum from W Africa whose sound can be changed in order to communicate different messages 話鼓（西非的一種可通過聲音變化傳遞不同信息的鼓）

ˌtalking ˈhead *noun* (*informal*) a person on television who talks straight to the camera（電視上的）發言者頭部特寫：*The election broadcast consisted largely of talking heads.* 有關選舉的電視廣播主要播放發言者的特寫鏡頭。

ˈtalking point *noun* **1** (*BrE*) a subject that is talked about or discussed by many people 話題；論題：*The judge's decision became a legal talking point.* 法官的判決成了法律界談論的中心。**2** (*NAmE*) an item that sb will speak about at a meeting, often one that supports a particular argument（常為支持某一論點的）論據

ˈtalking shop *noun* (*BrE, disapproving*) a place where there is a lot of discussion and argument but no action is taken（只討論而無行動的）清談俱樂部

ˈtalking-to *noun* [sing.] (*informal*) a serious talk with sb who has done sth wrong 訓斥；申斥；責備；斥責：*to give sb a good talking-to* 狠狠訓斥某人一頓

ˈtalk radio *noun* [U] radio programmes in which sb discusses a particular subject with people who telephone the radio station to give their opinions 電台聽眾熱線節目；扣應節目

ˈtalk show *noun* **1** (*especially NAmE*) (*BrE* also **ˈchat show**) a television or radio programme in which famous people are asked questions and talk in an informal way about their work and opinions on various topics（電視或電台的）訪談節目：*a talk-show host* 訪談節目主持人 **2** a television or radio programme in which a PRESENTER introduces a particular topic which is then discussed by the audience（電視或電台的）觀眾討論節目，聽眾討論節目

talk·time /ˈtɔːktaɪm/ *noun* [U] the amount of time that a mobile/cell phone can be used for calls without needing more power or more payments（手機的）通話時間，基本通話時間

tall 🔑 /tɔːl/ *adj.* (**tall·er**, **tall·est**)
1 🔑 (of a person, building, tree, etc. 人、建築物、樹木等) having a greater than average height 高的；高大的：*She's tall and thin.* 她身材高瘦。◇ *tall chimneys* 高高的煙囱 ◇ *the tallest building in the world* 世界上最高的建築物 ◇ *a tall glass of iced tea* 一大杯冰茶 OPP **short** **2** 🔑 used to describe or ask about the height of sb/sth（用以表示或詢問高度）有…高，身高：*How tall are you?* 你身高多少？◇ *He's six feet tall and weighs 200 pounds.* 他身高六英尺，體重 200 磅。➲ note at HIGH ▸ **tall·ness** *noun* [U]

IDM **stand ˈtall** (*especially NAmE*) to show that you are proud and able to deal with anything 趾高氣揚；昂然挺立 **be a ˌtall ˈorder** (*informal*) to be very difficult to do 難以辦到；要求苛刻 ➲ more at OAK, WALK *v.*

tall·boy /ˈtɔːlbɔɪ/ (*BrE*) (*NAmE* **high·boy**) *noun* a tall piece of furniture with drawers, used for storing clothes in（帶抽屜的）高衣櫃

tal·low /ˈtæləʊ; *NAmE* -loʊ/ *noun* [U] animal fat used for making CANDLES, soap, etc.（用以製造蠟燭、肥皂等的）動物油脂

ˌtall ˈpoppy syndrome *noun* [U] (*informal, especially AustralE*) the fact of criticizing people who are richer or

T

more successful than others 高罌粟綜合症（批評富有或成功的人）；仇富症；紅眼病

ˌtall ˈstory (*especially BrE*) (*NAmE* usually **ˌtall ˈtale**) *noun* a story that is difficult to believe because what it describes seems exaggerated and not likely to be true 無稽之談；荒誕不經的故事

tally /ˈtæli/ *noun, verb*

■ ***noun*** (*pl.* **-ies**) a record of the number or amount of sth, especially one that you can keep adding to 記錄；積分表；賬： *He hopes to improve on his tally of three goals in the past nine games.* 他希望提高在過去九場比賽中打進三球的紀錄。◇ ***Keep a tally** of how much you spend while you're away.* 在外出期間，把你的花費都記錄下來。

■ ***verb*** (**tal·lies**, **tally·ing**, **tal·lied**, **tal·lied**) **1** [I] **~ (with sth)** to be the same as or to match another person's account of sth, another set of figures, etc. （說法、數字等）與…符合（或一致）；吻合 SYN **match up**： *Her report of what happened tallied exactly with the story of another witness.* 她對於事情的敍述和另一個證人的說法完全吻合。 **2** [T] **~ sth (up)** to calculate the total number, cost, etc. of sth 計算（總的數目、成本等）；合計

ˌtally-ˈho *exclamation* used in hunting for telling the dogs that a FOX has been seen 呔嗬（狩獵時的吆喝聲，示意獵狗發現了狐狸）

the Tal·mud /ˈtælmʊd; *NAmE* also ˈtɑːl-/ *noun* [sing.] a collection of ancient writings on Jewish law and traditions 《塔木德經》（猶太古代法典） ▸ **Tal·mud·ic** /ˌtælˈmʊdɪk; -ˈmjuːd-; *NAmE* also ˌtɑːl-/ *adj.*

talon /ˈtælən/ *noun* a long sharp curved nail on the feet of some birds, especially BIRDS OF PREY (= birds that kill other creatures for food) （某些鳥類，尤指猛禽的）爪 ➲ **VISUAL VOCAB** page V12

taluk /ˈtɑːlʊk/ (also **taluka** /ˈtɑːlʊkɑː/) *noun* (in some countries in S Asia) a smaller division of a district that governs itself （一些南亞國家的）自治小區

tam·ar·ind /ˈtæmərɪnd/ *noun* a tropical tree that produces fruit, also called tamarinds, that are often preserved and used in Asian cooking 羅望子樹，酸豆（熱帶樹木）；羅望子果，酸豆（常用於亞洲式烹調）

tam·bour /ˈtæmbʊə(r); *NAmE* -bʊr/ *noun* a type of drum 鼓

tam·bour·ine /ˌtæmbəˈriːn/ *noun* a musical instrument that has a round wooden frame, sometimes covered with plastic or skin, with metal discs around the edge. To play it you shake it or hit it with your hand. 鈴鼓（蒙有塑料或皮面，鼓幫裝有金屬圓片，搖動或用手擊打發聲） ➲ **VISUAL VOCAB** page V35

tame /teɪm/ *adj., verb*

■ ***adj.*** (**tamer**, **tam·est**) **1** (of animals, birds, etc. 動物、鳥等) not afraid of people, and used to living with them 養馴的；馴服的 OPP **wild** **2** (*informal*) not interesting or exciting 平淡無奇的；枯燥乏味的： *You'll find life here pretty tame after New York.* 這裏的生活相當枯燥，與紐約形成對比。 **3** (*informal*) (of a person 人) willing to do what other people ask 聽使喚的；温順的： *I have a tame doctor who'll always give me a sick note when I want a day off.* 我的醫生對我百依百順，我想要休一天假時，他總會給我開病假條。 ▸ **tame·ly** *adv.* **tame·ness** *noun* [U]

■ ***verb*** **~ sth** to make sth tame or easy to control 馴化；馴服；使易於控制： *Lions can never be completely tamed.* 獅子永遠不能被完全馴化。◇ *She made strenuous efforts to tame her anger.* 她竭力壓制心頭怒火。

tamer /ˈteɪmə(r)/ *noun* (usually in compounds 通常構成複合詞) a person who trains wild animals 馴獸師；馴養者： *a lion-tamer* 馴獅人

Tamil /ˈtæmɪl/ *noun* **1** [C] a member of a race of people living in Tamil Nadu in southern India and in Sri Lanka 泰米爾人（居住在印度南部泰米爾納德邦和斯里蘭卡） **2** [U] the language of the Tamils 泰米爾語 ▸ **Tamil** *adj.*

Tam·many Hall /ˌtæməni ˈhɔːl/ *noun* a dishonest political organization that had a lot of influence in New York City in the 19th and early 20th centuries (sometimes used to refer to any dishonest political organization) 坦曼尼協會（19 世紀和 20 世紀初期操縱美國紐約市政界的腐敗政治組織，有時泛指腐敗政治組織）

tam-o'shanter /ˌtæməˈʃæntə(r)/ *noun* a round hat made of wool with a small ball made of wool in the centre, originally worn in Scotland 蘇格蘭寬頂羊毛圓帽（中央綴絨球）

tam·oxi·fen /təˈmɒksɪfen; *NAmE* -ˈmɑːks-/ *noun* [U] (*medical* 醫) a drug that is used especially to treat breast cancer 三苯氧胺，他莫昔芬（尤用於治療乳腺癌）

tamp /tæmp/ *verb* **~ sth (down)** to press sth down firmly, especially into a closed space 搗實；壓實；塞緊

Tam·pax™ /ˈtæmpæks/ *noun* [C, U] (*pl.* **Tam·pax**) a type of TAMPON 丹碧絲（衞生棉條）

tam·per /ˈtæmpə(r)/ *verb*

PHR V **ˈtamper with sth** to make changes to sth without permission, especially in order to damage it 篡改，擅自改動，胡亂擺弄（尤指有意破壞） SYN **interfere with**： *Someone had obviously tampered with the brakes of my car.* 顯然有人鼓搗過我汽車的剎車。

ˈtamper-proof *adj.* something that is **tamper-proof** is specially designed so that it cannot be easily changed or damaged 防更改的；防損毀的： *a tamper-proof identity card* 防塗改身分卡

tamp·ing /ˈtæmpɪŋ/ *adj.* (*WelshE, informal*) very angry 非常憤怒的

tam·pon /ˈtæmpɒn; *NAmE* -pɑːn/ *noun* a specially shaped piece of cotton material that a woman puts inside her VAGINA to absorb blood during her PERIOD （婦女用的）月經棉條，衞生栓 ➲ compare SANITARY TOWEL

tan /tæn/ *verb, noun, adj., abbr.*

■ ***verb*** (**-nn-**) **1** [I, T] **~ (sb/sth)** if a person or their skin tans or is **tanned**, they become brown as a result of spending time in the sun （使）曬成褐色，曬黑 **2** [T] **~ sth** to make animal skin into leather by treating it with chemicals 鞣（革）；硝（皮） IDM see HIDE *n.*

■ ***noun*** **1** [U] a yellowish-brown colour 棕黃色；黃褐色 **2** (also **sun·tan**) [C] the brown colour that sb with pale skin goes when they have been in the sun 曬成棕褐膚色；曬成的棕褐色： *to get a tan* 曬黑

■ ***adj.*** yellowish brown in colour 棕褐色的；棕黃色的

■ ***abbr.*** (*mathematics* 數) TANGENT 正切

tan·dem /ˈtændəm/ *noun* a bicycle for two riders, one behind the other 雙座自行車；雙人自行車 ➲ **VISUAL VOCAB** page V51

IDM **in ˈtandem (with sb/sth)** a thing that works or happens **in tandem** with sth else works together with it or happens at the same time as it 並行；並駕齊驅；同時實行

tan·doori /tænˈdʊəri; *NAmE* -ˈdʊri/ *noun* [U] (often used as an adjective 常用作形容詞) a method of cooking meat on a long straight piece of metal (called a SPIT) in a CLAY oven, originally used in S Asia 唐杜里烹飪法（源自南亞，將肉插在金屬棒上在泥灶中烘烤）： *tandoori chicken* 唐杜里雞 ◇ *a tandoori restaurant* 唐杜里餐館

tang /tæŋ/ *noun* [usually sing.] a strong sharp taste or smell 強烈味道；刺鼻氣味： *the tang of lemons* 清爽的檸檬味 ▸ **tangy** /ˈtæŋi/ *adj.*： *a refreshing tangy lemon flavour* 清新濃郁的檸檬香味

tan·gent /ˈtændʒənt/ *noun* **1** (*geometry* 幾何) a straight line that touches the outside of a curve but does not cross it 切線 ➲ **VISUAL VOCAB** page V71 **2** (*abbr.* **tan**) (*mathematics* 數) the RATIO of the length of the side opposite an angle in a RIGHT-ANGLED triangle to the length of the side next to it 正切 ➲ compare COSINE, SINE

IDM **fly/go off at a ˈtangent** (*BrE*) (*NAmE* **go off on a ˈtangent**) (*informal*) to suddenly start saying or doing sth that does not seem to be connected to what has gone before 突然轉換話題；突然改變行動

tan·gen·tial /tænˈdʒenʃl/ *adj.* **1** (*formal*) having only a slight or indirect connection with sth 稍微沾邊的；離題的；不相干的： *a tangential argument* 牽強附會的論點

T

2 (*geometry* 幾何) of or along a tangent 正切的；切線的 ▸ **tan·gen·tial·ly** *adj.*

tan·ger·ine /ˌtændʒəˈriːn; *NAmE* ˈtændʒəriːn/ *noun* **1** [C] a type of small sweet orange with loose skin that comes off easily 橘 **2** [U] a deep orange-yellow colour 橘黃色；橘紅色 ▸ **tan·ger·ine** *adj.*：*a tangerine evening gown* 橘紅色的女晚禮服

tangi /ˈtæŋi/ *noun* (*NZE*) a Maori funeral, or meal that is held after the ceremony（毛利人的）葬禮，輓宴

tan·gible /ˈtændʒəbl/ *adj.* **1** [usually before noun] that can be clearly seen to exist 有形的；實際的；真實的：***tangible benefits/improvements/results, etc.*** 實際的好處、改進、效果等 ◇ ***tangible assets*** (= a company's buildings, machinery, etc.) 有形資產 **2** that you can touch and feel 可觸摸的；可觸知的；可感知的：*The tension between them was* ***almost tangible****.* 他們之間的緊張關係幾乎讓人都感覺得出來。**OPP** **intangible** ▸ **tan·gibly** /ˈtændʒəbli/ *adv.*

tan·gle /ˈtæŋgl/ *noun, verb*

■ ***noun*** **1** a twisted mass of threads, hair, etc. that cannot be easily separated（線、毛髮等的）纏結的一團，亂團，亂糟糟的一堆：*a tangle of branches* 盤繞在一起的樹枝 ◇ *Her hair was a mass of tangles.* 她的頭髮亂糟糟的。**2** a state of confusion or lack of order 混亂；紛亂：*His financial affairs are in a tangle.* 他的財務一塌糊塗。**3** (*informal*) a disagreement or fight 糾紛；不和；爭執；打架

■ ***verb*** [T, I] **~ (sth) up** to twist sth into an untidy mass; to become twisted in this way 使纏結；糾結；亂作一團：*She had tangled up the sheets on the bed as she lay tossing and turning.* 她在牀上翻來覆去，把被單弄得亂成一團。

PHR V **ˈtangle with sb/sth** to become involved in an argument or a fight with sb/sth 爭論；爭吵；打架

tan·gled /ˈtæŋgld/ *adj.* **1** twisted together in an untidy way 纏結的；混亂的；紊亂的：*tangled hair/bed clothes* 凌亂的頭髮／牀上用品 **2** complicated, and not easy to understand 複雜的；糾纏不清的：*tangled financial affairs* 錯綜複雜的財務

tango /ˈtæŋgəʊ; *NAmE* -goʊ/ *noun, verb*

■ ***noun*** (*pl.* **-os** /-gəʊz; *NAmE* -goʊz/) a fast S American dance with a strong beat, in which two people hold each other closely; a piece of music for this dance 探戈舞；探戈舞曲

■ ***verb*** (**tango·ing**, **tan·goed**, **tan·goed**) [I] to dance the tango 跳探戈舞

IDM **it takes ˈtwo to tango** (*informal*) used to say that two people or groups, and not just one, are responsible for sth that has happened (usually sth bad)（常指壞事）一個巴掌拍不響，雙方都有責任

T

tank 🔑 /tæŋk/ *noun, verb*

■ ***noun*** **1** 🔑 a large container for holding liquid or gas（貯放液體或氣體的）箱，槽，罐：*a hot water tank* 熱水箱 ◇ *a fuel tank* 燃料箱 ◇ *a fish tank* (= for keeping fish in) 魚缸 ➲ **VISUAL VOCAB** pages V40, V51 ➲ see also SEPTIC TANK, THINK TANK **2** 🔑 (also **tank·ful** /-fʊl/) the contents of a tank or the amount it will hold 箱（或桶等）所裝之物；一箱（或一桶等）的量：*We drove there and back on one tank of petrol.* 我們開車去那裏來回用了一油箱汽油。**3** 🔑 a military vehicle covered with strong metal and armed with guns. It can travel over very rough ground using wheels that move inside metal belts. 坦克 **4** (*IndE*) an artificial pool, lake or RESERVOIR（人工）水池，湖，水庫

■ ***verb*** **1** [I] (*NAmE*) (of a company or a product 公司或產品) to fail completely 徹底失敗；破產；倒閉：*The company's shares tanked on Wall Street.* 這家公司的股票在華爾街徹底崩盤了。**2** [T, I] **~ (sth)** (*NAmE, sport* 體) to lose a game, especially deliberately（尤指故意）輸掉比賽：*She was accused of tanking the match.* 有人指責她故意輸掉這場比賽。

PHR V **ˌtank (sth) ˈup** (*NAmE*) to fill a car with petrol/gas 給（汽車）加油：*He tanked up and drove off.* 他給汽車加滿油開走了。◇ *We stopped to tank the car up.* 我們停下來給汽車加油。

tank·ard /ˈtæŋkəd; *NAmE* -ərd/ *noun* a large, usually metal, cup with a handle, that is used for drinking beer from（通常為金屬的）單柄大酒杯，啤酒杯

ˌtanked ˈup (*BrE*) (*NAmE* **tanked**) *adj.* (*informal*) very drunk 喝得爛醉的

ˈtank engine *noun* a steam engine that carries its own fuel and water inside, rather than using another small truck（自帶燃料的）水櫃蒸汽機車

tank·er /ˈtæŋkə(r)/ *noun* a ship or lorry/truck that carries oil, gas or petrol/gas in large quantities 運送大量液體或氣體的輪船（或卡車）；油輪；罐車；油槽車：*an oil tanker* 油輪 ➲ **VISUAL VOCAB** page V57 ➲ see also SUPERTANKER

tank·ini /ˌtæŋˈkiːni/ *noun* a SWIMSUIT in two pieces, consisting of a short top without sleeves and the bottom half of a BIKINI 袒基尼（兩件套泳裝，包括無袖短上衣和比基尼下褲）

ˈtank top *noun* **1** (*BrE*) a sweater without sleeves 坎肩 **2** (*NAmE*) a piece of clothing like a T-SHIRT without sleeves 汗背心

ˈtank tread *noun* (*especially NAmE*) (also **ˈCaterpillar track™** especially in *BrE*) *noun* a metal belt fastened around the wheels of a heavy vehicle, used for travelling over rough or soft ground（重型機動車使用的）坦克履帶，越障防陷履帶 ➲ **VISUAL VOCAB** page V58

tanned /tænd/ (also **sun·tanned**) *adj.* having a brown skin colour as a result of being in the sun 皮膚曬成褐色的；曬黑的

tan·ner /ˈtænə(r)/ *noun* a person whose job is to TAN animal skins to make leather 鞣皮工；硝皮匠；製革工人

tan·nery /ˈtænəri/ *noun* (*pl.* **-ies**) a place where animal skins are TANNED and made into leather 鞣皮廠；皮革廠

tan·nie /ˈtʌni/ *noun* (*SAfrE, informal*) **1** an aunt; a friendly form of address for a woman who is older than you 姑媽；姨媽；伯母；（用作稱呼）大媽，大娘 **2** (sometimes *disapproving*) a woman, especially one with old-fashioned views or tastes 婦人；（尤指）古板的女人

tan·nin /ˈtænɪn/ (also **ˌtannic ˈacid**) *noun* [U] a yellowish or brownish substance found in the BARK of some trees and the fruit of many plants, used especially in making leather, ink and wine 單寧；單寧酸；鞣質 ▸ **tan·nic** /ˈtænɪk/ *adj.*

Tan·noy™ /ˈtænɔɪ/ *noun* (*BrE*) a system with LOUDSPEAKERS used for giving information in a public place 塔諾伊擴音系統：*to make an announcement over the Tannoy* 通過塔諾伊擴音系統發佈通知

tan·tal·ize (*BrE* also **-ise**) /ˈtæntəlaɪz/ *verb* **~ sb/sth** to make a person or an animal want sth that they cannot have or do（以可望而不可即之物）逗引，招惹，使乾着急 ▸ **tan·tal·iz·ing**, **-is·ing** *adj.*：*The tantalizing aroma of fresh coffee wafted towards them.* 新鮮咖啡那誘人的香味向他們飄來。◇ *a* ***tantalizing glimpse*** *of the future* 對未來令人嚮往的展望 **tan·tal·iz·ing·ly**, **-is·ing·ly** *adv.*：*The branch was tantalizingly out of reach.* 夠不到那樹枝，讓人乾着急。

tan·ta·lum /ˈtæntələm/ *noun* [U] (*symb.* **Ta**) a chemical element. Tantalum is a hard silver-grey metal used in the production of electronic parts and of metal plates and pins for connecting broken bones. 鉭

tan·ta·mount /ˈtæntəmaʊnt/ *adj.* **~ to sth** (*formal*) having the same bad effect as sth else 無異於；等於；效果與…一樣壞：*If he resigned it would be tantamount to admitting that he was guilty.* 他若辭職就等於承認自己有錯。

tan·tra /ˈtæntrə/ *noun* **1** [C] an ancient Hindu or Buddhist text 坦陀羅（古印度教或佛教的經文）**2** [U] behaviour based on these texts, including prayer and MEDITATION 坦陀羅神秘修煉；密教修行 ▸ **tan·tric** /ˈtæntrɪk/ *adj.*

tan·trum /ˈtæntrəm/ *noun* a sudden short period of angry, unreasonable behaviour, especially in a child（尤指兒童）耍脾氣，使性子：*to* ***have/throw a tantrum*** 發脾氣 ◇ *Children often have* ***temper tantrums***

at the age of two or thereabouts. 兒童在兩歲左右經常愛使性子。

Taoi·seach /ˈtiːʃəx/ *noun* the Prime Minister of the Irish Republic（愛爾蘭共和國）總理

Tao·ism /ˈdaʊɪzəm; ˈtaʊ-/ *noun* [U] a Chinese philosophy based on the writings of Lao-tzu 道教 ▶ **Tao·ist** /ˈdaʊɪst; ˈtaʊ-/ *noun, adj.*

tap 0▬ /tæp/ *verb, noun*

■ ***verb*** (-pp-) **1** 0▬ [I, T] to hit sb/sth quickly and lightly 輕敲；輕拍；輕叩： **~ (away) (at sth)** *Someone tapped at the door.* 有人輕輕叩門。◇ *He was busy tapping away at his computer.* 他埋頭敲着電腦鍵盤。◇ **~ sb/sth** *Ralph tapped me on the shoulder.* 拉爾夫輕輕地拍了拍我的肩膀。 **2** 0▬ [T, I] **~ (sth)** if you **tap** your fingers, feet, etc. or they **tap**, you hit them gently against a table, the floor, etc., for example to the rhythm of music（用…）輕輕叩擊： *He kept tapping his fingers on the table.* 他不停地用手指輕輕敲着桌子。◇ *The music set everyone's feet tapping.* 樂曲使得每個人都用腳輕輕打起拍子來。 **3** [T, I] to make use of a source of energy, knowledge, etc. that already exists 利用，開發，發掘（已有的資源、知識等）： **~ sth** *We need to tap the expertise of the people we already have.* 我們需要利用我們現有人員的專業知識。◇ **~ into sth** *The movie seems to tap into a general sentimentality about animals.* 這部電影似乎在激發人們對動物的普遍憐惜之情。 **4** [T] **~ sth** (*especially BrE*) to fit a device to a telephone so that sb's calls can be listened to secretly（在電話上）安裝竊聽器，搭線竊聽： *He was convinced his phone was being tapped.* 他確信自己的電話在被人竊聽。 ➲ see also WIRETAPPING **5** [T] **~ sth** to cut into a tree in order to get liquid from it 在（樹）上切口（導出液體） **6** [T, usually passive] **~ sb** (*NAmE*) to choose sb to do a particular job 委任；指定（某人做某事）： *Richards has been tapped to replace the retiring chairperson.* 理查茲獲得委任接替行將退任的主席。 **7** [T] **~ sth** (*phonetics* 語音) to produce a TAP (6) 發輕拍音 SYN **flap**

PHR V **ˈtap sb for sth** (*BrE, informal*) to persuade sb to give you sth, especially money 向…索要，向…乞討（尤指錢） **ˌtap sth↔ˈin/ˈout** to put information, numbers, letters, etc. into a machine by pressing buttons 輸入，輸出（信息、數字、字母等）： *Tap in your PIN number.* 輸入你的個人身分識別號碼。 **ˌtap sth↔ˈout 1** to hit a surface gently to the rhythm of music（跟着音樂節奏）輕輕打拍子： *She tapped out the beat on the table.* 她輕擊桌面打着拍子。 **2** to write sth using a computer or a mobile/cell phone（用計算機或移動電話）寫，輸入，鍵入： *I tapped out a text message to Mandy.* 我給曼迪發了一條短信。

■ ***noun*** **1** 0▬ (*especially BrE*) (*NAmE* usually **fau·cet**) [C] a device for controlling the flow of water from a pipe into a bath/BATHTUB or SINK 水龍頭；旋塞： *bath taps* 浴缸水龍頭 ◇ *the* **hot/cold tap** (= the tap that hot/cold water comes out of) 熱水/冷水龍頭 ◇ ***Turn the tap on/off.*** 打開/關上龍頭。◇ *Don't leave the tap running.* 別把水龍頭開着白白流水。◇ *the sound of a* **dripping tap** 水龍頭滴答的漏水聲 ➲ picture at PLUG ➲ VISUAL VOCAB pages V24, V25 ➲ see also TAP WATER **2** [C] a device for controlling the flow of liquid or gas from a pipe or container 龍頭；旋塞： *a gas tap* 煤氣閥門 ◇ *beer taps* 啤酒旋塞 **3** 0▬ [C] a light hit with your hand or fingers 輕擊；輕拍；輕敲；輕扣： *a* **tap at/on** *the door* 輕輕的叩門 ◇ *He felt a tap on his shoulder and turned round.* 他覺得有人輕輕拍他的肩膀便轉過身來。 **4** [C] an act of fitting a device to a telephone so that sb's telephone calls can be listened to secretly 電話竊聽；搭線竊聽： *a phone tap* 電話竊聽 **5** [U] = TAP-DANCING **6** [C] (*phonetics* 語音) a speech sound which is produced by striking the tongue quickly and lightly against the part of the mouth behind the upper front teeth. The /t/ in *later* in American English and the /r/ in *very* in some British accents are examples of taps. 輕拍音 SYN **flap**

IDM **on ˈtap 1** available to be used at any time 可隨時使用的： *We have this sort of information on tap.* 我們可隨時向您提供這種資料。 **2** beer that is **on tap** is in a BARREL with a tap on it （啤酒）裝在有旋塞的桶裏的，散裝的 **3** (*NAmE*) something that is **on tap** is being discussed or prepared and will happen soon 協商中；準備中；即將發生

tapas /ˈtæpəs; -pæs/ *noun* [pl.] (from *Spanish*) small amounts of a variety of Spanish dishes, served with drinks in a bar 塔帕斯（酒吧中和飲料一起供應的各種西班牙風味小吃）

ˈtap dance *noun* [U, C] a style of dancing in which you tap the rhythm of the music with your feet, wearing special shoes with pieces of metal on the heels and toes 踢踏舞 ▶ **ˈtap dancer** *noun* **ˈtap-dancing** (also **tap**) *noun* [U]

tape 0▬ AW /teɪp/ *noun, verb*

■ ***noun*** **1** 0▬ [U] a long narrow strip of MAGNETIC material that is used for recording sounds, pictures or information 磁帶；錄音帶；錄像帶 ➲ see also MAGNETIC TAPE, VIDEOTAPE **2** 0▬ [C] a CASSETTE that contains sounds, or sounds and pictures, that have been recorded 錄了音的盒式磁帶；錄了像的盒式磁帶： *a* ***blank tape*** (= a tape that has nothing recorded on it) 空白盒式磁帶 ◇ *I lent her my Bob Marley tapes.* 我把我的鮑勃•馬利音樂帶借給了她。◇ *Police seized various books and tapes.* 警方扣留了各種圖書和磁帶。 **3** 0▬ [U] a long narrow strip of material with a sticky substance on one side that is used for sticking things together 膠帶；膠條： ***adhesive/sticky tape*** 黏膠帶 ➲ see also INSULATING TAPE, MASKING TAPE, SCOTCH TAPE, SELLOTAPE **4** [C, U] a narrow strip of material that is used for tying things together or as a label（捆、繫物品或作標記的）狹帶，帶子，線帶，窄布條： *The papers were in a pile, tied together with a tape.* 報紙叠成一摞，用帶子捆了起來。 ➲ see also RED TAPE, TICKER TAPE **5** [C] a long narrow strip of material that is stretched across the place where a race will finish （賽跑場地的）終點線： *the finishing tape* 終點線 **6** [C] = TAPE MEASURE

■ ***verb*** **1 ~ sb/sth** to record sb/sth on MAGNETIC tape using a special machine 把…錄在磁帶上： *Private conversations between the two had been taped and sent to a newspaper.* 這兩個人的私下談話被錄下音來送給了一家報紙。 **2 ~ sth (up)** to fasten sth by sticking or tying it with tape 用膠帶粘住；用帶子繫緊： *Put it in a box and tape it up securely.* 把這個放進盒子裏，再用帶子繫牢。 **3 ~ sth + adv./prep.** to stick sth onto sth else using sticky tape 用膠帶粘貼： *Someone had taped a message on the door.* 有人用膠帶把字條貼在了門上。 **4 ~ sth (up)** (*NAmE*) to tie a bandage firmly around an injury or a wound 用繃帶包紮： *That's a nasty cut—come on, we'll get it all taped up.* 傷口很嚴重，快，咱們用繃帶把它包紮起來。

IDM **have (got) sb/sth ˈtaped** (*BrE, informal*) to understand sb/sth completely and to have learned how to deal with them/it successfully 徹底瞭解；摸清楚…的底細： *He can't fool me—I've got him taped.* 他休想騙我，我把他的底細摸得一清二楚。

ˈtape measure (also **tape**, **ˈmeasuring tape**) *noun* a long narrow strip of plastic, cloth or FLEXIBLE metal that has measurements marked on it and is used for measuring the length of sth 捲尺；皮尺

taper /ˈteɪpə(r)/ *verb, noun*

■ ***verb*** [I, T] to become gradually narrower; to make sth become gradually narrower （使）逐漸變窄： *The tail tapered to a rounded tip.* 尾部越來越細，最後成了個圓尖。◇ **~ sth** *The pots are wide at the base and tapered at the top.* 這些壺底部粗，頂部細。

PHR V **ˌtaper ˈoff** to become gradually less in number, amount, degree, etc. （數量、程度等）逐漸減少： *The number of applicants for teaching posts has tapered off.* 申請做教學工作的人數越來越少。 **ˌtaper sth↔ˈoff** to make sth become gradually less in number, amount, degree, etc. 使（數目等）逐漸減少；降低…程度： *They are gradually tapering off production of the older models.* 他們在逐步減少生產舊型號的產品。

■ ***noun*** **1** a long thin piece of wood, paper, etc. that is used for lighting fires or lamps （點火用的）木條，紙媒 **2** a long thin CANDLE 細長蠟燭 **3** [usually sing.] the way that sth gradually decreases in size, becoming thinner 漸減；逐漸縮小（或變細）

T

ˈtape-record *verb* **~ sth** to record sth on tape 用磁帶錄製： *a tape-recorded interview* 錄音訪談

ˈtape recorder *noun* a machine that is used for recording and playing sounds on tape 錄音機

ˈtape recording *noun* something that has been recorded on tape 磁帶錄音；磁帶錄像： *a tape recording of the interview* 訪談錄音

tape·script /ˈteɪpskrɪpt/ *noun* the printed text of a recording of speech 錄音文本

tap·es·try /ˈtæpəstri/ *noun* [C, U] (*pl.* **-ies**) a picture or pattern that is made by WEAVING coloured wool onto heavy cloth; the art of doing this 壁毯；掛毯；織錦；繡帷： *medieval tapestries* 中世紀的壁毯 ◇ *tapestry cushions* 織錦沙發靠背墊 ◇ *crafts such as embroidery and tapestry* 諸如刺繡和織錦之類的手工藝 ▶ **tap·es·tried** *adj.* ： *tapestried walls* 掛有繡帷的牆

tape·worm /ˈteɪpwɜːm; *NAmE* -wɜːrm/ *noun* a long flat WORM that lives in the INTESTINES of humans and animals 絛蟲

ˈtap-in *noun* (in sport 體育運動) an easy light hit of the ball into the goal or hole from a close position 近距離輕鬆進球；輕撥入籃： *The pass left Tevez with a simple tap-in.* 這個傳球使特維斯輕鬆破門。

tapi·oca /ˌtæpiˈəʊkə; *NAmE* -ˈoʊkə/ *noun* [U] hard white grains obtained from the CASSAVA plant, often cooked with milk to make a DESSERT (= a sweet dish) 木薯澱粉

tapir /ˈteɪpə(r)/ *noun* an animal like a pig with a long nose, that lives in Central and S America and SE Asia 貘（生活在中南美洲和東南亞的長鼻豬狀動物）

ˌtap-ˈpenalty *noun* (in RUGBY 橄欖球) a situation where a player is allowed a free kick of the ball because the other team has broken a rule, and chooses to touch it lightly with the foot then immediately pick it up 輕踢罰球

tap·root /ˈtæpruːt/ *noun* the main root of a plant that grows straight downwards and produces smaller side roots （植物的）直根，主根

ˈtap water *noun* [U] water supplied through pipes to taps/faucets in a building 自來水： *Is the tap water safe to drink?* 這自來水喝了不會鬧病吧？

tar /tɑː(r)/ *noun, verb*

■ ***noun*** [U] **1** a thick black sticky liquid that becomes hard when cold. Tar is obtained from coal and is used especially in making roads. 焦油；焦油瀝青；柏油 **2** a substance similar to tar that is formed by burning TOBACCO （煙草點燃後產生的）煙鹼，尼古丁： *low-tar cigarettes* 尼古丁含量低的捲煙 **IDM** see SPOIL *v.*

■ ***verb*** (**-rr-**) **~ sth** to cover sth with tar 用瀝青塗抹；用柏油鋪： *a tarred road* 柏油路

IDM **tar and ˈfeather sb** to put tar on sb then cover them with feathers, as a punishment 把…渾身塗上瀝青並粘上羽毛（作為懲罰）；嚴懲 **be tarred with the same ˈbrush (as sb)** to be thought to have the same faults, etc. as sb else 被認為是一路貨色；被看成一丘之貉

tara·ma·sa·lata /ˌtærəməsəˈlɑːtə/ *noun* [U] (*BrE*) a type of Greek food made from fish eggs 希臘紅魚子泥色拉；魚子醬

ta·ran·tula /təˈræntʃələ/ *noun* a large spider covered with hair that lives in hot countries. Some types of tarantula have a poisonous bite. 塔蘭托毒蛛

tardy /ˈtɑːdi; *NAmE* ˈtɑːrdi/ *adj.* **~ (in doing sth)** (*formal*) slow to act, move or happen; late in happening or arriving 行動緩慢的；拖拉的；遲緩的；遲到的： *The law is often tardy in reacting to changing attitudes.* 法律對變化中的觀念常常反應遲緩。◇ *people who are tardy in paying their bills* 拖延付賬的人 ◇ (*NAmE*) *to be tardy for school* 上學遲到 ▶ **tar·dily** /ˈtɑːdɪli; *NAmE* ˈtɑːrd-/ *adv.* **tar·di·ness** *noun* [U]

tare /teə(r); *NAmE* ter/ *noun* (*literary* or *technical* 術語) a plant growing where you do not want it 莠草；雜草；雜生植物 **SYN** weed

Synonyms 同義詞辨析

target

objective • goal • object • end

These are all words for sth that you are trying to achieve. 以上各詞均指目標、目的。

target a result that you try to achieve 指試圖達到的目標、指標： *Set yourself targets that you can reasonably hope to achieve.* 給自己制訂有望達到的指標。◇ *attainment targets in schools* 學校的成績目標

objective (*rather formal*) something that you are trying to achieve 指正努力達到的目標、目的： *What is the main objective of this project?* 這個項目的主要目標是什麼？

goal something that you hope to achieve 指希望達到的目標、目的： *He continued to pursue his goal of becoming an actor.* 他繼續追求他成為演員的目標。

TARGET, OBJECTIVE OR GOAL? 用 target、objective 還是 goal？

A **target** is usually officially recorded in some way, for example by an employer or by a government committee. It is often specific, and in the form of figures, such as number of sales or exam passes, or a date. People often set their own **objectives**: these are things that they wish to achieve, often as part of a project or a talk they are giving. **Goals** are often long-term, and relate to people's life and career plans or the long-term plans of a company or organization. * target 通常為以某種方式正式記錄的目標，如由雇主或政府委員會等制訂，常為具體的數字，如銷售量、考試及格率或日期等；objective 通常指為自己制訂的、希望達到的目標，常為某一項目或發言的一部份；goal 通常指長遠目標，與人生和職業規劃或公司、機構的長遠規劃有關。

object the purpose of sth; sth that you plan to achieve 指目的、目標、宗旨： *The object is to educate people about road safety.* 目的就是教育大眾注意交通安全。

end something that you plan to achieve 指計劃達到的目的、目標： *He joined the society for political ends.* 他為了政治目的加入了這個協會。◇ *That's only OK if you believe that **the end justifies the means*** (= bad methods of doing sth are acceptable if the final result is good). 如果你認為只要目的正確可以不擇手段，那勉強是可以接受的。**NOTE** **End** is usually used in the plural or in particular fixed expressions. * end 常用複數或用於某些固定短語中。

PATTERNS

- to work **towards** a(n) target/objective/goal
- an **ambitious/major/long-term/short-term/future** target/objective/goal
- **economic/financial/business** targets/objectives/goals
- to **set/agree on/identify/reach/meet/exceed** a(n) target/objective/goal
- to **achieve** a(n) target/objective/goal/end

tar·get 0- **AW** /ˈtɑːɡɪt; *NAmE* ˈtɑːrɡɪt/ *noun, verb*

■ ***noun*** **1** 0- a result that you try to achieve 目標；指標： *business goals and targets* 經營目的和指標 ◇ *attainment targets* 成績目標 ◇ ***Set yourself targets** that you can reasonably hope to achieve.* 給自己制訂有望達到的指標。◇ *to **meet/achieve a target*** 完成 / 達到目標 ◇ *a **target date** of April 2012* * 2012 年 4 月這一預定日期 ◇ *The university will **reach its target** of 5 000 students next September.* 這所大學將於下個九月達到在校學生 5 000 人的目標。◇ *The new sports complex is **on target** to open in June.* 新建的體育中心將在六月份如期開放。◇ *a **target area/audience/group*** (= the particular area, audience, etc. that a product, programme, etc. is aimed at) 目標範圍 / 觀眾 / 群體 ➲ COLLOCATIONS at BUSINESS **2** 0- an object, a person or a place that people aim at when attacking （攻擊的）目標，對象： *They bombed military* *and civilian targets.* 他們轟炸了軍事和民用目標。◇ **~ for sb/sth** *Doors and windows are an* ***easy target*** *for burglars.* 門窗被竊賊作為入室的目標容易得手。◇ *It's a* ***prime target*** (= an obvious target) *for terrorist attacks.* 這是恐怖分子攻擊的首要目標。◇ **~ of sth** (*figurative*) *He's become the target of a lot of criticism recently.* 他最近成了眾矢之的。 **3** an object that people practise shooting at, especially a round board with circles on it 靶；靶子：*to aim at a target* 瞄準靶子 ◇ *to* ***hit/miss the target*** 中／脫靶 ◇ ***target practice*** 射擊練習 ➲ VISUAL VOCAB page V40

■ ***verb*** (**tar·get·ing**, **tar·get·ed**, **tar·get·ed**) [usually passive] **1 ~ sb/sth** to aim an attack or a criticism at sb/sth 把…作為攻擊目標；把…作為批評的對象：*The missiles were mainly targeted at the United States.* 導彈主要瞄準的是美國。◇ *The company has been targeted by animal rights groups for its use of dogs in drugs trials.* 這家公司因用狗做藥物試驗而成為動物保護團體批評的對象。 **2 ~ sb** to try to have an effect on a particular group of people 面向，把…對準（某群體）：*The campaign is clearly targeted at the young.* 這個宣傳計劃顯然是針對青年人的。◇ *a new magazine that targets single men* 以單身男士為讀者對象的新雜誌

'target language *noun* (*linguistics* 語言) **1** (also **'object language**) a language into which a text is being translated（翻譯的）譯文語言，譯入語 **2** a foreign language that sb is learning（外語學習的）目標語言，對象語言，所學語

tar·iff /'tærɪf/ *noun* **1** a tax that is paid on goods coming into or going out of a country 關稅 ➲ SYNONYMS at TAX ➲ COLLOCATIONS at INTERNATIONAL **2** a list of fixed prices that are charged by a hotel or restaurant for rooms, meals, etc., or by a company for a particular service（旅館、餐廳或服務公司的）價目表，收費表 **3** (*BrE, law* 律) a level of punishment for sb who has been found guilty of a crime 量刑標準

Tar·mac™ /'tɑːmæk; *NAmE* 'tɑːrmæk/ *noun* [U] **1** (also *less frequent* **tar·mac·adam** /ˌtɑːmə'kædəm; *NAmE* ˌtɑːrm-/) (*NAmE* also **black·top**) a black material used for making road surfaces, that consists of small stones mixed with TAR 塔瑪克柏油碎石（用作鋪築路面材料） **2 the tarmac** an area with a Tarmac surface, especially at an airport 柏油碎石路面；柏油碎石鋪的停機坪（或跑道）：*Three planes were standing on the tarmac, waiting to take off.* 三架飛機停在跑道上，等候起飛。

tar·mac /'tɑːmæk; *NAmE* 'tɑːrmæk/ *verb* (**-ck-**) (*NAmE* also **blacktop**) **~ sth** to cover a surface with Tarmac 以柏油碎石鋪築（路面）：*tarmacked roads* 柏油碎石路面

tarn /tɑːn; *NAmE* tɑːrn/ *noun* a small lake in the mountains 冰川湖；山中小湖

tar·na·tion /tɑː'neɪʃn; *NAmE* tɑːr'n-/ *exclamation* (*old-fashioned, especially NAmE*) a word that people use to show that they are annoyed with sb/sth（表示惱怒）該死，討厭

tar·nish /'tɑːnɪʃ; *NAmE* 'tɑːrnɪʃ/ *verb, noun*

■ ***verb*** **1** [I, T] if metal **tarnishes** or sth **tarnishes** it, it no longer looks bright and shiny（使）失去光澤，暗淡：*The mirrors had tarnished with age.* 這些鏡子因年深日久而照影不清楚。◇ **~ sth** *The silver candlesticks were tarnished and dusty.* 銀燭台都發烏了，滿是灰塵。 **2** [T] **~ sth** to spoil the good opinion people have of sb/sth 玷污，敗壞，損壞（名聲等） SYN **taint**：*He hopes to improve the newspaper's somewhat tarnished public image.* 他希望改善報紙略有受損的公眾形象。

■ ***noun*** [sing., U] a thin layer on the surface of a metal that makes it look dull and not bright（金屬表面上的）暗銹

tarot /'tærəʊ; *NAmE* -roʊ/ *noun* [sing., U] a set of special cards with pictures on them, used for telling sb what will happen to them in the future 塔羅紙牌（用於占卜）

tar·paulin /tɑː'pɔːlɪn; *NAmE* tɑːr'p-/ (also *NAmE informal* **tarp**) *noun* [C, U] a large sheet made of heavy WATERPROOF material, used to cover things with and to keep rain off 柏油帆布；（防水）油布

tar·ra·gon /'tærəgən/ *noun* [U] a plant with leaves that have a strong taste and are used in cooking as a HERB 龍蒿（用於烹調） ➲ VISUAL VOCAB page V32

tarry /'tæri/ *verb* (**tar·ries**, **tarry·ing**, **tar·ried**, **tar·ried**) [I] (*old use* or *literary*) to stay in a place, especially when you ought to leave; to delay coming to or going from a place 逗留；耽擱 SYN **linger**

tar·sal /'tɑːsl; *NAmE* 'tɑːrsl/ *noun* (*anatomy* 解) one of the small bones in the ankle and upper foot 跗骨（踝和腳上部的小骨）

tart /tɑːt; *NAmE* tɑːrt/ *noun, adj., verb*

■ ***noun*** **1** [C, U] an open PIE filled with sweet food such as fruit 甜果餡餅：*a strawberry tart* 草莓餡餅 ➲ compare FLAN, QUICHE **2** [C] (*BrE, informal, disapproving*) a woman who you think behaves or dresses in a way that is immoral and is intended to make men sexually excited 放蕩的女人；騷貨 ➲ see also TARTY **3** [C] (*slang*) a PROSTITUTE 妓女；野雞

■ ***adj.*** **1** having an unpleasant sour taste 酸的；酸澀的：*tart apples* 酸蘋果 **2** [usually before noun] (of remarks, etc. 話語等) quick and unkind 尖酸的；刻薄的；辛辣的：*a tart reply* 尖刻的答覆 SYN **sharp** ▸ **tart·ly** *adv.*：*'Too late!' said my mother tartly.* "早幹什麼去了！"我母親刻薄地說。 **tart·ness** *noun* [U]

■ ***verb***

PHR V **ˌtart yourself 'up** (*informal*) (especially of a woman 尤指女人) to make yourself more attractive by putting on nice clothes, jewellery, make-up, etc. 打扮得花枝招展；濃妝豔抹 **ˌtart sth↔'up** (*informal*) to decorate or improve the appearance of sth, often in a way that other people do not think is attractive 把…裝飾得俗氣；把…弄得花裏胡哨

tar·tan /'tɑːtn; *NAmE* 'tɑːrtn/ *noun* **1** [U, C] a pattern of squares and lines of different colours and widths that cross each other at an angle of 90°, used especially on cloth, and originally from Scotland（尤指源自蘇格蘭織物的）花格圖案，方格花紋：*a tartan rug* 花格小地毯 ➲ VISUAL VOCAB page V61 **2** [C] a tartan pattern connected with a particular group of families (= a CLAN) in Scotland（與蘇格蘭某家族有關的）花格圖案，方格花紋：*the MacLeod tartan* 麥克勞德花格圖案 **3** [U] cloth, especially made of wool, that has a tartan pattern 花格布料；（尤指）蘇格蘭格呢 ➲ compare PLAID

tar·tar /'tɑːtə(r); *NAmE* 'tɑːrt-/ *noun* **1** [U] a hard substance that forms on teeth 牙石；牙垢 **2** [C] (*old-fashioned*) a person in a position of authority who is very bad-tempered 暴君；脾氣暴躁的掌權者

tar·tare sauce (*NAmE* **tar·tar sauce**) /ˌtɑːtə 'sɔːs; *NAmE* ˌtɑːrtər/ *noun* [U] a thick cold white sauce made from MAYONNAISE, chopped onions and CAPERS, usually eaten with fish 韃靼醬，蛋黃沙司（用蛋黃醬、碎洋蔥和刺山柑調製而成，通常為吃魚的作料）

tar·tar·ic acid /tɑːˌtærɪk 'æsɪd; *NAmE* tɑːrˌt-/ *noun* [U] (*chemistry* 化) a type of acid that is found in GRAPES that are not ready to eat 酒石酸（存在於葡萄中）

tarty /'tɑːti; *NAmE* 'tɑːrti/ *adj.* (*disapproving*) (of a woman 女人) dressing or behaving in a way that is intended to attract sexual attention 風騷的；放蕩的

Tar·zan /'tɑːzæn; *NAmE* 'tɑːrz-/ *noun* a man with a very strong body 泰山（健壯的男子） ORIGIN From the novel *Tarzan of the Apes* by Edgar Rice Burroughs about a man who lived with wild animals. 源自埃德加•賴斯•巴勒斯的小說《人猿泰山》，其中的男主人公和野獸共同生活。

taser /'teɪzə(r)/ *noun* a gun that fires DARTS that give a person a small electric shock and makes them unable to move for a short time 電擊槍（發射電脈衝，使人暫時不能動彈）

task AW /tɑːsk; *NAmE* tæsk/ *noun, verb*

■ ***noun*** **1** a piece of work that sb has to do, especially a hard or unpleasant one（尤指艱巨或令人厭煩的）任務，工作：*to* ***perform/carry out/complete/undertake a task*** 執行／完成／承擔任務 ◇ ***a daunting/an impossible/a formidable/an unenviable, etc. task*** 令人望而生畏、不可能完成、艱巨、令人為難等的任務 ◇ ***a thankless task*** (= an unpleasant one that nobody wants to do and nobody thanks you for doing) 吃力不

T

討好的工作 ◇ *Our first task is to set up a communications system.* 我們的首項任務是架設通信系統。◇ *Detectives are now faced with **the task of** identifying the body.* 偵探現在面臨辨認屍體這項任務。◇ *Getting hold of this information was **no easy task*** (= was difficult). 把這一情報搞到手絕不是件輕而易舉的事。 **2** an activity which is designed to help achieve a particular learning goal, especially in language teaching（尤指語言教學中旨在幫助達到某一學習目的的）活動： *task-based learning* 任務型學習

IDM **take sb to 'task (for/over sth)** to criticize sb strongly for sth they have done 嚴厲地責備；申斥；訓斥

■ *verb* [usually passive] **~ sb (with sth)** *(formal)* to give sb a task to do 交給某人（任務）；派給某人（工作）

Synonyms 同義詞辨析

task

duties • mission • job • chore

These are all words for a piece of work that sb has to do. 以上各詞均指任務、工作。

task a piece of work that sb has to do, especially a difficult or unpleasant one 尤指艱巨或令人厭煩的任務、工作： *Our first task will be to set up a communications system.* 我們的首項任務是架設通信系統。

duties tasks that are part of your job 指職責、任務： *Your duties will include setting up a new computer system.* 你的職責將包括建立一個新的計算機系統。

mission an important official job that a person or group of people is given to do, especially when they are sent to another country 指官方使命、使團的使命： *They undertook a **fact-finding mission** in the region.* 他們承擔了在該地區核查事實的工作。

job a piece of work that sb has to do 指一項任務、一件工作： *I've got various jobs around the house to do.* 我在家裏有各種各樣的活兒要幹。

TASK OR JOB? 用 task 還是 job？

A **task** may be more difficult than a **job** and require you to think carefully about how you are going to do it. A **job** may be sth small that is one of several jobs that you have to do, especially in the home; or a **job** can be sth that takes a long time and is boring and/or needs a lot of patience. * task 可能比 job 艱巨，需要仔細思考如何去做；job 可指許多要做的事情中的一件小事，尤指家務活；job 有時指費時、沉悶或需要極大耐心的工作。

chore a task that you have to do regularly, especially one that you do in the home and find unpleasant or boring 指日常事務、例行工作、尤指令人厭煩或無聊的家務活： *household chores* 家務雜活

PATTERNS

- the task/mission/job/chore **of** (**doing**) sth
- (a) **daily/day-to-day** task/duties/job/chore
- (a) **routine** task/duties/mission/job/chore
- (a/an) **easy/difficult** task/mission/job
- (a) **household/domestic** task/duties/job/chore
- to **do** a task/a job/the chores
- to **finish** a task/a mission/a job/the chores
- to **give sb** a task/their duties/a mission/a job/a chore

'task force *noun* **1** a military force that is brought together and sent to a particular place 特遣部隊 **2** a group of people who are brought together to deal with a particular problem（為解決某問題而成立的）特別工作組

task·mas·ter /'tɑːskmɑːstə(r); *NAmE* 'tæskmæstər/ *noun* a person who gives other people work to do, often work that is difficult 工頭；監工；監督人： *She was **a hard taskmaster**.* 她是個嚴厲的工頭。

tassel 穗

tas·sel /'tæsl/ *noun* a bunch of threads that are tied together at one end and hang from CUSHIONS, curtains, clothes, etc. as a decoration（靠墊、窗簾、衣服等的）流蘇，穗，纓

tas·selled *(BrE)* (*US* **tas·seled**) /'tæsld/ *adj.* decorated with tassels 飾有流蘇的；帶穗的；有纓的

taste 0→ /teɪst/ *noun, verb*

■ *noun*

▸ **FLAVOUR** 味 **1** 0→ [C, U] the particular quality that different foods and drinks have that allows you to recognize them when you put them in your mouth 味道；滋味： *a **salty/bitter/sweet, etc. taste*** 鹹味、苦味、甜味等 ◇ *I don't like the taste of olives.* 我不喜歡橄欖的味道。◇ *This dish has an unusual combination of tastes and textures.* 這道菜的味道和口感搭配得很奇特。◇ *The soup has very little taste.* 這湯沒什麼味道。

▸ **SENSE** 感覺官能 **2** 0→ [U] the sense you have that allows you to recognize different foods and drinks when you put them in your mouth 味覺： *I've lost my sense of taste.* 我嚐不出味道。

▸ **SMALL QUANTITY** 少量 **3** 0→ [C, usually sing.] a small quantity of food or drink that you try in order to see what it is like 少許嚐的東西；一口；一點兒： *Just have a taste of this cheese.* 嚐一點兒這種奶酪吧。

▸ **SHORT EXPERIENCE** 短暫經歷 **4** [sing.] a short experience of sth 體驗；嘗試： *This was my **first taste** of live theatre.* 這是我初次在現場看戲。◇ *Although we didn't know it, this incident was **a taste of things to come**.* 儘管當時我們並不知道，但這件事是後來一系列事件的開端。

▸ **ABILITY TO CHOOSE WELL** 判斷力 **5** 0→ [U] a person's ability to choose things that people recognize as being of good quality or appropriate 鑒賞力；欣賞力： *He has very **good taste** in music.* 他有很高的音樂欣賞力。◇ *They've got more money than taste.* 他們有錢，但品味不高。◇ *The room was furnished with taste.* 這個房間佈置得很雅致。

▸ **WHAT YOU LIKE** 喜好 **6** 0→ [C, U] what a person likes or prefers 愛好；志趣： **~ (for sth)** *That trip gave me a taste for foreign travel.* 那次旅遊使我產生了去國外旅行的興趣。◇ **~ (in sth)** *She has very expensive tastes in clothes.* 她講究穿高檔的服裝。◇ *The colour and style is **a matter of personal taste**.* 顏色和式樣是個人愛好問題。◇ *Modern art is not **to everyone's taste**.* 現代藝術不見得適合每個人的口味。◇ *There are trips to suit all tastes.* 有適合各種喜好的旅遊。

IDM **be in bad, poor, the worst possible, etc. 'taste** to be offensive and not at all appropriate 趣味低級；粗俗；不得體： *Most of his jokes were in very poor taste.* 他的笑話大多粗俗不堪。**be in good, the best possible, etc. 'taste** to be appropriate and not at all offensive 適度；得體 **leave a bad/nasty 'taste in the mouth** (of events or experiences 事件或經歷) to make you feel disgusted or ashamed afterwards 使後來感到厭惡（或羞恥）；留下壞印象 **to 'taste** in the quantity that is needed to make sth taste the way you prefer 按口味；適量： *Add salt and pepper to taste.* 適量放鹽和胡椒粉。 ➲ more at ACCOUNT *v.*, ACQUIRE, MEDICINE

■ *verb* (not used in the progressive tenses 不用於進行時)

▸ **HAVE FLAVOUR** 有味道 **1** 0→ *linking verb* to have a particular flavour 有…味道： **+ adj.** *It tastes sweet.* 這有甜味兒。◇ **~ of sth** *The ice tasted of mint.* 這刨冰有薄荷味兒。◇ **~ like sth** *This drink tastes like sherry.* 這種酒味道像雪利酒。 **2 -tasting** (in adjectives 構成形容詞)

having a particular flavour 有…味道的：*foul-tasting medicine* 難吃的藥

▸ **RECOGNIZE FLAVOUR** 辨味 **3** [T] **~ sth** (often used with *can* or *could* 常與 can 或 could 連用) to be able to recognize flavours in food and drink 嚐出，品出（食品或飲料的味道）：*You can taste the garlic in this stew.* 在這燉肉裏你可以嚐出大蒜的味道。

▸ **TEST FLAVOUR** 嚐味 **4** [T] **~ sth** to test the flavour of sth by eating or drinking a small amount of it 嚐，品（味道）**SYN** **try**：*Taste it and see if you think there's enough salt in it.* 你嚐嚐看這夠不夠鹹。

▸ **EAT/DRINK** 吃；喝 **5** [T] **~ sth** to eat or drink food or liquid 吃；喝：*I've never tasted anything like it.* 我從來沒有吃過像這樣的東西。

▸ **HAVE SHORT EXPERIENCE** 有短暫經歷 **6** [T] **~ sth** to have a short experience of sth, especially sth that you want more of 淺嚐；嚐到甜頭：*He had tasted freedom only to lose it again.* 他剛嚐到了自由的甜頭，卻又失去了。

'taste bud *noun* [usually pl.] one of the small structures on the tongue that allow you to recognize the flavours of food and drink 味蕾

taste·ful /'teɪstfl/ *adj.* (especially of clothes, furniture, decorations, etc. 尤指衣服、傢具、裝飾等) attractive and of good quality and showing that the person who chose them can recognize good things 高雅的；雅致的；優美的 ▸ **taste·ful·ly** /-fəli/ *adv.*：*The bedroom was tastefully furnished.* 這臥室佈置得很雅致。

taste·less /'teɪstləs/ *adj.* **1** having little or no flavour 無味的；不可口的：*tasteless soup* 淡而無味的湯 **2** offensive and not appropriate 不雅的；粗俗的；不得體的；煞風景的：*tasteless jokes* 粗俗的笑話 **3** showing a lack of the ability to choose things that people recognize as attractive and of good quality 俗氣的；格調低的 ▸ **taste·less·ly** *adv.* **taste·less·ness** *noun* [U]

taster /'teɪstə(r)/ *noun* **1** a person whose job is to judge the quality of wine, tea, etc. by tasting it 試味員；品酒師；品茶員 **2** (*informal, especially BrE*) a small example of sth for you to try in order to see if you would like more of it （供嘗試的）小樣品

-tastic /'tæstɪk/ *suffix* (in adjectives 構成形容詞) (*BrE, informal*) used to emphasize that sb/sth of a particular type is extremely good （某類人或物品中）極好的：*We have a toptastic line-up of stars for you tonight.* 今晚我們為您請來了最佳明星陣容。◇ *Try this new choctastic recipe!* 試試這種特別美味的巧克力新烹飪法吧！➲ see also POPTASTIC

tast·ing /'teɪstɪŋ/ *noun* an event at which people can try different kinds of food and drink, especially wine, in small quantities 品嚐會：*a wine tasting* 品酒會

tasty /'teɪsti/ *adj.* (**tasti·er**, **tasti·est**) **1** (*approving*) having a strong and pleasant flavour 美味的；可口的；好吃的：*a tasty meal* 美餐 ◇ *something tasty to eat* 好吃的東西 **2** (*BrE, informal*, sometimes *offensive*) a word that some men use about women that they think are sexually attractive 風騷的，有味道的，性感的（男子用以形容性感女子）▸ **tasti·ness** *noun* [U]

tat /tæt/ *noun* [U] (*BrE, informal*) goods that are cheap and of low quality 劣質貨 ➲ see also TIT FOR TAT

ta-ta /ˌtæ 'tɑː/ *exclamation* (*BrE, informal*) goodbye 再見：*Ta-ta for now!* 回頭見！

tat·ami /tə'tɑːmi; 'tætəmi/ *noun* (from *Japanese*) a traditional Japanese floor covering made from dried RUSHES 榻榻米（燈芯草日本地蓆）

tater /'teɪtə(r)/ *noun* [usually pl.] (*slang*) a potato 土豆；馬鈴薯；洋芋

tat·tered /'tætəd; *NAmE* -tərd/ *adj.* old and torn; in bad condition 破爛的；破舊的；襤褸的；破裂的：*tattered clothes* 破舊的衣服 ◇ (*figurative*) *tattered relationships* 破裂了的關係 ◇ (*figurative*) *the hotel's tattered reputation* 旅館的敗壞的名聲

tat·ters /'tætəz; *NAmE* -tərz/ *noun* [pl.] clothes or pieces of cloth that are badly torn 破爛的衣服；破衣爛布 **IDM** **in tatters** **1** torn in many places 破爛不堪；破破爛爛：*His clothes were in tatters.* 他的衣服破舊不堪。 **2** ruined or badly damaged 被毀壞的；破敗的；坍塌的 **SYN** **in shreds**：*Her reputation was in tatters.* 她已名譽掃地。◇ *The government's education policy lies in tatters.* 政府的教育政策徹底破產了。

tat·tie /'tæti/ *noun* (*ScotE, informal*) a potato 馬鈴薯；土豆；洋芋

tat·tle /'tætl/ *verb* [I] **~ (on sb) (to sb)** (*informal, disapproving, especially NAmE*) to tell sb, especially sb in authority, about sth bad that sb else has done 向當權者告發；（就某人不端行為）打小報告 **SYN** **tell on sb**

tat·tle·tale /'tætlteɪl/ (*NAmE*) (*BrE* **tell·tale**) *noun* (*informal, disapproving*) a child who tells an adult what another child has done wrong 向大人告另一個孩子狀的小孩；小告密者

tat·too /tə'tuː; *NAmE* tæ'tuː/ *noun, verb*

■ ***noun*** (*pl.* **-oos**) **1** a picture or design that is marked permanently on a person's skin by making small holes in the skin with a needle and filling them with coloured ink 文身；（在皮膚上刺的）花紋：*His arms were covered in tattoos.* 他的胳膊上刺滿了花紋。➲ COLLOCATIONS at FASHION **2** (*especially BrE*) an outdoor show by members of the armed forces that includes marching, music and military exercises 野外軍事表演（包括齊步前進、軍樂和軍事演習）**3** [usually sing.] a rapid and continuous series of taps or hits, especially on a drum as a military signal 連續急促的敲擊；（尤指軍事上的）回營號，擊鼓號

■ ***verb*** to mark sb's skin with a tattoo 將花紋刺在…上；給…文身：**~ A on B** *He had a heart tattooed on his shoulder.* 他讓人給他在肩膀上刺了一顆心形圖案。◇ **~ B (with A)** *His shoulder was tattooed with a heart.* 他的肩膀上刺了一顆心形圖案。

tat·too·ist /tə'tuːɪst; *NAmE* tæ't-/ *noun* a person who draws tattoos on people's skin, as a job 紋身師；刺青師

tatty /'tæti/ *adj.* (*informal, especially BrE*) (**tat·tier**, **tat·ti·est**) in a bad condition because it has been used a lot or has not been cared for well 襤褸的；破爛的；破敗的；邋遢的 **SYN** **shabby**：*a tatty carpet* 破舊的地毯

tau /tɔː; taʊ/ *noun* the 19th letter of the Greek alphabet (Τ, τ) 希臘字母表的第 19 個字母

taught *past tense, past part.* of TEACH

taunt /tɔːnt/ *verb, noun*

■ ***verb*** **~ sb** to try to make sb angry or upset by saying unkind things about them, laughing at their failures, etc. 辱罵；嘲笑；諷刺；奚落：*The other kids continually taunted him about his size.* 其他孩子不斷地恥笑他的個頭兒。

■ ***noun*** an insulting or unkind remark that is intended to make sb angry or upset 嘲笑（或諷刺、奚落等）的言辭：*Black players often had to endure racist taunts.* 黑人運動員經常得忍受種族歧視性的奚落。

taupe /təʊp; *NAmE* toʊp/ *noun* [U] a brownish-grey colour 褐灰色 ▸ **taupe** *adj.*

taur·ine /'tɔːriːn/ *noun* [U] an acid substance which is sometimes used in drinks that are designed to make you feel more active 牛磺酸，氨基乙磺酸（用於飲料，可提神）

Taurus /'tɔːrəs/ *noun* **1** [U] the second sign of the ZODIAC, the BULL 黃道第二宮；金牛宮；金牛（星）座 **2** [sing.] a person born when the sun is in this sign, that is between 21 April and 21 May 屬金牛座的人（約出生於 4 月 21 日至 5 月 21 日）▸ **Taur·ean** /'tɔːriən/ *noun, adj.*

taut /tɔːt/ *adj.* **1** stretched tightly 拉緊的；繃緊的：*Keep the rope taut.* 保持把繩子拉緊。 **2** showing that you are anxious or TENSE 顯得緊張的（或焦慮的、不安的等）：*Her face was taut and pale.* 她神色緊張，臉色蒼白。**3** (of a person or their body 人或人體) with firm muscles; not fat 肌肉結實的；不虛胖的：*His body was solid and taut.* 他身體結實，肌肉發達。 **4** (of a piece of writing, etc. 文章等) tightly controlled, with no unnecessary parts in it 結構嚴謹的；緊湊的 ▸ **taut·ly** *adv.* **taut·ness** *noun* [U]

taut·en /'tɔːtn/ *verb* [I, T] **~ (sth)** to become taut; to make sth taut （使）拉緊，繃緊

tau·tol·ogy /tɔː'tɒlədʒi; *NAmE* -'tɑːl-/ *noun* [U, C] a statement in which you say the same thing twice in

T

different words, when this is unnecessary, for example 'They spoke in turn, one after the other.' 同義反複；贅述 ▸ **tauto·logic·al** /ˌtɔːtəˈlɒdʒɪkl; *NAmE* -ˈlɑːdʒ-/ *adj.* **tau·tolo·gous** /tɔːˈtɒləgəs; *NAmE* -ˈtɑːl-/ *adj.*

tav·ern /ˈtævən; *NAmE* -vərn/ *noun* (*old use* or *literary*) a pub or an INN 酒館；小旅店；客棧

taw·dry /ˈtɔːdri/ *adj.* (*disapproving*) **1** intended to be bright and attractive but cheap and of low quality 俗麗而不值錢的；俗氣的；花裏胡哨的：*tawdry jewellery* 俗麗便宜的首飾 **2** involving low moral standards; extremely unpleasant or offensive 粗俗的；下流的；卑鄙的；卑污的：*a tawdry affair* 卑鄙下流的勾當 ▸ **taw·dri·ness** *noun* [U]

tawny /ˈtɔːni/ *adj.* brownish-yellow in colour 黃褐色的；茶色的：*the lion's tawny mane* 獅子的黃褐色鬃毛

ˈ**tawny owl** *noun* a reddish-brown or grey European BIRD OF PREY (= a bird that kills other creatures for food) of the OWL family 灰林鴞（產於歐洲的一種紅褐色或灰色的鴞科猛禽）

Synonyms 同義詞辨析

tax

duty • customs • tariff • rates

These are all words for money that you have to pay to the government. 以上各詞均指稅款。

tax money that you have to pay to the government so that it can pay for public services 指稅、稅款：*income tax* 所得稅 ◇ *tax cuts* 稅款削減

duty a tax that you pay on things that you buy, especially those that you bring into a country 指購物稅項，尤指進口貨物交納的關稅：*The company has to pay customs duties on all imports.* 該公司須為所有進口貨物繳納關稅。

customs tax that is paid when goods are brought in from other countries 指關稅、進口稅

tariff a tax that is paid on goods coming into or going out of a country, often in order to protect industry from cheap imports 指（為使國內工業免遭廉價進口商品衝擊而徵收的）關稅：*A general tariff was imposed on foreign imports.* 國外進口貨物當時按普通稅率徵稅。

rates (in Britain) a tax paid by businesses to a local authority for land and buildings that they use, and in the past also paid by anyone who owned a house 指（英國地方政府徵收的）房地產稅、房產稅：*Business rates are very high in the city centre.* 市中心的商業房產稅非常高。

PATTERNS

- (a) tax/duty/tariff/rates **on** sth
- to pay an amount of money **in** tax/duty/customs/rates
- to **pay** (a) tax/duty/customs/tariff/rates
- to **collect** taxes/duties/rates
- to **increase/raise/reduce** taxes/duty/tariffs/rates
- to **cut** taxes/duties/rates
- to **impose** a tax/duty/tariff
- to **put** a tax/duty **on** sth

T

tax 0━ /tæks/ *noun, verb*

■ ***noun*** 0━ [C, U] money that you have to pay to the government so that it can pay for public services. People pay tax according to their income and businesses pay tax according to their profits. Tax is also often paid on goods and services. 稅；稅款：*to* ***raise/cut taxes*** 增加／削減稅收 ◇ ***tax increases/cuts*** 稅款的增加／削減 ◇ *changes in* ***tax rates*** 稅率的變化 ◇ *to pay over £1 000* ***in tax*** 繳納 1 000 多英鎊的稅款 ◇ *profits* ***before/after tax*** 稅前／稅後利潤 ◇ **~ on sth** *a tax on cigarettes* 香煙稅 ➲ COLLOCATIONS at ECONOMY ➲ see also CORPORATION TAX, COUNCIL TAX, DIRECT TAX, INDIRECT TAX, INHERITANCE TAX, POLL TAX, ROAD TAX, SALES TAX, STEALTH TAX, VALUE ADDED TAX, WITHHOLDING TAX

■ ***verb*** **1** 0━ **~ sb/sth** to put a tax on sb/sth; to make sb pay tax 對…徵稅；課稅；使納稅：*Any interest payments are taxed as part of your income.* 利息所得作為你收入的一部份要予以徵稅。◇ *His declared aim was to tax the rich.* 他宣佈他的目的是向富人徵稅。 **2 ~ sth** (*BrE*) to pay tax on a vehicle so that you may use it on the roads 繳納車輛牌照稅：*The car is taxed until July.* 這輛汽車的牌照稅繳納到了七月。 **3 ~ sb/sth** to need a great amount of physical or mental effort 使負重擔；使受壓力；使大傷腦筋：*The questions did not tax me.* 那些問題沒有讓我費腦筋。◇ *The problem is currently* ***taxing the brains*** *of the nation's experts* (= making them think very hard). 目前這個問題使得全國的專家大傷腦筋。

PHR V ˈ**tax sb with sth** (*formal*) to accuse sb of doing sth wrong（就某事）指責，責備，譴責…：*I taxed him with avoiding his responsibility as a parent.* 我指責他逃避做父親的責任。

tax·able /ˈtæksəbl/ *adj.* (of money 錢) that you have to pay tax on 應納稅的；應課稅的：*taxable income* 應課稅的收入

tax·ation /tækˈseɪʃn/ *noun* [U] **1** money that has to be paid as taxes 稅；稅款；稅金；稅收：*to reduce taxation* 減稅 **2** the system of collecting money by taxes 稅制；徵稅；課稅：*changes in the taxation structure* 稅制結構的變化

ˈ**tax avoidance** *noun* [U] ways of paying only the smallest amount of tax that you legally have to（合法）避稅 ➲ compare TAX EVASION

ˈ**tax bracket** (*BrE* also ˈ**tax band**) *noun* a range of different incomes on which the same rate of tax must be paid 稅率等級，稅級（同一稅率的納稅收入等級段）：*There are now only two tax brackets—22% and 40%.* 現在納稅收入只有兩個納稅檔次：22% 和 40%。

ˈ**tax break** *noun* a special advantage or reduction in taxes that the government gives to particular people or organizations 賦稅優惠；減稅

ˈ**tax collector** *noun* a person whose job is collecting the tax that people must pay on the money they earn 收稅員；稅務員

ˈ**tax credit** *noun* **1** money that is taken off your total tax bill 稅收抵免 **2** money provided by the government to people who need financial help, especially if they have children or are on a low income（尤指政府向有子女或低收入者提供的）補助金，救濟金

ˌ**tax-deˈduct·ible** *adj.* (of costs 費用) that can be taken off your income before the amount of tax that you have to pay is calculated 可減免課稅的，應稅收益額減免的（在計算所得稅時可予以扣除）

ˌ**tax-deˈferred** *adj.* (*NAmE*) that you only pay tax on later 延遲納稅的；延稅的：*a tax-deferred savings plan* 延稅儲蓄計劃

ˈ**tax disc** *noun* = ROAD FUND LICENCE

ˈ**tax dodge** *noun* (*informal*) a way of paying less tax, legally or illegally（合法或非法的）規避納稅 ▸ ˈ**tax dodger** *noun*

ˈ**tax evasion** *noun* [U] the crime of deliberately not paying all the taxes that you should pay（非法）逃稅；偷稅；漏稅 ➲ compare TAX AVOIDANCE

ˌ**tax-eˈxempt** *adj.* that is not taxed 免稅的：*tax-exempt savings* 免收利息所得稅的存款

ˈ**tax exile** *noun* a rich person who has left their own country and gone to live in a place where the taxes are lower 跨境避稅者，越國避稅者（為少繳稅而移居較低稅地區的富人）

ˌ**tax-ˈfree** *adj.* (of money, goods, etc. 錢、貨物等) that you do not have to pay tax on 免稅的；不納稅的：*a tax-free allowance* 免稅額 ▸ ˌ**tax-ˈfree** *adv.*

ˈ**tax haven** *noun* a place where taxes are low and where people choose to live or officially register their companies because taxes are higher in their own countries 避稅地，避稅港（人們願意居住或註冊公司的低稅率地方）

taxi 0-ᵣ /ˈtæksi/ *noun, verb*
■ *noun* **1** 0-ᵣ (also **cab**, **taxi·cab**) a car with a driver that you pay to take you somewhere. Taxis usually have METERS which show how much money you have to pay. 出租汽車；計程車；的士：*a* ***taxi driver/ride*** 出租汽車司機；乘出租車出行 ◇ *We'd better* ***take a taxi***. 我們最好乘出租車。◇ *I came home* ***by taxi***. 我是坐出租車回家的。◇ *to* ***order/hail/call a taxi*** 要／招呼／叫出租車 ➲ VISUAL VOCAB page V58 **2** in some places in Africa, a small bus with a driver that you pay to take you somewhere. Taxis usually have fixed routes and stop wherever passengers need to get on or off.（非洲某些地方行走固定路線、乘客可隨時上下的）小公共汽車，小巴士 ➲ see also DALA-DALA, MATATU
■ *verb* (**taxi·ing**, **tax·ied**, **tax·ied**) [I] (of a plane 飛機) to move slowly along the ground before taking off or after landing（起飛前或降落後在地面上）滑行

taxi·der·mist /ˈtæksɪdɜːmɪst; *NAmE* -dɜːrm-/ *noun* a person whose job is taxidermy 動物標本剝製師

taxi·dermy /ˈtæksɪdɜːmi; *NAmE* -dɜːrmi/ *noun* [U] the art of STUFFING dead animals, birds and fish with a special material so that they look like living ones and can be displayed 動物標本剝製術（將動物充填以支撐物，以表現出其生前外形）

tax·ing /ˈtæksɪŋ/ *adj.* needing a great amount of physical or mental effort 繁重的；費力的；傷腦筋的 SYN **demanding**：*a taxing job* 繁重的工作 ◇ *This shouldn't be too taxing for you.* 這對你來說不至於太費勁。➲ SYNONYMS at DIFFICULT

ˈ**tax inspector** *noun* (*BrE*) = INSPECTOR OF TAXES

ˈ**taxi rank** (*BrE*) (also ˈ**taxi stand** *NAmE, BrE*) *noun* a place where taxis park while they are waiting for passengers 出租汽車站；計程車停車處 ➲ VISUAL VOCAB pages V2, V3

ˈ**taxi squad** *noun* (in AMERICAN FOOTBALL 美式足球) **1** a group of players who practise with the first team but who do not play in games（不參加比賽的）陪練球隊 **2** four extra players on a team who play when other players are injured（統稱四名）替補隊員

taxi·way /ˈtæksiweɪ/ *noun* the hard path that a plane uses as it moves to and from the RUNWAY (= the hard surface where planes take off and land)（飛機的）滑行道

tax·man /ˈtæksmæn/ *noun* (*pl.* **-men** /-men/) **1 the taxman** [sing.] (*informal*) a way of referring to the government department that is responsible for collecting taxes 稅務部門；稅務機關：*He had been cheating the taxman for years.* 多年來他一直欺騙稅務部門。**2** [C] a person whose job is to collect taxes 收稅員；稅務員

tax·ono·mist /tækˈsɒnəmɪst; *NAmE* -ˈsɑːnə-/ *noun* a person who studies or is skilled in taxonomy 分類學家

tax·onomy /tækˈsɒnəmi; *NAmE* -ˈsɑːnə-/ *noun* (*pl.* **-ies**) **1** [U] the scientific process of CLASSIFYING things (= arranging them into groups) 分類學：*plant taxonomy* 植物分類學 **2** [C] a particular system of CLASSIFYING things 分類法；分類系統 ► **taxo·nom·ic** /ˌtæksəˈnɒmɪk; *NAmE* -ˈnɑːmɪk/ *adj.*

tax·pay·er /ˈtækspeɪə(r)/ *noun* a person who pays tax to the government, especially on the money that they earn 納稅人

ˈ**tax relief** (also **relief**) *noun* [U] a reduction in the amount of tax you have to pay 稅款減免

ˈ**tax return** *noun* an official document in which you give details of the amount of money that you have earned so that the government can calculate how much tax you have to pay 納稅申報單

ˈ**tax shelter** *noun* a way of using or investing money so that you can legally avoid paying tax on it 避稅方法（如用於消費、投資）

ˈ**tax year** *noun* (*BrE*) = FINANCIAL YEAR

tay·berry /ˈteɪbəri; *NAmE* -beri/ *noun* (*pl.* **-ies**) a dark red soft fruit that is a combination of a BLACKBERRY and a RASPBERRY 泰莓（黑莓和懸鉤子的雜交果實）

TB *abbr.* **1** /ˌtiː ˈbiː/ TUBERCULOSIS **2** (in writing 書寫形式) TERABYTE

Tb (also **Tbit**) *abbr.* (in writing 書寫形式) TERABIT

TBA /ˌtiː biː ˈeɪ/ *abbr.* (used in notices about events 用於通告) to be announced 待宣佈；待發表：*party with live band (TBA)* 樂隊現場伴奏的社交聚會（待公佈）

ˈ**T-bar** *noun* **1** (also ˈ**T-bar lift**) a machine which pulls two people up a mountain on SKIS together 丁字形吊椅（能同時送兩人上山滑雪）**2** a T-shaped strip of leather, etc. on a shoe（鞋子上的）丁字形皮條（等）

TBC /ˌtiː biː ˈsiː/ *abbr.* (used in notices about events 用於通告) to be confirmed 待確認：*The four-day course will run from March 8–11 (TBC).* 這門四天的課程將從 3 月 8 日進行到 11 日（待確認）。

ˈ**T-bill** *abbr.* (*NAmE, informal*) = TREASURY BILL

ˈ**T-bone steak** *noun* a thick slice of beef containing a bone in the shape of a T 帶骨牛排；T 字骨牛排

tbsp (also **tbs**) *abbr.* (*pl.* **tbsp** or **tbsps**) TABLESPOONFUL 一餐匙，一湯匙（的量）：*Add 3 tbsp sugar.* 加三湯匙的糖。

TCP/IP /ˌtiː siː ˌpiː aɪ ˈpiː/ *abbr.* (*computing* 計) transmission control protocol/Internet protocol (a system that controls the connection of computers to the Internet) * TCP/IP 協議，傳輸控制協議，網際協議（控制計算機接入互聯網的系統）

TD /ˌtiː ˈdiː/ *noun* the abbreviation for 'Teachta Dála', 'Member of the Dáil' (a member of the LOWER HOUSE of the parliament of the Republic of Ireland)（愛爾蘭共和國的）眾議院議員，下議院議員（全寫為 Teachta Dála，英語為 Member of the Dáil）

te (*BrE*) (*NAmE* **ti**) /tiː/ *noun* (*music* 音) the 7th note of a MAJOR SCALE 大調音階的第 7 音

tea 0-ᵣ /tiː/ *noun*
1 0-ᵣ [U] the dried leaves (called TEA LEAVES) of the tea bush 茶葉 ➲ see also GREEN TEA **2** 0-ᵣ [U] a hot drink made by pouring boiling water onto tea leaves. It may be drunk with milk or lemon and/or sugar added.（沏好的）茶：*a* ***cup/mug/pot of tea*** 一杯／一茶缸子／一壺茶 ◇ ***lemon/iced tea*** 檸檬茶；冰茶 ◇ *Would you like tea or coffee?* 你喝茶還是喝咖啡？◇ *Do you take sugar in your tea?* 你的茶裏放糖嗎？**3** 0-ᵣ [C] a cup of tea 一杯茶：*Two teas, please.* 請來兩杯茶。**4** [U, C] a hot drink made by pouring boiling water onto the leaves of other plants（用其他植物的葉子沏的）熱飲料：***camomile/mint/herb, etc. tea*** 蘋果菊花茶、薄荷茶、藥草茶等 ➲ see also BEEF TEA **5** [U, C] the name used by some people in Britain for the cooked meal eaten in the evening, especially when it is eaten early in the evening 晚點，便餐（英國人傍晚時吃）：*You can have your tea as soon as you come home from school.* 你放學一回到家就可以吃晚點。➲ compare DINNER, SUPPER **6** [U, C] (*BrE*) a light meal eaten in the afternoon or early evening, usually with SANDWICHES and/or biscuits and cakes and with tea to drink 茶點（在下午或傍晚，通常喝茶時還有三明治、餅乾和蛋糕）➲ note at MEAL ➲ see also CREAM TEA, HIGH TEA
IDM **not for all the tea in ˈChina** (*old-fashioned*) not even for a great reward 無論報酬多高都不；無論有多大好處都不：*I wouldn't do your job. Not for all the tea in China!* 我才不做你的那份工作。有天大的好處也不幹！➲ more at CUP *n.*

ˈ**tea bag** *noun* a small thin paper bag containing tea leaves, which you pour boiling water onto in order to make tea 袋泡茶；茶包

ˈ**tea break** *noun* (*BrE*) a short period of time when people stop working and drink tea, coffee, etc. 喝茶休息時間；工間休息時間

ˈ**tea caddy** (also **caddy**) *noun* (*especially BrE*) a small box with a lid that you keep tea in 茶葉盒；茶葉罐

tea·cake /ˈtiːkeɪk/ *noun* (*BrE*) a small flat round cake made of a bread-like mixture, usually containing dried fruit 茶點餅（扁平狀，常含有乾果）：*toasted teacakes* 烘烤的茶點餅

T

tea·cart /ˈtiːkɑːt; *NAmE* -kɑːrt/ (also **ˈtea wagon**) (both *US*) (*BrE* **ˈtea trolley**) *noun* a small table on wheels that is used for serving drinks and food 茶車；上菜車

ˈtea ceremony *noun* a Japanese ceremony in which tea is served and drunk according to complicated rules 茶道（日本沏茶和飲茶的禮儀）

Vocabulary Building 詞彙擴充

Teach and teachers 教與教師

Verbs 動詞

- **teach** *John teaches French at the local school.* 約翰在當地學校教法語。◇ *She taught me how to change a tyre.* 她教會了我換輪胎。
- **educate** *Our priority is to educate people about the dangers of drugs.* 我們首先要做的是教育人們認識毒品的危險。
- **instruct** *Members of staff should be instructed in the use of fire equipment.* 應該指導全體職員學會使用消防設備。
- **train** *She's a trained midwife.* 她是受過專門訓練的助產士。◇ *He's training the British Olympic swimming team.* 他在訓練英國的奧運游泳隊。
- **coach** *He's the best football player I've ever coached.* 他是我訓練過的最出色的足球運動員。◇ *She coaches some of the local children in maths.* (*BrE*) 她給當地一些孩子輔導數學。
- **tutor** *She tutors some of the local children in math.* (*NAmE*) 她給當地一些孩子輔導數學。

Nouns 名詞

- **teacher** *school/college teachers* 學校 / 大學教師
- **instructor** *a swimming/science instructor* 游泳教練；科學教員
- **trainer** *a horse trainer* 馴馬師 ◇ *Do you have a personal trainer?* 你有私人教練嗎？
- **coach** *a football coach* 足球教練
- **tutor** *tutors working with migrant children* 教移民孩子的家庭教師

T

teach 🔑 /tiːtʃ/ *verb* (**taught**, **taught** /tɔːt/)
1 🔑 [I, T] to give lessons to students in a school, college, university, etc.; to help sb learn sth by giving information about it 教（課程）；講授；教授：*She teaches at our local school.* 她在我們當地的學校任教。◇ *He taught for several years before becoming a writer.* 他教了幾年書之後才成為作家。◇ **~ sth** *I'll be teaching history and sociology next term.* 下學期我教歷史和社會學。◇ (*NAmE*) *to **teach school*** (= teach in a school) 當學校教師 ◇ **~ sth to sb** *He teaches English to advanced students.* 他教高年級學生英語。◇ **~ sb sth** *He teaches them English.* 他教他們英語。 **2** 🔑 [T] to show sb how to do sth so that they will be able to do it themselves 教；訓練：**~ (sb to do) sth** *Could you teach me to do that?* 你能教我幹那活兒嗎？◇ **~ sb how, what, etc. …** *My father taught me how to ride a bike.* 我父親教會了我騎自行車。 **3** 🔑 [T] to make sb feel or think in a different way 教育；教導；使懂得（情理）：**~ sb to do sth** *She taught me to be less critical of other people.* 她教育我不要太苛求於人。◇ **~ (sb) that …** *My parents taught me that honesty was always the best policy.* 我父母教導我，誠實永遠是處世的最佳原則。◇ **~ sb sth** *Our experience as refugees taught us many valuable lessons.* 我們流亡的經歷給了我們許多寶貴的教訓。 **4** [T, no passive] (*informal*) to persuade sb not to do sth again by making them suffer so much that they are afraid to do it 使引以為戒；懲戒：**~ sb to do sth** *Lost all your money? **That'll teach you** to gamble.* 你把錢都輸光了？這是賭博給你的教訓。◇ *I'll teach you to call* (= punish you for calling) *me a liar!* 你要說我撒謊，我就對你不客氣！◇ **~ sb sth** *The accident **taught me a lesson** I'll never forget.* 這次事故給了我一個終生難忘的教訓。

IDM **teach your grandmother to suck ˈeggs** (*BrE, informal*) to tell or show sb how to do sth that they can already do well, and probably better than you can 教奶奶嘬雞蛋；在能人面前逞強；班門弄斧 **(you can't) teach an old dog new ˈtricks** (*saying*) (you cannot) successfully make people change their ideas, methods of work, etc., when they have had them for a long time 老大（不）可教；（無法）改變人們長時間形成的思想（或做事方法等） **teach to the ˈtest** to teach students only what is necessary in order to pass a particular test, rather than help them develop a range of skills 應試教育；為考試而教學

teach·able /ˈtiːtʃəbl/ *adj.* **1** (of a subject 科目) that can be taught 適於教學的；可傳授的 **2** (of a person 人) able to learn by being taught 可教的；能學的；善學的

teach·er 🔑 /ˈtiːtʃə(r)/ *noun*
a person whose job is teaching, especially in a school 教師；教員；老師；先生：*a **history/science, etc. teacher*** 歷史、理科等教師 ◇ *primary school teachers* 小學教師 ◇ *There is a growing need for qualified teachers of Business English.* 對合格的商務英語教師的需求日益增長。 ➲ note at TEACH

ˌteacher ˈtraining *noun* [U] the process of teaching or learning the skills you need to be a teacher in a school 教師培訓；師資培訓 ▶ **ˌteacher ˈtrainer** *noun*：*experienced teachers and teacher trainers* 有經驗的教師和培訓師資的教師

ˈtea chest *noun* (*BrE*) a large light wooden box lined with metal in which tea is transported. Tea chests are sometimes used for transporting personal possessions, for example, when moving to another home. 茶葉箱（運輸茶葉用的大木箱，搬家時可裝個人物品）

ˈteach-in *noun* an informal lecture and discussion on a subject of public interest（以時事等為題的）宣講會，座談會

teach·ing 🔑 /ˈtiːtʃɪŋ/ *noun*
1 🔑 [U] the work of a teacher 教學；授課；指導：*She wants to go into teaching* (= make it a career). 她想從事教學工作。◇ *the teaching profession* 教學職業 **2** 🔑 [C, usually pl., U] the ideas of a particular person or group, especially about politics, religion or society, that are taught to other people 教導；學說；教義；教誨：*the teachings of Lenin* 列寧的學說 ◇ *views that go against traditional Christian teaching* 與傳統基督教教義相違的觀點

ˈteaching assistant *noun* **1** a person who is not a qualified teacher who helps a teacher in a school 教學助理 **2** (*abbr.* **TA**) (both *NAmE*) (also **ˈteaching fellow** *US, BrE*) a GRADUATE student who teaches UNDERGRADUATE classes at a university or college, takes discussion or practical classes, marks written work, etc. 助教（擔任本科生教學、組織討論、上實踐課、批改作業等工作的研究生）

ˈteaching practice (*BrE*) (*NAmE* **ˌstudent ˈteaching**) *noun* [U] the part of a course for people who are training to become teachers which involves teaching classes of students 教學實習

ˈtea cloth *noun* (*BrE*) = TEA TOWEL

ˈtea cosy (*BrE*) (*NAmE* **ˈtea cozy**) *noun* a cover placed over a TEAPOT in order to keep the tea warm 茶壺套；茶壺保溫罩

tea·cup /ˈtiːkʌp/ *noun* a cup in which tea is served 茶杯 **IDM** see STORM *n.*

ˈtea dance *noun* a social event held in the afternoon, especially in the past, at which people dance, drink tea, and eat a small meal（尤指舊時的）下午茶舞會

teak /tiːk/ *noun* [U] the strong hard wood of a tall Asian tree, used especially for making furniture 柚木（尤用以製造傢具）

tea·ket·tle /ˈtiːketl/ *noun* a metal container with a lid, handle and a SPOUT, used for boiling water 燒水壺

teal /tiːl/ *noun* **1** [C] (*pl.* **teal**) a small wild DUCK 水鴨；短頸野鴨 **2** [U] (*especially NAmE*) a bluish-green colour 藍綠色

'tea leaf *noun* a small piece of a dried leaf of the tea bush; used especially in the plural to describe what is left at the bottom of a cup or pot after the tea has been made 茶葉；茶葉渣

tea·light /'tiːlaɪt/ *noun* a small CANDLE that is used for decoration and which often gives off a pleasant smell 茶蠟，工藝茶蠟（蠟燭小，有些散發香味）

team 0→ AW /tiːm/ *noun, verb*

■ *noun* [C+sing./pl. v.] **1** 0→ a group of people who play a particular game or sport against another group of people（遊戲或運動的）隊：*a **football/baseball, etc. team*** 足球隊、棒球隊等 ◇ *a **team event*** (= one played by groups of people rather than individual players) 團體比賽項目 ◇ (*BrE*) *Whose team are you in?* 你是哪個隊的？◇ (*NAmE*) *Whose team are you on?* 你是哪個隊的？◇ *The team is/are not playing very well this season.* 這個隊本賽季狀態不佳。 **2** 0→ a group of people who work together at a particular job（一起工作的）組，班：*the sales team* 推銷小組 ◇ *a **team leader/member*** 隊長／員 ◇ *A team of experts has/have been called in to investigate.* 一個專家小組已應召來進行調查。 **3** two or more animals that are used together to pull a CART, etc.（同拉一輛車等的）一組牲畜，聯畜

■ *verb* [usually passive] **~ sb/sth (with sb/sth)** to put two or more things or people together in order to do sth or to achieve a particular effect 使互相配合；使協作；使合作：*He was teamed with his brother in the doubles.* 他被安排和哥哥搭檔參加雙打。

PHR V **,team 'up (with sb)** to join with another person or group in order to do sth together 合作；（與某人）結成一隊 **,team sb/sth 'up (with sb)** to put two or more people or things together in order to do sth or to achieve a particular effect 使互相配合；使協作；使合作

'team handball *noun* [U] (*US*) = HANDBALL (1)

team·mate /'tiːmmeɪt/ *noun* a member of the same team or group as yourself 同隊隊員；隊友

'team player *noun* a person who is good at working as a member of a team, usually in their job 善於與團隊合作的成員

,team 'spirit *noun* [U] (*approving*) the desire and willingness of people to work together and help each other as part of a team 合作精神；集體精神；團隊精神

team·ster /'tiːmstə(r)/ *noun* (*NAmE*) a person whose job is driving a truck 卡車司機 SYN **truck driver**

team·work /'tiːmwɜːk; *NAmE* -wɜːrk/ *noun* [U] the activity of working well together as a team 協同工作；配合：*She stressed the importance of good teamwork.* 她強調了團隊合作的重要性。

'tea party *noun* a social event at which people eat cake, drink tea, etc. in the afternoon（午後的）茶會，茶話會

tea·pot /'tiːpɒt; *NAmE* -pɑːt/ *noun* a container with a SPOUT, a handle and a lid, used for making and serving tea 茶壺 ➲ VISUAL VOCAB page V25 IDM see TEMPEST

tear[1] 0→ /teə(r); *NAmE* ter/ *verb, noun* ➲ see also TEAR[2]

■ *verb* (**tore** /tɔː(r)/, **torn** /tɔːn; *NAmE* tɔːrn/)

▸ DAMAGE 損壞 **1** 0→ [T, I] to damage sth by pulling it apart or into pieces or by cutting it on sth sharp; to become damaged in this way 撕裂；撕碎；扯破；戳破 SYN **rip**：**~ (sth) (+ adv./prep.)** *I tore my jeans on the fence.* 我的牛仔褲被籬笆掛破了。◇ *I tore a hole in my jeans.* 我的牛仔褲掛了個窟窿。◇ *He tore the letter in two.* 他把信撕成兩半。◇ *a torn handkerchief* 撕破的手帕 ◇ *Careful—the fabric tears very easily.* 小心，這種織物一撕就破。◇ **~ sth + adj.** *I tore the package open.* 我把包裹撕開。 **2** [T] **~ sth in sth** to make a hole in sth by force 撕開，劃成，刺出，扯開（裂口或洞）SYN **rip**：*The blast tore a hole in the wall.* 牆被炸開了個洞。

▸ REMOVE FROM STH/SB 移開 **3** 0→ [T] **~ sth + adv./prep.** to remove sth from sth else by pulling it roughly or violently 拉掉；撕掉；拔掉；扯掉 SYN **rip**：*The storm nearly tore the roof off.* 暴風雨差一點兒把屋頂掀掉。◇ *I tore another sheet from the pad.* 我從本子上又撕下一張紙。◇ *He tore his clothes off* (= took them off quickly and carelessly) *and dived into the lake.* 他把衣服從身上扯下，一頭跳入湖中。 **4** [T] to pull yourself/sb away by force from sb/sth that is holding you or them 掙開；拽開；奪去；揪走：**~ yourself/sb from sb/sth** *She tore herself from his grasp.* 她掙脫了他緊緊抓着她的手。◇ **~ yourself/sb + adj.** *He tore himself free.* 他掙脫了。

▸ INJURE MUSCLE 損傷肌肉 **5** [T] **~ sth** to injure a muscle, etc. by stretching it too much 拉傷；拽傷：*a torn ligament* 拉傷的韌帶

▸ MOVE QUICKLY 快速移動 **6** [I] **+ adv./prep.** to move somewhere very quickly or in an excited way 飛跑；狂奔；疾馳：*He tore off down the street.* 他沿大街飛奔。◇ *A truck tore past the gates.* 卡車從大門前疾馳而過。

▸ -TORN 受…傷害 **7** (in adjectives 構成形容詞) very badly affected or damaged by sth 深受…之苦的；飽經…摧殘的：*to bring peace to a strife-torn country* 給一個飽經變亂創傷的國家帶來和平 ◇ *a strike-torn industry* 深受罷工困擾的行業 ➲ see also WAR-TORN

IDM **tear sb/sth a'part, to 'shreds, to 'bits, etc.** to destroy or defeat sb/sth completely or criticize them or it severely 徹底毀滅；徹底打敗；嚴厲批評：*We tore the other team apart in the second half.* 我們在下半場把對方球隊打得落花流水。◇ *The critics tore his last movie to shreds.* 影評家把他最近的一部影片說得一無是處。 **,tear at your 'heart | ,tear your 'heart out** (*formal*) to strongly affect you in an emotional way 使傷心；使心如刀絞；使愁腸寸斷 **tear your 'hair (out)** (*informal*) to show that you are very angry or anxious about sth（因發怒、焦急而）撕扯自己的頭髮：*She's keeping very calm—anyone else would be tearing their hair out.* 她依舊泰然自若，換作別人早急壞了。 **(be in) a tearing 'hurry/'rush** (*especially BrE*) (to be) in a very great hurry 匆忙；急匆匆；風風火火 **be torn (between A and B)** to be unable to decide or choose between two people, things or feelings（在兩者間）難以選擇，左右為難：*I was torn between my parents and my friend.* 我在父母和朋友之間左右為難。 **tear sb 'off a strip | tear a 'strip off sb** (*BrE, informal*) to speak angrily to sb who has done sth wrong 怒斥；把…罵得狗血噴頭 **,that's 'torn it** (*BrE, informal*) used to say that sth has happened to spoil your plans（表示計劃受挫）這可糟了 ➲ more at HEART, LIMB, LOOSE *adj.*, PIECE *n.*, SHRED *n.*

PHR V **,tear sb↔a'part/'up** to make sb feel very unhappy or worried 使不快；使擔心 SYN **rip sb apart**：*It tears me apart to think I might have hurt her feelings.* 一想到我可能傷害了她的感情，我就感到痛心。 **,tear sth↔a'part 1** to destroy sth violently, especially by pulling it to pieces 撕毀；撕碎：*The dogs tore the fox apart.* 幾條狗把那隻狐狸撕成了碎片。 **2** to make people in a country, an organization or other place fight or argue with each other 使四分五裂；使分崩離析：*Racial strife is tearing our country apart.* 種族衝突把我們國家搞得四分五裂。 **3** to search a place, making it look untidy and causing damage 把（某處）搜索得凌亂不堪：*They tore the room apart, looking for money.* 他們為了找錢，把房間翻得亂七八糟。 SYN **rip sth apart** **'tear at sth** to pull or cut sth violently so that it tears 撕裂；扯開；撕破：*He tore at the meat with his bare hands.* 他只憑兩隻手就把肉撕碎了。 **,tear yourself a'way (from sth) | ,tear sth a'way (from sth)** to leave somewhere even though you would prefer to stay there; to take sth away from somewhere 依依不捨地離開；忍痛離去；把…拿走：*Dinner's ready, if you can tear yourself away from the TV.* 開飯了，別捨不得離開電視。◇ *She was unable to tear her eyes away from him* (= could not stop looking at him). 她戀戀不捨地望着他。 **,tear sth↔'down** to pull or knock down a building, wall, etc. 拆毀，拆除（建築物、牆等）SYN **demolish** **,tear 'into sb/sth 1** to attack sb/sth physically or with words 攻擊；襲擊；痛斥；抨擊 **2** to start doing sth with a lot of energy 積極投入：*They tore into their food as if they were starving.* 他們狼吞虎嚥地吃起飯來，好像餓壞了似的。 **,tear sb↔'up** = TEAR SB APART **,tear sth↔'up** 0→ to destroy a document, etc. by tearing it into pieces 撕毀，撕碎（文件等）SYN **rip sth up**：*She tore up all the letters he had sent her.* 她把他寄給她的信都撕了。◇ (*figurative*) *He accused the leader of tearing up the party's manifesto* (= of ignoring it). 他譴責領導人無視黨的宣言。

T

■ **noun** a hole that has been made in sth by tearing 破洞；裂口；裂縫：*This sheet has a tear in it.* 這條牀單上有個破洞。**IDM** see WEAR *n.*

tear² /tɪə(r); *NAmE* tɪr/ *noun* [usually pl.] ➲ see also TEAR¹
a drop of liquid that comes out of your eye when you cry 眼淚；淚珠；淚水：*A tear rolled down his face.* 一滴眼淚沿他的面頰流下來。◇ *She left the room* ***in tears*** (= crying). 她哭着離開了房間。◇ *He suddenly* ***burst into tears*** (= began to cry). 他突然放聲大哭起來。◇ *As he listened to the music, his* ***eyes filled with tears.*** 他聽着音樂，眼睛裏噙着淚水。◇ *Their story will* ***move you to tears*** (= make you cry). 他們的故事會使你感動得落淚。◇ *They* ***reduced her to tears*** (= made her cry, especially by being cruel or unkind). 他們弄得她哭起來了。◇ *Ann* ***wiped a tear*** *from her eye.* 安擦去眼裏的淚水。◇ *The memory* ***brought a tear to her eye*** (= made her cry). 她想起這事便熱淚盈眶。◇ *Most of the audience was* ***on the verge of tears.*** 大多數觀眾都快流淚了。◇ *I was* ***close to tears*** *as I told them the news.* 我告訴他們這一消息時都快要哭了出來。◇ *Desperately she* ***fought back the tears*** (= tried not to cry). 她竭力忍住沒讓眼淚流出來。◇ *to* ***shed tears*** *of happiness* 喜極而泣 ◇ *tears of pain, joy, etc.* 痛苦、喜悦等的淚水 ◇ *The* ***tears welled up*** *in his eyes.* 他熱淚盈眶。▶ **teary** /ˈtɪəri; *NAmE* ˈtɪri/ *adj.*：*teary eyes* 淚眼 ◇ *a teary smile/goodbye* 含淚的微笑；揮淚告別 **IDM** see BLOOD *n.*, BORED, CROCODILE, END *v.*

tear·away /ˈteərəweɪ; *NAmE* ˈter-/ *noun* (*BrE, informal*) a young person who is difficult to control and often does stupid, dangerous and/or illegal things 小流氓；阿飛；不良青年

tear·drop /ˈtɪədrɒp; *NAmE* ˈtɪrdrɑːp/ *noun* a single tear that comes from your eye 淚珠

tear duct /ˈtɪə dʌkt; *NAmE* ˈtɪr/ *noun* a tube through which tears pass from the tear GLANDS to the eye, or from the eye to the nose 淚管 ➲ VISUAL VOCAB page V59

tear·ful /ˈtɪəfl; *NAmE* ˈtɪrfl/ *adj.* **1** (of a person 人) crying, or about to cry 哭泣的；含淚的：*She suddenly became very tearful.* 她突然痛哭流涕。**2** (of an event, etc. 事件等) at which people feel emotional and cry 令人傷心的；催人淚下的：*a tearful farewell* 揮淚送別 ▶ **tear·ful·ly** /-fəli/ *adv.* **tear·ful·ness** *noun* [U]

tear gas /ˈtɪə ɡæs; *NAmE* ˈtɪr/ *noun* [U] a gas that makes your eyes sting and fill with tears, used by the police or army to control crowds 催淚瓦斯；催淚性毒氣

tear-jerker /ˈtɪə dʒɜːkə(r); *NAmE* ˈtɪr dʒɜːrkər/ *noun* (*informal*) a film/movie, story, etc. that is designed to make people feel sad 催人淚下的電影（或故事等）；"催淚彈" **SYN** **weepy**

T

tear-off /ˈteər ɒf; *NAmE* ˈter ɔːf; ɑːf/ *adj.* [only before noun] relating to sth that can be removed by being torn off, especially part of a sheet of paper（紙片等）可撕下的：*a tear-off slip* 可撕下的紙條

ˈtea room (also **ˈtea shop**) *noun* (*BrE*) a restaurant in which tea, coffee, cakes and SANDWICHES are served 茶室；茶館

tear-stained /ˈtɪə steɪnd; *NAmE* ˈtɪr/ *adj.* (especially of sb's face or cheeks 尤指臉或面頰) wet with tears 佈滿淚痕的；淚水漣漣的

tease /tiːz/ *verb, noun*

■ **verb** **1** [I, T] **~ (sb)** | **~ (sb) + speech** to laugh at sb and make jokes about them, either in a friendly way or in order to annoy or embarrass them 取笑；戲弄；揶揄；尋開心：*Don't get upset—I was only teasing.* 別不高興，我只是在逗你玩。◇ *I used to get teased about my name.* 過去別人總拿我的名字開玩笑。**2** [T] **~ sth** to annoy an animal, especially by touching it, pulling its tail, etc. 招惹，逗弄（動物）**3** [I, T] **~ (sb)** (*disapproving*) to make sb sexually excited, especially when you do not intend to have sex with them 挑逗，撩撥（異性）**4** [T] **~ sth (+ adv./prep.)** to pull sth gently apart into separate pieces 梳理：*to tease wool into strands* 把羊毛梳成縷 **5** (*NAmE*) (*BrE* **back·comb**) [T] **~ sth** to COMB your hair in the opposite direction to the way it grows so that it looks thicker 倒梳（頭髮）使之蓬起

PHR V ˌ**tease sth↔ˈout** **1** to remove knots from hair, wool, etc. by gently pulling or brushing it 梳理，梳通（毛髮等）**2** to spend time trying to find out information or the meaning of sth, especially when this is complicated or difficult 探討；深入研究；梳理清楚：*The teacher helped them tease out the meaning of the poem.* 老師幫助他們弄清楚那首詩的含義。

■ **noun** [usually sing.] **1** a person who likes to play tricks and jokes on other people, especially by telling them sth that is not true or by not telling them sth that they want to know 愛戲弄人的人；逗弄者；取笑者 **2** an act that is intended as a trick or joke 戲弄；捉弄；取笑 **3** (*disapproving*) a person who pretends to be attracted to sb, makes them sexually excited and then refuses to have sex with them 賣弄風騷的人；勾引人者

tea·sel (also **tea·zle**) /ˈtiːzl/ *noun* a plant which has large flowers with SPIKES, used in the past for brushing cloth to give it a smooth surface 川續斷，起絨草（舊時用以使織物表面起絨）

teaser /ˈtiːzə(r)/ *noun* **1** (*informal*) a difficult problem or question 難題；棘手的問題 ➲ see also BRAIN-TEASER **2** (also **ˈteaser ad**) an advertisement for a product that does not mention the name of the product or say much about it but is intended to make people interested and likely to pay attention to later advertisements 前導廣告，懸念式廣告（含蓄而引人好奇）

ˈtea set (*BrE*) (also **ˈtea service** *NAmE, BrE*) *noun* a set consisting of a TEAPOT, sugar bowl, cups, plates, etc., used for serving tea（一套）茶具

ˈtea shop *noun* (*BrE*) = TEA ROOM

teas·ing·ly /ˈtiːzɪŋli/ *adv.* **1** in a way that is intended to make sb feel embarrassed, annoyed, etc. 戲弄地；取笑地 **2** in a way that suggests sth and makes sb want to know more 激起好奇心地 **3** in a way that is intended to make sb sexually excited 挑逗地；撩撥地

tea·spoon /ˈtiːspuːn/ *noun* **1** a small spoon for putting sugar into tea and other drinks 茶匙；小匙 ➲ VISUAL VOCAB page V22 **2** (also **tea·spoon·ful** /-fʊl/) (*abbr.* **tsp**) the amount a teaspoon can hold 一茶匙（的量）：*Add two teaspoons of salt.* 加兩小匙鹽。

teat /tiːt/ *noun* **1** (*BrE*) (*NAmE* **nip·ple**) the rubber part at the end of a baby's bottle that the baby sucks in order to get milk, etc. from the bottle 奶嘴；橡膠乳頭 **2** one of the parts of a female animal's body that the young animals suck in order to get milk（雌獸的）乳頭，奶頭

tea·time /ˈtiːtaɪm/ *noun* [U] (*BrE*) the time during the afternoon or early evening when people have the meal called tea（下午或傍晚的）用茶點的時間

ˈtea towel (also **ˈtea cloth**) (both *BrE*) (*NAmE* **dish·towel**) *noun* a small towel used for drying cups, plates, knives, etc. after they have been washed（擦拭已洗茶具的）茶巾，抹布 ➲ VISUAL VOCAB page V25

ˈtea tree *noun* a small Australian and New Zealand tree. The oil from its leaves can be used to treat wounds and skin problems. 澳洲茶樹（產於澳大利亞和新西蘭，葉油可用於處理傷口和皮膚病）

ˈtea trolley (*BrE*) (*US* **ˈtea·cart**, **ˈtea wagon**) *noun* a small table on wheels that is used for serving drinks and food 茶具車

tea·zle *noun* = TEASEL

tebi·bit /ˈtebibɪt/ *noun* (*abbr.* **Tib**, **Tibit**) (*computing* 計) = TERABIT (2)

tebi·byte /ˈtebibaɪt/ *noun* (*abbr.* **TiB**) (*computing* 計) = TERABYTE (2)

tech /tek/ *noun* (*BrE, informal*) = TECHNICAL COLLEGE ➲ see also HIGH-TECH, LOW-TECH

techie (also **techy**) /ˈteki/ *noun* (*pl.* **-ies**) (*informal*) a person who is expert in or enthusiastic about technology, especially computers 科技通；科技迷；（尤指）電腦通，電腦迷

tech·ne·tium /tekˈniːʃɪəm/ *noun* [U] (*symb.* **Tc**) a chemical element. Technetium is found naturally as a product of URANIUM or made artificially from MOLYBDENUM. 鎝

tech·nical 0→ AW /ˈteknɪkl/ *adj.*
1 0→ [usually before noun] connected with the practical use of machinery, methods, etc. in science and industry 技術的；技能的；工藝的：*We offer free technical support for those buying our software.* 我們向購買我們軟件的顧客免費提供技術支持。◇ *a technical education* 技術教育 ◇ *technical drawing* (= especially taught as a school subject) 技術製圖（尤指學校教學科目） **2** 0→ [usually before noun] connected with the skills needed for a particular job, sport, art, etc. 專門技術的；技巧的；技藝的：*Skaters score extra points for technical complexity.* 滑冰運動員技巧難度大者獲得額外加分。 **3** 0→ connected with a particular subject and therefore difficult to understand if you do not know about that subject 專科的；專業的：*The article is full of* ***technical terms****.* 這篇文章滿篇皆是專業術語。◇ *The guide is too technical for a non-specialist.* 這份手冊對非專業人員來說太專業化了。 **4** 0→ [only before noun] connected with the details of a law or set of rules 訴訟程序性的；技術性的：*Their lawyers spent days arguing over technical details.* 他們的律師花了好幾天時間辯論訴訟程序細則。

ˈtechnical college (also *BrE informal* **tech**) *noun* a college where students can study mainly practical subjects 工學院

ˌtechnical ˈfoul *noun* (in BASKETBALL 籃球) an act of breaking certain rules of the game, especially ones relating to fair play 技術犯規（尤指違反公平比賽）

ˌtechnical ˈhitch *noun* a temporary problem or difficulty, especially one caused by a piece of machinery or equipment 暫時性問題（或困難）；（尤指）技術故障，機件故障

tech·ni·cal·ity /ˌteknɪˈkæləti/ *noun* (*pl.* **-ies**) **1** **technicalities** [pl.] the small details of how to do sth or how sth works 技術性細節 **2** a small detail in a law or set of rules, especially one that does not seem fair 訴訟程序性細節，技術性細則（尤指似乎不合理的）：*She was released* ***on a technicality*** (= because of a small detail in the law). 根據訴訟程序上的一個細則，她獲釋了。

ˌtechnical ˈknockout *noun* (in BOXING 拳擊運動) a victory when the opponent is still standing but is unable to continue fighting 技術得勝，技術性擊倒（對手依然站立但已無法繼續比賽）

tech·nic·al·ly AW /ˈteknɪkli/ *adv.* **1** according to the exact meaning, facts etc. 根據確切意義地；嚴格按照事實地：***Technically*** (***speaking***), *the two countries are still at war.* 嚴格說來，這兩國仍在交戰。◇ *It is still* ***technically possible*** *for them to win* (= but it seems unlikely). 從理論上講，他們仍有獲勝的可能性。 **2** in a way that is connected with the skills needed for a particular job, sport, art, etc. 在專業上；在技巧上；在技藝上：*As a musician, she is technically accomplished.* 作為樂師，她演奏藝術精湛。 **3** in a way that is connected with the practical use of machinery, methods, etc. in science and industry 在技術上；在技能上；在工藝上：*a technically advanced society* 科技先進的社會 ◇ *In those days recording sound was not* ***technically possible****.* 在那個時候，錄音在技術上是不可能的。

ˌtechnical supˈport (also *informal* **ˌtech supˈport**) *noun* **1** [U] technical help that a company gives to customers using their computers or other products （公司為用戶提供的）技術支持，技術支援：*All our software licences include technical support.* 我們的軟件證書均包含技術支持。 **2** [U+sing./pl. v.] a department in a company that provides technical help to its workers or customers （公司的）技術支持部，技術支援部：*I called tech support and they fixed it.* 我給技術支持部打了電話，他們修好了。

tech·ni·cian /tekˈnɪʃn/ *noun* **1** a person whose job is keeping a particular type of equipment or machinery in good condition 技術員；技師：*laboratory technicians* 實驗室技術員 **2** a person who is very skilled at the technical aspects of an art, a sport, etc. （藝術、體育等的）技巧精湛者，精於技巧者

Tech·ni·color™ /ˈteknɪkʌlə(r)/ *noun* [U] a process of producing colour film, as used in cinema films/movies 特藝色彩色電影印片法；特藝彩色

tech·ni·col·our (*especially US* **tech·ni·color**) /ˈteknɪkʌlə(r)/ *noun* [U] (*informal*) the state of having many bright colours 鮮豔的色彩；五彩繽紛：*The rooms were painted in* ***glorious technicolour****.* 這些房間被粉刷得絢麗多彩。

tech·ni·kon /ˈteknɪkɒn; *NAmE* -kɑːn/ (also *informal* **tech**) *noun* (*SAfrE*) a type of college or university that teaches mainly practical subjects 技術學院；職業技術大學

tech·nique 0→ AW /tekˈniːk/ *noun*
1 0→ [C] a particular way of doing sth, especially one in which you have to learn special skills 技巧；技藝；工藝：*The artist combines different techniques in the same painting.* 這位藝術家在同一幅畫中把不同的畫法結合在一起。◇ *marketing techniques* 營銷技巧 **2** 0→ [U, sing.] the skill with which sb is able to do sth practical 技術；技能：*Her technique has improved a lot over the past season.* 在過去的一個賽季裏，她的技術大有長進。

techno /ˈteknəʊ; *NAmE* -noʊ/ *noun* [U] a type of fast, electronic dance music, typically with little or no singing 泰克諾音樂（一種節奏快、通常無歌聲相伴的電子舞曲）

techno- /ˈteknəʊ; *NAmE* -noʊ/ *combining form* (in nouns, adjectives and adverbs 構成名詞、形容詞和副詞) connected with technology 科技的；技術的；工藝的：*technophobe* (= a person who is afraid of technology) 技術恐懼者

tech·no·bab·ble /ˈteknəʊbæbl; *NAmE* -noʊ-/ *noun* [U] (*informal, disapproving*) words or expressions connected with computers and technology that are difficult for ordinary people to understand 技術囈語（普通人難以理解）

tech·no·cracy /tekˈnɒkrəsi; *NAmE* -ˈnɑːk-/ *noun* [U, C] (*pl.* **-ies**) a social or political system in which people with scientific knowledge have a lot of power 技術專家治國制度；技術專家政治

tech·no·crat /ˈteknəkræt/ *noun* an expert in science, engineering, etc. who has a lot of power in politics and/or industry 技術專家官員；技術官僚 ► **tech·no·crat·ic** /ˌteknəˈkrætɪk/ *adj.* [usually before noun]

tech·nolo·gist /tekˈnɒlədʒɪst; *NAmE* -ˈnɑːl-/ *noun* an expert in technology 技術專家；工藝師

tech·nol·ogy 0→ AW /tekˈnɒlədʒi; *NAmE* -ˈnɑːl-/ *noun* (*pl.* **-ies**)
1 0→ [U, C] scientific knowledge used in practical ways in industry, for example in designing new machines 科技；工藝；工程技術；技術學；工藝學：*science and technology* 科學技術 ◇ *recent advances in medical technology* 醫療技術的新發展 ◇ *to make use of the most modern technologies* 利用最現代的技術 ➲ see also HIGH TECHNOLOGY, INFORMATION TECHNOLOGY **2** 0→ [U] machinery or equipment designed using technology 技術性機器（或設備）：*The company has invested in the latest technology.* 這家公司已在最新技術設備方面投資。 ► **tech·no·logic·al** AW /ˌteknəˈlɒdʒɪkl; *NAmE* -ˈlɑːdʒ-/ *adj.*：*technological advances* 科技進步 ◇ *technological change* 科技改革 ◇ *a major technological breakthrough* 重大科技突破 **tech·no·logic·al·ly** AW /-kli/ *adv.*：*technologically advanced* 技術上先進的

tech·no·phile /ˈteknəʊfaɪl; *NAmE* -noʊ-/ *noun* a person who is enthusiastic about new technology 新技術愛好者；新科技迷

tech·no·phobe /ˈteknəʊfəʊb; *NAmE* -noʊfoʊb/ *noun* a person who is afraid of, dislikes or avoids new technology 懼怕（或厭惡、逃避）新科技的人；科技恐懼者

ˈtech support *noun* (*informal*) = TECHNICAL SUPPORT

techy = TECHIE

tec·ton·ic /tekˈtɒnɪk; *NAmE* -ˈtɑːnɪk/ *adj.* [only before noun] (*geology* 地) connected with the structure of the earth's surface 地殼構造的 ➲ see also PLATE TECTONICS

teddy bear /ˈtedi beə(r); *NAmE* ber/ (*BrE* also **teddy** *pl.* **-ies**) *noun* a soft toy BEAR 泰迪熊（一種柔軟的填充玩具熊） ➲ **VISUAL VOCAB** page V37

T

'Teddy boy (also *informal* **ted** /ted/) *noun* (in Britain in the 1950s * 20 世紀 50 年代的英國) a member of a group of young men who liked ROCK AND ROLL music and who had their own style of dressing (usually wearing narrow trousers/pants, long jackets and pointed shoes) 阿飛（常穿緊身褲、長上衣、尖皮鞋，並熱衷於搖滾樂的青年男子）

te·di·ous /'tiːdiəs/ *adj.* lasting or taking too long and not interesting 冗長的；囉嗦的；單調乏味的；令人厭煩的 SYN **boring**：*The journey soon became tedious.* 那次旅行不久就變得乏味起來。◇ *We had to listen to the tedious details of his operation.* 我們不得不聽他嘮叨他那次行動繁瑣的細節。⊃ SYNONYMS at BORING ▸ **te·di·ous·ly** *adv.* **te·di·ous·ness** *noun* [U]

te·dium /'tiːdiəm/ *noun* [U] the quality of being boring 單調乏味；冗長；囉嗦 SYN **boredom**：*She longed for something to relieve the tedium of everyday life.* 她渴望有什麼事情能排解她日常生活中的煩悶。

tee /tiː/ *noun, verb*

■ ***noun*** **1** a flat area on a GOLF COURSE from which players hit the ball（高爾夫球場的）發球區，開球處：*to drive off from the first tee* 從第一發球區開球 ◇ *a tee shot* 開球處擊球 **2** a small piece of plastic or wood that you stick in the ground to support a GOLF ball before you hit it（高爾夫球）球座 IDM see T

■ ***verb*** (**teed**, **teed**)

PHR V **,tee 'off** to hit a GOLF ball from a tee, especially at the start of a match（尤指比賽開始時從高爾夫球座上）發球，開球 **,tee sb↔'off** (*NAmE, informal*) to make sb angry or annoyed 使生氣；使發火；使心煩 **,tee sth↔'up** | **,tee 'up** to prepare to hit a GOLF ball by placing it on a tee（把高爾夫球置於球座上）準備擊球

teed off /,tiːd 'ɒf; *NAmE* 'ɔːf; 'ɑːf/ *adj.* (*NAmE, informal*) annoyed or angry 給惹怒的；生氣的

tee-hee /,tiː 'hiː/ *noun* used to represent the sound of a quiet laugh（竊笑聲）嘻嘻，嘿嘿

teem /tiːm/ *verb* [I] (usually **be teeming**) (of rain 雨) to fall heavily 傾注；傾瀉 SYN **pour**：*The rain was teeming down.* 大雨傾盆而下。◇ ***It was teeming with*** *rain.* 大雨如注。

PHR V **'teem with sth** (usually **be 'teeming with sth**) to be full of people, animals, etc. moving around 充滿，遍佈，到處都是（移動着的人、動物等）：*The streets were teeming with tourists.* 大街上遊人如鯽。◇ *a river teeming with fish* 盛產魚的河流

teem·ing /'tiːmɪŋ/ *adj.* present in large numbers; full of people, animals, etc. that are moving around 大量的；充滿（移動着的人、動物等）的；擁擠的：*teeming insects* 成群結隊的昆蟲 ◇ *the teeming streets of the city* 熙熙攘攘的城市街道

teen·age /'tiːneɪdʒ/ (also *informal* **teen** especially in *NAmE*) *adj.* [usually before noun] between 13 and 19 years old; connected with people of this age 十幾歲的（指 13 至 19 歲）；青少年的：*teenage girls/boys* 十幾歲的少女／少年 ◇ *teenage rebellion* 青少年的叛逆行為 ◇ *teen magazines* 青少年雜誌

teen·aged /'tiːneɪdʒd/ *adj.* between 13 and 19 years old 十幾歲的（指 13 至 19 歲的）；青少年的：*They have two teenaged daughters.* 他們有兩個十幾歲的女兒。

teen·ager /'tiːneɪdʒə(r)/ (also *informal* **teen** especially in *NAmE*) *noun* a person who is between 13 and 19 years old（13 至 19 歲之間的）青少年，少年，少女：*a magazine aimed at teenagers* 以青少年為對象的雜誌

teens /tiːnz/ *noun* [pl.] the years of a person's life when they are between 13 and 19 years old 十幾歲（13 至 19 歲之間）：*She began writing poetry* ***in her teens.*** 她從十幾歲開始寫詩。◇ *to be in your* ***early/late teens*** 現年十三四／十八九歲

teeny /'tiːni/ *adj.* (*informal*) (**teen·ier**, **teeni·est**) **1** (also **teeny-weeny** /,tiːni 'wiːni/, **teensy** /'tiːnzi/, **teensy-weensy** /,tiːnzi 'wiːnzi/) very small 很小的；極小的 SYN **tiny 2** connected with people between 13 and 19 years old 十幾歲青少年的：*teeny magazines* 青少年雜誌

teeny-bopper /'tiːni bɒpə(r); *NAmE* bɑːp-/ *noun* (*old-fashioned, informal*) a young girl between the ages of about 10 and 13, who is very interested in pop music, fashionable clothes, etc. 時髦少女（喜好流行音樂和時髦服裝，年齡在 10 至 13 歲之間）

tee·pee = TEPEE

'tee shirt = T-SHIRT

tee·ter /'tiːtə(r)/ *verb* [I] to stand or move in an unsteady way so that you look as if you are going to fall 搖晃；蹣跚行走；踉蹌；搖搖欲墜：*She teetered after him in her high-heeled shoes.* 她穿着高跟鞋一步三晃地跟在他後面走。

IDM **teeter on the 'brink/'edge of sth** to be very close to a very unpleasant or dangerous situation 處在（災難或危險）的邊緣；瀕臨：*The country is teetering on the brink of civil war.* 這個國家正處在內戰的邊緣。

'teeter-totter *noun* (*NAmE*) = SEE-SAW *n.* (1)

teeth *pl.* of TOOTH

teethe /tiːð/ *verb* [I] when a baby **is teething**, its first teeth are starting to grow（幼兒）出牙，長牙

'teething troubles (also **'teething problems**) *noun* [pl.] small problems that a company, product, system, etc. has at the beginning（公司、產品、系統等的）初期遇到的小問題；創業階段遇到的小麻煩

tee·total /tiː'təʊtl; *NAmE* -'toʊtl/ *adj.* never drinking alcohol 從不飲酒的；滴酒不沾的：*He's strictly teetotal.* 他絕對是滴酒不沾。▸ **tee·total·ism** *noun* [U]

tee·total·ler (*BrE*) (*US* **tee·total·er**) /,tiː'təʊtlə(r); *NAmE* -'toʊ-/ *noun* a person who does not drink alcohol 不飲酒的人；滴酒不沾的人

TEFL /'tefl/ *abbr.* (*BrE*) teaching English as a foreign language 作為外語的英語教學

Tef·lon™ /'teflɒn; *NAmE* 'teflɑːn/ *noun, adj.*

■ ***noun*** [U] a substance used especially to cover the inside of cooking pans, that stops food from sticking to them 特氟隆，聚四氟乙烯（不粘鍋塗層材料）

■ ***adj.*** (especially of a politician 尤指從政者) still having a good reputation after making a mistake or doing sth that is not legal 扳不倒的（犯錯誤或違法後聲譽不受損）：*The Teflon Prime Minister has survived another crisis.* 不倒翁首相又挺過了一次危機。

tel. (also **Tel.**) *abbr.* (in writing 書寫形式) telephone number 電話號碼

telco /'telkəʊ; *NAmE* -koʊ/ *noun* (*pl.* **-os**) (used especially in newspapers 尤用於報章) a TELECOMMUNICATIONS company 電信公司：*Telcos were struggling to make money from broadband services.* 各家電信公司那時正努力通過寬帶業務贏利。

tele- /'teli/ *combining form* (in nouns, verbs, adjectives and adverbs 構成名詞、動詞、形容詞和副詞) **1** over a long distance; far 遠距離的；遠的：*telepathy* 傳心術 ◇ *telescopic* 望遠的 **2** connected with television 電視的：*teletext* 圖文電視 **3** done using a telephone 通過電話的：*telesales* 電話銷售

tele·bank·ing /'telibæŋkɪŋ/ *noun* [U] = TELEPHONE BANKING

tele·cam·era /'telikæmərə/ *noun* a video camera used in VIDEOCONFERENCING（用於視頻會議的）電視攝影機，遠距離攝影機

tele·cast /'telikɑːst; *NAmE* -kæst/ *noun* (*especially NAmE*) a broadcast on television 電視廣播；電視節目 ▸ **tele·cast** *verb* (**tele·cast**, **tele·cast**) [usually passive]：**~ sth** *The event will be telecast simultaneously to nearly 150 cities.* 這一盛事將向近 150 個城市同時進行電視廣播。 **tele·cast·er** *noun*

tele·com·mu·ni·ca·tions /,telikə,mjuːnɪ'keɪʃnz/ (also *informal* **tele·coms** /'telikɒmz; *NAmE* -kɑːmz/) *noun* [pl.] the technology of sending signals, images and messages over long distances by radio, telephone, television, SATELLITE, etc. 電信；電訊：*technological developments in telecommunications* 電信技術的發展 ◇ *the telecommunications industry* 電信業 ▸ **tele·com·mu·ni·ca·tion** (also *informal* **tele·com** /'telikɒm; *NAmE* -kɑːm/) *adj.* [only before noun]：*a telecommunication company* 電信公司

T

tele·com·mute /ˌtelikə'mjuːt/ *verb* [I] to work from home, communicating with your office, customers and others by telephone, email, etc. 家庭辦公，遠距離工作（通過電話、電子郵件等與辦公室、顧客等進行聯繫） ▸ **tele·com·muter** *noun* SYN **teleworker** **tele·com·mut·ing** *noun* [U] SYN **teleworking**

tele·con·fer·ence /'telikɒnfərəns; *NAmE* -kɑːn-/ *noun* a conference or discussion at which members are in different places and speak to each other using telephone and video connections 電話會議；電信會議；遠程會議 ▸ **tele·con·fer·ence** *verb* [I] **tele·con·fer·enc·ing** /'telikɒnfərənsɪŋ; *NAmE* -kɑːn-/ *noun* [U]

tele·cot·tage /'telikɒtɪdʒ; *NAmE* -kɑːt-/ *noun* a room or small building in a countryside area that is filled with computer equipment for the use of people living in the area（公用）鄉間電腦室，鄉間計算機屋

tele·film /'telifɪlm/ *noun* a film/movie that is made specially to be shown on television 電視影片

tele·gen·ic /ˌtelɪ'dʒenɪk/ *adj.* a **telegenic** person looks good on television（人）適於拍攝電視的，適於上電視鏡頭的

tele·gram /'telɪɡræm/ *noun* a message sent by TELEGRAPH and then printed and given to sb 電報（用電信號傳遞的信息）

tele·graph /'telɪɡrɑːf; *NAmE* -ɡræf/ *noun, verb*

■ ***noun*** [U] a method of sending messages over long distances, using wires that carry electrical signals 電報（通信方式）

■ ***verb*** **1** [I, T] ~ (**sth**) to send a message by telegraph 打電報；用電報發送（電文）；電告 **2** [T] ~ **sth** to make it clear to people what you are going to do, often without intending to（無意中）流露（思想），泄露（動機）

tele·graph·ic /ˌtelɪ'ɡræfɪk/ *adj.* connected with sending messages by telegraph 電報的；電報發送的：*You will need to arrange a telegraphic transfer from your bank to ours.* 你們得安排由你方銀行將錢款電匯給我方銀行。

'telegraph pole (*BrE*) (*NAmE* **'telephone pole**) *noun* a tall wooden pole used for carrying telephone or telegraph wires high above the ground（電話或電報線路的）電線杆

tel·eg·raphy /tə'leɡrəfi/ *noun* [U] the process of sending messages by telegraph 電報通訊術

tele·kin·esis /ˌtelɪkɪ'niːsɪs; *BrE* also -kaɪ'n-/ *noun* [U] the ability to move objects without touching them, using mental powers 心靈致動；心靈遙感

tele·mark /'telɪmɑːk; *NAmE* -mɑːrk/ *noun* [U] (in SKIING or SKI JUMPING 滑雪或跳台滑雪) a style of turning or landing with one SKI forward and bent knees 弓步式轉彎；弓步單橇向前着地

tele·mar·ket·ing /'telimɑːkɪtɪŋ; *NAmE* -mɑːrk-/ (*BrE* also **tele·sales**) *noun* [U] a method of selling things and taking orders for sales by telephone 電話銷售；電話推銷

tele·mat·ics /ˌtelɪ'mætɪks/ *noun* [U] the use or study of technology which allows information to be sent over long distances using computers 計算機信息通訊（學）；遠程信息處理（學）；遠程資訊

tele·meter /'telimiːtə(r)/ *noun* (*technical* 術語) a device for sending, receiving and measuring scientific data over a long distance 遙測裝置；遙測儀 ▸ **tele·meter** *verb*：~ **sth** (**to sth**) *Data from these instruments is telemetered to the laboratory.* 從這些儀器得到的數據用遙測儀傳送到實驗室。

tel·em·etry /tə'lemətri/ *noun* [U] (*technical* 術語) the process of using special equipment to send, receive and measure scientific data over long distances 遙測術；遠距離測量術

tele·ology /ˌtiːli'ɒlədʒi; *NAmE* -'ɑːlə-/ *noun* [U, sing.] (*philosophy* 哲) the theory that events and developments are meant to achieve a purpose and happen because of that 目的論（認為事物的發生和發展都是為了達到一定目的）▸ **teleo·logic·al** /ˌtiːliə'lɒdʒɪkl; *NAmE* -'lɑːdʒ-/ *adj.*

tele·op·er·ate /ˌteli'ɒpəreɪt; *NAmE* -'ɑːpə-/ *verb* ~ **sth** (**from sth**) to operate a machine which is not in the same place as you 遠程操縱，遙控（機器）：*Equipment on the space station is teleoperated from earth.* 空間站上的設備是從地球遙控的。

tele·path·ic /ˌtelɪ'pæθɪk/ *adj.* **1** using telepathy 用傳心術的；心靈感應的：*telepathic communication* 心靈感應交流 **2** (of a person 人) able to communicate by telepathy 會傳心術的；有心靈感應的：*How do I know what he's thinking? I'm not telepathic!* 我怎麼知道他在想什麼？我又不會傳心術！▸ **tele·path·ic·al·ly** /-kli/ *adv.*

tel·ep·athy /tə'lepəθi/ *noun* [U] the direct communication of thoughts or feelings from one person to another without using speech, writing, or any other normal method 傳心術；通靈術；心靈感應

tele·phone 0→ /'telɪfəʊn; *NAmE* -foʊn/ *noun, verb*

■ ***noun*** **1** 0→ [C, U] a system for talking to sb else over long distances, using wires or radio; a machine used for this 電話；電話系統；電話機：*The* ***telephone rang*** *and Pat answered it.* 電話響起，帕特接了。◇ *You can reserve seats* ***over the telephone***. 你可以打電話預訂座位。◇ *I need to* ***make a telephone call***. 我得打個電話。◇ ***telephone lines/networks/services*** 電話線路 / 網絡 / 業務 ➲ COLLOCATIONS at PHONE **2** 0→ [C] the part of the telephone that you hold in your hand and speak into 電話聽筒 SYN **handset**, **receiver** ➲ see also PHONE *n.* (2)

IDM **be on the 'telephone 1** to be using the telephone 在打電話；在通電話：*He's on the telephone at the moment.* 他正在打電話。◇ *You're wanted* (= sb wants to speak to you) *on the telephone.* 有人打電話找你。 **2** (*BrE*) to have a telephone in your home or place of work（在家裏或工作單位）裝有電話機的：*We're not on the telephone at the cottage.* 我們的鄉間別墅沒有安裝電話。

■ ***verb*** 0→ [I, T] (*formal, especially BrE*) to speak to sb by telephone 給某人打電話 SYN **call**, **phone**：*Please write or telephone for details.* 欲知詳情，請來信或電話聯繫。◇ *He telephoned to say he'd be late.* 他來電話說要晚到一會兒。◇ ~ **sth** *You can telephone your order 24 hours a day.* 一天 24 小時你都可以打電話訂購。◇ *I was about to telephone the police.* 我正要給警察打電話。➲ note at PHONE

ˌtelephone 'banking (also **'tele·bank·ing**) *noun* [U] activities relating to your bank account, which you do using the telephone 電話銀行業務

'telephone booth *noun* = PHONE BOOTH

'telephone box *noun* (*BrE*) = PHONE BOX

'telephone directory (also **'phone book**, **'telephone book**) *noun* a book that lists the names, addresses and telephone numbers of people in a particular area 電話號碼簿；電話簿：*to look up a number in the telephone directory* 在電話簿裏查電話號碼

'telephone exchange (also **exchange**) *noun* a place where telephone calls are connected so that people can speak to each other 電話交換台；總機；電話局

'telephone kiosk *noun* (*BrE*) = PHONE BOX

'telephone number (also **'phone number**) *noun* the number of a particular telephone, that you use when you make a call to it 電話號碼

'telephone pole (*NAmE*) (*BrE* **'telegraph pole**) *noun* a tall wooden pole used for carrying telephone or telegraph wires high above the ground（電話或電報線路的）電線杆

'telephone tapping (also **'phone tapping**) *noun* [U] the practice of connecting a piece of equipment to a telephone in order to listen secretly to other people's telephone conversations 電話竊聽

tel·eph·on·ist /tə'lefənɪst/ *noun* (*BrE*) = OPERATOR (2)

tel·eph·ony /tə'lefəni/ *noun* [U] the process of sending messages and signals by telephone 電話通訊

tele·photo lens /ˌtelifəʊtəʊ 'lenz; *NAmE* -foʊtoʊ/ *noun* a camera LENS that produces a large image of an object that is far away and allows you to take photographs of it 攝遠鏡頭；遠距離照相鏡頭

tele·port /'telipɔːt; *NAmE* -pɔːrt/ *verb* [I, T] ~ (**sb/sth**) (usually in SCIENCE FICTION) to move sb/sth immediately from one place to another a distance away, using

T

special equipment; to be moved in this way（通常見於科幻作品）（被）遠距離傳送：*The search party was teleported down to the planet's surface.* 搜索隊給傳送到那星球的表面。▶ **tele·por·ta·tion** /ˌtelipɔːˈteɪʃn; *NAmE* -pɔːrˈt-/ *noun* [U]

tele·print·er /ˈteliprɪntə(r)/ (*NAmE* also **tele·type·writer**) *noun* a machine that prints out TELEX messages that have been typed in another place and sent by telephone lines 電傳打印機

tele·prompt·er /ˈteliprɒmptə(r); *NAmE* -prɑːm-/ (*especially NAmE*) (*BrE* also **Auto·cue™**) *noun* a device used by people who are speaking in public, especially on television, which displays the words that they have to say 電子提詞器，自動提示器，講詞提示板（尤用於電視講話時向說話人提示講詞）

tele·sales /ˈteliseɪlz/ (*BrE*) (also **tele·mar·ket·ing** *NAmE*, *BrE*) *noun* [U] a method of selling things and taking orders for sales by telephone 電話銷售；電話推銷

tele·scope /ˈtelɪskəʊp; *NAmE* -skoʊp/ *noun, verb*

▪ ***noun*** a piece of equipment shaped like a tube, containing LENSES, that you look through to make objects that are far away appear larger and nearer 望遠鏡：*to look at the stars through a telescope* 用望遠鏡觀察星星 ➲ picture at BINOCULARS ➲ see also RADIO TELESCOPE

▪ ***verb*** **1** [I, T] **~ (sth)** to become shorter, or make sth shorter, by sliding sections inside one another（使）疊套縮短，疊縮 **2** [T] **~ sth (into sth)** to reduce sth so that it happens in less time 縮短，精簡，壓縮（成…）：*Three episodes have been telescoped into a single programme.* 三集的內容被濃縮成了一個單獨的節目。

tele·scop·ic /ˌtelɪˈskɒpɪk; *NAmE* -ˈskɑːpɪk/ *adj.* **1** connected with or using a telescope; making things look larger as a telescope does 望遠鏡的；望遠的；放大的：*a rifle with a telescopic sight* 裝有望遠瞄準器的步槍 **2** made of sections that can slide into each other to make the object longer or shorter 可伸縮的；套疊的；套筒的：*a telescopic aerial* 可伸縮天線 ▶ **tele·scop·ic·al·ly** /-kli/ *adv.*

tele·shop·ping /ˈteliʃɒpɪŋ; *NAmE* -ʃɑːp-/ *noun* [U] shopping that is done using the telephone or television 電話（或電視）購物

tele·text /ˈtelitekst/ *noun* [U] a service providing written news and information using television 圖文電視；電視文字廣播：*See if the results are* ***on teletext***. 看看結果是否上了圖文電視。

tele·thon /ˈteləθɒn; *NAmE* -θɑːn/ *noun* a very long television show, broadcast to raise money for charity（為募捐播放的）長時間的電視節目，馬拉松式電視節目

tele·type·writer /ˌteliˈtaɪpraɪtə(r)/ *noun* (*NAmE*) = TELEPRINTER

tele·van·gel·ist /ˌtelɪˈvændʒəlɪst/ *noun* (especially in the US) a person who appears regularly on television to try to persuade people to become Christians and to give money 電視福音佈道者（在美國尤指定期在電視上勸人加入基督教及捐款者）▶ **tele·van·gel·ism** *noun* [U]

tele·vise /ˈtelɪvaɪz/ *verb* [usually passive] **~ sth** to broadcast sth on television 用電視播送：*a televised debate* 電視播送的辯論 ◇ *to televise a novel* 電視播送小說 ◇ *The speech will be televised live.* 這次演講將由電視直播。

tele·vi·sion 🔑 /ˈtelɪvɪʒn/ *noun* (*abbr.* **TV**)
1 🔑 (also **ˈtelevision set**) (also *BrE informal* **telly**) [C] a piece of electrical equipment with a screen on which you can watch programmes with moving pictures and sounds 電視機：*a* ***colour television*** 彩色電視機 ◇ *a* ***widescreen television*** 寬屏幕電視機 ◇ *a* ***plasma screen***

Collocations 詞語搭配

Television 電視

Watching 觀看

- **watch** television/TV/a show/(*BrE*) a programme/(*NAmE*) a program/a documentary/a pilot/a rerun/a repeat 看電視／電視節目／紀實電視節目／試播節目／重播的電視節目
- **see** (*especially BrE*) an ad/(*especially NAmE*) a commercial/the news/the weather 看廣告／新聞／天氣節目
- **catch/miss** a show/a programme/a program/an episode/the news 看／錯過電視節目／電視連續劇的一集／新聞節目
- **pick up/reach for/grab** the remote (control) 拿起／伸手去拿／抓起遙控器
- **change/switch** channel 換頻道
- **surf** (**through**)/(*especially NAmE*) **flip through**/(*especially BrE*) **flick through** the channels 快速瀏覽電視頻道
- **sit in front of/switch on/switch off/turn on/turn off** the television/the TV/the TV set 坐在電視機前；開／關電視
- **have/install** satellite (TV)/cable (TV)/a satellite dish 有／安裝衛星電視／有線電視／衛星電視碟形天線

Showing 播放

- **show** a programme/a documentary/an ad/a commercial 播放電視節目／紀實電視節目／廣告
- **screen** a programme/a documentary 播放電視節目／紀實電視節目
- **run** an ad/a commercial 播放廣告
- **broadcast**/(*especially NAmE*) **air/repeat** a show/a programme/a documentary/an episode/a series 播放／重播電視節目／紀實電視節目／電視連續劇的一集／系列節目
- **go out/air/be recorded** live 現場直播／錄製
- **attract/draw** (**in**)/**pull** (**in**) viewers 吸引觀眾
- **be a hit with** viewers/audiences/critics 受到電視觀眾／觀眾／評論家的喜愛
- **get** (low/high) ratings 有（低／高）收視率

Appearing 演出

- **be on/appear on** television/TV/a TV show 在電視上／電視節目中露面
- **take part in** a phone-in/a game show/a quiz show/a reality TV show 參與熱線直播節目／遊戲節目／智力遊戲節目／電視真人秀
- **host** a show/a programme/series/a game show/a quiz show/a talk show/(*BrE*) a chat show 主持電視節目／系列節目／遊戲節目／智力遊戲節目／訪談節目
- **be/become/work as** a (*BrE*) TV presenter/talk-show host/sports commentator/anchorman/(*BrE*) newsreader 是／成為／當電視節目主持人／訪談節目主持人／體育運動實況解說員／新聞節目主持人／新聞播音員
- **read/present** the news 播報新聞
- **appear/perform** live (on TV)（在電視上）現場表演

Programme-making 節目製作

- **do/film/make** a show/a programme/a documentary/an episode/a pilot/a series/an ad/a commercial 拍攝電視節目／紀實電視節目／電視連續劇的一集／試播節目／系列節目／廣告
- **work on** a soap (opera)/a pilot (episode)/a sitcom 製作肥皂劇／試播節目（的一集）／情景喜劇
- **write/produce** a drama/sitcom/spin-off/comedy series 寫／拍攝戲劇／情景喜劇／電視系列劇的派生作品／喜劇連續劇

T

television 等離子電視機 ◇ *to* ***turn the television on/off*** 打開／關閉電視機 **2** (also *BrE informal* **telly**) [U] the programmes broadcast on television 電視節目；電視：*We don't do much in the evenings except* ***watch television.*** 我們在晚上除了看電視不怎麼幹別的事。 **3** [U] the system, process or business of broadcasting television programmes 電視系統；電視學；電視廣播業：***satellite/terrestrial/cable/digital television*** 衛星／地面／有線／數字電視系統 ◇ *the television news* 電視新聞 ◇ *a television documentary* 電視紀錄片 ◇ ***a television company/presenter*** 電視廣播公司／節目主持人 ◇ *I'd like to work* ***in television*** (= for a television company). 我希望從事電視廣播事業。 ➲ see also CABLE TELEVISION, CLOSED-CIRCUIT TELEVISION

IDM **on (the) 'television** (also *informal* **on TV**) (also *BrE informal* **on the 'telly**) being broadcast by television; appearing in a television programme 電視播放的；上電視的；在電視上露面的：*What's on television tonight?* 今晚有什麼電視節目？ ◇ *Is there anything good on the telly tonight?* 今晚電視有好節目嗎？ ◇ *It was on TV yesterday.* 昨天電視上播放了它。 ◇ *I recognize you. Aren't you on television?* 我認出你來了。你不是常上電視嗎？

tele·vis·ual /ˌteliˈvɪʒuəl/ *adj.* relating to or suitable for television 電視的；適於電視的：*a major televisual event* 電視播放的大型活動

tele·work·ing /ˈteliwɜːkɪŋ; *NAmE* -wɜːrk-/ *noun* [U] (*BrE*) the practice of working from home, communicating with your office, customers and others by telephone, email, etc. 遠程工作，遠程操作（在家裏工作，利用電話、電子郵件等與辦公室、客戶等聯繫） **SYN** **telecommuting** ▸ **tele·worker** *noun* **SYN** **telecommuter**

telex /ˈteleks/ *noun, verb*

■ ***noun*** **1** [U] an international system of communication in which messages are typed on a special machine and sent by the telephone system 電傳系統 **2** [C] a message sent or received by telex 電傳；用戶電報 **3** [C] (*informal*) a machine for sending and receiving messages by telex 電傳機；電傳收發機

■ ***verb*** [I, T] **~ (sth)** to send a message by telex 發電傳；以電傳發出（電文）

tell /tel/ *verb* (**told, told** /təʊld; *NAmE* toʊld/)

▸ **GIVE INFORMATION 提供信息** **1** [T] (of a person 人) to give information to sb by speaking or writing 告訴；告知：**~ sth to sb** *He told the news to everybody he saw.* 他逢人便講這個消息。 ◇ **~ sb sth** *He told everybody he saw the news.* 他逢人便講這個消息。 ◇ *Did she tell you her name?* 她告訴你她的姓名了嗎？ ◇ ***What did I tell you?*** (= you should have listened to my advice) 我跟你說什麼來着？ ◇ **~ sb (about sth)** *Why wasn't I told about the accident?* 為什麼沒人把這次事故告訴我？ ◇ **~ sb/yourself (that)** … *They've told us (that) they're not coming.* 他們已跟我們說過不來了。 ◇ ***I kept telling myself*** *(that) everything was OK.* 我不住告訴自己一切都沒問題。 ◇ *Are you telling me you didn't have any help with this?* (= I don't believe what you have said) 你是說在這件事情上你沒有得到過任何幫助嗎？ ◇ **~ sb where, what, etc.** … *Tell me where you live.* 告訴我你住哪兒？ ◇ **~ sb + speech** *'I'm ready to go now,' he told her.* "我現在可以走了。" 他對她說。 ➲ note at SAY **2** [T] (of some writing, an instrument, a sign, etc. 文章、儀器、標記等) to give information about sth 提供（情況）；說明；顯示：**~ sb sth** *The advertisement told us very little about the product.* 這則廣告提供的產品情況很少。 ◇ **~ sb how, where, etc.** … *This gauge tells you how much fuel you have left.* 這油表顯示還剩有多少燃料。 ◇ **~ sb (that)** … *The sound of his breathing told her (that) he was asleep.* 她從他呼吸的聲音中聽出來他睡着了。

▸ **EXPRESS IN WORDS 用言語表達** **3** [T] to express sth in words 講述；說；表達：**~ sth** *to* ***tell stories/jokes/lies*** 講故事；說笑話；撒謊 ◇ *Are you sure you're* ***telling the truth?*** 你說的真是實話嗎？ ◇ **~ sb how, what, etc.** … ***I can't tell you*** *how happy I am.* 我無法向你表達我多麼高興。

▸ **SECRET 秘密** **4** [I] (*informal*) to let sb know a secret 泄露（秘密）；告發：*Promise you won't tell.* 你要保證不往外講。 ◇ *'Who are you going out with tonight?'* ***'That would be telling!'*** (= it's a secret) "你今晚要和誰約會？" "那可不能講！"（是個秘密）

▸ **ORDER 命令** **5** [T] to order or advise sb to do sth 命令；指示；吩咐：**~ sb/yourself to do sth** *He was told to sit down and wait.* 有人吩咐他坐下等着。 ◇ *There was a sign telling motorists to slow down.* 有一個讓司機減速的指示牌。 ◇ *I kept telling myself to keep calm.* 我不斷叮囑自己要保持冷靜。 ◇ **~ sb sth** *Do what I tell you.* 你要照我的吩咐做。 ◇ **~ sb** *Children must* ***do as they're told.*** 孩子們必須聽話。 ◇ **~ sb what, when, etc.** … *Don't tell me what to do!* 別跟我說該怎麼辦！ ◇ **~ sb (that)** … *The doctor told me (that) I should eat less fat.* 醫生囑咐我要少吃油膩。 ➲ SYNONYMS at ORDER ➲ note at SAY

▸ **KNOW/JUDGE 知道；判斷** **6** [I, T] (not used in the progressive tenses 不用於進行時) to know, see or judge sth correctly 知道；看出；確切地判斷：*I think he's happy.* ***It's hard to tell.*** 我想他是幸福的。這很難說。 ◇ ***As far as I can tell,*** *she's enjoying the course.* 據我判斷，她喜歡這門課程。 ◇ **~ (that)** … *I could tell (that) he was angry from his expression.* 從他的表情我看得出他生氣了。 ◇ **~ how, if, etc.** … *'That's not an original.' 'How can you tell?'* "那不是正本。" "你怎麼知道的？" ◇ *The only way to tell if you like something is by trying it.* 要判定是否喜歡一件東西，唯一的辦法是試一試。

▸ **DISTINGUISH 辨別** **7** [T] (not used in the progressive tenses or in the passive 不用於進行時或被動語態) to distinguish one thing or person from another 識別；分辨；區分；辨認：**~ sth** *It was hard to* ***tell the difference between*** *the two versions.* 很難分辨出這兩個版本有什麼區別。 ◇ **~ A from B** *Can you tell Tom from his twin brother?* 你能分得出湯姆和他的孿生弟弟嗎？ ◇ **~ A and B apart** *It's difficult to* ***tell them apart.*** 很難把他們區分開來。 ◇ **~ which, what, etc.** … *The kittens look exactly alike—how can you* ***tell which is which?*** 這些小貓看上去一模一樣，你怎麼能分辨出哪隻是哪隻呢？

▸ **HAVE EFFECT 有影響** **8** [I] **~ (on sb)** to have an effect on sb/sth, especially a bad one 產生效果，發生影響（尤指負面影響）：*The strain was beginning to tell on the rescue team.* 過度的疲勞開始讓救援隊吃不消了。

IDM **all 'told** with all people, etc. counted and included 合計；總共：*There are 52 people coming, all told.* 總共有52人要來。 **don't 'tell me** (*informal*) used to say that you know or can guess what sb is going to say, especially because it is typical of them（用以表示知道或猜得出他人要說什麼）不至於…吧，別又要說…了吧：*Don't tell me you were late again!* 你不至於又遲到了吧！ **I/I'll ˌtell you 'what** (*informal*) used to introduce a suggestion 我的建議是；聽我說：*I'll tell you what—let's stay in instead.* 聽我說，咱們還是待在家裏吧。 **I 'tell you | I can 'tell you | I'm 'telling you** (*informal*) used to emphasize what you are saying, especially when it is surprising or difficult to believe 我可以肯定地說；我敢說；確實：*It isn't cheap, I can tell you!* 我敢說，這並不便宜！ ◇ *I'm telling you, that's exactly what she said.* 我可以肯定地說，那正是她的原話。 **I 'told you (so)** (*informal*) used when sth bad has happened, to remind sb that you warned them about it and they did not listen to you 我提醒過你要出事；不聽好人言，吃虧在眼前 **ˌlive, etc. to ˌtell the 'tale** to survive a difficult or dangerous experience so that you can tell others what really happened 幸免於難之後向人講述真實經歷 **tell a 'different story/tale** to give some information that is different from what you expect or have been told 說的情況迥然不同；講出來的是另一回事 **tell its own tale/story** to explain itself, without needing any further explanation or comment 不言而喻；不釋自明；無須解釋：*Her face told its own story.* 看她的面部表情，就什麼都明白了。 **'tell me** (*informal*) used to introduce a question（用以引出問題）告訴我，跟我說實話：*Tell me, have you had lunch yet?* 跟我說實話，你吃過午餐沒有？ **'tell me about it** (*informal*) used to say that you understand what sb is talking about and have had the same experience 你算說對了；的確：*'I get so annoyed with Steve!' 'Tell me about it. He drives me crazy.'* "史蒂夫把我煩透了！" "你算說對了。他快把我逼瘋了。" **tell me a'nother!** (*informal*) used to tell sb that you do not believe what they have said 不見得吧；我不相信；別瞎扯 **tell 'tales (about sth/on sb)** (*BrE*) to tell sb about sth that another person has done wrong

T

揭人短處；說長道短 ➲ related noun TELLTALE **tell the 'time** (*BrE*) (*NAmE* **tell 'time**) to read the time from a clock, etc. (根據鐘錶等) 說出時間；報時： *She's only five—she hasn't learnt to tell the time yet.* 她才五歲，還沒有學會看鐘錶。**tell sb where to get 'off/where they can get 'off** (*BrE, informal*) to make it clear to sb that you will no longer accept their bad behaviour 警告某人的行為不可容忍；不吃某人的這一套 **tell sb where to 'put/'stick sth | tell sb what they can 'do with sth** (*informal*) to make it clear to sb that you are angry and are rejecting what they are offering you 別來這一套；讓某人收起…的一套 **there's no 'telling** used to say that it is impossible to know what happened or will happen 無法知道；難以預料： *There's no telling how they'll react.* 說不準他們會有什麼反應。**to tell (you) the 'truth** (*informal*) used when admitting sth 說實話；老實說；說真的： *To tell the truth, I fell asleep in the middle of her talk.* 說實話，我在她講話過程中睡着了。**you can never 'tell | you never can 'tell** (*saying*) you can never be sure, for example because things are not always what they appear to be 誰也拿不準；誰也說不清；很難說 **you're telling 'me!** (*informal*) I completely agree with you 我完全同意；的確如此 ➲ more at HEAR, KISS *v.*, LITTLE *adj.*, THING, TIME *n.*, TRUTH

PHR V **,tell a'gainst sb** (*BrE, formal*) to be a disadvantage to sb 對…不利： *Her lack of experience told against her.* 她缺乏經驗對她不利。**'tell of sth** (*formal* or *literary*) to make sth known; to give an account of sth 公佈；說明： *notices telling of the proposed job cuts* 公佈擬裁員的通知 **,tell sb↔'off (for sth/for doing sth)** 🔑 (*informal*) to speak angrily to sb for doing sth wrong 責備；斥責；責罵；數落 **SYN** **scold**： *I told the boys off for making so much noise.* 孩子們太吵，我把他們訓斥了一頓。◇ *Did you get told off?* 你捱罵了沒有？➲ related noun TELLING-OFF **'tell on sb** (*informal*) to tell a person in authority about sth bad that sb has done 告發；打…的小報告；告…的狀： *Promise not to tell on me!* 答應我，別告發我！

,tell-'all *adj.* [only before noun] (of a book, an interview in a newspaper or magazine, etc. 書或報刊上的訪談錄等) in which sb, usually sb famous, admits sth that may shock people 坦白的，和盤托出的 (通常指名人)： *a tell-all book/memoir/autobiography* 自我爆料的書／回憶錄／自傳

tell·er /'telə(r)/ *noun* **1** a person whose job is to receive and pay out money in a bank (銀行的) 出納，出納員 **2** a machine that pays out money automatically 出納機；提款機： *automatic teller machines* 自動取款機 **3** a person whose job is to count votes, especially in a parliament (尤指議會投票時的) 計票員 **4** (usually in compounds 通常構成複合詞) a person who tells stories, etc. 說…的人；敍述者；講故事的人；說書人： *a foul-mouthed teller of lies* 滿嘴髒話的撒謊者 ➲ see also FORTUNE-TELLER, STORYTELLER

tell·ing /'telɪŋ/ *adj.* **1** having a strong or important effect; effective 強有力的；有明顯效果的；顯著的： *a telling argument* 有力的論據 **2** showing effectively what sb/sth is really like, but often without intending to 生動的；顯露真實面目的，說明問題的 (通常並非有意)： *The number of homeless people is a telling comment on the state of society.* 無家可歸者的數量是社會狀況的生動寫照。▸ **tell·ing·ly** *adv.*

,telling-'off *noun* [usually sing.] (*pl.* **,tellings-'off**) (*BrE, informal*) the act of speaking angrily to sb, especially a child, because they have done sth bad (尤指對兒童的) 責備，責罵，數落，嗔怪

tell·tale /'telteɪl/ *adj., noun*

■ **adj.** [only before noun] showing that sth exists or has happened 暴露實情的；能說明問題的： *telltale clues/marks/signs/sounds* 能說明問題的種種線索／痕跡／跡象／聲響 ◇ *The telltale smell of cigarettes told her that he had been in the room.* 那股明顯的香煙味告訴她，他曾在這房間裏待過。

■ **noun** (*BrE*) (*NAmE* **tat·tle·tale**) (*informal, disapproving*) a child who tells an adult what another child has done wrong 向大人告另一個孩子狀的小孩兒；小告密者

tel·lur·ium /te'ljʊəriəm; *NAmE* te'lʊr-/ *noun* [U] (*symb.* **Te**) a chemical element. Tellurium is a shiny silver-white substance that breaks easily, found in SULPHIDE ORES. 碲

telly /'teli/ *noun* (*pl.* **-ies**) (*BrE, informal*) **1** [C] a television set 電視機 **SYN** **TV**： *He spends most evenings just sitting in front of the telly.* 他大部份晚上的時間都坐在電視機前。**2** [U] the programmes broadcast on television 電視節目 **SYN** **TV**： *daytime telly* 日間電視節目 ◇ *Is there anything good **on telly**?* 電視上有好的節目嗎？◇ *I don't want to **watch telly**.* 我不想看電視。

tel·net /'telnet/ *noun* [U] (*computing* 計) a computer system which allows you to use data and programs on another computer; a connection made using this system 遠程登陸系統，遠程登陸接線 (允許用戶使用主機數據和程序) ▸ **tel·net** *verb* (**-tt-**) [I, T] **~ (to) sth | ~ in**

Tel·ugu /'teləgu:/ *noun* [U] a language spoken in Andhra Pradesh in SE India 泰盧固語 (印度東南部安得拉邦的語言)

tem·blor /'temblə(r)/ *noun* (*NAmE*) an EARTHQUAKE (= a sudden, violent shaking of the earth's surface) 地震

tem·er·ity /tə'merəti/ *noun* [U] (*formal*) extremely confident behaviour that people are likely to consider rude 魯莽；冒失；蠻勇： *He **had the temerity to** call me a liar!* 他竟敢說我撒謊！

temp /temp/ *noun, verb, abbr.*

■ **noun** a temporary employee in an office 臨時雇員；臨時工

■ **verb** [I] (*informal*) to do a temporary job or a series of temporary jobs 打臨時工；做臨時工作；打零工： *I've been temping for an employment agency.* 我一直在一家職業介紹所做臨時工。➲ COLLOCATIONS at JOB

■ **abbr.** (also **temp.** especially in *NAmE*) temperature 溫度： *max temp 17 °C* 最高溫度 17 攝氏度

tem·per /'tempə(r)/ *noun, verb*

■ **noun** **1** [C, usually sing., U] if sb has a **temper**, they become angry very easily 脾氣；易怒的性情： *a violent/short/quick, etc. temper* 烈性子、急性子、火性子等 ◇ *He must learn to **control his temper**.* 他得學會捺住性子。◇ *She broke the plates in a **fit of temper**.* 她一氣之下把盤子摔碎了。◇ *After an hour of waiting, **tempers began to fray*** (= people began to get angry). 等了一個小時後，大夥兒開始冒火了。**2** [C, usually sing.] a short period of feeling very angry 怒氣；火氣；陣怒： *to **fly into a temper*** 勃然大怒 ◇ *She says awful things when she's **in a temper**.* 她一發脾氣說話就難聽。**3** [C] the way that you are feeling at a particular time 心情；情緒；性情；心境 **SYN** **mood**： *Come back when you're in a better temper.* 心情好些時再回來。◇ *to be **in a bad/foul, etc. temper*** 心情不好、很壞等 **4 -tempered** (in adjectives 構成形容詞) having a particular type of temper 有…脾氣的；心情…的： ***good-/bad-tempered*** 脾氣好的／壞的 ◇ *a sweet-tempered child* 性情溫和的小孩 **HELP** You will find other compounds ending in **-tempered** at their place in the alphabet. 其他以 -tempered 結尾的複合詞可在各字母中的適當位置查到。

IDM **lose/keep your 'temper (with sb)** to fail/manage to control your anger 發脾氣；忍住怒火： *She lost her temper with a customer and shouted at him.* 她對一位顧客發了脾氣，衝着人家大喊大叫。◇ *I struggle to keep my temper with the kids when they misbehave.* 孩子們淘氣時，我強捺住性子不發脾氣。➲ more at QUICK *adj.*

■ **verb** **1 ~ sth (with sth)** (*formal*) to make sth less severe by adding sth that has the opposite effect 使緩和；使溫和： *Justice must be tempered with mercy.* 法外尚需施恩。**2 ~ sth** (*technical* 術語) to make metal as hard as it needs to be by heating and then cooling it 使 (金屬) 回火

tem·pera /'tempərə/ *noun* [U] a kind of paint in which the colour is mixed with egg and water; a method of painting that uses this kind of paint 蛋彩畫顏料 (用顏料與雞蛋和水調和而成)；蛋彩畫法

tem·pera·ment /'temprəmənt/ *noun* **1** [C, U] a person's or an animal's nature as shown in the way they behave or react to situations or people (人或動物的) 氣質，性情，性格，稟性： *to have an artistic temperament* 有藝術家的氣質 ◇ *a horse with an excellent temperament* 性情溫順的馬 ◇ *She's a dreamer and a romantic **by***

temperament. 她生性異想天開，浪漫多情。 **2** [U] the tendency to get emotional and excited very easily and behave in an unreasonable way 易衝動；（性情）暴躁；喜怒無常：*an actor given to displays of temperament* 性情喜怒無常的演員

tem·pera·men·tal /ˌtemprəˈmentl/ *adj.* **1** (*usually disapproving*) having a tendency to become angry, excited or upset easily, and to behave in an unreasonable way 喜怒無常的；容易激動的；反覆無常的：*You never know what to expect with her. She's so temperamental.* 你永遠說不清她要幹什麼。她一時一變。◇ (*figurative*) *The printer's being temperamental this morning.* 今天上午這台打印機時好時壞。 **2** connected with sb's nature and personality 氣質的；性情的；性格的：*They are firm friends in spite of temperamental differences.* 他們儘管性格不同，但仍然友情甚篤。 ▸ **tem·pera·men·tal·ly** /-təli/ *adv.*：*I'm temperamentally unsuited to this job.* 我的性格不適合這種工作。

tem·per·ance /ˈtempərəns/ *noun* [U] **1** (*old-fashioned*) the practice of not drinking alcohol because of your moral or religious beliefs（由於道德或宗教信仰而實行的）戒酒，禁酒，滴酒不沾 **2** (*formal*) the practice of controlling your behaviour, the amount you eat, etc., so that it is always reasonable 自我克制；克己；節慾；節食 SYN **moderation**

tem·per·ate /ˈtempərət/ *adj.* **1** [usually before noun] (*technical* 術語) (of a climate or region 氣候或地區) having a mild temperature without extremes of heat or cold 氣候溫和的；溫帶的 **2** (*formal*) behaving in a calm and controlled way 溫和的；心平氣和的；自我克制的 OPP **intemperate** ▸ **tem·per·ate·ly** *adv.*

ˈtemperate zone *noun* [C, usually sing.] (*technical* 術語) an area of the Earth that is not near the EQUATOR or the South or North Pole 溫帶

tem·pera·ture 🔑 /ˈtemprətʃə(r); *NAmE* also -tʃʊr/ *noun* [C, U] (*abbr.* **temp**)

1 🔑 the measurement in degrees of how hot or cold a thing or place is 溫度；氣溫：***high/low temperatures*** 高／低溫 ◇ *a* ***fall/drop in temperature*** 氣溫下降 ◇ *a* ***rise in temperature*** 氣溫升高 ◇ *The temperature has risen (by) five degrees.* 溫度升高了五度。◇ *Heat the oven to a temperature of 200°C* (= degrees CENTIGRADE). 使烤箱的溫度升至200攝氏度。◇ *Some places have had temperatures in the 40s* (= over 40° CENTIGRADE). 有些地方氣溫曾經超過40攝氏度。 ➲ see also ABSOLUTE TEMPERATURE, ROOM TEMPERATURE **2** 🔑 the measurement of how hot sb's body is 體溫：*to* ***take sb's temperature*** (= measure the temperature of sb's body using a special instrument) 量體溫 ◇ (*BrE*) *Does he* ***have a temperature*** (= is it higher than normal, because of illness)? 他發燒嗎？◇ *She's* ***running a temperature*** (= it is higher than normal). 她在發燒。◇ *He's in bed with a temperature of 40°.* 他臥病在牀，高燒40攝氏度。 ➲ compare FEVER (1) HELP In *NAmE* you can *take sb's temperature* but in the other examples the word **fever** is used. 在美式英語中可以用 take sb's temperature，但在其他幾個例句中用 fever 一詞。

IDM **raise/lower the ˈtemperature** to increase/decrease the amount of excitement, emotion, etc. in a situation 升／降溫；增加／減少熱烈程度等：*His angry refusal to agree raised the temperature of the meeting.* 他憤然拒不同意，使得會議的氣氛緊張起來。

tem·pest /ˈtempɪst/ *noun* (*formal* or *literary*) a violent storm 大風暴；暴風雨；暴風雪

IDM **a tempest in a ˈteapot** (*NAmE*) (*BrE* **a storm in a ˈteacup**) a lot of anger or worry about sth that is not important 茶杯裏的風暴；大驚小怪；小題大做

tem·pes·tu·ous /temˈpestʃuəs/ *adj.* **1** (*formal*) full of extreme emotions 激烈的；狂暴的；騷動的 SYN **stormy**：*a tempestuous relationship* 衝突不斷的關係 **2** (*formal* or *literary*) caused by or affected by a violent storm 狂風暴雨的；大風暴的 SYN **stormy**：*tempestuous seas* 波濤洶湧的大海

tem·plate /ˈtempleɪt/ *noun* **1** a shape cut out of a hard material, used as a model for producing exactly the same shape many times in another material 樣板；模板；型板 **2** a thing that is used as a model for producing other similar examples 樣板；模框；標準：*If you need to write a lot of similar letters, set up a template on your computer.* 如果你需要寫許多類似的信件，就在計算機上設一個模板。

tem·ple /ˈtempl/ *noun* **1** a building used for the worship of a god or gods, especially in religions other than Christianity（尤指非基督教的）廟宇，寺院，神殿，聖堂：*the Temple of Diana at Ephesus* 以弗所的狄安娜神廟 ◇ *a* ***Buddhist/Hindu/Sikh temple*** 佛教／印度教／錫克教廟宇 ◇ (*NAmE*) *to go to temple* (= to a service in a SYNAGOGUE, where Jews worship) 去會堂禮拜 ➲ COLLOCATIONS at RELIGION **2** each of the flat parts at the sides of the head, at the same level as the eyes and higher 太陽穴；鬢角；顳顬；顳部：*He had black hair, greying at the temples.* 他的頭髮是黑色的，但兩鬢已見斑白。 ➲ VISUAL VOCAB page V59

tempo /ˈtempəʊ; *NAmE* -poʊ/ *noun* [C, U] (*pl.* **-os** or, in sense 1, *technical* 術語 **tempi** /ˈtempiː/) **1** the speed or rhythm of a piece of music（樂曲的）速度，拍子，節奏：*a* ***slow/fast tempo*** 慢／快速 ◇ *It's a difficult piece, with numerous changes of tempo.* 這支曲子節奏變化多，難度很大。 **2** the speed of any movement or activity（運動或活動的）速度，節奏 SYN **pace**：*the increasing tempo of life in Western society* 西方社會日益加速的生活節奏

tem·poral /ˈtempərəl/ *adj.* **1** (*formal*) connected with the real physical world, not spiritual matters 世間的；世俗的；現世的：*Although spiritual leader of millions of people, the Pope has no temporal power.* 教宗雖然是億萬人的精神領袖，但沒有絲毫的世俗權力。 **2** (*formal*) connected with or limited by time 時間的：*a universe which has spatial and temporal dimensions* 有時空維度的宇宙 **3** (*anatomy* 解) near the TEMPLE(S) at the side of the head 太陽穴的；顳的：*the right temporal lobe of the brain* 大腦右顳葉

tem·por·ary 🔑 AW /ˈtemprəri; *NAmE* -pəreri/ *adj.* lasting or intended to last or be used only for a short time; not permanent 短暫的；暫時的；臨時的：*temporary relief from pain* 短暫的解痛 ◇ *I'm looking for some* ***temporary work.*** 我在找個臨時工作。◇ *They had to move into* ***temporary accommodation.*** 他們不得不搬進臨時住所。◇ *a* ***temporary measure/solution/arrangement*** 臨時措施／解決辦法／安排 ◇ *More than half the staff are temporary.* 半數以上的職員是臨時雇員。 OPP **permanent** ▸ **tem·por·ar·ily** 🔑 AW /ˈtemprərəli; *NAmE* ˌtempəˈrerəli/ *adv.*：*We regret this service is temporarily unavailable.* 我們很抱歉暫時不能提供這一服務。 **tem·por·ari·ness** *noun* [U]

tem·por·ize (*BrE* also **-ise**) /ˈtempəraɪz/ *verb* [I] (*formal*) to delay making a decision or giving a definite answer, in order to gain time 拖延時間（不迅速作決定等）

tempt /tempt/ *verb* **1** to attract sb or make sb want to do or have sth, even if they know it is wrong 引誘；誘惑：**~ sb (into sth/into doing sth)** *I was tempted by the dessert menu.* 甜食菜單饞得我垂涎欲滴。◇ *Don't tempt thieves by leaving valuables clearly visible.* 別把貴重物品放在顯眼處招賊。◇ **~ sb to do sth** *I was tempted to take the day off.* 我動了心，想那一天休假。 **2** to persuade or try to persuade sb to do sth that you want them to do, for example by offering them sth 勸誘；鼓動；慫恿；利誘：**~ sb (into sth/into doing sth)** *How can we tempt young people into engineering?* 我們怎麼才能吸引年輕人學習工程學呢？◇ **~ sb to do sth** *Nothing would tempt me to live here.* 什麼也吸引不了我到這裏居住。

IDM **tempt ˈfate/ˈprovidence** to do sth too confidently in a way that might mean that your good luck will come to an end 玩命；冒險；魯莽

temp·ta·tion /tempˈteɪʃn/ *noun* **1** [C, U] the desire to do or have sth that you know is bad or wrong 引誘；誘惑：*the temptation of easy profits* 輕而易舉獲利的誘惑 ◇ *to* ***give way to/yield to temptation*** 經不住誘惑 ◇ *I couldn't* ***resist the temptation*** *to open the letter.* 我抑制不住好奇心把信打開了。◇ *Don't* ***put temptation in her way*** *by offering her a cigarette.* 別遞煙來引誘她。 **2** [C] a thing that makes sb want to do or have sth that

T

they know is bad or wrong 煽誘人的事物：*An expensive bicycle is a temptation to thieves.* 高檔自行車對竊賊是個誘惑。

tempt·er /ˈtemptə(r)/ *noun* a person who tries to persuade sb to do sth, especially sth bad or wrong 引誘者；誘惑者

tempt·ing /ˈtemptɪŋ/ *adj.* something that is **tempting** is attractive, and makes people want to have it, do it, etc. 吸引人的；誘人的；有吸引力的：*It was a tempting offer.* 這是個誘人的提議。◊ *That cake looks very tempting.* 那蛋糕的樣子讓人嘴饞。◊ *It's tempting to speculate about what might have happened.* 大家不禁猜測，到底發生了什麼事。▶ **tempt·ing·ly** *adv.*

temp·tress /ˈtemptrəs/ *noun* (*old-fashioned* or *humorous*) a woman who TEMPTS sb, especially one who deliberately makes a man want to have sex with her 勾引人的女人；蕩婦

tem·pura /ˈtempʊrə; temˈpuːrə/ *noun* [U, C] a Japanese dish consisting of pieces of vegetables or fish that have been fried in BATTER (= a mixture of flour, egg and water) 天麩羅（日本麪拖油炸蔬菜或魚）

ten 0ꟷ /ten/ *number*
10 十 **HELP** There are examples of how to use numbers at the entry for **five**. 數詞用法示例見 five 條。
IDM **ˌten out of ˈten (for sth)** (*BrE*, often *ironic*) used to say that sb has guessed sth correctly or done sth very well 完全正確；得滿分：*Not brilliant, Robyn, but I'll give you ten out of ten for effort.* 做得不算頂好，羅賓，但要論賣力氣我給你打滿分。**ˌten to ˈone** very probably 十之八九；非常可能：*Ten to one he'll be late.* 十之八九他會遲到。

ten·able /ˈtenəbl/ *adj.* **1** (of a theory, an opinion, etc. 理論、想法等) easy to defend against attack or criticism 說得過去的；站得住腳的：*a tenable position* 說得過去的觀點 ◊ *The old idea that this work was not suitable for women was no longer tenable.* 這種工作不適合婦女的舊想法再也站不住腳了。**OPP** **untenable** **2** [not before noun] (of a job, position, etc., especially in a university 尤指大學中的工作、職位等) that can be held for a particular period of time 可保有，可保持，可擔任（一段時間）：*The lectureship is tenable for a period of three years.* 講師這一職務任期三年。

ten·acious /təˈneɪʃəs/ *adj.* (*formal*) **1** that does not stop holding sth or give up sth easily; determined 緊握的；不鬆手的；堅持的：*a tenacious grip* 緊握 ◊ *She's a tenacious woman. She never gives up.* 她是個堅毅的人，從不放棄。◊ *The party has kept its tenacious hold on power for more than twenty years.* 這個政黨已牢牢掌握大權二十多年。**2** continuing to exist, have influence, etc. for longer than you might expect 頑強的；堅忍不拔的 **SYN** **persistent**：*a tenacious illness* 頑症 ▶ **ten·acious·ly** *adv.*：*Though seriously ill, he still clings tenaciously to life.* 他雖然病情嚴重，但仍然頑強地活着。**ten·acity** /təˈnæsəti/ *noun* [U]：*They competed with skill and tenacity.* 他們競爭靠的是技術和頑強意志。

ten·ancy /ˈtenənsi/ *noun* (*pl.* **-ies**) **1** [C] (*BrE*) a period of time that you rent a house, land, etc. for（房屋、土地等的）租用期限，租賃期限，租期：*a three-month tenancy* 三個月的租期 ◊ *a tenancy agreement* 租賃協議 ➲ COLLOCATIONS at HOUSE **2** [C, U] the right to live or work in a building or on land that you rent（房屋或土地的）租用，租賃：*They had taken over the tenancy of the farm.* 他們承租了那個農場。

ten·ant /ˈtenənt/ *noun, verb*
■ ***noun*** a person who pays rent for the use of a room, building, land, etc. to the person who owns it 房客；租戶；佃戶：*They had evicted their tenants for non-payment of rent.* 他們趕走了未交房租的房客。◊ *The decorating was done by a previous tenant.* 裝修是一位前房客搞的。◊ *tenant farmers* (= ones who do not own their own farms) 佃農 ➲ COLLOCATIONS at HOUSE
■ ***verb*** [usually passive] **~ sth** to live or work in a place as a tenant（作為租賃者）居住，工作：*a tenanted farm* 租種的農場

tench /tentʃ/ *noun* (*pl.* **tench**) a European FRESHWATER fish 丁鱥（歐洲的一種淡水魚）

tend 0ꟷ /tend/ *verb*
1 0ꟷ [I] **~ to do sth** to be likely to do sth or to happen in a particular way because this is what often or usually happens 往往會；常常就：*Women tend to live longer than men.* 女人往往比男人長壽。◊ *When I'm tired, I tend to make mistakes.* 我累了就容易出錯。◊ *It tends to get very cold here in the winter.* 這裏冬天往往會很冷。◊ *People **tend to think** that the problem will never affect them.* 人們往往認為這個問題絕不會影響到他們。➲ LANGUAGE BANK at GENERALLY **2** [I] **~ (to/towards sth)** to take a particular direction or often have a particular quality 趨向；走向；傾向；趨於：*His views tend towards the extreme.* 他的觀點趨於偏激。◊ *Prices have tended downwards over recent years.* 近年來物價趨於下降。**3** [T, I] to care for sb/sth 照料；照管；護理：**~ sb/sth** *a shepherd tending his sheep* 照看羊的牧人 ◊ *Doctors and nurses tended the injured.* 醫生和護士護理受傷者。◊ *well-tended gardens* 精心照料的花園 ◊ **~ to sb/sth** *Ambulance crews were tending to the injured.* 救護車上的救護人員在照料受傷者。**4** [T] **~ sth** (*NAmE*) to serve customers in a store, bar, etc. 招待，侍候，照顧，照料（商店、酒吧等的顧客）：*He had a job **tending bar** in San Francisco.* 他在舊金山做酒吧服務員。

ten·dency 0ꟷ /ˈtendənsi/ *noun* (*pl.* **-ies**)
1 0ꟷ [C] if sb/sth has a particular **tendency**, they are likely to behave or act in a particular way 傾向；偏好；性情：*to **display** artistic, etc. **tendencies*** 顯示出對藝術等的偏好 ◊ **~ (for sb/sth) (to do sth)** *I **have a tendency** to talk too much when I'm nervous.* 我緊張時總愛嘮叨。◊ *There is a tendency for this disease to run in families.* 這種疾病易在家族裏遺傳。◊ **~ (to/towards sth)** *She has a strong natural tendency towards caution.* 她天生喜歡小心謹慎。**2** 0ꟷ [C] **~ (for sb/sth) (to do sth)** | **~ (to/towards sth)** a new custom that is starting to develop 趨勢；趨向 **SYN** **trend**：*There is a growing tendency among employers to hire casual staff.* 雇主雇用臨時職員有增加的趨勢。**3** [C+sing./pl. v.] (*BrE*) a group within a larger political group, whose views are more extreme than those of the rest of the group（政黨內的）極端派別

ten·den·tious /tenˈdenʃəs/ *adj.* (*formal*, usually *disapproving*) (of a speech, piece of writing, theory, etc. 演講、文章、理論等) expressing a strong opinion that people are likely to disagree with 傾向性的；有偏見的；有爭議的 **SYN** **controversial** ▶ **ten·den·tious·ly** *adv.* **SYN** **controversially** **ten·den·tious·ness** *noun* [U]

ten·der /ˈtendə(r)/ *adj., noun, verb*
■ ***adj.*** (**ten·derer**, **ten·derest**) **HELP** **More tender** and **most tender** are also common. * more tender 和 most tender 也常用。**1** kind, gentle and loving 和善的；溫柔的；親切的；慈愛的：*tender words* 親切的話語 ◊ *What he needs now is a lot of **tender loving care*** (= sympathetic treatment). 他現在需要的是充分的關心和愛護。**2** (of food 食物) easy to bite through and cut 嫩的；柔軟的：*This meat is extremely tender.* 這肉嫩得很。**OPP** **tough 3** (of part of the body 身體部位) painful when you touch it 疼痛的；一觸即痛的 **SYN** **sore** **4** easily hurt or damaged 易損壞的；纖弱的；脆弱的 **SYN** **delicate**：*tender young plants* 嬌嫩的幼苗 ▶ **ten·der·ly** *adv.* **ten·der·ness** *noun* [U]
IDM **at a ˌtender ˈage** | **at the tender age of ...** used in connection with sb who is still young and does not have much experience 在少不更事的…歲時；在不諳世故的…歲上：*He left home at the tender age of 15.* 他 15 歲離家，還少不更事。◊ *She shouldn't be having to deal with problems like this **at such a tender age**.* 她小小年紀涉世未深，實在無須處理這樣的問題。
■ ***noun*** **1** a formal offer to supply goods or do work at a stated price 投標 **SYN** **bid**：*Cleaning services have been **put out to tender*** (= companies have been asked to make offers to supply these services). 清潔工作已經對外招標。◊ *a competitive tender* 具有競爭力的投標 **2** a truck attached to a steam engine, carrying fuel and water（蒸汽機車的）煤水車 **3** a small boat, used for carrying people or goods between a larger boat and land（在大船和口岸之間載運人或貨物的）供應船，補給船，交通船

■ *verb* **1** [I] **~ (for sth)** to make a formal offer to supply goods or do work at a stated price 投標： *Local firms were invited to tender for the building contract.* 當地的公司被邀請投標承包建築工程。 **2** [T] **~ sth (to sb)** (*formal*) to offer or give sth to sb 提議；提供；提出： *He has* ***tendered his resignation*** *to the Prime Minister.* 他已向首相遞交辭呈。

tend·er·foot /ˈtendəfʊt; *NAmE* -dərf-/ *noun* (*pl.* **tend·er·feet** or **tend·er·foots**) (*NAmE, informal*) a person who is new to sth and not experienced 新手；初學者 **SYN** **greenhorn**

ˌtender-ˈhearted *adj.* having a kind and gentle nature 善良的；心腸軟的；有惻隱之心的

ten·der·ize (*BrE* also **-ise**) /ˈtendəraɪz/ *verb* **~ sth** to make meat softer and easier to cut and eat by preparing it in a particular way 使（肉）變嫩；使（肉）變軟

ten·der·loin /ˈtendəlɔɪn; *NAmE* -dərl-/ *noun* [U] good quality meat from the back or side of a cow or pig （牛、豬的）裏脊肉，嫩腰肉

ten·don /ˈtendən/ *noun* a strong band of TISSUE in the body that joins a muscle to a bone 腱 ➲ COLLOCATIONS at INJURY

ten·dril /ˈtendrəl/ *noun* **1** a thin curling STEM that grows from a climbing plant. A plant uses tendrils to attach itself to a wall or other support. （攀緣植物的）捲鬚 ➲ VISUAL VOCAB page V11 **2** (*literary*) a thin curling piece of sth such as hair 捲鬚狀物（如鬈髮）

tene·ment /ˈtenəmənt/ *noun* a large building divided into flats/apartments, especially in a poor area of a city （尤指城市貧困區的）經濟公寓，廉租公寓： *a tenement block* 經濟住宅街區

tenet /ˈtenɪt/ *noun* (*formal*) one of the principles or beliefs that a theory or larger set of beliefs is based on 原則；信條；教義： *one of the* ***basic/central tenets*** *of Christianity* 基督教的基本／主要信條之一

ten·fold /ˈtenfəʊld; *NAmE* -foʊld/ *adj., adv.* ➲ -FOLD

ˌten-gallon ˈhat *noun* a large hat with a broad BRIM, traditionally worn by COWBOYS 高頂寬邊帽（傳統牛仔帽）

ten·ner /ˈtenə(r)/ *noun* (*BrE, informal*) £10 or a ten-pound note 十英鎊；十英鎊鈔票： *You can have it for a tenner.* 你出十英鎊，這就歸你了。

ten·nis /ˈtenɪs/ (also *formal* **ˌlawn ˈtennis**) *noun* [U] a game in which two or four players use RACKETS to hit a ball backwards and forwards across a net on a specially marked COURT 網球 ➲ VISUAL VOCAB page V45： *to play tennis* 打網球 ◇ *a* ***tennis player/tournament/club/court*** 網球運動員／錦標賽／俱樂部／場

ˌtennis ˈelbow *noun* [U] painful swelling of the elbow caused by too much repeated twisting of the arm 網球肘（胳膊經常扭動引起的肘部腫痛）

ˈtennis racket (also **ˈtennis rac·quet**) *noun* the RACKET that you use when you play tennis 網球拍

ˈtennis shoe (*NAmE* also **athˈletic shoe**) *noun* a sports shoe that is made of strong cotton cloth or leather 網球鞋

tenon /ˈtenən/ *noun* (*technical* 術語) an end of a piece of wood that has been cut to fit into a MORTISE so that the two are held together 雄榫；凸榫；榫舌

tenor /ˈtenə(r)/ *noun, adj.*

■ *noun* **1** [C] a man's singing voice with a range just below the lowest woman's voice; a man with a tenor voice 男高音；男高音歌手 ➲ compare ALTO *n.*, BARITONE (1), BASS[1] *n.* (2), COUNTERTENOR **2** [sing.] a musical part written for a tenor voice 男高音部 **3** [sing.] **the ~ of sth** (*formal*) the general character or meaning of sth 大意；要旨；要領： *I was encouraged by the general tenor of his remarks.* 他的話中的要點使我深受鼓舞。

■ *adj.* [only before noun] (of a musical instrument 樂器) with a range of notes similar to that of a tenor voice 次中音的： *a tenor saxophone* 次中音薩克斯管 ➲ compare ALTO *adj.*, BASS[1] *adj.*, SOPRANO *adj.*

ˌten ˈpence (also **ˌten pence ˈpiece**, **10p** /ˌten ˈpiː/) *noun* a British coin worth ten pence 十便士硬幣： *Have you got a ten pence piece?* 你有一枚十便士的硬幣嗎？

ten·pin /ˈtenpɪn/ *noun* **1** [C] any of the ten bottle-shaped objects that players try to knock over in the game of TENPIN BOWLING （十柱保齡球戲中的）瓶形滾柱，木瓶 **2 ten·pins** [U] (*NAmE*) = TENPIN BOWLING

ˌtenpin ˈbowling (*NAmE* also **ten·pins**) *noun* [U] a game in which players try to knock over tenpins by rolling a heavy ball at them, played indoors, especially in a BOWLING ALLEY 十柱保齡球戲 ➲ VISUAL VOCAB page V40 ➲ compare SKITTLE

tense **AW** /tens/ *adj., noun, verb*

■ *adj.* **1** (of a person 人) nervous or worried, and unable to relax 神經緊張的；擔心的；不能鬆弛的： *He's a very tense person.* 他是個神經非常緊張的人。◇ *She sounded tense and angry.* 她的聲音聽起來又氣又急。 **2** (of a situation, an event, a period of time, etc. 形勢、事件、時期等) in which people have strong feelings such as worry, anger, etc. that often cannot be expressed openly 令人緊張的（或焦慮的、滿腹憤懣的等）： *I spent a tense few weeks waiting for the results of the tests.* 等候測試結果的這幾個星期裏我寢食不安。◇ *The atmosphere in the meeting was getting more and more tense.* 會議的氣氛越來越緊張。 **3** (of a muscle or other part of the body 肌肉或身體部位) tight rather than relaxed 繃緊的；不鬆弛的： *A massage will relax those tense muscles.* 按摩會使緊張的肌肉鬆弛。 **4** (of wire, etc. 金屬絲等) stretched tightly 拉緊的；繃緊的 **SYN** **taut** **5** (*phonetics* 語音) (of a speech sound 語音) produced with the muscles of the speech organs stretched tight 緊的；緊音性的 **OPP** **lax** ▶ **tense·ly** **AW** *adv.* **tense·ness** *noun* [U]

■ *noun* (*grammar* 語法) any of the forms of a verb that may be used to show the time of the action or state expressed by the verb （動詞的）時，時態： *the* ***past/present/future tense*** 過去／現在／將來時態

■ *verb* [T, I] if you **tense** your muscles, or you or your muscles **tense**, they become tight and stiff, especially because you are not relaxed （使肌肉）拉緊，繃緊： **~ sth/yourself (up)** *She tensed her muscles in anticipation of the blow.* 眼看要捱打，她繃緊了肌肉。◇ *He tensed himself, listening to see if anyone had followed him.* 他繃緊神經，仔細聽是否有人跟踪自己。◇ **~ (up)** *His muscles tensed as he got ready to run.* 他準備起跑時肌肉繃緊了。◇ *She tensed, hearing the strange noise again.* 再次聽到那個奇怪的聲音，她緊張起來。

IDM **be/get tensed ˈup** to become or feel nervous or worried so that you cannot relax 變得神經緊張；變得焦慮不安

ten·sile /ˈtensaɪl; *NAmE* ˈtensl/ *adj.* (*technical* 術語) **1** [only before noun] used to describe the extent to which sth can stretch without breaking 張力的；拉力的；抗張的： *the* ***tensile strength*** *of rope* 繩索的抗拉強度 **2** that can be drawn out or stretched 可拉長的；能伸長的；可延展的： *tensile cable* 可伸延的電纜

ten·sion 0‑w **AW** /ˈtenʃn/ *noun, verb*

■ *noun* **1** 0‑w [U, C, usually pl.] **~ (between A and B)** a situation in which people do not trust each other, or feel unfriendly towards each other, and which may cause them to attack each other 緊張局勢（或關係、狀況）： *There is mounting tension along the border.* 邊境局勢日趨緊張。◇ ***international/racial/political tensions*** 國際緊張局勢；種族間的緊張關係；政治上的緊張狀況 **2** [C, U] **~ (between A and B)** a situation in which the fact that there are different needs or interests causes difficulties 矛盾；對立： *There is often a tension between the aims of the company and the wishes of the employees.* 公司的目標和雇員的願望之間經常存在矛盾。 **3** 0‑w [U] a feeling of anxiety and stress that makes it impossible to relax （情緒上的）緊張，煩躁： ***nervous tension*** 神經緊張 ◇ *We laughed and that helped* ***ease the tension***. 我們笑了，因而使緊張的情緒緩和下來。 ➲ SYNONYMS at PRESSURE **4** [U] the feeling of fear and excitement that is created by a writer or a film/movie director（作家或電影導演製造的）緊張氣氛： *dramatic tension* 扣人心弦的

T

緊張氣氛 ◇ *As the movie progresses the tension builds.* 隨着電影劇情的發展，氣氛越來越緊張。 **5** [U] the state of being stretched tight; the extent to which sth is stretched tight 拉伸；張力；拉緊狀態；繃緊程度：*muscular tension* 肌肉繃緊 ◇ *Adjust the string tension of your tennis racket to suit your style of playing.* 調節網球拍的網張力，以配合你的打法。 ➲ see also SURFACE TENSION

■ ***verb* ~ sth** (*technical* 術語) to make a wire, sail, etc. tight and stretched（使金屬線、帆等）拉緊，繃緊

ten·sor /ˈtensə(r); -sɔː(r)/ *noun* (*anatomy* 解) a muscle that TIGHTENS or stretches part of the body 張肌

tent 🔑 /tent/ *noun* a shelter made of a large sheet of CANVAS, NYLON, etc. that is supported by poles and ropes fixed to the ground, and is used especially for camping 帳篷；帳棚：*to* ***put up/take down a tent*** 搭帳篷；拆帳篷 ◇ *to* ***pitch*** (= put up) ***a tent*** 搭帳篷 ◇ *Food will be served in the* ***hospitality tent*** (= for example at an outdoor show). 招待帳篷將有食物供應。 ➲ see also A-FRAME TENT, DOME TENT, FRAME TENT, OXYGEN TENT, PUP TENT, RIDGE TENT, WALL TENT

ten·tacle /ˈtentəkl/ *noun* **1** [C] a long thin part of the body of some creatures, such as SQUID, used for feeling or holding things, for moving or for getting food 觸角；觸手；觸鬚：(*figurative*) *Tentacles of fear closed around her body.* 恐懼的陰影籠罩着她。 ➲ VISUAL VOCAB page V13 **2 tentacles** [pl.] (usually *disapproving*) the influence that a large place, organization or system has and that is hard to avoid（大的地方、組織或系統難以避免的）影響，束縛，約束：*The tentacles of satellite television are spreading even wider.* 衞星電視的影響正日益擴大。

ten·ta·tive /ˈtentətɪv/ *adj.* **1** (of an arrangement, agreement, etc. 安排、協議等) not definite or certain because you may want to change it later 不確定的；不肯定的；暫定的：*We made a* ***tentative arrangement*** *to meet on Friday.* 我們暫定星期五見面。◇ *tentative conclusions* 初步結論 **2** not behaving or done with confidence 躊躇的；猶豫不定的；不果斷的 SYN **hesitant**：*a tentative greeting* 怯聲怯氣的問候 ◇ *I'm taking the first* ***tentative steps*** *towards fitness.* 我試探性地開始實施健身計劃。 ▸ **ten·ta·tive·ly** *adv.* **ten·ta·tive·ness** *noun* [U]

tent·ed /ˈtentɪd/ *adj.* consisting of tents; like a tent 由帳篷組成的；帳篷狀的：*a tented village* 帳篷村

ten·ter·hooks /ˈtentəhʊks; *NAmE* -tərh-/ *noun* [pl.]
IDM **(be) on ˈtenterhooks** (*NAmE* also **be on ˌpins and ˈneedles**) (to be) very anxious or excited while you are waiting to find out sth or see what will happen 坐立不安；如坐針氈：*I've been on tenterhooks all week waiting for the results.* 整個星期我都在坐立不安，等待結果出來。 ORIGIN From **tenterhook**, a hook which in the past was used to keep material stretched on a drying frame during manufacture. 源自 tenterhook（拉幅鈎），是過去把生產中的布料綳在乾燥架上的一種鈎子。

tenth 🔑 /tenθ/ *ordinal number, noun*
■ ***ordinal number*** 🔑 10th 第十 HELP There are examples of how to use ordinal numbers at the entry for **fifth**. 序數詞用法示例見 fifth 條。
■ ***noun*** 🔑 each of ten equal parts of sth 十分之一
IDM see POSSESSION

ˈtent peg *noun* = PEG *n.* (2) ➲ picture at PEG

tenu·ous /ˈtenjuəs/ *adj.* **1** so weak or uncertain that it hardly exists 脆弱的；微弱的；縹緲的：*a tenuous hold on life* 命若游絲 ◇ *His links with the organization turned out to be, at best, tenuous.* 最後證實他與這個組織的關係充其量不過是不即不離罷了。 **2** extremely thin and easily broken 纖細的；薄的；易斷的 ▸ **tenu·ous·ly** *adv.*

ten·ure /ˈtenjə(r)/ *noun* [U] **1** the period of time when sb holds an important job, especially a political one; the act of holding an important job（尤指重要政治職務的）任期，任職：*his four-year tenure as President* 他的四年總統任期 ◇ *She knew that tenure of high political office was beyond her.* 她知道自己與顯赫的政治地位無緣。 **2** the right to stay permanently in your job, especially as a teacher at a university（尤指大學教師的）終身職位，長期聘用：*It's still extremely difficult to get tenure.* 要取得終身職位仍然極其困難。 **3** the legal right to live in a house or use a piece of land（房地產的）保有權，保有期

ten·ured /ˈtenjəd; *NAmE* -jərd/ *adj.* [usually before noun] **1** (of an official job 公職) that you can keep permanently 終身的；長期保有的：*a tenured post* 終身職位 **2** (of a person, especially a teacher at a university 尤指大學教師) having the right to keep their job permanently 獲終身聘用的；享有終身職位的：*a tenured professor* 終身教授

tepee (also **tee·pee**) /ˈtiːpiː/ *noun* a type of tall tent shaped like a CONE, used by Native Americans in the past（美洲印第安人舊時使用的）圓錐形帳篷 ➲ see also WIGWAM

tepid /ˈtepɪd/ *adj.* **1** slightly warm, sometimes in a way that is not pleasant 不冷不熱的；微溫的；溫吞的 SYN **lukewarm**：*tepid tea* 溫吞的茶 ◇ *a tepid bath* 溫水浴 ➲ SYNONYMS at COLD **2** not enthusiastic 不熱情的；不熱烈的 SYN **lukewarm**：*The play was greeted with tepid applause.* 這台戲只得到了零落的掌聲。

te·quila /təˈkiːlə/ *noun* **1** [U] a strong alcoholic drink made in Mexico from a tropical plant 龍舌蘭酒，特奎拉酒（墨西哥產的一種烈性酒） **2** [C] a glass of tequila 一杯龍舌蘭酒

tera- /ˈterə/ *combining form* (in nouns; used in units of measurement 構成名詞，用於計量單位) **1** 10^{12}, or 1 000 000 000 000 萬億，太（拉）（十進制，等於 1 000 000 000 000） **2** 2^{40}, or 1 099 511 627 776 太（拉）（二進制，等於 1 099 511 627 776）

tera·bit /ˈterəbɪt/ *noun* (*abbr.* **Tb**, **Tbit**) (*computing* 計) **1** a unit of computer memory or data, equal to one million million, or 10^{12} (= 1 000 000 000 000) BITS 萬億比特，太比特（十進制計算機內存或數據單位，等於 1 000 000 000 000 比特） **2** (also **tebi·bit**) a unit of computer memory or data, equal to 2^{40} (= 1 099 511 627 776) BITS 太比特（二進制計算機內存或數據單位，等於 1 099 511 627 776 比特）

tera·byte /ˈterəbaɪt/ *noun* (*abbr.* **TB**) (*computing* 計) **1** a unit of computer memory or data, equal to one million million, or 10^{12} (= 1 000 000 000 000) BYTES 萬億字節，太字節（十進制計算機內存或數據的單位，等於 1 000 000 000 000 字節） **2** (also **tebi·byte**) a unit of computer memory or data, equal to 2^{40} (= 1 099 511 627 776) BYTES 太字節（二進制計算機內存或數據的單位，等於 1 099 511 627 776 字節）

ter·bium /ˈtɜːbiəm; *NAmE* ˈtɜːrb-/ *noun* [U] (*symb.* **Tb**) a chemical element. Terbium is a silver-white metal used in LASERS, X-RAYS and television TUBES. 鋱

ter·cen·ten·ary /ˌtɜːsenˈtiːnəri; *NAmE* ˌtɜːrsenˈtenəri/ *noun* (*pl.* **-ies**) the 300th anniversary of sth 三百週年紀念：*the tercentenary of the school's foundation* 建校三百週年紀念 ◇ *tercentenary celebrations* 三百週年慶典

ter·gi·ver·sate /ˈtɜːdʒɪvəseɪt; ˌtɜːdʒɪˈvɜːseɪt; *NAmE* tərˈdʒɪvərseɪt; ˈtɜːrdʒɪvərseɪt/ *verb* (*formal*) **1** [I] to make statements that deliberately hide the truth or that avoid answering a question directly（說話）含糊其詞，支吾，迴避事實 **2** [I] to stop being loyal to one person, group, or religion and begin to support another 改變立場；背叛；變節 ▸ **ter·gi·ver·sa·tion** /ˌtɜːdʒɪvəˈseɪʃn; *NAmE* ˌtɜːrdʒɪvərˈseɪʃn/ *noun* [U]

teri·yaki /ˌteriˈjɑːki; *BrE* also -ˈjæki/ *noun* [U, C] a Japanese dish consisting of meat or fish that has been left in a sweet sauce and then cooked 照燒（日本烹調方法，將肉或魚加甜味醬汁燒烤）

term 🔑 /tɜːm; *NAmE* tɜːrm/ *noun, verb*
■ ***noun*** ➲ see also TERMS **1** 🔑 [C] a word or phrase used as the name of sth, especially one connected with a particular type of language 詞語；術語；措辭：*a* ***technical/legal/scientific, etc. term*** 技術、法律、科學等術語 ◇ *a term of abuse* 咒罵用語 ◇ *'Register' is the term commonly used to describe different levels of formality in language.* "語域"是一個術語，通常用以描述語言中用語的正式程度。 ➲ SYNONYMS at WORD ➲ LANGUAGE BANK at DEFINE **2** 🔑 (*NAmE* also **tri·mes·ter**) [C, U] (especially in Britain) one of the three periods in the year during

T

which classes are held in schools, universities, etc. 學期（尤用於英國，學校一年分三個學期）：*the* ***spring/summer/autumn/fall term*** 春季／夏季／秋季學期◇ *Many students now have paid employment* ***during term.*** 現在許多學生在上學期間就從事有薪工作。◇ (*BrE*) *It's nearly the* ***end of term.*** 學期快要結束了。◇ (*NAmE*) *the* ***end of the term*** 期終 ➲ see also SEMESTER, TERMLY, TERM-TIME **3** 🔑 [C] a period of time for which sth lasts; a fixed or limited time 期；期限；任期：*during the president's first* ***term of/in office*** 在總統的首屆任期內◇ *He faces a maximum* ***prison/jail term*** *of 25 years.* 他面臨 25 年的最高刑期。◇ *a long term of imprisonment* 長期監禁 **4** [sing.] (*formal*) the end of a particular period of time, especially one for which an agreement, etc. lasts 到期；期滿：*the term of the loan* 貸款期限◇ *His life had reached its natural term.* 他已盡其天年。(*medical* 醫) *The pregnancy went to* ***full term*** (= lasted the normal length of time). 那次懷孕到了足月。**5** [C] (*mathematics* 數) each of the various parts in a series, an EQUATION, etc. （數列、方程等的）項

IDM **in terms of | in ... terms** ➲ IN TERMS OF at TERMS **in the 'long/'short/'medium term** used to describe what will happen a long, short, etc. time in the future 長／短／中期內：*Such a development seems unlikely, at least in the short term* (= it will not happen for quite a long time). 這樣的發展看來可能性不大，起碼短期之內應當如此。➲ see also LONG-TERM, MEDIUM-TERM, SHORT-TERM

■ ***verb*** [often passive] **~ sb/sth + noun/adj.** (*formal*) to use a particular name or word to describe sb/sth 把…稱為；把…叫做：*At his age, he can hardly be termed a young man.* 到了這個年紀，他稱不上是年輕人了。◇ *REM sleep is termed 'active' sleep.* 快速眼動睡眠稱作"主動"睡眠。

ter·ma·gant /ˈtɜːməɡənt; *NAmE* ˈtɜːrm-/ *noun* (*formal*) a woman who is very strict or who tries to tell people what to do, in an unpleasant way 苛刻的女人；專橫的女人

ter·min·al **AW** /ˈtɜːmɪnl; *NAmE* ˈtɜːrm-/ *noun, adj.*

■ ***noun*** **1** a building or set of buildings at an airport where air passengers arrive and leave 航空站；航空終點站：*A second terminal was opened in 2008.* 第二個航空站是 2008 年開始運營的。**2** a place, building or set of buildings where journeys by train, bus or boat begin or end （火車、公共汽車或船的）終點站：*a* ***railway/bus/ferry terminal*** 鐵路／公共汽車終點站；渡船碼頭 **3** (*computing* 計) a piece of equipment, usually consisting of a keyboard and a screen that joins the user to a central computer system 終端；終端機 **4** (*technical* 術語) a point at which connections can be made in an electric CIRCUIT （電路的）端子，線接頭：*a* ***positive/negative terminal*** 正極／負極端子

■ ***adj.*** **1** (of an illness or a disease 疾病) that cannot be cured and will lead to death, often slowly 晚期的；不治的；致命的：*He has terminal lung cancer.* 他患有晚期肺癌。◇ *The illness is usually terminal.* 這種病通常為不治之症。◇ (*figurative*) *She's suffering from terminal* (= very great) *boredom.* 她現在感到煩得要死。**2** (of a person 人) suffering from an illness that cannot be cured and will lead to death 病危的；臨終的；晚期的：*a terminal patient* 晚期病人 **3** certain to get worse and come to an end 不可救藥的；無可挽回的：*The industry* ***is in terminal decline.*** 這個行業每況愈下，一蹶不振。**4** [only before noun] (*formal* or *technical* 術語) at the end of sth 末端的；末梢的：*a terminal branch of a tree* 樹頂枝條◇ *terminal examinations* (= at the end of a course, etc.) 期終考試 ▸ **ter·min·al·ly** /-nəli/ *adv.*：*a hospice for the terminally ill* 臨終病人安養所◇ *a terminally dull film* 索然寡味的影片

ter·min·ate **AW** /ˈtɜːmɪneɪt; *NAmE* ˈtɜːrm-/ *verb* (*formal*) **1** [I, T] to end; to make sth end （使）停止，結束，終止：*Your contract of employment terminates in December.* 你的聘約十二月份到期。◇ **~ sth** *The agreement was terminated immediately.* 那項協議立即被終止了。◇ *to terminate a pregnancy* (= to perform or have an ABORTION) 終止妊娠（墮胎）**2** [I] (of a bus or train 公共汽車或火車) to end a journey/trip 到達終點站：*This train terminates at London Victoria.* 這趟列車的終點站是倫敦維多利亞火車站。

ter·min·ation **AW** /ˌtɜːmɪˈneɪʃn; *NAmE* ˌtɜːrm-/ *noun* **1** [U, C] (*formal*) the act of ending sth; the end of sth 結束；終止；末端；端：*Failure to comply with these conditions will result in termination of the contract.* 違反這些條件將導致合同終止。**2** [C] (*medical* 醫) a medical operation to end a PREGNANCY at an early stage 終止妊娠 **SYN** **abortion**

ter·min·ology /ˌtɜːmɪˈnɒlədʒi; *NAmE* ˌtɜːrməˈnɑːl-/ *noun* (*pl.* **-ies**) **1** [U, C] the set of technical words or expressions used in a particular subject （某學科的）術語：*medical terminology* 醫學術語 ➲ SYNONYMS at LANGUAGE **2** [U] words used with particular meanings 有特別含義的用語；專門用語：*The disagreement arose over a different use of terminology.* 分歧的緣起在於專門用語使用的不同。➲ SYNONYMS at LANGUAGE ▸ **ter·mino·logic·al** /ˌtɜːmɪnəˈlɒdʒɪkl; *NAmE* ˌtɜːrmənəˈlɑːdʒ-/ *adj.*

ter·minus /ˈtɜːmɪnəs; *NAmE* ˈtɜːrm-/ *noun* (*pl.* **ter·mini** /ˈtɜːmɪnaɪ; *NAmE* ˈtɜːrm-/) the last station at the end of a railway/railroad line or the last stop on a bus route （鐵路或公共汽車路線的）終點站

ter·mite /ˈtɜːmaɪt; *NAmE* ˈtɜːrm-/ *noun* an insect that lives in organized groups, mainly in hot countries. Termites do a lot of damage by eating the wood of trees and buildings. 白蟻：*a termite colony* 白蟻群

term·ly /ˈtɜːmli; *NAmE* ˈtɜːrm-/ *adj.* (*BrE*) happening in each of the periods that the school or college year is divided into 每學期的：*termly reports* 學期成績報告單

'term paper *noun* (in an American school or college) a long piece of written work that a student does on a subject that is part of a course of study （美國學校或大學的）學期論文

terms /tɜːmz; *NAmE* tɜːrmz/ *noun* [pl.] **1** the conditions that people offer, demand or accept when they make an agreement, an arrangement or a contract （協議、合同等的）條件，條款：*peace terms* 和平條件◇ ***Under the terms of the agreement,*** *their funding of the project will continue until 2015.* 根據協議條款，他們為這個項目提供資金，將延續到 2015 年。◇ *They failed to agree on the terms of a settlement.* 他們未能就和解的條件達成協議。◇ *These are the* ***terms and conditions*** *of your employment.* 這些是聘用你的條件。**2** conditions that you agree to when you buy, sell, or pay for sth; a price or cost （交易的）條件；價錢；費用：*to buy sth* ***on easy terms*** (= paying for it over a long period) 按分期付款方式購買◇ *My terms are £20 a lesson.* 每教一堂課我收費 20 英鎊。**3** a way of expressing yourself or of saying sth 表達方式；措辭；說法：*We wish to protest in* ***the strongest possible terms*** (= to say we are very angry). 我們想要以最強硬的措辭抗議。◇ *I'll try to explain in simple terms.* 我會盡量講得通俗易懂。◇ *The letter was brief, and* ***couched in*** *very polite* ***terms.*** 這封信內容簡短，措辭特別客氣。➲ SYNONYMS at LANGUAGE

IDM **be on good, friendly, bad, etc. 'terms (with sb)** to have a good, friendly, etc. relationship with sb（與某人）關係好（或友好、不好等）：*I had no idea that you and he were on such intimate terms* (= were such close friends). 我還不知道你和他的關係這麼密切。◇ *He is still on excellent terms with his ex-wife.* 他仍然和前妻保持着極好的關係。◇ *I'm on* ***first-name terms*** *with my boss now* (= we call each other by our first names). 現在我和老闆交情很好，相互直呼其名。**come to 'terms (with sb)** to reach an agreement with sb; to find a way of living or working together （與某人）達成協議，妥協 **come to 'terms with sth** to accept sth unpleasant by learning to deal with it 遷就順從；接受（令人不快的事物）；適應（困難的處境）：*She is still coming to terms with her son's death.* 她還沒有完全從兒子死亡的陰影中走出來。**in terms of 'sth | in ... terms** used to show what aspect of a subject you are talking about or how you are thinking about it 談及；就…而言；在…方面：*The job is great in terms of salary, but it has its disadvantages.* 就薪金而言，這個工作倒是挺不錯的，但也有一些不利之處。◇ *What does this mean in terms of cost?* 就費用而言，這意味着什麼？◇ *In practical terms this law*

T

may be difficult to enforce. 實際上，這條法規可能很難實施。◇ *The decision was disastrous in political terms.* 從政治上來看，這個決定是災難性的。◇ *He's talking in terms of starting a completely new career.* 他正在談論開創全新的事業。 **on your own 'terms | on sb's 'terms** according to the conditions that you or sb else decides 按照自己的條件；根據…的主張：*I'll only take the job on my own terms.* 我只會按照自己的條件接受這份工作。◇ *I'm not doing it on your terms.* 我不會按你的條件辦的。 ➲ more at CONTRADICTION, EQUAL, SPEAK, UNCERTAIN

ˌterms of 'reference *noun* [pl.] the limits that are set on what an official committee or report has been asked to do （委員會或報告的）受委託權限，受權調查範圍：*The matter, they decided, lay outside the commission's terms of reference.* 他們認定這個問題不在委員會受託權限之內。

'term-time *noun* [U] (*BrE*) the period of time when classes are held at a school, college, or university, as opposed to the holidays/vacations 學期（與假期相對而言） ▸ **'term-time** *adj.* [only before noun]：*Please give your term-time address.* 請提供你上學期間的住址。

tern /tɜːn; *NAmE* tɜːrn/ *noun* a bird with long pointed wings and a tail with two points that lives near the sea 燕鷗

ter·race /'terəs/ *noun* **1** [C] (*BrE*) (often in the names of streets 常用於街名) a continuous row of similar houses that are joined together in one block （相同的一排）排房，排屋：*12 Albert Terrace* 艾伯特排房 12 號 **2** [C] a flat, hard area, especially outside a house or restaurant, where you can sit, eat and enjoy the sun （尤指房屋或餐館外的）露天平台，陽台：*a sun terrace* 陽台 ◇ *a roof terrace* 屋頂平台 ◇ *All rooms have a balcony or terrace.* 所有的房間都有陽台或露台。 ➲ see also PATIO **3 terraces** [pl.] (*BrE*) the wide steps at a football (SOCCER) ground where people can stand to watch the game （足球場的）階梯看台 **4** [C] one of a series of flat areas of ground that are cut into the side of a hill like steps so that crops can be grown there 梯田；階地

ter·raced /'terəst/ *adj.* **1** (*BrE*) used to describe houses that form part of a terrace, or streets with houses in terraces 排房的；排屋的；（街道）有排房的：*a terraced cottage* 排房式小屋 ◇ *terraced housing* 排屋式住房 ◇ *terraced streets* 兩旁是排房的街道 **2** (of a slope or the side of a hill 斜坡或山坡) having a series of flat areas of ground like steps cut into it 梯田形的；階地狀的

ˌterraced 'house (also *less frequent* **ˌterrace 'house**) (both *BrE*) (*NAmE* **'row house, town·house**) *noun* a house that is one of a row of houses that are joined together on each side （成排相連房屋中的）一棟排房 ➲ **VISUAL VOCAB** page V16

ter·ra·cing /'terəsɪŋ/ *noun* [U] **1** (*BrE*) an area with wide steps at a football (SOCCER) ground where people can stand to watch the game （足球場的）階梯看台區 **2** a slope or the side of a hill that has had flat areas like steps cut into it 階梯狀坡地；階梯形山坡

terra·cotta /ˌterə'kɒtə; *NAmE* -'kɑːtə/ *noun* [U] **1** reddish-brown CLAY that has been baked but not GLAZED, used for making pots, etc. （無釉的）赤陶土，赤陶 **2** a reddish-brown colour 赤褐色；土紅色

terra firma /ˌterə 'fɜːmə; *NAmE* 'fɜːrmə/ *noun* [U] (from *Latin*, usually *humorous*) safe dry land, as contrasted with water or air 安全的陸地，堅實的大地（與水和空中相對而言） SYN **dry land**：*After two days at sea, it was good to be back on terra firma again.* 在海上度過兩天之後，又回到使人覺得堅實的陸地，真是愜意。

terra·form /'terəfɔːm; *NAmE* -fɔːrm/ *verb* **~ sth** to make a planet more like Earth, so that people can live on it 將（行星）地球化（以適合人類居住）

ter·rain /tə'reɪn/ *noun* [C, U] used to refer to an area of land when you are mentioning its natural features, for example, if it is rough, flat, etc. 地形；地勢；地帶：***difficult/rough/mountainous, etc. terrain*** 難以通過的地帶、崎嶇不平的地形、山地等 ➲ **SYNONYMS** at COUNTRY

ter'rain park *noun* an outdoor area with special features designed for winter sports, especially SNOWBOARDING (= moving over snow on a special board) 地形公園（為滑雪板等戶外冬季運動特別設計的場地）

terra·pin /'terəpɪn/ *noun* a small TURTLE (= a REPTILE with a hard round shell), that lives in warm rivers and lakes in N America 水龜（生活在北美溫帶江河湖泊中） ➲ compare TORTOISE

ter·rar·ium /te'reəriəm; *NAmE* -'rer-/ *noun* a glass container for growing plants in or for keeping small animals such as TURTLES or snakes in 生物育養箱；玻璃花園

ter·res·trial /tə'restriəl/ *adj.* **1** (*technical* 術語) (of animals and plants 動植物) living on the land or on the ground, rather than in water, in trees or in the air 陸地的；陸棲的；陸生的 **2** connected with the planet Earth 地球的；地球上的：*terrestrial life* 地球上的生物 ➲ compare CELESTIAL, EXTRATERRESTRIAL **3** (of television and broadcasting systems 電視和廣播系統) operating on earth rather than from a SATELLITE 陸地上的，地面上的（與衛星相對而言）

Synonyms 同義詞辨析

terrible

awful • horrible • dreadful • vile • horrendous

These words all describe sth that is very unpleasant.
以上各詞均指事物令人不快。

terrible very bad or unpleasant; making you feel unhappy, frightened, upset, ill, guilty or disapproving 指糟透了的、非常討厭的、令人極不快的、可怕的、駭人的：*What terrible news!* 多麼駭人聽聞的消息！◇ *That's a terrible thing to say!* 說這話太難聽了！

awful (*rather informal*) very bad or unpleasant; used to describe sth that you do not like or that makes you feel depressed, ill, guilty or disapproving 指很壞的、極討厭的（用以形容令人沮喪、不舒服、內疚或不高興的事物）：*That's an awful colour.* 那顏色難看得很。◇ *The weather last summer was awful.* 剛過去的夏季天氣真糟糕。

horrible (*rather informal*) very unpleasant; used to describe sth that you do not like 指極壞的、十分討厭的（用以形容令人不快的事物）：*The coffee tasted horrible.* 這咖啡難喝極了。

dreadful (*rather informal, especially BrE*) very bad or unpleasant; used to describe sth that you do not like or that you disapprove of 指糟糕透頂的、討厭的（用以形容令人不快或反對的事物）：*What dreadful weather!* 多麼討厭的天氣！

vile (*informal*) extremely bad or unpleasant 指糟糕透頂的、可惡的、極壞的：*There was a vile smell coming from the room.* 房間裏傳來令人惡心的氣味。◇ *He was in a vile mood.* 他的心情壞極了。

horrendous (*rather informal*) extremely unpleasant and unacceptable 指討厭得難以容忍的：*The traffic around the city was horrendous.* 城裏的交通糟透了。

PATTERNS

- terrible/awful/horrible/dreadful **for** sb
- a(n) terrible/awful/horrible/dreadful/vile **thing**
- a(n) terrible/awful/horrible/vile **smell**
- terrible/awful/horrible/dreadful/vile/horrendous **conditions**
- terrible/awful/horrible/dreadful/vile **weather**
- terrible/awful/dreadful **news**

ter·rible 🔑 /'terəbl/ *adj.*
1 🔑 very unpleasant; making you feel very unhappy, upset or frightened 非常討厭的；令人極不快的；可怕的：*a terrible experience* 令人極不愉快的經歷 ◇ *What terrible news!* 多麼駭人聽聞的消息！◇ *I've just had a terrible thought.* 我剛剛產生了一個可怕的念頭。 **2** 🔑 causing great harm or injury; very serious 危害極

大的；造成極大傷害的；非常嚴重的： *a terrible accident* 重大事故 ◇ *He had suffered terrible injuries.* 他受了重傷。**3** [not before noun] unhappy or ill/sick 不痛快；身體不舒服： *I feel terrible—I think I'll go to bed.* 我覺得難受，想去睡覺了。 **4** (*informal*) of very bad quality; very bad 劣質的；劣等的；拙劣的： *a terrible meal* 劣等餐食 ◇ *Your driving is terrible!* 你的駕駛技術真是糟糕透了！ **5** [only before noun] used to show the great extent or degree of sth bad 極度的；極其嚴重的： *a terrible mistake* 嚴重的錯誤 ◇ *to be in terrible pain* 處於極度痛苦之中 ◇ *The room was in a terrible mess.* 房間裏髒亂不堪。◇ (*informal*) *I had a terrible job* (= it was very difficult) *to persuade her to come.* 為勸她來，我費盡了口舌。

ter·ribly /ˈterəbli/ *adv.* **1** (*especially BrE*) very 非常；很： *I'm terribly sorry—did I hurt you?* 非常抱歉，我傷着您了嗎？◇ *It's terribly important for parents to be consistent.* 父母要做到始終如一，這是極為重要的。 **2** very much; very badly 非常地；很厲害地： *I miss him terribly.* 我非常思念他。◇ *They suffered terribly when their son was killed.* 兒子遇難之後，他們悲痛欲絕。◇ *The experiment went terribly wrong.* 這次實驗出了大問題。

ter·rier /ˈteriə(r)/ *noun* a small active dog. There are many types of terrier. 㹴（一種活潑的小狗） ➲ see also BULL TERRIER, PIT BULL TERRIER, YORKSHIRE TERRIER

ter·rif·ic /təˈrɪfɪk/ *adj.* **1** (*informal*) excellent; wonderful 極好的；絕妙的；了不起的： *I feel absolutely terrific today!* 我今天的感覺真是好極了！◇ *She's doing a terrific job.* 她活兒幹得真棒。 ➲ SYNONYMS at GREAT **2** (*informal*) very large; very great 很大的；巨大的；異乎尋常的： *I've got a terrific amount of work to do.* 我有大量的工作要做。◇ *We drove along at a terrific speed.* 我們以極快的速度驅車行駛。

ter·rif·ic·al·ly /təˈrɪfɪkli/ *adv.* (*informal*) extremely (usually used about positive qualities) 極其，非常（通常用於正面性質）： *terrifically exciting* 極其令人興奮

ter·ri·fied /ˈterɪfaɪd/ *adj.* very frightened 恐懼；很害怕： **~ (of sb/sth)** *to be terrified of spiders* 懼怕蜘蛛 ◇ **~ (of doing sth)** *I'm terrified of losing you.* 我真害怕失去你。◇ **~ (that …)** *He was terrified (that) he would fall.* 他很害怕會跌倒。◇ **~ (at sth)** *She was terrified at the thought of being alone.* 她一想到孤零零的獨自一人就驚恐不安。 ➲ SYNONYMS at AFRAID IDM see WIT

ter·rify /ˈterɪfaɪ/ *verb* (**ter·ri·fies**, **ter·ri·fy·ing**, **ter·ri·fied**, **ter·ri·fied**) **~ sb** to make sb feel extremely frightened 使恐懼；使十分害怕；使驚嚇： *Flying terrifies her.* 她害怕坐飛機。 ➲ SYNONYMS at FRIGHTEN ▸ **ter·ri·fy·ing** *adj.* : *It was a terrifying experience.* 那是一次可怕的經歷。 **ter·ri·fy·ing·ly** *adv.*

ter·rine /teˈriːn/ *noun* [U, C] a soft mixture of finely chopped meat, fish, etc. pressed into a container and served cold, especially in slices as the first course of a meal（罐裝）肉糜，魚醬

Ter·ri·tor·ial /ˌterəˈtɔːriəl/ *noun* (in Britain) a member of the Territorial Army（英國）本土防衛義勇軍士兵

ter·ri·tor·ial /ˌterəˈtɔːriəl/ *adj.* **1** connected with the land or sea that is owned by a particular country 領土的： *territorial disputes* 領土爭端 ◇ *Both countries feel they have territorial claims to* (= have a right to own) *the islands.* 兩個國家都認為對這些島嶼擁有主權。 **2** (of animals, birds, etc. 動物、鳥等) guarding and defending an area of land that they believe to be their own 地盤性的： *territorial instincts* 地盤性本能 ◇ *Cats are very territorial.* 貓的地盤性很強。 ▸ **ter·ri·tori·al·ity** /ˌterəˌtɔːriˈæləti/ *noun* [U] : *the instinctive territoriality of some animals* 一些動物本能的地盤性 **ter·ri·tori·al·ly** *adv.* : *The country was trying to expand territorially.* 這個國家在設法擴張領土。

the ˌTerritorial ˈArmy *noun* [sing.+sing./pl. v.] (*abbr.* **TA**) (in Britain) a military force of people who are not professional soldiers but who train as soldiers in their free time（英國）本土防衛義勇軍，國防義勇軍

ˌterritorial ˈwaters *noun* [pl.] the parts of a sea or an ocean which are near a country's coast and are legally under its control 領海

ter·ri·tory /ˈterətri; *NAmE* -tɔːri/ *noun* (*pl.* **-ies**) **1** [C, U] land that is under the control of a particular country or ruler 領土；版圖；領地： ***enemy/disputed/foreign territory*** 敵方 / 有爭議的 / 外國領土 ◇ *occupied territories* 被佔領的土地 ◇ *They have refused to allow UN troops to be stationed in their territory.* 他們拒不允許聯合國部隊駐紮在他們的國土上。 ➲ COLLOCATIONS at WAR **2** [C, U] an area that one person, group, animal, etc. considers as their own and defends against others who try to enter it（個人、群體、動物等佔據的）領域，管區，地盤： *Mating blackbirds will defend their territory against intruders.* 烏鶇交配時會保護自己的地盤，不允許外來者侵入。◇ (*figurative*) *This type of work is* ***uncharted territory*** *for us.* 我們從未涉足過這類工作。◇ (*figurative*) *Legal problems are Andy's territory* (= he deals with them). 法律問題由安迪負責處理。 **3** [C, U] an area of a town, country, etc. that sb has responsibility for in their work or another activity（某人負責的）地區： *Our representatives cover a very large territory.* 我們的代理人負責的地區很廣。 **4** [U] a particular type of land（某類）地區；（某種）地方： *unexplored territory* 未勘察地區 **5** (also **Territory**) [C] a country or an area that is part of the US, Australia or Canada but is not a state or PROVINCE（美國）準州；（澳大利亞）地區；（加拿大）地區： *Guam and American Samoa are US territories.* 關島和美屬薩摩亞是美國的準州。
IDM **ˌcome/ˌgo with the ˈterritory** to be a normal and accepted part of a particular job, situation, etc. 成為必然的部份（或結果）： *She has to work late most days, but in her kind of job that goes with the territory.* 她在大部份日子裏都得工作到很晚，但根據她的工作性質，這是不可避免的。 ➲ more at NEUTRAL *adj.*

ter·ror /ˈterə(r)/ *noun* **1** [U, sing.] a feeling of extreme fear 驚恐；恐懼；驚駭： *a feeling of* ***sheer/pure terror*** 膽戰心驚 ◇ *Her eyes were wild with terror.* 她的眼睛裏充滿了恐懼。◇ *People fled from the explosion* ***in terror***. 人們驚恐地逃離了爆炸現場。◇ *She* ***lives in terror of*** (= is constantly afraid of) *losing her job.* 她一直膽戰心驚地害怕丟了工作。◇ *Some women have a terror of losing control in the birth process.* 有些婦女懼怕在分娩過程中難以自制。◇ (*literary*) *The very name of the enemy* ***struck terror into*** *their hearts.* 他們一聽到敵人的名字就心驚膽戰。 ➲ SYNONYMS at FEAR **2** [C] a person, situation or thing that makes you very afraid 可怕的人；恐怖的事；可怕的情況： *These street gangs have become the terror of the neighbourhood.* 這些街頭少年團夥使得周圍鄰里談之色變。◇ *Death* ***holds no terrors for*** (= does not frighten or worry) *me.* 死神是嚇不倒我的。◇ *The terrors of the night were past.* 夜間那些恐怖的事情都已經成為過去。 **3** [U] violent action or the threat of violent action that is intended to cause fear, usually for political purposes（通常出於政治目的）恐怖行動，恐怖 SYN **terrorism** : *a campaign of terror* 恐怖運動 ◇ *terror tactics* 恐怖手段 ➲ see also REIGN OF TERROR **4** [C] (*informal*) a person (usually a child) or an animal that causes you trouble or is difficult to control 討厭鬼；小搗蛋： *Their kids are real little terrors.* 他們的小孩都是十足的討厭鬼。

ter·ror·ism /ˈterərɪzəm/ *noun* [U] the use of violent action in order to achieve political aims or to force a government to act 恐怖主義： *an act of terrorism* 恐怖主義行動 ➲ COLLOCATIONS at CRIME

ter·ror·ist /ˈterərɪst/ *noun* a person who takes part in terrorism 恐怖主義者；恐怖分子： *The terrorists are threatening to blow up the plane.* 恐怖分子揚言要炸毀飛機。◇ *a* ***terrorist attack/bomb/group*** 恐怖分子的襲擊 / 炸彈 / 團體

ter·ror·ize (*BrE* also **-ise**) /ˈterəraɪz/ *verb* to frighten and threaten people so that they will not oppose sth or will do as they are told 恐嚇；恫嚇；威脅： **~ sb** *drug dealers terrorizing the neighbourhood* 使附近地區人心惶惶的毒品販子 ◇ **~ sb into doing sth** *People were terrorized into leaving their homes.* 人們在恫嚇之下離開家園。

ˈterror-stricken *adj.* extremely frightened 膽戰心驚的；驚恐萬狀的

terry /ˈteri/ *noun* [U] a type of soft cotton cloth that absorbs liquids and has a surface covered with raised

LOOPS of thread, used especially for making towels 毛圈棉織物（多用以做毛巾）

terse /tɜːs; *NAmE* tɜːrs/ *adj.* using few words and often not seeming polite or friendly 簡要的；簡短生硬的：*a terse style* 生硬冷漠的風格 ◇ *The President issued a terse statement denying the charges.* 總統發表了一份簡短的聲明，否認那些指控。▶ **terse·ly** *adv.* **terse·ness** *noun* [U]

ter·tiary /ˈtɜːʃəri; *NAmE* ˈtɜːrʃieri; -ʃəri/ *adj.* third in order, rank or importance 第三的；第三位的；第三級的：*the tertiary sector* (= the area of industry that deals with services rather than materials or goods) 第三產業部門 ◇ (*BrE*) *tertiary education* (= at university or college level) 高等教育 ➲ compare PRIMARY (3), SECONDARY (3)

ˈtertiary ˈcollege *noun* (in Britain) a college that provides education for people aged 16 and older, but that is not a university 職業專科學校（英國為 16 歲以上的人提供教育的學院，但並非大學）

ˈtertiary ˈindustry (also **ˈservice industry**) *noun* [U, C] (*economics* 經) the part of a country's economy that provides services 第三產業；服務業 ➲ compare PRIMARY INDUSTRY, SECONDARY INDUSTRY

tery·lene™ /ˈterəliːn/ *noun* [U] (*BrE*) a light strong artificial material, used for making clothes, etc. 滌綸；聚酯纖維

TESL /ˈtesl/ *abbr.* teaching English as a second language 作為第二語言的英語教學

TESOL /ˈtiːsɒl; ˈtesɒl; *NAmE* -sɑːl; -sɔːl/ *abbr.* **1** teaching English to speakers of other languages 對母語為非英語人士的英語教學 **2** (*NAmE*) teachers of English to speakers of other languages (an organization of teachers) 國際英語教師協會

tes·sel·lated /ˈtesəleɪtɪd/ *adj.* (*technical* 術語) made from small flat pieces arranged in a pattern 鑲嵌鋪面小塊的；鑲嵌花樣的：*a tessellated pavement* 嵌花鋪面

test 0→ /test/ *noun, verb*

■ *noun*

▸ **OF KNOWLEDGE/ABILITY** 知識；能力 **1** 0→ an examination of sb's knowledge or ability, consisting of questions for them to answer or activities for them to perform 測驗；考查：*an IQ/intelligence/aptitude test* 智商／智力／能力傾向測驗 ◇ *to **take a test*** 參加測驗 ◇ (*BrE*) *to **do a test*** 參加測驗 ◇ **~ (on sth)** *a test on irregular verbs* 不規則動詞測驗 ◇ *to **pass/fail a test*** 通過／沒有通過測驗 ◇ (*BrE*) *a good mark **in the test*** 測驗中取得的高分 ◇ (*NAmE*) *a good grade **on the test*** 優良的測驗成績 ➲ COLLOCATIONS at EDUCATION ➲ note at EXAM (1) ➲ see also DRIVING TEST

▸ **OF HEALTH** 健康 **2** 0→ a medical examination to discover what is wrong with you or to check the condition of your health （醫療上的）檢查，化驗，檢驗：*a test for AIDS* 艾滋病化驗 ◇ *an eye test* 眼睛檢查 ◇ *a pregnancy test* 妊娠檢驗 ◇ *When can I get my **test results**?* 我什麼時候可以拿到化驗結果？➲ see also BLOOD TEST, BREATH TEST

▸ **OF MACHINE/PRODUCT, ETC.** 機器、產品等 **3** 0→ an experiment to discover whether or how well sth works, or to find out more information about it 試驗；測試：*laboratory tests* 實驗室測試 ◇ *a nuclear test* 核試驗 ◇ *Tests have shown high levels of pollutants in the water.* 測試顯示水中污染物質的含量很高。◇ *I'll run a diagnostic test to see why the server keeps crashing.* 我要做診斷測試，弄清為什麼服務器總是不斷地發生故障。➲ see also ACID TEST, BLIND TEST, FIELD TEST, MEANS TEST, ROAD TEST

▸ **OF STRENGTH, ETC.** 實力等 **4** a situation or an event that shows how good, strong, etc. sb/sth is 檢驗；考驗：*The local elections will be a good test of the government's popularity.* 地方選舉將是檢驗政府是否得人心的一個很好的試金石。

▸ **IN CRICKET, ETC.** 板球等 **5 Test** = TEST MATCH

IDM **put sb/sth to the ˈtest** to put sb/sth in a situation which will show what their or its true qualities are 使受考驗；使受檢驗：*His theories have never really been put to the test.* 他的理論從未真正經受過檢驗。 **stand the test of ˈtime** to prove to be good, popular, etc. over a long period of time 經得起時間的考驗 ➲ more at TEACH *v.*

■ *verb*

▸ **KNOWLEDGE/ABILITY** 知識；能力 **1** 0→ [T, I] to find out how much sb knows, or what they can do by asking them questions or giving them activities to perform 測驗；考查：**~ sb (on sth)** *Children are tested on core subjects at ages 7, 11 and 14.* 兒童在 7、11 和 14 歲時要接受核心課程的測驗。◇ **~ (sth)** *We test your English before deciding which class to put you in.* 我們測驗過你的英語後再決定把你分在哪一班。◇ *Schools use various methods of testing.* 學校採用各種各樣的測試方法。 **2** [I] **~ well/badly** to perform well/badly in a test of knowledge or ability 在知識或能力測試中表現不錯／糟糕：*students who tested well in reading* 閱讀測試考得好的學生

▸ **HEALTH** 健康 **3** 0→ [T, I] to examine the blood, a part of the body, etc. to find out what is wrong with a person, or to check the condition of their health 試驗；檢查；化驗：**~ sb/sth** *to test sb's eyesight/hearing* 檢查某人的視力／聽力 ◇ **~ sb/sth for sth** *The doctor tested him for hepatitis.* 醫生對他進行了肝炎病檢查。◇ **+ adj. (for sth)** *to **test positive/negative*** 化驗呈陽性／陰性 ◇ *Two athletes tested positive for steroids.* 兩名運動員的類固醇試驗呈陽性。

▸ **MACHINE/PRODUCT, ETC.** 機器、產品等 **4** 0→ [T] to use or try a machine, substance, etc. to find out how well it works or to find out more information about it 試驗；檢驗；測試：**~ sth** *Test your brakes regularly.* 要定期檢驗剎車。◇ **~ sth on sb/sth** *Our beauty products are not tested on animals.* 我們的美容產品不進行動物試驗。◇ **~ sth for sth** *The water is regularly tested for purity.* 水的純度定期受到檢測。◇ **~ sth out** *They opened a single store in Europe to test out the market.* 他們在歐洲開了一家商店，檢驗一下市場情況。➲ see also FIELD-TEST **5** [I] **~ well/badly** (of a machine or product) to perform well/badly in a test of how well it works （機器或產品）測試結果良好／很差：*The ad had tested badly with consumers.* 測試結果表明消費者對這則廣告的評價很差。

▸ **STRENGTH, ETC.** 實力等 **6** [T] **~ sb/sth** to be difficult and therefore need all your strength, ability, etc. 考驗；檢驗：*The long climb tested our fitness and stamina.* 那次長距離爬山是對我們健康狀況和耐力的考驗。➲ see also TESTING *n.*

IDM **test the ˈwaters** to find out what the situation is before doing sth or making a decision 摸清底細 ➲ more at TRIED

PHR V **ˈtest for sth | ˈtest sth for sth** to examine sth to see if a particular substance, etc. is present 化驗；檢驗；測試鑒定某物：*testing for oil* 化驗確定是否含油 ◇ *The software has been tested for viruses.* 這個軟件已經過是否有病毒的測試。

test·able /ˈtestəbl/ *adj.* that can be tested 可檢驗的；可試驗的；可驗證的：*testable hypotheses* 可驗證的假説

tes·ta·ment /ˈtestəmənt/ *noun* (*formal*) **1** [C, usually sing., U] **~ (to sth)** a thing that shows that sth else exists or is true 證據；證明 **SYN** **testimony** *The new model is a testament to the skill and dedication of the workforce.* 這種新型產品顯示了全體員工的技術水平和敬業精神。 **2** [C] = WILL *n.* (3)：*This is the last will and testament of ...* 這是…的臨終遺囑 ➲ see also NEW TESTAMENT, OLD TESTAMENT

ˈtest ban *noun* an agreement between countries to stop testing nuclear weapons 禁止核試驗協定：*a test ban treaty* 禁止核試驗條約

ˈtest bed *noun* a piece of equipment used for testing new machinery, especially aircraft engines 試驗台；（尤指飛機發動機的）試驗台架：(*figurative*) *The country is an ideal test bed for emerging technologies.* 這個國家是一個理想的新興技術試驗場。

ˈtest case *noun* a legal case or other situation whose result will be used as an example when decisions are being made on similar cases in the future （判決同類案件可援用的）判例

ˈtest drive *noun* an occasion when you drive a vehicle that you are thinking of buying so that you can see how well it works and if you like it （對想購買的車進行）試驗駕駛，試車 ▶ **ˈtest-drive** *verb* **~ sth**

test·er /ˈtestə(r)/ *noun* **1** a person or thing that tests sth 測試員；試驗員；測試器；測試儀：*testers of new* *software* 新軟件測試員 **2** a small container of a product, such as PERFUME, that you can try in a shop/store to see if you like it（商店裏的）小包裝試用品（如香水）

tes·tes *pl.* of TESTIS

'test flight *noun* a flight during which an aircraft or part of its equipment is tested（飛機的）試飛

tes·ticle /'testɪkl/ *noun* either of the two organs that produce SPERM, located in a bag of skin below the PENIS 睾丸 ▸ **tes·ticu·lar** /tes'tɪkjələ(r)/ *adj.* [only before noun]: *testicular cancer* 睾丸癌

test·ify /'testɪfaɪ/ *verb* (**testi·fies**, **testi·fy·ing**, **testi·fied**, **testi·fied**) **1** [I, T] to make a statement that sth happened or that sth is true, especially as a witness in court（尤指出庭）作證：**~ (against/for sb)** *She refused to testify against her husband.* 她拒絕出庭作證指控丈夫。◇ *There are several witnesses who will testify for the defence.* 有幾名證人願意為被告作證。◇ **~ about sth** *He was summoned to testify before a grand jury about his role in the affair.* 他被傳喚出庭在大陪審團前就他在這一事件中的角色作證。◇ **~ to sth/to doing sth** *Evans testified to receiving $200 000 in bribes.* 埃文斯出庭證實了收受 20 萬元賄賂的事情。◇ **~ (that) ...** *He testified (that) he was at the theatre at the time of the murder.* 他作證聲稱兇殺案發生時自己正在劇院。◇ **+ speech** *'I was approached by a man I did not recognize,' she testified.* "一個我不認識的男人和我接洽過。" 她作供說。**2** [T] **~ (that) ...** (*formal*) to say that you believe sth is true because you have evidence of it 證實；證明：*Too many young people are unable to write or spell well, as employers will testify.* 寫作或拼寫不好的年輕人太多了，這一點雇主都會證明。**3** [I] (*especially NAmE*) to express your belief in God publicly 見證（上帝的存在）

PHR V **'testify to sth** (*formal*) to show or be evidence that sth is true 作為某事的證明；表明；說明 **SYN** **evidence**：*The film testifies to the courage of ordinary people during the war.* 這部電影表明了老百姓在戰爭期間的英勇。

tes·ti·mo·nial /ˌtestɪ'məʊniəl; *NAmE* -'moʊ-/ *noun* **1** a formal written statement, often by a former employer, about sb's abilities, qualities and character; a formal written statement about the quality of sth 證明信；介紹信；推薦信：*a glowing testimonial* 充滿讚譽的推薦信 ◇ *The catalogue is full of testimonials from satisfied customers.* 這份商品目錄滿篇皆是稱心顧客的讚辭。**2** a thing that is given or done to show admiration for sb or to thank sb 感謝信；紀念品；獎品；獎狀：*a testimonial game* (= to raise money for a particular player) 紀念賽（為某位運動員籌款）

tes·ti·mony /'testɪməni; *NAmE* -moʊni/ *noun* (*pl.* **-ies**) **1** [U, sing.] **~ (to sth)** (*formal*) a thing that shows that sth else exists or is true 證據；證明 **SYN** **testament**：*This increase in exports* **bears testimony to** *the successes of industry.* 出口增長證明了工業的成功。◇ *The pyramids are an eloquent testimony to the ancient Egyptians' engineering skills.* 金字塔是古埃及人非凡工程技術的明鑒。**2** [C, U] a formal written or spoken statement saying what you know to be true, usually in court 證詞；證言；口供：*a sworn testimony* 宣誓證詞 ◇ *Can I refuse to give testimony?* 我能拒絕作證嗎？

test·ing /'testɪŋ/ *noun, adj.*

■ **noun** [U] the activity of testing sb/sth in order to find sth out, see if it works, etc. 試驗；測試；檢查：*nuclear testing* 核試驗 ◇ *testing and assessment in education* 教育測試與評估

■ **adj.** (of a problem or situation 問題或情況) difficult to deal with and needing particular strength or abilities 棘手的；傷腦筋的；難應付的

'testing ground *noun* **1** a place or situation used for testing new ideas and methods to see if they work（新思想、新方法的）試驗場，試點 **2** a place used for testing machines, etc. to see if they work correctly（機器等的）試驗場：*a piece of land in use as a tank testing ground* 用作坦克試驗場的一塊土地

tes·tis /'testɪs/ *noun* (*pl.* **tes·tes** /-tiːz/) (*anatomy* 解) a TESTICLE 睾丸

'Test match (also **Test**) *noun* a CRICKET or RUGBY match played between the teams of two different countries, usually as part of a series of matches on a tour（板球或橄欖球的）各國家隊間的決賽階段比賽

tes·tos·ter·one /te'stɒstərəʊn; *NAmE* te'stɑːstəroʊn/ *noun* a HORMONE (= chemical substance produced in the body) that causes men to develop the physical and sexual features that are characteristic of the male body 睾酮；睾丸素 ➲ compare OESTROGEN, PROGESTERONE

'test pilot *noun* a pilot whose job is to fly aircraft in order to test their performance（檢驗飛機性能的）試飛員

ˌtest 'run *noun* = TRIAL RUN

'test tube *noun* a small glass tube, closed at one end, that is used in scientific experiments 試管 ➲ VISUAL VOCAB page V70

'test-tube baby *noun* a baby that grows from an egg that is FERTILIZED outside the mother's body and then put back inside to continue developing normally 試管嬰兒 ➲ see also IN VITRO

testy /'testi/ *adj.* easily annoyed or irritated 易怒的；暴躁的 **SYN** **irritable** ▸ **test·ily** /-ɪli/ *adv.*：*'Leave me alone,' she said testily.* "別管我。" 她不耐煩地說。

tet·anus /'tetənəs/ *noun* [U] a disease in which the muscles, especially the JAW muscles, become stiff, caused by bacteria entering the body through cuts or wounds 破傷風

tetchy /'tetʃi/ *adj.* bad-tempered; likely to get angry easily or without good reason 易怒的；暴躁的；動輒發怒的 **SYN** **irritable** ▸ **tetch·ily** /-ɪli/ *adv.*

tête-à-tête /ˌteɪt ɑː 'teɪt/ *noun* (from *French*) a private conversation between two people 兩人密談；兩人私語；促膝談心

tether /'teðə(r)/ *verb, noun*

■ ***verb*** **~ sth (to sth)** to tie an animal to a post so that it cannot move very far 拴（牲畜）

■ ***noun*** a rope or chain used to tie an animal to sth, allowing it to move around in a small area（拴牲畜的）拴繩，拴鏈 **IDM** see END *n.*

tetra·he·dron /ˌtetrə'hiːdrən; -'hed-/ *noun* (*geometry* 幾何) a solid shape with four flat sides that are triangles 四面體 ➲ VISUAL VOCAB page V71

tet·ral·ogy /te'trælədʒi/ *noun* (*pl.* **-ies**) a group of four books, films/movies, etc. that have the same subject or characters 四部曲；四聯劇

Tetra Pak™ /'tetrə pæk/ *noun* a type of cardboard container in which milk or other drinks are sold 利樂包裝紙盒（用於包裝牛奶等）

Teut·on·ic /tjuː'tɒnɪk; *NAmE* tuː'tɑːnɪk/ *adj.* [usually before noun] (*informal*, often *disapproving*) showing qualities considered typical of German people 德意志民族特點的；日耳曼人風格的：*The preparations were made with Teutonic thoroughness.* 各項準備工作均以日耳曼人縝密的精神完成。

Tex-Mex /ˌteks 'meks/ *adj.* [only before noun] connected with the variety of Mexican cooking, music, etc. that is found in Texas and the SW part of the US 美國 — 墨西哥烹調的；美國 — 墨西哥音樂的；美國 — 墨西哥的

text 🔑 **AW** /tekst/ *noun, verb*

■ ***noun*** **1** 🔑 [U] the main printed part of a book or magazine, not the notes, pictures, etc.（書籍或雜誌的）正文，本文（並非附註、圖片等）：*My job is to lay out the text and graphics on the page.* 我的工作是設計頁面上的正文和圖表。**2** 🔑 [U] any form of written material 文本；文檔：*a computer that can process text* 能處理文本的電腦 ◇ *printed text* 打印的文本 **3** [C] = TEXT MESSAGE **4** 🔑 [C] the written form of a speech, a play, an article, etc. 演講稿；劇本；文稿：*The newspaper had printed the full text of the president's speech.* 報紙刊登了總統演講的全文。**5** 🔑 [C] a book, play, etc., especially one studied for an exam（尤指為了考試而學習的）課本，教科書，劇本：*a literary text* 文學課本 ◇ (*BrE*) *'Macbeth' is a* **set text** *this year.* 《麥克佩斯》是今年指定的必讀劇目。➲ COLLOCATIONS at LITERATURE **6** 🔑 [C] a piece of writing that you have to answer questions about in an exam or a lesson（考試或一課書中賴以回答問題的）文章 **SYN** **passage**：*Read the text carefully and then answer the questions.* 先仔細閱讀文章，然後再回答問題。**7** [C] (*NAmE*) = TEXTBOOK：*medical texts* 醫學課本 **8** [C] a sentence or short passage from the Bible that is read out and discussed by sb, especially during a religious service（尤指宗教儀式上引用的）《聖經》經文

■ ***verb*** [T, I] to send sb a written message using a mobile/cell phone（用手機給某人）發短信：**~ (sb)** *Text me when you're on your way.* 路上給我發短信吧。◇ *Kids seem to be texting non-stop these days.* 現在的孩子好像不停地發短信。◇ **~ sb sth** *I'll text you the final score.* 我會發短信告訴你最終的比分。➲ see also SMS, TEXT-MESSAGE

text·book /ˈtekstbʊk/ *noun, adj.*

■ ***noun*** (*NAmE* also **text**) a book that teaches a particular subject and that is used especially in schools and colleges 教科書；課本；教材：*a* ***school/medical/history, etc. textbook*** 學校、醫學、歷史等教科書 ➲ VISUAL VOCAB page V70

■ ***adj.*** [only before noun] used to describe sth that is done exactly as it should be done, in the best possible way 規範的；標準的：*a* ***textbook example*** *of how the game should be played* 這項比賽的標準示範

ˈtext editor *noun* (*computing* 計) a system or program that allows you to make changes to text 文本編輯系統（或程序）；文字編輯器

texter /ˈtekstə(r)/ *noun* (*especially BrE*) a person who sends TEXT MESSAGES 發送（手機）短信息的人；簡訊發送者

tex·tile /ˈtekstaɪl/ *noun* **1** [C] any type of cloth made by WEAVING or knitting 紡織品：*a factory producing a range of textiles* 生產一系列紡織品的工廠 ◇ *the textile industry* 紡織工業 ◇ *a textile designer* 紡織品設計師 ➲ note at FABRIC **2** **textiles** [pl.] the industry that makes cloth 紡織業

ˈtext message (also **text**) *noun* a written message that you send using a mobile/cell phone（手機）短信息；短信：*Send a text message to this number to vote.* 請發短信到此號碼參加投票。➲ COLLOCATIONS at PHONE ▸ **ˈtext-message** (also **text**) *verb* [T, I]：**~ (sb) (sth)** *I text-messaged him to say we were waiting in the pub.* 我發短信告訴他我們在酒吧裏等候。**ˈtext-messaging** (also **text·ing**) *noun* [U]

ˌtext-to-ˈspeech *noun* (*abbr.* **TTS**) [U] (*computing* 計) a computer program that converts text into spoken language 文本語音轉換程序；語音朗讀程序；文字至語音轉換程式：*text-to-speech software* 文本語音轉換軟件 ◇ *a TTS package* 語音朗讀軟件包

T

text·ual **AW** /ˈtekstʃuəl/ *adj.* [usually before noun] connected with or contained in a text 文本的；篇章的：*textual analysis* 文本分析 ◇ *textual errors* 文本錯誤

tex·tural /ˈtekstʃərəl/ *adj.* (*technical* 術語) relating to texture 質地的；紋理的：*the textural characteristics of the rocks* 岩石的紋理特徵

tex·ture /ˈtekstʃə(r)/ *noun* [C, U] **1** the way a surface, substance or piece of cloth feels when you touch it, for example how rough, smooth, hard or soft it is 質地；手感：*the soft texture of velvet* 天鵝絨柔軟的質地 ◇ *She uses a variety of different colours and textures in her wall hangings.* 她懸掛的帷幔色彩和質地多姿多彩。**2** the way food or drink tastes or feels in your mouth, for example whether it is rough, smooth, light, heavy, etc. 口感：*The two cheeses were very different in both taste and texture.* 這兩種奶酪的味道和口感大不相同。**3** the way that different parts of a piece of music or literature are combined to create a final impression（音樂或文學的）諧和統一感，神韻：*the rich texture of the symphony* 這首交響曲優美和諧的樂感

tex·tured /ˈtekstʃəd; *NAmE* -tʃərd/ *adj.* with a surface that is not smooth, but has a particular texture 起紋理的；質地不平的：*textured wallpaper* 起紋理的壁紙

ˌtextured ˈvegetable protein *noun* (*abbr.* **TVP**) a substance that looks like meat, but which is made from SOYA BEANS 結構性植物蛋白，植物組織蛋白，素肉（用大豆製成）

TFT /ˌtiː ef ˈtiː/ *noun* a piece of technology used to make flat screens for computers, mobile phones/cell phones, etc. (the abbreviation for thin film transistor) 薄膜晶體管，薄膜電晶體（全寫為 thin film transistor，電腦、手機等的平面屏幕製造技術）：*a 17 in TFT screen* * 17 英寸薄膜晶體管顯示器

TG /ˌtiː ˈdʒiː/ *abbr.* TRANSFORMATIONAL GRAMMAR 轉換語法

-th *suffix* **1** (in ordinal numbers 構成序數詞)：*sixth* 第六 ◇ *fifteenth* 第十五 ◇ *hundredth* 第一百 **2** (in nouns 構成名詞) the action or process of（表示動作或過程）：*growth* 生長

thali /ˈtɑːli/ *noun* (*IndE*) **1** a metal plate on which food is served 金屬餐盤 **2** a set meal at a restaurant（印度餐廳）套餐

thal·ido·mide /θəˈlɪdəmaɪd/ *noun* [U] a SEDATIVE drug which was used until the 1960s, when it was discovered that if given to pregnant women, it prevented some babies from developing normal arms and legs 沙利度胺，反應停，酞胺哌啶酮（一種鎮定藥，20 世紀 60 年代發現孕婦服用後會導致胎兒四肢畸形而被禁用）

thal·lium /ˈθæliəm/ *noun* [U] (*symb.* **Tl**) a chemical element. Thallium is a soft silver-white metal whose COMPOUNDS are very poisonous. 鉈

than 🔑 /ðən; *rare strong form* ðæn/ *prep., conj.*

1 🔑 used to introduce the second part of a comparison（用以引出比較的第二部份）比：*I'm older than her.* 我比她年齡大。◇ *There was more whisky in it than soda.* 那裏面的威士忌比蘇打水多。◇ *He loves me more than you do.* 他比你更愛我。◇ *It was much better than I'd expected.* 這比我預料的要好得多。◇ *You should know better than to behave like that.* 你應當明白事理，不該那麼不懂規矩。◇ *I'd rather email than phone, if that's OK by you.* 如果你認為可以的話，我想發電郵而不打電話。**2** 🔑 **more/less/fewer, etc. ~** used for comparing amounts, numbers, distances, etc.（比較數量、距離等）多於，小於，少於：*It never takes more than an hour.* 所用的時間從不會超過一個小時。◇ *It's less than a mile to the beach.* 離海灘不足一英里遠。◇ *There were fewer than twenty people there.* 那裏有不到二十個人。**3** used in expressions showing that one thing happens straight after another（表示一事緊跟另一事發生）就：***No sooner*** *had I sat down* ***than*** *there was a loud knock on the door.* 我剛坐下就有人大聲敲門。◇ ***Hardly*** *had we arrived* ***than*** *the problems started.* 我們剛到，問題就來了。**IDM** see OTHER *adj.*

thang /θæŋ/ *noun* (*NAmE, informal*) a way of saying or writing the word 'thing', that represents the pronunciation of the southern US 東西，事物（用於說話或書寫，表示美國南方對 thing 一詞的發音）

thank 🔑 /θæŋk/ *verb*

to tell sb that you are grateful for sth 謝謝，感謝（某人）；（為某事）道謝：**~ sb for sth** *I must write and thank Mary for the present.* 我得寫信感謝瑪麗送給我這份禮物。◇ *In his speech, he thanked everyone for all their hard work.* 他在講話中感謝大家各盡其力。◇ **~ sb for doing sth** *She said goodbye and thanked us for coming.* 她向我們道別，並感謝我們的光臨。◇ **~ sb** *There's no need to thank me—I enjoyed doing it.* 不必謝我，我樂意效勞。

IDM **have sb to thank (for sth)** used when you are saying who is responsible for sth 責怪；由…負責；多虧；歸功於：*I have my parents to thank for my success.* 我的成功歸功於我的父母。**I'll thank you for sth/to do sth** (*formal*) used to tell sb that you are annoyed and do not want them to do sth（用以表示惱火，不讓人做某事）請你…：*I'll thank you to mind your own business.* 請你少管閒事。**thank ˈGod/ˈgoodness/ˈheaven(s) (for sth)** 🔑 used to say that you are pleased about sth 謝天謝地：*Thank God you're safe!* 謝天謝地，你平安無事！◇ *'Thank goodness for that!' she said with a sigh of relief.* "這可要謝天謝地！"她寬慰地舒了一口氣。**HELP** Some people find the phrase **thank God** offensive. 有人認為 thank God 這一短語含冒犯意。**thank your lucky ˈstars** to feel very grateful and lucky about sth 真走運；吉星高照 **sb won't ˈthank you for sth** used to say that sb will not be pleased or will be annoyed about sth 某人會因而生氣：*John won't thank you for interfering.* 你插手，約翰必定十分惱火。

thank·ful /ˈθæŋkfl/ *adj.* [not usually before noun] pleased about sth good that has happened, or sth bad that has not happened 感謝；感激；欣慰：~ (**to do sth**) *I was thankful to see they'd all arrived safely.* 看到他們都平安到達，我感到欣慰。◇ ~ (**for sth**) *He wasn't badly hurt—that's something to be thankful for.* 他的傷不重，這倒是值得慶幸。◇ ~ (**that** ...) *I was thankful that he hadn't been hurt.* 他沒有受傷，我感到很欣慰。**IDM** see SMALL *adj.*

thank·ful·ly /ˈθæŋkfəli/ *adv.* **1** used to show that you are pleased that sth good has happened or that sth bad has been avoided （用以表示高興）幸虧 **SYN** **fortunately**：*There was a fire in the building, but thankfully no one was hurt.* 大樓失火了，但幸好沒有傷着人。**2** in a pleased or grateful way 高興地；感激地：*I accepted the invitation thankfully.* 我愉快地接受了邀請。

thank·less /ˈθæŋkləs/ *adj.* unpleasant or difficult to do and unlikely to bring you any rewards or thanks from anyone 讓人不領情的；徒勞無益的；吃力不討好的：*Sometimes being a mother and a housewife felt like* ***a thankless task.*** 做母親和家庭主婦有時使人覺得好像是個受累不討好的差使。

thanks 0‑w /θæŋks/ *exclamation, noun*

■ ***exclamation*** ➲ see also THANK YOU **1** 0‑w used to show that you are grateful to sb for sth they have done（表示感激）感謝，謝謝：~ (**for doing sth**) *Thanks for lending me the money.* 多謝您借錢給我。◇ ~ (**for sth**) ***Many thanks*** *for your support.* 多謝您的支持。◇ *'How are you?' 'Fine, thanks* (= thanks for asking).' "你好嗎？""好，謝謝。" **2** 0‑w a polite way of accepting sth that sb has offered you（接受好意）好的，謝謝：*'Would you like a coffee?' 'Oh, thanks.'* "來杯咖啡好嗎？""好的，謝謝。" ◇ *'Here's the change.'* ***'Thanks very much.'*** "這是找你的零錢。""非常感謝。" **3** 0‑w **no thanks** a polite way of refusing sth that sb has offered you（婉言謝絕）不用了，謝謝：*'Would you like some more?' 'No thanks.'* "再要一點兒嗎？""不要了，謝謝。"

■ ***noun*** 0‑w [pl.] ~ (**to sb**) (**for sth**) words or actions that show that you are grateful to sb for sth 感謝；感激；謝意 **SYN** **gratitude**：*How can I ever express my thanks to you for all you've done?* 對你所做的一切，我怎麼才能表達謝意？◇ *Thanks are due to all those who worked so hard for so many months.* 感謝這麼多月來辛勤工作的每一個人。◇ *She murmured her thanks.* 她低聲道謝。➲ see also VOTE OF THANKS

IDM **no thanks to sb/sth** despite sb/sth; with no help from sb/sth 雖然；並非由於；不歸功於：*We managed to get it finished in the end—no thanks to him* (= he didn't help). 我們終於把這件事完成了，但這沒有他的什麼功勞。**thanks a lot** **1** 0‑w used to show that you are very grateful to sb for sth they have done（表示非常感激）多謝：*Thanks a lot for all you've done.* 多謝你所做的一切。**2** (*ironic*) used to show that you are annoyed that sb has done sth because it causes trouble or difficulty for you（表示惱怒）多謝了：*'I'm afraid I've finished all the milk.' 'Well, thanks a lot!'* "對不起，我把牛奶都喝光了。""哦，多謝了！" **thanks to sb/sth** 0‑w (sometimes *ironic*) used to say that sth has happened because of sb/sth 幸虧；由於；因為：*It was all a great success—thanks to a lot of hard work.* 由於盡心竭力，這才大獲成功。◇ *Everyone knows about it now, thanks to you!* 多虧了你，現在大家都知道了！

thanks·giv·ing /ˌθæŋksˈɡɪvɪŋ/ *noun* **1 Thanksgiving** (**Day**) [U, C] a public holiday in the US (on the fourth Thursday in November) and in Canada (on the second Monday in October), originally to give thanks to God for the HARVEST and for health 感恩節（美國定為十一月的第四個星期四，加拿大定為十月的第二個星期一，均為公休日）：*We always eat turkey on Thanksgiving.* 我們過感恩節時總是吃火雞。◇ *Are you going home for Thanksgiving?* 你回家過感恩節嗎？➲ compare HARVEST FESTIVAL **2** [U] (*formal*) the expression of thanks to God 感恩（於上帝）

ˈthank you 0‑w *exclamation, noun*

■ ***exclamation*** ➲ see also THANKS **1** 0‑w used to show that you are grateful to sb for sth they have done（表示感激）謝謝你：~ (**for sth**) *Thank you for your letter.* 謝謝你的來信。◇ ~ (**for doing sth**) ***Thank you very much*** *for sending the photos.* 非常感謝你寄給我這些照片。**2** 0‑w a polite way of accepting sth that sb has offered you（接受好意）好，謝謝你：*'Would you like some help with that?' 'Oh, thank you.'* "這事你需要幫忙嗎？""需要，謝謝你。" **3** 0‑w **no thank you** a polite way of refusing sth that sb has offered you（婉言謝絕）不用了，謝謝你：*'Would you like some more cake?' 'No thank you.'* "你要再來點兒蛋糕嗎？""不要了，謝謝你。" **4** used at the end of a sentence to tell sb firmly that you do not need their help or advice（用於句末，堅決表示不需要幫助或勸告）謝謝：*'Shall I do that?' 'I can do it myself, thank you.'* "我來幹好嗎？""我自己能幹，謝謝。"

■ ***noun*** 0‑w [usually sing.] ~ (**to sb**) (**for sth**) an act, a gift, a comment, etc. intended to thank sb for sth they have done 感謝；謝意；酬謝；謝辭：*The actor sent a big thank you to all his fans for their letters of support.* 這位演員向所有來信表示支持的崇拜者表示萬分感謝。◇ *She took the money without so much as a thank you.* 她接過錢，連一聲謝謝都沒說。◇ *a thank-you letter* 感謝信

that 0‑w *det., pron., conj., adv.*

■ ***det.*** /ðæt/ (*pl.* **those** /ðəʊz; *NAmE* ðoʊz/) **1** 0‑w used for referring to a person or thing that is not near the speaker or as near to the speaker as another（指較遠的人或事物）那，那個：*Look at that man over there.* 瞧那邊的那個男子。◇ *How much are those apples at the back?* 後邊那些蘋果什麼價錢？**2** 0‑w used for referring to sb/sth that has already been mentioned or is already known about（指已提到過或已知的人或事物）那，那個：*I was living with my parents at that time.* 那時候我和父母住在一起。◇ *That incident changed their lives.* 那次事件改變了他們的生活。◇ *Have you forgotten about that money I lent you last week?* 你忘記上星期我借給你的那筆錢了吧？◇ *That dress of hers is too short.* 她那件連衣裙太短了。

■ ***pron.*** /ðæt/ (*pl.* **those** /ðəʊz; *NAmE* ðoʊz/) **1** 0‑w used for referring to a person or thing that is not near the speaker, or not as near to the speaker as another（指較遠的人或事物）那，那個：*Who's that?* 那是誰？◇ *That's Peter over there.* 那邊那個人是彼得。◇ *Hello. Is that Jo?* 喂，是喬嗎？◇ *That's a nice dress.* 那件連衣裙很漂亮。◇ *Those look riper than these.* 那些看上去比這些熟一些。**2** 0‑w used for referring to sb/sth that has already been mentioned, or is already known about（指已提到過或已知的人或事物）那，那個：*What can I do about that?* 這事我可怎麼辦？◇ *Do you remember when we went to Norway? That was a good trip.* 你記得我們什麼時候去挪威嗎？那次旅行真不錯。◇ *That's exactly what I think.* 我正是那麼想的。**3** (*formal*) used for referring to people or things of a particular type（特指）那，那種，那些：*Those present were in favour of change.* 在座的人都贊成變革。◇ *There are those who say* (= some people say) *she should not have got the job.* 有些人說她本不該得到這份工作。◇ *Salaries are higher here than those in my country.* 這裏的薪水比我國的高。**4** 0‑w /ðət; *rare strong form* ðæt/ (*pl.* **that**) used as a relative pronoun to introduce a part of a sentence which refers to the person, thing or time you have been talking about（用作關係代詞，引導從句）：*Where's the letter that came yesterday?* 昨天來的信在哪兒？◇ *Who was it that won the US Open?* 在美國公開賽上獲勝的是誰？◇ *The watch* (*that*) *you gave me keeps perfect time.* 您給我的那隻錶走得很準。◇ *The people* (*that*) *I spoke to were very helpful.* 我交談過的人都很肯幫忙。◇ *It's the best novel* (*that*) *I've ever read.* 這是我讀過的最佳小說。◇ *We moved here the year* (*that*) *my mother died.* 我們是我母親去世那年搬來的。**HELP** In spoken and informal written English **that** is nearly always left out when it is the object of the verb or is used with a preposition. 在英語口語和非正式的書面語中，作為動詞賓語或與介詞連用的 that 一般都省略。

T

IDM **and (all) 'that** (*BrE, informal*) and everything else connected with an activity, a situation, etc. 等等；以及諸如此類的事物 **SYN** **and so on**：*Did you bring the contract and (all) that?* 合同什麼的你都帶來了嗎？ **that is (to say)** used to say what sth means or to give more information 也就是說；即；換句話說：*He's a local government administrator, that is to say a civil servant.* 他是地方政府的行政官員，也就是文官。◇ *You'll find her very helpful—if she's not too busy, that is.* 你會覺得她很肯幫忙，那是說如果她不太忙的話。 ➲ LANGUAGE BANK at I.E. **ˌthat's 'it** (*informal*) **1** 🗝 used to say that sb is right, or is doing sth right （表示某人正確或做得對）就是這樣，正是如此，對啦：*No, the other one … that's it.* 不，另一個…就是它。◇ *That's it, carry on!* 對啦！繼續！ **2** 🗝 used to say that sth is finished, or that no more can be done （表示已完成或再也沒有可做的了）好了，就這樣吧：*That's it, the fire's out now.* 好了，現在火滅了。◇ *That's it for now, but if I get any news I'll let you know.* 現在就這些，如果再得到消息，我就通知你。◇ *A week to go, and that's it!* 還有一週，就完事了！ **3** used to say that you will not accept sth any longer （表示不再接受）行了，夠了：*That's it, I've had enough!* 夠了，我受夠了！ **4** 🗝 used to talk about the reason for sth （表示理由）就是這個問題，就是這麼回事：*So that's it—the fuse had gone.* 問題就出在這裏，保險絲燒斷了。◇ *You don't love me any more, is that it?* 你不再愛我啦，是不是這樣？ **ˌthat's 'that** (*informal*) used to say that your decision cannot be changed （表示決定不能更改）就是這樣，就這樣定了：*Well I'm not going, and that's that.* 好啦，我不去，就這麼定了。

■ **conj.** /ðət; *rare strong form* ðæt/ **1** 🗝 used after some verbs, adjectives and nouns to introduce a new part of the sentence （用於某些動詞、形容詞和名詞後，引出從句）：*She said (that) the story was true.* 她說這件事是真的。◇ *It's possible (that) he has not received the letter.* 可能他還沒有收到那封信。◇ *The fact (that) he's older than me is not relevant.* 他比我年紀大這一事實無關緊要。 **HELP** In spoken and informal written English **that** is usually left out after reporting verbs and adjectives. It is less often left out after nouns. 在英語口語和非正式的書面語中，在引出間接引語的動詞和形容詞之後的 that 通常省略，而在名詞後的則一般不省略。 **2** 🗝 **so … that …** used to express a result （表示結果）如此…以至：*She was so tired (that) she couldn't think straight.* 她累得昏頭昏腦。 **HELP** In informal English **that** is often left out. 在非正式英語中，that 常被省略。 **3** (*literary*) used for expressing a hope or a wish （表示希望或願望）多麼：*Oh that I could see him again!* 啊，我多麼想能再看到他！

■ **adv.** /ðæt/ **1** used when saying how much or showing how long, big, etc. sth is with your hands （以手勢表示長度、大小等時用）那樣，那麼：*I can't walk that far* (= as far as that). 我走不了那麼遠。◇ *It's about that long.* 大約有那麼長。 **2** **not (all) ~** not very, or not as much as has been said 不很；不那麼：*It isn't all that cold.* 天沒那麼冷。◇ *There aren't that many people here.* 這裏並沒有那麼多人。 **3** (*BrE, informal*) used to emphasize how much （用以強調程度）那麼：*I was that scared I didn't know what to do.* 我非常害怕，以至不知如何是好。

T

tha·ta·way /ˈðætəweɪ/ *adv.* (*informal*) in that direction 朝那邊；向那邊：*They went thataway!* 他們往那邊走了！

thatch /θætʃ/ *noun, verb*

■ **noun** **1** [U, C] dried STRAW, REEDS, etc. used for making a roof; a roof made of this material （作為屋頂材料的）茅草，稻草，蘆葦；茅草屋頂；草屋頂：*a roof made of thatch* 茅草屋頂 ◇ *The thatch was badly damaged in the storm.* 茅草屋頂在暴風雨中遭到嚴重破壞。 **2** [sing.] **~ of hair** (*informal*) thick hair on sb's head 濃密的頭髮

■ **verb** **~ sth** to cover the roof of a building with thatch 用茅草蓋屋頂 ▸ **thatched** *adj.*：*They live in a thatched cottage.* 他們住在茅舍裏。 ➲ VISUAL VOCAB page V16

thatch·er /ˈθætʃə(r)/ *noun* a person whose job is thatching roofs 蓋茅草屋頂的人

Thatch·er·ite /ˈθætʃəraɪt/ *adj.* connected with or supporting the policies of the former British Prime Minister, Margaret Thatcher (= thought of as being right-wing) （支持）英國前首相撒切爾夫人政策的；（支持）右翼政策的 ▸ **Thatch·er·ite** *noun*

thaw /θɔː/ *verb, noun*

■ **verb** **1** [I] **~ (out)** (of ice and snow 冰雪) to turn back into water after being frozen （結冰後）解凍，融化，融解 **SYN** **melt** **OPP** **freeze** **2** [I] when **it thaws** or is **thawing**, the weather becomes warm enough to melt snow and ice 天氣暖和得使冰雪融化（或解凍）：*It's starting to thaw.* 天氣轉暖，冰雪開始融化了。 **3** [I, T] **~ (sth) (out)** to become, or to let frozen food become, soft or liquid ready for cooking （使冷凍食品）化凍 ➲ compare DEFROST (1), DE-ICE, UNFREEZE (1)：*Leave the meat to thaw completely before cooking.* 讓凍肉完全化凍後再烹煮。 **4** [I, T] **~ (sth) (out)** to become, or make sth become, a normal temperature after being very cold （使）回到正常溫度，變暖：*I could feel my ears and toes start to thaw out.* 我覺得耳朵和腳趾暖和過來了。 **5** [I] **~ (out)** to become more friendly and less formal 變得友好（或隨和、不拘束）：*Relations between the two countries thawed a little after the talks.* 談判後兩國關係緩和了些。

■ **noun** **1** [C, usually sing.] a period of warmer weather following one of cold weather, causing snow and ice to melt 解凍時期；融化季節 **2** [sing.] **~ (in sth)** a situation in which the relations between two enemy countries become more friendly （敵對國家之間）關係緩和

the 🗝 /ðə; ði; *strong form* ðiː/ *definite article*

1 🗝 used to refer to sb/sth that has already been mentioned or is easily understood （指已提到或易領會到的人或事物）：*There were three questions. The first two were relatively easy but the third one was hard.* 有三個問題。頭兩個相對容易，第三個困難。◇ *There was an accident here yesterday. A car hit a tree and the driver was killed.* 昨天這裏發生了一起事故。一輛小轎車撞到樹上，駕車的人死了。◇ *The heat was getting to be too much for me.* 天氣熱得快讓我受不了。◇ *The nights are getting longer.* 夜越來越長。 **2** 🗝 used to refer to sb/sth that is the only, normal or obvious one of their kind （指獨一無二的、正常的或不言而喻的人或事物）：*the Mona Lisa*《蒙娜麗莎》◇ *the Nile* 尼羅河 ◇ *the Queen* 女王 ◇ *What's the matter?* 怎麼回事？◇ *The phone rang.* 電話鈴響了。◇ *I patted her on the back.* 我拍了拍她的背。◇ *How's the* (= your) *baby?* 寶寶好嗎？ **3** 🗝 used when explaining which person or thing you mean （解說時用）：*the house at the end of the street* 街盡頭的房子 ◇ *The people I met there were very friendly.* 我在那裏遇到的人很友善。◇ *It was the best day of my life.* 這是我一生中最美好的一天。◇ *You're the third person to ask me that.* 你是第三個問我那件事的人。◇ *Friday the thirteenth* 十三號，星期五 ◇ *Alexander the Great* 亞歷山大大帝 **4** 🗝 used to refer to a thing in general rather than a particular example （用以泛指）：*He taught himself to play the violin.* 他自學拉小提琴。◇ *The dolphin is an intelligent animal.* 海豚是聰明的動物。◇ *They placed the African elephant on their endangered list.* 他們把非洲大象列為瀕危動物。◇ *I heard it on the radio.* 我從收音機裏聽到了這件事。◇ *I'm usually out during the day.* 白天我通常不在家。 **5** 🗝 used with adjectives to refer to a thing or a group of people described by the adjective （與形容詞連用，指事物或統稱的人）：*With him, you should always expect the unexpected.* 在他身上你應隨時料到有意想不到的事情發生。◇ *the unemployed* 失業者 ◇ *the French* 法國人 **6** 🗝 used before the plural of sb's last name to refer to a whole family or a married couple （用於姓氏的複數形式前，指家庭或夫婦）：*Don't forget to invite the Jordans.* 別忘了邀請喬丹一家。 **7** enough of sth for a particular purpose （指特定用途的事物）足夠，恰好：*I wanted it but I didn't have the money.* 我想買那東西，但錢不夠。 **8** 🗝 used with a unit of measurement to mean 'every' （與計量單位連用）每，一：*My car does forty miles to the gallon.* 我的車每加侖汽油跑四十英里。◇ *You get paid by the hour.* 你領的是時薪。 **9** used with a unit of time to mean 'the present' （與時間單位連用）當前的，本，此：*Why not have the dish of the day?* 何不試一下今天的精選菜？◇ *She's flavour of the month with him.* 她是他眼下的紅人。 **10** /ðiː/ used, stressing *the*, to show that the person or thing referred to is famous or important （重讀，表示所指的為知名或重要的人或事物）：*Sheryl Crow? Not* '*the Sheryl Crow?* 謝里爾・克羅？莫不是大名鼎鼎的謝里爾・克羅？◇ *At that time London was* '*the place to be.* 那時候倫敦是不可不去的地方。

IDM **the more, less, etc. ..., the more, less, etc. ...** used to show that two things change to the same degree（用以表示兩個事物按照同一程度變化）越…越，愈…愈：*The more she thought about it, the more depressed she became.* 她越想這事越沮喪。◇ *The less said about the whole thing, the happier I'll be.* 對整個事情議論得越少，我越高興。

the·atre (*especially US* **theater**) /ˈθɪətə(r); *NAmE* ˈθiːətər/ *noun*
1 [C] a building or an outdoor area where plays and similar types of entertainment are performed 戲院；劇場；露天劇場：*Broadway theatres* 百老匯的劇院 ◇ *an open-air theatre* 露天劇場 ◇ *How often do you* **go to the theatre**? 你多久看一次戲？➲ VISUAL VOCAB pages V2, V3 ➲ see also LECTURE THEATRE **2** (also ˈ**movie theater**) (both *NAmE*) (*BrE* **cin·ema**) [C] a building in which films/movies are shown 電影院；影廳 **3** [U] plays considered as entertainment 戲劇：*an evening of live music and theatre* 現場演奏音樂戲劇晚會 ◇ (*BrE*) *I like music, theatre and cinema.* 我喜歡音樂、戲劇和電影。◇ *current ideas about what makes good theatre* (= what makes good entertainment when performed) 對何謂好戲劇的普遍看法 **4** [U] (also **the theatre** [sing.]) the work of writing, producing and acting in plays 戲劇工作；劇作；演出；上演：*I want to work in theatre.* 我想從事戲劇工作。◇ *He was essentially a man of the theatre.* 他基本上是個戲劇人。 **5** [C, U] (*BrE*) = OPERATING THEATRE：*a theatre sister* (= a nurse who helps during operations) 手術室護士長 ◇ *He's still* **in theatre**. 他仍在接受手術。 **6** [C, usually sing.] ~ (**of war, etc.**) (*formal*) the place in which a war or fighting takes place 戰場；戰區

theatre·goer (*especially US* **theater·goer**) /ˈθɪətəɡəʊə(r); *NAmE* ˈθiːətərɡoʊər/ (also **play·goer**) *noun* a person who goes regularly to the theatre 經常去戲院看戲的人；愛看戲的人 ▸ **theatre·going** (*especially US* **theater·going**) *adj.*：*the theatregoing public* 經常看戲的公眾

ˌ**theatre-in-the-ˈround** (*especially US* ˌ**theater-in-the-ˈround**) *noun* [U] a way of performing plays on a stage which is surrounded by the audience 圓形劇場式演出

ˈ**theatre nurse** (*BrE*) (*NAmE* ˈ**scrub nurse**) *noun* a nurse with special training, who helps during operations 手術室護士

the·at·ri·cal /θiˈætrɪkl/ *adj.* **1** [only before noun] connected with the theatre 戲劇的；演劇的；劇場的：*a theatrical agent* 演員經紀人 **2** (often *disapproving*) (of behaviour 舉止) exaggerated in order to attract attention or create a particular effect 演戲似的；誇張的；戲劇性的：*a theatrical gesture* 戲劇性的姿勢 ▸ **the·at·ri·cal·ly** /-kli/ *adv.*

the·at·ri·cal·ity /θiˌætrɪˈkæləti/ *noun* [U] the exaggerated quality of sth that is intended to attract attention or create a particular effect 戲劇性；誇張

the·at·ri·cals /θiˈætrɪklz/ *noun* [pl.] **1** performances of plays 戲劇演出：*amateur theatricals* 業餘戲劇演出 **2** (also **the·at·rics** especially in *NAmE*) behaviour that is exaggerated and emotional in order to attract attention 戲劇化動作；矯揉造作

thee /ðiː/ *pron.* (*old use* or *dialect*) a word meaning 'you', used when talking to only one person who is the object of the verb（第二人稱單數的賓格）你：*We beseech thee, O Lord.* 主啊，我們懇求您。➲ compare THOU

theft /θeft/ *noun* [U, C] ~ (**of sth**) the crime of stealing sth from a person or place 偷；偷竊；盜竊罪：*car theft* 偷盜汽車 ◇ *Police are investigating the theft of computers from the company's offices.* 警方正在調查這家公司辦公室裏的計算機失竊案。➲ compare BURGLARY, ROBBERY ➲ see also IDENTITY THEFT, THIEF

their /ðeə(r); *NAmE* ðer/ *det.*
(the possessive form of *they* * they 的所有格形式) **1** of or belonging to them 他們的；她們的；它們的：*Their parties are always fun.* 他們的聚會總是樂趣橫生。◇ *Which is their house?* 哪座房子是他們的？ **2** used instead of *his* or *her* to refer to a person whose sex is not mentioned or not known（在提及性別不詳的人時，用以代替 his 或 her）：*If anyone calls, ask for their number so I can call them back.* 如有人打電話來，問問他們的電話號碼，這樣我可以回電話。➲ note at GENDER

theirs /ðeəz; *NAmE* ðerz/ *pron.*
(the possessive form of *they* * they 的所有格形式) of or belonging to them 他們的，她們的，它們的（所有物）：*Theirs are the children with very fair hair.* 他們的孩子是那些長着滿頭金髮的。◇ *It's a favourite game of theirs.* 這是他們最喜愛的遊戲。

the·ism /ˈθiːɪzəm/ *noun* [U] belief in the existence of God or gods 有神論 OPP **atheism**

them /ðəm; *strong form* ðem/ *pron.*
(the object form of *they* * they 的賓格) **1** used when referring to people, animals or things as the object of a verb or preposition, or after the verb *be* 他們；她們；它們：*Tell them the news.* 把這消息告訴他們。◇ *What are you doing with those matches? Give them to me.* 你拿那些火柴做什麼？把它們交給我。◇ *Did you eat all of them?* 你都吃光了嗎？◇ *It's them.* 是他們。 **2** used instead of *him* or *her* to refer to a person whose sex is not mentioned or not known（指性別不詳的人時，用以代替 him 或 her）：*If anyone comes in before I get back, ask them to wait.* 如果在我回來之前有人來，就請他等一等。

the·mat·ic AW /θɪˈmætɪk; θiː-/ *adj.* [usually before noun] connected with the theme or themes of sth 題目的；主題的；專題的：*the thematic structure of a text* 文本的主題結構 ▸ **the·mat·ic·al·ly** AW /-kli/ *adv.*：*The books have been grouped thematically.* 這些書籍已按專題進行了分類。

theˌmatic ˈrole (also ˈ**theta role**) *noun* (*linguistics* 語言) the function that a noun phrase has in relation to a verb, for example AGENT or PATIENT 解元角色，主題角色（指與動詞相關的名詞短語的功能，如施動者或受動者）

theme AW /θiːm/ *noun, adj.*
■ *noun* **1** the subject or main idea in a talk, piece of writing or work of art（演講、文章或藝術作品的）題目，主題，主題思想：*North American literature is the main theme of this year's festival.* 北美文學是今年藝術節的主題。◇ *The President stressed a favourite campaign theme—greater emphasis on education.* 總統強調了最受人歡迎的競選主題 —— 更加重視教育。◇ *The naked male figure was always the central theme of Greek art.* 男性裸體畫像總是希臘藝術的中心主題。◇ *The stories are all* **variations on the theme** *of unhappy marriage.* 這些故事講來講去無非是這樣那樣的不幸婚姻。➲ COLLOCATIONS at LITERATURE **2** (*music* 音) a short tune that is repeated or developed in a piece of music（樂曲的）主題，主旋律 **3** = THEME MUSIC：*the theme from 'The Godfather'*《教父》的主題音樂 **4** (*old-fashioned, NAmE*) a short piece of writing on a particular subject, done for school（學生的）作文 **5** (*linguistics* 語言) the part of a sentence or clause that contains information that is not new to the reader or audience（句子的）主位；詞幹；主題 ➲ compare RHEME
■ *adj.* (*BrE*) ~ **pub/bar/restaurant, etc.** a pub, bar, etc. that is designed to reflect a particular subject or period of history（反映某主題或歷史時期的）主題酒館（或酒吧、餐館等）：*an Irish theme pub* 愛爾蘭主題酒館

themed /θiːmd/ *adj.* [usually before noun] (*BrE*) (of an event or a place of entertainment 事件或娛樂地點) designed to reflect a particular subject or period of history 特定主題的；特定歷史時期的：*a themed restaurant* 以特定主題裝飾的餐館

ˈ**theme music** *noun* [U] (also **theme**, ˈ**theme song**, ˈ**theme tune** [C]) music that is played at the beginning and end and/or is often repeated in a film/movie, television programme, etc.（電影、電視節目的）主題音樂 ➲ compare SIGNATURE TUNE

ˈ**theme park** *noun* a large park where people go to enjoy themselves, for example by riding on large machines such as ROLLER COASTERS, and where much

T

of the entertainment is connected with one subject or idea 主題樂園（娛樂項目大多圍繞一個主題的大型公園）：*a western-style theme park* 西部風格主題樂園

them·self /ðəm'self/ *pron.* (the reflexive form of *they*) used instead of *himself* or *herself* to refer to a person whose sex is not mentioned or not known（they 的反身形式，用以代替 himself 或 herself，指稱性別不明確的人）他自己，她自己：*Does anyone here consider themself a good cook?* 這裏有人覺得自己烹飪很拿手嗎？ **HELP** Although **themself** is fairly common, especially in spoken English, many people think it is not correct. * themself 很常見，特別是在英語口語中，但很多人認為不正確。

them·selves /ðəm'selvz/ *pron.*
1 (the reflexive form of *they* * they 的反身形式) used when people or animals performing an action are also affected by it 他們自己；她們自己；它們自己：*They seemed to be enjoying themselves.* 他們好像玩得非常高興。◇ *The children were arguing amongst themselves.* 孩子們在相互爭論。◇ *They've bought themselves a new car.* 他們給自己買了一輛新車。 **2** used to emphasize *they* or a plural subject（用以強調 they 或複數主語）他們（或她們、它們）親自，他們（或她們、它們）本身：*They themselves had had a similar experience.* 他們本身就曾有過類似的經歷。◇ *Don and Julie paid for it themselves.* 唐和朱莉他們親自付的款。 **3** used instead of *himself* or *herself* to refer to a person whose sex is not mentioned or not known（指性別不詳的人時，用以代替 himself 或 herself）：*There wasn't anyone who hadn't enjoyed themselves.* 沒有人不盡興。 **HELP** Although this use of **themselves** is fairly common, especially in spoken English, many people think it is not correct. * themselves 的這一用法相當普遍，尤其在英語口語中，但許多人認為並不正確。
IDM **(all) by them'selves** **1** alone; without anyone else（他們）獨自，單獨：*They wanted to spend the evening by themselves.* 他們想要單獨度過這個夜晚。 **2** without help（他們）獨立地：*They did the cooking by themselves.* 他們自己做了飯。 **(all) to them'selves** for them alone; not shared with anyone 只供他們自己用

then /ðen/ *adv., adj.*
■ ***adv.*** **1** used to refer to a particular time in the past or future（指過去）當時，那時；（指將來）到那時，屆時：*Life was harder then because neither of us had a job.* 那時生活比較艱苦，因為我倆都沒有工作。◇ *Things were very different* ***back then.*** 以前那個時候情況大不相同。◇ *She grew up in Zimbabwe, or Rhodesia as it then was.* 她生長在津巴布韋，當時該地叫羅得西亞。◇ *I saw them at Christmas but haven't heard a thing* ***since then.*** 我在聖誕節見到過他們，但之後沒聽到過什麼消息。◇ *I've been invited too, so I'll see you then.* 我也接到邀請，我們到那時見。◇ *There's a room free in Bob's house next week but you can stay with us* ***until then.*** 下星期鮑勃家有一個房間空着，不過在那之前你可以和我們住在一起。◇ *Call again next week. They should have reached a decision* ***by then.*** 下星期再來電話。到那時他們應該已作出決定了。◇ ***Just then*** (= at that moment) *there was a knock at the door.* 就在那時有人敲門了。◇ *She left in 1984 and* ***from then on*** *he lived alone.* 她於 1984 年離去，從那時起他便獨自一人生活。◇ *I took one look at the car and offered to buy it* ***there and then/then and there*** (= immediately). 我只看了那輛汽車一眼，就當即表示要買下來。 **2** used to introduce the next item in a series of actions, events, instructions, etc. 然後；接着；其後；後來：*He drank a glass of whisky, then another and then another.* 他喝了杯威士忌，接着又喝了一杯，然後又喝了一杯。◇ *First cook the onions, then add the mushrooms.* 先炒洋蔥，然後放進蘑菇。◇ *We lived in France and then Italy before coming back to England.* 我們在返回英格蘭之前，先住在法國，後來住在意大利。 ➲ LANGUAGE BANK at PROCESS **3** used to show the logical result of a particular statement or situation 那麼；因此；既然如此：*If you miss that train then you'll have to get a taxi.* 如果你錯過那趟火車，那就得坐出租汽車。◇ *'My wife's got a job in Glasgow.' 'I take it you'll be moving, then.'* "我妻子在格拉斯哥找了份工作。" "既然如此，我想你要搬家了。" ◇ *'You haven't done anything to upset me.' 'So what's wrong, then?'* "你沒有做使我煩心的事。" "那你是怎麼啦？" ◇ *Why don't you hire a car? Then you'll be able to visit more of the area.* 你怎麼不租輛汽車？那樣的話，你可以多參觀些地方。 **4** used to introduce additional information 另外；還有；再者；而且：*She's been very busy at work* ***and then*** *there was all that trouble with her son.* 她工作一直很忙，另外還有兒子的一大堆麻煩事。 **5** (*formal*) used to introduce a summary of sth that has just been said 總之：*These, then, are the main areas of concern.* 總之，這些是人們主要關注的方面。 **6** used to show the beginning or end of a conversation, statement, etc.（表示交談、陳述等的開始或結束）那麼：*Right then, where do you want the table to go?* 那好吧，你要把桌子放在哪裏呢？◇ *'I really have to go.' 'OK. Bye, then.'* "我真該走了。" "好，那就再見吧。" ◇ *OK then, I think we've just about covered everything on the agenda.* 就這樣吧，我想我們幾乎已把議程上所有的事項都討論過了。
IDM **... and 'then some** (*informal*) used to emphasize the large amount or number of sth, and to say that you have not mentioned everything 而且還要多；而且遠不止這些：*There are Indian, Chinese, Mexican, Thai restaurants ... and then some!* 有印度、中國、墨西哥、泰國餐館…，而且還有很多其他國家的餐館！ **but 'then | then a'gain | but then a'gain** (*informal*) used to introduce additional information or information that contrasts with sth that has just been said（引出另外情況或相對照的情況）不過，可是話又說回來了：*She was early, but then again, she always is.* 她到得早，不過話又說回來了，她總是早到。◇ *'So you might accept their offer?' 'Yes, then again I might not.'* "這麼說你也許會接受他們的提議了？" "是的，不過也可能不接受。" ➲ more at NOW *adv.*
■ ***adj.*** [only before noun] used to describe sb who had a particular title, job, etc. at the time in the past that is being discussed 當時（任職等）的：*That decision was taken by the then president.* 那個決定是由當時的總統作出的。

thence /ðens/ *adv.* (*old use* or *formal*) from that place; following that 從那裏；然後；隨之：*They made their way from Spain to France and thence to England.* 他們從西班牙去了法國，再從那裏去了英國。◇ *He was promoted to manager, thence to a partnership in the firm.* 他被提升為經理，然後又成了公司的合夥人。

thence·forth /ˌðens'fɔːθ; *NAmE* -'fɔːrθ/ (also **thence·for·ward** /ˌðens'fɔːwəd; *NAmE* -'fɔːrwərd/) *adv.* (*old use* or *formal*) starting from that time 從那時起；此後

theo- /'θiːəʊ; *NAmE* 'θiːoʊ/ *combining form* (in nouns, adjectives and adverbs 構成名詞、形容詞和副詞) connected with God or a god 上帝的；神的

the·oc·racy /θi'ɒkrəsi; *NAmE* θi'ɑːk-/ *noun* (*pl.* **-ies**) **1** [U] government of a country by religious leaders 神權政治；僧侶政體 **2** [C] a country that is governed by religious leaders 神權國；神權政治國家 ▸ **theo·crat·ic** /ˌθiːə'krætɪk/ *adj.*：*theocratic rule* 神權統治

the·odo·lite /θi'ɒdəlaɪt; *NAmE* θi'ɑːd-/ *noun* a piece of equipment used by SURVEYORS for measuring angles 經緯儀

theo·lo·gian /ˌθiːə'ləʊdʒən; *NAmE* -'loʊ-/ *noun* a person who studies theology 神學家；神學研究者

the·ology /θi'ɒlədʒi; *NAmE* -'ɑːlə-/ *noun* (*pl.* **-ies**) **1** [U] the study of religion and beliefs 神學；宗教學；宗教信仰學：*a degree in Theology* 神學學位 ◇ *a theology student* 研究神學的人 **2** [C] a set of religious beliefs 宗教信仰：*the theologies of the East* 東方的種種宗教信仰 ▸ **theo·logic·al** /ˌθiːə'lɒdʒɪkl; *NAmE* -'lɑːdʒ-/ *adj.*：(*BrE*) *a theological college* 神學院 ◇ (*NAmE*) *a theological seminary* 神學（修）院 **theo·logic·al·ly** /-kli/ *adv.*

the·orem /'θɪərəm; *NAmE* 'θiːə-; 'θɪr-/ *noun* (*technical* 術語) a rule or principle, especially in mathematics, that can be proved to be true（尤指數學）定理 ➲ COLLOCATIONS at SCIENTIFIC

the·or·etic·al **AW** /ˌθɪə'retɪkl; *NAmE* ˌθiːə-/ *adj.* [usually before noun] **1** concerned with the ideas and principles on which a particular subject is based, rather than with practice and experiment 理論上的：*a theoretical* *approach* 理論研究方法 ◇ *theoretical physics* 理論物理 ◇ *The first year provides students with a sound theoretical basis for later study.* 第一年為學生以後的學習奠定堅實的理論基礎。 OPP **experimental, practical** **2** that could possibly exist, happen or be true, although this is unlikely 理論上存在的；假設的： *It's a theoretical possibility.* 這是理論上存在的可能性。 ▸ **the·or·etic·al·ly** AW /-kli/ *adv.*： *theoretically sound conclusions* 理論上無懈可擊的結論 ◇ *It is theoretically possible for him to overrule their decision, but highly unlikely.* 按理說他可以否定他們的決定，但是可能性很小。

the·or·ist AW /ˈθɪərɪst; *NAmE* ˈθiːə-; ˈθɪr-/ (also **the·or·et·ician** /ˌθɪərəˈtɪʃn; *NAmE* ˌθiːə-; ˌθɪr-/) *noun* a person who develops ideas and principles about a particular subject in order to explain why things happen or exist 理論家；理論工作者

the·or·ize (*BrE* also **-ise**) /ˈθɪəraɪz; *NAmE* ˈθiːə-/ *verb* [I, T] **~ (about/on sth)** | **~ sth** | **~ that** ... to suggest facts and ideas to explain sth; to form a theory or theories about sth 從理論上說明；形成理論；理論化： *The study theorizes about the role of dreams in peoples' lives.* 這項研究從理論上說明了夢在人們一生中的作用。 ▸ **the·or·iz·ing, -is·ing** *noun* [U]

the·ory 0-w AW /ˈθɪəri; *NAmE* ˈθɪri; ˈθiːəri/ *noun* (*pl.* **-ies**)
1 0-w [C, U] a formal set of ideas that is intended to explain why sth happens or exists 學說；論；說： *According to the theory of relativity, nothing can travel faster than light.* 根據相對論，任何東西都無法超越光速。 ➲ COLLOCATIONS at SCIENTIFIC **2** 0-w [U] the principles on which a particular subject is based 理論；原理；原則： *the theory and practice of language teaching* 語言教學理論與實踐 **3** 0-w [C] **~ (that ...)** an opinion or idea that sb believes is true but that is not proved（未證明的）意見；看法；推測： *I have this theory that most people prefer being at work to being at home.* 依我看，多數人喜歡工作而不願待在家裏。
IDM **in ˈtheory** 0-w used to say that a particular statement is supposed to be true but may in fact be wrong 理論上；按理說： *In theory, these machines should last for ten years or more.* 從理論上講，這些機器應能用十年以上。◇ *That sounds fine in theory, but have you really thought it through?* 這話聽起來很有道理，但是你真正全面考慮過沒有？

the·oso·phy /θiˈɒsəfi; *NAmE* θiˈɑːs-/ *noun* **1** [U, C] a religious system of thought that tries to know God by means of MEDITATION, prayer, etc. 神智學（通過直接體驗以認識上帝） **2** **Theosophy** [U] the belief of a religious group, the Theosophical Society, started in New York in 1875 神智學會信仰（該會於 1875 年在紐約成立）

thera·peut·ic /ˌθerəˈpjuːtɪk/ *adj.* **1** [usually before noun] designed to help treat an illness 治療的；醫療的；治病的： *the therapeutic properties of herbs* 草藥的醫療效用 **2** helping you to relax 有助於放鬆精神的： *Painting can be very therapeutic.* 繪畫可以使人放鬆。 ▸ **thera·peut·ic·al·ly** /-kli/ *adv.*

thera·peut·ics /ˌθerəˈpjuːtɪks/ *noun* [U] the branch of medicine concerned with the treatment of diseases 治療學

ther·ap·ist /ˈθerəpɪst/ *noun* **1** (especially in compounds 尤用於構成複合詞) a specialist who treats a particular type of illness or problem, or who uses a particular type of treatment（某治療法的）治療專家： *a speech therapist* 語言治療師 ◇ *a beauty therapist* 美容師 ➲ see also OCCUPATIONAL THERAPIST, PHYSIOTHERAPIST **2** = PSYCHOTHERAPIST

ther·apy /ˈθerəpi/ *noun* (*pl.* **-ies**) **1** [U, C] the treatment of a physical problem or an illness 治療；療法： *Most leukaemia patients undergo some sort of* ***drug therapy*** (= treatment using drugs). 大多數白血病患者都會接受某種藥物治療。◇ ***alternative/complementary/natural therapies*** (= treatments that do not use traditional drugs) 替代 / 補充 / 自然療法 ➲ COLLOCATIONS at ILL **2** [U] = PSYCHOTHERAPY： *a therapy group* 心理治療小組 ◇ *She's* ***in therapy***. 她在接受心理治療。 ➲ see also CHEMOTHERAPY, GROUP THERAPY, HORMONE REPLACEMENT THERAPY, OCCUPATIONAL THERAPY, PHYSIOTHERAPY, RADIOTHERAPY, RETAIL THERAPY, SPEECH THERAPY

Thera·vada /ˌθerəˈvɑːdə/ (also ˌ**Thera**ˌ**vada** ˈ**Buddhism**) *noun* [U] one of the two major forms of Buddhism 上座部（佛教部派） ➲ compare MAHAYANA

there 0-w /ðeə(r); *NAmE* ðer/ *adv., exclamation*
■ ***adv.*** **1** 0-w **there is, are, was, were, etc.** used to show that sth exists or happens（表示存在或發生）： *There's a restaurant around the corner.* 拐角處有一家餐館。◇ *There are two people waiting outside.* 有兩個人正在外面等候。◇ *Has there been an accident?* 出過事故嗎？◇ *I don't want there to be any misunderstanding.* 我不希望有任何誤解。◇ *There seemed to be no doubt about it.* 此事似乎毫無疑問。◇ *There comes a point where you give up.* 有時候你總得放棄。◇ *There remains the problem of finance.* 財政問題仍然存在。◇ *Suddenly there was a loud bang.* 突然發出砰的一聲巨響。◇ (*informal*) *There's only four days left.* 只剩下四天了。◇ (*literary*) ***There once was*** *a poor farmer who had four sons.* 從前有一個貧苦的農夫，他有四個兒子。 **2** 0-w in, at or to that place or position 在那裏；到那裏；往那裏： *We went on to Paris and stayed there eleven days.* 我們接着去了巴黎，在那裏停留了十一天。◇ *I hope we get there in time.* 我希望我們及時到達那裏。◇ *It's there, right in front of you!* 在那兒，就在你前面！◇ ***There it is****—just behind the chair.* 可找到它了，就在椅子後面。◇ *'Have you seen my pen?' 'Yes, it's* ***over there****.'* "你看見我的筆了嗎？" "看見了，就在那兒。" ◇ *There are a lot of people* ***back there*** (= behind) *waiting to get in.* 後面有許多人等着進來。◇ *I'm not going* ***in there****—it's freezing!* 我不打算到那裏面去，太冷了！◇ *We're* ***almost there*** (= we have almost arrived). 我們差不多快到了。◇ *Can I get* ***there and back*** *in a day?* 我去那裏一天內能打來回嗎？◇ *I left in 2008 and I haven't been* ***back there*** *since.* 我於 2008 年離開那裏，從那以後再也沒有回去過。◇ *Hello, is Bob there please?* (= used when calling sb on the phone) 喂，請問鮑勃在嗎？◇ *I took one look at the car and offered to buy it* ***there and then/then and there*** (= immediately). 我只看了那輛汽車一眼，便當即表示要買下來。 **3** 0-w existing or available 存在的；現有的；可得到的： *I went to see if my old school was still there.* 我去看過母校是否依然存在。◇ *The money's there if you need it.* 你若需要用錢就來取好了。 **4** at that point (in a story, an argument, etc.)（故事、辯論等）在那一點上： *'I feel ...' There she stopped.* "我覺得…" 她說到那兒停了下來。◇ *I don't agree with you there.* 在那一點上，我不敢與你苟同。 **5** used to attract sb's attention（用以引起注意）： *Hello, there!* 喂，你好！◇ *You there! Come back!* 說你呢！回來！◇ ***There you are!*** *I've been looking for you everywhere.* 原來你在這兒！我到處都把你找遍了。 **6** used to attract sb's attention to a particular person, thing or fact（用以引起對某人、事物或事實的注意）： *There's the statue I was telling you about.* 那就是我跟你們講過的塑像。◇ *That woman there is the boss's wife.* 那邊那個女人是老闆的太太。◇ ***There goes*** *the last bus* (= we've just missed it). 最後一班公共汽車剛開走了。◇ ***There goes*** *the phone* (= it's ringing). 聽，電話鈴響了。◇ (*humorous*) ***There goes*** *my career!* (= my career is ruined) 我的前程就這麼給毀了！◇ *So,* ***there you have it****: that's how it all started.* 就這樣，你瞧：這就是整個事件的起因。 **7** **~ to do sth** used to show the role of a person or thing in a situation（表示人或事物在某一情況中的作用）： *The fact is, they're there to make money.* 真實的情況是，他們去那兒是為了賺錢。
IDM ˌ**been** ˈ**there**, ˌ**done** ˈ**that** (*informal*) used to show that you think a place or an activity is not very interesting or impressive because you have already experienced it（表示已去過某地或做過某事而不再感興趣）沒意思，沒勁，乏味：*Not Spain again! Been there, done that, got the T-shirt.* 別再去西班牙了！去過那兒了，連紀念 T 恤都買了，沒勁。 **be** ˈ**there for sb** to be available if sb wants to talk to you or if they need help 隨叫隨到；不離…左右： *You know I'll always be there for you.* 你知道我將永遠在你左右。 **by** ˈ**there** (*WelshE*) there; to there 在那裏；到那裏；往那裏： *He's over by there.* 他在那兒。

T

have been there be'fore (*informal*) to know all about a situation because you have experienced it 全都知道；親身經歷過 **not all 'there** (*informal*) not very intelligent, especially because of mental illness 傻傻乎乎；呆頭呆腦 **,so 'there!** (*informal*) used to show that you are determined not to change your attitude or opinion 就是這樣；我主意已定；沒什麼可商量的： *Well, you can't have it, so there!* 好啦，不給你了，就是這樣！ **,there it 'is** (*informal*) that is the situation 情況就是這樣： *It's crazy, I know, but there it is.* 我知道，那很瘋狂，不過情況就是如此。 **'there's a good boy, girl, dog, etc.** (*informal*) used to praise or encourage small children or animals（用以誇獎或勉勵幼兒、動物）乖，乖孩子： *Finish your lunch, there's a good boy.* 把午飯吃完，乖孩子。 **there's lovely, nice, etc.** (*WelshE*) used to say that sth has a particular quality（表示有某種特性）真可愛，太好了 **,there's 'sth for you** (*informal*) used to say that sth is a very good example of sth 這才叫；這才稱得上： *She visited him every day he was in the hospital. There's devotion for you.* 他住醫院時，她每天都去探望他。這才叫做盡心盡力。◇ (*ironic*) *He didn't even say thank you. There's gratitude for you!* 他連個謝字都沒說。瞧，這就是對你的感激！ **,there or therea'bouts** (*BrE, informal*) used to say that sth is very good, even if it is not perfect（表示即使不完美也很好）差不多： *At the end of the tournament, he'll be there or thereabouts* (= he may not win, but he will be one of the best players). 錦標賽結束時，他不拔頭籌也差不到哪裏去。 **,there, 'there!** (*informal*) used to persuade a small child to stop crying or being upset（勸說小孩不要啼哭或沮喪）好了，好了： *There, there! Never mind, you'll soon feel better.* 好了，好了！不要緊，你很快就會感到好一些了。 **,there you 'are** (also **,there you 'go**) (*informal*) **1** 0-ᵘ used when giving sb a thing they want or have asked for 給你；這就是你要的；拿去吧： *There you are—that'll be £3.80, please.* 喏，給您，請付 3 英鎊 80 便士。◇ *OK, there you go.* 好，給你。 **2** used when explaining or showing sth to sb（解釋或示範時用）這就行了，就是這樣： *You switch on, push in the DVD and there you are!* 你打開開關，把 DVD 推進去就行了！◇ *There you are! I told you it was easy!* 瞧，就是這樣！我跟你說過這很容易！ **3** used when you are talking about sth that happens in a typical way or about a situation that cannot be changed（某事的發生方式）一貫如此；（某狀況）無可更改： *There you go—that's what they're like.* 瞧，他們就是這個樣子。◇ *I know it's not ideal but there you go …* 我知道這並不理想，但只好這樣啦… **,there you go a'gain** (*informal*) used to criticize sb when they behave in a way that is typical of them（批評對方的一貫作風）你又來這一套了： *There you go again—jumping to conclusions.* 你又犯老毛病了，太快下結論了。 ➲ more at HERE *adv.*

T

■ *exclamation* used to express satisfaction that you were right about sth or to show that sth annoys you（表示因說中某事而感到滿意或表示煩惱）你瞧，好啦，得啦： *There now! What did I tell you?* (= you can see that I was right) 你瞧！我跟你說什麼來着？◇ *There! That didn't hurt too much, did it?* 怎麼樣，那不太痛吧？◇ *There! You've gone and woken the baby!* 瞧！你一去就把孩子弄醒了！

there·abouts /ˌðeərəˈbaʊts; *NAmE* ˌðerə-/ *adv.* (usually used after *or* 通常用於 or 之後) **1** near the place mentioned 在那附近： *He comes from Leeds or thereabouts.* 他是利茲或其附近的人。 **2** used to say that a particular number, quantity, time, etc. is not exact（數量、時間等）大約，左右，上下： *They paid $100 000 or thereabouts for the house.* 他們買那房子花了大約 10 萬元。 **IDM** see THERE *adv.*

there·after /ˌðeərˈɑːftə(r); *NAmE* ˌðerˈæf-/ *adv.* (*formal*) after the time or event mentioned 之後；此後；以後： *She married at 17 and gave birth to her first child shortly thereafter.* 她 17 歲結婚，之後不久便生了第一個孩子。 ➲ compare HEREAFTER (2)

there·by **AW** /ˌðeəˈbaɪ; *NAmE* ˌðerˈbaɪ/ *adv.* (*formal*) used to introduce the result of the action or situation mentioned 因此；由此；從而： *Regular exercise strengthens the heart, thereby reducing the risk of heart attack.* 經常鍛煉可以增強心臟機能，從而減少心臟病發作的危險。

there·fore 0-ᵘ /ˈðeəfɔː(r); *NAmE* ˈðerf-/ *adv.* used to introduce the logical result of sth that has just been mentioned 因此；所以；因而： *He's only 17 and therefore not eligible to vote.* 他只有 17 歲，因此沒有投票選舉的資格。◇ *There is still much to discuss. We shall, therefore, return to this item at our next meeting.* 要討論的問題還有很多。所以，我們將在下次會議上再討論這項議題。

Language Bank 用語庫

therefore

Ways of saying 'For this reason …' "因此" 的種種表達方法

- Today's children eat more junk food and get less exercise than previous generations of children. It is not surprising, **therefore**, that rates of childhood obesity are on the increase. 當今的孩子比過去幾代人吃的垃圾食品更多，鍛煉更少。因此，肥胖兒童的比例逐漸升高並不奇怪。
- Children who grow up on a diet of junk food find it difficult to change this habit later in life. It is essential, **therefore**, that parents encourage healthy eating from an early age. 吃垃圾食品長大的孩子發現在日後的生活中很難改變這個習慣。因此，父母從孩子幼年開始就倡導健康飲食非常重要。
- Children who grow up on a diet of junk food find it difficult to change this habit later in life. **For this reason,/This is why** it is essential that children eat healthily from an early age. 吃垃圾食品長大的孩子在日後的生活中很難改變這個習慣。因此，孩子從幼年開始就健康飲食非常重要。
- Eating habits formed in childhood tend to continue into adult life. **Thus**, the best way to prevent heart disease among adults is to encourage healthy eating from an early age. 孩童時期形成的飲食習慣往往會延續到成年。因此，預防成年人心臟疾病的最好方法就是從小鼓勵健康飲食。
- Eating habits formed in childhood tend to continue into adult life, **hence** the importance of encouraging healthy eating from an early age. 孩童時期形成的飲食習慣往往會延續到成年。因此，從小鼓勵健康飲食尤為重要。

➲ Language Banks at BECAUSE OF, CAUSE, CONSEQUENTLY, EMPHASIS, VITAL

there·from /ðeəˈfrɒm; *NAmE* ˌðerˈfrʌm/ *adv.* (*formal* or *law* 律) from the thing mentioned 由此；從那裏： *The committee will examine the agreement and any problems arising therefrom.* 委員會將審查這項協議和由此引起的問題。

there·in /ˌðeərˈɪn; *NAmE* ˌðer-/ *adv.* (*law* 律 or *formal*) in the place, object, document, etc. mentioned 在那裏，在其中（指提及的地點、物體、文件等）： *The insurance policy covers the building and any fixtures contained therein.* 保險單為這座大樓及其中所有的設施保了險。 **IDM** **therein lies …** used to emphasize the result or consequence of a particular situation 那一點就是；那方面便是；…就在那裏： *He works extremely hard and therein lies the key to his success.* 他工作極其努力，這就是他成功的關鍵。

there·of /ˌðeərˈɒv; *NAmE* ˌðerˈʌv/ *adv.* (*law* 律 or *formal*) of the thing mentioned 在其中；由此： *Is the property or any part thereof used for commercial activity?* 這一財產或其中任何部份是用於商業活動嗎？

there·on /ˌðeərˈɒn; *NAmE* ˌðerˈɑːn; -ˈɔːn/ *adv.* (*law* 律 or *formal*) on the thing mentioned 以…為根據；由…而產生： *a meeting to discuss the annual accounts and the auditors' report thereon* 討論年度賬目及其審計報告的會議

there's /ðeəz; *NAmE* ðerz/ *short form* **1** there is **2** there has

there·to /ˌðeə'tuː; *NAmE* ˌðer'tuː/ *adv.* (*law* 律 or *formal*) to the thing mentioned 附之；隨之：*The lease entitles the holder to use the buildings and any land attached thereto.* 本租約持有人有權使用此建築物以及所附屬的土地。

there·under /ˌðeər'ʌndə(r); *NAmE* ˌðer-/ *adv.* (*law* 律 or *formal*) under the thing mentioned 在其下；據此：*This savings plan is only available under the Finance Act 1990 and any regulations made thereunder.* 這項儲蓄計劃只根據《1990 年金融法案》及其下設規定提供。

there·upon /ˌðeərə'pɒn; *NAmE* ˌðerə'pɑːn/ *adv.* (*formal*) **1** immediately after the situation mentioned; as a direct result of the situation mentioned 立即；隨即；因此；於是：*The audience thereupon rose cheering to their feet.* 觀眾隨即起立歡呼。 **2** on the thing mentioned 在其上：*a large notice with black letters printed thereupon* 印有黑體字的大幅告示

there·with /ˌðeə'wɪð; -'wɪθ; *NAmE* ˌðer'w-/ *adv.* (*old use* or *formal*) **1** with or in the thing mentioned 與此；與之 **2** soon or immediately after that 隨即；立即

therm /θɜːm; *NAmE* θɜːrm/ *noun* a unit of heat, used in Britain for measuring a gas supply 撒姆（英國用以計量煤氣的熱量單位）

ther·mal /'θɜːml; *NAmE* 'θɜːrml/ *adj., noun*

■ ***adj.*** [only before noun] **1** (*technical* 術語) connected with heat 熱的；熱量的：*thermal energy* 熱能 **2** (of clothing 衣服) designed to keep you warm by preventing heat from escaping from the body 保暖的；防寒的：*thermal underwear* 保暖內衣褲 **3** (of streams, lakes, etc. 溪水、湖泊等) in which the water has been naturally heated by the earth 溫暖的；熱的：*thermal springs* 溫泉 ▸ **ther·mal·ly** /-əli/ *adv.*

■ ***noun*** **1** [C] a rising current of warm air used, for example, by a GLIDER to gain height 上升的熱氣流 **2 thermals** [pl.] (*especially BrE*) warm underwear that prevents heat from escaping from the body 保暖內衣褲

ˌthermal 'imaging *noun* [U] (*technical* 術語) the process of producing an image of sth or finding out where sth is, using the heat that comes from it 熱成像（利用物體所散發的熱量形成圖像或定位）：*Rescue teams are using thermal imaging to locate survivors of the earthquake.* 救援隊伍正利用熱成像確定地震幸存者的位置。

thermo- /'θɜːməʊ; *NAmE* -moʊ/ *combining form* (in nouns, adjectives and adverbs 構成名詞、形容詞和副詞) connected with heat 熱的：*thermonuclear* 熱核的 ◇ *thermometer* 溫度計

thermo·dynam·ics /ˌθɜːməʊdaɪ'næmɪks; *NAmE* ˌθɜːrmoʊ-/ *noun* [U] the science that deals with the relations between heat and other forms of energy 熱力學：*the laws of thermodynamics* 熱力學定律 ▸ **thermo·dynam·ic** *adj.*

therm·om·eter /θə'mɒmɪtə(r); *NAmE* θər'mɑːm-/ *noun* an instrument used for measuring the temperature of the air, a person's body, etc. 溫度計；寒暑表；體溫計：*a thermometer reading* 溫度計讀數

thermo·nuclear /ˌθɜːməʊ'njuːkliə(r); *NAmE* ˌθɜːrmoʊ'nuːk-/ *adj.* connected with nuclear reactions that only happen at very high temperatures 熱核的

thermo·plas·tic /ˌθɜːməʊ'plæstɪk; *NAmE* ˌθɜːrmoʊ-/ *noun* [U] (*technical* 術語) a plastic material that can be easily shaped and bent when it is heated, and that becomes hard when it is cooled 熱塑（性）塑料

Ther·mos™ /'θɜːməs; *NAmE* 'θɜːrməs/ (*BrE* also **'Thermos flask**) (*NAmE* also **'Thermos bottle**) *noun* a particular kind of VACUUM FLASK (= a container like a bottle with double walls with a VACUUM between them, used for keeping liquids hot or cold) 瑟姆斯保溫瓶；真空瓶；冰瓶 ➲ compare FLASK (2)

the thermo·sphere /'θɜːməsfɪə(r); *NAmE* 'θɜːrməsfɪr/ *noun* [sing.] (*technical* 術語) the region of the atmosphere above the MESOSPHERE 熱層

thermo·stat /'θɜːməstæt; *NAmE* 'θɜːrm-/ *noun* a device that measures and controls the temperature of a machine or room, by switching the heating or cooling system on and off as necessary 溫度自動調節器；恆温器 ▸ **thermo·stat·ic** /ˌθɜːmə'stætɪk; *NAmE* ˌθɜːrm-/ *adj.* [only before noun] **thermo·stat·ic·al·ly** /-kli/ *adv.*

the·saurus /θɪ'sɔːrəs/ *noun* (*pl.* **the·sauri** /θɪ'sɔːraɪ/ or **the·saur·uses** /-rəsɪz/) a book that lists words in groups that have similar meanings 分類詞典；同義詞詞典

these ➲ THIS

thesis AW /'θiːsɪs/ *noun* (*pl.* **theses** /'θiːsiːz/) **1 ~ (on sth)** a long piece of writing completed by a student as part of a university degree, based on their own research 論文；畢業論文；學位論文 **2** a statement or an opinion that is discussed in a logical way and presented with evidence in order to prove that it is true 命題；論題：*These latest findings support the thesis that sexuality is determined by nature rather than choice.* 這些最新發現證實了性別特徵取決於自然而不是選擇這一論點。 ➲ COLLOCATIONS at SCIENTIFIC

thes·pian /'θespiən/ *noun* (often *humorous*) an actor 演員 ▸ **thes·pian** *adj.*

theta /'θiːtə/ *noun* the 8th letter of the Greek alphabet (Θ, θ) 希臘字母表的第 8 個字母

'theta role *noun* = THEMATIC ROLE

they 🔑 /ðeɪ/ *pron.*

(used as the subject of a verb 用作動詞主語) **1** 🔑 people, animals or things that have already been mentioned or are easily identified 他們；她們；它們：*'Where are John and Liz?' 'They went for a walk.'* "約翰和利茲在哪兒？" "他們去散步了。" ◇ *They* (= the things you are carrying) *go on the bottom shelf.* 這些東西放在架子的底層。 **2** 🔑 used instead of *he* or *she* to refer to a person whose sex is not mentioned or not known（用以代替 he 或 she，指性別不詳的人）：*If anyone arrives late they'll have to wait outside.* 誰要是遲到，他就得在外面等着。 ➲ note at GENDER **3** 🔑 people in general （泛指）人們，人人，眾人：*The rest, as they say, is history.* 其餘的就盡人皆知，不須贅述了。 **4** 🔑 people in authority or experts 權威人士；上面（指負責人）；專家：*They cut my water off.* 管事的把水給我掐了。◇ *They now say that red wine is good for you.* 現在專家説喝紅葡萄酒對人有好處。

they'd /ðeɪd/ *short form* **1** they had **2** they would

they'll /ðeɪl/ *short form* they will

they're /ðeə(r); *NAmE* ðer; *NAmE weak form* ðər/ *short form* they are

they've /ðeɪv/ *short form* they have

thia·mine (also **thia·min**) /'θaɪəmɪn; -miːn/ *noun* [U] a VITAMIN of the B group, found in grains, BEANS and LIVER 硫胺素（B 類維生素，存在於穀物、豆子和肝臟中）

thick 🔑 /θɪk/ *adj., noun, adv.*

■ ***adj.*** (**thick·er, thick·est**)

▸ **DISTANCE BETWEEN SIDES** 厚度 **1** 🔑 having a larger distance between opposite sides or surfaces than other similar objects or than normal 厚的；粗的：*a thick slice of bread* 一片厚麪包 ◇ *a thick book* (= one that has a lot of pages) 一本厚書 ◇ *a thick coat* (= one made of heavy cloth) 厚大衣 ◇ *thick fingers* 粗手指 ◇ *Everything was covered with a thick layer of dust.* 所有的東西都覆蓋着厚厚的一層灰塵。 **2** 🔑 used to ask about or state the distance between opposite sides or surfaces （詢問或説明厚度）有…厚：*How thick are the walls?* 這些牆有多厚？◇ *They're two feet thick.* 它們兩英尺厚。

▸ **HAIR/FUR/TREES** 毛髮；毛皮；樹木 **3** 🔑 growing closely together in large numbers 濃密的；稠密的；茂密的：*thick dark hair* 濃密的黑髮 ◇ *a thick forest* 茂密的森林

▸ **LIQUID** 液體 **4** 🔑 not flowing very easily 濃的；黏稠的：*thick soup* 濃湯 ◇ *The effect will be ruined if the paint is too thick.* 塗料太稠就會破壞效果。

▸ **FOG/SMOKE/AIR** 霧；煙；空氣 **5** 🔑 difficult to see through; difficult to breathe in 能見度低的；濃的；陰霾的；渾濁的；不透氣的：*The plane crashed in thick fog.* 飛機在大霧中墜毀。◇ *thick smoke* 濃煙 ◇ **~ with sth** *The air was thick with dust.* 空氣由於灰塵瀰漫而悶塞。◇

T

(*figurative*) *The atmosphere was thick with tension.* 氣氛緊張得使人透不過氣來。
▸ WITH LARGE NUMBER/AMOUNT 大量 **6 ~ with sb/sth** having a large number of people or a large amount of sth in one place 擁滿；擠滿；充滿；瀰漫：*The beach was thick with sunbathers.* 海灘上密密麻麻都是曬太陽的人。
▸ STUPID 愚蠢 **7** (*BrE, informal*) (of a person 人) slow to learn or understand things 遲鈍的；愚笨的：*Are you thick, or what?* 你是傻還是怎麼啦？
▸ ACCENT 口音 **8** (sometimes *disapproving*) easily recognized as being from a particular country or area 濃重的；明顯的 SYN **strong**：*a thick Brooklyn accent* 濃重的布魯克林口音
▸ VOICE 嗓音 **9 ~ (with sth)** deep and not as clear as normal, especially because of illness or emotion 嘶啞的，不清的（尤指因疾病或激動所致）：*His voice was thick with emotion.* 他激動得話都說不清楚。
▸ FRIENDLY WITH SB 友好 **10 ~ (with sb)** (*informal*) very friendly with sb, especially in a way that makes other people suspicious 親密的；十分友好的；過於親近的：*You seem to be very thick with the boss!* 你好像和老闆走得挺近的！➲ see also THICKLY (3), THICKNESS
IDM **give sb/get a thick 'ear** (*BrE, informal*) to hit sb/be hit on the head as a punishment 打耳光；捱耳光 **(as) thick as 'thieves** (*informal*) (of two or more people 兩個或以上的人) very friendly, especially in a way that makes other people suspicious 非常友好；親密無間；過從甚密 **(as) thick as two short 'planks** (*BrE, informal*) (of a person 人) very stupid 笨得像木頭人；笨到極點 **a thick 'head** (*informal*) a physical condition in which your head is painful or you cannot think clearly as a result of an illness or of drinking too much alcohol （由於疾病或飲酒過量）暈頭脹腦，稀裏糊塗 **your thick 'head** (*informal*) used to show that you are annoyed that sb does not understand sth （認為某人理解慢而惱火）笨腦瓜，木頭腦瓜：*When will you get it into your thick head that I don't want to see you again!* 你那木頭腦瓜什麼時候才會明白我不想再見到你呢？ **a ˌthick 'skin** the ability to accept criticism, insults, etc. without becoming upset 厚臉皮；不計較面子 OPP **a thin skin** ➲ see also THICK-SKINNED ➲ more at BLOOD *n.*, GROUND *n.*
■ *noun* [U]
IDM **in the 'thick of sth** involved in the busiest or most active part of sth 在…最繁忙的時候；處於…最活躍部份；在密集處 **through ˌthick and 'thin** even when there are problems or difficulties 不顧艱難險阻；赴湯蹈火；同甘共苦：*He's supported the team for over ten years through thick and thin.* 十多年來，在任何情況下他都支持這個隊。
■ *adv.* (**thick·er**, **thick·est**) in a way that produces a wide piece or deep layer of sth 厚厚地：*Make sure you cut the bread nice and thick.* 你一定要把麪包片切得厚厚的。
IDM **lay it on 'thick** (*informal*) to talk about sb/sth in a way that makes them or it seem much better or much worse than they really are; to exaggerate sth 誇大其詞地褒貶；露骨地吹捧；過分貶低：*Praise them when necessary, but don't lay it on too thick.* 必要時要表揚他們，但不能言過其實。 **thick and 'fast** quickly and in large quantities 又快又多；頻頻：*Questions were coming at them thick and fast.* 問題鋪天蓋地向他們而來。

thick·en /ˈθɪkən/ *verb* [I, T] to become thicker; to make sth thicker （使）變厚，變濃，變稠：*Stir until the sauce has thickened.* 不停地攪拌醬汁，直到攪稠為止。◊ *It was a dangerous journey through thickening fog.* 旅途中霧越來越大，險象環生。◊ **~ sth** *Thicken the stew with flour.* 給燉肉汁勾芡。IDM see PLOT *n.*

thick·en·er /ˈθɪkənə(r)/ *noun* a substance used to make a liquid thicker 增稠劑：*paint thickeners* 油漆稠化劑

thicket /ˈθɪkɪt/ *noun* **1** a group of bushes or small trees growing closely together 灌木叢；樹叢 **2** a large number of things that are not easy to understand or separate 錯綜複雜；盤根錯節

thick·head /ˈθɪkhed/ (also **thicko**) *noun* (*BrE, informal*) a stupid person 傻瓜；笨蛋；呆子

thick·head·ed /ˌθɪkˈhedɪd/ *adj.* stupid 愚蠢的；笨的

thick·ly 🔑 /ˈθɪkli/ *adv.*
1 🔑 in a way that produces a wide piece or deep layer of sth 厚厚地：*thickly sliced bread* 切成厚片的麪包 ◊ *Apply the paint thickly in even strokes.* 塗顏料要厚，筆畫要勻。 **2 ~ wooded, populated, etc.** having a lot of trees, people, etc. close together （樹木、人口等）茂密，稠密 **3** in a deep voice that is not as clear as normal, especially because of illness or emotion 聲音不清地，沙啞地（尤指因疾病或激動）

thick·ness 🔑 /ˈθɪknəs/ *noun*
1 🔑 [U, C] the size of sth between opposite surfaces or sides 厚；厚度；粗 SYN **width**：*Use wood of at least 12 mm thickness.* 使用至少 12 毫米厚的木材。◊ *The board is available in four thicknesses.* 現有四種不同厚度的木板可供使用。 **2** [C] **~ (of sth)** a layer of sth 層：*The jacket was lined with a double thickness (= two layers) of fabric.* 這件短上衣有兩層襯裏。

Vocabulary Building 詞彙擴充

Saying that somebody is thin 形容人瘦

Thin is the most usual word. * thin 為最常用詞：*Steve is tall and thin and has brown hair.* 史蒂是瘦高個兒，長着棕色的頭髮。 It is sometimes used with a negative meaning. 該詞有時含貶義：*Mother looked thin and tired after her long illness.* 久病之後，母親看上去很憔悴。

The following words all express praise or admiration. 下列詞語均含有褒義：

- **Slim** means pleasantly thin. It is often used to describe women who have controlled their weight by diet or exercise. * slim 意為苗條、修長，常用以形容以節食或鍛煉來控制體重的女子：*She has a beautifully slim figure.* 她的身材十分苗條。
- A **slender** girl or woman is thin and graceful. * slender 指女性身材苗條、纖細、修長。
- A **lean** man is thin and fit. * lean 指男子瘦而健康。
- **Willowy** describes a woman who is attractively tall and thin. * willowy 指女子身材高挑，婀娜多姿。

The following words are more negative in their meaning. 下列詞語貶義較重：

- **Skinny** means very thin, often in a way that is not attractive. * skinny 意為瘦得皮包骨、乾瘦：*a skinny little kid* 瘦骨嶙峋的小孩
- **Bony** describes parts of the body when they are so thin that the bones can be seen. * bony 指人體某部位瘦得骨頭突出：*the old man's bony hands* 這老人骨瘦如柴的雙手
- **Scrawny** suggests that a person is thin, weak and not attractive. * scrawny 指人乾癟、骨瘦如柴：*a scrawny old woman* 骨瘦如柴的老婦
- **Gaunt** describes a person who is a little too thin and looks sad or ill. * gaunt 指人消瘦、憔悴。
- **Underweight** is used in medical contexts to describe people who are too thin because they are ill or have not had enough food. * underweight 在醫學上指人因疾病或飢餓而達不到標準體重：*Women who smoke risk giving birth to underweight babies.* 抽煙的婦女生出的嬰兒可能會體重不足。
- **Emaciated** describes a serious condition resulting from illness or lack of food. * emaciated 指因疾病或飢餓而枯瘦、消瘦。
- **Anorexic** is a medical term, but is now also used informally to describe a girl or woman who is so thin that you are worried about them. * anorexic（患厭食症的）是醫學術語，不過現在作為非正式用語亦指女孩或女人瘦得可憐。

It is more acceptable to talk to somebody about how thin or slim they are than about how fat they are. 說人瘦或苗條比說人胖更容易讓人接受。

➲ note at FAT

thicko /ˈθɪkəʊ; *NAmE* -oʊ/ *noun* (*pl.* **-os**) (*BrE, informal*) = THICKHEAD

thick·set /θɪkˈset/ *adj.* (especially of a man 尤指男子) having a strong heavy body 身體粗壯的；膀闊腰圓的；虎背熊腰的

ˌthick-ˈskinned *adj.* **1** (of a person 人) not easily upset by criticism or unkind comments 厚臉皮的；不計較臉面的；（對批評或侮辱）麻木不仁的 **2** (of fruit 水果) having a thick skin 皮厚的 OPP **thin-skinned**

thief 0-w /θiːf/ *noun* (*pl.* **thieves** /θiːvz/) a person who steals sth from another person or place 賊；小偷；竊賊：*a* ***car/jewel, etc. thief*** 偷汽車、珠寶等的竊賊 ➲ COLLOCATIONS at CRIME ➲ see also THEFT IDM see HONOUR *n.*, THICK *adj.*

thiev·ing /ˈθiːvɪŋ/ *noun* [U] (*informal*) the act of stealing things 偷竊 ▸ **thiev·ing** *adj.*：(*informal*) *You've no right to take that, you thieving swine!* 你沒有權利把那拿走，你這個貪心的賊！

thigh /θaɪ/ *noun* **1** the top part of the leg between the knee and the hip 大腿；股 ➲ COLLOCATIONS at PHYSICAL ➲ VISUAL VOCAB page V59 **2** the top part of the leg of a chicken, etc., cooked and eaten 食用的雞（等的）大腿

ˈthigh bone *noun* the large thick bone in the top part of the leg between the hip and the knee 股骨 SYN **femur** ➲ VISUAL VOCAB page V59

thim·ble /ˈθɪmbl/ *noun* a small metal or plastic object that you wear on the end of your finger to protect it when sewing 頂針；針箍

thimble·ful /ˈθɪmblfʊl/ *noun* a very small amount of a liquid, especially alcohol 少量液體（尤指酒）

thin 0-w /θɪn/ *adj.*, *adv.*, *verb*

■ ***adj.*** (**thin·ner**, **thin·nest**)

▸ NOT THICK 薄；細 **1** 0-w having a smaller distance between opposite sides or surfaces than other similar objects or than normal 薄的；細的：*Cut the vegetables into thin strips.* 把菜切成細條。◊ *A number of thin cracks appeared in the wall.* 牆上出現了許多細裂縫。◊ *The body was hidden beneath a thin layer of soil.* 屍體被埋藏在薄薄的一層土下面。◊ *a thin blouse* (= of light cloth) 薄薄的女襯衫 ➲ see also PAPER-THIN ➲ SYNONYMS at NARROW

▸ NOT FAT 瘦 **2** 0-w (of a person or part of the body 人或身體部位) (sometimes *disapproving*) not covered with much flesh 瘦的：*He was tall and thin, with dark hair.* 他又高又瘦，滿頭黑髮。◊ *She was looking pale and thin.* 她面黃肌瘦。◊ *He is as* ***thin as a rake*** (= very thin). 他骨瘦如柴。◊ *thin legs* 細腿

▸ HAIR 毛髮 **3** 0-w not growing closely together or in large amounts 稀少的；稀疏的：*thin grey hair* 稀疏的花白頭髮

▸ LIQUID 液體 **4** 0-w containing more liquid than is normal or expected 稀薄的；淡的 SYN **runny**：*The sauce was thin and tasteless.* 這醬汁淡而無味。

▸ SMOKE 煙 **5** fairly easy to see through 能見度較高的；稀薄的：*They fought their way through where the smoke was thinner.* 他們掙扎着從煙霧稀薄的地方逃了出去。

▸ AIR 空氣 **6** containing less OXYGEN than normal 稀薄的；含氧少的

▸ SOUND 聲音 **7** (*disapproving*) high and weak 微弱的；尖細的；有氣無力的：*Her thin voice trailed off into silence.* 她的聲音越來越弱直至毫無聲息。

▸ SMILE 微笑 **8** not sincere or enthusiastic 不真心實意的；冷淡的：*He gave a thin smile.* 他淡然一笑。

▸ LIGHT 光 **9** not very bright 微弱的；暗淡的：*the thin grey light of dawn* 淺灰色的晨曦

▸ POOR QUALITY 劣質 **10** of poor quality; lacking an important quality 質量差的；空乏的；拙劣的：*a thin excuse* (= one that people are not likely to believe) 站不住腳的藉口 ◊ *Their arguments all sound a little thin to me.* 他們的論據我聽起來都覺得有點兒缺乏說服力。

▸ **thin·ness** /ˈθɪnnəs/ *noun* [U] ➲ see also THINLY

IDM **be skating/walking on thin ˈice** to be taking a risk 履薄冰；冒風險 **disappear, vanish, etc. into thin ˈair** to disappear suddenly in a mysterious way 消失得無影無踪；不翼而飛；悄然而逝 **have a thin ˈtime (of it)** (*BrE, informal*) to have many problems or difficulties to deal with; to not be successful 遇到許多麻煩；過得不順 **out of thin ˈair** from nowhere or nothing, as if by magic 憑空；無中生有地 **the thin end of the ˈwedge** (*especially BrE*) an event or action that is the beginning of sth more serious and/or unpleasant（不好的事物的）端倪，冰山一角 **thin on ˈtop** (*informal*) without much hair on the head 頭髮稀疏；謝頂：*He's starting to get a little thin on top* (= he's losing his hair). 他開始有點謝頂了。 **a ˌthin ˈskin** the lack of ability to accept criticism, insults, etc. without becoming upset 臉皮薄；顧及臉面 SYN **sensitive** OPP **a thick skin** ➲ see also THIN-SKINNED (1) ➲ more at GROUND *n.*, LINE *n.*, SPREAD *v.*, THICK *adj.*, WEAR *v.*

■ ***adv.*** (**thin·ner**, **thin·nest**) in a way that produces a thin piece or layer of sth 薄薄地：*Don't spread it too thin.* 不要塗得太薄。◊ *I like my bread sliced thin.* 我喜歡吃切成薄片的麪包。

■ ***verb*** (**-nn-**)

▸ LIQUID 液體 **1** [T] **~ sth** (**down**) (**with sth**) to make a liquid less thick or strong by adding water or another substance（摻水等）使稀薄，使變淡：*Thin the paint with water.* 用水把顏料調稀。

▸ OF HAIR 毛髮 **2** [I] to become less thick 變稀疏；變稀少：*a middle-aged man with thinning hair* 頭髮逐漸稀少的中年男子

▸ BECOME LESS THICK 變稀少 **3** [I, T] to become less thick or fewer in number; to make sth less thick or fewer, for example by removing some things or people （使）變稀薄，變稀疏，變少：*The clouds thinned and the moon shone through.* 雲層漸稀，透出了月光。◊ **~ out** *The crowd had thinned out and only a few people were left.* 人群漸漸散去，只剩下幾個人。◊ **~ sth** (**out**) *Thin out the seedlings to about 10cm apart.* 把秧苗間成相隔 10 厘米。

thine /ðaɪn/ *pron.*, *det.* (*old use*)

■ ***pron.*** a word meaning 'yours', used when talking to only one person（第二人稱單數的物主代詞）你的（所有物）

■ ***det.*** the form of *thy* that is used before a vowel or 'h', meaning 'your'（第二人稱所有格單數 thy 的另一種形式，用於元音或 h 前）你的

thing 0-w /θɪŋ/ *noun*

▸ OBJECT 物體 **1** 0-w [C] an object whose name you do not use because you do not need to or want to, or because you do not know it 東西；物：*Can you pass me that thing over there?* 把那邊那個東西遞給我好嗎？◊ *She's very fond of sweet things* (= sweet foods). 她非常喜歡吃甜食。◊ *He's just bought one of those exercise things.* 他剛買了一副體育器械。◊ *Turn that thing off while I'm talking to you!* 我在跟你說話，把那個玩意兒關掉！ **2** 0-w [C] an object that is not alive in the way that people and plants are 物件；物品；事物：*Don't treat her like that—she's a person, not a thing!* 別那樣對待她，她是人，不是物件！◊ *He's good at making things with his hands.* 他善於手工製作物品。◊ *She took no interest in the people and things around her.* 她對周圍的人和事毫無興趣。

▸ POSSESSIONS/EQUIPMENT 所有物；設備 **3** 0-w **things** [pl.] (rather *informal*) objects, clothing or tools that belong to sb or are used for a particular purpose（個人的）用品，衣服；（某種）用具：*Shall I help you pack your things?* 我幫你打點行裝好嗎？◊ *Bring your swimming things with you.* 隨身帶上游泳用品。◊ *I'll just clear away the breakfast things.* 我這就收拾早餐餐具。◊ *Put your things* (= coat, etc.) *on and let's go.* 把你的衣服穿上，咱們就走。

▸ ANYTHING 任何東西 **4 a thing** [sing.] used with negatives to mean 'anything' in order to emphasize what you are saying 任何東西（用於否定句，加強語氣）：*I haven't got a thing to wear!* 我沒有一件可穿的衣服！◊ *There wasn't a thing we could do to help.* 沒有什麼我們能幫得上忙的。◊ *Ignore what he said—it* ***doesn't mean a thing.*** 別理睬他說的話，他那都是瞎說。

▸ FACT/EVENT/SITUATION/ACTION 事實；事件；情況；行為 **5** 0-w [C] a fact, an event, a situation or an action; what sb says or thinks 事實；事件；情況；行為；話語；想法：*There are a lot of things she doesn't know about me.* 我有很多情況她都不瞭解。◊ *There's another thing I'd like to ask you.* 還有一件事我想問你。◊ *A terrible thing*

T

happened last night. 昨天夜裏發生了一件可怕的事情。◇ He found **the whole thing** (= the situation) very boring. 他覺得這件事情非常無聊。◇ I've got loads of things to do today. 今天我有許多事要做。◇ **The main thing** to remember is to switch off the burglar alarm. 最要緊的是記住關掉防盜報警器的開關。◇ I like camping, climbing and **that sort of thing**. 我喜歡露營、爬山之類的活動。◇ She said **the first thing** that came into her head. 她想到了什麼就說什麼。◇ 'Why did you tell her our secret?' 'I did **no such thing**!' "你為什麼把我們的秘密告訴她？" "我沒幹過這種事！" ◇ Let's forget **the whole thing** (= everything). 咱們把所有事情都忘掉吧。 **6** **things** [pl.] (rather *informal*) the general situation, as it affects sb 形勢；局面；情況；事態： Things haven't gone entirely to plan. 事態沒有完全按照計劃發展。◇ (*informal*) Hi, Jane! **How are things?** 喂，簡，近來怎麼樣？◇ **Think things over** before you decide. 先把情況考慮周全再做決定。◇ **As things stand** at present, he seems certain to win. 據目前情況看，他似乎勝券在握。◇ **All things considered** (= considering all the difficulties or problems), she's done very well. 通盤考慮起來，她幹得很好。◇ Why do you make things so difficult for yourself? 你為什麼這樣跟自己過不去？ ➲ SYNONYMS at SITUATION

▸ **WHAT IS NEEDED/RIGHT** 需要的／合適的事物 **7** [C, usually sing.] what is needed or socially acceptable 需要的東西；適當的東西；合適的東西： You need something to cheer you up—I know just the thing! 你需要點什麼使你高興起來，我知道什麼正合你的需要！◇ to say **the right/wrong thing** 說得體的／不得體的話 ◇ The best thing to do is to apologize. 道歉方是上策。

▸ **THINGS OF PARTICULAR TYPE** 某種類型的事物 **8** **things** [pl.] (*formal*) (followed by an adjective 後接形容詞) all that can be described in a particular way 所有…的事物；凡是…的東西： She loves all things Japanese. 凡是日本的東西她都喜歡。

▸ **CREATURE** 生物 **9** [C] (used with an adjective 與形容詞連用) a living creature 生物；有生命的東西： All living things are composed of cells. 所有的生物都由細胞組成。

▸ **PERSON/ANIMAL** 人；動物 **10** [C] (with an adjective 與形容詞連用) (*informal*) used to talk to or about a person or an animal, to show how you feel about them （指人或動物，帶感情色彩）人，傢伙，東西： You silly thing! 你這個蠢貨！◇ You must be starving, you poor things. 你們一定是餓壞了，你們這些可憐的傢伙。◇ The cat's very ill, poor old thing. 這貓病得很厲害，真可憐。

IDM **A is 'one thing, B is a'nother | it's 'one thing to do A, it's a'nother thing to do B** B is very different from A, for example it is more difficult, serious or important …是一回事，…是另一回事；…和…截然不同： Romance is one thing, marriage is quite another. 愛情是一回事，婚姻卻是另一回事。◇ It's one thing to tease your sister, but it's another to hit her. 逗你妹妹玩是一回事，但打她那就另當別論了。 **ˌall/ˌother things being 'equal** if the conditions stay the same; if other conditions are the same 如果所有條件保持不變；如果其他情況一樣： All things being equal, we should finish the job tomorrow. 一切照常的話，我們明天應該完成這項工作。 **and 'things (like 'that)** (*informal*) used when you do not want to complete a list 等等；之類： She likes nice clothes and things like that. 她喜歡漂亮衣服之類的東西。◇ I've been busy shopping and things. 我一直忙於購物之類的事情。 **be all things to all 'men/'people** **1** (of people 人) to please everyone by changing your attitudes or opinions to suit different people 使人人高興；八面玲瓏 **2** (of things 事物) to be understood or used in different ways by different people 仁者見仁，智者見智 **come to/be the same 'thing** to have the same result or meaning 結果相同；意義相同 **be a 'good thing (that) …** to be lucky that … 幸運的是；幸虧： It's a good thing we got here early. 幸虧我們早到了這兒。 **be no bad 'thing (that) …** used to say that although sth seems to be bad, it could have good results 並不是壞事；或許是好事： We didn't want the press to get hold of the story, but it might be no bad thing. 我們本不想讓新聞界知道這事，但是知道了也許並非是壞事。 **be onto a good 'thing** to have found a job, situation or style of life that is pleasant or easy 找到稱心的工作；過上舒心的日子；混得不錯 **'do things to sb** (*informal*) to have a powerful emotional effect on sb 使某人十分激動；震撼某人： That song just does things to me. 一聽到那首歌我就激動不已。 **do your own 'thing** (*informal*) to do what you want to do or what interests you, without thinking about other people; to be independent 做自己想做的事；照自己的意願行事；獨立自主；自行其事 **ˌfirst/ˌlast 'thing** early in the morning/late in the evening 一早／晚上最後（要做的事）： I need the report on my desk first thing Monday morning. 星期一一早這個報告就得放在我的辦公桌上。 **ˌfirst things 'first** (often *humorous*) the most important matters must be dealt with first 要事先辦： We have a lot to discuss, but, first things first, let's have a cup of coffee! 我們有許多事要討論，不過急事先辦，咱們先喝杯咖啡吧！ **for 'one thing** used to introduce one of two or more reasons for doing sth （用以引出兩個以上的理由之一）一來，一方面： 'Why don't you get a car?' 'Well, for one thing, I can't drive!' "你為什麼不買輛汽車呢？" "啊，首先，我不會開車！" **have a 'thing about sb/sth** (*informal*) to have a strong like or dislike of sb/sth in a way that seems strange or unreasonable（莫名其妙地）對…有好感，對…有偏見： She has a thing about men with beards. 她對留鬍子的男人有強烈的感覺。 **it isn't my, his, etc. 'thing** it isn't sth that you really enjoy or are interested in 這不是我（或他等）真正喜歡的東西；並非…所好 **it's a … thing** (*informal*) it is sth that only a particular group understands 這是…的事（只有某群體才理解的）： You wouldn't know what it means—it's a girl thing. 你不會知道那是什麼意思，那是女孩子家的事。 **know/tell sb a 'thing or two (about sb/sth)** (*informal*) to know/tell sb some useful, interesting or surprising information about sb/sth 瞭解／透露有用的（或有趣的、意外的）信息；有所瞭解／披露；見多識廣： She's been married five times, so she knows a thing or two about men! 她結過五次婚，所以對男人有所瞭解。 **make a (big) 'thing of/about sth** (*informal*) to make sth seem more important than it really is 小題大做；大驚小怪；故弄玄虛 **not know, etc. the first thing a'bout sth/sb** to know nothing at all about sth/sb 對…一無所知；對…一竅不通 **not ˌquite the 'thing** **1** not considered socially acceptable 不太合時宜；不太時興；不得體： It wouldn't be quite the thing to turn up in running gear. 穿着跑步的運動服出現在這場合可不大成體統。 **2** (*old-fashioned*) not healthy or normal 身體不舒服；感到不適 **(just) ˌone of those 'things** used to say that you do not want to discuss or think about sth bad or unpleasant that has happened, but just accept it 命中注定的事；難免的倒霉事；不可挽回的事： It wasn't your fault. It was just one of those things. 不是你的錯。這是命中注定的事。 **ˌone (damned/damn) thing after a'nother** (*informal*) used to complain that a lot of unpleasant things keep happening to you （抱怨時用）倒霉事一樁接一樁 **ˌone thing leads to a'nother** used to suggest that the way one event or action leads to others is so obvious that it does not need to be stated （暗示事情的發展過程顯而易見）一來二去，自然而然： He offered me a ride home one night, and, well, one thing led to another and now we're married! 一天晚上他讓我搭車回家，唔，就這樣自然發展，我們現在結婚了！ **be 'seeing/'hearing things** (*informal, humorous*) to imagine that you can see or hear sth that is in fact not there 產生幻覺 **there's only ˌone thing 'for it** there is only one possible course of action 這只有一個辦法 **these ˌthings are sent to 'try us** (*saying*) used to say that you should accept an unpleasant situation or event because you cannot change it （表示無法改變，應該接受）這些都是對我們的考驗（或試煉） **the ˌthing 'is** (*informal*) used to introduce an important fact, reason or explanation 事實是；主要原因是： I'm sorry my assignment isn't finished. The thing is, I've had a lot of other work this week. 對不起，我的任務沒完成。主要原因是我這星期有許多其他工作要做。 **the ˌthing (about/with sth/sb) 'is** used to introduce a problem about sth/sb …的問題是： The thing with Karl is, he's always late. 卡爾的問題是，他總是遲到。 **the (whole) … thing** (*informal*) a situation or an activity of the type mentioned （純粹的）…事；（完全是）…的活動： She really didn't want to be involved in the whole family *thing.* 她實在不想捲入這整件家事中。 **ˌthings that go ˌbump in the ˈnight** (*informal, humorous*) used to refer to GHOSTS and other SUPERNATURAL things that cannot be explained 夜裏奇異可怕的響聲；鬼魂；超自然現象 **too ˈmuch of a good thing** used to say that, although sth is pleasant, you do not want to have too much of it 好事多了也覺得膩 **(what) with ˌone thing and aˈnother** (*informal*) because you have been busy with various problems, events or things you had to do 因為事情一個接着一個；由於忙得不可開交： *I completely forgot her birthday, what with one thing and another.* 因為忙得不可開交，我把她的生日忘得一乾二淨。➲ more at CHANCE *n.*, CLOSE² *adj.*, CLOSE² *adv.*, DAY, DECENT, DONE *adj.*, EASY *adv.*, NATURE, NEAR *adj.*, ONLY *adj.*, OVERDO, PUSH *v.*, REAL *adj.*, SCHEME *n.*, SHAPE *n.*, SURE *adj.*, TURN *v.*, WAY *n.*, WORK *v.*

Synonyms 同義詞辨析

things

stuff • property • possessions • junk • belongings • goods • valuables

These are all words for objects or items, especially ones that you own or have with you at a particular time. 以上各詞均指東西、物品，尤指個人擁有或隨身攜帶的物件。

things (*rather informal*) objects, clothing or tools that you own or that are used for a particular purpose 指個人擁有或作特定用途的物品、衣服、用具： *Shall I help you pack your things?* 我幫你打點行裝好嗎？◇ *Bring your swimming things.* 隨身帶上游泳用品。

stuff [U] (*informal*) used to refer to a group of objects when you do not know their names, when the names are not important or when it is obvious what you are talking about 指名稱不詳、名稱無關緊要或所指明確的東西、物品、玩意兒： *Where's all my stuff?* 我那些東西都哪兒去了？

property [U] (*rather formal*) a thing or things that are owned by sb 指所有物、財產、財物： *This building is government property.* 這座大樓是政府的財產。◇ *Be careful not to damage other people's property.* 小心別損壞別人的財物。

possessions things that you own, especially sth that can be moved 指個人財產、私人物品： *Prisoners were allowed no personal possessions except letters and photographs.* 囚犯除信件和照片外不允許有任何私人物品。

junk [U] things that are considered useless or of little value 指無用的東西、無價值的東西： *I've cleared out all that old junk from the attic.* 我把閣樓裏所有的廢舊雜物都清除乾淨了。

belongings possessions that can be moved, especially ones that you have with you at a particular time 指動產，尤指隨身物品： *Please make sure you have all your belongings with you when leaving the plane.* 請確保在下飛機前帶好所有的隨身物品。

goods (*technical* or *rather formal*) possessions that can be moved 指動產、（可搬運的）私人財產： *He was found guilty of* ***handling stolen goods.*** 他被判犯銷贓罪。

valuables things that are worth a lot of money, especially small personal things such as jewellery or cameras 尤指私人的貴重物品（如首飾、相機等）： *Never leave cash or other valuables lying around.* 現金或其他貴重物品請勿亂放。

PATTERNS

- **personal** things/stuff/property/possessions/belongings
- to **collect/gather/pack** (up) your things/stuff/possessions/belongings
- to **search** sb's/your/the things/stuff/property/belongings
- to **go through** sb's/your/the things/stuff/belongings

thing·ummy /ˈθɪŋəmi/ *noun* (*pl.* **-ies**) (also **thing·ama·bob** /ˈθɪŋəməbɒb; *NAmE* -bɑːb/, **thing·uma·jig** /ˈθɪŋəmədʒɪɡ/, **thingy**) (*informal*) used to refer to a person or thing whose name you do not know or have forgotten, or which you do not want to mention （指不知、或忘記、或不想提及其名）某某，那個人，那東西： *It's one of those thingummies for keeping papers together.* 那是存放文件的玩意兒。◇ *Is thingummy going to be there? You know, that woman from the Sales Department?* 某某人會去那兒嗎？你知道，就是銷售部的那個女的。

thingy /ˈθɪŋi/ *noun* (*pl.* **-ies**) = THINGUMMY

Vocabulary Building 詞彙擴充

Other words for thing 表示事物的其他詞

Instead of using the word **thing**, try to use more precise and interesting words, especially in formal written English. 盡量使用更貼切和有意思的詞代替 thing，尤其在正式的書面語中。

- **aspect** *That was the most puzzling aspect of the situation.* (*… the most puzzling thing about …*) 那是整個局勢中最令人費解的一面。
- **attribute** *Curiosity is an essential attribute for a journalist.* (*… an essential thing for a journalist to have.*) 好奇心是新聞記者的基本素質。
- **characteristic** *This bird has several interesting characteristics.* (*There are several interesting things about this bird.*) 這種鳥有幾個有趣的特徵。
- **detail** *I want to know every detail of what happened.* (*… everything about …*) 我想瞭解所發生事情的全部詳情。
- **feature** *Noise is a familiar feature of city life.* (*… a familiar thing in city life.*) 噪音是城市生活的常見特徵。
- **issue** *She has campaigned on many controversial issues.* (*… many controversial things.*) 她就許多具爭議性的問題參加過運動。
- **matter** *We have several important matters to deal with at this meeting.* (*… several important things …*) 我們有幾個重要問題要在這次會議上處理。
- **point** *That's a very interesting point you made.* (*… a very interesting thing you said.*) 你提出的這個意見非常值得重視。
- **subject** *The book covers a number of subjects.* (*… a number of things.*) 本書涉及幾個課題。
- **topic** *We discussed a wide range of topics.* (*… a wide range of things.*) 我們就廣泛的話題進行了討論。
- **trait** *Her generosity is one of her most attractive traits.* (*… one of the most attractive things about her.*) 慷慨大方是她最具魅力的個性之一。
- Don't use **thing** after an adjective when the adjective can be used on its own. 形容詞可單獨使用時，切勿在後面加 thing：*Having your own computer is very useful.* 自己有一台計算機用處很大。◇ ~~*Having your own computer is a very useful thing.*~~
- It is often more natural to use words like **something**, **anything**, etc. instead of **thing**. 以 something、anything 等詞代替 thing 使用常常更自然： *I have something important to tell you.* 我有重要的事情要告訴你。◇ ~~*I have an important thing to tell you.*~~ ◇ *Do you want anything else?* 你還想要點別的什麼嗎？◇ ~~*Do you want any other thing?*~~
- It is more natural to say **a lot**, **a great deal**, **much**, etc. rather than **many things**. * a lot、a great deal、much 等詞比 many things 說起來更自然： *I have so much to tell you.* 我要對你講的事情太多了。◇ ~~*I have so many things to tell you.*~~ ◇ *She knows a lot about basketball.* 她對籃球很有研究。◇ ~~*She knows many things about basketball.*~~

T

Synonyms 同義詞辨析

think

believe • feel • reckon • be under the impression

These words all mean to have an idea that sth is true or possible or to have a particular opinion about sb/sth. 以上各詞均含以為、認為之意。

think to have an idea that sth is true or possible, although you are not completely certain; to have a particular opinion about sb/sth 指認為、以為： *Do you think (that) they'll come?* 你認為他們會來嗎？ ◇ *Well, I like it. What do you think?* 嗯，我喜歡這個。你認為怎麼樣？

believe to have an idea that sth is true or possible, although you are not completely certain; to have a particular opinion about sb/sth 指認為、以為： *Police believe (that) the man may be armed.* 警方認為那個人可能攜有武器。

THINK OR BELIEVE? 用 think 還是 believe？

When you are expressing an idea that you have or that sb has of what is true or possible, **believe** is more formal than **think**. It is used especially for talking about ideas that other people have; **think** is used more often for talking about your own ideas. 表達自己或別人認為真實或有可能的想法時，believe 較 think 正式。believe 尤用於別人的想法；think 較常用於自己的想法： *Police believe ...* 警方認為… ◇ *I think ...* 我認為… When you are expressing an opinion, **believe** is stronger than **think** and is used especially for matters of principle; **think** is used more for practical matters or matters of personal taste. 表達意見時，believe 語氣較 think 強烈，尤用於原則性事情；think 多用於實際事情或個人喜好。

feel to have a particular opinion about sth that has happened or about what you/sb ought to do 指認為（已發生的事情…）、相信（應該…）： *We all felt (that) we were unlucky to lose.* 我們都認為輸了是運氣不好。

reckon (*informal*) to think that sth is true or possible 指認為、以為： *I reckon (that) I'm going to get that job.* 我認為我會得到那份工作。

be under the impression that ... to have an idea that sth is true 指以為某事…： *I was under the impression that the work had already been completed.* 我還以為已經完工了呢。

PATTERNS

- to think/believe/feel/reckon/be under the impression **that** ...
- **It is** thought/believed/reckoned **that** ...
- to **be** thought/believed/felt/reckoned **to be** sth
- to think/believe/feel sth **about** sb/sth
- to **sincerely/honestly/seriously/mistakenly** think/believe/feel

T

think 0-π /θɪŋk/ *verb, noun*

■ *verb* (**thought**, **thought** /θɔːt/)

▸ **HAVE OPINION/BELIEF** 有看法／信念 **1** 0-π [T, I] (not used in the progressive tenses 不用於進行時) to have a particular idea or opinion about sth/sb; to believe sth 認為；以為： **~ (that)** ... *Do you think (that) they'll come?* 你認為他們會來嗎？ ◇ *I thought I heard a scream.* 我好像聽到了一聲尖叫。 ◇ *I didn't think you liked sports.* 我原以為你不喜好運動。 ◇ ***Am I right in thinking** that you used to live here?* 我想你過去在這裏住過，對嗎？ ◇ *I think this is their house, but I'm not sure.* 我想這是他們的家，但不敢肯定。 ◇ *He ought to resign, I think.* 我看他應該辭職。 ◇ *We'll need about 20 chairs, **I should think**.* 我看我們需要大約 20 把椅子。 ◇ **it is thought that** ... ***It was** once **thought that** the sun travelled around the earth.* 人們曾經認為太陽繞着地球轉。 ◇ **~ sth (about sth)** *What did you think about the idea?* 你原先認為這個想法怎麼樣？ ◇ *Well, I like it. **What do you think?*** 嗯，我喜歡這個想法。你認為怎麼樣？ ◇ **~ so** *'Will we make it in time?' '**I think so.**'* "我們會及時完成嗎？" "我想會的。" ◇ *'Is he any good?' '**I don't think so.**'* "他怎麼樣？" "我認為一般。" ◇ **~ sb/sth + adj.** ***I think it** highly unlikely that I'll get the job.* 我認為我得到這份工作的可能性極小。 ◇ *She thought him kind and generous.* 她認為他寬厚仁慈。 ◇ **sb/sth is thought to be sb/sth** *He's thought to be one of the richest men in Europe.* 他被認為是歐洲最富有的人之一。 ➲ LANGUAGE BANK at ACCORDING TO, OPINION

▸ **USE MIND** 動腦筋 **2** 0-π [I, T] to use your mind to consider sth, to form connected ideas, to try to solve problems, etc. 想；思考；思索；思想： *Are animals able to think?* 動物能思考嗎？ ◇ *Let me think* (= give me time before I answer). 讓我想一想。 ◇ **~ (about sth)** *I can't tell you now—I'll have to **think about it**.* 我現在無法告訴你，我得考慮一下。 ◇ *She **had thought** very **deeply** about this problem.* 她曾經對這個問題深深思考過。 ◇ *All he ever thinks about is money.* 他滿腦子想的只是錢。 ◇ *I'm sorry, **I wasn't thinking*** (= said when you have upset or offended sb accidentally). 對不起，我太冒昧了。 ◇ **~ what, how, etc.** ... *He was trying to think what to do.* 他在努力想辦法。 **3** 0-π [T] (usually used in the progressive tenses 通常用於進行時) to have ideas, words or images in your mind 想；琢磨： **~ sth** *You're very quiet. What are you thinking?* 你一聲不吭，在想什麼？ ◇ **~ what, how, etc.** ... *I was just thinking what a long way it is.* 我剛才在琢磨路途太遠了。 ◇ **+ speech** *'I must be crazy,' she thought.* "我準是瘋了。" 她想。

▸ **IMAGINE** 想像 **4** 0-π [T, no passive, I] to form an idea of sth; to imagine sth 猜想；想像；試想： **~ where, how, etc.** ... *We couldn't think where you'd gone.* 我們猜想不出來你到哪裏去了。 ◇ *Just think how nice it would be to see them again.* 試想一下要是能再見到他們該有多好。 ◇ **~ (that)** ... *I can't think (that) he would be so stupid.* 我不能想像他會這麼蠢。 ◇ **~ (sth)** ***Just think**—we'll be lying on the beach this time tomorrow.* 想想看，明天這個時候我們就躺在海灘上了。 ◇ *If I'm late home, my mother always **thinks the worst**.* 如果我回家晚了，我母親總是往最壞處想。 ◇ *Try to **think yourself into** the role.* 盡量發揮想像力，使自己進入角色。 ➲ SYNONYMS at IMAGINE

▸ **EXPECT** 預料 **5** 0-π [T] to expect sth 料想；預料；預期： **~ (that)** ... *I never thought (that) I'd see her again.* 我從未料想到還會見到她。 ◇ *The job took longer than we thought.* 這項工作用的時間比我們預想的多。 ◇ *You'd think she'd have been grateful for my help* (= but she wasn't). 你還期望她會對我的幫助感恩戴德呢。 ◇ **~ to do sth** (*formal*) *Who would have thought to find you here?* 誰會料到你在這兒呢？

▸ **IN A PARTICULAR WAY** 以某種方式 **6** [I, T] (*informal*) [no passive] to think in a particular way or on a particular subject 只想；一心想；對…着迷： **+ adj.** *Let's think positive.* 咱們往好的方面想吧。 ◇ *You need to **think big*** (= aim to achieve a lot). 你要敢想。 ◇ **~ sth** *If you want to make money, you've got to think money.* 你要想賺錢，就得一門心思琢磨錢。

▸ **SHOWING ANGER/SURPRISE** 表示生氣／吃驚 **7** [T] **~ (that)** ... used in questions to show that you are angry or surprised（用於問句，表示生氣或吃驚）： *What do you think you're doing?* 你以為你在幹什麼？

▸ **BEING LESS DEFINITE/MORE POLITE** 不太肯定；較為婉轉 **8** [T, I] used to make sth you say sound less definite or more polite（用於使話語不太肯定或較為婉轉）： **~ (that)** ... *I thought we could go out tonight.* 我本想我們今晚可以出去。 ◇ *Twenty guests are enough, I would have thought.* 我覺得二十位客人就夠了。 ◇ ***Do you think** you could open the window?* 請打開窗子好嗎？ ◇ **~ so** *'You've made a mistake.' 'I don't think so.'* "你出錯了。" "我想不會吧。"

▸ **INTEND** 打算 **9** [T, I] **~ (that** ...) to intend sth; to have a plan about sth 打算；想要；計劃： *I think I'll go for a swim.* 我想去游泳。 ◇ *I'm thinking in terms of about 70 guests at the wedding.* 我打算邀請 70 位嘉賓參加婚禮。

▸ **REMEMBER** 記憶 **10** [T] to remember sth; to have sth come into your mind 記得；想起： **~ to do sth** *I didn't think* (= it did not occur to me) *to tell her.* 我沒有想到要告訴她。 ◇ **~ where, what, etc.** ... *I can't think where I put the keys.* 我想不起把鑰匙放在哪兒了。

IDM **come to 'think of it** used when you suddenly remember sth or realize that it might be important（用於突然想起某事或認識到其重要性）想起來了，的確：*Come to think of it, he did mention seeing you.* 想起來了，他確實提到看見過你。 **I ˌdon't 'think so** (*informal*) used to say very strongly that you do not agree with sth, or that sth is not possible 我想並非如此；我不這樣認為；根本不可能：*Me? Fail? I don't think so.* 我？失敗？我可不這樣認為。 **if/when you 'think about it** used to draw attention to a fact that is not obvious or has not previously been mentioned（用以引起對不明顯或未曾提到過的事情的注意）你想想看：*It was a difficult situation, when you think about it.* 仔細想來，當時處境是很困難的。 **I 'thought as much** that is what I expected or suspected 我早料到了；果然不出我所料：*'He said he'd forgotten.' 'I thought as much.'* "他說忘了。" "果然不出我所料。" **ˌthink aˈgain** to consider a situation again and perhaps change your idea or intention 重新考慮後另作打算（常指最終改變主意） **think aˈloud/out 'loud** to say what your thoughts are as you have them 自言自語；邊想邊說；進行有聲思考 **think 'better of it/of doing sth** to decide not to do sth after thinking further about it 深思熟慮後決定不做；一想又改變主意 **SYN** **reconsider**：*Rosie was about to protest but thought better of it.* 羅西剛要抗議，但又一想決定作罷。 **think (the) 'better of sb** to have a higher opinion of sb 對某人有較高的評價：*She has behaved appallingly—I must say I thought better of her.* 她的行為太惡劣了，看來我過去是高看了她。 **think nothing 'of it** (*formal*) used as a polite response when sb has said sorry to you or thanked you 別在意；沒什麼；別客氣 **think 'nothing of sth/of doing sth** to consider an activity to be normal and not particularly unusual or difficult 不把…當一回事；對…等閒視之；覺得…無所謂：*She thinks nothing of walking thirty miles a day.* 她認為一天步行三十英里不足為奇。 **think on your 'feet** to be able to think and react to things very quickly and effectively without any preparation 思維敏捷；反應迅速 **ˌthink out of the 'box** to think about sth, or how to do sth, in a way that is new, different or shows imagination 跳出框框想問題；另闢蹊徑 **'think straight** to think in a clear or logical way 思路清晰 **think 'twice about sth/about doing sth** to think carefully before deciding to do sth 三思而行；慎重考慮後再決定：*You should think twice about employing someone you've never met.* 雇用素不相識的人應三思而行。 **think the world, highly, a lot, not much, poorly, little, etc. of sb/sth** to have a very good, poor, etc. opinion of sb/sth 對…評價高（或不高）：*He thinks the world of his daughter.* 他非常器重女兒。◇ *I don't think much of her idea.* 我認為她的主意不怎麼樣。 **to think (that ...)** used to show that you are surprised or shocked by sth（表示驚訝）想想看，想想…吧：*To think that my mother wrote all those books and I never knew!* 想想看，我母親寫了那麼多部書，我竟然一無所知！ ➲ more at FIT *adj.*, GREAT *adj.*, ILL *adv.*, LET *v.*, LIKE *v.*, OWN *v.*

PHR V **'think about/of sb/sth** 🔑 **1** to consider sb/sth when you are doing or planning sth 考慮到；關心；替…着想：*Don't you ever think about other people?* 難道你就從來沒有考慮過別人？ **2** to consider doing sth 考慮，打算（做某事） **SYN** **contemplate**：**~ doing sth** *She's thinking of changing her job.* 她在考慮換工作。 **ˌthink aˈhead (to sth)** to think about a future event or situation and plan for it 預先考慮；預想；預先計劃 **ˌthink 'back (to sth)** to think about sth that happened in the past 回想；追憶：*I keep thinking back to the day I arrived here.* 我不斷回想起剛到這兒那一天的情景。 **ˌthink for yourˈself** to form your own opinions and make decisions without depending on others 獨立思考；自行決定 **'think of sth/sb 1** 🔑 to have an image or idea of sth/sb in your mind 想像到；對…有想法：*When I said that I wasn't thinking of anyone in particular.* 我說那話時，並沒有想到任何具體的人。 **2** 🔑 to create an idea in your imagination 想出；構思出：*Can anybody think of a way to raise money?* 誰能想出個集資的辦法？ ◇ *Have you thought of a name for the baby yet?* 你想好給孩子起什麼名字沒有？ **3** 🔑 [no passive] (used especially with *can* 尤與 can 連用) to remember sth/sb 記得；想起：*I can think of at least three occasions when he arrived late.* 我記得他至少遲到過三次。◇ *I can't think of her name at the moment.* 我一時想不起她的名字。 **'think of sb/sth as sb/sth** 🔑 to consider sb/sth in a particular way 把…看作；把…視為：*I think of this place as my home.* 我把這個地方當成了家。◇ *She is thought of as a possible director.* 人們認為她有可能成為董事。 ➲ see also WELL THOUGHT OF **'think of sth** to imagine an actual or a possible situation 想一想；想像：*Just think of the expense!* 想想這筆開銷吧！◇ **~ doing sth** *I couldn't think of letting you take the blame* (= I would not allow that to happen). 我沒想到過讓你承擔責任。 **ˌthink sth↔'out** to consider or plan sth carefully 認真考慮；仔細盤算：*It's a very well thought out plan.* 這個計劃考慮得十分周密。 **ˌthink sth↔'over** 🔑 to consider sth carefully, especially before reaching a decision（尤指在作決定前）仔細考慮，慎重思考：*He'd like more time to think things over.* 他希望有更多的時間把情況考慮周詳。 **ˌthink sth↔'through** to consider a problem or a possible course of action fully 充分考慮；全盤考慮；想透 **ˌthink sth↔'up** 🔑 (*informal*) to create sth in your mind 想出；發明 **SYN** **devise, invent**：*Can't you think up a better excuse than that?* 難道你就想不出一個比這更好的藉口？

■ ***noun*** [sing.]

IDM **have a 'think (about sth)** (*informal*) to think carefully about sth in order to make a decision about it 想一想，琢磨一下（以便作決定）：*I'll have a think and let you know tomorrow.* 我要好好想一想，明天告訴你。 **you've got another think 'coming** (*informal*) used to tell sb that they are wrong about sth and must change their plans or opinions 你還得想一想；你得改變計劃（或主意）

think·able /ˈθɪŋkəbl/ *adj.* [not before noun] that you can imagine as a possibility 可以想像；想像得到：*Such an idea was scarcely thinkable ten years ago.* 十年前，這樣的想法幾乎是難以想像的。 **OPP** **unthinkable**

think·er /ˈθɪŋkə(r)/ *noun* **1** a person who thinks seriously, and often writes about important things, such as philosophy or science 思想家：*Einstein was one of the greatest thinkers of the 20th century.* 愛因斯坦是 20 世紀最偉大的思想家之一。 **2** a person who thinks in a particular way 思想…的人：*a clear thinker* 思路清晰的人

think·ing 🔑 /ˈθɪŋkɪŋ/ *noun, adj.*

■ ***noun*** [U] **1** 🔑 the process of thinking about sth 思想；思考；思維：*I had to do some quick thinking.* 我得迅速思考一番。 ➲ see also LATERAL THINKING, WISHFUL THINKING **2** 🔑 ideas or opinions about sth 想法；見解：*What is the current thinking on this question?* 目前對這個問題的看法是什麼？◇ *She explained the thinking behind the campaign.* 她解釋了發動這場運動的想法。

IDM see WAY *n.*

■ ***adj.*** [only before noun] intelligent and able to think seriously about things 思想的；有理智的；有思考力的：*the thinking woman's magazine* 理性婦女的雜誌

'thinking cap *noun*

IDM **put your 'thinking cap on** (*informal*) to try to solve a problem by thinking about it 動腦筋；通過思考努力解決問題

'think tank *noun* a group of experts who provide advice and ideas on political, social or economic issues（政治、社會、經濟問題的）智囊團，智庫，專家小組

thin·ly /ˈθɪnli/ *adv.* **1** in a way that produces a thin piece or layer of sth 細；瘦；薄：*Slice the potatoes thinly.* 把土豆切成薄片。 **2** with only a few things or people spread over a place so that there is a lot of space between them 稀疏；稀少：*a thinly populated area* 人煙稀少的地區 **3** in a way that is not sincere or enthusiastic 冷淡；冷漠：*She smiled thinly.* 她淡然一笑。 **4** in a way that does not hide the truth very well 容易識破的；顯而易見的 **SYN** **barely**：*The novel is a thinly disguised autobiography.* 這部小說讓人一眼就可以看出是部自傳。

thin·ner /ˈθɪnə(r)/ *noun* [U, C] a substance that is added to paint, VARNISH, etc. to make it less thick（塗料、清漆等的）稀料，稀釋劑

T

thin-'skinned *adj.* **1** easily upset by criticism or insults 臉皮薄的；（對批評或侮辱）易生氣的 **2** (of fruit 水果) having a thin skin 皮薄的 OPP **thick-skinned**

third /θɜːd; *NAmE* θɜːrd/ *ordinal number, noun*

■ ***ordinal number*** 3rd 第三 HELP There are examples of how to use ordinal numbers at the entry for **fifth**. 序數詞用法示例見 fifth 條。

IDM **third time 'lucky** (*US* also **third time is the 'charm**) used when you have failed to do sth twice and hope that you will succeed the third time（但願）第三次交好運；過一過二不過三

■ ***noun*** **1** each of three equal parts of sth 三分之一 ➲ LANGUAGE BANK at PROPORTION **2 ~ (in sth)** a level of university degree at British universities, that is lower than average 三等學位（英國大學中低於平均水平的學位）➲ compare FIRST *n.* (4), SECOND *n.* (7)

the ˌthird 'age *noun* [sing.] (*BrE*) the period of your life between MIDDLE AGE and OLD AGE, when you are still active 第三齡（中年和老年之間依然活躍的年齡段）

ˌthird 'class *noun* **1** [U, sing.] (especially in the past) the cheapest and least comfortable part of a train, ship, etc.（尤指舊時火車、輪船等的）三等座，三等艙 **2** [U] (in the US) the class of mail used for sending advertisements, etc. 第三類郵件（在美國用以郵寄廣告等）**3** [U, sing.] the lowest standard of degree given by a British university 第三等學位（英國大學頒發的最低標準學位）

'third-class *adj.* **1** (especially in the past) connected with the cheapest and least comfortable way of travelling on a train, ship, etc. 三等的（尤指舊時火車座位、輪船艙位等）**2** (in the US) connected with the class of mail used to send advertisements, etc. 第三類的（美國郵件等級）**3** [only before noun] used to describe the lowest standard of degree given by a British university 第三等的（英國大學學位）**4** (*disapproving*) (of people 人) less important than other people 第三等的；卑微的：*They are treated as third-class citizens.* 他們被當成三等公民對待。▸ **ˌthird 'class** *adv.*：*to travel third class* 乘坐三等艙

third de'gree *noun* [sing.]

IDM **give sb the ˌthird de'gree** (*informal*) to question sb for a long time and in a thorough way; to use threats or violence to get information from sb 對某人逼供（或疲勞詢問、刑訊）

ˌthird-de'gree *adj.* **1 ~ burns** burns of the most serious kind, affecting TISSUE below the skin 三度（燒傷）**2** (*NAmE*) **~ murder, assault, robbery, etc.** murder, etc. of the least serious of three kinds 第三等級（謀殺、人身侵犯或搶劫等）➲ compare FIRST-DEGREE, SECOND-DEGREE

T

'third-generation *adj.* (*abbr.* **3G**) **1** used to describe technology that has been developed to send data to mobile phones/cell phones, etc. at much higher speeds than were possible before 第三代移動通信技術的 **2** used to describe any technology that is being developed that is more advanced than the earlier two stages 第三代技術的

third·ly /'θɜːdli; *NAmE* 'θɜːrd-/ *adv.* used to introduce the third of a list of points you want to make in a speech or piece of writing（用於講話或文章中列舉事項）第三，第三點：*Thirdly, I would like to say that …* 第三，我想說…

ˌthird 'party *noun* (*law* 律 or *formal*) a person who is involved in a situation in addition to the two main people involved 第三人；第三方；第三當事人；第三者

ˌthird-party in'surance *noun* [U] insurance that COVERS (= protects) you if you injure sb or damage sb's property 第三者保險，第三責任險（保障受保人於被追討賠償時的損失）

the ˌthird 'person *noun* [sing.] **1** (*grammar* 語法) a set of pronouns and verb forms used by a speaker to refer to other people and things 第三人稱（代詞及動詞形式）：*'They are' is the third person plural of the verb 'to be'.* * they are 是動詞 to be 的第三人稱複數形式。**2** a way of writing a novel, etc. as the experience of sb else, using third person forms 第三人稱（寫作方法）：*a book written* ***in the third person*** 以第三人稱寫的書 ➲ compare THE FIRST PERSON, THE SECOND PERSON

ˌthird-'rate *adj.* of very poor quality 劣質的；三等的；三流的 SYN **inferior**：*a third-rate actor* 三流演員

the Third Reich /ˌθɜːd 'raɪk; 'raɪx; *NAmE* ˌθɜːrd/ *noun* [sing.] the Nazi rule of Germany between 1933 and 1945 第三帝國（1933 至 1945 年間的德國納粹政權）

ˌthird 'way *noun* [sing.] a course of action or political policy that is between two extreme positions 第三條道路（介乎兩種極端立場之間的行動方案或政策）

the ˌThird 'World *noun* [sing.] a way of referring to the poor or developing countries of Africa, Asia and Latin America, which is sometimes considered offensive 第三世界：*the causes of poverty and injustice in the Third World* 第三世界貧窮和不公正的原因 ◇ *Third-World debt* 第三世界債務 ➲ compare FIRST WORLD

thirst /θɜːst; *NAmE* θɜːrst/ *noun, verb*

■ ***noun*** **1** [U, sing.] the feeling of needing or wanting a drink 口渴；乾渴感：*He quenched his thirst with a long drink of cold water.* 他喝了好多冷水解渴。◇ *She woke up with a raging thirst and a headache.* 她醒來後，感到頭痛，口渴難忍。**2** [U] the state of not having enough water to drink 渴；乾渴：*Thousands are dying of thirst.* 成千上萬的人都乾渴得奄奄一息。**3** [sing.] **~ (for sth)** a strong desire for sth 渴望；渴求 SYN **craving**：*a thirst for knowledge* 如飢似渴的求知慾

■ ***verb*** [I] (*old use*) to be thirsty 渴；想喝水

PHR V **'thirst for sth** (*literary*) to feel a strong desire for sth 渴望；渴求 SYN **crave**：*She thirsted for power.* 她渴望擁有權力。

thirsty /'θɜːsti; *NAmE* 'θɜːrsti/ *adj.* (**thirst·ier, thirsti·est**) **1** needing or wanting to drink 渴的；口渴的：*We were hungry and thirsty.* 我們又飢又渴。◇ *Digging is* ***thirsty work*** (= makes you thirsty). 挖地是個使人口渴的活。**2 ~ for sth** having a strong desire for sth 渴望；渴求；熱望 SYN **hungry**：*He is thirsty for power.* 他拚命想掌權。**3** (of plants, fields, etc. 植物、田地等) dry; in need of water 乾旱的；缺水的 ▸ **thirst·ily** /-ɪli/ *adv.*：*Paul drank thirstily.* 保羅渴得拚命喝水。

thir·teen /ˌθɜː'tiːn; *NAmE* ˌθɜːr't-/ *number* 13 十三 ▸ **thir·teenth** /ˌθɜː'tiːnθ; *NAmE* ˌθɜːr't-/ *ordinal number, noun* HELP There are examples of how to use ordinal numbers at the entry for **fifth**. 序數詞用法示例見 fifth 條。

thirty /'θɜːti; *NAmE* 'θɜːrti/

1 *number* 30 三十 **2** *noun* **the thirties** [pl.] numbers, years or temperatures from 30 to 39 三十幾；三十年代 ▸ **thir·ti·eth** /'θɜːtiəθ; *NAmE* 'θɜːrt-/ *ordinal number, noun* HELP There are examples of how to use ordinal numbers at the entry for **fifth**. 序數詞用法示例見 fifth 條。

IDM **in your 'thirties** between the ages of 30 and 39 * 30 多歲

this /ðɪs/ *det., pron., adv.*

■ ***det., pron.*** (*pl.* **these** /ðiːz/) **1** used to refer to a particular person, thing or event that is close to you, especially compared with another（指較近的人或事物）這，這個：*How long have you been living in this country?* 你在這個國家居住多久啦？◇ *Well, make up your mind. Which do you want? This one or that one?* 哎，拿定主意。你要哪一個？這個還是那個？◇ *I think you'll find these more comfortable than those.* 我想你會覺得這些比那些更舒適。◇ *Is this your bag?* 這是你的包嗎？**2** used to refer to sth/sb that has already been mentioned（指已提到過的人或事物）這，這個：*There was a court case resulting from this incident.* 這一事件引起一宗案件。◇ *The boy was afraid and the dog had sensed this.* 男孩害怕了，狗已經察覺到這一點。◇ *What's this I hear about you getting married?* 我聽說你結婚了，這是怎麼回事？**3** used for introducing sb or showing sth to sb（介紹人或展示事物時用）這，這樣：*Hello, this is Maria Diaz* (= on the telephone). 喂，我是瑪麗亞・迪亞茲。◇ *Jo, this is Kate* (= when you are introducing them). 喬，這位是凱特。◇ *This is the captain speaking.* 我是船長。◇ *Listen to this.* 聽聽這件事。◇ *Do it like this* (= in the way I am showing you). 照這樣去做。**4** used with periods of time related to the present（與和現在

有關的一段時間連用）今，本，這個，現在：*this week/month/year* 本週；本月；今年 ◇ *I saw her this morning* (= today in the morning). 今天早晨我見到過她。◇ *Do you want me to come this Tuesday* (= Tuesday of this week) *or next Tuesday?* 你要我本週二還是下週二來？◇ *Do it **this minute*** (= now). 現在就做。◇ *He never comes to see me **these days*** (= now, as compared with the past). 近來他一直不來看我。 **5 ~ sth of sb's** (*informal*) used to refer to sb/sth that is connected with a person, especially when you have a particular attitude towards it or them（尤指說話者抱有既定看法的人或事物）…的這個（或這些）：*These new friends of hers are supposed to be very rich.* 她的這些新朋友想必都很富有。 **6** (*informal*) used when you are telling a story or telling sb about sth（述說時用）有個：*There was this strange man sitting next to me on the plane.* 在飛機上有個奇怪的人坐在我身旁。◇ *I've been getting these pains in my chest.* 我胸部一直有一些疼痛感。

IDM **ˌthis and ˈthat | ˌthis, ˌthat and the ˈother** (*informal*) various things or activities 這樣那樣；各種事情；各種各樣的活動：*'What did you talk about?' 'Oh, this and that.'* "你們談什麼來着？" "噢，無所不談。"

■ ***adv.*** to this degree; so 這樣；這麼：*It's about this high* (= as high as I am showing you with my hands). 大約有這麼高。◇ *I didn't think we'd get this far.* 我未曾想到我們會走得這麼遠。

this·tle /ˈθɪsl/ *noun* a wild plant with leaves with sharp points and purple, yellow or white flowers made up of a mass of narrow PETALS pointing upwards. The thistle is the national symbol of Scotland. 薊（野生植物，葉有刺，花呈紫色、黃色或白色，為蘇格蘭民族象徵） ➲ VISUAL VOCAB page V11

thistle·down /ˈθɪsldaʊn/ *noun* [U] a very light soft substance that contains THISTLE seeds and is blown from THISTLES by the wind 薊種子冠毛

thither /ˈðɪðə(r)/ *adv.* (*old use*) to or towards that place 到那裏；向那裏 **IDM** see HITHER

tho' *adv.* an informal spelling of 'though'（though 的非正式拼法）

thong /θɒŋ; *NAmE* θɔːŋ; θɑːŋ/ *noun* **1** a narrow strip of leather that is used to fasten sth or as a WHIP（用以繫物或做皮鞭的）皮條 **2** a pair of women's KNICKERS or men's UNDERPANTS that has only a very narrow strip of cloth, like a string, at the back（背後為繩子一樣窄條的）內褲；丁字內褲 **3** (*NAmE, AustralE, NZE*) = FLIP-FLOP

thorax /ˈθɔːræks/ *noun* (*pl.* **thor·axes** or **thor·aces** /ˈθɔːrəsiːz/) **1** (*anatomy* 解) the part of the body that is surrounded by the RIBS, between the neck and the waist 胸；胸腔 **2** the middle section of an insect's body, to which the legs and wings are attached（昆蟲的）胸，胸部 ➲ VISUAL VOCAB page V13 ▸ **thor·acic** /θɔːˈræsɪk/ *adj.* [only before noun]

thor·ium /ˈθɔːriəm/ *noun* [U] (*symb.* **Th**) a chemical element. Thorium is a white RADIOACTIVE metal used as a source of nuclear energy. 釷（放射性化學元素）

thorn /θɔːn; *NAmE* θɔːrn/ *noun* **1** a small sharp pointed part on the STEM of some plants, such as ROSES（玫瑰之類植物的）刺，棘刺 ➲ VISUAL VOCAB page V11 **2** a tree or bush that has thorns 帶刺的樹；荊棘 ➲ see also BLACKTHORN, HAWTHORN **3** (*phonetics* 語音) the letter that was used in Old English and Icelandic to represent the sounds /θ/ and /ð/ and later written as *th* 刺形符，字母 ð（古英語和古冰島語用的字母，表示 /θ/ 和 /ð/ 的發音，後書寫為 th）

IDM **a thorn in sb's ˈflesh/ˈside** a person or thing that repeatedly annoys sb or stops them from doing sth 不斷讓人煩心的人（或事）；肉中刺；眼中釘

thorny /ˈθɔːni; *NAmE* ˈθɔːrni/ *adj.* (**thorn·ier**, **thorni·est**) **1** [usually before noun] causing difficulty or disagreement 棘手的；麻煩的；引起爭議的 **SYN** **knotty**：*a thorny question/issue/problem* 棘手的問題 **2** having thorns 有刺的；多刺的：*a thorny bush* 有刺的灌木

thor·ough 🔑 /ˈθʌrə; *NAmE* ˈθɜːroʊ/ *adj.* **1** 🔑 done completely; with great attention to detail 徹底的；完全的；深入的；細緻的：*a thorough knowledge of the subject* 對這一學科的透徹瞭解 ◇ *The police carried out a thorough investigation.* 警方展開了全面的調查。 **2** 🔑 [not usually before noun] (of a person 人) doing things very carefully and with great attention to detail 仔細周到；工作縝密：*She's very thorough and conscientious.* 她勤勤懇懇，一絲不苟。 **3** (*BrE, informal*) used to emphasize how bad or annoying sb/sth is 十足的；徹頭徹尾的；完完全全的 **SYN** **complete**：*Everything was in a thorough mess.* 一切都是亂七八糟的。 ▸ **thor·ough·ness** *noun* [U]：*I was impressed by the thoroughness of the report.* 那份報告全面深入，給我留下了深刻的印象。◇ *I admire his thoroughness.* 我欽佩他辦事認真仔細。

thor·ough·bred /ˈθʌrəbred; *NAmE* ˈθɜːroʊb-/ *noun* an animal, especially a horse, of high quality, that has parents that are both of the same breed 純種動物，良種動物（尤指馬） ▸ **thor·ough·bred** *adj.*：*a thoroughbred mare* 純種母馬

thor·ough·fare /ˈθʌrəfeə(r); *NAmE* ˈθɜːroʊfer/ *noun* a public road or street used by traffic, especially a main road in a city or town 大街；大道；通衢

thor·ough·going /ˌθʌrəˈɡəʊɪŋ; *NAmE* ˌθɜːroʊˈɡoʊɪŋ/ *adj.* [only before noun] **1** very thorough; looking at every detail 徹底的；仔細的：*a thoroughgoing revision of the text* 對文本認真仔細的校訂 **2** complete 完全的；全面的；徹底的：*a thoroughgoing commitment to change* 對變革的全面承諾

thor·ough·ly 🔑 /ˈθʌrəli; *NAmE* ˈθɜːr-/ *adv.* **1** 🔑 very much; completely 非常；極其；徹底；完全：*We thoroughly enjoyed ourselves.* 我們玩得痛快極了。◇ *I'm thoroughly confused.* 我完全給搞糊塗了。◇ *a thoroughly professional performance* 地道的專業表演 **2** 🔑 completely and with great attention to detail 徹底；仔細；縝密：*Wash the fruit thoroughly before use.* 把水果仔細清洗過後再用。◇ *The work had not been done very thoroughly.* 這工作做得不太認真。

those ➲ THAT

thou /ðaʊ/ *pron.* (*old use* or *dialect*) a word meaning 'you', used when talking to only one person who is the subject of the verb（用作第二人稱單數動詞的主語）你，汝；爾 ➲ compare THEE

though 🔑 /ðəʊ; *NAmE* ðoʊ/ *conj., adv.*

■ ***conj.*** **1** 🔑 despite the fact that 雖然；儘管；即使 **SYN** **although**：*Anne was fond of Tim, though he often annoyed her.* 安妮喜歡蒂姆，雖然他經常使她心煩。◇ *Though she gave no sign, I was sure she had seen me.* 儘管她沒有示意，我還是確信她看見了我。◇ *His clothes, though old and worn, looked clean and of good quality.* 他的衣服雖然很舊，但看上去乾乾淨淨，質地很好。◇ *Strange though it may sound, I was pleased it was over.* 儘管聽起來也許很奇怪，但我很高興這都結束了。 **2** 🔑 used to add a fact or an opinion that makes the previous statement less strong or less important（用於主句後，引出補充說明，使語氣變弱）不過，可是，然而：*They're very different, though they did seem to get on well when they met.* 他們大不相同，可是見面後好像還確實相處得不錯。◇ *He'll probably say no, though it's worth asking.* 他很可能會拒絕，不過問一下有益無損。 ➲ note at ALTHOUGH **IDM** see AS *conj.*, EVEN *adv.*

■ ***adv.*** 🔑 used especially at the end of a sentence to add a fact or an opinion that makes the previous statement less strong or less important（尤用於句末補充說明，使語氣減弱）不過，可是，然而：*Our team lost. It was a good game though.* 我們隊輸了，可是這也不失為一場好球。◇ *'Have you ever been to Australia?' 'No. I'd like to, though.'* "你去過澳大利亞嗎？" "沒有，不過我很想去。" ➲ note at ALTHOUGH

thought 🔑 /θɔːt/ *noun*

▸ STH YOU THINK 所想之事 **1** 🔑 [C] something that you think of or remember 想法；看法；主意；記憶：**~ of (sb/sth) doing sth** *I don't like the thought of you walking home alone.* 我不喜歡你一個人步行回家。◇ **~ of sth** *The **very thought of** it makes me feel sick.* 一想到這事就使我惡心。◇ **~ (that …)** *She was struck by the sudden thought that he might already have left.* 她突然想到他可能已經離去。◇ *I've just **had a thought*** (= an idea). 我剛想到一個主意。◇ *Would Mark be able to help? **It's just a thought.***

T

馬克能幫忙嗎？僅僅是想到這一點而已。◇ *'Why don't you try the other key?' '**That's a thought!**'* "你為什麼不試試另一把鑰匙？" "這倒是個主意！" ◇ *I'd like to hear your thoughts on the subject.* 我想聽聽你對這個問題的看法。

▸ **MIND/IDEAS** 心思；思想 **2** 🔑 **thoughts** [pl.] a person's mind and all the ideas that they have in it when they are thinking 心思；思想：*My thoughts turned to home.* 我想家了。

▸ **PROCESS/ACT OF THINKING** 思維過程；思考 **3** [U] the power or process of thinking 思考能力；思維過程；思考；思維：*A good teacher encourages independence of thought.* 好的教師鼓勵獨立思考。◇ *She was **lost in thought*** (= concentrating so much on her thoughts that she was not aware of her surroundings). 她陷入沉思。**4** 🔑 [U] the act of thinking seriously and carefully about sth 考慮；深思 **SYN** **consideration**：*I've given the matter careful thought.* 我對這件事認真考慮過了。◇ *Not enough thought has gone into this essay.* 這篇文章很膚淺。

▸ **CARE/WORRY** 關心；憂慮 **5** [C] **~ (for sb/sth)** a feeling of care or worry 關心；關懷；顧慮；憂慮：***Spare a thought** for those without enough to eat this winter.* 請關心一下今冬食不果腹的人。◇ ***Don't give it another thought*** (= to tell sb not to worry after they have said they are sorry). 別多想了（讓道了歉的人不再擔心）。◇ ***It's the thought that counts*** (= used to say that sb has been very kind even if they have only done sth small or unimportant). 有這份心意就好。

▸ **INTENTION** 意向 **6** [U, C] an intention or a hope of doing sth 意圖；打算；希望；念頭：**~ (of doing sth)** *She had given up all thought of changing her job.* 她打消了所有變換工作的念頭。◇ **~ (of sth)** *He acted with no thoughts of personal gain.* 他這樣做根本沒有考慮個人得失。

▸ **IN POLITICS/SCIENCE, ETC.** 政治、科學等 **7** [U] ideas in politics, science, etc. connected with a particular person, group or period of history 思想；思潮：*feminist thought* 女權主義思想 ➲ see also THINK *v.*

IDM **have ˌsecond ˈthoughts** to change your opinion after thinking about sth again（經考慮後）改變想法；（轉念一想）改變主意 **on ˈsecond ˈthoughts** (*BrE*) (*NAmE* **on ˈsecond ˈthought**) used to say that you have changed your opinion（表示已改變想法）又一想，轉念一想：*I'll wait here. No, on second thoughts, I'll come with you.* 我就在這兒等。不，再一想，我還是跟你一起走。 **without a second ˈthought** immediately; without stopping to think about sth further 立即；馬上；不假思索：*He dived in after her without a second thought.* 他不假思索地隨她跳入水中。➲ more at COLLECT *v.*, FOOD, PAUSE *n.*, PENNY, PERISH, SCHOOL *n.*, TRAIN *n.*, WISH *n.*

thought·crime /ˈθɔːtkraɪm/ *noun* [U, C] an idea or opinion that is considered socially unacceptable or criminal 思想罪（被認為社會不接受或構成犯罪的想法或觀點） **ORIGIN** From George Orwell's novel *Nineteen Eighty-Four.* 源自喬治•奧威爾所著小說《一九八四》。

thought·ful /ˈθɔːtfl/ *adj.* **1** quiet, because you are thinking 沉思的；深思的；思考的：*He looked thoughtful.* 他一臉沉思的神情。◇ *They sat in thoughtful silence.* 他們坐着，沉思不語。**2** (*approving*) showing that you think about and care for other people 體貼的；關心別人的；關切的 **SYN** **considerate, kind**：*It was very thoughtful of you to send the flowers.* 你送花來，想得真周到。**3** showing signs of careful thought 縝密思考過的；深思熟慮的：*a player who has a thoughtful approach to the game* 對這場比賽縝密研究過對策的運動員 ▸ **thought·ful·ly** /-fəli/ *adv.*：*Martin looked at her thoughtfully.* 馬丁若有所思地望着她。◇ *She used the towel thoughtfully provided by her host.* 她用了主人特意為她準備的毛巾。 **thought·ful·ness** *noun* [U]

thought·less /ˈθɔːtləs/ *adj.* (*disapproving*) not caring about the possible effects of your words or actions on other people 粗心大意的；欠考慮的；輕率的 **SYN** **inconsiderate**：*a thoughtless remark* 欠考慮的話 ▸ **thought·less·ly** *adv.* **thought·less·ness** *noun* [U]

ˈthought police *noun* [pl.] a group of people who are seen as trying to control people's ideas and stop them from having their own opinions 思想警察（被認為試圖控制他人思想、禁止獨立觀點的集體）

ˈthought-provok·ing *adj.* making people think seriously about a particular subject or issue 發人深省的；引人深思的

thou·sand 🔑 /ˈθaʊznd/ *number* (*abbr.* K)
1 🔑 1 000 一千 **HELP** You say **a, one, two, etc. thousand** without a final 's' on 'thousand'. **Thousands (of ...)** can be used if there is no number or quantity before it. Always use a plural verb with **thousand** or **thousands**, except when an amount of money is mentioned. * thousand 與數詞 a、one、two 等連用時，後面不加 s。若前面沒有數目或數量，可用 thousands (of ...)。除指金額外，thousand 和 thousands 均用複數動詞：*Four thousand (people) are expected to attend.* ◇ *Two thousand (pounds) was withdrawn from the account.* **2** 🔑 **a thousand** or **thousands (of ...)** (usually *informal*) a large number 數以千計的；成千上萬的；許許多多的：*There were thousands of people there.* 那裏有成千上萬的人。**3** **the thousands** the numbers from 1 000 to 9 999 * 1 000 到 9 999 間的數目；千位數：*The cost ran into the thousands.* 成本達到千位數。**HELP** There are more examples of how to use numbers at the entry for **hundred**. 更多數詞用法示例見 hundred 條。**IDM** see BAT *v.*

thou·sandth 🔑 /ˈθaʊznθ/ *ordinal number, noun*
▪ ***ordinal number*** 🔑 1 000th 第一千：*the city's thousandth anniversary* 這座城市的一千週年紀念
▪ ***noun*** 🔑 each of one thousand parts of sth 千分之一：*a/one thousandth of a second* 千分之一秒

thrall /θrɔːl/ *noun*
IDM **in (sb's/sth's) ˈthrall | in ˈthrall to sb/sth** (*literary*) controlled or strongly influenced by sb/sth 受…控制；深受…影響

thrash /θræʃ/ *verb, noun*
▪ ***verb*** **1** [T] **~ sb/sth** to hit a person or an animal many times with a stick, etc. as a punishment（作為懲罰用棍子等）抽打，連續擊打 **SYN** **beat** **2** [I, T] to move or make sth move in a violent or uncontrolled way（使）激烈扭動，翻來覆去：**~ (about/around)** *Someone was thrashing around in the water, obviously in trouble.* 有人在水裏亂撲騰，顯然遇到了危險。◇ **~ sth (about/around)** *A whale was thrashing the water with its tail.* 一條鯨魚不住地用尾巴擊水。◇ *She thrashed her head from side to side.* 她把頭搖得像撥浪鼓似的。**3** [T] **~ sb/sth** (*informal, especially BrE*) to defeat sb very easily in a game（賽事中）輕易擊敗，一舉戰勝：*Scotland thrashed England 5–1.* 蘇格蘭隊以 5:1 大勝英格蘭隊。➲ compare WHIP *v.* (5)

PHR V **ˌthrash sth↔ˈout** (*informal*) to discuss a situation or problem thoroughly in order to decide sth 徹底討論，反覆討論（以便作出決定）

▪ ***noun*** **1** [U] a type of loud rock music 快節奏重金屬搖滾樂 **2** [C] (*old-fashioned, informal*) a party with music and dancing 載歌載舞的聚會

thrash·ing /ˈθræʃɪŋ/ *noun* **1** an act of hitting sb very hard, especially with a stick 棒打；毆打；痛打：*to **give sb/get a thrashing*** 痛打某人一頓；捱了一頓痛打 **2** (*informal*) a severe defeat in a game（比賽）大敗，慘敗

thread 🔑 /θred/ *noun, verb*
▪ ***noun*** **1** 🔑 [U, C] a thin string of cotton, wool, silk, etc. used for sewing or making cloth（棉、毛、絲等的）線：*a needle and thread* 針線 ◇ *a robe embroidered with gold thread* 用金線繡的長袍 ◇ *the delicate threads of a spider's web* 蜘蛛網的纖絲 ➲ picture at ROPE ➲ VISUAL VOCAB page V41 **2** [C] an idea or a feature that is part of sth greater; an idea that connects the different parts of sth 線索；脈絡；思緒；思路；貫穿的主線：*A common thread runs through these discussions.* 這些討論都貫穿着一條共同的主線。◇ *The author skilfully draws together the different threads of the plot.* 作者嫻熟地把情節的各種線索串聯在一起。◇ *I **lost the thread** of the argument* (= I could no longer follow it). 我再跟不上這論證的思路了。**3** [C] **~ (of sth)** a long thin line of sth 線狀物；細細的一條：*A thread of light emerged from the keyhole.* 從鎖眼裏透出一絲光亮。**4** [C] (*computing* 計) a series

of connected messages on a MESSAGE BOARD on the Internet which have been sent by different people（互聯網留言板上帖子的）系列相關信息，鏈式消息 **5** [C] the raised line that runs around the length of a screw and that allows it to be fixed in place by twisting 螺紋 ➲ VISUAL VOCAB page V20 **6 threads** [pl.] (*old-fashioned, NAmE, slang*) clothes 衣服 IDM see HANG *v.*, PICK *v.*

■ *verb* **1** [T] **~ sth (+ adv./prep.)** to pass sth long and thin, especially thread, through a narrow opening or hole 穿（針）；紉（針）；穿過：*to thread a needle (with cotton)*（用棉線）紉針 ◇ *to thread cotton through a needle* 用棉線紉針 ◇ *A tiny wire is threaded through a vein to the heart.* 一根細金屬絲從靜脈裏穿到心臟。**2** [I, T] to move or make sth move through a narrow space, avoiding things that are in the way（使）穿過；通過；穿行 SYN **pick your way**：**+ adv./prep.** *The waiters threaded between the crowded tables.* 服務員穿行在擁擠的餐桌之間。◇ **~ your way + adv./prep.** *It took me a long time to thread my way through the crowd.* 我花了很長時間才從人群中擠過去。**3** [T] **~ sth (onto sth)** to join two or more objects together by passing sth long and thin through them 穿成串；串在一起：*to thread beads (onto a string)*（在繩子上）把珠子串起來 **4** [T] **~ sth** to pass film, tape, string, etc. through parts of a piece of equipment so that it is ready to use 給…裝入（膠片、磁帶、絲弦等）**5** [T, usually passive] **~ sth (with sth)** to sew or twist a particular type of thread into sth 用…線縫；把…線絞入：*a robe threaded with gold and silver* 用金銀線縫的長袍

thread·bare /ˈθredbeə(r); *NAmE* -ber/ *adj.* **1** (of cloth, clothing, etc. 織物、衣服等) old and thin because it has been used a lot 穿舊的；磨薄的；破舊的：*a threadbare carpet* 磨薄了的地毯 **2** (of an argument, excuse, etc. 論點、藉口等) that does not have much effect, especially because it has been used too much 老一套的；陳腐的

thread·ed /ˈθredɪd/ *adj.* (*technical* 術語) (of a screw, etc. 螺釘等) having a THREAD *n.* (5) 有螺紋的

ˈthread vein *noun* a very thin VEIN, especially one that can be seen through the skin（尤指透過皮膚可見的）毛細血管

thread·worm /ˈθredwɜːm; *NAmE* -wɜːrm/ *noun* a small thin WORM that lives in the INTESTINES of humans and animals 線蟲；蟯蟲

threat 🔑 /θret/ *noun*

1 🔑 [C, U] **~ (to do sth)** a statement in which you tell sb that you will punish or harm them, especially if they do not do what you want 威脅；恐嚇：*to make threats against sb* 對某人進行威脅 ◇ *She is prepared to* ***carry out her threat*** *to resign.* 她以辭職作為要挾，已準備好付諸行動。◇ *He received* ***death threats*** *from right-wing groups.* 他收到了右翼團體的死亡恐嚇。◇ *crimes involving violence or the threat of violence* 涉及暴力或暴力威脅的罪行 **2** 🔑 [U, C, usually sing.] the possibility of trouble, danger or disaster 壞事發生的可能：*These ancient woodlands are* ***under threat*** *from new road developments.* 新道路的開發可能對這些古老的林地造成破壞。◇ *There is a real threat of war.* 確有戰爭的徵兆。**3** 🔑 [C, usually sing.] **~ (to sth)** a person or thing that is likely to cause trouble, danger, etc. 構成威脅的人；形成威脅的事物：*He is unlikely to be a threat to the Spanish player in the final.* 相信他不會在決賽中對這位西班牙運動員形成威脅。◇ *Drugs* ***pose a major threat to*** *our society.* 毒品成為對社會的一大威脅。

threat·en 🔑 /ˈθretn/ *verb*

1 🔑 [T] to say that you will cause trouble, hurt sb, etc. if you do not get what you want 揚言要；威脅；恐嚇：**~ sb** *They broke my windows and threatened me.* 他們砸碎我的窗子並威脅我。◇ **~ sb with sth** *The attacker threatened them with a gun.* 襲擊者用槍威脅他們。◇ *He was threatened with dismissal if he continued to turn up late for work.* 他受到警告，如果繼續上班遲到，就被辭退。◇ **~ sth** *The threatened strike has been called off.* 揚言要進行的罷工被取消了。◇ **~ to do sth** *The hijackers threatened to kill one passenger every hour if their demands were not met.* 劫機者要挾說，如果他們的要求得不到滿足，他們每過一小時就殺死一名乘客。◇ **~ that ...** *They threatened that passengers would be killed.* 他們要挾說要殺死乘客。**2** 🔑 [I, T] to seem likely to happen or cause sth unpleasant 預示凶兆；有…危險：*A storm was threatening.* 暴風雨即將來臨。◇ **~ to do sth** *This dispute threatens to split the party.* 這一分歧可能會造成黨的分裂。◇ **~ sth** *The clouds threatened rain.* 烏雲密佈預示大雨將至。**3** 🔑 [T] **~ sth** to be a danger to sth 危及；對…構成威脅 SYN **endanger, put at risk**：*Pollution is threatening marine life.* 污染正危及海洋生物。

threat·en·ing 🔑 /ˈθretnɪŋ/ *adj.*

1 🔑 expressing a threat of harm or violence 威脅的；恐嚇的 SYN **menacing**：*threatening letters* 恐嚇信 ◇ *threatening behaviour* 威脅行為 **2** 🔑 (of the sky, clouds, etc. 天空、雲等) showing that bad weather is likely 陰沉沉的；烏雲密佈的：*The sky was dark and threatening.* 天空烏雲密佈，陰沉沉的。▸ **threat·en·ing·ly** *adv.*：*He glared at her threateningly.* 他氣勢洶洶地瞪着她。

three 🔑 /θriː/ *number*

3 三 HELP There are examples of how to use numbers at the entry for **five**. 數詞用法示例見 five 條。

IDM **the three ˈRs** (*old-fashioned*) reading, writing and ARITHMETIC, thought to be the most important parts of a child's education 初等教育三要素（被視為兒童教育最重要部份的讀、寫、算）➲ more at TWO

ˌthree-card ˈtrick *noun* a game in which players bet money on which is the queen out of three cards lying face down 三牌猜王后（賭博戲，參加者猜三張正面朝下的紙牌中哪一張為王后）

ˌthree-ˈcornered *adj.* [usually before noun] **1** having three corners 三角形的；有三個角的；三隅的：*a three-cornered hat* 三角帽 **2** involving three people or groups 有三人參加的；有三個組的：*a three-cornered contest* 三方競爭

ˌthree-ˈD (also **3-D**) *noun* [U] the quality of having, or appearing to have, length, width and depth (= three DIMENSIONS) 三維；三度；立體：*These glasses allow you to see the film in three-D.* 這副眼鏡讓你能看立體電影。◇ *a three-D image* 立體視像

ˌthree-day eˈventing *noun* = EVENTING

ˌthree-diˈmension·al *adj.* having, or appearing to have, length, width and depth 三維的；立體的；三度空間的；有立體感的：*three-dimensional objects* 立體物體

three·fold /ˈθriːfəʊld; *NAmE* -foʊld/ *adj., adv.* ➲ -FOLD

ˌthree ˈfourths *noun* [pl.] (*US*) = THREE QUARTERS

three-legged race /ˌθriː ˈlegɪd reɪs/ *noun* a race in which people taking part run in pairs, the right leg of one runner being tied to the left leg of the other 二人三足賽跑，綁腿賽跑（參賽者兩人一組，一人的右腿和另一人的左腿綁在一起）

ˌthree-line ˈwhip *noun* (in Britain) a written notice to Members of Parliament from their party leaders telling them that they must be present at a particular vote and must vote in a particular way 緊急通知（英國政黨領袖要求其議員必須參加投票和如何投票的書面通知）

ˌthree-ˈpeat *noun* (*NAmE*) (used especially in newspapers 尤用於報章) an occasion when a person or team wins a competition for the third time, especially in sport（尤指在同一個體育比賽中的）第三次獲勝，三連冠，三連霸 ▸ **ˌthree-ˈpeat** *verb* [I]

three·pence /ˌθriːˈpens; *formerly* ˈθrepəns/ *noun* [U] (*BrE*) the sum of three old pence（舊時的）三便士

three·penny bit /ˌθrepəni ˈbɪt/ (also **ˌthree·penny ˈpiece**) *noun* a British coin in use until 1971, worth three old pence 三便士硬幣（1971 年已停止使用的英國硬幣）

ˌthree-ˈpiece *adj.* [only before noun] consisting of three separate parts or pieces 三件一套的；由三部份組成的：*a* ***three-piece suit*** (= a set of clothes consisting of trousers/pants, a jacket and a WAISTCOAT/VEST) 三件式套服（包括褲子、上衣和背心）◇ (*BrE*) *a* ***three-piece suite*** (= a set of three pieces of furniture, usually a SOFA and two ARMCHAIRS) 三件一套的傢具（通常為一張長沙發和兩張單人沙發）

T

ˌthree-point ˈturn *noun* a method of turning a car in a small space so that it faces in the opposite direction, by driving forwards, then backwards, then forwards again, in a series of curves 三點轉向（汽車在狹窄場所轉彎掉頭的方法，先向前，再後退，再向前進）

ˌthree-ˈquarter *adj.* [only before noun] used to describe sth which is three quarters of the usual size 四分之三的：*a three-quarter length coat* 七分長大衣

ˌthree ˈquarters (*US* also **ˌthree ˈfourths**) *noun* **~ (of sth)** three of the four equal parts into which sth may be divided 四分之三：*three quarters of an hour* 四十五分鐘

ˌthree-ring ˈcircus *noun* [sing.] (*NAmE, informal*) a place or situation with a lot of confusing or amusing activity 有各種娛樂活動的場所；大型熱鬧的演出

three·some /ˈθriːsəm/ *noun* **1** [C+sing./pl. v.] a group of three people 三人一組；三人小組 **2** [C] an occasion when three people have sex together 三人性愛

ˈthree-star *adj.* [usually before noun] **1** having three stars in a system that measures quality. The highest standard is usually represented by four or five stars.（質量）三星級的：*a three-star hotel* 三星級賓館 **2** (*NAmE*) having the third-highest military rank, and wearing uniform which has three stars on it（軍銜）三星的：*a three-star general* 三星上將

ˌthree-ˈway *adj.* [only before noun] happening or working in three ways or directions, or between three people 三方面的；三向的；三人參加的：*a three-way switch* 三路開關 ◇ *a three-way discussion* 三人談

thren·ody /ˈθrenədi/ *noun* (*pl.* **-ies**) (*technical* 術語) a song, poem or other expression of great sadness for sb who has died or for sth that has ended 輓歌；哀歌；悲詩；哀悼

thresh /θreʃ/ *verb* **1** [T] **~ sth** to separate grains of rice, WHEAT, etc. from the rest of the plant using a machine or, especially in the past, by hitting it with a special tool（用機器）使脱粒；（尤指舊時手持工具）打稻，打麥 ➲ COLLOCATIONS at FARMING **2** [I, T] **~ (sth)** to make, or cause sth to make, uncontrolled movements （使）劇烈扭動，翻滾 SYN **thrash** ▶ **thresh·ing** *noun* [U]：*a threshing machine* 脱粒機

thresh·old /ˈθreʃhəʊld; *NAmE* -hoʊld/ *noun* **1** the floor or ground at the bottom of a DOORWAY, considered as the entrance to a building or room 門檻；門口：*She stood hesitating on the threshold.* 她站在門口，猶豫不決。◇ *He stepped across the threshold.* 他邁過門檻。 **2** the level at which sth starts to happen or have an effect 閾；界；起始點：*He has a low **boredom threshold*** (= he gets bored easily). 他極易感到乏味。◇ *I have a high **pain threshold*** (= I can suffer a lot of pain before I start to react). 我的忍痛力很高。◇ *My earnings are just above the **tax threshold*** (= more than the amount at which you start paying tax). 我的收入剛剛超過徵税起點。 **3** [usually sing.] the point just before a new situation, period of life, etc. begins 開端；起點；入門：*She felt as though she was **on the threshold of** a new life.* 她覺得好像就要開始新生活了。

threw *past tense of* THROW

thrice /θraɪs/ *adv.* (*old use* or *formal*) three times 三次；三倍

thrift /θrɪft/ *noun* [U] **1** (*approving*) the habit of saving money and spending it carefully so that none is wasted 節約；節儉 ➲ see also SPENDTHRIFT **2** a wild plant with bright pink flowers that grows by the sea/ocean 海石竹（海邊野生植物，花鮮豔，呈粉紅色）

ˈthrift shop (also **ˈthrift store**) (both *NAmE*) (*BrE* **ˈcharity shop**) *noun* a shop/store that sells clothes and other goods given by people to raise money for a charity 慈善商店（通過出售捐贈的衣物等募集慈善基金）

thrifty /ˈθrɪfti/ *adj.* (*approving*) careful about spending money and not wasting things 節約的；節儉的 SYN **frugal**

thrill /θrɪl/ *noun, verb*

■ ***noun*** **1** a strong feeling of excitement or pleasure; an experience that gives you this feeling 震顫感；興奮感；興奮；激動；令人興奮的經歷：**~ (to do sth)** *It gave me a big **thrill** to meet my favourite author in person.* 能見到我最喜歡的作者本人使我感到興奮不已。◇ **~ (of doing sth)** *the thrill of catching a really big fish* 捉到一條很大的魚的興奮經歷 ◇ *She gets an obvious thrill out of performing.* 她顯然從表演中得到一種興奮感。**2** a sudden strong feeling that produces a physical effect 一陣強烈的感覺：*A thrill of alarm ran through him.* 一陣驚恐的感覺傳遍他的全身。

IDM **(the) thrills and ˈspills** (*informal*) the excitement that is involved in dangerous activities, especially sports （危險活動，尤指體育運動的）緊張和刺激

■ ***verb*** **~ sb** to excite or please sb very much 使非常興奮；使非常激動：*This band has thrilled audiences all over the world.* 這支樂隊使全世界的觀眾狂熱痴迷。◇ *I was thrilled by your news.* 你的消息使我興奮極了。

PHR V **ˈthrill to sth** (*formal*) to feel very excited at sth 對…感到非常興奮（或激動）

thrilled /θrɪld/ *adj.* very excited and pleased 非常興奮；極為激動：**~ (about/at/with sth)** *He was thrilled at the prospect of seeing them again.* 他一想到有望再次見到他們便欣喜若狂。◇ **~ (to do sth)** *I was thrilled to be invited.* 我有幸受到邀請，感到非常興奮。◇ **~ (that ...)** (*BrE*) *She was **thrilled to bits*** (= extremely pleased) *that he'd been offered the job.* 她得知他得到了這份工作簡直樂不可支。◇ *'Are you pleased?' 'I'm thrilled.'* "你高興嗎？" "我太興奮了。" ➲ SYNONYMS at GLAD

thrill·er /ˈθrɪlə(r)/ *noun* a book, play or film/movie with an exciting story, especially one about crime or SPYING（尤指關於罪案或間諜的）驚險小説（或戲劇、電影）

thrill·ing /ˈθrɪlɪŋ/ *adj.* exciting and enjoyable 驚險的；緊張的；扣人心弦的；令人興奮不已的：*a thrilling experience/finish* 激動人心的經歷／結局 ➲ SYNONYMS at EXCITING ▶ **thrill·ing·ly** *adv.*

ˈthrill ride *noun* a ride at an AMUSEMENT PARK that makes you feel very excited and frightened at the same time（遊樂園的）驚險刺激乘騎，飛轉

thrive /θraɪv/ *verb* [I] to become, and continue to be, successful, strong, healthy, etc. 興旺發達；繁榮；蓬勃發展；旺盛；茁壯成長 SYN **flourish**：*New businesses thrive in this area.* 新企業在這一地區蓬勃興起。◇ *These animals rarely thrive in captivity.* 這些動物欄養起來很少會肥壯。▶ **thriv·ing** *adj.*：*a thriving industry* 興盛的行業

PHR V **ˈthrive on sth** to enjoy sth or be successful at sth, especially sth that other people would not like 以某事為樂，因某事而有成（尤指別人不喜歡的事物）：*He thrives on hard work.* 他以苦幹為樂事。

throat 0-w /θrəʊt; *NAmE* θroʊt/ *noun* **1** 0-w a passage in the neck through which food and air pass on their way into the body; the front part of the neck 咽喉；喉嚨；頸前部：*a sore throat* 咽喉痛 ◇ *A sob caught in his throat.* 他泣不成聲。◇ *He held the knife to her throat.* 他拿刀子頂着她的喉嚨。◇ *Their throats had been cut.* 他們的咽喉被割斷了。➲ VISUAL VOCAB page V59 **2 -throated** (in adjectives 構成形容詞) having the type of throat mentioned 有…喉嚨的；嗓子…的：*a deep-throated roar* 低沉的咆哮 ◇ *a red-throated diver* 紅喉潛鳥 ➲ see also CUT-THROAT

IDM **be at each other's ˈthroats** (of two or more people, groups, etc. 兩個以上的人或群體等) to be fighting or arguing with each other 打架鬥毆；激烈爭吵；吵架 **cut your own ˈthroat** to do sth that is likely to harm you, especially when you are angry and trying to harm sb else（尤指生氣和要加害於人時）自食惡果，卡自己的脖子，自尋死路 **force/thrust/ram sth down sb's ˈthroat** (*informal*) to try to force sb to listen to and accept your opinions in a way that they find annoying 強加於人；強迫接受（觀點） ➲ more at CLEAR *v.*, FROG, JUMP *v.*, LUMP *n.*, STICK *v.*

throaty /ˈθrəʊti; *NAmE* ˈθroʊti/ *adj.* sounding low and rough 聲音低沉的；嘶啞的：*a throaty laugh* 嘎嘎的笑聲 ◇ *the throaty roar of the engines* 發動機的低沉轟鳴聲 ▶ **throat·ily** /-ɪli/ *adv.*

T

throb /θrɒb; *NAmE* θrɑːb/ *verb, noun*

■ ***verb*** (**-bb-**) **1** [I] **~ (with sth)** (of a part of the body 身體部位) to feel a series of regular painful movements （有規律地）抽動，抽痛：*His head throbbed painfully.* 他的頭一抽一跳地痛。◇ *My feet were throbbing after the long walk home.* 我走了很長的路回到家後，雙腳陣陣作痛。➲ SYNONYMS at HURT **2** [I] to beat or sound with a strong, regular rhythm （強烈有節奏地）跳動，搏動，震響 SYN **pulsate**：*The ship's engines throbbed quietly.* 船上的發動機有節奏地輕輕震動。◇ *a throbbing drumbeat* 咚咚的擊鼓聲 ◇ *The blood was throbbing in my veins.* 血液在我的靜脈中有節律地湧動着。◇ **~ with sth** (*figurative*) *His voice was throbbing with emotion.* 他的聲音激動得顫抖。

■ ***noun*** (also **throb·bing**) [sing.] a strong regular beat; a feeling of pain that you experience as a series of strong beats （強烈有規律的）跳動；陣陣的疼痛：*the throb of the machines* 機器有節奏的顫動 ◇ *My headache faded to a dull throbbing.* 我的頭痛逐漸減輕，後來變得微微抽痛。➲ see also HEART-THROB

throes /θrəʊz; *NAmE* θroʊz/ *noun* [pl.] violent pains, especially at the moment of death （尤指死亡時的）劇痛：*The creature went into its death throes.* 這小生命到了臨終疼痛階段。

IDM **in the throes of sth/of doing sth** in the middle of an activity, especially a difficult or complicated one 正在做，正忙於（尤指困難或複雜的活動）：*The country was in the throes of revolutionary change.* 國家正處於革命動盪中。

throm·bosis /θrɒmˈbəʊsɪs; *NAmE* θrɑːmˈboʊ-/ *noun* [C, U] (*pl.* **throm·boses** /-siːz/) (*medical* 醫) a serious condition caused by a blood CLOT (= a thick mass of blood) forming in a blood VESSEL (= tube) or in the heart 血栓形成 ➲ see also CORONARY THROMBOSIS, DEEP VEIN THROMBOSIS

throne /θrəʊn; *NAmE* θroʊn/ *noun* **1** [C] a special chair used by a king or queen to sit on at ceremonies （國王、女王的）御座，寶座 **2 the throne** [sing.] the position of being a king or queen 王位；王權；帝位：*Queen Elizabeth* ***came/succeeded to the throne*** *in 1952.* 伊麗莎白女王於 1952 年即位／登基。◇ *when Henry VIII was* ***on the throne*** (= was king) 亨利八世在位時

IDM see POWER *n.*

throng /θrɒŋ; *NAmE* θrɔːŋ; θrɑːŋ/ *noun, verb*

■ ***noun*** (*literary*) a crowd of people 聚集的人群；一大群人：*We pushed our way through the throng.* 我們擠過人群。

■ ***verb*** [I, T] (*literary*) to go somewhere or be present somewhere in large numbers 群集；擁塞；擁向：**+ adv./prep.** *The children thronged into the hall.* 孩子們擁進了大廳。◇ **~ to do sth** *People are thronging to see his new play.* 人們成群結隊地去看他的新戲。◇ **~ sth** *Crowds thronged the stores.* 各商店都擠滿了人。

PHR V ˈ**throng with sb/sth** | **be** ˈ**thronged with sb/sth** to be full of people, cars, etc. 擠滿（人、汽車等）：*The cafes were thronging with students.* 小餐館裏都擠滿了學生。◇ *The streets were thronged with people.* 條條大街都擠滿了人。

throt·tle /ˈθrɒtl; *NAmE* ˈθrɑːtl/ *verb, noun*

■ ***verb*** **~ sb** to attack or kill sb by squeezing their throat in order to stop them from breathing 使窒息；掐死；勒死 SYN **strangle**：*He throttled the guard with his bare hands.* 他徒手掐死了衛兵。◇ (*humorous*) *I like her, although I could cheerfully throttle her at times* (= because she is annoying). 我喜歡她，雖然她有時煩得讓人想把她掐死。◇ (*figurative*) *The city is being throttled by traffic.* 這座城市的交通擁擠不堪。

PHR V ˌ**throttle (sth)** ˈ**back/**ˈ**down/**ˈ**up** to control the supply of fuel or power to an engine in order to reduce/increase the speed of a vehicle 調節油門；減／加速：*I throttled back as we approached the runway.* 我們靠近跑道時，我減速了。

■ ***noun*** a device that controls the amount of fuel that goes into the engine of a vehicle, for example the ACCELERATOR in a car 節流閥；節流桿；風門；風門桿：*He drove along* ***at full throttle*** (= as fast as possible). 他全速駕車行駛。

through 0-w /θruː/ *prep., adv., adj.*

■ ***prep.*** HELP For the special uses of **through** in phrasal verbs, look at the entries for the verbs. For example **get through sth** is in the phrasal verb section at **get**. * through 在短語動詞中的特殊用法見有關動詞詞條。如 get through sth 在詞條 get 的短語動詞部份。 **1** 0-w from one end or side of sth/sb to the other 從…一端至另一端；穿過；貫穿：*The burglar got in through the window.* 盜賊是從窗戶進來的。◇ *The bullet went straight through him.* 子彈從他身上穿了過去。◇ *Her knees had gone through* (= made holes in) *her jeans.* 她的膝蓋把牛仔褲磨破了。◇ *The sand ran through* (= between) *my fingers.* 沙子從我的手指縫間漏了下去。◇ *The path led through the trees to the river.* 這條小路穿過樹林通向河邊。◇ *The doctor pushed his way through the crowd.* 醫生擠過人群。◇ *The Charles River flows through Boston.* 查爾斯河流經波士頓。 **2 see, hear, etc. ~ sth** to see, hear, etc. sth from the other side of an object or a substance 透過…看到；隔着…聽到：*I couldn't hear their conversation through the wall.* 我隔牆聽不到他們的交談。◇ *He could just make out three people through the mist.* 透過薄霧他勉強能看出有三個人。 **3** 0-w from the beginning to the end of an activity, a situation or a period of time 自始至終；從頭到尾：*The children are too young to sit through a concert.* 這些孩子年紀太小，音樂會沒完就坐不住了。◇ *He will not live through the night.* 他活不過今天晚上了。◇ *I'm halfway through* (= reading) *her second novel.* 她的第二部小說我看了一半了。 **4** 0-w past a barrier, stage or test 通過（障礙、階段或測試）；穿過：*Go through this gate, and you'll see the house on your left.* 你穿過這道大門，就看到左面的房子了。◇ *He drove through a red light* (= passed it when he should have stopped). 他開車闖了紅燈。◇ *First I have to get through the exams.* 首先我必須通過這些考試。◇ *The bill had a difficult passage through Parliament.* 這項提案費了一番周折才在議會上通過。◇ *I'd never have got through it all* (= a difficult situation) *without you.* 假如沒有您，我是絕對渡不過這個難關的。 **5** 0-w (also *informal* **thru**) (both *NAmE*) until, and including 直至，一直到（所指時間包括在內）：*We'll be in New York Tuesday through Friday.* 我們從星期二到星期五將一直待在紐約。➲ note at INCLUSIVE **6** 0-w by means of; because of 以；憑藉；因為；由於：*You can only achieve success through hard work.* 你得孜孜不倦方能成功。◇ *It was through him* (= as a result of his help) *that I got the job.* 我全靠他的幫助才找到這份工作。◇ *The accident happened through no fault of mine.* 發生事故並不是我的過錯。

■ ***adv.*** HELP For the special uses of **through** in phrasal verbs, look at the entries for the verbs. For example **carry sth through** is in the phrasal verb section at **carry**. * through 在短語動詞中的特殊用法見有關動詞詞條。如 carry sth through 在詞條 carry 的短語動詞部份。 **1** 0-w from one end or side of sth to the other 從一端到另一端；通過：*Put the coffee in the filter and let the water run through.* 把咖啡放入過濾器裏讓水流過。◇ *The tyre's flat—the nail has gone right through.* 輪胎癟了，讓釘子扎穿了。◇ *The onlookers stood aside to let the paramedics through.* 圍觀的人閃開一條路，讓醫務輔助人員通過。◇ *The flood was too deep to drive through.* 洪水太深，汽車開不過去。 **2** 0-w from the beginning to the end of a thing or period of time 自始至終；從頭至尾：*Don't tell me how it ends—I haven't read it all the way through yet.* 先別告訴我書的結尾，我還沒有看完呢。◇ *I expect I'll struggle through until payday.* 我想我會捱到發薪日的。 **3** 0-w past a barrier, stage or test 通過（障礙、階段或測試）：*The lights were red but he drove straight through.* 紅燈亮着，但他開車闖了過去。◇ *Our team is through to* (= has reached) *the semi-finals.* 我們隊打進了半決賽。 **4** 0-w travelling through a place without stopping or without people having to get off one train and onto another 直達；逕直：*'Did you stop in Oxford on the way?' 'No, we drove straight through.'* "你路經牛津時停車了嗎？" "沒有，我一直開過來的。" ◇ *This train goes straight through to York.* 這列火車直達約克。 **5** 0-w connected by telephone （電話）接通着：*Ask to be* ***put through*** *to me personally.* 請接線員

T

把電話直接接給我本人。◇ *I tried to call you but I couldn't get through.* 我給你打電話了，可是怎麼也打不通。**6** used after an adjective to mean 'completely'（用於形容詞後）完全，徹底：*We got wet through.* 我們渾身上下都濕透了。

IDM **,through and 'through** completely; in every way 完全；徹底；地地道道；徹頭徹尾：*He's British through and through.* 他是地地道道的英國人。

■ ***adj.*** **1** [only before noun] **through** traffic travels from one side of a place to the other without stopping（交通旅行）直達的，直通的，聯運的，全程的 **2** [only before noun] a **through** train takes you to the final place you want to get to and you do not have to get off and get on another train（火車）直達的，直通的 **3** [only before noun] a **through** road or route is open at both ends and allows traffic to travel from one end to the other（道路或路線）直通的：*The village lies on a busy through road.* 那村莊坐落在一條繁忙的直達公路上。◇ ***No through road*** (= the road is closed at one end). 此路不通。**4** [not before noun] **~ (with sth/sb)** (*especially NAmE*) used to show that you have finished using sth or have ended a relationship with sb（使用）完成，結束；（關係）了結，斷絕：*Are you through with that newspaper?* 你看完那份報紙了嗎？◇ *Todd and I are through.* 托德和我吹了。

through·out /θruːˈaʊt/ *prep.* **1** in or into every part of sth 各處；遍及：*They export their products to markets throughout the world.* 他們把產品出口到世界各地的市場。**2** during the whole period of time of sth 自始至終；貫穿整個時期：*The museum is open daily throughout the year.* 這個博物館一年到頭每天都開放。▸ **through·out** *adv.*：*The house was painted white throughout.* 這所房子全都粉刷成了白色。◇ *The ceremony lasted two hours and we had to stand throughout.* 儀式進行了兩個小時，我們自始至終都得站着。

through·put /ˈθruːpʊt/ *noun* [U, C, usually sing.] (*technical* 術語) the amount of work that is done, or the number of people that are dealt with, in a particular period of time（某一時期內的）生產量，接待人數

through·way = THRUWAY

throw /θrəʊ; *NAmE* θroʊ/ *verb, noun*

■ ***verb*** (**threw** /θruː/, **thrown** /θrəʊn; *NAmE* θroʊn/)

▸ **WITH HAND** 用手 **1** [T, I] to send sth from your hand through the air by moving your hand or arm quickly 投；擲；拋；扔：**~ (sth)** *Stop throwing stones at the window!* 別朝窗戶扔石頭了！◇ *She threw the ball up and caught it again.* 她把球拋起來又接住。◇ *They had a competition to see who could throw the furthest.* 他們舉行了一場比賽，看誰投得最遠。◇ **~ sth to sb** *Don't throw it to him, give it to him!* 別扔給他，遞給他！◇ **~ sb sth** *Can you throw me that towel?* 請把那條毛巾扔給我好嗎？

▸ **PUT CARELESSLY** 漫不經心地放置 **2** [T] **~ sth + adv./prep.** to put sth in a particular place quickly and carelessly 摔；丟；扔：*Just throw your bag down over there.* 把你的袋子就扔到那邊吧。

▸ **MOVE WITH FORCE** 用力移動 **3** [T] to move sth suddenly and with force 猛推；使勁撞：**~ sth + adv./prep.** *The boat was thrown onto the rocks.* 那條船觸礁了。◇ *The sea throws up all sorts of debris on the beach.* 大海把各種殘骸碎片都沖上海灘。◇ **~ sth + adj.** *I threw open the windows to let the smoke out.* 我猛力推開窗子，讓煙散出去。

▸ **PART OF BODY** 身體部位 **4** [T] **~ sth/yourself + adv./prep.** to move your body or part of it quickly or suddenly 猛動（頭、臂、腿）；挺起（胸）；仰起（頭）；揮動（拳頭、手臂）：*He threw back his head and roared with laughter.* 他猛地仰起頭哈哈大笑起來。◇ *I ran up and threw my arms around him.* 我跑上前去，張開雙臂把他摟在懷裏。◇ *Jenny threw herself onto the bed.* 珍妮一頭倒在牀上。

▸ **MAKE SB FALL** 使人摔倒 **5** [T] **~ sb** to make sb fall quickly or violently to the ground 使迅猛地摔倒在地：*Two riders were thrown* (= off their horses) *in the second race.* 有兩名騎手在第二場賽馬中從馬上摔了下來。

▸ **INTO PARTICULAR STATE** 處於某種狀態 **6** [T, usually passive] **~ sb/sth + adv./prep.** to make sb/sth be in a particular state 使處於，使陷入（某種狀態）：*Hundreds were thrown out of work.* 數以百計的人遭到解雇。◇ *We were thrown into confusion by the news.* 我們被那消息弄得驚慌失措。◇ *The problem was suddenly thrown into sharp focus.* 這個問題突然引起人們的密切關注了。

▸ **DIRECT STH AT SB/STH** 指向某人／事物 **7** [T] **~ sth on/at sb/sth** to direct sth at sb/sth 把…對準；向…作出；對…施加：*to throw doubt on the verdict* 對判決產生懷疑 ◇ *to throw the blame on someone* 委過於人 ◇ *to throw accusations at someone* 對某人大加指責 ◇ *He threw the question back at me* (= expected me to answer it myself). 他反過來問我這個問題。

▸ **UPSET** 使煩惱 **8** [T] **~ sb** (*informal*) to make sb feel upset, confused, or surprised 使心煩意亂；使困惑；使驚奇：*The news of her death really threw me.* 她的噩耗確實令我震驚。

▸ **DICE** 色子 **9** [T] **~ sth** to roll a DICE or let it fall after shaking it; to obtain a particular number in this way 擲（色子）；擲出（色子的點數）：*Throw the dice!* 擲色子！◇ *He threw three sixes in a row.* 他一連擲出三個六點。

▸ **CLAY POT** 泥壺 **10** [T] **~ sth** (*technical* 術語) to make a CLAY pot, dish, etc. on a POTTER'S WHEEL（在陶鈞上）把…拉製成坯：*a hand-thrown vase* 手工拉製的陶瓶

▸ **LIGHT/SHADE** 光；影 **11** [T] **~ sth (+ adv./prep.)** to send light or shade onto sth 照射（光線）；投射（陰影）：*The trees threw long shadows across the lawn.* 樹木在草坪上投下長長的影子。

▸ **YOUR VOICE** 嗓音 **12** [T] **~ your voice** to make your voice sound as if it is coming from another person or place 使變音；使嗓音聽起來像來自他人（或別處）**SYN** **project**

▸ **A PUNCH** 一拳 **13** [T] **~ a punch** to hit sb with your FIST 揮拳猛擊；出拳

▸ **SWITCH/HANDLE** 開關；操作桿 **14** [T] **~ sth** to move a switch, handle, etc. to operate sth 按動，扳動，推動（開關、操作桿等）

▸ **BAD-TEMPERED BEHAVIOUR** 發脾氣 **15** [T] **~ sth** to have a sudden period of bad-tempered behaviour, violent emotion, etc. 突然發作（脾氣等）：*She'll throw a fit if she finds out.* 她要是發現了，一定會大發雷霆。◇ *Children often throw tantrums at this age.* 兒童在這個年齡經常犯脾氣。

▸ **A PARTY** 聚會 **16** [T] **~ a party** (*informal*) to give a party 舉行聚會

▸ **IN SPORTS/COMPETITIONS** 體育運動；比賽 **17** [T] **~ sth** (*informal*) to deliberately lose a game or contest that you should have won 故意輸掉（本應獲勝的比賽或競賽）：*He was accused of having thrown the game.* 他被指責故意放水，輸掉了這場比賽。

IDM Idioms containing **throw** are at the entries for the nouns and adjectives in the idioms, for example **throw your hat into the ring** is at **hat**. 含 throw 的習語，都可在該等習語中的名詞及形容詞相關詞條找到，如 throw your hat into the ring 在詞條 hat 下。

PHR V **,throw sth↔a'side** to reject sth such as an attitude, a way of life, etc. 拒絕接受（某種看法、生活方式等）**'throw yourself at sth/sb** **1** to rush violently at sth/sb 衝向（人或物）；向…猛撲過去 **2** (*informal, disapproving*) (usually of a woman 通常指女人) to be too enthusiastic in trying to attract a sexual partner 撒嬌；獻媚；勾引 **,throw sth↔a'way** **1** (also **,throw sth↔'out**) to get rid of sth that you no longer want 扔掉；丟棄；拋棄：*I don't need that—you can throw it away.* 我不需要那東西，你可以把它扔了。◇ *That old chair should be thrown away.* 那把舊椅子應該扔掉了。**2** to fail to make use of sth; to waste sth 失去；錯過；浪費；白費：*to throw away an opportunity* 失去機會 ➲ see also THROWAWAY **,throw sth 'back at sb** to remind sb of sth they have said or done in the past, especially to upset or annoy them（尤指為使人煩惱）使想起，提醒，重提 **,throw sb 'back on sth** [usually passive] to force sb to rely on sth because nothing else is available 迫使依靠（因別無他物）：*There was no TV so we were thrown back on our own resources* (= had to entertain ourselves). 沒有電視機，所以我們只好自娛自樂了。**,throw sth↔'in** **1** to include sth with what you are selling or offering, without increasing the price（不提

高售價或報價的）奉送，額外贈送：*You can have the piano for $200, and I'll throw in the stool as well.* 你花 200 元就可以買走這架鋼琴，另外奉送這張琴凳。 **2** to add a remark to a conversation 加插評語（或感歎句等）：*Jack threw in the odd encouraging comment.* 傑克難得加了一句鼓勵的話。 **,throw yourself/sth 'into sth** to begin to do sth with energy and enthusiasm 投身於；熱衷於；積極從事 **,throw sth/sb↔'off 1** to manage to get rid of sth/sb that is making you suffer, annoying you, etc. 擺脱；甩掉：*to throw off a cold/your worries/your pursuers* 治好傷風；消除憂慮；甩掉追捕者 **2** to take off a piece of clothing quickly and carelessly 匆匆脱掉，拽下，扯掉（衣服）：*She entered the room and threw off her wet coat.* 她一進屋就脱掉了濕漉漉的大衣。 **,throw sth↔'on** to put on a piece of clothing quickly and carelessly 匆匆穿上（衣服）：*She just threw on the first skirt she found.* 她找到一件裙子就匆忙穿上。**,throw sth↔'open (to sb) 1** to allow people to enter or visit a place where they could not go before（對…）開放；允許…進入 **2** to allow people to discuss sth, take part in a competition, etc. 允許…公開（討論）；允許…參加（競賽）：*The debate will be thrown open to the audience.* 這次辯論將允許觀眾參加。 **,throw sb↔'out (of ...)** 🔑 to force sb to leave a place 攆走；轟走；逐出：*You'll be thrown out if you don't pay the rent.* 你不付房租就會被攆出去。 **,throw sth↔'out 1** to say sth in a way that suggests you have not given it a lot of thought 脱口而出；隨口説：*to throw out a suggestion* 隨口提出建議 **2** to decide not to accept a proposal, an idea, etc. 拒不接受，否決（建議、想法等） **3** = THROW STH AWAY **4** to produce smoke, light, heat, etc. 冒（煙）；發（光）；散發出（熱）：*a small fire that threw out a lot of heat* 散發出大量熱量的小火爐 **5** to confuse sth or make it wrong 使混淆不清；打亂；使出錯：*Our calculations of the cost of our trip were thrown out by changes in the exchange rate.* 我們旅行費用的預算因為匯率變動而完全打亂了。 **,throw sb 'over** (*old-fashioned*) to stop being friends with sb or having a romantic relationship with them 同某人絕交；拋棄某人 **,throw sb↔to'gether** [often passive] to bring people into contact with each other, often unexpectedly 使不期而遇；使意外聚在一起：*Fate had thrown them together.* 命運使他們聚在一起。 **,throw sth↔to'gether** to make or produce sth in a hurry 匆忙拼湊成；倉促製出：*I threw together a quick meal.* 我匆匆做了一頓便飯。 **,throw 'up** to VOMIT 嘔吐 **SYN be sick**：*The smell made me want to throw up.* 這味道使得我想嘔吐。 **,throw sth↔'up 1** to VOMIT food 嘔出（食物）**SYN sick up**：*The baby's thrown up her dinner.* 女嬰把吃的東西吐了出來。 **2** to make people notice sth 使顯眼；使引起注意：*Her research has thrown up some interesting facts.* 她的研究有些很有意思的發現。 **3** to build sth suddenly or in a hurry 突然建造；匆忙建造：*They're throwing up new housing estates all over the place.* 他們在這一帶突然建起了新的居住區。 **4** to leave your job 辭職：*to throw up your career* 放棄事業

■ ***noun* 1** the act of throwing sth, especially a ball or DICE 拋；扔；摔；投（球）；擲（色子）：*a well-aimed throw* 準確的投擲 ◇ *It's your throw* (= it's your turn to throw the dice). 輪到你擲（色子）了。◇ *He threw me to the ground with a judo throw.* 他用柔道摔法把我摔倒在地。 **2** the distance which sth is thrown 投擲的距離：*a javelin throw of 57 metres* * 57 米遠的標槍投擲 **3** a loose cloth cover that can be thrown over a SOFA, etc.（沙發等的）套，罩 ➲ **VISUAL VOCAB** page V21

IDM **$100, £50, etc. a 'throw** (*informal*) used to say how much items cost each 每件價格為；每件值：*The tickets for the dinner were £50 a throw.* 餐券每張 50 英鎊。➲ more at STONE *n.*

throw·away /ˈθrəʊəweɪ; *NAmE* ˈθroʊ-/ *adj.* [only before noun] **1 ~ line/remark/comment** something you say quickly without careful thought, sometimes in order to be funny 脱口而出的；順嘴説出的；開玩笑的：*She was very upset at what to him was just a throwaway remark.* 對他來説這只是隨口説説而已，而她聽了卻很不高興。 **2** (of goods, etc. 貨品等) produced cheaply and intended to be thrown away after use 用後丟棄的；一次性使用的 **SYN disposable**：*throwaway products* 一次性使用的產品 ◇ *We live in a throwaway society* (= a society in which things are not made to last a long time). 我們生活在一次性物品充斥的社會。

throw·back /ˈθrəʊbæk; *NAmE* ˈθroʊ-/ *noun* [usually sing.] **~ (to sth)** a person or thing that is similar to sb/sth that existed in the past 返祖者；返祖；返祖型的東西：*The car's design is a throwback to the 1960s.* 這種汽車的設計回到了 20 世紀 60 年代。

throw·er /ˈθrəʊə(r); *NAmE* ˈθroʊ-/ *noun* a person who throws sth 投擲者；投手：*a discus thrower* 鐵餅運動員 ➲ see also FLAME-THROWER

'throw-in *noun* (in football (SOCCER) and RUGBY 足球和橄欖球) the act of throwing the ball back onto the playing field after it has gone outside the area 擲界外球；擲邊線球

thrown *past part.* of THROW

'throw pillow (*NAmE*) (*BrE* **'scatter cushion**) *noun* a small CUSHION that can be placed on furniture, on the floor, etc. for decoration（散放的）小裝飾墊 ➲ **VISUAL VOCAB** page V21

thru (*NAmE, informal*) = THROUGH *prep.* (5)

thrush /θrʌʃ/ *noun* **1** [C] a bird with a brown back and brown spots on its chest 鶇（一種背部為褐色、胸部有褐色斑點的鳥）：*a song thrush* 歌鶇 **2** [U] an infectious disease that affects the mouth and throat 鵝口瘡；真菌性口炎 **3** [U] (*BrE*) (*NAmE* **'yeast infection**) an infectious disease that affects the VAGINA 唸珠菌陰道炎

Synonyms 同義詞辨析

throw

toss • hurl • fling • chuck • lob • bowl • pitch

These words all mean to send sth from your hand through the air. 以上各詞均含扔、投、擲、拋之義。

throw to send sth from your hand or hands through the air 指投、擲、拋、扔：*Some kids were throwing stones at the window.* 有些孩子在朝窗戶扔石頭。 ◇ *She threw the ball and he caught it.* 她把球拋出來，他接住了。

toss to throw sth lightly or carelessly 指輕輕或漫不經心地扔、拋、擲：*She tossed her jacket onto the bed.* 她把她的短上衣丟到牀上。

hurl to throw sth violently in a particular direction 指猛扔、猛投、猛摔：*Rioters hurled a brick through the car's windscreen.* 暴徒把一塊磚猛地扔向汽車，砸破了擋風玻璃。

fling to throw sb/sth somewhere with a lot of force, especially because you are angry or in a hurry 尤指生氣地或急匆匆地用力扔、擲、拋、丟：*She flung the letter down onto the table.* 她把信摔在桌子上。

chuck (*especially BrE, informal*) to throw sth carelessly 指隨便扔、拋：*I chucked him the keys.* 我把鑰匙扔給了他。

lob (*informal*) to throw sth so that it goes high through the air 指往空中高扔、高拋、高擲：*They were lobbing stones over the wall.* 他們在朝牆那邊扔石頭。

bowl (in cricket) to throw the ball to the batsman（板球）指把球投給擊球員

pitch (in baseball) to throw the ball to the batter（棒球）指把球投給擊球員

PATTERNS

- to throw/toss/hurl/fling/chuck/lob/bowl/pitch sth **at/to** sb/sth
- to throw/toss/fling/chuck sth **aside/away**
- to throw/toss/hurl/fling/chuck/lob/bowl/pitch a **ball**
- to throw/toss/hurl/fling/chuck **stones/rocks/a brick**
- to throw/toss/hurl/fling sth **angrily**
- to throw/toss sth **casually/carelessly**

thrust /θrʌst/ *verb, noun*

■ *verb* (**thrust**, **thrust**) **1** [T, I] to push sth/sb suddenly or violently in a particular direction; to move quickly and suddenly in a particular direction 猛推；衝；搡；擠；塞：**~ sth/sb/yourself + adv./prep.** *He thrust the baby into my arms and ran off.* 他把嬰兒往我懷裏一塞就跑了。◇ *She thrust her hands deep into her pockets.* 她把雙手深深插進口袋裏。◇ (*figurative*) *He tends to thrust himself forward too much.* 他這個人太好強。◇ **+ adv./prep.** *She thrust past him angrily and left.* 她氣呼呼地從他身旁擠過去走了。**2** [I, T] **~ (at sb) (with sth)** | **~ (sth at sb)** to make a sudden strong forward movement at sb with a weapon, etc. 刺；戳：*He thrust at me with a knife.* 他拿刀向我刺來。◇ *a thrusting movement* 衝刺動作 **IDM** see THROAT

PHR V **ˌthrust sth↔aˈside** to refuse to listen to sb's complaints, comments, etc. 置之一旁；置之不理：*All our objections were thrust aside.* 我們所有的異議都被置之不理。**ˈthrust sth/sb on/upon sb** to force sb to accept or deal with sth/sb that they do not want 把…強加於；強迫…接受；強人所難：*She was annoyed at having three extra guests suddenly thrust on her.* 突然又來了三位不速之客要她接待，她感到很惱火。

■ *noun* **1 the thrust** [sing.] the main point of an argument, a policy, etc.（論據、政策等的）要點，要旨，重點：*The thrust of his argument was that change was needed.* 他的論據要點是改革是必要的。**2** [C] a sudden strong movement that pushes sth/sb forward 猛推；刺；戳；插：*He killed her with a thrust of the knife.* 他把她一刀刺死了。**3** [U] (*technical* 術語) the force that is produced by an engine to push a plane, ROCKET, etc. forward（發動機推動飛機、火箭等的）推力，驅動力 **IDM** see CUT *n.*

thrust·er /ˈθrʌstə(r)/ *noun* a small engine used to provide extra force, especially on a SPACECRAFT 助力器；（尤指航天器的）推進器，加速器

thru·way (also **through·way**) /ˈθruːweɪ/ *noun* (*NAmE*) used in the names of some FREEWAYS (= important roads across or between states)（用於某些跨州或州際高速公路的名稱中）過境道路，直達道路：*the New York State Thruway* 紐約州直達高速公路

thud /θʌd/ *noun, verb*

■ *noun* a sound like the one which is made when a heavy object hits sth else 砰的一聲；撲通一聲：*His head hit the floor with a dull thud.* 他的頭砰的一聲撞在了地板上。

■ *verb* (**-dd-**) **1** [I, T] **~ (sth) + adv./prep.** to fall or hit sth with a low dull sound 砰地落下；颼的一聲擊中：*His arrow thudded into the target.* 他的箭噗的一聲射中靶子。**2** [I] (*literary*) (especially of the heart 尤指心臟) to beat strongly 有力地跳動；怦怦地跳

thug /θʌg/ *noun* a violent person, especially a criminal 惡棍；暴徒；罪犯：*a gang of thugs* 一夥暴徒 ▸ **thug·gish** /ˈθʌgɪʃ/ *adj.*：*thuggish brutality* 殘忍的暴行

thug·gery /ˈθʌgəri/ *noun* [U] (*formal*) violent, usually criminal, behaviour 暴行；罪惡行徑

thu·lium /ˈθuːliəm; *BrE* also ˈθjuː-/ *noun* [U] (*symb.* **Tm**) a chemical element. Thulium is a soft silver-white metal. 銩

thumb 🔑 /θʌm/ *noun, verb*

■ *noun* **1** 🔑 the short thick finger at the side of the hand, slightly apart from the other four 拇指：*She still **sucks her thumb** when she's worried.* 她在憂慮時仍然會吸吮大拇指。➲ VISUAL VOCAB page V59 ➲ see also GREEN THUMB **2** 🔑 the part of a glove that covers the thumb（手套的）拇指部份：*There's a hole in the thumb.* 手套的拇指上有個窟窿。

IDM **be all (ˌfingers and) ˈthumbs** to be awkward with your hands so that you drop things or are unable to do sth 笨手笨腳；笨拙；手指不靈活 **hold ˈthumbs** (*SAfrE*) to hope that your plans will be successful or that sth will take place in the way that you want it to 希望（計劃）成功；期望如願以償：*Let's hold thumbs that you get the job.* 我們期望你如願得到這份工作啊。**thumbs ˈup/ˈdown** (*informal*) used to show that sth has been accepted/rejected or that it is/is not a success 翹拇指（表示接受或成功）；拇指向下（表示拒絕或不成功）：*Their proposals **were given the thumbs down**.* 他們的建議遭到拒絕。◇ *It looks like it's thumbs up for their latest album.* 看樣子他們的最新歌曲專集成功了。**ORIGIN** In contests in ancient Rome the public put their thumbs up if they wanted a gladiator to live, and down if they wanted him to be killed. 在古羅馬的角鬥中，公眾若希望角鬥士活就豎起拇指朝上，若希望他被殺死就伸出拇指朝下。**under sb's ˈthumb** (of a person 人) completely controlled by sb 完全受人支配；受制於人 ➲ more at RULE *n.*, SORE *adj.*, TWIDDLE *v.*

■ *verb* **1** [I, T] to make a signal with your thumb to passing drivers to ask them to stop and take you somewhere 翹起拇指請求搭乘（過路汽車）；示意請求搭便車：**+ adv./prep.** *He had thumbed all across Europe.* 他搭乘便車遊遍了歐洲。◇ (*BrE*) **~ a lift** *We managed to thumb a lift with a lorry driver.* 我們豎起拇指招呼過路的卡車司機讓我們搭便車。◇ (*NAmE*) **~ a ride** *We managed to thumb a ride with a truck driver.* 我們豎起拇指招呼過路的卡車司機讓我們搭便車。**2** [T] **~ sth (+ adv./prep.)** to touch or move sth with your thumb 用拇指摸；用拇指撥：*She thumbed off the safety catch of her pistol.* 她用拇指打開了手槍的保險栓。➲ see also WELL THUMBED

IDM **thumb your ˈnose at sb/sth** to make a rude sign with your thumb on your nose; to show that you have no respect for sb/sth 嗤之以鼻；蔑視：*The company just thumbs its nose at the legislation on pollution.* 這家公司完全不把污染立法放在眼裏。

PHR V **ˈthumb through sth** to turn the pages of a book quickly in order to get a general idea of what is in it 快速翻閱

ˈthumb drive *noun* (*NAmE*) = FLASH DRIVE

ˈthumb index *noun* a series of cuts in the edge of a book, with letters of the alphabet on them, to help you to find the section that you want more easily 拇指頁標；書邊標目；書邊挖月索引

thumb·nail /ˈθʌmneɪl/ *noun* **1** the nail on the thumb 拇指甲 **2** (also **ˌthumbnail ˈimage**) (*computing* 計) a very small picture on a computer screen which shows you what a larger picture looks like, or what a page of a document will look like when you print it 索引圖像；（打印預覽）略圖

ˌthumbnail ˈsketch *noun* a short description of sth, giving only the main details 簡略描述

ˈthumb piano (also **sansa**) *noun* an African musical instrument consisting of a row of metal strips, that you play with your fingers and thumbs 拇指鋼琴（非洲樂器，由一排金屬簧片組成）

thumb·print /ˈθʌmprɪnt/ *noun* the mark made by the pattern of lines on the top of a person's thumb 拇指紋印

thumb·screw /ˈθʌmskruː/ *noun* an instrument that was used in the past for TORTURING people by crushing their thumbs 拇指夾（舊時的一種刑具）

thumb·suck /ˈθʌmsʌk/ *noun* [C, usually sing., U] (*SAfrE*, *informal*, often *disapproving*) a guess or estimate 猜測；估計：*Their sales projections are a total thumbsuck.* 他們的銷售量預測純屬估計。

thumb·tack /ˈθʌmtæk/ (also **tack**) (both *NAmE*) (*BrE* **ˈdrawing pin**) *noun* a short pin with a large round flat head, used especially for fastening paper to a board or wall 圖釘 ➲ VISUAL VOCAB page V69

thump /θʌmp/ *verb, noun*

■ *verb* **1** [T, I] **~ (sb/sth) (+ adv./prep.)** to hit sb/sth hard, especially with your closed hand 重擊；狠打；（尤指用拳）捶擊：*He thumped the table angrily.* 他憤怒地用拳捶擊桌子。◇ *She couldn't get her breath and had to be thumped on the back.* 她喘不上氣來，不得不讓人捶背。◇ (*informal*) *I'll thump you if you say that again.* 你若再說這話，我就把你揍扁。◇ (*figurative*) *He thumped out a tune* (= played it very loudly) *on the piano.* 他在鋼琴上猛力彈奏了一支曲子。**2** [I, T] to fall on or hit a surface hard, with a loud dull sound; to make sth do this（使）撞擊，嘭地發出悶響：**+ adv./prep.** *A bird thumped against the window.* 一隻鳥兒咚的一聲撞在窗上。◇ **~ sth + adv./prep.** *He thumped the report down on my desk.* 他嘭的一聲把報告摔在我的辦公桌上。

3 [I] to beat strongly 強有力地跳動；怦怦地跳：*My heart was thumping with excitement.* 我激動得心怦怦跳。➲ see also TUB-THUMPING

■ ***noun*** **1** the sound of sth heavy hitting the ground or another object 重擊聲；碰撞聲：*There was a thump as the truck hit the bank.* 卡車撞在馬路邊坡上，發出砰的一聲巨響。 **2** (*BrE, informal*) an act of hitting sb/sth hard 重擊；捶擊：*She gave him a thump on the back.* 她在他背上重重打了一拳。

thump·ing /'θʌmpɪŋ/ *adj.* [only before noun] (*informal*) very big 很大的；巨大的 SYN **huge**：*a thumping majority* 壓倒的多數 ▸ **thump·ing** *adv.*：(*BrE*) *He told us a thumping great lie.* 他對我們撒了一個彌天大謊。

thun·der /'θʌndə(r)/ *noun, verb*

■ ***noun*** [U] **1** the loud noise that you hear after a flash of LIGHTNING, during a storm 雷；雷聲：*the rumble of distant thunder* 遠處雷聲隆隆 ◇ *a clap/crash/roll of thunder* 一聲霹靂；一聲巨雷；雷聲隆隆 ◇ *Thunder crashed in the sky.* 霹靂在空中炸響。➲ COLLOCATIONS at WEATHER **2** a loud noise like thunder 雷鳴般的響聲；轟隆聲：*the thunder of hooves* 隆隆的馬蹄聲 IDM see FACE *n.*, STEAL *v.*

■ ***verb*** **1** [I] when **it thunders**, there is a loud noise in the sky during a storm 打雷 **2** [I] to make a very loud deep noise 發出雷鳴般響聲；轟隆隆地響 SYN **roar**：*A voice thundered in my ear.* 一個震耳欲聾的聲音在我耳邊響起。◇ *thundering traffic* 轟隆隆的來往車輛 **3** [I] **+ adv./prep.** to move very fast and with a loud deep noise 轟隆隆地快速移動 SYN **roar**：*Heavy trucks kept thundering past.* 重型卡車不斷地隆隆駛過。 **4** [T] **~ sth + adv./prep.** (*informal*) to make sth move somewhere very fast 使快速移動：*Essien thundered the ball past the goalie.* 埃辛砰地一腳將球踢過了守門員。 **5** [I, T] (*literary*) to shout, complain, etc. very loudly and angrily 怒喝；大聲斥責：**~ (sth)** *He thundered against the evils of television.* 他大聲譴責電視的種種壞處。◇ **+ speech** *'Sit still!' she thundered.* "坐着別動！" 她怒喝道。

thun·der·bolt /'θʌndəbəʊlt; *NAmE* 'θʌndərboʊlt/ *noun* a flash of LIGHTNING that comes at the same time as the noise of THUNDER and that hits sth 雷電；霹靂：*The news hit them like a thunderbolt* (= was very shocking). 這個消息猶如晴天霹靂使他們大為震驚。

thun·der·box /'θʌndəbɒks; *NAmE* 'θʌndərbɑːks/ *noun* (*old-fashioned, BrE, informal*) a toilet, especially a simple one（簡易）便桶，馬桶

thun·der·clap /'θʌndəklæp; *NAmE* -dərk-/ *noun* a loud crash made by THUNDER 雷聲；霹靂

thun·der·cloud /'θʌndəklaʊd; *NAmE* -dərk-/ *noun* a large dark cloud that produces THUNDER and LIGHTNING during a storm 雷雨雲

thun·der·ous /'θʌndərəs/ *adj.* (*formal*) **1** very loud 雷鳴般的；聲音很大的 SYN **deafening**：*thunderous applause* 雷鳴般的掌聲 **2** looking very angry 怒容滿面的；面色陰沉的；怒氣沖沖的：*his thunderous expression* 他那氣勢洶洶的表情 ▸ **thun·der·ous·ly** *adv.*

thun·der·storm /'θʌndəstɔːm; *NAmE* 'θʌndərstɔːrm/ *noun* a storm with THUNDER and LIGHTNING and usually very heavy rain 雷雨；雷暴；雷雨交加

thun·der·struck /'θʌndəstrʌk; *NAmE* -dərs-/ *adj.* [not usually before noun] (*formal*) extremely surprised and shocked 大吃一驚 SYN **amazed**

thun·dery /'θʌndəri/ *adj.* (of weather 天氣) with THUNDER; suggesting that THUNDER is likely 有雷的；可能要打雷的

Thurs·day 🔑 /'θɜːzdeɪ; -di; *NAmE* 'θɜːrz-/ *noun* [C, U] (*abbr.* **Thur.**, **Thurs.**) the day of the week after Wednesday and before Friday 星期四 HELP To see how **Thursday** is used, look at the examples at **Monday**. * Thursday 的用法見詞條 Monday 下的示例。 ORIGIN From the Old English for 'day of thunder', translated from Latin *Jovis dies* 'Jupiter's day'. Jupiter was the god associated with thunder. 源自古英語，原意為 day of thunder（打雷日），古英語則譯自拉丁文 Jovis dies（Jupiter's day）。Jupiter（朱庇特）為雷神。

thus 🔑 /ðʌs/ *adv.* (*formal*)

1 🔑 in this way; like this 以此方式；如此；這樣：*Many scholars have argued thus.* 許多學者都這樣論證過。◇ *The universities have expanded, thus allowing many more people the chance of higher education.* 大學擴招了，這樣就使更多人能有機會接受高等教育。 **2** 🔑 as a result of sth just mentioned 因此；從而；所以 SYN **hence, therefore**：*He is the eldest son and thus heir to the title.* 他是長子，因此是這個封號的繼承人。◇ *We do not own the building. Thus, it would be impossible for us to make any major changes to it.* 我們不是這棟樓房的房主，因此不能對它進行大改動。➲ LANGUAGE BANK at THEREFORE IDM see FAR *adv.*

thwack /θwæk/ *verb* **~ sb/sth** to hit sb/sth hard, making a short loud sound 重擊；拍打；使勁打 ▸ **thwack** *noun*：*the thwack of bat on ball* 球拍擊球

thwart /θwɔːt; *NAmE* θwɔːrt/ *verb* [often passive] to prevent sb from doing what they want to do 阻止；阻撓；對…構成阻力 SYN **frustrate**：**~ sth** *to thwart sb's plans* 阻撓某人的計劃 ◇ **~ sb (in sth)** *She was thwarted in her attempt to take control of the party.* 她控制這個政黨的企圖受阻了。

thy /ðaɪ/ (also **thine** before a vowel) *det.* (*old use*) a word meaning 'your', used when talking to only one person（用作第二人稱單數所有格形式）你的：*Honour thy father and thy mother.* 要孝敬父母。

thyme /taɪm/ *noun* [U] a plant with small leaves that have a sweet smell and are used in cooking as a HERB 百里香（一種植物，葉小，有香味，可作烹飪調味品）➲ VISUAL VOCAB page V32

thy·mus /'θaɪməs/ (also **'thymus gland**) *noun* (*anatomy* 解) an organ in the neck that produces LYMPHOCYTES (= cells to fight infection) 胸腺

thy·roid /'θaɪrɔɪd/ (also **'thyroid gland**) *noun* (*anatomy* 解) a small organ at the front of the neck that produces HORMONES that control the way in which the body grows and functions 甲狀腺

thy·self /ðaɪ'self/ *pron.* (*old use* or *dialect*) a word meaning 'yourself', used when talking to only one person（用作第二人稱單數反身代詞）你自己

ti (*NAmE*) (*BrE* **te**) /tiː/ *noun* (*music* 音) the 7th note of a MAJOR SCALE 大調音階的第 7 音

tiara /ti'ɑːrə/ *noun* a piece of jewellery like a small crown decorated with PRECIOUS STONES, worn by a woman, for example a princess, on formal occasions 冠狀頭飾（女子用，如公主在正式場合戴的鑲有寶石的王冠式頭飾）

TiB *abbr.* (in writing 書寫形式) TEBIBYTE

Tib *abbr.* (also **Tibit**) (in writing 書寫形式) TEBIBIT

tibia /'tɪbiə/ *noun* (*pl.* **tib·iae** /-biiː/) (*anatomy* 解) the SHIN BONE 脛骨 ➲ VISUAL VOCAB page V59 ➲ see also FIBULA

tic /tɪk/ *noun* a sudden quick movement of a muscle, especially in your face or head, that you cannot control（尤指面部或頭部肌肉的）抽搐

tick /tɪk/ *verb, noun*

■ ***verb*** **1** [I] (of a clock, etc. 鐘錶等) to make short, light, regular repeated sounds to mark time passing 發出滴答聲；滴答地走時：*In the silence we could hear the clock ticking.* 寂靜中，我們能聽到鐘錶滴答作響。◇ *a ticking bomb* 滴答作響的定時炸彈 ◇ **~ away** *While we waited the taxi's meter kept ticking away.* 我們等候時，出租汽車的計程器一直在滴答滴答地走着。 **2** [T] (*BrE*) (*NAmE* **check**) **~ sth** to put a mark (✓) next to an item on a list, an answer, etc. 標記號；打上鉤；打對號：*Please tick the appropriate box.* 請在適合的方框內打鉤。◇ *Tick 'yes' or 'no' to each question.* 在每個問題的 "是" 或 "否" 旁打鉤。◇ *I've ticked the names of the people who have paid.* 我在已付款者的姓名旁畫了鉤。

IDM **,tick all the/sb's 'boxes** (*BrE, informal*) to do exactly the right things to please sb 投其所好；迎合眾人／某人的喜好：*This is a movie that ticks all the boxes.* 這是一部適合眾人口味的影片。 **what makes sb 'tick** what makes sb behave in the way that they do 使某人

T

這樣做的原因：*I've never really understood what makes her tick.* 我從未真正弄懂她為什麼這麼做。

PHR V **,tick a'way/'by/'past** (of time 時間) to pass 過去；流逝：*I had to get to the airport by two, and the minutes were ticking away.* 我必須在兩點前趕到機場，但是時間一分一秒地過去了。 **,tick sth↔a'way** (of a clock, etc. 鐘錶等) to mark the time as it passes 標示時間流逝：*The clock ticked away the minutes.* 鐘錶顯示時間一分一秒地過去。 **,tick sb↔'off 1** (*BrE, informal*) to speak angrily to sb, especially a child, because they have done sth wrong 責備，斥責，責罵（尤指犯錯的孩子） **SYN** **tell off** ➲ related noun TICKING OFF **2** (*NAmE, informal*) to make sb angry or annoyed 使生氣；使煩惱 **,tick sb/sth 'off** (*BrE*) (*NAmE* **,check sb/sth 'off**) to put a mark (✓) beside a name or an item on a list to show that sth has been dealt with 給…畫上鉤；給…打核對號 **,tick 'over** (*BrE*) (usually used in the progressive tenses 通常用於進行時) **1** (of an engine 發動機) to run slowly while the vehicle is not moving 空轉；慢速運轉 **SYN** **idle 2** (of a business, a system, an activity, etc. 企業、系統、活動等) to keep working slowly without producing or achieving much（沒有進展地）徐緩運作：*Just **keep things ticking over** while I'm away.* 在我外出期間，維持現狀就行。

■ ***noun*** **1** [C] (*BrE*) (*NAmE* **'check mark**, **check**) a mark (✓) put beside a sum or an item on a list, usually to show that it has been checked or done or is correct 核對號；對號；鉤號；記號：***Put a tick** in the appropriate box if you would like further information about any of our products.* 如想進一步瞭解我們任何產品的情況，請在適當的方框內打鉤。 ➲ compare CROSS *n.* (1), X *symb.* (4) **2** [C] a small insect that bites humans and animals and sucks their blood. There are several types of tick, some of which can carry diseases. 蜱，壁蝨，扁蝨（吸血寄生蟲，有些種類能傳播疾病）：*a tick bite* 蜱叮咬之處 ➲ VISUAL VOCAB page V13 **3** (also **tick·ing**) [U] a short, light, regularly repeated sound, especially that of a clock or watch（尤指鐘錶的）滴答聲：*The only sound was the soft tick of the clock.* 唯一的響聲是鐘錶輕輕的滴答聲。 **4** [C] (*BrE, informal*) a moment 一會兒；一瞬間；一剎那；片刻：*Hang on a tick!* 等一會，別掛斷電話！◇ *I'll be with you in two ticks.* 我馬上就來。 **5** [U] (*old-fashioned, BrE, informal*) permission to delay paying for sth that you have bought 賒賬；賒欠；賒購 **SYN** **credit**：*Can I have these **on tick**?* 我可以賒購這些東西嗎？

tick·box /ˈtɪkbɒks; *NAmE* -bɑːks/ *noun* (*BrE*) = CHECKBOX

tick·er /ˈtɪkə(r)/ *noun* **1** = NEWS TICKER **2** (*old-fashioned, informal*) a person's heart（人的）心臟

'ticker tape *noun* [U] (*especially NAmE*) (in the past) long narrow strips of paper with information, for example STOCK MARKET prices, printed on them by a special TELEGRAPH machine（舊時電傳打字機用的）紙帶：*a **ticker-tape parade** in the streets of New York* (= an occasion when people throw pieces of paper as part of a celebration, for example in honour of a famous person) 紐約街道上的拋紙帶迎賓式

ticket 🔑 /ˈtɪkɪt/ *noun, verb*

■ ***noun*** **1** 🔑 **~ (for/to sth)** a printed piece of paper that gives you the right to travel on a particular bus, train, etc. or to go into a theatre, etc. 票；券；車票；戲票；入場券：*a **bus/theatre/plane, etc. ticket*** 公共汽車票、戲票、飛機票等 ◇ *free tickets to the show* 演出的免費入場券 ◇ *Tickets are available from the Arts Centre at £5.00.* 藝術中心有票，每張 5 英鎊。◇ *a **ticket office/machine/collector*** 售票處；自動售票機；收票員 ◇ (*figurative*) *She hoped that getting this job would finally be her **ticket to success**.* 她希望得到這份工作終將會使她踏上成功之途。 ➲ picture at LABEL ➲ see also MEAL TICKET (2), RETURN TICKET, SEASON TICKET **2** 🔑 a printed piece of paper with a number or numbers on it, that you buy in order to have the chance of winning a prize if the number or numbers are later chosen 獎券；彩票：*a **lottery/raffle ticket*** 彩票 ◇ *There are three winning tickets.* 有三張中獎的彩票。 **3** 🔑 a label that is attached to sth in a shop/store giving details of its price, size, etc.（商店中標明貨物價格、尺碼等的）標籤 **4** an official notice that orders you to pay a FINE because you have done sth illegal while driving or parking your car（交通違章）通知單，罰款單 **SYN** **fine**：*a **parking/speeding ticket*** 違章停車／超速駕駛罰款單 **5** [usually sing.] (*especially NAmE*) a list of candidates that are supported by a particular political party in an election（政黨在選舉中所支持的）候選人名單：*She ran for office on the Democratic ticket.* 她作為民主黨的候選人參加競選。 ➲ see also DREAM TICKET

IDM **be 'tickets** (*SAfrE, informal*) be the end 結束；終結：*It's tickets for the team that loses.* 落敗的球隊就此止步。 **just the 'ticket** (*BrE* also **just the 'job**) (*informal, approving*) exactly what is needed in a particular situation 正需要的東西；求之不得的東西 **'that's the ticket** (*old-fashioned, BrE, informal*) used to say that sth is just what is needed or that everything is just right 所需要的東西；一切正好 ➲ more at SPLIT *v.*

■ ***verb*** **1 ~ sth/sb** (*technical* 術語) to produce and sell tickets for an event, a trip, etc.; to give sb a ticket 售票；給…門票；送票：*Passengers can now be ticketed electronically.* 旅客現在可以電子購票。 **2** [usually passive] **~ sb** (*especially NAmE*) to give sb an official notice that orders them to pay a FINE because they have done sth illegal while driving or parking a car 發出交通違章通知單：*Park illegally, and you're likely to be ticketed.* 違章停車就可能收到罰款單。

ticket·ed /ˈtɪkɪtɪd/ *adj.* [usually before noun] a **ticketed** event is one for which you need a ticket to get in 須憑票入場的：*The museum holds both free and ticketed events.* 博物館舉辦的活動既有免費入場的，也有憑票入場的。

IDM **be 'ticketed for sth** (*especially NAmE*) to be intended for a particular purpose 被指定為；被委派為

ticket·ing /ˈtɪkɪtɪŋ/ *noun* [U] the process of producing and selling tickets 售票：*ticketing systems* 售票系統

'ticket tout *noun* (*BrE*) = TOUT (3)

tickety-boo /ˌtɪkəti ˈbuː/ *adj.* [not before noun] (*old-fashioned, BrE, informal*) very good or successful, with no problems 非常好；妥當

tick·ing /ˈtɪkɪŋ/ *noun* [U] a type of strong cotton cloth that is often striped, used especially for making MATTRESS and PILLOW covers（尤指做牀墊和枕芯套的）結實條紋棉布

,ticking 'off *noun* [sing.] (*old-fashioned, BrE, informal*) the act of telling sb that they have done sth to make you angry 斥責；責罵；申斥 **SYN** **telling off**

tickle /ˈtɪkl/ *verb, noun*

■ ***verb*** **1** [T, I] **~ (sb/sth)** to move your fingers on a sensitive part of sb's body in a way that makes them laugh 呵癢；胳肢：*The bigger girls used to chase me and tickle me.* 比我高大的女孩過去總是追趕着胳肢我。◇ *Stop tickling!* 別胳肢了！ **2** [T, I] **~ (sth)** to produce a slightly uncomfortable feeling in a sensitive part of the body; to have a feeling like this（使）發癢：*His beard was tickling her cheek.* 他的鬍鬚扎得她的面頰癢癢的。◇ *My throat tickles.* 我嗓子發癢。◇ *a tickling cough* 癢咳 **3** [T] to amuse and interest sb 逗樂；使高興；使感興趣；使滿足：**~ sb/sth** *to tickle sb's imagination* 滿足某人的想像力 ◇ **~ sb to do sth** *I was tickled to discover that we'd both done the same thing.* 我高興地發現我倆在做同樣的事。

IDM **be tickled 'pink** (*informal*) to be very pleased or amused 高興極了；非常開心 **tickle sb's 'fancy** (*informal*) to please or amuse sb 使覺得好玩；使開心：*See if any of these tickle your fancy.* 看看這些中是否有你喜歡的。

■ ***noun*** [usually sing.] **1** an act of tickling sb 呵癢；胳肢：*She gave the child a little tickle.* 她輕輕地胳肢孩子。 **2** a slightly uncomfortable feeling in a part of your body 癢；癢感：*to have a tickle in your throat* (= that makes you want to cough) 喉嚨裏發癢 **IDM** see SLAP *n.*

tick·lish /ˈtɪklɪʃ/ *adj.* **1** (of a person 人) sensitive to being tickled 怕癢的；易癢的：*Are you ticklish?* 你怕癢嗎？ **2** (*informal*) (of a situation or problem 情況或問題) difficult to deal with, and possibly embarrassing 難對付的；難處理的；棘手的 **SYN** **awkward 3** (of a cough

咳嗽) that irritates your throat 使喉嚨發癢的：*a dry ticklish cough* 喉嚨發癢的乾咳

tick-tock /ˌtɪk ˈtɒk; *NAmE* ˌtɪk ˈtɑːk/ *noun* [usually sing.] used to describe the sound of a large clock TICKING（大時鐘的）滴答聲

ticky-tacky /ˌtɪki ˈtæki/ *noun* [U] (*NAmE, informal*) building material that is cheap and of low quality 廉價劣質建築材料 ▶ **ticky-tacky** *adj.*

tic-tac-toe (also **tick-tack-toe**) /ˌtɪk tæk ˈtəʊ; *NAmE* ˈtoʊ/ (*NAmE*) (*BrE* ˌ**noughts and ˈcrosses**) *noun* [U] a simple game in which two players take turns to write Os or Xs in a set of nine squares. The first player to complete a row of three Os or three Xs is the winner. 井字遊戲，圈叉遊戲（二人輪流在井字形九格中畫 O 或 X，先將三個 O 或 X 連成一線者為勝）➲ VISUAL VOCAB page V39

tidal /ˈtaɪdl/ *adj.* connected with TIDES (= the regular rise and fall of the sea) 潮汐的；有潮的：*tidal forces* 潮汐力 ◊ *a tidal river* 感潮河

ˌ**tidal ˈwave** *noun* **1** a very large ocean wave that is caused by a storm or an EARTHQUAKE, and that destroys things when it reaches the land 潮汐波；潮浪；海嘯 **2 ~ (of sth)** a sudden increase in a particular feeling, activity or type of behaviour（情感或事物發展的）高漲階段；高潮；浪潮；熱潮：*a tidal wave of crime* 犯罪高潮

tid·bit /ˈtɪdbɪt/ (*NAmE*) (*BrE* **tit·bit**) *noun* a small special piece of food 小片食物 SYN **morsel**

tid·dler /ˈtɪdlə(r)/ *noun* (*BrE, informal*) a very small fish 小魚

tid·dly /ˈtɪdli/ *adj.* (*BrE, informal*) **1** slightly drunk 微醉的；有醉意的 **2** very small 微小的 SYN **tiny**

tiddly·winks /ˈtɪdliwɪŋks/ *noun* [U] a game in which players try to make small plastic discs jump into a cup by pressing them on the edge with a larger disc 挑圓片遊戲（用大圓片壓小圓片的邊緣使其彈入杯狀容器）

tide /taɪd/ *noun, verb*

■ ***noun*** **1** [C, U] a regular rise and fall in the level of the sea, caused by the pull of the moon and sun; the flow of water that happens as the sea rises and falls 潮；潮汐；潮水：*the ebb and flow of the tide* 海潮的漲落 ◊ *The* ***tide is in/out****.* 漲／退潮了。◊ *Is the tide coming in or going out?* 是在漲潮還是在落潮？◊ *The body was washed up on the beach by the tide.* 屍體被潮水沖上了海灘。➲ see also HIGH TIDE, LOW TIDE, NEAP TIDE, SPRING TIDE **2** [C, usually sing.] the direction in which the opinion of a large number of people seems to be moving 潮流；趨勢；動向：*It takes courage to speak out against the tide of opinion.* 跟輿論趨向唱反調需要勇氣。**3** [C, usually sing.] a large amount of sth unpleasant that is increasing and is difficult to control（難以控制的）惡潮，怒潮：*There is anxiety about the* ***rising tide*** *of crime.* 犯罪率日益增長令人憂慮。**4** [sing.] **~ of sth** a feeling that you suddenly have that gets stronger and stronger 高漲的情緒：*A tide of rage surged through her.* 一股怒火燃遍她的全身。**5 -tide** [sing.] (*old use*) (in compounds 構成複合詞) a time or season of the year 時節；季節：*Christmastide* 聖誕節節期

IDM **go, swim, etc. with/against the ˈtide** to agree with/oppose the attitudes or opinions that most other people have 順應／逆潮流；趕／反潮流 **the ˈtide turned | turn the ˈtide** used to say that there is a change in sb's luck or in how successful they are being 轉變運氣；改變形勢

■ ***verb***

PHR V ˌ**tide sb ˈover (sth)** [no passive] to help sb during a difficult period by providing what they need 幫助某人渡過（困難時期）；協助某人克服（困難）：*Can you lend me some money to tide me over until I get paid?* 你能借些錢給我幫我湊合到發薪日嗎？

tide·line /ˈtaɪdlaɪn/ *noun* a line left or reached by the sea when the tide is at its highest point（海灘上的）漲潮線

tide·mark /ˈtaɪdmɑːk; *NAmE* -mɑːrk/ *noun* **1** a line that is made by the sea on a beach at the highest point that the sea reaches（海灘上的）高潮痕 **2** (*BrE, informal*) a line that is left around the inside of a bath/BATHTUB by dirty water（污水在浴缸內側留下的一圈）垢痕

ˈ**tide pool** (*NAmE*) (*BrE* ˈ**rock pool**) *noun* a small amount of water that collects between the rocks by the sea/ocean（海邊）岩石區潮水潭 ➲ VISUAL VOCAB page V5

tide·water /ˈtaɪdwɔːtə(r)/ *noun* **1** [C] (*NAmE*) an area of land at or near the coast 濱海地區；沿海低地 **2** [U, C] water that is brought by the TIDE 潮水

tid·ings /ˈtaɪdɪŋz/ *noun* [pl.] (*old-fashioned* or *humorous*) news 消息；音訊；音信：*I am the bearer of* ***good tidings****.* 我帶來了好消息。◊ *He brought* ***glad tidings****.* 他帶來了喜訊。

tidy 🔑 /ˈtaɪdi/ *adj., verb, noun*

■ ***adj.*** (**tidi·er, tidi·est**) **1** 🔑 (*especially BrE*) arranged neatly and with everything in order 整潔的；整齊的；井然有序的；井井有條的：*a tidy desk* 整潔的書桌 ◊ *She keeps her flat very* ***tidy****.* 她把她的單元房間保持得很整潔。◊ *I like everything to be* ***neat and tidy****.* 我喜歡一切都井井有條。OPP **untidy** **2** 🔑 (*especially BrE*) keeping things neat and in order 愛整潔的；愛整齊的：*I'm a tidy person.* 我這個人講究整潔。◊ *tidy habits* 愛整齊的習慣 OPP **untidy** **3** [only before noun] (*informal*) a **tidy** amount of money is fairly large 高額的；可觀的 SYN **considerable**：*It must have cost a tidy sum.* 這準花了相當大的一筆錢。◊ *a tidy profit* 可觀的利潤 ▶ **tidi·ly** *adv.*：*The room was very tidily arranged.* 這房間佈置得整整齊齊。**tidi·ness** *noun* [U]

■ ***verb*** 🔑 (**tidies, tidy·ing, tidied, tidied**) [I, T] (*especially BrE*) to make sth look neat by putting things in the place where they belong 使整潔；使整齊；使有條理；整理：*I spent all morning cleaning and tidying.* 我用了整個上午的時間清掃整理。◊ **~ up** *When you cook, could you please tidy up after yourself.* 請你在做飯時隨手收拾乾淨。◊ **~ sth (up)** *to tidy (up) a room* 整理房間

PHR V ˌ**tidy sth↔aˈway** (*BrE*) to put things in the place where they belong, especially where they cannot be seen, so that a room appears tidy 收拾起來；拾掇起 ˌ**tidy sth↔ˈup** to arrange or deal with sth so that it is well or correctly finished 收拾妥；整理好：*I tidied up the report before handing it in.* 我把報告整理好後才呈交。

■ ***noun*** (*pl.* **-ies**) (*BrE*) (especially in compounds 尤用於構成複合詞) a container for putting small objects in, in order to keep a place tidy 盛零碎物品的容器：*a desk tidy* 案頭文具盒

tie 🔑 /taɪ/ *verb, noun*

■ ***verb*** (**ties, tying, tied, tied**)

▸ **FASTEN WITH STRING/ROPE** 用線／繩紮牢 **1** 🔑 [T] **~ sth (+ adv./prep.)** to attach or hold two or more things together using string, rope, etc.; to fasten sb/sth with string, rope, etc.（用線、繩等）繫，拴，綁，捆，束：*She tied the newspapers in a bundle.* 她把報紙紮成一捆。◊ *He had to tie her hands together.* 他不得不把她的雙手綁在一起。◊ *They tied him to a chair with cable.* 他們用電纜把他綁在一把椅子上。◊ *Shall I tie the package or tape it?* 我把這個包裹捆起來還是貼膠帶？◊ *I tie back my hair when I'm cooking.* 我做飯時把頭髮束在後面。**2** 🔑 [T] **~ sth + adv./prep.** to fasten sth to or around sth else 將…繫在…上；束緊；繫牢；捆綁：*She tied a label on to the suitcase.* 她把籤條繫在衣箱上。**3** 🔑 [T] **~ sth** to make a knot in a piece of string, rope, etc.（在線、繩上）打結，繫扣：*to tie a ribbon* 繫絲帶 ◊ *Can you help me tie my tie?* 你能幫我打領帶嗎？◊ *Tie up your shoelaces!* 把你的鞋帶繫好！◊ *I tied a knot in the rope.* 我在繩子上打了個結。**4** [I] (**+ adv./prep.**) to be closed or fastened with a knot, etc. 打結繫牢；繫上：*The skirt ties at the waist.* 裙子在腰部束緊。

▸ **CONNECT/LINK** 連接；聯繫 **5** [T, usually passive] **~ sb/sth (to sth/sb)** to connect or link sb/sth closely with sb/sth else 連接；聯合；使緊密結合：*Pay increases are tied to inflation.* 提高工資和通貨膨脹緊密相關。◊ *The house is tied to the job, so we'll have to move when I retire.* 這房子是為工作提供的，所以我退休後我們就得搬家。

▸ **RESTRICT** 限制 **6** [T, usually passive] to restrict sb and make them unable to do everything they want to 束縛；約束；限制：**~ sb** *to be tied by a contract* 受合同

T

的約束 ◇ **~ sb to sth** *I want to work but I'm tied to the house with the baby.* 我想工作，但卻被孩子拴在家裏。◇ **~ sb to doing sth** *I don't want to be tied to coming home at a particular time.* 我不想受按鐘點回家的束縛。

▸ **IN GAME/COMPETITION** 比賽；競賽 **7** [I, T] (of two teams, etc. 兩個隊等) to have the same number of points 打成平局；得分相同 **SYN** draw : **~ (with sb)** *England tied 2–2 with Germany in the first round.* 在第一輪比賽中英格蘭隊與德國隊以 2:2 打成平局。◇ **~ for sth** *They tied for second place.* 他們並列第二名。◇ **~ sth** *The scores are tied at 3–3.* 比分為 3:3 平。◇ *Last night's vote was tied.* 昨晚的表決得票相同。

▸ **MUSIC** 音樂 **8** [T] **~ sth** to join notes with a tie 用連結線連接（音符）➲ see also TONGUE-TIED

IDM **tie sb/yourself (up) in 'knots** to become or make sb very confused（使）大惑不解，糊塗 **,tie one 'on** (*old-fashioned, NAmE, slang*) to get very drunk 喝醉；喝得爛醉 **,tie the 'knot** (*informal*) to get married 結婚；結成夫妻 ➲ more at APRON, HAND *n.*

PHR V **,tie sb 'down (to sth/to doing sth)** to restrict sb's freedom, for example by making them accept particular conditions or by keeping them busy 限制；束縛；牽制：*Kids tie you down, don't they?* 孩子們把你給拖累住了吧？◇ *I don't want to tie myself down to coming back on a particular date.* 我不想限定自己在哪一天回來。 **,tie 'in (with sth)** to match or agree with sth 與…相配；與…相符：*This evidence ties in closely with what we already know.* 這一證據和我們已掌握的情況完全相符。 **,tie 'in (with sth)** | **,tie sth↔'in (with sth)** to link sth or be linked to sth; to happen, or arrange for sth to happen, at the same time as sth else（使）連接在一起，同時進行：*The concert will tie in with the festival of dance taking place the same weekend.* 音樂會將和週末舉行的舞蹈會演同時進行。➲ related noun TIE-IN **,tie sth↔'off** to put a knot in the end of sth; to close sth with string, thread, etc. 結紮；（用繩子、線等）封口：*to tie off a rope* 在繩子頭上打結 ◇ *to tie off an artery* 結紮動脈血管 **,tie 'up** | **,tie sth↔'up** **1** 🔑 to attach a boat to a fixed object with a rope（使船隻）繫泊，停靠：*We tied up alongside the quay.* 我們把船停靠在碼頭邊上。◇ *We tied the boat up.* 我們把船停泊妥當。 **2** 🔑 to close sth with a knot; to be closed or fastened with a knot 繫緊；捆牢；拴住；紮緊：*to tie up a garbage bag* 紮緊垃圾袋 **,tie sb↔'up** **1** 🔑 to tie sb's arms and legs tightly so that they cannot move or escape 把某人捆綁起來：*The gang tied up a security guard.* 那群歹徒把一名保安人員捆綁起來。 **2** [usually passive] to keep sb busy so that they have no time for other things 把…纏住；使不能分身：*I'm tied up in a meeting until 3.* 我開會直到 3 點鐘才能脫身。 **,tie sth↔'up** **1** 🔑 to attach an animal to sth with a rope, chain, etc.（用繩索等把動物）拴住，拴到…上：*He left his dog tied up to a tree.* 他把狗拴在了樹上。 **2** [usually passive] to connect or link sth to sth else 把…聯繫起來；使與…有關係：*Her behaviour is tied up with her feelings of guilt.* 她的行為與她的罪惡感有關。➲ related noun TIE-UP (2) **3** [often passive] to invest money so that it is not easily available for use 佔用，擱死（資金）：*Most of the capital is tied up in property.* 大部份資金都投在了房地產上無法動用。 **4** to deal with all the remaining details of sth 完成；處理完：*We are hoping to tie up the deal by tomorrow.* 我們希望能在明天前達成交易。◇ *I went into the office for an hour to* ***tie up any loose ends*** (= finish remaining small jobs). 我去了辦公室一個小時，把未了結的零星事務處理完。

■ ***noun***

▸ **CLOTHES** 衣服 **1** 🔑 (*NAmE* also **neck·tie**) a long narrow piece of cloth worn around the neck, especially by men, with a knot in front 領帶：*a* ***collar and tie*** 繫着領帶 ◇ *a striped silk tie* 帶條紋的真絲領帶 ➲ **VISUAL VOCAB** page V61 ➲ see also BLACK TIE, BOW TIE, OLD SCHOOL TIE, WHITE TIE

▸ **FOR FASTENING** 捆紮 **2** a piece of string or wire used for fastening or tying sth 繩子；金屬絲；線：*ties for closing plastic bags* 封塑料袋用的捆紮繩

▸ **CONNECTION** 連接 **3** 🔑 [usually pl.] a strong connection between people or organizations 聯繫；關係；紐帶：*family ties* 家族關係 ◇ *the ties of friendship* 友誼的紐帶 ◇ *economic ties* 經濟聯繫 ◇ *The firm has close ties with an American corporation.* 這家商行與一家美國公司關係密切。

▸ **RESTRICTION** 限制 **4** a thing that limits sb's freedom of action 束縛；約束；限制；牽累：*He was still a young man and he did not want any ties.* 他還年輕，不想有任何束縛。

▸ **IN GAME/COMPETITION** 比賽；競賽 **5** a situation in a game or competition when two or more players have the same score 平局；得分相同；不分勝負：*The match ended in a tie.* 這場比賽以平局結束。➲ compare DRAW *n.* (2) **6** (*BrE*) a sports match, especially a football (SOCCER) match, that is part of a larger competition（尤指足球）淘汰賽：*the first leg of the Cup tie between Leeds and Roma* 利茲隊和羅馬隊在優勝杯淘汰賽中的第一輪比賽

▸ **MUSIC** 音樂 **7** a curved line written over two notes of the same PITCH (= how high or low a note is) to show that they are to be played or sung as one note 延音線；延音連接線 ➲ picture at MUSIC

▸ **ON RAILWAY** 鐵路 **8** (*NAmE*) (*BrE* **sleep·er**) one of the heavy pieces of wood or concrete on which the rails on a railway/railroad track are laid（鐵路）枕木，軌枕 ➲ **VISUAL VOCAB** page V58

tie·break /ˈtaɪbreɪk/ (*BrE*) (*NAmE* **tie·break·er**) *noun* (in TENNIS 網球) a period of extra play to decide who is the winner of a SET when both players have won six games 平分決勝局；搶七局

tie·breaker /ˈtaɪbreɪkə(r)/ *noun* **1** (*NAmE*) (*BrE* **tie-break**) (in TENNIS 網球) a period of extra play to decide who is the winner of a SET when both players have won six games 平分決勝局；搶七局 **2** an extra question in a competition to decide who is the winner when two or more of those taking part have equal scores 平分決勝比賽；（競賽中比分相同時附加的）決勝負問題

tied /taɪd/ *adj.* [only before noun] (*BrE*) (of a house 房屋) rented to sb on the condition that they work for the owner 只租給雇工居住的：*a tied cottage on a farm* 農場裏租給雇工的農舍

,tied 'house *noun* (*BrE*) a pub that is owned by a particular BREWERY (= a company that produces beer) and that mainly sells the beer which that brewery produces 酒廠酒吧（啤酒廠開設，主要賣自製啤酒）➲ compare FREE HOUSE

'tie-dye *verb* **~ sth** to make patterns on cloth by tying knots in it or tying string around it before you put it in a DYE, so that some parts receive more colour than others 紮染（織物）

'tie-in *noun* a product such as a book or toy that is connected with a new film/movie, television programme, etc.（與新上演的電影或電視節目等）相關的產品，有關的書籍，有聯繫的玩具

tie·pin /ˈtaɪpɪn/ (*NAmE* also **'tie tack**) *noun* a small decorative pin that is worn on a tie to keep it in place 領帶扣針；領帶別針

tier /tɪə(r); *NAmE* tɪr/ *noun* **1** a row or layer of sth that has several rows or layers placed one above the other 排；層：*a wedding cake with three tiers* 三層的結婚蛋糕 ◇ *The seating is arranged* ***in tiers***. 座位是一級級排列的。 **2** one of several levels in an organization or a system 階層；等級：*We have introduced an extra tier of administration.* 我們額外增加了一層管理。◇ *a two-tier system of management* 兩級管理制

tiered /tɪəd; *NAmE* tɪrd/ *adj.* **1** arranged in tiers 成排的；分層的：*tiered seating* 成排的座位 **2** **-tiered** (in compounds 構成複合詞) having the number of tiers mentioned …層的；…排的；…級的：*a two-tiered system* 兩級系統

'tie-up *noun* **1** **~ (with sb/sth)** (*BrE*) an agreement between two companies to join together（兩家公司的）聯合，合作：*They're negotiating a tie-up with Ford.* 他們正在與福特公司洽談合作事宜。 **2** **~ (between A and B)** (*BrE*) a connection between two or more things 聯繫；關係；關聯：*a tie-up between politics and economics* 政治和經濟之間的關係 **3** (*especially NAmE*) a situation in which sth stops working or moving forward 停頓；停滯不前：*a traffic tie-up* 交通阻塞

T

TIFF /tɪf/ *noun* [U, C] (*computing* 計) the abbreviation for 'tagged image file format' (a form in which images can be stored and shown on a computer; an image created in this form) 標籤式圖像文件格式，TIFF 格式，TIFF 圖像（全寫為 tagged image file format）

tiff /tɪf/ *noun* (*informal*) a slight argument between close friends or lovers （朋友或情人之間的）爭執，拌嘴，口角，吵嘴： *to have a tiff with sb* 與某人口角

tif·fin /ˈtɪfɪn/ *noun* [U] (*old-fashioned* or *IndE*) a small meal, especially lunch 簡易飯菜；（尤指）午餐

tig /tɪg/ *noun* [U] (*BrE*) = TAG (6)

tiger /ˈtaɪgə(r)/ *noun* a large wild animal of the cat family, that has yellowish fur with black lines (= STRIPES) and lives in parts of Asia 虎；老虎： *She **fought like a tiger** to be able to keep her children.* 她勇猛搏鬥，以便能保住她的孩子。 ➲ compare TIGRESS ➲ see also PAPER TIGER

ˌtiger eˈconomy *noun* the economy of a country that is growing very quickly 小龍經濟（指飛速發展的國家的經濟）

tiger·ish /ˈtaɪgərɪʃ/ *adj.* like a tiger, especially in being aggressive or showing great energy 像虎的；兇猛有力的

tight 0‑‑ /taɪt/ *adj.*, *adv.*

■ *adj.* (**tight·er**, **tight·est**)

▸ **FIRM** 牢固 **1** 0‑‑ held or fixed in position firmly; difficult to move or undo 牢固的；緊的；不鬆動的；難解開的： *He kept **a tight grip** on her arm.* 他緊緊握住她的胳膊。 ◇ *She twisted her hair into a tight knot.* 她把頭髮緊緊地挽了個髮髻。 ◇ *The screw was so tight that it wouldn't move.* 螺絲釘太緊，擰不開。

▸ **CLOTHES** 衣服 **2** 0‑‑ fitting closely to your body and sometimes uncomfortable 緊身的；緊貼的： *She was wearing a tight pair of jeans.* 她穿着一條緊身牛仔褲。 ◇ *These shoes are much too tight.* 這雙鞋太緊了。 ◇ *The new sweater was a **tight fit**.* 這件新毛衣很貼身。 OPP **loose** ➲ see also SKINTIGHT

▸ **CONTROL** 控制 **3** 0‑‑ very strict and firm 嚴密的；嚴格的；嚴厲的： *to **keep tight control** over sth* 對某事嚴加控制 ◇ *We need tighter security at the airport.* 我們需要在機場實行更加嚴密的安全措施。

▸ **STRETCHED** 拉伸 **4** 0‑‑ stretched or pulled so that it cannot stretch much further 拉緊的；繃緊的： *The rope was stretched tight.* 這繩子拉得很緊。

▸ **CLOSE TOGETHER** 緊密靠攏 **5** [usually before noun] with things or people packed closely together, leaving little space between them 裝緊的；密集的；擠滿的： *There was a tight group of people around the speaker.* 演講人周圍嚴嚴實實地擠了一群人。 ◇ *With six of us in the car it was **a tight squeeze**.* 小轎車裏坐了我們六個人，擠得很。

▸ **MONEY/TIME** 金錢；時間 **6** difficult to manage with because there is not enough 緊的；拮据的；不寬裕的： *We have a very tight budget.* 我們的預算很緊。 ◇ *The president has a tight schedule today.* 總統今天的日程排滿了。

▸ **EXPRESSION/VOICE** 表情；嗓音 **7** looking or sounding anxious, upset, angry, etc. 顯得緊張的；忐忑不安的；生氣的： *'I'm sorry,' she said, with a tight smile.* "對不起。" 她勉強一笑說。 ➲ see also UPTIGHT (1)

▸ **PART OF BODY** 身體部位 **8** feeling painful or uncomfortable because of illness or emotion （由於疾病或情感）疼痛的，不適的，憋氣的 SYN **constricted**： *He complained of having a tight chest.* 他主訴胸部憋悶。 ◇ *Her throat felt tight, just looking at her baby.* 她喉嚨哽咽得說不出話來，只是看着她的嬰兒。

▸ **RELATIONSHIP** 關係 **9** having a close relationship with sb else or with other people 親密的；緊密的；密切的： *It was a tight community and newcomers were not welcome.* 這個社區很團結，不歡迎新來的人。 ➲ see also TIGHT-KNIT

▸ **BEND/CURVE** 彎曲；曲線 **10** curving suddenly rather than gradually 急轉的；陡的： *The driver slowed down at a tight bend in the road.* 駕駛員在道路急轉彎處慢了下來。 ◇ *The plane flew around in a tight circle.* 飛機繞着小圈盤旋。

▸ **CONTEST/RACE** 競賽；賽跑 **11** with runners, teams, etc. that seem to be equally good 勢均力敵的；不相上下的；旗鼓相當的 SYN **close**： *a tight race* 勢均力敵的賽跑

▸ **NOT GENEROUS** 不慷慨 **12** (*informal, disapproving*) not wanting to spend much money; not generous 小氣的；吝嗇的；不大方的 SYN **mean**： *He's very tight with his money.* 他花錢很摳門兒。

▸ **DRUNK** 喝醉 **13** [not usually before noun] (*old-fashioned, informal*) drunk 喝醉；醉醺醺 SYN **tipsy**

▸ **-TIGHT** 密封 **14** (in compounds 構成複合詞) not allowing the substance mentioned to enter 不漏…的；不透…的；防…的： *measures to make your home weathertight* 使你家防風雨的措施 ➲ see also AIRTIGHT, WATERTIGHT (1)

▸ **tight·ness** *noun* [U]

IDM **to keep a tight ˈrein on sb/sth** to control sb/sth carefully or strictly 對…嚴加控制（或約束）；牢牢駕馭 **run a tight ˈship** to organize sth in a very efficient way, controlling other people very closely 管理有方；嚴加控制 **a tight ˈspot/ˈcorner** a very difficult or dangerous situation 困境；險境

■ *adv.* (**tight·er**, **tight·est**) closely and firmly; tightly 緊緊地；牢固地： ***Hold tight!*** 抓緊了！ ◇ *My suitcase was packed tight.* 我的衣箱塞得滿滿的。 ◇ *His fists were clenched tight.* 他緊握雙拳。 IDM see SIT, SLEEP *v.*

Which Word? 詞語辨析

tight / tightly

■ **Tight** and **tightly** are both adverbs that come from the adjective **tight**. They have the same meaning, but **tight** is often used instead of **tightly** after a verb, especially in informal language, and in compounds.
* tight 和 tightly 均為源自形容詞 tight 的副詞，意思相同，但在動詞後，尤其在非正式用語和複合詞中，常用 tight 代替 tightly： *packed tight* 擠得緊緊的 ◇ *a tight-fitting lid* 嚴實的蓋子 Before a past participle **tightly** is used. 過去分詞前用 tightly： *clusters of tightly packed flowers* 一簇簇密集的花

ˈtight-arse *noun* (*informal, disapproving*) **1** (*BrE*) a person who does not like spending money 吝嗇鬼；鐵公雞 **2** (*BrE*) (*NAmE* **ˈtight-ass**) a person who controls their emotions and actions very carefully and does not like to break the rules 拘謹的人；拘泥的人 ▸ **ˈtight-arsed** (*BrE*) (*NAmE* **ˈtight-assed**) *adj.*

tight·en /ˈtaɪtn/ *verb* **1** [I, T] to become or make sth become tight or tighter （使）變緊，更加牢固： **~ (up)** *The rope holding the boat suddenly tightened and broke.* 繫船的繩子突然繃斷了。 ◇ *His mouth tightened into a thin line.* 他的嘴抿成了一道細縫。 ◇ **~ sth (up)** *to tighten a lid/screw/rope/knot* 擰緊蓋子／螺釘；繃緊繩子；打緊結 ◇ *The nuts weren't properly tightened and the wheel came off.* 螺母沒擰緊，輪子脫落了。 ◇ *She tightened her grip on his arm.* 她抓他的手臂抓得更緊了。 **2** [T] **~ sth** to make sth become stricter 使更加嚴格；加強： *to tighten security* 加強安全措施 OPP **loosen**

IDM **tighten your ˈbelt** to spend less money because there is less available 勒緊腰帶（省吃儉用） ➲ SYNONYMS at SAVE

PHR V **ˌtighten ˈup (on sth)** to become stricter or more careful 變得更加嚴格（或小心）： *Laws on gambling have tightened up recently.* 有關賭博的法律最近變得更加嚴厲。 ◇ *The police are tightening up on under-age drinking.* 警方正在採取更加嚴厲的措施對付未成年人飲酒的問題。

ˌtight ˈend *noun* (in AMERICAN FOOTBALL 美式足球) an attacking player who plays close to the TACKLE 邊鋒

ˌtight-ˈfisted *adj.* not willing to spend or give much money 吝嗇的；小氣的 SYN **mean, stingy**

ˌtight-ˈfitting *adj.* that fits very tightly or closely 緊身的；貼身的 SYN **close-fitting**： *a tight-fitting skirt* 緊身裙子

ˈtight head *noun* (in RUGBY 橄欖球) the player in the front row of a team in the SCRUM who is furthest from where the ball is put in 並列爭球前邊鋒

T

ˌtight-ˈknit (also **ˌtightly-ˈknit**) *adj.* (of a family or community 家族或社區) with all the members having strong friendly relationships with one another 關係密切的；緊密團結的：*a tight-knit mining community* 緊密團結的礦業界

ˌtight-ˈlipped *adj.* **1** not willing to talk about sth 口緊的；緘口不語的；守口如瓶的 **2** keeping your lips pressed firmly together, especially because you are angry about sth 雙唇緊閉的（尤指因生氣）

tight·ly /ˈtaɪtli/ *adv.* closely and firmly; in a tight manner 緊緊地；牢固地；緊密地：*Her eyes were tightly closed.* 她的雙眼緊閉着。◇ *He held on tightly to her arm.* 他緊緊抓住她的手臂。◇ *a tightly packed crowd of tourists* 擠得嚴嚴實實的旅遊人群 ➲ note at TIGHT

tight·rope /ˈtaɪtrəʊp; *NAmE* -roʊp/ *noun* a rope or wire that is stretched tightly high above the ground and that performers walk along, especially in a CIRCUS（尤指馬戲團表演用的）繃緊的繩索，繃緊的鋼絲：*a tightrope walker* 走鋼絲演員

IDM **tread/walk a ˈtightrope** to be in a difficult situation in which you do not have much freedom of action and need to be extremely careful about what you do 身處困境；如履薄冰

tights /taɪts/ *noun* [pl.] **1** (*BrE*) (*NAmE* **panty·hose**) a piece of clothing made of very thin cloth that fits closely over a woman's hips, legs and feet（女用）連褲襪，緊身褲：*a pair of tights* 一條連褲襪 ➲ compare STOCKING (1) **2** a piece of clothing similar to tights but made of thicker cloth, worn especially by dancers（尤指舞蹈演員穿的）緊身衣褲

tight·wad /ˈtaɪtwɒd; *NAmE* -wɑːd/ *noun* (*NAmE, informal*) a person who hates to spend or give money 吝嗇鬼；小氣鬼；守財奴 **SYN** **miser**

tig·ress /ˈtaɪɡrəs/ *noun* a female TIGER 雌老虎

tike *noun* = TYKE

tikka /ˈtɪkə; *BrE* also ˈtiːkə/ *noun* [U, C] a spicy S Asian dish consisting of pieces of meat or vegetables which have been left in a sauce and then cooked 帝卡燒焗肉片（或蔬菜）（南亞菜肴，將肉片或蔬菜用醬汁醃後烹煮而成）：*chicken tikka* 帝卡燒焗雞肉片

til, ˈtil ➲ UNTIL

tilak /ˈtɪlæk/ *noun* a mark on the FOREHEAD of a Hindu, worn as a religious symbol or for decoration（印度教教徒標在前額代表教派或作裝飾的）吉祥記

til·apia /tɪˈlæpiə; -ˈleɪp-; *NAmE* -ˈlɑːp-/ *noun* (*pl.* **tilapia** or **tilapias**) [C, U] a FRESHWATER fish found in hot countries that is used for food 羅非魚，吳郭魚

tilde /ˈtɪldə/ *noun* **1** the mark (~) placed over letters in some languages and some vowels in the International Phonetic Alphabet to show how they should be pronounced, as in *España*, *São Paulo* and *penchant* /ˈpɒ̃ʃɒ̃/ 腭化符號（~）（置於某些語言的字母和國際音標中某些元音符號之上，表示發音方法）**2** (also **ˌswung ˈdash**) the mark (~), used in this dictionary in some parts of an entry to represent the word in blue type at the top of the entry 波浪號，代字號（在本詞典詞條的某些義項內用以代表首詞）

tile /taɪl/ *noun, verb*

■ *noun* **1** a flat, usually square, piece of baked CLAY, carpet or other material that is used in rows for covering walls and floors（貼牆或鋪地用的）瓷磚，地磚，小方地毯，片狀材料：*ceramic floor tiles* 陶瓷地磚 ◇ *carpet tiles* 小方地毯 **2** a piece of baked CLAY that is used in rows for covering roofs（鋪屋頂的）瓦，瓦片 ➲ VISUAL VOCAB page V17 **3** any of the small flat pieces that are used in particular board games（棋盤遊戲的）棋子 **IDM** see NIGHT

■ *verb* **1** ~ **sth** to cover a surface with tiles 鋪瓦；鋪地磚；貼瓷磚：*a tiled bathroom* 鋪瓷磚的浴室 **2** ~ **sth** (*computing* 計) to arrange several windows on a computer screen so that they fill the screen but do not cover each other 平鋪顯示，並列顯示，瓦片式顯示（視窗）

tiler /ˈtaɪlə(r)/ *noun* a person whose job is to lay tiles 磚瓦匠；鋪瓦工；貼磚工

til·ing /ˈtaɪlɪŋ/ *noun* [U] **1** an area covered with tiles 瓷磚面；地磚面；瓦屋頂 ➲ VISUAL VOCAB page V24 **2** the work of covering a floor, wall, etc. with tiles 蓋瓦；貼瓷磚；鋪地磚

till /tɪl/ *conj., prep., noun, verb*

■ *conj., prep.* = UNTIL：*We're open till 6 o'clock.* 我們營業到 6 點鐘。◇ *Can't you wait till we get home?* 難道你就不能等我們回到家嗎？◇ *Just wait till you see it. It's great.* 你就等着直到看見它吧。好看極了。**HELP** **Till** is generally felt to be more informal than **until** and is used much less often in writing. At the beginning of a sentence, **until** is usually used. 一般認為 till 不如 until 正式，在書面語中不常用。句首通常用 until。

■ *noun* **1** (*BrE*) = CASH REGISTER **2** (*BrE, informal*) the place where you pay for goods in a large shop/store（大商店中的）交款處，收銀枱：*Please pay at the till.* 請在交款處付款。◇ *a long queue at the till* 收款處的長隊 **3** (*especially NAmE*) the drawer where the money is put in a CASH REGISTER（現金出納機的）放錢的抽屜 **IDM** see FINGER *n.*

■ *verb* ~ **sth** (*old use*) to prepare and use land for growing crops 耕作；犁地

till·age /ˈtɪlɪdʒ/ *noun* [U] (*old-fashioned*) **1** the process of preparing and using land for growing crops 耕地（包括整地和土壤中耕）**2** land that is used for growing crops 耕地

till·er /ˈtɪlə(r)/ *noun* a bar that is used to turn the RUDDER of a small boat in order to steer it（小船的）舵柄 ➲ compare HELM

tilt /tɪlt/ *verb, noun*

■ *verb* **1** [I, T] to move, or make sth move, into a position with one side or end higher than the other（使）傾斜，傾側 **SYN** **tip**：(+ **adv./prep.**) *Suddenly the boat tilted to one side.* 小船突然傾向一側。◇ *The seat tilts forward, when you press this lever.* 按這個控制柄，座位就向前傾斜。◇ ~ **sth** (+ **adv./prep.**) *His hat was tilted slightly at an angle.* 他的帽子有點歪。◇ *She tilted her head back and looked up at me with a smile.* 她仰起頭含笑看着我。**2** [T, I] ~ **(sth/sb) (in favour of/away from sth/sb)** to make sth/sb change slightly so that one particular opinion, person, etc. is preferred or more likely to succeed than another; to change in this way 使傾向於；使向…傾斜；偏向：*The conditions may **tilt the balance** in favour of the Kenyan runners.* 這些條件可能對肯尼亞賽跑運動員有利。◇ *Popular opinion has **tilted in favour** of the socialists.* 公眾輿論已倒向社會黨人一邊。

IDM **tilt at ˈwindmills** to waste your energy attacking imaginary enemies 攻擊假想敵；庸人自擾 **ORIGIN** From Cervantes' novel *Don Quixote*, in which the hero thought that the windmills he saw were giants and tried to fight them. 源自塞萬提斯的長篇小說《堂吉訶德》，書中的主人公認為他看到的風車是巨人，於是與之展開搏鬥。

PHR V **ˈtilt at sb/sth** (*BrE*) to attack sb/sth in speech or writing 抨擊；攻擊 **ˈtilt at sth** (*BrE*) to try to win sth 力爭贏得某物：*He was tilting at the top prize.* 他在力爭奪魁。

■ *noun* **1** a position in which one end or side of sth is higher than the other; an act of tilting sth to one side 傾斜；傾側：*The table is at a slight tilt.* 這桌子有點兒傾斜。◇ *He answered with a tilt of his head.* 他歪着頭回答。**2** an attempt to win sth or defeat sb（意欲贏得某物或戰勝某人的）企圖，嘗試：*She aims to **have a tilt** at the world championship next year.* 她的目標是明年問鼎世界冠軍。

IDM **(at) full ˈtilt/ˈpelt** as fast as possible 全速；儘快

tim·ber /ˈtɪmbə(r)/ *noun* **1** [U] trees that are grown to be used in building or for making things（用於建築或製作物品的）樹木，林木；用材林：*the timber industry* 林木業 **2** [U] (*especially BrE*) (*NAmE* usually **lum·ber**) wood that is prepared for use in building, etc.（建築等用的）木材，木料：*houses built of timber* 木屋 **3** [C, usually pl.] a long heavy piece of wood used in building a house or ship（建造房屋用的）大木料，棟木；（造船用的）肋材：*roof timbers* 房檁 **4** **timber!** used to warn people

T

that a tree that has been cut is about to fall（砍伐樹木時說）倒啦，小心大樹倒下

tim·bered /ˈtɪmbəd; *NAmE* -bərd/ *adj.* built of timbers; with a FRAMEWORK of timbers 木製的；木結構的 ➲ see also HALF-TIMBERED

ˈtim·ber yard (*BrE*) (*NAmE* **lum·ber·yard**) *noun* a place where wood for building, etc. is stored and sold 木料場；貯木場

timbre /ˈtæmbə(r)/ *noun* (*formal*) the quality of sound that is produced by a particular voice or musical instrument 音質；音色；音品

Tim·buktu (also **Tim·buctoo**) /ˌtɪmbʌkˈtuː/ *noun* a place that is very far away 遙遠的地方 **ORIGIN** From the name of a town in northern Mali. 源自馬里北部城鎮廷巴克圖。

time 🗝 /taɪm/ *noun, verb*

■ **noun** ➲ see also TIMES

▸ **MINUTES/HOURS/YEARS, ETC.** 分鐘、小時、年等 **1** 🗝 [U] what is measured in minutes, hours, days, etc.（以分鐘、小時、天等計量的）時間：*The changing seasons mark the* ***passing of time****.* 寒來暑往，斗轉星移。◇ *A visit to the museum will take you* ***back in time*** *to the 1930s.* 參觀這家博物館就會使你回到 20 世紀 30 年代。◇ *time and space* 時間和空間 ◇ ***As time went by*** *we saw less and less of each other.* 隨着時間的過去，我們見面越來越少。◇ *Perceptions change* ***over time*** (= as time passes). 觀念隨着時間的流逝而變化。➲ see also FATHER TIME **2** 🗝 [U] the time shown on a clock in minutes and hours（鐘錶所顯示的）時間，鐘點，時刻：***What time is it/What's the time?*** 幾點了？◇ *Do you have the time?* 你知道現在幾點了嗎？◇ (*BrE*) ***What time do you make it?*** 你說現在幾點了？◇ (*NAmE*) ***What time do you have?*** 你知道現在幾點了嗎？◇ *The time is now half past ten.* 現在是十點半。◇ (*BrE*) *Can she* ***tell the time*** *yet* (= say what time it is by looking at a clock)? 她會看鐘錶了嗎？◇ (*NAmE*) *Can she* ***tell time*** *yet?* 她會看鐘錶了嗎？◇ *My watch* ***keeps perfect time*** (= always shows the correct time). 我的錶走得很準。◇ *Look at the time! We'll be late.* 看幾點了！我們要遲到了。◇ ***This time tomorrow*** *I'll be in Canada.* 明天這個時候我就在加拿大了。 **3** 🗝 [U] the time measured in a particular part of the world（世界某一地區所計量的）時，時間：*Greenwich Mean Time* 格林尼治時間 ◇ *6 o'clock* ***local time*** 當地時間 6 點鐘 ➲ see also STANDARD TIME, SUMMER TIME **4** 🗝 [U, C] the time when sth happens or when sth should happen（某事發生或應該發生的）時間，時候：*What time do you finish work?* 你什麼時候下班？◇ *The baby loves bath time.* 這嬰兒喜歡洗澡的時候。◇ **~ (to do sth)** *I think it's time to go to bed.* 我想該睡覺了。◇ **~ (for sth)** *It's time for lunch.* 午餐時間到了。◇ **~ (that)** … *It's time the kids were in bed.* 孩子們該睡覺了。◇ ***By the time*** *you get there the meeting will be over.* 等你到了那裏的時候，會議就該結束了。◇ *A computer screen shows arrival and departure times.* 電腦屏幕顯示出到達和離開的時間。◇ *The train arrived right* ***on time*** (= at exactly the correct time). 火車準點到達。◇ *You'll feel differently about it* ***when the time comes*** (= when it happens). 到時候你就會有不同的感受了。➲ see also ANY TIME, CLOSING TIME, DRIVE TIME, NIGHT-TIME, OPENING TIME

▸ **PERIOD** 時間段 **5** 🗝 [U] **~ (to do sth)** an amount of time; the amount of time available to work, rest, etc. 一段時間；（可用於工作、休息等的）一段時間：*Allow plenty of time to get to the airport.* 預留足夠的時間到達機場。◇ *I can probably* ***make the time*** *to see them.* 我大概能騰出時間去看望他們。◇ *It* ***takes time*** *to make changes in the law.* 修改法律還有待時日。◇ *We have* ***no time to lose*** (= we must hurry). 我們不能耽誤時間了！◇ *He spends most of his time working.* 他把大部份時間都花在工作上。◇ *She doesn't have much* ***free/spare time****.* 她沒有多少空餘時間。◇ *What a* ***waste of time****!* 太浪費時間了！◇ *I didn't finish the test—****I ran out of time****.* 我沒答完試卷，我的時間不夠了。◇ ***Time's up****—have you worked out the answer yet?* 時間到了，你得出答案了沒有？◇ *He never takes any* ***time off*** (= time spent not working). 他從不休息。◇ *Jane's worked here* ***for some time*** (= for a fairly long period of time). 簡在這兒工作已經有好些時候了。◇ *Do it now please—not in three hours' time* (= three hours from now). 請現在就幹，而不是三個小時之後。◇ *The journey time is two hours.* 旅程時間為兩個小時。➲ see also RESPONSE TIME **6** 🗝 **a time** [sing.] a period of time, either long or short, during which you do sth or sth happens（或長或短的）一段時間：*His injuries will* ***take a long time*** *to heal.* 他的傷需要很長一段時間才能好。◇ *I lived in Egypt* ***for a time****.* 我在埃及住過一陣子。◇ *The early morning is the best* ***time of day****.* 清晨是一天最好的時光。◇ *Her parents died* ***a long time ago****.* 她的父母很早以前就去世了。◇ ***At one time*** (= at a period of time in the past) *Emily was my best friend.* 埃米莉一度是我最好的朋友。◇ *Mr Curtis was the manager* ***in my time*** (= when I was working there). 我在那裏工作時，柯蒂斯先生是經理。 **7** 🗝 [U, pl.] a period of history connected with particular events or experiences in people's lives 時期；時代；年代；世道：*The movie is set* ***at the time of*** *the Russian Revolution.* 這部電影以俄國革命時期為背景。◇ *in ancient times* 在古代 ◇ *the violent times we live in* (= the present period of history) 我們生逢的亂世 ◇ *Times are hard for the unemployed.* 對失業者來說，時世艱難。◇ ***Times have changed*** *since Grandma was young.* 世易時移，現在已不是祖母年輕時那會兒了。➲ see also OLD-TIME

▸ **OCCASION/EVENT** 次；事件 **8** 🗝 [C] an occasion when you do sth or when sth happens 次；回：***Every time*** *I hear that song I feel happy.* 我每次聽到那首歌都感到很愉快。◇ ***Next time*** *you're here let's have lunch together.* 下次你到這裏來，咱們一起吃午飯。◇ *He failed his driving test three times.* 他考了三次駕駛執照都沒通過。◇ *He's determined to pass* ***this time****.* 這一回他決心要考及格。◇ *When was the* ***last time*** *you saw her?* 你上次是什麼時候見到她的？◇ ***How many times*** (= how often) *do I have to tell you not to do that?* 我得要跟你說多少回不要做那種事？◇ (*especially NAmE*) *I remember* ***one time*** (= once) *we had to abandon our car in the snow.* 我記得有一次我們迫於無奈把汽車丟棄在雪地裏。◇ (*formal*) ***At no time did*** *I give my consent to the plan.* 我從未同意過這項計劃。 **HELP** To talk about the first or the last time you do sth, use **the first/last time (that) I …** . 談論第一次或最後一次做什麼事情，可以說 the first/last time (that) I … : *This is the first time (that) I've been to London.* ◇ ~~*This is the first time for me to go to London.*~~ ◇ *That was the last time (that) I saw her.* **9** 🗝 [C] an event or occasion that you experience in a particular way（以某種方式經歷的）事件，時刻：*Did you* ***have a good time*** *in Spain?* 你在西班牙過得愉快嗎？◇ *I had an awful time in the hospital.* 我在醫院的日子可真難熬。

▸ **FOR RACE** 賽跑 **10** [C, U] how long sb takes to run a race or complete an event（完成賽跑或競賽項目的）所用時間：*The winner's time was 11.6 seconds.* 獲勝者的時間是 11.6 秒。◇ *She completed the 500 metres* ***in record time*** (= faster than any previous runner). 她以破紀錄的時間跑完了 500 米。◇ *one of the fastest times ever* 歷來最快的成績之一

▸ **IN MUSIC** 音樂 **11** [U] the number of beats in a BAR/MEASURE of music 拍子；節拍：*This piece is in four-four time.* 這首樂曲為四分之四拍。◇ *a slow waltz time* 緩慢的華爾茲節拍 ◇ *The conductor* ***beat time*** *with a baton.* 指揮用指揮棒打拍子。 **12** [U] the correct speed and rhythm of a piece of music（樂曲正確的）速度，節奏：*Try and dance* ***in time to*** *the music* (= with the same speed and rhythm). 要跟上音樂的節奏跳舞。◇ *Clap your hands to* ***keep time*** (= sing or move with the correct speed and rhythm). 拍手以保持節奏。◇ *to play* ***in/out of time*** (= follow/not follow the correct speed and rhythm) 演奏得合 / 不合節奏 ◇ *He always plays in perfect time.* 他演奏的節奏總是準確無誤。➲ see also BIG TIME *n.*, SMALL-TIME

IDM **(and) about ˈtime (ˈtoo)** | **(and) not before ˈtime** used to say that sth should have happened before now 早該發生；早該如此 **against ˈtime** if you do sth **against time**, you do it as fast as you can because you do not have much time 爭分奪秒；搶時間：*They're working against time to try and get people out of the rubble alive.* 他們正在爭分奪秒工作，設法把人們從瓦礫中活着救出來。 **ahead of/behind ˈtime** earlier/later than was expected 提前；拖後：*We finished 15 minutes ahead of time.* 我們提前 15 分鐘完成。 **ahead of your ˈtime**

having advanced or new ideas that other people use or copy later 超越時代的；有超前意識的；具有前瞻性的 **all the 'time | the whole 'time 1** 🔑 during the whole of a particular period of time（在某段時間內）一直，始終：*The letter was in my pocket all the time* (= while I was looking for it). 這信一直在我的口袋裏。**2** 🔑 very often; repeatedly 經常；總是；老是：*She leaves the lights on all the time.* 她總是讓燈亮着。**at all 'times** 🔑 always 總是；隨時；永遠：*Our representatives are ready to help you at all times.* 我們的代表隨時準備幫助你。**at the 'best of times** even when the circumstances are very good 即使在最好的情況下：*He's never very happy at the best of times—he'll be much worse now!* 他即使在情緒最好的時候也從未很高興過，現在就更糟了！**at the same 'time 1** 🔑 at one time; together 同時；一起：*She was laughing and crying at the same time.* 她又哭又笑。**2** 🔑 used to introduce a contrasting fact, etc. that must be considered（用以引出必須予以考慮的相對情況）同時，也，然而，不過：*You have to be firm, but at the same time you should try and be sympathetic.* 你必須要嚴格，不過也應盡量懷有同情心。**at a 'time** 🔑 separately or in groups of two, three, etc. on each occasion 每次；逐一；依次：*We had to go and see the principal one at a time.* 我們得逐一去見校長。◇ *She ran up the stairs two at a time.* 她一步兩階地跑上樓梯。**at 'my, 'your, 'his, etc. time of life** at the age you are (especially when you are not young) 在…這樣的年紀（尤指不年輕時）：*Eyesight doesn't get any better at my time of life.* 到我這把年紀，視力絕不會變好的。**at 'times** 🔑 sometimes 有時；間或：*He can be really bad-tempered at times.* 他有的時候脾氣可真壞。**before my, your, his, etc. 'time 1** happening before you were born or can remember or before you lived, worked, etc. somewhere 在…出生（或記事、在世、工作等）之前：*'Were you taught by Professor Pascal?' 'No, he was before my time.'* "帕斯卡爾教授教過你嗎？""沒有，他教書時我還沒有入校呢。"**2** before the usual time in sb's life when sth happens 過早；提前 **SYN** **prematurely**：*She got old before her time.* 她過早地衰老了。**behind the 'times** old-fashioned in your ideas, methods, etc.（思想、方法等）落伍，過時，陳舊 **do 'time** (*informal*) to spend time in prison 坐牢；蹲監獄 **every 'time** whenever there is a choice 無論何時；一有機會：*I don't really like cities—give me the countryside every time.* 我不太喜歡城市，一有機會就讓我去鄉村吧。**for the time 'being** for a short period of time but not permanently 暫時；眼下：*You can leave your suitcase here for the time being.* 你可以暫時把衣箱留在這兒。**from ,time to 'time** 🔑 occasionally but not regularly 不時；有時；偶爾；間或：*She has to work at weekends from time to time.* 她偶爾週末還得工作。**have a lot of time for sb/sth** (*informal, especially BrE*) to like and be interested in sb/sth 喜歡；對…感興趣；願意為…花時間 **have no time for sb/sth | not have much time for sb/sth** (*informal*) to dislike sb/sth 不喜歡；討厭；不願為…花時間：*I have no time for lazy people like Steve.* 我討厭像史蒂夫這樣的懶漢。**have the ,time of your 'life** (*informal*) to enjoy yourself very much 過得很快樂；玩得痛快 **have time on your 'hands | have time to 'kill** (*informal*) to have nothing to do or not be busy 無所事事；沒事可幹；閒着 **in good 'time** early; with enough time so that you are not in a hurry 及早；有足夠的時間 **(all) in good 'time** (*informal*) used to say that sth will be done or will happen at the appropriate time and not before 會按時做（或出現）；不消多久：*Be patient, Emily! All in good time.* 埃米莉，別急！快好了。**in (less than/next to) 'no time** so soon or so quickly that it is surprising 短暫（或快）得令人吃驚；立刻；馬上；一會兒：*The kids will be leaving home in no time.* 孩子們很快就要離開家了。**in 'time** after a period of time when a situation has changed 經過一段時間之後；遲早；最後；終於 **SYN** **eventually**：*They learned to accept their stepmother in time.* 過了一段時間之後他們便學會了接受他們的繼母。**in time (for sth/to do sth)** 🔑 not late; with enough time to be able to do sth 來得及；及時：*Will we be in time for the six o'clock train?* 我們來得及趕上六點鐘的那趟火車嗎？◇ *The ambulance got there just in time* (= to save sb's life). 救護車正好及時趕到那裏。**in your own (good) 'time** (*informal*) when you are ready and not sooner 在準備停當時：*Don't hassle him! He'll do it in his own good time.* 別嘮嘮叨叨地煩他了！他準備好時就會做的。**in your own time** in your free time and not when you usually work or study 在業餘時間；在空閒時 **it's a,bout/,high 'time** 🔑 (*informal*) used to say that you think sb should do sth soon 差不多 / 現在是…的時候了：*It's about time you cleaned your room!* 你該打掃自己的房間了！**keep up/move with the 'times** to change and develop your ideas, way of working, etc. so that you do what is modern and what is expected 跟上時代；跟着潮流 **make good, etc. 'time** to complete a journey quickly 在路上花的時間很短：*We made excellent time and arrived in Spain in two days.* 我們一路很順當，兩天後就到了西班牙。**'many a time | 'many's the time (that) ...** (*old-fashioned*) many times; frequently 多次；常常；屢屢 **,nine times out of 'ten | ,ninety-,nine times out of a 'hundred** used to say that sth is usually true or almost always happens 十有八九；幾乎總是：*Nine times out of ten she gives the right answer.* 她的答案十有八九是對的。**(and) not before 'time** = (AND) ABOUT TIME (TOO) **not give sb the ,time of 'day** to refuse to speak to sb because you do not like or respect them 對某人厭棄不睬：*Since the success of her novel, people shake her hand who once wouldn't have given her the time of day.* 自從她的小說獲得成功之後，曾經懶得答理她的人也跟她握起手來。**(there is) no time like the 'present** (*saying*) now is the best time to do sth, not in the future 現在是做…的最佳時機；現在不做更待何時 **of all 'time** that has ever existed 自古以來；有史以來；從未有過：*Many rated him the best singer of all time.* 許多人認為他是有史以來最優秀的歌手。➲ see also ALL-TIME **take your 'time (over sth) | take your 'time to do sth/doing sth 1** 🔑 to use as much time as you need without hurrying 從容不迫；慢慢來：*There's no rush—take your time.* 別着急，慢慢來。**2** used to say you think sb is late or is too slow in doing sth 遲到；慢慢騰騰；磨磨蹭蹭：*You certainly took your time getting here!* 你真是姍姍來遲啊！**take time 'out** to spend some time away from your usual work or activity in order to rest or do sth else instead 抽出時間（暫停工作或活動）；忙裏偷閒：*She is taking time out from her music career for a year.* 她將抽出一年的時間，暫不從事音樂事業。➲ SYNONYMS at REST **,time after 'time | ,time and (,time) a'gain** often; on many or all occasions 一次又一次；一再；屢屢；總是：*You will get a perfect result time after time if you follow these instructions.* 如果你遵循這些用法說明，每次都會得到最佳的效果。**time and a 'half** one and a half times the usual rate of pay 通常工資的一倍半 ➲ see also DOUBLE TIME **time 'flies** (*saying*) time seems to pass very quickly 時間過得真快；光陰似箭；時光飛逝：*How time flies! I've got to go now.* 時間過得真快！現在我得走了。◇ *Time has flown since the holiday began.* 假日一開始，時間就過得飛快。**ORIGIN** This phrase is a translation of the Latin 'tempus fugit'. 此短語譯自拉丁文 tempus fugit。**time is 'money** (*saying*) time is valuable, and should not be wasted 時間就是金錢；一寸光陰一寸金 **time is on your 'side** used to say that sb can wait for sth to happen or can wait before doing sth 有的是時間（等待某事發生或做某事）**(the) next, first, second, etc. time 'round** on the next, first, etc. occasion that the same thing happens 同樣的事情下次（或第一次等）發生時：*He repeated none of the errors he'd made first time round.* 他沒有重複過首次所犯下的任何錯誤。◇ *This time round it was not so easy.* 這一次這事可就不那麼容易了。**time 'was (when) ...** (*old-fashioned*) used to say that sth used to happen in the past 曾經有那麼個時候…；那年頭… **time (alone) will 'tell | only time will 'tell** (*saying*) used to say that you will have to wait for some time to find out the result of a situation（只有）時間會證明：*Only time will tell if the treatment has been successful.* 只有時間才能證明這種療法是否成功。**the whole 'time** = ALL THE TIME ➲ more at BEAT *v.*, BIDE, BORROW, BUY *v.*, CALL *v.*, COURSE *n.*, DAY, DEVIL, EASY *adj.*, FIRST *det.*, FORTH, FULLNESS, GAIN *v.*, GIVE *v.*, HARD *adj.*, HIGH *adj.*, KILL *v.*, LONG *adj.*, LOST, LUCK *n.*, MARK *v.*, MATTER *n.*, MOVE *v.*, NICK *n.*, NINETY, OLD,

ONCE *adv.*, PASS *v.*, RACE *n.*, SIGN *n.*, STITCH *n.*, SWEET *adj.*, THIN *adj.*, THIRD *ordinal number*, WHALE

■ ***verb***

▸ **ARRANGE TIME 安排時間** **1** [often passive] to arrange to do sth or arrange for sth to happen at a particular time 為…安排時間；選擇…的時機： **~ sth (for sth)** *She timed her arrival for shortly after 3.* 她定在 3 點鐘剛過到達。◇ *Their request was **badly timed*** (= it was made at the wrong time). 他們的要求提出的時機不對。◇ *'I hope we're not too early.' 'You couldn't have timed it better!'* "我希望我們沒有到得太早。" "你們來的時間再合適不過了。" ◇ **~ sth to do sth** *Publication of his biography was **timed to coincide with** his 70th birthday celebrations.* 他的自傳特別安排在他的 70 壽誕慶典時出版。

▸ **MEASURE TIME 計量時間** **2** to measure how long it takes for sth to happen or for sb to do sth 計時；測定…所需的時間： **~ sth (at sth)** *The winner was timed at 20.4 seconds.* 獲勝者用的時間為 20.4 秒。◇ **~ how long …** *Time how long it takes you to answer the questions.* 記一下自己回答這些問題所需的時間。

▸ **IN SPORT 體育運動** **3 ~ sth** to hit or kick a ball at a particular moment in a sports game 在某一時刻擊球（或踢球）： *She timed the pass perfectly.* 她傳球的時機掌握得恰到好處。◇ *a beautifully timed shot* 時機把握得絕妙的一擊 ➲ see also ILL-TIMED, MISTIME, TIMING, WELL TIMED

PHR V **ˌtime ˈout | ˌtime sth ˈout** (of a computer program or task) to turn off, or turn sth off, automatically after a particular length of time even if the user has not finished（計算機程序或任務）超時自動關閉： *My satellite connection timed out—it was so frustrating.* 我的衛星連接超時自動斷開了，真令人沮喪。

ˌtime-and-ˈmotion study *noun* a study to find out how efficient a company's working methods are 時間與動作研究（為估計生產或工作效率）

ˈtime bomb *noun* **1** a bomb that can be set to explode at a particular time 定時炸彈 **2** a situation that is likely to cause serious problems in the future 潛在危險；隱患： *Rising unemployment is a political time bomb for the government.* 日益嚴重的失業問題對政府來說是一枚政治上的定時炸彈。

ˈtime capsule *noun* a container that is filled with objects that people think are typical of the time they are living in. It is buried so that it can be discovered by people in the future. 時代文物貯藏器（收藏具有時代特徵的物品）

ˈtime card *noun* (*especially NAmE*) a piece of card on which the number of hours that sb has worked are recorded, usually by a machine 考勤卡；工作時間記錄卡

ˈtime clock *noun* a special clock that records the exact time that sb starts and finishes work 考勤鐘；上下班計時鐘

ˈtime-consuming *adj.* taking or needing a lot of time 費時的；耗時間的： *a difficult and time-consuming process* 困難而又費時的過程

ˈtime frame *noun* the length of time that is used or available for sth（用於某事的）一段時間

ˈtime-honoured (*especially US* **-honored**) *adj.* respected because it has been used or done for a long time 古老而受到尊重的；歷史悠久的；由來已久的： *They showed their approval in the time-honoured way* (= by clapping, for example). 他們以傳統的方式表示同意。

time·keep·er /ˈtaɪmkiːpə(r)/ *noun* a person who records the time that is spent doing sth, for example at work or at a sports event（工作或運動比賽等的）時間記錄員，計時員

IDM **be a good/bad ˈtimekeeper** to be regularly on time/late for work 經常按時 / 不按時上班

time·keep·ing /ˈtaɪmkiːpɪŋ/ *noun* [U] **1** a person's ability to arrive in time for things, especially work（尤指上班的）準時，守時 **2** the activity of recording the time sth takes 計時

ˈtime lag (also **lag**, **ˈtime lapse**) *noun* the period of time between two connected events（兩件相關事件的）時間間隔，時滯： *There is a long time lag between when I do the work and when I get paid.* 我做工作和領薪水之間相隔很長一段時間。

ˈtime-lapse *adj.* [only before noun] (of photography 攝影) using a method in which a series of individual pictures of a process are shown together so that sth that really happens very slowly is shown as happening very quickly 延時拍攝的： *a time-lapse sequence of a flower opening* 一組延時拍攝花蕾開放的鏡頭

time·less /ˈtaɪmləs/ *adj.* (*formal*) **1** not appearing to be affected by the passing of time or by changes in fashion 不受時間影響的；無時間性的；永不過時的： *her timeless beauty* 她的永恒的美麗 **2** existing or continuing for ever 永存的；永遠的；永恒的；永久的 **SYN** **unending**： *timeless eternity* 萬古長存 ▸ **time·less·ly** *adv.* **time·less·ness** *noun* [U]

ˈtime limit *noun* the length of time within which you must do or complete sth 時限；期限；限期： *We have to set a time limit for the work.* 我們得為這項工作規定個期限。◇ *The work must be completed within a certain time limit.* 這項工作必須在一定期限內完成。

time·line /ˈtaɪmlaɪn/ *noun* a horizontal line that is used to represent time, with the past towards the left and the future towards the right 時間線，時線（用以表示時間的水平線，左邊表示過去，右邊表示未來）

ˈtime lock *noun* **1** a lock with a device which prevents it from being opened until a particular time 定時鎖 **2** (*computing* 計) part of a program which stops the program operating after a particular time 定時鎖程序塊，鎖時程序塊，定時鎖定程式（使程序停止運行）

time·ly /ˈtaɪmli/ *adj.* happening at exactly the right time 及時的；適時的 **SYN** **opportune**： *A nasty incident was prevented by the timely arrival of the police.* 警察的及時到來阻止了一次嚴重事故。◇ *This has been **a timely reminder** to us all.* 對我們大家來說這個提醒非常及時。 **OPP** **untimely** ▸ **time·li·ness** *noun* [U]

ˈtime machine *noun* (in SCIENCE FICTION stories 科幻小說) a machine that enables you to travel in time to the past or the future 時間機器（能使人往返於過去或未來）

time·out /ˈtaɪmaʊt/ *noun* **1** (*NAmE*) a short period of rest during a sports game（體育比賽中的）暫停 **2** (*computing* 計) an occasion when a process or program is automatically stopped after a certain amount of time because it has not worked successfully 超時；（自動）暫停

time·piece /ˈtaɪmpiːs/ *noun* (*formal*) a clock or watch 鐘；錶

ˌtime-ˈpoor *adj.* having very little or no free time because you work all the time 缺乏空閒時間的： *products for customers who are time-poor but cash-rich* 面向沒閒暇但有錢的顧客的產品

timer /ˈtaɪmə(r)/ *noun* (often in compounds 常構成複合詞) a device that is used to measure the time that sth takes; a device that starts or stops a machine working at a particular time 時計；計時器；跑錶；定時器： *an oven timer* 烤箱定時器 ➲ VISUAL VOCAB page V26 ➲ see also EGG TIMER, OLD-TIMER

ˈtime-release *adj.* [usually before noun] releasing an active substance, for example a drug, a little at a time（藥等）逐漸釋放的，緩釋的

times /taɪmz/ **1** *prep.* (*informal*) multiplied by 乘以： *Five times two is/equals ten* (5 × 2 = 10). 五乘以二等於十。 **2** *noun* [pl.] used in comparisons to show how much more, better, etc. sth is than sth else（用於比較）倍： *three times as long as sth* 某物的三倍長 ◇ *three times longer than sth* 比某物長兩倍 ◇ *three times the length of sth* 三倍於某物的長度 ➲ LANGUAGE BANK at PROPORTION

ˈtime-saving *adj.* [usually before noun] that reduces the amount of time it takes to do sth 節省時間的；省時的： *time-saving devices* 省時裝置

time·scale /ˈtaɪmskeɪl/ *noun* the period of time that it takes for sth to happen or be completed（事情發生或完成所需要的）一段時間，期限： *What's the timescale for the project?* 這個項目的工期是多長？

T

ˈtime-server *noun* (*disapproving*) a person who does as little work as possible in their job because they are just waiting until they leave for another job or retire 等待時間過去的人（離職或退休前苟且偷安）；混日子的人 ▶ **ˈtime-serving** *adj., noun* [U]

time·share /ˈtaɪmʃeə(r); *NAmE* -ʃer/ *noun* **1** (also **ˈtime-sharing**) [U] an arrangement in which several people own a holiday/vacation home together and each uses it at a different time of the year 分時使用度假房的辦法：*timeshare apartments* 分時度假用的套房 **2** [C] a holiday/vacation home that you own in this way 分時使用的度假房：*They have a timeshare in Florida.* 他們在佛羅里達有一套分時使用的度假房。

ˈtime sheet *noun* a piece of paper on which the number of hours that sb has worked are recorded 考勤表；工作時間記錄單

ˈtime signal *noun* a sound or sounds that show the exact time of day, especially a series of short high sounds that are broadcast on the radio（尤指收音機播放的）報時信號

ˈtime signature *noun* (*music* 音) a sign at the start of a piece of music, usually in the form of numbers, showing the number of beats in each BAR/MEASURE（樂譜開頭的）拍號 ➲ picture at MUSIC

ˈtime span *noun* a period of time 一段時間；時段：*These changes have occurred over a long time span.* 這些變化經過了很長一段時間才形成。

ˈtime switch *noun* a switch that can be set to start and stop a machine working automatically at a particular time（自動）計時開關，定時開關：*The heating is on a time switch.* 暖氣靠定時開關自動供熱。

time·table 0➡ /ˈtaɪmteɪbl/ *noun, verb*

■ **noun** **1** 0➡ (*especially BrE*) (*NAmE* usually **sched·ule**) a list showing the times at which particular events will happen 時間表；時刻表：*a* ***bus/train timetable*** (= when they arrive and leave) 公共汽車／火車時刻表 ◇ *We have a new timetable each term* (= showing the times of each class in school). 我們每個學期都有新的課程表。◇ *Sport is no longer so important in the school timetable* (= all the subjects that are taught at schools). 體育課在學校的課程表上已不再是重點課。**2** 0➡ a plan of when you expect or hope particular events to happen 預定計劃；時間安排 SYN **schedule**：*I have a busy timetable this week* (= I have planned to do many things). 這個星期我的時間安排得很緊。◇ *The government has set out its timetable for the peace talks.* 政府已制訂出和平談判的時間表。➲ note at AGENDA

■ **verb** [usually passive] **~ sth (for sth)** (*especially BrE*) to arrange for sth to take place at a particular time 為…安排時間 SYN **schedule**：*A series of discussion groups have been timetabled for the afternoons.* 一系列小組討論已安排在幾個下午進行。▶ **time·tab·ling** *noun* [U]

ˈtime trial *noun* (in cycle racing and some other sports 自行車賽等體育運動) a race in which the people who are taking part race on their own in as fast a time as possible, instead of racing against each other at the same time 計時賽

ˈtime warp *noun* an imaginary situation, described for example in SCIENCE FICTION, in which it is possible for people or things from the past or the future to move to the present 時間錯位（如科幻小說中所描寫，過去或將來的人或事都可能移到現在）

IDM **be (stuck) in a ˈtime warp** not having changed at all from a time in the past although everything else has 停留在過去（毫無變化）

ˈtime-wasting *noun* [U] **1** the act of wasting time 浪費時間 **2** (*BrE*) (in sport 體育運動) the act of playing more slowly towards the end of a game to prevent the opposing team from scoring（比賽接近結束時為阻止對手得分的）拖延時間 ➲ compare RUN DOWN/OUT THE CLOCK at CLOCK *n.* ▶ **ˈtime-waster** *noun*

ˈtime-worn *adj.* old and used a lot, and therefore damaged, or no longer useful or interesting 陳舊的；陳腐的；日久用壞的

ˈtime zone *noun* one of the 24 areas that the world is divided into, each with its own time that is one hour earlier than that of the time zone immediately to the east 時區

timid /ˈtɪmɪd/ *adj.* shy and nervous; not brave 羞怯的；膽怯的；缺乏勇氣的：*He stopped in the doorway, too timid to go in.* 他在門口停住了腳步，不好意思進去。◇ *They've been rather timid in the changes they've made* (= they've been afraid to make any big changes). 他們對所進行的變革一直小心翼翼。◇ *a timid voice* 羞怯的聲音 ▶ **tim·id·ity** /tɪˈmɪdəti/ *noun* [U] **tim·id·ly** *adv.*

tim·ing /ˈtaɪmɪŋ/ *noun* **1** [U, C] the act of choosing when sth happens; a particular point or period of time when sth happens or is planned 定時；時間的選擇；（事情發生或計劃安排的）特定時間：*The timing of the decision was a complete surprise.* 選擇那個時間作決定，完全出人意料。◇ *Please check your flight timings carefully.* 請仔細核對航班時間。**2** [U] the skill of doing sth at exactly the right time 時機的掌握；火候的把握：*an actor with a great sense of comic timing* 一位深諳把握時機引人發笑的演員 ◇ *Your timing is perfect. I was just about to call you.* 你來得正是時候。我剛想要給你打電話。**3** [U] the repeated rhythm of sth; the skill of producing this 節奏；掌握節奏的技巧：*She played the piano confidently but her timing was not good.* 她鋼琴彈得很自信，但是節奏掌握得不好。**4** [U] (*technical* 術語) the rate at which an electric SPARK is produced in a vehicle's engine in order to make it work（汽車發動機的）點火時間控制

tim·or·ous /ˈtɪmərəs/ *adj.* (*literary* or *formal*) nervous and easily frightened 羞怯的；膽怯的；畏怯的 SYN **timid** ▶ **tim·or·ous·ly** *adv.*

tim·pani /ˈtɪmpəni/ (also *informal* **timps** /tɪmps/) *noun* [pl.] a set of large metal drums (also called KETTLEDRUMS) in an ORCHESTRA（管弦樂隊的）定音鼓 ▶ **tim·pan·ist** *noun*

tin 0➡ /tɪn/ *noun*

1 0➡ [U] (*symb.* **Sn**) a chemical element. Tin is a soft silver-white metal that is often mixed with other metals or used to cover them to prevent them from RUSTING. 錫：*a tin mine* 錫礦 ◇ *a tin box* 錫盒 **2** 0➡ [C] (also **ˌtin ˈcan**) (both *BrE*) (also **can** *NAmE, BrE*) **~ (of sth)** a metal container in which food and drink is sold; the contents of one of these containers 罐；罐頭盒；罐頭：*a tin of beans* 一罐青豆 ◇ *Next, add two tins of tomatoes.* 然後，加兩罐番茄。➲ VISUAL VOCAB page V33 **3** 0➡ [C] (*BrE*) (also **can** *NAmE, BrE*) **~ (of sth)** a metal container with a lid, in the shape of a CYLINDER, in which paint, glue, etc. is sold and stored; the contents of one of these containers（盛塗料、膠水等的）馬口鐵罐，白鐵桶；罐裝物：*a tin of varnish* 一罐清漆 ◇ *The bedroom needed three tins of paint* (= in order to paint it). 臥室用了三桶塗料。**4** [C] a metal container with a lid used for keeping food in 金屬食品盒：*a biscuit/cake/cookie tin* 餅乾／蛋糕／曲奇餅盒 ➲ VISUAL VOCAB page V33 **5** [C] (*BrE*) (*NAmE* **pan**) a metal container used for cooking food in 烘焙用的金屬器皿；烤盤；烤模：*a cake tin* 蛋糕烤盤 ➲ VISUAL VOCAB page V27

IDM **(it) does (eˌxactly) what it says on the ˈtin** (*informal, saying*) used to say that sth is as good or effective as it claims to be, or that it really does what it claims to do. This expression is especially used when you are comparing publicity and advertisements with actual products.（尤用於比較廣告宣傳和實際產品）和所說的一樣好，名副其實：*I paid £150 for this camera and am more than happy with it. It does exactly what it says on the tin!* 我花 150 英鎊買了這架照相機，真是十分令人滿意。它和廣告所說的別無二致！

ˌtin ˈcan *noun* = TIN (2)

tinc·ture /ˈtɪŋktʃə(r)/ *noun* [C, U] (*technical* 術語) a substance dissolved in alcohol for use as a medicine 酊；酊劑

tin·der /ˈtɪndə(r)/ *noun* [U] dry material, especially wood or grass, that burns easily and can be used to light a fire 引火物；火絨；火種：*The fire started late Saturday in tinder-dry grass near the Snake River.* 大火是星期六晚些時候在斯內克河附近乾枯的草地上燃起的。

T

tin·der·box /ˈtɪndəbɒks; *NAmE* ˈtɪndərbɑːks/ *noun* **1** a box containing dry material, used in the past for lighting a fire（舊時點火用的）火絨盒，引火盒 **2** (*formal*) a situation that is likely to become dangerous 一觸即發的形勢

tine /taɪn/ *noun* (*technical* 術語) any of the points or sharp parts of, for example, a fork or the ANTLERS of a DEER（叉子等的）尖頭，尖齒；（鹿角的）分叉 ➲ VISUAL VOCAB page V22

tin·foil /ˈtɪnfɔɪl/ *noun* [U] metal made into very thin sheets, that is used for wrapping food, etc.（包裹食物等用的）錫箔，錫紙

tinge /tɪndʒ/ *verb, noun*

■ ***verb*** [usually passive] **1 ~ sth (with sth)** to add a small amount of colour to sth（輕微地）給…着色，給…染色：*white petals tinged with blue* 略帶藍色的白花瓣 **2 ~ sth (with sth)** to add a small amount of a particular emotion or quality to sth 使略帶…感情（或性質）：*a look of surprise tinged with disapproval* 帶有幾分不滿的驚奇神情

■ ***noun*** [usually sing.] a small amount of a colour, feeling or quality 微量，少許，一絲，幾分（顏色、感情或性質）：*to feel a tinge of envy* 感到幾分妒忌 ◇ *There was a faint pink tinge to the sky.* 天空略帶一點淡淡的粉紅色。➲ SYNONYMS at COLOUR

tin·gle /ˈtɪŋɡl/ *verb, noun*

■ ***verb*** **1** [I] (of a part of your body 身體部位) to feel as if a lot of small sharp points are pushing into it 感到刺痛：*The cold air made her face tingle.* 冷空氣凍得她的臉發痛。◇ *a tingling sensation* 刺痛感 ➲ SYNONYMS at HURT **2** [I] **~ with sth** to feel an emotion strongly 強烈地感到：*She was still tingling with excitement.* 她仍然興奮不已。

■ ***noun*** [usually sing.] (also **ting·ling** [sing., U]) **1** a slight stinging or uncomfortable feeling in a part of your body 刺痛感 **2** an exciting or uncomfortable feeling of emotion 激動感；興奮感；震顫：*to feel a tingle of excitement* 感到一陣激動

tin·gly /ˈtɪŋɡli/ *adj.* causing or experiencing a slight feeling of tingling 引起（或感到）輕微刺痛的：*a tingly sensation* 刺痛感

tin·ker /ˈtɪŋkə(r)/ *noun, verb*

■ ***noun*** (in the past) a person who travelled from place to place, selling or repairing things（舊時走街串巷的）小爐匠，補鍋匠，白鐵匠

■ ***verb*** [I] **~ (with sth)** to make small changes to sth in order to repair or improve it, especially in a way that may not be helpful（尤指不起作用地）小修補，小修理

tin·kle /ˈtɪŋkl/ *noun, verb*

■ ***noun*** [usually sing.] **1** (also **tink·ling** [sing., U]) a light high ringing sound 丁零聲；噹啷響：*the tinkle of glass breaking* 玻璃破碎發出的噹啷聲 **2** (*old-fashioned, BrE, informal*) a telephone call 電話通話 **3** (*BrE, informal*) an act of URINATING 撒尿；小便：*to have a tinkle* 撒尿

■ ***verb*** [I, T] **~ (sth)** to make a series of light high ringing sounds; to make sth produce this sound（使）發出叮噹聲，丁零響：*A bell tinkled as the door opened.* 房門一開，鈴聲丁零響了。◇ *tinkling laughter* 銀鈴般的笑聲

tinned /tɪnd/ (*BrE*) (also **canned** *NAmE, BrE*) *adj.* (of food 食物) preserved in a can 罐裝的：*tinned fruit* 罐頭水果

tin·nitus /ˈtɪnɪtəs/ *noun* [U] (*medical* 醫) an unpleasant condition in which sb hears ringing in their ears 耳鳴

tinny /ˈtɪni/ *adj., noun*

■ ***adj.*** (*especially BrE, disapproving*) **1** having a high thin sound like small pieces of metal hitting each other（聲音）尖細的，尖聲尖氣的，如金屬片碰撞聲般的 **2** having a taste like metal 有金屬味的：*The beer tasted tinny.* 這啤酒喝起來有金屬味。

■ ***noun*** (also **tin·nie**) (*pl.* **-ies**) (*AustralE, NZE, informal*) a can of beer 一罐啤酒

ˈ**tin opener** (*BrE*) (also ˈ**can opener** *NAmE, BrE*) *noun* a kitchen UTENSIL (= a tool) for opening tins of food 開罐器；罐頭刀；罐頭起子 ➲ VISUAL VOCAB page V26

ˌ**Tin Pan ˈAlley** *noun* [U] (*old-fashioned, informal*) people who write and publish popular songs 流行歌曲作者和發行人 **ORIGIN** From the name of the part of New York where many such people worked in the past. 源自舊時紐約的流行歌曲作者和發行人聚集區名稱。

tin·plate /ˈtɪnpleɪt/ *noun* [U] a metal material made from iron and steel and covered with a layer of tin 鍍錫鐵皮；馬口鐵

tin·pot /ˈtɪnpɒt; *NAmE* -pɑːt/ *adj.* [only before noun] (*BrE, disapproving*) (especially of a leader or government 尤指領導人或政府) not important and of little worth or use 無足輕重的；不起作用的：*a tinpot dictator* 領導無方的獨裁者

tin·sel /ˈtɪnsl/ *noun* [U] strips of shiny material like metal, used as decorations, especially at Christmas（尤指聖誕節時裝飾用的）光片，金屬箔，金屬絲

Tin·sel·town /ˈtɪnsltaʊn/ *noun* [U] (*informal*) a way of referring to Hollywood in California, the centre of the US movie industry 星光熠熠之城（指位於加利福尼亞州的美國電影業中心好萊塢）

tint /tɪnt/ *noun, verb*

■ ***noun*** **1** a shade or small amount of a particular colour; a faint colour covering a surface 色調；淡色彩；（一層）淡色，淺色：*leaves with red and gold autumn tints* 金秋時節略呈紅黃色的樹葉 ◇ *the brownish tint of an old photo* 舊照片的淡褐色 ➲ SYNONYMS at COLOUR **2** an artificial colour used to change the colour of your hair; the act of colouring the hair with a tint 染髮劑；染髮：*a blond tint* 金黃色染髮劑 ◇ *to have a tint* 染髮

■ ***verb*** **1** [usually passive] **~ sth (with sth)** to add a small amount of colour to sth 為…輕微染色；給…略微着色 **2 ~ sth** to change the colour of sb's hair with a tint 染（髮）▸ **tint·ed** *adj.*：*tinted glasses* 有色眼鏡

ˌ**T-interˈsec·tion** (*NAmE*) (*BrE* ˈ**T-junction**) *noun* a place where one road joins another but does not cross it, so that the roads form the shape of the letter T 丁字路口

tin·tin·nabu·la·tion /ˌtɪntɪnæbjuˈleɪʃn/ *noun* [U, C] (*formal*) a ringing sound 叮噹聲；丁零聲

ˌ**tin ˈwhistle** (also ˌ**penny ˈwhistle**) *noun* a simple musical instrument like a short pipe with six holes, that you play by blowing 六孔小笛；六孔哨

tiny 🔑 /ˈtaɪni/ *adj.* (**tini·er**, **tini·est**) very small in size or amount 極小的；微小的；微量的：*a tiny baby* 纖弱的嬰兒 ◇ *Only a tiny minority hold such extreme views.* 只有極少數人持這樣極端的觀點。**IDM** see PATTER *n.*

-tion ➲ -ION

tip 🔑 /tɪp/ *noun, verb*

■ ***noun***

▸ END OF STH 末端 **1** 🔑 the thin pointed end of sth 尖端；尖兒；端：*the tips of your fingers* 手指尖 ◇ *the tip of your nose* 你的鼻尖 ◇ *the northern tip of the island* 島的北端 ➲ see also FINGERTIP **2** 🔑 a small part that fits on or over the end of sth（裝在頂端的）小部件：*a walking stick with a rubber tip* 帶橡皮頭的手杖 ➲ see also FELT-TIP PEN, FILTER TIP

▸ ADVICE 建議 **3** 🔑 a small piece of advice about sth practical 指點；實用的提示 **SYN** hint：**~ (on/for doing sth)** *handy tips for buying a computer* 購買電腦幾點有用的提示 ◇ **~ (on/for sth)** *useful tips on how to save money* 幾個省錢的竅門兒 **4** (*informal*) a secret or expert piece of advice about what the result of a competition, etc. is likely to be, especially about which horse is likely to win a race（尤指有關賽馬的）內幕消息，指點：*a hot tip for the big race* 賽馬大賽的最新內幕消息 **5** (*NAmE*) (also ˈ**tip-off** especially in *BrE*) (*informal*) secret information that sb gives, for example to the police, to warn them about an illegal activity that is going to happen 秘密情報；密報；線報：*The man was arrested after an anonymous tip.* 這男子被匿名舉報後被捕。

▸ EXTRA MONEY 額外的錢 **6** 🔑 a small amount of extra money that you give to sb, for example sb who serves you in a restaurant 小費；小賬：*to* ***leave a tip*** 留小費 ◇ *He* ***gave*** *the waiter* ***a*** *generous* ***tip****.* 他給了服務員很多小費。

▸ FOR RUBBISH 垃圾 **7** (*BrE*) a place where you can take rubbish/garbage and leave it 垃圾場；垃圾堆

T

▸ **UNTIDY PLACE** 髒亂處 **8** (*BrE, informal, disapproving*) an untidy place 髒亂的地方 **SYN dump**：*Their flat is a tip!* 他們的寓所簡直是個豬窩！

IDM **on the tip of your 'tongue** if a word or name is **on the tip of your tongue**, you are sure that you know it but you cannot remember it 話在嘴邊上（卻一時想不起來）**the tip of the 'iceberg** only a small part of a much larger problem（問題的）冰山一角，端倪

■ ***verb*** (-pp-)

▸ **LEAN/POUR/PUSH AT AN ANGLE** 傾斜地倚／倒／推 **1** [I, T] to move so that one end or side is higher than the other; to move sth into this position（使）傾斜，傾倒，翻覆 **SYN tilt**：(**+ adv./prep.**) *The boat tipped to one side.* 船向一邊傾斜。◇ *The seat tips forward to allow passengers into the back.* 座位向前放倒，好讓乘客進入車的後部。◇ **~ sth** (**+ adv./prep.**) *She tipped her head back and laughed loudly.* 她把頭一仰，哈哈大笑起來。**2** [T] **~ sth/sb + adv./prep.** to make sth/sb come out of a container or its/their position by holding or lifting it/them at an angle 倒出；傾倒；傾覆：*She tipped the dirty water down the drain.* 她把髒水倒入了下水道。◇ *The bus stopped abruptly, nearly tipping me out of my seat.* 公共汽車突然剎車，差點兒把我從座位上甩出去。**3** [T] **~ sth + adv./prep.** to touch sth lightly so that it moves in a particular direction 輕觸；輕碰：*The goalkeeper just managed to tip the ball over the crossbar.* 守門員剛好把球捅出球門的橫梁。

▸ **LEAVE RUBBISH** 丟垃圾 **4** [I, T] **~ (sth)** (*BrE*) to leave rubbish/garbage somewhere outdoors in order to get rid of it（在戶外）倒垃圾：*'No tipping.'* (= for example, on a notice) "此處禁止倒垃圾。"

▸ **GIVE EXTRA MONEY** 額外付款 **5** [I, T] to give sb an extra amount of money to thank them for sth they have done for you as part of their job 給小費；付小賬：*Americans were always welcome because they tended to tip heavily.* 美國人總是受歡迎，因為他們往往給很多小費。◇ **~ sb** *Did you remember to tip the waiter?* 你記得給服務員小費了嗎？◇ **~ sb sth** *She tipped the porter a dollar.* 她給了行李工一元的小費。

▸ **PREDICT SUCCESS** 預測成功 **6** [T] (*especially BrE*) to say in advance that sb/sth will be successful 預言…獲勝；事先說…會成功：**~ sb/sth (for sth)** *The band is being tipped for the top.* 人們看好這支樂隊將位居榜首。◇ **~ sb/sth as sth** *The senator has been tipped by many as a future president.* 許多人猜測這位參議員將會繼任總統。◇ **~ sb/sth to do sth** *The actor is tipped to win an Oscar for his performance.* 這位演員因表演出色而被認為有望獲得奧斯卡獎。

▸ **COVER END** 覆蓋端頭 **7** [T, usually passive] **~ sth (with sth)** to cover the end or edge of sth with a colour, a substance, etc.（用顏色、物質等）覆蓋…的末端，遮蓋…的邊：*The wings are tipped with yellow.* 翅膀的尖端呈黃色。

IDM **it is/was 'tipping (it) down** (*BrE, informal*) it is/was raining heavily 大雨傾盆；大雨如注 **tip the 'balance/'scales** (also **swing the 'balance**) to affect the result of sth in one way rather than another 使天平傾斜；使結果傾向某方；起決定性作用：*In an interview, smart presentation can tip the scales in your favour.* 在面試中，機敏的表現是一種有利的條件。**tip your 'hand** (*NAmE*) (*BrE* **show your 'hand/'cards**) to make your plans or intentions known 攤牌；讓對方摸着底細；公開自己的意圖 **tip the scales at sth** to weigh a particular amount 重量為：*He tipped the scales at just over 80 kilos.* 他稱得體重剛過 80 公斤。**tip sb the 'wink | tip the 'wink to sb** (*BrE, informal*) to give sb secret information that they can use to gain an advantage for themselves 給某人密送情報 ➲ more at HAT

PHR V **,tip sb↔'off (about sth)** (*informal*) to warn sb about sth that is going to happen, especially sth illegal 暗中警告，私下告誡，密報（尤指非法的事情）：*Three men were arrested after police were tipped off about the raid.* 警方獲得有關襲擊的密報後，逮捕了三個人。◇ **~ that …** *They were tipped off that he might be living in Wales.* 他們探得風聲他可能住在威爾士。➲ related noun TIP-OFF **,tip 'up/'over | ,tip sth↔'up/'over** to fall or turn over; to make sth do this（使）跌倒，傾覆：*The mug tipped over, spilling hot coffee everywhere.* 杯子倒了，熱咖啡濺得到處都是。◇ *We'll have to tip the sofa up to get it through the door.* 我們必須把沙發翻轉過來才能搬過房門。

'tip-off *noun* (*especially BrE*) (*NAmE* usually **tip**) (*informal*) secret information that sb gives, for example to the police, to warn them about an illegal activity that is going to happen 舉報；密告：*The man was arrested after an anonymous tip-off.* 有人匿名舉報後，那個人被抓了起來。

tip·per /'tɪpə(r)/ *noun* **1** (used with an adjective 與形容詞連用) a person who gives sb a TIP (= a small amount of extra money to thank them for doing sth as part of their job) of the size mentioned 給…小費者；給賞錢者：*She says that Americans are usually big tippers.* 她說美國人通常給小費很大方。**2** (also **'tipper lorry/truck**) a lorry/truck with a container part that can be moved into a sloping position so that its load can slide off at the back 翻斗卡車；自卸貨卡車

tip·pet /'tɪpɪt/ *noun* a long piece of fur worn in the past by a woman around the neck and shoulders, with the ends hanging down in front; a similar piece of clothing worn by judges, priests, etc. 蒂皮特披巾（舊時的女式毛皮披巾）；（法官、教士等所披的）黑色聖帶

Tipp-Ex™ /'tɪpeks/ *noun* [U] (*BrE*) a liquid, usually white, that you use to cover mistakes that you make when you are writing or typing, and that you can write on top of; a type of CORRECTION FLUID 迪美斯修正液；修正液 ▸ **tip·pex** *verb*：**~ sth (out)** *I tippexed out the mistakes.* 我用修正液塗改了錯誤。

'tipping point *noun* the point at which the number of small changes over a period of time reaches a level where a further small change has a sudden and very great effect on a system or leads to an idea suddenly spreading quickly among a large number of people（個案積累終成大趨勢的）引爆點，爆發點

tip·ple /'tɪpl/ *noun, verb*

■ ***noun*** [usually sing.] (*informal, especially BrE*) an alcoholic drink 含酒精飲料：*His favourite tipple was rum and lemon.* 他最愛喝的飲料是朗姆酒加檸檬汁。

■ ***verb*** [I, T] **~ (sth)** (*informal, especially BrE*) to drink alcohol 飲酒 ▸ **tip·pler** /'tɪplə(r)/ *noun*

tip·ster /'tɪpstə(r)/ *noun* **1** a person who tells you, often in exchange for money, which horse is likely to win a race, so that you can bet on it and win money 提供賽馬情報的人（常指販賣情報者）**2** (*especially NAmE*) a person who gives information to the police about a crime or criminal（犯罪行為等的）舉報者，告密者

tipsy /'tɪpsi/ *adj.* (*informal*) slightly drunk 微醉的；略有醉意的 **SYN tight**

tip·toe /'tɪptəʊ; *NAmE* -toʊ/ *noun, verb*

■ ***noun***

IDM **on 'tiptoe/'tiptoes** standing or walking on the front part of your foot, with your heels off the ground, in order to make yourself taller or to move very quietly 踮着腳；躡手躡腳：*She had to stand on tiptoe to reach the top shelf.* 她得踮着腳才能夠到頂層擱架。◇ *We crept around on tiptoes so as not to disturb him.* 我們躡手躡腳地在周圍走動，以免驚動他。

■ ***verb*** [I] (**+ adv./prep.**) to walk using the front parts of your feet only, so that other people cannot hear you 踮着腳走；躡手躡腳地走：*I tiptoed over to the window.* 我踮着腳走到窗前。

,tip-'top *adj.* [usually before noun] (*informal*) excellent 極好的；頭等的；一流的：*The house is **in tip-top condition**.* 這座房子的狀況沒得挑。

'tip-up *adj.* (of a seat 座位) moving up into a vertical position when nobody is sitting in it（無人坐時）自動上翻的，自動收起的

tir·ade /taɪ'reɪd; *NAmE* 'taɪreɪd/ *noun* **~ (against sb/sth)** a long angry speech criticizing sb/sth or accusing sb of sth（批評或指責性的）長篇激烈講話：*She launched into a tirade of abuse against politicians.* 她發表了長篇演說，憤怒地譴責政客。

tire 0-π /ˈtaɪə(r)/ *verb, noun*
■ **verb** [I, T] ~ (**sb**) to become tired and feel as if you want to sleep or rest; to make sb feel this way （使）疲勞，疲倦，困倦： *Her legs were beginning to tire.* 她的雙腿開始感到累了。◇ *He has made a good recovery but still tires easily.* 他已康復得不錯，但仍然容易感到疲勞。
IDM **never tire of doing sth** to do sth a lot, especially in a way that annoys people 不厭其煩地做： *He went to Harvard—as he never tires of reminding us.* 他上過哈佛，他總是不厭其煩地一再提醒我們這一點。
PHR V **ˈtire of sth/sb** to become bored with sth/sb or begin to enjoy it/them less 對…感到厭倦；對…膩煩： *They soon tired of the beach and went for a walk.* 他們很快對海灘膩煩了，便去散步。 **ˌtire sb/yourself ˈout** 0-π to make sb/yourself very tired 使感到筋疲力盡；使感到疲憊不堪 ➲ see also TIRED
■ **noun** 0-π (*NAmE*) (*BrE* **tyre**) a thick rubber ring that fits around the edge of a wheel of a car, bicycle, etc. 輪胎： *a* **front tire** 前胎 ◇ *a* **back/rear tire** 後胎 ◇ *to pump up a tire* 給輪胎打氣 ◇ *a* **flat/burst/punctured tire** 癟了的／爆了的／扎了的輪胎 ◇ **bald/worn tires** 磨平的／磨損的輪胎 ◇ *to check your tire pressure* 檢查輪胎氣壓 ➲ VISUAL VOCAB pages V51, V52 ➲ see also SPARE TYRE (1)

tired 0-π /ˈtaɪəd; *NAmE* ˈtaɪərd/ *adj.*
1 0-π feeling that you would like to sleep or rest; needing rest 疲倦的；疲勞的；困倦的 SYN **weary**： *to* **be/look/feel tired** 感到／顯得／覺得疲憊 ◇ *I'm too tired even to think.* 我累得連想也不願意想。◇ *They were cold, hungry and* **tired out** (= very tired). 他們又冷又餓，疲憊不堪。◇ *tired feet* 疲勞的雙腳 **2** 0-π feeling that you have had enough of sb/sth because you no longer find them/it interesting or because they make you angry or unhappy 厭倦；厭煩： **~ of sb/sth** *I'm sick and tired of all the arguments.* 我對所有這些爭論煩透了。◇ **~ of doing sth** *She was tired of hearing about their trip to India.* 她聽膩了他們的印度之行。 **3** boring because it is too familiar or has been used too much 陳舊的；陳腐的；陳詞濫調的： *He always comes out with the same tired old jokes.* 他總是講些千篇一律老掉牙的笑話。
▸ **tired·ly** *adv.*： *He shook his head tiredly.* 他厭倦地搖了搖頭。 **tired·ness** *noun* [U] ➲ see also DOG-TIRED

ˈtire iron *noun* (*NAmE*) a metal tool for taking tyres off wheels 拆輪胎棒

tire·less /ˈtaɪələs; *NAmE* ˈtaɪərləs/ *adj.* (*approving*) putting a lot of hard work and energy into sth over a long period of time 不知疲倦的；不覺疲勞的；精力充沛的 SYN **indefatigable**： *a tireless campaigner for human rights* 不屈不撓的人權運動參與者 ▸ **tire·less·ly** *adv.*

tire·some /ˈtaɪəsəm; *NAmE* ˈtaɪərsəm/ *adj.* making you feel annoyed 討厭的；令人厭煩的；煩人的 SYN **annoying**： *Buying a house can be a very tiresome business.* 買房子有時是件很麻煩的事。◇ *The children were being very tiresome.* 這些孩子非常討人嫌。▸ **tire·some·ly** *adv.*

tir·ing 0-π /ˈtaɪərɪŋ/ *adj.*
making you feel the need to sleep or rest 令人困倦的；使人疲勞的；累人的 SYN **exhausting**： *It had been a long tiring day.* 這一天讓人感到又累又長。

'tis /tɪz/ *short form* (*old use*) it is

tis·sue /ˈtɪʃuː; *BrE* also ˈtɪsjuː/ *noun* **1** [U] (also **tissues** [pl.]) a collection of cells that form the different parts of humans, animals and plants （人、動植物細胞的）組織： **muscle/brain/nerve, etc. tissue** 肌肉、大腦、神經等組織 ◇ *scar tissue* 瘢痕組織 **2** [C] a piece of soft paper that absorbs liquids, used especially as a HANDKERCHIEF （尤指用作手帕的）紙巾，手巾紙： *a box of tissues* 一盒紙巾 **3** (also **ˈtissue paper**) [U] very thin paper used for wrapping and packing things that break easily （用於包裝易碎物品的）薄紙，綿紙
IDM **a ˌtissue of ˈlies** (*literary*) a story, an excuse, etc. that is full of lies 一派謊言

tit /tɪt/ *noun* **1** [usually pl.] (also **titty**) (*taboo, slang*) a woman's breast or NIPPLE （女人的）奶子，奶頭，乳頭 **2** (*BrE, slang*) a stupid person 蠢貨；笨蛋；窩囊廢 **3** a small European bird. There are several types of tit. 山雀： *a great tit* 大山雀 ➲ see also BLUE TIT

Titan /ˈtaɪtn/ (also **titan**) *noun* (*formal*) a person who is very large, strong, intelligent or important 巨人；高人；偉人 ORIGIN From the **Titans**, who in Greek mythology were the older gods who were defeated in a battle with Zeus. 源自提坦諸神（Titans），在希臘神話中被宙斯打敗的眾巨神。

ti·tan·ic /taɪˈtænɪk/ *adj.* (*formal*) very large, important, strong or difficult 巨大的；極重要的；強大的；極艱巨的： *a titanic struggle between good and evil* 善與惡之間的一場大搏鬥

ti·tan·ium /tɪˈteɪniəm/ *noun* [U] (*symb.* **Ti**) a chemical element. Titanium is a silver-white metal used in making various strong light materials. 鈦

tit·bit /ˈtɪtbɪt/ (*BrE*) (*NAmE* **tid·bit**) *noun* **1** a small special piece of food 小片食物 SYN **morsel**： *She had saved a few titbits for her cat.* 她給貓留了點好吃的東西。 **2** a small but interesting piece of news 花絮；趣聞；佚事 SYN **snippet**： *titbits of gossip* 蜚短流長

titch /tɪtʃ/ *noun* (*BrE, informal* often *humorous*) used as a way of talking about or addressing a very small person （用於談論或稱呼）小不點兒，娃兒

titchy /ˈtɪtʃi/ *adj.* (*BrE, informal*) very small 很小的

ˌtit for ˈtat *noun* [U] a situation in which you do sth bad to sb because they have done the same to you 以牙還牙；針鋒相對；一報還一報： *the routine tit for tat when countries expel each other's envoys* 國家相互驅逐對方使節這種慣常的報復行動 ◇ *tit-for-tat assassinations by rival gangs* 敵對團夥冤冤相報的暗殺

tithe /taɪð/ *noun* **1** (in the past) a tenth of the goods that sb produced or the money that they earned, that was paid as a tax to support the Church （舊時按固定比例給教會的）什一稅 **2** (in some Christian Churches today) a tenth of a person's income, that they give to the Church （現在某些教友按收入的十分之一給基督教教會的）什一捐獻

tit·il·late /ˈtɪtɪleɪt/ *verb* [I, T] (often *disapproving*) to interest or excite sb, especially in a sexual way 使興奮；煽情；煽動情慾： *titillating pictures* 煽動情慾的圖畫 ◇ **~ sth** *a story intended to titillate the imagination of the public* 意欲煽動公眾想像力的故事 ▸ **tit·il·la·tion** /ˌtɪtɪˈleɪʃn/ *noun* [U]

titi·vate /ˈtɪtɪveɪt/ *verb* **~ sth** to improve the appearance of sb/sth by making small changes 打扮；裝扮；裝點： *She titivated her hair in the mirror.* 她對着鏡子梳理頭髮。

title 0-π /ˈtaɪtl/ *noun, verb*
■ **noun** **1** 0-π [C] the name of a book, poem, painting, piece of music, etc. （書、詩歌、圖畫、樂曲等的）名稱，標題，題目： *His poems were published under the title of 'Love and Reason'.* 他的詩是以《愛情與理智》為題發表的。◇ *the* **title track** *from their latest CD* (= the song with the same title as the disc) 他們最新 CD 的同名主打歌 ◇ *She has sung the* **title role** *in 'Carmen'* (= the role of Carmen in that OPERA). 她在《卡門》中演唱卡門的角色。 **2** [C] a particular book or magazine （書刊的）一種，一本： *The company publishes twenty new titles a year.* 這家公司一年出版二十種新書。 **3** 0-π [C] a word in front of a person's name to show their rank or profession, whether or not they are married, etc. （人名前表示地位、職業、婚否等的）稱號，頭銜，職稱，稱謂： *The present duke inherited the title from his father.* 現在的公爵承襲的是他父親的爵位。◇ *Give your name and title* (= Mr, Miss, Ms, Dr, etc.). 報出你的姓名和稱謂。 ➲ note at NAME **4** 0-π [C] a name that describes a job 職位名稱；職稱： *The official title of the job is 'Administrative Assistant'.* 這個職位的正式名稱為“行政助理”。 **5** [C] the position of being the winner of a competition, especially a sports competition （競賽、體育比賽的）冠軍： *the world heavyweight title* 重量級世界拳擊冠軍 ◇ *She has three world titles.* 她已獲得三項世界冠軍。 **6** [U, C] **~ (to sth/to do sth)** (*law* 律) the legal right to own sth, especially land or property; the document that shows you have this right （尤指土地或財產的）所有權，所有權憑證，房地契

T

■ ***verb*** [usually passive] **~ sth + noun** to give a book, piece of music, etc. a particular name （給書、樂曲等）加標題，定題目：*Their first album was titled 'Made in Valmez'.* 他們的第一張專輯定名為 Made in Valmez。

'title bar *noun* (*computing* 計) a bar at the top of a computer screen, which shows the name of the program and file that is on the screen （計算機屏幕頂端的）標題欄

titled /ˈtaɪtld/ *adj.* having a title such as Lord, LADY, etc. 有頭銜的；有爵位的

'title deed *noun* [usually pl.] a legal document proving that sb is the owner of a particular house, etc. 房契；產權契約；所有權憑證

'title-holder *noun* **1** a person or team that has defeated all the other people or teams taking part in an important competition 冠軍；冠軍得主：*the current Olympic title-holder* 本屆奧林匹克運動會冠軍 **2** (*technical* 術語) (*NAmE*) the legal owner of sth 法定所有人；合法所有人

'title page *noun* a page at the front of a book that has the title and the author's name on it （書的）標題頁，書名頁，扉頁

ti·trate /taɪˈtreɪt; tɪ-/ *verb* **~ sth** (*chemistry* 化) to find out how much of a particular substance is in a liquid by measuring how much of another substance is needed to react with it 滴定測量（液體中的物質） ▸ **ti·tra·tion** /-ˈtreɪʃn/ *noun* [U]

tit·ter /ˈtɪtə(r)/ *verb* [I] to laugh quietly, especially in a nervous or embarrassed way （尤指緊張或尷尬地）傻笑，嗤嗤地笑，竊笑 SYN **giggle** ▸ **tit·ter** *noun*

tittle-tattle /ˈtɪtl tætl/ *noun* [U] (*informal, disapproving*) unimportant talk, usually not true, about other people and their lives 閒聊；蜚短流長；張家長李家短 SYN **gossip**

titty /ˈtɪti/ *noun* (*pl.* **-ies**) (*slang*) = TIT (1)

titu·lar /ˈtɪtjulə(r); *NAmE* -tʃə-/ *adj.* [only before noun] **1** (*formal*) having a particular title or status but no real power or authority 名義上的；有名無實的；徒有虛名的 SYN **nominal**：*the titular head of state* 名義上的國家元首 **2** the **titular** character of a book, play, film/movie, etc. is the one mentioned in the title 標題的；被用作標題的 SYN **eponymous**

tizzy /ˈtɪzi/ (also **tizz** /tɪz/) *noun* [sing.] (*informal*) a state of nervous excitement or confusion 緊張；慌張；慌亂：*She was in a real tizzy before the meeting.* 她在會前感到心慌意亂。

T

'T-junction (*BrE*) (*NAmE* **ˌT-interˈsection**) *noun* a place where one road joins another but does not cross it, so that the roads form the shape of the letter T 丁字路口

TLC /ˌtiː el ˈsiː/ *noun* [U] (*informal*) the abbreviation for 'tender loving care' (care that you give sb to make them feel better) 悉心照料（全寫為 tender loving care）：*What he needs now is just rest and a lot of TLC.* 他現在需要的只是休息和充分的親切關懷。

Tlin·git /ˈtlɪŋɡɪt/ *noun* (*pl.* **Tlin·git** or **Tlin·gits**) a member of a Native American people, many of whom live in the US state of Alaska 特林吉特人（美洲土著，很多居於美國阿拉斯加州）

TM /ˌtiː ˈem/ *abbr.* **1** TRADEMARK **2** (*US* **T.M.**) TRANSCENDENTAL MEDITATION

tme·sis /ˈtmiːsɪs/ *noun* [U, C] (*pl.* **tme·ses** /-siːz/) (*linguistics* 語言) the use of a word or words in the middle of another word, for example 'abso-bloody-lutely' 分割插入法（在詞的中間插入其他詞，如 abso-bloody-lutely）；插詞

TNT /ˌtiː en ˈtiː/ *noun* [U] a powerful EXPLOSIVE 三硝基甲苯；梯恩梯；黃色炸藥

to 🔑 /*before consonants* tə; *before vowels* tu; *strong form* tuː/ *prep., infinitive marker, adv.*

■ ***prep.*** HELP For the special uses of **to** in phrasal verbs, look at the entries for the verbs. For example **see to sth** is in the phrasal verb section at **see**. * to 在短語動詞中的特殊用法見有關動詞詞條。如 see to sth 在詞條 see 的短語動詞部份。 **1** 🔑 in the direction of sth; towards sth 向，朝，往，對着（某方向或某處）：*I walked to the office.* 我朝辦公室走去。◇ *It fell to the ground.* 它掉到了地上。◇ *It was on the way to the station.* 那是在去火車站的路上。◇ *He's going to Paris.* 他就要去巴黎了。◇ *my first visit to Africa* 我對非洲的第一次訪問 ◇ *He pointed to something on the opposite bank.* 他指向對岸的某樣東西。◇ *Her childhood was spent travelling from place to place.* 她的童年是在不斷遷移中度過的。 **2** 🔑 **~ the sth (of sth)** located in the direction mentioned from sth 位於…方向：*Place the cursor to the left of the first word.* 把光標置於第一個單詞的左方。◇ *There are mountains to the north.* 北面有山。 **3** 🔑 as far as sth 到，達（某處）：*The meadows lead down to the river.* 牧場一直延伸到河邊。◇ *Her hair fell to her waist.* 她的長髮一直垂到腰部。 **4** 🔑 reaching a particular state 到，達（某種狀態）：*The vegetables were cooked to perfection.* 這些蔬菜燒的火候恰到好處。◇ *He tore the letter to pieces.* 他把信撕碎了。◇ *She sang the baby to sleep.* 她唱着歌把孩子哄睡了。◇ *The letter reduced her to tears* (= made her cry). 那封信讓她落淚了。◇ *His expression changed from amazement to joy.* 他的表情由驚變喜。 **5** 🔑 used to show the end or limit of a range or period of time （表示範圍或一段時間的結尾或界限）到，至：*a drop in profits from $105 million to around $75 million* 利潤從 1.05 億元降到 7 500 萬元左右 ◇ *I'd say he was 25 to 30 years old* (= approximately 25 or 30 years old). 我猜他在 25 至 30 歲之間。◇ *I like all kinds of music from opera to reggae.* 我喜歡各種音樂，從歌劇到雷蓋都喜歡。◇ *We only work from Monday to Friday.* 我們僅從星期一工作到星期五。◇ *I watched the programme from beginning to end.* 這個節目我從頭看到了尾。 **6** 🔑 before the start of sth 在…開始之前；離，差：*How long is it to lunch?* 離吃午飯還有多久？◇ (*especially BrE*) *It's five to ten* (= five minutes before ten o'clock). 現在是十點差五分。 **7** 🔑 used to show the person or thing that receives sth （引出接受者）給，予，向：*He gave it to his sister.* 他把那給了他的妹妹。◇ *I'll explain to you where everything goes.* 我會向你解釋所有東西的擺放位置。◇ *I am deeply grateful to my parents.* 我對父母是感恩戴德。◇ *Who did she address the letter to?* 那封信她是寫給誰的？◇ (*formal*) *To whom did she address the letter?* 那封信她是寫給誰的？ **8** 🔑 used to show the person or thing that is affected by an action （引出受事者或受體）對於，關於：*She is devoted to her family.* 她深深愛着自己的家庭。◇ *What have you done to your hair?* 你怎麼把頭髮弄成這個樣子？ **9** 🔑 used to show that two things are attached or connected （表示兩件事物相接或相連）：*Attach this rope to the front of the car.* 把這繩子繫在小轎車的前面。 **10** 🔑 used to show a relationship between one person or thing and another （表示兩人或事物之間的關係）屬於，歸於，關於，對於：*She's married to an Italian.* 她嫁給了一個意大利人。◇ *the Japanese ambassador to France* 日本駐法大使 ◇ *the key to the door* 這個門的鑰匙 ◇ *the solution to this problem* 解決這個問題的辦法 **11** 🔑 directed towards; concerning 指向；關於：*It was a threat to world peace.* 這是對世界和平的威脅。◇ *She made a reference to her recent book.* 她提到了自己最近的那本書。 **12** 🔑 used to introduce the second part of a comparison or RATIO （引出比較或比率的第二部份）比：*I prefer walking to climbing.* 我喜歡散步多於喜歡爬山。◇ *The industry today is nothing to what it once was.* 這一行業的現狀與昔日的盛況相比微不足道。◇ *We won by six goals to three.* 我們以六比三獲勝。 **13** 🔑 used to show a quantity or rate （表示數量或比率）等於，每，一：*There are 2.54 centimetres to an inch.* 一英寸等於 2.54 厘米。◇ *This car does 30 miles to the gallon.* 這輛汽車每加侖汽油可行駛 30 英里。 ➲ compare PER **14** 🔑 in honour of sb/sth 向…表示敬意：*a monument to the soldiers who died in the war* 陣亡將士紀念碑 ◇ *Let's drink to Julia and her new job.* 讓咱們為朱莉婭和她的新工作乾杯。 **15** while sth else is happening or being done 伴隨；隨同：*He left the stage to prolonged applause.* 他在經久不息的掌聲中退下了舞台。 **16** used after verbs of movement to mean 'with the intention of giving sth' （用於表示動作的動詞之後）為了給，以提供：*People rushed to her rescue and picked* *her up.* 人們衝上前來把她救起。**17** 🔑 used to show sb's attitude or reaction to sth（表示態度或反應）適合，符合，致使：*His music isn't really to my taste.* 他的音樂不太合我的口味。◇ *To her astonishment, he smiled.* 使她驚訝的是，他笑了。**18** 🔑 used to show what sb's opinion or feeling about sth is（表示看法或感覺）按…的看法，據…認為：*It sounded like crying to me.* 在我聽來這像哭。

■ ***infinitive marker*** **HELP** **To** is often used before the base form of a verb to show that the verb is in the infinitive. The infinitive is used after many verbs and also after many nouns and adjectives. * to 常用於原形動詞之前，表示該動詞為不定式。不定式用於許多動詞之後，也用於許多名詞和形容詞之後。**1** 🔑 used to show purpose or intention（表示目的或意圖）：*I set out to buy food.* 我動身去買吃的。◇ *I am going to tell you a story.* 我要給你們講一個故事。◇ *She was determined to do well.* 她決心要做好。◇ *His aim was to become president.* 他的目的是當總統。◇ *To be honest with you, I don't remember what he said.* 跟你說實話，我不記得他說過什麼了。**2** 🔑 used to show the result of sth（表示結果）：*She managed to escape.* 她設法逃走了。◇ *It was too hot to go out.* 天太熱，不能出去。◇ *He couldn't get close enough to see.* 他無法靠近看個清楚。**3** 🔑 used to show the cause of sth（表示原因）：*I'm sorry to hear that.* 我聽到這消息很難過。**4** 🔑 used to show an action that you want or are advised to do（表示想做或讓做的事情）：*I'd love to go to France this summer.* 今年夏天我想去法國。◇ *The leaflet explains how to apply for a place.* 這本小冊子介紹如何申請職位。◇ *I don't know what to say.* 我不知道說什麼好。**HELP** **To** can also be used without a following verb when the missing verb is easy to understand. * to 後面的動詞可以容易推斷出來時也可省略：*He asked her to come but she said she didn't want to.* **5** 🔑 used to show sth that is known or reported about a particular person or thing（表示已知或轉述的事情）：*The house was said to be haunted.* 據說這座房子裏鬧鬼。**6** 🔑 used to show that one action immediately follows another（表示一個動作緊跟另一動作）：*I reached the station only to find that my train had already left.* 我到了車站，卻發現我要搭乘的火車已經開走了。**7 am, is, are, was, were ~** used to show that you must or should do sth 必須；一定；應該：*You are not to talk during the exam.* 考試期間不許說話。◇ *She was to be here at 8.30 but she didn't arrive.* 她應該在 8:30 到這裏，但是沒有到。

■ ***adv.*** (usually of a door 通常指門) in or into a closed position 關着；關閉；關上：*Push the door to.* 推門關上。➲ see also TOING

IDM **,to and 'fro** backwards and forwards 往返地；來回地：*She rocked the baby to and fro.* 她來回搖動着嬰兒。**HELP** For the special uses of **to** in phrasal verbs, look at the entries for the verbs. For example **set to** is in the phrasal verb section at **set**. * to 在短語動詞中的特殊用法見有關動詞詞條。如 set to 在詞條 set 的短語動詞部份。

toad /təʊd; *NAmE* toʊd/ *noun* **1** a small animal like a FROG but with a drier and less smooth skin, that lives on land but breeds in water (= is an AMPHIBIAN) 蟾蜍；癩蛤蟆 ➲ VISUAL VOCAB page V13 **2** (*informal, disapproving*) an unpleasant person 討厭的人；使人惡心的人

,toad-in-the-'hole *noun* [U] a British dish of SAUSAGES cooked in BATTER 裹麪糊烤香腸（一種英國菜）

toad·stool /'təʊdstu:l; *NAmE* 'toʊd-/ *noun* a FUNGUS with a round flat or curved head and a short STEM. Many types of toadstool are poisonous. 傘菌；毒菌；毒蕈；毒蘑菇 ➲ compare MUSHROOM *n.*

toady /'təʊdi; *NAmE* 'toʊdi/ *noun, verb*

■ ***noun*** (*pl.* **-ies**) (*informal, disapproving*) a person who treats sb more important with special kindness or respect in order to gain their favour or help 諂媚者；馬屁精 **SYN** **sycophant**

■ ***verb*** (**toad·ies**, **toady·ing**, **toad·ied**, **toad·ied**) [I] **~ (to sb)** (*disapproving*) to treat sb more important with special kindness or respect in order to gain their favour or help 拍馬；奉承；諂媚

toast /təʊst; *NAmE* toʊst/ *noun, verb*

■ ***noun*** **1** [U] slices of bread that have been made brown and crisp by heating them on both sides in a toaster or under a GRILL 烤麪包片；吐司：*cheese on toast* 烤麪包片加奶酪 ◇ *a piece of toast* 一塊烤麪包片 ◇ *two **slices/rounds of toast*** 兩片 / 兩整片烤麪包片 ➲ see also FRENCH TOAST **2** [C] **~ (to sb/sth)** the act of a group of people wishing sb happiness, success, etc. by drinking a glass of sth, especially alcohol, at the same time 乾杯；祝酒；敬酒：*I'd like to **propose a toast** to the bride and groom.* 我提議為新娘新郎乾杯。◇ *The committee **drank a toast** to the new project.* 委員會為這項新計劃乾杯。**3** [sing.] **the ~ of ...** a person who is praised by a lot of people in a particular place because of sth that they have done well（在某領域）廣受讚譽的人，有口皆碑的人：*The performance made her the toast of the festival.* 她的演出使她在會演中備受推崇。

IDM **be 'toast** (*informal, especially NAmE*) to be likely to die or be destroyed 會死；要完蛋：*One mistake and you're toast.* 要是出一次錯，你就完了。

■ ***verb*** **1** [T] **~ sb/sth** to lift a glass of wine, etc. in the air and drink it at the same time as other people in order to wish sb/sth success, happiness, etc. 為…舉杯敬酒；為…乾杯：*The happy couple were toasted in champagne.* 人們舉起香檳酒為這對幸福的伉儷乾杯。◇ *We toasted the success of the new company.* 我們為新公司的成功乾杯。**2** [T, I] **~ (sth)** to make sth, especially bread, turn brown by heating it in a toaster or close to heat; to turn brown in this way 烤（尤指麪包）；把…烤得焦黃：*a toasted sandwich* 烤過的三明治 ◇ *Place under a hot grill until the nuts have toasted.* 把這些堅果放在高溫烤架下面烤熟。➲ COLLOCATIONS at COOKING **3** [T] **~ sth** to warm a part of your body by placing it near a fire 烤火；取暖；使暖和

toast·er /'təʊstə(r); *NAmE* 'toʊ-/ *noun* an electrical machine that you put slices of bread in to make toast（電的）烤麪包片器；吐司爐 ➲ VISUAL VOCAB page V25

toastie /'təʊsti; *NAmE* 'toʊsti/ *noun* (*BrE*) a SANDWICH that has been TOASTED 烤三明治；吐司三明治

'toasting fork *noun* a fork with a long handle used for TOASTING bread in front of a fire 烤麪包長叉

toast·mas·ter /'təʊstmɑ:stə(r); *NAmE* 'toʊstmæstər/ *noun* a person who introduces the speakers at a formal dinner and calls for people to drink sth together in honour of particular people (= proposes TOASTS) 宴會主持人；致祝酒辭的人

toasty /'təʊsti; *NAmE* 'toʊ-/ *adj.* (*especially NAmE*) warm and comfortable 暖烘烘的；温暖舒適的

to·bacco /tə'bækəʊ; *NAmE* -koʊ/ *noun* [U, C] (*pl.* **-os**) the dried leaves of the tobacco plant that are used for making cigarettes, smoking in a pipe or chewing 煙葉；煙草：*The government imposed a ban on tobacco advertising* (= the advertising of cigarettes and all other forms of tobacco). 政府禁止做煙草廣告。

to·bac·con·ist /tə'bækənɪst/ *noun* **1** a person who owns, manages or works in a shop/store selling cigarettes, tobacco for pipes, etc. 煙草店老闆；煙草商 **2** **to·bac·con·ist's** (*pl.* **to·bac·con·ists**) a shop/store that sells cigarettes, tobacco, etc. 煙草店：*There's a tobacconist's on the corner.* 街角處有一家煙草店。

to·bog·gan /tə'bɒgən; *NAmE* -'bɑ:g-/ *noun, verb*

■ ***noun*** a long light narrow SLEDGE (= a vehicle that slides over snow) sometimes curved up in front, used for sliding down slopes 長雪橇；平底長雪橇

■ ***verb*** [I] to travel down a slope on snow or ice using a toboggan 坐長雪橇滑行 ▸ **to·bog·gan·ing** *noun* [U]

toc·cata /tə'kɑ:tə/ *noun* a piece of music for a keyboard instrument which includes difficult passages designed to show the player's skill 托卡塔（用鍵盤樂器演奏的樂曲，其中有的樂段難度很大，以顯示演奏者的技藝）

toc·sin /'tɒksɪn; *NAmE* 'tɑ:k-/ *noun* (*old use*) a warning bell or signal 警鐘；警戒信號

T

tod /tɒd; *NAmE* tɑːd/ *noun*
IDM **on your 'tod** (*old-fashioned, BrE, informal*) on your own; alone 獨自；單獨

today /təˈdeɪ/ *adv., noun*
■ ***adv.*** **1** on this day 在今天；在今日：*I've got a piano lesson later today.* 今天晚些時候我有一堂鋼琴課。◇ *The exams start **a week today/today week*** (= one week from now). 考試於下週的今天開始。**2** at the present period 現在；當今；當代 **SYN** **nowadays**：*Young people today face a very difficult future at work.* 如今的年輕人面臨着充滿困難的工作前景。
■ ***noun*** [U] **1** this day 今天；今日：*Today is her tenth birthday.* 今天是她的十歲生日。◇ *The review is in today's paper.* 這篇評論刊登在今天的報紙上。◇ *I'm leaving a week from today.* 我下週的今天動身。**2** the present period of time 現在；當今；當代：*today's young people* 當代青年

tod·dle /ˈtɒdl; *NAmE* ˈtɑːdl/ *verb* **1** [I] when a young child who has just learnt to walk **toddles**, he/she walks with short, unsteady steps（幼兒學步時）搖搖擺擺地走，蹣跚行走 **2** [I] **+ adv./prep.** (*informal*) to walk or go somewhere 步行；去：*She toddles down to the park most afternoons.* 多數下午她都遛達着去公園。◇ *I locked the door and then toddled off to bed.* 我鎖上房門，然後就上牀睡覺去了。

tod·dler /ˈtɒdlə(r); *NAmE* ˈtɑːd-/ *noun* a child who has only recently learnt to walk 學步的兒童；剛學會走路的孩子

toddy /ˈtɒdi; *NAmE* ˈtɑːdi/ *noun* [C, U] (*pl.* **-ies**) a drink made with strong alcohol, sugar, hot water and sometimes spices 托迪酒（用烈酒加熱水、糖或香料等調配而成）

tod·ger /ˈtɒdʒə(r); *NAmE* ˈtɑːdʒər/ *noun* (*BrE, informal*) a man's PENIS 陰莖

to-do /təˈduː/ *noun* [sing.] (*informal, becoming old-fashioned*) unnecessary excitement or anger about sth 忙亂；喧嚷；大驚小怪；吵吵嚷嚷 **SYN** **fuss**：*What a to-do!* 真是太大驚小怪了！

toe /təʊ; *NAmE* toʊ/ *noun, verb*
■ ***noun*** **1** one of the five small parts that stick out from the foot 腳趾：*the **big/little toe*** (= the largest/smallest toe) 大／小腳趾 ◇ *I stubbed my toe on the step.* 我的腳趾踢在了台階上。◇ *Can you **touch your toes**?* (= by bending over while keeping your legs straight) 你彎腰夠得着你的腳趾麼？ ➲ VISUAL VOCAB page V59 **2** the part of a sock, shoe, etc. that covers the toes（襪、鞋等的）足尖部 ➲ VISUAL VOCAB page V64 **3 -toed** (in adjectives 構成形容詞) having the type or number of toes mentioned 有…腳趾的：*open-toed sandals* 露腳趾的涼鞋 ◇ *a three-toed sloth* 三趾樹懶 ➲ see also PIGEON-TOED
IDM **keep sb on their 'toes** to make sure that sb is ready to deal with anything that might happen by doing things that they are not expecting（通過出其不意的行動）使保持警覺：*Surprise visits help to keep the staff on their toes.* 突擊巡察有助於使員工不致懈怠偷懶。**make sb's 'toes curl** to make sb feel embarrassed or uncomfortable 使人尷尬；使人難為情 ➲ see also TOE-CURLING ➲ more at DIG *v.*, DIP *v.*, HEAD *n.*, STEP *v.*, TOP *n.*, TREAD *v.*
■ ***verb***
IDM **toe the 'line** (*NAmE* also **toe the 'mark**) to say or do what sb in authority tells you to say or do, even if you do not share the same opinions, etc. 順從當局（或集體）；遵循…路線：*to toe the party line* 遵循黨的路線

toe·cap /ˈtəʊkæp; *NAmE* ˈtoʊ-/ *noun* a piece of metal or leather that covers the front part of a shoe or boot to make it stronger（鞋或靴尖的）外包頭

'toe-curling *adj.* (*informal*) extremely embarrassing because of being very bad or silly 令人無地自容的；丟人現眼的 ▸ **'toe-curling·ly** *adv.*：*a toe-curlingly awful movie* 非常令人反感的電影

TOEFL™ /ˈtəʊfl; *NAmE* ˈtoʊfl/ *abbr.* Test of English as a Foreign Language (a test of a person's level of English that is taken in order to go to a university in the US) 作為外語的英語測驗，托福考試（為上美國大學而進行的英語水平測試）

toe·hold /ˈtəʊhəʊld; *NAmE* ˈtoʊhoʊld/ *noun* **1** a position in a place or an activity which you hope will lead to more power or success 初步的地位；立足點：*The firm is anxious to gain a toehold in Europe.* 這家公司急於在歐洲找個立腳點。**2** a very small hole or space on a CLIFF, just big enough to put your foot in when you are climbing（攀登時可放進腳去的）小立足點，小支撐點

TOEIC™ /ˈtəʊɪk; *NAmE* ˈtoʊɪk/ *noun* [U] the abbreviation for 'Test of English for International Communication' (a test that measures your ability to read and understand English if it is not your first language) 國際交流英語測試，托業考試（全寫為 Test of English for International Communication，作為外語的英語閱讀和理解能力測試）

toe·nail /ˈtəʊneɪl; *NAmE* ˈtoʊ-/ *noun* the nail on a toe 趾甲 ➲ VISUAL VOCAB page V59

toe·rag /ˈtəʊræɡ; *NAmE* ˈtoʊ-/ *noun* (*BrE, slang*) used as a rude and offensive way of addressing sb you do not like or that you are angry with 渾蛋；廢物

'toe-tapping *adj.* (*informal*) (of music 音樂) lively and making you want to move your feet 歡快的；輕鬆明快的

toey /ˈtəʊi; *NAmE* ˈtoʊi/ *adj.* (*AustralE, NZE, informal*) (of a person or an animal) nervous or not able to keep still（人或動物）神經緊張的，焦急不安的，躁動的

toff /tɒf; *NAmE* tɑːf/ *noun* (*BrE, informal*) a disapproving way of referring to sb from a high social class 紈絝子弟；花花公子

tof·fee /ˈtɒfi; *NAmE* ˈtɔːfi; ˈtɑːfi/ *noun* [U, C] a hard sticky sweet/candy made by heating sugar, butter and water together and allowing it to cool 太妃糖；乳脂糖
IDM **can't do sth for 'toffee** (*old-fashioned, BrE, informal*) if sb **can't do sth for toffee**, they are very bad at doing it 做某事很糟糕；不能勝任某事：*He can't dance for toffee!* 他根本不會跳舞！

'toffee apple (*BrE*) (*NAmE* **'candy apple**) *noun* an apple covered with a thin layer of hard toffee and fixed on a stick 太妃蘋果（外塗奶油乳脂，用籤子插起）

'toffee-nosed *adj.* (*old-fashioned, BrE, informal*) behaving as if you are better than other people, especially those of a lower social class 勢利眼的；妄自尊大的；目空一切的 **SYN** **snobbish**

tofu /ˈtəʊfuː; *NAmE* ˈtoʊfuː/ (also **'bean curd**) *noun* [U] a soft white substance that is made from SOYA and used in cooking, often instead of meat 豆腐

tog /tɒɡ; *NAmE* tɑːɡ/ *noun, verb*
■ ***noun*** (*BrE*) **1 togs** [pl.] (*informal, becoming old-fashioned*) clothes, especially ones that you wear for a particular purpose（尤指專用的）衣服，服裝：*running togs* 跑步裝 **2** a unit for measuring the warmth of DUVETS, etc. 托格（顯示羽絨被褥等保暖性的熱阻計量單位）
■ ***verb*** (**-gg-**)
IDM **be ˌtogged 'out/'up (in sth)** (*informal*) to be wearing clothes for a particular activity or occasion 穿着（適合某種活動或場合）的服裝：*They were all togged up in their skiing gear.* 他們全都身着滑雪服。

toga /ˈtəʊɡə; *NAmE* ˈtoʊɡə/ *noun* a loose outer piece of clothing worn by the citizens of ancient Rome 托加袍（古羅馬市民穿的寬鬆大袍）

to·gether /təˈɡeðə(r)/ *adv., adj.*
■ ***adv.*** **HELP** For the special uses of **together** in phrasal verbs, look at the entries for the verbs. For example **pull yourself together** is in the phrasal verb section at **pull**. * together 在短語動詞中的特殊用法見有關動詞詞條。如 pull yourself together 在詞條 pull 的短語動詞部份。 **1** with or near to sb/sth else; with each other 在一起；共同：*We grew up together.* 我們是在一塊兒長大的。◇ *Together they climbed the dark stairs.* 他們一起登上黑洞洞的樓梯。◇ *Get all the ingredients together before you start cooking.* 把所有的材料放在一起再開始烹飪。◇ *Stay **close together**—I don't want anyone to get lost.* 緊緊靠在一起，我不想把誰給丟了。**2** so that two or more things touch or are joined to or combined with each other 以使接觸（或相結合）；到一起：*He rubbed his hands together in satisfaction.* 他滿意地擦搓着

雙手。◇ *She nailed the two boards together.* 她把兩塊木板釘在了一起。◇ *Mix the sand and cement together.* 把沙子和水泥混合在一起。◇ ***Taken together**, these factors are highly significant.* 這些因素綜合起來看就很重要了。◇ *He has **more** money **than the rest of** us **put together**.* 他的錢比我們所有人的加在一起還多。 **3** ⚷ (of two people 兩個人) in a close relationship, for example a marriage 關係密切；有婚姻關係：*They split up after ten years together.* 他們在一起生活了十年之後分手了。 **4** ⚷ in or into agreement 一致；協調：*After the meeting the two sides in the dispute were no closer together.* 會面之後，爭論的雙方立場差距依然如故。 **5** ⚷ at the same time 同時；一起；一齊：*They both spoke together.* 他們兩人同時發言。◇ (*informal*) ***All together now:** 'Happy birthday to you …'* 現在大家一齊唱："祝你生日快樂…" **6 for hours, days, etc. ~** (*formal*) for hours, days, etc. without stopping 接連…地；連續…地；…不間斷地：*She sat for hours together just staring into space.* 她連續幾個小時坐在那裏怔怔地望着前面。

IDM **together with** **1** ⚷ including 包括…在內：*Together with the Johnsons, there were 12 of us in the villa.* 包括約翰遜一家在內，別墅裏總共有我們 12 個人。 **2** ⚷ in addition to; as well as 加之；和；連同；同…一起：*I sent my order, together with a cheque for £40.* 我把訂單連同一張 40 英鎊的支票一起寄出去。

■ ***adj.*** (*informal, approving*) (of a person 人) well organized and confident 自信而妥實的：*He's incredibly together for someone so young.* 他這個人年紀輕輕，辦事如此穩當，真是了不起。

to·gether·ness /tə'geðənəs; *NAmE* -ðərn-/ *noun* [U] the happy feeling you have when you are with people you like, especially family and friends （尤指家庭或朋友的）和睦相處，親密無間，團結友愛

tog·gle /'tɒgl; *NAmE* 'tɑːgl/ *noun, verb*

■ ***noun*** **1** a short piece of wood, plastic, etc. that is put through a LOOP of thread to fasten sth, such as a coat or bag, instead of a button （大衣或袋子等上木質或塑料的）栓扣釘，棒形鈕扣，套索扣 ➲ VISUAL VOCAB page V63 **2** (also **'toggle switch**) (*computing* 計) a key on a computer that you press to change from one style or operation to another, and back again 轉換鍵；切換鍵

■ ***verb*** [I, T] (*computing* 計) to press a key or set of keys on a computer keyboard in order to turn a feature on or off, or to move from one program, etc. to another （兩種狀態之間）切換，轉換：**~ (between A and B)** *He toggled between the two windows.* 他在兩個窗口之間來回切換。◇ **~ sth** *This key toggles various views of the data.* 按此鍵可切換數據的各種視圖。

'toggle switch *noun* **1** an electrical switch which you move up and down or backwards and forwards 撥動開關；扳扭開關；肘節開關 **2** (*computing* 計) = TOGGLE (2)

toil /tɔɪl/ *verb, noun*

■ ***verb*** (*formal*) **1** [I] to work very hard and/or for a long time, usually doing hard physical work （長時間）苦幹，辛勤勞作 SYN **slave away** **2** [I] **+ adv./prep.** to move slowly and with difficulty 艱難緩慢地移動；跋涉 SYN **slog**：*They toiled up the hill in the blazing sun.* 他們冒着炎炎烈日艱難地一步一步爬上山岡。▶ **toil·er** *noun*

■ ***noun*** [U] (*formal* or *literary*) hard unpleasant work that makes you very tired 苦工；勞累的工作：*a life of hardship and toil* 艱難勞苦的一生 ➲ see also TOILS

toi·let ⚷ /'tɔɪlət/ *noun*

1 ⚷ [C] a large bowl attached to a pipe that you sit on or stand over when you get rid of waste matter from your body 坐便器；抽水馬桶：*Have you flushed the toilet?* 你沖廁所了嗎？◇ (*BrE*) *I need to **go to the toilet*** (= use the toilet). 我得去趟洗手間。◇ *a toilet seat* 馬桶座圈◇ *toilet facilities* 衞生間設備◇ *Do you **need the toilet?*** 你需要用洗手間嗎？ ➲ VISUAL VOCAB page V24 **2** ⚷ (*BrE*) (*NAmE* **bath·room**) [C] a room containing a toilet 廁所；衞生間；盥洗室：*Every flat has its own bathroom and toilet.* 每套公寓都帶有洗澡間和盥洗室。◇ *Who's in the toilet?* 誰在用廁所？ **3** ⚷ (*BrE*) [C] (also **toi·lets** [pl.]) a room or small building containing several toilets, each in a separate smaller room （有幾個分隔坐便器的）廁所間，廁所：*public toilets* 公共廁所◇ *Could you tell me where the ladies' toilet is, please?* 請問哪裏有女廁所？ **4** [U] (*old-fashioned*) the process of washing and dressing yourself, arranging your hair, etc. 梳洗；打扮

> **British/American 英式/美式英語**
>
> **toilet / bathroom**
>
> ■ In *BrE*, but not in *NAmE*, the room that has a toilet in it is usually referred to as a **toilet**. This room in people's houses can also be called the **lavatory**, or informally, the **loo**. An extra downstairs toilet in a house can be called the **cloakroom**. In public places, especially on signs, the words **toilets**, **Gents** (for men's toilets) or **Ladies** (for women's toilets) are used for a room or small building containing several toilets. You might also see **WC** or **Public Conveniences** on some signs. 在英式英語而非美式英語中，廁所一般稱為 toilet，住宅中的廁所亦可稱為 lavatory 或（非正式用法）loo。住宅樓下附加的廁所可叫做 cloakroom。在公共場所，尤其在指示牌上，toilets、Gents（男廁所）或 Ladies（女廁所）指有幾個小間的廁所。有的指示牌亦可能用 WC 或 Public Conveniences。
>
> ■ In *NAmE* the room that contains a toilet is usually called the **bathroom**, never the **toilet**. A room with a toilet in a public place can also be called a **restroom**, **ladies' room**, **women's room** or **men's room**. **Washroom** is also used, especially in Canada. 在美式英語中，廁所一般稱為 bathroom，從不叫 toilet。公共廁所亦可稱為 restroom、ladies' room、women's room 或 men's room，還可用 washroom，尤其是在加拿大。

'toilet bag *noun* (*BrE*) = SPONGE BAG

'toilet paper (also **'toilet tissue**) *noun* [U] thin soft paper used for cleaning yourself after you have used the toilet 衞生紙；手紙：*a roll of toilet paper* 一捲衞生紙 ➲ VISUAL VOCAB page V24

toi·let·ries /'tɔɪlətriz/ *noun* [pl.] things such as soap or TOOTHPASTE that you use for washing, cleaning your teeth, etc. （香皂、牙膏等）洗漱用品 ➲ VISUAL VOCAB page V24

'toilet roll *noun* (*BrE*) a roll of toilet paper 衞生紙捲；手紙捲 ➲ picture at ROLL

'toiletry bag (*NAmE*) (*BrE* **'sponge bag**, **'toilet bag**, **wash·bag**) *noun* a small bag for holding your soap, TOOTHBRUSH, etc. when you are travelling 盥洗用品袋 ➲ VISUAL VOCAB page V24

'toilet soap *noun* [U, C] soap that you use for washing yourself 香皂

'toilet-train *verb* [usually passive] **~ sb** to teach a small child to use the toilet 訓練（幼兒）上廁所 ▶ **'toilet-trained** *adj.* **'toilet-training** *noun* [U]

'toilet water *noun* [U, C] a kind of PERFUME (= a pleasant smelling liquid for the skin) that has water added to it and is not very expensive 花露水

toils /tɔɪlz/ *noun* [pl.] (*formal* or *literary*) if you are caught in **the toils** of an unpleasant feeling or situation, you cannot escape from it 牢籠；羅網 SYN **snare**

toing /'tuːɪŋ/ *noun*

IDM **,toing and 'froing** **1** movement or travel backwards and forwards between two or more places 來回運動；往返旅行；來來往往：*All this toing and froing between London and New York takes it out of him.* 這樣沒完沒了地在倫敦和紐約之間來回奔波使得他疲憊不堪。 **2** a lot of unnecessary or repeated activity or discussion 翻來覆去地做（或討論）；忙亂；折騰：*After a great deal of toing and froing, I decided not to change jobs after all.* 好一番折騰之後，我最終決定還是不換工作。

toke /təʊk; *NAmE* toʊk/ *noun* (*informal*) an act of breathing in smoke from a cigarette containing MARIJUANA 吸一口（大麻煙） ▶ **toke** *verb* [I]

T

token /ˈtəʊkən; *NAmE* ˈtoʊ-/ *noun, adj.*

■ ***noun*** **1** a round piece of metal or plastic used instead of money to operate some machines or as a form of payment（用以啟動某些機器或用作支付方式的）代幣，專用輔幣：*a parking token* 停車專用輔幣 **2** (*BrE*) a piece of paper that you pay for and that sb can exchange for sth in a shop/store 代價券：*a £20* ***book/record/gift token*** 價值 20 英鎊的書券 / 唱片券 / 禮物券 **3** a piece of paper that you can collect when you buy a particular product and then exchange for sth 贈券；禮券：*Collect six tokens for a free T-shirt.* 收集到六張禮券可以換一件 T 恤衫。 **4** something that is a symbol of a feeling, a fact, an event, etc.（感覺、事實、事件等的）象徵，標誌，表示，信物 SYN **expression, mark**：*Please accept this small gift* ***as a token of*** *our gratitude.* 區區薄禮，以表謝忱，請笑納。

IDM **by the same ˈtoken** for the same reasons 由於同樣的原因；同樣地：*The penalty for failure will be high. But, by the same token, the rewards for success will be great.* 失敗就要付出沉重的代價，同樣，成功就會獲得很大的回報。

■ ***adj.*** [only before noun] **1** involving very little effort or feeling and intended only as a way of showing other people that you think sb/sth is important, when really you are not sincere 裝樣子的；裝點門面的；敷衍的：*The government has only made a token gesture towards helping the unemployed.* 政府只不過是做做樣子表示了一下對失業者的幫助。◇ *There was one token woman on the committee* (= a woman who is included in the group to make it look as if women are always included, although that is not true). 委員會中有一位裝點門面的女性委員。 **2** done as a symbol to show that you are serious about sth and will keep a promise or an agreement or do more later 象徵性的；作為標誌的：*The government agreed to send a small token force to the area.* 政府同意派遣一小支象徵性的部隊到那一地區。◇ *a one-day token strike* 一天的象徵性罷工 **3** (of a small amount of money 小額款項) that you pay or charge sb only as a symbol, because a payment is expected 象徵性支付的 SYN **nominal**：*We charge only a token fee for use of the facilities.* 我們對使用這些設施只收取象徵性的費用。

token·ism /ˈtəʊkənɪzəm; *NAmE* ˈtoʊ-/ *noun* [U] (*disapproving*) the fact of doing sth only in order to do what the law requires or to satisfy a particular group of people, but not in a way that is really sincere 裝點門面；表面文章；敷衍了事；應付差事：*Appointing one woman to the otherwise all-male staff could look like tokenism.* 給原本清一色的男職員隊伍增派一位女性會顯得是裝點門面。

T

to·kol·oshe /ˈtɒkɒlɒʃ; *NAmE* ˈtɑːkəlɑːʃ/ *noun* (*SAfrE*) an evil imaginary creature that some people believe can harm you while you are sleeping 托克洛希（傳說中能趁人睡眠時進行傷害的邪惡精靈）

Tok Pisin /ˌtɒk ˈpɪzən; -sən; *NAmE* ˌtɑːk/ (also **Pidgin**) *noun* [U] a CREOLE language based on English, used in Papua New Guinea 新美拉尼西亞語（巴布亞新幾內亞使用的一種以英語為基礎的克里奧爾語）

told *past tense, past part.* of TELL

tol·er·able /ˈtɒlərəbl; *NAmE* ˈtɑːl-/ *adj.* (*formal*) **1** fairly good, but not of the best quality 尚好的；過得去的；還可以的 SYN **reasonable**：*a tolerable degree of success* 說得過去的成功 **2** that you can accept or bear, although unpleasant or painful 可接受的；可忍受的；可容忍的 SYN **bearable**：*At times, the heat was barely tolerable.* 有時天氣炎熱得幾乎令人難以忍受。 OPP **intolerable** ▸ **tol·er·ably** /ˈtɒlərəbli; *NAmE* ˈtɑːl-/ *adv.*：*He plays the piano tolerably (well).* 他鋼琴彈得還算不錯。

tol·er·ance /ˈtɒlərəns; *NAmE* ˈtɑːl-/ *noun* **1** [U] **~ (of/for sb/sth)** the willingness to accept or TOLERATE sb/sth, especially opinions or behaviour that you may not agree with, or people who are not like you 忍受；容忍；寬容；寬恕：*She had no tolerance for jokes of any kind.* 她容不得開任何玩笑。◇ *religious tolerance* 宗教上的包容 ◇ *a reputation for tolerance towards refugees* 對難民寬容的美譽 ➲ see also ZERO TOLERANCE OPP **intolerance** **2** [C, U] **~ (to sth)** the ability to suffer sth, especially pain, difficult conditions, etc. without being harmed 忍耐力；忍受性；耐力；耐量：*tolerance to cold* 耐寒力 ◇ *Tolerance to alcohol decreases with age.* 酒量隨年齡的增大而減少。 **3** [C, U] (*technical* 術語) the amount by which the measurement of a value can vary without causing problems 公差；容限：*They were working to a tolerance of 0.0001 of a centimetre.* 他們在按 0.0001 厘米的公差加工。

tol·er·ant /ˈtɒlərənt; *NAmE* ˈtɑːl-/ *adj.* **1 ~ (of/towards sb/sth)** able to accept what other people say or do even if you do not agree with it 忍受的；容忍的；寬容的：*He has a very tolerant attitude towards other religions.* 他對其他宗教持非常包容的態度。 **2 ~ (of sth)** (of plants, animals or machines 植物、動物或機器) able to survive or operate in difficult conditions 能在困難條件下生存（或操作）的；能耐…的：*The plants are tolerant of frost.* 這些植物耐霜。 OPP **intolerant** ▸ **tol·er·ant·ly** *adv.*

tol·er·ate /ˈtɒləreɪt; *NAmE* ˈtɑːl-/ *verb* **1** to allow sb to do sth that you do not agree with or like 容許，允許（不同意或不喜歡的事物）SYN **put up with**：**~ sth** *Their relationship was tolerated but not encouraged.* 他們的關係得到了允許，但不宜鼓勵。◇ *This sort of behaviour will not be tolerated.* 這種行為是不能容許的。◇ **~ (sb/sth) doing/being/having sth** *She refused to tolerate being called a liar.* 她拒不接受被稱為撒謊者。 **2 ~ sb/sth** to accept sb/sth that is annoying, unpleasant, etc. without complaining 忍受；容忍；包容 SYN **put up with**：*There is a limit to what one person can tolerate.* 一個人的容忍是有限度的。◇ *I don't know how you tolerate that noise!* 我不知道你怎麼能忍受那樣的噪音！ **3 ~ sth** to be able to be affected by a drug, difficult conditions, etc. without being harmed （對藥物）有耐受性；能經受（困難條件）：*She tolerated the chemotherapy well.* 她對這次化療的耐受力很強。◇ *Few plants will tolerate sudden changes in temperature.* 很少植物經受得住氣溫的突然變化。

tol·er·ation /ˌtɒləˈreɪʃn; *NAmE* ˌtɑːl-/ *noun* [U] a willingness to allow sth that you do not like or agree with to happen or continue 忍受；容忍；寬容；容許 SYN **tolerance**：*religious toleration* 宗教上的寬容

toll /təʊl; *NAmE* toʊl/ *noun, verb*

■ ***noun*** **1** [C] money that you pay to use a particular road or bridge （道路、橋梁的）通行費：*motorway tolls* 高速公路通行費 ◇ *a* ***toll road/bridge*** 收費道路 / 橋梁 ➲ SYNONYMS at RATE **2** [C, usually sing.] the amount of damage or the number of deaths and injuries that are caused in a particular war, disaster, etc. （戰爭、災難等造成的）毀壞；傷亡人數：*The official* ***death toll*** *has now reached 7 000.* 官方公佈的死亡人數現已達 7 000 人。◇ *the war's growing casualty toll* 不斷增長的戰爭傷亡人數 **3** [sing.] the sound of a bell ringing with slow regular strokes （緩慢而有規律的）鐘聲 **4** [C] (*NAmE*) a charge for a telephone call that is calculated at a higher rate than a local call 長途電話費

IDM **take a heavy ˈtoll (on sb/sth)** | **take its ˈtoll (on sb/sth)** to have a bad effect on sb/sth; to cause a lot of damage, deaths, suffering, etc. 產生惡果；造成重大損失（或傷亡、災難等）：*Illness had taken a heavy toll on her.* 疾病對她的身體造成極大的損害。◇ *The recession is taking its toll on the housing markets.* 經濟衰退使住房市場遭受着重大損失。

■ ***verb*** [I, T] when a bell **tolls** or sb **tolls** it, it is rung slowly many times, especially as a sign that sb has died （緩慢而有規律地）敲（鐘）；（尤指）鳴（喪鐘）：**~ (for sb)** *The Abbey bell tolled for those killed in the war.* 大教堂為戰爭中的死難者鳴鐘。◇ **~ sth** *The bell tolled the hour.* 鳴鐘報時。◇ (*figurative*) *The revolution* ***tolled the death knell*** (= signalled the end) *for the Russian monarchy.* 那場革命敲響了俄國君主制的喪鐘。

toll·booth /ˈtəʊlbuːð; *NAmE* ˈtoʊlbuːθ/ *noun* a small building by the side of a road where you pay to drive on a road, go over a bridge, etc. （道路、橋梁的）收費亭，收費站

ˌtoll-ˈfree *adj.* (*NAmE*) (of a telephone call to an organization or a service 打給機構或服務部門的電話) that you do not have to pay for 免費的：*a toll-free number* 免費電話號碼 ➲ see also FREEPHONE

toll·house cookie /ˌtəʊlhaʊs ˈkʊki; *NAmE* ˌtoʊl-/ *noun* (*US*) a crisp sweet biscuit/cookie that contains small pieces of chocolate 碎粒巧克力曲奇

ˈtoll plaza *noun* (*US*) a row of TOLLBOOTHS across a road（道路上的）收費站，收費區，收費廣場

Tom /tɒm; *NAmE* tɑːm/ *noun*
IDM **any/every ˌTom, ˌDick or ˈHarry** (usually *disapproving*) any ordinary person rather than the people you know or people who have special skills or qualities（不熟悉或無特長的）任何人；閒人；生人：*We don't want any Tom, Dick or Harry using the club bar.* 我們不想隨便讓什麼人都來使用會所的酒吧。

tom /tɒm; *NAmE* tɑːm/ *noun* = TOMCAT

toma·hawk /ˈtɒməhɔːk; *NAmE* ˈtɑːm-/ *noun* a light AXE used by Native Americans 印第安戰斧（美洲土著的一種工具）

to·mato 0-w /təˈmɑːtəʊ; *NAmE* təˈmeɪtoʊ/ *noun* [C, U] (*pl.* **-oes**)
a soft fruit with a lot of juice and shiny red skin that is eaten as a vegetable either raw or cooked 番茄；西紅柿：*a bacon, lettuce and tomato sandwich* 熏肉生菜番茄三明治 ◇ *sliced tomatoes* 番茄片 ◇ *tomato plants* 番茄植株 ➲ VISUAL VOCAB page V31

tomb /tuːm/ *noun* a large grave, especially one built of stone above or below the ground 墳墓；塚

tom·bola /tɒmˈbəʊlə; *NAmE* tɑːmˈboʊlə/ *noun* [U, C] (*BrE*) a game in which you buy tickets with numbers on them. If the number on your ticket is the same as the number on one of the prizes, you win the prize. "翻筋斗" 賭戲（一種抽彩搖獎法）

tom·boy /ˈtɒmbɔɪ; *NAmE* ˈtɑːm-/ *noun* a young girl who enjoys activities and games that are traditionally considered to be for boys 假小子，野丫頭（喜歡男孩玩意兒的女孩子）

tomb·stone /ˈtuːmstəʊn; *NAmE* -stoʊn/ *noun* a large, flat stone that lies over a grave or stands at one end, that shows the name, age, etc. of the person buried there 墓碑 ➲ compare GRAVESTONE, HEADSTONE

tom·cat /ˈtɒmkæt; *NAmE* ˈtɑːm-/ (also **tom**) *noun* a male cat 公貓；雄貓

tome /təʊm; *NAmE* toʊm/ *noun* (*formal*) a large heavy book, especially one dealing with a serious topic（尤指嚴肅的）大部頭書，巨著

tom·fool /ˌtɒmˈfuːl; *NAmE* ˌtɑːm-/ *noun* (*old-fashioned*) a silly person 傻瓜；笨蛋 ▶ **tom·fool** *adj.* [only before noun]

tom·fool·ery /tɒmˈfuːləri; *NAmE* tɑːm-/ *noun* [U] (*old-fashioned*) silly behaviour 愚蠢的行為 SYN **foolishness**

Tommy /ˈtɒmi; *NAmE* ˈtɑːmi/ *noun* (*old use, informal*) a British soldier 英國兵

ˈtommy gun *noun* a type of SUB-MACHINE GUN 湯普森衝鋒槍

tommy·rot /ˈtɒmirɒt; *NAmE* ˈtɑːmirɑːt/ *noun* [U] (*old-fashioned*) nonsense 廢話；胡說

tom·og·raphy /təˈmɒɡrəfi; *NAmE* -ˈmɑːɡ-/ *noun* [U] a way of producing an image of the inside of the human body or a solid object using X-RAYS or ULTRASOUND 體層攝影（利用 X 射線和超聲波清楚顯示體內結構）

to·mor·row 0-w /təˈmɒrəʊ; *NAmE* təˈmɔːroʊ; -ˈmɑːr-/ *adv., noun*
■ ***adv.*** on or during the day after today 在明天；在明日：*I'm off now. See you tomorrow.* 我走了。明天見。◇ *She's leaving tomorrow.* 她明天就走了。◇ (*especially BrE*) *They arrive **a week tomorrow/tomorrow week*** (= after a week, starting from tomorrow). 他們將於從明天算起一星期後到達。IDM see JAM *n.*
■ ***noun*** [U] **1** 0-w the day after today 明天；明日：*Today is Tuesday, so tomorrow is Wednesday.* 今天是星期二，那麼明天就是星期三。◇ ***tomorrow afternoon/morning/night/evening*** 明天下午 / 上午 / 夜裏 / 晚上 ◇ *I'll see you **the day after tomorrow**.* 我們後天見。◇ *The announcement will appear in tomorrow's newspapers.* 這份通告將於明日見報。◇ *I want it done by tomorrow.* 我希望這件事在明天以前做好。**2** 0-w the future 未來；將來；來日：

Who knows what changes tomorrow may bring? 誰知道將來會有什麼變化？◇ *Tomorrow's workers will have to be more adaptable.* 未來的工人必須具有更強的適應性。
IDM **do sth as if/like there's no toˈmorrow** to do sth a lot or as though you do not care what effects it will have 不顧後果地一個勁…：*I ate as if there was no tomorrow.* 我狼吞虎嚥地吃着。◇ *She spends money like there's no tomorrow.* 她拚命花錢，就像過了今天沒有明天似的。

ˈtom-tom *noun* a tall narrow drum that you play with your hands 桶子鼓；咚咚鼓 ➲ VISUAL VOCAB page V35

ton 0-w /tʌn/ *noun*
1 0-w [C] (*pl.* **tons** or **ton**) a unit for measuring weight, in Britain 2 240 pounds (**long ton**) and in the US 2 000 pounds (**short ton**) 噸（英國為 2 240 磅，即長噸；美國為 2 000 磅，即短噸）：(*informal*) *What have you got in this bag? It weighs a ton!* 你這口袋裏裝的是什麼？重死了！➲ compare TONNE **2** [C] a unit for measuring the size of a ship. 1 ton is equal to 100 CUBIC feet. 註冊噸，噸位（船舶大小的計量單位，1 噸等於 100 立方英尺）**3 tons** [pl.] (*informal*) a lot 大量；許多：*They've got tons of money.* 他們腰纏萬貫。◇ *I've still got tons to do.* 我還有許多事要做。**4 a/the ton** (*BrE, informal*) 100, especially when connected with a speed of 100 miles per hour * 100；（尤指）每小時 100 英里的速度：*He was caught doing a ton.* 他被發現以每小時 100 英里的速度行車。
IDM **like a ton of ˈbricks** (*informal*) very heavily; very severely 非常沉重；極為嚴厲：*Disappointment hit her like a ton of bricks.* 她大失所望。◇ *They **came down on him like a ton of bricks*** (= criticized him very severely). 他們狠狠批評了他一頓。

tonal /ˈtəʊnl; *NAmE* ˈtoʊnl/ *adj.* **1** (*technical* 術語) relating to tones of sound or colour 音調的；聲調的；色調的 **2** (*music* 音) having a particular KEY 調性的 OPP **atonal** ▶ **tonal·ly** *adv.*

ton·al·ity /təʊˈnæləti; *NAmE* toʊ-/ *noun* [U, C] (*pl.* **-ies**) (*music* 音) the quality of a piece of music that depends on the KEY in which it is written 調性

tone 0-w /təʊn; *NAmE* toʊn/ *noun, verb*
■ ***noun***
▸ OF VOICE 腔調 **1** 0-w [C] the quality of sb's voice, especially expressing a particular emotion 語氣；口氣；腔調；口吻：*speaking in **hushed/low/clipped/measured, etc. tones*** 以壓低、低沉、短促、緩慢謹慎等的語調講話 ◇ *a conversational tone* 交談的語氣 ◇ *a tone of surprise* 驚奇的口氣 ◇ *Don't speak to me in that **tone of voice*** (= in that unpleasant way). 別用那種口吻跟我講話。◇ *There's no need to **take that tone** with me—it's not my fault we're late.* 不必那樣跟我拿腔拿調的。我們來晚了，可不是我的錯。
▸ CHARACTER/ATMOSPHERE 特徵；氣氛 **2** 0-w [sing.] the general character and attitude of sth such as a piece of writing, or the atmosphere of an event 風格；特色；氣氛；情調：*The overall tone of the book is gently nostalgic.* 這本書整體格調是溫情的懷舊。◇ *She **set the tone for** the meeting with a firm statement of company policy.* 她堅定地說明了公司的方針，為會議定下了調子。◇ *Trust you to **lower the tone** of the conversation* (= for example by telling a rude joke). 管保你會降低談話的格調（如講粗俗的笑話）。◇ *The article was moderate **in tone** and presented both sides of the case.* 這篇文章基調溫和，不偏不倚。
▸ OF SOUND 聲音 **3** 0-w [C] the quality of a sound, especially the sound of a musical instrument or one produced by electronic equipment（尤指樂器或電子音響設備的）音質，音色：*the full rich tone of the trumpet* 小號飽滿嘹亮的音色 ◇ *the volume and tone controls on a car stereo* 汽車立體聲系統音量和音質的控制裝置
▸ COLOUR 顏色 **4** [C] a shade of a colour 色調；明暗；影調：*a carpet in warm tones of brown and orange* 棕色和橘黃色的暖色調地毯
▸ OF MUSCLES/SKIN 肌肉；皮膚 **5** [U] how strong and firm your muscles or skin are（肌肉）結實度，健壯度；（皮膚）柔韌性：*how to improve your **muscle/skin tone*** 如何使肌肉發達 / 皮膚柔韌

T

▸ **ON TELEPHONE 電話** **6** [C] a sound heard on a telephone line（打電話時聽到的）聲音信號：(*BrE*) *the* ***dialling tone*** 撥號音 ◇ (*NAmE*) *the* ***dial tone*** 撥號音 ◇ *Please speak after the tone* (= for example as an instruction on an answering machine). 聽到信號後請講話。

▸ **IN MUSIC 音樂** **7** (*BrE*) (*US* **'whole step**) [C] one of the five longer INTERVALS in a musical SCALE, for example the INTERVAL between C and D or between E and F♯ 全音 ➲ compare SEMITONE, STEP *n.* (10)

▸ **PHONETICS 語音學** **8** [C] the PITCH (= how high or low a sound is) of a syllable in speaking（說話的）聲調，音調：*a* ***rising/falling tone*** 升調；降調 **9** a particular PITCH pattern on a syllable in languages such as Chinese, that can be used to distinguish different meanings（字的）聲調；字調

▸ **-TONED 有…音調** **10** (in adjectives 構成形容詞) having the type of tone mentioned 有…音調的（或音質的、色調的）：*a bright-toned soprano* 聲音嘹亮的女高音 ◇ *olive-toned skin* 黃褐色的皮膚

■ ***verb***

▸ **MUSCLES/SKIN 肌肉；皮膚** **1** [T] **~ sth (up)** to make your muscles, skin, etc. firmer and stronger 使更健壯；使更結實；使更有力：*Massage will help to tone up loose skin under the chin.* 按摩有助於使頦下鬆弛的皮膚柔韌起來。◇ *a beautifully toned body* 優美矯健的身體

▸ **COLOUR 顏色** **2** [I] **~ (in) (with sth)** (*BrE*) to match the colour of sth 與…協調；與…相配：*The beige of his jacket toned (in) with the cream shirt.* 他那夾克的米黃色與乳白色的襯衫非常協調。

PHR V **,tone sth↔'down** **1** to make a speech, an opinion, etc. less extreme or offensive 使（講話、意見等）緩和；使溫和：*The language of the article will have to be toned down for the mass market.* 這篇文章的措辭必須緩和一下以適合大眾市場。 **2** to make a colour less bright 使（顏色）柔和

,tone-'deaf *adj.* unable to hear the difference between musical notes 不能辨別音高的

'tone language *noun* a language in which differences in TONE *n.* (9) can change the meaning of words 聲調語言（聲調變化構成不同的語意）

tone·less /'təʊnləs; *NAmE* 'toʊn-/ *adj.* (of a voice, etc. 聲音等) dull or flat; not expressing any emotion or interest 單調的；呆板的；沉悶的 ▸ **tone·less·ly** *adv.*

'tone poem *noun* a piece of music that is intended to describe a place or express an idea 音詩（文學性的管弦樂曲）

toner /'təʊnə(r); *NAmE* 'toʊ-/ *noun* [U, C] **1** a type of ink used in machines that print or photocopy（打印機或複印機使用的）墨粉 **2** a liquid or cream used for making the skin on your face firm and smooth 護膚油；美容霜

T

'tone unit (also **'tone group**) *noun* (*phonetics* 語音) the basic unit of INTONATION in a language which consists of one or more syllables with a complete PITCH movement 語調單位（即有完整音高變化的一個或多個音節）

tongs /tɒŋz; *NAmE* tɔːŋz; tɑːŋz/ *noun* [pl.] **1** a tool with two long parts that are joined at one end, used for picking up and holding things 夾剪；夾具；鉗子；燒瓶鉗：*a pair of tongs* 一把夾剪 ➲ VISUAL VOCAB pages V26, V27, V70 **2** (also **'curling tongs**) (both *BrE*) (*NAmE* **curling iron**) a tool that is heated and used for curling hair 燙髮鉗；捲髮鉗 **IDM** see HAMMER *n.*

tongue 0━ /tʌŋ/ *noun, verb*

■ ***noun*** **1** 0━ [C] the soft part in the mouth that moves around, used for tasting, swallowing, speaking, etc. 舌；舌頭：*He clicked his tongue to attract their attention.* 他咂嘴發出嘖嘖聲以吸引他們的注意。◇ *She ran her tongue over her lips.* 她用舌頭舔着嘴唇。◇ *It's very rude to* ***stick your tongue out*** *at people.* 向別人吐舌頭是非常不禮貌的。 ➲ VISUAL VOCAB page V59 **2** [U, C] the tongue of some animals, cooked and eaten 口條：*a slice of ox tongue* 一片牛口條 **3** [C] (*formal* or *literary*) a language 語言：*None of the tribes speak the same tongue.* 這些部落所說的語言都不相同。◇ *I tried speaking to her in her native tongue.* 我試着用她的本族語和她說話。➲ see also MOTHER TONGUE **4** [sing.] a particular way of speaking 說話方式：*He has a sharp tongue.* 他說話尖酸刻薄。◇ (*formal*) *I'll thank you to* ***keep a civil tongue in your head*** (= speak politely). 請你說話講究禮貌。➲ see also SILVER TONGUE **5** **-tongued** (in adjectives 構成形容詞) speaking in the way mentioned 有…說話方式的；說話…的：*sharp-tongued* 說話尖刻的 **6** [C] a long narrow piece of leather under the LACES on a shoe 鞋舌 ➲ VISUAL VOCAB page V64 **7** [C] **~ (of sth)** (*literary*) something that is long and narrow and shaped like a tongue 舌狀物：*a tongue of flame* 火舌

IDM **get your 'tongue around/round sth** to pronounce a difficult word correctly 正確發出（難讀單詞）的音 **,hold your 'tongue/'peace** (*old-fashioned*) to say nothing although you would like to give your opinion 忍住不說；保持緘默 **roll/slip/trip off the 'tongue** to be easy to say or pronounce 容易說（或發音）；順口：*It's not a name that exactly trips off the tongue, is it?* 這個名字叫起來繞口，是不是？ **set 'tongues wagging** (*informal*) to cause people to start talking about sb's private affairs 惹得滿城風雨；使議論紛紛；招閒話 **with your tongue in your 'cheek | with tongue in 'cheek** if you say sth **with your tongue in your cheek**, you are not being serious and mean it as a joke 說說而已；半開玩笑地 ➲ more at BITE *v.*, FIND *v.*, LOOSE *adj.*, LOOSEN, SLIP *n.*, TIP *n.*, WATCH *v.*

■ ***verb*** **1 ~ sth** to stop the flow of air into a wind instrument with your tongue in order to make a note 吹奏（管樂器） **2 ~ sth** to LICK sth with your tongue 舔

,tongue and 'groove *noun* [U] wooden boards that have a long cut along one edge and a long RIDGE along the other, which are used to connect them together 企口接合板；舌槽接合板

'tongue depressor (*NAmE*) (*BrE* **spat·ula**) *noun* a thin flat instrument that doctors use for pressing the tongue down when they are examining sb's throat 壓舌板；壓舌器（醫生診症用）

,tongue-in-'cheek *adj.* not intended seriously; done or said as a joke 言不由衷的；隨便說說的；開玩笑的：*a tongue-in-cheek remark* 一句戲言 ▸ **,tongue-in-'cheek** *adv.*：*The offer was made almost tongue-in-cheek.* 這種提議差不多只是說說而已。

'tongue-tied *adj.* not able to speak because you are shy or nervous（因害羞或緊張）張口結舌的，說不出話來的

'tongue-twister *noun* a word or phrase that is difficult to say quickly or correctly, such as 'She sells sea shells on the seashore.' 繞口令

tonic /'tɒnɪk; *NAmE* 'tɑːn-/ *noun* **1** (also **'tonic water**) [U, C] a clear FIZZY drink (= with bubbles in it) with a slightly bitter taste, that is often mixed with a strong alcoholic drink, especially GIN or VODKA 奎寧水，湯力水（一種味微苦、常加於烈性酒中的有氣飲料）：*a gin and tonic* 一杯杜松子酒奎寧水 **2** [C] a medicine that makes you feel stronger and healthier, taken especially when you feel tired 補藥；滋補品：*herbal tonics* 滋補草藥 **3** [C, U] a liquid that you put on your hair or skin in order to make it healthier 護髮液；護膚液：*skin tonic* 護膚液 **4** [C, usually sing.] (*old-fashioned*) anything that makes people feel healthier or happier 使精神振奮的東西：*The weekend break was just the tonic I needed.* 週末休息正是我所需要的養精蓄銳的機會。 **5** [C] (*music* 音) the first note of a SCALE of eight notes 主音（自然音階中的第一音） **6** (also **,tonic 'syllable**) [C] (*phonetics* 語音) the syllable in a TONE UNIT on which a change in PITCH takes place 語調音節，語調核心（區別音高變化的音節）

,tonic ,sol-'fa *noun* = SOL-FA

ton·ify /'təʊnɪfaɪ; *NAmE* 'toʊn-/ *verb* (**toni·fies**, **toni·fy·ing**, **toni·fied**, **toni·fied**) **~ sth** to make a part of the body firmer, smoother and stronger, by exercise or by applying special creams, etc.（通過鍛煉或塗特殊的護膚霜等）提高肌肉張力

to·night 0━ /tə'naɪt/ *adv., noun*

■ ***adv.*** on or during the evening or night of today 在今夜；在今晚：*Will you have dinner with me tonight?* 今天晚上和我一起吃飯好嗎？◇ *It's cold tonight.* 今天晚上很冷。

■ ***noun*** [U] the evening or night of today 今夜；今晚：*Here are tonight's football results.* 現在報告今晚足球比賽的結果。◇ *Tonight will be cloudy.* 今天夜間多雲。

ton·nage /ˈtʌnɪdʒ/ *noun* [U, C] **1** the size of a ship or the amount it can carry, expressed in tons （表示船舶大小或載重量的）噸位 **2** the total amount that sth weighs （某物的）總重量

tonne 0-w /tʌn/ (*pl.* **tonnes** or **tonne**) (also ˌ**metric ˈton**) *noun* a unit for measuring weight, equal to 1 000 kilograms 公噸（等於 1 000 公斤）: *a record grain harvest of 236m tonnes* * 2.36 億公噸創紀錄的穀物收穫量 ◇ *a 17-tonne truck* * 17 噸卡車 ➲ compare TON (1)

ton·sil /ˈtɒnsl; *NAmE* ˈtɑːnsl/ *noun* either of the two small organs at the sides of the throat, near the base of the tongue 扁桃體: *I've had my tonsils out* (= removed). 我的扁桃體已被切除了。 ➲ VISUAL VOCAB page V59

ton·sil·lec·tomy /ˌtɒnsəˈlektəmi; *NAmE* ˌtɑːn-/ *noun* (*pl.* **-ies**) (*medical* 醫) a medical operation to remove the TONSILS 扁桃體切除術

ton·sil·litis /ˌtɒnsəˈlaɪtɪs; *NAmE* ˌtɑːn-/ *noun* [U] an infection of the tonsils in which they become swollen and sore 扁桃體炎

ton·sure /ˈtɒnʃə(r); *NAmE* ˈtɑːn-/ *noun* the part of a MONK's or priest's head that has been shaved （僧侶或教士的）頭頂剃光部位

Tony /ˈtəʊni; *NAmE* ˈtoʊni/ *noun* (*pl.* **Tonys**) an award given in the US for achievement in the theatre 托尼獎（美國的舞台劇成就獎）

tony /ˈtəʊni; *NAmE* ˈtoʊni/ *adj.* (*NAmE, informal*, becoming *old-fashioned*) fashionable and expensive 豪華的；時興而昂貴的

too 0-w /tuː/ *adv.*
1 0-w used before adjectives and adverbs to say that sth is more than is good, necessary, possible, etc. （用於形容詞和副詞前）太，過於，過度: *He's **far too** young to go on his own.* 他年紀太小，不能獨自一人去。 ◇ *This is too large a helping for me/This helping is too large for me.* 這一份太多，我吃不了。 ◇ *Is it too much to ask for a little quiet?* 請略微安靜一點兒，這個要求過分嗎？ ◇ *The dress was too tight for me.* 這件連衣裙我穿太窄了。 ◇ *It's too late to do anything about it now.* 現在進行任何補救都為時太晚。 ◇ *Accidents like this happen **all too*** (= much too) *often.* 這類事故發生得太頻繁了。 **2** 0-w (usually placed at the end of a clause 通常置於句末) also; as well 也；又；還: *Can I come too?* 我也可以來嗎？ ◇ *When I've finished painting the bathroom, I'm going to do the kitchen too.* 我油漆完浴室後，還要油漆廚房。 ➲ note at ALSO ➲ see also ME-TOO **3** used to comment on sth that makes a situation worse （評說某事物使情況更糟）而且，還: *She broke her leg last week—and on her birthday too!* 她上星期把腿摔斷了，而且還是在她生日那一天！ **4** 0-w very 很；非常: *I'm not too sure if this is right.* 這是否正確，我沒有太大把握。 ◇ *I'm just going out—I won't be too long.* 我正要出去，用不了多長時間。 ◇ *She's **none too*** (= not very) *clever.* 她不很聰明。 **5** used to emphasize sth, especially your anger, surprise or agreement with sth （用以強調生氣、驚奇或同意等）: *'He did apologize eventually.' 'I should think so too!'* "他終於道歉了。" "我想他應該如此！" ◇ *'She gave me the money.' 'About time too!'* "她把那錢給我了。" "早該這樣！"

IDM **be too ˈmuch (for sb)** 0-w to need more skill or strength than you have; to be more difficult, annoying, etc. than you can bear 非…力所能及；非…所能忍受 ➲ more at RIGHT *adj.*

took *past tense* of TAKE

tool 0-w /tuːl/ *noun, verb*
■ *noun* **1** 0-w an instrument such as a hammer, SCREWDRIVER, SAW, etc. that you hold in your hand and use for making things, repairing things, etc. 工具: *garden tools* 園藝工具 ◇ *a cutting tool* 切削工具 ◇ *power tools* (= using electricity) 電動工具 ◇ *Always select the right tool for the job.* 一定要選對幹活的工具。 ➲ VISUAL VOCAB page V20 **2** 0-w a thing that helps you to do your job or to achieve sth （有助於做工或完成某事的）用具，器具，手段，方法: *research tools like questionnaires* 問卷之類的研究方法 ◇ *The computer is now an invaluable tool for the family doctor.* 計算機現在是家庭醫生非常有用的工具。 ◇ *Some of them carried the guns which were **the tools of their trade*** (= the things they needed to do their job). 他們有些人攜帶着噴槍，那是幹他們那一行的器具。 **3** a person who is used or controlled by another person or group 受人利用的人；工具: *The prime minister was an unwitting tool of the president.* 首相不知不覺被總統利用了。 **4** (*taboo, slang*) a PENIS 雞巴；陰莖 IDM see DOWN *v.*
■ *verb* [I] + adv./prep. (*NAmE, informal*) to drive around in a vehicle 驅車兜風；駕車到處跑
PHR V ˌ**tool ˈup** | ˌ**tool sb/sth**↔ˈ**up** (*technical* 術語) to get or provide sb/sth with the equipment, etc. that is necessary to do or produce sth 獲得（或提供）必要的設備；給…配置裝備: *The factory is not tooled up to produce this type of engine.* 這家工廠還沒有裝置生產這類發動機的設備。

tool·bar /ˈtuːlbɑː(r)/ *noun* (*computing* 計) a row of symbols (= ICONS) on a computer screen that show the different things that you can do with a particular program （計算機屏幕上的）工具欄，工具列

tool·box /ˈtuːlbɒks; *NAmE* -bɑːks/ *noun* a box with a lid for keeping tools in 工具箱 ➲ VISUAL VOCAB page V20

tooled /tuːld/ *adj.* (of leather 皮革) decorated with patterns made with a special heated tool 熱燙花的；壓花的

tool·kit /ˈtuːlkɪt/ *noun* **1** a set of tools in a box or bag （裝在箱子或包裹的）一套工具；工具箱；工具包 **2** (*computing* 計) a set of software tools 配套軟件；軟件包；工具箱 **3** the things that you need in order to achieve sth 配備用品；裝備

tool·maker /ˈtuːlmeɪkə(r)/ *noun* a person or company that makes tools, especially ones used in industry （尤指工業用）工具製造者，工具製造廠 ▶ **tool·mak·ing** /ˈtuːlmeɪkɪŋ/ *noun* [U]

toonie /ˈtuːni/ *noun* (*CanE*) the Canadian two-dollar coin 兩加元硬幣

toot /tuːt/ *noun, verb*
■ *noun* a short high sound made by a car horn or a whistle （喇叭、哨子等發出的）嘟嘟聲: *She gave a sharp toot on her horn.* 她高聲按響了喇叭。
■ *verb* [I, T] (*especially BrE*) when a car horn **toots** or you **toot** it, it makes a short high sound （汽車喇叭）發出短促尖銳的聲音，發出嘟嘟聲: *the sound of horns tooting* 鳴喇叭的聲音 ◇ ~ **sth** *Toot your horn to let them know we're here.* 按按喇叭，告訴他們我們到了。
IDM see HORN *n.*

tooth 0-w /tuːθ/ *noun* (*pl.* **teeth** /tiːθ/)
1 0-w any of the hard white structures in the mouth used for biting and chewing food 牙；齒: *I've just **had a tooth out** at the dentist's.* 我剛在牙科診所拔了一顆牙。 ◇ *to **brush/clean your teeth*** 刷牙 ◇ ***tooth decay*** 齲齒 ◇ *She answered **through clenched teeth*** (= opening her mouth only a little because of anger). 她咬牙切齒地回答。 ◇ *The cat **sank its teeth into** his finger.* 那隻貓狠狠咬住了他的手指。 ➲ COLLOCATIONS at PHYSICAL ➲ VISUAL VOCAB page V59 ➲ see also BUCK TEETH, FALSE TEETH, MILK TOOTH, WISDOM TOOTH **2** a narrow pointed part that sticks out of an object 齒狀部份；齒: *the teeth on a saw* 鋸齒 ➲ VISUAL VOCAB page V63 ➲ see also FINE-TOOTH COMB

IDM **cut your teeth on sth** to do sth that gives you your first experience of a particular type of work 從…中獲得初步經驗；初次涉足 **cut a ˈtooth** (of a baby 嬰兒) to grow a new tooth 出牙；長出新牙 **get your ˈteeth into sth** (*informal*) to put a lot of effort and enthusiasm into sth that is difficult enough to keep you interested 專注於，全力投入（有一定難度的事）: *Choose an essay topic that you can really get your teeth into.* 選擇一個你可以真正悉心鑽研的論文題目。 **have ˈteeth** (*BrE, informal*) (of an organization, a law, etc. 組織、法律等) to be powerful and effective 具有強大威力；有殺傷力 **in the teeth of sth** **1** despite problems, opposition, etc. 不管，不顧，儘管遇到（困難、反對等）: *The new policy was adopted in the teeth of fierce criticism.* 新政策儘管受到強烈的批評，但還是被採用了。 **2** in the direction that a strong wind is coming from 頂着，迎着

T

（強風）：*They crossed the bay in the teeth of a howling gale.* 他們頂着呼嘯的狂風渡過了海灣。 **set sb's 'teeth on edge** (of a sound or taste 聲音或味道) to make sb feel physically uncomfortable 使感到身體不舒服：*Just the sound of her voice sets my teeth on edge.* 我一聽到她的聲音就渾身不舒服。➲ more at ARMED, BARE *v.*, BIT, EYE *n.*, EYE TEETH, FIGHT *v.*, GNASH, GRIT *v.*, HELL, KICK *v.*, KICK *n.*, LIE[2] *v.*, LONG *adj.*, RED *adj.*, SKIN *n.*, SWEET *adj.*

tooth·ache /ˈtuːθeɪk/ *noun* [U, C, usually sing.] a pain in your teeth or in one tooth 牙痛：(*BrE*) *I've got toothache.* 我牙疼。◇ (*NAmE, BrE*) *I've got a toothache.* 我牙疼。

tooth·brush /ˈtuːθbrʌʃ/ *noun* a small brush for cleaning your teeth 牙刷 ➲ VISUAL VOCAB page V24

toothbrush mous'tache *noun* a short MOUSTACHE cut with square corners（理成方形的）牙刷鬍子

toothed /tuːθt; tuːðd/ *adj.* [only before noun] **1** (*technical* 術語) having teeth 有齒的：*a toothed whale* 齒鯨 **2 -toothed** (in compounds 構成複合詞) having the type of teeth mentioned 有…齒的：*a gap-toothed smile* 露出稀疏的牙齒咧着嘴笑

the 'tooth fairy *noun* [sing.] an imaginary creature that is said to take away a tooth that a small child leaves near his or her bed at night and to leave a coin there in its place 牙仙子（傳說會取去幼兒脫落並放於牀邊的乳齒，在原處留下一枚錢幣）

tooth·less /ˈtuːθləs/ *adj.* **1** having no teeth 無牙的；無齒的：*a toothless old man* 沒牙的老頭 ◇ *She gave us a toothless grin.* 她張開沒牙的嘴巴對我們笑了笑。**2** having no power or authority 人微言輕的；沒有權威的；不起作用的

tooth·paste /ˈtuːθpeɪst/ *noun* [U] a substance that you put on a brush and use to clean your teeth 牙膏 ➲ VISUAL VOCAB page V24

tooth·pick /ˈtuːθpɪk/ *noun* a short pointed piece of wood or plastic used for removing bits of food from between the teeth 牙籤

tooth·some /ˈtuːθsəm/ *adj.* (*humorous*) (of food 食物) tasting good 美味的；可口的 SYN tasty

toothy /ˈtuːθi/ *adj.* a **toothy** smile shows a lot of teeth（笑時）露齒的，多齒的

too·tle /ˈtuːtl/ *verb* (*informal*) **1** [I] + *adv./prep.* to walk, drive, etc. somewhere without hurrying 信步；閒逛；遛達；不慌不忙地開車 **2** [I, T] ~ (**sth**) to produce a series of notes by blowing into a musical instrument 吹奏（樂器）

toot·sies /ˈtʊtsɪz/ *noun* [pl.] (*informal*) (used by or when speaking to young children 兒語) toes or feet 腳趾；腳

T

top 0→ /tɒp; *NAmE* tɑːp/ *noun, adj., verb*

■ *noun*

▸ HIGHEST POINT 最高點 **1** 0→ [C] the highest part or point of sth 頂；頂部；頂端：*She was standing* ***at the top*** *of the stairs.* 她站在樓梯的頂端。◇ *Write your name at the top.* 把你的姓名寫在上端。◇ *The title is* ***right at the top*** *of the page.* 標題就在頁面的頂端。◇ *He filled my glass* ***to the top.*** 他把我的杯子斟得滿滿的。◇ *We climbed to the* ***very top*** *of the hill.* 我們爬到了山的最高點。◇ *Snow was falling on the mountain tops.* 山頂上正在下雪。◇ (*BrE*) *the top of the milk* (= the cream that rises to the top of a bottle of milk) 牛奶表面的奶皮 ◇ *The wind was blowing in the tops of the trees.* 風兒吹拂着樹梢。➲ see also ROOFTOP, TREETOP

▸ UPPER SURFACE 上層表面 **2** 0→ [C] the upper flat surface of sth 表面；上面：*Can you polish the top of the table?* 請把桌面擦亮好嗎？◇ *a desk top* 桌面 ➲ see also HARDTOP, ROLL-TOP DESK, TABLETOP

▸ HIGHEST RANK 最高等級 **3** 0→ [sing.] **the ~ (of sth)** the highest or most important rank or position 最高的級別；最重要的職位：*He's at the top of his profession.* 他正處於事業的巔峰。◇ *She is determined to make it to the top* (= achieve fame or success). 她決心要出人頭地。◇ *They finished the season at the top of the league.* 他們打完這個賽季之後積分高居聯賽的榜首。◇ *We have a lot of things to do, but packing is at the* ***top of the list.*** 我們有許多事情要做，但首先是打點行裝。◇ *This decision came from the top.* 這個決定是由最高領導作出的。

▸ FARTHEST POINT 最遠點 **4** 0→ [sing.] **the ~ of sth** the end of a street, table, etc. that is farthest away from you or from where you usually come to it 盡頭；遠端：*I'll meet you at the top of Thorpe Street.* 我會和你在索普大街的盡頭碰面。

▸ OF PEN/BOTTLE 筆；瓶子 **5** 0→ [C] a thing that you put on the end of sth to close it 帽；蓋；塞：*Where's the top of this pen?* 這支筆的筆帽在哪兒？◇ *a bottle with a screw top* 帶螺旋蓋兒的瓶子 ➲ SYNONYMS at LID ➲ VISUAL VOCAB page V33

▸ CLOTHING 衣服 **6** 0→ [C] a piece of clothing worn on the upper part of the body 上衣：*I need a top to go with this skirt.* 我需要一件上衣來配這條裙子。◇ *a* ***tracksuit/pyjama/bikini top*** 運動服上衣；睡衣／比基尼泳裝的上部 ➲ see also CROP TOP

▸ LEAVES OF PLANT 植物的葉子 **7** [C, usually pl.] the leaves of a plant that is grown mainly for its root（根菜作物的）莖葉：*Remove the green tops from the carrots.* 去掉胡蘿蔔的綠葉。

▸ AMOUNT OF MONEY 款額 **8 tops** [pl.] (*BrE*) used after an amount of money to show that it is the highest possible（用於款額後）最高額：*It couldn't have cost more than £50, tops.* 這東西的價格最高不會超過 50 英鎊。

▸ BEST 最好 **9 tops** [pl.] (*old-fashioned, informal*) a person or thing of the best quality 最優秀的人；最好的東西；精華：*Among sports superstars she's (the) tops.* 她在超級體育明星中獨佔鰲頭。◇ *In the survey the Brits come out tops for humour.* 這項調查顯示，英國人的幽默是首屈一指的。

▸ TOY 玩具 **10** [C] a child's toy that spins on a point when it is turned round very quickly by hand or by a string 陀螺：*She was so confused—her mind was* ***spinning like a top.*** 她如墜五里霧中，被搞得暈頭轉向。➲ see also BIG TOP

IDM **at the top of the 'tree** in the highest position or rank in a profession or career（在行業、事業中）高居首位，處於頂峰 **at the top of your 'voice** as loudly as possible 高聲地；放聲地；扯着喉嚨地：*She was screaming at the top of her voice.* 她在聲嘶力竭地尖叫。 **come out on 'top** to win a contest or an argument（在比賽或辯論中）名列前茅，先拔頭籌：*In most boardroom disputes he tends to come out on top.* 在大多數董事會議的辯論中，他往往佔據上風。 **from ˌtop to 'bottom** going to every part of a place in a very thorough way 從上到下；徹底地：*We cleaned the house from top to bottom.* 我們把房子徹底打掃了一遍。 **from ˌtop to 'toe** completely; all over 從頭到腳；渾身上下；全部：*She was dressed in green from top to toe.* 她從頭到腳穿了一身綠。 **get on 'top of sb** to be too much for sb to manage or deal with 使吃不消；使應接不暇：*All this extra work is getting on top of him.* 這麼多的額外工作快使他吃不消了。 **get on 'top of sth** to manage to control or deal with sth 設法駕馭；處理：*How will I ever get on top of all this work?* 我究竟怎樣才處理得了這麼多的工作？ **off the ˌtop of your 'head** (*informal*) just guessing or using your memory, without taking time to think carefully or check the facts 單憑猜測（或記憶）；信口地；不假思索地：*I can't remember the name off the top of my head, but I can look it up for you.* 我一時想不起這個名字，不過我可以給你查一查。 **on 'top 1** 0→ on the highest point or surface 在上面；在頂部：*a cake with cream on top* 上面澆有奶油的蛋糕 ◇ *Stand on top and look down.* 站在頂上俯視。◇ *He's going bald on top* (= on the top of his head). 他歇頂了。**2** in a leading position or in control 處於領先地位；控制局面：*She remained on top for the rest of the match.* 在比賽的餘下部份她一直領先。**3** in addition 另外；加之：*Look, here's 30 dollars, and I'll buy you lunch on top.* 瞧，這是給你的 30 塊錢，另外我還要給你買午餐。 **on top of sth/sb 1** 0→ on, over or covering sth/sb 在…上面；在…上方；覆蓋着：*Books were piled on top of one another.* 書籍一本一本地摞在一起。◇ *Many people were crushed when the building collapsed on top of them.* 那座樓房倒塌時砸傷了下面許多人。**2** 0→ in addition to sth 除…之外：*He gets commission on top of his salary.* 他除了薪金之外還拿佣金。◇ *On top of everything else,* *my car's been stolen.* 我所有的東西都被盜，連汽車也給偷走了。 **3** very close to sth/sb 緊挨着；與…緊靠着：*We were all living on top of each other in that tiny apartment.* 我們都擠着住在那套小小的公寓裏。 **4** in control of a situation 控制着；掌握着：*Do you think he's really on top of his job?* 你認為他真的能做好他的工作嗎？ **on ˌtop of the ˈworld** very happy or proud 歡天喜地；心滿意足；非常自豪 **ˌover the ˈtop** (*abbr.* OTT) (*informal, especially BrE*) done to an exaggerated degree and with too much effort 過分；過火；過頭：*His performance is completely over the top.* 他的表演完全過火了。◇ *an over-the-top reaction* 過頭的反應 **ˌtake sth from the ˈtop** (*informal*) to go back to the beginning of a song, piece of music, etc. and repeat it 從頭再唱（或再奏等）：*OK, everybody, let's take it from the top.* 好，咱們大家從頭再唱一遍。 **up ˈtop** (*BrE, informal*) used to talk about a person's intelligence（指人的智力）頭腦，腦子：*He hasn't got much up top* (= he isn't very intelligent). 他沒有多少腦子。➲ more at BLOW *v.*, HEAP *n.*, PILE *n.*, THIN *adj.*

■ ***adj.*** [usually before noun] **1** 🔑 highest in position, rank or degree（位置、級別或程度）最高的：*He lives on the top floor.* 他住在頂層。◇ *She kept her passport in the top drawer.* 她把護照存放在最上層抽屜裏。◇ *He's one of the top players in the country.* 他是國內最優秀的運動員之一。◇ *She got the top job.* 她得到了那個最高職位。◇ *He finished top in the exam.* 他考試得了第一名。◇ *She got top marks for her essay.* 她的論文得了最高分。◇ *They're top of the league.* 他們是聯賽的領頭羊。◇ *The athletes are all on top form* (= performing their best). 運動員都處於最佳競技狀態。◇ *Welfare reform is a top priority for the government.* 福利改革是政府的當務之急。◇ *The car was travelling at top speed.* 那輛汽車全速行駛。 **2** (*BrE, informal*) very good 很好的；極棒的；頂呱呱的：*He's a top bloke.* 他是個大好人。

■ ***verb*** (**-pp-**)

▸ **BE MORE** 多出 **1 ~ sth** to be higher than a particular amount 高於，超過（某一數量）：*Worldwide sales look set to top $1 billion.* 全球銷售額看來很可能要超過 10 億元。

▸ **BE THE BEST** 是最好 **2 ~ sth** to be in the highest position on a list because you are the most successful, important, etc. 居…之首；為…之冠：*The band topped the charts for five weeks with their first single.* 這支樂隊的第一張單曲唱片有五個星期高居最暢銷流行音樂唱片榜首。

▸ **PUT ON TOP** 置於頂端 **3** [usually passive] **~ sth (with sth)** to put sth on the top of sth else 把（某物）放在…的上面：*fruit salad topped with cream* 上面澆了奶油的水果色拉

▸ **SAY/DO STH BETTER** 說／做得更好 **4 ~ sth** to say or do sth that is better, funnier, more impressive, etc. than sth that sb else has said or done in the past 勝過，優於，壓倒（前人所做）：*I'm afraid the other company has topped your offer* (= offered more money). 很抱歉，另一家公司出價比你們高。

▸ **KILL YOURSELF** 自殺 **5 ~ yourself** (*BrE, informal*) to kill yourself deliberately 自殺

▸ **CLIMB HILL** 爬山 **6 ~ sth** (*literary*) to reach the highest point of a hill, etc. 到達山頂；達到頂端

IDM **to top/cap it ˈall** (*informal*) used to introduce the final piece of information that is worse than the other bad things that you have just mentioned 更有甚者；最糟糕的是 **ˌtop and ˈtail sth** (*BrE*) to cut the top and bottom parts off fruit and vegetables to prepare them to be cooked or eaten 去掉（水果、蔬菜）的兩端；砍掉…的兩頭

PHR V **ˌtop sth↔ˈoff (with sth)** to complete sth successfully by doing or adding one final thing 以…圓滿結束；用…完成 **ˌtop ˈout (at sth)** if sth **tops out** at a particular price, speed, etc. it does not rise any higher（價格、速度等）達到頂點，到最高點：*Inflation topped out at 12%.* 通貨膨脹達到了 12% 這個最高點。 **ˌtop sth↔ˈup** (*especially BrE*) **1** to fill a container that already has some liquid in it with more liquid 裝滿，注滿（未滿的容器）：*Top the car up with oil before you set off.* 出發前給車加滿油。◇ *Top the oil up before you set off.* 出發前加滿油。 **2** to increase the amount of sth to the level you want or need 補足；將…增加到所需的量：*She relies on tips to top up her wages.* 她靠小費彌補工資的不足。◇ (*BrE*) *I need to top up my mobile phone* (= pay more money so you can make more calls). 我需要給手機充值。➲ related noun TOP-UP (1) **ˌtop sb ˈup** (*especially BrE*) to fill sb's glass or cup with sth more to drink 給…的杯子斟滿（飲料）：*Can I top you up?* 把你的杯子加滿好嗎？➲ related noun TOP-UP (2)

topaz /ˈtəʊpæz; *NAmE* ˈtoʊ-/ *noun* [C, U] a clear yellow SEMI-PRECIOUS stone 黃玉：*a topaz ring* 黃玉戒指

ˌtop ˈbrass *noun* [sing.+sing./pl. v.] (*BrE, informal*) = BRASS (5)

ˌtop-ˈclass *adj.* of the highest quality or standard 頭等的；第一流的；頂級的：*a top-class performance* 頂級的表演

top·coat /ˈtɒpkəʊt; *NAmE* ˈtɑːpkoʊt/ *noun* **1** the last layer of paint put on a surface（油漆等的）外塗層 ➲ compare UNDERCOAT **2** (*old-fashioned*) an OVERCOAT 大衣

ˌtop ˈdog *noun* [usually sing.] (*informal*) a person, group or country that is better than all the others, especially in a situation that involves competition（尤指競爭中的）奪魁者，優勝者

ˌtop ˈdollar *noun*

IDM **pay, earn, charge, etc. top ˈdollar** (*informal*) pay, earn, charge, etc. a lot of money 支付（或賺得、收取等）一大筆錢：*If you want the best, you have to pay top dollar.* 你想要最好的，就得花大錢。◇ *We can help you get top dollar when you sell your house.* 您賣房子我們能幫您賣個好價錢。

ˌtop-ˈdown *adj.* **1** (of a plan, project, etc. 計劃、項目等) starting with a general idea to which details are added later 從總體到具體的；自上而下的；先總後分的 ➲ compare BOTTOM-UP **2** starting from or involving the people who have higher positions in an organization（組織或機構中）自上而下的，與高層有關的：*a top-down management style* 自上而下的管理方式

ˌtop ˈdrawer *noun* [sing.] if sb/sth is out of **the top drawer**, they are of the highest social class or of the highest quality（社會地位的）最上層，最高層；精華 ▸ **ˌtop-ˈdrawer** *adj.*

topee = TOPI

ˌtop-ˈend *adj.* [only before noun] among the best, most expensive, etc. examples of sth 最高檔的；最昂貴級的；最高級的：*Many people are upgrading their mobiles to top-end models.* 很多人不斷將手機升級到最高端的款式。

ˌtop-ˈflight *adj.* of the highest quality; the best or most successful 第一流的；最高檔的；最佳的；最成功的

ˌtop ˈgear *noun* [U] (*BrE*) the highest gear in a vehicle（車輛變速器的）最高擋：*They cruised along **in top gear**.* 他們駕車高速行駛。◇ (*figurative*) *Her career is moving into top gear.* 她的事業正如日中天。

ˌtop-ˈgrossing *adj.* [only before noun] earning more money than other similar things or people 賺錢最多的；收入最高的：*the top-grossing movie of 2009* * 2009 年票房收入最高的影片

ˌtop ˈhat (also *informal* **top·per**) *noun* a man's tall black or grey hat, worn with formal clothes on very formal occasions 高頂禮帽 ➲ VISUAL VOCAB page V65

ˌtop-ˈheavy *adj.* **1** too heavy at the top and therefore likely to fall 上部過重的；頭重腳輕的 **2** (of an organization 組織) having too many senior staff compared to the number of workers 高級職員過多的；將多兵少的

ˌtop-ˈhole *adj.* (*old-fashioned, BrE, informal*) excellent 極好的；很棒的

topi (also **topee**) /ˈtəʊpi; *NAmE* ˈtoʊpi; toʊˈpiː/ *noun* a light hard hat worn to give protection from the sun in very hot countries 遮陽帽；通草帽

topi·ary /ˈtəʊpiəri; *NAmE* ˈtoʊpieri/ *noun* [U] the art of cutting bushes into shapes such as birds or animals 林木造型藝術；綠雕塑術

topic 🔑 **AW** /ˈtɒpɪk; *NAmE* ˈtɑːp-/ *noun* a subject that you talk, write or learn about 話題；題目；標題：*The main **topic of conversation** was Tom's new girlfriend.* 交談的主要話題是湯姆的新女友。◇ *The*

T

article covered a wide range of topics. 這篇文章討論了一系列廣泛的論題。

IDM **on topic** (*NAmE*) appropriate or relevant to the situation 切題：*Keep the text short and on topic.* 文章要簡短切題。◇ *Let's get back on topic.* 我們回到正題上來吧。

top·ic·al **AW** /ˈtɒpɪkl; *NAmE* ˈtɑːp-/ *adj.* **1** connected with sth that is happening or of interest at the present time 有關時事的；當前關注的；熱門話題的：*a topical joke/reference* 時事笑話；提及熱門話題 ◇ *topical events* 當前人們所關注的事件 **2** (*medical* 醫) connected with, or put directly on, a part of the body（身體）局部的，表面的 ▸ **top·ic·al·ity** /ˌtɒpɪˈkæləti; *NAmE* ˌtɑːp-/ *noun* [U, sing.]

top·knot /ˈtɒpnɒt; *NAmE* ˈtɑːpnɑːt/ *noun* a way of arranging your hair in which it is tied up on the top of your head 頂髻

top·less /ˈtɒpləs; *NAmE* ˈtɑːp-/ *adj.* (of a woman 女人) not wearing any clothes on the upper part of the body so that her breasts are not covered 上身裸露的；不穿上裝的：*a topless model* 上身裸露的模特兒 ◇ *a topless bar* (= where the female staff are topless) 女招待不穿上裝的酒吧 ▸ **top·less** *adv.*：*to sunbathe topless* 裸露着上身沐日光浴

ˌtop-ˈlevel *adj.* [only before noun] involving the most important or best people in a company, an organization or a sport（公司、機構或某項運動中）最重要的，最優秀的：*a top-level meeting* 最高級會談 ◇ *top-level tennis* 頂級網球比賽

top·most /ˈtɒpməʊst; *NAmE* ˈtɑːpmoʊst/ *adj.* [only before noun] (*formal*) highest 最高的；最上面的：*the topmost branches of the tree* 樹頂的枝丫

ˌtop-ˈnotch *adj.* (*informal*) excellent; of the highest quality 最好的；卓越的；第一流的

ˌtop of the ˈrange (*BrE*) (*NAmE* **ˌtop of the ˈline**) *adj.* [usually before noun] used to describe the most expensive of a group of similar products（同類產品中）最昂貴的，最高價的：*Our equipment is top of the range.* 我們的設備是最昂貴的。◇ *our top-of-the-range model* 我們最昂貴的產品型號

top·og·raphy /təˈpɒɡrəfi; *NAmE* təˈpɑːɡ-/ *noun* [U] (*technical* 術語) the physical features of an area of land, especially the position of its rivers, mountains, etc.; the study of these features 地形；地貌；地勢；地形學：*a map showing the topography of the island* 這個島的地形圖 ▸ **topo·graph·ic·al** /ˌtɒpəˈɡræfɪkl; *NAmE* ˌtɑːpə-/ (also **topo·graph·ic** /ˌtɒpəˈɡræfɪk; *NAmE* ˌtɑːpə-/) *adj.*：*a topographical map/feature* 地形圖；地貌特徵 **topo·graph·ic·al·ly** /-kli/ *adv.*

top·ology /təˈpɒlədʒi; *NAmE* -ˈpɑːl-/ *noun* [U, C] (*technical* 術語) the way the parts of sth are arranged and related（事物的）結構，構相：*The Canadian banking topology is relatively flat, with a few large banks controlling the entire market.* 加拿大銀行業結構相對簡單，由幾家大銀行控制着整個市場。

topo·nym /ˈtɒpənɪm; *NAmE* ˈtɑːp-/ *noun* (*technical* 術語) a place name 地名

topos /ˈtɒpɒs; *NAmE* ˈtoʊpɑːs; ˈtɑːp-/ *noun* (*pl.* **topoi** /ˈtɒpɔɪ; *NAmE* ˈtoʊ-; ˈtɑː-/) (*technical* 術語) a traditional subject or idea in literature（文學的）傳統主題，傳統觀念

top·per /ˈtɒpə(r); *NAmE* ˈtɑːp-/ *noun* (*informal*) = TOP HAT

top·ping /ˈtɒpɪŋ; *NAmE* ˈtɑːp-/ *noun* [C, U] a layer of food that you put on top of a dish, cake, etc. to add flavour or to make it look nice（菜肴、蛋糕等上的）澆汁，澆料，配料，佐料

top·ple /ˈtɒpl; *NAmE* ˈtɑːpl/ *verb* **1** [I, T] to become unsteady and fall down; to make sth do this（使）失去平衡而墜落，倒塌，倒下：**+ adv./prep.** *The pile of books toppled over.* 那一摞書倒了。◇ **~ sb/sth + adv./prep.** *He brushed past, toppling her from her stool.* 他經過時蹭了她一下，使她從凳子上摔了下來。**2** [T] **~ sb/sth** to make sb lose their position of power or authority 打倒；推翻；顛覆 **SYN** **overthrow**：*a plot to topple the President* 推翻總統的陰謀

ˌtop-ˈranking *adj.* [only before noun] of the highest rank, status or importance in an organization, a sport, etc.（組織、運動等中）最高級的，最重要的

ˌtop-ˈrated *adj.* [only before noun] most popular with the public 最受歡迎的；一流的：*a top-rated TV show* 最受歡迎的電視節目

top·sail /ˈtɒpseɪl; ˈtɒpsl; *NAmE* ˈtɑːpseɪl; ˈtɑːpsl/ *noun* [usually sing.] the sail attached to the upper part of the MAST of a ship 上桅帆

ˌtop ˈsecret *adj.* that must be kept completely secret, especially from other governments（尤指對他國政府）最高機密的，絕密的：*This information has been classified top secret.* 這一情報被歸為絕密類別。◇ *top-secret documents* 絕密文件

ˌtop-ˈshelf *adj.* [only before noun] **1** (*BrE*) including pictures of naked people and/or sexual acts 含色情內容的：*top-shelf magazines/DVDs* 色情雜誌／影碟 **2** (*especially NAmE*) of the highest class 一流的：*It is a top-shelf law firm.* 那是一家頂級律師事務所。

top·side /ˈtɒpsaɪd; *NAmE* ˈtɑːp-/ *noun* [U] (*BrE*) a piece of beef that is cut from the upper part of the leg 牛上股肉

top·soil /ˈtɒpsɔɪl; *NAmE* ˈtɑːp-/ *noun* [U] the layer of soil nearest the surface of the ground 表土；表土層 ➲ compare SUBSOIL

top·spin /ˈtɒpspɪn; *NAmE* tɑːp-/ *noun* [U] (*sport* 體) the fast forward spinning movement that a player can give to a ball by hitting or throwing it in a special way（球的）上旋

topsy-turvy /ˌtɒpsi ˈtɜːvi; *NAmE* ˌtɑːpsi ˈtɜːrvi/ *adj.* (*informal*) in a state of great confusion 亂七八糟的；雜亂無章的；顛三倒四的：*Everything's topsy-turvy in my life at the moment.* 現在我的生活全都被打亂了。

ˌtop ˈtable (*BrE*) (*NAmE* **ˌhead ˈtable**) *noun* the table at which the most important guests sit at a formal dinner（正式宴會上的）主桌

the ˌtop ˈten *noun* [pl.] the ten pop records that have sold the most copies in a particular week（某星期）流行音樂十大暢銷唱片

ˈtop-up *noun* (*BrE*) **1** a payment that you make to increase the amount of money, etc. to the level that is needed 附加付款：*a phone top-up* (= to buy more time for calls) 電話充值費 ◇ *Students will have to pay top-up fees* (= fees that are above the basic level). 學生必須交附加費用。**2** (*informal*) an amount of a drink that you add to a cup or glass in order to fill it again（重新斟滿杯子的）補充飲料：*Can I give anyone a top-up?* 我來給哪位添酒好嗎？

ˈtop-up card *noun* a card that you buy for a mobile/cell phone so that you can make more calls to the value of the card 手機充值卡

toque /təʊk; *NAmE* toʊk/ *noun* **1** a woman's small hat 托克小女帽；無邊女帽 **2** (*CanE*) a close-fitting hat made of wool, sometimes with a ball of wool on the top 絨線保暖帽，絨線無邊帽（有時頂部飾絨球）

tor /tɔː(r)/ *noun* a small hill with rocks at the top, especially in parts of SW England（尤指英格蘭西南部的）突岩

Torah /ˈtɔːrɑː; tɔːˈrɑː/ *noun* (usually **the Torah**) (in Judaism 猶太教) the law of God as given to Moses and recorded in the first five books of the Bible 托拉，律法書，梅瑟五書，摩西五經（《聖經》中的首五卷）

torch /tɔːtʃ; *NAmE* tɔːrtʃ/ *noun, verb*

■ *noun* **1** (*BrE*) (also **flash·light** *NAmE, BrE*) a small electric lamp that uses batteries and that you can hold in your hand 手電筒：*Shine the torch on the lock while I try to get the key in.* 我插鑰匙時，請用手電筒照着鎖頭。**2** (*NAmE*) = BLOWTORCH **3** a long piece of wood that has material at one end that is set on fire and that people carry to give light 火炬；火把：*a flaming torch* 燃燒着的火炬 ◇ *the Olympic torch* 奧林匹克火炬 ◇ (*figurative*) *They struggled to keep the torch of idealism and hope alive.* 他們為使理想主義和希望的火炬不熄滅而奮鬥。

IDM **put sth to the ˈtorch** (*literary*) to set fire to sth deliberately 將…付之一炬 ➲ more at CARRY

■ ***verb*** **~ sth** to set fire to a building or vehicle deliberately in order to destroy it 放火燒，縱火燒（建築物或汽車）

torch·light /ˈtɔːtʃlaɪt; *NAmE* ˈtɔːrtʃ-/ *noun* [U] the light that is produced by an electric torch or by burning torches 手電筒光；火炬的光亮

ˈ**torch song** *noun* a type of sad romantic song about feelings of love for a person who does not share those feelings 單戀情歌；情殤曲；失戀情歌 ▸ ˈ**torch singer** *noun*

tore *past tense* of TEAR

torea·dor /ˈtɒriədɔː(r); *NAmE* ˈtɔːr-/ *noun* a man, especially one riding a horse, who fights BULLS to entertain people, for example in Spain （西班牙等地、尤指騎馬的）鬥牛士

tor·ment *noun, verb*

■ ***noun*** /ˈtɔːment; *NAmE* ˈtɔːrm-/ [U, C] (*formal*) extreme suffering, especially mental suffering; a person or thing that causes this （尤指精神上的）折磨，痛苦；苦難之源 **SYN** **anguish**：*the cries of a man* ***in torment*** 一個備受折磨的人的喊叫聲 ◇ *She suffered years of mental torment after her son's death.* 兒子去世後，她多年悲痛欲絕。◇ *The flies were a terrible torment.* 蒼蠅一度肆虐。

■ ***verb*** /tɔːˈment; *NAmE* tɔːrˈm-/ **1 ~ sb** (*formal*) to make sb suffer very much 使備受折磨；使痛苦；煩擾 **SYN** **plague**：*He was tormented by feelings of insecurity.* 他苦於沒有安全感。 **2 ~ sb/sth** to annoy a person or an animal in a cruel way because you think it is amusing 戲弄；捉弄；糾纏 **SYN** **torture**

tor·ment·or /tɔːˈmentə(r); *NAmE* tɔːrˈm-/ *noun* (*formal*) a person who causes sb to suffer 折磨人的人；折磨者

torn *past part.* of TEAR

tor·nado /tɔːˈneɪdəʊ; *NAmE* tɔːrˈneɪdoʊ/ *noun* (*pl.* **-oes** or **-os**) a violent storm with very strong winds which move in a circle. There is often also a long cloud which is narrower at the bottom than the top. 龍捲風；旋風 ➲ **COLLOCATIONS** at WEATHER

tor·pedo /tɔːˈpiːdəʊ; *NAmE* tɔːrˈpiːdoʊ/ *noun, verb*

■ ***noun*** (*pl.* **-oes**) a long narrow bomb that is fired under the water from a ship or SUBMARINE and that explodes when it hits a ship, etc. 魚雷

■ ***verb*** (**tor·pe·does**, **tor·pe·do·ing**, **tor·pe·doed**, **tor·pe·doed**) **1 ~ sth** to attack a ship or make it sink using a torpedo 用魚雷襲擊（或擊沉） **2 ~ sth** to completely destroy the possibility that sth could succeed 徹底破壞，完全摧毀（某事成功的可能性）：*Her comments had torpedoed the deal.* 她的一番話使得那筆交易徹底告吹。

tor·pid /ˈtɔːpɪd; *NAmE* ˈtɔːrpɪd/ *adj.* (*formal*) not active; with no energy or enthusiasm 不活潑的；遲鈍的；有氣無力的；懶散的 **SYN** **lethargic**

tor·por /ˈtɔːpə(r); *NAmE* ˈtɔːrp-/ *noun* [U, sing.] (*formal*) the state of not being active and having no energy or enthusiasm 遲鈍；死氣沉沉；懶散 **SYN** **lethargy**：*In the heat they sank into a state of torpor.* 炎熱的天氣使得他們委靡不振。

torque /tɔːk; *NAmE* tɔːrk/ *noun* [U] (*technical* 術語) a twisting force that causes machinery, etc. to ROTATE (= turn around) （使機器等旋轉的）轉矩

tor·rent /ˈtɒrənt; *NAmE* ˈtɔːr-; ˈtɑːr-/ *noun* **1** a large amount of water moving very quickly 急流；激流；湍流；洪流：*After the winter rains, the stream becomes a* ***raging torrent****.* 冬雨過後，溪流湍急。◇ *The rain was coming down* ***in torrents****.* 大雨如注。 **2** a large amount of sth that comes suddenly and violently 迸發；連發；狂潮 **SYN** **deluge**：*a torrent of abuse/criticism* 連珠炮似的謾罵 / 批評 ◇ *a torrent of words* 滔滔不絕的話語

tor·ren·tial /təˈrenʃl/ *adj.* (of rain 雨) falling in large amounts 傾瀉的；如注的

tor·rid /ˈtɒrɪd; *NAmE* ˈtɔːr-; ˈtɑːr-/ *adj.* [usually before noun] **1** full of strong emotions, especially connected with sex and love （尤指情愛）熱烈的，狂熱的，熱情洋溢的 **SYN** **passionate**：*a torrid love affair* 狂熱的戀情 **2** (*formal*) (of a climate or country 氣候或國家) very hot or dry 炎熱而乾燥的；酷熱的；灼熱的：*a torrid summer* 酷熱的夏季 **3** (*BrE*) very difficult 艱難的：*They face a torrid time in tonight's game.* 他們在今晚的比賽中面臨一場惡戰。

ˈ**torrid zone** *noun* [sing.] (*technical* 術語) an area of the earth near the EQUATOR 熱帶 **SYN** **the tropics**

tor·sion /ˈtɔːʃn; *NAmE* ˈtɔːrʃn/ *noun* [U] (*technical* 術語) twisting, especially of one end of sth while the other end is held fixed （物體等一端固定的）扭轉

torso /ˈtɔːsəʊ; *NAmE* ˈtɔːrsoʊ/ *noun* (*pl.* **-os**) **1** the main part of the body, not including the head, arms or legs （身體的）軀幹 **SYN** **trunk** **2** a statue of a torso 軀幹雕像

tort /tɔːt; *NAmE* tɔːrt/ *noun* [C, U] (*law* 律) something wrong that sb does to sb else that is not criminal, but that can lead to action in a CIVIL court 侵權行為（不構成刑事犯罪但可引起民事訴訟）

torte /ˈtɔːtə; tɔːt; *NAmE* ˈtɔːrtə; tɔːrt/ *noun* [C, U] a large cake filled with a mixture of cream, chocolate, fruit, etc. 奶油巧克力水果大蛋糕

tor·tilla /tɔːˈtiːə; *NAmE* tɔːrˈt-/ *noun* (from *Spanish*) **1** a thin Mexican PANCAKE made with CORN (MAIZE) flour or WHEAT flour, usually eaten hot and filled with meat, cheese, etc. 墨西哥薄餡餅（用玉米麵或白麵製成，通常加肉、奶酪等為餡，熱食） **2** a Spanish dish made with eggs and potatoes fried together 西班牙土豆炒雞蛋

torˈtilla chip *noun* a small flat hard piece of food, often shaped like a triangle, made from CORN (MAIZE) 脆玉米片（通常為三角形）

tor·toise /ˈtɔːtəs; *NAmE* ˈtɔːrtəs/ *noun* a REPTILE with a hard round shell, that lives on land and moves very slowly. It can pull its head and legs into its shell. 陸龜；龜 ➲ **VISUAL VOCAB** page V13 ➲ compare TERRAPIN, TURTLE (2)

tor·toise·shell /ˈtɔːtəsʃel; ˈtɔːtəʃel; *NAmE* ˈtɔːrt-/ *noun* **1** [U] the hard shell of a TURTLE, especially the type with orange and brown marks, used for making COMBS and small decorative objects 龜甲；龜板；玳瑁殼 **2** (*NAmE* also ˈ**calico cat**) [C] a cat with black, brown, orange and white fur （毛色為黃褐黑白相間的）家貓 **3** [C] a BUTTERFLY with orange and brown marks on its wings （翅膀帶黃褐色斑點的）蛺蝶

tor·tu·ous /ˈtɔːtʃuəs; *NAmE* ˈtɔːrtʃ-/ *adj.* [usually before noun] (*formal*) **1** (usually *disapproving*) not simple and direct; long, complicated and difficult to understand 拐彎抹角的；含混不清的；冗長費解的 **SYN** **convoluted**：*tortuous language* 含混不清的語言 ◇ *the long, tortuous process of negotiating peace* 漫長而曲折的和平談判過程 **2** (of a road, path, etc. 道路、小路等) full of bends 彎彎曲曲的；逶迤的；蜿蜒的 **SYN** **winding** ▸ **tor·tu·ous·ly** *adv.*

tor·ture /ˈtɔːtʃə(r); *NAmE* ˈtɔːrtʃ-/ *noun, verb*

■ ***noun*** [U, C] **1** the act of causing sb severe pain in order to punish them or make them say or do sth 拷打；拷問；酷刑：*Many of the refugees have suffered torture.* 許多難民都遭受過拷打。◇ *the use of torture* 施酷刑 ◇ *terrible instruments of torture* 可怕的刑訊工具 ◇ *His confessions were made* ***under torture****.* 他被屈打成招。◇ *I heard stories of gruesome tortures in prisons.* 我聽說過監獄裏令人毛骨悚然的刑訊。 **2** (*informal*) mental or physical suffering; sth that causes this （精神上或肉體上的）折磨，痛苦；折磨人的事物：*The interview was sheer torture from start to finish.* 這次面試從頭至尾使人備受煎熬。

■ ***verb*** [often passive] **1** to hurt sb physically or mentally in order to punish them or make them tell you sth 拷打；拷問；嚴刑逼供：**~ sb** *Many of the rebels were captured and tortured by secret police.* 反叛者中許多人被捕並遭受到秘密警察的酷刑。◇ **~ sb into doing sth** *He was tortured into giving them the information.* 他受不住酷刑被迫向他們供出了情報。 **2 ~ sb** to make sb feel extremely unhappy or anxious 使痛苦；使苦惱；使焦急；使受煎熬 **SYN** **torment**：*He spent his life tortured* *by the memories of his childhood.* 童年的記憶使他痛苦了一輩子。 ▸ **tor·turer** /ˈtɔːtʃərə(r); *NAmE* ˈtɔːrtʃ-/ *noun*

tor·tured /ˈtɔːtʃəd; *NAmE* ˈtɔːrtʃərd/ *adj.* [only before noun] suffering severely; involving a lot of suffering and difficulty 遭受重創的；飽受煎熬的： *a tortured mind* 飽受煎熬的心靈

Tory /ˈtɔːri/ *noun* (*pl.* **-ies**) (*informal*) a member or supporter of the British Conservative party 英國保守黨黨員（或支持者）： *The Tories* (= the Tory party) *lost the election.* 英國保守黨在選舉中失敗。 ▸ **Tory** *adj.* [usually before noun]： *the Tory party* 英國保守黨 ◇ *Tory policies* 英國保守黨的政策 **Tory·ism** *noun* [U]

tosa /ˈtəʊsə; *NAmE* ˈtoʊ-/ *noun* a large strong dog originally kept for fighting 土佐鬥犬

tosh /tɒʃ; *NAmE* tɑːʃ/ *noun* [U] (*old-fashioned, BrE, slang*) nonsense 胡說；廢話 SYN **rubbish**

toss /tɒs; *NAmE* tɔːs; tɑːs/ *verb, noun*

■ *verb*

▸ THROW 扔 **1** [T] to throw sth lightly or carelessly（輕輕或漫不經心地）扔，拋，擲： **~ sth + adv./prep.** *I tossed the book aside and got up.* 我把書丟在一邊，站了起來。 ◇ **~ sth to sb** *He tossed the ball to Anna.* 他把球拋給了安娜。 ◇ **~ sb sth** *He tossed Anna the ball.* 他把球拋給了安娜。 ➲ SYNONYMS at THROW

▸ YOUR HEAD 頭 **2** [T] **~ sth** to move your head suddenly upwards, especially to show that you are annoyed or impatient 甩（頭，以表示惱怒或不耐煩）： *She just tossed her head and walked off.* 她頭一甩，走開了。

▸ SIDE TO SIDE/UP AND DOWN 左右；上下 **3** [I, T] to move or make sb/sth move from side to side or up and down（使）搖擺，揮動，顛簸： *Branches were tossing in the wind.* 樹枝隨風搖曳。 ◇ *I couldn't sleep but kept **tossing and turning** in bed all night.* 我徹夜在牀上輾轉反側不能成眠。 ◇ **~ sb/sth** *Our boat was being tossed by the huge waves.* 我們的船隨着巨浪顛簸。

▸ IN COOKING 烹調 **4** [T] **~ sth** to shake or turn food in order to cover it with oil, butter, etc. 搖勻；翻動（以沾油、奶酪等）： *Drain the pasta and toss it in melted butter.* 把麪條的湯控乾，在溶化了的黃油裏攪拌。 **5** [T] **~ a pancake** (*BrE*) to throw a PANCAKE upwards so that it turns over in the air and you can fry the other side 把（煎餅）顛起翻面

▸ COIN 硬幣 **6** [T, I] to throw a coin in the air in order to decide sth, especially by guessing which side is facing upwards when it lands（為…）擲硬幣決定；擲幣猜邊兒 SYN **flip** ： **~ sth** *Let's **toss a coin**.* 咱們擲硬幣猜邊兒決定吧。 ◇ (*especially BrE*) **~ (sb) for sth** *There's only one ticket left—I'll toss you for it.* 只剩一張票，我來與你擲幣決定給誰。 ◇ (*BrE*) **~ up (for sth)** *We tossed up to see who went first.* 我們擲硬幣決定誰先去。 ◇ (*BrE*) **~ up between A and B** (*figurative*) *He had to toss up between* (= decide between) *paying the rent or buying food.* 他不得不在付房租和買食品之間作出決定。 ➲ related noun TOSS-UP

PHR V **ˌtoss ˈoff | ˌtoss sb/yourself ˈoff** (*BrE, taboo, slang*) to give yourself sexual pleasure by rubbing your sex organs; to give sb sexual pleasure by rubbing their sex organs 手淫；對某人行手淫 SYN **masturbate** **ˌtoss sth↔ˈoff** (*BrE*) to produce sth quickly and without much thought or effort 未經思索（或費力）很快做好

■ *noun* [usually sing.]

▸ OF COIN 硬幣 **1** an act of throwing a coin in the air in order to decide sth 擲硬幣決定： *The final result was decided **on/by the toss of a coin**.* 最後的結果是擲硬幣決定的。 ◇ ***to win/lose the toss*** (= to guess correctly/wrongly which side of a coin will face upwards when it lands on the ground after it has been thrown in the air) 猜中／猜錯所擲硬幣朝上的一面

▸ OF HEAD 頭 **2 ~ of your head** an act of moving your head suddenly upwards, especially to show that you are annoyed or impatient 向上甩頭，猛仰頭（尤指表示惱怒或不耐煩）： *She dismissed the question with a toss of her head.* 她一揚頭，對這一問題不予理睬。

▸ THROW 扔 **3** an act of throwing sth, especially in a competition or game（尤指比賽或遊戲中）投擲： *a toss of 10 metres* * 10 米遠的投擲

IDM **not give a ˈtoss (about sb/sth)** (*BrE, slang*) to not care at all about sb/sth 毫不介意；滿不在乎 ➲ more at ARGUE

toss·er /ˈtɒsə(r); *NAmE* ˈtɔːs-; ˈtɑːs-/ *noun* (*BrE, slang*) a stupid or unpleasant person 蠢貨；傻蛋；討厭鬼

toss·pot /ˈtɒspɒt; *NAmE* ˈtɔːspɑːt; ˈtɑːspɑːt/ *noun* (*BrE, slang*) an offensive word for an unpleasant or stupid person（含冒犯意）討厭鬼，蠢貨

ˈtoss-up *noun* [sing.] (*informal*) a situation in which either of two choices, results, etc. is equally possible（兩種選擇、結果等的）同樣可能，均等機會： *'Have you decided on the colour yet?' '**It's a toss-up** between the blue and the green.'* "你決定了要什麼顏色沒有？" "在藍色和綠色之間實在難以割捨。"

tot /tɒt; *NAmE* tɑːt/ *noun, verb*

■ *noun* **1** (*informal*) a very young child 幼兒 **2** (*especially BrE*) a small amount of a strong alcoholic drink in a glass 小杯烈酒

■ *verb* (**-tt-**)

PHR V **ˌtot sth↔ˈup** (*informal, especially BrE*) to add together several numbers or amounts in order to calculate the total 把…加起來；計算…的總和 SYN **add up**

total 0→ /ˈtəʊtl; *NAmE* ˈtoʊtl/ *adj., noun, verb*

■ *adj.* [usually before noun] **1** 0→ being the amount or number after everyone or everything is counted or added together 總的；總計的；全體的；全部的： *the total profit* 利潤總額 ◇ *This brought the total number of accidents so far this year to 113.* 這使得今年迄今為止發生事故的總數達到 113 起。 ◇ *The club has a total membership of 300.* 這家俱樂部的成員總數為 300 人。 **2** 0→ including everything 徹底的；完全的 SYN **complete** ： *The room was in total darkness.* 房間裏一片漆黑。 ◇ *They wanted a total ban on handguns.* 他們要求徹底禁止擁有手槍。 ◇ *The evening was a total disaster.* 晚會徹底搞砸了。 ◇ *I can't believe you'd tell a total stranger about it!* 我不能相信你會把這事告訴一個素昧平生的人！

■ *noun* the amount you get when you add several numbers or amounts together; the final number of people or things when they have all been counted 總數；總額；合計；總計： *You got 47 points on the written examination and 18 on the oral, making a total of 65.* 你筆試得了 47 分，口試得了 18 分，總分 65 分。 ◇ *His businesses are worth a combined total of $3 billion.* 他的企業加在一起總值 30 億元。 ◇ *Out of a total of 15 games, they only won 2.* 在總共 15 場比賽中，他們只勝了 2 場。 ◇ *The repairs came to over £500 **in total*** (= including everything). 修理費總共 500 多英鎊。 ➲ see also GRAND TOTAL, RUNNING TOTAL, SUM TOTAL

■ *verb* (**-ll-**, *US* also **-l-**) **1 ~ sth** to reach a particular total 總數達；共計： *Imports totalled $1.5 billion last year.* 去年的進口總額達 15 億元。 **2 ~ sth/sb (up)** to add up the numbers of sth/sb and get a total 把…加起來；計算…的總和： *Each student's points were totalled and entered in a list.* 每個學生的總分都已計算出來並列入表中。 **3 ~ sth** (*informal, especially NAmE*) to damage a car very badly, so that it is not worth repairing it 徹底毀壞（汽車） ➲ see also WRITE STH OFF (2) at WRITE

to·tali·tar·ian /təʊˌtæləˈteəriən; *NAmE* toʊˌtæləˈter-/ *adj.* (*disapproving*) (of a country or system of government 國家或政府體制) in which there is only one political party that has complete power and control over the people 極權主義的 ▸ **to·tali·tar·ian·ism** /-ɪzəm/ *noun* [U]

to·tal·ity /təʊˈtæləti; *NAmE* toʊ-/ *noun* [C, U] (*formal*) the state of being complete or whole; the whole number or amount 全體；全部；整個；總數；總額： *The seriousness of the situation is difficult to appreciate **in its totality**.* 很難從全局上理解局勢的嚴重性。

to·tal·iza·tor (*BrE* also **-isa·tor**) /ˈtəʊtəlaɪzeɪtə(r); *NAmE* ˈtoʊt-/ (also **to·tal·izer**, **-iser** /ˈtəʊtəlaɪzə(r); *NAmE* ˈtoʊt-/) *noun* a device for showing the number and amount of bets put on a race 賭金數額顯示器（用於賽馬等）

to·tal·ly 0→ /ˈtəʊtəli; *NAmE* ˈtoʊ-/ *adv.* completely 完全；全部地；整個地： *They come from totally different cultures.* 他們來自完全不同的文化。 ◇ *I'm still not totally convinced that he knows what he's doing.* 我仍然不完全相信他明白自己在幹什麼。 ◇ *This behaviour is totally unacceptable.* 這種行為是完全不能接受的。 ◇

T

(*informal, especially NAmE*) 'She's so cute!' 'Totally!' (= I agree) "她真是精明過人！" "一點不錯！" ◇ (*informal*) *It's a totally awesome experience.* 這是個棒極了的經歷。

,total ,quality 'management *noun* [U] (*abbr.* **TQM**) a system of management that considers that every employee in an organization is responsible for keeping the highest standards in every aspect of the company's work 全面質量管理，全面品質管理（認為機構中每個雇員都有責任在各方面按最高標準工作的管理體系）

tote /təʊt; *NAmE* toʊt/ *noun, verb*

■ ***noun*** **1** (also **the Tote**) [sing.] a system of betting on horses in which the total amount of money that is bet on each race is divided among the people who bet on the winners（賽馬的）賭金計算系統 **2** (also **'tote bag**) [C] (*NAmE*) a large bag for carrying things with you 大手提袋；大提包

■ ***verb*** **1 ~ sth** (*informal, especially NAmE*) to carry sth, especially sth heavy 攜帶，搬運（尤指重物）：*We arrived, toting our bags and suitcases.* 我們背着提包拎着衣箱到了那裏。 **2 -toting** (in adjectives 構成形容詞) carrying the thing mentioned 攜帶…的：*gun-toting soldiers* 持槍的士兵

totem /'təʊtəm; *NAmE* 'toʊ-/ *noun* an animal or other natural object that is chosen and respected as a special symbol of a community or family, especially among Native Americans; an image of this animal, etc.（尤指美洲土著的）圖騰；圖騰形象 ▸ **to·tem·ic** /təʊ'temɪk; *NAmE* toʊ-/ *adj.*：*totemic animals* 圖騰動物

'totem pole *noun* **1** a tall wooden pole that has symbols and pictures (called TOTEMS) CARVED or painted on it, traditionally made by Native Americans 圖騰柱 **2** (*NAmE, informal*) a range of different levels in an organization, etc.（機構等內的）等級，級別：*I didn't want to be* ***low man on the totem pole*** *for ever.* 我不想永遠當小人物。

t'other /'tʌðə(r)/ *adj., pron.* (*BrE, dialect*) the other（兩者中的）另一個；其餘的：*I saw it t'other day.* 幾天前我見過它。◇ *They were talking of this, that and t'other.* 他們談這，談那，無所不談。

toto ➲ IN TOTO

tot·ter /'tɒtə(r); *NAmE* 'tɑːt-/ *verb* **1** [I] (**+ adv./prep.**) to walk or move with weak unsteady steps, especially because you are drunk or ill/sick 蹣跚；踉蹌；跌跌撞撞 SYN **stagger** **2** [I] to be weak and seem likely to fall 搖搖欲墜；搖搖晃晃：*the tottering walls of the castle* 古城堡搖搖欲墜的牆壁 ◇ (*figurative*) *a tottering dictatorship* 瀕臨瓦解的獨裁統治

totty /'tɒti; *NAmE* 'tɑːti/ *noun* [U] (*BrE, slang*) sexually attractive women (an expression used by men, and usually offensive to women) 騷貨；浪貨

tou·can /'tuːkæn/ *noun* a tropical American bird that is black with some areas of very bright feathers, and that has a very large beak 鵎鵼，巨嘴鳥（分佈於美洲熱帶地區，羽毛鮮豔，喙很大）

touch 🔑 /tʌtʃ/ *verb, noun*

■ ***verb***

▸ **WITH HAND/PART OF BODY** 用手或身體部位 **1** 🔑 [T] **~ sb/sth** to put your hand or another part of your body onto sb/sth 觸摸；碰：*Don't touch that plate—it's hot!* 別碰那個盤子，燙手！◇ *Can you touch your toes?* (= bend and reach them with your hands) 你彎腰夠得着你的腳趾麼？◇ *I touched him lightly on the arm.* 我輕輕碰了碰他的手臂。◇ *He has hardly touched the ball all game.* 他整場比賽幾乎沒摸到過球。◇ (*figurative*) *I must do some more work on that article—I haven't touched it all week.* 我還得在那篇文章上再下點兒工夫，我整整一個星期沒有碰它了。

▸ **NO SPACE BETWEEN** 無間隙 **2** 🔑 [I, T] (of two or more things, surfaces, etc. 兩個或以上的東西、表面等) to be or come so close together that there is no space between 接觸；觸及：*Make sure the wires don't touch.* 一定不要讓金屬線搭在一起。◇ **~ sth** *Don't let your coat touch the wet paint.* 你的外衣別蹭着還沒有乾的油漆。◇ *His coat was so long it was almost touching the floor.* 他的大衣太長，差不多拖到地上了。

▸ **MOVE STH/HIT SB** 移動東西；打人 **3** 🔑 [T] (often in negative sentences 常用於否定句) **~ sth/sb** to move sth, especially in such a way that you damage it; to hit or harm sb 移動；碰到；打（人）；使受傷：*I told you not to touch my things.* 我告訴過你不要動我的東西。◇ *He said I kicked him, but I never touched him!* 他說我踢他了，可是我從來就沒碰過他！

▸ **AFFECT SB/STH** 影響某人／某事物 **4** 🔑 [T] **~ sb/sth** (**to do sth**) to make sb feel upset or sympathetic 感動；觸動；使同情：*Her story touched us all deeply.* 她的故事使我們大家深受感動。 **5** [T] **~ sb/sth** (*old-fashioned* or *formal*) to affect or concern sb/sth 影響；與…有關：*These are issues that touch us all.* 這些問題與我們大家都有關係。

▸ **EAT/DRINK/USE** 吃；喝；用 **6** [T] (usually in negative sentences 通常用於否定句) **~ sth** to eat, drink or use sth 吃；喝；使用：*You've hardly touched your food.* 你沒怎麼吃東西啊。◇ *He hasn't touched the money his aunt left him.* 他還沒動過他姑媽留給他的錢。

▸ **EQUAL SB** 與…等同 **7** [T] (usually in negative sentences 通常用於否定句) **~ sb** to be as good as sb in skill, quality, etc. 與…媲美；比得上；抵得過：*No one can touch him when it comes to interior design.* 在室內設計方面，沒有人能比得上他。

▸ **REACH LEVEL** 達到水平 **8** [T] **~ sth** to reach a particular level, etc. 達到（某一水平等）：*The speedometer was touching 90.* 速度表顯示時速達 90 英里。

▸ **BE INVOLVED WITH** 被牽涉 **9** [T] **~ sth/sb** to become connected with or work with a situation or person 與…有關；從事；與…共事：*Everything she touches turns to disaster.* 什麼事她一插手就會糟糕。◇ *His last two movies have been complete flops and now no studio will touch him.* 他的前兩部電影徹底失敗了，現在沒有製片廠願意用他。

▸ **OF SMILE** 微笑 **10** [T] **~ sth** to be seen on sb's face for a short time（在臉上）閃現，掠過：*A smile touched the corners of his mouth.* 他的嘴角閃現出一絲笑意。

IDM **be touched with sth** to have a small amount of a particular quality 略微帶點兒；輕微呈現：*His hair was touched with grey.* 他的頭髮有些斑白。 **not touch sb/sth with a 'bargepole** (*BrE*) (*NAmE* **not touch sb/sth with a ten-foot 'pole**) (*informal*) to refuse to get involved with sb/sth or in a particular situation 決不與…有任何牽扯；拒不牽扯到…中去 **touch 'base (with sb)** (*informal*) to make contact with sb again 再次聯繫 **touch 'bottom** **1** to reach the ground at the bottom of an area of water 觸到水底 **2** (*BrE*) to reach the worst possible state or condition 到最壞境況；到最低點；跌到谷底 **,touch 'wood** (*BrE*) (*NAmE* **,knock on 'wood**) (*saying*) used when you have just mentioned some way in which you have been lucky in the past, to avoid bringing bad luck（表示希望繼續走好運）：*I've been driving for over 20 years and never had an accident—touch wood!* 我開車 20 多年從來沒出過車禍，但願好運常在！ ➲ more at CHORD, FORELOCK, HAIR, NERVE *n.*, RAW *n.*

PHR V **,touch 'down** **1** (of a plane, SPACECRAFT, etc. 飛機、航天器等) to make contact with the ground as it lands 着陸；降落：(*figurative*) *Tornadoes touched down in Alabama and Louisiana.* 龍捲風在亞拉巴馬州和路易斯安那州登陸了。 ➲ related noun TOUCHDOWN (1) **2** (in RUGBY 橄欖球) to score a TRY by putting the ball on the ground behind the other team's goal line（在對方球門線後）持球觸地得分，底線得分 ➲ related noun TOUCHDOWN (2) **'touch sb for sth** (*informal*) to persuade sb to give or lend you sth, especially money 向…要，勸說…借給（尤指錢） **,touch sth↔'off** to make sth begin, especially a difficult or violent situation 觸發，引發，引起（困難或暴力的局面） **'touch on/upon sth** to mention or deal with a subject in only a few words, without going into detail 談及；提及：*In his speech he was only able to touch on a few aspects of the problem.* 他在演講中只能涉及這個問題的幾個方面。 **,touch sb↔'up** (*BrE, informal*) to touch sb sexually, usually in a way that is not expected or welcome（常指強行猥褻地）觸摸 SYN **grope** **,touch sth↔'up** to improve sth by changing or adding to it slightly（稍加）修飾，潤色，修改：*She was busy touching up her make-up in the mirror.* 她正忙着對着鏡子補妝。

T

■ *noun*

▸ **SENSE 感覺 1** [U] the sense that enables you to be aware of things and what they are like when you put your hands and fingers on them 觸覺；觸感：*the sense of touch* 觸覺

▸ **WITH HAND/PART OF BODY 用手或身體部位 2** [C, usually sing.] an act of putting your hand or another part of your body onto sb/sth 觸摸；觸；碰：*The gentle touch of his hand on her shoulder made her jump.* 他的手輕輕地觸了一下她肩膀便使她跳了起來。◇ *All this information is readily available **at the touch of a button*** (= by simply pressing a button). 這麼多的資料一按鍵便可毫不費力地查到。◇ *This type of engraving requires a delicate touch.* 這種雕刻要求手法輕巧。

▸ **WAY STH FEELS 給人的感覺 3** [sing.] the way that sth feels when you put your hand or fingers on it or when it comes into contact with your body 觸摸時的感覺：*The body was cold **to the touch**.* 這具屍體摸上去是冰冷的。◇ *material with a smooth silky touch* 摸起來光滑得像絲綢一樣的料子 ◇ *He could not bear the touch of clothing on his sunburnt skin.* 他忍受不住衣服磨蹭他那被太陽灼傷的皮膚。

▸ **SMALL DETAIL 細節 4** [C] a small detail that is added to sth in order to improve it or make it complete 修飾；潤色；裝點：*I spent the morning **putting the finishing touches to** the report.* 我花了一個上午為這個報告做最後的潤色。◇ *Meeting them at the airport was a nice touch.* 到機場迎接他們是一個妙着。

▸ **WAY OF DOING STH 辦事方法 5** [sing.] a way or style of doing sth 作風；風格；手法：*She prefers to answer any fan mail herself for a more personal touch.* 她喜歡針對每一位崇拜者的來信，親自予以回覆。◇ *Computer graphics will give your presentation the professional touch.* 計算機繪圖將會使你的演示具有專業特色。◇ *He couldn't find his magic touch with the ball today* (= he didn't play well). 他今天施展不出神奇的運球技巧。◇ *This meal is awful. I think I'm **losing my touch*** (= my ability to do sth). 這頓飯太難吃了。我想我的烹調技藝在走下坡路。

▸ **SMALL AMOUNT 微量 6** [C, usually sing.] **~ of sth** a very small amount 一點兒；少許 SYN **trace**：*There was a touch of sarcasm in her voice.* 她的話音中有點兒譏諷的意味。

▸ **SLIGHTLY 輕微 7 a touch** [sing.] slightly; a little 輕微；稍許：*The music was a touch too loud for my liking.* 這音樂有點太吵，不合我的口味。

▸ **IN FOOTBALL/RUGBY 足球；橄欖球 8** [U] the area outside the lines that mark the sides of the playing field 邊線以外的區域：*He kicked the ball into touch.* 他把球踢出了邊線。

IDM **be, get, keep, etc. in 'touch (with sb)** to communicate with sb, especially by writing to them or telephoning them（與…）有（或進行、保持等）聯繫：*Are you still in touch with your friends from college?* 你和大學的同學還有聯繫嗎？◇ *Thanks for showing us your products—we'll be in touch.* 謝謝給我們介紹你們的產品，我們將會保持聯繫。◇ *I'm trying to get in touch with Jane. Do you have her number?* 我正在設法和簡取得聯繫。你有她的電話號碼嗎？◇ *Let's keep in touch.* 咱們保持聯繫。◇ *I'll put you in touch with someone in your area.* 我將安排你和你那個地區的一個人進行聯繫。 **be, keep, etc. in 'touch (with sth)** to know what is happening in a particular subject or area 瞭解（某課題或領域的情況）：*It is important to keep in touch with the latest research.* 及時掌握最新研究情況很重要。 **be out of 'touch (with sb)** to no longer communicate with sb, so that you no longer know what is happening to them 失去聯繫；不再瞭解（某人的）情況 **be, become, etc. out of 'touch (with sth)** to not know or understand what is happening in a particular subject or area 不再瞭解，不懂得（某課題或領域）的情況：*Unfortunately, the people making the decisions are out of touch with the real world.* 令人遺憾的是，制訂決策的人不瞭解實情。 **an easy/a soft 'touch** (*informal*) a person that you can easily persuade to do sth, especially to give you money（尤指在錢財方面）有求必應的人，耳根子軟的人：*Unfortunately, my father is no soft touch.* 可惜，我父親並非有求必應。 **lose 'touch (with sb/sth) 1** to no longer have any contact with sb/sth 失去聯繫：*I've lost touch with all my old friends.* 我與所有的老朋友都失去了聯繫。 **2** to no longer understand sth, especially how ordinary people feel 不再瞭解（尤指一般人的想法）➲ more at COMMON *adj.*, KICK *v.*, LIGHT *adj.*

,touch-and-'go *adj.* [not usually before noun] (*informal*) used to say that the result of a situation is uncertain and that there is a possibility that sth bad or unpleasant will happen 不確定；無把握；很難說；吉凶未卜：*She's fine now, but it was touch-and-go for a while* (= there was a possibility that she might die). 她現在好了，可是她曾一度病危。

touch·down /ˈtʌtʃdaʊn/ *noun* **1** [C, U] the moment when a plane or SPACECRAFT lands（飛機或宇宙飛船的）着陸，降落，接地 SYN **landing 2** [C] (in RUGBY 橄欖球) an act of scoring points by putting the ball down on the area of ground behind the other team's GOAL LINE（在對方球門線後）持球觸地 **3** [C] (in AMERICAN FOOTBALL 美式足球) an act of scoring points by crossing the other team's GOAL LINE while carrying the ball, or receiving the ball when you are over the other team's GOAL LINE 持球越過對方球門線；在對方球門線上接球

tou·ché /ˈtuːʃeɪ; *NAmE* tuːˈʃeɪ/ *exclamation* (from *French*) used during an argument or a discussion to show that you accept that sb has answered your comment in a clever way and has gained an advantage by making a good point（承認對方言之有理，答話切中要害）一針見血，一語破的

touched /tʌtʃt/ *adj.* [not before noun] **1** feeling happy and grateful because of sth kind that sb has done; feeling emotional about sth 感激；受感動；激動：**~ (by sth)** *She was touched by their warm welcome.* 她對他們的熱烈歡迎十分感動。◇ *She was touched by the plight of the refugees.* 難民的困境使她受到觸動。◇ **~ (that ...)** *I was touched that he still remembered me.* 他仍然記得我，使我十分感動。 **2** (*old-fashioned, informal*) slightly crazy 神經兮兮；瘋瘋癲癲

,touch 'football *noun* [U] (*NAmE*) a type of AMERICAN FOOTBALL in which touching is used instead of TACKLING 觸身式橄欖球（利用身體接觸而不是擒抱的美式足球）➲ compare FLAG FOOTBALL

touch·ing /ˈtʌtʃɪŋ/ *adj.* causing feelings of pity or sympathy; making you feel emotional 令人同情的；感人的；動人的 SYN **moving**：*It was a touching story that moved many of us to tears.* 那是一個讓我們許多人落淚的動人故事。▸ **touch·ing·ly** *adv.*

'touch judge *noun* (in RUGBY 橄欖球) a LINESMAN 邊線裁判員；巡邊員；司線員

touch·line /ˈtʌtʃlaɪn/ *noun* a line that marks the side of the playing field in football (SOCCER), RUGBY, etc.（足球、橄欖球等場地的）邊線

'touch pad *noun* (*computing* 計) a device which you touch in different places in order to operate a program（操作程序的）觸摸板，觸控板

touch·paper /ˈtʌtʃpeɪpə(r)/ *noun* a piece of paper that burns slowly, that you light in order to start a FIREWORK burning（焰火的）火硝紙，導火紙

'touch screen *noun* (*computing* 計) a computer screen which allows you to give instructions to the computer by touching areas on it（計算機）觸摸屏，觸控式螢幕

touch·stone /ˈtʌtʃstəʊn; *NAmE* -stoʊn/ *noun* [usually sing.] **~ (of/for sth)** (*formal*) something that provides a standard against which other things are compared and/or judged 試金石；檢驗標準：*the touchstone for quality* 檢驗質量的標準

'Touch-Tone™ *adj.* (of a telephone or telephone system 電話或電話系統) producing different sounds when different numbers are pushed 塔奇通按鈕式撥號的

'touch-type *verb* [I] to type without having to look at the keys of a TYPEWRITER or keyboard（不看鍵盤）按指法打字；盲打

'touch-up *noun* a quick improvement made to the appearance or condition of sth 潤色；修飾；裝點：*My lipstick needed a touch-up.* 我的口紅需要補一下。

touchy /ˈtʌtʃi/ *adj.* (**touch·ier**, **touchi·est**) **1** [not usually before noun] **~ (about sth)** (of a person 人) easily upset or offended 易煩惱；易生氣；易怒 **SYN** **sensitive**：*He's a little touchy about his weight.* 他有點忌諱別人說他胖。**2** [usually before noun] (of a subject 課題) that may upset or offend people and should therefore be dealt with carefully 敏感性的；需要小心處理的；棘手的 **SYN** **delicate, sensitive** ▶ **touchi·ness** *noun* [U]

ˌtouchy-ˈfeely *adj.* (*informal, usually disapproving*) expressing emotions too openly 露骨地表示情感的

tough /tʌf/ *adj., noun, verb*

■ ***adj.*** (**tough·er, tough·est**)

▸ **DIFFICULT 困難 1** having or causing problems or difficulties 艱苦的；艱難的；棘手的：*a tough childhood* 苦難的童年 ◇ *It was a tough decision to make.* 那是個很難做的決定。◇ *She's been having* ***a tough time of it*** (= a lot of problems) *lately.* 她最近的日子一直很難熬。◇ *He faces the toughest test of his leadership so far.* 他面臨迄今為止對自己的領導工作最嚴峻的考驗。◇ *It can be tough trying to juggle a career and a family.* 要事業家庭兩不誤，有時會很艱難。

▸ **STRICT/FIRM 嚴格；強硬 2** demanding that particular rules be obeyed and showing a lack of sympathy for any problems or suffering that this may cause 嚴厲的；強硬的；無情的：**~ (on sb/sth)** *Don't be too tough on him—he was only trying to help.* 別對他要求過嚴，他只是想幫忙。◇ **~ (with sb/sth)** *It's about time teachers started to* ***get tough with*** *bullies.* 現在教師該對橫行霸道的學生開始採取嚴厲措施了。◇ *The school* ***takes a tough line on*** (= punishes severely) *cheating.* 學校對作弊行為的懲罰很嚴厲。**OPP** **soft**

▸ **STRONG 強壯 3** strong enough to deal successfully with difficult conditions or situations 堅強的；健壯的；能吃苦耐勞的；堅韌不拔的：*a tough breed of cattle* 健壯型的牛 ◇ *He's not tough enough for a career in sales.* 他幹推銷這一行缺少足夠的韌勁。◇ *She's a* ***tough cookie/customer*** (= sb who knows what they want and is not easily influenced by other people). 她是個有主見的人。**4** (of a person 人) physically strong and likely to be violent 剽悍的；粗暴的；粗野的：*You think you're so tough, don't you?* 你以為自己夠厲害的，是不是？◇ *He plays the* ***tough guy*** *in the movie.* 他在電影中扮演硬漢。

▸ **MEAT 肉 5** difficult to cut or chew 難切開的；嚼不爛的；老的 **OPP** **tender**

▸ **NOT EASILY DAMAGED 不易損壞 6** not easily cut, broken, torn, etc. 堅固的；不易切開（或打破、撕破等）的：*a tough pair of shoes* 一雙結實的鞋子 ◇ *The reptile's skin is tough and scaly.* 這種爬行動物的皮膚堅韌並帶有鱗片。

▸ **UNFORTUNATE 不幸 7 ~ (on sb)** (*informal*) unfortunate for sb in a way that seems unfair 不幸的；倒霉的：*It was tough on her being dropped from the team like that.* 她就這樣被隊裏刷了下來，真是倒霉。◇ (*ironic*) *'I can't get it finished in time.' 'Tough!* (= I don't feel sorry about it.)' "我無法按時完成。" "活該倒霉！"

▶ **tough·ly** *adv.* **tough·ness** *noun* [U]

IDM **(as) tough as old ˈboots | (as) tough as ˈnails** (*informal*) **1** very strong and able to deal successfully with difficult conditions or situations 很強壯；堅韌不拔；雷打不動 **2** not feeling or showing any emotion 鐵石心腸；不為所動 **tough ˈluck** (*informal*) **1** (*BrE*) used to show sympathy for sth unfortunate that has happened to sb（表示同情）真不幸，真不走運：*'I failed by one point.' 'That's tough luck.'* "我差一分沒及格。" "運氣真不好。" **2** (*ironic*) used to show that you do not feel sorry for sb who has a problem（表示並不同情）該你倒霉：*'If you take the car, I won't be able to go out.' 'Tough luck!'* "如果你把車開走，我就出不去了。" "該你倒霉！" ➲ more at ACT *n.*, GOING *n.*, HANG *v.*, NUT *n.*, TALK *v.*

■ ***noun*** (*old-fashioned, informal*) a person who regularly uses violence against other people 粗暴的人；暴徒；惡棍

■ ***verb***

PHR V **ˌtough sth↔ˈout** to stay firm and determined in a difficult situation 堅持；挺過：*You're just going to have to* ***tough it out.*** 你只好硬着頭皮撐到底了。

tough·en /ˈtʌfn/ *verb* **1** [T, I] **~ (sth) (up)** to become or make sth stronger, so that it is not easily cut, broken, etc.（使）堅硬，堅固：*toughened glass* 鋼化玻璃 **2** [T] **~ sth (up)** to make sth such as laws or rules stricter 加強，強化（法律、規定等）：*The government is considering toughening up the law on censorship.* 政府正在考慮強化書報電影審查方面的法律。**3** [T] **~ sb (up)** to make sb stronger and more able to deal with difficult situations 使更堅強；使堅韌

toughie /ˈtʌfi/ *noun* (*informal*) **1** a person who is determined and not easily frightened 堅定勇敢的人；無畏的人 **2** a very difficult choice or question 艱難的選擇；難題

ˌtough ˈlove *noun* [U] the fact of helping sb who has problems by dealing with them in a strict way because you believe it is good for them 嚴厲的愛（為幫助而嚴厲對待有問題的人）

ˌtough-ˈminded *adj.* dealing with problems and situations in a determined way without being influenced by emotions 堅定理智的；堅强面對現實的 **SYN** **hard-headed**

tou·pee /ˈtuːpeɪ; *NAmE* tuːˈpeɪ/ (also *informal* **rug** especially in *NAmE*) *noun* a small section of artificial hair, worn by a man to cover an area of his head where hair no longer grows（男用）小型遮禿假髮

tour /tʊə(r); tɔː(r); *NAmE* tʊr/ *noun, verb*

■ ***noun* 1 ~ (of/round/around sth)** a journey made for pleasure during which several different towns, countries, etc. are visited 旅行；旅遊：*a* ***walking/sightseeing, etc. tour*** 徒步、觀光等旅行 ◇ *a* ***coach tour*** *of northern France* 乘長途汽車在法國北部旅遊 ◇ *a* ***tour operator*** (= a person or company that organizes tours) 旅遊經營商 ➲ SYNONYMS at TRIP ➲ COLLOCATIONS at TRAVEL ➲ see also PACKAGE TOUR, WHISTLE-STOP **2** an act of walking around a town, building, etc. in order to visit it 遊覽；參觀；觀光：*We were given a* ***guided tour*** (= by sb who knows about the place) *of the palace.* 我們由導遊帶領參觀遊覽了那座宮殿。◇ *a* ***tour guide*** 導遊 ◇ *a* ***tour of inspection*** (= an official visit of a factory, classroom, etc. made by sb whose job is to check that everything is working as expected) 視察 **3** an official series of visits made to different places by a sports team, an ORCHESTRA, an important person, etc. 巡迴比賽（或演出等）；巡視：*The band is currently on a nine-day tour of France.* 這支樂隊目前正在法國進行九天的巡迴演出。◇ *The band is* ***on tour*** *in France.* 這支樂隊正在法國巡迴演出。◇ *a concert tour* 巡迴音樂會 ◇ *The Prince will visit Boston on the last leg* (= part) *of his American tour.* 親王美國之行的最後一站是波士頓。◇ *The soldiers all used to do a six-month* ***tour of duty*** *in Northern Ireland.* 士兵過去都要在北愛爾蘭服役六個月。

■ ***verb*** [T, I] to travel around a place, for example on holiday/vacation, or to perform, to advertise sth, etc. 在…旅遊；在…巡迴演出（或做宣傳廣告等）：**~ sth** *He toured America with his one-man show.* 他在美國進行了個人巡迴演出。◇ *She toured the country promoting her book.* 她在全國巡迴推銷自己的書。◇ **~ around sth** *We spent four weeks touring around Europe.* 我們花了四個星期周遊歐洲。

tour de force /ˌtʊə də ˈfɔːs; *NAmE* ˌtʊr də ˈfɔːrs/ *noun* (*pl.* **tours de force** /ˌtʊə də ˈfɔːs; *NAmE* ˌtʊr də ˈfɔːrs/) (from *French*) an extremely skilful performance or achievement 絕技；特技；傑作：*a cinematic tour de force* 電影傑作

Tour·ette's syn·drome /tʊˈrets sɪndrəʊm; *NAmE* -droʊm/ *noun* [U] (*medical* 醫) a DISORDER of the nerves in which a person makes a lot of small movements and sounds that they cannot control, including using swear words 圖洛特氏綜合症，妥瑞症（特徵為不自主而反複出現的肌肉痙攣和發聲）

tour·ism /ˈtʊərɪzəm; ˈtɔːr-; *NAmE* ˈtʊr-/ *noun* [U] the business activity connected with providing accommodation, services and entertainment for people who are visiting a place for pleasure 旅遊業；觀光業：*The area is heavily dependent on tourism.* 這個地區非常依賴旅遊業。◇ *the tourism industry* 旅遊業 ➲ COLLOCATIONS at TRAVEL ➲ see also AGRITOURISM

T

tour·ist 0-π /ˈtʊərɪst; ˈtɔːr-; *NAmE* ˈtʊr-/ *noun*
1 0-π a person who is travelling or visiting a place for pleasure 旅遊者；觀光者；遊客：*busloads of foreign tourists* 一輛輛滿載外國觀光客的旅遊車 ◇ *a popular* ***tourist attraction/destination/resort*** 為遊客所喜愛的旅遊景點／目的地／勝地 ◇ *the* ***tourist industry/sector*** 旅遊業／部門 ◇ *Further information is available from the local* ***tourist office***. 進一步詳情可向當地的旅遊辦事處查詢。➲ COLLOCATIONS at TRAVEL **2** (*BrE*) a member of a sports team that is playing a series of official games in a foreign country（在國外參加）巡迴比賽的運動隊隊員

ˈtourist class *noun* [U] the cheapest type of ticket or accommodation that is available on a plane or ship or in a hotel（飛機、輪船的）二等艙（或票），經濟艙（或票）；（旅館的）旅遊客房，最便宜的客房

ˈtourist trap *noun* (*informal, disapproving*) a place that attracts a lot of tourists and where food, drink, entertainment, etc. is more expensive than normal 敲遊客竹槓的地方

tour·isty /ˈtʊərɪsti; ˈtɔːr-; *NAmE* ˈtʊr-/ *adj.* (*informal, disapproving*) attracting or designed to attract a lot of tourists 吸引很多遊客的；為吸引遊客設計的：*Jersey is the most touristy of the islands.* 這些島嶼中就數澤西島最能吸引遊客。◇ *a shop full of touristy souvenirs* 擺滿旅遊紀念品的商店

tour·na·ment /ˈtʊənəmənt; ˈtɔːn-; ˈtɜːn-; *NAmE* ˈtʊrn-; ˈtɜːrn-/ *noun* **1** (*NAmE less frequent* **tour·ney**) a sports competition involving a number of teams or players who take part in different games and must leave the competition if they lose. The competition continues until there is only the winner left. 錦標賽；聯賽：*a* ***golf/squash/tennis, etc. tournament*** 高爾夫球、壁球、網球等錦標賽 **2** a competition in the Middle Ages between soldiers on HORSEBACK fighting to show courage and skill（中世紀的）騎士比武

tour·ney /ˈtʊəni; ˈtɜːni; *NAmE* ˈtʊrni; ˈtɜːrni/ *noun* (*NAmE*) = TOURNAMENT (1)

tour·ni·quet /ˈtʊənɪkeɪ; *NAmE* ˈtɜːrnəkət/ *noun* a piece of cloth, etc. that is tied tightly around an arm or a leg to stop the loss of blood from a wound（紮在手臂或腿上的）止血帶

tou·sle /ˈtaʊzl/ *verb* [usually passive] **~ sth** to make sb's hair untidy 弄亂（頭髮）；使蓬亂 ▸ **tou·sled** *adj.*：*a boy with blue eyes and tousled hair* 頭髮蓬亂的藍眼睛男孩

tout /taʊt/ *verb, noun*
■ *verb* **1** [T] **~ sb/sth (as sth)** to try to persuade people that sb/sth is important or valuable by praising them/it 標榜；吹捧；吹噓：*She's being touted as the next leader of the party.* 她被吹捧為該黨的下一任領導人。**2** [I, T] (*especially BrE*) to try to persuade people to buy your goods or services, especially by going to them and asking them directly 兜售；招徠：**~ (for sth)** *the problem of unlicensed taxi drivers touting for business at airports* 沒有執照的出租汽車司機在機場攬生意的問題 ◇ **~ sth** *He's busy touting his client's latest book around London publishers.* 他正忙於向倫敦多家出版商兜售他的委託人的一部新書。**3** [I, T] (*BrE*) (*NAmE* **scalp**) **~ (sth)** to sell tickets for a popular event illegally, at a price that is higher than the official price, especially outside a theatre, STADIUM, etc.（尤指在劇院、體育場等外）倒賣高價票，賣黑市票
■ *noun* (also **ˈticket tout**) (both *BrE*) (*NAmE* **scalp·er**) a person who buys tickets for concerts, sports events, etc. and then sells them to other people at a higher price（音樂會、體育比賽等的）賣高價票的人，票販子

tout court /ˌtuː ˈkʊə(r); ˈkɔː(r); *NAmE* ˈkʊr/ *adv.* (from *French*) simply, with nothing to add 簡單地；僅僅：*It was a lie, tout court.* 那只不過是謊言。

tow /təʊ; *NAmE* toʊ/ *verb, noun*
■ *verb* **~ sth (away)** to pull a car or boat behind another vehicle, using a rope or chain（用繩索或鏈條）拖，拉，牽引，拽：*Our car was towed away by the police.* 我們的汽車被警察拖走了。➲ SYNONYMS at PULL ➲ see also TOW BAR, TOW ROPE
■ *noun* [sing.] an act of one vehicle pulling another vehicle using a rope or chain（車、船等的）牽引，拽引：*The car broke down and we had to get somebody to give us a tow.* 汽車拋錨了，我們只得讓人拖走。◇ *a tow truck* 牽引車
IDM **in tow** **1** (*informal*) if you have sb **in tow**, they are with you and following closely behind 緊隨着；陪伴着：*She turned up with her mother in tow.* 她露面了，後面緊跟着她的母親。**2** if a ship is taken **in tow**, it is pulled by another ship（船）被拖着走

to·wards 0-π /təˈwɔːdz; *NAmE* tɔːrdz/ (also **to·ward** /təˈwɔːd; *NAmE* tɔːrd/especially in *NAmE*) *prep.*
1 0-π in the direction of sb/sth 向；朝；對着：*They were heading towards the German border.* 他們正前往德國邊界。◇ *She had her back towards me.* 她背對着我。**2** 0-π getting closer to achieving sth 趨向，接近，將近（完成某事）：*This is a first step towards political union.* 這是走向政治上聯合的第一步。**3** 0-π close or closer to a point in time 接近，將近（某一時間）：*towards the end of April* 將近四月底 **4** 0-π in relation to sb/sth 對；對於；關於：*He was warm and tender towards her.* 他對她既熱情又溫柔。◇ *our attitude towards death* 我們對死亡的態度 **5** with the aim of obtaining sth, or helping sb to obtain sth 以…為目標（或目的）；用於：*The money will go towards a new school building* (= will help pay for it). 這筆資金將用於修建新校舍。

ˈtow bar *noun* a bar fixed to the back of a vehicle for TOWING (= pulling) another vehicle（用以牽引拖車的）牽引桿，拖桿

towel 0-π /ˈtaʊəl/ *noun, verb*
■ *noun* a piece of cloth or paper used for drying things, especially your body 毛巾；手巾；抹布；紙巾：*Help yourself to a clean towel.* 請隨便拿一條乾淨毛巾用。◇ *a* ***hand/bath towel*** (= a small/large towel) 手巾；浴巾 ◇ *a* ***beach towel*** (= a large towel used for lying on in the sun) 沙灘太陽浴巾 ◇ *a* ***kitchen towel*** (= a piece of paper from a roll that you use to clean up liquid, etc. in the kitchen) 廚房用清潔紙巾 ➲ VISUAL VOCAB page V24 ➲ see also PAPER TOWEL, SANITARY TOWEL, TEA TOWEL
IDM **throw in the ˈtowel** (*informal*) to admit that you have been defeated and stop trying 認輸；承認失敗；放棄努力
■ *verb* (**-ll-**, *NAmE* also **-l-**) **~ yourself/sb/sth (down)** to dry yourself/sb/sth with a towel 用毛巾擦乾

towel·ling (*BrE*) (*US* **towel·ing**) /ˈtaʊəlɪŋ/ *noun* [U] a type of soft cotton cloth that absorbs liquids, used especially for making towels 毛巾布；毛巾料：*a towelling bathrobe* 毛巾布浴衣

ˈtowel rail (*BrE*) (*NAmE* **ˈtowel rack**) *noun* a bar or frame for hanging towels on in a bathroom 毛巾架 ➲ VISUAL VOCAB page V24

tower 0-π /ˈtaʊə(r)/ *noun, verb*
■ *noun* **1** 0-π a tall narrow building or part of a building, especially of a church or castle 塔；建築物的塔形部份；（尤指教堂或城堡的）塔樓：*a* ***clock/bell tower*** 鐘樓 ◇ *the Tower of London* 倫敦塔 ◇ *the Eiffel Tower* 埃菲爾鐵塔 **2** (often in compounds 常構成複合詞) a tall structure used for sending television or radio signals（電視或無線電信號的）發射塔：*a television tower* 電視塔 **3** (usually in compounds 通常構成複合詞) a tall piece of furniture used for storing things 高櫃；高架子：*a CD tower* 光盤櫃 ➲ see also CONTROL TOWER, COOLING TOWER, IVORY TOWER, WATCHTOWER, WATER TOWER
IDM **a ˌtower of ˈstrength** a person that you can rely on to help, protect and comfort you when you are in trouble（危難時的）可依靠的人，主心骨
■ *verb*
PHR V **ˌtower ˈover/aˈbove sb/sth** **1** to be much higher or taller than the people or things that are near 遠高於，高聳於（附近的人或物）：*The cliffs towered above them.* 懸崖峭壁高聳於他們上方。◇ *He towered over his classmates.* 他的個兒比班裏其他同學高出一大截。**2** to be much better than others in ability, quality, etc.（在能力、品質等方面）勝過，遠遠超過（其他）：*She towers over other dancers of her generation.* 她遠遠超過同時代的舞蹈演員。

ˈ**tower block** *noun* (*BrE*) a very tall block of flats/apartments or offices 高層建築；公寓大樓；辦公大樓

tower·ing /ˈtaʊərɪŋ/ *adj.* [only before noun] **1** extremely tall or high and therefore impressive 高大的；高聳的；屹立的： *towering cliffs* 高聳的懸崖 **2** of extremely high quality 卓越的；傑出的；出色的： *a towering performance* 出色的表演 **3** (of emotions 情感) extremely strong 強烈的；激烈的： *a towering rage* 勃然大怒

tow·line /ˈtəʊlaɪn; *NAmE* ˈtoʊ-/ *noun* = TOW ROPE

town 0‑m /taʊn/ *noun*
1 0‑m [C, U] a place with many houses, shops/stores, etc. where people live and work. It is larger than a village but smaller than a city. 鎮；市鎮；集鎮： *a university town* 大學城 ◇ *They live in a rough part of town.* 他們居住在一個社會秩序混亂的城區。◇ *The nearest town is ten miles away.* 最近的集鎮離這裏有十英里遠。◇ *We spent a month in the French town of Le Puy.* 我們在一個叫勒皮的法國小鎮裏待了一個月。➲ see also SMALL-TOWN **HELP** You will find other compounds ending in **town** at their place in the alphabet. 其他以 town 結尾的複合詞可在各字母中的適當位置查到。 **2** 0‑m **the town** [sing.] the people who live in a particular town （某一市鎮的）居民，市民： *The whole town is talking about it.* 全鎮的人都在議論這件事。 **3** 0‑m [U] the area of a town where most of the shops/stores and businesses are （城鎮的）商業區： *Can you give me a lift into town?* 我可以搭你的車到商業區去嗎？➲ see also DOWNTOWN, MIDTOWN, OUT-OF-TOWN, UPTOWN **4** [U] (*especially NAmE*) a particular town where sb lives and works or one that has just been referred to （生活、工作或剛提到的）城鎮： *I'll be in town next week if you want to meet.* 如果你想見面的話，我下個星期在城裏。◇ *He married a girl from out of town.* 他娶了一個外地姑娘。➲ see also OUT-OF-TOWN **5** [sing., U] life in towns or cities as opposed to life in the country 城市生活（與鄉村生活相對）： *Pollution is just one of the disadvantages of living in the town.* 污染只是生活在城裏的不利條件之一。

IDM **go to ˈtown (on sth)** (*informal*) to do sth with a lot of energy, enthusiasm, etc., especially by spending a lot of money （尤指花大錢）大幹一番 **(out) on the ˈtown** (*informal*) visiting restaurants, clubs, theatres, etc. for entertainment, especially at night （尤指夜裏）去娛樂場所玩： *a night on the town* 去娛樂場所作樂的夜晚 ◇ *How about going out on the town tonight?* 今晚出去痛痛快快地玩一玩怎麼樣？➲ more at GAME *n.*, MAN *n.*, PAINT *v.*

ˌ**town and ˈgown** *noun* [U] the relationship between the people who live permanently in a town where there is a university and the members of the university 大學城居民與師生的關係

ˌ**town ˈcentre** *noun* (*BrE*) the main part of a town, where the shops/stores are 市中心；（城鎮的）商業中心 ➲ compare DOWNTOWN

ˌ**town ˈclerk** *noun* **1** (*NAmE*) a public officer in charge of the records of a town 鎮書記員（主管檔案） **2** (*BrE*) in the past, the person who was the secretary of, and gave legal advice to, the local government of a town （舊時的）鎮政府秘書兼法律顧問

ˌ**town ˈcrier** (also **crier**) *noun* (in the past) a person whose job was to walk through a town shouting news, official ANNOUNCEMENTS, etc. （舊時沿街高聲傳報消息等的）街頭公告員

townee = TOWNIE (1)

ˌ**town ˈhall** *noun* a building containing local government offices and, in Britain, usually a hall for public

Collocations 詞語搭配

Town and country 城鎮與鄉村

Town 城鎮

- **live in** a city/a town/an urban environment/(informal) a concrete jungle/the suburbs/shanty towns/slums 住在城裏／鎮上／城區／混凝土叢林／郊區／棚戶區／貧民窟
- **live** (*especially NAmE*) downtown/in the downtown area/(*BrE*) in the city centre 住在市中心
- **enjoy/like** the hectic pace of life/the hustle and bustle of city life 喜歡忙碌的生活節奏／城市生活的熱鬧
- **cope with** the stress/pressure of urban life 應對城市生活的壓力
- **get caught up in** the rat race 捲入大城市裏為財富、權力等的瘋狂追逐中
- **prefer/seek** the anonymity of life in a big city 更喜歡／追求大城市裏人與人互不相識的生活
- **be drawn by/resist** the lure of the big city 被大城市的誘惑所吸引；抵禦大城市的誘惑
- **head for** the bright lights (of the big city/New York) 奔向（大城市／紐約）五光十色的生活
- **enjoy/love** the vibrant/lively nightlife 享受／喜愛充滿生機的夜生活
- **have/be close to** all the amenities 擁有／緊靠各種便利設施
- **be surrounded by** towering skyscrapers/a soulless urban sprawl 被高聳入雲的摩天大樓／毫無生氣的城市拓展區所包圍
- **use/travel by/rely on** (*BrE*) public transport/(*NAmE*) public transportation 使用／出行乘坐／依賴公共交通
- **put up with/get stuck in/sit in** massive/huge/heavy/endless/constant traffic jams 忍受／陷入大面積／嚴重的／沒完沒了的／持續的交通堵塞
- **tackle/ease/reduce/relieve/alleviate** the heavy/severe traffic congestion 處理／減緩嚴重的交通堵塞
- **be affected/choked/damaged by** pollution 受到污染的影響；被污染嗆得透不過氣；受到污染的傷害

Country 鄉村

- **live** in a village/the countryside/an isolated area/a rural backwater/(*informal*) the sticks 住在村裏／鄉村／偏僻的地區／落後的鄉村／偏遠的鄉村地區
- **enjoy/like** the relaxed/slower pace of life 享受／喜歡悠閒／緩慢的生活節奏
- **enjoy/love/explore** the great outdoors 享受／喜歡／探索藍天碧野
- **look for/find/get/enjoy** a little peace and quiet 尋找／找到／得到／享受一點寧靜與安寧
- **need/want** to get back/closer to nature 需要／想要回去／接近大自然
- **be surrounded by** open/unspoilt/picturesque countryside 四周被空曠的／未被污染的／風景如畫的鄉村環繞
- **escape/quit/get out of/leave** the rat race 逃離／退出城市中你死我活的競爭
- **seek/achieve** a better/healthy work-life balance 尋求／達到工作與生活更好的／健康的平衡
- **downshift** to a less stressful life 選擇壓力較小的生活
- **seek/start** a new life in the country 在鄉村尋求／開始一種新的生活
- (*BrE, informal*) **up sticks/** (*NAmE, informal*) **pull up stakes** and move to/head for … 突然遷居到…
- **create/build/foster** a strong sense of community 樹立／培養強烈的社群意識
- **depend on/be employed in/work in** agriculture 依賴／從事農業
- **live off/farm/work** the land 靠土地為生；耕種土地
- **tackle/address** the problem of rural unemployment 解決農村失業問題

meetings, concerts, etc. 鎮公所；市政廳；（英國）市鎮集會所

ˈtown house *noun* **1** (*BrE*) a house in a town owned by sb who also has a house in the country（另有鄉村住房者的）城市住宅 **2** (*BrE*) a tall narrow house in a town that is part of a row of similar houses 排房：*an elegant Georgian town house* 一套具有喬治王朝時期風格的典雅排房 ➲ VISUAL VOCAB page V16 **3** (usually **ˈtownhouse**) (*NAmE*) = ROW HOUSE

townie /ˈtaʊni/ *noun* (*disapproving*) **1** (also **townee**) a person who lives in or comes from a town or city, especially sb who does not know much about life in the countryside（尤指不瞭解鄉村生活的）城裏人 **2** (*NAmE*) a person who lives in a town with a college or university but does not attend or work at it（大學城中不上大學或不在大學工作的）居民，老百姓 **3** (*BrE, informal*) a member of a group of young people who live in a town, all wear similar clothes, such as TRACKSUITS and caps, and often behave badly 阿飛，城市小流氓（穿着類似，行為不端）

ˌtown ˈmeeting *noun* a meeting when people in a town come together to discuss problems that affect the town and to give their opinions on various issues 鎮民大會

ˌtown ˈplanner *noun* = PLANNER (1)

ˌtown ˈplanning (also **plan·ning**) *noun* [U] the control of the development of towns and their buildings, roads, etc. so that they can be pleasant and convenient places for people to live in; the subject that studies this 城鎮規劃；城鎮規劃學

town·scape /ˈtaʊnskeɪp/ *noun* **1** what you see when you look at a town, for example from a distance 城市風景；城鎮景觀：*an industrial townscape* 工業城市景象 **2** (*technical* 術語) a picture of a town 城鎮風景畫 ➲ compare LANDSCAPE *n.* (2), SEASCAPE

town·ship /ˈtaʊnʃɪp/ *noun* **1** (in South Africa in the past) a town or part of a town that black people had to live in, and where only black people lived（舊時南非的）黑人城鎮，黑人居住區 **2** (in the US or Canada) a division of a county that is a unit of local government 鎮區（美國和加拿大縣以下一級的地方政府）

towns·people /ˈtaʊnzpiːpl/ (also **towns·folk** /ˈtaʊnsfəʊk; *NAmE* -foʊk/) *noun* [pl.] people who live in towns, not in the countryside; the people who live in a particular town 鎮民；市民；城裏人；（某一城鎮的）居民

tow·path /ˈtəʊpɑːθ; *NAmE* ˈtoʊpæθ/ *noun* a path along the bank of a river or CANAL, that was used in the past by horses pulling boats (called BARGES) 縴道，縴路（舊時河流沿岸馬拉駁船所走的路）

ˈtow rope (also **tow·line**) *noun* a rope that is used for pulling sth along, especially a vehicle 縴繩；拖纜；拖索

ˈtow truck (*especially NAmE*) (*BrE* usually **ˈbreakdown truck**) *noun* a truck that is used for taking cars away to be repaired when they have had a breakdown（把故障車輛拖去修理的）牽引車 ➲ VISUAL VOCAB page V57

tox·ae·mia (*BrE*) (*NAmE* **tox·emia**) /tɒkˈsiːmiə; *NAmE* tɑːk-/ *noun* [U] (*medical* 醫) infection of the blood by harmful bacteria 毒血症 SYN **blood poisoning**

toxic /ˈtɒksɪk; *NAmE* ˈtɑːk-/ *adj.* **1** containing poison; poisonous 有毒的；引起中毒的：***toxic chemicals/fumes/gases/substances*** 有毒的化學品／煙霧／氣體／物質 ◇ *to dispose of **toxic waste*** 處理有毒廢料 ◇ *Many pesticides are **highly toxic**.* 許多殺蟲劑毒性很大。 **2 ~ debt/loan/asset/investment** a level of debt or high-risk investment that causes very serious problems for a bank or other financial institution 有毒的（指能引致銀行或其他金融機構出現嚴重問題的高水平債務或高風險投資） **3** [usually before noun] (*informal*) (of a person 人) having a very unpleasant personality, especially in the way they like to control and influence other people in a dishonest way 卑鄙無恥的；（尤指）愛擺佈人的

tox·icity /tɒkˈsɪsəti; *NAmE* tɑːk-/ *noun* (*pl.* **-ies**) (*technical* 術語) **1** [U] the quality of being poisonous; the extent to which sth is poisonous 毒性；毒力：*substances with high levels of toxicity* 毒性大的物質 **2** [C] the effect that a poisonous substance has 毒性作用；毒性反應：*Minor toxicities of this drug include nausea and vomiting.* 這種藥的輕微毒性反應包括惡心和嘔吐。

toxi·col·ogy /ˌtɒksɪˈkɒlədʒi; *NAmE* ˌtɑːksɪˈkɑːl-/ *noun* [U] the scientific study of poisons 毒理學；毒物學 ▸ **toxi·colo·gical** /ˌtɒksɪkəˈlɒdʒɪkl; *NAmE* ˌtɑːksɪkəˈlɑːdʒɪkl/ *adj.* **toxi·colo·gist** /-dʒɪst/ *noun*

ˌtoxic ˈshock syndrome *noun* [U] a serious illness in women caused by harmful bacteria in the VAGINA, connected with the use of TAMPONS 中毒性休克綜合症

toxin /ˈtɒksɪn; *NAmE* ˈtɑːk-/ *noun* a poisonous substance, especially one that is produced by bacteria in plants and animals 毒素（尤指生物體自然產生的毒物）

toxo·plas·mo·sis /ˌtɒksəʊplæzˈməʊsɪs; *NAmE* ˌtɑːksoʊplæzˈmoʊsɪs/ *noun* [U] (*medical* 醫) a disease that can be dangerous to a baby while it is still in its mother's body, caught from infected meat, soil, or animal FAECES 弓形體病（對胎兒有害，由感染病菌的肉、土壤或動物糞便傳染）

toy 0➛ /tɔɪ/ *noun, adj., verb*

■ ***noun*** **1** 0➛ an object for children to play with 玩具：***cuddly/soft toys*** 令人想摟抱的／軟玩具 ◇ *The children were playing happily with their toys.* 孩子們正高興地玩着玩具。 ➲ VISUAL VOCAB page V37 **2** an object that you have for enjoyment or pleasure rather than for a serious purpose 玩物；玩意兒 SYN **plaything**：*executive toys* 行政人員的玩意兒 ◇ *His latest toy is the electric drill he bought last week.* 他的新玩意兒是他上星期買的電鑽。

■ ***adj.*** [only before noun] **1** 0➛ made as a copy of a particular thing and used for playing with 玩具的；作玩具的：*a toy car* 玩具汽車 ◇ *toy soldiers* 玩具士兵 **2** (of a dog 狗) of a very small breed 個頭很小的；小體型品種的：*a toy poodle* 小鬈毛狗

■ ***verb***

PHR V **ˈtoy with sth 1** to consider an idea or a plan, but not very seriously and not for a long time 不太認真地考慮；把…當兒戲 SYN **flirt with**：*I did briefly **toy with the idea of** living in France.* 我確實稍稍有過定居法國的念頭。 **2** to play with sth and move it around carelessly or without thinking 玩耍；戲弄；擺弄：*He kept toying nervously with his pen.* 他一直精神緊張地擺弄着鋼筆。 ◇ *She hardly ate a thing, just toyed with a piece of cheese on her plate.* 她幾乎沒吃一點東西，只是撥弄着碟子裏的一塊奶酪。

ˈtoy boy *noun* (*BrE*) (*NAmE* **ˈboy toy**) (*informal, humorous*) a woman's male lover who is much younger than she is（比情婦年輕得多的）小情夫，小男友

toyi-toyi /ˈtɔɪ tɔɪ/ *noun* [U] (*SAfrE*) a type of dance or march, used as a form of protest, in which you repeatedly move one leg up and down followed by the other 托弋托弋舞（或遊行）（作為抗議示威，左右交替踢腿）

TQM /ˌtiː kjuː ˈem/ *abbr.* TOTAL QUALITY MANAGEMENT 全面質量管理；全面品質管理

trace 0➛ AW /treɪs/ *verb, noun*

■ ***verb*** **1** 0➛ **~ sb/sth (to sth)** to find or discover sb/sth by looking carefully for them/it 查出；找到；發現；追踪 SYN **track down**：*We finally traced him to an address in Chicago.* 我們終於追查到他在芝加哥的一個地址。 **2** 0➛ **~ sth (back) (to sth)** to find the origin or cause of sth 追溯；追究：*She could trace her family tree back to the 16th century.* 她能把本族家譜追溯到 16 世紀。 ◇ *The leak was eventually traced to a broken seal.* 最後查出泄漏是由於密封處破裂所致。 ◇ *The police traced the call* (= used special electronic equipment to find out who made the telephone call) *to her ex-husband's number.* 警方用追踪裝置查出是她前夫的電話號碼打出的電話。 **3 ~ sth (from sth) (to sth)** to describe a process or the development of sth 描繪（事物的過程或發展）；追述；記述：*Her book traces the town's history from Saxon times to the present day.* 她的書描述的是這個市鎮從撒克遜時代到現在的歷史。 **4 ~ sth (out)** to draw a line or lines on a surface 畫（線）：*She traced a line in the sand.* 她在沙地上畫了一條線。 **5 ~ sth** to follow the shape or outline of sth 繪出，勾畫出（輪廓）：*He traced the route on the map.* 他在地圖上勾畫出了路線。◇ *A tear traced a path down her cheek.* 一滴眼淚沿着她的面頰流了下來。 **6 ~ sth** to copy a map, drawing, etc. by drawing on transparent paper (= TRACING PAPER) placed over it（用透明紙覆蓋在地圖、繪畫等上）複製，描摹

■ ***noun*** **1** 0-π [C, U] a mark, an object or a sign that shows that sb/sth existed or was present 痕跡；遺跡；蹤跡：*It's exciting to discover traces of earlier civilizations.* 發現以前文明的遺跡，真令人興奮。◇ *Police searched the area but found* ***no trace of*** *the escaped prisoners.* 警方搜索了那一地區，但未發現越獄逃犯的任何蹤跡。◇ *Years of living in England had eliminated* ***all trace of*** *her American accent.* 她因多年居住在英國，美國口音已蕩然無存。◇ *The ship had vanished* ***without (a) trace.*** 那艘船消失得無影無踪。 **2** 0-π [C] **~ of sth** a very small amount of sth 微量；少許：*The post-mortem revealed traces of poison in his stomach.* 驗屍發現他胃中有微量毒物。◇ *She spoke without a trace of bitterness.* 她說話時一點兒也不傷感。 **3** [C] (*technical* 術語) a line or pattern on paper or a screen that shows information that is found by a machine 描記圖；軌跡；跡線；掃描線：*The trace showed a normal heart rhythm.* 描記圖顯示心率正常。 **4** [C] **~ on sb/sth** a search to find out information about the identity of sb/sth, especially what number a telephone call was made from（對信息的）跟踪，追踪：*The police ran a trace on the call.* 警察對那通電話進行了追踪。 **5** [C, usually pl.] one of the two long pieces of leather that fasten a CARRIAGE or CART to the horse that pulls it 挽繩；套繩 IDM see KICK *v.*

trace·able AW /'treɪsəbl/ *adj.* **~ (to sb/sth)** if sth is **traceable**, you can find out where it came from, where it has gone, when it began or what its cause was 可追溯的；可追踪的；可追本溯源的：*Most telephone calls are traceable.* 大多數電話都可查出是從哪裏打來的。

'trace element *noun* **1** a chemical substance that is found in very small amounts 痕量元素 **2** a chemical substance that living things, especially plants, need only in very small amounts to be able to grow well 微量元素（生物，尤指植物，生長所需要的微量的化學物質）

tracer /'treɪsə(r)/ *noun* **1** a bullet or SHELL (= a kind of bomb) that leaves a line of smoke or flame behind it 曳光彈 **2** (*technical* 術語) a RADIOACTIVE substance that can be seen in the human body and is used to find out what is happening inside the body 示踪劑；同位素指示劑

tra·cery /'treɪsəri/ *noun* (*pl.* **-ies**) **1** [U] (*technical* 術語) a pattern of lines and curves in stone on the top part of some church windows 窗花格（某些教堂窗戶頂部的石製花飾） **2** [U, C, usually sing.] (*literary*) an attractive pattern of lines and curves 精美花飾圖案

trachea /trə'ki:ə; *NAmE* 'treɪkiə/ *noun* (*pl.* **trach·eas** or **trach·eae** /-ki:i:/) (*anatomy* 解) the tube in the throat that carries air to the lungs 氣管 SYN **windpipe** ➲ VISUAL VOCAB page V59

trache·ot·omy /ˌtræki'ɒtəmi; *NAmE* ˌtreɪki'ɑ:t-/ *noun* (*pl.* **-ies**) (*medical* 醫) a medical operation to cut a hole in sb's trachea so that they can breathe 氣管切開術

tra·cing /'treɪsɪŋ/ *noun* a copy of a map, drawing, etc. that you make by drawing on a piece of transparent paper placed on top of it 描摹；摹圖；描圖

'tracing paper *noun* [U] strong transparent paper that is placed on top of a drawing, etc. so that you can follow the lines with a pen or pencil in order to make a copy of it 描圖紙；摹圖紙

track 0-π /træk/ *noun, verb*

■ ***noun***

▸ **ROUGH PATH** 崎嶇不平的小路 **1** 0-π [C] a rough path or road, usually one that has not been built but that has been made by people walking there（人踩出的）小道，小徑：*a muddy track through the forest* 穿過森林的泥濘小徑 ➲ VISUAL VOCAB pages V4, V5 ➲ see also CART TRACK

▸ **MARKS ON GROUND** 地面上的痕跡 **2** 0-π [C, usually pl.] marks left by a person, an animal or a moving vehicle（人、動物或車輛留下的）足跡，踪跡；車轍：*We followed the bear's tracks in the snow.* 我們跟着熊在雪地上留下的足跡走。◇ *tyre tracks* 輪胎印跡

▸ **FOR TRAIN** 火車 **3** 0-π [C, U] rails that a train moves along 軌道：***railway/railroad tracks*** 鐵路軌道 ◇ *India has thousands of miles of track.* 印度有數千英里的鐵道。 **4** 0-π [C] (*NAmE*) a track with a number at a train station that a train arrives at or leaves from（火車站的）站台：*The train for Chicago is on track 9.* 開往芝加哥的列車停靠在 9 號站台。 ➲ note at PLATFORM

▸ **FOR RACES** 賽跑 **5** 0-π [C] a piece of ground with a special surface for people, cars, etc. to have races on（賽跑、賽車等的）跑道：*a running track* 賽跑跑道 ◇ *a Formula One Grand Prix track* (= for motor racing) 一級方程式大獎賽賽道 ➲ see also DIRT TRACK (2), TRACK AND FIELD

▸ **DIRECTION/COURSE** 方向；路線 **6** [C] the path or direction that sb/sth is moving in（移動的）路徑，路線，方向：*Police are* ***on the track of*** (= searching for) *the thieves.* 警察正在追踪竊賊。◇ *She is on the* ***fast track*** *to promotion* (= will get it quickly). 她現在升遷在望。 ➲ see also ONE-TRACK MIND

▸ **ON TAPE/CD** 錄音磁帶；光盤 **7** 0-π [C] a piece of music or song on a record, tape or CD（唱片、錄音磁帶或光盤的）一首樂曲，一首歌曲：*a track from their latest album* 他們最新唱片專輯裏的一首歌曲 **8** [C] part of a tape, CD or computer disk that music or information can be recorded on（錄音磁帶、光盤或計算機磁盤的）音軌，聲道：*a sixteen track recording studio* 十六聲道錄音室 ◇ *She sang on the backing track.* 她是唱和聲的。 ➲ see also SOUNDTRACK

▸ **FOR CURTAIN** 幕簾 **9** [C] a pole or rail that a curtain moves along（幕簾的）滑軌，滑道

▸ **ON LARGE VEHICLE** 大型車輛 **10** [C] a continuous belt of metal plates around the wheels of a large vehicle such as a BULLDOZER that allows it to move over the ground（推土機等的）履帶

IDM **ˌback on 'track** going in the right direction again after a mistake, failure, etc. 重新步入正確軌道；恢復正常：*I tried to get my life back on track after my divorce.* 離婚之後我力圖使生活恢復正常。 **be ˌon 'track** to be doing the right thing in order to achieve a particular result 步入正軌；做法對頭：*Curtis is on track for the gold medal.* 柯蒂斯正踏上奪取金牌之途。 **keep/lose track of sb/sth** to have/not have information about what is happening or where sb/sth is 瞭解 / 不瞭解…的動態；與…保持 / 失去聯繫：*Bank statements help you keep track of where your money is going.* 銀行賬單有助於你瞭解你的資金使用情況。◇ *I lost all track of time* (= forgot what time it was). 我完全忘了時間。 **make 'tracks** (*informal*) to leave a place, especially to go home 離去（尤指回家） **on the right/wrong 'track** thinking or behaving in the right/wrong way 思路對頭 / 不對頭；做法對路 / 不對路 **stop/halt sb in their 'tracks | stop/halt/freeze in your 'tracks** to suddenly make sb stop by frightening or surprising them; to suddenly stop because sth has frightened or surprised you（使由於恐懼或吃驚）突然止步；（使）怔住：*The question stopped Alice in her tracks.* 這個問題問得艾麗斯張口結舌無以答對。 ➲ more at BEAT *v.*, COVER *v.*, HOT *adj.*, WRONG *adj.*

■ ***verb***

▸ **FOLLOW** 跟隨 **1** [T, I] **~ (sb/sth)** to find sb/sth by following the marks, signs, information, etc., that they have left behind them 跟踪；追踪：*hunters tracking and shooting bears* 追踪射獵熊的獵人 **2** [T] **~ sb/sth | ~ where, how, etc. …** to follow the movements of sb/sth, especially by using special electronic equipment（尤指用特殊電子設備）跟踪，追踪：*We continued tracking the plane on our radar.* 我們繼續用雷達追踪那架飛機。 **3** [T] **~ sb/sth | ~ where, how, etc. …** to follow the progress or development of sb/sth 跟踪（進展情況）：*The research project involves tracking the careers of 400 graduates.* 這個研究項目對 400 名畢業生的事業發展情況進行跟踪調查。 ➲ see also FAST-TRACK

▸ **OF CAMERA** 攝影機 **4** [I] **+ adv./prep.** to move in relation to the thing that is being filmed 跟踪攝影；移動攝影：

T

The camera eventually tracked away. 攝影機最終將鏡頭推遠。
▸ **SCHOOL STUDENTS** 學校學生 **5** (*NAmE*) = STREAM (4)
▸ **LEAVE MARKS** 留下痕跡 **6** [T] **~ sth (+ adv./prep.)** (*especially NAmE*) to leave dirty marks behind you as you walk 留下（髒）足跡：*Don't track mud on my clean floor.* 別在我乾淨的地板上踩上泥腳印。
PHR V **,track sb/sth↔'down** to find sb/sth after searching in several different places 搜尋到；跟踪找到；追查到 **SYN** **trace**：*The police have so far failed to track down the attacker.* 警方至今未能追捕到攻擊者。

,track and 'field (*NAmE*) (*BrE* **ath·let·ics**) *noun* sports that people compete in, such as running and jumping 田徑運動 ➲ **VISUAL VOCAB** pages V46, V47

track·ball /ˈtrækbɔːl/ (also **'tracker ball, roller·ball**) *noun* (*computing* 計) a device containing a ball that is used instead of a mouse to move the CURSOR around the screen 軌跡球；跟踪球；光標運動球

track·er /ˈtrækə(r)/ *noun* a person who can find people or wild animals by following the marks that they leave on the ground 追踪者；跟踪者；追踪人（或野獸）的人

'tracker ball *noun* (*computing* 計) = TRACKBALL

'tracker dog *noun* a dog that has been trained to help the police find people or EXPLOSIVES（受過訓練協助搜尋人或炸藥的）警犬

'track event *noun* [usually pl.] a sports event that is a race run on a track, rather than jumping or throwing sth 徑賽項目 ➲ **VISUAL VOCAB** page V47 ➲ compare FIELD EVENT

'tracking station *noun* a place where people follow the movements of aircraft, etc. in the sky by RADAR or radio（用雷達或無線電追踪飛機等動向的）跟踪站

'track·less trol·ley (*US*) (*BrE* **trol·ley·bus**) *noun* a bus driven by electricity from a cable above the street 無軌電車

'track record *noun* all the past achievements, successes or failures of a person or an organization（個人或組織的）業績記錄：*He has a proven track record in marketing.* 他有可靠的銷售業績記錄。

track·suit /ˈtræksuːt/ (also **'jogging suit**) *noun* a warm loose pair of trousers/pants and matching jacket worn for sports practice or as informal clothes（運動練習時或作便衣穿的）寬鬆暖和的衣褲；運動服 ➲ compare SHELL SUIT

tract /trækt/ *noun* **1** (*biology* 生) a system of connected organs or TISSUES along which materials or messages pass（連通身體組織或器官的）道，束：*the digestive tract* 消化道 ◊ *a nerve tract* 神經束 **2** an area of land, especially a large one 大片土地；地帶 **SYN** **stretch**：*vast tracts of forest* 大片大片的森林 **3** (sometimes *disapproving*) a short piece of writing, especially on a religious, moral or political subject, that is intended to influence people's ideas（尤指宣揚宗教、倫理或政治的）短文，傳單，小冊子

tract·able /ˈtræktəbl/ *adj.* (*formal*) easy to deal with or control 易處理的；易駕馭的 **SYN** **manageable** **OPP** **intractable** ▸ **tract·abil·ity** /ˌtræktəˈbɪləti/ *noun* [U]

'tract house (also **'tract home**) *noun* (*NAmE*) a modern house built on an area of land where a lot of other similar houses have also been built（設計類似的）住宅區房屋

trac·tion /ˈtrækʃn/ *noun* [U] **1** the action of pulling sth along a surface; the power that is used for doing this 牽引；拖拉；牽引力；拉力 **2** a way of treating a broken bone in your body that involves using special equipment to pull the bone gradually back into its correct place 牽引（使體內斷骨復位的療法）：*He spent six weeks* **in traction** *after he broke his leg.* 他腿部骨折後做了六個星期的牽引治療。**3** the force that stops sth, for example the wheels of a vehicle, from sliding on the ground（車輪等對地面的）附着摩擦力

'traction engine *noun* a vehicle, driven by steam or DIESEL oil, used in the past for pulling heavy loads（舊時用以拖重物的）牽引機車，牽引車

trac·tor /ˈtræktə(r)/ *noun* **1** a powerful vehicle with two large and two smaller wheels, used especially for pulling farm machinery 拖拉機；牽引機 ➲ **VISUAL VOCAB** pages V2, V3, V58 **2** (*NAmE*) the front part of a tractor-trailer, where the driver sits（牽引式掛車的）牽引車，拖車頭 ➲ **VISUAL VOCAB** page V57

'tractor-trailer (also **'trailer truck**) *noun* (*NAmE*) a large lorry/truck with two sections, one in front where the driver sits and one behind for carrying goods. The sections are connected by a FLEXIBLE joint so that the tractor-trailer can turn corners more easily. 牽引式掛車；鉸接式卡車；載重拖車 ➲ **VISUAL VOCAB** page V57 ➲ see also ARTICULATED

trad /træd/ (also *less frequent* **'trad jazz**) (both *BrE*) *noun* [U] traditional JAZZ in the style of the 1920s, with free playing (= IMPROVISATION) against a background of fixed rhythms and combinations of notes 傳統爵士樂（有 20 世紀 20 年代的風格、固定的節奏及和聲，可即興發揮）➲ see also DIXIELAND

trad·able (also **trade·able**) /ˈtreɪdəbl/ *adj.* (*technical* 術語) that you can easily buy and sell or exchange for money or goods 可買賣的；可交易的 **SYN** **marketable**

trade 🔑 /treɪd/ *noun, verb*
■ ***noun*** **1** 🔑 [U] the activity of buying and selling or of exchanging goods or services between people or countries 貿易；買賣；商業；交易：***international/foreign trade*** 國際／對外貿易 ◊ *Trade between the two countries has increased.* 兩國之間的貿易增長了。◊ *the international trade in oil* 國際石油貿易 ◊ *the* ***arms/drugs, etc. trade*** 軍火、毒品等交易 ➲ **COLLOCATIONS** at BUSINESS, INTERNATIONAL ➲ see also BALANCE OF TRADE, FAIR-TRADE, FREE TRADE **2** 🔑 [C] a particular type of business 行業；職業；生意：*the* ***building/food/tourist, etc. trade*** 建築業、食品業、旅遊業等 ◊ *He works in the* ***retail trade*** (= selling goods in shops/stores). 他做零售工作。➲ see also RAG TRADE **3** **the trade** [sing.+sing./pl. v.] a particular area of business and the people or companies that are connected with it 同業；同行；同人：*They offer discounts to the trade* (= to people who are working in the same business). 他們對同行業的人給予折扣。◊ *a* ***trade magazine/journal*** 行業雜誌／期刊 ➲ see also STOCK-IN-TRADE **4** 🔑 [U, C] the amount of goods or services that you sell 營業額；交易量 **SYN** **business**：*Trade was very good last month.* 上月的交易量很大。**5** 🔑 [U, C] a job, especially one that involves working with your hands and that requires special training and skills（尤指手工）職業；手藝；行當：*He was a carpenter* ***by trade***. 他以木工為業。◊ *When she leaves school, she wants to learn a trade.* 她畢業後想學一門手藝。◊ *She was surrounded by* ***the tools of her trade*** (= everything she needs to do her job). 她周圍都是她幹活用的工具。➲ **SYNONYMS** at WORK **IDM** see JACK *n.*, PLY *v.*, ROARING, TRICK *n.*
■ ***verb*** **1** 🔑 [I, T] to buy and sell things 做買賣；做生意；從事貿易：**~ (in sth) (with sb)** *The firm openly traded in arms.* 這家公司公開買賣軍火。◊ *Early explorers traded directly with the Indians.* 早期的探險者與印第安人直接進行交易。◊ *trading partners* (= countries that you trade with) 貿易夥伴 ◊ **~ sth (with sb)** *Our products are now traded worldwide.* 我們的產品現在銷往世界各地。**2** [I] to exist and operate as a business or company 營業；營運：*The firm has now ceased trading.* 這家商行現已停業。◊ **~ as sb/sth** *They traded as 'Walker and Son'.* 他們以「沃克父子公司」之名營業。**3** [I, T] **~ (sth)** to be bought and sold, or to buy and sell sth, on a STOCK EXCHANGE（在證券交易所）交易，買賣：*Shares were trading at under half their usual value.* 那些股份以低於通常價值的一半買賣。**4** [T] to exchange sth that you have for sth that sb else has 互相交換；以物易物：**~ (sb) sth** *to* ***trade secrets/insults/jokes*** 互換秘密；對罵；互說笑話 ◊ **~ sth for sth** *She traded her posters for his CD.* 她以海報換取他的光盤。◊ **~ sth with sb** *I wouldn't mind* ***trading places*** *with her for a day.* 我不介意和她掉換一天位置。
PHR V **'trade at sth** (*US*) to buy goods or shop at a particular store 在（某商店）購物 **,trade 'down** to

spend less money on things than you used to 降低消費：*Shoppers are trading down and looking for bargains.* 到商店買東西的人都降低消費，尋找減價貨。 **ˌtrade sth↔ˈin** to give sth used as part of the payment for sth new 以舊物折價換新物；折價貼換：*He traded in his old car for a new Mercedes.* 他把舊汽車折價添錢買了輛新奔馳。➲ related noun TRADE-IN **ˌtrade sth↔ˈoff (against/for sth)** to balance two things or situations that are opposed to each other 權衡；平衡；使協調：*They were attempting to trade off inflation against unemployment.* 他們正力求在通貨膨脹和失業之間進行協調。➲ related noun TRADE-OFF **ˈtrade on sth** (*disapproving*) to use sth to your own advantage, especially in an unfair way（為私利不公正地）利用 SYN **exploit**: *They trade on people's insecurity to sell them insurance.* 他們利用人們的不安全感向他們推銷保險。 **ˌtrade ˈup** **1** to sell sth in order to buy sth more expensive 賣次買好；（賣掉原有的以便）買更貴的東西：*We're going to trade up to a larger house.* 我們打算賣掉房子，再買一座大點的。 **2** to give sth you have used as part of the payment for sth more expensive 以舊物折價添錢買較貴的東西；折價貼換

ˈtrade balance *noun* = BALANCE OF TRADE

ˈtrade deficit (also **ˈtrade gap**) *noun* [usually sing.] a situation in which the value of a country's imports is greater than the value of its exports 外貿逆差；貿易赤字

the ˌTrade Deˈscriptions Act *noun* [sing.] (in Britain) a law that states that goods must be described honestly when they are advertised or sold 商品說明法（英國規定商品出售或做廣告必須如實說明）：*You could get them under the Trade Descriptions Act for that!* 你可以根據《商品說明法》將他們繩之以法。

ˈtrade fair (also **ˈtrade show**) *noun* an event at which many different companies show and sell their products 商品展銷會；商品交易會

ˈtrade-in *noun* a method of buying sth by giving a used item as part of the payment for a new one; the used item itself 折舊貼換交易；以舊折價換新；折價舊物：*the trade-in value of a car* 一輛汽車的以舊換新抵價 ◇ *Do you have a trade-in?* 你有折價的舊物品嗎？➲ see also PART EXCHANGE

trade·mark /ˈtreɪdmɑːk; *NAmE* -mɑːrk/ *noun* **1** (*abbr.* **TM**) a name, symbol or design that a company uses for its products and that cannot be used by anyone else 商標：*'Big Mac' is McDonald's best-known trademark.* "巨無霸"是麥當勞最著名的商標。 **2** a special way of behaving or dressing that is typical of sb and that makes them easily recognized（人的行為或衣着的）特徵，標記

ˈtrade name *noun* **1** = BRAND NAME **2** a name that is taken and used by a company for business purposes（公司的）商號，牌號，字號

ˈtrade-off *noun* **~ (between sth and sth)** the act of balancing two things that are opposed to each other（在相互對立的兩者間的）權衡，協調：*a trade-off between increased production and a reduction in quality* 對產量增加和質量下降的權衡

trader /ˈtreɪdə(r)/ *noun* a person who buys and sells things as a job 商人；經商者；買賣人；證券交易人：***small/independent/local traders*** 小的／獨立的／當地的商人 ◇ ***bond/currency traders*** 債券／貨幣交易人

ˈtrade route *noun* (in the past) the route that people buying and selling goods used to take across land or sea（舊時的）商隊路線，商船航線

ˈtrade school *noun* (*NAmE*) a school where students go to learn a trade 中等職業學校

ˌtrade ˈsecret *noun* a secret piece of information that is known only by the people at a particular company 商業秘密：*The recipe for their drink is a closely guarded trade secret.* 他們飲料的配方是嚴格保守的商業秘密。

ˈtrade show *noun* = TRADE FAIR

trades·man /ˈtreɪdzmən/ *noun* (*pl.* **-men** /-mən/) **1** a person whose job involves going to houses to sell or deliver goods 上門推銷商；送貨員 **2** (*especially BrE*) a person who sells goods, especially in a shop/store 售貨的商人；店主 SYN **shopkeeper** **3** (*especially NAmE*) a skilled person, especially one who makes things by hand 工匠；手藝人

trades·people /ˈtreɪdzpiːpl/ *noun* [pl.] **1** people whose job involves selling goods or services, especially people who own a shop/store（統稱）商人，商店主人 **2** people whose job involves training and special skills, for example CARPENTERS 手藝人；工匠

the ˌTrades ˌUnion ˈCongress *noun* [sing.] = TUC

ˌtrade ˈsurplus *noun* a situation in which the value of a country's exports is greater than the value of its imports 外貿盈餘；貿易順差

ˌtrade ˈunion (*BrE* also **ˌtrades ˈunion**) *noun* = UNION (1) ▶ **ˌtrade ˈunionism** *noun* [U]：*the history of trade unionism* 工會主義的歷史

ˌtrade ˈunionist (also **ˌtrades ˈunionist**, **union·ist**) *noun* a member of a trade/labor union 工會會員

ˈtrade-up *noun* a sale of an object in order to buy sth similar but better and more expensive 賣次買好；以次換好的買賣

ˈtrade winds *noun* [pl.] strong winds that blow all the time towards the EQUATOR and then to the west 信風，貿易風（穩定吹向赤道再向西）

trad·ing 0-m /ˈtreɪdɪŋ/ *noun* [U] the activity of buying and selling things 貿易；經商；營業；交易：*new laws on Sunday trading* (= shops being open on Sundays) 關於星期日營業的新法律 ◇ *Supermarkets everywhere reported excellent trading in the run-up to Christmas.* 各地超級市場報告說聖誕節前生意火爆。◇ *Shares worth $8 million changed hands during a day of hectic trading.* 當日交投活躍，股票轉手市值達 800 萬元。

ˈtrading card *noun* (*especially NAmE*) one of a set of cards, often showing sports players or other famous people on them, that children collect and exchange with one another 集換式卡牌（兒童收集並相互交換的運動員或明星等卡牌）

ˈtrading estate *noun* (*BrE*) an area of land, often on the edge of a city or town, where there are a number of businesses and small factories（城鎮邊緣的）工商業區 ➲ compare INDUSTRIAL ESTATE

ˈtrading floor *noun* an area in a STOCK EXCHANGE or bank where shares and other SECURITIES are bought and sold（證券交易所或銀行的）交易大廳

ˈtrading post *noun* a small place in an area that is a long way from any town, used as a centre for buying and selling goods (especially in N America in the past)（尤指北美舊時偏遠地區的）貿易站

trad·ition 0-m AW /trəˈdɪʃn/ *noun* [C, U] a belief, custom or way of doing sth that has existed for a long time among a particular group of people; a set of these beliefs or customs 傳統；傳統的信仰（或風俗）：***religious/cultural, etc. traditions*** 宗教、文化等傳統 ◇ *This region is* ***steeped in tradition.*** 這個地區有着深厚的傳統。◇ *The company has a* ***long tradition*** *of fine design.* 這家公司的優秀設計歷史悠久。◇ *The British are said to love tradition* (= to want to do things in the way they have always been done). 據說英國人熱愛傳統。◇ *They* ***broke with tradition*** (= did things differently) *and got married quietly.* 他們打破傳統，毫不聲張地結了婚。◇ ***By tradition,*** *children play tricks on 1 April.* 按照傳統風俗，兒童在 4 月 1 日搗亂戲弄別人。◇ *There's a tradition in our family that we have a party on New Year's Eve.* 我們家有個傳統，新年除夕要辦家庭聚會。◇ *He's a politician* ***in the tradition of*** (= similar in style to) *Kennedy.* 他是位具有肯尼迪風格的政治家。

trad·ition·al 0-m AW /trəˈdɪʃənl/ *adj.* **1** 0-m being part of the beliefs, customs or way of life of a particular group of people, that have not changed for a long time 傳統的；習俗的；慣例的：*traditional dress* 傳統服裝 ◇ ***It's traditional*** *in America to eat turkey on Thanksgiving Day.* 感恩節時吃火雞是美國的傳統。 **2** 0-m (sometimes *disapproving*) following older methods and ideas rather than modern or different ones 傳統

T

的；因襲的；守舊的 SYN **conventional**：*traditional methods of teaching* 傳統的教學方法 ◇ *Their marriage is very traditional.* 他們的婚姻十分守舊。▶ **trad·ition·al·ly** AW /-ʃənəli/ *adv.*：*The festival is traditionally held in May.* 這個節日按照傳統是在五月份過的。◇ *Housework has traditionally been regarded as women's work.* 家務歷來被視為女性的工作。

trad·ition·al·ism /trəˈdɪʃənəlɪzəm/ *noun* [U] the belief that customs and traditions are more important for a society than modern ideas 傳統主義（認為傳統習俗比現代思想對社會更重要）

trad·ition·al·ist AW /trəˈdɪʃənəlɪst/ *noun* a person who prefers tradition to modern ideas or ways of doing things 傳統主義者 ▶ **trad·ition·al·ist** *adj.*

ˈtrad jazz *noun* [U] = TRAD

tra·duce /trəˈdjuːs; *NAmE* -ˈduːs/ *verb* **~ sb** (*formal*) to say things about sb that are unpleasant or not true 誹謗；中傷；詆譭 SYN **slander**

traf·fic /ˈtræfɪk/ *noun, verb*

■ ***noun*** [U] **1** the vehicles that are on a road at a particular time 路上行駛的車輛；交通：***heavy/rush-hour traffic*** 繁忙的／高峰時刻的交通 ◇ ***local/through traffic*** 當地／過境車輛 ◇ *There's always a lot of traffic at this time of day.* 每天這個時候總是有很多來往車輛。◇ *They were stuck* ***in traffic*** *and missed their flight.* 他們遇到了塞車，沒趕上班機。◇ *a plan to reduce* ***traffic congestion*** 減少交通擁塞的計劃 ◇ ***traffic police*** (= who control traffic on a road or stop drivers who are breaking the law) 交通警察 ◇ *The delay is due simply to the* ***volume of traffic.*** 延誤完全是因為交通擁擠。➲ COLLOCATIONS at DRIVING **2** the movement of ships, trains, aircraft, etc. along a particular route（沿固定路線的）航行，行駛，飛行：*transatlantic traffic* 橫渡大西洋的航行 ◇ *air traffic control* 空中交通管制 **3** the movement of people or goods from one place to another 運輸；人流；貨流：***commuter/freight/passenger traffic*** 市郊間上下班運輸；貨運；客運 ◇ *the traffic of goods between one country and another* 一國與另一國間的貨物運輸 **4** the movement of messages and signals through an electronic communication system 信息流量；通信（量）：*the computer servers that manage global Internet traffic* 管理全球互聯網通信的計算機服務器 **5 ~ (in sth)** illegal trade in sth（非法的）交易，買賣：*the traffic in firearms* 非法軍火交易

■ ***verb*** (-ck-)

PHR V **ˈtraffic in sth** to buy and sell sth illegally（非法）進行…交易，做…買賣：*to traffic in drugs* 買賣毒品 ▶ **traf·fick·er** *noun*：*a drugs trafficker* 毒品販子 **traf·fick·ing** *noun* [U]：*drug trafficking* 販毒

T

ˈtraffic calming *noun* [U] (*BrE*) ways of making roads safer, especially for people who are walking or riding bicycles, by building raised areas, etc. to make cars go more slowly 道路安全措施，減緩機動車速措施（如在馬路設置凸面使車輛減速，保障行人及騎自行車者的安全）

ˈtraffic circle (also **ro·tary**) (both *NAmE*) (*BrE* **round·about**) *noun* a place where two or more roads meet, forming a circle that all traffic must go around in the same direction（交通）環島

ˈtraffic cone *noun* = CONE *n.* (3)

ˈtraffic island (*BrE* also **island**, **ref·uge**) (*US* also **ˈsafety island**) *noun* an area in the middle of a road where you can stand and wait for cars to go past until it is safe for you to cross 安全島（供行人避讓車輛）

ˈtraffic jam *noun* a long line of vehicles on a road that cannot move or that can only move very slowly 堵車；交通阻塞：*We were* ***stuck in a traffic jam.*** 我們遇上了交通阻塞。➲ COLLOCATIONS at DRIVING

ˈtraffic light *noun* [C] (also **ˈtraffic lights** [pl.]) (*NAmE* also **stop·lights** [pl.]) a signal that controls the traffic on a road, by means of red, orange and green lights that show when you must stop and when you can go 交通信號燈：*Turn left at the traffic lights.* 在交通信號燈處向左拐。➲ VISUAL VOCAB pages V2, V3

ˈtraffic warden *noun* (*BrE*) a person whose job is to check that people do not park their cars in the wrong place or for longer than is allowed, and to report on those who do or tell them that they have to pay a FINE（處理違章停車的）交通管理員

tra·gedian /trəˈdʒiːdiən/ *noun* (*formal*) **1** a person who writes tragedies for the theatre 悲劇作家 **2** an actor in tragedies 悲劇演員

tra·gedy /ˈtrædʒədi/ *noun* [C, U] (*pl.* **-ies**) **1** a very sad event or situation, especially one that involves death 悲慘的事；不幸；災難；慘案：***It's a tragedy*** *that she died so young.* 她英年早逝是一大悲哀。◇ ***Tragedy struck*** *the family when their son was hit by a car and killed.* 這個家庭慘遭不幸，他們的兒子被汽車撞死了。◇ *The whole affair* ***ended in tragedy.*** 整個事件以悲劇而告終。**2** a serious play with a sad ending, especially one in which the main character dies; plays of this type 悲劇；悲劇作品：*Shakespeare's tragedies* 莎士比亞的悲劇 ◇ *Greek tragedy* 希臘悲劇 ➲ compare COMEDY (1)

tra·gic /ˈtrædʒɪk/ *adj.* **1** making you feel very sad, usually because sb has died or suffered a lot 悲慘的；悲痛的；可悲的：*He was killed in a tragic accident at the age of 24.* 他 24 歲時在一次悲慘的事故中喪命。◇ *Cuts in the health service could have tragic consequences for patients.* 減少公共醫療衞生服務可能對病人造成悲慘的後果。◇ *It would be tragic if her talent remained unrecognized.* 若她一直懷才不遇，那就可悲了。**2** [only before noun] connected with tragedy (= the style of literature) 悲劇的：***a tragic actor/hero*** 悲劇演員／男主角 ▶ **tra·gic·al·ly** /-kli/ *adv.*：*Tragically, his wife was killed in a car accident.* 他的妻子在車禍中不幸身亡。◇ *He died tragically young.* 他英年早逝。

ˌtragic ˈirony *noun* [U] (*technical* 術語) a technique in literature in which a character's actions or thoughts are known to the reader or audience but not to the other characters in the story 悲劇性諷刺（故事中某個人物的行為或想法為讀者或觀眾所知卻不為故事中其他人物所知的表現手法）

tragi·com·edy /ˌtrædʒiˈkɒmədi; *NAmE* -ˈkɑːm-/ *noun* [C, U] (*pl.* **-ies**) **1** a play that is both funny and sad; plays of this type 悲喜劇；悲喜劇作品 **2** an event or a situation that is both funny and sad 悲喜交加的事情（或局面）▶ **tragi·com·ic** /-ˈkɒmɪk; *NAmE* -ˈkɑːm-/ *adj.*

trail /treɪl/ *noun, verb*

■ ***noun*** **1** a long line or series of marks that is left by sb/sth（長串的）痕跡，蹤跡，足跡：*a trail of blood* 一連串血跡 ◇ *tourists who* ***leave a trail*** *of litter everywhere they go* 一路亂丟垃圾的遊客 ◇ *The hurricane left a trail of destruction behind it.* 颶風過後滿目瘡痍。**2** a track, sign or smell that is left behind and that can be followed, especially in hunting（尤指打獵時跟蹤的）蹤跡，足跡，臭跡：*The hounds were following the fox's trail.* 獵犬追踪着狐狸的氣味。◇ *The police are still* ***on the trail of*** *the escaped prisoner.* 警方仍在追捕逃犯。◇ *Fortunately the* ***trail was still warm*** (= clear and easy to follow). 慶幸的是痕跡仍然清晰可循。◇ *The* ***trail had gone cold.*** 臭跡已經消失了。**3** a path through the countryside（鄉間的）小路，小徑：*a trail through the forest* 穿過森林的小路 ➲ see also NATURE TRAIL **4** a route that is followed for a particular purpose（特定）路線，路徑：*a* ***tourist trail*** (= of famous buildings) 遊覽路線 ◇ *politicians on the* ***campaign trail*** (= travelling around to attract support) 進行巡迴宣傳的政治人物 IDM see BLAZE *v.*, HIT *v.*, HOT *adj.*

■ ***verb*** **1** [T, I] to pull sth behind sb/sth, usually along the ground; to be pulled along in this way（被）拖，拉：**~ sth** *A jeep trailing a cloud of dust was speeding in my direction.* 一輛吉普車拖着一股揚塵，朝我疾馳而來。◇ *I trailed my hand in the water as the boat moved along.* 我把手放在水裏，讓小船拖着往前划行。◇ **(+ adv./prep.)** *The bride's dress trailed behind her.* 新娘的結婚禮服拖在身後。**2** [I] **+ adv./prep.** to walk slowly because you are tired or bored, especially behind sb else（尤指跟在他人後面）疲憊地走，沒精打采地慢走，磨蹭：*The kids trailed around after us while we shopped for clothes.* 我們在商店買衣服時，孩子們無精打采地跟在後面。**3** [I, T] (used especially in the progressive tenses 尤用於進行時) to be losing a game or other contest（在比賽或其他競

賽中）落後，失利，失敗： *United were trailing 2–0 at half-time.* 聯隊在上半場結束時以 0:2 落後。◇ **~ by sth** *We were trailing by five points.* 我們落後五分。◇ **~ in sth** *This country is still trailing badly in scientific research.* 這個國家在科研方面仍然大大滯後。◇ **~ sb/sth** *The Conservatives are trailing Labour in the opinion polls.* 在民意測驗中保守黨的支持率落後於工黨。 **4** [T] **~ sb/sth** to follow sb/sth by looking for signs that show you where they have been 跟踪；追踪： *The police trailed Dale for days.* 警方跟踪了戴爾多日。 **5** [I] to grow or hang downwards over sth or along the ground; to move downwards over sth 蔓生；蔓延；沿…向下移動： *trailing plants* 蔓生植物 ◇ *He had tears trailing down his cheeks.* 他的眼淚順着雙頰流了下來。

PHR V **,trail a'way/'off** (of sb's speech 話語) to become gradually quieter and then stop 聲音逐漸減弱到停止；逐漸消失： *His voice trailed away to nothing.* 他的聲音越來越小，最後消失了。◇ **+ speech** *'I only hope ...', she trailed off.* "我只希望…"她的聲音越來越小，最後聽不到了。

'trail bike *noun* a light motorcycle that can be used on rough ground 越野摩托車；越野機車

trail·blazer /'treɪlbleɪzə(r)/ *noun* a person who is the first to do or discover sth and so makes it possible for others to follow 創始人；先驅；拓荒者；開路先鋒 ➲ compare BLAZE A TRAIL at BLAZE *v.* ▶ **trail·blaz·ing** *adj.* [usually before noun]： *trailblazing scientific research* 創新的科學研究

trail·er /'treɪlə(r)/ *noun* **1** a truck, or a container with wheels, that is pulled by another vehicle 拖車；掛車： *a car towing a trailer with a boat on it* 拖着一輛載有小船的拖車的小汽車 ➲ VISUAL VOCAB page V58 ➲ see also TRACTOR-TRAILER **2** (*NAmE*) (*BrE* **mobile home**) a vehicle without an engine, that can be pulled by a car or truck or used as a home or an office when it is parked （拖車式）活動房屋，活動工作室： *a trailer park* (= an area where trailers are parked and used as homes) 拖車式活動房屋停車場 ➲ VISUAL VOCAB page V16 **3** (*NAmE*) = MOBILE HOME (1) **4** (*especially BrE*) (*NAmE* usually **preview**) a series of short scenes from a film/movie or television programme, shown in advance to advertise it（電影或電視節目的）預告片 ➲ SYNONYMS at ADVERTISEMENT

'trailer trash *noun* [U] (*NAmE, informal, offensive*) a way of referring to poor white people from a low social class 旅行車垃圾（指地位低下的貧困白人）

'trailer truck *noun* (*NAmE*) = TRACTOR-TRAILER

,trailing 'edge *noun* (*technical* 術語) the rear edge of sth moving, especially an aircraft wing （移動物體，尤指機翼的）後緣 ➲ VISUAL VOCAB page V53

train 0→ /treɪn/ *noun, verb*

■ *noun* **1** 0→ a railway/railroad engine pulling a number of coaches/cars or trucks, taking people and goods from one place to another 火車；列車： *to get on/off a train* 上／下火車 ◇ *I like travelling **by train**.* 我喜歡乘火車旅行。◇ *a **passenger/commuter/goods/freight train*** 客運／市郊通勤／貨運列車 ◇ *to **catch/take/get the train** to London* 趕上／乘坐／搭乘開往倫敦的火車 ◇ *a **train journey/driver*** 火車旅程／司機 ◇ *You have to **change trains** at Reading.* 你得在雷丁倒車。 ➲ VISUAL VOCAB page V58 ➲ see also GRAVY TRAIN, ROAD TRAIN, WAGON TRAIN **2** a number of people or animals moving in a line 列隊行進的人（或動物）；隊列；行列： *a camel train* 駱駝隊 **3** [usually sing.] a series of events or actions that are connected 一系列相關的事情（或行動）： *His death set in motion a **train of events** that led to the outbreak of war.* 他的死引發了一系列的事件，從而導致了戰爭的爆發。 **4** the part of a long formal dress that spreads out on the floor behind the person wearing it 拖裾，裙裾（長禮服的曳地部份）

IDM **bring sth in its 'train** (*formal*) to have sth as a result 帶來…後果： *Unemployment brings great difficulties in its train.* 失業帶來了重重困難。 **in sb's 'train** (*formal*) following behind sb 跟隨…之後： *In the train of the rich and famous came the journalists.* 記者蜂擁在豪紳名流之後。 **set sth in 'train** (*formal*) to prepare or start sth 安排；準備；開始： *That telephone call set in train a whole series of events.* 那通電話把一整套事項安排好了。 **a train of 'thought** the connected series of thoughts that are in your head at a particular time 思路；思緒： *The phone ringing interrupted my train of thought.* 電話鈴聲打斷了我的思路。

■ *verb* **1** 0→ [T, I] to teach a person or an animal the skills for a particular job or activity; to be taught in this way 訓練；培訓；接受訓練： **~ sb/sth** *badly trained staff* 缺乏訓練的員工 ◇ **~ sb/sth to do sth** *They train dogs to sniff out drugs.* 他們訓練狗嗅出毒品。◇ **~ (sb) (as/in/for sth)** *He trained as a teacher before becoming an actor.* 他在成為演員之前受過師資培訓。◇ *All members of the team have trained in first aid.* 全隊隊員都接受過急救培訓。◇ **~ to do/be sth** *Sue is training to be a doctor.* 蘇正在接受醫生培訓。 **2** 0→ [I, T] to prepare yourself/sb for a particular activity, especially a sport, by doing a lot of exercise; to prepare a person or an animal in this way 進行…訓練；（尤指）進行體育鍛煉；訓練（人或動物）： **~ (for/in sth)** *athletes training for the Olympics* 為迎戰奧林匹克運動會而進行訓練的運動員 ◇ **~ sb/sth (for/in sth)** *She trains horses.* 她是馴馬的。◇ *He trains the Olympic team.* 他訓練奧林匹克隊。 **3** [T] to develop a natural ability or quality so that it improves 教育；培養…的能力（或素質）： **~ sth** *An expert with a trained eye will spot the difference immediately.* 訓練有素眼光敏銳的專家會馬上發現差別所在。◇ **~ sth to do sth** *You can train your mind to think positively.* 你可以培養自己有樂觀思想的能力。 **4** [T] **~ sth (around/along/up, etc.)** to make a plant grow in a particular direction 使（植物）朝某方向生長；修整： *Roses had been trained around the door.* 玫瑰被修整得圍繞着門口生長。

PHR V **'train sth at/on sb/sth** to aim a gun, camera, light, etc. at sb/sth 把（槍口、照相機、燈光等）瞄準，對準

train·ee /,treɪ'niː/ *noun* a person who is being taught how to do a particular job 接受培訓者；實習生；見習生： *a management trainee* 管理培訓生 ◇ *a trainee teacher* 實習教師 ➲ COLLOCATIONS at JOB

train·er /'treɪnə(r)/ *noun* **1** (also **'training shoe**) (both *BrE*) (*NAmE* **sneak·er**) [usually pl.] a shoe that you wear for sports or as informal clothing 運動鞋；便鞋： *a pair of trainers* 一雙運動鞋 ➲ VISUAL VOCAB page V64 ➲ see also CROSS-TRAINER **2** a person who teaches people or animals to perform a particular job or skill well, or to do a particular sport 教員；馴獸師；教練員： *teacher trainers* 培訓師資的教員 ◇ *a racehorse trainer* 賽馬馴馬師 ◇ *Her trainer had decided she shouldn't run in the race.* 她的教練決定她不應參加賽跑。 ➲ see also PERSONAL TRAINER

train·ing 0→ /'treɪnɪŋ/ *noun* [U] **1** 0→ **~ (in sth/in doing sth)** the process of learning the skills that you need to do a job 訓練；培訓： *staff training* 職工培訓 ◇ *Few candidates had received any training in management.* 沒有幾個應聘者接受過管理培訓。◇ *a training course* 培訓課程 ➲ COLLOCATIONS at EDUCATION, JOB **2** 0→ the process of preparing to take part in a sports competition by doing physical exercises （為參加體育比賽而進行的）訓練，鍛煉： *to be **in training** for a race* 在進行賽跑訓練

'training college *noun* (*BrE*) a college that trains people for a job or profession 專科學院；職業（培訓）學院： *a police training college* 警察學院

'training shoe *noun* (*BrE*) = TRAINER (1)

'training wheels (*NAmE*) (*BrE* **sta·bil·izers**) *noun* [pl.] small wheels that are fitted at each side of the back wheel on a child's bicycle to stop it from falling over （兒童自行車後輪兩側的）輔助輪 ➲ VISUAL VOCAB page V51

train·man /'treɪnmən/ *noun* (*pl.* **-men** /-mən/) (*NAmE*) a member of the team of people operating a train 列車員；乘務員

'train set *noun* a toy train, together with the track that it runs on, a toy station, etc. 玩具火車（包括鐵軌、車站等成套玩具）

T

train·spot·ter /ˈtreɪnspɒtə(r); *NAmE* -spɑːt-/ *noun* (*BrE*) **1** a person who collects the numbers of railway engines as a hobby （作為業餘愛好）收集機車號碼的人 **2** (*disapproving*) a person who is interested in the details of a subject that other people think are boring 過分注重細節的人 ▸ **ˈtrain·spot·ting** *noun* [U]

traipse /treɪps/ *verb* [I] **+ adv./prep.** (*informal*) to walk somewhere slowly when you are tired and unwilling 疲憊地走；拖沓地行走；磨蹭

trait /treɪt/ *noun* a particular quality in your personality （人的個性的）特徵，特性，特點：*personality traits* 個性特點

trai·tor /ˈtreɪtə(r)/ *noun* **~ (to sb/sth)** a person who gives away secrets about their friends, their country, etc. 背叛者；叛徒；賣國賊：*He was seen as a traitor to the socialist cause.* 他被視為社會主義事業的叛徒。◇ *She denied that she had* ***turned traitor*** (= become a traitor). 她否認自己叛變了。

trai·tor·ous /ˈtreɪtərəs/ *adj.* (*formal*) giving away secrets about your friends, your country, etc. 背叛的；叛國的；賣國的 ▸ **trai·tor·ous·ly** *adv.*

tra·jec·tory /trəˈdʒektəri/ (*pl.* **-ies**) *noun* (*technical* 術語) the curved path of sth that has been fired, hit or thrown into the air （射體在空中的）軌道，彈道，軌跡，流軌：*a missile's trajectory* 導彈的彈道 ◇ (*figurative*) *My career seemed to be on a downward trajectory.* 我的事業似乎在走下坡路。

tram /træm/ (also **tram·car**) (both *BrE*) (*US* **street·car**, **trol·ley**) *noun* a vehicle driven by electricity, that runs on rails along the streets of a town and carries passengers 有軌電車：*a tram route* 有軌電車路線 ➲ VISUAL VOCAB page V58

tram·lines /ˈtræmlaɪnz/ *noun* [pl.] **1** the rails in the street that trams run on 電車軌道 **2** (*BrE*) (*NAmE* **alley**) (*informal*) the pair of parallel lines on a TENNIS or BADMINTON COURT that mark the extra area that is used when four people are playing （網球或羽毛球雙打時）球場兩側的加線

tram·mel /ˈtræml/ *verb* (**-ll-**, *especially US* **-l-**) [often passive] **~ sb/sth** (*formal*) to limit sb's freedom of movement or activity 限制，束縛，阻礙（某人的活動自由） SYN **restrict** ➲ compare UNTRAMMELLED

tramp /træmp/ *noun, verb*

■ ***noun*** **1** (also **hobo**) [C] a person with no home or job who travels from place to place, usually asking people in the street for food or money 流浪漢；流浪乞丐 **2** [sing.] **the ~ of sb/sth** the sound of sb's heavy steps 沉重的腳步聲：*the tramp of marching feet* 行進中沉重的腳步聲 **3** [C, usually sing.] a long walk 長途步行；徒步旅行 SYN **trek**：*We had a long tramp home.* 我們是經過長途跋涉回家的。 **4** (*old-fashioned, NAmE, disapproving*) a woman who has many sexual partners 淫婦；蕩婦

■ ***verb*** (also *NAmE informal* **tromp**) [I, T] to walk with heavy or noisy steps, especially for a long time（尤指長時間地）重步行走，踏，踩：(**+ adv./prep.**) *We tramped across the wet grass to look at the statue.* 我們踏過濕漉漉的草地去看那座雕像。◇ *the sound of tramping feet* 沉重的腳步聲 ◇ **~ sth** *She's been tramping the streets looking for a job.* 她一直在大街上四處奔走尋找工作。

tram·ple /ˈtræmpl/ *verb* **1** [T, I] to step heavily on sb/sth so that you crush or harm them/it with your feet 踩碎；踩傷；踐踏：**~ sb/sth** *People were* ***trampled underfoot*** *in the rush for the exit.* 有人在拚命湧向出口時被踩在腳下。◇ *He was* ***trampled to death*** *by a runaway horse.* 他被一匹脫韁的馬踩死了。◇ **~ sb/sth down** *The campers had trampled the corn down.* 野營的人踐踏了莊稼。◇ **~ on/over sth** *Don't trample on the flowers!* 勿踏花草！ **2** [I] **~ (on/over) sb/sth** to ignore sb's feelings or rights and treat them as if they are not important 踐踏，摧殘（人權、心靈等）：*The government is trampling on the views of ordinary people.* 政府在踐踏民意。

tram·po·line /ˈtræmpəliːn/ *noun, verb*

■ ***noun*** a piece of equipment that is used in GYMNASTICS for doing jumps in the air. It consists of a sheet of strong material that is attached by springs to a frame. 蹦牀，跳牀，彈牀（體操器械） ➲ VISUAL VOCAB page V37

■ ***verb*** [I] to jump on a trampoline 在蹦牀上彈跳 ▸ **tram·po·lin·ing** *noun* [U]

tram·way /ˈtræmweɪ/ *noun* the rails that form the route for a TRAM 有軌電車軌道

trance /trɑːns; *NAmE* træns/ *noun* **1** [C] a state in which sb seems to be asleep but is aware of what is said to them, for example if they are HYPNOTIZED 昏睡狀態；催眠狀態：*to* ***go/fall into a trance*** 進入／陷入昏睡狀態 **2** [C] a state in which you are thinking so much about sth that you do not notice what is happening around you 出神；發呆 SYN **daze 3** (also **ˈtrance music**) [U] a type of electronic dance music with HYPNOTIC rhythms and sounds 迷幻音樂

tranche /trɑːnʃ/ *noun* (*finance* 財) (*BrE*) one of the parts into which an amount of money or a number of shares in a company is divided （款額或股份的）一份，一部份

tranny (also **tran·nie**) /ˈtræni/ *noun* (*pl.* **-ies**) (*informal*) **1** a TRANSSEXUAL or TRANSVESTITE 變性者；易性癖者；易裝癖者 **2** (*especially BrE*) a TRANSISTOR radio 晶體管收音機；電晶體收音機 **3** a TRANSPARENCY (1) 幻燈片；透明正片

tran·quil /ˈtræŋkwɪl/ *adj.* (*formal*) quiet and peaceful 安靜的；平靜的；安寧的 SYN **serene**：*a tranquil scene* 靜謐的景象 ◇ *the tranquil waters of the lake* 平靜無波的湖水 ◇ *She led a tranquil life in the country.* 她過着恬靜的鄉村生活。 ▸ **tran·quil·lity** (*BrE*) (*NAmE* also **tran·quil·ity**) /træŋˈkwɪləti/ *noun* [U] **tran·quil·ly** *adv.*

tran·quil·lize (also **-ise**) (both *BrE*) (*NAmE* **tran·quil·ize**) /ˈtræŋkwəlaɪz/ *verb* **~ sb/sth** to make a person or an animal calm or unconscious, especially by giving them a drug (= a TRANQUILLIZER) （尤指用鎮定劑）使平靜，使安定

tran·quil·lizer (also **-iser**) (both *BrE*) (*NAmE* **tran·quil·izer**) /ˈtræŋkwəlaɪzə(r)/ *noun* a drug used to reduce anxiety 安定藥；鎮靜劑：*She's on* (= is taking) *tranquillizers.* 她在服用鎮靜劑。

trans- /trænz-; træns-/ *prefix* **1** (in adjectives 構成形容詞) across; beyond 橫穿；通過；超越：*transatlantic* 橫渡大西洋的 ◇ *transcontinental* 橫貫大陸的 **2** (in verbs 構成動詞) into another place or state 進入（另一地方）；成為（另一狀態）：*transplant* 移植 ◇ *transform* 轉變

trans·act /trænˈzækt/ *verb* [T, I] **~ (sth) (with sb)** (*formal*) to do business with a person or an organization （與人或組織）做業務，做交易：*buyers and sellers transacting business* 進行交易的買方和賣方

trans·ac·tion /trænˈzækʃn/ *noun* **1** [C] **~ (between A and B)** a piece of business that is done between people, especially an act of buying or selling （一筆）交易，業務，買賣 SYN **deal**：*financial transactions between companies* 公司之間的財務往來 ◇ *commercial transactions* 商業交易 **2** [U] **~ of sth** (*formal*) the process of doing sth 辦理；處理：*the transaction of government business* 處理政府事務

trans·at·lan·tic /ˌtrænzətˈlæntɪk/ *adj.* [only before noun] **1** crossing the Atlantic Ocean 橫渡大西洋的；橫越大西洋的：*a transatlantic flight* 橫越大西洋的飛行 **2** connected with countries on both sides of the Atlantic Ocean 大西洋兩岸國家的：*a transatlantic alliance* 大西洋兩岸國家聯盟 **3** on or from the other side of the Atlantic Ocean 在大西洋彼岸的；來自大西洋彼岸的：*to speak with a transatlantic accent* 說話帶大西洋對岸的口音

trans·ceiver /trænˈsiːvə(r)/ *noun* a radio that can both send and receive messages 無線電收發兩用機

tran·scend /trænˈsend/ *verb* **~ sth** (*formal*) to be or go beyond the usual limits of sth 超出，超越（通常的界限） SYN **exceed**

tran·scend·ent /trænˈsendənt/ *adj.* (*formal*) going beyond the usual limits; extremely great 卓越的；傑出的；極其偉大的 ▸ **tran·scend·ence** /-dəns/ *noun* [U]：*the transcendence of God* 上帝的至高無上

tran·scen·den·tal /ˌtrænsenˈdentl/ *adj.* [usually before noun] going beyond the limits of human knowledge, experience or reason, especially in a religious or spiritual way（尤指宗教或精神方面）超凡的，玄奧的：*a transcendental experience* 超凡的感受

ˌtranscenˌdental mediˈtation (*BrE*) (*NAmE* **Transcendental Meditation™**) *noun* [U] (*abbr.* **TM**) a method of making yourself calm by thinking deeply in silence and repeating a special phrase to yourself many times 超脱禪定法（靜思默唸真言）

trans·con·tin·en·tal /ˌtrænzˌkɒntɪˈnentl; ˌtræns-; *NAmE* -ˌkɑːn-/ *adj.* crossing a continent 橫貫大陸的；穿越大陸的：*a transcontinental railway/railroad* 橫貫大陸的鐵路

tran·scribe /trænˈskraɪb/ *verb* **1** to record thoughts, speech or data in a written form, or in a different written form from the original 記錄；抄錄；把…轉成（另一種書寫形式）：**~ sth** *Clerks transcribe everything that is said in court.* 書記員把在法庭上所有的話都記錄在案。◇ *The interview was recorded and then transcribed.* 採訪談話先錄了音，然後再抄錄出來。◇ **~ sth into sth** *How many official documents have been transcribed into Braille for blind people?* 有多少官方文件已經轉成盲文供盲人閱讀？ **2 ~ sth** (*technical* 術語) to show the sounds of speech using a special PHONETIC alphabet 用音標標音 **3 ~ sth (for sth)** to write a piece of music in a different form so that it can be played by another musical instrument or sung by another voice 改編（樂曲，以適合其他樂器或聲部）：*a piano piece transcribed for the guitar* 為吉他改編的鋼琴曲

tran·script /ˈtrænskrɪpt/ *noun* **1** (also **tran·scrip·tion**) a written or printed copy of words that have been spoken 抄本；謄本；打印本：*a transcript of the interview* 採訪內容的文字稿 **2** (*especially NAmE*) an official record of a student's work that shows the courses they have taken and the marks/grades they have achieved 學生成績報告單

tran·scrip·tion /trænˈskrɪpʃn/ *noun* **1** [U] the act or process of representing sth in a written or printed form 抄寫；謄寫；打印：*errors made in transcription* 抄寫錯誤 ◇ *phonetic transcription* 標音 **2** [C] = TRANSCRIPT (1)：*The full transcription of the interview is attached.* 現附上採訪記錄文本的全文。 **3** [C] something that is represented in writing 書面標註的事物：*This dictionary gives phonetic transcriptions of all headwords.* 本詞典所有詞目都註出了音標。 **4** [C] a change in the written form of a piece of music so that it can be played on a different instrument or sung by a different voice（樂曲的）改編

trans·ducer /trænzˈdjuːsə(r); træns-; *NAmE* -ˈduːsər/ *noun* (*technical* 術語) a device for producing an electrical signal from another form of energy such as pressure 換能器；變換器

tran·sept /ˈtrænsept/ *noun* (*architecture* 建) either of the two wide parts of a church shaped like a cross, that are built at RIGHT ANGLES to the main central part（十字形教堂的）耳堂 ➲ compare NAVE

tran·sex·ual = TRANSSEXUAL

ˌtrans-fatty ˈacid (also **ˌtrans-ˈfat**) *noun* [C, U] a type of fat produced when oils are changed by a chemical process into solids, for example to make MARGARINE. Trans-fatty acids are believed to encourage the harmful development of CHOLESTEROL. 反式脂肪酸：*foods that are low in trans-fatty acids* 低反式脂肪酸食物 ➲ see also MONOUNSATURATED FAT, POLYUNSATURATED FAT, SATURATED FAT, UNSATURATED FAT

trans·fer 🗝 **AW** *verb, noun*

■ *verb* /trænsˈfɜː(r)/ (**-rr-**)

▸ **TO NEW PLACE** 到新地方 **1** 🗝 [I, T] to move from one place to another; to move sth/sb from one place to another（使）轉移，搬遷：**~ (from …) (to …)** *The film studio is transferring to Hollywood.* 這家電影製片廠正遷往好萊塢。◇ (*especially NAmE*) *If I spend a semester in Madrid, will my credits transfer?* 如果我在馬德里上一學期的課，我的學分能轉過來嗎？◇ **~ sth/sb (from …) (to …)** *How can I transfer money from my bank account to his?* 怎麼才能把我賬戶上的錢轉到他的賬戶上呢？◇ *The patient was transferred to another hospital.* 患者轉送到了另一家醫院。◇ (*especially NAmE*) *I couldn't transfer all my credits from junior college.* 我無法把我在專科學校的所有學分都轉過來。

▸ **TO NEW JOB/SCHOOL/SITUATION** 到新的工作／學校／環境 **2** 🗝 [I, T] to move from one job, school, situation, etc. to another; to arrange for sb to move（使）調動；轉職；轉學；改變（環境）：**~ (from …) (to …)** *Children usually transfer to secondary school at 11 or 12.* 兒童通常在 11 或 12 歲時升讀中學。◇ *He transferred to UCLA after his freshman year.* 他讀完大學一年級後，轉學到加利福尼亞大學洛杉磯分校。◇ **~ sb (from …) (to …)** *Ten employees are being transferred from the sales department.* 十名雇員已調離銷售部。

▸ **FEELING/DISEASE/POWER** 感覺；疾病；權力 **3** [T, I] **~ (sth) (from …) (to …)** if you **transfer** a feeling, a disease, or power, etc., or if it **transfers** from one person to another, the second person has it, often instead of the first 轉移（感情）；傳染（疾病）；讓與，轉讓（權力等）：*Joe had already transferred his affections from Lisa to Cleo.* 喬已移情別戀，把愛意從莉薩轉移到了克利奧身上。◇ *This disease is rarely transferred from mother to baby* (= so that the baby has it as well as the mother). 這種疾病很少由母親傳給嬰兒。

▸ **PROPERTY** 財產 **4** [T] **~ sth (to sb)** to officially arrange for sth to belong to sb else or for sb else to control sth 轉讓；讓與 **SYN** **sign over**：*He transferred the property to his son.* 他把財產轉讓給了兒子。

▸ **IN SPORT** 體育運動 **5** [I, T] (*especially BrE*) to move, or to move sb, to a different sports team, especially a professional football (SOCCER) team 轉會，使轉會（尤指職業足球隊）：**~ (from …) (to …)** *He transferred to Everton for £6 million.* 他以 600 萬英鎊的轉會費轉到埃弗頓隊。◇ **~ sb (from …) (to …)** *He was transferred from Spurs to Arsenal for a huge fee.* 他以巨額轉會費從熱刺隊轉到阿森納隊。

▸ **TO NEW VEHICLE** 換乘交通工具 **6** [I, T] to change to a different vehicle during a journey; to arrange for sb to change to a different vehicle during a journey（使在旅途中）轉乘，換乘，倒車：**~ (from …) (to …)** *I transferred at Bahrain for a flight to Singapore.* 我在巴林轉乘飛往新加坡的班機。◇ **~ sb (from …) (to …)** *Passengers are transferred from the airport to the hotel by taxi.* 旅客自機場改乘出租汽車到旅館。

▸ **INFORMATION/MUSIC, ETC.** 信息、音樂等 **7** 🗝 [T, I] to copy information, music, an idea, etc. from one method of recording or presenting it to another; to be recorded or presented in a different way 轉存，轉錄（資料、音樂等）；改編：**~ sth (from sth) (to sth)** *You can transfer data to a memory stick in a few seconds.* 你可以在幾秒鐘內將數據轉存到記憶棒。◇ **~ (from sth) (to sth)** *The novel does not transfer well to the movies.* 這部小說不太適宜改編成電影。

■ *noun* /ˈtrænsfɜː(r)/

▸ **CHANGE OF PLACE/JOB/SITUATION** 地點／工作／環境的改變 **1** 🗝 [U, C] the act of moving sb/sth from one place, group or job to another; an occasion when this happens 搬遷；轉移；調動；變換：*electronic **data transfer*** 電子數據傳輸 ◇ *the transfer of currency from one country to another* 貨幣從一國到另一國的匯劃 ◇ *He has asked for a transfer to the company's Paris branch.* 他要求調到公司的巴黎分部。◇ *After the election there was a swift **transfer of power**.* 大選之後權力迅速交接。

▸ **IN SPORT** 體育運動 **2** [U, C] the act of moving a sports player from one club or team to another（運動員）轉會：*It was the first goal he had scored since his transfer from Chelsea.* 這是他從切爾西隊轉會過來之後的第一記入球。◇ *a transfer fee* 轉會費 ◇ *to be **on the transfer list*** (= available to join another club) 在轉會名單上

▸ **CHANGE OF VEHICLE** 轉車 **3** [U, C] an act of changing to a different place, vehicle or route when you are travelling（旅途中的）中轉，換乘，改變路線：*The transfer from the airport to the hotel is included in the price.* 票價包括從機場轉車到旅館的費用。

▸ **TRAIN/BUS TICKET** 火車／公共汽車票 **4** [C] (*NAmE*) a ticket that allows a passenger to continue their journey on another bus or train 轉車票；換乘票

▸ **PICTURE** 圖畫 **5** [C] (*especially BrE*) (*NAmE* usually **decal**) a picture or design that can be removed from a piece of paper and stuck onto a surface, for example by being pressed or heated 轉印圖畫，轉印圖案（利用擠壓或加熱，可從紙上轉印到物體的表面） ▸ PSYCHOLOGY 心理學 **6** [U] (*psychology* 心) the process of using behaviour which has already been learned in one situation in a new situation 遷移（將已習得的行為在新的情況下應用） ➲ see also LANGUAGE TRANSFER

trans·fer·able AW /træns'fɜːrəbl/ *adj.* that can be moved from one place, person or use to another 可轉移的；可調動的；可轉讓的；可轉錄的；可中轉的：*This ticket is not transferable* (= it may only be used by the person who has bought it). 此票不得轉讓。◇ *We aim to provide our students with **transferable skills*** (= that can be used in different jobs). 我們的目的是讓學生掌握可用於不同工作的技術。 ▸ **trans·fer·abil·ity** /ˌtrænsˌfɜːrə'bɪləti/ *noun* [U]

trans·fer·ence AW /'trænsfərəns; *NAmE* træns'fɜːrəns/ *noun* [U] (*technical* 術語 or *formal*) the process of moving sth from one place, person or use to another 轉移；轉遞；調動；轉讓：*the transference of heat from the liquid to the container* 熱量從液體到容器的傳導

trans·fer·ral /træns'fɜːrəl/ *noun* [U] the action of transferring sth or sb 轉移；調動；轉換

'transfer student *noun* (*NAmE*) a student at a college or university who has completed classes at another college or university after leaving high school（大學）轉學生

trans·fig·ure /træns'fɪgə(r); *NAmE* -gjər/ *verb* [often passive] **~ sb/sth** (*literary*) to change the appearance of a person or thing so that they look more beautiful 使改觀；美化…的外表 ▸ **trans·fig·ur·ation** /ˌtrænsˌfɪgə'reɪʃn; *NAmE* -gjə'r-/ *noun* [U]

trans·fix /træns'fɪks/ *verb* [usually passive] **~ sb** to make sb unable to move because they are afraid, surprised, etc. 使（因恐懼、驚愕等而）動彈不得；使驚呆 SYN **paralyse**：*Luisa stood transfixed with shock.* 盧薩大吃一驚，站在那裏呆若木雞。

trans·form 0ᵛ AW /træns'fɔːm; *NAmE* -'fɔːrm/ *verb* **1** 0ᵛ **~ sth/sb (from sth) (into sth)** to change the form of sth 使改變形態 SYN **convert**：*The photochemical reactions transform the light into electrical impulses.* 光化學反應使光變為電脈衝。 **2** 0ᵛ **~ sth/sb (from sth) (into sth)** to completely change the appearance or character of sth, especially so that it is better 使改變外觀（或性質）；使改觀：*A new colour scheme will transform your bedroom.* 新的色彩調配將使你的臥室煥然一新。◇ *It was an event that would transform my life.* 那是能夠徹底改變我一生的一件事。

trans·form·ation AW /ˌtrænsfə'meɪʃn; *NAmE* -fər'm-/ *noun* **1** [C, U] a complete change in sb/sth（徹底的）變化，改觀，轉變，改革：*The way in which we work has **undergone a complete transformation** in the past decade.* 在過去的十年裏，我們的工作方式經歷了徹底的變革。◇ *What a transformation! You look great.* 真是判若兩人！你看上去真神氣。◇ **~ (from sth) (to/into sth)** *the country's transformation from dictatorship to democracy* 這個國家由獨裁到民主的轉變 **2** [U] used in South Africa to describe the process of making institutions and organizations more DEMOCRATIC（用於南非）民主改革：*a lack of transformation in the private sector* 在私營部門缺乏民主改革 ▸ **trans·form·ation·al** /-ʃənl/ *adj.*

ˌtransforˌmational 'grammar *noun* [U] (*abbr.* TG) (*linguistics* 語言) a type of grammar that describes a language as a system that has a deep structure which changes in particular ways when real sentences are produced 轉換語法（將語言描述為有深層結構的系統，在產出真實句子時按特定方式轉換）

trans·form·er /træns'fɔːmə(r); *NAmE* -'fɔːrm-/ *noun* a device for reducing or increasing the VOLTAGE of an electric power supply, usually to allow a particular piece of electrical equipment to be used 變壓器

trans·fu·sion /træns'fjuːʒn/ *noun* [C, U] **1** = BLOOD TRANSFUSION **2 ~ of sth** the act of investing extra money in a place or an activity that needs it 追加投資；（資金的）注入：*The project badly needs a transfusion of cash.* 這個項目急需追加現金投資。 ▸ **trans·fuse** *verb*：**~ sth (into sb/sth)** *to transfuse blood into a patient* 給病人輸血

trans·gen·der /trænz'dʒendə(r); træns-/ *adj.* relating to TRANSSEXUALS and TRANSVESTITES 變性（者）的；易性癖（者）的；易裝癖（者）的：*transgender issues* 關於變性的有爭議的問題 ▸ **trans·gen·dered** *adj.*

trans·gen·ic /ˌtrænz'dʒenɪk; 'træns'dʒenɪk/ *adj., noun* (*biology* 生)

■ ***adj.*** (of a plant or an animal 植物或動物) having GENETIC material introduced from another type of plant or animal 轉基因的 SYN **genetically modified**：*transgenic crops* 轉基因作物 ▸ **trans·gen·ic·ally** /-kli/ *adv.*

■ ***noun*** **1 trans·gen·ics** [pl.] the study or practice of creating transgenic plants or animals 轉基因學；轉基因（做法） **2** [C] a transgenic plant or animal 轉基因植物（或動物）

trans·gress /trænz'gres; træns-/ *verb* **~ sth** (*formal*) to go beyond the limit of what is morally or legally acceptable 越軌；違背（道德）；違犯（法律） ▸ **trans·gres·sion** /trænz'greʃn; træns-/ *noun* [C, U] **trans·gres·sor** *noun*

trans·hu·mance /træns'hjuːməns; *NAmE* trænz-/ *noun* [U] (*technical* 術語) the practice of moving animals to different fields in different seasons, for example to higher fields in summer and lower fields in winter 季節遷移（畜牧形式）

tran·si·ent /'trænziənt; *NAmE* 'trænʃnt/ *adj., noun*

■ ***adj.*** (*formal*) **1** continuing for only a short time 短暫的；轉瞬即逝的 SYN **fleeting, temporary**：*the transient nature of speech* 言語的即逝性 **2** staying or working in a place for only a short time, before moving on 暫住的；過往的；臨時的：*a city with a large transient population* (= of students, temporary workers, etc.) 有大量流動人口的城市 ▸ **tran·si·ence** /-əns/ *noun* [U]：*the transience of human life* 人生的短暫

■ ***noun*** (*especially NAmE*) a person who stays or works in a place for only a short time, before moving on 暫住某地的人；過往旅客；臨時工

tran·sis·tor /træn'zɪstə(r); -'sɪst-/ *noun* **1** a small electronic device used in computers, radios, televisions, etc. for controlling an electric current as it passes along a CIRCUIT 晶體管 **2** (also **tranˌsistor 'radio**) (also *informal* **tranny** especially in *BrE*) a small radio with transistors 晶體管收音機

tran·sit AW /'trænzɪt; -sɪt/ *noun, verb*

■ ***noun*** **1** [U] the process of being moved or carried from one place to another 運輸；運送；搬運；載運：*The cost includes transit.* 成本中包括運費。◇ *goods damaged **in transit*** 在運輸中損壞的貨物 ◇ *transit times* 運送時間 **2** [U, C, usually sing.] the act of going through a place on the way to somewhere else 通過；經過；通行；過境；中轉：*the transit lounge at Vienna airport* 維也納機場中轉候機室 ◇ *a **transit visa*** (= one that allows a person to pass through a country but not to stay there) 過境簽證 **3** [U] (*NAmE*) the system of buses, trains, etc. which people use to travel from one place to another 交通運輸系統：*the city's **mass/public transit** system* 城市的公共交通運輸系統

■ ***verb*** [T, I] **~ (sth)** to pass across or through an area 穿過；經過；越過：*The ship is currently transiting the Gulf of Mexico.* 這艘船現在正穿越墨西哥灣。

'transit camp *noun* a camp that provides temporary accommodation for REFUGEES 臨時難民營

tran·si·tion AW /træn'zɪʃn; -'sɪʃn/ *noun* [U, C] the process or a period of changing from one state or condition to another 過渡；轉變；變革；變遷：**~ (from sth) (to sth)** *the transition from school to full-time work* 從學校到全日工作的過渡階段 ◇ *He will remain head of state during the **period of transition** to democracy.* 在向民主政權過渡時期，他仍將是國家首腦。◇ **~ (between A and B)** *We need to ensure a smooth transition between the old system and the new one.* 我們需要確保新舊制度的平穩過渡。◇ *This course is useful for students who are **in transition*** (= in the process of changing) *from one training programme to another.* 對轉換培訓項目的學生來說，這一課程很有用。 ▸ **tran·si·tion·al** AW /-ʃənl/

T

adj. : *a transitional period* 過渡時期 ◇ *a transitional government* 過渡政府

tran'sition metal (also **tran'sition element**) *noun* (*chemistry* 化) one of the group of metals in the centre of the PERIODIC TABLE (= a list of all the chemical elements) which form coloured COMPOUNDS and often act as CATALYSTS (= substances that make chemical reactions happen faster) 過渡金屬（位於元素週期表中心的一組金屬元素，可形成有色化合物，常作為催化劑）

tran·si·tive /'trænsətɪv/ *adj.* (*grammar* 語法) (of verbs 動詞) used with a DIRECT OBJECT 及物的 : *In 'She wrote a letter', the verb 'wrote' is transitive and the word 'letter' is the direct object.* 在 She wrote a letter 一句中，動詞 wrote 是及物動詞，letter 一詞是直接賓語。 OPP **intransitive** ▸ **tran·si·tive·ly** *adv.* : *The verb is being used transitively.* 這個動詞在此用作及物動詞。

tran·si·tiv·ity /ˌtrænsə'tɪvəti; ˌtrænz-/ *noun* [U] (*grammar* 語法) the fact of whether a particular verb is TRANSITIVE or INTRANSITIVE（動詞的）及物性

tran·si·tory AW /'trænsətri; *NAmE* -tɔːri/ *adj.* (*formal*) continuing for only a short time 暫時的；片刻的；轉瞬即逝的 SYN **fleeting**, **temporary** : *the transitory nature of his happiness* 他的幸福曇花一現

'Transit van™ *noun* (*BrE*) a type of large van that is used for delivering goods, carrying equipment, etc. 貨運車；全順車

trans·late 0-m /træns'leɪt; trænz-/ *verb* **1** 0-m [T, I] to express the meaning of speech or writing in a different language 翻譯；譯 : **~ sth (from sth) (into sth)** *He translated the letter into English.* 他把這封信譯成了英文。◇ *Her books have been translated into 24 languages.* 她的書被譯成了 24 種語言。◇ *Can you help me translate this legal jargon into plain English?* 你能幫助我用淺顯易懂的英語來說明這一法律術語嗎？◇ **~ sth (as sth)** *'Suisse' had been wrongly translated as 'Sweden'.* * Suisse 被錯譯成 Sweden（瑞典）。◇ **~ (from sth) (into sth)** *I don't speak Greek so Dina offered to translate for me.* 我不懂希臘語，於是戴娜主動給我翻譯。◇ *My work involves translating from German.* 我的工作包括德語翻譯。 **2** 0-m [I] to be changed from one language to another 被翻譯；被譯成 : *Most poetry does not translate well.* 詩歌大多翻譯不好。◇ **~ as sth** *The Welsh name translates as 'Land's End'.* 這個威爾士語的地名可譯成"蘭茲角"。 **3** [T, I] to change sth, or to be changed, into a different form（使）轉變，變為 : **~ sth (into sth)** *It's time to translate words into action.* 是把言語化為行動的時候了。◇ **~ into sth** *I hope all the hard work will translate into profits.* 我希望所有的辛勤勞動都會有回報。 **4** [T, I] **~ (sth) (as sth)** to understand sth in a particular way or give sth a particular meaning（以某種方式）理解；給予（某種含義）SYN **interpret** : *the various words and gestures that we translate as love* 我們理解為愛的各種言語和姿勢

trans·la·tion 0-m /træns'leɪʃn; trænz-/ *noun* **1** 0-m [U] **~ (from sth) (into sth)** | **~ (of sth) (into sth)** the process of changing sth that is written or spoken into another language 翻譯；譯 : *an error in translation* 誤譯 ◇ *He specializes in translation from Danish into English.* 他專門從事把丹麥文譯成英文的工作。◇ *The book loses something **in translation**.* 此書在翻譯過程中丟失了一些原意。◇ *The irony is **lost in translation**.* 原文的反語用法在翻譯中丟失了。 **2** 0-m [C, U] a text or work that has been changed from one language into another 譯文；譯本；譯作 : *The usual translation of 'glasnost' is 'openness'.* * glasnost 一詞通常譯為 openness（公開性）。◇ *a **rough translation*** (= not translating everything exactly) 粗略的翻譯 ◇ *a **literal translation*** (= following the original words exactly) 直譯 ◇ *a **free translation*** (= not following the original words exactly) 意譯 ◇ *a **word-for-word translation*** 字字對應的翻譯 ◇ *I have only read Tolstoy **in translation**.* 我只讀過托爾斯泰作品的譯本。◇ *a copy of Dryden's translation of the Aeneid* 一本德萊頓翻譯的史詩《埃涅阿斯紀》 **3** [U] **~ (of sth) into sth** the process of changing sth into a different form 轉變；轉化 : *the translation of theory into practice* 從理論到實踐的轉化

trans·la·tor /træns'leɪtə(r); trænz-/ *noun* a person who translates writing or speech into a different language, especially as a job（尤指專職）翻譯，譯員，譯者，翻譯家 : *She works as a translator of technical texts.* 她的工作是科技翻譯。 ⊃ compare INTERPRETER (1)

trans·lit·er·ate /træns'lɪtəreɪt; trænz-/ *verb* **~ sth (into/as sth)** (*formal*) to write words or letters using letters of a different alphabet or language 移譯；音譯 ▸ **trans·lit·er·ation** /ˌtrænsˌlɪtə'reɪʃn; ˌtrænz-/ *noun* [C, U]

trans·lu·cent /træns'luːsnt; trænz-/ *adj.* (*formal*) allowing light to pass through but not transparent 半透明的 ▸ **trans·lu·cence** /-sns/ (also **trans·lu·cency** /-snsi/) *noun* [U]

trans·mi·gra·tion /ˌtrænzmaɪ'greɪʃn; ˌtræns-/ *noun* [U] the passing of a person's soul after their death into another body（死後靈魂的）轉生，轉世

trans·mis·sion AW /træns'mɪʃn; trænz-/ *noun* (*formal*) **1** [U] the act or process of passing sth from one person, place or thing to another 傳送；傳遞；傳達；傳播；傳染 SYN **transfer** : *the transmission of the disease* 這種疾病的傳播 ◇ *the risk of transmission* 傳染的危險 **2** [U] the act or process of sending out an electronic signal or message or of broadcasting a radio or television programme（電子信號或信息的）發射，發送；（電台或電視節目的）播送 : *the transmission of computer data along telephone lines* 計算機數據沿電話線的傳輸 ◇ *a break in transmission* (= of a radio or television broadcast) *due to a technical fault* 技術故障造成的播送中斷 **3** [C] a radio or television message or broadcast（電台或電視）信息，廣播 : *a live transmission from Sydney* 來自悉尼的現場直播 **4** [U, C] the system in a vehicle by which power is passed from the engine to the wheels（車輛的）傳動裝置，變速器

trans·mit AW /træns'mɪt; trænz-/ *verb* (**-tt-**) **1** [T, I] **~ (sth) (from ...) (to ...)** to send an electronic signal, radio or television broadcast, etc. 傳送；輸送；發射；播送 : *signals transmitted from a satellite* 從衛星傳送來的信號 ◇ *The ceremony was transmitted live by satellite to over fifty countries.* 典禮通過衛星向五十多個國家進行了實況轉播。◇ *a short-wave radio that can transmit as well as receive* 收發兩用的短波無線電裝置 **2** [T] (*formal*) to pass sth from one person to another 傳播；傳染 SYN **transfer** : **~ sth** *sexually transmitted diseases* 性傳播疾病 ◇ **~ sth to sb** *Parents can unwittingly transmit their own fears to their children.* 父母自己的恐懼有可能在無意中感染了孩子。 **3** [T] **~ sth** (*technical* 術語) to allow heat, light, sound, etc. to pass through 傳（熱、聲等）；透（光等）；使通過 SYN **conduct**

trans·mit·ter /træns'mɪtə(r); trænz-/ *noun* **1** a piece of equipment used for sending electronic signals, especially radio or television signals（尤指電台或電視信號的）發射機，發射台，發報台 ⊃ compare RECEIVER (2) **2 ~ of sth** (*formal*) a person or thing that transmits sth from one person or thing to another 傳送者；傳輸者；傳播者；傳染媒介 : *Emphasis was placed on the school as a transmitter of moral values.* 人們強調學校為道德價值觀的傳輸者。

trans·mog·rify /trænz'mɒgrɪfaɪ; ˌtræns-; *NAmE* -'mɑːg-/ *verb* (**trans·mog·ri·fies**, **trans·mog·ri·fy·ing**, **trans·mog·ri·fied**, **trans·mog·ri·fied**) **~ sb/sth** (often *humorous*) to change sb/sth completely, especially in a surprising way（尤指出乎意料地）使完全改變 SYN **transform** ▸ **trans·mog·ri·fi·ca·tion** /ˌtrænzˌmɒgrɪfɪ'keɪʃn; ˌtræns-; *NAmE* -ˌmɑːg-/ *noun* [U]

trans·mute /trænz'mjuːt; træns-/ *verb* [T, I] **~ (sth) (into sth)** (*formal*) to change, or make sth change, into sth different（使）變化，變質，變形 SYN **transform** : *It was once thought that lead could be transmuted into gold.* 有人曾經認為鉛可以變成黃金。 ▸ **trans·mu·ta·tion** /ˌtrænzmjuː'teɪʃn; ˌtræns-/ *noun* [C, U]

trans·nation·al /ˌtrænz'næʃnəl; ˌtræns-/ *adj.* (*business* 商) existing in or involving many different countries 跨國的；多國的 : *transnational corporations* 跨國公司

tran·som /ˈtrænsəm/ *noun* **1** a bar of wood or stone across the top of a door or window（門窗上端的）横檔，横楣 **2** (*NAmE*) = FANLIGHT

trans·par·ency /trænsˈpærənsi/ *noun* (*pl.* **-ies**) **1** (also *informal* **tranny**) [C] a picture printed on a piece of film, usually in a frame, that can be shown on a screen by shining light through the film 幻燈片；透明正片 **SYN** **slide**：*an overhead transparency* (= used with an OVERHEAD PROJECTOR) 高射投影透明正片 **2** [U] the quality of sth, such as glass, that allows you to see through it 透明；透明性 **3** [U] the quality of sth, such as an excuse or a lie, that allows sb to see the truth easily 顯而易見；一目瞭然：*They were shocked by the transparency of his lies.* 他們感到震驚的是他竟睜着眼睛説瞎話。**4** [U] the quality of sth, such as a situation or an argument, that makes it easy to understand 易懂；清楚；透明度：*a need for greater transparency in legal documents* 對法律文件更簡明易懂的需求 ◇ *The police reforms will ensure greater transparency and accountability.* 警察機構的改革將確保更大程度的透明度和問責性。

trans·par·ent 🔑 /trænsˈpærənt/ *adj.* **1** 🔑 (of glass, plastic, etc. 玻璃、塑料等) allowing you to see through it 透明的；清澈的：*The insect's wings are almost transparent.* 這昆蟲的翅膀幾乎是透明的。**OPP** **opaque** **2** (of an excuse, a lie, etc. 藉口、謊言等) allowing you to see the truth easily 易識破的；易看穿的；顯而易見的 **SYN** **obvious**：*a man of transparent honesty* 顯然很誠實的人 ◇ *a transparent attempt to buy votes* 明顯收買選票的企圖 ◇ *Am I that transparent?* (= are my intentions that obvious?) 我的動機看來那麼明顯嗎？**3** (of language, information, etc. 語言、信息等) easy to understand 易懂的：*a campaign to make official documents more transparent* 簡化公文語言的運動 **OPP** **opaque** ▸ **trans·par·ent·ly** *adv.*：*transparently obvious* 顯而易見

tran·spir·ation /ˌtrænspɪˈreɪʃn/ *noun* [U] (*biology* 生) the process of water passing out from the surface of a plant or leaf 蒸騰作用，蒸散作用（植物或葉子表面水分的散失過程）➲ compare PERSPIRATION

tran·spire /trænˈspaɪə(r)/ *verb* (*formal*) **1** [T] (not usually used in the progressive tenses 通常不用於進行時) **~ that …** if **it transpires that** sth has happened or is true, it is known or has been shown to be true 公開；透露；為人所知：*It transpired that the gang had had a contact inside the bank.* 據報這夥歹徒在銀行裏有內應。◇ *This story, it later transpired, was untrue.* 後來得知，此事純屬憑空假造。**2** [I] to happen 發生：*You're meeting him tomorrow? Let me know what transpires.* 你明天和他見面嗎？把見面的情況告訴我。**3** [I, T] **~ (sth)** (*biology* 生) when plants or leaves **transpire**, water passes out from their surface （植物）水分蒸發，蒸騰

T

trans·plant *verb, noun*

▪ **verb** /trænsˈplɑːnt; trænz-; *NAmE* -ˈplænt/ **1 ~ sth (from sb/sth) (into sb/sth)** to take an organ, skin, etc. from one person, animal, part of the body, etc. and put it into or onto another 移植（器官、皮膚等）：*Surgeons have successfully transplanted a liver into a four-year-old boy.* 外科醫生成功地給一個四歲的男孩移植了肝臟。◇ *Patients often reject transplanted organs.* 患者經常排斥移植的器官。➲ compare IMPLANT *v.* (2) **2 ~ sth** to move a growing plant and plant it somewhere else 移栽，移種，移植（植物）**3 ~ sb/sth (from …) (to …)** (*formal*) to move sb/sth to a different place or environment 使遷移；使移居：*Japanese production methods have been transplanted into some British factories.* 日本的生產方法已被引進到一些英國的工廠。▸ **trans·plan·ta·tion** /ˌtrænsplɑːnˈteɪʃn; ˌtrænz-; *NAmE* -plæn-/ *noun* [U]：*liver transplantation* 肝臟移植 ◇ *the transplantation of entire communities overseas* 整個整個社群向海外的遷移

▪ **noun** /ˈtrænsplɑːnt; ˈtrænz-; *NAmE* -plænt/ **1** [C, U] a medical operation in which a damaged organ, etc. is replaced with one from another person（器官等的）移植：*to have a heart transplant* 接受心臟移植 ◇ *a transplant operation* 移植手術 ◇ *a shortage of suitable kidneys for transplant* 適合移植的腎臟的短缺 ➲ COLLOCATIONS at ILL **2** [C] an organ, etc. that is used in a transplant operation 移植器官：*There is always a chance that the body will reject the transplant.* 身體總是有排斥移植器官的可能。➲ compare IMPLANT *n.*

tran·spon·der /trænsˈpɒndə(r); *NAmE* -ˈpɑːn-/ *noun* (*technical* 術語) a piece of equipment that receives radio signals and automatically sends out another signal in reply 發射機應答器；詢問機；轉發器

trans·port 🔑 **AW** *noun, verb*

▪ **noun** /ˈtrænspɔːt; *NAmE* -spɔːrt/ **1** 🔑 (*especially BrE*) (*NAmE* usually **trans·por·ta·tion**) [U] a system for carrying people or goods from one place to another using vehicles, roads, etc. 交通運輸系統：***air/freight/road transport*** 空運；貨運；路運 ◇ *the government's transport policy* 政府的交通運輸政策 ➲ see also PUBLIC TRANSPORT **2** 🔑 (*BrE*) (*NAmE* **trans·por·ta·tion**) [U] a vehicle or method of travel 交通車輛；運輸工具；旅行方式：*Applicants must have their own transport.* 申請人必須有自己的交通工具。◇ *Transport to and from the airport is included in the price.* 價格中包括往返機場的交通費。◇ *His bike is his only **means of transport**.* 自行車是他唯一的代步工具。**3** 🔑 [U] (*especially BrE*) (also **trans·por·ta·tion** *NAmE, BrE*) the activity or business of carrying goods from one place to another using lorries/trucks, trains, etc. 運輸；運送；輸送；搬運：*The goods were damaged during transport.* 貨物在運輸期間受損。◇ *controls on the transport of nuclear waste* 運輸核廢料的管制措施 **4** [C] a ship, plane or lorry/truck used for carrying soldiers, supplies, etc. from one place to another（運送部隊、給養等的）運輸船，運輸機，運輸卡車 **5 transports** [pl.] **~ of sth** (*literary*) strong feelings and emotions 強烈的情感；激情；激動：*to be in transports of delight* 興高采烈

▪ **verb** /trænˈspɔːt; *NAmE* -ˈspɔːrt/ **1** 🔑 **~ sth/sb (+ adv./prep.)** to take sth/sb from one place to another in a vehicle（用交通工具）運輸，運送，輸送：*to transport goods/passengers* 運送貨物／旅客 **2** 🔑 **~ sth (+ adv./prep.)** to move sth somewhere by means of a natural process（以自然方式）運輸，輸送，傳播 **SYN** **carry**：*The seeds are transported by the wind.* 這些種子是由風傳播的。◇ *Blood transports oxygen around the body.* 血把氧氣輸送到全身。**3 ~ sb (+ adv./prep.)** to make sb feel that they are in a different place, time or situation 使產生身臨其境的感覺：*The book transports you to another world.* 這本書會把你帶到另一個世界。**4 ~ sb (+ adv./prep.)** (in the past) to send sb to a far away place as a punishment（舊時）流放：*British convicts were transported to Australia for life.* 英國的囚犯被終生流放到澳大利亞。

trans·port·able /trænˈspɔːtəbl; *NAmE* -ˈspɔːrt-/ *adj.* [not usually before noun] that can be carried or moved from one place to another, especially by a vehicle 可運輸；可運送；可輸送

trans·por·ta·tion 🔑 **AW** /ˌtrænspɔːˈteɪʃn; *NAmE* -pɔːrˈt-/ *noun* [U]
1 (*especially NAmE*) = TRANSPORT *n.* (1)：*the transportation industry* 運輸業 ◇ *public transportation* (= the system of buses, trains, etc. provided for people to travel from one place to another) 公共交通運輸系統 ◇ *The city is providing free transportation to the stadium from downtown.* 本市現在提供從市中心到體育場的免費交通。◇ *the transportation of heavy loads* 重載運輸 ◇ *transportation costs* 運費 **2** (in the past) the act of sending criminals to a place that is far away as a form of punishment（舊時的）流放

ˈ**transport cafe** *noun* (*BrE*) a CAFE at the side of a main road that serves cheap food and is used mainly by lorry/truck drivers（供長途卡車司機用餐的）路邊小餐館 ➲ compare TRUCK STOP

trans·port·er **AW** /trænˈspɔːtə(r); *NAmE* -ˈspɔːrt-/ *noun* a large vehicle used for carrying heavy objects, for example other vehicles 大型載重運輸車：*a car transporter* 裝運汽車的運輸車 ➲ VISUAL VOCAB page V57

trans·pose /trænˈspəʊz; *NAmE* -ˈspoʊz/ *verb* [often passive] **1 ~ sth** (*formal*) to change the order of two or more things 使掉換順序 **SYN** **reverse** **2 ~ sth (from sth) (to sth)** (*formal*) to move or change sth to a different place or environment or into a different form 使轉移；使換位；使變形 SYN **transfer**： *The director transposes Shakespeare's play from 16th century Venice to present-day England.* 導演把莎士比亞的戲劇從 16 世紀的威尼斯改成當代的英國。 **3 ~ sth** (*music* 音) to write or play a piece of music or a series of notes in a different key 使（樂曲）變調，移調 ▶ **trans·pos·ition** /ˌtrænspəˈzɪʃn/ *noun* [C, U]

trans·sex·ual (also **tran·sex·ual**) /trænzˈsekʃuəl; træns-/ (also *informal* **tranny**) *noun* a person who feels emotionally that they want to live, dress, etc. as a member of the opposite sex, especially one who has a medical operation to change their sexual organs 易性癖者；（經外科手術後的）變性人

tran·sub·stan·ti·ation /ˌtrænsəbˌstænʃiˈeɪʃn/ *noun* [U] the belief that the bread and wine of the COMMUNION service become the actual body and blood of Jesus Christ after they have been BLESSED, even though they still look like bread and wine 實體變換，體變（指麪餅和葡萄酒經祝聖後變成基督的體血，只留下餅酒的外形）

trans·verse /ˈtrænzvɜːs; ˈtræns-; *NAmE* -vɜːrs/ *adj.* [usually before noun] (*technical* 術語) placed across sth 橫（向）的；橫斷的；橫切的 SYN **diagonal**： *A transverse bar joins the two posts.* 一根橫杆連接着兩根立柱。

ˌtransverse ˈwave *noun* (*technical* 術語) a wave that VIBRATES at 90° to the direction in which it is moving 橫波 ➲ compare LONGITUDINAL WAVE

trans·vest·ite /trænzˈvestaɪt; træns-/ (also *informal* **tranny**) *noun* a person, especially a man, who enjoys dressing as a member of the opposite sex 有異性裝扮癖的人，易裝癖者（尤指男性） ▶ **trans·vest·ism** /trænzˈvestɪzəm; træns-/ *noun* [U]

trap 🔑 /træp/ *noun, verb*

■ ***noun***

▸ FOR ANIMALS 動物 **1** 🔑 a piece of equipment for catching animals（捕捉動物的）陷阱，羅網，夾，捕捉器： *a fox with its leg in a trap* 被夾子夾住腿的狐狸 ◇ *A trap was laid, with fresh bait.* 陷阱設置好，還投放了新誘餌。 ➲ see also MOUSETRAP

▸ TRICK 計謀 **2** 🔑 a clever plan designed to trick sb, either by capturing them or by making them do or say sth that they did not mean to do or say 圈套；詭計： *She had **set a trap** for him and he had walked straight into it.* 她給他設下圈套，他就逕直鑽了進去。 ➲ see also BOOBY TRAP, RADAR TRAP, SAND TRAP, TOURIST TRAP

▸ BAD SITUATION 惡劣處境 **3** [usually sing.] an unpleasant situation from which it is hard to escape（難以逃脫的）困境，牢籠： *the unemployment trap* 失業的困境 ◇ *Some women see marriage as a trap.* 有些婦女把婚姻視作圍城。 ➲ see also DEATHTRAP, POVERTY TRAP

▸ CARRIAGE 馬車 **4** a light CARRIAGE with two wheels, pulled by a horse 雙輪輕便馬車： *a pony and trap* 一匹小馬拉的雙輪輕便馬車

▸ MOUTH 嘴 **5** (*slang*) mouth 嘴；口 SYN **gob**： *Shut your trap!* (= a rude way of telling sb to be quiet) 閉上你的臭嘴！ ◇ *to keep your trap shut* (= to not tell a secret) 嘴上有把門兒的

▸ FOR RACING DOG 賽狗 **6** a CAGE from which a GREYHOUND (= a type of dog) is let out at the start of a race 隔欄（賽狗開始時把狗從中放出）

▸ IN GOLF 高爾夫球 **7** (*NAmE*) = BUNKER *n.* (3)

IDM **to fall into/avoid the trap of doing sth** to do/avoid doing sth that is a mistake but which seems at first to be a good idea 掉進／避免掉進陷阱： *Parents often fall into the trap of trying to do everything for their children.* 家長經常一廂情願地極力為子女操辦一切。 ➲ more at SPRING *v.*

■ ***verb*** (-pp-)

▸ IN DANGEROUS/BAD SITUATION 處境危險／惡劣 **1** 🔑 [often passive] **~ sb (+ adv./prep.)** to keep sb in a dangerous place or bad situation that they want to get out of but cannot 使落入險境；使陷入困境： *Help! I'm trapped!* 救命啊！我給困住了！ ◇ *They were trapped in the burning building.* 他們被困在燃燒着的樓房裏。 ◇ *We became trapped by the rising floodwater.* 我們被上漲的洪水困住了。 ◇ *He was trapped in an unhappy marriage.* 他陷入不幸的婚姻之中。 ◇ *I feel trapped in my job.* 我覺得被工作纏住了。

▸ PART OF BODY/CLOTHING 身體／衣服部位 **2** 🔑 **~ sth (+ adv./prep.)** to have part of your body, your clothing, etc. held in a place so tightly that you cannot remove it and it may be injured or damaged 卡住；夾住；絆住；纏住： *I trapped my coat in the car door.* 我的外衣被汽車門夾住了。 ◇ *The pain was caused by a trapped nerve.* 這疼痛是由於神經受抑制引起的。

▸ CATCH 捕捉 **3 ~ sth** to catch or keep sth in a place and prevent it from escaping, especially so that you can use it 收集；吸收： *Solar panels trap energy from the sun.* 太陽能電池板吸收太陽能。 **4** 🔑 **~ sb/sth (+ adv./prep.)** to force sb/sth into a place or situation that they cannot escape from, especially in order to catch them 把…逼進，迫使…進入（不能逃脫的地方）： *The escaped prisoners were eventually trapped in an underground garage and recaptured.* 越獄逃犯終於給追逼到地下汽車庫，再次被捕。 **5 ~ sth** to catch an animal in a trap 設陷阱捕捉，用捕捉器捕捉（動物）： *Raccoons used to be trapped for their fur.* 人們過去經常獵取浣熊，以獲得其毛皮。

▸ TRICK 計謀 **6 ~ sb (into sth/into doing sth)** to trick sb into sth 使陷入圈套；使中計；使上當： *He felt he had been trapped into accepting the terms of the contract.* 他覺得自己是中了圈套才接受這合同條款的。

trap·door /ˈtræpdɔː(r)/ *noun* a small door in a floor or ceiling 地板門；（天花板上的）活板門，通風門，活動天窗

trap·eze /trəˈpiːz; *NAmE* træ-/ *noun* a wooden or metal bar hanging from two pieces of rope high above the ground, used especially by CIRCUS performers（尤指馬戲團演員使用的）高空鞦韆，吊架： *a trapeze artist* 高空鞦韆表演者

tra·pez·ium /trəˈpiːziəm/ *noun* (*pl.* **tra·pez·iums** or **tra·pezia** /trəˈpiːziə/) (*geometry* 幾何) **1** (*BrE*) (*NAmE* **trap·ez·oid**) a flat shape with four straight sides, one pair of opposite sides being parallel and the other pair not parallel 梯形 ➲ VISUAL VOCAB page V71 **2** (*NAmE*) (*BrE* **trap·ez·oid**) a flat shape with four straight sides, none of which are parallel 不規則四邊形

trap·ez·oid /ˈtræpəzɔɪd/ *noun* (*geometry* 幾何) **1** (*BrE*) (*NAmE* **tra·pez·ium**) a flat shape with four straight sides, none of which are parallel 不規則四邊形 ➲ VISUAL VOCAB page V71 **2** (*NAmE*) (*BrE* **tra·pez·ium**) a flat shape with four straight sides, one pair of opposite sides being parallel and the other pair not parallel 梯形

trap·per /ˈtræpə(r)/ *noun* a person who traps and kills animals, especially for their fur 捕殺動物者（尤指為獲取毛皮）

trap·pings /ˈtræpɪŋz/ *noun* [pl.] **~ (of sth)** (*formal*, especially *disapproving*) the possessions, clothes, etc. that are connected with a particular situation, job or social position（與某一處境、職業或社會地位有關的）身外之物，標誌，服裝： *They enjoyed all the trappings of wealth.* 他們享有所有象徵財富的東西。

Trap·pist /ˈtræpɪst/ *adj.* belonging to a group of MONKS who have very strict rules, including a rule that they must not speak 特拉普派的（有嚴格教規，包括緘口苦修的修道士組織） ▶ **Trap·pist** *noun*

trash /træʃ/ *noun, verb*

■ ***noun*** [U] **1** (*NAmE*) things that you throw away because you no longer want or need them 廢物；垃圾 ➲ note at RUBBISH **2** (*informal, disapproving*) objects, writing, ideas, etc. that you think are of poor quality 劣質品；拙劣的作品；糟粕；謬論： *What's this trash you're watching?* 你看的這個烏七八糟的節目是什麼？ ◇ (*especially BrE*) *He's talking trash* (= nonsense). 他在胡說八道。 **3** (*NAmE, informal*) an offensive word used to describe people that you do not respect 窩囊廢；廢物；沒出息的人： ***white trash*** (= poor white people, especially those living in the southern US) 貧賤的白人 ➲ see also TRAILER TRASH

■ ***verb*** (*informal*) **1 ~ sth** to damage or destroy sth 損壞；毀壞：*The band was famous for trashing hotel rooms.* 這個樂隊以破壞旅館房間出名。 **2 ~ sth/sb** to criticize sth/sb very strongly 抨擊；譴責 **3 ~ sth** (*NAmE*) to throw away sth that you do not want 丟棄；把…拋棄： *I'm leaving*

T

my old toys here—if you don't want them, just trash them. 我把我的舊玩具留在這裏，你不要就扔掉好了。

ˈ**trash can** *noun* (*NAmE*) **1** (*BrE* ˈ**litter bin**) a container for people to put rubbish/garbage in, in the street or in a public building （街道上或公共建築物裏的）垃圾箱，廢物箱 **2** = GARBAGE CAN

ˈ**trash talk** (also ˈ**trash talking**) *noun* [U] (*NAmE, informal*) a way of talking which is intended to make sb, especially an opponent, feel less confident 垃圾言論（為令對手等喪失自信心）；打擊對手士氣的言論 ➲ compare SLEDGING (2)

trashy /ˈtræʃi/ *adj.* (*informal*) (**trash·ier, trashi·est**) of poor quality; with no value 蹩腳的；無價值的 SYN **rubbishy**：*trashy TV shows* 無聊的電視節目

trat·toria /ˌtrætəˈriːə/ *noun* (from *Italian*) an Italian restaurant serving simple food 意大利餐館（或便餐店）

trauma /ˈtrɔːmə; *NAmE* ˈtraʊmə/ *noun* **1** [U] (*psychology* 心) a mental condition caused by severe shock, especially when the harmful effects last for a long time 精神創傷 **2** [C, U] an unpleasant experience that makes you feel upset and/or anxious 痛苦經歷；挫折：*She felt exhausted after the traumas of recent weeks.* 她經受了最近幾個星期的痛苦之後感到精疲力竭。 **3** [U, C] (*medical* 醫) an injury 損傷；外傷：*The patient suffered severe brain trauma.* 患者的大腦受到嚴重損傷。

trau·mat·ic /trɔːˈmætɪk; *NAmE* traʊˈm-/ *adj.* **1** extremely unpleasant and causing you to feel upset and/or anxious 痛苦的；極不愉快的：*a traumatic experience* 不幸的經歷 ◇ *Divorce can be traumatic for everyone involved.* 離婚對所有相關的人都會造成痛苦。 **2** [only before noun] (*psychology* 心 or *medical* 醫) connected with or caused by trauma 創傷的；外傷的；損傷的：*traumatic amnesia* 創傷性遺忘 ➲ see also POST-TRAUMATIC STRESS DISORDER ▸ **trau·mat·ic·al·ly** /-kli/ *adv.*

trau·ma·tize (*BrE* also **-ise**) /ˈtrɔːmətaɪz; *NAmE* ˈtraʊm-/ *verb* [usually passive] **~ sb** to shock and upset sb very much, often making them unable to think or work normally 使受精神創傷

trav·ail /ˈtræveɪl; trəˈveɪl/ *noun* [U, pl.] (*old use* or *literary*) an unpleasant experience or situation that involves a lot of hard work, difficulties and/or suffering 艱苦勞動；煎熬；艱辛；痛苦

travel 0➡ /ˈtrævl/ *verb, noun*

■ *verb* (**-ll-**, *especially US* **-l-**) **1** 0➡ [I, T] to go from one place to another, especially over a long distance 長途行走；旅行；遊歷：*to travel around the world* 周遊世界 ◇ *I go to bed early if I'm travelling the next day.* 如果第二天去

Collocations 詞語搭配

Travel and tourism 旅遊和旅遊業

Holidays/vacations 假期

- **have/take** (*BrE*) a holiday/(*NAmE*) a vacation/a break/a day off/(*BrE*) a gap year 休假；短期休假；休一天假；休空缺年假
- **go on/be on** holiday/vacation/leave/honeymoon/safari/a trip/a tour/a cruise/a pilgrimage 去／在度假／休假／度蜜月／遊獵／旅遊／觀光／乘船遊覽／朝聖
- **go** backpacking/camping/hitchhiking/sightseeing 去背包旅行／露營／搭順風車旅行／觀光遊覽
- **plan** a trip/a holiday/a vacation/your itinerary 計劃旅行／假期／行程
- **book** accommodation/a hotel room/a flight/tickets 預訂住宿／酒店房間／航班／票
- **have/make/cancel** a reservation/(*especially BrE*) booking 預訂；取消預訂
- **rent** a villa/(*both BrE*) a holiday home/a holiday cottage 租一座度假別墅／一個度假住所／一座度假小別墅
- (*especially BrE*) **hire**/(*especially NAmE*) **rent** a car/bicycle/oped 租借一輛汽車／自行車／機器腳踏車
- **stay in** a hotel/a bed and breakfast/a youth hostel/a villa/(*both BrE*) a holiday home/a caravan 住在酒店／提供住宿和早餐的旅館／青年旅舍／度假別墅／度假住所／旅行拖車裏
- **cost/charge $100 a/per night for** a single/double/twin/standard/(*BrE*) en suite room 單人房／雙人房／標間／套房一晚花費／要價 100 元
- **check into/out of** a hotel/a motel/your room 入住／結賬離開酒店／汽車旅館／房間
- **pack/unpack** your suitcase/bags 把東西裝進手提箱／旅行包；取出手提箱／旅行包裏的東西
- **call/order** room service 打電話叫／叫客房服務
- **cancel/cut short** a trip/holiday/vacation 取消／縮短旅程／假期

Foreign travel 出國旅行

- **apply for/get/renew** a/your passport 申請／拿到／續簽護照
- **take out/buy/get** travel insurance 獲得／購買／取得旅遊保險
- **catch/miss** your plane/train/ferry/connecting flight 趕上／錯過飛機／火車／渡船／轉乘航班
- **fly (in)/travel in** business/economy class 乘坐商務／經濟艙飛行／旅行
- **make/have** a brief/two-day/twelve-hour stopover/(*NAmE also*) layover in Hong Kong 在香港作短暫的／兩天的／十二小時的中途停留
- **experience/cause/lead to** delays 遇上／引起／導致延誤
- **check (in)/collect/get/lose** (your) (*especially BrE*) luggage/(*especially NAmE*) baggage 托運／取／弄丟行李
- **be charged for/pay** excess baggage 被收取／支付超重行李費
- **board/get on/leave/get off** the aircraft/plane/ship/ferry 上／下飛機／船／渡船
- **taxi down/leave/approach/hit/overshoot** the runway 在跑道上滑行；離開／接近／降落在／衝出跑道
- **experience/hit/encounter** severe turbulence 遇到強烈的氣流
- **suffer from/recover from/get over your** jet lag/travel sickness 遭受時差反應／暈車；從時差反應／暈車恢復過來；克服時差反應／暈車

The tourist industry 旅遊業

- **attract/draw/bring** tourists/visitors 吸引遊客
- **encourage/promote/hurt** tourism 鼓勵／促進／損害旅遊業
- **promote/develop** ecotourism 促進／發展生態旅遊
- **build/develop/visit** a tourist/holiday/(*especially BrE*) seaside/beach/ski resort 建立／開發／參觀旅遊／假日／海濱／海灘／滑雪勝地
- **work for/be operated by** a major hotel chain 就職於一家大型連鎖酒店；由一家大型連鎖酒店經營
- **be served by/compete with** low-cost/(*especially NAmE*) low-fare/budget airlines 由廉價航空公司提供服務；與廉價航空公司競爭
- **book sth through/make a booking through/use** a travel agent 通過旅行社預訂；利用旅行社
- **contact/check with** your travel agent/tour operator 聯繫旅行社；向旅行社咨詢
- **book/be on/go on** a package deal/holiday/tour 預訂／進行／去套餐旅遊
- **buy/bring back** (tacky/overpriced) souvenirs 購買／帶回（低劣的／定價過高的）紀念品

T

旅行我就早睡。◇ *I love travelling by train.* 我喜歡乘火車旅行。◇ *We always travel first class.* 我們總坐頭等艙旅行。◇ *We travelled to California for the wedding.* 我們到加利福尼亞州去參加婚禮。◇ *When I finished college I went* ***travelling*** *for six months* (= spent time visiting different places). 我大學畢業後在外旅行了六個月。◇ **~ sth** *He travelled the length of the Nile in a canoe.* 他乘獨木舟遊完尼羅河的全程。◇ *I travel 40 miles to work every day.* 我每天奔波 40 英里去上班。 **2** [I] (+ **adv./prep.**) to go or move at a particular speed, in a particular direction, or a particular distance（以某速度、朝某方向或在某距離內）行進，轉送，傳播：*to travel at 50 miles an hour* 以每小時 50 英里的速度行進 ◇ *Messages travel along the spine from the nerve endings to the brain.* 信息從神經末梢沿脊柱傳送到大腦。◇ *News travels fast these days.* 如今消息傳播得很快。 **3** [I] (of food, wine, an object, etc. 食物、葡萄酒、物體等) to be still in good condition after a long journey 經長途運輸仍不變質；經得住長途運輸：*Some wines do not travel well.* 有些葡萄酒經不住長途運輸。 **4** [I] (+ **adv./prep.**) (of a book, an idea, etc. 書籍、思想等) to be equally successful in another place and not just where it began 盛行各地；廣為流傳：*Some writing travels badly in translation.* 有些作品經翻譯後不流傳。 **5** [I] to go fast 走得快；快速行進：*Their car can really travel!* 他們的車開得可真快！ **6** [I] (in BASKETBALL 籃球) to move while you are holding the ball, in a way that is not allowed 持球走；（帶球）走步

IDM **travel 'light** to take very little with you when you go on a trip 輕裝上路

■ ***noun*** **1** [U] the act or activity of travelling 旅行；旅遊；遊歷：***air/rail/space, etc. travel*** 乘飛機、乘火車、乘航天器等 ◇ *travel expenses* 旅費 ◇ *The job involves a considerable amount of* ***foreign travel***. 這個工作要經常出差去國外。◇ *the travel industry* 旅遊業 ◇ *travel sickness* 暈車 ◇ *a* ***travel bag/clock*** (= for use when travelling) 旅行包 / 鐘 ◇ *The pass allows* ***unlimited travel*** *on all public transport in the city.* 持有乘車證可乘坐市內所有的公共交通工具，次數不限。 **2** **travels** [pl.] time spent travelling, especially in foreign countries and for pleasure（出國）旅遊，旅行：*The novel is based on his travels in India.* 這部長篇小說是根據他的印度之行寫成的。◇ *When are you off* ***on your travels*** (= going travelling)? 你們什麼時候動身外出旅行？

'travel agency *noun* a company that arranges travel and/or accommodation for people going on a holiday/vacation or journey 旅行社

'travel agent *noun* **1** a person or business whose job is to make arrangements for people wanting to travel, for example buying tickets or arranging hotel rooms 旅行代辦人；旅行代理商 ➲ COLLOCATIONS at TRAVEL **2** **travel agent's** (*pl.* **travel agents**) a shop/store where you can go to arrange a holiday/vacation, etc. 旅行社：*He works in a travel agent's.* 他在一家旅行社工作。➲ see also TRAVEL AGENCY

trav·ela·tor (also **trav·ola·tor**) /'trævəleɪtə(r)/ *noun* a moving path, especially at an airport（尤指機場的）自動人行道

trav·elled (*especially US* **trav·eled**) /'trævld/ *adj.* (usually in compounds 通常構成複合詞) **1** (of a person 人) having travelled the amount mentioned 有過…次旅行的；到過…地方的：*a much-travelled man* 見多識廣的人 **2** (of a road, etc. 路等) used the amount mentioned（常有人或不常有人）走的：*The path was steeper and less travelled than the previous one.* 這條小路比剛才那條陡，走的人少。

trav·el·ler (*especially US* **trav·el·er**) /'trævələ(r)/ *noun* **1** a person who is travelling or who often travels 旅行者；旅遊者；旅客；遊客：*She is a frequent traveller to Belgium.* 她經常到比利時去旅行。◇ *He passed the time chatting with fellow travellers.* 他與同行的旅客閒聊消磨時間。➲ see also COMMERCIAL TRAVELLER **2** (*BrE*) a person who does not live in one place but travels around, especially as part of a group（尤指結隊而行的）漂泊者：*New Age travellers* 經常遷移的新時代人 **HELP** **Traveller** is used especially to talk about travelling people of Irish origin, but is also used as a word for all travelling people, including people from the ROMANI community. * traveller 尤指經常遷移的愛爾蘭裔人，但也可泛指包括吉卜賽人在內的所有經常遷移的人。➲ compare GYPSY

'traveller's cheque (*US* **'traveler's check**) *noun* a cheque for a fixed amount, sold by a bank or TRAVEL AGENT, that can be exchanged for cash in foreign countries 旅行支票

trav·el·ling (*especially US* **trav·el·ing**) /'trævəlɪŋ/ *adj.*, *noun*

■ ***adj.*** [only before noun] **1** going from place to place 旅行的；巡迴的；流動的：*a* ***travelling circus/exhibition/performer, etc.*** 巡迴馬戲團、展覽、表演者等 ◇ *the travelling public* 旅遊愛好者們 ◇ (*BrE*) ***travelling people*** (= people who have no fixed home, especially those living in a community that moves from place to place, also known as 'travellers') 不斷遷移的人 **2** used when you travel 旅行用的：*a travelling clock* 旅行鐘

■ ***noun*** [U] the act of travelling 旅行：*The job requires a lot of travelling.* 這個工作要求經常出差。◇ *a* ***travelling companion*** 旅伴

,travelling 'salesman (*especially US* **,traveling 'salesman**) *noun* (*old-fashioned*) = SALES REPRESENTATIVE

trav·el·ogue (*NAmE* also **trav·elog**) /'trævəlɒg; *NAmE* -lɔːg; -lɑːg/ *noun* a film/movie, broadcast or piece of writing about travel 旅行紀錄片；旅遊廣播節目；遊記

'travel-sick *adj.* (*BrE*) feeling sick because you are travelling in a vehicle 暈車的；暈船的；暈機的 ▸ **'travel-sickness** (*BrE*) (also **'motion sickness** *NAmE*, *BrE*) *noun* [U]

tra·verse *verb*, *noun*

■ ***verb*** /trə'vɜːs; *NAmE* -'vɜːrs/ **~ sth** (*formal* or *technical* 術語) to cross an area of land or water 橫過；橫越；穿過；橫渡

■ ***noun*** /'trævɜːs; *NAmE* -vɜːrs/ (in mountain climbing 爬山) an act of moving sideways or walking across a steep slope, not climbing up or down it; a place where this is possible or necessary（在陡坡上的）側向移動，橫過，橫越；可橫越的地方

trav·esty /'trævəsti/ *noun* (*pl.* **-ies**) **~ (of sth)** something that does not have the qualities or values that it should have, and as a result is often shocking or offensive 嘲弄；歪曲 **SYN** **parody**：*The trial was a* ***travesty of justice***. 這一審判是對正義的嘲弄。

trav·ola·tor = TRAVELATOR

trawl /trɔːl/ *verb*, *noun*

■ ***verb*** **1** [T, I] to search through a large amount of information or a large number of people, places, etc. looking for a particular thing or person 查閱（資料）；搜集，搜羅，網羅（人或物）：**~ sth (for sth/sb)** *She trawled the shops for bargains.* 她到各商店搜羅便宜貨。◇ **~ (through sth) (for sth/sb)** *The police are trawling through their files for similar cases.* 警方正在檔案中查閱類似案件。 **2** [I] **~ (for sth)** to fish for sth by pulling a large net with a wide opening through the water 用拖網捕魚

■ ***noun*** **1** a search through a large amount of information, documents, etc.（對資料、文件等的）查閱：*A quick trawl through the newspapers yielded five suitable job adverts.* 快速翻閱一下報紙便找到五則適合的招聘廣告。 **2** (also **'trawl net**) a large net with a wide opening, that is dragged along the bottom of the sea by a boat in order to catch fish（海上捕魚用的）拖網

trawl·er /'trɔːlə(r)/ *noun* a fishing boat that uses large nets that it drags through the sea behind it 拖網漁船

tray /treɪ/ *noun* **1** a flat piece of wood, metal or plastic with raised edges, used for carrying or holding things, especially food 盤；托盤：*He brought her breakfast in bed on a tray.* 他把早餐用托盤給她送到牀上。◇ *She came in with a tray of drinks.* 她端着一托盤飲料走進來。◇ *a tea tray* 茶盤 **2** (often in compounds 常構成複合詞) a shallow plastic box, used for various purposes（各種用途的）淺塑料盒：*a seed tray* (= for planting seeds in) 育苗盤 ◇ *a cat's litter tray* 貓的便盆 ➲ VISUAL VOCAB

T

pages V33, V69 ➲ see also BAKING TRAY at BAKING SHEET, IN TRAY, OUT TRAY

TRC /ˌtiː ɑː ˈsiː; *NAmE* ɑːr/ *abbr.* Truth and Reconciliation Commission (an organization that was established in South Africa to investigate how people had been treated unfairly in the past) 真相與和解委員會（南非組織，調查以往的不公平待遇事件）

treach·er·ous /ˈtretʃərəs/ *adj.* **1** that cannot be trusted; intending to harm you 不可信任的；背叛的；奸詐的 **SYN** **deceitful**：*He was weak, cowardly and treacherous.* 他軟弱、膽怯、奸詐。◇ *lying, treacherous words* 陰險的謊話 **2** dangerous, especially when seeming safe 有潛在危險的：*The ice on the roads made driving conditions treacherous.* 路上的冰對駕車構成了隱患。▶ **treach·er·ous·ly** *adv.*

treach·ery /ˈtretʃəri/ *noun* [U, C] (*pl.* **-ies**) behaviour that involves not being loyal to sb who trusts you; an example of this 背叛；變節；背信棄義：*an act of treachery* 背叛行為

trea·cle /ˈtriːkl/ *noun* [U] (*BrE*) **1** (*NAmE* **mo·las·ses**) a thick black sweet sticky liquid produced when sugar is REFINED (= made pure), used in cooking （製糖時產生的）糖漿，糖蜜 **2** = GOLDEN SYRUP：*a treacle tart* 糖蜜餡餅

trea·cly /ˈtriːkli/ *adj.* **1** (*BrE*) like treacle 像糖漿的；糖蜜似的：*a treacly brown liquid* 糖漿狀的棕色液體 **2** expressing feelings of love in a way that seems false or exaggerated 虛情假意的；過分多情的：*treacly music* 甜膩膩的音樂

tread /tred/ *verb, noun*

■ *verb* (**trod** /trɒd; *NAmE* trɑːd/, **trod·den** /ˈtrɒdn; *NAmE* ˈtrɑːdn/ or **trod**) **1** [I] **~ (on/in/over sth/sb)** (*especially BrE*) to put your foot down while you are stepping or walking 踩；踏；踐踏：*Ouch! You trod on my toe!* 唉喲！你踩着我的腳指頭了！◇ *Careful you don't tread in that puddle.* 小心，別踩着那水坑。 **2** [T] **~ sth (+ adv./prep.)** to crush or press sth with your feet 踩碎；踐踏 **SYN** **trample**：*Don't tread ash into the carpet!* 別把煙灰踩進地毯裏！◇ *The wine is still made by treading grapes in the traditional way.* 這種葡萄酒仍然是以傳統的方法踩碎葡萄釀製的。 **3** [T, I] **~ (sth)** (*formal* or *literary*) to walk somewhere 行走；步行；走：*Few people had trod this path before.* 以前沒有多少人走過這條小路。◇ *He was treading quietly and cautiously.* 他躡手躡腳地走着。

IDM **tread ˈcarefully, ˈwarily, etc.** to be very careful about what you do or say 小心謹慎地說；小心翼翼地做：*The government will have to tread very carefully in handling this issue.* 政府在處理這個問題時須慎之又慎。 **ˌtread a difficult, dangerous, solitary, etc. ˈpath** to choose and follow a particular way of life, way of doing sth, etc. 走一條困難、危險、孤獨等的人生道路（指選擇特定的生活方式或處事方法）：*A restaurant has to tread the tricky path between maintaining quality and keeping prices down.* 餐館必須在保證質量和價格低廉之間走出一條困難的折衷之路。 **ˌtread on sb's ˈheels** to follow sb closely 緊隨某人之後；步人後塵 **ˌtread on sb's ˈtoes** (*especially BrE*) (*NAmE* usually **ˌstep on sb's ˈtoes**) (*informal*) to offend or annoy sb, especially by getting involved in sth that is their responsibility 激怒，得罪，冒犯（尤指因插手他人職責） **ˌtread ˈwater 1** to keep yourself vertical in deep water by moving your arms and legs 踩水（擺動四肢使身體在深水中保持直立） **2** to make no progress while you are waiting for sth to happen 躡足不前；徘徊觀望 ➲ more at FOOL *n.*, LINE *n.*, TIGHTROPE

■ *noun* **1** [sing.] the way that sb walks; the sound that sb makes when they walk 步法；步態；腳步聲：*I heard his heavy tread on the stairs.* 我聽到他在樓梯上的沉重腳步聲。 **2** [C, U] the raised pattern on the surface of a tyre on a vehicle （輪胎的）胎面；外胎花紋：*The tyres were worn below the legal limit of 1.6 mm of tread.* 這些輪胎磨損得已低於胎面 1.6 毫米的法定厚度。 **3** [C] the upper surface of a step or stair （台階或樓梯的）踏步板，梯面，踏面 ➲ picture at STAIRCASE ➲ compare RISER (2)

treadle /ˈtredl/ *noun* (especially in the past) a device worked by the foot to operate a machine （尤指舊時驅動機器的）踏板

tread·mill /ˈtredmɪl/ *noun* **1** [sing.] work or a way of life that is boring or tiring because it involves always doing the same things 枯燥無味的工作（或生活方式）：*I'd like to escape the office treadmill.* 我想擺脫辦公室的枯燥工作。 **2** [C] (especially in the past) a large wheel turned by the weight of people or animals walking on steps around its inside edge, and used to operate machinery （尤指舊時由人或牲畜踩動踏板使之轉動的）踏車 **3** [C] an exercise machine that has a moving surface that you can walk or run on while remaining in the same place （鍛煉身體的）跑步機，走步機 ➲ VISUAL VOCAB page V42

trea·son /ˈtriːzn/ (also **ˌhigh ˈtreason**) *noun* [U] the crime of doing sth that could cause danger to your country, such as helping its enemies during a war 危害國家罪，叛國罪（如戰時通敵） ▶ **treas·on·able** /ˈtriːzənəbl/ *adj.*：*a treasonable act* 叛國行為

treas·ure /ˈtreʒə(r)/ *noun, verb*

■ *noun* **1** [U] a collection of valuable things such as gold, silver and jewellery 金銀財寶；珠寶；財富：*buried treasure* 埋藏的財寶 ◇ *a pirate's treasure chest* 海盜的財寶箱 **2** [C, usually pl.] a highly valued object 極貴重的物品；珍寶；寶物；珍品：*the priceless art treasures of the Uffizi Gallery* 烏菲齊美術館收藏的無價藝術瑰寶 **3** [sing.] a person who is much loved or valued 備受寵愛（或珍愛）的人；心肝寶貝兒

■ *verb* **~ sth** to have or keep sth that you love and that is extremely valuable to you 珍視；珍愛；珍重；珍藏 **SYN** **cherish**：*I treasure his friendship.* 我珍重他的友誼。◇ *This ring is my most treasured possession.* 這枚戒指是我最珍愛的財產。

ˈtreasure house *noun* a place that contains many valuable or interesting things 寶庫；寶地：*The area is a treasure house of archaeological relics.* 這個地區是古文物遺跡的寶庫。

ˈtreasure hunt *noun* a game in which players try to find a hidden prize by answering a series of questions that have been left in different places 尋寶遊戲（回答問題以獲得匿藏的獎品）

treas·urer /ˈtreʒərə(r)/ *noun* a person who is responsible for the money and accounts of a club or an organization （俱樂部或組織的）司庫，會計，出納，財務主管

ˈtreasure trove *noun* **1** [U, C, usually sing.] valuable things that are found hidden and whose owner is unknown 無主財寶 **2** [C, usually sing.] a place, book, etc. containing many useful or beautiful things 寶藏，寶庫（貯藏珍寶、知識等）

treas·ury /ˈtreʒəri/ *noun* (*pl.* **-ies**) **1** **the Treasury** [sing.+sing./pl. v.] (in Britain, the US and some other countries) the government department that controls public money （英國、美國和其他一些國家的）財政部 **2** [C] a place in a castle, etc. where valuable things are stored （城堡等中的）金銀財寶庫，寶庫

ˈtreasury bill (also *informal* **ˈT-bill**) *noun* a type of investment sold by the US government in which a fixed amount of money is paid back on a certain date （美國）短期國庫券

treat 🔑 /triːt/ *verb, noun*

■ *verb*

▸ BEHAVE TOWARDS SB/STH 對待 **1** 🔑 to behave in a particular way towards sb/sth 以…態度對待；以…方式對待：**~ sb/sth (with sth)** *to treat people with respect/consideration/suspicion, etc.* 對人尊敬、體諒、懷疑等 ◇ *Treat your keyboard with care and it should last for years.* 小心使用你的鍵盤，這樣就可以使用很多年。◇ **~ sb/sth like sth** *My parents still treat me like a child.* 我父母仍然把我當成孩子。◇ **~ sb/sth as sth** *He was treated as a hero on his release from prison.* 他獲釋出獄時被當成英雄看待。

▸ CONSIDER 考慮 **2** 🔑 **~ sth as sth** to consider sth in a particular way 把…看作；把…視為：*I decided to* *treat his remark as a joke.* 我決定把他的話當作戲言。 **3** ~ **sth + adv./prep.** to deal with or discuss sth in a particular way 處理；討論： *The question is treated in more detail in the next chapter.* 下一章中對這一問題有更詳盡的闡述。

▸ **ILLNESS/INJURY** 疾病；損傷 **4** ~ **sb** (**for sth**) (**with sth**) to give medical care or attention to a person, an illness, an injury, etc. 醫治；治療： *She was treated for sunstroke.* 她因中暑而接受治療。◇ *The condition is usually treated with drugs and a strict diet.* 這種病通常用藥物和嚴格控制飲食進行治療。 ➲ COLLOCATIONS at INJURY

▸ **USE CHEMICAL** 用化學品 **5** ~ **sth** (**with sth**) to use a chemical substance or process to clean, protect, preserve, etc. sth（利用化學物質或反應）處理，保護，保存： *to treat crops with insecticide* 給莊稼噴灑殺蟲劑 ◇ *wood treated with preservative* 經過防腐處理的木材

▸ **PAY FOR STH ENJOYABLE** 花錢享受 **6** ~ **sb/yourself** (**to sth**) to pay for sth that sb/you will enjoy and that you do not usually have or do 招待；款待；請（客）；買（可享受的東西）： *She treated him to lunch.* 她請他吃午飯。◇ *Don't worry about the cost—I'll treat you.* 別擔心費用，我來替你付。◇ *I'm going to treat myself to a new pair of shoes.* 我打算給自己買雙新鞋。

▸ **treat·able** *adj.*： *a treatable infection* 能治療的傳染病

IDM **treat sb like 'dirt** (*informal*) to treat sb with no respect at all 視某人如糞土；把…視為草芥；蔑視

PHR V **'treat sb to sth** to entertain sb with sth special 用…招待；以…款待： *The crowd were treated to a superb display of tennis.* 觀眾看了一場非常精彩的網球賽，大飽眼福。

■ ***noun*** something very pleasant and enjoyable, especially sth that you give sb or do for them 樂事；樂趣；款待： *We took the kids to the zoo* ***as a*** *special* ***treat***. 我們特地帶孩子們到動物園去，讓他們開心一下。◇ *You've never been to this area before? Then you're in for a real treat.* 你以前從來沒有到過這一地區？那麼你一定會喜之不盡。◇ *When I was young chocolate was a treat.* 我年輕的時候，吃巧克力是一種難得的享受。◇ *Let's go out for lunch—****my treat*** (= I will pay). 咱們到外面去吃午餐，我請客。 ➲ SYNONYMS at PLEASURE

IDM **a 'treat** (*BrE, informal*) extremely well or good 極為有效；棒極了： *His idea worked a treat* (= was successful). 他的主意極為奏效。 ➲ more at TRICK *n.*

trea·tise /'triːtɪs; -tɪz/ *noun* ~ (**on sth**) (*formal*) a long and serious piece of writing on a particular subject（專題）論文

treat·ment /'triːtmənt/ *noun*

1 [U, C] ~ (**for sth**) something that is done to cure an illness or injury, or to make sb look and feel good 治療；療法；診治；護理： *He is receiving treatment for shock.* 他正在接受休克治療。◇ *She is* ***responding well to treatment***. 她經過治療大有起色。◇ *to require* ***hospital/medical treatment*** 需要住院／藥物治療 ◇ *There are various treatments available for this condition.* 對這種病情有各種療法。◇ *Guests at the health spa receive a range of beauty treatments.* 客人在健身水療館可接受各種美容服務。 ➲ COLLOCATIONS at ILL **2** [U] a way of behaving towards or dealing with a person or thing 對待；待遇： *the brutal treatment of political prisoners* 對獄中政治犯的殘酷虐待 ◇ *Certain city areas have been singled out for special treatment.* 某些城區已劃出要進行特別治理。 **3** [U, C] a way of dealing with or discussing a subject, work of art, etc. 處理；討論；論述： *Shakespeare's treatment of madness in 'King Lear'* 莎士比亞在《李爾王》中對瘋癲的處理手法 **4** [U, C] a process by which sth is cleaned, or protected against sth（淨化或防治）處理，加工： *a sewage* ***treatment plant*** 污水處理廠 ◇ ~ **for sth** *an effective treatment for dry rot* 防治乾腐病的有效方法

treaty /'triːti/ *noun* (*pl.* **-ies**) a formal agreement between two or more countries（國家之間的）條約，協定： *the Treaty of Rome* 《羅馬條約》◇ *a peace treaty* 和平協定 ◇ *to* ***draw up/sign/ratify a treaty*** 起草／簽署／正式批准條約 ◇ *Under* ***the terms of the treaty***, *La Rochelle was ceded to the English.* 根據這個條約的條款，拉羅謝爾割讓給了英國人。 ➲ COLLOCATIONS at WAR

treble /'trebl/ *noun, verb, det., adj.*

■ ***noun*** **1** [U] the high tones or part in music or a sound system（音樂或音響系統的）高音，高音部： *to turn up the treble on the stereo* 把立體聲唱機的高音音量調大 ➲ compare BASS[1] *n.* (1) **2** [C] a child's high voice; a boy who sings with a treble voice 童聲高音；唱高音的男童歌手 ➲ compare SOPRANO *n.* **3** [sing.] a musical part written for a treble voice 高音聲部 **4** [sing.] (*BrE*) three successes in a row 三連勝： *The victory completed a treble for the horse's owner.* 這次勝利使得馬主獲得三連勝。

■ ***verb*** [I, T] to become, or to make sth, three times as much or as many（使）成三倍，增加兩倍 **SYN** **triple**： *Cases of food poisoning have trebled in the last two years.* 在過去的兩年裏，食物中毒事件增加了兩倍。◇ ~ **sth** *He trebled his earnings in two years.* 他在兩年間收入增加了兩倍。

■ ***det.*** [usually before noun] three times as much or as many 三倍的；三重的： *Capital expenditure was treble the 2007 level.* 資本支出是 2007 年的三倍。

■ ***adj.*** [only before noun] high in tone 高音的；高聲的： *a treble voice* 高嗓音 ◇ *the* ***treble clef*** (= the symbol in music showing that the notes following it are high) 高音譜號 ➲ picture at MUSIC ➲ compare BASS[1] *adj.*

tree /triː/ *noun*

a tall plant that can live a long time. Trees have a thick central wooden TRUNK from which branches grow, usually with leaves on them. 樹；樹木；喬木： *an oak tree* 橡樹 ◇ *to* ***plant a tree*** 植樹 ◇ *to* ***chop/cut down a tree*** 伐／砍倒一棵樹 ◇ *They followed a path through the trees.* 他們沿着林間小路走着。 ➲ COLLOCATIONS at LIFE ➲ VISUAL VOCAB page V10 ➲ compare BUSH (1), SHRUB ➲ see also BAY TREE, CHRISTMAS TREE, FAMILY TREE, GUM TREE, PLANE TREE

IDM **be out of your 'tree** (*informal*) to be behaving in a crazy or stupid way, perhaps because of drugs or alcohol（藥物或酒精等引起的）發瘋，發傻 ➲ more at APPLE, BARK *v.*, FOREST, GROW, TOP *n.*, WOOD

'tree diagram *noun* a diagram with lines that divide more and more as you move to lower levels to show the relationships between processes, people etc.（表示層級關係的）樹形圖

'tree house *noun* a structure built in the branches of a tree, usually for children to play on 樹上小屋（搭建在樹枝間，通常供兒童遊戲用）

'tree-hugger *noun* (*informal, usually disapproving*) a person who cares very much about the environment and tries to protect it 抱樹人，環保狂（指過度熱衷環保的人）

tree·less /'triːləs/ *adj.* without trees 無樹木的： *a treeless plain* 沒有樹木的平原

tree·line /'triːlaɪn/ *noun* [sing.] a level of land, for example on a mountain, above which trees will not grow 林木線（山上等樹木生長的上限）

'tree structure *noun* (*computing* 計) a diagram that uses lines that divide into more and more lines to show the various levels of a computer program, and how each part relates to a part in the level above（計算機程序的）樹形結構圖

'tree surgeon (also *formal* **ar·bor·ist**) *noun* a person whose job is treating trees that are damaged or have a disease, especially by cutting off branches, to try to preserve them 樹木修補者；樹木修整專家 ▸ **'tree surgery** *noun* [U]

tree·top /'triːtɒp; *NAmE* -tɑːp/ *noun* [usually pl.] the branches at the top of a tree 樹梢： *birds nesting in the treetops* 在樹梢上築巢的鳥

tre·foil /'trefɔɪl; 'triːfɔɪl/ *noun* **1** (*technical* 術語) a plant whose leaves are divided into three similar parts, for example CLOVER 三葉草；三葉植物 **2** a decoration or a design shaped like a trefoil leaf 三葉形裝飾（或圖案）

trek /trek/ *noun, verb*

■ ***noun*** **1** a long, hard walk lasting several days or weeks, especially in the mountains 長途跋涉，艱難的旅程

T

（尤指在山區） **2** (*informal*) a long walk 遠距離行走 **SYN** **tramp**：*It's a long trek into town.* 到商業區去要走很長的路。

■ ***verb*** (-kk-) **1** [I] (+ **adv./prep.**) (*informal*) to make a long or difficult journey, especially on foot （尤指徒步）長途跋涉：*I hate having to trek up that hill with all the groceries.* 我很不願意得帶着這麼多吃用雜物爬上那個山頭。 **2** (also **go trekking**) [I] (+ **adv./prep.**) to spend time walking, especially in mountains and for enjoyment and interest （尤指在山中）遠足，徒步旅行：*We went trekking in Nepal.* 我們去尼泊爾徒步旅行。◇ *During the expedition, they trekked ten to thirteen hours a day.* 在探險期間，他們每天都要走十到十三個小時。➲ see also PONY-TREKKING

trel·lis /ˈtrelɪs/ *noun* [C, U] a light frame made of long narrow pieces of wood that cross each other, used to support climbing plants （支撐攀緣植物的）棚，架 ➲ VISUAL VOCAB page V16

trem·ble /ˈtrembl/ *verb*, *noun*

■ ***verb*** **1** [I] **~ (with sth)** to shake in a way that you cannot control, especially because you are very nervous, excited, frightened, etc. （因緊張、激動、驚慌等）顫抖，哆嗦，抖動，戰慄：*My legs were trembling with fear.* 我嚇得雙腿直發抖。◇ *Her voice trembled with excitement.* 她激動得聲音顫抖。◇ *He opened the letter with trembling hands.* 他雙手哆嗦着把信打開。 **2** [I] to shake slightly 顫動；輕輕搖晃 **SYN** **quiver**：*leaves trembling in the breeze* 在微風中搖曳的樹葉 **3** [I] to be very worried or frightened 極擔心；焦慮；恐懼：*I tremble at the thought of having to make a speech.* 我一想到得發表演講心裏就發怵。

■ ***noun*** [C, usually sing.] (also **trem·bling** [C, U]) a feeling, movement or sound of trembling 顫抖；戰慄；哆嗦：*a tremble of fear* 恐懼引起的顫抖 ◇ *She tried to control the trembling in her legs.* 她竭力控制住顫抖的雙腿。

trem·bly /ˈtrembli/ *adj.* (*informal*) shaking from fear, cold, excitement, etc. 發抖的；戰慄的；哆嗦的

tre·men·dous /trəˈmendəs/ *adj.* **1** very great 巨大的；極大的 **SYN** **huge**：*a tremendous explosion* 巨大的爆炸聲 ◇ *A tremendous amount of work has gone into the project.* 大量的工作已投入到這項工程。 **2** extremely good 極好的；精彩的；了不起的 **SYN** **remarkable**：*It was a tremendous experience.* 這是個了不起的經歷。▸ **tre·men·dous·ly** *adv.*：*tremendously exciting* 極其令人興奮

trem·olo /ˈtreməlәʊ; *NAmE* -loʊ/ *noun* (*pl.* **-os**) (*music* 音) a special effect in singing or playing a musical instrument made by repeating the same note or two notes very quickly （演唱或樂器演奏的）顫音，震音

tremor /ˈtremə(r)/ *noun* **1** a small EARTHQUAKE in which the ground shakes slightly 輕微地震；小震；微震：*an earth tremor* 地動 **2** a slight shaking movement in a part of your body caused, for example, by cold or fear （由於寒冷或恐懼引起的）顫抖，戰慄，哆嗦 **SYN** **quiver**：*There was a slight tremor in his voice.* 他的聲音略微有點兒顫抖。

tremu·lous /ˈtremjələs/ *adj.* (*literary*) shaking slightly because you are nervous; causing you to shake slightly （因緊張）顫抖的，戰慄的；使打戰的；使顫動的 **SYN** **trembling**：*a tremulous voice* 顫抖的聲音 ◇ *He was in a state of tremulous excitement.* 他激動得直發抖。▸ **tremu·lous·ly** *adv.*

trench /trentʃ/ *noun* **1** a long deep hole dug in the ground, for example for carrying away water 溝；渠 **2** a long deep hole dug in the ground in which soldiers can be protected from enemy attacks (for example in northern France and Belgium in the First World War) 戰壕；壍壕：*life in the trenches* 第一次世界大戰期間的戰壕生活 ◇ *trench warfare* 壍壕戰 **3** (also ˌ**ocean ˈtrench**) a long deep narrow hole in the ocean floor 海溝；大洋溝

tren·chant /ˈtrentʃənt/ *adj.* (*formal*) (of criticism, remarks, etc. 批評、言語等) expressed strongly and effectively, in a clear way 尖銳的；有效的；鮮明的 **SYN** **incisive** ▸ **tren·chant·ly** *adv.*

ˈ**trench coat** *noun* a long loose coat, worn especially to keep off rain, with a belt and pockets in the style of a military coat （軍裝式帶口袋和繫帶的）雨衣，大衣

trench·er /ˈtrentʃə(r)/ *noun* a wooden plate used in the past for serving food （舊時端飯菜用的）大木盤

ˌ**trench ˈfoot** *noun* [U] a painful condition of the feet, in which the flesh begins to decay and die, caused by being in mud or water for too long 壕溝足（因在泥水中時間過長而造成足部皮肉壞死）

trend 🔑 **AW** /trend/ *noun*

a general direction in which a situation is changing or developing 趨勢；趨向；傾向；動態；動向：***economic/social/political trends*** 經濟 / 社會 / 政治趨勢 ◇ **~ (towards sth)** *There is a **growing trend** towards earlier retirement.* 提早退休者有增加的趨勢。◇ **~ (in sth)** ***current trends*** *in language teaching* 當前語言教學的趨勢 ◇ ***a downward/an upward trend*** *in sales* 銷售額下滑 / 上升的趨勢 ◇ *You seem to have **set*** (= started) *a new **trend**.* 看來你們是開了一個新風氣。◇ *This trend is being **reversed*** (= is going in the opposite direction). 這種傾向正在向相反的方向轉變。◇ *One region is attempting to **buck*** (= oppose or resist) *the **trend** of economic decline.* 有一個地區試圖在經濟衰退的趨勢中逆流而上。◇ *The **underlying trend** of inflation is still upwards.* 通貨膨脹的潛在趨勢仍然是上升的。➲ LANGUAGE BANK at FALL

trend·set·ter /ˈtrendsetə(r)/ *noun* (often *approving*) a person who starts a new fashion or makes it popular 新潮倡導者；創新風的人 ▸ **trend·set·ting** *adj.* [only before noun]

trendy /ˈtrendi/ *adj.*, *noun*

■ ***adj.*** (**trend·ier**, **trendi·est**) (*informal*) very fashionable 時髦的；趕時髦的：*trendy clothes* 時髦的衣服 ▸ **trend·ily** *adv.* **trendi·ness** *noun* [U]

■ ***noun*** (*pl.* **-ies**) (*BrE*, *informal*, usually *disapproving*) a trendy person 趕時髦的人；盲從潮流的人：*young trendies from art college* 藝術院校時髦的年輕人

trepi·da·tion /ˌtrepɪˈdeɪʃn/ *noun* [U] (*formal*) great worry or fear about sth unpleasant that may happen 驚恐；恐懼；驚惶；不安

tres·pass /ˈtrespəs/ *verb*, *noun*

■ ***verb*** **1** [I] **~ (on sth)** to enter land or a building that you do not have permission or the right to enter 擅自進入，非法侵入（他人的土地或建築物）：*He told me I was trespassing on private land.* 他說我在擅闖私人土地。 **2** [I] (*old use*) to do sth wrong 做錯事

PHR V ˈ**trespass on sth** (*formal*) to make unfair use of sb's time, help, etc. 濫用，不公正地利用（別人的時間、幫助等） **SYN** **encroach on**：*I mustn't trespass on your time any longer.* 我不能再佔用你的時間了。

■ ***noun*** **1** [U, C] an act of trespassing on land 非法侵入（他人土地） **2** [C] (*old use*) something that you do that is morally wrong 罪過 **SYN** **sin**

tres·pass·er /ˈtrespəsə(r)/ *noun* a person who goes onto sb's land without their permission 不法進入者：*The notice read: 'Trespassers will be prosecuted.'* 告示上寫着"非請莫入，違者必究"。

tresses /ˈtresɪz/ *noun* [pl.] (*literary*) a woman's long hair （女性的）長髮 **SYN** **locks**

tres·tle /ˈtresl/ *noun* a wooden or metal structure with two pairs of sloping legs. Trestles are used in pairs to support a flat surface, for example the top of a table. （放置桌面等成對的）支架，條凳

ˈ**trestle table** *noun* a table that consists of a wooden top supported by trestles 支架枱；擱板桌

trews /truːz/ *noun* [pl.] trousers/pants, especially when they are made of TARTAN （尤指格子呢的）褲子，短褲

trey /treɪ/ *noun* (in BASKETBALL 籃球) a shot that scores three points 三分球

tri- /traɪ/ *combining form* (in nouns and adjectives 構成名詞和形容詞) three; having three 三；有三的：*tricycle* 三輪腳踏車 ◇ *triangular* 三角的

triad /ˈtraɪæd/ *noun* **1** (*formal*) a group of three related people or things 三人組合；三位一體；三件一套 **2** (also

Triad) a Chinese secret organization involved in criminal activity 三合會（中國秘密犯罪組織）

tri·age /ˈtriːɑːʒ; *NAmE* triːˈɑːʒ/ *noun* [U] (in a hospital 醫院) the process of deciding how seriously ill/sick or injured a person is, so that the most serious cases can be treated first 患者鑒別分類；傷員鑒別分類；治療類選法

trial 0-m /ˈtraɪəl/ *noun, verb*

■ ***noun***

▸ LAW 法律 **1** 0-m [U, C] a formal examination of evidence in court by a judge and often a JURY, to decide if sb accused of a crime is guilty or not（法院的）審訊，審理，審判：*a murder trial* 謀殺案的審理 ◇ *He's **on trial** for murder.* 他因涉嫌謀殺罪而受審。◇ *She will **stand trial/go on trial** for fraud.* 她因涉嫌詐騙將受到審判。◇ *The men were arrested but not **brought to trial**.* 這些人已被逮捕但並未送交法院審判。◇ *The case never **came to trial**.* 這個案件從未開庭審理。◇ *She is awaiting trial on corruption charges.* 她因被控貪污正等候審判。◇ *He did not receive a fair trial.* 他沒有受到公正的審判。◇ *She was detained without trial.* 她未經審訊便被羈押。➲ COLLOCATIONS at JUSTICE

▸ TEST 試驗 **2** 0-m [C, U] the process of testing the ability, quality or performance of sb/sth, especially before you make a final decision about them（對能力、質量、性能等的）試驗，試用：*The new drug is undergoing clinical trials.* 這種新藥正在進行臨牀試驗。◇ *She agreed to employ me for **a trial period**.* 她同意試用我一段時間。◇ *The system was introduced **on a trial basis** for one month.* 這個制度已引進試行一個月。◇ *a **trial separation*** (= of a couple whose marriage is in difficulties) 試驗性分居 ◇ *We had the machine **on trial** for a week.* 這台機器我們已經試用了一個星期。◇ *a **trial of strength*** (= a contest to see who is stronger) 實力的較量 ➲ COLLOCATIONS at SCIENTIFIC

▸ IN SPORT 體育運動 **3** [C, usually pl.] (*BrE*) (*NAmE* **try·out**) a competition or series of tests to find the best players for a sports team or an important event 預賽；選拔賽：*Olympic trials* 奧林匹克運動會選拔賽

▸ FOR ANIMALS 動物 **4** [C, usually pl.] an event at which animals compete or perform 比賽；表演：*horse trials* 馬匹比賽

▸ DIFFICULT EXPERIENCE 艱難經歷 **5** [C] an experience or a person that causes difficulties for sb 令人傷腦筋的事；惹麻煩的人；考驗：*the **trials and tribulations** of married life* 婚姻生活的考驗與磨煉 ◇ **~ to sb** *She was a sore trial to her family at times.* 她有時讓家人傷透了腦筋。

IDM ˌ**trial and ˈerror** the process of solving a problem by trying various methods until you find a method that is successful 反複試驗；不斷摸索：*Children learn to use computer programs **by trial and error**.* 兒童通過反複摸索才學會運用計算機程序。

■ ***verb*** (**-ll-**, *NAmE* **-l-**) [T, I] **~ (sth)** (*BrE*) to test the ability, quality or performance of sth to see if it will be effective or successful 測試（能力、質量、性能等）；試驗；試用

ˈ**trial balloon** *noun* (*especially NAmE*) something that you say or do to find out what people think about a course of action before you take it 試探性言論（或行動）

ˌ**trial ˈrun** (also ˌ**test ˈrun**) *noun* a test of how well sth new works, so that you can see if any changes are necessary（對新事物的）初步試驗，試行

tri·angle 0-m /ˈtraɪæŋɡl/ *noun*

1 0-m a flat shape with three straight sides and three angles; a thing in the shape of a triangle 三角形；三角形物體：(*BrE*) *a right-angled triangle* 直角三角形 ◇ (*NAmE*) *a right triangle* 直角三角形 ◇ *Cut the sandwiches into triangles.* 把三明治切成三角形。➲ VISUAL VOCAB page V71 **2** a simple musical instrument that consists of a long piece of metal bent into the shape of a triangle, that you hit with another piece of metal 三角鐵（打擊樂器）➲ VISUAL VOCAB page V35 **3** a situation involving three people in a complicated relationship 三角關係：*a love triangle* 三角戀愛 ➲ see also ETERNAL TRIANGLE **4** (*NAmE*) (*BrE* ˈ**set square**) an instrument for drawing straight lines and angles, made from a flat piece of plastic or metal in the shape of a triangle with one angle of 90° 三角板；三角尺

tri·angu·lar /traɪˈæŋɡjələ(r)/ *adj.* **1** shaped like a triangle 三角的；三角形的 **2** involving three people or groups 涉及三人的；三組的；三方面的：*a triangular contest in an election* 競選中三位候選人的角逐

tri·angu·la·tion /traɪˌæŋɡjuˈleɪʃn/ *noun* [U] (*technical* 術語) a method of finding out distance and position, usually on a map, by measuring the distance between two fixed points and then measuring the angle from each of these to the third point（通常在地圖上做的）三角測量，三角定位

triˌanguˈlation point *noun* = TRIG POINT

tri·ath·lon /traɪˈæθlən/ *noun* a sporting event in which people compete in three different sports, usually swimming, cycling and running 三項全能運動；鐵人三項賽 ➲ compare BIATHLON, DECATHLON, HEPTATHLON, PENTATHLON

tri·bal /ˈtraɪbl/ *noun, adj.*

■ ***adj.*** [usually before noun] connected with a tribe or tribes 部落的；部族的：*tribal art* 部落藝術 ◇ *tribal leaders* 部落首領

■ ***noun*** a member of a tribe, especially in S Asia（尤指南亞的）部落成員

tri·bal·ism /ˈtraɪbəlɪzəm/ *noun* [U] **1** behaviour, attitudes, etc. that are based on being loyal to a tribe or other social group 部落習性；種族意識；部落主義 **2** the state of being organized in a tribe or tribes 部落制度

ˈ**tri-band** *adj.* (of a mobile phone/cell phone) able to use three different ranges of radio waves so that it can be used in different regions of the world（手機）三頻的

tribe /traɪb/ *noun* **1** (sometimes *offensive*) (in developing countries) a group of people of the same race, and with the same customs, language, religion, etc., living in a particular area and often led by a chief 部落：*tribes living in remote areas of the Amazonian rainforest* 居住在亞馬孫河雨林偏遠地區的部落 **2** (usually *disapproving*) a group or class of people, especially of one profession（尤指同一職業的）一夥（人），一幫（人），一類（人）：*He had a sudden outburst against the whole tribe of actors.* 他突然對所有的演員非常反感。**3** (*biology* 生) a group of related animals or plants（動物或植物的）群，族：*a tribe of cats* 貓族 **4** (*informal* or *humorous*) a large number of people 大群；大幫；大批：*One or two of the grandchildren will be there, but not the whole tribe.* 一兩個孫子孫女會去那裏，但並不是所有的人。

tribes·man /ˈtraɪbzmən/, **tribes·woman** /ˈtraɪbzwʊmən/ *noun* (*pl.* **-men** /-mən/, **-women** /-wɪmɪn/) a member of a tribe 部落成員

tribes·people /ˈtraɪbzpiːpl/ *noun* [pl.] the people who belong to a particular tribe 部落成員

tribu·la·tion /ˌtrɪbjuˈleɪʃn/ *noun* [C, U] (*literary* or *humorous*) great trouble or suffering 憂患；苦難；磨難；痛苦：*the tribulations of modern life* 現代生活的苦惱

tri·bu·nal /traɪˈbjuːnl/ *noun* [C+sing./pl. v.] a type of court with the authority to deal with a particular problem or disagreement 特別法庭；裁判所：*an international war crimes tribunal* 國際戰爭罪法庭 ◇ *a military tribunal* 軍事法庭 ➲ see also INDUSTRIAL TRIBUNAL

trib·une /ˈtrɪbjuːn/ *noun* **1** an official elected by the people in ancient Rome to defend their rights; a popular leader（古羅馬由平民選出的）保民官；受擁戴的領袖 **2** a raised area that sb stands on to make a speech in public（公開演講的）講壇

tribu·tary /ˈtrɪbjətri; *NAmE* -teri/ *noun* (*pl.* **-ies**) a river or stream that flows into a larger river or a lake（流入大河或湖泊的）支流 ➲ VISUAL VOCAB pages V4, V5 ▸ **tribu·tary** *adj.* [only before noun]：*a tributary stream* 支流

trib·ute /ˈtrɪbjuːt/ *noun* **1** [U, C] **~ (to sb)** an act, a statement or a gift that is intended to show your respect or admiration, especially for a dead person（尤指對死者的）致敬，頌辭；悼念；致哀；弔唁禮物：*At her funeral her oldest friend **paid tribute to** her life and work.* 在葬

T

禮上，與她相識最久的老朋友對她的一生和工作給予了高度的讚揚。◇ *This book is a fitting tribute to the bravery of the pioneers.* 本書是對先驅們大無畏精神恰如其分的獻禮。◇ *floral tributes* (= gifts of flowers at a funeral) 葬禮獻花 **2** [sing.] **~ to sth/sb** showing the good effects or influence of sth/sb（良好效果或影響的）體現，顯示：*His recovery is a tribute to the doctors' skill.* 他的康復充分顯示了各位醫生高超的醫術。 **3** [U, C] (especially in the past) money given by one country or ruler to another, especially in return for protection or for not being attacked（尤指舊時一國向他國交納的）貢品，貢金

'tribute band *noun* a group of musicians who play the music of a famous band and copy the way they look and sound 翻唱樂隊；致敬樂隊

trice /traɪs/ *noun*
IDM **in a 'trice** very quickly or suddenly 轉眼之間；彈指一揮間；瞬息間 **SYN** **in an instant**：*He was gone in a trice.* 轉眼之間他就沒影兒了。

tri·ceps /ˈtraɪseps/ *noun* (*pl.* **tri·ceps**) the large muscle at the back of the top part of the arm 三頭肌 ➲ compare BICEPS

tri·cera·tops /traɪˈserətɒps; *NAmE* -tɑːps/ *noun* (*pl.* **tri·cera·tops** or **tri·cera·topses**) a large DINOSAUR with two large horns and one small horn on its very large head 三角（恐）龍

trich·ology /trɪˈkɒlədʒi; *NAmE* -ˈkɑːl-/ *noun* [U] the study of the hair and SCALP 毛髮學；髮理學 ▸ **trich·olo·gist** /trɪˈkɒlədʒɪst; *NAmE* -ˈkɑːl-/ *noun*

trick 0┳ /trɪk/ *noun, verb, adj.*

■ ***noun***

▸ **STH TO CHEAT SB 用以騙人** **1** 0┳ something that you do to make sb believe sth which is not true, or to annoy sb as a joke 詭計；花招；騙局；把戲：*They had to think of a trick to get past the guards.* 他們只好想出個計謀騙過崗哨。◇ *The kids are always* ***playing tricks on*** *their teacher.* 孩子們經常要些花招戲弄老師。➲ see also CONFIDENCE TRICK, DIRTY TRICK

▸ **STH CONFUSING 令人困惑的事** **2** 0┳ something that confuses you so that you see, understand, remember, etc. things in the wrong way 引起錯覺（或記憶紊亂）的事物：*One of the problems of old age is that your memory can start to* ***play tricks*** *on you.* 老年人的問題之一是記憶可能紊亂起來。◇ *Was there somebody standing there or was it* ***a trick of the light****?* 是真的有人站在那兒還是光線引起的錯覺？

▸ **ENTERTAINMENT 娛樂** **3** 0┳ a clever action that sb/sth performs as a way of entertaining people 戲法；把戲：*He amused the kids with conjuring tricks.* 他變戲法逗得孩子們直樂。◇ *a card trick* 紙牌戲法 ➲ see also HAT-TRICK

▸ **GOOD METHOD 好方法** **4** [usually sing.] a way of doing sth that works well; a good method 技巧；訣竅；竅門：***The trick is*** *to pick the animal up by the back of its neck.* 竅門在於抓住動物的後脖頸把它提起來。◇ *He used the old trick of attacking in order to defend himself.* 他採用了以攻為守的老招數。

▸ **IN CARD GAMES 紙牌遊戲** **5** the cards that you play or win in a single part of a card game 一圈；一墩；一圈所打（或贏）的牌：*I won six tricks in a row.* 我接連贏了六墩牌。

IDM **a bag/box of 'tricks** (*informal*) a set of methods or equipment that sb can use 一套措施；全部法寶 **be up to your (old) 'tricks** (*informal, disapproving*) to be behaving in the same bad way as before 故技重演；要老花招 **do the 'trick** (*informal*) to succeed in solving a problem or achieving a particular result 奏效；起作用；達到目的：*I don't know what it was that did the trick, but I am definitely feeling much better.* 我不知道是什麼起的作用，但是我確實覺得好多了。 **every trick in the 'book** every available method, whether it is honest or not 無所不用其極；渾身解數：*He'll try every trick in the book to stop you from winning.* 他將使盡渾身解數阻止你取勝。 **have a 'trick, some more 'tricks, etc. up your sleeve** to have an idea, some plans, etc. that you keep ready to use if it becomes necessary 袖藏玄機；胸有成竹；自有錦囊妙計 **,trick or 'treat** said by children who visit people's houses at Halloween and threaten to play tricks on people who do not give them sweets/candy 是請吃糖，還是想遭殃（萬聖節時兒童挨家索要糖果用語，揚言若不給糖就搗亂戲弄別人） **the ,tricks of the 'trade** the clever ways of doing things, known and used by people who do a particular job or activity（某一行業或活動的）絕招，絕活，門道，生意經 **,turn a 'trick** (*NAmE, slang*) to have sex with sb for money 接客賣淫 ➲ more at MISS *v.*, TEACH

■ ***verb*** 0┳ to make sb believe sth which is not true, especially in order to cheat them 欺騙；欺詐：**~ sb** *I'd been tricked and I felt stupid.* 我被人騙了，覺得自己真傻。◇ **~ your way + adv./prep.** *He managed to trick his way past the security guards.* 他想方設法騙過保安員獲得通行。➲ SYNONYMS at CHEAT

PHR V **,trick sb 'into sth/into doing sth** to make sb do sth by means of a trick 騙某人做某事：*He tricked me into lending him £100.* 他騙我借給了他 100 英鎊。 **,trick sb 'out of sth** to get sth from sb by means of a trick 從某人處騙走某物：*She was tricked out of her life savings.* 她被騙走了一生的積蓄。 **,trick sb/sth↔'out (in/with sth)** (*literary*) to dress or decorate sb/sth in a way that attracts attention 打扮（或裝飾）得引人注目

■ ***adj.*** [only before noun] **1** intended to trick sb 意在欺騙的；容易使人上當的：*It was a* ***trick question*** (= one to which the answer seems easy but actually is not). 那是個容易使人上當的問題。◇ *It's all done using* ***trick photography*** (= photography that uses clever techniques to show things that do not actually exist or are impossible). 這都是利用特技攝影產生的假象。 **2** (*NAmE*) (of part of the body 身體部位) weak and not working well 虛弱有毛病的：*a trick knee* 膝軟

trick·ery /ˈtrɪkəri/ *noun* [U] the use of dishonest methods to trick people in order to achieve what you want 欺騙；欺詐；耍花招；招搖撞騙 **SYN** **deception**

trickle /ˈtrɪkl/ *verb, noun*

■ ***verb*** **1** [I, T] to flow, or to make sth flow, slowly in a thin stream（使）滴，淌，小股流淌：**(+ adv./prep.)** *Tears were trickling down her cheeks.* 眼淚順着她的面頰流了下來。◇ **~ sth (+ adv./prep.)** *Trickle some oil over the salad.* 往色拉上滴些油。 **2** [I, T] **~ (sth) + adv./prep.** to go, or to make sth go, somewhere slowly or gradually（使）慢慢走，緩慢移動：*People began trickling into the hall.* 人們開始緩步進入大廳。◇ *News is starting to trickle out.* 消息漸漸傳了出來。

PHR V **,trickle 'down** (especially of money 尤指錢) to spread from rich to poor people through the economic system of a country（經國家經濟體制）由富人向窮人滴流

■ ***noun*** **1** a small amount of liquid, flowing slowly 細流；涓流 **2** [usually sing.] **~ (of sth)** a small amount or number of sth, coming or going slowly 稀稀疏疏緩慢來往的東西：*a steady trickle of visitors* 三三兩兩絡繹不絕的遊客

'trickle-down *noun* [U] the theory that if the richest people in society become richer, this will have a good effect on poorer people as well, for example by creating more jobs 下層受惠論，滴漏理論（富人愈富應能惠及窮人）

trick·ster /ˈtrɪkstə(r)/ *noun* a person who tricks or cheats people 騙子

tricksy /ˈtrɪksi/ *adj.* (*informal*, usually *disapproving*) using ideas and methods that are intended to be clever but are too complicated 過於精密的

tricky /ˈtrɪki/ *adj.* (**trick·ier**, **tricki·est**) **1** (rather *informal*) difficult to do or deal with 難辦的；難對付的：*a tricky situation* 微妙的局勢 ◇ *Getting it to fit exactly is a* ***tricky business****.* 使這完全合適是件很難做到的事。◇ *The equipment can be tricky to install.* 這設備安裝起來可能很費事。 **2** (of people 人) clever but likely to trick you 狡猾的；詭計多端的 **SYN** **crafty**

tri·col·our (*US* **tri·color**) /ˈtrɪkələ(r); *NAmE* ˈtraɪkʌlər/ *noun* [C] a flag which has three bands of different colours, especially the French and Irish national flags 三色旗（尤指法國和愛爾蘭的國旗）

T

tri·cycle /ˈtraɪsɪkl/ (also *informal* **trike**) *noun* a vehicle similar to a bicycle, but with one wheel at the front and two at the back 三輪腳踏車 ➲ VISUAL VOCAB page V51

tri·dent /ˈtraɪdnt/ *noun* a weapon used in the past that looks like a long fork with three points 三叉戟（舊時武器）

tried /traɪd/ *adj.* ➲ see also TRY *v.*

IDM **ˌtried and ˈtested/ˈtrusted** (*BrE*) (*NAmE* **ˌtried and ˈtrue**) that you have used or relied on in the past successfully 經過考驗的；可靠的；可信賴的：*a tried and tested method for solving the problem* 解決這個問題的可靠辦法

tri·en·nial /traɪˈeniəl/ *adj.* happening every three years 每三年一次的；每三年的

trier /ˈtraɪə(r)/ *noun* a person who tries very hard at what they are doing and does their best 工作盡心盡力的人；勤勤懇懇的人

trifle /ˈtraɪfl/ *noun, verb*

■ *noun* **1** **a trifle** [sing.] (used as an adverb 用作副詞) (*formal* or *humorous*) slightly 稍微；一點兒：*She seemed a trifle anxious.* 她似乎有點兒焦急。 **2** [C] something that is not valuable or important 小事；瑣事；不值錢的東西：*$1 000 is a mere trifle to her.* * 1 000 元對她來說不過是區區小數。 **3** [C, U] (*BrE*) a cold DESSERT (= a sweet dish) made from cake and fruit with wine and/or jelly poured over it, covered with CUSTARD and cream 蛋奶水果鬆蛋糕，屈萊弗（在蛋糕和水果上澆葡萄酒或果凍，上覆蛋奶凍等）

■ *verb*

PHR V **ˈtrifle with sb/sth** (*formal*) (used especially in negative sentences 尤用於否定句) to treat sb/sth without genuine respect 怠慢；小看：*He is not a person to be trifled with.* 他這個人怠慢不得。

trif·ling /ˈtraɪflɪŋ/ *adj.* (*formal*) small and not important 瑣碎的；微不足道的；無足輕重的；不重要的 SYN **trivial**：*trifling details* 瑣碎細節

trig·ger AW /ˈtrɪɡə(r)/ *noun, verb*

■ *noun* **1** the part of a gun that you press in order to fire it（槍的）扳機：*to **pull/squeeze the trigger*** 扣扳機 ◇ *He kept his finger on the trigger.* 他的手指一直勾着扳機。 **2** ~ (**for sth**) | ~ (**to sth/to do sth**) something that is the cause of a particular reaction or development, especially a bad one（尤指引發不良反應或發展的）起因，誘因：*The trigger for the strike was the closure of yet another factory.* 觸發這次罷工的是再有一家工廠關閉。 **3** the part of a bomb that causes it to explode 觸發器；引爆器：*nuclear triggers* 核引爆器

■ *verb* **1** ~ **sth** (**off**) to make sth happen suddenly 發動；引起；觸發 SYN **set off**：*Nuts can trigger off a violent allergic reaction.* 堅果可以引起嚴重的過敏反應。 **2** ~ **sth** to cause a device to start functioning 開動；起動 SYN **set off**：*to trigger an alarm* 觸發警報器

ˈtrigger-happy *adj.* (*informal, disapproving*) too willing and quick to use violence, especially with guns 以開槍為樂的；好鬥的；愛動武的；動輒開槍的

trig·onom·etry /ˌtrɪɡəˈnɒmətri; *NAmE* -ˈnɑːm-/ *noun* [U] the type of mathematics that deals with the relationship between the sides and angles of triangles 三角學 ▸ **trig·ono·met·ric** /ˌtrɪɡənəˈmetrɪk/ (also **trig·ono·met·ric·al** /-kl/) *adj.*

trig point /ˈtrɪɡ pɔɪnt/ (also **triˌanguˈlation point**) *noun* (*technical* 術語) a position on a high place used as a REFERENCE POINT, especially by people who make and use maps. It is usually marked on the ground by a short stone PILLAR.（地圖製作和使用者設的）三角測量點，三角參照點

tri·graph /ˈtraɪɡrɑːf; *NAmE* -ɡræf/ *noun* (*linguistics* 語言) a combination of three letters representing one sound, for example 'sch' in German 三合字母；三字母一音

trike /traɪk/ *noun* (*informal*) = TRICYCLE

tri·lat·eral /ˌtraɪˈlætərəl/ *adj.* involving three groups of people or three countries 三邊的；三方的：*trilateral talks* 三方會談 ➲ compare BILATERAL, MULTILATERAL, UNILATERAL

trilby /ˈtrɪlbi/ *noun* (*pl.* **-ies**) (*especially BrE*) a man's soft hat with a narrow BRIM and the top part pushed in from front to back（男用）軟氈帽 ➲ VISUAL VOCAB page V65

tri·lin·gual /ˌtraɪˈlɪŋɡwəl/ *adj.* **1** able to speak three languages equally well 會說三種語言的：*He is trilingual in English, Spanish and Danish.* 他能講英語、西班牙語和丹麥語三種語言。 **2** using three languages; written in three languages 使用三種語言的；用三種語言寫的：*trilingual education* 三語教育 ◇ *a trilingual menu* 三語菜單

trill /trɪl/ *noun, verb*

■ *noun* **1** a repeated short high sound made, for example, by sb's voice or by a bird（人的）顫聲，短促尖聲；（鳥的）啼囀，唧唧啾啾 **2** (*music* 音) the sound made when two notes next to each other in the musical SCALE are played or sung quickly several times one after the other 顫音 **3** (also **roll**) (*phonetics* 語音) a sound, usually an /r/, produced by making the tongue VIBRATE against a part of the mouth 顫音

■ *verb* **1** [I] to make repeated short high sounds（連續）發顫音，發短促的響聲 SYN **warble**：*A phone trilled on the desk.* 辦公桌上的電話丁零零地響了。◇ *The canary was trilling away happily.* 那隻金絲雀唧唧啾啾地歡唱個不停。 **2** [T] **+ speech** to say sth in a high cheerful voice 歡快地高聲說 SYN **warble**：*'How wonderful!' she trilled.* "太妙了！" 她高興地喊道。 **3** [T] ~ **sth** (*phonetics* 語音) to pronounce an 'r' sound by making a trill (3) 發 r 顫音 ➲ compare ROLL *v.* (10)

tril·lion /ˈtrɪljən/ *number* **1** 🔑 1 000 000 000 000; one million million 萬億；兆 HELP You say **a, one, two, several, etc. trillion** without a final 's' on 'trillion'. **Trillions (of …)** can be used if there is no number or quantity before it. Always use a plural verb with **trillion** or **trillions**. 說 a, one, two, several, etc. trillion 時，trillion 後面不加 s。若前面沒有數目或數量，可用 trillions (of …)。trillion 和 trillions 均用複數動詞。 **2** 🔑 **a trillion** or **trillions (of …)** (*informal*) a very large amount 大量；無數 HELP There are more examples of how to use numbers at the entry for **hundred**. 更多數詞用法示例見 hundred 條。 **3** (*old-fashioned, BrE*) one million million million; 1 000 000 000 000 000 000 百萬兆

tri·lo·bite /ˈtraɪləʊbaɪt; *NAmE* ˈtraɪlə-/ *noun* a small sea creature that lived millions of years ago and is now a FOSSIL 三葉蟲（生活於幾百萬年前的小型海洋生物，已成化石）

tril·ogy /ˈtrɪlədʒi/ *noun* (*pl.* **-ies**) a group of three books, films/movies, etc. that have the same subject or characters（書籍、電影等的）三部曲；三部劇

trim /trɪm/ *verb, noun, adj.*

■ *verb* (**-mm-**) **1** ~ **sth** to make sth neater, smaller, better, etc., by cutting parts from it 修剪；修整：*to trim your hair* 理髮 ◇ *to trim a hedge (back)* 修剪樹籬 ◇ (*figurative*) *The training budget had been trimmed by £10 000.* 培訓預算削減了 1 萬英鎊。 **2** ~ **sth** (**off sth**) | ~ **sth** (**off/away**) to cut away unnecessary parts from sth 切去，割掉，剪下，除去（不必要的部份）：*Trim any excess fat off the meat.* 把多餘的肥膘從肉上切掉。◇ *I trimmed two centimetres off the hem of the skirt.* 我把裙子的下襬剪短了兩厘米。 **3** [usually passive] ~ **sth** (**with sth**) to decorate sth, especially around its edges 裝飾，修飾，點綴（尤指某物的邊緣）：*gloves trimmed with fur* 毛皮鑲邊的手套

IDM **ˌtrim your ˈsails** **1** to arrange the sails of a boat to suit the wind so that the boat moves faster 隨風揚帆；見風轉舵 **2** to reduce your costs 減少開支；削減費用

PHR V **ˌtrim ˈdown** | **ˌtrim sth↔ˈdown** to become smaller in size; to make sth smaller（使）變小；縮減：*Using the diet he's trimmed down from 90 kilos to 70.* 通過控制飲食，他的體重從 90 公斤減到了 70 公斤。

■ *noun* **1** [C, usually sing.] an act of cutting a small amount off sth, especially hair（尤指毛髮的）修剪：*a wash and trim* 洗頭理髮 ◇ *The hedge needs a trim.* 這樹籬得修剪了。 **2** [U, sing.] material that is used to decorate clothes, furniture, cars, etc., especially along the edges, by being a different colour, etc.（衣服、傢具、汽車等

T

的）飾物，邊飾，裝飾配件：*The car is available with black or red trim* (= the colour of the seats). 這款汽車的座椅有黑紅兩種顏色。◇ *a blue jacket with a white trim* 鑲有白邊的藍色上衣

IDM **in (good, etc.) 'trim** (*informal*) in good condition or order 狀態良好；健康極佳；井然有序：*He **keeps in trim** by running every day.* 他每天跑步保持身體健康。◇ *The team need to **get in trim** for the coming season.* 這個球隊需要為下個賽季做好準備。

■ *adj.* **1** (of a person 人) looking thin, healthy and attractive 苗條的；修長的；健康優雅的：*She has kept very trim.* 她的身材保持得很苗條。◇ *a trim figure* 修長的身材 **2** neat and well cared for 整齊的；精心照管的；井然有序的 SYN **well kept**：*a trim garden* 精心管理的花園

tri·maran /ˈtraɪməræn/ *noun* a fast sailing boat like a CATAMARAN, but with three HULLS instead of two 三體帆船

tri·mes·ter /traɪˈmestə(r)/ *noun* **1** (*medical* 醫) a period of three months during the time when a woman is pregnant 妊娠的三月期（醫學上將妊娠期分為三期，每一期為三個月）：*the first trimester of pregnancy* 妊娠的頭三個月 **2** (*NAmE*) = TERM *n.* (2)：*The school year is divided into three trimesters.* 一學年分三個學期。➲ compare SEMESTER

trim·mer /ˈtrɪmə(r)/ *noun* a machine for cutting the edges of bushes, grass and HEDGES（樹叢、花草、樹籬的）修剪機：*a hedge-trimmer* 樹籬修剪機

trim·ming /ˈtrɪmɪŋ/ *noun* **1 trimmings** (*NAmE* also **fixings**) [pl.] the extra things that it is traditional to have for a special meal or occasion（菜肴的）配料；額外的事物：*a splendid feast of turkey with **all the trimmings*** 備有各種配料的豐盛火雞大餐 **2 trimmings** [pl.] the small pieces of sth that are left when you have cut sth 修剪下來的東西；剪屑：*hedge trimmings* 樹籬修剪下來的碎枝葉 **3** [U, C, usually pl.] material that is used to decorate sth, for example along its edges 裝飾材料；鑲邊飾物：*a white blouse with blue trimming* 有藍色飾邊的白襯衫

trin·ity /ˈtrɪnəti/ *noun* [sing.] **1 the Trinity** (in Christianity 基督教) the union of Father, Son and HOLY SPIRIT as one God 三位一體（聖父、聖子及聖靈合為上帝）**2** (*formal*) a group of three people or things 三人小組；三件一套；三合一

trin·ket /ˈtrɪŋkɪt/ *noun* a piece of jewellery or small decorative object that is not worth much money（價值不高的）小首飾，小裝飾物

trio /ˈtriːəʊ; *NAmE* ˈtriːoʊ/ *noun* (*pl.* **-os**) **1** [C+sing./pl. v.] a group of three people or things 三人小組；三件一套；三合一 ➲ compare DUO (1) **2** [C+sing./pl. v.] a group of three musicians or singers who play or sing together 三重奏樂團；三重唱組合 **3** [C] a piece of music for three musicians or singers 三重奏（曲）；三重唱（曲）：*a trio for piano, oboe and bassoon* 鋼琴、雙簧管及大管三重奏 ➲ compare DUET

T

trip 0ꟷ /trɪp/ *noun, verb*

■ *noun* **1** 0ꟷ a journey to a place and back again, especially a short one for pleasure or a particular purpose（尤指短程往返的）旅行，旅遊，出行：*Did you have a good trip?* 你旅行順利嗎？◇ *We **went on a trip** to the mountains.* 我們到山裏去旅遊了。◇ *a **day trip*** (= lasting a day) 一日遊 ◇ *a **boat/coach trip*** 乘船／長途汽車旅行 ◇ *a **business/school/shopping trip*** 出差；學校旅行；去商場購物 ◇ *They **took a trip** down the river.* 他們沿河往下游旅行。◇ *We had to **make several trips** to bring all the equipment over.* 我們往返了幾次才把全部設備運過來。➲ COLLOCATIONS at TRAVEL ➲ see also EGO TRIP, FIELD TRIP, ROUND TRIP **2** (*slang*) the experience that sb has if they take a powerful drug that affects the mind and makes them imagine things（服用毒品後所產生的）幻覺，迷幻感受：*an acid* (= LSD) *trip* 迷幻藥產生的幻覺 **3** an act of falling or nearly falling down, because you hit your foot against sth 絆；絆倒 IDM see GUILT *n.*

■ *verb* (**-pp-**) **1** 0ꟷ [I] to catch your foot on sth and fall or almost fall 絆；絆倒：*She tripped and fell.* 她絆了一下摔倒了。◇ **~ over/on sth** *Someone will trip over that cable.* 有人會讓那條電纜絆倒的。◇ **~ over/up** *Be careful you don't trip up on the step.* 你小心別在台階上絆倒了。**2** 0ꟷ [T] **~ sb** (*BrE* also **trip sb up**) to catch sb's foot and make them fall or almost fall 將…絆倒；使跌倒：*As I passed, he stuck out a leg and tried to trip me up.* 我經過時，他伸出腿來想把我絆倒。**3** [I] **+ adv./prep.** (*literary*) to walk, run or dance with quick light steps 腳步輕快地走（或跑、跳舞）：*She said goodbye and tripped off along the road.* 她說了聲再見就連蹦帶跳地沿路走了。**4** [T] **~ sth** to release a switch, etc. or to operate sth by doing so 觸發（開關）；（鬆開開關）開動：*to trip a switch* 打開開關 ◇ *Any intruders will trip the alarm.* 任何非法入室者都會觸響報警器。**5** [I] (*informal*) to be under the influence of a drug that makes you HALLUCINATE（服用毒品後）產生幻覺 IDM see MEMORY LANE, TONGUE *n.*

PHR V **ˌtrip ˈup | ˌtrip sb↔ˈup** to make a mistake; to deliberately make sb do this（故意使）犯錯誤：*Read the questions carefully, because the examiners sometimes try to trip you up.* 要仔細把問題看清楚，因為出卷人有時故意讓你出錯。

tri·par·tite /traɪˈpɑːtaɪt; *NAmE* -ˈpɑːrt-/ *adj.* [usually before noun] (*formal*) having three parts or involving three people, groups, etc. 有三部份的；涉及三人的；三方參加的

tripe /traɪp/ *noun* [U] **1** the LINING of a cow's or pig's stomach, eaten as food 食用牛肚（或豬肚）；百葉 **2** (*informal*) something that sb says or writes that you think is nonsense or not of good quality 廢話；胡說；拙劣的文章 SYN **garbage, rubbish**

ˈtrip hop *noun* [U] a type of dance music, which is a mixture of HIP HOP and REGGAE, has a slow beat, and is intended to create a relaxed atmosphere 迷幻舞曲（結合嘻哈和雷蓋音樂元素、節奏緩慢）

triple /ˈtrɪpl/ *adj., verb*

■ *adj.* [only before noun] **1** having three parts or involving three people or groups 三部份的；三人的；三組的：*a triple heart bypass operation* 心臟三處分流手術 ◇ *a triple alliance* 三方同盟 ◇ *They're showing a **triple bill** of horror movies* (= three horror movies one after the other). 他們正在連演三部恐怖片。**2** three times as much or as many as sth 三倍的；三重的：*The amount of alcohol in his blood was triple the legal maximum.* 他血液中的酒精含量為法定最高限量的三倍。◇ *Its population is about triple that of Venice.* 它的人口大約是威尼斯的三倍。▸ **triply** /ˈtrɪpli/ *adv.*

■ *verb* [I, T] **~ (sth)** to become, or to make sth, three times as much or as many 成為三倍；使增至三倍 SYN **treble**：*Output should triple by next year.* 到明年產量應增至三倍。

the ˈtriple jump *noun* [sing.] a sporting event in which people try to jump as far forward as possible with three jumps. The first jump lands on one foot, the second on the other, and the third on both feet. 三級跳遠

trip·let /ˈtrɪplət/ *noun* **1** one of three children born at the same time to the same mother 三胞胎中的一個 **2** (*music* 音) a group of three equal notes to be played or sung in the time usually taken to play or sing two of the same kind 三連音

trip·li·cate /ˈtrɪplɪkət/ *noun*

IDM **in ˈtriplicate 1** done three times 做過三次：*Each sample was tested in triplicate.* 每種樣品都做過三次檢驗。**2** (of a document 文件) copied twice, so that there are three copies in total 一式三份 ➲ compare DUPLICATE *n.*

tri·pod /ˈtraɪpɒd; *NAmE* -pɑːd/ *noun* a support with three legs for a camera, TELESCOPE, etc.（照相機、望遠鏡等的）三腳架 ➲ VISUAL VOCAB page V70

trip·per /ˈtrɪpə(r)/ *noun* (*BrE*) a person who is visiting a place for a short time for pleasure（短程）旅遊者：*a day tripper* 一日遊者

trip·tych /ˈtrɪptɪk/ *noun* (*technical* 術語) a picture that is painted or CARVED on three pieces of wood placed side by side, especially one over an ALTAR in a church 三連畫；三聯雕刻；（尤指）三摺聖像畫

trip·wire /ˈtrɪpwaɪə(r)/ *noun* a wire that is stretched close to the ground as part of a device for catching sb/sth if they touch it 絆索；絆網

tri·reme /ˈtraɪriːm/ *noun* a long flat ship with three rows of OARS on each side, used in war by the ancient Greeks and Romans（古希臘和羅馬人的）三層划槳戰船

tri·shaw /ˈtraɪʃɔː/ *noun* a light vehicle with three wheels and PEDALS, used in SE Asia to carry passengers（東南亞載客用的）三輪腳踏車

trite /traɪt/ *adj.* (of a remark, an opinion, etc. 言語、想法等) dull and boring because it has been expressed so many times before; not original 老生常談的；陳腐的；老一套的 SYN **banal** ▶ **trite·ly** *adv.* **trite·ness** *noun* [U]

Synonyms 同義詞辨析

trip

journey • tour • expedition • excursion • outing • day out

These are all words for an act of travelling to a place. 以上各詞均指旅行、旅遊。

trip an act of travelling from one place to another, and usually back again 通常指往返的旅行： *a business trip* 出差 ◇ *a five-minute trip by taxi* 五分鐘的出租車車程

journey an act of travelling from one place to another, especially when they are a long way apart 尤指長途旅行： *a long and difficult journey across the mountains* 漫長而艱難的翻山旅行

TRIP OR JOURNEY? 用 trip 還是 journey？

A **trip** usually involves you going to a place and back again; a **journey** is usually one-way. A **trip** is often shorter than a **journey**, although it does not have to be. * trip 通常為往返旅行，journey 通常為單程旅行。trip 的行程常較 journey 短，但並非一定如此： *a trip to New York* 去紐約的旅行 ◇ *a round-the-world trip* 環球旅行 It is often short in time, even if it is long in distance. **Journey** is more often used when the travelling takes a long time and is difficult. In North American English **journey** is not used for short trips. 即使距離遠，trip 所花時間常常不長。如果旅程長且艱難較常用 journey。在美式英語中，journey 不用以指短途旅行： *(BrE) What is your journey to work like?* 你上班的路程如何？

tour a journey made for pleasure during which several different places are visited 指旅行、旅遊： *a tour of Bavaria* 巴伐利亞之旅

expedition an organized journey with a particular purpose, especially to find out about a place that is not well known 指遠征、探險、考察： *the first expedition to the South Pole* 首次去南極的探險

excursion a short trip made for pleasure, especially one that has been organized for a group of people 尤指集體遠足、短途旅行： *We went on an all-day excursion to the island.* 我們到島上去遊覽了一整天。

outing a short trip made for pleasure or education, usually with a group of people and lasting no more than a day 指集體出外遊玩或學習，通常不超過一天： *The children were on a day's outing from school.* 孩子們離校遊覽了一天。

day out a trip to somewhere for a day, especially for pleasure 指一日遊： *We had a day out at the beach.* 我們在海灘玩了一天。

PATTERNS

- a(n) **foreign/overseas** trip/journey/tour/expedition
- a **bus/coach/train/rail** trip/journey/tour
- to **go on** a(n) trip/journey/tour/expedition/excursion/outing/day out
- to **set out/off on** a(n) trip/journey/tour/expedition/excursion
- to **make** a(n) trip/journey/tour/expedition/excursion

tri·tium /ˈtrɪtiəm/ *noun* [U] (*symb.* **T**) an ISOTOPE (= a different form) of hydrogen with a mass that is three times that of the usual isotope 氚（氫的同位素）

tri·umph /ˈtraɪʌmf/ *noun, verb*

■ ***noun*** **1** [C, U] a great success, achievement or victory 巨大成功；重大成就；偉大勝利： *one of the greatest triumphs of modern science* 現代科學最重大的成就之一 ◇ **~ over sb/sth** *It was a personal triumph over her old rival.* 這是她對老對頭的個人勝利。 **2** [U] the feeling of great satisfaction or joy that you get from a great success or victory（巨大成功或勝利的）心滿意足，喜悅，狂喜： *a shout of triumph* 喜悅的歡呼聲 ◇ *The winning team returned home **in triumph**.* 球隊凱旋而歸。 **3** [sing.] **a ~ (of sth)** an excellent example of how successful sth can be（成功的）典範，楷模： *Her arrest was a triumph of international cooperation.* 她的被捕是國際合作的成果。

■ ***verb*** [I] **~ (over sb/sth)** to defeat sb/sth; to be successful 打敗；戰勝；成功： *As is usual in this kind of movie, good triumphs over evil in the end.* 像這類電影的一貫結局一樣，善良戰勝了邪惡。 ◇ *France triumphed 3–0 in the final.* 法國隊在決賽中以 3:0 獲勝。

tri·umph·al /traɪˈʌmfl/ *adj.* [usually before noun] done or made in order to celebrate a great success or victory 慶祝成功（或勝利）的；凱旋的

tri·umph·al·ism /traɪˈʌmfəlɪzəm/ *noun* [U] (*disapproving*) behaviour that celebrates a victory or success in a way that is too proud and intended to upset the people you have defeated 耀武揚威；揚揚得意 ▶ **tri·umph·al·ist** *adj.*

tri·umph·ant /traɪˈʌmfənt/ *adj.* **1** very successful in a way that causes great satisfaction 高奏凱歌的；大獲全勝的；巨大成功的： *They emerged triumphant in the September election.* 他們在九月份的選舉中大獲全勝。 **2** showing great satisfaction or joy about a victory or success 歡欣鼓舞的；揚揚得意的；耀武揚威的： *a triumphant smile* 得意揚揚的笑容 ▶ **tri·umph·ant·ly** *adv.*

tri·um·vir·ate /traɪˈʌmvərət/ *noun* (*formal*) a group of three powerful people or groups who control sth together 三人領導小組；三人統治集團；三方執政集團

trivet /ˈtrɪvɪt/ *noun* a metal stand that you can put a hot dish, etc. on（墊熱菜盤等用的）金屬架

trivia /ˈtrɪviə/ *noun* [U] **1** unimportant matters, details or information 瑣事；細枝末節： *We spent the whole evening discussing domestic trivia.* 我們整個晚上談論家庭瑣事。 **2** (usually in compounds 通常構成複合詞) facts about many subjects that are used in a game to test people's knowledge（智力測驗比賽用的）各種科目的知識： *a trivia quiz* 知識面寬的問答比賽

triv·ial /ˈtrɪviəl/ *adj.* not important or serious; not worth considering 不重要的；瑣碎的；微不足道的： *a trivial detail* 細枝末節 ◇ *I know it **sounds trivial**, but I'm worried about it.* 我知道這事聽起來微不足道，但我還是放心不下。 ◇ *I'll try to fix it—but it's not trivial* (= it may be difficult to fix). 我會設法修好，不過這並非易事。 ▶ **trivi·al·ly** /-iəli/ *adv.*

trivi·al·ity /ˌtrɪviˈæləti/ *noun* (*pl.* **-ies**) (*disapproving*) **1** [C] a matter that is not important 瑣事；小事： *I don't want to waste time on trivialities.* 我不想把時間浪費在一些瑣碎小事上。 **2** [U] the state of being unimportant or dealing with unimportant things 微不足道；瑣碎；無足輕重： *His speech was one of great triviality.* 他的講話根本無足輕重。

trivi·al·ize (*BrE* also **-ise**) /ˈtrɪviəlaɪz/ *verb* **~ sth** (usually *disapproving*) to make sth seem less important, serious, difficult, etc. than it really is 使顯得瑣碎（或不重要、不難等）；輕視 ▶ **trivi·al·iza·tion**, **-isa·tion** /ˌtrɪviəlaɪˈzeɪʃn; *NAmE* -ləˈz-/ *noun* [U]

tro·chee /ˈtrəʊkiː; *NAmE* ˈtroʊkiː/ *noun* (*technical* 術語) a unit of sound in poetry consisting of one strong or long syllable followed by one weak or short syllable（詩的）揚抑格，長短格 ▶ **tro·cha·ic** /trəʊˈkeɪɪk; *NAmE* troʊ-/ *adj.*

trod *past tense* of TREAD

trod·den *past part.* of TREAD

T

trog /trɒg; *NAmE* trɑːg/ *noun* (*BrE, informal*) a person with bad social skills and low intelligence 不受歡迎的人；呆子

trog·lo·dyte /ˈtrɒglədaɪt; *NAmE* ˈtrɑːg-/ *noun* a person living in a CAVE, especially in PREHISTORIC times（尤指史前時期的）穴居人 SYN **cave dweller**

troika /ˈtrɔɪkə/ *noun* (*formal*) a group of three politicians or countries working together 三人領導小組；三頭政治；三鉅頭；三國集團

troil·ism /ˈtrɔɪlɪzəm/ *noun* [U] sexual activity involving three people 三方性愛

Tro·jan /ˈtrəʊdʒən; *NAmE* ˈtroʊ-/ *noun, adj.* a person from the ancient city of Troy in Asia Minor（小亞細亞古城）特洛伊人

IDM **work like a ˈTrojan** (*old-fashioned*) to work very hard 埋頭苦幹；賣力幹活

ˌTrojan ˈhorse *noun* **1** a person or thing that is used to trick an enemy in order to achieve a secret purpose 特洛伊木馬；（來自外部的）顛覆分子（或活動） **2** (*computing* 計) a computer program that seems to be helpful but that is, in fact, designed to destroy data, etc. 特洛伊木馬程序（一種欺騙程序，看來有用，實際卻旨在毀壞數據等） ORIGIN From the story in which the ancient Greeks hid inside a hollow wooden statue of a horse in order to enter the city of their enemies, Troy. 源自傳說，古希臘人為了潛入敵城特洛伊而藏在空心的木馬中。

troll /trɒl; trəʊl; *NAmE* troʊl/ *noun, verb*

■ ***noun*** **1** (in Scandinavian stories) a creature that looks like an ugly person. Some trolls are very large and evil, others are small and friendly but like to trick people.（斯堪的納維亞傳說中的）山精，巨怪，友善頑皮的侏儒 **2** (*informal*) a message to a discussion group on the Internet that sb deliberately sends to make other people angry; a person who sends a message like this "投餌"，惡意挑釁的帖子（在互聯網討論組張貼）；"投餌"人；發挑釁帖子的人

■ ***verb*** **1** [I] **~ (for sth)** (*especially NAmE*) to catch fish by pulling a line with BAIT on it through the water behind a boat 曳繩釣（魚）；拖釣 **2** [T, I] (*informal*) to search for or try to get sth 搜查；搜索；設法得到： **~ sth for sth** *He trolled the Internet for advice on the disease.* 他搜索互聯網尋求治療這種病的建議。◇ **~ for sth** *Both candidates have been trolling for votes.* 兩個候選人一直都在拉票。

trol·ley /ˈtrɒli; *NAmE* ˈtrɑːli/ *noun* **1** (*BrE*) (*NAmE* **cart**) a small vehicle with wheels that can be pushed or pulled along and is used for carrying things 手推車；手拉車： *a* ***shopping/supermarket/luggage trolley*** 購物／超市／行李手推車 ➲ VISUAL VOCAB page V33 **2** (*BrE*) (*US* **cart, wagon**) a small table on very small wheels, used for carrying or serving food or drink（運或送食品、飲料的）小推車，枱車： *a drinks trolley* 飲料車 ◇ *a tea trolley* 茶具車 **3** (*US*) = STREETCAR

IDM **off your ˈtrolley** (*BrE, informal*) crazy; stupid 失去理智；瘋瘋癲癲；愚蠢

trol·ley·bus /ˈtrɒlibʌs; *NAmE* ˈtrɑːl-/ (*BrE*) (*US* **ˈtrackless trolley**) *noun* a bus driven by electricity from a cable above the street 無軌電車

ˈtrolley car *noun* (*old-fashioned, US*) = STREETCAR

trol·lop /ˈtrɒləp; *NAmE* ˈtrɑːləp/ *noun* (*old-fashioned, offensive*) **1** a woman who has many sexual partners 蕩婦；娼婦 **2** a woman who is very untidy 邋遢的女人；懶婆娘

trom·bone /trɒmˈbəʊn; *NAmE* trɑːmˈboʊn/ *noun* a large BRASS musical instrument that you blow into, with a sliding tube used to change the note 長號；伸縮長號 ➲ VISUAL VOCAB page V34

trom·bon·ist /trɒmˈbəʊnɪst; *NAmE* trɑːmˈboʊ-/ *noun* a person who plays the trombone 長號手

tromp /trɒmp; *NAmE* trɑːmp/ *verb* (*NAmE, informal*) = TRAMP

trompe l'œil /ˌtrɒmp ˈlɔɪ; *NAmE* ˌtrɔːmp/ *noun* (*pl.* **trompe l'œils** /ˌtrɒmp ˈlɔɪ; *NAmE* ˌtrɔːmp/) (from *French*) a painting or design intended to make the person looking at it think that it is a real object 視幻覺畫，視幻覺圖（逼真和寫實達到亂真程度）

troop /truːp/ *noun, verb*

■ ***noun*** **1 troops** [pl.] soldiers, especially in large groups 軍隊；部隊；士兵： *They announced the withdrawal of 12 000 troops from the area.* 他們宣佈從這個地區撤軍 12 000 人。◇ *The president decided to* ***send in the troops.*** 總統決定派駐軍隊。◇ *Russian troops* 俄國軍隊 ➲ COLLOCATIONS at WAR **2** [C] one group of soldiers, especially in tanks or on horses 連隊；坦克連；騎兵連： (*figurative*) *A troop of guests was moving towards the house.* 一群客人朝那房子走去。 **3** [C] a local group of SCOUTS 童子軍中隊 ▸ **troop** *adj.* [only before noun]： *troop movements* (= of soldiers) 部隊的調動

■ ***verb*** [I] **+ adv./prep.** (used with a plural subject 與複數主語連用) to walk somewhere together as a group 成群結隊而行；列隊行進： *After lunch we all trooped down to the beach.* 午餐後我們都成群結隊走向海灘。

troop·er /ˈtruːpə(r)/ *noun* **1** a soldier of low rank in the part of an army that uses tanks or horses 坦克兵；騎兵 **2** (*NAmE*) = STATE TROOPER IDM see SWEAR

troop·ship /ˈtruːpʃɪp/ *noun* a ship used for transporting soldiers 部隊運輸船；運兵船

trop ➲ DE TROP

trope /trəʊp; *NAmE* troʊp/ *noun* (*technical* 術語) a word or phrase that is used in a way that is different from its usual meaning in order to create a particular mental image or effect. METAPHORS and SIMILES are tropes. 轉義詞語；比喻詞語

troph·ic /ˈtrəʊfɪk; ˈtrɒf-; *NAmE* ˈtroʊfɪk/ *adj.* (*biology* 生) **1** relating to feeding, and to the food necessary for growth 營養的；營養有關的 **2** (of a HORMONE or its effect 荷爾蒙或其作用) causing the release of another HORMONE or other substance into the blood 引起其他荷爾蒙（或物質）分泌的；有分泌作用的

ˌtrophic ˈlevel *noun* (*technical* 術語) each of several levels in an ECOSYSTEM (= all the plants and animals in a particular area and their relationship with their surroundings). Each level consists of living creatures that share the same function in the FOOD CHAIN and get their food from the same source.（生態系統的）營養級

trophy /ˈtrəʊfi; *NAmE* ˈtroʊfi/ *noun, adj.*

■ ***noun*** (*pl.* **-ies**) **1** an object such as a silver cup that is given as a prize for winning a competition（頒發給競賽獲勝者的）獎品，獎杯 ➲ picture at MEDAL **2 Trophy** used in the names of some competitions and races in which a trophy is given to the winner（用於比賽或賽跑名稱）獎，獎杯 **3** an object that you keep to show that you were successful in sth, especially hunting or war（尤指狩獵或戰爭中獲得的）紀念品，戰利品

■ ***adj.*** [only before noun] **~ building/art/girlfriend, etc.** (*informal, disapproving*) an impressive or beautiful thing or person that you have in order to make other people admire you 炫耀的；擺闊的；招搖的： *We don't need a trophy building for our business.* 我們的企業不需要豪華奢侈的建築。

ˈtrophy wife *noun* (*informal, disapproving*) a young attractive woman who is married to an older man and thought of as a trophy (= sth that shows that you are successful and impress other people)（年長男人用以炫耀的）寶貝嬌妻

trop·ic /ˈtrɒpɪk; *NAmE* ˈtrɑːpɪk/ *noun* **1** [C, usually sing.] one of the two imaginary lines drawn around the world 23° 26′ north (**the Tropic of Cancer**) or south (**the Tropic of Capricorn**) of the EQUATOR 回歸線（北回歸線稱作 the Tropic of Cancer，南回歸線稱作 the Tropic of Capricorn） **2 the tropics** [pl.] the area between the two tropics, which is the hottest part of the world 熱帶；熱帶地區 SYN **the torrid zone**

trop·ic·al 0→ /ˈtrɒpɪkl; *NAmE* ˈtrɑːp-/ *adj.* coming from, found in or typical of the tropics 熱帶的；來自熱帶的；產於熱帶的： *tropical fish* 熱帶魚 ◇ *tropical Africa* 熱帶非洲 ◇ *a tropical island* 位於熱帶地區的島

T

tro·pism /ˈtrəʊpɪzəm; ˈtrɒp-; *NAmE* ˈtroʊpɪzəm/ *noun* [U] (*biology* 生) the action of a living thing turning all or part of itself in a particular direction, towards or away from sth such as a source of light（生物的）向性

the tropo·sphere /ˈtrɒpəsfɪə(r); *NAmE* ˈtroʊpəsfɪr; ˈtrɑːp-/ *noun* [sing.] (*technical* 術語) the lowest layer of the earth's atmosphere, between the surface of the earth and about 6-10 kilometres above the surface 對流層（大氣的最低層，在地球表面和 6 至 10 公里上空之間）

trot /trɒt; *NAmE* trɑːt/ *verb*, *noun*

■ ***verb*** (-tt-) **1** [I] (of a horse or its rider 馬或騎馬者) to move forward at a speed that is faster than a walk and slower than a CANTER 快步；疾走；小跑 **2** [T] **~ sth** to ride a horse in this way 騎馬小跑：*She trotted her pony around the field.* 她騎着小馬繞場慢跑。**3** [I] **+ adv./prep.** (of a person or an animal 人或動物) to run or walk fast, taking short quick steps 小步快跑；碎步急行：*The children trotted into the room.* 孩子們小跑着進了房間。**4** [I] **+ adv./prep.** (*informal*) to walk or go somewhere 步行；走；到…去：*The guide led the way and we trotted along behind him.* 嚮導在前面帶路，我們跟在他的後面走。**IDM** see HOT *adj.*

PHR V **ˌtrot sth↔ˈout** (*informal*, *disapproving*) to give the same excuses, facts, explanations, etc. for sth that have often been used before 重複，翻出（老一套的藉口、事實、解釋等）：*They trotted out the same old excuses for the lack of jobs in the area.* 他們又用那老一套的藉口解釋這個地區缺少就業機會的問題。

■ ***noun*** **1** [sing.] a trotting speed, taking short quick steps（指速度）慢跑，小跑，小步快跑，疾走：*The horse slowed to a trot.* 那馬放慢速度在小跑。◇ *The girl **broke into a trot** and disappeared around the corner.* 那姑娘突然小步跑了起來，拐過街角不見了。**2** [C] a period of trotting（指活動）小跑；一陣小跑

IDM **on the ˈtrot** (*BrE*, *informal*) **1** one after the other 接連地；接二連三；一個接着一個 **SYN** **in succession**：*They've now won three games on the trot.* 他們現在已經連勝三場比賽。**2** busy all the time 忙個不停：*I've been on the trot all day.* 我一整天忙得不可開交。

troth /trəʊθ; *NAmE* trɑːθ/ *noun* **IDM** see PLIGHT *v.*

Trot·sky·ist /ˈtrɒtskiɪst; *NAmE* ˈtrɑːt-/ (also **Trot·sky·ite** /ˈtrɒtskiaɪt; *NAmE* ˈtrɑːt-/) *noun* a supporter of the political ideas of Leon Trotsky, especially that SOCIALISM should be introduced all over the world by means of revolution 托洛茨基分子 ▸ **Trot·sky·ist** (also **Trot·sky·ite**) *adj.*

trot·ter /ˈtrɒtə(r); *NAmE* ˈtrɑːt-/ *noun* **1** a pig's foot, especially when cooked and eaten as food（尤指煮熟供食用的）豬蹄，豬腳 **2** a horse that has been trained to TROT fast in races（受過快步馬賽訓練的）快步馬

trou·ba·dour /ˈtruːbədɔː(r)/ *noun* (*literary*) a writer and performer of songs or poetry (after the French travelling performers of the 11th-13th centuries) 遊吟詩人（因 11–13 世紀法國的巡迴表演者而得名）

trouble 🔑 /ˈtrʌbl/ *noun*, *verb*

■ ***noun***

▸ **PROBLEM/WORRY 問題；憂慮** **1** 🔑 [U, C] a problem, worry, difficulty, etc. or a situation causing this 問題；憂慮；困難；苦惱：*We **have trouble** getting staff.* 我們在招聘雇員方面有困難。◇ *He could **make trouble for me** if he wanted to.* 他要是想找麻煩就能給我找麻煩。◇ **~ (with sb/sth)** ***The trouble with you is** you don't really want to work.* 你的問題在於你並不是很想工作。◇ *We've never **had** much **trouble with** vandals around here.* 我們這一帶從來沒有多少破壞公物的問題。◇ ***Her trouble is** she's incapable of making a decision.* 她的問題是自己沒有能力做決定。◇ ***The trouble is*** (= what is difficult is) *there aren't any trains at that time.* 麻煩的是當時沒有火車。◇ ***The only trouble is** we won't be here then.* 唯一的麻煩是到那時我們就不在這兒了。◇ *No, I don't know his number—I have quite enough trouble remembering my own.* 不，我不知道他的號碼，我光記自己的號碼就夠困難的了。◇ *financial troubles* 財政困難 ◇ *She was on the phone for an hour telling me her troubles.* 她在電話上用了一個小時向我傾訴她的種種煩惱。◇ *Our troubles aren't over yet.* 我們的麻煩還沒有完呢。➲ see also TEETHING TROUBLES

▸ **ILLNESS/PAIN 疾病；疼痛** **2** 🔑 [U] illness or pain 疾病；疼痛：*back trouble* 背痛 ◇ *I've been having trouble with my knee.* 我一直膝蓋痛。➲ SYNONYMS at ILLNESS

▸ **WITH MACHINE 機器** **3** 🔑 [U] something that is wrong with a machine, vehicle, etc.（機器、車輛等的）故障：*mechanical trouble* 機械故障

▸ **DIFFICULT/VIOLENT SITUATION 困難／暴力局面** **4** 🔑 [U] a situation that is difficult or dangerous; a situation in which you can be criticized or punished 困境；險境；可能受到批評（或處罰）的情形：*The company **ran into trouble** early on, when a major order was cancelled.* 這家公司早些時候有一個大訂單被撤銷，因此陷入了困境。◇ *A yachtsman **got into trouble** off the coast and had to be rescued.* 一個駕駛帆船的人在海上遇險須要救援。◇ *If I don't get this finished in time, I'll be **in trouble**.* 我如不按時把這完成就要倒霉了。◇ *He's **in trouble with** the police.* 他犯事落入了警察的手裏。◇ *My brother was always **getting me into trouble** with my parents.* 以前我弟弟經常連累我遭父母的責難。**5** 🔑 [U] an angry or violent situation 紛爭；動亂；騷亂：*The police were expecting trouble after the match.* 警方預料比賽後會有騷亂。◇ *If you're not in by midnight, there'll be trouble* (= I'll be very angry). 你要是半夜前不回家，我就讓你有好戲看。◇ *He had to throw out a few drunks who were causing trouble in the bar.* 他不得不轟走幾個在酒吧裏鬧事的醉鬼。

▸ **EXTRA EFFORT 額外努力** **6** 🔑 [U] **~ (to sb)** extra effort or work 額外努力（或工作）；煩擾；打擾；麻煩 **SYN** **bother**：*I don't want to **put you to a lot of trouble**.* 我不想給你添很多的麻煩。◇ *I'll get it if you like, that will **save you the trouble of** going out.* 如果你願意的話我去取，省得你還得出去。◇ *Making your own yogurt **is more trouble than it's worth**.* 自己做酸奶很麻煩，不值得。◇ *She **went to a lot of trouble** to find the book for me.* 她不辭勞苦把書給我找到了。◇ *He thanked me for my trouble and left.* 他感謝我盡了力便走了。◇ *Nothing is ever **too much trouble** for her* (= she's always ready to help). 她從不把麻煩當回事。◇ *I can call back later—it's **no trouble*** (= I don't mind). 我可以過一會兒回電話，沒關係。◇ *I hope the children weren't too much trouble.* 我希望這些孩子沒有太煩人。

▸ **IN NORTHERN IRELAND 北愛爾蘭** **7** **the Troubles** [pl.] the time of political and social problems in Northern Ireland, especially after 1968, when there was violence between Catholics and Protestants about whether Northern Ireland should remain part of the UK 動亂時期（尤指 1968 年後，天主教徒和新教徒之間就北愛爾蘭是否應繼續附屬於英國而引發的暴力衝突）

IDM **get sb into ˈtrouble** (*old-fashioned*) to make a woman who is not married pregnant 使…未婚先孕 **give (sb) (some, no, any, etc.) ˈtrouble** to cause problems or difficulties 給（或沒有給）…造成麻煩（或煩惱、困難）：*My back's been giving me a lot of trouble lately.* 我的後背最近一直疼痛。◇ *The children didn't give me any trouble at all when we were out.* 我們外出時孩子們一點兒也沒給我添麻煩。**look for ˈtrouble** to behave in a way that is likely to cause an argument, violence, etc. 自找麻煩；自尋煩惱；自討苦吃：*Drunken youths hang around outside looking for trouble.* 喝醉的年輕人在街頭遊蕩，酗酒滋事。**take trouble over/with sth** | **take trouble doing/to do sth** to try hard to do sth well 盡心盡力地做；費力地做：*They take a lot of trouble to find the right person for the right job.* 他們竭力尋找適合做這項工作的人。**take the trouble to do sth** to do sth even though it involves effort or difficulty 不辭辛勞地做；不厭其煩地做 **SYN** **make the effort**：*She didn't even take the trouble to find out how to spell my name.* 她嫌麻煩，甚至連我的姓名如何拼寫都不想搞清楚。**a trouble ˌshared is a trouble ˈhalved** (*saying*) if you talk to sb about your problems and worries, instead of keeping them to yourself, they seem less serious 煩惱可以分擔（向人傾訴，愁苦就會減少）➲ more at ASK *v.*

■ ***verb***

▸ **MAKE SB WORRIED 使憂慮** **1** [T] **~ sb** to make sb worried or upset 使憂慮；使煩惱；使苦惱：*What is it that's troubling you?* 是什麼事使得你愁眉苦臉？

▸ **DISTURB 打擾** **2** [T] (often used in polite requests 常用於客氣的請求) to disturb sb because you want to ask them sth 勞駕；費神；麻煩 SYN **bother** : **~ sb** *Sorry to trouble you, but could you tell me the time?* 對不起打擾您一下，請問幾點了？◇ **~ sb with sth** *I don't want to trouble the doctor with such a small problem.* 我不想為了這個小毛病麻煩醫生。◇ (*formal*) **~ sb to do sth** *Could I trouble you to open the window, please?* 勞駕，請您把窗戶打開好嗎？

▸ **MAKE EFFORT 努力** **3** [I] **~ to do sth** (*BrE, formal*) (usually used in negative sentences 通常用於否定句) to make an effort to do sth 費神；費事；費力 SYN **bother** : *He rushed into the room without troubling to knock.* 他連門也懶得敲就闖進屋去。

▸ **CAUSE PAIN 造成痛苦** **4** [T] **~ sb** (of a medical problem 健康問題) to cause pain 使疼痛；折磨：*My back's been troubling me again.* 我的背又在一直疼了。IDM see POUR

troubled /ˈtrʌbld/ *adj.* **1** (of a person 人) worried and anxious 憂慮的；煩惱的；不安的：*She looked into his troubled face.* 她仔細打量着他那張佈滿愁容的臉。**2** (of a place, situation or time 地方、局勢或時間) having a lot of problems 麻煩多的；混亂的；擾亂的：*a troubled marriage* 坎坷的婚姻◇ *We live in* ***troubled times.*** 我們生逢亂世。

trouble·maker /ˈtrʌblmeɪkə(r)/ *noun* a person who often causes trouble, especially by involving others in arguments or encouraging them to complain about people in authority 麻煩製造者；搬弄是非者；搗亂者；鬧事者

trouble·shoot /ˈtrʌblʃuːt/ *verb* **1** [I, T] **~ (sth)** to analyse and solve serious problems for a company or other organization（為公司、機構等）分析解決（難題）**2** [I, T] **~ (sth)** (*computing* 計) to identify and correct faults in a computer system 檢修，排除（系統錯誤）▸ **trouble·shoot·ing** *noun* [U]

trouble·shoot·er /ˈtrʌblʃuːtə(r)/ *noun* a person who helps to solve problems in a company or an organization（公司或組織中）解決困難者

trouble·some /ˈtrʌblsəm/ *adj.* causing trouble, pain, etc. over a long period of time 令人煩惱的；討厭的；令人痛苦的 SYN **annoying, irritating** : *a troublesome cough/child/problem* 煩人的咳嗽；讓人心煩的孩子；棘手的問題

ˈtrouble spot *noun* a place or country where trouble often happens, especially violence or war 不安定的地區；動亂的國家；（尤指）經常發生暴力（或戰爭）的地方

trough /trɒf; *NAmE* trɔːf/ *noun* **1** [C] a long narrow open container for animals to eat or drink from 槽；飼料槽；飲水槽 **2** **the trough** [sing.] (*informal*) if you say that people have their noses **in the trough**, you mean that they are trying to get a lot of money for themselves 錢槽；錢眼 **3** [C] (*technical* 術語) a long narrow region of low air pressure between two regions of higher pressure 低壓槽；槽形低壓 ➲ compare RIDGE *n.* (3) **4** [C] a period of time when the level of sth is low, especially a time when a business or the economy is not growing 低谷；（企業或經濟的）低潮，蕭條階段：*There have been* ***peaks and troughs*** *in the long-term trend of unemployment.* 長期以來失業率一直時起時伏。**5** [C] a low area between two waves in the sea, or two hills（海浪間的）波谷；（小山間的）槽谷，盆狀窪地

trounce /traʊns/ *verb* **~ sb** (*formal*) to defeat sb completely 徹底打敗；擊潰：*Brazil trounced Italy 5–1 in the final.* 在決賽中巴西隊以 5:1 狂勝意大利隊。

troupe /truːp/ *noun* [C+sing./pl. v.] a group of actors, singers, etc. who work together（演員、歌手等的）班子，表演團

trouper /ˈtruːpə(r)/ *noun* (*informal*) an actor or other person who has a lot of experience and who you can depend on 角兒；台柱子演員；可靠的人；主心骨

trou·ser *verb* **~ sth** (*BrE, informal*) to take or earn an amount of money 收受；賺得 SYN **pocket**

trou·sers 0‐ /ˈtraʊzəz; *NAmE* -zərz/ (*especially BrE*) (*NAmE* usually **pants**) *noun* [pl.] a piece of clothing that covers the body from the waist down and is divided into two parts to cover each leg separately 褲子：*a pair of grey trousers* 一條灰褲子 ◇ *I was still* ***in short trousers*** (= still only a boy) *at the time.* 我那時還在穿着短褲呢（仍然是個男孩）。◇ *He dropped his trousers.* 他脫了褲子。➲ VISUAL VOCAB page V61 ▸ **trou·ser** *adj.* [only before noun] : *trouser pockets* 褲兜 IDM see CATCH *v.*, WEAR *v.*

ˈtrouser suit (*BrE*) (*NAmE* **pant·suit**) *noun* a woman's suit of jacket and trousers/pants（女子的）衣褲套裝

trous·seau /ˈtruːsəʊ; *NAmE* -soʊ/ *noun* (*pl.* **trous·seaus** or **trous·seaux** /-səʊz; *NAmE* -soʊz/) (*old-fashioned*) the clothes and other possessions collected by a woman who is soon going to get married, to begin her married life with 嫁妝；妝奩

trout /traʊt/ *noun* **1** [C, U] (*pl.* **trout**) a common FRESHWATER fish that is used for food. There are several types of trout. 鮭；鮭鱒魚；鱒魚：*rainbow trout* 虹鱒◇ *trout fishing* 捕鱒魚◇ *Shall we have trout for dinner?* 我們正餐吃鱒魚好嗎？➲ VISUAL VOCAB page V12 **2** [C, usually sing.] (usually **old trout**) (*informal, disapproving*) a bad-tempered or annoying old woman 惡婆子；討厭的老太婆

trove /trəʊv; *NAmE* troʊv/ *noun* ➲ TREASURE TROVE

trowel /ˈtraʊəl/ *noun* **1** a small garden tool with a curved blade for lifting plants and digging holes 小鏟子（園藝工具）➲ VISUAL VOCAB page V19 **2** a small tool with a flat blade, used in building for spreading CEMENT or PLASTER（抹泥灰或砂漿用的）瓦刀，鏝刀，抹子

IDM **lay it on with a ˈtrowel** (*informal*) to talk about sb/sth in a way that makes them or it seem much better or much worse than they really are; to exaggerate sth 過分地吹捧；言過其實；過分貶低：*He was laying the flattery on with a trowel.* 他吹捧得天花亂墜。

troy /trɔɪ/ *noun* [U] a system for measuring PRECIOUS METALS and PRECIOUS STONES 金衡制（用於稱量貴重金屬和寶石）

tru·ancy /ˈtruːənsi/ *noun* [U] the practice of staying away from school without permission 曠課；逃學

tru·ant /ˈtruːənt/ *noun* a child who stays away from school without permission 曠課的小學生 ▸ **tru·ant** *verb* [I] : *A number of pupils have been truanting regularly.* 不少小學生一直經常曠課。

IDM **play ˈtruant** (*BrE*) (*NAmE, old-fashioned, informal* **play ˈhooky**) to stay away from school without permission 曠課；逃學 ➲ COLLOCATIONS at EDUCATION ➲ see also BUNK OFF at BUNK *v.*, SKIVE

truce /truːs/ *noun* an agreement between enemies or opponents to stop fighting for an agreed period of time; the period of time that this lasts 停戰協定；休戰；停戰期：*to* ***call/break a truce*** 宣佈休戰；破壞停戰協定 ➲ COLLOCATIONS at WAR

truck 0‐ /trʌk/ *noun, verb*

■ ***noun*** 0‐ **1** (*especially NAmE*) (*BrE* also **lorry**) a large vehicle for carrying heavy loads by road 卡車；貨運汽車：*a truck driver* 卡車司機 ➲ COLLOCATIONS at DRIVING ➲ VISUAL VOCAB page V57 **2** (*BrE*) (*NAmE* **car**) an open railway vehicle for carrying goods or animals（鐵路上運送貨物或動物的）敞篷車，無蓋車皮：*a cattle truck* 敞篷運牛車廂 **3** a vehicle that is open at the back, used for carrying goods, soldiers, animals, etc.（運送貨物、士兵、動物等後面敞開的）載重汽車：*a delivery/garbage/farm truck* 送貨車；垃圾車；農用卡車 **4** a vehicle for carrying things, that is pulled or pushed by hand（運送東西的）手推車，手拉車 ➲ see also FORKLIFT TRUCK, PICKUP TRUCK at PICKUP *n.* (1), SALT TRUCK

IDM **have/want no truck with sb/sth** (*BrE*) to refuse to deal with sb; to refuse to accept or consider sth 拒不與…打交道；拒不接受；拒不考慮：*We in this party will have no truck with illegal organizations.* 我們黨的成員絕不與非法組織有來往。

■ ***verb*** **~ sth (+ adv./prep.)** (*especially NAmE*) to take sth somewhere by truck 用卡車裝運 ▸ **truck·ing** *noun* [U] : *trucking companies* 貨車運輸公司

truck·er /ˈtrʌkə(r)/ *noun* (*especially NAmE*) a person whose job is driving a truck 卡車司機

ˈ**truck farm** (*US*) (*BrE* ˌ**market ˈgarden**) *noun* a type of farm where vegetables are grown for sale 蔬菜農場 ▸ ˈ**truck farmer** *noun* ˈ**truck farming** *noun* [U]

truck·load /ˈtrʌkləʊd; *NAmE* -loʊd/ *noun* **~ (of sb/sth)** the amount of sb/sth that fills a truck (often used to express the fact that an amount is large) 貨車荷載；一卡車（的量）；大量

ˈ**truck stop** *noun* (*NAmE*) a place at the side of a main road where lorry/truck drivers can stop for a time and can rest, get sth to eat, etc. 長途卡車服務站；公路小餐館 ➲ compare TRANSPORT CAFE

trucu·lent /ˈtrʌkjələnt/ *adj.* (*formal, disapproving*) tending to argue or be bad-tempered; slightly aggressive 愛爭吵的；粗暴的；好鬥的；尋釁的 ▸ **trucu·lence** /-ləns/ *noun* [U] **trucu·lent·ly** *adv.*

trudge /trʌdʒ/ *verb, noun*

■ ***verb*** [I] to walk slowly or with heavy steps, because you are tired or carrying sth heavy（因疲勞或負重而）步履沉重地走，緩慢地走，費力地走：**+ noun** *He trudged the last two miles to the town.* 他步履艱難地走完最後兩英里到了城裏。◇ **+ adv./prep.** *The men trudged up the hill, laden with supplies.* 這些人背着補給品疲憊地往山上爬。

■ ***noun*** [sing.] a long tiring walk 徒步跋涉；疲憊的長途步行

true 🗝 /truː/ *adj., adv., noun*

WORD FAMILY
true *adj.* (≠ untrue)
truth *noun*
truthful *adj.* (≠ untruthful)
truthfully *adv.*
truly *adv.*

■ ***adj.*** (**truer**, **tru·est**)

▸ CORRECT 正確 **1** 🗝 connected with facts rather than things that have been invented or guessed 符合事實的；確實的；如實的：*Indicate whether the following statements are* ***true or false****.* 標出下列說法是對還是錯。◇ *Is it true she's leaving?* 她要走是真的嗎？◇ *All the rumours turned out to be true.* 所有的傳聞結果都確有其事。◇ *That's not strictly* (= completely) *true.* 那不完全正確。◇ *The novel is based on* ***a true story****.* 這部小說是根據真人真事寫成的。◇ *His excuse just doesn't* ***ring*** (= sound) ***true****.* 他的藉口聽起來就是不真實。◇ *Unfortunately, these findings do not* ***hold true*** (= are not valid) *for women and children.* 遺憾的是，這些調查結果不適用於婦女和兒童。◇ *The music is dull and uninspiring, and* ***the same is true of*** *the acting.* 音樂沉悶枯燥毫不動人，表演也是。◇ *You never spoke a truer word* (= used to emphasize that you agree with what sb has just said). 你說的一點不假。**OPP untrue**

▸ REAL 真正 **2** 🗝 real or exact, especially when this is different from how sth seems 實質的，真正的（而非表面上的）：*the true face of war* (= what it is really like rather than what people think it is like) 戰爭的真實面目 ◇ *The true cost of these experiments to the environment will not be known for years to come.* 這些實驗對環境造成的確切代價在未來數年內是看不見的。◇ *He reveals his true character to very few people.* 他沒有向什麼人顯露過他的真實性格。**3** 🗝 [usually before noun] having the qualities or characteristics of the thing mentioned 名副其實的；真正的：*It was true love between them.* 他們是真心相愛。◇ *He's a true gentleman.* 他是個正人君子。◇ *The painting is a masterpiece in the truest sense of the word.* 這幅畫是名副其實的傑作。◇ *He is credited with inventing the first true helicopter.* 他被認為是發明第一架真正的直升機的人。

▸ ADMITTING FACT 承認事實 **4** 🗝 used to admit that a particular fact or statement is correct, although you think that sth else is more important（承認事實或說法正確，但有更重要的考慮）確實，的確：*It's true that he could do the job, but would he fit in with the rest of the team?* 他確實能做這項工作，但他是否能和團隊其他人配合得好呢？◇ *'We could get it cheaper.' 'True, but would it be as good?'* "我們可以買得再便宜一點兒。" "話是這麼說，但是質量是不是一樣好呢？" ➲ LANGUAGE BANK at NEVERTHELESS

▸ LOYAL 忠實 **5** showing respect and support for a particular person or belief in a way that does not change, even in different situations 忠誠的；忠心耿耿的；忠實的：*a true friend* 忠實的朋友 ◇ **~ to sth** *She has always been true to herself* (= done what she thought was good, right, etc.). 她一貫堅持按自己的信念辦事。◇ *He was* ***true to his word*** (= did what he promised to do). 他信守諾言。

▸ ACCURATE 精確 **6 ~ (to sth)** being an accurate version or copy of sth 精確的；與正本無異的；逼真的：*The movie is not true to the book.* 這部電影並非忠於原著。**7** [not usually before noun] (*old-fashioned* or *literary*) straight and accurate 正而準：*His aim was true* (= he hit the target). 他瞄得很準。

IDM **come ˈtrue** 🗝 (of a hope, wish, etc. 希望、願望等) to become reality 實現；成為現實：*Winning the medal was like* ***a dream come true****.* 獲得這枚獎牌好比夢想成真。**too ˌgood to be ˈtrue** used to say that you cannot believe that sth is as good as it seems 好得難以令人相信：*'I'm afraid you were quoted the wrong price.' 'I thought it was too good to be true.'* "很抱歉，給你報錯價了。" "我也覺得價格低得難以令人置信。" **your true ˈcolours** (often *disapproving*) your real character, rather than the one that you usually allow other people to see 本性；本來面目 **true to ˈform** used to say that sb is behaving in the way that you expect them to behave, especially when this is annoying 跟往常一樣；一如既往；合乎本性 **true to ˈlife** (of a book, film/movie, etc. 書、電影等) seeming real rather than invented 真實的；逼真的；維妙維肖；活靈活現 ➲ more at RING² *v.*, TRIED

■ ***adv.*** (*old-fashioned* or *literary*)

▸ STRAIGHT 逕直 **1** in a direct line 筆直地；不偏不斜地：*The arrow flew straight and true to the target.* 箭不偏不斜地朝靶子飛去。

▸ CORRECTLY 正確地 **2 speak ~** to tell the truth 直言相告；實話實說：*He had spoken truer than he knew.* 他說得比他知道的還確切。

■ ***noun***

IDM ˌ**out of ˈtrue** if an object is **out of true**, it is not straight or in the correct position 歪七扭八；位置不正；偏斜

Synonyms 同義詞辨析

true

right • correct

These words all describe sth that cannot be doubted as fact and includes no mistakes. 以上各詞均指某事屬實、真確、真實。

true connected with facts rather than things that have been invented or guessed 指合乎事實的、確實的、如實的：*Are the following statements* ***true or false****?* 下列說法是對還是錯？◇ *Is it* ***true*** *(****that****) she's leaving?* 她要走是真的嗎？

right that is true and cannot be doubted as a fact 指正確的、真實的：*I got about half the answers right.* 我的回答約有一半是正確的。◇ *What's the right time?* 現在的準確時間是幾點？

correct right according to the facts and without any mistakes 指準確無誤的、正確的：*Only one of the answers is correct.* 這些答案中只有一個是正確的。◇ *Check that all the details are correct.* 檢查所有這些細節是否準確無誤。

RIGHT OR CORRECT? 用 right 還是 correct？

Correct is more formal than **right** and is more likely to be used in official or formal instructions or documents.
* correct 較 right 正式，更多用於官方或正式的說明或文件中。

PATTERNS

- right/correct **about** sb/sth
- the true/right/correct **answer**
- the right/correct **time**

ˌ**true-ˈblue** *adj.* **1** (*BrE*) strongly supporting the British Conservative Party（英國）堅決支持保守黨的，忠於保守黨的：*true-blue Tory voters* 忠於保守黨的投票人

T

2 (*especially NAmE*) being a loyal supporter of a particular person, group, principle, etc.; being a typical example of sth（對人、團體、原則等）忠貞不渝的，堅定不移的；典型的；有代表性的：*a true-blue Californian* 典型的加利福尼亞州人

ˌtrue-ˈlife *adj.* [only before noun] a **true-life** story is one that actually happened rather than one that has been invented 真人真事的；確有其事的；寫實的

ˌtrue ˈnorth *noun* [U] north according to the earth's AXIS (= the imaginary line through the earth's centre from north to south) 真北（以地軸北極為正北）➲ compare MAGNETIC NORTH

truf·fle /ˈtrʌfl/ *noun* **1** an expensive type of FUNGUS that grows underground, used in cooking 塊菌（生長於地下，可食用，價格昂貴）**2** a soft round sweet/candy made of chocolate 圓形巧克力軟糖

trug /trʌg/ *noun* a shallow BASKET used for carrying garden tools, plants, etc.（裝園藝用具、植物等的）淺筐

tru·ism /ˈtruːɪzəm/ *noun* a statement that is clearly true and does not therefore add anything interesting or important to a discussion 不言而喻的道理；自明之理；老生常談

truly 🔑 /ˈtruːli/ *adv.*
1 🔑 used to emphasize that a particular statement, feeling, etc. is sincere or genuine（用於說法、感覺等）真誠地，誠懇地，衷心地：*I'm truly sorry that things had to end like this.* 事情落到這樣的結局，我從內心裏感到歉疚。**2** 🔑 used to emphasize a particular quality（指性質）真正，確實：*a truly memorable occasion* 的確值得紀念的盛事 **3** 🔑 used to emphasize that a particular description is accurate or correct（指描述）確切，準確，精確，確實：*a truly democratic system of government* 真正的民主政體 ◇ (*informal*) *Well,* ***really and truly****, things were better than expected.* 啊，情況的的確確比預計的要好。

IDM **yours truly** **1** 🔑 **Yours Truly** (*NAmE, formal*) used at the end of a formal letter before you sign your name（用於正式信函末尾署名前）**2** (*informal, often humorous*) I/me 鄙人：*Steve came first, Robin second, and yours truly came last.* 史蒂夫最先，羅賓第二，鄙人最後。➲ more at WELL *adv.*

trump /trʌmp/ *noun, verb*
■ *noun* **1** (also **ˈtrump card**) [C] (in some card games) a card that belongs to the SUIT (= one of the four sets in a PACK/DECK of cards) that has been chosen for a particular game to have a higher value than the other three suits（某些紙牌遊戲的一張）王牌，主牌，將牌：*I played a trump and won the trick.* 我打出一張主牌，贏了那一墩。**2 trumps** [U+sing./pl. v.] (in some card games) the SUIT that has been chosen for a particular game to have a higher value than the other three suits（某些紙牌遊戲的）王牌花色，主牌花色：*What's trumps?* 王牌是什麼？◇ *Clubs are trumps.* 梅花是主牌。

IDM **ˌcome up/ˌturn up ˈtrumps** to do what is necessary to make a particular situation successful, especially when this is sudden or unexpected 打出王牌；做有助於獲得（意外）成功的事：*I didn't honestly think he'd pass the exam but he came up trumps on the day.* 說實話我以為他考試及不了格，但是那天他發揮出色，考得不錯。

■ *verb* **1 ~ sth (with sth)** (in some card games 某些紙牌遊戲) to play a trump card that beats sb else's card 出王牌贏（牌）；出王牌壓掉（他人的牌）**2 ~ sth/sb** to beat sth that sb says or does by saying or doing sth even better 贏；勝過；打敗

PHR V **ˌtrump sth↔ˈup** to make up a false story about sb/sth, especially accusing them of doing sth wrong 誣陷；捏造；編造：*She was arrested on a trumped-up charge.* 她以莫須有的罪名被捕。

ˈtrump card *noun* **1** = TRUMP (1) **2** something that gives you an advantage over other people, especially when they do not know what it is and you are able to use it to surprise them 王牌；絕招；殺手鐧

T

trump·ery /ˈtrʌmpəri/ *noun* [U] (*old-fashioned*) objects of little value 實際價值低的東西 ▸ **trump·ery** *adj.*

trum·pet /ˈtrʌmpɪt/ *noun, verb*
■ *noun* **1** a BRASS musical instrument made of a curved metal tube that you blow into, with three VALVES for changing the note 小號；喇叭 ➲ VISUAL VOCAB page V34 **2** a thing shaped like a trumpet, especially the open flower of a DAFFODIL 喇叭形物；（尤指）綻開的水仙花 ➲ VISUAL VOCAB page V11 **IDM** see BLOW *v.*
■ *verb* **1** [T] **~ sth (as sth)** | **+ speech** to talk about sth publicly in a proud or enthusiastic way 宣揚；鼓吹；吹噓：*to trumpet somebody's achievements* 吹噓某人的成就 ◇ *Their marriage was trumpeted as the wedding of the year.* 他們的聯姻被宣揚成年度婚禮。**2** [I] (especially of an ELEPHANT 尤指大象) to make a loud noise 吼叫

trum·pet·er /ˈtrʌmpɪtə(r)/ *noun* a person who plays a trumpet 號手；號兵；小號吹奏者

trun·cate /trʌŋˈkeɪt; *NAmE* ˈtrʌŋkeɪt/ *verb* [usually passive] **~ sth** (*formal*) to make sth shorter, especially by cutting off the top or end 截短，縮短，刪節（尤指掐頭或去尾）：*My article was published in truncated form.* 我的文章以節錄的形式發表了。▸ **trun·ca·tion** *noun* [U, C]

trun·cheon /ˈtrʌntʃən/ (also **baton**) (both *especially BrE*) (*NAmE* usually **night·stick**) *noun* a short thick stick that police officers carry as a weapon 警棍

trun·dle /ˈtrʌndl/ *verb* **1** [I, T] **~ (sth) + adv./prep.** to move or roll somewhere slowly and noisily; to move sth slowly and noisily, especially sth heavy, with wheels（使緩慢、轟鳴地）移動，滾動：*A train trundled across the bridge.* 一列火車隆隆駛過大橋。**2** [I] **+ adv./prep.** (of a person 人) to walk slowly with heavy steps 沉重緩慢地走

PHR V **ˌtrundle sth↔ˈout** (*disapproving, especially BrE*) to mention or do sth that you have often mentioned or done before 重提某事；故技重演：*A long list of reasons was trundled out to justify their demands.* 他們重複一大串理由，說明他們的要求正當。

trunks 樹幹；象鼻；大箱子；（男式）游泳褲

trunk /trʌŋk/ *noun* **1** [C] the thick main STEM of a tree, that the branches grow from 樹幹 ➲ VISUAL VOCAB page V10 **2** (*NAmE*) (*BrE* **boot**) [C] the space at the back of a car that you put bags, cases, etc. in（汽車後部的）行李箱 ➲ VISUAL VOCAB page V52 **3** [C] the long nose of an ELEPHANT 象鼻 ➲ VISUAL VOCAB page V12 **4 trunks** [pl.] = SWIMMING TRUNKS **5** [C] a large strong box with a lid used for storing or transporting clothes, books, etc. 大箱子；大衣箱 ➲ VISUAL VOCAB page V64 **6** [C, usually sing.] the main part of the human body apart from the head, arms and legs（人的）軀幹 ➲ see also TORSO (1)

ˈtrunk call *noun* (*old-fashioned, BrE*) a telephone call to a place that is a long distance away but in the same country（國內）長途電話

ˈtrunk road *noun* (*BrE*) an important main road 公路幹線；幹道

truss /trʌs/ *noun, verb*
■ *noun* **1** a special belt with a thick piece of material, worn by sb suffering from a HERNIA in order to support the muscles 疝帶（疝病患者所用）**2** a frame made of pieces of wood or metal used to support a roof, bridge, etc.（支撐屋頂、橋梁等的）構架，桁架
■ *verb* **1 ~ sb/sth (up)** to tie up sb's arms and legs so that they cannot move 把（人的雙臂和雙腿）捆緊，縛牢

2 ~ sth to tie the legs and wings of a chicken, etc. before it is cooked（在烹煮雞等前）把腿和翅膀束緊

trust 0‑m /trʌst/ *noun, verb*

■ ***noun* 1** 0‑m [U] **~ (in sb/sth)** the belief that sb/sth is good, sincere, honest, etc. and will not try to harm or trick you 相信；信任；信賴：*Her trust in him was unfounded.* 她對他的信任毫無道理。◇ *a partnership* ***based on trust*** 建立在互相信任基礎上的合夥關係◇ *It has taken years to* ***earn their trust***. 花了好多年才贏得他們的信任。◇ *If you* ***put your trust in*** *me, I will not let you down.* 你要是信賴我，我就不會讓你失望。◇ *She will not* ***betray your trust*** (= do sth that you have asked her not to do). 她不會辜負你對她的信任。◇ *He was appointed to a* ***position of trust*** (= a job involving a lot of responsibility, because people trust him). 他被委以重任。**2** [C, U] (*law* 律) an arrangement by which an organization or a group of people has legal control of money or property that has been given to sb, usually until that person reaches a particular age; an amount of money or property that is controlled in this way 委託；信託；信託財產：*He* ***set up a trust*** *for his children.* 他為子女安排好了信託財產。◇ *The money will be* ***held in trust*** *until she is 18.* 這筆錢將由人代管到她 18 歲為止。◇ *Our fees depend on the value of the trust.* 我們的費用視信託金額而定。➲ see also UNIT TRUST **3** [C] (*law* 律) an organization or a group of people that invests money that is given or lent to it and uses the profits to help a charity 受託基金機構；受託團體：*a charitable trust* 慈善基金機構 **4** [C] (*business* 商) (*especially NAmE*) a group of companies that work together illegally to reduce competition, control prices, etc. 托拉斯（為減少競爭、操縱價格等而非法聯合的企業組織）：*anti-trust laws* 反托拉斯法

IDM **in sb's 'trust | in the trust of sb** being taken care of by sb 由某人保管（或照管）：*The family pet was left in the trust of a neighbour.* 這家的寵物委託鄰居代管。 **take sth on 'trust** to believe what sb says even though you do not have any proof or evidence to show that it is true 聽信；輕信；貿然相信

■ ***verb* 1** to have confidence in sb; to believe that sb is good, sincere, honest, etc. 信任；信賴；相信（某人的善良、真誠等）：**~ sb** *She trusts Alan implicitly.* 她絕對信任艾倫。◇ **~ sb to do sth** *You can trust me not to tell anyone.* 你可以相信我不會跟任何人講。 **2 ~ sth** to believe that sth is true or correct or that you can rely on it 相信；認為可靠：*He trusted her judgement.* 他相信她的判斷力。◇ *Don't trust what the newspapers say!* 別相信報紙上的話！ **3 ~ (that) …** (*formal*) to hope and expect that sth is true 想；希望；期望：*I trust (that) you have no objections to our proposals?* 我想你不反對我們的建議吧？

IDM **not trust sb an 'inch** to not trust sb at all 對…根本不相信 **trust 'you, 'him, 'her, etc. (to do sth)** (*informal*) used when sb does or says sth that you think is typical of them（認為某人言行一貫如此時說）管保，保證：*Trust John to forget Sue's birthday!* 管保約翰會把蘇的生日忘了！➲ more at TRIED

PHR V **'trust in sb/sth** (*formal*) to have confidence in sb/sth; to believe that sb/sth is good and can be relied on 相信；信任；信賴：*She needs to trust more in her own abilities.* 她需要更加相信自己的能力。 **'trust to sth** [no passive] to put your confidence in sth such as luck, chance, etc. because there is nothing else to help you 依靠，依賴（運氣、機會等）：*I stumbled along in the dark, trusting to luck to find the right door.* 我摸黑跌跌撞撞地往前走，希望憑運氣能找對門。 **'trust sb with sth/sb** to give sth/sb to a person to take care of because you believe they would be very careful with it/them 託付；託交；把…委託給某人照管：*I'd trust her with my life.* 她是我可以性命相託的人。

trust·ee /trʌ'stiː/ *noun* **1** a person or an organization that has control of money or property that has been put into a TRUST for sb（財產的）受託人 **2** a member of a group of people that controls the financial affairs of a charity or other organization（慈善事業或其他機構的）受託人

trustee·ship /trʌ'stiːʃɪp/ *noun* [U, C] **1** the job of being a trustee 受託人職責 **2** the responsibility for governing a particular region, given to a country by the United

Synonyms 同義詞辨析

trust

depend on sb/sth • rely on sb/sth • count on sb/sth • believe in sb

These words all mean to believe that sb/sth will do what you hope or expect of them or that what they tell you is correct or true. 以上各詞均含相信、信任、信賴之意。

trust to believe that sb is good, honest, sincere, etc. and that they will do what you expect of them or do the right thing; to believe that sth is true or correct 指相信、信任、信賴：*You can trust me not to tell anyone.* 你可以相信我不會跟任何人講。◇ *Don't trust what you read in the newspapers!* 別相信你在報紙上讀到的！

depend on/upon sb/sth (often used with *can/cannot/could/could not*) to trust sb/sth to do what you expect or want, to do the right thing, or to be true or correct（常與 can/cannot/could/could not 連用）指相信、信賴、指望：*He was the sort of person you could depend on.* 他是你可以信賴的人。◇ *Can you depend on her version of what happened?* 你相信她對所發生事情的描述嗎？

rely on/upon sb/sth (used especially with *can/cannot/could/could not* and *should/should not*) to trust sb/sth to do what you expect or want, or to be honest, correct or good enough（尤與 can/cannot/could/could not 和 should/should not 連用）指信任、信賴：*Can I rely on you to keep this secret?* 我能相信你會保守這個秘密嗎？◇ *You can't rely on any figures you get from them.* 你不能相信從他們那兒得到的任何數據。

TRUST, DEPEND OR RELY ON/UPON SB/STH? 用 trust、depend 還是 rely on/upon sb/sth？

You can **trust** a person but not a thing or system. You can **trust** sb's *judgement* or *advice*, but not their support. You can **depend on** sb's *support*, but not their judgement or advice. **Rely on/upon sb/sth** is used especially with *you can/could* or *you should* to give advice or a promise. * trust 的賓語可以是人，但不能是物或制度；trust 後還可接 sb's judgement 或 advice，但不能接 sb's support；depend on 後可跟 sb's support，但不能跟 sb' s judgement 或 advice；rely on/upon sb/sth 尤與 you can/could 或 you should 連用，以給予建議或承諾：~~*I don't really rely on his judgement.*~~ ◇ *You can't really rely on his judgement.* 你不能真的相信他的判斷。

count on sb/sth (often used with *can/cannot/could/could not*) to be sure that sb will do what you need them to do, or that sth will happen as you want it to happen（常與 can/cannot/could/could not 連用）指可信賴、依靠、指望（某人做某事）、確信（某事會發生）：*I'm counting on you to help me.* 我就靠你幫我啦。◇ *We can't count on the good weather lasting.* 我們不能指望這樣好的天氣會持久。

believe in sb to feel that you can trust sb and/or that they will be successful 指信賴、信任、相信某人會成功：*They need a leader they can believe in.* 他們需要一個可以信賴的領導。

PATTERNS

- to trust/depend on/rely on/count on sb/sth **to do sth**
- to trust/believe **in** sb/sth
- to trust/rely on **sb's advice/judgement**
- to depend on/rely on/count on **sb's support**
- to **completely** trust/depend on/rely on/believe in sb/sth

T

Nations Organization; a region that is governed by another country in this way 託管（聯合國委託某一國家管理某一地區）；託管地區

ˈtrust fund *noun* money that is controlled for sb by an organization or a group of people 信託基金

trust·ing /ˈtrʌstɪŋ/ *adj.* tending to believe that other people are good, honest, etc. 輕信的；輕易信賴別人的：*If you're too trusting, other people will take advantage of you.* 如果你過於輕信，其他人就會打你的主意。▸ **trust·ing·ly** *adv.*

ˈtrust territory *noun* a region governed by the United Nations Organization or by another country that has been chosen by the United Nations Organization（聯合國或其委託國家的）託管領地

trust·worthy /ˈtrʌstwɜːði; *NAmE* -wɜːrði/ *adj.* that you can rely on to be good, honest, sincere, etc. 值得信任的；可信賴的；可靠的 SYN **reliable** ▸ **trust·worthi·ness** *noun* [U]

trusty /ˈtrʌsti/ *adj., noun*

■ ***adj.*** [only before noun] (*old use* or *humorous*) that you have had a long time and have always been able to rely on（長期以來）可信任的，可信賴的；忠實的 SYN **reliable**：*a trusty friend* 忠實的朋友 ◇ *She spent years touring Europe with her trusty old camera.* 她帶着她那架忠心耿耿的照相機在歐洲周遊多年。

■ ***noun*** (*pl.* **-ies**) (*informal*) a prisoner who is given special advantages because of good behaviour 模範囚犯（由於表現好而受到優待）

truth 🗝 /truːθ/ *noun* (*pl.* **truths** /truːðz/)

1 🗝 **the truth** [sing.] the true facts about sth, rather than the things that have been invented or guessed 真相；實情；事實；真實情況：*Do you think she's **telling the truth**?* 你認為她在講實話嗎？◇ *We are determined to get at (= discover) the truth.* 我們決心查出真相。◇ ***The truth (of the matter) is** we can't afford to keep all the staff on.* 實際情況是我們無力繼續聘用所有的職員。◇ *I don't think you are telling me **the whole truth** about what happened.* 我認為你沒有把事情的全部真相都告訴我。**2** 🗝 [U] the quality or state of being based on fact 真實；真實性：*There is no truth in the rumours.* 這些謠言毫無根據。◇ *There is not **a grain of truth** in what she says.* 她說的沒有一句真話。OPP **falsity** **3** [C] a fact that is believed by most people to be true 真理：*universal truths* 普遍真理 ◇ *She was forced to face up to a few unwelcome truths about her family.* 她不得不正視有關她家的幾樁尷尬事。➲ compare UNTRUTH (1) ➲ see also HALF-TRUTH, HOME TRUTH

IDM **if (the) ˌtruth be ˈknown/ˈtold** used to tell sb the true facts about a situation, especially when these are not known by other people（用於說出真相）說實話，說真的，老實說 **in ˈtruth** (*formal*) used to emphasize the true facts about a situation（強調真實情況）的確，事實上：*She laughed and chatted but was, in truth, not having much fun.* 她雖然又是笑又是侃，但實際上玩得並不開心。**ˌnothing could be ˌfurther from the ˈtruth** used to say that a fact or comment is completely false 大錯特錯；假到極點；荒謬絕倫 **to tell (you) the ˈtruth** (*informal*) used when admitting sth（承認某事）說實話，老實說：*To tell you the truth, I'll be glad to get home.* 說實話，能回家我會很高興。**ˌtruth is stranger than ˈfiction** (*saying*) used to say that things that actually happen are often more surprising than stories that are invented 現實比虛構更不可思議 **(the) ˌtruth will ˈout** (*saying*) used to say that people will find out the true facts about a situation even if you try to keep them secret 真相終將大白於天下；紙包不住火；終會水落石出 ➲ more at BEND *v.*, ECONOMICAL, MOMENT

ˈtruth drug *noun* a drug that is believed to be able to put sb into a state where they will answer questions with the truth 吐真藥；坦白藥

truth·ful /ˈtruːθfl/ *adj.* **1 ~ (about sth)** (of a person 人) saying only what is true 誠實；講真話，坦率 SYN **honest**：*They were less than truthful about their part in the crime.* 他們對自己在這次犯罪中所擔當的角色講的絕非實情。◇ *Are you being completely truthful with me?* 你跟我講的全是真話嗎？**2** (of a statement 陳述) giving the true facts about sth 真實的；如實的：*a truthful answer* 坦誠的回答 OPP **untruthful** ▸ **truth·ful·ly** /-fəli/ *adv.*：*She answered all their questions truthfully.* 她如實回答了他們的所有問題。**truth·ful·ness** *noun* [U]

try 🗝 /traɪ/ *verb, noun*

■ ***verb*** (**tries**, **try·ing**, **tried**, **tried**) **1** 🗝 [I, T] to make an attempt or effort to do or get sth 試圖；想要；設法；努力：*I don't know if I can come but I'll try.* 我不知道是否能來，但我盡可能來。◇ **~ to do sth** *What are you trying to do?* 你想要做什麼？◇ *I tried hard not to laugh.* 我強忍住不笑出來。◇ **~ your best/hardest (to do sth)** *She tried her best to solve the problem.* 她盡了最大的努力解決這個問題。◇ *Just try your hardest.* 請盡力而為吧。HELP In spoken English **try** can be used with **and** plus another verb, instead of with **to** and the infinitive. 英語口語中，try 可以和 and 加另一動詞連用，而不和 to 及動詞不定式連用：*I'll try and get you a new one tomorrow.* ◇ *Try and finish quickly.* In this structure, only the form **try** can be used, not **tries**, **trying** or **tried**. 在這一結構中，只能用 try 的形式，而不能用 tries、trying 或 tried。**2** 🗝 [T] to use, do or test sth in order to see if it is good, suitable, etc. 試；試用；試做；試驗：**~ sth** *Have you tried this new coffee? It's very good.* 你嚐過這種新咖啡嗎？好極啦。◇ *'Would you like to try some raw fish?' 'Why not? **I'll try anything once!**'* "你想嚐點兒生魚片嗎？" "好哇，我什麼都想嚐一點兒！" ◇ *Have you ever tried windsurfing?* 你玩過帆板運動嗎？◇ ***Try these shoes for size**—they should fit you.* 試試這雙鞋的大小，你穿應該合腳。◇ *She tried the door, but it was locked.* 她推了推那扇門，但門鎖着。◇ **~ doing sth** *John isn't here. Try phoning his home number.* 約翰不在這兒。給他家裏打電話試試看。HELP Notice the difference between **try to do sth** and **try doing sth**: *You should try to eat more fruit.* means 'You should make an effort to eat more fruit.'; *You should try eating more fruit.* means 'You should see if eating more fruit will help you' (to feel better, for example). 注意 try to do sth 和 try doing sth 的區別：You should try to eat more fruit 意思是：你應該盡量多吃些水果；而 You should try eating more fruit 意思是：你應該試試多吃些水果（看看身體是不是會好些）。**3** [T] to examine evidence in court and decide whether sb is innocent or guilty 審理；審訊；審判：**~ sb (for sth)** *He was tried for murder.* 他因謀殺罪而受審。◇ **~ sth** *The case was tried before a jury.* 此案是由陪審團參加審理的。

IDM **ˌnot for want/lack of ˈtrying** used to say that although sb has not succeeded in sth, they have tried very hard 並非努力不夠；已經盡力了：*They haven't won a game yet, but it isn't for want of trying.* 他們還沒贏過一場比賽，但並不是由於拚勁不足。**try your ˈhand (at sth)** to do sth such as an activity or a sport for the first time 初試身手 **ˌtry it ˈon (with sb)** (*BrE, informal, disapproving*) **1** to behave badly towards sb or try to get sth from them, even though you know this will make them angry 對…粗野無禮；耍弄；向…行騙：*Children often try it on with new teachers.* 兒童經常設法戲弄新來的老師。**2** to try to start a sexual relationship with sb 試圖與（某人）發生性關係 **try your ˈluck (at sth)** to do sth that involves risk or luck, hoping to succeed 碰運氣：*My grandparents emigrated to Canada to try their luck there.* 我的祖父母移民到加拿大去碰碰運氣。**try sb's ˈpatience** to make sb feel impatient 使忍無可忍；使不耐煩 ➲ more at DAMNEDEST, LEVEL *adj.*, THING

PHR V **ˈtry for sth** to make an attempt to get or win sth 試圖獲得；力爭贏得 **ˌtry sth↔ˈon** 🗝 to put on a piece of clothing to see if it fits and how it looks 試穿（衣物）：*Try the shoes on before you buy them.* 鞋子要先穿上試一試再買。**ˌtry ˈout for sth** (*especially NAmE*) to compete for a position or place in sth, or to be a member of a team 參加…選拔（或試演）：*She's trying out for the school play.* 她正在參加學校戲劇演員甄選。➲ related noun TRYOUT **ˌtry sb/sth↔ˈout (on sb)** 🗝 to test or use sb/sth in order to see how good or effective they are 試用（某人）；測試；試驗：*They're trying out a new presenter for the show.* 他們正在為這個節目試用一名新的主持人。➲ related noun TRYOUT

T

■ *noun* (*pl.* **tries**) **1** [usually sing.] an act of trying to do sth 嘗試；試圖；努力 **SYN** **attempt**: *I doubt they'll be able to help but it's* **worth a try** (= worth asking them). 我不敢肯定他們能夠幫得上忙，但不妨試一試。◇ **~ (at sth/at doing sth)** *Why don't you* **have a try** *at convincing him?* 為什麼你不試試說服他？◇ (*NAmE*) *The US negotiators decided to* **make another try at** *reaching a settlement.* 美國的談判者決定再作一番努力，力爭達成和解。◇ *I don't think I'll be any good at tennis, but I'll* **give it a try**. 我不認為我有打網球的特長，但是我會試一試。◇ (*informal*) *'What's that behind you?' '***Nice try** (= at making me turn round)*, but you'll have to do better than that!'* "看你身後是什麼？" "好個鬼花招，不過你耍的手法還不夠高明！" **2** (in RUGBY 橄欖球) an act of scoring points by touching the ground behind your opponents' GOAL LINE with the ball 在對方球門線後帶球觸地；持球觸地得分: *to score a try* 帶球觸地得分

ˌtry-and-ˈbuy *adj.* [only before noun] (especially of computer programs and equipment 尤指計算機程序和設備) that can be used free for a limited period of time, during which you can decide whether you want to buy it or not 先試後買的

try·ing /ˈtraɪɪŋ/ *adj.* annoying or difficult to deal with 令人厭煩的；難對付的: *These are trying times for all of us.* 對我們所有人來說，這是最難熬的時期。

try·out /ˈtraɪaʊt/ *noun* **1** an act of testing how good or effective sb/sth is before deciding whether to use them in the future 檢查衡量潛力；考核潛力 **2** (*NAmE*) (*BrE* **trial**) a competition or series of tests to find the best players for a sports team or an important event 預賽；選拔賽

tryst /trɪst/ *noun* (*literary* or *humorous*) a secret meeting between lovers （情人的）約會，幽會

tsar (also **tzar**, **czar**) /zɑː(r)/ *noun* **1** the title of the EMPEROR of Russia in the past 沙皇（舊時俄國皇帝的稱號）: *Tsar Nicholas II* 沙皇尼古拉二世 **2** (in compounds 構成複合詞) (*informal*) an official whose job is to advise the government on policy in a particular area （在某領域向政府提供有關政策的建議的）政府顧問，政府高級官員: (*BrE*) *a drugs tsar* 毒品問題顧問 ◇ (*NAmE*) *a drug tsar* 毒品問題顧問

tsar·ina (also **tzar·ina**, **czar·ina**) /zɑːˈriːnə/ *noun* the title of the EMPRESS of Russia in the past（舊時俄國的）女沙皇，沙皇皇后

tsar·ism (also **tzar·ism**, **czar·ism**) /ˈzɑːrɪzəm/ *noun* [U] the Russian system of government by a tsar, which existed before 1917 （1917 年之前的）俄國沙皇政體 ▸ **tsar·ist** (also **tzar·ist**, **czar·ist**) *noun, adj.*

tsetse fly /ˈtsetsi flaɪ/ *noun* an African fly that bites humans and animals and sucks their blood and can spread a disease called SLEEPING SICKNESS 舌蠅，采采蠅（叮咬人和動物吸血傳染昏睡病的非洲蒼蠅）

ˈT-shirt (also **ˈtee shirt**) *noun* an informal shirt with short sleeves and no COLLAR or buttons, or just a few buttons at the top * T 恤衫；短袖汗衫 ➲ VISUAL VOCAB page V63

tsk tsk /ˌtəsk ˈtəsk/ *exclamation* used in writing to represent the sound you make with your tongue when you disapprove of something （用於書寫，表示不贊成）嘖嘖: *So you were out drinking again last night were you? Tsk tsk!* 這麼說你昨晚又外出喝酒了，對嗎？嘖嘖！

tsotsi /ˈtsɒtsi; *NAmE* ˈtsɑːt-/ *noun* (*SAfrE*) a young black criminal 黑人少年犯

Tsotsi·taal /ˈtsɒtsitɑːl; *NAmE* ˈtsɑːt-/ *noun* [U] (*SAfrE*) a simple form of language that includes words from Afrikaans and African languages, used especially between young black people in cities or TOWNSHIPS 南非塔爾語（包含南非荷蘭語和非洲語言中一些詞彙的簡單語言，尤用於非洲城鎮年輕黑人之間）

tsp *abbr.* (*pl.* **tsp** or **tsps**) TEASPOONFUL 一茶匙（的量）: *1 tsp chilli powder* 一茶匙辣椒粉

ˈT-square *noun* a plastic or metal instrument in the shape of a T for drawing or measuring RIGHT ANGLES (= of 90°) 丁字尺；曲尺

tsu·nami /tsuːˈnɑːmi/ *noun* (from *Japanese*) an extremely large wave in the sea caused, for example, by an EARTHQUAKE 海嘯；海震 **SYN** **tidal wave**

tub /tʌb/ *noun* **1** a large round container without a lid, used for washing clothes in, growing plants in, etc. 盆；桶: *There were tubs of flowers on the balcony.* 陽台上有一盆盆的花。 **2** a small wide, usually round, plastic or paper container with a lid, used for food, etc.（塑料或紙的）飯盒，食品盒: *a tub of margarine* 一盒人造黃油 ➲ VISUAL VOCAB page V33 **3** (*informal, especially NAmE*) = BATHTUB: *They found her lying in the tub.* 他們發現她躺在浴缸裏。 ➲ see also HOT TUB

tuba /ˈtjuːbə; *NAmE* ˈtuːbə/ *noun* a large BRASS musical instrument that you play by blowing, and that produces low notes 大號（低音銅管樂器） ➲ VISUAL VOCAB page V34

tubal /ˈtjuːbl; *NAmE* ˈtuːbl/ *adj.* (*medical* 醫) connected with the FALLOPIAN TUBES 輸卵管的: *a tubal pregnancy* 輸卵管妊娠

tubby /ˈtʌbi/ *adj.* (*informal*) (of a person 人) short and slightly fat 矮胖的 **SYN** **stout**

tube 🔑 /tjuːb; *NAmE* tuːb/ *noun*

▸ **PIPE** 管 **1** 🔑 [C] a long hollow pipe made of metal, plastic, rubber, etc., through which liquids or gases move from one place to another （金屬、塑料、橡皮等製成的）管，管子 ➲ see also CATHODE RAY TUBE, INNER TUBE, TEST TUBE **2** 🔑 [C] a hollow object in the shape of a pipe or tube 管狀物: *a bike's inner tube* 自行車內胎 ◇ *the cardboard tube from the centre of a toilet roll* 手紙捲中央的硬紙管

▸ **CONTAINER** 容器 **3** 🔑 [C] **~ (of sth)** a long narrow container made of soft metal or plastic, with a lid, used for holding thick liquids that can be squeezed out of it （由軟金屬或塑料製成的帶蓋的、盛膏狀物的）軟管: *a tube of toothpaste* 一管牙膏 ➲ VISUAL VOCAB page V33 **4** (*AustralE, informal*) a can of beer 一罐啤酒: *a tube of lager* 一罐拉格啤酒

▸ **PART OF BODY** 身體部位 **5** [C] a part inside the body that is shaped like a tube and through which air, liquid, etc. passes 管狀器官；管；道: *bronchial tubes* 支氣管 ➲ VISUAL VOCAB page V59 ➲ see also FALLOPIAN TUBE

▸ **UNDERGROUND RAILWAY** 地下鐵道 **6** (also **The Tube™**) [sing.] (*BrE*) the underground railway system in London 倫敦地下鐵道: *a* **tube station/train** 地鐵車站／列車 ◇ *We came* **by tube**. 我們乘地鐵來的。 ➲ note at UNDERGROUND

▸ **TELEVISION** 電視 **7 the tube** [sing.] (*NAmE, informal*) the television 電視；電視機

▸ **IN EAR** 耳朵 **8** (*NAmE*) (*BrE* **grom·met**) [C] a small tube placed in a child's ear in order to DRAIN liquid from it 鼓室通氣管；中耳引流管

IDM **go down the ˈtube/ˈtubes** (*informal*) (of a plan, company, situation, etc. 計劃、公司、情況等) to fail 失敗；落空；完蛋；吹了: *The education system is going down the tubes.* 這種教育體系就要垮台了。

tuber /ˈtjuːbə(r); *NAmE* ˈtuː-/ *noun* the short thick round part of an underground STEM or root of some plants, such as potatoes, which stores food and from which new plants grow 塊莖（某些植物的肉質地下莖） ▸ **tu·ber·ous** /ˈtjuːbərəs; *NAmE* ˈtuː-/ *adj.*

tu·ber·cle /ˈtjuːbəkl; *NAmE* ˈtuːb-/ *noun* **1** (*anatomy* 解, *biology* 生) a small round lump, especially on a bone or on the surface of an animal or plant 結節；疣粒；小塊莖 **2** (*medical* 醫) a small swollen area in the lung caused by TUBERCULOSIS （肺）結核結節

tu·ber·cu·losis /tjuːˌbɜːkjuˈləʊsɪs; *NAmE* tuːˌbɜːrkjəˈloʊsɪs/ *noun* [U] (*abbr.* **TB**) a serious infectious disease in which swellings appear on the lungs and other parts of the body 結核病 ▸ **tu·ber·cu·lar** /tjuːˈbɜːkjələ(r); *NAmE* tuːˈbɜːrk-/ *adj.*: *a tubercular infection* 結核病感染

ˈtube top (*NAmE*) (*BrE* **ˈboob tube**) *noun* a piece of women's clothing that is made of cloth that stretches and covers the chest （女人的）緊身平口胸衣

'tube well *noun* a pipe with holes in the sides near the end, that is put into the ground and used with a PUMP operated by hand to bring water up from under the ground 管井

tub·ing /ˈtjuːbɪŋ; *NAmE* ˈtuːbɪŋ/ *noun* [U] metal, plastic, etc. in the shape of a tube 管；管狀物；金屬管；塑料管： *a length of copper tubing* 一截銅管 ➲ VISUAL VOCAB page V70

'tub-thumping *noun* [U] (*BrE, disapproving*) the act of giving your opinions about sth in a loud and aggressive way 慷慨激昂的演講；大吹大擂的宣揚 ▸ **'tub-thumping** *adj.*

tu·bu·lar /ˈtjuːbjələ(r); *NAmE* ˈtuː-/ *adj.* **1** made of tubes or of parts that are shaped like tubes 管子構成的；有管狀部份的： *a tubular metal chair* 用金屬管做的椅子 **2** shaped like a tube 管狀的

,tubular 'bells *noun* [pl.] a musical instrument which sounds like a set of bells, consisting of a row of hanging metal tubes that are hit with a stick 管鐘（打擊樂器，由一排懸掛的金屬管組成）

TUC /ˌtiː juː ˈsiː/ *abbr.* Trades Union Congress (an organization to which many British TRADE/LABOR UNIONS belong) 英國職工大會（統轄英國多個工會）

tuck /tʌk/ *verb, noun*

■ ***verb*** **1 ~ sth + adv./prep.** to push, fold or turn the ends or edges of clothes, paper, etc. so that they are held in place or look neat 把（衣服、紙張等的邊緣）塞進，摺疊，捲起： *She tucked up her skirt and waded into the river.* 她撩起裙子蹚水走進河裏。◇ *The sheets should be tucked in neatly* (= around the bed). 牀單的四邊應整整齊齊地掖在褥墊下面。◇ *Tuck the flap of the envelope in.* 把信封的口蓋塞進信封裏。 **2 ~ sth + adv./prep.** to put sth into a small space, especially to hide it or keep it safe or comfortable 把…塞進狹窄的空間；把…藏入；收藏： *She tucked her hair (up) under her cap.* 她把頭髮攏起來塞進帽子裏。◇ *He sat with his legs tucked up under him.* 他盤着腿坐着。◇ *The letter had been tucked under a pile of papers.* 那封信壓在了一摞文件下面。 **3 ~ sth + adv./prep.** to cover sb with sth so that they are warm and comfortable 用…蓋住；用…圍緊；用…裹嚴： *She tucked a blanket around his legs.* 她拿一條毯子把他的雙腿裹好。

PHR V **,tuck sth↔a'way 1 be tucked away** to be located in a quiet place, where not many people go 坐落在，位於（僻靜的地方）： *The shop is tucked away down a backstreet.* 這家店鋪位於一條僻靜的小巷。 **2** to hide sth somewhere or keep it in a safe place 收藏起；使隱藏： *She kept his letters tucked away in a drawer.* 她把他的來信收藏在抽屜裏。◇ *They have thousands of pounds tucked away in a savings account.* 他們把幾千英鎊存在一個儲蓄賬戶上。 **3** (*BrE, informal*) to eat a lot of food 大吃；拚命吃；暴食 **,tuck sb 'in/'up** to make sb feel comfortable in bed by pulling the covers up around them 把…的被子掖好： *I tucked the children in and said goodnight.* 我給孩子們蓋好被子說晚安。 **,tuck 'in | ,tuck 'into sth** (*BrE, informal*) to eat a lot of food, especially when it is done quickly and with enthusiasm 痛快地吃；狼吞虎嚥地吃： *Come on, tuck in everyone!* 來呀，大家痛痛快快地吃吧！◇ *He was tucking into a huge plateful of pasta.* 他在狼吞虎嚥地吃一大盤意大利麪。

■ ***noun*** **1** [C] a fold that is sewn into a piece of clothing or cloth, either for decoration or to change the shape of it （衣服或織物的）褶，打褶 **2** [C] (*informal*) a medical operation in which skin and/or fat is removed to make sb look younger or thinner 減肥手術 **3** [U] (*old-fashioned, BrE, informal*) food, especially sweets, etc. eaten by children at school 食物，零食（尤指兒童在學校吃的糖果等）

tuck·er /ˈtʌkə(r)/ *noun* [U] (*AustralE, NZE, informal*) food 食物 **IDM** see BIB

Tudor /ˈtjuːdə(r); *NAmE* ˈtuː-/ *adj.* connected with the time when kings and queens from the Tudor family ruled England (1485-1603)（英格蘭）都鐸王朝時代的： *Tudor architecture* 都鐸式建築

Tues·day 🔑 /ˈtjuːzdeɪ; -di; *NAmE* ˈtuː-/ *noun* [C, U] (*abbr.* **Tue.**, **Tues.**) the day of the week after Monday and before Wednesday 星期二 **HELP** To see how **Tuesday** is used, look at the examples at **Monday**. * Tuesday 的用法見詞條 Monday 下的示例。 **ORIGIN** Originally translated from the Latin for 'day of Mars' *dies Marti* and named after the Germanic god *Tiw*. 譯自拉丁文 dies Marti，原意為 day of Mars（戰神日），以日耳曼神 Tiw（蒂烏）命名。

tuft /tʌft/ *noun* **~ (of sth)** a number of pieces of hair, grass, etc. growing or held closely together at the base （在底部叢生或聚集的）一綹毛髮，一叢草

tuft·ed /ˈtʌftɪd/ *adj.* [usually before noun] having a tuft or tufts; growing in tufts 成束的；成簇的；叢生的；簇生的： *a tufted carpet* 簇絨地毯 ◇ *a tufted duck* 冠鳧

tug /tʌg/ *verb, noun*

■ ***verb*** (-gg-) **1** [I, T] to pull sth hard, often several times （常為幾次用力）拉，拖，拽： **~ (at/on sth)** *She tugged at his sleeve to get his attention.* 她拽了拽他的袖子引起他的注意。◇ (*figurative*) *a sad story that* ***tugs at your heartstrings*** (= makes you feel sad) 令人心酸的故事 ◇ **~ sth** *The baby was tugging her hair.* 嬰兒直扯她的頭髮。◇ **~ sth + adj.** *He tugged the door open.* 他用力拉開了門。 **2** [T] **~ sth + adv./prep.** to pull sth hard in a particular direction （朝某一方向用力）拉，拖，拽： *He tugged the hat down over his head.* 他把帽子往下拉了拉遮住臉。 ➲ SYNONYMS at PULL **IDM** see FORELOCK

■ ***noun*** **1** (also **tug·boat** /ˈtʌgbəʊt; *NAmE* -boʊt/) a small powerful boat for pulling ships, especially into a HARBOUR or up a river 拖船 ➲ VISUAL VOCAB page V54 **2** a sudden hard pull （突然的）猛拉，猛拽： *I felt a tug at my sleeve.* 我覺得有人用力拽了一下我的袖子。◇ *She gave her sister's hair a sharp tug.* 她猛地使勁扯了一下她姐姐的頭髮。 **3** [usually sing.] a sudden strong emotional feeling 一股強烈的感情： *a tug of attraction* 一陣強烈的吸引

,tug of 'love *noun* [sing.] (*BrE, informal*) a situation in which a child's parents are divorced or no longer living together and are fighting over who the child should live with （離異或分居父母對孩子的）監護權爭奪

,tug of 'war *noun* [sing., U] **1** a sporting event in which two teams pull at opposite ends of a rope until one team drags the other over a line on the ground 拔河 **2** a situation in which two people or groups try very hard to get or keep the same thing （兩人或兩組的）激烈爭奪

tu·ition /tjuˈɪʃn; *NAmE* tu-/ *noun* [U] **1 ~ (in sth)** (*formal*) the act of teaching sth, especially to one person or to people in small groups （尤指對個人或小組的）教學，講授，指導： *She received private tuition in French.* 她由私人教授法語。 ➲ COLLOCATIONS at EDUCATION **2** (also **tu'ition fees** [pl.]) the money that you pay to be taught, especially in a college or university （尤指大專院校的）學費

tulip /ˈtjuːlɪp; *NAmE* ˈtuː-/ *noun* a large, brightly coloured spring flower, shaped like a cup, on a tall STEM 鬱金香 ➲ VISUAL VOCAB page V11

tulle /tjuːl; *NAmE* tuːl/ *noun* [U] a type of soft fine cloth made of silk, NYLON, etc. and full of very small holes, used especially for making VEILS and dresses 絹網，絲網，眼紗，網眼織物（尤用以製作面紗或連衣裙）

tum /tʌm/ *noun* (*BrE, informal*) a person's stomach or the area around the stomach 胃；肚子

tum·ble /ˈtʌmbl/ *verb, noun*

■ ***verb*** **1** [I, T] **~ (sb/sth) + adv./prep.** to fall downwards, often hitting the ground several times, but usually without serious injury; to make sb/sth fall in this way （使）跌倒，摔倒，滾落，翻滾下來： *He slipped and tumbled down the stairs.* 他腳一滑滾下了樓梯。 **2** [I] **~ (down)** to fall suddenly and in a dramatic way 倒塌；坍塌： *The scaffolding came tumbling down.* 腳手架突然倒塌。◇ (*figurative*) *World records tumbled at the last Olympics.* 在上屆奧林匹克運動會上世界紀錄大幅下滑。 ➲ see also TUMBLEDOWN **3** [I] to fall rapidly in value or amount（價格或數量）暴跌，驟降：*The price of oil is still tumbling.* 油價仍在急遽下跌。 **4** [I] **+ adv./prep.** to move or fall somewhere in a relaxed, uncontrolled, or noisy way 翻滾；打滾；翻騰；輕鬆地倒下：*A group of noisy children tumbled out of the bus.* 一群吵吵嚷嚷的孩子一窩蜂地下了公共汽車。◇ *Thick golden curls tumbled down over her shoulders.* 厚厚的金色鬈髮垂在她的肩上。 **5** [I] to perform ACROBATICS on the floor, especially SOMERSAULTS (= a jump in which you turn over completely in the air) 表演雜技；翻跟頭；（尤指）做空翻動作

PHR V **'tumble to sth/sb** (*BrE, informal*) to suddenly understand sth or be aware of sth 頓悟；突然意識到

■ ***noun*** **1** [C, usually sing.] a sudden fall 跌倒；滾落；暴跌：*The jockey **took a nasty tumble** at the third fence.* 騎師在第三道柵欄處給重重摔下馬來。◇ *Share prices **took a sharp tumble** following news of the merger.* 合併消息傳出，股價隨即暴跌。➲ see also ROUGH AND TUMBLE **2** [sing.] **~ (of sth)** an untidy group of things 混亂的一堆；雜亂不堪的一團：*a tumble of blond curls* 蓬亂的金色鬈髮

tumble·down /'tʌmbldaʊn/ *adj.* [usually before noun] (of a building 建築物) old and in a poor condition so that it looks as if it is falling down 破敗不堪的；搖搖欲墜的 **SYN** **dilapidated**

,tumble 'dryer (also **,tumble-'drier**) (both *BrE*) *noun* a machine that uses hot air to dry clothes after they have been washed 滾筒式（衣服）烘乾機 ➲ compare SPIN DRYER

tum·bler /'tʌmblə(r)/ *noun* **1** a glass for drinking out of, with a flat bottom, straight sides and no handle or STEM（無柄無腳、平底直壁的）玻璃杯 ➲ **VISUAL VOCAB** page V22 **2** (also **tum·bler·ful** /-fʊl/) the amount held by a tumbler 一平底玻璃杯（的量） **3** (*old-fashioned*) an ACROBAT who performs SOMERSAULTS (= a jump in which you turn over completely in the air) 翻筋斗雜技演員

tumble·weed /'tʌmblwi:d/ *noun* [U] a plant that grows like a bush in the desert areas of N America and Australia. In the autumn/fall, it breaks off just above the ground and is blown around like a ball by the wind. 風滾草（生長於北美和澳洲沙漠地區，秋季在地面處折落，隨風像球一樣到處滾動）

tum·bril /'tʌmbrəl/ *noun* an open vehicle used for taking people to their deaths at the GUILLOTINE during the French Revolution（法國大革命期間押送囚犯去斷頭台的）死囚車

tu·mes·cent /tju:'mesnt; *NAmE* tu:-/ *adj.* (*formal*) (especially of parts of the body 尤指身體部位) larger than normal, especially as a result of sexual excitement（尤指由於性衝動而）脹大的 **SYN** **swollen** ► **tu·mes·cence** /-sns/ *noun* [U]

tummy /'tʌmi/ *noun* (*pl.* **-ies**) (*informal*) (used especially by children or when speaking to children 尤為兒語或對兒童說話時用) the stomach or the area around the stomach 胃；肚子：*Mum, my tummy hurts.* 媽媽，我肚子痛。◇ *to have (a) tummy ache* 肚子痛 ◇ *a **tummy bug/upset*** (= an illness when you feel sick or VOMIT) 反胃

'tummy button *noun* (*BrE, informal*) = NAVEL

tu·mour (*especially US* **tu·mor**) /'tju:mə(r); *NAmE* 'tu:-/ *noun* a mass of cells growing in or on a part of the body where they should not, usually causing medical problems 瘤；腫瘤；腫塊：*a brain tumour* 腦瘤 ◇ *a **benign/malignant*** (= harmless/harmful) ***tumour*** 良性／惡性腫瘤

tu·mult /'tju:mʌlt; *NAmE* 'tu:-/ *noun* [U, C, usually sing.] (*formal*) **1** a confused situation in which there is usually a lot of noise and excitement, often involving large numbers of people 騷亂；騷動；混亂；喧譁 **2** a state in which your thoughts or feelings are confused 心煩意亂；思緒不寧

tu·mul·tu·ous /tju:'mʌltʃuəs; *NAmE* tu:-/ *adj.* [usually before noun] **1** very loud; involving strong feelings, especially feelings of approval 嘈雜的；喧囂的；熱烈的；歡騰的：*tumultuous applause* 熱烈的歡呼聲 ◇ *a **tumultuous reception/welcome*** 熱情的接待；熱烈的歡迎 **2** involving a lot of change and confusion and/or violence 動盪的；動亂的；狂暴的 **SYN** **tempestuous**：*the tumultuous years of the English Civil War* 英國內戰的動亂年代

tu·mu·lus /'tju:mjələs; *NAmE* 'tu:-/ *noun* (*pl.* **tu·muli** /-laɪ/) (*technical* 術語) a large pile of earth built over the grave of an important person in ancient times 塚；（古墓的）墳頭

tun /tʌn/ *noun* (*old-fashioned*) a large round wooden container for beer, wine, etc. 大酒桶；大啤酒桶 **SYN** **barrel**

tuna /'tju:nə; *NAmE* 'tu:nə/ *noun* [C, U] (*pl.* **tuna** or **tunas**) (also **'tuna fish**) (*BrE* also *less frequent* **tunny**) a large sea fish that is used for food 金槍魚：*fishing for tuna* 捕金槍魚 ◇ *tuna steaks* 金槍魚排 ◇ *a tin/can of tuna in vegetable oil* 一罐植物油浸金槍魚罐頭

tun·dra /'tʌndrə/ *noun* [U] the large flat Arctic regions of northern Europe, Asia and N America where no trees grow and where the soil below the surface of the ground is always frozen 凍原，苔原（樹木不生，底土常年冰凍的北極地區）

tune 0-w /tju:n; *NAmE* tu:n/ *noun, verb*

■ ***noun*** 0-w [C] a series of musical notes that are sung or played in a particular order to form a piece of music 曲調；曲子：*He was humming a familiar tune.* 他低聲哼着一支熟悉的小曲。◇ *I don't know the title but I recognize the tune.* 我不知道曲名，但聽得出這曲調。◇ *It was a catchy tune* (= song). 這是一首悅耳易記的曲子。◇ *a football song sung **to the tune of*** (= using the tune of) *'When the saints go marching in'* 用《聖者的行進》的曲調唱的足球歌 ➲ **COLLOCATIONS** at MUSIC ➲ see also SIGNATURE TUNE, THEME TUNE at THEME MUSIC

IDM **be ,in/,out of 'tune (with sb/sth)** to be/not be in agreement with sb/sth; to have/not have the same opinions, feelings, interests, etc. as sb/sth（與…）協調／不協調，一致／不一致，融洽／不融洽：*These proposals are perfectly in tune with our own thoughts on the subject.* 這些建議與我們在這個問題上的想法完全一致。◇ *The President is out of tune with public opinion.* 總統與公眾輿論大唱反調。 **,in/,out of 'tune** to be/not be singing or playing the correct musical notes to sound pleasant 音調正確／不正確；演奏合調／走調：*None of them could sing in tune.* 他們中沒有一個人能唱得合調。◇ *The piano is out of tune.* 鋼琴音走調了。 **to the tune of sth** (*informal*) used to emphasize how much money sth has cost（用於強調）總額達，總數為：*The hotel has been refurbished to the tune of a million dollars.* 這家旅館重新裝修花費達一百萬元。➲ more at CALL *v.*, CHANGE *v.*, DANCE *v.*, PAY *v.*, SING

■ ***verb*** **1 ~ sth** to adjust a musical instrument so that it plays at the correct PITCH（為樂器）調音，校音：*to tune a guitar* 給吉他調弦 **2 ~ sth** to adjust an engine so that it runs smoothly and as well as possible 調整，調節（發動機） **3** [usually passive] **~ sth (in) (to sth)** to adjust the controls on a radio or television so that you can receive a particular programme or channel（給收音機、電視等）調諧，調頻道：*The radio was tuned (in) to the BBC World Service.* 收音機調到了英國廣播公司國際廣播電台。◇ (*informal*) ***Stay tuned*** *for the news coming up next.* 別轉台，下面的新聞馬上就來。 **4 ~ sth (to sth)** to prepare or adjust sth so that it is suitable for a particular situation 調整；使協調；使適合：*His speech was tuned to what the audience wanted to hear.* 他在演講中專講聽眾愛聽的話。

PHR V **,tune 'in (to sth)** to listen to a radio programme or watch a television programme 收聽（收音機廣播節目）；收看（電視節目） **,tune 'in to sb/sth** to become aware of other people's thoughts and feelings, etc. 理解，體諒（他人的思想感情等） **,tune 'out | ,tune sb/sth↔'out** to stop listening to sth 不理睬；思想開小差：*When she started talking about her job, he just tuned out.* 在她開始談她工作的時候，他走神了。 **,tune 'up | ,tune sth↔'up** to adjust musical instruments so that they can play together（樂隊等為樂器）調音，定弦：*The orchestra was tuning up as we entered the hall.* 我們進入音樂廳時，管弦樂隊正在調音。

T

,tuned 'in *adj.* [not before noun] **~ (to sth)** aware of what is happening in a particular situation（對情況）瞭解，掌握： *The resort is tuned in to the tastes of young and old alike.* 這個度假勝地適合各種口味，老少皆宜。

tune·ful /'tjuːnfl; *NAmE* 'tuːnfl/ *adj.* having a pleasant tune or sound 音調優美的；聲音悅耳的 **OPP** **tuneless** ▸ **tune·ful·ly** /-fəli/ *adv.* **tune·ful·ness** *noun* [U]

tune·less /'tjuːnləs; *NAmE* 'tuːn-/ *adj.* not having a pleasant tune or sound 不好聽的；不成曲調的；沒腔沒調的 **OPP** **tuneful** ▸ **tune·less·ly** *adv.*

tuner /'tjuːnə(r); *NAmE* 'tuː-/ *noun* **1** (especially in compounds 尤用於構成複合詞) a person who tunes musical instruments, especially pianos（樂器的）調音者，調弦者；（尤指）鋼琴調音師 **2** the part of a radio, television, etc. that you move in order to change the signal and receive the radio or television station that you want（收音機、電視機等的）調諧鈕，調諧鍵 **3** an electronic device that receives a radio signal and sends it to an AMPLIFIER so that it can be heard（接收無線電信號傳輸到放大器的）調諧器

tune·smith /'tjuːnsmɪθ; *NAmE* 'tuːn-/ *noun* (*informal*) a person who writes popular music 流行音樂作曲家

tung·sten /'tʌŋstən/ *noun* [U] (*symb.* **W**) a chemical element. Tungsten is a very hard silver-grey metal, used especially in making steel and in FILAMENTS for LIGHT BULBS. 鎢

tunic /'tjuːnɪk; *NAmE* 'tuː-/ *noun* **1** a loose piece of clothing covering the body down to the knees, usually without sleeves, as worn in ancient Greece and Rome（古希臘、古羅馬時期長及膝的）短袍 **2** a piece of women's clothing like a tunic, that reaches to the hips and is worn over trousers/pants or a skirt（長及臀部，罩於褲或裙外的）女式寬上衣 **3** (*BrE*) a tightly fitting jacket worn as part of a uniform by police officers, soldiers, etc.（警察、士兵等的）緊身制服上衣

'tuning fork *noun* a small metal instrument with two long parts joined together at one end, that produces a particular musical note when you hit it and is used in TUNING musical instruments 音叉

'tuning peg *noun* = PEG *n.* (4) ➲ picture at PEG

tun·nel 🔑 /'tʌnl/ *noun, verb*

■ ***noun*** **1** 🔑 a passage built underground, for example to allow a road or railway/railroad to go through a hill, under a river, etc. 地下通道；地道；隧道： *a* ***railway/railroad tunnel*** 鐵路隧道 ◇ *the Channel Tunnel* 英吉利海峽隧道 ➲ see also WIND TUNNEL **2** an underground passage made by an animal（動物的）洞穴通道

IDM see LIGHT *n.*

T

■ ***verb*** (**-ll-**, *NAmE* also **-l-**) [I, T] to dig a tunnel under or through the ground 開鑿隧道；挖地道： **+ adv./prep.** *The engineers had to tunnel through solid rock.* 工程師須要在堅實的岩石中開鑿隧道。◇ **~ your way + adv./prep.** *The rescuers tunnelled their way in to the trapped miners.* 救援人員挖地道通向那些被困的礦工。

,tunnel 'vision *noun* [U] **1** (*medical* 醫) a condition in which sb cannot see things that are not straight ahead of them 視野狹窄（只能看正前方的人或物）**2** (*disapproving*) an inability to see or understand all the aspects of a situation, an argument, etc. instead of just one part of it 一孔之見；井蛙之見

tunny /'tʌni/ *noun* (*pl.* **tunny**) (*BrE*) = TUNA

tup·pence (also **two·pence**) /'tʌpəns/ *noun* [U] (*BrE, informal*) the sum of two pence 兩便士

IDM **not care/give 'tuppence for sb/sth** to think that sb/sth is not important or that they have no value 認為…無關緊要；認為…沒有價值

tup·penny /'tʌpəni/ *adj.* [only before noun] (*BrE, informal*) = TWOPENNY

Tup·per·ware™ /'tʌpəweə(r); *NAmE* 'tʌpərwer/ *noun* [U] plastic containers used mainly for storing food 特百惠塑料容器（主要用於貯存食物）

tur·ban /'tɜːbən; *NAmE* 'tɜːrbən/ *noun* **1** a long piece of cloth wound tightly around the head, worn, for example, by Muslim or Sikh men（穆斯林或錫克教男教徒等用的）包頭巾 **2** a woman's hat that looks like a turban（女用）頭巾帽 ▸ **tur·baned** /'tɜːbənd; *NAmE* 'tɜːrb-/ *adj.*： *turbaned Sikhs* 包着頭巾的錫克教徒

tur·bid /'tɜːbɪd; *NAmE* 'tɜːrbɪd/ *adj.* (*formal*) (of liquid 液體) full of mud, dirt, etc. so that you cannot see through it 渾濁的；污濁不清的 **SYN** **muddy** ▸ **tur·bid·ity** /tɜː'bɪdəti; *NAmE* tɜːr'b-/ *noun* [U]

tur·bine /'tɜːbaɪn; *NAmE* 'tɜːrb-/ *noun* a machine or an engine that receives its power from a wheel that is turned by the pressure of water, air or gas 渦輪機；汽輪機 ➲ see also WIND TURBINE

turbo·char·ger /'tɜːbəʊtʃɑːdʒə(r); *NAmE* 'tɜːrboʊtʃɑːrdʒər/ (also **turbo** *pl.* **-os**) *noun* a system driven by a turbine that gets its power from an engine's EXHAUST gases. It sends the mixture of petrol/gas and air into the engine at high pressure, making it more powerful. 渦輪增壓器；透平增壓器 ▸ **turbo·charge** *verb*： **~ sth** *turbocharged engines* 渦輪增壓發動機

turbo·jet /'tɜːbəʊdʒet; *NAmE* 'tɜːrboʊ-/ *noun* **1** a TURBINE engine that produces forward movement by forcing out a stream of hot air and gas behind it 渦輪噴氣發動機 **2** a plane that gets its power from this type of engine 渦輪噴氣飛機

turbo·prop /'tɜːbəʊprɒp; *NAmE* 'tɜːrboʊprɑːp/ *noun* **1** a TURBINE engine that produces forward movement by turning a PROPELLER (= a set of spinning blades) 渦輪螺旋槳發動機 **2** a plane that gets its power from this type of engine 渦輪螺旋槳飛機

tur·bot /'tɜːbət; *NAmE* 'tɜːrbət/ *noun* [C, U] (*pl.* **tur·bot** or **tur·bots**) a large flat European sea fish that is used for food 大菱鮃（產於歐洲的一種可食用比目魚）

tur·bu·lence /'tɜːbjələns; *NAmE* 'tɜːrb-/ *noun* [U] **1** a situation in which there is a lot of sudden change, confusion, disagreement and sometimes violence 騷亂；動亂；動盪；混亂 **SYN** **upheaval** **2** a series of sudden and violent changes in the direction that air or water is moving in（空氣和水的）湍流，渦流，紊流： *We experienced severe turbulence during the flight.* 我們在飛行中遇到了強烈的氣流。➲ COLLOCATIONS at TRAVEL

tur·bu·lent /'tɜːbjələnt; *NAmE* 'tɜːrb-/ *adj.* [usually before noun] **1** in which there is a lot of sudden change, confusion, disagreement and sometimes violence 動盪的；動亂的；騷動的；混亂的： *a short and turbulent career in politics* 短暫動盪的政治生涯 ◇ *a turbulent part of the world* 世界上動盪不安的地區 **2** (of air or water 空氣或水) changing direction suddenly and violently 洶湧的；猛烈的；湍動的： *The aircraft is designed to withstand turbulent conditions.* 這架飛機是為經受猛烈的氣流而設計的。◇ ***a turbulent sea/storm*** (= caused by turbulent water/air) 波濤洶湧的大海；狂風暴雨 **3** (of people 人) noisy and/or difficult to control 騷動的；混亂而難以控制的 **SYN** **unruly**： *a turbulent crowd* 騷動的人群

turd /tɜːd; *NAmE* tɜːrd/ *noun* (*taboo, slang*) **1** a lump of solid waste from the BOWELS 糞塊；糞球；糞團： *dog turds* 狗屎堆 **2** an offensive word for an unpleasant person 臭狗屎（對不喜歡的人的冒犯語）

tur·een /tju'riːn; tə'riːn/ *noun* a large deep dish with a lid, used for serving vegetables or soup（盛菜或湯的）有蓋海碗；湯碗

turf /tɜːf; *NAmE* tɜːrf/ *noun, verb*

■ ***noun*** (*pl.* **turfs** or **turves** /tɜːvz; *NAmE* tɜːrvz/) **1** [U, C] short grass and the surface layer of soil that is held together by its roots; a piece of this that has been cut from the ground and is used especially for making LAWNS (= the area of grass in a garden/yard) 草皮；（鋪草坪用的）草皮塊： *newly laid turf* 新鋪的草皮 ◇ *(especially BrE) the hallowed turf of Wimbledon, etc.* (= the grass used for playing a sport on) 溫布爾登等給視為神聖的運動場草皮 **2** [U, C] PEAT that is cut to be used as fuel; a piece of this 泥煤；泥炭；泥煤塊；泥炭塊 **3** **the turf** [sing.] the sport of horse racing 賽馬 **4** [U] **sb's ~** (*informal, especially NAmE*) the place where sb lives and/or works, especially when they think of it as their own（自己的）地盤，勢力範圍： *He feels more confident on* ***home turf***. 他在主場感到更有信心。

■ *verb* **~ sth** to cover an area of ground with turf 用草皮覆蓋

PHR V ˌ**turf sb ˈout (of sth)** | ˌ**turf sb ˈoff (sth)** (*BrE, informal*) to make sb leave a place, an organization, etc. 趕出，驅逐出（地方、組織等） SYN **throw out**：*He was turfed out of the party.* 他已被驅逐出黨。◇ *The boys were turfed off the bus.* 男孩們被趕下了公共汽車。

ˈ**turf accountant** *noun* (*BrE, formal*) = BOOKMAKER

ˈ**turf war** *noun* a violent disagreement between two groups of people about who should control a particular area, activity or business （地盤、勢力範圍等的）爭奪戰；地盤之爭：*a vicious turf war between rival gangs of drug dealers* 對立販毒團夥之間的猛烈火拚

tur·gid /ˈtɜːdʒɪd; *NAmE* ˈtɜːrdʒɪd/ *adj.* (*formal*) **1** (of language, writing, etc. 語言、文章等) boring, complicated and difficult to understand 枯燥無味的；晦澀難懂的 **2** swollen; containing more water than usual 腫脹的；膨脹的；腫大的：*the turgid waters of the Thames* 上漲的泰晤士河水

tur·ista /tuˈrɪstə/ *noun* [U] (*NAmE, informal*) DIARRHOEA that is suffered by sb who is visiting a foreign country （外地）旅行者腹瀉；水土不服造成的腹瀉

tur·key /ˈtɜːki; *NAmE* ˈtɜːrki/ *noun* (*pl.* **-eys**) **1** [C] a large bird that is often kept for its meat, eaten especially at Christmas in Britain and at Thanksgiving in the US 吐綬雞；火雞 ➲ **VISUAL VOCAB** page V12 **2** [U] meat from a turkey 火雞肉：*roast turkey* 烤火雞肉 **3** [C] (*NAmE, informal*) a failure 失敗：*His latest movie is a real turkey.* 他最近的那部電影是一大敗筆。 **4** [C] (*NAmE, informal*) a stupid or useless person 笨蛋；草包 ➲ see also COLD TURKEY IDM see TALK *v.*

ˈ**turkey shoot** *noun* (*informal, especially NAmE*) a battle or contest in which one side is much stronger than the other and able to win very easily 一邊倒的戰爭（或比賽）

Turk·ish /ˈtɜːkɪʃ; *NAmE* ˈtɜːrkɪʃ/ *adj., noun*

■ *adj.* from or connected with Turkey 土耳其的

■ *noun* [U] the language of Turkey 土耳其語

ˌ**Turkish ˈbath** *noun* a type of bath in which you sit in a room full of hot steam, have a MASSAGE and then a cold shower or bath; a building where this treatment takes place 土耳其浴；蒸汽浴；蒸汽浴室

ˌ**Turkish ˈcoffee** *noun* [U, C] very strong, usually very sweet, black coffee 土耳其咖啡（通常很甜，不加牛奶）

ˌ**Turkish deˈlight** *noun* [U, C] a sweet/candy made from a substance like jelly that is flavoured with fruit and covered with fine white sugar 土耳其軟糖，拌砂軟糖（一種外粘白糖面的膠質糖果）

tur·meric /ˈtɜːmərɪk; *NAmE* ˈtɜːrm-/ *noun* [U] a yellow powder made from the root of an Asian plant, used in cooking as a spice, especially in CURRY 薑黃根粉（用作烹飪調料，尤用於做咖喱） ➲ **VISUAL VOCAB** page V32

tur·moil /ˈtɜːmɔɪl; *NAmE* ˈtɜːrm-/ *noun* [U, sing.] a state of great anxiety and confusion 動亂；騷動；混亂；焦慮 SYN **confusion**：***emotional/mental/political turmoil*** 紛亂的情緒；精神上的混亂；政治動亂 ◇ *His statement threw the court* ***into turmoil***. 他的陳述使得法庭陷入一片混亂。◇ *Her mind was* ***in (a) turmoil***. 她心亂如麻。

turn 0-π /tɜːn; *NAmE* tɜːrn/ *verb, noun*

■ *verb*

▸ **MOVE ROUND** 轉動 **1** 0-π [I, T] to move or make sth move around a central point （使）轉動，旋轉：*The wheels of the car began to turn.* 汽車的輪子開始轉動起來。◇ *I can't get the screw to turn.* 我擰不動這個螺絲釘。◇ **~ sth (+ adv./prep.)** *He turned the key in the lock.* 他轉動鑰匙開鎖。◇ *She turned the wheel sharply to the left.* 她猛地向左打方向盤。

▸ **CHANGE POSITION/DIRECTION** 改變位置 / 方向 **2** 0-π [I, T] to move your body or part of your body so as to face or start moving in a different direction 轉身；扭轉（身體部位）：*We turned and headed for home.* 我們轉身朝家走去。◇ *She turned to look at me.* 她轉過頭來看着我。◇ **+ adv./prep.** *He turned back to his work.* 他回去繼續工作。◇ *I turned away and looked out of the window.* 我扭過臉去望着窗外。◇ **~ sth (+ adv./prep.)** *He turned his back to the wall.* 他轉身背對着牆。◇ *She turned her head away.* 她把頭扭向別處。 ➲ see also TURN OVER **3** 0-π [T] **~ sth + adv./prep.** to move sth so that it is in a different position or facing a different direction 翻轉；翻動；把…翻過來：*She turned the chair on its side to repair it.* 她把椅子翻轉過來修理。◇ *Turn the sweater inside out before you wash it.* 你把針織套衫裏面翻過來再洗。 ➲ see also TURN OVER **4** 0-π [I, T] to change the direction you are moving or travelling in; to make sth change the direction it is moving in（使）改變方向；轉彎：**~ (into sth)** *He turned into a narrow street.* 他拐進了一條狹窄的街道。◇ **~ sth** *The man* ***turned the corner*** *and disappeared.* 那男人轉過街角就沒影了。◇ **~ sth into sth** *I turned the car into the car park.* 我轉彎把汽車開進了停車場。 **5** 0-π [I] (+ **adv./prep.**) (of a road or river 道路或河流) to curve in a particular direction 轉向；轉彎：*The road turns to the left after the church.* 這條路過了教堂之後向左轉彎。

▸ **AIM/POINT** 瞄準；指向 **6** [T, I] to aim or point sth in a particular direction 朝着；向…方向；對準：**~ sth (on/to sb/sth/yourself)** *Police turned water cannon on the rioters.* 警察把高壓水槍對準了鬧事者。◇ *He turned the gun on himself.* 他把槍口對準了自己。◇ *She looked at him then turned her attention back to me.* 她看了看他，然後又把注意力轉回到我的身上。◇ **~ to sb/sth/yourself** *His thoughts turned to his dead wife.* 他想起了自己已故的妻子。

▸ **OF TIDE IN SEA** 海潮 **7** [I] to start to come in or go out 開始漲（或落）：*The tide is turning—we'd better get back.* 漲潮了，我們最好回去吧。

▸ **LET SB/STH GO** 鬆開 **8** [T] to make or let sb/sth go into a particular place or state（使）鬆開，釋放：**~ sth + adv./prep.** *They turned the horse into the field.* 他們把馬鬆開放到牧場裏。◇ **~ sth + adj.** *to turn the dogs loose* 把狗隻放開

▸ **FOLD** 摺疊 **9** [T] **~ sth + adv./prep.** to fold sth in a particular way 摺起；翻轉：*She turned down the blankets and climbed into bed.* 她掀開毯子爬上牀去。◇ *He turned up the collar of his coat and hurried out into the rain.* 他豎起大衣領子，冒雨匆匆走了。

▸ **CARTWHEEL/SOMERSAULT** 側手翻；筋斗 **10** [T, no passive] **~ sth** to perform a movement by moving your body in a circle 表演（身體旋轉動作）：*to turn cartwheels/somersaults* 做側手翻；翻筋斗

▸ **PAGE** 書頁 **11** 0-π [T, I] if you **turn** a page of a book or magazine, you move it so that you can read the next page 翻，翻動（書頁）：**~ sth** *He sat turning the pages idly.* 他坐在那裏無所事事地翻着書。◇ **~ to sth** *Turn to p.23.* 翻到第 23 頁。

▸ **GAME** 比賽 **12** [I, T] **~ (sth) (around)** if a game **turns** or sb **turns** it, it changes the way it is developing so that a different person or team starts to win（使）逆轉

▸ **BECOME** 變成 **13** 0-π *linking verb* to change into a particular state or condition; to make sth do this（使）變成，成為：**+ adj.** *The leaves were turning brown.* 葉子變了褐色。◇ *The weather has turned cold.* 天氣變得寒冷了。◇ *He turned nasty when we refused to give him the money.* 我們不給他錢時，他變得窮兇極惡。◇ *He decided to* ***turn professional***. 他決定轉為職業人員。◇ **~ sth + adj.** *The heat turned the milk sour.* 炎熱的天氣使得牛奶變酸了。◇ **+ noun** *She turned a deathly shade of white when she heard the news.* 她聽到這個消息時面如死灰。◇ *He's a lawyer turned politician* (= he used to be a lawyer but is now a politician). 他以前是個律師，現在成為政治家了。 ➲ **SYNONYMS** at BECOME

▸ **AGE/TIME** 年齡；時間 **14** *linking verb* (not used in the progressive tenses 不用於進行時) **+ noun** to reach or pass a particular age or time 到達，超過（某一年齡或時間）：*She turns 21 in June.* 她到六月份就滿 21 歲了。◇ *It's turned midnight.* 已過了午夜。

▸ **STOMACH** 胃 **15** [I, T] **~ (your stomach)** when your stomach **turns** or sth **turns** your stomach, you feel as though you will VOMIT 作嘔；惡心；使（胃）不適

▸ **WOOD** 木材 **16** [T] **~ sth** to shape sth on a LATHE （在車牀上）車削：*to turn a chair leg* 在車牀上車椅子腿 ◇ *turned boxes and bowls* 車削成的盒和碗

IDM Most idioms containing **turn** are at the entries for the nouns and adjectives in the idioms, for example **not turn a hair** is at **hair**. 大多數含 turn 的習語，都可

在該等習語中的名詞及形容詞相關詞條找到，如 not turn a hair 在詞條 hair 下。 **as it/things turned ˈout** as was shown or proved by later events 正如後來表明的；果然如此；果不其然： *I didn't need my umbrella, as it turned out* (= because it didn't rain). 我果然沒用上我的傘。 **be well, badly, etc. turned ˈout** to be well, badly, etc. dressed 穿着打扮得好（或不好等） **turn round/around and do sth** (*informal*) used to report what sb says or does, when this is surprising or annoying（用以報告令人吃驚或不快的言行）竟會： *How could she turn round and say that, after all I've done for her?* 我為她做了這麼多，她怎麼竟會說出那種話來？

PHR V **ˌturn aˈgainst sb | ˌturn sb aˈgainst sb** to stop or make sb stop being friendly towards sb（使）與…反目成仇，變得敵對： *She turned against her old friend.* 她與老朋友翻臉了。◇ *After the divorce he tried to turn the children against their mother.* 他離婚後企圖教唆子女反對他們的母親。

ˌturn aˈround/ˈround | ˌturn sb/sth aˈround/ˈround 🔑 to change position or direction so as to face the other way; to make sb/sth do this（使）翻身，轉身，翻轉： *Turn around and let me look at your back.* 轉過身去讓我看看你的後背。◇ *I turned my chair round to face the fire.* 我把椅子轉過來面向火爐。 **ˌturn aˈround/ˈround | ˌturn sth↔aˈround/ˈround** if a business, economy, etc. **turns around** or sb **turns it around**, it starts being successful after it has been unsuccessful for a time（使企業、經濟等）好轉，扭轉，有起色 ➲ related noun TURNAROUND

ˌturn sb↔aˈway (from sth) to refuse to allow sb to enter a place 把某人拒之門外；不准某人進入： *Hundreds of people were turned away from the stadium* (= because it was full). 體育場滿座，數百人被拒之門外。◇ *They had nowhere to stay so I couldn't turn them away.* 他們無處安身，所以我不能把他們打發走。

ˌturn ˈback | ˌturn sb/sth↔ˈback 🔑 to return the way you have come; to make sb/sth do this（使）原路返回，往回走： *The weather became so bad that they had to turn back.* 天氣變得非常惡劣，他們不得不循原路折回。◇ (*figurative*) *We said we would do it—there can be no turning back.* 我們說過要幹這事，不能反悔。◇ *Our car was turned back at the border.* 我們的汽車在邊境被擋了回來。 ➲ SYNONYMS at RETURN

ˌturn sb/sth↔ˈdown 🔑 to reject or refuse to consider an offer, a proposal, etc. or the person who makes it 拒絕，頂回（提議、建議或提議人）： *Why did she turn down your invitation?* 她為什麼謝絕你的邀請？◇ *He has been turned down for ten jobs so far.* 他迄今申請了十份工作都遭到拒絕。◇ *He asked her to marry him but she turned him down.* 他請求她嫁給他，但是她回絕了。

ˌturn sth↔ˈdown 🔑 to reduce the noise, heat, etc. produced by a piece of equipment by moving its controls 把…調低；關小： *Please turn the volume down.* 請把音量調低些。◇ **+ adj.** *He turned the lights down low.* 他把燈光調得暗了一些。

ˌturn ˈin **1** to face or curve towards the centre 朝內；向內拐： *Her feet turn in.* 她的兩腳呈內八字。 **2** (*old-fashioned*) to go to bed 上牀睡覺 **ˌturn sb↔ˈin** (*informal*) to take sb to the police or sb in authority because they have committed a crime 把…扭送（到警察局）；使自首： *She threatened to turn him in to the police.* 她揚言要把他交給警方。◇ *He decided to turn himself in.* 他決定到警察局去自首。 **ˌturn sth↔ˈin** **1** to give back sth that you no longer need 交還，退還（不再需要的東西）： *You must turn in your pass when you leave the building.* 你離開大樓時必須交還通行證。 **2** (*especially NAmE*) to give sth to sb in authority 上交；呈交；提交： *They turned in a petition with 80 000 signatures.* 他們遞交了一份有 8 萬人簽名的請願書。◇ *I haven't even turned in Monday's work yet.* 我連星期一的作業還沒交呢。 **3** to achieve a score, performance, profit, etc. 取得（分數）；完成（表演）；獲得（利潤）： *The champion turned in a superb performance to retain her title.* 上屆冠軍表現十分出色，衛冕成功。 **ˌturn ˈin on yourself** to become too concerned with your own problems and stop communicating with others 忙於自己的事情而不與人交往；閉門謝客

ˌturn (from sth) ˈinto sth 🔑 to become sth 變成某事物： *Our dream holiday turned into a nightmare.* 我們夢想的假日變成了一場噩夢。◇ *In one year she turned from a problem child into a model student.* 一年內，她從問題兒童變成了模範學生。 **ˌturn sb/sth (from sth) ˈinto sth** 🔑 to make sb/sth become sth 使（從…）變成： *Ten years of prison had turned him into an old man.* 十年大獄使他變成了一個老頭。◇ *The prince was turned into a frog by the witch.* 王子被女巫變成了一隻青蛙。

ˌturn ˈoff | ˌturn ˈoff sth [no passive] to leave a road in order to travel on another 拐彎；轉入另一條路： *Is this where we turn off?* 這兒是我們換道的地方嗎？◇ *The jet began to turn off the main runway.* 那架噴氣式飛機開始拐出主跑道。 **ˌturn ˈoff** (*informal*) to stop listening to or thinking about sb/sth 不再聽；不再想： *I couldn't understand the lecture so I just turned off.* 我聽不懂講課，所以也就不聽了。 **ˌturn sb↔ˈoff** **1** to make sb feel bored or not interested 使厭煩；使失去興趣： *People had been turned off by both candidates in the election.* 大選中的兩位候選人都讓人覺得掃興。 **2** to stop sb feeling sexually attracted; to make sb have a feeling of disgust 使（異性）失去興趣；使厭惡 ➲ related noun TURN-OFF **ˌturn sth↔ˈoff** 🔑 to stop the flow of electricity, gas, water, etc. by moving a switch, button, etc. 關掉，截斷（電流、煤氣、水等）： *to turn off the light* 關上燈◇ *Please turn the television off before you go to bed.* 睡覺前請關上電視。

ˈturn on sb to attack sb suddenly and unexpectedly 突然攻擊： *The dogs suddenly turned on each other.* 那兩條狗突然互相撕咬了起來。◇ *Why are you all turning on me* (= criticizing or blaming me)? 你們怎麼突然都衝我來了？ **ˈturn on sth** [no passive] **1** (*BrE*) to depend on sth 依靠；依…而定；取決於： *Much turns on the outcome of the current peace talks.* 事情主要取決於當前和談的結果。 **2** [no passive] to have sth as it main topic 以…為主題： *The discussion turned on the need to raise standards.* 這次討論的主要議題是提高標準的必要性。 **ˌturn sb↔ˈon** (*informal*) to make sb excited or interested, especially sexually 使性興奮；使感興趣： *Jazz has never really turned me on.* 我對爵士樂從未真正產生過興趣。◇ *She gets turned on by men in uniform.* 她看到穿制服的男人就慾火攻心。 ➲ related noun TURN-ON **ˌturn sb ˈon (to sth)** (*informal*) to make sb become interested in sth or to use sth for the first time 使對…感興趣；使首次使用： *He turned her on to jazz.* 他使她對爵士樂產生了興趣。 **ˌturn sth↔ˈon** 🔑 to start the flow of electricity, gas, water, etc. by moving a switch, button, etc. 接通（電流、煤氣、水等）；打開： *to turn on the heating* 打開供熱系統◇ *I'll turn the television on.* 我來打開電視機。◇ (*figurative*) *He really knows how to* ***turn on the charm*** (= suddenly become pleasant and attractive). 他確實懂得如何一展魅力。

ˌturn ˈout **1** to be present at an event 出席（某項活動）；在場： *A vast crowd turned out to watch the procession.* 有一大群人出來觀看遊行隊伍。 ➲ related noun TURNOUT **2** (used with an adverb or adjective, or in questions with *how* 與副詞或形容詞連用，或用於以 how 引導的疑問句) to happen in a particular way; to develop or end in a particular way …地發展（或發生）；結果…： *Despite our worries everything turned out well.* 儘管我們都很擔心，結果一切都順利。◇ *You never know how your children will turn out.* 很難說子女將來的發展怎樣。◇ **+ adj.** *If the day turns out wet, we may have to change our plans.* 如果那天下雨的話，我們可能得改變計劃。 **3** to point away from the centre 向外；朝外： *Her toes turn out.* 她的腳趾向外撇。 **4** 🔑 to be discovered to be; to prove to be 原來是；證明是；結果是： **~ that …** *It turned out that she was a friend of my sister.* 她原來是我姐姐的朋友。◇ **~ to be/have sth** *The job turned out to be harder than we thought.* 這工作結果比我們想像的要難。◇ *The house they had offered us turned out to be a tiny apartment.* 他們向我們提供的房子原來是很小的公寓套間。 **ˌturn sb/sth↔ˈout** to produce sb/sth 製造；生產；培養出： *The factory turns out 900 cars a week.* 這家工廠每週生產 900 輛汽車。 **ˌturn sb ˈout (of/from sth)** to force sb to leave a place 趕走；逐出；攆走 **ˌturn sth↔ˈout** **1** to switch a light or a source of heat off 關掉（燈或熱源）；熄滅： *Remember to turn out the lights when you* *go to bed.* 臨睡前別忘了關燈。 **2** (*BrE*) to clean sth thoroughly by removing the contents and organizing them again 騰空；徹底清理： *to turn out the attic* 把閣樓騰空清掃 **3** to empty sth, especially your pockets 弄空，掏淨（尤指口袋） **4** to make sth point away from the centre 使向外；使朝外： *She turned her toes out.* 她把腳趾向外撇。

ˌturn ˈover 1 🔑 to change position so that the other side is facing towards the outside or the top 翻身；翻轉： *If you turn over you might find it easier to get to sleep.* 你若翻個身也許入睡容易些。◇ *The car skidded and turned over.* 汽車打滑向一側翻倒了。◇ (*figurative*) *The smell made my stomach turn over* (= made me feel sick). 這氣味讓我反胃。 **2** (of an engine 發動機) to start or to continue to run 發動；轉動；繼續運轉 **3** to change to another channel when you are watching television 變換（電視頻道） **ˌturn ˈover sth** to do business worth a particular amount of money in a particular period of time 營業額為…；做金額為…的生意： *The company turns over £3.5 million a year.* 這家公司一年的營業額為 350 萬英鎊。 ➲ related noun TURNOVER **ˌturn sth↔ˈover 1** 🔑 to make sth change position so that the other side is facing towards the outside or the top 使翻個兒；使翻轉： *Brown the meat on one side, then turn it over and brown the other side.* 把肉的一面烤黃，然後翻轉過來，再烤另一面。 **2** to think about sth carefully 認真思考；深思熟慮： *She kept turning over the events of the day in her mind.* 她腦子裏不斷琢磨當天發生的事。 **3** (of a shop/store 商店) to sell goods and replace them 週轉；銷貨和進貨： *A supermarket will turn over its stock very rapidly.* 超級市場的貨物週轉得很快。 ➲ related noun TURNOVER **4** (*informal*) to steal from a place 從…偷竊： *Burglars had turned the house over.* 盜賊把這所房子盜竊一空。 **5** to make an engine start running 發動（引擎） **ˌturn sb↔ˈover to sb** to deliver sb to the control or care of sb else, especially sb in authority 移交，送交（他人看管，尤指當局）： *Customs officials turned the man over to the police.* 海關官員把那個男子移交給警方看管。 **ˌturn sth↔ˈover to sb** to give the control of sth to sb 把…移交給（他人管理）： *He turned the business over to his daughter.* 他把這個企業交給了女兒管理。 **ˌturn sth↔ˈover to sth** to change the use or function of sth 改變，轉變（用途或功能）： *The factory was turned over to the manufacture of aircraft parts.* 這家工廠轉產飛機部件。

ˈturn to sb/sth 🔑 to go to sb/sth for help, advice, etc. 向…求助（或尋求指教等）： *She has nobody she can turn to.* 她求助無門。

ˌturn ˈup 1 🔑 to be found, especially by chance, after being lost（尤指失去後偶然）被發現，被找到： *Don't worry about the letter—I'm sure it'll turn up.* 別為那封信擔心，我相信會找到的。 **2** 🔑 (of a person 人) to arrive 到達；來到；露面： *We arranged to meet at 7.30, but she never turned up.* 我們約好 7:30 碰頭，但她根本沒露面。 **3** (of an opportunity 機會) to happen, especially by chance 偶然出現；到來： *He's still hoping something* (= for example, a job or a piece of luck) *will turn up.* 他仍然在希望會有機會出現。 ➲ related noun TURN-UP **ˌturn sth↔ˈup 1** 🔑 to increase the sound, heat, etc. of a piece of equipment 開大，調高（音量、熱量等）： *Could you turn the TV up?* 你能把電視機的音量開大些嗎？◇ **+ adj.** *The music was turned up loud.* 音樂的音量開大了。 **2** (*BrE*) to make a piece of clothing shorter by folding and sewing it up at the bottom 將（衣服的底邊）摺起縫好；改短 OPP **let down** ➲ related noun TURN-UP **3** to find sth 找到；發現： *Our efforts to trace him turned up nothing.* 我們辛辛苦苦跟踪他，卻無功而返。

■ ***noun*** [C]

▸ **MOVEMENT 活動 1** 🔑 an act of turning sb/sth around 轉動；旋動： *Give the handle a few turns.* 轉動幾下把手。

▸ **OF ROAD/VEHICLE 道路；車輛 2** 🔑 a change in direction in a vehicle（車輛的）轉彎，轉向： ***Make a left/right turn*** *into West Street.* 向左／右拐入西大街。 ➲ see also THREE-POINT TURN, U-TURN **3** (*especially NAmE*) (*BrE* also **turn·ing**) a place where a road leads away from the one you are travelling on 岔路口；拐彎處；轉彎處 **4** a bend or corner in a road（道路的）彎道，轉彎處： *a lane full of* ***twists and turns*** 彎彎曲曲的小巷

▸ **TIME 時間 5** 🔑 the time when sb in a group of people should or is allowed to do sth（依次輪到的）機會： *When it's your turn, take another card.* 輪到你時，再抓一張牌。◇ *Please* ***wait your turn.*** 請等着輪到你。◇ ***Whose turn is it*** *to cook?* 輪到誰做飯了？◇ *Steve* ***took a turn*** *driving while I slept.* 我睡覺時，史蒂夫接着開車。

▸ **CHANGE 變化 6** an unusual or unexpected change in what is happening（異乎尋常或意外的）變化，轉變： *a surprising* ***turn of events*** 意想不到的事態變化 ◇ *His health has* ***taken a turn for the*** *worse* (= suddenly got worse). 他的健康狀況突然惡化。◇ *Events took a dramatic turn in the weeks that followed.* 在以後的幾週裏，事態急轉直下。◇ *The book is,* ***by turns,*** *funny and very sad.* 這部書時而妙趣橫生，時而悲悲戚戚。 ➲ see also ABOUT-TURN

▸ **PERFORMANCE 表演 7** a short performance or piece of entertainment such as a song, etc. 短小節目： *Everyone got up on stage to do a turn.* 每個人都登台表演了一個小節目。 ➲ see also STAR TURN

▸ **WALK 步行 8** (*old-fashioned*) a short walk 散步；轉一圈： *We took a turn around the park.* 我們在公園裏轉了一圈。

▸ **ILLNESS 疾病 9** (*old-fashioned*) a feeling of illness（疾病的）一陣發作；不適感： *a funny turn* (= a feeling that you may faint) 感到一陣暈眩

IDM **at every ˈturn** everywhere or every time you try and do sth 處處；事事；每次： *At every turn I met with disappointment.* 我事事都不順心。 **(do sb) a good ˈturn** (to do) sth that helps sb（為某人做）好事，善事；（做）有助於某人的事： *Well, that's my good turn for the day.* 好啦，這就是我今天做的好事。 **done to a ˈturn** (*BrE*) cooked for exactly the right amount of time 烹調得恰到火候 **give sb a ˈturn** (*old-fashioned*) to frighten or shock sb 使大吃一驚；嚇某人一跳 **in ˈturn 1** 🔑 one after the other in a particular order 依次；輪流；逐個： *The children called out their names in turn.* 孩子們逐一自報姓名。 **2** as a result of sth in a series of events 相應地；轉而： *Increased production will, in turn, lead to increased profits.* 增加生產會繼而增加利潤。 **ˌone good ˌturn deserves aˈnother** (*saying*) you should help sb who has helped you 善須善報；要以德報德；好人應得好報 **on the ˈturn** (*especially BrE*) going to change soon 即將變化： *His luck is on the turn.* 他就要時來運轉了。 **speak/talk ˌout of ˈturn** to say sth that you should not because it is the wrong situation or because it offends sb 說話出格（或冒失、魯莽、不合時宜） **take ˈturns (in sth/to do sth)** 🔑 (*BrE* also **take it in ˈturns**) if people **take turns** or **take it in turns** to do sth, they do it one after the other to make sure it is done fairly 依次；輪流： *The male and female birds take turns in sitting on the eggs.* 雄鳥和雌鳥輪流伏窩。◇ *We take it in turns to do the housework.* 我們輪流做家務。 **the ˌturn of the ˈcentury/ˈyear** the time when a new century/year starts 世紀之交；新年伊始；辭舊迎新之際： *It was built at the turn of the century.* 這是在世紀之交修建的。 **a ˌturn of ˈmind** a particular way of thinking about things 思維方式；思想方法 **a ˌturn of ˈphrase** a particular way of describing sth 措辭；表達方式；描述方式 **a ˌturn of the ˈscrew** an extra amount of pressure, CRUELTY, etc. added to a situation that is already difficult to bear or understand 雪上加霜 **a ˌturn of ˈspeed** a sudden increase in your speed or rate of progress; the ability to suddenly increase your speed 突然加速；加快進度；突然加快的能力： *He put on an impressive turn of speed in the last lap.* 他在最後一圈猛然加速。 ➲ more at HAND *n.*, SERVE *v.*

turn·about /ˈtɜːnəbaʊt; *NAmE* ˈtɜːrn-/ *noun* [sing.] **~ (in sth)** a sudden and complete change in sb/sth 突變；一百八十度的大轉彎；變卦 SYN **reversal**

turn·around /ˈtɜːnəraʊnd; *NAmE* ˈtɜːrn-/ (*BrE* also **turn·round**) *noun* [usually sing.] **1** the amount of time it takes to unload a ship or plane at the end of one journey and load it again for the next one（輪船、飛機的）終點裝卸時間 **2** the amount of time it takes to do a piece of work that you have been given and return it（接活到交活之間的）週轉期，時限 **3** a situation in which sth

T

changes from bad to good 好轉；起色；轉機：*a turnaround in the economy* 經濟好轉 **4** a complete change in sb's opinion, behaviour, etc.（觀點、行為等的）徹底轉變

turn·coat /ˈtɜːnkəʊt; *NAmE* ˈtɜːrnkoʊt/ *noun* (*disapproving*) a person who leaves one political party, religious group, etc. to join one that has very different views 叛徒；變節者；叛逆

turn·ing /ˈtɜːnɪŋ; *NAmE* ˈtɜːrnɪŋ/ (*BrE*) (also **turn** *NAmE, BrE*) *noun* a place where a road leads away from the one you are travelling on 岔路口；拐彎處；轉彎處：*Take the first turning on the right.* 在第一個路口向右拐。◇ *I think we must have taken a wrong turning somewhere.* 我覺得我們一定是在什麼地方拐錯了路。

ˈturning circle *noun* the smallest circle that a vehicle can turn around in（車輛掉頭用的）最小轉向圓，最小回轉圓

ˈturning point *noun* **~ (in sth)** the time when an important change takes place, usually with the result that a situation improves 轉折點；轉機；轉捩點：*The promotion **marked a turning point in** her career.* 這次提升標誌着她事業上的轉折點。

tur·nip /ˈtɜːnɪp; *NAmE* ˈtɜːrnɪp/ *noun* [C, U] **1** a round white, or white and purple, root vegetable 蔓菁；蕪菁 ➲ VISUAL VOCAB page V31 **2** (*ScotE*) = SWEDE ➲ VISUAL VOCAB page V31

turn·key /ˈtɜːnkiː; *NAmE* ˈtɜːrn-/ *adj.* (especially of computer systems 尤指計算機系統) complete and ready to use immediately 交鑰匙的；完整並可立即使用的

ˈturn-off *noun* **1** a place where a road leads away from another larger or more important road 岔道；支路：*We missed the turn-off for the airport.* 我們錯過了通往機場的岔道。 **2** [usually sing.] (*informal*) a person or thing that people do not find interesting, attractive or sexually exciting 掃興的人（或事）；厭煩的人（或事）；引不起性慾的人（或物）：*The city's crime rate is a serious turn-off to potential investors.* 這個城市的犯罪率使得潛在的投資者望而卻步。◇ *I find beards a real turn-off.* 我覺得鬍子確實令人厭惡。

ˈturn-on *noun* [usually sing.] (*informal*) a person or thing that people find sexually exciting 引起性慾的人（或物）

turn·out /ˈtɜːnaʊt; *NAmE* ˈtɜːrn-/ *noun* [C, usually sing., U] **1** the number of people who attend a particular event 出席人數；到場人數：*This year's festival attracted a record turnout.* 今年的節日吸引的參加者之多創了紀錄。 **2** the number of people who vote in a particular election 投票人數：*a **high/low/poor turnout*** 參加投票的人數很多／很少／寥寥無幾 ◇ *a 60% turnout of voters* * 60% 的投票率

turn·over /ˈtɜːnəʊvə(r); *NAmE* ˈtɜːrnoʊ-/ *noun* **1** [C, usually sing., U] **~ (of sth)** the total amount of goods or services sold by a company during a particular period of time（一定時期內的）營業額，成交量：*an annual turnover of $75 million* * 7 500 萬元的年營業額 ◇ *a fall in turnover* 營業額的下降 ➲ COLLOCATIONS at BUSINESS **2** [sing.] **~ (of sb)** the rate at which employees leave a company and are replaced by other people 人事變更率；人員調整率：*a high turnover of staff* 很高的人員變更率 **3** [sing.] **~ (of sth)** the rate at which goods are sold in a shop/store and replaced by others（商店的）貨物週轉率，銷售比率：*a fast turnover of stock* 快速的存貨週轉 **4** [C] a small PIE in the shape of a triangle or half a circle, filled with fruit or jam 三角餡餅，半圓餡餅（以水果或果醬作餡）

turn·pike /ˈtɜːnpaɪk; *NAmE* ˈtɜːrn-/ (also **pike**) (both *NAmE*) *noun* a wide road, where traffic can travel fast for long distances and that drivers must pay a TOLL to use 收費公路

turn·round /ˈtɜːnraʊnd; *NAmE* ˈtɜːrn-/ *noun* (*BrE*) = TURNAROUND

ˈturn signal (*NAmE*) (*BrE* **in·di·ca·tor**) (also *informal* **blink·er** *NAmE, BrE*) *noun* a light on a vehicle that flashes to show that the vehicle is going to turn left or right 轉向燈；方向燈 ➲ VISUAL VOCAB page V52

turn·stile /ˈtɜːnstaɪl; *NAmE* ˈtɜːrn-/ *noun* a gate at the entrance to a public building, STADIUM, etc. that turns in a circle when pushed, allowing one person to go through at a time 旋轉柵門（常設於公共建築、體育場等入口處）➲ picture at STILE

turn·table /ˈtɜːnteɪbl; *NAmE* ˈtɜːrn-/ *noun* **1** the round surface on a RECORD PLAYER that you place the record on to be played（唱機上的）唱盤 **2** a large round surface that is able to move in a circle and onto which a railway/railroad engine is driven in order to turn it to go in the opposite direction（鐵路機車的）轉台，旋車盤

ˈturn-up *noun* (*BrE*) **1** (*NAmE* **cuff**) [C] the bottom of the leg of a pair of trousers/pants that has been folded over on the outside（褲腳的）外翻邊，外捲邊 **2** [sing.] (*informal*) something surprising or unexpected that happens 奇異的事；意想不到的事：*He actually offered to help? That's **a turn-up for the books!*** 他居然提出要幫忙？這真是太陽從西邊出來了！

tur·pen·tine /ˈtɜːpəntaɪn; *NAmE* ˈtɜːrp-/ (also *informal* **turps** /tɜːps; *NAmE* tɜːrps/) *noun* [U] a clear liquid with a strong smell, used especially for making paint thinner and for cleaning paint from brushes and clothes 松脂；松節油

tur·pi·tude /ˈtɜːpɪtjuːd; *NAmE* ˈtɜːrpətuːd/ *noun* [U] (*formal*) very immoral behaviour 墮落；卑鄙；邪惡 SYN **wickedness**

tur·quoise /ˈtɜːkwɔɪz; *NAmE* ˈtɜːrk-/ *noun* **1** [C, U] a blue or greenish-blue SEMI-PRECIOUS stone 綠松石：*a turquoise brooch* 綠松石胸針 **2** [U] a greenish-blue colour 綠松石色；青綠色 ▸ **tur·quoise** *adj.*：*a turquoise dress* 一條青綠色的連衣裙

tur·ret /ˈtʌrət; *NAmE* ˈtɜːrət/ *noun* **1** a small tower on top of a wall or building, especially a castle（尤指城堡的）塔樓，角樓 ➲ VISUAL VOCAB page V15 **2** a small metal tower on a ship, plane or TANK that can usually turn around and from which guns are fired（戰艦、飛機或坦克的）迴轉炮塔，旋轉槍架

tur·ret·ed /ˈtʌrətɪd; *NAmE* ˈtɜːr-/ *adj.* [usually before noun] having one or more turrets 有塔樓的；有角樓的

tur·tle /ˈtɜːtl; *NAmE* ˈtɜːrtl/ *noun* **1** (*NAmE* also **ˈsea turtle**) a large REPTILE with a hard round shell, that lives in the sea 海龜 ➲ VISUAL VOCAB page V13 **2** (*NAmE, informal*) any REPTILE with a large shell, for example a TORTOISE or TERRAPIN（任何種類的）龜；陸龜；水龜；鱉

IDM **turn ˈturtle** (of a boat 船) to turn over completely while sailing（在航行中）傾覆，翻

ˈturtle dove *noun* a wild DOVE (= a type of bird) with a pleasant soft call, thought to be a very loving bird 斑鳩

turtle·neck /ˈtɜːtlnek; *NAmE* ˈtɜːrtl-/ *noun* **1** (also **ˌturtleneck ˈsweater**) a sweater with a high part fitting closely around the neck 高領套頭衫 **2** (*NAmE*) (*BrE* **ˈpolo neck**) a high round COLLAR made when the neck of a piece of clothing is folded over; a piece of clothing with a polo neck 高圓翻領；高圓翻領衣服 ➲ VISUAL VOCAB page V63

turves *pl.* of TURF

tusk /tʌsk/ *noun* either of the long curved teeth that stick out of the mouth of ELEPHANTS and some other animals（象和某些其他動物的）長牙 ➲ VISUAL VOCAB page V12 ➲ see also IVORY (1)

tus·sle /ˈtʌsl/ *noun, verb*

■ ***noun*** **~ (for/over sth)** a short struggle, fight or argument especially in order to get sth 扭打，爭鬥，爭執（尤指為了爭得物品）：*He was injured during a tussle for the ball.* 他在爭球時受了傷。

■ ***verb*** [I] **~ (with sb/sth)** to fight or compete with sb/sth, especially in order to get sth 扭打，爭鬥（尤指為了爭奪物品）：*The children were tussling with one another for the ball.* 孩子們在你搶我奪地爭球。

tus·sock /ˈtʌsək/ *noun* a small area of grass that is longer and thicker than the grass around it（比周圍的草密而高的）草叢 ▸ **tus·socky** *adj.*：*tussocky grass* 叢生草

tut /tʌt/ (also **ˌtut-ˈtut**) *exclamation, noun* used as the written or spoken way of showing the sound that people make when they disapprove of sth（作書面語或口語，表示不贊成的咂嘴聲）嘖嘖：*Tut-tut, I expected better of you.* 嘖嘖，我沒想到你會這樣。◇ *tut-tuts of disapproval* 不同意的嘖嘖聲 ▸ **tut** (also **ˌtut-ˈtut**) *verb* (**-tt-**) [I]： *He tut-tutted under his breath.* 他輕聲咂咂嘴。

tutee /tjuːˈtiː; *NAmE* tuː-/ *noun* a person who is taught or given advice by a TUTOR 受輔導者；受指導者

tu·tel·age /ˈtjuːtəlɪdʒ; *NAmE* ˈtuː-/ *noun* [U] (*formal*) **1** the teaching and instruction that one person gives to another 教導；指導；輔導 **SYN** **tuition** **2** the state of being protected or controlled by another person, organization or country（人、組織、國家等給予的）保護，監護，託管： *parental tutelage* 家長的監護

tutor /ˈtjuːtə(r); *NAmE* ˈtuː-/ *noun, verb*

■ ***noun*** **1** a private teacher, especially one who teaches an individual student or a very small group 家庭教師；私人教師 **2** (*especially BrE*) a teacher whose job is to pay special attention to the studies or health, etc. of a student or a group of students 導師；指導教師： *his history tutor* 他的歷史導師 ◇ *He was my* ***personal tutor*** *at university.* 他是我大學時的個人指導教師。◇ *She's in my* ***tutor group*** *at school.* 她在學校裏是指導我的那個小組的成員。 **3** (*BrE*) a teacher, especially one who teaches adults or who has a special role in a school or college（負責成人教育或在學校裏有特別任務的）教師： *a part-time adult education tutor* 兼職的成人教育教師 **4** (*NAmE*) an assistant LECTURER in a college（大專院校的）助教 **5** a book of instruction in a particular subject, especially music 課本；（尤指）音樂課本： *a violin tutor* 小提琴課本

■ ***verb*** **1** [T] **~ sb** (**in sth**) to be a tutor to an individual student or a small group; to teach sb, especially privately 教；任課；指導；進行單獨（或小組）輔導；任…的私人教師： *He tutors students in mathematics.* 他教學生數學。 **2** [I] to work as a tutor 當家庭教師；任大學導師： *Her work was divided between tutoring and research.* 她的工作分為導師工作和研究工作。

tu·tor·ial /tjuːˈtɔːriəl; *NAmE* tuː-/ *noun, adj.*

■ ***noun*** **1** a period of teaching in a university that involves discussion between an individual student or a small group of students and a tutor（大學導師的）個別輔導時間，輔導課 **2** a short book or computer program that gives information on a particular subject or explains how sth is done 教程；輔導材料；使用說明書： *An online tutorial is provided.* 在線輔導可供查閱。

■ ***adj.*** connected with the work of a tutor 導師的；私人教師的；輔導的： *tutorial staff* 輔導人員 ◇ (*BrE*) *a tutorial college* (= a private school that prepares students for exams) 私立考試輔導學校

tutti-frutti /ˌtuːti ˈfruːti/ *noun* [U] a type of ice cream that contains pieces of fruit of various kinds 什錦水果冰淇淋

tutu /ˈtuːtuː/ *noun* a BALLET dancer's skirt made of many layers of material. Tutus may be either short and stiff, sticking out from the waist, or long and bell-shaped. 芭蕾舞裙

tu-whit, tu-whoo /təˌwɪt təˈwuː/ *noun* used to represent the sound that an OWL makes（貓頭鷹的叫聲）嘟噫－嘟呼

tux·edo /tʌkˈsiːdəʊ; *NAmE* -doʊ/ *noun* (*pl.* **-os**) (also *informal* **tux** /tʌks/) (*especially NAmE*) **1** (*BrE* also **ˈdinner suit**) a black or white jacket and trousers/pants, worn with a BOW TIE at formal occasions in the evening（配蝶形領結的）成套無尾晚禮服 **2** (*BrE* also **ˈdinner jacket**) a black or white jacket worn with a BOW TIE at formal occasions in the evening（配蝶形領結的）晚禮服上衣，無尾禮服上衣 **ORIGIN** From Tuxedo Park in New York, where it was first worn. 源自紐約的塔克西多公園，此處最早有人穿這種服裝。

TV 🔑 /ˌtiː ˈviː/ *noun* [C, U] television 電視；電視機： *What's* ***on TV*** *tonight?* 今晚電視有什麼節目？◇ *We're buying a new TV with the money.* 我們要用這筆錢買一台新電視機。◇ *Almost all homes have at least one* ***TV set***. 差不多每家都至少有一台電視機。◇ *All rooms have a bathroom and colour TV.* 所有的房間都有洗澡間和彩色電視機。◇ ***a TV series/show/programme*** 電視系列片／節目 ◇ ***satellite/cable/digital TV*** 衛星／有線／數字電視 ◇ *She's a highly paid TV presenter.* 她是高薪電視節目主持人。➲ COLLOCATIONS at TELEVISION ➲ VISUAL VOCAB page V21 ➲ see also PAY TV

ˌTV ˈdinner *noun* a meal that you can buy already cooked and prepared, that you only have to heat up before you can eat it（加熱即可食用的）方便快餐，熟食快餐

TVP™ /ˌtiː ˌviː ˈpiː/ *abbr.* TEXTURED VEGETABLE PROTEIN

twad·dle /ˈtwɒdl; *NAmE* ˈtwɑːdl/ *noun* [U] (*old-fashioned, informal*) something that has been said or written that you think is stupid and not true 胡說八道；蠢話；廢話；拙劣的文字 **SYN** **nonsense**

twain /tweɪn/ *number* (*old use*) two 二

IDM **never the ˌtwain shall ˈmeet** (*saying*) used to say that two things are so different that they cannot exist together 二者永遠合不到一起；涇渭分明；大相逕庭

twang /twæŋ/ *noun, verb*

■ ***noun*** [usually sing.] **1** used to describe a way of speaking, usually one that is typical of a particular area and especially one in which the sounds are produced through the nose as well as the mouth 鼻音（通常指方言） **2** a sound that is made when a tight string, especially on a musical instrument, is pulled and released（樂器等的）撥弦聲

■ ***verb*** [I, T] to make a sound like a tight wire or string being pulled and released; to make sth do this 彈撥；（使）發出彈撥聲，發出嘣的一聲： *The bed springs twanged.* 這牀的彈簧嘣嘣響。◇ **~ sth** *Someone was twanging a guitar in the next room.* 隔壁有人在彈吉他。

'twas /twɒz; *NAmE* twʌz/ *abbr.* (*literary*) it was * it was 的縮寫

twat /twæt; twɒt; *NAmE* twɑːt/ *noun* (*taboo, slang, especially BrE*) **1** an offensive word for an unpleasant or stupid person 討厭鬼；蠢材 **2** an offensive word for the outer female sex organs 屄

tweak /twiːk/ *verb, noun*

■ ***verb*** **1 ~ sth** to pull or twist sth suddenly 扭；擰；扯： *She tweaked his ear playfully.* 她擰他的耳朵逗着玩兒。 **2 ~ sth** to make slight changes to a machine, system, etc. to improve it 稍稍調整（機器、系統等）： *I think you'll have to tweak these figures a little before you show them to the boss.* 我想你得略微改動一下這些數字再讓老闆過目。

■ ***noun*** **1** a sharp pull or twist 扭；擰；扯： *She gave his ear a tweak.* 她擰了一下他的耳朵。 **2** a slight change that you make to a machine, system, etc. to improve it（對機器、系統等的）輕微調整

twee /twiː/ *adj.* (*BrE, informal, disapproving*) very pretty, in a way that you find unpleasant and silly; appearing SENTIMENTAL 矯揉造作的；花裏胡哨的；故作多情的： *The room was decorated with twee little pictures of animals.* 這個房間裏掛滿了花哨的動物小圖片。

tweed /twiːd/ *noun* **1** [U] a type of thick rough cloth made of wool that has small spots of different coloured thread in it（雜色）粗花呢： *a tweed jacket* 粗花呢短上衣 **2 tweeds** [pl.] clothes made of tweed 粗花呢服裝

Tweedle·dum and Tweedle·dee /ˌtwiːdlˈdʌm ən twiːdlˈdiː/ *noun* [pl.] two people or things that are not different from each other 無差別的兩個人（或事物）；半斤八兩 **ORIGIN** From two characters in *Through the Looking Glass* by Lewis Carroll who look the same and say the same things. 源自劉易斯・卡羅爾所著小說《鏡中世界》中的兩個角色。

tweedy /ˈtwiːdi/ *adj.* **1** made of or looking like tweed 粗花呢製的；像粗花呢的： *a tweedy jacket* 粗花呢夾克 **2** (*BrE, informal, often disapproving*) used to describe the sort of person who often wears tweeds and therefore shows that they belong to the social class of rich people who live in the country（經常身穿呢子衣服）鄉紳的，鄉紳派頭的

tween /twiːn/ (also **tween·er** *especially BrE* **tween·ager** /ˈtwiːneɪdʒə(r)/) *noun* a child between the ages of about 10 and 12 * 10 至 12 歲之間的少年 **SYN** **pre-teen**

T

tween·er /ˈtwiːnə(r)/ *noun* **1** = TWEEN **2** a person or thing that is between two categories, classes or age groups 介乎兩者之間的人（或事物）：*The film is a tweener, neither indie nor mainstream.* 這部影片既非獨立製作，也不屬於主流，而是介於兩者之間。

tweet /twiːt/ *noun, verb*
■ *noun* **1** the short high sound made by a small bird（小鳥的）唧啾，吱喳 **2** (also **twitter**) a message sent using the Twitter SOCIAL NETWORKING service 運用推特社交網絡發送的信息
■ *verb* = TWITTER (1), (3)

tweet·er /ˈtwiːtə(r)/ *noun* a LOUDSPEAKER for reproducing the high notes in a SOUND SYSTEM（音響系統的）高頻揚聲器 ➲ compare WOOFER

tweez·ers /ˈtwiːzəz; *NAmE* -ərz/ *noun* [pl.] a small tool with two long thin parts joined together at one end, used for picking up very small things or for pulling out hairs 鑷子；小夾鉗：*a pair of tweezers* 一把鑷子 ➲ VISUAL VOCAB page V24

ˌTwelfth ˈNight *noun* [U] **1** January 6th, the day of the Christian festival of EPIPHANY 主顯節，顯現節（1 月 6 日，基督教節日）**2** the evening of January 5th, the day before EPIPHANY, which traditionally marks the end of Christmas celebrations 主顯節前夕，顯現節前夕（1 月 5 日夜，傳統上標誌着聖誕期的結束）

twelve 🔑 /twelv/ *number*
12 十二 ▸ **twelfth** 🔑 /twelfθ/ *ordinal number, noun* **HELP** There are examples of how to use ordinal numbers at the entry for **fifth**. 序數詞用法示例見 fifth 條。

twelve·month /ˈtwelvmʌnθ/ *noun* [sing.] (*old use*) a year 十二個月；一年

ˈtwelve-note (also **do·deca·phon·ic**, **ˈtwelve-tone**) *adj.* [only before noun] (*music* 音) used to describe a system of music which uses the twelve notes in the scale equally rather than using a particular KEY 十二音體系的

twenty 🔑 /ˈtwenti/
1 🔑 *number* 20 二十 **2** *noun* **the twenties** [pl.] numbers, years or temperatures from 20 to 29 二十幾；二十年代 ▸ **twen·ti·eth** 🔑 /ˈtwentiəθ/ *ordinal number, noun* **HELP** There are examples of how to use ordinal numbers at the entry for **fifth**. 序數詞用法示例見 fifth 條。
IDM **in your ˈtwenties** between the ages of 20 and 29 * 20 多歲

ˌtwenty-ˈfirst *noun* [sing.] (*informal, especially BrE*) a person's 21st birthday and the celebrations for this occasion * 21 歲生日；21 歲生日慶典

ˌtwenty-ˌfour ˈseven (also **24/7**) *adv.* (*informal*) twenty-four hours a day, seven days a week (used to mean 'all the time') 一天二十四小時，一星期七天（用以表示"全天候"）：*He's on duty twenty-four seven.* 他不分晝夜地天天上班。

ˌtwenty ˈpence (also **ˌtwenty pence ˈpiece**, **20p** /ˌtwenti ˈpiː/) *noun* a British coin worth 20 pence * 20 便士硬幣：*You need two 20ps for the machine.* 你得往這機器裏放兩枚 20 便士的硬幣。

ˌtwenty-ˌtwenty ˈvision (also **20/20 vision**) *noun* [U] the ability to see perfectly 絕好的視力

ˈtwere /twɜː(r)/ *abbr.* (*old use*) it were * it were 的縮寫

twerp /twɜːp; *NAmE* twɜːrp/ *noun* (*old-fashioned, informal*) a stupid or annoying person 笨蛋；討厭鬼

twice 🔑 /twaɪs/ *adv.*
1 🔑 two times; on two occasions 兩次；兩遍：*I don't know him well; I've only met him twice.* 我跟他不熟悉，只見過兩次面。◇ *They go there* ***twice a week/month/year***. 他們每星期／每月／每年去那裏兩次。◇ *a* ***twice-monthly/yearly*** *newsletter* 半月／半年刊的簡訊 **2** 🔑 double in quantity, rate, etc. 兩倍：*an area twice the size of Wales* 兩倍於威爾士大小的地區 ◇ *Cats sleep twice as much as people.* 貓睡覺的時間比人長一倍。◇ *At 56 he's twice her age.* 他 56 歲，年齡比她大一倍。
IDM **twice ˈover** not just once but twice 不止一次，而是兩次：*There was enough of the drug in her stomach to kill her twice over.* 她胃中的藥物足夠毒死她兩次的。➲ more at LIGHTNING *n.*, ONCE *adv.*, THINK *v.*

twid·dle /ˈtwɪdl/ *verb, noun*
■ *verb* [I, T] (*BrE*) to twist or turn sth with your fingers often because you are nervous or bored（常因緊張或無聊）旋弄，擺弄，捻弄（物件）：**~ with sth** *He twiddled with the radio knob until he found the right programme.* 他轉動了一會收音機旋鈕才找到了合意的節目。◇ **~ sth** *She was twiddling the ring on her finger.* 她擺弄着手指上的戒指。
IDM **twiddle your thumbs** **1** to move your thumbs around each other with your fingers joined together 抱手旋弄大拇指 **2** to do nothing while you are waiting for sth to happen（等待之際）無所事事
■ *noun* **1** (*BrE*) a twist or turn 擰；轉動：*a twiddle of the knob* 轉動一下旋鈕 **2** a decorative twist in a pattern, piece of music, etc.（圖案等的）修飾性曲線，螺旋形線條；（樂曲的）裝飾音：*twiddles on the clarinet* 單簧管的裝飾音

twid·dly /ˈtwɪdli/ *adj.* (*BrE, informal*) detailed or complicated 瑣碎的；繁雜的 **SYN** **fiddly**

twig /twɪɡ/ *noun, verb*
■ *noun* a small very thin branch that grows out of a larger branch on a bush or tree 細枝；小枝；嫩枝 ➲ VISUAL VOCAB page V10
■ *verb* (**-gg-**) [I, T] **~ (sth) | ~ what … | ~ (that) …** (*BrE, informal*) to suddenly understand or realize sth（突然地）懂得，理解，明白，意識到：*Haven't you twigged yet?* 難道你還不明白？◇ *I finally twigged what he meant.* 我終於弄明白了他的意思。

twi·light /ˈtwaɪlaɪt/ *noun, adj.*
■ *noun* [U] **1** the faint light or the period of time at the end of the day after the sun has gone down 暮色；薄暮；黃昏：*It was hard to see him clearly* ***in the twilight***. 在朦朧的暮色中很難看清他。◇ *We went for a walk along the beach* ***at twilight***. 黃昏時分我們沿着海灘散步。**2 the ~ (of sth)** the final stage of sth when it becomes weaker or less important than it was 沒落時期；衰退期；晚期：*the twilight years* (= the last years of your life) 暮年
■ *adj.* [only before noun] **1** (*formal*) used to describe a state in which things are strange and mysterious, or where things are kept secret and do not seem to be part of the real world 奇妙神秘的；虛幻的：*the* ***twilight world of*** *the occult* 魔法的虛幻世界 ◇ *They lived in the* ***twilight zone*** *on the fringes of society.* 他們生活在社會邊緣的陰暗之處。**2** used to describe a situation or area of thought that is not clearly defined（局面或思想領域）朦朧的，模糊的，界限不清的

twi·lit /ˈtwaɪlɪt/ *adj.* (*literary*) lit by twilight 暮色蒼茫的；昏暗朦朧的

twill /twɪl/ *noun* [U] a type of strong cloth that is made in a particular way to produce a surface of raised DIAGONAL lines 斜紋布：*a cotton twill skirt* 斜紋布裙子

ˈtwill /twɪl/ *abbr.* (*old use*) it will * it will 的縮寫

twin 🔑 /twɪn/ *noun, verb, adj.*
■ *noun* **1** 🔑 one of two children born at the same time to the same mother 孿生兒之一；雙胞胎之一：*She's expecting twins.* 她懷着雙胞胎。➲ COLLOCATIONS at CHILD ➲ see also CONJOINED TWIN, FRATERNAL TWIN, IDENTICAL TWIN, SIAMESE TWIN **2** one of two similar things that make a pair 一對相像的事物之一
■ *verb* (**-nn-**) **1** [usually passive] **~ sth (with sth)** to make a close relationship between two towns or areas 使結成姊妹城市；使結成友好地區：*Oxford is twinned with Bonn in Germany.* 牛津和德國的波恩結成了友好城市。**2 ~ sth (with sth)** to join two people or things closely together 使（兩人或兩事物）緊密結合；使偶合；使相連：*The opera twins the themes of love and death.* 這齣歌劇把愛與死的主題緊密結合在一起。
■ *adj.* [only before noun] **1** 🔑 used to describe one of a pair of children who are twins 孿生之一的；雙胞胎之一的：***twin boys/girls*** 孿生男孩／女孩 ◇ ***a twin brother/sister*** 孿生兄弟／姐妹中的一個 **2** used to describe two things that are used as a pair 成對的；成雙的：*a ship with*

T

twin propellers 有雙螺旋槳的船 **3** used to describe two things that are connected, or present or happening at the same time 雙重的；雙聯的；兩個同時發生的：*The prison service has the twin goals of punishment and rehabilitation.* 監獄有懲罰和改造雙重目的。

ˌtwin ˈbed *noun* **1** [usually pl.] one of a pair of single beds in a room （成對的）一張單人牀：*Would you prefer twin beds or a double?* 你們喜歡一對單人牀還是一張雙人牀？ **2** (*NAmE*) (*BrE* **ˌsingle ˈbed**) a bed big enough for one person 單人牀：*sheets to fit a twin bed* 單人牀的牀單 ➲ **VISUAL VOCAB** page V23

ˌtwin-ˈbedded *adj.* (of a room 房間) having two single beds in it 有兩張單人牀的

ˌtwin ˈbedroom *noun* a room in a hotel, etc. that has two single beds （旅館等的）有兩張單人牀的房間

twine /twaɪn/ *noun, verb*

■ **noun** [U] strong string that has two or more STRANDS (= single thin pieces of thread or string) twisted together （兩股或多股的）線，繩；合股線；麻繩

■ **verb** [I, T] **~ (sth) around/round/through/in sth** to wind or twist around sth; to make sth do this （使）盤繞，纏繞，圍繞：*ivy twining around a tree trunk* 纏繞在樹幹上的藤蔓 ◇ *She twined her arms around my neck.* 她用雙臂摟着我的脖子。

ˌtwin-ˈengined *adj.* (of an aircraft 飛機) having two engines 雙發動機的；雙引擎的

twinge /twɪndʒ/ *noun* **1** a sudden short feeling of pain （一陣）劇痛，刺痛：*He **felt a twinge** in his knee.* 他感到膝蓋一陣劇痛。 **2 ~ (of sth)** a sudden short feeling of an unpleasant emotion （一陣）不快，難過，痛苦：*a twinge of disappointment* 一陣失望

twin·kle /ˈtwɪŋkl/ *verb, noun*

■ **verb 1** [I] to shine with a light that keeps changing from bright to faint to bright again 閃耀；閃爍：*Stars twinkled in the sky.* 星星在天空中閃爍。◇ *twinkling lights in the distance* 遠處閃耀的點點燈光 ➲ **SYNONYMS** at SHINE **2** [I] **~ (with sth)** | **~ (at sb)** if your eyes **twinkle**, you have a bright expression because you are happy or excited （眼睛因高興或興奮）閃光，發亮：*twinkling blue eyes* 閃閃發亮的藍眼睛 ◇ *Her eyes twinkled with merriment.* 她高興得雙眸閃閃發亮。

■ **noun** [sing.] **1** an expression in your eyes that shows you are happy or amused about sth（眼睛的）閃亮；欣喜的神情：*He looked at me with a **twinkle in his eye**.* 他目光熠熠地望着我。 **2** a small light that keeps changing from bright to faint to bright again 閃爍；閃耀；閃光：*the twinkle of stars* 星星的閃爍 ◇ *the twinkle of the harbour lights in the distance* 遠處港口燈光的閃爍

twink·ling /ˈtwɪŋklɪŋ/ *noun* [sing.] (*old-fashioned, informal*) a very short time 瞬間；轉眼；一眨眼；一剎那

IDM **in the ˌtwinkling of an ˈeye** very quickly 瞬息之間；轉眼之間 **SYN** **in an instant**

twin·set /ˈtwɪnset/ *noun* (*BrE*) a woman's matching sweater and CARDIGAN that are designed to be worn together 女式套裝毛衣（配套穿的套頭和開襟毛衣）

ˌtwin ˈtown *noun* one of two towns in different countries that have a special relationship with each other （不同國家間）結成姊妹城的兩個城市之一：*a visit to Lyon, Birmingham's twin town in France* 對伯明翰在法國的友好城市里昂的訪問

twirl /twɜːl; *NAmE* twɜːrl/ *verb, noun*

■ **verb 1** [I, T] **~ (sb) (around/round)** to move or dance round and round; to make sb do this （使）旋轉，轉動：*She twirled around in front of the mirror.* 她對着鏡子轉動身子。◇ *He held her hand and twirled her around.* 他牽着她的手，讓她旋轉。 **2** [T] **~ sth (around/about)** to make sth turn quickly and lightly round and round 使輕快地轉動；使旋轉 **SYN** **spin**：*He twirled his hat in his hand.* 他快速旋轉着手裏的帽子。◇ *She sat twirling the stem of the glass in her fingers.* 她坐在那裏用手指捻動着高腳酒杯的柄腳。 **3** [T] **~ sth** to twist or curl sth with your fingers （用手指）纏繞，盤繞，捲曲：*He kept twirling his moustache.* 他不停地用手指捲鬍鬚。

■ **noun** the action of a person spinning around once （人）旋轉一週：*Kate **did a twirl** in her new dress.* 凱特穿着新連衣裙轉了一圈。

twist 🔑 /twɪst/ *verb, noun*

■ **verb**

▸ **BEND INTO SHAPE** 彎曲成形 **1** 🔑 [T] **~ sth (into sth)** to bend or turn sth into a particular shape 使彎曲，使扭曲（成一定形狀）：*Twist the wire to form a circle.* 把鐵絲彎成一個環。 **2** 🔑 [T, I] to bend or turn sth into a shape or position that is not normal or natural; to be bent or turned in this way （使）彎曲變形，扭曲變形：**~ sth (+ adv./prep.)** *He grabbed me and twisted my arm behind my back.* 他抓住我，把我的胳膊扭到背後。◇ **(+ adv./prep.)** *Her face twisted in anger.* 她氣得臉都變形了。

▸ **TURN BODY** 轉動身體 **3** [T, I] to turn part of your body around while the rest stays still 扭轉，轉動（身體部位）：**~ sth (+ adv./prep.)** *He twisted his head around to look at her.* 他扭過頭去看她。◇ **(+ adv./prep.)** *She twisted in her chair when I called her name.* 我喚她的名字時，她坐在座椅上轉過身來。 **4** 🔑 [I, T] to turn your body with quick sharp movements and change direction often （猛地將身體）轉動，旋轉，扭動：*I **twisted and turned** to avoid being caught.* 我左躲右閃免得被捉住。◇ **+ adv./prep.** *She tried unsuccessfully to twist free.* 她試圖掙脫身子，但無濟於事。◇ **~ sth/yourself + adv./prep.** *He managed to twist himself round in the restricted space.* 他設法在有限的空間內轉過身來。

▸ **TURN WITH HAND** 用手轉動 **5** 🔑 [T] **~ sth (+ adv./prep.)** to turn sth around in a circle with your hand （用手）轉動，旋轉：*Twist the knob to the left to open the door.* 向左轉動手柄把門打開。◇ *Nervously I twisted the ring on my finger.* 我緊張地轉動着手指上的戒指。

▸ **OF ROADS/RIVERS** 道路；河流 **6** 🔑 [I] to bend and change direction often 曲折；蜿蜒；盤旋：*The road **twists and turns** along the coast.* 道路沿着海濱蜿蜒曲折。◇ *narrow twisting streets* 狹窄彎曲的街道 ◇ *a twisting staircase* 盤旋而上的樓梯

▸ **ANKLE/WRIST/KNEE** 踝；腕；膝 **7** 🔑 [T] **~ sth** to injure part of your body, especially your ankle, wrist or knee, bending it in an awkward way 扭傷；崴傷：*She fell and twisted her ankle.* 她摔了一下，把腳崴了。

▸ **WIND AROUND** 纏繞 **8** 🔑 [T] **~ sth (+ adv./prep.)** to wind sth around or through an object 使纏繞；繚繞；盤繞：*She twisted a scarf around her head.* 她用一條圍巾裹住了頭。◇ *The telephone cable has **got twisted*** (= wound around itself). 電話線纏繞在一起了。 **9** 🔑 [I] **~ (round/around sth)** to move or grow by winding around sth 蠕動；盤繞；纏繞生長：*A snake was twisting around his arm.* 一條蛇纏繞在他的手臂上。

▸ **FACTS** 事實 **10** [T] **~ sth** to deliberately change the meaning of what sb has said, or to present facts in a particular way, in order to benefit yourself or harm sb else （故意）歪曲，曲解 **SYN** **misrepresent**：*You always twist everything I say.* 你總是歪曲我說的每一句話。◇ *The newspaper was accused of twisting the facts.* 這家報紙被指責歪曲事實。

▸ **THREADS** 線 **11** [T] **~ sth (into sth)** to turn or wind threads, etc. together to make sth longer or thicker 捻，搓，絞（線等）：*They had twisted the sheets into a rope and escaped by climbing down it.* 他們把牀單絞成繩子，緣繩而下逃走了。

IDM **twist sb's ˈarm** (*informal*) to persuade or force sb to do sth 勸說；強迫；生拉硬拽；施加壓力 ➲ more at KNIFE *n.*, LITTLE FINGER

PHR V **ˌtwist sth↔ˈoff** to turn and pull sth with your hand to remove it from sth 擰開；扭脫：*I twisted off the lid and looked inside.* 我擰開蓋子往裏面看。◇ *a twist-off top* 一擰即開的蓋兒

■ **noun**

▸ **ACTION OF TURNING** 旋轉 **1** 🔑 [C] the action of turning sth with your hand, or of turning a part of your body 轉動；旋轉；搓；捻；擰；扭動：*She gave the lid another twist and it came off.* 她又擰了一下，蓋兒開了。◇ *He gave a shy smile and a little twist of his head.* 他羞怯地笑了笑，略微扭了一下頭。

▸ **UNEXPECTED CHANGE** 意外變化 **2** 🔑 [C] an unexpected change or development in a story or situation （故事或情況的）轉折，轉變，突然變化：*the twists and turns of*

T

his political career 他政治生涯的一波三折 ◇ *The story has taken another twist.* 故事情節再一次變化。◇ *The disappearance of a vital witness added a* ***new twist*** *to the case.* 一名重要證人失踪，令訴訟出現了新的變數。◇ *By a curious* ***twist of fate*** *we met again only a week or so later.* 由於命運巧妙的安排，大約只過了一週我們又相逢了。

▸ **IN ROAD/RIVER 道路；河流 3** [C] a sharp bend in a road or river 急轉彎處；曲折處：*The car followed the* ***twists and turns*** *of the mountain road.* 汽車沿着彎彎曲曲的山路行駛。

▸ **SHAPE 形狀 4** [C] a thing that has been twisted into a particular shape 螺旋狀的東西；捲曲物；捻合成的東西：*mineral water with a twist of lemon* 加了一片檸檬的礦泉水

▸ **DANCE 舞蹈 5 the twist** [sing.] a fast dance that was popular in the 1960s, in which you twist from side to side 扭擺舞（盛行於 20 世紀 60 年代）

IDM **round the bend/twist** (*informal, especially BrE*) crazy 發瘋；瘋狂：*She's gone completely round the twist.* 她完全瘋了。➲ more at KNICKERS

twist·ed /ˈtwɪstɪd/ *adj.*

1 bent or turned so that the original shape is lost 扭曲的；彎曲的；變形的：*After the crash the car was a mass of twisted metal.* 那輛車撞成了一堆扭曲的廢鐵。◇ *a twisted ankle* (= injured by being turned suddenly) 扭傷的踝關節 ◇ *She gave a small twisted smile.* 她不自然地微微一笑。➲ picture at CURVED **2** (of a person's mind or behaviour 人的思想或行為) not normal; strange in an unpleasant way 怪僻的；偏執的：*Her experiences had left her* ***bitter and twisted.*** 她的經歷使她變得憤憤不平，性情乖僻。

twist·er /ˈtwɪstə(r)/ *noun* (*NAmE, informal*) a violent storm that is caused by a powerful spinning column of air 旋風；龍捲風 **SYN** **tornado**

twisty /ˈtwɪsti/ *adj.* (especially of a road 尤指道路) having many bends or turns 彎彎曲曲的；蜿蜒曲折的 **SYN** **winding, zigzag**

twit /twɪt/ *noun* (*informal, especially BrE*) a silly or annoying person 笨蛋；傻瓜；討厭鬼

twitch /twɪtʃ/ *verb, noun*

■ *verb* **1** [I, T] **~ (sth)** if a part of your body **twitches**, or if you **twitch** it, it makes a sudden quick movement, sometimes one that you cannot control 痙攣；抽搐；抽動：*Her lips twitched with amusement.* 她忍俊不禁地顫動着嘴唇。◇ *The cats watched each other, their tails twitching.* 兩隻貓晃動着尾巴彼此對視着。**2** [T, I] **~ (sth)** to give sth a short sharp pull; to be pulled in this way 急拉；猛拽；猛地被扯動：*He twitched the package out of my hands.* 他猛地從我手中拽走了包裹。◇ *The curtains twitched as she rang the bell.* 她按鈴時窗簾被猛地拉動了一下。

■ *noun* **1** a sudden quick movement that you cannot control in one of your muscles 痙攣；抽搐；抽動：*She has a twitch in her left eye.* 她左眼跳了一下。◇ *a nervous twitch* 神經性抽搐 **2** a sudden quick movement or feeling 閃動；晃動；急拉；（一陣）感覺：*He greeted us with a mere twitch of his head.* 他只晃了一下頭算是和我們打過招呼。◇ *At that moment she felt the first twitch of anxiety.* 那一刻她第一次感到一陣焦慮。

twitch·er /ˈtwɪtʃə(r)/ *noun* (*BrE, informal*) a person who is very keen on finding and watching rare birds 觀鳥癡，賞鳥迷（熱衷發現和觀賞珍稀鳥類）

twitchy /ˈtwɪtʃi/ *adj.* (*informal*) **1** nervous or anxious about sth 神經緊張的；焦急的；焦慮不安的 **SYN** **jittery** **2** making sudden quick movements 抽搐的；抽動的；痙攣的

Twit·ter™ /ˈtwɪtə(r)/ *noun* [U] a SOCIAL NETWORKING service that allows you to send out short regular messages about what you are doing, that people can access on the Internet or on their mobile/cell phones 推特（通過互聯網或用手機訪問並發送即時短信息的社交網絡服務）➲ compare MICROBLOGGING, TWEET *n.* (2)

twit·ter /ˈtwɪtə(r)/ *verb, noun*

■ *verb* **1** (also **tweet**) [I] when birds **twitter**, they make a series of short high sounds（鳥）啁啾，吱喳，啁啾 **2** [I, T] **~ (on) (about sth)** | **+ speech** (*especially BrE*) to talk quickly in a high excited voice, especially about sth that is not very important 唧唧喳喳地說話 **3** (also **tweet**) [I, T] **~ (sth)** to send a message using the Twitter SOCIAL NETWORKING service 運用推特社交網絡發送信息

■ *noun* [sing.] **1** (also **twit·tering**) a series of short high sounds that birds make（鳥的）啁啾聲，吱吱叫聲 **2** (*informal*) a state of nervous excitement 興奮；緊張；激動 **3** = TWEET *n.* (2)

'twixt /twɪkst/ *prep.* (*old use*) between 在…中間；在…之間 **IDM** see SLIP *n.*

two /tuː/ *number*

2 二 **HELP** There are examples of how to use numbers at the entry for **five**. 數詞用法示例見 five 條。

IDM **a 'day, 'moment, 'pound, etc. or two** one or a few days, moments, pounds, etc. 一兩天（或一會兒、一兩鎊等）：*May I borrow it for a day or two?* 這個我可以借用一兩天嗎？ **fall between two 'stools** (*BrE*) to fail to be or to get either of two choices, both of which would have been acceptable 兩頭落空；雞飛蛋打 **in 'two** in or into two pieces or halves 一分為二；成兩半：*He broke the bar of chocolate in two and gave me half.* 他把巧克力掰成兩半，給了我一塊。 **in ˌtwos and 'threes** two or three at a time; in small numbers 三三兩兩；稀稀拉拉：*People arrived in twos and threes.* 人們三三兩兩地到了。 **it takes two to do sth** (*saying*) one person cannot be completely responsible for sth 雙方都有責任；一個巴掌拍不響：*You can't put all the blame on him. It takes two to make a marriage.* 你不能全責怪他，結婚是兩個人的事。 **not have two beans, brain cells, etc. to rub to'gether** (*informal*) to have no money; to be very stupid, etc. 不名一文（或沒有腦子等） **put ˌtwo and ˌtwo to'gether** to guess the truth from what you see, hear, etc. 根據所見所聞推斷：*He's inclined to* ***put two and two together and make five*** (= reaches the wrong conclusion from what he sees, hears, etc.). 他愛捕風捉影，聽風就是雨。 **that makes 'two of us** (*informal*) I am in the same position or I agree with you 我也一樣；我也有同感：*'I'm tired!' 'That makes two of us!'* "我累了！" "我也是一樣！" **two ˌsides of the same 'coin** used to talk about two ways of looking at the same situation 同一事物的兩個方面 ➲ more at MIND *n.*, SHAKE *n.*

'two-bit *adj.* [only before noun] (*informal, especially NAmE*) not good or important 不好的；微不足道的；不重要的：*She wanted to be more than just a two-bit secretary.* 她並不想只做個人微言輕的小秘書。

ˌtwo 'bits *noun* [pl.] (*old-fashioned, NAmE, informal*) 25 cents（貨幣）25 分

ˌtwo-di'mension·al *adj.* flat; having no depth; appearing to have only two DIMENSIONS 平面的；無深度的；二度空間的；二維的：*a two-dimensional drawing* 平面圖 ◇ (*figurative*) *The novel was criticized for its two-dimensional characters* (= that did not seem like real people). 這部小說被評為人物缺乏深度之作。

ˌtwo-'edged *adj.* **1** (of a blade, knife, etc. 刃、刀等) having two sharp edges for cutting 雙刃的；雙鋒的 **2** having two possible meanings or results, one good and one bad 有好壞兩種含義（或結果）的；雙關的；有利有弊的：*a two-edged remark* 雙關語 ◇ *Fame can be* ***a two-edged sword.*** 名聲是把雙刃劍。

ˌtwo-'faced *adj.* (*informal, disapproving*) not sincere; not acting in a way that supports what you say that you believe; saying different things to different people about a particular subject 兩面派的；言行不一的；陰一套陽一套的 **SYN** **hypocritical**

ˌtwo 'fingers *noun* [pl.] (*BrE, informal*) a sign that you make by holding up your hand with the inside part facing towards you and making a V-shape with your first and second fingers (used as a way of being rude to other people)（手心向裏，表示侮蔑的）V 字形手勢：*I gave him the two fingers.* 我對他做了一個侮辱性的手勢。➲ compare V-SIGN

two·fold /ˈtuːfəʊld; *NAmE* -foʊld/ *adj.* (*formal*) **1** consisting of two parts 由兩部份組成的；有兩部份的： *The problem was twofold.* 這個問題分兩個部份。 **2** twice as much or as many 兩倍的： *a twofold increase in demand* 需求增加了一倍 ▸ **two·fold** *adv.*: *Her original investment has increased twofold.* 她原先的投資已經增加到兩倍。

ˌtwo-ˈhanded *adj.* using or needing both hands 用雙手的；需要雙手的： *a two-handed backhand* (= in TENNIS) 雙手握拍反手擊球 ◇ *a two-handed catch* 用雙手接的球

ˌtwo-ˈhander *noun* (*especially BrE*) a play that is written for only two actors 雙人物戲劇

twonk /twɒŋk; *NAmE* twɑːŋk/ *noun* (*BrE, slang*) a stupid person 傻瓜；笨蛋

ˌtwo ˈpence (also **ˌtwo pence ˈpiece**, **2p** /ˌtuː ˈpiː/) *noun* a British coin worth two pence （英國的）兩便士硬幣

two·pence /ˈtʌpəns/ *noun* (*BrE*) = TUPPENCE

two·penny (also *informal* **tup·penny**) /ˈtʌpəni; *NAmE* also ˈtuːpeni/ *adj.* (*BrE*) costing or worth two old pence 值兩舊便士的： *a twopenny stamp* 一枚兩便士的郵票

ˌtwo-ˈpiece *noun* a set of clothes consisting of two matching pieces of clothing, for example a skirt and jacket or trousers/pants and a jacket 兩件一套的衣服；兩件式 ▸ **ˌtwo-ˈpiece** *adj.*： *a two-piece suit* 兩件式西裝

ˈtwo-ply *adj.* (of wool, wood or other material 毛線、木材或其他材料) with two threads or thicknesses 雙股的；雙層的

ˌtwo-ˈseater *noun* a vehicle, an aircraft or a piece of furniture with seats for two people 雙座車輛（或飛機、傢具） ➲ VISUAL VOCAB page V21

two·some /ˈtuːsəm/ *noun* a group of two people who do sth together （共事的）兩人組 SYN **pair**

ˈtwo-star *adj.* [usually before noun] **1** having two stars in a system that measures quality. The highest standard is usually represented by four or five stars. （質量）兩星級的： *a two-star hotel* 兩星級賓館 **2** (*NAmE*) having the fourth-highest military rank, and wearing uniform which has two stars on it （軍銜）兩星的

ˈtwo-step *noun* a dance with long, sliding steps; the music for this dance 兩步舞；兩步舞曲

ˈtwo-stroke *adj.* (of an engine or vehicle 發動機或車輛) with a PISTON that makes two movements, one up and one down, in each power CYCLE 二衝程的 ➲ compare FOUR-STROKE

ˈtwo-time *verb* **~ sb** (*informal*) to not be faithful to a person you have a relationship with, especially a sexual one, by having a secret relationship with sb else at the same time 對（情人或愛人）不忠： *Are you sure he's not two-timing you?* 你肯定他沒有背着你另有所愛？ ▸ **ˈtwo-timer** *noun*

ˈtwo-tone *adj.* [only before noun] having two different colours or sounds 兩色的；雙音的

'twould /twʊd/ *abbr.* (*old use*) it would * it would 的縮寫

ˌtwo-ˌup ˌtwo-ˈdown *noun* (*BrE, informal*) a house with two rooms on the bottom floor and two bedrooms upstairs 兩上兩下的房屋（樓下兩室，樓上兩卧室）

ˌtwo-ˈway *adj.* [usually before noun] **1** moving in two different directions; allowing sth to move in two different directions 雙行的；雙向的： *two-way traffic* 雙向交通 ◇ *two-way trade* 雙向貿易 ◇ *a two-way switch* (= that allows electric current to be turned on or off from either of two points) 雙路開關 **2** (of communication between people 人際交流) needing equal effort from both people or groups involved 相互的；彼此的；有來有往的： *Friendship is a two-way process.* 友誼是一種相互的關係。 **3** (of radio equipment, etc. 無線電設備等) used both for sending and receiving signals 收發兩用的

ˌtwo-way ˈmirror *noun* a piece of glass that is a mirror on one side, but that you can see through from the other 單向透明玻璃鏡（一面是鏡子，但從鏡後可看到鏡前面）

ty·coon /taɪˈkuːn/ *noun* a person who is successful in business or industry and has become rich and powerful （企業界的）大亨，鉅頭，鉅子： *a* **business/property/media tycoon** 產業大亨；房地產鉅頭；傳媒鉅子

tyke (also **tike**) /taɪk/ *noun* (*informal*) **1** a small child, especially one who behaves badly 小孩子；小淘氣；小調皮鬼 **2** (*BrE*) a person from Yorkshire 約克郡人

tym·pa·num /ˈtɪmpənəm/ *noun* (*pl.* **tym·pa·nums** or **tym·pana** /ˈtɪmpənə/) (*anatomy* 解) the EARDRUM 鼓膜；耳膜

type 🔑 /taɪp/ *noun, verb*

■ ***noun*** **1** 🔑 [C] **~ (of sth)** a class or group of people or things that share particular qualities or features and are part of a larger group; a kind or sort 類型；種類： *different racial types* 不同的人種 ◇ *a rare blood type* 罕見的血型 ◇ *There are three main types of contract(s).* 有三種主要的合同。 ◇ *Bungalows are a type of house.* 平房是一種房屋。 ◇ *She mixes with all types of people.* 她和各種類型的人打交道。 ◇ *She mixes with people of all types.* 她和各種類型的人打交道。 ◇ *I love this type of book.* 我喜歡這類書籍。 ◇ *I love these types of books.* 我喜歡這些種類的書籍。 ◇ (*informal*) *I love these type of books.* 我愛讀這些種類的書籍。 ◇ *What do you charge for this type of work?* 這種活你收多少錢？ ◇ *What do you charge for work of this type?* 這種活你收多少錢？ ◇ *It is the first car of its type to have this design feature.* 這是同類型汽車中首部具備這種設計特點的。 **2** [sing.] (*informal*) a person of a particular character, with particular features, etc. 具有某種特徵的人；典型： *She's the artistic type.* 她是藝術家一類的人。 ◇ *He's not the type to be unfaithful.* 他不是背信棄義的那種人。 ◇ *She's* **not my type** (= not the kind of person I am usually attracted to). 她不是我喜歡的那種人。 **3** **-type** (in adjectives 構成形容詞) having the qualities or features of the group, person or thing mentioned 屬於…類型的；具有…特徵的： *a police-type badge* 一枚警徽 ◇ *a continental-type cafe* 有歐洲大陸特色的小餐館 **4** [U] letters that are printed or typed （印刷或打印的）文字，字體，字型： *The type was too small for me to read.* 這種印刷文字太小，我看不清。 ◇ *The important words are in bold type.* 重點詞是用黑體字印刷的。

■ ***verb*** **1** 🔑 [I, T] to write sth using a computer or TYPEWRITER （用計算機或打字機）打字： *How fast can you type?* 你打字有多快？ ◇ *typing errors* 打字錯誤 ◇ **~ sth (out/in/up)** *This letter will need to be typed* (*out*) *again.* 這封信需要再打一遍。 ◇ *Type* (*in*) *the filename, then press 'Return'.* 鍵入文件名稱，再按"返回"鍵。 ◇ *Has that report been* **typed up** *yet?* 那份報告打出來沒有？ **2** [T] **~ sb/sth** (*technical* 術語) to find out the group or class that a person or thing belongs to 測定…的類型；分型；定型： *Blood samples were taken from patients for typing.* 已採集患者的血樣供測定血型用。

type·cast /ˈtaɪpkɑːst; *NAmE* -kæst/ *verb* (**type·cast**, **type·cast**) [usually passive] **~ sb (as sth)** if an actor is **typecast**, he or she is always given the same kind of character to play 讓（演員）總演同一類型的角色： *She didn't want to be typecast as a dumb blonde.* 她不想總是演傻乎乎的金髮女郎一類的角色。

type·face /ˈtaɪpfeɪs/ *noun* a set of letters, numbers, etc. of a particular design, used in printing （印刷用的）字體： *I'd like the heading to be in a different typeface from the text.* 我希望標題和正文使用不同的字體。

type·script /ˈtaɪpskrɪpt/ *noun* [C, U] a copy of a text or document that has been typed （打印出的）文稿，文件；打字稿

type·set·ter /ˈtaɪpsetə(r)/ *noun* a person, machine or company that prepares a book, etc. for printing 排字工人；排字機；排字公司 ▸ **type·set** *verb* (**type·set·ting**, **type·set**, **type·set**)： **~ sth** *Pages can now be typeset on-screen.* 現在可以屏幕排版。 **type·set·ting** *noun* [U]： *computerized typesetting* 計算機排版

type·writer /ˈtaɪpraɪtə(r)/ *noun* a machine that produces writing similar to print. It has keys that you press to make metal letters or signs hit a piece of paper through a strip of cloth covered with ink. 打字機 ➲ see also TYPIST

T

type·writ·ing /ˈtaɪpraɪtɪŋ/ *noun* = TYPING

type·writ·ten /ˈtaɪprɪtn/ *adj.* written using a typewriter or computer（用打字機或計算機）打字的，打印的

ty·phoid /ˈtaɪfɔɪd/ (also *less frequent* ˌ**typhoid ˈfever**) *noun* [U] a serious infectious disease that causes fever, red spots on the chest and severe pain in the BOWELS, and sometimes causes death 傷寒：*a typhoid epidemic* 傷寒的流行

ty·phoon /taɪˈfuːn/ *noun* a violent tropical storm with very strong winds 颱風 ➲ compare CYCLONE, HURRICANE

ty·phus /ˈtaɪfəs/ *noun* [U] a serious infectious disease that causes fever, headaches, purple marks on the body and often death 斑疹傷寒

typ·ical 🔑 /ˈtɪpɪkl/ *adj.*
1 🔑 having the usual qualities or features of a particular type of person, thing or group 典型的；有代表性的 SYN **representative**：*a typical Italian cafe* 典型的意大利式小餐館 ◇ *This is a typical example of Roman pottery.* 這是一件典型的羅馬陶器。◇ **~ of sb/sth** *This meal is typical of local cookery.* 這是有當地風味的飯菜。◇ **~ for sb/sth** *The weather at the moment is not typical for July.* 現在的天氣並不是七月份常有的。OPP **atypical** **2** 🔑 happening in the usual way; showing what sth is usually like 一貫的；平常的 SYN **normal**：*A typical working day for me begins at 7.30.* 我的工作日一般在 7:30 開始。OPP **untypical** **3** 🔑 **~ (of sb/sth)** (often *disapproving*) behaving in the way that you expect 不出所料；特有的：*It was typical of her to forget.* 她這個人就是愛忘事。◇ *He spoke with typical enthusiasm.* 他以其特有的熱情講話。◇ (*informal*) *She's late again—typical!* 她又遲到了，一貫如此！

typ·ic·al·ly 🔑 /ˈtɪpɪkli/ *adv.*
1 🔑 used to say that sth usually happens in the way that you are stating 通常；一般：*The factory typically produces 500 chairs a week.* 這家工廠通常每週生產 500 把椅子。◇ *A typically priced meal will be around $10.* 一餐通常的價格為 10 元左右。**2** 🔑 in a way that shows the usual qualities or features of a particular type of person, thing or group 典型地；具有代表性地：*typically American hospitality* 美國人特有的殷勤好客 ◇ *Mothers typically worry about their children.* 母親總愛掛念自己的子女。**3** 🔑 in the way that you expect sb/sth to behave 不出所料；果然：*Typically, she couldn't find her keys.* 她果然又找不着自己的鑰匙了。◇ *He was typically modest about his achievements.* 他一如既往，對自己的成就很謙虛。

T

typ·ify /ˈtɪpɪfaɪ/ *verb* (**typi·fies**, **typi·fy·ing**, **typi·fied**, **typi·fied**) (not usually used in the progressive tenses 通常不用於進行時) **1 ~ sth** to be a typical example of sth 作為…的典型；是…的典範：*clothes that typify the 1960s* * 20 世紀 60 年代典型的服裝 ◇ *the new style of politician, typified by the Prime Minister* 以首相為代表的新型政治家風格 **2 ~ sth** to be a typical feature of sth 成為…的特徵：*the haunting guitar melodies that typify the band's music* 反映這個樂隊音樂特色的縈繞心頭的吉他樂曲

typ·ing /ˈtaɪpɪŋ/ (also *less frequent* **type·writ·ing**) *noun* [U] **1** the activity or job of using a TYPEWRITER or computer to write sth（用打字機或計算機）打字：*to do the typing* 打字 ◇ *typing errors* 打印錯誤 ◇ *a* **typing pool** (= a group of people who share a company's typing work) 打字小組 **2** writing that has been done on a TYPEWRITER or computer（用打字機或計算機打的）打字稿，文稿

typ·ist /ˈtaɪpɪst/ *noun* **1** a person who works in an office typing letters, etc. 打字員 **2** a person who uses a TYPEWRITER or computer keyboard（用打字機或計算機鍵盤的）打字者：*I'm quite a fast typist.* 我打字相當快。

typo /ˈtaɪpəʊ; *NAmE* -poʊ/ *noun* (*pl.* **-os**) (*informal*) a small mistake in a typed or printed text 打字（或排印）文稿的小錯誤

typ·og·raph·er /taɪˈpɒɡrəfə(r); *NAmE* -ˈpɑːɡ-/ *noun* a person who is skilled in typography 印刷工人；排字工

typ·og·raphy /taɪˈpɒɡrəfi; *NAmE* -ˈpɑːɡ-/ *noun* [U] the art or work of preparing books, etc. for printing, especially of designing how text will appear when it is printed 印刷術；排印；版面設計 ▸ **typo·graph·ic·al** /ˌtaɪpəˈɡræfɪkl/ (also **typo·graph·ic** /ˌtaɪpəˈɡræfɪk/) *adj.*：*a typographical error* 排印錯誤 ◇ *typographic design* 印刷版面設計 **typo·graph·ic·al·ly** /-kli/ *adv.*

typ·ology /taɪˈpɒlədʒi; *NAmE* -ˈpɑːl-/ *noun* (*pl.* **-ies**) (*technical* 術語) a system of dividing things into different types 類型學

tyr·an·nical /tɪˈrænɪkl/ (also *formal* **tyr·an·nous** /ˈtɪrənəs/) *adj.* using power or authority over people in an unfair and cruel way 暴君的；專橫的；殘暴的 SYN **autocratic**, **dictatorial**

tyr·an·nize (*BrE* also **-ise**) /ˈtɪrənaɪz/ *verb* [T, I] to use your power to treat sb in a cruel or unfair way 對…施行暴政；專橫地對待：**~ sb/sth** *a father tyrannizing his children* 專橫地對待子女的父親 ◇ **~ over sb/sth** *a political leader who tyrannizes over his people* 對人民施行暴政的政治頭領 ➲ see also TYRANT

tyr·an·no·saur /tɪˈrænəsɔː(r); taɪ-/ (also **tyr·an·no·saurus** /tɪˌrænəˈsɔːrəs/) *noun* a very large DINOSAUR that stood on two legs, had large powerful JAWS and two short front legs 霸王龍

tyr·anny /ˈtɪrəni/ *noun* [U, C] (*pl.* **-ies**) **1** unfair or cruel use of power or authority 暴虐；專橫；苛政；專政：*a victim of oppression and tyranny* 壓迫和暴政的受害者 ◇ *The children had no protection against the tyranny of their father.* 孩子們無法抵禦其父的虐待。◇ *the tyrannies of Nazi rule* 納粹統治的暴行 ◇ (*figurative*) *These days it seems we must all submit to the tyranny of the motor car.* 如今，似乎所有人都離不開汽車了。**2** the rule of a tyrant; a country under this rule 暴君統治；暴君統治的國家 SYN **dictatorship**：*Any political system refusing to allow dissent becomes a tyranny.* 任何不允許不同政見的政治體制都會變成專制。

tyr·ant /ˈtaɪrənt/ *noun* a person who has complete power in a country and uses it in a cruel and unfair way 暴君；專制君主；暴虐的統治者 SYN **dictator**：*The country was ruled by a succession of tyrants.* 這個國家接連遭受暴君的統治。◇ (*figurative*) *His boss is a complete tyrant.* 他的老闆是個不折不扣的暴君。

tyre 🔑 (*BrE*) (*NAmE* **tire**) /ˈtaɪə(r)/ *noun*
a thick rubber ring that fits around the edge of a wheel of a car, bicycle, etc. 輪胎：*a* ***front tyre*** 前胎 ◇ *a* ***back/rear tyre*** 後胎 ◇ *to pump up a tyre* 給輪胎打氣 ◇ *a* ***flat/burst/punctured tyre*** 癟了的／爆了的／扎了的輪胎 ◇ ***bald/worn tyres*** 磨平的／磨損的輪胎 ➲ COLLOCATIONS at DRIVING ➲ VISUAL VOCAB pages V51, V52 ➲ see also SPARE TYRE

tyro /ˈtaɪrəʊ; *NAmE* -roʊ/ *noun* (*pl.* **-os**) a person who has little or no experience of sth or is beginning to learn sth 初學者；新手；生手 SYN **novice**

tzar, **tzar·ina**, **tzar·ism**, **tzar·ist** = TSAR, TSARINA, TSARISM, TSARIST

Uu

U /juː/ *noun, abbr.*

■ ***noun*** (also **u**) [C, U] (*pl.* **Us, U's, u's** /juːz/) the 21st letter of the English alphabet 英語字母表的第 21 個字母：*'Under' begins with (a) U/'U'.* * under 一詞以字母 u 開頭。➲ see also U-BOAT, U-TURN

■ ***abbr.*** (*BrE*) universal (the label of a film/movie that is suitable for anyone including children) * U 類影片（適合所有觀眾）：*Aladdin, certificate U* * U 類電影《阿拉丁》

'U-bend *noun* a section of pipe shaped like a U, especially one that carries away used water（尤指污水管的）U 形彎頭，馬蹄彎頭，U 形管

uber- (also **über-**) /ˈuːbə(r)/ *combining form* (from *German, informal*) (in nouns and adjectives 構成名詞和形容詞) of the greatest or best kind; to a very large degree 最好的；超級的：*His girlfriend was a real uber-babe, with long blonde hair and a big smile.* 他的女友是個超級靚妞，一頭長長的金髮，臉上帶着燦爛的笑容。◇ *This stylish new restaurant is futuristic and uber-cool.* 這家時尚的新餐館設計極其超前，真是超酷。

ubi·qui·tous /juːˈbɪkwɪtəs/ *adj.* [usually before noun] (*formal* or *humorous*) seeming to be everywhere or in several places at the same time; very common 似乎無所不在的；十分普遍的：*the ubiquitous bicycles of university towns* 大學城裏處處可見的自行車 ◇ *the ubiquitous movie star, Tom Hanks* 盡人皆知的影星湯姆 • 漢克斯 ▸ **ubi·qui·tous·ly** *adv.* **ubi·quity** /juːˈbɪkwəti/ *noun* [U]：*the ubiquity of the mass media* 大眾傳媒的無所不在

'U-boat *noun* a German SUBMARINE (= a ship that can travel underwater)（德國）U 潛艇

ubuntu /ʊˈbʊntuː/ *noun* [U] (*SAfrE*) the idea that people are not only individuals but live in a community and must share things and care for each other 班圖精神，社團關愛精神（生活在集體中，大家必須分享物品並互相關心）

u.c. *abbr.* (in writing 書寫形式) UPPER CASE

UCAS /ˈjuːkæs/ *abbr.* (in Britain) Universities and Colleges Admissions Service (an official organization that deals with applications to study at universities and colleges)（英國）高校招生服務處

UDA /juː diː ˈeɪ/ *abbr.* Ulster Defence Association (an illegal military organization in Northern Ireland that wants Northern Ireland to remain part of the UK) 北愛爾蘭防務協會（非法軍事組織，主張北愛爾蘭繼續屬於英國）

udder /ˈʌdə(r)/ *noun* an organ shaped like a bag that produces milk and hangs underneath the body of a cow, GOAT, etc.（母牛、母羊等的）乳房

UDR /juː diː ˈɑː(r)/ *abbr.* Ulster Defence Regiment (a branch of the British army in Northern Ireland, now forming part of the Royal Irish Regiment) 北愛爾蘭防衛軍（英軍的一部份）

UEFA /juˈeɪfə/ *abbr.* Union of European Football Associations 歐足聯；歐洲足球協會聯合會

U-ey /ˈjuːi/ *noun* (*informal, especially AustralE*) a turn of 180° that a vehicle makes so that it can move forwards in the opposite direction（汽車等的）U 形轉彎，180 度轉彎 SYN **U-turn**

UFO (also **ufo**) /juː ef ˈəʊ; ˈjuːfəʊ; *NAmE* juː ef ˈoʊ; ˈjuːfoʊ/ *noun* (*pl.* **UFOs** or **ufos**) the abbreviation for 'Unidentified Flying Object' (a strange object that some people claim to have seen in the sky and believe is a SPACECRAFT from another planet) 幽浮，不明飛行物（全寫為 Unidentified Flying Object）➲ compare FLYING SAUCER

ufol·ogy /juːˈfɒlədʒi; *NAmE* -ˈfɑːl-/ *noun* [U] the study of UFOs 不明飛行物學；幽浮學

ugali /uːˈɡɑːli/ *noun* [U] (*EAfrE*) a type of food made with flour from CORN (MAIZE) or MILLET, usually eaten with meat or vegetable STEW 蒸玉米粉糰，蒸黍粉糕（通常和燉肉或蔬菜一起吃）

ugh (also **urgh**) *exclamation* the way of writing the sound (/ɜː/ /ʊx/) that people make when they think that sth is disgusting or unpleasant（表示厭惡或不快）咳，呸：*Ugh! How can you eat that stuff?* 咳！你怎麼能吃那玩意兒呢？

Ugli™ /ˈʌɡli/ (also **'Ugli fruit**) *noun* a large CITRUS fruit with a rough, yellowish-orange skin and sweet flesh with a lot of juice 醜橘（大柑橘類水果，果皮粗糙，呈淡橙色，果肉甜而多汁）

ugly 🗝 /ˈʌɡli/ *adj.* (**ug·lier, ugli·est**)
1 🗝 unpleasant to look at 醜陋的；難看的 SYN **unattractive**：*an ugly face* 醜陋的面孔 ◇ *an ugly building* 難看的建築 **2** 🗝 (of an event, a situation, etc. 事件、局勢等) unpleasant or dangerous; involving threats or violence 令人不快的；危險的；險惡的；兇險的：*an ugly incident* 危險事件 ◇ *There were ugly scenes in the streets last night as rioting continued.* 昨晚暴亂持續之際，街上險象環生。▸ **ugli·ness** *noun* [U] IDM see REAR *v.* (4), SIN *n.* (3)

ˌugly 'duckling *noun* a person or thing that at first does not seem attractive or likely to succeed but that later becomes successful or much admired 醜小鴨（初似平庸後來出眾的人或事物）ORIGIN From the title of a story by Hans Christian Andersen, in which a young swan thinks it is an ugly young duck until it grows up into a beautiful adult swan. 源自安徒生童話，講述一隻小天鵝一直認為自己是隻醜小鴨，長大後卻變成了美麗的天鵝。

uh *exclamation* the way of writing the sound /ʌ/ or /ɜː/ that people make when they are not sure about sth, when they do not hear or understand sth you have said, or when they want you to agree with what they have said（表示不肯定、不清楚或徵求同意）嗯，唔：*Uh, yeah, I guess so.* 嗯，對，我想是這樣。◇ *'Are you ready yet?' 'Uh? Oh. Yes.'* "你準備好了嗎？" "嗯？噢，好了。" ◇ *We can discuss this another time, uh?* 這事咱們以後再說，嗯？

UHF /juː eɪtʃ ˈef/ *abbr.* ultra-high frequency (a range of radio waves used for high-quality radio and television broadcasting) 超高頻

'uh-huh *exclamation* the way of writing the sound that people make when they understand or agree with what you have said, when they want you to continue or when they are answering 'Yes'（表示理解、贊同、希望對方繼續或作肯定答覆）嗯，哦，喔，啊：*'Did you read my note?' 'Uh-huh.'* "你看了我的條子沒有？" "嗯。"

'uh-oh (also **'oh-oh**) *exclamation* the way of writing the sound that people make when they want to say that they have done sth wrong or that they think there will be trouble（表示做錯了事或感到有麻煩）哎喲，哦唷：*Uh-oh. I forgot to write that letter.* 哦唷，我忘了寫那封信了。◇ *Uh-oh! Turn the TV off. Here comes Dad!* 哎喲！把電視關掉！爸爸來了！

UHT /juː eɪtʃ ˈtiː/ *abbr.* (*BrE*) ultra heat treated. UHT milk has been heated to a very high temperature in order to make it last for a long time. 經高溫處理

uh-uh *exclamation* the way of writing the sound /ˈʌ ʌ/ that people make when they are answering 'No' to a question（表示不同意）哼，嘘

uja·maa /ˌʊdʒæˈmɑː/ *noun* [U] (in Tanzania) SOCIALISM（坦桑尼亞）烏賈馬，社會主義

UK (also **U.K.** especially in *US*) /juː ˈkeɪ/ *abbr.* UNITED KINGDOM

uku·lele /juːkəˈleɪli/ *noun* a musical instrument with four strings, like a small GUITAR 尤克萊利琴（四弦小吉他）

ulcer /ˈʌlsə(r)/ *noun* a sore area on the outside of the body or on the surface of an organ inside the body which is painful and may BLEED or produce a poisonous substance 潰瘍：*a stomach ulcer* 胃潰瘍 ➲ see also MOUTH ULCER

ul·cer·ate /ˈʌlsəreɪt/ *verb* [I, T, usually passive] **~ (sth)** (*medical* 醫) to become, or make sth become, covered with ulcers （使）形成潰瘍，潰爛 ▸ **ul·cer·ation** /ˌʌlsəˈreɪʃn/ *noun* [U, C]

ulna /ˈʌlnə/ *noun* (*pl.* **ulnae** /-niː/) (*anatomy* 解) the longer bone of the two bones in the lower part of the arm between the elbow and the wrist, on the side opposite the thumb 尺骨 ➲ see also RADIUS (3) ➲ VISUAL VOCAB page V59

ul·ter·ior /ʌlˈtɪəriə(r); *NAmE* -ˈtɪr-/ *adj.* [only before noun] (of a reason for doing sth 行事的理由) that sb keeps hidden and does not admit 隱秘的；不可告人的；秘密的；矢口否認的：*She must have some **ulterior motive** for being nice to me—what does she really want?* 她對我這麼好，一定別有用心。她到底想幹什麼呢？

ul·tim·ate 0⊸ AW /ˈʌltɪmət/ *adj., noun*

■ ***adj.*** [only before noun] **1** 0⊸ happening at the end of a long process 最後的；最終的；終極的 SYN **final**：*our **ultimate goal/aim/objective/target*** 我們最終的目的／目標 ◇ *We will accept ultimate responsibility for whatever happens.* 無論出什麼事情，我們願承擔全部責任。◇ *The ultimate decision lies with the parents.* 最後的決定權握在父母手中。 **2** 0⊸ most extreme; best, worst, greatest, most important, etc. 極端的；最好（或壞、偉大、重要等）的：*This race will be the ultimate test of your skill.* 這次競賽將是對你的技能的最大考驗。◇ *Silk sheets are the ultimate luxury.* 絲綢牀單乃是極度的奢侈品。 **3** from which sth originally comes 根本的；基本的；基礎性的 SYN **basic**, **fundamental**：*the ultimate truths of philosophy and science* 哲學與科學的終極原理

■ ***noun*** [sing.] **the ~ in sth** (*informal*) the best, most advanced, greatest, etc. of its kind 最好（或先進、偉大等）的事物；極品；精華：*the ultimate in modern design* 現代設計的最高代表

ˈultimate fighting™ (also **ˈextreme fighting**) *noun* [U] a sport that combines different styles of fighting such as BOXING, WRESTLING and MARTIAL ARTS and in which there are not many rules 終極搏擊，終極格鬥（結合拳擊、摔跤和武術等，規則不多）

ul·tim·ate·ly 0⊸ AW /ˈʌltɪmətli/ *adv.*

1 0⊸ in the end; finally 最終；最後；終歸：*Ultimately, you'll have to make the decision yourself.* 最終你還是得自己拿主意。◇ *A poor diet will ultimately lead to illness.* 不均衡的飲食終將導致疾病。 **2** at the most basic and important level 最基本地；根本上：*All life depends ultimately on oxygen.* 一切生命歸根到底都要依賴氧氣。

ul·ti·matum /ˌʌltɪˈmeɪtəm/ *noun* (*pl.* **ul·ti·matums** or **ul·ti·ma·ta**) a final warning to a person or country that if they do not do what you ask, you will use force or take action against them 最後通牒：*to issue an ultimatum* 發出最後通牒

ultra /ˈʌltrə/ *noun* a person who holds extreme views, especially in politics （尤指政治上的）過激分子，極端主義者

U

ultra- /ˈʌltrə/ *prefix* (in adjectives and nouns 構成形容詞和名詞) extremely; beyond a particular limit 極；超過某限度：*ultra-modern* 超現代的 ◇ *ultraviolet* 紫外線的 ➲ compare INFRA-

ˌultra-high ˈfrequency *noun* [U] = UHF

ultra·light /ˈʌltrəlaɪt/ (*NAmE*) (*BrE* **micro·light**) *noun* a very small light aircraft for one or two people 超輕型飛機 ➲ VISUAL VOCAB page V53

ultra·mar·ine /ˌʌltrəməˈriːn/ *noun* [U] a bright blue colour 群青色；佛青色

ultra·short /ˌʌltrəˈʃɔːt; *NAmE* -ˈʃɔːrt/ *adj.* (of radio waves 無線電波) having a very short WAVELENGTH (shorter than 10 metres), with a FREQUENCY greater than 30 MEGAHERTZ 超短的 ➲ compare LONG WAVE, MEDIUM WAVE, SHORT WAVE

ultra·son·ic /ˌʌltrəˈsɒnɪk; *NAmE* -ˈsɑːn-/ *adj.* [usually before noun] (of sounds 聲音) higher than humans can hear 超聲的；超音的：*ultrasonic waves* 超聲波

ultra·sound /ˈʌltrəsaʊnd/ *noun* **1** [U] sound that is higher than humans can hear 超聲；超音 **2** [U, C] a medical process that produces an image of what is inside your body 超聲波掃描檢查：*Ultrasound showed she was expecting twins.* 超聲波掃描顯示她懷了雙胞胎。

ultra·vio·let /ˌʌltrəˈvaɪələt/ (*abbr.* **UV**) *adj.* [usually before noun] (*physics* 物) of or using ELECTROMAGNETIC waves that are just shorter than those of VIOLET light in the SPECTRUM and that cannot be seen 紫外線的；利用紫外線的：*ultraviolet rays* (= that cause the skin to go darker) 紫外線 ◇ *an ultraviolet lamp* 紫外線燈 ➲ compare INFRARED

ulu·late /ˈjuːljʊleɪt; ˈʌljʊleɪt; *NAmE* ˈʌljəl-/ *verb* [I] (*literary*) to give a long cry 嚎叫；大叫；長嘯 SYN **wail** ▸ **ulu·la·tion** /-leɪʃn/ *noun* [U, C]

um *exclamation* the way of writing the sound /ʌm/ or /əm/ that people make when they hesitate, or do not know what to say next （表示猶豫或說話中間停頓）嗯，呃，姆：*Um, I'm not sure how to ask you this ….* 嗯，我不知道該怎麼問你這個…

umami /uːˈmɑːmi/ *noun* [U] a taste found in some foods that is neither sweet, sour, bitter nor salty 鮮味：*Tomatoes have lots of umami.* 西紅柿味道特鮮。

umber /ˈʌmbə(r)/ *noun* [U] a dark brown or yellowish-brown colour used in paints （油漆中用的）棕土，赭土

um·bil·ical cord /ʌmˌbɪlɪkl ˈkɔːd; *NAmE* ˈkɔːrd/ *noun* a long piece of TISSUE that connects a baby to its mother before it is born and is cut at the moment of birth 臍帶

um·bil·icus /ʌmˈbɪlɪkəs; ˌʌmbɪˈlaɪkəs/ *noun* (*pl.* **um·bil·ici** /ʌmˈbɪlɪsaɪ; ˌʌmbɪˈlaɪsaɪ; -kaɪ/ or **um·bil·icuses**) (*technical* 術語) the NAVEL 臍；肚臍

umbra /ˈʌmbrə/ *noun* (*pl.* **um·bras** or **um·brae** /ˈʌmbriː/) (*technical* 術語) **1** the darkest part of a shadow 本影（影子中光源完全照射不到的部份） **2** the area on the earth or the moon which is the darkest during an ECLIPSE （日蝕或月蝕期間地球或月球的）本影 ➲ compare PENUMBRA (2)

um·brage /ˈʌmbrɪdʒ/ *noun*

IDM **take ˈumbrage (at sth)** (*formal* or *humorous*) to feel offended, insulted or upset by sth, often without a good reason 認為受到冒犯（或羞辱）；（無故）感到不安 SYN **take offence**

um·brella 0⊸ /ʌmˈbrelə/ *noun*

1 0⊸ (also *BrE informal* **brolly**) an object with a round folding frame of long straight pieces of metal covered with material, that you use to protect yourself from the rain or from hot sun 傘；雨傘；陽傘：*I put up my umbrella.* 我撐開傘。◇ *colourful beach umbrellas* 五彩繽紛的海灘遮陽傘 ➲ compare PARASOL (2), SUNSHADE (1) **2** a thing that contains or includes many different parts or elements 綜合體；總體；整體：*Many previously separate groups are now operating under the umbrella of a single authority.* 許多原本分散的團體現歸一個單一的機構領導。◇ *an **umbrella organization/group/fund*** 綜合機構／團體／基金 ◇ *'Contact sports' is an **umbrella term** for a variety of different sports.* "接觸式運動"是多種不同體育運動的總稱。 **3** a country or system that protects people 保護國（或體系）；保護傘；庇護

um·faan /ʊmˈfɑːn/ *noun* (*pl.* **um·faans** or **ba·fana** /bɑːˈfɑːnə/) (*SAfrE*) **1** a young black man who is not married 未婚黑人男青年 **2** a young black boy 黑人男孩

um·laut /ˈʊmlaʊt/ *noun* the mark placed over a vowel in some languages to show how it should be pronounced, as over the *u* in the German word *für* （元音的）變音符 ➲ compare ACUTE ACCENT, CIRCUMFLEX, GRAVE², TILDE (1)

UMPC /juː em piː ˈsiː/ *noun* (*computing* 計) a very small computer that is easy to carry, often with a touch screen and sometimes without a physical keyboard (the abbreviation for 'ultra-mobile personal computer') 超移動個人電腦，超級移動電腦（全寫為 ultra-mobile personal computer，便攜式小型電腦，常帶觸控屏，有時不帶實體鍵盤）

um·pire /ˈʌmpaɪə(r)/ *noun, verb*

■ ***noun*** (also *NAmE informal* **ump**) (in sports such as TENNIS and BASEBALL 網球、棒球等體育運動) a person whose job is to watch a game and make sure that rules are not broken 裁判員 ➲ compare REFEREE (1)

■ *verb* [I, T] to act as an umpire 做裁判員；當裁判：*We need someone to umpire.* 我們得找個人當裁判。◇ **~ sth** *to umpire a game of baseball* 做棒球賽裁判

ump·teen /ˌʌmp'tiːn/ *det.* (*informal*) very many 大量；很多：*I've told this story umpteen times.* 這個故事我已講了無數次了。▸ **ump·teen** *pron.*：*Umpteen of them all arrived at once.* 他們大夥都一塊兒來了。 **ump·teenth** /ˌʌmp'tiːnθ/ *det.*：*'This is crazy,' she told herself for the* ***umpteenth time*** (= she had done it many times before). "這簡直瘋了！" 她已無數次這般地自言自語着。

UN (also **U.N.** especially in *US*) /juː 'en/ *abbr.* United Nations (an association of many countries that aims to help economic and social conditions improve and to solve political problems in the world in a peaceful way) 聯合國：*the UN Security Council* 聯合國安理會 ◇ *a UN peacekeeping plan* 聯合國維和計劃

un- /ʌn/ *prefix* **1** (in adjectives, adverbs and nouns 構成形容詞、副詞和名詞) not; the opposite of 不；未；非；反：*unable* 不能 ◇ *unconsciously* 無意識地 ◇ *untruth* 謬誤 **2** (in verbs that describe the opposite of a process 構成表示相反過程的動詞)：*unlock* 開鎖 ◇ *undo* 解開

'un /ən/ *pron.* (*BrE, informal*) a way of saying or writing 'one' (等於 one)：*That was a good 'un.* 那個東西不錯。◇ *The little 'uns* (= the small children) *couldn't keep up.* 小不點兒跟不上了。

un·abashed /ˌʌnə'bæʃt/ *adj.* not ashamed, embarrassed or affected by people's disapproval, when other people would be 不在乎的；不害羞的；不難為情的 **OPP** **abashed** ▸ **un·abashed·ly** /-ʃɪdli/ *adv.*

un·abated /ˌʌnə'beɪtɪd/ *adj.* [not usually before noun] (*formal*) without becoming any less strong 不減；未變弱：*The rain* ***continued unabated***. 雨勢一直沒減弱。

un·able 🔑 /ʌn'eɪbl/ *adj.* [not before noun] **~ to do sth** (rather *formal*) not having the skill, strength, time, knowledge, etc. to do sth 沒有所需技能（或力量、時間、知識等）；未能；無法：*He lay there, unable to move.* 他躺在那裏動彈不得。◇ *I tried to contact him but was unable to.* 我試着跟他聯繫，卻沒聯繫上。 **OPP** **able**

un·abridged /ˌʌnə'brɪdʒd/ *adj.* (of a novel, play, speech, etc. 小說、戲劇、講演等) complete, without being made shorter in any way（版本）完整的；未刪節的 **OPP** **abridged**

un·ac·cent·ed /ʌn'æksentɪd/ *adj.* **1** (of sb's speech 講話) having no regional or foreign accent 不帶地方（或外國）口音的；無口音的 **2** (*phonetics* 語音) (of a syllable 音節) having no stress 非重讀的

un·accept·able 🔑 /ˌʌnək'septəbl/ *adj.* that you cannot accept, allow or approve of 不能接受（或允許、同意）的：*Such behaviour is totally unacceptable in a civilized society.* 這種行為在文明社會是完全不能接受的。◇ *Noise from the factory has reached an unacceptable level.* 工廠的噪聲達到了難以容忍的地步。 **OPP** **acceptable** ▸ **un·accept·ably** /-bli/ *adv.*：*unacceptably high levels of unemployment* 奇高的失業率

un·accom·pan·ied **AW** /ˌʌnə'kʌmpənid/ *adj.* **1** (*formal*) without a person going together with sb/sth 無人陪伴（或同行）的：*No unaccompanied children allowed.* 無大人帶領的兒童不許進入。◇ ***unaccompanied luggage/baggage*** (= travelling separately from its owner) 託運的行李 **2** (*music* 音) performed without anyone else playing or singing at the same time 無伴奏的；無伴唱的：*a sonata for unaccompanied violin* 無伴奏小提琴奏鳴曲 **3** (*formal*) **~ by sth** not together with a particular thing 沒有；不伴有：*Mere words, unaccompanied by any violence, cannot amount to an assault.* 只有言語而未伴隨暴力不能算侵犯人身。

un·account·able /ˌʌnə'kaʊntəbl/ *adj.* (*formal*) **1** impossible to understand or explain 無法理解的；難以解釋的 **SYN** **inexplicable**：*For some unaccountable reason, the letter never arrived.* 不知何故，那封信始終未寄到。 **2 ~ (to sb/sth)** not having to explain or give reasons for your actions to anyone 無須解釋（或說明）的；不負責的：*Too many government departments are unaccountable to the general public.* 有太多的政府部門不對社會大眾負責。 **OPP** **accountable**

un·account·ably /ˌʌnə'kaʊntəbli/ *adv.* (*formal*) in a way that is very difficult to explain; without any obvious reason 難以解釋地；莫名其妙地；無明顯原因地 **SYN** **inexplicably**：*He has been unaccountably delayed.* 他被莫名其妙地耽誤了。

un·account·ed for /ˌʌnə'kaʊntɪd fɔː(r)/ *adj.* [not before noun] **1** a person or thing that is **unaccounted for** cannot be found and people do not know what has happened to them or it 下落不明；失踪：*At least 300 civilians are unaccounted for after the bombing raids.* 遭轟炸襲擊之後，至少有 300 名平民下落不明。 **2** not explained 未解釋；未說明：*In the story he gave the police, half an hour was left unaccounted for.* 他對警察的陳述中有半個小時的事情未交代清楚。

un·accus·tomed /ˌʌnə'kʌstəmd/ *adj.* (*formal*) **1 ~ to sth/to doing sth** not in the habit of doing sth; not used to sth 不習慣；不適應：*He was unaccustomed to hard work.* 他不習慣艱苦工作。◇ *I am unaccustomed to being told what to do.* 我沒有聽人使喚的習慣。 **2** [usually before noun] not usual, normal or familiar 反常的；不一般的；不熟悉的：*The unaccustomed heat made him weary.* 反常的炎熱令他虛弱無力。 **OPP** **accustomed**

un·achiev·able /ˌʌnə'tʃiːvəbl/ *adj.* that you cannot manage to reach or obtain 難以達到的；無法獲得的：*unachievable goals* 難以實現的目標 **OPP** **achievable**

un·acknow·ledged /ˌʌnək'nɒlɪdʒd; *NAmE* -'nɑːl-/ *adj.* **1** not receiving the thanks or praise that is deserved 未得到應有的感激（或讚賞）的：*Her contribution to the research went largely unacknowledged.* 她對這項研究的貢獻大都被忽略了。 **2** that people do not admit as existing or true; that people are not aware of 不被承認存在（或真實）的；未被意識到的：*unacknowledged feelings* 下意識的感情 **3** not publicly or officially recognized 未得到公開（或正式）承認的；非正式的：*the unacknowledged leader of the group* 這個團體非正式任命的首領

un·ac·quaint·ed /ˌʌnə'kweɪntɪd/ *adj.* **~ (with sth/sb)** (*formal*) not familiar with sth/sb; having no experience of sth 不熟悉；無經驗：*visitors unacquainted with local customs* 不諳當地風俗的遊客 **OPP** **acquainted**

un·adjust·ed /ˌʌnə'dʒʌstɪd/ *adj.* (*statistics* 統計) (of figures 數字) not adjusted according to particular facts or circumstances 未調整的；調整前的：*Unadjusted figures which do not take tourism into account showed that unemployment fell in July.* 不含旅遊業的調整前數字表明七月份失業率下降。

un·adorned /ˌʌnə'dɔːnd; *NAmE* -'dɔːrnd/ *adj.* (*formal*) without any decoration 不加裝飾的；簡樸的 **SYN** **simple**：*The walls were plain and unadorned.* 牆壁樸素無華。

un·adul·ter·ated /ˌʌnə'dʌltəreɪtɪd/ *adj.* **1** [usually before noun] you use **unadulterated** to emphasize that sth is complete or total 完全的；十足的；不折不扣的 **SYN** **undiluted**：*For me, the holiday was sheer unadulterated pleasure.* 對我來說，這個假期是百分之百的賞心樂事。 **2** not mixed with other substances; not ADULTERATED 純的；不摻雜質的 **SYN** **pure**：*unadulterated foods* 未摻雜其他物質的食物

un·ad·ven·tur·ous /ˌʌnəd'ventʃərəs/ *adj.* not willing to take risks or try new and exciting things 不願冒險（或嘗試新奇事物）的 **SYN** **cautious** **OPP** **adventurous**

un·affect·ed **AW** /ˌʌnə'fektɪd/ *adj.* **1 ~ (by sth)** not changed or influenced by sth; not affected by sth 未被改變的；未受影響的；無動於衷的：*People's rights are unaffected by the new law.* 新法規沒有影響人民的權利。◇ *Some members of the family may remain unaffected by the disease.* 這家族有些人可能不會受到這種疾病的影響。 **2** (*approving*) (of a person or their behaviour 人或其行為) natural and sincere 真誠自然的；真摯的；不做作的 **OPP** **affected**

un·affili·ated /ˌʌnə'fɪlieɪtɪd/ *adj.* **~ (with sth)** not belonging to or connected with a political party or a large organization 獨立的；無黨派（或組織）的 **SYN** **independent** **OPP** **affiliated**

U

un·afford·able /ˌʌnəˈfɔːdəbl; *NAmE* -əˈfɔːrd-/ *adj.* costing so much that people do not have enough money to pay for it 買不起的；負擔不起的：*Health insurance is now unaffordable for many people.* 如今很多人買不起健康保險。**OPP affordable**

un·afraid /ˌʌnəˈfreɪd/ *adj.* [not before noun] (*formal*) not afraid or nervous; not worried about what might happen 不害怕；不畏懼；不緊張；無顧忌：**~ (of sth)** *She was unafraid of conflict.* 她不怕發生衝突。◇ **~ (to do sth)** *He's unafraid to speak his mind.* 他勇於説出心裏話。

un·aid·ed **AW** /ʌnˈeɪdɪd/ *adj.* (*formal*) without help from anyone or anything 無外援的；獨力的：*He can now walk unaided.* 他現在能獨自行走了。

un·ali·en·able /ʌnˈeɪliənəbl/ *adj.* = INALIENABLE

un·alloyed /ˌʌnəˈlɔɪd/ *adj.* (*formal*) not mixed with anything else, such as negative feelings 純真的；純粹的 **SYN pure**：*unalloyed joy* 純粹的快樂

un·alter·able **AW** /ʌnˈɔːltərəbl/ *adj.* (*formal*) that cannot be changed 不可更改的；無法改變的 **SYN immutable**：*the unalterable laws of the universe* 不可改變的宇宙法則

un·altered **AW** /ʌnˈɔːltəd; *NAmE* -tərd/ *adj.* that has not changed or been changed 未改變的；未被改變的：*This practice has* ***remained unaltered*** *for centuries.* 這種習俗已延續了數百年未變。

un·am·bigu·ous **AW** /ˌʌnæmˈbɪɡjuəs/ *adj.* clear in meaning; that can only be understood in one way 意思清楚的；明確的；毫不含糊的；無歧義的：*an unambiguous statement* 明確的陳述 ◇ *The message was clear and unambiguous—'Get out!'* 這其中的含義明確無疑——"滾開！" **OPP ambiguous** ▶ **un·am·bigu·ous·ly** **AW** *adv.*

un·am·bi·tious /ˌʌnæmˈbɪʃəs/ *adj.* **1** (of a person 人) not interested in becoming successful, rich, powerful, etc. 無抱負的；無名利心的 **2** not involving a lot of effort, time, money, etc. or anything new 不費功夫（或時間、金錢等）的；不鋪張的：*an unambitious plan* 平凡的計劃 **OPP ambitious**

ˌun-Aˈmerican *adj.* against American values or interests 與美國人價值（或興趣）相反的；非美國的

unan·im·ity /juːnəˈnɪməti/ *noun* [U] complete agreement about sth among a group of people 一致同意；全體贊同

unani·mous /juˈnænɪməs/ *adj.* **1** if a decision or an opinion is **unanimous**, it is agreed or shared by everyone in a group （決定或意見）一致的，一致同意的：*a unanimous vote* 全體一致的表決 ◇ *unanimous support* 一致的擁護 ◇ *The decision was not unanimous.* 這項決定沒有得到一致通過。**2 ~ (in sth)** if a group of people are **unanimous**, they all agree about sth （團體）意見一致的，一致同意某事的：*Local people are unanimous in their opposition to the proposed new road.* 當地居民一致反對擬建的新公路。▶ **unani·mous·ly** *adv.*：*The motion was passed unanimously.* 這動議獲一致通過。

un·announced /ˌʌnəˈnaʊnst/ *adj.* happening without anyone being told or warned in advance 未通知的；未預告的；未打招呼的：*She just turned up unannounced on my doorstep.* 她未打招呼就來到我家門口了。◇ *an unannounced increase in bus fares* 公共汽車票價未經公告的上漲

un·answer·able /ʌnˈɑːnsərəbl; *NAmE* ʌnˈæn-/ *adj.* **1** an **unanswerable** argument, etc. is one that nobody can question or disagree with 無可爭辯的；不容反對的 **SYN irrefutable**：*They presented an unanswerable case for more investment.* 他們提出了一個無可爭辯的理由，要求增加投資。**2** an **unanswerable** question is one that has no answer or that you cannot answer 無答案的；無法回答的

un·answered /ʌnˈɑːnsəd; *NAmE* -sərd/ *adj.* **1** (of a question, problem, etc. 提問、問題等) that has not been answered 未回答的；未解答的；懸而未決的：*Many questions about the crime* ***remain unanswered.*** 這樁罪行涉及的許多問題仍然沒有答案。**2** (of a letter, telephone call, etc. 信函、電話等) that has not been replied to 未回覆（或答覆）的：*unanswered letters* 未答覆的信件

un·antici·pated **AW** /ˌʌnænˈtɪsɪpeɪtɪd/ *adj.* (*formal*) that you have not expected or predicted; that you have not anticipated 沒想到的；未預料到的：*unanticipated costs* 預料之外的費用

un·apolo·get·ic /ˌʌnəˌpɒləˈdʒetɪk; *NAmE* -ˌpɑːl-/ *adj.* not saying that you are sorry about sth, even in situations in which other people might expect you to 不致歉的；不道歉的 **OPP apologetic** ▶ **un·apolo·get·ic·al·ly** /-kli/ *adv.*

un·appeal·ing /ˌʌnəˈpiːlɪŋ/ *adj.* not attractive or pleasant 不誘人的；無魅力的；令人不快的：*The room was painted in an unappealing shade of brown.* 這屋子漆成了難看的棕色。◇ *The prospect of studying for another five years was distinctly unappealing.* 未來還需要再學五年真是讓人厭煩。**OPP appealing**

un·appe·tiz·ing (*BrE* also **-is·ing**) /ʌnˈæpɪtaɪzɪŋ/ *adj.* (of food 食物) unpleasant to eat; looking as if it will be unpleasant to eat 難吃的；倒胃口的；看似難吃的 **OPP appetizing**

un·appre·ci·ated **AW** /ˌʌnəˈpriːʃieɪtɪd/ *adj.* [not usually before noun] not having your work or your qualities recognized and enjoyed by other people; not appreciated 無人賞識；不被欣賞；無人感激：*He was in a job where he felt unappreciated and undervalued.* 他以前的工作未讓他感到受賞識和重視。

un·approach·able **AW** /ˌʌnəˈprəʊtʃəbl; *NAmE* -ˈproʊ-/ *adj.* (of a person 人) unfriendly and not easy to talk to 不友好的；難接近的；不好説話的 **OPP approachable**

un·argu·able /ʌnˈɑːɡjuəbl; *NAmE* -ˈɑːrɡ-/ *adj.* (*formal*) that nobody can disagree with 無可爭辯的；不容置疑的：*unarguable proof* 不容置疑的證據 ➲ compare ARGUABLE (2) ▶ **un·argu·ably** *adv.*：*She is unarguably one of the country's finest athletes.* 她無疑是全國最優秀的運動員之一。

un·armed /ˌʌnˈɑːmd; *NAmE* ˌʌnˈɑːrmd/ *adj.* **1** not carrying a weapon 不帶武器的；非武裝的：*unarmed civilians* 沒有武裝的平民 **2** not involving the use of weapons 不使用武器的；徒手的：*The soldiers were trained in* ***unarmed combat.*** 士兵接受徒手格鬥訓練。**OPP armed**

un·ashamed /ˌʌnəˈʃeɪmd/ *adj.* feeling no shame or embarrassment about sth, especially when people might expect you to 不害臊的；不感覺難為情的 ➲ compare ASHAMED ▶ **un·ashamed·ly** /ˌʌnəˈʃeɪmɪdli/ *adv.*：*She wept unashamedly.* 她不顧羞恥地哭了起來。◇ *an unashamedly sentimental song* 一首誇張的傷感歌曲

un·asked /ˌʌnˈɑːskt; *NAmE* ˌʌnˈæskt/ *adj.* **1** an **unasked** question is one that you have not asked even though you would like to know the answer 沒發問的；未出口的 **2** without being invited or asked 未獲邀請的；未被問及的：*He came to the party unasked.* 他未經邀請就來參加聚會了。◇ *She brought him, unasked, the relevant file.* 她主動把有關案卷帶給了他。

unˈasked-for *adj.* that has not been asked for or requested 未經要求的；非請求的：*unasked-for advice* 主動提出的建議

un·assail·able /ˌʌnəˈseɪləbl/ *adj.* (*formal*) that cannot be destroyed, defeated or questioned 無法摧毀的；不可戰勝的；不容置疑的：*The party now has an unassailable lead.* 這個黨的領先地位現在堅不可摧。◇ *Their ten-point lead puts the team in an almost unassailable position.* 他們以十分領先的優勢使整個球隊處於難以撼動的地位。

un·assigned **AW** /ˌʌnəˈsaɪnd/ *adj.* not given to or reserved for any particular person or purpose 未分配的；未保留的

un·assist·ed **AW** /ˌʌnəˈsɪstɪd/ *adj.* not helped by anyone or anything 無人幫助的；不靠外援的；獨力的 **SYN unaided**：*She could not move unassisted.* 她不能夠獨力活動。

un·assum·ing /ˌʌnəˈsjuːmɪŋ; *NAmE* ˌʌnəˈsuː-/ *adj.* (*approving*) not wanting to draw attention to yourself or to your abilities or status 不愛出風頭的；不愛炫耀的；謙遜的 **SYN modest**

un·attached AW /ˌʌnəˈtætʃt/ *adj.* **1** not married or involved in a romantic relationship 未婚的；單身的；未戀愛的 SYN **single**：*He was still unattached at the age of 34.* 他 34 歲時還是單身。 **2** not connected with or belonging to a particular group or organization 不屬於團體或組織的；無所屬的；無黨派的；獨立的 ➲ compare ATTACHED (1)

un·attain·able AW /ˌʌnəˈteɪnəbl/ *adj.* impossible to achieve or reach 無法得到的；難以達到的：*an unattainable goal* 難以達到的目標 OPP **attainable**

un·attend·ed /ˌʌnəˈtendɪd/ *adj.* (*formal*) without the owner present; not being watched or cared for 主人不在場的；無人看管（或照料）的：*unattended vehicles* 無人看管的車輛 ◇ *Never leave young children unattended.* 對幼兒切不可疏於看管。

un·attract·ive /ˌʌnəˈtræktɪv/ *adj.* **1** not attractive or pleasant to look at 不悅目的；不漂亮的；難看的：*an unattractive brown colour* 難看的棕色 **2** not good, interesting or pleasant 不好的；無趣的；令人反感的：*one of the unattractive aspects of the free market economy* 自由市場經濟糟糕的一個方面 OPP **attractive** ▸ **un·attract·ive·ly** *adv.*

un·author·ized (*BrE* also **-ised**) /ʌnˈɔːθəraɪzd/ *adj.* without official permission 未經許可（或批准）的：*No access for unauthorized personnel.* 未經允許不得入內。 OPP **authorized**

un·avail·able AW /ˌʌnəˈveɪləbl/ *adj.* [not usually before noun] **~ (to sb/sth)** **1** that cannot be obtained 無法得到；難以獲得：*Such luxuries are unavailable to ordinary people.* 此等奢侈品普通百姓是難以獲得的。 **2** not able or not willing to see, meet or talk to sb 不能（或不願）見面；不能（或不願）交談：*The minister was* ***unavailable for comment.*** 部長無暇接受訪問作出評論。 OPP **available** ▸ **un·avail·abil·ity** *noun* [U]

un·avail·ing /ˌʌnəˈveɪlɪŋ/ *adj.* (*formal*) without success 徒勞的；無成果的 SYN **unsuccessful**：*Their efforts were unavailing.* 他們的努力都付諸東流。

un·avoid·able /ˌʌnəˈvɔɪdəbl/ *adj.* impossible to avoid or prevent 無法避免的；難以預防的：*unavoidable delays* 不可避免的延誤 OPP **avoidable** ▸ **un·avoid·ably** /-əbli/ *adv.*：*I was unavoidably delayed.* 我無奈被耽擱了。

un·aware AW /ˌʌnəˈweə(r); *NAmE* -ˈwer/ *adj.* [not before noun] not knowing or realizing that sth is happening or that sth exists 不知道；沒意識到；未察覺：**~ of sth** *He was completely unaware of the whole affair.* 他對整件事情一無所知。 ◇ **~ that …** *She was unaware that I could see her.* 她沒想到我能看見她。 OPP **aware** ▸ **un·aware·ness** *noun* [U]

un·awares /ˌʌnəˈweəz; *NAmE* -ˈwerz/ *adv.* **1** when not expected 猝然；出其不意地；冷不防：*The camera had* ***caught her unawares.*** 她毫無防備地被拍攝下來。 ◇ *The announcement* ***took me unawares.*** 這項聲明令我感到意外。 ◇ *She came upon him unawares when he was searching her room.* 他在翻她屋子時，冷不防被她撞見了。 **2** (*formal*) without noticing or realizing 不留神地；未注意到；不知不覺地：*He slipped unawares into sleep.* 他不知不覺地睡着了。

un·bal·ance /ˌʌnˈbæləns/ *verb* **1 ~ sth** to make sth no longer balanced, for example by giving too much importance to one part of it 使不平衡；使失去均衡 **2 ~ sb/sth** to make sb/sth unsteady so that they are likely to fall down 使失去重心（或平衡）；使傾覆 **3 ~ sb** to make sb slightly crazy or mentally ill 使心理不平衡；使精神失常

un·bal·anced /ˌʌnˈbælənst/ *adj.* **1** [not usually before noun] (of a person 人) slightly crazy; mentally ill 心理不平衡；精神失常 **2** [usually before noun] giving too much or too little importance to one part or aspect of sth 不持平的；偏頗的；失衡的：*an unbalanced article* 持論偏頗的文章 ◇ *an unbalanced diet* 不均衡的飲食

unban /ˌʌnˈbæn/ *verb* (**-nn-**) **~ sth** to allow sth that was banned before 開放；解禁 OPP **ban**

un·bear·able /ʌnˈbeərəbl; *NAmE* -ˈber-/ *adj.* too painful, annoying or unpleasant to deal with or accept 難耐的；無法接受的；難以處理的 SYN **intolerable**：*The heat was becoming unbearable.* 炎熱開始變得難以忍受。 ◇ *unbearable pain* 無法忍受的疼痛 ◇ *He's been unbearable since he won that prize.* 他得獎以後變得很難相與。 OPP **bearable** ▸ **un·bear·ably** /-əbli/ *adv.*：*unbearably hot* 酷熱難當

un·beat·able /ʌnˈbiːtəbl/ *adj.* **1** (of a team, player, etc. 團隊、運動員等) impossible to defeat 難以擊敗的；打不垮的 SYN **invincible** **2** (of prices, value, etc. 價格、價值等) impossible to improve 已達極限的；難以競爭的：*unbeatable offers* 最優惠的報價

un·beat·en /ʌnˈbiːtn/ *adj.* (*sport* 體) not having been defeated 未嘗敗績的；未敗過的：*The team are unbeaten in their last four games.* 這個隊在最近的四場比賽中從未失敗過。 ◇ *They will be putting their* ***unbeaten record*** *to the test next Saturday.* 下週六他們的不敗紀錄將要受到考驗。

un·be·com·ing /ˌʌnbɪˈkʌmɪŋ/ *adj.* (*formal*) **1** not suiting a particular person 不合適的；不相稱的 SYN **unflattering**：*She was wearing an unbecoming shade of purple.* 她穿着一身不相配的紫色衣服。 **2 ~ (to/of sb)** not appropriate or acceptable 不恰當；不得體；不可接受 SYN **inappropriate**：*He was accused of conduct unbecoming to an officer.* 他被譴責行為有失官員身分。 OPP **becoming**

un·be·fit·ting /ˌʌnbɪˈfɪtɪŋ/ *adj.* **~ (of/for/to sb/sth)** (*formal*) not suitable or good enough for sb/sth 不合適；不適宜；不得體：*His behaviour is unbefitting of a university professor.* 他的行為與大學教授的身分不相符。 ◇ *The amount of litter in the streets is unbefitting for a historic city.* 街道上垃圾之多與歷史名城不協調。

un·be·known /ˌʌnbɪˈnəʊn; *NAmE* -ˈnoʊn/ (also *less frequent* **un·be·knownst** /ˌʌnbɪˈnəʊnst; *NAmE* -ˈnoʊnst/) *adj.* **~ to sb** (*formal*) without the person mentioned knowing 瞞着；背着：*Unbeknown to her they had organized a surprise party.* 他們瞞着她為她籌備了一個意外驚喜的聚會。

un·belief /ˌʌnbɪˈliːf/ *noun* [U] (*formal*) lack of belief, or the state of not believing, especially in God, a religion, etc. （對上帝的）不相信；無（宗教）信仰 ➲ compare BELIEF (3), DISBELIEF

un·believ·able /ˌʌnbɪˈliːvəbl/ *adj.* **1** (*informal*) used to emphasize how good, bad or extreme sth is 非常好（或壞、極端）的；難以置信的；驚人的 SYN **incredible**：*We had an unbelievable* (= very good) *time in Paris.* 我們在巴黎的日子快活極了。 ◇ *Conditions in the prison camp were unbelievable* (= very bad). 集中營的生活條件糟糕透了。 ◇ *The cold was unbelievable* (= it was extremely cold). 天氣冷極了。 ◇ ***It's unbelievable that*** (= very shocking) *they have permitted this trial to go ahead.* 令人震驚的是他們竟允許進行這項審訊。 **2** very difficult to believe and unlikely to be true 難以相信的；不真實的 SYN **incredible**：*I found the whole story bizarre, not to say unbelievable.* 我覺得整個事件經過荒誕不經，更不用說不可信了。 ▸ **un·believ·ably** *adv.*：*unbelievably bad/good* 壞得／好得令人難以置信 ◇ *Unbelievably it actually works.* 難以相信的是，它確實有效。

un·believer /ˌʌnbɪˈliːvə(r)/ *noun* (*formal*) a person who does not believe, especially in God, a religion, etc. 無（宗教）信仰的人；（尤指）不信上帝的人 OPP **believer**

un·believ·ing /ˌʌnbɪˈliːvɪŋ/ *adj.* (*formal*) feeling or showing that you do not believe sb/sth 不相信的；懷疑的：*She stared at us with unbelieving eyes.* 她用疑惑的眼睛看着我們。 ◇ *He gazed at the letter, unbelieving.* 他兩眼盯着信，滿腹狐疑。

un·bend /ˌʌnˈbend/ *verb* (**un·bent**, **un·bent** /ˌʌnˈbent/) **1** [I] to relax and become less strict or formal in your behaviour or attitude （在行為或態度上）放鬆；變得無拘束；隨和 **2** [T, I] **~ (sth)** to make sth that was bent become straight; to become straight 拉直；抻直；變直

un·bend·ing /ˌʌnˈbendɪŋ/ *adj.* (often *disapproving*) unwilling to change your opinions, decisions, etc. 頑固的；固執的；倔強的 SYN **inflexible**

un·biased AW (also **un·biassed**) /ʌnˈbaɪəst/ *adj.* fair and not influenced by your own or sb else's opinions,

U

desires, etc. 公正的；不偏不倚的；無偏見的 SYN **impartial**：*unbiased advice* 客觀的忠告 ◇ *an unbiased judge* 公正的法官 OPP **biased**

un·bid·den /ʌnˈbɪdn/ *adj.* (*literary*) (usually used after the verb 通常置於動詞後) without being asked, invited or expected 未經要求；未被邀請；擅自 SYN **unasked**：*He walked into the room unbidden.* 他逕自走進了屋子。

un·bleached /ʌnˈbliːtʃt/ *adj.* not made whiter by the use of chemicals; not bleached 未漂白的：*unbleached flour* 未經漂白的麪粉

un·blem·ished /ʌnˈblemɪʃt/ *adj.* (*formal*) not spoiled, damaged or marked in any way 完好的；無損的；無污點的：*He had an unblemished reputation.* 他的名聲白璧無瑕。◇ *her pale unblemished skin* 她那白皙光潔的皮膚

un·blink·ing /ʌnˈblɪŋkɪŋ/ *adj.* (*formal*) if sb has an **unblinking stare** or looks with **unblinking eyes**, they look very steadily at sth and do not BLINK 不眨眼的；目不轉睛的 ▸ **un·blink·ing·ly** *adv.*

un·block /ˌʌnˈblɒk; *NAmE* -ˈblɑːk/ *verb* **~ sth** to clean sth, for example a pipe, by removing sth that is blocking it 疏通（管道等）；清除障礙

un·born /ˌʌnˈbɔːn; *NAmE* -ˈbɔːrn/ *adj.* [usually before noun] not yet born 未出世的；未出生的：*her unborn baby* 她未出世的寶寶

un·bound·ed /ʌnˈbaʊndɪd/ *adj.* (*formal*) having, or seeming to have, no limits（似）無限的；無盡的；無窮的 SYN **boundless, infinite**：*her unbounded energy* 她的無限精力

un·bowed /ˌʌnˈbaʊd/ *adj.* (*literary*) not defeated or not ready to accept defeat 不敗的；不屈的；不服輸的：*The losing team left the field* ***bloody but unbowed.*** 那支隊一番苦戰下離開球場，雖敗猶榮。

un·break·able /ʌnˈbreɪkəbl/ *adj.* impossible to break 無法打破的；牢不可破的 SYN **indestructible**：*This new material is virtually unbreakable.* 這種新材料實際上是不碎的。OPP **breakable**

un·bridge·able /ʌnˈbrɪdʒəbl/ *adj.* an **unbridgeable** gap or difference between two people or groups or their opinions is one that cannot be closed or made less wide（分歧、意見等）無法彌合的；無法溝通的

un·bridled /ʌnˈbraɪdld/ *adj.* [usually before noun] (*formal*) not controlled and therefore extreme 無節制的；奔放的；極端的：*unbridled passion* 奔放的激情

un·broken /ʌnˈbrəʊkən; *NAmE* -ˈbroʊ-/ *adj.* **1** not interrupted or disturbed in any way 連續的；不間斷的：*a single unbroken line* 一條連續的線 ◇ *30 years of virtually unbroken peace* 持續將近 30 年的和平 ◇ *my first night of unbroken sleep since the baby was born* 自孩子出世以來我睡的頭一個囫圇覺 **2** (of a record in a sport, etc. 體育運動等的紀錄) that has not been improved on 未改寫的；未被打破的；未被超過的

U

un·buckle /ˌʌnˈbʌkl/ *verb* **~ sth** to undo the BUCKLE of a belt, shoe, etc. 解開，鬆開（皮帶、鞋子等）的扣

un·bur·den /ˌʌnˈbɜːdn; *NAmE* -ˈbɜːrdn/ *verb* **1 ~ yourself/sth (of sth) (to sb)** (*formal*) to talk to sb about your problems or sth you have been worrying about, so that you feel less anxious 傾訴；訴說；訴苦：*She needed to unburden herself to somebody.* 她需要找個人訴訴心裏的苦衷。**2 ~ sb/sth (of sth)** to take sth that causes a lot of work or worry away from sb/sth 給…解除（負擔）；分憂 OPP **burden**

un·but·ton /ˌʌnˈbʌtn/ *verb* **~ sth** to undo the buttons on a piece of clothing 解開鈕扣：*He unbuttoned his shirt.* 他解開襯衣扣子。OPP **button (up)**

un·but·toned /ˌʌnˈbʌtnd/ *adj.* informal and relaxed 非正式的；輕鬆的；無拘束的：*Staff respond well to her unbuttoned style of management.* 職工對她灑脫的管理風格反應很好。

unˈcalled for *adj.* (of behaviour or remarks 行為或言論) not fair or appropriate 不公允的；不適當的；不恰當的 SYN **unnecessary**：*His comments were uncalled for.* 他的評論有失公允。◇ *uncalled-for comments* 不恰當的言論

un·canny /ʌnˈkæni/ *adj.* strange and difficult to explain 異常的；難以解釋的 SYN **weird**：*I had an uncanny feeling I was being watched.* 我有種被人監視的奇怪感覺。◇ *It was uncanny really, almost as if she knew what I was thinking.* 真是不可思議，她好像知道我在想什麼似的。▸ **un·can·nily** /-ɪli/ *adv.*：*He looked uncannily like someone I knew.* 他酷似我認識的一個人。

unˈcared for *adj.* not taken care of 無人照看的 SYN **neglected**：*The garden looked uncared for.* 這花園似乎無人管理。◇ *an uncared-for garden* 一個無人照料的花園

un·car·ing /ʌnˈkeərɪŋ; *NAmE* -ˈker-/ *adj.* (*disapproving*) not sympathetic about the problems or suffering of other people 冷漠的；無同情心的 SYN **callous** OPP **caring**

un·ceas·ing /ʌnˈsiːsɪŋ/ *adj.* (*formal*) continuing all the time 持續不斷的；連綿不絕的 SYN **incessant**：*unceasing efforts* 不懈的努力 ◇ *Planes passed overhead with unceasing regularity.* 每隔一段時間總有飛機從頭頂飛過。▸ **un·ceas·ing·ly** *adv.*：*Snow fell unceasingly.* 飛雪連綿。

un·cen·sored /ʌnˈsensəd; *NAmE* -sərd/ *adj.* (of a report, film/movie, etc. 報告、電影等) not CENSORED (= having had parts removed that are not considered suitable for the public) 未作刪剪的；未經審查的：*an uncensored newspaper article* 一篇未經刪剪的報紙文章

un·cere·mo·ni·ous /ˌʌnˌserəˈməʊniəs; *NAmE* -ˈmoʊ-/ *adj.* (*formal*) done roughly and rudely 粗暴無禮的；粗野的：*He was bundled out of the room with unceremonious haste.* 他被粗暴地轟出屋外。➲ compare CEREMONIOUS

un·cere·mo·ni·ous·ly /ˌʌnˌserəˈməʊniəsli; *NAmE* -ˈmoʊ-/ *adv.* (*formal*) in a rough or rude way, without caring about a person's feelings 粗野地；粗暴無禮地：*They dumped his belongings unceremoniously on the floor.* 他們粗暴地把他的物品摔到地板上。

un·cer·tain 0➜ /ʌnˈsɜːtn; *NAmE* ʌnˈsɜːrtn/ *adj.* **1** 0➜ [not before noun] **~ (about/of sth)** feeling doubt about sth; not sure 無把握；猶豫；拿不準：*They're both uncertain about what to do.* 他們兩人都拿不定主意該怎麼辦。◇ *I'm still uncertain of my feelings for him.* 我仍不能肯定我對他的感情。OPP **certain** **2** 0➜ likely to change, especially in a negative or unpleasant way 多變的；難預料的：*Our future looks uncertain.* 我們似乎前途渺茫。◇ *a man of uncertain temper* 脾氣令人捉摸不透的男人 **3** 0➜ not definite or decided 不確定的；未決定的 SYN **unclear**：*It is uncertain what his role in the company will be.* 他在公司擔當什麼職務尚未決定。**4** not confident 信心不足的；遲疑的 SYN **hesitant**：*The baby took its first uncertain steps.* 寶寶邁出了最初蹣跚的腳步。

IDM **in ˌno unˌcertain ˈterms** clearly and strongly 明確有力地；毫不含糊地：*I told him what I thought of him in no uncertain terms.* 我直言不諱地說出了我對他的看法。

un·cer·tain·ly /ʌnˈsɜːtnli; *NAmE* -ˈsɜːrtn-/ *adv.* without confidence 猶豫地；遲疑地 SYN **hesitantly**：*They smiled uncertainly at one another.* 他們猶豫地相視而笑。

un·cer·tainty /ʌnˈsɜːtnti; *NAmE* -ˈsɜːrtn-/ *noun* (*pl.* **-ies**) **1** [U] the state of being uncertain 猶豫；遲疑；無把握：*There is considerable uncertainty about the company's future.* 這家公司的前景相當渺茫。◇ *He had an air of uncertainty about him.* 他顯出將信將疑的神情。**2** [C] something that you cannot be sure about; a situation that causes you to be or feel uncertain 拿不定的事；令人無把握的局面：*life's uncertainties* 人生的不可知因素 ◇ *the uncertainties of war* 戰爭帶來的不確定性

un·chal·lenge·able /ʌnˈtʃælɪndʒəbl/ *adj.* that cannot be questioned or argued with; that cannot be challenged 不可爭辯的；不容置辯的；不可挑戰的：*unchallengeable evidence* 無可置辯的證據

un·chal·lenged /ʌnˈtʃælɪndʒd/ *adj.* **1** not doubted; accepted without question; not challenged 不被懷疑的；完全接受的；沒有異議的：*She could not allow such a claim to* ***go unchallenged.*** 她不能對這樣的要求聽任不管。**2** (of a ruler or leader, or their position 統治者、領袖或其地位) not opposed by anyone 無人反對的；穩固的：*He is in a position of unchallenged authority.* 他擁有絕對的權威。**3** without being stopped and asked to explain who you are, what you are doing, etc. 無阻擋的；未受盤查的：*I walked into the building unchallenged.* 我暢行無阻地走進大樓。

un·change·able /ʌn'tʃeɪndʒəbl/ *adj.* that cannot be changed 不可改變的：*unchangeable laws* 不變的定律 ➲ compare CHANGEABLE

un·changed /ʌn'tʃeɪndʒd/ *adj.* [not usually before noun] that has stayed the same and not changed 不變；沒有變化：*My opinion remains unchanged.* 我的看法一如既往。

un·chan·ging /ʌn'tʃeɪndʒɪŋ/ *adj.* that always stays the same and does not change 永恆的；不變的：*unchanging truths* 永恆的真理

un·char·ac·ter·is·tic /ˌʌnˌkærəktə'rɪstɪk/ *adj.* **~ (of sb)** not typical of sb; not the way sb usually behaves（指人的行為）非典型的；非通常的；表現奇怪的：*The remark was quite uncharacteristic of her.* 這話很不像是她說的。**OPP** **characteristic** ▸ **un·char·ac·ter·is·tic·al·ly** /-kli/ *adv.*：*The children had been uncharacteristically quiet.* 孩子們顯得異樣的安靜。

un·char·it·able /ʌn'tʃærɪtəbl/ *adj.* unkind and unfair in the way that you judge people 刻薄的；苛刻的；冷酷的：*uncharitable thoughts* 刻薄的想法 **OPP** **charitable** ▸ **un·char·it·ably** /-əbli/ *adv.*

un·chart·ed **AW** /ˌʌn'tʃɑːtɪd; *NAmE* -'tʃɑːrt-/ *adj.* [usually before noun] **1** that has not been visited or investigated before; not familiar 人跡罕至的；無人涉足的；陌生的：*They set off into the country's uncharted interior.* 他們出發前往這個國家人跡罕至的內陸。◇ (*figurative*) *The party is sailing in* ***uncharted waters*** (= a situation it has not been in before). 這個黨面臨一種嶄新的局勢。◇ (*figurative*) *I was moving into* ***uncharted territory*** (= a completely new experience) *with this relationship.* 這個關係讓我開始體驗到全新的事物。**2** not marked on a map 地圖上未繪出（或未標明）的：*The ship hit an uncharted rock.* 船撞在海圖上未標示的岩石上。

un·checked /ˌʌn'tʃekt/ *adj.* if sth harmful is **unchecked**, it is not controlled or stopped from getting worse 不加約束的；不受限制的；放任的：*The fire was allowed to burn unchecked.* 大火肆虐，不受控制。◇ *The rise in violent crime must not* ***go unchecked***. 暴力犯罪的增長必須加以制止。◇ *The plant will soon choke ponds and waterways if* ***left unchecked***. 如不控制這種植物的生長，池塘和水道很快就要被阻塞。

un·chris·tian /ˌʌn'krɪstʃən/ *adj.* not showing the qualities you expect of a Christian; not kind or thinking about other people's feelings 無基督教徒品質的；不慈善的；不為他人着想的 **OPP** **christian**

un·civil /ʌn'sɪvl/ *adj.* (*formal*) not polite 失禮的；粗魯的 **OPP** **civil** ➲ see also INCIVILITY

un·civ·il·ized (*BrE* also **-ised**) /ʌn'sɪvəlaɪzd/ *adj.* (*disapproving*) **1** (of people or their behaviour 人或其行為) not behaving in a way that is acceptable according to social or moral standards 不合社會（或道德）規範的；無教養的 **2** (of people or places 人或地方) not having developed a modern culture and way of life 未開化的；遠離文明的：*I have worked in the wildest and most uncivilized parts of the world.* 我曾在世界上最荒涼、最原始的地區工作過。**OPP** **civilized**

un·claimed /ʌn'kleɪmd/ *adj.* that nobody has claimed as belonging to them or being owed to them 無人認領的；無人索取的

un·clas·si·fied /ʌn'klæsɪfaɪd/ *adj.* **1** (of documents, information, etc. 文件、信息等) not officially secret; available to everyone 非機密的；公開的 **OPP** **classified** **2** (*technical* 術語) that has not been CLASSIFIED as being the member of a particular group 未分類的；無類別的：(*BrE*) *A high proportion of candidates get low or unclassified grades* (= their work is not good enough to receive a grade). 有很大部份的考生得分很低甚或不獲評分。**3** (*BrE*) (of a road 道路) not large or important enough to be given a number（因並非大路而）未編號的

uncle 🔑 /'ʌŋkl/ *noun*
1 🔑 the brother of your mother or father; the husband of your aunt 舅父；叔父；伯父；姑父；姨父：*Uncle Ian* 伊恩叔叔 ◇ *I'm going to visit my uncle.* 我要去看我舅舅。◇ *I've just become an uncle* (= because your brother/sister has had a baby). 我剛當上叔叔（或舅舅）。**2** used by children, with a first name, to address a man who is a close friend of their parents（兒童用語，稱呼父母的同輩朋友）叔叔，伯伯 **IDM** see BOB

un·clean /ˌʌn'kliːn/ *adj.* **1** (*formal*) dirty and therefore likely to cause disease 骯髒的，不潔淨的（因而容易致病）：*unclean water* 不清潔的水 **OPP** **clean** **2** considered to be bad, immoral or not pure in a religious way, and therefore not to be touched, eaten, etc. 邪惡的；不潔的；（宗教上所指）不潔淨的 **SYN** **impure**：*unclean thoughts* 邪念 ◇ *unclean food* 不潔的食物

un·clear /ˌʌn'klɪə(r); *NAmE* -'klɪr/ *adj.* **1** not clear or definite; difficult to understand or be sure about 不清楚的；不確定的；難以掌握的：*His motives are unclear.* 他的用意不明。◇ *It is unclear whether there is any damage.* 有無損壞尚不清楚。◇ *Your diagrams are unclear.* 你的圖表不清楚。**2 ~ (about sth) | ~ (as to sth)** not fully understanding sth 不完全明白；不理解 **SYN** **uncertain**：*I'm unclear about what you want me to do.* 我不太明白你要我做什麼。

ˌUncle 'Sam *noun* (*informal*) a way of referring to the United States of America or the US government (sometimes shown as a tall man with a white beard and a tall hat) 山姆大叔（指美國或美國政府，有時被塑造成留白鬚、戴大禮帽的高個子男人）：*He owed $20 000 in tax to Uncle Sam.* 他欠美國政府 2 萬元稅款。

ˌUncle 'Tom *noun* (*taboo, offensive*) sometimes used in the past to refer to a black man who wants to please or serve white people 湯姆大叔（舊時有時用以指想討好或侍奉白人的黑人男子）**ORIGIN** From a character in the novel *Uncle Tom's Cabin* by Harriet Beecher Stowe. 源自哈麗雅特 • 比徹 • 斯托所著長篇小說《湯姆叔叔的小屋》中的人物。

un·clothed /ˌʌn'kləʊðd; *NAmE* -kloʊðd/ *adj.* (*formal*) not wearing any clothes 赤裸的；裸體的；一絲不掛的 **SYN** **naked** **OPP** **clothed**

un·clut·tered /ˌʌn'klʌtəd; *NAmE* -tərd/ *adj.* (*approving*) not containing too many objects, details or unnecessary items 簡潔的；整潔的；利落的 **SYN** **tidy** **OPP** **cluttered**

un·coil /ˌʌn'kɔɪl/ *verb* [I, T] to become or make sth straight after it has been wound or twisted round in a circle（使盤捲的東西）展開，打開；拉直：*The snake slowly uncoiled.* 蛇慢慢地展開了盤着的身體。◇ **~ sth/itself** *to uncoil a rope* 打開盤捲的繩索

un·col·oured (*especially US* **un·col·ored**) /ˌʌn'kʌləd; *NAmE* -ərd/ *adj.* with no colour; with no colour added 無色的；不加色的

un·combed /ˌʌn'kəʊmd; *NAmE* -'koʊmd/ *adj.* (of hair 頭髮) that has not been brushed or COMBED; very untidy 未梳理的；蓬亂的

un·com·fort·able 🔑 /ʌn'kʌmftəbl; *BrE* also -fət-; *NAmE* also -fərt-/ *adj.*
1 🔑 (of clothes, furniture, etc. 衣服、傢具等) not letting you feel physically comfortable; unpleasant to wear, sit on, etc. 使人不舒服的；令人不舒適的：*uncomfortable shoes* 不舒適的鞋子 ◇ *I couldn't sleep because the bed was so uncomfortable.* 這牀太不舒服了，我睡不着覺。**OPP** **comfortable** **2** 🔑 not feeling physically relaxed, warm, etc. 感到難受的；感覺不舒服（或不暖和等）的：*I was sitting in an extremely uncomfortable position.* 我坐着的姿勢難受極了。◇ *She still finds it uncomfortable to stand without support.* 她仍覺得沒有支撐站着不太舒服。**OPP** **comfortable** **3** 🔑 anxious, embarrassed or afraid and unable to relax; making you feel like this（使）焦慮的；尷尬的；害怕的；不自在的：*He looked distinctly uncomfortable when the subject was mentioned.* 提到這個話題，他顯然局促不安起來。◇ *There was an uncomfortable silence.* 有一種令人不安的寂靜。**OPP** **comfortable** **4** unpleasant or difficult to deal with 棘手的；麻煩的；難處理的：*an uncomfortable fact* 令人頭痛的事實 ◇ *I had the uncomfortable feeling that it was my fault.* 我內心惴惴不安，覺得那是我的過錯。

un·com·fort·ably /ʌnˈkʌmftəbli; BrE also -fət-; NAmE also -fərt-/ *adv.* **1** in a way that makes you feel anxious or embarrassed; in a way that shows you are anxious or embarrassed 令人不安（或尷尬）地；顯得不安（或尷尬）地：*I became uncomfortably aware that no one else was laughing.* 我難堪地意識到別人都沒有笑。◇ *Her comment was uncomfortably close to the truth.* 她的評論逼近真相，令人局促不安。◇ *He shifted uncomfortably in his seat when I mentioned money.* 我提到錢時，他便坐不住了。 **2** in a way that is not physically comfortable 不舒服地；難受地：*I was feeling uncomfortably hot.* 我覺得酷熱難當。◇ *She perched uncomfortably on the edge of the table.* 她將就坐在桌邊上，非常難受。

un·com·mit·ted /ˌʌnkəˈmɪtɪd/ *adj.* **~ (to sb/sth)** not having given or promised support to a particular person, group, belief, action, etc. 未作承諾的；未表態的：*The party needs to canvass the uncommitted voters.* 這個黨需要向未表明態度的選民游説拉票。➲ compare COMMITTED

un·com·mon /ʌnˈkɒmən; NAmE -ˈkɑːm-/ *adj.* **1** not existing in large numbers or in many places 不常有的；罕見的；稀罕的 **SYN** **unusual, rare**：*an uncommon occurrence* 不尋常的事情 ◇ *Side effects from the drug are uncommon.* 這藥很少有副作用。◇ *It is **not uncommon** for college students to live at home.* 大學生住在家裏並不少見。◇ *Red squirrels are uncommon in England.* 紅松鼠在英格蘭很少見。 **OPP** **common 2** (*formal* or *literary*) unusually large in degree or amount; great 程度深的；特別大的 **SYN** **remarkable**：*She showed uncommon pleasure at his arrival.* 他的到來令她異常歡喜。

un·com·mon·ly /ʌnˈkɒmənli; NAmE -ˈkɑːm-/ *adv.* (*formal*) **1** to an unusual degree; extremely 極其；極端地；非凡地：*an uncommonly gifted child* 一個天賦異稟的兒童 **2** not often; not usually 不經常；罕見；不平常：*Not uncommonly, there is a great deal of rain in August.* 八月份降雨量大並非異常。

un·com·mu·ni·ca·tive **AW** /ˌʌnkəˈmjuːnɪkətɪv/ *adj.* (*disapproving*) (of a person 人) not willing to talk to other people or give opinions 不愛説話的；寡言少語的；緘默的 **SYN** **taciturn** **OPP** **communicative**

un·com·peti·tive /ˌʌnkəmˈpetətɪv/ *adj.* (*business* 商) not cheaper or better than others and therefore not able to compete equally 無競爭力的；競爭力弱的：*an uncompetitive industry* 無競爭力的行業 ◇ *uncompetitive prices* 缺乏競爭力的價格 **OPP** **competitive**

un·com·plain·ing /ˌʌnkəmˈpleɪnɪŋ/ *adj.* (*approving*) not saying that you are unhappy about a difficult or unpleasant situation; not saying that you are in pain 任勞任怨的；不抱怨的 ► **un·com·plain·ing·ly** *adv.*

un·com·pleted /ˌʌnkəmˈpliːtɪd/ *adj.* that has not been finished 未完成的；未竟的；未竣工的：*an uncompleted project* 未完成的項目

U

un·com·pli·cated /ʌnˈkɒmplɪkeɪtɪd; NAmE -ˈkɑːm-/ *adj.* simple; without any difficulty or confusion 簡單的；率真的；容易的；不混亂的 **SYN** **straightforward**：*an easygoing, uncomplicated young man* 一個隨和、率直的男青年 ◇ *Why can't I have an uncomplicated life?* 我為什麼不能過一種簡樸的生活？ **OPP** **complicated**

un·com·pli·men·tary /ˌʌnˌkɒmplɪˈmentri; NAmE -ˌkɑːm-/ *adj.* rude or insulting 無禮的；貶抑的；污辱性的：*uncomplimentary remarks* 不客氣的話 ➲ compare COMPLIMENTARY (2)

un·com·pre·hend·ing /ˌʌnˌkɒmprɪˈhendɪŋ; NAmE -ˌkɑːm-/ *adj.* (*formal*) (of a person 人) not understanding a situation or what is happening 不理解的；茫然的；不領會的 ► **un·com·pre·hend·ing·ly** *adv.*：*She looked at him uncomprehendingly.* 她一臉茫然地注視着他。

un·com·prom·is·ing /ʌnˈkɒmprəmaɪzɪŋ; NAmE -ˈkɑːm-/ *adj.* unwilling to change your opinions or behaviour 不讓步的；不妥協的；強硬的：*an uncompromising attitude* 強硬的態度 ◇ *He has a reputation for being tough and uncompromising.* 他的嚴厲和強硬態度是出了名的。► **un·com·prom·is·ing·ly** *adv.*

un·con·cealed /ˌʌnkənˈsiːld/ *adj.* [usually before noun] (of an emotion, etc. 感情等) that you do not try to hide 不掩飾的；不隱藏的；明顯的 **SYN** **obvious**：*unconcealed curiosity* 表露無遺的好奇心

un·con·cern /ˌʌnkənˈsɜːn; NAmE -ˈsɜːrn/ *noun* [U] (*formal*) a lack of care, interest or worry about sth that other people would care about 冷漠；不關心；無興趣 **SYN** **indifference**：*She received the news with apparent unconcern.* 她接到這消息時顯然無動於衷。➲ compare CONCERN *n.* (1)

un·con·cerned /ˌʌnkənˈsɜːnd; NAmE -ˈsɜːrnd/ *adj.* **1 ~ (about/by sth)** not worried or anxious about sth because you feel it does not affect you or is not important 冷淡的；漠視的；漫不經心的：*He drove on, apparently unconcerned about the noise the engine was making.* 他繼續駕車前進，對發動機發出的噪聲顯然毫不在意。 **2 ~ (with sb/sth)** not interested in sth 不關心的；無興趣的：*Young people are often unconcerned with political issues.* 青年人對政治問題往往漠不關心。 **OPP** **concerned** ► **un·con·cern·ed·ly** /ˌʌnkənˈsɜːnɪdli/ *adv.*

un·con·di·tion·al /ˌʌnkənˈdɪʃənl/ *adj.* without any conditions or limits 無條件的；無限制的；絕對的：*the **unconditional surrender** of military forces* 軍隊的無條件投降 ◇ *She gave her children **unconditional love**.* 她將愛毫無保留地給了她的孩子。 **OPP** **conditional** ► **un·con·di·tion·al·ly** /-ʃənəli/ *adv.*

un·con·di·tioned /ˌʌnkənˈdɪʃnd/ *adj.* (*psychology* 心) (of behaviour 行為) not trained or influenced by experience; natural 非培養的；本性的；先天的；無條件的：*an unconditioned response* 無條件反射

un·con·fined **AW** /ˌʌnkənˈfaɪnd/ *adj.* (*formal*) not limited in space, range or amount 不受限制的；無限的：*The animals have unconfined access to pasture.* 這些動物是散養的。◇ *When the news came through joy was unconfined.* 聽到消息時無比喜悦。

un·con·firmed /ˌʌnkənˈfɜːmd; NAmE -ˈfɜːrmd/ *adj.* that has not yet been proved to be true or confirmed 未經證實的；未被認可的；未確認的：*unconfirmed rumours* 未證實的傳言 ◇ *Unconfirmed reports said that at least six people had been killed.* 未經證實的報道稱至少有六人喪生。

un·con·gen·ial /ˌʌnkənˈdʒiːniəl/ *adj.* (*formal*) **1** (of a person 人) not pleasant or friendly; not like yourself 不友善的；性情不相投的：*uncongenial company* 脾氣不相投的同伴 **2 ~ (to sb)** (of a place, job, etc. 地方、工作等) not pleasant; not making you feel relaxed; not suitable for your personality 不愉快的；令人緊張的；不適宜的：*an uncongenial atmosphere* 不和諧的氣氛 **3 ~ (to sth)** not suitable for sth; not encouraging sth 不適合的；不利的：*The religious climate at the time was uncongenial to new ideas.* 當時的宗教氣候容不得新思想。 **OPP** **congenial**

un·con·nect·ed /ˌʌnkəˈnektɪd/ *adj.* not related or connected in any way 不相關的；無聯繫的：*The two crimes are apparently unconnected.* 這兩起犯罪顯然沒有關聯。◇ **~ with/to sth** *My resignation was totally unconnected with recent events.* 我的辭職與最近的事件毫不相干。

un·con·quer·able /ʌnˈkɒŋkərəbl; NAmE -ˈkɑːŋ-/ *adj.* too strong to be defeated or changed 不可戰勝的；堅不可摧的；難以改變的 **SYN** **invincible**

un·con·scion·able /ʌnˈkɒnʃənəbl; NAmE -ˈkɑːn-/ *adj.* [usually before noun] (*formal*) **1** (of an action, etc. 行動等) so bad, immoral, etc. that it should make you feel ashamed 違背良心的 **2** (often *humorous*) too great, large, long, etc. 過分的；過於大（或多、長等）的 **SYN** **excessive**

un·con·scious 0→ /ʌnˈkɒnʃəs; NAmE -ˈkɑːn-/ *adj.*, *noun*

■ ***adj.*** **1** 0→ in a state like sleep because of an injury or illness, and not able to use your senses 無知覺的；昏迷的；不省人事的：*She was **knocked unconscious**.* 她被打昏了。◇ *They found him lying unconscious on the floor.* 他們發現他暈倒在地板上。 **2** 0→ (of feelings, thoughts, etc. 感情、思想等) existing or happening without you realizing or being aware; not deliberate or controlled

無意識的；自然流露的：*unconscious desires* 自然流露的慾望 ◇ *The brochure is full of unconscious humour.* 這本小冊子妙趣橫生。➲ compare SUBCONSCIOUS *adj.* **3** 🔑 **~ of sb/sth** not aware of sb/sth; not noticing sth; not conscious 未察覺；未意識到；未注意 SYN **oblivious to**：*She is unconscious of the effect she has on people.* 她沒有察覺自己對大眾的影響。◇ *He was quite unconscious of the danger.* 他絲毫沒有意識到危險。OPP **conscious**

■ *noun* **the unconscious** [sing.] (*psychology* 心) the part of a person's mind with thoughts, feelings, etc. that they are not aware of and cannot control but which can sometimes be understood by studying their behaviour or dreams 無意識（不察覺的心理活動）➲ compare SUBCONSCIOUS

un·con·scious·ly /ʌn'kɒnʃəsli; *NAmE* -'kɑːn-/ *adv.* without being aware 無意地；不知不覺地：*Perhaps, unconsciously, I've done something to offend her.* 我也許無意中做了什麼得罪她的事。OPP **consciously**

un·con·scious·ness /ʌn'kɒnʃəsnəs; *NAmE* -'kɑːn-/ *noun* [U] a state like sleep caused by injury or illness, when you are unable to use your senses 昏迷；無知覺狀態：*He had lapsed into unconsciousness.* 他陷入了昏迷狀態。

un·con·sid·ered /ˌʌnkən'sɪdəd; *NAmE* -ərd/ *adj.* (*formal*) not thought about, or not thought about with enough care 未經（或欠）考慮的；未經深思熟慮的：*I came to regret my unconsidered remarks.* 我對我那些考慮不周的言辭開始感到後悔。

un·con·sol·able /ˌʌnkən'səʊləbl; *NAmE* -'soʊl-/ *adj.* = INCONSOLABLE ▸ **un·con·sol·ably** /-əbli/ *adv.* = INCONSOLABLY

un·con·sti·tu·tion·al AW /ˌʌnˌkɒnstɪ'tjuːʃənl; *NAmE* -kɑːnstə'tuː-/ *adj.* not allowed by the CONSTITUTION of a country, a political system or an organization 違背憲法的；違反憲章（或章程）的 OPP **constitutional** ▸ **un·con·sti·tu·tion·al·ly** /-ʃənəli/ *adv.*

un·con·strained AW /ˌʌnkən'streɪnd/ *adj.* not restricted or limited 不受約束的；自由的：*unconstrained growth* 自然生長 ➲ see also CONSTRAIN (2)

un·con·tam·in·ated /ˌʌnkən'tæmɪneɪtɪd/ *adj.* not harmed or spoilt by sth (for example, dangerous substances) 未被損害的；未受污染的：*uncontaminated water* 未被污染的水 OPP **contaminated**

un·con·ten·tious /ˌʌnkən'tenʃəs/ *adj.* (*formal*) not likely to cause disagreement between people 沒有（或不容易）引起爭議的：*The proposal is relatively uncontentious.* 這個建議並沒有什麼重大的爭議。OPP **contentious**

un·con·test·ed /ˌʌnkən'testɪd/ *adj.* without any opposition or argument 無爭議的；無人反對的：*an uncontested election/divorce* 無爭議的選舉／離婚 ◇ *These claims have not* **gone uncontested**. 這些說法並非無人提出異議。

un·con·trol·lable /ˌʌnkən'trəʊləbl; *NAmE* -'troʊ-/ *adj.* that you cannot control or prevent 無法控制的；難以防止的；禁不住的：*an uncontrollable temper* 控制不住的脾氣 ◇ *uncontrollable bleeding* 止不住的流血 ◇ *I had an uncontrollable urge to laugh.* 我忍不住想笑。◇ *The ball was uncontrollable.* 球控制不住了。◇ *He's an uncontrollable child* (= he behaves very badly and cannot be controlled). 他是個難以管教的孩子。▸ **un·con·trol·lably** /-əbli/ *adv.*：*She began shaking uncontrollably.* 她不由自主地哆嗦起來。

un·con·trolled 🔑 /ˌʌnkən'trəʊld; *NAmE* -'troʊld/ *adj.* **1** 🔑 (of emotions, behaviour, etc. 感情、行為等) that sb cannot control or stop 抑制不住的；無法制止的：*uncontrolled anger* 克制不住的憤怒 ◇ *The thoughts rushed into my mind uncontrolled.* 各種想法如潮水般湧上我的心頭。**2** 🔑 that is not limited or managed by law or rules 不受法律（或規則）制約的；無序的：*the uncontrolled growth of cities* 城市的無規劃發展 ◇ *uncontrolled dumping of toxic wastes* 有毒廢棄物的胡亂棄置 ➲ compare CONTROLLED (2)

un·con·tro·ver·sial AW /ˌʌnˌkɒntrə'vɜːʃl; *NAmE* ˌʌnkɑːntrə'vɜːrʃl/ *adj.* not causing, or not likely to cause, any disagreement 無爭議的；不會引起不和的：*an uncontroversial opinion* 無爭議的意見 ◇ *He chose an uncontroversial topic for his speech.* 他為自己的演講選擇了一個不會引起爭議的話題。OPP **controversial** ➲ compare NON-CONTROVERSIAL

un·con·ven·tion·al AW /ˌʌnkən'venʃənl/ *adj.* (often *approving*) not following what is done or considered normal or acceptable by most people; different and interesting 不因循守舊的；不因襲的；新奇的 SYN **unorthodox**：*an unconventional approach to the problem* 解決這個問題的非常規方法 ◇ *unconventional views* 新奇的觀點 OPP **conventional** ▸ **un·con·ven·tion·al·ity** /ˌʌnkənvenʃə'næləti/ *noun* [U] **un·con·ven·tion·al·ly** /-ʃənəli/ *adv.*

un·con·vinced AW /ˌʌnkən'vɪnst/ *adj.* not believing or not certain about sth despite what you have been told 不信服的；未被說服的：**~ (of sth)** *I* **remain unconvinced** *of the need for change.* 我仍懷疑改革的必要性。◇ **~ (by sth)** *She seemed unconvinced by their promises.* 她似乎不相信他們的許諾。◇ **~ (that …)** *The jury were unconvinced that he was innocent.* 陪審團不相信他是無辜的。OPP **convinced**

un·con·vin·cing /ˌʌnkən'vɪnsɪŋ/ *adj.* not seeming true or real; not making you believe that sth is true 似乎不真實的；不令人信服的；難以相信的：*I find the characters in the book very unconvincing.* 我覺得書中的人物很不真實。◇ *She managed a weak, unconvincing smile.* 她勉強擠出一絲笑意。OPP **convincing** ▸ **un·con·vin·cing·ly** *adv.*

un·cooked /ˌʌn'kʊkt/ *adj.* not cooked 未烹煮的；生的 SYN **raw**：*Eat plenty of uncooked fruit and vegetables.* 要多吃新鮮水果和生蔬菜。

un·cool /ˌʌn'kuːl/ *adj.* (*informal*) not considered acceptable by fashionable young people 不時髦的；不帥的；不瀟灑的；不"酷"的 OPP **cool**

un·co·opera·tive /ˌʌnkəʊ'ɒpərətɪv; *NAmE* -koʊ'ɑːp-/ *adj.* not willing to be helpful to other people or do what they ask 不願合作的；不願配合的 SYN **unhelpful** OPP **cooperative**

un·co·or·din·ated /ˌʌnkəʊ'ɔːdɪneɪtɪd; *NAmE* -koʊ'ɔːrd-/ *adj.* **1** if a person is **uncoordinated**, they are not able to control their movements well, and are therefore not very skilful at some sports and physical activities 動作不協調的；不靈便的；手腳笨拙的 **2** (of movements or parts of the body 動作或身體部位) not controlled; not moving smoothly or together 不協調的；不靈活的 **3** (of plans, projects, etc. 計劃、項目等) not well organized; with no thought for how the different parts work together 不縝密的；無通盤安排的；缺乏全面考慮的

un·cork /ˌʌn'kɔːk; *NAmE* -'kɔːrk/ *verb* **~ sth** to open a bottle by removing the CORK from the top 打開瓶塞 OPP **cork**

un·cor·rob·or·ated /ˌʌnkə'rɒbəreɪtɪd; *NAmE* -'rɑːb-/ *adj.* (of a statement or claim 聲明或要求) not supported by any other evidence; not having been CORROBORATED 無確證的；未經證實的 SYN **unconfirmed**

un·count·able /ʌn'kaʊntəbl/ (also **ˌnon-'count**) *adj.* (*grammar* 語法) a noun that is **uncountable** cannot be made plural or used with *a* or *an*, for example *water*, *bread* and *information*（名詞）不可數的 OPP **countable** ➲ compare COUNTLESS

ˌuncount noun *noun* (*grammar* 語法) an uncountable noun 不可數名詞 OPP **count noun**

un·couple /ˌʌn'kʌpl/ *verb* **~ sth (from sth)** to remove the connection between two vehicles, two parts of a train, etc. 使（車輛、車廂等）分離；分開（連在一起的兩個）

un·couth /ʌn'kuːθ/ *adj.* (of a person or their behaviour 人或其行為) rude or socially unacceptable 粗魯的；無禮的；無教養的 SYN **coarse**：*uncouth laughter* 粗野的笑聲 ◇ *an uncouth young man* 一個無教養的年輕人

un·cover /ʌn'kʌvə(r)/ *verb* **1 ~ sth** to remove sth that is covering sth 揭開蓋子：*Uncover the pan and let the soup simmer.* 揭開鍋蓋，讓湯再慢火煨一下。**2 ~ sth** to discover sth that was previously hidden or secret 發現；

揭露；揭發： *Police have uncovered a plot to kidnap the President's son.* 警方發現了一起綁架總統之子的陰謀。

un·covered /ʌnˈkʌvəd; *NAmE* -ərd/ *adj.* not covered by anything 裸露的；暴露的；無覆蓋的： *His head was uncovered.* 他光着頭。

un·crit·ic·al /ʌnˈkrɪtɪkl/ *adj.* (usually *disapproving*) not willing to criticize sb/sth or to judge whether sb/sth is right or wrong 不願批評的；不置可否的；不得罪人的： *Her uncritical acceptance of everything I said began to irritate me.* 我說什麼她都不論對錯一概接受，這倒惹我不耐煩起來。 OPP **critical** ▸ **un·crit·ic·al·ly** /-ɪkli/ *adv.*

un·crowd·ed /ʌnˈkraʊdɪd/ *adj.* not full of people 不擁擠的；人少的： *The beach was pleasantly uncrowded.* 海灘上人不多，很是愜意。 OPP **crowded**

un·crowned /ˌʌnˈkraʊnd/ *adj.* (of a king or queen 國君) not yet CROWNED 尚未加冕的

IDM **the ˌuncrowned ˈking/ˈqueen (of sth)** the person considered to be the best, most famous or successful in a particular place or area of activity 無冕之王（某地區或領域中最傑出的人）

unc·tion /ˈʌŋkʃn/ *noun* [U] **1** the act of pouring oil on sb's head or another part of their body as part of an important religious ceremony（宗教上的）傅油禮 ➲ see also EXTREME UNCTION **2** (*formal, disapproving*) behaviour or speech that is not sincere and that expresses too much praise or admiration of sb 虛情假意的行為（或講話）；奉承；甜言蜜語

unc·tu·ous /ˈʌŋktjuəs; *NAmE* -tʃuəs/ *adj.* (*formal, disapproving*) friendly or giving praise in a way that is not sincere and which is therefore unpleasant 諂媚的；油滑的；拍馬奉迎的 ▸ **unc·tu·ous·ly** *adv.*

un·culti·vated /ʌnˈkʌltɪveɪtɪd/ *adj.* (of land 土地) not used for growing crops 未經耕作的；未開墾的 OPP **cultivated**

un·cul·tured AW /ʌnˈkʌltʃəd; *NAmE* -tʃərd/ *adj.* (of people 人) not well educated; not able to understand or enjoy art, literature, etc. 缺乏教養的；不文雅的；粗俗的 OPP **cultured**

un·curl /ˌʌnˈkɜːl; *NAmE* -ˈkɜːrl/ *verb* [I, T] to become straight, or to make sth become straight, after being in a curled position（使由盤捲姿勢）伸直；抻直： *The snake slowly uncurled.* 那條蛇慢慢地伸開了蜷縮的身子。◇ **~ sth/itself** *The cat uncurled itself and jumped off the wall.* 那貓伸直了腰跳下牆頭。 OPP **curl up**

uncut /ˌʌnˈkʌt/ *adj.* **1** left to grow; not cut short 未割的；未剪的： *The uncut grass came up to her waist.* 未割的草齊了她的腰。 **2** (of a book, film/movie, etc. 書籍、電影等) left in its complete form; without any parts removed; not CENSORED 未刪節的；未刪剪的；未審查的： *the original uncut version* 未刪節的原版 **3** (of a PRECIOUS STONE 寶石) not shaped by cutting 未雕琢的；未加工的： *uncut diamonds* 未雕琢的鑽石 **4** not cut into separate pieces 未切開的；完整的： *an uncut loaf of bread* 一整條未切的麵包

un·dam·aged /ʌnˈdæmɪdʒd/ *adj.* not damaged or spoilt 未損壞的；未毀壞的： *There was a slight collision but my car was undamaged.* 雖有輕微碰撞，但我的汽車沒有損壞。◇ *He emerged from the court case with his reputation undamaged.* 他挺過了官司，名聲沒有受損。

un·dated /ˌʌnˈdeɪtɪd/ *adj.* **1** without a date written or printed on it 未註日期的： *an undated letter* 一封沒寫日期的信 **2** of which the date is not known 日期不明的；時間不詳的： *undated archaeological remains* 時間未確定的考古遺跡 ➲ compare DATED

un·daunt·ed /ʌnˈdɔːntɪd/ *adj.* [not usually before noun] (*formal*) still enthusiastic and determined, despite difficulties or disappointment 頑強；百折不撓；堅強不屈 SYN **undeterred**： *He seemed undaunted by all the opposition to his idea.* 儘管他的思想屢遭非難，他似乎仍然百折不撓。

un·decided /ˌʌndɪˈsaɪdɪd/ *adj.* [not usually before noun] **1** not having made a decision about sb/sth 未拿定主意；猶豫不決： **~ (about sb/sth)** *I'm still undecided (about) who to vote for.* 我還拿不定主意投誰的票。◇ **~ (as to sth)** *He was undecided as to what to do next.* 他對下一步要做什麼猶豫不決。 **2** not having been decided 尚未被確定；懸而未決： *The venue for the World Cup remains undecided.* 世界杯的舉辦地點尚未確定。 ➲ compare DECIDED (2)

un·declared /ˌʌndɪˈkleəd; *NAmE* -ˈklerd/ *adj.* not admitted to; not stated in an open way; not having been declared 未承認的；未聲明的；未申報的： *No income should remain undeclared.* 一切收入均應申報。◇ *Undeclared goods* (= that the customs are not told about) *may be confiscated.* 未報關的物品可能被沒收。

un·defeat·ed /ˌʌndɪˈfiːtɪd/ *adj.* (especially in sport 尤用於體育運動) not having lost or been defeated 不敗的；未嘗敗績的： *They are undefeated in 13 games.* 他們 13 場比賽未被打敗過。◇ *the undefeated world champion* 全勝的世界冠軍

un·defend·ed /ˌʌndɪˈfendɪd/ *adj.* **1** not protected or guarded 不設防的；不加防禦的 SYN **unprotected**： *undefended borders* 不設防邊界 **2** if a case in court is **undefended**, no defence is made against it 無抗辯的；不作辯護的

un·defined AW /ˌʌndɪˈfaɪnd/ *adj.* not made clear or definite 未闡明的；未限定的： *The money was lent for an undefined period of time.* 這筆錢無限期借出。

un·de·lete /ˌʌndɪˈliːt/ *verb* [T, I] **~ (sth)** (*computing* 計) to cancel an action of DELETING a document, a file, text, etc. on a computer, so that it appears again 取消刪除；恢復（已刪除的文件等）

un·demand·ing /ˌʌndɪˈmɑːndɪŋ/ *adj.* **1** not needing a lot of effort or thought 不費力的；不費神的；輕鬆容易的： *an undemanding job* 輕鬆的工作 **2** (of a person 人) not asking for a lot of attention or action from other people 不強求的；不要求照顧的；隨和的 OPP **demanding**

un·demo·crat·ic /ˌʌndeməˈkrætɪk/ *adj.* against or not acting according to the principles of DEMOCRACY 不民主的；專横的；霸道的： *undemocratic decisions* 專制的決定 ◇ *an undemocratic regime* 專制政權 OPP **democratic** ▸ **un·demo·crat·ic·al·ly** /-kli/ *adv.*： *an undemocratically elected government* 非民選政府 ◇ *He was accused of acting undemocratically.* 他被指責作風專制。

un·demon·stra·tive /ˌʌndɪˈmɒnstrətɪv; *NAmE* -ˈmɑːn-/ *adj.* not showing feelings openly, especially feelings of affection 喜怒不形於色的；不流露感情的 OPP **demonstrative**

un·deni·able AW /ˌʌndɪˈnaɪəbl/ *adj.* true or certain; that cannot be denied 不可否認的；確鑿的 SYN **indisputable**： *He had undeniable charm.* 他具有不可否認的魅力。◇ *It is an undeniable fact that crime is increasing.* 犯罪在增長是無可爭辯的事實。 OPP **deniable** ▸ **undeni·ably** /-əbli/ *adv.*： *undeniably impressive* 公認地感人

under /ˈʌndə(r)/ *prep., adv., adj.*

■ *prep.* **1** in, to or through a position that is below sth 在（或到、通過）…下面： *Have you looked under the bed?* 你看了牀底下沒有？◇ *She placed the ladder under* (= just lower than) *the window.* 她把梯子立在窗戶下面。◇ *The dog squeezed under the gate and ran into the road.* 狗從門底下鑽出去，跑到大路上去了。 **2** below the surface of sth; covered by sth 在…表面下；由…覆蓋着： *The boat lay under several feet of water.* 那條船沉在水下好幾英尺處。 **3** less than; younger than 少於；小於；不足；比…年輕： *an annual income of under £10 000* 不到 1 萬英鎊的年收入 ◇ *It took us under an hour.* 這事花了我們不到一小時。◇ *Nobody under 18 is allowed to buy alcohol.* 未滿 18 歲者不得買酒。 **4** used to say who or what controls, governs or manages sb/sth 由…控制（或管理、經營）： *The country is now under martial law.* 這個國家目前在戒嚴中。◇ *The coinage was reformed under Elizabeth I* (= when she was queen). 英國幣制在伊麗莎白一世時代作了改革。◇ *She has a staff of 19 working under her.* 她手下有 19 個職員工作。◇ *Under its new conductor, the orchestra has established an international reputation.* 在新指揮的領導下，這個樂團建立了國際聲譽。 **5** according to an agreement, a law or a system 根據，按照（協議、法律或制度）： *Six suspects are being held under the Prevention of Terrorism Act.*

U

根據《防止恐怖法》，六個嫌疑人被拘押。◇ *Under the terms of the lease you had no right to sublet the property.* 按租約條款的規定，你無權轉租這房產。◇ *Is the television still under guarantee?* 這台電視機還在保修期內嗎？ **6** 🔑 experiencing a particular process 在…過程中：*The hotel is still under construction.* 旅館還在興建中。◇ *The matter is under investigation.* 此事正在調查中。 **7** 🔑 affected by sth 由…造成；受…影響：*The wall collapsed under the strain.* 牆壁因承受不了重壓而坍塌了。◇ *I've been feeling under stress lately.* 我最近感到壓力很大。◇ *I'm under no illusions about what hard work this will be.* 對於這項工作的辛苦，我從不存錯誤的幻想。◇ *You'll be under anaesthetic, so you won't feel a thing.* 你將被麻醉，所以什麼也感覺不到。 **8** using a particular name 用，以（某一名字）：*She also writes under the pseudonym of Barbara Vine.* 她也用芭芭拉•瓦因的化名從事寫作。 **9** found in a particular part of a book, list, etc. 在…項下；在（書等中的）某部份：*If it's not under 'sports', try looking under 'games'.* 如果在"體育運動"項下查不到，就試試"遊戲"項吧。

■ **adv.** **1** 🔑 below sth 在下面：*He pulled up the covers and crawled under.* 他揭開被子鑽到裏面。 **2** 🔑 below the surface of water 在水下：*She took a deep breath and stayed under for more than a minute.* 她深吸了一口氣，然後潛水一分多鐘。◇ *The boat was going under fast.* 小船正迅速下沉。 **3** 🔑 less; younger 少於；小於；較年輕：*prices of ten dollars and under* 十元及以下的價格 ◇ *children aged 12 and under* * 12 歲及以下的兒童 **4** in or into an unconscious state 在昏迷中；陷入昏迷狀態：*He felt himself going under.* 他覺得自己將要昏厥。

■ **adj.** [only before noun] lower; underneath 較低的；下面的：*the under layer* 下面的一層 ◇ *the under surface of a leaf* 葉子的背面

under- /ˈʌndə(r)/ *prefix* **1** (in nouns and adjectives 構成名詞和形容詞) below; beneath 在下面；在…之下：*undergrowth* 灌木叢 ◇ *undercover* 暗中的 **2** (in nouns 構成名詞) lower in age or rank（年齡）較小；（級別）較低：*the under-fives* 五歲以下的兒童 ◇ *an undergraduate* 大學生 **3** (in adjectives and verbs 構成形容詞和動詞) not enough 不足；未：*underripe* 未成熟的 ◇ *undercooked* 未煮熟的

under·achieve /ˌʌndərəˈtʃiːv/ *verb* [I] to do less well than you could do, especially in school work（尤指學習上）未發揮水平，未展現實力 ▸ **under·achieve·ment** *noun* [U] **under·achiever** *noun*

under·age /ˈʌndəreɪdʒ/ *adj.* [only before noun] done by people who are too young by law 未達到法定年齡的人所做的；未成年人的：*underage drinking* 未成年飲酒 ➲ see also AGE

under·arm /ˈʌndərɑːm; *NAmE* -ɑːrm/ *adj., adv.*

■ **adj.** **1** [only before noun] connected with a person's ARMPIT 腋窩的；腋下的：***underarm hair/deodorant/sweating*** 腋毛；腋下除臭劑；腋下出汗 **2** an **underarm** throw of a ball is done with the hand kept below the level of the shoulder 下手（或低手）投球的 ➲ compare OVERARM

■ **adv.** if you throw, etc. **underarm**, you throw keeping your hand below the level of your shoulder 下手地，低手地（投球等）➲ compare OVERARM

under·belly /ˈʌndəbeli; *NAmE* -dərb-/ *noun* [sing.] **1** the weakest part of sth that is most easily attacked 脆弱點；薄弱環節：*The trade deficit remains the **soft underbelly** of the US economy.* 貿易赤字仍是美國經濟的軟肋。 **2** the underneath part of an animal（動物的）下腹部，腩：(*figurative*) *He became familiar with the dark underbelly of life in the city* (= the parts that are usually hidden). 他逐漸熟悉都市生活的陰暗面。

under·bid /ˌʌndəˈbɪd; *NAmE* -dərˈb-/ *verb* (**under·bid·ding**, **under·bid**, **under·bid**) **~ sb/sth** to make a lower bid than sb else, for example when trying to win a contract 投標出價低於（競爭對手）

under·brush /ˈʌndəbrʌʃ; *NAmE* -dərb-/ (*NAmE*) (*BrE* **under·growth**) *noun* [U] a mass of bushes and plants that grow close together under trees in woods and forests（林木下的）下層灌木叢

under·car·riage /ˈʌndəkærɪdʒ; *NAmE* -dərk-/ (also **ˈlanding gear**) *noun* the part of an aircraft, including the wheels, that supports it when it is landing and taking off（飛行器的）起落架 ➲ VISUAL VOCAB page V53

under·charge /ˌʌndəˈtʃɑːdʒ; *NAmE* ˌʌndərˈtʃɑːrdʒ/ *verb* [I, T] **~ (sb) (for sth)** to charge too little for sth, usually by mistake（因疏忽）少收…的款項 OPP **overcharge**

under·class /ˈʌndəklɑːs; *NAmE* ˈʌndərklæs/ *noun* [sing.] a social class that is very poor and has no status 社會底層；貧困階層：*The long-term unemployed are becoming a new underclass.* 長期失業的人正形成新的貧困階層。

under·class·man /ˌʌndəˈklɑːsmən; *NAmE* -dərˈklæs-/, **under·class·woman** /ˌʌndəˈklɑːswʊmən; *NAmE* -dərˈklæs-/ *noun* (*pl.* **-men** /-mən/, **-women** /-wɪmɪn/) (in the US) a student in the first or second year of HIGH SCHOOL or college 低年級學生（美國中學或大學一、二年級的學生）➲ compare UPPERCLASSMAN

under·clothes /ˈʌndəkləʊðz; *NAmE* ˈʌndərkloʊðz/ *noun* [pl.] (also **under·cloth·ing** /-kləʊðɪŋ; *NAmE* -kloʊ-/ [U]) (*formal*) = UNDERWEAR

under·coat /ˈʌndəkəʊt; *NAmE* ˈʌndərkoʊt/ *noun* [C, U] a layer of paint under the final layer; the paint used for making this 底塗層；內塗層；底層塗料 ➲ compare TOPCOAT (1)

under·cook /ˌʌndəˈkʊk; *NAmE* -dərˈk-/ *verb* [usually passive] **~ sth** to not cook sth for long enough, with the result that it is not ready to eat 未煮透

under·cover /ˌʌndəˈkʌvə(r); *NAmE* -dərˈk-/ *adj.* [usually before noun] working or done secretly in order to find out information for the police, a government, etc. 秘密工作的；暗中做的；私下進行的：*an **undercover agent*** 密探 ◇ *an **undercover operation/investigation*** 秘密行動／調查 ▸ **under·cover** *adv.*：*The illegal payments were discovered by a journalist **working undercover**.* 這些非法付款是一位暗中查訪的新聞記者發現的。

under·cur·rent /ˈʌndəkʌrənt; *NAmE* -dərkɜːr-/ *noun* **~ (of sth)** a feeling, especially a negative one, that is hidden but whose effects are felt 潛在的情緒（尤指負面的）SYN **undertone**：*I detect an undercurrent of resentment towards the new proposals.* 我察覺到對新提案有一股潛在的不滿情緒。

under·cut *verb, noun*

■ **verb** /ˌʌndəˈkʌt; *NAmE* ˌʌndərˈkʌt/ (**under·cut·ting**, **under·cut**, **under·cut**) **1 ~ sb/sth** to sell goods or services at a lower price than your COMPETITORS 削價競爭；以低於（競爭對手）的價格做生意：*to undercut sb's prices* 以低於對手的價格求售 ◇ *We were able to undercut our European rivals by 5%.* 我們能以低於我們的歐洲對手 5% 的價格出售。 **2 ~ sb/sth** to make sb/sth weaker or less likely to be effective 削弱；使降低效力 SYN **undermine**：*Some members of the board were trying to undercut the chairman's authority.* 委員會的某些成員試圖削弱主席的權力。

■ **noun** /ˈʌndəkʌt; *NAmE* ˈʌndərkʌt/ a way of cutting sb's hair in which the hair is left quite long on top but the hair on the lower part of the head is cut much shorter 大蓋兒頭髮型；帽盔式髮型；華蓋式髮型

under·devel·oped /ˌʌndədɪˈveləpt; *NAmE* -dərdɪ-/ *adj.* (of a country, society, etc. 國家、社會等) having few industries and a low standard of living 工業不發達的；生活水平低的；低度開發的 ➲ compare DEVELOPED (1), DEVELOPING, UNDEVELOPED (2) HELP 'A **developing** country' is now the usual expression. 現在常用 developing country（發展中國家）。▸ **under·devel·op·ment** *noun* [U]

under·dog /ˈʌndədɒg; *NAmE* ˈʌndərdɔːg; -dɑːg/ *noun* a person, team, country, etc. that is thought to be in a weaker position than others and therefore not likely to be successful, win a competition, etc. 處於劣勢的人（或團隊、國家等）；弱者；比賽前不被看好者：*Before the game we were definitely the underdogs.* 我們在賽前絕對不被看好。◇ *In politics, he was a champion of the underdog* (= always fought for the rights of weaker people). 在政治上，他總是為弱勢群體爭取權益。 OPP **overdog**

U

under·done /ˌʌndəˈdʌn; NAmE -dərˈd-/ *adj.* not completely cooked 未煮熟的；欠火的 ➲ compare WELL DONE, OVERDONE (3)

under·employed /ˌʌndərɪmˈplɔɪd/ *adj.* not having enough work to do; not having work that makes full use of your skills and abilities 未充分就業的（指就業不足、沒有足夠的工作可做，或所做的工作未能充分發揮技能）

under·esti·mate AW *verb, noun*

■ *verb* /ˌʌndərˈestɪmeɪt/ **1 ~ sth | ~ what, how, etc. ...** to think or guess that the amount, cost or size of sth is smaller than it really is 低估；對…估計不足：*to underestimate the cost of the project* 低估項目的成本 ◇ *We underestimated the time it would take to get there.* 我們低估了抵達那裏所需的時間。**2 ~ sb/sth** to not realize how good, strong, determined, etc. sb really is 對…認識不足（或重視不夠）；低估；輕視：*Never underestimate your opponent.* 決不可低估你的對手。OPP **overestimate** ➲ compare UNDERRATE

■ *noun* /ˌʌndərˈestɪmət/ (also **under·esti·ma·tion** /ˌʌndərˌestɪˈmeɪʃn/ [C, U]) an estimate about the size, cost, etc. of sth that is too low 低估；輕視：*My guess of 400 proved to be a serious underestimate.* 我猜 400，結果證明是嚴重的低估。OPP **overestimate**

under·expose /ˌʌndərɪkˈspəʊz; NAmE -ˈspoʊz/ *verb* [usually passive] **~ sth** to allow too little light to reach the film when you take a photograph 使曝光不足 OPP **overexpose**

under·fed /ˌʌndəˈfed; NAmE -dərˈf-/ *adj.* having had too little food to eat 食物不足的；沒吃飽的 SYN **malnourished** OPP **overfed**

under·floor /ˌʌndəˈflɔː(r); NAmE -dərˈf-/ *adj.* [only before noun] placed underneath the floor 在地板下面的：*underfloor heating* 設在地板下面的供暖系統

under·foot /ˌʌndəˈfʊt; NAmE -dərˈf-/ *adv.* under your feet; on the ground where you are walking 在腳下；在（腳下的）地面上：*The ground was dry and firm underfoot.* 腳下踩的土地又乾又硬。◇ *I was nearly **trampled underfoot** by the crowd of people rushing for the door.* 衝向大門的人群險些把我踩在腳下。

under·fund·ed /ˌʌndəˈfʌndɪd; NAmE -dərˈf-/ *adj.* (of an organization, a project, etc. 機構、項目等) not having enough money to spend, with the result that it cannot function well 資金不足的；缺乏資金的：***seriously/chronically underfunded*** 嚴重／長期缺乏資金

under·gar·ment /ˈʌndəɡɑːmənt; NAmE -dərɡɑːrm-/ *noun* (*old-fashioned* or *formal*) a piece of underwear 內衣

under·go AW /ˌʌndəˈɡəʊ; NAmE ˌʌndərˈɡoʊ/ *verb* (**under·goes** /-ˈɡəʊz; NAmE -ˈɡoʊz/, **under·went** /-ˈwent/, **under·gone** /-ˈɡɒn; NAmE -ˈɡɔːn; -ˈɡɑːn/) **~ sth** to experience sth, especially a change or sth unpleasant 經歷，經受（變化、不快的事等）：*to **undergo** tests/trials/repairs* 經受考驗；接受檢修 ◇ *My mother **underwent** major **surgery** last year.* 我母親去年動過大手術。◇ *Some children **undergo** a complete **transformation** when they become teenagers.* 一些兒童進入少年期會完全變了另一個人。

U

under·gradu·ate /ˌʌndəˈɡrædʒuət; NAmE -dərˈɡ-/ *noun* a university or college student who is studying for their first degree 本科生：*a first-year undergraduate* 大學一年級學生 ◇ *an **undergraduate course/student/degree*** 大學本科課程／學生／學位 ➲ note at STUDENT

under·ground ⚷ *adj., adv., noun*

■ *adj.* /ˌʌndəˈɡraʊnd; NAmE -dərˈɡ-/ [only before noun] **1** ⚷ under the surface of the ground 地下的；地面以下的：*underground passages/caves/streams* 地下通道／洞穴／溪流 ◇ *underground cables* 地下電纜 ➲ compare OVERGROUND **2** operating secretly and often illegally, especially against a government 秘密的，非法的，暗中的，地下的（尤指反政府的）：*an underground resistance movement* 地下抵抗運動

■ *adv.* /ˌʌndəˈɡraʊnd; NAmE -dərˈɡ-/ **1** ⚷ under the surface of the ground 在地下；在地面下：*Rescuers found victims trapped several feet underground.* 營救人員發現有受難者被困在地下幾英尺處。◇ *toxic waste buried deep underground* 深埋在地下的有毒廢棄物 **2** in or into a secret place in order to hide from the police, the government, etc. 隱蔽地；隱匿地：*He **went underground** to avoid arrest.* 他隱藏起來以防被捕。

■ *noun* /ˈʌndəɡraʊnd; NAmE -dərɡ-/ **1** (often **the Underground**) (*BrE*) (*NAmE* **sub·way**) [sing.] an underground railway/railroad system in a city（城市的）地下鐵路系統，地鐵：*underground stations* 地鐵車站 ◇ *the London Underground* 倫敦地鐵 ◇ *I always travel by underground.* 我總是乘地鐵。➲ VISUAL VOCAB page V58 ➲ compare METRO *n.* (1), TUBE (6) **2 the underground** [sing.+sing./pl. v.] a secret political organization, usually working against the government of a country 秘密政治組織；（反政府）地下組織

British/American 英式／美式英語

underground / subway / metro / tube

- A city's underground railway/railroad system is usually called the **underground** (often **the Underground**) in *BrE* and the **subway** in *NAmE*. Speakers of *BrE* also use **subway** for systems in American cities and **metro** for systems in other European countries. **The Metro** is the name for the systems in Paris and Washington, D.C. London's system is often called **the Tube**. 城市的地鐵系統在英式英語中通常稱為 underground（常作 the Underground），在美式英語中為 subway。說英式英語的人指美國城市的地鐵亦用 subway，而指其他歐洲國家的地鐵則用 metro。the Metro 為巴黎和華盛頓市的地鐵名稱；倫敦的地鐵通常稱作 the Tube。

the ˌunderground eˈconomy (*NAmE*) (*BrE* **the ˌblack eˈconomy**) *noun* [sing.] business activity or work that is done without the knowledge of the government or other officials so that people avoid paying tax on the money they earn 地下經濟活動；黑市經濟

under·growth /ˈʌndəɡrəʊθ; NAmE ˈʌndərɡroʊθ/ (*BrE*) (*NAmE* **under·brush**) *noun* [U] a mass of bushes and plants that grow close together under trees in woods and forests 下層灌木叢（指林木下的）：*They used their knives to clear a path through the dense undergrowth.* 他們用刀在濃密的灌木叢中劈開一條小路。◇ *The murder weapon was found concealed in undergrowth.* 殺人兇器被發現藏在灌木叢中。

under·hand /ˌʌndəˈhænd; NAmE -dərˈh-/ (also *less frequent* **under·hand·ed** /-ˈhændɪd/) *adj.* (*disapproving*) secret and dishonest 秘密的；陰險的；狡詐的；卑鄙的：*I would never have expected her to behave in such an underhand way.* 我從未想到她的行為竟如此陰險。

under·in·sured /ˌʌndərɪnˈʃʊəd; -ˈʃɔːd; NAmE -ˈʃʊrd/ *adj.* not having enough insurance protection 保險（額）不足的

under·lay /ˈʌndəleɪ; NAmE ˈʌndərleɪ/ *noun* [U, C] a layer of thick material placed under a carpet to protect it 地毯襯墊

under·lie AW /ˌʌndəˈlaɪ; NAmE ˌʌndərˈlaɪ/ *verb* (**under·lying**, **under·lay** /-ˈleɪ/, **under·lain** /-ˈleɪn/) [no passive] **~ sth** (*formal*) to be the basis or cause of sth 構成…的基礎；作為…的原因：*These ideas underlie much of his work.* 他的作品大部份都是以這些主題思想為基礎。◇ *It is a principle that underlies all the party's policies.* 這是貫穿該黨各項政策的一條準則。➲ see also UNDERLYING

under·line /ˌʌndəˈlaɪn; NAmE -dərˈl-/ (also **under·score** especially in *NAmE*) *verb* **1 ~ sth** to draw a line under a word, sentence, etc. 在（詞語等下）畫線；畫底線標出 **2** to emphasize or show that sth is important or true 強調；突現：**~ sth** *The report underlines the importance of pre-school education.* 這份報告強調學前教育的重要性。◇ **~ how, what, etc. ...** *Her question underlined how little she understood him.* 她的問題表明她多麼不瞭解他。◇ **~ that ...** *The report underlined that the project enjoyed considerable support in both countries.* 這份報告強調該項目得到兩國的極大支持。◇ **it is underlined that ...**

It should be underlined that these are only preliminary findings. 需要強調的是，這些只是初步的研究結果。

under·ling /ˈʌndəlɪŋ; *NAmE* ˈʌndərlɪŋ/ *noun* (*disapproving*) a person with a lower rank or status 走卒；嘍囉；手下；下屬 SYN **minion**

under·lying AW /ˌʌndəˈlaɪɪŋ; *NAmE* -dərˈl-/ *adj.* [only before noun] **1** important in a situation but not always easily noticed or stated clearly 根本的；潛在的；隱含的：*The underlying assumption is that the amount of money available is limited.* 隱含的假定是可用的資金有限。◇ *Unemployment may be an underlying cause of the rising crime rate.* 失業可能是犯罪率攀升的潛在原因。 **2** existing under the surface of sth else 表面下的；下層的：*the underlying rock formation* 地表下的岩石結構 ➲ see also UNDERLIE

under·manned /ˌʌndəˈmænd; *NAmE* -dərˈm-/ *adj.* (of a hospital, factory, etc. 醫院、工廠等) not having enough people working in order to be able to function well 人手不足的；編制不足的；缺編的 SYN **understaffed** OPP **overmanned**

under·men·tioned /ˌʌndəˈmenʃnd; *NAmE* -dərˈm-/ *adj.* (*BrE, formal*) used in a book or document to refer to sth that is mentioned later（用於書或文件）下述的

under·mine /ˌʌndəˈmaɪn; *NAmE* -dərˈm-/ *verb* **1 ~ sth** to make sth, especially sb's confidence or authority, gradually weaker or less effective 逐漸削弱（信心、權威等）；使逐步減少效力：*Our confidence in the team has been seriously undermined by their recent defeats.* 他們最近的幾次失敗已嚴重動搖了我們對該隊的信心。◇ *This crisis has undermined his position.* 這場危機已損害了他的地位。 **2 ~ sth** to make sth weaker at the base, for example by digging under it 從根基處破壞；挖…的牆腳

under·neath 🔑 /ˌʌndəˈniːθ; *NAmE* -dərˈn-/ *prep., adv., noun*

■ ***prep., adv.*** **1** 🔑 under or below sth else, especially when it is hidden or covered by the thing on top 在…底下；隱藏（或掩蓋）在下面：*The coin rolled underneath the piano.* 硬幣滾到了鋼琴底下。◇ *This jacket's too big, even with a sweater underneath.* 即使裏面穿一件毛衣，這件外套也太大了。 **2** 🔑 used to talk about sb's real feelings or character, as opposed to the way they seem to be（指真實的感情或性格）在…表象之下：*Underneath her cool exterior she was really very frightened.* 她外表冷靜，其實內心十分害怕。◇ *He seems bad-tempered, but he's very soft-hearted underneath.* 他表面脾氣暴躁，實則菩薩心腸。

■ ***noun*** **the underneath** [sing.] the lower surface or part of sth（物體的）下表面，底面，底部，下部：*She pulled the drawer out and examined the underneath carefully.* 她拉開抽屜仔細查看底部。

under·nour·ished /ˌʌndəˈnʌrɪʃt; *NAmE* -dərˈnɜːr-/ *adj.* in bad health because of a lack of food or a lack of the right type of food 營養不良的；缺乏營養的 SYN **malnourished**：*severely undernourished children* 嚴重營養不良的兒童 ▶ **under·nour·ish·ment** /-ˈnʌrɪʃmənt; *NAmE* -ˈnɜːr-/ *noun* [U]

under·paid /ˌʌndəˈpeɪd; *NAmE* -dərˈp-/ *adj.* not paid enough for the work you do 報酬過低的；酬不抵勞的：*Nurses complain of being* ***overworked and underpaid.*** 護士抱怨工作勞累過度而報酬過低。

under·pants /ˈʌndəpænts; *NAmE* -dərp-/ *noun* [pl.] **1** (also *informal* **pants**) (*BrE*) a piece of men's underwear worn under their trousers/pants（男用）內褲，襯褲 **2** (*NAmE*) a piece of underwear worn by men or women under trousers/pants, a skirt, etc.（男、女）內褲，襯褲

under·pass /ˈʌndəpɑːs; *NAmE* ˈʌndərpæs/ *noun* a road or path that goes under another road or railway/railroad track 下層通道，地下通道（在另一條道路或鐵路之下）➲ compare OVERPASS

under·pay /ˌʌndəˈpeɪ; *NAmE* -dərˈp-/ *verb* (**under·paid**, **under·paid** /-peɪd/) [usually passive] **~ sb** to pay sb too little money, especially for their work 給…報酬過低；少付工資 OPP **overpay**

under·per·form /ˌʌndəpəˈfɔːm; *NAmE* ˌʌndərpərˈfɔːrm/ *verb* [I] to not be as successful as was expected 發揮不夠；表現不理想

under·pin /ˌʌndəˈpɪn; *NAmE* -dərˈp-/ *verb* (**-nn-**) **1 ~ sth** (*formal*) to support or form the basis of an argument, a claim, etc. 加強，鞏固，構成（基礎等）：*The report is underpinned by extensive research.* 這份報告以廣泛的研究為基礎。 **2 ~ sth** (*technical* 術語) to support a wall by putting metal, concrete, etc. under it 加固（牆）基 ▶ **under·pin·ning** *noun* [C, U]

under·play /ˌʌndəˈpleɪ; *NAmE* -dərˈp-/ *verb* **~ sth** (*especially BrE*) to make sth seem less important than it really is 低調處理；降低…的重要性 SYN **play down, downplay** OPP **overplay**

under·pre·pared /ˌʌndəprɪˈpeəd; *NAmE* ˌʌndərprɪˈperd/ *adj.* not having done enough preparation for sth you have to do 準備不充分的；準備不足的

under·priced /ˌʌndəˈpraɪst; *NAmE* -dərˈp-/ *adj.* something that is **underpriced** is sold at a price that is too low and less than its real value 定價過低的

under·priv·il·eged /ˌʌndəˈprɪvəlɪdʒd; *NAmE* -dərˈp-/ *adj.* **1** [usually before noun] having less money and fewer opportunities than most people in society 在社會中處於弱勢的；貧苦的；機遇少的；底層的 SYN **disadvantaged**：*underprivileged sections of the community* 社區的弱勢階層 ◇ ***educationally/socially underprivileged*** *groups* 教育上／社會上處於弱勢地位的群體 ➲ compare PRIVILEGED (1) **2 the underprivileged** *noun* [pl.] people who are underprivileged 弱勢群體；貧困階層

under·rate /ˌʌndəˈreɪt/ *verb* **~ sb/sth** to not recognize how good, important, etc. sb/sth really is 過低評價；低估：*He's seriously underrated as a writer.* 他是被嚴重低估的一位作家。◇ *an underrated movie* 一部未得到應有評價的電影 ➲ compare OVERRATE, UNDERESTIMATE (2)

ˌunder-reˈhearsed *adj.* (of a play or other performance 戲劇或其他表演) that has not been prepared and practised enough 排演不夠的；練習過少的；準備不充分的

ˌunder-ˌrepreˈsent·ed *adj.* not having as many representatives as would be expected or needed 代表人數不夠的；代表名額不足的：*Women are under-represented at senior levels in business.* 商界高層的女性代表不足。

ˌunder-ˌreˈsourced AW *adj.* not provided with as much money or as many staff, materials, etc. as are needed 缺乏資源的；資金（或人手、材料等）不足的：*Nurses are overstretched and the hospital is seriously under-resourced.* 護士超負荷工作，醫院人手嚴重不足。

under·score *verb, noun*

■ ***verb*** /ˌʌndəˈskɔː(r); *NAmE* -dərˈs-/ (*especially NAmE*) = UNDERLINE (1)

■ ***noun*** /ˈʌndəskɔː(r); *NAmE* -dərs-/ (*computing* 計) the symbol (_) that is used to draw a line under a letter or word and used in computer commands and in Internet addresses 下畫線，底線（用於字母下畫線或計算機命令和互聯網地址中）

under·sea /ˈʌndəsiː; *NAmE* ˈʌndərsiː/ *adj.* [only before noun] found, used or happening below the surface of the sea 海面下的；海底的：*undersea cables/earthquakes* 海底電纜／地震

under·sec·re·tary /ˌʌndəˈsekrətri; *NAmE* ˌʌndərˈsekrəteri/ *noun* (*pl.* **-ies**) **1** (in Britain) a senior CIVIL SERVANT in charge of one part of a government department（英國）政務次官 ➲ compare PERMANENT UNDERSECRETARY **2** (in Britain) a junior minister who reports to the minister in charge of a government department（英國）副大臣，次長 **3** (in the US) an official of high rank in a government department, directly below a member of a cabinet（美國）副部長，副國務卿

under·sell /ˌʌndəˈsel; *NAmE* ˌʌndərˈsel/ *verb* (**un·der·sold**, **un·der·sold** /-ˈsəʊld; *NAmE* -ˈsoʊld/) **1 ~ sth** to sell goods or services at a lower price than your COMPETITORS 以低於（競爭者）的價格出售；競價銷售 **2 ~ sth** to sell sth at a price lower than its real value 賠本出售；壓價銷售 **3 ~ sb/sth/yourself** to make people think that sb/sth is not as good or as interesting as they really are 降低人們對…的印象；貶損：*Don't undersell yourself at the interview.* 面試時不可過分自謙。

U

under·shirt /ˈʌndəʃɜːt; *NAmE* ˈʌndərʃɜːrt/ (*NAmE*) (*BrE* **vest**) *noun* a piece of underwear worn under a shirt, etc. next to the skin（襯衣等裏面貼身穿的）背心，汗衫 ➲ compare SINGLET

under·shoot /ˌʌndəˈʃuːt; *NAmE* -dərˈʃ-/ *verb* (**under·shot**, **under·shot**) [I, T] **~ (sth)** (of an aircraft 飛機) to land before reaching the RUNWAY 未達跑道着陸 ▸ **under·shoot** *noun*

Synonyms 同義詞辨析

understand

see • get • follow • grasp • comprehend

These words all mean to know or realize sth, for example why sth happens, how sth works or what sth means. 以上各詞均含懂得、理解、認識到之義。

understand to know or realize the meaning of words, a language, what sb says, etc. to know or realize how or why sth happens, how it works or why it is important 指懂、理解、領會（詞義、語言、話語等），瞭解、認識到、明白（事情如何或為何發生、如何起作用或為何重要等）：*I don't understand the instructions.* 我不懂這些指令的意思。◊ *Doctors still don't understand much about the disease.* 醫生對這種疾病還瞭解不多。

see to understand what is happening, what sb is saying, how sth works or how important sth is 指理解、明白、領會（正在發生的事、某人的話、某事如何起作用或重要性如何）：*'It opens like this.' 'Oh, I see.'* "這樣就打開了。" "哦，我明白了。" ◊ *Oh yes, **I see what you mean**.* 噢，我明白你的意思了。

get (*informal*) to understand a joke, what sb is trying to tell you, or a situation that they are trying to describe 指理解、明白（笑話、某人試圖告知的事或描述的情況）：*She didn't get the joke.* 她聽不懂那個笑話。◊ *I don't get you.* 我搞不懂你的意思。

follow to understand an explanation, a story or the meaning of sth 指理解、明白（說明、故事、意思）：*Sorry—I don't quite follow.* 對不起，我不太聽懂你的話。◊ *The plot is almost impossible to follow.* 故事情節幾乎叫人不明所以。

grasp to come to understand a fact, an idea or how to do sth 指理解、領會、領悟、明白（事實、想法或如何做某事）：*They failed to grasp the importance of his words.* 他們沒有理解他的話的重要性。

UNDERSTAND OR GRASP? 用 understand 還是 grasp？

You can use **understand** or **grasp** for the action of realizing the meaning or importance of sth for the first time. 第一次意識到某事的意義或重要性可用 understand 或 grasp：*It's a difficult concept for children to understand/grasp.* 對孩子來說，這是一個很難理解的概念。 Only **understand** can be used to talk about languages, words or writing. 只有 understand 可用於理解語言、詞彙或文章等：~~*I don't grasp French/the instructions.*~~

comprehend (often used in negative statements) (*formal*) to understand a fact, idea or reason（常用於否定句中）指理解、領悟、明白（事實、想法或原因）：*The concept of infinity is almost impossible for the human mind to comprehend.* 無窮的概念幾乎是人類的大腦無法理解的。

PATTERNS

- to understand/see/get/follow/grasp/comprehend **what/why/how …**
- to understand/see/grasp/comprehend **that …**
- to understand/see/get/grasp **the point/idea** (of sth)
- to be **easy/difficult/hard** to understand/see/follow/grasp/comprehend
- to **fully** understand/see/grasp/comprehend sth

under·shorts /ˈʌndəʃɔːts; *NAmE* ˈʌndərʃɔːrts/ *noun* [pl.] (*NAmE*) UNDERPANTS that are worn by men（男用）內褲，襯褲

under·side /ˈʌndəsaɪd; *NAmE* -dərs-/ *noun* the side or surface of sth that is underneath 下側；底面；底部；下表面 SYN **bottom**

the under·signed /ˌʌndəˈsaɪnd; *NAmE* -dərˈs-/ *noun* (*pl.* **the under·signed**) (*formal*) the person who has signed that particular document（文件的）簽字人，具名人，簽署人：*We, the undersigned, agree to …* 我們，本文件的具名人，同意…

under·sized /ˌʌndəˈsaɪzd; *NAmE* -dərˈs-/ *adj.* not as big as normal 小於正常（或一般）的

under·skirt /ˈʌndəskɜːt; *NAmE* ˈʌndərskɜːrt/ *noun* a skirt that is worn under another skirt as underwear 襯裙

under·sold *past tense, past part.* of UNDERSELL

under·spend /ˌʌndəˈspend; *NAmE* -dərˈs-/ *verb* (**under·spent**, **under·spent**) [I, T] to not spend enough money on sth 花費不足；對…投資不夠：**~ (on sth)** *The inquiry found that the company had seriously underspent on safety equipment.* 調查發現，公司對安全設備的投資嚴重不足。◊ **~ sth** *We've underspent our budget this year.* 我們今年的花費少於預算。 ▸ **under·spend** /ˈʌndəspend; *NAmE* ˈʌndərs-/ *noun* [sing.]：(*BrE*) *a £1 million underspend* 少花的 100 萬英鎊

under·staffed /ˌʌndəˈstɑːft; *NAmE* ˌʌndərˈstæft/ *adj.* [not usually before noun] not having enough people working and therefore not able to function well 人員不足；人手太少 SYN **undermanned** OPP **overstaffed**

under·stand 🔑 /ˌʌndəˈstænd; *NAmE* -dərˈs-/ *verb* (**under·stood**, **under·stood** /-ˈstʊd/) (not used in the progressive tenses 不用於進行時)

> **WORD FAMILY**
> **understand** *verb* (≠ misunderstand)
> **understandable** *adj.*
> **misunderstood** *adj.*
> **understanding** *adj.*, *noun* (≠ misunderstanding)

▸ **MEANING** 意思 **1** 🔑 [T, I] to know or realize the meaning of words, a language, what sb says, etc. 懂；理解；領會：**~ (sth)** *Can you understand French?* 你懂法語嗎？◊ *Do you understand the instructions?* 你懂得這些指令的意思嗎？◊ *She didn't understand the form she was signing.* 她弄不懂她正在簽署的表格。◊ *I'm not sure that I understand. Go over it again.* 我不敢說我搞懂了。請再來一遍吧。◊ *I don't want you doing that again. Do you understand?* 我不許你再這樣做。你聽明白了嗎？◊ **~ what …** *I don't understand what he's saying.* 我不明白他在說些什麼。

▸ **HOW STH WORKS/HAPPENS** 運作；發生 **2** 🔑 [T, I] to know or realize how or why sth happens, how it works or why it is important 瞭解；認識到；明瞭：**~ (sth)** *Doctors still don't understand much about the disease.* 醫生對這種疾病仍瞭解不多。◊ *No one is answering the phone—I can't understand it.* 沒人接電話，我不知道是怎麼回事。◊ **~ why, what, etc. …** *I could never understand why she was fired.* 我怎麼也不明白她為何被解雇。◊ **~ sb/sth doing sth** *I just can't understand him taking the money.* 我真想不通他為什麼會偷錢。◊ (*formal*) *I just can't understand his taking the money.* 我真想不通他為什麼會偷錢。◊ **~ that …** *He was the first to understand that we live in a knowledge economy.* 他最早認識到我們正處於知識經濟的時代。

▸ **KNOW SB** 瞭解某人 **3** 🔑 [T, I] to know sb's character, how they feel and why they behave in the way they do 瞭解；諒解；體諒：**~ sb** *Nobody understands me.* 沒有人瞭解我。◊ *He doesn't understand women at all.* 他根本就不瞭解女性。◊ **~ what, how, etc. …** *They understand what I have been through.* 他們對我的遭遇很同情。◊ **~ (that …)** *I quite understand that you need some time alone.* 我很理解你需要獨自靜一會。◊ *If you want to leave early, I'm sure he'll understand.* 如果你想早些離開，我相信他會體諒的。◊ **~ sb doing sth** *I quite understand you needing some time alone.* 我很理解你需要獨自靜一會。

▸ **THINK/BELIEVE** 認為；相信 **4** [T] (*formal*) to think or believe that sth is true because you have been told that it is 得知；據信；認為：**~ (that) …** *I understand (that) you wish to see the manager.* 我聽說您想見經理。◊ *Am*

U

I to understand that you refuse? 你是告訴我你拒絕了？◇ **~ sb/sth to be/have sth** *The Prime Minister is understood to have been extremely angry about the report.* 據說首相對這份報告大為惱火。◇ **it is understood that …** *It is understood that the band are working on their next album.* 據說這個樂隊正在錄製他們的下一張專輯。

▸ BE AGREED 得到贊同 **5** [T] **it is understood that …** to agree sth with sb without it needing to be said 默認；默許；不言而喻：*I thought it was understood that my expenses would be paid.* 我原以為對方已同意支付我的費用。

▸ MISSING WORD 省略的字 **6** [T, usually passive] **~ sth** to realize that a word in a phrase or sentence is not expressed and to supply it in your mind 領會；清楚；推斷出：*In the sentence 'I can't drive', the object 'a car' is understood.* 在 I can't drive 一句中，可推測出賓語 a car 被省略了。

IDM **ˌmake yourself underˈstood** to make your meaning clear, especially in another language（尤指用另一種語言）把自己的意思說清楚：*He doesn't speak much Japanese but he can make himself understood.* 他不大會講日語，不過尚能勉強表達意思。➲ more at GIVE *v.*

under·stand·able /ˌʌndəˈstændəbl; *NAmE* -dərˈs-/ *adj.* **1** (of behaviour, feelings, reactions, etc. 行為、感情、反應等) seeming normal and reasonable in a particular situation 合情理的；正常的；可以理解的 SYN **natural**：*Their attitude is **perfectly understandable**.* 他們的態度是完全可以理解的。◇ *It was an understandable mistake to make.* 那是一個情有可原的失誤。 **2** (of language, documents, etc. 語言、文件等) easy to understand 易懂的 SYN **comprehensible**：*Warning notices must be readily understandable.* 警告性標示必須明白易懂。

under·stand·ably /ˌʌndəˈstændəbli; *NAmE* -dərˈs-/ *adv.* in a way that seems normal and reasonable in a particular situation 可以理解地；正常地；合乎情理地 SYN **naturally**：*They were understandably disappointed with the result.* 他們對結果感到失望是可以理解的。

under·stand·ing 0‒ /ˌʌndəˈstændɪŋ; *NAmE* -dərˈs-/ *noun, adj.*

■ ***noun*** **1** 0‒ [U, sing.] **~ (of sth)** the knowledge that sb has about a particular subject or situation 理解；領悟；瞭解：*The committee has little or no understanding of the problem.* 委員會對這個問題瞭解不多或根本不瞭解。◇ *The existence of God is beyond human understanding* (= humans cannot know whether God exists or not). 上帝的存在與否是超出人類所能理解的。 **2** 0‒ [C, usually sing.] an informal agreement（非正式的）協議：*We finally **came to an understanding** about what hours we would work.* 我們最終就工作時間問題取得了一致意見。◇ *We have this understanding that nobody talks about work over lunch.* 我們有個默契：吃午飯時誰也不許談工作。 **3** 0‒ [U, sing.] the ability to understand why people behave in a particular way and the willingness to forgive them when they do sth wrong 理解；諒解；體諒：*We must tackle the problem with sympathy and understanding.* 我們必須以同情和諒解的態度來處理這個問題。◇ *We are looking for a better understanding between the two nations.* 我們正在尋求兩國間的進一步瞭解。 **4** 0‒ [U, C] **~ (of sth)** the particular way in which sb understands sth 理解；看法；解釋；意見 SYN **interpretation**：*My understanding of the situation is …* 我對形勢的看法是… ◇ *The statement is open to various understandings.* 這個聲明可以有各種不同的詮釋。

IDM **on the understanding that …** (*formal*) used to introduce a condition that must be agreed before sth else can happen 條件是…：*They agreed to the changes on the understanding that they would be introduced gradually.* 他們同意這些改革，條件是須要逐步進行。

■ ***adj.*** showing sympathy for other people's problems and being willing to forgive them when they do sth wrong 善解人意的；富有同情心的；體諒人的 SYN **sympathetic**：*She has very understanding parents.* 她的父母對她非常寬容。▸ **under·stand·ing·ly** *adv.*

under·state /ˌʌndəˈsteɪt; *NAmE* -dərˈs-/ *verb* **~ sth** to state that sth is smaller, less important or less serious than it really is 輕描淡寫；避重就輕地說：*It would be a mistake to understate the seriousness of the problem.* 對問題的嚴重性輕描淡寫是錯誤的。OPP **overstate**

under·stated /ˌʌndəˈsteɪtɪd; *NAmE* -dərˈs-/ *adj.* (*approving*) if a style, colour, etc. is **understated**, it is pleasing and elegant in a way that is not too obvious 淡雅的；素雅的；柔和的；不過分的 SYN **subtle**

under·state·ment /ˈʌndəsteɪtmənt; *NAmE* -dərs-/ *noun* **1** [C] a statement that makes sth seem less important, impressive, serious, etc. than it really is 保守的說法；不充分的敘述：*To say we were pleased is an understatement* (= we were extremely pleased). 說我們高興，那是輕描淡寫。◇ *'These figures are a bit disappointing.' 'That's got to be **the understatement of the year**.'* "這些數字有點令人失望。" "那一定是本年度最保守的說法了。" **2** [U] the practice of making things seem less impressive, important, serious, etc. than they really are 淡化；低調說法：*typical English understatement* 典型的英國式低調說法 ◇ *He always goes for subtlety and understatement in his movies.* 他總是在自己的電影中運用細膩刻畫和淡化手法。OPP **overstatement**

under·stood *past tense, past part.* of UNDERSTAND

under·study /ˈʌndəstʌdi; *NAmE* -dərs-/ *noun, verb*

■ ***noun*** (*pl.* **-ies**) **~ (to sb)** an actor who learns the part of another actor in a play so that they can play that part if necessary 候補演員；替角

■ ***verb*** (**under·stud·ies**, **under·study·ing**, **under·stud·ied**, **under·stud·ied**) **~ sb/sth** to learn a part in a play as an understudy; to act as an understudy to sb 排練當候補演員；做替角

under·take AW /ˌʌndəˈteɪk; *NAmE* -dərˈt-/ *verb* (**under·took** /-ˈtʊk/, **under·taken** /-ˈteɪkən/) (*formal*) **1 ~ sth** to make yourself responsible for sth and start doing it 承擔；從事；負責：*to **undertake a task/project*** 承擔一個任務／項目 ◇ *University professors both teach and **undertake research**.* 大學教授既要教學又要從事研究工作。◇ *The company has announced that it will undertake a full investigation into the accident.* 公司已經宣佈將對這次事故進行全面調查。 **2 ~ to do sth | ~ that …** to agree or promise that you will do sth 承諾；允諾；答應：*He undertook to finish the job by Friday.* 他答應星期五或之前完成這一工作。

under·taker /ˈʌndəteɪkə(r); *NAmE* -dərt-/ (also *formal* **ˈfuneral director**) (*NAmE* also **mor·ti·cian**) *noun* a person whose job is to prepare the bodies of dead people to be buried or CREMATED, and to arrange funerals 殯葬承辦人；殯儀服務員

under·tak·ing AW /ˌʌndəˈteɪkɪŋ; *NAmE* -dərˈt-/ *noun* **1** [C] a task or project, especially one that is important and/or difficult（重大或艱巨的）任務，項目，事業；企業 SYN **venture**：*He is interested in buying the club as a commercial undertaking.* 他有意購買那個俱樂部作為投資。◇ *In those days, the trip across country was a dangerous undertaking.* 那個時期，越野旅行是一件危險的事情。 **2** [C] (*formal*) an agreement or a promise to do sth 承諾；保證；許諾；答應：**~ (to do sth)** *a government undertaking to spend more on education* 政府增加教育經費的承諾◇ **~ (that …)** *The landlord gave a written undertaking that the repairs would be carried out.* 房東書面保證將進行維修。 **3** /ˈʌndəteɪkɪŋ; *NAmE* -dərt-/ [U] the business of an undertaker 殯儀業；喪葬業

ˌunder-the-ˈcounter *adj.* (*informal*) illegal 枱面下的；非法的；私下的；暗中的

under·tone /ˈʌndətəʊn; *NAmE* ˈʌndərtoʊn/ *noun* **~ (of sth)** a feeling, quality or meaning that is not expressed directly but is still noticeable from what sb says or does 蘊涵的感情（或特質、意思）；寓意；弦外之音 SYN **undercurrent**：*His soft words contained an undertone of warning.* 他溫和的話中蘊涵着警告之意。◇ *The play does not have the political undertones of the novel.* 這部戲沒有小說的那種政治寓意。➲ compare OVERTONE

IDM **in an ˈundertone | in ˈundertones** in a quiet voice 低聲地；小聲地

under·took AW *past tense* of UNDERTAKE

U

under·tow /ˈʌndətəʊ; *NAmE* ˈʌndərtoʊ/ *noun* [usually sing.] **1** a current in the sea or ocean that moves in the opposite direction to the water near the surface 底流；水下逆流：*The children were carried out to sea by the strong undertow.* 強大的回流把孩子們捲到海裏去了。**2 ~ (of sth)** a feeling or quality that influences people in a particular situation even though they may not really be aware of it 潛在的傾向（或特質）；感染力

under·trial /ˈʌndətraɪəl; *NAmE* ˈʌndərt-/ *noun* (*IndE*) a person who has been charged with a crime 審訊中的人：*The undertrials will appear in court next week.* 候審者將於下週出庭。

under·used /ˌʌndəˈjuːzd; *NAmE* -dərˈj-/ (also *formal* **under·util·ized**) *adj.* not used as much as it could or should be 未充分利用的；浪費的 ▸ **under·use** /ˌʌndəˈjuːs; *NAmE* -dərˈj-/ (also *formal* **under·util·iza·tion**) *noun* [U]

under·util·ized (*BrE* also **-ised**) /ˌʌndəˈjuːtəlaɪzd; *NAmE* -dərˈj-/ *adj.* (*formal*) = UNDERUSED ▸ **under·util·iza·tion, -isa·tion** /ˌʌndəjuːtəlaɪˈzeɪʃn; *NAmE* -dərˌjuːtələˈz-/ *noun* [U] = UNDERUSE

under·value /ˌʌndəˈvæljuː; *NAmE* -dərˈv-/ *verb* [usually passive] **~ sb/sth** to not recognize how good, valuable or important sb/sth really is 低估；對…認識不足；輕視：*Education is currently undervalued in this country.* 現在這個國家對教育重視不夠。◇ *He believes his house has been undervalued.* 他認為自己的房子估值太低。OPP **overvalue**

under·water 🔑 /ˌʌndəˈwɔːtə(r); *NAmE* -dərˈw-/ *adj.* [only before noun] found, used or happening below the surface of water 水下的；用於水下的；水下發生的：*underwater creatures* 水生動物 ◇ *an underwater camera* 水下攝影機 ▸ **under·water** 🔑 *adv.*：*Take a deep breath and see how long you can stay underwater.* 深吸一口氣，看你能在水裏待多久。

under·way /ˌʌndəˈweɪ; *NAmE* -dərˈw-/ *adj.* [not before noun]

IDM **underway** = UNDER WAY at WAY

under·wear 🔑 /ˈʌndəweə(r); *NAmE* ˈʌndərwer/ *noun* [U] (also *formal* **under·clothes, under·cloth·ing**) clothes that you wear under other clothes and next to the skin 內衣；襯衣：*She packed one change of underwear.* 她打行李時帶了一套換洗的內衣。

under·weight /ˌʌndəˈweɪt; *NAmE* -dərˈw-/ *adj.* (especially of a person 尤指人) weighing less than the normal or expected weight 體重不足的；未達到正常體重的：*She is a few pounds underweight for* (= in relation to) *her height.* 就其身高而言，她的體重還差幾磅。OPP **overweight** ➲ COLLOCATIONS at DIET

under·went *past tense* of UNDERGO

U

under·whelmed /ˌʌndəˈwelmd; *NAmE* -dərˈw-/ *adj.* (*informal, humorous*) not impressed with or excited about sth at all 無動於衷的；毫不激動的：*We were distinctly underwhelmed by the director's speech.* 主任的講話顯然令我們感覺索然無味。➲ compare OVERWHELMED

under·whelm·ing /ˌʌndəˈwelmɪŋ; *NAmE* -dərˈw-/ *adj.* (*informal, humorous*) not impressing or exciting you at all 平庸的；索然無味的：*the contrast between his overwhelming guitar-playing and his underwhelming singing* 他那激昂的吉他演奏與其味同嚼蠟的歌唱之間的反差

under·wired /ˌʌndəˈwaɪəd; *NAmE* ˌʌndərˈwaɪərd/ (*BrE*) (*NAmE* **under·wire** /ˌʌndəˈwaɪə(r); *NAmE* ˌʌndərˈwaɪər/) *adj.* (of a BRA 胸罩) having a thin metal strip sewn into the bottom half of each CUP to improve the shape 鋼托式的（罩杯下半部縫金屬撐條）；用金屬條定型的

under·world /ˈʌndəwɜːld; *NAmE* ˈʌndərwɜːrld/ *noun* [sing.] **1** the people and activities involved in crime in a particular place 黑社會；黑道；犯罪集團：*the criminal underworld* 罪惡的黑社會 ◇ *the Glasgow underworld* 格拉斯哥的黑社會 **2 the underworld** (in MYTHS and LEGENDS, for example those of ancient Greece 神話、傳說中的) the place under the earth where people are believed to go when they die 陰間；冥府；陰曹地府

under·write /ˌʌndəˈraɪt; *NAmE* -dərˈr-/ *verb* (**under·wrote** /-ˈrəʊt; *NAmE* -ˈroʊt/, **under·writ·ten** /-ˈrɪtn/) (*technical* 術語) **1 ~ sth** to accept financial responsibility for an activity so that you will pay for special costs or for losses it may make 承擔經濟責任（包括支付特別費用或損失）**2 ~ sth** to accept responsibility for an insurance policy so that you will pay money in case loss or damage happens 承擔保險責任；承保 **3 ~ sth** to agree to buy shares that are not bought by the public when new shares are offered for sale 包銷，承銷（未獲認購的新發行股份）

under·writer /ˈʌndəraɪtə(r)/ *noun* **1** a person or organization that underwrites insurance policies, especially for ships （尤指船隻的）承保人，保險商 **2** a person whose job is to estimate the risks involved in a particular activity and decide how much sb must pay for insurance 核保人（對投保項目進行風險評估並決定保險費率）

un·des·cend·ed /ˌʌndɪˈsendɪd/ *adj.* (*medical* 醫) (of a TESTICLE 睾丸) staying inside the body instead of moving down normally into the SCROTUM 未下降（入陰囊）的；內隱的

un·deserved /ˌʌndɪˈzɜːvd; *NAmE* -ˈzɜːrvd/ *adj.* that sb does not deserve and therefore unfair 不應得的；冤枉的；不公正的：*The criticism was totally undeserved.* 這批評純屬冤枉人。◇ *an undeserved victory* 不該得到的勝利 ▸ **un·deserv·ed·ly** /-dɪˈzɜːvɪdli; *NAmE* -ˈzɜːrv-/ *adv.*

un·deserv·ing /ˌʌndɪˈzɜːvɪŋ; *NAmE* -ˈzɜːrv-/ *adj.* **~ (of sth)** (*formal*) not deserving to have or receive sth 不夠格的；不相當的；不配的：*He was undeserving of her affections.* 他不配得到她的愛。OPP **deserving**

un·desir·able /ˌʌndɪˈzaɪərəbl/ *adj., noun*

■ *adj.* not wanted or approved of; likely to cause trouble or problems 不想要的；不得人心的；易惹麻煩的：***undesirable consequences/effects*** 不良後果／影響 ◇ *It would be highly undesirable to increase class sizes further.* 再增加班級人數，是大家都極不願意的。◇ *prostitution and other undesirable practices* 賣淫和其他不良勾當 OPP **desirable** ▸ **un·desir·ably** /-əbli/ *adv.*

■ *noun* [usually pl.] a person who is not wanted in a particular place, especially because they are considered dangerous or criminal 不受歡迎的人；不良分子：*He's been mixing with drug addicts and other undesirables.* 他一直跟癮君子和其他不良分子混在一起。

un·detect·able /ˌʌndɪˈtektəbl/ *adj.* impossible to see or find 看不見的；察覺不出的；發現不了的：*The sound is virtually undetectable to the human ear.* 這聲音實際上是人耳難以聽得到的。OPP **detectable**

un·detect·ed /ˌʌndɪˈtektɪd/ *adj.* not noticed by anyone 未被注意的：*How could anyone break into the palace undetected?* 怎麼會有人神不知、鬼不覺地潛入皇宮呢？◇ *The disease often* ***goes/remains undetected*** *for many years.* 這種疾病經常潛伏多年而不被察覺。

un·deterred /ˌʌndɪˈtɜːd; *NAmE* -ˈtɜːrd/ *adj.* if sb is **undeterred** by sth, they do not allow it to stop them from doing sth 頑強的；堅毅的；不屈不撓的

un·devel·oped /ˌʌndɪˈveləpt/ *adj.* **1** (of land 土地) not used for farming, industry, building, etc. 未開墾的；未利用的；未開發的 **2** (of a country 國家) not having modern industries, and with a low standard of living 不發達的；落後的 **3** not grown to full size 發育不良的；未充分發育的：*undeveloped limbs* 發育不全的四肢 ➲ compare UNDERDEVELOPED

un·did *past tense* of UNDO

un·dies /ˈʌndiz/ *noun* [pl.] (*informal*) underwear 內衣；襯衣

un·dif·fer·en·ti·ated /ˌʌndɪfəˈrenʃieɪtɪd/ *adj.* having parts that you cannot distinguish between; not split into different parts or sections 無法區分的；分不開的；一體的：*a view of society as an undifferentiated whole* 認為社會是一個統一整體的觀點 ◇ *an undifferentiated target audience* 不分類的目標觀眾

un·dig·ni·fied /ʌnˈdɪɡnɪfaɪd/ *adj.* causing you to look silly and to lose the respect of other people 不像樣的；不成體統的；不體面的；不莊重的：*There was an undignified* *scramble for the best seats.* 大家爭搶最好的位子，真是有失體統。**OPP** **dignified**

un·diluted /ˌʌndaɪˈluːtɪd; *BrE* also -ˈljuːtɪd/ *adj.* **1** (of a liquid 液體) not made weaker by having water added to it; not having been DILUTED 未摻水的；未稀釋的 **2** (of a feeling or quality 感情或品質) not mixed or combined with anything and therefore very strong 真摯的；純潔的；濃烈的；醇厚的 **SYN** **unadulterated**

un·dimin·ished **AW** /ˌʌndɪˈmɪnɪʃt/ *adj.* that has not become smaller or weaker 未減少的；未衰的；未減弱的：*They continued with undiminished enthusiasm.* 他們熱情依舊地繼續着。

un·dis·charged /ˌʌndɪsˈtʃɑːdʒd; *NAmE* -ˈtʃɑːrdʒd/ *adj.* (*law* 律) an **undischarged** BANKRUPT is a person who has been officially stated to be bankrupt by a court but who still has to pay his or her debts（破產者）未清償債務的

un·dis·cip·lined /ʌnˈdɪsəplɪnd/ *adj.* lacking control and organization; behaving badly 無組織紀律的；沒規矩的；缺乏管教的 **OPP** **disciplined**

un·dis·closed /ˌʌndɪsˈkləʊzd; *NAmE* -ˈkloʊzd/ *adj.* not made known or told to anyone; not having been DISCLOSED 未披露的；未公開的；保密的：*He was paid an undisclosed sum.* 他得到了一筆數目不詳的款項。

un·dis·cov·ered /ˌʌndɪsˈkʌvəd; *NAmE* -ərd/ *adj.* that has not been found or noticed; that has not been discovered 未找到（或注意到）的；未被發現的：*a previously undiscovered talent* 以前沒被發掘的天才

un·dis·guised /ˌʌndɪsˈɡaɪzd/ *adj.* (especially of a feeling 尤指感情) that you do not try to hide from other people; not DISGUISED 坦誠的；率直的；不加掩飾的：*a look of undisguised admiration* 不加掩飾的仰慕神情

un·dis·mayed /ˌʌndɪsˈmeɪd/ *adj.* [not before noun] (*formal*) not worried or frightened by sth unpleasant or unexpected 處變不驚；不驚恐；鎮定 **SYN** **undaunted**

un·dis·puted /ˌʌndɪˈspjuːtɪd/ *adj.* **1** that cannot be questioned or proved to be false; that cannot be DISPUTED 不容置疑的；毫無疑問的；不可爭辯的 **SYN** **irrefutable**：*undisputed facts* 不容置疑的事實 **2** that everyone accepts or recognizes 廣為接受的；公認的：*the undisputed champion of the world* 公認的世界冠軍

un·dis·tin·guished /ˌʌndɪˈstɪŋɡwɪʃt/ *adj.* not very interesting, successful or attractive 乏味的；平凡的；無特色的；不吸引人的：*an undistinguished career* 平凡的職業生涯 **OPP** **distinguished**

un·dis·turbed /ˌʌndɪˈstɜːbd; *NAmE* -ˈstɜːrbd/ *adj.* **1** [not usually before noun] not moved or touched by anyone or anything 未被移動（或觸及）**SYN** **untouched**：*The treasure had lain undisturbed for centuries.* 那份珍寶安然無恙地存放了幾個世紀。**2** not interrupted by anyone 未受驚擾的；未被打擾的 **SYN** **uninterrupted**：*She succeeded in working undisturbed for a few hours.* 她終於得以安安靜靜地工作了幾個小時。**3** [not usually before noun] **~ (by sth)** not affected or upset by sth 平靜；鎮定；泰然自若 **SYN** **unconcerned**：*He seemed undisturbed by the news of her death.* 他對她的死訊似乎無動於衷。➲ compare DISTURBED (3)

un·div·ided /ˌʌndɪˈvaɪdɪd/ *adj.* **1** not split into smaller parts; not divided 未劃分的；未分開的；完整的：*an undivided Church* 未分立支派的教會 **2** [usually before noun] total; complete; not divided 完全的；全部的；專注的：*undivided loyalty* 赤膽忠心 ◇ *You must be prepared to give the job your* ***undivided attention***. 你必須準備好全心全意地投入工作。

undo 🔑 /ʌnˈduː/ *verb* (**un·does** /ʌnˈdʌz/, **un·did** /ʌnˈdɪd/, **un·done** /ʌnˈdʌn/)

1 🔑 **~ sth** to open sth that is fastened, tied or wrapped 打開；解開；拆開：*to* ***undo a button/knot/zip, etc.*** 解開鈕扣、解開繩結、拉開拉鎖等 ◇ *to* ***undo a jacket/shirt, etc.*** 解開上衣、襯衫等 ◇ *I undid the package and took out the books.* 我打開包裹取出書來。**OPP** **do up** **2 ~ sth** to cancel the effect of sth 消除，取消，廢止（某事的影響）：*He undid most of the good work of the previous manager.* 他把前任經理的大部份功績都毀掉了。◇ *It's not too late to try and* ***undo*** *some of* ***the damage***. 想辦法補救部份損失還為時不晚。◇ *UNDO* (= a command on a computer that cancels the previous action) 撤銷（計算機的還原指令）**3** [usually passive] **~ sb/sth** (*formal*) to make sb/sth fail 打敗；挫敗：*The team was undone by the speed and strength of their opponents.* 這個隊伍被對手的速度和體力打敗了。

un·dock /ʌnˈdɒk; *NAmE* -ˈdɑːk/ *verb* **~ sth** (*computing* 計) to remove a computer from a DOCKING STATION 使出塢 **OPP** **dock**

un·docu·ment·ed /ˌʌnˈdɒkjumentɪd; *NAmE* -ˈdɑːk-/ *adj.* **1** not supported by written evidence 無書面證據的：*undocumented accusations* 無書面證據的指控 **2** not having the necessary documents, especially permission to live and work in a foreign country 無必要證件的；（尤指在外國）無居住證的，無執照的：*undocumented immigrants* 無證移民

un·do·ing /ʌnˈduːɪŋ/ *noun* [sing.] the reason why sb fails at sth or is unsuccessful in life 失敗的原因 **SYN** **downfall**：*That one mistake was his undoing.* 他一失足即成千古恨。

un·done /ʌnˈdʌn/ *adj.* [not usually before noun] **1** (especially of clothing 尤指衣服) not fastened or tied 未扣；未繫；鬆開：*Her blouse had* ***come undone***. 她的襯衫扣鬆開了。**2** (especially of work 尤指工作) not finished 未完成；未竟：*Most of the work had been left undone.* 大部份工作還沒有做完。**3** (*old use*) (of a person 人) defeated and without any hope for the future 完蛋；一蹶不振；無出頭之日

un·doubt·ed /ʌnˈdaʊtɪd/ *adj.* [usually before noun] used to emphasize that sth exists or is definitely true 無疑的；確實的；千真萬確的 **SYN** **indubitable**：*She has an undoubted talent as an organizer.* 她的確有組織才能。
▶ **un·doubt·ed·ly** *adv.*：*There is undoubtedly a great deal of truth in what he says.* 他所說的的確大部份都是實情。

undreamed-of /ʌnˈdriːmd ɒv; *NAmE* ʌv/ (also **undreamt-of** /ʌnˈdremt ɒv; *NAmE* ʌv/ especially in *BrE*) *adj.* much more or much better than you thought was possible 意想不到的；做夢都沒想到的：*undreamed-of success* 意想不到的成功

un·dress /ʌnˈdres/ *verb, noun*

■ ***verb*** [I, T] to take off your clothes; to remove sb else's clothes（給…）脫衣服：*She undressed and got into bed.* 她解衣上牀了。◇ **~ sb** *to undress a child* 給小孩脫衣服 ◇ *He* ***got undressed*** *in a small cubicle next to the pool.* 他在游泳池旁的小更衣室裏脫掉了衣服。**OPP** **dress**

■ ***noun*** [U] (*formal*) the fact of sb wearing no, or few, clothes 裸體；赤身：*He appeared at the window in a* ***state of undress***. 他光着身子出現在窗前。

un·dressed /ʌnˈdrest/ *adj.* [not usually before noun] not wearing any clothes 赤裸；一絲不掛：*She began to* ***get undressed*** (= remove her clothes). 她開始脫去衣服。**OPP** **dressed**

un·drink·able /ʌnˈdrɪŋkəbl/ *adj.* not good or pure enough to drink 不適合飲用的；不能喝的 **OPP** **drinkable**

undue /ˌʌnˈdjuː; *NAmE* ˌʌnˈduː/ *adj.* [only before noun] (*formal*) more than you think is reasonable or necessary 不適當的；過分的；過度的 **SYN** **excessive**：*They are taking undue advantage of the situation.* 他們過分利用了這種情勢。◇ *The work should be carried out without undue delay.* 進行這項工作不得有不當的延誤。◇ *We did not want to put any undue pressure on them.* 我們並不想給他們施加過多的壓力。➲ compare DUE *adj.* (6)

un·du·late /ˈʌndjuleɪt; *NAmE* -dʒə-/ *verb* [I] (*formal*) to go or move gently up and down like waves 起伏；波動；盪漾：*The countryside undulates pleasantly.* 原野起伏，景色宜人。

un·du·la·tion /ˌʌndjuˈleɪʃn; *NAmE* -dʒə-/ *noun* [C, U] a smooth curving shape or movement like a series of waves 波浪形；起伏；波動；盪漾

un·duly /ˌʌnˈdjuːli; *NAmE* ˌʌnˈduːli/ *adv.* (*formal*) more than you think is reasonable or necessary 過分；過度；不適當地 **SYN** **excessively**：*He did not sound unduly worried at the prospect.* 他的口氣聽上去對前景並不十分

U

擔憂。◇ *The levels of pollution in this area are unduly high.* 本地區的污染程度過高。◇ *The thought did not disturb her unduly.* 這個想法並沒有讓她過分煩惱。➲ compare DULY (1)

un·dying /ʌn'daɪɪŋ/ *adj.* [only before noun] lasting for ever 永恆的；永久的；不朽的 **SYN** **eternal**：*undying love* 永恆的愛

un·earned /ˌʌn'ɜːnd; *NAmE* ˌʌn'ɜːrnd/ *adj.* [usually before noun] used to describe money that you receive but do not earn by working 非勞動所得的：*Declare all* ***unearned income.*** 一切非勞動所得的收入都要申報。

un·earth /ʌn'ɜːθ; *NAmE* ʌn'ɜːrθ/ *verb* **1 ~ sth** to find sth in the ground by digging 挖掘；發掘；使出土 **SYN** **dig up**：*to unearth buried treasures* 挖掘地下埋藏的珍寶 **2 ~ sth** to find or discover sth by chance or after searching for it（偶然或經搜尋）發現，找到 **SYN** **dig up**：*I unearthed my old diaries when we moved house.* 我們搬家時我偶然發現了自己以前的日記。◇ *The newspaper has unearthed some disturbing facts.* 報紙揭發了一些令人不安的真相。

un·earth·ly /ʌn'ɜːθli; *NAmE* -'ɜːrθ-/ *adj.* [usually before noun] very strange; not natural and therefore frightening 怪異的；異常的；非自然的；恐怖的：*an unearthly cry* 令人毛骨悚然的喊聲 ◇ *an unearthly light* 奇異的光

IDM **at an unearthly 'hour** (*informal*) very early, especially when this is annoying 很早；過分的早：*The job involved getting up at some unearthly hour to catch the first train.* 這工作需要起大早趕頭班火車。

un·ease /ʌn'iːz/ (also **un·easi·ness** /ʌn'iːzinəs/) *noun* [U, sing.] the feeling of being worried or unhappy about sth 不安；憂慮 **SYN** **anxiety**：*a deep* ***feeling/sense of unease*** 深刻的憂慮感／憂患意識 ◇ *There was a growing unease about their involvement in the war.* 對他們捲入戰爭感到日益不安。◇ *He was unable to hide his unease at the way the situation was developing.* 他無法掩飾對局勢演變的憂慮。

un·easy /ʌn'iːzi/ *adj.* **1** feeling worried or unhappy about a particular situation, especially because you think that sth bad or unpleasant may happen or because you are not sure that what you are doing is right 擔心的；憂慮的；不安的 **SYN** **anxious**：*an uneasy laugh* 不自然的大笑 ◇ **~ about sth** *He was beginning to feel distinctly uneasy about their visit.* 他對他們的造訪明顯地感到不安起來。◇ **~ about doing sth** *She felt uneasy about leaving the children with them.* 把孩子託付給他們，她心裏七上八下的。➲ SYNONYMS at WORRIED **2** not certain to last; not safe or settled 不穩定的；靠不住的；不確定的：*an uneasy peace* 不會持久的和平 ◇ *The two sides eventually reached an uneasy compromise.* 雙方最終達成了暫時的妥協。**3** that does not enable you to relax or feel comfortable 令人不安的；令人不舒服的；不安穩的：*She woke from an* ***uneasy sleep*** *to find the house empty.* 她睡得不安穩，醒來時發現屋子裏空無一人。**4** used to describe a mixture of two things, feelings, etc. that do not go well together 不和諧的；不協調的；矛盾的：*an* ***uneasy mix*** *of humour and violence* 幽默與暴力的矛盾組合 ◇ *Old farmhouses and new villas stood together in uneasy proximity.* 破舊的農舍與嶄新的別墅比肩而立，很不協調。▶ **un·eas·ily** /ʌn'iːzɪli/ *adv.*：*I wondered uneasily what he was thinking.* 我惴惴不安，不知他到底有什麼心事。◇ *She shifted uneasily in her chair.* 她忐忑不安地在椅子上移動。◇ *His socialist views* ***sit uneasily*** *with his huge fortune.* 他擁有大量財富，這與他的社會主義觀點格格不入。

U

un·eat·able /ʌn'iːtəbl/ *adj.* (of food 食物) not good enough to be eaten 不能吃的；不宜食用的 ➲ see also INEDIBLE

un·eat·en /ʌn'iːtn/ *adj.* not eaten 未吃的：*Bill put the uneaten food away.* 比爾把沒吃的食物收了起來。

un·eco·nom·ic /ˌʌnˌiːkə'nɒmɪk; ˌʌnˌek-; *NAmE* -'nɑːm-/ *adj.* **1** (of a business, factory, etc. 企業、工廠等) not making a profit 不贏利的；不賺錢的 **SYN** **unprofitable**：*uneconomic industries* 不賺錢的行業 **OPP** **economic** **2** = UNECONOMICAL

un·eco·nom·ic·al **AW** /ˌʌnˌiːkə'nɒmɪkl; ˌʌnˌek-; *NAmE* -'nɑːm-/ (also **un·eco·nom·ic**) *adj.* **~ (to do sth)** using too much time or money, or too many materials, and therefore not likely to make a profit 浪費的；不節儉的；不經濟的：*It soon proved uneconomical to stay open 24 hours a day.* 每天 24 小時營業很快便能證明是不經濟的。**OPP** **economical**

un·edify·ing /ʌn'edɪfaɪɪŋ/ *adj.* (*formal, especially BrE*) unpleasant in a way that makes you feel disapproval 討厭的；令人厭惡的；有傷風化的：*the unedifying sight of the two party leaders screeching at each other* 兩黨魁猜猜對吠的討厭情景 ➲ compare EDIFYING

un·edu·cated /ʌn'edʒukeɪtɪd/ *adj.* having had little or no formal education at a school; showing a lack of education 未受教育的；未教化的；缺乏教養的：*an uneducated workforce* 缺乏教育的勞動力 ◇ *an uneducated point of view* 無知的觀點 ➲ compare EDUCATED (2)

un·elect·ed /ˌʌnɪ'lektɪd/ *adj.* not having been chosen by people in an election 未當選的；落選的：*unelected bureaucrats* 未當選的官僚

un·emo·tion·al /ˌʌnɪ'məʊʃənl; *NAmE* -'moʊ-/ *adj.* not showing your feelings 不露感情的；不動聲色的；平靜的：*an unemotional speech* 心平氣和的講話 ◇ *She seemed very cool and unemotional.* 她顯得十分冷靜。**OPP** **emotional** ▶ **un·emo·tion·al·ly** *adv.*

un·employ·able /ˌʌnɪm'plɔɪəbl/ *adj.* lacking the skills or qualities that you need to get a job 不宜雇用的（因缺乏所需技能或資質不足）**OPP** **employable**

un·employed 🗝 /ˌʌnɪm'plɔɪd/ *adj.* without a job although able to work 失業的；待業的；下崗的 **SYN** **jobless**：*How long have you been unemployed?* 你失業多久了？◇ *an unemployed builder* 失業的建築工人 ➲ COLLOCATIONS at UNEMPLOYMENT ▶ **the un·employed** 🗝 *noun* [pl.]：*a programme to get the* ***long-term unemployed*** *back to work* 協助長期失業者恢復工作的計劃 ◇ *I've joined the ranks of the unemployed* (= I've lost my job). 我加入了失業者的行列。

un·employ·ment 🗝 /ˌʌnɪm'plɔɪmənt/ *noun* [U] **1** 🗝 the fact of a number of people not having a job; the number of people without a job 失業；失業人數：*an area of* ***high/low unemployment*** 失業率高／低的地區 ◇ ***rising/falling unemployment*** 上升的／下降的失業率 ◇ *It was a time of* ***mass unemployment.*** 曾經有大批人失業。◇ *measures to help* ***reduce/tackle unemployment*** 旨在減少失業／緩解失業情況的措施 ◇ *the* ***level/rate of unemployment*** 失業人數；失業率 ◇ ***unemployment benefit/statistics*** 失業補貼／統計資料 ➲ COLLOCATIONS at ECONOMY **2** 🗝 the state of not having a job 無業；沒有工作：*Thousands of young people are facing* ***long-term unemployment.*** 成千上萬的青年正面臨長期待業狀況。➲ compare EMPLOYMENT (1) **3** (*US*) = UNEMPLOYMENT BENEFIT：*Since losing his job, Mike has been collecting unemployment.* 自從丟了工作之後，馬克一直在領取失業救濟金。

unem'ployment benefit (*BrE*) (*US* **unem,ployment compen'sation**, **unemployment**) *noun* [U] (also **unem'ployment benefits** [pl.]) money paid by the government to sb who is unemployed 失業補貼（或津貼）；失業救濟金：*people on* (= receiving) *unemployment benefit* 領取失業救濟金的人 ◇ *Applications for unemployment benefits dropped last month.* 上個月申請失業津貼的人數下降了。➲ see also JOBSEEKER'S ALLOWANCE

un·en·cum·bered /ˌʌnɪn'kʌmbəd; *NAmE* -bərd/ *adj.* **1** not having or carrying anything heavy or anything that makes you go more slowly 無負擔的；沒有阻礙的；不受妨礙的 **2** (of property 地產) not having any debts left to be paid 沒有作為抵押的

un·end·ing /ʌn'endɪŋ/ *adj.* seeming to last for ever 無盡的；源源不斷的；不竭的：*a seemingly unending supply of money* 似乎源源不斷的資金供應

un·en·dur·able /ˌʌnɪn'djʊərəbl; *NAmE* -'dʊr-/ *adj.* (*formal*) too bad, unpleasant, etc. to bear 無法容忍的；難以忍受的 **SYN** **unbearable**：*unendurable pain* 難以忍受的痛苦

un·envi·able /ʌnˈenviəbl/ *adj.* [usually before noun] difficult or unpleasant; that you would not want to have 艱難的；討厭的；不值得羨慕的：*She was given the* ***unenviable task*** *of informing the losers.* 讓她去通知失敗的人，真不是什麼好差事。OPP **enviable**

un·equal /ʌnˈiːkwəl/ *adj.* **1** [usually before noun] in which people are treated in different ways or have different advantages in a way that seems unfair 不平等的；不均衡的；不公平的 SYN **unfair**：*an unequal distribution of wealth* 財富的分配不均 ◇ *an unequal contest* 不公平競爭 **2 ~ (in sth)** different in size, amount, etc.（面積、數量等）不相等的，不同的：*The sleeves are unequal in length.* 這兩隻衣袖不一樣長。◇ *The rooms upstairs are of unequal size.* 樓上的房間大小不同。**3 ~ to sth** (*formal*) not capable of doing sth 力所不及；不勝任：*She felt unequal to the task she had set herself.* 她覺得難以完成給自己定下的任務。OPP **equal** ▸ **un·equal·ly** /-kwəli/ *adv.*

un·equalled (*US* **un·equaled**) /ʌnˈiːkwəld/ *adj.* better than all others 無比的；無雙的；出類拔萃的 SYN **unparalleled**：*an unequalled record of success* 空前的成功紀錄

un·equivo·cal /ˌʌnɪˈkwɪvəkl/ *adj.* (*formal*) expressing your opinion or intention very clearly and firmly 表達明確的；毫不含糊的；斬釘截鐵的 SYN **unambiguous**：*an unequivocal rejection* 明確的拒絕 ◇ *The answer was an unequivocal 'no'.* 回答是個乾脆利落的"不"字。OPP **equivocal** ➲ SYNONYMS at PLAIN (1) ▸ **un·equivo·cal·ly** /-kəli/ *adv.*

un·err·ing /ʌnˈɜːrɪŋ/ *adj.* always right or accurate 萬無一失的；一貫正確（或精確）的 SYN **unfailing**：*She had an unerring instinct for a good business deal.* 她有天生擅長做生意的本事。▸ **un·err·ing·ly** *adv.*

Collocations 詞語搭配

Unemployment 失業

Losing your job 失業

- **lose** your job 失業
- (*BrE*) **become/be made** redundant 被裁減
- **be offered/take** voluntary redundancy/early retirement 被要求／選擇自願裁員／提前退休
- **face/be threatened with** dismissal/(*BrE*) the sack/(*BrE*) compulsory redundancy 面臨被解職／被裁／強制裁員；受到解職／被裁／強制裁員的威脅
- **dismiss/fire/**(*especially BrE*) **sack** an employee/a worker/a manager 解雇雇員／工人／經理
- **lay off** staff/workers/employees 解雇員工／工人／雇員
- (*AustralE, NZE, SAfrE*) **retrench** workers 縮減人員
- **cut/reduce/downsize/slash** the workforce 裁減員工
- (*BrE*) **make** staff/workers/employees redundant 裁員

Being unemployed 失業；待業；下崗

- **be** unemployed/out of work/out of a job 失業
- **seek/look for** work/employment 找工作
- **be on/collect/draw/get/receive** (*both BrE*) unemployment benefit/jobseeker's allowance 領取失業補助金
- **be/go/live/sign** (*BrE, informal*) on the dole 領取失業救濟金
- **claim/draw/get** (*BrE, informal*) the dole 領取失業救濟金
- **be on/qualify for** (*NAmE*) unemployment (compensation) 領取／有資格領取失業補償金
- **be/go/live/depend** (*NAmE*) on welfare 靠社會保障金過活
- **collect/receive** (*NAmE*) welfare 領取社會保障金
- **combat/tackle/cut/reduce** unemployment 防止／解決／減少失業

UNESCO /juːˈneskəʊ; *NAmE* -koʊ/ (also **Unesco**) *abbr.* United Nations Educational, Scientific and Cultural Organization 聯合國教科文組織；聯合國教育、科學及文化組織

un·eth·ic·al AW /ʌnˈeθɪkl/ *adj.* not morally acceptable 不道德的：*unethical behaviour* 不道德行為 OPP **ethical** ▸ **un·eth·ic·al·ly** /-kli/ *adv.*

un·even /ʌnˈiːvn/ *adj.* **1** not level, smooth or flat 凹凸不平的；不平坦的：*The floor felt uneven under his feet.* 他覺得腳下的地板高低不平。OPP **even** **2** not following a regular pattern; not having a regular size and shape 無定型的；不規則的；無規律的 SYN **irregular**：*Her breathing was quick and uneven.* 她的呼吸急促不勻。◇ *uneven teeth* 不整齊的牙齒 OPP **even** **3** not having the same quality in all parts 質量不穩定的：*an uneven performance* (= with some good parts and some bad parts) 時好時壞的表現 **4** (of a contest or match 競爭或比賽) in which one group, team or player is much better than the other 實力懸殊的；一邊倒的；不在同一水平的 SYN **unequal** OPP **even** **5** organized in a way that is not regular and/or fair 不均衡的；不公平的；不規則的 SYN **unequal**：*an uneven distribution of resources* 資源的不均衡分配 OPP **even** ▸ **un·even·ly** *adv.* **un·even·ness** *noun* [U]

unˌeven ˈbars (*NAmE*) (*BrE* **asymˌmetric ˈbars**) *noun* [pl.] two bars on posts of different heights that are used by women for doing GYMNASTIC exercises on 高低槓（女子體操器械）

un·event·ful /ˌʌnɪˈventfl/ *adj.* in which nothing interesting, unusual or exciting happens 平淡無奇的；平凡的；缺乏刺激的：*an uneventful life* 平淡的一生 OPP **eventful** ▸ **un·event·ful·ly** /-fəli/ *adv.*：*The day passed uneventfully.* 這一天平平淡淡地過去了。

un·ex·cep·tion·able /ˌʌnɪkˈsepʃənəbl/ *adj.* **1** (*formal*) not giving any reason for criticism 無可指責的；無從挑剔的；無懈可擊的：*a man of unexceptionable character* 一個品格完美的男子 **2** (*informal*) not very new or exciting 不新奇的；不刺激的；不令人振奮的

un·ex·cep·tion·al /ˌʌnɪkˈsepʃənl/ *adj.* not interesting or unusual 乏味的；平常的；不突出的；普通的 SYN **unremarkable** ➲ compare EXCEPTIONAL

un·ex·cit·ing /ˌʌnɪkˈsaɪtɪŋ/ *adj.* not interesting; boring 枯燥的；乏味的；無聊的 OPP **exciting**

un·ex·pect·ed 🔑 /ˌʌnɪkˈspektɪd/ *adj.* if sth is **unexpected**, it surprises you because you were not expecting it 出乎意料的；始料不及的：*an unexpected result* 意想不到的結果 ◇ *an unexpected visitor* 不速之客 ◇ *The announcement was not* ***entirely unexpected***. 這個通告並非完全出乎意料。▸ **the unexpected** 🔑 *noun* [sing.]：*Police officers must be prepared for the unexpected.* 警察必須隨時準備應付意外事件。**un·ex·pect·ed·ly** 🔑 *adv.*：*They had arrived unexpectedly.* 他們意外地到達了。◇ *an unexpectedly large bill* 出乎意料的高額賬單 ◇ *The plane was unexpectedly delayed.* 飛機意外地延誤了。◇ *Not unexpectedly, most local business depends on tourism.* 並非出人意料的是，當地的大部份生意依靠旅遊業。**un·ex·pect·ed·ness** *noun* [U] ➲ compare EXPECT (4), EXPECTED

un·ex·pired /ˌʌnɪkˈspaɪəd; *NAmE* -ˈspaɪərd/ *adj.* [usually before noun] (of an agreement or a period of time 協議或限期) still valid; not yet having come to an end or EXPIRED 有效的；未過期的

un·ex·plained /ˌʌnɪkˈspleɪnd/ *adj.* for which the reason or cause is not known; that has not been explained 原因不詳的；未解釋的；未說明的：*an unexplained mystery* 解釋不清的奧妙 ◇ *He died in unexplained circumstances.* 他死因不明。

un·ex·ploded /ˌʌnɪkˈspləʊdɪd; *NAmE* -ˈsploʊ-/ *adj.* [only before noun] (of a bomb, etc. 炸彈等) that has not yet exploded 未爆炸的

un·ex·plored /ˌʌnɪkˈsplɔːd; *NAmE* -ˈsplɔːrd/ *adj.* **1** (of a country or an area of land 國家或地域) that nobody has investigated or put on a map; that has not been

U

explored 無人涉足的；未畫進地圖的；未經勘察的 **2** (of an idea, a theory, etc. 想法、理論等) that has not yet been examined or discussed thoroughly 未經徹底研究（或探討）的

un·ex·pressed /ˌʌnɪk'sprest/ *adj.* (of a thought, a feeling or an idea 思想、感情或意見) not shown or made known in words, looks or actions; not expressed 未表現出的；未表達的；未表示的

un·ex·pur·gated /ʌn'ekspəgeɪtɪd; *NAmE* -pərg-/ *adj.* (of a text) complete and containing all the original material, even if it is offensive （文稿）未經刪節的：*This is the full unexpurgated version of the diaries.* 這是日記的足本。

un·fail·ing /ʌn'feɪlɪŋ/ *adj.* that you can rely on to always be there and always be the same 可靠的；一貫的；永久的：*unfailing support* 一貫的支持 ◇ *She fought the disease with* ***unfailing good humour.*** 她始終抱樂觀態度同疾病鬥爭。 ▸ **un·fail·ing·ly** *adv.*：*unfailingly loyal/polite* 一貫地忠心耿耿／彬彬有禮

un·fair 0‑w /ˌʌn'feə(r); *NAmE* -'fer/ *adj.* not right or fair according to a set of rules or principles; not treating people equally 不公正的；不公平的；待人不平等的 SYN **unjust**：*unfair criticism* 不公正的批評 ◇ **~ (on/to sb)** *It seems unfair on him to make him pay for everything.* 讓他承擔一切費用似乎對他不公平。 ◇ *It would* ***be unfair*** *not to let you have a choice.* 不讓你有所選擇是不公平的。 ◇ *They had been given an* ***unfair advantage.*** 他們得到了不公正的好處。 ◇ ***unfair dismissal*** (= a situation in which sb is illegally dismissed from their job) 不公平解雇 ◇ *measures to prevent unfair competition between member countries* 防止成員國之間不公平競爭的措施 ◇ *Life seems so unfair sometimes.* 人生有時似乎非常不公平。 ◇ *It's so unfair!* 這太不公平了！ OPP **fair** ▸ **un·fair·ly** 0‑w *adv.*：*She claims to have been unfairly dismissed.* 她聲言遭到無理解雇。 ◇ *The tests discriminate unfairly against older people.* 這些測驗使年紀較大的人受到歧視。 **un·fair·ness** *noun* [U]

un·faith·ful /ʌn'feɪθfl/ *adj.* **~ (to sb)** having sex with sb who is not your husband, wife or usual partner 不忠的；通姦的：*Have you ever been unfaithful to him?* 你對他是否有過不忠行為？ OPP **faithful** ▸ **un·faith·ful·ness** *noun* [U]

un·famil·iar /ˌʌnfə'mɪliə(r)/ *adj.* **1** that you do not know or recognize 陌生的；不熟悉的；不認識的：*She felt uneasy in the unfamiliar surroundings.* 她在陌生的環境中感到局促不安。 ◇ **~ to sb** *Please highlight any terms that are unfamiliar to you.* 請把你們不熟悉的用語都標示出來。 **2 ~ with sth** not having any knowledge or experience of sth 無…的知識（或經驗）：*an introductory course for students who are unfamiliar with computers* 為不瞭解計算機的學生開設的入門課程 OPP **familiar** ▸ **un·famili·ar·ity** /ˌʌnfəˌmɪli'ærəti/ *noun* [U]

U

un·fash·ion·able /ʌn'fæʃnəbl/ *adj.* not popular or fashionable at a particular time 不時興的；不時髦的；過時的：*an unfashionable part of London* 倫敦一個偏僻的角落 ◇ *unfashionable ideas* 守舊的思想 OPP **fashionable** ▸ **un·fash·ion·ably** *adv.*：*a man with unfashionably long hair* 留着過時長髮的男人

un·fas·ten /ʌn'fɑːsn; *NAmE* ʌn'fæsn/ *verb* **~ sth** to undo sth that is fastened 解開；鬆開；打開：*to unfasten a belt/button, etc.* 解開皮帶、鈕扣等 OPP **fasten**

un·fath·om·able /ʌn'fæðəməbl/ *adj.* (*formal*) **1** too strange or difficult to be understood 難以理解的；莫測高深的：*an unfathomable mystery* 難以解釋的奧秘 **2** if sb has an **unfathomable** expression, it is impossible to know what they are thinking （表情）難以琢磨的，微妙的

un·favour·able (*especially US* **un·favor·able**) /ʌn'feɪvərəbl/ *adj.* (*formal*) **1 ~ (for/to sth)** (of conditions, situations, etc. 條件、形勢等) not good and likely to cause problems or make sth more difficult 不利的；有害的：*The conditions were unfavourable for agriculture.* 這些條件不利於農業。 ◇ *an unfavourable exchange rate* 不利的匯率 **2** showing that you do not approve of or like sb/sth 不贊成的；否定的；不喜歡的：*an unfavourable comment* 負面的評論 ◇ *The documentary presents him in a very* ***unfavourable light.*** 這部紀錄片從十分負面的角度來描繪他。 ◇ *an* ***unfavourable comparison*** (= one that makes one thing seem much worse than another) 使相形見絀的比較 OPP **favourable** ▸ **un·favour·ably** (*BrE*) (*NAmE* **un·favor·ably**) *adv.*：*In this respect, Britain* ***compares unfavourably*** *with other European countries.* 在這方面，英國比歐洲其他各國要遜色。

un·fazed /ʌn'feɪzd/ *adj.* (*informal*) not worried or surprised by sth unexpected that happens 未受干擾；不覺擔憂 OPP **fazed**

un·feas·ible /ʌn'fiːzəbl/ *adj.* not possible to do or achieve 不可行的；難以實現的 OPP **feasible**

un·feel·ing /ʌn'fiːlɪŋ/ *adj.* not showing care or sympathy for other people 漠不關心的；無情的；無憐憫心的

un·feigned /ʌn'feɪnd/ *adj.* (*formal*) real and sincere 真誠的；真摯的；不虛偽的 SYN **genuine**：*unfeigned admiration* 由衷的欽佩

un·fenced /ʌn'fenst/ *adj.* (of a road or piece of land 道路或土地) without fences beside or around it 無護欄的；無圍欄的

un·fet·tered /ʌn'fetəd; *NAmE* -tərd/ *adj.* (*formal*) not controlled or restricted 無限制的；不受約束的；自由的：*an unfettered free market* 不受約束的自由市場

un·filled /ʌn'fɪld/ *adj.* **1** if a job or position is **unfilled**, nobody has been chosen for it （職位）空缺的 **2** if a pause in a conversation is **unfilled**, nobody speaks （談話中）停頓的 **3** an **unfilled** cake has nothing inside it （糕餅）無餡的 **4** (*especially NAmE*) if an order for goods is **unfilled**, the goods have not been supplied （訂單）未交貨的

un·fin·ished /ʌn'fɪnɪʃt/ *adj.* not complete; not finished 未做完的；未完成的：*We have some* ***unfinished business*** *to settle.* 我們還有些沒做完的事要處理。

unfit /ʌn'fɪt/ *adj.* **1** not of an acceptable standard; not suitable 不合格的；不適合的；不適宜的：**~ (for sth)** *The housing was* ***unfit for human habitation.*** 這種住房不適合居住。 ◇ *The food on offer was* ***unfit for human consumption.*** 那些特價食品不適宜讓人食用。 ◇ **~ (to eat, drink, live in, etc.)** *This water is unfit to drink.* 這水不宜飲用。 ◇ *Most of the buildings are unfit to live in.* 這些樓房多數不適合居住。 ◇ **~ (to do sth)** *They described him as unfit to govern.* 他們認為他這個人不適合做管治工作。 ◇ (*technical* 術語) *Many of the houses were condemned as unfit.* 這些房屋有許多被宣佈為不適宜居住。 ◇ (*technical* 術語) *The court claims she is an unfit mother.* 法庭聲稱她是個不稱職的母親。 **2** not capable of doing sth, for example because of illness （因病等）不能做某事，不宜做事：**~ for sth** *He's still unfit for work.* 他還不宜工作。 ◇ **~ to do sth** *The company's doctor found that she was unfit to carry out her normal work.* 公司的醫生認為，她不宜從事正常工作。 **3** (*especially BrE*) (of a person 人) not in good physical condition; not fit, because you have not taken exercise 健康狀況欠佳；身體狀態差：*The captain is still unfit and will miss tonight's game.* 隊長身體狀態仍不好，將不會出戰今晚的比賽。 OPP **fit** ▸ **un·fit·ness** *noun* [U]

un·fit·ted /ʌn'fɪtɪd/ *adj.* **~ for sth | ~ to do sth** (*formal*) not suitable for sth 不適於；不適合：*She felt herself unfitted for marriage.* 她覺得自己不適宜結婚。

un·flag·ging /ˌʌn'flægɪŋ/ *adj.* [usually before noun] remaining strong; not becoming weak or tired 蓬勃的；不鬆懈的；不減弱的；不倦的 SYN **tireless**：*unflagging energy* 無窮的精力

un·flap·pable /ˌʌn'flæpəbl/ *adj.* (*informal*) able to stay calm in a difficult situation 鎮定的；冷靜的 SYN **imperturbable**

un·flat·ter·ing /ʌn'flætərɪŋ/ *adj.* making sb/sth seem worse or less attractive than they really are 貶損的；有損形象的；不恭維的：*an unflattering dress* 難看的連衣裙 ◇ *unflattering comments* 貶抑的評論 OPP **flattering**

un·flinch·ing /ʌn'flɪntʃɪŋ/ *adj.* remaining strong and determined, even in a difficult or dangerous situation

不屈不撓的；果敢的；堅定的；不畏縮的 SYN **steadfast**：*unflinching loyalty* 堅貞不渝的忠誠 ◇ *an unflinching stare* 毫不畏懼的注視 ▸ **un·flinch·ing·ly** *adv.* ➲ see also FLINCH

un·focused (also **un·focussed**) /ʌnˈfəʊkəst; *NAmE* -ˈfoʊ-/ *adj.* **1** (especially of eyes 尤指眼睛) not looking at a particular thing or person; not having been focused 目光分散的；漫不經心的：*an unfocused look* 茫然的神情 **2** (of plans, work, etc. 計劃、工作等) not having a clear aim or purpose; not well organized or clear 目的不明確的；組織不嚴密的；鬆散的：*The research is too unfocused to have any significant impact.* 這一次的研究太零散，難以發揮重大的作用。◇ *unfocused questions* 漫無邊際的問題

un·fold /ʌnˈfəʊld; *NAmE* ʌnˈfoʊld/ *verb* **1** [T, I] **~ (sth)** to spread open or flat sth that has previously been folded; to become open and flat （使）展開；打開：*to unfold a map* 展開地圖 ◇ *She unfolded her arms.* 她張開雙臂。OPP **fold** **2** [I, T] to be gradually made known; to gradually make sth known to other people （使）逐漸展現；展示；透露：*The audience watched as* ***the story unfolded*** *before their eyes.* 觀眾注視着劇情逐漸地展開。◇ **~ sth (to sb)** *She unfolded her tale to us.* 她向我們傾吐了她的故事。

un·forced /ʌnˈfɔːst; *NAmE* ʌnˈfɔːrst/ *adj.* **1** (especially in sports 尤用於體育運動) an **unforced** error is one that you make by playing badly, not because your opponent has caused you to make a mistake by their skilful play （失誤）自己造成的，非受迫性的 **2** natural; done without effort 自然的；輕易的；不費力的：*unforced humour* 自然的幽默

un·fore·see·able /ˌʌnfɔːˈsiːəbl; *NAmE* -fɔːrˈs-/ *adj.* that you cannot predict or FORESEE 無法預見的；難以預測的：*Building a dam here could have* ***unforeseeable consequences*** *for the environment.* 在這裏修建水壩可能會對環境造成無法預料的後果。OPP **foreseeable**

un·fore·seen /ˌʌnfɔːˈsiːn; *NAmE* -fɔːrˈs-/ *adj.* that you did not expect to happen 未想到的；始料不及的 SYN **unexpected**：***unforeseen delays/problems*** 意外的延誤／問題 ◇ *The project was running late owing to* ***unforeseen circumstances.*** 這個項目因意外情況而拖延了。➲ compare FORESEE

un·for·get·table /ˌʌnfəˈɡetəbl; *NAmE* -fərˈɡ-/ *adj.* if sth is **unforgettable**, you cannot forget it, usually because it is so beautiful, interesting, enjoyable, etc. 難以忘懷的；令人難忘的 SYN **memorable** ➲ compare FORGETTABLE

un·for·giv·able /ˌʌnfəˈɡɪvəbl; *NAmE* -fərˈɡ-/ *adj.* if sb's behaviour is **unforgivable**, it is so bad or unacceptable that you cannot forgive the person 不可原諒的；難以饒恕的 SYN **inexcusable** OPP **forgivable** ▸ **un·for·giv·ably** *adv.*

un·for·giv·ing /ˌʌnfəˈɡɪvɪŋ; *NAmE* -fərˈɡ-/ *adj.* (*formal*) **1** (of a person 人) unwilling to forgive other people when they have done sth wrong 不饒人的；不寬容的；不肯原諒的 OPP **forgiving** **2** (of a place, situation, etc. 地方、局面等) unpleasant and causing difficulties for people 讓人為難的；難應付的；棘手的

un·formed /ˌʌnˈfɔːmd; *NAmE* ˌʌnˈfɔːrmd/ *adj.* (*formal*) not fully developed 發展不充分的；未成形的；不成熟的：*unformed ideas* 不成熟的意見

un·forth·com·ing /ˌʌnfɔːθˈkʌmɪŋ; *NAmE* -fɔːrθ-/ *adj.* not wanting to help or give information about sth 不願幫忙的；口緊的；不露口風的 SYN **reticent**：*He was very unforthcoming about what had happened.* 他對發生的事守口如瓶。OPP **forthcoming**

un·for·tu·nate 0-w /ʌnˈfɔːtʃənət; *NAmE* -ˈfɔːrtʃ-/ *adj., noun*

■ ***adj.*** **1** 0-w having bad luck; caused by bad luck 不幸的；倒霉的 SYN **unlucky**：*He was unfortunate to lose in the final round.* 他不幸在最後一輪輸了。◇ *It was an unfortunate accident.* 那是一次不幸的事故。OPP **fortunate** **2** 0-w (*formal*) if you say that a situation is **unfortunate**, you wish that it had not happened or that it had been different 令人遺憾的；可惜的 SYN **regrettable**：*She described the decision as 'unfortunate'.* 她把這項決定說成是"令人遺憾"。◇ *It was unfortunate that he couldn't speak English.* 可惜他不會講英語。◇ *You're putting me in a* ***most unfortunate*** *position.* 你正在把我推入十分可悲的處境。➲ LANGUAGE BANK at IMPERSONAL **3** embarrassing and/or offensive 令人尷尬的；不適當的；得罪人的：*It was an unfortunate choice of words.* 那是一種不恰當的措辭。

■ ***noun*** (*literary*) a person who does not have much luck, money, etc. 不幸的人：*one of life's unfortunates* 人生中的不幸者之一

un·for·tu·nate·ly 0-w /ʌnˈfɔːtʃənətli; *NAmE* -ˈfɔːrtʃ-/ *adv.*

used to say that a particular situation or fact makes you sad or disappointed, or gets you into a difficult position 不幸地；遺憾地；可惜地；可悲地 SYN **regrettably**：*Unfortunately, I won't be able to attend the meeting.* 真可惜我不能參加這次會議。◇ *I can't make it, unfortunately.* 很遺憾，我來不及。◇ *Unfortunately for him, the police had been informed and were waiting outside.* 算他倒霉，警察已接到報告，就在外邊等着。◇ *It won't be finished for a few weeks. Unfortunately!* 這工作得過幾週才能完成。很遺憾！OPP **fortunately**

un·found·ed AW /ʌnˈfaʊndɪd/ *adj.* not based on reason or fact 莫須有的；無端的；沒理由的；不依據事實的：***unfounded allegations/rumours, etc.*** 缺乏依據的指稱、無中生有的謠言等 ◇ *Speculation about a divorce* ***proved*** *totally* ***unfounded.*** 有關離婚的猜測證實純屬無稽之談。

un·freeze /ˌʌnˈfriːz/ *verb* (**un·froze** /-ˈfrəʊz; *NAmE* -ˈfroʊz/, **un·frozen** /-ˈfrəʊzn; *NAmE* -ˈfroʊzn/) **1** [T, I] **~ (sth)** if you **unfreeze** sth that has been frozen or very cold, or it **unfreezes**, it melts or warms until it reaches a normal temperature （使）解凍，化凍，融化 ➲ compare DEFROST (1), DE-ICE, THAW (3) **2** [T] **~ sth** to remove official controls on money or an economy 解凍；解除（對資金的凍結或經濟方面的限制）：*The party plans to unfreeze some of the cash held by local government.* 這個黨計劃將地方政府凍結的一部份現款解凍。OPP **freeze**

un·friend·ly 0-w /ʌnˈfrendli/ *adj.*

not kind or pleasant to sb 不友好的；冷漠的；有敵意的：*an unfriendly atmosphere* 不友好的氣氛 ◇ **~ (to/towards sb)** *There's no need to be so unfriendly towards them.* 沒必要對他們這麼不客氣。◇ *the use of* ***environmentally unfriendly*** *products* (= that harm the environment) 危害環境的產品的使用 OPP **friendly** ▸ **un·friend·li·ness** *noun* [U]

un·ful·filled /ˌʌnfʊlˈfɪld/ *adj.* **1** (of a need, wish, etc. 需要、願望等) that has not been satisfied or achieved 未滿足的；未實現的；未兌現的：***unfulfilled ambitions/hopes/promises, etc.*** 未實現的抱負、希望、諾言等 **2** if a person feels **unfulfilled**, they feel that they could achieve more in their life or work 壯志未酬的；宏圖未展的 OPP **fulfilled**

un·ful·fil·ling /ˌʌnfʊlˈfɪlɪŋ/ *adj.* not causing sb to feel satisfied and useful 不能使人感到滿足的；不令人稱心的：*an unfulfilling job* 不能令人感到滿足的工作

un·funny /ʌnˈfʌni/ *adj.* not funny or amusing, especially when sth is supposed to be funny 索然無味的；沒意思的；無趣的：*The show was deeply unfunny.* 這場演出毫無趣味。

un·furl /ˌʌnˈfɜːl; *NAmE* ˌʌnˈfɜːrl/ *verb* [I, T] when sth that is curled or rolled tightly **unfurls**, or you **unfurl** it, it opens （使捲緊的東西）打開，展開：*The leaves slowly unfurled.* 葉子慢慢地展開了。◇ **~ sth** *to unfurl a flag* 展開旗子

un·fur·nished /ʌnˈfɜːnɪʃt; *NAmE* -ˈfɜːrn-/ *adj.* without furniture 無傢具的：*We rented an unfurnished apartment.* 我們租了一套不帶傢具的公寓。OPP **furnished**

un·gain·ly /ʌnˈɡeɪnli/ *adj.* moving in a way that is not smooth or elegant 笨手笨腳的；（舉止）不雅觀的，難看的 SYN **awkward**：*He was a tall, ungainly boy of 18.* 他是個個子高而笨拙的 18 歲小伙子。

un·gentle·man·ly /ʌnˈdʒentlmənli/ *adj.* (of a man's behaviour 男子的行為) not polite or pleasant; not acceptable 不禮貌的；無教養（或風度）的 OPP **gentlemanly**

U

un·glam·or·ous /ʌnˈglæmərəs/ *adj.* not attractive or exciting; dull 無魅力的；不刺激的；枯燥的：*an unglamorous job* 乏味的工作 OPP **glamorous**

un·glued /ˌʌnˈgluːd/ *adj.*

IDM **come unˈglued** (*NAmE, informal*) **1** to become very upset 十分煩惱；心情煩亂 **2** if a plan, etc. **comes unglued**, it does not work successfully（計劃等）不順利，效果不佳

un·god·ly /ʌnˈgɒdli; *NAmE* -ˈgɑːd-/ *adj.* (*old-fashioned*) not showing respect for God; evil 褻瀆神靈的；不敬神的；邪惡的 OPP **godly**

IDM **at an ungodly ˈhour** very early or very late and therefore annoying 一大早（或很晚）；在十分不便的時間

un·gov·ern·able /ʌnˈgʌvənəbl; *NAmE* -ˈgʌvərn-/ *adj.* **1** (of a country, region, etc. 國家、地區等) impossible to govern or control 無法管治的；難以控制的 **2** (*formal*) (of a person's feelings 感情) impossible to control 抑制不住的；無法控制的 SYN **uncontrollable**：*ungovernable rage* 難以抑制的暴怒

un·gra·cious /ʌnˈgreɪʃəs/ *adj.* (*formal*) not polite or friendly, especially towards sb who is being kind to you（尤指對別人的善意）不客氣的，失禮的 OPP **gracious** ▸ **un·gra·cious·ly** *adv.*

un·gram·mat·ical /ˌʌngrəˈmætɪkl/ *adj.* not following the rules of grammar 違反語法規則的；不合語法的 OPP **grammatical**

un·grate·ful /ʌnˈgreɪtfl/ *adj.* not showing or expressing thanks for sth that sb has done for you or given to you 不領情的；忘恩負義的 OPP **grateful** ▸ **un·grate·ful·ly** /-fəli/ *adv.*

un·guard·ed /ʌnˈgɑːdɪd; *NAmE* -ˈgɑːrd-/ *adj.* **1** not protected or watched 無防備的；無警戒的；無保護的：*The museum was unguarded at night.* 這個博物館夜裏無人看守。◇ *an unguarded fire* (= that has nothing to stop people from burning themselves on it) 無防護設施的火堆 **2** (of a remark, look, etc. 話語、神情等) said or done carelessly, at a time when you are not thinking about the effects of your words or are not paying attention 不小心的；不謹慎的；不留神的：*an unguarded remark* 輕率的言論 ◇ *It was something I'd let out **in an unguarded moment**.* 那是我一不留神說漏了嘴的話。➲ compare GUARDED

un·guent /ˈʌŋgwənt/ *noun* [C, U] (*formal*) a soft substance that is used for rubbing onto the skin to heal it 藥膏；軟膏

un·gu·late /ˈʌŋgjʊlət; -leɪt/ *noun* (*technical* 術語) any animal which has HOOFS, such as a cow or horse 有蹄類動物

un·hand /ˌʌnˈhænd/ *verb* **~ sb** (*old-fashioned* or *humorous*) to release a person that you are holding 放開某人的手

un·hap·pily /ʌnˈhæpɪli/ *adv.* **1** in an unhappy way 難過地；快快不樂地：*He sighed unhappily.* 他難過地歎息了一聲。 **2** used to say that a particular situation or fact makes you sad or disappointed 遺憾地；不幸地；可惜地 SYN **unfortunately**：*Unhappily, such good luck is rare.* 遺憾的是，這樣的好運太少了。◇ *His wife, unhappily, died five years ago.* 他的妻子不幸於五年前去世了。OPP **happily**

un·happy 🔑 /ʌnˈhæpi/ *adj.* (**un·hap·pier, un·happi·est**) HELP **More unhappy** and **most unhappy** are also common. * more unhappy 和 most unhappy 也常用。
1 🔑 not happy; sad 不快樂的；不幸福的；悲傷的：*to **be/look/seem/sound unhappy*** 感到／看來／似乎／聽起來不愉快 ◇ *an unhappy childhood* 不快樂的童年 ◇ *I didn't realize but he was **deeply unhappy** at that time.* 我沒有察覺到他那時非常不開心。 **2** 🔑 **~ (about/at/with sth)** not pleased or satisfied with sth 不悅的；不高興的；不滿的：*They were unhappy with their accommodation.* 他們對住處不滿意。◇ *He was unhappy at being left out of the team.* 他對未能入選球隊感到不高興。 **3** (*formal*) unfortunate or not suitable 不幸的；不適當的：*an unhappy coincidence* 不幸的巧合 ◇ *It was an unhappy choice of words.* 那樣用詞是不適當的。▸ **un·hap·pi·ness** *noun* [U]

un·harmed /ʌnˈhɑːmd; *NAmE* ʌnˈhɑːrmd/ *adj.* not injured or damaged; not harmed 未受傷的；未受損害的

UNHCR /ˌjuː en ˌeɪtʃ siː ˈɑː(r)/ *abbr.* United Nations High Commission for Refugees (an organization whose function is to help and protect REFUGEES) 聯合國難民事務高級專員辦事處

un·healthy /ʌnˈhelθi/ *adj.* **1** not having good health; showing a lack of good health 不健康的；虛弱的：*They looked poor and unhealthy.* 他們看起來貧病交加。◇ *unhealthy skin* 不健康的皮膚 ◇ *His eyeballs were an unhealthy yellow.* 他的眼球是不健康的蠟黃色。**2** harmful to your health; likely to make you ill/sick 損害健康的；會致病的：*unhealthy living conditions* 有礙健康的生活條件 ◇ *an **unhealthy diet/lifestyle*** 不良的飲食／生活方式 **3** not normal and likely to be harmful 反常的；不良的；有害的 SYN **unwholesome**：*He had an unhealthy interest in disease and death.* 他對疾病與死亡有一種病態的興趣。OPP **healthy** ▸ **un·health·ily** /-ɪli/ *adv.*

un·heard /ʌnˈhɜːd; *NAmE* ʌnˈhɜːrd/ *adj.* **1** that nobody pays attention to 無人理會的；未被注意的：*Their protests **went unheard**.* 他們的抗議無人理會。 **2** not listened to or heard 未被聽的；未聽到的：*a previously unheard tape of their conversations* 以前未聽過的他們談話的錄音帶

unheard-of /ʌnˈhɜːd ɒv; *NAmE* ʌnˈhɜːrd ʌv/ *adj.* that has never been known or done; very unusual 前所未聞的；空前的；很反常的：*He'd dyed his hair, which was almost unheard-of in the 1960s.* 他染了頭髮，這在 20 世紀 60 年代是罕見的事。◇ *It is almost unheard-of for a new band to be offered such a deal.* 一支新樂隊得到這樣的待遇，幾乎是空前的。

un·heat·ed /ʌnˈhiːtɪd/ *adj.* having no form of heating 無供暖設施的；無暖氣的：*an unheated bathroom* 無暖氣的浴室 OPP **heated**

un·heed·ed /ʌnˈhiːdɪd/ *adj.* (*formal*) that is heard, seen or noticed but then ignored 遭視而不見的；遭聽而不聞的；被忽視的：*Her warning **went unheeded**.* 她的警告沒有引起重視。➲ compare HEED

un·help·ful /ʌnˈhelpfl/ *adj.* not helpful or useful; not willing to help sb 無益的；無用的；不願幫助的：*an unhelpful response* 於事無補的反應 ◇ *The taxi driver was being very unhelpful.* 那個出租車司機不肯幫忙。OPP **helpful** ▸ **un·help·ful·ly** /-fəli/ *adv.*

un·her·ald·ed /ʌnˈherəldɪd/ *adj.* (*formal*) not previously mentioned; happening without any warning 未曾提及的；突如其來的；突然發生的

un·hesi·tat·ing /ʌnˈhezɪteɪtɪŋ/ *adj.* done or given immediately and confidently 果斷的；堅決的；毫不遲疑的：*He gave an unhesitating 'yes' when asked if he would go through the experience again.* 問到是否願意再有一次這樣的經歷時，他毫不遲疑地表示願意。▸ **un·hesi·tat·ing·ly** *adv.*

un·hin·dered /ʌnˈhɪndəd; *NAmE* -dərd/ *adj.* without anything stopping or preventing the progress of sb/sth 不受阻擋的；沒有障礙的：*She had unhindered access to the files.* 她可任意直接存取檔案。◇ *He was able to **pass unhindered** through several military checkpoints.* 他暢行無阻地通過了好幾處軍事檢查站。➲ see also HINDER

un·hinge /ʌnˈhɪndʒ/ *verb* [usually passive] **~ sb** to make sb mentally ill 使精神失常（或錯亂）

un·hitch /ʌnˈhɪtʃ/ *verb* **~ sth** to undo sth that is tied to sth else 解開；分開；卸掉：*to unhitch a trailer* 卸掉拖車 ➲ see also HITCH (4)

un·holy /ʌnˈhəʊli; *NAmE* -ˈhoʊ-/ *adj.* **1** dangerous; likely to be harmful 危險的；有害的：*an **unholy alliance** between the medical profession and the pharmaceutical industry* 醫療界與醫藥業的不當聯盟 **2** not respecting the laws of a religion 不守教規的；褻瀆神明的；罪惡的 OPP **holy 3** [only before noun] (*informal*) used to emphasize how bad sth is 過分的；極端的；無法容忍的：*She wondered how she had got into this unholy mess.* 她不知道自己如何弄得如此狼狽不堪。

un·hook /ʌnˈhʊk/ *verb* **~ sth (from sth)** to remove sth from a hook; to undo the hooks on clothes, etc. 從鉤子

上取下；解開（衣物等）的鉤子：*He unhooked his coat from the door.* 他從門上取下外衣。◇ *She unhooked her bra.* 她解開了胸罩。

un·hur·ried /ʌnˈhʌrid; *NAmE* -ˈhɜːr-/ *adj.* (*formal*) relaxed and calm; not done too quickly 從容的；不慌不忙的 **OPP** **hurried** ▸ **un·hur·ried·ly** *adv.*：*Lynn walked unhurriedly into the kitchen.* 林恩不慌不忙地走進了廚房。

un·hurt /ʌnˈhɜːt; *NAmE* ʌnˈhɜːrt/ *adj.* [not before noun] not injured or harmed 未受傷；未受傷害；平安；安然無恙 **SYN** **unharmed**：*He escaped from the crash unhurt.* 他平安逃過了這場車禍。**OPP** **hurt**

un·hygien·ic /ˌʌnhaɪˈdʒiːnɪk; *NAmE* usually -ˈdʒen-/ *adj.* not clean and therefore likely to cause disease or infection 不清潔的；不衛生的；易致病（或感染）的 **OPP** **hygienic**

uni /ˈjuːni/ *noun* (*BrE, informal*) university 大學：*friends from uni* 大學校友 ◇ *Where were you **at uni**?* 你在哪兒上的大學？

uni- /ˈjuːni/ *combining form* (in nouns, adjectives and adverbs 構成名詞、形容詞和副詞) one; having one 單；獨；一：*uniform* 制服 ◇ *unilaterally* 單方面地

uni·cam·eral /ˌjuːnɪˈkæmərəl/ *adj.* (*technical* 術語) (of a parliament 議會) that has only one main governing body 單院的；一院（制）的

UNICEF /ˈjuːnɪsef/ *abbr.* United Nations Children's Fund (an organization within the United Nations that helps to take care of the health and education of children all over the world) 聯合國兒童基金會

uni·cel·lu·lar /ˌjuːnɪˈseljələ(r)/ *adj.* (*biology* 生) (of a living thing 生物) consisting of only one cell 單細胞的：*unicellular organisms* 單細胞生物

uni·corn /ˈjuːnɪkɔːn; *NAmE* -kɔːrn/ *noun* (in stories) an animal like a white horse with a long straight horn on its head （傳說中的）獨角獸

uni·cycle /ˈjuːnɪsaɪkl/ (also **mono·cycle**) *noun* a vehicle that is similar to a bicycle but that has only one wheel 獨輪腳踏車 ➲ VISUAL VOCAB page V51

un·iden·ti·fi·able **AW** /ˌʌnaɪˈdentɪfaɪəbl/ *adj.* impossible to identify 無法辨認的；難以確認的：*He had an unidentifiable accent.* 他的口音難以識別。◇ *Many of the bodies were unidentifiable except by dental records.* 許多屍體若不是靠牙科病歷就無法辨認。**OPP** **identifiable**

un·iden·ti·fied /ˌʌnaɪˈdentɪfaɪd/ *adj.* not recognized or known; not identified 未知的；不明的；未確認的：*an unidentified virus* 尚未確定的病毒 ◇ *The painting was sold to an unidentified American dealer* (= his or her name was not given). 這幅畫賣給了一名未披露姓名的美國商人。

Unifiˈcation Church *noun* a religious and political organization begun in Korea in 1954 by Sun Myung Moon 統一教團（1954 年由文鮮明成立於韓國的宗教與政治組織）

uni·form 0‑w **AW** /ˈjuːnɪfɔːm; *NAmE* -fɔːrm/ *noun, adj.*

■ ***noun*** **1** 0‑w [C, U] the special set of clothes worn by all members of an organization or a group at work, or by children at school 制服；校服：*a **military/police/nurse's uniform*** 軍裝；警服；護士制服 ◇ *soldiers **in uniform*** 穿制服的軍人 ◇ *The hat is part of the **school uniform**.* 帽子是校服的一部份。◇ *Do you have to **wear uniform**?* 你非得穿制服不可嗎？ **2** [C, usually sing., U] (*NAmE*) (*BrE* **strip**) the clothes worn by the members of a sports team when they are playing （運動隊）隊服：*a striped baseball uniform* 條紋棒球服 ◇ *the team's **away uniform*** (= that they use when playing games away from home) 該隊的客場隊服 **3** [sing., U] the type of clothes that a person or group usually wears 清一色服裝；統一服裝：*my standard teenage uniform of sweatshirt and jeans* 我少年時代標準的衣着：運動衫和牛仔褲

■ ***adj.*** 0‑w not varying; the same in all parts and at all times 一致的；統一的；一律的：*uniform rates of pay* 統一的薪資標準 ◇ *The walls were a uniform grey.* 牆壁一律都是灰色。◇ *Growth has not been uniform across the country.* 全國各地的發展程度不一。◇ *uniform lines of terraced houses* (= they all looked the same) 整齊的一列列排房 ▸ **uni·form·ity** **AW** /ˌjuːnɪˈfɔːməti/ *noun* [U, sing.]：*They tried to ensure uniformity across the different departments.* 他們努力保證各部門之間的統一。◇ *the drab uniformity of the houses* 這些房屋的千篇一律 **uni·form·ly** **AW** *adv.*：*The principles were applied uniformly across all the departments.* 這些原則統一適用於所有部門。◇ *The quality is uniformly high.* 質量一律很高。◇ *Pressure must be uniformly distributed over the whole surface.* 壓力必須均勻分佈於整個表面。

uni·formed /ˈjuːnɪfɔːmd; *NAmE* -fɔːrmd/ *adj.* wearing a uniform 穿制服的：*a uniformed chauffeur* 穿制服的司機

unify **AW** /ˈjuːnɪfaɪ/ *verb* (**uni·fies**, **uni·fy·ing**, **uni·fied**, **uni·fied**) **~ sth** to join people, things, parts of a country, etc. together so that they form a single unit 統一；使成一體；使一元化：*The new leader hopes to unify the country.* 新領袖希望把國家統一起來。◇ *the task of unifying Europe* 統一歐洲的大業 ◇ *a unified transport system* 統一的運輸體系 ▸ **uni·fi·ca·tion** **AW** /ˌjuːnɪfɪˈkeɪʃn/ *noun* [U]：*the unification of Germany* 德國的統一

uni·lat·eral /ˌjuːnɪˈlætrəl/ *adj.* done by one member of a group or an organization without the agreement of the other members 單方的：*a unilateral decision* 單方面的決定 ◇ *a unilateral declaration of independence* 單方面宣佈獨立 ◇ *They were forced to take unilateral action.* 他們被迫採取單方面行動。◇ *They had campaigned vigorously for **unilateral nuclear disarmament*** (= when one country gets rid of its nuclear weapons without waiting for other countries to do the same). 他們曾致力於單方面裁減核武器運動。➲ compare BILATERAL (1), MULTILATERAL (1), TRILATERAL ▸ **uni·lat·eral·ly** /-rəli/ *adv.*

uni·lat·eral·ism /ˌjuːnɪˈlætrəlɪzəm/ *noun* [U] belief in or support of unilateral action, especially the policy of getting rid of nuclear weapons without waiting for other countries to do the same 單邊主義（信仰和支持單方面行動，尤指單方面銷毀核武器的政策） ▸ **uni·lat·eral·ist** *noun*：*the defeat of the unilateralists on nuclear disarmament* 核武器裁軍單邊主義者的失敗 **uni·lat·eral·ist** *adj.*：*unilateralist defence policy* 單邊主義防禦政策

un·imagin·able /ˌʌnɪˈmædʒɪnəbl/ *adj.* (*formal*) impossible to think of or to believe exists; impossible to imagine 難以置信的；不可想像的：*unimaginable wealth* 難以想像的財富 ◇ *This level of success would have been unimaginable just last year.* 取得這樣的成就，這在僅僅一年前都是不敢想像的。**OPP** **imaginable** ▸ **un·imagin·ably** *adv.*

un·imagina·tive /ˌʌnɪˈmædʒɪnətɪv/ *adj.* lacking in original or new ideas 無創意的；缺乏想像力的 **SYN** **dull**：*an unimaginative solution to a problem* 毫無創意的解決方法 ◇ *a boring unimaginative man* 一個乏味、沒有想像力的男人 **OPP** **imaginative**

un·im·paired /ˌʌnɪmˈpeəd; *NAmE* -ˈperd/ *adj.* (*formal*) not damaged or spoiled 未被損壞的；未毀壞的：*Although he's ninety, his mental faculties remain unimpaired.* 他雖年屆九旬，但頭腦仍然清晰。**OPP** **impaired**

un·im·peach·able /ˌʌnɪmˈpiːtʃəbl/ *adj.* (*formal, approving*) that you cannot doubt or question 不容置疑的；無可指摘的；無可懷疑的：*evidence from an unimpeachable source* 來源可靠的證據

un·im·peded /ˌʌnɪmˈpiːdɪd/ *adj.* (*formal*) with nothing blocking or stopping sb/sth 無障礙的；無阻擋的：*an unimpeded view of the bay* 一覽無餘的海灣風光 ◇ *free and unimpeded trade* 自由順暢的貿易

un·im·port·ant 0‑w /ˌʌnɪmˈpɔːtnt; *NAmE* -ˈpɔːrtnt/ *adj.*

not important 不重要的；次要的；無足輕重的：*unimportant details* 細枝末節 ◇ ***relatively/comparatively unimportant*** 相對／比較次要的 ◇ *They dismissed the problem as unimportant.* 他們認為這個問題無關緊要而不予理會。◇ *This consideration was not unimportant.* 這項考慮並非無關緊要。◇ *I was just a young girl from a small town and I felt very unimportant.* 當時我只是個從小鎮出來的小女孩，自覺十分渺小。▸ **un·im·port·ance** *noun* [U]

un·im·pressed /ˌʌnɪmˈprest/ *adj.* **~ (by/with sb/sth)** not thinking that sb/sth is particularly good, interesting, etc.; not impressed by sb/sth 印象平平的；無深刻印象的

un·im·pres·sive /ˌʌnɪmˈpresɪv/ *adj.* ordinary; not special in any way 普通的；平庸的；毫無特色的：*His academic record was unimpressive.* 他的學業成績平平。 OPP **impressive**

un·inflect·ed /ˌʌnɪnˈflektɪd/ *adj.* (*linguistics* 語言) (of a word or language 詞或語言) not changing its form to show different functions in grammar 無屈折變化的；無屈折的

un·in·forma·tive /ˌʌnɪnˈfɔːmətɪv; *NAmE* -ˈfɔːrm-/ *adj.* not giving enough information 不詳細的；信息不足的：*The reports of the explosion were brief and uninformative.* 有關爆炸事件的報道很簡略，未及詳情。 OPP **informative**

un·in·formed /ˌʌnɪnˈfɔːmd; *NAmE* -ˈfɔːrmd/ *adj.* having or showing a lack of knowledge or information about sth 知識（或信息）貧乏的；蒙昧的；無知的：*an uninformed comment/criticism* 無知的話語 / 批評 ◇ *The public is generally uninformed about these diseases.* 大眾對這些疾病普遍知之甚少。 OPP **informed**

un·in·hab·it·able /ˌʌnɪnˈhæbɪtəbl/ *adj.* not fit to live in; impossible to live in 不宜居住的；無法居住的：*The building was totally uninhabitable.* 這棟大樓根本沒法住人。 OPP **habitable**

un·in·hab·it·ed /ˌʌnɪnˈhæbɪtɪd/ *adj.* with no people living there; not INHABITED 無人居住的；無人煙的；荒涼的：*an uninhabited island* 荒島

un·in·hib·it·ed /ˌʌnɪnˈhɪbɪtɪd/ *adj.* behaving or expressing yourself freely without worrying about what other people think 縱情的；無拘無束的；隨心所欲的 SYN **unrestrained**：*uninhibited dancing* 縱情的舞蹈 OPP **inhibited**

the un·initi·ated /ˌʌnɪˈnɪʃieɪtɪd/ *noun* [pl.] people who have no special knowledge or experience of sth 無專門知識（或經驗）的人；門外漢；外行：*To the uninitiated the system seems too complicated.* 對外行而言，這個系統似乎過於複雜。 ▸ **un·initi·ated** *adj.*

un·in·jured AW /ʌnˈɪndʒəd; *NAmE* -dʒərd/ *adj.* [not usually before noun] not hurt or injured in any way 安然無恙；毫無損傷 SYN **unhurt**：*They escaped from the crash uninjured.* 他們安然逃過了撞車事故。

un·in·spired /ˌʌnɪnˈspaɪəd; *NAmE* -ˈspaɪərd/ *adj.* not original or exciting 無創意的；不激勵人心的；乏味的 SYN **dull** OPP **inspired**

un·in·spir·ing /ˌʌnɪnˈspaɪərɪŋ/ *adj.* not making people interested or excited 不吸引人的；不令人鼓舞的：*The view from the window was uninspiring.* 窗外的景色平凡無奇。 OPP **inspiring**

un·in·stall /ˌʌnɪnˈstɔːl/ *verb* **~ sth** (*computing* 計) to remove a program from a computer 卸載（程序）；移除（程式）：*Uninstall any programs that you no longer need.* 將不再需要的程序全部卸載。

un·in·sur·able /ˌʌnɪnˈʃʊərəbl; -ˈʃɔːrə-; *NAmE* -ˈʃʊrə-/ *adj.* something that is **uninsurable** cannot be given insurance because it involves too much risk （因風險太大而）不可予以保險的

un·in·sured /ˌʌnɪnˈʃʊəd; -ˈʃɔːd; *NAmE* -ˈʃʊrd/ *adj.* not having insurance; not covered by insurance 未保險的；無保險的：*an uninsured driver* 沒有保險的駕駛員 ◇ *an uninsured claim* 未保過險的索賠

un·in·tel·li·gent AW /ˌʌnɪnˈtelɪdʒənt/ *adj.* not intelligent 愚笨的；遲鈍的；不聰明的：*He was not unintelligent, but he was lazy.* 他並非不聰明，不過就是懶。

un·in·tel·li·gible /ˌʌnɪnˈtelɪdʒəbl/ *adj.* impossible to understand 難以理解的；難懂的 SYN **incomprehensible**：*She turned away and muttered something unintelligible.* 她轉向一旁，嘴裏不知咕噥些什麼。◇ **~ to sb** *A lot of the jargon they use is unintelligible to outsiders.* 他們所用的大量行話是外人聽不懂的。 OPP **intelligible** ▸ **un·in·tel·li·gib·ly** /-əbli/ *adv.*

un·in·tend·ed /ˌʌnɪnˈtendɪd/ *adj.* an **unintended** effect, result or meaning is one that you did not plan or intend to happen 非計劃的；無意的；無心的

un·in·ten·tion·al /ˌʌnɪnˈtenʃənl/ *adj.* not done deliberately, but happening by accident 無意的；非故意的；偶然的：*Perhaps I misled you, but it was quite unintentional* (= I did not mean to). 也許我誤導了你，但那絕不是有意的。 OPP **intentional** ▸ **un·in·ten·tion·al·ly** /-ʃənəli/ *adv.*：*They had unintentionally provided wrong information.* 他們無意中提供了錯誤的信息。

un·inter·est·ed /ʌnˈɪntrəstɪd; -trest-/ *adj.* **~ (in sb/sth)** not interested; not wanting to know about sb/sth 不感興趣的；冷淡的；漠不關心的：*He was totally uninterested in sport.* 他對體育運動毫無興趣。◇ *She seemed cold and uninterested.* 她似乎很冷漠且不感興趣。 ➲ note at INTERESTED (1)

un·inter·est·ing /ʌnˈɪntrəstɪŋ; -trest-/ *adj.* not attracting your attention or interest; not interesting 不吸引人的；無趣的；無聊的 ➲ note at INTERESTED

un·inter·rupt·ed /ˌʌnˌɪntəˈrʌptɪd/ *adj.* not stopped or blocked by anything; continuous and not interrupted 不受阻擋的；不間斷的；持續不斷的：*We had an uninterrupted view of the stage.* 我們能清楚地看見舞台。◇ *eight hours of uninterrupted sleep* 八個小時未受干擾的睡眠 ◇ *We managed to eat our meal uninterrupted by phone calls.* 我們總算吃了一頓沒有電話打攪的安生飯。

un·in·vited /ˌʌnɪnˈvaɪtɪd/ *adj.* doing sth or going somewhere when you have not been asked or invited to, especially when sb does not want you to 未經要求的；未獲邀請的；不速而至的：*uninvited guests at a party* 聚會上的不速之客 ◇ *He turned up uninvited.* 他不請自到了。

un·in·vit·ing /ˌʌnɪnˈvaɪtɪŋ/ *adj.* not attractive or pleasant 無吸引力的；不誘人的：*The water looked cold and uninviting.* 這水看上去涼冰冰的，讓人不敢下去。 OPP **inviting**

un·in·volved AW /ˌʌnɪnˈvɒlvd; *NAmE* -ˈvɑːlvd/ *adj.* **~ (in/with sth)** not taking part in sth; not connected with sb/sth, especially on an emotional level（尤指感情方面）不投入的，不相關的：*My mum was distant and cold and very uninvolved in my life.* 我媽媽疏遠冷漠，對我的生活全不介入。 OPP **involved**

union 0‑ /ˈjuːniən/ *noun*
1 0‑ (also ˌ**trade** ˈ**union**) (*BrE* also ˌ**trades** ˈ**union**) (*NAmE* also ˈ**labor union**) [C] an organization of workers, usually in a particular industry, that exists to protect their interests, improve conditions of work, etc. 工會：*I've **joined the union**.* 我已經加入工會。◇ *a **union member*** 工會會員 **2** 0‑ [C] an association or a club for people or organizations with the same interest 協會；聯合會；會社；俱樂部：*the Scottish Rugby Union* 蘇格蘭橄欖球協會 ➲ see also STUDENTS' UNION (2) **3** 0‑ [C] a group of states or countries that have the same central government or that agree to work together 同盟；聯盟；聯邦：*the former Soviet Union* 前蘇維埃聯邦 ◇ *the European Union* 歐洲聯盟 **4 Union** [sing.] the US (used especially at the time of the Civil War)（尤指內戰時期的）美利堅合眾國，美國：*the Union and the Confederacy* 合眾國與南部邦聯 ◇ *the State of the Union address by the President* 美國總統向國會發表的國情咨文 **5** 0‑ [U, sing.] the act of joining two or more things together; the state of being joined together; the act of two people joining together 聯合；結合；合併：*a summit to discuss economic and monetary union* 商討經濟和金融合作的高峰會議 ◇ *Northern Ireland's union with Britain* 北愛爾蘭同英國的聯合 ◇ *sexual union* 性結合 **6** [C] (*old-fashioned*) a marriage 結為夫妻；婚姻：*Their union was blessed with six children.* 他們婚後幸得六個兒女。

union·ist /ˈjuːniənɪst/ *noun* **1** = TRADE UNIONIST **2 Union·ist** a person who believes that Northern Ireland should stay part of the United Kingdom 統一主義者，統一派（主張北愛爾蘭繼續為英國的一部份）**3 Union·ist** a supporter of the Union during the Civil War in the US （美國內戰時期的）合眾國擁護者，合眾派成員 ▸ **union·ism** /ˈjuːniənɪzəm/ *noun* [U]

union·ize (*BrE* also **-ise**) /ˈjuːniənaɪz/ *verb* [T, I] **~ (sth)** to organize people to become members of a TRADE/LABOR UNION; to become a member of a trade/labor union 組織(或成立)工會;加入工會: *a unionized workforce* 有工會組織的勞動力 ◇ *They were forbidden to unionize.* 他們被禁止成立工會。 ▸ **union·iza·tion, -isa·tion** /ˌjuːniənaɪˈzeɪʃn; *NAmE* -nəˈz-/ *noun* [U]

the ˌUnion ˈJack *noun* [sing.] the name for the national flag of the United Kingdom 聯合王國國旗;英國國旗

unique 0‑ AW /juˈniːk/ *adj.*
1 0‑ being the only one of its kind 唯一的;獨一無二的: *Everyone's fingerprints are unique.* 每個人的指紋都是獨一無二的。 HELP You can use **absolutely**, **totally** or **almost** with **unique** in this meaning. 作此義時可用 absolutely、totally 或 almost 修飾 unique。 **2** 0‑ very special or unusual 獨特的;罕見的: *a unique talent* 奇才 ◇ *The preview offers a unique opportunity to see the show without the crowds.* 預展提供了看展覽但不擁擠的難得機會。◇ *The deal will put the company in a unique position to export goods to Eastern Europe.* 這項協議給予這家公司向東歐輸出商品的特殊地位。 HELP You can use **more, very**, etc. with **unique** in this meaning. 作此義時可用 more、very 等修飾 unique。 **3** 0‑ **~ (to sb/sth)** belonging to or connected with one particular person, place or thing (某人、地或事物)獨具的,特有的: *an atmosphere that is unique to New York* 紐約所獨具的氣氛 ◇ *The koala is unique to Australia.* 樹袋熊是澳大利亞獨有的。 ▸ **unique·ly** AW *adv.*: *Her past experience made her uniquely suited to lead the campaign.* 她以往的經歷使她格外適合領導這場運動。◇ *The UK, uniquely, has not had to face the problem of mass unemployment.* 唯有英國無須面對大量失業的問題。◇ *He was a uniquely gifted teacher.* 他是個天賦異稟的天才教師。 **unique·ness** AW *noun* [U]: *The author stresses the uniqueness of the individual.* 這位作者強調個人的獨特性。

uni·sex /ˈjuːnɪseks/ *adj.* intended for or used by both men and women 男女皆宜的;不分性別的: *a unisex hair salon* 男女美髮店 ◇ *unisex jeans* 男女都能穿的牛仔褲

uni·son /ˈjuːnɪsn/ *noun*
IDM **in ˈunison (with sb/sth)** **1** if people do or say sth **in unison**, they all do it at the same time (做事、說話)一起,一齊 **2** if people or organizations are working **in unison**, they are working together, because they agree with each other 一致行動;協調地 **3** (*music* 音) if singers or musicians sing or play **in unison**, they sing or play notes at the same PITCH or at one or more OCTAVES apart (歌唱或演奏)一齊,同音,同度

unit 0‑ /ˈjuːnɪt/ *noun*
▸ SINGLE THING 單個事物 **1** 0‑ a single thing, person or group that is complete by itself but can also form part of sth larger 單獨的事物(或人、群體);單位;單元: *The cell is the unit of which all living organisms are composed.* 細胞是構成一切生物的單位。◇ *The* ***basic unit*** *of society is the family.* 社會的基本單位是家庭。 **2** (*business* 商) a single item of the type of product that a company sells 一件(商品);單位: *The game's selling price was $15 per unit.* 這遊戲的售價為每套 15 元。◇ *What's the* ***unit cost***? 單位成本是多少錢?
▸ GROUP OF PEOPLE 群體 **3** 0‑ a group of people who work or live together, especially for a particular purpose 班組;小隊: ***army/military/police units*** 陸軍 / 軍事 / 警察分隊 ◇ *Medical units were operating in the disaster area.* 醫療小組正在災區工作。
▸ IN HOSPITAL 醫院 **4** 0‑ a department, especially in a hospital, that provides a particular type of care or treatment 科;病區: *the intensive care unit* 重症監護室 ◇ *a maternity unit* 婦產科
▸ FURNITURE 傢具 **5** 0‑ a piece of furniture, especially a cupboard, that fits with and matches others of the same type 配套傢具組件;(尤指)成套傢具中的櫃子: *a fitted kitchen with white units* 用白色組件的廚房 ◇ ***floor/wall units*** 地板 / 牆壁組合件 ◇ ***bedroom/kitchen/storage units*** 臥室 / 廚房 / 貯藏室組合設備 ⇨ VISUAL VOCAB page V25
▸ MEASUREMENT 計量 **6** **~ (of sth)** a fixed quantity, etc. that is used as a standard measurement 單位;單元: *a* ***unit of time/length/weight*** 時間 / 長度 / 重量單位 ◇ *a* ***unit of currency****, such as the euro or the dollar* 貨幣單位,如歐元或美元 ◇ *Women are advised not to drink more than fourteen units of alcohol per week.* 建議婦女每週飲酒不超過十四個酒精單位。
▸ SMALL MACHINE 小機器 **7** a small machine that has a particular purpose or is part of a larger machine 裝置;機件;部件;元件: *a waste disposal unit* 廢物銷毀器 ◇ *the central processing unit of a computer* 電腦的中央處理器
▸ IN TEXTBOOK 課本 **8** one of the parts into which a TEXTBOOK or a series of lessons is divided 單元;課: *The present perfect is covered in Unit 8.* 現在完成時在第 8 單元講解。
▸ FLAT/APARTMENT/HOUSE 公寓;住宅 **9** (also **ˈhome unit**) (*AustralE, NZE*) a single flat/apartment or house in a building or group of buildings containing a number of them (一)套;單元
▸ NUMBER 數字 **10** any whole number from 0 to 9 個位數: *a column for the tens and a column for the units* 十位數欄和個位數欄

Uni·tar·ian /ˌjuːnɪˈteəriən; *NAmE* -ˈter-/ *noun* a member of a Christian Church that does not believe in the TRINITY and has no formal teachings 神體一位派信徒,獨神論派信徒(屬於不信仰三位一體的基督教派別) ▸ **Uni·tar·ian** *adj.* **Uni·tar·ian·ism** /-ɪzəm/ *noun* [U]

uni·tary /ˈjuːnətri; *NAmE* -teri/ *adj.* **1** (*technical* 術語) (of a country or an organization 國家或機構) consisting of a number of areas or groups that are joined together and are controlled by one government or group 集中的;統一的;中央集權制的: *a single unitary state* 單一中央集權制國家 ◇ (*BrE*) *a* ***unitary authority*** (= a type of local council, introduced in some areas from 1995 to replace existing local governments which consisted of county and district councils) 單一管理區(1995 年起在某些地區實行,由此成立的地方委員會取代原有的郡、區政府) **2** (*formal*) single; forming one unit 單一的;形成單一個體的

unite 0‑ /juˈnaɪt/ *verb*
1 0‑ [I] to join together with other people in order to do sth as a group (為某事)聯合,聯手,團結: **~ in sth** *Local resident groups have* ***united in opposition*** *to the plan.* 當地居民團體已聯合起來反對這項計劃。◇ **~ in doing sth** *We will unite in fighting crime.* 我們將聯手打擊犯罪。◇ **~ (behind/against sb/sth)** *Will they unite behind the new leader?* 他們會團結支持新領導人嗎?◇ *Nationalist parties united to oppose the government's plans.* 民族主義黨派聯合反對政府的計劃。 **2** 0‑ [T, I] to make people or things join together to form a unit; to join together (與某人或集體)聯結,聯合;統一: **~ (sb/sth)** *A special bond unites our two countries.* 一種特殊的紐帶把我們兩國聯結起來。◇ *His aim was to unite Italy.* 他的目標是統一意大利。◇ *The two countries united in 1887.* 兩國於 1887 年合併。◇ **~ (sb/sth) (with sb/sth)** *She unites keen business skills with a charming personality.* 她兼具敏銳的商業技能和個人魅力。

united 0‑ /juˈnaɪtɪd/ *adj.*
1 0‑ (of countries 國家) joined together as a political unit or by shared aims 聯合的;統一的: *the United States of America* 美利堅合眾國 ◇ *efforts to build a united Europe* 建立統一歐洲的努力 **2** 0‑ (of people or groups 人或群體) in agreement and working together 和諧的;一致的;團結的: *We need to become a more united team.* 我們要成為一支更加團結的隊伍。◇ *They are united in their opposition to the plan.* 他們一致反對這個計劃。◇ *We should present* ***a united front*** (= an appearance of being in agreement with each other). 我們要表現得團結一致。 **3** used in the names of some teams and companies (用於團隊和公司名稱): *Manchester United* 曼徹斯特聯隊 ◇ *United Distillers* 聯合釀造公司

the Uˌnited ˈFree Church *noun* [sing.] a church formed in Scotland in 1900 from the union of the Free Church of Scotland and the United Presbyterian Church (蘇格蘭)聯合自由長老會(1900 年由蘇格蘭自由長老會和聯合長老會聯合於蘇格蘭成立)

the Uˌnited ˈKingdom *noun* [sing.] (*abbr.* **(the) UK**) England, Scotland, Wales and Northern Ireland (considered as a political unit) 英國,聯合王國(由英格蘭、蘇格蘭、威爾士和北愛爾蘭組成的政治實體)

U

the U,nited 'Nations *noun* [sing.+sing./pl. v.] (*abbr.* **(the) UN**) an association of many countries which aims to improve economic and social conditions and to solve political problems in the world in a peaceful way 聯合國

the ,United Nations Se'curity Council *noun* = SECURITY COUNCIL

,United ,Press Inter'national *noun* (*abbr.* **UPI**) a US company that collects news and sells it to newspapers and radio and television stations 合眾國際社（美國的私營通訊社）

the U,nited 'States (of A'merica) *noun* (*abbr.* **(the) US, (the) USA**) a large country in N America consisting of 50 states and the District of Columbia 美國；美利堅合眾國 HELP Although **United States** is sometimes found with a plural verb after it, this is quite rare and it is much more common to use a singular verb. * United States 後有時用複數動詞，但很罕見，用單數動詞要常見得多。 ➲ note at AMERICAN

,unit 'trust (*BrE*) (*NAmE* **'mutual fund**) *noun* a company that offers a service to people by investing their money in various different businesses 單位信託投資公司（代客戶進行不同組合的投資）

unity /'juːnəti/ *noun* (*pl.* **-ies**) **1** [U, sing.] the state of being in agreement and working together; the state of being joined together to form one unit 團結一致；聯合；統一：*European unity* 歐洲的統一 ◇ *a plea for unity within the party* 要求黨內團結的呼籲 ◇ *unity of purpose* 目標一致 OPP **disunity** **2** [U] (in art, etc. 藝術等) the state of looking or being complete in a natural and pleasing way 完整；完美；和諧；協調：*The design lacks unity.* 這項設計整體不夠協調。 **3** [C] (in literature and theatre 文學、戲劇) any of the principles of CLASSICAL OR NEOCLASSICAL theatre that restrict the action of a play to a single story, day and place（情節、時間和地點的）統一性，一致性；三一律：*the unities of action, time and place* 要求情節、時間和地點一致的三一律 **4** [sing.] (*formal*) a single thing that may consist of a number of different parts 統一體；聯合體；整體：*If society is to exist as a unity, its members must have shared values.* 社會若要成為一個統一的群體，它的成員就必須有共同的價值觀。 **5** [U] (*mathematics* 數) the number one（數目或數字）一

Univ. *abbr.* (in writing) University（書寫形式）大學

uni·ver·sal /,juːnɪ'vɜːsl; *NAmE* -'vɜːrsl/ *adj.* **1** done by or involving all the people in the world or in a particular group 普遍的；全體的；全世界的；共同的：*Such problems are a universal feature of old age.* 這類問題是老年人的通病。◇ *Agreement on this issue is almost universal.* 這個問題幾乎取得全體一致的意見。◇ ***universal suffrage*** (= the right of all the people in a country to vote) 普選權 **2** true or right at all times and in all places 普遍存在的；廣泛適用的：*universal facts about human nature* 人性的普遍現象 ▸ **uni·ver·sal·ity** /,juːnɪvɜː'sæləti; *NAmE* -vɜːr's-/ *noun*：*the universality of religious experience* 宗教行為的普遍性

,uni,versal 'grammar *noun* [U, C] (*linguistics* 語言) the set of rules that is thought to be able to describe all languages 普遍語法（據信能夠描述所有語言的一系列規則）

,uni,versal 'indicator *noun* (*chemistry* 化) a substance that changes colour when another substance touches it, indicating whether it is an acid or an ALKALI 通用指示劑（通過顏色變化顯示物質的酸鹼性）

uni·ver·sal·ly /,juːnɪ'vɜːsəli; *NAmE* -'vɜːrs-/ *adv.* **1** by everyone 全體地；一致地；共同地：*to be universally accepted* 得到普遍接受 **2** everywhere or in every situation 到處；隨時隨地；在各種情況下：*This treatment is not universally available.* 這種療法不是到處都有的。◇ *The theory does not apply universally.* 這個理論並非放之四海而皆準。

uni·verse 🔑 /'juːnɪvɜːs; *NAmE* -vɜːrs/ *noun* **1** 🔑 **the universe** [sing.] the whole of space and everything in it, including the earth, the planets and the stars 宇宙；天地萬物；萬象：*theories of how the universe began* 關於宇宙形成的各種理論 **2** [C] a system of stars, planets, etc. in space outside our own（已知宇宙以外的）宇宙：*The idea of a parallel universe is hard to grasp.* 認為另有一個平行宇宙的概念是很難理解的。◇ *He lives in a little universe of his own.* 他生活在自己的小天地裏。 **3** [sing.] a set of experiences of a particular type（某種）經驗體系：*the moral universe* 道德體系

uni·ver·sity 🔑 /,juːnɪ'vɜːsəti; *NAmE* -'vɜːrs-/ *noun* [C, U] (*pl.* **-ies**) (*abbr.* **Univ.**) an institution at the highest level of education where you can study for a degree or do research（綜合性）大學；高等學府：*Is there a university in this town?* 這座城市有沒有大學？◇ *Ohio State University* 俄亥俄州立大學 ◇ *the University of York* 約克大學 ◇ *York University* 約克大學 ◇ (*BrE*) *Both their children are **at university**.* 他們的兩個孩子都在上大學。◇ (*BrE*) *He's hoping to **go to university** next year.* 他希望明年能上大學。◇ ***a university course/degree/lecturer*** 大學課程／學位／講師 ➲ COLLOCATIONS at EDUCATION ➲ note at COLLEGE ➲ see also STATE UNIVERSITY

IDM **the university of 'life** (*informal*) the experience of life thought of as giving sb an education, instead of the person gaining formal qualifications 人生大學（生活體驗，相對於正式學歷）：*a degree from the university of life* 人生大學學位

Unix™ /'juːnɪks/ *noun* [U] (*computing* 計) an OPERATING SYSTEM which can be used by many people at the same time * Unix 操作系統（可供多人同時使用）

un·just /,ʌn'dʒʌst/ *adj.* not deserved or fair 不公平的；不公正的；非正義的：*an unjust law* 不公正的法律 OPP **just** ▸ **un·just·ly** *adv.*：*She felt that she had been unjustly treated.* 她覺得自己受到了不公平的待遇。

un·jus·ti·fi·able /ʌn'dʒʌstɪfaɪəbl/ *adj.* (of an action 行動) impossible to excuse or accept because there is no good reason for it 不可原諒的；無法接受的；無正當理由的 SYN **indefensible**：*an unjustifiable delay* 無理的拖延 OPP **justifiable** ▸ **un·jus·ti·fi·ably** /-əbli/ *adv.*

un·jus·ti·fied AW /ʌn'dʒʌstɪfaɪd/ *adj.* not fair or necessary 不公正的；不正當的；不必要的 SYN **unwarranted**：*The criticism was wholly unjustified.* 這樣的批評完全是不公平的。 OPP **justified**

un·kempt /,ʌn'kempt/ *adj.* (*formal*) (especially of sb's hair or general appearance 尤指頭髮或外貌) not well cared for; not neat or tidy 不整潔的；凌亂的；不修邊幅的 SYN **dishevelled**：*greasy, unkempt hair* 油乎乎亂蓬蓬的頭髮

un·kind 🔑 /,ʌn'kaɪnd/ *adj.* **~ (to sb/sth) (to do sth)** unpleasant or unfriendly; slightly cruel 不友善的；不親切的；不客氣的；刻薄的：*an unkind remark* 不友善的話 ◇ *He was never actually unkind to them.* 其實他從沒有對他們不好。◇ *It would be unkind to go without him.* 甩掉他那就太不夠朋友了。 OPP **kind** ▸ **un·kind·ly** *adv.*：*'That's your problem,' she remarked unkindly.* "那是你的問題。" 她刻薄地說。 **un·kind·ness** *noun* [U]

un·know·able /ʌn'nəʊəbl; *NAmE* -'noʊ-/ *adj.* (*formal*) that cannot be known 無法知道的；不可知的：*a distant, unknowable divine power* 遙遠不可知的神力

un·know·ing /ʌn'nəʊɪŋ; *NAmE* -'noʊ-/ *adj.* [usually before noun] (*formal*) not aware of what you are doing or what is happening 沒意識到的；未察覺的；無知的：*He was the unknowing cause of all the misunderstanding.* 他無意中引起了這一切誤會。 ➲ compare KNOWING ▸ **un·know·ing·ly** *adv.*：*She had unknowingly broken the rules.* 她無意中犯了規。

un·known 🔑 /,ʌn'nəʊn; *NAmE* -'noʊn/ *adj.*, *noun*

■ *adj.* **1** 🔑 **~ (to sb)** not known or identified 未知的；不詳的；未被確認的：*a species of insect previously unknown to science* 科學上以前尚未瞭解的一種昆蟲 ◇ *He was trying, **for some unknown reason**, to count the stars.* 不知何故，他試圖數星星。◇ *The man's identity remains unknown.* 這名男子的身分還是個謎。 **2** 🔑 (of people 人) not famous or well known 不出名的；無名的：*an unknown actor* 沒有名氣的演員 ◇ *The author is virtually unknown outside Poland.* 在波蘭以外，這位作者實際上鮮為人知。 **3** 🔑 never happening or existing 從未發

生的；從不存在的：*The disease is as yet unknown in Europe* (= there have been no cases there). 這種疾病至今尚未在歐洲出現過。◇ *It was **not unknown for** people to have to wait several hours* (= it happened sometimes). 人們得等幾個小時的事時有發生。

IDM **an ˌunknown ˈquantity** a person or thing whose qualities or abilities are not yet known 未知數（指尚不清楚，有待證實的人或事物） **unknown to sb** without the person mentioned being aware of it …尚不知道；把…蒙在鼓裏：*Unknown to me, he had already signed the agreement.* 他背着我已簽了協議。

■ ***noun*** **1 the unknown** [sing.] places or things that are not known about 未知的地方（或事物）：*a journey into the unknown* 探險之旅 ◇ *a fear of the unknown* 對未知事物的恐懼 **2** [C] a person who is not well known 無名者；不出名的人：*A young unknown played the leading role.* 演主角的是一個名不見經傳的年輕人。**3** [C] a fact or an influence that is not known 不明的情況；未知的因素：*There are so many unknowns in the proposal.* 這項提案中的未知數太多了。**4** [C] (*mathematics* 數) a quantity that does not have a known value 未知數；未知量：*X and Y in the equation are both unknowns.* 等式中的 X 和 Y 都是未知數。

the ˌUnknown ˈSoldier *noun* [sing.] a soldier who has been killed in a war, whose body has not been identified, and who is buried in special ceremony. The **Unknown Soldier** is a symbol for all the soldiers killed in a particular war or in wars generally 無名戰士（在特別葬禮上埋葬的陣亡無名軍人，象徵某場或所有戰爭中的陣亡將士）：*the tomb of the Unknown Soldier* 無名戰士墓

un·lace /ʌnˈleɪs/ *verb* **~ sth** to undo the LACES of shoes, clothes, etc. 解開（鞋子、衣服等）的帶子 **OPP** **lace up**

un·laden /ˌʌnˈleɪdn/ *adj.* (*technical* 術語) (of a vehicle 車輛等) not loaded 未負載的；空車的：*a vehicle with an unladen weight of 3 000 kg* 淨重 3 噸的汽車 ➲ compare LADEN (1)

un·law·ful /ʌnˈlɔːfl/ *adj.* (*formal*) not allowed by the law 不合法的；非法的；違法的 **SYN** **illegal** **OPP** **lawful** ▸ **un·law·ful·ly** /-fəli/ *adv.*

unˌlawful ˈkilling *noun* (*law* 律) a murder or other killing which is considered a crime, for example when a person dies because sb is careless 非法殺人（包括因疏忽導致他人死亡）：*The two police officers were accused of unlawful killing.* 這兩名警員被控非法殺人。

un·lead·ed /ˌʌnˈledɪd/ *adj.* (of petrol/gas 汽油或燃氣) not containing LEAD and therefore less harmful to the environment 無鉛的；不含鉛的 **OPP** **leaded** ▸ **un·lead·ed** *noun* [U]：*Unleaded is cheaper than diesel.* 無鉛汽油比柴油便宜。

un·learn /ˌʌnˈlɜːn; *NAmE* ˌʌnˈlɜːrn/ *verb* **~ sth** to deliberately forget sth that you have learned, especially sth bad or wrong 故意忘卻（尤指錯事或壞事）；拋棄：*You'll have to unlearn all the bad habits you learned with your last piano teacher.* 你必須丟掉你的前任鋼琴老師所教的一切壞習慣。

un·leash /ʌnˈliːʃ/ *verb* **~ sth (on/upon sb/sth)** to suddenly let a strong force, emotion, etc. be felt or have an effect 發泄；突然釋放；使爆發：*The government's proposals unleashed a storm of protest in the press.* 政府的提案引發了新聞界的抗議浪潮。

un·leav·ened /ˌʌnˈlevnd/ *adj.* (of bread 麪包) made without any YEAST and therefore flat 未發酵的；不加酵母的；死麪的 ➲ see also LEAVEN *n.*

un·less 🔑 /ənˈles/ *conj.*
1 🔑 used to say that sth can only happen or be true in a particular situation 除非；除非在…情況下：*You won't get paid for time off unless you have a doctor's note.* 除非你有醫生證明，否則你不上班便拿不到工資。◇ *I won't tell them—not unless you say I can.* 我絕不告訴他們，除非你允許。◇ *Unless I'm mistaken, she was back at work yesterday.* 除非是我記錯了，她是昨天回來上班的。◇ *He hasn't got any hobbies—unless you call watching TV a hobby.* 他沒有什麼愛好，除非你把看電視也稱作愛好。**2** 🔑 used to give the only situation in which sth will not happen or be true 若非；如果不：*I sleep with the window open unless it's really cold.* 天氣若不很冷，我總開着窗戶睡覺。◇ *Unless something unexpected happens, I'll see you tomorrow.* 如果不出意外，我明天去看你。◇ *Have a cup of tea—unless you'd prefer a cold drink?* 喝杯茶吧，還是你喜歡冷飲？**HELP** **Unless** is used to talk about a situation that could happen, or something that could be true, in the future. If you know that something has not happened or that sth is not true, use **if … not**. 指將來可能發生或可能真實的情況用 unless。如果知道沒有發生或不真實則用 if … not：*If you weren't always in such a hurry* (= but you are), *your work would be much better.* ◇ ~~*Your work would be much better unless you were always in such a hurry.*~~

un·let·tered /ˌʌnˈletəd; *NAmE* -tərd/ *adj.* (*formal*) unable to read 不識字的；文盲的

un·licensed **AW** /ʌnˈlaɪsnst/ *adj.* without a licence 無執照的；無許可證的：*an unlicensed vehicle* 無牌照車子 **OPP** **licensed**

un·like 🔑 /ˌʌnˈlaɪk/ *prep., adj.*
■ ***prep.*** **1** 🔑 different from a particular person or thing 不像；與…不同：*Music is quite unlike any other art form.* 音樂與其他藝術形式迥然不同。◇ *The sound was **not unlike** that of birds singing.* 這聲音有點像鳥鳴。**2** 🔑 used to contrast sb/sth with another person or thing（用於對比）與…不同：*Unlike most systems, this one is very easy to install.* 本系統與多數系統不同，極易安裝。➲ LANGUAGE BANK at CONTRAST **3** 🔑 not typical of sb/sth 非…的特徵：*It's very unlike him to be so late.* 遲到這麼久可實在不像他平時的作風。**OPP** **like**
■ ***adj.*** 🔑 [not before noun] (of two people or things 兩個人或事物) different from each other 不同；不像；相異：*They are both teachers. Otherwise they are quite unlike.* 他們兩位都是教師；除此之外他們迥然不同。➲ compare ALIKE *adj.*, LIKE *adj.*

un·like·ly 🔑 /ʌnˈlaɪkli/ *adj.* (**un·like·lier**, **un·likeli·est**)
HELP **More unlikely** and **most unlikely** are the usual forms. 常用 more unlikely 和 most unlikely。
1 🔑 not likely to happen; not probable 不大可能發生的：**~ (to do sth)** *The project seemed unlikely to succeed.* 這個項目似乎難以成功。◇ **~ (that …)** *It's most* (= very) *unlikely that she'll arrive before seven.* 她極不可能在七點前到達。◇ ***In the unlikely event of** a problem arising, please contact the hotel manager.* 萬一出現問題，請找旅館經理。**2** [only before noun] not the person, thing or place that you would normally think of or expect 非心目中的；非想像的：*He seems a most unlikely candidate for the job.* 他似乎是最不適合擔任這項工作的人選。◇ *They have built hotels in the most unlikely places.* 他們把旅館建在最冷門的地方。**3** 🔑 [only before noun] difficult to believe 難以相信的；不能信服的 **SYN** **implausible**：*She gave me an unlikely explanation for her behaviour.* 她對自己行為的解釋很難令我信服。**OPP** **likely** ▸ **un·like·li·hood** /ʌnˈlaɪklihʊd/ **un·like·li·ness** /-nəs/ *noun* [U]

un·lim·it·ed /ʌnˈlɪmɪtɪd/ *adj.* as much or as many as is possible; not limited in any way 盡量多的；任意多的；無限制的：*The ticket gives you unlimited travel for seven days.* 憑本車票在七日內可自由乘車不受限制。◇ *The court has the power to impose an unlimited fine for this offence.* 法庭有權對這一違法行為罰款，額度不受限制。◇ *You will be allowed unlimited access to the files.* 你可以無限制使用這些檔案。

un·lined /ˌʌnˈlaɪnd/ *adj.* **1** not marked with lines 無線條的；無皺紋的：*unlined paper/skin* 無横格的紙；無皺紋的皮膚 **2** (of a piece of clothing, etc. 衣服等) made without an extra layer of cloth on the inside 無襯裏的 **OPP** **lined**

un·list·ed /ˌʌnˈlɪstɪd/ *adj.* **1** not on a published list, especially of STOCK EXCHANGE prices 未列表公佈的；（尤指證券）未掛牌的，未上市的：*an unlisted company* 非上市公司 **2** (of a telephone number 電話號碼) not listed in the public telephone book, at the request of the owner of the telephone. The telephone company will not give unlisted numbers to people who ask for them. 未登入電話簿的 ➲ see also EX-DIRECTORY

U

unlit /ˌʌnˈlɪt/ *adj.* **1** dark because there are no lights or the lights are not switched on 黑暗的；無燈光的： *an unlit passage* 無燈光的通道 **2** not yet burning 未點燃的： *an unlit cigarette* 未點燃的香煙 OPP **lighted**

un·load /ˌʌnˈləʊd; NAmE ˌʌnˈloʊd/ *verb*
1 [T, I] to remove things from a vehicle or ship after it has taken them somewhere（從車、船上）卸，取下： **~ sth from sth** *Everyone helped to unload the luggage from the car.* 大家都幫着從汽車上卸行李。◊ **~ (sth)** *This isn't a suitable place to unload the van.* 這個地方不適宜卸車。◊ *The truck driver was waiting to unload.* 卡車司機在等着卸貨。OPP **load** **2** [T] **~ sth** to remove the contents of sth after you have finished using it, especially the bullets from a gun or the film from a camera 拆掉，退出，取出（子彈或膠捲等）OPP **load** **3** [T] **~ sth/sb (on/onto sb)** (*informal*) to pass the responsibility for sb/sth to sb else 推卸（責任）；甩掉（包袱）： *It's his problem, not something he should unload onto you.* 那是他的事，他不該把問題甩給你。**4** [T] **~ sth (on/onto sb/sth)** (*informal*) to get rid of or sell sth, especially sth illegal or of bad quality 脱手，賣掉（尤指非法物品或次品）： *They want to unload their shares at the right price.* 他們想在價格合適的時候賣掉股票。

un·lock /ˌʌnˈlɒk; NAmE ˌʌnˈlɑːk/ *verb* **1 ~ sth** to undo the lock of a door, window, etc., using a key（用鑰匙）開…的鎖： *to unlock the door* 打開門鎖 OPP **lock** **2 ~ sth** to discover sth and let it be known 發現；揭示；揭開： *The divers hoped to unlock some of the secrets of the seabed.* 潛水員希望揭開海底的一些秘密。

un·locked /ˌʌnˈlɒkt; NAmE ˌʌnˈlɑːkt/ *adj.* not locked 未鎖的： *Don't leave your desk unlocked.* 請不要忘記鎖好辦公桌。

unlooked-for /ʌnˈlʊkt fɔː(r)/ *adj.* (*formal*) not expected 沒想到的；不期的；意外的： *unlooked-for developments* 意料之外的發展

un·loose /ˌʌnˈluːs/ (also **un·loosen** /ʌnˈluːsn/) *verb* **~ sth** (*old-fashioned or formal*) to make sth loose 鬆開；解開： *He unloosed his tie.* 他鬆開了領帶。

un·loved /ˌʌnˈlʌvd/ *adj.* (*formal*) not loved by anyone 無人喜歡（或疼愛）的： *unloved children* 無人疼愛的孩子

un·love·ly /ʌnˈlʌvli/ *adj.* (*formal*) not attractive 不好看的；不動人的；不美觀的： *an unlovely building* 不美觀的建築物

un·luck·ily /ʌnˈlʌkɪli/ *adv.* unfortunately; as a result of bad luck 不幸地；遺憾地；倒霉地： *He was injured in the first game and unluckily missed the final.* 他第一場比賽就受了傷，遺憾地未能參加決賽。OPP **luckily**

un·lucky /ʌnˈlʌki/ *adj.* (**un·luck·ier**, **un·lucki·est**)
HELP You can also use **more unlucky** and **most unlucky**. 亦可用 more unlucky 和 most unlucky。
1 ~ (to do sth) having bad luck or happening because of bad luck; not lucky 不幸的；倒霉的；不順利的 SYN **unfortunate**： *He was very unlucky not to win.* 他不幸輸了。◊ *By some unlucky chance, her name was left off the list.* 倒霉的是，名單上漏掉了她的名字。**2 ~ (to do sth)** causing bad luck 不吉利的；晦氣的： *Some people think it's unlucky to walk under a ladder.* 有些人認為從梯子下面走過不吉利。◊ *Thirteen is often considered an unlucky number.* 十三常被認為是不吉利的數字。OPP **lucky**

un·made /ˌʌnˈmeɪd/ *adj.* **1** an **unmade** bed is not ready for sleeping in because the sheets, etc. have not been arranged neatly（牀）未鋪好的 **2** (*BrE*) an **unmade** road does not have a hard smooth surface（道路）未鋪路面的

un·man·age·able /ʌnˈmænɪdʒəbl/ *adj.* difficult or impossible to control or deal with 難以控制（或處理）的；無法對付的 OPP **manageable**

un·man·ly /ʌnˈmænli/ *adj.* (*formal*) not having the qualities that are admired or expected in a man 非男子漢的；無男子氣概的 OPP **manly**

un·manned /ˌʌnˈmænd/ *adj.* if a machine, a vehicle, a place or an activity is **unmanned**, it does not have or need a person to control or operate it 無（需）人操作的；無（需）人控制的；自控的： *an unmanned spacecraft* 無人駕駛宇宙飛船 ◊ *an unmanned Mars mission* 無人火星探測計劃 OPP **manned**

un·man·ner·ly /ʌnˈmænəli; NAmE -nərli/ *adj.* (*formal*) not having or showing good manners; not polite 沒有禮貌的；沒教養的

un·marked /ʌnˈmɑːkt; NAmE ʌnˈmɑːrkt/ *adj.* **1** without a sign or words to show what or where sth is 無標誌的；無標記的；無記號的： *an unmarked police car* 無標識的警車 ◊ *He was buried in an unmarked grave.* 他埋在一處無名塚下。➲ compare MARKED (1) **2** (*especially BrE*) (of a player in a team game, especially football (SOCCER) 比賽隊員，尤指足球員) with no player from the other team staying close to prevent them from getting the ball 無人盯防的： *He headed the ball to the unmarked Gray.* 他把球頂給了無人盯防的格雷。**3** (*linguistics* 語言) (of a word or form of a word 詞或詞形) not showing any particular feature or style, such as being formal or informal 無標記的 OPP **marked**

un·mar·ried /ˌʌnˈmærid/ *adj.* not married 未婚的；獨身的 SYN **single**： *an unmarried mother* 未婚母親

un·mask /ˌʌnˈmɑːsk; NAmE ˌʌnˈmæsk/ *verb* **~ sb/sth** to show the true character of sb, or a hidden truth about sth 使露出真相；揭露；暴露 SYN **expose**： *to unmask a spy* 揭發間諜

un·matched /ˌʌnˈmætʃt/ *adj.* **~ (by sb/sth)** (*formal*) better than all others 無雙的；無比的： *He had a talent unmatched by any other politician of this century.* 他的才華是本世紀其他政壇人物所望塵莫及的。

un·mem·or·able /ʌnˈmemərəbl/ *adj.* that cannot be remembered because it was not special 容易遺忘（或忘懷）的 OPP **memorable**

un·men·tion·able /ʌnˈmenʃənəbl/ *adj.* [usually before noun] too shocking or embarrassing to be mentioned or spoken about 不可提及的；不宜述說的；難以啟齒的： *an unmentionable disease* 羞於啟齒的疾病

unmet /ˌʌnˈmet/ *adj.* (*formal*) (of needs, etc. 需要等) not satisfied 未滿足的： *a report on the unmet needs of elderly people* 有關老年人生活所需不足的報告

un·mind·ful /ʌnˈmaɪndfl/ *adj.* **~ of sb/sth** (*formal*) not giving thought or attention to sb/sth 不注意的；不留心的；漫不經心的 OPP **mindful**

un·miss·able /ʌnˈmɪsəbl/ *adj.* that you must not miss because it is so good 不能錯過的；不可失掉的： *an unmissable opportunity* 不能錯過的良機

un·mis·tak·able (also *less frequent* **un·mis·take·able**) /ˌʌnmɪˈsteɪkəbl/ *adj.* that cannot be mistaken for sb/sth else 不會弄錯的；確定無疑的；清楚明白的： *Her accent was unmistakable.* 她的口音是很明顯的。◊ *the unmistakable sound of gunfire* 清清楚楚的槍炮聲 ► **un·mis·tak·ably** (also *less frequent* **un·mis·take·ably**) /-əbli/ *adv.*： *His accent was unmistakably British.* 他明顯地操英國口音。

un·miti·gated /ʌnˈmɪtɪɡeɪtɪd/ *adj.* [only before noun] used to mean 'complete', usually when describing sth bad 完全的，十足的，徹底的（通常指壞事）SYN **absolute**： *The evening was an unmitigated disaster.* 這一晚完全是一場災難。➲ see also MITIGATE

un·modi·fied AW /ˌʌnˈmɒdɪfaɪd; NAmE ˈmɑːd-/ *adj.* not MODIFIED 未更改的；未修改的

un·mol·est·ed /ˌʌnməˈlestɪd/ *adj.* [not usually before noun] (*formal*) not disturbed or attacked by sb; not prevented from doing sth 不受打攪（或攻擊）；未受阻撓；不被干涉

un·moti·vated AW /ˌʌnˈməʊtɪveɪtɪd; NAmE -ˈmoʊ-/ *adj.* **1** not having interest in or enthusiasm for sth, especially work or study（尤指對工作或學習）缺乏動機的，不感興趣的，無熱情的： *unmotivated students* 缺乏動力的學生 **2** without a reason or MOTIVE 無緣由的；無動機的： *an unmotivated attack* 無緣無故的攻擊 OPP **motivated**

un·moved /ˌʌnˈmuːvd/ *adj.* **~ (by sth)** not feeling pity or sympathy, especially in a situation where it would be

U

normal to do so 冷漠的；無同情心的；無動於衷的：*Alice seemed totally unmoved by the whole experience.* 艾麗斯似乎對整個經過十分冷漠。◇ *She pleaded with him but he remained unmoved.* 她苦苦哀求，可是他仍無動於衷。

un·mov·ing /ʌnˈmuːvɪŋ/ *adj.* (*formal*) not moving 不動的；靜止的：*He stood, unmoving, in the shadows.* 他一動不動地站在陰暗處。

un·music·al /ˌʌnˈmjuːzɪkl/ *adj.* **1** (of a sound 聲音) unpleasant to listen to 難聽的；刺耳的；不悦耳的：*His voice was harsh and unmusical.* 他的聲音刺耳難聽。**2** (of a person 人) unable to play or enjoy music 不擅長音樂的；對音樂無興趣的 **OPP** **musical**

un·named /ˌʌnˈneɪmd/ *adj.* whose name is not given or not known 未披露姓名的；不知姓名的：*information from an unnamed source* 不願透露姓名的人提供的消息 ◇ *Two casualties, as yet unnamed, are still in the local hospital.* 兩個尚不知姓名的傷者仍在當地醫院。

un·nat·ural /ʌnˈnætʃrəl/ *adj.* **1** different from what is normal or expected, or from what is generally accepted as being right 不自然的；勉強的；反常的：*It seems unnatural for a child to spend so much time alone.* 一個孩子獨自一人待那麼長時間似乎有點反常。◇ *There was an unnatural silence and then a scream.* 一陣反常的寂靜，接着便是一聲尖叫。◇ *unnatural sexual practices* 反常的性行為 ◇ *He gave an unnatural smile* (= that did not seem genuine). 他勉強笑了笑。**2** different from anything in nature 不正常的；怪異的：*Her leg was bent at an unnatural angle.* 她的腿彎曲的角度反常。◇ *an unnatural death* (= one not from natural causes) 非正常死亡 **OPP** **natural** ▸ **un·nat·ur·al·ly** /-rəli/ *adv.*：*She was, **not unnaturally**, very surprised at the news.* 這消息自然讓她大吃一驚。◇ *His eyes were unnaturally bright.* 他的眼睛異常明亮。

un·neces·sary 🔑 /ʌnˈnesəsəri; *NAmE* -seri/ *adj.* **1** 🔑 not needed; more than is needed 不需要的；不必要的；多餘的 **SYN** **unjustified**：*unnecessary expense* 不必要的花費 ◇ *They were found guilty of causing unnecessary suffering to animals.* 他們因虐待動物而被判有罪。◇ *All this fuss is **totally unnecessary**.* 這場紛擾是完全可以避免的。**OPP** **necessary** **2** 🔑 (of remarks, etc. 言語等) not needed in the situation and likely to be offensive 不必要（且容易開罪於人）的 **SYN** **uncalled for**：*That last comment was a little unnecessary, wasn't it?* 那最後一點評論有點多餘，是吧？▸ **un·neces·sar·ily** /ʌnˈnesəsərəli; *NAmE* ˌʌnˌnesəˈserəli/ *adv.*：*There's no point worrying him unnecessarily.* 沒有必要讓他過於擔心。◇ *unnecessarily complicated instructions* 過分複雜的指令

un·nerve /ˌʌnˈnɜːv; *NAmE* ˌʌnˈnɜːrv/ *verb* **~ sb** to make sb feel nervous or frightened or lose confidence 使緊張；使恐懼；使喪失信心：*His silence unnerved us.* 他的沉默令我們心裏發慌。◇ *She appeared strained and a little unnerved.* 她看起來神色不安，有點心慌。▸ **un·nerv·ing** *adj.* **un·nerv·ing·ly** *adv.*

un·noticed /ˌʌnˈnəʊtɪst; *NAmE* -ˈnoʊ-/ *adj.* [not before noun] not seen or noticed 未被看見；未受到注意；被忽視：*His kindness did not **go unnoticed** by his staff.* 他的厚道員工瞭然於心。

un·num·bered /ˌʌnˈnʌmbəd; *NAmE* -bərd/ *adj.* not marked with a number; not NUMBERED 未編號的；未標號的：*unnumbered seats* 未編號的座位

UNO /ˌjuː en ˈəʊ; *NAmE* ˈoʊ; ˈjuːnəʊ; *NAmE* -noʊ/ *abbr.* United Nations Organization 聯合國組織 ➲ see also UNITED NATIONS

un·ob·jec·tion·able /ˌʌnəbˈdʒekʃənəbl/ *adj.* (*formal*) (of an idea, etc. 看法等) that you can accept 可以接受的；無異議的 **SYN** **acceptable**

un·ob·served /ˌʌnəbˈzɜːvd; *NAmE* -ˈzɜːrvd/ *adj.* without being seen 不被看見（或發現）的：*It's not easy for somebody to get into the building unobserved.* 進入這棟大樓而不被發現很不容易。

un·ob·tain·able **AW** /ˌʌnəbˈteɪnəbl/ *adj.* [not usually before noun] that cannot be obtained 得不到；無法達到 **OPP** **obtainable**

un·ob·tru·sive /ˌʌnəbˈtruːsɪv/ *adj.* (*formal*, often *approving*) not attracting unnecessary attention 不張揚的；不招搖的：*The service at the hotel is efficient and unobtrusive.* 那旅館的服務既有效率，又沉穩低調。**OPP** **obtrusive** ▸ **un·ob·tru·sive·ly** *adv.*：*Dora slipped unobtrusively in through the back door.* 多拉悄悄地從後門溜了進去。

un·occu·pied /ˌʌnˈɒkjupaɪd; *NAmE* -ˈɑːk-/ *adj.* **1** empty, with nobody living there or using it 空着的；閒置的；無人佔用的：*an unoccupied house* 閒置的房屋 ◇ *I sat down at the nearest unoccupied table.* 我在最近的一張空桌旁坐了下來。**2** (of a region or country 地區或國家) not controlled by foreign soldiers 未淪陷的；未被敵人佔領的：*unoccupied territory* 未淪陷的領土 **OPP** **occupied**

un·offi·cial /ˌʌnəˈfɪʃl/ *adj.* **1** that does not have permission or approval from sb in authority 未經正式批准的；非官方的；非正式的：*an unofficial agreement/strike* 未經批准的協議／罷工 ◇ *Unofficial estimates put the figure at over two million.* 非官方的估計數字為 200 萬以上。**2** that is not part of sb's official business 非公事的；私事的；私人的：*The former president paid an unofficial visit to China.* 前總統到中國進行了私人訪問。**OPP** **official** ▸ **un·offi·cial·ly** /-ʃəli/ *adv.*

un·opened /ʌnˈəʊpənd; *NAmE* -ˈoʊ-/ *adj.* not opened yet 未開啟的；未打開的：*The letter was returned unopened.* 信被原封不動地退回了。

un·opposed /ˌʌnəˈpəʊzd; *NAmE* -ˈpoʊzd/ *adj.* [not usually before noun] not opposed or stopped by anyone 無人反對；無阻撓：*The party leader was re-elected unopposed.* 這個黨派的領袖再次順利當選。

un·organ·ized (*BrE* also **-ised**) /ʌnˈɔːɡənaɪzd; *NAmE* -ˈɔːrɡ-/ *adj.* **1** (of workers 工人) without a TRADE/LABOR UNION or other organization to represent or support them 沒有工會的；沒有成立組織的 **2** = DISORGANIZED **3** not having been organized 無組織的；無系統的；雜亂無章的：*unorganized data* 雜亂的數據 ➲ compare ORGANIZED

un·ortho·dox /ʌnˈɔːθədɒks; *NAmE* ʌnˈɔːrθədɑːks/ *adj.* different from what is usual or accepted 非正統的；非傳統的；不正規的：*unorthodox methods* 非正統的方法 **OPP** **orthodox** ➲ compare HETERODOX

un·pack /ˌʌnˈpæk/ *verb* **1** [T, I] **~ (sth)** to take things out of a suitcase, bag, etc. 打開（箱、包等）取；從（箱、包等中）取出：*I unpacked my bags as soon as I arrived.* 我一到達就打開行李袋，把東西取出來。◇ *She unpacked all the clothes she needed and left the rest in the case.* 她取出所有要穿的衣服，其餘的都留在箱子裏。◇ *She went to her room to unpack.* 她回到自己的房間打開行李取出衣物。**OPP** **pack** **2** [T] **~ sth** to separate sth into parts so that it is easier to understand 分析；剖析：*to unpack a theory* 剖析一個理論

un·paid /ˌʌnˈpeɪd/ *adj.* **1** not yet paid 未付的；未償付的：*unpaid bills* 未付的賬單 **2** done or taken without payment 無償的；不付報酬的：*unpaid work* 無償勞動 ◇ *unpaid leave* 不帶薪的休假 **OPP** **paid** **3** (of people 人) not receiving payment for work that they do 不領報酬的；義務的：*unpaid volunteers* 不領報酬的志願者 **OPP** **paid**

un·pal·at·able /ʌnˈpælətəbl/ *adj.* **~ (to sb)** **1** (of facts, ideas, etc. 事實、意見等) unpleasant and not easy to accept 令人不快的；難以接受的 **SYN** **distasteful**：*Only then did I learn the unpalatable truth.* 直到那時我才得知令人難以接受的真相。**2** not pleasant to taste 難吃的；不可口的：*unpalatable food* 難吃的食物 **OPP** **palatable**

un·par·al·leled **AW** /ʌnˈpærəleld/ *adj.* (*formal*) used to emphasize that sth is bigger, better or worse than anything else like it 無比的；無雙的；空前的；絕無僅有的 **SYN** **unequalled**：*It was an unparalleled opportunity to develop her career.* 這是她發展自己的事業的絕好機會。◇ *The book has enjoyed a success unparalleled in recent publishing history.* 這本書在近期出版史上是空前的成功。➲ compare PARALLEL *v.*

un·par·don·able /ʌnˈpɑːdnəbl; *NAmE* -ˈpɑːrd-/ *adj.* that cannot be forgiven or excused 不可饒恕的；不可原諒的 **SYN** **unforgivable, inexcusable** **OPP** **pardonable**

U

un·par·lia·men·tary /ˌʌnˌpɑːləˈmentri; *NAmE* -ˌpɑːrl-/ *adj.* against the accepted rules of behaviour in a parliament 違反議會行為準則的；違反議會慣例的：*unparliamentary language* 不適於在議會使用的言語

un·pat·ri·ot·ic /ˌʌnˌpætriˈɒtɪk; *NAmE* -ˌpeɪtriˈɑːt-/ *adj.* not supporting your own country 無愛國心的；不愛國的 **OPP patriotic**

un·per·turbed /ˌʌnpəˈtɜːbd; *NAmE* ˌʌnpərˈtɜːrbd/ *adj.* not worried or anxious 不擔憂的；平靜的；鎮靜的；鎮定的：*She seemed unperturbed by the news.* 她聽到這消息似乎並不驚慌。**OPP perturbed**

un·pick /ʌnˈpɪk/ *verb* **~ sth** to take out STITCHES from a piece of sewing or knitting 拆去…的縫線；拆（編織物）的針腳

un·placed /ˌʌnˈpleɪst/ *adj.* (*BrE*) not one of the first three to finish in a race or competition （速度比賽或競爭）未進入前三名的，未獲名次的

un·planned /ˌʌnˈplænd/ *adj.* not planned in advance 未計劃（或籌劃）的；意外的：*an unplanned pregnancy* 意外懷孕

un·play·able /ˌʌnˈpleɪəbl/ *adj.* (*especially BrE*) not able to be played; impossible to play on or with （樂曲）無法演奏的；（球）接不住的；（運動場）不能用於比賽的：*The ball was unplayable* (= it was hit so well that it was impossible to hit it back). 那個球沒法接。➲ compare PLAYABLE (2)

un·pleas·ant 🔑 /ʌnˈpleznt/ *adj.*
1 🔑 not pleasant or comfortable 令人不快的；不舒服的 **SYN disagreeable**：*an unpleasant experience* 不愉快的經歷 ◇ *The minerals in the water made it unpleasant to drink.* 水裏的礦物質使得這水挺難喝的。**2** 🔑 **~ (to sb)** not kind, friendly or polite 不和藹的；不客氣的；不禮貌的：*He was very unpleasant to me.* 他對我很兇。◇ *She said some very unpleasant things about you.* 她說了你一些壞話。**OPP pleasant** ▸ **un·pleas·ant·ly** *adv.*：*The drink is very sweet, but not unpleasantly so.* 這飲料非常甜，但並不膩。◇ *He laughed unpleasantly.* 他笑得令人討厭。

un·pleas·ant·ness /ʌnˈplezntnəs/ *noun* [U] bad feeling or arguments between people 不和；反目；爭執

un·plug /ˌʌnˈplʌɡ/ *verb* **(-gg-) ~ sth** to remove the plug of a piece of electrical equipment from the electricity supply 拔掉…的電源插頭 **OPP plug sth in**

Un·plugged™ /ˌʌnˈplʌɡd/ *adj.* (sometimes after noun 有時用於名詞後) (of pop or ROCK music or musicians 流行樂、搖滾樂或音樂人) performed or performing with ACOUSTIC rather than electric instruments 不插電的（用原音樂器）：*an Unplugged concert* 不插電音樂會 ◇ *Bob Dylan Unplugged* 鮑勃 • 迪倫不插電演出

un·pol·luted /ˌʌnpəˈluːtɪd/ *adj.* that has not been POLLUTED (= made dirty by harmful substances) 未被污染的；乾淨的

un·popu·lar /ʌnˈpɒpjələ(r); *NAmE* -ˈpɑːp-/ *adj.* not liked or enjoyed by a person, a group or people in general 沒人緣的；不受歡迎的；不得人心的：*an unpopular choice* 不普遍的選擇 ◇ *an unpopular government* 不得人心的政府 ◇ **~ with/among sb** *The proposed increase in income tax proved **deeply unpopular** with the electorate.* 增加所得稅的建議令選民十分不滿。**OPP popular** ▸ **un·popu·lar·ity** /ˌʌnˌpɒpjuˈlærəti; *NAmE* -ˌpɑːp-/ *noun* [U]：*the growing unpopularity of the military regime* 軍政府日益不得人心

un·pre·ced·ent·ed **AW** /ʌnˈpresɪdentɪd/ *adj.* that has never happened, been done or been known before 前所未有的；空前的；沒有先例的：*The situation is unprecedented in modern times.* 這種情況在現代還沒有出現過。▸ **un·pre·ced·ent·ed·ly** *adv.*：*a period of unprecedentedly high food prices* 食物空前昂貴的時期

un·pre·dict·able **AW** /ˌʌnprɪˈdɪktəbl/ *adj.* **1** that cannot be predicted because it changes a lot or depends on too many different things 無法預言的；不可預測的；難以預料的：*unpredictable weather* 變幻莫測的天氣 ◇ *The result is entirely unpredictable.* 結果是完全無法預料的。**2** if a person is **unpredictable**, you cannot predict how they will behave in a particular situation （人）善變的，難以捉摸的 **OPP predictable** ▸ **un·pre·dict·abil·ity** **AW** /ˌʌnprɪˌdɪktəˈbɪləti/ *noun* [U]：*the unpredictability of the English weather* 英國天氣的變幻莫測 **un·pre·dict·ably** *adv.*

un·pre·ju·diced /ʌnˈpredʒədɪst/ *adj.* not influenced by an unreasonable fear or dislike of sth/sb; willing to consider different ideas and opinions 公正的；無成見的；無偏見的；一視同仁的 **OPP prejudiced**

un·pre·medi·tated /ˌʌnpriːˈmedɪteɪtɪd/ *adj.* (*formal*) (of a crime or bad action 罪行或惡行) not planned in advance 非預謀的；非事先策劃的 **OPP premeditated**

un·pre·pared /ˌʌnprɪˈpeəd; *NAmE* -ˈperd/ *adj.* **1 ~ (for sth)** not ready or not expecting sth 無準備的；沒有預料的；無防備的：*She was totally unprepared for his response.* 她對他的反應毫無準備。**2 ~ (to do sth)** (*formal*) not willing to do sth 不樂意的；不情願的；不甘心的：*She was unprepared to accept that her marriage was over.* 她不願相信她的婚姻已經結束。**OPP prepared**

un·pre·pos·sess·ing /ˌʌnˌpriːpəˈzesɪŋ/ *adj.* (*formal*) not attractive; not making a good or strong impression 不討人喜歡的；不吸引人的；讓人無良好（或深刻）印象的 **SYN unattractive** ➲ compare PREPOSSESSING

un·pre·ten·tious /ˌʌnprɪˈtenʃəs/ *adj.* (*approving*) not trying to appear more special, intelligent, important, etc. than you really are 謙虛謹慎的；不事張揚的；不愛炫耀的 **OPP pretentious**

un·prin·cipled **AW** /ʌnˈprɪnsəpld/ *adj.* (*formal*) without moral principles 不道德的 **SYN dishonest** **OPP principled**

un·print·able /ʌnˈprɪntəbl/ *adj.* (of words or comments 語言或評論) too offensive or shocking to be printed and read by people （因冒犯或令人震驚）不宜刊印的，不宜發表的 **OPP printable**

un·prob·lem·at·ic /ˌʌnˌprɒbləˈmætɪk; *NAmE* -ˌprɑːb-/ (also *less frequent* **un·prob·lem·at·ic·al** /-ɪkl/) *adj.* not having or causing problems 沒有問題的；不惹麻煩的 **OPP problematic** ▸ **un·prob·lem·at·ic·al·ly** /-kli/ *adv.*

un·pro·duct·ive /ˌʌnprəˈdʌktɪv/ *adj.* not producing very much; not producing good results 產量少的；效果不佳的；無益的：*unproductive land* 貧瘠的土地 ◇ *an unproductive meeting* 事倍功半的會議 ◇ *I've had a very unproductive day.* 我這一天什麼事都沒幹成。**OPP productive** ▸ **un·pro·duct·ive·ly** *adv.*

un·pro·fes·sion·al /ˌʌnprəˈfeʃənl/ *adj.* not reaching the standard expected in a particular profession 未達專業水平的；違反職業道德的：*She was found guilty of unprofessional conduct.* 她因違反職業道德而被判罪。**OPP professional** ➲ compare NON-PROFESSIONAL ▸ **un·pro·fes·sion·al·ly** /-ʃənəli/ *adv.*

un·prof·it·able /ʌnˈprɒfɪtəbl; *NAmE* -ˈprɑːf-/ *adj.* **1** not making enough financial profit 不盈利的；無利可圖的：*unprofitable companies* 不賺錢的公司 **2** (*formal*) not bringing any advantage 無益的；沒好處的 **OPP profitable** ▸ **un·prof·it·ably** /-əbli/ *adv.*

un·prom·is·ing /ʌnˈprɒmɪsɪŋ; *NAmE* -ˈprɑːm-/ *adj.* not likely to be successful or show good results 不樂觀的；難有好結果的 **OPP promising**

un·prompt·ed /ʌnˈprɒmptɪd; *NAmE* -ˈprɑːm-/ *adj.* said or done without sb asking you to say or do it 主動的；自發的：*Quite unprompted, Sam started telling us exactly what had happened that night.* 薩姆完全出於主動，開始把那天夜裏發生的事一一向我們說了出來。➲ see also PROMPT

un·pro·nounce·able /ˌʌnprəˈnaʊnsəbl/ *adj.* (of a word, especially a name 詞語，尤指名字) too difficult to pronounce 難發音的；拗口的 **OPP pronounceable**

un·pro·tect·ed /ˌʌnprəˈtektɪd/ *adj.* **1** not protected against being hurt or damaged 未受保護的；未設防的 **2** not covered to prevent it from causing damage or injury 無防護罩的；無掩護的：*Machinery was often unprotected and accidents were frequent.* 機器常裸露着，因此事故頻仍。**3** (of sex 性交) done without using a CONDOM 未用避孕套的；無防護的

un·proven /ʌn'pruːvn/ *adj.* not proved or tested 未驗證的；未經檢驗的： *unproven theories* 未證實的理論 ➲ compare PROVEN

un·pro·voked /ˌʌnprə'vəʊkt; *NAmE* -'voʊkt/ *adj.* (especially of an attack 尤指攻擊) not caused by anything the person being attacked has said or done 未受挑釁的；無端的： *an act of unprovoked aggression* 無端的侵犯行為 ◇ *Her angry outburst was totally unprovoked.* 她暴跳如雷完全是無理取鬧。 ➲ see also PROVOKE (2)

un·pub·lished AW /ʌn'pʌblɪʃt/ *adj.* not published 未出版的；未發表的；未公開的： *an unpublished novel* 未出版的小説

un·pun·ished /ʌn'pʌnɪʃt/ *adj.* not punished 未受懲罰的： *He promised that the murder would not **go unpunished**.* 他保證不會讓兇手逍遙法外。

un·put·down·able /ˌʌnpʊt'daʊnəbl/ *adj.* (*informal*) (of a book 書) so exciting or interesting that you cannot stop reading it 使人着迷的；扣人心弦的

un·quali·fied /ˌʌn'kwɒlɪfaɪd; *NAmE* -'kwɑːl-/ *adj.* **1** not having the right knowledge, experience or qualifications to do sth 不合格的；沒資格的： *an unqualified instructor* 不合格的教員 ◇ **~ to do sth** *I feel unqualified to comment on the subject.* 我覺得沒有資格對此事發表意見。 ◇ **~ for sth** *He was totally unqualified for his job as a senior manager.* 他擔任高級經理職務完全不夠格。 **2** /ʌn'kwɒlɪfaɪd/ [usually before noun] complete; not limited by any negative qualities 完全的；絕對的；無保留的；無限制條件的： *The event was not an unqualified success.* 這件事並非百分之百的成功。 ◇ *I gave her my unqualified support.* 我全力支持她。 OPP **qualified**

un·quench·able /ʌn'kwentʃəbl/ *adj.* (*formal*) that cannot be satisfied 滿足不了的；止不住的： *He had an **unquenchable thirst** for life.* 他有着極其強烈的求生慾。 ➲ see also QUENCH

un·ques·tion·able /ʌn'kwestʃənəbl/ *adj.* (*formal*) that cannot be doubted 無疑的；無可非議的；確實的： *a man of unquestionable honesty* 絕對誠實的人 OPP **questionable** ▸ **un·ques·tion·ably** /-əbli/ *adv.*： *It was unquestionably a step in the right direction.* 這無疑是朝正確方向邁出的一步。

un·ques·tioned /ʌn'kwestʃənd/ *adj.* (*formal*) **1** so obvious that it cannot be doubted 顯而易見的；無可爭議的；毋庸置疑的；公認的： *His courage remains unquestioned.* 他的勇敢仍然不容置疑。 **2** accepted as right or true without really being considered 不假思索而認可的；盲目接受的： *an unquestioned assumption* 盲目接受的假設

un·ques·tion·ing /ʌn'kwestʃənɪŋ/ *adj.* (*formal*) done or given without asking questions, expressing doubt, etc. 不加質詢的；不表示懷疑（等）的： *unquestioning obedience* 絕對的服從 ▸ **un·ques·tion·ing·ly** *adv.*

un·quiet /ˌʌn'kwaɪət/ *adj.* [usually before noun] (*literary*) not calm; anxious and RESTLESS 不平靜的；焦躁不安的；心神不寧的

un·quote /ˌʌn'kwəʊt; *NAmE* ˌʌn'kwoʊt/ *noun* IDM see QUOTE *v.*

un·ravel /ʌn'rævl/ *verb* (**-ll-**, *US* **-l-**) **1** [T, I] **~ (sth)** if you **unravel** threads that are twisted, WOVEN or knitted, or if they **unravel**, they become separated（把纏或織在一起的線）解開，拆散，鬆開： *I unravelled the string and wound it into a ball.* 我把繩子解開並繞成一個球。 **2** [I] (of a system, plan, relationship, etc. 系統、計劃、關係等) to start to fail or no longer stay together as a whole 解體；崩潰；瓦解 **3** [T, I] **~ (sth)** to explain sth that is difficult to understand or is mysterious; to become clearer or easier to understand 闡釋；説明；澄清；變得清楚易懂： *The discovery will help scientists unravel the mystery of the Ice Age.* 這一發現將有助於科學家揭開冰川時代的奧秘。

un·read /ˌʌn'red/ *adj.* (of a book, etc. 書籍等) that has not been read 未讀的；未閱的： *a pile of unread newspapers* 一摞未看的報紙

un·read·able /ʌn'riːdəbl/ *adj.* **1** (of a book, etc. 書籍等) too dull or difficult to be worth reading（因枯燥晦澀而）不值一讀的，難以卒讀的 **2** = ILLEGIBLE **3** if sb's face or expression is **unreadable**, you cannot tell what they are thinking or feeling（面部表情）揣摩不透的，難以捉摸的 **4** (*computing* 計) (of a computer file, disk, etc. 計算機文件、磁盤等) containing information that a computer is not able to read 無法讀取的；打不開的

un·real /ˌʌn'rɪəl; *NAmE* ˌʌn'riːəl/ *adj.* **1** so strange that it is more like a dream than reality 奇異的；虛幻的；夢幻般的： *The party began to take on an unreal, almost nightmarish quality.* 聚會開始呈現出虛幻、近乎夢魘般的氣氛。 **2** not related to reality 不真實的；脱離現實的 SYN **unrealistic**： *Many people have unreal expectations of what marriage will be like.* 許多人對婚姻生活抱有不切實際的憧憬。 **3** (*informal*) used to say that you like sth very much or that sth surprises you（表示十分喜愛或驚訝）： *'That's unreal!' she laughed.* "這怎麼可能！"她笑了起來。 ▸ **un·real·ity** /ˌʌnri'æləti/ *noun* [U]

un·real·is·tic /ˌʌnrɪə'lɪstɪk; *NAmE* -riːə-/ *adj.* not showing or accepting things as they are 不切實際的；不實事求是的： *unrealistic expectations* 不切實際的期望 ◇ ***It is unrealistic to** expect them to be able to solve the problem immediately.* 指望他們能夠立即解決問題是不現實的。 OPP **realistic** ▸ **un·real·is·tic·al·ly** *adv.*： *These prices are unrealistically high.* 這些價格高得離譜。

un·real·ized (*BrE* also **-ised**) /ˌʌn'riːəlaɪzd; *BrE* also -'rɪəl-/ *adj.* **1** not achieved or created 未實現的；未完成的；未成為現實的： *an unrealized ambition* 沒有實現的抱負 ◇ *Their potential is unrealized.* 他們沒有發揮出潛力。 **2** (*finance* 財) not sold or changed into the form of money 未變現的： *unrealized assets* 未變現資產

un·rea·son·able 0-π /ʌn'riːznəbl/ *adj.* not fair; expecting too much 不合理的；不公正的；期望過高的： *The job was beginning to make unreasonable demands on his free time.* 他的閒暇時間開始被工作過分地侵佔了。 ◇ *The fees they charge are not unreasonable.* 他們的收費還算合理。 ◇ ***It would be unreasonable to** expect somebody to come at such short notice.* 要求人家隨傳隨到，太不近人情了吧。 ◇ *He was being totally unreasonable about it.* 他在這件事上蠻不講理。 OPP **reasonable** ▸ **un·rea·son·able·ness** *noun* [U] **un·rea·son·ably** /-əbli/ *adv.*

un·rea·son·ing /ʌn'riːzənɪŋ/ *adj.* [usually before noun] (*formal*) not based on facts or reason 沒根據的；缺乏理性的；無緣無故的 SYN **irrational**： *unreasoning fear* 無端的恐懼

un·rec·og·niz·able (*BrE* also **-is·able**) /ˌʌnrekəg'naɪzəbl/ *adj.* (of a person or thing 人或事物) so changed or damaged that you do not recognize them or it 變得（或損壞得）難以辨認的；無法識別的： *He was unrecognizable without his beard.* 他刮掉鬍子，無人認得出他了。 OPP **recognizable**

un·rec·og·nized (*BrE* also **-ised**) /ʌn'rekəgnaɪzd/ *adj.* **1** that people are not aware of or do not realize is important 未被意識到的；被忽略的；不受重視的： *The problem of ageism in the workplace often **goes unrecognized**.* 工作場所的年齡歧視問題常被忽視。 **2** (of a person 人) not having received the admiration they deserve for sth that they have done or achieved 被埋沒的；未得到賞識的

un·re·con·struct·ed /ˌʌnriːkən'strʌktɪd/ *adj.* [only before noun] (*disapproving*) (of people and their beliefs 人及信仰) not having changed, although the situation they are in has changed 僵化的；頑固守舊的；不順應形勢的

un·re·cord·ed /ˌʌnrɪ'kɔːdɪd; *NAmE* -'kɔːrd-/ *adj.* not written down or recorded 未寫下的；未記錄的；未錄音的： *Many crimes **go unrecorded**.* 許多罪行都未記錄在案。

un·re·fined /ˌʌnrɪ'faɪnd/ *adj.* **1** (of a substance 物質) not separated from the other substances that it is combined with in its natural form 未精製的；未提煉的： *unrefined sugar* 原糖 **2** (of a person or their behaviour 人或行為) not polite or educated 粗俗的；不文雅的；缺乏教養的 OPP **refined**

U

un·re·gen·er·ate /ˌʌnrɪˈdʒenərət/ *adj.* (*formal*) not trying to change your bad habits or bad behaviour 惡習不改的；不思悔改的

un·regu·lated AW /ˌʌnˈregjuleɪtɪd/ *adj.* not controlled by laws or regulations 不受法規約束的；不受管制的

un·re·lated /ˌʌnrɪˈleɪtɪd/ *adj.* **1** not connected; not related to sth else 無關聯的；不相關的 SYN **unconnected**：*The two events were totally unrelated.* 這兩件事互不相干。 **2** (of people, animals, etc. 人、動物等) not belonging to the same family 不屬於同一家族（或同一科等）的；無親緣關係的 OPP **related**

un·re·lent·ing /ˌʌnrɪˈlentɪŋ/ *adj.* (*formal*) **1** (of an unpleasant situation 令人不快的局面) not stopping or becoming less severe 持續的；不緩和的；勢頭不減的 SYN **relentless**：*unrelenting pressure* 持續不斷的壓力 ◇ *The heat was unrelenting.* 炎熱沒有減弱的跡象。 **2** if a person is **unrelenting**, they continue with sth without considering the feelings of other people 不留情的 SYN **relentless**：*He was unrelenting in his search for the truth about his father.* 他不顧一切地搜集有關他父親的事實真相。 ▶ **un·re·lent·ing·ly** *adv.*

un·re·li·able AW /ˌʌnrɪˈlaɪəbl/ *adj.* that cannot be trusted or depended on 不可靠的；不能信賴的：*The trains are notoriously unreliable.* 火車不準點是出了名的。◇ *He's totally unreliable as a source of information.* 他提供的消息完全不可信。OPP **reliable** ▶ **un·re·li·abil·ity** /ˌʌnrɪˌlaɪəˈbɪləti/ *noun* [U]：*the unreliability of some statistics* 某些統計資料的不可靠性

un·re·lieved /ˌʌnrɪˈliːvd/ *adj.* (*formal*) (of an unpleasant situation 令人不快的情況) continuing without changing 持續不變的；未緩和的

un·re·mark·able /ˌʌnrɪˈmɑːkəbl; *NAmE* -ˈmɑːrk-/ *adj.* ordinary; not special or remarkable in any way 一般的；平常的；平凡的；平庸的：*an unremarkable life* 平淡的生活

un·re·marked /ˌʌnrɪˈmɑːkt; *NAmE* -ˈmɑːrkt/ *adj.* (*formal*) not noticed 未被注意：*His absence **went unremarked**.* 沒有人注意到他不在場。

un·re·mit·ting /ˌʌnrɪˈmɪtɪŋ/ *adj.* (*formal*) never stopping 不停的；不懈的；持續不斷的：*unremitting hostility* 從未化解的敵視 ▶ **un·re·mit·ting·ly** *adv.*：*unremittingly gloomy weather* 持續的陰沉天氣

un·re·peat·able /ˌʌnrɪˈpiːtəbl/ *adj.* **1** too offensive or shocking to be repeated（因冒犯或令人震驚）不宜重提的，不堪重複的：*He called me several unrepeatable names.* 他罵了我幾句不堪入耳的話。 **2** that cannot be repeated or done again 不可重複的；不能重演的：*an unrepeatable experience* 不可重複的經歷 OPP **repeatable**

un·re·pent·ant /ˌʌnrɪˈpentənt/ *adj.* showing no shame about your actions or beliefs 不思悔改的；不悔悟的；頑固不化的 OPP **repentant** ▶ **un·re·pent·ant·ly** *adv.*

U

un·re·port·ed /ˌʌnrɪˈpɔːtɪd; *NAmE* -ˈpɔːrt-/ *adj.* not reported to the police or sb in authority or to the public 未舉報的；未報告的；未報道的：*Many cases of bullying go unreported.* 很多恐嚇案件都沒有人告發。

un·rep·re·sen·ta·tive /ˌʌnˌreprɪˈzentətɪv/ *adj.* **~ (of sb/sth)** not typical of a group of people or things and therefore not useful as a source of information about that group 不典型的；無代表性的 SYN **untypical**：*an unrepresentative sample* 缺乏代表性的樣品 OPP **representative**

un·re·quit·ed /ˌʌnrɪˈkwaɪtɪd/ *adj.* (*formal*) (of love 愛情) not returned by the person that you love 沒有回報的；單方面的；單相思的 ➲ compare REQUITE

un·re·served /ˌʌnrɪˈzɜːvd; *NAmE* -ˈzɜːrvd/ *adj.* **1** (of seats in a theatre, etc. 劇院的座位等) not paid for in advance; not kept for the use of a particular person 未被預訂的；非保留的 **2** (*formal*) complete and without any doubts 完全的；徹底的；無保留的：*He offered us his unreserved apologies.* 他誠懇地向我們道了歉。

un·re·served·ly /ˌʌnrɪˈzɜːvɪdli; *NAmE* -ˈzɜːrv-/ *adv.* completely; without hesitating or having any doubts 完全地；坦誠地；無條件地；無保留地：*We apologize unreservedly for any offence we have caused.* 若有得罪，我們深表歉意。

un·re·solved AW /ˌʌnrɪˈzɒlvd; *NAmE* -ˈzɑːlvd; -ˈzɔːlvd/ *adj.* (*formal*) (of a problem or question 問題或提問) not yet solved or answered; not having been resolved 未克服的；未解答的；未解決的

un·re·spon·sive AW /ˌʌnrɪˈspɒnsɪv; *NAmE* -ˈspɑːn-/ *adj.* **~ (to sth)** (*formal*) not reacting to sb/sth; not giving the response that you would expect or hope for 無反應的；未答覆的；反應遲鈍的：*a politician who is unresponsive to the mood of the country* 對國民情緒毫無反應的政客 OPP **responsive**

un·rest /ʌnˈrest/ *noun* [U] a political situation in which people are angry and likely to protest or fight 動盪；動亂；騷動：***industrial/civil/social/political/popular unrest*** 工業／平民／社會／政治／民眾動亂 ◇ *There is **growing unrest** in the south of the country.* 這個國家的南方日益動盪不安。➲ COLLOCATIONS at WAR

un·re·strained AW /ˌʌnrɪˈstreɪnd/ *adj.* (*formal*) not controlled; not having been RESTRAINED 無節制的；放縱的；不加制約的：*unrestrained aggression* 肆無忌憚的侵犯

un·re·strict·ed AW /ˌʌnrɪˈstrɪktɪd/ *adj.* not controlled or limited in any way 沒有限制的 SYN **unlimited**：*We have unrestricted access to all the facilities.* 我們可隨意使用一切設施。OPP **restricted**

un·re·ward·ed /ˌʌnrɪˈwɔːdɪd; *NAmE* -ˈwɔːrd-/ *adj.* not receiving the success that you are trying to achieve 無回報的；未果的；未獲成功的：*Real talent often **goes unrewarded**.* 真正的人才常被埋沒。

un·re·ward·ing /ˌʌnrɪˈwɔːdɪŋ; *NAmE* -ˈwɔːrd-/ *adj.* (of an activity, etc. 活動等) not bringing feelings of satisfaction or achievement 不令人滿足的；未能給人成就感的 OPP **rewarding**

un·ripe /ˌʌnˈraɪp/ *adj.* not yet ready to eat（食物）未成熟的：*unripe fruit* 未熟的水果 OPP **ripe**

un·rivalled (*especially BrE*) (*NAmE* usually **un·rivaled**) /ʌnˈraɪvld/ *adj.* (*formal*) better or greater than any other 無與倫比的；無雙的 SYN **unsurpassed**

un·roll /ʌnˈrəʊl; *NAmE* ʌnˈroʊl/ *verb* **1** [T, I] **~ (sth)** if you **unroll** paper, cloth, etc. that was in a roll or if it **unrolls**, it opens and becomes flat（使紙張、織物等）展開，攤開，鋪開：*We unrolled our sleeping bags.* 我們打開了睡袋。➲ compare ROLL *v.* (5) **2** [I] (of events 事情) to happen one after another in a series 相繼出現；連續發生：*We watched the events unroll before the cameras.* 我們眼看着事態的發展一一呈現在鏡頭前。

un·round·ed /ˌʌnˈraʊndɪd/ *adj.* (*phonetics* 語音) (of a speech sound 語音) pronounced with the lips not forming a narrow round shape 非圓唇的 OPP **rounded**

un·ruf·fled /ʌnˈrʌfld/ *adj.* (of a person 人) calm 平靜的；鎮定的；沉着的 SYN **unperturbed**：*He remained unruffled by their accusations.* 對於他們的指控他處之泰然。

un·ruled /ˌʌnˈruːld/ *adj.* (of paper 紙) not having printed lines on it 未印橫格的；無平行線的

un·ruly /ʌnˈruːli/ *adj.* difficult to control or manage 難以控制（或管理）的；難以駕馭的 SYN **disorderly**：*an unruly class* 難管教的班級 ◇ *unruly behaviour* 無法無天的行為 ◇ *unruly hair* (= difficult to keep looking neat) 難梳理的頭髮 ▶ **un·ru·li·ness** *noun* [U]

un·sad·dle /ʌnˈsædl/ *verb* **1** [T, I] **~ (sth)** to take the saddle off a horse 給（馬）解鞍；卸馬鞍 **2** [T] **~ sb** to throw a rider off 把…掀下馬；使落馬 SYN **unseat**

un·safe /ʌnˈseɪf/ *adj.* **1** (of a thing, a place or an activity 東西、地方或活動) not safe; dangerous 不安全的；危險的：*The roof was declared unsafe.* 已宣佈屋頂有安全隱患。◇ *It was considered unsafe to release the prisoners.* 釋放這些囚犯被認為是危險的。◇ *unsafe sex* (= for example, sex without a CONDOM) 不安全的性行為 **2** (of people 人) in danger of being harmed 身處險境的：*He felt unsafe and alone.* 他感到既危險又孤單。 **3** (*BrE, law* 律) (of a decision in a court of law 法庭判決) based on evidence that may be false or is not good enough 證據

不可靠（或不足）的：*Their convictions were declared unsafe.* 先前給他們的定罪已經宣佈證據不足。OPP **safe**

un·said /ʌn'sed/ *adj.* [not before noun] thought but not spoken（想到卻）未說出：*Some things are better* ***left unsaid***. 有些事情還是不說出來好。

un·sale·able (also **un·sal·able**) /ʌn'seɪləbl/ *adj.* that cannot be sold, because it is not good enough or because nobody wants to buy it 無銷路的；難以售出的 OPP **saleable**

un·salt·ed /ʌn'sɔːltɪd; *BrE* also -'sɒlt-; *NAmE* -'sɑːlt-/ *adj.* (especially of food 尤指食物) without added salt 未放鹽的；不加鹽的：*unsalted butter* 無鹽黃油

un·sani·tary /ʌn'sænətri; *NAmE* -teri/ *adj.* (*especially NAmE*) = INSANITARY

un·sat·is·fac·tory /ˌʌnˌsætɪs'fæktəri/ *adj.* not good enough 不夠好的；不能令人滿意的 SYN **inadequate, unacceptable** OPP **satisfactory** ▸ **un·sat·is·fac·tor·ily** /-tərəli/ *adv.*

un·sat·is·fied /ʌn'sætɪsfaɪd/ *adj.* **1** (of a need, demand, etc. 需要、要求等) not dealt with 未處理的；未解決的；未滿足的 **2** (of a person 人) not having got what you hoped; not having had enough of sth 不如意的；失望的；未得到滿足的 ➲ compare DISSATISFIED, SATISFIED (1)

un·sat·is·fy·ing /ˌʌn'sætɪsfaɪɪŋ/ *adj.* not giving you any satisfaction 不令人滿意（或感到滿足）的 OPP **satisfying**：*a shallow, unsatisfying relationship* 淡薄而不令人滿意的關係

un·sat·ur·ated fat /ʌnˌsætʃəreɪtɪd 'fæt/ *noun* [U, C] a type of fat found in nuts, seeds and vegetable oils that does not encourage the harmful development of CHOLESTEROL 不飽和脂肪：*Avocados are high in unsaturated fat.* 油梨富含不飽和脂肪。➲ see also MONOUNSATURATED FAT, POLYUNSATURATED FAT, SATURATED FAT, TRANS-FATTY ACID

un·savoury (*especially US* **un·savory**) /ʌn'seɪvəri/ *adj.* unpleasant or offensive; not considered morally acceptable 討厭的；無禮的；聲名狼藉的；不道德的：*an unsavoury incident* 令人厭惡的事件 ◇ *Her friends are all pretty unsavoury characters.* 她的朋友盡是些不三不四的人。

un·scathed /ʌn'skeɪðd/ *adj.* [not before noun] not hurt 未受傷害；未受傷 SYN **unharmed**：*The hostages* ***emerged*** *from their ordeal* ***unscathed***. 各人質歷盡磨難後安然生還。

un·sched·uled AW /ʌn'ʃedjuːld; *NAmE* ʌn'skedʒuːld/ *adj.* that was not planned in advance 未事先計劃的；非計劃中的 SYN **unplanned**：*an unscheduled stop* 計劃外的停頓

un·sci·en·tif·ic /ˌʌnˌsaɪən'tɪfɪk/ *adj.* (often *disapproving*) not scientific; not done in a careful, logical way 不科學的；非科學的；違背科學方法的：*an unscientific approach to a problem* 非科學的解決問題方式 ➲ compare NON-SCIENTIFIC

un·scram·ble /ˌʌn'skræmbl/ *verb* **1 ~ sth** to change a word, message, television signal, etc. that has been sent in a code so that it can be read or understood 使（信息、信號等）還原；譯出（密碼）；解碼 OPP **scramble 2 ~ sth** to arrange sth that is confused or in the wrong order in a clear correct way 整理；清理；使條理化

un·screw /ˌʌn'skruː/ *verb* **1** [T, I] **~ (sth)** to undo sth by twisting or turning it; to become undone in this way（被）旋鬆，擰開：*I can't unscrew the lid of this jar.* 這個瓶蓋兒我擰不開。**2** [T] **~ sth** to take the screws out of sth 擰下…的螺絲：*You'll have to unscrew the handles to paint the door.* 要漆這扇門，你得把門把手上的螺絲擰開拿下來。

un·script·ed /ʌn'skrɪptɪd/ *adj.* (of a speech, broadcast, etc. 講演、廣播等) not written or prepared in detail in advance 無底稿的；未詳細準備的 OPP **scripted**

un·scru·pu·lous /ʌn'skruːpjələs/ *adj.* without moral principles; not honest or fair 不道德的；無道德原則的；不誠實的；不公正的 SYN **unprincipled**：*unscrupulous methods* 不公正的方法 OPP **scrupulous** ▸ **un·scru·pu·lous·ly** *adv.* **un·scru·pu·lous·ness** *noun* [U]

un·sea·son·able /ʌn'siːznəbl/ *adj.* unusual for the time of year 不合季節的；違反時令的：*unseasonable weather* 反常的天氣 OPP **seasonable** ▸ **un·sea·son·ably** /-əbli/ *adv.*：*unseasonably warm* 反常地溫暖

un·sea·son·al /ʌn'siːzənl/ *adj.* not typical of or not suitable for the time of year 無季節特徵的；不合節令的：*unseasonal weather* 不合節令的異常天氣 OPP **seasonal**

un·seat /ˌʌn'siːt/ *verb* **1 ~ sb** to remove sb from a position of power 罷免；解除職務；趕下台 **2 ~ sb** to make sb fall off a horse or bicycle 使掉下馬（或自行車）：*The horse unseated its rider at the first fence.* 馬在過第一道籬障時把騎手掀了下來。

un·seed·ed /ʌn'siːdɪd/ *adj.* not chosen as a SEED in a sports competition, especially in TENNIS 未被列為種子選手的；（尤指網球運動員）非種子的：*unseeded players* 非種子選手 OPP **seeded**

un·see·ing /ˌʌn'siːɪŋ/ *adj.* (*literary*) not noticing or really looking at anything although your eyes are open 心不在焉地看着的 ▸ **un·see·ing·ly** *adv.*：*They stared unseeingly at the wreckage.* 他們看着殘骸發愣。

un·seem·ly /ʌn'siːmli/ *adj.* (*old-fashioned* or *formal*) (of behaviour, etc. 行為等) not polite or suitable for a particular situation 不禮貌的；不得體的；不相宜的 SYN **improper** OPP **seemly**

un·seen /ˌʌn'siːn/ *adj.* **1** that cannot be seen 看不見的；無形的：*unseen forces* 無形的力量 ◇ *He was killed by a single shot from an unseen soldier.* 一個埋伏的士兵一槍就把他打死了。◇ *I managed to slip out of the room unseen.* 我總算偷偷地溜出了屋子。**2** not previously seen 前所未見的；未被發現的：*unseen dangers* 未預見的危險 ◇ *The exam consists of an essay and an* ***unseen translation***. 考試包括一篇作文和一篇即席翻譯。IDM see SIGHT *n.* (1)

un·self·con·scious /ˌʌnself'kɒnʃəs; *NAmE* -'kɑːn-/ *adj.* not worried about or aware of what other people think of you 不管（或不注意）別人看法的；不怯場的；大方自然的 OPP **self-conscious** ▸ **un·self·con·scious·ly** *adv.*

un·self·ish /ʌn'selfɪʃ/ *adj.* giving more time or importance to other people's needs, wishes, etc. than to your own 無私的；忘我的；不謀私利的 SYN **selfless**：*unselfish motives* 無私的動機 OPP **selfish** ▸ **un·self·ish·ly** *adv.* **un·self·ish·ness** *noun* [U]

un·sen·ti·men·tal /ˌʌnˌsentɪ'mentl/ *adj.* not having or expressing emotions such as love or pity; not allowing such emotions to influence what you do 沒有（或不流露）感情的；不感情用事的 OPP **sentimental**

un·ser·vice·able /ʌn'sɜːvɪsəbl; *NAmE* -'sɜːrv-/ *adj.* not suitable to be used 不適用的；不正常運轉的 OPP **serviceable**

un·set·tle /ˌʌn'setl/ *verb* **~ sb** to make sb feel upset or worried, especially because a situation has changed 使心神不寧；擾亂；使擔憂：*Changing schools might unsettle the kids.* 轉學可能會讓孩子心情不能安穩。

un·set·tled /ʌn'setld/ *adj.* **1** (of a situation 形勢) that may change; making people uncertain about what might happen 多變的；不安定的；不平穩的；動盪不安的：*These were difficult and unsettled times.* 那是個艱難而動盪的時期。◇ *The weather has been very unsettled* (= it has changed a lot). 天氣一直變幻莫測。**2** not calm or relaxed 不鎮靜的；心緒不寧的；不安的：*They all felt restless and unsettled.* 他們都感到焦躁不安。**3** (of an argument, etc. 爭論等) that continues without any agreement being reached 無休止的；未解決的 SYN **unresolved 4** (of a bill, etc. 賬單等) not yet paid 未支付的；未付清的

un·set·tling /ʌn'setlɪŋ/ *adj.* making you feel upset, nervous or worried 令人不安（或緊張、擔憂）的

un·shaded /ˌʌn'ʃeɪdɪd/ *adj.* (of a source of light 光源) without a SHADE or other covering 無（燈）罩的；無遮蔽的：*an unshaded light bulb* 沒有燈罩的電燈泡

un·shak·able (*BrE* also **un·shake·able**) /ʌn'ʃeɪkəbl/ *adj.* (of a feeling or an attitude 感情或態度) that cannot be changed or destroyed 不能改變的；不可動搖的；堅定不移的；堅不可摧的 SYN **firm**

U

un·shaken /ˌʌnˈʃeɪkən/ *adj.* **~ (in sth)** not having changed a particular feeling or attitude 堅定的；未動搖的： *They remain unshaken in their loyalty.* 他們仍然忠貞不渝。

un·shaven /ˌʌnˈʃeɪvn/ *adj.* not having shaved or been shaved recently 未刮臉的；未剃鬚的： *He looked pale and unshaven.* 他面色蒼白，鬍子也沒刮。◇ *his unshaven face* 他那張沒刮的臉 ➲ compare SHAVEN

un·sight·ly /ʌnˈsaɪtli/ *adj.* not pleasant to look at 難看的；不雅觀的；不悅目的 **SYN** **ugly**

un·skilled /ˌʌnˈskɪld/ *adj.* not having or needing special skills or training 無特長的；無（需）特別技能的；無（需）專門訓練的： *unskilled manual workers* 非熟練體力勞動者 ◇ *unskilled work* 無需特別技能的工作 **OPP** **skilled**

un·smil·ing /ʌnˈsmaɪlɪŋ/ *adj.* (*formal*) not smiling; looking unfriendly 不苟言笑的；表情冷漠的： *His eyes were hard and unsmiling.* 他目光嚴厲冷峻。 ▸ **un·smil·ing·ly** *adv.*

un·soci·able /ʌnˈsəʊʃəbl; *NAmE* -ˈsoʊ-/ *adj.* **1** not enjoying the company of other people; not friendly 不愛交際的；不合群的 **OPP** **sociable** **2** = UNSOCIAL

un·social /ˌʌnˈsəʊʃl; *NAmE* ˌʌnˈsoʊʃl/ (also *less frequent* **un·soci·able**) (*BrE*) *adj.* outside the normal times of working 非正常工作時間的；正常工作時間以外的： *I work long and unsocial hours.* 我工作時間長，且在非正常時間上班。

un·sold /ˌʌnˈsəʊld; *NAmE* ˌʌnˈsoʊld/ *adj.* not bought by anyone 未售出的；無人購買的： *Many of the houses remain unsold.* 這些房屋有許多尚未售出。

un·soli·cit·ed /ˌʌnsəˈlɪsɪtɪd/ *adj.* not asked for and sometimes not wanted 未經要求的；自發的；自我推薦的： *unsolicited advice* 主動提出的忠告

un·solved /ˌʌnˈsɒlvd; *NAmE* ˌʌnˈsɑːlvd/ *adj.* not having been solved 未解決的；未破解的： *an* ***unsolved murder/mystery/problem*** 未破案的謀殺事件；未解開的謎團；未解決的問題

un·sophis·ti·cated /ˌʌnsəˈfɪstɪkeɪtɪd/ *adj.* **1** not having or showing much experience of the world and social situations 單純的；閱歷淺的；涉世不深的；不諳世故的： *unsophisticated tastes* 單純的愛好 **2** simple and basic; not complicated 基本的；簡單的；不複雜的 **SYN** **crude**： *unsophisticated equipment* 簡單的基本設備 **OPP** **sophisticated**

un·sorted /ˌʌnˈsɔːtɪd; *NAmE* -ˈsɔːrt-/ *adj.* not sorted, or not arranged in any particular order 未分類的；未排序的： *a pile of unsorted papers* 一沓未整理的文件

un·sound /ˌʌnˈsaʊnd/ *adj.* **1** not acceptable; not holding acceptable views 不穩妥的；觀點不正確的： *ideologically unsound* 意識上不妥 ◇ *The use of disposable products is considered ecologically unsound.* 使用一次性產品被認為是沒有顧及對生態的影響。 **2** containing mistakes; that you cannot rely on 有錯誤的；靠不住的 **SYN** **unreliable**： *The methods used were unsound.* 所使用的方法不可靠。 **3** (of a building, etc. 建築物等) in poor condition; weak and likely to fall down 破舊的；搖搖欲墜的： *The roof is* ***structurally unsound.*** 這屋頂結構不牢固。 **OPP** **sound** ▸ **un·sound·ness** *noun* [U]

IDM **of ˌunsound ˈmind** (*law* 律) not responsible for your actions because of a mental illness 精神失常，神志不清（無須對自己的行為負責）

un·spar·ing /ʌnˈspeərɪŋ; *NAmE* -ˈsper-/ *adj.* **~ (in sth)** (*formal*) **1** not caring about people's feelings 無情的；嚴厲的： *She is unsparing in her criticism.* 她批評人毫不留情。◇ *an unsparing portrait of life in the slums* 對貧民窟生活無情的摹寫 **2** giving or given generously 慷慨的；大方的；不吝嗇的： *He won his mother's unsparing approval.* 他贏得了母親毫無保留的贊同。 ➲ compare SPARING ▸ **un·spar·ing·ly** *adv.*

un·speak·able /ʌnˈspiːkəbl/ *adj.* (*literary*, usually *disapproving*) that cannot be described in words, usually because it is so bad 難以說出口的；不堪入耳的 **SYN** **indescribable** ▸ **un·speak·ably** /-əbli/ *adv.*

un·speci·fied **AW** /ˌʌnˈspesɪfaɪd/ *adj.* not stated clearly or definitely; not having been SPECIFIED 未說明的；不明確的： *The story takes place at an unspecified date.* 故事發生的日期不明。

un·spec·tacu·lar /ˌʌnspekˈtækjələ(r)/ *adj.* not exciting or special 平凡的；平淡的；普通的： *He had a steady but unspectacular career.* 他的事業穩定但平淡無奇。

un·spoiled /ˌʌnˈspɔɪld/ (*BrE* also **un·spoilt** /ˌʌnˈspɔɪlt/) *adj.* (*approving*) **1** (of a place 地方) beautiful because it has not been changed or built on 有自然美的；未遭破壞的 **2** (of a person 人) not made unpleasant, bad-tempered, etc. by being praised too much 未被寵壞的；未被捧殺的 **OPP** **spoilt**

un·spoken /ˌʌnˈspəʊkən; *NAmE* -ˈspoʊ-/ *adj.* (*formal*) not stated; not said in words but understood or agreed between people 未說出的；未表達的；默契的；心照不宣的 **SYN** **unstated**： *an unspoken assumption* 隱含的假定 ◇ *Something unspoken hung in the air between them.* 他們之間有些心照不宣的事還沒有解決。

un·sport·ing /ˌʌnˈspɔːtɪŋ; *NAmE* -ˈspɔːrt-/ *adj.* (*disapproving*) not fair or generous in your behaviour or treatment of others, especially of an opponent in a game 不公平的；不光明正大的；（尤指）缺乏體育道德的 **OPP** **sporting**

un·sports·man·like /ˌʌnˈspɔːtsmənlaɪk; *NAmE* -ˈspɔːrts-/ *adj.* (*disapproving*) not behaving in a fair, generous and polite way, especially when playing a sport or game 沒有運動員風範的，無體育精神的（尤指體育比賽中不光明磊落、無氣度）： *unsportsmanlike conduct* 有失運動員風度的行為

un·stable **AW** /ʌnˈsteɪbl/ *adj.* **1** likely to change suddenly 不穩定的；易變的；變化莫測的 **SYN** **volatile**： *The political situation remains highly unstable.* 政局仍然十分動盪。 **2** if people are **unstable**, their behaviour and emotions change often and suddenly because their minds are upset（行為、情緒）反覆無常的，不穩定的 ➲ **SYNONYMS** at MENTALLY **3** likely to move or fall 易動（或倒下）的；不穩固的 **4** (*technical* 術語) (of a substance 物質) not staying in the same chemical or ATOMIC state 不穩定的；能衰變的： *chemically unstable* 化學上不穩定的 **OPP** **stable** ➲ see also INSTABILITY

un·stated /ʌnˈsteɪtɪd/ *adj.* (*formal*) not stated; not said in words but understood or agreed between people 未說出的；未用語言表達的；心照不宣的 **SYN** **unspoken**： *Their reasoning was based on a set of unstated assumptions.* 他們的推理是以一系列未說明的假定為基礎的。

un·steady 🔑 /ʌnˈstedi/ *adj.*
1 🔑 not completely in control of your movements so that you might fall 站不穩的；搖晃的： *She is still a little* ***unsteady on her feet*** *after the operation.* 手術以後她還有點站不穩。 **2** 🔑 shaking or moving in a way that is not controlled 顫抖的；抖動的： *an unsteady hand* 顫抖的手 **OPP** **steady** ▸ **un·stead·ily** /-ɪli/ *adv.* **un·steadi·ness** *noun* [U]

un·stint·ing /ʌnˈstɪntɪŋ/ *adj.* given or giving generously 慷慨的；大方的；無限的： *unstinting support* 全力的支持 ◇ **~ in sth** *They were unstinting in their praise.* 他們讚不絕口。 ▸ **un·stint·ing·ly** *adv.*

un·stop·pable /ʌnˈstɒpəbl; *NAmE* -ˈstɑːp-/ *adj.* that cannot be stopped or prevented 無法遏止的；不能防止的： *an unstoppable rise in prices* 無法遏止的價格上漲 ◇ *On form, the team was simply unstoppable.* 若狀態良好，這個隊伍簡直勢不可當。

un·stressed **AW** /ˌʌnˈstrest/ *adj.* (*phonetics* 語音) (of a syllable 音節) pronounced without emphasis 非重讀的；輕讀的 **OPP** **stressed**

un·struc·tured **AW** /ʌnˈstrʌktʃəd; *NAmE* -tʃərd/ *adj.* without structure or organization 結構淩亂的；無條理的；紊亂的

un·stuck /ˌʌnˈstʌk/ *adj.*
IDM **ˌcome unˈstuck** **1** to become separated from sth it was stuck or fastened to 未粘住；脫離；鬆開： *The flap of the envelope had come unstuck.* 信封的封口沒粘牢，張開了。 **2** (*BrE, informal*) (of a person, plan, etc. 人、計劃等) to fail completely, with bad results 徹底失敗；一敗塗地

un·sub·scribe /ˌʌnsəb'skraɪb/ *verb* [I, T] **~ (from sth)** | **~ sb/sth** (*computing* 計) to remove your email address from an Internet MAILING LIST 取消收取網上電郵的登記；取消訂閱

un·sub·stan·ti·ated /ˌʌnsəb'stænʃieɪtɪd/ *adj.* (*formal*) not proved to be true by evidence 未經證實的；未被證明的 SYN **unsupported**：*an unsubstantiated claim/rumour, etc.* 未經證實的説法、傳言等

un·suc·cess·ful /ˌʌnsək'sesfl/ *adj.* not successful; not achieving what you wanted to 不成功的；失敗的；落空的：*His efforts to get a job proved unsuccessful.* 他求職的努力都落空了。◇ *They were unsuccessful in meeting their objectives for the year.* 他們未能達到年度目標。◇ *She made several unsuccessful attempts to see him.* 她幾次想見他都未如願。OPP **successful** ▸ **un·suc·cess·ful·ly** *adv.*

un·suit·able /ʌn'suːtəbl; *BrE* also -'sjuː-/ *adj.* **~ (for sb/sth)** not right or appropriate for a particular person, purpose or occasion 不適當的；不適宜的；不合適的：*He was wearing shoes that were totally unsuitable for climbing.* 他穿了一雙完全不適合登山的鞋子。OPP **suitable** ▸ **un·suit·abil·ity** *noun* [U] **un·suit·ably** *adv.*：*They were unsuitably dressed for the occasion.* 他們的穿着在那種場合很不得體。

un·suit·ed /ʌn'suːtɪd; *BrE* also -'sjuː-/ *adj.* **1 ~ (to/for sth)** | **~ (to do sth)** not having the right or necessary qualities for sth 不合格的；不勝任的；不適宜的：*He is unsuited to academic work.* 他不適合做學術工作。◇ *She was totally unsuited for the job.* 她根本不能勝任這項工作。 **2** if two people are **unsuited** to each other they do not have the same interests, etc. and are therefore not likely to make a good couple （人）志趣不相投的，不相配的，不般配的 OPP **suited**

un·sul·lied /ʌn'sʌlid/ *adj.* (*literary*) not spoiled by anything; still pure or in the original state 未被玷污的；保持潔淨的；純潔的 SYN **unspoiled**

un·sung /ˌʌn'sʌŋ/ *adj.* [usually before noun] (*formal*) not praised or famous but deserving to be 被埋沒的；未被頌揚的：*the unsung heroes of the war* 戰爭中的無名英雄

un·sup·port·ed /ˌʌnsə'pɔːtɪd; *NAmE* -'pɔːrt-/ *adj.* **1** (of a statement, etc. 聲明等) not proved to be true by evidence 未經證實的 SYN **unsubstantiated**：*Their claims are unsupported by research findings.* 他們的説法並未能得到研究結果的證實。 **2** not helped or paid for by sb/sth else 無資助的；自力更生的：*She has brought up three children unsupported.* 她獨力將三個孩子撫養成人。 **3** not physically supported 無支撐物的：*Sections of the structure have been left unsupported.* 這個結構有幾部份沒有支撐。

un·sure /ˌʌn'ʃʊə(r); -'ʃɔː(r); *NAmE* -'ʃʊr/ *adj.* [not before noun] **1** not certain of sth; having doubts 無把握；不確知；猶豫：**~ about/of sth** *There were a lot of things I was unsure about.* 有許多事情我沒把握。◇ **~ how, what, etc. …** *I was unsure how to reply to this question.* 我拿不準該如何回答這個問題。◇ **~ of/as to how, what, etc. …** *He was unsure of what to do next.* 他對下一步該做什麼猶豫不定。◇ *They were unsure as to what the next move should be.* 下一步該做什麼他們心裏沒底。 **2 ~ (of yourself)** lacking confidence in yourself 缺乏自信：*Like many women, deep down she was unsure of herself.* 和許多女性一樣，她心底裏缺乏自信。OPP **sure**

un·sur·passed /ˌʌnsə'pɑːst; *NAmE* ˌʌnsər'pæst/ *adj.* (*formal*) better or greater than any other 無比的；卓絕的；出類拔萃的 SYN **unrivalled**

un·sur·prised /ˌʌnsə'praɪzd; *NAmE* -sər'p-/ *adj.* [not usually before noun] not surprised 不覺得驚奇：*She appeared totally unsurprised at the news.* 她對這消息一點都不顯得驚奇。

un·sur·pris·ing /ˌʌnsə'praɪzɪŋ; *NAmE* -sər'p-/ *adj.* not causing surprise 不令人驚訝的；不足為奇的 OPP **surprising** ▸ **un·sur·pris·ing·ly** *adv.*：*Unsurprisingly, the plan failed.* 果然不出所料，計劃失敗了。

un·sus·pect·ed /ˌʌnsə'spektɪd/ *adj.* not predicted or known; that you were not previously aware of 未預料到的；未知的；未覺察到的

un·sus·pect·ing /ˌʌnsə'spektɪŋ/ *adj.* [usually before noun] feeling no suspicion; not aware of danger or of sth bad 毫不懷疑的；無危險意識的；無戒備心的：*He had crept up on his unsuspecting victim from behind.* 他從背後悄悄逼近了那毫無戒備的受害者。

un·sus·tain·able AW /ˌʌnsə'steɪnəbl/ *adj.* that cannot be continued at the same level, rate, etc. 不能持續的；無法維持的：*unsustainable growth* 難以持續的增長 OPP **sustainable**

un·sweet·ened /ˌʌn'swiːtnd/ *adj.* (of food or drinks 食物或飲料) without sugar or a similar substance having been added 未加糖的；未加甜味素的

un·swerv·ing /ʌn'swɜːvɪŋ; *NAmE* -'swɜːrv-/ *adj.* (*formal*) strong and not changing or becoming weaker 堅定的；不懈的；始終如一的：***unswerving loyalty/support, etc.*** 始終如一的忠誠、支持等

un·sym·pa·thet·ic /ˌʌnˌsɪmpə'θetɪk/ *adj.* **1 ~ (to/towards sb)** not feeling or showing any sympathy 無同情心的；不表示同情的；冷漠的：*I told him about the problem but he was totally unsympathetic.* 我把麻煩事告訴了他，但他完全無動於衷。 **2 ~ (to/towards sth)** not in agreement with sth; not supporting an idea, aim, etc. （與…）不一致的；有分歧的；（與某意見、目的等）相違的：*The government was unsympathetic to public opinion.* 政府違背了民意。 **3** (of a person 人) not easy to like; unpleasant 不招人喜歡的 OPP **sympathetic** ▸ **un·sym·pa·thet·ic·al·ly** /-kli/ *adv.*：*'You've only got yourself to blame,' she said unsympathetically.* "你只能怪你自己。" 她冷漠地説。

un·sys·tem·at·ic /ˌʌnˌsɪstə'mætɪk/ *adj.* not organized into a clear system 無系統的；紊亂的；雜亂無章的 OPP **systematic** ▸ **un·sys·tem·at·ic·al·ly** *adv.*

un·taint·ed /ʌn'teɪntɪd/ *adj.* **~ (by sth)** (*formal*) not damaged or spoiled by sth unpleasant; not TAINTED 未受損害的；未被污染的；未被玷污的

un·tal·ent·ed /ʌn'tæləntɪd/ *adj.* without a natural ability to do sth well 無天賦的；沒有特別天分的 OPP **talented**

un·tamed /ˌʌn'teɪmd/ *adj.* allowed to remain in a wild state; not changed, controlled or influenced by anyone; not TAMED 野性的；未馴服的；未受抑制的；未調教的

un·tan·gle /ˌʌn'tæŋgl/ *verb* **1 ~ sth (from sth)** to undo string, hair, wire, etc. that has become twisted or has knots in it 解開，鬆開（結子等） **2 ~ sth** to make sth that is complicated or confusing easier to deal with or understand 整理；理清

un·tapped /ˌʌn'tæpt/ *adj.* available but not yet used 未利用的；未開發的；蘊藏的：*untapped reserves of oil* 未開採的石油貯量

un·ten·able /ʌn'tenəbl/ *adj.* (*formal*) (of a theory, position, etc. 理論、地位等) that cannot be defended against attack or criticism 難以捍衞的；站不住腳的；不堪一擊的：*His position had become untenable and he was forced to resign.* 他的地位已難以維持，因此他被迫辭職。OPP **tenable**

un·test·ed /ˌʌn'testɪd/ *adj.* not tested; of unknown quality or value 未經試驗（或考驗）的

un·think·able /ʌn'θɪŋkəbl/ *adj.* **~ (for sb) (to do sth)** | **~ (that …)** impossible to imagine or accept 難以想像的；不可思議的；難以置信的 SYN **inconceivable**：*It was unthinkable that she could be dead.* 她竟然去世了，真是很難相信。OPP **thinkable** ▸ **the un·think·able** *noun* [sing.]：*Suddenly the unthinkable happened and he drew out a gun.* 突然，難以相信的事情發生了，他拔出了手槍。◇ *The time has come to **think the unthinkable*** (= consider possibilities that used to be unacceptable). 現在該開始考慮以前不予考慮的事情了。

un·think·ing /ʌn'θɪŋkɪŋ/ *adj.* (*formal*) not thinking about the effects of what you do or say; not thinking much about serious things 不計後果的；考慮不周的；不動腦筋的 SYN **thoughtless** ▸ **un·think·ing·ly** *adv.*

un·tidy 0‑π /ʌn'taɪdi/ *adj.* (**un·tidi·er**, **un·tidi·est**)
1 0‑π not neat or well arranged; in a state of confusion 不整潔的；不整齊的；凌亂的：*an untidy desk* 凌亂的辦公桌 ◇ *untidy hair* 蓬亂的頭髮 **2** 0‑π (of a person 人) not keeping things neat or well organized 無條理的；不修邊幅的：*Why do you have to be so untidy?* 你為什麼非得這麼邋遢？ **OPP** **tidy** ▸ **un·tidi·ly** /-ɪli/ *adv.* **un·tidi·ness** *noun* [U]

untie /ʌn'taɪ/ *verb* **~ sth** to undo a knot in sth; to undo sth that is tied 解開…的結；打開：*to untie a knot* 解開繩結 ◇ *I quickly untied the package and peeped inside.* 我迅速拆開包裹，往裏瞥了一眼。◇ *He untied the rope and pushed the boat into the water.* 他解開纜繩，把小船推入水中。

until 0‑π /ən'tɪl/ *conj., prep.* (also *informal* **till**, **til**, **'til**) up to the point in time or the event mentioned 到…時；直到…為止：*Let's wait until the rain stops.* 咱們等雨停了吧。◇ *Until she spoke I hadn't realized she wasn't English.* 直到她開口說話我才知道她不是英國人。◇ *You're not going out until you've finished this.* 你沒把這事做完就不准出去。◇ *Until now I have always lived alone.* 直到現在，我一直獨自生活。◇ *They moved here in 2009. Until then they'd always been in the London area.* 他們 2009 年搬到這裏，之前一直住在倫敦地區。◇ *He continued working* ***up until*** *his death.* 他一直工作到去世。◇ *The street is full of traffic* ***from morning till night.*** 街上從早到晚車水馬龍。◇ *You can stay on the bus until London* (= until you reach London). 你可以不用下車，直到公車到達倫敦為止。

un·time·ly /ʌn'taɪmli/ *adj.* (*formal*) **1** happening too soon or sooner than is normal or expected 過早的；不到時間的；突然的 **SYN** **premature**：*She met a tragic and* ***untimely death*** *at 25.* 她於 25 歲時不幸猝然離世。**2** happening at a time or in a situation that is not suitable 不合時宜的；不適時的 **SYN** **ill-timed**：*His interruption was untimely.* 他的插話不是時候。**OPP** **timely**

un·tir·ing /ʌn'taɪərɪŋ/ *adj.* (*approving*) continuing to do sth for a long period of time with a lot of effort and/or enthusiasm 不知疲勞的；孜孜不倦的；堅持不懈的 **SYN** **tireless**

un·titled /ˌʌn'taɪtld/ *adj.* (of a work of art 藝術品) without a title 無題的（表示不標明題目或沒有名稱）

unto /'ʌntə; 'ʌntu/ *prep.* (*old use*) **1** to or towards sb/sth 朝；向；到；對：*The angel appeared unto him in a dream.* 天使在夢中出現在他面前。**2** until a particular time or event 直到；到…為止：*The knights swore loyalty unto death.* 騎士們宣誓至死效忠。

un·told /ˌʌn'təʊld; *NAmE* ˌʌn'toʊld/ *adj.* **1** [only before noun] used to emphasize how large, great, unpleasant, etc. sth is 難以形容的（大、惡劣等） **SYN** **immeasurable**：*untold misery/wealth* 極度的痛苦；巨額財富 ◇ *These gases cause* ***untold damage*** *to the environment.* 這些氣體對環境造成難以估計的破壞。**2** (of a story 故事) not told to anyone 未講過的；未敘述的

un·touch·able /ʌn'tʌtʃəbl/ *adj., noun*
▪ *adj.* **1** a person who is **untouchable** is in a position where they are unlikely to be punished or criticized 不可處罰（或批評）的；管不了的：*Given his political connections, he thought he was untouchable.* 他有一些政界關係，所以自認為誰也管不了他。**2** that cannot be touched or changed by other people 不可觸及（或改變）的：*The department's budget is untouchable.* 這個部門的預算是不容變動的。**3** (in India in the past) belonging to or connected with the Hindu social class (or CASTE) that was considered by other classes to be the lowest（舊時印度）賤民的，不可接觸者的
▪ *noun* (often **Untouchable**) (in India in the past) a member of a Hindu social class (or CASTE) that was considered by other classes to be the lowest（舊時印度）賤民，不可接觸者

un·touched /ʌn'tʌtʃt/ *adj.* [not usually before noun] **1 ~ (by sth)** not affected by sth, especially sth bad or unpleasant; not damaged 未受影響；未被損害；原封未動：*The area has remained relatively untouched by commercial development.* 相對而言，這個地區至今沒有受到商業開發的影響。**2** (of food or drink 食物或飲料) not eaten or drunk 未食用（或飲用）；未動：*She left her meal untouched.* 她的飯連動都沒動。**3** not changed in any way 未改變；未修改：*The final clause in the contract will be left untouched.* 合同的最後一項條款將不作改動。

un·to·ward /ˌʌntə'wɔːd; *NAmE* ʌn'tɔːrd/ *adj.* unusual and unexpected, and usually unpleasant 異常的；意外的；不幸的；棘手的：*That's the plan—unless* ***anything untoward*** *happens.* 計劃就這麼定了，除非出現異常情況。◇ *He had noticed* ***nothing untoward.*** 他沒有注意到有何特殊情況。

un·trained /ˌʌn'treɪnd/ *adj.* **~ (in sth)** not trained to perform a particular job or skill; without formal training in sth 沒有訓練的；未經正規培訓的：*untrained in keyboard skills* 未經鍵盤操作技能訓練的 ◇ *untrained teachers* 未經正規培訓的教師 ◇ ***To the untrained eye,*** *the products look remarkably similar.* 這些產品在沒有受過專門訓練的人看來幾乎一模一樣。

un·tram·melled (*especially US* **un·tram·meled**) /ʌn'træmld/ *adj.* **~ (by sth)** (*formal*) not restricted or limited by sth 不受限制的；無拘束的；自由自在的 ➲ compare TRAMMEL

un·treat·ed /ˌʌn'triːtɪd/ *adj.* **1** not receiving medical treatment 沒有接受治療的：*If untreated, the illness can become severe.* 若不加以治療，病情就可能會變得很嚴重。**2** (of substances 物質) not made safe by chemical or other treatment 未處理的：*untreated sewage* 未處理的污水 **3** (of wood 木材) not treated with substances to preserve it 未經防護處理的

un·tried /ˌʌn'traɪd/ *adj.* **1** without experience of doing a particular job 沒有經驗的：*She chose two untried actors for the leading roles.* 她選了兩個沒有經驗的演員飾演主角。**2** not yet tried or tested to discover if it works or is successful 未檢驗的；未經考驗（或試驗）的 **SYN** **untested**：*This is a new and relatively untried procedure.* 這是個未經多少試驗的新程序。

un·true /ʌn'truː/ *adj.* **1** not true; not based on facts 不真實的；假的；無事實根據的：*These accusations are totally untrue.* 這些指控純屬捏造。◇ *an untrue claim* 不真實的說法 ◇ *It* ***is untrue to say*** *that something like this could never happen again.* 說這類事情再也不會發生是毫無事實根據的。**2 ~ (to sb/sth)** (*formal*) not loyal to sb/sth 不忠實的；不忠誠的 **SYN** **unfaithful**：*If he agreed to their demands, he would have to be untrue to his own principles.* 假使答應他們的要求，他就得背叛自己的原則。**OPP** **true**

un·trust·worthy /ʌn'trʌstwɜːði; *NAmE* -wɜːrði/ *adj.* that cannot be trusted 不可靠的；不能信賴（或信任）的 **OPP** **trustworthy**

un·truth /ˌʌn'truːθ/ *noun* (*pl.* **un·truths** /ˌʌn'truːðz; -'truːθs/) **1** [C] (*formal*) a lie. People often say 'untruth' to avoid saying 'lie'.（lie 的委婉說法）妄語，謊語，假話 ➲ compare TRUTH (1) **2** [U] the state of being false 虛偽；虛假；不真實

un·truth·ful /ʌn'truːθfl/ *adj.* saying things that you know are not true 說謊的；不說實話的 **OPP** **truthful** ▸ **un·truth·ful·ly** /-fəli/ *adv.*

un·turned /ˌʌn'tɜːnd; *NAmE* ˌʌn'tɜːrnd/ *adj.* **IDM** see STONE *n.*

un·tutored /ˌʌn'tjuːtəd; *NAmE* ˌʌn'tuːtərd/ *adj.* (*formal*) not having been formally taught about sth 未接受正規教育的；未受過正式訓練的

un·typ·ical /ʌn'tɪpɪkl/ *adj.* **~ (of sb/sth)** not typical 不典型的；無代表性的；無特徵的：*an untypical example* 非典型的例子 ◇ *Schools in this area are quite untypical of schools in the rest of the country.* 這個地區的學校根本不能代表全國其他地區的學校。◇ *All in all, it had been a* ***not untypical*** *day* (= it had been very like other days). 總而言之，那一天平平常常，並沒有什麼特別。**OPP** **typical** ➲ compare ATYPICAL ▸ **un·typ·ic·al·ly** *adv.*

un·usable /ˌʌn'juːzəbl/ *adj.* in such a bad condition or of such low quality that it cannot be used（破得或差得）不能使用的；破爛不堪的 **OPP** **usable**

un·used¹ /ˌʌnˈjuːzd/ *adj.* not being used at the moment; never having been used 沒用着的；閒着的；未用過的 ➲ compare DISUSED

un·used² /ʌnˈjuːst/ *adj.* not having much experience of sth and therefore not knowing how to deal with it; not used to sth 經驗少；不習慣；不熟悉；不慣於：**~ to sth** *This is an easy routine, designed for anyone who is unused to exercise.* 這是一套簡單的固定動作，是為不常鍛煉的人設計的。◇ **~ to doing sth** *She was unused to talking about herself.* 她不習慣談論自己。OPP **used**

un·usual 0→ /ʌnˈjuːʒuəl; -ʒəl/ *adj.*
1 0→ different from what is usual or normal 特別的；不尋常的；罕見的 SYN **uncommon**：*It's unusual for the trees to flower so early.* 這種樹這麼早開花很少見。◇ *She has a very unusual name.* 她的名字很特別。◇ *It's not unusual for young doctors to work a 70-hour week* (= it happens often). 年輕的醫生每週工作 70 小時並不罕見。**2** 0→ different from other similar things and therefore interesting and attractive 獨特的；與眾不同的；別致的：*an unusual colour* 特別的顏色

un·usual·ly 0→ /ʌnˈjuːʒuəli; -ʒəli/ *adv.*
1 0→ used before adjectives to emphasize that a particular quality is greater than normal（置於形容詞前，用以強調）特別地，極，非常：*unusually high levels of radiation* 超高的輻射強度 ◇ *an unusually cold winter* 異常寒冷的冬天 **2** 0→ used to say that a particular situation is not normal or expected 不尋常地；意想不到地：*Unusually for him, he wore a tie.* 他破例打了一條領帶。

un·utter·able /ʌnˈʌtərəbl/ *adj.* [only before noun] (*formal*) used to emphasize how great a particular emotion or quality is 難以言表的；說不出的：*unutterable sadness* 無法形容的悲傷 ▸ **un·utter·ably** /-əbli/ *adv.*

un·var·nished /ʌnˈvɑːnɪʃt; *NAmE* -ˈvɑːrn-/ *adj.* **1** [only before noun] (*formal*) with nothing added 不加掩飾的；質樸的；坦率的：*It was the plain unvarnished truth.* 這是簡單確鑿的事實。**2** (of wood, etc. 木材等) not covered with VARNISH 未加塗層的；未塗清漆的

un·vary·ing /ʌnˈveərɪŋ; *NAmE* -ˈveri-; -ˈværi-/ *adj.* (*formal*) never changing 從無變化的；固定的；恆久的：*an unvarying routine* 不變的常規

un·veil /ˌʌnˈveɪl/ *verb* **1 ~ sth** to remove a cover or curtain from a painting, statue, etc. so that it can be seen in public for the first time 為…揭幕；揭開…上的覆蓋物；拉開…的帷幔：*The Queen unveiled a plaque to mark the official opening of the hospital.* 女王主持揭幕式，標誌着醫院正式啟用。**2 ~ sth** to show or introduce a new plan, product, etc. to the public for the first time（首次）展示，介紹，推出；將…公諸於眾 SYN **reveal**：*They will be unveiling their new models at the Motor Show.* 他們將在汽車大展上首次推出自己的新型汽車。

un·voiced /ˌʌnˈvɔɪst/ *adj.* **1** thought about but not expressed in words（想法）未用語言表達的，未說出的 **2** (*phonetics* 語音) (of consonants 輔音) produced without moving your VOCAL CORDS; not VOICED 清音的；不帶聲的 SYN **voiceless**：*unvoiced consonants such as 'p' and 't'* 清輔音如 /p/ 和 /t/

un·waged /ˌʌnˈweɪdʒd/ *adj.* (*BrE*) **1** (of a person 人) not earning money by working 無工資收入的；不掙錢的 OPP **waged** **2** (of work 工作) for which you are not paid 無償的；無報酬的 SYN **unpaid** **3 the unwaged** *noun* [pl.] people who are unwaged 無工作報酬者

un·want·ed /ˌʌnˈwɒntɪd; *NAmE* -ˈwɑːnt-; -ˈwɔːnt-/ *adj.* that you do not want 不需要的；多餘的；不受歡迎的；無用的：*unwanted advice* 多餘的勸告 ◇ *unwanted pregnancies* 意外懷孕 ◇ *It is very sad when children feel unwanted* (= feel that other people do not care about them). 小孩覺得沒有人愛是很悲慘的。

un·war·rant·ed /ʌnˈwɒrəntɪd; *NAmE* -ˈwɔːr-; -ˈwɑːr-/ *adj.* (*formal*) not reasonable or necessary; not appropriate 不合理的；不必要的；無正當理由的；不適當的 SYN **unjustified**：*Much of the criticism was totally unwarranted.* 這種批評基本上是毫無道理的。

un·wary /ʌnˈweəri; *NAmE* -ˈweri/ *adj.* **1** [only before noun] not aware of the possible dangers or problems of a situation and therefore likely to be harmed in some way 不警覺的；不提防的 ➲ compare WARY **2 the unwary** *noun* [pl.] people who are unwary 粗心的人；不警覺的人：*The stock market is full of traps for the unwary.* 對無風險意識的人而言，股票市場充滿了陷阱。

un·washed /ˌʌnˈwɒʃt; *NAmE* -ˈwɔːʃt; -ˈwɑːʃt/ *adj.* not washed; dirty 未洗滌的；骯髒的：*a pile of unwashed dishes* 一堆未洗的碟子 ◇ *Their clothes were dirty and their hair unwashed.* 他們衣服骯髒，頭髮未洗。

un·waver·ing /ʌnˈweɪvərɪŋ/ *adj.* (*formal*) not changing or becoming weaker in any way 不動搖的；堅定的；始終如一的：*unwavering support* 堅定不移的支持 ▸ **un·waver·ing·ly** *adv.*

un·wel·come /ʌnˈwelkəm/ *adj.* not wanted 不需要的；不受歡迎的；多餘的：*an unwelcome visitor* 不受歡迎的訪客 ◇ *To avoid attracting unwelcome attention he kept his voice down.* 為避免引起不必要的注意，他把聲音壓低了。OPP **welcome**

un·wel·com·ing /ʌnˈwelkəmɪŋ/ *adj.* **1** (of a person 人) not friendly towards sb who is visiting or arriving（對造訪者）不親切的，不熱情的，冷淡的 **2** (of a place 地方) not attractive; looking uncomfortable to be in 不愜意的；不能引起親切感的；不溫馨的 OPP **welcoming**

un·well /ʌnˈwel/ *adj.* [not before noun] (rather *formal*) ill/sick 有恙；染病；不適；不舒服：*She said she was feeling unwell and went home.* 她說她感覺不舒服回家了。OPP **well**

un·whole·some /ˌʌnˈhəʊlsəm; *NAmE* -ˈhoʊl-/ *adj.* **1** harmful to health; not looking healthy 有損健康的；不健康的；不衞生的 **2** that you consider unpleasant or not natural 令人不快的；討厭的；不自然的 SYN **unhealthy** OPP **wholesome**

un·wieldy /ʌnˈwiːldi/ *adj.* **1** (of an object 東西) difficult to move or control because of its size, shape or weight 笨重的；笨拙的；不靈巧的 SYN **cumbersome** **2** (of a system or group of people 體制或團體) difficult to control or organize because it is very large or complicated 難控制（或操縱、管理）的；運轉不靈的；尾大不掉的

un·will·ing 0→ /ʌnˈwɪlɪŋ/ *adj.*
1 0→ [not usually before noun] **~** (**to do sth**) not wanting to do sth and refusing to do it 不情願；不願意：*They are unwilling to invest any more money in the project.* 他們不想在這個項目上再增加投資。◇ *She was unable, or unwilling, to give me any further details.* 她不能，或不願意，向我提供進一步的細節。**2** [only before noun] not wanting to do or be sth, but forced to by other people 勉強的；無奈的；迫不得已的 SYN **reluctant**：*an unwilling hero* 自己不願卻被抬舉的英雄 ◇ *He became the unwilling object of her attention.* 他受到她的青睞實非所願。OPP **willing** ▸ **un·will·ing·ly** 0→ *adv.* **un·will·ing·ness** *noun* [U]

un·wind /ˌʌnˈwaɪnd/ *verb* (**un·wound**, **un·wound** /ˌʌnˈwaʊnd/) **1** [T, I] **~** (**sth**) (**from sth**) to undo sth that has been wrapped into a ball or around sth 解開，打開，鬆開（捲繞之物）：*to unwind a ball of string* 解開一團繩 ◇ *He unwound his scarf from his neck.* 他從脖子上解下圍巾。◇ *The bandage gradually unwound and fell off.* 繃帶逐漸鬆開脫落了。**2** [I] to stop worrying or thinking about problems and start to relax 放鬆；輕鬆 SYN **relax, wind down**：*Music helps me unwind after a busy day.* 音樂使我在忙碌一天後得以放鬆。

un·wise /ˌʌnˈwaɪz/ *adj.* **~** (**to do sth**) showing a lack of good judgement 愚蠢的；不明智的；輕率的 SYN **foolish**：*It would be unwise to comment on the situation without knowing all the facts.* 不全面瞭解情況就對局勢妄加評論是不明智的。◇ *an unwise investment* 不明智的投資 OPP **wise** ▸ **un·wise·ly** *adv.*：*Perhaps unwisely, I agreed to help.* 我同意幫忙，這也許太輕率了。

un·wit·ting /ʌnˈwɪtɪŋ/ *adj.* [only before noun] not aware of what you are doing or of the situation you are involved in 不知情的；糊裏糊塗的；無意的：*He became an unwitting accomplice in the crime.* 他糊裏糊塗地成了犯罪的幫兇。◇ *She was the unwitting cause of the argument.* 她無意中引起了這場爭執。

U

un·wit·ting·ly /ʌnˈwɪtɪŋli/ *adv.* without being aware of what you are doing or the situation that you are involved in 糊裏糊塗地；茫然；無意地：*She had broken the law unwittingly, but still she had broken it.* 她並非故意犯法，但畢竟是犯了法。 OPP **wittingly**

un·wont·ed /ʌnˈwəʊntɪd; *NAmE* -ˈwoʊn-/ *adj.* (*formal*) not usual or expected 不平常的；異常的；罕見的；沒想到的：*He spoke with unwonted enthusiasm.* 他講話顯得出人意料的熱心。

un·work·able /ʌnˈwɜːkəbl; *NAmE* -ˈwɜːrk-/ *adj.* not practical or possible to do successfully 不切實際的；難以實行的；行不通的：*an unworkable plan* 不切實際的計劃 ◇ *The law as it stands is unworkable.* 照現在的情形，這條法律是難以執行的。 OPP **workable**

un·world·ly /ʌnˈwɜːldli; *NAmE* -ˈwɜːrld-/ *adj.* **1** not interested in money or the things that it buys 不慕金錢的；對錢財無興趣的 **2** lacking experience of life 不諳世故的；天真的 SYN **naive** OPP **worldly** **3** having qualities that do not seem to belong to this world 非現世的；非塵世的；超凡的：*The landscape had a stark, unworldly beauty.* 那景色有一種簡樸、超凡的美。

un·wor·ried /ʌnˈwʌrid; *NAmE* -ˈwɜːr-/ *adj.* [not usually before noun] (*formal*) not worried; calm; relaxed 坦然；平靜；輕鬆：*She appeared unworried by criticism.* 她看上去並不在乎挨批評。

un·worthy /ʌnˈwɜːði; *NAmE* ʌnˈwɜːrði/ *adj.* (*formal*) **1** ~ (**of sth**) not having the necessary qualities to deserve sth, especially respect 不值得（尊重）的；不配的：*He considered himself unworthy of the honour they had bestowed on him.* 他認為自己不配得到大家賦予他的榮譽。 OPP **worthy** **2** ~ (**of sb**) not acceptable from sb, especially sb who has an important job or high social position 格格不入的；不能接受的；（與…的身分）不相稱的 SYN **unbefitting** : *Such opinions are unworthy of educated people.* 知識分子發表這樣的言論有失身分。
▸ **un·worthi·ness** *noun* [U] : *feelings of unworthiness* 自卑感

un·wound *past tense, past part.* of UNWIND

un·wrap /ʌnˈræp/ *verb* (**-pp-**) **~ sth** to take off the paper, etc. that covers or protects sth 打開（或解開、拆開）…的包裝：*Don't unwrap your present until your birthday.* 生日禮物要等到你生日那天才可打開。 OPP **wrap up**

un·writ·ten /ˌʌnˈrɪtn/ *adj.* **1** ~ **law, rule, agreement, etc.** a law, etc. that everyone knows about and accepts even though it has not been made official 非書面的，不成文的，慣常的（法律、規定、協議等）：*an unwritten understanding that nobody leaves before five o'clock* 五點鐘之前誰都不離開的默契 **2** (of a book, etc. 書等) not yet written 未寫的；未寫完的：*The photographs were to be included in his as yet unwritten autobiography.* 這些照片準備要收入他那尚未寫的自傳之中。

U

un·yield·ing /ʌnˈjiːldɪŋ/ *adj.* (*formal*) **1** if a person is **unyielding**, they are not easily influenced and they are unlikely to change their mind 堅定的；頑強不屈的；固執的 SYN **inflexible** **2** an **unyielding** substance or object does not bend or break when pressure is put on it 不彎曲的；堅固的

unzip /ˌʌnˈzɪp/ *verb* (**-pp-**) **1** [T, I] ~ (**sth**) if you **unzip** a piece of clothing, a bag, etc., or if it **unzips**, you open it by undoing the ZIP that fastens it 拉開…的拉鎖；…的拉鎖被拉開 OPP **zip up** **2** [T] ~ **sth** (*computing* 計) to return a file to its original size after it has been COMPRESSED (= made smaller)（文件）解壓縮 SYN **decompress** OPP **zip**

up 0~ /ʌp/ *adv., prep., adj., verb, noun*

■ **adv.** HELP For the special uses of **up** in phrasal verbs, look at the entries for the verbs. For example **break up** is in the phrasal verb section at **break**. * up 在短語動詞中的特殊用法見有關動詞詞條。如 break up 在詞條 break 的短語動詞部份。 **1** 0~ towards or in a higher position 向（或在）較高位置；向上；在上面：*He jumped up from his chair.* 他從椅子上跳起來。◇ *The sun was already up* (= had risen) *when they set off.* 他們出發時太陽已經升起了。◇ *They live up in the mountains.* 他們住在山區。◇ *It didn't take long to put the tent up.* 沒用多長時間就搭完帳篷了。◇ *I pinned the notice up on the wall.* 我把通知釘在牆上了。◇ *Lay the cards face up* (= facing upwards) *on the table.* 把紙牌正面朝上擺在桌子上。◇ *You look nice with your hair up* (= arranged on top of or at the back of your head). 你把頭髮向上梳很好看。◇ ***Up you come!*** (= said when lifting a child) 舉高高嘍！ **2** 0~ to or at a higher level 向（或在）較高水平；加大；增高：*She turned the volume up.* 她把音量調大了。◇ *Prices are still going up* (= rising). 物價還在上漲。◇ *United were 3–1 up at half-time.* 半場結束時，聯隊以 3:1 領先。◇ *The wind is getting up* (= blowing more strongly). 風漸漸大起來了。◇ *Sales are **well up on** last year.* 銷量比去年大幅增加。 ➲ LANGUAGE BANK at INCREASE **3** 0~ to the place where sb/sth is 朝（某人或某物）的方向；向…的地方：*A car drove up and he got in.* 一輛汽車開過來，他就上了車。◇ *She went straight up to the door and knocked loudly.* 她逕直走到門前大聲敲門。 **4** to or at an important place, especially a large city 到，朝，在（重要地方，尤指大城市）：*We're going up to New York for the day.* 我們要上紐約一天。◇ (*BrE, formal*) *His son's up at Oxford* (= Oxford University). 他兒子在上牛津大學。 **5** 0~ to a place in the north of a country 向（國家北部的地方）；向（北方）：*They've moved **up north**.* 他們已搬到北部去了。◇ *We drove up to Inverness to see my father.* 我們開車北上因弗內斯去看我父親。 **6** 0~ into pieces or parts 成碎片；分開：*She tore the paper up.* 她把紙撕得粉碎。◇ *They've had the road up* (= with the surface broken or removed) *to lay some pipes.* 他們挖開了路面以便敷設管線。◇ *How shall we divide up the work?* 我們怎麼分工呢？ **7** 0~ completely 完全；徹底地：*We ate all the food up.* 我們把食物吃光了。◇ *The stream has dried up.* 小溪已經乾涸了。 **8** so as to be formed or brought together（以便）形成，聚攏：*The government agreed to set up a committee of inquiry.* 政府同意成立一個調查委員會。◇ *She gathered up her belongings.* 她收拾起她的私人物品。 **9** 0~ so as to be finished or closed（以便）完結，關閉：*I have some paperwork to finish up.* 我有些文案工作要做完。◇ *Do your coat up; it's cold.* 把上衣扣上，天涼了。 **10** 0~ (of a period of time 一段時間) finished; over 已結束；已過去：*Time's up. Stop writing and hand in your papers.* 時間到了。不要再寫了，把試卷交上來。 **11** 0~ out of bed 未上牀；起牀：*I stayed up late* (= did not go to bed until late) *last night.* 我昨晚熬夜了。◇ (*BrE*) *He's **up and about** again after his illness.* 他病癒後又能起來活動了。 **12** 0~ (*informal*) used to say that sth is happening, especially sth unusual or unpleasant（尤指異常或不愉快的事情）發生，出現：*I could tell **something was up** by the looks on their faces.* 從他們的臉色我就看出發生什麼事了。◇ ***What's up?*** (= What is the matter?) 怎麼回事？◇ ***What's up with** him? He looks furious.* 他怎麼了？他看上去怒氣沖沖。◇ *Is anything up? You can tell me.* 出什麼事了嗎？跟我說吧。 HELP In *NAmE* **What's up?** can just mean 'What's new?' or 'What's happening?'. There may not be anything wrong. 在美式英語中，what's up 可以是 what's new 或 what's happening 的意思，可能沒有什麼不對頭的事。

IDM **be up to sb** 0~ to be sb's duty or responsibility; to be for sb to decide 是…的職責（或責任）；由…決定：*It's not up to you to tell me how to do my job.* 還輪不到你來告訴我怎麼做我的事。◇ *Shall we eat out or stay in? It's up to you.* 咱們是到外面吃飯還是待在家裏？你決定吧。 **not be ˈup to much** (*BrE*) to be of poor quality; to not be very good 質量差；不很好：*His work isn't up to much.* 他的活兒做得不怎麼樣。 **up against sth** (*informal*) facing problems or opposition 遇到問題；遭到反對：*Teachers are up against some major problems these days.* 老師們最近面臨着一些重大問題。◇ *She's really **up against it*** (= in a difficult situation). 她確實陷入了困境。 **ˌup and ˈdown** **1** 0~ moving upwards and downwards 起伏；上下波動：*The boat bobbed up and down on the water.* 小船在水面顛簸。 **2** 0~ in one direction and then in the opposite direction 來回；往復：*She was pacing up and down in front of her desk.* 她在辦公桌前踱來踱去。 **3** sometimes good and sometimes bad 時好時壞：*My relationship with him was up and down.* 我跟他的關係忽冷忽熱。 **4** (*NAmE, informal*) if you swear **up and down** that sth is true, you say that it is definitely true 絕對地；肯定地；完全地 **,up and 'running** (of a system, for example a computer system 系統，如計算機系統) working; being used 在運轉；在使用中： *By that time the new system should be up and running.* 到那時這個新系統應該會運轉起來了。 **up before sb/sth** appearing in front of sb in authority for a judgement to be made about sth that you have done 到…面前接受裁決；出庭受審： *He came up before the local magistrate for speeding.* 他因超速駕駛到當地法庭受審。 **up for sth 1** on offer for sth 提供作…： *The house is up for sale.* 這所房子正待出售。 **2** being considered for sth, especially as a candidate 正被考慮，被提名（作候選人等）： *Two candidates are up for election.* 有兩位候選人被提名參選。 **3** (*informal*) willing to take part in a particular activity 願意參與（某活動）： *We're going clubbing tonight. Are you **up for it**?* 我們今晚去夜總會，你願意來嗎？ **'up there** (*informal*) among or almost the best, worst, most important, etc.（是或差不多是最好、最差、最重要等）之列，之一： *It may not have been the worst week of my life but it's up there.* 這可能不是我一生中最糟糕的一週，但也差不遠了。◇ *OK, it's not my absolute dream, but it's up there.* 是的，那不是我的終極夢想，不過也差不遠了。 **up to sth 1** 🔑 as far as a particular number, level, etc. 到達（某數量、程度等）；至多有： *I can take up to four people* (= but no more than four) *in my car.* 我的汽車最多能帶四個人。◇ *The temperature went up to 35°C.* 氣温上升到了 35 攝氏度。 **2** 🔑 (also **up until sth**) not further or later than sth; until sth 直到；不多於；不遲於： *Read up to page 100.* 讀到第 100 頁。◇ *Up to now he's been very quiet.* 到目前為止，他一直很安靜。 **3** as high or as good as sth 與…一樣高（或好）： *Her latest book isn't up to her usual standard.* 她的新作沒有達到她平常的水準。 **4** (also **up to doing sth**) physically or mentally capable of sth （體力或智力上）能勝任： *He's not up to the job.* 他無法勝任這項工作。◇ *I don't feel up to going to work today.* 我覺得不舒服，今天不能去上班。 **5** (*informal*) doing sth, especially sth bad 正在幹，從事着（尤指壞事）；在搗鬼： *What's she up to?* 她在搞什麼鬼？◇ *What've you been up to?* 你一直在搞什麼名堂？◇ *I'm sure he's **up to no good*** (= doing sth bad). 我敢說他在打什麼壞主意。

■ ***prep.* 1** 🔑 to or in a higher position somewhere 向，在（較高位置）： *She climbed up the flight of steps.* 她爬上了那層台階。◇ *The village is further up the valley.* 村莊在山谷的更深處。 **2** 🔑 along or further along a road or street 沿着；順着： *We live just up the road, past the post office.* 我們就住在路的前面，剛過郵局的地方。 **3** 🔑 towards the place where a river starts 向…上游；溯流而上： *a cruise up the Rhine* 乘船沿萊茵河溯流而上

IDM **up and down sth** in one direction and then in the opposite direction along sth 沿…來來回回： *I looked up and down the corridor.* 我來回掃視着走廊。 **,up 'yours!** (*taboo, slang*) an offensive way of being rude to sb, for example because they have said sth that makes you angry（憤怒地回應）去你的

■ ***adj.* 1** [only before noun] directed or moving upwards 向上的；往上移動的： *an up stroke* 上提筆畫 ◇ *the up escalator* 上行自動扶梯 **2** [not before noun] (*informal*) cheerful; happy or excited 高興；快樂；激動： *The mood here is resolutely up.* 這裏的氣氛十分熱鬧。 **3** [not before noun] (of a computer system 計算機系統) working 在運行： *Our system should be up by this afternoon.* 到今天下午，我們的電腦系統應該運行起來了。

■ ***verb*** (-pp-) **1** [I] **up and ...** (*informal* or *humorous*) to suddenly move or do sth unexpected 突然移動；突然做（意想不到的事）： *He **upped and left** without telling anyone.* 他突然起身不辭而別。 **2** [T] **~ sth** to increase the price or amount of sth 提高…的價格（或數量） **SYN** **raise**： *The buyers upped their offer by £1 000.* 買方把出價增加了 1 000 英鎊。

IDM **,up 'sticks** (*BrE*) (*NAmE* **,pull up 'stakes**) (*informal*) to suddenly move from your house and go to live somewhere else 突然遷居 ➲ more at ANTE

■ ***noun***

IDM **on the 'up** increasing or improving 在增長；在改善中： *Business confidence is on the up.* 商業信心有增強趨勢。 **on the ,up and 'up** (*informal*) **1** (*BrE*) becoming more and more successful 蒸蒸日上；日益興旺；越來越好： *The club has been on the up and up since the beginning of the season.* 從本季開始，這個俱樂部便日益欣欣向榮。 **2** (*NAmE*) = ON THE LEVEL at LEVEL *n.*： *The offer seems to be on the up and up.* 這一提議似乎是坦誠可信的。 **,ups and 'downs** the mixture of good and bad things in life or in a particular situation or relationship 浮沉；興衰；榮辱

up- /ʌp/ *prefix* (in adjectives, verbs and related nouns 構成形容詞、動詞和相關的名詞) higher; upwards; towards the top of sth 更高；向上；朝頂部： *upland* 高地 ◇ *upturned* 向上翹的 ◇ *upgrade* 升級 ◇ *uphill* 上坡

,up-'anchor *verb* [I] (of a ship or its CREW 輪船或船員) to raise the ANCHOR from the water in order to be ready to sail 起錨（準備開航）

,up-and-'coming *adj.* likely to be successful and popular in the future 有前途的；前程似錦的： *up-and-coming young actors* 前程似錦的年輕演員

up·beat /'ʌpbiːt/ *adj.* (*informal*) positive and enthusiastic; making you feel that the future will be good 樂觀的；快樂的；積極向上的 **SYN** **optimistic**： *The tone of the speech was upbeat.* 這次講話的語氣頗為樂觀。◇ *The meeting ended on an upbeat note.* 會議在樂觀的氣氛中結束。 **OPP** **downbeat**

up·braid /ʌp'breɪd/ *verb* **~ sb (for sth/for doing sth)** (*formal*) to criticize sb or speak angrily to them because you do not approve of sth that they have said or done 申斥；訓斥；責罵 **SYN** **reproach**

up·bring·ing /'ʌpbrɪŋɪŋ/ *noun* [sing., U] the way in which a child is cared for and taught how to behave while it is growing up 撫育；養育；教養；培養： *to have had a sheltered upbringing* 受到呵護的養育 ◇ *He was a Catholic by upbringing.* 他因受家庭薰陶，從小就是個天主教徒。

UPC /juː piː 'siː/ *abbr.* (*NAmE, technical* 術語) Universal Product Code 通用產品代碼；通用商品條碼： *The Universal Product Code symbol, also known as the 'barcode', is printed on products for sale and contains information that a computer can read.* 通用產品代碼符號，亦稱"條形碼"，印在出售的商品上，其中含有計算機能識別的信息。

up·chuck /'ʌptʃʌk/ *verb* [I, T] **~ (sth)** (*NAmE, informal*) to VOMIT 嘔吐

up·com·ing /'ʌpkʌmɪŋ/ *adj.* [only before noun] (*especially NAmE*) going to happen soon 即將發生（或來臨）的： *the upcoming presidential election* 即將舉行的總統選舉 ◇ *a single from the band's upcoming album* 選自該樂隊即將發行的專輯的一首單曲

,up-'country *adj.* [only before noun] connected with an area of a country that is not near large towns 內地的；偏遠的；偏僻的 ► **,up-'country** *adv.*

up·date *verb, noun*

■ ***verb*** /,ʌp'deɪt/ **1 ~ sth** to make sth more modern by adding new parts, etc. 使現代化；更新： *It's about time we updated our software.* 我們的軟件應該更新了。 **2** to give sb the most recent information about sth; to add the most recent information to sth 向…提供最新信息；給…增加最新信息 **SYN** **bring up to date**： **~ sb (on sth)** *I called the office to update them on the day's developments.* 我給辦公室打電話告訴他們當天最新的發展。◇ **~ sth** *Our records are regularly updated.* 我們的記錄定期更新。

■ ***noun*** /'ʌpdeɪt/ **1 ~ (on sth)** a report or broadcast that gives the most recent information about sth; a new version of sth containing the most recent information 最新報道；最新消息；最新進展： *a news update* 最新新聞報道 **2** (*computing* 計) the most recent improvements to a computer program that are sent to users of the program（計算機程序的）更新，最新校正數據

upend /ʌp'end/ *verb* **~ sb/sth** to turn sb/sth upside down 翻倒；倒放；使顛倒： *The bicycle lay upended in a ditch.* 自行車翻倒在一條小水溝裏。

up·field /,ʌp'fiːld/ *adv.* (*sport* 體) towards your opponent's end of the playing field 向前場；朝前場

up·front /ˌʌpˈfrʌnt/ *adj.* **1 ~ (about sth)** not trying to hide what you think or do 坦率的；誠實的；直爽的 SYN **honest, frank**：*He's been upfront about his intentions since the beginning.* 他從一開始就坦白說出了他的意圖。 **2** [only before noun] paid in advance, before other payments are made 預付的；預交的：*There will be an upfront fee of 4%.* 將收取 4% 的預付費。 ➲ see also UP FRONT at FRONT

up·grad·ation /ˌʌpgreɪˈdeɪʃn; ˌʌpgrəˈd-/ *noun* [U] (*IndE*) the fact of UPGRADING sth 升級；改善；提高：*the upgradation of civic facilities in large cities* 大城市市政設施的改進

up·grade /ˌʌpˈgreɪd/ *verb* [often passive] **1 ~ sth** to make a piece of machinery, computer system, etc. more powerful and efficient 使（機器、計算機系統等）升級；提高；改進 **2 ~ sb (to sth)** to give sb a more important job 提升；提拔 SYN **promote** **3 ~ sb (to sth)** to give sb a better seat on a plane, room in a hotel, etc. than the one that they have paid for 提高（飛機乘客、旅館住客等的）待遇；優待 **4 ~ sth** to improve the condition of a building, etc. in order to provide a better service 提高（設施、服務等的）檔次；改善；使升格：*to upgrade the town's leisure facilities* 改善鎮裏的休閒設施 ➲ compare DOWNGRADE (1) ▸ **up·grade** /ˈʌpgreɪd/ *noun*

up·heav·al /ʌpˈhiːvl/ *noun* [C, U] a big change that causes a lot of confusion, worry and problems 劇變；激變；動亂；動盪 SYN **disruption**：*the latest upheavals in the education system* 最近教育制度上的種種變更 ◇ *I can't face the upheaval of moving house again.* 我無法忍受再次搬家的折騰。◇ *a period of emotional upheaval* 情緒波動很大的時期

up·hill /ˌʌpˈhɪl/ *adj., adv.*

■ *adj.* **1** sloping upwards 上坡的：*an* **uphill** *climb/slope* 向上的攀爬；上坡 ◇ *The last part of the race is all uphill.* 賽跑的最後一段全是上坡路。 OPP **downhill** **2 ~ battle, struggle, task, etc.** an argument or a struggle that is difficult to win and takes a lot of effort over a long period of time 漫長而艱難的，費力的（戰鬥、鬥爭、任務等）

■ *adv.* towards the top of a hill or slope 向山上；朝上坡方向：*We cycled uphill for over an hour.* 我們騎自行車爬了一個多小時的坡。◇ *The path slopes steeply uphill.* 小徑直上陡峭的山坡。 OPP **downhill**

up·hold /ʌpˈhəʊld; *NAmE* -ˈhoʊld/ *verb* (**up·held, up·held** /-ˈheld/) **1 ~ sth** to support sth that you think is right and make sure that it continues to exist 支持，維護（正義等）：*We have a duty to uphold the law.* 維護法律是我們的責任。 **2 ~ sth** (especially of a court of law 尤指法庭) to agree that a previous decision was correct or that a request is reasonable 維持（原判）；受理（申訴）：*to* **uphold** *a conviction/an appeal/a complaint* 維持原判；受理上訴 / 申訴 ▸ **up·hold·er** *noun*：*an upholder of traditional values* 支持傳統價值觀的人

up·hol·ster /ʌpˈhəʊlstə(r); *NAmE* -ˈhoʊl-/ *verb* [usually passive] **~ sth (in sth)** to cover a chair, etc. with soft material (= PADDING) and cloth 為（椅子等）裝軟墊（或套子等）

up·hol·ster·er /ʌpˈhəʊlstərə(r); *NAmE* -ˈhoʊl-/ *noun* a person whose job is to upholster furniture 傢具裝飾商

up·hol·stery /ʌpˈhəʊlstəri; *NAmE* -ˈhoʊl-/ *noun* [U] **1** soft covering on furniture such as ARMCHAIRS and SOFAS 傢具裝飾品（或襯墊等） **2** the process or trade of UPHOLSTERING 傢具裝飾；傢具裝飾業

UPI /juː piː ˈaɪ/ *abbr.* UNITED PRESS INTERNATIONAL

up·keep /ˈʌpkiːp/ *noun* [U] **1 ~ (of sth)** the cost or process of keeping sth in good condition 保養（費）；維修（費） SYN **maintenance**：*Tenants are responsible for the upkeep of rented property.* 承租人應負責維修租用的房產。 **2 ~ (of sb/sth)** the cost or process of giving a child or an animal the things that they need 撫養（費）；餵養（成本）：*He makes payments to his ex-wife for the upkeep of their children.* 他向前妻支付子女的撫養費。

U

up·land /ˈʌplənd/ *noun* [usually pl.] an area of high land that is not near the coast（內陸）高地；山地 ▸ **up·land** *adj.* [only before noun]：*upland agriculture* 山區農業

up·lift *noun, verb*

■ *noun* /ˈʌplɪft/ [U, sing.] **1** the fact of sth being raised or of sth increasing 提高；抬高；增長；增加：*an uplift in sales* 銷售的增長 ◇ *an uplift bra* (= that raises the breasts) 挺高式乳罩 **2** a feeling of hope and happiness 振奮；鼓舞：*The news gave them a much needed uplift.* 這消息給他們帶來了及時的鼓舞。 **3** (also **up·thrust**) (*geology* 地) the process or result of land being moved to a higher level by movements inside the earth（地殼的）隆起，上升

■ *verb* /ˌʌpˈlɪft/ **~ sb** (*formal*) to make sb feel happier or give sb more hope 鼓勵；激勵；使振奮

up·lift·ed /ˌʌpˈlɪftɪd/ *adj.* **1** [not before noun] feeling happy and full of hope 興沖沖；意氣昂揚 **2** (*literary*) lifted upwards 抬起的；昂起的；舉起的：*a sea of uplifted faces* 一張張揚起的臉

up·lift·ing /ˌʌpˈlɪftɪŋ/ *adj.* making you feel happier or giving you more hope 令人振奮的；鼓舞人心的；催人奮進的：*an uplifting experience/speech* 令人振奮的經歷 / 演說

up·light·er /ˈʌplaɪtə(r)/ (also **up·light** /ˈʌplaɪt/) *noun* a lamp in a room that is designed to send light upwards 上射燈 ➲ compare DOWNLIGHTER

up·link /ˈʌplɪŋk/ *noun* (*technical* 術語) a communications link to a SATELLITE（衛星通信的）上行鏈路，上行線

up·load *verb, noun*

■ *verb* /ˌʌpˈləʊd; *NAmE* -ˈloʊd/ **~ sth** (*computing* 計) to move data to a larger computer system from a smaller one 上載；上傳 OPP **download** ➲ COLLOCATIONS at EMAIL

■ *noun* /ˈʌpləʊd; *NAmE* -loʊd/ (*computing* 計) data that has been moved to a larger computer system from a smaller one 上載（或上傳）的數據 OPP **download**

up·mar·ket /ˌʌpˈmɑːkɪt; *NAmE* -ˈmɑːrk-/ (*BrE*) (*NAmE* **up·scale**) *adj.* [usually before noun] designed for or used by people who belong to a high social class or have a lot of money 高檔的；高級的：*an upmarket restaurant* 高級餐廳 OPP **downmarket** ▸ **ˌupˈmarket** (*BrE*) (*NAmE* **ˌupˈscale**) *adv.*：*The company has been forced to move more upmarket.* 這家公司被迫進一步轉向高端市場。

upon 0-w /əˈpɒn; *NAmE* əˈpɑːn; əˈpɔːn/ *prep.*

1 0-w (*formal, especially BrE*) = ON：*The decision was based upon two considerations.* 這一決定是基於兩種考慮的。 HELP Although the word **upon** has the same meaning as **on**, it is usually used in more formal contexts or in phrases such as *once upon a time* and *row upon row of seats*. * upon 與 on 同義，但通常用於較正式的場合或 once upon a time 和 row upon row of seats 等短語中。 **2 ... upon ...** used to emphasize that there is a large number or amount of sth（強調數目或數量大）：*mile upon mile of dusty road* 綿延數英里塵土飛揚的道路 ◇ *thousands upon thousands of letters* 成千上萬封信件

IDM **(almost) uˈpon you** if sth in the future is **almost upon you**, it is going to arrive or happen very soon 近在咫尺；即將來臨：*The summer season was almost upon them again.* 轉眼間他們又要過夏天了。 ➲ more at ONCE *adv.*

upper 0-w /ˈʌpə(r)/ *adj., noun*

■ *adj.* [only before noun] **1** 0-w located above sth else, especially sth of the same type or the other of a pair 上邊的，上面的，上層的（尤指同類或一對中的一個）：*the upper lip* 上嘴唇 ◇ *the upper deck* 上層甲板 **2** 0-w at or near the top of sth 上部的；靠上部的：*the upper arm* 上臂 ◇ *the upper slopes of the mountain* 靠近山頂的斜坡 ◇ *a member of the upper middle class* 中上層社會的人 ◇ *salaries at the upper end of the pay scale* 工資級別最高的薪金 ◇ *There is an upper limit of £20 000 spent on any one project.* 任何項目都有一個 2 萬英鎊的經費上限。 **3** (of a place 地方) located away from the coast, on high ground or towards the north of an area 內陸的；高地的；向北部的：*the upper reaches of the river* 河流的上游 OPP **lower**

IDM **gain, get, have, etc. the ˌupper ˈhand** to get an advantage over sb so that you are in control of a particular situation 佔上風；處於有利地位；有優勢；有控制權 ➲ more at STIFF *adj.*

■ ***noun*** [usually pl.] **1** the top part of a shoe that is attached to the SOLE 鞋幫；靴面：*shoes with leather uppers* 皮鞋 ➲ VISUAL VOCAB page V64 **2** (*informal*) a drug that makes you feel excited and full of energy 興奮劑 ➲ compare DOWNER (1)

IDM **on your 'uppers** (*BrE, informal*) having very little money 手頭拮据；困窘

ˌupper 'case *noun* [U] capital letters (= the large form of letters, for example A, B, C rather than a, b, c) 大寫字母：*Headings should be in upper case.* 標題應該大寫。➲ compare LOWER CASE ► **ˌupper 'case** *adj.*：*upper-case letters* 大寫字母

ˌupper 'chamber *noun* = UPPER HOUSE

the ˌupper 'class *noun* [sing.] (also **the ˌupper 'classes** [pl.]) the groups of people that are considered to have the highest social status and that have more money and/or power than other people in society 上流社會；上等階層：*a member of the upper class/upper classes* 上流社會人士 ► **ˌupper 'class** *adj.*：*Her family is very upper class.* 她家世顯赫。◇ *an upper-class accent* 上流社會的腔調 ➲ compare LOWER CLASS, MIDDLE CLASS, WORKING CLASS

upper·class·man /ˌʌpəˈklɑːsmən; *NAmE* ˌʌpərˈklæs-/, **upper·class·woman** /ˌʌpəˈklɑːswʊmən; *NAmE* ˌʌpərˈklæs-/ *noun* (*pl.* **-men** /-mən/, **-women** /-wɪmɪn/) (in the US) a student in the last two years of HIGH SCHOOL or college 高年級學生（美國中學或大學的最後兩個年級的學生）➲ compare UNDERCLASSMAN

the ˌupper 'crust *noun* [sing.+sing./pl. v.] (*informal*) the people who belong to the highest social class 上流社會的人；上層人士；達官顯貴 SYN **aristocracy** ► **ˌupper-'crust** *adj.*

upper·cut /ˈʌpəkʌt; *NAmE* ˈʌpərkʌt/ *noun* (in boxing 拳擊運動) a way of hitting sb on the chin, in which you bend your arm and move your hand upwards 上鈎拳

ˌupper 'house (also **ˌupper 'chamber**) (also **ˌsecond 'chamber** especially in *BrE*) *noun* [sing.] one of the parts of a parliament in countries which have a parliament that is divided into two parts. In Britain it is the House of Lords and in the US it is the Senate. 上議院；（英國）貴族院；（美國）參議院 ➲ compare LOWER HOUSE

upper·most /ˈʌpəməʊst; *NAmE* ˈʌpərmoʊst/ *adj., adv.*

■ ***adj.*** **1** [usually before noun] (*formal*) higher or nearer the top than other things 最高的；最上端的；最上面的：*the uppermost branches of the tree* 樹頂端的枝椏 **2** [not usually before noun] more important than other things in a particular situation 最重要；最關鍵：*These thoughts were **uppermost in my mind**.* 我心裏想得最多的就是這些事。

■ ***adv.*** (*formal*) in the highest position; facing upwards 處於最高位置；面向上地：*Place the material on a flat surface, shiny side uppermost.* 把材料放在平面上，有光的一面朝上。

'upper school *noun* (*BrE*) a school, or the classes in a school, for older students, usually between the ages of 14 and 18 高中，高中班（通常為 14 至 18 歲的學生而設）➲ compare LOWER SCHOOL, MIDDLE SCHOOL

up·pity /ˈʌpəti/ *adj.* (*old-fashioned, informal*) behaving as if you are more important than you really are, especially when this means that you refuse to obey orders 傲慢的；自視甚高（而不服從）的

up·raised /ˌʌpˈreɪzd/ *adj.* lifted upwards 舉起的；揚起的：*She strode towards them, her fist upraised.* 她舉着拳頭，大步邁向他們。

up·right /ˈʌpraɪt/ *adj., adv., noun*

■ ***adj.*** **1** (of a person 人) not lying down, and with the back straight rather than bent 直立的；挺直的：*an upright posture* 直立的姿勢 ◇ *Gradually raise your body into an upright position.* 慢慢起身，成直立狀態。**2** placed in a vertical position 豎直的；直立的；垂直的：*Keep the bottle upright.* 保持瓶子直立。◇ *an upright freezer* (= one that is taller than it is wide) 立式冰櫃 ◇ *an upright piano* (= one with vertical strings) 一台立式鋼琴 **3** (of a person 人) behaving in a moral and honest way 正直的；誠實的；規矩的 SYN **upstanding**：*an upright citizen* 正直的公民 IDM see BOLT *adv.*

■ ***adv.*** in or into a vertical position 豎立着；垂直着：*She sat upright in bed.* 她挺直地坐在牀上。◇ *He managed to pull himself upright.* 他設法挺直了身子。

■ ***noun*** **1** a long piece of wood, metal or plastic that is placed in a vertical position, especially in order to support sth （支撐用的）直柱，立柱，立放構件 **2** = UPRIGHT PIANO

up·right·ness /ˈʌpraɪtnəs/ *noun* [U] behaviour or attitudes that are very moral and honest 正直的行為（或態度）；誠實；公正

ˌupright pi'ano (also **up·right**) *noun* a piano in which the strings are vertical 立式鋼琴 ➲ VISUAL VOCAB page V36 ➲ compare GRAND PIANO, SPINET (1)

up·ris·ing /ˈʌpraɪzɪŋ/ *noun* ~ (**against sth**) a situation in which a group of people join together in order to fight against the people who are in power 起義；暴動；造反 SYN **rebellion, revolt**：*an armed uprising against the government* 反政府的武裝起義 ◇ *a **popular uprising*** (= by the ordinary people of the country) 平民暴動 ◇ *to **crush/suppress an uprising*** 粉碎 / 鎮壓暴動

up·river /ˌʌpˈrɪvə(r)/ *adv.* = UPSTREAM

up·roar /ˈʌprɔː(r)/ *noun* [U, sing.] **1** a situation in which people shout and make a lot of noise because they are angry or upset about sth 吵鬧；喧囂；叫喊：*The room was **in** (**an**) **uproar**.* 屋子裏一片嘈雜。◇ *Her comments provoked (an) uproar from the audience.* 她的評論激起了聽眾的鼓噪。 **2** a situation in which there is a lot of public criticism and angry argument about sth that sb has said or done 騷動；怨憤 SYN **outcry**：*The article caused (an) uproar.* 這篇文章引起了軒然大波。

up·roari·ous /ʌpˈrɔːriəs/ *adj.* [usually before noun] **1** in which there is a lot of noise and people laugh or shout a lot 喧鬧的；熱烈的；吵吵嚷嚷的：*an uproarious party* 熱鬧的聚會 **2** extremely funny 滑稽的；極可笑的；令人捧腹的：*an uproarious story* 令人捧腹的故事 ► **up·roari·ous·ly** *adv.*：*The audience laughed uproariously.* 觀眾哄然大笑。◇ *uproariously funny* 滑稽得令人捧腹

up·root /ˌʌpˈruːt/ *verb* **1** [T] **~ sth** to pull a tree, plant, etc. out of the ground 將…連根拔起 **2** [I, T] to leave a place where you have lived for a long time; to make sb do this （使）離開家園（或熟悉的地方等）：*We decided to uproot and head for Scotland.* 我們決定遷往蘇格蘭。◇ **~ yourself/sb** *If I accept the job, it will mean uprooting my family and moving to Italy.* 如果我接受了這份工作，那將意味着我得舉家搬遷到意大利去。

up·rush /ˈʌprʌʃ/ *noun* [sing.] **~ of sth** (*formal*) a sudden feeling of sth such as joy or fear （快樂或懼怕等感覺的）突發，突湧：*an uprush of joy* 湧上心頭的一陣喜悅

ups-a-daisy /ˈʊpsə deɪzi; ˈʌpsə/ *exclamation* = UPSY-DAISY

up·scale /ˌʌpˈskeɪl/ (*NAmE*) (*BrE* **up·mar·ket**) *adj.* [usually before noun] designed for or used by people who belong to a high social class or have a lot of money 高檔的；高級的 OPP **downscale** ► **ˌup'scale** (*NAmE*) (*BrE* **ˌup-'market**) *adv.*

up·sell /ˈʌpsel/ *verb* (**upsold, upsold** /ˈʌpsəʊld; *NAmE* -soʊld/) [I] (*business* 商) to persuade a customer to buy more products or a more expensive product than they originally intended 向上端推銷（指勸說顧客購買更多或更貴的產品）：*You can usually upsell to about half the customers.* 通常可以說服大約一半的顧客掏更多的錢買東西。► **up·sell·ing** /ˈʌpselɪŋ/ *noun* [U]：(*business* 商) *You can make great profits from upselling.* 可以通過向上端推銷賺取很高的收益。

upset 0- *verb, adj., noun*

■ ***verb*** /ʌpˈset/ (**up·set·ting, upset, upset**) **1** 0- to make sb/yourself feel unhappy, anxious or annoyed 使煩惱；使心煩意亂；使生氣 SYN **distress**：**~ sb/yourself** *This decision is likely to upset a lot of people.* 這項決定很可能會使許多人悻然不快。◇ *Don't upset yourself about it—let's just forget it ever happened.* 你別為這事煩惱了，咱們就只當它沒發生過。◇ **it upsets sb that …** *It upset him* that nobody had bothered to tell him about it. 讓他不高興的是，誰也沒把這件事告訴他。◇ **it upsets sb to do sth** *It upsets me to think of her all alone in that big house.* 想到她孤身一人守着那所大房子，我就感到不舒服。 **2 ~ sth** to make a plan, situation, etc. go wrong 打亂；攪亂：*He arrived an hour late and upset all our arrangements.* 他遲到了一個小時，把我們的一切安排都打亂了。 **3 ~ sb's stomach** to make sb feel sick after they have eaten or drunk sth 使（腸胃）不適 **4 ~ sth** to make sth fall over by hitting it by accident 打翻；碰倒；使傾覆：*She stood up suddenly, upsetting a glass of wine.* 她驀然起身，碰倒了一杯酒。

IDM **upset the 'apple cart** to cause problems for sb or spoil their plans, arrangements, etc. 製造麻煩；打亂計劃（或安排等）

■ ***adj.*** /ˌʌp'set/ **1** [not before noun] **~ (about sth)** | **~ (that …)** unhappy or disappointed because of sth unpleasant that has happened 難過；不高興；失望；沮喪：*There's no point getting upset about it.* 犯不着為此事難過。 **2** **an ˌupset 'stomach** an illness in the stomach that makes you feel sick or have DIARRHOEA 腸胃不適；腹瀉

■ ***noun*** /'ʌpset/ **1** [U] a situation in which there are problems or difficulties, especially when these are unexpected（意外的）混亂，困擾，麻煩：*The company has survived the recent upset in share prices.* 這家公司撐過了最近股價的動盪。◇ *His health has not been improved by all the upset at home.* 家中的紛亂使他的健康毫無起色。 **2** [C] (in a competition 競賽) a situation in which a person or team beats the person or team that was expected to win 意外的結果；爆冷門 **3** [C] an illness in the stomach that makes you feel sick or have DIARRHOEA 腸胃病；腹瀉：*a stomach upset* 拉肚子 **4** [U, C] feelings of unhappiness and disappointment caused by sth unpleasant that has happened 不痛快；煩悶；失望；苦惱：*It had been the cause of much emotional upset.* 那便是使人情緒一落千丈的原因。

up·set·ting /ʌp'setɪŋ/ *adj.* making you feel unhappy, anxious or annoyed 令人不快（或憂慮、苦惱）的：*an upsetting experience* 令人苦惱的經歷

up·shift /'ʌpʃɪft/ *verb* [I] (*NAmE*) to change into a higher gear in a vehicle 換高擋（開車等加速）

the up·shot /'ʌpʃɒt; *NAmE* -ʃɑːt/ *noun* [sing.] the final result of a series of events 最後結果；結局 **SYN** **outcome**：*The upshot of it all was that he left college and got a job.* 事情的結局是，他離開學院並投身工作了。

up·side /'ʌpsaɪd/ *noun* [sing.] the more positive aspect of a situation that is generally bad（糟糕局面的）好的一面，光明的一面，正面 **OPP** **downside**

ˌupside 'down *adv.* in or into a position in which the top of sth is where the bottom is normally found and the bottom is where the top is normally found 顛倒；倒轉；翻轉：*The canoe floated upside down on the lake.* 獨木舟底朝天漂浮在湖面上。 **OPP** **right side up** ▸ **ˌupside 'down** *adj.* [not usually before noun]：*The painting looks like it's upside down to me.* 在我看來這幅畫好像是上下顛倒了。

IDM **turn sth ˌupside 'down** **1** to make a place untidy when looking for sth 把…翻得亂七八糟；使凌亂不堪：*The police turned the whole house upside down looking for clues.* 警察為查找線索把整所房子翻得亂七八糟。 **2** to cause large changes and confusion in a person's life 給（某人生活）造成大的變化（或混亂）：*His sudden death turned her world upside down.* 他的遽然離世使她的生活完全亂套了。

up·si·lon /ʌp'saɪlən; 'ʊpsɪlɒn; *NAmE* 'ʊpsɪlɑːn/ *noun* the 20th letter of the Greek alphabet (Υ, υ) 希臘字母表的第 20 個字母

up·skill /'ʌpskɪl/ *verb* [T, I] **~ (sb)** (*business* 商) to teach sb new skills; to learn new skills（使）提高技能；（使）學習新技能：*The company has invested heavily in upskilling its workforce.* 公司在提高勞動員工的技能方面投資很大。▸ **up·skill·ing** /'ʌpskɪlɪŋ/ *noun* [U]

up·stage /ˌʌp'steɪdʒ/ *adv., adj., verb*
■ ***adv., adj.*** at or towards the back of the stage in a theatre 在（或向）舞台後部（的） **OPP** **downstage**
■ ***verb* ~ sb** to say or do sth that makes people notice you more than the person that they should be interested in 搶…的鏡頭；把對…的注意吸引過來：*She was furious at being upstaged by her younger sister.* 她被妹妹搶去風頭，感到氣憤不已。

up·stairs /ˌʌp'steəz; *NAmE* -'sterz/ *adv., noun*
■ ***adv.*** up the stairs; on or to a floor of a house or other building higher than the one that you are on 在（或向）樓上；在（或向）上一層：*The cat belongs to the people who live upstairs.* 這貓是樓上人家的。◇ *I carried her bags upstairs.* 我把她的包拿到樓上。◇ *She went upstairs to get dressed.* 她上樓換衣服去了。 **OPP** **downstairs** ▸ **up·stairs** *adj.* [only before noun]：*an upstairs room* 樓上的房間 **IDM** see KICK *v.*
■ ***noun*** [sing.] the floor or floors in a building that are above the ground floor 二樓；二樓以上各層；樓上：*We've converted the upstairs into an office.* 我們把樓上改成了辦公室。 **OPP** **downstairs**

up·stand·ing /ˌʌp'stændɪŋ/ *adj.* [usually before noun] (*formal*) behaving in a moral and honest way 正直的；正派的；誠實的 **SYN** **upright**：*an upstanding member of the community* 群體中正直的一分子

IDM **be up'standing** (*BrE, formal*) used in a formal situation to tell people to stand up（用於正式場合）請起立：*Ladies and gentlemen, please be upstanding and join me in a toast to the bride and groom.* 各位來賓，請大家起立，我們一起為新娘新郎乾一杯。

up·start /'ʌpstɑːt; *NAmE* -stɑːrt/ *noun* (*disapproving*) a person who has just started in a new position or job but who behaves as if they are more important than other people, in a way that is annoying 自命不凡的新上任者；狂妄自大的新手

up·state /ˌʌp'steɪt/ *adv.* (*US*) in or to a part of a state that is far from its main cities, especially a northern part 在（或向）州的鄉野地區（尤指北部）：*They retired and went to live upstate.* 他們退休後移居到州的鄉野地區去了。 ▸ **up·state** *adj.* [only before noun]：*upstate New York* 紐約的北部

up·stream /ˌʌp'striːm/ (also *less frequent* **up·river**) *adv.* **~ (of/from sth)** along a river, in the opposite direction to the way in which the water flows 向（或在）上游；逆流：*The nearest town is about ten miles upstream.* 最近的城鎮大約在沿河向上十英里處。◇ *upstream of/from the bridge* 在橋的上游 **OPP** **downstream**

up·surge /'ʌpsɜːdʒ; *NAmE* -sɜːrdʒ/ *noun* [usually sing.] (*formal*) a sudden large increase in sth 急劇上升；飆升；猛增：**~ (in sth)** *an upsurge in violent crime* 暴力犯罪的猛增 ◇ **~ (of sth)** *a recent upsurge of interest in his movies* 最近他的電影掀起的一陣熱潮

up·swell /'ʌpswel/ (also **up·swell·ing** /'ʌpswelɪŋ/) *noun* [sing.] **~ of sth** (*formal*) an increase in sth, especially a feeling（尤指感覺的）增加，上漲，上湧：*a huge upswell of emotion* 膨脹的激情

up·swept /'ʌpswept/ (also **'swept-up**) *adj.* curved or sloping upwards 向上彎曲的；向上傾斜的：*an upswept moustache* 翹鬍子

up·swing /'ʌpswɪŋ/ *noun* [usually sing.] **~ (in sth)** a situation in which sth improves or increases over a period of time 改進；改善；上升；進步 **SYN** **upturn**：*an upswing in economic activity* 經濟活動的增加 ◇ *an upswing in the team's fortunes* 這支隊伍鴻運高照

upsy-daisy /'ʊpsi deɪzi; 'ʌpsi/ (also **ups-a-daisy**, **oops-a-daisy**) *exclamation* said when you have made a mistake, dropped sth, fallen down, etc. or when sb else has（自己或他人出錯、掉東西、摔倒等時說）天哪，哎呀

up·take /'ʌpteɪk/ *noun* [U, sing.] **1 ~ (of sth)** the use that is made of sth that has become available（對現有東西的）使用，利用，應用：*There has been a high uptake of the free training.* 免費培訓有很多人參加。 **2 ~ (of sth)** (*technical* 術語) the process by which sth is taken into a body or system; the rate at which this happens 吸收；吸收速度：*the uptake of oxygen by muscles* 肌肉對氧氣的吸收

IDM **be ˌquick/ˌslow on the ˈuptake** (*informal*) to be quick/slow to understand sth 領悟得快／慢：*Is he always this slow on the uptake?* 他總是理解得這麼慢嗎？

up·tempo /ˈʌptempəʊ; *NAmE* -poʊ/ *adj.* (especially of music 尤指音樂) fast 快節奏的；節奏漸快的：*uptempo dance tunes* 快節奏舞曲

up·thrust /ˈʌpθrʌst/ *noun* [U] **1** (*physics* 物) the force with which a liquid or gas pushes up against an object that is floating in it（液體或氣體對漂浮物的）上推 **2** (*geology* 地) = UPLIFT (3)

up·tick /ˈʌptɪk/ *noun* (*economics* 經) (*NAmE*) a small increase in the level or value of sth（程度或價值的）小幅上升：*The futures market is showing an uptick.* 期貨市場正小幅上揚。 OPP **downtick**

up·tight /ˌʌpˈtaɪt/ *adj.* **~ (about sth)** (*informal*) **1** anxious and/or angry about sth 緊張不安的；憤怒的：*Relax! You're getting too uptight about it.* 輕鬆點兒！你對這事太緊張了。 **2** (*especially NAmE*) nervous about showing your feelings 局促的；拘謹的；緊張的：*an uptight teenager* 腼腆的少年

up·time /ˈʌptaɪm/ *noun* [U] the time during which a machine, especially a computer, is working（計算機等的）運行時間 OPP **downtime**

ˌup to ˈdate *adj.* **1** modern; fashionable 現代的；最新的；時髦的；新式的：*This technology is bang up to date* (= completely modern). 這項技術是最新式的。◇ *up-to-date clothes* 時髦服裝 ◇ *up-to-date equipment* 最新的設備 **2** having or including the most recent information 擁有（或包含）最新信息的：*We are keeping up to date with the latest developments.* 我們保持掌握最新的發展情況。◇ *up-to-date records* 最新的記錄 ◇ *She* ***brought him up to date*** *with what had happened.* 她讓他知道最新的情況。 ➲ see also OUT OF DATE (1)

ˌup-to-the-ˈminute *adj.* [usually before noun] **1** having or including the most recent information 最新的；時新的；即時的：*up-to-the-minute news* 最新消息 **2** modern; fashionable 現代化的；時髦的；流行的：*up-to-the-minute designs* 最時髦的設計 ➲ see also UP TO THE MINUTE at MINUTE *n.*

up·town /ˌʌpˈtaʊn/ *adv.*, *adj.* (*NAmE*)

▪ ***adv.*** in or to the parts of a town or city that are away from the centre, where people live 離開市中心；在（或向）市郊：*They live in an apartment uptown.* 他們住在市郊的一套公寓。◇ *We walked uptown a couple of blocks until we found a cab.* 我們向市郊走了好幾條街才找到一輛出租車。 ➲ compare DOWNTOWN, MIDTOWN

▪ ***adj.*** **1** [only before noun] in, to or typical of the parts of a town or city that are away from the centre, where people live 在（或向）市郊住宅區的；市郊住宅區的：*an uptown train* 開往市郊住宅區的火車 **2** typical of an area of a town or city where people have a lot of money 富人區的：*uptown prices* 富人區的價格 ◇ *an uptown girl* 富人區的姑娘

up·trend /ˈʌptrend/ *noun* [sing.] (*NAmE*) a situation in which business activity or performance increases or improves over a period of time（商業活動的）上升趨勢，改善，增強，活躍 OPP **downtrend**

up·turn /ˈʌptɜːn; *NAmE* -tɜːrn/ *noun* [usually sing.] **~ (in sth)** a situation in which sth improves or increases over a period of time 回升；好轉；改善；提高 SYN **upswing**：*an upturn in the economy* 經濟的好轉 ◇ *The restaurant trade is on the upturn.* 餐廳業正在復蘇。 OPP **downturn**

up·turned /ˌʌpˈtɜːnd; *NAmE* ˌʌpˈtɜːrnd/ *adj.* [usually before noun] **1** pointing or facing upwards 向上翹的；面朝上的：*an upturned nose* (= that curves upwards at the end) 翹鼻子 ◇ *She looked down at the sea of upturned faces.* 她俯視着一大片仰起的臉孔。 **2** turned upside down 顛倒的；翻轉的；倒着的：*She sat on an upturned box.* 她坐在一個倒放的箱子上。

uPVC /ˌjuː ˌpiː ˌviː ˈsiː/ *noun* [U] the abbreviation for 'unplasticized polyvinyl chloride' (a strong plastic used to make window frames and pipes) 未增塑聚氯乙烯，未塑化聚氯乙烯（全寫為 unplasticized polyvinyl chloride，用以製作窗框和管子的堅固塑料）

up·ward 0┳ /ˈʌpwəd; *NAmE* -wərd/ *adj.* [only before noun]

1 0┳ pointing towards or facing a higher place 向上的；朝上的；向高處的：*an upward gaze* 舉目凝望 **2** increasing in amount or price（數量、價格）上升的，上漲的，增長的：*an upward movement in property prices* 房地產價格的上升 OPP **downward**

ˌupwardly ˈmobile *adj.* moving towards a higher social position, usually in which you become richer 走向上層社會的；走向富裕的；步步高升的：*upwardly mobile immigrant groups* 步步高升的移民群體 ◇ *an upwardly mobile lifestyle* 日益闊綽的生活方式 ▶ **ˌupward moˈbility** *noun* [U]

up·wards 0┳ /ˈʌpwədz; *NAmE* -wərdz/ (*especially BrE*) (also **up·ward** especially in *NAmE*) *adv.*

1 0┳ towards a higher place or position 向上；向高處：*A flight of steps led upwards to the front door.* 一段台階往上通向正門。◇ *Place your hands on the table with the palms facing upwards.* 把手放在桌子上，手心朝上。 OPP **downwards 2** towards a higher amount or price（數量、價格）上升，上漲，提高：*Bad weather forced the price of fruit upwards.* 惡劣的天氣迫使水果價格上漲。◇ *The budget has been revised upwards.* 預算已經上調。 OPP **downwards 3 ~ of sth** more than the amount or number mentioned 在…以上；大於；超過：*You should expect to pay upwards of £50 for a hotel room.* 住宿飯店，每個房間預計至少要 50 英鎊。

up·wind /ˌʌpˈwɪnd/ *adv.* in the opposite direction to the way in which the wind is blowing 逆風；頂風：*to sail upwind* 逆風行船 ◇ *The house was upwind of the factory and its smells* (= the wind did not blow the smells towards the house). 這房子坐落在工廠的上風處，聞不到工廠的氣味。 OPP **downwind** ▶ **up·wind** *adj.*

ur- /ʊə(r); *NAmE* ʊr/ *prefix* (*formal*) earliest or original 最早的；原始的

ur·an·ium /juˈreɪniəm/ *noun* [U] (*symb.* **U**) a chemical element. Uranium is a heavy, silver-white, RADIOACTIVE metal, used mainly in producing nuclear energy. 鈾（放射性化學元素）

Ura·nus /ˈjʊərənəs; jʊˈreɪnəs; *NAmE* ˈjʊr-; jʊˈr-/ *noun* the planet in the SOLAR SYSTEM that is 7th in order of distance from the sun 天王星

urban 0┳ /ˈɜːbən; *NAmE* ˈɜːrbən/ *adj.* [usually before noun]

1 0┳ connected with a town or city 城市的；都市的；城鎮的：*damage to both urban and rural environments* 對城鄉環境的破壞 ◇ *urban areas* 城鎮地區 ◇ *urban life* 城市生活 ◇ *urban development* (= the process of building towns and cities or making them larger) 城市發展 ◇ ***urban renewal/regeneration*** (= the process of improving the buildings, etc. in the poor parts of a town or city) 城市環境更新 ◇ *efforts to control* ***urban sprawl*** (= the spread of city buildings into the countryside) 控制城市向鄉村延伸的努力 ➲ compare RURAL **2** connected with types of music such as RHYTHM AND BLUES and REGGAE that are played by black musicians 都市音樂的，城市音樂的（如節奏布魯斯音樂、雷蓋音樂）：*today's urban music scene* 當今的城市音樂圈 ◇ *urban radio shows* 城市音樂廣播節目

ur·bane /ɜːˈbeɪn; *NAmE* ɜːrˈb-/ *adj.* (especially of a man 尤指男子) good at knowing what to say and how to behave in social situations; appearing relaxed and confident 溫文儒雅的；練達的；從容不迫的 ▶ **ur·bane·ly** *adv.* **ur·ban·ity** /ɜːˈbænəti; *NAmE* ɜːrˈb-/ *noun* [U]

ur·ban·ite /ˈɜːbənaɪt; *NAmE* ˈɜːrb-/ *noun* a person who lives in a town or city 城市居民

ur·ban·ized (*BrE* also **-ised**) /ˈɜːbənaɪzd; *NAmE* ˈɜːrb-/ *adj.* **1** (of an area, a country, etc. 地區、國家等) having a lot of towns, streets, factories, etc. rather than countryside 城市化的 **2** (of people 人) living and working in towns and cities rather than in the country 生活於城市的；在都市工作的：*an increasingly urbanized society* 城鎮居民日益增加的社會 ▶ **ur·ban·iza·tion**, **-isa·tion** /ˌɜːbənaɪˈzeɪʃn; *NAmE* ˌɜːrbənəˈz-/ *noun* [U]

ˌurban ˈmyth (also **ˌurban ˈlegend**) *noun* a story about an amusing or strange event that is supposed to have happened, which is often repeated and which many people believe is true 都市傳奇（街談巷議的傳聞或趣事）

ur·chin /ˈɜːtʃɪn; *NAmE* ˈɜːrtʃɪn/ *noun* **1** (*old-fashioned*) a young child who is poor and dirty, often one who has no home 貧窮骯髒的兒童；流浪兒：*a dirty little street urchin* 骯髒的街頭小乞丐 **2** = SEA URCHIN

Urdu /ˈʊədu:; ˈɜːdu:; *NAmE* ˈʊrdu:; ˈɜːrdu:/ *noun* [U] the official language of Pakistan, also widely used in India 烏爾都語（巴基斯坦的官方語言，印度也通用）

-ure *suffix* (in nouns 構成名詞) the action, process or result of …的行動（或過程、結果等）：*closure* 關閉 ◇ *failure* 失敗

urea /jʊˈri:ə/ *noun* [U] (*technical* 術語) a clear substance containing NITROGEN that is found especially in URINE 尿素；脲

ur·ethra /jʊˈri:θrə/ *noun* (*anatomy* 解) the tube that carries liquid waste out of the body. In men and male animals SPERM also flows along this tube. 尿道 ▸ **ur·eth·ral** *adj.* [only before noun]

ur·eth·ritis /ˌjʊərəˈθraɪtɪs; *NAmE* ˌjʊr-/ *noun* [U] (*medical* 醫) infection of the urethra 尿道炎

urge 0➡ /ɜːdʒ; *NAmE* ɜːrdʒ/ *verb, noun*

■ *verb* **1** 0➡ to advise or try hard to persuade sb to do sth 敦促；催促；力勸：**~ sb to do sth** *She urged him to stay.* 她力勸他留下。◇ **~ that …** *The report urged that all children be taught to swim.* 這份報告呼籲給所有的兒童教授游泳。◇ **~ (sb) + speech** *'Why not give it a try?' she urged (him).* "為什麼不試一試呢？"她敦促（他）道。➲ SYNONYMS at RECOMMEND **2** 0➡ **~ sth (on/upon sb)** to recommend sth strongly 大力推薦；竭力主張：*The situation is dangerous and the UN is urging caution.* 局勢岌岌可危，聯合國力主謹慎行事。 **3 ~ sb/sth + adv./prep.** (*formal*) to make a person or an animal move more quickly and/or in a particular direction, especially by pushing or forcing them 驅趕；鞭策：*He urged his horse forward.* 他策馬前行。

PHR V **ˌurge sb↔ˈon** to encourage sb to do sth or support them so that they do it better 鼓勵；激勵；為…加油：*She could hear him urging her on as she ran past.* 她跑過他面前時，聽到他在為她加油。

■ *noun* 0➡ a strong desire to do sth 強烈的慾望；衝動：*sexual urges* 性衝動 ◇ **~ to do sth** *I had a sudden urge to hit him.* 我突然很想揍他一頓。

ur·gent 0➡ /ˈɜːdʒənt; *NAmE* ˈɜːrdʒ-/ *adj.*

1 0➡ that needs to be dealt with or happen immediately 緊急的；緊迫的；迫切的 **SYN** **pressing**：*an urgent appeal for information* 緊急呼籲提供信息 ◇ *a problem that requires urgent attention* 需要緊急處理的問題 ◇ *'Can I see you for a moment?' 'Is it urgent?'* "我能見你一下嗎？""有急事嗎？" ◇ *Mark the message 'urgent', please.* 請在通知上註明"急件"。◇ *The law is* ***in urgent need of*** *reform.* 這項法律亟待修訂。 **2** 0➡ showing that you think that sth needs to be dealt with immediately 催促的；急切的：*an urgent whisper* 急切的耳語 ▸ **ur·gen·cy** /-dʒənsi/ *noun* [U, sing.]：*This is a matter of some urgency.* 這件事相當緊迫。◇ *The attack added a new urgency to the peace talks.* 這次攻擊事件使和平談判愈加緊迫。 **ur·gent·ly** *adv.*：*New equipment is urgently needed.* 急需新設備。◇ *I need to speak to her urgently.* 我得馬上跟她談談。◇ *'We must find him,' she said urgently.* "我們必須找到他。"她急切地說。

urgh /ɜx; *NAmE* ərx/ *exclamation* = UGH：*Urgh! There's a dead fly in my coffee!* 呸！我的咖啡裏有隻死蒼蠅！

ur·inal /jʊəˈraɪnl; ˈjʊərɪnl; *NAmE* ˈjʊrənl/ *noun* a type of toilet for men that is attached to the wall; a room or building containing urinals（男用）小便池，小便器；男廁所

urin·ary /ˈjʊərɪnəri; *NAmE* ˈjʊrəneri/ *adj.* [usually before noun] (*medical* 醫) connected with URINE or the parts of the body through which it passes 尿的；泌尿的；泌尿器官的

urin·ate /ˈjʊərɪneɪt; *NAmE* ˈjʊrən-/ *verb* [I] (*formal* or *technical* 術語) to get rid of URINE from the body 排尿；小便 ▸ **urin·ation** /ˌjʊərɪˈneɪʃn; *NAmE* ˌjʊrəˈn-/ *noun* [U]

urine /ˈjʊərɪn; -raɪn; *NAmE* ˈjʊrən/ (also *informal* **wee** especially in *BrE*) *noun* [U] the waste liquid that collects in the BLADDER and that you pass from your body 尿；小便

URL /ˌjuː ɑːr ˈel/ *abbr.* (*computing* 計) uniform/universal resource locator (the address of a WORLD WIDE WEB page) 統一資源定位地址；URL 地址

urn /ɜːn; *NAmE* ɜːrn/ *noun* **1** a tall decorated container, especially one used for holding the ASHES of a dead person 甕；（尤指）骨灰缸 **2** a large metal container with a tap, used for making and/or serving tea or coffee（帶龍頭的）茶水桶，咖啡桶：*a tea urn* 茶水桶

ur·ology /jʊəˈrɒlədʒi; *NAmE* jʊˈrɑːl-/ *noun* [U] (*medical* 醫) the scientific study of the URINARY system 泌尿學 ▸ **uro·logic·al** /ˌjʊərəˈlɒdʒɪkl; *NAmE* ˌjʊrəˈlɑːdʒ-/ *adj.* **ur·olo·gist** /-dʒɪst/ *noun*

Ursa Major /ˌɜːsə ˈmeɪdʒə(r); *NAmE* ˌɜːrsə/ (also **the ˌGreat ˈBear**) *noun* [sing.] (*astronomy* 天) a large group of stars that can be clearly seen from the northern HEMISPHERE 大熊（星）座

Ursa Minor /ˌɜːsə ˈmaɪnə(r); *NAmE* ˌɜːrsə/ (also **the ˌLittle ˈBear**) *noun* [sing.] a group of stars that can be clearly seen from the northern HEMISPHERE and that includes the POLE STAR 小熊（星）座

ur·sine /ˈɜːsaɪn; *NAmE* ˈɜːrs-/ *adj.* [usually before noun] (*technical* 術語 or *literary*) connected with BEARS; like a bear 與熊有關的；像熊的

ur·ti·caria /ˌɜːtɪˈkeəriə; *NAmE* ˌɜːrtɪˈkeriə/ (also **nettle-rash**, **hives**) *noun* [U] (*medical* 醫) red spots on the skin that ITCH (= make you want to scratch), caused by an ALLERGIC reaction, for example to certain foods 蕁麻疹

US (also **U.S.** especially in *US*) /ˌjuː ˈes/ *abbr.* UNITED STATES (OF AMERICA)：*She became a US citizen.* 她成了美國公民。◇ *the US dollar* 美元

us 0➡ /əs; *strong form* ʌs/ *pron.*

(the object form of *we* * we 的賓格) **1** 0➡ used when the speaker or writer and another or others are the object of a verb or preposition, or after the verb *be* 我們：*She gave us a picture as a wedding present.* 她贈給我們一幅畫作結婚禮物。◇ *We'll take the dog with us.* 我們要把狗帶上。◇ *Hello, it's us back again.* 嘿！我們又回來了。 **2** (*BrE, informal*) me 我：*Give us the newspaper, will you?* 把報紙給我好嗎？

USA (also **U.S.A.** especially in *US*) /ˌjuː es ˈeɪ/ *abbr.* UNITED STATES OF AMERICA：*Do you need a visa for the USA?* 你需要美國簽證嗎？

us·able /ˈjuːzəbl/ *adj.* that can be used; in good enough condition to be used 能用的；可用的；適用的：*The bike is rusty but usable.* 自行車生銹了，但還能騎。◇ *How can we display this data in a usable form?* 我們如何把這些數據以實用形式展示出來呢？ **OPP** **unusable**

USAF /ˌjuː es eɪ ˈef/ *abbr.* United States Air Force 美國空軍

usage /ˈjuːsɪdʒ; ˈjuːz-/ *noun* **1** [U, C] the way in which words are used in a language（詞語的）用法，慣用法：*current English usage* 當代英語慣用法 ◇ *It's not a word* ***in common usage***. 這不是一個常用詞。 **2** [U] the fact of sth being used; how much sth is used 使用；利用；利用率：*land usage* 土地的利用 ◇ *Car usage is predicted to increase.* 汽車的使用率預計會增長。

USB /ˌjuː es ˈbiː/ *abbr.* (*computing* 計) universal serial bus (the system for connecting other pieces of equipment to a computer) 通用串行總線，通用序列匯流排（連接計算機外接設備的系統）：*All new PCs now have USB sockets.* 新的個人計算機現在都有通用串行總線插孔。◇ *a USB port* 通用串行總線端口

USˈB drive (also *informal* **USˈB stick**) *noun* = FLASH DRIVE ➲ VISUAL VOCAB page V66

USCIS /ˌjuː es siː aɪ ˈes/ *abbr.* United States Citizenship and Immigration Services (the US government department that deals with people from other countries who want to visit or live in the US or to become a US citizen, part of the Department of Homeland Security) 美國公民及移民事務署（隸屬美國國土安全部）

use verb, noun

■ **verb** /juːz/ (**used**, **used** /juːzd/) **1** [T] to do sth with a machine, a method, an object, etc. for a particular purpose 使用；利用；運用：**~ sth** *Can I use your phone?* 我可以用一下你的電話嗎？◇ *Have you ever used this software before?* 你以前用過這套軟件嗎？◇ *How often do you use* (= travel by) *the bus?* 你多長時間坐一次公共汽車？◇ *They were able to achieve a settlement without using military force.* 他們沒有訴諸武力就解決了問題。◇ *I have some information you may be able to use* (= to get an advantage from). 我有些可能對你有用的信息。◇ **~ sth for sth/for doing sth** *The blue files are used for storing old invoices.* 藍色卷宗是用來存放舊發票的。◇ **~ sth to do sth** *Police used tear gas to disperse the crowds.* 警察用了催淚瓦斯驅散人群。◇ **~ sth as sth** *The building is currently being used as a warehouse.* 這所房子目前用作倉庫。◇ *You can't keep using your bad back as an excuse.* 你不能老拿腰疼當託辭呀。 **2** [T] **~ sth** to take a particular amount of a liquid, substance, etc. in order to achieve or make sth 消耗：*This type of heater uses a lot of electricity.* 這種加熱器耗電量很大。◇ *I hope you haven't used all the milk.* 希望你沒有把牛奶都用掉了。 **3** [T] **~ sth** to say or write particular words or a particular type of language 說，寫，使用（詞語或語言）：*The poem uses simple language.* 這首詩用語簡單。◇ *That's a word I never use.* 那是我從來不用的字眼。◇ *You have to use the past tense.* 要使用過去時。 **4** [T] **~ sb** (*disapproving*) to be kind, friendly, etc. to sb with the intention of getting an advantage for yourself from them（施展手段）利用（別人） SYN **exploit**：*Can't you see he's just **using you for his own ends**?* 你難道看不出他在利用你謀求私利嗎？◇ *I felt used.* 我覺得被人利用了。 **5** [T, I] **~ (sth)** to take illegal drugs 吸（毒）；服用（毒品）：*Most of the inmates have used drugs at some point in their lives.* 大多數囚犯都在人生的某個階段服用過毒品。◇ (*slang*) *She's been using since she was 13.* 她從 13 歲起就吸毒。

IDM **I, you, etc. could use sth** (*informal*) used to say that you would like to have sth very much 恨不得；巴不得；非常想：*I think we could all use a drink after that!* 我想我們在事情辦完之後都得痛快地喝一杯！ **use your 'head** (*BrE* also **use your 'loaf**) (*informal*) used to tell sb to think about sth, especially when they have asked for your opinion or said sth stupid 你動動腦子；你仔細想想：*'Why don't you want to see him again?' 'Oh, use your head!'* "你為什麼不願再見到他？" "唔，你好好想想吧！" ORIGIN From rhyming slang, in which **loaf of bread** stands for 'head'. 源自同韻俚語 loaf of bread，代表 head 的意思。

PHR V **ˌuse sth↔'up** to use all of sth so that there is none left 用盡；吃光：*Making soup is a good way of using up leftover vegetables.* 把剩下的蔬菜全部用來做湯是個好主意。

■ **noun** /juːs/ **1** [U, sing.] the act of using sth; the state of being used 用；使用；得到利用：*A ban was imposed on the use of chemical weapons.* 化學武器已被禁止使用。◇ *The software is designed for use in schools.* 這個軟件是為學校應用設計的。◇ *I'm not sure that this is the most valuable use of my time.* 我不能肯定我的時間這樣來安排是最有價值的。◇ *The chapel was built in the 12th century and is still **in use** today.* 這座小教堂建於 12 世紀，今天仍在使用。◇ *The bar is **for the use of** members only.* 酒吧僅供會員使用。 **2** [C, U] a purpose for which sth is used; a way in which sth is or can be used 用途；功能；用法：*I'm sure you'll think of a use for it.* 我相信你會給這東西找到用途的。◇ *This chemical has a wide range of industrial uses.* 這種化學製品在工業上用途廣泛。 ➲ see also SINGLE-USE **3** [U] **~ (of sth)** the right or opportunity to use sth, for example sth that belongs to sb else 使用權；使用的機會：*I have the use of the car this week.* 這輛汽車本週歸我使用。 **4** [U] the ability to use your mind or body 運用頭腦（或身體）的能力；功能：*He lost the use of his legs* (= became unable to walk) *in an accident.* 他在一次事故中失去了雙腿的功能。

IDM **be no 'use (to sb)** (also *formal* **be of no 'use**) to be useless 無用：*You can throw those away—they're no use to anyone.* 那些東西你可以扔了，它們對誰都沒用。 **be of 'use (to sb)** (*formal*) to be useful 有用；有幫助：*Can I be of any use* (= can I help)? 有什麼要我幫忙的嗎？ **come into/go out of, etc. 'use** to start/stop being used 開始／停止使用：*When did this word come into common use?* 這個詞是什麼時候普遍使用起來的？ **have its/their/your 'uses** (*informal*, often *humorous*) to be useful sometimes 有時用得着的；偶爾可派上用場：*I know you don't like him, but he has his uses.* 我知道你不喜歡他，但他有時還用得着。 **have no 'use for sb** to dislike sb 討厭（或憎惡）…的人：*I've no use for people who don't make an effort.* 我厭惡那些不努力的人。 **have no 'use for sth** to not need sth 不需要；用不着 **it's no 'use (doing sth) | what's the 'use (of doing sth)?** used to say that there is no point in doing sth because it will not be successful or have a good result 沒有意義；沒有用處：*What's the use of worrying about it?* 為此事操心有什麼用呢？◇ *It's no use—I can't persuade her.* 沒用，我勸不了她。 **make 'use of sth/sb** to use sth/sb, especially in order to get an advantage 使用；利用（以謀私利等）：*We could make better use of our resources.* 我們可以更有效地利用我們的資源。 **put sth to good 'use** to be able to use sth for a purpose, and get an advantage from doing so 有效使用（或利用）：*She'll be able to put her languages to good use in her new job.* 她在新工作中應該可以好好運用她會的各種語言。

used[1] /juːst/ *adj.*
familiar with sth because you do it or experience it often 習慣於；適應：**~ to doing sth** *I'm not used to eating so much at lunchtime.* 我不習慣午飯吃那麼多。◇ **~ to sth** *I found the job tiring at first but I soon **got used to** it.* 起初我覺得這份工作很累人，但很快就習慣了。 ➲ note at USED TO

used[2] /juːzd/ *adj.* [usually before noun]
that has belonged to or been used by sb else before 用過的；舊的；二手的 SYN **second-hand**：*used cars* 二手汽車

Which Word? 詞語辨析

used to / be used to

- Do not confuse **used to do sth** with **be used to sth**. 不要混淆 used to do sth 與 be used to sth。
- You use **used to do sth** to talk about something that happened regularly or was the case in the past, but is not now. * used to do sth 指過去慣常做某事，而現在則不了：*I used to smoke, but I gave up a couple of years ago.* 我以前抽煙，但幾年前就戒掉了。
- You use **be used to sth/to doing sth** to talk about something that you are familiar with so that it no longer seems new or strange to you. * be used to sth/to doing sth 指習慣於、適應於：*We're used to the noise from the traffic now.* 現在我們已經適應車輛往來的噪音了。◇ *I'm used to getting up early.* 我習慣早起。 You can also use **get used to sth**. 亦可用 get used to sth：*Don't worry—you'll soon get used to his sense of humour.* 別擔心，你不久就會適應他的幽默感。◇ *I didn't think I could ever get used to living in a big city after living in the country.* 我覺得我在農村住了之後就無法適應大城市的生活了。

used to /ˈjuːst tə; *before vowels and finally* ˈjuːst tu/ *modal verb* (*negative* **didn't use to** /-juːs/, *BrE* also *old-fashioned* or *formal* **used not to** *short form* **usedn't to** /ˈjuːsnt tə; *before vowels and finally* ˈjuːsnt tu/)
used to say that sth happened continuously or frequently during a period in the past（用於過去持續或經常發生的事）曾經：*I used to live in London.* 我曾經在倫敦居住過。◇ *We used to go sailing on the lake in summer.* 從前的夏天，我們經常泛舟湖上。◇ *I didn't use to like him much when we were at school.* 以前我們是同學時，我並不太喜歡他。◇ *You used to see a lot of her, didn't you?* 你過去常見她吧？ ➲ note at MODAL

Grammar Point 語法說明

used to

- Except in negatives and questions, the correct form is **used to**. 除在否定句和疑問句中之外，正確的形式為 used to：*I used to go there every Saturday.* 我以前每星期六都去那兒。◇ ~~*I use to go there every Saturday.*~~
- To form questions, use *did*. 構成疑問句用 did：*Did she use to have long hair?* 她過去留長髮嗎？Note that the correct spelling is **use to**, not 'used to'. 注意：正確的拼寫為 use to，而非 used to。
- The negative form is usually **didn't use to**, but in *BrE* this is quite informal and is not usually used in writing. 否定式通常為 didn't use to，但在英式英語中，此形式相當口語化，通常不用於書面語中。
- The negative form **used not to** (*rather formal*) and the question form **used you to …?** (*old-fashioned and very formal*) are only used in *BrE*, usually in writing. 否定式 used not to（相當正式）和疑問式 used you to …?（過時且非常正式）只用於英式英語，而且通常作書面語。

use·ful 🔑 /ˈjuːsfl/ *adj.* **1** 🔑 that can help you to do or achieve what you want 有用的；有益的；實用的；有幫助的：*a useful gadget* 有用的小器具 ◇ **~ (to do sth)** *It can be useful to write a short summary of your argument first.* 先把你的論點綱要寫下來可能會有幫助。◇ **~ (to sb)** *He might be useful to us.* 我們也許用得上他。◇ **~ (for sth/for doing sth)** *These plants are particularly useful for brightening up shady areas.* 這些植物特別有助於讓背陰的地方明亮起來。◇ *Don't just sit watching television—**make yourself useful!*** 別光坐着看電視，幫一下忙吧！◇ *This information could **prove useful**.* 這條信息往後也許有用。◇ *Your knowledge of German may **come in useful*** (= be useful in a particular situation). 你的德文知識可能會派上用場。◇ *Some products can be recycled at the end of their useful life.* 有些產品過了有效使用年限後是可以回收再利用的。**2** (*BrE, informal*) good; of the right standard 好的；合格的 SYN **competent**：*He's a very useful player.* 他是個很棒的運動員。▸ **use·ful·ly** /-fəli/ *adv.*：*The money could be more usefully spent on new equipment.* 這筆錢用來購置新設備可能會更有價值。

use·ful·ness /ˈjuːsfəlnəs/ *noun* [U] the fact of being useful or possible to use 有用；實用；可用性：*There are doubts about the usefulness of these tests.* 這些試驗是否有用，人們有所保留。◇ *The building has outlived its usefulness.* 這座樓房已超過使用年限了。

U

use·less 🔑 /ˈjuːsləs/ *adj.* **1** 🔑 not useful; not doing or achieving what is needed or wanted 無用的；無效的；無價值的：*This pen is useless.* 這支筆沒用了。◇ **~ (to do sth)** *He knew it was useless to protest.* 他知道抗議是徒勞的。◇ **~ (doing sth)** *It's useless worrying about it.* 為這事擔心無濟於事。◇ *She tried to work, but it was useless* (= she wasn't able to). 她很想做事，但力不從心。**2 ~ (at sth/at doing sth)** (*informal*) not very good at sth; not able to do things well 差勁的；不行的；不擅長的：*I'm useless at French.* 我的法語不太行。◇ *Don't ask her to help. She's useless.* 別求她幫忙。她沒那個能耐。▸ **use·less·ly** *adv.* **use·less·ness** *noun* [U]

Use·net /ˈjuːznet/ *noun* [U] (*computing* 計) a service on the Internet used by groups of users who email each other because they share a particular interest * Usenet 網，用戶網絡（志趣相投的用戶用以互發電郵）

user 🔑 /ˈjuːzə(r)/ *noun* **1** 🔑 a person or thing that uses sth 使用者；用戶：*road users* 道路的使用者 ◇ *computer software users* 電腦軟件用戶 ◇ *a user manual* 使用說明書 ➲ see also END-USER **2** (*slang*) a person who uses illegal drugs 癮君子；吸毒者

ˈuser fee *noun* (*NAmE*) a tax on a service that is provided for the public 使用費（某些稅捐）

ˌuser-ˈfriend·ly *adj.* easy for people who are not experts to use or understand 方便非專業用戶的；便於使用的；易於掌握的 ▸ **ˌuser-ˈfriendli·ness** *noun* [U]

ˈuser group *noun* a group of people who use a particular thing and who share information about it, especially people who share information about computers on the Internet 用戶組，使用者群組（使用同一產品或服務並交流信息）

user·name /ˈjuːzəneɪm; *NAmE* -zərn-/ *noun* (*computing* 計) the name you use in order to be able to use a computer program or system （使用計算機程序或系統時用以識別身分的）用戶名：*Please enter your username.* 請鍵入你的用戶名。

usher /ˈʌʃə(r)/ *noun, verb*

■ ***noun*** **1** a person who shows people where to sit in a church, public hall, etc. 引座員 **2** an official who has special responsibilities in court, for example allowing people in and out of the court （法院的）傳達員，門衛，門房 **3** a friend of the BRIDEGROOM at a wedding, who has special duties 男儐相

■ ***verb* ~ sb + adv./prep.** to take or show sb where they should go 把…引往；引導；引領：*The secretary ushered me into his office.* 秘書把我領進他的辦公室。➲ SYNONYMS at TAKE

PHR V **ˌusher sth↔ˈin** (*formal*) to be the beginning of sth new or to make sth new begin 開創；開始；開啟：*The change of management ushered in fresh ideas and policies.* 更換領導班子帶來了新思想和新政策。

ush·er·ette /ˌʌʃəˈret/ *noun* (*especially BrE*) a woman whose job is to lead people to their seats in a theatre or cinema/movie theater 女引座員

USN /juː es ˈen/ *abbr.* United States Navy 美國海軍

USP /juː es ˈpiː/ *noun* (*business* 商) the abbreviation for unique selling proposition or unique selling point (a feature of a product or service that makes it different from all the others that are available and is a reason for people to choose it) 獨特賣點（全寫為 unique selling proposition 或 unique selling point，指產品或服務與眾不同而吸引顧客的特色）：*You need to come up with a USP.* 你得想出個獨特的賣點來。

USS /juː es ˈes/ *abbr.* United States Ship (used before the name of a ship in the US navy) 美國船（用於美國海軍艦船的名稱前）：*USS Oklahoma* 美國軍艦俄克拉何馬號

USSR /juː es es ˈɑː(r)/ *abbr.* (the former) Union of Soviet Socialist Republics （前）蘇聯，蘇維埃社會主義共和國聯盟

usual 🔑 /ˈjuːʒuəl; -ʒəl/ *adj.* **1** 🔑 that happens or is done most of the time or in most cases 通常的；尋常的；慣常的 SYN **normal**：*She made all the usual excuses.* 她淨找了些司空見慣的藉口。◇ *He came home later than usual.* 他回家比平時晚了些。◇ *She sat in her usual seat at the back.* 她坐在後排平時慣坐的位子上。◇ *He didn't sound like his usual happy self.* 他聽起來不像平常那個樂天派了。◇ **~ (for sb/sth) (to do sth)** ***It is usual to*** *start a speech by thanking everybody for coming.* 講話前先感謝大家光臨，這是慣例。➲ compare UNUSUAL (1) **2 the usual** *noun* [sing.] (*informal*) what usually happens; what you usually have, especially the drink that you usually have 慣常的事物；（尤指）常喝的飲料

IDM **as usual** 🔑 in the same way as what happens most of the time or in most cases 照例；照舊；像往常一樣：*Steve, as usual, was the last to arrive.* 史蒂夫照例來得最晚。◇ *As usual at that hour, the place was deserted.* 跟平常那個時刻一樣，那地方空蕩蕩的。◇ *Despite her problems, she carried on working as usual.* 儘管她有困難，她照樣繼續工作。➲ more at BUSINESS, PER

usu·al·ly 🔑 /ˈjuːʒuəli; -ʒəli/ *adv.* in the way that is usual or normal; most often 通常地；正常地；一般地；經常地：*I'm usually home by 6 o'clock.* 我一般 6 點鐘回到家。◇ *We usually go by car.* 我們通常開汽車去。◇ *How long does the journey usually take?* 這段旅程通常需要多長時間？

us·urer /ˈjuːʒərə(r)/ *noun* (*old-fashioned, disapproving*) a person who lends money to people at unfairly high rates of interest 放高利貸者

us·uri·ous /juːˈʒʊəriəs; *NAmE* juːˈʒʊr-/ *adj.* (*formal*) lending money at very high rates of interest 放高利貸的；收取高利的

usurp /juːˈzɜːp; *NAmE* -ˈzɜːrp/ *verb* **~ sb/sth** (*formal*) to take sb's position and/or power without having the right to do this 篡奪；侵權 ▶ **usurp·ation** /ˌjuːzɜːˈpeɪʃn; *NAmE* -zɜːrˈp-/ *noun* [U, C] **usurp·er** *noun*

usury /ˈjuːʒəri/ *noun* [U] (*old-fashioned, disapproving*) the practice of lending money to people at unfairly high rates of interest 放高利貸；高利盤剝

Utd *abbr.* UNITED

Ute /juːt/ *noun* (*pl.* **Ute** or **Utes**) a member of a Native American people many of whom live in the US states of Colorado and Utah 猶他人（美洲土著，很多居於美國科羅拉多州和猶他州）

ute /juːt/ *noun* (*AustralE, NZE, informal*) a vehicle with low sides and no roof at the back used, for example, by farmers（農用）小卡車，輕型貨車 SYN **pickup**

uten·sil /juːˈtensl/ *noun* (*formal*) a tool that is used in the house（家庭）用具，器皿；傢什：***cooking/kitchen utensils*** 炊具；廚房用具 ➲ VISUAL VOCAB page V26

uterus /ˈjuːtərəs/ *noun* (*anatomy* 解) the organ in women and female animals in which babies develop before they are born 子宮 SYN **womb** ▶ **uter·ine** /ˈjuːtəraɪn/ *adj.* [only before noun] ➲ see also INTRAUTERINE DEVICE

utili·tar·ian /ˌjuːtɪlɪˈteəriən; *NAmE* -ˈter-/ *adj.* **1** (*formal*) designed to be useful and practical rather than attractive 實用的；功利的；實惠的 **2** (*philosophy* 哲) based on or supporting the ideas of utilitarianism 實用主義的；功利主義的

utili·tar·ian·ism /ˌjuːtɪlɪˈteəriənɪzəm; *NAmE* -ˈter-/ *noun* [U] (*philosophy* 哲) the belief that the right course of action is the one that will produce the greatest happiness of the greatest number of people 功利主義

util·ity AW /juːˈtɪləti/ *noun, adj.*

■ ***noun*** (*pl.* **-ies**) **1** [C] (*especially NAmE*) a service provided for the public, for example an electricity, water or gas supply 公用事業：*the administration of* ***public utilities*** 公共事業的管理 ➲ COLLOCATIONS at HOUSE **2** [U] (*formal*) the quality of being useful 實用；效用；有用 SYN **usefulness** **3** [C] (*computing* 計) a piece of computer software that performs a particular task 應用程序；實用程序；公用程序

■ ***adj.*** [only before noun] that can be used for several different purposes 多用途的；多效用的；多功能的：*an all-round utility player* (= one who can play equally well in several different positions in a sport) 全面型選手

uˈtility room *noun* a room, especially in a private house, that contains large pieces of equipment such as a WASHING MACHINE, FREEZER, etc. 雜物室，雜用間（放置洗衣機、電冰箱等大體積家用器具）

uˈtility vehicle (also **uˈtility truck**) *noun* a small truck with low sides designed for carrying light loads 輕載小卡車；輕型貨車

util·ize (*BrE* also **-ise**) AW /ˈjuːtəlaɪz/ *verb* **~ sth** (**as sth**) (*formal*) to use sth, especially for a practical purpose 使用；利用；運用；應用 SYN **make use of**：*The Romans were the first to utilize concrete as a building material.* 羅馬人首先使用混凝土作建築材料。◇ *The resources at our disposal could have been better utilized.* 我們所掌握的資源本來可以利用得更好，獲得更高的效益。▶ **util·iza·tion, -isa·tion** AW /ˌjuːtəlaɪˈzeɪʃn; *NAmE* -ləˈz-/ *noun* [U]

ut·most /ˈʌtməʊst; *NAmE* -moʊst/ *adj., noun*

■ ***adj.*** (also *less frequent* **ut·ter·most**) [only before noun] greatest; most extreme 最大的；極度的：*This is a matter of the utmost importance.* 這是個極其重要的問題。◇ *You should study this document with the utmost care.* 你對這份文件的研究應該慎之又慎。

■ ***noun*** [sing.] the greatest amount possible 最大量；最大限度；極限；最大可能：*Our resources are strained to the utmost.* 我們的資源極端緊缺。◇ *He* ***did his utmost*** (= tried as hard as possible) *to persuade me not to go.* 他使盡渾身解數勸我別去。

uto·pia /juːˈtəʊpiə; *NAmE* -ˈtoʊ-/ (also **Utopia**) *noun* [C, U] an imaginary place or state in which everything is perfect 烏托邦；空想的完美境界 ORIGIN From the title of a book by Sir Thomas More, which describes a place like this. 源自托馬斯 • 莫爾爵士所著的書名，書中描繪了這樣一個地方。

uto·pian /juːˈtəʊpiən; *NAmE* -ˈtoʊ-/ (also **Utopian**) *adj.* having a strong belief that everything can be perfect, often in a way that does not seem to be realistic or practical 烏托邦的；空想完美主義的：*utopian ideals* 不切實際的理想 ◇ *a utopian society* 烏托邦式社會 ▶ **uto·pian·ism** (also **Utopianism**) *noun* [U]

utter /ˈʌtə(r)/ *adj., verb*

■ ***adj.*** [only before noun] used to emphasize how complete sth is 完全的；十足的；徹底的：*That's complete and utter nonsense!* 那純屬一派胡言！◇ *To my utter amazement she agreed.* 令我大感意外的是，她同意了。◇ *He felt an utter fool.* 他覺得自己蠢到家了。▶ **ut·ter·ly** *adv.*：*We're so utterly different from each other.* 我們之間有着天壤之別。◇ *She utterly failed to convince them.* 她根本沒有說服他們。

■ ***verb*** **~ sth** (*formal*) to make a sound with your voice; to say sth 出聲；說；講：*to utter a cry* 發出喊叫聲 ◇ *She did not* ***utter a word*** *during lunch* (= said nothing). 進午餐時，她一言未發。

ut·ter·ance /ˈʌtərəns/ *noun* (*formal*) **1** [U] the act of expressing sth in words 用言語的表達；說話：*to give utterance to your thoughts* 把你的想法說出來 **2** [C] something that you say 話語；言論：*one of her few recorded public utterances* 她僅有的幾次公開講話錄音之一

ut·ter·most /ˈʌtəməʊst; *NAmE* ˈʌtərmoʊst/ *adj., noun* [sing.] = UTMOST

ˈU-turn *noun* **1** a turn of 180° that a vehicle makes so that it can move forwards in the opposite direction（汽車等的）U 形轉彎，180 度轉彎：*to* ***do/make a U-turn*** 作 180 度轉彎 **2** (*informal*) a complete change in policy or behaviour, usually one that is embarrassing（政策、行為上令人尷尬的）徹底轉變，180 度大轉變

UUP /ˌjuː juː ˈpiː/ *abbr.* Ulster Unionist Party (a political party in Northern Ireland that wants it to remain part of the United Kingdom) 北愛爾蘭統一黨（主張北愛爾蘭為英國的一部份）

UV /ˌjuː ˈviː/ *abbr.* ULTRAVIOLET 紫外線的；利用紫外線的：*UV radiation* 紫外輻射

UVA /ˌjuː viː ˈeɪ/ *noun* [U] ULTRAVIOLET, RAYS that are relatively long 長波紫外線；紫外線 A：*UVA rays* 長波紫外線

UVB /ˌjuː viː ˈbiː/ *noun* [U] ULTRAVIOLET, RAYS that are relatively short 中波紫外線；紫外線 B：*UVB rays* 中波紫外線

UVC /ˌjuː viː ˈsiː/ *noun* [U] ULTRAVIOLET, RAYS that are very short and do not get through the OZONE LAYER 短波紫外線，紫外線 C（不能穿過臭氧層）：*UVC radiation* 短波紫外輻射

uvula /ˈjuːvjələ/ *noun* (*pl.* **uvu·lae** /-liː/) (*anatomy* 解) a small piece of flesh that hangs from the top of the inside of the mouth just above the throat 小舌；懸雍垂 ➲ VISUAL VOCAB page V59

uvu·lar /ˈjuːvjələ(r)/ *adj.* (*phonetics* 語音) (of a consonant 輔音) produced by placing the back of the tongue against or near the uvula 小舌（部位發出）的

ux·or·ial /ʌkˈsɔːriəl/ *adj.* (*formal*) connected with a wife 與妻子有關的

Uzi™ /ˈuːzi/ *noun* a type of SUB-MACHINE GUN designed in Israel 烏齊衝鋒槍（以色列設計）

Vv

V /viː/ *noun, abbr., symbol*

■ ***noun*** (also **v**) (*pl.* **Vs**, **V's**, **v's** /viːz/) **1** [C, U] the 22nd letter of the English alphabet 英語字母表的第 22 個字母：*'Violin' begins with (a) V/'V'.* * violin 一詞以字母 v 開頭。 **2** a thing shaped like a V * V 形物：*Ahead was the deep V of a gorge with water pouring down it.* 前面是陡深的 V 字形峽谷，水流傾瀉而下。➲ see also V-CHIP, V-NECK, V-SIGN

■ ***abbr.*** (in writing) VOLT(S)（書寫形式）伏，伏特：*a 1.5 V battery* * 1.5 伏電池

■ ***symbol*** (also **v**) the number 5 in ROMAN NUMERALS（羅馬數字）5

v *abbr.* **1** (also **vs** especially in *NAmE*) (in sport or in a legal case 體育運動或法律案件) VERSUS (= against) 對；對抗：*England v West Indies* 英格蘭隊對西印度群島隊 ◇ *the State vs Kramer* (= a case in a court of law) 州政府訴克雷默案 **2** (in writing 書寫形式) (*BrE, informal*) very 很；非常；十分：*I was v pleased to get your letter.* 來信收到，很高興。 **3** VIDE

vac /væk/ *noun* (*BrE, informal*) a university vacation（大學的）假期

va·cancy /ˈveɪkənsi/ *noun* (*pl.* **-ies**) **1** [C] a job that is available for sb to do（職位的）空缺；空職；空額：***job vacancies*** 職位空缺 ◇ *a temporary vacancy* 臨時空缺 ◇ **~ (for sb/sth)** *vacancies for bar staff* 酒吧職員的空缺 ◇ *to **fill a vacancy*** 填補空額 ➲ SYNONYMS at JOB **2** [C] a room that is available in a hotel, etc.（旅館等的）空房，空間：*I'm sorry, we have no vacancies.* 對不起，我們這裏客滿。 **3** [U] lack of interest or ideas 無興趣；無主意；空虛 SYN **emptiness**：*the vacancy of her expression* 她那茫然若失的表情

va·cant /ˈveɪkənt/ *adj.* **1** (of a seat, hotel room, house, etc. 座位、旅館房間、房屋等) empty; not being used 空着的；未被佔用的 SYN **unoccupied**：*vacant properties* 未被佔用的房地產 ◇ *The seat next to him was vacant.* 他旁邊的座位空着。◇ (*especially NAmE*) *a **vacant lot*** (= a piece of land in a city that is not being used) 一塊閒置的地皮 ➲ compare ENGAGED (4), OCCUPIED (1) **2** (*formal*) if a job in a company is **vacant**, nobody is doing it and it is available for sb to take（職位）空缺的：*When the post finally fell (= became) vacant, they offered it to Fiona.* 這個職位最終空出來之後，他們給了菲奧納。◇ (*BrE*) ***Situations Vacant*** (= a section in a newspaper where jobs are advertised) 招聘廣告欄目 **3** (of a look, an expression, etc. 目光、表情等) showing no sign that the person is thinking of anything 無神的；呆滯的；茫然的；若有所失的：*a vacant look* 呆滯的目光 ▶ **va·cant·ly** *adv.*：*to stare vacantly* 茫然瞪視

ˌvacant posˈsession *noun* [U] (*BrE, technical* 術語) the fact of owning a house that is empty because the people who lived there have moved out 交吉的地產

vac·ate /vəˈkeɪt; veɪˈk-; *NAmE* also ˈveɪkeɪt/ *verb* (*formal*) **1 ~ sth** to leave a building, seat, etc., especially so that sb else can use it 搬出，騰出，空出（建築物、座位等）：*Guests are requested to vacate their rooms by noon on the day of departure.* 房客務請在離開之日的中午以前騰出房間。 **2 ~ sth** to leave a job, position of authority, etc. so that it is available for sb else 辭（職）；讓（位）

vac·ation 0-w /vəˈkeɪʃn; veɪˈk-/ *noun, verb*

■ ***noun*** **1** 0-w [C] (in Britain) one of the periods of time when universities or courts of law are closed; (in the US) one of the periods of time when schools, colleges, universities or courts of law are closed（英國大學的）假期；（美國學校的）假期；（法庭的）休庭期：*the **Christmas/Easter/summer vacation*** 聖誕節／復活節假期；暑假 ◇ (*BrE*) *the **long vacation*** (= the summer vacation) 暑假 ➲ see also VAC **2** 0-w (*NAmE*) (*BrE* **holi·day**) [U, C] a period of time spent travelling or resting away from home 度假：*They're **on vacation** in Hawaii right now.* 他們此時正在夏威夷度假。◇ *You look tired—you should **take a vacation**.* 你看上去很累，應該休假了。◇ *The job includes two weeks' paid vacation.* 這份工作包括兩週的帶薪假期。◇ *a **vacation home*** 度假之家 ➲ COLLOCATIONS at TRAVEL ➲ note at HOLIDAY

■ ***verb*** [I] (*NAmE*) (*BrE* **holi·day**) to spend a holiday somewhere 度假；休假：*They are currently vacationing in Florida.* 他們目前正在佛羅里達州度假。

vac·ation·er /vəˈkeɪʃnə(r); veɪˈk-/ (*NAmE*) (*BrE* **holi·day-maker**) *noun* a person who is visiting a place on holiday/vacation 度假者

vac·cin·ate /ˈvæksɪneɪt/ *verb* [often passive] **~ sb (against sth)** to give a person or an animal a vaccine, especially by INJECTING it, in order to protect them against a disease 給…接種疫苗：*I was vaccinated against tetanus.* 我接種了破傷風疫苗。➲ COLLOCATIONS at ILL ➲ compare IMMUNIZE, INOCULATE ▶ **vac·cin·ation** /ˌvæksɪˈneɪʃn/ *noun* [C, U]：*Make sure your vaccinations are up to date.* 一定要接種最新的疫苗。◇ *vaccination against typhoid* 傷寒疫苗的接種

vac·cine /ˈvæksiːn; *NAmE* vækˈsiːn/ *noun* [C, U] a substance that is put into the blood and that protects the body from a disease 疫苗；菌苗：*a measles vaccine* 麻疹疫苗 ◇ *There is no vaccine against HIV infection.* 現在還沒有防止感染艾滋病病毒的疫苗。

vacil·late /ˈvæsəleɪt/ *verb* [I] (*formal*) to keep changing your opinion or thoughts about sth, especially in a way that annoys other people 觀點（或立場等）搖擺；動搖 SYN **waver** ▶ **va·cil·la·tion** /ˌvæsəˈleɪʃn/ *noun* [U, C]

vacu·ity /vəˈkjuːəti/ *noun* [U] (*formal*) lack of serious thought or purpose 空虛；茫然；缺乏思考

vacu·ole /ˈvækjuəʊl; *NAmE* -oʊl/ *noun* **1** (*biology* 生) a small space within a cell, usually filled with liquid（細胞內的）液泡，泡 **2** (*medical* 醫) a small hole in the TISSUE of the body, usually caused by disease（身體組織中由疾病等造成的）空泡

vacu·ous /ˈvækjuəs/ *adj.* (*formal*) showing no sign of intelligence or sensitive feelings 空洞的；空洞無物的：*a vacuous expression* 茫然的表情 ▶ **vacu·ous·ly** *adv.* **vacu·ous·ness** *noun* [U]

vac·uum /ˈvækjuəm/ *noun, verb*

■ ***noun*** **1** a space that is completely empty of all substances, including all air or other gas 真空：*a vacuum pump* (= one that creates a vacuum) 真空泵 ◇ ***vacuum-packed*** *foods* (= in a package from which most of the air has been removed) 真空包裝的食品 **2** [usually sing.] a situation in which sb/sth is missing or lacking 真空狀態；空白；空虛：*His resignation has created a vacuum which cannot easily be filled.* 他的引退造成了難以填補的空白。 **3** [usually sing.] the act of cleaning sth with a vacuum cleaner（用真空吸塵器所做的）清潔，清掃：*to give a room a quick vacuum* 用吸塵器把房間迅速清掃一下

IDM **in a ˈvacuum** existing separately from other people, events, etc. when there should be a connection 與世隔絕；脫離實際：*This kind of decision cannot ever be made in a vacuum.* 這種決定絕不能脫離實際。

■ ***verb*** [T, I] **~ (sth)** to clean sth using a vacuum cleaner 用真空吸塵器清掃 SYN **hoover**：*Have you vacuumed the stairs?* 你用吸塵器清掃樓梯了嗎？

ˈvacuum cleaner (*BrE* also **Hoover™**) *noun* an electrical machine that cleans floors, carpets, etc. by sucking up dirt and dust 真空吸塵器 ➲ VISUAL VOCAB page V20

ˈvacuum flask (also **flask**) (both *BrE*) (*US* **ˈvacuum bottle**) *noun* a container like a bottle with double walls with a vacuum between them, used for keeping liquids hot or cold 真空瓶；保溫瓶；熱水瓶；冰瓶 ➲ compare THERMOS

vade mecum /ˌvɑːdi ˈmeɪkəm/ *noun* (from *Latin, formal*) a book or written guide which you keep with you all the time, because you find it helpful（常備的）手冊，便覽

vaga·bond /ˈvæɡəbɒnd; *NAmE* -bɑːnd/ *noun* (*old-fashioned, disapproving*) a person who has no home or job and who travels from place to place 流浪漢；無業遊民；漂泊者

va·gar·ies /ˈveɪgəriz/ *noun* [pl.] (*formal*) changes in sb/sth that are difficult to predict or control 奇思遐想；游移不定；變幻莫測

va·gina /vəˈdʒaɪnə/ *noun* the passage in the body of a woman or female animal between the outer sex organs and the WOMB 陰道 ▶ **va·ginal** /vəˈdʒaɪnl/ *adj.* **va·gi·nal·ly** *adv.*

va·grancy /ˈveɪgrənsi/ *noun* [U] (*law* 律) the crime of living on the streets and BEGGING (= asking for money) from people 流浪罪；流浪行乞

va·grant /ˈveɪgrənt/ *noun* (*formal* or *law* 律) a person who has no home or job, especially one who BEGS (= asks for money) from people 無業遊民；流浪者；（尤指）乞丐 ▶ **va·grant** *adj.*

vague /veɪg/ *adj.* (**vaguer**, **vaguest**) **1** not clear in a person's mind（思想上）不清楚的，含糊的，不明確的，模糊的：*to have a* ***vague impression/memory/recollection*** *of sth* 對某事印象／記憶模糊 ◇ *They had only a* ***vague idea*** *where the place was.* 他們只是大概知道那個地方的位置。 **2 ~ (about sth)** not having or giving enough information or details about sth 不具體的；不詳細的；粗略的：*She's a little vague about her plans for next year.* 她對她明年的計劃不怎麼明確。◇ *The politicians made vague promises about tax cuts.* 政界人物的減稅承諾言辭含混。◇ *He was accused of being deliberately vague.* 他被指責為故意含糊其詞。◇ *We had only a vague description of the attacker.* 我們只有那個襲擊者的粗略描述。 **3** (of a person's behaviour 人的行為) suggesting a lack of clear thought or attention 茫然的；糊塗的；心不在焉的 SYN **absent-minded**：*His vague manner concealed a brilliant mind.* 他大智若愚。 **4** not having a clear shape 不清楚的；模糊的；朦朧的 SYN **indistinct**：*In the darkness they could see the vague outline of a church.* 他們在黑暗中能看到一座教堂的朦朧輪廓。 ▶ **vague·ness** *noun* [U]

vague·ly /ˈveɪgli/ *adv.* **1** in a way that is not detailed or exact 不詳細地；含糊地；不確切地：*a vaguely worded statement* 措辭含糊的聲明 ◇ *I can vaguely remember my first day at school.* 我還依稀記得我第一天上學的情景。 **2** slightly 略微；稍微：*There was something vaguely familiar about her face.* 她有點兒面熟。◇ *He was vaguely aware of footsteps behind him.* 他彷彿意識到背後有腳步聲。 **3** in a way that shows that you are not paying attention or thinking clearly 心不在焉地：*He smiled vaguely, ignoring her questions.* 他漫不經心地笑了笑，沒有理會她的問題。

vain /veɪn/ *adj.* **1** that does not produce the result you want 徒勞的；枉然的；無結果的 SYN **useless**：*She closed her eyes tightly* ***in a vain attempt*** *to hold back the tears.* 她緊閉雙眼，卻無法忍住眼淚。◇ *I knocked loudly* ***in the vain hope*** *that someone might answer.* 我敲門敲得很響，希望有人應聲，卻是徒然。 **2** (*disapproving*) too proud of your own appearance, abilities or achievements 自負的；自視過高的 SYN **conceited**：*She's too vain to wear glasses.* 她太愛虛榮，不肯戴眼鏡。 ➲ see also VANITY (1)

IDM **in ˈvain** without success 枉費心機；徒勞無益；白費力氣：*They tried in vain to persuade her to go.* 他們極力勸說她去，但枉費了一番口舌。◇ *All our efforts were in vain.* 我們的所有努力都付諸東流了。 ➲ more at NAME *n.*

vain·glori·ous /ˌveɪnˈglɔːriəs/ *adj.* (*literary, disapproving*) too proud of your own abilities or achievements 自負的；自命不凡的；自吹自擂的 ▶ **vain·glory** /ˌveɪnˈglɔːri/ *noun* [U]

vain·ly /ˈveɪnli/ *adv.* without success 徒勞地；不成功地；白費力地：*He shouted after them, vainly trying to attract their attention.* 他在他們的後面高喊，想引起他們的注意，卻是徒勞。

val·ance /ˈvæləns/ *noun* **1** a narrow piece of cloth like a short curtain that hangs around the frame of a bed, under a shelf, etc.（牀架等四周的）短帷幔，布簾 ➲ VISUAL VOCAB page V23 **2** (*especially NAmE*) = PELMET

vale /veɪl/ *noun* (*old use* or *literary*) (also used in modern place names 也用於現代地名) a valley 谷；山谷：*a wooded vale* 樹木茂密的山谷 ◇ *the Vale of the White Horse* 懷特霍斯谷

val·edic·tion /ˌvælɪˈdɪkʃn/ *noun* [C, U] (*formal*) the act of saying goodbye, especially in a formal speech（尤指正式演講中的）告別，告別辭

val·edic·tor·ian /ˌvælɪdɪkˈtɔːriən/ *noun* (*NAmE*) the student who has the highest marks/grades in a particular group of students and who gives the valedictory speech at a GRADUATION ceremony（畢業典禮上）致告別辭的最優生

val·edic·tory /ˌvælɪˈdɪktəri/ *adj.* [usually before noun] (*formal*) connected with saying goodbye, especially at a formal occasion（尤在正式場合）告別的，告辭的：*a valedictory speech* 告別演說

va·lency /ˈveɪlənsi/ *noun* [C, U] (*pl.* **-ies**) (also **va·lence** /ˈveɪləns/ especially in *NAmE*) **1** (*chemistry* 化) a measurement of the power of an atom to combine with others, by the number of HYDROGEN atoms it can combine with or DISPLACE 價；化合價；原子價：*Carbon has a valency of 4.* 碳的化合價是 4 價。 **2** (*linguistics* 語言) the number of GRAMMATICAL elements that a word, especially a verb, combines with in a sentence 組配數限，配價（一個詞，尤指動詞，在句子中結合的語法成分的數目）

val·en·tine /ˈvæləntaɪn/ *noun* **1** (also **ˈvalentine card**) a card that you send to sb that you love on St Valentine's Day (14 February), often without putting your name on it（在 2 月 14 日常以匿名寄送的）聖瓦倫廷節情人卡 **2** a person that you send a valentine to（收受聖瓦倫廷節賀卡的）情人

ˈValentine's Day ➲ ST VALENTINE'S DAY

val·er·ian /vəˈlɪəriən; *NAmE* -ˈlɪr-/ *noun* [U] a drug obtained from the root of a plant with the same name, used to make people feel calmer 纈草（從纈草根提取的鎮定藥）

valet *noun, verb*

■ ***noun*** /ˈvæleɪ; ˈvælɪt; *NAmE* also væˈleɪ/ **1** a man's personal servant who takes care of his clothes, serves his meals, etc.（照管男子衣食等的）貼身僕人，僕從 **2** (*BrE*) a hotel employee whose job is to clean the clothes of hotel guests（旅館中）為顧客洗衣服的服務員 **3** (*NAmE*) a person who parks your car for you at a hotel or restaurant（旅館或餐廳）為顧客停車的服務員

■ ***verb*** /ˈvælɪt/ **1** [T] **~ sth** (*BrE*) to clean a person's car thoroughly, especially on the inside 徹底清洗（尤指車內）：*a car valeting service* 清洗汽車服務 **2** [I] to perform the duties of a valet 侍候；服侍

Val·halla /vælˈhælə/ *noun* [U] (in ancient Scandinavian stories 古斯堪的納維亞神話) a palace in which some chosen men who had died in battle went to live with the god Odin for ever 瓦爾哈拉殿堂（陣亡將士與奧丁神永久生活的宮殿）

vali·ant /ˈvæliənt/ *adj.* (especially *literary*) very brave or determined 英勇的；勇敢的；果敢的；堅定的 SYN **courageous**：*valiant warriors* 勇敢的武士 ◇ *She made* ***a valiant attempt*** *not to laugh.* 她試圖強忍住不笑出來。 ▶ **vali·ant·ly** *adv.*

valid 🔑 AW /ˈvælɪd/ *adj.*

1 🔑 that is legally or officially acceptable（法律上）有效的；（正式）認可的：*a valid passport* 有效的護照 ◇ *a bus pass valid for 1 month* 公共汽車月票 ◇ *They have a valid claim to compensation.* 他們有要求賠償的合法權利。 **2** based on what is logical or true 符合邏輯的；合理的；有根據的；確鑿的：*She had valid reasons for not supporting the proposals.* 她有充分的理由不支持這些建議。◇ *The point you make is perfectly valid.* 你提出的論點完全站得住腳。 **3** (*computing* 計) that is accepted by the system 有效的；系統認可的：*a valid password* 有效密碼 OPP **invalid** ▶ **val·id·ly** AW *adv.*：*The contract had been validly drawn up.* 這份合同已依據法律草擬妥當。

val·id·ate AW /ˈvælɪdeɪt/ *verb* (*formal*) **1 ~ sth** to prove that sth is true 證實；確認；確證：*to validate a theory* 證實理論 OPP **invalidate** **2 ~ sth** to make sth legally valid 使生效；使有法律效力：*to validate a contract* 使合同生效 OPP **invalidate** **3 ~ sth** to state officially that sth is useful and of an acceptable standard 批准；

V

確認…有效；認可：*Check that their courses have been validated by a reputable organization.* 要確保他們的課程獲得有聲望機構的承認。▶ **val·id·ation** AW /ˌvælɪˈdeɪʃn/ *noun* [U, C]

val·id·ity AW /vəˈlɪdəti/ *noun* [U] **1** the state of being legally or officially acceptable（法律上的）有效，合法性；（正式的）認可：*The period of validity of the agreement has expired.* 本協議的有效期已過。**2** the state of being logical and true 符合邏輯；正當；正確：*We had doubts about the validity of their argument.* 我們對他們的論點的正確性有過懷疑。

val·ise /vəˈliːz; *NAmE* vəˈliːs/ *noun* (*old-fashioned*) a small bag for carrying clothes, used when you are travelling（裝衣服的）小旅行包

Val·ium™ /ˈvæliəm/ *noun* [U] a drug used to reduce anxiety 瓦利姆鎮定藥

Val·kyrie /ˈvælkɪri; vælˈkɪəri; *NAmE* vælˈkɪri; -ˈkaɪri/ *noun* (in ancient Scandinavian stories 古斯堪的納維亞神話) one of the twelve female servants of the god Odin, who selected men who had been killed in battle and took them to VALHALLA 瓦爾基里（奧丁神十二侍女之一，負責挑選陣亡者並帶到瓦爾哈拉殿堂）

val·ley 🔑 /ˈvæli/ *noun* an area of low land between hills or mountains, often with a river flowing through it; the land that a river flows through 谷；山谷；溪谷；流域：*a small town set in a valley* 坐落在溪谷中的小鎮 ◇ *a wooded valley* 樹木茂盛的山谷 ◇ *the valley floor* 谷底 ◇ *the Shenandoah Valley* 謝南多厄谷 ➲ VISUAL VOCAB pages V4, V5

ˈValley Girl *noun* (*NAmE, informal*) a girl from a rich family who is only interested in things like shopping, thought to be typical of one of those living in the San Fernando Valley of California 谷地富家女（只熱衷於購物等，被認為是加利福尼亞州聖費爾南多谷地富家女的典型）

val·our (*especially US* **valor**) /ˈvælə(r)/ *noun* [U] (*literary*) great courage, especially in war（尤指戰爭中的）英勇，勇氣 SYN **bravery** ▶ **val·or·ous** /ˈvælərəs/ *adj.* IDM see DISCRETION

Synonyms 同義詞辨析

valuable

precious • priceless • irreplaceable

These words all describe sth that is worth a lot of money or very important to sb. 以上各詞均用以形容物品值錢、寶貴。

valuable worth a lot of money 指值錢的、貴重的：*The thieves took three pieces of valuable jewellery.* 竊賊盜走了三件貴重的首飾。

precious rare and worth a lot of money; loved or valued very much 指珍稀的、珍貴的、寶貴的：*a precious Chinese vase, valued at half a million pounds* 價值 50 萬英鎊的稀世中國花瓶 ◇ *precious memories of our time together* 我們共度時光的珍貴回憶

priceless extremely valuable; loved or valued very much 指無價的、極珍貴的、極寶貴的：*a priceless collection of antiques* 價值連城的古文物收藏

irreplaceable too valuable or special to be replaced 指因貴重或獨特而不能替代的

PATTERNS

- valuable/precious/priceless/irreplaceable **possessions**
- valuable/precious/priceless **antiques/jewels/jewellery**

V

valu·able 🔑 /ˈvæljuəbl/ *adj.*
1 🔑 ~ (**to sb/sth**) very useful or important 很有用的；很重要的；寶貴的：*a valuable experience* 寶貴的經驗 ◇ *The book provides valuable information on recent trends.* 此書就近來的發展趨勢提供了寶貴的信息。◇ *This advice was to **prove valuable**.* 這忠告證明是有益的。**2** 🔑 worth a lot of money 很值錢的；貴重的：*valuable antiques* 貴重的古玩 ◇ *Luckily, nothing valuable was stolen.* 幸運的是，沒有貴重物品失竊。OPP **valueless, worthless** ➲ compare INVALUABLE, PRICELESS (1)

valu·ables /ˈvæljuəblz/ *noun* [pl.] things that are worth a lot of money, especially small personal things such as jewellery, cameras, etc.（尤指私人的）貴重物品 ➲ SYNONYMS at THING

valu·ation /ˌvæljuˈeɪʃn/ *noun* [C, U] **1** a professional judgement about how much money sth is worth; its estimated value（專業）估價；估定的價值；估值：*Surveyors carried out a valuation of the property.* 鑒定人員對這處房產作了估價。◇ *Experts set a high valuation on the painting.* 專家對這幅畫估價很高。◇ *land valuation* 土地的估價 **2** (*formal*) a judgement about how useful or important sth is; its estimated importance 評價；評估：*She puts a high valuation on trust between colleagues.* 她很看重同事間的信任。

value 🔑 /ˈvæljuː/ *noun, verb*

WORD FAMILY
value *noun, verb*
valuable *adj.*
invaluable *adj.* (≠ valueless)
valuables *noun*

■ ***noun***

▸ **HOW MUCH STH IS WORTH** 價值 **1** 🔑 [U, C] how much sth is worth in money or other goods for which it can be exchanged（商品）價值：*to **go up/rise/increase in value*** 升值 ◇ *to **go down/fall/drop in value*** 貶值 ◇ *rising property values* 上漲中的房地產價值 ◇ *The winner will receive a prize to the **value of** £1 000.* 獲勝者將得到價值為 1 000 英鎊的獎項。◇ *Sports cars tend to **hold their value** well.* 跑車往往很能保值。➲ SYNONYMS at PRICE ➲ see also MARKET VALUE, STREET VALUE **2** 🔑 [U] (*especially BrE*) how much sth is worth compared with its price（與價格相比的）值，划算程度：*to be **good/excellent value*** (= worth the money it costs) 很／極為合算 ◇ *to be **bad/poor value*** (= not worth the money it costs) 不上算；不值 ◇ *Larger sizes give the best **value for money**.* 較大尺寸的最划算。

▸ **BEING USEFUL/IMPORTANT** 有用；重要 **3** 🔑 [U] the quality of being useful or important 用途；積極作用 SYN **benefit**：*The value of regular exercise should not be underestimated.* 經常鍛煉的好處不應低估。◇ *The arrival of canals was **of great value** to many industries.* 運河的出現對許多行業具有重大的意義。◇ *to **be of little/no value** to sb* 對某人沒什麼／毫無幫助 ◇ *This ring has great **sentimental value** for me.* 這枚戒指對我來說很有紀念意義。◇ *I suppose it has a certain **novelty value*** (= it's interesting because it's new). 我覺得這有一定的新意。◇ *food with a high nutritional value* 營養價值高的食物 ◇ *The story has very little news value.* 這件事沒有什麼新聞價值。

▸ **BELIEFS** 信念 **4** 🔑 **values** [pl.] beliefs about what is right and wrong and what is important in life 是非標準；生活準則；價值觀：*moral values* 道德信條 ◇ *a return to traditional values in education, such as firm discipline* 恢復傳統的教育準則，如嚴格的紀律 ◇ *The young have a completely different **set of values** and expectations.* 年輕人有一整套截然不同的價值觀和期望。

▸ **MATHEMATICS** 數學 **5** [C] the amount represented by a letter or symbol 值；數值：*Let y have the value 33.* 假設 y 的值為 33。

■ ***verb***

▸ **CONSIDER IMPORTANT** 認為重要 **1** 🔑 (not used in the progressive tenses 不用於進行時) to think that sb/sth is important 重視；珍視：**~ sb/sth** (**as sth**) *I really value him as a friend.* 我真的把他視為好朋友。◇ **~ sb/sth** (**for sth**) *The area is valued for its vineyards.* 這個地區因它的葡萄園而受到重視。◇ *a valued member of staff* 職工中受重視的一員

▸ **DECIDE WORTH** 決定價值 **2** 🔑 [usually passive] **~ sth** (**at sth**) to decide that sth is worth a particular amount of money 給…估價；給…定價：*The property has been valued at over $2 million.* 這處房地產估價為 200 多萬元。

ˌvalue ˈadded tax *noun* [U] = VAT

ˌvalue-ˈfree *adj.* not influenced by personal opinions 不受主觀價值影響的；客觀的

'value judgement (also **'value judgment** especially in *NAmE*) *noun* [C, U] (sometimes *disapproving*) a judgement about how good or important sth is, based on personal opinions rather than facts（根據主觀意見的）價值判斷

,value-'laden *adj.* influenced by personal opinions 受主觀價值影響的；主觀的：*'Freedom fighter' is a value-laden word.*"自由戰士"是個帶有主觀判斷的詞。

value·less /'væljuːləs/ *adj.* (*formal*) without value or worth 沒有價值的；不值錢的 SYN **worthless** OPP **valuable**

valuer /'væljuːə(r)/ *noun* a person whose job is to estimate how much property, land, etc. is worth（房地產等的）估價人

valve /vælv/ *noun* **1** a device for controlling the flow of a liquid or gas, letting it move in one direction only 閥；閥門；活門；氣門 ➲ VISUAL VOCAB page V51 **2** a structure in the heart or in a VEIN that lets blood flow in one direction only（心臟或血管的）瓣膜 **3** a device in some BRASS musical instruments for changing the note（銅管樂器的）閥鍵，活塞 ➲ VISUAL VOCAB page V34

vam·oose /və'muːs/ *verb* [I] (*old-fashioned, informal*) to leave quickly 匆匆離去；迅速走開；開溜

vamp /væmp/ *noun* (*old-fashioned, disapproving*) a sexually attractive woman who tries to control men 妖婦（利用色相控制男性）

vam·pire /'væmpaɪə(r)/ *noun* (in stories 傳說) a dead person who leaves his or her grave at night to suck the blood of living people 吸血鬼（夜間走出墳墓吸吮活人血的遊魂）

'vampire bat *noun* a S American BAT (= an animal like a mouse with wings) that sucks the blood of other animals 吸血蝠（產於美洲熱帶，吸吮其他動物的血）

vam·pir·ism /'væmpaɪərɪzəm/ *noun* [U] the behaviour or practices of VAMPIRES 吸血鬼行為；吸血

van 0→ /væn/ *noun*
1 0→ a covered vehicle with no side windows in its back half, usually smaller than a lorry/truck, used for carrying goods or people 客貨車；廂式送貨車：*a furniture van* 運傢具的貨車 ◇ *a police van* (= for carrying police officers or prisoners) 警車 ◇ *a delivery van* 送貨車 ◇ *a van driver* 客貨車司機 ➲ VISUAL VOCAB page V57 **2** (*NAmE*) a covered vehicle with side windows, usually smaller than a lorry/truck, that can carry about twelve passengers 麵包車（通常為 12 座左右）**3** (*BrE*) a closed coach/car on a train for carrying bags, cases, etc. or mail（鐵路上運送包裹、郵件等的）車廂：*a luggage van* 裝運行李的車廂
IDM **in the 'van** (*BrE, formal*) at the front or in the leading position 處於前沿；處於領先地位

van·adium /və'neɪdiəm/ *noun* [U] (*symb.* **V**) a chemical element. Vanadium is a soft poisonous silver-grey metal that is added to some types of steel to make it stronger. 釩

'van conversion *noun* (*US*) = CONVERSION VAN

van·dal /'vændl/ *noun* a person who deliberately destroys or damages public property 故意破壞公物者

van·dal·ism /'vændəlɪzəm/ *noun* [U] the crime of destroying or damaging sth, especially public property, deliberately and for no good reason 故意破壞公共財物罪；恣意毀壞他人財產罪：*an act of vandalism* 恣意破壞公共財物的行為 ➲ COLLOCATIONS at CRIME

van·dal·ize (*BrE* also **-ise**) /'vændəlaɪz/ *verb* [usually passive] **~ sth** to damage sth, especially public property, deliberately and for no good reason 故意破壞，肆意破壞（尤指公共財物）

vane /veɪn/ *noun* a flat blade that is moved by wind or water and is part of the machinery in a WINDMILL, etc.（風車等的）翼，葉片，輪葉 ➲ see also WEATHERVANE

van·guard /'vængɑːd; *NAmE* -gɑːrd/ *noun* (usually **the vanguard**) [sing.] **1** the leaders of a movement in society, for example in politics, art, industry, etc.（政治、藝術、工業等社會活動的）領導者，先鋒，先驅者：*The company is proud to be* ***in the vanguard of*** *scientific progress.* 這家公司以處於科學發展的領先地位而自豪。**2** the part of an army, etc. that is at the front when moving forward to attack the enemy 先頭部隊；前衛；尖兵 OPP **rearguard**

van·illa /və'nɪlə/ *noun, adj.*
■ ***noun*** [U] a substance obtained from the BEANS of a tropical plant, also called vanilla, used to give flavour to sweet foods, for example ice cream 香草醛，香草香精（從熱帶植物香子蘭豆中提取，用於冰淇淋等甜食）：(*BrE*) *vanilla essence* 香子蘭精 ◇ (*NAmE*) *vanilla extract* 香子蘭精 ◇ (*BrE*) *a vanilla pod* 香子蘭莢果 ◇ (*NAmE*) *a vanilla bean* 香子蘭豆
■ ***adj.*** **1** flavoured with vanilla 有香子蘭香味的；香草味的：*vanilla ice cream* 香草冰淇淋 **2** (*informal, especially NAmE*) ordinary; not special in any way 普通的；尋常的；毫無特色的：*The city is pretty much plain vanilla.* 這座城市相當一般化。

van·il·lin /və'nɪlɪn/ *noun* [U] a strong-smelling chemical which gives VANILLA its smell 香草醛；香蘭素

van·ish /'vænɪʃ/ *verb* **1** [I] to disappear suddenly and/or in a way that you cannot explain（莫名其妙地）突然消失：*The magician vanished in a puff of smoke.* 魔術師在一股煙霧中突然不見了。◇ *My glasses seem to have vanished.* 我的眼鏡似乎不翼而飛了。◇ *He* ***vanished without trace.*** 他消失得無影無踪。**2** [I] to stop existing 不復存在；消亡；絕跡：*the vanishing woodlands of Europe* 瀕於絕跡的歐洲林地 ◇ *All hopes of a peaceful settlement had now vanished.* 和平解決的全部希望現已化為泡影。IDM see ACT *n.*, FACE *n.*

'vanishing point *noun* [usually sing.] (*technical* 術語) the point in the distance at which parallel lines appear to meet 滅點；消失點

van·ity /'vænəti/ *noun* (*pl.* **-ies**) **1** [U] (*disapproving*) too much pride in your own appearance, abilities or achievements 自負；自大；虛榮；虛榮心：*She had no personal vanity* (= about her appearance). 她對自己的相貌毫不自負。➲ see also VAIN **2** [U] (*literary*) the quality of being unimportant, especially compared with other things that are important（尤指與其他重大事物相比）渺小，無所謂，不重要：*the vanity of human ambition in the face of death* 個人抱負在死亡面前的微不足道 **3** **vanities** [pl.] behaviour or attitudes that show people's vanity 自負的行為；虛榮的態度；過分的驕傲：*Politics is too often concerned only with the personal vanities of politicians.* 政治常常僅與政界人士的個人虛榮有關。**4** (also **'vanity table**) [C] (*NAmE*) = DRESSING TABLE

'vanity case *noun* a small bag or case with a mirror in it, used for carrying make-up 小化妝包；小梳妝盒

'vanity unit *noun* (*BrE*) a WASHBASIN fixed into a flat surface with cupboards underneath（下帶櫥櫃的）組合式盥洗盆，嵌入式盥洗盆 ➲ VISUAL VOCAB page V24

van·quish /'væŋkwɪʃ/ *verb* **~ sb/sth** (*literary*) to defeat sb completely in a competition, war, etc. 完全征服；徹底擊敗；戰勝 SYN **conquer**

the van·quished /'væŋkwɪʃt/ *noun* [pl.] (*literary*) people who have been completely defeated in a competition, war, etc. 戰敗者；被完全征服的人；敗陣者

vant·age point /'vɑːntɪdʒ pɔɪnt; *NAmE* 'væn-/ (also *formal* **vant·age**) *noun* a position from which you watch sth; a point in time or a situation from which you consider sth, especially the past（觀察事物的）有利地點；（尤指考慮舊時事物的）有利時刻，有利形勢：*The cafe was a good vantage point for watching the world go by.* 從這家小餐館能清楚地看到世事的變遷。◇ *From the vantage point of the present, the war seems to have achieved nothing.* 依目前的情況來看，這場戰爭似乎一無所獲。

vapid /'væpɪd/ *adj.* (*formal*) lacking interest or intelligence 乏味的；枯燥的；愚蠢的 SYN **dull** ▶ **vap·id·ity** /və'pɪdəti/ *noun* [U]

vapor (*NAmE*) = VAPOUR

va·por·ize (*BrE* also **-ise**) /'veɪpəraɪz/ *verb* [I, T] **~ (sth)** (*technical* 術語) to turn into gas; to make sth turn into

V

gas （使）汽化，蒸發 ▸ **va·por·iza·tion**, **-isa·tion** /ˌveɪpəraɪˈzeɪʃn; NAmE -rəˈz-/ *noun* [U]

va·por·ous /ˈveɪpərəs/ *adj.* (*formal*) full of vapour; like vapour 充滿蒸氣的；似蒸氣的：*clouds of vaporous air* 團團濛濛霧氣

va·pour (*especially US* **vapor**) /ˈveɪpə(r)/ *noun* [C, U] a mass of very small drops of liquid in the air, for example steam 蒸氣；潮氣；霧氣：*water vapour* 水蒸氣

ˈvapour trail (*especially US* **ˈva·por trail**) *noun* the white line that is left in the sky by a plane （飛機在高空留下的）水汽尾跡，凝結尾跡，拉煙

va·pour·ware (*especially US* **va·por·ware**) /ˈveɪpəweə(r); NAmE -pərwer/ *noun* [U] (*computing* 計) a piece of software or other computer product that has been advertised but is not available to buy yet, either because it is only an idea or because it is still being written or designed 霧件，霧體（已做廣告但尚未上市的計算機程序或產品）

vari·abil·ity AW /ˌveəriəˈbɪləti; NAmE ˌver-; ˌvær-/ *noun* [U] the fact of sth being likely to vary 可變性；易變性；反覆不定：*climatic variability* 氣候的多變性 ◇ *a degree of variability in the exchange rate* 匯率的變化幅度

vari·able AW /ˈveəriəbl; NAmE ˈver-; ˈvær-/ *adj.*, *noun*

■ *adj.* **1** often changing; likely to change 多變的；易變的；變化無常的 SYN **fluctuating**：*variable temperatures* 變化不定的氣溫 ◇ *The acting is of variable quality* (= some of it is good and some of it is bad). 表演時好時壞。➲ compare INVARIABLE **2** able to be changed 可更改的；可變的：*The drill has variable speed control.* 這鑽機有變速控制。◇ *variable lighting* 亮度可調的照明設備 ▸ **vari·ably** AW /-iəbli/ *adv.*

■ *noun* a situation, number or quantity that can vary or be varied 可變情況；變量；可變因素：*With so many variables, it is difficult to calculate the cost.* 有這麼多的可變因素，很難計算出成本。◇ *The temperature remained constant while pressure was a variable in the experiment.* 做這實驗時溫度保持不變，但壓力可變。OPP **constant**

vari·ance AW /ˈveəriəns; NAmE ˈver-; ˈvær-/ *noun* [U, C] (*formal*) the amount by which sth changes or is different from sth else 變化幅度；差額：*variance in temperature* 溫差 ◇ *a note with subtle variances of pitch* 音高有細微變化的音符

IDM **at ˈvariance (with sb/sth)** (*formal*) disagreeing with or opposing sb/sth 看法不一；矛盾；衝突：*These conclusions are totally at variance with the evidence.* 這些結論與證據完全相悖。

vari·ant AW /ˈveəriənt; NAmE ˈver-; ˈvær-/ *noun* ~ **(of/on sth)** a thing that is a slightly different form or type of sth else 變種；變體；變形：*This game is a variant of baseball.* 這種運動是由棒球演變而來的。▸ **vari·ant** *adj.*：*variant forms of spelling* 不同的拼寫形式

V

vari·ation 0-m AW /ˌveəriˈeɪʃn; NAmE ˌver-/ *noun*

1 0-m [C, U] ~ **(in/of sth)** a change, especially in the amount or level of sth （數量、水平等的）變化，變更，變異：*The dial records very slight variations in pressure.* 該刻度盤能顯示很微小的壓力變化。◇ *Currency exchange rates are always subject to variation.* 貨幣的兑換率總在波動。◇ ***regional/seasonal variation*** (= depending on the region or time of year) 地區性／季節性變化 **2** 0-m [C] ~ **(on sth)** a thing that is different from other things in the same general group 變異的東西；變種；變體：*This soup is a spicy variation on a traditional favourite.* 這種湯是在一種受歡迎的傳統湯羹中加了香料。**3** [C] ~ **(on sth)** (*music* 音) any of a set of short pieces of music based on a simple tune repeated in a different and more complicated form 變奏；變奏曲：*a set of variations on a theme by Mozart* 以莫扎特某一樂曲為主題的一組變奏曲 ◇ (*figurative*) *His numerous complaints are all* ***variations on a theme*** (= all about the same thing). 他的滿腹牢騷說來道去都是為了一件事。

vari·cose vein /ˌværɪkəʊs ˈveɪn; NAmE -koʊs/ *noun* a VEIN, especially one in the leg, which has become swollen and painful （尤指腿部的）靜脈曲張

var·ied 0-m AW /ˈveərid; NAmE ˈverid; ˈvær-/ *adj.* (usually *approving*)

1 0-m of many different types 各種各樣的；形形色色的；不相同的：*varied opinions* 各種不同的意見 ◇ *a wide and varied selection of cheeses* 種類繁多的可供選購的奶酪 **2** 0-m not staying the same, but changing often 變化的；多變的；不同的：*He led a full and varied life.* 他過着豐富多彩的生活。

varie·gated /ˈveəriəgeɪtɪd; ˈveərɪg-; NAmE ˈver-/ *adj.* **1** (*technical* 術語) having spots or marks of a different colour 斑駁的；有斑點的：*a plant with variegated leaves* 斑葉植物 ➲ VISUAL VOCAB page V11 **2** (*formal*) consisting of many different types of thing or person 五花八門的；形形色色的

var·iety 0-m /vəˈraɪəti/ *noun* (*pl.* **-ies**)

1 0-m [sing.] ~ **(of sth)** several different sorts of the same thing （同一事物的）不同種類，多種式樣：*There is* ***a wide variety of*** *patterns to choose from.* 有種類繁多的圖案可供選擇。◇ *He resigned for a variety of reasons.* 他由於種種原因辭職了。◇ *This tool can be used in a variety of ways.* 這一工具有多種用途。◇ *I was impressed by the variety of dishes on offer.* 所供應的菜肴之豐盛讓我歎服。HELP A plural verb is needed after **a (large, wide, etc.) variety of ...** . 在 a (large, wide, etc.) variety of ... 之後謂語動詞要用複數。**2** 0-m [U] the quality of not being the same or not doing the same thing all the time 變化；多樣化；多變性 SYN **diversity**：*We all need variety in our diet.* 我們都需要飲食多樣化。◇ *We want more variety in our work.* 我們希望我們的工作多變點兒花樣。**3** 0-m [C] ~ **(of sth)** a type of a thing, for example a plant or language, that is different from the others in the same general group （植物、語言等的）變種，變體；異體；品種：*Apples come in a great many varieties.* 蘋果的品種繁多。◇ *a rare variety of orchid* 蘭花的稀有品種 ◇ *different varieties of English* 各類英語 ◇ *My cooking is of the 'quick and simple' variety.* 我做飯菜屬於既快捷又簡單的那一類。**4** (*NAmE* also **vaude·ville**) [U] a form of theatre or television entertainment that consists of a series of short performances, such as singing, dancing and funny acts 綜藝節目（包括歌舞、雜耍等的舞台演出或電視節目）：*a* ***variety show/theatre*** 綜藝節目／劇場

IDM **variety is the spice of ˈlife** (*saying*) new and exciting experiences make life more interesting 經歷豐富多彩才令生活充滿樂趣

vaˈriety meats *noun* [pl.] (*NAmE*) = OFFAL

vaˈriety store *noun* (*old-fashioned*, *NAmE*) a shop/store that sells a wide range of goods at low prices （廉價）雜貨店，雜貨鋪

vari·fo·cals /ˈveərɪfəʊklz; NAmE ˈverɪfoʊklz/ *noun* [pl.] a pair of glasses in which each LENS varies in thickness from the upper part to the lower part. The upper part is for looking at things at a distance, and the lower part is for looking at things that are close to you. 變焦眼鏡，漸進眼鏡（鏡片由上至下用於看遠、近距離的東西）➲ compare BIFOCALS ▸ **vari·focal** *adj.* ➲ compare BIFOCAL at BIFOCALS

vari·ous 0-m /ˈveəriəs; NAmE ˈver-; ˈvær-/ *adj.*

1 0-m several different 各種不同的；各種各樣的 SYN **diverse**：*Tents come in various shapes and sizes.* 帳篷有各種各樣的形狀和大小。◇ *She took the job for various reasons.* 她由於種種原因接受了這份工作。◇ *There are various ways of doing this.* 做這一工作的方法有很多。**2** (*formal*) having many different features 具有多種特徵的；多姿多彩的 SYN **diverse**：*a large and various country* 一個多姿多彩的大國

vari·ous·ly /ˈveəriəsli; NAmE ˈver-; ˈvær-/ *adv.* (*formal*) in several different ways, usually by several different people 以各種方式；不同地：*He has been* ***variously described*** *as a hero, a genius and a bully.* 他被描述為英雄、天才、惡霸，不一而足。◇ *The cost has been variously estimated at between £10 million and £20 million.* 對成本的估計眾說紛紜，從 1 000 萬英鎊到 2 000 萬英鎊不等。

var·mint /ˈvɑːmɪnt; NAmE ˈvɑːrm-/ *noun* (*old-fashioned*, *informal*) **1** a person, especially a child, who causes trouble 惹是生非的人；（尤指）頑童，小淘氣 **2** a wild animal, especially a FOX, that causes problems 害獸（尤指狐狸）

var·nish /ˈvɑːnɪʃ; *NAmE* ˈvɑːrnɪʃ/ *noun, verb*

■ ***noun*** [U, C] a liquid that is painted onto wood, metal, etc. and that forms a hard shiny transparent surface when it is dry 清漆；罩光漆；凡立水；指甲油 ➲ VISUAL VOCAB page V60 ➲ see also NAIL VARNISH at NAIL POLISH

■ ***verb*** to put varnish on the surface of sth 給…塗清漆；上清漆；塗指甲油： **~ sth** *The doors are then stained and varnished.* 這些門還要染色塗清漆。◇ (*BrE*) *Josie was sitting at her desk, varnishing her nails.* 喬西坐在書桌旁，塗着指甲油。◇ **~ sth + noun** *Her nails were varnished a brilliant shade of red.* 她的指甲上塗了一層鮮亮的紅指甲油。

var·sity /ˈvɑːsəti; *NAmE* ˈvɑːrs-/ *noun, adj.*

■ ***noun*** [C, U] (*pl.* **-ies**) **1** (*NAmE*) the main team that represents a college or HIGH SCHOOL, especially in sports competitions （尤指體育比賽中大中學校的）代表隊，校隊 **2** (*BrE, old use* or *IndE* or *SAfrE*) university 大學： *She's still at varsity.* 她還在上大學。

■ ***adj.*** [only before noun] (*BrE, informal*) used when describing activities connected with the universities of Oxford and Cambridge, especially sports competitions （常用於牛津和劍橋兩大學的體育比賽）大學的： *the varsity match* 大學體育比賽

vary 0➡ AW /ˈveəri; *NAmE* ˈveri; ˈværi/ *verb* (**vary·ing**, **var·ied**, **var·ied**)

> **WORD FAMILY**
> vary *verb*
> varied *adj.*
> variable *adj.*
> variation *noun*
> various *adj.*
> variety *noun*

1 0➡ [I] **~ (in sth)** (of a group of similar things 一組類似的事物) to be different from each other in size, shape, etc. （大小、形狀等）相異，不同，有別 SYN **differ**： *The students' work varies considerably in quality.* 學生作業的質量甚是參差不齊。◇ *The quality of the students' work varies considerably.* 學生作業的質量甚是參差不齊。◇ *New techniques were introduced with* ***varying degrees of*** *success.* 引進新技術的成功程度不盡相同。 **2** 0➡ [I] to change or be different according to the situation（根據情況）變化，變更，改變： **~ with sth** *The menu varies with the season.* 菜單隨季節而變動。◇ **~ according to sth** *Prices vary according to the type of room you require.* 價格隨要求的房間類型而有所變化。◇ **~ from sth to sth** | **~ (between A and B)** *Class numbers vary between 25 and 30.* 班級的數目從 25 到 30 不等。◇ *'What time do you start work?' '****It varies.****'* "你幾點鐘開始工作？" "沒準兒。" **3** 0➡ [T] **~ sth** to make changes to sth to make it slightly different （略為）變更，改變： *The job enables me to vary the hours I work.* 這項工作使我能夠調整工作時間。

vas·cu·lar /ˈvæskjələ(r)/ *adj.* [usually before noun] (*technical* 術語) of or containing VEINS (= the tubes that carry liquids around the bodies of animals and plants) 血管的；脈管的；維管的

vas def·er·ens /ˌvæs ˈdefərenz/ *noun* (*pl.* **vasa def·er·en·tia** /ˌveɪsə defəˈrenʃiə/) (*anatomy* 解) the tube through which SPERM pass from the TESTIS on their way out of the body 輸精管

vase /vɑːz; *NAmE* veɪs; veɪz/ *noun* a container made of glass, etc., used for holding cut flowers or as a decorative object 花瓶；裝飾瓶：*a vase of flowers* 一瓶花 ➲ VISUAL VOCAB page V21

vas·ec·tomy /vəˈsektəmi/ *noun* (*pl.* **-ies**) (*medical* 醫) a medical operation to remove part of each of the tubes in a man's body that carry SPERM, after which he is not able to make a woman pregnant 輸精管切除術

Vas·el·ine™ /ˈvæsəliːn/ *noun* [U] a thick soft clear substance that is used on skin to heal or protect it, or as a LUBRICANT to stop surfaces from sticking together 凡士林

vaso·con·stric·tion /ˌveɪzəʊkənˈstrɪkʃn; *NAmE* -zoʊ-/ *noun* [U] (*biology* 生 or *medical* 醫) a process in which BLOOD VESSELS become narrower, which tends to increase BLOOD PRESSURE 血管收縮（而導致血壓增高）

vaso·di·lation /ˌveɪzəʊdaɪˈleɪʃn; *NAmE* -zoʊ-/ *noun* [U] (*biology* 生 or *medical* 醫) a process in which BLOOD VESSELS become wider, which tends to reduce BLOOD PRESSURE 血管舒張（而導致血壓降低）

vas·sal /ˈvæsl/ *noun* **1** a man in the Middle Ages who promised to fight for and be loyal to a king or other powerful owner of land, in return for being given land to live on 封臣，家臣（中世紀為國王或其他權貴效忠的受封者） **2** a country that depends on and is controlled by another country 附庸國；屬國

vast 0➡ /vɑːst; *NAmE* væst/ *adj.* extremely large in area, size, amount, etc. 遼闊的；巨大的；龐大的；大量的 SYN **huge**： *a vast area of forest* 莽莽蒼蒼的森林 ◇ *a vast crowd* 一大群人 ◇ *a vast amount of information* 大量信息 ◇ *At dusk bats appear* ***in vast numbers.*** 蝙蝠於傍晚時分大批出現。◇ *His business empire was vast.* 他的企業規模龐大。◇ *In* ***the vast majority*** *of cases, this should not be a problem.* 在絕大多數情況下，這應該不成問題。 ▶ **vast·ness** *noun* [U, C]： *the vastness of space* 太空的浩瀚無垠

vast·ly /ˈvɑːstli; *NAmE* ˈvæstli/ *adv.* very much 非常；很： *I'm a vastly different person now.* 我現在已判若兩人了。◇ *The quality of the training has vastly improved.* 訓練的質量已經大幅度提高。

VAT /ˌviː eɪ ˈtiː; væt/ *noun* [U] (*BrE*) the abbreviation for 'value added tax' (a tax that is added to the price of goods and services) 增值稅（全寫為 value added tax）： *Prices include VAT.* 價格中含增值稅。◇ *£27.50 + VAT* * 27.50 英鎊加增值稅

vat /væt/ *noun* a large container for holding liquids, especially in industrial processes （尤指工業用）大桶，大盆，甕，缸，罐： *distilling vats* 蒸餾罐 ◇ *a vat of whisky* 一大桶威士忌

Vati·can /ˈvætɪkən/ *noun* **the Vatican** **1** [sing.] the group of buildings in Rome where the POPE lives and works 梵蒂岡（羅馬教宗居住和辦公的地方） **2** [sing. +sing./pl. v.] the centre of government of the Roman Catholic Church 梵蒂岡（羅馬天主教教廷）

vaude·ville /ˈvɔːdəvɪl/ *noun* [U] **1** (*NAmE*) = VARIETY (4) **2** (*BrE* also **ˈmusic hall**) a type of entertainment popular in the late 19th and early 20th centuries, including singing, dancing and comedy （流行於 19 世紀末 20 世紀初的）歌舞雜耍表演

ˈvaudeville theater (*NAmE*) (*BrE* **ˈmusic hall**) *noun* a theatre used for popular entertainment in the late 19th and early 20th centuries 歌舞雜耍戲院

vault /vɔːlt/ *noun, verb*

■ ***noun*** **1** a room with thick walls and a strong door, especially in a bank, used for keeping valuable things safe （尤指銀行的）金庫，保險庫 **2** a room under a church or in a CEMETERY, used for burying people （教堂的）地下墓室；（墳地的）墓穴 **3** a roof or ceiling in the form of an ARCH or a series of ARCHES 拱頂；穹隆 **4** a jump made by vaulting 撐物跳高；撐杆跳 ➲ see also POLE VAULT

■ ***verb*** [I, T] to jump over an object in a single movement, using your hands or a pole to push you （用手支撐或撐杆）跳躍，騰躍： **~ over sth** *She vaulted over the gate and ran up the path.* 她用手一撐躍過柵欄門沿着小路跑去。◇ **~ sth** *to vault a fence* 躍過籬笆牆 ➲ see also POLE VAULT

vault·ed /ˈvɔːltɪd/ *adj.* (*architecture* 建) made in the shape of an ARCH or a series of ARCHES; having a ceiling or roof of this shape 拱形的；有拱頂的： *a vaulted ceiling/cellar* 拱形天花板／地窖 ➲ VISUAL VOCAB page V14

vault·ing /ˈvɔːltɪŋ/ *noun* [U] (*architecture* 建) a pattern of ARCHES in a ceiling or roof （天花板或屋頂的）拱形結構

ˈvaulting horse (also **horse**) *noun* a large object with legs, and sometimes handles, that GYMNASTS use to vault over （體操器械）跳馬

vaunt·ed /ˈvɔːntɪd/ *adj.* [usually before noun] (*formal*) proudly talked about or praised as being very good, especially when this is not deserved 被吹噓的；被誇耀的： *Their* ***much vaunted*** *reforms did not materialize.* 他們大肆吹噓的改革並沒有實現。

V

va-va-voom /ˌvɑː vɑː ˈvuːm; ˌvæ væ/ *noun* [U] (*informal*) the quality of being exciting or sexually attractive 令人興奮的特性；性感 **ORIGIN** First used in the 1950s in the US to represent the sound of a car engine running. * 20 世紀 50 年代在美國首次使用，表示汽車發動機運轉的聲音。

VC /ˌviː ˈsiː/ *noun* [sing.] the abbreviation for 'Victoria Cross' (a MEDAL for special courage that is given to members of the British and Commonwealth armed forces) 維多利亞十字勳章（全寫為 Victoria Cross，授予英國和聯邦軍隊中特別英勇的官兵）：*He was awarded the VC.* 他榮獲維多利亞十字勳章。◇ *Col James Blunt VC* 維多利亞十字勳章獲得者詹姆斯 • 布倫特上校

ˈV-chip *noun* a computer chip in a television RECEIVER that can be programmed to block material that contains sex and violence 頻道鎖碼，V 芯片，暴力晶片（裝入電視接收器阻斷含有色情和暴力內容的節目）

VCR /ˌviː siː ˈɑː(r)/ *noun* (*especially NAmE*) the abbreviation for 'video cassette recorder' (a machine which is used to play videos or to record programmes from a television) 錄像機（全寫為 video cassette recorder）：*Don't forget to program the VCR.* 別忘了對錄像機進行預設。

VD /ˌviː ˈdiː/ *abbr.* VENEREAL DISEASE

VDU /ˌviː diː ˈjuː/ (*BrE*) (*NAmE* **VDT** /ˌviː diː ˈtiː/) *noun* the abbreviation for 'visual display unit/video display terminal' (a machine with a screen like a television that displays information from a computer) 直觀顯示器，視頻顯示終端（全寫為 visual display unit/video display terminal，用以顯示計算機信息）

veal /viːl/ *noun* [U] meat from a CALF (= a young cow) 小牛肉；牛犢肉

vec·tor /ˈvektə(r)/ *noun* **1** (*mathematics* 數) a quantity that has both size and direction 矢量；向量：*Acceleration and velocity are both vectors.* 加速度和速度都是矢量。➲ compare SCALAR **2** (*biology* 生) an insect, etc. that carries a particular disease from one living thing to another（傳染疾病的）介體，載體 **3** (*technical* 術語) a course taken by an aircraft（航空器的）航線

Veda /ˈveɪdə; ˈviːdə/ *noun* an ancient holy text of Hinduism《吠陀》（印度教古經文）

Vedic /ˈveɪdɪk; ˈviːd-/ *adj., noun*
- **adj.** relating to the Vedas《吠陀》有關的
- **noun** [U] the language of the Vedas 吠陀梵語

vee·jay /ˈviː dʒeɪ/ *noun* = VIDEO JOCKEY

veep /viːp/ *noun* (*NAmE, informal*) VICE-PRESIDENT 副總統

veer /vɪə(r); *NAmE* vɪr/ *verb* **1** [I] **+ adv./prep.** (especially of a vehicle 尤指車輛) to change direction suddenly 突然變向；猛然轉向 **SYN** **swerve**：*The bus veered onto the wrong side of the road.* 公共汽車突然駛入了逆行道。**2** [I] **+ adv./prep.** (of a conversation or way of behaving or thinking 說話、行為或思想) to change in the way it develops 偏離；改變；轉變：*The debate veered away from the main topic of discussion.* 爭論脱離了討論的主題。◇ *His emotions veered between fear and anger.* 他的情緒變化不定，一會兒恐懼一會兒生氣。**3** [I] **+ adv./prep.** (*technical* 術語) (of the wind 風) to change direction 改變方向：*The wind veered to the west.* 風向轉西。

veg /vedʒ/ *noun, verb*
- **noun** [U, C] (*pl.* **veg**) (*BrE, informal*) a vegetable or vegetables 蔬菜：*a fruit and veg stall* 水果蔬菜攤位 ◇ *He likes the traditional **meat and two veg** for his main meal.* 他主餐喜歡傳統的一葷兩素。
- **verb** (**-gg-**)

PHR V **ˌveg ˈout** (*informal*) to relax by doing sth that needs very little effort, for example watching television 消遣；休閒

vegan /ˈviːɡən/ *noun* a person who does not eat any animal products such as meat, milk or eggs. Some vegans do not use animal products such as silk or leather. 嚴格素食主義者（不吃肉、奶、蛋等，有的不用動物產品）

Vege·bur·ger™ /ˈvedʒibɜːɡə(r); *NAmE* -bɜːrɡ-/ *noun* = VEGGIE BURGER

Vege·mite™ /ˈvedʒɪmaɪt/ *noun* [U] (*AustralE, NZE*) a dark substance made from YEAST, spread on bread, etc. 維吉米特黑醬（用酵母製成，塗於麪包等上）

vege·table 🔑 /ˈvedʒtəbl/ *noun*
1 🔑 (also *informal* **veg·gie** especially in *NAmE*) a plant or part of a plant that is eaten as food. Potatoes, BEANS and onions are all vegetables. 蔬菜：***green vegetables*** (= for example CABBAGE) 綠色蔬菜 ◇ ***root vegetables*** (= for example CARROTS) 塊根蔬菜 ◇ *a salad of raw vegetables* 生菜色拉 ◇ *a **vegetable garden/patch/plot*** 菜園；菜畦；菜地 ◇ *vegetable matter* (= plants in general) 植物質 ➲ VISUAL VOCAB page V31 ➲ compare ANIMAL *n.* (3), FRUIT *n.* (1), MINERAL (1) **2** (*BrE* also **cab·bage**) a person who is physically alive but not capable of much mental or physical activity, for example because of an accident or illness 植物人：*Severe brain damage turned him into a vegetable.* 嚴重的腦損傷使他變成了植物人。**3** a person who has a boring life 生活單調乏味的人：*Since losing my job I've been a vegetable.* 失業以來我感到百無聊賴。

vege·tal /ˈvedʒətl/ *adj.* (*formal*) connected with plants 植物有關的

vege·tar·ian /ˌvedʒəˈteəriən; *NAmE* -ˈter-/ (also *BrE informal* **veg·gie**) *noun* a person who does not eat meat or fish 素食者；吃素的人：*Is she a vegetarian?* 她是素食者嗎？➲ compare FRUITARIAN, HERBIVORE ▶ **vege·tar·ian** *adj.*：*Are you vegetarian?* 你只吃素食嗎？◇ *a vegetarian diet* (= with no meat or fish in it) 素食食譜 ◇ *a vegetarian restaurant* (= that serves no meat or fish) 素食餐館 **vege·tar·ian·ism** /-ɪzəm/ *noun* [U]

vege·tate /ˈvedʒəteɪt/ *verb* [I] (of a person 人) to spend time doing very little and feeling bored 過無聊生活；無所用心

vege·tated /ˈvedʒəteɪtɪd/ *adj.* having the amount of plant life mentioned 有…植物的；植物…的：*a **densely/sparsely vegetated** area* 植物茂密的／稀疏的地區

vege·ta·tion /ˌvedʒəˈteɪʃn/ *noun* [U] plants in general, especially the plants that are found in a particular area or environment（統稱）植物；（尤指某地或環境的）植被，植物群落，草木：*The hills are covered in lush green vegetation.* 這片丘嶺草木茂盛，鬱鬱葱葱。

vege·ta·tive /ˈvedʒɪtətɪv; *NAmE* -teɪtɪv/ *adj.* **1** relating to plant life 植物的；植物性的 **2** (*medical* 醫) (of a person 人) alive but showing no sign of brain activity 植物人狀態的 ➲ see also PERSISTENT VEGETATIVE STATE

veg·gie /ˈvedʒi/ *noun* (*informal*) **1** (*BrE*) = VEGETARIAN：*He's turned veggie* (= become a vegetarian). 他改吃素了。**2** (*especially NAmE*) = VEGETABLE (1) ▶ **veg·gie** *adj.*

ˈveggie burger (also **Vege·bur·ger™**) *noun* a BURGER made with vegetables, especially BEANS, instead of meat 素漢堡包

vehe·ment /ˈviːəmənt/ *adj.* showing very strong feelings, especially anger（感情）強烈的，激烈的；（尤指）憤怒的 **SYN** **forceful**：*a **vehement denial/attack/protest, etc.*** 強烈的否認、攻擊、抗議等 ◇ *He had been vehement in his opposition to the idea.* 他一直強烈反對這一主張。▶ **vehe·mence** /-məns/ *noun* [U] **vehe·ment·ly** *adv.*：*The charge was vehemently denied.* 這一指責遭到了斷然否認。

ve·hicle 🔑 **AW** /ˈviːəkl; *NAmE* also ˈviːhɪkl/ *noun*
1 🔑 (rather *formal*) a thing that is used for transporting people or goods from one place to another, such as a car or lorry/truck 交通工具；車輛：*motor vehicles* (= cars, buses, lorries/trucks, etc.) 機動車輛 ◇ *Are you the driver of this vehicle?* 你是這輛汽車的駕駛員嗎？◇ *rows of parked vehicles* 一排排停放的車輛 ➲ VISUAL VOCAB pages V57, V58 **2 ~ (for sth)** something that can be used to express your ideas or feelings or as a way of achieving sth（賴以表達思想、感情或達到目的的）手段，工具：*Art may be used as a vehicle for propaganda.* 藝術可以用作宣傳的工具。◇ *The play is an ideal vehicle for her talents.* 這部戲是她施展才華的理想機會。

ve·hicu·lar /vəˈhɪkjələ(r); *NAmE* viːˈh-/ *adj.* (*formal*) intended for vehicles or consisting of vehicles 供車輛等使用的；車輛的；運輸工具的：*vehicular access* 車輛入口 ◇ *The road is closed to vehicular traffic.* 此路禁止車輛通行。

veil /veɪl/ *noun, verb*

■ ***noun*** **1** a covering of very thin transparent material worn, especially by women, to protect or hide the face, or as part of a hat, etc.（尤指女用的）面紗，面罩：*a bridal veil* 新娘的面紗 **2** a piece of cloth worn by NUNS over the head and shoulders （修女的）頭巾 **3** [sing.] (*formal*) something that stops you from learning the truth about a situation 掩飾；掩蓋；藉口；託辭：*Their work is carried out behind a veil of secrecy.* 他們的工作是在秘密掩護下進行的。◇ *It would be better to* ***draw a veil*** *over what happened next* (= not talk about it). 最好把之後發生的事情掩蓋起來。 **4** [sing.] (*formal*) a thin layer that stops you from seeing sth 薄薄的遮蓋層：*The mountain tops were hidden beneath a veil of mist.* 山頂籠罩在薄霧中。

IDM **take the 'veil** (*old-fashioned*) to become a NUN 當修女

■ ***verb*** **1 ~ sth/yourself** to cover your face with a veil 戴面紗；戴面罩 **2 ~ sth** (*literary*) to cover sth with sth that hides it partly or completely 遮掩；掩飾 SYN **shroud**：*A fine drizzle began to veil the hills.* 濛濛的細雨漸漸籠罩了群山。

veiled /veɪld/ *adj.* **1** not expressed directly or clearly because you do not want your meaning to be obvious 含蓄的；掩飾的：*a* ***thinly veiled*** *threat* 幾乎不加掩飾的威脅 ◇ *She made a* ***veiled reference to*** *his past mistakes.* 她含蓄地提到了他過去所犯的錯誤。 **2** wearing a veil 戴面紗的；蒙面的：*a mysterious veiled woman* 戴面紗的神秘女人

vein /veɪn/ *noun* **1** [C] any of the tubes that carry blood from all parts of the body towards the heart 靜脈：*the jugular vein* 頸靜脈 ➲ compare ARTERY (1) ➲ see also DEEP VEIN THROMBOSIS, VARICOSE VEIN **2** [C] any of the very thin tubes that form the frame of a leaf or an insect's wing 葉脈；翅脈 **3** [C] a narrow strip of a different colour in some types of stone, wood and cheese 紋理；紋路；條紋 **4** [C] a thin layer of minerals or metal contained in rock 礦脈；礦脈牀；礦層；岩脈：*a vein of gold* 金礦脈 SYN **seam** **5** [sing.] **~ (of sth)** an amount of a particular quality or feature in sth （某種素質或特徵的）量：*They had tapped a rich vein of information in his secretary.* 他們從他的秘書那裏摸到了大量信息。 **6** [sing., U] a particular style or manner 風格；方式：*A number of other people commented* ***in a similar vein.*** 其他一些人也以類似的腔調評論。◇ *'And that's not all,' he continued in angry vein.* "那還不算全部呢。"他生氣地繼續說道。

veined /veɪnd/ *adj.* having or marked with veins or thin lines 有靜脈的；有葉脈的；有翅脈的；有紋理的：*thin blue-veined hands* 青筋暴突的瘦弱的雙手 ◇ *veined marble* 有紋理的大理石

vein·ing /'veɪnɪŋ/ *noun* [U] a pattern of veins or thin lines 靜脈紋；紋理：*the blue veining in Gorgonzola cheese* 戈爾貢佐拉乾酪的藍紋

vein·ous /'veɪnəs/ *adj.* (*technical* 術語) having VEINS that are very noticeable 靜脈明顯的

velar /'viːlə(r)/ *noun* (*phonetics* 語音) a speech sound made by placing the back of the tongue against or near the back part of the mouth, for example /k/ or /g/ in the English words *key* and *go* 軟腭音，舌面後音（如 /k/ 或 /g/） ▸ **velar** *adj.*

Vel·cro™ /'velkrəʊ; *NAmE* -kroʊ/ *noun* [U] a material for fastening clothes, etc. with two different surfaces, one rough and one smooth, that stick to each other when they are pressed together 維可牢搭扣；尼龍搭扣；魔術貼 ➲ VISUAL VOCAB page V63

veld /velt/ *noun* [U] (in South Africa) flat open land with grass and no trees 斐勒得（南非的無樹草原） ➲ compare PAMPAS, PRAIRIE, SAVANNAH, STEPPE

vel·lum /'veləm/ *noun* [U] **1** material made from the skin of a sheep, GOAT or CALF, used for making book covers and, in the past, for writing on （書封或舊時書寫用的）羊皮紙，犢皮紙 **2** smooth cream-coloured paper used for writing on 仿羊皮紙；仿犢皮紙

vel·oci·rap·tor /vəˌlɒsɪ'ræptə(r); *NAmE* -ˌlɑːs-/ *noun* a small DINOSAUR that moved fairly quickly 迅掠龍；疾走龍

vel·ocity /və'lɒsəti; *NAmE* -'lɑːs-/ *noun* [U, C] (*pl.* **-ies**) **1** (*technical* 術語) the speed of sth in a particular direction （沿某一方向的）速度：*the velocity of light* 光速 ◇ *to* ***gain/lose velocity*** 加 / 減速 ◇ *a* ***high-velocity*** *rifle* 高速步槍 **2** (*formal*) high speed 高速；快速：*Jaguars can move with an astonishing velocity.* 美洲豹跑起來速度驚人。

velo·drome /'velədrəʊm; *NAmE* -droʊm/ *noun* a track or building used for cycle racing （自行車或摩托車的）賽車場

vel·our /və'lʊə(r); *NAmE* və'lʊr/ *noun* [U] a type of silk or cotton cloth with a thick soft surface like VELVET 絲絨；拉絨織物；維羅絨

velum /'viːləm/ *noun* (*pl.* **vela** /'viːlə/) (*anatomy* 解) a layer of TISSUE that covers sth, especially the soft PALATE inside the mouth 罩膜；緣膜

vel·vet /'velvɪt/ *noun* [U] a type of cloth made from silk, cotton or NYLON, with a thick soft surface 絲絨；立絨；經絨；天鵝絨：*a velvet dress* 天鵝絨連衣裙 ◇ *velvet curtains/drapes* 天鵝絨窗簾 / 帷幕 IDM see IRON *adj.*

vel·vet·een /ˌvelvə'tiːn/ *noun* [U] a type of cotton cloth that looks like VELVET but is less expensive 棉絨；平絨；縴絨

vel·vety /'velvəti/ *adj.* pleasantly smooth and soft 光滑柔軟的；柔和的：*velvety skin* 柔軟的皮膚 ◇ *a velvety red wine* 醇厚的紅葡萄酒

vena cava /ˌviːnə 'keɪvə/ *noun* (*pl.* **venae cavae** /ˌviːniː 'keɪviː/) (*anatomy* 解) either of the two VEINS that take blood without OXYGEN in it towards the heart 腔靜脈

venal /'viːnl/ *adj.* (*formal*) prepared to do dishonest or immoral things in return for money 貪贓枉法的；見利忘義的 SYN **corrupt**：*venal journalists* 唯利是圖的記者 ▸ **ve·nal·ity** /viː'næləti/ *noun* [U]

vend /vend/ *verb* **~ sth** (*formal*) to sell sth 售賣

ven·detta /ven'detə/ *noun* **1** a long and violent disagreement between two families or groups, in which people are murdered in return for previous murders 家族世仇；團夥仇殺 SYN **feud** **2 ~ (against sb)** a long argument or disagreement in which one person or group does or says things to harm another 積怨；宿怨；長期不和：*He has accused the media of pursuing a vendetta against him.* 他指責媒體長期跟他過不去。◇ *She conducted a* ***personal vendetta*** *against me.* 她對我有宿仇。

vending machine /'vendɪŋ məʃiːn/ *noun* a machine from which you can buy cigarettes, drinks, etc. by putting coins into it （出售香煙、飲料等的）投幣式自動售貨機

vend·or /'vendə(r)/ *noun* **1** a person who sells things, for example food or newspapers, usually outside on the street 小販；攤販：*street vendors* 街頭小販 **2** (*formal*) a company that sells a particular product （某種產品的）銷售公司：*software vendors* 軟件銷售商 **3** (*law* 律) a person who is selling a house, etc. （房屋等的）賣主 ➲ compare SELLER (1)

ven·eer /və'nɪə(r); *NAmE* və'nɪr/ *noun, verb*

■ ***noun*** **1** [C, U] a thin layer of wood or plastic that is glued to the surface of cheaper wood, especially on a piece of furniture 飾面薄板，薄片鑲飾（尤用於傢具上） **2** [sing.] **~ (of sth)** (*formal*) an outer appearance of a particular quality that hides the true nature of sb/sth 虛假的外表；虛飾：*Her veneer of politeness began to crack.* 她那彬彬有禮的偽裝開始露餡兒了。

■ ***verb*** **~ sth (with/in sth)** to cover the surface of sth with a veneer of wood, etc. （用薄片鑲飾等）飾面，覆蓋

ven·er·able /'venərəbl/ *adj.* **1** (*formal*) **venerable** people or things deserve respect because they are old, important, wise, etc. （因年高、顯要、智慧等）令人尊重的，值得敬重的，受敬佩的：*a venerable old man* 德高望重的老人 ◇ *a venerable institution* 令人仰慕的機構 **2 the Venerable ...** [only before noun] (in the Anglican Church) a title of respect used when talking about an ARCHDEACON （對聖公會吏長的尊稱）尊者：*the*

V

Venerable Martin Roberts 尊者馬丁 • 羅伯茨 **3 the Venerable …** [only before noun] (in the Roman Catholic Church) a title given to a dead person who is very holy but who has not yet been made a SAINT 真福（天主教會對列入聖品前的已故聖潔者的尊稱）

ven·er·ate /ˈvenəreɪt/ *verb* **~ sb/sth (as sth)** (*formal*) to have and show a lot of respect for sb/sth, especially sb/sth that is considered to be holy or very important 敬重；崇敬；敬仰 **SYN** **revere** ▸ **ven·er·ation** /ˌvenəˈreɪʃn/ *noun* [U]： *The relics were objects of veneration.* 這些聖人遺物是備受敬奉之物。

ven·ereal /vəˈnɪəriəl; *NAmE* -ˈnɪr-/ *adj.* [only before noun] relating to diseases spread by sexual contact 性病的；性交傳染的： *a venereal infection* 性傳染病

veˌnereal diˈsease *noun* [C, U] (*abbr.* **VD**) a disease that is caught by having sex with an infected person 性病

ven·etian blind /vəˌniːʃn ˈblaɪnd/ *noun* a BLIND for a window that has flat horizontal plastic or metal strips going across it that you can turn to let in as much light as you want 百葉窗簾 ➲ VISUAL VOCAB page V21

ven·geance /ˈvendʒəns/ *noun* [U] (*formal*) the act of punishing or harming sb in return for what they have done to you, your family or friends 報復；報仇；復仇 **SYN** **revenge**： *a desire for vengeance* 復仇心 ◇ **~ on/upon sb** *to take vengeance on sb* 對某人進行報復 ◇ *He swore vengeance on his child's killer.* 他發誓要找殺害他孩子的兇手報仇。

IDM **with a ˈvengeance** (*informal*) to a greater degree than is expected or usual 程度更深地；出乎意料地： *She set to work with a vengeance.* 她加倍努力地工作起來。

venge·ful /ˈvendʒfl/ *adj.* (*formal*) showing a desire to punish sb who has harmed you 心存報復的；圖謀復仇的 ▸ **venge·ful·ly** /-fəli/ *adv.*

ve·nial /ˈviːniəl/ *adj.* [usually before noun] (*formal*) (of a SIN or mistake 罪過或錯誤) not very serious and therefore able to be forgiven 輕微而可原諒的

ven·ison /ˈvenɪsn; -zn/ *noun* [U] meat from a DEER 鹿肉

Venn diagram 文氏圖

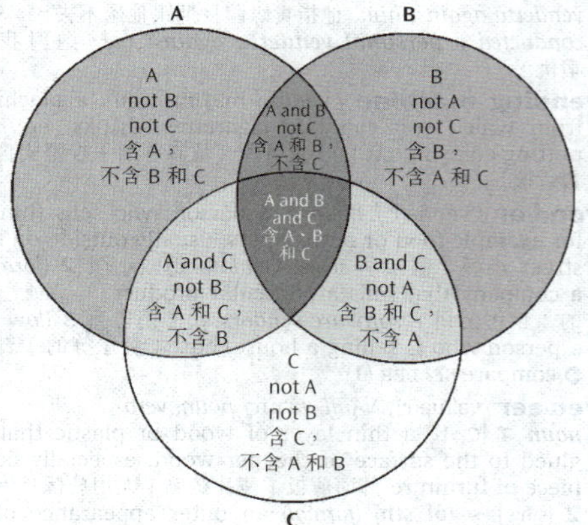

Venn dia·gram /ˈven daɪəgræm/ *noun* (*mathematics* 數) a picture showing SETS (= groups of things that have a shared quality) as circles that cross over each other, to show which qualities the different sets have in common 文氏圖（將集表示為相交的圓，以顯示不同集之間的共同性質）

venom /ˈvenəm/ *noun* [U] **1** the poisonous liquid that some snakes, spiders, etc. produce when they bite or sting you（毒蛇、蜘蛛等分泌的）毒液 **2** (*formal*) strong bitter feeling; hatred and a desire to hurt sb 惡毒；怨恨；惡意；歹心： *a look of pure venom* 惡狠狠的樣子 **IDM** see SPIT *v.*

ven·om·ous /ˈvenəməs/ *adj.* **1** (of a snake, etc. 蛇等) producing venom 分泌毒液的；有毒的 **2** (*formal*) full of bitter feeling or hatred 惡毒的；惡意的；充滿仇恨的： *a venomous look* 惡狠狠的樣子 ▸ **ven·om·ous·ly** *adv.*

ven·ous /ˈviːnəs/ *adj.* (*technical* 術語) of or contained in VEINS (= the tubes that carry liquids around the bodies of animals and plants) 靜脈的；靜脈中的；葉脈的： *venous blood* 靜脈血

vent /vent/ *noun, verb*

▪ ***noun*** **1** an opening that allows air, gas or liquid to pass out of or into a room, building, container, etc.（空氣、氣體、液體的）出口，進口，漏孔： ***air/heating vents*** 通氣孔；熱風孔 ➲ VISUAL VOCAB page V52 ➲ compare REGISTER *n.* (4) **2** (*technical* 術語) the opening in the body of a bird, fish, REPTILE or other small animal, through which waste matter is passed out（鳥、魚等小動物的）肛門 **3** a long thin opening at the bottom of the back or side of a coat or jacket（大衣等的）衩口，開衩，背衩

IDM **give (full) vent to sth** (*formal*) to express a feeling, especially anger, strongly（充分）表達；（淋漓盡致地）發泄： *She gave full vent to her feelings in a violent outburst.* 她大發脾氣以宣泄情緒。

▪ ***verb*** **~ sth (on sb)** (*formal*) to express feelings, especially anger, strongly 表達，發泄（感情，尤指憤怒）： *He vented his anger on the referee.* 他把氣撒在裁判身上。

ven·ti·late /ˈventɪleɪt/ *verb* **1 ~ sth** to allow fresh air to enter and move around a room, building, etc. 使（房間、建築物等）通風；使通氣： *a well-ventilated room* 通風良好的房間 ◇ *The bathroom is ventilated by means of an extractor fan.* 這個浴室使用抽風扇通風。 **2 ~ sth** (*formal*) to express your feelings or opinions publicly 公開表達（感情或意見）**SYN** **air** ▸ **ven·ti·lation** /ˌventɪˈleɪʃn/ *noun* [U]： *a ventilation shaft* 通風井 ◇ *Make sure that there is adequate ventilation in the room before using the paint.* 在使用油漆前確保室內通風充足。

ven·ti·la·tor /ˈventɪleɪtə(r)/ *noun* **1** a device or an opening for letting fresh air come into a room, etc. 通風設備；通風口 **2** a piece of equipment with a PUMP that helps sb to breathe by sending air in and out of their lungs 通氣機；呼吸器： *He was put on a ventilator.* 給他戴上了呼吸器。

ven·tral /ˈventrəl/ *adj.* [only before noun] (*biology* 生) on or connected with the part of a fish or an animal that is underneath (or that in humans faces forward) 腹的；腹部的；腹側的： *a fish's ventral fin* 魚的腹鰭 ➲ VISUAL VOCAB page V12

ven·tricle /ˈventrɪkl/ *noun* (*anatomy* 解) **1** either of the two lower spaces in the heart that PUMP blood to the LUNGS or around the body 心室 ➲ compare AURICLE (1) **2** any hollow space in the body, especially one of four main hollow spaces in the brain（體內的）室，腔；（尤指）腦室

ven·trilo·quism /venˈtrɪləkwɪzəm/ *noun* [U] the art of speaking without moving your lips and of making it look as if your voice is coming from another person 腹語術，口技（嘴唇不動、聲音像來自他人的發聲技巧） ▸ **ven·trilo·quist** /venˈtrɪləkwɪst/ *noun*： *Entertainment included a ventriloquist.* 演出的包括一名口技表演者。◇ *a ventriloquist's dummy* 表演口技用的傀儡

ven·ture 0‑π /ˈventʃə(r)/ *noun, verb*

▪ ***noun*** a business project or activity, especially one that involves taking risks（尤指有風險的）企業，商業，投機活動，經營項目 **SYN** **undertaking**： *A disastrous business venture lost him thousands of dollars.* 一個徹底失敗的經營項目使他損失嚴重。 ➲ see also JOINT VENTURE

▪ ***verb*** **1** 0‑π [I] **+ adv./prep.** to go somewhere even though you know that it might be dangerous or unpleasant 敢於去（危險或令人不快的地方）： *They ventured nervously into the water.* 他們緊張地硬着頭皮下水。◇ *He's never ventured abroad in his life.* 他一生中從來不敢出國。 **2** [T] (*formal*) to say or do sth in a careful way, especially because it might upset or offend sb 小心地說，謹慎地做（尤指會使人煩惱或不快的事）： **~ sth** *She*

V

hardly dared to venture an opinion. 她幾乎不敢亮明觀點。◇ **~ to do sth** *I ventured to suggest that she might have made a mistake.* 我小心地提醒說她可能出了差錯。◇ **+ speech** *'And if I say no?' she ventured.* "那麼我要是說不呢？" 她試探說。◇ **~ that ...** *He ventured that the data might be flawed.* 他大膽地推測說數據可能有誤差。 **3** [T] **~ sth** (**on sth**) to risk losing sth valuable or important if you are not successful at sth 冒着（失去貴重或重要的東西）的危險 SYN **gamble**： *It was wrong to venture his financial security on such a risky deal.* 他以自己穩定的財政作賭注去做風險這麼大的交易是錯誤的。

IDM **nothing 'ventured, nothing 'gained** (*saying*) used to say that you have to take risks if you want to achieve things and be successful 不敢冒險就一事無成；不入虎穴，焉得虎子

PHR V **'venture into/on sth** to do sth, even though it involves risks 冒險做： *This is the first time the company has ventured into movie production.* 這是這家公司首次涉足電影製作。

'venture capital *noun* [U] (*business* 商) money that is invested in a new company to help it develop, which may involve a lot of risk 風險資本（投入新公司的資金，風險很大） ➲ compare WORKING CAPITAL

'Venture Scout (*BrE*) (*US* **Ex'plorer Scout**) *noun* a member of the senior branch of the SCOUT ASSOCIATION for young people between the ages of 15 or 16 and 20 深資童軍，奮進童子軍（15 或 16 歲至 20 歲）

ven·ture·some /'ventʃəsəm; *NAmE* -tʃərs-/ *adj.* (*formal* or *literary*) willing to take risks 大膽的；好冒險的 SYN **daring**

venue /'venjuː/ *noun* a place where people meet for an organized event, for example a concert, sporting event or conference 活動場地（如音樂廳、體育比賽場館、會場）： *The band will be playing at 20 different venues on their UK tour.* 這個樂隊在英國巡迴演出期間將在 20 個不同的地點演出。◇ *Please note the change of venue for this event.* 請注意：這次比賽易地進行。 ➲ SYNONYMS at PLACE

Venus /'viːnəs/ *noun* the planet in the SOLAR SYSTEM that is second in order of distance from the sun, between Mercury and the earth 金星；太白星

Venus fly·trap /ˌviːnəs 'flaɪtræp/ *noun* a small CARNIVOROUS (= flesh-eating) plant with leaves that trap insects by closing quickly around them 捕蠅草（用葉子捕捉後消化昆蟲）

ver·acity /və'ræsəti/ *noun* [U] (*formal*) the quality of being true; the habit of telling the truth 真實；真實性；誠實 SYN **truth, truthfulness**： *They questioned the veracity of her story.* 他們質疑她所述事情的真實性。

ver·anda (also **ver·an·dah**) /və'rændə/ *noun* **1** (*especially BrE*) (*NAmE* usually **porch**) a platform with an open front and a roof, built onto the side of a house on the ground floor （房屋底層有頂半敞的）走廊，遊廊： *After dinner, we sat talking on the veranda.* 飯後我們坐在遊廊上交談。 **2** (*AustralE, NZE*) a roof over the part of the street where people walk in front of a shop/store （店鋪面街上方的）遮簷，遊廊 SYN **awning**

verb /vɜːb; *NAmE* vɜːrb/ *noun* (*grammar* 語法) a word or group of words that expresses an action (such as *eat*), an event (such as *happen*) or a state (such as *exist*) 動詞： ***regular/irregular verbs*** 規則 / 不規則動詞 ◇ ***transitive/intransitive verbs*** 及物 / 不及物動詞 ➲ see also PHRASAL VERB

ver·bal /'vɜːbl; *NAmE* 'vɜːrbl/ *adj.* **1** relating to words 文字的；言語的；詞語的： *The job applicant must have good verbal skills.* 應聘這份工作的人必須具有良好的語言表達技能。◇ *non-verbal communication* (= expressions of the face, GESTURES, etc.) 非語言交際 **2** spoken, not written 口頭（而非書面）的： *a **verbal agreement/warning*** 口頭協議 / 警告 ◇ *verbal instructions* 口頭指示 ➲ compare ORAL *adj.* (1) **3** (*grammar* 語法) relating to verbs 動詞的： *a verbal noun* 動名詞

ver·bal·ize (*BrE* also **-ise**) /'vɜːbəlaɪz; *NAmE* 'vɜːrb-/ *verb* [T, I] **~** (**sth**) (*formal*) to express your feelings or ideas in words 用言語（或文字）表達 SYN **put into words**： *He's a real genius but he has difficulty verbalizing his ideas.* 他確實是個天才，可是難以用語言表達他的思想。

ver·bal·ly /'vɜːbəli; *NAmE* 'vɜːrb-/ *adv.* in spoken words and not in writing or actions 口頭上（而非書面或行動上）： *The company had received complaints both verbally and in writing.* 這家公司收到了口頭和書面的投訴。

ver·ba·tim /vɜː'beɪtɪm; *NAmE* vɜːr'b-/ *adj., adv.* exactly as spoken or written 一字不差的（地）；逐字的（地） SYN **word for word**： *a verbatim report* 一字不差的報告 ◇ *He reported the speech verbatim.* 他逐字報道了那篇講話。

ver·bena /vɜː'biːnə; *NAmE* vɜːr'b-/ *noun* [U, C] a garden plant with bright flowers 馬鞭草（庭院花卉，花鮮豔）

ver·bi·age /'vɜːbiɪdʒ; *NAmE* 'vɜːrb-/ *noun* [U] (*formal, disapproving*) the use of too many words, or of more difficult words than are needed, to express an idea 連篇累贅；晦澀難懂

ver·bose /vɜː'bəʊs; *NAmE* vɜːr'boʊs/ *adj.* (*formal, disapproving*) using or containing more words than are needed 冗長的；囉嗦的；嘮叨的 SYN **long-winded**： *a verbose speaker/style* 囉裏囉嗦的演講者；長篇大論 ▸ **ver·bos·ity** /vɜː'bɒsəti; *NAmE* vɜːr'bɑːs-/ *noun* [U]

ver·dant /'vɜːdnt; *NAmE* 'vɜːrdnt/ *adj.* (*literary*) (of grass, plants, fields, etc. 草、植物、田地等) fresh and green 嫩綠的；碧綠的；青翠的

ver·dict /'vɜːdɪkt; *NAmE* 'vɜːrd-/ *noun* **1** a decision that is made by a JURY in court, stating if sb is considered guilty of a crime or not （陪審團的）裁定，裁決，裁斷： *Has the jury **reached a verdict**?* 陪審團作出裁定了嗎？◇ *The jury **returned a verdict*** (= gave a verdict) *of guilty.* 陪審團作出了有罪的裁決。 ➲ COLLOCATIONS at JUSTICE ➲ see also MAJORITY VERDICT, OPEN VERDICT **2 ~** (**on sth/sb**) a decision that you make or an opinion that you give about sth, after you have tested it or considered it carefully （經過檢驗或認真考慮後的）決定，結論，意見： *The coroner **recorded a verdict** of accidental death.* 驗屍官得出了意外死亡的結論。◇ *The panel will **give their verdict** on the latest video releases.* 專題組將就最近發行的錄像提出他們的意見。◇ *Well, what's your verdict?* 那麼，你有何意見呢？

ver·di·gris /'vɜːdɪgriː; -griːs; *NAmE* 'vɜːrd-/ *noun* [U] the greenish substance which forms, for example on roofs, when COPPER reacts with the air 銅綠，鹼性碳酸銅（銅遇空氣發生反應形成）

ver·dure /'vɜːdjə(r); *NAmE* 'vɜːrd-/ *noun* [U] (*literary*) thick green plants growing in a particular place 青蔥的草木；鬱鬱蔥蔥的植物

verge /vɜːdʒ; *NAmE* vɜːrdʒ/ *noun, verb*

■ ***noun*** (*BrE*) a piece of grass at the edge of a path, road, etc. （路邊的）小草地，綠地： *a grass verge* 長了草的路邊 ➲ compare SOFT SHOULDER

IDM **on/to the verge of sth/of doing sth** very near to the moment when sb does sth or sth happens 瀕於；接近於；行將： *He was on the verge of tears.* 他差點兒哭了出來。◇ *They are on the verge of signing a new contract.* 他們即將簽訂一份新的合同。

■ ***verb***

PHR V **'verge on sth** to be very close to an extreme state or condition 極接近；瀕於 SYN **border on sth**： *Some of his suggestions verged on the outrageous.* 他的一些建議都快到了荒唐的地步。

ver·ger /'vɜːdʒə(r); *NAmE* 'vɜːrdʒ-/ *noun* (*especially BrE*) an official whose job is to take care of the inside of a church and to perform some simple duties during church services 教堂司事

ver·ify /'verɪfaɪ/ *verb* (**veri·fies, veri·fy·ing, veri·fied, veri·fied**) (*formal*) **1** to check that sth is true or accurate 核實；查對；核準： **~ sth** *We have no way of verifying his story.* 我們無法核實他的說法。◇ **~ that ...** *Please verify that there is sufficient memory available before loading the program.* 請在核實有足夠的內存後再安裝程序。◇ **~ whether, what, etc. ...** *I'll leave you to verify whether these claims are true.* 我讓你來查核這些說法是否屬實。 **2 ~ sth | ~ that ...** to show or say that sth is true or accurate 證明；證實 SYN **confirm**： *Her version of events was verified by neighbours.* 她對這些事件的說

V

法已得到鄰居的證實。▸ **veri·fi·able** /ˈverɪfaɪəbl/ *adj.*：*a verifiable fact* 可核實的事實 **veri·fi·ca·tion** /ˌverɪfɪˈkeɪʃn/ *noun* [U]：*the verification of hypotheses* 對假說的證實

ver·ily /ˈverɪli/ *adv.* (*old use*) really; truly 真正地；真實地

veri·sim·ili·tude /ˌverɪsɪˈmɪlɪtjuːd; *NAmE* -tuːd/ *noun* [U] (*formal*) the quality of seeming to be true or real 貌似真實；逼真 SYN **authenticity**：*To add verisimilitude, the stage is covered with sand for the desert scenes.* 為了更加逼真，舞台上鋪滿了沙子作為沙漠的場景。

ver·it·able /ˈverɪtəbl/ *adj.* [only before noun] (*formal* or *humorous*) a word used to emphasize that sb/sth can be compared to sb/sth else that is more exciting, more impressive, etc. 十足的；名副其實的；不折不扣的 SYN **positive**：*The meal that followed was a veritable banquet.* 隨後擺上的飯菜儼然是一桌宴席。

ver·ity /ˈverəti/ *noun* (*pl.* **-ies**) **1** [usually pl.] (*formal*) a belief or principle about life that is accepted as true（關於生命的）信念，準則，真理：*the* ***eternal verities*** *of life* 生命永恆的真理 **2** [U] (*old use*) truth 真理；客觀事實

vermi·celli /ˌvɜːmɪˈtʃeli; *NAmE* ˌvɜːrm-/ *noun* [U] **1** PASTA in the shape of very thin sticks, often broken into small pieces and added to soups 意大利細麪條（常折碎做湯等） **2** (*BrE*) small pieces of chocolate in the shape of very thin sticks broken into pieces, used to decorate cakes 碎條巧克力（用以裝飾糕點）

ver·mil·ion /vəˈmɪliən; *NAmE* vərˈm-/ *adj.* bright red in colour 鮮紅的；朱紅的 ▸ **ver·mil·ion** *noun* [U]

ver·min /ˈvɜːmɪn; *NAmE* ˈvɜːrmɪn/ *noun* [pl.] **1** wild animals or birds that destroy plants or food, or attack farm animals and birds 害獸；害鳥：*On farms the fox is considered vermin and treated as such.* 在農場裏狐狸被當成有害動物來對待。 **2** insects that live on the bodies of animals and sometimes humans 體外寄生蟲；害蟲：*The room was crawling with vermin.* 這房間裏蝨蚤橫行。 **3** (*disapproving*) people who are very unpleasant or dangerous to society 蟊賊；歹徒；害人蟲

ver·min·ous /ˈvɜːmɪnəs; *NAmE* ˈvɜːrm-/ *adj.* (*formal*) covered with vermin 有害蟲的；佈滿寄生蟲的

ver·mouth /ˈvɜːməθ; *NAmE* vərˈmuːθ/ *noun* [U] a strong wine, flavoured with HERBS and spices, often mixed with other drinks as a COCKTAIL 味美思酒，苦艾酒（以多種香草製成，常用以調配雞尾酒）

ver·nacu·lar /vəˈnækjələ(r); *NAmE* vərˈn-/ *noun* **1** (usually **the vernacular**) [sing.] the language spoken in a particular area or by a particular group, especially one that is not the official or written language 方言；土語 **2** [U] (*technical* 術語) a style of ARCHITECTURE concerned with ordinary houses rather than large public buildings（建築的）民間風格 ▸ **ver·nacu·lar** *adj.*

ver·nal /ˈvɜːnl; *NAmE* ˈvɜːrnl/ *adj.* [only before noun] (*formal* or *literary*) connected with the season of spring 春季的：*the vernal equinox* 春分

V

ver·nis·sage /ˌvɜːnɪˈsɑːʒ; *NAmE* ˌvɜːrn-/ *noun* (*pl.* **ver·nis·sages** /ˌvɜːnɪˈsɑːʒ; *NAmE* ˌvɜːrn-/) an occasion when a few invited people can look at paintings before they go on show to the public（畫展開幕前的）特邀來賓觀摩

ver·ruca /vəˈruːkə/ (*BrE*) (*NAmE* **ˈplantar wart**) *noun* a small hard lump like a WART on the bottom of the foot, which can be easily spread from person to person（長在腳底上，容易傳染的）疣

ver·sa·tile /ˈvɜːsətaɪl; *NAmE* ˈvɜːrsətl/ *adj.* (*approving*) **1** (of a person 人) able to do many different things 多才多藝的；有多種技能的；多面手的：*He's a versatile actor who has played a wide variety of parts.* 他是個多才多藝的演員，扮演過各種各樣的角色。 **2** (of food, a building, etc. 食物、建築物等) having many different uses 多用途的；多功能的：*Eggs are easy to cook and are an extremely versatile food.* 雞蛋容易烹煮，怎麼做着吃都行。 ▸ **ver·sa·til·ity** /ˌvɜːsəˈtɪləti; *NAmE* ˌvɜːrs-/ *noun* [U]：*She is a designer of extraordinary versatility.* 她是位特別多才多藝的設計師。

verse /vɜːs; *NAmE* vɜːrs/ *noun* **1** [U] writing that is arranged in lines, often with a regular rhythm or pattern of RHYME 詩；韻文 SYN **poetry**：*Most of the play is written in verse, but some of it is in prose.* 這劇本大部份是用韻文寫的，不過有一些是用散文。 ➲ see also BLANK VERSE, FREE VERSE **2** [C] a group of lines that form a unit in a poem or song 詩節；歌曲的段落：*a hymn with six verses* 一首六節的讚美詩 **3 verses** [pl.] (*old-fashioned*) poetry 詩：*a book of comic verses* 打油詩集 **4** [C] any one of the short NUMBERED divisions of a chapter in the Bible（《聖經》的）節 IDM see CHAPTER

versed /vɜːst; *NAmE* vɜːrst/ *adj.* **~ in sth** having a lot of knowledge about sth, or skill at sth 精通的；熟練的 SYN **expert in**, **practised in**：*He was* ***well versed in*** *employment law.* 他精通雇傭法。

ver·si·fi·ca·tion /ˌvɜːsɪfɪˈkeɪʃn; *NAmE* ˌvɜːrs-/ *noun* [U] (*formal*) the art of writing poetry in a particular pattern; the pattern in which poetry is written 詩格；詩律；詩體；韻律

vers·ify /ˈvɜːsɪfaɪ; *NAmE* ˈvɜːrs-/ *verb* (**ver·si·fies**, **ver·si·fy·ing**, **ver·si·fied**, **ver·si·fied**) [I, T] **~ (sth)** (*formal*, sometimes *disapproving*) to write sth in verse 以詩體寫 ▸ **ver·si·fier** *noun*

ver·sion 0‑ AW /ˈvɜːʃn; -ʒn; *NAmE* ˈvɜːrʒn/ *noun* **1** 0‑ a form of sth that is slightly different from an earlier form or from other forms of the same thing 變體；變種；型式：*There are two versions of the game, a long one and a short one.* 這遊戲有兩個版本，一長一短。◇ *the* ***latest version*** *of the software package* 軟件包的最新版本 ◇ *the* ***de luxe/luxury version*** 豪華型 ➲ see also BETA VERSION **2** 0‑ a description of an event from the position of a particular person or group of people（從不同角度的）說法，描述：*She gave us her version of what had happened that day.* 她向我們描述了她認為那天發生的事情。◇ *Their versions of how the accident happened conflict.* 他們對事故發生情況的說法相互矛盾。 ➲ SYNONYMS at REPORT **3** 0‑ a film/movie, play, piece of music, etc. that is based on a particular piece of work but is in a different form, style or language（電影、劇本、樂曲等的）版本，改編形式，改寫本：*the film version of 'War and Peace'* 根據《戰爭與和平》改編的電影 ◇ *The English version of the novel is due for publication next year.* 這部小說的英文譯本預定明年出版。 ➲ see also AUTHORIZED VERSION, COVER VERSION

verso /ˈvɜːsəʊ; *NAmE* ˈvɜːrsoʊ/ *noun* (*pl.* **-os**) (*technical* 術語) the page on the left side of an open book（書的）左頁，偶數頁；（書頁的）背面 OPP **recto**

ver·sus /ˈvɜːsəs; *NAmE* ˈvɜːrsəs/ *prep.* (*abbr.* **v**, **vs**) **1** (*sport* 體 or *law* 律) used to show that two teams or sides are against each other（表示兩隊或雙方對陣）對，訴，對抗：*It is France versus Brazil in the final.* 決賽是法國隊對巴西隊。◇ *in the case of the State versus Ford* 在州政府訴福特公司的案件中 **2** used to compare two different ideas, choices, etc.（比較兩種不同想法、選擇等）與…相對，與…相比：*It was the promise of better job opportunities versus the inconvenience of moving away and leaving her friends.* 那是較好的就業前景與搬走並遠離朋友的不便之間的矛盾。

ver·tebra /ˈvɜːtɪbrə; *NAmE* ˈvɜːrt-/ *noun* (*pl.* **ver·te·brae** /-reɪ; -riː/) any of the small bones that are connected together to form the SPINE 椎骨；脊椎 ➲ VISUAL VOCAB page V59 ▸ **ver·te·bral** *adj.* [only before noun]

ver·te·brate /ˈvɜːtɪbrət; *NAmE* ˈvɜːrt-/ *noun* (*technical* 術語) any animal with a BACKBONE, including all MAMMALS, birds, fish, REPTILES and AMPHIBIANS 脊椎動物（包括所有哺乳動物、鳥類、魚類、爬行動物和兩棲動物） ➲ compare INVERTEBRATE ▸ **ver·te·brate** *adj.*

ver·tex /ˈvɜːteks; *NAmE* ˈvɜːrt-/ *noun* (*pl.* **ver·ti·ces** /-tɪsiːz/ or **ver·texes**) **1** (*geometry* 幾何) a point where two lines meet to form an angle, especially the point of a triangle or CONE opposite the base（三角形或錐形的）角頂；頂點 ➲ VISUAL VOCAB page V71 **2** (*technical* 術語) the highest point or top of sth 至高點；頂點

ver·ti·cal 0‑ /ˈvɜːtɪkl; *NAmE* ˈvɜːrt-/ *adj.*, *noun*

■ *adj.* **1** 0‑ (of a line, pole, etc. 線、杆等) going straight up or down from a level surface or from top to bottom in a picture, etc. 豎的；垂直的；直立的

SYN **perpendicular** : *the vertical axis of the graph* 圖的縱軸 ◇ *The cliff was almost vertical.* 那懸崖幾乎是筆陡的。◇ *There was a vertical drop to the ocean.* 至海洋有一段垂直落差。➲ compare HORIZONTAL **2** having a structure in which there are top, middle and bottom levels 縱向的 : *a vertical flow of communication* 上下級縱向交流 ▸ **ver·ti·cal·ly** /-kli/ *adv.*

■ ***noun*** (usually **the vertical**) a vertical line or position 垂直線；垂直位置 SYN **perpendicular** : *The wall is several degrees off the vertical.* 這堵牆傾斜了有好幾度。

ver·tigin·ous /vɜː'tɪdʒɪnəs; *NAmE* vɜːr't-/ *adj.* (*formal*) causing a feeling of vertigo 引起眩暈的 SYN **dizzying** : *From the path there was a vertiginous drop to the valley below.* 從小路向谷底望去令人眩暈。

ver·tigo /'vɜːtɪɡəʊ; *NAmE* 'vɜːrtɪɡoʊ/ *noun* [U] the feeling of DIZZINESS and fear, and of losing your balance, that is caused in some people when they look down from a very high place（從高處俯視時感到的）眩暈，頭暈目眩

verve /vɜːv; *NAmE* vɜːrv/ *noun* [U, sing.] energy, excitement or enthusiasm 精力；激情；熱情；熱忱 SYN **gusto** : *It was a performance of verve and vitality.* 這是一場充滿激情與活力的演出。

Grammar Point 語法説明

very / very much

- **Very** is used with adjectives, past participles used as adjectives, and adverbs. * very 與形容詞、作形容詞的過去分詞或副詞連用 : *I am very hungry.* 我很餓。◇ *I was very pleased to get your letter.* 收到你的信我非常高興。◇ *You played very well.* 你演得很好。 But notice this use 但注意 : *I'm* ***very much afraid*** *that your son may be involved in the crime.* 我非常擔憂，你兒子可能與這樁罪案有牽連。
- **Very** is not used with past participles that have a passive meaning. **Much**, **very much** or **greatly** (*formal*) are usually used instead. 含被動意義的過去分詞不與 very 連用，而通常用 much、very much 或 greatly（正式用語）: *Your help was very much appreciated.* 非常感謝您的幫助。◇ *He was much loved by everyone.* 他深受大家的愛戴。◇ *She was greatly admired.* 她很受讚賞。
- **Very** is used to emphasize superlative adjectives. * very 用以強調形容詞最高級 : *my very best work* 我最好的工作 ◇ *the very youngest children* 這些最小的孩子 However, with comparative adjectives **much**, **very much**, **a lot**, etc. are used. 形容詞比較級則用 much、very much、a lot 等 : *Your work is very much better.* 你的工作要好得多。◇ *much younger children* 小得多的孩子
- **Very** is not used with adjectives and adverbs that already have an extreme meaning. You are more likely to use an adverb such as *absolutely*, *completely*, etc. 含極端意義的形容詞和副詞不用 very，而常用 absolutely、completely 等副詞 : *She was absolutely furious.* 她憤怒極了。◇ *I'm completely exhausted.* 我完全筋疲力盡了。◇ *You played really brilliantly.* 你的表現真是棒極了。
- **Very** is not used with verbs. Use **very much** instead. 動詞不用 very，而用 very much : *We enjoyed staying with you very much.* 我們非常喜歡待在你這裏。

very 🔑 /'veri/ *adv., adj.*

■ ***adv.*** (*abbr.* **v**) **1** 🔑 used before adjectives, adverbs and determiners to mean 'in a high degree' or 'extremely'（置於形容詞、副詞和限定詞前）很，非常，十分，極 : *very small* 很小 ◇ *very quickly* 極快 ◇ *Very few people know that.* 很少有人知道那件事。◇ *Thanks very much.* 非常感謝。◇ *'Do you like it?' 'Yeah, I do.* ***Very much.****'* "你喜歡嗎？" "是的，我喜歡，非常喜歡。" ◇ *'Is it what you expected?' 'Oh yes,* ***very much so****.'* "這是你所期望的嗎？" "啊，是的，非常期望如此。" ◇ *'Are you busy?' 'Not very.'* "你忙嗎？" "不太忙。" ◇ *The new building has been very much admired.* 這座新建築物是人見人誇。◇ *I'm* ***not very*** (= not at all) *impressed.* 我覺得並不怎麼樣。◇ *I'm* ***very very*** *grateful.* 我萬分感激。**2** 🔑 used to emphasize a superlative adjective or before *own*（強調形容詞最高級或置於 own 前）完全，十足 : *They wanted the* ***very best*** *quality.* 他們要最好的質量。◇ *Be there by six* ***at the very latest****.* 至遲不要超過六點到達那裏。◇ *At last he had his* ***very own*** *car* (= belonging to him and to nobody else). 他終於有了完全屬於他自己的汽車。**3 the ~ same** exactly the same 完全同樣；完全同一 : *Mario said the very same thing.* 馬里奧説的完全是同一件事。

■ ***adj.*** [only before noun] **1** used to emphasize that you are talking about a particular thing or person and not about another（特指人或事物）正是的，恰好的，同一的 SYN **actual** : *Those were her very words.* 這些都是她的原話。◇ *He might be phoning her* ***at this very moment****.* 他也許這會兒正在給她打電話呢。◇ *That's* ***the very thing*** *I need.* 那正是我需要的東西。**2** used to emphasize an extreme place or time（強調極限的地點或時間）最…的，極端的，十足的 : *It happens at the very beginning of the book.* 這事發生在書的一開頭。**3** used to emphasize a noun（加強名詞的語氣）僅僅的，唯獨的，甚至於 SYN **mere** : *The* ***very thought of*** *drink made him feel sick.* 他一想到酒就覺得惡心。◇ *'I can't do that!' she gasped, appalled at* ***the very idea****.* "那事我可不能幹！" 她一聽到這個想法便吃驚地倒抽着冷氣。IDM see EYE *n.*

ˌvery high 'frequency *noun* [U] = VHF

Very light /'veri laɪt/ *noun* a bright coloured light that is fired from a gun as a signal from a ship that it needs help（船上發出的）求援閃光信號彈

ves·icle /'vesɪkl/ *noun* **1** (*biology* 生) a small bag or hollow structure in the body of a plant or an animal（動植物體內的）泡，囊 **2** (*medical* 醫) a small swelling filled with liquid under the skin 水泡 SYN **blister**

ves·pers /'vespəz; *NAmE* -pərz/ *noun* [U] the service of evening prayer in some Christian Churches（基督教某些教派的）晚課，晚禱 ➲ compare EVENSONG, MATINS

ves·sel /'vesl/ *noun* **1** (*formal*) a large ship or boat 大船；輪船 : *ocean-going vessels* 遠洋輪船 **2** (*old use* or *technical* 術語) a container used for holding liquids, such as a bowl, cup, etc.（盛液體的）容器，器皿 : *a Bronze Age drinking vessel* 青銅器時代的飲具 **3** a tube that carries blood through the body of a person or an animal, or liquid through the parts of a plant（人或動物的）血管，脈管；（植物的）導管 ➲ see also BLOOD VESSEL

vest /vest/ *noun, verb*

■ ***noun*** **1** (*BrE*) (*NAmE* **under·shirt**) a piece of underwear worn under a shirt, etc. next to the skin（襯衣等裏面貼身穿的）背心，汗衫 : *a cotton vest* 棉汗衫 ➲ compare SINGLET **2** a special piece of clothing that covers the upper part of the body 坎肩；（外面穿的）背心 : *a bullet-proof vest* 防彈背心 ◇ *a running vest* 賽跑背心 **3** (*NAmE*) (*BrE* **waist·coat**) a short piece of clothing with buttons down the front but no sleeves, usually worn over a shirt and under a jacket, often forming part of a man's suit（西服的）背心 ➲ VISUAL VOCAB page V61

■ ***verb***

PHR V **'vest in sb/sth** (*law* 律) (of power, property, etc. 權力、財產等) to belong to sb/sth legally（合法地）屬於，歸屬 **'vest sth in sb | 'vest sb with sth** [often passive] (*formal*) **1** to give sb the legal right or power to do sth 授予，賦予，給予（合法權利或權力）: *Overall authority is vested in the Supreme Council.* 一切權力屬於最高議會。◇ *The Supreme Council is vested with overall authority.* 最高議會擁有一切權力。**2** to make sb the legal owner of land or property 使合法擁有（土地或財產）

ˌvested 'interest *noun* **~ (in sth)** a personal reason for wanting sth to happen, especially because you get some advantage from it 既得利益 : *They have a vested interest in keeping the club as exclusive as possible.* 他們希望俱樂部盡可能地限制會員加入以從中受益。◇ *Vested interests* (= people with a vested interest) *are opposing the plan.* 既得利益集團在反對這項計劃。

V

ves·ti·bule /ˈvestɪbjuːl/ *noun* **1** (*formal*) an entrance hall of a large building , for example where hats and coats can be left 前廳，門廳（如可放衣帽處） **2** (*technical* 術語) a space at the end of a coach/car on a train that connects it with the next coach/car 通過台（列車兩個車廂間的連接處）

ves·tige /ˈvestɪdʒ/ *noun* (*formal*) **1** a small part of sth that still exists after the rest of it has stopped existing 殘留部份；遺跡 **SYN** **trace**： *the **last vestiges** of the old colonial regime* 舊殖民制度最後的殘餘 **2** usually used in negative sentences, to say that not even a small amount of sth exists（通常用於否定句）絲毫，一點兒： *There's not a vestige of truth in the rumour.* 這個謠傳毫無真實可言。

ves·tigial /veˈstɪdʒiəl/ *adj.* [usually before noun] (*formal* or *technical* 術語) remaining as the last small part of sth that used to exist 殘留的；殘餘的；退化的： *vestigial traces of an earlier culture* 早期文化的遺跡 ◇ *It is often possible to see the vestigial remains of rear limbs on some snakes.* 在某些蛇身上常可看到退化後肢的痕跡。

vest·ment /ˈvestmənt/ *noun* [usually pl.] a piece of clothing worn by a priest during church services（司祭在禮拜儀式上穿的）祭衣，祭服

ves·try /ˈvestri/ *noun* (*pl.* **-ies**) a room in a church where a priest prepares for a service by putting on special clothes and where various objects used in worship are kept（教堂的）祭衣室 **SYN** **sacristy**

vet /vet/ *noun, verb*

■ ***noun*** **1** (*especially BrE*) (*NAmE* usually **vet·er·in·ar·ian**) (also *BrE formal* **ˈveterinary surgeon**) a person who has been trained in the science of animal medicine, whose job is to treat animals who are sick or injured 獸醫 **2 vet's** (*pl.* **vets**) the place where a vet works 獸醫診所： *I've got to take the dog to the vet's tomorrow.* 明天我得把狗帶到獸醫診所去診治。 **3** (*NAmE, informal*) = VETERAN (2)： *a Vietnam vet* 參加過越戰的老兵

■ ***verb*** (**-tt-**) (*BrE*) **1 ~ sb** to find out about a person's past life and career in order to decide if they are suitable for a particular job 審查（某人過去的生活和職業） **SYN** **screen**： *All candidates are carefully vetted for security reasons.* 由於安全的緣故，所有的求職申請人都要經過嚴格的審查。 ➲ see also POSITIVE VETTING **2 ~ sth** to check the contents, quality, etc. of sth carefully 仔細檢查，審查（內容、質量等） **SYN** **screen**： *All reports are vetted before publication.* 所有報道都要經過仔細檢查後才能發表。

vetch /vetʃ/ *noun* [U, C] a plant of the PEA family. There are several types of vetch, one of which is used as food for farm animals. 巢菜，野豌豆（有一種可作飼料）

vet·eran /ˈvetərən/ *noun* **1** a person who has a lot of experience in a particular area or activity 經驗豐富的人；老手： *the veteran American actor, Clint Eastwood* 美國資深演員克林特 • 伊斯特伍德 **2** (also *NAmE informal* **vet**) a person who has been a soldier, sailor, etc. in a war 退伍軍人；老兵；老戰士；老水兵： *war veterans* 經歷過戰爭的老戰士 ◇ *a Vietnam vet* 越戰退伍軍人

ˌveteran ˈcar *noun* (*BrE*) a car made before 1916 老爺車（1916 年以前生產的汽車） ➲ compare VINTAGE *adj.* (2)

ˈVeterans Day *noun* a holiday in the US on 11 November, in honour of members of the armed forces and others who have died in war 退伍軍人節（美國紀念陣亡將士的日子，定於 11 月 11 日） ➲ see also MEMORIAL DAY, REMEMBRANCE SUNDAY

vet·er·in·ar·ian /ˌvetərɪˈneəriən; *NAmE* -ˈner-/ *noun* (*NAmE*) = VET *n.* (1)

vet·er·in·ary /ˈvetnri; ˈvetrənəri; *NAmE* ˈvetəreneri/ *adj.* [only before noun] connected with caring for the health of animals 獸醫的：***veterinary medicine/science*** 獸醫學

ˈveterinary surgeon *noun* (*BrE, formal*) = VET *n.* (1)

veto /ˈviːtəʊ; *NAmE* -toʊ/ *noun, verb*

■ ***noun*** (*pl.* **-oes**) **1** [C, U] the right to refuse to allow sth to be done, especially the right to stop a law from being passed or a decision from being taken 否決權： *The British government used its veto to block the proposal.* 英國政府行使其否決權阻止了這項提案。◇ *to have the **power/right of veto*** 有否決權 ◇ *the use of the presidential veto* 總統否決權的行使 **2** [C] **~ (on sth/on doing sth)** an occasion when sb refuses to allow sth to be done 拒絕認可；禁止 **SYN** **ban**： *For months there was a veto on employing new staff.* 有好幾個月禁止雇用新職員。

■ ***verb*** (**ve·toes**, **veto·ing**, **ve·toed**, **ve·toed**) **1 ~ sth** to stop sth from happening or being done by using your official authority (= by using your veto) 行使否決權；拒絕認可；禁止： *Plans for the dam have been vetoed by the Environmental Protection Agency.* 修建大壩的計劃已被環境保護局否決。 ➲ COLLOCATIONS at POLITICS **2 ~ sth** to refuse to accept or do what sb has suggested 拒不接受；反對；否定 **SYN** **rule out**： *I wanted to go camping but the others quickly vetoed that idea.* 我想去野營，但這個想法很快遭到了其他人的反對。

vex /veks/ *verb* **~ sb** (*old-fashioned* or *formal*) to annoy or worry sb 使惱火；使煩惱；使憂慮 ▶ **vex·ing** *adj.*： *a vexing problem* 令人煩惱的問題

vex·ation /vekˈseɪʃn/ *noun* (*old-fashioned* or *formal*) **1** [U] the state of feeling upset or annoyed 煩惱；惱火；傷腦筋；心煩意亂 **2** [C] a thing that upsets or annoys you 令人心煩（或惱火）的事

vex·atious /vekˈseɪʃəs/ *adj.* (*old-fashioned* or *formal*) making you feel upset or annoyed 使人煩惱的；令人惱火的

vexed /vekst/ *adj.* **1 ~ question/issue** a problem that is difficult to deal with （問題等）棘手的，傷腦筋的 **SYN** **thorny**： *The conference spent days discussing the vexed question of border controls.* 會議花了幾天的時間討論邊境管制這個難題。 **2 ~ (at/with sb/sth)** (*old-fashioned*) upset or annoyed （人）惱火，煩惱，傷腦筋

VHF /ˌviː eɪtʃ ˈef/ *abbr.* very high frequency (a range of radio waves used for high-quality broadcasting) 甚高頻，特高頻（用於高質量廣播的無線電波段）

VHS™ /ˌviː eɪtʃ ˈes/ *abbr.* video home system (a system used by VIDEO RECORDERS and some CAMCORDERS) 家用錄像系統；VHS 系統

via 🔑 **AW** /ˈvaɪə; ˈviːə/ *prep.* **1** 🔑 through a place 經由，經過（某一地方）： *We flew home via Dubai.* 我們乘飛機經迪拜回國。 **2** by means of a particular person, system, etc. 通過，憑藉（某人、系統等）： *I heard about the sale via Jane.* 我從簡那裏聽說了這次大減價。◇ *The news programme came to us via satellite.* 新聞節目是通過衛星傳送到我們這裏來的。

vi·able /ˈvaɪəbl/ *adj.* **1** that can be done; that will be successful 可實施的；切實可行的 **SYN** **feasible**： *a **viable option/proposition*** 切實可行的選擇／提議 ◇ *There is no **viable alternative**.* 沒有其他可行的措施。◇ *to be **commercially/politically/financially/economically viable*** 在商業上／政治上／財政上／經濟上可行 **2** (*biology* 生) capable of developing and surviving independently 能獨立發展的；能獨立生存的；可生長發育的： *viable organisms* 可存活的生物 ▶ **via·bil·ity** /ˌvaɪəˈbɪləti/ *noun* [U]： *commercial viability* 商業上的可行性

via·duct /ˈvaɪədʌkt/ *noun* a long high bridge, usually with ARCHES, that carries a road or railway/railroad across a river or valley 高架橋（通常有拱，橫跨河道或山谷連通公路或鐵路） ➲ VISUAL VOCAB page V14

Viagra™ /vaɪˈæɡrə/ *noun* [U] a drug used to treat IMPOTENCE in men 萬艾可，威爾剛，“偉哥”（一種治療陽痿的藥物）

vial /ˈvaɪəl/ *noun* (*especially NAmE*) = PHIAL

vibes /vaɪbz/ *noun* [pl.] **1** (also *formal* **vi·bra·tions**) (also **vibe** [sing.]) (*informal*) a mood or an atmosphere produced by a particular person, thing or place 情緒；氣氛；氛圍： ***good/bad vibes*** 好／壞情緒 ◇ *The vibes weren't right.* 這氣氛不對頭。 **2** = VIBRAPHONE： *a jazzy vibes backing* 爵士樂的顫音琴伴奏

vi·brant /ˈvaɪbrənt/ *adj.* **1** full of life and energy 充滿生機的；生氣勃勃的；精力充沛的 **SYN** **exciting**： *a vibrant city* 充滿生機的城市 ◇ *Thailand is at its most vibrant during the New Year celebrations.* 在歡度新年期

間，泰國舉國歡騰。 **2** (of colours 顏色) very bright and strong 鮮豔的；醒目的 SYN **brilliant**： *The room was decorated in vibrant reds and yellows.* 那房間是由鮮豔的紅黃兩色裝飾的。 ➲ SYNONYMS at BRIGHT **3** (of music, sounds, etc. 音樂、聲音等) loud and powerful 響亮的；洪亮的；強勁的： *vibrant rhythms* 強有力的節奏 ▸ **vi·brancy** /-brənsi/ *noun* [U] **vi·brant·ly** *adv.*

vi·bra·phone /ˈvaɪbrəfəʊn; *NAmE* -foʊn/ *noun* [C] (also *informal* **vibes** [pl.]) a musical instrument used especially in JAZZ, that has two rows of metal bars that you hit, and a motor that makes them vibrate 顫音琴（常用於爵士樂）

vi·brate /vaɪˈbreɪt; *NAmE* usually ˈvaɪbreɪt/ *verb* [I, T] to move or make sth move from side to side very quickly and with small movements （使）振動，顫動，擺動： **~ (sth)** *Every time a train went past the walls vibrated.* 每當火車駛過，這些牆都會震動。◇ **~ with sth** *The atmosphere seemed to vibrate with tension.* 氣氛似乎緊張得發顫。

vi·bra·tion /vaɪˈbreɪʃn/ *noun* **1** [C, U] a continuous shaking movement or feeling 震動；顫動；抖動；（感情的）共鳴： *We could feel the vibrations from the trucks passing outside.* 我們可以感到外面卡車經過時的顫動。◇ *a reduction in the level of vibration in the engine* 發動機震動程度的下降 **2 vibrations** [pl.] (*formal*) = VIBES (1)

vi·brato /vɪˈbrɑːtəʊ; *NAmE* -toʊ/ *noun* [U, C] (*pl.* **-os**) (*music* 音) a shaking effect in singing or playing a musical instrument, made by rapid slight changes in PITCH (= how high or low a sound is) （演唱或演奏的）顫音效果，顫音

vi·bra·tor /vaɪˈbreɪtə(r)/ *noun* an electrical device that produces a continuous shaking movement, used in MASSAGE or for sexual pleasure （用於按摩或產生性快感的）顫動按摩器，震動器

vicar /ˈvɪkə(r)/ *noun* **1** (*especially BrE*) an Anglican priest who is in charge of a church and the area around it (called a PARISH) （聖公會的）代牧，教區牧師 **2** (*NAmE*) a priest in the US Episcopal Church （美國聖公會的）牧師 ➲ compare CURATE[1], MINISTER *n.* (2), PRIEST (1), RECTOR (1)

vic·ar·age /ˈvɪkərɪdʒ/ *noun* a vicar's house 代牧住宅

vic·ari·ous /vɪˈkeəriəs; *NAmE* vaɪˈker-/ *adj.* [only before noun] felt or experienced by watching or reading about sb else doing sth, rather than by doing it yourself 間接感受到的： *He got a vicarious thrill out of watching his son score the winning goal.* 他看着兒子射入獲勝的一球，也同樣感到欣喜若狂。 ▸ **vic·ari·ous·ly** *adv.*

vice /vaɪs/ *noun* **1** [U] criminal activities that involve sex or drugs （與性或毒品有關的）罪行： *plain-clothes detectives from the vice squad* 取締性或毒品犯罪行動隊的便衣偵探 **2** [U, C] evil or immoral behaviour; an evil or immoral quality in sb's character 惡行；不道德行為；墮落；邪惡： *The film ended most satisfactorily: vice punished and virtue rewarded.* 這部電影的結尾皆大歡喜：邪惡受到懲治，美德得到報償。◇ *Greed is a terrible vice.* 貪婪是一種惡習。◇ (*humorous*) *Cigarettes are my only vice.* 我唯一的罪過就是愛抽煙。 **3** (*BrE*) (*NAmE* **vise**) [C] a tool with two metal blocks that can be moved together by turning a screw. The vice is used to hold an object firmly while work is done on it. 台鉗；虎鉗： *He held my arm in a* ***vice-like*** (= very firm) ***grip***. 他的手像虎鉗一樣緊緊抓住了我的手臂。 ➲ VISUAL VOCAB page V20

vice- /vaɪs/ *combining form* (in nouns and related adjectives 構成名詞和相關的形容詞) next in rank to sb and able to represent them or act for them 副；代理： *vice-captain* 副艦長

ˌvice ˈadmiral *noun* an officer of very high rank in the navy 海軍中將

ˌvice ˈchancellor *noun* the head of a university in Britain, who is in charge of the work of running the university. (Compare the CHANCELLOR, who is the official head of a university but only has duties at various ceremonies.) （英國大學）校長

ˌvice-ˈpresident *noun* (*abbr.* **VP**) **1** the person below the president of a country in rank, who takes control of the country if the president is not able to 副總統；國家副主席 **2** (*NAmE*) a person in charge of a particular part of a business company （商業公司的）副總裁，副總經理： *the vice-president of sales* 負責銷售的副總裁 ▸ **ˌvice-presiˈdential** *adj.* [usually before noun]

vice·roy /ˈvaɪsrɔɪ/ *noun* (often used as a title 常用作頭銜) (in the past) a person who was sent by a king or queen to govern a COLONY （舊時受君主委派管治殖民地的）總督

vice versa /ˌvaɪs ˈvɜːsə; ˌvaɪsi; *NAmE* ˈvɜːrsə/ *adv.* used to say that the opposite of what you have just said is also true 反過來也一樣；反之亦然： *You can cruise from Cairo to Aswan or vice versa* (= also from Aswan to Cairo). 你可以乘船從開羅遊覽到阿斯旺，也可以從阿斯旺遊覽到開羅。

the vicin·ity /vəˈsɪnəti/ *noun* [sing.] the area around a particular place 周圍地區；鄰近地區；附近： *Crowds gathered* ***in the vicinity of*** *Trafalgar Square.* 成群結隊的人聚集在特拉法爾加廣場周圍。◇ *There is no hospital* ***in the immediate vicinity***. 附近沒有醫院。

vi·cious /ˈvɪʃəs/ *adj.* **1** violent and cruel 狂暴的；殘酷的 SYN **brutal**： *a vicious attack* 猛烈的攻擊 ◇ *a vicious criminal* 兇殘的罪犯 ◇ *She has a vicious temper.* 她性情暴虐。 **2** (of animals 動物) aggressive and dangerous 兇猛危險的：*a vicious dog* 惡犬 **3** (of an attack, criticism, etc. 攻擊、批評等) full of hatred and anger 充滿仇恨的；嚴厲的： *She wrote me a vicious letter.* 她給我寫了一封嚴厲的信。 **4** (*informal*) very bad or severe 惡劣的；嚴重的： *a vicious headache* 劇烈的頭痛 ◇ *a vicious spiral of rising prices* 物價的惡性持續上漲 ▸ **vi·cious·ly** *adv.* **vi·cious·ness** *noun* [U]： *Police were shocked by the viciousness of the assault.* 警方對這一攻擊的殘忍感到震驚。

ˌvicious ˈcircle *noun* [sing.] a situation in which one problem causes another problem which then makes the first problem worse 惡性循環 ➲ compare VIRTUOUS CIRCLE

vi·cis·si·tude /vɪˈsɪsɪtjuːd; *NAmE* -tuːd/ *noun* [usually pl.] (*formal*) one of the many changes and problems in a situation or in your life, that you have to deal with 變遷；人生的沉浮；興衰枯榮

vic·tim 0━ /ˈvɪktɪm/ *noun*

1 0━ a person who has been attacked, injured or killed as the result of a crime, a disease, an accident, etc. 受害者；罹難者；罹病者；犧牲品： ***murder/rape, etc. victims*** 謀殺案、強姦案等受害者 ◇ ***accident/earthquake/famine, etc. victims*** 事故、地震、饑荒等的罹難者 ◇ ***AIDS/cancer/stroke, etc. victims*** 艾滋病、癌症、中風等患者 ◇ *victims of crime* 犯罪的受害者 ◇ *She was the* ***innocent victim*** *of an arson attack.* 她是一起縱火案的無辜受害者。◇ *Schools are the latest victims of cuts in public spending.* 學校是削減公共開支的最新的犧牲品。 **2** 0━ a person who has been tricked 受騙者；上當的人 SYN **target**： *They were the victims of a cruel hoax.* 他們成了一大騙局的上當受騙者。 ➲ see also FASHION VICTIM **3** an animal or a person that is killed and offered as a SACRIFICE 為祭祀殺死的動物（或人）；祭品；犧牲： *a sacrificial victim* 祭品

IDM **fall ˈvictim (to sth)** (*formal*) to be injured, damaged or killed by sth 受傷；受損；被害

vic·tim·ize (*BrE* also **-ise**) /ˈvɪktɪmaɪz/ *verb* [often passive] **~ sb** to make sb suffer unfairly because you do not like them, their opinions, or sth that they have done （不正當地）使受害，使受苦： *For years the family had been victimized by racist neighbours.* 多年來這家人因鄰居懷有種族偏見而飽受欺凌。◇ *The union claimed that some of its members had been victimized for taking part in the strike.* 工會聲稱有些會員因參加罷工而受到迫害。 ▸ **vic·tim·iza·tion, -isa·tion** /ˌvɪktɪmaɪˈzeɪʃn; *NAmE* -məˈz-/ *noun* [U]

vic·tim·less /ˈvɪktɪmləs/ *adj.* a **victimless** crime is one in which nobody seems to suffer or be harmed （犯罪行為）無受害人的，不侵害他人的

ˌvictim supˈport *noun* [U] a service provided by the police that helps people who are victims of crime 受害人援助（警方提供）

vic·tor /ˈvɪktə(r)/ *noun* (*literary*) the winner of a battle, competition, game, etc. 勝利者；獲勝者

Vic·toria Cross /vɪkˌtɔːriə ˈkrɒs; *NAmE* ˈkrɔːs/ *noun* (*abbr.* **VC**) a MEDAL for special courage that is given to members of the British and Commonwealth armed forces 維多利亞十字勳章（授予英勇的英國及英聯邦軍人）

Vic·tor·ian /vɪkˈtɔːriən/ *adj., noun*

■ ***adj.*** **1** connected with the period from 1837 to 1901 when Queen Victoria ruled Britain （英國）維多利亞女王時代（1837–1901 年）的：*Victorian architecture* 維多利亞女王時代的建築 ◇ *the Victorian age* 維多利亞時代 **2** having the attitudes that were typical of society during Queen Victoria's REIGN 持維多利亞時代觀點的：*Victorian attitudes to sex* (= being easily shocked by sexual matters) 維多利亞時代的性愛觀 ◇ *She advocated a return to Victorian values* (= hard work, pride in your country, etc.). 她提倡恢復維多利亞時代的價值觀念。

■ ***noun*** a British person who was alive during the period from 1837 to 1901, when Queen Victoria ruled 維多利亞時代的英國人

Vicˌtoria ˈsponge *noun* [C, U] a type of SPONGE CAKE that is made with fat in the mixture 維多利亞海綿蛋糕

vic·tori·ous /vɪkˈtɔːriəs/ *adj.* having won a victory; that ends in victory 勝利的；獲勝的；戰勝的 **SYN** **successful, triumphant**：*the victorious army/team* 勝利之師；獲勝的隊 ◇ **~ in sth** *He **emerged victorious** in the elections.* 他在競選中脫穎而出獲得勝利。▸ **vic·tori·ous·ly** *adv.*

vic·tory 0→ /ˈvɪktəri/ *noun* (*pl.* **-ies**) [C, U] **~ (over/against sb/sth)** success in a game, an election, a war, etc. 勝利；成功：*the team's 3–2 victory against Poland* 該隊以 3:2 戰勝波蘭隊 ◇ *to **win a victory*** 獲得勝利 ◇ *a **decisive/narrow victory*** 決定性的勝利；險勝 ◇ *an election victory* 選舉勝利 ◇ *She is confident of victory in Saturday's final.* 她對在星期六決賽中取得勝利充滿信心。◇ ***victory celebrations/parades*** 勝利的慶祝活動／遊行 ➲ see also MORAL VICTORY
IDM **roar, romp, sweep, etc. to victory** to win sth easily 輕易取勝；大獲全勝：*He swept to victory in the final of the championship.* 他在錦標賽的決賽中輕而易舉地獲勝。

vict·ual·ler /ˈvɪtlə(r)/ (also **ˌlicensed ˈvictualler**) *noun* (*BrE, law* 律) a person who is legally allowed to sell alcoholic drinks 持證售酒者

vict·uals /ˈvɪtlz/ *noun* [pl.] (*old-fashioned*) food and drink 飲食；食物及飲料

vi·cuña /vɪˈkuːnjə/ *noun* a wild animal with a long neck and very soft wool, which lives in S America. Vicuñas are related to LLAMAS. 駱馬（產於南美的駱駝科動物）；南美駝馬

V

vide /ˈviːdeɪ/ *verb* (*abbr.* **v**) **~ sth** used (meaning 'see') as an instruction in books to tell the reader to look at a particular book, passage, etc. for more information （指示語，用於書等中）參見，參閱，另見

video 0→ /ˈvɪdiəʊ; *NAmE* -oʊ/ *noun, verb*

■ ***noun*** (*pl.* **-os**) **1** 0→ (also **video·tape**) [U, C] a type of MAGNETIC tape used for recording moving pictures and sound; a box containing this tape, also called a **video cassette** 錄像帶；盒式錄像帶：*The movie will be released **on video** in June.* 這部電影的錄像帶將於六月份發行。◇ *Do we have a **blank video**?* 我們有空白錄像帶嗎？ **2** 0→ [U] a system of recording moving pictures and sound, either using VIDEOTAPE or a DIGITAL method of storing data 錄像系統：*A wedding is the perfect subject for video.* 婚禮是極好的錄像主題。◇ *the use of video in schools* 學校對電影電視錄像的使用 **3** 0→ [C] a copy of a film/movie, programme, etc. that is recorded on VIDEOTAPE（指製品）錄像，錄影：*a video of 'ET'*《外星人》的錄像帶 ◇ *a **home video*** (= not a professional one) 家庭錄像 ◇ *a **video shop/store*** 錄像帶商店 ➲ COLLOCATIONS at CINEMA **4** (also **ˈmusic video**) [C] a short film made by a pop or rock band to be shown with a song when it is played on television 音樂短片 **5** (also **ˈvideo clip**) [C] a short film or recording of an event, made using DIGITAL technology and viewed on a computer, especially over the Internet 視頻；視頻剪輯：*The school made a short **promotional video**.* 學校錄製了一條宣傳短片。◇ *Upload your videos and share them with friends and family online.* 上傳你的視頻，與朋友和家人在線分享。 **6** [C] (*BrE*) = VIDEO CASSETTE RECORDER：*to **programme the video** to record the football match* 預調錄像機錄下足球賽

■ ***verb*** (also *formal* **video·tape**) **~ sth/sb** (*especially BrE*) to record a television programme using a VIDEO CASSETTE RECORDER; to film sb/sth using a video camera 錄電視節目；給…錄像：*Did you remember to video that programme?* 你記得錄那個節目了嗎？◇ *Videoing students can be a useful teaching exercise.* 給學生錄像可以成為有用的教學活動。

ˈvideo arcade *noun* a place where you can play video games on machines that you use coins to operate（投幣式）錄像遊戲廳，電子遊戲機室

ˈvideo camera *noun* a special camera for making video films 攝像機 ➲ see also CAMCORDER

ˈvideo card (also **ˈgraphics adapter**) *noun* (*computing* 計) a device that allows images to be shown on a computer screen 視頻卡；顯示卡

ˌvideo caˈssette recorder *noun* (*abbr.* **VCR**) (also **video**, **ˌvideo caˈssette player**, **ˈvideo recorder**) a piece of equipment that you use to record and play films/movies and TV programmes on video 錄像機

video·con·fer·en·cing /ˈvɪdiəʊkɒnfərənsɪŋ; *NAmE* ˈvɪdioʊkɑːn-/ *noun* [U] a system that enables people in different parts of the world to have a meeting by watching and listening to each other using video screens 視頻會議；視像會議

ˈvideo diary *noun* a series of video recordings made by sb over a period of time, in which they record their experiences, thoughts and feelings 錄影日記；影音日記

video·disc /ˈvɪdiəʊdɪsk; *NAmE* -oʊ-/ *noun* [U, C] a plastic disc that you can record films/movies and programmes on, for showing on a television screen 視盤；影碟 ➲ see also DVD

ˈvideo game *noun* a game in which you press buttons to control and move images on a screen 電子遊戲

ˈvideo jockey (also **VJ**, **vee-jay**) *noun* a person who introduces music videos on television 電視音樂節目主持人

ˌvideo ˈnasty *noun* (*BrE, informal*) a video film/movie that shows offensive scenes of sex and violence 黃色錄像片；暴力電視片

video·phone /ˈvɪdiəʊfəʊn; *NAmE* -oʊfoʊn/ *noun* a type of telephone with a screen that enables you to see the person you are talking to 可視電話；電視電話；視像電話

video·tape /ˈvɪdiəʊteɪp; *NAmE* -oʊ-/ *noun, verb*

■ ***noun*** [U, C] = VIDEO *n.* (1)

■ ***verb*** **~ sth** (*formal*) = VIDEO：*a videotaped interview* 錄像訪談

video·tex /ˈvɪdiəʊteks; *NAmE* -oʊ-/ *noun* [U] (*US*) = VIEWDATA

vie /vaɪ/ *verb* (**vying** /ˈvaɪɪŋ/, **vied**, **vied**) [I] (*formal*) to compete strongly with sb in order to obtain or achieve sth 激烈競爭；爭奪 **SYN** **compete**：**~ (with sb) (for sth)** *She was surrounded by men all vying for her attention.* 她周圍盡是爭相博得她青睞的男子。◇ *a row of restaurants vying with each other for business* 彼此爭搶生意的一排飯館 ◇ **~ (to do sth)** *Screaming fans vied to get closer to their idol.* 尖聲喊叫的崇拜者爭先恐後地湧向他們的偶像。

view 0→ /vjuː/ *noun, verb*

■ ***noun***

▸ **OPINION** 想法 **1** 0→ [C] a personal opinion about sth; an attitude towards sth（個人的）看法，意見，見解；態度：*to have **different/conflicting/opposing views*** 有不同的／矛盾的／相反的觀點 ◇ *to have **strong** political **views*** 持強硬的政治觀點 ◇ **~ (about/on sth)** *His views on the subject were well known.* 他對這個問題的看法眾所周知。◇ *This evidence **supports the view** that there is too* *much violence on television.* 這一證據證實了人們認為電視節目中有太多暴力的看法。◇ *We* ***take the view*** *that it would be wrong to interfere.* 我們所持的態度是：干涉是錯誤的。◇ ***In my view*** *it was a waste of time.* 依我看，這是浪費時間。◇ *What is needed is a frank* ***exchange of views.*** 需要的是坦誠地交換意見。➲ see also POINT OF VIEW ➲ **LANGUAGE BANK** at ACCORDING TO, OPINION

▸ **WAY OF UNDERSTANDING** 理解方式 **2** [sing.] **~ (of sth)** a way of understanding or thinking about sth（理解或思維的）方法，方式：*He has an optimistic view of life.* 他樂觀地看待人生。◇ *the Christian view of the world* 基督教的世界觀◇ *The traditional view was that marriage was meant to last.* 傳統的觀念是結成夫妻就要白頭到老。➲ see also WORLD VIEW

▸ **WHAT YOU CAN SEE** 可看到的東西 **3** [U, sing.] used when you are talking about whether you can see sth or whether sth can be seen in a particular situation 觀看；看；視野；視域；視線：*The lake soon* ***came into view.*** 那湖很快映入眼簾。◇ *The sun disappeared* ***from view.*** 太陽看不見了。◇ *There was nobody* ***in view.*** 一個人也看不見。◇ *Sit down—you're blocking my view.* 坐下，你擋住我的視線了。◇ *I didn't have a good view of the stage.* 我看不清舞台。➲ note at SIGHT **4** [C] what you can see from a particular place or position, especially beautiful countryside（從某處看到的）景色，風景；（尤指）鄉間美景：*There were magnificent views of the surrounding countryside.* 四周鄉間的景色壯觀秀麗。◇ *The view from the top of the tower was spectacular.* 從塔頂遠眺景色蔚為壯觀。◇ *a* ***sea/mountain view*** 海／山景 ◇ *I'd like a room with a view.* 我想要一個可以觀看風景的房間。

▸ **PHOTOGRAPH/PICTURE** 照片；圖畫 **5** [C] a photograph or picture that shows an interesting place or scene 風景照；風景畫：*a book with views of Paris* 一本巴黎風光畫冊

▸ **CHANCE TO SEE STH** 觀看的機會 **6** (also **view·ing**) [C] a special chance to see or admire sth（一次）觀看；一睹；一覽：*a* ***private view*** (= for example, of an art exhibition) 畫展預展

IDM **have, etc. sth in 'view** (*formal*) to have a particular aim, plan, etc. in your mind 心中有…目的（或打算等）**SYN** **have sth in mind** **in full 'view (of sb/sth)** completely visible, directly in front of sb/sth 完全看得見；在眼皮底下：*He was shot in full view of a large crowd.* 他在眾目睽睽之下被人槍殺了。**in view of sth** (*formal*) considering sth 鑒於；考慮到；由於：*In view of the weather, the event will now be held indoors.* 由於天氣的緣故，這項賽事將在室內進行。**on 'view** being shown in a public place so that people can look at it 在展出；陳列着；展覽着 **with a view to sth/to doing sth** (*formal*) with the intention or hope of doing sth 為了；指望：*He's painting the house with a view to selling it.* 他在粉刷房子，想把它賣掉。➲ more at BIRD *n.*, DIM *adj.*, HEAVE *v.*, LONG *adj.*

■ *verb*

▸ **THINK ABOUT STH** 思考 **1** to think about sb/sth in a particular way 把…視為；以…看待：**~ (sb/sth as sth)** *When the car was first built, the design was viewed as highly original.* 這種車剛造出時，其設計被認為是獨具匠心。◇ *How do you view your position within the company?* 你如何看待自己在公司中的位置？◇ **~ sb/sth with sth** *She viewed him with suspicion.* 她以懷疑的目光看待他。➲ **SYNONYMS** at REGARD

▸ **LOOK AT STH** 看 **2** **~ sth** (*formal*) to look at sth, especially when you look carefully 看；觀看；（尤指）仔細察看：*People came from all over the world to view her work.* 人們從世界各地湧來欣賞她的作品。◇ *A viewing platform gave stunning views over the valley.* 從觀景台向山谷望去，景色之壯觀令人歎為觀止。➲ **SYNONYMS** at LOOK **3** **~ sth** (*formal*) to visit a house, etc. with the intention of buying or renting it 查看，察看（房子等，以便購買或租用）：*The property can only be viewed by appointment.* 察看這處房產須預約。

▸ **WATCH TV, FILM/MOVIE** 看電視／電影 **4** **~ sth** (*formal*) to watch television, a film/movie, etc. 看，觀看（電視、電影等）：*The show has a viewing audience of six million* (= six million people watch it). 這個節目有六百萬觀眾觀看。◇ *an opportunity to view the movie before it goes on general release* 在公開放映之前觀看這部影片的機會 ➲ note at LOOK

Synonyms 同義詞辨析

view

sight • scene • panorama

These are all words for a thing that you can see, especially from a particular place. 以上各詞均指景色，尤指從某處看到的風景。

view what you can see from a particular place or position, especially beautiful natural scenery 指從某處看到的景色、風景，尤指自然美景：*The cottage had a delightful sea view.* 這小屋可以看到宜人的海景。

sight a thing that you see or can see, especially sth that is impressive or unusual 指看見或看得見的事物、景象，尤指壯觀、奇特的景象：*It's a spectacular sight as the flamingos lift into the air.* 一群紅鸛飛向空中，景象十分壯觀。

scene a view that you see, especially one with people and/or animals moving about and doing things 指景象、景色，尤指有人和／或動物活動的風光：*It was a delightful rural scene.* 那是賞心悅目的鄉村風光。

panorama a view of a wide area of land 指全景：*The tower offers a breathtaking panorama of Prague.* 從塔上可看到壯麗的布拉格全景。

PATTERNS

- a view/panorama **of** sth
- a **beautiful/breathtaking** view/sight/scene/panorama
- a **magnificent/spectacular** view/sight/panorama
- to **take in** the view/sight/scene
- to **admire** the view/sight

view·data /ˈvjuːdeɪtə; *NAmE* also -dætə/ (*US* also **video·tex**) *noun* [U] an information system in which computer data is sent along telephone lines and shown on a television screen 視傳，視傳系統（通過電話線路傳輸計算機數據並在電視屏上顯示）

view·er /ˈvjuːə(r)/ *noun* **1** a person watching television 電視觀眾：*The programme attracted millions of viewers.* 這個節目吸引了數百萬電視觀眾。➲ **COLLOCATIONS** at TELEVISION **2** a person who looks at or considers sth 觀看者；觀察者：*Some of her art is intended to shock the viewer.* 她的某些藝術作品旨在震撼觀賞者。◇ *viewers of the current political scene* 當前政治局面的觀察家 **3** a device for looking at SLIDES (= photographs on special film), for example a small box with a light in it（幻燈片）觀看器；幻燈機

viewer·ship /ˈvjuːəʃɪp; *NAmE* ˈvjuːər-/ *noun* [usually sing.] the number or type of people who watch a particular television programme or television channel（電視節目或頻道的）觀眾人數，觀眾類型

view·find·er /ˈvjuːfaɪndə(r)/ *noun* the part of a camera that you look through to see the area that you are photographing（照相機的）取景器

view·point /ˈvjuːpɔɪnt/ *noun* **1** **~ (on sth)** a way of thinking about a subject 觀點；看法 **SYN** **point of view**：*Try looking at things from a different viewpoint.* 試試從不同的角度觀察事物。◇ *She will have her own viewpoint on the matter.* 她對這個問題會有她自己的看法。◇ *From a practical viewpoint, I'd advise you not to go.* 從實際角度考慮，我勸你不要去。**2** a direction or place from which you look at sth 角度 **SYN** **angle**：*The artist has painted the scene from various viewpoints.* 那位畫家從各種角度把這一景色畫了下來。➲ see also POINT OF VIEW

V

view·port /ˈvjuːpɔːt; *NAmE* -pɔːrt/ *noun* **1** (*computing* 計) an area inside a frame on a screen, for viewing information（電腦屏幕的）視點，視埠 **2** a window in a SPACECRAFT（宇宙飛船的）觀察窗，觀察孔

vigil /ˈvɪdʒɪl/ *noun* [C, U] a period of time when people stay awake, especially at night, in order to watch a sick person, say prayers, protest, etc.（看望病人、禱告、抗議等的）不眠時間；（尤指）值夜，守夜祈禱：*His parents **kept a** round-the-clock **vigil** at his bedside.* 他父母日夜守護在他的牀邊。

vigi·lant /ˈvɪdʒɪlənt/ *adj.* (*formal*) very careful to notice any signs of danger or trouble 警覺的；警惕的；警戒的；謹慎 **SYN** **alert**, **watchful**：*A pilot must remain vigilant at all times.* 飛行員必須隨時保持警惕。▸ **vigi·lance** /-əns/ *noun* [U] **SYN** **watchfulness**：*She stressed the need for constant vigilance.* 她強調必須時常保持警惕。**vigi·lant·ly** *adv.*

vigi·lante /ˌvɪdʒɪˈlænti/ *noun* (sometimes *disapproving*) a member of a group of people who try to prevent crime or punish criminals in their community, especially because they think the police are not doing this（尤指認為警方不力而自發組織的）治安會會員 ▸ **vigi·lant·ism** /ˌvɪdʒɪˈlæntɪzəm/ *noun* [U]

vi·gnette /vɪnˈjet/ *noun* (*formal*) **1** a short piece of writing or acting that clearly shows what a particular person, situation, etc. is like（清晰展示人物特徵、局勢等的）短文，簡介，花絮；（表演）片段，小品 **2** a small picture or drawing, especially on the first page of a book（尤指書扉頁上的）小花飾，小插圖

vig·or·ous /ˈvɪɡərəs/ *adj.* **1** very active, determined or full of energy 充滿活力的；果斷的；精力充沛的 **SYN** **energetic**：*a vigorous campaign against tax fraud* 堅決打擊騙稅的運動 ◇ *a vigorous opponent of the government* 堅決反對政府的人 ◇ *Take **vigorous exercise** for several hours a week.* 每週做幾個小時劇烈運動。**2** strong and healthy 強壯的；強健的：*a vigorous young man* 身強力壯的年輕人 ◇ *This plant is a vigorous grower.* 這種植物生長起來茂盛茁壯。▸ **vig·or·ous·ly** *adv.*

vig·our (*especially US* **vigor**) /ˈvɪɡə(r)/ *noun* [U] energy, force or enthusiasm 精力；力量；活力；熱情 **SYN** **vitality**：*He worked with renewed vigour and determination.* 他將重燃起來的活力和熱情投入到工作中。

Vi·king /ˈvaɪkɪŋ/ *noun* a member of a race of Scandinavian people who attacked and sometimes settled in parts of NW Europe, including Britain, in the 8th to the 11th centuries 維金人，維京人，北歐海盜（斯堪的納維亞部落成員，8–11 世紀時劫掠英國等西北歐部份地區，有時在當地定居）

vile /vaɪl/ *adj.* (**viler**, **vil·est**) **1** (*informal*) extremely unpleasant or bad 糟糕透頂的；可惡的；極壞的 **SYN** **disgusting**：*a vile smell* 令人惡心的氣味 ◇ *The weather was really vile most of the time.* 天氣大部份時間都糟糕得很。◇ *He was in a vile mood.* 他的心情壞極了。➲ SYNONYMS at TERRIBLE **2** (*formal*) morally bad; completely unacceptable 邪惡的；令人完全不能接受的 **SYN** **wicked**：*the vile practice of taking hostages* 扣押人質的卑劣行徑 ▸ **vile·ly** /ˈvaɪlli/ *adv.* **vile·ness** *noun* [U]

vil·ify /ˈvɪlɪfaɪ/ *verb* (**vili·fies**, **vili·fy·ing**, **vili·fied**, **vili·fied**) **~ sb/sth (as sth)** | **~ sb/sth (for sth/for doing sth)** (*formal*) to say or write unpleasant things about sb/sth so that other people will have a low opinion of them 污衊；誹謗；詆譭；中傷 **SYN** **malign**, **revile** ▸ **vili·fi·ca·tion** /ˌvɪlɪfɪˈkeɪʃn/ *noun* [U]：*the vilification of single parents by right-wing politicians* 右翼政客對單親父母的詆譭

villa /ˈvɪlə/ *noun* **1** (*BrE*) a house where people stay on holiday/vacation 度假別墅：*We rented a holiday villa in Spain.* 我們在西班牙租了一座假日別墅。**2** a house in the country with a large garden, especially in southern Europe（尤指南歐的）鄉間莊園 **3** (*BrE*) a large house in a town（城內的）豪宅：*a Victorian villa in North London* 倫敦北部的維多利亞式豪宅 **4** (in Roman times 古羅馬時代) a country house or farm with land attached to it（附有土地的）鄉間宅第，別墅，莊園

vil·lage 🔑 /ˈvɪlɪdʒ/ *noun* **1** 🔑 [C] a very small town located in a country area 村莊；村鎮：*We visited towns and villages all over Spain.* 我們走遍了西班牙的城鎮和村莊。◇ *a **fishing/mountain/seaside village*** 漁村；山村；濱海村 ◇ (*especially BrE*) *the village shop* 鄉村商店 ◇ *Her books are about village life.* 她的書是關於鄉村生活的。➲ VISUAL VOCAB page V3 **HELP** Do not use **village** to talk about small towns in the US. In *NAmE* **village** is used for a small place in another country that seems more old-fashioned than a town in the US. 在美國說小村鎮不用 village。在美式英語中，village 用於指其他國家看似比美國小村鎮古老的小地方。**2** 🔑 **the village** [sing.] (*especially BrE*) the people who live in a village 鄉村居民；村民：*The whole village was invited to the party.* 全村的人都獲邀參加聚會。

ˌvillage ˈidiot *noun* a person in a village who is thought to be stupid; a stupid person 愚笨的村人；蠢人

vil·la·ger /ˈvɪlɪdʒə(r)/ *noun* a person who lives in a village 村民；鄉村居民；鄉下人

vil·lain /ˈvɪlən/ *noun* **1** the main bad character in a story, play, etc.（小說、戲劇等中的）主要反面人物，反派主角，壞人：*He often plays the part of the villain.* 他經常扮演反面人物。**2** a person who is morally bad or responsible for causing trouble or harm 惡棍；壞蛋：*the heroes and villains of the 20th century* * 20 世紀的英雄豪傑與罪魁禍首 ◇ *Industrialized nations are the real environmental villains.* 工業化國家是破壞環境的真正元兇。**3** (*BrE, informal*) a criminal 罪犯

IDM **the ˈvillain of the piece** (especially *humorous*) the person or thing that is responsible for all the trouble in a situation 元兇；禍首；癥結

vil·lain·ous /ˈvɪlənəs/ *adj.* [usually before noun] (*formal*) very evil; very unpleasant 邪惡的；可憎的

vil·lainy /ˈvɪləni/ *noun* [U] (*formal* or *humorous*) immoral or cruel behaviour 邪惡行為；罪惡

vil·lein /ˈvɪleɪn/ *noun* (in the Middle Ages) a poor man who had to work for a richer man in return for a small piece of land to grow food on（中世紀的）農奴，隸農

vil·lus /ˈvɪləs/ *noun* (*pl.* **villi** /ˈvɪlaɪ; -liː/) (*biology* 生) any one of the many small thin parts shaped like fingers that stick out from some surfaces on the inside of the body (for example in the INTESTINE). Villi increase the area of these surfaces so that substances can be absorbed by the body more easily. 絨毛（在小腸內壁等）

vim /vɪm/ *noun* [U] (*old-fashioned, informal*) energy 精力；活力；力量

vin·ai·grette /ˌvɪnɪˈɡret/ *noun* [U] a mixture of oil, VINEGAR and various HERBS, etc., used to add flavour to a salad 色拉調味汁（用油、醋和各種香草等混合而成）**SYN** **French dressing**

vin·da·loo /ˌvɪndəˈluː/ *noun* [U, C] (*pl.* **-oos**) a very spicy Indian dish, usually containing meat or fish 辛辣咖喱肉，辛辣咖喱魚（印度菜肴）：*lamb vindaloo* 辛辣咖喱羊肉

vin·di·cate /ˈvɪndɪkeɪt/ *verb* (*formal*) **1 ~ sth** to prove that sth is true or that you were right to do sth, especially when other people had a different opinion 證實；證明有理 **SYN** **justify**：*I have every confidence that this decision will be fully vindicated.* 我完全相信這一決定的正確性將得到充分證明。**2 ~ sb** to prove that sb is not guilty when they have been accused of doing sth wrong or illegal 澄清（責難或嫌疑）；證明（某人）無罪（責）：*New evidence emerged, vindicating him completely.* 新證據出現了，證明他完全是無辜的。▸ **vin·di·ca·tion** /ˌvɪndɪˈkeɪʃn/ *noun* [U, sing.]：*Anti-nuclear protesters regarded the Chernobyl accident as a clear vindication of their campaign.* 反核示威者認為，切爾諾貝利核電站核泄漏事故清楚地表明他們的反核運動是正確的。

vin·dic·tive /vɪnˈdɪktɪv/ *adj.* trying to harm or upset sb, or showing that you want to, because you think that they have harmed you 想復仇的；報復性的；懷恨的 **SYN** **spiteful**：*He accused her of being vindictive.* 他指

V

責她存心報復。◇ *a vindictive comment* 報復性的言論 ▶ **vin·dic·tive·ly** *adv.* **vin·dic·tive·ness** *noun* [U]

vine /vaɪn/ *noun* **1** a climbing plant that produces GRAPES 葡萄藤：*grapes on the vine* 藤上的葡萄 ◇ *vine leaves* 葡萄葉 ➲ see also GRAPEVINE **2** any climbing plant with long thin STEMS; one of these STEMS 藤本植物；攀緣植物；藤；藤蔓

vin·egar /ˈvɪnɪɡə(r)/ *noun* [U] a liquid with a bitter taste made from MALT (= a type of grain) or wine, used to add flavour to food or to preserve it 醋：*malt/wine vinegar* 麥芽／葡萄酒醋 ◇ *onions pickled in vinegar* 用醋泡製的洋葱 ➲ see also BALSAMIC VINEGAR

vin·egary /ˈvɪnɪɡəri/ *adj.* having a taste or smell that is typical of vinegar 醋的；酸的；有醋味的：*a vinegary wine* 酸葡萄酒

vine·yard /ˈvɪnjəd; *NAmE* -jərd/ *noun* a piece of land where GRAPES are grown in order to produce wine; a business that produces wine from the GRAPES it grows in a vineyard（為釀酒而種植的）葡萄園；（以自產葡萄進行生產的）葡萄酒廠 ➲ **VISUAL VOCAB** pages V2 ,V3 ➲ compare WINERY

vino /ˈviːnəʊ; *NAmE* -noʊ/ *noun* [U] (*informal, humorous*) wine 葡萄酒；果酒

vin·tage /ˈvɪntɪdʒ/ *noun, adj.*

■ *noun* **1** the wine that was produced in a particular year or place; the year in which it was produced 特定年份（或地方）釀製的酒；釀造年份：*the 1999 vintage* * 1999 年釀製的葡萄酒 ◇ *2005 was a particularly fine vintage.* * 2005 年是特別好的釀酒年份。 **2** [usually sing.] the period or season of gathering GRAPES for making wine 採摘葡萄釀酒的期間（或季節）；葡萄收穫期（或季節）：*The vintage was later than usual.* 這次葡萄的收穫季節比往常晚。

■ *adj.* [only before noun] **1** **vintage** wine is of very good quality and has been stored for several years（葡萄酒）優質的，上等的，佳釀的 **2** (*BrE*) (of a vehicle 車輛) made between 1919 and 1930 and admired for its style and interest 古色古香的（指 1917–1930 年間製造，車型和品味受人青睞的）➲ compare VETERAN CAR **3** typical of a period in the past and of high quality; the best work of the particular person（過去某個時期）典型的，優質的；（某人的）最佳作品的：*a collection of vintage designs* 優秀設計選編 ◇ *vintage TV drama* 最佳電視劇 ◇ *The opera is vintage Rossini.* 這部歌劇是羅西尼的最佳代表作。 **4** **~ year** a particularly good and successful year 成績卓著的一年；成功的一年：*2008 was not a vintage year for the movies.* * 2008 年對電影業來說不是個好年景。

vint·ner /ˈvɪntnə(r)/ *noun* (*old-fashioned, formal*) a person whose business is buying and selling wines or a person who grows GRAPES and makes wine 葡萄酒商；葡萄酒釀製者

vinyl /ˈvaɪnl/ *noun* [U] **1** a strong plastic that can bend easily, used for making wall, floor and furniture coverings, book covers, and, especially in the past, records 乙烯基；乙烯基塑料；（尤指舊時）壓製唱片的塑料 **2** records made of vinyl, in contrast to CDs 乙烯基唱片；黑膠唱片：*My dad had to buy CDs of all the albums he already owned on vinyl.* 我爸爸就是要買他已有的所有黑膠唱片的 CD 版。

viol /ˈvaɪəl/ *noun* an early type of musical instrument with strings, shaped like a VIOLIN 維奧爾琴（一種早期的拉弦樂器）

viola /viˈəʊlə; *NAmE* -ˈoʊ-/ *noun* a musical instrument with strings, that you hold under your chin and play with a BOW. A viola is larger than a VIOLIN and plays lower notes. 中提琴：*a viola player* 中提琴手 ➲ **VISUAL VOCAB** page V34

vio·late AW /ˈvaɪəleɪt/ *verb* **1** **~ sth** (*formal*) to go against or refuse to obey a law, an agreement, etc. 違反，違犯，違背（法律、協議等）SYN **flout**：*to violate international law* 違反國際法 **2** **~ sth** (*formal*) to disturb or not respect sb's peace, PRIVACY, etc. 侵犯（隱私等）；使人不得安寧；攪擾：*She accused the press photographers of violating her privacy.* 她指責新聞攝影記者侵犯了她的隱私。 **3** **~ sth** to damage or destroy a holy or special place 褻瀆，污損（神聖之地）SYN **desecrate**：*to violate a grave* 褻瀆墳墓 **4** **~ sb** (*literary or old-fashioned*) to force sb to have sex 強姦；姦污 SYN **rape** ▶ **vio·la·tion** AW /ˌvaɪəˈleɪʃn/ *noun* [U, C]：*They were in open violation of the treaty.* 他們公然違反條約。◇ *gross violations of human rights* 對人權的粗暴踐踏 **vio·la·tor** *noun*

vio·lence 0- /ˈvaɪələns/ *noun* [U]

1 0- violent behaviour that is intended to hurt or kill sb 暴力；暴行：***crimes/acts/threats of violence*** 暴力犯罪／行為／威脅 ◇ **~ (against sb)** *He condemned the protesters' use of violence against the police.* 他譴責抗議者對警察使用暴力。◇ ***domestic violence*** (= between family members) 家庭暴力 ◇ *Why do they always have to* ***resort to violence****?* 為什麼他們總是非要訴諸暴力不可呢？◇ ***Violence broke out/erupted*** *inside the prison last night.* 昨晚監獄裏發生了暴力事件。◇ *Is there too much sex and violence on TV?* 電視上有太多的色情和暴力嗎？ **2** 0- physical or emotional force and energy 狂熱；激情；激烈的力量：*The violence of her feelings surprised him.* 她感情之強烈使他吃驚。

vio·lent 0- /ˈvaɪələnt/ *adj.*

1 0- involving or caused by physical force that is intended to hurt or kill sb 暴力的；強暴的：***violent crime*** 暴力犯罪 ◇ *Students were involved in violent clashes with the police.* 學生和警察發生了暴力衝突。◇ *He met with a* ***violent death*** (= he was murdered, killed in a fight, etc.). 他遭暴力致死。◇ *Her husband was a violent man.* 她丈夫是個粗暴的人。◇ *The crowd suddenly* ***turned violent****.* 人群中突然有人開始大打出手。◇ *Children should not be allowed to watch violent movies* (= that show a lot of violence). 不應允許兒童看暴力電影。 **2** 0- showing or caused by very strong emotion 感情強烈的；激情的；由激情引起的：*There was a violent reaction from the public.* 公眾的反應強烈。 **3** 0- very strong and sudden 猛烈的；劇烈的；強烈的 SYN **intense, severe**：*I took a violent dislike to him.* 我很討厭他。◇ *a violent explosion* 劇烈的爆炸 ◇ *a violent change* 急劇的變化 ◇ *a violent headache* 劇烈的頭痛 **4** (of a colour 顏色) extremely bright 強烈的；鮮豔奪目的：*Her dress was a violent pink.* 她的連衣裙是非常鮮豔的粉紅色。

vio·lent·ly 0- /ˈvaɪələntli/ *adv.*

1 0- with great energy or strong movement, especially caused by a strong emotion such as fear or hatred 強烈地；激烈地：*She shook her head violently.* 她拚命搖頭。◇ *to shiver violently* 劇烈地顫抖 **2** 0- very strongly or severely 猛烈地；厲害地：*He was violently sick.* 他病得很厲害。◇ *They are violently opposed to the idea.* 他們強烈反對這個想法。 **3** 0- in a way that involves physical violence 兇猛地；兇狠地；強烈地：*The crowd reacted violently.* 人群反應強烈。

vio·let /ˈvaɪələt/ *noun* **1** [C] a small wild or garden plant with purple or white flowers with a sweet smell that appear in spring 紫羅蘭 **2** [U] a bluish-purple colour 藍紫色；紫羅蘭色：*dressed in violet* 身着藍紫色衣服的 ▶ **vio·let** *adj.*：*violet eyes* 藍紫色的眼睛 IDM see SHRINK *v.*

vio·lin /ˌvaɪəˈlɪn/ *noun* a musical instrument with strings, that you hold under your chin and play with a BOW 小提琴：*Brahms' violin concerto* 勃拉姆斯的小提琴協奏曲 ➲ **VISUAL VOCAB** page V34 ➲ compare VIOLA ➲ see also FIDDLE *n.* (1)

vio·lin·ist /ˌvaɪəˈlɪnɪst/ *noun* a person who plays a violin 小提琴手；小提琴演奏者

vio·list *noun* **1** /viˈəʊlɪst; *NAmE* -ˈoʊl-/ a person who plays a VIOLA 中提琴手；中提琴演奏者 **2** /ˈvaɪəlɪst/ a person who plays a VIOL 維奧爾琴手；維奧爾琴演奏者

vio·lon·cello /ˌvaɪələnˈtʃeləʊ; *NAmE* -loʊ/ *noun* (*pl.* **-os**) (*formal*) = CELLO

VIP /ˌviː aɪ ˈpiː/ *noun* the abbreviation for 'Very Important Person' (a famous or important person who is treated in a special way) 要人，貴賓（全寫為 Very Important Person）SYN **celebrity, dignitary**：*the VIP lounge* 貴賓廳 ◇ *to get* ***the VIP treatment*** 得到貴賓待遇

V

viper /ˈvaɪpə(r)/ *noun* **1** a small poisonous snake 蝰蛇（一種小毒蛇） **2** (*formal*) a person who harms other people 毒如蛇蠍的人；險惡的人

vir·ago /vɪˈrɑːɡəʊ; *NAmE* -ɡoʊ/ *noun* (*pl.* **-os**) (*literary, disapproving*) a woman who is aggressive and tries to tell people what to do 愛支使人的女性；潑婦；悍婦

viral /ˈvaɪrəl/ *adj.* like or caused by a virus 病毒的；病毒性的；病毒引起的： *a **viral infection*** 病毒性感染 ◇ *a **viral email*** (= that is sent on from one person to others, who then send it on again) 傳播病毒郵件

ˈviral marketing *noun* [U] a way of advertising in which information about a company's products or services is sent by email to people who then send it on by email to other people they know 病毒式營銷（通過互聯網用戶之間的電郵進行廣告宣傳）

vir·gin /ˈvɜːdʒɪn; *NAmE* ˈvɜːrdʒ-/ *noun, adj.*

■ ***noun*** **1** [C] a person who has never had sex 處女；童男 **2 the (Blessed) Virgin** [sing.] the Virgin Mary, mother of Jesus Christ 童貞瑪利亞（耶穌之母） **3** [C] a person who has no experience of a particular activity 無…經驗的人；新手： *a political virgin* 無政治經驗的人 ◇ *an Internet virgin* 網絡新手

■ ***adj.*** **1** [usually before noun] in its original pure or natural condition and not changed, touched or spoiled 未開發的；原始狀態的；天然的；未改變的；未觸動的： ***virgin forest/land/territory*** 原始森林；處女地；未開發地區 ◇ ***virgin snow*** (= fresh and not marked) 新雪 **2** [only before noun] with no sexual experience 處女的；貞潔的；童貞的： *a virgin bride* 貞潔的新娘 ◇ *the **virgin birth*** (= the belief that Mary was a virgin before and after giving birth to Jesus) 聖母瑪利亞童貞生子

vir·gin·al /ˈvɜːdʒɪnl; *NAmE* ˈvɜːrdʒ-/ *adj.* of or like a virgin; pure and innocent 處女（般）的；童貞的；貞潔的；純真的： *She was dressed in virginal white.* 她穿了一身潔白無瑕的衣服。

Vir·ginia creep·er /vəˌdʒɪniə ˈkriːpə(r); *NAmE* vərˈdʒ-/ *noun* [U, C] a climbing plant, often grown on walls, with large leaves that turn red in the autumn/fall 五葉地錦，弗吉尼亞爬山虎（常蔓生於牆上，葉大，秋季變成紅色）

vir·gin·ity /vəˈdʒɪnəti; *NAmE* vərˈdʒ-/ *noun* [U] the state of being a virgin 處女狀態；童貞；原始狀態： *He **lost his virginity*** (= had sex for the first time) *when he was 18.* 他在 18 歲時失去童貞。

Virgo /ˈvɜːɡəʊ; *NAmE* ˈvɜːrɡoʊ/ *noun* **1** [U] the 6th sign of the ZODIAC, the VIRGIN 黃道第六宮；室女宮；室女（星）座 **2** [C] (*pl.* **-os**) a person born when the sun is in this sign, that is between 23 August and 23 September, approximately 屬室女座的人（約出生於 8 月 23 日至 9 月 23 日）

vir·id·ian /vɪˈrɪdiən/ *noun* [U] (*technical* 術語) a bluish-green PIGMENT used in art; the colour of this pigment 鉻綠（顏料）；鉻綠色；青綠色

vir·ile /ˈvɪraɪl; *NAmE* ˈvɪrəl/ *adj.* (usually *approving*) **1** (of men 男子) strong and full of energy, especially sexual energy 強壯的；精力充沛的；（尤指）性機能強的 **2** having or showing the strength and energy that is considered typical of men 有陽剛之氣的；有男子氣概的；雄渾的： *a virile performance* 雄壯的演奏 ◇ *virile athleticism* 雄健的體魄

vir·il·ity /vəˈrɪləti/ *noun* [U] **1** sexual power in men（男性的）性功能，生殖力： *displays of male virility* 男子生殖力的表現 ◇ *a need to prove his virility* 證明他有生殖能力的需要 **2** strength or energy 力量；活力： *economic virility* 經濟活力

vir·ology /vaɪˈrɒlədʒi; *NAmE* -ˈrɑːl-/ *noun* [U] the scientific study of viruses and the diseases caused by them 病毒學 ▸ **vir·olo·gist** /vaɪˈrɒlədʒɪst; *NAmE* -ˈrɑːl-/ *noun*

vir·tual AW /ˈvɜːtʃuəl; *NAmE* ˈvɜːrtʃ-/ *adj.* [only before noun] **1** almost or very nearly the thing described, so that any slight difference is not important 很接近的；幾乎…的；事實上的；實際上的；實質上的： *The country was sliding into a state of virtual civil war.* 這個國家實際上正逐漸進入內戰狀態。 ◇ *The company has a virtual monopoly in this area of trade.* 這家公司實質上已經壟斷了這種貿易。 ◇ *He married a virtual stranger.* 他娶了一個幾乎素不相識的女子。 **2** made to appear to exist by the use of computer software, for example on the Internet（通過計算機軟件，如在互聯網上）模擬的，虛擬的： *New technology has enabled development of an online 'virtual library'.* 新技術已經使在線"虛擬圖書館"的發展成為可能。

vir·tu·al·ly 🔑 AW /ˈvɜːtʃuəli; *NAmE* ˈvɜːrtʃ-/ *adv.* **1** 🔑 almost or very nearly, so that any slight difference is not important 幾乎；差不多；事實上；實際上： *to be virtually impossible* 幾乎是不可能的 ◇ ***Virtually all** students will be exempt from the tax.* 差不多所有的學生都會獲得豁免此稅項。 ◇ *He virtually admitted he was guilty.* 他實際上已承認自己有罪。 ◇ *This year's results are virtually the same as last year's.* 今年的結果幾乎和去年的一樣。 **2** (*computing* 計) by the use of computer software that makes sth appear to exist; using VIRTUAL REALITY technology 模擬；虛擬；以模擬現實技術

ˌvirtual ˈmemory (also **ˌvirtual ˈstorage**) *noun* [U] (*computing* 計) extra memory that is automatically created when all the normal memory is being used 虛擬存貯（器）；虛擬記憶體

ˌvirtual reˈality *noun* [U] images created by a computer that appear to surround the person looking at them and seem almost real（計算機創造的）虛擬現實，擬境，虛擬時空

ˌvirtual ˈworld *noun* images, sounds and text used by a computer to create a world where people can communicate with each other, play games and pretend to live another life（計算機）虛擬世界

vir·tue /ˈvɜːtʃuː; *NAmE* ˈvɜːrtʃuː/ *noun* **1** [U] (*formal*) behaviour or attitudes that show high moral standards 高尚的道德；正直的品性；德行： *He led a life of virtue.* 他過着高尚的生活。 ◇ *She was certainly no **paragon of virtue**!* 她決不是道德高尚的典範！ **2** [C] a particular good quality or habit 美德；優秀品質；良好習慣： *Patience is not one of her virtues, I'm afraid.* 恐怕她不具有耐心這一美德。 **3** [C, U] an attractive or useful quality 優點；長處；用處 SYN **advantage**： *The plan **has the virtue of** simplicity.* 這項計劃的優點是簡單。 ◇ *He was extolling the virtues of the Internet.* 他讚揚了互聯網的長處。 ◇ *They could see **no virtue in** discussing it further.* 他們看不到再討論下去有什麼用處。

IDM **by/in virtue of sth** (*formal*) by means of or because of sth 憑藉；依靠；由於；因為： *She got the job by virtue of her greater experience.* 她由於經驗較為豐富而得到了那份工作。 **make a ˌvirtue of neˈcessity** to manage to gain an advantage from sth that you have to do and cannot avoid 不得已而力爭有所得 **ˌvirtue is its own reˈward** (*saying*) the reward for acting in a moral or correct way is the knowledge that you have done so, and you should not expect more than this, for example praise from other people or payment 施恩無他圖，有德便是報；美德本身就是成果 ➲ more at EASY *adj.*

vir·tu·os·ity /ˌvɜːtʃuˈɒsəti; *NAmE* ˌvɜːrtʃuˈɑːs-/ *noun* [U] (*formal*) a very high degree of skill in performing or playing（表演或演奏方面的）高超技藝，精湛演技： *technical virtuosity* 技術的嫻熟 ◇ *a performance of breathtaking virtuosity* 技藝令人叫絕的演出

vir·tu·oso /ˌvɜːtʃuˈəʊsəʊ; -ˈəʊzəʊ; *NAmE* ˌvɜːrtʃuˈoʊsoʊ; -ˈoʊzoʊ/ *noun, adj.*

■ ***noun*** (*pl.* **vir·tu·osos** or **vir·tu·osi** /-siː; -ziː/) a person who is extremely skilful at doing sth, especially playing a musical instrument 技藝超群的人；（尤指）演奏家： *a piano virtuoso* 鋼琴演奏家

■ ***adj.*** [only before noun] showing extremely great skill 技藝精湛的；技巧超群的： *a virtuoso performance* 技藝精湛的表演 ◇ *a virtuoso pianist* 鋼琴大師

vir·tu·ous /ˈvɜːtʃuəs; *NAmE* ˈvɜːrtʃ-/ *adj.* **1** (*formal*) behaving in a very good and moral way 品行端正的；品德高的；有道德的 SYN **irreproachable**： *a wise and virtuous man* 博學多識的君子 ◇ *She lived an entirely virtuous life.* 她一生品行端正。 **2** (*disapproving* or *humorous*) claiming to behave better or have higher moral standards than other people 自命不凡的；自命清

V

高的：*He was feeling virtuous because he had finished and they hadn't.* 因為他完成了而他們沒有，他自以為了不起。▸ **vir·tu·ous·ly** *adv.*

ˌvirtuous ˈcircle *noun* (*formal*) a series of events in which each one seems to increase the good effects of the previous one 良性循環 ➲ compare VICIOUS CIRCLE

viru·lent /ˈvɪrələnt; -rjəl-/ *adj.* **1** (of a disease or poison 疾病或毒物) extremely dangerous or harmful and quick to have an effect 致命的；惡性的；劇毒的 **2** (*formal*) showing strong negative and bitter feelings 狠毒的；惡毒的；不共戴天的：*virulent criticism* 惡意的批評 ◇ *virulent nationalism* 不共戴天的民族主義 ▸ **viru·lence** /-ləns/ *noun* [U] **viru·lent·ly** *adv.*

virus 🔑 /ˈvaɪrəs/ *noun*
1 🔑 a living thing, too small to be seen without a MICROSCOPE, that causes infectious disease in people, animals and plants 病毒；濾過性病毒：*the flu virus* 流感病毒 ◇ *a virus infection* 病毒感染 ➲ COLLOCATIONS at ILL, LIFE **2** 🔑 (*informal*) a disease caused by a virus 病毒性疾病；病毒病：*There's a virus going around the office.* 辦公室裏流行着一種病毒性疾病。 **3** 🔑 instructions that are hidden within a computer program and are designed to cause faults or destroy data（計算機程序中的）病毒 ➲ COLLOCATIONS at EMAIL ➲ see also VIRAL

visa /ˈviːzə/ *noun* a stamp or mark put in your passport by officials of a foreign country that gives you permission to enter, pass through or leave their country（護照的）簽證：*to* ***apply for a visa*** 申請簽證 ◇ *an* ***entry/tourist/transit/exit visa*** 入境／旅遊／過境／出境簽證

vis·age /ˈvɪzɪdʒ/ *noun* (*literary*) a person's face（人的）臉，面容

vis-à-vis /ˌviːz ɑː ˈviː/ *prep.* (from *French*) **1** in relation to 關於；對於：*Britain's role vis-à-vis the United States* 英國對美國的作用 **2** in comparison with 和…相比；與…相較：*It was felt that the company had an unfair advantage vis-à-vis smaller companies elsewhere.* 人們感到這家公司與其他地方的小公司相比佔有不公平的優勢。

vis·cera /ˈvɪsərə/ *noun* [pl.] (*anatomy* 解) the large organs inside the body, such as the heart, lungs and stomach 內臟；臟腑

vis·ceral /ˈvɪsərəl/ *adj.* **1** (*literary*) resulting from strong feelings rather than careful thought（未經過認真思考而）出自內心的，發自肺腑的：*She had a visceral dislike of all things foreign.* 凡是外國的東西，她都打心眼兒裏討厭。 **2** (*technical* 術語) relating to the viscera 內臟的；臟腑的

vis·cid /ˈvɪsɪd/ *adj.* (*formal* or *technical* 術語) sticky and SLIMY 黏稠的；黏質的：*the viscid lining of the intestine* 腸黏膜

vis·cose /ˈvɪskəʊz; -kəʊs; *NAmE* -koʊs; -koʊz/ *noun* [U] (*especially BrE*) a chemical made from CELLULOSE, used to make FIBRES which can be used to make clothes, etc. 黏膠

vis·count /ˈvaɪkaʊnt/ *noun* (in Britain) a NOBLEMAN of a rank below an EARL and above a BARON 子爵（英國貴族，低於伯爵而高於男爵）

vis·count·cy /ˈvaɪkaʊntsi/ *noun* the rank or position of a viscount 子爵爵位（或地位）

vis·count·ess /ˈvaɪkaʊntəs/ *noun* **1** a woman who has the rank of a VISCOUNT 女子爵 **2** the wife of a VISCOUNT 子爵夫人

vis·cous /ˈvɪskəs/ *adj.* (*technical* 術語) (of a liquid 液體) thick and sticky; not flowing freely 黏稠的；黏滯的 ▸ **vis·cos·ity** /vɪˈskɒsəti; *NAmE* -ˈskɑːs-/ *noun* [U]

vise (*NAmE*) (*BrE* **vice**) /vaɪs/ *noun* [C] a tool with two metal blocks that can be moved together by turning a screw. The vise is used to hold an object firmly while work is done on it. 台鉗；老虎鉗：*He held my arm in a* ***vise-like*** (= very firm) ***grip***. 他的手像老虎鉗一樣緊緊抓住了我的手臂。➲ VISUAL VOCAB page V20

visi·bil·ity AW /ˌvɪzəˈbɪləti/ *noun* [U] **1** how far or well you can see, especially as affected by the light or the weather 可見度；能見度；能見距離：***good/poor/bad/zero visibility*** 能見度高／低／差／為零 ◇ *Visibility was down to about 100 metres in the fog.* 霧中的能見距離降到了大約 100 米。◇ *The car has excellent* ***all-round visibility*** (= you can see what is around you very easily from it). 這輛車四周的視野極好。 **2** the fact or state of being easy to see 可見性；明顯性：***high visibility*** *equipment for cyclists* 騎自行車人配備的高可見性的設備 ◇ *The advertisements were intended to increase the company's visibility in the marketplace* (= to make people more aware of their products and services). 那些廣告旨在使這家公司在市場中更加引人注目。

vis·ible 🔑 AW /ˈvɪzəbl/ *adj.*
1 🔑 that can be seen 看得見的；可見的：*The house is* ***clearly visible*** *from the beach.* 從海灘可以清楚地看到那所房子。◇ *Most stars are not* ***visible to the naked eye***. 大多數星星肉眼看不見。 **2** 🔑 that is obvious enough to be noticed 明顯的；能注意到的 SYN **obvious**：*visible benefits* 顯而易見的實惠 ◇ *a visible police presence* 明顯有警察在場 ◇ *He showed no visible sign of emotion.* 他絲毫不露聲色。◇ *She made a visible effort to control her anger.* 看得出她竭力控制自己不發火。➲ compare INVISIBLE

ˌvisible miˈnority *noun* (*CanE*) a group whose members are clearly different in race from those of the majority race in a society 顯性少數民族（與佔社會主體的種族明顯不同）

vis·ibly AW /ˈvɪzəbli/ *adv.* in a way that is easily noticeable 易察覺地；明顯地：*He was visibly shocked.* 看得出他大為震驚。◇ *She paled visibly at the news.* 她聽到這消息時臉色明顯地變得蒼白。

vi·sion 🔑 AW /ˈvɪʒn/ *noun*
1 🔑 [U] the ability to see; the area that you can see from a particular position 視力；視野：*to have* ***good/perfect/poor/blurred/normal vision*** 視力好／極好／差／模糊／正常 ◇ ***20–20 vision*** (= the ability to see perfectly) * 20–20 的視力 ◇ *Cats have good* ***night vision***. 貓在夜間視力好。◇ *The couple moved outside her* ***field of vision***. 這對夫婦離開了她的視野。◇ *He glimpsed something on the edge of his vision.* 他斜眼瞥見了點什麼。➲ note at SIGHT ➲ see also TUNNEL VISION **2** 🔑 [C] an idea or a picture in your imagination 想像；幻象：*He had a vision of a world in which there would be no wars.* 他幻想有一個沒有戰爭的世界。◇ *I* ***had visions*** *of us getting hopelessly lost.* 我想像我們完全迷失了方向。 **3** 🔑 [C] a dream or similar experience, especially of a religious kind 夢幻；幻象；神示；異象：*The idea came to her in a vision.* 她在神示中想到了這個主意。 **4** 🔑 [U] the ability to think about or plan the future with great imagination and intelligence 想像力；眼力；遠見卓識 SYN **foresight**：*a leader of vision* 有遠見的領袖 **5** [C] **a ~ (of sth)** (*literary*) a person of great beauty or who shows the quality mentioned 俊男；天仙；有…氣質的人：*She was a vision in white lace.* 她穿着鑲白色網眼紗邊的衣服美極了。◇ *a vision of loveliness* 可愛的人 **6** [U] the picture on a television or cinema/movie theater screen（電視或影院屏幕的）影像，畫面：*We apologize for the loss of vision.* 很抱歉沒法顯示畫面。

vi·sion·ary /ˈvɪʒənri; *NAmE* -ʒəneri/ *adj., noun*
■ ***adj.*** **1** (*approving*) original and showing the ability to think about or plan the future with great imagination and intelligence 有眼力的；有創見的；有遠見卓識的：*a visionary leader* 有遠見卓識的領袖 **2** relating to dreams or strange experiences, especially of a religious kind 夢幻的；耽於幻想的；（尤指）宗教異象的；神示的：*visionary experiences* 異象體驗
■ ***noun*** (*pl.* **-ies**) (usually *approving*) a person who has the ability to think about or plan the future in a way that is intelligent or shows imagination 有眼力的人；有遠見卓識的人

visit 🔑 /ˈvɪzɪt/ *verb, noun*
■ ***verb*** **1** 🔑 [T] **~ sb/sth** to go to see a person or a place for a period of time 訪問；拜訪；看望；參觀：*She went to visit relatives in Wales.* 她去威爾士看望親戚了。◇ *The Prime Minister is visiting Japan at the moment.* 首相目前正在訪問日本。◇ *You should visit your dentist at least twice a year.* 你應該每年至少去看兩次牙科醫生。 **2** 🔑 [T] **~ sth** (*computing* 計) to go to a website on the Internet 訪問（互聯網上的網站）：*For more information, visit*

V

our website. 欲知詳情，請訪問我們的網站。 **3** [I, T] to stay somewhere for a short time（短暫地）作客，逗留：*We don't live here. We're just visiting.* 我們不住在這裏，只作短期停留。◇ **~ sth** *The lake is also visited by seals in the summer.* 夏天也有海豹游到這湖裏來。 **4** [T] **~ sth** to make an official visit to sb, for example to perform checks or give advice 視察；巡視：*government inspectors visiting schools* 視察學校的政府檢察員

PHR V **'visit sth on/upon sb/sth** (*old use*) to punish sb/sth 對…進行懲罰：*The sins of the fathers are visited upon the children* (= children are blamed or suffer for what their parents have done). 父輩造的孽報應到子女頭上。 **'visit with sb** (*NAmE*) to spend time with sb, especially talking socially 與某人聊天；與某人閒談：*Come and visit with me some time.* 找個時間來跟我聊聊吧。

■ **noun** **1** **~ (to sb/sth) (from sb)** an occasion or a period of time when sb goes to see a place or person and spends time there 訪問；參觀；遊覽；逗留；看望：*It's my first visit to New York.* 這是我第一次訪問紐約。◇ *They're on an* ***exchange visit*** *to France.* 他們到法國進行互訪。◇ *If you have time,* ***pay a visit to*** *the local museum.* 你若有空，參觀一下當地的博物館。◇ *We had a visit from the police last night.* 昨晚警察來我們家了。◇ *Is this a* ***social visit****, or is it business?* 這是社交性的拜訪，還是業務性的？◇ *a visit to the doctor* 看醫生 ◇ (*BrE*) *a* ***home visit*** (= when your doctor visits you) 上門出診 ➲ see also FLYING VISIT **2** (*computing* 計) an occasion when sb looks at a website on the Internet（到網站的）訪問：*Visits to our website have doubled in a year.* 我們網站的訪問人次一年內翻了一番。 **3** **~ (with sb)** (*NAmE, informal*) an occasion when two or more people meet to talk in an informal way 碰頭；會面

vis·it·ation /ˌvɪzɪˈteɪʃn/ *noun* **1** [U] (*NAmE*) the right of a parent who is divorced or separated from his or her partner to visit a child who is living with the partner（離婚父母對子女的）探視權：*She is seeking more liberal visitation with her daughter.* 她正在尋求對女兒更自由的探視權。◇ *visitation rights* 探視子女的權利 ➲ compare ACCESS *n.* (2) **2** [C, U] **~ (of/from sb/sth)** (*formal*) an official visit, especially to check that rules are being obeyed and everything is as it should be 視察；巡視 **3** [C] **~ (of/from sb/sth)** (*formal*) an unexpected appearance of sth, for example a GHOST（神靈等的）顯現，顯示，出現 **4** [C] **~ (of sth)** (*formal*) a disaster that is believed to be a punishment from God（視為上帝懲罰的）天災，災難，災禍：*a visitation of plague* 天降瘟疫

vis·it·ing /ˈvɪzɪtɪŋ/ *adj.* [only before noun] a **visiting** professor or lecturer is one who is teaching for a fixed period at a particular university or college, but who normally teaches at another one（指教授或講師）客座的

'visiting card (*BrE*) (*NAmE* **'calling card**) (also **card** *BrE, NAmE*) *noun* (especially in the past) a small card with your name on it which you leave with sb after, or instead of, a formal visit（尤指舊時訪客留下或其他人用以表示到訪的）名片 ➲ compare BUSINESS CARD

vis·it·or /ˈvɪzɪtə(r)/ *noun* **~ (to …)** a person who visits a person or place 來訪者；訪問者；參觀者；遊客：*We've got visitors coming this weekend.* 本週末我們有客人來訪。◇ *Do you get many visitors?* 來探望你的人多嗎？◇ *She's a frequent visitor to the US.* 她經常去美國。◇ *The theme park attracts 2.5 million visitors a year.* 這個主題樂園每年吸引 250 萬遊客。◇ *How can we attract more visitors to our website?* 我們如何才能吸引更多人訪問我們的網站呢？ ➲ see also HEALTH VISITOR

'visitors' book *noun* a book in which visitors write their names, addresses and sometimes comments, for example, at a hotel or place of public interest 來客登記簿；來賓留言簿；遊客意見簿

visor /ˈvaɪzə(r)/ *noun* **1** a part of a helmet that can be pulled down to protect the eyes and face（頭盔上的）面甲，面罩，護面 ➲ VISUAL VOCAB page V65 **2** a curved piece of plastic, etc. worn on the head above the eyes to protect them from the sun 遮陽帽舌 **3** a small piece of plastic, etc. inside the front window of a car that can be pulled down to protect the driver's eyes from the sun（汽車內擋風玻璃上方的）遮陽板 ➲ VISUAL VOCAB page V52 **4** (*NAmE*) = BILL *n.* (9)

vista /ˈvɪstə/ *noun* **1** (*literary*) a beautiful view, for example, of the countryside, a city, etc.（農村、城市等的）景色，景觀 SYN **panorama** **2** (*formal*) a range of things that might happen in the future（未來可能發生的）一系列情景，一連串事情 SYN **prospect**：*This new job could open up whole new vistas for her.* 這項新工作可能給她開闢全新的前景。

vis·ual AW /ˈvɪʒuəl/ *adj., noun*

■ **adj.** of or connected with seeing or sight 視力的；視覺的：*I have a very good visual memory.* 我過目不忘。◇ *the visual arts* 視覺藝術 ◇ *The building makes a tremendous visual impact.* 這棟建築物給人以極其深刻的視覺印象。▶ **visu·al·ly** AW *adv.*：***visually handicapped/impaired*** 有視力障礙的；視力受損的 ◇ *visually exciting* 視覺上令人興奮

■ **noun** a picture, map, piece of film, etc. used to make an article or a talk easier to understand or more interesting 視覺資料（指説明性的圖片、影片等）：*He used striking visuals to get his point across.* 他用醒目的視覺資料解釋他的觀點。

ˌvisual 'aid *noun* [usually pl.] a picture, video, etc. used in teaching to help people to learn or understand sth 直觀教具；視覺資料 ➲ WRITING TUTOR page WT21

ˌvisual di'splay unit *noun* (*computing* 計) = VDU

ˌvisual 'field *noun* (*technical* 術語) = FIELD OF VISION

visu·al·ize (*BrE* also **-ise**) AW /ˈvɪʒuəlaɪz/ *verb* to form a picture of sb/sth in your mind 使形象化；想像；構思；設想 SYN **imagine**：**~ sb/sth/yourself (as sth)** *Try to visualize him as an old man.* 盡量設想他是一位老人。◇ **~ what, how, etc. …** *I can't visualize what this room looked like before it was decorated.* 我想像不出這個房間在裝修之前是什麼樣子。◇ **~ sb/sth/yourself doing sth** *It can help to visualize yourself making your speech clearly and confidently.* 設想自己口齒清晰和充滿信心地演講是很有助益的。◇ **~ doing sth** *She couldn't visualize climbing the mountain.* 她想像不出如何攀登這座大山。▶ **visu·al·iza·tion, -isa·tion** AW /ˌvɪʒuəlaɪˈzeɪʃn; *NAmE* -ləˈz-/ *noun* [U, C]

vita /ˈviːtə/ *noun* (*US*) = CURRICULUM VITAE (2)

Language Bank 用語庫

vital

Saying that something is necessary 表達某事是必要的

- **It is vital that** journalists can verify the accuracy of their reports. 新聞記者能夠核實其報道的準確性，這一點至關重要。
- Journalists play a **vital/crucial** role in educating the public. 新聞記者對教育公眾起着極其重要的作用。
- Public trust is a **crucial** issue for all news organizations. 對所有新聞機構來説，公眾的信任是至關重要的問題。
- The ability to write well is **essential** for any journalist. 好的筆頭功夫對任何一個新聞記者都是非常重要的。
- The Internet has become an **indispensable** tool for reporters. 互聯網已經成為記者不可或缺的工具。
- In journalism, accuracy is **paramount**./… is **of paramount importance**. 在新聞工作中，準確至關重要。
- **It is imperative that** journalists maintain the highest possible standards of reporting. 新聞記者的當務之急是盡可能保持最高水平的報道。

➲ Synonyms at ESSENTIAL

➲ Language Banks at EMPHASIS, IMPERSONAL

V

vital 0-w /'vaɪtl/ *adj.*
1 0-w necessary or essential in order for sth to succeed or exist 必不可少的；對…極重要的： **~ (for sth)** *the vitamins that are vital for health* 保持健康必不可少的維生素 ◇ **~ (to sth)** *Good financial accounts are vital to the success of any enterprise.* 妥善的財務賬目對任何公司的成功都是極其重要的。◇ *Reading is **of vital importance** in language learning.* 閱讀在語言學習中至關重要。◇ *The police play **a vital role** in our society.* 警察在我們的社會中起着極其重要的作用。◇ **~ that …** ***It is vital that** you keep accurate records when you are self-employed.* 幹個體的要準確記錄賬目，這十分重要。◇ **~ to do sth** *It was vital to show that he was not afraid.* 最重要的是要表現出他毫無畏懼。 ➲ SYNONYMS at ESSENTIAL ➲ LANGUAGE BANK at EMPHASIS, IMPERSONAL **2** [only before noun] connected with or necessary for staying alive 生命的；維持生命所必需的：*the **vital organs*** (= the brain, heart, lungs, etc.) 活命器官 **3** (of a person 人) full of energy and enthusiasm 生氣勃勃的；充滿生機的；熱情洋溢的 SYN **dynamic**

vi·tal·ity /vaɪ'tæləti/ *noun* [U] energy and enthusiasm 生命力；活力；熱情 SYN **vigour**：*She is bursting with vitality and new ideas.* 她朝氣蓬勃，滿腦子新主意。

vi·tal·ly /'vaɪtəli/ *adv.* extremely; in an essential way 極其；絕對：*Education is **vitally important** for the country's future.* 教育對國家的未來是至關重要的。

the vi·tals /'vaɪtlz/ *noun* [pl.] (*old-fashioned* or *humorous*) the organs of the body that are essential for staying alive, for example the brain, heart, lungs, etc. （維持生命的）重要器官

ˌvital ˈsign *noun* [usually pl.] (*medical* 醫) a measurement that shows that sb is alive, such as the rate of their breathing, their body temperature or their HEARTBEAT 生命體徵，生命徵象（如呼吸、體溫、心搏等）

ˌvital staˈtistics *noun* [pl.] **1** figures that show the number of births and deaths in a country 生命統計，人口動態統計（顯示一國出生和死亡的人口數字） **2** (*BrE, informal*) the measurements of a woman's chest, waist and hips 女子三圍尺寸

vita·min /'vɪtəmɪn; *NAmE* 'vaɪt-/ *noun* a natural substance found in food that is an essential part of what humans and animals eat to help them grow and stay healthy. There are many different vitamins. 維生素；維他命：*breakfast cereals enriched with vitamins* 增加了維生素的穀物早餐食品 ◇ *vitamin deficiency* 維生素缺乏 ◇ *vitamin pills* 維生素丸 ➲ COLLOCATIONS at DIET

ˌvitamin ˈC (also **asˌcorbic ˈacid**) *noun* [U] a vitamin found in fruits such as oranges and lemons, and in green vegetables 維生素 C，維他命 C，抗壞血酸（存在於柑橘、檸檬等水果和綠色蔬菜）：*Oranges are rich in vitamin C.* 柑橘裏含有豐富的維生素 C。

viti·ate /'vɪʃieɪt/ *verb* [usually passive] **~ sth** (*formal*) to spoil or reduce the effect of sth 使失效；削弱效用

viti·cul·ture /'vɪtɪkʌltʃə(r); 'vaɪt-/ *noun* [U] (*technical* 術語) the science or practice of growing GRAPES 葡萄栽培學；葡萄栽培術；葡萄栽培

vit·re·ous /'vɪtriəs/ *adj.* (*technical* 術語) hard, shiny and transparent like glass 玻璃質的；玻璃狀的；透明的：*vitreous enamel* 玻璃釉

ˌvitreous ˈhumour (*especially US* **ˌvitreous ˈhumor**) *noun* [U] (*anatomy* 解) the transparent jelly-like substance inside the eye （眼睛的）玻璃體液，玻璃狀液 ➲ compare AQUEOUS HUMOUR

vit·rify /'vɪtrɪfaɪ/ *verb* (**vit·ri·fies, vit·ri·fy·ing, vit·ri·fied, vit·ri·fied**) [I, T] **~ (sth)** (*technical* 術語) to change or make sth change into glass, or a substance like glass 使成玻璃（狀物質）；使玻璃化 ▶ **vit·ri·fi·ca·tion** /ˌvɪtrɪfɪ'keɪʃn/ *noun* [U]

vit·riol /'vɪtriəl/ *noun* [U] (*formal*) very cruel and bitter comments or criticism 尖刻無情的話（或批評） SYN **abuse**

vit·ri·ol·ic /ˌvɪtri'ɒlɪk; *NAmE* -'ɑːlɪk/ *adj.* (*formal*) (of language or comments 言語或評論) full of anger and hatred 憤怒的；惡意的；尖酸刻薄的 SYN **bitter**：*The newspaper launched a vitriolic attack on the president.* 這家報紙對總統發起了一場惡意的攻擊。

vitro ➲ IN VITRO

vi·tu·per·ation /vɪˌtjuːpə'reɪʃn; *NAmE* vaɪˌtuː-/ *noun* [U] (*formal*) cruel and angry criticism 辱罵；斥責；責罵 SYN **abuse** ▶ **vi·tu·pera·tive** /vɪ'tjuːpərətɪv; *NAmE* vaɪ'tuːpəreɪtɪv/ *adj.*：*a vituperative attack* 謾罵式的攻擊

viva[1] /'viːvə/ *exclamation* used for expressing support for sb or sth （表示擁護）萬歲

viva[2] /'vaɪvə/ *noun* (*BrE*) = VIVA VOCE

viv·ace /vɪ'vɑːtʃeɪ/ *noun* (*music* 音) (from *Italian*) a piece of music to be played in a quick lively way 活板音樂 ▶ **viv·ace** *adv., adj.*

viv·acious /vɪ'veɪʃəs; *NAmE* also vaɪ'v-/ *adj.* (*approving*) (especially of a woman 尤指女子) having a lively, attractive personality 可愛的；活潑的；動人的：*He had three pretty, vivacious daughters.* 他有三個活潑漂亮的女兒。 ▶ **viv·acious·ly** *adv.* **viv·acity** /vɪ'væsəti; *NAmE* also vaɪ'v-/ *noun* [U]：*He was charmed by her beauty and vivacity.* 他被她的美麗與活潑迷住了。

viv·ar·ium /vaɪ'veəriəm; vɪ'v-; *NAmE* -'ver-/ *noun* (*pl.* **viv·ar·ia** /vaɪ'veəriə; vɪ'v-; *NAmE* -'ver-/) a container for keeping live animals in, especially for scientific study 生態缸（用於飼養動物作科研用途等）

viva voce /ˌvaɪvə 'vəʊtʃi; *NAmE* 'voʊtʃi/ (*BrE* also **viva**) *noun* (from *Latin*) a spoken exam, especially in a British university （尤指英國大學的）口試

vive la dif·fer·ence /ˌviːv lɑː ˌdɪfə'rɒns; *NAmE* -'rɑːns/ *exclamation* (from *French, humorous*) used to show that you think it is good that there is a difference between two people or things, especially a difference between men and women （尤用以贊同男女有別）差別萬歲

vivid /'vɪvɪd/ *adj.* **1** (of memories, a description, etc. 記憶、描述等) producing very clear pictures in your mind 清晰的；生動的；逼真的 SYN **graphic**：*vivid memories* 清晰的記憶 ◇ *He gave a vivid account of his life as a fighter pilot.* 他生動地描述了他那戰鬥機飛行員的生活。 **2** (of light, colours, etc. 光、顏色等) very bright 鮮明的；耀眼的；鮮豔的；強烈的：*vivid blue eyes* 碧藍的眼睛 ➲ SYNONYMS at BRIGHT **3** (of sb's imagination 人的想像) able to form pictures of ideas, situations, etc. easily in the mind 豐富的 ▶ **viv·id·ly** *adv.*：*I vividly remember the day we first met.* 我對我們第一次相見的那天記憶猶新。 **viv·id·ness** *noun* [U]：*the vividness of my dream* 我的夢境的清晰逼真

viv·ip·ar·ous /vɪ'vɪpərəs/ *adj.* (*biology* 生) (of an animal 動物) producing live babies from its body rather than eggs 胎生的 ➲ compare OVIPAROUS, OVOVIVIPAROUS

vivi·sec·tion /ˌvɪvɪ'sekʃn/ *noun* [U] the practice of doing experiments on live animals for medical or scientific research 活體解剖

vivo ➲ IN VIVO

vixen /'vɪksn/ *noun* **1** a female FOX (= a wild animal of the dog family) 雌狐 **2** (*old-fashioned*) an unpleasant and bad-tempered woman 潑婦；悍婦；母夜叉

viz. /vɪz/ *adv.* (*formal, especially BrE*) used to introduce a list of things that explain sth more clearly or are given as examples 即；就是 SYN **namely**：*four major colleges of surgery, viz. London, Glasgow, Edinburgh and Dublin* 四所主要的外科學院，即倫敦、格拉斯哥、愛丁堡和都柏林

viz·ier /vɪ'zɪə(r); *NAmE* vɪ'zɪr/ (also **wazir**) *noun* an important official in some Muslim countries in the past 維齊（舊時某些穆斯林國家的高官）

VJ /ˌviː dʒeɪ/ *abbr.* = VIDEO JOCKEY

VLE /ˌviː el 'iː/ *noun* (*BrE*) the abbreviation for 'virtual learning environment' (a software system for teaching and learning using the Internet) 虛擬學習環境（全寫為 virtual learning environment，利用互聯網教學的軟件系統）

'V-neck *noun* an opening for the neck in a piece of clothing shaped like the letter V; a piece of clothing with a V-neck * V 形領；V 字領；雞心領；V 形領服裝：*a V-neck sweater* 雞心領套衫 ◇ *a navy V-neck* 一件海軍藍

V

的 V 形領衣服 ➲ VISUAL VOCAB page V63 ➲ picture at NECK ▶ ˈV-necked *adj.*：*a V-necked sweater* 雞心領套衫

VOA /ˌviː əʊ ˈeɪ; *NAmE* oʊ/ *abbr.* VOICE OF AMERICA

vo·cabu·lary 🔑 /vəˈkæbjələri; *NAmE* -leri/ *noun* [C, U] (*pl.* -ies)

1 🔑 all the words that a person knows or uses（某人掌握或使用的）詞彙，詞彙量：*to have a* ***wide/limited vocabulary*** 詞彙量大／有限 ◇ *your* ***active vocabulary*** (= the words that you use) 你的常用詞彙 ◇ *your* ***passive vocabulary*** (= the words that you understand but don't use) 你的不常用詞彙 ◇ *Reading will increase your vocabulary.* 閱讀會增加你的詞彙量。◇ *The word 'failure' is not in his vocabulary* (= for him, failure does not exist). 在他的詞典中沒有"失敗"這個詞。➲ SYNONYMS at LANGUAGE ➲ see also DEFINING VOCABULARY **2** 🔑 all the words in a particular language（某一語言的）詞彙，詞彙量：*When did the word 'bungalow' first enter the vocabulary?* * bungalow 一詞何時進入（英語）詞彙中的？➲ SYNONYMS at LANGUAGE **3** the words that people use when they are talking about a particular subject（某學科中所使用的）詞彙：*The word has become part of advertising vocabulary.* 這個單詞已經成了廣告用語。➲ SYNONYMS at LANGUAGE **4** (also *informal* **vocab** /ˈvəʊkæb; *NAmE* ˈvoʊkæb/) a list of words with their meanings, especially in a book for learning a foreign language（尤指外語教科書中附有釋義的）詞彙表

vocal /ˈvəʊkl; *NAmE* ˈvoʊkl/ *adj., noun*

■ ***adj.*** **1** [only before noun] connected with the voice 嗓音的；發聲的：*vocal music* 聲樂 ◇ *the vocal organs* (= the tongue, lips, etc.) 發聲器官 ➲ SYNONYMS at SPOKEN **2** telling people your opinions or protesting about sth loudly and with confidence 大聲表達的；直言不諱的：*He has been very vocal in his criticism of the government's policy.* 他對政府政策的批評一直是直言不諱。◇ *The protesters are a small but vocal minority.* 抗議者人數不多但敢於直言。

■ ***noun*** [usually pl.] the part of a piece of music that is sung, rather than played on a musical instrument（樂曲中的）歌唱部份，聲樂部份：*backing vocals* 伴唱 ◇ *In this recording Armstrong himself is* ***on vocals****.* 在這個錄音中阿姆斯特朗親自領唱。

ˌvocal ˈcords *noun* [pl.] the thin strips of TISSUE in the throat that are moved by the flow of air to produce the voice 聲帶

vo·cal·ic /vəʊˈkælɪk; *NAmE* voʊ-/ *adj.* (*phonetics* 語音) relating to or consisting of a vowel or vowels 元音的；元音性的；母音的 ➲ compare CONSONANTAL

vo·cal·ist /ˈvəʊkəlɪst; *NAmE* ˈvoʊ-/ *noun* a singer, especially in a pop, rock or JAZZ band（尤指流行音樂、搖滾樂或爵士樂樂隊的）歌手，歌唱者：*a* ***lead/guest/backing vocalist*** 領唱／特邀／伴唱歌手 ➲ compare INSTRUMENTALIST

V

vo·cal·iza·tion (*BrE* also **-isa·tion**) /ˌvəʊkəlaɪˈzeɪʃn; *NAmE* ˌvoʊkələˈzeɪʃn/ *noun* (*formal*) **1** [C] a word or sound that is produced by the voice 說出的話；嗓音；歌聲：*the vocalizations of animals* 動物發出的聲音 **2** [U] the process of producing a word or sound with the voice 說話；發聲；唱歌；發嗓音

vo·cal·ize (*BrE* also **-ise**) /ˈvəʊkəlaɪz; *NAmE* ˈvoʊ-/ *verb* (*formal*) **1** [T] **~ sth** to use words to express sth 用言語表達 SYN **articulate, express**：*Showing children pictures sometimes helps them to vocalize their ideas.* 讓兒童看圖畫有時有助於他們用言語表達思想。**2** [I, T] **~ (sth)** to say or sing sounds or words 說（話）；唱（歌）；哼；發聲：*Your baby will begin to vocalize long before she can talk.* 你的寶寶遠在會說話之前就會開始咿呀發聲。

vo·cal·ly /ˈvəʊkəli; *NAmE* ˈvoʊ-/ *adv.* **1** in a way that uses the voice 用嗓音；口頭上：*to communicate vocally* 口頭交流 **2** by speaking in a loud and confident way 大聲地；直言不諱地：*They protested vocally.* 他們直言不諱地提出了抗議。

vo·ca·tion /vəʊˈkeɪʃn; *NAmE* voʊ-/ *noun* **1** [C] a type of work or way of life that you believe is especially suitable for you（認為特別適合自己的）工作，職業，生活方式 SYN **calling**：*Nursing is not just a job—it's a vocation.* 護理不僅僅是一項工作，而且還是一種職業。◇ *She believes that she has found her true vocation in life.* 她相信自己找到了真正適合自己的生活方式。◇ *You missed your vocation—you should have been an actor.* 你幹錯行了，你本該當演員。➲ COLLOCATIONS at JOB **2** [C, U] **~ (for sth)** a belief that a particular type of work or way of life is especially suitable for you（認為某種工作或生活方式特別適合自己的）信心，使命感：*He has a vocation for teaching.* 他是教書的材料。◇ *She is a doctor with a strong sense of vocation.* 她是一位具有強烈使命感的醫生。**3** [C, U] a belief that you have been chosen by God to be a priest or NUN 聖召；神召：*a vocation to the priesthood* 司鐸聖召

vo·ca·tion·al /vəʊˈkeɪʃənl; *NAmE* voʊ-/ *adj.* connected with the skills, knowledge, etc. that you need to have in order to do a particular job 職業的；職業技術的；業務知識的：***vocational education/qualifications/training*** 職業教育／資格／培訓

voˈcational school *noun* [C, U] (in the US) a school that teaches skills that are necessary for particular jobs（美國）職業學校，技術學校

voca·tive /ˈvɒkətɪv; *NAmE* ˈvɑːk-/ *noun* (*grammar* 語法) (in some languages 用於某些語言) the form of a noun, a pronoun or an adjective used when talking to a person or thing 呼格；呼格詞；呼語 ➲ compare ABLATIVE, ACCUSATIVE, DATIVE, GENITIVE, NOMINATIVE ▶ **voca·tive** *adj.*：*the vocative case* 呼格

vo·cif·er·ous /vəˈsɪfərəs; *NAmE* voʊˈs-/ *adj.* (*formal*) expressing your opinions or feelings in a loud and confident way 大聲疾呼的；喧嚷的；大叫大嚷的 SYN **strident**：*vociferous protests* 高聲的抗議 ◇ *a vociferous critic of the president's stance* 猛烈批評總統所持態度的人 ▶ **vo·cif·er·ous·ly** *adv.*：*to complain vociferously* 大聲地抱怨

vodka /ˈvɒdkə; *NAmE* ˈvɑːdkə/ *noun* **1** [U] a strong clear alcoholic drink, made from grain, originally from Russia 伏特加（原產於俄國的烈性酒）**2** [C] a glass of vodka 一杯伏特加酒：*I'll have a vodka and lime.* 我要喝一杯酸橙伏特加。

vogue /vəʊg; *NAmE* voʊg/ *noun* [C, usually sing., U] **~ (for sth)** a fashion for sth 流行；時髦；風行；風尚：*the vogue for child-centred education* 以孩子為中心的教育潮流 ◇ *Black is* ***in vogue*** *again.* 黑色又成了流行色。➲ COLLOCATIONS at FASHION

voice 🔑 /vɔɪs/ *noun, verb*

■ ***noun***

▸ SOUND FROM MOUTH 口中發出的聲音 **1** 🔑 [C, U] the sound or sounds produced through the mouth by a person speaking or singing 嗓音；說話聲；歌唱聲：*I could hear voices in the next room.* 我能聽到隔壁說話的聲音。◇ *to speak* ***in a deep/soft/loud/quiet, etc. voice*** 低沉地說、輕柔地說、大聲地說、輕聲地說等 ◇ *'I promise,' she said in a* ***small voice*** (= a quiet, shy voice). "我答應。"她小聲說。◇ *to* ***raise/lower your voice*** (= to speak louder/more quietly) 提高／壓低嗓門 ◇ ***Keep your voice down*** (= speak quietly). 說話輕一些。◇ *Don't take that* ***tone of voice*** *with me!* 別用那種腔調和我說話。◇ *Her voice shook with emotion.* 她激動得聲音顫抖。◇ *'There you are,' said a voice behind me.* "你來啦。"我身後一個聲音說道。◇ *When did his* ***voice break*** (= become deep like a man's)? 他的嗓音什麼時候變粗的？◇ *He was suffering from flu and had* ***lost his voice*** (= could not speak). 他患了流感，嗓子啞了。◇ *She has a good singing voice.* 她有一副很好的歌喉。◇ *She was* ***in good voice*** (= singing well) *at the concert tonight.* 她在今晚的音樂會上唱得不錯。

▸ -VOICED 嗓音… **2** (in adjectives 構成形容詞) having a voice of the type mentioned 有…嗓音的；嗓音…的：*low-voiced* 嗓門低的 ◇ *squeaky-voiced* 嗓音尖細的

▸ OPINION 看法 **3** 🔑 [sing.] **~ (in sth)** the right to express your opinion and influence decisions 發言權；發表意見的權利；影響：*Employees should* ***have a voice*** *in the decision-making process.* 雇員在決策的過程中應該有發

言權。**4** [C] a particular attitude, opinion or feeling that is expressed; a feeling or an opinion that you become aware of inside yourself 呼聲；意見；態度；心聲：*He pledged that his party would listen to the voice of the people.* 他保證他的政黨願意傾聽人民的呼聲。◇ *Very few* ***dissenting voices*** *were heard on the right of the party.* 在黨的右翼聽不到什麼不同的政見。◇ *the* ***voice of reason/sanity/conscience*** 理性的／理智的／良心的聲音 ◇ *'Coward!' a tiny* ***inner voice*** *insisted.* "膽小鬼！"內心一把小聲音堅持說。
▸ **GRAMMAR** 語法 **5** [sing.] **the active/passive ~** the form of a verb that shows whether the subject of a sentence performs the action (*the active voice*) or is affected by it (*the passive voice*) 主動／被動語態
▸ **PHONETICS** 語音學 **6** [U] sound produced by movement of the VOCAL CORDS used in the pronunciation of vowels and some consonants 濁音（聲帶震動發出的元音和某些輔音）➲ see also VOICED, VOICELESS
IDM **give voice to sth** to express your feelings, worries, etc. 表露心聲；表白心跡 **make your 'voice heard** to express your feelings, opinions, etc. in a way that makes people notice and consider them（為引起他人注意）發表意見，表達感情 **with ˌone 'voice** as a group; with everyone agreeing 異口同聲；眾口一詞：*The various opposition parties speak with one voice on this issue.* 在這個問題上各反對黨派眾口一詞。➲ more at FIND *v.*, SOUND *n.*, STILL *adj.*, TOP *n.*
■ ***verb***
▸ **GIVE OPINION** 發表意見 **1 ~ sth** to tell people your feelings or opinions about sth 表示，表達，吐露（感情或意見）：*to* ***voice complaints/criticisms/doubts/objections, etc.*** 表示不滿、批評、懷疑、異議等 ◇ *A number of parents have* ***voiced concern*** *about their children's safety.* 一些家長對他們子女的安全表示了擔心。
▸ **PHONETICS** 語音學 **2 ~ sth** to produce a sound with a movement of your VOCAL CORDS as well as your breath 發濁音；發嗓音 ➲ compare UNVOICED (2), VOICELESS

'voice box *noun* the area at the top of the throat that contains the VOCAL CORDS 聲匣；喉 **SYN** **larynx**

voiced /vɔɪst/ *adj.* (*phonetics* 語音) (of consonants 輔音) produced by moving your VOCAL CORDS. For example, the consonants /b/, /d/ and /g/ are voiced. 濁音性的；帶聲的 **OPP** **unvoiced**

voice·less /'vɔɪsləs/ *adj.* (*phonetics* 語音) (of consonants 輔音) produced without moving your VOCAL CORDS. For example, the consonants /p/, /t/ and /k/ are voiceless. 清音的 **SYN** **unvoiced** **OPP** **voiced**

voice·mail /'vɔɪsmeɪl/ *noun* [U] an electronic system which can store telephone messages, so that sb can listen to them later 語音信箱；電話留言

the ˌVoice of A'merica *noun* [sing.] (*abbr.* **VOA**) an official US government service that broadcasts news and other programmes in English and many other languages around the world 美國之音（廣播電台）

'voice-over *noun* information or comments in a film/movie, television programme, etc. that are given by a person who is not seen on the screen（電影或電視節目）解說，畫外音：*She earns a lot of money doing voice-overs for TV commercials.* 她為電視廣告作解說收入很高。

voice·print /'vɔɪsprɪnt/ *noun* (*technical* 術語) a printed record of a person's speech, showing the different FREQUENCIES and lengths of sounds as a series of waves 聲紋（顯示個人說話聲音頻率和長度的打印記錄）

'voice recognition *noun* [U] **1** technology that allows a computer to identify a voice（計算機）語音識別 **2** = SPEECH RECOGNITION

void /vɔɪd/ *noun, adj., verb*
■ ***noun*** [usually sing.] (*formal* or *literary*) a large empty space 空間；空白；真空；空虛：*Below him was nothing but a black void.* 他下面只是一片漆黑。◇ (*figurative*) *The void left by his mother's death was never filled.* 他母親死後留下的空虛感永遠沒能填補上。
■ ***adj.*** **1 ~ of sth** (*formal*) completely lacking sth 缺乏；沒有 **SYN** **devoid**：*The sky was void of stars.* 天空沒有一顆星星。**2** (*law* 律) (of a contract, an agreement etc.) not valid or legal 無效的：*The agreement was declared void.* 本協議已宣佈無效。**3** (*formal*) empty 空的；空空如也的：*void spaces* 空位 **IDM** see NULL
■ ***verb*** **1 ~ sth** (*law* 律) to state officially that sth is no longer valid 使無效；宣佈…作廢；取消 **SYN** **invalidate, nullify** **2 ~ sth** (*formal*) to empty waste matter from the BLADDER or BOWELS 排泄，排放（大小便）

'void deck *noun* (*SEAsianE*) the ground floor of a block of flats/apartments, which is left empty and is usually for the use of all the people who live in the building 公寓樓大堂（在底層，常為公用）

voile /vɔɪl/ *noun* [U] a type of cloth made of cotton, wool or silk that is almost transparent, used for making clothes 巴里紗（用以製衣的一種棉、毛或絲的近乎透明的織物）

VoIP /vɔɪp/ (also **ˌIP te'lephony**) *noun* [U] the abbreviation for 'voice over Internet protocol' (a telephone system that allows users to make and receive calls using the Internet) * IP 電話，網絡電話（通過互聯網來傳送語音的電話系統，全寫為 voice over Internet protocol）

vol. **AW** *abbr.* VOLUME *n.* 卷；冊：*the Complete Works of Byron Vol. 2* 《拜倫全集》第 2 卷

vola·tile /'vɒlətaɪl; *NAmE* 'vɑːlətl/ *adj.* **1** (often *disapproving*) (of a person or their moods 人或其情緒) changing easily from one mood to another 易變的；無定性的；無常性的：*a highly volatile personality* 反覆無常的個性 **2** (of a situation 情況) likely to change suddenly; easily becoming dangerous 可能急劇波動的；不穩定的；易惡化的 **SYN** **unstable**：*a highly volatile situation from which riots might develop* 可能會出現動亂的極不穩定的局勢 ◇ *a volatile exchange rate* 劇烈波動的匯率 **3** (*technical* 術語) (of a substance 物質) that changes easily into a gas 易揮發的；易發散的：*Petrol is a volatile substance.* 汽油是揮發性物質。▸ **vola·til·ity** /ˌvɒlə'tɪləti; *NAmE* ˌvɑːl-/ *noun* [U]

vol-au-vent /'vɒl ə vɒ̃; *NAmE* ˌvɔːl oʊ 'vɑ̃ː/ *noun* (*BrE*, from *French*) a small round case of light PASTRY filled with meat, fish, etc. in a cream sauce, often eaten with your fingers at parties 酥皮餡餅（以肉、魚等加奶油作餡的小圓千層酥）

vol·can·ic /vɒl'kænɪk; *NAmE* vɑːl-; vɔːl-/ *adj.* caused or produced by a volcano 火山的；火山引起的；火山產生的：*volcanic rocks* 火山岩 ◇ *volcanic eruptions* 火山噴發

vol·cano /vɒl'keɪnəʊ; *NAmE* vɑːl'keɪnoʊ; vɔːl'keɪnoʊ/ *noun* (*pl.* **-oes** or **-os**) a mountain with a large opening at the top through which gases and LAVA (= hot liquid rock) are forced out into the air, or have been in the past 火山：*An active volcano may erupt at any time.* 活火山會隨時噴發。◇ *a dormant volcano* (= one that is not active at present) 休眠火山 ◇ *an extinct volcano* (= one that is no longer active) 死火山

vol·can·ology /ˌvɒlkə'nɒlədʒi; *NAmE* ˌvɑːlkə'nɑːl-; ˌvɔːlkə'nɑːl-/ (also **vul·can·ology**) *noun* [U] the scientific study of volcanoes 火山學

vole /vəʊl; *NAmE* voʊl/ *noun* a small animal like a mouse or RAT that lives in fields or near rivers 田鼠 ➲ see also WATER VOLE

vol·ition /və'lɪʃn; *NAmE* also voʊ'l-/ *noun* [U] (*formal*) the power to choose sth freely or to make your own decisions 意志力；自願選擇；自行決斷 **SYN** **free will**：*They left entirely* ***of their own volition*** (= because they wanted to). 他們完全是自願離開的。

vol·ley /'vɒli; *NAmE* 'vɑːli/ *noun, verb*
■ ***noun*** **1** (in some sports, for example TENNIS or football (SOCCER) 某些體育運動，如網球或足球) a hit or kick of the ball before it touches the ground 截擊空中球；凌空擊球（或踢球）：*She hit a forehand volley into the net.* 她正手截擊球未過網。**2** a lot of bullets, stones, etc. that are fired or thrown at the same time（子彈的）群射，齊發；（石塊的）齊投：*A volley of shots rang out.* 一排子彈呼嘯而出。◇ *Police fired a volley over the heads of the crowd.* 警察朝人群頭頂上方射出一排子彈。**3** a lot of questions, comments, insults, etc. that are directed at sb quickly one after the other（質問、評論、辱罵等

的）接連發出 SYN **torrent**： *She faced a volley of angry questions from her mother.* 她受到母親一連串憤怒的質問。

■ *verb* [T, I] **~ (sth)** (in some sports, for example TENNIS or football (SOCCER) 某些體育運動，如網球或足球) to hit or kick the ball before it touches the ground 攔截（空中球）；截擊；凌空抽射：*He volleyed the ball into the back of the net.* 他凌空一腳把球踢入網窩。

vol·ley·ball /ˈvɒlibɔːl; *NAmE* ˈvɑːl-; ˈvɔːl-/ *noun* [U] a game in which two teams of six players use their hands to hit a large ball backwards and forwards over a high net while trying not to let the ball touch the ground on their own side 排球運動 ➲ see also BEACH VOLLEYBALL

volt /vəʊlt; vɒlt; *NAmE* voʊlt/ *noun* (*abbr.* **V**) a unit for measuring the force of an electric current 伏，伏特（電壓單位）：*a high security fence with 5 000 volts passing through it* 有 5 000 伏電流通過的森嚴鐵絲網

volt·age /ˈvəʊltɪdʒ; *NAmE* ˈvoʊlt-/ *noun* [U, C] electrical force measured in volts 電壓；伏特數：***high/low voltage*** 高／低壓

volte-face /ˌvɒlt ˈfɑːs; *NAmE* ˌvɔːlt/ *noun* [sing.] (*formal*) a complete change of opinion or plan（意見或計劃的）大轉變，完全轉變 SYN **about-turn**： *This represents a volte-face in government thinking.* 這代表着政府觀點的徹底轉變。

volt·meter /ˈvəʊltmiːtə(r); *NAmE* ˈvoʊlt-/ *noun* an instrument for measuring VOLTAGE 伏特計；電壓表

vol·uble /ˈvɒljʊbl; *NAmE* ˈvɑːljə-/ *adj.* (*formal*) **1** talking a lot, and with enthusiasm, about a subject 健談的；滔滔不絕的：*Evelyn was very voluble on the subject of women's rights.* 伊夫林談起女權這個話題口若懸河。**2** expressed in many words and spoken quickly 流利的；明快的：*voluble protests* 振振有詞的抗議 ▸ **vol·ubly** /ˈvɒljʊbli; *NAmE* ˈvɑːljə-/ *adv.*

vol·ume 🔑 AW /ˈvɒljuːm; *NAmE* ˈvɑːl-; -jəm/ *noun* **1** 🔑 [U, C] the amount of space that an object or a substance fills; the amount of space that a container has 體積；容積；容量：*How do you measure the volume of a gas?* 你如何計量氣體的體積？◇ *jars of different volumes* 不同容量的罐子 **2** 🔑 [U, C] the amount of sth 量；額：*the **sheer volume** (= large amount) of business* 大量業務◇ *This work has grown in volume recently.* 這項工作的量最近增加了。◇ *New roads are being built to cope with the increased volume of traffic.* 正在修建新的道路以應付增加了的交通量。◇ *Sales volumes fell 0.2% in June.* 六月份的銷售額下降了 0.2%。**3** 🔑 [U] the amount of sound that is produced by a television, radio, etc. 音量；響度：*to **turn the volume up/down*** 把音量調大／小 **4** 🔑 [C] (*abbr.* **vol.**) a book, that is part of a series of books（成套書籍中的）一卷，一冊：*an encyclopedia in 20 volumes* 一套 20 卷的百科全書 **5** [C] (*formal*) a book 書：*a library of over 50 000 volumes* 藏書 5 萬多冊的圖書館◇ *a slim volume of poetry* 薄薄的一本詩集 **6** [C] (*abbr.* **vol.**) a series of different issues of the same magazine, especially all the issues for one year 卷，合訂本（同一雜誌的一系列期刊，尤指一年的）：*'New Scientist' volume 142, number 3* 《新科學家》第 142 卷第 3 號 IDM see SPEAK

vo·lu·min·ous /vəˈluːmɪnəs/ *adj.* (*formal*) **1** (of clothing 衣服) very large; having a lot of cloth 肥大的；寬鬆的；用布料多的 SYN **ample**： *a voluminous skirt* 肥大的裙子 **2** (of a piece of writing, a book, etc. 文章、書等) very long and detailed 浩繁的；大部頭的；長篇的；冗長的 **3** (of a container, piece of furniture, etc. 容器、傢具等) very large 很大的：*I sank down into a voluminous armchair.* 我一下子坐在了寬大的扶手椅裏。▸ **vo·lu·min·ous·ly** *adv.*

volu·mize (*BrE* also **-ise**) /ˈvɒljʊmaɪz; *NAmE* ˈvɑːl-/ *verb* **~ sth** to make hair look thicker 使（頭髮）顯得濃密；使（頭髮）豐盈 ▸ **volu·mizer** /ˈvɒljʊmaɪzə(r); *NAmE* ˈvɑːl-/ *noun*

vol·un·tar·ily AW /ˈvɒləntrəli; *NAmE* ˌvɑːlənˈterəli/ *adv.* **1** willingly; without being forced 自願地；自動地；主動地：*He was not asked to leave—he went voluntarily.* 沒人讓他走，是他主動走的。**2** without payment; free 無償地；義務地：*The fund is voluntarily administered.* 這個基金是無償管理的。

vol·un·tary AW /ˈvɒləntri; *NAmE* ˈvɑːlənteri/ *adj., noun*

■ *adj.* **1** done willingly, not because you are forced 自願的；志願的；主動的；自告奮勇的：*a voluntary agreement* 自願協議◇ *Attendance on the course is purely voluntary.* 聽這門課純粹是自願的。◇ *to pay **voluntary contributions** into a pension fund* 自願向退休基金交款◇ (*BrE*) *He took **voluntary redundancy**.* 他選擇了自願裁汰。OPP **compulsory** **2** [usually before noun] (of work 工作) done by people who choose to do it without being paid 自願性的；無償的；義務性的：*I do some **voluntary work** at the local hospital.* 我在當地醫院從事一些義務性工作。◇ *She works there on a **voluntary basis**.* 她自願在那裏無償工作。◇ ***voluntary services/bodies/agencies/organizations*** (= organized, controlled or supported by people who choose to do this and are usually not paid) 義務性服務／團體／機構／組織◇ ***the voluntary sector*** (= organizations which are set up to help people and which do not make a profit, for example charities) 志願機構 **3** [only before noun] (of a person 人) doing a job without wanting to be paid for it 自願的；志願的；義務的；自發的：*a voluntary worker* 志願工作者 **4** (*technical* 術語) (of movements of the body 人體活動) that you can control 隨意的；可以控制的 OPP **involuntary**

■ *noun* (*pl.* **-ies**) a piece of music played before, during or after a church service, usually on an organ 儀式終始曲，即興曲（通常用風琴在教堂禮拜儀式前後或期間演奏）

ˌVoluntary ˌService Overˈseas *noun* [U] (*abbr.* **VSO**) a British charity that sends skilled people such as doctors and teachers to work in other countries as volunteers 海外志願者服務社（英國外派醫生、教師等技術人士的慈善機構）

vol·un·teer AW /ˌvɒlənˈtɪə(r); *NAmE* ˌvɑːlənˈtɪr/ *noun, verb*

■ *noun* **1** a person who does a job without being paid for it 義務工作者；志願者：*volunteer helpers* 無償援助者◇ *Schools need volunteers to help children to read.* 學校需要義務工作者幫助兒童閱讀。**2** a person who offers to do sth without being forced to do it 自告奮勇者；主動做某事的人：*Are there any volunteers to help clear up?* 有自願幫助清掃的人嗎？**3** a person who chooses to join the armed forces without being forced to join 志願兵；義勇兵 ➲ compare CONSCRIPT *n.*

■ *verb* **1** [I, T] to offer to do sth without being forced to do it or without getting paid for it 自願做；義務做；無償做：**~ to do sth** *Jill volunteered to organize a petition.* 吉爾自告奮勇組織請願。◇ **~ (for/as sth)** *Several staff members volunteered for early retirement.* 幾位職員自願提前退休。◇ **~ sth (for/as sth)** *He volunteered his services as a driver.* 他自願服務充當司機。**2** [T] **~ sth** | **+ speech** to suggest sth or tell sb sth without being asked 主動建議（或告訴）：*to volunteer advice* 主動提出忠告 **3** [I] **~ (for sth)** | **~ to do sth** to join the army, etc. without being forced to 自願參軍；當志願兵：*to volunteer for military service* 自願服兵役 **4** [T] **~ sb (for/as sth)** | **~ sb to do sth** to suggest sb for a job or an activity, even though they may not want to do it（未經當事人同意）舉薦：*They volunteered me for the job of interpreter.* 他們擅自指定由我擔任口頭翻譯。

the ˌVolunteer Reˈserve Forces *noun* [pl.] the parts of the British armed forces for people who are volunteers and train in their free time so they can be used in a national emergency（英國）志願兵員預備役部隊

vo·lup·tu·ary /vəˈlʌptʃuəri; *NAmE* -ueri/ *noun* (*pl.* **-ies**) (*formal*, usually *disapproving*) a person who enjoys physical, especially sexual, pleasures very much 驕奢淫逸者；縱慾者

vo·lup·tu·ous /vəˈlʌptʃuəs/ *adj.* **1** (*formal*) (of a woman 女人) attractive in a sexual way with large breasts and hips 體態豐滿的；性感的；肉感的 SYN **buxom**： *a voluptuous woman* 體態豐滿的女人◇ *a voluptuous body* 豐滿性感的身體 **2** (*literary*) giving you physical pleasure 令人舒服的；舒適的 SYN **sensual**： *voluptuous perfume*

V

芬芳馥郁的香水 ▶ **vo·lup·tu·ous·ly** *adv.* **vo·lup·tu·ous·ness** *noun* [U]

vomit /ˈvɒmɪt; *NAmE* ˈvɑːm-/ *verb, noun*

■ ***verb*** (also *informal* ˌ**throw** ˈ**up**) [I, T] to bring food from the stomach back out through the mouth 嘔；吐；嘔吐 **SYN** **be sick**：*The smell made her want to vomit.* 那氣味使得她想要吐。◇ **~ sth up** *He had vomited up his supper.* 他把晚飯吃的東西都吐了出來。◇ **~ sth** *The injured man was vomiting blood.* 那受傷的人在吐血。➲ see also SICK *v.*

■ ***noun*** [U] food from the stomach brought back out through the mouth 嘔吐物

voo·doo /ˈvuːduː/ *noun* [U] a religion that is practised especially in Haiti and involves magic and WITCHCRAFT 伏都教，巫毒教（尤指在海地奉行的一種宗教，涉及魔法和巫術）

vor·acious /vəˈreɪʃəs/ *adj.* (*formal*) **1** eating or wanting large amounts of food 飯量大的；貪吃的；狼吞虎嚥的 **SYN** **greedy**：*a voracious eater* 貪吃的人 ◇ *to have a* ***voracious appetite*** 胃口極大 **2** wanting a lot of new information and knowledge（對信息、知識）渴求的；求知慾強的 **SYN** **avid**：*a voracious reader* 求知慾極強的讀者 ◇ *a boy with a voracious and undiscriminating appetite for facts* 一個如飢似渴地尋求事實的男孩 ▶ **vor·acious·ly** *adv.* **vor·acity** /vəˈræsəti/ *noun* [U]

vor·tex /ˈvɔːteks; *NAmE* ˈvɔːrt-/ *noun* (*pl.* **vor·texes** or **vor·ti·ces** /-tɪsiːz/) **1** (*technical* 術語) a mass of air, water, etc. that spins around very fast and pulls things into its centre 低渦；渦旋 **SYN** **whirlpool**, **whirlwind** **2** (*literary*) a very powerful feeling or situation that you cannot avoid or escape from 感情（或局勢）的漩渦：*They were caught up in a whirling vortex of emotion.* 他們陷入了感情漩渦。

vo·tary /ˈvəʊtəri; *NAmE* ˈvoʊt-/ *noun* (*pl.* **-ies**) **~ of sb/sth** (*formal*) a person who worships or loves sb/sth 仰慕者；愛好者；信仰者：*a votary of John Keats* 約翰•濟慈的崇拜者

vote 0→ /vəʊt; *NAmE* voʊt/ *noun, verb*

■ ***noun*** **1** 0→ [C] **~ (for/against sb/sth)** a formal choice that you make in an election or at a meeting in order to choose sb or decide sth 選票；票：*There were 21 votes for and 17 against the motion, with 2 abstentions.* 這項動議有 21 票贊成，17 票反對，2 票棄權。◇ *The motion was passed by 6 votes to 3.* 這項動議以 6 票對 3 票獲得通過。◇ *The chairperson has the* ***casting/deciding vote****.* 主席可投決定票。◇ *The Green candidate won over 3 000 of the 14 000* ***votes cast****.* 綠黨候選人在 14 000 張投票總數中獲得了 3 000 多張選票。 **2** 0→ [C] **~ (on sth)** an occasion when a group of people vote on sth 投票；選舉；表決：*to* ***have/take a vote*** *on an issue* 就一問題進行表決 ◇ *The issue was* ***put to the vote****.* 這一問題被付諸表決。◇ *The vote was unanimous.* 表決一致通過。➲ SYNONYMS at ELECTION **3** 0→ **the vote** [sing.] the total number of votes in an election 投票總數；選票總數：*She obtained 40% of the vote.* 她獲得 40% 的選票。◇ *The party increased their share of the vote.* 這個政黨得票份額有所增長。**4** 0→ **the vote** [sing.] the vote given by a particular group of people, or for a particular party, etc.（某一群體的）投票總數；（某一政黨等的）得票總數：*the student vote* 學生的投票總數 ◇ *the Labour vote* 工黨得票總數 **5** 0→ **the vote** [sing.] the right to vote, especially in political elections（尤指政治選舉中的）投票權，選舉權，表決權：*In Britain and the US, people get the vote at 18.* 在英國和美國，國民 18 歲開始有選舉權。➲ see also BLOCK VOTE

Collocations 詞語搭配

Voting in elections 在選舉中投票

Running for election 參加選舉

- **conduct/hold** an election/a referendum 舉行選舉／全民公決
- (*especially NAmE*) **run for** office/election/governor/mayor/president/the White House 競選公職；參加競選；競選州長／市長／總統／美國總統
- (*especially BrE*) **stand for** election/office/Parliament/the Labour Party/a second term 參加競選；競選公職／議會議員；當工黨候選人；競選連任
- **hold/call/contest** a general/national election 舉行／要求／角逐大選／全國選舉
- **launch/run** a presidential election campaign 開始總統競選活動
- **support/back** a candidate 支持候選人
- **sway/convince/persuade** voters/the electorate 說服選民／全體選民
- **appeal to/attract/woo/target** (*NAmE*) swing voters/(*BrE*) floating voters 吸引游離選民；尋求游離選民的支持；瞄準游離選民
- **fix/rig/steal** an election/the vote 操縱選舉；暗中舞弊獲取選票

Voting 投票

- **go to/be turned away from** (*especially BrE*) a polling station/(*NAmE*) a polling place 去／被拒絕進入投票站投票
- **cast** a/your vote/ballot (for sb) 投（某人）一票
- **vote for** the Conservative candidate/the Democratic party 投票給保守黨候選人／民主黨
- **mark/spoil** your ballot paper 在選票上做標記；投廢票
- **count** (*BrE*) the postal votes/(*especially NAmE*) the absentee ballots 清點郵寄選票數
- **go to/be defeated at** the ballot box 去投票箱投票；競選失敗
- **get/win/receive/lose** votes 贏得／失去選票
- **get/win** (60% of) the popular/black/Hispanic/Latino/Muslim vote 贏得大眾／黑人／西班牙裔美國人／居住在美國的拉丁美洲人／穆斯林（60%）的選票
- **win** the election/(*in the US*) the primaries/a seat in Parliament/a majority/power 贏得大選／（美國的）初選／議會中的一個席位／多數票／權力
- **lose** an election/the vote/your majority/your seat 在選舉中失敗；失去多數人的支持／席位
- **win/come to power in** a landslide (victory) (= with many more votes than any other party) 以壓倒多數的選票獲勝／掌權
- **elect/re-elect sb** (as) mayor/president/an MP/senator/congressman/congresswoman 選舉／再度選舉某人為市長／總統／議員／參議員／國會議員／國會女議員

Taking power 掌權

- **be sworn** into office/in as president 宣誓就職／就任總統
- **take/administer** (*in the US*) the oath of office（美國）宣誓就職；聽取就職宣誓
- **swear/take** (*in the UK*) an/the oath of allegiance（英國）宣誓效忠
- **give/deliver** (*in the US*) the president's inaugural address 發表（美國）總統就職演說
- **take/enter/hold/leave** office 就職；任職；離職
- **appoint sb** (as) ambassador/governor/judge/minister 任命某人為大使／州長／法官／部長
- **form** a government/a cabinet 組建政府／內閣
- **serve** two terms as prime minister/in office 任兩屆總理；兩屆任職

➲ more collocations at ECONOMY, POLITICS

■ *verb* **1** 🔑 [I, T] to show formally by marking a paper or raising your hand which person you want to win an election, or which plan or idea you support 投票（贊成／反對）；表決（支持／不支持）；選舉：**~ (for/against sb/sth)** *Did you vote for or against her?* 你投了她的贊成票還是反對票？◇ *How did you vote at the last election?* 在上次選舉中你是怎麼投的票？◇ **~ in favour of sth** *Over 60% of members voted in favour of* (= for) *the motion.* * 60% 以上的成員對這一動議投了贊成票。◇ **~ (on sth)** *We'll listen to the arguments on both sides and then vote on it.* 我們將先聽取雙方的論點，然後再表決。◇ *Only about half of the electorate bothered to vote.* 只有約半數的選民參加了投票。◇ **~ sth** *We voted Democrat in the last election.* 我們在上次選舉中投了民主黨的票。◇ **~ to do sth** *Parliament voted to set up an independent inquiry into the matter.* 議會表決對這個問題進行獨立調查。➲ COLLOCATIONS at POLITICS **2** 🔑 [T, usually passive] **~ sb/sth + noun** to choose sb/sth for a position or an award by voting 選出，推舉（某人擔任某職）；表決（授獎給某人）：*He was voted most promising new director.* 他當選為最有前途的新導演。**3** [T, usually passive] **~ sth + noun** to say that sth is good or bad 表明，認為，公認（某事好或壞）：*The event was voted a great success.* 大家認為這項活動很成功。**4** [T] **~ sb/yourself sth** to agree to give sb/yourself sth by voting 投票同意：*The directors have just voted themselves a huge pay increase.* 董事們剛剛投票同意給他們自己大幅度提高工資。**5** [T] **~ (that)** ... to suggest sth or support a suggestion that sb has made 提議；建議；支持（建議）：*I vote (that) we go out to eat.* 我提議我們到外面去吃飯。

IDM **ˌvote with your ˈfeet** to show what you think about sth by going or not going somewhere 用腳投票（用去或不去某處表示想法）：*Shoppers voted with their feet and avoided the store.* 購物者對那家商店避而遠之。

PHR V **ˌvote sb/sth↔ˈdown** to reject or defeat sb/sth by voting for sb/sth else 投票否決；投票擊敗 **ˌvote sb ˈin | ˌvote sb ˈinto/ˈonto sth** to choose sb for a position by voting 投票選出…任職：*He was voted in as treasurer.* 他當選為司庫。◇ *She was voted onto the board of governors.* 她獲選入董事會。**ˌvote sb ˈout | ˌvote sb ˈout of/ˈoff sth** to dismiss sb from a position by voting 投票免去…的職務：*He was voted out of office.* 經投票他被免去了職務。**ˌvote sth↔ˈthrough** to bring a plan, etc. into effect by voting for it 投票通過（計劃等）：*A proposal to merge the two companies was voted through yesterday.* 兩家公司合併的建議已於昨日投票通過。

ˌvote of ˈconfidence *noun* [usually sing.] a formal vote to show that people support a leader, a political party, an idea, etc.（表示支持領導人、政黨、看法等的）信任票

ˌvote of ˌno ˈconfidence *noun* [usually sing.] a formal vote to show that people do not support a leader, a political party, an idea, etc.（表示不支持領導人、政黨、看法等的）不信任票

ˌvote of ˈthanks *noun* [usually sing.] a short formal speech in which you thank sb for sth and ask other people to join you in thanking them 謝辭

voter /ˈvəʊtə(r); *NAmE* ˈvoʊ-/ *noun* a person who votes or has the right to vote, especially in a political election（尤指政治性選舉的）投票人，選舉人，有選舉權的人：*A clear majority of voters were in favour of the motion.* 絕大多數選民贊成這一動議。◇ *Only 60% of eligible voters actually used their vote.* 只有 60% 的符合資格的投票人行使了選舉權。➲ COLLOCATIONS at VOTE ➲ see also FLOATING VOTER, SWING VOTER

vot·ing /ˈvəʊtɪŋ; *NAmE* ˈvoʊ-/ *noun* [U] the action of choosing sb/sth in an election or at a meeting 投票；選舉；表決：*He was eliminated in the first round of voting.* 他在第一輪投票中被淘汰。◇ *Voting will take place on May 1.* 投票將於 5 月 1 日進行。◇ *tactical voting* 有策略的投票 ◇ *to be of voting age* 到了選舉年齡

ˈvoting booth *noun* (*especially NAmE*) = POLLING BOOTH

ˈvoting machine *noun* a machine in which votes can be recorded automatically, used, for example, in the US 選票計算機；投票記錄機；計票機

vo·tive /ˈvəʊtɪv; *NAmE* ˈvoʊ-/ *adj.* [usually before noun] (*technical* 術語) presented to a god as a sign of thanks（向上帝）還願的，表示謝恩的：*votive offerings* 還願奉獻物

vouch /vaʊtʃ/ *verb*

PHR V **ˈvouch for sb/sth** (*formal*) to say that you believe that sb will behave well and that you will be responsible for their actions 替…擔保（或保證）：*Are you willing to vouch for him?* 你願意為他擔保嗎？◇ *I can vouch for her ability to work hard.* 我保證她能夠努力工作。**ˈvouch for sth** (*formal*) to say that you believe that sth is true or good because you have evidence for it（因有證據而）為…作證 **SYN** **confirm**：*I was in bed with the flu. My wife can vouch for that.* 我患流感臥牀休息了。我的妻子可為此作證。

vouch·er /ˈvaʊtʃə(r)/ *noun* a printed piece of paper that can be used instead of money to pay for sth, or that allows you to pay less than the usual price of sth 代幣券；票券：*a voucher for a free meal* 免費用餐券 ◇ *a travel voucher* 旅遊券 ◇ *This discount voucher entitles you to 10% off your next purchase.* 憑這張優惠券你下次購物可打九折。➲ see also LUNCHEON VOUCHER

vouch·safe /ˌvaʊtʃˈseɪf/ *verb* **~ sth (to sb)** | **~ sb sth** | **~ that** ... | **+ speech** (*old-fashioned* or *formal*) to give, offer or tell sth to sb, especially in order to give them a special advantage 給予…，告知…（尤指為給特別的好處）：*He vouchsafed to me certain family secrets.* 讓我知道了某些家庭秘密。

vow /vaʊ/ *noun, verb*

■ *noun* a formal and serious promise, especially a religious one, to do sth（尤指宗教的）誓，誓言，誓約：*to* ***make/take a vow*** 立／發誓 ◇ *to* ***break/keep a vow*** 違反／履行誓約 ◇ *to break your* ***marriage vows*** 背棄婚姻誓約 ◇ *Nuns take* ***a vow of*** *chastity.* 修女矢發貞潔願。➲ COLLOCATIONS at MARRIAGE

■ *verb* to make a formal and serious promise to do sth or a formal statement that is true 起誓；立誓；發誓：**~ to do sth** *She vowed never to speak to him again.* 她發誓再也不和他說話了。◇ **~ (that)** ... *He vowed (that) he had not hurt her.* 他起誓他沒有傷害過她。◇ **~ sth** *They vowed eternal friendship.* 他們立誓要友誼長存。◇ **+ speech** *'I'll be back,' she vowed.* "我會回來的。" 她發誓道。

vowel /ˈvaʊəl/ *noun* (*phonetics* 語音) **1** a speech sound in which the mouth is open and the tongue is not touching the top of the mouth, the teeth, etc., for example /ɑː, e, ɔː/ 元音；母音：*vowel sounds* 元音 ◇ *Each language has a different vowel system.* 每種語言都有不同的元音系統。**2** a letter that represents a vowel sound. In English the vowels are a, e, i, o, and u. 元音字母 ➲ compare CONSONANT ➲ see also DIPHTHONG

vox pop /ˌvɒks ˈpɒp; *NAmE* ˌvɑːks ˈpɑːp/ *noun* [C, U] (*BrE, informal*) the opinion of members of the public, especially when it is broadcast or published（尤指廣播或發表的）公眾輿論

voy·age /ˈvɔɪɪdʒ/ *noun, verb*

■ *noun* a long journey, especially by sea or in space 航行；（尤指）航海，航天：*an around-the-world voyage* 環球航行 ◇ *a voyage in space* 航天 ◇ *The Titanic sank on its* ***maiden voyage*** (= first journey). 泰坦尼克號首航便沉沒了。◇ (*figurative*) *Going to college can be a voyage of self-discovery.* 上大學可以算作自我發現之行。

■ *verb* [I] **+ adv./prep.** (*literary*) to travel, especially in a ship and over a long distance 航行；遠行；（尤指）遠航

voy·ager /ˈvɔɪɪdʒə(r)/ *noun* (*old-fashioned* or *literary*) a person who goes on a long journey, especially by ship to unknown parts of the world 航行者；遠行者；（尤指）遠航探險者

voy·eur /vwaɪˈɜː(r); vɔɪˈɜː(r)/ *noun* (*disapproving*) **1** a person who gets pleasure from secretly watching other people have sex 窺淫癖者（喜歡窺視他人性行為）**2** a person who enjoys watching the problems and private lives of others 刺探隱秘者（喜歡刺探他人的問題或私生活）▶ **voy·eur·ism** /vwaɪˈɜːrɪzəm; vɔɪˈɜː-/ *noun* [U] **voy·eur·is·tic** /ˌvwaɪəˈrɪstɪk; ˌvɔɪəˈr-/ *adj.*：*a voyeuristic interest in other people's lives* 對他人生活懷有窺秘癖的興趣

VP /ˌviː ˈpiː/ *abbr.* VICE-PRESIDENT 副總統；副總裁

vroom /vruːm/ *noun* [U] used to represent the loud sound made by a vehicle moving very fast（車輛高速行駛時發出的）嗚的一聲：*Vroom! A sports car roared past.* 嗚的一聲，一輛跑車疾駛而過。

vs *abbr.* (*especially NAmE*) VERSUS

ˈ**V-sign** *noun* a sign that you make by holding up your hand and making a V-shape with your first and second fingers. When the PALM (= inside part) of your hand is facing away from you, the sign means 'victory'; when the palm is facing towards you the sign is used as a way of being rude to other people. * V 字形手勢（手心向外表示勝利，手心向內表示侮辱）➲ compare TWO FINGERS

VSO /ˌviː es ˈəʊ; *NAmE* ˈoʊ/ *abbr.* VOLUNTARY SERVICE OVERSEAS

VTOL /ˌviː tiː əʊ ˈel; *NAmE* oʊ/ *abbr.* vertical take-off and landing (used to refer to an aircraft that can take off and land by going straight up or straight down)（飛機）垂直起降

vul·can·ized (*BrE* also **-ised**) /ˈvʌlkənaɪzd/ *adj.* (*technical* 術語) (of rubber 橡膠) treated with SULPHUR at great heat to make it stronger 經硫化處理的；經硬化的

vul·can·ology /ˌvʌlkəˈnɒlədʒi; *NAmE* -ˈnɑːl-/ *noun* [U] = VOLCANOLOGY

vul·gar /ˈvʌlɡə(r)/ *adj.* **1** not having or showing good taste; not polite, elegant or well behaved 庸俗的；粗俗的；粗野的；不雅的 **SYN** **coarse, in bad taste**：*a vulgar man* 粗俗的男人 ◇ *vulgar decorations* 俗裏俗氣的裝飾 ◇ *She found their laughter and noisy games coarse and rather vulgar.* 她覺得他們的笑聲和吵吵鬧鬧的遊戲趣味低下，俗不可耐。 **2** rude and likely to offend 粗野的；粗魯的；下流的 **SYN** **crude**：*vulgar jokes* 低俗的笑話 ▸ **vul·gar·ly** *adv.*：*He eyed her vulgarly.* 他色迷迷地瞅着她。

ˌ**vulgar ˈfraction** *noun* (*BrE*) a FRACTION (= a number less than one) that is shown as numbers above and below a line 普通分數：*¾ and ⅝ are vulgar fractions.* * ¾ 和 ⅝ 均為普通分數。➲ compare DECIMAL FRACTION at DECIMAL *n.*

vul·gar·ian /vʌlˈɡeəriən; *NAmE* -ˈɡer-/ *noun* (*formal*) a person who does not have polite manners or good taste 粗俗的人；庸俗的人

vul·gar·ism /ˈvʌlɡərɪzəm/ *noun* (*formal*) a rude word or expression, especially one relating to sex（尤指與性有關的）粗鄙詞語

vul·gar·ity /vʌlˈɡærəti/ *noun* [U, C] the fact of being rude or not having good taste; a rude object, picture, etc. 庸俗；粗野；下流；庸俗的物品（或圖畫等）：*She was offended by the vulgarity of their jokes.* 他們那些粗俗的笑話使她大為不快。◇ *a pornographic magazine full of vulgarities* 充滿下流圖片的色情雜誌

vul·gar·ize (*BrE* also **-ise**) /ˈvʌlɡəraɪz/ *verb* **~ sth** (*formal, disapproving*) to spoil sth by changing it so that it is more ordinary than before and not of such a high standard 使庸俗化；使通俗化 ▸ **vul·gar·iza·tion, -isa·tion** /ˌvʌlɡəraɪˈzeɪʃn; *NAmE* -rəˈz-/ *noun* [U]

ˌ**vulgar ˈLatin** *noun* [U] the spoken form of Latin which was used in the western part of the Roman Empire 民間拉丁語（羅馬帝國西部使用的拉丁口語）

the Vul·gate /ˈvʌlɡeɪt; -ɡət/ *noun* [sing.] the main Latin version of the Bible prepared in the late 4th century《聖經》拉丁通行本（完成於 4 世紀後期）

vul·ner·able /ˈvʌlnərəbl/ *adj.* **~ (to sb/sth)** weak and easily hurt physically or emotionally（身體上或感情上）脆弱的，易受…傷害的：*to be vulnerable to attack* 易受攻擊 ◇ *She looked very vulnerable standing there on her own.* 她獨自站在那裏看上去弱不禁風。◇ *In cases of food poisoning, young children are especially vulnerable.* 遇到食物中毒，幼兒尤其容易受危害。◇ *The sudden resignation of the financial director put the company in a very* ***vulnerable position.*** 財務部主任的突然辭職使得這家公司岌岌可危。 ▸ **vul·ner·abil·ity** /ˌvʌlnərəˈbɪləti/ *noun* [U]：**~ (of sb/sth) (to sth)** *financial vulnerability* 在財政上易受打擊 ◇ *the vulnerability of newborn babies to disease* 新生嬰兒容易患病 **vul·ner·ably** /-əbli/ *adv.*

vul·pine /ˈvʌlpaɪn/ *adj.* (*formal*) of or like a FOX 狐狸的；狐狸似的；狡猾的

vul·ture /ˈvʌltʃə(r)/ *noun* **1** a large bird, usually without feathers on its head or neck, that eats the flesh of animals that are already dead 兀鷲；禿鷲：***vultures circling/wheeling*** *overhead* 在頭頂上空盤旋的兀鷲 ➲ VISUAL VOCAB page V12 **2** a person who hopes to gain from the troubles or sufferings of other people 乘人之危的人；趁火打劫的人

vulva /ˈvʌlvə/ *noun* (*anatomy* 解) the outer opening of the female sex organs 外陰；女陰

vuvu·zela™ /ˌvuːvuːˈzeɪlə/ *noun* (*SAfrE*) a long plastic instrument in the shape of a TRUMPET, that makes a very loud noise when you blow it and is popular with football fans in South Africa 嗚嗚祖拉，巫巫茲拉（南非足球迷使用的塑料長喇叭）

vying *pres. part.* of VIE

W w

W /ˈdʌbljuː/ *noun, abbr.*

■ ***noun*** (also **w**) [C, U] (*pl.* **Ws**, **W's**, **w's** /ˈdʌbljuːz/) the 23rd letter of the English alphabet 英語字母表的第 23 個字母：*'Water' begins with (a) W/'W'.* * water 一詞以字母 w 開頭。

■ ***abbr.*** **1** west; western 西方（的）；西部（的）**2** WATT 瓦；瓦特：*a 100W light bulb* * 100 瓦的電燈泡

W-2 form /ˌdʌbljuː ˈtuː fɔːm; *NAmE* fɔːrm/ *noun* (in the US) an official document that an employer gives to an employee that shows the amount of pay and tax for the year（美國雇主發給雇員的）全年薪資和納稅表

wack /wæk/ *adj.* (*informal, especially US*) **1** very bad; not of good quality 很差的；劣質的：*That movie was really wack.* 那齣電影糟透了。**2** very strange 很奇怪的；怪異的

wacko /ˈwækəʊ; *NAmE* -koʊ/ *adj., noun* (*informal*)

■ ***adj.*** crazy; not sensible 古怪的；發瘋的；不理智的：*wacko opinions* 古怪的看法

■ ***noun*** (*pl.* **-os** or **-oes**) (*especially NAmE*) a crazy person 瘋子

wacky (also **whacky**) /ˈwæki/ *adj.* (**wack·ier**, **wacki·est**) (*informal*) funny or amusing in a slightly crazy way 古怪的；滑稽可笑的；瘋瘋癲癲的 SYN **zany**：*wacky ideas* 滑稽可笑的想法 ◇ *Some of his friends are pretty **wild and wacky** characters.* 他的一些朋友是那種放蕩不羈又怪裏怪氣的人。

wad /wɒd; *NAmE* wɑːd/ *noun, verb*

■ ***noun*** **1** a thick pile of pieces of paper, paper money, etc. folded or rolled together（紙張、鈔票等的）捲，沓，捆：*He pulled a thick wad of £10 notes out of his pocket.* 他從衣袋裏掏出厚厚的一沓面額 10 英鎊的鈔票。◇ (*BrE, slang*) *They had a wad/wads of money* (= a large amount). 他們有大把大把的錢。**2** a mass of soft material, used for blocking sth or keeping sth in place 用以填塞（或填襯等）的軟材料；填料；填絮；襯料：*The nurse used a wad of cotton wool to stop the bleeding.* 護士用了一團脫脂棉止血。

■ ***verb*** (**-dd-**) **1 ~ sth** (**up**) (*especially NAmE*) to fold or press sth into a tight wad 將…揉成團；使成沓；使成捲 **2 ~ sth** to fill sth with soft material for warmth or protection（用柔軟的材料）填塞，填充，襯墊

wad·ding /ˈwɒdɪŋ; *NAmE* ˈwɑːd-/ *noun* [U] soft material that you wrap around things to protect them（柔軟的）填料，填絮，襯墊

wad·dle /ˈwɒdl; *NAmE* ˈwɑːdl/ *verb* [I] (+ **adv./prep.**) to walk with short steps, swinging from side to side, like a DUCK（鴨子似地）蹣跚行走，搖擺地行走 ▶ **wad·dle** *noun* [sing.]：*She walked with a waddle.* 她走起路來步履蹣跚。

wade /weɪd/ *verb* **1** [I, T] to walk with an effort through sth, especially water or mud 跋涉，涉，蹚（水或淤泥等）：(+ **adv./prep.**) *He waded into the water to push the boat out.* 他蹚進水裏把船推出來。◇ *Sometimes they had to wade waist-deep through mud.* 有時他們得通過齊腰深的泥漿。◇ **~ sth** *They waded the river at a shallow point.* 他們在水淺處蹚過河。**2** (*NAmE*) (*BrE* **pad·dle**) [I] to walk or stand with no shoes or socks in shallow water in the sea, a lake, etc. 蹚水；赤足涉水

PHR V **ˌwade ˈin** | **ˌwade ˈinto sth** (*informal*) to enter a fight, a discussion or an argument in an aggressive or not very sensitive way 強行加入，介入，插手（打架、討論、爭論等）：*The police waded into the crowd with batons.* 警察揮舞着警棍衝入人群。◇ *You shouldn't have waded in with all those unpleasant accusations.* 你本不該插一槓子，橫加指責，讓人難受。**ˌwade ˈinto sb** (*informal*) to attack sb with words in an angry aggressive way 抨擊 **ˌwade ˈthrough sth** [no passive] to deal with or read sth that is boring and takes a lot of time 艱難地處理；費力地閱讀：*I spent the whole day wading through the paperwork on my desk.* 我一整天都在伏案處理文件。

wader /ˈweɪdə(r)/ *noun* **1** (also **ˈwading bird**) [C] any of several different types of bird with long legs that feed in shallow water 涉禽；涉水鳥 **2 waders** [pl.] long rubber boots that reach up to your THIGH, that you wear for standing in water, especially when fishing（涉水捕魚等穿的）高筒防水膠靴：*a pair of waders* 一雙高筒防水膠靴

wadi /ˈwɒdi; *NAmE* ˈwɑːdi/ *noun* (in the Middle East and N Africa) a valley or channel that is dry except when it rains（中東和北非僅在雨後才有水的）乾谷，乾河谷

ˈwading pool (*NAmE*) (*BrE* **ˈpaddling pool**) *noun* a shallow swimming pool for children to play in, especially a small plastic one that you fill with water（尤指塑料的小型）淺水池，嬉水池

wafer /ˈweɪfə(r)/ *noun* **1** a thin crisp light biscuit/cookie, often eaten with ice cream 威化餅，薄脆餅（常與冰淇淋同吃）**2** a very thin round piece of special bread given by the priest during COMMUNION 聖餅；聖體；麪餅 **3 ~ (of sth)** a very thin piece of sth 薄片

ˌwafer-ˈthin *adj.* very thin 很薄的 ➲ compare PAPER-THIN

waf·fle /ˈwɒfl; *NAmE* ˈwɑːfl; ˈwɔːfl/ *noun, verb*

■ ***noun*** **1** [C] a crisp flat cake with a pattern of squares on both sides, often eaten with sweet sauce, cream, etc. on top 華夫餅，蛋奶烘餅（兩面有方塊圖案，常塗以糖漿、奶油等）：*a waffle iron* (= for making waffles with) 蛋奶烘餅烤模 **2** [U] (*BrE, informal*) language that uses a lot of words but does not say anything important or interesting 胡扯；廢話連篇：*The report is just full of waffle.* 這份報告只是一大堆廢話。

■ ***verb*** **1** [I] **~ (on) (about sth)** (*BrE, informal, disapproving*) to talk or write using a lot of words but without saying anything interesting or important 胡扯；耍貧嘴；絮叨；胡寫：*The principal waffled on about exam results but no one was listening.* 校長絮絮叨叨地談着考試結果，但是誰也沒有聽進去。**2** [I] **~ (on/over sth)** (*NAmE, informal*) to be unable to decide what to do about sth or what you think about sth 拿不定主意；三心二意：*The senator was accused of waffling on major issues.* 人們指責參議員在主要問題上立場模糊。

waft /wɒft; *NAmE* wɑːft; wæft/ *verb, noun*

■ ***verb*** [I, T] to move, or make sth move, gently through the air（隨風）飄盪；使飄盪；吹拂 SYN **drift**：**+ adv./prep.** *The sound of their voices wafted across the lake.* 他們的聲音飄過湖面傳到了另一邊。◇ *Delicious smells wafted up from the kitchen.* 香噴噴的味道從廚房飄了出來。◇ **~ sth + adv./prep.** *The scent of the flowers was wafted along by the breeze.* 微風傳花香。

■ ***noun*** (*formal*) a smell or a line of smoke carried through the air 一陣，一股（在空氣中飄盪的味或煙）：*wafts of perfume/smoke* 陣陣香氣；縷縷青煙

Wag /wæg/ *noun* (*BrE, informal*) one of a group of 'wives and girlfriends' of famous men, especially members of a sports team（名人的，尤指運動隊明星的）妻子女友團成員：*Wags at the World Cup* 世界杯足球賽中的太太女友團

wag /wæg/ *verb, noun*

■ ***verb*** (**-gg-**) **1** [T, I] **~ (sth)** if a dog **wags** its tail, or its tail **wags**, its tail moves from side to side several times（狗）搖，擺動（尾巴）；（狗尾巴）搖，擺動 **2** [T] **~ sth** to shake your finger or your head from side to side or up and down, often as a sign of disapproval 擺動，搖（頭或手指，常表示不贊成）**3** [T] **~ sth** (*AustralE, NZE*) to stay away from school without permission 逃學：*to wag school* 逃學 IDM see TAIL *n.*, TONGUE *n.*

■ ***noun*** **1** (*old-fashioned, especially BrE*) a person who enjoys making jokes 老開玩笑的人；愛鬧着玩的人 SYN **joker** **2** a wagging movement 搖擺；擺動

wage 0━ /weɪdʒ/ *noun, verb*

■ ***noun*** 0━ [sing.] (also **wages** [pl.]) a regular amount of money that you earn, usually every week, for work or services（通常指按週領的）工資，工錢：*wages of £200 a week* 一星期 200 英鎊的工資 ◇ *a **weekly wage** of £200* 週薪 200 英鎊 ◇ ***wage cuts*** 減薪 ◇ *a **wage increase** of 3%* * 3% 的加薪 ◇ (*BrE*) *a **wage rise** of 3%* * 3% 的加薪 ◇ ***wage demands/claims/settlements*** 增加工資的要求；

W

工資解決協議 ◇ *Wages are paid on Fridays.* 每星期五發工資。◇ *There are extra benefits for people on* ***low wages.*** 低薪者有額外補助。◇ *The staff have agreed to a voluntary* ***wage freeze*** (= a situation in which wages are not increased for a time). 全體員工已經同意自願凍結工資。➲ **SYNONYMS** at INCOME ➲ **COLLOCATIONS** at FINANCE ➲ compare SALARY ➲ see also LIVING WAGE, MINIMUM WAGE

■ ***verb*** to begin and continue a war, a battle, etc. 開始，發動，進行，繼續（戰爭、戰鬥等）：**~ sth** *The rebels have waged a guerrilla war since 2007.* 叛亂分子自 2007 年以來一直在進行游擊戰。◇ **~ sth against/on sb/sth** *He alleged that a press campaign was being waged against him.* 他聲稱有人正在對他發起新聞攻勢。

waged /weɪdʒd/ *adj.* **1** (of a person 人) having regular paid work 領工資的；有定期付酬工作的：*waged workers* 有固定工作者 **2** (of work 工作) for which you are paid 支取工資的；帶薪的：*waged employment* 有酬雇用 **3 the waged** *noun* [pl.] people who have regular paid work 工薪族；（統稱）拿工資的人 **OPP unwaged**

ˈwage earner *noun* a person who earns money, especially a person who works for wages 掙錢的人；掙工資的人：*We have two wage earners in the family.* 我們家有兩個人掙錢。

ˈwage packet *noun* (*BrE*) = PAY PACKET

wager /ˈweɪdʒə(r)/ *noun, verb*

■ ***noun*** (*old-fashioned* or *formal*) an arrangement to risk money on the result of a particular event 打賭 **SYN bet**

■ ***verb*** (*old-fashioned* or *formal*) **1** [I, T] to bet money 打賭；押（賭注）**SYN bet**：**~ on sth** *She always wagered on an outsider.* 她總是把賭注押在不大可能獲勝的馬上。◇ **~ sth (on sth)** *to wager £50 on a horse* 在一匹馬上押 50 英鎊的賭注 ◇ **~ sth/sb that …** *I had wagered a great deal of money that I would beat him.* 我下了大賭注打賭，這次比賽我會贏他的。 **2** [T] **~ (that) …** used to say that you are so confident that sth is true or will happen that you would be willing to bet money on it 打賭；打包票 **SYN bet**：*I'll wager that she knows more about it than she's saying.* 我敢打賭，她知道的比她說的要多。

wag·gish /ˈwæɡɪʃ/ *adj.* (*old-fashioned*) funny, clever and not serious 詼諧的；打趣的：*waggish remarks* 俏皮話

wag·gle /ˈwæɡl/ *verb* [T, I] **~ (sth)** (*informal*) to make sth move with short movements from side to side or up and down; to move in this way （使）上下移動，來回擺動：*Can you waggle your ears?* 你能讓耳朵來回動嗎？ ▶ **wag·gle** *noun*

Wag·ner·ian /vɑːɡˈnɪəriən; *NAmE* -ˈnɪr-/ *adj.* **1** related to the music of the German COMPOSER Richard Wagner; typical of this music 瓦格納樂曲的，瓦格納作品風格的（指德國作曲家理查德 • 瓦格納）**2** (*humorous*) very big or great, or in a style that is too serious or exaggerated 巨大的；極大的；過於嚴肅（或誇張）的：*a hangover of Wagnerian proportions* 強烈的宿醉反應

wagon /ˈwæɡən/ *noun* **1** (*BrE*) (*NAmE* **ˈfreight car**) a railway/railroad truck for carrying goods （鐵路）貨車車廂，車皮 **2** (*BrE* also **wag·gon**) a vehicle with four wheels, pulled by horses or OXEN and used for carrying heavy loads 四輪載重馬車（或牛車） **3** (also **cart**) (both *NAmE*) (*BrE* **trol·ley**) a small table on very small wheels, used for carrying or serving food or drink （運送食品、飲料的）小推車，柏車 ➲ see also BANDWAGON, STATION WAGON

IDM be/go on the ˈwagon (*informal*) to not drink alcohol, either for a short time or permanently （短期或永久地）不喝酒，戒酒，滴酒不沾

wag·on·load /ˈwæɡənləʊd; *NAmE* -loʊd/ *noun* an amount of goods carried on a wagon 貨車車廂載荷；馬車載荷

ˈwagon train *noun* a long line of WAGONS and horses, used by people travelling west in N America in the 19th century （19 世紀美國人向西部遷移的）馬拉篷車隊

wag·tail /ˈwæɡteɪl/ *noun* a small bird with a long tail that moves up and down when the bird is walking 鶺鴒（走動時長尾上下擺動）

wah-wah /ˈwɑː wɑː/ *noun* [U] (*music* 音) a special effect made on electric musical instruments, especially the GUITAR, which varies the quality of the sound （尤指吉他等電子樂器發出的）"哇哇"音響效果

waif /weɪf/ *noun* a small thin person, usually a child, who looks as if they do not have enough to eat 瘦小的人；（通常指）面黃肌瘦的小孩：*the* ***waifs and strays*** *of our society* (= people with no home) 我們社會的棄兒 ▶ **ˈwaif-like** *adj.*：*waif-like young girls* 面黃肌瘦的女孩子

wail /weɪl/ *verb, noun*

■ ***verb*** **1** [I] to make a long loud high cry because you are sad or in pain （因悲傷或疼痛）哭號，慟哭：*The little girl was wailing miserably.* 那小女孩難過得號啕大哭。◇ *women wailing and weeping* 痛哭流涕的婦女 **2** [T, I] to cry or complain about sth in a loud high voice 大聲呼叫；哀號；高聲抱怨 **SYN moan**：**+ speech** *'It's broken,' she wailed.* "打碎了。"她大聲叫道。◇ **~ (about sth)** *There's no point wailing about something that happened so long ago.* 事情早已發生，痛哭流涕也於事無補。 **3** [I] (of things 物) to make a long high sound 發出長而高的聲音；呼嘯：*Ambulances raced by with sirens wailing.* 救護車高聲鳴笛疾馳而過。 ▶ **wail·ing** *noun* [sing., U]：*a high-pitched wailing* 高聲哭號

■ ***noun*** a long loud high cry expressing pain or sadness; a sound similar to this （疼痛或悲傷時發出的）號啕，哀號 **SYN moan**：*a wail of despair* 絕望的哀號 ◇ *the distant wail of sirens* 遠處警報器的鳴響

wains·cot /ˈweɪnskət/ *noun* (*old use*) = SKIRTING BOARD

waist 🔑 /weɪst/ *noun*

1 🔑 the area around the middle of the body between the RIBS and the hips, often narrower than the areas above and below 腰；腰部；腰圍：*He put his arm around her waist.* 他摟住了她的腰。◇ *She was paralysed* ***from the waist down*** (= in the area below her waist). 她從腰部以下都癱瘓了。◇ *The workmen were* ***stripped to the waist*** (= wearing no clothes on the top half of their bodies). 工人光着上身。➲ **COLLOCATIONS** at PHYSICAL ➲ **VISUAL VOCAB** page V59 **2** 🔑 the part of a piece of clothing that covers the waist （衣服的）腰部，腰：*a skirt with an elasticated waist* 腰部有鬆緊帶的裙子 **3 -waisted** (in adjectives 構成形容詞) having the type of waist mentioned 有…腰身的；腰身…的：*a high-waisted dress* 高腰連衣裙

waist·band /ˈweɪstbænd/ *noun* the strip of cloth that forms the waist of a piece of clothing, especially at the top of a skirt or trousers/pants 衣服腰；腰頭；（尤指）裙腰，褲腰：*an elasticated waistband* 鬆緊腰身

waist·coat /ˈweɪskəʊt; *NAmE* usually ˈweskət; *NAmE* also ˈweɪskoʊt/ (*BrE*) (*NAmE* **vest**) *noun* a short piece of clothing with buttons down the front but no sleeves, usually worn over a shirt and under a jacket, often forming part of a man's suit （西服的）背心 ➲ **VISUAL VOCAB** page V61

ˌwaist-ˈdeep *adj., adv.* up to the waist 齊腰深（的）；上至腰部（的）：*The water was waist-deep.* 水齊腰深。◇ *We waded waist-deep into the muddy water.* 我們蹚進齊腰深的泥水裏。

ˌwaist-ˈhigh *adj., adv.* high enough to reach the waist 齊腰高（的）；高至腰部（的）：*waist-high grass* 齊腰高的草 ◇ *The grass had grown waist-high.* 草長得齊腰高了。

waist·line /ˈweɪstlaɪn/ *noun* **1** the amount that a person measures around the waist, used to talk about how fat or thin they are 腰圍：*an expanding waistline* 逐漸增大的腰圍 **2** the place on a piece of clothing where your waist is （衣服的）腰部，腰 **SYN waist**

wait 🔑 /weɪt/ *verb, noun*

■ ***verb*** **1** 🔑 [I, T] to stay where you are or delay doing sth until sb/sth comes or sth happens 等；等待；等候：*She rang the bell and waited.* 她按鈴後等候着。◇ **+ adv./prep.** *Have you been waiting long?* 你等了很久了嗎？◇ *I've been waiting (for) twenty minutes.* 我等了二十分鐘。◇ *I'll wait outside until the meeting's over.* 我會在外面等到會議結束。◇ **~ for sb/sth** *Wait for me!* 等等我！◇ **~ for sb/sth to do sth** *We're waiting for the rain to stop before we go out.* 我們要等到雨停了再出去。◇ **~ to do sth**

W

Hurry up! We're waiting to go. 快點兒，我們等着走呢。◇ **~ your turn** *You'll just have to wait your turn* (= wait until your turn comes). 你得等着輪到你才行。 **2** [I, T] to hope or watch for sth to happen, especially for a long time （尤指長期地）希望，盼望，期待：**~ (for sth)** *Leeds United had waited for success for eighteen years.* 利茲聯隊企盼奪冠已經十八年了。◇ *This is just the opportunity I've been waiting for.* 這正是我一直在期待的機會。◇ **~ for sb/sth to do sth** *He's waiting for me to make a mistake.* 他正盼着我出錯呢。◇ **~ your chance** *I waited my chance and slipped out when no one was looking.* 我等待時機，趁沒人注意時溜了出去。 **3 be waiting** [I] (of things 事物) to be ready for sb to have or use 準備妥；在手邊；可得到；可使用：**~ (for sb)** *There's a letter waiting for you at home.* 家裏有你一封信。◇ **~ to do sth** *The hotel had a taxi waiting to collect us.* 旅館召了輛出租車等着接我們。 **4** [I] to be left to be dealt with at a later time because it is not urgent 推遲；擱置；延緩：*I've got some calls to make but they **can wait** until tomorrow.* 我有幾個電話要打，不過可以等到明天再說。

IDM **an ˌaccident/a diˌsaster waiting to ˈhappen** a thing or person that is very likely to cause danger or a problem in the future because of the condition it is in or the way they behave 隱患 **I, they, etc. can't ˈwait/can hardly ˈwait** used when you are emphasizing that sb is very excited about sth or keen to do it （我、他們等）迫不及待：*The children **can't wait for** Christmas to come.* 孩子們等聖誕節都等不及了。◇ *I can hardly wait to see him again.* 我迫不及待地想再次見到他。 **keep sb ˈwaiting** to make sb have to wait or be delayed, especially because you arrive late （尤指因遲到）讓人等候，使人耽擱：*I'm sorry to have kept you waiting.* 對不起，讓你久等了。 **ˌwait and ˈsee** used to tell sb that they must be patient and wait to find out about sth later 耐心等待；等着瞧：*We'll just have to wait and see—there's nothing we can do at the moment.* 我們只得等等看，眼下沒有法子。◇ *a wait-and-see policy* 等待觀望的政策 ◇ *'Where are we going?' 'Wait and see!'* "我們到哪裏去？""等着瞧吧！" **wait at ˈtable** (*formal*) to serve food to people, for example at a formal meal 伺候進餐；（往飯桌上）端飯上菜 **ˈwait for it** (*informal, especially BrE*) **1** used to say that you are about to tell sb sth that is surprising or amusing （要說出令人吃驚或高興的事情）聽着，聽好了：*They're off on a trip, to—wait for it—the Maldives!* 他們出去旅行了，去的地方是，聽好了，馬爾代夫！ **2** used to tell sb not to start doing sth yet, but to wait until you tell them （讓人在得到通知前別做某事）等候通知 **wait a minute/moment/second** **1** to wait for a short time 等一會兒；稍等一下：*Can you wait a second while I make a call?* 你能等一會兒讓我打個電話嗎？ **2** used when you have just noticed or remembered sth, or had a sudden idea （剛注意到、想起某事或突然想出了主意）且慢，等一等：*Wait a minute—this isn't the right key.* 等一等，不是這把鑰匙。 **wait on sb hand and ˈfoot** (*disapproving*) to take care of sb's needs so well that they do not have to do anything for themselves 過分照顧；讓…飯來張口，衣來伸手 **wait ˈtables** (*NAmE*) to work serving food to people in a restaurant （在餐館）端盤子，招待顧客 **ˈwait till/until …** (*informal*) used to show that you are very excited about telling or showing sth to sb （興奮地表示或展示某事物）等到…吧：*Wait till you see what I've found!* 你等着看看我發現了什麼吧！ **what are we ˈwaiting for?** (*informal*) used to suggest that you should all start doing what you have been discussing （建議都應開始去做商議中的事）我們還在等什麼呢 **what are you ˈwaiting for?** (*informal*) used to tell sb to do sth now rather than later （讓人馬上就幹而不要往後拖）你還等什麼呢：*If the car needs cleaning, what are you waiting for?* 如果這輛汽車需要清洗，你還在等什麼呢？ **(just) you ˈwait** used to emphasize a threat, warning or promise （用以加強威脅、警告或允諾的語氣）你就等着吧，你就等着瞧：*I'll be famous one day, just you wait!* 我有朝一日會出名的，你就等着瞧吧！ ➲ more at DUST *n.*, WING *n.*

PHR V **ˌwait aˈbout/aˈround** to stay in a place, with nothing particular to do, for example because you are expecting sth to happen or sb to arrive 白白等着；空等 **ˌwait beˈhind** (*especially BrE*) to stay after other people have gone, especially to speak to sb privately 等到他人走後留下來（尤指為與人私下談話） **ˌwait ˈin** (*BrE*) to stay at home because you are expecting sb to come, telephone, etc. 在家等候（人、電話等） **ˈwait on sb** to act as a servant to sb, especially by serving food to them 伺候，服侍，招待（尤指進餐） **ˈwait on sth/sb** (*informal, especially NAmE*) to wait for sth to happen before you do or decide sth 等待…（才採取行動或作出決定）：*She is waiting on the result of a blood test.* 她在等驗血結果。 **ˌwait sth↔ˈout** to wait until an unpleasant event has finished 等待（令人不快的事情）結束：*We sheltered in a doorway to wait out the storm.* 我們躲避在一個門洞裏等候暴風雨過去。 **ˌwait ˈup** (*NAmE*) used to ask sb to stop or go more slowly so that you can join them 等一等，慢點走（以便自己趕上） **ˌwait ˈup (for sb)** to wait for sb to come home at night before you go to bed 熬夜，不睡覺（等人回家）

▪ ***noun*** [usually sing.] **~ (for sb/sth)** an act of waiting; an amount of time waited 等候；等待；等待的時間：*We had **a long wait** for the bus.* 我們等公共汽車等了很長時間。◇ *He now faces an agonizing two-month wait for the test results.* 他現在要苦苦等待兩個月才能拿到測驗結果。

IDM see LIE¹ *v.*

wait·er /ˈweɪtə(r)/ (*feminine* **wait·ress**) *noun* a person whose job is to serve customers at their tables in a restaurant, etc. （餐館等的）服務員，侍者：*I'll ask the waitress for the bill.* 我要讓女服務員拿賬單來。◇ *Waiter, could you bring me some water?* 服務員，給我送點兒水來好嗎？ ➲ note at GENDER ➲ see also DUMB WAITER, SERVER (4)

wait·ing /ˈweɪtɪŋ/ *noun* [U] **1** the fact of staying where you are or delaying doing sth until sb/sth comes or sth happens 等候；等待：***No waiting*** (= on a sign at the side of the road, telling vehicles that they must not stop there). 禁止停車（路牌指示） **2** the fact of working as a waiter or waitress 當侍者；當服務員 ➲ see also WAITRESSING

ˈwaiting game *noun* [sing.] a policy of waiting to see how a situation develops before you decide how to act 伺機而動的策略

ˈwaiting list *noun* a list of people who are waiting for sth such as a service or medical treatment that is not yet available （服務或醫療的）等候者名單：*There are no places available right now but I'll **put you on a waiting list**.* 現時沒有空位，但我會把你列入等候者名單的。◇ *There's a waiting list to join the golf club.* 等着加入高爾夫球俱樂部的有一長隊人呢。◇ (*BrE*) *The government has promised to cut hospital waiting lists.* 政府已許諾減少排隊看病的人數。

ˈwaiting room *noun* a room where people can sit while they are waiting, for example for a bus or train, or to see a doctor or dentist 等候室；候車室；候診室

ˈwait list *noun* (*NAmE*) = WAITING LIST：*She was on a wait list for a liver transplant.* 她的名字當時在肝移植等候者名單上。

ˈwait-list *verb* **~ sb** (*NAmE*) to put sb's name on a WAITING LIST 列入等候者名單：*He's been wait-listed for a football scholarship to Stanford.* 他的名字在上斯坦福大學的足球獎學金等候者名單上。

wait·person /ˈweɪtpɜːsn; *NAmE* -pɜːrsn/ *noun* (*pl.* **-persons**) (*NAmE*) a person whose job is to serve customers at their tables in a restaurant, etc. （餐館等的）服務員；侍應生

wait·ress /ˈweɪtrəs/ *noun* ➲ WAITER

wait·ress·ing /ˈweɪtrəsɪŋ/ *noun* [U] the job of being a waitress 女服務員工作：*I did some waitressing when I was a student.* 我當學生時做過侍應生。

wait·staff /ˈweɪtstɑːf; *NAmE* -stæf/ *noun* [U] (*NAmE*) the people whose job is to serve customers at their tables in a restaurant, etc. （統稱，餐館等的）服務人員；全體侍應生

waive /weɪv/ *verb* **~ sth** to choose not to demand sth in a particular case, even though you have a legal or official right to do so 放棄（權利、要求等） **SYN** **forgo**

waiver /ˈweɪvə(r)/ *noun* (*law* 律) a situation in which sb gives up a legal right or claim; an official document stating this（對合法權利或要求的）棄權；棄權聲明

wake 0-π /weɪk/ *verb*, *noun*

■ ***verb*** (**woke** /wəʊk/, **woken** /ˈwəʊkən/) **1** 0-π [I, T] to stop sleeping; to make sb stop sleeping 醒；醒來；喚醒；弄醒：**~ (up)** *What time do you usually wake up in the morning?* 通常你早晨幾點鐘醒？◇ *I always wake early in the summer.* 我夏天總是醒得早。◇ *Wake up! It's eight o'clock.* 醒醒吧！已經八點鐘了。◇ **~ to sth** (*formal*) *They woke to a clear blue sky.* 他們醒來時天空碧藍。◇ **~ from sth** (*formal*) *She had just woken from a deep sleep.* 她剛從熟睡中醒來。◇ **~ to do sth** *He woke up to find himself alone in the house.* 他醒來時發現屋裏只有他一個人。◇ **~ sb (up)** *Try not to wake the baby up.* 盡量別把孩子弄醒。◇ *I was woken by the sound of someone moving around.* 有人來回走動的響聲把我吵醒了。➲ note at AWAKE **2** [T] **~ sth** (*literary* or *formal*) to make sb remember sth or feel sth again 喚起（記憶）；使再次感覺到：*The incident woke memories of his past sufferings.* 這件事喚起了他對往昔苦難的回憶。

IDM **wake ˌup and smell the ˈcoffee** (*informal*) (usually in orders 通常用於命令) used to tell sb to become aware of what is really happening in a situation, especially when this is sth unpleasant 要清醒面對現實

PHR V **ˌwake ˈup** to become more lively and interested 活躍起來；更感興趣：*Wake up and listen!* 打起精神注意聽！➲ see also WAKE *v.* (1) **ˌwake sb↔ˈup** to make sb feel more lively 使活躍；使清醒：*A cold shower will soon wake you up.* 你沖個涼水澡，很快就清醒了。◇ *The class needs waking up.* 應該讓這個班活躍起來。➲ see also WAKE *v.* (1) **ˌwake ˈup to sth** to become aware of sth; to realize sth 意識到；認識到：*He hasn't yet woken up to the seriousness of the situation.* 他還沒有意識到形勢的嚴重性。

■ ***noun*** **1** an occasion before or after a funeral when people gather to remember the dead person, traditionally held the night before the funeral to watch over the body before it is buried（葬禮前的）守夜；守靈 **2** the track that a boat or ship leaves behind on the surface of the water（船隻航行時的）尾流，航跡 ➲ VISUAL VOCAB page V5

IDM **in the wake of sb/sth** coming after or following sb/sth 隨…之後而來；跟隨在…後：*There have been demonstrations on the streets in the wake of the recent bomb attack.* 在近來的轟炸之後，大街上隨即出現了示威遊行。◇ *A group of reporters followed in her wake.* 一群記者跟隨在她的身後。◇ *The storm left a trail of destruction in its wake.* 暴風雨過處滿目瘡痍。

wake·board·ing /ˈweɪkbɔːdɪŋ; *NAmE* -bɔːrd-/ *noun* [U] the sport of riding on a short wide board called a **wake-board** while being pulled along through the water by a fast boat 尾流滑水（有快艇牽引，用尾波板進行）▶ **wake·board** *verb* [I] ➲ VISUAL VOCAB page V50

wake·ful /ˈweɪkfl/ *adj.* (*formal*) **1** not sleeping; unable to sleep 失眠的；不能入睡的 SYN **sleepless**：*He lay wakeful all night.* 他躺在牀上徹夜未眠。**2** (of a period at night 夜間一段時間) spent with little or no sleep 沒怎麼睡的；不眠的 SYN **sleepless**：*She had spent many wakeful nights worrying about him.* 她度過了許多不眠之夜，為他擔心。▶ **wake·ful·ness** *noun* [U]

waken /ˈweɪkən/ *verb* (*formal*) **1** [I, T] to wake, or make sb wake, from sleep 醒來；睡醒；喚醒；弄醒：**~ (up)** *The child had just wakened.* 這孩子剛醒。◇ **~ sb (up)** *I was wakened by a knock at the door.* 敲門聲把我吵醒了。➲ note at AWAKE **2** [T] **~ sth** to make sb remember sth or feel sth again 喚起（記憶）；使感覺到：*The dream wakened a forgotten memory.* 那夢喚起了一段忘卻的記憶。

ˈwake-up call *noun* **1** a telephone call that you arrange to be made to you at a particular time, for example in a hotel, in order to wake you up 催醒電話；叫早電話：*I asked for a wake-up call at 6.30 a.m.* 我請他們在早晨 6:30 打電話叫醒我。**2** an event that makes people realize that there is a problem that they need to do sth about 讓人警醒的事：*These riots should be a wake-up call for the government.* 這些暴亂該為政府敲響警鐘了。

wakey-wakey /ˌweɪki ˈweɪki/ *exclamation* (*BrE*, *informal*, *humorous*) used to tell sb to wake up（用以叫醒別人）醒醒

wak·ing /ˈweɪkɪŋ/ *adj.* [only before noun] used to describe time when you are awake 醒着的；不眠的：*She spends all her waking hours caring for her mother.* 她不睡覺的時候都在照看母親。▶ **wak·ing** *noun* [U]：*the dreamlike state between waking and sleeping* 似睡非睡的夢境狀態

Wal·dorf salad /ˌwɔːldɔːf ˈsæləd; *NAmE* -dɔːrf/ *noun* [U, C] a salad made from apples, nuts, CELERY and MAYONNAISE (= sauce made with egg and oil) 沃爾多夫色拉（用蘋果、果仁、芹菜、蛋黃醬製作而成）

Vocabulary Building 詞彙擴充

Ways of walking 走路的方式

- **creep** *He could hear someone creeping around downstairs.* 他聽得見有人在樓下躡手躡腳走來走去的聲音。
- **limp** *One player limped off the field with a twisted ankle.* 一個球員拖着扭傷的腳踝一瘸一拐地走下場。
- **pace** *I found him in the corridor nervously pacing up and down.* 我看到他在走廊裏焦慮不安地走來走去。
- **pad** *She spent the morning padding about the house in her slippers.* 她一個早上都穿着拖鞋在房子裏輕輕地走來走去。
- **plod** *They wearily plodded home through the rain.* 他們冒着雨疲憊而吃力地走回家。
- **shuffle** *The queue gradually shuffled forward.* 排隊等候的人慢慢向前挪動。
- **stagger** *They staggered out of the pub, completely drunk.* 他們喝得醉醺醺的，踉踉蹌蹌地走出了酒館。
- **stomp** *She stomped out of the room, slamming the door behind her.* 她噔噔地走出了屋子，隨手砰的一聲把門關上。
- **stroll** *Families were strolling around the park.* 遊人一家一家地在公園四處漫步。
- **tiptoe** *They tiptoed upstairs so they wouldn't wake the baby.* 他們踮着腳上樓，以免吵醒嬰兒。
- **trudge** *We trudged up the hill.* 我們步履艱難地一步一步往山上爬。

walk 0-π /wɔːk/ *verb*, *noun*

■ ***verb*** **1** 0-π [I, T] to move or go somewhere by putting one foot in front of the other on the ground, but without running 走；行走；步行：*The baby is just learning to walk.* 這孩子剛學走路。◇ *'How did you get here?' 'I walked.'* "你怎麼到這兒來的？" "我走路來的。" ◇ **+ adv./prep.** *He walked slowly away from her.* 他慢慢地從她身旁走開。◇ *The door opened and Jo walked in.* 門開了，喬走了進來。◇ *She missed the bus and had to walk home.* 她沒趕上公共汽車，只好步行回家。◇ *The school is* ***within*** *easy* ***walking distance of*** *the train station.* 學校離火車站不遠，不費勁就走到了。◇ **~ sth** *Children here walk several miles to school.* 這裏的孩子去上學要步行好幾英里。**2** 0-π (also **go walking**) (both *especially BrE*) [I, T] to spend time walking for pleasure 徒步旅行；散步：(**+ adv./prep.**) *We're going walking in the mountains this summer.* 今年夏天我們打算到山裏去徒步旅行。◇ *I walked across Scotland with a friend.* 我和一個朋友徒步穿越了蘇格蘭。◇ **~ sth** *They love walking the moors.* 他們喜歡到沼澤地散步。**3** [T] **~ sb + adv./prep.** to go somewhere with sb on foot, especially in order to make sure they get there safely 陪伴…走；護送…走：*He always walked her home.* 他經常護送她走回家。**4** [T] **~ sth + adv./prep.** to take an animal for a walk; to make an animal walk somewhere 牽着（動物）走；遛；趕着…走：*They walk their dogs every day.*

W

他們每天遛狗。➲ SYNONYMS at TAKE **5** [I] (*informal*) to disappear; to be taken away 不翼而飛；被盜走：*Lock up any valuables. Things tend to walk here* (= be stolen). 把貴重物品鎖起來。這裏的東西常會不翼而飛。 **6** [I] (*literary*) (of a GHOST 鬼魂) to appear 出現；出沒；顯靈

IDM **run before you can 'walk** to do things that are difficult, without learning the basic skills first 不會走就跑；沒掌握基本功就做難事 **walk the 'beat** (of police officers 警察) to walk around the area that they are responsible for 在轄區執勤巡邏 **walk 'free** to be allowed to leave court, etc., without receiving any punishment 獲無罪釋放 **'walk it** (*informal*) **1** to go somewhere on foot instead of in a vehicle 徒步前往 **2** (*BrE*) to easily achieve sth that you want 輕易獲得；輕易取勝：*It's not a difficult exam. You'll walk it!* 這次考試不難。你會輕鬆通過的！ **walk sb off their 'feet** (*informal*) to make sb walk so far or so fast that they are very tired 使走得筋疲力盡 **walk off the 'job** (*NAmE*) to stop working in order to go on strike（離開崗位）罷工 **walk the 'plank** (in the past) to walk along a board placed over the side of a ship and fall into the sea, as a punishment 走跳板（舊時強迫受害人在置於船舷外的跳板上行走而致落水） **walk the 'streets** to walk around the streets of a town or city（在城鎮裏）穿街走巷；在大街上閒逛：*Is it safe to walk the streets alone at night?* 夜間獨自一人在大街上行走安全嗎？ **walk 'tall** to feel proud and confident 昂首闊步；趾高氣揚 **ˌwalk the 'walk** (*informal*, *approving*) to act in a way that shows people you are really good at what you do, and not just good at talking about it 言行一致：*You can talk the talk but can you walk the walk?* 你說得頭頭是道，可是你做得到嗎？ ➲ more at AIR *n.*, AISLE, LINE *n.*, MEMORY LANE, THIN *adj.*, TIGHTROPE

PHR V **ˌwalk a'way (from sb/sth)** to leave a difficult situation or relationship, etc. instead of staying and trying to deal with it（從困難的處境或關係中）脫身，一走了之 **ˌwalk a'way with sth** (*informal*) to win or obtain sth easily 輕易取勝；輕易獲得：*She walked away with the gold medal.* 她輕鬆地摘走了金牌。 **ˌwalk 'in on sb/sth** to enter a room when sb in there is doing sth private and does not expect you 冷不丁進屋撞見 **ˌwalk 'into sth** (*informal*) **1** to become involved in an unpleasant situation, especially because you were not sensible enough to avoid it 不意落入，不明智地陷入（不愉快的境地）：*I realized I'd walked into a trap.* 我意識到自己稀裏糊塗落入了陷阱。 **2** to succeed in getting a job very easily 輕易獲得（工作） **ˌwalk 'into sth/sb** to crash into sth/sb while you are walking, for example because you do not see them 走路時撞着（人或東西） **ˌwalk 'off** to leave a person or place suddenly because you are angry or upset 憤然離去；拂袖而去 **ˌwalk sth↔'off** to go for a walk after a meal so that you feel less full 散步消食：*We walked off a heavy Sunday lunch.* 我們星期日午餐吃得特別多，散散步幫助消化。 **ˌwalk 'off with sth** (*informal*) **1** to win sth easily 輕易取勝 **2** to take sth that is not yours; to steal sth 順手牽羊；順便偷走 **ˌwalk 'out** (*informal*) (of workers 工人) to stop working in order to go on strike（離開崗位）罷工 ➲ related noun WALKOUT **ˌwalk 'out (of sth)** 🔑 to leave a meeting, performance, etc. suddenly, especially in order to show your disapproval 突然離去，退場，退席（尤為表示異議） **ˌwalk 'out (on sb)** (*informal*) to suddenly leave sb that you are having a relationship with and that you have a responsibility for 遺棄，拋棄，捨棄，離開（某人） **SYN** **desert**：*How could she walk out on her kids?* 她怎麼能遺棄自己的孩子呢？ **ˌwalk 'out (on sth)** (*informal*) to stop doing sth that you have agreed to do before it is completed 半途而廢；半截撂挑子：*I never walk out on a job half done.* 我做工作從不半途而廢。 **ˌwalk (all) 'over sb** (*informal*) **1** to treat sb badly, without considering them or their needs 苛刻對待：*She'll always let him walk all over her.* 她對他總是逆來順受。**2** to defeat sb easily 輕而易舉地打敗；輕取 ➲ related noun WALKOVER **ˌwalk sb 'through sth** to help sb learn or become familiar with sth, by showing them each stage of the process in turn（循序漸進地）教；逐步引導：*She walked me through a demonstration of the software.* 她一步步地給我演示軟件。 ➲ related noun WALK-THROUGH **ˌwalk 'up (to sb/sth)** 🔑 to walk towards sb/sth, especially in a confident way（尤指自信地）向…走去，走近

■ ***noun*** **1** 🔑 [C] a journey on foot, usually for pleasure or exercise 行走；步行；徒步旅行；散步：*Let's **go for a walk**.* 咱們去散散步吧。◇ *I like to have a walk in the evenings.* 我喜歡在晚上散步。◇ *She's **taken the dog for a walk**.* 她帶着狗去散步了。◇ *He set out on the long walk home.* 他動身走很長的路回家了。◇ *The office is ten minutes' walk from here.* 從這裏去辦公室要步行十分鐘。◇ *a ten-minute walk* 步行十分鐘的路程 ◇ *It's only a short walk to the beach.* 步行到海灘沒多遠。 **2** 🔑 [C] a path or route for walking, usually for pleasure; an organized event when people walk for pleasure 散步的小路；步行的路徑；（為遊玩而組織的）徒步旅行：*a circular walk* 環形步行路徑 ◇ *There are some interesting walks in the area.* 這一帶有一些有趣的小徑。◇ *a guided walk around the farm* 由嚮導引路繞農場走一圈 **3** [sing.] a way or style of walking; the act or speed of walking rather than running 步態；步行速度：*I recognized him by his walk.* 我根據他走路的樣子認出了他。◇ *The horse slowed to a walk.* 那匹馬慢下來緩步而行。 **4** [C] (*NAmE*) a SIDEWALK or path 人行道；小路

IDM **a ˌwalk in the 'park** (*informal*) a thing that is very easy to do or deal with 易事；輕而易舉的事：*The role isn't exactly a walk in the park.* 這個角色絕非閒庭散步。 **a walk of 'life** a person's job or position in society 行業；職業；地位；階層 **SYN** **background**：*She has friends from all walks of life.* 她在社會各界中都有朋友。

walk·about /'wɔːkəbaʊt/ *noun* **1** (*BrE*) an occasion when an important person walks among ordinary people to meet and talk to them（要人的）出巡 **2** (*AustralE*) a journey (originally on foot) that is made by an Australian Aboriginal in order to live in the traditional manner（澳大利亞土著為回歸傳統生活而進行的）短期叢林流浪

IDM **go 'walkabout** **1** (*informal*) to be lost or not where you should be 迷路；丟失：*My rucksack seems to have gone walkabout.* 我的旅行包好像是丟了。 **2** (of an Australian Aboriginal) to go into the country away from white society in order to live in the traditional manner（澳大利亞土著遠離白人社會到鄉間）進行叢林漫遊

walk·er /'wɔːkə(r)/ *noun* **1** (*especially BrE*) a person who walks, usually for pleasure or exercise 步行者；散步的人；徒步旅行者：*The coastal path is a popular route for walkers.* 這條海濱小路是散步者很喜歡走的路徑。 **2 a fast, slow, etc. ~** a person who walks fast, slow, etc. 走路快（或慢等）的人 **3** (*NAmE*) (*BrE* **Zim·mer frame™**, *informal* **Zim·mer**) a metal frame that people use to help them to walk, for example people who are old or who have sth wrong with their legs 助行器：*He now needs a walker to get around.* 他現在走動需要助行架。 ➲ picture at FRAME **4** (*NAmE*) (*BrE* **'baby walker**) a frame with wheels and a HARNESS for a baby who can walk around a room, supported by the frame（幼兒）學步車

walk·ies /'wɔːkiz/ *noun* [pl.] (*BrE*, *informal*) a walk with a dog 遛狗：*to go for walkies* 去遛狗

walkie-talkie /ˌwɔːki 'tɔːki/ *noun* (*informal*) a small radio that you can carry with you and use to send or receive messages 步話機；無線電通話機

'walk-in *adj.* [only before noun] **1** large enough to walk into 大得能走進去的：*a walk-in closet* 小貯藏室 **2** not arranged in advance; where you do not need to arrange a time in advance 未經預約的；無須事先約定的：*a walk-in interview* 未經預約的訪談 ◇ *a walk-in clinic* 無需預約的診所

walk·ing 🔑 /'wɔːkɪŋ/ *noun*, *adj.*

■ ***noun*** [U] **1** 🔑 (*especially BrE*) the activity of going for walks in the countryside for exercise or pleasure 行走；步行；散步；徒步旅行：*to **go walking*** 去散步 ◇ *walking boots* 便靴 ◇ *a walking holiday in Scotland* 蘇格蘭的徒步旅行假日 ➲ see also POWER WALKING **2** the sport of walking a long distance as fast as possible without running 競走

■ ***adj.*** [only before noun] (*informal*) used to describe a human or living example of the thing mentioned 似人的；活的：*She's a walking dictionary* (= she knows a lot of words). 她是部活字典。

ˈwalking bus *noun* (in Britain) a way for a group of children to walk safely in a group with an adult to and from school, along a route that passes by the children's homes 步行巴士（英國小學生由成人帶領，結隊步行安全上學和回家）

ˈwalking papers *noun* [pl.] (*NAmE, informal*) the letter or notice dismissing sb from a job 解雇函；解雇通知書

ˈwalking stick (also **stick** especially in *BrE*) *noun* a stick that you carry and use as a support when you are walking 手杖；拐棍 ➲ picture at STICK

the ˌwalking ˈwounded *noun* [pl.] people who have been injured in a battle or an accident but who are still able to walk （戰爭或事故中）能走路的傷員

Walk·man™ /ˈwɔːkmən/ *noun* (*pl.* **-mans** /-mənz/) a type of PERSONAL STEREO 隨身聽（小型立體聲音響）

ˈwalk-on *adj.* **~ part/role** used to describe a very small part in a play or film/movie, without any words to say （指戲劇或電影中無台詞的）小角色，龍套角色

walk·out /ˈwɔːkaʊt/ *noun* **1** a sudden strike by workers （突然的）罷工 **2** the act of suddenly leaving a meeting as a protest against sth （為表示抗議而突然的）退場，退席

walk·over /ˈwɔːkəʊvə(r)/ *noun* an easy victory in a game or competition（比賽或競賽中的）輕易取得的勝利

ˈwalk-through *noun* **1** an occasion when you practise a performance, etc. without an audience being present 排演；排練；彩排 **2** a careful explanation of the details of a process 逐步解釋

ˈwalk-up *noun* (*NAmE*) a tall building with stairs but no lift/elevator; an office or a flat/apartment in such a building 無電梯的大樓；無電梯大樓中的辦公室（或公寓套房）

walk·way /ˈwɔːkweɪ/ *noun* a passage or path for walking along, often outside and raised above the ground（常為戶外高出地面的）人行通道，走道

wall 🔑 /wɔːl/ *noun, verb*

■ ***noun*** **1** 🔑 a long vertical solid structure, made of stone, brick or concrete, that surrounds, divides or protects an area of land 城牆；圍牆：*The fields were divided by stone walls.* 這些田地由石牆分隔。◇ *He sat on the wall and watched the others playing.* 他坐在牆頭上看別人玩耍。 ➲ VISUAL VOCAB page V17 ➲ see also SEA WALL **2** 🔑 any of the vertical sides of a building or room 牆；壁；牆壁：*I'm going to paint the walls white and the ceiling pink.* 我打算把牆壁刷成白色，把天花板刷成粉紅色。◇ *Hang the picture **on the wall** opposite the window.* 把這張畫掛在對着窗的牆上。◇ *She leaned against the wall.* 她倚靠着牆。 ➲ COLLOCATIONS at DECORATE **3** something that forms a barrier or stops you from making progress 屏障；隔閡；壁壘：*The boat struck a solid wall of water.* 船撞上一道水幕。◇ *The investigators were confronted by a **wall of silence**.* 調查人員碰了壁，問誰誰都默不作聲。 **4** the outer layer of sth hollow such as an organ of the body or a cell of an animal or a plant （身體器官或動植物細胞等的）外壁：*the abdominal wall* 腹腔壁 ◇ *the wall of an artery* 動脈血管壁

IDM **go to the ˈwall** (*informal*) (of a company or an organization 公司或機構) to fail because of lack of money（因缺少資金）走投無路，失敗，破產，陷於絕境 **off the ˈwall** (*informal*) unusual and amusing; slightly crazy 奇妙的；有點兒出格的：*Some of his ideas are really off the wall.* 他有些想法真是十分新奇。◇ *off-the-wall ideas* 奇妙的想法 **up the ˈwall** (*informal*) crazy or angry 發狂；憤怒：*That noise is driving me up the wall.* 那噪音讓我都快瘋了。◇ *I mustn't be late or Dad will go up the wall.* 我不能晚了，否則爸爸會發脾氣的。 **ˌwalls have ˈears** (*saying*) used to warn people to be careful what they say because other people may be listening 隔牆有耳 ➲ more at BACK *n.*, BOUNCE *v.*, BRICK *n.*, FLY *n.*, HIT *v.*, FOUR, HANDWRITING, HEAD *n.*, WRITING

■ ***verb*** [usually passive] **~ sth** to surround an area, a town, etc. with a wall or walls 用牆把…圍住：*a walled city* 有城牆的城市

PHR V **ˌwall sth↔ˈin** [usually passive] to surround sth/sb with a wall or barrier 把（人或東西）圍到屏障等裏面 **ˌwall sth↔ˈoff** [usually passive] to separate one place or area from another with a wall 用牆把…隔開 **ˌwall sb↔ˈup** [usually passive] to keep sb as a prisoner behind walls 把…關在大牆後；監禁 **ˌwall sth↔ˈup** [usually passive] to fill an opening with a wall, bricks, etc. so that you can no longer use it （用牆、磚等把通路）堵住，封死

wal·laby /ˈwɒləbi; *NAmE* ˈwɑːl-/ *noun* (*pl.* **-ies**) an Australian animal like a small KANGAROO, that moves by jumping on its strong back legs and keeps its young in a POUCH (= a pocket of skin) on the front of the mother's body 沙袋鼠（袋鼠科動物，產於澳大利亞）

wal·lah /ˈwɒlə; *NAmE* ˈwɑːlə/ *noun* (*informal* or *IndE*) a person connected with a particular job 與…工作有關的人；從事…工作的人：*office wallahs* 辦公室人員

ˈwall anchor (*NAmE*) (*BrE* **Rawl·plug™**, **ˈwall plug**) *noun* a small plastic tube, closed at one end, that you put into a wall to hold a screw （塑料製）牆錨；牆栓

wall·chart /ˈwɔːltʃɑːt; *NAmE* -tʃɑːrt/ *noun* a large piece of paper on which there is information, fixed to a wall for people to look at 掛圖

wall·cov·er·ing /ˈwɔːlkʌvərɪŋ/ *noun* [U, C] WALLPAPER or cloth used to decorate the walls in a room 覆蓋牆壁的裝飾；壁紙；牆布

wal·let 🔑 /ˈwɒlɪt; *NAmE* ˈwɑːl-; ˈwɔːl-/ *noun*

1 🔑 (*NAmE* also **bill·fold**) a small flat folding case made of leather or plastic used for keeping paper money and credit cards in （放鈔票、信用卡的）錢包，皮夾子 ➲ VISUAL VOCAB page V64 **2** (*BrE*) a flat leather, plastic or cardboard case for carrying documents in （攜帶文件用的）皮夾，塑料夾，硬紙夾：*a document wallet* 文件夾

wall·flower /ˈwɔːlflaʊə(r)/ *noun* **1** a garden plant with yellow, orange or red flowers with a sweet smell that appear in late spring 桂竹香（一種園藝植物，暮春開花，呈黃、橙或紅色） **2** (*informal*) a person who does not dance at a party because they do not have sb to dance with or because they are too shy （舞會或聚會上因無舞伴或靦腆）待在一旁的人，壁花

wall·ing /ˈwɔːlɪŋ/ *noun* [U] **1** material from which a wall is built 砌牆的材料：*stone walling* 砌牆石料 **2** the act or skill of building a wall or walls 砌牆；壘牆；壘牆技術：*a firm that does paving and walling* 從事鋪路砌牆的公司

ˌwall-ˈmounted *adj.* fixed onto a wall 固定在牆上的：*wall-mounted lights* 壁燈

wal·lop /ˈwɒləp; *NAmE* ˈwɑːl-/ *noun, verb*

■ ***noun*** [sing.] (*informal*) a heavy powerful hit 痛打；猛擊

■ ***verb*** (*informal*) **1 ~ sb/sth** to hit sb/sth very hard 痛打；猛擊 SYN **thump** **2 ~ sb/sth** to defeat sb completely in a contest, match, etc. （在競賽、比賽等中）徹底擊敗，大勝 SYN **thrash**：*We walloped them 6–0.* 我們以 6:0 把他們打得落花流水。

wal·lop·ing /ˈwɒləpɪŋ; *NAmE* ˈwɑːl-/ *noun, adj.* (*informal*)

■ ***noun*** [usually sing.] **1** a heavy defeat 大敗；慘敗：*Our team got a real walloping last week.* 我們隊上星期一敗塗地。 **2** an act of hitting sb very hard several times, often as a punishment （連續）痛打，狠揍

■ ***adj.*** [only before noun] very big 很大的；巨大的：*They had to pay a walloping great fine.* 他們不得不繳一大筆罰款。

wal·low /ˈwɒləʊ; *NAmE* ˈwɑːloʊ/ *verb, noun*

■ ***verb*** **1** [I] **~ (in sth)** (of large animals or people 大動物或人) to lie and roll about in water or mud, to keep cool or for pleasure （為保持涼爽或嬉戲在爛泥、水裏）打滾，翻滾：*hippos wallowing in the river* 在河裏打滾的河馬 ◇ *He loves to wallow in a hot bath after a game.* 他在比賽後喜歡泡個熱水澡。 **2** [I] **~ in sth** (often *disapproving*) to enjoy sth that causes you pleasure 沉湎；放縱：*She wallowed in the luxury of the hotel.* 她沉湎於旅館豪華奢侈的享樂之中。◇ ***to wallow in despair/self-pity*** (= to think about your unhappy feelings all the time and seem to be enjoying them) 陷入絕望；顧影自憐

■ ***noun*** [sing.] an act of wallowing（在爛泥或水裏的）打滾嬉戲，翻滾：*pigs having a wallow in the mud* 在爛泥中打滾的豬

W

ˈwall painting *noun* a picture painted straight onto the surface of a wall 壁畫

wall·paper /ˈwɔːlpeɪpə(r)/ *noun, verb*
■ ***noun*** [U] **1** thick paper, often with a pattern on it, used for covering the walls and ceiling of a room 壁紙；牆紙：*wallpaper paste* 貼壁紙用的糨糊 ◇ *a roll of wallpaper* 一捲壁紙 ◇ *to hang wallpaper* 貼壁紙 ➲ COLLOCATIONS at DECORATE **2** (*computing* 計) the background pattern or picture that you choose to have on the screen of your computer, mobile/cell phone, etc.（計算機、手機屏幕上的）壁紙，桌面背景
■ ***verb*** (also **paper**) [T, I] **~ (sth)** to put wallpaper onto the walls of a room 往（屋裏牆上）貼壁紙

ˈwall plug *noun* = RAWLPLUG

ˈWall Street *noun* [U] the US financial centre and STOCK EXCHANGE in New York City (used to refer to the business that is done there) 華爾街（美國紐約金融中心和證券交易所所在地）：*Share prices fell on Wall Street today.* 今日紐約證券交易所的股價下跌。◇ *Wall Street responded quickly to the news.* 華爾街對這一消息反應迅速。

ˈwall tent (*NAmE*) (*BrE* **ˈframe tent**) *noun* a large tent with a roof and walls that do not slope much 框架式大帳篷（篷頂和篷壁形成的坡度很小）➲ compare DOME TENT, RIDGE TENT

ˌwall-to-ˈwall *adj.* [only before noun] **1** covering the floor of a room completely 覆蓋整個地板的：***wall-to-wall carpets/carpeting*** 鋪滿整個地板的地毯 ➲ VISUAL VOCAB page V23 **2** (*informal*) continuous; happening or existing all the time or everywhere 連續的；無時不在的；到處存在的：*wall-to-wall TV sports coverage* 連續的電視體育報道

wally /ˈwɒli; *NAmE* ˈwɔːli; ˈwɑːli/ *noun* (*pl.* **-ies**) (*BrE, informal*) a stupid person 傻瓜；笨蛋；白痴

wal·nut /ˈwɔːlnʌt/ *noun* **1** [C] the light brown nut of the walnut tree that has a rough surface and a hard round shell in two halves 核桃；胡桃 ➲ VISUAL VOCAB page V32 **2** (also **ˈwalnut tree**) [C] the tree on which walnuts grow 核桃樹；胡桃樹 **3** [U] the brown wood of the walnut tree, used in making furniture 核桃木；胡桃木

wal·rus /ˈwɔːlrəs/ *noun* an animal like a large SEAL (= a sea animal with thick fur, that eats fish and lives around coasts), that has two long outer teeth called TUSKS and lives in Arctic regions 海象（形似海豹，獠牙較長，棲息在北極海域）

ˌwalrus mouˈstache *noun* (*informal*) a long thick MOUSTACHE that hangs down on each side of the mouth 海象鬍子（濃密且兩端下垂的唇上長鬍鬚）

Walter Mitty /ˌwɔːltə(r) ˈmɪti/ *noun* a person who imagines that their life is full of excitement and adventures when it is in fact just ordinary 幻想多彩生活的人
ORIGIN From the name of the main character in James Thurber's story *The Secret Life of Walter Mitty*. 源自詹姆斯•瑟伯所著小說《沃爾特•米蒂的秘密生活》中主角的名字。

W

waltz /wɔːls; wɔːlts/ *noun, verb*
■ ***noun*** a dance in which two people dance together to a regular rhythm; a piece of music for this dance 華爾茲舞；華爾茲舞曲；圓舞曲：*to dance a/the waltz* 跳華爾茲舞 ◇ *a Strauss waltz* 施特勞斯圓舞曲
■ ***verb*** **1** [I, T] to dance a waltz 跳華爾茲舞：**(+ adv./prep.)** *I watched them waltzing across the floor.* 我望着他們跳着華爾茲滑過地板。◇ **~ sb + adv./prep.** *He waltzed her around the room.* 他帶着她滿屋跳華爾茲舞。**2** [I] **+ adv./prep.** (*informal*) to walk or go somewhere in a very confident way 大搖大擺地走：*I don't like him waltzing into the house as if he owned it.* 我不喜歡他像房主似地大搖大擺走進屋來。 **3** [I] **~ (through sth)** to complete or achieve sth without any difficulty 輕易完成；輕而易舉地取得：*The recruits have waltzed through their training.* 新招收的成員輕鬆順利地完成了訓練。
PHR V **ˌwaltz ˈoff (with sth/sb)** (*informal*) to leave a place or person in a way that is very annoying, often taking sth that is not yours 令人討厭地離開（常帶走不屬於自己的東西）：*He just waltzed off with my car!* 他順手牽羊開走了我的汽車！

WAN /wæn/ *noun* (*pl.* **WANs**) (*computing* 計) the abbreviation for 'wide area network' (a system in which computers in different places are connected, usually over a large area) 廣域網（全寫為 wide area network，將大範圍內不同地方的電腦聯網的系統）➲ compare LAN

wan /wɒn; *NAmE* wɑːn/ *adj.* looking pale and weak 蒼白無力的；無血色的；憔悴的：*his grey, wan face* 他那蒼白憔悴的面孔 ◇ *She gave me a wan smile* (= showing no energy or enthusiasm). 她勉強向我微微一笑。▸ **wanly** *adv.*：*He smiled wanly.* 他慘然一笑。

wan·anchi /ˌwʌnʌˈmtʃi/ *noun* [pl.] (*EAfrE*) people; the public 人們；公眾

wand /wɒnd; *NAmE* wɑːnd/ *noun* **1** (also **ˌmagic ˈwand**) a straight thin stick that is held by sb when performing magic or magic tricks 魔杖：*The fairy waved her wand and the table disappeared.* 那仙女魔杖一揮，桌子不翼而飛。◇ *You can't expect me to just* ***wave a (magic) wand*** *and make everything all right again.* 你不能指望我揮動一下魔杖，便一切又平安無事了。**2** any object in the shape of a straight thin stick 棍；棒；杆；杖：*a mascara wand* 睫毛膏棒 ➲ VISUAL VOCAB page V60

wan·der 🔑 /ˈwɒndə(r); *NAmE* ˈwɑːn-/ *verb, noun*
■ ***verb*** **1** 🔑 [I, T] to walk slowly around or to a place, often without any particular sense of purpose or direction 閒逛；漫遊；遊蕩：**+ adv./prep.** *She wandered aimlessly around the streets.* 她在大街上漫無目的地到處遊蕩。◇ *We wandered back towards the car.* 我們遛達着回到汽車那裏。◇ **~ sth** *The child was found wandering the streets alone.* 那孩子被發現獨自在大街上瞎轉。**2** 🔑 [I] to move away from the place where you ought to be or the people you are with 偏離（正道）；走失；離散 SYN **stray**：**~ away/off** *The child wandered off and got lost.* 那孩子走散後迷路了。◇ **~ from/off sth** *They had wandered from the path into the woods.* 他們離開小路消失在樹林裏。**3** 🔑 [I] (of a person's mind or thoughts 人的思想或想法) to stop being directed on sth and to move without much control to other ideas, subjects, etc. 走神；神志恍惚；（思想）開小差 SYN **drift**：*It's easy to be distracted and* ***let your attention wander.*** 很容易走神分散了注意力。◇ *Try not to* ***let your mind wander.*** 盡量別讓你的思想開小差。◇ **~ away, back, to, etc. sth** *Her thoughts wandered back to her youth.* 她浮想聯翩，思緒回到了青春歲月。 **4** [I] (of a person's eyes 人的眼睛) to move slowly from looking at one thing to looking at another thing or in other directions 慢慢地移開：*She* ***let her gaze wander.*** 她東瞅瞅西望望。◇ **+ adv./prep.** *His eyes wandered towards the photographs on the wall.* 他的目光慢慢地移向牆上的照片。 **5** [I] **(+ adv./prep.)** (of a road or river 道路或河流) to curve instead of following a straight course 蜿蜒；迂迴曲折：*The road wanders along through the hills.* 這條路蜿蜒曲折地穿過丘陵。
■ ***noun*** 🔑 [sing.] a short walk in or around a place, usually with no special purpose 遊蕩；遛達；閒逛；徘徊：*I went to the park and had a wander around.* 我去公園轉了一圈。

wan·der·er /ˈwɒndərə(r); *NAmE* ˈwɑːn-/ *noun* a person who keeps travelling from place to place with no permanent home 漂泊者；漫遊者；流浪者

wan·der·ings /ˈwɒndərɪŋz; *NAmE* ˈwɑːn-/ *noun* [pl.] (*literary*) journeys from place to place, usually with no special purpose 漫遊；流浪；漂泊

wan·der·lust /ˈwɒndəlʌst; *NAmE* ˈwɑːndərl-/ *noun* [U] (from *German*) a strong desire to travel 漫遊癖；旅行癖

wane /weɪn/ *verb, noun*
■ ***verb*** **1** [I] to become gradually weaker or less important 衰落；衰敗；敗落；減弱 SYN **decrease, fade**：*Her enthusiasm for the whole idea was waning rapidly.* 她對整個想法的熱情迅速冷淡了下來。 **2** [I] (of the moon 月亮) to appear slightly smaller each day after being round and full 缺；虧 OPP **wax** IDM see WAX *v.*
■ ***noun*** [sing.]
IDM **on the ˈwane** becoming smaller, less important or less common 變小；衰落；減弱；敗落 SYN **declining**：

Her popularity has been on the wane for some time. 她的人氣一段時間以來江河日下。

wan·gle /ˈwæŋgl/ *verb* (*informal*) to get sth that you or another person wants by persuading sb or by a clever plan 把…弄到手；設法獲得；搞：**~ sth** *She had wangled an invitation to the opening night.* 她弄到了一張首映之夜的請柬。◇ *We should be able to* **wangle it** *so that you can start tomorrow.* 我們應該能設法安排你明天啟程。◇ *He managed to* **wangle his way** *onto the course.* 他終於設法修讀了這一科目。◇ **~ sth from/out of sb** *I'll try to wangle some money out of my parents.* 我要設法從父母那裏哄出些錢來。◇ **~ sb sth** *He had wangled her a seat on the plane.* 他為她弄到了一個飛機上的座位。

wank /wæŋk/ *verb, noun*

■ ***verb*** [I] (*BrE, taboo, slang*) to MASTURBATE 行手淫

■ ***noun*** [usually sing.] (*BrE, taboo, slang*) an act of MASTURBATION 手淫

wank·er /ˈwæŋkə(r)/ *noun* (*BrE, taboo, slang*) an offensive word used to insult sb, especially a man, and to show anger or dislike 無能者，下流坯子（尤用以侮辱男性）：*a bunch of wankers* 一群下流坯子

wanna /ˈwɒnə; *NAmE* ˈwɔːnə; ˈwɑːnə/ (*informal, non-standard*) the written form of the word some people use to mean 'want to' or 'want a', which is not considered to be correct 要，想要個（書寫形式，有人用以表示 want to 或 want a。此用法被視為不正確）：*I wanna go.* 我想走。◇ *Wanna drink?* (= Do you want …) 要杯飲料嗎？ **HELP** You should not write this form, unless you are copying somebody's speech. 除非轉述他人話語，否則不宜寫成這種形式。

wan·nabe /ˈwɒnəbi; *NAmE* ˈwɑːn-; ˈwɔːn-/ *noun* (*informal, disapproving*) a person who behaves, dresses, etc. like sb famous because they want to be like them （名人的）崇拜模仿者

More About 補充說明

offers and invitations 提議和邀請

- **Would you like …?** is the most usual polite question form for offers and invitations, especially in *BrE*. * Would you like …? 是最常見的禮貌提議和邀請疑問式，尤用於英式英語：*Would you like a cup of coffee?* 喝杯咖啡好嗎？
- **Do you want …?** is less formal and more direct. It is more common in *NAmE* than in *BrE*. * Do you want …? 較非正式且更直接，在美式英語中比在英式英語中常見：*We're going to a club tonight. Do you want to come with us?* 今晚我們要去俱樂部，你想和我們一起去嗎？
- **Would you care …?** is very formal and now sounds old-fashioned. * Would you care …? 很正式，聽起來顯得過時。

want 0‑ᴡ /wɒnt; *NAmE* wɑːnt; wɔːnt/ *verb, noun*

■ ***verb*** [T] (not usually used in the progressive tenses 通常不用於進行時)

▸ **WISH** 希望 **1** 0‑ᴡ to have a desire or a wish for sth 要；想要；希望：**~ sth** *Do you want some more tea?* 你再要點兒茶嗎？◇ *She's always wanted a large family.* 她一直希望有一個大家庭。◇ ***All I want is*** *the truth.* 我只想知道實情。◇ *Thanks for the present—it's* ***just what I wanted.*** 感謝贈我這份禮物，這正是我想要的。◇ *I can do whatever I want.* 我想幹什麼就可以幹什麼。◇ ***The last thing I wanted was to*** *upset you.* 我最不希望做的事就是惹你不高興。◇ *The party wants her as leader.* 這個政黨希望由她做領袖。◇ **~ (to do sth)** *What do you want to do tomorrow?* 明天你想做什麼？◇ *'It's time you did your homework.' 'I don't want to!'* "你該做作業了。""我就是不想做！"◇ *There are two points which I wanted to make.* 我想要指出的有兩點。◇ ***I just wanted*** *to know if everything was all right.* 我只是想知道是否一切都好。◇ (*informal*) *You can come too,* ***if you want.*** 如果你想來也可以來。◇ **~ sb/sth to do sth** *Do you want me to help?* 你要我幫忙嗎？◇ *We didn't want this to happen.* 我們並不希望發生這樣的事情。◇ *I want it (to be) done as quickly as possible.* 我希望這件事儘快完成。 **HELP** Notice that you cannot say 'want that …'. 注意不能說 want that …：~~*I want that you do it quickly.*~~ When the infinitive is used after **want**, it must have **to**. * want 後用不定式時，必須有 to：~~*I want study in America.*~~ ◇ **~ sb/sth doing sth** *I don't want you coming home so late.* 我不希望你這麼晚回家。◇ **~ sb/sth + adj.** *Do you want your coffee black or white?* 你的咖啡裏加不加奶？

▸ **NEED** 需要 **2** 0‑ᴡ (*informal*) to need sth 需要：**~ sth** *We'll want more furniture for the new office.* 我們的新辦公室需要添些傢具。◇ *What this house wants is a good clean.* 這房子需要好好打掃一下。◇ **~ doing sth** *The plants want watering daily.* 這些植物需要天天澆水。◇ **~ to be/have sth** *The plants want to be watered daily.* 這些植物需要天天澆水。 **3** [usually passive] **~ sb (+ adv./prep.)** to need sb to be present in the place or for the purpose mentioned 需要…在場：*She's wanted immediately in the director's office.* 她得馬上到主任辦公室去。◇ *Excuse me, you're wanted on the phone.* 對不起，有你的電話。 ⊃ see also WANTED

▸ **SHOULD/OUGHT TO** 應該 **4 ~ to do sth** (*informal*) used to give advice to sb, meaning 'should' or 'ought to'（用於提出建議）應該：*If possible, you want to avoid alcohol.* 你應盡可能避免飲酒。◇ *He wants to be more careful.* 他應多加小心。◇ *You don't want to do it like that.* 你不應那樣做。

▸ **FEEL SEXUAL DESIRE** 有性慾 **5 ~ sb** to feel sexual desire for sb 對…有性慾

▸ **LACK** 缺少 **6 ~ sth** (*formal*) to lack sth 缺少；缺乏 **SYN** **be short of**：*He doesn't want courage.* 他有的是勇氣。

IDM **not want to ˈknow (about sth)** (*informal*) to take no interest in sth because you do not care about it or it is too much trouble 不想知道；不願理會：*I've tried to ask her advice, but she doesn't want to know* (= about my problems). 我嘗試向她請教，但她卻不願理會。◇ *'How much was it?'* ***'You don't want to know'*** (= it is better if you don't know). "這要多少錢？""你還是不知道的好。" **want ˈrid of sb/sth** (*BrE, informal*) to want to be free of sb/sth that has been annoying you or that you do not want 想擺脫；想甩掉：*Are you trying to say you want rid of me?* 你是在說要甩掉我嗎？ **what do you ˈwant?** used to ask sb in a rude or angry way why they are there or what they want you to do （語帶指責）你在這裏幹什麼；你要我幹什麼 ⊃ more at NONE *pron.*, PART *n.*, TRUCK *n.*, WASTE *v.*, WAY *n.*

PHR V **ˈwant for sth** (especially in negative sentences 尤用於否定句) (*formal*) to lack sth that you really need 缺少，短缺（真正需要的東西）：*He's ensured that his children will* ***want for nothing*** (= will have everything they need). 他得到保證他的子女將什麼也不會缺少。 **want sth from/out of sth/sb** to hope to get sth from a particular experience or person 希望從…中得到：*I had to discover what I really wanted out of life.* 我得弄清楚我確實要從生活中得到什麼。◇ *What do you want from me?* 你要從我這裏得到什麼？ **ˌwant ˈin/ˈout** (*informal, especially NAmE*) to want to come in or out of a place 想進來（或出去）：*The dog wants in.* 那條狗想進來。 **ˌwant ˈin | ˌwant ˈin/ˈinto sth** (*informal*) to want to be involved in sth 想要參與；希望涉足：*He wants in on the deal.* 他希望參與這宗交易。 **ˌwant ˈout | ˌwant ˈout of sth** (*informal*) to want to stop being involved in sth 想要退出：*Jenny was fed up. She wanted out.* 珍妮厭倦了，她想要退出。

■ ***noun*** (*formal*)

▸ **STH YOU NEED** 需要的東西 **1** [C, usually pl.] something that you need or want 需要的東西；想望的東西：*She spent her life pandering to the wants of her children.* 她一生都在設法滿足子女的需要。

▸ **LACK** 缺少 **2** [U, sing.] **~ of sth** (*formal*) a situation in which there is not enough of sth; a lack of sth 缺少；缺乏；不足：*a want of adequate medical facilities* 缺少足夠的醫療設施

▸ **BEING POOR** 貧窮 **3** [U] (*formal*) the state of being poor, not having food, etc. 貧窮；貧困；匱乏：*Visitors to the slums were clearly shocked to see so many families living* ***in want.*** 到過貧民窟的人看到有這麼多的家庭生活在貧苦之中顯然震驚不已。

IDM **for (the) want of sth** because of a lack of sth; because sth is not available 因為缺乏…：*The project failed for want of financial backing.* 這個項目由於缺少財政支援而告吹。◇ *We call our music 'postmodern' for the want of a better word.* 由於沒有更合適的詞來表達，我們把我們的音樂稱作"後現代風格"。**in want of sth** (*formal*) needing sth 需要（某事物）：*The present system is in want of a total review.* 目前的系統需要全面的復查。**not for (the) want of doing sth** used to say that if sth is not successful, it is not because of a lack of effort 並非辦事不力：*If he doesn't manage to convince them, it won't be for **want of trying*** (= he has tried hard). 如果他沒能使他們信服，這倒不是由於努力不夠。

'want ads *noun* [pl.] (*NAmE*) = CLASSIFIED ADVERTISEMENTS

Collocations 詞語搭配

War and peace 戰爭與和平

Starting a war 開戰

- **declare/make/wage** war (on sb/sth)（向…）宣戰／挑起戰爭／發動戰爭
- **go to** war (against/with sb)（向…）開戰
- **cause/spark/provoke/foment/quell** unrest 引起／平息騷亂
- **incite/lead/crush/suppress** a revolt/rebellion 煽動／領導／鎮壓起義／叛亂
- **launch/mount/carry out** a surprise/terrorist attack 發起／實施突然／恐怖襲擊
- **prevent/halt/represent** an escalation of the conflict 防止／阻止／表明衝突升級
- **be torn apart by/be on the brink of** civil war 被內戰搞得四分五裂；瀕於內戰
- **enter/invade/occupy** sb's territory 進入／侵略／佔領某人的領土
- **lead/launch/resist/repel** an invasion 領導／發起／抵制／擊退武裝入侵

Military operations 軍事行動

- **adopt/develop/implement/pursue** a military strategy 採用／發展／實施／執行軍事戰略
- **carry out/execute/perform** military operations/manoeuvres/(*especially US*) maneuvers 執行軍事行動／軍事演習
- **send/deploy/station/pull back/withdraw** troops 派遣／部署／派駐／撤回部隊
- **go on/fly/carry out** a reconnaissance/rescue mission 進行／駕機執行／執行偵察／營救任務
- **train/equip/deploy** army/military/combat units 訓練／裝備／部署陸軍／軍事／作戰分隊
- **lead/launch/conduct** a raid/a surprise attack/an (air/airborne/amphibious) assault (on sb) 領導／發起／實施（對某人的）突然襲擊／（空中／空投部隊／登陸）攻擊
- **employ/use** guerrilla tactics 採用游擊戰術
- **conduct/wage** biological/guerrilla warfare 進行／發動生物戰／游擊戰
- **fight/crush/defeat** the rebels/the insurgency 設法戰勝／鎮壓／挫敗叛亂者／叛亂
- **suffer/inflict** a crushing defeat 遭受慘敗；大獲全勝
- **achieve/win** a decisive victory 贏得決定性的勝利
- **halt/stop** the British/German/Russian advance 阻止英國／德國／俄國的前進
- **order/force** a retreat 命令／強迫撤退

Fighting 作戰

- **join/serve in** the army/navy/air force 加入陸軍／海軍／空軍；在陸軍／海軍／空軍部隊服役
- **be/go/remain/serve** on active duty 在服現役
- **serve/complete/return from** a tour of duty 在服役；服役完畢；服役歸來
- **be sent** to the front (line) 被派往前線
- **attack/strike/engage/defeat/kill/destroy** the enemy 襲擊／攻擊敵人；與敵人交戰；擊敗／殺死／消滅敵人
- **see/report/be engaged in** heavy fighting 目睹／報道／參與激戰
- **call for/be met with** armed resistance 要求／遭遇武裝抵抗
- **come under** heavy/machine-gun/mortar fire 冒着激烈的／機關槍的／迫擊炮的射擊
- **fire** a machine-gun/mortar shells/rockets (at sb/sth)（對…）發射機關槍／迫擊炮彈／火箭彈
- **shoot** a rifle/a pistol/bullets/missiles 步槍／手槍射擊；發射子彈／導彈
- **launch/fire** a cruise/ballistic/anti-tank missile 發射巡航／彈道／反坦克導彈
- **use** biological/chemical/nuclear weapons 使用生物／化學／核武器
- **inflict/suffer/sustain** heavy losses/casualties 遭受慘重損失／傷亡
- **be hit/killed by** enemy/friendly/artillery fire 被敵軍／友軍／炮火擊中／射死
- **become/be held as** a prisoner of war 成為戰俘；作為戰俘被監禁

Civilians in war 戰爭中的平民

- **harm/kill/target/protect** innocent/unarmed civilians 傷害／殺死／瞄準／保護無辜的／手無寸鐵的平民
- **cause/avoid/limit/minimize** civilian casualties/collateral damage 導致／避免／限制／最大限度減少平民傷亡／附帶性破壞
- **impose/enforce/lift** a curfew 強制實行／解除宵禁
- **engage in/be a victim of** ethnic cleansing 參與種族清洗；成為種族清洗的受害者
- **be sent to** an internment/a concentration camp 被送到俘虜拘留營／集中營
- **accept/house/resettle** refugees fleeing from war 接受／收容／安置戰爭難民
- **fear/threaten** military/violent reprisals 害怕／揚言要軍事／暴力報復
- **commit/be accused of** war crimes/crimes against humanity/genocide 犯／被指控犯戰爭罪／反人類罪／種族滅絕罪

Making peace 和解

- **make/bring/win/achieve/maintain/promote** peace 促使／帶來／贏得／實現／保持／促進和平
- **call for/negotiate/broker/declare** a ceasefire/a temporary truce 要求／商談／協商／宣佈停戰／暫時休戰
- **sign** a ceasefire agreement 簽署停戰協議
- **call for/bring/put an end to** hostilities 要求發動／引發／結束戰爭
- **demand/negotiate/accept** the surrender of sb/sth 強烈要求／商討／接受…投降
- **establish/send (in)** a peacekeeping force 建立／派遣維和部隊
- **negotiate/conclude/ratify/sign/accept/reject/break/violate** a peace treaty 商討／達成／正式批准／簽署／接受／拒絕／破壞／違反和平協定

W

want·ed /ˈwɒntɪd; NAmE ˈwɑːn-/ *adj.* being searched for by the police, in connection with a crime 受通緝的：*He is wanted by the police in connection with the deaths of two people.* 他因與兩條人命有關而受到警方通緝。◇ *Italy's most wanted man* 意大利頭號通緝犯

want·ing /ˈwɒntɪŋ; NAmE ˈwɑːn-; ˈwɔːn-/ *adj.* [not before noun] (*formal*) **1 ~ (in sth)** not having enough of sth 缺少；缺乏；不足 SYN **lacking**：*The students were certainly not wanting in enthusiasm.* 學生們當然不乏熱情。**2 ~ (in sth)** not good enough 欠缺；不夠好；不令人滿意：*This explanation is wanting in many respects.* 這一解釋在很多方面不能令人滿意。◇ *The new system was tried and **found wanting**.* 這一新系統經測試發現不夠好。

wan·ton /ˈwɒntən; NAmE ˈwɑːn-/ *adj.* (*formal*) **1** [usually before noun] causing harm or damage deliberately and for no acceptable reason 惡意的；不懷好意的；恣意的：*wanton destruction* 肆意破壞 ◇ *a wanton disregard for human life* 全然不顧人的死活 **2** (*old-fashioned, disapproving*) (usually of a woman 通常指女人) behaving in a very immoral way; having many sexual partners 淫蕩的；淫亂的；水性楊花的 ▸ **wan·ton·ly** *adv.* **wan·ton·ness** *noun* [U]

WAP /wæp/ *abbr.* wireless application protocol (a technology that links devices such as mobile phones/cell phones to the Internet) 無線應用協議（一項能使手機等上網的技術）：*a WAP-enabled phone* 可無線上網的電話

wap·iti /ˈwɒpɪti; NAmE ˈwɑːp-/ *noun* (*pl.* **wap·iti**) (*NAmE* also **elk**) a very large N American DEER 美洲赤鹿 ➲ picture at ELK

war 0‑ /wɔː(r)/ *noun*

1 0‑ [U, C] a situation in which two or more countries or groups of people fight against each other over a period of time 戰爭；戰爭狀態：*the Second World War* 第二次世界大戰 ◇ *the threat of (a) nuclear war* 核戰爭威脅 ◇ *to **win/lose a/the war*** 戰勝；戰敗 ◇ *the **war between** England and Scotland* 英格蘭和蘇格蘭之間的戰爭 ◇ *England's **war with/against** Scotland* 英格蘭和／對蘇格蘭的戰爭 ◇ *It was the year Britain **declared war on** Germany.* 那是英國對德國宣戰的那一年。◇ *Social and political problems led to **the outbreak*** (= the beginning) ***of war**.* 社會和政治問題導致了戰爭的爆發。◇ *Where were you living when **war broke out**?* 戰爭爆發時你住在哪兒？◇ *The government does not want to **go to war*** (= start a war) *unless all other alternatives have failed.* 除非所有其他方法都行不通，否則政府不希望開戰。◇ *How long have they been **at war**?* 他們交戰有多長時間了？◇ *a **war hero*** 戰鬥英雄 ◇ (*formal*) *In the Middle Ages England **waged war** on France.* 在中世紀，英國向法國發動了戰爭。◇ *More troops are being despatched to the **war zone**.* 更多的部隊被派往作戰地區。◇ (*formal*) *the **theatre of war*** (= the area in which fighting takes place) 戰區 ➲ see also CIVIL WAR, COLD WAR, COUNCIL OF WAR, PHONEY WAR, POST-WAR, PRISONER OF WAR, WARRING, WORLD WAR **2** 0‑ [C, U] a situation in which there is aggressive competition between groups, companies, countries, etc.（群體、公司、國家之間的）競爭，鬥爭，對抗，衝突：*the class war* 階級鬥爭 ◇ *a trade war* 貿易戰 ➲ see also PRICE WAR **3** 0‑ [U, sing.] **~ (against/on sb/sth)** a fight or an effort over a long period of time to get rid of or stop sth unpleasant （為消滅有害事物的）長期鬥爭；頑強抵禦：*The government **has declared war on** drug dealers.* 政府已向販毒分子宣戰。◇ *We seem to be winning the war against crime.* 我們在撲滅罪行方面似乎已做出成績。➲ SYNONYMS at CAMPAIGN

IDM **have been in the ˈwars** (*informal*) to have been injured in a fight or an accident 打架受傷；在事故中受傷：*You look like you've been in the wars—who gave you that black eye?* 看樣子你打架受傷了，是誰把你打得鼻青眼腫？ **a ˌwar of ˈnerves** an attempt to defeat your opponents by putting pressure on them so that they lose courage or confidence 神經戰（利用心理壓力摧毀對方的鬥志） **a ˌwar of ˈwords** a bitter argument or disagreement over a period of time between two or more people or groups 舌戰；論戰：*the political war of words over tax* 有關稅收問題的政治論戰 ➲ more at FAIR *adj.*

war·ble /ˈwɔːbl; NAmE ˈwɔːrbl/ *verb* **1** [T, I] **~ (sth)** | **+ speech** (*humorous*) to sing, especially in a high voice that is not very steady （尤指用顫音高聲）唱：*He warbled his way through the song.* 整個歌曲他是用高顫音唱的。**2** [I, T] **~ (sth)** (of a bird 鳥) to sing with rapidly changing notes 囀鳴 ▸ **war·ble** *noun*

warb·ler /ˈwɔːblə(r); NAmE ˈwɔːrb-/ *noun* a small bird. There are many types of warbler, some of which have a musical call. 鶯（有些能發出悅耳的囀鳴）

war·chalk·ing /ˈwɔːtʃɔːkɪŋ; NAmE ˈwɔːr-/ *noun* [U] (*informal*) the action of drawing a symbol on the wall of a building to show that you can get a free Internet connection near that place 免費上網標記（在牆上標示附近可免費上網）

ˈwar chest *noun* an amount of money that a government or an organization has available to spend on a particular plan, project, etc. 專用款項；專款

ˈwar crime *noun* a cruel act that is committed during a war and is against the international rules of war 戰爭罪行（違反國際戰爭公約的戰時行為）

ˈwar criminal *noun* a person who has committed war crimes 戰犯

ˈwar cry *noun* a word or phrase that is shouted by people fighting in a battle in order to give themselves courage and to frighten the enemy （作戰時鼓舞士氣的）喊殺聲，吶喊聲

ward /wɔːd; NAmE wɔːrd/ *noun, verb*

■ ***noun*** **1** a separate room or area in a hospital for people with the same type of medical condition 病房；病室：***a maternity/surgical/psychiatric/children's, etc. ward*** 產科、外科、精神科、兒科等病房 ◇ *He worked as a nurse **on the** children's **ward**.* 他在兒科病房當護士。**2** (in Britain) one of the areas into which a city is divided and which elects and is represented by a member of the local council （英國城市中可選出一位地方議員的）區，選區 **3** (*law* 律) a person, especially a child, who is under the legal protection of a court or another person (called a GUARDIAN) 受監護人（受法院或監護人保護的人，尤指兒童）：*The child was made a **ward of court**.* 這個孩子由法院監護。

■ ***verb***

PHR V **ˌward sb/sth↔ˈoff** to protect or defend yourself against danger, illness, attack, etc. 防止，避免，抵禦（危險、疾病、攻擊等）：*to ward off criticism* 受到批評後為自己開脫 ◇ *She put up her hands to ward him off.* 她舉起雙手把他擋開。

-ward (also *less frequent* **-wards**) *suffix* (in adjectives 構成形容詞) in the direction of 向…的：*backward* 向後的 ◇ *eastward* 向東的 ◇ *homeward* 回家去的 ▸ **-wards** (also **-ward** especially in *NAmE*) (in adverbs 構成副詞)：*onwards* 向前 ◇ *forwards* 向前

ˈwar dance *noun* a dance that is performed by members of some peoples, for example before battle or to celebrate a victory 戰舞（某些民族在戰前動員或祝捷時跳）

war·den /ˈwɔːdn; NAmE ˈwɔːrdn/ *noun* **1** a person who is responsible for taking care of a particular place and making sure that the rules are obeyed 管理人；看守人；監護人：*a forest warden* 護林員 ◇ (*BrE*) *the warden of a youth hostel* 青年旅舍的管理員 ➲ see also CHURCHWARDEN, DOG WARDEN, GAME WARDEN, TRAFFIC WARDEN **2** (*especially NAmE*) the person in charge of a prison 監獄長 **3** (in Britain) a title given to the head of some colleges and institutions （英國）學院院長，協會會長，機構主管：*the Warden of Wadham College, Oxford* 牛津大學沃德姆學院院長

war·der /ˈwɔːdə(r); NAmE ˈwɔːrd-/ (*feminine* **ward·ress** /ˈwɔːdrəs; NAmE ˈwɔːrd-/) *noun* (*BrE*) a person who guards prisoners in a prison （監獄的）看守；獄吏 ➲ compare GUARD *n.* (1)

W

ward·robe /ˈwɔːdrəʊb; *NAmE* ˈwɔːrdroʊb/ *noun* **1** a large cupboard for hanging clothes in which is either a piece of furniture or (in British English) built into the wall 衣櫃；衣橱；（英國）放置衣物的壁櫥：*a fitted wardrobe* 入牆衣櫃 ➲ **VISUAL VOCAB** page V23 ➲ compare CLOSET *n.* **2** [usually sing.] the clothes that a person has （一個人的）全部衣物：*everything you need for your summer wardrobe* 需要的所有夏裝 ➲ **COLLOCATIONS** at FASHION **3** [usually sing.] the department in a theatre or television company that takes care of the clothes that actors wear （劇院或電視公司的）服裝部，戲裝保管室

ˈwardrobe mistress, **ˈwardrobe master** *noun* a person whose job is to take care of the clothes that the actors in a theatre company, etc. wear on stage （劇團等的）服裝保管員

ward·room /ˈwɔːdruːm; -rʊm; *NAmE* ˈwɔːrd-/ *noun* a room in a ship, especially a WARSHIP, where the officers live and eat （尤指軍艦上的）軍官起居室，軍官餐廳

-wards ➲ -WARD

ward·ship /ˈwɔːdʃɪp; *NAmE* ˈwɔːrd-/ *noun* [U] (*law* 律) the fact of a child being cared for by a GUARDIAN (= a person who is not his or her parent) or of being protected by a court （監護人或法院對兒童的）監護，保護 ➲ see also WARD *n.* (3)

ware /weə(r); *NAmE* wer/ *noun* **1** [U] (in compounds 構成複合詞) objects made of the material or in the way or place mentioned 用某材料（或以某方式、在某地）製造的物品：*ceramic ware* 陶瓷製品 ◇ *a collection of local ware* 一批當地器皿 ◇ *basketware* 籃筐製品 ➲ see also EARTHENWARE, FLATWARE, GLASSWARE, SILVERWARE **2** [U] (in compounds 構成複合詞) objects used for the purpose or in the room mentioned 作…用的器皿；…室的物品：*bathroom ware* 浴室用品 ◇ *ornamental ware* 裝飾品 ◇ *homeware* 家居用品 ➲ see also KITCHENWARE, TABLEWARE **3 wares** [pl.] (*old-fashioned*) things that sb is selling, especially in the street or at a market （尤指小商販在大街上或市場裏出售的）物品：*He travelled from town to town selling his wares.* 他走鄉串鎮出售自己的貨品。

ware·house /ˈweəhaʊs; *NAmE* ˈwerh-/ *noun* a building where large quantities of goods are stored, especially before they are sent to shops/stores to be sold 倉庫；貨棧；貨倉 ➲ **VISUAL VOCAB** page V15

ware·hous·ing /ˈweəhaʊzɪŋ; *NAmE* ˈwerh-/ *noun* [U] the practice or business of storing things in a warehouse 倉貯；倉貯業

war·fare /ˈwɔːfeə(r); *NAmE* ˈwɔːrfer/ *noun* [U] **1** the activity of fighting a war, especially using particular weapons or methods 戰；作戰；戰爭：***air/naval/guerrilla, etc. warfare*** 空戰、海戰、游擊戰等 ◇ *countries engaged in warfare* 參戰國 ➲ **COLLOCATIONS** at WAR ➲ see also BIOLOGICAL WARFARE, CHEMICAL WARFARE, GERM WARFARE **2** the activity of competing in an aggressive way with another group, company, etc. （群體、公司等之間的）鬥爭，競爭，衝突：***class/gang warfare*** 階級／幫派鬥爭 ◇ *The debate soon degenerated into open warfare.* 爭論很快惡化，演變成了公開的論戰。➲ see also PSYCHOLOGICAL WARFARE

war·farin /ˈwɔːfərɪn; *NAmE* ˈwɔːrf-/ *noun* [U] a substance that is used as a poison to kill RATS and also for people as a medicine to make the blood thinner, for example in the treatment of THROMBOSIS 華法林；苄丙酮香豆素（用作抗凝血劑）

ˈwar game *noun* **1** a practice battle that is used to test military plans and equipment 作戰演習；軍事演習 **2** a game or activity in which imaginary battles are fought, for example by moving models of soldiers, ships, etc. around on a table, or on a computer 戰爭遊戲（用模型士兵、戰艦等在桌面或計算機上進行）

ˈwar gaming *noun* [U] the activity of playing war games (2) 戰爭遊戲

war·head /ˈwɔːhed; *NAmE* ˈwɔːrhed/ *noun* the EXPLOSIVE part of a MISSILE （導彈的）彈頭：*nuclear warheads* 核彈頭

war·horse /ˈwɔːhɔːs; *NAmE* ˈwɔːrhɔːrs/ *noun* **1** (in the past) a large horse used in battle （舊時）軍馬，戰馬 **2** (*informal*) an old soldier or politician who has a lot of experience 久經沙場的老兵；老練的政治家

wari·ly, **wari·ness** ➲ WARY

war·like /ˈwɔːlaɪk; *NAmE* ˈwɔːrl-/ *adj.* (*formal*) **1** aggressive and wanting to fight 好戰的；好鬥的；尚武的 SYN **belligerent**：*a warlike nation* 好戰的民族 **2** connected with fighting wars 戰爭的；與戰爭有關的；軍事的 SYN **military**：*warlike preparations* 戰備

war·lock /ˈwɔːlɒk; *NAmE* ˈwɔːrlɑːk/ *noun* a man who is believed to have magic powers, especially evil ones （尤指邪惡的）男巫，術士

war·lord /ˈwɔːlɔːd; *NAmE* ˈwɔːrlɔːrd/ *noun* (*disapproving*) the leader of a military group that is not official and that fights against other groups within a country or an area 軍閥

warm 0→ /wɔːm; *NAmE* wɔːrm/ *adj.*, *verb*, *noun*, *adv.*

■ ***adj.*** (**warm·er**, **warm·est**)

▸ **AT PLEASANT TEMPERATURE** 溫度宜人 **1** 0→ at a fairly high temperature in a way that is pleasant, rather than being hot or cold 溫暖的；暖和的：*a warm breeze* 和煦的微風 ◇ *Wash the blouse in warm soapy water.* 這件女襯衫要用溫的肥皂水洗。◇ *It's **nice and warm** in here.* 這裏暖烘烘的。◇ *Are you warm enough?* 你夠暖和嗎？◇ *The children jumped up and down to **keep warm**.* 孩子們上下跳動保持身體暖和。◇ *You'll be as **warm as toast** in here.* 你在這裏會感到暖烘烘的。

▸ **CLOTHES/BUILDINGS** 衣服；建築物 **2** 0→ keeping you warm or staying warm in cold weather 保暖的；保溫的：*a warm pair of socks* 一雙暖和的襪子 ◇ *This sleeping bag is very warm.* 這條睡袋很暖和。◇ *a warm house* 溫暖的房屋

▸ **FRIENDLY** 友善 **3** 0→ showing enthusiasm and/or affection; friendly 溫情的；熱心的；友好的：*His smile was warm and friendly.* 他的微笑熱情而友好。◇ *The speaker was given **a warm welcome/reception**.* 演講者受到熱烈的歡迎。◇ *Please send her my warmest congratulations.* 請代我向她致以最熱烈的祝賀。

▸ **COLOURS** 顏色 **4** (of colours 顏色) containing red, orange or yellow, which creates a pleasant, comfortable and relaxed feeling or atmosphere 暖色調的：*The room was decorated in warm shades of red and orange.* 這房間是用紅和橙的這些暖色調裝飾的。

▸ **IN GAME** 遊戲 **5** [not before noun] used to say that sb has almost guessed the answer to sth or that they have almost found sb/sth that has been hidden 即將猜中；接近答案；即將找到：*Keep guessing—you're getting warmer.* 接着猜，你離答案越來越近了。

▸ **warm·ly** *adv.*：*They were warmly dressed in coats and scarves.* 他們身着大衣，圍着圍巾，穿得暖暖和和。◇ *The play was warmly received by the critics.* 評論家對這齣戲反應熱烈。➲ see also WARMTH

■ ***verb***

▸ **MAKE/BECOME WARM** （使）變暖 **1** 0→ [T, I] to make sth/sb warm or warmer; to become warm or warmer （使）溫暖，變暖和：**~ sth/sb/yourself (up)** *I'll warm up some milk.* 我來熱些牛奶。◇ *Come in and warm yourself by the fire.* 進來烤火暖和暖和吧。◇ *The alcohol warmed and relaxed him.* 這酒使他渾身發暖輕鬆起來。◇ **~ (up)** *As the climate warms (up) the ice caps will melt.* 隨着氣候變暖，冰冠將融化。

▸ **BECOME FRIENDLY** 變得友好 **2** [I, T] **~ (sb)** to become more friendly, loving, etc.; to make sb feel or become more friendly, loving, etc. （使）變得更友好，變得更溫情 ➲ see also GLOBAL WARMING, HOUSE-WARMING

IDM **warm the ˈcockles (of sb's ˈheart)** (*BrE*) to make sb feel happy or sympathetic 使人內心感到高興（或同情）➲ more at DEATH

PHR V **ˌwarm ˈdown** to do gentle exercises to help your body relax after doing a particular sport or activity （在體育運動或活動後）做放鬆運動 ➲ related noun WARM-DOWN **ˈwarm to/towards sb** to begin to like sb 開始喜歡上（某人）：*I warmed to her immediately.* 我立即喜歡上了她。 **ˈwarm to/towards sth** to become more interested in or enthusiastic about sth 對…更加感興趣（或熱衷）: *The speaker was now warming to her theme.* 演講者就她的主題越講越起勁。 **ˌwarm ˈup** 1 to prepare for physical exercise or a performance by doing gentle exercises or practice（為體育活動或表演）做適應性練習，做準備活動；熱身 ➲ related noun WARM-UP 2 (of a machine, an engine, etc. 機器、發動機等) to run for a short time in order to reach the temperature at which it will operate well 暖機；預熱 **ˌwarm ˈup | ˌwarm sb/sth↔ˈup** to become more lively or enthusiastic; to make sb/sth more lively or enthusiastic（使）活躍起來，熱情起來: *The party soon warmed up.* 聚會很快活躍起來。 **ˌwarm sth↔ˈup** to heat previously cooked food again for eating 把（冷飯菜）熱一熱

■ ***noun***

▸ PLACE 地方 **the warm** [sing.] a place where the temperature is warm 暖和的地方: *Come inside into the warm.* 進來暖和暖和。

■ ***adv.*** (**warm·er, warm·est**) (*informal*) in a way that makes you feel warm 使人暖和地；溫暖地 SYN **warmly**: ***Wrap up warm*** *before you go outside!* 穿得暖和些再出去！

ˌwarm-ˈblooded *adj.* (of animals 動物) having a warm blood temperature that does not change if the temperature around them changes 溫血的；恒溫的 ➲ compare COLD-BLOODED (2), HOT-BLOODED

ˈwarm-down *noun* [usually sing.] a series of gentle exercises that you do to help your body relax after doing a particular sport or activity（鍛煉後的）緩和運動，放鬆運動，收操

warm·er /ˈwɔːmə(r); *NAmE* ˈwɔːrm-/ *noun* (especially in compounds 尤用於構成複合詞) a piece of clothing, a device, etc. that warms sb/sth 保温衣；保温器；加熱器: *a plate warmer* 暖盤器 ➲ see also LEG WARMER

ˌwarm-ˈhearted *adj.* (of a person 人) kind, friendly and sympathetic 熱心腸的；友好的；富有同情心的 ➲ compare COLD-HEARTED

warm·ing /ˈwɔːmɪŋ; *NAmE* ˈwɔːrmɪŋ/ *noun* [U] the process of making sth, or of becoming, warm or warmer 加溫；溫暖；暖和；變暖: *atmospheric warming* 大氣層變暖 ➲ see also GLOBAL WARMING ▸ **warm·ing** *adj.*: *the warming rays of the sun* 暖融融的太陽光線 ◇ *a warming drink* 熱飲

ˈwarming pan *noun* a metal container with a long handle that, in the past, was filled with hot coals and used to warm beds（舊時的）長柄炭爐，長柄暖牀器

war·mon·ger /ˈwɔːmʌŋɡə(r); *NAmE* ˈwɔːrm-/ *noun* (*formal, disapproving*) a person, especially a politician or leader, who wants to start a war or encourages people to start a war 戰爭販子 ▸ **war·mon·ger·ing** *noun* [U] **war·mon·ger·ing** *adj.* [only before noun]

warmth /wɔːmθ; *NAmE* wɔːrmθ/ *noun* [U]
1 the state or quality of being warm, rather than hot or cold 溫暖；暖和: *She felt the warmth of his arms around her.* 她感到了他雙臂摟着她的溫暖。◇ *The animals huddled together for warmth.* 那些動物依偎在一起取暖。◇ *He led the child into the warmth and safety of the house.* 他把這孩子領到家裏享受温暖和安全。 2 the state or quality of being enthusiastic and/or friendly 熱情；友情: *They were touched by the warmth of the welcome.* 他們受到了熱情歡迎，很感動。

ˈwarm-up *noun* [usually sing.] 1 a short practice or a series of gentle exercises that you do to prepare yourself for doing a particular sport or activity（體育運動等前的）適應性活動，準備活動；熱身練習: *warm-up exercises* 熱身練習 2 a short performance of music, comedy, etc. that is intended to prepare the audience for the main show 暖場表演（正式表演開始前上演的短小音樂、喜劇等節目）: *a warm-up act* 暖場表演

warn /wɔːn; *NAmE* wɔːrn/ *verb*
1 [T, I] to tell sb about sth, especially sth dangerous or unpleasant that is likely to happen, so that they can avoid it 提醒注意（可能發生的事）；使警惕: **~ sb** *I tried to warn him, but he wouldn't listen.* 我設法提醒過他，可他就是不聽。◇ *If you're thinking of getting a dog,* ***be warned****—they take a lot of time and money.* 如果你

想養條狗，有話說在前頭，那可既費時間又費錢。◇ **~ (sb) about/against sb/sth** *He warned us against pickpockets.* 他提醒我們要提防小偷。◇ **~ (sb) of sth** *Police have warned of possible delays.* 警方已經通知交通可能受阻。◇ **~ (sb) that ...** *She was warned that if she did it again she would lose her job.* 她被警告說如果她再這樣做就會丟掉工作。◇ **~ sb what, how, etc. ...** *I had been warned what to expect.* 有人事先告訴過我要出什麼事。◇ **~ (sb) + speech** *'Beware of pickpockets,' she warned (him).* "當心扒手。" 她提醒（他）道。 2 [I, T] to strongly advise sb to do or not to do sth in order to avoid danger or punishment 勸告（使有所防備）；警告；告誡 SYN **advise**: **~ (sb) against/about sth** *The guidebook warns against walking alone at night.* 這本指南告誡夜間不要單獨行走。◇ **~ sb (to do sth)** *He warned Billy to keep away from his daughter.* 他警告比利離他女兒遠點。 3 [T] **~ sb (for sth)** (in sport, etc. 體育運動等) to give sb an official warning after they have broken a rule 警告: *The referee warned him for dangerous play.* 裁判作出警告，表示他有危險動作。

PHR V **ˌwarn sb ˈoff (sth)** 1 to tell sb to leave or stay away from a place or person, especially in a threatening way（尤指以威脅的方式）叫…離開，告誡…不要靠近: *The farmer warned us off his land when we tried to camp there.* 我們想在那裏露營時，農場主警告我們不得靠近他的土地。 2 to advise sb not to do sth or to stop doing sth 勸…不要做；建議…停止做: **~ doing sth** *We were warned off buying the house.* 有人勸我們不要購買這所房子。

warn·ing /ˈwɔːnɪŋ; *NAmE* ˈwɔːrn-/ *noun*
1 [C, U] a statement, an event, etc. telling sb that sth bad or unpleasant may happen in the future so that they can try to avoid it（就可能發生的意外等提出的）警告，警示；先兆: *Doctors* ***issued a warning against*** *eating any fish caught in the river.* 醫生發出警告不要吃在那條河裏捕的魚。◇ *to give sb* ***fair/advance/adequate warning*** *of sth* 就某事向某人發出充分的／預先的／足夠的警告 ◇ *The bridge collapsed* ***without (any) warning.*** 那座橋在沒有任何先兆的情況下坍塌了。◇ *Let me give you* ***a word of warning.*** 我來提醒你一句。◇ *a government* ***health warning*** 政府關於健康的忠告 ➲ see also EARLY WARNING 2 [C] a statement telling sb that they will be punished if they continue to behave in a particular way（就將要遭受的處罰等提出的）警告，警戒 SYN **caution**: *to give sb a* ***verbal/written/final warning*** 向某人發出口頭／書面／最後警告 ▸ **warn·ing** *adj.* [only before noun]: *She had ignored the* ***warning signs*** *of trouble ahead.* 她沒有理會警示前方危險的標誌。◇ *Police fired a number of* ***warning shots.*** 警方多次鳴槍警告。◇ ***Warning bells began to ring*** (= it was a sign that sth was wrong) *when her letters were returned unopened.* 當她的信原封不動被退回時，不祥之感就來了。

ˌwarning ˈtriangle *noun* (*BrE*) a red triangle that a driver puts on the road next to his or her car as a warning to other drivers when the car has stopped because of a fault, an accident, etc.（發生故障或車禍等使用的）三角警示架，三角警示牌

warp /wɔːp; *NAmE* wɔːrp/ *verb, noun*

■ ***verb*** 1 [I, T] **~ (sth)** to become, or make sth become, twisted or bent out of its natural shape, for example because it has become too hot, too damp, etc.（使）扭曲，彎曲，變形: *The window frames had begun to warp.* 窗框已經開始變形。 2 [T] **~ sth** to influence sb so that they begin to behave in an unacceptable or shocking way 使（行為等）不合情理；使乖戾: *His judgement was warped by prejudice.* 他因偏見而判斷有誤。

■ ***noun*** **the warp** [sing.] (*technical* 術語) the threads on a LOOM (= a machine used for making cloth) that other threads are passed over and under in order to make cloth（織布機上的）經線，經紗 ➲ compare WEFT ➲ see also TIME WARP

war·paint /ˈwɔːpeɪnt; *NAmE* ˈwɔːrp-/ *noun* [U] 1 paint that some peoples, for example Native American peoples, put on their bodies and faces before fighting

W

a battle（美國土著等）出征前塗在身上和臉上的顏料 **2** (*informal, humorous*) make-up, especially when it is thick or bright（尤指濃重的）化妝

war·path /ˈwɔːpɑːθ; *NAmE* ˈwɔːrpæθ/ *noun*
IDM **(be/go) on the ˈwarpath** (*informal*) (to be) angry and wanting to fight or punish sb（怒不可遏）準備開火

warped /wɔːpt; *NAmE* wɔːrpt/ *adj.* **1** (*disapproving*) (of a person 人) having ideas that most people think are strange or unpleasant 思想反常的；乖戾的：*a warped mind* 扭曲的心靈 ◇ *a warped sense of humour* 畸形的幽默感 **2** bent or twisted and not in the normal shape 彎曲的；扭曲的；變形的

war·plane /ˈwɔːpleɪn; *NAmE* ˈwɔːrp-/ *noun* a military plane that is designed for fighting in the air or dropping bombs 軍用飛機（戰鬥機、轟炸機等）

ˈwarp speed *noun* [sing.] (*informal, humorous*) a very fast speed 極高速 **ORIGIN** From the US television series *Star Trek*, in which a 'warp drive' allowed space travel at speeds faster than the speed of light. 源自美國電視系列片《星艦迷航》，其中的"曲相推進"能使空間旅行速度超過光速。

war·rant /ˈwɒrənt; *NAmE* ˈwɔːr-; ˈwɑːr-/ *noun, verb*
■ ***noun*** **1** [C] a legal document that is signed by a judge and gives the police authority to do sth 執行令；授權令：*an arrest warrant* 逮捕證 ◇ **~ for sth** *They **issued a warrant** for her arrest.* 當局發出了逮捕她的令狀。◇ **~ to do sth** *They had a warrant to search the house.* 他們有搜查這座房子的搜查令。➲ see also DEATH WARRANT, SEARCH WARRANT **2** [C] **~ (for sth)** a document that gives you the right to receive money, services, etc.（接受款項、服務等的）憑單，許可證 **3** [U] **~ (for sth/for doing sth)** (*formal*) (usually in negative sentences 通常用於否定句) an acceptable reason for doing sth（做某事的）正當理由，依據：*There is no warrant for such criticism.* 這種批評毫無根據。
■ ***verb*** (*formal*) to make sth necessary or appropriate in a particular situation 使有必要；使正當；使恰當 **SYN** **justify**：**~ sth** *Further investigation is clearly warranted.* 進一步調查顯然是必要的。◇ **~ (sb/sth) doing sth** *The situation scarcely warrants their/them being dismissed.* 這種情況很難證明解雇他們是正當的。➲ see also UNWARRANTED
IDM **I/I'll warrant (you)** (*old-fashioned*) used to tell sb that you are sure of sth and that they can be sure of it too 我給你打保票；我向你保證

ˈwarrant officer *noun* a member of one of the middle ranks in the army, the British AIR FORCE and the US navy 准尉（陸軍、英國空軍和美國海軍的中級軍銜）：*Warrant Officer Gary Owen* 加里•歐文准尉

war·ranty /ˈwɒrənti; *NAmE* ˈwɔːr-; ˈwɑːr-/ *noun* (*pl.* **-ies**) [C, U] a written agreement in which a company selling sth promises to repair or replace it if there is a problem within a particular period of time（商品）保用單 **SYN** **guarantee**：*The television comes with a full two-year warranty.* 這台電視機有整兩年的保修期。◇ *Is the car still **under warranty**?* 這輛汽車仍在保修期內嗎？

W

war·ren /ˈwɒrən; *NAmE* ˈwɔːr-; ˈwɑːr-/ *noun* = RABBIT WARREN：(*figurative*) *The offices were a warren of small rooms and passages.* 這些辦公室房間小，通道窄。

war·ring /ˈwɔːrɪŋ/ *adj.* [only before noun] involved in a war 戰爭的；交戰的；敵對的：*A ceasefire has been agreed by the country's three warring factions.* 這個國家的交戰三方已達成停火協議。

war·rior /ˈwɒriə(r); *NAmE* ˈwɔːr-/ *noun* (*formal*) (especially in the past) a person who fights in a battle or war（尤指舊時的）武士，勇士，鬥士：*a warrior nation* (= whose people are skilled in fighting) 善戰的民族 ◇ *a Zulu warrior* 祖魯人的勇士

war·ship /ˈwɔːʃɪp; *NAmE* ˈwɔːrʃɪp/ *noun* a ship used in war 軍艦；艦艇

wart /wɔːt; *NAmE* wɔːrt/ *noun* **1** a small hard lump that grows on your skin and that is caused by a virus 疣；瘊子；肉贅 **2** (*NAmE*) = VERRUCA
IDM **ˌwarts and ˈall** (*informal*) including all the bad or unpleasant features of sb/sth 包括所有的缺點；不隱瞞缺點；不遮醜：*She still loves him, warts and all.* 她仍然愛他，不管他有什麼缺點。

wart·hog /ˈwɔːthɒg; *NAmE* ˈwɔːrthɑːg/ *noun* an African wild pig with two large outer teeth called TUSKS and lumps like warts on its face 疣豬（非洲野豬，有一對獠牙，臉部有肉贅）

war·time /ˈwɔːtaɪm; *NAmE* ˈwɔːrt-/ *noun* [U] the period during which a country is fighting a war 戰時：*Different rules applied in wartime.* 戰時實施不同的規定。
▸ **war·time** *adj.* [only before noun]：*Fruit was a luxury in wartime Britain.* 在戰時的英國，水果是一種奢侈品。
➲ compare PEACETIME

ˈwar-torn *adj.* [only before noun] a **war-torn** country or area is severely affected by the fighting that is taking place there 受戰爭嚴重破壞的；飽受戰爭蹂躪的

warty /ˈwɔːti; *NAmE* ˈwɔːrti/ *adj.* covered with WARTS 有疣的；長着瘊子的

ˈwar widow *noun* a woman whose husband was killed in a war 戰爭遺孀

wary /ˈweəri; *NAmE* ˈweri/ *adj.* (*comparative* **wari·er**, *no superlative*) careful when dealing with sb/sth because you think that there may be a danger or problem（對待人或事物時）小心的，謹慎的，留神的，小心翼翼的 **SYN** **cautious**：**~ (of sb/sth)** *Be wary of strangers who offer you a ride.* 提防那些主動讓你搭車的陌生人。◇ **~ (of doing sth)** *She was wary of getting involved with him.* 她唯恐和他有牽連。◇ *He gave her a wary look.* 他留意地看了她一眼。◇ *The police will need to **keep a wary eye on** this area of town* (= watch it carefully, in case there is trouble). 警方必須密切注意這一帶城區。
➲ compare UNWARY (1) ▸ **wari·ly** /-rəli/ *adv.*：*The cat eyed him warily.* 那隻貓警惕地注視着他。 **wari·ness** *noun* [U]：*feelings of wariness* 小心謹慎 ◇ *There was a wariness in her tone.* 她的語氣中透出一絲謹慎。

was /wəz; *strong form* wɒz; *NAmE* wʌz/ ➲ BE

was·abi /wəˈsɑːbi/ *noun* [U] (from *Japanese*) a root vegetable with a strong taste like HORSERADISH, used in Japanese cooking, especially with raw fish 山嵛菜（辣味塊根蔬菜，尤用於生魚等日本食物）

wash 🔑 /wɒʃ; *NAmE* wɑːʃ; wɔːʃ/ *verb, noun*
■ ***verb*** **1** 🔑 [T] to make sth/sb clean using water and usually soap 洗；洗滌：**~ sth/sb** *These jeans need washing.* 這條牛仔褲該洗了。◇ *to wash the car* 洗車 ◇ *to wash your hands* 洗手 ◇ *Wash the fruit thoroughly before eating.* 把水果徹底洗乾淨後再吃。◇ **~ sth from sth** *She washed the blood from his face.* 她把他臉上的血洗掉。◇ **~ sth/sb + adj.** *The beach had been washed clean by the tide.* 海灘讓潮水沖刷得乾乾淨淨。➲ SYNONYMS at CLEAN
2 🔑 [I, T] (*especially BrE*) to make yourself clean using water and usually soap 洗澡；洗臉；洗手：*I washed and changed before going out.* 我洗了個澡，換好衣服，然後才出去。◇ **~ yourself** *She was no longer able to wash herself.* 她再也不能給自己洗澡了。 **3** [I] **(+ adv./prep.)** (of clothes, cloth, etc. 衣服、織物等) to be able to be washed without losing colour or being damaged 耐洗；洗後不褪色（或破損）：*This sweater washes well.* 這件套衫很耐洗。 **4** [I, T] (of water 水) to flow or carry sth/sb in a particular direction（向着某一方向）流動；沖向：**+ adv./prep.** *Water washed over the deck.* 水從甲板上流過。◇ **~ sth/sb + adv./prep.** *Pieces of the wreckage were **washed ashore**.* 沉船殘骸的碎片被沖到了岸上。◇ *He was **washed overboard** by a huge wave.* 一個巨浪把他從船上掀進海裏。
IDM **wash your dirty linen in ˈpublic** (*BrE, disapproving*) to discuss your personal affairs in public, especially sth embarrassing 公開談論個人的事；（尤指）家醜外揚
wash your ˈhands of sb/sth to refuse to be responsible for or involved with sb/sth 拒絕對…負責；脫離關係；洗手不幹：*When her son was arrested again she washed her hands of him.* 她的兒子再次被捕，她就與他脫離了關係。 **sth won't/doesn't ˈwash (with sb)** used to say that sb's explanation, excuse, etc. is not valid or that you/sb else will not accept it（解釋、藉口等）對某人來說站不住腳，令某人不能接受：*That excuse simply won't wash with me.* 那種託辭根本不能令我信服。

PHR V **ˌwash sb/sth↔aˈway** (of water 水) to remove or carry sb/sth away to another place 沖掉；沖走：*Part of the path had been washed away by the sea.* 部份小路已被海浪沖壞。**ˌwash sth↔ˈdown (with sth)** **1** to clean sth large or a surface with a lot of water 沖洗，沖刷（大件物品或表面）：*Wash down the walls before painting them.* 先把牆沖洗後再粉刷。**2** to drink sth after, or at the same time as, eating sth 配着食物喝（飲料）：*For lunch we had bread and cheese, washed down with beer.* 我們午餐吃的是麵包和奶酪，喝的是啤酒。**ˌwash ˈoff** to be removed from the surface of sth or from clothes by washing 被沖洗掉；被洗掉：*Those grease stains won't wash off.* 那些油漬洗不掉。**ˌwash sth↔ˈoff (sth)** to remove sth from the surface of sth or from clothes by washing（從某物表面或衣服上）沖洗掉，洗掉：*Wash that mud off your boots before you come in.* 先把你靴子上的泥沖洗掉再進來。**ˌwash ˈout** (of a dirty mark 污跡) to be removed from clothes by washing（從衣服上）被洗掉：*These ink stains won't wash out.* 這些墨漬洗不掉。**ˌwash sth↔ˈout** **1** to wash the inside of sth to remove dirt, etc. 洗淨，清洗（某物的內部）：*to wash out empty bottles* 把空瓶子裏面洗乾淨 **2** to remove a substance from sth by washing 把…洗掉：*Wash the dye out with shampoo.* 用洗髮劑把染髮劑洗掉。**3** (of rain 雨) to make a game, an event, etc. end early or prevent it from starting 使（比賽等）提前結束；阻止…的舉行：*The game was completely washed out.* 這場比賽因下雨根本無法進行。➲ related noun WASHOUT **ˌwash ˈover sb** **1** (also **ˌwash ˈthrough sb**) (*literary*) (of a feeling 感覺) to suddenly affect sb strongly, so that they are not aware of anything else 衝動；升騰：*Waves of nausea washed over him.* 他突然感到陣陣惡心。**2** to happen to or around sb without affecting them（周圍發生的事情）對…無多大影響：*She manages to let criticism just wash over her.* 她克服了別人批評所造成的影響。**ˌwash ˈup** **1** (*BrE*) (also **do the dishes** *NAmE, BrE*) to wash plates, glasses, etc. after a meal 洗刷飯後的杯盤等 ➲ related noun WASHING-UP **2** (*NAmE*) to wash your face and hands 洗臉和手：*Go and get washed up.* 去洗洗臉和手。**ˌwash sth↔ˈup** **1** (*BrE*) to wash dishes after a meal 洗刷（吃飯用過的盤子等）：*I didn't wash up the pans.* 我沒有刷鍋。**2** (of water 水) to carry sth onto land 把…沖到陸地上：*The body was found washed up on a beach.* 有人發現屍體被沖上了海灘。

■ ***noun*** **1** [C, usually sing.] (*especially BrE*) an act of cleaning sb/sth using water and usually soap 洗；洗滌；清洗；洗刷：*These towels are ready for a wash.* 這些毛巾需要洗了。◇ *I'll just* **have a** *quick* **wash** *before dinner.* 我只是很快地洗一洗就吃飯。◇ *I'm doing a dark wash* (= washing all the dark clothes together). 我在集中洗深色的衣服。◇ *Your shirt's* **in the wash** (= being washed or waiting to be washed). 你的襯衣正在洗。◇ *My sweater shrank in the wash.* 我的套衫洗後縮水了。◇ *That blouse shouldn't look like that after only two washes.* 那件女襯衫只洗過兩水，不應該變成這個樣子。➲ see also CAR WASH **2** **the wash** [sing.] an area of water that has waves and is moving a lot, especially after a boat has moved through it; the sound made by this（尤指船過後划出的）水流，波浪；波浪拍打聲：*The dinghy was rocked by the wash of a passing ferry.* 駛過的渡船掀起的波浪把小艇沖得搖搖晃晃。◇ *They listened to the wash of waves on the beach.* 他們聽着波浪拍擊海灘的聲音。**3** [C] a thin layer of a liquid, especially paint, that is put on a surface 薄塗層（尤指塗料）：*The walls were covered with a pale yellow wash.* 牆壁刷了一層薄的淺黃色塗料。➲ see also WHITEWASH *n.* (1) **4** [C, U] a liquid containing soap, used for cleaning your skin 肥皂液：*an antiseptic skin wash* 抗菌淨膚液 ➲ see also MOUTHWASH

IDM **it will (all) come out in the ˈwash** (*informal*) **1** used to say that the truth about a situation will be made known at some time in the future 終將水落石出；將會真相大白 **2** used to make sb less anxious by telling them that any problems or difficulties will be solved in the future（用以勸人不要太着急）問題終會解決的，困難將會被克服的

wash·able /ˈwɒʃəbl; *NAmE* ˈwɑːʃ-; ˈwɔːʃ-/ *adj.* that can be washed without being damaged 可洗的；耐洗的：*machine washable* (= that can be washed in a washing machine) 可用洗衣機洗的

wash·bag /ˈwɒʃbæg; *NAmE* ˈwɔːʃ-; ˈwɑːʃ-/ *noun* (*BrE*) = SPONGE BAG

wash·basin /ˈwɒʃbeɪsn; *NAmE* ˈwɑːʃ-; ˈwɔːʃ-/ (also **basin**) (both *especially BrE*) (also **sink** *NAmE, BrE*) (*NAmE* also **wash·bowl**) *noun* a large bowl that has taps/faucets and is fixed to the wall in a bathroom, used for washing your hands and face in（浴室內固定在牆上有水龍頭的）洗臉盆 ➲ VISUAL VOCAB page V24

wash·board /ˈwɒʃbɔːd; *NAmE* ˈwɑːʃbɔːrd; ˈwɔːʃ-/ *noun* a board with a surface with RIDGES on it, used in the past for rubbing clothes on when washing them; a similar board played as a musical instrument（洗衣用）搓板；（打擊樂器）刮板

wash·cloth /ˈwɒʃklɒθ; *NAmE* ˈwɑːʃklɔːθ; ˈwɔːʃ-/ (*NAmE*) (*BrE* **flan·nel**, **face·cloth**) *noun* a small piece of cloth used for washing yourself（洗擦身體用的）小毛巾

wash·day /ˈwɒʃdeɪ; *NAmE* ˈwɑːʃ-; ˈwɔːʃ-/ (also **ˈwashing day**) *noun* the day in sb's house when the clothes, etc. are washed, especially when this happens on the same day each week（尤指每週固定的）洗衣日

ˌwashed ˈout *adj.* **1** (of cloth, clothes or colours 織物、衣服或顏色) no longer brightly coloured, often as a result of frequent washing（洗後）褪色的：*She didn't like jeans that looked too washed out.* 她不喜歡看起來褪色厲害的牛仔褲。◇ *a pair of washed-out old jeans* 一條洗得褪了色的舊牛仔褲 ◇ *The walls were a washed-out blue colour.* 牆壁是一種褪了色的藍色。**2** (of a person 人) pale and tired 蒼白無力的；疲憊的 **SYN** **exhausted**：*He always looks washed out at the end of the week.* 他在週末總是滿臉倦色。

ˌwashed ˈup *adj.* (*informal*) no longer successful and unlikely to succeed again in the future（事業等）告吹的，完蛋：*Her singing career was all washed up by the time she was 27.* 她到 27 歲時歌唱生涯就告終了。

wash·er /ˈwɒʃə(r); *NAmE* ˈwɑːʃ-; ˈwɔːʃ-/ *noun* **1** a small flat ring made of rubber, metal or plastic placed between two surfaces, for example under a NUT (2) to make a connection tight（螺母等的）墊圈，墊片；襯墊 ➲ VISUAL VOCAB page V20 **2** (*informal*) a WASHING MACHINE 洗衣機 ➲ see also DISHWASHER

ˌwasher-ˈdryer *noun* an electric machine that washes and dries clothes, etc. 洗衣烘乾機

ˌwasher-ˈup *noun* (*BrE, informal*) a person who washes dishes 洗碟子的人

wash·er·wom·an /ˈwɒʃəwʊmən; *NAmE* ˈwɑːʃər-; ˈwɔːʃər-/ *noun* (*pl.* **-women** /-wɪmɪn/) a woman in the past whose job was to wash clothes, etc. for other people（舊時的）洗衣女工

wash·ing /ˈwɒʃɪŋ; *NAmE* ˈwɑːʃ-; ˈwɔːʃ-/ *noun* [U] **1** the act of cleaning sth using water and usually soap 洗；洗滌；洗刷；沖洗：*a gentle shampoo for frequent washing* 供經常洗髮用的柔性洗髮劑 ◇ *I* **do the washing** (= wash the clothes) *in our house.* 我在家裏洗衣服。➲ see also BRAINWASHING at BRAINWASH **2** (*BrE*) clothes, sheets, etc. that are waiting to be washed, being washed or have just been washed 待洗的（或正在洗的、剛洗過的）衣物：*a pile of dirty washing* 一堆待洗的髒衣物 ◇ *Would you* **hang the washing out** (= hang it outside to dry)? 你把剛洗過的衣服晾在外面好嗎？

ˈwashing day *noun* = WASHDAY

ˈwashing line *noun* (*BrE*) = CLOTHES LINE

ˈwashing machine *noun* an electric machine for washing clothes 洗衣機

ˈwashing powder *noun* [U] (*BrE*) soap or DETERGENT in the form of powder for washing clothes 洗衣粉

ˈwashing soda *noun* [U] = SODIUM CARBONATE

ˌwashing-ˈup (*BrE*) *noun* [U] **1** the act of washing plates, glasses, pans, etc. after a meal（飯後）刷洗餐具：*If you cook, I'll* **do the washing-up**. 如果你做飯，我就洗碗。

W

◇ *a washing-up bowl* 洗碟盆 **2** the dirty plates, glasses, pans, etc. that have to be washed after a meal（飯後的）待洗餐具：*The sink was still full of last night's washing-up.* 洗滌槽裏仍然擺滿了昨天晚上沒洗刷的餐具。

washing-'up liquid *noun* [U] (*BrE*) liquid soap for washing dishes, pans, etc.（刷洗餐具的）洗滌液

wash·out /'wɒʃaʊt; *NAmE* 'wɑːʃ-; 'wɔːʃ-/ *noun* (*informal*) an event, etc. that is a complete failure, especially because of rain 因雨取消的事；徹底失敗的事情

wash·room /'wɒʃruːm; -rʊm; *NAmE* 'wɑːʃ-; 'wɔːʃ-/ *noun* (*old-fashioned, NAmE*) a toilet/bathroom, especially one that is in a public building（尤指公共建築物內的）洗手間，廁所

wash·stand /'wɒʃstænd; *NAmE* 'wɑːʃ-; 'wɔːʃ-/ *noun* (especially in the past) a special table in a bedroom that holds a BASIN for washing yourself in（尤指舊時卧室內的）盥洗台

wash·tub /'wɒʃtʌb; *NAmE* 'wɑːʃ-; 'wɔːʃ-/ *noun* (in the past) a large metal container for washing clothes, etc. in（舊時的）洗衣盆

wasn't /'wɒznt; *NAmE* also 'wʌznt/ ➲ BE

Wasp /wɒsp; *NAmE* wɑːsp/ (also **WASP**) *noun* (*especially NAmE*, usually *disapproving*) the abbreviation for 'White Anglo-Saxon Protestant' (a white American whose family originally came from northern Europe and is therefore thought to be from the most powerful section of society) 白種盎格魯—撒克遜裔新教徒（全寫為 White Anglo-Saxon Protestant，祖先為來自北歐的白種人，被認為是美國社會中勢力最強大的族群）：*a privileged Wasp background* 享有特權的盎格魯 — 撒克遜裔白人新教徒出身

wasp /wɒsp; *NAmE* wɑːsp/ *noun* a black and yellow flying insect that can sting 黃蜂；胡蜂：*a wasp sting* 黃蜂螫傷 ◇ *a wasps' nest* 黃蜂窩 ➲ VISUAL VOCAB page V13

wasp·ish /'wɒspɪʃ; *NAmE* 'wɑːs-/ *adj.* (*formal*) bad-tempered and unpleasant 暴躁的；易怒的 SYN **irritable** ▸ **wasp·ish·ly** *adv.*

was·sail /'wɒseɪl; *NAmE* 'wɑːs-/ *verb* (*old use*) **1** [I] to enjoy yourself by drinking alcohol with others 與人飲酒狂歡；縱酒歡鬧 **2** [I] to go from house to house at Christmas time singing CAROLS（挨戶唱歌）報聖誕佳音 ▸ **was·sail·er** *noun*

wast·age /'weɪstɪdʒ/ *noun* **1** [U, sing.] **~ (of sth)** the fact of losing or destroying sth, especially because it has been used or dealt with carelessly 耗費；損耗；浪費：*It was a new production technique aimed at minimizing wastage.* 這是一項旨在使損耗減至最低的新生產技術。**2** [U] the amount of sth that is wasted 損耗量；耗費量；浪費量：*There is little wastage from a lean cut of meat.* 瘦肉的廢棄部份很少。**3** [U] (*BrE*) the loss of employees because they stop working or move to other jobs; the number of students who do not finish a particular course of study（雇員的）減員；（學生的）流失人數：*Half of the posts will be lost through **natural wastage**.* 有一半的職位通過自然減員將會丟失。◇ *student wastage rates* 學生流失率

W

waste 🔑 /weɪst/ *verb, noun, adj.*

■ *verb*

▸ NOT USE WELL 使用不當 **1** 🔑 to use more of sth than is necessary or useful 浪費；濫用：**~ sth** *to waste time/food/energy* 浪費時間／食物／能源 ◇ **~ sth on sth** *Why waste money on clothes you don't need?* 為什麼浪費錢買你不需要的衣服呢？◇ **~ sth (in) doing sth** *She **wasted no time** in rejecting the offer* (= she rejected it immediately). 她當即拒絕了提議。◇ *You're **wasting your time** trying to explain it to him* (= because he will not understand). 你跟他解釋是在浪費時間。**2 ~ sth (on sb/sth)** to give, say, use, etc. sth good where it is not valued or used in the way that it should be 白費；糟蹋：*Don't waste your sympathy on him—he got what he deserved.* 別把你的同情心白白浪費在他的身上，他是咎由自取。◇ *Her comments were not wasted on Chris* (= he understood what she meant). 她對克里斯的一席話沒有白費。**3** 🔑 [usually passive] to not make good or full use of sb/sth 未充分利用；使…屈才：**~ sb/sth** *It was a wasted opportunity.* 這白白浪費了一次機會。◇ **~ sb/sth as sth** *You're wasted as a sales manager—you should have been an actor.* 你當銷售經理屈才了，你本應該做演員。

▸ KILL SB 殺人 **4 ~ sb** (*informal, especially NAmE*) to get rid of sb, usually by killing them 幹掉；把…廢了；殺死

▸ DEFEAT SB 打敗 **5 ~ sb** (*NAmE, informal*) to defeat sb very badly in a game or competition（遊戲或比賽中）大勝，把…打得落花流水

IDM **waste your 'breath** to say sth that nobody takes any notice of 白費唇舌 **,waste not, 'want not** (*saying*) if you never waste anything, especially food or money, you will always have it when you need it 勤儉節約，吃穿不缺

PHR V **,waste a'way** (of a person 人) to become thin and weak, especially because of illness（尤指因病）變得瘦弱 SYN **become emaciated**

■ *noun*

▸ NOT GOOD USE 非充分利用 **1** 🔑 [U, sing.] **~ (of sth)** the act of using sth in a careless or unnecessary way, causing it to be lost or destroyed 浪費；濫用：*I hate unnecessary waste.* 我憎恨不必要的浪費。◇ *It seems such a waste to throw good food away.* 把好的食物扔掉似乎太浪費了。◇ *I hate to see good food **go to waste*** (= be thrown away). 我不願看到好好的食物被扔掉。◇ *The report is critical of the department's waste of resources.* 報告批評了這個部門對資源的浪費。◇ *What a waste of paper!* 多麼浪費紙啊！**2** 🔑 [sing.] a situation in which it is not worth spending time, money, etc. on sth 白費；糟蹋：*These meetings are a complete **waste of time**.* 這些會議完全是白費時間。◇ *They believe the statue is a waste of taxpayers' money.* 他們認為這座雕像糟蹋了納稅人的錢。

▸ MATERIALS 材料 **3** 🔑 [U] (also **wastes** [pl.]) materials that are no longer needed and are thrown away 廢料；廢物；棄物；垃圾：***household/industrial waste*** 生活垃圾；工業廢料 ◇ *toxic wastes* 有毒廢物 ◇ ***waste disposal*** (= the process of getting rid of waste) 廢物處理 **4** (also **,waste 'matter**) [U] material that the body gets rid of as solid or liquid material 糞便：*The farmers use both animal and human waste as fertilizer.* 農民把牲畜和人類的糞便都用作肥料。

▸ LAND 土地 **5 wastes** [pl.] (*formal*) a large area of land where there are very few people, animals or plants 人煙稀少的地區；荒蕪地區；荒原：*the frozen wastes of Siberia* 西伯利亞的凍土荒原

IDM **a waste of 'space** (*informal*) a person who is useless or no good at anything 無用的人；幹什麼都不行的人；廢物；飯桶

■ *adj.* [usually before noun]

▸ LAND 土地 **1** 🔑 not suitable for building or growing things on and therefore not used 荒蕪的；廢棄的 SYN **derelict**：*The car was found on a piece of waste ground.* 那輛車是在一塊荒地裏發現的。

▸ MATERIALS 材料 **2** 🔑 no longer needed for a particular process and therefore thrown away 廢棄的；丟棄的；無用的：*waste plastic* 廢塑料

IDM **lay sth 'waste | lay 'waste (to) sth** (*formal*) to destroy a place completely 徹底毀壞（某地）；把…夷為平地

waste·bas·ket /'weɪstbɑːskɪt; *NAmE* -bæs-/ (*NAmE*) (*BrE* **,waste-'paper basket**) *noun* a BASKET or other container for waste paper, etc. 廢紙簍；廢紙箱 ➲ picture at BASKET ➲ VISUAL VOCAB pages V21, V69

'waste bin *noun* (*BrE*) a container that you put rubbish/garbage in 垃圾箱；垃圾桶

wasted /'weɪstɪd/ *adj.* **1** [only before noun] (of an action 行動) unsuccessful because it does not produce the result you wanted 徒勞無功的；白費的：*We had a wasted trip—they weren't in.* 我們白跑了一趟，他們不在。**2** too thin, especially because of illness（尤指因病）瘦骨嶙峋的，瘦弱的：*thin wasted legs* 枯瘦的雙腿 **3** (*slang*) strongly affected by alcohol or drugs（飲酒或吸毒後）極度迷醉的

'waste-disposal unit (also **'waste disposer**) *noun* (*NAmE* usually **'garbage dis·posal, dis·posal**) a machine connected to the waste pipe of a kitchen SINK, for cutting food waste into small pieces 廢物處理機（裝於廚房水槽的污水管上，用以切碎食物垃圾）

waste·ful /ˈweɪstfl/ *adj.* using more of sth than is necessary; not saving or keeping sth that could be used 浪費的；揮霍的：*The whole process is wasteful and inefficient.* 整個程序既浪費又效率低。◇ **~ of sth** *an engine that is wasteful of fuel* 費燃料的發動機 ▸ **waste·ful·ly** /-fəli/ *adv.* **waste·ful·ness** *noun* [U]

waste·land /ˈweɪstlænd/ *noun* [C, U] an area of land that cannot be used or that is no longer used for building or growing things on 荒地；荒原；不毛之地：*industrial wasteland* 工業廢地 ◇ *the desert wastelands of Arizona* 亞利桑那州的荒漠 ◇ (*figurative*) *The mid 1970s are seen as a cultural wasteland for rock music.* * 20 世紀 70 年代中期被視為搖滾樂的文化荒漠。

ˌwaste ˈpaper *noun* [U] paper that is not wanted and is thrown away 廢紙

ˌwaste-ˈpaper basket (*BrE*) (*NAmE* **waste·basket**) *noun* a BASKET or other container for waste paper, etc. 廢紙簍；廢紙箱 ➲ picture at BASKET ➲ **VISUAL VOCAB** pages V21, V69

ˈwaste product *noun* a useless material or substance produced while making sth else 工業垃圾；（生產中的）無用副產品

waster /ˈweɪstə(r)/ *noun* **1** (often in compounds 常構成複合詞) a person or thing that uses too much of sth in an unnecessary way 浪費…的人；耗費…的東西：*He's a time-waster.* 他總是浪費時間。 **2** (*informal, disapproving*) a person who is useless or no good at anything 廢物；無用的人；飯桶；酒囊飯袋

waste·water /ˈweɪstwɔːtə(r); *NAmE* also -wɑːt-/ *noun* [U] (*especially NAmE*) used water that contains waste substances from homes, factories and farms 廢水：*municipal water and wastewater systems* 市政用水和廢水系統 ◇ *a wastewater treatment plant* 廢水處理廠 ➲ compare SEWAGE

wast·ing /ˈweɪstɪŋ/ *adj.* a **wasting** disease or illness is one that causes sb to gradually become weaker and thinner（指疾病）消耗性的，使消瘦的，使虛弱的

wast·rel /ˈweɪstrəl/ *noun* (*literary*) a lazy person who spends their time and/or money in a careless and stupid way 花花公子；浪蕩子；二流子

watch 🔑 /wɒtʃ; *NAmE* wɑːtʃ/ *verb, noun*

■ *verb* **1** 🔑 [T, I] to look at sb/sth for a time, paying attention to what happens 看；注視；觀看；觀察：**~ sb/sth** *to watch television/a football game* 看電視／足球比賽 ◇ **~ sth for sth** *He watched the house for signs of activity.* 他注視着那所房子裏的動靜。◇ **~ (for sth)** *He watched for signs of activity in the house.* 他注視着那所房子裏的動靜。◇ *'Would you like to play?' 'No thanks—I'll just watch.'* "你想玩嗎？""不啦，謝謝。我就看看好了。" ◇ *We watched to see what would happen next.* 我們注視着下一步要發生的事情。◇ **~ what, how, etc. …** *Watch what I do, then you try.* 你注意看我的動作，然後試着做。◇ **~ sb/sth doing sth** *She watched the kids playing in the yard.* 她看着孩子們在院子裏玩。◇ **~ sb/sth do sth** *They watched the bus disappear into the distance.* 他們注視着公共汽車消失在遠方。 ➲ **SYNONYMS** at LOOK **2** 🔑 [T] **~ sb/sth (for sb)** to take care of sb/sth for a short time（短時間）照看，看護，照管：*Could you watch my bags for me while I buy a paper?* 我去買份報紙，你能替我照看一下我的包嗎？ **3** 🔑 (*BrE* also **mind**) [T] (*informal*) to be careful about sth 小心；當心；留意：**~ sth/yourself** *Watch yourself!* (= be careful, because you're in a dangerous situation) 當心！◇ *Watch your bag—there are thieves around.* 小心你的提包，這裏有小偷。◇ *I have to **watch every penny*** (= be careful what I spend). 我必須掂量着花每一分錢。◇ *Watch your head on the low ceiling.* 天花板很低，當心別碰着頭。◇ **~ where, what, etc. …** *Hey, watch where you're going!* 嘿，瞧着點路！

IDM **watch the ˈclock** (*disapproving*) to be careful not to work longer than the required time; to think more about when your work will finish than about the work itself 盯着鐘錶（算計着不超過規定的工作時間，或只盼望下班而無心工作）➲ see also CLOCK-WATCHER **a watched ˌpot never ˈboils** (*saying*) used to say that when you are impatient for sth to happen, time seems to pass very slowly 心急水不開（越心急，時間過得越慢）**ˈwatch it** (*informal*) used as a warning to sb to be careful 當心；留神；注意 **watch your ˈmouth/ˈtongue** to be careful what you say in order not to offend sb or make them angry 說話當心；嘴上留個把門的 **watch the ˈtime** to be sure that you know what the time is, so that you finish sth at the correct time, or are not late for sth 注意時間（以便按時完成或到達）：*I'll have to watch the time. I need to leave early today.* 我得看着點時間。今天我要早走。 **watch this ˈspace** (*informal*) used in orders, to tell sb to wait for more news about sth to be announced（用於命令）等待下面發表的消息：*I can't tell you any more right now, but watch this space.* 目前我不能跟你多說，等着聽下面發表的消息吧。 **watch the ˈworld go by** to relax and watch people in a public place 閒看人來人往；靜觀眾生百態：*We sat outside a cafe, watching the world go by.* 我們坐在一家小餐館外面，望着眼前來來往往的人們。➲ more at LANGUAGE, STEP *n.*

PHR V **ˈwatch for sb/sth** to look and wait for sb/sth to appear or for sth to happen 觀察等待（某人出現或發生某事）：*The cat was on the wall, watching for birds.* 那隻貓在牆上伺機捕捉鳥兒。 **ˌwatch ˈout** 🔑 (*informal*) used to warn sb about sth dangerous 小心；留神；注意：*Watch out! There's a car coming!* 小心！汽車來了！ **ˌwatch ˈout for sb/sth** **1** 🔑 to make an effort to be aware of what is happening, so that you will notice if anything bad or unusual happens 密切注意；留意：*The cashiers were asked to watch out for forged banknotes.* 出納員接到要求，要注意偽鈔。 **2** to be careful of sth 小心；當心：*Watch out for the stairs—they're steep.* 小心樓梯，這些台階很陡。 **ˌwatch ˈover sb/sth** (*formal*) to take care of sb/sth; to guard and protect sb/sth 照管；監督；保護

■ *noun* **1** 🔑 [C] a type of small clock that you wear on your wrist, or (in the past) carried in your pocket 錶；手錶；（舊時的）懷錶：*She kept looking anxiously at her watch.* 她焦急不安地一個勁兒看錶。◇ *My watch is fast/slow.* 我的錶快／慢了。➲ picture at CLOCK ➲ see also STOPWATCH, WRISTWATCH **2** [sing., U] the act of watching sb/sth carefully in case of possible danger or problems 注意；注視；監視；觀察：*The police have **mounted a watch** outside the hotel.* 警方已在旅館外面佈置人監視。◇ *I'll **keep watch** while you go through his papers* (= watch and warn you if somebody is coming). 你查閱他的文件，我來放哨。◇ *The government is **keeping a close watch** on how the situation develops.* 政府正在密切注視着形勢的發展。➲ see also NEIGHBOURHOOD WATCH **3** [C, U] a fixed period of time, usually while other people are asleep, during which sb watches for any danger so that they can warn others, for example on a ship; the person or people who do this（如在船上）值班（人）；警戒（人）；守夜（人）：*I'm **on first watch**.* 我值第一班。◇ *I go **on watch** in an hour.* 我一個小時後值班。➲ see also NIGHTWATCHMAN

IDM **be on the ˈwatch (for sb/sth)** to be looking carefully for sb/sth that you expect to see, especially in order to avoid possible danger 小心提防；警戒：*Be on the watch for thieves.* 要提防小偷。➲ more at CLOSE² *adj.*

watch·able /ˈwɒtʃəbl; *NAmE* ˈwɑːtʃ-/ *adj.* (*informal*) entertaining or pleasant to watch 值得一看的

watch·band /ˈwɒtʃbænd; *NAmE* ˈwɑːtʃ-/ (*NAmE*) (*BrE* **ˈwatch strap**) *noun* a thin strip of leather, etc. for fastening your watch around your wrist 錶帶

watch·dog /ˈwɒtʃdɒg; *NAmE* ˈwɑːtʃdɔːg/ *noun* a person or group of people whose job is to check that companies are not doing anything illegal or ignoring people's rights（監督公司活動及監護人們權利的）監察人，監察團體：*a consumer watchdog* 消費者監察人 ➲ compare GUARD DOG

watch·er /ˈwɒtʃə(r); *NAmE* ˈwɑːtʃ-/ *noun* (often in compounds 常構成複合詞) a person who watches and studies sb/sth regularly …觀察家；…觀察員：*an industry/a market watcher* 行業／市場觀察員 ➲ see also BIRDWATCHER, CLOCK-WATCHER

watch·ful /ˈwɒtʃfl; *NAmE* ˈwɑːtʃ-/ *adj.* paying attention to what is happening in case of danger, accidents, etc. 注意的；警惕的；提防的：*Her expression was watchful and alert.* 她露出一副察言觀色、處處提防的表情。◇ *His mother **kept a watchful eye on** him.* 他的母親特別留心他。◇ *The children played **under the watchful eye of** their teacher.* 孩子們在老師的看護下玩耍。▶ **watch·ful·ly** /-fəli/ *adv.* **watch·ful·ness** *noun* [U]

ˌ**watching** ˈ**brief** *noun* [sing.] the task of watching a group, especially a political organization, to make sure that it is doing everything it should and nothing wrong or illegal（尤指對政治組織的）監視，監督

watch·maker /ˈwɒtʃmeɪkə(r); *NAmE* ˈwɑːtʃ-/ *noun* a person who makes and repairs watches and clocks as a job 鐘錶匠；鐘錶製造人；修錶匠

watch·man /ˈwɒtʃmən; *NAmE* ˈwɑːtʃ-/ *noun* (*pl.* **-men** /-mən/) (*old-fashioned*) a man whose job is to guard a building, for example a bank, an office building or a factory, especially at night（夜間）保安員，看守人，警衛員 ➲ see also NIGHTWATCHMAN

ˈ**watch strap** (*BrE*) (*NAmE* ˈ**watch·band**) *noun* a thin strip of leather, etc. for fastening your watch around your wrist 錶帶

watch·tower /ˈwɒtʃtaʊə(r); *NAmE* ˈwɑːtʃ-/ *noun* a tall tower from which soldiers, etc. watch when they are guarding a place 瞭望塔；崗樓

watch·word /ˈwɒtʃwɜːd; *NAmE* ˈwɑːtʃwɜːrd/ *noun* a word or phrase that expresses sb's beliefs or attitudes, or that explains what sb should do in a particular situation 口號；標語；格言：*Quality is our watchword.* 質量是我們的口號。

water 0-m /ˈwɔːtə(r); *NAmE* also ˈwɑːt-/ *noun, verb*

■ *noun* **1** 0-m [U] a liquid without colour, smell or taste that falls as rain, is in lakes, rivers and seas, and is used for drinking, washing, etc. 水：*a glass of water* 一杯水 ◇ ***drinking water*** 飲用水 ◇ *water pollution* 水污染 ◇ ***clean/dirty water*** 淨水；髒水 ◇ *water shortages* 缺水 ◇ *There is hot and cold **running water** in all the bedrooms.* 所有的卧室裏都有冷熱自來水。➲ see also BATHWATER **2** 0-m [U] an area of water, especially a lake, river, sea or ocean 大片的水；水域；（尤指）江，河，湖，海：*We walked down to the water's edge.* 我們步行到水邊去。◇ *She fell into the water.* 她失足落水。◇ ***shallow/deep water*** 淺／深水域 ◇ *In the lagoon the water was calm.* 環礁湖裏風平浪靜。➲ see also BACKWATER (1), BREAKWATER **3** 0-m **waters** [pl.] the water in a particular lake, river, sea or ocean（某一江、河、湖、海的）水域：*the grey waters of the River Clyde* 克萊德河灰濛濛的河水 ◇ *This species is found in **coastal waters** around the Indian Ocean.* 在環印度洋沿岸的海域有這一物種。**4** 0-m [U] the surface of a mass of water（一片）水面：*She dived under the water.* 她潛入水下。◇ *The leaves floated on the water.* 葉片漂浮在水面上。➲ see also UNDERWATER **5** **waters** [pl.] an area of sea or ocean belonging to a particular country（某個國家的）領海，海域：*We were still in British waters.* 我們仍在英國的領海上。◇ *fishing in international waters* 在國際海域捕魚 ➲ see also TERRITORIAL WATERS **6** **waters** [pl.] **murky, uncharted, stormy, dangerous, etc.** ~ used to describe a situation, usually one that is difficult, dangerous or not familiar 不明朗（或未知的、困難、危險等）局面：*The conversation got into the murky waters of jealousy and relationships.* 交談進入到愛妒交織的複雜話題。◇ *The government has warned of stormy waters ahead.* 政府已告誡說，以後的局勢將很嚴峻。**HELP** There are many other compounds ending in **water**. You will find them at their place in the alphabet. 以 water 結尾的複合詞還有很多，可在各字母中的適當位置查到。

IDM **by water** (*formal*) using a boat or ship 乘船；由水路 **it's (all) water under the ˈbridge** used to say that sth happened in the past and is now forgotten or no longer important 已成往事；往事雲煙 **like ˈwater** (*informal*) in large quantities 大量地：*He spends money like water.* 他揮霍無度。**not hold ˈwater** (*informal*) if an argument, an excuse, a theory, etc. does not **hold water**, you cannot believe it（論點、藉口、理論等）站不住腳，不合情理 **sb's ˈwaters break** when a pregnant woman's **waters break**, the liquid in her WOMB passes out of her body just before the baby is born 羊水破（即將分娩） **(like) water off a ˌduck's ˈback** (*informal*) used to say that sth, especially criticism, has no effect on sb/sth（像）耳邊風；水過鴨背：*I can't tell my son what to do; it's water off a duck's back with him.* 我無法告訴我兒子該做什麼，他根本聽不進去。➲ more at BLOOD *n.*, BLOW *v.*, COLD *adj.*, DEAD *adj.*, DEEP *adj.*, DIP *v.*, DUCK *n.*, FISH *n.*, HEAD *n.*, HELL, HORSE *n.*, HOT *adj.*, PASS *v.*, POUR, STILL *adj.*, TEST *v.*, TREAD *v.*

■ *verb* **1** [T] **~ sth** to pour water on plants, etc. 給…澆水；灌溉：*to water the plants/garden* 給花草／花園澆水 **2** [I] (of the eyes 眼睛) to become full of tears 充滿眼淚：*The smoke made my eyes water.* 煙熏得我直流眼淚。**3** [I] (of the mouth 嘴) to produce SALIVA 流口水：*The smells from the kitchen made our mouths water.* 廚房裏的香味饞得我們直流口水。**4** [T] **~ sth** to give water to an animal to drink 給…水喝；飲（動物）：*to water the horses* 飲馬 ◇ (*humorous*) *After a tour of the grounds, the guests were **fed and watered**.* 客人們遊覽場地之後，給招待得酒足飯飽。**5** [T, usually passive] **~ sth** (*technical* 術語) (of a river, etc. 河流等) to provide an area of land with water 流經；給（某地）供水：*The valley is watered by a stream.* 這山谷有一條小溪流過。**6** [T] **~ sth** to add water to an alcoholic drink 往（酒裏）摻水；給…加水：*watered wine* 摻了水的葡萄酒

PHR V ˌ**water sth**↔ˈ**down** **1** to make a liquid weaker by adding water 加水沖淡（液體）；摻水稀釋 **SYN** **dilute** **2** [usually passive] to change a speech, a piece of writing, etc. in order to make it less strong or offensive 緩和（說話、文章等的）語氣；使變得輕描淡寫 **SYN** **dilute**

the ˈ**Water Bearer** *noun* [sing.] = AQUARIUS

water·bed /ˈwɔːtəbed; *NAmE* ˈwɔːtərb-; ˈwɑːt-/ *noun* a bed with a rubber or plastic MATTRESS that is filled with water 水牀（鋪橡膠或塑料充水牀墊的牀）

water·bird /ˈwɔːtəbɜːd; *NAmE* ˈwɔːtərbɜːrd; ˈwɑːt-/ *noun* a bird that lives near and walks or swims in water, especially rivers or lakes（尤指江河湖泊中的）水鳥，水禽

ˈ**water biscuit** *noun* (*BrE*) a thin crisp plain biscuit, usually eaten with butter and/or cheese 薄脆餅乾（通常加黃油、奶酪食用）

water·board·ing /ˈwɔːtəbɔːdɪŋ; *NAmE* ˈwɔːtərbɔːrd-; ˈwɑːt-/ *noun* [U] a way of trying to force sb to give you information by pouring water onto their face while making them lie on their back, so that they feel as if they are DROWNING 水刑（仰卧溺水體驗逼供）

water·borne /ˈwɔːtəbɔːn; *NAmE* ˈwɔːtərbɔːrn; ˈwɑːt-/ *adj.* spread or carried by water 水傳播的；水源傳染的；經水路的：*cholera and other waterborne diseases* 霍亂等經水傳染疾病 ◇ *waterborne goods* 水運貨物 ➲ compare AIRBORNE (2)

ˈ**water buffalo** *noun* (*pl.* **water buf·falo** or **water buf·faloes**) a large Asian animal of the cow family, used for pulling vehicles and farm equipment in tropical countries 印度水牛（作為挽畜和耕畜）

ˈ**water butt** (*BrE*) (*NAmE* ˈ**rain barrel**) *noun* a large BARREL for collecting rain as it flows off a roof（接房簷雨水的）大水桶 ➲ VISUAL VOCAB page V19

ˈ**water cannon** *noun* a machine that produces a powerful flow of water, used by the police to control crowds of people 水炮（警方用以驅散人群）

the ˈ**Water Carrier** *noun* [sing.] = AQUARIUS

ˈ**water chestnut** *noun* the thick round white root of a tropical plant that grows in water, often used in Chinese cooking 荸薺

ˈ**water clock** *noun* (in the past) a clock that used the flow of water to measure time 水鐘，漏壺（舊時利用水流計時）

ˈ**water closet** *noun* (*abbr.* **WC**) (*old-fashioned*) a toilet 盥洗室；廁所

water·col·our (*especially US* **water·color**) /ˈwɔːtəkʌlə(r); *NAmE* ˈwɔːtərk-; ˈwɑːt-/ *noun* **1** **watercolours** [pl.] paints that you mix with water, not oil, and use for painting pictures 水彩（顏料）➲ COLLOCATIONS at ART **2** [C] a picture painted with these paints 水彩畫

water·col·our·ist (*especially US* **water·col·or·ist**) /ˈwɔːtəkʌlərɪst; *NAmE* ˈwɔːtər-/ *noun* a person who paints with watercolours 水彩畫作者；水彩畫家

ˈwater-cooled *adj.* (of machines, etc. 機器等) cooled using water 水冷的

ˈwater cooler *noun* **1** a machine, for example in an office, that cools water and supplies it for drinking 飲水冷卻器 **2** used when referring to a place where office workers talk in an informal way, for example near the water cooler 職員聊天處（飲水冷卻器附近等的辦公室人員閒談處）：*It was a story they'd shared around the water cooler.* 這件事成為他們工作之餘閒聊的談資。

water·course /ˈwɔːtəkɔːs; *NAmE* ˈwɔːtərkɔːrs; ˈwɑːt-/ *noun* (*technical* 術語) a stream or an artificial channel for water 河道；水道；溝渠；渠道

water·cress /ˈwɔːtəkres; *NAmE* ˈwɔːtərk-; ˈwɑːt-/ *noun* [U] a water plant with small round green leaves and thin STEMS. It has a strong taste and is often eaten raw in salads. 水田芥，豆瓣菜，西洋菜（水生植物，有辛香味）

ˌwatered ˈsilk *noun* [U] a type of shiny silk cloth with a pattern on it that looks like water in waves 波紋綢

water·fall /ˈwɔːtəfɔːl; *NAmE* ˈwɔːtərf-; ˈwɑːt-/ *noun* a place where a stream or river falls from a high place, for example over a CLIFF or rock 瀑布 ➲ VISUAL VOCAB pages V4, V5

ˈwater feature *noun* an artificial area of water, or structure with water flowing through it, which is intended to make a garden more attractive and interesting（花園中的）人工水景 ➲ VISUAL VOCAB page V19

ˈwater fountain *noun* (*NAmE*) = DRINKING FOUNTAIN

water·fowl /ˈwɔːtəfaʊl; *NAmE* ˈwɔːtərf-; ˈwɑːt-/ *noun* [usually pl.] (*pl.* **water·fowl**) a bird that can swim and lives near water, especially a DUCK or GOOSE 水鳥；水禽（尤指鴨或鵝）

water·front /ˈwɔːtəfrʌnt; *NAmE* ˈwɔːtərf-; ˈwɑːt-/ *noun* [usually sing.] a part of a town or an area that is next to water, for example in a HARBOUR 濱水路；濱水區；碼頭區：*a waterfront apartment* 一套濱水公寓

ˈwater gun *noun* (*NAmE*) = WATER PISTOL

water·hole /ˈwɔːtəhəʊl; *NAmE* ˈwɔːtərhoʊl; ˈwɑːt-/ (also **ˈwatering hole**) *noun* a place in a hot country, where animals go to drink（熱帶國家動物飲水的）水坑，水池

ˈwater ice *noun* [U, C] (*BrE*) = SORBET

ˈwatering can *noun* a metal or plastic container with a handle and a long SPOUT, used for pouring water on plants（澆花草用的）灑水壺，噴壺 ➲ VISUAL VOCAB page V19

ˈwatering hole *noun* **1** = WATERHOLE **2** (*informal, humorous*) a bar or place where people go to drink 酒吧；酒館

ˈwatering place *noun* (*old-fashioned*) a town with a natural supply of MINERAL WATER where people go for their health 礦泉療養地 SYN **spa**

ˈwater jump *noun* an area of water that horses or runners have to jump over in a race or competition（障礙賽馬或賽跑等中需越過的）水溝障礙

water·less /ˈwɔːtələs; *NAmE* ˈwɔːtərləs; ˈwɑːt-/ *adj.* with no water 無水的；乾的：*a waterless barren region* 乾旱的荒蕪地區

ˈwater level *noun* [U, C] the height that the surface of a mass of water rises or falls to, or the height it is at 水準；水位；水平

ˈwater lily *noun* a plant that floats on the surface of water, with large round flat leaves and white, yellow or pink flowers 睡蓮

water·line /ˈwɔːtəlaɪn; *NAmE* ˈwɔːtərl-; ˈwɑːt-/ *noun* **the waterline** [sing.] the level that the water reaches along the side of a ship（船的）吃水線，水線

water·logged /ˈwɔːtəlɒgd; *NAmE* ˈwɔːtərlɔːgd; ˈwɑːt-/ *adj.* **1** (of soil, a field, etc. 土壤、田地等) so full of water that it cannot hold any more and becomes flooded 水浸的；水澇的；水淹的：*They couldn't play because the pitch was waterlogged.* 因球場泡水他們未能進行比賽。 **2** (of a boat, etc. 船等) so full of water that it can no longer float 進水滿艙的；浸滿水下沉的

Water·loo /ˌwɔːtəˈluː; *NAmE* ˌwɔːtərˈluː; ˈwɑːt-/ *noun* [sing.] **sb's ~** a final defeat for sb 最終的失敗；毀滅性打擊：*This was the point at which he was to **meet his Waterloo**.* 這就是他最終失敗之處。 ORIGIN From the battle of **Waterloo** in 1815, in which the British (under the Duke of Wellington) and the Prussians finally defeated Napoleon. 源自 1815 年的滑鐵盧戰役。在那場戰役中，英國人（在威靈頓公爵的率領下）和普魯士人最終打敗了拿破侖。

ˈwater main *noun* a large underground pipe that supplies water to buildings, etc. 給水幹管；總水管

water·mark /ˈwɔːtəmɑːk; *NAmE* ˈwɔːtərmɑːrk; ˈwɑːt-/ *noun* a symbol or design in some types of paper, which can be seen when the paper is held against the light（紙張上的）水印 ➲ see also HIGH-WATER MARK, LOW-WATER MARK

ˈwater meadow *noun* [usually pl.] a field near a river that is often flooded（河邊經常讓水淹的）浸水草地，草甸

water·melon /ˈwɔːtəmelən; *NAmE* ˈwɔːtərm-; ˈwɑːt-/ *noun* [C, U] a type of large MELON with hard, dark green skin, red flesh and black seeds 西瓜 ➲ VISUAL VOCAB page V30

water·mill /ˈwɔːtəmɪl; *NAmE* ˈwɔːtərm-; ˈwɑːt-/ *noun* a MILL next to a river in which the machinery for GRINDING grain into flour is driven by the power of the water turning a wheel 水磨；水力磨粉機

ˈwater moccasin *noun* = COTTONMOUTH

ˈwater pistol (*NAmE* also **ˈwater gun**, **ˈsquirt gun**) *noun* a toy gun that shoots water 玩具噴水手槍

ˈwater polo *noun* [U] a game played by two teams of people swimming in a swimming pool. Players try to throw a ball into the other team's goal. 水球運動

ˈwater power *noun* [U] power produced by the movement of water, used to drive machinery or produce electricity 水力；水能

water·proof /ˈwɔːtəpruːf; *NAmE* ˈwɔːtərp-; ˈwɑːt-/ *adj., noun, verb*

■ ***adj.*** that does not let water through or that cannot be damaged by water 不透水的；防水的；耐水的：*waterproof clothing* 防水衣 ◇ *a waterproof camera* 防水照相機

■ ***noun*** [usually pl.] a piece of clothing made from material that does not let water through 防水衣物；雨衣：*You'll need waterproofs* (= a waterproof jacket and trousers/pants). 你會用得着雨衣褲的。

■ ***verb*** **~ sth** to make sth waterproof 使不透水；使防水

ˈwater rat *noun* = WATER VOLE

ˈwater-repellent *adj.* a material, etc. that is **water-repellent** is specially treated so that water runs off it rather than going into it（材料等經處理後）拒水的，防水的：*a water-repellent coating* 防水塗層

ˈwater-resist·ant *adj.* that does not let water through easily 有抗水作用的；防水的：*a water-resistant jacket* 防水上衣

water·shed /ˈwɔːtəʃed; *NAmE* ˈwɔːtərʃed; ˈwɑːt-/ *noun* **1** [C] **~ (in sth)** an event or a period of time that marks an important change 轉折點，分界線，分水嶺（標誌着重大變化的事件或時期）：*The middle decades of the 19th century marked a watershed in Russia's history.* * 19 世紀中葉標誌着俄國歷史的轉折點。 **2** [C] a line of high land where streams on one side flow into one river, and streams on the other side flow into a different river 分水線；分水嶺；分水界 **3 the watershed** [sing.] (in Britain) the time before which programmes that are not considered suitable for children may not be shown on television（英國）兒童不宜節目可在電視上播放的起始時間：*the 9 o'clock watershed* 可開播兒童不宜電視節目的晚上 9 點鐘時限

water·side /ˈwɔːtəsaɪd; *NAmE* ˈwɔːters-; ˈwɑːt-/ *noun* [sing.] the area at the edge of a river, lake, etc. 水邊；

W

河邊；湖濱；海濱： *They strolled down to the waterside.* 他們漫步向水邊走去。◇ *a waterside cafe* 一家水濱小餐館

water·ski /ˈwɔːtəskiː; *NAmE* ˈwɔːtərs-; ˈwɑːt-/ *verb, noun*

■ ***verb*** [I] to SKI on water while being pulled by a fast boat 作水橇滑水 ▸ **water·ski·ing** *noun* [U]： *We snorkelled and did some waterskiing.* 我們去浮潛，並玩了一會兒水橇運動。➲ VISUAL VOCAB page V50

■ ***noun*** either of the pair of long flat boards on which a person stands in order to waterski 滑水橇

ˈwater softener *noun* [U, C] a device or substance that removes particular minerals, especially CHALK, from water 硬水軟化器；軟水劑

ˈwater sports *noun* [pl.] sports that are done on or in water, for example sailing and WATERSKIING 水上運動

water·spout /ˈwɔːtəspaʊt; *NAmE* ˈwɔːtərs-; ˈwɑːt-/ *noun* a column of water that is pulled up from the sea during a storm by a rapidly spinning column of air 水龍捲；海龍捲

ˈwater strider (*NAmE*) (*BrE* **ˈpond skater**) *noun* an insect which moves quickly across the surface of water 黽蝽；水黽

ˈwater supply *noun* [C, U] the water provided for a town, an area or a building; the act of or system for supplying water to a town, etc. 給水；供水；給水系統；供水系統： ***a clean/contaminated water supply*** 潔淨的／受污染的水源◇ *to improve the water supply to rural villages* 改善鄉村供水系統

ˈwater table *noun* [usually sing.] (*technical* 術語) the level at and below which water is found in the ground 地下水位

water·tight /ˈwɔːtətaɪt; *NAmE* ˈwɔːtərt-; ˈwɑːt-/ *adj.* **1** that does not allow water to get in or out 不透水的；防水的；水密的： *a watertight container* 不漏水的容器 **2** (of an excuse, a plan, an argument, etc. 藉口、計劃、論點等) carefully prepared so that it contains no mistakes, faults or weaknesses 嚴密的；無懈可擊的；天衣無縫的： *a watertight alibi* 無法駁倒的不在犯罪現場證據◇ *The case has to be made watertight.* 案由必須做到無懈可擊。

ˈwater tower *noun* a tall structure with a tank of water at the top from which water is supplied to buildings in the area around it（自來）水塔

ˈwater vole (*BrE*) (also **ˈwater rat**) *noun* an animal like a RAT that swims and lives in a hole beside a river or lake 水鼷，水田鼠，水鼠（穴居於溪流、湖泊旁）

water·way /ˈwɔːtəweɪ; *NAmE* ˈwɔːtərw-; ˈwɑːt-/ *noun* a river, CANAL, etc. along which boats can travel 水路；航道： *inland waterways* 內河航道◇ *a navigable waterway* 可通航的水路

water·wheel /ˈwɔːtəwiːl; *NAmE* ˈwɔːtərw-; ˈwɑːt-/ *noun* a wheel turned by the movement of water, used, especially in the past, to drive machinery（尤指舊時的）水輪，水車

ˈwater wings *noun* [pl.] (*old-fashioned*) a pair of plastic bags filled with air that children wear on their arms when they learn to swim（兒童學游泳時套在胳膊上的）雙翼式浮水袋

water·works /ˈwɔːtəwɜːks; *NAmE* ˈwɔːtərwɜːrks; ˈwɑːt-/ *noun* (*pl.* **water·works**) **1** [C+sing./pl. v.] a building with machinery for supplying water to an area 自來水廠 **2** [pl.] (*informal* or *humorous*) the organs of the body through which URINE (= waste water) is passed（人體的）排水系統；泌尿系統

IDM **turn on the ˈwaterworks** (*informal, disapproving*) to start crying, especially in order to get sympathy or attention 開始哭鼻子（尤指為博得同情或引人關注）

watery /ˈwɔːtəri; *NAmE* ˈwɑːt-/ *adj.* **1** of or like water; containing a lot of water 水的；似水的；含水的；水分很多的： *a watery fluid* 稀薄的流體◇ *His eyes were red and watery.* 他兩眼發紅，淚水汪汪。◇ (*literary*) *She was rescued from a* ***watery grave*** (= saved from DROWNING). 她從龍王爺那裏被救了回來。 **2** weak and/or pale 虛弱的；蒼白無力的： *a watery sun* 慘淡的太陽◇ *His eyes were a watery blue.* 他的眼睛是淡藍色的。◇ *a watery smile* (= weak and without much feeling) 淡然一笑 **3** (of food, drink, etc. 食物、飲料等) containing too much water; thin and having no taste 水分過多的；稀薄無味的： *watery soup* 稀薄無味的湯

Wat·ford /ˈwɒtfəd; *NAmE* ˈwɑːtfərd/ *noun* (*BrE*) a town in Hertfordshire, north of London, that is considered to mark the northern limit of the area of London and SE England. The expression **north of Watford** means the parts of Britain outside this area. 沃特福德（赫特福德郡城鎮，被視為倫敦地區和英格蘭東南部北界限的標誌）： *civil servants who seem to think the world ends north of Watford* 似乎把沃特福德以北當作天涯海角的公務員

watt /wɒt; *NAmE* wɑːt/ *noun* (*abbr.* **W**) a unit for measuring electrical power 瓦，瓦特（電功率單位）： *a 60-watt light bulb* * 60 瓦的電燈泡

watt·age /ˈwɒtɪdʒ; *NAmE* ˈwɑːt-/ *noun* [U] (*technical* 術語) an amount of electrical power expressed in watts 瓦數；瓦特數

wat·tle /ˈwɒtl; *NAmE* ˈwɑːtl/ *noun* **1** [U] sticks twisted together as a material for making fences, walls, etc. 編條結構（用於編築籬笆、圍牆等）： *walls made of* ***wattle and daub*** 泥笆牆 **2** [C] a piece of red skin that hangs down from the throat of a bird such as a TURKEY（火雞等禽類喉部的）紅色肉垂 **3** [C, U] (*especially AustralE*) a name for various types of ACACIA tree 金合歡樹

wave 0-m /weɪv/ *noun, verb*

■ ***noun***

▸ **OF WATER** 水 **1** 0-m [C] a raised line of water that moves across the surface of the sea, ocean, etc. 海浪；波浪；波濤： *Huge* ***waves were breaking*** *on the shore.* 巨浪拍打着海岸。◇ *Surfers flocked to the beach to* ***ride the waves.*** 衝浪者集聚到海灘去衝浪。◇ *the gentle sound of* ***waves lapping*** 波浪輕輕拍打的聲音◇ *Children were playing* ***in the waves.*** 孩子們在海浪中嬉戲。◇ *Seagulls bobbed* ***on the waves.*** 海鷗隨浪花一起一伏地漂浮在水面。◇ *The wind made little waves on the pond.* 風吹得池水起了漣漪。➲ VISUAL VOCAB pages V4, V5 ➲ see also TIDAL WAVE (1)

▸ **OF ACTIVITY/FEELING** 活動；感覺 **2** 0-m [C] a sudden increase in a particular activity or feeling 洶湧的行動（或思想）態勢；心潮；風潮： ***a wave of opposition/protest/violence, etc.*** 反對、抗議、暴力等的浪潮◇ *a* ***crime wave*** 犯罪潮◇ *A wave of fear swept over him.* 一陣恐懼傳遍他的全身。◇ *Guilt and horror flooded her* ***in waves.*** 歉疚和恐懼一陣陣湧上她的心頭。◇ *A wave of panic spread through the crowd.* 一陣恐慌傳遍人群。➲ see also BRAINWAVE, HEATWAVE

▸ **LARGE NUMBER** 大量 **3** 0-m [C] a large number of people or things suddenly moving or appearing somewhere 湧現的人（或事物）；湧動的人（或物）： *Wave after wave of aircraft passed overhead.* 一批又一批飛機從上空掠過。➲ see also NEW WAVE

▸ **MOVEMENT OF ARM/HAND/BODY** 臂／手／身體的動作 **4** 0-m [C] a movement of your arm and hand from side to side 揮臂；揮手；招手；擺手： *She declined the offer with a wave of her hand.* 她擺了擺手謝絕了這一提議。◇ *He* ***gave us a wave*** *as the bus drove off.* 公共汽車開走時他向我們揮了揮手。 **5 the wave** (*NAmE*) (*BrE* **ˌMexican ˈwave**) [sing.] a continuous movement that looks like a wave on the sea, made by a large group of people, especially people watching a sports game, when one person after another stands up, raises their arms, and then sits down again 人浪（尤指體育比賽中看台上的觀眾依次站起坐下而形成的波浪狀場面）

▸ **OF HEAT/SOUND/LIGHT** 熱；聲；光 **6** 0-m [C] the form that some types of energy such as heat, sound, light, etc. take as they move 波；波狀運動： ***radio/sound/ultrasonic waves*** 無線電波；聲波；超聲波 ➲ see also AIRWAVES, LONG WAVE, MEDIUM WAVE, MICROWAVE *n.* (2), SHOCK WAVE (1), SHORT WAVE, SOUND WAVE

▸ **IN HAIR** 頭髮 **7** [C] if a person's hair has **a wave** or **waves**, it is not straight but curls slightly 拳曲；波浪 ➲ see also PERMANENT WAVE

▸ **SEA** 海洋 **8 the waves** [pl.] (*literary*) the sea 大海 ➲ see also WAVY

IDM **make ˈwaves** (*informal*) to be very active in a way that makes people notice you, and that may sometimes cause problems 咋咋呼呼；大肆張揚 ➲ more at CREST *n.*, RIDE *v.*

■ ***verb***

▸ **MOVE HAND/ARM 揮動手／臂** **1** 🔑 [I, T] to move your hand or arm from side to side in the air in order to attract attention, say hello, etc. 揮手；招手；擺手；揮臂：*The people on the bus waved and we waved back.* 公共汽車上的人揮手致意，我們也向他們揮手。◇ **~ at/to sb** *Why did you wave at him?* 你為什麼向他招手？◇ **~ sth (about/around)** *A man in the water was shouting and waving his arms around frantically.* 水裏有個人大喊大叫，拚命擺動着雙臂。◇ **~ sth at sb** *She waved her hand dismissively at the housekeeper.* 她輕蔑地朝客房服務員揮了揮手。◇ **~ sb sth** *My mother was crying as I **waved her goodbye**.* 我向母親揮手告別時她哭了。◇ **~ sth to sb** *My mother was crying as I **waved goodbye** to her.* 我向母親揮手告別時她哭了。 **2** 🔑 [I, T] to show where sth is, show sb where to go, etc. by moving your hand in a particular direction 揮手指引，揮手示意（方向）：**+ adv./prep.** *She waved vaguely in the direction of the house.* 她含糊地朝房子的方向揮了揮手。◇ **~ sth/sb + adv./prep.** *'He's over there,' said Ali, **waving a hand** towards some trees.* "他在那兒。"阿里説着朝幾棵樹揮了揮手。◇ *I showed my pass to the security guard and he waved me through.* 我向保安員出示了通行證，他揮手讓我通過。 **3** 🔑 [T] to hold sth in your hand and move it from side to side 揮舞，揮動（手中之物）：**~ sth** *Crowds lined the route, waving flags and cheering.* 人群沿路線排成行，揮舞着旗子歡呼。◇ **~ sth + adv./prep.** *'I'm rich!' she exclaimed, waving the money under his nose.* "我發財了！"她在他的鼻子下面舞動着鈔票喊道。

▸ **MOVE FREELY 自由移動** **4** 🔑 [I] to move freely and gently, for example in the wind, while one end or side is held in position（一端固定地）飄揚，飄動，搖晃，起伏：*The flag waved in the breeze.* 旗子在微風中飄揚。

▸ **HAIR 頭髮** **5** [I] to curl slightly 略呈波形；拳曲：*His hair waves naturally.* 他天生一頭鬈髮。 **6** [T] **~ sth** to make sb's hair curl slightly 使…略呈波形；燙（髮）：*She's had her hair waved.* 她燙髮了。

IDM **like waving a red flag in front of a 'bull** (*US*) (*BrE* **a red rag to a 'bull**) something that is likely to make sb very angry 鬥牛的紅布；激起人怒火的事物 ➲ more at FLAG *n.*

PHR V **ˌwave sth↔aˈside/aˈway** to not accept sth because you do not think it is necessary or important 對…置之不理；不理會 **SYN** **dismiss**：*My objections to the plan were waved aside.* 我對這項計劃的反對意見未被理會。 **ˌwave sth/sb↔ˈdown** to signal to a vehicle or its driver to stop by waving your hand 對（汽車或司機）揮手示意停下；揮手叫停 **ˌwave sb↔ˈoff** to wave goodbye to sb as they are leaving 揮手送別

wave·band /ˈweɪvbænd/ *noun* = BAND *n.* (6)：*a radio set with medium and short wavebands* 中短波段收音機

ˌwave-cut ˈplatform *noun* (*technical* 術語) an area of land between the CLIFFS and the sea which is covered by water when the sea is at its highest level 浪蝕台，波蝕台地（懸崖和海之間的地面，漲潮時被水覆蓋）

wave·form /ˈweɪvfɔːm; *NAmE* -fɔːrm/ *noun* (*physics* 物) a curve showing the shape of a wave at a particular time 波形

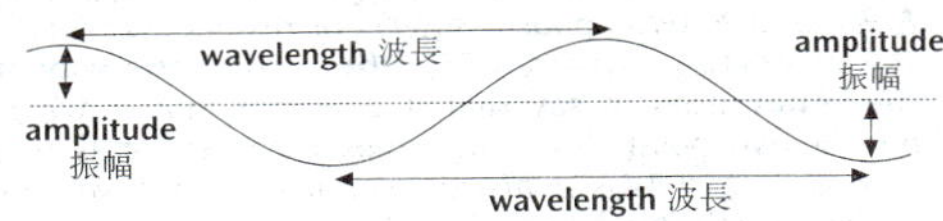

wave·length /ˈweɪvleŋθ/ *noun* **1** the distance between two similar points on a wave of energy, such as light or sound 波長 **2** the size of a radio wave that is used by a particular radio station, etc. for sending signals or broadcasting programmes（廣播電台等使用的）頻道，波道

IDM **be on the same ˈwavelength | be on sb's ˈwavelength** (*informal*) to have the same way of thinking or the same ideas or feelings as sb else 具有（與他人）相同的思路；合拍；與…所見略同

wave·let /ˈweɪvlət/ *noun* (*literary*) a small wave on the surface of a lake, the sea or the ocean（湖面或海面的）鱗波，漣漪

ˈwave machine *noun* a machine that makes waves in the water in a swimming pool（游泳池內的）造波機

waver /ˈweɪvə(r)/ *verb* **1** [I] to be or become weak or unsteady 減弱；動搖；顫抖：*His voice wavered with emotion.* 他激動得嗓音發抖。◇ *Her determination never wavered.* 她的決心從未動搖過。◇ *She never wavered in her determination to succeed.* 她要取得成功的決心從未動搖過。 **2** [I] **~ (between A and B) | ~ (on/over sth)** to hesitate and be unable to make a decision or choice 躊躇；猶豫不決；舉棋不定 **SYN** **hesitate**：*She's wavering between buying a house in the city or moving away.* 她舉棋不定，不知是在這個城市裏買所房子，還是遷居他處。 **3** [I] (especially of light 尤指光) to move in an unsteady way 搖曳；閃爍；忽明忽暗 ▸ **waver·er** /ˈweɪvərə(r)/ *noun*：*The strength of his argument convinced the waverers.* 他以有力的論據説服了那些搖擺不定的人。

wavy /ˈweɪvi/ *adj.* (**wavi·er, wavi·est**) having curves; not straight 起伏不平的；波浪形的；拳曲的：*brown wavy hair* 棕色鬈髮 ◇ *a pattern of wavy lines* 波浪形線條圖案 ➲ picture at CURVED

wax /wæks/ *noun, verb*

■ ***noun*** [U] **1** a solid substance that is made from BEESWAX or from various fats and oils and used for making CANDLES, polish, models, etc. It becomes soft when it is heated. 蠟；蜂蠟；動物蠟；植物蠟；石蠟：*styling wax for the hair* 定型髮蠟 ◇ *floor wax* 地板蠟 ◇ *wax crayons* 蠟筆 ◇ *wax polish* 上光蠟 ➲ see also PARAFFIN WAX, SEALING WAX **2** a soft sticky yellowish substance that is found in your ears 耳垢；耳屎

IDM see BALL *n.*

■ ***verb*** **1** [T] **~ sth** to polish sth with wax 給…打蠟 **2** [T, usually passive] **~ sth** to cover sth with wax 給…上蠟；給…塗蠟：*waxed paper* 蠟紙 ◇ *a waxed jacket* 上過蠟的夾克 **3** [T, often passive] **~ sth** to remove hair from a part of the body using wax 用蠟除去…上的毛：*to wax your legs/to have your legs waxed* 用蠟除去你腿上的毛 **4** [I] (of the moon 月亮) to seem to get gradually bigger until its full form is visible 漸圓；漸滿 **OPP** **wane** **5** [I] **+ lyrical, eloquent, sentimental, etc.** (*formal*) to become LYRICAL, etc. when speaking or writing 説話變得（熱情、雄辯、傷感等）起來：*He waxed lyrical on the food at the new restaurant.* 他對這家新餐館的菜肴越説越來勁。

IDM **ˌwax and ˈwane** (*literary*) to increase then decrease in strength, importance, etc. over a period of time（力量、重要性等）興衰枯榮，盛衰；陰晴圓缺

ˈwax bean *noun* (*NAmE*) a type of BEAN that is a long thin yellow POD, cooked and eaten whole as a vegetable 黃莢種菜豆；黃刀豆；蠟豆

ˈwaxed paper (*NAmE* also **ˈwax paper**) *noun* [U] paper covered with a thin layer of wax, used to wrap food or when cooking（包裝食品或烹飪用的）蠟紙

waxen /ˈwæksn/ *adj.* **1** (*formal*) made of wax 蠟的；蠟製的；塗蠟的：*waxen images* 蠟像 **2** (*literary*) pale and looking ill/sick 蒼白的；病態的：*a waxen face* 蒼白的臉

ˈwax paper *noun* (*NAmE*) = GREASEPROOF PAPER, WAXED PAPER

wax·work /ˈwækswɜːk; *NAmE* -wɜːrk/ *noun* **1** a model of a person that is made of wax 蠟像；蠟人 **2** **wax·works** (*pl.* **wax·works**) (*especially BrE*) (*NAmE* usually **ˈwax museum**) a museum where you can see wax models of famous people 蠟像館

waxy /ˈwæksi/ *adj.* made of wax; looking or feeling like wax 蠟製的；似蠟的；質地光滑的

way 🔑 /weɪ/ *noun, adv.*

■ ***noun***

▸ **METHOD/STYLE 方法；方式** **1** 🔑 [C] a method, style or manner of doing sth 方法；手段；途徑；方式：**~ to do sth** *That's not **the right way** to hold a pair of scissors.*

W

那樣拿剪刀不對。◇ (*informal, disapproving*) ***That's no way** to speak to your mother!* 不能那樣跟你媽媽說話！◇ **~ of doing sth** *I'm not happy with this way of working.* 我不喜歡這種工作方法。◇ **~ (that …)** *It's not what you say, it's the way that you say it.* 問題不在於你說什麼，而在於你怎麼說。◇ ***I hate the way** she always criticizes me.* 我討厭她一貫批評我的方式。◇ *I told you we should have done it **my way**!* 我跟你說過我們原本應該用我的方法來做這事。◇ *Infectious diseases can be acquired in several ways.* 傳染病的感染途徑有幾種。◇ *I generally get what I want **one way or another*** (= by some means). 我一般總能想方設法得到我想要的東西。➲ see also THIRD WAY

▸ **BEHAVIOUR 行為 2** [C] a particular manner or style of behaviour 作風；風度；樣子：*They grinned at her **in a friendly way**.* 他們友好地對她咧嘴笑了笑。◇ ***It was not his way** to admit that he had made a mistake.* 承認自己犯了錯誤可不是他一貫的作風。◇ *Don't worry, if she seems quiet—**it's just her way**.* 如果她看上去不愛說話，別擔心，她就是這麼個人。◇ *He was showing off, **as is the way** with adolescent boys.* 他在炫耀，青春期的男孩都是這個樣子。**3 ways** [pl.] the typical way of behaving and living of a particular group of people（群體的）行為方式，生活方式，習俗：*After ten years I'm used to the strange British ways.* 十年之後，我習慣了英國人的奇異習俗。

▸ **ROUTE/ROAD 路線；道路 4** [C, usually sing.] **~ (from …) (to …)** a route or road that you take in order to reach a place 路線；路；道路：*the **best/quickest/shortest way** from A to B* 從甲地到乙地最好的／最快的／最近的路線 ◇ *Can you **tell me the way** to Leicester Square?* 你能告訴我去萊斯特廣場的路嗎？◇ *to **ask sb the way*** 向某人問路 ◇ *We went the **long way round**.* 我們繞了一個大圈子。**5** [C, usually sing.] the route along which sb/sth is moving; the route that sb/sth would take if there was nothing stopping them/it 行進路線；通路：***Get out of my way!** I'm in a hurry.* 讓開！我有急事。◇ *Riot police with shields were blocking the demonstrators' way.* 手持盾牌的防暴警察堵住了示威者的路。◇ *We fought our way through the dense vegetation.* 我們在茂密的植被中開出一條通路。◇ *Unfortunately they ran into a snowstorm along the way.* 他們不幸在途中遇上了暴風雪。➲ see also RIGHT OF WAY **6** [C] a road, path or street for travelling along 路；小徑；街道：*There's a way across the fields.* 有一條路穿過田地。➲ see also FREEWAY, HIGHWAY, MOTORWAY, RAILWAY (1), WATERWAY **7 Way** used in the names of streets（用於街道名稱）路，道：*106 Headley Way* 黑德利路 106 號

▸ **DIRECTION 方向 8** [C, usually sing.] **which, this, that, etc. ~** a particular direction; in a particular direction 某方向；往某方向：*Which way did they go?* 他們往哪邊去了？◇ *We just missed a car coming **the other way**.* 我們剛錯過一輛從那邊開過來的汽車。◇ *Look **both ways*** (= look left and right) *before crossing the road.* 橫過馬路前要朝左右兩邊看一看。◇ *Make sure that sign's **the right way up**.* 一定不要把這招牌掛顛倒了。◇ *Kids were running **this way and that*** (= in all directions). 孩子們四處奔跑。◇ *They decided to split the money four ways* (= between four different people). 他們決定把錢分成四份。◇ (*figurative*) *Which way* (= for which party) *are you going to vote?* 你打算投哪邊的票？➲ see also EACH WAY, ONE-WAY, THREE-WAY, TWO-WAY

▸ **FOR ENTERING/LEAVING 進入；離去 9** [C, usually sing.] a means of going into or leaving a place, such as a door or gate 出入通道；門口：*the **way in/out*** 入口；出口 ◇ *They escaped out the back way.* 他們從後門逃走了。➲ see also COMPANIONWAY

▸ **DISTANCE/TIME 距離；時間 10** [sing.] (also *NAmE informal* **ways**) a distance or period of time between two points（兩點之間的）距離，時間段：*A little way up on the left is the Museum of Modern Art.* 前面不遠左手邊就是現代藝術博物館。◇ *September was **a long way off**.* 那時離九月份還有很長一段時間。◇ (*figurative*) *The area's wine industry still has **a way to go** to full maturity.* 這個地區的釀酒業還遠遠沒有完全成熟。◇ *You came **all this way** to see us?* 你大老遠地跑來看我們？◇ (*NAmE, informal*) *We still have **a ways to go**.* 我們還有很大的差距。

▸ **AREA 地區 11** [sing.] (*informal*) an area, a part of a country, etc. 地區；地帶：*I think he lives somewhere **over** London **way**.* 我想他住在倫敦附近。◇ *I'll stop by and see you next time I'm **down your way**.* 下次我去你那一帶時會順道去看你的。

▸ **ASPECT 方面 12** [C] a particular aspect of sth 方面 **SYN** **respect**：*I have changed in every way.* 我已經完完全全變了。◇ *It's been quite a day, **one way and another*** (= for several reasons). 從幾方面看，這是不尋常的一天。

▸ **CONDITION/STATE 情況；狀態 13** [sing.] a particular condition or state 情況；狀態：*The economy's **in a bad way**.* 經濟狀況很糟。◇ *I don't know how we're going to manage, **the way things are**.* 按目前這樣的情況，我不知道我們要如何應付。

IDM **across the 'way** (*BrE* also **over the 'way**) on the other side of the street, etc. 在街對面；在…對面：*Music blared from the open window of the house across the way.* 從街對面那棟房子開着的窗戶裏傳出嘈雜的音樂聲。**,all the 'way 1** (also **the ,whole 'way**) during the whole journey/period of time 一路上；自始至終：*She didn't speak a word to me all the way back home.* 回家的一路上，她沒對我說過一句話。**2** completely; as much as it takes to achieve what you want 完全地；無保留地：*I'm fighting him all the way.* 我在全力和他對抗。◇ *You can feel that the audience is with her all the way.* 你可以感覺到聽眾完全支持她。**(that's/it's) always the 'way** (*informal*) used to say that things often happen in a particular way, especially when it is not convenient（表示經常如此，尤用於貶義）總是這樣，老是 **any way you 'slice it** (*NAmE, informal*) however you choose to look at a situation 無論你如何看待 **'be/be 'born/be 'made that way** (of a person 人) to behave or do things in a particular manner because it is part of your character 天性如此；生下就這樣：*It's not his fault he's so pompous—he was born that way.* 他如此自命不凡並不是他的錯，他天生就是這種性格。**be ,set in your 'ways** to have habits or opinions that you have had for a long time and that you do not want to change 積習難改；秉性難移；執拗 **by the 'way** (also **by the 'by/'bye**) (*informal*) used to introduce a comment or question that is not directly related to what you have been talking about 順便提一下；捎帶說一聲；附帶問一句：*By the way, I found that book you were looking for.* 順便提一下，我找到了你在尋找的那本書。◇ *What's the time, by the way?* 順便問一句，幾點鐘了？◇ *Oh by the way, if you see Jackie, tell her I'll call her this evening.* 啊，對了，你要是看到傑基，告訴她我今晚給她打電話。**by way of sth** by a route that includes the place mentioned 路經；經過；經由 **SYN** **via**：*The artist recently arrived in Paris from Bulgaria by way of Vienna.* 這位藝術家最近從保加利亞途經維也納到了巴黎。◇ *She came to TV by way of drama school.* 她是唸過戲劇學校後到電視台的。**by way of/in the way of sth** as a form of sth; for sth; as a means of sth 作為…的形式；為了；作為…的手段：*He received £600 by way of compensation from the company.* 他得到那家公司 600 英鎊的賠償。◇ *She rolled her eyes by way of an answer and left.* 她轉動了一下眼睛作為回答就走了。**come your 'way** to happen to you by chance, or when you were not expecting it 意外落在…頭上；偶爾發生在…身上：*He took whatever came his way.* 無論什麼事落到他的頭上，他都認了。**cut both/two 'ways** (of an action, argument, etc. 行動、論點等) to have two opposite effects or results 兩面都行得通（或說得通）；有利也有弊 **either way** | **one way or the other** used to say that it does not matter which one of two possibilities happens, is chosen or is true 兩者都一樣：*Was it his fault or not? Either way, an explanation is due.* 是他的錯或不是？無論是不是，都得有個解釋。◇ *We could meet today or tomorrow—I don't mind one way or the other.* 我們可以在今天或明天見面，哪一天對我都行。**every 'which way** (*informal*) in all directions 四面八方；向各處：*Her hair tumbled every which way.* 她的頭髮亂得像雞窩。**get into/out of the way of (doing) sth** to become used to doing sth/to lose the habit of doing sth 養成（或丟掉）…的習慣：*The women had got into the way of going up on the deck every evening.* 這些女人養成了每天晚上到甲板上去的習慣。**get in the way of** to prevent sb from doing sth;

W

to prevent sth from happening 擋…的路；妨礙：*He wouldn't allow emotions to get in the way of him doing his job.* 他不會讓感情妨礙自己的工作。**get/have your own 'way** to get or do what you want, especially when sb has tried to stop you 一意孤行；為所欲為：*She always gets her own way in the end.* 她最後總是一意孤行。**give 'way** to break or fall down 斷裂；倒塌；塌陷：*The pillars gave way and a section of the roof collapsed.* 這些立柱坍塌了，一部份屋頂墜落下來。◇ *Her numb leg gave way beneath her and she stumbled clumsily.* 她那麻木了的腿一軟，她便重重地摔了一跤。**give 'way (to sb/sth) 1** to stop resisting sb/sth; to agree to do sth that you do not want to do 屈服；退讓；讓步：*He refused to give way on any of the points.* 他拒絕在任何一點上讓步。**2** (*BrE*) to allow sb/sth to be or go first 讓…在先；讓…先行：*Give way to traffic already on the roundabout.* 讓已上環狀交叉路的車輛先行。**give way to sth 1** to allow yourself to be very strongly affected by sth, especially an emotion 讓自己陷於（某種情緒等）：*Flinging herself on the bed, she gave way to helpless misery.* 她一頭撲倒在牀上，痛苦不堪。**2** to be replaced by sth 被…代替：*The storm gave way to bright sunshine.* 暴風雨過後陽光燦爛。**go all the 'way (with sb)** (*informal*) to have full SEXUAL INTERCOURSE with sb（與某人）盡情地性交 **go a long/some way towards doing sth** to help very much/a little in achieving sth（對做某事）幫助很大／不大，作用很大／不大：*The new law goes a long way towards solving the problem.* 新的法律十分有助於解決這一問題。**go out of your 'way (to do sth)** to make a special effort to do sth 特地；格外努力：*He would always go out of his way to be friendly towards her.* 他總是特意向她表示友好。**go your own 'way** to do as you choose, especially when sb has advised you against it 一意孤行；我行我素：*It's best to let her go her own way if you don't want a fight.* 你要不想吵架的話，最好是隨她去好了。**go sb's way 1** to travel in the same direction as sb 與…同路：*I'm going your way—I'll walk with you.* 咱們同路，我和你一起走。**2** (of events 事情) to go well for you; to be in your favour 進行順利；對…有利：*By the third round he knew the fight was going his way.* 拳擊打到第三輪，他知道形勢對自己很有利。**go the way of all 'flesh** (*saying*) to die 長逝；走向人生終點 **have it your 'own way!** (*informal*) used to say in an angry way that although you are not happy about sth that sb has said, you are not going to argue 隨你的便好了：*Oh OK, then. Have it your own way.* 啊，好啦。隨你的便吧。**have it/things/everything your 'own way** to have what you want, especially by opposing other people 為所欲為；一意孤行 **have a way of doing sth** used to say that sth often happens in a particular way, especially when it is out of your control …是常有的事（尤指無法控制的事）：*First love affairs have a way of not working out.* 第一次戀愛常常不成功。**have a way with sb/sth** to be good at dealing with sb/sth 善於應付；善於處理；有辦法對付：*He has a way with small children.* 他很會逗小孩。◇ *She has a way with words* (= is very good at expressing herself). 她善於辭令。**have/want it 'both ways** to have or want to have the advantages of two different situations or ways of behaving that are impossible to combine（想）兩全其美：*You can't have it both ways. If you can afford to go out all the time, you can afford to pay off some of your debts.* 你不可能做到兩全其美。如果你有錢整天外出玩樂，就能還掉一部份債。**have your (wicked) way with sb** (*old-fashioned, humorous*) to persuade sb to have sex with you 把…勾到手 **in a big/small way** on a large/small scale 大／小規模地：*The new delivery service has taken off in a big way.* 新的遞送服務迅速走紅。◇ *Many people are investing in a small way in the stock market.* 許多人都在小量地向證券市場投資。**in ˌmore ways than 'one** used to show that a statement has more than one meaning（所說的話）不止一個意思；在很多方面：*With the first goal he used his head in more ways than one.* 他進第一個球時從多方面動了腦筋。**in her, his, its, etc. (own) 'way** in a manner that is appropriate to or typical of a person or thing but that may seem unusual to other people 以…的特有方式：*I expect she does love you in her own way.* 我想她的確是以她特有的方式愛你。**in a 'way | in 'one way | in 'some ways** to some extent; not completely 在某種程度上；不完全地：*In a way it was one of our biggest mistakes.* 從某種意義上來說，這是我們所犯的最大錯誤之一。**in the/sb's 'way** 🔑 stopping sb from moving or doing sth 妨礙；擋着…的路：*You'll have to move—you're in my way.* 你得挪一挪，你擋了我的路。◇ *I left them alone, as I felt I was in the way.* 我留下他們單獨在一起，因為我覺得我礙他們的事。**in the way of sth** used in questions and negative sentences to talk about the types of sth that are available（用於問句或否定句）關於，就…而言：*There isn't much in the way of entertainment in this place.* 這個地方沒有多少娛樂活動。**keep/stay out of sb's 'way** 🔑 to avoid sb 規避；避開；躲開 **look the other 'way** to deliberately avoid seeing sb/sth 故意避而不看：*Prison officers know what's going on, but look the other way.* 獄警知道出了什麼事，但扭過頭去裝作沒看見。**lose your 'way 1** 🔑 to become lost 迷失方向；迷路：*We lost our way in the dark.* 我們在黑暗中迷了路。**2** to forget or move away from the purpose or reason for sth 忘記宗旨；背離…的意圖：*I feel that the project has lost its way.* 我覺得這個項目已經背離了原來的意圖。**make your 'way (to/towards sth)** to move or get somewhere; to make progress 去；前往；到…地方去；前進：*Will you be able to* ***make your own way*** *to the airport* (= get there without help, a ride, etc.)? 你能自己去機場嗎？◇ *Is this your plan for* ***making your way in the world****?* 這就是你要獲得成功的計劃嗎？**make 'way (for sb/sth)** to allow sb/sth to pass; to allow sb/sth to take the place of sb/sth 讓…通過；給…讓路；讓出位置：*Make way for the Lord Mayor!* 給市長大人讓路！◇ *Tropical forest is felled to make way for grassland.* 熱帶森林被砍伐，騰出地方做草地。**ˌmy way or the 'highway** (*NAmE, informal*) used to say that sb else has either to agree with your opinion or to leave 要麼聽我的，要麼走人 **(there are) no two ways a'bout it** (*saying*) used to show that you are certain about sth 肯定無疑；別無他途：*It was the wrong decision—there are no two ways about it.* 這是錯誤的決定，毫無疑問。**(there is) ˌno 'way** 🔑 (*informal*) used to say that there is no possibility that you will do sth or that sth will happen 不可能；決不；不行；沒門兒：*'Do you want to help?' 'No way!'* "你想幫忙嗎？" "沒門！" ◇ *No way am I going to drive them there.* 我無論如何都不會開車把他們送到那裏去。◇ *There's no way we could afford that sort of money.* 我們無論如何都花不起那種錢。**on your/the/its 'way 1** 🔑 going or coming 即將去（或來）；就要去（或來）：*I'd better be on my way* (= I must leave) *soon.* 我最好還是快點兒走。◇ *The letter should be on its way to you.* 那封信該快到你那裏了。**2** 🔑 during the journey 在路上；在行進中：*He stopped for breakfast on the way.* 他中途停下吃早點。◇ *She grabbed her camera and bag on her way out.* 她出門時一把抓起照相機和提包。**3** (of a baby 嬰兒) not yet born 尚未出生的：*They've got three kids and one on the way.* 他們有三個孩子，還有一個尚未出生。**the ˌother way 'round 1** 🔑 in the opposite position, direction or order 顛倒過來；相反；反過來：*I think it should go on the other way round.* 我想這應該以相反的方式繼續下去。**2** 🔑 the opposite situation 相反的情況：*I didn't leave you. It was the other way round* (= you left me). 我沒有離開你。是你離開了我。**ˌout of the 'way 1** 🔑 no longer stopping sb from moving or doing sth 不再擋路；不再礙事：*I moved my legs out of the way so that she could get past.* 我挪開腿讓她過去。◇ *I didn't say anything until Dad was out of the way.* 我直到爸爸不再干涉之後才說話。**2** finished; dealt with 結束；處理完：*Our region is poised for growth once the election is out of the way.* 大選一結束，我們地區就準備發展。**3** used in negative sentences to mean 'unusual'（用於否定句）奇特的，不尋常的，罕見的：*She had obviously noticed nothing out of the way.* 她顯然沒發現異常情況。➲ see also OUT-OF-THE-WAY **ˌout of your 'way** not on the route that you planned to take 不在計劃走的路線上：*I'd love a ride home—if it's not out of your way.* 我很想搭你的車回家，如果這不叫你繞路的話。**see your 'way ('clear) to doing sth/to do sth** to find that it is possible or convenient to do sth 覺得有可能做某事；認為便於做某事：*Small*

W

builders cannot see their way clear to take on many trainees. 小建築商認為不可能招收很多見習生。 **see which way the 'wind is blowing** to get an idea of what is likely to happen before doing sth 看看風向；觀察勢頭；摸清可能發生的情況 **(not) stand in sb's 'way** to (not) prevent sb from doing sth（不）妨礙別人：*If you believe you can make her happy, I won't stand in your way.* 如果你相信你能使她幸福，我不會妨礙你的。 **that's the way the cookie 'crumbles** (*informal*) that is the situation and we cannot change it, so we must accept it 情況就是這樣；沒有別的辦法 **there's more than ˌone way to skin a 'cat** (*saying, humorous*) there are many different ways to achieve sth（要做成某事）方法不止一個，有的是辦法 **to 'my way of thinking** in my opinion 我認為；依我看；依我之見 **under 'way** (also **under-way**) having started 已經開始；在進行中：*Preparations are well under way for a week of special events in May.* 五月份特別活動週的準備工作已經順利開展。 **a/the/sb's way of 'life** 🗝 the typical pattern of behaviour of a person or group（個人或群體的）特有的行為模式，典型生活方式：*the American way of life* 美國人的生活方式 **the ˌway of the 'world** the way that most people behave; the way that things happen, which you cannot change 大多數人的行為模式；世道；事情發生的規律：*The rich and powerful make the decisions—that's the way of the world.* 有錢有勢者說了算，這就是世道。 **ˌways and 'means** the methods and materials available for doing sth（做某事現有的）方法和資源，手段和財力：*ways and means of raising money* 籌資辦法 **a way 'into sth** (also **a way 'in to sth**) something that allows you to join a group of people, an industry, etc. that it is difficult to join, or to understand sth that it is difficult to understand（加入難以進入的群體、行業等的）敲門磚；（弄懂難以理解事物的）竅門，訣竅 **the way to sb's 'heart** the way to make sb like or love you 贏得某人喜愛的辦法；攻心策：*The way to a man's heart is through his stomach* (= by giving him good food). 取得男人歡心的方法就是讓他吃好。 **way to 'go!** (*NAmE, informal*) used to tell sb that you are pleased about sth they have done 幹得好：*Good work, guys! Way to go!* 夥計們，活兒不錯！幹得好！ **ˌwork your 'way through college, round the world, etc.** to have a job or series of jobs while studying, travelling, etc. in order to pay for your education, etc. 勤工儉學；半工半讀；邊掙錢邊周遊世界 **ˌwork your way 'through sth** to do sth from beginning to end, especially when it takes a lot of time or effort 自始至終做（尤指耗費時間或力量的事）：*She worked her way through the pile of documents.* 她從頭至尾處理了那一堆文件。 **ˌwork your way 'up** to move regularly to a more senior position in a company 逐步升職；按部就班晉升：*He worked his way up from messenger boy to account executive.* 他從送信員一步一步晉升為客戶經理。 ➲ more at CHANGE *v.*, CLAW *v.*, CLEAR *v.*, DOWNHILL *adj.*, EASY *adj.*, ERROR, FAMILY *n.*, FEEL *v.*, FIND *v.*, HARD *adj.*, HARM *n.*, HEAD *n.*, KNOW *v.*, LAUGH *v.*, LIE² *v.*, LONG *adj.*, MEND *v.*, MIDDLE *adj.*, OPEN *v.*, ORDINARY, PARTING *n.*, PAVE, PAY *v.*, PICK *v.*, RUB *v.*, SEPARATE *adj.*, SHAPE *n.*, SHOW *v.*, SMOOTH *v.*, SWEET *adj.*, SWING *v.*, TALK *v.*, WELL *adv.*, WILL *n.*, WRONG *adj.*

■ ***adv.*** 🗝 **1** (used with a preposition or an adverb 與介詞或副詞連用) very far; by a large amount 很遠；大量：*She finished the race **way ahead** of the other runners.* 她遙遙領先於其他選手跑到終點。◇ *I must be going home; it's **way past** my bedtime.* 我得回家了，早過了我的就寢時間了。◇ *The price is **way above** what we can afford.* 這價格大大超過了我們的支付能力。◇ *They live **way out** in the suburbs.* 他們住在很偏遠的郊區。◇ *This skirt is* way (= a lot) *too short.* 這條裙子太短了。◇ *I guessed that there would be a hundred people there, but I was **way out*** (= wrong by a large amount). 我估計那裏會有一百人，但是我大錯特錯了。 **2** (used with an adjective 與形容詞連用) (*informal, especially NAmE*) very 非常；極其：*Things just got way difficult.* 事情變得太困難了。◇ *I'm way glad to hear that.* 聽到這個消息，我太高興了。

IDM **'way back (in …)** a long time ago 很久以前：*I first met him way back in the 80s.* 我和他初次見面早在八十年代。

way·farer /ˈweɪfeərə(r); *NAmE* -fer-/ *noun* (*old-fashioned or literary*) a person who travels from one place to another, usually on foot（徒步）旅行者

way·lay /weɪˈleɪ/ *verb* (**way·laid**, **way·laid** /-ˈleɪd/) **~ sb** to stop sb who is going somewhere, especially in order to talk to them or attack them 攔截（尤其是為了談話或襲擊）；攔路：*I got waylaid on my way here.* 我在來這裏的路上遭到了攔路搶劫。

way·mark /ˈweɪmɑːk; *NAmE* -mɑːrk/ *noun* (*BrE*) a mark or sign on a route in the countryside to show the way to people who are walking, etc.（鄉間步道等的）路標：*Turn right where you see a waymark arrow.* 看到箭頭路標就向右轉。 ▸ **way·marked** /-mɑːkt; *NAmE* -mɑːrkt/ *adj.*：*waymarked routes* 有路標的路線

ˌway ˈout *noun* **1** (*BrE*) a door used for leaving a building（建築物的）出口 **SYN** **exit** **2** a way of escaping from a difficult situation（困境的）出路：*She was in a mess and could see no way out.* 她陷入困境，找不到出路。

IDM **on the way 'out** **1** as you are leaving 在離開的途中 **2** going out of fashion 開始過時

ˌway-'out *adj.* (*old-fashioned, informal*) unusual or strange 稀奇的；非傳統的；前衛的 **SYN** **weird**：*way-out ideas* 離奇的想法

way·point /ˈweɪpɔɪnt/ *noun* **1** a place where you stop during a journey（旅途中的）停留處 **2** (*technical* 術語) the COORDINATES, checked by a computer, of each stage of a flight or journey by sea 航路點（飛行或航海每一階段的坐標點）

-ways *suffix* (in adjectives and adverbs 構成形容詞和副詞) in the direction of 在…方向（的）；朝…方向（的）：*lengthways* 縱向的 ◇ *sideways* 向一側的

the ˌWays and 'Means Committee *noun* [sing. +sing./pl. v.] a group of members of the US House of Representatives which makes suggestions about laws concerning tax and trade in order to provide money for the US government 美國眾議院籌款委員會，美國眾議院歲入委員會（就稅收和貿易法規提出建議以便為政府提供資金）

way·side /ˈweɪsaɪd/ *noun* [sing.] the area at the side of a road or path 路邊；路旁：*a wayside inn* 路邊的客店 ◇ *wild flowers growing by the wayside* 路旁長的野花

IDM **fall by the 'wayside** to fail or be unable to make progress 半途而廢；中輟

'way station *noun* (*especially NAmE*) a place where people stop to eat or rest during a long journey（長途旅行中的）小站，小飯館

way·ward /ˈweɪwəd; *NAmE* -wərd/ *adj.* (*formal*) difficult to control 難以控制的；任性的；倔強的 **SYN** **head-strong**：*a wayward child* 任性的孩子 ◇ *wayward emotions* 反覆無常的情緒 ▸ **way·ward·ness** *noun* [U]

wazir /wəˈzɪə(r); *NAmE* -ˈzɪr/ *noun* = VIZIER

wazoo /wæˈzuː/ *noun* (*US, slang*) a person's bottom (the part they sit on) or ANUS 屁股；屁眼

IDM **ˌout/ˌup the wa'zoo** in large numbers or amounts 數目很大；大量

Wb *abbr.* WEBER

WC /ˌdʌbljuː ˈsiː/ *noun* (*BrE*) (on signs and doors in public places) toilet (the abbreviation for 'water closet') 盥洗室，廁所（全寫為 water closet，見於公共場所的指示牌和廁所門上）

w/c *abbr.* (used in writing 書寫形式) (*BrE*) week commencing (the week that begins on the date mentioned) 從（提到之）日開始的一週：*the schedule for w/c 19 November* 從 11 月 19 日開始一週的日程

we 🗝 /wi; *strong form* wiː/ *pron.* (used as the subject of a verb 用作動詞的主語) **1** 🗝 I and another person or other people; I and you 我們；咱們：*We've moved to Atlanta.* 我們已經搬到亞特蘭大了。◇ *We'd* (= the company would) *like to offer you the job.* 我們公司想聘你做這一工作。◇ *Why don't we go and see it together?* 咱們為什麼不一起去看看呢？ **2** 🗝 people in general 人們：*We should take more care of our historic buildings.* 我們應該更加愛護有歷史意義的建築。 ➲ see also ROYAL 'WE'

weak /wiːk/ *adj.* (**weaker**, **weakest**)
▸ **NOT PHYSICALLY STRONG** 身體虛弱 **1** not physically strong 虛弱的；無力的：*She is still weak after her illness.* 她病後仍然虛弱。◇ *His legs felt weak.* 他覺得兩腿發軟。◇ *She suffered from a weak heart.* 她心臟不太好。
▸ **LIKELY TO BREAK** 易破 **2** that cannot support a lot of weight; likely to break 不牢固的；易損壞的；易破的：*That bridge is too weak for heavy traffic.* 那座橋不太牢固，承受不住過多的車輛。
▸ **WITHOUT POWER** 沒有能力 **3** easy to influence; not having much power 易受影響的；懦弱的；軟弱無力的：*a weak and cowardly man* 一個懦弱膽怯的男子 ◇ ***In a weak moment*** (= when I was easily persuaded) *I said she could borrow the car.* 我一時心軟，同意她借用汽車。◇ *a weak leader* 軟弱的領導人 ◇ *The unions have always been weak in this industry.* 在這個行業，工會一直沒有權威。
▸ **POOR/SICK PEOPLE** 窮／病人 **4 the weak** *noun* [pl.] people who are poor, sick or without power 窮人；病人；弱者
▸ **CURRENCY/ECONOMY** 貨幣；經濟 **5** not FINANCIALLY strong or successful 疲軟的；蕭條的：*a weak currency* 疲軟的貨幣 ◇ *The economy is very weak.* 經濟十分蕭條。
▸ **NOT GOOD AT STH** 不善於 **6** not good at sth 不善於；不擅長；（能力）弱的：*a weak team* 弱隊 ◇ **~ in sth** *I was always weak in the science subjects.* 我總是學不好理科。
▸ **NOT CONVINCING** 欠缺說服力 **7** that people are not likely to believe or be persuaded by 不能令人信服的；不能說服人的 SYN **unconvincing**：*weak arguments* 無說服力的論據 ◇ *I enjoyed the movie but I thought the ending was very weak.* 我喜歡這部電影，但是覺得結尾很牽強。
▸ **HARD TO SEE/HEAR** 難以看見／聽到 **8** not easily seen or heard 微弱的；隱約的：*a weak light/signal/sound* 微弱的光線／信號／聲音
▸ **WITHOUT ENTHUSIASM** 缺乏熱情 **9** done without enthusiasm or energy 淡漠的；無活力的；無生氣的：*a weak smile* 淡淡的微笑 ◇ *He made a weak attempt to look cheerful.* 他有氣無力地擺出高興的樣子。
▸ **LIQUID** 液體 **10** a **weak** liquid contains a lot of water 稀的；稀薄的；稀釋的：*weak tea* 淡茶
▸ **POINT/SPOT** 點；處 **11 ~ point/spot** the part of a person's character, an argument, etc. that is easy to attack or criticize 弱點；缺點；不足之處：*The team's weak points are in defence.* 這個隊的弱點在防守。◇ *He knew her weak spot where Steve was concerned.* 他瞭解她在與史蒂夫有關事情方面的缺點。
▸ **GRAMMAR** 語法 **12** a **weak** verb forms the past tense and past participle by adding a regular ending and not by changing a vowel. In English this is done by adding *-d*, *-ed* or *-t* (for example *walk, walked*)（動詞）規則的，弱（變化）的
▸ **PHONETICS** 語音學 **13** (of the pronunciation of some words 某些單詞的發音) used when there is no stress on the word. For example, the weak form of *and* is /ən/ or /n/, as in *bread and butter* /ˌbred n ˈbʌtə(r)/. 輕讀的；非重讀的 OPP **strong**
IDM **ˌweak at the ˈknees** (*informal*) hardly able to stand because of emotion, fear, illness, etc.（因激動、恐懼、疾病等）兩腿發軟：*His sudden smile made her go weak at the knees.* 他突然笑了笑，使得她兩膝發軟。 **the weak link (in the ˈchain)** the point at which a system or an organization is most likely to fail 薄弱環節 ➲ more at SPIRIT *n.*

weak·en /ˈwiːkən/ *verb* **1** [T, I] **~ (sb/sth)** to make sb/sth less strong or powerful; to become less strong or powerful（使）虛弱，衰弱；減弱；削弱：*The team has been weakened by injury.* 這個隊因傷實力減弱。◇ *The new evidence weakens the case against her.* 新的證據削弱了訴她的案由。◇ *His authority is steadily weakening.* 他的權威日趨減弱。 OPP **strengthen** **2** [T, I] **~ (sth)** to make sth less physically strong; to become less physically strong 使強度減弱；削弱：*The explosion had weakened the building's foundations.* 爆炸鬆動了這座樓房的地基。◇ *She felt her legs weaken.* 她覺得兩腿無力。 **3** [I, T] to become or make sb become less determined or certain about sth 使（肯定程度）減弱；動搖；猶豫：*You must not agree to do it. Don't weaken.* 你們一定不能同意做這件事。別心軟。◇ **~ sth** *Nothing could weaken his resolve to continue.* 什麼也不能削弱他繼續下去的決心。

ˈweak force *noun* (*technical* 術語) one of the four FUNDAMENTAL FORCES in the universe, which is produced between PARTICLES in an atom 弱力（宇宙四種基本力之一，產生於原子中的粒子之間）➲ see also ELECTROMAGNETISM, GRAVITY (1), STRONG FORCE

ˌweak-ˈkneed *adj.* (*informal*) lacking courage or strength 缺乏勇氣的；意志薄弱的；不堅決的

weak·ling /ˈwiːklɪŋ/ *noun* (*disapproving*) a person who is not physically strong 瘦弱的人；弱不禁風的人

weak·ly /ˈwiːkli/ *adv.* in a weak way 虛弱地；軟弱無力地；懦弱地；冷淡地：*She **smiled weakly** at them.* 她勉強朝他們笑笑。◇ *'I'm not sure about it,' he said weakly.* "這我說不準。"他支吾說。

weak·ness /ˈwiːknəs/ *noun*
1 [U] lack of strength, power or determination 軟弱；虛弱；疲軟；衰弱；懦弱：*The sudden weakness in her legs made her stumble.* 她突然兩腿發軟踉蹌了一下。◇ *the weakness of the dollar against the pound* 美元對英鎊的疲軟 ◇ *He thought that crying was a **sign of weakness**.* 他認為哭是懦弱的表現。 OPP **strength** **2** [C] a weak point in a system, sb's character, etc.（系統、性格等的）弱點，缺點，不足：*It's important to know your own **strengths and weaknesses**.* 瞭解自己的優缺點很重要。◇ *Can you spot the weakness in her argument?* 你能指出她論點中的不足之處嗎？ OPP **strength** **3** [C, usually sing.] **~ (for sth/sb)** difficulty in resisting sth/sb that you like very much（對人或事物的）迷戀，無法抗拒：*He has a weakness for chocolate.* 他愛吃巧克力。

weal /wiːl/ *noun* a sore red mark on sb's skin where they have been hit（捱打造成的）紅腫傷痕

wealth /welθ/ *noun*
1 [U] a large amount of money, property, etc. that a person or country owns 錢財；財產；財物；財富：*a person of wealth and influence* 有錢有勢的人 ◇ *His personal wealth is estimated at around $100 million.* 他個人的財產估計為 1 億元左右。◇ *the **distribution of wealth** in Britain* 英國財富的分配 ➲ COLLOCATIONS at FINANCE **2** [U] the state of being rich 富有；富裕；富足：*The purpose of industry is to create wealth.* 勤勞的目的是致富。◇ *Good education often depends on wealth.* 良好的教育經常依靠良好的經濟條件。 **3** [sing.] **~ of sth** a large amount of sth 大量；豐富；眾多；充裕：*a wealth of information* 大量的信息 ◇ *The new manager brings **a great wealth of experience** to the job.* 新任經理為這項工作帶來了豐富的經驗。➲ compare RICHNESS

wealthy /ˈwelθi/ *adj.* (**wealth·ier**, **wealthi·est**) **1** having a lot of money, possessions, etc. 富有的；富裕的；富饒的 SYN **rich**：*a wealthy nation* 富國 ◇ *The couple are said to be fabulously wealthy.* 據說這對夫婦家財萬貫。◇ *They live in a wealthy suburb of Chicago.* 他們住在芝加哥郊區的一處富人區。➲ SYNONYMS at RICH **2 the wealthy** *noun* [pl.] people who are rich 富人；有錢人；闊人

wean /wiːn/ *verb* **~ sb/sth (off/from sth)** to gradually stop feeding a baby or young animal with its mother's milk and start feeding it with solid food 使（嬰兒或動物幼崽）斷奶
PHR V **ˈwean sb off/from sth** to make sb gradually stop doing or using sth 使逐漸戒除某些習慣（或使用某些東西）：*The doctor tried to wean her off sleeping pills.* 醫生設法使她逐漸停止服用安眠藥片。 **ˈwean sb on sth** [usually passive] to make sb experience sth regularly, especially from an early age 使…經常經歷（尤指從早年）：*He was weaned on a diet of rigid discipline and duty.* 他自幼受到嚴格紀律和職責的約束。

weapon /ˈwepən/ *noun*
1 an object such as a knife, gun, bomb, etc. that is used for fighting or attacking sb 武器；兵器；兇器：*nuclear weapons* 核武器 ◇ *a **lethal/deadly weapon*** 致命武器 ◇ *The police still haven't found the **murder weapon**.* 警方仍未找到謀殺的兇器。◇ *He was charged with carrying an **offensive weapon**.* 他被指控攜帶攻擊性武器。

➲ COLLOCATIONS at WAR ➲ see also BIOLOGICAL WEAPON, CHEMICAL WEAPON **2** something such as knowledge, words, actions, etc. that can be used to attack or fight against sb/sth 武器，手段，工具（指用作攻擊或鬥爭的知識、言語、行動等）: *Education is the only weapon to fight the spread of the disease.* 教育是戰勝這一疾病蔓延的唯一手段。◇ *Guilt is the* ***secret weapon*** *for the control of children.* 愧疚是控制兒童的秘密武器。 IDM see DOUBLE-EDGED

weap·on·ize (*BrE* also **-ise**) /ˈwepənaɪz/ *verb* **~ sth** to make sth suitable for use as a weapon 使適合用作武器；使武器化: *They may have weaponized quantities of anthrax.* 他們可能已將大量炭疽製成了武器。▸ **weap·on·iza·tion, -isa·tion** /ˌwepənaɪˈzeɪʃn; *NAmE* -nəˈz-/ *noun* [U]

ˌweapon of ˌmass deˈstruction *noun* (*abbr.* **WMD**) a weapon such as a nuclear weapon, a CHEMICAL WEAPON or a BIOLOGICAL WEAPON that can cause a lot of destruction and kill many people 大規模殺傷性武器（如核武器、化學武器和生物武器）

weap·on·ry /ˈwepənri/ *noun* [U] all the weapons of a particular type or belonging to a particular country or group（總稱某一類型或某國、某組織的）武器，兵器: *high-tech weaponry* 高科技武器 ◇ *US weaponry* 美國的軍械

wear /weə(r); *NAmE* wer/ *verb*, *noun*

■ ***verb*** (**wore** /wɔː(r)/, **worn** /wɔːn; *NAmE* wɔːrn/)

▸ **CLOTHING/DECORATION** 衣服；飾物 **1** [T] **~ sth** to have sth on your body as a piece of clothing, a decoration, etc. 穿；戴；佩戴: *She was wearing a new coat.* 她穿了一件新外衣。◇ *Do I have to wear a tie?* 我得繫領帶嗎？◇ *Was she wearing a seat belt?* 她繫着座椅安全帶嗎？◇ *He wore glasses.* 他戴着眼鏡。◇ *All delegates must wear a badge.* 所有代表都要佩戴徽章。◇ *She always wears black* (= black clothes). 她總是穿黑色衣服。 ➲ COLLOCATIONS at FASHION

▸ **HAIR** 鬚髮 **2** [T] to have your hair in a particular style; to have a beard or MOUSTACHE 蓄，留（髮、鬚等）: **~ sth + adj.** *She wears her hair long.* 她梳着長髮。◇ **~ sth** *to wear a beard* 留鬍鬚

▸ **EXPRESSION ON FACE** 面部表情 **3** [T] **~ sth** to have a particular expression on your face 流露，面帶，呈現（某種神態）: *He wore a puzzled look on his face.* 他臉上流露出迷惑不解的神情。◇ *His face wore a puzzled look.* 他臉上流露出迷惑不解的神情。

▸ **DAMAGE WITH USE** 用壞 **4** [I, T] to become, or make sth become thinner, smoother or weaker through continuous use or rubbing 磨損；消耗；用舊: *The carpets are starting to wear.* 地毯漸漸磨壞了。◇ **+ adj.** *The sheets have worn thin.* 牀單已經磨薄了。◇ **~ sth + adj.** *The stones have been worn smooth by the constant flow of water.* 不停的流水把這些石頭沖刷得很光滑。**5** [T] **~ sth + adv./prep.** to make a hole, path, etc. in sth by continuous use or rubbing 穿破；磨出（洞）；踩出（路）；沖出（溝）: *I've* ***worn holes*** *in all my socks.* 我把我所有的襪子都穿破了。

▸ **STAY IN GOOD CONDITION** 保持良好狀況 **6** [I] **~ well** to stay in good condition after being used for a long time 耐用；耐穿；耐磨；耐久: *That carpet is wearing well, isn't it?* 這地毯很耐用，是不是？◇ (*figurative, humorous*) *You're wearing well—only a few grey hairs!* 你一點兒都不顯老，只是有幾根灰白頭髮！

▸ **ACCEPT/ALLOW** 接受；允許 **7** [T] (usually used in questions and negative sentences 通常用於問句和否定句) **~ sth** (*BrE, informal*) to accept or allow sth, especially sth that you do not approve of 接受，容許（尤指不贊成的事物）

IDM **wear your ˌheart on your ˈsleeve** to allow your feelings to be seen by other people 讓感情外露；把心事掛在臉上 **wear ˈthin** to begin to become weaker or less acceptable 開始變弱；變得不受歡迎；變得興趣索然: *These excuses are wearing a little thin* (= because we've heard them so many times before). 這些託辭讓人聽得有點兒膩煩。**wear the ˈtrousers** (*BrE*) (*NAmE* **wear the ˈpants**) (often *disapproving*) (especially of a woman 尤指女人) to be the person in a marriage or other relationship who makes most of the decisions（在婚姻等關係中）處於支配的位置，起指揮的作用 ➲ more at CAP *n.*

PHR V **ˌwear aˈway | ˌwear sth↔aˈway** to become, or make sth become, gradually thinner or smoother by continuously using or rubbing it（因重複使用或磨擦而）變薄，變光滑；磨薄；磨光: *The inscription on the coin had worn away.* 鑄在這枚硬幣上的文字已磨平了。◇ *The steps had been worn away by the feet of thousands of pilgrims.* 成千上萬的朝聖者把台階踏得磨損了。 **ˌwear ˈdown | ˌwear sth↔ˈdown** to become, or make sth become, gradually smaller or smoother by continuously using or rubbing it（因重複使用或磨擦而）變小，變光滑；磨短: *Notice how the tread on this tyre has worn down.* 注意這個輪胎的花紋磨損的程度。 **ˌwear sb/sth↔ˈdown** to make sb/sth weaker or less determined, especially by continuously attacking or putting pressure on them or it over a period of time（尤指通過不斷攻擊或施加壓力）使衰弱，使意志薄弱: *Her persistence paid off and she eventually wore me down.* 她鍥而不捨取得成功，終於使我服輸了。 **ˌwear ˈoff** to gradually disappear or stop 逐漸消失；消逝；逐漸停止: *The effects of the drug will soon wear off.* 這麻醉藥品的作用將很快消失。 **ˌwear ˈon** (of time 時間) to pass, especially in a way that seems slow 慢慢地過去；（光陰）荏苒: *As the evening wore on, she became more and more nervous.* 隨着夜色漸深，她越來越緊張。 **ˌwear ˈout | ˌwear sth↔ˈout** to become, or make sth become, thin or no longer able to be used, usually because it has been used too much（因使用過度而）磨薄；穿破；磨損；用壞: *He wore out two pairs of shoes last year.* 去年他穿壞了兩雙鞋。 **ˌwear yourself/sb ˈout** to make yourself/sb feel very tired 使疲乏；使筋疲力盡；使厭煩: *The kids have totally worn me out.* 孩子們簡直把我煩透了。◇ *You'll wear yourself out if you carry on working so hard.* 你要是繼續這樣拚命工作，身體會吃不消的。

■ ***noun*** [U]

▸ **CLOTHING** 衣服 **1** (usually in compounds 通常構成複合詞) used especially in shops/stores to describe clothes for a particular purpose or occasion（尤用於商店）…時穿的衣服，…裝: ***casual/evening, etc. wear*** 便裝、晚禮服等 ◇ ***children's/ladies' wear*** 童裝；女裝 ➲ see also FOOTWEAR, MENSWEAR, SPORTSWEAR, UNDERWEAR **2** the fact of wearing sth 衣着；穿着；穿戴；佩戴: *casual clothes for everyday wear* 平時穿的休閒服 ◇ *These woollen suits are not designed for wear in hot climates.* 這些毛料西服不是設計為炎熱氣候下穿着的。 ➲ SYNONYMS at CLOTHES

▸ **USE** 使用 **3** the amount or type of use that sth has over a period of time 使用量（或形式）；耐用性；經久性: *You should get years of wear out of that carpet.* 那條地毯你可使用很多年。

▸ **DAMAGE** 損壞 **4** the damage or loss of quality that is caused when sth has been used a lot（因使用過度而）磨損；用壞；耗損: *His shoes were beginning to show signs of wear.* 他那雙鞋看樣子快穿壞了。

IDM **ˌwear and ˈtear** the damage to objects, furniture, property, etc. that is the result of normal use（正常使用造成的）磨損，損耗，損壞: *The insurance policy does not cover damage caused by normal wear and tear.* 保險單不保正常使用所造成的壞損。 ➲ more at WORSE *n.*

wear·able /ˈweərəbl; *NAmE* ˈwer-/ *adj.* (of clothes, etc. 衣服等) pleasant and comfortable to wear; suitable to be worn 穿戴舒適的；可穿戴的；適於穿戴的

wear·er /ˈweərə(r); *NAmE* ˈwer-/ *noun* the person who is wearing sth; a person who usually wears the thing mentioned 穿戴者；佩戴人；常穿戴…的人: *The straps can be adjusted to suit the wearer.* 這些背帶可進行調整以適合使用者。◇ *contact lens wearers* 戴隱形眼鏡的人

wear·ing /ˈweərɪŋ; *NAmE* ˈwer-/ *adj.* that makes you feel very tired mentally or physically 令人精疲力竭的；使人疲倦的；令人厭煩的 SYN **exhausting**

weari·some /ˈwɪərisəm; *NAmE* ˈwɪr-/ *adj.* (*formal*) that makes you feel very bored and tired 乏味的；令人疲勞的；使人厭倦的 SYN **tedious**

weary /ˈwɪəri; *NAmE* ˈwɪri/ *adj.*, *verb*

■ ***adj.*** (**weari·er**, **weari·est**) **1** very tired, especially after you have been working hard or doing sth for a long time（尤指長時間努力工作後）疲勞的，疲倦的，疲憊

W

的：*a weary traveller* 疲憊不堪的旅行者 ◇ *She suddenly felt old and weary.* 她突然感到了衰老和疲倦。◇ *a weary sigh* 疲倦的歎息 **2** (*literary*) making you feel tired or bored 使人疲勞的；使人厭煩的：*a weary journey* 使人疲乏的旅程 **3 ~ of sth/of doing sth** (*formal*) no longer interested in or enthusiastic about sth (對…) 不再感興趣，不再熱心，感到不耐煩：*Students soon grow weary of listening to a parade of historical facts.* 學生們很快便對聽連串史實厭煩起來。▶ **wear·ily** /ˈwɪərəli; NAmE ˈwɪr-/ *adv.*：*He closed his eyes wearily.* 他疲憊地閉上了眼睛。**weari·ness** *noun* [U]

■ ***verb*** (**wear·ies**, **weary·ing**, **wear·ied**, **wear·ied**) **1** [T] **~ sb** (*formal*) to make sb feel tired 使疲勞；使疲倦 SYN **tire** **2** [I] **~ of sth/of doing sth** to lose your interest in or enthusiasm for sth (對…) 失去興趣，失去熱情 SYN **tire**：*She soon wearied of his stories.* 她很快就厭煩了他的故事。

weasel /ˈwiːzl/ *noun, verb*

■ ***noun*** a small wild animal with reddish-brown fur, a long thin body and short legs. Weasels eat smaller animals. 鼬；黃鼠狼

■ ***verb*** (-ll-, *NAmE* -l-)

PHR V **ˌweasel ˈout (of sth)** (*informal, disapproving, especially NAmE*) to avoid doing sth that you ought to do or have promised to do 逃避，推諉 (責任或已作出的承諾)：*He's now trying to weasel out of our agreement.* 他現在正設法逃避在我們協議中應承擔的義務。

ˈweasel word *noun* [usually pl.] (*informal, disapproving*) a word that has little meaning, or more than one meaning, that you use when you want to avoid saying sth in a clear or direct way 滑頭話；含糊其詞的話；推諉詞

wea·ther 0⊸ /ˈweðə(r)/ *noun, verb*

■ ***noun*** [U] **1** 0⊸ the condition of the atmosphere at a particular place and time, such as the temperature, and if there is wind, rain, sun, etc. 天氣；氣象：***hot/cold/wet/fine/summer/windy, etc. weather*** 炎熱、寒冷、下雨、晴朗、夏天、颳風等的天氣 ◇ *Did you have **good weather** on your trip?* 你旅途中天氣好嗎？◇ *I'm not going out in this weather!* 這種天氣我不會出門的！◇ *There's going to be **a change in the weather**.* 天氣將有變化。◇ *if **the weather holds/breaks*** (= if the good weather continues/changes) 如果天氣還是這麼好／變壞 ◇ *The weather is very changeable at the moment.* 現時天氣變化無常。◇ *'Are you going to the beach tomorrow?' 'It depends on the weather.'* "你明天打算去海灘嗎？" "那要看天氣而定。" ◇ *We'll have the party outside, **weather permitting*** (= if it doesn't rain). 天氣允許的話，我們就在室外舉行這次聚會。◇ ***a weather map/chart*** 氣象圖 ◇ *a weather report* 氣象報告 **2** 0⊸ **the weather** (*informal*) a report of what the weather will be like, that is on the radio or television, or in the newspapers 氣象預報：*to listen to the weather* 收聽氣象預報

IDM **in ˈall weathers** (*BrE*) in all kinds of weather, good and bad 不論天氣好壞；風雨無阻：*She goes out jogging in all weathers.* 無論天氣好壞，她都出去慢跑鍛煉。**keep a ˈweather eye on sb/sth** to watch sb/sth carefully in case you need to take action 對…隨時留意；對…小心提防 **under the ˈweather** (*informal*) if you are or feel **under the weather**, you feel slightly ill/sick and not as well as usual 略有不適；不得勁 ⊃ more at BRASS, HEAVY *adj.*

Collocations 詞語搭配

The weather 天氣

Good weather 好天氣

- **be bathed in/bask in/be blessed with/enjoy** bright/brilliant/glorious sunshine 沐浴着／享受着明媚的／燦爛的陽光
- the sun **shines/warms sth/beats down (on sth)** 太陽照耀着／温暖着／照射在…
- the sunshine **breaks/streams through sth** 陽光穿過…
- fluffy/wispy clouds **drift across the sky** 絨毛般的／一縷縷雲彩在空中飄過
- a gentle/light/stiff/cool/warm/sea breeze **blows in/comes in off the sea** 微風／輕風／強風／涼爽的風／暖風／海風從海上吹來
- the snow **crunches beneath/under sb's feet/boots** 積雪在…腳下／靴子下嘎吱作響

Bad weather 壞天氣

- thick/dark/storm clouds **form/gather/roll in/cover the sky/block out the sun** 厚厚的雲層／烏雲／暴風雲形成／聚集／大量聚集／遮住天空／擋住太陽
- the sky **darkens/turns black** 天空變暗／變黑
- a fine mist **hangs in the air** 一絲薄霧瀰漫在空氣中
- a dense/heavy/thick fog **rolls in** 濃霧滾滾而來
- the rain **falls/comes down (in buckets/sheets)/pours down** 下雨了；大雨傾盆而下；大雨滂沱
- snow **falls/comes down/covers sth** 雪花飄落／覆蓋着…
- the wind **blows/whistles/howls/picks up/whips through sth/sweeps across sth** 風颳／嗖嗖地颳／呼嘯而過／愈颳愈大／颳過…／掠過…
- strong/gale-force winds **blow/gust (up to 80 mph)** 狂風大作 (高達每小時 80 英里的速度)
- a storm **is approaching/is moving inland/hits/strikes/rages** 暴風雨即將降臨／向內陸／移動／來臨／襲來／肆虐
- thunder **rolls/rumbles/sounds** 雷聲隆隆
- (forked/sheet) lightning **strikes/hits/flashes** (叉狀的／片狀的) 閃電襲來／閃過
- a (blinding/snow) blizzard **hits/strikes/blows/rages** (令人目眩的) 暴風雪襲來／大作／肆虐
- a tornado **touches down/hits/strikes/destroys sth/rips through sth** 龍捲風襲擊／摧毀…／撕裂…
- **forecast/expect/predict** rain/snow/a category-four hurricane 預報有雨／雪／四級颶風
- (*NAmE*) **pour (down)**/ (*BrE*) **pour (down) with rain** 下瓢潑大雨
- **get caught in/seek shelter from/escape** the rain 遇上下雨；尋找避雨處；躲雨
- **be covered/shrouded in** mist/a blanket of fog 籠罩在霧靄之中／厚厚的一層霧中
- **be in for/brave/shelter from** a/the storm 即將遇到／勇敢面對／躲避暴風雨
- **hear** rolling/distant thunder 聽到隆隆的／遠處的雷聲
- **be battered/buffeted by** strong winds 遭受強風肆虐；被強風吹得左右搖擺
- (*BrE*) **be blowing** a gale 在颳大風
- **battle against/brave** the elements 與惡劣天氣搏鬥；冒着風雨

The weather improves 天氣好轉

- the sun **breaks through the clouds** 太陽破雲而出
- the sky **clears/brightens (up)/lightens (up)** 天放晴了
- the clouds **part/clear** 烏雲散去
- the rain **stops/lets up/holds off** 雨停了／小了／延遲了
- the wind **dies down** 風逐漸平息
- the storm **passes** 暴風雨過去了
- the mist/fog **lifts/clears** 薄霧／霧消散了

■ *verb* **1** [I, T] to change, or make sth change, colour or shape because of the effect of the sun, rain or wind（因受風吹、日曬、雨淋等，使）褪色，變色，變形：*This brick weathers to a warm pinkish-brown colour.* 這塊磚經日曬雨淋褪成了帶粉紅的暖褐色。◇ **~ sth** *Her face was weathered by the sun.* 她的臉曬黑了。**2** [T] **~ sth** to come safely through a difficult period or experience 經受住，平安地渡過（困難）：*The company just managed to weather the recession.* 這家公司勉強渡過了衰退期。◇ *She refuses to resign, intending to* ***weather the storm*** (= wait until the situation improves again). 她拒絕辭職，想要經受住這次風暴的考驗。

'weather balloon *noun* a BALLOON that carries instruments into the atmosphere to measure weather conditions 氣象氣球

'weather-beaten *adj.* [usually before noun] (especially of a person or their skin 尤指人或人的皮膚) rough and damaged because the person spends a lot of time outside（因風吹日曬）粗糙的，曬黑的，受損的

wea·ther·board /ˈweðəbɔːd; *NAmE* ˈweðərbɔːrd/ (also **clap·board** especially in *NAmE*) *noun* one of a series of long, narrow, horizontal pieces of wood, each with one edge thicker than the other. They are fixed to the outside walls of a house with the bottom of one over the top of the one below, to cover the wall and protect it from rain and wind 封簷板；風雨板：*a weatherboard house* 安裝了封簷板的房屋 ► **'wea·ther·boarded** *adj.* **'wea·ther·board·ing** *noun* [U]

'weather centre (*BrE*) (*US* **'weather bureau**) *noun* a place where information about the weather is collected and reports are prepared 氣象局；氣象站

weathercock 風信雞

wea·ther·cock /ˈweðəkɒk; *NAmE* ˈweðərkɑːk/ *noun* a WEATHERVANE in the shape of a male chicken (called a COCK or ROOSTER)（公雞形）風向標；風信雞

'weather forecast (also **fore·cast**) *noun* a description, for example on the radio or television, of what the weather will be like tomorrow or for the next few days 天氣預報

wea·ther·ing /ˈweðərɪŋ/ *noun* [U] the action of sun, rain or wind on rocks, making them change shape or colour（岩石的）風化

wea·ther·ize (*BrE* also **-ise**) /ˈweðəraɪz/ *verb* **~ sth** (*NAmE*) to protect a building against the effects of cold weather, for example by providing INSULATION 使（建築物）提供禦寒性能

wea·ther·man /ˈweðəmæn; *NAmE* -ðərm-/ (*pl.* **-men** /-men/), **wea·ther·girl** /ˈweðəgɜːl; *NAmE* -ðərgɜːrl/ *noun* (*informal*) a person on radio or television whose job is describing the weather and telling people what it is going to be like 氣象播音員

wea·ther·proof /ˈweðəpruːf; *NAmE* -ðərp-/ *adj.* that is not affected by weather; that protects sb/sth from wind and rain 不受氣候影響的；全天候的；防風雨的：*The finished roof should be weatherproof for years.* 修過的屋頂若干年內不會漏雨。◇ *a weatherproof jacket* 風雨短上衣

'weather station *noun* a place where weather conditions are studied and recorded 氣象站

'weather strip (*NAmE*) (*BrE* **'draught excluder**) *noun* a piece of material that helps to prevent cold air coming through a door, window, etc.（門窗等的）擋風簾

wea·ther·vane /ˈweðəveɪn; *NAmE* -ðərv-/ *noun* a metal object on the roof of a building that turns easily in the wind and shows which direction the wind is blowing from 風向標；風標 ➲ see also WEATHERCOCK

weave /wiːv/ *verb, noun*

■ *verb* (**wove** /wəʊv; *NAmE* woʊv/, **woven** /ˈwəʊvn; *NAmE* ˈwoʊvn/) **HELP** In sense 4 **weaved** is used for the past tense and past participle. 作第 4 義時過去時和過去分詞用 weaved。 **1** [T, I] to make cloth, a carpet, a BASKET, etc. by crossing threads or strips across, over and under each other by hand or on a machine called a LOOM（用手或機器）編，織：**~ A from B** *The baskets are woven from strips of willow.* 這些籃子是用柳條編的。◇ **~ B into A** *The strips of willow are woven into baskets.* 用柳條編成籃子。◇ **~ sth together** *threads woven together* 織在一起的線 ◇ **~ (sth)** *Most spiders weave webs that are almost invisible.* 大多數蜘蛛可結成幾乎看不見的網。◇ *She is skilled at spinning and weaving.* 她是紡織能手。**2** [T] **~ A (out of/from B)** | **~ B (into A)** to make sth by twisting flowers, pieces of wood, etc. together（用…）編成：*She deftly wove the flowers into a garland.* 她靈巧地把花編成了一個花環。**3** [T] to put facts, events, details, etc. together to make a story or a closely connected whole（把…）編成，編纂成，編造（故事等）：**~ (sth into) sth** *to weave a narrative* 編故事 ◇ **~ sth together** *The biography weaves together the various strands of Einstein's life.* 這部傳記把愛因斯坦一生的各個方面編纂成書。**4** (**weaved**, **weaved**) [I, T] to move along by running and changing direction continuously to avoid things that are in your way 迂迴行進，穿行（以避開障礙）：**+ adv./prep.** *She was weaving in and out of the traffic.* 她在來往的車輛中穿來穿去。◇ *The road weaves through a range of hills.* 這條路在群山中繞來繞去。◇ **~ your way + adv./prep.** *He had to weave his way through the milling crowds.* 他不得不在來回亂轉的人群中穿梭而行。

IDM **weave your 'magic** | **weave a 'spell (over sb)** (*especially BrE*) to perform or behave in a way that is attractive or interesting, or that makes sb behave in a particular way（對某人）施展魔力；發揮（對某人的）影響力：*Will Ronaldo be able to weave his magic against Italy on Wednesday?* 羅納爾多星期三能施展其魔力擊敗意大利隊嗎？

■ *noun* the way in which threads are arranged in a piece of cloth that has been woven; the pattern that the threads make 編法；織法；編織式樣

weaver /ˈwiːvə(r)/ *noun* a person whose job is weaving cloth 織布工；編織工

'weaver bird *noun* a tropical bird that builds large nests by weaving sticks and pieces of grass together in a complicated way 織布鳥，織巢鳥（棲息於熱帶，以用枝條和草築巢著名）

web 🔑 /web/ *noun*

1 🔑 [C] = SPIDER'S WEB：*A spider had spun a perfect web outside the window.* 蜘蛛在窗外結了一張完整的網。➲ **VISUAL VOCAB** page V13 **2** 🔑 [C] a complicated pattern of things that are closely connected to each other 網狀物；網絡；錯綜複雜的事物：*a web of streets* 縱橫交錯的街道 ◇ *We were caught in a* ***tangled web*** *of relationships.* 我們陷入了錯綜複雜的人際關係網絡。**3** 🔑 **the Web** (also **the web**) [sing.] = WORLD WIDE WEB：*I found the information* ***on the Web***. 我在互聯網上找到了這條消息。➲ **COLLOCATIONS** at EMAIL **4** [C] a piece of skin that joins the toes of some birds and animals that swim, for example DUCKS and FROGS 蹼

Web 2.0 /ˌweb tuː pɔɪnt ˈəʊ; *NAmE* ˈoʊ/ *noun* [U] the developments in the way that people use the Internet that allow users free access and give them more control over the information 互聯網 2.0（指互聯網應用方式的新發展，允許用戶免費上網並對信息有更多的支配權）

web·bed /webd/ *adj.* [only before noun] a bird or an animal (such as a DUCK or FROG) that has **webbed feet** has pieces of skin between the toes 有蹼的 ➲ VISUAL VOCAB page V12

web·bing /ˈwebɪŋ/ *noun* [U] strong strips of cloth that are used to make belts, etc., and to support the seats of chairs, etc.（用以製作帶子等的）帶狀結實織物

web·cam (*NAmE* **Web·cam™**) /ˈwebkæm/ *noun* a video camera that is connected to a computer so that what it records can be seen on a website as it happens 網絡攝像機；網絡攝影機；網路攝影機 ➲ VISUAL VOCAB page V66

web·cast /ˈwebkɑːst; *NAmE* ˈwebkæst/ *noun* a live broadcast that is sent out on the Internet 網絡直播

ˈ**Web-enabled** *adj.* able to be connected to and used with the Internet 能上網的：*a Web-enabled interface* 網絡接口界面

weber /ˈveɪbə(r)/ *noun* (*abbr.* **Wb**) (*physics* 物) a unit for measuring the amount of MAGNETIC force that passes through a point in a MAGNETIC FIELD 韋伯（磁通量單位）

web·head /ˈwebhed/ *noun* (*informal*) a person who uses the Internet a lot 網迷；網蟲

webli·og·raphy /ˌwebliˈɒɡrəfi; *NAmE* -ˈɑːɡ-/ *noun* (*pl.* **-ies**) a list of websites or electronic works about a particular subject that have been used by a person writing an article, etc. 網絡參考書目；網路書目：*a Poe webliography* 愛倫•坡網絡書目 ◇ *a selected webliography on new Irish poetry* 愛爾蘭新詩網絡參考目錄

web·log /ˈweblɒɡ; *NAmE* -lɔːɡ; -lɑːɡ/ *noun* = BLOG

web·master /ˈwebmɑːstə(r); *NAmE* -mæs-/ *noun* (*computing* 計) a person who is responsible for particular pages of information on the World Wide Web（萬維網）站點管理員

ˈ**web page** *noun* a document that is connected to the World Wide Web and that anyone with an Internet connection can see, usually forming part of a website 網頁：*We learned how to create and register a new web page.* 我們學會了如何製作和註冊一個新網頁。

web·site 🔑 /ˈwebsaɪt/ *noun*
a place connected to the Internet, where a company or an organization, or an individual person, puts information 網站：*I found this information **on their website**.* 我在他們的網站上發現了這一信息。◇ *For current prices please **visit our website**.* 有關目前的價格，請訪問我們的網站。 ➲ COLLOCATIONS at EMAIL ➲ VISUAL VOCAB page V68

web·zine /ˈwebziːn/ *noun* a magazine published on the Internet, not on paper 網絡雜誌；網路雜誌

wed /wed/ *verb* (**wed·ded**, **wed·ded** or **wed**, **wed**) [I, T] (not used in the progressive tenses 不用於進行時) (*old-fashioned* or used in newspapers 過時用法或用於報章) to marry 結婚；娶；嫁：*The couple plan to wed next summer.* 這倆人計劃在夏天結婚。◇ **~ sb** *Rock star to wed top model* (= in a newspaper HEADLINE). 搖滾歌星與頂級名模結成伉儷。

we'd /wiːd; wid/ *short form* **1** we had **2** we would

wed·ded /ˈwedɪd/ *adj.* **1 ~ to sth** (*formal*) if you are **wedded** to sth, you like or support it so much that you are not willing to give it up 執著；獻身；全力以赴：*She's wedded to her job.* 她專心致志地工作。 **2** [usually before noun] (*old-fashioned* or *formal*) legally married（在法律上）已婚的，已完婚的：*your **lawfully wedded** husband* 你的合法丈夫 ◇ *to live together in **wedded bliss*** 一起過着幸福美滿的婚姻生活 **3** [not before noun] **~ (to sth)** (*formal* or *literary*) combined or united with sth 結合在一起；融為一體

wed·ding 🔑 /ˈwedɪŋ/ *noun*
a marriage ceremony, and the meal or party that usually follows it 婚禮；結婚慶典：*a **wedding present*** 結婚禮物 ◇ *a **wedding ceremony/reception*** 結婚典禮；婚宴 ◇ *Have you been invited to their wedding?* 他們有沒有邀請你參加婚禮？◇ *She looked beautiful on her **wedding day**.* 她在自己的婚禮上看來很漂亮。◇ *All her friends could hear **wedding bells*** (= they thought she would soon get married). 所有的朋友彷彿已聽到了她婚禮的鐘聲。 ➲ COLLOCATIONS at MARRIAGE ➲ see also DIAMOND WEDDING, GOLDEN WEDDING, SHOTGUN WEDDING, SILVER WEDDING, WHITE WEDDING

ˈ**wedding anniversary** *noun* the celebration every year of the date when two people were married 結婚紀念日：*Today's our wedding anniversary.* 今天是我們的結婚紀念日。

ˈ**wedding band** *noun* a wedding ring in the form of a plain band, usually of gold 結婚戒指（通常為金質淨面） ➲ VISUAL VOCAB page V65

ˈ**wedding breakfast** *noun* (*BrE*, *formal*) a special meal after a marriage ceremony 婚宴

ˈ**wedding cake** *noun* [C, U] a cake covered with ICING, and usually with several layers, eaten at a wedding party 結婚蛋糕

ˈ**wedding dress** *noun* a dress that a woman wears at her wedding, especially a long white one 婚紗

ˈ**wedding ring** *noun* a ring that is given during a marriage ceremony and worn afterwards to show that you are married 結婚戒指 ➲ VISUAL VOCAB page V65

ˈ**wedding tackle** *noun* [U] (*BrE*, *slang*) a man's sexual organs 雞巴；陽具

wedge /wedʒ/ *noun*, *verb*
■ ***noun* 1** a piece of wood, rubber, metal, etc. with one thick end and one thin pointed end that you use to keep a door open, to keep two things apart, or to split wood or rock 楔子；三角木：*He hammered the wedge into the crack in the stone.* 他用錘子把楔子砸入石縫裏。◇ (*figurative*) *I don't want to **drive a wedge** between the two of you* (= to make you start disliking each other). 我不想在你們倆中間挑起不和。 **2** something that is shaped like a wedge or that is used like a wedge 楔形物；用作楔子的東西：*a wedge of cake* 一角蛋糕 ◇ *shoes with wedge heels* 坡跟鞋 ➲ VISUAL VOCAB page V64 **3** a GOLF CLUB that has the part that you hit the ball with shaped like a wedge（擊高爾夫球的）楔形鐵頭球棒 IDM see THIN *adj.*
■ ***verb* 1 ~ sth + adv./prep.** to put or squeeze sth tightly into a narrow space, so that it cannot move easily 將…擠入（或塞進、插入） SYN **jam**：*The boat was now wedged between the rocks.* 船卡在了岩石之間。◇ *She wedged herself into the passenger seat.* 她擠進了旅客座椅中。 **2 ~ sth (+ adj.)** to make sth stay in a particular position, especially open or shut, by placing sth against it 把…楔牢（或楔住）：*to wedge the door open* 用楔子卡住門讓它開着

ˈ**wedge issue** *noun* (*NAmE*) an important and difficult political issue, used by a political party to draw supporters away from an opposing party 楔子問題，楔子議題（政黨藉以離間對手支持者的重大政治難題）

wedgie /ˈwedʒi/ *noun* (*informal*) an act of lifting sb up by his/her underwear, usually done as a joke 抓着內褲提起某人（作為玩笑）

wed·lock /ˈwedlɒk; *NAmE* -lɑːk/ *noun* [U] (*old-fashioned* or *law* 律) the state of being married 婚姻；已婚狀態：*children born **in/out of wedlock*** (= whose parents are/are not married) 婚生／非婚生子女

Wed·nes·day 🔑 /ˈwenzdeɪ; -di/ *noun* [C, U] (*abbr.* **Wed.**, **Weds.**)
the day of the week after Tuesday and before Thursday 星期三 HELP To see how **Wednesday** is used, look at the examples at **Monday**. * Wednesday 的用法見詞條 Monday 下的示例。 ORIGIN Originally translated from the Latin for 'day of Mercury' *Mercurii dies* and named after the Germanic god *Odin*. 譯自拉丁文 Mercurii dies，原意為 day of Mercury（水星日），以日耳曼神 Odin（奧丁）命名。

wee /wiː/ *adj.*, *noun*, *verb*
■ ***adj.*** (*informal*) **1** (*especially ScotE*) very small in size 很小的；極小的：*a wee girl* 嬌小的女孩 **2** small in amount; little 微量的；很少的；一丁點兒的：*Just a wee drop of milk for me.* 給我一丁點兒奶就行。◇ *I felt **a wee bit** guilty about it.* 我對此覺得有點兒愧疚。

IDM **the wee small 'hours** (*ScotE*) (*NAmE* **the wee 'hours**) = THE SMALL/EARLY HOURS at HOUR

▪ **noun** (also **'wee-wee**) (*informal, especially BrE*) (often used by young children or when you are talking to them 常用作兒語) **1** [sing.] an act of passing liquid waste (called URINE) from your body 尿尿；撒尿： *to do/have a wee* 尿尿 **2** [U] = URINE： *a puddle of wee* 一灘尿

▪ **verb** (also **'wee-wee**) [I] (*informal, especially BrE*) (often used by young children or when you are talking to them 常用作兒語) to pass liquid waste (called URINE) from the body 尿尿；撒尿： *Do you need to wee?* 你要撒尿嗎？

weed /wi:d/ *noun, verb*

▪ **noun** **1** [C] a wild plant growing where it is not wanted, especially among crops or garden plants 雜草，野草（尤指莊稼或花園中的）： *The yard was overgrown with weeds.* 這座庭院雜草叢生。 **2** [U] any wild plant without flowers that grows in water and forms a green floating mass 水草 **3 the weed** [sing.] (*humorous*) TOBACCO or cigarettes 煙草；煙葉；香煙；煙捲： *I wish I could give up the weed* (= stop smoking). 但願我能把煙戒掉。 **4** [U] (*informal*) the drug CANNABIS 大麻煙 **5** [C] (*BrE, informal, disapproving*) a person with a weak character or body 懦弱的人；體弱的人

▪ **verb** [T, I] **~ (sth)** to take out weeds from the ground 除（地面的）雜草： *I've been weeding the flower beds.* 我一直在除花壇裏的雜草。

PHR V **,weed sth/sb↔'out** to remove or get rid of people or things from a group because they are not wanted or are less good than the rest 清除，剔除，淘汰（不需要的或較差的人或物）

weed·kill·er /'wi:dkɪlə(r)/ *noun* [U, C] a substance that is used to destroy weeds 除草劑；除莠劑

weedy /'wi:di/ *adj.* (**weed·ier**, **weedi·est**) **1** (*BrE, informal, disapproving*) having a thin weak body 瘦弱的；弱不禁風的： *a weedy little man* 瘦弱矮小的男子 **2** full of or covered with weeds 雜草叢生的；長滿雜草的

,Wee 'Free *noun* a member of the part of the Free Church of Scotland that did not join with the United Presbyterian Church in 1900 to form the United Free Church（1900 年未與蘇格蘭聯合長老會聯合成立聯合自由長老會的）蘇格蘭自由長老會少數派成員

Wee·juns™ /'wi:dʒənz/ *noun* [pl.] (*US*) MOCCASIN style shoes 樂芙鞋（一種軟幫皮鞋）

week 🔑 /wi:k/ *noun*

1 🔑 a period of seven days, either from Monday to Sunday or from Sunday to Saturday 週；星期；禮拜： ***last/this/next week*** 上／本／下星期◇ *It rained all week.* 整個星期都在下雨。◇ *What* ***day of the week*** *is it?* 今天星期幾？◇ *He comes to see us* ***once a week.*** 他每週來看望我們一次。 **2** 🔑 any period of seven days 一週；七天的時間： *a* ***two-week*** *vacation* 兩週假期◇ *The course lasts five weeks.* 這門課程為期五週。◇ ***a week ago*** *today* (= seven days ago) 一週前的今天◇ *She'll be back* ***in a week.*** 她一週後回來。 **3** 🔑 the five days other than Saturday and Sunday（除星期六和星期日以外的）五天： *They live in town* ***during the week*** *and go to the country for the weekend.* 他們從星期一到星期五住在城裏，週末到鄉下去。◇ (*BrE*) *I never have the time to go out* ***in the week.*** 我從星期一到星期五從來沒有時間外出參加社交活動。 **4** 🔑 the part of the week when you go to work 工作週（一個星期中的工作時間）： *a 35-hour week* * 35 小時的工作週◇ *The firm is introducing a shorter* ***working week.*** 這家公司要採用較短的週工作時間。

IDM **today, tomorrow, Monday, etc. 'week** (*BrE*) (also **a ,week (from) to'day, etc.** *NAmE, BrE*) seven days after the day that you mention 一週後的今天（或明天、星期一等）： *I'll see you Thursday week.* 我們下星期四見。 **,week after 'week** 🔑 (*informal*) continuously for many weeks 一個星期又一個星期；一週接一週；一連數週： *Week after week the drought continued.* 乾旱持續了好多個星期。 **,week by 'week** 🔑 as the weeks pass 一個星期一個星期地；每過一週： *Week by week he grew a little stronger.* 每過一星期他都更健壯一點兒。 **week ,in, week 'out** happening every week 一週又一週；每個星期都；每週均無例外： *Every Sunday, week in, week out, she goes to her parents for lunch.* 她每個星期天都毫無例外地到她父母那裏吃午飯。 **a ,week next/on/this 'Monday, etc.** | **a ,week to'morrow, etc.** 🔑 (*BrE*) (also **a ,week from 'Monday, etc.** *NAmE, BrE*) seven days after the day that you mention 一週後的今天（或明天、星期一等）： *It's my birthday a week on Tuesday.* 一週後的星期二是我的生日。 **a ,week 'yesterday, last 'Monday, etc.** 🔑 (*especially BrE*) seven days before the day that you mention 一個星期前的昨天（或那個星期一等）： *She started work a week yesterday.* 她在一個星期前的昨天就開始工作了。 ➲ more at OTHER *adj.*

week·day /'wi:kdeɪ/ *noun* any day except Saturday and Sunday 週日（星期一至星期五的任何一天）： *The centre is open from 9 a.m. to 6 p.m. on weekdays.* 本中心星期一至星期五上午 9 點至下午 6 點開放。 ▸ **week·days** *adv.*： *open weekdays from 9 a.m. to 6 p.m.* 星期一至星期五上午 9 點至下午 6 點開放

week·end 🔑 /,wi:k'end; *NAmE* 'wi:kend/ *noun, verb*

▪ **noun** **1** 🔑 Saturday and Sunday 星期六和星期日；週末： *Are you doing anything* ***over the weekend?*** 你在週末做些什麼？◇ *Have a good weekend!* 週末愉快！◇ *It happened* ***on the weekend of*** *24 and 25 April.* 事情發生在 4 月 24 日和 25 日那個週末。◇ (*BrE*) *The office is closed* ***at the weekend.*** 本辦事處星期六和星期日不辦公。◇ (*especially NAmE*) *The office is closed* ***on the weekend.*** 本辦事處星期六和星期日不辦公。◇ (*BrE, informal*) *I like to go out* ***on a weekend.*** 我喜歡週末外出參加社交活動。◇ *We go skiing most weekends in winter.* 我們在冬天的週末大多去滑雪。 ➲ see also DIRTY WEEKEND, LONG WEEKEND **2** 🔑 Saturday and Sunday, or a slightly longer period, as a holiday/vacation 星期六和星期日（或略長一點的）假日： *He won a weekend for two in Rome.* 他贏得雙人去羅馬度週末的獎項。◇ *a weekend break* 週末假日

▪ **verb** [I] **+ adv./prep.** to spend the weekend somewhere（在某處）過週末；度週末： *They're weekending in Paris.* 他們正在巴黎度週末。

week·end·er /,wi:k'endə(r)/ *noun* **1** a person who visits or lives in a place only on Saturdays and Sundays 週末遊人（或來客等） **2** (*AustralE, informal*) a house in the country that people go to for weekends and holidays/vacations 週末度假屋（供度週末或假日用的鄉間房屋）

,weekend 'warrior *noun* (*NAmE*) a person who works all week, especially in an office or other indoor job, and uses the weekends to go out and do more active and/or dangerous physical activities 週末戰士（僅在週末外出參加劇烈驚險體育活動的人，尤指室內工作者）

'week-long *adj.* lasting for a week 持續一星期的；為期一週的： *a week-long visit to Rome* 到羅馬進行為期一週的訪問◇ *week-long courses* 為期一週的課程

week·ly 🔑 /'wi:kli/ *adj., noun*

▪ **adj.** happening, done or published once a week or every week 每週的： *weekly meetings* 週會◇ *a weekly magazine* 週刊 ▸ **week·ly** *adv.*： *Employees are paid weekly.* 雇員按週領工資。◇ *The newspaper is published twice weekly.* 這份報紙每週出版兩次。

▪ **noun** (*pl.* **-ies**) a newspaper or magazine that is published every week 週報；週刊

week·night /'wi:knaɪt/ *noun* any night of the week except Saturday, Sunday and sometimes Friday night 週日夜晚（除星期六和星期日以外的任何夜晚，有時亦不含星期五晚上）： *I have to stay in on weeknights.* 除了星期六和星期日外我每天夜裏都得待在家裏。

weenie /'wi:ni/ *noun* (*NAmE, informal*) **1** (*disapproving*) a person who is not strong, brave or confident 懦弱的人；窩囊廢 **SYN** **wimp**： *Don't be such a weenie!* 別這麼窩囊！ **2** = FRANKFURTER **3** (*slang*) a word for a PENIS, used especially by children 小雞雞（指陰莖，尤用於兒語）

weeny /'wi:ni/ *adj.* (**ween·ier**, **weeni·est**) (*informal*) extremely small 極小的 **SYN** **tiny**： *Weren't you just a weeny bit scared?* 難道你就一點兒都不害怕嗎？ ➲ see also TEENY (1)

weep /wi:p/ *verb, noun*

▪ **verb** (**wept**, **wept** /wept/) **1** [I, T] (*formal or literary*) to cry, usually because you are sad（通常因悲傷）哭泣，流淚：

She started to weep uncontrollably. 她不由自主地哭了起來。◇ ***I could have wept** thinking about what I'd missed.* 想到所失去的東西，我真想痛哭一場。◇ **~ for/with sth** *He wept for joy.* 他高興得流淚了。◇ **~ at/over sth** *I do not weep over his death.* 他死了我也不哭。◇ **~ sth** *She wept bitter tears of disappointment.* 她失望得痛哭流涕。◇ **~ to do sth** *I wept to see him looking so sick.* 看到他病成那個樣子我愴然淚下。◇ **+ speech** *'I'm so unhappy!' she wept.* "我好難過啊！" 她哭着說道。 **2** [I] (usually used in the progressive tenses 通常用於進行時) (of a wound 傷口) to produce liquid 流出，滲出（液體）: *His legs were covered with weeping sores* (= sores which had not healed). 他的雙腿有多處紅腫流膿的傷口。
■ ***noun*** [sing.] an act of crying 哭泣；落淚: *Sometimes you feel better for a good weep.* 有時候你痛痛快快哭上一場就會覺得好受些。

weep·ing /'wi:pɪŋ/ *adj.* [only before noun] (of some trees 某些樹木) with branches that hang downwards 有下垂枝條的: *a **weeping willow/fig/birch*** 垂柳；枝條下垂的無花果樹 / 樺樹

weepy /'wi:pi/ *adj., noun*
■ ***adj.*** (*informal*) sad and tending to cry easily 悲傷欲哭的；眼淚汪汪的；動不動就哭的: *She was feeling tired and weepy.* 她感到累得想哭。
■ ***noun*** (also **weepie**) (*pl.* **-ies**) (*informal*) a sad film/movie or play that makes you want to cry 催人淚下的電影（或戲劇）；令人傷感的電影（或戲劇） SYN **tear-jerker**

wee·vil /'wi:vl/ *noun* a small insect with a hard shell, that eats grain, nuts and other seeds and destroys crops 象鼻蟲，象甲，豆象（吃穀物、堅果和種子，危害作物的小甲蟲）

'wee-wee *noun, verb* = WEE

the weft /weft/ (also *less frequent* **the woof**) *noun* [sing.] the threads that are twisted under and over the threads that are held on a LOOM (= a frame or machine for making cloth)（織布機上的）緯線，緯紗 ➲ compare WARP *n.*

weigh 0➡ /weɪ/ *verb*
1 0➡ *linking verb* (**+ noun**) to have a particular weight 有…重；重: *How much do you weigh* (= how heavy are you)? 你體重多少？◇ *She weighs 60 kilos.* 她體重為 60 公斤。◇ *These cases **weigh a ton*** (= are very heavy). 這些箱子重得很。 **2** 0➡ [T] **~ sb/sth/yourself** to measure how heavy sb/sth is, usually by using SCALES 稱重量，量體重（通常用磅秤）: *He weighed himself on the bathroom scales.* 他用浴室磅秤稱稱體重。◇ *She weighed the stone in her hand* (= estimated how heavy it was by holding it). 她用手掂了掂那塊石頭的重量。 **3** [T] to consider sth carefully before making a decision 認真考慮；權衡；斟酌: **~ sth (up)** *You must weigh up the pros and cons* (= consider the advantages and disadvantages of sth). 你必須權衡利弊。◇ *She weighed up all the evidence.* 她慎重地考慮了所有的證據。◇ **~ (up) sth against sth** *I weighed the benefits of the plan against the risks involved.* 我認真考慮了這個計劃的優點和有關的風險。 **4** [I] **~ (with sb) (against sb/sth)** to have an influence on sb's opinion or the result of sth（對看法或結果）有影響；有分量: *His past record **weighs heavily** against him.* 他過去的記錄對他很不利。 **5** [T] **~ anchor** to lift an ANCHOR out of the water and into a boat before sailing away 起（錨）
IDM **weigh your 'words** to choose your words carefully so that you say exactly what you mean 推敲；斟酌字句
PHR V **,weigh sb↔'down** to make sb feel worried or anxious 使煩惱；使焦慮；使憂心忡忡 SYN **burden**: *The responsibilities of the job are weighing her down.* 這項工作的責任壓得她喘不過氣來。◇ *He is weighed down with guilt.* 他由於內疚而心神不定。 **,weigh sb/sth↔'down** to make sb/sth heavier so that they are not able to move easily 壓得…難以移動；壓彎: *I was weighed down with baggage.* 我被行李壓得走不動路。 **,weigh 'in (at sth)** to have your weight measured, especially before a contest, race, etc.（尤指賽前）量體重: *Both boxers weighed in at several pounds below the limit.* 兩個拳擊手賽前量的體重都比規定限度少幾磅。 ➲ related noun WEIGH-IN **,weigh 'in (with sth)** (*informal*) to join in a discussion, an argument, an activity, etc. by saying sth important, persuading sb, or doing sth to help（在討論、辯論等中）發表有分量的意見，發揮作用: *We all weighed in with our suggestions.* 我們都提出了有分量的建議。◇ *Finally the government weighed in with financial aid.* 最後政府提供了財政支援。 **'weigh on sb/sth** to make sb anxious or worried 加重…的思想負擔；使焦慮不安；使擔憂: *The responsibilities **weigh heavily** on him.* 他肩負重任，寢食不安。◇ *Something was weighing on her mind.* 她心事重重。 **,weigh sth↔'out** to measure an amount of sth by weight 稱出（一定重量的東西）: *She weighed out a kilo of flour.* 她稱出一千克麪粉。 **,weigh sb↔'up** to form an opinion of sb by watching or talking to them（通過觀察或談話）形成對…的看法，品評

weigh·bridge /'weɪbrɪdʒ/ *noun* a machine for weighing vehicles and their loads, usually with a platform onto which the vehicle is driven 橋秤，地秤，地磅，稱量台（用以稱車等及裝載量）

'weigh-in *noun* the occasion when the weight of a BOXER, JOCKEY, etc. is checked officially（對拳擊手、騎師等正式的）稱體重

'weighing machine *noun* a machine for weighing large objects or for weighing people in a public place 稱量機；衡器

weight 0➡ /weɪt/ *noun, verb*
■ ***noun***
▸ **BEING HEAVY** 重 **1** 0➡ [U, C] how heavy sb/sth is, which can be measured in, for example, kilograms or pounds 重量；分量: *It is about 76 kilos **in weight**.* 這東西重約 76 千克。◇ *Bananas are sold by weight.* 香蕉按重量出售。◇ *In the wild, this fish can reach a weight of 5lbs.* 這種魚在自然生存環境中可以長到 5 磅重。◇ *She is trying to **lose weight*** (= become less heavy and less fat). 她正在設法減肥。◇ *He's **put on/gained weight*** (= become heavier and fatter) *since he gave up smoking.* 他戒煙後體重增加了。◇ *Sam has a weight problem* (= is too fat). 薩姆太胖了。◇ *No more for me. I have to **watch my weight**.* 我不再吃了。我得控制體重。 ➲ COLLOCATIONS at DIET ➲ see also OVERWEIGHT, UNDERWEIGHT **2** 0➡ [U] the fact of being heavy 重: *He staggered a little **under the weight of** his backpack.* 他身上的背包壓得他有點步履蹣跚。◇ *I just hoped the branch would **take my weight**.* 我只是希望樹枝經得住我的體重。◇ *The pillars have to support the weight of the roof.* 這些立柱必須支撐起屋頂的重量。◇ *Don't put any weight on that ankle for at least a week.* 至少要一個星期別讓那個腳踝承重。 ➲ see also DEADWEIGHT
▸ **HEAVY OBJECT** 重物 **3** 0➡ [C] an object that is heavy 重物: *The doctor said he should not lift heavy weights.* 醫生說他不應舉重物。 **4** [C] an object used to keep sth in position or as part of a machine（用於固定某物或用作機器部件的）重體，重物: *weights on a fishing line* 釣線上的墜 ➲ see also PAPERWEIGHT
▸ **RESPONSIBILITY/WORRY** 責任；憂心 **5** [sing.] **~ (of sth)** a great responsibility or worry 重任；重擔；重壓；壓力 SYN **burden**: *The full weight of responsibility falls on her.* 全部的重任都落在了她的肩上。◇ *The news was certainly a **weight off my mind*** (= I did not have to worry about it any more). 這個消息真是去掉了我心裏的重擔。◇ *Finally telling the truth was **a great weight off my shoulders**.* 最後講了實話使我如釋重負。
▸ **INFLUENCE/STRENGTH** 影響；實力 **6** [U] importance, influence or strength 重要性；影響力；實力: *The many letters of support **added weight** to the campaign.* 許多聲援信增加了這場運動的影響力。◇ *The President has now offered to **lend** his **weight to** the project.* 總統現已主動表示支持這個項目。◇ *Your opinion **carries weight** with the boss.* 你的意見對老闆有影響。◇ *How can you ignore **the sheer weight of** medical opinion?* 你怎麼能忽視醫生意見的絕對重要性呢？◇ *The weight of evidence against her is overwhelming.* 對她不利的證據確鑿，無法抵賴。
▸ **FOR MEASURING/LIFTING** 測量；舉重 **7** [C, U] a unit or system of units by which weight is measured 重量單位；衡制: *tables of weights and measures* 度量衡表◇ ***imperial/metric weight*** 英制 / 公制重量 **8** [C] a piece of metal that is known to weigh a particular amount and is used to measure the weight of sth, or lifted by people

W

to improve their strength and as a sport 砝碼；秤砣；秤錘；槓鈴片；啞鈴：*a set of weights* 一組砝碼◇ *She lifts weights as part of her training.* 舉槓鈴是她鍛煉的一部份。◇ *He does a lot of **weight training**.* 他進行大量的舉重訓練。

IDM **take the weight off your feet** (*informal*) to sit down and rest, especially when you are tired（尤指疲乏時）坐下歇歇腳，坐下喘口氣：*Come and sit down and take the weight off your feet for a while.* 來坐下歇一會兒吧。 **throw your 'weight about/around** (*informal*) to use your position of authority or power in an aggressive way in order to achieve what you want 仗勢欺人；盛氣淩人 **throw/put your weight behind sth** to use all your influence and power to support sth 鼎力支持；全力相助 **weight of 'numbers** the combined power, strength or influence of a group 人多勢眾；團隊力量（或影響）：*They won the argument by sheer weight of numbers.* 他們純粹靠人多勢眾在爭論中獲勝。 ➲ more at GROAN v., PULL v., PUNCH v., WORTH adj.

■ *verb*

▸ **ATTACH HEAVY OBJECT** 附上重物 **1 ~ sth (down) (with sth)** to attach a weight to sth in order to keep it in the right position or make it heavier 在…上加重量；使負重；（用重物）固定：*The fishing nets are weighted with lead.* 這些漁網是靠鉛墜下沉的。

▸ **GIVE IMPORTANCE** 重視 **2** [usually passive] **~ sth** to give different values to things to show how important you think each of them is compared with the others 使加權：*The results of the survey were weighted to allow for variations in the sample.* 這次調查的結果進行了加權處理，以包容樣本中的偏差。◇ *a **weighted vote*** (= one that is worth more than a single vote) 加權選票◇ (*NAmE*) *a **weighted grade*** (= given at school for a course that is more advanced or harder and so has a higher value) 加權分數

weight·ed /'weɪtɪd/ *adj.* [not before noun] arranged in such a way that a particular person or thing has an advantage or a disadvantage 有利（或不利）於 **SYN** **biased**：**~ towards sb/sth** *The proposal is weighted towards smaller businesses.* 這項提議對小型企業有利。◇ **~ against sb/sth** *Everything seemed weighted against them.* 一切似乎都與他們過不去。◇ **~ in favour of sb/sth** *The course is heavily weighted in favour of engineering.* 這門課程非常側重於工程學。

weight·ing /'weɪtɪŋ/ *noun* **1** [U] (*BrE*) extra money that you get paid for working in a particular area because it is expensive to live there（發放給在生活費用高的地區工作的人的）額外津貼，生活補貼 **2** [C, U] a value that you give to each of a number of things to show how important it is compared with the others 加權值：*Each of the factors is given a weighting on a scale of 1 to 10.* 每種因素按 1 至 10 之間的數值加權。◇ *Each question in the exam has equal weighting.* 考試中每道題的分值相等。

weight·less /'weɪtləs/ *adj.* having no weight or appearing to have no weight, for example because there is no GRAVITY 無重量的；似無重量的；失重的：*Astronauts work in weightless conditions.* 宇航員在失重的條件下工作。▸ **weight·less·ness** *noun* [U]

weight·lift·ing /'weɪtlɪftɪŋ/ *noun* [U] the sport or activity of lifting heavy weights 舉重 ▸ **weight·lift·er** *noun*

weighty /'weɪti/ *adj.* (**weight·ier**, **weighti·est**) (*formal*) **1** important and serious 嚴重的；重要的；重大的：*weighty matters* 重大事情 **2** heavy 重的；沉重的：*a **weighty volume/tome*** 大部頭書 ▸ **weight·ily** /-ɪli/ *adv.* **weighti·ness** *noun* [U]

weir /wɪə(r); *NAmE* wɪr/ *noun* a low wall or barrier built across a river in order to control the flow of water or change its direction 堰；攔河壩；導流壩

weird /wɪəd; *NAmE* wɪrd/ *adj.*, *verb*

■ *adj.* (**weird·er**, **weird·est**) **1** very strange or unusual and difficult to explain 奇異的；不尋常的；怪誕的 **SYN** **strange**：*a weird dream* 離奇的夢◇ *She's a really weird girl.* 她真是個古怪的女孩。◇ *He's got some weird ideas.* 他有些怪念頭。◇ *It's really weird seeing yourself on television.* 看到自己上了電視感覺怪怪的。◇ *the **weird and wonderful** creatures that live beneath the sea* 奇異美麗的海底生物 **2** strange in a mysterious and frightening way 離奇的；詭異的 **SYN** **eerie**：*She began to make weird inhuman sounds.* 她開始發出可怕的非人的聲音。▸ **weird·ly** *adv.*：*The town was weirdly familiar.* 這個城鎮怪面熟的。 **weird·ness** *noun* [U]

■ *verb*

PHR V **,weird sb 'out** (*informal*) to seem strange or worrying to sb and make them feel uncomfortable 使感到奇怪；使感到煩惱；使感到不舒服：*The whole concept really weirds me out.* 這整個想法讓我覺得十分怪異。

weirdo /'wɪədəʊ; *NAmE* 'wɪrdoʊ/ *noun* (*pl.* **-os** /-əʊz/) (*informal, disapproving*) a person who looks strange and/or behaves in a strange way（長相或行為）古怪的人；怪人

welch /weltʃ; welʃ/ *verb* = WELSH

wel·come 🔑 /'welkəm/ *verb, adj., noun, exclamation*

■ *verb* **1** 🔑 [T, I] to say hello to sb in a friendly way when they arrive somewhere（打招呼）歡迎（某人的到來）：**~ (sb)** *They were at the door to welcome us.* 他們在門口迎接我們。◇ *a welcoming smile* 歡迎的微笑◇ **~ sb to sth** *It is a pleasure to welcome you to our home.* 很高興歡迎您光臨舍下。 **2** 🔑 [T] **~ sb** to be pleased that sb has come or has joined an organization, activity, etc. 歡迎（新來的人）；迎新：*They **welcomed** the new volunteers **with open arms*** (= with enthusiasm). 他們熱烈歡迎這些新的志願者。 **3** 🔑 [T] **~ sth** to be pleased to receive or accept sth 樂意接納；欣然接受：*I'd welcome any suggestions.* 任何建議我都會愉快地接受。◇ *I **warmly welcome** this decision.* 我熱烈歡迎這一決定。◇ *In general, the changes they had made were to be welcomed.* 總的來說，他們所作的這些變動都會被欣然接受。

■ *adj.* **1** 🔑 that you are pleased to have, receive, etc. 令人愉快的；受歡迎的：*a welcome sight* 賞心悅目的景象◇ *Your letter was very welcome.* 很高興收到你的信。◇ *The fine weather **made a welcome change**.* 天氣轉晴，令人心曠神怡。 **2** 🔑 (of people 人) accepted or wanted somewhere 受歡迎的；受款待的：*Children are always welcome at the hotel.* 兒童在旅館裏總是受到款待。◇ *Our neighbours **made us welcome** as soon as we arrived.* 我們一到就受到了鄰居們的歡迎。◇ *I had the feeling we were not welcome at the meeting.* 我有種感覺，人家並不歡迎我們參加這個會議。 **3** 🔑 **~ to do sth** (*informal*) used to say that you are happy for sb to do sth if they want to（表示樂於讓某人做某事）可隨意：*They're welcome to stay here as long as they like.* 他們在這裏願意住多久就住多久。 **4 ~ to sth** (*informal*) used to say that you are very happy for sb to have sth because you definitely do not want it（表示十分樂於讓他人取去自己不想要的事物）儘管…好了：*It's an awful job. If you want it, you're **welcome to it**!* 這事真難辦。你要是想做就交給你做好了！

IDM **you're 'welcome** 🔑 used as a polite reply when sb thanks you for sth 別客氣；不用謝；哪裏話：*'Thanks for your help.' 'You're welcome.'* "多謝你的幫助。" "別客氣。"

■ *noun* **1** 🔑 [C, U] something that you do or say to sb when they arrive, especially sth that makes them feel you are happy to see them 迎接；接待；歡迎：*Thank you for your **warm welcome**.* 感謝你們的熱情接待。◇ *The winners were **given an enthusiastic welcome** when they arrived home.* 獲勝者凱旋而歸時受到了熱烈歡迎。◇ *a **speech/smile of welcome*** 歡迎辭；歡迎的微笑◇ *to receive a **hero's welcome*** 受到英雄般的歡迎 **2** [C] the way that people react to sth, which shows their opinion of it（表明看法的）反應方式，對待，接受：*This new comedy deserves a **warm welcome**.* 這齣新喜劇值得受到熱烈歡迎。◇ *The proposals were **given a** cautious **welcome** by the trade unions.* 這些建議得到了工會審慎的接受。

IDM **outstay/overstay your 'welcome** to stay somewhere as a guest longer than you are wanted 做客太久而不再受歡迎

■ *exclamation* 🔑 used as a GREETING to tell sb that you are pleased that they are there 歡迎：*Welcome home!* 歡迎歸來！◇ *Welcome to Oxford!* 歡迎您來到牛津！◇

Good evening everybody. Welcome to the show! 諸位，晚上好。歡迎觀看本次演出！

ˈwelcome mat *noun*

IDM **lay, put, roll, etc. out the ˈwelcome mat (for sb)** (*especially NAmE*) to make sb feel welcome; to try to attract visitors, etc. 使感到受歡迎；設法吸引（客人等）

wel·com·ing /ˈwelkəmɪŋ/ *adj.* **1** (of a person 人) friendly towards sb who is visiting or arriving（對來訪或到達的人）歡迎的，熱情的，友好的 **2** (of a place 地方) attractive and looking comfortable to be in 令人感到愜意的；舒適的 **OPP** **unwelcoming**

weld /weld/ *verb, noun*

■ ***verb*** **1** [T, I] to join pieces of metal together by heating their edges and pressing them together 焊接；熔接；鍛接：**~ (sth)** *to weld a broken axle* 焊接一條斷裂的軸 ◇ **~ A (on) (to B)** *The car has had a new wing welded on.* 這輛汽車焊上了一塊新擋泥板。◇ **~ A and B (together)** *All the parts of the sculpture have to be welded together.* 這件雕塑所有的部件都必須焊接在一起。**2** [T] to unite people or things into a strong and effective group 使緊密結合；使連成整體：**~ sb/sth into sth** *They had welded a bunch of untrained recruits into an efficient fighting force.* 他們把一群未經訓練的新兵組織成了一支有戰鬥力的部隊。◇ **~ sth together** *The crisis helped to weld the party together.* 這場危機促使整個黨緊密地團結在一起。

■ ***noun*** a joint made by welding 焊接點；焊接處

weld·er /ˈweldə(r)/ *noun* a person whose job is welding metal 焊工

wel·fare **AW** /ˈwelfeə(r); *NAmE* -fer/ *noun* [U] **1** the general health, happiness and safety of a person, an animal or a group（個體或群體的）幸福，福祉，安康 **SYN** **well-being**：*We are concerned about the child's welfare.* 我們關注那個孩子的福祉。**2** practical or financial help that is provided, often by the government, for people or animals that need it（政府給予的）福利：*The state is still the main provider of welfare.* 政府仍然是福利的主要提供者。◇ *child welfare* 兒童福利 ◇ *a social welfare programme* 社會福利計劃 ◇ ***welfare provision/services/work*** 福利供給／機構／工作 **3** (*especially NAmE*) (*BrE* also **ˌsocial seˈcurity**) money that the government pays regularly to people who are poor, unemployed, sick, etc. 社會保障金（政府定期向貧窮、失業、患病等人員發放）：*They would rather work than live* ***on welfare***. 他們寧願工作而不願靠社會保障金過活。➲ COLLOCATIONS at UNEMPLOYMENT

ˌwelfare ˈstate *noun* **1** (often **the Welfare State**) [usually sing.] a system by which the government provides a range of free services to people who need them, for example medical care, money for people without work, care for old people, etc. 福利制度（由政府向有需要的人提供各種免費服務，如醫療、失業救濟金、對老人的照顧等）**2** [C] a country that has such a system 福利國家

wel·kin /ˈwelkɪn/ *noun* [U] (*literary* or *old use*) the sky or heaven 天空；蒼穹

IDM **let/make the welkin ˈring** to make a very loud noise 響徹雲霄

Grammar Point 語法說明

well

- Compound adjectives beginning with **well** are generally written with no hyphen when they are used alone after a verb, but with a hyphen when they come before a noun. 以 well 開頭的複合形容詞單獨用於動詞後一般不用連字符，但用於名詞前要用連字符：*She is well dressed.* 她衣着入時。◇ *a well-dressed woman* 穿着考究的女人 The forms without hyphens are given in the entries in the dictionary, but forms with hyphens can be seen in some examples. 本詞典的詞條給出了無連字符的形式，有連字符的形式則可在某些例句中見到。
- The comparative and superlative forms of these are usually formed with **better** and **best**. 這些複合形容詞的比較級和最高級通常由 better 和 best 構成：*better-known poets* 較著名的詩人 ◇ *the best-dressed person in the room* 這屋裏穿着最考究的人

well 🔑 /wel/ *adv., adj., exclamation, noun, verb*

■ ***adv.*** (**bet·ter** /ˈbetə(r)/, **best** /best/) **1** 🔑 in a good, right or acceptable way 好；對；令人滿意地：*The kids all behaved well.* 孩子們都很有禮貌。◇ *The conference was very well organized.* 這次會議組織得很好。◇ ***Well done!*** (= expressing admiration for what sb has done) 幹得好！◇ *His campaign was not* ***going well***. 他的競選活動進展得不順利。◇ *These animals make very good pets if treated well* (= with kindness). 這些動物受到愛護就會很溫順。◇ *People* ***spoke well of*** (= spoke with approval of) *him.* 人們對他的評價很高。◇ *She* ***took it*** *very* ***well*** (= did not react too badly), *all things considered.* 總的說來，她承受得還挺不錯。◇ *They lived well* (= in comfort and spending a lot of money) *and were generous with their money.* 他們生活優裕，花錢大方。◇ *She was determined to marry well* (= marry sb rich and/or with a high social position). 她決意嫁給有錢有勢的人。**2** 🔑 thoroughly and completely 完全地；徹底地；全部地：*Add the lemon juice and mix well.* 加進檸檬汁並攪拌均勻。◇ *The surface must be well prepared before you start to paint.* 一定要把表面打磨好再開始粉刷。◇ *How well do you know Carla?* 你跟卡拉有多熟？◇ *He's well able to take care of himself.* 他完全能夠自理。◇ (*BrE, informal*) *I was well annoyed, I can tell you.* 我跟你說吧，我那時氣壞了。**3** 🔑 to a great extent or degree 很；相當；大大地；遠遠地：*He was driving at well over the speed limit.* 他當時開車的速度遠遠超過了限制。◇ *a well-loved tale* 深受喜愛的故事 ◇ *The castle is* ***well worth*** *a visit.* 這座城堡很值得參觀。◇ *He liked her* ***well enough*** (= to a reasonable degree) *but he wasn't going to make a close friend of her.* 他夠喜歡她的，但並不打算和她結為密友。**4** **can/could well** easily 容易地；輕鬆地：*She could well afford to pay for it herself.* 她自己完全買得起。**5** **can/could/may/might well** probably 很可能：*You may well be right.* 你很可能是對的。◇ ***It may well be that*** *the train is delayed.* 火車很可能晚點了。**6** **can/could/may/might well** with good reason 有充分理由；合理地：***I can't very well*** *leave now.* 我現在離開不太合適。◇ ***I couldn't very well*** *refuse to help them, could I?* 我沒有理由拒絕幫助他們，是不是？◇ *'What are we doing here?' '****You may well ask*** (= I don't really know either).' "我們在這裏幹什麼呢？" "你算問對了（我也不知道）。"

IDM **as well (as sb/sth)** 🔑 in addition to sb/sth; too 除…之外；也；還：*Are they coming as well?* 他們也來嗎？◇ *They sell books as well as newspapers.* 他們既賣報也賣書。◇ *She is a talented musician as well as being a photographer.* 她不但是個攝影師而且還是個天才的音樂家。➲ note at ALSO **be doing ˈwell** 🔑 to be getting healthier after an illness; to be in good health after a birth（病後）康復，恢復良好；（產後）平安，健康：*Mother and baby are doing well.* 母子平安。**(you, etc.) may/might as well be hanged/hung for a ˌsheep as (for) a ˈlamb** (*saying*) if you are going to be punished for doing sth wrong, whether it is a big or small thing, you may as well do the big thing 與其偷羊羔被絞死，不如偷隻羊；一不做，二不休 **be well on the way to sth/doing sth** to have nearly achieved sth and be going to achieve it soon 即將達到；將要成就：*She is well on the way to recovery.* 她就要康復了。◇ *He is well on the way to establishing himself among the top ten players in the world.* 他很快就會成為排名世界前十位的選手。**be ˌwell ˈout of sth** (*BrE, informal*) to be lucky that you are not involved in sth 幸運地與…無關；幸虧沒有捲入 **be ˌwell ˈup in sth** to know a lot about sth 精通；熟悉：*He's well up in all the latest developments.* 他對所有的最新發展情況都瞭如指掌。**do ˈwell** 🔑 to be successful 成功：*Jack is doing very well at school.* 傑克在學校裏學習成績斐然。**do ˈwell by sb** to treat sb generously 善待；慷慨對待 **do ˈwell for yourself** to become successful or rich 成功；發家致富 **do ˈwell out of sb/sth** to make a profit or get money from sb/sth 獲利於；從…中獲取錢財 **do ˈwell to do sth** to be sensible or wise to do sth 做…明智（或聰明）：*He* ***would do well to*** *concentrate more on his work.* 他最好還是更加集中精力在工作上。◇ *You did well to sell when the price was high.* 你在價

錢高的時候出售，真明智。 **leave/let well a'lone** (*BrE*) (*NAmE* **let well enough a'lone**) to not get involved in sth that does not concern you 不管閒事；事不關己高高掛起：*When it comes to other people's arguments, it's better to leave well alone.* 遇到別人爭論時，最好別插嘴。 **may/might (just) as well do sth** to do sth because it seems best in the situation that you are in, although you may not really want to do it 做…倒也無妨；只好做（某事）：*If no one else wants it, we might as well give it to him.* 如果沒人要這個，我們不妨給他吧。 **,well and 'truly** (*informal*) completely 完全；徹底：*By that time we were well and truly lost.* 那時候我們已經完全迷路了。 **'well away** (*BrE, informal*) **1** having made good progress 有很大進步；大有進展：*If we got Terry to do that, we'd be well away.* 假若我們讓特里幹這事，我們就會有很大成績。 **2** drunk or fast asleep 酒醉；沉睡 **,well 'in (with sb)** (*informal*) to be good friends with sb, especially sb important 是某人（尤指要人）的好友：*She seems to be well in with all the right people.* 她似乎和所有大人物都關係很好。 ➲ more at BLOODY[1], FUCKING, JOLLY *adv.*, KNOW *v.*, MEAN *v.*, PRETTY *adv.*

■ ***adj.*** (**bet·ter** /ˈbetə(r)/, **best** /best/) **1** 🔑 [not usually before noun] in good health 健康；身體好：*I don't **feel** very **well**.* 我覺得身體不太好。◇ *Is she well enough to travel?* 她身體怎麼樣，能夠旅行嗎？◇ ***Get well soon!*** (= for example, on a card) 願早日康復！◇ *I'm better now, thank you.* 我現在好些了，謝謝您。◇ (*informal*) *He's not a well man.* 他身體不太好。 **2** [not before noun] in a good state or position 狀態良好；情況良好：*It seems that **all is not well** at home.* 看來家中並非事事如意。◇ ***All's well that ends well*** (= used when sth has ended happily, even though you thought it might not). 結果好就算一切都好。 **3** [not before noun] (**as**) **~ (to do sth)** sensible; a good idea 明智；可取；好主意：*It would be **just as well** to call and say we might be late.* 還是打個電話說一聲我們可能到得晚些比較好。◇ (*formal*) *It would be well to start early.* 最好還是早點動身。

IDM **,all very 'well (for sb) (to do sth)** (*informal*) used to criticize or reject a remark that sb has made, especially when they are trying to make you feel happier about sth（用於批評或反駁）某人儘可做某事：*It's all very well for you to say it doesn't matter, but I've put a lot of work into this and I want it to be a success.* 你說這無所謂當然容易，可是我卻已經花費很大力氣而且想要取得成功。 **,all well and 'good** (*informal*) quite good but not exactly what is wanted 好倒是好（但並不完全合乎心意）：*That's all well and good, but why didn't he call her to say so?* 那好倒是好，可是他為什麼不給她打電話這樣說呢？

■ ***exclamation*** **1** 🔑 used to express surprise, anger or relief（表示驚奇、憤怒或寬慰）哎呀，喲，啊，好啦：***Well, well—I would never have guessed it!*** 喲，喲，我怎麼也不會猜到那兒去！◇ ***Well, really! What a thing to say!*** 啊，真是的！這麼說太不像話了！◇ *Well, thank goodness that's over!* 好啦，謝天謝地，這件事總算過去了！ **2** 🔑 used to show that you accept that sth cannot be changed（承認某事不可改變）唉，好吧：*Well, it can't be helped.* 唉，這沒有辦法。◇ *'We lost.' 'Oh, well. Better luck next time.'* "我們輸了。" "啊，算了。願下次交好運。" **3** 🔑 used to agree to sth, rather unwillingly（勉強同意）嗯，好吧：*Well, I suppose I could fit you in at 3.45.* 好吧，我想可以在 3:45 見你。◇ *Oh, **very well**, then, if you insist.* 啊，那好吧，如果你堅持的話。 **4** 🔑 used when continuing a conversation after a pause（停頓後繼續交談）唔，這個，噢：*Well, as I was saying ...* 噢，我剛才是說… **5** 🔑 used to say that sth is uncertain（表示不肯定）哦：*'Do you want to come?' 'Well, I'm not sure.'* "你想來嗎？" "哦，我還說不準。" **6** 🔑 used to show that you are waiting for sb to say sth（等待別人說話）嘿，唔：*Well? Are you going to tell us or not?* 嗯？你想不想告訴我們？ **7** 🔑 used to mark the end of a conversation（結束交談）就這樣，好啦：*Well, I'd better be going now.* 就這樣，我現在該走了。 **8** 🔑 used when you are pausing to consider your next words（說話時稍微停頓）對了，噢：*I think it happened, well, towards the end of last summer.* 我想事情發生在，對了，快到上個夏末的時候。 **9** used when you want to correct or change sth that you have just said（糾正或改變剛說過的話時用）：*There were thousands of people there—well, hundreds, anyway.* 那裏有數以千計的人，噢，至少幾百人。

IDM **well I 'never ('did)!** (*old-fashioned*) used to express surprise（表示驚奇）喲，我可從未做過（或聽說過）這樣的事 ➲ more at SAY *v.*

■ ***noun*** **1** a deep hole in the ground from which people obtain water. The sides of wells are usually covered with brick or stone and there is usually some covering or a small wall at the top of the well. 井；水井 **2** = OIL WELL **3** a narrow space in a building that drops down from a high to a low level and usually contains stairs or a lift/elevator 樓梯井；電梯井道 ➲ see also STAIRWELL **4** (*BrE*) the space in front of the judge in a court, where the lawyers sit（法庭中的）律師席

■ ***verb*** **1** [I] **~ (up)** (of a liquid 液體) to rise to the surface of sth and start to flow 湧出；冒出；流出；溢出：*Tears were welling up in her eyes.* 她熱淚盈眶。 **2** [I] **~ (up)** (*literary*) (of an emotion 情感) to become stronger 湧起；迸發：*Hate welled up inside him as he thought of the two of them together.* 他一想到他們倆在一起就恨得咬牙切齒。

we'll /wiːl; wɪl/ *short form* **1** we will **2** we shall

,well ad'justed *adj.* (of a person 人) able to deal with people, problems and life in general in a normal, sensible way 能適應環境的；能自如地待人接物的；穩重的 ➲ compare MALADJUSTED

,well ad'vised *adj.* [not before noun] **~ (to do sth)** acting in the most sensible way 審慎；穩妥：*You **would be well advised to** tackle this problem urgently.* 你還是抓緊處理這個問題為好。 ➲ compare ILL-ADVISED

,well ap'pointed *adj.* (*formal*) having all the necessary equipment; having comfortable and attractive furniture, etc. 設備齊全的；陳設講究的

,well at'tended *adj.* attended by a lot of people 有許多人出席的；座無虛席的：*a well-attended conference* 與會者甚多的會議

,well 'balanced *adj.* **1** containing a sensible variety of the sort of things or people that are needed 很均衡的；很均勻的：*a well-balanced diet* 均衡的飲食 ◇ *The team was not well balanced.* 這個隊的隊員配備得不是很均衡。 **2** (of a person or their behaviour 人或其行為) sensible and emotionally in control 通情達理的；頭腦清醒的；情緒穩定的：*His response was well balanced.* 他的反應很沉着。

,well be'haved *adj.* behaving in a way that other people think is polite or correct 彬彬有禮的；行為端正的：*a well-behaved child* 規規矩矩的孩子 ◇ *The audience was surprisingly well behaved.* 觀眾令人出奇地守秩序。

'well-being *noun* [U] general health and happiness 健康；安樂；康樂：***emotional/physical/psychological well-being*** 情緒／身體／心理健康 ◇ *to have **a sense of well-being*** 有一種心曠神怡的感覺

,well 'born *adj.* (*formal*) from a rich family or a family of high social class 出身高貴的；出身名門的

,well 'bred *adj.* (*old-fashioned, formal*) having or showing good manners; typical of a high social class 有教養的；有涵養的；知書達理的；高貴的：*a well-bred young lady* 一位有教養的少女 ◇ *She was too well bred to show her disappointment.* 她很有涵養，沒有表露出她的失望。 **OPP** **ill-bred**

,well 'built *adj.* **1** (of a person 人) with a solid, strong body 身強力壯的；體格健美的 **2** (of a building or machine 建築或機器) strongly made 結實的；堅固的

,well con'nected *adj.* (*formal*) (of a person 人) having important or rich friends or relatives 與達官豪富有親友關係的；社會關係強固的

,well 'cut *adj.* (of clothes 衣服) made well and therefore probably expensive 做工精細的；考究的

,well de'fined *adj.* easy to see or understand 易於辨認理解的；明確的；規定得清楚的；界限分明的：*well-defined rules* 明確的規則 ◇ *These categories are not well defined.* 這些類別劃分得不太明確。 **OPP** **ill-defined**

,well de'veloped *adj.* fully developed; fully grown 發育良好的；完善的；健全的：*He had a well-developed sense of his own superiority.* 他的個人優越感十足。

Synonyms 同義詞辨析

well

all right • OK • fine • healthy • strong • fit

These words all describe sb who is not ill and is in good health. 以上各詞均形容人健康、身體好。

well [not usually before noun] (*rather informal*) in good health 指健康、身體好： *I'm not feeling very well.* 我感覺身體不太好。◇ *Is he well enough to travel?* 他身體怎麼樣，能夠旅行嗎？ **NOTE** **Well** is used especially to talk about your own health, to ask sb about their health or to make a comment on it. * well 尤用以談自己的健康、詢問別人的健康或談論身體情況。

all right [not before noun] (*rather informal*) not feeling ill; not injured 指感覺身體還好、沒有生病、沒有受傷： *Are you feeling all right?* 你感覺還好嗎？

OK [not before noun] (*informal*) not feeling ill; not injured 指感覺身體還好、沒有生病、沒有受傷： *She says she's OK now, and will be back at work tomorrow.* 她說她現在身體還可以，明天就回來上班。

ALL RIGHT OR OK? 用 all right 還是 OK？

These words are slightly less positive than the other words in this group. They are both used in spoken English to talk about not actually being ill or injured, rather than being positively in good health. Both are rather informal but **OK** is slightly more informal than **all right**. 上述兩詞比同組其他詞的肯定含意稍弱一些，兩詞均用於英語口語中，指沒有生病、安然無恙，而非確定身體健康；兩詞均相當非正式，不過 OK 較 all right 還要非正式些。

fine [not before noun] (not used in negative statements) (*rather informal*) completely well （不用於否定句）指身體很好、健康： *'How are you?' 'Fine, thanks.'* "你好嗎？" "很好，謝謝。" **NOTE** **Fine** is used especially to talk about your health, especially when sb asks you how you are. It is also used to talk about sb's health when you are talking to sb else. Unlike **well** it is not often used to ask sb about their health or make a comment on it. * fine 尤用於回應別人的詢問，表示自己身體很健康；與人談話時，亦可用以指另一人身體健康。與 well 不一樣，fine 通常不用於詢問別人的身體狀況或者談論身體情況： ~~*Are you keeping fine?*~~

healthy in good health and not likely to become ill 指健康、健壯： *Keep healthy by exercising regularly.* 經常鍛煉以保持健康。

strong in good health and not suffering from an illness 指健康、身體好： *After a few weeks she was feeling stronger.* 幾週之後她感覺身體好些了。 **NOTE** **Strong** is often used to talk about becoming healthy again after an illness. * strong 常用以指病後恢復健康。

fit (*especially BrE*) in good physical health, especially because you take regular physical exercise 指健壯，尤指因經常鍛煉而身體健康： *I go swimming every day in order to keep fit.* 我每天游泳以保持健康。

PATTERNS

- all right/OK/fit **for** sth
- all right/OK/fit **to do sth**
- to **feel/look** well/all right/OK/fine/healthy/strong/fit
- to **keep** (sb) well/healthy/fit
- **perfectly** well/all right/OK/fine/healthy/fit
- **physically** well/healthy/strong/fit

ˌwell disˈposed *adj.* **~ (towards/to sb/sth)** having friendly feelings towards sb or a positive attitude towards sth 和善親切的；懷有好感的 **OPP** **ill-disposed**

ˌwell ˈdocumented *adj.* having a lot of written evidence to prove, support or explain it 證據充分的；有大量文件證明的： *The problem is well documented.* 這個問題有很多依據。◇ *well-documented facts* 證據充分的事實

ˌwell ˈdone *adj.* (of food, especially meat 食物，尤指肉) cooked thoroughly or for a long time 熟透的；煮透了的；燒爛了的： *He prefers his steak well done.* 他喜歡吃煎得熟透的牛排。 ➲ compare RARE (3), UNDERDONE

ˌwell ˈdressed *adj.* wearing fashionable or expensive clothes 衣着入時的；穿着講究的： *This is what today's well-dressed man is wearing.* 這是當今時髦男子的穿着。

ˌwell ˈearned *adj.* much deserved 完全應得的；理當有的；當之無愧的： *a well-earned rest* 應有的休息

ˌwell enˈdowed *adj.* **1** (*informal, humorous*) (of a woman 女人) having large breasts 乳房大的 **2** (*informal, humorous*) (of a man 男人) having large GENITALS 陰莖大的；生殖器大的 **3** (of an organization 組織) having a lot of money 資金充足的： *well-endowed colleges* 資金充足的學院

ˌwell eˈstablished *adj.* having a respected position, because of being successful, etc. over a long period 地位穩固的；樹立起聲譽的；得到確認的： *a well-established firm* 久享盛譽的商行 ◇ *He is now well established in his career.* 他現在已經在事業上穩住了根基。

ˌwell ˈfed *adj.* having plenty of good food to eat regularly 吃得好的；營養足的： *well-fed family pets* 餵得肥肥胖胖的家庭寵物 ◇ *The animals all looked well fed and cared for.* 這些動物看上去都得到了精心的飼養和照料。

ˌwell ˈformed *adj.* (of sentences 句子) written or spoken correctly according to the rules of grammar 符合語法規則的；結構完整的

ˌwell ˈfounded (also *less frequent* **ˌwell ˈgrounded**) *adj.* having good reasons or evidence to cause or support it 理由充足的；有根據的；有事實依據的： *well-founded suspicions* 有根據的懷疑 ◇ *His fear turned out to be well founded.* 他的恐懼證明是有道理的。 **OPP** **ill-founded**

ˌwell ˈgroomed *adj.* (of a person 人) looking clean, neat and carefully dressed 整潔且衣着得體的

ˌwell ˈgrounded *adj.* **1 ~ in sth** having a good training in a subject or skill 功底深的；基礎扎實的 **2** = WELL FOUNDED

ˌwell ˈheeled *adj.* (*informal*) having a lot of money 有錢的；富有的 **SYN** **rich, wealthy**

ˌwell ˈhung *adj.* **1** (of meat 肉) having been left for several days before being cooked in order to improve the flavour 適度風乾的 **2** (of a man 男子) (*informal*) having a large PENIS 大陰莖的；生殖器碩大下垂的

ˌwell inˈformed *adj.* having or showing knowledge or information about many subjects or about one particular subject 見多識廣的；消息靈通的；知識淵博的： *a well-informed decision* 有見識的決定 **OPP** **ill-informed**

wel·ling·ton /ˈwelɪŋtən/ (also **ˌwellington ˈboot**, *informal* **welly**) (all *BrE*) (*NAmE* **ˌrubber ˈboot**) *noun* one of a pair of long rubber boots, usually reaching almost up to the knee, that you wear to stop your feet getting wet 威靈頓長筒靴；及膝膠靴： *a pair of wellingtons* 一雙高筒膠靴 ➲ VISUAL VOCAB page V64

ˌwell inˈtentioned *adj.* intending to be helpful or useful but not always succeeding very well 出於好心的，好心好意的，善意的（但往往事與願違） **SYN** **well meaning**

ˌwell ˈkept *adj.* **1** kept neat and in good condition 保持整齊的；妥善保管的；悉心照料的： *well-kept gardens* 照料得井井有條的花園 **2** (of a secret 秘密) known only to a few people 保守得好的；嚴守的

ˌwell ˈknown 0‑w *adj.*

1 0‑w known about by a lot of people 眾所周知的；著名的；出名的 **SYN** **famous**： *a well-known actor* 著名演員 ◇ *His books are not well known.* 他寫的書不太有名。

2 0‑w (of a fact 事實) generally known and accepted 為人所熟知的（或熟悉的、認可的）： *It is a well-known fact that caffeine is a stimulant.* 咖啡因是興奮劑，這是人所共知的事實。

ˌwell ˈmannered *adj.* (*formal*) having good manners 行為端正的；舉止得當的；有禮貌的 SYN **polite** OPP **ill-mannered**

ˌwell ˈmatched *adj.* able to live together, play or fight each other, etc. because they are similar in character, ability, etc. 匹配的；相匹敵的；不相上下的：*a well-matched couple* 天生的一對 ◇ *The two teams were well matched.* 這兩個隊勢均力敵。

ˌwell ˈmeaning *adj.* intending to do what is right and helpful but often not succeeding 出於好心的，好心好意的，善意的（但常事與願違）SYN **well intentioned**：*a well-meaning attempt to be helpful* 嘗試幫忙的善意舉動 ◇ *He's very well meaning.* 他用心良苦。

ˌwell ˈmeant *adj.* done, said, etc. in order to be helpful but often not succeeding 本意良好的，出於好心的，善意的（但常事與願違）：*well-meant comments* 善意的批評 ◇ *His offer was well meant.* 他的提議是出於好心。

well·ness /ˈwelnəs/ *noun* [U] (*especially NAmE*) the state of being healthy 健康

ˌwell-ˈnigh *adv.* (*formal*) almost 幾乎；差不多；可謂：*Defence was well-nigh impossible against such opponents.* 遇到這樣的對手幾乎防不勝防。

ˌwell ˈoff *adj.* **1** (*comparative* **better ˈoff**) having a lot of money 富有的；富裕的 SYN **rich**：*a well-off family* 富裕家庭 ◇ *They are much better off than us.* 他們比我們富得多。➲ SYNONYMS at RICH **2** (*comparative* **better ˈoff**, *superlative* **best ˈoff**) in a good situation 境況良好：*I've got my own room so I'm well off.* 我有自己的房間，所以還不錯。◇ *Some people don't know when they're well off.* 有些人身在福中不知福。OPP **badly off**

IDM **be well ˈoff for sth** (*BrE*) to have enough of sth（某事物）充裕：*We're well off for jobs around here* (= there are many available). 我們這裏工作機會很多。

ˌwell ˈoiled *adj.* operating smoothly and well 運轉順暢的；一帆風順的：*The system ran like a well-oiled machine.* 這個系統運行得就像一台上了油的機器。

ˌwell ˈpaid *adj.* earning or providing a lot of money 報酬（或薪金）豐厚的：*well-paid managers* 高薪經理 ◇ *The job is very well paid.* 這個職位工資很高。

ˌwell preˈserved *adj.* not showing many signs of age; kept in good condition 不顯老的；保養得好的

ˌwell ˈread *adj.* having read many books and therefore having gained a lot of knowledge 博覽群書的；博學的

ˌwell ˈrounded *adj.* **1** having a variety of experiences and abilities and a fully developed personality 全才的；通才的；全面發展的：*well-rounded individuals* 全面發展的人 **2** providing or showing a variety of experience, ability, etc. 全面的；面面俱到的：*a well-rounded education* 通才教育 **3** (of a person's body 人體) pleasantly round in shape 豐滿的

ˌwell ˈrun *adj.* managed smoothly and well 運轉良好的；經營得好的：*a well-run hotel* 經營良好的旅館

ˌwell ˈspoken *adj.* having a way of speaking that is considered correct or elegant 言語得體的；談吐文雅的

W

well·spring /ˈwelsprɪŋ/ *noun* (*literary*) a supply or source of a particular quality, especially one that never ends（永不枯竭的）源泉，來源

ˌwell ˈthought of *adj.* respected, admired and liked 受敬重的；令人欽佩的；受喜愛的：*Their family has always been well thought of around here.* 他們家在這一帶一直頗受敬重。

ˌwell thought ˈout *adj.* carefully planned 經過深思熟慮的；計劃周密的

ˌwell ˈthumbed *adj.* a **well-thumbed** book has been read many times（書）被翻舊了的，翻閱過很多遍的

ˌwell ˈtimed *adj.* done or happening at the right time or at an appropriate time 適時的；不早不晚的 SYN **timely**：*a well-timed intervention* 及時的介入 ◇ *Your remarks were certainly well timed.* 你的話說得確實正是時候。OPP **ill-timed**

ˌwell-to-ˈdo *adj.* having a lot of money 有錢的；富有的；富裕的 SYN **rich, wealthy**：*a well-to-do family* 富裕家庭 ◇ *They're very well-to-do.* 他們很闊綽。

ˌwell ˈtravelled (*BrE*) (*NAmE* **ˌwell ˈtraveled**) *adj.* **1** (of a person 人) having travelled to many different places 旅行經歷豐富的；去過很多地方的 **2** (of a route 路線) used by a lot of people 交通頻繁的；人流量大的

ˌwell ˈtried *adj.* used many times before and known to be successful 屢試不爽的；屢屢證明行之有效的：*a well-tried method* 屢試不爽的方法

ˌwell ˈtrodden *adj.* (*formal*) (of a road or path 道路或小徑) much used 常有人走的

ˌwell ˈturned *adj.* (*formal*) expressed in an elegant way 措辭優雅的：*a well-turned phrase* 文雅的言辭

ˌwell ˈused *adj.* used a lot 使用得多的；頻繁使用的：*a well-used path* 行人很多的小路

ˈwell-wisher *noun* a person who wants to show that they support sb and want them to be happy, successful, etc.（以行動）表示祝願者

ˌwell ˈworn *adj.* **1** worn or used a lot or for a long time 破舊的；破爛不堪的；使用很久的：*a well-worn jacket* 穿得破舊了的夾克 ◇ *Most British visitors beat a well-worn path to the same tourist areas of the US.* 大多數英國遊客總沿着一條老路線參觀相同的美國旅遊景點。**2** (of a phrase, story, etc. 短語、故事等) heard so often that it does not sound interesting any more 聽膩了的；使用過多的；陳腐的 SYN **hackneyed**

welly /ˈweli/ *noun, verb*

■ *noun* (*pl.* **-ies**) (*BrE, informal*) = WELLINGTON：*a pair of green wellies* 一雙綠色的長筒靴

IDM **give it some ˈwelly** (*BrE, informal*) to use a lot of physical effort 用很大的力氣

■ *verb* (**wel·lies, welly·ing, wel·lied, wel·lied**) **~ sth (+ adv./prep.)** (*BrE, informal*) to hit or kick sth very hard 重擊；猛踢：*He wellied the ball over the bar.* 他一腳猛射，球從橫梁上飛出。

Welsh /welʃ/ *noun, adj.*

■ *noun* **1** [U] the Celtic language of Wales 威爾士語：*Do you speak Welsh?* 你說威爾士語嗎？ **2 the Welsh** [pl.] the people of Wales 威爾士人

■ *adj.* of or connected with Wales, its people or its language 威爾士的；威爾士人的；威爾士語的：*Welsh poetry* 威爾士詩歌

welsh /welʃ/ (also **welch**) *verb* [I] **~ (on sb/sth)** (*disapproving, informal*) to not do sth that you have promised to do, for example to not pay money that you owe 說話不算數；賴賬；耍賴皮：*'I'm not in the habit of welshing on deals,' said Don.* 唐說："我做生意沒有說話不算數的習慣。"

the ˌWelsh Asˈsembly (also **the ˌNational Asˌsembly for ˈWales**) *noun* [sing.] the group of people who are elected as a government for Wales with limited independence from the British Parliament that includes the power to make certain laws 威爾士議會

ˌWelsh ˈdresser *noun* (*BrE*) = DRESSER

ˌWelsh ˈrarebit (also **rare·bit**) *noun* [U] (*BrE*) a hot dish of cheese melted on TOAST 威爾士乾酪吐司（麵包片上澆有熔化奶酪）

welt /welt/ *noun* a raised mark on the skin where sth has hit or rubbed you（撞擊或擦傷所致的）紅腫 SYN **weal**

Welt·an·schau·ung /ˈveltænʃaʊʊŋ/ *noun* (*pl.* **Welt·an·schau·ung·en** /-ən/) (from *German, formal*) a particular philosophy or view of life 世界觀；人生觀

wel·ter /ˈweltə(r)/ *noun* [sing.] **~ of sth** (*formal*) a large and confusing amount of sth 雜亂的一堆：*a welter of information* 一大堆雜亂的信息

wel·ter·weight /ˈweltəweɪt; *NAmE* -tərw-/ *noun* a BOXER weighing between 61 and 67 kilograms, heavier than a LIGHTWEIGHT 次中量級拳擊手（體重在 61 至 67 公斤之間）：*a welterweight champion* 次中量級拳擊冠軍

wench /wentʃ/ *noun* (*old use* or *humorous*) a young woman 少婦；少女

wend /wend/ *verb* [T, I] **~ (your way)** (+ **adv./prep.**) (*old use* or *literary*) to move or travel slowly somewhere（緩慢

地）走，去，行，往： *Leo wended his way home through the wet streets.* 利奧沿着潮濕的街道緩緩地朝家走去。

Wendy house /'wendi haʊs/ *noun* (*BrE*) = PLAYHOUSE (2)

went *past tense* of GO

wept *past tense, past part.* of WEEP

were /wə(r); *strong form* wɜː(r)/ ➲ BE

we're /wɪə(r); *NAmE* wɪr/ *short form* we are

weren't /wɜːnt/ *short form* were not

were·wolf /'weəwʊlf; *NAmE* 'werw-/ *noun* (*pl.* **-wolves** /-wʊlvz/) (in stories) a person who sometimes changes into a WOLF, especially at the time of the full moon（傳說中，尤指在月圓時）變成狼的人，狼人

Wer·nicke's area /'wɜːnɪkəz eəriə; 'veənɪkəz; *NAmE* 'wɜːrnɪkəz eriə; 'vern-/ *noun* (*anatomy* 解) an area in the brain concerned with understanding language 韋尼克區（大腦中的語言理解區）

west 0➡ /west/ *noun, adj., adv.*

■ ***noun*** [U, sing.] (*abbr.* **W**) **1** 0➡ (usually **the west**) the direction that you look towards to see the sun go down; one of the four main points of the COMPASS 西；西方：*Which way is west?* 哪邊是西？◇ *Rain is spreading from the west.* 雨正從西邊襲來。◇ *He lives **to the west of*** (= further west than) *the town.* 他住在這個城鎮以西的地方。➲ picture at COMPASS ➲ compare EAST, NORTH, SOUTH **2** 0➡ **the West** Europe, N America and Canada, contrasted with Eastern countries 西方（與東方國家相對照的歐洲和北美）：*I was born in Japan, but I've lived in the West for some years now.* 我出生在日本，但已在西方居住了一些年了。**3 the West** (*NAmE*) the western side of the US 美國西部：*the history of the American West* 美國西部的歷史 ➲ see also MIDWEST, WILD WEST **4 the West** (in the past) Western Europe and N America, when contrasted with the Communist countries of Eastern Europe（舊時與共產黨執政的東歐國家相對照的）西方國家，西歐及北美：*East-West relations* 東西方關係

■ ***adj.*** [only before noun] (*abbr.* **W**) **1** 0➡ in or towards the west 西方的；向西的；西部的：*West Africa* 西非 ◇ *the west coast of Scotland* 蘇格蘭西海岸 **2** 0➡ a west wind blows from the west 西風的；西方吹來的 ➲ compare WESTERLY

■ ***adv.*** 0➡ towards the west 向西；朝西：*This room faces west.* 這個房間朝西。

west·bound /'westbaʊnd/ *adj.* travelling or leading towards the west 西行的；向西的：*westbound traffic* 西行車輛 ◇ *the westbound carriageway of the motorway* 高速公路的西行車道

the ˌWest 'Coast *noun* [sing.] the states on the west coast of the US, especially California 美國西海岸諸州（尤指加利福尼亞州）

the 'West Country *noun* [sing.] the counties in the south-west of England 英格蘭西南部諸郡

the ˌWest 'End *noun* [sing.] the western area of central London where there are many theatres, shops/stores and hotels 西倫敦，倫敦西區（即倫敦市中心西部的戲院、商店和旅館聚集區）

west·er·ly /'westəli; *NAmE* -ərli/ *adj., noun*

■ ***adj.*** **1** [only before noun] in or towards the west 西方的；向西的；西部的：*travelling in a westerly direction* 向西行進 **2** [usually before noun] (of winds 風) blowing from the west 從西方吹來的：*westerly gales* 從西面颳來的大風 ➲ compare WEST

■ ***noun*** (*pl.* **-ies**) a wind that blows from the west 西風：*light westerlies* 微微的西風

west·ern 0➡ /'westən; *NAmE* -ərn/ *adj., noun*

■ ***adj.*** **1** 0➡ [only before noun] (*abbr.* **W**) (also **Western**) located in the west or facing west 西方的；向西的；西部的：*western Spain* 西班牙西部 ◇ *Western Europe* 西歐 ◇ *the western slopes of the mountain* 山的西坡 **2** 0➡ (usually **Western**) connected with the west part of the world, especially Europe and N America 西方的；西方國家的；（尤指）歐美的：*Western art* 西方藝術 ➲ see also COUNTRY AND WESTERN

■ ***noun*** a film/movie or book about life in the western US in the 19th century, usually involving COWBOYS（描寫19 世紀美國西部，尤指有關牛仔生活的）西部電影，西部小説

west·ern·er /'westənə(r); *NAmE* -ərn-/ *noun* **1** a person who comes from or lives in the western part of the world, especially western Europe or N America 西方人；（尤指）歐美人 **2 Westerner** a person who was born in or who lives in western Canada or the US（加拿大或美國）西部人

west·ern·iza·tion (*BrE* also **-isa·tion**) /ˌwestənaɪ'zeɪʃn; *NAmE* -ərnə'z-/ *noun* [U] the process of becoming westernized 西方化；西化；歐美化

west·ern·ize (*BrE* also **-ise**) /'westənaɪz; *NAmE* -ərn-/ *verb* [usually passive] **~ sth** to bring ideas or ways of life that are typical of western Europe and N America to other countries 使西方化；使歐美化：*The islands have been westernized by the growth of tourism.* 旅遊業的增長已經使這些島嶼西方化了。▸ **west·ern·ized, -ised** *adj.*：*a westernized society* 西方化了的社會

west·ern·most /'westənməʊst; *NAmE* -ərnmoʊst/ *adj.* located furthest west 最西的；最西端的；最西部的：*the westernmost tip of the island* 島的最西端

the West Indies /ˌwest 'ɪndɪz; -diːz/ *noun* [pl.] several groups of islands between the Caribbean and the Atlantic, that include the Antilles and the Bahamas 西印度群島（位於加勒比海和大西洋之間，包括安的列斯群島和巴哈馬群島）▸ **ˌWest 'Indian** *adj.* **ˌWest 'Indian** *noun*

West·min·ster /'westmɪnstə(r)/ *noun* [U] the British parliament and government 威斯敏斯特（英國議會及政府）：*The rumours were still circulating at Westminster.* 當時謠言依然在英國議會和政府流傳。**ORIGIN** From the name of the part of London with the Houses of Parliament, Downing Street and many government offices. 源自倫敦威斯敏斯特區，為英國議會大廈、唐寧街及許多政府機關所在地。

ˌwest-north-'west *noun* [sing.] (*abbr.* **WNW**) the direction at an equal distance between west and north-west 西西北；西北西 ▸ **ˌwest-north-'west** *adv.*

the 'West Side *noun* [sing.] the western part of Manhattan in New York City which includes Broadway and Central Park 曼哈頓西區（在美國紐約市，包括百老匯和中央公園）

ˌwest-south-'west *noun* [sing.] (*abbr.* **WSW**) the direction at an equal distance between west and south-west 西西南；西南西 ▸ **ˌwest-south-'west** *adv.*

west·wards /'westwədz; *NAmE* -wərdz/ (also **west·ward**) *adv.* towards the west 向西；朝西：*to turn westwards* 向西轉 ▸ **west·ward** *adj.*：*in a westward direction* 方向朝西

wet 0➡ /wet/ *adj., verb, noun*

■ ***adj.*** (**wet·ter**, **wet·test**) **1** 0➡ covered with or containing liquid, especially water 潮的；濕的；潮濕的：*wet clothes* 濕衣服 ◇ *wet grass* 濕草 ◇ *You'll **get wet*** (= in the rain) *if you go out now.* 你要是現在出去會被淋濕的。◇ *Try not to get your shoes wet.* 盡量別弄濕了鞋子。◇ *His face was wet with tears.* 他淚流滿面。◇ *We were all **soaking wet*** (= extremely wet). 我們都成了落湯雞。◇ *Her hair was still **dripping wet**.* 她的頭髮仍然濕淋淋的。◇ *My shirt was **wet through*** (= completely wet). 我的襯衣濕透了。**2** 0➡ (of weather, etc. 天氣等) with rain 有雨的；下雨的：*a wet day* 下雨天 ◇ *a wet climate* 多雨的氣候 ◇ ***It's wet** outside.* 外邊下雨了。◇ *It's going to be wet tomorrow.* 明天有雨。◇ *It was the wettest October for many years.* 這是多年來下雨最多的一個十月份。**3** 0➡ (of paint, ink, etc. 油漆、墨水等) not yet dry 尚未乾的：*Keep off! Wet paint.* 油漆未乾，請勿靠近！**4** if a child or its NAPPY/DIAPER is **wet**, its nappy/diaper is full of URINE（兒童）尿濕了尿布的；（尿布）尿濕的 **5** (*BrE*) (of a person 人) (*informal, disapproving*) lacking a strong character 窩囊的；沒有骨氣的 **SYN** **feeble**, **wimpish**：*'Don't be so wet,' she laughed.* "別這麼窩囊。" 她笑道。

▸ **wetly** *adv.* **wet·ness** *noun* [U]

IDM **all 'wet** (*NAmE, informal*) completely wrong 完全錯的；大錯特錯 **(still) ˌwet behind the 'ears** (*informal,*

W

disapproving) young and without much experience 乳臭未乾；少不更事；沒見過世面 SYN **naive** ➲ more at FOOT *n.*

■ ***verb*** (**wet·ting**, **wet**, **wet** or **wet·ting**, **wet·ted**, **wet·ted**) **~ sth** to make sth wet 使潮濕；把…弄濕：*Wet the brush slightly before putting it in the paint.* 把刷子弄濕點再去沾油漆。

IDM **wet the/your 'bed** [no passive] to URINATE in your bed by accident 尿牀：*It is quite common for small children to wet their beds.* 小孩尿牀是常有的事。 **'wet yourself | wet your 'pants/'knickers** [no passive] to URINATE in your underwear by accident 尿褲子

■ ***noun*** **1 the wet** [sing.] wet weather; rain 雨天；雨：*Come in out of the wet.* 快進來，別淋着。 **2** [U] liquid, especially water 液體；（尤指）水：*The dog shook the wet from its coat.* 狗抖掉了毛上的水。 **3** [C] (*BrE, disapproving*) a conservative politician who supports MODERATE policies rather than extreme ones 保守黨溫和派成員：*Tory wets* 保守黨的溫和派 **4** [C] (*BrE, informal, disapproving*) a person who lacks a strong character 窩囊廢；軟骨頭 SYN **wimp**

Synonyms 同義詞辨析

wet

moist • damp • soaked • drenched • saturated

These words all describe things covered with or full of liquid, especially water. 以上各詞均形容物體等潮的、濕的。

wet covered with or full of liquid, especially water 指潮的、濕的、潮濕的：*The car had skidded on the wet road.* 汽車在濕路上打滑了。◇ *You'll get wet* (= in the rain) *if you go out now.* 你現在出去就會被淋濕。

moist slightly wet, often in a way that is pleasant or useful 指微濕的、濕潤的、潤澤的，常指是舒適或有益的：*a lovely rich moist cake* 可愛的鬆軟味濃的蛋糕

damp slightly wet, often in a way that is unpleasant 指微濕的、潮濕的、濕度大的，常指令人不舒服的：*The cottage was cold and damp.* 這小屋又冷又濕。

soaked (*rather informal*) very wet 指濕透了：*You're soaked through!* (= completely wet) 你都濕透了！

drenched very wet 指濕透了：*We were caught in the storm and came home drenched to the skin.* 我們遇上了暴雨，回到家時渾身濕透了。

SOAKED OR DRENCHED? 用 soaked 還是 drenched？

Both of these words can be used with *with* or *in*. 上述兩詞均可與 with 或 in 連用：*soaked/drenched with/in sweat/blood* 大汗淋漓；浸透了鮮血 **Soaked** but not usually **drenched** can also be used before a noun. * soaked 亦可用於名詞前，drenched 通常不這樣用：*their soaked clothes* 他們濕透了的衣服 ◇ ~~*their drenched clothes*~~

saturated very wet 指濕透、浸透：*The ground is completely saturated: it would be pointless to plant anything.* 地已經浸透，種什麼東西都是白搭。

PATTERNS

- wet/moist/damp/soaked/drenched/saturated **with** sth
- soaked/drenched **in** sth
- sb's **coat/shirt/shoes/clothes/hair** is/are wet/damp/soaked/drenched
- wet/moist/damp/saturated **ground/earth**
- to **get** wet/moist/damp/soaked/drenched/saturated

wet·back /'wetbæk/ *noun* (*US, taboo, slang*) an offensive word for a Mexican person, especially one who enters the US illegally 濕背人（從墨西哥到美國的移民，尤指偷渡者）

,wet 'blanket *noun* (*informal, disapproving*) a person who is not enthusiastic about anything and who stops other people from enjoying themselves 潑冷水的人；掃興的人

'wet dock *noun* a place for ships to stay in order to be repaired, have goods put onto them, etc., in which there is enough water for the ship to float 濕船塢 ➲ compare DRY DOCK

,wet 'dream *noun* a sexually exciting dream that a man has that results in an ORGASM 夢遺；（夢中）遺精

'wet fish *noun* [U] (*BrE*) fresh raw fish for sale in a shop, etc.（供出售的）鮮魚

wet·land /'wetlənd/ *noun* [C, U] (also **wetlands** [pl.]) an area of wet land 濕地；沼澤地：*The wetlands are home to a large variety of wildlife.* 濕地是多種野生動物的棲息地。 ▸ **wet·land** *adj.* [only before noun]：*wetland birds* 沼澤地區的鳥

'wet look *noun* [sing.] the appearance of hair being shiny and wet, obtained by using hair GEL or by treating it with chemicals（頭髮的）濕潤亮澤，濕亮感 ▸ **'wet-look** *adj.*：*wet-look hair gel* 保濕亮髮膠

'wet nurse *noun* (usually in the past) a woman employed to feed another woman's baby with her own breast milk（通常指舊時的）奶媽，乳母

'wet room *noun* (*BrE*) a bathroom in which the shower is not separated from the rest of the room 非乾濕分離衞生間；淋浴洗手間

wet·suit /'wetsu:t; *BrE* also -sju:t/ *noun* a piece of clothing made of rubber that fits the whole body closely, worn by people swimming underwater or sailing 潛水衣 ➲ VISUAL VOCAB page V40

wet·ware /'wetweə(r); *NAmE* -wer/ *noun* [U] (*computing* 計) the human brain, considered as a computer program or system 濕件，濕體（被視為計算機程序或系統的人腦）

we've /wi:v; wiv/ *short form* we have

whack /wæk/ *verb, noun*

■ ***verb*** **1 ~ sb/sth** (*informal*) to hit sb/sth very hard 猛打；重擊；狠揍：*She whacked him with her handbag.* 她用手提包狠狠地打他。◇ *James whacked the ball over the net.* 詹姆斯猛力把球擊過網去。 **2 ~ sth + adv./prep.** (*informal*) to put sth somewhere without much care 草草放下：*Just whack your bags in the corner.* 就把你的包丟在角落裏吧。 **3 ~ sb** (*NAmE, slang*) to murder sb 謀殺

■ ***noun*** [usually sing.] (*informal*) **1** the act of hitting sb/sth hard; the sound made by this 重擊；重擊聲：*He gave the ball a good whack.* 他猛擊了一下球。◇ *I heard the whack of the bullet hitting the wood.* 我聽到子彈砰的一聲擊中了木頭。 **2** (*BrE*) a share of sth; an amount of sth 份兒；一份；量：*Don't leave all the work to her. Everyone should do their fair whack.* 別把所有的工作都讓她做。大家應合理地分擔一下。◇ *You have to pay the full whack. There are no reductions.* 你得付全額。沒有折扣。◇ *He charges **top whack*** (= the highest amount possible). 他索要最高價。

IDM **out of 'whack** (*informal, especially NAmE*) **1** no longer correct or working properly 不對頭；有毛病；運行不正常：*The system is clearly out of whack.* 這個系統明顯是運行不正常。◇ *All the traveling had thrown my body out of whack.* 這一路旅行已經使我的身體出了毛病。 **2** not agreeing with or the same as sth else 不一致；不一樣：*Expectations and reality got out of whack.* 期望和現實之間出現了差距。

whacked /wækt/ (also **,whacked 'out**) *adj.* [not usually before noun] (*BrE, informal*) very tired 筋疲力盡；累垮了：*I'm whacked!* 我累死了！

whack·ing /'wækɪŋ/ (also **'whacking great**) *adj.* (*BrE, informal*) used to emphasize how big or how much sth is（強調體積或數額）巨大的，極大的 SYN **whopping**：*a whacking great hole in the roof* 房頂上一個巨大的窟窿 ◇ *They were fined a whacking £100 000.* 他們被罰了 10 萬英鎊的巨款。

whacko (also **wacko**) /'wækəʊ; *NAmE* -koʊ/ *adj.* (*informal*) crazy 瘋狂的；發狂的

whacky = WACKY

whale /weɪl/ *noun* a very large animal that lives in the sea and looks like a very large fish. There are several types of whale, some of which are hunted. 鯨：*whale meat* 鯨肉 ➲ see also BLUE WHALE, KILLER WHALE, PILOT WHALE, SPERM WHALE

IDM **have a 'whale of a time** (*informal*) to enjoy yourself very much; to have a very good time 玩得很痛快；過得非常快活

whale·bone /ˈweɪlbəʊn; *NAmE* -boʊn/ *noun* [U] a thin hard substance found in the upper JAW of some types of whale, used in the past to make some clothes stiffer 鯨鬚，鯨骨（幾種鯨上腭的角質薄片，舊時用以支撐衣服）

whaler /ˈweɪlə(r)/ *noun* **1** a ship used for hunting whales 捕鯨船 **2** a person who hunts whales 捕鯨人

whal·ing /ˈweɪlɪŋ/ *noun* [U] the activity or business of hunting and killing WHALES 捕鯨（業）；鯨加工（業）

wham /wæm/ *exclamation* (*informal*) **1** used to represent the sound of a sudden, loud hit （突然的重擊聲）砰，嘭：*The bombs went down—wham!—right on target.* 炸彈落了下來，砰！正好擊中目標。 **2** used to show that sth that is unexpected has suddenly happened （表示意外的事情突然發生）：*I saw him yesterday and—wham!—I realized I was still in love with him.* 我昨天看到他了。我猛地一下子意識到我仍然愛着他。

whammy /ˈwæmi/ *noun* (*pl.* **-ies**) (*informal*) an unpleasant situation or event that causes problems for sb/sth 晦氣；倒霉事：*With this government we've had a **double whammy** of tax increases and benefit cuts.* 自從這任政府上台以來，我們又是增加稅收又是減少補貼，倒了雙倍的霉。 **ORIGIN** From the 1950s American cartoon *Li'l Abner*, in which one of the characters could **shoot a whammy** (put a curse on sb) by pointing a finger with one eye open, or a **double whammy** with both eyes open. 源自 20 世紀 50 年代美國的漫畫《利爾 • 阿布納》。其中一個人物睜一隻眼時用手指指着可施一個詛咒，睜兩隻眼睛可施兩個詛咒。

wha·nau /ˈfɑːnaʊ/ *noun* (*pl.* **wha·nau**) (*NZE*) a family or community of related families who live together in the same area （生活在同一地區的）大家庭，家族

wharf /wɔːf; *NAmE* wɔːrf/ *noun* (*pl.* **wharves** /wɔːvz; *NAmE* wɔːrvz/ or **wharfs**) a flat structure built beside the sea or a river where boats can be tied up and goods unloaded 碼頭

what 🔑 /wɒt; *NAmE* wɑːt; wʌt/ *pron., det.*
1 🔑 used in questions to ask for particular information about sb/sth 什麼：*What is your name?* 你叫什麼名字？◇ *What* (= what job) *does he do?* 他是做什麼工作的？◇ *What time is it?* 現在什麼時候了？◇ *What kind of music do you like?* 你喜歡什麼音樂？ ➲ compare WHICH (1)
2 🔑 the thing or things that; whatever …的事物；無論什麼；凡是…的事物：*What you need is a good meal.* 你需要的是一頓美餐。◇ *Nobody knows what will happen next.* 沒有人知道接下來將會發生什麼事。◇ *I spent what little time I had with my family.* 我僅有的一點兒時間都和家人在一起度過了。 **3** 🔑 used to say that you think that sth is especially good, bad, etc. 多麼；真；太：*What awful weather!* 天氣太糟糕了！◇ *What a beautiful house!* 多麼漂亮的房子啊！

IDM **and 'what not | and what 'have you** (*informal*) and other things of the same type 以及其他同樣的東西；諸如此類：*It's full of old toys, books and what not.* 這裏全都是舊玩具、書籍，以及諸如此類的東西。 **get/give sb what 'for** (*BrE, informal*) to be punished/punish sb severely（受到）嚴懲；（被）痛打一頓，申斥一頓：*I'll give her what for if she does that again.* 她若再這樣做，看我怎麼收拾她。 **or 'what** (*informal*) **1** used to emphasize your opinion （強調看法）：*Is he stupid or what?* 他真是傻透了。 **2** used when you are not sure about sth （表示不肯定）還是別的什麼：*I don't know if he's a teacher or what.* 我不知道他是個教師還是別的什麼。◇ *Are we going now or what?* 我們現在走還是不走？ **what?** (*informal*) **1** 🔑 used when you have not heard or have not understood sth （沒聽見或沒聽懂時說）什麼：*What? I can't hear you.* 什麼？我聽不見你說話。 **2** 🔑 used to show that you have heard sb and to ask what they want （聽到對方的話並問他們要什麼）什麼事，要什麼：*'Mummy!' 'What?' 'I'm thirsty.'* "媽咪！" "什麼事？" "我口渴。" **3** 🔑 used to express surprise or anger （驚訝或憤怒時說）什麼，竟有這種事，真的：*'It will cost $500.' 'What?'* "這東西要花 500 元。" "真的？" ◇ *'I asked her to marry me.' '**You what?**'* "我向她求婚了。" "你說什麼？" **'what about ...?** (*informal*) **1** 🔑 used to make a suggestion （提出建議）…怎麼樣：*What about a trip to France?* 到法國去旅遊一趟如何？ **2** 🔑 used to introduce sb/sth into the conversation （用以引出話題）…怎麼樣：*What about you, Joe? Do you like football?* 你怎麼樣，喬？你喜歡足球嗎？ **'what-d'you-call-him/-her/-it/-them | 'what's-his/-her/-its/-their-name** used instead of a name that you cannot remember （記不得名字時說）你叫他（或她、它、他們）什麼來着：*She's just gone out with old what-d'you-call-him.* 她剛和老…，你叫他什麼來着，一塊出去的。 **what for?** 🔑 for what purpose or reason? 為何目的；為何理由：*What is this tool for?* 這個工具是幹什麼用的？◇ *What did you do that for* (= why did you do that)? 你為何做那事？◇ *'I need to see a doctor.' 'What for?'* "我得去看醫生。" "看什麼病？" **what if ...?** 🔑 what would happen if? 要是…會怎麼樣呢：*What if the train is late?* 火車要是晚點會怎麼樣呢？◇ *What if she forgets to bring it?* 要是她忘記帶來，會怎麼樣呢？ **what 'of it?** (*informal*) used when admitting that sth is true, to ask why it should be considered important（承認某事屬實，想知道為何重要）那又怎麼樣呢，那有什麼關係呢：*Yes, I wrote the article. What of it?* 是的，文章是我寫的。那又怎麼樣呢？ **what's ˌup with 'that?** (*especially NAmE*) used to suggest that sth you have heard is a stupid idea or does not make sense 那是什麼回事（表示聽到的話愚蠢或無聊）：*They dropped their best player. What's up with that?* 他們把最佳隊員棄用了。那是什麼回事？ **what's 'what** (*informal*) what things are useful, important, etc. 什麼事物有用（或重要等）：*She certainly knows what's what.* 她當然知道輕重緩急。 **what's with sb?** (*NAmE, informal*) used to ask why sb is behaving in a strange way （詢問某人為何行為古怪）…怎麼啦：*What's with you? You haven't said a word all morning.* 你怎麼啦？整個上午你一句話都沒說。 **what's with sth?** (*NAmE, informal*) used to ask the reason for sth （詢問原因）為什麼，怎麼：*What's with all this walking? Can't we take a cab?* 怎麼就這麼一直走？難道我們就不能打輛出租車嗎？ **what with sth** used to list the various reasons for sth （列舉各種理由）由於，因為：*What with the cold weather and my bad leg, I haven't been out for weeks.* 由於天氣很冷，我的腿又不好，我已經好幾個星期沒有出門了。

whatch·am·acall·it /ˈwɒtʃəməkɔːlɪt; *NAmE* ˈwɑːt-; ˈwʌt-/ *noun* (*informal*) used when you cannot think of the name of sth （想不起名稱時說）叫什麼來着：*Have you got a whatchamacallit? You know ... a screwdriver?* 你有一把…叫什麼來着的？你知道的…螺絲刀？

what·ever 🔑 /wɒtˈevə(r); *NAmE* wət-; wɑːt-/ *det., pron., adv.*

▪ ***det., pron.*** **1** 🔑 any or every; anything or everything 任何；每一；任何事物；一切事物：*Take whatever action is needed.* 採取任何必要的行動。◇ *Do whatever you like.* 你喜歡做什麼就做什麼。 **2** 🔑 used when you are saying that it does not matter what sb does or what happens, because the result will be the same （表示做什麼或發生什麼都沒關係，因結果都一樣）無論什麼，不管什麼：*Whatever decision he made I would support it.* 無論他作出什麼決定我都會支持的。◇ *You have our support, whatever you decide.* 不管你做何決定，都會得到我們的支持。 **3** (*especially BrE*) used in questions to express surprise or confusion（用於問句，表示驚訝或困惑）到底是什麼，究竟是什麼：*Whatever do you mean?* 你究竟是什麼意思？◇ *Chocolate-flavoured carrots! **Whatever next?*** 巧克力味的胡蘿蔔！接下來到底還想吃什麼？ **4** (*informal, ironic*) used as a reply to tell sb that you do not care what happens or that you are not interested in what they are talking about（用於回應，表示不在乎或不感興趣）或許吧，無所謂：*'You should try a herbal remedy.' 'Yeah, whatever.'* "你應該試一試草藥療法。" "是啊，或許吧。" **5** (*informal*) used to say that you do not mind what you do, have, etc. and that anything is acceptable （表示不在乎，什麼都可接受）什麼都可以：*'What would* *you like to do today?' 'Whatever.'* "今天你想做什麼呢？" "做什麼都可以。"

IDM **or what'ever** (*informal*) or sth of a similar type 諸如此類；等等：*It's the same in any situation: in a prison, hospital or whatever.* 這在什麼場合都一樣：在監獄、醫院或諸如此類的地方。 **what'ever you do** used to warn sb not to do sth under any circumstances（警告某人決不要做某事）無論如何：*Don't tell Paul, whatever you do!* 無論如何都不要告訴保羅！

■ *adv.* **1** (also **what·so·ever**) **no, nothing, none, etc. ~** not at all; not of any kind 一點兒都（不）；絲毫（不）；什麼都（沒有）：*They received no help whatever.* 他們沒有得到一點兒幫助。◇ *'Is there any doubt about it?' 'None whatsoever.'* "對此有懷疑嗎？" "絲毫沒有。" **2** (*informal*) used to say that it does not matter what sb does, or what happens, because the result will be the same 不管發生什麼：*We told him we'd back him whatever.* 我們告訴他，在任何情況下我們都會支持他。

what·not /ˈwɒtnɒt; *NAmE* ˈwɑːtnɑːt/ *noun* [U] **and ~** (*informal*) used when you are referring to sth, but are not being exact and do not mention its name（由於拿不準而不指名：某種東西，不可名狀的東西：*It's a new firm. They make toys and whatnot.* 這是家新的公司。他們製作玩具和別的小玩意兒。

whats·it /ˈwɒtsɪt; *NAmE* ˈwɑːt-; ˈwʌt-/ *noun* (*informal, especially BrE*) used when you cannot think of the word or name you want, or do not want to use a particular word（想不起名稱或不想指明時說）什麼來着，某某玩意兒：*I've got to make a whatsit for the party. That's it—a flan.* 我得給聚會製作一個什麼東西來着。想起來了，一個果餡餅。

wheat /wiːt/ *noun* [U] a plant grown for its grain that is used to produce the flour for bread, cakes, PASTA, etc.; the grain of this plant 小麥；小麥籽：*wheat flour* 小麥製的麵粉 ➲ COLLOCATIONS at FARMING ➲ VISUAL VOCAB page V32

IDM **sort out/separate the ˌwheat from the ˈchaff** to distinguish useful or valuable people or things from ones that are not useful or have no value 識別優劣；分清好壞；去蕪存菁

the ˈWheat Belt *noun* [sing.] the western central region of the US including the Great Plains where wheat is an important crop 小麥帶（包括大平原在內的美國中西部小麥產區）

wheat·germ /ˈwiːtdʒɜːm; *NAmE* -dʒɜːrm/ *noun* [U] the centre of the wheat grain, which is especially good for your health 麥芽；小麥胚芽

wheat·meal /ˈwiːtmiːl/ *noun* [U] a type of flour made from wheat, that uses more of the grain than WHITE FLOUR 小麥粉；全麥麵粉

whee /wiː/ *exclamation* used to express excitement（激動時發出的聲音）喲，啊

whee·dle /ˈwiːdl/ *verb* (*disapproving*) to persuade sb to give you sth or do sth by saying nice things that you do not mean（用言語）哄 SYN **coax**：**~ sth (out of sb)** *The kids can always wheedle money out of their father.* 孩子們總是能從父親那裏哄出錢來。◇ **~ sb into doing sth** *She wheedled me into lending her my new coat.* 她用花言巧語哄我把新大衣借給了她。◇ **+ speech** *'Come on, Em,' he wheedled.* "快點，愛瑪。" 他哄道。

W

wheel 0‑ /wiːl/ *noun, verb*

■ *noun*

▸ **ON/IN VEHICLES** 車輛 **1** 0‑ [C] one of the round objects under a car, bicycle, bus, etc. that turns when it moves 輪；車輪；輪子：*He braked suddenly, causing the front wheels to skid.* 他猛然剎車，使得前車輪打滑了。◇ *One of the boys was pushing the other along in a little box* ***on wheels***. 一個男孩用下面裝着輪子的小箱子推着另一個男孩。 **2** 0‑ [C, usually sing.] the round object used to steer a car, etc. or ship（汽車等的）方向盤；（輪船的）舵輪：*This is the first time I've sat* ***behind the wheel*** *since the accident.* 這是出車禍以來我頭一次坐在方向盤前。◇ *A car swept past with Laura* ***at the wheel***. 勞拉駕車疾馳而過。◇ *Do you want to* ***take the wheel*** (= drive) *now?* 你現在想開車嗎？ ➲ see also HELM, STEERING WHEEL **3 wheels** [pl.] (*informal*) a car 汽車：*At last he had his own wheels.* 他終於有了自己的汽車。

▸ **IN MACHINE** 機器 **4** 0‑ [C] a flat round part in a machine 機輪：*gear wheels* 齒輪 ➲ see also CARTWHEEL, CATHERINE WHEEL, FERRIS WHEEL, MILL WHEEL, SPINNING WHEEL, WATERWHEEL

▸ **ORGANIZATION/SYSTEM** 組織；系統 **5 wheels** [pl.] **~ (of sth)** an organization or a system that seems to work like a complicated machine that is difficult to understand 錯綜複雜的機構（或系統）：***the wheels of bureaucracy/commerce/government, etc.*** 複雜的官僚、商務、政府等機構 ◇ *It was Rob's idea. I merely* ***set the wheels in motion*** (= started the process). 這是羅布的主意。我只不過是讓它運作起來而已。

▸ **-WHEELED** 有…輪 **6** (in adjectives 構成形容詞) having the number or type of wheels mentioned 有…輪的：*a sixteen-wheeled lorry* 十六輪大卡車

▸ **-WHEELER** 有…輪子的車 **7** (in nouns 構成名詞) a car, bicycle, etc. with the number of wheels mentioned 有…輪子的汽車（或自行車等）：*a three-wheeler* 三輪機動車

IDM **ˌwheels within ˈwheels** a situation which is difficult to understand because it involves complicated or secret processes and decisions 錯綜複雜；盤根錯節：*There are wheels within wheels in this organization—you never really know what is going on.* 這個機構裏錯綜複雜，你永遠搞不清到底是怎麼回事。➲ more at COG, GREASE *v.*, OIL *v.*, REINVENT, SHOULDER *n.*, SPOKE

■ *verb*

▸ **MOVE STH WITH WHEELS** 用輪子移動 **1** [T] **~ sth (+ adv./prep.)** to push or pull sth that has wheels 推（或拉）有輪之物：*She wheeled her bicycle across the road.* 她推着自行車穿過了馬路。 **2** [T] **~ sb/sth (+ adv./prep.)** to move sb/sth that is in or on sth that has wheels 用有輪之物推動（或拉動、移動）…：*The nurse wheeled him along the corridor.* 護士推着他沿樓道走。

▸ **MOVE IN CIRCLE** 旋轉 **3** [I] **(+ adv./prep.)** to move or fly in a circle 轉動；旋轉；打轉；盤旋：*Birds wheeled above us in the sky.* 鳥兒在我們上空盤旋。

▸ **TURN QUICKLY** 快速轉向 **4** [I, T] to turn quickly or suddenly and face the opposite direction; to make sb/sth do this（使）迅速轉身，猛然轉身：**(+ adv./prep.)** *She wheeled around and started running.* 她突然轉身就跑。◇ **~ sb/sth (+ adv./prep.)** *He wheeled his horse back to the gate.* 他突然掉轉馬頭返回到大門。

IDM **ˌwheel and ˈdeal** (usually used in the progressive tenses 通常用於進行時) to do a lot of complicated deals in business or politics, often in a dishonest way（在商界或政界）工於心計；（以不正當的方式）進行紛繁複雜的交易，周旋

PHR V **ˌwheel sth↔ˈout** to show or use sth to help you do sth, even when it has often been seen or heard before 故伎重演：*They wheeled out the same old arguments we'd heard so many times before.* 他們又彈起了我們聽過多次的老調。

ˈwheel arch *noun* a space in the body of a vehicle over a wheel, shaped like an ARCH 車輪拱罩部份；輪拱

wheel·bar·row /ˈwiːlbærəʊ; *NAmE* -roʊ/ (also **bar·row**) *noun* a large open container with a wheel and two handles that you use outside to carry things 獨輪車；手推車 ➲ VISUAL VOCAB page V19

wheel·base /ˈwiːlbeɪs/ *noun* [sing.] (*technical* 術語) the distance between the front and back wheels of a car or other vehicle（汽車或其他機動車輛的）軸距；（機車的）輪組定距

wheel·chair /ˈwiːltʃeə(r); *NAmE* -tʃer/ *noun* a special chair with wheels, used by people who cannot walk because of illness, an accident, etc. 輪椅：*Does the hotel have* ***wheelchair access***? 這家旅館有輪椅通道嗎？◇ *He's been* ***confined to a wheelchair*** *since the accident.* 他從車禍以後就離不開輪椅了。◇ *wheelchair users* 坐輪椅的人

ˈwheel clamp *noun* (*BrE*) = CLAMP *n.* (2), DENVER BOOT

wheeler-dealer /ˌwiːlə ˈdiːlə(r)/ *noun* (*informal*) a person who does a lot of complicated deals in business or politics, often in a dishonest way（商界或政界的）工於心計的人，進行複雜交易的人

wheel·house /ˈwiːlhaʊs/ *noun* a small CABIN with walls and a roof on a ship where the person steering stands at the wheel（船上的）操舵室，駕駛室

wheelie /ˈwiːli/ *noun* (*informal*) a trick that you can do on a bicycle or motorcycle by balancing on the back wheel, with the front wheel off the ground（騎自行車或摩托車將前輪抬起的）後輪支撐車技：*to do a wheelie* 做自行車前輪抬起後輪平衡的特技

ˈwheelie bin *noun* (*BrE, informal*) a large container with a lid and wheels, that you keep outside your house and use for putting rubbish in（帶蓋的）有輪大垃圾筒

wheel·wright /ˈwiːlraɪt/ *noun* a person whose job is making and repairing wheels, especially wooden ones 車輪修造工（尤指木輪的）

wheeze /wiːz/ *verb, noun*

■ ***verb*** [I, T] to breathe noisily and with difficulty 喘；喘息；喘鳴：*He was coughing and wheezing all night.* 他整夜又咳嗽又喘。◇ **+ speech** *'I have a chest infection,' she wheezed.* "我胸部受到了感染。"她呼哧呼哧地說。

■ ***noun*** [usually sing.] **1** the high whistling sound that your chest makes when you cannot breathe easily 喘息聲；喘鳴聲；呼吸發出的哨音；呼哧呼哧聲 **2** (*old-fashioned, BrE, informal*) a clever trick or plan 花招；計謀

wheezy /ˈwiːzi/ *adj.* making the high whistling sound that your chest makes when you cannot breathe easily 喘息的；喘鳴的；氣喘吁吁的；呼哧呼哧響的：*I'm wheezy today.* 我今天感到喘不上氣來。◇ *a wheezy cough* 喘鳴性咳 ▸ **wheez·ily** /-ɪli/ *adv.* **wheezi·ness** *noun* [U]

whelk /welk/ *noun* a small SHELLFISH that can be eaten 蛾螺（有些可食用）

whelp /welp/ *noun, verb*

■ ***noun*** (*technical* 術語) a young animal of the dog family; a PUPPY or CUB 小狗；幼犬；（犬科動物的）幼獸

■ ***verb*** [I, T] **~** (sth) (*formal*) (of a female dog 母狗) to give birth to a PUPPY or PUPPIES 下（崽）；產（仔）

when 🔑 /wen/ *adv., pron., conj.*

■ ***adv.*** **1** 🔑 (used in questions 用於問句) at what time; on what occasion 什麼時候；何時；什麼情況下；什麼場合下：*When did you last see him?* 你上次什麼時候見到他的？◇ *When can I see you?* 我什麼時候可以見你？◇ *When* (= in what circumstances) *would such a solution be possible?* 什麼情況下可以這麼解決？ **2** 🔑 used after an expression of time to mean 'at which' or 'on which'（用於時間的表達方式之後）在那時，其時：*Sunday is the only day when I can relax.* 星期日是我唯一可以休息的日子。◇ *There are times when I wonder why I do this job.* 有時候我也不明白自己為什麼要幹這個工作。 **3** 🔑 at which time; on which occasion 其時；當時；當場：*The last time I went to Scotland was in May, when the weather was beautiful.* 我上次去蘇格蘭是在五月份，那時的天氣好極了。

■ ***pron.*** 🔑 what/which time 什麼時候；何時：*Until when can you stay?* 你可以待到什麼時候？◇ *'I've got a new job.' 'Since when?'* "我有了份新工作。" "什麼時候開始的？"

■ ***conj.*** **1** 🔑 at or during the time that 在…時候；當…時；在…期間：*I loved history when I was at school.* 我上學時喜歡歷史。 **2** 🔑 after 在…之後：*Call me when you've finished.* 你完成後就打電話給我。 **3** 🔑 at any time that; whenever 在任何…時候：*Can you spare five minutes when it's convenient?* 方便時能佔用你五分鐘時間嗎？ **4** 🔑 just after which 一…就；剛…就：*He had just drifted off to sleep when the phone rang.* 他剛睡着電話鈴就響了。 **5** 🔑 considering that 考慮到；既然：*How can they expect to learn anything when they never listen?* 既然他們從不聽講，他們怎麼能指望學到東西呢？ **6** although 雖然；然而；可是：*She claimed to be 18, when I know she's only 16.* 她自稱是 18 歲，可是我知道她才 16 歲。 IDM see AS *conj.*

whence /wens/ *adv.* (*old use*) from where 從何處；從哪裏：*They returned whence they had come.* 他們從哪裏來又回到哪裏去了。

when·ever 🔑 /wenˈevə(r)/ *conj., adv.*

■ ***conj.*** **1** 🔑 at any time that; on any occasion that 在任何…的時候；無論何時；在任何…的情況下：*You can ask for help whenever you need it.* 你如果需要幫助隨時可以提出來。 **2** 🔑 every time that 每當；每次：*Whenever she comes, she brings a friend.* 她每次來都帶着個朋友。◇ *The roof leaks whenever it rains.* 屋頂每逢下雨就漏。◇ *We try to help* ***whenever possible.*** 只要有可能我們都盡量幫忙。 **3** used when the time when sth happens is not important 別的什麼時候（也可以）；任何時間（都行）：*'When do you need it by?' 'Saturday or Sunday. Whenever.'* "你什麼時候需要這個東西？" "星期六或星期日。哪一天都行。" ◇ *It's not urgent—we can do it next week or whenever.* 這不着急，我們可以在下星期或別的什麼時候做。

■ ***adv.*** used in questions to mean 'when', expressing surprise（用於問句，表示驚奇）究竟什麼時候：*Whenever did you find time to do all that cooking?* 你怎麼有時間做了這麼多菜？

where 🔑 /weə(r); *NAmE* wer/ *adv., conj.*

■ ***adv.*** **1** 🔑 in or to what place or situation 在哪裏；到哪裏；處於哪種情形：*Where do you live?* 你住在哪兒？◇ *I wonder where they will take us to.* 我不知道他們要把我們帶到哪裏去。◇ *Where* (= at what point) *did I go wrong in my calculations?* 我計算中什麼地方出了差錯？◇ *Where* (= in what book, newspaper, etc.) *did you read that?* 你在哪兒讀到這個的？◇ *Just where* (= to what situation or final argument) *is all this leading us?* 這一切到底是要將我們引向何處？ **2** 🔑 used after words or phrases that refer to a place or situation to mean 'at, in or to which'（用於表示地點或情況的詞語後）在那（地方），到那（地方）：*It's one of the few countries where people drive on the left.* 這是為數不多的幾個靠左行駛的國家之一。 **3** 🔑 the place or situation in which 在那裏；在該處；在該情況下：*We then moved to Paris, where we lived for six years.* 我們隨後移居巴黎，在那裏住了六年。

■ ***conj.*** (in) the place or situation in which （在）…的地方；（在）…情況下：*This is where I live.* 這是我住的地方。◇ *Sit where I can see you.* 坐在我能看到你的地方。◇ *Where people were concerned, his threshold of boredom was low.* 涉及人的事情，他便極易感到厭煩。◇ *That's where* (= the point in the argument at which) *you're wrong.* 這就是你的錯誤所在。

where·abouts *noun, adv.*

■ ***noun*** /ˈweərəbaʊts; *NAmE* ˈwer-/ [U+sing./pl. v.] the place where sb/sth is （人或物）所在的地方；下落；行踪：*His whereabouts are/is still unknown.* 他仍下落不明。

■ ***adv.*** /ˌweərəˈbaʊts; *NAmE* ˌwer-/ used to ask the general area where sb/sth is （用以詢問大概的地方）在什麼地方，在哪裏：*Whereabouts did you find it?* 你在哪兒找到它的？

where·as 🔑 AW /ˌweərˈæz; *NAmE* ˌwer-/ *conj.* **1** 🔑 used to compare or contrast two facts（用以比較或對比兩個事實）然而，但是，儘管：*Some of the studies show positive results, whereas others do not.* 有一些研究結果令人滿意，然而其他的則不然。 ➲ LANGUAGE BANK at CONTRAST **2** (*law* 律) used at the beginning of a sentence in an official document to mean 'because of the fact that ...'（用於正式文件中句子的開頭）鑒於

where·by AW /weəˈbaɪ; *NAmE* wer-/ *adv.* (*formal*) by which; because of which 憑此；藉以；由於：*They have introduced a new system whereby all employees must undergo regular training.* 他們採用了新的制度，所有的雇員都必須接受正規的培訓。

where·fore /ˈweəfɔː(r); *NAmE* ˈwerf-/ *noun* IDM see WHY *n.*

where·in /weərˈɪn; *NAmE* wer-/ *adv., conj.* (*formal*) in which place, situation or thing; in what way 其中；在那裏；在那種情況下；以什麼方式：*Wherein lies the difference between conservatism and liberalism?* 保守主義和自由主義的區別在哪裏？

where·of /weərˈɒv; *NAmE* werˈʌv/ *conj.* (*old use* or *humorous*) of what or which 關於什麼；關於那個：*I know whereof I speak* (= I know a lot about what I am talking about). 我知道自己在說些什麼。

where·upon /ˌweərəˈpɒn; *NAmE* ˌwerəˈpɑːn/ *conj.* (*formal*) and then; as a result of this 然後；於是；隨之；據此；因此：*He told her she was a liar, whereupon she walked out.* 他對她說她在說謊，她便憤然而去。

wher·ever /weər'evə(r); *NAmE* wer-/ *conj., adv.*

■ **conj.** **1** in any place 在任何地方：*Sit wherever you like.* 你愛坐在哪兒就坐哪兒。◇ *He comes from Boula, **wherever that may be*** (= I don't know where it is). 他的原籍是布拉，管它在什麼地方呢。**2** in all places that 在…的各個地方；各處；處處 SYN **everywhere**：*Wherever she goes, there are crowds of people waiting to see her.* 她所到之處都有成群的人等着見她。**3** in all cases that 在所有…的情況下 SYN **whenever**：*Use wholegrain breakfast cereals **wherever possible**.* 只要有可能就用全穀物早餐食品。

IDM **or wher'ever** (*informal*) or any other place 或其他任何地方：*tourists from Spain, France or wherever* 來自西班牙、法國或任何別的地方的遊客

■ **adv.** used in questions to mean 'where', expressing surprise（用於問句，表示驚訝）究竟在哪裏，究竟到哪兒：*Wherever can he have gone to?* 他究竟會到哪兒去了呢？

the where·withal /'weəwɪðɔːl; *NAmE* 'werw-/ *noun* [sing.] **~ (to do sth)** the money, things or skill that you need in order to be able to do sth（做某事的）所需資金，必要的設備，所需技術：*They lacked the wherewithal to pay for the repairs.* 他們缺少維修費。

whet /wet/ *verb* (-tt-) **~ sth** to increase your desire for or interest in sth 刺激…的慾望；增強…的興趣：*The book will **whet your appetite** for more of her work.* 你看了這本書就會更想多讀她的著作。

whether /'weðə(r)/ *conj.*

1 used to express a doubt or choice between two possibilities（表示遲疑或兩個可能性之間的選擇）是否：*He seemed undecided **whether** to go **or** stay.* 他似乎還沒有決定去留。◇ *It remains to be seen **whether or not** this idea can be put into practice.* 這一想法能否付諸實踐還有待於觀察。◇ *I asked him **whether** he had done it all himself **or whether** someone had helped him.* 我問過他這都是他自己做的還是有人幫他做的。◇ *I'll see whether she's at home* (= or not at home). 我來看看她在不在家。◇ *It's doubtful whether there'll be any seats left.* 看來未必還有座位。➲ note at IF **2** used to show that sth is true in either of two cases（表示兩種情況都真實）是…（還是），或者…（或者），不管…（還是）：*You are entitled to a free gift whether you accept our offer of insurance or not.* 無論你接不接受我們的保險提議，你都可以免費得到一份禮物。◇ *I'm going **whether** you like it **or not**.* 不管你願意不願意，我都要走了。◇ ***Whether or not** we're successful, we can be sure that we did our best.* 不管成功與否，我們確已盡了最大努力。

whet·stone /'wetstəʊn; *NAmE* -stoʊn/ *noun* a stone that is used to make tools, knives and weapons sharp 磨刀石

whew /hwjuː; fjuː/ *exclamation* a sound that people make to show that they are surprised or RELIEVED about sth or that they are very hot or tired（驚訝、寬慰或感到很熱、疲勞時發出的聲音）哟，噢：*Whew—and I thought it was serious!* 嚯，我原以為它有多麼嚴重呢！◇ *Ten grand? Whew!* 一萬英鎊？哟！➲ compare PHEW

W

whey /weɪ/ *noun* [U] the thin liquid that is left from sour milk after the solid part (called CURDS) has been removed 乳清，乳水（酸奶中的凝乳去掉後剩下的含水成分）

which /wɪtʃ/ *pron., det.*

1 used in questions to ask sb to be exact about one or more people or things from a limited number 哪一個；哪一些：*Which is better exercise—swimming or tennis?* 游泳和網球，哪種運動比較好？◇ *Which of the applicants has got the job?* 哪一位應聘者得到了這份工作？◇ *Which of the patients have recovered?* 哪些患者已經康復了？◇ *Which way is the wind blowing?* 風朝哪個方向颳？➲ compare WHAT (1) **2** used to be exact about the thing or things that you mean（明確所指的事物）…的那個，…的那些：*Houses which overlook the lake cost more.* 俯瞰湖泊的房子要價高些。◇ *It was a crisis for which she was totally unprepared.* 這是一場她完全沒有防備的危機。HELP **That** can be used instead of **which** in this meaning, but it is not used immediately after a preposition：*It was a crisis **that** she was totally unprepared **for**.* 此義中 that 可代替 which，但 that 不能緊跟在介詞之後：It was a crisis that she was totally unprepared for. **3** used to give more information about sth（進一步提供有關某事物的信息）那個，那些：*His best movie, which won several awards, was about the life of Gandhi.* 他最優秀的電影，就是榮獲幾項大獎的那一部，是關於甘地生平的。◇ *Your claim ought to succeed, **in which case** the damages will be substantial.* 你的索賠應當能成功，假如這樣的話，損害賠償金將會相當可觀。HELP **That** cannot be used instead of **which** in this meaning. * which 在此義中不能用 that 替代。

IDM ˌ**which is** ˈ**which** used to talk about distinguishing one person or thing from another（區分人或事物）誰是誰，哪個是哪個：*The twins are so alike I can't tell which is which.* 這一對雙胞胎長得一模一樣，我分不清誰是誰。

which·ever /wɪtʃ'evə(r)/ *det., pron.* **1** used to say what feature or quality is important in deciding sth（表示什麼特徵或品質在作決定時重要）…的那個，…的那些：*Choose whichever brand you prefer.* 挑選你喜歡的那個品牌。◇ *Pensions should be increased annually in line with earnings or prices, whichever is the higher.* 養老金每年應該按照收入或物價中升幅較高的那一項增長。◇ *Whichever of you gets here first will get the prize.* 你們誰第一個到達這裏誰就獲獎。**2** used to say that it does not matter which, as the result will be the same 無論哪個；無論哪些：*It takes three hours, whichever route you take.* 無論你走哪一條路都需要三個小時。◇ *The situation is an awkward one, **whichever way you look at it**.* 無論從哪一方面看，這個局面都很尷尬。◇ *Whichever they choose, we must accept their decision.* 無論他們如何選擇，我們都必須接受他們的決定。

whiff /wɪf/ *noun, verb*

■ **noun** [usually sing.] **1 ~ (of sth)** a smell, especially one that you only smell for a short time 一點兒氣味；一股氣味：*a whiff of cigar smoke* 一股雪茄煙味 ◇ *He caught a whiff of perfume as he leaned towards her.* 他探身靠近她時聞到一股香水味。**2 ~ (of sth)** a slight sign or feeling of sth 輕微的跡象（或感覺）；一點點；些許：*a whiff of danger* 一點點危險 **3** (*NAmE*) (in GOLF or BASEBALL 高爾夫球或棒球) an unsuccessful attempt to hit the ball 揮空棒（擊球未中）

■ **verb** **1** [I] (*BrE, informal*) to smell bad 有臭味；發臭 **2** [I] (*NAmE*) (in GOLF or BASEBALL 高爾夫球或棒球) to try without success to hit the ball 揮空棒（擊球未中）

whiffy /'wɪfi/ *adj.* (*BrE, informal*) smelling bad 難聞的；發臭的

Whig /wɪɡ/ *noun* in Britain in the past, a member of a party that supported progress and reform and that later became the Liberal Party 輝格黨黨員（屬於英國舊時的激進黨派，自由黨的前身）

while /waɪl/ *conj., noun, verb*

■ **conj.** (also *formal* **whilst** /waɪlst/ especially in *BrE*) **1** during the time that sth is happening 在…期間；當…的時候 SYN **when**：*We must have been burgled while we were asleep.* 我們睡覺時一定讓賊入室偷了。◇ *Her parents died while she was still at school.* 她還在讀書時父母就去世了。◇ *While I was waiting at the bus stop, three buses went by in the opposite direction.* 我在公共汽車站等車時，對向駛過了三輛公共汽車。**2** at the same time as sth else is happening 與…同時：*You can go swimming while I'm having lunch.* 我吃午飯時你可以去游泳。◇ *shoes mended while you wait* 在你等候的時候修的鞋 **3** used to contrast two things（對比兩件事物）…而，…然而：*While Tom's very good at science, his brother is absolutely hopeless.* 湯姆很擅長理科，而他的弟弟絕對是不可救藥。➲ LANGUAGE BANK at CONTRAST **4** (used at the beginning of a sentence 用於句首) although; despite the fact that ... 雖然；儘管：*While I am willing to help, I do not have much time available.* 儘管我願意幫忙，但是沒有多少時間。➲ LANGUAGE BANK at NEVERTHELESS **5** (*NEngE*) until 到…時；直到…為止：*I waited while six o'clock.* 我一直等到了六點鐘。

IDM ˌ**while you're/I'm etc.** ˈ**at it** used to suggest that sb could do sth while they are doing sth else 趁做某事的時候；順便；順帶：*'I'm just going to buy some postcards.'*

'Can you get me some stamps while you're at it?' "我正想去買明信片。" "你能順便給我買些郵票嗎？"

■ **noun** [sing.] a period of time 一段時間；一會兒： *They chatted **for a while**.* 他們聊了一會兒。◇ *I'll be back in **a little while*** (= a short time). 我一會兒就回來。◇ *I haven't seen him for **quite a while*** (= a fairly long time). 我有好一陣子沒有見到他了。◇ *They walked back together, talking **all the while*** (= all the time). 他們一起邊走邊聊着回去的。 **IDM** see ONCE *adv.*, WORTH *adj.*

■ **verb**

PHR V **,while sth↔a'way** to spend time in a pleasant lazy way 逍遙自在地度過，消磨（時間）： *We whiled away the time reading and playing cards.* 我們靠看書和玩紙牌消磨時間。

whim /wɪm/ *noun* [C, U] a sudden wish to do or have sth, especially when it is sth unusual or unnecessary 心血來潮；一時的興致；突發的奇想： *He was forced to pander to **her every whim**.* 她每次心血來潮他都不得不依隨她。◇ *We bought the house **on a whim**.* 我們一時衝動買了這所房子。◇ *My duties seem to change daily **at the whim of** the boss.* 我的職責似乎隨着老闆的興致每天改變。◇ *the whims of fashion* 時尚的變化多端◇ *She hires and fires people **at whim**.* 她隨心所欲地雇用人和解雇人。

whim·per /'wɪmpə(r)/ *verb, noun*

■ **verb** [I, T] to make low, weak crying noises; to speak in this way 抽泣；嗚咽；啜泣；泣訴；抽搭着說： *The child was lost and began to whimper.* 那孩子迷了路，抽抽搭搭地哭起來。◇ **+ speech** *'Don't leave me alone,' he whimpered.* "別丟下我不管。" 他嗚咽着說。

■ **noun** a low weak cry that a person or an animal makes when they are hurt, frightened or sad 抽泣；嗚咽聲

whim·si·cal /'wɪmzɪkl/ *adj.* unusual and not serious in a way that is either amusing or annoying 異想天開的；想入非非的；心血來潮的；滑稽可笑的： *to have a whimsical sense of humour* 有離奇的幽默感◇ *Much of his writing has a whimsical quality.* 他的大部份作品都很出奇。▸ **whim·si·cal·ly** /-kli/ *adv.*

whimsy /'wɪmzi/ *noun* [U] a way of thinking or behaving, or a style of doing sth that is unusual and not serious, in a way that is either amusing or annoying 怪念頭；古怪可笑的舉動；吊兒郎當；隨心所欲

whine /waɪn/ *verb, noun*

■ **verb** **1** [I, T] (**+ speech**) | **~ that ...** to complain in an annoying, crying voice 哭哭啼啼；哭嚷： *Stop whining!* 別哭哭啼啼的！◇ *'I want to go home,' whined Toby.* "我要回家。" 托比哭嚷道。➲ **SYNONYMS** at COMPLAIN **2** [I] to make a long high unpleasant sound because you are in pain or unhappy 哀鳴；慘叫： *The dog whined and scratched at the door.* 那狗嗷嗷地叫着抓門。 **3** [I] (of a machine 機器) to make a long high unpleasant sound 嘎嘎響；嗖嗖響；嘎吱嘎吱響 ▸ **whiny** *adj.* : *a whiny voice/tone* 哭哭啼啼的聲音／語氣◇ *a whiny kid/brat* 哭哭啼啼的小孩／小子

■ **noun** [usually sing.] **1** a long high sound that is usually unpleasant or annoying 嘎吱聲；吱吱聲；嘎嘎聲： *the steady whine of the engine* 發動機不停的嘎吱聲 **2** a long high cry that a child or dog makes when it is hurt or wants sth （兒童發出的）哭喊聲；（狗發出的）號叫聲 **3** a high tone of voice that you use when you complain about sth 抱怨的語調

whinge /wɪndʒ/ *verb* (*pres. part.* **whinge·ing** or **whing·ing**) [I] **~ (about sb/sth)** (*BrE, informal, disapproving*) to complain in an annoying way 絮絮叨叨地抱怨： *She's always whingeing about how unfair everything is.* 她總是嘟囔着說一切都太不公平了。▸ **whinge** *noun* **whin·ger** *noun*

whinny /'wɪni/ *verb* (**whin·nies**, **whinny·ing**, **whin·nied**, **whin·nied**) [I] (of a horse 馬) to make a quiet NEIGH 輕聲嘶鳴 ▸ **whinny** *noun* (*pl.* **-ies**)

whip /wɪp/ *noun, verb*

■ **noun** **1** [C] a long thin piece of rope or leather, attached to a handle, used for making animals move or punishing people 鞭子： *He cracked his whip and the horse leapt forward.* 他甩了個響鞭，馬兒就奮蹄向前奔去。 **2** [C] an official in a political party who is responsible for making sure that party members attend and vote in important government debates 紀律委員，黨鞭（在政黨中負責確保黨員出席政府重要辯論並表決）： *the chief whip* 組織秘書長 **3** [C] a written instruction telling members of a political party how to vote on a particular issue （政黨發給黨員的）投票通知書，投票指示 ➲ see also THREE-LINE WHIP **4** [U, C] a sweet dish made from cream, eggs, sugar and fruit mixed together 攪打奶油甜食（用奶油、雞蛋、糖和水果攪打而成）

IDM **have/hold, etc. the 'whip hand (over sb/sth)** to be in a position where you have power or control over sb/sth 執掌大權；執鞭在手 ➲ more at CRACK *v.*, FAIR *adj.*

■ **verb** (**-pp-**) **1** [T] **~ sb/sth** to hit a person or an animal hard with a whip, as a punishment or to make them go faster or work harder 鞭打；鞭策；以鞭打責罰；鞭笞 **2** [I, T] to move, or make sth move, quickly and suddenly or violently in a particular direction （使朝某一方向）猛然移動： **+ adv./prep.** *A branch whipped across the car window.* 一條樹枝突然劃過車窗。◇ *Her hair whipped around her face in the wind.* 她的頭髮隨風在臉際飄拂。◇ **~ sth** *The waves were being whipped by 50 mile an hour winds.* 時速 50 英里的大風捲起了波浪。 **3** [T] **~ sth + adv./prep.** to remove or pull sth quickly and suddenly （突然迅速地）除去，拉動，抽出： *She whipped the mask off her face.* 她刷地一下子把臉上的面具摘掉了。◇ *The man whipped out a knife.* 那個人突然抽出一把刀來。 **4** [T] to stir cream, etc. very quickly until it becomes stiff 攪打（奶油等）： **~ sth** *Serve the pie with **whipped cream**.* 端上加了攪打奶油的餡餅。◇ **~ sth up** *Whip the egg whites up into stiff peaks.* 把蛋白打得起稠尖兒。➲ **VISUAL VOCAB** page V28 **5** [T] **~ sb/sth** (*NAmE, informal*) to defeat sb very easily in a game （在比賽中）輕而易舉地擊敗： *The team whipped its opponents by 35 points.* 這個隊以 35 分的優勢輕鬆擊敗對手。➲ compare THRASH *v.* (3) **6** [T] **~ sth** (*BrE, informal*) to steal sth 偷；盜竊

PHR V **,whip 'through sth** (*informal*) to do or finish sth very quickly 匆匆做；迅速完成： *We whipped through customs in ten minutes.* 我們十分鐘便辦完了海關手續。

,whip sb/sth↔'up **1** to deliberately try and make people excited or feel strongly about sth 激發；激勵；煽動 **SYN** **rouse**： *The advertisements were designed to whip up public opinion.* 設計這些廣告是為了激起公眾的輿論。◇ *He was a speaker who could really **whip up a crowd**.* 他是個真正有感召力的演說者。 **2** to quickly make a meal or sth to eat 匆匆做（飯等）： *She whipped up a delicious lunch for us in 15 minutes.* 她用了 15 分鐘就給我們備好了一頓可口的午餐。

whip·lash /'wɪplæʃ/ *noun* **1** [C, usually sing.] a hit with a whip 鞭打 **2** [U] = WHIPLASH INJURY： *He was very bruised and suffering from whiplash.* 他滿身青腫，而且頸部過度屈伸受傷。

'whiplash injury *noun* [C, U] (also **whip·lash**) a neck injury caused when your head moves forward and back suddenly, especially in a car accident 揮鞭傷，鞭打損傷（尤指車禍造成的頸部過度屈伸損傷）

whip·per·snap·per /'wɪpəsnæpə(r); *NAmE* 'wɪpərs-/ *noun* (*old-fashioned, informal*) a young and unimportant person who behaves in a way that others think is too confident and rude 狂妄小子

whip·pet /'wɪpɪt/ *noun* a small thin dog, similar to a GREYHOUND, that can run very fast and is often used for racing 小靈狗（類似靈䁖，常用於賽狗）

whip·ping /'wɪpɪŋ/ *noun* [usually sing.] an act of hitting sb with a whip, as a punishment 鞭打，鞭笞（作為懲罰）

'whipping boy *noun* a person who is often blamed or punished for things other people have done 代人受過者；替罪羊；出氣筒

'whipping cream *noun* [U] cream that becomes thicker when it is stirred quickly (= WHIPPED) 攪打奶油

whip·poor·will /'wɪpəwɪl; *NAmE* -pərw-/ *noun* a brown N American bird with a cry that sounds like its name 三聲夜鷹；"嚎破威"

ˈwhip-round *noun* (*BrE, informal*) if a group of people have a **whip-round**, they all give money so they can buy sth for sb 湊份子

whir (*especially NAmE*) = WHIRR

whirl /wɜːl; *NAmE* wɜːrl/ *verb, noun*

■ **verb** **1** [I, T] to move, or make sb/sth move, around quickly in a circle or in a particular direction （使）旋轉，迴旋，打轉 **SYN** **spin**：(+ **adv./prep.**) *Leaves whirled in the wind.* 落葉在風中旋轉。◇ *She whirled around to face him.* 她猛地轉過身子面對着他。◇ *the whirling blades of the helicopter* 直升機旋轉着的槳葉 ◇ **~ sb/sth (+ adv./prep.)** *Tom whirled her across the dance floor.* 湯姆擁着她從舞池的一邊旋轉到另一邊。 **2** [I] if your mind, thoughts, etc. **whirl**, you feel confused and excited and cannot think clearly（頭腦、思想等）混亂不清，激動，恍惚 **SYN** **reel**：*I couldn't sleep—my mind was whirling from all that had happened.* 我睡不着，所發生的一切一直在腦子裏轉來轉去。◇ *So many thoughts whirled around in her mind.* 她思緒萬千，腦子裏亂作一團。

■ **noun** [sing.] **1** a movement of sth spinning round and round 旋轉；迴旋；急轉：*a whirl of dust* 塵土飛揚 ◇ (*figurative*) *Her mind was* **in a whirl** (= in a state of confusion or excitement). 她腦子裏亂糟糟的。 **2** a number of activities or events happening one after the other 接連不斷的活動；紛至沓來的事件：*Her life was one long whirl of parties.* 她的生活就是接連不斷的聚會。◇ *It's easy to get caught up in the* **social whirl**. 很容易被紛繁的社交活動纏得脫不開身。

IDM **give sth a ˈwhirl** (*informal*) to try sth to see if you like it or can do it 試一試

whirli·gig /ˈwɜːliɡɪɡ; *NAmE* ˈwɜːrl-/ *noun* **1** something that is very active and always changing 活躍多變的事物；經常變換的東西；變遷：*the whirligig of fashion* 時尚的千變萬化 **2** (*old-fashioned*) a MERRY-GO-ROUND at a FAIRGROUND for children to ride on 旋轉木馬

whirl·pool /ˈwɜːlpuːl; *NAmE* ˈwɜːrl-/ *noun* **1** a place in a river or the sea where currents of water spin round very fast（河水或海水的）漩渦 **SYN** **eddy**：(*figurative*) *She felt she was being dragged into a whirlpool of emotion.* 她覺得自己被捲入了感情的漩渦。 **2** (also ˌ**whirlpool ˈbath**) a special bath/ BATHTUB or swimming pool for relaxing in, in which the water moves in circles 渦流浴缸；渦流游泳池 ➲ see also JACUZZI

whirl·wind /ˈwɜːlwɪnd; *NAmE* ˈwɜːrl-/ *noun, adj.*

■ **noun** **1** a very strong wind that moves very fast in a spinning movement and causes a lot of damage 旋風；旋流 **2** a situation or series of events where a lot of things happen very quickly 一片忙亂：*To recover from the divorce, I threw myself into a whirlwind of activities.* 為了從離婚中恢復過來，我馬不停蹄地投身於一系列的活動。

■ **adj.** [only before noun] happening very fast 快速的；匆匆忙忙的；旋風似的：*a whirlwind romance* 旋風式戀愛 ◇ *a whirlwind tour of America* 旋風式的美國之行

whirr (*especially BrE*) (*NAmE* usually **whir**) /wɜː(r)/ *verb, noun*

W

■ **verb** (**-rr-**) [I] to make a continuous low sound like the parts of a machine moving 嗡嗡地響；呼呼地響：*The clock began to whirr before striking the hour.* 鐘在打點前先嘎啦嘎啦地響起來。

■ **noun** (also **whir·ring**) [usually sing.] a continuous low sound, for example the sound made by the regular movement of a machine or the wings of a bird 嗡嗡聲；呼呼聲：*the whirr of a motor* 發動機的嗡嗡聲 ◇ *There was a whirring of machinery.* 有機器發出的嗡嗡聲。

whisk /wɪsk/ *verb, noun*

■ **verb** **1 ~ sth** to mix liquids, eggs, etc. into a stiff light mass, using a fork or special tool 攪打，攪動（液體、雞蛋等）**SYN** **beat**：*Whisk the egg whites until stiff.* 把蛋白攪打稠。 **2 ~ sb/sth + adv./prep.** to take sb/sth somewhere very quickly and suddenly 匆匆帶走；迅速送走：*Jamie whisked her off to Paris for the weekend.* 傑米匆匆把她帶到巴黎去度週末。◇ *The waiter whisked away the plates before we had finished.* 服務員沒等我們吃完就匆忙把盤子端走了。

■ **noun** a kitchen UTENSIL (= a tool) for stirring eggs, etc. very fast 打蛋器；攪拌器：*an electric whisk* 電動攪拌器 ➲ VISUAL VOCAB pages V25, V26, V28

whis·ker /ˈwɪskə(r)/ *noun* **1** [C] any of the long stiff hairs that grow near the mouth of a cat, mouse, etc.（貓、鼠等的）鬚 **2 whiskers** [pl.] (*old-fashioned* or *humorous*) the hair growing on a man's face, especially on his cheeks and chin 絡腮鬍子；連鬢鬍子 ➲ VISUAL VOCAB page V12

IDM **be, come, etc. within a whisker of sth/doing sth** (*BrE*) to almost do sth 幾乎要做；險些要做：*They came within a whisker of being killed.* 他們險些丟了性命。 **by a ˈwhisker** by a very small amount 差一點兒 ➲ more at CAT

whis·kered /ˈwɪskəd; *NAmE* -kərd/ (also **whis·kery** /ˈwɪskəri/) *adj.* having whiskers 有絡腮鬍子的；有鬚的

whisky (*BrE*) (*US, IrishE* **whis·key**) /ˈwɪski/ *noun* (*pl.* **whis·kies, whis·keys**) **1** [U, C] a strong alcoholic drink made from MALTED grain. It is sometimes drunk with water and/or ice. 威士忌：*a bottle of whisky* 一瓶威士忌 ◇ *Scotch whisky* 蘇格蘭威士忌 ◇ *highland whiskies* 高地威士忌 ➲ see also BOURBON, SCOTCH **2** [C] a glass of whisky 一杯威士忌：*a whisky and soda* 一杯加蘇打水的威士忌 ◇ *Two whiskies, please.* 請來兩杯威士忌。➲ see also SCOTCH

whis·per 🔑 /ˈwɪspə(r)/ *verb, noun*

■ **verb** **1** 🔑 [I, T] to speak very quietly to sb so that other people cannot hear what you are saying 耳語；低語；私語；小聲說 **SYN** **murmur**：*Don't you know it's rude to whisper?* 難道你不知道竊竊私語是不禮貌的嗎？◇ **~ about sth** *What are you two whispering about?* 你們兩人在低聲說些什麼？◇ **+ speech** *'Can you meet me tonight?' he whispered.* "你今晚能和我見面嗎？" 他小聲問。◇ **~ sth (to sb)** *She leaned over and whispered something in his ear.* 她探過身去附耳跟他說了些什麼。◇ **~ (to sb) that …** *He whispered to me that he was afraid.* 他低聲對我說他害怕。 **2** [T, often passive] **~ that … | it is whispered that …** to say or suggest sth about sb/sth in a private or secret way 私下說；秘密告訴；悄聲暗示：*It was whispered that he would soon die and he did.* 有人私下說他將不久於人世，他果然死了。 **3** [I] (**+ adv./prep.**) (*literary*) (of leaves, the wind, etc. 葉子、風等) to make a soft, quiet sound 沙沙作響；發颯颯聲

■ **noun** **1** 🔑 a low quiet voice or the sound it makes 耳語（聲）；低語（聲）；私語（聲）**SYN** **murmur**：*They spoke* **in whispers**. 他們在交頭接耳。◇ *Her voice dropped to a whisper.* 她壓低聲音小聲說話。➲ see also STAGE WHISPER **2** (also **whis·per·ing**) (*literary*) a soft sound 輕柔的聲音 **SYN** **murmur**：*I could hear the whispering of the sea.* 我聽見大海在輕聲訴說。 **3** a piece of news that is spread by being talked about but may not be true 傳言；謠傳 **SYN** **rumour**：*I've heard whispers that he's leaving.* 我聽人傳說他要走。

ˈwhispering campaign *noun* an attempt to damage sb's reputation by saying unpleasant things about them and passing this information from person to person 散佈流言蜚語；造謠中傷

whist /wɪst/ *noun* [U] a card game for two pairs of players in which each pair tries to win the most cards 惠斯特（一種由兩對遊戲者玩的紙牌遊戲）

whis·tle 🔑 /ˈwɪsl/ *noun, verb*

■ **noun** **1** 🔑 a small metal or plastic tube that you blow to make a loud high sound, used to attract attention or as a signal 哨子：*The referee finally* **blew the whistle** *to stop the game.* 主裁判終於吹停了比賽。➲ see also TIN WHISTLE **2** 🔑 the sound made by blowing a whistle 哨子聲：*He scored the winning goal just seconds before the final whistle.* 他就在終場哨聲前的幾秒鐘內打進了制勝的一球。 **3** 🔑 the sound that you make by forcing your breath out when your lips are closed 口哨：*a shrill whistle* 尖厲的口哨聲 ➲ see also WOLF WHISTLE **4** 🔑 the high loud sound produced by air or steam being forced through a small opening, or by sth moving quickly through the air 汽笛聲；警笛聲；呼嘯聲 **5** a piece of equipment that makes a high loud sound when air or steam is forced through it 汽笛：*The train whistle blew as we left the station.* 我們離開車站時火車的汽笛響了。

◇ *a factory whistle* 工廠的汽笛 IDM see BLOW *v.*, CLEAN *adj.*

■ **verb** **1** [T, I] to make a high sound or a musical tune by forcing your breath out when your lips are closed 吹口哨；打呼哨： ~ **(sth)** *to whistle a tune* 用口哨吹曲子 ◇ *He whistled in amazement.* 他驚愕地吹了個口哨。◇ *The crowd booed and whistled as the player came onto the field.* 那隊員上場時，人群又是發出呸呸聲又是吹口哨。◇ ~ **to sb/sth** *She whistled to the dog to come back.* 她打了個呼哨把狗喚回來。◇ ~ **at sb/sth** *Workmen whistled at her as she walked past.* 當她走過時工人向她吹口哨。 **2** [I] to make a high sound by blowing into a whistle 吹哨子： *The referee whistled for a foul.* 裁判吹哨子示意有人犯規。**3** [I] (of a KETTLE or other machine 燒水壺或機器) to make a high sound 鳴叫；呼嘯；發出笛聲： *The kettle began to whistle.* 燒水壺嗚嗚地響了起來。◇ *The microphone was making a strange whistling sound.* 擴音器發出一種奇怪的哨音。 **4** [I] + **adv./prep.** to move quickly, making a high sound 呼嘯而行；嗖嗖地移動： *The wind whistled down the chimney.* 風颼颼地灌進煙囱。◇ *A bullet whistled past his ear.* 子彈嗖的一聲從他耳邊飛過。 **5** [I] (of a bird 鳥) to make a high sound 囀鳴；啁啾

IDM **sb can 'whistle for sth** (*BrE, informal*) used to say that you are not going to give sb sth that they have asked for（表示不給他人所要的東西）得不到，空指望

'whistle-blower *noun* (used especially in newspapers 尤用於報章) a person who informs people in authority or the public that the company they work for is doing sth wrong or illegal（公司等處）檢舉揭發舞弊內情的人

'whistle-stop *adj.* [only before noun] visiting a lot of different places in a very short time 走馬觀花的；浮光掠影的： *to go on a* ***whistle-stop tour*** *of Europe* 到歐洲各地作走馬看花的觀光◇ *politicians on a whistle-stop election campaign* 在各地進行蜻蜓點水式競選宣傳的政治人物

Whit /wɪt/ *adj.* connected with Whitsun 聖靈降臨節的；聖神降臨節的： *Whit Monday* 聖靈降臨節後的第一個星期一

whit /wɪt/ *noun* [sing.] (*old-fashioned*) (usually in negative sentences 通常用於否定句) a very small amount 一點點；很少量；絲毫 SYN **jot**

IDM **not a 'whit | not one 'whit** not at all; not the smallest amount 絲毫不；一點不

white /waɪt/ *adj., noun*

■ **adj.** (**whiter**, **whit·est**) **1** having the colour of fresh snow or of milk 白的；白色的： *a crisp white shirt* 一件挺括的白襯衫◇ *white bread* 白麪包◇ *a set of perfect white teeth* 一副潔白無瑕的牙齒◇ *His hair was* ***as white as snow.*** 他頭髮雪白。◇ *The horse was almost* ***pure white*** *in colour.* 那匹馬幾乎是純白色。 **2** belonging to or connected with a race of people who have pale skin 白種人的；白人的： *white middle-class families* 白人中產階級家庭◇ *She writes about her experiences as a black girl in a predominantly white city.* 她寫的是自己身為一個黑人姑娘在以白人為主的城市裏的經歷。 **3** (of the skin 皮膚) pale because of emotion or illness 臉色蒼白的： *white with shock* 震驚得臉色發白◇ *She* ***went white as a sheet*** *when she heard the news.* 她聽到這消息時臉色變得煞白。 **4** (*BrE*) (of tea or coffee 茶或咖啡) with milk added 加牛奶的： *Two white coffees, please.* 請來兩杯加牛奶的咖啡。◇ *Do you take your coffee black or white?* 你喝咖啡加不加牛奶？ ➲ compare BLACK *adj.* (4) ▶ **white·ness** *noun* [U, sing.]

■ **noun** **1** [U] the colour of fresh snow or of milk 白色；雪白；乳白： *the pure white of the newly painted walls* 新粉刷的牆壁的純白色◇ *She was dressed all in white.* 她穿着一身白色的衣服。 **2** [C, usually pl.] a member of a race or people who have pale skin 白種人；白人 **3** [U, C] white wine 白葡萄酒： *Would you like red or white?* 你喜歡喝紅葡萄酒還是白葡萄酒？◇ *a very dry white* 特乾白葡萄酒 **4** [C, U] the part of an egg that surrounds the YOLK (= the yellow part) 蛋白；蛋清： *Use the whites of two eggs.* 用兩個雞蛋的蛋清。 **5** [C, usually pl.] the white part of the eye 眼白；白眼珠： *The whites of her eyes were bloodshot.* 她的白眼珠佈滿血絲。➲ VISUAL VOCAB page V59 **6** **whites** [pl.] white clothes, sheets, etc. when they are separated from coloured ones to be washed 要洗滌的白色衣服（或牀單等）： (*BrE*) *Don't wash whites and coloureds together.* 別把白色衣服和帶顏色的衣服一塊洗。◇ (*NAmE*) *Don't wash whites and colors together.* 別把白色衣服和帶顏色的衣服一起洗。 **7** **whites** [pl.] white clothes worn for playing some sports 白色運動服： ***cricket/tennis whites*** 白色板球／網球運動服 IDM see BLACK *n.*

IDM **,whiter than 'white** (of a person 人) completely honest and morally good 完全誠實清白；純潔無瑕： *The government must be seen to be whiter than white.* 政府須讓人覺得是清正廉潔的。

white·bait /ˈwaɪtbeɪt/ *noun* [pl.] very small young fish of several types that are fried and eaten whole 小鮮魚，銀魚（可食用）

,white 'blood cell (also **'white cell**) (also *technical* 術語 **leuco·cyte**) *noun* (*biology* 生) any of the clear cells in the blood that help to fight disease 白細胞；白血球

white·board /ˈwaɪtbɔːd; *NAmE* -bɔːrd/ *noun* a large board with a smooth white surface that teachers, etc. write on with special pens 白色書寫板；白板 ➲ VISUAL VOCAB page V70 ➲ compare BLACKBOARD

,white 'bread *noun* [U] bread made with WHITE FLOUR 白麪麪包；精粉麪包

'white-bread *adj.* [only before noun] (*NAmE, informal*) ordinary and traditional 普通的；一般傳統的： *a white-bread town* 普普通通的老鎮

white·caps /ˈwaɪtkæps/ (*NAmE*) (*BrE* **,white 'horses**) *noun* [pl.] waves in the sea or ocean with white tops on them（海上的）白浪，白頭浪

,white 'Christmas *noun* a Christmas during which there is snow on the ground 白色聖誕節（地面有雪）

,white-'collar *adj.* [usually before noun] working in an office, rather than in a factory, etc.; connected with work in offices 白領的；文職的；腦力勞動的： *white-collar workers* 白領工作者◇ *a white-collar job* 白領工作◇ *white-collar crime* (= in which office workers steal from their company, etc.) 白領犯罪 ➲ compare BLUE-COLLAR, PINK-COLLAR

,white 'dwarf *noun* (*astronomy* 天) a small star that is near the end of its life and is very DENSE (= solid and heavy) 白矮星（光度小，處於演化末期的一類恒星）

,white 'elephant *noun* [usually sing.] a thing that is useless and no longer needed, although it may have cost a lot of money 昂貴而無用之物： *The new office block has become an expensive white elephant.* 這座新辦公大樓成了昂貴的擺設。 ORIGIN From the story that in Siam (now Thailand) the king would give a white elephant as a present to somebody that he did not like. That person would have to spend all their money on looking after the rare animal. 源自下面的故事：在暹羅（今泰國），國王總是賜給他不喜歡的人一頭白象。這個人就得花掉所有的錢飼養這隻稀有動物。

,white 'fish *noun* [U, C] (*pl.* **white fish**) fish with pale flesh 白魚

,white 'flag *noun* [usually sing.] a sign that you accept defeat and wish to stop fighting 白旗（承認失敗並願意停戰的標誌）： *to* ***raise/show/wave the white flag*** 舉起／打出／搖動白旗

,white 'flight *noun* [U] (*US*) a situation where white people who can afford it go to live outside the cities because they are worried about crime in city centres 白人遷移（白人因擔心市中心的治安而到郊區居住）

,white 'flour *noun* [U] flour made from WHEAT grains, from which most of the BRAN (= outer covering) and WHEATGERM (= centre part) have been removed 白麪；精麥粉

'white goods *noun* [pl.] large pieces of electrical equipment in the house, such as WASHING MACHINES, etc. 白色家電；大件家用電器 ➲ compare BROWN GOODS

White·hall /ˈwaɪthɔːl/ *noun* **1** [U] a street in London where there are many government offices 懷特霍爾（倫敦的一條街，政府機關所在地） **2** [sing.+sing./pl. v.] a way of referring to the British Government 白廳（指英國

政府）：*Whitehall are/is refusing to comment.* 白廳拒絕發表評論。

ˌwhite ˈheat *noun* [U] the very high temperature at which metal looks white 白熱；白熾

ˌwhite ˈhope *noun* [sing.] (*informal*) a person who is expected to bring success to a team, an organization, etc.（團隊、組織等）被寄予厚望的人：*He was once the* ***great white hope*** *of British boxing.* 他一度曾是英國拳擊的希望所在。

ˌwhite ˈhorses (*BrE*) (*NAmE* **white·caps**) *noun* [pl.] waves in the sea or ocean with white tops on them（大海中的）白浪

ˌwhite-ˈhot *adj.* **1** (of metal or sth burning 金屬或燃燒物) so hot that it looks white 白熱的；白熾的 **2** very strong and INTENSE 白熱化的；極其激烈的

the ˈWhite House *noun* [sing.] **1** the official home of the President of the US in Washington, DC 白宮（美國總統官邸，位於首都華盛頓）**2** the US President and his or her officials 白宮（指美國總統或美國政府）：*The White House has issued a statement.* 白宮已經發表了一項聲明。◇ *White House aides* 總統助手

ˌwhite ˈknight *noun* a person or an organization that rescues a company from being bought by another company at too low a price 白武士，白衣騎士（把公司從不利的收購建議中挽救出來的個人或機構）

ˌwhite-ˈknuckle ride *noun* a ride at a FAIRGROUND that makes you feel very excited and frightened at the same time 令人既興奮又緊張的遊樂場乘行

ˌwhite ˈlie *noun* a harmless or small lie, especially one that you tell to avoid hurting sb（尤指為避免傷害他人感情的）善意的謊言，小謊

ˌwhite ˈlight *noun* [U] ordinary light that has no colour 白光

ˌwhite ˈmeat *noun* [U] **1** meat that is pale in colour when it has been cooked, such as chicken 白肉（烹煮後呈白色的肉，如雞肉）➲ compare RED MEAT **2** pale meat from the breast of a chicken or other bird that has been cooked（雞或其他禽類的）熟胸脯肉

whiten /ˈwaɪtn/ *verb* [I, T] to become white or whiter; to make sth white or whiter（使）變白，變得更白：*He gripped the wheel until his knuckles whitened.* 他緊緊握住方向盤，握得指關節都變白了。◇ **~ sth** *Snow had whitened the tops of the trees.* 大雪把樹冠變成了白色。

ˌwhite ˈnoise *noun* [U] unpleasant noise, like the noise that comes from a television or radio that is turned on but not TUNED IN 白噪聲（整個頻道範圍內的噪聲）

ˈwhite-out *noun* weather conditions in which there is so much snow or cloud that it is impossible to see anything 乳白天空（雪大或雲重而看不見東西）➲ see also WITEOUT

the ˌwhite ˈpages *noun* [pl.] a telephone book (on white paper), or a section of a book, that lists the names, addresses and telephone numbers of people living in a particular area 白頁（分區電話簿）

ˌWhite ˈPaper *noun* (in Britain) a government report that gives information about sth and explains government plans before a new law is introduced（英國）白皮書 ➲ compare GREEN PAPER

ˌwhite ˈpepper *noun* [U] a greyish-brown powder made from dried BERRIES (called PEPPERCORNS), used to give flavour to food 白胡椒粉

ˌwhite ˈsauce *noun* [U] a thick sauce made from butter, flour and milk 白沙司，白醬，白汁（用黃油、麪粉和牛奶調製而成）**SYN** **béchamel**

ˌwhite ˈspirit *noun* [U] (*BrE*) a clear liquid made from petrol/gas, used as a cleaning substance or to make paint thinner 石油溶劑油；稀釋劑

ˌwhite ˈstick *noun* a long thin white stick carried by blind people to help them walk around without knocking things and to show others that they are blind 白色手杖（用以探索障礙物和表示用者為失明人）

ˌwhite ˈtie *noun* a man's white BOW TIE, also used to mean very formal evening dress for men（男用）白領結，正式晚禮服：*dressed in white tie and tails* 身穿燕尾服打着白領結

ˌwhite-ˈtie *adj.* (of social occasions 社交場合) very formal, when men are expected to wear white BOW TIES and jackets with TAILS 非常正式的；要求男士穿燕尾晚禮服打白領結的：*Is it a white-tie affair?* 這是個穿夜禮服的聚會嗎？

ˌwhite-ˈvan man *noun* (*BrE, informal*) used to refer to the sort of man who drives a white van in an aggressive way, thought of as a symbol of the rude and sometimes violent way in which some men behave today 白色貨車司機（借喻粗魯瘋狂的男子）

white·wall /ˈwaɪtwɔːl/ *noun* **1** (*BrE* also ˌ**whitewall ˈtyre**) (*NAmE* also **whitewall tire**) a tyre with a white line going round it for decoration 白圈輪胎 **2 white-walls** [pl.] (*especially US*) the shaved area at the sides of the head when the hair is cut in a very short style（鍋蓋短髮側面的）剃頭圈

white·wash /ˈwaɪtwɒʃ; *NAmE* -wɑːʃ; -wɔːʃ/ *noun, verb*

■ ***noun*** **1** [U] a mixture of CHALK or LIME and water, used for painting houses and walls white（粉刷用的）石灰水，白塗料 **2** [U, sing.] (*disapproving*) an attempt to hide unpleasant facts about sb/sth 粉飾；掩蓋 **SYN** **cover-up**：*The opposition claimed the report was a whitewash.* 反對派聲稱這份報告文過飾非。**3** [C, usually sing.] (*informal*) (in sport) a victory in every game in a series（在體育比賽中接連擊敗對手的）全勝：*a 7–0 whitewash* * 7:0 全勝 ◇ *a whitewash victory* 大獲全勝

■ ***verb*** **1 ~ sth** to cover sth such as a wall with whitewash 粉刷（牆壁等）；刷石灰水 **2 ~ sb/sth** (*disapproving*) to try to hide unpleasant facts about sb/sth; to try to make sth seem better than it is 掩飾；粉飾：*His wife had wanted to whitewash his reputation after he died.* 他妻子在他死後本來想粉飾他的名聲。**3 ~ sb/sth** (*especially BrE*) (in sport 體育運動) to defeat an opponent in every game in a series（在系列比賽中）完全擊敗，完勝

ˌwhite ˈwater *noun* [U] **1** a part of a river that looks white because the water is moving very fast over rocks（河水湍急流過岩石時呈現的）碎浪水花，白色水域：*a stretch of white water* 一片白色水域 ◇ *white-water rafting* 激流皮划艇運動 ➲ VISUAL VOCAB page V50 **2** a part of the sea or ocean that looks white because it is very rough and the waves are high（海洋的）白色水域，驚濤駭浪的水域

ˌwhite ˈwedding *noun* a traditional wedding, especially in a church, at which the BRIDE wears a white dress（尤指在教堂舉行的）新娘穿白色禮服的傳統婚禮

ˌwhite ˈwine *noun* **1** [U, C] pale yellow wine 白葡萄酒；淺黃色果酒：*a bottle of dry white wine* 一瓶乾白葡萄酒 ◇ *chilled white wine* 冰鎮白葡萄酒 **2** [C] a glass of white wine 一杯白葡萄酒 ➲ compare RED WINE, ROSÉ

ˌwhite ˈwitch *noun* a person who does magic that does not harm other people 行善女巫；行善巫師

whitey /ˈwaɪti/ *noun* (*slang*) an offensive word for a white person, used by black people（黑人用語，含冒犯意）白人，白鬼

whither /ˈwɪðə(r)/ *adv., conj.* **1** (*old use*) where; to which 哪裏；何處；到何處：*Whither should they go?* 他們應往何處去？◇ *They did not know whither they should go.* 他們不知何去何從。◇ *the place whither they were sent* 他們被送往的地方 **2** (*formal*) used to ask what is likely to happen to sth in the future（詢問將可能發生什麼）怎樣的情況，怎樣的前途：*Whither modern architecture?* 現代建築何去何從？

whit·ing /ˈwaɪtɪŋ/ *noun* [C, U] (*pl.* **whit·ing**) a small sea fish with white flesh that is used for food 牙鱈（一種肉為白色可食用的小海魚）

whit·ish /ˈwaɪtɪʃ/ *adj.* fairly white in colour 發白的；稍白的：*a bird with a whitish throat* 白喉鳥

Whit·sun /ˈwɪtsn/ *noun* [U, C] the 7th Sunday after Easter and the days close to it 聖靈降臨節，聖神降臨節（復活節後的第 7 個星期日前後幾天）

ˌWhit ˈSunday *noun* [U, C] (*BrE*) = PENTECOST (1)

Whit·sun·tide /ˈwɪtsntaɪd/ *noun* [U] the week or days close to Whit Sunday 聖神降臨週；聖靈降臨節週末

whit·tle /ˈwɪtl/ *verb* to form a piece of wood, etc. into a particular shape by cutting small pieces from it 把（木頭等）削成…：**~ A (from B)** *He whittled a simple toy from the piece of wood.* 他把那塊木頭削成了一個簡易的玩具。◇ **~ B (into A)** *He whittled the piece of wood into a simple toy.* 他把那塊木頭削成了一個簡易的玩具。

PHR V **ˌwhittle sth↔aˈway** to make sth gradually decrease in value or amount 削減，減少，降低（…的價值或數量）**ˌwhittle sth↔ˈdown** to reduce the size or number of sth 減少，縮減（…的大小或數目）：*I finally managed to whittle down the names on the list to only five.* 我最後總算把名單上的名字減少到了只有五個。

whizz (*especially BrE*) (also **whiz** especially in *NAmE*) /wɪz/ *verb, noun*

■ ***verb*** (*informal*) **1** [I] **+ adv./prep.** to move very quickly, making a high continuous sound 嗖地移動；飛速行駛：*A bullet whizzed past my ear.* 一顆子彈嗖的一聲從我耳邊飛過。◇ *He whizzed down the road on his motorbike.* 他騎着摩托車呼嘯着沿路絕塵而去。**2** [I] **+ adv./prep.** to do sth very quickly 快速地做；匆匆地幹：*She whizzed through the work.* 她麻利地把活幹完了。

■ ***noun*** (*informal*) a person who is very good at sth 能手；善於…的人：*She's a whizz at crosswords.* 她填縱橫字謎很在行。

ˈwhizz-kid (*especially BrE*) (*NAmE* usually **ˈwhiz-kid**) *noun* (*informal*) a person who is very good and successful at sth, especially at a young age 神童；有為青年：*financial whizz-kids* 金融方面年輕有為的人物

whizzy /ˈwɪzi/ *adj.* (**whiz·zier**, **whiz·ziest**) (*informal*) having features that make use of advanced technology 採用先進技術的：*a whizzy new hand-held computer* 技術先進的新型掌上電腦

WHO /ˌdʌblju: eɪtʃ ˈəʊ; *NAmE* ˈoʊ/ *abbr.* World Health Organization (an international organization that aims to fight and control disease) 世界衞生組織

who 0‑ /hu:/ *pron.*

1 0‑ used in questions to ask about the name, identity or function of one or more people（詢問姓名、身分或職務）誰，什麼人：*Who is that woman?* 那個女的是誰？◇ *I wonder who that letter was from.* 我不知道是誰來的信。◇ *Who are you phoning?* 你在給誰打電話？◇ *Who's the money for?* 這是給誰的錢？**2** 0‑ used to show which person or people you mean（表示所指的人）：*The people who called yesterday want to buy the house.* 昨天打電話來的人想買這座房子。◇ *The people (who) we met in France have sent us a card.* 我們在法國結識的人給我們寄來了一張賀卡。**3** 0‑ used to give more information about sb（進一步提供有關某人的信息）：*Mrs Smith, who has a lot of teaching experience at junior level, will be joining the school in September.* 史密斯太太將在九月份加入這所學校，她在初級教育方面頗有經驗。◇ *And then Mary, who we had been talking about earlier, walked in.* 隨後瑪麗走了進來，我們剛才還在談論她呢。➲ compare WHOM

IDM **who am ˈI, who are ˈyou, etc. to do sth?** used to ask what right or authority sb has to do sth …憑什麼；…有什麼資格：*Who are you to tell me I can't park here?* 你憑什麼不讓我在這兒停車？**who's ˈwho** people's names, jobs, status, etc. 誰是誰；人們的情況（姓名、工作、身分等）：*You'll soon find out who's who in the office.* 你很快就會瞭解辦公室裏每個人的情況。➲ see also WHO'S WHO

whoa /wəʊ; *NAmE* woʊ/ *exclamation* used as a command to a horse, etc. to make it stop or stand still（吆喝馬等停下或不動的口令）吁

who'd /hu:d/ *short form* **1** who had **2** who would

who·dun·nit (*BrE*) (also **who·dun·it** *NAmE, BrE*) /ˌhu:ˈdʌnɪt/ *noun* (*informal*) a story, play, etc. about a murder in which you do not know who did the murder until the end（在結尾時才能知道誰是謀殺犯的）偵探小說，偵探戲劇

who·ever 0‑ /hu:ˈevə(r)/ *pron.*

1 0‑ the person or people who; any person who …的那個人（或那些人）；…的任何人：*Whoever says that is a liar.* 說那話的人都是騙子。◇ *Send it to whoever is in charge of sales.* 把這寄給負責銷售的人。**2** 0‑ used to say that it does not matter who, since the result will be the same 無論誰；不管什麼人：*Come out of there, whoever you are.* 不管你是誰，從那裏出來吧。◇ *I don't want to see them, whoever they are.* 無論他們是誰，我都不想見。**3** used in questions to mean 'who', expressing surprise（用於問句，表示驚訝）究竟是誰，到底是誰：*Whoever heard of such a thing!* 究竟有誰聽說過這種事！

whole 0‑ /həʊl; *NAmE* hoʊl/ *adj., noun, adv.*

■ ***adj.*** **1** 0‑ [only before noun] full; complete 全部的；整體的；完全的；所有的：*He spent the whole day writing.* 他整整寫了一天。◇ *We drank a whole bottle each.* 我們每人都喝了整整一瓶。◇ *The whole country (= all the people in it) mourned her death.* 舉國都在為她的逝世哀悼。◇ *Let's forget the **whole thing**.* 咱們徹底忘掉這件事吧。◇ *She wasn't telling the **whole truth**.* 她沒有把實情都講出來。**2** 0‑ [only before noun] used to emphasize how large or important sth is（強調大小或重要性）整個的，全部的：*We offer a whole variety of weekend breaks.* 我們提供的週末假日活動豐富多彩，一應俱全。◇ *I can't afford it—that's **the whole point**.* 我買不起，這就是全部的理由。**3** 0‑ not broken or damaged 完整的；完好無損的 **SYN** **in one piece**：*Owls usually swallow their prey whole* (= without chewing it). 貓頭鷹通常把獵物囫圇吞下。➲ note at HALF ▸ **whole·ness** *noun* [U] ➲ see also WHOLLY

IDM Most idioms containing **whole** are at the entries for the nouns and verbs in the idioms, for example **go the whole hog** is at **hog**. 大多數含 whole 的習語，都可在該等習語中的名詞及動詞相關詞條找到，如 go the whole hog 在詞條 hog 下。**a ˈwhole lot** 0‑ (*informal*) very much; a lot 非常；很多：*I'm feeling a whole lot better.* 我覺得好得多了。**a ˈwhole lot (of sth)** 0‑ (*informal*) a large number or amount 許許多多；大量：*There were a whole lot of people I didn't know.* 有許多人我都不認識。◇ *I lost a whole lot of money.* 我丟了好多錢。**the ˌwhole ˈlot** 0‑ everything; all of sth 一切；全部；所有：*I've sold the whole lot.* 我把所有的東西都賣了。

■ ***noun*** **1** 0‑ [C] a thing that is complete in itself 整個；整體：*Four quarters make a whole.* 四個四分之一構成一個整體。◇ *The subjects of the curriculum form a coherent whole.* 課程中的科目構成了一個連貫的整體。**2** 0‑ [sing.] **the ~ of sth** all that there is of sth 全部；全體；所有：*The effects will last for the whole of his life.* 這些將會持續影響他的一生。➲ note at HALF

IDM **as a ˈwhole** 0‑ as one thing or piece and not as separate parts 作為一個整體；總體上：*The festival will be great for our city and for the country as a whole.* 這次慶典活動對我們城市乃至整個國家都將是意義重大的。**on the whole** 0‑ considering everything; in general 總的說來；大體上；基本上：*On the whole, I'm in favour of the idea.* 大體說來，我贊成這個想法。

■ ***adv.*** **~ new/different/other ...** (*informal*) completely new/different 全新的；完全不同的：*It's a whole new world out here.* 這兒是一個全新的世界。◇ *That's a whole other story.* 那完全是另外一回事。

whole·food /ˈhəʊlfu:d; *NAmE* ˈhoʊl-/ *noun* [U] (also **wholefoods** [pl.]) food that is considered healthy because it is in a simple form, has not been REFINED, and does not contain artificial substances（未經加工且不含人造添加劑的）全營養食物；全天然食物

whole·grain /ˈhəʊlgreɪn; *NAmE* ˈhoʊl-/ *adj.* made with or containing whole grains, for example of WHEAT 含全穀物的；全穀物製作的

whole·heart·ed /ˌhəʊlˈhɑ:tɪd; *NAmE* ˌhoʊlˈhɑ:rtəd/ *adj.* (*approving*) complete and enthusiastic 全心全意的；赤誠的：*The plan was given wholehearted support.* 這項計劃得到了全心全意的支持。▸ **whole·heart·ed·ly** *adv.*：*to agree wholeheartedly* 完全同意

whole·meal /ˈhəʊlmi:l; *NAmE* ˈhoʊl-/ (*BrE*) (also **whole-wheat** *NAmE, BrE*) *adj.* **wholemeal/wholewheat** bread or flour contains the whole grains of WHEAT, etc. including the HUSK 全麥的

W

ˈwhole note (*NAmE*) (*BrE* **semi·breve**) *noun* (*music* 音) a note that lasts as long as four CROTCHETS/QUARTER NOTES 全音符 ➲ picture at MUSIC

ˌwhole ˈnumber *noun* (*mathematics* 數) a number that consists of one or more units, with no FRACTIONS (= parts of a number less than one) 整數

whole·sale /ˈhəʊlseɪl; *NAmE* ˈhoʊl-/ *adj.* [only before noun] **1** connected with goods that are bought and sold in large quantities, especially so they can be sold again to make a profit 批發的；躉售的： *wholesale prices* 批發價格 ➲ compare RETAIL¹ *n.* **2** (especially of sth bad 尤指負面的事物) happening or done to a very large number of people or things 大規模的： *the wholesale slaughter of innocent people* 對無辜人民的大屠殺 ▸ **whole·sale** *adv.*： *We buy the building materials wholesale.* 我們批量購買建築材料。◇ *These young people die wholesale from heroin overdoses.* 這些年輕人因過量吸海洛因大批死亡。

whole·sal·ing /ˈhəʊlseɪlɪŋ; *NAmE* ˈhoʊl-/ *noun* [U] the business of buying and selling goods in large quantities, especially so they can be sold again to make a profit 批發業 ➲ compare RETAILING ▸ **whole·saler** *noun*： *fruit and vegetable wholesalers* 水果和蔬菜批發商

whole·some /ˈhəʊlsəm; *NAmE* ˈhoʊl-/ *adj.* **1** good for your health 有益健康的： *fresh, wholesome food* 有益健康的新鮮食品 **2** morally good; having a good moral influence 有道德的；有良好道德影響的： *It was clean wholesome fun.* 這是健康有益的玩樂。 OPP **unwhole·some** ▸ **whole·some·ness** *noun* [U]

ˈwhole step (*US*) (*BrE* **tone**) *noun* (*music* 音) one of the five longer INTERVALS in a musical SCALE, for example the INTERVAL between C and D or between E and F# 全音

whole·wheat /ˈhəʊlwiːt; *NAmE* ˈhoʊl-/ (*BrE* also **whole·meal**) *adj.* **wholewheat** bread or flour contains the whole grains of WHEAT, etc. including the HUSK 全麥的

who'll /huːl/ *short form* who will

whol·ly /ˈhəʊlli; *NAmE* ˈhoʊlli/ *adv.* (*formal*) completely 完全；全面；整體地 SYN **totally**： *wholly inappropriate behaviour* 完全失當的行為 ◇ *The government is not wholly to blame for the recession.* 這次衰退不能完全怨政府。

whom 0⁻ /huːm/ *pron.* (*formal*) used instead of 'who' as the object of a verb or preposition（與 who 同義，作為動詞或介詞的賓語）誰，什麼人： *Whom did they invite?* 他們邀請誰了？◇ *To whom should I write?* 我應該把信寫給誰？◇ *The author whom you criticized in your review has written a reply.* 你在評論中批評的那位作者已經回信答覆了。◇ *Her mother, in whom she confided, said she would support her unconditionally.* 她所信賴的母親說將無條件地支持她。

whom·ever /ˌhuːmˈevə(r)/, **whom·so·ever** /ˌhuːmsəʊˈevə(r); *NAmE* -soʊ-/ *pron.* (*literary*) used instead of 'whoever' as the object of a verb or preposition（與 whoever 同義，作為動詞或介詞的賓語）誰，無論誰： *He was free to marry whomever he chose.* 他看上了誰就可以和誰結婚。

whoop /wuːp; huːp/ *noun, verb*

■ ***noun*** a loud cry expressing joy, excitement, etc.（高興、激動等時的）高喊，大叫： *whoops of delight* 高興的喊叫

■ ***verb*** [I] to shout loudly because you are happy or excited（因高興或激動）高喊，喊叫

IDM **ˌwhoop it ˈup** /wuːp; *NAmE* wʊp/ (*informal*) **1** to enjoy yourself very much with a noisy group of people 歡鬧；狂歡作樂 **2** (*NAmE*) to make people excited or enthusiastic about sth 使群情振奮；使歡欣鼓舞

whoo·pee /wʊˈpiː/ *exclamation, noun*

■ ***exclamation*** used to express happiness（表示高興）哈哈： *Whoopee, we've won!* 哈哈，我們贏了！

■ ***noun*** [U]

IDM **make ˈwhoopee** (*old-fashioned, informal*) to celebrate in a noisy way 狂歡慶祝

ˈwhoopee cushion *noun* a rubber CUSHION that makes a noise like a FART when sb sits on it, used as a joke 放屁座墊，屁袋（坐上去發出放屁聲，開玩笑用）

whoop·ing cough /ˈhuːpɪŋ kɒf; *NAmE* kɔːf/ *noun* [U] an infectious disease, especially of children, that makes them cough and have difficulty breathing 百日咳

whoops /wʊps/ *exclamation* **1** used when sb has almost had an accident, broken sth, etc.（險些出事故或造成小失誤時說）哎喲： *Whoops! Careful, you almost spilt coffee everywhere.* 哎喲！小心點，你差點把咖啡灑得到處都是。 **2** used when you have done sth embarrassing, said sth rude by accident, told a secret, etc.（做了尷尬事或失言後說）唉：*Whoops, you weren't supposed to hear that.* 唉，你不該聽到這事的。

whoosh /wʊʃ; wuːʃ/ *noun, verb*

■ ***noun*** [usually sing.] (*informal*) the sudden movement and sound of air or water rushing past（風吹）呼呼；（水流）嘩嘩： *a whoosh of air* 呼的一口氣 ◇ *There was a whoosh as everything went up in flames.* "呼"的一聲，一切都毀於火海。

■ ***verb*** [I] + **adv./prep.** (*informal*) to move very quickly with the sound of air or water rushing（空氣）呼呼地移動；（水）嘩嘩地流

whop·per /ˈwɒpə(r); *NAmE* ˈwɑːp-/ *noun* (*informal*) **1** something that is very big for its type 特大的（或碩大的）東西： *Pete has caught a whopper* (= a large fish). 皮特捕到了一條特大的魚。 **2** a lie 謊言；瞎話： *She's told some whoppers about her past.* 關於她的過去，她說了些謊話。

whop·ping /ˈwɒpɪŋ; *NAmE* ˈwɑːp-/ (also **ˈwhopping great**) *adj.* [only before noun] (*informal*) very big 巨大的；很大的： *The company made a whopping 75 million dollar loss.* 公司遭受了 7 500 萬元的巨額損失。

whore /hɔː(r)/ *noun* **1** (*old-fashioned*) a female PROSTITUTE 娼妓；妓女 **2** (*taboo*) an offensive word used to refer to a woman who has sex with a lot of men 亂搞男女關係的女人；破鞋

who're /ˈhuːə(r)/ *short form* who are

Grammar Point 語法說明

whom

- **Whom** is not used very often in spoken English. **Who** is usually used as the object pronoun, especially in questions. 在英語口語中，whom 不常用，通常用 who 作賓格代詞，尤其在疑問句中： *Who did you invite to the party?* 你邀請了哪些人來參加聚會？
- The use of **whom** as the pronoun after prepositions is very formal. * whom 作代詞置於介詞後的用法非常正式： *To whom should I address the letter?* 這封信我該寫給誰呢？◇ *He asked me with whom I had discussed it.* 他問我和誰討論過此事。 In spoken English it is much more natural to use **who** and put the preposition at the end of the sentence. 在英語口語中，疑問詞用 who，將介詞置於句末更自然： *Who should I address the letter to?* 這封信我該寫給誰呢？◇ *He asked me who I had discussed it with.* 他問我和誰討論過此事。
- In defining relative clauses the object pronoun **whom** is not often used. You can either use **who** or **that**, or leave out the pronoun completely. 在限定性關係從句中，賓格代詞 whom 不常用，可用 who 或 that 或乾脆省去代詞： *The family (who/that/whom) I met at the airport were very kind.* 我在機場接的這家人非常友好。
- In non-defining relative clauses **who** or, more formally, **whom** (but not *that*) is used and the pronoun cannot be left out. 在非限定性關係從句中，要用 who 或更正式的 whom（但不能用 that），而且此代詞不能省略： *Our doctor, who/whom we all liked very much, retired last week.* 我們的醫生上週退休了，我們都很愛戴他。 This pattern is not used very much in spoken English. 此句型在英語口語中不很常用。

whore·house /ˈhɔːhaʊs; *NAmE* ˈhɔːrh-/ *noun* (*old-fashioned*) a BROTHEL (= a place where people pay to have sex) 妓院

whor·ing /ˈhɔːrɪŋ/ *noun* [U] (*old-fashioned*) the activity of having sex with a PROSTITUTE 嫖妓；嫖娼；宿娼

whorl /wɜːl; *NAmE* wɜːrl/ *noun* **1** a pattern made by a curved line that forms a rough circle, with smaller circles inside bigger ones 螺旋狀圖案；螺紋：*the whorls on your fingertips* 你指紋的渦 **2** (*technical* 術語) a ring of leaves, flowers, etc. around the STEM of a plant 輪，輪生體（環生於植物莖部的葉、花等）

who's /huːz/ *short form* **1** who is **2** who has

whose /huːz/ *det., pron.*
1 used in questions to ask who sth belongs to（用於問句）誰的：*Whose house is that?* 那是誰的房子？◇ *I wonder whose this is.* 我不知道這是誰的。 **2** used to say which person or thing you mean（特指）那個人的，那一個的，其：*He's a man whose opinion I respect.* 他是我尊重其意見的人。◇ *It's the house whose door is painted red.* 這就是那所門戶塗成紅色的房子。 **3** used to give more information about a person or thing（進一步提供信息時用）：*Isobel, whose brother he was, had heard the joke before.* 伊澤貝爾，就是他的弟弟，以前曾經聽說過這個笑話。

who·so·ever /ˌhuːsəʊˈevə(r); *NAmE* -soʊ-/ *pron.* (*old use*) = WHOEVER

ˌwho's ˈwho *noun* a list or book of facts about famous people 名人一覽表；名人錄：*The list of delegates attending read like a who's who of the business world.* 與會代表名單讀起來像個商界名人錄。 ORIGIN From the reference book *Who's Who*, which gives information about many well-known people and what they have done. 源自彙集眾多名人及其事跡的參考書《名人錄》。

who've /huːv/ *short form* who have

whup /wʌp/ *verb* **(-pp-)** **~ sb/sth** (*informal, especially US*) to defeat sb easily in a game, a fight, an election, etc.（在比賽、鬥爭、選舉等中）輕易打敗對方

why /waɪ/ *adv., exclamation, noun*
■ ***adv.*** **1** used in questions to ask the reason for or purpose of sth（用於問句）為什麼，為何：*Why were you late?* 你為什麼遲到？◇ *Tell me why you did it.* 告訴我你為什麼這樣做。◇ *'I would like you to go.' '**Why me?**'* "我希望你去。" "為什麼要我去呢？" ◇ (*informal*) ***Why oh why*** *do people keep leaving the door open?* 人們到底為什麼總敞着門呢？ **2** used in questions to suggest that it is not necessary to do sth（反問，表示不必）何必：*Why get upset just because you got one bad grade?* 何必因為一次成績不好就想不開呢？◇ *Why bother to write? We'll see him tomorrow.* 還費事寫信幹什麼？我們明天就見到他了。 **3** used to give or talk about a reason（說明理由）為什麼，…的原因：*That's why I left so early.* 這就是我早早離去的原因。◇ *I know you did it—I just want to know why.* 我知道這是你幹的，我只是想知道為什麼。◇ ***The reason why*** *the injection needs repeating every year is that the virus changes.* 每年需要重新注射的原因是這病毒經常變化。
IDM **why ˈever** used in questions to mean 'why', expressing surprise（用於問句，語帶驚訝）究竟為什麼：*Why ever didn't you tell us before?* 你為什麼不早告訴我們呢？ **ˌwhy ˈnot?** used to make or agree to a suggestion（提出或贊同建議）為什麼不呢，好哇：*Why not write to her?* 為什麼不給她寫信呢？◇ *'Let's eat out.' '**Why not?**'* "咱們到外邊吃去吧。" "好哇。" ◇ ***Why don't*** *we go together?* 我們為什麼不一起去呢？
■ ***exclamation*** (*old-fashioned* or *NAmE*) used to express surprise, lack of patience, etc.（驚訝、不耐煩等時說）哎呀，呦，喲，嗨：*Why Jane, it's you!* 呦，簡，是你呀！◇ *Why, it's easy—a child could do it!* 嗨，這容易得很，連小孩子都幹得了！
■ ***noun***
IDM **the ˌwhys and (the) ˈwherefores** the reasons for sth 理由；原因；緣故：*I had no intention of going into the whys and the wherefores of the situation.* 我無意深入調查這一情況的來龍去脈。

WI *abbr.* **1** West Indies 西印度群島 **2** /ˌdʌbljuː ˈaɪ/ Women's Institute (a British women's organization in which groups of women meet regularly to take part in various activities) 婦女協會

Wicca /ˈwɪkə/ *noun* [U] a modern form of WITCHCRAFT, practised as a religion（現代）巫術宗教 ► **Wic·can** /ˈwɪkən/ *adj.*

wick /wɪk/ *noun, verb*
■ ***noun*** **1** the piece of string in the centre of a CANDLE which you light so that the candle burns 燭芯 ➲ VISUAL VOCAB page V22 **2** the piece of material in an oil lamp which absorbs the oil and which you light so that the lamp burns 燈芯
IDM **get on sb's ˈwick** (*BrE, informal*) to annoy sb 激怒（某人）；招惹（某人）
■ ***verb*** **~ sth (away)** (of a material) to take small drops of liquid from an area and move them away（指材料）吸乾，吸取，吸走：*Wool socks wick away sweat.* 羊毛襪吸汗。

wicked /ˈwɪkɪd/ *adj., noun*
■ ***adj.*** (**wick·ed·er**, **wick·ed·est**) HELP You can also use **more wicked** and **most wicked**. 亦可用 more wicked 和 most wicked。 **1** morally bad 邪惡的；缺德的 SYN **evil**：*a wicked deed* 傷天害理的行為 ◇ *stories about a wicked witch* 關於邪惡女巫的故事 **2** (*informal*) slightly bad but in a way that is amusing and/or attractive 淘氣的；調皮的；惡作劇的 SYN **mischievous**：*a wicked grin* 調皮的咧嘴一笑 ◇ *Jane has a wicked sense of humour.* 簡有一種惡作劇的幽默感。 **3** dangerous, harmful or powerful 危險的；有害的；強大的：*He has a wicked punch.* 他出拳兇猛。◇ *a wicked-looking knife* 寒光四射的刀 **4** (*slang*) very good 極好的；很棒的：*This song's wicked.* 這支歌太棒了。 ► **wick·ed·ly** *adv.*：*Martin grinned wickedly.* 馬丁頑皮地咧嘴笑了笑。◇ *a wickedly funny comedy* 惡作劇式的滑稽喜劇 ◇ *a wickedly sharp blade* 寒光四射的利刃 **wick·ed·ness** *noun* [U]
■ ***noun*** **the wicked** [pl.] people who are wicked 惡人；邪惡的人
IDM **(there's) no peace/rest for the ˈwicked** (usually *humorous*) used when sb is complaining that they have a lot of work to do（工作太多時說）惡人決無平安

wicker /ˈwɪkə(r)/ *noun* [U] thin sticks of wood twisted together to make BASKETS, furniture, etc.（編製筐籃、傢具等用的）柳條，枝條：*a wicker chair* 柳條椅

wick·er·work /ˈwɪkəwɜːk; *NAmE* ˈwɪkərwɜːrk/ *noun* [U] BASKETS, furniture, etc. made from wicker 柳條編製品

wicket /ˈwɪkɪt/ *noun* (in CRICKET 板球) **1** either of the two sets of three vertical sticks (called STUMPS) with pieces of wood (called BAILS) lying across the top. The BOWLER tries to hit the wicket with the ball. 三柱門 ➲ VISUAL VOCAB page V44 **2** the area of ground between the two wickets 兩個三柱門之間的場地
IDM **keep ˈwicket** to act as a WICKETKEEPER 防守三柱門 ➲ more at STICKY *adj.*

ˈwicket gate *noun* a small gate, especially one at the side of a larger one（尤指大門旁的）小門，便門，旁門

wicket·keep·er /ˈwɪkɪtkiːpə(r)/ (also *BrE informal* **keep·er**) *noun* (in CRICKET 板球) a player who stands behind the WICKET in order to stop or catch the ball 三柱門守門員；捕手 ➲ VISUAL VOCAB page V44

wide /waɪd/ *adj., adv., noun*

> **WORD FAMILY**
> wide *adj., adv.*
> widely *adv.*
> widen *verb*
> width *noun*

■ ***adj.*** (**wider**, **wid·est**)
► FROM ONE SIDE TO THE OTHER 從一邊到另一邊 **1** measuring a lot from one side to the other 寬的；寬闊的：*a wide river* 寬闊的河 ◇ *Sam has a wide mouth.* 薩姆有一張大嘴。◇ *a jacket with wide lapels* 寬翻領夾克衫 ◇ *Her face broke into a **wide grin**.* 她滿臉堆笑。 OPP **narrow** ➲ see also WIDTH **2** measuring a particular distance from one side to the other …寬的；寬度為…的：***How wide*** *is that stream?* 那條小溪有多寬？◇ *It's about 2 metres wide.* 它大約 2 米寬。◇ *The road was just wide enough for two vehicles to pass.* 這條路的寬度剛好能讓兩輛車開過。

W

▸ LARGE NUMBER/AMOUNT 大量 **3** 🔑 including a large number or variety of different people or things; covering a large area 大量的；廣泛的；範圍大的： *a wide range/choice/variety of goods* 一系列品種繁多的 / 大量可供選擇的 / 各種各樣的貨品 ◇ *Her music appeals to a wide audience.* 她的音樂吸引了大批的聽眾。◇ *Jenny has a wide circle of friends.* 珍妮交友甚廣。◇ *a manager with wide experience of industry* 在工業方面經驗豐富的經理 ◇ *It's the best job in **the whole wide world**.* 這是整個大千世界中最好的工作。◇ *The incident has received wide coverage in the press.* 這個事件已被新聞界廣泛報道。◇ *The festival attracts people from a wide area.* 這個藝術節吸引了四面八方的人。

▸ DIFFERENCE/GAP 差距；缺口 **4** 🔑 very big 很大的： *There are wide variations in prices.* 價格的變動很大。

▸ GENERAL 廣泛 **5** (only used in the comparative and superlative 僅用於比較級和最高級) general; not only looking at details 一般的；廣泛的： *the wider aims of the project* 該計劃更廣義的宗旨 ◇ *We are talking about education **in its widest sense**.* 我們在討論最廣義的教育。

▸ EYES 眼睛 **6** fully open 睜大的；全張開的： *She stared at him with wide eyes.* 她睜大了眼睛瞪着他。

▸ NOT CLOSE 距離遠 **7 ~ (of sth)** far from the point aimed at 遠離目標： *Her shot was wide (of the target).* 她的槍打飛了靶。

▸ -WIDE 全…範圍 **8** (in adjectives and adverbs 構成形容詞和副詞) happening or existing in the whole of a country, etc. 全（國等）範圍的： *a nationwide search* 全國性的搜查 ◇ *We need to act on a Europe-wide scale.* 我們得在全歐洲範圍內採取行動。

IDM **give sb/sth a wide 'berth** to not go too near sb/sth; to avoid sb/sth 對…避而遠之；退避三舍： *He gave the dog a wide berth.* 他遠遠避開那條狗。 **wide of the 'mark** not accurate 不準確；離譜： *Their predictions turned out to be wide of the mark.* 後來發現他們的預測結果太離譜了。

■ *adv.* (**wider**, **wid·est**) as far or fully as possible 盡可能遠地；充分地： *The door was **wide open**.* 門四敞大開。◇ *The championship is still **wide open*** (= anyone could win). 誰將獲得冠軍還難以預料。◇ *She had a fear of **wide-open spaces**.* 身處開闊的空地中會使她感到害怕。◇ *He stood with his legs **wide apart**.* 他站在那裏，兩腿大張。◇ *In a few seconds she was **wide awake**.* 片刻之間她完全醒來。◇ ***Open** your mouth **wide**.* 把嘴張大。

IDM see CAST *v.*, FAR *adv.*

■ *noun* (*sport* 體) a ball that has been BOWLED (= thrown) where the BATSMAN or BATTER cannot reach it（板球）歪球，壞球

,wide-angle 'lens *noun* a camera LENS that can give a wider view than a normal lens 廣角透鏡

'wide boy *noun* (*BrE, informal, disapproving*) a man who makes money in dishonest ways 騙錢者

,wide-'eyed *adj* **1** with your eyes fully open because of fear, surprise, etc.（因恐懼、驚訝等）睜大眼睛的： *She stared at him in wide-eyed amazement.* 她睜大眼睛驚訝地注視着他。 **2** having little experience and therefore very willing to believe, trust or accept sb/sth 天真的 SYN **naive**

wide·ly 🔑 /ˈwaɪdli/ *adv.*

1 🔑 by a lot of people; in or to many places 普遍地；廣泛地；範圍廣地： *a widely held belief* 普遍持有的信念 ◇ *The idea is now widely accepted.* 這個思想現在已獲得普遍接受。◇ *He has travelled widely in Asia.* 他在亞洲許多地方旅遊過。◇ *Her books are **widely read*** (= a lot of people read them). 她寫的書有眾多的讀者。◇ *He's an educated, **widely-read** man* (= he has read a lot of books). 他這個人有教養，博覽群書。 **2** 🔑 to a large degree; a lot 很大程度上；大大地： *Standards vary widely.* 程度參差不齊。

widen /ˈwaɪdn/ *verb* **1** [I, T] to become wider; to make sth wider（使）變寬；加寬；拓寬；放寬： *Her eyes widened in surprise.* 她驚訝地睜大了眼睛。◇ **~ into sth** *Here the stream widens into a river.* 溪水在這裏變寬，成了一條河。◇ **~ sth** *They may have to widen the road to cope with the increase in traffic.* 他們可能得拓寬這條道路以適應車輛的增多。 **2** [I, T] to become larger in degree or range; to make sth larger in degree or range（使）擴展，程度加深，範圍擴大： *the widening gap between rich and poor* 貧富之間日益擴大的差距 ◇ **~ sth** *We plan to widen the scope of our existing activities by offering more language courses.* 我們計劃通過開設更多的語言課程以擴大我們現有的活動範圍。◇ *The legislation will be widened to include all firearms.* 這項法規的範圍將擴大到包括所有的槍支。

Synonyms 同義詞辨析

wide / broad

These adjectives are frequently used with the following nouns. 以上形容詞常與下列名詞連用：

wide ~	broad ~
street	shoulders
river	back
area	smile
range	range
variety	agreement
choice	outline

■ **Wide** is the word most commonly used to talk about something that measures a long distance from one side to the other. **Broad** is more often used to talk about parts of the body. (Although **wide** can be used with *mouth*.) * wide 為最普通用語，指寬闊。broad 較常用以指身體部位寬、闊。（不過 wide 可與 mouth 連用。）It is used in more formal or written language to describe the features of the countryside, etc. * broad 在較正式或書面語中指鄉村景物遼闊、開闊： *a broad river* 寬闊的河流 ◇ *a broad stretch of meadowland* 一片遼闊的草原

■ Both **wide** and **broad** can be used to describe something that includes a large variety of different people or things. * wide 和 broad 均可用以表示人或事物種類很多： *a wide/broad range of products* 各種各樣的產品 **Broad**, but not **wide**, can be used to mean 'general' or 'not detailed'. * broad 可表示大概、粗略、不詳細，wide 無此意： *All of us are in broad agreement on this matter.* 我們大家就此事基本達成一致意見。

,wide-'ranging *adj.* including or dealing with a large number of different subjects or areas 覆蓋面廣的；內容廣泛的： *The commission has been given wide-ranging powers.* 委員會被授予的權限很廣。◇ *a wide-ranging discussion* 廣泛的討論

wide·screen /ˈwaɪdskriːn/ *noun* [U] a way of presenting images on television with the width a lot greater than the height（電視）寬屏幕模式，寬螢幕 SYN **letterbox**： *a widescreen TV* 寬屏電視

wide·spread AW /ˈwaɪdspred/ *adj.* existing or happening over a large area or among many people 分佈廣的；普遍的；廣泛的： *widespread damage* 廣泛的損壞 ◇ *The plan received widespread support throughout the country.* 這項計劃得到了全國的普遍支持。

widg·eon = WIGEON

widget /ˈwɪdʒɪt/ *noun* **1** (*informal*) used to refer to any small device that you do not know the name of（不知名的）小器物，小裝置，小玩意兒 **2** (*business* 商) a product that does not exist, used as an example of a typical product when making calculations 典型產品（並不真實存在，作計算之用）： *Company A produces two million widgets a year.* * A 公司年產 200 萬件產品。 **3** (*computing* 計) a small box on a web page that delivers changing information, such as news items or weather reports, while the rest of the page remains the same 微件，控件，掛件（網頁上顯示不時更新的信息的小窗口）

widow /ˈwɪdəʊ; *NAmE* ˈwɪdoʊ/ *noun, verb*

■ *noun* a woman whose husband has died and who has not married again 寡婦；遺孀

■ *verb* **be widowed** if sb **is widowed**, their husband or wife has died 使喪偶；使成為寡婦（或鰥夫）：*She was widowed when she was 35.* 她 35 歲時就守了寡。
▸ **widowed** *adj.*：*his widowed father* 他鰥居的父親

wid·ow·er /ˈwɪdəʊə(r); *NAmE* ˈwɪdoʊ-/ *noun* a man whose wife has died and who has not married again 鰥夫

widow·hood /ˈwɪdəʊhʊd; *NAmE* ˈwɪdoʊ-/ *noun* [U] the state or period of being a widow or widower 寡居（期）；鰥居（期）

ˌwidow's ˈpeak *noun* hair growing in the shape of a V on sb's FOREHEAD（額前的）V 形髮尖 ➲ VISUAL VOCAB page V60

width 0‑ /wɪdθ; wɪtθ/ *noun*
1 0‑ [U, C] the measurement from one side of sth to the other; how wide sth is 寬度；廣度：*It's about 10 metres **in width**.* 它寬約 10 米。◇ *The terrace runs **the full width of** the house.* 露台和房子一般寬。◇ *The carpet is available in different widths.* 這款地毯有各種寬度可供選擇。 **2** [C] a piece of material of a particular width 某一寬度的材料：*You'll need two widths of fabric for each curtain.* 每個窗簾你需要兩塊這樣寬的布料。 **3** [C] the distance between the two long sides of a swimming pool（游泳池兩長邊之間的）池寬：*How many widths can you swim?* 你在游泳池裏橫向能游幾個來回？ ➲ compare LENGTH (1)

width·ways /ˈwɪdθweɪz; ˈwɪtθ-/ *adv.* along the width and not the length 橫向地；橫着：*Cut the cake in half widthways.* 將這個蛋糕橫着切成兩半。 ➲ compare LENGTHWAYS

wield /wiːld/ *verb* **1 ~ sth** to have and use power, authority, etc. 擁有，運用，行使，支配（權力等）：*She wields enormous power within the party.* 她操縱着黨內大權。 **2 ~ sth** to hold sth, ready to use it as a weapon or tool 揮，操，使用（武器、工具等） SYN **brandish**：*He was wielding a large knife.* 他揮舞着一把大刀。

wie·ner /ˈwiːnə(r)/ *noun* (*NAmE*) **1** = FRANKFURTER **2** (*slang*) a word for a PENIS, used especially by children 小雞雞（指陰莖，尤用於兒語）

wife 0‑ /waɪf/ *noun* (*pl.* **wives** /waɪvz/)
the woman that a man is married to; a married woman 妻子；太太；夫人；已婚婦女：*the doctor's wife* 醫生的太太 ◇ *She's his second wife.* 她是他的第二個妻子。◇ *an increase in the number of working wives* 已婚職業婦女人數的增加 ➲ COLLOCATIONS at MARRIAGE ➲ see also FISHWIFE, HOUSEWIFE, MIDWIFE, TROPHY WIFE IDM see HUSBAND *n.*, OLD, WORLD

wife·ly /ˈwaɪfli/ *adj.* (*old-fashioned* or *humorous*) typical or expected of a wife 妻子特有（或應有）的；作為人妻的；已婚婦女的：*wifely duties* 妻子的責任

ˈwife-swapping *noun* [U] (*informal*) the practice of exchanging sexual partners between a group of married couples 換妻（數對夫妻聚集交換性伴侶的活動）

Wi-fi™ /ˈwaɪ faɪ/ *noun* [U] (*computing* 計) the abbreviation for 'wireless fidelity' (a system for sending data over computer networks using radio waves instead of wires) 無線保真（全寫為 wireless fidelity，用無線電波而非網線在計算機網絡傳輸數據的系統）

wig /wɪg/ *noun, verb*
■ *noun* a piece of artificial hair that is worn on the head, for example to hide the fact that a person is BALD, to cover sb's own hair, or by a judge and some other lawyers in some courts of law 假髮
■ *verb* (-gg-)
PHR V **ˌwig ˈout** (*NAmE, informal*) to become very excited, very anxious or angry about sth; to go crazy 變得激動（或焦慮、生氣）；發狂

wig·eon (also **widg·eon**) /ˈwɪdʒən/ *noun* (*pl.* **wig·eon**, **widg·eon**) a type of wild DUCK 赤頸鴨

wig·gle /ˈwɪgl/ *verb, noun*
■ *verb* [I, T] (*informal*) **~ sth** to move from side to side or up and down in short quick movements; to make sth move in this way（使）扭動，擺動，搖動，起伏 SYN **wriggle**：*He removed his shoes and wiggled his toes.* 他脱掉鞋子，扭動着腳趾。◇ *Her bottom wiggled as she walked past.* 她屁股一扭一扭地走了過去。
■ *noun* a small movement from side to side or up and down（輕微的）擺動，扭動，搖動，起伏

ˈwiggle room *noun* [U] (*informal*) the chance to change sth or to understand it in a different way 迴旋餘地；空子：*The buyer still has some wiggle room when the deal is under contract.* 根據合同，買方在交易時仍有一定的迴旋餘地。◇ *The amendment leaves no wiggle room for lawmakers.* 修正案沒有給立法者留下漏洞。

wig·gly /ˈwɪgli/ *adj.* (*informal*) (of a line 線) having many curves in it 彎彎曲曲的；波浪形的；起伏的 SYN **wavy**

wight /waɪt/ *noun* (*literary* or *old use*) **1** a GHOST or other spirit 鬼；幽靈 **2** (especially following an adjective 尤用於形容詞之後) a person, considered in a particular way …的人：*a poor wight* 可憐鬼

wig·wam /ˈwɪgwæm; *NAmE* -wɑːm/ *noun* a type of tent, shaped like a DOME or CONE, used by Native Americans in the past（舊時印第安人使用的圓頂或錐形的）棚屋 ➲ see also TEPEE

wiki /ˈwɪki/ *noun* a website that allows any user to change or add to the information it contains 維基（允許用戶修改或添加信息的網站）：*There's a wiki page hosted by the conference where you can share ideas and information.* 大會建立了維基網頁，供大家交流想法和共享信息。

wilco /ˈwɪlkəʊ; *NAmE* -koʊ/ *exclamation* people say **Wilco!** in communication by radio to show that they agree to do sth（無線電用語）照辦，遵辦

wild 0‑ /waɪld/ *adj., noun*
■ *adj.* (**wild·er**, **wild·est**)
▸ ANIMALS/PLANTS 動植物 **1** 0‑ living or growing in natural conditions; not kept in a house or on a farm 自然生長的；野的；野生的：***wild animals/flowers*** 野生動物；野花 ◇ *a wild rabbit* 野兔 ◇ *wild strawberries* 野草莓 ◇ *The plants **grow wild** along the banks of rivers.* 沿河兩岸生長着野生植物。
▸ SCENERY/LAND 風景；土地 **2** 0‑ in its natural state; not changed by people 天然的；荒涼的；荒蕪的：*wild moorland* 荒涼的高沼地
▸ OUT OF CONTROL 失去控制 **3** 0‑ lacking discipline or control 缺乏管教的；無法無天的；放蕩的：*The boy is wild and completely out of control.* 這男孩缺乏管教，簡直是完全失控。◇ *He had a wild look in his eyes.* 他的眼神很不安分。
▸ FEELINGS 感情 **4** 0‑ full of very strong feeling 感情熾烈的：*wild laughter* 開懷大笑 ◇ *The crowd **went wild**.* 群情激昂。◇ *It makes me wild* (= very angry) *to see such waste.* 看到這種浪費現象讓我非常生氣。
▸ NOT SENSIBLE 不合情理 **5** 0‑ not carefully planned; not sensible or accurate 盲目的；瞎抓的：*He made a wild guess at the answer.* 他胡亂猜了個答案。◇ *wild accusations* 無端的指責
▸ EXCITING 激動 **6** (*informal*) very good, enjoyable or exciting 很棒的；高興的；令人激動的：*We had a wild time in New York.* 我們在紐約玩得痛快極了。
▸ ENTHUSIASTIC 熱情 **7 ~ about sb/sth** (*informal*) very enthusiastic about sb/sth 熱衷於…；狂熱：*She's totally wild about him.* 她對他簡直是着了迷。◇ *I'm not wild about the idea.* 我對這個想法不太感興趣。
▸ WEATHER/SEA 天氣；海洋 **8** affected by storms and strong winds 狂暴的；暴風雨的 SYN **stormy**：*a wild night* 暴風雨之夜 ◇ *The sea was wild.* 大海波濤洶湧。
▸ **wild·ness** *noun* [U] ➲ see also WILDLY
IDM **beyond sb's wildest ˈdreams** far more, better, etc. than you could ever have imagined or hoped for 做夢都沒想到；遠遠出乎所料；大大超出希望 **not/never in sb's wildest ˈdreams** used to say that sth has happened in a way that sb did not expect at all（表示完全出乎意料）做夢都沒有，從來沒有想到：*Never in my wildest dreams did I think I'd meet him again.* 我連做夢都沒想到會再見他。 **run ˈwild 1** to grow or develop freely without any control 變得荒蕪；自由生長；任其發展：*The ivy has run wild.* 常春藤長瘋了。◇ *Let your **imagination run wild** and be creative.* 讓你的想像力自由馳騁發揮創意吧。 **2** if children or animals **run wild**, they behave as they like because nobody is controlling

them 恣意妄為；變得狂野 **wild 'horses would not drag, make, etc. sb (do sth)** used to say that nothing would prevent sb from doing sth or make them do sth they do not want to do 任何事情都不能阻止（或促使某人做某事）；八匹馬拉不了某人回頭 ➲ more at sow¹

■ ***noun* 1 the wild** [sing.] a natural environment that is not controlled by people 自然環境；野生狀態：*The bird is too tame now to survive **in the wild**.* 這隻鳥養得太溫馴了，現在很難在野生環境中生存。 **2 the wilds** [pl.] areas of a country far from towns or cities, where few people live 偏遠地區；人煙稀少的地區：*the wilds of Alaska* 阿拉斯加人煙稀少的地區 ◊ (*humorous*) *They live on a farm somewhere out **in the wilds**.* 他們住在邊遠地區的一個農場裏。

ˌwild 'boar *noun* = BOAR

'wild card *noun* **1** (in card games 紙牌遊戲) a card that has no value of its own and takes the value of any card that the player chooses（由持牌人自由決定牌值的）百搭派，變牌 **2** (*sport* 體) an opportunity for sb to play in a competition when they have not qualified in the usual way; a player who enters a competition in this way "百搭"式參賽，"百搭"式參賽選手，"外卡"參賽，"外卡"選手（指沒有正常參賽資格而參賽） **3** (*computing* 計) a symbol that has no meaning of its own and can represent any letter or number 通配符 **4** a person or thing whose behaviour or effect is difficult to predict 難以預測的人（或事物）；未知因素；未知數

wild·cat /'waɪldkæt/ *adj., verb, noun*

■ ***adj.*** [only before noun] **1** a **wildcat strike** happens suddenly and without the official support of a TRADE/LABOR UNION（罷工）未經工會同意的，突然自發進行的 **2** (of a business or project 企業或項目) that has not been carefully planned and that will probably not be successful; that does not follow normal standards and methods（計劃不周密而）不穩妥的；不按正常標準的

■ ***verb*** (**-tt-**) [I] (*NAmE*) to look for oil in a place where nobody has found any yet 勘探石油 ▶ **wild·cat·ter** *noun*

■ ***noun*** a type of small wild cat that lives in mountains and forests 野貓（生活在山區或森林裏）

wilde·beest /'wɪldəbiːst/ *noun* (*pl.* **wilde·beest**) (also **gnu**) a large ANTELOPE with curved horns 牛羚；角馬：*a herd of wildebeest* 一群牛羚

wil·der·ness /'wɪldənəs; *NAmE* -dərn-/ *noun* [usually sing.] **1** a large area of land that has never been developed or used for growing crops because it is difficult to live there 未開發的地區；荒無人煙的地區；荒野：*The Antarctic is the world's last great wilderness.* 南極洲是世界上最後一個大荒原。◊ (*NAmE*) *a **wilderness area*** (= one where it is not permitted to build houses or roads)（政府劃定的）保留自然環境面貌地區 ◊ (*figurative*) *the barren wilderness of modern life* 現代生活貧瘠的荒漠 **2** a place that people do not take care of or control 荒蕪的地方；雜草叢生處：*Their garden is a wilderness of grass and weeds.* 他們的花園雜草叢生。

IDM in the 'wilderness no longer in an important position, especially in politics 在野；不再當政（或掌權）

W

wild·fire /'waɪldfaɪə(r)/ *noun* [U] **IDM** see SPREAD *v.*

wild·fowl /'waɪldfaʊl/ *noun* [pl.] birds that people hunt for sport or food, especially birds that live near water such as DUCKS and GEESE（尤指生活在水邊被人獵食的）野禽，野鴨，野鵝

ˌwild 'goose chase *noun* a search for sth that is impossible for you to find or that does not exist, that makes you waste a lot of time 徒勞的尋找；白費力氣的追逐

wild·life /'waɪldlaɪf/ *noun* [U] animals, birds, insects, etc. that are wild and live in a natural environment 野生動物；野生生物：*Development of the area would endanger wildlife.* 開發這一地區將會危及到野生生物。◊ *a **wildlife habitat/sanctuary*** 野生動物棲息地／保護區

wild·ly 🔑 /'waɪldli/ *adv.* **1** 🔑 in a way that is not controlled 失控地；紊亂地：*She looked wildly around for an escape.* 她環顧四周，拚命尋找逃路。◊ *His heart was beating wildly.* 他的心臟劇烈地跳着。 **2** 🔑 extremely; very 極其；非常：*The story had been wildly exaggerated.* 這件事被過分地誇大了。◊ *It is not a wildly funny play.* 這並不是一齣太滑稽的戲劇。

the ˌWild 'West *noun* [sing.] the western states of the US during the years when the first Europeans were settling there, used especially when you are referring to the fact that there was not much respect for the law there 荒野西部，西大荒（開拓時期，尤指尚無法制的美國西部）

wiles /waɪlz/ *noun* [pl.] clever tricks that sb uses in order to get what they want or to make sb behave in a particular way 花招；詭計；奸計

wil·ful (*especially BrE*) (*NAmE* usually **will·ful**) /'wɪlfl/ *adj.* (*disapproving*) **1** [usually before noun] (*formal, disapproving* or *law* 律) (of a bad or harmful action 不友好或有害行為) done deliberately, although the person doing it knows that it is wrong 故意的；有意的；成心的：*wilful damage* 蓄意破壞 **2** determined to do what you want; not caring about what other people want 任性的；固執的；倔強的 **SYN headstrong**：*a wilful child* 任性的孩子 ▶ **wil·ful·ly** /-fəli/ *adv.* **wil·ful·ness** *noun* [U]

will 🔑 /wɪl/ *modal verb, verb, noun*

■ ***modal verb*** (*short form* **'ll** /l/, *negative* **will not**, *short form* **won't** /wəʊnt; *NAmE* woʊnt/, *pt* **would** /wəd/; *strong form* wʊd/, *short form* **'d** /d/, *negative* **would not**, *short form* **wouldn't** /'wʊdnt/) **1** 🔑 used for talking about or predicting the future（談及將來）：*You'll be in time if you hurry.* 你要是抓緊一點兒就會來得及。◊ *How long will you be staying in Paris?* 你將在巴黎待多久？◊ *Fred said he'd be leaving soon.* 弗雷德說他很快就要走了。◊ *By next year all the money will have been spent.* 到明年所有的錢都將花光了。 **2** 🔑 used for showing that sb is willing to do sth（表示願意）願，要，會，定要：*I'll check this letter for you, if you want.* 你要是願意，我會給你查查這封信的。◊ *They won't lend us any more money.* 他們不願再借給我們錢了。◊ *He wouldn't come—he said he was too busy.* 他不願來，他說他太忙。◊ *We said we would keep them.* 我們說過要保存它們的。 **3** 🔑 used for asking sb to do sth（煩勞別人做事時用）：*Will you send this letter for me, please?* 請你替我把這封信寄出去行嗎？◊ *You'll water the plants while I'm away, won't you?* 我外出的時候請你給花草澆澆水，行不行？◊ *I asked him if he wouldn't mind calling later.* 我問他能否過會兒再來電話。 **4** 🔑 used for ordering sb to do sth（命令時用）：*You'll do it this minute!* 你現在就要做這事！◊ *Will you be quiet!* 安靜點兒！ **5** 🔑 used for stating what you think is probably true（含有肯定的意思）：*That'll be the doctor now.* 這會兒準是醫生來了。◊ *You'll have had dinner already, I suppose.* 我想，到時候你大概已經吃過飯了。 **6** 🔑 used for stating what is generally true（敍述一般真理）：*If it's made of wood it will float.* 這要是木材做的就能浮在水面上。◊ *Engines won't run without lubricants.* 沒有潤滑油發動機就不能運轉。 **7** 🔑 used for stating what is true or possible in a particular case（敍述在某種情況下是真實或可能的事）：*This jar will hold a kilo.* 這個罐子能盛一千克。◊ *The door won't open!* 那扇門就是打不開！ **8** 🔑 used for talking about habits（談及習慣）：*She'll listen to music, alone in her room, for hours.* 她總是獨自一個人在屋裏聽音樂，一聽就是幾個小時。◊ *He would spend hours on the telephone.* 他一打電話往往就是幾個小時。 **HELP** If you put extra stress on the word **will** or **would** in this meaning, it shows that the habit annoys you. 在此義中如果重讀 will 或 would，即表示這一習慣令人惱火：*He 'will comb his hair at the table, even though he knows I don't like it.* ➲ note at MODAL, SHALL

■ ***verb*** (*third person sing. pres. t.* **will**) [I] (only used in the simple present tense 僅用於簡單現在時) (*old-fashioned* or *formal*) to want or like 想要；希望；願意；喜歡：*Call it what you will, it's still a problem.* 不管怎麼說，這仍然是個問題。

■ ***verb* 1** to use the power of your mind to do sth or to make sth happen 立定志向；決心；決意：**～ sth** *As a child he had thought he could fly, if he willed it enough.* 他小時候曾經以為，只要有足夠決心，想要飛就能飛起來。◊ **～ sb/sth to do sth** *She willed her eyes to stay open.* 她使勁睜着眼睛。◊ *He willed himself not to panic.* 他竭

力讓自己不要恐慌。 **2 ~ sth | ~ that …** (*old use*) to intend or want sth to happen 想要（某事發生）: *They thought they had been victorious in battle because God had willed it.* 他們以為自己打了勝仗是上帝的旨意。 **3** to formally give your property or possessions to sb after you have died, by means of a WILL *n.* (3) 立遺囑將（財產等）贈與（某人）；立遺囑贈與: **~ sb sth** *Joe had willed them everything he possessed.* 喬把自己擁有的一切都遺贈給了他們。◇ **~ sth (to sb)** *Joe had willed everything he possessed to them.* 喬把自己擁有的一切都遺贈給了他們。

■ ***noun*** **1** [C, U] the ability to control your thoughts and actions in order to achieve what you want to do; a feeling of strong determination to do sth that you want to do 意志；毅力；自制力: *to have a **strong will*** 有堅強的意志◇ *to have **an iron will/a will of iron*** 有鋼鐵般的意志◇ *Her decision to continue shows great strength of will.* 她決心堅持下去，顯示出了很大的意志力。◇ *In spite of what happened, he never lost **the will to live**.* 儘管如此遭遇，他從未喪失活下去的意志。◇ *The meeting turned out to be a **clash of wills**.* 這次會議結果成了一次意志的角力。◇ *She always wants to impose her will on other people* (= to get what she wants). 她總是想把自己的意志強加於人。➲ see also FREE WILL, WILLPOWER **2** [sing.] what sb wants to happen in a particular situation 意願；心願: *I don't want to go against your will.* 我不想違背您的意願。◇ (*formal*) *It is God's will.* 這是上帝的旨意。 **3** (also **tes·ta·ment**) [C] a legal document that says what is to happen to sb's money and property after they die 遺囑: *I ought to **make a will**.* 我應該立份遺囑。◇ *My father left me the house in his will.* 我父親在遺囑中把這所房子遺贈給了我。➲ see also LIVING WILL **4 -willed** (in adjectives 構成形容詞) having the type of will mentioned 有…意志的；…毅力的: *a strong-willed young woman* 意志堅強的年輕女子◇ *weak-willed greedy people* 意志薄弱而貪婪的人

IDM **against your 'will** when you do not want to 不情願地；違心地: *I was forced to sign the agreement against my will.* 我被迫違心地簽了這份協議。 **at 'will** whenever or wherever you like 任意；隨意: *They were able to come and go at will.* 他們能夠來去自由。 **where there's a ˌwill there's a 'way** (*saying*) if you really want to do sth then you will find a way of doing it 有志者事竟成 **with a 'will** in a willing and enthusiastic way 願意地；熱情地；樂意地 **with the ˌbest will in the 'world** used to say that you cannot do sth, even though you really want to 儘管已盡心竭力；儘管真心願意: *With the best will in the world I could not describe him as a good father.* 儘管我心裏極想美言幾句，卻怎麼也不能說他是位好父親。

will·ful (*NAmE*) = WILFUL

wil·lie = WILLY

the wil·lies /ˈwɪliz/ *noun* [pl.] (*informal*) if sth **gives you the willies**, you are frightened by it or find it unpleasant 心裏發毛；滿心不自在

will·ing /ˈwɪlɪŋ/ *adj.*
1 [not usually before noun] **~ (to do sth)** not objecting to doing sth; having no reason for not doing sth 願意；樂意: *They keep a list of people (who are) willing to work nights.* 他們有一份願意夜間工作的人的名單。◇ *I'm **perfectly willing** to discuss the problem.* 我十分樂意討論這個問題。 **2** [usually before noun] ready or pleased to help and not needing to be persuaded; done or given in an enthusiastic way 自願的；樂於相助的；積極肯幹的: ***willing helpers/volunteers*** 主動幫忙的人；志願工作者◇ *willing support* 自願的支持◇ *She's very willing.* 她非常積極肯幹。 **OPP** **unwilling** ▸ **will·ing·ly** *adv.*: *People would willingly pay more for better services.* 有好一些的服務，人們是願意多花錢的。◇ *'Will you help me?' 'Willingly.'* "請幫幫我好嗎？" "當然可以。" **will·ing·ness** *noun* [U, sing.] **IDM** see GOD, SHOW *v.*, SPIRIT

will-o'-the-wisp /ˌwɪl ə ðə ˈwɪsp/ *noun* [usually sing.] **1** a thing that is impossible to obtain; a person that you cannot depend on 難以捉摸的人（或事物）；鏡花水月；虛無之物 **2** a blue light that is sometimes seen at night on soft wet ground and is caused by natural gases burning 磷火；鬼火

wil·low /ˈwɪləʊ; *NAmE* ˈwɪloʊ/ *noun* **1** [C] a tree with long thin branches and long thin leaves, that often grows near water 柳；柳樹 ➲ **VISUAL VOCAB** page V10 ➲ see also PUSSY WILLOW **2** [U] the wood of the willow tree, used especially for making CRICKET BATS 柳木（常用以製作板球拍）

wil·lowy /ˈwɪləʊi; *NAmE* ˈwɪloʊi/ *adj.* (*approving*) (of a person, especially a woman 人，尤指女人) tall, thin and attractive 修長苗條的；婀娜多姿的

will·power /ˈwɪlpaʊə(r)/ *noun* [U] the ability to control your thoughts and actions in order to achieve what you want to do 意志力

willy (also **wil·lie**) /ˈwɪli/ *noun* (*pl.* **-ies**) (*BrE, informal*) a word for a PENIS, used especially by children or when speaking to children 小雞雞（尤作兒童用語）➲ see also WILLIES

willy-nilly /ˌwɪli ˈnɪli/ *adv.* (*informal*) **1** whether you want to or not 不管願意不願意；無論想要不想要: *She was forced willy-nilly to accept the company's proposals.* 她被迫無奈接受了公司的提議。 **2** in a careless way without planning 隨意地；亂糟糟地: *Don't use your credit card willy-nilly.* 別拿着你的信用卡隨便花。

wilt /wɪlt/ *verb* **1** [I, T] **~ (sth)** if a plant or flower **wilts**, or sth **wilts** it, it bends towards the ground because of the heat or a lack of water （使）枯萎，凋謝，蔫 **SYN** **droop** **2** [I] (*informal*) to become weak or tired or less confident 變得委靡不振；發蔫；變得又累又乏；失去自信 **SYN** **flag**: *The spectators were wilting visibly in the hot sun.* 看得出觀眾在炎熱的陽光下快支撐不住了。◇ *He was wilting under the pressure of work.* 他被工作壓得喘不過氣來。 **3 thou wilt** (*old use*) used to mean 'you will', when talking to one person （同一個人談話時用，即 you will）

wilt·ed /ˈwɪltɪd/ *adj.* **wilted** vegetable leaves, for example LETTUCE leaves, have been cooked for a short time and then used in a salad （菜葉）稍煮的，焯水的

wily /ˈwaɪli/ *adj.* (**wili·er**, **wili·est**) clever at getting what you want, and willing to trick people 狡猾的；詭計多端的；愛捉弄人的 **SYN** **cunning**: *The boss is a wily old fox.* 老闆是個狡猾的老狐狸。

wimp /wɪmp/ *noun, verb*
■ ***noun*** (*informal, disapproving*) a person who is not strong, brave or confident 懦夫；窩囊廢 **SYN** **weed** ▸ **wimp·ish** (also **wimpy**) *adj.*: *wimpish behaviour* 懦弱的行為
■ ***verb***
PHR V **ˌwimp ˈout (of sth)** (*informal, disapproving*) to not do sth that you intended to do because you are too frightened or not confident enough to do it 畏縮而不敢做；怯而不做

wim·ple /ˈwɪmpl/ *noun* a head covering made of cloth folded around the head and neck, worn by women in the Middle Ages and now by some NUNS （中世紀婦女和當今某些修女戴的）溫帕爾頭巾

win /wɪn/ *verb, noun*
■ ***verb*** (**win·ning**, **won**, **won** /wʌn/) **1** [I, T] to be the most successful in a competition, race, battle, etc. （在比賽、賽跑、戰鬥等中）獲勝，贏: *Which team won?* 哪個隊贏了？◇ **~ at sth** *to **win at cards/chess, etc.*** 贏牌、贏棋等◇ **~ against sb/sth** *France won by six goals to two against Denmark.* 法國隊以六比二戰勝丹麥隊。◇ **~ sth** *to **win an election/a game/a war, etc.*** 贏得選舉、比賽、戰爭等◇ *She loves to win an argument.* 她喜歡在辯論中獲勝。 **2** [T] to get sth as the result of a competition, race, election, etc. （在比賽、賽跑、選舉等中）贏得，奪取，獲得，摔得: **~ sth** *Britain won five gold medals.* 英國奪取了五塊金牌。◇ *He won £3 000 in the lottery.* 他中彩得了 3 000 英鎊。◇ *How many states did the Republicans win?* 共和黨在多少個州的選舉中獲勝？◇ **~ sth from sb** *The Conservatives won the seat from Labour in the last election.* 在上次選舉中保守黨從工黨手中奪得了這個議席。◇ **~ yourself/sb sth** *You've won yourself a trip to New York.* 你贏得了一次紐約之旅。 **3** [T] **~ sth** to achieve or get sth that you want, especially by your own efforts （尤指通過自己的努力）取得，獲得:

W

They are trying to **win support for** *their proposals.* 他們在努力爭取人們支持他們的建議。◇ *The company has won a contract to supply books and materials to schools.* 這家公司得到了一份向學校供應圖書資料的合同。◇ *She won the admiration of many people in her battle against cancer.* 她在與癌症的對抗中贏得了許多人的欽佩。➲ see also NO-WIN, WINNER, WINNING, WIN-WIN

IDM **you, he, etc. ˌcan't 'win** (*informal*) used to say that there is no acceptable way of dealing with a particular situation 怎麼做都不討好；沒有令人滿意的方法 **you can't win them 'all | you 'win some, you 'lose some** (*informal*) used to express sympathy for sb who has been disappointed about sth（用於勉慰）一個人不可能事事都成功，有所得就有所失 **'you win** (*informal*) used to agree to what sb wants after you have failed to persuade them to do or let you do sth else（被迫表示同意時說）你贏了，我服輸了：*OK, you win, I'll admit I was wrong.* 行，你贏了。我承認我錯了。**win (sth) ˌhands 'down** (*informal*) to win sth very easily 輕易取得；唾手可得 **win sb's 'heart** to make sb love you 贏得（某人）的愛 **ˌwin or 'lose** whether you succeed or fail 不論成敗；不管輸贏；無論勝負：*Win or lose, we'll know we've done our best.* 無論勝負，我們都知道自己已盡了最大努力。➲ more at DAY, SPUR *n.*

PHR V **ˌwin sb↔a'round/'over/'round (to sth)** to get sb's support or approval by persuading them that you are right 贏得…的支持；說服；把…爭取過來：*She's against the idea but I'm sure I can win her over.* 她反對這一想法，但我相信我能把她爭取過來。**ˌwin sth/sb↔'back** to get or have again sth/sb that you had before 重新獲得；把…爭取回來：*The party is struggling to win back voters who have been alienated by recent scandals.* 這個政黨正盡力把最近因醜聞而疏遠的選民爭取回來。**ˌwin 'out/'through** (*informal*) to be successful despite difficulties（克服困難）終獲成功：*It won't be easy but we'll win through in the end.* 這並不容易，但我們最終會獲得成功。

■ ***noun*** a victory in a game, contest, etc.（在比賽、競賽等中的）勝利：*two wins and three defeats* 兩勝三負 ◇ *They have not had a win so far this season.* 他們這一賽季迄今還沒有贏過一場。◇ *France swept to a 6–2 win over Denmark.* 法國隊以 6:2 狂勝丹麥隊。

wince /wɪns/ *verb* [I] **~ (at sth)** to suddenly make an expression with your face that shows that you are feeling pain or embarrassment（因痛苦或尷尬）齜牙咧嘴，皺眉蹙額：*He winced as a sharp pain shot through his left leg.* 他左腿一陣劇痛疼得他直齜牙咧嘴。◇ *I still wince when I think about that stupid thing I said.* 我想到我說過的蠢話時仍懊悔不已。▸ **wince** *noun* [usually sing.]：*a wince of pain* 痛得齜牙咧嘴

winch /wɪntʃ/ *noun, verb*

■ ***noun*** a machine for lifting or pulling heavy objects using a rope or chain 絞車；捲揚機

■ ***verb*** **~ sb/sth + adv./prep.** to lift sb/sth up into the air using a winch（用絞車）吊起，拉起

Win·ches·ter /ˈwɪntʃɪstə(r)/ (also **ˌWinchester 'rifle**) *noun* a type of long gun that fires several bullets one after the other 溫切斯特連發步槍

wind¹ 🔑 /wɪnd/ *noun, verb* ➲ see also WIND²

■ ***noun*** **1** 🔑 [C, U] (also **the wind**) air that moves quickly as a result of natural forces 風；氣流：***strong/high winds*** 強勁的風；大風 ◇ ***gale-force winds*** 大風級的風 ◇ *a* ***light wind*** 微風 ◇ *a* ***north/south/east/west wind*** 北風；南風；東風；西風 ◇ *a* ***chill/cold/biting wind*** *from the north* 冷颼颼的／寒冷的／刺骨的北風 ◇ *The wind is blowing from the south.* 颳的是南風。◇ *The trees were swaying* ***in the wind****.* 樹在風中搖晃。◇ ***A gust of wind*** *blew my hat off.* 一陣風把我的帽子颳掉了。◇ *The weather was hot, without a* ***breath of wind****.* 天氣炎熱，連一絲風都沒有。◇ *The wall gives some protection from the* ***prevailing wind****.* 這堵牆擋着常颳的風，起到一些保護作用。◇ *The wind is getting up* (= starting to blow strongly). 風勢越來越大。◇ *The wind has dropped* (= stopped blowing strongly). 風勢已經減弱。◇ ***wind speed/direction*** 風速；風向 ➲ **COLLOCATIONS** at WEATHER ➲ see also CROSSWIND, DOWNWIND, HEADWIND, TAILWIND, TRADE WIND, WINDY **2** (*BrE*) (*NAmE* **gas**) [U] air that you swallow with food or drink; gas that is produced in your stomach or INTESTINES that makes you feel uncomfortable（隨食物或飲料）吞下的氣；胃氣；腸氣：*I can't eat beans—they give me wind.* 我不能吃豆子，吃了肚子就脹氣。◇ *Try to bring the baby's wind up.* 設法讓嬰兒噯氣。**3** [U] breath that you need when you do exercise or blow into a musical instrument（運動或吹奏樂器時的）呼吸：*I need time to get my wind back after that run.* 我跑過之後需要時間喘口氣。◇ *He kicked Gomez in the stomach, knocking the wind out of him.* 他踢了戈梅斯的肚子，把他踢得喘不上氣來。➲ see also SECOND WIND **4** [U+sing./pl. v.] (also **winds** [pl.]) the group of musical instruments in an ORCHESTRA that produce sounds when you blow into them; the musicians who play those instruments（管弦樂團的）管樂器，管樂器組：*music for wind and strings* 管弦樂 ◇ *The wind section played beautifully.* 管樂組吹奏得很動聽。➲ compare WOODWIND

IDM **break 'wind** to release gas from your BOWELS through your ANUS 放屁 **get 'wind of sth** (*informal*) to hear about sth secret or private 聽到…的風聲；獲悉…的秘密消息 **get/have the 'wind up (about sth)** (*informal*) to become/be frightened about sth 因…害怕（或憂慮）**in the 'wind** about to happen soon, although you do not know exactly how or when 即將發生；在醞釀中 **like the 'wind** very quickly 一陣風似地；飛快地 **put the 'wind up sb** (*BrE, informal*) to make sb frightened 使害怕；使驚嚇 **take the 'wind out of sb's sails** (*informal*) to make sb suddenly less confident or angry, especially when you do or say sth that they do not expect 出其不意地打擊某人的信心；突然減輕某人的怒氣 **a wind/the winds of 'change** (used especially by journalists 常作新聞用語) an event or a series of events that has started to happen and will cause important changes or results 改革之風；變化的趨向：*A wind of change was blowing through the banking world.* 銀行界颳起了改革之風。➲ more at CAUTION *n.*, FOLLOWING, ILL *adj.*, SAIL *v.*, STRAW, WAY *n.*

■ ***verb*** **1** [usually passive] **~ sb** to make sb unable to breathe easily for a short time 使喘不過氣來；使喘大氣：*He was momentarily winded by the blow to his stomach.* 他的肚子上捱了一擊，一時喘不過氣來。**2 ~ sb** (*BrE*) to gently hit or rub a baby's back to make it BURP (= release gas from its stomach through its mouth)（輕拍嬰兒後背）使噯氣 **SYN** **burp** ➲ see also LONG-WINDED

wind² 🔑 /waɪnd/ *verb* ➲ see also WIND¹ (**wound, wound** /waʊnd/)

1 🔑 [I, T] (of a road, river, etc. 路、河等) to have many bends and twists 蜿蜒；曲折而行；迂迴：**+ adv./prep.** *The path wound down to the beach.* 這條小路彎彎曲曲通向海灘。◇ **~ its way + adv./prep.** *The river winds its way between two meadows.* 這條河蜿蜒流經兩個牧場之間。➲ see also WINDING **2** 🔑 [T] **~ sth + adv./prep.** to wrap or twist sth around itself or sth else 捲纏；纏繞；繞成團：*He wound the wool into a ball.* 他把毛線纏繞成一團。◇ *Wind the bandage around your finger.* 用繃帶把你的手指包紮起來。**3** 🔑 [T, I] to make a clock or other piece of machinery work by turning a KNOB, handle, etc. several times; to be able to be made to work in this way 給（鐘錶等）上發條；（通過轉動把手等）操作；可上發條；可通過轉動把手（等）操作：**~ sth (up)** *He had forgotten to wind his watch.* 他忘了給錶上發條了。◇ **~ up** *It was one of those old-fashioned gramophones that winds up.* 那是一台上弦的老式留聲機。➲ see also WIND-UP **4** 🔑 [T, I] to operate a tape, film, etc. so that it moves nearer to its ending or starting position 捲繞，倒（磁帶、膠捲等）：**~ sth forward/back** *He wound the tape back to the beginning.* 他把磁帶倒到了開頭。◇ **~ forward/back** *Wind forward to the bit where they discover the body.* 往前繞片，繞到他們發現屍體的那一截。**5** [T] **~ sth** to turn a handle several times 轉動（把手）：*You operate the trapdoor by winding this handle.* 你要轉動這個手柄來操縱活動天窗。**IDM** see LITTLE FINGER ▸ **wind** *noun*：*Give the handle another couple of winds.* 再轉動兩下手柄。

PHR V **ˌwind 'down 1** (of a person 人) to rest or relax after a period of activity or excitement 喘口氣；喘息

W

一下 SYN unwind **2** (of a piece of machinery 機器) to go slowly and then stop 慢下來後停住 **,wind sth↔'down 1** to bring a business, an activity, etc. to an end gradually over a period of time 使（業務、活動等）逐步結束：*The government is winding down its nuclear programme.* 政府在逐步取消核計劃。**2** to make sth such as the window of a car move downwards by turning a handle, pressing a button, etc. 把（汽車窗玻璃等）搖下：*Can I wind my window down?* 我可以把我這邊的窗戶搖下來嗎？**,wind 'up** (*informal*) (of a person 人) to find yourself in a particular place or situation 以…告終（或終結）：*I always said he would wind up in prison.* 我以前一直說他終歸要進班房。◇ **~ doing sth** *We eventually wound up staying in a little hotel a few miles from town.* 我們最後在離城幾英里的一家小旅館裏落腳。◇ **+ adj.** *If you take risks like that you'll wind up dead.* 你要是冒那種險就會把命賠上。**,wind 'up | ,wind sth↔'up** to bring sth such as a speech or meeting to an end 結束（講話、會議等）：*The speaker was just winding up when the door was flung open.* 演講者剛要結束講話時門突然被推開了。◇ *If we all agree, let's wind up the discussion.* 如果我們大家都同意，咱們就結束討論吧。**,wind sb↔'up** (*BrE, informal*) to deliberately say or do sth in order to annoy sb 惹…生氣；戲弄：*Calm down! Can't you see he's only winding you up?* 別激動！難道你看不出他只是在氣你嗎？◇ *That can't be true! You're winding me up.* 那不會是真的！你在故意氣我。➲ related noun WIND-UP **,wind sth↔'up 1** to stop running a company, business, etc. and close it completely 關閉（公司、企業等）；（完全）停止營業 **2** to make sth such as the window of a car move upwards by turning a handle, pressing a button, etc. 把（汽車窗玻璃等）搖上

wind·bag /'wɪndbæg/ *noun* (*informal, disapproving*) a person who talks too much, and does not say anything important or interesting 夸夸其談的人；空話連篇的人；話匣子

wind-blown /'wɪnd bləʊn; *NAmE* bloʊn/ *adj.* **1** carried from one place to another by the wind 被風吹的；隨風飄的 **2** made untidy by the wind 被風颳亂的；被風吹散的：*wind-blown hair* 被風吹亂的頭髮

wind·break /'wɪndbreɪk/ *noun* a row of trees, a fence, etc. that provides protection from the wind 防風林；擋風籬；擋風牆；風障

wind·cheat·er /'wɪndtʃiːtə(r)/ (*old-fashioned, BrE*) (*NAmE* **wind·break·er** /'wɪndbreɪkə(r)/) *noun* a jacket designed to protect you from the wind 防風夾克；風衣

wind chill /'wɪnd tʃɪl/ *noun* [U] the effect of low temperature combined with wind on sb/sth 風寒（與風速相關的冷卻作用）：*Take the* ***wind-chill factor*** *into account.* 把風寒指數考慮進去。

wind chimes /'wɪnd tʃaɪmz/ *noun* [pl.] a set of hanging pieces of metal, etc. that make a pleasant ringing sound in the wind 風鈴；風鐸

wind-down /'waɪnd daʊn/ (also **,winding-'down**) *noun* [sing.] a gradual reduction in activity as sth comes to an end 逐漸減少至終止；逐步結束：*The wind-down of the company was handled very efficiently.* 公司處理逐步縮減直至關閉的事宜效率很高。

wind·er /'waɪndə(r)/ *noun* a device or piece of machinery that winds sth, for example sth that winds a watch or the film in a camera 纏繞器；捲簧器；捲線機

wind·fall /'wɪndfɔːl/ *noun* **1** an amount of money that sb/sth wins or receives unexpectedly 意外之財；意外獲得的東西：*The hospital got a sudden windfall of £300 000.* 這家醫院獲得了一筆 30 萬英鎊的意外款項。◇ *windfall profits* 意外的利潤 ◇ *The government imposed a* ***windfall tax*** (= a tax on profits to be paid once only, not every year) *on some industries.* 政府對某些行業徵收暴利稅。**2** a fruit, especially an apple, that the wind has blown down from a tree 風吹落的果子（尤指蘋果）

wind farm /'wɪnd fɑːm; *NAmE* fɑːrm/ *noun* an area of land on which there are a lot of WINDMILLS or WIND TURBINES for producing electricity 風力發電場 ➲ COLLOCATIONS at ENVIRONMENT

wind gauge /'wɪnd geɪdʒ/ *noun* = ANEMOMETER

the Win·dies /'wɪndɪz; -diːz/ *noun* [pl.] (*informal*) the West Indian CRICKET team 西印度群島板球隊

wind·ing /'waɪndɪŋ/ *adj.* having a curving and twisting shape 曲折的；彎曲的；蜿蜒的：*a long and winding road* 漫長而曲折的道路

winding-down /,waɪndɪŋ 'daʊn/ *noun* = WIND DOWN

winding sheet /'waɪndɪŋ ʃiːt/ *noun* (especially in the past) a piece of cloth that a dead person's body was wrapped in before it was buried（尤指舊時的）裹屍布 SYN **shroud**

wind instrument /'wɪnd ɪnstrəmənt/ *noun* any musical instrument that you play by blowing 管樂器；吹奏樂器 ➲ compare BRASS (2), WOODWIND

wind·lass /'wɪndləs/ *noun* a type of WINCH (= a machine for lifting or pulling heavy objects) 絞盤；捲揚機；轆轤

wind·less /'wɪndləs/ *adj.* (*formal*) without wind 無風的；平靜的：*a windless day* 風平浪靜的一天 OPP **windy**

wind machine /'wɪnd məʃiːn/ *noun* **1** a machine used in the theatre or in films/movies that blows air to give the effect of wind（劇院或電影用的）造風機，風力效果機 **2** a machine used in ORCHESTRAS to produce the sound of wind（管弦樂隊的）風聲器，風鳴器

wind·mill /'wɪndmɪl/ *noun* **1** a building with machinery for GRINDING grain into flour that is driven by the power of the wind turning long arms (called SAILS) 風車磨房 ➲ **VISUAL VOCAB** pages V2, V3 **2** a tall thin structure with parts that turn round, used to change the power of the wind into electricity（通過轉動將風能轉化為電能的）風車 **3** (*BrE*) (*NAmE* **pin·wheel**) a toy with curved plastic parts that form the shape of a flower which turns round on the end of a stick when you blow on it 玩具風車 IDM see TILT *v.*

win·dow 0→ /'wɪndəʊ; *NAmE* 'wɪndoʊ/ *noun*

1 0→ an opening in the wall or roof of a building, car, etc., usually covered with glass, that allows light and air to come in and people to see out; the glass in a window 窗；窗戶；窗口；窗玻璃：*She* ***looked out of the window.*** 她向窗外看去。◇ *to* ***open/close the window*** 打開／關上窗戶 ◇ *the* ***bedroom/car/kitchen, etc. window*** 卧室、汽車、廚房等的窗戶 ◇ *a broken window* 破碎的窗玻璃 ➲ **VISUAL VOCAB** pages V17, V52 ➲ see also BAY WINDOW, DORMER WINDOW, FRENCH WINDOW, PICTURE WINDOW, ROSE WINDOW, SASH WINDOW **2** 0→ = SHOP WINDOW：*I saw the dress I wanted* ***in the window.*** 我在櫥窗裏看到了我想買的連衣裙。◇ *a window display* 櫥窗陳列 **3** 0→ an area within a frame on a computer screen, in which a particular program is operating or in which information of a particular type is shown（計算機屏幕的）窗口，視窗：*to* ***create/open a window*** 建立／打開窗口 ➲ **VISUAL VOCAB** page V68 **4** 0→ a small area of sth that you can see through, for example to talk to sb or read sth on the other side 牆上（或信封等上）開的窗形的口；透明窗口：*There was a long line of people at the box-office window.* 在售票處窗口外排了一長隊人。◇ *The address must be clearly visible through the window of the envelope.* 從信封的透明窗必須能夠看清楚地址。 **5** [sing.] **~ on/into sth** a way of seeing and learning about sth 瞭解信息的渠道；窗口：*Television is a sort of* ***window on the world.*** 電視是瞭解世界的窗口。◇ *It gave me an intriguing window into the way people live.* 這為我提供了一個瞭解人們的生活方式的有趣窗口。 **6** a time when there is an opportunity to do sth, although it may not last long 一絲機會；短暫的時機：*We now have a small* ***window of opportunity*** *in which to make our views known.* 我們現在有一線機會使人瞭解我們的觀點。

IDM **fly/go out (of) the 'window** (*informal*) to stop existing; to disappear completely 化為烏有；消失殆盡：*As soon as the kids arrived, order went out of the window.* 孩子們一到，一切就都亂了套。

'window box *noun* a long narrow box outside a window, in which plants are grown 窗口花壇；窗欄花箱 ➲ **VISUAL VOCAB** page V17

ˈwindow cleaner *noun* a person whose job is to clean windows 擦窗工

ˈwindow dressing *noun* [U] **1** the art of arranging goods in shop/store windows in an attractive way 櫥窗裝飾藝術；櫥窗設計藝術 **2** (*disapproving*) the fact of doing or saying sth in a way that creates a good impression but does not show the real facts 裝飾門面；弄虛作假：*The reforms are seen as window dressing.* 這些改革被視為是裝飾門面。

ˈwindow ledge *noun* = WINDOWSILL

win·dow·less /ˈwɪndəʊləs; *NAmE* -doʊ-/ *adj.* without windows 無窗的：*a tiny, windowless cell* 一間沒有窗戶的斗室

win·dow·pane /ˈwɪndəʊpeɪn; *NAmE* -doʊ-/ *noun* a piece of glass in a window （一塊）窗玻璃 ➲ VISUAL VOCAB page V17

ˈwindow shade *noun* (*NAmE*) = BLIND *n.* (1)

ˈwindow-shopping *noun* [U] the activity of looking at the goods in shop/store windows, usually without intending to buy anything 瀏覽櫥窗（通常無意購買）：*to go window-shopping* 去逛街瀏覽櫥窗 ➲ COLLOCATIONS at SHOPPING

win·dow·sill /ˈwɪndəʊsɪl; *NAmE* ˈwɪndoʊ-/ (also **sill**, **ˈwindow ledge**) *noun* a narrow shelf below a window, either inside or outside 窗沿；窗台：*Place the plants on a sunny windowsill.* 把這些植物放在陽光充足的窗台上。➲ VISUAL VOCAB page V17

wind·pipe /ˈwɪndpaɪp/ *noun* the tube in the throat that carries air to the lungs 氣管 SYN **trachea** ➲ VISUAL VOCAB page V59

wind·screen /ˈwɪndskriːn/ (*BrE*) (*NAmE* **wind·shield**) *noun* the window across the front of a vehicle （機動車前面的）擋風玻璃 ➲ COLLOCATIONS at DRIVING ➲ VISUAL VOCAB page V52

ˈwindscreen wiper (*BrE*) (*NAmE* **ˈwindshield wiper**) (also **wiper** *BrE, NAmE*) *noun* a blade with a rubber edge that moves across a windscreen to make it clear of rain, snow, etc. 擋風玻璃刮水器；風擋雨雪刷；雨刮器 ➲ VISUAL VOCAB page V52

wind·shield /ˈwɪndʃiːld/ *noun* **1** (*NAmE*) (*BrE* **wind·screen**) the window across the front of a vehicle（機動車前面的）擋風玻璃，風擋 ➲ VISUAL VOCAB page V52 **2** a glass or plastic screen that provides protection from the wind, for example at the front of a motorcycle （摩托車等前面的）擋風玻璃，風擋

wind·sock /ˈwɪndsɒk; *NAmE* -sɑːk/ *noun* a tube made of soft material, open at both ends, that hangs at the top of a pole, to show the direction of the wind 風向袋

wind·storm /ˈwɪndstɔːm; *NAmE* -stɔːrm/ *noun* (*NAmE*) a storm where there is very strong wind but little rain or snow 風暴

wind·surf·er /ˈwɪndsɜːfə(r); *NAmE* -sɜːrf-/ *noun* **1** (also **sail·board** *BrE, NAmE*) a long narrow board with a sail, that you stand on and sail across water on 帆板 **2** a person on a windsurfer 帆板運動員

wind·surf·ing /ˈwɪndsɜːfɪŋ; *NAmE* -sɜːrf-/ (also **board·sail·ing**) *noun* [U] the sport of sailing on water standing on a windsurfer 帆板運動：*to go windsurfing* 去做帆板運動 ➲ VISUAL VOCAB page V50 ▸ **wind·surf** *verb* [I]：*Most visitors come to sail or windsurf.* 遊客大多是來進行帆船或帆板運動的。

wind·swept /ˈwɪndswept/ *adj.* **1** (of a place 地方) having strong winds and little protection from them 受大風吹的；當風的：*the windswept Atlantic coast* 受大風侵襲的大西洋海岸 **2** looking as though you have been in a strong wind 似被風吹散的；亂蓬蓬的：*windswept hair* 凌亂的頭髮

wind tunnel /ˈwɪnd tʌnl/ *noun* a large tunnel where aircraft, etc. are tested by forcing air past them （試驗飛機等用的）風洞，風道

wind turbine /ˈwɪnd tɜːbaɪn; *NAmE* tɜːrb-/ *noun* a type of modern WINDMILL used for producing electricity 風力渦輪（發電）機 ➲ VISUAL VOCAB page V8

wind-up /ˈwaɪnd ʌp/ *adj., noun*

■ *adj.* [only before noun] **1** that you operate by turning a key or handle 裝有發條的；用手柄操作的：*an old-fashioned wind-up gramophone* 裝有發條的老式留聲機 **2** intended to bring sth to an end 意欲結束的；終了的；收場的：*a wind-up speech* 結束語

■ *noun* (*BrE, informal*) something that sb says or does in order to be deliberately annoying, especially as a joke 戲弄人或惹人氣惱的言語（或行動）

wind·ward /ˈwɪndwəd; *NAmE* -wərd/ *adj., noun*

■ *adj.* on the side of sth from which the wind is blowing 向風的；迎風的；頂風的；上風的：*the windward side of the boat* 船向風的一側 OPP **leeward** ➲ see also LEE (1) ▸ **wind·ward** *adv.* OPP **leeward**

■ *noun* [U] the side or direction from which the wind is blowing 向風面；迎風面；上風面：*to sail to windward* 迎風航行 ➲ compare LEEWARD

windy /ˈwɪndi/ *adj.* (**wind·ier**, **windi·est**) **1** (of weather, etc. 天氣等) with a lot of wind 多風的；風大的：*a windy day* 大風天 OPP **windless** **2** (of a place 地方) getting a lot of wind 當風的；受大風吹的：*windy hills* 當風的丘陵 **3** (*informal, disapproving*) (of speech 講話) involving speaking for longer than necessary and in a way that is complicated and not clear 夸夸其談的；空話連篇的；空洞無物的

the ˌWindy ˈCity *noun* [sing.] a name for the US city of Chicago 風城（美國芝加哥市的別稱）

wine 0‑ /waɪn/ *noun, verb*

■ *noun* **1** 0‑ [U, C] an alcoholic drink made from the juice of GRAPES that has been left to FERMENT. There are many different kinds of wine. 葡萄酒：*a bottle of wine* 一瓶葡萄酒 ◇ *a glass of* ***dry/sweet wine*** 一杯乾／甜葡萄酒 ◇ ***red/rosé/white wine*** 紅／玫瑰紅／白葡萄酒 ◇ ***sparkling wine*** 汽酒 ➲ see also TABLE WINE **2** [U, C] an alcoholic drink made from plants or fruits other than GRAPES （用植物或除葡萄以外的水果釀製的）酒，果酒：*elderberry/rice wine* 接骨木果酒；米酒 **3** [U] (also **wine ˈred**) a dark red colour 紫紅色；深紅色

■ *verb*

IDM **ˌwine and ˈdine (sb)** to go to restaurants, etc. and enjoy good food and drink; to entertain sb by buying them good food and drink （去餐館等）大吃大喝；用酒宴款待：*The firm spent thousands wining and dining potential clients.* 這家公司成千上萬地花費在大擺酒宴款待潛在的客戶上。

ˈwine bar *noun* a bar or small restaurant where wine is the main drink available （主要供應葡萄酒的）酒吧，小酒館

ˈwine cellar (also **cel·lar**) *noun* an underground room where wine is stored; the wine stored in this room 酒窖；貯藏在酒窖裏的酒

ˌwine ˈcooler *noun* **1** (*NAmE*) a drink made with wine, fruit juice, ice and SODA WATER （用葡萄酒、果汁、冰和蘇打水製成的）冰鎮果酒飲料 **2** **ˈwine cooler** a container for putting a bottle of wine in to cool it 鎮酒冰壺

ˈwine farm *noun* (*SAfrE*) a VINEYARD (= a place where GRAPES are grown for making wine) （種植釀酒用葡萄的）葡萄園

ˈwine glass *noun* a glass for drinking wine from （飲葡萄酒用的）玻璃酒杯 ➲ VISUAL VOCAB page V22

wine·grow·er /ˈwaɪngrəʊə(r); *NAmE* -groʊ-/ *noun* a person who grows GRAPES for wine （釀酒）葡萄園主

ˈwine gum *noun* (*BrE*) a small fruit-flavoured sweet/candy 果味橡皮糖

ˈwine list *noun* a list of wines available in a restaurant （餐館供應的）酒單 ➲ COLLOCATIONS at RESTAURANT

wine·maker /ˈwaɪnmeɪkə(r)/ *noun* a person who produces wine 葡萄酒釀造者；葡萄酒生產者 ▸ **wine·mak·ing** /ˈwaɪnmeɪkɪŋ/ *noun* [U]

win·ery /ˈwaɪnəri/ *noun* (*pl.* **-ies**) (*especially NAmE*) a place where wine is made 葡萄酒廠；釀酒廠 ➲ compare VINEYARD

W

ˌ**wine ˈvinegar** *noun* [U] VINEGAR which is made from wine rather than from grain or apples 葡萄酒醋

wing 0→ /wɪŋ/ *noun, verb*

■ ***noun***

▸ **OF BIRD/INSECT 鳥；昆蟲 1** 0→ [C] one of the parts of the body of a bird, insect or BAT that it uses for flying（鳥、昆蟲或蝙蝠）翅膀，翼：*The swan* ***flapped its wings*** *noisily.* 天鵝大聲地拍打着翅膀。◇ *wing feathers* 翅膀上的羽毛 ➲ **VISUAL VOCAB** pages V12, V13

▸ **OF PLANE 飛機 2** 0→ [C] one of the large flat parts that stick out from the side of a plane and help to keep it in the air when it is flying（飛行器的）翅膀；機翼 ➲ **VISUAL VOCAB** page V53

▸ **OF BUILDING 建築物 3** [C] one of the parts of a large building that sticks out from the main part 側翼部份；側廳；耳房；廂房：*the east wing* 東翼樓 ◇ *the new wing of the hospital* 與醫院一側相連的新樓房

▸ **OF CAR 汽車 4** (*BrE*) (*NAmE* **fend·er**) [C] a part of a car that is above a wheel 擋泥板；翼子板：*There was a dent in the nearside wing.* 左邊擋泥板上有一個凹痕。➲ **VISUAL VOCAB** page V52

▸ **OF ORGANIZATION 組織 5** [C] one section of an organization that has a particular function or whose members share the same opinions（起某種作用或持相同觀點的）派，翼 SYN **arm**：*the radical wing of the party* 這個政黨中的激進派 ◇ *the political wing of the National Resistance Army* 國民抵抗軍的政治組織 ➲ see also LEFT WING (1), RIGHT WING (1)

▸ **IN FOOTBALL/HOCKEY 足球；曲棍球 6** [C] = WINGER ➲ see also LEFT WING (2), RIGHT WING (2) **7** [C] the far left or right side of the sports field（運動場地的）遠端邊側：*He plays on the wing.* 他踢邊鋒。

▸ **IN THEATRE 劇院 8 the wings** [pl.] the area at either side of the stage that cannot be seen by the audience（舞台上觀眾看不到的）邊廂，翼部，側面

IDM **get your ˈwings** to pass the exams that mean you are allowed to fly a plane 獲得飛行資格；通過飛行考試 **(waiting) in the ˈwings** ready to take over a particular job or be used in a particular situation when needed 準備接替某工作；準備就緒 **on a ˌwing and a ˈprayer** with only a very slight chance of success 只有一線成功的可能 **on the ˈwing** (*literary*) (of a bird, insect, etc. 鳥、昆蟲等) flying 飛行中的；飛着的 **take sb under your ˈwing** to take care of and help sb who has less experience of sth than you 呵護；庇護；把…置於卵翼之下 **take ˈwing** (*literary*) (of a bird, insect, etc. 鳥、昆蟲等) to fly away 展翅飛翔；飛走：(*figurative*) *Her imagination took wing.* 她發揮了海闊天空的想像。➲ more at CLIP *v.*, SPREAD *v.*

■ ***verb***

▸ **FLY 飛 1** [T, I] **~ (its way) + adv./prep.** (*literary*) to fly somewhere 飛；飛行：*A solitary seagull winged its way across the bay.* 一隻孤零零的海鷗飛過了海灣。

▸ **GO QUICKLY 快走 2** [T] **~ its way + adv./prep.** to be sent somewhere very quickly 被迅速送往：*An application form will be winging its way to you soon.* 申請表不久將送達你處。

IDM **ˈwing it** (*informal*) to do sth without planning or preparing it first 臨時應付；即興；匆匆拼湊 SYN **improvise**：*I didn't know I'd have to make a speech—I just had to wing it.* 我不知道還得講話，只好臨場即興發揮說點什麼。

ˈ**wing back** *noun* (in football (SOCCER) 足球) a player who plays near the edge of the field and who both attacks and defends 防守型邊鋒；翼衛

ˈ**wing chair** *noun* a comfortable chair that has a high back with pieces pointing forwards at the sides 翼狀靠背扶手椅

ˌ**wing ˈcollar** *noun* a high stiff shirt COLLAR for men, worn with formal clothes（男子正式服裝的）翼領，燕子領

ˈ**wing commander** *noun* an officer of high rank in the British AIR FORCE（英國空軍的）空軍中校：*Wing Commander Brian Moore* 空軍中校布賴恩 • 穆爾

wing·ding /ˈwɪŋdɪŋ/ *noun* (*old-fashioned, NAmE, informal*) a party 聚會

winged /wɪŋd/ *adj.* **1** having wings 有翅膀的；有翼的：*winged insects* 有翼昆蟲 OPP **wingless 2 -winged** (in adjectives 構成形容詞) having the number or type of wings mentioned 有…隻翅膀的；有…翅膀的：*a long-winged bird* 長翼鳥

wing·er /ˈwɪŋə(r)/ *noun* (also **wing**) (*sport* 體) either of the attacking players who play towards the side of the playing area in sports such as football (SOCCER) or HOCKEY（足球、曲棍球等）邊鋒隊員

wing·less /ˈwɪŋləs/ *adj.* (especially of insects 尤指昆蟲) without wings 無翅的；無翼的 OPP **winged**

ˈ**wing mirror** (*BrE*) (*NAmE* **ˈside-view mirror**) *noun* a mirror that sticks out from the side of a vehicle and allows the driver to see behind the vehicle（車輛）側翼後視鏡 ➲ **VISUAL VOCAB** page V52

ˈ**wing nut** *noun* a NUT (2) for holding things in place, which has parts that stick out at the sides so that you can turn it easily 翼形螺母；元寶螺母；蝶形螺帽

wing·span /ˈwɪŋspæn/ *noun* the distance between the end of one wing and the end of the other when the wings are fully stretched 翼展；翼幅：*a bird with a two-foot wingspan* 翼幅為兩英尺的鳥

wing·tips /ˈwɪŋtɪps/ *noun* [pl.] (*NAmE*) strong leather shoes that fasten with LACES and have an extra piece of leather with small holes in it over the toe 翼形飾孔皮鞋（鞋頭有帶孔蓋飾）

wink /wɪŋk/ *verb, noun*

■ ***verb*** **1** [I] **~ (at sb)** to close one eye and open it again quickly, especially as a private signal to sb, or to show sth is a joke 眨一隻眼，眨眼示意（尤指使眼色或表示開玩笑）：*He winked at her and she knew he was thinking the same thing that she was.* 他衝她眨了眨眼，她便知道他的想法和她一樣。➲ compare BLINK **2** [I] to shine with an unsteady light; to flash on and off 閃爍；明滅 SYN **blink**：*We could see the lights of the ship winking in the distance.* 我們看見船在遠方忽明忽暗地閃着燈光。

PHR V **ˈwink at sth** to pretend that you have not noticed sth, especially sth bad or illegal（尤指對壞事）視而不見；睜一隻眼閉一隻眼

■ ***noun*** an act of winking, especially as a signal to sb 眨一隻眼；眨眼示意；眼色：*He gave her a knowing wink.* 他向她會意地眨了一下眼睛。➲ see also FORTY WINKS

IDM **not get/have a ˈwink of sleep** | **not sleep a ˈwink** to not be able to sleep 沒合一下眼；不能入睡：*I didn't get a wink of sleep last night.* 我昨天一夜都沒合眼。◇ *I hardly slept a wink.* 我幾乎連個盹都沒打。➲ more at NOD *n.*, NUDGE *n.*, TIP *v.*

win·kle /ˈwɪŋkl/ *noun, verb*

■ ***noun*** (*BrE*) (also **peri·win·kle** *NAmE, BrE*) a small SHELLFISH, like a SNAIL, that can be eaten 濱螺，蛾螺，玉黍螺（可食用）

■ ***verb*** (*BrE, informal*)

PHR V **ˌwinkle sth/sb↔ˈout (of sth)** to get sth/sb out of a place or position, especially when this is not easy to do（從…處）挖出，掏出；迫使…離開（某地方或位置）**ˌwinkle sth ˈout of sb** to get information from sb, especially with difficulty 從…套出（實情等）SYN **extract**：*She always manages to winkle secrets out of people.* 她總是能從別人那裏探聽出秘密。

Win·ne·bago™ /ˌwɪnɪˈbeɪɡəʊ; *NAmE* -ɡoʊ/ *noun* (*NAmE*) (*pl.* **Win·ne·bago** or **-os**) a large vehicle designed for people to live and sleep in when they are camping; a type of RV 溫內巴戈露營車；探險野營車

win·ner 0→ /ˈwɪnə(r)/ *noun*

1 0→ a person, a team, an animal, etc. that wins sth 獲勝的人（或隊、動物等）；優勝者：*The winners of the competition will be announced next month.* 競賽的獲勝者將於下月公佈。◇ *There are no winners in a divorce* (= everyone suffers). 離婚的人都是兩敗俱傷。**2** [usually sing.] (*informal*) a thing or person that is successful or likely to be successful 成功者；可能成功的人（或事物）：*I think your idea is a winner.* 我認為你的想法能夠成功。◇ *The design is very good. We could be* ***onto a winner*** (= we may do or produce sth successful). 這設

W

計很好。我們的產品可能會成功。 **3** [sing.] (*sport* 體) a goal or point that causes a team or a person to win a game 致勝的一記入球；贏得比賽的一分： *Rooney scored the winner after 20 minutes* 魯尼在 20 分鐘後射入了致勝的一球。 ➲ compare LOSER **IDM** see PICK *v.*

win·ning 🔑 /ˈwɪnɪŋ/ *adj.*
1 🔑 [only before noun] that wins or has won sth, for example a race or competition 獲勝的；贏的： *the winning horse* 獲勝的馬 ◇ *the winning goal* 制勝的一記入球 **2** [usually before noun] attractive in a way that makes other people like you 吸引人的；動人的；迷人的；可愛的： *a winning smile* 動人的微笑 ▶ **win·ning·ly** *adv.*
IDM see CARD *n.*

win·ning·est /ˈwɪnɪŋɪst/ *adj.* (*NAmE, informal*) having won the most games, races or competitions 贏得最多比賽項目的： *the winningest coach in the history of the US national team* 美國國家隊歷史上贏得最多項比賽的教練

ˈwinning post *noun* (*especially BrE*) a post that shows where the end of a race is 終點柱： *to be first past the winning post* 第一個跑過終點柱

win·nings /ˈwɪnɪŋz/ *noun* [pl.] money that sb wins in a competition or game or by gambling（比賽、賭博中）贏得的錢

win·now /ˈwɪnəʊ; *NAmE* -noʊ/ *verb* **~ sth** to blow air through grain in order to remove its outer covering (called the CHAFF) 簸，揚，風選（以去掉穀殼）
PHR V ˌ**winnow sb/sth ˈout (of sth)** (*formal*) to remove people or things from a group so that only the best ones are left 篩選；遴選；選拔 **SYN** **sift out**

wino /ˈwaɪnəʊ; *NAmE* -noʊ/ *noun* (*pl.* **-os**) (*informal*) a person who drinks a lot of cheap alcohol and who has no home（無家可歸的）酒鬼

win·some /ˈwɪnsəm/ *adj.* (*formal*) (of people or their manner 人或其舉止) pleasant and attractive 討人喜歡的；惹人喜愛的；楚楚動人的 **SYN** **engaging**： *a winsome smile* 莞爾一笑 ▶ **win·some·ly** *adv.*

win·ter 🔑 /ˈwɪntə(r)/ *noun, verb*
■ ***noun*** 🔑 [U, C] the coldest season of the year, between autumn/fall and spring 冬天；冬季： *a* ***mild/severe/hard winter*** 暖冬；嚴冬；隆冬 ◇ *Our house can be very cold* ***in*** *(****the****)* ***winter***. 我們的房子到了冬天有時會非常冷。 ◇ *They worked on the building all through the winter.* 他們整個冬天都在建造這座大樓。 ◇ *We went to New Zealand last winter.* 我們去年冬天去了新西蘭。 ◇ *the* ***winter months*** 冬季的月份 ◇ *a* ***winter coat*** 過冬的大衣 **IDM** see DEAD *n.*
■ ***verb*** [I] (+ **adv./prep.**) to spend the winter somewhere 過冬： *Many British birds winter in Africa.* 許多英國的鳥在非洲過冬。 ➲ compare OVERWINTER

ˌwinter ˈsports *noun* [pl.] sports that people do on snow or ice 冬季運動（指雪上和冰上的運動） ➲ VISUAL VOCAB page V48

win·ter·time /ˈwɪntətaɪm; *NAmE* -tərt-/ *noun* [U] the period of time when it is winter 冬季；冬天；冬令： *The days are shorter in (the) wintertime.* 冬季白天較短。

W

win·try /ˈwɪntri/ *adj.* **1** typical of winter; cold 冬天的；冬令的；寒冷的： *wintry weather* 冬季的天氣 ◇ *a wintry landscape* 冬景 ◇ ***wintry showers*** (= of snow) 冬季的陣雪 **2** not friendly 冷漠的；冷冰冰的 **SYN** **frosty**： *a wintry smile* 冷冷一笑

ˌwin-ˈwin *adj.* [only before noun] (of a situation 局面) in which there is a good result for each person or group involved 對各方都有益的；雙贏的： *This is a* ***win-win situation*** *all around.* 這是一個各得其所的局面。

wipe /waɪp/ *verb, noun*
■ ***verb*** **1** to rub sth against a surface, in order to remove dirt or liquid from it; to rub a surface with a cloth, etc. in order to clean it 擦；拭；抹；揩；蹭： **~ sth (on sth)** *Please wipe your feet on the mat.* 請在墊子上蹭一蹭腳。 ◇ *He wiped his hands on a clean towel.* 他用一塊乾淨的手巾擦了擦雙手。 ◇ **~ sth with sth** *She was sniffing and wiping her eyes with a tissue.* 她邊抽泣邊用手巾紙拭擦眼淚。 ◇ **~ sth + adj.** *He wiped his plate clean with a piece of bread.* 他用一塊麵包把碟子擦乾淨。 **2** to remove dirt, liquid, etc. from sth by using a cloth, your hand, etc.（用布、手等）擦乾淨，抹掉： **~ sth (from/off sth)** *He wiped the sweat from his forehead.* 他擦去額頭上的汗。 ◇ (*figurative*) *Wipe that stupid smile off your face.* 別那麼傻笑啦。 ◇ **~ sth away/off/up** *She wiped off her make-up.* 她把化的妝擦掉了。 ◇ *Use that cloth to wipe up the mess.* 用那塊布把髒東西擦掉。 **3** to remove information, sound, images, etc. from a computer, tape or video 消除，抹去（計算機、磁帶或錄像帶上的信息等） **SYN** **erase**： **~ sth off (sth)** *You must have wiped off that programme I recorded.* 你一定是把我錄製的節目給抹掉了。 ◇ **~ sth** *Somebody had wiped all the tapes.* 有人把所有磁帶上錄製的內容都抹掉了。 **4** to deliberately forget an experience because it was unpleasant or embarrassing 抹去（舊事） **SYN** **erase**： **~ sth from sth** *I tried to wipe the whole episode from my mind.* 我設法把這整個經歷從心中抹掉。 ◇ **~ sth out** *You can never wipe out the past.* 你永遠不能把過去一筆勾銷。
IDM **wipe sb/sth off the ˌface of the ˈearth | wipe sth off the ˈmap** to destroy or remove sb/sth completely 使…從地球上消失；徹底消除 **wipe the slate ˈclean** to agree to forget about past mistakes or arguments and start again with a relationship 把以往過錯一筆勾銷；一消前愆；捐棄前嫌 ➲ more at FLOOR *n.*
PHR V ˌ**wipe sth↔ˈdown** to clean a surface completely, using a wet cloth（用濕布）徹底揩擦乾淨： *She took a cloth and wiped down the kitchen table.* 她拿了一塊布把廚房桌面擦得乾乾淨淨。 **wipe sth off sth** to remove sth from sth 從…除掉（或抹掉）： *Billions of pounds were wiped off share prices today.* 今天的股票價格下挫造成數十億英鎊的損失。 ˌ**wipe ˈout** (*informal*) to fall over, especially when you are doing a sport such as SKIING or SURFING（尤指做滑雪或衝浪等體育運動時）跌倒，翻跌下來 ˌ**wipe sb↔ˈout** (*informal*) to make sb extremely tired 使疲憊不堪： *All that travelling has wiped her out.* 一路舟車辛勞讓她疲憊不堪。 ➲ see also WIPED OUT ˌ**wipe sb/sth↔ˈout** [often passive] to destroy or remove sb/sth completely 徹底消滅；全部摧毀： *Whole villages were wiped out by the earthquake.* 地震把整座整座的村莊夷為平地。 ◇ *Last year's profits were virtually wiped out.* 去年的利潤幾乎全都賠光了。 ◇ *a campaign to wipe out malaria* 消滅瘧疾的運動 ➲ related noun WIPEOUT
■ ***noun*** **1** an act of cleaning sth using a cloth 擦；揩；拭： *Can you give the table a quick wipe?* 你把桌子快速擦一下行嗎？ **2** a special piece of thin cloth or soft paper that has been treated with a liquid and that you use to clean away dirt and bacteria（濕）抹布，紙巾： *Remember to take nappies and* ***baby wipes***. 記住帶尿布和嬰兒的濕紙巾。

ˌwiped ˈout *adj.* [not before noun] (*informal*) extremely tired 十分疲勞；筋疲力盡： *You look wiped out.* 你看上去疲憊不堪。

wipe·out /ˈwaɪpaʊt/ *noun* (*informal*) **1** [U, C] complete destruction, failure or defeat 全部摧毀；徹底失敗： *The party faces virtual wipeout in the election.* 這個政黨在選舉中面臨着近乎全軍覆滅。 ◇ *a 5-0 wipeout* * 5 比 0 的大敗 **2** [C] a fall from a SURFBOARD（從衝浪板上的）跌倒，翻跌

wiper /ˈwaɪpə(r)/ *noun* = WINDSCREEN WIPER

wire 🔑 /ˈwaɪə(r)/ *noun, verb*
■ ***noun*** **1** 🔑 [U, C] metal in the form of thin thread; a piece of this 金屬絲；金屬線；一段金屬絲（或線）： *a coil of copper wire* 一捲銅絲 ◇ *a wire basket* 金屬絲編織籃 ◇ *The box was fastened with a rusty wire.* 那個箱子是用生銹的鐵絲捆紮的。 ➲ picture at CORD ➲ see also BARBED WIRE, HIGH WIRE, TRIPWIRE **2** 🔑 [C, U] a piece of wire that is used to carry an electric current or signal 電線；導線： *overhead wires* 架空電線 ◇ *fuse wire* 保險絲 ◇ *The telephone wires had been cut.* 電話線被割斷了。 ➲ see also HOT-WIRE **3 the wire** [sing.] a wire fence 金屬絲編製的柵欄；鐵絲網： *Three prisoners escaped by crawling under the wire.* 三個囚犯從鐵絲網柵欄下鑽出去越獄了。 **4** [C] (*informal, especially NAmE*) = TELEGRAM： *We sent a wire asking him to join us.* 我們給他發了一份電報請他加入我們的行列。 ➲ see also WIRY
IDM **get your ˈwires crossed** (*informal*) to become confused about what sb has said to you so that you

think they meant sth else 誤會（別人的意思）**go, come, etc. (right) down to the 'wire** (*informal*) if you say that a situation goes **down to the wire**, you mean that the result will not be decided or known until the very end 直到最後才見分曉 ➲ more at LIVE² *adj.*, PULL *v.*

■ ***verb*** **1 ~ sth (up)** to connect a building, piece of equipment, etc. to an electricity supply using wires 用導線給（建築物、設備等）接通電源：*Make sure the plug is wired up correctly.* 插頭一定要接對。 **2 ~ sb/sth up (to sth)** | **~ sb/sth to sth** to connect sb/sth to a piece of equipment, especially a TAPE RECORDER or computer system 將…連接到（磁帶錄音機、計算機等設備）：*He was wired up to a police tape recorder.* 他被連接到了警方的錄音機上。 **3 ~ sth (for sth)** to put a special device somewhere in order to listen secretly to other people's conversations 給…安裝竊聽器 SYN **bug**：*The room had been wired for sound.* 這個房間已經裝上了竊聽器。 **4** (*especially NAmE*) to send sb a message by TELEGRAM 給（某人）打電報：**~ sth (to sb)** *He wired the news to us.* 他打電報把這個消息通知了我們。◇ **~ sb (sth)** *He wired us the news.* 他打電報把這個消息通知了我們。 **5** to send money from one bank to another using an electronic system 給（某人）電匯：**~ sth (to sb)** *The bank wired the money to her.* 銀行將錢電匯給了她。◇ **~ sb sth** *The bank wired her the money.* 銀行將錢電匯給了她。 **6 ~ sth** to join things together using wire 用金屬絲把…連在一起

'wire cutters *noun* [pl.] a tool for cutting wire 鋼絲鉗：*a pair of wire cutters* 一把鋼絲鉗 ➲ VISUAL VOCAB page V20

wired /'waɪəd; *NAmE* 'waɪərd/ *adj.* **1** connected to a system of computers（與計算機系統）聯網的，連線的：*Many colleges now have wired dormitories.* 現在許多大學的學生宿舍已經聯網。 **2** (of glass, material, etc. 玻璃、材料等) containing wires that make it strong or stiff（為使堅挺或堅固）內含金屬絲的，夾絲的 **3** (*informal*) excited or nervous; not relaxed 興奮的；緊張不安的 **4** (*informal, especially NAmE*) under the influence of alcohol or an illegal drug（受酒精或毒品影響而）迷醉的

'wire fraud *noun* [U, C] FRAUD (= dishonest ways of getting money) using computers and telephones（利用計算機或電話的）遠程詐騙（罪）

wire·less /'waɪələs; *NAmE* 'waɪərləs/ *noun, adj.*

■ ***noun*** **1** [C] (*old-fashioned, especially BrE*) a radio 無線電收音機：*I heard it on the wireless.* 我是從無線電收音機裏聽到的。 **2** [U] a system of sending and receiving signals 無線電發射和接收系統；無線電報：*a message sent by wireless* 用無線電報發出的信息

■ ***adj.*** not using wires 無線的：*wireless communications* 無線通信 ▸ **wire·less·ly** *adv.*

,wire 'netting *noun* [U] wire that is twisted into a net, used especially for fences 金屬絲網（尤用作柵欄）

wire·pull·er /'waɪəpʊlə(r); *NAmE* 'waɪər-/ *noun* (*NAmE*) a person who is able to control or influence events without people realizing it 幕後牽線者；背後操縱者

'wire service *noun* (*especially NAmE*) an organization that supplies news to newspapers and to radio and television stations 新聞通訊社；電訊社

'wire strippers *noun* [pl.] a tool for removing the plastic covering from electric wires（電線）剝皮鉗

wire·tap·ping /'waɪətæpɪŋ; *NAmE* 'waɪərt-/ *noun* [U] the act of secretly listening to other people's telephone conversations by attaching a device to the telephone line（用秘密連線方法）竊聽電話 ▸ **wire·tap** *verb* (-pp-) **~ sth** **wire·tap** *noun*：*the use of illegal wiretaps* 非法使用竊聽電話 ➲ see also TAP *v.* (4)

,wire 'wool *noun* [U] (*BrE*) = STEEL WOOL

wir·ing /'waɪərɪŋ/ *noun* [U] the system of wires that is used for supplying electricity to a building or machine（給建築物或機器供電的）線路：*to check the wiring* 檢查線路 ◇ *a wiring diagram* 線路圖

wiry /'waɪəri/ *adj.* (**wiri·er**, **wiri·est**) **1** (of a person 人) thin but strong 瘦而結實的 SYN **sinewy**：*a wiry little man* 清瘦結實的小個男子 **2** (of hair, plants, etc. 頭髮、植物等) stiff and strong; like wire 硬而結實的；像金屬絲的

wis·dom /'wɪzdəm/ *noun* [U] **1** the ability to make sensible decisions and give good advice because of the experience and knowledge that you have 智慧；才智；精明：*a woman of great wisdom* 才女 ◇ *words of wisdom* 至理名言 **2 ~ of sth/of doing sth** how sensible sth is 明智：***I question the wisdom of*** *giving a child so much money.* 我對給孩子這麼多錢是否明智懷有疑問。 **3** the knowledge that a society or culture has gained over a long period of time（社會或文化長期積累的）知識，學問：*the collective wisdom of the Native American people* 美洲原住民的集體智慧

IDM **conventional/received 'wisdom** the view or belief that most people hold 大多數人的看法；普遍信念：*Conventional wisdom has it that riots only ever happen in cities.* 人們普遍認為，只有城市裏才發生暴亂。 **in his/her/its, etc. (infinite) 'wisdom** used when you are saying that you do not understand why sb has done sth（表示不理解他人的無知）以其（無限的）智慧：*The government in its wisdom has decided to support the ban.* 政府竟愚蠢到決定支持這項禁令。 ➲ more at PEARL

'wisdom tooth *noun* any of the four large teeth at the back of the mouth that do not grow until you are an adult 智牙；智齒

wise 0⁻ /waɪz/ *adj., verb*

■ ***adj.*** (**wiser**, **wis·est**) **1** 0⁻ (of people 人) able to make sensible decisions and give good advice because of the experience and knowledge that you have 充滿智慧的；明智的；英明的；明察善斷的：*a wise old man* 智叟 ◇ *I'm* ***older and wiser*** *after ten years in the business.* 在商界混了十年之後，我變得老成聰明了。 **2** 0⁻ (of actions and behaviour 行動和行為) sensible; based on good judgement 明智的；高明的；有判斷力的 SYN **prudent**：*a wise decision* 明智的決定 ◇ ***It was very wise to*** *leave when you did.* 你那時離開非常明智。◇ *The wisest course of action is just to say nothing.* 最明智的做法就是緘默不言。◇ *I was grateful for her wise counsel.* 我感激她為我指點迷津。 ▸ **wise·ly** *adv.*：*She nodded wisely.* 她聰明地點了點頭。◇ *He wisely decided to tell the truth.* 他明智地決定實話實說。

IDM **be none the 'wiser** | **not be any the 'wiser** **1** to not understand sth, even after it has been explained to you（解釋之後）依然不懂，仍不明白：*I've read the instructions, but I'm still none the wiser.* 我看了用法說明，但仍然弄不明白。 **2** to not know or find out about sth bad that sb has done 不知道，發現不了（某人做的壞事）：*If you put the money back, no one will be any the wiser.* 只要你把錢放回去，誰都不會察覺。 **be ,wise after the e'vent** (often *disapproving*) to understand sth, or realize what you should have done, only after sth has happened 事後聰明；馬後炮 **be/get 'wise to sb/sth** (*informal*) to become aware that sb is being dishonest 明白，察覺（某人的不軌行為）：*He thought he could fool me but I got wise to him.* 他以為能耍得了我，其實我清楚他是怎麼一號人。 **put sb 'wise (to sth)** (*informal*) to inform sb about sth 告訴…（內情）；使…知道

■ ***verb***

PHR V **,wise 'up (to sth)** (*informal*) to become aware of the unpleasant truth about a situation 意識到，覺察（令人不愉快的實情）

-wise *suffix* (in adjectives and adverbs 構成形容詞和副詞) **1** in the manner or direction of 以…方式；朝…方向：*likewise* 同樣 ◇ *clockwise* 順時針方向 **2** (*informal*) concerning 關於；在…方面：*Things aren't too good businesswise.* 業務方面的情況不太好。

wise·acre /'waɪzeɪkə(r)/ *noun* (*old-fashioned, informal, especially NAmE*) a person who is annoying because they are very confident and think they know a lot 自以為無所不知的人；自以為是的人

wise·crack /'waɪzkræk/ *noun* (*informal*) a clever remark or joke 俏皮話；風涼話 ▸ **wise·crack** *verb* [I, T]：(**+ speech**) *He plays a wisecracking detective.* 他扮演一位滿嘴俏皮話的偵探。

'wise guy *noun* **1** (*informal, disapproving, especially NAmE*) a person who speaks or behaves as if they know more than other people 自以為無所不知的人；萬事通

W

SYN **know-all** 2 (*US, slang*) a member of the Mafia 黑手黨成員

ˈwise woman *noun* (*old use*) a woman with knowledge of traditional medicines and magic （深諳傳統醫術和幻術的）神婆，巫婆

wish /wɪʃ/ *verb, noun*

■ *verb* **1** [T] (not usually used in the present progressive tense 通常不用於現在進行時) to want sth to happen or to be true even though it is unlikely or impossible 希望（不大可能的事）發生；懷着（不可能實現的）願望：**~ (that)** … *I wish I were taller.* 我要是個子高一些就好了。◊ (*BrE* also) *I wish I was taller.* 我要是個子高一些就好了。◊ *I wish I hadn't eaten so much.* 我倒希望我沒有吃這麼多。◊ *'Where is he now?' '**I only wish** I knew!'* "他現在在哪兒？" "我要是知道就好了！" ◊ *I wish you wouldn't leave your clothes all over the floor.* 我真希望你不把衣服丟得滿地都是。 HELP 'That' is nearly always left out, especially in speech. 尤其在口語中 that 幾乎總是給省略掉。◊ **~ sb/sth/yourself + adj.** *He's dead and it's no use wishing him alive again.* 他死了，希望他死而復生是無濟於事的。◊ **~ sb/sth/yourself + adv./prep.** *She wished herself a million miles away.* 她恨不得自己遠在百萬英里之外。 **2** [I, T] (*especially BrE, formal*) to want to do sth; to want sth to happen 希望（做某事）；想要（某事發生）：*You may stay until morning, **if you wish**.* 如果你願意，你可以一直待到早晨。◊ *'I'd rather not talk now.' '(**Just**) **as you wish**.'* "現在我最好還是不說話。" "悉聽尊便。" ◊ **~ to do sth** *This course is designed for people wishing to update their computer skills.* 這門課程是為想要提高電腦技術的人而設的。◊ *I wish to speak to the manager.* 我想跟經理說話。◊ *I don't wish* (= I don't mean) *to be rude, but could you be a little quieter?* 我不想無禮，但請你安靜一點兒好嗎？◊ **~ sb sth** *She could not believe that he wished her harm.* 她不能相信他希望她受到傷害。◊ **~ sb/sth to do sth** *He was not sure whether he wished her to stay or go.* 他說不準他到底是希望她留下還是走開。 **3** [I] **~ (for sth)** to think very hard that you want sth, especially sth that can only be achieved by good luck or magic 盼望；企求；想要：*She shut her eyes and wished for him to get better.* 她閉上眼睛盼禱他好起來。◊ *If you wish really hard, maybe you'll get what you want.* 心誠則靈。◊ *It's no use wishing for the impossible.* 企求不可能的事情是徒勞無益的。◊ *He has everything he could possibly wish for.* 他可能想要的一切東西他都有了。 **4** [T] to say that you hope that sb will be happy, lucky, etc. 祝；祝願：**~ sb sth** *I wished her a happy birthday.* 我祝她生日快樂。◊ *Wish me luck!* 祝我交好運吧！◊ **~ sb well** *We wish them both well in their retirement.* 我們祝願他們兩位退休後頤養天年。

IDM **I ˈwish!** (*informal*) used to say that sth is impossible or very unlikely, although you wish it were possible 但願如此（但不可能或不大可能） SYN **if only**：*'You'll have finished by tomorrow.' 'I wish!'* "你到明天就完成了。" "但願如此！"

PHR V **ˌwish sth aˈway** to try to get rid of sth by wishing it did not exist 從心裏竭力擺脫；希望…不再存在 **ˈwish sb/sth on sb** (*informal*) (used in negative sentences 用於否定句) to want sb to have sth unpleasant 想讓…有（不愉快的事）：*I wouldn't wish something like that on my worst enemy.* 即使是我的死對頭，我也不想他出那樣的事。

■ *noun* **1** [C] a desire or a feeling that you want to do sth or have sth 願望；希望：**~ (to do sth)** *She expressed a wish to be alone.* 她表示希望沒有人打擾她。◊ *He **had no wish to** start a fight.* 他無意挑釁。◊ *His dearest wish* (= what he wants most of all) *is to see his grandchildren again.* 他最大的願望是能再次見到自己的孫子孫女。◊ **~ for sth** *I can understand her wish for secrecy.* 我可以理解她想保守秘密的願望。◊ **~ that** … *It was her dying wish that I should have it.* 她的臨終願望是把這東西留給我。 **2** [C] a thing that you want to have or to happen 想要的東西；希望的事：*to carry out sb's wishes* 實現某人的願望 ◊ *I'm sure that you will get your wish.* 我相信你會心想事成。◊ *She married **against** her parents' **wishes**.* 她違背父母的願望嫁給了別人。 ➲ see also DEATH WISH **3** [C] an attempt to make sth happen by thinking hard about it, especially in stories when it often happens by magic 願；心願：*Throw some money in the fountain and **make a wish**.* 往噴泉裏扔些錢，許個願。◊ *The genie granted him three wishes.* 精靈准許他表達三個心願。◊ *The prince's **wish came true**.* 王子的願望實現了。 **4** **wishes** [pl.] **~ (for sth)** used especially in a letter or card to say that you hope that sb will be happy, well or successful （書信或賀卡等中的）祝願，祝福：*We all send our **best wishes** for the future.* 我們都對未來致以最好的祝願。◊ *Give my good wishes to the family.* 請替我向全家致意。◊ ***With best wishes*** (= for example, at the end of a letter) 祝好（如信中結尾語）

IDM **if wishes were ˌhorses, beggars would/might ˈride** (*saying*) wishing for sth does not make it happen 想有不見得就有；願望不等於事實 **your wish is my comˈmand** (*humorous*) used to say that you are ready to do whatever sb asks you to do 悉聽閣下吩咐 **the wish is father to the ˈthought** (*saying*) we believe a thing because we want it to be true 希望什麼就相信什麼

Grammar Point 語法說明

wish

- After the verb **wish** in sense 1, a past tense is always used in a *that* clause. 動詞 wish 作第 1 義時，後面的 that 從句總是用過去時：*Do you wish (that) you **had** a better job?* 你希望有個更好的工作嗎？ In more formal English, especially in *NAmE*, many people use *were* after *I, he, she, it* instead of *was*. 在更正式的英語，尤其是美式英語中，許多人在 I、he、she、it 之後用 were，而不用 was：*I wish he **were** here tonight.* 要是他今晚在這兒就好了。

wish·bone /ˈwɪʃbəʊn; *NAmE* -boʊn/ *noun* a V-shaped bone between the neck and breast of a chicken, DUCK, etc. When the bird is eaten, this bone is sometimes pulled apart by two people, and the person who gets the larger part can make a wish. 叉骨，如願骨（吃家禽等時兩人將頸與胸之間的 V 形骨拉開，得大塊骨者可許願）

ˌwishful ˈthinking *noun* [U] the belief that sth that you want to happen is happening or will happen, although this is actually not true or very unlikely 不實際的幻想；一廂情願：*I've got a feeling that Alex likes me, but that might just be wishful thinking.* 我感覺亞歷克斯喜歡上我了，但那可能只是我一廂情願的想法。

ˈwishing well *noun* a WELL that people drop a coin into and make a wish （投幣）許願井

ˈwish list *noun* (*informal*) all the things that you would like to have, or that you would like to happen 希望一覽表（指所有希望得到的東西或全部希望發生的事情）

wishy-washy /ˈwɪʃi wɒʃi; *NAmE* -wɑːʃi; -wɔːʃi/ *adj.* (*informal, disapproving*) **1** not having clear or firm ideas or beliefs （思想或信仰）稀裏糊塗的，不清楚的，不堅定的：*a wishy-washy liberal* 不堅定的自由主義者 **2** not bright in colour （顏色）淺的，淡的：*a wishy-washy blue* 淡淡的藍色

wisp /wɪsp/ *noun* **~ (of sth)** **1** a small, thin piece of hair, grass, etc. （頭髮、草等的）小縷，小綹，小把，小束 **2** a long thin line of smoke or cloud （煙、雲等的）一縷

wispy /ˈwɪspi/ *adj.* consisting of small, thin pieces; not thick 一綹綹的；一縷縷的；成束的；纖細的：*wispy hair/clouds* 一縷縷頭髮／雲彩 ◊ *a wispy beard* 一綹綹鬍鬚

wis·teria /wɪˈstɪəriə; *NAmE* -ˈstɪr-/ (also **wis·taria** /wɪˈsteəriə; *NAmE* -ˈster-/) *noun* [U] a climbing plant with bunches of pale purple or white flowers that hang down 紫藤屬植物

wist·ful /ˈwɪstfl/ *adj.* thinking sadly about sth that you would like to have, especially sth in the past that you can no longer have 傷感的；（對已不可能發生之事）徒然神往的：*a wistful smile* 傷感的微笑 ► **wist·ful·ly** /-fəli/ *adv.*：*She sighed wistfully.* 她傷感地歎息。◊ *'If only I had known you then,' he said wistfully.* "要是我那時認識你就好了。" 他癡往地說道。 **wist·ful·ness** *noun* [U]

wit /wɪt/ *noun* **1** [U, sing.] the ability to say or write things that are both clever and amusing 措辭巧妙的能力；風趣；才思：*to have a* ***quick/sharp/dry/ready wit*** 才思敏捷；敏銳機智；假裝正經的詼諧；頭腦機敏 ◇ *a woman of wit and intelligence* 才思敏捷、聰穎的女子 ◇ *a book full of the* ***wit and wisdom*** *of his 30 years in politics* 一本有關他 30 年政治生涯中才思與智慧的書 **2** [C] a person who has the ability to say or write things that are both clever and amusing 才思敏捷說話詼諧的人；機智幽默的人：*a well-known wit and raconteur* 一位聞名遐邇、妙語連珠的故事大王 **3 wits** [pl.] your ability to think quickly and clearly and to make good decisions 理解力；穎悟力；頭腦；智力：*He needed all his wits to find his way out.* 他需要絞盡腦汁找到出路。◇ *The game was a long* ***battle of wits***. 這場遊戲是長時間的鬥智。◇ *Kate paused and* ***gathered her wits***. 凱特停下來恢復一下理智。◇ *a chance to* ***pit your wits against*** (= compete with, using your intelligence) *our quiz champion* 利用你的智慧同我們的知識競賽冠軍進行較量的機會 **4 -witted** (in adjectives 構成形容詞) having the type of intelligence mentioned 有…智慧的；頭腦…的：*a quick-witted group of students* 一群頭腦聰明的學生 **5** [U] **~ to do sth** the intelligence or good sense to know what is the right thing to do（正確判斷的）能力，智力；明智：*At least you had the wit to ask for help.* 你起碼還能意識到要求救。◇ *It should not be* ***beyond the wit of man*** *to resolve this dispute.* 解決這一糾紛應當是人力所能及的事。➲ see also WITLESS

WORD FAMILY
wit *noun*
witty *adj.*
witticism *noun*
outwit *verb*

IDM **be at your wits' 'end** to be so worried by a problem that you do not know what to do next 智窮計盡；全然不知所措 **be frightened/scared/terrified out of your 'wits** to be very frightened 嚇得魂不附體 **have/keep your 'wits about you** to be aware of what is happening around you and ready to think and act quickly 時刻保持頭腦冷靜；隨機應變 **to 'wit** (*old-fashioned, formal*) you use **to wit** when you are about to be more exact about sth that you have just referred to 也就是說；即：*Pilot error, to wit failure to follow procedures, was the cause of the accident.* 飛行員的失誤，即沒有遵守操作程序，是事故的原因。➲ more at LIVE[1]

witch /wɪtʃ/ *noun* **1** a woman who is believed to have magic powers, especially to do evil things. In stories, she usually wears a black pointed hat and flies on a BROOMSTICK. 女巫；巫婆 **2** (*disapproving*) an ugly unpleasant old woman 醜老太婆 IDM see BREW *n.*

witch·craft /'wɪtʃkrɑːft; *NAmE* -kræft/ *noun* [U] the use of magic powers, especially evil ones 巫術；（尤指）妖術，魔法

'witch doctor *noun* (especially in Africa) a person who is believed to have special magic powers that can be used to heal people（尤指非洲的）巫醫 ➲ compare MEDICINE MAN

'witch hazel *noun* [U] a liquid that is used for treating injuries on the skin 金縷梅酊劑（用於治療皮膚創傷）

'witch-hunt *noun* (usually *disapproving*) an attempt to find and punish people who hold opinions that are thought to be unacceptable or dangerous to society（對被認為持不為社會所接受或危及社會政見者的）搜捕，政治迫害

the 'witching hour *noun* [sing.] the time, late at night, when it is thought that magic things can happen 半夜三更；魔幻之事發生的時刻

Wite·out™ /'waɪtaʊt/ *noun* [U] (*NAmE*) a white liquid that you use to cover mistakes that you make when you are writing or typing, and that you can write on top of; a type of CORRECTION FLUID 惠陶特修正液 ➲ see also WHITE-OUT

with 🔑 /wɪð; wɪθ/ *prep.*
HELP For the special uses of **with** in phrasal verbs, look at the entries for the verbs. For example **bear with sb/sth** is in the phrasal verb section at **bear**. * with 在短語動詞中的特殊用法見有關動詞詞條。如 bear with sb/sth 在詞條 bear 的短語動詞部份。 **1** 🔑 in the company or presence of sb/sth 和…在一起；和；同；跟：*She lives with her parents.* 她同父母住在一起。◇ *I have a client with me right now.* 我現在有個客戶。◇ *a nice steak with a bottle of red wine* 一份美味牛排再加上一瓶紅葡萄酒 **2** 🔑 having or carrying sth 有；具有；帶有：*a girl with* (= who has) *red hair* 一位紅髮女郎 ◇ *a jacket with a hood* 帶風帽的短上衣 ◇ *He looked at her with a hurt expression.* 他帶着受傷害的神情看着她。◇ *They're both in bed with flu.* 他們雙雙患流感臥病在牀。◇ *a man with a suitcase* 提衣箱的男子 **3** 🔑 using sth 用；使用；以；藉：*Cut it with a knife.* 用刀把它切開。◇ *It is treated with acid before being analysed.* 對它先用酸處理再進行分析。 **4** 🔑 used to say what fills, covers, etc. sth（表示以某物填充、覆蓋等）：*The bag was stuffed with dirty clothes.* 袋子裏塞滿了髒衣服。◇ *Sprinkle the dish with salt.* 在這盤菜上撒上鹽。 **5** 🔑 in opposition to sb/sth; against sb/sth 與…對立；反對：*to fight with sb* 與某人打架 ◇ *to play tennis with sb* 與某人打網球 ◇ *at war with a neighbouring country* 與鄰國交戰 ◇ *I had an argument with my boss.* 我跟老闆吵了一架。 **6** 🔑 concerning; in the case of 關於；對於；對…來說：*Be careful with the glasses.* 小心這些玻璃杯。◇ *Are you pleased with the result?* 你對結果滿意嗎？◇ *Don't be angry with her.* 別生她的氣。◇ *With these students it's pronunciation that's the problem.* 對這些學生來說，成問題的是發音。 **7** 🔑 used when considering one fact in relation to another（涉及一事與另一事的關係）：*She won't be able to help us with all the family commitments she has.* 她有這麼多家務事，幫不了我們。◇ *It's much easier compared with last time.* 這與上次相比容易得多。 **8** 🔑 including 包括；還有：*The meal with wine came to $20 each.* 包括酒這頓飯每人 20 塊錢。◇ *With all the lesson preparation I have to do I work 12 hours a day.* 加上必須的備課在內，我每天工作 12 個小時。 **9** 🔑 used to show the way in which sb does sth（表示行為方式）：*He behaved with great dignity.* 他舉止莊重威嚴。◇ *She sleeps with the window open.* 她愛開着窗戶睡覺。◇ *Don't stand with your hands in your pockets.* 站着的時候別把雙手插在口袋裏。 **10** 🔑 because of; as a result of 因為；由於；作為…的結果：*She blushed with embarrassment.* 她難為情得臉紅了。◇ *His fingers were numb with cold.* 他的手指凍麻了。 **11** 🔑 because of sth and as it happens 由於；隨着：*The shadows lengthened with the approach of sunset.* 隨着太陽西沉，影子越來越長。◇ *Skill comes with practice.* 熟能生巧。 **12** in the same direction as sth 與…方向一致；順着：*Marine mammals generally swim with the current.* 海洋哺乳動物一般順水而游。 **13** 🔑 used to show who has possession of or responsibility for sth 由…持有；由…負責：*The keys are with reception.* 鑰匙在服務枱。◇ *Leave it with me.* 把這交給我吧。 **14** 🔑 employed by; using the services of 為…工作；受雇於；利用…的服務：*She acted with a touring company for three years.* 她在一巡迴劇團裏演出了三年。◇ *I bank with HSBC.* 我的錢存在匯豐銀行裏。 **15** showing separation from sth/sb（表示分離）：*I could never part with this ring.* 我永遠也不摘掉這枚戒指。◇ *Can we dispense with the formalities?* 我們可以免去這些客套嗎？ **16** despite sth 雖然；儘管：*With all her faults I still love her.* 儘管她有種種缺點，我依然愛着她。 **17** used in exclamations（用於感歎）：*Off to bed with you!* 你給我睡覺去！◇ *Down with school!* 取締學校！

IDM **be 'with me/you** (*informal*) to be able to understand what sb is talking about 能理解…講的話：*Are you with me?* 你明白我說的話嗎？◇ *I'm afraid I'm not quite with you.* 對不起，我不太懂你的意思。 **be 'with sb (on sth)** to support sb and agree with what they say 支持；與…站在一起；同意…說的話：*We're all with you on this one.* 在這個問題上我們都支持你。 **'with it** (*informal*) **1** knowing about current fashions and ideas 時新；時髦 SYN **trendy**：*Don't you have anything more with it to wear?* 難道你沒有更時髦一點兒的衣服穿？ **2** understanding what is happening around you 明白周圍情況；敏感 SYN **alert**：*You don't seem very with it today.* 你今天腦瓜子似乎不太管用。 **with 'that** straight after that; then 緊接着；隨即；然後：*He muttered a few words of apology and with that he left.* 他低聲嘰咕了幾句道歉的話，然後就走了。

with·draw /wɪðˈdrɔː; wɪθˈd-/ *verb* (**with·drew** /-ˈdruː/, **with·drawn** /-ˈdrɔːn/)
1 [I, T] to move back or away from a place or situation; to make sb/sth do this （使）撤回，撤離 SYN **pull out**：*Government troops were forced to withdraw.* 政府部隊被迫撤走了。◇ **~ (sb/sth) (from sth)** *Both powers withdrew their forces from the region.* 兩個大國都把部隊撤離了這個地區。◇ *She withdrew her hand from his.* 她把手從他的手裏抽了回來。 **2** [T] to stop giving or offering sth to sb 停止提供；不再給予：**~ sth** *Workers have threatened to withdraw their labour* (= go on strike). 工人揚言要罷工。◇ *He withdrew his support for our campaign.* 他停止了對我們運動的支持。◇ **~ sth from sth** *The drug was* **withdrawn from sale** *after a number of people suffered serious side effects.* 這藥因許多人服後產生嚴重副作用而被停止銷售。 **3** [I, T] to stop taking part in an activity or being a member of an organization; to stop sb/sth from doing these things （使）退出：**~ (from sth)** *There have been calls for Britain to withdraw from the EU.* 一直有人要求英國退出歐盟。◇ **~ sb/sth (from sth)** *The horse had been withdrawn from the race.* 那匹馬被停賽了。 **4** [T] **~ sth (from sth)** to take money out of a bank account 提，取（銀行賬戶中的款）：*I'd like to withdraw £250 please.* 勞駕，我想提取 250 英鎊。➲ COLLOCATIONS at FINANCE **5** [T] **~ sth** (*formal*) to say that you no longer believe that sth you previously said is true 收回，撤回，撤銷（說過的話）SYN **retract**：*The newspaper withdrew the allegations the next day.* 這家報紙第二天收回了這些說法。 **6** [I] **~ (from sth) (into sth/yourself)** to become quieter and spend less time with other people 脫離（社會）；不與人交往：*She's beginning to withdraw into herself.* 她開始變得不愛與人交往了。

with·draw·al /wɪðˈdrɔːəl; wɪθˈd-/ *noun* **1** [U, C] the act of moving or taking sth away or back 撤走；收回；取回：*the withdrawal of support* 不再支持◇ *the withdrawal of the UN troops from the region* 聯合國部隊從該地區的撤離◇ *the withdrawal of a product from the market* 從市場上收回一種產品 **2** [U] the act of no longer taking part in sth or being a member of an organization 不再參加；退出（組織）：*his withdrawal from the election* 他從選舉中的退出◇ *a campaign for Britain's withdrawal from the EU* 爭取英國退出歐盟的運動 **3** [C] the act of taking an amount of money out of your bank account （從銀行賬戶中）提款，取款：*You can* **make withdrawals** *of up to $250 a day.* 你一天可以從銀行賬戶中提取最多不超過 250 元。➲ COLLOCATIONS at FINANCE **4** [U] the period of time when sb is getting used to not taking a drug that they have become ADDICTED to, and the unpleasant effects of doing this 戒毒過程；脫癮期：*I got* **withdrawal symptoms** *after giving up smoking.* 我戒煙之後出現了脫癮症狀。 **5** [C, usually sing., U] the act of saying that you no longer believe that sth you have previously said is true（對說過的話的）收回，撤回 SYN **retraction**：*The newspaper published a withdrawal the next day.* 報紙第二天發表了撤銷聲明。 **6** [U] (*psychology* 心) the behaviour of sb who wants to be alone and does not want to communicate with other people 孤僻

with·drawn /wɪðˈdrɔːn/ *adj.* not wanting to talk to other people; extremely quiet and shy 沉默寡言的；怕羞的；內向的

wither /ˈwɪðə(r)/ *verb* **1** [I, T] **~ (sth)** if a plant **withers** or sth **withers** it, it dries up and dies （使）枯萎，凋謝：*The grass had withered in the warm sun.* 這些草在溫暖的陽光下枯死了。 **2** [I] **~ (away)** to become less or weaker, especially before disappearing completely 萎縮；（尤指漸漸）破滅，消失：*All our hopes just withered away.* 我們所有的希望都漸漸破滅了。

withered /ˈwɪðəd; *NAmE* -ərd/ *adj.* [usually before noun] **1** (of plants 植物) dried up and dead 乾枯的；枯萎的 SYN **shrivelled**：*withered leaves* 枯葉 **2** (of people 人) looking old because they are thin and weak and have very dry skin 衰老憔悴的；枯槁的；乾癟的 **3** (of parts of the body 身體部位) thin and weak and not fully developed because of disease 瘦弱的；發育不良的；病態的：*withered limbs* 乾癟的四肢

wither·ing /ˈwɪðərɪŋ/ *adj.* (of a look, remark, etc. 神情、話語等) intended to make sb feel silly or ashamed 尖刻的；使人難堪的；令人無地自容的：*withering scorn* 使人難堪的輕蔑◇ *She gave him a withering look.* 她極其蔑視地看了他一眼。▸ **wither·ing·ly** *adv.*

with·ers /ˈwɪðəz; *NAmE* -ərz/ *noun* [pl.] the highest part of a horse's back, between its shoulders 鬐甲（馬肩胛骨間隆起部份）

with·hold /wɪðˈhəʊld; wɪθˈh-; *NAmE* -ˈhoʊld/ *verb* (**with·held**, **with·held** /-ˈheld/) **~ sth (from sb/sth)** (*formal*) to refuse to give sth to sb 拒絕給；不給 SYN **keep back**：*She was accused of withholding information from the police.* 她被指控對警方知情不報。

with'holding tax *noun* [C, U] (in the US) an amount of money that an employer takes out of sb's income as tax and pays directly to the government （美國由雇主從員工收入中扣除並直接交給政府的）須扣稅款 ➲ compare PAY AS YOU EARN

with·in /wɪˈðɪn/ *prep., adv.*
■ ***prep.*** **1** before a particular period of time has passed; during a particular period of time 不出（某段時間）；在（某段時間）之內：*You should receive a reply within seven days.* 你會在七天之內收到答覆。◇ *The ambulance arrived* **within minutes of** *the call being made.* 打電話後幾分鐘內救護車就到了。◇ *Two elections were held* **within the space of** *a year.* 在一年的時間之內舉行了兩次選舉。 **2** not further than a particular distance from sth 不出（某段距離）；在（某段距離）之間：*a house within a mile of the station* 離車站不到一英里的一所房子◇ *Is it* **within walking distance?** 那裏步行走得到嗎？ **3** inside the range or limits of sth 不出（某範圍或限度）；在（某範圍）之內：*That question is not within the scope of this talk.* 那個問題不在本次會談範圍之內。◇ *We are now within range of enemy fire.* 我們現在處於敵人的火力射程以內。◇ *He finds it hard to live within his income* (= without spending more than he earns). 他覺得靠自己的收入生活難以為繼。 **4** (*formal*) inside sth/sb 在…裏；在…內部：*The noise seems to be coming from within the building.* 吵鬧聲像是從樓房裏傳出來的。◇ *There is discontent within the farming industry.* 農業界內部存在不滿。
■ ***adv.*** (*formal*) inside 在裏面；在內部：*Cleaner required. Apply within.* (= on a sign) 招聘清潔工。應聘者請進。

with·out /wɪˈðaʊt/ *prep., adv.*
■ ***prep.*** **1** not having, experiencing or showing sth 沒有；缺乏：*They had gone two days without food.* 他們兩天沒吃東西。◇ *He found the place without difficulty.* 他毫不費力地找到了那地方。◇ *She spoke without much enthusiasm.* 她說話冷冰冰的。 **2** not in the company of sb 不和…在一起；無…相伴：*Don't go without me.* 別甩下我就走。 **3** not using or taking sth 不用；不拿；不帶：*Can you see without your glasses?* 你不戴眼鏡能看見嗎？◇ *Don't go out without your coat.* 別不穿大衣就出去。 **4** not doing the action mentioned 不（做某事）；無；沒：**~ doing sth** *He left without saying goodbye.* 他不辭而別。◇ *You can't make an omelette without breaking eggs.* 你不可能不打破雞蛋就做成煎蛋捲。◇ ***Without wanting to*** *criticize, I think you could have done better.* (= used before you make a critical comment) 我不是想要批評誰，只是認為你本可以做得更好一些。◇ **~ sb doing sth** *The party was organized without her knowing anything about it.* 聚會已操辦妥當，她卻一無所知。
■ ***adv.*** not having or showing sth 沒有；缺乏：*Do you want a room with a bath or one without?* 你要不要帶洗澡間的房間？◇ *If there's none left we'll have to* **do without.** 如果沒有剩餘的我們就只得將就了。◇ *I'm sure we'll* **manage without.** 我相信我們能湊合的。

ˌwith-ˈprofit (also **ˌwith-ˈprofits**) *adj.* (*BrE*) used to describe an insurance policy or an investment where the amount paid includes a share in the company's profits （保單或投資）分紅的，共享利潤的

with·stand /wɪðˈstænd; wɪθˈs-/ *verb* (**with·stood**, **with·stood** /-ˈstʊd/) **~ sth** (*formal*) to be strong enough not to be hurt or damaged by extreme conditions, the use of force, etc. 承受；抵住；頂住；經受住 SYN **resist, stand up to**：*The materials used have to be able to withstand high temperatures.* 所使用的材料必須能夠耐高温。◇ *They had withstood siege, hunger and deprivation.* 他們經受了圍困、飢餓和貧窮。

wit·less /ˈwɪtləs/ *adj.* silly or stupid; not sensible 愚蠢的；不明事理的 SYN **foolish**
IDM **be scared/bored ˈwitless** (*informal*) to be extremely frightened or bored 被嚇破了膽；乏味得要命

Synonyms 同義詞辨析

witness

observer • onlooker • passer-by • bystander • eyewitness

These are all words for a person who sees sth happen. 以上各詞均指目睹事情發生的人。

witness a person who sees sth happen and is able to describe it to other people; a person who gives evidence in a court of law 指目擊者、見證人、證人：*Police have appealed for witnesses to the accident.* 警方呼籲這起事故的目擊者出來作證。

observer a person who sees sth happen 指觀察者、目擊者：*According to observers, the plane exploded shortly after take-off.* 據目擊者說，飛機起飛後不久就爆炸了。

onlooker a person who watches sth that is happening but is not involved in it 指旁觀者：*A crowd of onlookers gathered at the scene of the crash.* 在撞車地點聚集了一大群圍觀者。

passer-by a person who is going past sb/sth by chance, especially when sth unexpected happens 指路人、過路的人，尤指意想不到的事發生時碰巧路過的：*Police asked passers-by if they had witnessed the accident.* 警察詢問過路的人是否目擊了這次事故。

bystander a person who is near and can see what is happening when sth such as an accident or fight takes place 指現場目擊者、旁觀者：*Three innocent **bystanders** were killed in the crossfire.* 三個無辜的旁觀者在交叉火力中喪生。

eyewitness a person who has seen a crime or accident and can describe it afterwards. 指犯罪或事故現場的目擊者、見證人

PATTERNS

- a(n) witness/observer/onlooker/passer-by/bystander/eyewitness **sees** sth
- a(n) observer/onlooker/passer-by/bystander **witnesses** sth

wit·ness 0‑π /ˈwɪtnəs/ *noun, verb*

■ *noun*

▸ PERSON WHO SEES STH 目睹者 **1** 0‑π (also **eye·wit·ness**) [C] a person who sees sth happen and is able to describe it to other people 目擊者；見證人：*Police have appealed for witnesses to the accident.* 警方呼籲這起事故的目擊者出來作證。◇ *a witness to the killing* 殺人案的目擊證人 ➲ COLLOCATIONS at CRIME, JUSTICE

▸ IN COURT 法庭上 **2** 0‑π [C] a person who gives evidence in court 證人：*a **defence/prosecution witness*** 被告的／原告的證人 ◇ *to appear as (a) **witness for the defence/prosecution*** 出庭為被告／原告作證

▸ OF SIGNATURE 簽名 **3** 0‑π [C] a person who is present when an official document is signed and who also signs it to prove that they saw this happen 見證人；連署人：*He was one of the witnesses at our wedding.* 他是我們婚禮的見證人之一。

▸ OF RELIGIOUS BELIEFS 宗教信仰 **4** [U] evidence of a person's strong religious beliefs, that they show by what they say and do in public 見證（以言行證實信仰） ➲ see also JEHOVAH'S WITNESS

IDM **be (a) ˈwitness to sth** **1** (*formal*) to see sth take place 目擊，看見（某事發生）：*He has been witness to a terrible murder.* 他目擊了一起殘忍的兇殺事件。 **2** to show that sth is true; to provide evidence for sth 證明…真實；為…提供證據：*His good health is a witness to the success of the treatment.* 他身體健康證明這種療法是成功的。 **bear/give ˈwitness (to sth)** to provide evidence of the truth of sth 為…作證；證明

■ *verb*

▸ SEE STH 看到 **1** 0‑π [T] **~ sth** to see sth happen (typically a crime or an accident) 當場看到，目擊（尤指罪行或事故）：*She was shocked by the violent scenes she had witnessed.* 她被親眼目睹的暴虐場面驚呆了。◇ *Police have appealed for anyone who witnessed the incident to contact them.* 警方呼籲凡是目擊這一事故的人與他們聯繫。◇ *We are now witnessing an unprecedented increase in violent crime.* 我們現在親眼看到暴力犯罪空前增多。 ➲ SYNONYMS at NOTICE

▸ OF TIME/PLACE 時間；地點 **2** [T] **~ sth** to be the place, period, organization, etc. in which particular events take place 是發生…的地點（或時間、組織等）；見證：*Recent years have witnessed a growing social mobility.* 近年來人們的社會流動性越來越大。◇ *The retail trade is witnessing a sharp fall in sales.* 零售業的銷售額在急劇下降。

▸ SIGNATURE 簽署 **3** [T] **~ sth** to be present when an official document is signed and sign it yourself to prove that you saw this happen（為正式文件的簽署）作證，連署：*to witness a signature* 為簽署作證

▸ BE SIGN/PROOF 跡象；證據 **4** [T, I, usually passive] to be a sign or proof of sth 是…的跡象；為…的證據：**~ sth** *There has been increasing interest in her life and work, **as witnessed by** the publication of two new biographies.* 從兩部新傳記的出版可以看出，人們對她的生活和工作越來越感興趣。◇ **~ to sth** *The huge attendance figures for the exhibition witness to a healthy interest in modern art.* 從展覽會參觀人數之多可以看出，人們對現代藝術具有濃厚興趣。 **5** [T] **~ sth** (*formal*) used when giving an example that proves sth you have just said（擺證據）…就是證據，看…就知道：*Authentic Italian cooking is very healthy—witness the low incidence of heart disease in Italy.* 正宗的意大利烹飪對健康非常有益，在意大利心臟病發病率低就是證據。

▸ TO RELIGIOUS BELIEFS 宗教信仰 **6** [I] **~ (to sth)** (*especially NAmE*) to speak to people about your strong religious beliefs（為宗教信仰）做見證 SYN **testify**

ˈ**witness box** (*BrE*) (*NAmE* ˈ**witness stand**) (also **stand** *BrE, NAmE*) *noun* the place in court where people stand to give evidence（法庭上的）證人席 ➲ COLLOCATIONS at JUSTICE

wit·ter /ˈwɪtə(r)/ *verb* [I] **~ (on) (about sth)** (*BrE, informal, usually disapproving*) to talk about sth unimportant and boring for a long time 嘮叨；夸夸其談：*What's he wittering on about?* 他在嘮叨什麼？

wit·ti·cism /ˈwɪtɪsɪzəm/ *noun* a clever and amusing remark 妙語；俏皮話；詼諧語

wit·ting·ly /ˈwɪtɪŋli/ *adv.* (*formal*) in a way that shows that you are aware of what you are doing 有意地；故意地；明知地 SYN **intentionally**：*It was clear that, wittingly or unwittingly, he had offended her.* 很顯然，不管是有意還是無意，他反正得罪了她。 OPP **unwittingly**

witty /ˈwɪti/ *adj.* (**wit·tier, wit·ti·est**) able to say or write clever, amusing things 言辭詼諧的；巧妙的；妙趣橫生的；機智的：*a witty speaker* 幽默的演講人 ◇ *a witty remark* 機智的話 ➲ SYNONYMS at FUNNY ▸ **wit·tily** *adv.* **wit·ti·ness** *noun* [U]

wives *pl.* of WIFE

wiz·ard /ˈwɪzəd; *NAmE* -ərd/ *noun* **1** (in stories) a man with magic powers（傳說中的）男巫，術士 **2** a person who is especially good at sth 行家；能手；奇才：*a **computer/financial, etc. wizard*** 計算機、金融等奇才 **3** (*computing* 計) a program that makes it easy to use another program or perform a task by giving you a series of simple choices 嚮導（程序）

wiz·ard·ry /ˈwɪzədri; *NAmE* -ərd-/ *noun* [U] a very impressive and clever achievement; great skill 傑出的成就；非

W

凡的才能： *electronic wizardry* 電子方面的非凡才能 ◇ *The second goal was sheer wizardry.* 第二記入球真是神奇。

wiz·ened /ˈwɪznd/ *adj.* looking smaller and having many folds and lines in the skin, because of being old（由於年老）乾癟的，多皺的，乾枯的 **SYN** **shrivelled**： *a wizened little man* 乾癟的小老頭 ◇ *wizened apples* 皺癟的蘋果

WLTM *abbr.* would like to meet (used in personal advertisements)（用於私人廣告）願意見面，希望見面

WMD /ˌdʌblju: em ˈdi:/ *abbr.* WEAPON OF MASS DESTRUCTION

woad /wəʊd; *NAmE* woʊd/ *noun* [U] a blue substance that people used to paint their bodies and faces with in ancient times 靛藍（古時人們用來塗染身體和臉）

wob·ble /ˈwɒbl; *NAmE* ˈwɑ:bl/ *verb, noun*

■ *verb* **1** [I, T] to move from side to side in an unsteady way; to make sth do this（使）搖擺，搖晃： *This chair wobbles.* 這把椅子不穩。◇ (*figurative*) *Her voice wobbled with emotion.* 她激動得聲音發顫。◇ **~ sth** *Don't wobble the table—I'm trying to write.* 別搖桌子，我在寫字呢。 **2** [I] **+ adv./prep.** to go in a particular direction while moving from side to side in an unsteady way 一搖一擺地走： *He wobbled off on his bike.* 他搖搖晃晃地騎着自行車走了。 **3** [I] to hesitate or lose confidence about doing sth 猶豫不決；信心動搖： *Yesterday the president showed the first signs of wobbling over the issue.* 昨天總統第一次在這個問題上表現得有些搖擺不定。

■ *noun* **1** [usually sing.] a slight unsteady movement from side to side 鬆動；搖晃： *The handlebars developed a wobble.* 這車把鬆動搖晃了。 **2** a moment when you hesitate or lose confidence about sth 猶豫不決；信心動搖： *The team is experiencing a mid-season wobble.* 這支隊正處於賽季中期的不穩定狀態。

wobble·board /ˈwɒblbɔ:d; *NAmE* ˈwɑ:blbɔ:rd/ *noun* a musical instrument consisting of a piece of board which is shaken to produce low sounds, originally played by Australian Aborigines 晃動板（原澳大利亞土著樂器，晃動發低音）

wob·bly /ˈwɒbli; *NAmE* ˈwɑ:bli/ *adj., noun*

■ *adj.* (*informal*) **1** moving in an unsteady way from side to side 搖擺的；搖搖晃晃的： *a chair with a wobbly leg* 一條腿不穩的椅子 ◇ *a wobbly tooth* 鬆動的牙齒 ◇ *He's still a bit wobbly after the operation* (= not able to stand firmly). 他動了手術之後仍然有點兒站不穩。 **2** not firm or confident 顫動的；不穩的；不自信的 **SYN** **shaky**： *the wobbly singing of the choir* 唱詩班發顫的歌聲 ◇ *The evening got off to a wobbly start.* 這次晚會一開始就不順當。

■ *noun*

IDM **throw a ˈwobbly** (*BrE, informal*) to suddenly become very angry or upset 勃然大怒；發脾氣

wodge /wɒdʒ; *NAmE* wɑ:dʒ/ *noun* **~ (of sth)** (*BrE, informal*) a large piece or amount of sth 大塊；大堆；大量： *a thick wodge of ten-pound notes* 厚厚一沓十英鎊鈔票

woe /wəʊ; *NAmE* woʊ/ *noun* (*old-fashioned* or *humorous*) **1** **woes** [pl.] the troubles and problems that sb has 麻煩；問題；困難： *financial woes* 財政困難 ◇ *Thanks for listening to my woes.* 謝謝您聽我訴說不幸的遭遇。 **2** [U] great unhappiness 痛苦；苦惱；悲傷；悲哀 **SYN** **misery**： *a tale of woe* 悲慘的故事

IDM **ˌwoe beˈtide sb** | **ˈwoe to sb** (*formal* or *humorous*) a phrase that is used to warn sb that there will be trouble for them if they do sth or do not do sth（用以警告某人會有麻煩）…就要倒霉，…將會遭殃： *Woe betide anyone who gets in her way!* 誰擋住她的路誰就會遭殃！ **ˌwoe is ˈme!** *exclamation* (*old use* or *humorous*) a phrase that is used to say that you are very unhappy 我好苦哇！

woe·be·gone /ˈwəʊbɪɡɒn; *NAmE* ˈwoʊbɪɡɔ:n; -ɡɑ:n/ *adj.* (*formal*) looking very sad（神情）悲傷的，憂傷的；愁眉苦臉的 **SYN** **miserable**： *a woebegone expression* 悲傷的表情

woe·ful /ˈwəʊfl; *NAmE* ˈwoʊfl/ *adj.* **1** [usually before noun] very bad or serious; that you disapprove of 糟糕的；嚴重的；不合意的 **SYN** **deplorable**： *She displayed a woeful ignorance of the rules.* 她對這些條例表現出可悲的無知。 **2** (*literary* or *formal*) very sad 悲慘的；憂傷的： *a woeful face* 憂傷的面孔 ◇ *woeful tales of broken romances* 破裂愛情的悲慘故事 ▸ **woe·ful·ly** /-fəli/ *adv.*

wog /wɒɡ; *NAmE* wɑ:ɡ/ *noun* **1** (*BrE, taboo, slang*) a very offensive word for a person who does not have white skin 外國佬（對有色人種的蔑稱） **2** (*AustralE, taboo, slang*) an offensive word for a person from southern Europe or whose parents came from southern Europe 南蠻子（對南歐人或其後裔的蔑稱） **3** (*AustralE, informal*) an illness, usually one that is not very serious 病；小病： *A flu wog struck.* 突患流感。

wok /wɒk; *NAmE* wɑ:k/ *noun* (from *Chinese*) a large pan shaped like a bowl, used for cooking food, especially Chinese food 炒菜鍋；鑊子 ➲ VISUAL VOCAB page V27

woke *past tense* of WAKE

woken *past part.* of WAKE

wolds /wəʊldz; *NAmE* woʊldz/ *noun* [pl.] used in the names of places in Britain for an area of high open land（用於英國的地名）丘陵： *the Yorkshire Wolds* 約克郡丘陵

wolf /wʊlf/ *noun, verb*

■ *noun* (*pl.* **wolves** /wʊlvz/) a large wild animal of the dog family, that lives and hunts in groups 狼： *a pack of wolves* 一群狼

IDM **keep the ˈwolf from the door** (*informal*) to have enough money to avoid going hungry; to stop sb feeling hungry 勉強度日；餬口 **throw sb to the ˈwolves** to leave sb to be roughly treated or criticized without trying to help or defend them 棄…於險境而不顧；見死不救 **a wolf in sheep's ˈclothing** a person who seems to be friendly or harmless but is really an enemy 披着羊皮的狼 ➲ more at CRY *v.*, LONE

■ *verb* **~ sth (down)** (*informal*) to eat food very quickly, especially by putting a lot of it in your mouth at once 大口地快吃；狼吞虎嚥 **SYN** **gobble**

wolf·hound /ˈwʊlfhaʊnd/ *noun* a very large tall dog with long hair and long legs, originally used for hunting wolves 獵狼犬： *an Irish wolfhound* 愛爾蘭獵狼犬

wolf·ish /ˈwʊlfɪʃ/ *adj.* (*formal*) like a wolf 似狼的： *wolfish yellow eyes* 狼一般的黃眼睛 ◇ (*figurative*) *a wolfish grin* (= showing sexual interest in sb) 淫蕩的露齒笑 ▸ **wolf·ish·ly** *adv.*

ˈwolf whistle *noun* a whistle with a short rising note and a long falling note, used by sb, usually a man, to show that they find sb else attractive, especially sb passing in the street 挑逗呼哨（尤指男子在街上向美貌女子吹的）： *She was fed up with the builders' wolf whistles each morning.* 每天早上都有建築工人衝她挑逗地吹口哨，她煩都煩死了。 ▸ **ˈwolf-whistle** *verb* [I, T] **~ (sb)**

wolverine /ˈwʊlvəri:n/ *noun* a wild animal that looks similar to a small bear, with short legs, long brown hair and a long tail. Wolverines live in cold, northern areas of Europe and North America. 狼獾

wolves *pl.* of WOLF

woman 0⊶ /ˈwʊmən/ *noun* (*pl.* **women** /ˈwɪmɪn/)

1 0⊶ [C] an adult female human 成年女子；婦女： *men, women and children* 男人、女人和兒童 ◇ *a 24-year-old woman* * 24 歲的女子 ◇ *I prefer to see a woman doctor.* 我希望讓女醫生給我看病。 **2** [U] female humans in general（泛指）女性：(*informal*) *She's all woman!* (= has qualities that are typical of women) 她是典型的女人！ **3** [C] (in compounds 構成複合詞) a woman who comes from the place mentioned or whose job or interest is connected with the thing mentioned 來自…（或做…、喜歡…等）的女子： *an Englishwoman* 英國女人 ◇ *a businesswoman* 女商人 ◇ *a Congresswoman* 女議員 ◇ *a horsewoman* 女騎師 ➲ note at GENDER **4** [C] a female worker, especially one who works with her hands（尤指做手工勞動的）女工： *We used to have a woman to do the cleaning.* 我們曾雇過一位女工打掃衛生。 **5** [sing.] (*old-fashioned*) a rude way of addressing a female person in an angry or important way（對女人無禮的稱呼）娘兒們：*Be quiet, woman!* 安靜，你這個臭娘兒們！ **6** [C] (sometimes *disapproving*) a wife or sexual partner 妻子；女朋友；女相好：*He's got a new woman in his life.* 他生命中又有了一個女人。➲ see also FALLEN WOMAN, KEPT WOMAN, OTHER WOMAN

IDM **be your own 'man/'woman** to act or think independently, not following others or being ordered 獨立自主：*Working for herself meant that she could be her own woman.* 獨立工作意味着她能夠自主。➲ more at HEART, HELL, HONEST, MAN *n.*, PART *n.*, POSSESSED, SUBSTANCE, WORLD

woman·hood /'wʊmənhʊd/ *noun* [U] (*formal*) **1** the state of being a woman, rather than a girl 成年女子的狀態：*He watched his daughters grow to womanhood.* 他看着自己的女兒們都長大成人了。**2** women in general（統稱）婦女：*the womanhood of this country* 這個國家的婦女 ➲ compare MANHOOD

woman·ish /'wʊmənɪʃ/ *adj.* (*disapproving*) (especially of a man 尤指男子) behaving in a way that is more suitable for a woman; more suitable for women than men 脂粉氣的；娘娘腔的；更適合女性的：*He has a womanish manner.* 他舉手投足像個女人。◇ *a womanish novel* 女性小說

woman·iz·ing (*BrE* also **-is·ing**) /'wʊmənaɪzɪŋ/ *noun* [U] (*disapproving*) the fact of having sexual relationships with many different women 玩弄女性；沉溺於女色 **SYN** **philandering** ▸ **woman·izer**, **-iser** *noun*

woman·kind /'wʊmənkaɪnd/ *noun* [U] (*old-fashioned, formal*) women in general（統稱）女人，女性 ➲ compare MANKIND

woman·ly /'wʊmənli/ *adj.* (*approving*) behaving, dressing, etc. in a way that people think is typical of or very suitable for a woman 女性特有的；女子般的；適合女人的 **SYN** **feminine**：*womanly qualities* 女子的特性 ◇ *a soft womanly figure* 婀娜多姿的體態 ▸ **woman·li·ness** *noun* [U]

womb /wu:m/ *noun* the organ in women and female animals in which babies develop before they are born 子宮 **SYN** **uterus**

wom·bat /'wɒmbæt; *NAmE* 'wɑ:m-/ *noun* an Australian animal like a small BEAR, that carries its young in a POUCH (= a pocket of skin) on the front of the mother's body 毛鼻袋熊（體形像熊的澳大利亞有袋動物）

women·folk /'wɪmɪnfəʊk; *NAmE* -foʊk/ *noun* [pl.] (*formal* or *humorous*) all the women in a community or family, especially one that is led by men（一個集體或家庭的，尤指由男人領導的）女人們，婦女們：*The male hunters brought back the food for their womenfolk to cook.* 男獵手們帶回食物讓他們的女人烹調。➲ compare MENFOLK

women's lib·ber /ˌwɪmɪnz 'lɪbə(r)/ *noun* (*old-fashioned, informal*, often *disapproving*) a person who supports Women's Liberation (2) 婦解分子；支持婦女解放運動的人

ˌwomen's libeˈration *noun* [U] (*old-fashioned*) **1** (also *informal* **women's lib** /ˌwɪmɪnz 'lɪb/) the freedom of women to have the same social and economic rights as men 婦女解放 **2** **Women's Liberation** (also *informal* **Women's Lib**) the movement that aimed to achieve equal social and economic rights for women 婦女解放運動

'women's studies *noun* [U+sing./pl. v.] the study of women and their role in history, literature and society 女性研究（研究女性及其在歷史、文學和社會中的作用）：*to major in women's studies.* 主修女性研究

womens·wear /'wɪmɪnzweə(r); *NAmE* -wer/ *noun* [U] (used especially in shops/stores) clothes for women（尤用於商店）女式服裝，女裝

won *past tense, past part.* of WIN

won·der 🔑 /'wʌndə(r)/ *verb, noun*

■ *verb* **1** 🔑 [T, I] to think about sth and try to decide what is true, what will happen, what you should do, etc. 想知道；想弄明白；琢磨：**~ who, where, etc. ...** *I wonder who she is.* 我在想她到底是誰。◇ *I was just beginning to wonder where you were.* 我剛才正琢磨你上哪兒了呢。◇ **~ (about sth)** *'Why do you want to know?' 'No particular reason. I was just wondering.'* "你為什麼想要知道？" "沒有特殊原因。我就是想搞清楚。" ◇ *We were wondering about next April for the wedding.* 我們尋思着下個四月舉行婚禮可好。◇ **+ speech** *'What should I do now?' she wondered.* "我現在該怎麼辦呢？" 她自忖道。**2** 🔑 [T] **~ if, whether ...** used as a polite way of asking a question or asking sb to do sth（禮貌地提問或請人做事時說）：*I wonder if you can help me.* 不知您是否能幫我的忙？◇ *I was wondering whether you'd like to come to a party.* 不知您能否來參加聚會。**3** [I, T] to be very surprised by sth 感到詫異；非常驚訝：**~ (at sth)** *She wondered at her own stupidity.* 她沒想到自己竟會這樣愚蠢。◇ (*BrE, informal*) *He's gone and left us to do all the work, **I shouldn't wonder*** (= I wouldn't be surprised if he had). 他走了，把所有的活都留給我們幹。我對此並不感到奇怪。◇ **~ (that) ...** *I wonder (that) he didn't hurt himself jumping over that wall.* 我納悶他怎麼從那牆上跳過去竟沒摔傷自己。◇ ***I don't wonder** you're tired. You've had a busy day.* 你累了，這我一點兒不奇怪。你已經忙了一整天。

■ *noun* **1** [U] a feeling of surprise and admiration that you have when you see or experience sth beautiful, unusual or unexpected 驚訝；驚奇；驚異；驚歎 **SYN** **awe**：*He retained a childlike sense of wonder.* 他仍然有一種孩子般的好奇感。◇ *She gazed down **in wonder** at the city spread below her.* 她俯視展現在眼前的城市，驚歎不已。**2** [C] something that fills you with surprise and admiration 奇跡；奇觀；奇事；奇妙之處 **SYN** **marvel**：*The Grand Canyon is one of the natural wonders of the world.* 大峽谷是世界自然奇觀之一。◇ *the wonders of modern technology* 現代技術的奇跡 ◇ *That's the wonder of poetry—you're always discovering something new.* 這就是詩的奇妙之處，你總有新的發現。◇ *the **Seven Wonders of the World*** (= the seven most impressive structures of the ancient world) 世界七大奇觀 **3** [sing.] (*informal*) a person who is very clever at doing sth; a person or thing that seems very good or effective 能人；奇才；有特效的東西：*Dita, you're a wonder! I would never have thought of doing that.* 蒂塔，你真神了！我從來想不到那樣做。◇ *Have you seen the **boy wonder** play yet?* 你看過那場神童表演沒有？◇ *a new wonder drug* 一種新的特效藥

IDM **do 'wonders (for sb/sth)** to have a very good effect on sb/sth（為某人或替某事）創造奇跡；產生神奇作用：*The news has done wonders for our morale.* 這消息大大振奮了我們的士氣。**(it's) no/little/small 'wonder (that) ...** it is not surprising 不足為奇；並不奇怪：*It is little wonder (that) she was so upset.* 她如此心煩意亂，並不奇怪。◇ (*informal*) *No wonder you're tired, you've been walking for hours.* 難怪你累了呢，你一直走了好幾個小時。**it's a 'wonder (that) ...** (*informal*) it is surprising or strange 令人驚奇的是；莫名其妙的是：*It's a wonder (that) more people weren't hurt.* 奇怪的是沒有更多的人受到傷害。**wonders will never 'cease** (*informal*, usually *ironic*) a phrase used to express surprise and pleasure at sth（表示驚喜）真是無奇不有，怪事何其多：*'I've cleaned my room.' 'Wonders will never cease!'* "我把我的房間打掃乾淨了。" "怎麼太陽從西邊出來了！" **work 'wonders** to achieve very good results 創造奇跡；取得優良的成績；產生良好的效果：*Her new diet and exercise programme has worked wonders for her.* 她新的飲食和鍛煉計劃對她產生了奇效。➲ more at CHINLESS, NINE

won·der·ful 🔑 /'wʌndəfl; *NAmE* -dərfl/ *adj.*

1 🔑 very good, pleasant or enjoyable 精彩的；絕妙的；令人高興的；使人愉快的：*a wonderful surprise* 驚喜 ◇ *We had a wonderful time last night.* 我們昨天夜裏過得非常愉快。◇ *You've all been **absolutely wonderful**!* 你們真是都太好了！◇ ***It's wonderful** to see you!* 看到你真叫人高興！**2** 🔑 making you feel surprise or admiration 令人驚奇的；令人讚歎的 **SYN** **remarkable**：*It's wonderful what you can do when you have to.* 在迫不得已時，人的潛能令人驚歎。➲ SYNONYMS at next page

won·der·ful·ly /'wʌndəfəli; *NAmE* -dərf-/ *adv.* (*formal*)

1 very; very well 非常；很好地：*The hotel is wonderfully comfortable.* 這家旅館非常舒適。◇ *Things have worked out wonderfully (well).* 事情的結果很不錯。**2** unusually; in a surprising way 異乎尋常地；令人驚奇地：*He's*

W

wonderfully fit for his age. 他年紀那麼大，可身體出奇地好。

won·der·ing·ly /ˈwʌndrɪŋli/ *adv.* (*formal*) in a way that shows surprise and/or admiration 顯得驚奇地；驚訝地；驚歎地：*She gazed at him wonderingly.* 她驚奇地瞅着他。

won·der·land /ˈwʌndəlænd; *NAmE* -dərl-/ *noun* [usually sing.] **1** an imaginary place in children's stories（童話中的）仙境，奇境 **2** a place that is exciting and full of beautiful and interesting things 非常奇妙的地方；極為美麗的地方

won·der·ment /ˈwʌndəmənt; *NAmE* -dərm-/ *noun* [U] (*formal*) a feeling of pleasant surprise or WONDER 驚喜；驚歎

won·drous /ˈwʌndrəs/ *adj.* (*literary*) strange, beautiful and impressive 奇異的；美好的；了不起的 **SYN** **wonderful** ▸ **won·drous·ly** *adv.*

wonga /ˈwɒŋgə; *NAmE* ˈwɑːŋgə/ *noun* [U] (*BrE, slang*) money 錢

wonk /wɒŋk; *NAmE* wɑːŋk/ *noun* (*especially US, informal, disapproving*) **1** a person who works too hard and is considered boring 一味苦幹的人；書呆子 **2** a person who takes too much interest in the details of political policy 死摳政策細枝末節的人：*the President's chief economic **policy wonk*** 總統的首席經濟問題策士

Synonyms 同義詞辨析

wonderful

lovely • delightful

These words all describe an experience, feeling or sight that gives you great pleasure. 以上各詞均指經歷、感覺或景象令人高興、使人愉快。

wonderful that you enjoy very much; that gives you great pleasure; extremely good 指使人愉快的、令人高興的、精彩的、絕妙的：*We had a wonderful time last night.* 我們昨天晚上過得非常愉快。◇ *The weather was absolutely wonderful.* 天氣好極了。

lovely (*rather informal, especially BrE*) that you enjoy very much; that gives you great pleasure; very attractive 指令人愉快的、有吸引力的、迷人的：*What a lovely day!* (= the weather is very good) 多麼好的天氣啊！◇ *It's been lovely having you here.* 有你在這兒真是太好了。

delightful that gives you great pleasure; very attractive 指令人愉快的、宜人的：*a delightful little fishing village* 宜人的小漁村

WONDERFUL, LOVELY OR DELIGHTFUL? 用 wonderful、lovely 還是 delightful？

All these words can describe times, events, places, sights, feelings and the weather. **Wonderful** can also describe a chance or ability. **Lovely** is the most frequent in spoken British English, but in North American English **wonderful** is the most frequent, both spoken and written. **Delightful** is used especially to talk about times, events and places. 以上各詞均可形容時光、活動、地方、景色、感覺和天氣。wonderful 亦可形容機會或能力。lovely 在英式英語口語中最常用，但在美式英語中，無論是口語還是書面語 wonderful 最常用。delightful 尤用以形容時光、活動和地方。

PATTERNS

- wonderful/lovely/delightful **weather/views/scenery**
- It's wonderful/lovely **to be/feel/find/have/know/see ...**
- **It would be** wonderful/lovely/delightful **if ...**
- It's wonderful/lovely **that ...**
- That **sounds** wonderful/lovely/delightful.
- **really/quite/absolutely** wonderful/lovely/delightful

wonky /ˈwɒŋki; *NAmE* ˈwɑːŋki/ *adj.* (*BrE, informal*) not steady; not straight 不穩的；搖晃的；歪斜的：*a wonky chair* 搖搖晃晃的椅子

wont /wəʊnt; *NAmE* wɔːnt/ *adj., noun*

■ **adj.** [not before noun] **~ (to do sth)** (*old-fashioned, formal*) in the habit of doing sth 習慣於 **SYN** **accustomed**：*He was wont to fall asleep after supper.* 他習慣吃完晚飯就睡覺。

■ **noun** [sing.] (*old-fashioned, formal*) something a person often does 慣常做法；習慣 **SYN** **habit**：*She got up early, as was her wont.* 她像慣常一樣起得很早。

won't /wəʊnt; *NAmE* woʊnt/ *short form* will not

won·ton /ˌwɒnˈtɒn; *NAmE* ˈwɑːntɑːn/ *noun* (from *Chinese*) a small piece of food wrapped in DOUGH, often served in Chinese soup or as DIM SUM 餛飩

woo /wuː/ *verb* **1 ~ sb** to try to get the support of sb 爭取…的支持；尋求…的贊同：*Voters are being wooed with promises of lower taxes.* 通過許諾減低稅收爭取選民。 **2 ~ sb** (*old-fashioned*) (of a man 男子) to try to persuade a woman to love him and marry him 追求（異性）；求愛 **SYN** **court**

wood 0⊶ /wʊd/ *noun*

1 0⊶ [U, C] the hard material that the TRUNK and branches of a tree are made of; this material when it is used to build or make things with, or as a fuel 木；木頭；木料；木材；木柴：*He chopped some wood for the fire.* 他劈了些柴燒火。◇ *a plank of wood* 一長條木板 ◇ *All the furniture was made of **wood**.* 這裏所有的傢具都是用木料製作的。◇ *a wood floor* 木地板 ◇ *furniture made of a variety of different woods* 用各種不同的木材製作的傢具 ➲ **VISUAL VOCAB** page V10 ➲ see also DEAD WOOD, HARDWOOD, SOFTWOOD, WOODEN, WOODY **2** 0⊶ [C] (also **woods** [pl.]) an area of trees, smaller than a forest 樹林；林地：*a large wood* 一大片樹林 ◇ *a walk in the woods* 在樹林中散步 ➲ **VISUAL VOCAB** page V3 ➲ see also WOODED **3** [C] a heavy wooden ball used in the game of BOWLS（草地滾球戲的）木瓶 **4** [C] a GOLF CLUB with a large head, that was usually made of wood in the past 木頭球棒（舊時通常有木製頂部的高爾夫球棒）➲ compare IRON *n.* (5)

IDM **not see the ˌwood for the ˈtrees** (*BrE*) (*NAmE* **not see the ˌforest for the ˈtrees**) to not see or understand the main point about sth, because you are paying too much attention to small details 見樹不見林 **not ˌout of the ˈwoods** (*informal*) not yet free from difficulties or problems 尚未擺脫困境；尚未渡過難關 ➲ more at KNOCK *v.*, NECK *n.*, TOUCH *v.*

wood·block /ˈwʊdblɒk; *NAmE* -blɑːk/ *noun* **1** each of the small flat pieces of wood that are fitted together to cover a floor（鋪地板用的）木條，木塊：*a woodblock floor* 木條地板 ➲ compare PARQUET **2** a piece of wood with a pattern cut into it, used for printing 木刻印版；版木

wood·carv·ing /ˈwʊdkɑːvɪŋ; *NAmE* -kɑːrv-/ *noun* [U, C] the process of shaping a piece of wood with a sharp tool; a decorative object made in this way 木雕；木雕品 ▸ **wood·carver** *noun*

wood·chuck /ˈwʊdtʃʌk/ (also **ground·hog**) *noun* a small N American animal of the SQUIRREL family 美洲旱獺，土撥鼠（北美洲松鼠科動物）

wood·cock /ˈwʊdkɒk; *NAmE* -kɑːk/ *noun* (*pl.* **wood·cock** or **wood·cocks**) a brown bird with a long straight beak, short legs and a short tail, hunted for food or sport 丘鷸，山鷸（長喙黃褐色獵禽）

wood·cut /ˈwʊdkʌt/ *noun* a print that is made from a pattern cut in a piece of wood 木版畫；木刻

wood·cut·ter /ˈwʊdkʌtə(r)/ *noun* (*old-fashioned*) a person whose job is cutting down trees 伐木工

wood·ed /ˈwʊdɪd/ *adj.* (of land 土地) covered with trees 長滿樹木的；樹木覆蓋的

wood·en 0⊶ /ˈwʊdn/ *adj.*

1 0⊶ [usually before noun] made of wood 木製的；木頭的：*a wooden box* 木箱 **2** not showing enough natural expression, emotion or movement 木頭似的；死板的；呆板的；木訥的 **SYN** **stiff**：*The actor playing the father was too wooden.* 飾演父親的演員太呆板。▸ **wood·en·ly**

adv. : *She speaks her lines very woodenly.* 她台詞唸得毫無表情。 **wood·en·ness** *noun* [U]

ˌwooden ˈspoon *noun* a spoon made of wood, used in cooking for stirring and mixing 木匙；木勺 ➲ VISUAL VOCAB page V26

IDM **get, win, take, etc. the ˌwooden ˈspoon** (*BrE, informal*) to come last in a race or competition（在賽跑或比賽中）獲得最後一名，成為末名

wood·land /ˈwʊdlənd/ *noun* [U, C] (also **wood·lands** [pl.]) an area of land that is covered with trees 樹林；林地；林區： *ancient woodland* 原始林區 ◇ *The house is fringed by fields and woodlands.* 這房子的周圍是田地和樹林。 ◇ *woodland walks* 林地小徑

wood·louse /ˈwʊdlaʊs/ *noun* (*pl.* **wood·lice** /ˈwʊdlaɪs/) a small grey creature like an insect, with a hard shell, that lives in decaying wood or damp soil 潮蟲 ➲ VISUAL VOCAB page V13

wood·man /ˈwʊdmən/ *noun* (*pl.* **-men** /-mən/) (also **woods·man**) a person who works or lives in a forest, taking care of and sometimes cutting down trees, etc. 護林人；伐木工；樵夫

wood·peck·er /ˈwʊdpekə(r)/ *noun* a bird with a long beak that it uses to make holes in trees when it is looking for insects to eat 啄木鳥

ˈwood pigeon *noun* a bird of the PIGEON family, that lives in woods and fields rather than in cities 林鴿；斑尾鴿

wood·pile /ˈwʊdpaɪl/ *noun* a pile of wood that will be used for fuel 木柴堆

ˈwood pulp *noun* [U] wood that has been broken into small pieces and crushed until it is soft. It is used for making paper. 木漿（用於造紙）

wood·shed /ˈwʊdʃed/ *noun* a small building for storing wood in, especially for fuel 木料間；（尤指）柴房，柴棚

woods·man /ˈwʊdzmən/ *noun* (*pl.* **-men** /-mən/) = WOODMAN

woodsy /ˈwʊdzi/ *adj.* (*informal, especially NAmE*) covered with trees; connected with woods 樹林覆蓋的；樹林的

wood·turn·ing /ˈwʊdtɜːnɪŋ; *NAmE* -tɜːrn-/ *noun* [U] the process of shaping a piece of wood by turning it against a sharp tool on a machine (called a LATHE) 木工車牀加工 ▸ **wood·turn·er** *noun*

wood·wind /ˈwʊdwɪnd/ *noun* [U+sing./pl. v.] (also **wood·winds** [pl.] especially in *NAmE*) the group of musical instruments in an ORCHESTRA that are mostly made of wood or metal and are played by blowing. FLUTES, CLARINETS and BASSOONS are all woodwind instruments.（管弦樂團的）木管樂器，木管樂器組： *the woodwind section of the orchestra* 管弦樂隊的木管樂器組 ➲ VISUAL VOCAB page V34 ➲ compare BRASS (2), PERCUSSION, STRING *n.* (6), WIND[1] *n.* (4), WIND INSTRUMENT

wood·work /ˈwʊdwɜːk; *NAmE* -wɜːrk/ *noun* [U] **1** things made of wood in a building or room, such as doors and stairs（建築物或房間的）木建部份，木構件，木製品： *The woodwork needs painting.* 木建部份需要上油漆。 ◇ (*BrE*) *He* ***hit the woodwork*** (= the wooden frame of the goal in the game of football/ SOCCER, etc.) *twice before scoring.* 他兩次射門擊中球門框之後，終得進球。 **2** (*BrE*) (also **ˈwood·work·ing** *NAmE, BrE*) the activity or skill of making things from wood 木工活；木工手藝

IDM **blend/fade into the ˈwoodwork** to behave in a way that does not attract any attention; to disappear or hide 默默無聞；銷聲匿跡；蟄伏 **come/crawl out of the ˈwoodwork** (*informal, disapproving*) if you say that sb **comes/crawls out of the woodwork**, you mean that they have suddenly appeared in order to express an opinion or to take advantage of a situation 突然露面；紛紛出籠： *When he won the lottery, all sorts of distant relatives came out of the woodwork.* 他博彩中獎後，八杆子打不着的親戚都突然來登門造訪。

wood·worm /ˈwʊdwɜːm; *NAmE* -wɜːrm/ *noun* **1** [C] a small WORM that eats wood, making a lot of small holes in it 木蛀蟲；木蠹 **2** [U] the damage caused by woodworms 木蛀蟲害；木蠹蟲害： *The beams are riddled with woodworm.* 這些木梁被蛀蟲蛀得都是洞。

woody /ˈwʊdi/ *adj.* **1** (of plants 植物) having a thick, hard STEM like wood 木本的；木質的 **2** covered with trees 長滿樹木的；樹木茂盛的： *a woody valley* 樹木茂盛的山谷 **3** having a smell like wood 像木頭味的

woof /wʊf/ *exclamation, verb, noun*

■ ***exclamation*** (*informal*) a word used to describe the loud noise that a dog makes（狗叫聲）汪汪： *'Woof! Woof!' he barked.* "汪！汪！"它叫着。 ▸ **woof** *verb* [I]

■ ***noun*** = WEFT

woof·er /ˈwuːfə(r)/ *noun* a LOUDSPEAKER for reproducing the low notes in a SOUND SYSTEM（音響系統的）低音揚聲器，低音喇叭 ➲ compare TWEETER

woo hoo /ˌwuː ˈhuː/ *exclamation* (*informal*) used when you are glad because sth happens that you enjoy 哦呵（表示高興）： *Woo hoo! The weekend is here.* 哇哈！到週末了。

wool 🔑 /wʊl/ *noun* [U]

1 🔑 the soft fine hair that covers the body of sheep, GOATS and some other animals（羊等的）絨，毛 **2** 🔑 long thick thread made from animal's wool, used for knitting 毛線；絨線： *a ball of wool* 一團毛線 ➲ VISUAL VOCAB page V41 **3** 🔑 cloth made from animal's wool, used for making clothes, etc. 毛料；毛織物： *This scarf is 100% wool.* 這條披肩是全毛的。◇ *pure new wool* 純新毛料 ◇ *a wool blanket* 毛毯 ➲ see also COTTON WOOL, DYED IN THE WOOL, LAMBSWOOL, STEEL WOOL, WIRE WOOL IDM see PULL *v.*

wool·len (*BrE*) (*NAmE* **wool·en**) /ˈwʊlən/ *adj.* **1** [usually before noun] made of wool 毛紡的；羊毛的；毛料的；毛線的： *a woollen blanket* 毛毯 ◇ *woollen cloth* 毛料 **2** [only before noun] involved in making cloth from wool 毛紡的；毛紡織業的： *the woollen industry* 毛紡業

wool·lens (*BrE*) (*NAmE* **wool·ens**) /ˈwʊlənz/ *noun* [pl.] clothes made of wool, especially knitted clothes（尤指針織的）毛衣

wool·ly /ˈwʊli/ *adj., noun*

■ ***adj.*** (*NAmE* also **wooly**) (**wool·lier**, **wool·li·est**) **1** covered with wool or with hair like wool 有毛覆蓋的；毛狀物覆蓋的： *woolly monkeys* 毛茸茸的猴子 **2** (*informal, especially BrE*) made of wool; like wool 毛製的；毛的；似毛的 SYN **woollen** ： *a woolly hat* 毛質的帽子 **3** (of people or their ideas, etc. 人或思想等) not thinking clearly; not clearly expressed 糊塗的；混亂的；模糊的 SYN **confused** ： *woolly arguments* 混亂的論點 ▸ **wool·li·ness** *noun* [U]

■ ***noun*** (*pl.* **-ies**) (*informal*) **1** (*BrE, becoming old-fashioned*) a piece of clothing made of wool, especially one that has been knitted 毛料衣服；（尤指針織的）毛線衣 **2** (*AustralE, NZE*) a sheep 羊

Woop Woop /ˈwʊp wʊp/ *noun* (*AustralE, informal*) a humorous name for a town or area that is a long way from a big city 偏遠城鎮（或地區）

woozy /ˈwuːzi/ *adj.* (*informal*) **1** feeling unsteady, confused and unable to think clearly 眩暈的；頭昏的；暈頭脹腦的 **2** (*especially NAmE*) feeling as though you might VOMIT 惡心的；要嘔吐的

wop /wɒp; *NAmE* wɑːp/ *noun* (*taboo, slang*) a very offensive word for a person from southern Europe, especially an Italian 南歐人；南蠻子；（尤指）意大利佬

Wor·ces·ter sauce /ˌwʊstə ˈsɔːs; *NAmE* ˌwʊstər/ (also **Wor·ces·ter·shire sauce** /ˌwʊstəʃə; *NAmE* ˌwʊstərʃɪr/) *noun* [U] a dark thin sauce made of VINEGAR, SOY SAUCE and spices 伍斯特沙司（用醋、醬油和香料調製而成）

word 🔑 /wɜːd; *NAmE* wɜːrd/ *noun, verb, exclamation*

■ ***noun***

▸ UNIT OF LANGUAGE 語言單位 **1** 🔑 [C] a single unit of language which means sth and can be spoken or written 單詞；詞；字： *Do not write more than 200 words.* 寫的東西不要超過 200 字。◇ *Do you know the words to this song?* 你知道這首歌的歌詞嗎？◇ *What's the Spanish* ***word for*** *'table'?* * table 一詞在西班牙語裏叫什麼？◇ *He was a true friend* ***in all senses of the word.***

W

從任何意義上來說他都是位真正的朋友。◇ *Tell me what happened **in your own words**.* 用你自己的話告訴我出了什麼事。◇ *I could hear every word they were saying.* 我可以聽到他們說的每一個字。◇ *He couldn't **find the words** to thank her enough.* 他找不出適當的話語來充分表達對她的感激之情。◇ ***Words fail me*** (= I cannot express how I feel). 我無法用語言來表達我的感情。◇ *There are no words to say how sorry we are.* 我們十分後悔，實在無以言喻。◇ *I can't remember her exact words.* 我記不清她的原話了。◇ *Angry **is not the word for it**—I was furious.* 說"生氣"都不夠，我是怒不可遏。➲ see also BUZZWORD, FOUR-LETTER WORD, HOUSEHOLD WORD, SWEAR WORD

▸ **STH YOU SAY** 說的話 **2** 🗝 [C] a thing that you say; a remark or statement 說的話；話語；言語：*Have **a word with** Pat and see what she thinks.* 和帕特談一談，看她是怎麼想的。◇ *Could I have a quick word with you* (= speak to you quickly)? 我能跟你很快地說句話嗎？◇ ***A word of warning**: read the instructions very carefully.* 警示：仔細閱讀說明。◇ *words of love* 情話 ◇ *She left **without a word*** (= without saying anything). 她一句話也沒說就走了。◇ *I don't believe a word of his story* (= I don't believe any of it). 他說的這件事我一句都不相信。◇ *a man **of few words*** (= who doesn't talk very much) 少言寡語的男子 ◇ *I'd like to say a few words about future plans.* 我想就今後的計劃說幾句。◇ *Remember—**not a word to*** (= don't tell) *Peter about any of this.* 記住，對彼得可要隻字不提這件事的任何情況。◇ *He **never breathed a word** of this to me.* 這事他從來沒向我透露過一點風聲。

▸ **PROMISE** 諾言 **3** 🗝 [sing.] a promise or guarantee that you will do sth or that sth will happen or is true 諾言；許諾；保證：***I give you my word*** *that this won't happen again.* 我向你保證這種事不會再次發生。◇ *I give you my **word of honour*** (= my sincere promise) ... 我向你莊嚴承諾… ◇ *We never doubted her word.* 我們從不懷疑她的許諾。◇ *We only **have his word for it** that the cheque is in the post.* 他只是向我們保證支票在郵寄之中。◇ *to **keep your word*** (= do what you promised) 遵守諾言 ◇ *He promised to help and **was as good as his word*** (= did what he promised). 他答應幫忙，並且說話算數。◇ *He's a **man of his word*** (= he does what he promises). 他是個守信用的人。◇ *I trusted her not to **go back on her word*** (= break her promise). 我相信她不會食言。◇ *I can't prove it—you'll have to **take my word for it*** (= believe me). 我無法證明此事，你就相信我好了。

▸ **INFORMATION/NEWS** 信息；消息 **4** [sing.] a piece of information or news 信息；消息：*There's been no word from them since before Christmas.* 自聖誕節前就一直沒有他們的消息。◇ *She **sent word** that she would be late.* 她捎信來說她要晚些來。◇ *If **word gets out** about the affair, he will have to resign.* 要是這一緋聞傳出去，他就得辭職。◇ ***Word has it that** she's leaving.* 據說她要走了。◇ *The **word is** they've split up.* 據說他們離異了。◇ *He likes to **spread the word** about the importance of healthy eating.* 他喜歡宣傳保健飲食的重要性。

▸ **BIBLE** 《聖經》 **5 the Word** (also **the ˌWord of ˈGod**) [sing.] the Bible and its teachings 《聖經》；福音

IDM **by ˌword of ˈmouth** because people tell each other and not because they read about it 口頭上；經口述：*The news spread by word of mouth.* 這消息是口頭傳開的。 **(right) from the word ˈgo** (*informal*) from the very beginning 從一開始 **(not) get a word in ˈedgeways** (*BrE*) (*NAmE* **(not) get a word in ˈedgewise**) (not) to be able to say anything because sb else is speaking too much （因別人說話太多）插（不上）嘴：*When Mary starts talking, no one else can get a word in edgeways.* 瑪麗講起話來，別人誰也插不上嘴。 **have a word in sb's ˈear** (*BrE*) to speak to sb privately about sth 和…說私話；與…密談 **have/exchange ˈwords (with sb) (about sth)** (*especially BrE*) to have an argument with sb （與某人）爭論，爭吵：*We've had words.* 我們吵過架。◇ *Words were exchanged.* 發生過爭吵了。 **in ˈother words** 🗝 used to introduce an explanation of sth 換句話說；也就是說；換言之：*They asked him to leave—in other words he was fired.* 他們請他走人，也就是說，他被解雇了。➲ LANGUAGE BANK at I.E. **(not) in so/as many ˈwords** (not) in exactly the same words as sb says were used （並非）一字不差地，原原本本地：*'Did she say she was sorry?' 'Not in so many words.'* "她道歉了沒有？" "沒有直截了當地說。" ◇ *He didn't approve of the plan and said so in as many words.* 他明確地說他不同意這計劃。 **in a ˈword** (*informal*) used for giving a very short, usually negative, answer or comment 簡言之；一句話；總之：*'Would you like to help us?' 'In a word, no.'* "你願意幫助我們嗎？" "一句話，不願意。" **in words of one ˈsyllable** using very simple language 用極其簡單的言語：*Could you say that again in words of one syllable?* 你能用很簡單的言語把這再說一遍嗎？ **the last/final word (on sth)** the last comment or decision about sth （對某事的）最後意見，最後決定：*He always **has** to **have the last word** in any argument.* 在任何爭論中總是得他最後說了算。 **(upon) my ˈword** (*old-fashioned*) used to show that you are surprised about sth （表示驚奇）哎呀，咦 **not have a good word to ˈsay for sb/sth** (*informal*) to never say anything good about sb/sth 從不說…的好話：*Nobody had a good word to say about him.* 沒有一個人說過他好。 **put in a (good) ˈword for sb** to praise sb to sb else in order to help them get a job, etc. 為某人說好話；替某人美言；推薦某人 **put ˈwords into sb's mouth** to suggest that sb has said sth when in fact they have not 硬說某人說過某些話 **say/give the ˈword** to give an order; to make a request 下命令；吩咐一下；提請求：*Just say the word, and I'll go.* 只要發句話，我就走。 **take sb at their ˈword** to believe exactly what sb says or promises 完全相信…的話（或許諾）；深信不疑 **take the ˈwords right out of sb's mouth** to say what sb else was going to say 說出…想要講的話 **too funny, silly, ridiculous, etc. for ˈwords** extremely funny, silly, ridiculous, etc. 有趣（或愚蠢、荒唐等）得難以言表；極其有趣（或愚蠢、荒唐等） **ˌword for ˈword** 🗝 in exactly the same words or (when translated) exactly equivalent words 一字不差地；（翻譯時）逐字地：*She repeated their conversation word for word to me.* 她一字不差地把他們的談話對我複述了一遍。◇ *a word-for-word translation* 逐字的翻譯 **sb's word is their ˈbond** somebody's promise can be relied on completely 一諾千金；言而有信 **words to that efˈfect** used to show that you are giving the general meaning of what sb has said rather than the exact words 諸如此類的話；大致是這個意思的話：*He told me to leave—or words to that effect.* 他叫我離開，或諸如此類的話。➲ more at ACTION *n.*, BANDY *v.*, DIRTY *adj.*, EAT, FAMOUS, HANG *v.*, LAST[1] *det.*, LOST, MINCE *v.*, MUM *adj.*, OPERATIVE *adj.*, PLAY *n.*, PRINT *v.*, WAR, WEIGH, WRITTEN

■ *verb* [often passive] **~ sth** to write or say sth using particular words 措辭；用詞：*How was the letter worded* (= what did it say exactly)? 這封信到底寫了些什麼？ ▸ **word·ed** *adj.*：*a carefully worded speech* 措辭嚴謹的演講 ◇ *a strongly worded letter of protest* 措辭強硬的抗議信

■ *exclamation* **word!** (*NAmE*) used to show that you accept or agree with what sb has just said （表示接受或同意別人剛說的話）就是，說得對

ˈword break (also **ˈword division**) *noun* (*technical* 術語) a point at which a word is split between two lines of text 斷字（一個單詞可在轉行時斷開的地方）

ˈword class *noun* (*grammar* 語法) one of the classes into which words are divided according to their grammar, such as noun, verb, adjective, etc. 詞類 **SYN** **part of speech**

word·ing /ˈwɜːdɪŋ; *NAmE* ˈwɜːrd-/ *noun* [U, C, usually sing.] the words that are used in a piece of writing or speech, especially when they have been carefully chosen 措辭；用詞：*The wording was deliberately ambiguous.* 這裏的措辭故意模棱兩可。➲ SYNONYMS at LANGUAGE

word·less /ˈwɜːdləs; *NAmE* ˈwɜːrd-/ *adj.* (*formal* or *literary*) **1** [usually before noun] without saying any words; silent 默默無言的；沉默的：*a wordless cry/prayer* 無言的痛哭；默默的禱告 **2** (of people 人) not saying anything 不語的；沉默寡言的 ▸ **word·less·ly** *adv.*

ˌword-ˈperfect (*BrE*) (*NAmE* **ˌletter-ˈperfect**) *adj.* able to remember and repeat sth exactly without making any mistakes 能背得一字不差的；能背得滾瓜爛熟的

Synonyms 同義詞辨析

word

term • phrase • expression • idiom

These are all words for a unit of language used to express sth. 以上各詞均為表達意思的語言單位。

word a single unit of language which means sth and can be spoken or written 指單詞、詞、字：*Do not write more than 200 words.* 寫的東西不要超過 200 字。◇ *He uses a lot of long words.* 他使用了很多長詞。

term (*rather formal*) a word or phrase used as the name of sth, especially one connected with a particular type of language 指詞語、術語、措辭：*technical/legal/scientific terms* 專門／法律／科學用語 ◇ *'Old man' is a slang term for 'father'.* * old man 為俚語，指父親。

phrase a group of words which have a particular meaning when used together 指短語、詞組、慣用法：*Who coined the phrase 'desktop publishing'?* 誰創造了 desktop publishing（桌面出版）這個詞組？ NOTE In grammar, a **phrase** is a group of words without a finite verb, especially one that forms part of a sentence: 'the green car' and 'on Friday morning' are phrases. 在語法上，phrase 指不含限定動詞、構成句子一部份的短語、詞組，如 the green car 和 on Friday morning 均為詞組。

expression a word or phrase 指詞語、措辭、表達方式：*He tends to use a lot of slang expressions that I've never heard before.* 他往往用許多我以前從未聽說過的俚語。

idiom a group of words whose meaning is different from the meanings of the individual words 指習語、成語、慣用語：*'Let the cat out of the bag' is an idiom meaning to tell a secret by mistake.* * let the cat out of the bag（讓貓從袋子裏跑出來）為成語，意為無意中泄露秘密。

PATTERNS

- a word/term **for** sth
- a **new** word/term/phrase/expression
- a **technical/colloquial** word/term/phrase/expression
- a **slang** word/term/phrase
- an **idiomatic** phrase/expression
- to **use** a(n) word/term/phrase/expression/idiom
- to **coin** a(n) word/term/phrase/expression
- a(n) word/term/phrase/expression/idiom **means** sth

word·play /ˈwɜːdpleɪ; *NAmE* ˈwɜːrd-/ *noun* [U] making jokes by using words in a clever or amusing way, especially by using a word that has two meanings, or different words that sound the same 巧妙的應答；雙關語 ➲ compare PUN

ˈ**word processing** *noun* [U] the use of a computer to create, store and print a piece of text, usually typed in from a keyboard（計算機）文字處理

ˈ**word processor** *noun* a computer that runs a word processing program and is usually used for writing letters, reports, etc. 文字處理機

word·search /ˈwɜːdsɜːtʃ; *NAmE* ˈwɜːrdsɜːrtʃ/ *noun* a game consisting of letters arranged in a square, containing several hidden words that you must find 文字搜索遊戲（從字母方格中找出隱藏的詞）➲ VISUAL VOCAB page V39

word·smith /ˈwɜːdsmɪθ; *NAmE* ˈwɜːrd-/ *noun* a person who is skilful at using words 詞語大師

wordy /ˈwɜːdi; *NAmE* ˈwɜːrdi/ *adj.* (usually *disapproving*) using too many words, especially formal ones 話多的；冗長的；囉嗦的 SYN **verbose**：*a wordy and repetitive essay* 一篇冗長繁複的文章 ▶ **wordi·ness** *noun* [U]

wore *past tense* of WEAR

work 0-w /wɜːk; *NAmE* wɜːrk/ *verb, noun*

■ *verb*

▸ **DO JOB/TASK 做工；執行任務** **1** 0-w [I] to do sth that involves physical or mental effort, especially as part of a job 做體力（或腦力）工作；勞動；幹活：*I can't work if I'm cold.* 我要是覺得冷就幹不了活。◇ **~ at sth** *I've been working at my assignment all day.* 我整天都在做作業。◇ **~ on sth** *He is working on a new novel.* 他正在寫一部新小說。◇ *She's outside, working on the car.* 她在外面修理汽車。◇ **+ noun** *Doctors often work very long hours.* 醫生經常長時間工作。 **2** 0-w [I] to have a job 受雇於；從事…工作：*Both my parents work.* 我父母都工作。◇ **~ for sb/sth** *She works for an engineering company.* 她在一家工程公司工作。◇ **~ in sth** *I've always worked in education.* 我一直從事教育工作。◇ **~ with sb/sth** *Do you enjoy working with children?* 你喜歡做兒童工作嗎？◇ **~ as sth** *My son is working as a teacher.* 我的兒子是當老師的。

▸ **MAKE EFFORT 努力** **3** [T] **~ yourself/sb + adv./prep.** to make yourself/sb work, especially very hard 使工作；（尤指）使賣力幹活：*She works herself too hard.* 她工作起來太不辭勞苦了。 **4** 0-w [I] to make efforts to achieve sth 爭取；力爭；努力取得：**~ for sth** *She dedicated her life to working for peace.* 她為爭取和平奉獻了自己的一生。◇ **~ to do sth** *The committee is working to get the prisoners freed.* 委員會正在設法營救那些被監禁的人出獄。

▸ **MANAGE 管理** **5** [T] **~ sth** to manage or operate sth to gain benefit from it 管理，經營（以獲利）：*to work the land* (= grow crops on it, etc.) 耕種土地 ◇ *He works a large area* (= selling a company's goods, etc.). 他負責一個大地區的工作。◇ (*figurative*) *She was a skilful speaker who knew how to* ***work a crowd*** (= to excite them or make them feel sth strongly). 她是個很有技巧的演講者，善於感召聽眾。

▸ **MACHINE/DEVICE 機器；裝置** **6** 0-w [I] to function; to operate 運轉；運行：*The phone isn't working.* 這部電話壞了。◇ *It works by electricity.* 這是電動的。◇ *Are they any closer to understanding how the brain works?* 他們對大腦功能的瞭解有進展嗎？ **7** [T] **~ sth** to make a machine, device, etc. operate 開動，操作（機器、裝置等）；使運作：*Do you know how to work the coffee machine?* 你會使用咖啡機嗎？◇ *The machine is worked by wind power.* 這台機器是以風力推動的。

▸ **HAVE RESULT/EFFECT 有結果／作用** **8** 0-w [I] to have the result or effect that you want 奏效；產生預期的結果（或作用）：*The pills the doctor gave me aren't working.* 醫生給我的藥片不管事。◇ *My plan worked, and I got them to agree.* 我的計劃奏效了，我讓他們同意了。◇ **~ on sb/sth** *His charm doesn't work on me* (= does not affect or impress me). 我不為他的魅力所動。 **9** [I] to have a particular effect 產生…作用：**~ against sb** *Your age can work against you in this job.* 你的年紀會妨礙你幹這個工作。◇ **~ in sb's favour** *Speaking Italian should work in his favour.* 會說意大利語應對他有好處。 **10** [T] **~ sth** to cause or produce sth as a result of effort 使奏效；（由於努力）造成，產生：*You can work miracles with very little money if you follow our home decoration tips.* 你要是按照我們的家居裝飾訣竅行事，可以用很少的錢就產生奇妙的效果。

▸ **USE MATERIAL 使用材料** **11** [T] to make a material into a particular shape or form by pressing, stretching, hitting it, etc.（通過壓擠、拉長、錘擊等）使成形，使定形：**~ sth** *to work clay* 製陶 ◇ *to work gold* 打製金器 ◇ **~ sth into sth** *to work the mixture into a paste* 把混合物調成糊狀 **12** [I] **~ in/with sth** (of an artist, etc. 藝術家等) to use a particular material to produce a picture or other item 用某種材料作畫（或編製、編織等）：*an artist working in oils* 油畫畫家 ◇ *a craftsman working with wool* 毛織手工藝人

▸ **OF PART OF FACE/BODY 臉／身體部位** **13** [I] (*formal*) to move violently 抽動；抽搐；顫動：*He stared at me in horror, his mouth working.* 他恐懼地盯着我，嘴在抽搐着。

▸ **MOVE GRADUALLY 逐漸移動** **14** [I, T] to move or pass to a particular place or state, usually gradually（逐漸地）

移動（到某位置）；（逐步）變成（某狀態）：**+ adv./prep.** *It will take a while for the drug to work out of your system.* 這藥需要一段時間才能從你體內排出。◇ **~ your way + adv./prep.** (*figurative*) *He worked his way to the top of his profession.* 他一步一步努力，終於成為行業內的翹楚。◇ **~ yourself/sth + adj.** *I was tied up, but managed to work myself free.* 我被捆綁起來，但設法掙脫了繩索。◇ **+ adj.** *The screw had **worked loose**.* 這螺絲釘鬆動了。

IDM Most idioms containing **work** are at the entries for the nouns and adjectives in the idioms, for example **work your fingers to the bone** is at **finger**. 大多數含 work 的習語，都可在該等習語中的名詞及形容詞相關詞條找到，如 work your fingers to the bone 在詞條 finger 下。 **'work it/things** (*informal*) to arrange sth in a particular way, especially by being clever（尤指巧妙地）辦成，辦妥：*Can you work it so that we get free tickets?* 你能不能為我們搞到些免費票？

PHR V **ˌwork aˈround/ˈround to sth/sb** to gradually turn a conversation towards a particular topic, subject, etc. 漸漸轉變（話題、主題等）：*It was some time before he worked around to what he really wanted to say.* 他東拉西扯了一會才繞到真正要說的事情上來。 **'work at sth** to make great efforts to achieve sth or do sth well 致力於；努力做：*He's working at losing weight.* 他正在努力減肥。◇ *Learning to play the piano isn't easy. You have to **work at it**.* 學彈鋼琴不容易，你非得下功夫不可。 **ˌwork sth 'in | work sth into sth** **1** to try to include sth 盡量包括；設法把…加進：*Can't you work a few more jokes into your speech?* 難道你就不能在講話中再增加幾句笑話嗎？ **2** to add one substance to another and mix them together 摻入；將…攪拌進：*Gradually work in the butter.* 逐漸摻進黃油。 **ˌwork sth↔'off** **1** to get rid of sth, especially a strong feeling, by using physical effort（通過消耗體力）宣泄感情：*She worked off her anger by going for a walk.* 她散散步氣就消了。 **2** to earn money in order to be able to pay a debt 工作以償債：*They had a large bank loan to work off.* 他們有一大筆銀行貸款需要償還。 **'work on sb** to try to persuade sb to agree to sth or to do sth 努力說服（使某人答應或做某事）：*He hasn't said he'll do it yet, but I'm working on him.* 他還沒說他會做這事，不過我正在設法說服他。 **'work on sth** to try hard to improve or achieve sth 努力改善（或完成）：*You need to work on your pronunciation a bit more.* 你需要再加把勁改進發音。◇ *'Have you sorted out a babysitter yet?' 'No, but **I'm working on it**.'* "你找到臨時看孩子的保母了嗎？" "還沒有，我正在找呢。" **ˌwork 'out** **1** 🔑 to train the body by physical exercise 鍛煉身體；做運動：*I work out regularly to keep fit.* 我經常做運動以保持健康。 ➲ related noun WORKOUT **2** 🔑 to develop in a successful way 成功地發展：*My first job didn't work out.* 我的第一份工作幹得不好。◇ *Things have worked out quite well for us.* 事情的結果對我們很不錯。 **ˌwork 'out (at sth)** if sth **works out** at sth, you calculate that it will be a particular amount 計算；計算出：**+ adj.** *It'll work out cheaper to travel by bus.* 算來還是乘公共汽車便宜些。 **ˌwork sb↔'out** (*BrE*) to understand sb's character 瞭解，理解（某人的性格）：*I've never been able to work her out.* 我從未能摸準她的秉性。 **ˌwork sth↔'out** **1** 🔑 to calculate sth 計算；算出：*to work out the answer* 計算出答案 **2** 🔑 (*especially BrE*) to find the answer to sth 找…的答案；解決 **SYN** **solve**：*to work out a problem* 解決問題 ◇ **~ what, where, etc. …** *Can you work out what these squiggles mean?* 你能辨認出這些潦草的字跡是什麼意思嗎？◇ *I couldn't work out where the music was coming from.* 我弄不清這音樂是從哪裏傳來的。 **3** 🔑 to plan or think of sth 計劃；思考：*I've worked out a new way of doing it.* 我想出了做這事的一個新方法。 **4** [usually passive] to remove all the coal, minerals, etc. from a mine over a period of time 挖盡，開採光（煤、礦產等）：*a worked-out silver mine* 開採光了的銀礦 **ˌwork sb↔'over** (*slang*) to attack sb and hit them, for example to make them give you information 拷問；逼供 **'work to sth** to follow a plan, schedule, etc. 按照（計劃、時間表等）；根據…行事：*to work to a budget* 按照預算辦事 ◇ *We're working to a very tight deadline* (= we have little time in which to do the work). 我們的工期很緊。 **'work towards sth** to try to reach or achieve a goal 努力達到，設法完成（目標） **ˌwork sth↔'up** to develop or improve sth with some effort 逐步發展；努力改進：*I can't work up any enthusiasm for his idea.* 我對他的想法怎麼也熱心不起來。◇ *She went for a long walk to work up an appetite.* 她為了增加食慾散了很長時間的步。 **ˌwork sb/yourself 'up (into sth)** to make sb/yourself reach a state of great excitement, anger, etc. 使激動；使發怒：*Don't work yourself up into a state about it. It isn't worth it.* 別為此大動肝火。這不值得。◇ *What are you so worked up about?* 什麼事使得你這麼激動？ **ˌwork sth 'up into sth** to bring sth to a more complete or more acceptable state 使完整；使完好；修整：*I'm working my notes up into a dissertation.* 我正在把我的筆記整理成一篇論文。 **ˌwork 'up to sth** to develop or move gradually towards sth, usually sth more exciting or extreme 逐步發展到，逐漸達到（更高或更深的程度）：*The music worked up to a rousing finale.* 樂曲漸變到一個激動人心的末樂章。◇ *I began by jogging in the park and worked up to running five miles a day.* 我開始在公園裏慢跑，後來逐漸增加到一天跑五英里。

■ ***noun***

▸ **JOB/TASK 工作；任務** **1** 🔑 [U] the job that a person does especially in order to earn money 工作；職業 **SYN** **employment**：*She had been **out of work*** (= without a job) *for a year.* 她已經失業一年了。◇ (*BrE*) *They are **in work*** (= have a job). 他們有工作。◇ *He **started work** as a security guard.* 他開始工作時做保安員。◇ *It is difficult to find work in the present economic climate.* 在目前這種經濟大氣候下很難找到工作。◇ *I'm still looking for work.* 我仍在找工作。◇ *She's planning to **return to work** once the children start school.* 她正計劃孩子一入學就恢復上班。◇ *What **line of work** are you in* (= what type of work do you do)? 你幹哪種工作？◇ ***before/after work*** (= in the morning/evening each day) 上班前；下班後 ◇ ***full-time/part-time/unpaid/voluntary work*** 全日制／兼職／無報酬的／志願工作 ➲ COLLOCATIONS at JOB, UNEMPLOYMENT **2** 🔑 [U] the duties that you have and the activities that you do as part of your job 職責；工作內容：*Police work is mainly routine.* 警察的工作主要都是按常規的。◇ *The accountant described his work to the sales staff.* 會計師向銷售部的職員介紹了自己的職責。 ➲ see also PIECEWORK, SOCIAL WORK **3** 🔑 [U] tasks that need to be done 工作；活計：*There is plenty of **work to be done** in the garden.* 花園裏有很多活要幹。◇ *Taking care of a baby is **hard work**.* 照看嬰兒是件苦差。◇ *I have some work for you to do.* 我有些事要你做。◇ *Stop talking and get on with your work.* 別說話了，繼續幹你們的活兒吧。 ➲ see also HOMEWORK, SCHOOLWORK **4** [U] materials needed or used for doing work, especially books, papers, etc. 工作所需的材料（或檔案等）：*She often brings work* (= for example, files and documents) *home with her from the office.* 她經常把辦公室裏的工作帶回家。◇ *His work was spread all over the floor.* 他工作的材料攤了一地。 ➲ see also PAPERWORK

▸ **PLACE OF JOB 工作地點** **5** 🔑 [U] (used without *the* 不與 the 連用) the place where you do your job 工作地點；工作單位；工作場所：*I **go to work** at 8 o'clock.* 我 8 點鐘去上班。◇ *When do you **leave for work**?* 你什麼時候去上班？◇ *The new legislation concerns health and safety **at work**.* 這項新法規涉及工作場所的健康與安全。◇ *I have to **leave work** early today.* 我今天得早點兒下班。◇ *Her friends **from work** came to see her in the hospital.* 她工作單位的朋友來醫院看望她。

▸ **EFFORT 努力** **6** 🔑 [U] the use of physical strength or mental power in order to do or make sth 工作；勞動：*She earned her grades through sheer **hard work**.* 她的學習成績完全是靠刻苦用功得來的。◇ *We **started work on** the project in 2009.* 我們從 2009 年開始幹這個項目。◇ *Work continues on renovating the hotel.* 修整這家旅館的工作在繼續。◇ *The work of building the bridge took six months.* 修建這座橋的工作用了六個月的時間。◇ *The art collection was his **life's work**.* 這些藝術品收藏是他一生的成就。◇ *She **set them to work** painting the fence.* 她讓他們刷圍牆。 ➲ see also DONKEY WORK, FIELDWORK

▸ **PRODUCT OF WORK 工作成果** **7** 🔑 [U] a thing or things that are produced as a result of work 工作成果；產品；作品：*She's an artist whose work I really admire.* 她這位藝術家的作品令我讚賞不已。◇ *Is this **all your own work***

(= did you do it without help from others)? 這件作品是你獨立完成的嗎？◇ *The book is a detailed and thorough **piece of work** covering all aspects of the subject.* 這本書包括了這一學科的方方面面，是一部縝密翔實的大作。

▸ **RESULT OF ACTION** 行動結果 **8** [U] the result of an action; what is done by sb 作為；行動結果：*The damage is clearly the work of vandals.* 這毀損顯然是些恣意破壞公物的人所為。

▸ **BOOK/MUSIC/ART** 書籍；音樂；藝術 **9** [C] a book, piece of music, painting, etc. 著作；作品：*the **collected/complete works** of Tolstoy* 托爾斯泰選集／全集 ◇ ***works of fiction/literature*** 小說／文學作品 ◇ *Beethoven's piano works* 貝多芬的鋼琴曲 ➲ compare OPUS ➲ see also WORK OF ART

▸ **BUILDING/REPAIRING** 修造 **10 works** [pl.] (often in compounds 常構成複合詞) activities involving building or repairing sth 建；修；修建：*roadworks* 道路施工 ◇ *They expanded the shipyards and started engineering works.* 他們擴建造船廠，開始了工程施工。➲ see also PUBLIC WORKS

▸ **FACTORY** 工廠 **11 works** (*pl.* **works**) [C+sing./pl. v.] (often in compounds 常構成複合詞) a place where things are made or industrial processes take place 工廠：*an engineering works* 機器製造廠 ◇ *a brickworks* 磚廠 ➲ SYNONYMS at FACTORY

▸ **PARTS OF MACHINE** 機器部件 **12 the works** [pl.] the moving parts of a machine, etc. （機器等的）活動部件 SYN **mechanism**

▸ **EVERYTHING** 所有的事物 **13 the works** [pl.] (*informal*) everything 所有的事物；全套物品：*We went to the chip shop and had the works: fish, chips, gherkins, mushy peas.* 我們去薯條店吃了套餐：炸魚、炸薯條、小黃瓜、豆泥。

▸ **PHYSICS** 物理 **14** [U] the use of force to produce movement 功；做功 ➲ see also JOULE

IDM **all ˌwork and no ˈplay (makes ˌJack a dull ˈboy)** (*saying*) it is not healthy to spend all your time working; you need to relax too 只工作不玩耍，聰明的孩子也變傻 **at ˈwork 1** having an effect on sth 起作用：*She suspected that secret influences were at work.* 她懷疑有些秘密勢力在作祟。**2** ~ (**on sth**) busy doing sth 忙着（做某事）：*He is still at work on the painting.* 他仍在忙着畫那幅畫。◇ *Danger—men at work.* 危險——有人施工。**get (down) to/set to ˈwork** to begin; to make a start 開始，着手（工作）：*We set to work on the outside of the house* (= for example, painting it). 我們從屋子的外部開始幹了起來。**give sb the ˈworks** (*informal*) to give or tell sb everything 給（或告訴）…一切 **ˌgood ˈworks** kind acts to help others 善行；善舉 **go/set about your ˈwork** to do/start to do your work 做（或着手做）自己的工作：*She went cheerfully about her work.* 她高高興興地做自己的工作。**have your ˈwork cut out** (*informal*) to be likely to have difficulty doing sth （做某事）可能有困難：*You'll have your work cut out to get there by nine o'clock.* 你九點鐘前趕到那裏可不容易。**in the ˈworks** something that is **in the works** is being discussed, planned or prepared and will happen or exist soon 在討論（或計劃、籌備等）中；在醞釀中 SYN **in the pipeline** **the work of a ˈmoment, ˈsecond, etc.** (*formal*) a thing that takes a very short time to do 即刻做完的事 ➲ more at DAY, DEVIL, DIRTY *adj.*, HAND *n.*, HARD *adj.*, JOB, LIGHT *adj.*, NASTY, NICE, SHORT *adj.*, SPANNER

work·able /ˈwɜːkəbl; *NAmE* ˈwɜːrk-/ *adj.* **1** (of a system, an idea, etc. 系統、想法等) that can be used successfully and effectively 可行的；行得通的 SYN **practical**：*a workable plan* 切實可行的計劃 **2** that you can shape, spread, dig, etc. 可成形（或延長、挖掘等）的：*Add more water until the dough is workable.* 往麪糰裏再加點兒水，直到能揉成形為止。**3** (of a mine, etc. 礦等) that can still be used and will make a profit 可開採的；可開發的

work·aday /ˈwɜːkədeɪ; *NAmE* ˈwɜːrk-/ *adj.* [usually before noun] (*formal*) ordinary; not very interesting 普通的；平凡的；平淡無奇的 SYN **everyday**

work·ahol·ic /ˌwɜːkəˈhɒlɪk; *NAmE* ˌwɜːrkəˈhɔːlɪk; -ˈhɑːl-/ *noun* (*informal*, usually *disapproving*) a person who works very hard and finds it difficult to stop working and do other things 工作狂；工作迷；醉心於工作的人

Synonyms 同義詞辨析

work

employment • career • profession • occupation • trade

These are all words for the work that sb does in return for payment, especially over a long period of time.
以上各詞均指有報酬的工作，尤指長期從事的職業。

work the job that sb does, especially in order to earn money 指工作、職業：*It's very difficult to find work at the moment.* 目前很難找到工作。

employment (*rather formal*) work, especially when it is done to earn money; the state of being employed or the situation in which people have work 指工作、職業、受雇、就業：*Only half the people here are in paid employment.* 這兒只有一半的人有拿工資的工作。

career the job or series of jobs that sb has in a particular area of work, usually involving more responsibility as time passes 指生涯、職業：*He had a very distinguished career in the Foreign Office.* 他在外交部有過一段光輝的事業。

profession a type of job that needs special training or skill, especially one that needs a high level of education 指需要專門技能（尤其是較高教育水平）的職業、專業：*He hopes to enter the medical profession.* 他希望能從事醫務工作。NOTE **The profession** is all the people who work in a particular profession. * the profession 統稱某專業的人、同行、同業：*the legal profession* 法律界 **The professions** are the traditional jobs that need a high level of education and training, such as being a doctor or lawyer. * the professions 統稱需要較高教育水平和訓練的傳統職業，如醫生、律師等。

occupation (*rather formal*) a job or profession 指工作、職業：*Please state your name, age, and occupation.* 請寫明姓名、年齡和職業。

trade a job, especially one that involves working with your hands and requires special training and skills 指行業，尤指手工職業、手藝、行當：*Carpentry is a highly skilled trade.* 木工是需要純熟技巧的職業。

PATTERNS

- **in/out of** work/employment
- (a) **full-time/part-time** work/employment/career/occupation
- **permanent/temporary** work/employment
- (a) **well-paid** work/employment/profession/occupation
- (a) **low-paid** work/employment/occupation
- to **look for/seek/find** work/employment/a career/an occupation
- to **get/obtain/give sb/offer sb/create/generate/provide** work/employment

work·around /ˈwɜːkəraʊnd; *NAmE* ˈwɜːrk-/ *noun* (*computing* 計) a way in which you can solve or avoid a problem when the most obvious solution is not possible 應變方法；變通方法

ˈwork basket *noun* (*old-fashioned*, *BrE*) a container for the things you need for sewing 針線筐

work·bench /ˈwɜːkbentʃ; *NAmE* ˈwɜːrk-/ (also **bench**) *noun* a long heavy table used for doing practical jobs, working with tools, etc. 工作枱

work·book /ˈwɜːkbʊk; *NAmE* ˈwɜːrk-/ (*BrE*) (*NAmE* **ˈexercise book**) *noun* a book with exercises in it, often with spaces for students to write answers in, to help them practise what they have learnt 練習冊；作業本 ➲ VISUAL VOCAB page V70

work·day /ˈwɜːkdeɪ; *NAmE* ˈwɜːrk-/ *noun* **1** (*NAmE*) (*BrE* **ˌworking ˈday**) the part of a day during which you work 工作日（一天中的工作時間）：*an 8-hour workday*

W

* 8 小時工作日 **2** = WORKING DAY (2)： *workday traffic* 平日的交通

ˌworked ˈup *adj.* [not before noun] **~ (about sth)** (*informal*) very excited or upset about sth 異常興奮；十分生氣：*There's no point in **getting worked up** about it.* 為此大發脾氣也無濟於事。

work·er /ˈwɜːkə(r); *NAmE* ˈwɜːrk-/ *noun* **1** (often in compounds 常構成複合詞) a person who works, especially one who does a particular kind of work 工作者；人員：*farm/factory/office workers* 農場/工廠工人；職員◇*rescue/aid/research workers* 救援/援助/研究人員◇***temporary/part-time/casual workers*** 臨時工；兼職工；零工◇***manual/skilled/unskilled workers*** 體力勞動者；熟練/非熟練工人 ➲ COLLOCATIONS at JOB ➲ see also GUEST WORKER, SEX WORKER, SOCIAL WORKER **2** [usually pl.] a person who is employed in a company or industry, especially sb who does physical work rather than organizing things or managing people 雇員；（尤指）勞工，工人：*Conflict between employers and workers intensified and the number of strikes rose.* 勞資矛盾加劇，罷工次數增多。◇*talks between workers and management* 勞資談判 **3** (usually after an adjective 通常置於形容詞後) a person who works in a particular way 幹活…的人：*a **hard/fast/quick/slow worker*** 做事努力/快/麻利/慢的人 **4** a female BEE that helps do the work of the group of bees but does not reproduce 工蜂 ➲ compare DRONE *n.* (3), QUEEN BEE (1) IDM see FAST *adj.*

ˈwork experience *noun* [U] **1** the work or jobs that you have done in your life so far 工作經歷：*The opportunities available will depend on your previous work experience and qualifications.* 能否有機會要看你的工作經歷和學歷。**2** (*BrE*) a period of time that a young person, especially a student, spends working in a company as a form of training（學生）實習 ➲ compare INTERNSHIP (1)

work·fare /ˈwɜːkfeə(r); *NAmE* ˈwɜːrkfer/ *noun* [U] a system in which unemployed people have to work in order to get money for food, rent, etc. from the government 工作福利制（領取福利金的失業者須要參與公益工作等）

work·force /ˈwɜːkfɔːs; *NAmE* ˈwɜːrkfɔːrs/ *noun* [C+sing./pl. v.] **1** all the people who work for a particular company, organization, etc. 全體員工 SYN **staff**：*The factory has a 1 000-strong workforce.* 這家工廠的職工多達千人。◇*Two thirds of the workforce is/are women.* 職工中的三分之二是婦女。➲ COLLOCATIONS at UNEMPLOYMENT **2** all the people in a country or an area who are available for work（國家或地區的）勞動力，勞動大軍，勞動人口：*A quarter of the local workforce is/are unemployed.* 本地四分之一的勞動力都失業了。

work·horse /ˈwɜːkhɔːs; *NAmE* ˈwɜːrkhɔːrs/ *noun* a person or machine that you can rely on to do hard and/or boring work 埋頭苦幹的人；老黃牛（指吃苦耐勞的人）；耐用的機器

work·house /ˈwɜːkhaʊs; *NAmE* ˈwɜːrk-/ (*BrE*) (also **poor·house** *NAmE, BrE*) *noun* (in Britain in the past) a building where very poor people were sent to live and given work to do（英國舊時的）濟貧院，勞動救濟所

W

work·ing /ˈwɜːkɪŋ; *NAmE* ˈwɜːrk-/ *adj., noun*

■ ***adj.*** [only before noun] **1** having a job for which you are paid 有工作的；有職業的 SYN **employed**：*the working population* 勞動人口◇*a **working mother*** 在職母親 ➲ see also HARD-WORKING **2** having a job that involves hard physical work rather than office work, studying, etc. 做工的；從事體力勞動的：*a **working man*** 工人◇*a working men's club* 工人俱樂部 **3** connected with your job and the time you spend doing it 工作上的；工作時間的：*long **working hours*** 長的工作時間◇*poor **working conditions*** 惡劣的工作環境◇*I have a good **working relationship** with my boss.* 我和老闆的工作關係很好。◇*She spent most of her **working life** as a teacher.* 她一生中大部份工作時間都當教師。◇*recent changes in **working practices*** 工作做法方面最近的變化 **4** a **working** breakfast or lunch is one at which you discuss business（早餐或午餐等）邊吃邊談公事的 **5** used as a basis for work, discussion, etc. but likely to be changed or improved in the future 初步的；暫定的：*a working theory* 初步的理論◇*Have you decided on a working title for your thesis yet?* 你選了論文的暫定題目嗎？ **6** if you have a **working** knowledge of sth, you can use it at a basic level 尚可應付工作的；基本夠用的 **7** the **working** parts of a machine are the parts that move in order to make it function（機械部件）操縱用的，用於啟動的 **8** a **working** majority is a small majority that is enough to enable a government to win votes in parliament and make new laws（議會票數）足夠多數的 IDM see ORDER *n.*

■ ***noun*** [usually pl.] **1 ~ (of sth)** the way in which a machine, a system, an organization, etc. works（機器、系統、組織等的）運作，工作方法：*an introduction to the workings of Congress* 對國會運作方式的介紹◇*the workings of the human mind* 人腦的活動方式◇*the machine's inner workings* 這台機器的內部運轉情況 **2** the parts of a mine or QUARRY where coal, metal, stone, etc. is or has been dug from the ground（礦山或採石場的）礦，巷道，作業區

ˌworking ˈcapital *noun* [U] (*business* 商) the money that is needed to run a business rather than the money that is used to buy buildings and equipment when starting the business 流動資本；運營資本；週轉資金 ➲ compare VENTURE CAPITAL

the ˌworking ˈclass *noun* [sing.+sing./pl. v.] (also **the ˌworking ˈclasses** [pl.]) the social class whose members do not have much money or power and are usually employed to do MANUAL work (= physical work using their hands) 工人階級：*the political party of the working class* 工人階級的政黨◇*The working class has/have rejected them in the elections.* 工人階級在選舉中沒有投他們的票。➲ compare MIDDLE CLASS, UPPER CLASS ▸ **ˌworking-ˈclass** *adj.*：*a working-class background* 工人階級出身

ˌworking ˈday *noun* (*BrE*) **1** (*NAmE* **work·day**) the part of a day during which you work 一天中的工作時間：*I spend most of my working day sitting at a desk.* 我一天之中大部份工作時間都坐在辦公桌旁。 **2** (also *less frequent* **work·day**) a day on which you usually work or on which most people usually work 工作日：*Sunday is a normal working day for me.* 星期日是我的正常工作日。◇*Thousands of working days were lost through strikes last year.* 去年因罷工損失了數以千計的工作日。◇*Allow two working days (= not Saturday or Sunday) for delivery.* 送貨需兩個工作日。

ˈworking girl *noun* (*informal*) **1** (becoming *old-fashioned*) a PROSTITUTE. People say 'working girl' to avoid saying 'prostitute'. 上班女郎（婉指妓女） **2** (sometimes *offensive*) a woman who has a paid job 勞動女子；女工；職業婦女

ˈworking paper *noun* **1** [C] a report written by a group of people chosen to study an aspect of law, education, health, etc.（委員會等的）研究報告 **2 working papers** [pl.] (in the US) an official document that enables sb under 16 years old or born outside the US to have a job（美國 16 歲以下或僑居者的）工作證，雇傭證書

ˈworking party (*BrE*) (also **ˈworking group** *NAmE, BrE*) *noun* [C+sing./pl. v.] **~ (on sth)** a group of people chosen to study a particular problem or situation in order to suggest ways of dealing with it（專題）調查委員會

ˌworking ˈweek (*BrE*) (*NAmE* **work·week**) *noun* the total amount of time that you spend at work during the week 一週的工作時間；工作週：*a 40-hour working week* * 40 個小時的工作週

ˌwork-life ˈbalance *noun* [sing.] the number of hours per week you spend working, compared with the number of hours you spend with your family, relaxing, etc. 工作與生活的平衡；勞逸結合：*Part-time working is often the best way to improve your work-life balance.* 兼職工作往往是更好地兼顧工作與生活的最佳途徑。

work·load /ˈwɜːkləʊd; *NAmE* ˈwɜːrkloʊd/ *noun* the amount of work that has to be done by a particular person or organization（某一人或組織的）工作量，工作負擔：*a heavy workload* 沉重的工作負擔◇*We have taken* *on extra staff to cope with the increased workload.* 我們已經額外雇用員工來應付增加了的工作量。 ➲ COLLOCATIONS at JOB

work·man /ˈwɜːkmən; *NAmE* ˈwɜːrk-/ *noun* (*pl.* **-men** /-mən/) **1** a man who is employed to do physical work 男工人；工匠 **2** (with an adjective 與形容詞連用) a person who works in the way mentioned 工作…的人：*a good/bad workman* 工作好的／差的人

work·man·like /ˈwɜːkmənlaɪk; *NAmE* ˈwɜːrk-/ *adj.* done, made, etc. in a skilful and thorough way but not usually very original or exciting 技術嫻熟（但無新意）的

work·man·ship /ˈwɜːkmənʃɪp; *NAmE* ˈwɜːrk-/ *noun* [U] the skill with which sb makes sth, especially when this affects the way it looks or works 手藝；技藝；工藝：*Our buyers insist on high standards of workmanship and materials.* 我們的買主對工藝和材料堅持要高標準。

work·mate /ˈwɜːkmeɪt; *NAmE* ˈwɜːrk-/ *noun* (*especially BrE*) a person that you work with, often doing the same job, in an office, a factory, etc. 一起工作的人；同事；工友 SYN **colleague**

ˌwork of ˈart *noun* (*pl.* **ˌworks of ˈart**) **1** a painting, statue, etc. 藝術品；（繪畫、雕塑等）藝術作品：*A number of priceless works of art were stolen from the gallery.* 美術館中許多價值連城的藝術品被盜。 **2** something that is attractive and skilfully made 令人賞心悅目的東西；精緻的物品：*The bride's dress was a work of art.* 新娘的禮服十分精美。

work·out /ˈwɜːkaʊt; *NAmE* ˈwɜːrk-/ *noun* a period of physical exercise that you do to keep fit 鍛煉：*She does a 20-minute workout every morning.* 她每天早晨做運動20分鐘。

ˈwork permit *noun* an official document that sb needs in order to work in a particular foreign country（國外就業）工作許可證

work·place /ˈwɜːkpleɪs; *NAmE* ˈwɜːrk-/ *noun* (often **the workplace**) [sing.] the office, factory, etc. where people work 工作場所：*the introduction of new technology into the workplace* 把新技術引進工廠

ˈwork placement *noun* [U, C] (*BrE*) = PLACEMENT (2)

ˈwork release *noun* [U] (*US*) a system that allows prisoners to leave prison during the day to go to work 監外就業（允許囚犯日間離開監獄外出工作的制度）

work·room /ˈwɜːkruːm; -rʊm; *NAmE* ˈwɜːrk-/ *noun* a room in which work is done, especially work that involves making things 工作室；工作間；作坊：*The jeweller has a workroom at the back of his shop.* 珠寶商在他的店鋪後面有一間工場。

works *noun* ➲ WORK

ˌworks ˈcouncil *noun* (*especially BrE*) a group of employees who represent all the employees at a factory, etc. in discussions with their employers over conditions of work 職工委員會（負責和雇主協商工作條件等）

work·sheet /ˈwɜːkʃiːt; *NAmE* ˈwɜːrk-/ *noun* **1** a piece of paper on which there is a series of questions and exercises to be done by a student（學生做的）活頁練習題 **2** a piece of paper on which work that has been done or has to be done is recorded 工作記錄（或進度）表

work·shop /ˈwɜːkʃɒp; *NAmE* ˈwɜːrkʃɑːp/ *noun* **1** a room or building in which things are made or repaired using tools or machinery 車間；工場；作坊 ➲ SYNONYMS at FACTORY **2** a period of discussion and practical work on a particular subject, in which a group of people share their knowledge and experience 研討會；講習班：*a drama workshop* 戲劇研討班 ◇ *a poetry workshop* 詩歌講習班 ➲ COLLOCATIONS at EDUCATION

ˈwork-shy *adj.* (*BrE, disapproving*) unwilling to work 不願工作的；怕幹活的；懶惰的 SYN **lazy**

work·space /ˈwɜːkspeɪs; *NAmE* ˈwɜːrk-/ *noun* **1** [U, C] a space in which to work, especially in an office（辦公室等的）工作場所 **2** [C] (*computing* 計) a place where information that is being used by one person on a computer network is stored（計算機網絡的）工作區

work·sta·tion /ˈwɜːksteɪʃn; *NAmE* ˈwɜːrk-/ *noun* the desk and computer at which a person works; one computer that is part of a computer network（計算機）工作站 ➲ VISUAL VOCAB page V69

work·top /ˈwɜːktɒp; *NAmE* ˈwɜːrktɑːp/ (also **ˈwork surface** both *BrE*) (*NAmE* **counter**, **counter·top**) *noun* a flat surface in a kitchen for preparing food on（廚房的）操作枱 ➲ VISUAL VOCAB page V25

ˌwork-to-ˈrule *noun* [usually sing.] a situation in which workers refuse to do any work that is not in their contracts, in order to protest about sth 按章工作（為表示抗議而拒絕做超出合同規定的工作） ➲ compare GO-SLOW

work·week /ˈwɜːkwiːk; *NAmE* ˈwɜːrk-/ (*NAmE*) (*BrE* **ˌworking ˈweek**) *noun* the total amount of time that you spend at work during the week 一週的工作時間；工作週

world 0-w /wɜːld; *NAmE* wɜːrld/ *noun*

▸ **THE EARTH/ITS PEOPLE** 地球；地球人 **1** 0-w **the world** [sing.] the earth, with all its countries, peoples and natural features 世界；地球；天下：*to sail **around the world*** 環球航行 ◇ *travelling (**all over**) **the world*** 周遊世界 ◇ *a map of the world* 世界地圖 ◇ *French is spoken in many **parts of the world**.* 世界上許多地方都說法語。◇ *Which is the largest city **in the world**?* 世界上最大的城市是哪個？◇ *He's the world's highest paid entertainer.* 他是世界上薪金最高的演藝人。◇ *a meeting of world leaders* 世界各國領導人大會 ◇ *campaigning for world peace* 發起世界和平運動 **2** 0-w [C, usually sing.] a particular part of the earth; a particular group of countries or people; a particular period of history and the people of that period 某地域（或民族、歷史時期等）的人類社會；世界：*the Arab world* 阿拉伯世界 ◇ *the English-speaking world* 講英語的地區 ◇ *the industrialized and developing worlds* 工業化國家和發展中國家 ◇ *the ancient/modern world* 古代／現代社會 ➲ see also FIRST WORLD, NEW WORLD, OLD WORLD, THIRD WORLD

▸ **ANOTHER PLANET** 另一顆行星 **3** [C] a planet like the earth（像地球的）星球，天體：*There may be other worlds out there.* 那裏可能有其他星球。

▸ **TYPE OF LIFE** 生命 **4** 0-w [C] the people or things belonging to a particular group or connected with a particular interest, job, etc. 按性質（或職業等）劃分的類別；界；界別：*the **animal/plant/insect world*** 動物界；植物界；昆蟲界 ◇ *the world of fashion* 時裝界 ◇ *stars from the sporting and artistic worlds* 體育和藝術界的眾明星 **5** 0-w [usually sing.] (usually used with an adjective 通常與形容詞連用) everything that exists of a particular kind; a particular kind of life or existence 某領域的一切事物；某種生活：***the natural world*** (= animals, plants, minerals, etc.) 自然界 ◇ *They are a couple in **the real world** as well as in the movie.* 他們在電影和現實生活中都是一對夫婦。◇ *The island is a world of brilliant colours and dramatic sunsets.* 這個島是個絢麗多彩、晚霞嬌妍的世界。◇ *They had little contact with the **outside world*** (= people and places that were not part of their normal life). 他們與外界沒有什麼聯繫。

▸ **PERSON'S LIFE** 人生 **6** 0-w [sing.] a person's environment, experiences, friends and family, etc. 生活環境；閱歷；生活圈子：*Parents are the most important people in a child's world.* 父母在兒童的天地裏是最重要的人。◇ *When his wife died, his entire world was turned upside down.* 他妻子死後，他的整個生活變得一塌糊塗。

▸ **SOCIETY** 社會 **7** 0-w [sing.] our society and the way people live and behave; the people in the world 社會；世情；世故；世人：*We live in a rapidly changing world.* 我們生活在瞬息萬變的社會裏。◇ *He's too young to understand **the ways of the world**.* 他還太年輕，不懂得處世之道。◇ *The **whole world** was waiting for news of the astronauts.* 全世界的人都在等待宇航員的消息。◇ *She felt that the world was against her.* 她覺得整個世界都在與她作對。◇ ***The eyes of the world** are on the President.* 世人的眼睛都在盯着總統。 **8** **the world** [sing.] a way of life where possessions and physical pleasures are important, rather than spiritual values 塵世；世俗；世事；世情：*monks and nuns renouncing the world* 棄絕俗世享樂的修道士和修女 ➲ see also OLDE WORLDE, OLD-WORLD

▸ **HUMAN EXISTENCE** 人類的生存 **9** [sing.] the state of human existence 人世；今世：*this world and the next* (= life on earth and existence after death) 今世和來世

IDM **be ˌall the ˈworld to sb** to be loved by and very important to sb 是…的最喜愛的人（或事物）；對…非常重要；是…的一切 **the best of ˈboth/ˈall possible worlds** the benefits of two or more completely different situations that you can enjoy at the same time 兩全其美；兩頭受益；旱澇保收：*If you enjoy the coast and the country, you'll get the best of both worlds on this walk.* 你要是喜歡海濱和鄉村，那麼這次散步你會一舉兩得。**be ˈworlds apart** to be completely different in attitudes, opinions, etc.（在態度、看法等方面）有天壤之別，截然不同 **come/go ˈdown/ˈup in the world** to become less/more important or successful in society 落泊；衰落；倒運；飛黃騰達；發跡；興盛 **come into the ˈworld** (*literary*) to be born 出生；降生人間 **do sb/sth the ˈworld of good** to make sb feel much better; to improve sth 使…感到好得多；對…大有好處；改善：*A change of job would do you the world of good.* 換一下工作會對你大有好處。**for all the world as if/though ...** | **for all the world like sb/sth** (*formal*) exactly as if ...; exactly like sb/sth 簡直像是；恰似：*She behaved for all the world as if nothing unusual had happened.* 看她的表現就像根本沒有發生過什麼大事似的。◇ *He looked for all the world like a schoolboy caught stealing apples.* 他那個樣子簡直就像偷蘋果時被當場抓住的小學生。**have the world at your ˈfeet** to be very successful and admired 功成名就；為世人仰慕 **how, why, etc. in the ˈworld** (*informal*) used to emphasize sth and to show that you are surprised or annoyed（用於強調，表示驚訝或不悅）到底，究竟：*What in the world did they think they were doing?* 他們到底認為自己在做什麼？**in an ideal/a perfect ˈworld** used to say that sth is what you would like to happen or what should happen, but you know it cannot 在理想狀態下：*In an ideal world we would be recycling and reusing everything.* 我們要是能回收並再利用所有的東西就再理想不過了。**in the ˈworld** 🔑 used to emphasize what you are saying（加強語氣）世界上，天下，根本，到底：*There's nothing in the world I'd like more than to visit New York.* 訪問紐約是我最想做的事。◇ *Don't rush—we've got* ***all the time in the world****.* 別急急忙忙的，我們有的是時間。◇ *You look as if you haven't got* ***a care in the world****!* 你看上去好像一絲牽掛都沒有！**(be/live) in a world of your ˈown** if you are **in a world of your own**, you are so concerned with your own thoughts that you do not notice what is happening around you（生活）在自己的小天地裏 **a man/woman of the ˈworld** a person with a lot of experience of life, who is not easily surprised or shocked 生活閱歷豐富的人；老成持重的人 **not for (all) the ˈworld** used to say that you would never do sth 絕不：*I wouldn't hurt you for the world.* 我絕不會傷害你。**the ... of this world** (*informal*) used to refer to people of a particular type …這類人：*We all envy the Bill Gateses of this world* (= the people who are as rich and successful as Bill Gates). 我們大家都羨慕比爾 • 蓋茨這樣的人。**ˌout of this ˈworld** (*informal*) used to emphasize how good, beautiful, etc. sth is 好（或美等）得不得了；非凡；呱呱叫：*The meal was out of this world.* 這頓飯簡直是沒治了。**see the ˈworld** to travel widely and gain wide experience 見多識廣；見世面 **set/put the world to ˈrights** to talk about how the world could be changed to be a better place 談論如何使世界變得更好：*We stayed up all night, setting the world to rights.* 我們一夜沒睡，談論着如何拯救世界。**set the ˈworld on fire** (*BrE* also **set the ˈworld alight**) (*informal*) (usually used in negative sentences 通常用於否定句) to be very successful and gain the admiration of other people 大獲成功；引起轟動：*He's never going to set the world on fire with his paintings.* 他的繪畫永遠不會引起轟動。**what is the world ˈcoming to?** used to express disapproval, surprise or shock, especially at changes in people's attitudes or behaviour 這個世界要變成什麼樣子了；這世道是怎麼了；太不像話：*When I listen to the news these days, I sometimes wonder what the world is coming to.* 我近來收聽新聞時，有時納悶這成了什麼世道了。**(all) the ˌworld and his ˈwife** (*BrE, informal, humorous*) everyone; a large number of people 人人；許多人 **a ˈworld away (from sth)** used to emphasize how different two things are（和…）截然不同，有天壤之別：*His new luxury mansion was a world away from the tiny house where he was born.* 他那座新的豪宅與他出生的小屋完全不能相比。**the ˌworld is your ˈoyster** there is no limit to the opportunities open to you 世界是屬於你的；你的前途無量 **a/the ˈworld of difference** (*informal*) used to emphasize how much difference there is between two things 完全不同；是兩碼事：*There's a world of difference between liking someone and loving them.* 喜歡一個人和愛一個人完全不是一回事。**the (whole) world ˈover** everywhere in the world 世界各地；全世界：*People are basically the same the world over.* 世界各地的人基本上都一樣。➲ more at BRAVE *adj.*, DEAD *adj.*, END *n.*, LOST, PROMISE *v.*, SMALL *adj.*, TOP *n.*, WATCH *v.*, WAY *n.*, WILL *n.*, WORST *n.*

the ˌWorld ˈBank *noun* [sing.] an international organization that lends money to countries who are members at times when they are in difficulty and need more money 世界銀行（向處於困境需要資助的成員國貸款的國際機構）

ˈworld-beater *noun* a person or thing that is better than all others 天下無雙的人（或事物）▸ **ˈworld-beating** *adj.*

ˌworld-ˈclass *adj.* as good as the best in the world 世界級的；世界上一流的：*a world-class athlete* 世界一流的運動員

the ˌWorld ˈCup *noun* (in sports 體育運動) a competition between national teams from all over the world, usually held every few years 世界杯比賽（通常為幾年一度）：*The next Rugby World Cup will take place in three years' time.* 下一屆橄欖球世界杯賽將於三年後舉行。

ˌworld ˈEnglish *noun* [U] the English language, used throughout the world for international communication, including all of its regional varieties, such as Australian, Indian and South African English 世界英語（通行於世界各地的國際交流英語，包括澳大利亞英語、印度英語、南非英語等地域變體）

ˌworld-ˈfamous *adj.* known all over the world 舉世聞名的；世界著名的：*a world-famous scientist* 世界著名的科學家 ◇ *His books are world-famous.* 他的著作舉世聞名。

ˌWorld ˈHeritage Site *noun* a natural or MAN-MADE place that is recognized as having great international importance and is therefore protected 世界遺產保護區

ˌworld ˈlanguage *noun* a language that is known or spoken in many countries 世界通用語；國際語言

world·ly /ˈwɜːldli; *NAmE* ˈwɜːrld-/ *adj.* (*literary*) **1** [only before noun] connected with the world in which we live rather than with spiritual things 塵世的；世俗的；世事的：*worldly success* 世俗的成就 ◇ *your* ***worldly goods*** (= the things that you own) 你個人的物品 **OPP** **spiritual** **2** having a lot of experience of life and therefore not easily shocked 生活經驗豐富的；老成持重的；世故的：*At 15, he was more worldly than his older cousins who lived in the country.* 他 15 歲時就比他那些居住在鄉村的表兄們懂人情世故了。**OPP** **unworldly** ▸ **world·li·ness** *noun* [U]

ˌworldly-ˈwise *adj.* having a lot of experience of life and therefore not easily shocked 善於處世的；老於世故的

ˈworld music *noun* [U] traditional music from non-Western countries; Western popular music that includes elements of traditional music from non-Western countries 世界音樂（非西方國家的傳統音樂以及具有這些音樂元素的西方流行音樂）

ˌworld ˈpower *noun* a powerful country that has a lot of influence in international politics 世界強國

the ˌWorld ˈSeries™ *noun* a series of BASEBALL games played every year between the winners of the American League and the National League 世界系列賽（美國棒球聯盟和全國棒球聯盟優勝者之間的年度比賽）

ˌworld ˈview *noun* a person's way of thinking about and understanding life, which depends on their beliefs

W

and attitudes 世界觀： *Your education is bound to shape your world view.* 一個人接受的教育必定會決定其世界觀的形成。

ˌworld ˈwar *noun* [C, U] a war that involves many countries 世界大戰

ˌWorld ˌWar ˈOne (also **ˌWorld ˌWar ˈI**) *noun* = FIRST WORLD WAR

ˌWorld ˌWar ˈTwo (also **ˌWorld ˌWar ˈII**) *noun* = SECOND WORLD WAR

ˈworld-weary *adj.* no longer excited by life; showing this 厭世的；厭棄人生的 SYN **jaded** ▶ **ˈworld-weariness** *noun* [U]

world·wide /ˈwɜːldwaɪd; *NAmE* ˈwɜːrld-/ *adj.* [usually before noun] affecting all parts of the world 影響全世界的；世界各地的： *an increase in worldwide sales* 全球銷售額的增長 ◇ *The story has attracted worldwide attention.* 這件事已經引起了全世界的關注。 ▶ **ˌworld·ˈwide** *adv.*： *We have 2 000 members worldwide.* 我們在全世界有 2 000 名成員。

the ˌWorld Wide ˈWeb (also **the Web**) *noun* (*abbr.* **WWW**) a system for finding information on the Internet, in which documents are connected to other documents using HYPERTEXT links 萬維網；環球信息網： *to browse a site on the World Wide Web* 在萬維網上瀏覽一個網站 ➲ VISUAL VOCAB page V68

worm /wɜːm; *NAmE* wɜːrm/ *noun, verb*

■ ***noun* 1** [C] a long thin creature with no bones or legs, that lives in soil 蠕蟲： *birds looking for worms* 覓食蠕蟲的鳥 ➲ see also EARTHWORM, LUGWORM **2 worms** [pl.] long thin creatures that live inside the bodies of humans or animals and can cause illness （人或動物體內的）寄生蟲；腸蟲： *The dog has worms.* 這條狗體內有寄生蟲。 ➲ see also HOOKWORM, TAPEWORM **3** [C] the young form of an insect when it looks like a short worm （昆蟲的）幼蟲： *This apple is full of worms.* 這個蘋果生滿了蟲子。 ➲ see also GLOW-WORM, SILKWORM, WOODWORM **4** [C] (*computing* 計) a computer program that is a type of virus and that spreads across a network by copying itself 蠕蟲；蠕蟲程序；蠕蟲病毒 **5** [C, usually sing.] (*informal, disapproving*) a person you do not like or respect, especially because they have a weak character and do not behave well towards other people 懦夫；可憐蟲

IDM **the ˌworm will ˈturn** (*saying*) a person who is normally quiet and does not complain will protest when the situation becomes too hard to bear 老實人被逼急了也要反抗；兔子急了也咬人 ➲ more at CAN[2] *n.*, EARLY *adj.*

■ ***verb* 1 ~ your way + adv./prep.** to use a twisting and turning movement, especially to move through a narrow or crowded place 蠕動，曲折行進（尤指通過狹窄或擁擠的地方）： *She wormed her way through the crowd to the reception desk.* 她在人群中左拐右繞走到服務枱。 **2 ~ sth** to give an animal medicine that makes worms pass out of its body in the FAECES 給（動物）驅腸蟲

PHR V **ˌworm your way/yourself ˈinto sth** (*disapproving*) to make sb like you or trust you, in order to gain some advantage for yourself 贏得歡心，騙取信任（以獲利） SYN **insinuate yourself**： *He managed to worm his way into her life.* 他設法騙取信任進入了她的生活。 **ˌworm sth ˈout of sb** (*informal*) to make sb tell you sth, by asking them questions in a clever way for a long period of time（慢慢地）從某人處套出話來；不斷套問： *We eventually wormed the secret out of her.* 我們最後從她口裏探聽出了秘密。

ˈworm-eaten *adj.* full of holes made by WORMS or WOODWORMS 蟲蛀的；蟲咬的；被蟲蛀成很多洞的

worm·ery /ˈwɜːməri; *NAmE* ˈwɜːrm-/ *noun* (*pl.* **-ies**) a container in which WORMS are kept, for example in order to produce COMPOST 飼蟲箱

worm·hole /ˈwɜːmhəʊl; *NAmE* ˈwɜːrmhoʊl/ *noun* **1** a hole made by a worm or young insect 蛀洞；蛀孔 **2** (*physics* 物) a possible connection between regions of SPACE-TIME that are far apart 蠕蟲洞（即相隔遙遠的時空區之間的可能連接）

worm·wood /ˈwɜːmwʊd; *NAmE* ˈwɜːrm-/ *noun* [U] a plant with a bitter flavour, used in making alcoholic drinks and medicines 蒿，洋艾（有些具苦味，可入藥或用來製苦艾酒等）

wormy /ˈwɜːmi; *NAmE* ˈwɜːrmi/ *adj.* containing WORMS 有蟲子的；有蛀蟲的： *a wormy apple* 生蟲的蘋果

worn /wɔːn; *NAmE* wɔːrn/ *adj.* **1** [usually before noun] (of a thing 物品) damaged or thinner than normal because it is old and has been used a lot 用壞的；用舊的；磨薄的： *an old pair of worn jeans* 一條破舊的牛仔褲 ◇ *The stone steps were worn and broken.* 這些石頭台階被磨平破裂了。 ➲ see also WELL WORN **2** (of a person 人) looking very tired 疲憊的；筋疲力盡的 SYN **weary**： *She came out of the ordeal looking thin and worn.* 她經歷過這場苦難後顯得憔悴不堪。 ➲ see also WEAR *v.*

ˌworn ˈout *adj.* **1** (of a thing 物品) badly damaged and/or no longer useful because it has been used a lot 破爛不堪的；廢舊的： *These shoes are worn out.* 這雙鞋破得不能再穿了。 ◇ *the gradual replacement of worn-out equipment* 破舊設備的逐漸更新 ◇ *a speech full of worn-out old clichés* 充滿老掉牙的陳詞濫調的演講 **2** [not usually before noun] (of a person 人) looking or feeling very tired, especially as a result of hard work or physical exercise 疲憊不堪；精疲力竭： *Can we sit down? I'm worn out.* 我們能坐下嗎？我都累壞了。 ➲ compare OUTWORN

wor·ried 0-w /ˈwʌrid; *NAmE* ˈwɜːr-/ *adj.* thinking about unpleasant things that have happened or that might happen and therefore feeling unhappy and afraid 擔心的；擔憂的；發愁的： *Don't look so worried!* 別這麼愁眉苦臉的！ ◇ **~ about sb/sth** *I'm not worried about her—she can take care of herself.* 我不為她擔心，她能照顧自己。 ◇ *Doctors are worried about the possible spread of the disease.* 醫生擔心這疾病可能會蔓延。 ◇ **~ by sth** *We're not too worried by these results.* 我們對這些結果並不太擔心。 ◇ **~ (that ...)** *The police are worried that the man may be armed.* 警方擔心那個人可能攜帶着武器。 ◇ *I was worried you wouldn't come.* 我還擔心你不來呢。 ◇ *Where have you been? I've been* ***worried sick*** (= extremely worried). 你到哪裏去了？我都擔心死了。 ◇ *Try not to* ***get worried.*** 盡量別擔憂。 ◇ *She gave me a worried look.* 她心事重重地看了我一眼。 ➲ SYNONYMS at next page ▶ **wor·ried·ly** *adv.*： *He glanced worriedly at his father.* 他憂心忡忡地瞥了他父親一眼。

IDM **you had me ˈworried** (*informal*) used to tell sb that you were worried because you had not understood what they had said correctly （誤會所致）你讓我虛驚一場： *You had me worried for a moment—I thought you were going to resign!* 你可讓我擔心了一陣子，我原以為你要辭職呢！

wor·rier /ˈwʌriə(r); *NAmE* ˈwɜːr-/ *noun* a person who worries a lot about unpleasant things that have happened or that might happen 愛擔憂的人；常發愁的人

wor·ri·some /ˈwʌrisəm; *NAmE* ˈwɜːr-/ *adj.* (*especially NAmE*) that makes you worry 令人擔心的；使人擔憂的

worry 0-w /ˈwʌri; *NAmE* ˈwɜːri/ *verb, noun*

■ ***verb*** (**wor·ries**, **worry·ing**, **wor·ried**, **wor·ried**) **1** 0-w [I] to keep thinking about unpleasant things that might happen or about problems that you have 擔心；擔憂；發愁： ***Don't worry.*** *We have plenty of time.* 不必擔心。我們有很多時間。 ◇ **~ about sb/sth** *Don't worry about me. I'll be all right.* 別為我擔憂。我會沒事的。 ◇ *He's always worrying about his weight.* 他總是為自己的體重發愁。 ◇ **~ over sb/sth** *There's no point in worrying over things you can't change.* 對改變不了的事情擔心也沒用。 ◇ **~ (that) ...** *I worry that I won't get into college.* 我擔心自己進不了大學。 **2** 0-w [T] to make sb/yourself anxious about sb/sth 使擔心；使擔憂；使發愁： **~ sb/yourself (about sb/sth)** *What worries me is how I am going to get another job.* 使我發愁的是如何再找到工作。 ◇ **~ sb/yourself + adj. (about sb/sth)** *He's* ***worried himself sick*** (= become extremely anxious) *about his daughter.* 他的女兒可把他愁壞了。 ◇ **it worries sb that ...** *It worries me*

W

that he hasn't come home yet. 他還沒有回家，這叫我放心不下。◇ **it worries sb to do sth** *It worried me to think what might happen.* 想到可能會發生的事情我就發愁了。**3** [T] to annoy or disturb sb 騷擾；煩擾；使不安寧：**~ sb** *The noise never seems to worry her.* 這噪音似乎從不讓她厭煩。◇ **~ sb with sth** *Don't keep worrying him with a lot of silly questions.* 別老用許多愚蠢的問題打擾他。**4** [T] **~ sth** (of a dog 狗) to attack animals, especially sheep, by chasing and/or biting them 攻擊，撕咬（動物，尤指羊）

IDM ˌ**not to ˈworry** (*informal, especially BrE*) it is not important; it does not matter 別擔心；不必發愁；沒關係：*Not to worry—I can soon fix it.* 別着急，我很快就能把它修理好。◇ *Not to worry—no harm done.* 別擔心，沒傷着。

PHR V ˈ**worry at sth 1** to bite sth and shake or pull it 咬；撕扯；搖晃；拉扯：*Rebecca worried at her lip.* 麗貝卡咬着嘴唇。◇ *He began to worry at the knot in the cord.* 他開始解繩子上的結。**2** to think about a problem a lot and try and find a solution 思考，苦想（解決辦法）

■ ***noun*** (*pl.* **-ies**) **1** [U] the state of worrying about sth 擔心；憂慮；發愁 SYN **anxiety**：*The threat of losing their jobs is a constant source of worry to them.* 丟掉工作的威脅常使他們憂心忡忡。◇ *to be frantic* ***with worry*** 愁得要命 **2** [C] something that worries you 令人擔憂的事；讓人發愁的事：*family/financial worries* 家庭中的/財務上的煩惱 ◇ **~ (about/over sth)** *worries about the future* 對未來的擔憂 ◇ **~ (for/to sb)** *Mugging is a real worry for many old people.* 行兇搶劫確實令許多老人心神不安。◇ *My only worry is that …* 唯一令我擔憂的是…

IDM ˈ**no worries!** (*informal*) it's not a problem; it's all right (often used as a reply when sb thanks you for sth) 沒什麼，不客氣，沒關係（常用以回答別人的道謝）

ˈ**worry beads** *noun* [pl.] small BEADS on a string that you move and turn in order to keep calm 排愁串珠，安神串珠（用手捻轉使自己鎮靜）

worry·ing /ˈwʌriŋ; *NAmE* ˈwɜːr-/ *adj.* that makes you worry 令人擔憂的；令人發愁的：*a worrying development* 令人擔憂的發展 ◇ *It must be worrying for you not to know where he is.* 你不知道他的下落一定很着急。◇ *It is particularly worrying that nobody seems to be in charge.* 特別令人擔憂的是，似乎沒有任何人在負責。◇ *It's been a* ***worrying time*** *for us all.* 我們大家一直憂心忡忡。▶ **worry·ing·ly** *adv.*：*worryingly high levels of radiation* 令人擔憂的強輻射 ◇ *Worryingly, the plan contains few details on how spending will be cut.* 令人擔憂的是，這項計劃中有關如何削減開支的細則很少。

worry·wart /ˈwʌriwɔːt; *NAmE* ˈwɜːriwɔːrt/ *noun* (*NAmE, informal*) a person who worries about unimportant things 自尋煩惱的人；愛發愁的人

wors /vɔːs; *NAmE* vɔːrs/ *noun* [U] (*SAfrE*) SAUSAGE 香腸；臘腸

worse /wɜːs; *NAmE* wɜːrs/ *adj., adv., noun*

■ ***adj.*** (comparative of *bad* * bad 的比較級) **1** of poorer quality or lower standard; less good or more unpleasant 更差的；更糟的；更壞的：*The rooms were awful and the food was worse.* 房間很糟糕，吃的更差。◇ *The weather* ***got worse*** *during the day.* 日間天氣變得更惡劣了。◇ *I've been to* ***far worse*** *places.* 我到過糟糕得多的地方。◇ **~ than sth** *The interview was* ***much worse than*** *he had expected.* 這次面試比他預計的要糟得多。◇ **~ than doing sth** *There's* ***nothing worse than*** *going out in the cold with wet hair.* 沒有比在大冷天頭髮濕着外出更糟糕的了。**2** **~ (than sth/doing sth)** more serious or severe 更嚴重的；更嚴厲的：*They were trying to prevent an* ***even worse*** *tragedy.* 他們正在設法避免更大的悲劇發生。◇ *The crisis was getting* ***worse and worse****.* 危機越來越嚴重了。◇ *Don't tell her that—you'll only* ***make things worse****.* 別把這事告訴她，你只會火上澆油。◇ *Never mind—it* ***could be worse*** (= although the situation is bad, it is not as bad as it might have been). 沒關係，原本可能還要更糟。**3** [not before noun] more ill/sick or unhappy 病情更重；健康惡化；更不愉快：*If he gets any worse we'll call the doctor.* 要是他的病情惡化，我們就請醫生。◇ *He told her she'd let them down and she felt* ***worse than ever****.* 他對她說，她讓他們失望了，於是她難過極了。

IDM **come off ˈworse** to lose a fight, competition, etc. or suffer more compared with others（戰鬥、比賽等）失敗，輸得更慘 **go from ˌbad to ˈworse** (of a bad condition, situation, etc. 不好的情況、局勢等) to get even worse 每況愈下；越來越糟 ˌ**worse ˈluck!** (*BrE, informal*) used to show that you are disappointed about sth（表示失望）倒霉，不幸，可惜：*I shall have to miss the party, worse luck!* 我參加不了這次聚會了，真倒霉！

➲ more at BARK *n.*, FATE

Synonyms 同義詞辨析

worried

concerned • nervous • anxious • uneasy

These words all describe feeling unhappy and afraid because you are thinking about unpleasant things that might happen or might have happened. 以上各詞均指感到不安、擔憂。

- **worried** thinking about unpleasant things that might happen or might have happened and therefore feeling unhappy and afraid 指因想到令人不快的事而擔心的、擔憂的
- **concerned** worried and feeling concern about sth 指擔心的、憂慮的

WORRIED OR CONCERNED? 用 worried 還是 concerned？

Concerned is usually used when you are talking about a problem that affects another person, society, the world, etc, while **worried** can be used for this or for more personal matters. * concerned 通常指對影響他人、社會、世界等問題的擔憂，而 worried 既可指對這類問題，也可指對個人問題的憂慮。

- **nervous** feeling worried about sth or slightly afraid of sth 指焦慮的、擔憂的、惶恐的
- **anxious** feeling worried or nervous about sth 指焦慮的、憂慮的、擔心的

WORRIED, NERVOUS OR ANXIOUS? 用 worried、nervous 還是 anxious？

Worried is the most frequent word to describe how you feel when you are thinking about a problem or something bad that might happen. **Anxious** can describe a stronger feeling and is more formal. **Nervous** is more often used to describe how you feel before you do something very important such as an exam or an interview, or something unpleasant or difficult. **Nervous** can describe sb's personality: *a very nervious girl* is often or usually nervous; *a worried girl* is worried on a particular occasion or about a particular thing. **Worried** describes her feelings, not her personality. **Anxious** may describe feelings or personality. * worried 最通用，表示對某個問題或可能發生的不幸有所擔憂。anxious 可指較強烈的擔憂和不安，且較正式。nervous 較常用以形容重要事情（如考試、面試）、令人不快或困難的事情發生前的緊張不安、戰戰兢兢。nervous 亦可指人的性格：a very nervious girl 指性格易緊張的女孩，而 a worried girl 指在某個時刻或對某事擔憂的女孩。worried 形容感覺而非性格，anxious 既可形容感覺也可形容性格。

- **uneasy** feeling worried or unhappy about a particular situation, especially because you think sth bad may happen or because you are not sure that what you are doing is right 指擔心的、憂慮的、不安的，尤其想到不幸的事情可能發生或不確定自己是否做得對

PATTERNS

- worried/concerned/nervous/anxious/uneasy **about (doing)** sth
- worried/concerned/anxious **for** sb/sth
- worried/concerned/nervous/anxious **that** …
- a(n) worried/concerned/nervous/anxious/uneasy **expression/look/smile**
- to **get** worried/nervous/anxious

W

■ ***adv.*** (comparative of *badly* * badly 的比較級) **1** 🗝 **~ (than sth)** less well 更壞；更差；更糟：*I didn't do it very well, but, if anything, he did it worse than I did.* 我幹得不太好，但其實他幹得比我還糟。**2** 🗝 **~ (than sth)** more seriously or severely 更嚴重；更厲害：*It's raining worse than ever.* 雨下得比以往都大。**3** 🗝 **~ (than sth)** used to introduce a statement about sth that is more serious or unpleasant than things already mentioned 更糟的是；更倒霉的是：*She'd lost her job. Even worse, she'd lost her house and her children, too.* 她丟了工作。更倒霉的是，她還失去了房子和孩子。

IDM **be ˌworse ˈoff (than sb/sth)** 🗝 to be poorer, unhappier, etc. than before or than sb else（比以前或其他人）更窮，更不愉快，更差：*The increase in taxes means that we'll be £30 a month worse off than before.* 稅收的增加意味着我們將比以前每月少掙 30 英鎊。**you can/could do worse than do sth** used to say that you think sth is a good idea 倒不如試做某事；你做某事倒不失可取：*If you want a safe investment, you could do a lot worse than put your money in a building society.* 你要想投資而不冒風險，倒不如把錢存到房屋互助協會。

■ ***noun*** [U] more problems or bad news 更多的問題；更壞的消息：*I'm afraid there is worse to come.* 恐怕更糟的還在後頭呢。

IDM **be none the ˈworse (for sth)** to not be harmed by sth 沒有受到（…的）不良影響：*The kids were none the worse for their adventure.* 孩子們沒有因歷險而受傷。**the ˌworse for ˈwear** (*informal*) **1** in a poor condition because of being used a lot 用舊的；用壞的 **2** drunk 喝醉的 ➲ more at BETTER *n.*, CHANGE *n.*

worsen /ˈwɜːsn; *NAmE* ˈwɜːrsn/ *verb* [I, T] to become or make sth worse than it was before（使）變得更壞，變得更糟，惡化 **SYN** **deteriorate**：*The political situation is steadily worsening.* 政治局勢在持續惡化。◇ *Her health has worsened considerably since we last saw her.* 自從我們上次見到她以來，她的身體差多了。◇ **~ sth** *Staff shortages were worsened by the flu epidemic.* 由於流感，職員短缺的情況更加嚴重了。▸ **worsen·ing** *noun* [sing.]：*a worsening of the international debt crisis* 國際債務危機的加劇 **worsen·ing** *adj.*：*worsening weather conditions* 正在變壞的天氣

wor·ship 🗝 /ˈwɜːʃɪp; *NAmE* ˈwɜːrʃɪp/ *noun, verb*

■ ***noun*** **1** 🗝 [U] the practice of showing respect for God or a god, by saying prayers, singing with others, etc.; a ceremony for this（對上帝或神的）崇拜，敬仰，禮拜：***an act/a place of worship*** 禮拜；禮拜場所 ◇ *ancestor worship* 對祖先的祭祀 ◇ *morning worship* (= a church service in the morning) 早晨的禮拜 **2** [U] a strong feeling of love and respect for sb/sth 崇拜；崇敬；愛慕 **SYN** **adoration** ➲ see also HERO WORSHIP **3** **His, Your, etc. Worship** [C] (*BrE*, *formal*) a polite way of addressing or referring to a MAGISTRATE or MAYOR（對治安官或市長的尊稱）閣下

■ ***verb*** (**-pp-**, *NAmE* also **-p-**) **1** 🗝 [T] **~ sb/sth** to show respect for God or a god, especially by saying prayers, singing, etc. with other people in a religious building 崇敬，崇拜（上帝或神）；（尤指在宗教場所）做禮拜 ➲ COLLOCATIONS at RELIGION **2** 🗝 [I] to go to a service in a religious building 到宗教場所參加禮拜：*We worship at St Mary's.* 我們在聖瑪利教堂做禮拜。◇ *He worshipped at the local mosque.* 他在當地的清真寺做禮拜。**3** 🗝 [T] **~ sb/sth** to love and admire sb very much, especially so much that you cannot see their faults 熱愛；愛慕，崇拜（尤指達到看不到缺點的地步）：*She worships her children.* 她極度疼愛自己的兒女。◇ *He worshipped her from afar* (= he loved her but did not tell her his feelings). 他暗戀着她。◇ *She **worships the ground he walks on**.* 她對他的愛達到痴迷的程度。

wor·ship·ful /ˈwɜːʃɪpfl; *NAmE* ˈwɜːrʃ-/ *adj.* [only before noun] **1** (*formal*) showing or feeling respect and admiration for sb/sth 崇敬的；敬重的；愛慕的 **2** **Worshipful** used in Britain in the titles of some MAYORS and some groups of CRAFTSMEN 尊敬的（英國用於某些市長和工匠團體的稱號中）：*the Worshipful Company of Goldsmiths*（倫敦）金業公會

wor·ship·per (*NAmE* also **wor·ship·er**) /ˈwɜːʃɪpə(r); *NAmE* ˈwɜːrʃ-/ *noun* a person who worships God or a god 崇拜上帝（或神）的人；做禮拜的人；敬神者；拜神者：*regular worshippers at St Andrew's Church* 經常到聖安德肋教堂做禮拜的人 ◇ (*figurative*) *sun worshippers lying on the beach* 躺在海灘上曬太陽的人們

worst 🗝 /wɜːst; *NAmE* wɜːrst/ *adj., adv., noun, verb*

■ ***adj.*** 🗝 (superlative of *bad* * bad 的最高級) of the poorest quality or lowest standard; worse than any other person or thing of a similar kind 最差的；最壞的；最糟的：*It was **by far the worst** speech he had ever made.* 這是他迄今發表過的最差的演講。◇ *What's the worst thing that could happen?* 情況最壞會怎麼樣？◇ *What she said confirmed my **worst fears*** (= proved they were right). 她的話證實了我最擔心的事。

IDM **be your ˌown worst ˈenemy** to be the cause of your own problems 自討苦吃；是自己問題的根源 **come off ˈworst** to lose a fight, competition, etc. or suffer more compared with others（在戰鬥、比賽等中）吃敗仗，輸得最慘

■ ***adv.*** 🗝 (superlative of *badly* * badly 的最高級) most badly or seriously 最壞；最糟；最嚴重：*He was voted the worst dressed celebrity.* 大家一致認為他是衣着最差的名人。◇ *Manufacturing industry was worst affected by the fuel shortage.* 製造業受燃料短缺的影響最為嚴重。◇ ***Worst of all**, I lost the watch my father had given me.* 最糟糕的是，我把父親送給我的錶丟了。

■ ***noun*** 🗝 **the worst** [sing.] the most serious or unpleasant thing that could happen; the part, situation, possibility, etc. that is worse than any other（可能發生的）最嚴重的事；最壞的部份（或情況、可能性等）：*The worst of the storm was over.* 最厲害的一陣風暴過去了。◇ *When they did not hear from her, they **feared the worst**.* 他們聽不到她的消息時，唯恐發生了最壞的事。◇ ***The worst of it** is that I can't even be sure if they received my letter.* 最糟糕的是，我甚至不能肯定他們是否收到了我的信。◇ *He was always optimistic, even when things were **at their worst**.* 他即使在情況最糟糕的時候也總是很樂觀。

IDM **at (the) ˈworst** 🗝 used for saying what is the worst thing that can happen（指可能出現的最壞情況）往最壞處說，充其量：*At the very worst, he'll have to pay a fine.* 在最壞的情況下，他得交罰款。**bring out the ˈworst in sb** to make sb show their worst qualities 使原形畢露；使表現出最壞的品質：*Pressure can bring out the worst in people.* 壓力可以使人現出原形。**do your ˈworst** (of a person 人) to do as much damage or be as unpleasant as possible 進行最大破壞；使盡最壞的招數：*Let them do their worst—we'll fight them every inch of the way.* 隨便他們幹什麼壞事吧，我們一定和他們拚到底。**get the ˈworst of it** to be defeated 遭遇失敗；吃敗仗：*He'd been in a fight and had obviously got the worst of it.* 他打架了，而且顯然是大敗而歸。**if the ˌworst comes to the ˈworst** (*NAmE* also **if ˌworst comes to ˈworst**) if the situation becomes too difficult or dangerous 如果發生最壞的事情；如果情況變得過於艱難（或危險）：*If the worst comes to the worst, we'll just have to sell the house.* 如果最壞的事發生，我們就只好把房子賣掉。**the worst of ˈall (possible) worlds** all the disadvantages of every situation 各種情況的所有不利因素

■ ***verb*** **~ sb** (*old-fashioned* or *formal*) [usually passive] to defeat sb in a fight, a contest or an argument（在打鬥、比賽或辯論中）打敗對方，戰勝 **SYN** **get the better of**

ˈworst-case *adj.* [only before noun] involving the worst situation that could happen 最壞情況的：*In the **worst-case scenario** more than ten thousand people might be affected.* 在最壞的情況下，有一萬多人可能會受到影響。

worst·ed /ˈwʊstɪd/ *noun* [U] a type of cloth made of wool with a smooth surface, used for making clothes 精紡毛料：*a grey worsted suit* 一套灰色的精紡毛料西服

worth 🗝 /wɜːθ; *NAmE* wɜːrθ/ *adj., noun*

■ ***adj.*** [not before noun] (used like a preposition, followed by a noun, pronoun or number, or by the *-ing* form of a verb 用法同介詞，後接名詞、代詞、數字或動詞的 -ing 形式) **1** 🗝 **~ sth** having a value in money, etc. 有…價值；值…錢：*Our house is worth about £100 000.* 我們的房子

W

大約值 10 萬英鎊。◇ *How much is this painting worth?* 這幅畫值多少錢？◇ *to be* ***worth a bomb/packet/fortune*** (= a lot of money) 值一大筆錢 ◇ *It isn't worth much.* 這不值多少錢。◇ *If you answer this question correctly, it's worth five points.* 答對了這道題可以得五分。➲ SYNONYMS at PRICE **2** used to recommend the action mentioned because you think it may be useful, enjoyable, etc.（指行動）值得，有價值：**~ sth** *The museum is certainly worth a visit.* 這家博物館的確值得參觀。◇ **~ doing sth** *This idea is* ***well worth*** *considering.* 這個想法很值得考慮。◇ *It's worth making an appointment before you go.* 去之前預約一下是值得的。**3** **~ sth/doing sth** important, good or enjoyable enough to make sb feel satisfied, especially when difficulty or effort is involved 值得（費周折）：*Was it worth the effort?* 這值得花費力氣嗎？◇ *The new house really wasn't worth all the expense involved.* 這座新房子確實不值這麼多的花費。◇ *The job involves a lot of hard work but* ***it's worth it.*** 這工作需要花費很大力氣，但是值得。◇ *The trip was expensive but it was* ***worth every penny.*** 這次旅行花費很大，但是花的每一分錢都不冤枉。➲ see also WORTHWHILE **4** **~ sth** (of a person 人) having money and possessions of a particular value 擁有…價值的財產：*He's worth £10 million.* 他擁有 1 000 萬英鎊的財產。

IDM **for ˌall sb/it is ˈworth** **1** with great energy, effort and determination 竭盡全力；拚命；十分堅定：*He was rowing for all he was worth.* 他在拚命地划船。**2** in order to get as much as you can from sb/sth 盡量（多得）；拚命（榨取）：*She is milking her success for all it's worth.* 她在利用自己的成功拚命撈好處。**for ˌwhat it's ˈworth** (*informal*) used to emphasize that what you are saying is only your own opinion or suggestion and may not be very helpful（所說的只是個人意見）無論管不管用，不論好壞：*I prefer this colour, for what it's worth.* 無論好壞，我喜歡這個顏色。**(the game is) not worth the ˈcandle** (*old-fashioned, saying*) the advantages to be gained from doing sth are not great enough, considering the effort or cost involved 得不償失；代價太高 **not worth the paper it's ˈwritten/ˈprinted on** (of an agreement or official document 協議或正式文件) having no value, especially legally, or because one of the people involved has no intention of doing what they said they would（尤指在法律上）毫無價值 **ˌworth your/its ˈsalt** deserving respect, especially because you do your job well 稱職；勝任：*Any teacher worth her salt knows that.* 凡稱職的教師都知道這一點。**ˌworth your/its ˌweight in ˈgold** very useful or valuable 非常有用；很有價值：*A good mechanic is worth his weight in gold.* 優秀的技工是不可多得的。**ˌworth sb's ˈwhile** interesting or useful for sb to do 對…有好處（或用處）；值得：*It will be worth your while to come to the meeting.* 你來參加會議對你會大有好處。◇ *He'll do the job if you* ***make it worth his while*** (= pay him well). 你要是給他的報酬豐厚，他會做這份工作的。➲ more at BIRD, JOB

■ ***noun*** [U] **1** **ten dollars', £40, etc. ~ of sth** an amount of sth that has the value mentioned 價值（十元、40 英鎊等）的東西：*The winner will receive ten pounds' worth of books.* 獲勝者將得到價值十英鎊的書籍。◇ *a dollar's worth of change* 一元的零錢 **2** **a week's, month's, etc. ~ of sth** an amount of sth that lasts a week, etc. 能用（一個星期、一個月等）的東西 **3** the financial, practical or moral value of sb/sth 價值；意義；作用：*Their contribution was of great worth.* 他們的貢獻具有偉大的意義。◇ *The activities help children to develop a sense of their own worth.* 這些活動有助於兒童培養自身的價值感。◇ *A good interview enables candidates to prove their worth* (= show how good they are). 好的面試可以讓求職者證明他們的價值。◇ *a personal net worth of $10 million* 價值 1 000 萬元的個人淨資產 **IDM** see CENT *n.*, MONEY

worth·less /ˈwɜːθləs; *NAmE* ˈwɜːrθ-/ *adj.* **1** having no practical or financial value 沒用的；無價值的：*Critics say his paintings are worthless.* 批評家說他的畫毫無價值。**OPP** **valuable** **2** (of a person 人) having no good qualities or useful skills 品質壞的；不中用的：*a worthless individual* 品質壞的人 ◇ *Constant rejections made him feel worthless.* 不斷地遭到拒絕使他覺得一無是處。▸ **worth·less·ness** *noun* [U]：*a sense of worthlessness* 沒有價值的感覺

worth·while /ˌwɜːθˈwaɪl; *NAmE* ˌwɜːrθ-/ *adj.* important, enjoyable, interesting, etc.; worth spending time, money or effort on 重要的；令人愉快的；有趣的；值得花時間（或花錢、努力等）：*It was in aid of a* ***worthwhile cause*** (= a charity, etc.) 這是在為高尚的事業盡一分力。◇ *The smile on her face made it all worthwhile.* 她臉上的笑容使得這一切都非常值得。◇ **~ for sb to do sth** *High prices in the UK* ***make it worthwhile*** *for buyers to look abroad.* 英國的高價足以使買主把視線轉向國外。◇ **~ to do sth** ***It is worthwhile to*** *include really high-quality illustrations.* 把真正高質量的插圖包括進去是值得的。◇ **~ doing sth** *It didn't seem worthwhile writing it all out again.* 把這再都寫出來似乎不必要。**HELP** This word can be written **worth while**, except when it is used before a noun. 除非用在名詞前，否則可寫成 worth while。

worthy /ˈwɜːði; *NAmE* ˈwɜːrði/ *adj., noun*

■ ***adj.*** (**wor·thier**, **wor·thi·est**) **1** **~ (of sb/sth)** (*formal*) having the qualities that deserve sb/sth 值得（或應得）…的：*to be worthy of attention* 值得注意 ◇ *A number of the report's findings are* ***worthy of note.*** 這份報告裏有些調查結果值得注意。◇ *No composer was considered worthy of the name until he had written an opera.* 作曲家直到寫出一部歌劇來才被認為是名副其實。◇ *a worthy champion* (= one who deserved to win) 當之無愧的冠軍 ◇ *He felt he was not worthy of her.* 他覺得他配不上她。**OPP** **unworthy** **2** [usually before noun] having qualities that deserve your respect, attention or admiration 值得尊敬的；值得注意的；值得敬仰的 **SYN** **deserving**：*The money we raise will be going to a very* ***worthy cause.*** 我們籌集的錢款將用於非常崇高的事業。◇ *a worthy member of the team* 一位優秀的隊員 **3** having good qualities but not very interesting or exciting 值得尊敬的，有價值的（但不太令人感興趣或激動的）：*her worthy but dull husband* 她那為人正派卻呆板的丈夫 **4** **~ of sb/sth** typical of what a particular person or thing might do, give, etc. 有（某人或事物）的典型特徵：*He gave a speech that was worthy of Martin Luther King.* 他做了一次典型的馬丁・路德・金式的演講。**5** **-worthy** (in compounds 構成複合詞) deserving, or suitable for, the thing mentioned 值得…的；適於…的：*trustworthy* 值得信任的 ◇ *roadworthy* 適於在公路上行駛的 ▸ **wor·thily** /-ɪli/ *adv.* **worthi·ness** *noun* [U]

■ ***noun*** (*pl.* **-ies**) (often *humorous*) an important person 要人；大人物；知名人士：*a meeting attended by local worthies* 當地知名人士參加的會議

wot (*BrE, non-standard*, often *humorous*) a way of writing 'what', used to show that sb is speaking very informal English（what 的一種寫法，表示說話者用極不正規的英語）什麼：*'Wot's going on?' he shouted.* "出了什麼事？"他喊道。

wotcha /ˈwɒtʃə; *NAmE* ˈwɑːtʃə/ *exclamation* (*BrE, informal*) used as a friendly way of saying hello to a person 你好；嗨：*Wotcha Dave—thanks for coming.* 你好，戴夫，謝謝光臨。

would /*strong form* wʊd; *weak form* wəd; əd/ *modal verb* (*short form* **'d** /d/, *negative* **would not**, *short form* **wouldn't** /ˈwʊdnt/)

1 used as the past form of *will* when reporting what sb has said or thought（will 的過去式，用於轉述）將，將會：*He said he would be here at eight o'clock* (= His words were: 'I will be there at eight o'clock.'). 他說他將在八點鐘到達這裏。◇ *She asked if I would help.* 她問我是否會幫忙。◇ *They told me that they probably wouldn't come.* 他們對我說他們多半不會來。**2** used for talking about the result of an event that you imagine（帶出想像的結果）：*She'd look better with shorter hair.* 她留短髮會顯得好看些。◇ *If you went to see him, he would be delighted.* 倘若你去看望他，他會高興的。◇ *Hurry up! It would be a shame to miss the beginning of the play.* 快點兒！要是錯過這齣戲的開場就太可惜了。◇ *She'd be a fool to accept it* (= if she accepted). 她倘若接受，那她就是個傻瓜。**3** used for describing a possible action or event that did not in fact happen, because sth else did not happen first（表示可能發生的事情沒有發生，是因

W

為之前另一件事沒有發生）就會：*If I had seen the advertisement in time I would have applied for the job.* 我要是及時看到了這則廣告，我就應聘那份工作了。◇ *They would never have met if she hadn't gone to Emma's party.* 她如果不去參加埃瑪的聚會，他們就永遠不會相會。 **4** **so that/in order that sb/sth ~** used for saying why sb does sth （說明動機）：*She burned the letters so that her husband would never read them.* 她把那些信都燒了以便永遠不讓她丈夫看見。 **5** **wish (that) sb/sth ~** used for saying what you want to happen （表達願望）會，將會：*I wish you'd be quiet for a minute.* 我希望你會安靜一會兒。 **6** used to show that sb/sth was not willing or refused to do sth （表示不願意）：*She wouldn't change it, even though she knew it was wrong.* 儘管她知道這錯了，她也不肯改變。◇ *My car wouldn't start this morning.* 今天早晨我的汽車怎麼也發動不起來。 **7** used to ask sb politely to do sth （客氣地請求）：***Would you mind** leaving us alone for a few minutes?* 你不介意讓我們單獨待一會兒吧？◇ *Would you open the door for me, please?* 請你給我開門好嗎？ **8** used in polite offers or invitations （客氣地建議或邀請）：***Would you like** a sandwich?* 您來一個三明治好嗎？◇ *Would you have dinner with me on Friday?* 請你星期五和我一起用餐好嗎？ **9** **~ like, love, hate, prefer, etc. sth/(sb) to do sth | ~ rather do sth/sb did sth** used to say what you like, love, hate, etc. （表示願意、喜歡、不願意等）：*I'd love a coffee.* 我想喝杯咖啡。◇ *I'd be only too glad to help.* 我非常願意幫忙。◇ *I'd hate you to think I was criticizing you.* 我可不願意讓你認為我是在批評你。◇ *I'd rather come with you.* 我倒願意和你一起去。◇ *I'd rather you came with us.* 我倒願意你和我們一塊兒去。 **10** **~ imagine, say, think, etc. (that) ...** used to give opinions that you are not certain about （提出拿不準的看法）：*I would imagine the job will take about two days.* 我猜想這工作大概需要兩天左右的時間吧。◇ *I'd say he was about fifty.* 我猜他五十歲上下。 **11** **I would ...** used to give advice （提出忠告）：***I wouldn't** have any more to drink, **if I were you**.* 我要是你的話，我就不會再喝酒了。 **12** used for talking about things that often happened in the past （帶出過去常見的情況）總是，老是 SYN **used to**：*When my parents were away, my grandmother would take care of me.* 我父母外出的時候，總是祖母照看我。◇ *He'd always be the first to offer to help.* 他總是第一個主動提出幫忙。 **13** (usually *disapproving*) used for talking about behaviour that you think is typical （帶出一貫的行為）總是，愛，好，就：*'She said it was your fault.' 'Well, **she would say that, wouldn't she?** She's never liked me.'* "她說這是你的錯。" "唉，她總是這麼說，不是嗎？她從來就沒有喜歡過我。" **14** **~ that ...** (*literary*) used to express a strong wish （用以表示強烈的願望）：*Would that he had lived to see it.* 他要是能活到看見這該多好哇。 ➲ note at MODAL, SHOULD

'would-be *adj.* [only before noun] used to describe sb who is hoping to become the type of person mentioned （形容想要成為…的人）未來的：*a would-be actor* 想要成為演員的人 ◇ *advice for would-be parents* 對即將成為父母的人的忠告

wound¹ /wuːnd/ *noun, verb* ➲ see also WOUND²

■ ***noun*** **1** an injury to part of the body, especially one in which a hole is made in the skin using a weapon （身體上的）傷，傷口；（武器造成的）傷：*a **leg/head, etc. wound*** 腿傷、頭傷等 ◇ *a **bullet/knife/gunshot/stab wound*** 槍傷；刀傷；槍傷；刺傷 ◇ *an old **war wound*** 戰爭中的舊傷 ◇ *The nurse **cleaned the wound**.* 護士清洗了傷口。◇ *The **wound healed** slowly.* 傷口癒合得很慢。◇ *He died from the wounds he had received to his chest.* 他由於胸部受傷而死亡。 ➲ SYNONYMS at INJURE ➲ COLLOCATIONS at INJURY ➲ see also FLESH WOUND **2** mental or emotional pain caused by sth unpleasant that has been said or done to you （心靈上的）傷，創傷：*After a serious argument, it can take some time for the wounds to heal.* 激烈爭吵之後的感情創傷需要一些時間才能癒合。◇ *Seeing him again **opened up old wounds**.* 再次見到他打開了舊的創傷。 IDM see LICK *v.*, REOPEN, RUB *v.*

■ ***verb*** [often passive] **1** **~ sb/sth** to injure part of the body, especially by making a hole in the skin using a weapon 使（身體）受傷；（用武器）傷害：*He had been wounded in the arm.* 他的手臂受過傷。 **2** **~ sb** to hurt sb's feelings 使（心靈）受傷；傷感情：*She felt **deeply wounded** by his cruel remarks.* 他那刻薄的話語使她感到深受傷害。

wound² /waʊnd/ *past tense, past part.* of WIND ➲ see also WOUND¹

wound·ed /ˈwuːndɪd/ *adj.*

1 injured by a weapon, for example in a war （身體）受傷的；負傷的：*wounded soldiers* 傷兵 ◇ ***seriously wounded*** 傷勢嚴重 ◇ *There were 79 killed and 230 wounded.* 有 79 人死亡，230 人受傷。 **2** feeling emotional pain because of sth unpleasant that sb has said or done （感情）受損害的，受傷害的：*wounded pride* 受到傷害的自尊心 **3** **the wounded** *noun* [pl.] people who are wounded, for example in a war 傷員；傷兵；傷號

wound·ing /ˈwuːndɪŋ/ *adj.* that hurts sb's feelings 傷感情的：*He found her remarks deeply wounding.* 他覺得她的話十分傷人。

wove *past tense* of WEAVE

woven *past part.* of WEAVE

wow /waʊ/ *exclamation, verb, noun*

■ ***exclamation*** (also **wowee** /ˌwaʊˈiː/) (*informal*) used to express great surprise or admiration （表示極大的驚奇或欽佩）哇，呀：*Wow! You look terrific!* 哇！你的樣子太酷了！

■ ***verb*** **~ sb (with sth)** (*informal*) to impress sb very much, especially with a performance （尤指以表演）博得…的稱讚，使喝彩，使叫絕：*He wowed audiences around the country with his new show.* 他以他的新節目博得了全國各地觀眾的交口稱讚。

■ ***noun*** **1** [sing.] (*informal*) a great success 極大的成功；一鳴驚人之舉：*Don't worry. You'll be a wow.* 別擔心。你會一鳴驚人的。 **2** [U] (*technical* 術語) gradual changes in the PITCH of sound played on a record or tape（唱片或錄音磁帶逐漸出現的）走調，失真，顫動 ➲ compare FLUTTER

ˈwow factor *noun* [sing.] (*informal*) the quality sth has of being very impressive or surprising to people 令人叫好的性質；使人驚奇的因素：*If you want to sell your house quickly, it needs a wow factor.* 若想很快把房子賣掉，就得找個賣點。

wow·ser /ˈwaʊzə(r)/ *noun* (*AustralE, NZE, informal*) **1** a person who criticizes people who are enjoying themselves 批評別人玩樂者；掃別人興的人 SYN **killjoy** **2** a person who does not drink alcohol 不喝酒的人 SYN **teetotaller**

WPC /ˌdʌbljuː piː ˈsiː/ *noun* (*BrE*) the abbreviation for 'woman police constable' (a woman police officer of the lowest rank) 女警察（全寫為 woman police constable，警銜最低的女警察）：*WPC (Linda) Green* （琳達）格林女警察

wpm *abbr.* words per minute 每分鐘字數；字 / 分鐘：*to type at 60 wpm* 每分鐘打 60 個字

WRAC /ræk; ˌdʌbljuː ɑːr eɪ ˈsiː/ *abbr.* (in Britain) Women's Royal Army Corps （英國）皇家陸軍婦女隊

wrack = RACK *v.*

WRAF /ræf; ˌdʌbljuː ɑːr eɪ ˈef/ *abbr.* (in Britain) Women's Royal Air Force （英國）皇家空軍婦女隊

wraith /reɪθ/ *noun* the GHOST of a person that is seen a short time before or after that person dies（臨終前後顯現的）活人靈魂，鬼魂 SYN **spectre**：*a wraith-like figure* (= a very thin, pale person) 瘦削蒼白、幽靈似的人

wran·gle /ˈræŋɡl/ *noun, verb*

■ ***noun*** **~ (with sb)(over sth) | ~ (between A and B)** an argument that is complicated and continues over a long period of time （長時間的）爭論，爭吵：*a legal wrangle between the company and their suppliers* 這家公司與各供貨商之間長期的法律糾紛 ▶ **wran·gling** *noun* [U, C]

■ ***verb*** [I] **~ (with sb) (over/about sth)** to argue angrily and usually for a long time about sth （通常為長時間地）爭吵，爭辯：*They're still wrangling over the financial details.* 他們仍在為財務細節爭吵。

W

wran·gler /ˈræŋɡlə(r)/ *noun* (*NAmE, informal*) a COWBOY or a COWGIRL, especially one who takes care of horses （尤指放馬的）牛仔，女牛仔

wrap /ræp/ *verb, noun*

■ ***verb*** (**-pp-**) **1** [T] **~ sth (up) (in sth)** to cover sth completely in paper or other material, for example when you are giving it as a present 包，裹（禮物等）：*He spent the evening wrapping up the Christmas presents.* 他花了一個晚上的時間把聖誕禮物都包了起來。◊ *individually wrapped chocolates* 單塊包裝的巧克力 ➲ see also GIFT-WRAP **2** [T] to cover sth/sb in material, for example in order to protect it/them 用…包裹（或包紮、覆蓋等）：**~ A (up) in B** *Wrap the meat in foil before you cook it.* 把肉用錫箔裹起來後再烹調。◊ *I wrapped the baby (up) in a blanket.* 我用毯子把嬰兒裹了起來。◊ **~ B round/around A** *I wrapped a blanket around the baby.* 我用毯子把嬰兒裹了起來。➲ see also SHRINK-WRAPPED **3** [T] **~ sth around/round sth/sb** to put sth firmly around sth/sb 用…纏繞（或圍緊）：*A scarf was wrapped around his neck.* 他的脖子上圍着一條圍巾。◊ *His arms were wrapped around her waist.* 他的雙臂緊緊環抱她的腰。 **4** [T, I] (*computing* 計) to cause text to be carried over to a new line automatically as you reach the end of the previous line; to be carried over in this way （使文字）換行：**~ sth (around/round)** *How can I wrap the text around?* 我怎麼才能使文本換行呢？◊ **~ (around/round)** *The text wraps around if it is too long to fit the screen.* 如果文本太長，在顯示屏放不下的話，會自動換行。➲ compare UNWRAP

IDM **be ˌwrapped ˈup in sb/sth** to be so involved with sb/sth that you do not pay enough attention to other people or things 專心致志於；全神貫注於；完全沉浸於 **SYN** **absorbed, engrossed** ➲ more at LITTLE FINGER

PHR V **ˌwrap ˈup | ˌwrap it ˈup** (*slang*) usually used as an order to tell sb to stop talking or causing trouble, etc. 住口；閉嘴；別再搗亂 **ˌwrap ˈup | ˌwrap sb/yourself ˈup** to put warm clothes on sb/yourself （使）穿得暖和：*She told them to* ***wrap up warm/warmly****.* 她叫他們穿暖和點。**ˌwrap sth↔ˈup** (*informal*) to complete sth such as an agreement or a meeting in an acceptable way 圓滿完成，順利結束（協議或會議等）：*That just about wraps it up for today.* 這就差不多給今天畫了個圓滿的句號。

■ ***noun*** **1** [C] a piece of cloth that a woman wears around her shoulders for decoration or to keep warm （女用）披肩，圍巾 **2** [U] paper, plastic, etc. that is used for wrapping things in 包裹（或包裝）材料：*We stock a wide range of cards and* ***gift wrap****.* 我們備有各種各樣的賀卡和禮品包裝材料。➲ see also PLASTIC WRAP **3** [sing.] used when making a film/movie to say that filming has finished （拍攝電影時）完成拍攝，停機：*Cut! That's a wrap.* 停！就拍攝到這兒。 **4** [C] a type of SANDWICH made with a cold TORTILLA rolled around meat or vegetables 墨西哥捲（用凍玉米薄餅裹肉或蔬菜而成的三明治）

IDM **under ˈwraps** (*informal*) being kept secret until some time in the future 保密；隱藏：*Next year's collection is still being kept under wraps.* 明年的時裝系列仍在保密之中。

W

ˈwrap-around *adj.* **1** curving or stretching round at the sides 彎曲（或伸展）至兩邊的：*wrap-around sunglasses* 面罩型太陽眼鏡 **2** (of a piece of clothing 衣服) having one part that is pulled over to cover another part at the front and then loosely fastened 圍裹式的：*a wrap-around skirt* 裹裙

wrap·arounds /ˈræpəraʊndz/ *noun* [pl.] a pair of SUNGLASSES that fit closely and curve round the sides of the head 面罩型太陽眼鏡

wrapped /ræpt/ *adj.* (*AustralE, informal*) extremely pleased 極高興的；十分滿意的：*The minister declared that he was wrapped.* 部長公開表示他特別滿意。

wrap·per /ˈræpə(r)/ *noun* **1** a piece of paper, plastic, etc. that is wrapped around sth, especially food, when you buy it in order to protect it and keep it clean （食品等的）包裝材料，包裝紙，包裝塑料：(*BrE*) *sweet wrappers* 糖果包裝紙 ◊ (*NAmE*) *candy wrappers* 糖果包裝紙 **2** (*WAfrE*) a piece of cloth that is worn as an item of clothing around the waist and legs （腰際和腿部的）圍裹式服裝

wrap·ping /ˈræpɪŋ/ *noun* [U] (also **wrappings** [pl.]) paper, plastic, etc. used for covering sth in order to protect it 包裝材料；包裝紙；包裝塑料：*She tore the cellophane wrapping off the box.* 她把包裝盒子的玻璃紙撕了下來。◊ *shrink wrapping* (= plastic designed to SHRINK around objects so that it fits them tightly) 收縮塑料薄膜 ◊ *The painting was still in its wrappings.* 那幅畫仍然包裝着。

ˈwrapping paper *noun* [U] coloured paper used for wrapping presents （包裝禮品的）彩色包裝紙：***a piece/sheet/roll of wrapping paper*** 一塊／一張／一捲彩色包裝紙

wrasse /ræs/ *noun* (*pl.* **wrasse** or **wrasses**) a sea fish with thick lips and strong teeth 隆頭魚

wrath /rɒθ; *NAmE* ræθ/ *noun* [U] (*old-fashioned* or *formal*) extreme anger 盛怒；震怒；怒火：*the wrath of God* 上帝的憤怒 ▸ **wrath·ful** /-fl/ *adj.* **wrath·ful·ly** *adv.*

wreak /riːk/ *verb* **~ sth (on sb)** (*formal*) to do great damage or harm to sb/sth 造成（巨大的破壞或傷害）：*Their policies would* ***wreak havoc*** *on the economy.* 他們的政策將對經濟造成巨大的破壞。◊ *He swore to* ***wreak vengeance*** *on those who had betrayed him.* 他發誓要對背叛他的人進行報復。

wreath /riːθ/ *noun* (*pl.* **wreaths** /riːðz/) **1** an arrangement of flowers and leaves, especially in the shape of a circle, placed on graves, etc. as a sign of respect for sb who has died 花圈（用於祭奠）：*The Queen* ***laid a wreath*** *at the war memorial.* 女王向陣亡將士紀念碑獻了花圈。 **2** an arrangement of flowers and/or leaves in the shape of a circle, traditionally hung on doors as a decoration at Christmas 花環（傳統上聖誕節時掛在門上）：*a holly wreath* 聖誕冬青花環 **3** a circle of flowers or leaves worn on the head, and used in the past as a sign of honour 花冠（舊時用作榮譽的象徵）：*a laurel wreath* 桂冠 **4** (*literary*) a circle of smoke, cloud, etc. （煙、雲等的）圈，繚繞

wreathe /riːð/ *verb* (*formal*) **1** [T, usually passive] **~ sth (in/with sth)** to surround or cover sth 環繞；覆蓋；籠罩：*The mountain tops were wreathed in mist.* 山頂籠罩在薄霧之中。◊ (*figurative*) *Her face was* ***wreathed in smiles*** (= she was smiling a lot). 她臉上樂開了花。 **2** [I] **+ adv./prep.** to move slowly and lightly, especially in circles 緩緩移動；盤繞；纏繞；縈繞 **SYN** **weave**：*smoke wreathing into the sky* 裊裊升空的煙

wreck /rek/ *noun, verb*

■ ***noun*** **1** a ship that has sunk or that has been very badly damaged 沉船；嚴重損毀的船 ➲ see also SHIPWRECK **2** a car, plane, etc. that has been very badly damaged in an accident （事故中）遭嚴重毀壞的汽車（或飛機等）：*Two passengers are still trapped in the wreck.* 有兩名乘客仍被困在失事的車輛裏。➲ SYNONYMS at CRASH **3** [usually sing.] (*informal*) a person who is in a bad physical or mental condition （身體或精神上）受到嚴重損傷的人：*Physically, I was a total wreck.* 從身體上說，我完全是一個廢人。◊ *The interview reduced him to* ***a nervous wreck****.* 這次面試使得他的精神高度緊張。 **4** (*informal*) a vehicle, building, etc. that is in very bad condition 狀況非常糟糕的車輛（或建築物等）：*The house was a wreck when we bought it.* 我們買下這座房子時，它破爛不堪。◊ (*figurative*) *They still hoped to salvage something from the wreck of their marriage.* 他們仍然希望從他們破碎的婚姻中挽回點什麼。 **5** (*NAmE*) = CRASH *n.* (1)：***a car/train wreck*** 汽車／火車失事

■ ***verb*** **1 ~ sth** to damage or destroy sth 破壞；損壞；毀壞：*The building had been wrecked by the explosion.* 那座樓房被炸毀了。◊ *The road was littered with wrecked cars.* 公路上到處都是被撞壞的汽車。 **2 ~ sth (for sb)** to spoil sth completely 毀滅；毀掉：*The weather wrecked all our plans.* 天氣把我們的計劃全都毀了。◊ *A serious injury nearly wrecked his career.* 一次重傷差點兒葬送了他的前程。 **3** [usually passive] **~ sth** to damage a ship so much that it sinks or can no longer sail 使（船舶）失事；使遇難；使下沉：*The ship was wrecked off the* *coast of France.* 那艘船在法國的沿岸失事。➲ see also SHIPWRECK

wreck·age /ˈrekɪdʒ/ *noun* [U] the parts of a vehicle, building, etc. that remain after it has been badly damaged or destroyed（車輛等的）殘骸；（建築物等的）廢墟：*A few survivors were pulled from the wreckage.* 從廢墟中扒出了幾個幸存者。◇ *Pieces of wreckage were found ten miles away from the scene of the explosion.* 從離爆炸現場十英里外的地方發現了殘骸碎片。◇ (*figurative*) *Could nothing be rescued from the wreckage of her dreams?* 難道從她那破滅的夢想中就找不出一絲希望了嗎？

wrecked /rekt/ *adj.* **1** [only before noun] having been wrecked 失事的；遇難的；毀壞的：*a wrecked ship/marriage* 遇難的船隻；破裂的婚姻 **2** [not before noun] (*BrE, slang*) very drunk 喝得爛醉

wreck·er /ˈrekə(r)/ *noun* **1** a person who ruins another person's plans, relationship, etc.（對他人計劃、關係等的）破壞者 **2** (*NAmE*) a vehicle used for moving other vehicles that have been damaged in an accident 救險車

ˈwrecking ball *noun* a heavy metal ball that swings from a CRANE and is used to hit a building to make it fall down（懸掛於吊車供拆除建築物用的）破碎球，落錘

wren /ren/ *noun* a very small brown bird 鷦鷯（形小，淺褐色）

wrench /rentʃ/ *verb, noun*

■ ***verb*** **1** [T, I] to pull or twist sth/sb/yourself suddenly and violently 猛拉；猛扭；猛擰 SYN **jerk**：**~ (sth/sb/yourself) + adv./prep.** *The bag was wrenched from her grasp.* 那隻包從她緊握的手裏被奪了出來。◇ *He grabbed Ben, wrenching him away from his mother.* 他抓住本，把他從他母親那裏一把搶走了。◇ (*figurative*) *Guy wrenched his mind back to the present.* 蓋伊的思緒猛地回到現在。◇ **~ (sth/sb/yourself) + adj.** *They wrenched the door open.* 他們猛地把門拉開了。◇ *She managed to wrench herself free.* 她終於設法掙脱出來。 **2** [T] **~ sth** to twist and injure a part of your body, especially your ankle or shoulder 扭傷（腳踝、肩膀等）SYN **twist**：*She wrenched her knee when she fell.* 她跌倒時把膝蓋扭傷了。 **3** [T, I] (*formal*) to make sb feel great pain or unhappiness, especially so that they make a sound or cry 使痛苦，使十分難過（尤指以致哭喊出聲）：**~ (sth) (from sb)** *His words wrenched a sob from her.* 他的話使得她難過得哭泣起來。◇ *a wrenching experience* 苦難的經歷 ◇ **~ at sth** *Her words wrenched at my heart.* 她的話使得我心如刀絞。➲ see also GUT-WRENCHING

■ ***noun*** **1** (*especially NAmE*) (*BrE* usually **span·ner**) [C] a metal tool with a specially shaped end for holding and turning things, including one which can be adjusted to fit objects of different sizes, also called a MONKEY WRENCH or an ADJUSTABLE SPANNER 扳鉗；扳手 ➲ **VISUAL VOCAB** page V20 **2** [sing.] pain or unhappiness that you feel when you have to leave a person or place that you love（離別的）痛苦，難受：*Leaving home was a terrible wrench for me.* 對我來說離開家是件十分痛苦的事。 **3** [C, usually sing.] a sudden and violent twist or pull 猛扭；猛拉：*She stumbled and gave her ankle a painful wrench.* 她絆了一跤，把腳踝崴得很痛。

IDM **throw a ˈwrench in/into sth** (*NAmE, informal*) = THROW A MONKEY WRENCH IN/INTO STH at MONKEY WRENCH

wrest /rest/ *verb*

PHR V **ˈwrest sth from sb/sth** (*formal*) **1** to take sth such as power or control from sb/sth with great effort 攫取，搶奪（權力）：*They attempted to **wrest control** of the town from government forces.* 他們企圖從政府軍手中奪取對這個城鎮的控制權。 **2** to take sth from sb that they do not want to give, suddenly or violently 搶，奪（物品）SYN **wrench**：*He wrested the gun from my grasp.* 他把槍從我手裏搶走了。

wres·tle /ˈresl/ *verb* **1** [I, T] to fight sb by holding them and trying to throw or force them to the ground, sometimes as a sport 摔跤：*As a boy he had boxed and wrestled.* 他小時候練過拳擊和摔跤。◇ **~ with sb** *Armed guards wrestled with the intruder.* 武裝警衛和闖入者扭打起來。◇ **~ sb (+ adv./prep.)** *Shoppers wrestled the raider to the ground.* 購物的人把搶劫者摔倒在地上。 **2** [I, T] to struggle to deal with sth that is difficult 奮力對付；努力處理；全力解決 SYN **battle, grapple**：**~ (with) sth** *She had spent the whole weekend wrestling with the problem.* 她整個週末都在絞盡腦汁處理這個問題。◇ *He wrestled with the controls as the plane plunged.* 飛機向下衝時，他竭力控制住操縱裝置。◇ **~ to do sth** *She has been wrestling to raise the money all year.* 她一年來一直在想方設法籌集這筆資金。

wrest·ler /ˈreslə(r)/ *noun* a person who takes part in the sport of wrestling 摔跤運動員

wrest·ling /ˈreslɪŋ/ *noun* [U] a sport in which two people fight by holding each other and trying to throw or force the other one to the ground 摔跤運動

wretch /retʃ/ *noun* **1** a person that you feel sympathy or pity for 不幸的人；可憐的人：*a poor wretch* 可憐的人 **2** (often *humorous*) an evil, unpleasant or annoying person 惡棍；壞蛋；無賴；無恥之徒

wretch·ed /ˈretʃɪd/ *adj.* **1** (of a person 人) feeling ill/sick or unhappy 感到不適的；難受的；不愉快的：*You look wretched—what's wrong?* 你看起來愁眉苦臉的，怎麼啦？◇ *I felt wretched about the way things had turned out.* 事情落了這麼個結局，我感到很難受。 **2** (*formal*) extremely bad or unpleasant 極壞的；惡劣的 SYN **awful**：*She had a wretched time of it at school.* 她上學時的日子十分難熬。◇ *The animals are kept in the most wretched conditions.* 這些動物的飼養條件極其惡劣。 **3** (*formal*) making you feel sympathy or pity 可憐的；悲慘的 SYN **pitiful**：*She finally agreed to have the wretched animal put down.* 她最後同意把這頭可憐的動物人道毀滅。 **4** [only before noun] (*informal*) used to show that you think that sb/sth is extremely annoying（表示憎惡）該死的，無法容忍的：*Is it that wretched woman again?* 這又是那個該死的女人吧？▸ **wretch·ed·ly** *adv.* **wretch·ed·ness** *noun* [U]

wrig·gle /ˈrɪgl/ *verb, noun*

■ ***verb*** **1** [I, T] to twist and turn your body or part of it with quick short movements 扭動身體；扭來扭去 SYN **wiggle**：**~ (about/around)** *The baby was wriggling around on my lap.* 嬰兒在我大腿上扭來扭去。◇ **~ sth** *She wriggled her toes.* 她扭動着腳趾。 **2** [I, T] to move somewhere by twisting and turning your body or part of it 蠕動；甩動而行；蜿蜒行進 SYN **squirm**：(**+ adv./prep.**) *The fish wriggled out of my fingers.* 那條魚從我指縫中一甩身溜走了。◇ **+ adj.** *She managed to wriggle free.* 她設法扭動着掙脱了。◇ **~ your way/yourself + adv./prep.** *They wriggled their way through the tunnel.* 他們在地道中蜿蜒行進。

PHR V **ˌwriggle ˈout of sth/out of doing sth** (*informal, disapproving*) to avoid doing sth that you should do, especially by thinking of clever excuses 耍滑不做，逃避（應做的事）：*He tried desperately to wriggle out of giving a clear answer.* 他竭力支支吾吾不給予明確的回答。

■ ***noun*** [usually sing.] an act of wriggling 扭動；蠕動；蜿蜒行進

wring /rɪŋ/ *verb* (**wrung**, **wrung** /rʌŋ/) **1 ~ sth (out)** to twist and squeeze clothes, etc. in order to get the water out of them 擰，絞，擰出，絞出（衣服等中的水）➲ picture at SQUEEZE **2 ~ sth** if you **wring** a bird's neck, you twist it in order to kill the bird 擰，扭（鳥的脖子，以將其殺死）

IDM **ˌwring sb's ˈhand** to squeeze sb's hand very tightly when you shake hands（握手時）攥緊…的手 **ˌwring your ˈhands** to hold your hands together, and twist and squeeze them in a way that shows you are anxious or upset, especially when you cannot change the situation（尤指出於焦急或煩惱）扭絞雙手 **ˌwring sb's ˈneck** (*informal*) when you say that you will **wring sb's neck**, you mean that you are very angry or annoyed with them（表示憤怒或氣惱）擰斷…的脖子，非掐死…不可

PHR V **ˈwring sth from/out of sb** to obtain sth from sb with difficulty, especially by putting pressure on them 從…處費力弄到；從…壓榨出 SYN **extract**

wring·er /ˈrɪŋə(r)/ *noun* = MANGLE
IDM **go through the ˈwringer** (*informal*) to have a difficult or unpleasant experience, or a series of them 受盡磨難；歷盡艱難

ˌwringing ˈwet *adj.* (especially of clothes 尤指衣服) very wet 很濕的；濕得能擰出水的

wrin·kle /ˈrɪŋkl/ *noun, verb*
■ **noun** **1** a line or small fold in your skin, especially on your face, that forms as you get older（尤指臉上的）皺紋：*There were fine wrinkles around her eyes.* 她眼角上出現了魚尾紋。➲ COLLOCATIONS at PHYSICAL **2** [usually pl.] a small fold that you do not want in a piece of cloth or paper（布或紙上的）皺褶，皺痕 SYN **crease**
■ **verb** **1** [T, I] to make the skin on your face form into lines or folds; to form lines or folds in this way（使臉上）起皺紋；皺起：**~ sth (up)** *She wrinkled up her nose in distaste.* 她厭惡地皺起鼻子。◇ *He wrinkled his brow in concentration.* 他全神貫注地鎖緊眉頭。◇ **~ (up)** *His face wrinkled in a grin.* 他咧嘴一笑滿臉都是皺紋。 **2** [I, T] **~ (sth)** to form raised folds or lines in an untidy way; to make sth do this（使）起皺褶：*Her stockings were wrinkling at the knees.* 她長襪的膝蓋處起了皺褶。

wrin·kled /ˈrɪŋkld/ *adj.* (of skin, clothing, etc. 皮膚、衣服等) having wrinkles 有皺紋的

wrink·ling /ˈrɪŋklɪŋ/ *noun* [U] the process by which WRINKLES form in the skin（皮膚）起皺紋

wrin·kly /ˈrɪŋkli/ *adj., noun*
■ **adj.** (*informal*) (of skin, clothing, etc. 皮膚、衣服等) having WRINKLES 皺的；有皺紋的
■ **noun** (*pl.* **-ies**) (*BrE, informal*) an offensive word for an old person, used by younger people（對老年人的冒犯稱呼）老皺皮

wrist 0‑‑ /rɪst/ *noun*
the joint between the hand and the arm 手腕；腕關節：*She's broken her wrist.* 她的腕關節骨折了。◇ *He wore a copper bracelet* **on his wrist**. 他腕上戴着隻銅手鐲。➲ VISUAL VOCAB page V59 **IDM** see SLAP *n.*

wrist·band /ˈrɪstbænd/ *noun* a strip of material worn around the wrist, as a decoration, to absorb sweat during exercise, or to show support for sth 腕帶；腕套；腕箍：*He was wearing an anti-racism wristband.* 他戴着一隻反種族歧視的腕帶。

wrist·watch /ˈrɪstwɒtʃ; *NAmE* -wɑːtʃ/ *noun* a watch that you wear on your wrist 手錶

writ /rɪt/ *noun, verb*
■ **noun** **~ (for sth) (against sb)** a legal document from a court telling sb to do or not to do sth（法庭的）令狀，書面命令：*The company has been* **served with a writ** *for breach of contract.* 這家公司因違約已接到法院令狀。◇ *We fully intend to* **issue a writ** *against the newspaper.* 我們一心想傳訊這家報紙。➲ see also HOLY WRIT
■ **verb** (*old use*) *past part.* of WRITE
IDM **ˌwrit ˈlarge** (*literary*) **1** easy to see or understand 顯而易見的；公然：*Mistrust was writ large on her face.* 她臉上明顯流露出不信任的神情。 **2** (used after a noun 用於名詞後) being a large or obvious example of the thing mentioned 明擺着；典型：*This is deception writ large.* 這是明目張膽的欺騙。

W

write 0‑‑ /raɪt/ *verb* (**wrote** /rəʊt; *NAmE* roʊt/, **writ·ten** /ˈrɪtn/)
▸ **LETTERS/NUMBERS** 字母；數字 **1** 0‑‑ [I, T] to make letters or numbers on a surface, especially using a pen or a pencil 書寫；寫字：*In some countries children don't start learning to* **read and write** *until they are six.* 有些國家的兒童到了六歲才開始讀書寫字。◇ **~ in/on/with sth** *Please write in pen on both sides of the paper.* 請用筆在紙的正反兩面書寫。◇ *I haven't got anything to write with.* 我沒有筆可以寫字。◇ **~ sth** *Write your name at the top of the paper.* 請把名字寫在紙的頂端。◇ *The teacher wrote the answers on the board.* 老師把答案寫了在黑板上。◇ *The 'b' had been wrongly written as a 'd'.* * b 錯寫成 d 了。
▸ **BOOK/MUSIC/PROGRAM** 書籍；音樂；程序 **2** 0‑‑ [T, I] to produce sth in written form so that people can read, perform or use it, etc. 寫作；作曲；編寫：**~ sth** *to write a novel/a song/an essay/a computer program, etc.* 寫小說、寫歌、寫散文、編電腦程序等 ◇ *Who was 'The Grapes of Wrath' written by?* 《憤怒的葡萄》是誰寫的？◇ *Which opera did Verdi write first?* 威爾地最早寫的是哪一部歌劇？◇ **~ sth about/on sth** *He hopes to write a book about his experiences one day.* 他希望有一天寫一部關於自己經歷的書。◇ *She had to write a report on the project.* 她必須就這個項目寫一份報告。◇ **~ (about sth)** *I wanted to travel and then write about it.* 我本想去旅行，然後把見聞寫下來。◇ *He writes for the 'New Yorker'* (= works as a writer). 他為《紐約客》雜誌撰稿。◇ *No decision has been made* **at the time of writing**. 寫這個的時候尚未作出決定。◇ **~ sb sth** *She wrote him several poems.* 她為他寫了幾首詩。
▸ **A LETTER** 信 **3** 0‑‑ [I, T] to put information, a message of good wishes, etc. in a letter and send it to sb 寫信：*Bye! Don't forget to write.* 再見！別忘了寫信。◇ *Can you write and confirm your booking?* 你能寫信來確認你的預訂項目嗎？◇ *I'm writing to enquire about language courses.* 特此致函詢問有關語言課程事宜。◇ **~ to sb** *She wrote to him in France.* 她給他往法國寫信。◇ **~ sth (to sb)** *I wrote a letter to the Publicity Department.* 我給宣傳部寫了一封信。◇ **~ sb sth** *I wrote the Publicity Department a letter.* 我給宣傳部寫了一封信。◇ **~ that ...** *She wrote that they were all fine.* 她信上說他們一切安好。◇ **~ sb** (*NAmE*) *Write me while you're away.* 你外出期間給我寫信。◇ **~ sb that ...** (*NAmE*) *He wrote me that he would be arriving Monday.* 他給我寫信說他將於星期一到達。◇ **~ doing sth** *They wrote thanking us for the present.* 他們寫信來感謝我們贈送的禮物。
▸ **STATE IN WRITING** 書面陳述 **4** 0‑‑ [T, I] to state the information or the words mentioned 寫道；（以文字）說：**~ that ...** *In his latest book he writes that the theory has since been disproved.* 他在最近的一部書裏寫道，那個理論後來已被證明不能成立。◇ **~ of sth** *Ancient historians wrote of a lost continent beneath the ocean.* 古代史學家寫過有關一個沉沒海底大陸的事跡。◇ **+ speech** *'Of all my books,' wrote Dickens, 'I like this the best.'* 狄更斯寫道："在我所有的書中，我最喜歡這本"。
▸ **CHEQUE/FORM** 支票；表格 **5** 0‑‑ [T] to put information in the appropriate places on a cheque or other form 開（支票等）；填寫（表格等）：**~ sth (out)** *to write out a cheque* 開一張支票 ◇ **~ sb (out) sth** *I'll write you a receipt.* 我來給你開一張收據。
▸ **COMPUTING** 計算機技術 **6** [T, I] **~ (sth) to/onto sth** to record data in the memory of a computer 將（數據）寫入（存貯器）：*An error was reported when he tried to write data to the file for the first time.* 當他第一次嘗試把數據寫入文檔時，報告說有錯。
▸ **OF PEN/PENCIL** 筆 **7** [I] to work correctly or in the way mentioned 好使；能使用；以…方式寫：*This pen won't write.* 這支鋼筆不好使。
IDM **be written all over sb's ˈface** (of a feeling 感情) to be very obvious to other people from the expression on sb's face 形之於色；表現得十分明顯：*Guilt was written all over his face.* 他滿臉愧疚。 **have sth/sb written all ˈover it/sb** (*informal*) to show clearly the quality mentioned or the influence of the person mentioned 明顯有（某性質）；顯然受到（某人影響）：*It was a performance with star quality written all over it.* 這次演出顯然明星氣派十足。◇ *This essay has got Mike written all over it.* 這篇散文儼然是邁克的手筆。 **nothing (much) to write ˈhome about** (*informal*) not especially good; ordinary 不特別好；很普通；一般 **that's all she ˈwrote** (*NAmE, informal*) used when you are stating that there is nothing more that can be said about sth or that sth is completely finished（表示沒有其他要說或某事已徹底結束）就這麼多，到此結束 ➲ more at WORTH *adj.*
PHR V **ˌwrite aˈway** = WRITE OFF/AWAY **ˌwrite ˈback (to sb)** 0‑‑ to write sb a letter replying to their letter（給某人）寫回信，覆信 SYN **reply**：*I'm afraid I never wrote back.* 我恐怕從未寫過回信。◇ *She wrote back saying that she couldn't come.* 她回信說她來不了。
ˌwrite sth↔ˈdown **1** 0‑‑ to write sth on paper, especially in order to remember or record it 寫下；記錄下：*Write down the address before you forget it.* 把地址記下來，免得忘了。 **2** (*business* 商) to reduce the value of ASSETS when stating it in a company's accounts 減記，

劃減（資產的賬面價值） ➲ related noun WRITE-DOWN **ˌwrite ˈin (to sb/sth) (for sth)** to write a letter to an organization or a company, for example to ask about sth or to express an opinion 致函（某機構）（表達意見等）：*I'll write in for more information.* 我要寫信索取更詳細的材料。 **ˌwrite sb/sth↔ˈin** (*NAmE, politics* 政) to add an extra name to your voting paper in an election in order to be able to vote for them （在選票上）寫上非候選人姓名 ➲ related noun WRITE-IN **ˌwrite sth ˈinto sth** to include a rule or condition in a contract or an agreement when it is made 把…寫入（合同或協議） **ˌwrite ˈoff/aˈway (to sb/sth) (for sth)** to write to an organization or a company, usually in order to ask them to send you sth 致函（某機構）（索取資料等） SYN **send off**：*I've written off for the catalogue.* 我已去函索取商品目錄。 **ˌwrite sth↔ˈoff 1** (*business* 商) to cancel a debt; to recognize that sth is a failure, has no value, etc. 註銷，銷記（賬項、資產等）：*to write off a debt/an investment* 註銷一筆債務 / 一項投資 **2** (*BrE*) to damage sth, especially a vehicle, so badly that it cannot be repaired 把（車輛等）毀壞，報廢 ➲ related noun WRITE-OFF ➲ see also TOTAL *v.* (3) **ˌwrite sb/sth↔ˈoff (as sth)** to decide that sb/sth is a failure or not worth paying any attention to 認定…失敗（或沒有價值、不可救藥等） SYN **dismiss** **ˌwrite sth↔ˈout** to write sth on paper, including all the details, especially a piece of work or an account of sth 把…全部寫出 ➲ see also WRITE (5) **ˌwrite sb↔ˈout (of sth)** to remove a character from a regular series on television or radio 去掉（系列電視劇或廣播劇中的角色） **ˌwrite sth↔ˈup** to record sth in writing in a full and complete form, often using notes that you made earlier （利用筆記等）詳細寫出：*to write up your notes/the minutes of a meeting* 把筆記 / 會議記錄整理好 ➲ related noun WRITE-UP

ˈwrite-back *noun* [C, U] (*business* 商) a situation where an ASSET gets a value which it was thought to have lost; an amount of money entered in the financial records because of this （對呆賬的）撥回；撥回資產的賬面值

ˈwrite-down *noun* (*business* 商) a reduction in the value of ASSETS, etc. （資產等賬面價值的）減記，劃減

ˈwrite-in *noun* (*US*) a vote for sb who is not an official candidate in an election, in which you write their name on your BALLOT PAPER 投給非候選人的票

ˈwrite-off *noun* **1** (*BrE*) a vehicle that has been so badly damaged in an accident that it is not worth spending money to repair it 報廢車輛 **2** [sing.] (*informal*) a period of time during which you do not achieve anything 無所作為的一段時間：*With meetings and phone calls, yesterday was a complete write-off.* 昨天都在開會和打電話，瞎忙了一天。 **3 ~ (of sth)** (*business* 商) an act of cancelling a debt and accepting that it will never be paid （債項的）註銷，銷記

ˌwrite-proˈtect *verb* **~ sth** (*computing* 計) to protect the information on a computer disk from being changed or DELETED (= destroyed) 給（磁盤信息）寫保護；設法防寫保護

writer 🔑 /ˈraɪtə(r)/ *noun*
1 🔑 a person whose job is writing books, stories, articles, etc. 作家；作者；著者：*writers of poetry* 詩人 ◊ *a **travel/cookery, etc. writer*** 遊記作家、寫菜譜的人等 **2** 🔑 a person who has written a particular thing 寫…的人；執筆者；撰寫人：*the writer of this letter* 寫這封信的人 **3** 🔑 (with an adjective 與形容詞連用) a person who forms letters in a particular way when they are writing 寫字…的人：*a messy writer* 書寫潦草的人

ˌwriter's ˈblock *noun* [U] a problem that writers sometimes have when they cannot think of what to write and have no new ideas （寫作人的）靈感障礙，神思枯竭，寫作筆障

ˌwriter's ˈcramp *noun* [U] a pain or stiff feeling in the hand caused by writing for a long time 書寫痙攣（長時間寫字造成的手部疼痛或僵硬感）

ˈwrite-up *noun* an article in a newspaper or magazine in which sb writes what they think about a new book, play, product, etc. （報刊上的）評論，評述，評介

writhe /raɪð/ *verb* [I] **~ (about/around) (in/with sth)** to twist or move your body without stopping, often because you are in great pain （常指因劇痛不停地）扭動，翻滾：*She was writhing around on the floor in agony.* 她痛得在地板上直打滾。◊ *The snake writhed and hissed.* 那蛇蠕動着，發出嘶嘶的聲音。◊ (*figurative*) *He was writhing* (= suffering a lot) *with embarrassment.* 他難堪得無地自容。

writ·ing 🔑 /ˈraɪtɪŋ/ *noun*
1 🔑 [U] the activity of writing, in contrast to reading, speaking, etc. 寫；書寫；寫作：*Our son's having problems with his **reading and writing*** (= at school) 我們兒子在讀寫方面有困難。◊ *a **writing case*** (= containing paper, pens, etc.) 文具盒 **2** 🔑 [U] the activity of writing books, articles, etc., especially as a job （專職）寫作；著書立說：*Only later did she discover a talent for writing.* 她到了較後期才發現自己的寫作天分。◊ *He is leaving the band to concentrate on his writing.* 他要離開樂隊去專職寫作。◊ ***creative writing*** 文學創作 ◊ ***feminist/travel, etc. writing*** 女權主義文章、遊記等的寫作 ➲ see also SONGWRITING **3** 🔑 [U] books, articles, etc. in general 著作；文字作品；文章：*The review is a brilliant piece of writing.* 這篇評論很精彩。**4** 🔑 **writings** [pl.] a group of pieces of writing, especially by a particular person or on a particular subject （某作家或專題的）著作，作品：*His experiences in India influenced his later writings.* 他在印度的經歷影響了他後來的著作。◊ *the writings of Hegel* 黑格爾的著作 **5** 🔑 [U] words that have been written or painted on sth （書寫或塗畫的）文字：*There was writing all over the desk.* 書桌上寫滿了字。 **6** 🔑 [U] the particular way in which sb forms letters when they write 筆跡；字跡；書法 SYN **handwriting**：*Who's this from? I don't recognize the writing.* 這是誰寫來的？我辨認不出筆跡。
IDM **in ˈwriting** 🔑 in the form of a letter, document, etc. (that gives proof of sth) 以書面形式（作為憑證）：*All telephone reservations must be confirmed in writing.* 所有的電話預訂必須以書面形式確認。◊ *Could you **put** your complaint **in writing**?* 你能把投訴的內容寫下來嗎？◊ *You must **get it in writing**.* 你必須用書面的形式。 **the ˌwriting is on the ˈwall | see the ˌwriting on the ˈwall** (*NAmE* also **the ˌhandwriting on the ˈwall**) (*saying*) used when you are describing a situation in which there are signs that sth is going to have problems or that it is going to be a failure （看出）厄運臨頭的預兆，不祥之兆：*It is amazing that not one of them saw the writing on the wall.* 令人吃驚的是他們就沒有一個人看出大難臨頭的預兆。 ORIGIN From the Bible story in which strange writing appeared on a wall during a feast given by King Belshazzar, predicting Belshazzar's death and the fall of his city. 源自《聖經》故事，伯沙撒國王大擺宴席時，牆上出現了奇怪的字跡，預言伯沙撒的死亡及其王國的覆滅。

ˈwriting paper *noun* [U] = NOTEPAPER

writ·ten 🔑 /ˈrɪtn/ *adj.*
1 🔑 [usually before noun] expressed in writing rather than in speech 書面的：*written instructions* 書面指示 **2** 🔑 [usually before noun] (of an exam, a piece of work, etc. 測驗、工作等) involving writing rather than speaking or practical skills 書面的；筆頭的：*a written test* 筆試 ◊ *written communication skills* 書面交流技巧 **3** 🔑 [only before noun] in the form of a letter, document, etc. and therefore official 以書信（或文件等）形式的；書面的；成文的；正式的：*a written apology* 書面道歉 ◊ *a written contract* 書面合同 ➲ see also WRITE *v.*
IDM **the ˌwritten ˈword** language expressed in writing rather than in speech 書面語：*the permanence of the written word* 書面語傳之久遠的特性

wrong 🔑 /rɒŋ; *NAmE* rɔːŋ/ *adj., adv., noun, verb*
■ ***adj.***
▸ NOT CORRECT 不正確 **1** 🔑 not right or correct 錯誤的；不對的；不正確的：*I got all the answers wrong.* 我的答案全都錯了。◊ *He was driving on the wrong side of the road.* 他開車行駛在道路逆行的一側。◊ *Sorry, I must have dialled the wrong number.* 對不起，我一定是撥錯電話號

W

碼了。◇ *You're holding the camera* ***the wrong way up!*** 你把照相機拿顛倒了！◇ *That picture is* ***the wrong way round.*** 那幅畫掛反了。OPP **right** 2 [not before noun] (of a person 人) not right about sth/sb 出錯；搞錯；有錯誤 SYN **mistaken**：*I think she lives at number 44, but I could be wrong.* 我想她是住在 44 號，不過我可能記錯了。◇ **~ (about sth/sb)** *You were wrong about Tom; he's not married after all.* 你把湯姆的情況搞錯了，他根本沒結婚。◇ **~ (to do sth)** *We were wrong to assume that she'd agree.* 我們錯誤地以為她會同意。◇ *She would* ***prove him wrong*** (= prove that he was wrong) *whatever happened.* 不論發生的是什麼事，她都會證明他是錯的。◇ (*informal*) *You think you've beaten me but* ***that's where you're wrong.*** 你以為已經贏了我了，可你錯就錯在這裏。◇ (*informal*) ***Correct me if I'm wrong*** (= I may be wrong) *but didn't you say you two knew each other?* 我若說錯了請你糾正，你不是說過你們彼此認識嗎？

▸ **CAUSING PROBLEMS** 造成問題 **3** [not before noun] causing problems or difficulties; not as it should be 引起問題（或麻煩）；有毛病；不正常：*Is anything wrong? You look worried.* 出了什麼事？看你愁眉苦臉的樣子。◇ *'What's wrong?' 'Oh, nothing.'* "哪兒不舒服？" "噢，沒事。" ◇ **~ with sb/sth** *There's something wrong with the printer.* 打印機出了故障。◇ *The doctor could find* ***nothing wrong*** *with him.* 醫生查不出他有什麼病。◇ *I* ***have something wrong with*** *my foot.* 我的腳有點兒不對勁。

▸ **NOT SUITABLE** 不適合 **4** [usually before noun] not suitable, right or what you need 不合適的；不適當的；不合意的：**~ (sth) (for sth)** *He's the wrong person for the job.* 他不適合做這項工作。◇ **~ (sth to do)** *I realized that it was the wrong thing to say.* 我意識到說這話不恰當。◇ *We don't want this document* ***falling into the wrong hands.*** 我們不想讓這份文件落入不對路的人手裏。◇ *It was his bad luck to be* ***in the wrong place at the wrong time*** (= so that he got involved in trouble without intending to). 算他倒霉，在錯誤的時間出現在錯誤的地方。

▸ **NOT MORALLY RIGHT** 不道德 **5** [not usually before noun] not morally right or honest 不道德；不義；不誠實：*This man has* ***done nothing wrong.*** 這位男子沒有做過不正當的事。◇ **~ (of/for sb) (to do sth)** *It is wrong to tell lies.* 說謊是不道德的。◇ *It was wrong of me to get so angry.* 我不該發這麼大脾氣。◇ **~ with sth/with doing sth** *What's wrong with eating meat?* 吃肉有什麼不對？◇ **~ that …** *It is wrong that he should not be punished for what he did.* 他的所作所為竟可不受懲罰，這太不公平了。

▸ **wrong·ness** *noun* [U] (*formal*)

IDM **from/on the ˌwrong side of the ˈtracks** from or living in a poor area or part of town 來自（城裏的）貧民區；住在貧窮的地區（或城區） **get (hold of) the ˌwrong end of the ˈstick** (*BrE, informal*) to understand sth in the wrong way 誤解；誤會 **on the ˌwrong side of the ˈlaw** in trouble with the police 違法 **take sth the wrong ˈway** to be offended by a remark that was not intended to be offensive 誤會本意良好的話 ➲ more at BACK *v.*, BARK *v.*, BED *n.*, FAR *adv.*, FOOT *n.*, NOTE *n.*, RUB *v.*, SIDE *n.*, TRACK *n.*

■ *adv.* (used after verbs 用於動詞之後) in a way that produces a result that is not correct or that you do not want 錯誤地；不正確；不對：*My name is spelt wrong.* 我的名字給拼錯了。◇ *The program won't load. What am I doing wrong?* 這程序安裝不了。我哪裏出錯了？◇ *I was trying to apologize but it* ***came out wrong*** (= what I said sounded wrong). 我是想要道歉，可是話一出口卻變了味兒。◇ *'I thought you were going out.' 'Well you must have* ***thought wrong,*** *then!'* "我原以為你要出去呢。" "啊，那你一定是想錯了！" OPP **right**

IDM **get sb ˈwrong** (*informal*) to not understand correctly what sb means 誤會，誤解，曲解（某人的意思）：***Don't get me wrong*** (= do not be offended by what I am going to say), *I think he's doing a good job, but …* 別誤解我，我認為他活兒幹得不錯，不過… **get sth ˈwrong** (*informal*) **1** to not understand a situation correctly 誤會，誤解，曲解（某事）：*No, you've got it all wrong. She's his wife.* 不，你完全誤會了。她是他的妻子。 **2** to make a mistake with sth 把…搞錯；把…弄錯：*I must have got the figures wrong.* 我一定是把數字給搞錯了。 **go ˈwrong 1** to make a mistake 犯錯誤；做錯事；搞錯；弄錯：*If you do what she tells you, you won't go far wrong.* 你要是按照她說的做，就不會出大差錯。◇ *Where did we go wrong with those kids* (= what mistakes did we make for them to behave so badly)? 我們在什麼地方把這些孩子慣壞了？ **2** (of a machine 機器) to stop working correctly 發生故障；出毛病：*My watch keeps going wrong.* 我的錶不斷地出毛病。 **3** to experience problems or difficulties 出現問題；遇到困難：*The relationship started to go wrong when they moved abroad.* 移居國外後，他們的關係開始出現問題了。◇ *What else can go wrong* (= what other problems are we going to have)? 還會出現什麼問題？ **you can't go ˈwrong (with sth)** (*informal*) used to say that sth will always be acceptable in a particular situation 絕對不會出錯；決不會有問題：*For a quick lunch you can't go wrong with pasta.* 想要吃一頓快捷的午餐，吃意大利麪準錯不了。➲ more at FOOT *n.*

■ *noun* **1** [U] behaviour that is not honest or morally acceptable 不義行為；欺騙行徑；惡行：*Children must be taught the difference between right and wrong.* 必須教兒童分清是非。◇ *Her son can* ***do no wrong*** *in her eyes.* 在她眼裏，她的兒子不可能做壞事。 **2** [C] (*formal*) an act that is not legal, honest or morally acceptable 犯罪；欺騙；罪惡：*It is time to forgive past wrongs if progress is to be made.* 如果想有進步，現在就該寬恕過去的罪過。OPP **right**

IDM **in the ˈwrong** responsible for an accident, a mistake, an argument, etc.（在事故、錯誤、爭論等中）有錯，應承擔責任：*The motorcyclist was clearly in the wrong.* 騎摩托車的人顯然對事故負有責任。 **two ˌwrongs don't make a ˈright** (*saying*) used to say that if sb does sth bad to you, the situation will not be improved by doing sth bad to them 怨怨相報永無完了；以牙還牙行不通 ➲ more at RIGHT *v.*

■ *verb* [usually passive] **~ sb** (*formal*) to treat sb badly or in an unfair way 不公正（或不誠實）對待：*He felt deeply wronged by the allegations.* 這些指控讓他感到深受冤枉。

Which Word? 詞語辨析

wrong / wrongly / wrongfully

- In informal language **wrong** can be used as an adverb instead of **wrongly**, when it means 'incorrectly' and comes after a verb or its object. 在非正式用法中，wrong 可作副詞代替 wrongly，表示錯誤地，置於動詞或動詞賓語之後：*My name was spelled wrong.* 我的名字拼錯了。◇ *I'm afraid you guessed wrong.* 恐怕你猜錯了。 **Wrongly** is used before a past participle or a *that* clause. * wrongly 用於過去分詞或 that 從句之前：*My name was wrongly spelt.* 我的名字拼錯了。◇ *She guessed wrongly that he was a teacher.* 她猜他是個教師猜錯了。
- **Wrongfully** is usually used in a formal legal situation with words like *convicted, dismissed and imprisoned.* * wrongfully 通常用於正式的法律場合，與 convicted、dismissed、imprisoned 等詞連用。

wrong·doer /ˈrɒŋduːə(r); *NAmE* ˈrɔːŋ-; ˈrɑːŋ-/ *noun* (*formal*) a person who does sth dishonest or illegal 做壞事的人；違法犯罪者；作惡者 SYN **criminal, offender**

wrong·doing /ˈrɒŋduːɪŋ; *NAmE* ˈrɔːŋ-/ *noun* [U, C] (*formal*) illegal or dishonest behaviour 不法行為；壞事；作惡；欺騙行徑 SYN **crime, offence**

ˌwrong-ˈfoot *verb* **~ sb** (*BrE*) to put sb in a difficult or embarrassing situation by doing sth that they do not expect 使措手不及；使窘態畢露：*It was an attempt to wrong-foot the opposition.* 這一舉動為的是讓對手措手不及。

wrong·ful /ˈrɒŋfl; *NAmE* ˈrɔːŋ-/ *adj.* [usually before noun] (*law* 律) not fair, morally right or legal 不公正的；不道德的；不合法的：*She decided to sue her employer*

W

for wrongful dismissal. 她決定起訴雇主非法解雇她。
▸ **wrong·ful·ly** /-fəli/ *adv.* : *to be wrongfully convicted/dismissed* 遭非法定罪 / 解雇 ➲ note at WRONG

Synonyms 同義詞辨析

wrong

false • mistaken • incorrect • inaccurate • misguided • untrue

These words all describe sth that is not right or correct, or sb who is not right about sth. 以上各詞均指錯誤、不正確、犯錯。

wrong not right or correct; (of a person) not right about sb/sth 指錯誤的、不正確的，（人）出錯、搞錯、有錯誤： *I got all the answers wrong.* 我的答案全都錯了。◇ *We were wrong to assume she'd agree.* 我們錯誤地以為她會同意。

false not true or correct; wrong because it is based on sth that is not true or correct 指不正確的、不真實的、錯誤的： *A whale is a fish.* ***True or false?*** 鯨魚是魚，對還是錯？◇ *She gave false information to the insurance company.* 她向保險公司提供了虛假信息。

mistaken wrong in your opinion or judgement; based on a wrong opinion or bad judgement 指意見或判斷不正確的、以錯誤的意見或判斷為基礎的： *You're completely mistaken about Jane.* 你對簡的看法完全錯了。

incorrect (*rather formal*) wrong according to the facts; containing mistakes 指與事實不符的、不準確的、不正確的： *Many of the figures were incorrect.* 這些數字有許多是不準確的。

inaccurate wrong according to the facts; containing mistakes 指與事實不符的、不準確的、不正確的： *The report was badly researched and quite inaccurate.* 這報告沒有經過認真調查，頗為失實。

INCORRECT OR INACCURATE? 用 incorrect 還是 inaccurate？

A fact, figure or spelling that is wrong is **incorrect**; information, a belief or a description based on incorrect facts can be **incorrect** or **inaccurate**; something that is produced, such as a film, report or map, that contains incorrect facts is **inaccurate**. 事實、數據或拼寫錯誤用 incorrect；以錯誤事實為基礎的信息、看法或描述可用 incorrect 或 inaccurate；影片、報告或地圖等製品與事實不符用 inaccurate。

misguided wrong because you have understood or judged a situation badly 指理解不當的、判斷失誤的： *In her misguided attempts to help, she only made the situation worse.* 她想幫忙，但做法不對頭，反把事情弄得更糟。

untrue not based on facts, but invented or guessed 指無事實根據的、捏造的、憑空猜想的： *These accusations are totally untrue.* 這些指控純屬捏造。

PATTERNS

- to be wrong/mistaken **about** sth
- wrong/false/mistaken/incorrect/inaccurate/untrue **information**
- a(n) false/mistaken/incorrect/inaccurate/misguided **belief**
- a(n) wrong/incorrect **answer**

ˌwrong-ˈheaded *adj.* having or showing bad judgement 判斷錯誤的；執迷不悟的： *wrong-headed beliefs* 錯誤的信念

wrong·ly 0━ /ˈrɒŋli; *NAmE* ˈrɔːŋ-/ *adv.* in a way that is unfair, immoral or not correct 不公正地；不道德地；錯誤地： *She was wrongly accused of stealing.* 她被誣告犯了偷盜罪。◇ *He assumed, wrongly, that she did not care.* 他誤以為她並不在乎。◇ *The sentence had been wrongly translated.* 這個句子翻譯錯了。◇ *They knew they had acted wrongly.* 他們知道他們做得不對。◇ ***Rightly or wrongly,*** *they felt they should have been better informed* (= I do not know whether they were right to feel this way). 不論對錯，他們覺得應該讓他們瞭解到更多的情況。➲ note at WRONG

wrote *past tense* of WRITE

wrought /rɔːt/ *verb* **~ sth** (*formal* or *literary*) (used only in the past tense 僅用於過去時) caused sth to happen, especially a change 使發生了，造成了（尤指變化）： *This century wrought major changes in our society.* 本世紀給我們的社會帶來了重大變革。◇ *The storm wrought havoc in the south.* 這場暴風雨在南方造成了巨大的災害。 **HELP** **Wrought** is an old form of the past tense of **work**. * wrought 是 work 過去時的舊式。

ˌwrought ˈiron *noun* [U] a form of iron used to make decorative fences, gates, etc. 鍛鐵；熟鐵： *The gates were made of wrought iron.* 這些大門是用熟鐵製成的。◇ *wrought-iron gates* 熟鐵門 ➲ compare CAST IRON

wrung *past tense, past part.* of WRING

wry /raɪ/ *adj.* [usually before noun] **1** showing that you are both amused and disappointed or annoyed 啼笑皆非的： *'At least we got one vote,' she said with a wry smile.* "我們起碼還得了一票。" 她苦笑着解嘲道。◇ *He pulled a wry face when I asked him how it had gone.* 我問他近況如何，他有些哭笑不得。 **2** amusing in a way that shows IRONY 挖苦的；諷刺的；揶揄的： *a wry comedy about family life* 關於家庭生活的諷刺喜劇 ◇ *a wry comment* 挖苦的評論 ◇ *wry humour* 冷嘲式的幽默 ▸ **wryly** *adv.* : *to smile wryly* 冷笑 **wry·ness** *noun* [U]

WTO /ˌdʌbljuː tiː ˈəʊ; *NAmE* ˈoʊ/ *abbr.* World Trade Organization (an international organization that encourages international trade and economic development, especially by reducing restrictions on trade) 世界貿易組織

Wu /wuː/ *noun* [U] a form of Chinese spoken in Jiangsu, Zhejiang and Shanghai 吳語（通行於江蘇、浙江和上海的漢語方言）

wun·der·kind /ˈwʊndəkɪnd; *NAmE* -dərk-/ *noun* (*pl.* **wunder·kind·er** /ˈwʊndəkɪndə(r); *NAmE* -dərk-/) (from *German*, sometimes *disapproving*) a person who is very successful at a young age 神童；少年得志者

Wur·litz·er™ /ˈwɜːlɪtsə(r); *NAmE* ˈwɜːrl-/ *noun* a large musical organ, especially one used in the cinemas/movie theaters of the 1930s（尤指 20 世紀 30 年代用於電影院的）沃利策管風琴

wuss /wʊs/ *noun* (*slang*) a person who is not strong or brave 懦夫；膿包： *Don't be such a wuss!* 別這麼軟弱！

WWW /ˌdʌbljuː dʌbljuː ˈdʌbljuː/ *abbr.* = WORLD WIDE WEB： *several useful WWW addresses* 幾個有用的萬維網網址

WYSIWYG /ˈwɪziwɪg/ *abbr.* (*computing* 計) what you see is what you get (what you see on the computer screen is exactly the same as will be printed) 所見即所得，直接可視數據（計算機屏上顯示的和打印出來的材料一樣）

X /eks/ (also **x**) *noun, symbol*

■ ***noun*** (*pl.* **Xs**, **X's**, **x's** /'eksɪz/) **1** [C, U] the 24th letter of the English alphabet 英語字母表的第 24 個字母：*'Xylophone' begins with (an) X/'X'.* * xylophone 一詞以字母 x 開頭。**2** [U] (*mathematics* 數) used to represent a number whose value is not mentioned（代表未知數）：*The equation is impossible for any value of x greater than 2.* 當 x 的值大於 2 時，這個等式不成立。**3** [U] a person, a number, an influence, etc. that is not known or not named 未知的人（或數、影響等）；未指明的人（或數、影響等）：*Let's suppose X knows what Y is doing.* 假設 X 知道 Y 正在幹什麼。➲ see also X CHROMOSOME, X-RATED, X-RAY

■ ***symbol*** **1** the number 10 in ROMAN NUMERALS（羅馬數字）10 **2** used to represent a kiss at the end of a letter, etc.（置於書信等的結尾，表示親吻）：*Love from Kathy XXX.* 愛你的凱西，吻你，吻你，吻你。**3** used to show a vote for sb in an election（在選舉中表示投給某人的一票）：*Write X beside the candidate of your choice.* 在你選擇的候選人旁邊打一個 X。**4** used to show that a written answer is wrong（表示書面答案是錯的）➲ compare TICK *n.* (1) **5** used to show position, for example on a map（用以標明方位，如在地圖上）：*X marks the spot.* * X 標出了所說的地點。

'X chromosome *noun* (*biology* 生) a SEX CHROMOSOME. Two X chromosomes exist in the cells of human females. In human males each cell has one X chromosome and one Y chromosome. * X 染色體

xenon /'zenɒn; 'zi:-; *NAmE* -nɑ:n/ *noun* [U] (*symb.* **Xe**) a chemical element. Xenon is a gas that is found in very small quantities in the air and is used in some special electric lamps. 氙；氙氣

xeno·pho·bia /,zenə'fəʊbiə; *NAmE* -'foʊ-/ *noun* [U] (*disapproving*) a strong feeling of dislike or fear of people from other countries 仇外，懼外（對外國人的厭惡或懼怕）：*a campaign against racism and xenophobia* 反對種族主義和仇外情緒的運動 ▸ **xeno·pho·bic** /-'fəʊbɪk; *NAmE* -'foʊ-/ *adj.*

xeno·trans·plan·ta·tion /,zi:nəʊ,trænsplɑ:n'teɪʃn; -,trænz-; *NAmE* ,zi:noʊ-; -plæn't-/ *noun* [U] (*medical* 醫) the process of taking organs from animals and putting them into humans for medical purposes（從動物到人體的）異種器官移植

Xerox™ /'zɪərɒks; *NAmE* 'zɪrɑ:ks/ *noun* a process for producing copies of letters, documents, etc. using a special machine; a copy made using this process 施樂複印；施樂複印件；全錄影印；全錄影印件：*a Xerox machine* 施樂複印機

xerox /'zɪərɒks; *NAmE* 'zɪrɑ:ks/ *verb* **~ sth** to make a copy of a letter, document, etc. by using Xerox or a similar process 複印；複製 **SYN** **photocopy**：*Could you xerox this letter, please?* 請複印一下這封信好嗎？

X factor /'eks fæktə(r)/ *noun* [sing.] a special quality, especially one that is essential for success and is difficult to describe 特質，X 因素（尤指獲得成功所必需又難以描述的素質）：*She certainly has the X factor that all great singers have.* 她確實具備所有偉大的歌唱家所擁有的特質。

Xhosa /'kɔ:sə; 'kəʊ-; *NAmE* 'koʊ-/ *noun* [U] a language spoken by the Xhosa people in South Africa（南非）科薩語

xi /saɪ; zaɪ; ksaɪ; gzaɪ/ *noun* the 14th letter of the Greek alphabet (Ξ, ξ) 希臘字母表的第 14 個字母

Xiang (also **Hsiang**) /ʃi:'æŋ/ *noun* [U] a form of Chinese spoken mainly in Hunan 湘語；湘方言；湖南話

-xion ➲ -ION

XL /,eks 'el/ *abbr.* extra large (used for sizes of things, especially clothes) 特大號（衣服尺碼等）：*an XL T-shirt* 一件特大號 T 恤衫

Xmas /'krɪsməs; 'eksməs/ *noun* [C, U] (*informal*) used as a short form of 'Christmas', usually in writing 聖誕節（Christmas 的縮寫）：*A merry Xmas to all our readers!* 祝廣大讀者聖誕快樂！

XML /,eks em 'el/ *abbr.* (*computing* 計) Extensible Mark-up Language (a system used for marking the structure of text on a computer, for example when creating website pages) 可擴展置標語言，可擴展標記語言（製作網頁等用的文本結構標記系統）

'X-rated *adj.* (especially of a film/movie 尤指電影) that people under 18 are not allowed to see because it contains sex and/or violence * X 級的，青少年不宜的（充斥性和／或暴力而禁止 18 歲以下的青少年觀看）

X-ray /'eks reɪ/ *noun, verb*

■ ***noun*** **1** [usually pl.] a type of RADIATION that can pass through objects that are not transparent and make it possible to see inside them * X 射線；X 光；愛克斯射線；愛克斯光：*an X-ray machine* (= one that produces X-rays) 愛克斯光機 **2** a photograph made by X-rays, especially one showing bones or organs in the body * X 光照片：*a chest X-ray* 胸部 X 光照片 ◇ *The doctor studied the X-rays of her lungs.* 醫生研究了她肺部的 X 光照片。◇ *to take an X-ray* 拍攝 X 光照片 **3** a medical examination using X-rays 用 X 射線進行的臨牀檢查：*I had to go for an X-ray.* 我得去做 X 光檢查。

■ ***verb*** **~ sth** to photograph and examine bones and organs inside the body, using X-rays 用 X 射線拍攝檢查：*He had to have his chest X-rayed.* 他得做胸部 X 光檢查。

xylem /'zaɪləm/ *noun* [U] (*biology* 生) the material in plants that carries water and minerals upwards from the root 木質部（植物中將水分和礦物質從根部向上輸送的組織）➲ compare PHLOEM

xylo·phone /'zaɪləfəʊn; *NAmE* -foʊn/ *noun* a musical instrument made of two rows of wooden bars of different lengths that you hit with two small sticks 木琴 ➲ compare GLOCKENSPIEL ➲ **VISUAL VOCAB** page V35

Yy

Y /waɪ/ *noun, abbr.*
■ ***noun*** (also **y**) (*pl.* **Ys**, **Y's**, **y's** /waɪz/) **1** [C, U] the 25th letter of the English alphabet 英語字母表的第 25 個字母：*'Year' begins with (a) Y/'Y'.* * year 一詞以字母 y 開頭。 **2** [U] (*mathematics* 數) used to represent a number whose value is not mentioned（代表未知數）：*Can the value of y be predicted from the value of x?* 能從 x 值推知 y 值嗎？ **3** [U] a person, a number, an influence, etc. that is not known or not named 未知的人（或數、影響等）；未指明的人（或數、影響等）：*Let's suppose X knows what Y is doing.* 假設 X 知道 Y 正在幹什麼。 ➲ see also Y CHROMOSOME, Y-FRONTS
■ ***abbr.*** **the Y** (*NAmE, informal*) YMCA, YWCA 基督教青年會；基督教女青年會
■ ***symbol*** the symbol for the chemical element YTTRIUM（化學元素）釔

-y *suffix* **1** (also **-ey**) (in adjectives 構成形容詞) full of; having the quality of 充滿…的；有…特性的：*dusty* 積滿灰塵的 ◇ *clayey* 像黏土的 **2** (in adjectives 構成形容詞) tending to 有…傾向的：*runny* 水分過多的 ◇ *sticky* 黏性的 **3** (in nouns 構成名詞) the action or process of …的動作（或過程）：*inquiry* 詢問 **4** (also **-ie**) (in nouns, showing affection 構成名詞，表示喜愛)：*doggy* 小狗 ◇ *daddy* 爸爸

ya /jə/ *pron., det.* (*informal, non-standard*) used in writing as a way of showing the way people sometimes pronounce the word 'you' or 'your' 你，你的（書寫時用，表示口語的 you 或 your）：*He said, 'I got something for ya.'* 他說："我有東西給你。"

yaar /jɑː; *NAmE* jɑːr/ *noun* (*IndE, informal*) (used as a friendly way of addressing sb) a friend（用作友好稱呼）朋友，夥計：*Let's go for a drink, yaar!* 咱們去喝一杯吧，朋友！

yacht /jɒt; *NAmE* jɑːt/ (*NAmE* also **sail·boat**) *noun* a large sailing boat, often also with an engine and a place to sleep on board, used for pleasure trips and racing 帆船；遊艇；快艇：*a* ***yacht club/race*** 帆船俱樂部／比賽 ◇ *a motor yacht* 摩托艇 ◇ *a luxury yacht* 豪華遊艇 ➲ VISUAL VOCAB page V56 ➲ compare DINGHY (1)

yacht·ing /'jɒtɪŋ; *NAmE* 'jɑːt-/ *noun* [U] the sport or activity of sailing or racing yachts 快艇（或帆船）運動

yachts·man /'jɒtsmən; *NAmE* 'jɑːt-/, **yachts·woman** /'jɒtswʊmən; *NAmE* 'jɑːt-/ *noun* (*pl.* **-men** /-mən/, **-women** /-wɪmɪn/) a person who sails a yacht for pleasure or as a sport 遊艇（或快艇）駕駛者；帆船比賽選手：*a round-the-world yachtsman* 駕駛帆船環球旅行的人

yack *verb* = YAK

yada yada yada (also **yadda yadda yadda**) /jædə jædə 'jædə/ *exclamation* (*NAmE, informal*) used when you are talking about sth to show that some of the details are not worth saying because they are not important or are boring or obvious 等等；如此這般：*His new girlfriend is attractive, funny, smart, yada yada yada.* 他的新女友有魅力、有趣、聰明，別的就不說了。

yah /jɑː/ *exclamation* **1** a way of writing 'yes' to show that the speaker has an upper-class accent 是，好（書寫時用，表示帶上流社會口音的 yes） **2** used to show that you have a low opinion of sb/sth（表示評價低）嘖，哎：*Yah, you missed!* 喂，你沒打中！

yahoo /'jɑːhuː; jə'huː/ *noun, exclamation*
■ ***noun*** (*pl.* **-oos**) (*disapproving*) a rude, noisy or violent person 粗人；野蠻人
■ ***exclamation*** /jɑː'huː; jæ'huː/ (*informal*) used to show that you are very happy（表示高興）哈哈，哇噻：*Yahoo, we did it!* 啊哈，我們成功了！

Yah·weh /'jɑːweɪ/ *noun* = JEHOVAH

yak /jæk/ *noun, verb*
■ ***noun*** an animal of the cow family, with long horns and long hair, that lives in central Asia 牦牛（生活於中亞）
■ ***verb*** (**-kk-**) (also **yack**) [I] (*informal, often disapproving*) to talk continuously about things that are not very serious or important 沒完沒了地說些無聊的話：*She just kept yakking on.* 她只是一個勁地東拉西扯。

yakka /'jækə/ *noun* [U] (*AustralE, NZE, informal*) work, especially of a hard physical kind 工作；艱苦勞作：*hard yakka* 沉重的體力活

Yale lock™ /'jeɪl lɒk; *NAmE* lɑːk/ *noun* (*BrE*) a type of lock that is often fitted in the front door of a house and which opens by using a flat key with a series of pointed edges 耶魯鎖（常裝於房屋大門，鑰匙呈扁平鋸齒狀）

y'all /jɔːl/ *pron.* = YOU-ALL

yam /jæm/ *noun* [C, U] the large root of a tropical plant that is cooked as a vegetable 薯蕷；山藥 ➲ VISUAL VOCAB page V31

yang /jæŋ/ *noun* [U] (from *Chinese*) (in Chinese philosophy) the bright active male principle of the universe（中國哲學）陽 ➲ compare YIN

Yank /jæŋk/ (also **Yan·kee**) *noun* (*BrE, informal*) an offensive word for a person from the US; an American（含冒犯意）美國佬；美國人

yank /jæŋk/ *verb* [T, I] (*informal*) to pull sth/sb hard, quickly and suddenly 猛拉；猛拽：**~ sth/sb (+ adv./prep.)** *He yanked her to her feet.* 他一下子把她拉起來。◇ **~ sth/sb + adj.** *I yanked the door open.* 我猛地把門拽開。◇ **(+ adv./prep.)** *Liz yanked at my arm.* 利茲猛地拉了一下我的胳膊。 ▶ **yank** *noun*：*She gave the rope a yank.* 她猛地拽了拽繩子。

Yan·kee /'jæŋki/ *noun* **1** (*NAmE*) a person who comes from or lives in any of the northern states of the US, especially New England 美國北方人；（尤指）新英格蘭人 **2** a soldier who fought for the Union (= the northern states) in the American Civil War（美國南北戰爭時的）北軍士兵 **3** (*BrE, informal*) = YANK

yap /jæp/ *verb* (**-pp-**) **1** [I] **~ (at sb/sth)** (especially of small dogs 尤指小狗) to BARK a lot, making a high, sharp and usually irritating sound（常指令人感到煩厭的高聲）吠叫：*The dogs yapped at his heels.* 幾隻狗跟在他後面汪汪亂叫。◇ *yapping dogs* 吠叫的狗 **2** [I] (*informal*) to talk in a silly, noisy and usually irritating way 哇哩哇啦地胡扯 ▶ **yap** *noun*

yard 🔑 /jɑːd; *NAmE* jɑːrd/ *noun*
1 🔑 (*BrE*) an area outside a building, usually with a hard surface and a surrounding wall 院子：*the prison yard* 監獄裏的院子 ◇ *The children were playing in the yard at the front of the school.* 孩子們在學校前面的空地上玩耍。 ➲ see also BACKYARD (2) **2** 🔑 (*NAmE*) (*BrE* **gar·den**) a piece of land next to or around your house where you can grow flowers, fruit, vegetables, etc., usually with a LAWN (= an area of grass)（住宅旁或周圍的）庭園，花園，果園，菜園 ➲ VISUAL VOCAB page V19 ➲ see also BACKYARD **3** 🔑 (usually in compounds 通常構成複合詞) an area of land used for a special purpose or business（某種用途的）區域，場地：*a boat yard* 船塢 HELP You will find other compounds ending in **yard** at their place in the alphabet. 其他以 yard 結尾的複合詞可在各字母中的適當位置查到。 ➲ SYNONYMS at FACTORY **4** 🔑 (*abbr.* **yd**) a unit for measuring length, equal to 3 feet (36 inches) or 0.9144 of a metre 碼（長度單位，等於 3 英尺（36 英寸）或 0.9144 米） **5** (*technical* 術語) a long piece of wood fastened to a MAST that supports a sail on a boat or ship 帆桁 IDM see INCH *n.*, NINE

yard·age /'jɑːdɪdʒ; *NAmE* 'jɑːrd-/ *noun* [C, U] (*technical* 術語) **1** size measured in yards or square yards 碼數；平方碼數 **2** (in AMERICAN FOOTBALL 美式足球) the number of yards that a team or player has moved forward（球隊或球員向前推進的）碼數

yard·arm /'jɑːdɑːm; *NAmE* 'jɑːrdɑːrm/ *noun* (*technical* 術語) either end of the long piece of wood fastened to a ship's MAST that supports a sail 帆桁端

Yardie /'jɑːdi; *NAmE* 'jɑːrdi/ *noun* (*BrE, informal*) (in the UK) a member of a group of criminals from Jamaica or the West Indies（英國）亞迪（牙買加或西印度群島的犯罪組織成員）

'yard sale *noun* (*NAmE*) a sale of things from sb's house, held in their yard 庭院拍賣會（在自家庭院售賣二手傢什）➲ see also GARAGE SALE

yard·stick /ˈjɑːdstɪk; *NAmE* ˈjɑːrd-/ *noun* **1** (*especially NAmE*) a ruler for measuring one yard 碼尺 **2** a standard used for judging how good or successful sth is（好壞或成敗的）衡量標準；準繩：*a yardstick by which to measure sth* 衡量某事物的標準 ◇ *Exam results are not the only yardstick of a school's performance.* 考試結果不是衡量學校水平的唯一標準。

yar·mulke (also **yar·mulka**) /ˈjɑːmʊlkə; *NAmE* ˈjɑːrm-/ (also **kippa**) *noun* a small round cap worn on top of the head by Jewish men; a type of SKULLCAP（猶太男子戴的）圓頂小帽；無簷便帽

yarn /jɑːn; *NAmE* jɑːrn/ *noun* **1** [U, C] thread that has been spun, used for knitting, making cloth, etc. 紗；紗線 ➲ VISUAL VOCAB page V41 **2** [C] (*informal*) a long story, especially one that is exaggerated or invented（尤指誇張的或編造的）長故事：*He used to* ***spin yarns*** (= tell stories) *about his time in the Army.* 他過去經常編造一些有關他在部隊時的離奇故事。 IDM see PITCH *v.*

yar·row /ˈjærəʊ; *NAmE* -roʊ/ *noun* [U, C] a plant with flat groups of many small white or pinkish flowers that have a strong smell 蓍草

yash·mak /ˈjæʃmæk/ *noun* a piece of cloth covering most of the face, worn by some Muslim women（穆斯林婦女戴的）面紗

yaw /jɔː/ *verb* [I] (*technical* 術語) (of a ship or plane 輪船或飛機) to turn to one side, away from a straight course, in an unsteady way 偏航 ▸ **yaw** *noun* [C, U]

yawl /jɔːl/ *noun* **1** a type of boat with sails 雙桅輕便帆船 **2** a ROWING BOAT carried on a ship 船載小划艇

yawn 0-w /jɔːn/ *verb, noun*

■ ***verb*** **1** 0-w [I] to open your mouth wide and breathe in deeply through it, usually because you are tired or bored 打哈欠：*He stood up, stretched and yawned.* 他站起身來，伸了個懶腰，打了個哈欠。 **2** [I] (of a large hole or an empty space 大的洞穴或空間) to be very wide and often frightening and difficult to get across 非常寬；難以逾越 SYN **gape**：*A crevasse yawned at their feet.* 他們的腳下是一條張開大口的裂縫。◇ (*figurative*) *There's a* ***yawning gap*** *between rich and poor.* 貧富之間有一條鴻溝。

■ ***noun*** **1** 0-w an act of yawning 哈欠：*She stifled another yawn and tried hard to look interested.* 她又忍住了哈欠，竭力顯出感興趣的樣子。 **2** [usually sing.] (*informal*) a boring event, idea, etc. 乏味的事情；無趣的想法：*The meeting was one big yawn from start to finish.* 這個會議自始至終都無聊透頂。

yaws /jɔːz/ *noun* [U] a tropical skin disease that causes large red swellings 雅司病（熱帶皮膚病，可導致皮膚嚴重腫脹）

yay /jeɪ/ *exclamation, adv.* (*informal, especially NAmE*)

■ ***exclamation*** used to show that you are very pleased about sth（表示滿意）吔：*I won! Yay!* 吔，我贏了！

■ ***adv.*** **1** to this degree 這麼；那麼；多麼 SYN **so**：*The fish I caught was yay big.* 我釣的魚有這麼大呢。 **2** to a high degree 非常；極其 SYN **extremely**：*Yay good movie!* 非常棒的電影！

'Y chromosome *noun* (*biology* 生) a SEX CHROMOSOME. In human males each cell has one X chromosome and one Y chromosome. In human females there is never a Y chromosome. * Y 染色體

yd *abbr.* (*pl.* **yds**) YARD 碼：*12 yds of silk* * 12 碼的絲綢

ye *pron., det.*

■ ***pron.*** /jiː; *weak form* ji/ (*old use* or *dialect*) a word meaning 'you', used when talking to more than one person 你們：*Gather ye rosebuds while ye may.* 花開堪折直須折。

■ ***det.*** /jiː/ a word meaning 'the', used in the names of pubs, shops, etc. to make them seem old（相當於 the，用於酒吧、商店等的名稱，以使其顯得古色古香）：*Ye Olde Starre Inn* 老斯塔爾酒店

yea /jeɪ/ *adv., noun* (*old use*) yes 是 ➲ compare NAY (2)

yeah 0-w /jeə/ *exclamation* (*informal*) yes 是的；對

IDM **,oh 'yeah?** used when you are commenting on what sb has just said（回應時用）哦，是嗎：*'We're off to France soon.' 'Oh yeah? When's that?'* "我們很快就要去法國了。" "哦，是嗎？什麼時候去呀？" ◇ *'I'm going to be rich one day.' 'Oh yeah?'* (= I don't believe you.) "總有一天我會發財的。" "哦，真的？" **,yeah, 'right** used to say that you do not believe what sb has just said, disagree with it, or are not interested in it（表示不相信、不同意或不感興趣）算了吧：*'You'll be fine.' 'Yeah, right.'* "你會沒事的。" "得了吧。"

year 0-w /jɪə(r); jɜː(r); *NAmE* jɪr/ *noun* (*abbr.* **yr**)

1 0-w (also **,calendar 'year**) [C] the period from 1 January to 31 December, that is 365 or 366 days, divided into 12 months 年；日曆年：*in the year 1865* 在 1865 年 ◇ *I lost my job earlier this year.* 今年早些時候，我失業了。◇ *Elections take place every year.* 每年都進行各項選舉。◇ *The museum is open* ***all*** (***the***) ***year round*** (= during the whole year). 博物館全年開放。➲ see also LEAP YEAR, NEW YEAR **2** 0-w [C] a period of 12 months, measured from any particular time 一年時間：*It's exactly a year since I started working here.* 我來這裏工作已經整整一年了。◇ *She gave up teaching three years ago.* 三年前，她放棄了教學工作。◇ *in the first year of their marriage* 在他們婚後第一年裏 ◇ *the pre-war/war/post-war years* (= the period before/during/after the war) 戰前的／戰爭的／戰後的年代 ◇ *I have happy memories of my years in Poland* (= the time I spent there). 在波蘭的歲月給我留下了美好的回憶。➲ see also GAP YEAR, LIGHT YEAR, OFF YEAR **3** 0-w [C] a period of 12 months connected with a particular activity 與某事相關的一年；年度：*the* ***academic/school year*** 學年 ◇ *the* ***tax year*** 課稅年度 ➲ see also FINANCIAL YEAR **4** [C] (*especially BrE*) (at a school, etc. 學校等) a level that you stay in for one year; a student at a particular level 年級；某年級的學生：*We started German in year seven.* 我們在七年級開始學習德語。◇ *a year-seven pupil* 七年級學生 ◇ *The first years do French.* 一年級學生學習法語。◇ *She was in my year at school.* 她上學時跟我同級。 **5** 0-w [C, usually pl.] age; time of life 年歲；年紀；年齡：*He was 14* ***years old*** *when it happened.* 這件事情發生的時候，他 14 歲。◇ *She looks young for her years.* 她看上去比她的年齡小。◇ *They were both only* ***20 years of age***. 他們兩人都只有 20 歲。◇ *a twenty-year-old man* 一名二十歲的男子 ◇ *He died in his sixtieth year.* 他是六十歲時去世的。◇ *She's* ***getting on in years*** (= is no longer young). 她已經上年紀了。 **6** 0-w **years** [pl.] (*informal*) a long time 很久；好長時間：*It's years since we last met.* 我們多年沒有見面了。◇ *They haven't seen each other* ***for years***. 他們彼此多年沒有見面了。◇ *That's the best movie I've seen* ***in years***. 那是我多年來看過的最好的電影。◇ *We've had a lot of fun* ***over the years***. 這些年來我們過得很開心。

IDM **man, woman, car, etc. of the 'year** a person or thing that people decide is the best in a particular field in a particular year 某年度最優秀人物（或事物） **not/never in a hundred, etc. 'years** (*informal*) used to emphasize that you will/would never do sth 永遠不；絕對不：*I'd never have thought of that in a million years.* 我永遠也想不出這個主意。 **put 'years on sb** to make sb feel or look older 使感到老邁；使顯得年老 **take 'years off sb** to make sb feel or look younger 使覺得（或顯得）年輕 **,year after 'year** every year for many years 年年；每年 **,year by 'year** as the years pass; each year 一年一年地；每年；年復一年：*Year by year their affection for each other grew stronger.* 年復一年，他們對彼此的愛愈加強烈。 **the year 'dot** (*BrE*) (*NAmE* **the year 'one**) (*informal*) a very long time ago 很久以前：*I've been going there every summer since the year dot.* 我從很久以前就每年夏天都去那裏。 **year 'in, year 'out** every year 年復一年；年年 **,year of 'grace | ,year of our 'Lord** (*formal*) any particular year after the birth of Christ 紀元某年；公元某年 **,year on 'year** (used especially when talking about figures, prices, etc. 尤用於統計數字、價格等) each year, compared with the last year 與前一年同期比較：*Spending has increased year on year.* 與去年同期

比較，開銷增加了。◇ *a year-on-year increase in spending* 開銷的年度增長 ➲ more at ADVANCED, DECLINE *v.*, DONKEY, SEVEN, TURN *n.*

year·book /ˈjɪəbʊk; *NAmE* ˈjɪrbʊk/ *noun* **1** a book published once a year, giving details of events, etc. of the previous year, especially those connected with a particular area of activity 年鑒；年刊 **2** (*especially NAmE*) a book that is produced by the senior class in a school or college, containing photographs of students and details of school activities （每年出版的）校刊；學校年刊

year·ling /ˈjɪəlɪŋ; *NAmE* ˈjɪrlɪŋ/ *noun* an animal, especially a horse, between one and two years old 一至兩歲的動物（尤指馬）；一歲（或兩歲）幼崽

ˌyear-ˈlong *adj.* [only before noun] continuing for a whole year 一整年的；持續一年的： *a year-long dispute* 持續一年的爭端

year·ly /ˈjɪəli; ˈjɜːli; *NAmE* ˈjɪrli/ *adj.* **1** happening once a year or every year 每年的；一年一次的： *Pay is reviewed on a yearly basis.* 工資每年審查一次。 **2** paid, valid or calculated for one year 年度的；一年的：*yearly income/interest* 年度收入；年利率 ▸ **year·ly** *adv.*： *The magazine is issued twice yearly* (= twice every year). 這份雜誌每年發行兩期。

yearn /jɜːn; *NAmE* jɜːrn/ *verb* [I] (*literary*) to want sth very much, especially when it is very difficult to get 渴望；渴求 SYN **long** ： **~ (for sth/sb)** *The people yearned for peace.* 人民渴望和平。◇ *There was a yearning look in his eyes.* 他兩眼流露出渴望的神情。◇ **~ to do sth** *She yearned to escape from her office job.* 她一心想着躲避辦公室裏的工作。

yearn·ing /ˈjɜːnɪŋ; *NAmE* ˈjɜːrnɪŋ/ *noun* [C, U] (*formal*) a strong and emotional desire 渴望；嚮往 SYN **longing** ： **~ (for sb/sth)** *a yearning for a quiet life* 對寧靜生活的嚮往 ◇ **~ (to do sth)** *She had no great yearning to go back.* 她並不十分想回去。 ▸ **yearn·ing·ly** *adv.*

ˌyear-ˈround *adj.* all through the year 全年的；整整一年的： *an island with year-round sunshine* 一年四季陽光燦爛的島

yeast /jiːst/ *noun* [U, C] a FUNGUS used in making beer and wine, or to make bread rise 酵母；酵母菌 ▸ **yeasty** *adj.*： *a yeasty smell* 發酵的氣味

ˈyeast extract *noun* [U] a black substance made from yeast, spread on bread, etc. 酵母膏 ➲ see also MARMITE

ˈyeast infection (*NAmE*) (*BrE* **thrush**) *noun* an infectious disease that affects the VAGINA 陰道炎

yebo /ˈjebɒ; *NAmE* -bɔː/ *exclamation* (*SAfrE, informal*) **1** yes 是；對 **2** hello 喂；你好： *Yebo Craig. Thanks for the email.* 你好，克雷格。謝謝你的電郵。

yell /jel/ *verb, noun*

■ *verb* [I, T] to shout loudly, for example because you are angry, excited, frightened or in pain 叫喊；大喊；吼叫： **~ (at sb/sth)** *He yelled at the other driver.* 他衝着另一位司機大叫。◇ **~ at sb to do sth** *She yelled at the child to get down from the wall.* 她喊着讓小孩從牆上下來。◇ **~ with sth** *They yelled with excitement.* 他們興奮得喊叫起來。◇ **~ out (in sth)** *She yelled out in pain.* 她疼得大聲喊叫。◇ **+ speech** *'Be careful!' he yelled.* 他大叫道："當心！" ◇ **~ sth (at sb/sth)** *The crowd yelled encouragement at the players.* 人群大聲叫喊着給運動員加油。◇ **~ out sth** *He yelled out her name.* 他大聲喊叫她的名字。 ➲ SYNONYMS at SHOUT

■ *noun* **1** a loud cry of pain, excitement, etc. 喊叫；叫嚷；大喊： *to let out/give a yell* 大喊一聲 ◇ *a yell of delight* 歡呼 **2** (*NAmE*) an organized shout of support for a team at a sports event （為運動隊加油的）吶喊，歡呼

yel·low 🗝 /ˈjeləʊ; *NAmE* ˈjeloʊ/ *adj., noun, verb*

■ *adj.* (**yel·lower, yel·lowest**) **1** 🗝 having the colour of lemons or butter 黃的；黃色的： *pale yellow flowers* 淡黃色的花朵 ◇ *a bright yellow waterproof jacket* 鮮黃色的防水夾克 **2** (*taboo*) an offensive word used to describe the light brown skin of people from some E Asian countries （輕蔑語）黃皮膚的，黃色人種的 **3** (*informal, disapproving*) easily frightened 膽怯的 SYN **cowardly** ▸ **yel·low·ness** *noun* [U, sing.]

■ *noun* 🗝 [U, C] the colour of lemons or butter 黃；黃色： *She was dressed in yellow.* 她穿着黃衣服。◇ *the reds and yellows of the trees* 紅色和黃色的樹葉

■ *verb* [I, T] **~ (sth)** to become yellow; to make sth become yellow （使）變黃

ˈyellow-belly *noun* (*old-fashioned, informal, disapproving*) a COWARD (= sb who is not brave) 膽小鬼；懦夫 ▸ **ˈyellow-bellied** *adj.* [usually before noun]

ˌyellow ˈcard *noun* (in football (SOCCER) 足球) a card shown by the REFEREE to a player as a warning about bad behaviour 黃牌（由裁判員出示，作為對犯規行為的警告） ➲ compare RED CARD

ˌyellow ˈfever *noun* [U] an infectious tropical disease that makes the skin turn yellow and often causes death 黃熱病（熱帶疾病，可導致死亡）

ˌyellow ˈflag *noun* **1** a type of yellow IRIS (= a flower) that grows near water 黃鳶尾；黃菖蒲 **2** a yellow flag on a ship showing that sb has or may have an infectious disease （表示船上有疫情而掛起的）檢疫旗，黃旗

yel·low·ham·mer /ˈjeləʊhæmə(r); *NAmE* -loʊ-/ *noun* a small bird, the male of which has a yellow head, neck and breast 黃鵐（雄性的頭、頸和胸黃色）

yel·low·ish /ˈjeləʊɪʃ; *NAmE* -loʊ-/ (also *less frequent* **yel·lowy** /ˈjeləʊi; *NAmE* -loʊ-/) *adj.* fairly yellow in colour 微黃色的；發黃的： *The paper had a yellowish tinge because it was so old.* 這份報紙很舊，已經有些發黃了。

ˌyellow ˈjournalism *noun* [U] (*US*) newspaper reports that are exaggerated and written to shock readers 黃色新聞（誇張或聳人聽聞的報章報道） ORIGIN From a comic strip *The Yellow Kid* that was printed in yellow ink to attract readers' attention. 源自以黃色油墨印刷以吸引讀者的連環畫《黃色小子》。

ˌyellow ˈline *noun* (in Britain) a yellow line painted at the side of a road to show that you can only park your car there at particular times or for a short time （英國路邊限制停車的）黃線： ***double yellow lines*** (= two lines that mean you cannot park there at all) 禁止停車的雙黃線

ˌYellow ˈPages™ (*BrE*) (*NAmE* **ˌyellow ˈpages**) *noun* [pl.] a book with yellow pages that gives a list of companies and organizations and their telephone numbers, arranged according to the type of services they offer 黃頁（分類商業電話號碼簿）

ˌyellow ˈribbon *noun* (in the US) a piece of yellow material that sb ties around a tree as a sign that they are thinking about sb who has gone away, especially a soldier fighting in a war, or sb taken as a HOSTAGE or prisoner, and that they hope that the person will soon return safely 黃絲帶（繫在樹上表示期盼親友，尤指參戰的士兵、人質或囚犯，能早日平安歸來）

yelp /jelp/ *verb* [I, T] (**+ speech**) to give a sudden short cry, usually of pain （因疼痛等）突然尖叫 ▸ **yelp** *noun*

yen /jen/ *noun* **1** (*pl.* **yen**) [C] the unit of money in Japan 日元（日本貨幣單位） **2 the yen** [sing.] (*finance* 財) the value of the yen compared with the value of the money of other countries 日元比價 **3** [C, usually sing.] **~ (for sth/to do sth)** a strong desire 強烈的慾望；渴望 SYN **longing** ： *I've always had a yen to travel around the world.* 我一直非常渴望周遊世界。

yeo·man /ˈjəʊmən; *NAmE* ˈjoʊ-/ *noun* (*pl.* **-men** /-mən/) **1** (in Britain in the past) a farmer who owned and worked on his land （英國舊時的）自耕農，自由民 **2** an officer in the US Navy who does mainly office work （美國海軍的）文書軍士

yeo·man·ry /ˈjəʊmənri; *NAmE* ˈjoʊ-/ *noun* [sing.+sing./pl. v.] **1** (in Britain in the past) the social class of farmers who owned their land （統稱英國舊時的）自耕農 **2** (in Britain in the past) farmers who became soldiers and provided their own horses （英國舊時的）攜馬當兵的農民

yeow /jiːˈaʊ/ *exclamation* (*informal*) used to express sudden pain （突然感到疼痛時發出的聲音）哎喲，啊唷

yep /jep/ *exclamation* (*informal*) used to say 'yes' (用以表示 yes)是的，好了：*'Are you ready?' 'Yep.'* "準備好了嗎？" "好了。"

yer /jə(r)/ *pron., det.* (*informal, non-standard*) used in writing as a way of showing the way people sometimes pronounce the word 'you' or 'your' (書寫時用，表示口語的 you 或 your)：*See yer when I get back.* 等我回來時再見吧。◇ *What's yer name?* 你叫什麼名字？

yes 0-π /jes/ *exclamation, noun*

■ ***exclamation*** **1** 0-π used to answer a question and say that sth is correct or true (答話時表示正確或真實)：*'Is this your car?' 'Yes, it is.'* "這是你的車嗎？" "對，是的。" ◇ *'Are you coming? Yes or no?'* "你來嗎？來還是不來？" **2** 0-π used to show that you agree with what has been said (表示同意所說的話)：*'I enjoyed her latest novel.' 'Yes, me too.'* "我喜歡她這本最新的小說。" "對，我也是。" ◇ *'It's an excellent hotel.' '**Yes, but** (= I don't completely agree) it's too expensive.'* "這家旅館好極了。" "是啊，但就是太貴了。" **3** 0-π used to disagree with sth negative that sb has just said (反駁否定的話)：*'I've never met her before.' 'Yes, you have.'* "我以前從沒見過她。" "不，你見過。" **4** 0-π used to agree to a request or to give permission (表示答應或許可)：*'Dad, can I borrow the car?' 'Yes, but be careful.'* "爸爸，我借用一下車好嗎？" "可以，不過要小心。" ◇ *We're hoping that they will **say yes to** our proposals.* 我們希望他們會同意我們的提議。 **5** 0-π used to accept an offer or invitation (接受提議或邀請)：*'Would you like a drink?' '**Yes, please/thanks.**'* "喝一杯好嗎？" "好吧，謝謝。" **6** 0-π used for asking sb what they want (詢問某人所需)：*Yes? How can I help you?* 有事嗎？我能幫你什麼忙？ **7** 0-π used for replying politely when sb calls you (禮貌地應答呼喚)：*'Waiter!' 'Yes, sir?'* "服務員！" "什麼事，先生？" **8** 0-π used to show that you have just remembered sth (表示剛想起某事)哦，對了：*Where did I put the keys? Oh, yes—in my pocket!* 我把鑰匙放在哪兒了？哦，對了，在我口袋裏！ **9** 0-π used to encourage sb to continue speaking (鼓勵某人繼續講)往下說：*'I'm going to Paris this weekend.' 'Yes …'* "我這週末要去巴黎。" "接着說。" **10** 0-π used to show that you do not believe what sb has said (表示不相信某人所言)真的：*'Sorry I'm late—the bus didn't come.' 'Oh yes?'* "對不起，我遲到了，巴士脫班。" "哦，是嗎？" **11** 0-π used to emphasize what you have just said (強調所說的話)一點不假：*Mrs Smith has just won £2 million—yes!—£2 million!* 史密斯夫人剛剛贏了 200 萬英鎊！一點沒假，整整 200 萬英鎊！ **12** 0-π used to show that you are excited or extremely pleased about sth that you have done or sth that has happened (感到興奮或高興時說)好啊：*'They've scored another goal.' 'Yes!!'* "他們又進了一球。" "太棒了！！" **13 yes, yes** used to show that you are impatient or irritated about sth (表示不耐煩或氣惱)得，得：*'Hurry up—it's late.' 'Yes, yes—I'm coming.'* "快點，來不及了。" "行了，行了，我就來。"

IDM **,yes and 'no** used when you cannot give a clear answer to a question 說不準；也是也不是：*'Are you enjoying it?' 'Yes and no.'* "你喜歡這個嗎？" "不好說。"

■ ***noun*** 0-π (*pl.* **yes·ses** or **yeses** /ˈjesɪz/) an answer that shows that you agree with an idea, a statement, etc.; a person who says 'yes' 表示同意的答覆；表示同意的人：*I need a simple yes or no to my questions.* 我的問題只需要簡單地回答是或不是。◇ *There will be two ballot boxes—one for yesses and one for noes.* 將設兩個投票箱：一個放贊成票，一個放反對票。◇ *I'll put you down as a yes.* 我把你看作贊同者。

yesh·iva /jəˈʃiːvə/ *noun* a college or school for Orthodox Jews 授業座(正統派猶太教育機構)

'yes-man *noun* (*pl.* **-men** /-men/) (*disapproving*) a person who always agrees with people in authority in order to gain their approval 應聲蟲；唯唯諾諾的人

yes·sir /ˈjesə(r); ˈjesɜː(r)/ *exclamation* (*informal, especially NAmE*) used to emphasize your opinion or say that you agree very strongly (表示強調)的確，完全同意：*Yessir, she was beautiful.* 的確，她很漂亮。

yes·ter·day 0-π /ˈjestədeɪ; ˈjestədi; *NAmE* -tərd-/ *adv., noun, adj.*

■ ***adv.*** on the day before today 在昨天：*They arrived yesterday.* 他們昨天到達。◇ *I can remember our wedding as if it were yesterday.* 我們的婚禮我記憶猶新，就像昨天一樣。◇ *Where were you yesterday morning?* 你昨天上午在哪兒？◇ *To think I was lying on a beach only **the day before yesterday**.* 想想吧，就在前天，我還躺在海灘上呢。**IDM** see BORN *v.*

■ ***noun*** [U] **1** 0-π the day before today 昨天：*Yesterday was Sunday.* 昨天是星期天。◇ *What happened at yesterday's meeting?* 昨天的會上發生了什麼事？ **2** 0-π (also **yes·ter·days** [pl.]) the recent past 不久前；近日；往昔：*Yesterday's students are today's employees.* 昨天還是學生，今天成了雇員。◇ *All her yesterdays had vanished without a trace.* 她的過去已經完全煙消雲散了。

■ ***adj.*** [not before noun] (*informal*, often *humorous*) no longer fashionable or new 過時：*Email—that's **so yesterday**!* 電子郵件，那太過時了！

yes·ter·year /ˈjestəjɪə(r); *NAmE* ˈjestərjɪr/ *noun* [U] (*old-fashioned* or *literary*) the past, especially a time when attitudes and ideas were different (尤指思想觀念有別於當今的)舊時，往昔，過去

yet 0-π /jet/ *adv., conj.*

■ ***adv.*** **1** 0-π used in negative sentences and questions to talk about sth that has not happened but that you expect to happen (用於否定句和疑問句，談論尚未發生但可能發生的事)：*(BrE) I haven't received a letter from him yet.* 我還沒有收到他的信呢。◇ *(NAmE) I didn't receive a letter from him yet.* 我還沒有收到過他的信。◇ *'Are you ready?' 'No, not yet.'* "你準備好了嗎？" "還沒有。" ◇ *We **have yet to** decide what action to take* (= We have not decided what action to take). 我們尚未決定採取何種行動。➲ note at ALREADY **2** 0-π (used in negative sentences 用於否定句) now; as soon as this 現在；即刻；馬上：*Don't go yet.* 先別走。◇ *We don't need to start yet.* 我們不必馬上開始。 **3** 0-π from now until the period of time mentioned has passed 從現在起直至某一時間；還：*He'll be busy for ages yet.* 他還要忙很長一段時間。◇ *They won't arrive for at least two hours yet.* 他們至少要過兩個小時才能到。 **4 could, might, may, etc. do sth ~** used to say that sth could, might, etc. happen in the future, even though it seems unlikely (表示將來可能發生，儘管現在似乎沒有可能)早晚，總有一天：*We may win yet.* 我們遲早會贏的。◇ *(formal) She could yet surprise us all.* 總有一天，她會讓我們都大吃一驚。 **5** 0-π **the best, longest, etc. sth ~ (done)** the best, longest, etc. thing of its kind made, produced, written, etc. until now/then 迄今為止，到當時為止(最好或最長等的)：*the most comprehensive study yet of his music* 迄今為止對他的音樂最為全面的研究 ◇ *It was the highest building yet constructed.* 這是到當時為止所建的最高的建築物。 **6** 0-π **~ another/more | ~ again** used to emphasize an increase in number or amount or the number of times sth happens (強調次數或數量的增加)：*snow, snow and yet more snow* 下雪，下雪，還要下雪 ◇ *yet another diet book* 又是一本關於節食的書 ◇ *Prices were cut **yet again*** (= once more, after many other times). 物價又再一次降低。 **7 ~ worse, more importantly, etc.** used to emphasize an increase in the degree of sth (= how bad, important, etc. it is) (強調程度的增加)更 **SYN** **even, still**：*a recent and yet more improbable theory* 一個新近提出的但更加不切實際的理論

IDM **as 'yet** 0-π until now or until a particular time in the past 直到現在；直至過去某時：*an as yet unpublished report* 一篇尚未發表的報告 ◇ *As yet little was known of the causes of the disease.* 當時人們對這種疾病的起因幾乎一無所知。

■ ***conj.*** 0-π despite what has just been said 但是；然而 **SYN** **nevertheless**：*It's a small car, yet it's surprisingly spacious.* 這輛汽車不大，然而卻出奇地寬敞。◇ *He has a good job, and yet he never seems to have any money.* 他有份好工作，然而他卻好像總也沒有錢。

yeti /ˈjeti/ (also **A,bominable 'Snowman**) *noun* a large creature like a BEAR or a man covered with hair, that some people believe lives in the Himalayan mountains

雪人（似人或似熊的巨大長毛動物，據傳生活在喜馬拉雅山）

yew /juː/ *noun* **1** [C, U] (also **'yew tree**) a small tree with dark green leaves and small red BERRIES 紫杉；紅豆杉 ➲ **VISUAL VOCAB** page V10 **2** [U] the wood of the yew tree 紫杉木

'Y-Fronts™ *noun* [pl.] (*BrE*) men's UNDERPANTS, with an opening in the front sewn in the shape of a Y upside-down * Y 前縫內褲（前縫呈倒 Y 形的男內褲）：*a pair of Y-Fronts* 一條 Y 前縫男內褲

YHA /ˌwaɪ eɪtʃ 'eɪ/ *abbr.* Youth Hostels Association (an organization that exists in many countries and provides cheap simple accommodation) 青年旅社協會

yid /jɪd/ *noun* (*taboo, slang*) a very offensive word for a Jewish person （蔑稱）猶太人，猶太佬

Yid·dish /'jɪdɪʃ/ *noun* [U] a Jewish language, originally used in central and eastern Europe, based on a form of German with words from Hebrew and several modern languages 意第緒語，依地語（猶太人的語言，起源於歐洲中部和東部，以德語為基礎，借用希伯來語和若干現代語言的詞語）▶ **Yid·dish** *adj.*

yield /jiːld/ *verb, noun*

■ ***verb*** **1** [T] **~ sth** to produce or provide sth, for example a profit, result or crop 出產（作物）；產生（收益、效益等）；提供：*Higher-rate deposit accounts yield good returns.* 高利率的存款會產生豐厚的收益。◇ *The research has yielded useful information.* 這項研究提供了有用的資料。◇ *trees that no longer yield fruit* 不再結果實的樹 **2** [I] (*formal*) to stop resisting sth/sb; to agree to do sth that you do not want to do 屈服；讓步 **SYN** **give way**：*After a long siege, the town was forced to yield.* 經過長時間的包圍，這座孤城被迫投降。◇ **~ to sth/sb** *He reluctantly yielded to their demands.* 他不情願地屈從於他們的要求。◇ *I yielded to temptation and had a chocolate bar.* 我經不住誘惑，吃了一大塊巧克力。 **3** [T] **~ sth/sb (up) (to sb)** (*formal*) to allow sb to win, have or take control of sth that has been yours until now 放棄；繳出 **SYN** **surrender**：*He refused to yield up his gun.* 他拒絕繳槍。◇ (*figurative*) *The universe is slowly yielding up its secrets.* 宇宙慢慢地展現出它的秘密。 **4** [I] to move, bend or break because of pressure （受壓）活動，變形，彎曲，折斷：*Despite our attempts to break it, the lock would not yield.* 這把鎖我們砸也砸不開。 **5** [I] **~ (to sb/sth)** (*NAmE, IrishE*) to allow vehicles on a bigger road to go first 給（大路上的車輛）讓路 **SYN** **give way**：*Yield to oncoming traffic.* 給迎面駛來的車輛讓路。◇ *a yield sign* 讓車標誌

PHR V **'yield to sth** (*formal*) to be replaced by sth 被…替代；為…所取代：*Barges yielded to road vehicles for transporting goods.* 在貨物運輸方面，駁船讓位給了公路車輛。

■ ***noun*** [C, U] the total amount of crops, profits, etc. that are produced 產量；產出；利潤：*a high crop yield* 作物豐收 ◇ *a reduction in milk yield* 牛奶產量的降低 ◇ *This will give a yield of 10% on your investment.* 這會給你的投資帶來 10% 的利潤。

yield·ing /'jiːldɪŋ/ *adj.* (*formal*) **1** (of a substance 物質) soft and easy to bend or move when you press it 柔軟的；易彎曲的；易變形的 **2** (of a person 人) willing to do what other people want 順從的；百依百順的 **3** (used with an adverb 與副詞連用) giving the amount of crops, profits, etc. mentioned 帶來…收成（或利潤等）的：***high/low yielding** crops* 高 / 低產量作物

yikes /jaɪks/ *exclamation* (*informal*) used to show that you are surprised or suddenly afraid （驚訝或突然害怕時說）呀，啊

yin /jɪn/ *noun* [U] (from *Chinese*) (in Chinese philosophy) the dark, not active, female principle of the universe （中國哲學）陰 ➲ compare YANG

yip·pee /jɪ'piː; *NAmE* 'jɪpi/ *exclamation* (*old-fashioned, informal*) used to show you are pleased or excited （高興或興奮時說）

ylang-ylang (also **ilang-ilang**) /ˌiːlæŋ 'iːlæŋ/ *noun* **1** [U] an oil from the flowers of a tropical tree, used in PERFUMES and AROMATHERAPY 伊蘭油（從熱帶伊蘭樹的花中提取，用於香水和芳香療法） **2** [U, C] a tree with yellow flowers from which this oil is obtained 伊蘭伊蘭；芳香樹；香依蘭；香水樹

YMCA /ˌwaɪ em siː 'eɪ/ (also *NAmE informal* **the Y**) *abbr.* Young Men's Christian Association (an organization that exists in many countries and provides accommodation and social and sports activities) 基督教青年會：*We stayed at the YMCA.* 我們住在基督教青年會。

yo /jəʊ; *NAmE* joʊ/ *exclamation* (*slang*) used by young people to say hello （年輕人的招呼語）喂，嘿

yob /jɒb; *NAmE* jɑːb/ (also **yobbo** /'jɒbəʊ; *NAmE* 'jɑːboʊ/ *pl.* **-os**) *noun* (*BrE, informal*) a rude, noisy and sometimes aggressive and violent boy or young man 粗野的男孩；粗俗橫蠻的青年男子 **SYN** **lout** ▶ **yob·bish** *adj.* [usually before noun]

yodel /'jəʊdl; *NAmE* 'joʊdl/ *verb, noun*

■ ***verb*** (**-ll-**, *especially US* **-l-**) [I, T] **~ (sth)** to sing or call in the traditional Swiss way, changing your voice frequently between its normal level and a very high level 用約德爾唱法歌唱（以瑞士傳統的真假嗓音交替歌唱）

■ ***noun*** a song or musical call in which sb yodels 約德爾唱法，約德爾歌曲（用真假嗓音交替歌唱）

yoga /'jəʊgə; *NAmE* 'joʊgə/ *noun* [U] **1** a Hindu philosophy that teaches you how to control your body and mind in the belief that you can become united with the spirit of the universe in this way 瑜伽派（印度哲學派別） **2** a system of exercises for your body and for controlling your breathing, used by people who want to become fitter or to relax 瑜伽術（健體和控制呼吸的鍛煉）➲ **VISUAL VOCAB** page V42 ▶ **yogic** /'jəʊgɪk; *NAmE* 'joʊ-/ *adj.*：*yogic techniques* 瑜伽技巧

yogi /'jəʊgi; *NAmE* 'joʊgi/ *noun* (*pl.* **yogis**) an expert in, or teacher of, the philosophy of yoga 瑜伽哲學專家（或導師）

yog·urt (also **yog·hurt**, **yog·hourt**) /'jɒgət; *NAmE* 'joʊgərt/ *noun* [U, C] a thick white liquid food, made by adding bacteria to milk, served cold and often flavoured with fruit; an amount of this sold in a small pot 酸奶；優格；一份酸奶：*natural yogurt* 原味酸奶 ◇ *There's a yogurt left if you're still hungry.* 如果你還餓的話，還有一份酸奶。◇ *a lemon yogurt* 檸檬酸奶

yoke /jəʊk; *NAmE* joʊk/ *noun, verb*

■ ***noun*** **1** [C] a long piece of wood that is fastened across the necks of two animals, especially OXEN, so that they can pull heavy loads 軛；（尤指）牛軛 **2** [sing.] (*literary or formal*) rough treatment or sth that restricts your freedom and makes your life very difficult to bear 奴役；束縛；枷鎖；羈絆：*the yoke of imperialism* 帝國主義的枷鎖 **3** [C] a piece of wood that is shaped to fit across a person's shoulders so that they can carry two equal loads 軛形扁擔 **4** [C] a part of a dress, skirt, etc. that fits around the shoulders or hips and from which the rest of the cloth hangs 上衣抵肩；裙（或褲）腰

■ ***verb*** **1** to join two animals together with a yoke; to attach an animal to sth with a yoke 用軛把（動物）套在一起；給（動物）上軛：**~ A and B together** *A pair of oxen, yoked together, was used.* 把兩頭牛用軛套在一起使喚。◇ **~ sth to sth** *an ox yoked to a plough* 用軛套在犁上的牛 **2** [usually passive] **~ A and B together** | **~ sth to sth** (*formal*) to bring two people, countries, ideas, etc. together so that they are forced into a close relationship （強行）使結合，使聯合：*The Hong Kong dollar was yoked to the American dollar for many years.* 港元多年來與美元掛鈎。

yokel /'jəʊkl; *NAmE* 'joʊkl/ *noun* (often *humorous*) if you call a person a **yokel**, you are saying that they do not have much education or understanding of modern life, because they come from the countryside 鄉巴佬；鄉下人

yolk /jəʊk; *NAmE* joʊk/ *noun* [C, U] the round yellow part in the middle of an egg 蛋黃：*Separate the whites from the yolks.* 將蛋清和蛋黃分開。

Yom Kip·pur /ˌjɒm 'kɪpə(r); kɪ'pʊə(r); *NAmE* ˌjɑːm kɪ'pʊr; ˌjɔːm/ *noun* [U] a Jewish religious holiday in September or October when people eat nothing all day and say prayers of PENITENCE in the SYNAGOGUE, also known as the Day of Atonement 贖罪日（猶太教的重大節日，在每年的九月或一月，人們於此日禁食並懺悔祈禱）

yomp /jɒmp; *NAmE* jɑːmp/ *verb* [I] + **adv./prep.** (*BrE, informal*) (of a soldier 軍人) to march with heavy equipment over rough ground 負重越野行軍；全副武裝跋涉 ▸ **yomp** *noun* *a 30-mile yomp* * 30 英里的負重越野行軍

yon /jɒn; *NAmE* jɑːn/ *det., adv.*
■ **det.** (*old use* or *dialect*) that 那；那個：*There's an old farm over yon hill.* 小山那邊有一個舊農場。
■ **adv.** IDM see HITHER

yon·der /ˈjɒndə(r); *NAmE* ˈjɑːn-/ *det.* (*old use* or *dialect*) that is over there; that you can see over there 那裏的；那邊的：*Let's rest under yonder tree.* 我們在那邊的樹下休息吧。▸ **yon·der** *adv.*：*Whose is that farm over yonder?* 那邊的農場是誰的？

yonks /jɒŋks; *NAmE* jɑːŋks/ *noun* [U] (*BrE, informal, becoming old-fashioned*) a long time 很長時間：*I haven't seen you for yonks!* 我很久沒見你了！

yoof /juːf/ *noun* [U] (*BrE, informal, humorous*) a non-standard spelling of 'youth', used to refer to young people as a group, especially as the group that particular types of entertainment, magazines, etc. are designed for（youth 的不規範拼寫，統稱）年輕人；年輕人目標群體 ▸ **yoof** *adj.* [only before noun]

yoo-hoo /ˈjuː huː/ *exclamation* (*informal, becoming old-fashioned*) used to attract sb's attention, especially when they are some distance away（尤用以引起遠處的人的注意）喲—嚯

yore /jɔː(r)/ *noun*
IDM **of 'yore** (*old use* or *literary*) long ago 很久以前：*in days of yore* 在很久以前

York·shire pud·ding /ˌjɔːkʃə ˈpʊdɪŋ; *NAmE* ˌjɔːrkʃər/ *noun* [U, C] a type of British food made from BATTER that is baked until it rises, traditionally eaten with ROAST beef 約克夏布丁（在英國習慣上和烤牛肉同食）

Yorkshire terrier /ˌjɔːkʃə ˈteriə(r); *NAmE* ˌjɔːrkʃər/ *noun* a very small dog with long brown and grey hair 約克夏㹴（棕灰兩色的長毛小狗）

Yor·uba /ˈjɒrʊbə; *NAmE* ˈjɔːrəbə/ *noun* [U] a language spoken by the Yoruba people of W Africa, especially in SW Nigeria 約魯巴語（非洲西部，尤其尼日利亞西南部的約魯巴人的語言）

you 🔑 /ju; *NAmE* jə; *strong form* juː/ *pron.*
1 🔑 used as the subject or object of a verb or after a preposition to refer to the person or people being spoken or written to 你；您；你們：*You said you knew the way.* 你說過你知道路的。◇ *I thought she told you.* 我以為她告訴你了。◇ *Can I sit next to you?* 我可以坐在你旁邊嗎？◇ *I don't think that hairstyle is you* (= it doesn't suit your appearance or personality). 我覺得那種髮型不適合你。 **2** 🔑 used with nouns and adjectives to speak to sb directly（與名詞及形容詞連用，直接稱呼某人）：*You girls, stop talking!* 你們這些女孩子，別說話了！◇ *You stupid idiot!* 你這個白痴！ **3** 🔑 used for referring to people in general（泛指任何人）：*You learn a language better if you visit the country where it is spoken.* 如果到說某種語言的國家去，就會把這種語言學得更好。◇ *It's a friendly place—people come up to you in the street and start talking.* 這個地方的人很友好，在街上走着就有人上來跟你攀談。

you-all /ˈjuː ɔːl/ (also **y'all**) *pron.* (*informal*) used especially in the southern US to mean *you* when talking to more than one person（尤用於美國南部）你們：*Have you-all brought swimsuits?* 你們都帶游泳衣了嗎？

you'd /juːd/ *short form* **1** you had **2** you would

you'll /juːl/ *short form* you will

young 🔑 /jʌŋ/ *adj., noun*
■ **adj.** (**young·er** /ˈjʌŋɡə(r)/, **young·est** /ˈjʌŋɡɪst/) **1** 🔑 having lived or existed for only a short time; not fully developed 幼小的；未成熟的：*young babies* 幼嬰 ◇ *a young country* 新成立的國家 ◇ *Caterpillars eat the young leaves of this plant.* 毛毛蟲吃這種植物的嫩葉。◇ *a young wine* 新釀的葡萄酒 ◇ *The night is* **still young** (= it has only just started). 夜晚剛剛開始。 OPP **old 2** 🔑 not yet old; not as old as others 年輕的；歲數不大的；相對年輕的：*young people* 年輕人 ◇ *talented young football players* 天才的年輕足球運動員 ◇ *I am the youngest of four sisters.* 我是四姐妹當中最小的。◇ ***In his younger days*** *he played rugby for Wales.* 他年輕的時候在威爾士隊踢橄欖球。◇ *I met the young Michelle Obama at Princeton.* 米歇爾•奧巴馬年輕的時候，我在普林斯頓見過她。◇ *Her grandchildren keep her young.* 她的孫子孫女讓她保持年輕。◇ *My son's thirteen but he's* **young for his age** (= not as developed as other boys of the same age). 我兒子十三歲了，但他比實際年齡顯得小。◇ *They* **married young** (= at an early age). 他們很早結婚。◇ *My mother* **died young**. 我母親去世得早。 OPP **old 3** 🔑 consisting of young people or young children; with a low average age 由年輕人（或兒童）構成的；青少年的；平均年齡小的：*They have a young family.* 他們家的孩子還小。◇ *a young audience* 青少年觀眾 **4** suitable or appropriate for young people 年輕人的；青年的；適合青年人的 SYN **youthful**：*young fashion* 年輕人的時尚 ◇ *The clothes she wears are much too young for her.* 她穿的衣服顯得過於年輕了。 **5 ~ man/lady/woman** used to show that you are angry or annoyed with a particular young person（對年輕人表示生氣或惱怒）：*I think you owe me an apology, young lady!* 小姐，我認為你應該向我道歉！ **6 the younger** used before or after a person's name to distinguish them from an older relative（用於姓名之前或之後，以區別於年長的親戚）：*the younger Kennedy* 年紀較輕的那位肯尼迪 ◇ (*BrE, formal*) *William Pitt the younger* 小威廉•皮特 ➲ compare THE ELDER at ELDER *adj.*, JUNIOR *adj.* (3)
IDM **be getting 'younger** (*informal*) used to say that people seem to be doing sth at a younger age than they used to, or that they seem younger because you are now older（表示做某事的人好像越來越年輕）：*The band's fans are getting younger.* 這支樂隊的歌迷越來越年輕了。◇ *Why do police officers seem to be getting younger?* 為什麼警察好像越來越年輕了？ **not be getting any 'younger** (*informal*) used when you are commenting that time is passing and that you are growing older 老了；歲月不饒人 **ˌyoung at 'heart** thinking and behaving like a young person even when you are old 人老心不老 ➲ more at OLD, ONLY *adv.*
■ ***noun*** [pl.] **1** 🔑 **the young** young people considered as a group（統稱）年輕人，青年人：*It's a movie that will appeal to the young.* 這部電影年輕人會感興趣。◇ *It's a book for* ***young and old alike***. 這本書老少咸宜。 **2** 🔑 young animals of a particular type or that belong to a particular mother 幼崽；幼獸；幼鳥：*a mother bird feeding her young* 餵養幼鳥的鳥媽媽

young·ish /ˈjʌŋɪʃ/ *adj.* fairly young 頗年輕的：*a youngish president* 相當年輕的總裁

ˌyoung of'fender *noun* (*BrE*) a criminal who, according to the law, is not yet an adult but no longer a child 少年犯：*a young offender institution* 少年犯管教所

ˌyoung 'person *noun* (*BrE, law* 律) a person between the ages of 14 and 17（14 至 17 歲的）青少年

young·ster /ˈjʌŋstə(r)/ *noun* (*informal*) a young person or a child 年輕人；少年；兒童：*The camp is for youngsters aged 8 to 14.* 這次夏令營是為 8 至 14 歲的少年兒童安排的。

ˌyoung 'thing *noun* (*informal*) a young adult 青年人：*bright young things working in the computer business* 在電腦行業工作的聰明的青年人

ˌyoung 'Turk *noun* (*old-fashioned*) a young person who wants great changes to take place in the established political system 少壯派激進分子

your 🔑 /jɔː(r); *NAmE* jʊr; *weak form* jə(r)/ *det.* (the possessive form of *you* * you 的所有格形式) **1** 🔑 of or belonging to the person or people being spoken or written to 你的；您的；你們的：*I like your dress.* 我喜歡你的連衣裙。◇ *Excuse me, is this your seat?* 對不起，這是您的座位嗎？◇ *The bank is on your right.* 銀行在你的右邊。 **2** 🔑 of or belonging to people in general（泛指）大家的，人們的：*Dentists advise you to have your teeth checked every six months.* 牙醫建議大家每六個月檢查一次牙齒。◇ *In Japan you are taught great respect for your* *elders.* 在日本，人們要學會非常尊敬長輩。 **3** (*informal*) used to show that sb/sth is well known or often talked about（指有名或經常被談論的人或事物）： *This is your typical English pub.* 這就是典型的英格蘭酒吧。◇ (*ironic, disapproving*) ***You and your bright ideas!*** 你的主意可真高明！ **4 Your** used in some titles, especially those of royal people（用於某些稱呼，尤指王室成員）： *Your Majesty* 陛下◇ *Your Excellency* 閣下

you're /jʊə(r); jɔː(r); *NAmE* jʊr; *NAmE weak form* jər/ *short form* you are

yours 0-w /jɔːz; *NAmE* jərz; jɔːrz; jʊrz/ *pron.*
1 0-w of or belonging to you 你的；您的；你們的：*Is that book yours?* 這是您的書嗎？◇ *Is she a friend of yours?* 她是你的朋友嗎？◇ *My hair is very fine. Yours is much thicker.* 我的頭髮很稀。你的頭髮密多了。 **2** 0-w (usually **Yours**) used at the end of a letter before signing your name（用於書信結尾的簽名前）： (*BrE*) ***Yours sincerely/faithfully*** 您的誠摯的／忠實的◇ (*NAmE*) ***Sincerely Yours*** 您的真摯的◇ (*NAmE*) ***Yours Truly*** 你的忠實的 **3** (*BrE, informal*) your home 你的住所： *Let's go back to yours after the show.* 演出結束後我們回你家。

your·self 0-w /jɔːˈself; *weak form* jə-; *NAmE* jər-; jɔːr-; jʊr-/ (*pl.* **your·selves** /-ˈselvz/) *pron.*
1 0-w (the reflexive form of *you* * you 的反身形式) used when the person or people being spoken to both cause and are affected by an action 你自己；您自己；你們自己： *Have you hurt yourself?* 你傷着自己了嗎？◇ *You don't seem quite yourself today* (= you do not seem well or do not seem as happy as usual). 你今天看上去好像不大舒服。◇ *Enjoy yourselves!* 祝你們玩得開心！ **2** 0-w used to emphasize the fact that the person who is being spoken to is doing sth（強調說話對象做某事）： *Do it yourself—I don't have time.* 你自己做吧，我沒時間。◇ *You can try it out for yourselves.* 你們可以親自試一試。◇ *You yourself are one of the chief offenders.* 你本人就是主犯之一。 **3** you 你；您： *We sell a lot of these to people like yourself.* 我們把許多這種東西賣給您這樣的人。◇ *'And yourself,' he replied, 'How are you?'* "你呢，" 他回應道，"你好嗎？"

IDM **(all) by your'self/your'selves** **1** alone; without anyone else（你／你們）獨自，單獨： *How long were you by yourself in the house?* 你自己一個人在屋裏待了多長時間？ **2** without help（你／你們）獨立地： *Are you sure you did this exercise by yourself?* 這個練習真是你自己做的嗎？ **(all) to your'self/your'selves** for only you to have, use, etc. 獨有；專用： *I'm going to be away next week so you'll have the office to yourself.* 我下週要出差，所以這個辦公室就歸你一個人使用了。 **be your'self** to act naturally 行為自然；不做作： *Don't act sophisticated—just be yourself.* 不要裝得老成持重，表現出你平常的樣子就行了。

youse (also **yous**) /juːz/ *pron.* (*non-standard, dialect*) a word meaning 'you', used when talking to more than one person 你們

youth 0-w /juːθ/ *noun* (*pl.* **youths** /juːðz/)
1 0-w [U] the time of life when a person is young, especially the time before a child becomes an adult 青年時期（尤指成年以前）：*He had been a talented musician in his youth.* 他年輕時很有音樂天才。 **2** 0-w [U] the quality or state of being young 年輕；青春；朝氣： *She brings to the job a rare combination of youth and experience.* 她很年輕，然而幹這份工作已有經驗，這是很難得的。 **3** 0-w [C] (often *disapproving*) a young man 青年男子；小伙子： *The fight was started by a gang of youths.* 這場打鬥是一夥少年挑起來的。 **4** 0-w (also **the youth**) [pl.] young people considered as a group（統稱）青年，年輕人： *the nation's youth* 全國青年◇ *the youth of today* 當代青年◇ *youth culture* 年輕人的文化◇ *youth unemployment* 青年失業問題

'youth club *noun* (in Britain) a club where young people can meet each other and take part in various activities（英國）青年俱樂部

ˌyouth 'custody *noun* [U] (*BrE*) a period of time when a young criminal is kept in a type of prison as a punishment 青少年犯的拘禁期： *He was sentenced to two years' youth custody.* 他被判處在少年犯拘留所拘禁兩年。◇ *a youth custody centre* 青少年犯拘留所

youth·ful /ˈjuːθfl/ *adj.* **1** typical of young people 年輕人的；青年的；青春的： *youthful enthusiasm/energy/inexperience* 青春的激情／活力；年輕人的幼稚 **2** young or seeming younger than you are 年輕的；顯得年輕的： *She's a very youthful 65.* 她 65 歲了，但顯得非常年輕。
▶ **youth·ful·ly** /-fəli/ *adv.* **youth·ful·ness** *noun* [U]

'youth hostel *noun* a building that provides cheap and simple accommodation and meals, especially to young people who are travelling 青年招待所，青年旅舍（為旅行的青年人提供廉價食宿） ➲ COLLOCATIONS at TRAVEL

'youth hostelling *noun* [U] (*BrE*) the activity of staying in different youth hostels and walking, etc. between them 在各地住青年招待所： *to go youth hostelling* 借助青年招待所到處去旅行

YouTube™ /ˈjuːtjuːb; *NAmE* ˈjuːtuːb/ *noun* [U] a website where people can watch and share short videos 視頻網站；影片分享網站

you've /juːv/ *short form* you have

yowl /jaʊl/ *verb* [I] to make a long loud cry that sounds unhappy 哭叫；號哭；號啕大哭 **SYN** **wail** ▶ **yowl** *noun*

'yo-yo *noun, verb, adj.*
■ ***noun*** (also **Yo Yo™**) (*pl.* **yo-yos**, **Yo Yos**) a toy that consists of two round pieces of plastic or wood joined together, with a piece of string wound between them. You put one end of the string around your finger and make the yo-yo go up and down. 悠悠球，溜溜球，搖搖（拉線使圓盤旋轉着沿線上下來回移動）： *He kept bouncing up and down **like a yo-yo**.* 他像一隻悠悠球似的不停地上竄下跳。
■ ***verb*** [I] (+ **adv./prep.**) to change repeatedly in size, amount, quality, etc. from one extreme to another 上下跳動；左右搖擺： *When I was young my weight yo-yoed between 140 and 190 pounds.* 我年輕時體重在 140 到 190 磅之間忽上忽下。
■ ***adj.*** [only before noun] changing repeatedly in size, amount, quality, etc. from one extreme to another 上下跳動的；左搖右擺的： *She worries about her pattern of yo-yo dieting.* 節食後體重反彈，再節食再反彈，她對這種模式很擔心。

yr (also **yr.** especially in *NAmE*) *abbr.* **1** (*pl.* **yrs**) YEAR(S)： *children aged 4–11 yrs* * 4 至 11 歲的兒童 **2** YOUR

yt·ter·bium /ɪˈtɜːbiəm; *NAmE* ɪˈtɜːrb-/ *noun* [U] (*symb.* **Yb**) a chemical element. Ytterbium is a silver-white metal used to make steel stronger and in some X-RAY machines. 鐿

yt·trium /ˈɪtriəm/ *noun* [U] (*symb.* **Y**) a chemical element. Yttrium is a grey-white metal used in MAGNETS. 釔

yuan /juˈɑːn/ *noun* (*pl.* **yuan**) the unit of money in China 元（中國貨幣單位） ➲ see also RENMINBI

yucca /ˈjʌkə/ *noun* a tropical plant with long stiff pointed leaves on a thick straight STEM, often grown indoors 絲蘭（葉劍形堅挺，常種於室內）

yuck (*BrE* also **yuk**) /jʌk/ *exclamation* (*informal*) used to show that you think sth is disgusting or unpleasant（表示憎厭）討厭，可惡： *It's filthy! Yuck!* 髒死了！真惡心！

yucky (*BrE* also **yukky**) /ˈjʌki/ *adj.* (*informal*) disgusting or very unpleasant 討厭的；令人生厭的；令人厭惡的： *yucky food* 難以下嚥的食物

Yue /jəˈweɪ; jʊˈeɪ/ *noun* = CANTONESE *n.* (1)

Yule /juːl/ *noun* [C, U] (*old use* or *literary*) the festival of Christmas 聖誕節

'yule log *noun* **1** a large LOG of wood traditionally burnt on Christmas Eve 聖誕節原木（傳統上在聖誕夜燒的大原木） **2** a chocolate cake in the shape of a LOG, traditionally eaten at Christmas 聖誕節原木（巧克力）蛋糕

Yule·tide /ˈjuːltaɪd/ *noun* [U, C] (*old use* or *literary*) the period around Christmas Day 聖誕節期間：*Yuletide food and drink* 聖誕食物和飲料

Y

yum /jʌm/ (also **ˌyum-ˈyum**) *exclamation* (*informal*) used to show that you think sth tastes or smells very nice（表示味道或氣味非常好）

yummy /ˈjʌmi/ *adj.* (*informal*) very good to eat 很好吃的 **SYN** **delicious**：*a yummy cake* 好吃的蛋糕

ˈyummy mummy *noun* (*pl.* **-ies**) (*BrE*, *informal*) an attractive young woman who is the mother of a young child or children 年輕漂亮的媽媽；辣媽：*celebrity yummy mummies* 年輕漂亮的名人媽媽

yup·pie (also **yuppy**) /ˈjʌpi/ *noun* (*pl.* **-ies**) (*informal*, often *disapproving*) a young professional person who lives in a city and earns a lot of money that they spend on expensive and fashionable things 雅皮士（城市中收入高、生活優裕的年輕專業人員）**ORIGIN** Formed from the first letters of the words 'young urban professional'. 由 young urban professional 的首字母組成。

yup·pify /ˈjʌpɪfaɪ/ *verb* (**yup·pi·fies**, **yup·pi·fy·ing**, **yup·pi·fied**, **yup·pi·fied**) [often passive] **~ sth** (*informal*, *disapproving*) to make sth such as an area of a city more expensive and fashionable, and attractive to yuppies 使（市區等）更華貴時髦；使雅皮士化；使雅痞化：*a yuppified area of London* 倫敦一處雅皮士化地區 ▸ **yup·pi·fi·ca·tion** /ˌjʌpɪfɪˈkeɪʃn/ *noun* [U]

yurt /jɜːt; *NAmE* jɜːrt/ *noun* a type of traditional tent used in Mongolia and Siberia 蒙古包（蒙古和西伯利亞的圓頂帳篷）

YWCA /ˌwaɪ dʌbljuː siː ˈeɪ/ (also *NAmE*, *informal* **the Y**) *abbr.* Young Women's Christian Association (an organization that exists in many countries and provides accommodation and social and sports activities) 基督教女青年會：*members of the YWCA* 基督教女青年會的會員

Y

Zz

Z (also **z**) /zed; *US* ziː/ *noun* (*pl.* **Zs**, **Z's**, **z's** /zedz; *US*ziːz/) **1** [C, U] the 26th and last letter of the English alphabet 英語字母表的第 26 個字母：*'Zebra' begins with (a) Z/'Z'.* * zebra 一詞以字母 z 開頭。 **2 Z's** [pl.] (*NAmE, informal, humorous*) sleep 睡覺；睡眠：*I need to **catch some Z's**.* 我需要睡一會兒。**IDM** see A *n.*

'Z angles *noun* = ALTERNATE ANGLES

zany /ˈzeɪni/ *adj.* (**zani·er**, **zani·est**) (*informal*) strange or unusual in an amusing way 古怪的；滑稽可笑的 **SYN** **wacky**：*zany humour* 古怪的幽默

zap /zæp/ *verb* (**-pp-**) (*informal*) **1** [T] to destroy, kill or hit sb/sth suddenly and with force（突然而猛烈地）毀壞，殺死，打擊：**~ sb/sth** *The monster **got zapped** by a flying saucer* (= in a computer game). 怪獸被飛碟殺死了。◇ *It's vital to zap stress fast.* 快速消除壓力非常重要。◇ **~ sb/sth with sth** *He jumped like a man who'd been zapped with 1 000 volts.* 他像受到 1 000 伏的電擊似的猛跳起來。**2** [I] **+ adv./prep.** to do sth very fast 很快地做；迅速做：*I'm zapping through* (= reading very fast) *some modern novels at the moment.* 我現在正在迅速地瀏覽一些現代小說。 **3** [I, T] **~ (sth)** to use the REMOTE CONTROL to change television channels quickly （用遙控器）快速變換頻道 **4** [I, T] **~ (sb/sth) + adv./prep.** to move, or make sb/sth move, very fast in the direction mentioned （使沿某方向）快速移動 **SYN** **zip**：*The racing cars zapped past us.* 賽車從我們身邊飛馳而過。

zap·per /ˈzæpə(r)/ *noun* (*informal*) **1** = REMOTE CONTROL (2) **2** a device or weapon that attacks or destroys sth quickly 滅殺器：*a bug zapper* 滅蟲器

ZAR *abbr.* the written abbreviation for the South African RAND (= the national money of South Africa) 南非蘭特（全寫為 South African Rand，書面語，即南非貨幣）：*All prices listed are in ZAR.* 所有價格都是用南非蘭特列出的。

zeal /ziːl/ *noun* [U, C] **~ (for/in sth)** (*formal*) great energy or enthusiasm connected with sth that you feel strongly about 熱情；激情：*her **missionary/reforming/religious/political zeal*** 她的傳教士般的／改革／宗教／政治熱情

zealot /ˈzelət/ *noun* (often *disapproving*) a person who is extremely enthusiastic about sth, especially religion or politics （尤指宗教或政治的）狂熱分子，狂熱者 **SYN** **fanatic**

zeal·ot·ry /ˈzelətri/ *noun* [U] (often *disapproving*) the attitude or behaviour of a zealot 狂熱分子的態度（或行為）：*religious zealotry* 宗教狂熱行為

zeal·ous /ˈzeləs/ *adj.* (*formal*) showing great energy and enthusiasm for sth, especially because you feel strongly about it 熱情的；熱烈的；充滿激情的：*a zealous reformer* 充滿激情的改革者 ▸ **zeal·ous·ly** *adv.*

zebra /ˈzebrə; ˈziːbrə/ *noun* (*pl.* **zebra** or **zebras**) an African wild animal like a horse with black and white lines (= STRIPES) on its body 斑馬

ˌzebra ˈcrossing *noun* (*BrE*) an area of road marked with broad black and white lines where vehicles must stop for people to walk across 斑馬線；斑馬紋行人穿越道 ➲ see also PEDESTRIAN CROSSING, PELICAN CROSSING

zebu /ˈziːbuː/ *noun* (*pl.* **zebus** or **zebu**) an animal of the cow family with long horns and a HUMP (= high part) on its back, kept on farms especially in hot climates 瘤牛

zeit·geist /ˈzaɪtɡaɪst/ *noun* [sing.] (from *German, formal*) the general mood or quality of a particular period of history, as shown by the ideas, beliefs, etc. common at the time 時代精神；時代思潮 **SYN** **spirit of the times**

Zen /zen/ *noun* [U] a Japanese form of Buddhism 日本禪宗

zen·ith /ˈzenɪθ/ *noun* **1** the highest point that the sun or moon reaches in the sky, directly above you 天頂（太陽或月亮在天空中的最高點） **2** (*formal*) the time when sth is strongest and most successful 鼎盛時期；頂峰 **SYN** **peak** **OPP** **nadir**

zephyr /ˈzefə(r)/ *noun* (*old-fashioned* or *literary*) a soft gentle wind 和風；微風

Zep·pelin /ˈzepəlɪn/ *noun* a German type of large AIRSHIP 齊柏林飛艇（源自德國的大型飛艇）

zero 🔑 /ˈzɪərəʊ; *NAmE* ˈzɪroʊ; ˈziː-/ *number, verb*

■ ***number*** **1** 🔑 (*pl.* **-os**) (*BrE* also **nought**) 0 零：*Five, four, three, two, one, zero ... We have lift-off.* 五、四、三、二、一、零… 我們升空了。 **2** 🔑 a temperature, pressure, etc. that is equal to zero on a scale（氣溫、壓力等的）零度，零點：*It was ten degrees below zero last night* (= −10°C). 昨天夜裏的氣溫是零下 10 攝氏度。◇ *The thermometer had fallen to zero.* 溫度計顯示溫度降到了零度。**3** 🔑 the lowest possible amount or level; nothing at all 最少量；最低點；最低程度；毫無：*I rated my chances as zero.* 我覺得我根本沒有機會。◇ *zero inflation* 零通脹

■ ***verb*** (**zer·oes**, **zero·ing**, **zer·oed**, **zer·oed**) **~ sth** to turn an instrument, control, etc. to zero 將（儀器、控制裝置等）調到零

PHR V **ˌzero ˈin on sb/sth** **1** to fix all your attention on the person or thing mentioned 集中全部注意力於：*They zeroed in on the key issues.* 他們集中討論了關鍵問題。 **2** to aim guns, etc. at the person or thing mentioned （用槍炮等）瞄準

ˌzero-ˈcarbon *adj.* in which the amount of CARBON DIOXIDE produced has been reduced to nothing or is balanced by actions that protect the environment 零碳的（指碳排放量減為零或通過環保行為抵銷的） **SYN** **carbon neutral**：*a zero-carbon house* 零碳環保住宅

ˌzero ˈgravity *noun* [U] (*abbr.* **ˌzero ˈG**) a state in which there is no GRAVITY, or where gravity has no effect, for example in space（太空等的）零重力狀態，失重狀態

ˌzero ˈgrazing *noun* [U] a farming method that involves keeping cows inside and bringing them cut grass, rather than letting them feed in the fields 零放牧（刈割牧草飼牛的圈養方式）

ˈzero hour *noun* [U] the time when an important event, an attack, etc. is planned to start 零時；發動（進攻等的）時刻

ˌzero-ˈrated *adj.* (*BrE, technical* 術語) (of goods, services, etc. 貨品、服務等) that you do not need to pay VAT (= value added tax) on 免付增值稅的

ˌzero-ˈsum game *noun* a situation in which what is gained by one person or group is lost by another person or group 一方得益一方受損的局面；得失相抵的情形

ˌzero ˈtolerance *noun* [U] the policy of applying laws very strictly so that people are punished even for offences that are not very serious 零容忍政策（指對輕微過失都不予放過的嚴厲執法政策）

zest /zest/ *noun* **1** [sing., U] **~ (for sth)** enjoyment and enthusiasm 熱情；狂熱 **SYN** **appetite**：*He had a great **zest for life**.* 他對生命有着極大的熱情。 **2** [U, sing.] the quality of being exciting, interesting and enjoyable 興奮；激動；有趣；愉快：*The slight risk added zest to the experience.* 冒了一點兒險使得這次經歷更加有趣。 **3** [U] the outer skin of an orange, a lemon, etc., when it is used to give flavour in cooking 柑橘外皮（包括檸檬或橙子等的外皮層，用於調味） ➲ compare PEEL *n.* (1), RIND (1), SKIN *n.* (4) ▸ **zest·ful** /-fl/ *adj.* **zesty** /ˈzesti/ *adj.*

zeta /ˈziːtə/ *noun* the 6th letter of the Greek alphabet (Ζ, ζ) 希臘字母表的第 6 個字母

zeug·ma /ˈzjuːɡmə; *NAmE* ˈzuːɡ-/ *noun* [C, U] (*technical* 術語) the use of a word which must be understood in two different ways at the same time in order to make sense, for example 'The bread was baking, and so was I.' 軛式搭配法，軛式修飾法（一個詞以不同的詞義同時與兩個詞搭配使用）

zig·gurat /ˈzɪɡəræt/ *noun* in ancient Mesopotamia, a tower with steps going up the sides, sometimes with a TEMPLE at the top 塔廟，廟塔（古代美索不達米亞的階梯式金字塔形建築）

zig·zag /ˈzɪɡzæɡ/ *noun, verb*

■ **noun** a line or pattern that looks like a series of letter W's as it bends to the left and then to the right again 鋸齒形線條（或形狀）；之字形：*The path descended the hill in a series of zigzags.* 小路順着山坡蜿蜒而下。▸ **zig·zag** *adj.* [only before noun]：*a zigzag line/path/pattern* 彎彎曲曲的線條／小路／形狀

■ **verb** (**-gg-**) [I] (**+ adv./prep.**) to move forward by making sharp sudden turns first to the left and then to the right 曲折前進：*The narrow path zigzags up the cliff.* 狹窄的路曲曲折折通向懸崖。

zilch /zɪltʃ/ *noun* [U] (*informal*) nothing 沒有；毫無：*I arrived in this country with zilch.* 我來到這個國家時身上一無所有。

zilla (also **zillah**) /ˈzɪlə/ *noun* (in S Asia) a district that has its own local government（南亞）行政專區

zil·lion /ˈzɪljən/ *noun* (*informal, especially NAmE*) a very large number 非常多：*There were zillions of people there.* 那裏人山人海。

Zim·mer frame™ /ˈzɪmə freɪm; *NAmE* ˈzɪmər/ (also *informal* **Zim·mer** /ˈzɪmə(r)/) (both *BrE*) (*NAmE* **walk·er**) *noun* a metal frame that people use to help them to walk, for example people who are old or who have sth wrong with their legs 齊默式助行架 ➲ picture at FRAME

zinc /zɪŋk/ *noun* **1** [U] (*symb.* **Zn**) a chemical element. Zinc is a bluish-white metal that is mixed with COPPER to produce BRASS and is often used to cover other metals to prevent them from RUSTING. 鋅 **2** [C] (*informal*) (in some places in Africa) a sheet of CORRUGATED iron that is used to make a roof, shelter, etc.（非洲某些地方用於搭建屋頂、棚子等的）波紋鐵板，瓦楞鐵板：*They built a temporary home out of zincs.* 他們用瓦楞鐵板搭建了一個臨時住所。

ˌzinc ˈoxide *noun* [U] (*symb.* **ZnO**) a substance used in creams as a treatment for certain skin conditions 氧化鋅（用於皮膚膏）

'zine (also **zine**) /ziːn/ *noun* (*informal*) a magazine, especially a FANZINE 雜誌（尤指愛好者雜誌）

zing /zɪŋ/ *verb, noun*

■ **verb** (*informal*) **1** [I, T] **~ (sth) + adv./prep.** to move or to make sth move very quickly, often with a high whistling sound（使）呼嘯疾行：*electrical pulses zinging down a wire* 迅速通過電線的電脈衝 **2** [T] **~ sb/sth (for/on sth)** (*NAmE*) to criticize sb strongly 嚴厲批評；斥責

■ **noun** [U] (*informal*) interest or excitement 興趣；激動；興奮 ▸ **zingy** *adj.*

zing·er /ˈzɪŋə(r)/ *noun* (*informal, especially NAmE*) a clever or amusing remark 妙語；有趣的話：*She opened the speech with a real zinger.* 她的開場白十分風趣。

Zion·ism /ˈzaɪənɪzəm/ *noun* [U] a political movement that was originally concerned with establishing an independent state for Jewish people, and is now concerned with developing the state of Israel 猶太復國運動；猶太復國主義；錫安主義 ▸ **Zion·ist** /ˈzaɪənɪst/ *noun, adj.*

zip /zɪp/ *noun, verb*

■ **noun 1** (also **ˈzip fastener**) (both *BrE*) (also **zip·per** *NAmE, BrE*) [C] a thing that you use to fasten clothes, bags, etc. It consists of two rows of metal or plastic teeth that you can pull together to close sth or pull apart to open it. 拉鏈；拉鎖：*to do up/undo/open/close a zip* 拉上／拉開拉鏈 ◇ *My zip's stuck.* 我的拉鏈卡住了。➲ VISUAL VOCAB page V63 **2** [U] (*informal*) energy or speed 能量；速度 **3** [sing.] (*informal, especially NAmE*) nothing 零；沒有；毫無：*We won four zip (= 4–0).* 我們以四比零獲勝。◇ *He said zip all evening.* 整個晚上他一聲不吭。

■ **verb** (**-pp-**) **1** [T] to fasten clothes, bags, etc. with a zip/zipper 拉上拉鏈：**~ sth** *I zipped and buttoned my jacket.* 我把夾克的拉鏈拉上，繫好扣子。◇ **~ sb/yourself into sth** *The children were safely zipped into their sleeping bags.* 孩子們都安安穩穩地躺在睡袋裏，拉鏈也給他們拉好了。◇ **~ sth + adj.** *He zipped his case shut.* 他拉上了箱子的拉鎖。➲ compare UNZIP **2** [I] **~ (up/together)** to be fastened with a zip/zipper 用拉鏈鎖上：*The sleeping bags can zip together.* 這些睡袋可用拉鏈連起來。**3** [I, T] **~ (sth) + adv./prep.** (*informal*) to move very quickly or to make sth move very quickly in the direction mentioned（使沿某方向）快速移動：*A sports car zipped past us.* 一輛跑車從我們身邊呼嘯而過。**4** [T] **~ sth** (*computing* 計) to COMPRESS a file (= make it smaller) 壓縮（文件）**OPP** **unzip**

PHR V **ˌzip ˈup | ˌzip sb/sth ˈup** to be fastened with a zip/zipper; to fasten sth with a zip/zipper 拉上拉鏈；拉上…的拉鏈：*This jacket zips up right to the neck.* 這件夾克的拉鏈一直拉到脖子。◇ *Shall I zip you up* (= fasten your dress, etc.)? 要我給你拉上拉鏈嗎？➲ compare UNZIP

ˈzip code (also **ZIP code**) (*US*) (*BrE, CanE* **post·code**) *noun* a group of letters and/or numbers that are used as part of an address so that post/mail can be separated into groups and delivered more quickly 郵政編碼；郵編

Ziploc bag™ /ˈzɪplɒk bæɡ; *NAmE* -lɑːk/ *noun* (*NAmE*) a small plastic bag for storing food, that has edges that seal when you press them together in order to keep the air out 齊普洛克保鮮袋；自封袋；夾鏈袋

zip·per /ˈzɪpə(r)/ (*especially NAmE*) (*BrE* also **zip**, **ˈzip fastener**) *noun* a thing that you use to fasten clothes, bags, etc. It consists of two rows of metal or plastic teeth that you can pull together to close sth or pull apart to open it. 拉鏈；拉鎖 ➲ VISUAL VOCAB page V63

zippy /ˈzɪpi/ *adj.* (**zip·pier**, **zip·pi·est**) (*informal*) **1** able to move very quickly 迅捷的；速度快的：*a zippy little car* 飛快的小汽車 **2** lively and exciting, especially in flavour 活潑的；（味道）清新濃郁的，提神的：*a wine with a zippy tang* 味道濃郁的葡萄酒

ˈzip-up *adj.* [only before noun] (*especially BrE*) (of clothing, a bag, etc. 衣服、袋子等) fastened with a zip/zipper 用拉鏈的：*a zip-up top* 拉鏈上衣

zir·co·nium /zɜːˈkəʊniəm; *NAmE* zɜːrˈkoʊ-/ *noun* [U] (*symb.* **Zr**) a chemical element. Zirconium is a hard silver-grey metal that does not CORRODE very easily. 鋯

zit /zɪt/ *noun* (*informal, especially NAmE*) a spot on the skin, especially on the face（尤指臉上的）丘疹 **SYN** **pimple** ➲ compare SPOT *n.* (3)

zith·er /ˈzɪðə(r)/ *noun* a musical instrument with a lot of metal strings stretched over a flat wooden box, that you play with your fingers or a PLECTRUM 齊特琴（匣式弦樂器，用手指或撥子演奏）

zo·diac /ˈzəʊdiæk; *NAmE* ˈzoʊ-/ *noun* **1 the zodiac** [sing.] the imaginary area in the sky in which the sun, moon and planets appear to lie, and which has been divided into twelve equal parts each with a special name and symbol 黃道帶（天球上的十二個等份區，各有其名稱和符號，日、月、行星分佈其中）：*the* ***signs of the zodiac*** 黃道十二宮 **2** [C] a diagram of these twelve parts, and signs that some people believe can be used to predict how the planets will influence our lives 黃道十二宮圖（用於占星術）▸ **zo·di·ac·al** /zəʊˈdaɪəkl; *NAmE* zoʊ-/ *adj.*

zom·bie /ˈzɒmbi; *NAmE* ˈzɑːmbi/ *noun* **1** (*informal*) a person who seems only partly alive, without any feeling or interest in what is happening 無生氣的人；麻木遲鈍的人 **2** (in some African and Caribbean religions and in horror stories) a dead body that has been made alive again by magic（某些非洲和加勒比地區的宗教及恐怖故事中）靠巫術起死回生的僵屍

zonal /ˈzəʊnl; *NAmE* ˈzoʊnl/ *adj.* (*technical* 術語) connected with zones; arranged in zones 地帶的；區域的；分成區的

zone 0━ /zəʊn; *NAmE* zoʊn/ *noun, verb*

■ **noun 1** 0━ an area or a region with a particular feature or use（有某特色或作用的）地區，地帶：*a* ***war/security/demilitarized, etc. zone*** 交戰區、安全區、非軍事區等 ◇ *an* ***earthquake/danger, etc. zone*** 地震帶、危險地帶等 ◇ *a* ***pedestrian zone*** (= where vehicles may not go) 步行區 ➲ see also NO-FLY ZONE, TIME ZONE, TWILIGHT **2** 0━ one of the areas that a larger area is divided into for the purpose of organization（規劃的）區域，分區：*postal charges to countries in zone 2* 到位於

Z

第 2 郵區的國家的郵資 **3** an area or a part of an object, especially one that is different from its surroundings（尤指有別於周圍的）區域，部份：*When the needle enters the red zone the engine is too hot.* 當指針進入紅色區域時，發動機就過熱了。◇ *the erogenous zones of the body* 身體的性慾發生區 ➲ see also CRUMPLE ZONE **4** one of the parts that the earth's surface is divided into by imaginary lines that are parallel to the EQUATOR（地球表面與赤道平行的）氣候帶：*the northern/southern temperate zone* 北／南温帶

IDM **in the 'zone** (*NAmE, informal*) in a state in which you feel confident and are performing at your best 處於最佳狀態：*When I'm in the zone, writing is the most satisfying thing in the world.* 當我狀態好的時候，寫作是世界上最讓我愉快的事。

■ ***verb*** [usually passive] **1 ~ sth (for sth)** to keep an area of land to be used for a particular purpose 將…劃作特殊區域；指定…為某項用途的區域：*The town centre was zoned for office development.* 鎮中心被劃定為寫字樓開發區。 **2 ~ sth** to divide an area of land into smaller areas 將…分成區（或劃成帶） ▸ **zon·ing** *noun* [U]

PHR V **ˌzone 'out** (*especially NAmE, informal*) to fall asleep, become unconscious or stop paying attention 入睡；失去知覺；走神：*I just zoned out for a moment.* 我剛睡着了一會兒。

zoned /zəʊnd; *NAmE* zoʊnd/ *adj.* **1** divided into areas designed for a particular use 劃成（特殊）區域的：*zoned housing land* 劃定為住宅區的土地 **2** (also **ˌzoned 'out**) (both *NAmE, informal*) not behaving or thinking normally because of the effects of a drug（由於毒品作用而）舉止怪異的，精神恍惚的，神志不清的

zonked /zɒŋkt; *NAmE* zɑːŋkt; zɔːŋkt/ *adj.* [not before noun] **~ (out)** (*slang*) extremely tired or suffering from the effects of alcohol or drugs 極度疲憊；筋疲力盡；醉酒；麻醉

zoo /zuː/ *noun* (*pl.* **zoos**) (also *formal* **ˌzoological 'garden(s)**) a place where many kinds of wild animals are kept for the public to see and where they are studied, bred and protected 動物園

zoo·keep·er /'zuːkiːpə(r)/ *noun* a person who works in a zoo, taking care of the animals 動物園管理員

zoo·logic·al /ˌzəʊə'lɒdʒɪkl; ˌzuːə'l-; *NAmE* ˌzoʊə'lɑːdʒ-/ *adj.* connected with the science of ZOOLOGY 動物學的

ˌzoological 'garden *noun* (also **ˌzoological 'gardens** [pl.]) (*formal*) = ZOO

zo·olo·gist /zəʊ'ɒlədʒɪst; zu'ɒl-; *NAmE* zoʊ'ɑːl-/ *noun* a scientist who studies zoology 動物學家

zo·ology /zəʊ'ɒlədʒi; zu'ɒl-; *NAmE* zoʊ'ɑːl-/ *noun* [U] the scientific study of animals and their behaviour 動物學 ➲ compare BIOLOGY (1), BOTANY

zoom /zuːm/ *verb, noun*

■ ***verb*** **1** [I] **+ adv./prep.** (*informal*) to move or go somewhere very fast 快速移動；迅速前往 **SYN** **rush, whizz**：*Traffic zoomed past us.* 車輛從我們身邊疾馳而過。◇ *For five weeks they zoomed around Europe.* 他們在歐洲各國馬不停蹄地奔波了五個星期。 **2** [I] **~ (up) (to …)** (*informal*) (of prices, costs, etc. 價格、費用等) to increase a lot quickly and suddenly 急劇增長；猛漲：*House prices have zoomed up this year.* 今年房屋價格飛漲。

PHR V **ˌzoom 'in/'out** (of a camera 攝影機或攝像機) to show the object that is being photographed from closer/further away, with the use of a ZOOM LENS（用變焦距鏡頭）拉近，推遠；使畫面放大（或縮小）：*The camera zoomed in on the actor's face.* 攝影機將演員的臉拉近了。

■ ***noun*** **1** [C] = ZOOM LENS：*a zoom shot* 用變焦距鏡頭拍的照片 **2** [sing.] the sound of a vehicle moving very fast（車輛等）疾馳的聲音

'zoom lens (also **zoom**) *noun* a camera LENS that you use to make the thing that you are photographing appear nearer to you or further away from you than it really is 變焦距鏡頭 ➲ VISUAL VOCAB page V41

zoot suit /'zuːt suːt; *BrE* also sjuːt/ *noun* a man's suit with wide trousers/pants and a long loose jacket with wide shoulders that was popular in the 1940s 佐特套裝（流行於 20 世紀 40 年代的男裝，褲管寬大、上衣長而寬鬆、肩寬）

zorb·ing /'zɔːbɪŋ; *NAmE* 'zɔːrb-/ *noun* [U] a sport in which sb is put inside a large transparent plastic ball which is then rolled along the ground or down hills 滾人球運動（人在大型透明塑料球中沿地面或山坡翻滾）

Zoro·ast·rian·ism /ˌzɒrəʊ'æstriənɪzəm; *NAmE* ˌzɔːroʊ-/ *noun* [U] a religion started in ancient Persia by Zoroaster, that teaches that there is one God and a continuing struggle in the world between forces of light and dark 瑣羅亞斯德教，拜火教（始於古代波斯，由瑣羅亞斯德創立，宣揚一神論，認為世界上存在光明與黑暗之間的永恆鬥爭） ▸ **Zoro·ast·rian** *noun, adj.* ➲ see also PARSEE

zuc·chini /zu'kiːni/ *noun* (*pl.* **zuc·chini** or **zuc·chi·nis**) (*NAmE*) (*BrE* **cour·gette**) a long vegetable with dark green skin and white flesh（深綠皮）西葫蘆 ➲ VISUAL VOCAB page V31

Zulu /'zuːluː/ *noun* **1** [C] a member of a race of black people who live in South Africa 祖魯人（南非的一個黑人種族的成員） **2** [U] the language spoken by Zulus and many other black South Africans 祖魯語 ▸ **Zulu** *adj.*

Zuni /'zuːni/ *noun* (*pl.* **Zuni** or **Zunis**) a member of a Native American people many of whom live in western New Mexico 祖尼人（美洲土著，很多居於新墨西哥州西部）

zwie·back /'zwiːbæk/ *noun* [U] (*NAmE*, from *German*) slices of sweet bread that are cooked again until they are dry and hard 烤乾麵包片

zy·deco /'zaɪdɪkəʊ; *NAmE* -koʊ/ *noun* [U] a type of dance music, originally played by black Americans in Louisiana 柴迪科舞曲（最早由美國路易斯安那州的黑人演奏）

zy·gote /'zaɪgəʊt; *NAmE* -goʊt/ *noun* (*biology* 生) a single cell that develops into a person or animal, formed by the joining together of a male and a female GAMETE (= a cell that is provided by each parent) 受精卵；合子

Oxford Writing Tutor
牛津寫作指南

Using the Oxford Advanced Learner's Dictionary to improve your writing
利用《牛津高階英語詞典》提高寫作水平

Whether you are writing a business email or a long research essay, your dictionary can be a powerful tool to assist you in becoming a better writer in English.
無論撰寫商業電子郵件或長篇研究論文，本詞典是有助於提高英語寫作水平的強效工具。

1. Using the main part of the dictionary
利用本詞典的正文部份

You can use the main A–Z of the dictionary to help you 本詞典的 A–Z 正文部份有助於：

- **Choose your words carefully.** Many words in English have similar or related meanings, but are used in different contexts or situations. **慎重選擇詞彙。** 英語中有許多詞語意思相近或相關，但語境或使用場合不同。

> Look carefully at the example sentences provided in the entries for words you want to use. Also look at any **synonyms notes, vocabulary notes** and **topic notes** to help you choose the most appropriate word. If you need academic vocabulary, look for the **AW** symbol.
> 仔細閱讀擬用單詞所在詞條中提供的例句，也要閱讀同義詞辨析說明、詞彙辨析說明和主題說明，以便選擇最恰當的詞。如果需要使用學術詞彙，請查找 **AW** 標識。

- **Combine words naturally and effectively.** In English, certain pairs of words go together and sound natural to native speakers (for example, *heavy rain*)—and others do not (~~*strong rain*~~). This is called **collocation**. Information on which words collocate with one another can be found in the example sentences in the dictionary entries.
搭配道地自然。 在英語中，有些詞必須搭配使用，母語為英語的人聽上去才道地自然（如 heavy rain）——而與其他詞搭配使用則變得不自然（~~strong rain~~）。這稱作詞語搭配。有關哪些詞相互搭配的情況可在本詞典詞條的例句中找到。

> Look up the key nouns you have used in your writing to check which verbs or adjectives are usually used with them.
> 在詞典中查閱寫作時所使用的主要名詞，弄清楚哪些動詞或形容詞通常與它們搭配。

- **Become more flexible.** Rather than repeating the same word or phrase many times in your work, try to find other ways to express your ideas. **表達方式更多樣。** 設法找到其他表達方式，而不是在文章中多次重複同一個詞或短語。

> Look for the **SYN** symbol to find synonyms and also study the **synonyms notes**. Look for **word families** and try using words in the same family that are different parts of speech (e.g. *different*, adjective and *differ*, verb). For example, you could write: *French **is different from** English in this respect.* You could also express this: *French **differs from** English in this respect.* 找到 **SYN** 標識下所列同義詞並研讀同義詞辨析說明。找到詞族，試着使用同一詞族中不同詞類的詞彙（如形容詞 different 和動詞 differ）。例如，可以寫：French **is different from** English in this respect.（在這方面法語有別於英語。）也可以寫：French **differs from** English in this respect.

- **Edit and check your work** 校訂和檢查作業 You can use your dictionary to check any problem areas such as spelling, parts of speech, irregular forms, grammar, phrasal verbs, and prepositions. 利用本詞典可檢查任何有問題之處，如拼寫、詞類、不規則形式、語法、短語動詞以及介詞。

2. Using the Writing Tutor 利用牛津寫作指南

In the following pages you will find examples of essays and practical types of writing that you can use as models for your own work. You will also find advice about planning, organizing and writing each type of text. 在本指南的餘下部份會提供參考範文和實用寫作體裁，還有關於各類文本謀篇佈局和寫作的建議。

- **Examples of written texts** 範文
  Look carefully at 仔細閱讀以下幾方面：
  - the structure and organization of the text 篇章結構和組織
  - the way ideas and paragraphs are linked 構思和段落銜接
  - the language and style 語言和文體
  - the notes on particular points 特別說明
- **Tips** 提示 These are quick reminders and advice to help when you are writing. 這部份提供寫作的便捷提醒和建議。
- **Language banks** give you some useful phrases that you can use in each type of writing. 用語庫提供了各類寫作中一些有用的短語。

> Check that you are familiar with these phrases and know how to use them correctly. 確保自己熟悉並知道如何正確使用這些短語。

You can add other phrases when you meet them in your reading. In the main part of the dictionary there are more notes like this which give you further phrases and examples to show you how to use them. (*For example, look at the note at 'however'.*) 也可以補充閱讀過程中遇到的其他短語。在本詞典的正文部份有更多類似的說明，提供了更多的短語和例子說明它們的用法，如 however 條的說明。

Contents 目錄

The writing process 寫作過程

Each individual writer has their own aims and needs and their own way of approaching various parts of the writing process. However, whether you are writing a short essay, an article, a report or a research paper, the overall process is generally the same. 每位作者都有自己的目的、需要以及對寫作過程各階段的處理方式。不過，無論是寫短文、文章、報告，還是寫研究論文，總體過程大致相同。

1 Preliminary Phase 準備階段

Ask yourself some planning questions that will help guide the rest of the process. 問自己一些有助於指引餘下過程的規劃性問題。

What is the purpose of this piece of writing? 這篇文章的目的是什麼？

For example 例如：

- To answer a specific essay, examination or research question 回答特定的論述題、考試題或研究課題
- To convince others of your point of view 說服他人相信你的觀點
- To communicate your knowledge or understanding to others, such as a teacher or an examiner 將自己的知識或看法告訴他人，比如老師或主考人

Who is my audience? 我的讀者是誰？

For example 例如：

- A teacher or professor 老師或教授
- Fellow students or colleagues 同學或同事
- An employer 僱主
- The general public 公眾

The answers (you may have more than one purpose or type of audience) will help you to choose the appropriate level of formality. They will also help you make decisions about the amount of research required, as well as the kinds of examples and supporting evidence you will use. 這些答案（可能有不止一個目的或一類讀者）會有助於選擇適當的正式程度，也有助於確定需要投入的研究工作量以及要引用何種例子和佐證。

2 Pre-Writing Phase 寫作前階段

Explore 探討

Brainstorm for ideas using whatever method suits you best 以任何適合自己的方式開動腦筋找靈感：

- Mind maps 畫出思維導圖
- Lists of interesting concepts, facts, questions, etc. 列出有趣的概念、事實、問題等
- Conversations with colleagues 與同事交談討論

Research 調查研究

Next, research your topic and gather information from a variety of sources 接下來，就論題進行調查研究並以各種渠道收集信息：

- Books and journals 書籍和報刊
- The media 媒體
- Websites 網站
- Interviews or questionnaires 訪談或問卷
- Scientific studies 科學研究

When you read sources, take detailed notes and keep an accurate record of each source. (*Look at page WT16.*) 閱讀原始資料時要做詳細筆記並準確記錄出處。（見 WT16 頁）

Organize 組織

After carrying out your research, you can draft a thesis (your main argument, statement or idea) to guide you. 完成調研之後可草擬論題（主要論點或想法）以引導寫作。

Then, using your notes, make a detailed outline of the logical plan of your essay, article or report to support this thesis, giving a structure to your writing before you begin to write. 然後，利用筆記圍繞這個論題對文章或報告的謀篇佈局列出詳細提綱，給文章設好框架再動筆寫。

- Decide roughly how many words you will give to each part of your essay/report. 確定論文/報告各個部份的大致字數。
- Collect or prepare any visual aids such as charts or diagrams that you might need. 收集或準備任何可能需要的視覺材料，如圖表或簡圖。

3 Writing Phase 寫作階段

In this phase, you will draft and revise several times until you have what you consider to be a final draft. 在這一階段，要起草並反複修改初稿，直到自己認為已經定稿。

Draft 初稿

Write your draft in formal sentences and paragraphs. 用正式的句子和段落寫初稿。

- Remain focused on your thesis main idea. If you do change this, go back and adapt your original plan to ensure that your essay/report continues to support the new thesis. 緊扣主要論點。如果一定要改變論點，那麼就回頭修改原提綱以確保論文/報告仍然支持新的論點。
- Follow your outline, modifying it if necessary. 按照提綱寫作，如果有必要可邊寫邊修改提綱。
- In early drafts, concentrate on structure rather than spelling and punctuation. 寫前幾稿時把注意力放在結構上，而不是拼寫和標點符號。

Review/Edit 檢查/修訂

In this step, you read your writing with a critical eye. 在這一步，用挑剔的眼光閱讀自己的文章。

In early drafts, ask yourself 檢查前幾稿時問自己：

- Have you answered the question or achieved your original purpose? 回答了問題或達到了最初的目的嗎？
- Have you introduced your subject, developed it logically and come to a conclusion? 介紹了主題、有邏輯地闡述主題並得出結論了嗎？
- Is your supporting evidence appropriate and complete? Do you need more examples, statistics or quotes? 佐證恰當並充分嗎？需要增加例子、統計數據或引文嗎？
- Have you used headings to help the reader, if appropriate? 適當運用標題方便讀者閱讀了嗎？
- Are the relationships between ideas clear and clearly signaled to the reader? 思路清楚嗎？清楚地向讀者表明了嗎？
- Is each part the right length for the demands of the topic – with no part too long? 各部份長度符合題目要求嗎？有沒有過長的部份？

In later drafts, ask yourself 檢查後幾稿時問自己：

- Have you used paragraph breaks well? 段落劃分得當嗎？
- Is the level of formality appropriate for your readers? 文體正式程度適合讀者嗎？
- Have you chosen your words carefully, using correct collocations? 選詞是否謹慎？搭配是否正確？
- Have you avoided repeating the same words or phrases too often (except technical terms)? 避免過多地重複相同的詞或短語（術語除外）了嗎？
- Have you met any word count requirements? 符合字數的要求嗎？

If possible, ask someone else to read your text. 如果有可能，請人讀一下你的文章。

After each review, return to the drafting step, revising and editing your writing as necessary. 每檢查一次都要回到撰寫草稿這一步，如果有必要就進行修改校正。

Using sources in essays 在文章中使用原始資料

Ask yourself 問自己：

Have you quoted or mentioned sources to support your points? 已引用或提及原始資料以支持自己的論點了嗎？

Have you used the citation style recommended by your teachers or institution? 已使用老師或學校所推薦的引文格式了嗎？

Have you listed your references in the style recommended? 按推薦使用的格式列出參考文獻了嗎？

(*Look also at page WT18.* 另見 WT18 頁。)

4 Presentation Phase
提交前最後檢查階段

Proofread 校對

When you have a final draft of your writing, you will need to read it once more to find and correct surface errors. 終稿完成之後需要再讀一遍，以便發現並改正字面錯誤。

Tip 提示

- Try to leave some time between your final draft and proofreading as you will find it easier to see your mistakes. 在完成終稿和校對之間盡量留出一段時間。這可以使你更容易看到自己的錯誤。

Check for 檢查

- Spelling 拼寫
- Punctuation 標點符號
- Grammatical mistakes 語法上的錯誤

You may find it helpful to ask someone else to proofread your final draft as a last step. 你會發現在最後階段時找人校對終稿很有幫助。

Format 格式

Check with your teacher or tutor how you should present your work in terms of 跟老師或導師弄清楚提交文章時所要求的格式：

- Font size 字體大小
- Margins 邊距
- Line spacing 行距

Examinations 考試

In an exam, you will not have time for all these stages, but your answers will be more successful if you 考試時不會有時間完成所有這些步驟，但通常可以：

- brainstorm ideas 開動腦筋找靈感
- organize and plan 組織和構思
- re-read, check and edit 重新閱讀、檢查和修訂

What makes writing formal?
撰寫正式文章的要素

Whatever type of text you are writing, your aim should always be to express your ideas clearly and in a way that your readers can easily understand. 無論寫何種體裁的文章，目標始終應該是清楚地、用讀者容易理解的方式闡述自己的思想。

When you read, notice the kind of language that is used in the type of writing you need to do. 閱讀時留意自己需要使用的寫作體裁的語言。

To make your writing more formal, consider 寫較正式的文章需要考慮：

1. **Word choice** 選詞
   - It is usually best to use standard English words and phrases, that is, those with no label in the dictionary. 通常最好使用標準的英語詞彙和短語，即本詞典中沒有標識的詞語。
   - Only use words and phrases marked *formal* if you are sure they are appropriate. 在確保合適的情況下，才用標示為“正式”的詞彙和短語。
   - Avoid anything marked *informal*, *slang*, *offensive*, etc. 避免任何標示為“非正式”、“俚語”、“冒犯”等的表達方式。
   - Use suitable synonyms for common words such as *do*, *put*, *get*, *make*. e.g. *Several operations* ***were carried out/performed*** (not *done*). 用適當的同義詞替代如 do、put、get、make 等常用詞。例如 Several operations **were carried out/performed** （不用 done）。
   - Words that are frequently used in academic writing are marked **AW** in the dictionary. 在本詞典中，學術文章中的常用詞標示為 **AW**。

2. **Short forms** 簡寫形式
   - Avoid contracted forms (e.g. *haven't, I'm*) and abbreviations (e.g. *ad – advertisement*). 避免使用縮寫形式（如 haven't、I'm）和縮略語（如 ad – advertisement）。

3. **Sentence structure** 句子結構

- In formal writing you are likely to be expressing complex ideas. To do this you will need to write sentences using relative pronouns (e.g. *which*, *that*), subordinating conjunctions (e.g. *although*, *because*, *if*) and coordinating conjunctions (e.g. *and*, *but*, *or*). 正式寫作中往往要表達複雜的思想，因此，需要使用關係代詞（如 which、that）、從屬連詞（如 although、because、if）和並列連詞（如 and、but、or）組句。
- Very long sentences with many clauses can be difficult to understand. Aim for **clarity**. 帶許多從句的長句會很難理解。要力求清楚。

Academic writing 學術寫作

This tends to be **impersonal** in style in order to be objective. This makes it sound formal. When you read in your subject, notice how the writers express themselves. The following points may help you in your writing 學術寫作在風格方面往往不涉及個人感情以表示客觀。這使它顯得正式。閱讀有關的專業文獻時，留意作者如何表達思想。以下幾點可能有助於你的寫作：

- Limit the use of the **first person pronouns** (*I* and *we*). Rather than *In this study I aim to* ..., write: *This study aims to* ... or *The aim of this study is to* ... Look at how *I* and *we* are used in your subject area. Avoid using *you*. 盡量不用第一人稱代詞（I 和 we）。寫：*This study aims to* ... 或 *The aim of this study is to* ...，而不要寫：*In this study I aim to* ...。看一下自己的專業領域中 I 和 we 的用法。避免使用 you。
- **Passive forms** are often used as they focus attention on the verb, not the person 被動形式強調動詞而不是人，因此經常使用。e.g. 如 *A study was conducted to see* ...; *It can be argued that* ...
- Patterns with **it and an adjective** are often used 經常使用 it + 形容詞這一模式：*It is clear that* ...; *It is necessary to* ...
- **Nouns** are often used as subjects of active verbs 名詞常用作主動動詞的主語：*The results show that* ...
- **Complex noun phrases** with prepositions are very common 後接介詞的複合名詞短語很常見：*The advantages of X are* ...; *the use of light treatment in 95 patients with* ...

Answering the question 回答問題

At all times, you must ensure that you really understand an examination question or assignment title and address all the required parts. 任何時候都要確保真正理解試題或作業題目，並解答所有需要解答的部份。

Questions can be considered in terms of three main components 可按三個主要組成部份考慮問題：

- **Topic** 主題
- **Scope and focus** 範圍和重點
- **Question type** 問題類型

Topic 主題

The topic(s) of the question will usually be clear from the question itself.
問題的主題通常看問題本身就一目瞭然。For example 例如：
Explain the process of photosynthesis. 解釋光合作用的過程。
When you write your answer think about why the examiner has chosen to ask about this topic.
解答時考慮一下出考題的人為什麼選擇問這個主題。

Scope and focus 範圍和重點

Often, the wording of the question will include a word or phrase that either limits or expands the topic in a very specific way. These phrases show you the focus of the question. 問題的措辭中往往包含明確的限定或詳述主題的詞或短語。這些短語顯示出問題的重點。
Try to avoid common mistakes, such as 盡量避免犯常見的錯誤，如：

- **Covering too broad an area.** For example, if the question asks about textile mills in the American South in the 1930s, think very carefully about including information about the 1920s or 1940s, or about textile mills in other parts of the country. 覆蓋面過寬。例如，如果問題是關於美國南部在 20 世紀 30 年代的紡織廠，那麼要十分慎重地考慮是否包括 20 世紀 20 年代和 40 年代的、或這個國家其他地區紡織廠的信息。
- **Writing with too narrow a focus.** For example, if you are asked about the impact of climate change on South America, you should not write about its impact only on Brazil.
寫作重點過窄。例如，如果問題是關於氣候變化對南美的影響，就不能只寫它對巴西的影響。
- **Including irrelevant information.** For example, if you are asked about using nuclear power as an energy source, you should not write about wind or solar power. 包含無關信息。例如，如果問題是關於使用核能作能源，就不能寫風能或太陽能。
- **Only answering half of the question.** For example, if the question asks *What other effects will a reduction in air travel have and will the advantages outweigh the disadvantages?* you need to discuss both questions. 解答問題不全面。例如，如果問題是「減少乘飛機會有什麼其他影響？會利大於弊嗎？」那麼就得對兩個問題都進行討論。

Question types 問題類型

The depth and type of information that you provide in your answer depends on the kind of question being asked. The table on the next page shows the key words that might appear in different types of questions. 回答問題時所提供信息的深度和類型取決於問題的類型。下頁的表格中顯示各類問題中可能出現的關鍵詞語。

IELTS Academic Writing 雅思考試學術寫作

- Task 1 任務 1：This is usually a combination of comprehension and analysis questions 通常結合了理解型與分析型的問題：*Summarize the information ... and make comparisons where relevant.*
- Task 2 任務 2：This is usually an evaluation question 通常為評價型問題：*At what age should young people be considered adults? Explain your position.*

1. Knowledge Questions 知識型問題

These ask you to recall important facts and are the simplest question.
此類問題要求背誦重要的事實，是最簡單的問題。

2. Comprehension Questions 理解型問題

These ask you to demonstrate your understanding of concepts. You must clearly show that you understand the ideas and theories that underlie the facts. 此類問題要求說明自己對概念的理解。必須清楚地表現出自己理解用以解釋事實的概念和理論。

3. Application Questions 應用型問題

Here you use your knowledge of facts and concepts to address a specific problem. These questions require you to move beyond simple recollection. 此處要利用自己對事實和概念的瞭解解決具體問題。回答此類問題不能局限於簡單的背誦資料。

4. Analysis Questions 分析型問題

These examine relationships between/among various facts and concepts.
此類問題探討各種事實和概念之間的關係。

5. Synthesis Questions 綜合型問題

These ask you to create a new product or structure in written form.
此類問題要求以書面形式建立新的產物或體系。

6. Evaluation Questions 評價型問題

These ask you to make value judgments and present your own opinions. This kind of question is very common in academic work. It is important to support your opinions by citing the work and views of experts in the field, if possible. 此類問題要求作出價值判斷並表達自己的看法，這在學術作業中很常見。盡可能引用該領域專家的著作和觀點來支持自己的看法，這很重要。

Question Types 問題類型

Level of Difficulty 難度

6. Evaluation Questions 評價型問題

Key verbs 關鍵動詞

- discuss 討論
- evaluate 評價
- compare 比較
- consider 考慮
- examine 檢查
- explore 探討
- comment (on) 評論
- justify 證明…正確
- appraise 評價
- weigh 權衡
- support 支持
- recommend 建議

Example 例如：
Discuss the argument that the use of force in self-defence is justifiable. 就用武力進行自衛是正當的這一論點進行討論。

5. Synthesis Questions 綜合型問題

Key verbs 關鍵動詞

- design 設計
- plan 規劃
- construct 構想
- create 建立
- compose 撰寫
- produce 製作
- develop 開發
- invent 發明
- combine 組合

Example 例如：
Design an experiment to investigate whether listening to music improves students' performance in their studies. 設計一個實驗以研究聽音樂能否提高學生的學習效率。

4. Analysis Questions 分析型問題

Key verbs 關鍵動詞

- analyze 分析
- compare 比較
- contrast 對比
- distinguish 區分
- differentiate 辨別
- subdivide 再分
- classify 分類
- categorize 歸類
- select 選擇
- infer 推斷
- prioritize 劃分優先順序

Example 例如：
Compare the merits of 'renting' and 'squatting' as solutions to housing problems for the poor in cities in the developing world. 比較"租房"和"偷住空房"作為發展中國家城市貧民住房問題的解決方法的各自優點。

3. Application Questions 應用型問題

Key verbs 關鍵動詞

- apply 應用
- show 說明
- solve 解決
- choose 選擇
- organize 組織
- generalize 概括
- prepare 準備
- relate (X to Y) 說明（X 和 Y 的）關係

Example 例如：
Show how a national minimum wage will affect levels of unemployment and total output.
說明國家最低工資將如何影響失業率和總產量。

2. Comprehension Questions 理解型問題

Key verbs 關鍵動詞

- explain 解釋
- summarize 概括
- illustrate 舉例說明
- restate 重新表述
- paraphrase 釋義
- give examples 舉例
- express 表述
- distinguish (between) （在…之間）區別
- trace 描述過程
- match 配對

Example 例如：
Give three examples of human activities that have major effects on our climate. 舉出三個例子說明人類活動對我們的氣候產生重大影響。

1. Knowledge Questions 知識型問題

Key verbs 關鍵動詞

- outline 概述
- define 界定
- describe 描述
- give 給出
- state 說明
- summarize 概括
- label 歸類
- identify 識別
- name 陳說
- list 列舉

Example 例如：
Define the term 'muscle tone' and describe how it can help good posture. 請界定術語"肌肉張力"並描述它如何能有助於保持良好的姿勢。

Writing a comparison essay 撰寫對比文

You may often need to **compare** and **contrast** things in exams, academic essays, work and everyday life. Here is an example of a comparison essay. 也許你在考試、寫學術論文、工作和日常生活中經常需要比較和對比事物。以下是一篇對比文範文。

Are private schools better than state schools? Discuss.

For parents, few things are more important than their child's education. In many countries, parents of school-age children can choose to send their child to a private school rather than to a state school.[1] In this essay, state schools are defined as those that do not charge tuition fees because they are funded and run by local or central government; private schools, on the other hand, are funded almost entirely by the fees that they charge.[2] Before deciding where to educate their child, parents need to examine the differences between the two types of school, particularly as regards the curriculum, the quality of tuition and student achievement.[3]

Private and state schools are comparable in some respects. Like state schools, private schools aim to develop the knowledge, skills and character of students, in order to prepare them for their future lives. Both types of school are also very similar in the way they organize their teaching and assessment, using terms or semesters with assessments at the end of the academic year.

Despite these similarities, there are a number of marked differences in the way that state and private schools operate. The range of subjects taught at state schools is largely limited by the demands of the national curriculum. In contrast, private schools can offer a greater choice of subjects, because they generally have more money to spend on equipment, technology and staff than state schools do.

Teachers working within the state system must have recognized teaching qualifications and are paid according to a national scale. Private schools, however, are in a position to offer higher salaries and may therefore be able to attract subject specialists who have considerable expertise in their field.

In general, it is true to say that while state schools have a high student-teacher ratio, private schools tend to offer smaller classes. This may lead to better discipline in private schools with the result that students may achieve somewhat higher academic standards.

It is clear, therefore, that there are significant differences between private and state schools, and that private schools may offer advantages.[1] The benefits of private schooling must, however, be balanced against the cost involved and each family's budget priorities.[2]

Paragraph 1—Introduction
第 1 段——引言

[1] Sentences 1 and 2 catch the reader's interest. 第 1、第 2 句引發讀者的興趣。

[2] The next sentence gives a definition of the two types of school. (Note: a definition is optional) 下一句給出兩種學校的定義。(註：定義並非是必需的)

[3] The 4th sentence indicates the scope of the essay and leads to the next paragraph. 第 4 句指出文章的範圍並引出下一段。

Paragraph 2—Similarities
第 2 段——相似點

Aims, teaching and assessment
目標、教學和評估

The writer notes 2 similarities here before emphasizing 5 differences in paragraphs 3–5.
在第 3 至 5 段強調 5 處差別之前，作者首先指出 2 個相似點。

Paragraph 3—Difference 1
第 3 段——差別之一

The curriculum 課程

Despite these similarities indicates that the writer is now going to list the differences. * Despite these similarities 表示作者即將列舉不同點。

Paragraph 4—Difference 2
第 4 段——差別之二

Quality of teachers 教師素質

Paragraph 5—Differences 3–5
第 5 段——差別三至五

Class size, discipline and academic standards 班級大小、紀律和學術水平

Paragraph 6—Conclusion
第 6 段——結論

[1] The first sentence summarizes the findings in paragraphs 2–5. 第 1 句歸納第 2–5 段的討論結果。

[2] The second sentence gives the writer's personal opinion. 第 2 句提出作者本人的看法。

Key 說明

Blue shows ways of introducing similarities 藍色表示介紹相似點的方式

Yellow shows ways of introducing contrasts 黃色表示介紹對比的方式

Collocations: adjectives + nouns 搭配：形容詞＋名詞

To find interesting and appropriate adjectives to use with nouns, look up the nouns in the dictionary: e.g. *difference*; *expertise*; *ratio*; *standard* 要找到與名詞連用的有趣而且恰當的形容詞，在本詞典中查閱有關名詞：如 difference、expertise、ratio、standard

Collocations: prepositions 搭配：介詞

To find the correct preposition to use after a verb or noun, look up the word in the dictionary: e.g. *difference*; *balance* 要找到動詞或名詞後接的正確的介詞，在本詞典中查閱這個詞：如 difference、balance

Preparing to write 準備寫作

- **Brainstorm ideas** about similarities and differences. For example, arrange points in a table 開動腦筋找出相似點和不同點。例如，將要點用表列出：

Characteristics 特點	State Schools 公立學校	Private Schools 私立學校	Similar or different? 相似還是不同？
Funding 資金來源	*Government* 政府	*Fees* 學費	*Different* 不同
Class size 班級大小	*Usually large* 通常較大	*Usually smaller* 通常較小	*Different* 不同

- **Highlight the similarities and the differences** and decide which are more important. For this essay the differences are more important. 突出顯示相似點和不同點並決定哪方面更重要。在範文中，不同點更重要。
- **Choose which points to include** in the essay and which to leave out. 選擇文章中哪些論點要包括在內和哪些要捨棄。
- Decide how to **define** the two things you are comparing. Here *funding* formed the basis of the definition. 決定如何定義所比較的兩個事物。在範文中 funding（資金來源）構成定義的基礎。
- Choose the **organization structure** (*see below*). Here **Type A1** was used. 選擇組織結構（見下）。範文使用了 A1 類。

<table>
<tr>
<td>

Shorter essays 短文

Type A1 * A1 類：to emphasize the **differences** 強調不同點

Introduction 引言

Similarities of X and Y * X 和 Y 的相似點

Differences between X and Y * X 和 Y 的不同點

Conclusion 結論

OR 或 **Type A2** * A2 類：To emphasize the **similarities**, reverse the second and third sections. 強調相似點時，將以上第二、三部份顛倒次序即可。

</td>
<td>

OR 或 **Type B1** * B1 類：

Introduction 引言

Characteristics of X * X 的特點

Characteristics of Y * Y 的特點

Show how Y is **similar** to or **different** from X 說明 Y 與 X 如何相似或不同。

Conclusion 結論

</td>
</tr>
<tr>
<td>

Longer essays 較長的文章

Type C1 * C1 類

Introduction 引言

Aspect 1 第一個方面：compare X and Y 比較 X 和 Y

Aspect 2 第二個方面：compare X and Y (and so on) 比較 X 和 Y（以此類推）

Conclusion 結論

</td>
<td>

OR 或

Type A1 or **A2** above. 上述 A1 或 A2 類。

</td>
</tr>
</table>

Language bank 用語庫

Similarities 相似	**Differences** 不同
X … Similarly, Y …	*X … On the other hand, Y … / Y, on the other hand, …*
Both X and Y …	*Unlike X, Y …*
X … Y also …	*X … In contrast, Y … / While X … , Y …*
Both + plural noun 複數名詞 … e.g. *Both types of school …*	*X … , while Y …*
Like X, Y … e.g. *Like state schools, private schools …*	*X … However, Y … / X … Y, however, …*
X and Y are similar in that they both …	*X differs from Y in terms of / with regard to …* (e.g. *their sources of funding.*)
X is similar to Y in terms of / with regard to …	*X is different from / contrasts with Y in that …*
X resembles Y in that they both …	*X … , whereas Y … / Whereas X … , Y …*
X is the same as Y.	

Being more precise 更加準確地比較：

Similarities 相似

X is almost / nearly / virtually / just / exactly / precisely *the same as Y.*

X and Y are very / rather / quite *similar.*

Differences 不同

X is slightly / a little / somewhat *smaller than Y.*

X is much / considerably *smaller than Y.*

X and Y are completely / totally / entirely / quite *different.*

X and Y are not quite / exactly / entirely *the same.*

Writing an argument essay 撰寫議論文

Many essays that you have to write, whether during your school or college course or in an examination, will require you to present a reasoned argument on a particular issue. This will often be based on your research into the topic, but some questions may ask you to give your opinion. In both cases your argument must be clearly organized and supported with information, evidence and reasons. The language tends to be formal and impersonal. 在學校學習或考試期間，許多要寫的文章要求就某一問題進行合乎邏輯的論述。這往往基於專題調查研究，但有些問題可能要求陳述己見。這兩種情況均要求論述組織清晰並有資料、證據和理由為依據。語言風格往往需要正式和客觀。

'Manned space missions should now be replaced with unmanned missions.' Discuss.

Paragraph 1—Introduction
第 1 段——引言

[1] Introduces the topic. 介紹主題。

[2] States the focus of the essay. 說明文章重點。

It is clear that the study of space and the planets is by nature expensive. Scientists and politicians must constantly attempt to balance costs with potential research benefits.[1] A major question to be considered is whether the benefits of manned space flight are worth the costs.[2]

Paragraph 2—Introduces the argument 第 2 段——介紹論點

The first point (manned missions are not cost effective) with a quote from an expert to give authority. 第一點（載人航天任務不划算）引用專家的話以增加權威性。

[1] This is a useful way to introduce a quotation. 這是很有用的引用方式。

For Nobel Prize-winning physicist Steven Weinberg the answer is clear. As he noted in 2007[1] in a lecture at the Space Telescope Science Institute in Baltimore. 'Human beings don't serve any useful function in space. They radiate heat, they're very expensive to keep alive, and unlike robotic missions, they have a natural desire to come back, so that anything involving human beings is enormously expensive.'

Paragraph 3—Development
第 3 段——論述

Reasons and data are given to support the writer's point of view. 給出理由和數據以支持作者的觀點。

Unmanned missions are much less expensive than manned, having no requirement for airtight compartments, food or life support systems. They are also lighter and therefore require less fuel and launch equipment. According to NASA, the 1992 manned Space Shuttle Endeavor cost $1.7 billion to build and requires approximately $450 million for each launch. In contrast, the entire unmanned Voyager mission from 1972 until 1989, when it observed Neptune, cost only $865 million.

Paragraph 4—Development
第 4 段——論述

Introduces the second point (unmanned projects are more scientifically productive). 介紹第二點（無人項目的科學效益更高）。

In addition to their relative cost effectiveness, unmanned projects generally yield a much greater volume of data. While manned flights have yet to extend beyond the orbit of Earth's moon, unmanned missions have explored almost our entire solar system, and have recently observed an Earth-like planet in a nearby solar system. Manned missions would neither be able to travel so far, be away so long, nor collect so much data while at the same time guaranteeing the astronauts' safe return.

Paragraph 5 — Counterargument
第 5 段——反方論點

[1] Presents the argument: *Some may argue* suggests that the writer will go on to argue against this position. 給出論點：Some may argue 表明作者將反駁這種觀點。

[2] Refutes it. *However* introduces the argument against [1]. 反駁。However 引出相反的論點。

Some may argue that only manned space flight possesses the ability to inspire and engage the general population, providing much-needed momentum for continued governmental funding and educational interest in mathematics and the sciences.[1] However, media coverage of recent projects such as the Mars Rover, the Titan moon lander, and the Hubble telescope's photographs of extrasolar planets demonstrates that unmanned missions clearly have the ability to attract and hold public interest.[2]

Paragraph 6—Conclusion
第 6 段——結論

Summarizes the writer's points and states his/her conclusion on the title. 歸納作者的論點並申明他／她關於這個主題的結論。

[1] *Thus* introduces the conclusion. * Thus 引出結論。

[2] *I would argue that* clearly shows the writer's position. * I would argue that 清楚地表明作者的立場。

Thus,[1] taking into account the lower cost, the greater quantity of data and widespread popular support, I would argue that[2] for now, at least, unmanned space missions undoubtedly yield the most value in terms of public spending.

Linking words and phrases guide the reader through the argument and show the writer's opinion. 銜接詞和短語在論證過程中引導讀者並表明作者的看法。

Adverbs can be used to show your opinion. 副詞可用來表達看法。

These phrases make the argument less personal and more objective. 這些短語使論述更加客觀。

Experts are quoted to support the argument. 引用專家的話支持論點。

Preparing to write 準備寫作

- Brainstorm your ideas on the question, read and research the topic (unless in an examination). Which do you think are the strongest arguments? Decide what your viewpoint will be. 針對問題開動腦筋搜羅想法，閱讀並搜集相關資料（考試時除外）。你認為哪些論據最有力？決定你將從哪個角度論述。
- Select 2 or 3 strong ideas on each side, with supporting examples, ideas or evidence. For some questions you can use evidence from your personal experience. 每個方面選 2 個或 3 個有說服力的論點，加上作為依據的例證、觀點或證據。有些問題可以用個人經歷作為證據。
- Decide how to organize your essay to persuade readers of your case. 決定如何組織文章以說服讀者。
- Note down some useful vocabulary on the topic. 記下有關論題的一些有用詞彙。

Structure 1 (used in the model essay) 結構一（用於範文中）	**Structure 2** 結構二
Introduction 引言	Introduction 引言
Arguments **for** your case + supporting evidence, examples or reasons 正方論點 + 作為依據的證據、例證或理由	Argument 1 論點一：+ supporting evidence, examples or reasons * + 作為依據的證據、例證或理由
Arguments **against** + evidence 反方論點 + 證據	Counterargument 反方論點
Evaluation of arguments 對論點的評論	Argument 2 論點二：+ supporting evidence, examples or reasons * + 作為依據的證據、例證或理由
Summary and conclusion 歸納總結	Counterargument (and so on) 反方論點（以此類推）
It is possible to reverse arguments for and against. 可以顛倒正方和反方論點的次序。	Evaluation of arguments 對論點的評論
	Summary and conclusion 歸納總結

Tips 提示

- Look carefully at the **title or question** and make sure you really answer it. 仔細閱讀題目或問題並確保真正作出解答。
- Use **general statements** to convey the main ideas, and then provide **evidence**, **examples**, **details** and **reasons** to support these statements. 概要說明主題思想，然後提供證據、例證、細節和理由作為依據。
- Use **paragraph divisions** and **connecting words and phrases** to make the structure of your essay clear to your readers. 劃分段落並使用銜接詞和短語，以便讀者對文章的結構一目瞭然。
- For **language** to help you structure your argument, look at the notes at 'addition', 'first'. 有關行文的語言，請查閱本詞典 addition 和 first 詞條下的用法說明。

Showing your position 説明立場

When you write an argument essay, you can show what your opinion is on the issue or question without using personal phrases such as *I think* ... or *In my opinion*, ... You can do this by choosing words carefully as you write. Some examples are given below. Look out for more in your reading. 寫議論文時，不使用 I think ... 或 In my opinion ... 之類涉及個人的短語也可以表明自己對問題的看法。可以邊寫邊仔細選詞。下面列出了一些例子，閱讀時再多找一些表達方式。

Language bank 用語庫

Adjectives 形容詞

important, major, serious, significant

e.g. *An **important** point to consider is ...; This was a **highly significant** discovery.*

Patterns with It + adjective * **It +** 形容詞句型

clear, likely, possible, surprising, evident

e.g. ***It is clear that** the study of space is expensive.*

important, difficult, necessary, possible, interesting

e.g. ***It is important to** consider the practical effects of these measures.*

Adverbs and phrases 副詞和短語

clearly, indeed, in fact, of course

generally, usually, mainly, widely

perhaps, probably, certainly, possibly

rarely, sometimes, often

e.g. ***Clearly**, this is a serious issue that deserves further study.*

*This book is **generally** held to be her greatest novel.*

Verbs 動詞

These help show how certain you are about a point or an argument. 以下動詞有助於説明對某個觀點或論點的確定性。

Modal verbs 情態動詞 : can, could; may, might; will, would (*the first of each pair is most certain* 每對情態動詞的第一個詞是用於表示最確定的)

Compare 比較 : *I **argue** that* ... (very certain 很確定). / *I **would argue** that* ... (not so certain 不太確定)

It + verb * **It +** 動詞 : It appears that, It seems that ...

It + passive verb * **It +** 動詞被動式 : It can be seen that ...; It should/must be noted/ emphasized that ...

Showing verbs 表明類動詞 : show, indicate, demonstrate, suggest, imply (*These have a non-human subject* 以非人類名詞作主語)

Arguing verbs 論説類動詞 : argue, suggest, consider, conclude (*These can have a human subject* e.g. *I* 可用人作主語，如 I)

Linking words and phrases 銜接詞和短語

Firstly (= *I have several points to make* 我有幾個論點要提出)

Furthermore ...; In addition, ... Moreover, ... (= *I have another important point* 我有另一個要點)

However, ... (*to introduce a counterargument* 引出反方論點)

Thus, ... Therefore, ... (*to introduce a conclusion* 引出結論)

Writing a longer essay or dissertation 撰寫長篇論文或學位論文

When you have a longer essay or dissertation to write, you will go through the same process of preparing and writing as for shorter essays. (*Look at page WT3.*) However, there are additional things to bear in mind. 撰寫長篇論文或學位論文時，其準備階段和寫作過程與短文一樣。(參見 WT3 頁。) 不過，還要注意另外的一些事項。

The title 題目

If your title or a question has been given to you, check that you understand exactly what it means. (*Pages WT7–9*). If you are writing the title yourself, choose a clear title with definite boundaries. 如果有指定的題目或問題，注意確切地弄懂其意思。(見 WT7–9 頁。) 如需自擬題目，就挑選一個清楚的、界定明確的題目。

Ask yourself 問自己：

- How can I define my subject so that it is not too wide in scope? 我如何界定自己的題目從而不過於寬泛？

e.g. **Not** 不說 *How does Dickens reflect Victorian society in his novels?* **but** 而說 *How does Little Dorrit reflect Dickens's view of Victorian society?*

Reading and research 閱讀和搜集資料：evaluate your sources 評估原始資料

The quality of your research will play a vital part in the success of your writing. Keep the question or title in mind when you look for source material in books, journals or websites. 搜集資料的質量對於寫作成功與否至關重要。搜集書籍、報刊或網站的原始資料時要始終記住問題或題目。

Ask yourself 問自己：

- Is the content relevant? 內容切題嗎？
- Is it reliable? Is it written by someone who is an expert in the field? 資料可靠嗎？是本領域的專家寫的嗎？
- Is it biased in any way? 有任何方面的偏見嗎？
- Is there evidence to support information on anonymous websites? 匿名網站的信息有依據嗎？

If you are using surveys, questionnaires, market research or other studies, look carefully at the statistics and consider if the results are valid and the conclusions justified. 如果採用民意調查、調查問卷、市場調查或其他研究方法，仔細審查統計數據並考慮結果是否可信，結論是否合理。

Making notes 做筆記

When you are reading, make clear, accurate notes which summarize the key points and main information. Keep a note of the full reference for your source (title, author, date, publisher and page numbers). 閱讀文獻時要清楚、準確地做筆記，筆記應歸納要點和主要信息。記下原始資料參考書目的完整信息（題目、作者、日期、出版社和頁碼）。

Ask yourself 問自己：

- Have I summarized the information accurately? 我對信息的歸納準確嗎？
- Is this part particularly useful? If so, have I written down the exact words used and the page number, so that I can quote it? 這部份特別有用嗎？如果是，那麼我有沒有一字不差地摘錄了內容和頁碼以便引用？

Planning and organizing 謀篇佈局

A long text is usually divided into sections with subheadings and it has a list of references or a bibliography at the end. 長篇文章通常劃分為帶小標題的章節，末尾列出參考書目。

When you plan your work, ask yourself
謀劃篇章時要問自己：

- How long should my text and each part be? 我的文章以及各部份應該寫多長？
- Have I organized my notes, grouping together writers who have made similar points? 我有沒有整理筆記、將觀點相似的作者歸到了一類？
- Do I agree with their opinions? 我同意他們的觀點嗎？
- What is the point I want to make to my readers? 我想對讀者説明什麼？
- What do I want my readers to know by the end? 我最終想讓讀者知道什麼？
- Have I planned what to write in the introduction, body and conclusion? 我對引言、主體部份和結論的內容有規劃嗎？

Using other people's ideas 引用他人的觀點

When you have finished writing, look carefully at how you have used other people's words and ideas. 文章完成之後，仔細看一下自己是如何引用他人的話和觀點的。

Ask yourself 問自己：

- Have I considered and discussed other people's ideas adequately? 我充分考慮和討論過他人的觀點嗎？
- Have I paraphrased their ideas accurately? 我對他們的觀點解釋得準確嗎？
- Have I made it clear which words/ideas are mine and whose words/ideas I have quoted? 我是否已清楚説明哪些話/觀點是我本人的，哪些話/觀點是引用的？
- Have I included in my list of references all the works I have used and referred to? 我的參考書目中已列出我所使用和參考過的所有文獻嗎？

Dissertations 學位論文

A dissertation may differ from a long essay in the way in which it is organized. Check with your tutor. A dissertation will usually have all or some of the following chapters or parts.
學位論文與長篇論文組織方式可能不同。可向導師核實。學位論文通常包括下列章節的全部或一部份：

- Title 標題
- Contents 目錄
- Abstract 摘要 (*a short text summarizing your dissertation* 摘寫論文要點的短文)
- Introductory chapter 序篇 (broad to narrow focus 焦點由寬到窄：*to give the background, justify your research, explain your approach, give major arguments and current ideas on your topic and show the structure of your dissertation* 給出研究背景、解釋研究理由、説明研究方法、提出主要論點和當前有關該論題的觀點，並説明論文結構)
- Review of the literature 文獻回顧
- Methodology 研究方法 (*how you carried out any empirical research* 你是如何進行實驗研究的)
- Results/findings 結果/發現
- Discussion 討論
- Conclusion 結論 (narrow to broad focus 焦點由窄到寬：*a summary of your arguments and an evaluation of your work; further research needed* 對自己論點的總結和研究的評價；所需的進一步研究)
- Bibliography or list of references 參考書目

Quoting and writing a bibliography
引述和列出參考書目

If you use the words or ideas of another person, you must always say where these have come from. If you do not, you might be accused of **plagiarism** (= copying another person's ideas or words and pretending that they are yours). 引用他人的話或觀點必須說明出處。如果不這麼做，就會被指控為剽竊（plagiarism，即是抄襲別人的觀點或說話當成自己的觀點或說話）。

Mention the author briefly in the essay and then at the end write a full reference in your **bibliography** or list of references. Different institutions have different styles for this, so check to see the method and punctuation to use, and be consistent. 在文中簡要提及作者，然後在參考書目中給出完整的參考信息。不同機構有不同的參考書目格式，所以要弄清楚應採用的方法和標點，並做到統一。

1. Author-date (Harvard) system
作者—日期（哈佛）格式

Used especially in social and physical sciences. 尤用於社會科學和自然科學。

In the essay or dissertation
文章或學位論文中

In your text, give the family name of the author or editor of the book or article you are referring to and the year of publication in brackets after your quotation or statement. 在正文中，將參考文獻的作者或編者的姓和出版年份放在引文或表述之後的括號內。For example 例如：

> Dialects are not inferior. Most linguists agree that 'a standard language is not linguistically better.' (Swan, 2005:52).
>
> Mason (1995) describes the procedure for a teacher to evaluate each student quickly during an oral presentation.

Give both authors if there are two, but if there are more, cite the first author and add 'et al.' (= and others). 有兩個作者時兩人均要列出，但超過兩個時，則列出第一作者後再加 et al.（…等人）：
(Mason and Wood 2008) or 或 (Mason *et al.*, 2008).

Give the full reference in your bibliography. 參考書目中列出完整的參考信息。

The bibliography 參考書目

In this system, it is often called **References** and is a list of the works that you have mentioned in your text. Give the full reference. 在本格式中，參考書目常稱作 References，指論文中所提到的文獻列表，給出完整的參考信息。

> Swan, Michael. (2005) *Grammar*. Oxford: Oxford University Press.

You need to write 需要寫：

- The surname of the author or editor, followed by the initials or first name 作者或編者的姓，後接名的首字母或名
- The year of publication in brackets 出版年份，置於括號內
- The title of the book, in *italics* or <u>underlined</u> 書名，用斜體或下畫線
- The edition number if it is not the first edition 版本，如果不是第一版的話
- The place of publication (sometimes omitted) 出版地（有時省略）
- The publisher 出版社

2. Footnote/endnote system
腳註／尾註格式

This is a common style to use in writing on arts subjects. One version is described here. 這是文科專業寫作中常用的格式。以下說明其中一種。

In the essay or dissertation
文章或學位論文中

Give details of the source in a numbered **footnote** at the bottom of the page, or at the end of the essay in an **endnote**. Put the same number in your text after the reference. 頁腳帶編號的腳註（footnote）或論文結尾處的尾註（endnote）註明文獻來源的詳細信息。正文參考部份之後標上同一編號：

> Phillips suggests that "parts of the city have remained untouched by the influences of modern life"[1]. He goes on to say that "it is unlike any city in the world"[2].

Footnote 腳註

[1] Patrick Phillips, *A Brief Guide to Rome* (London: Spire Press, 2001) p.36.

If your next quote is from the same source you can just write **ibid**. and the page number. 如果下一引文出處相同，就只寫 ibid. 和頁碼：

[2] ibid. p.38

Later references can be shorter. 之後的參考信息可簡短些：

[23] Phillips, *Guide to Rome*, pp.56–60

The bibliography 參考書目

Give a full list of references at the end of your text, in alphabetical order by the authors' names. Use this order. 論文末列出完整參考書目，按作者姓氏的字母順序編排。用以下順序：

Phillips, Patrick, *A Brief Guide to Rome*. London: Spire Press, 2001

Other examples 其他示例

These apply to both systems, but in the author-date system, the year will go after the author's name. 這些對於兩種格式均適用，但在作者—日期格式中，出版年份置於作者名之後。

Books 書籍

If the book is **edited** 如果是編的書：

Wehmeier, S. ed. *Oxford Advanced Learner's Dictionary*. 7th ed. Oxford: Oxford University Press, 2005

For an **article** in an edited book or journal 文集或期刊中的文章：

Johns, A.M., and T. Dudley-Evans, 'English for Specific Purposes: International in Scope, Specific in Purpose', *TESOL Quarterly* 25 (2), 1991, 297–314.

Newspaper articles 報紙上的文章

Fennell, E. 'How is the recession hitting lawyers?' *The Times*, 31 July 2008, p.54.

Electronic resources 電子資源

Include as much detail as you can find. 盡量列出所有能找到的信息

In your **text**, cite by author if known, otherwise by title or URL, and the year if possible. 在正文中，如果知道作者就按作者引用，否則就按標題或 URL 地址引用，如果可能的話就給出年份：(Directgov, 2008).

In your **bibliography** give the author, the title, volume/page, type of medium, date and publishing organization. Provide the URL and the date you last accessed the page. 在參考書目中列出作者、標題、卷/頁碼、媒體類型、年份和出版機構。提供 URL 地址和最後登錄網頁的日期：

Directgov. 2008.<http://www.direct.gov.uk/en/index.htm> accessed 27 October 2009.

Oral presentations 口頭報告

You may have to give an oral presentation or talk as part of your academic course, for an examination or at work. In many ways, preparing a talk is similar to preparing an essay. The guidelines below apply to most types of talk. 作為學業課程的一部份、在考試或工作中，你都可能必須作口頭報告或演講。準備演講在很多方面類似擬定文稿。以下指導原則適用於大多數類型的演講。

Preparing an oral presentation 準備口頭報告

Good preparation is the most important factor for a successful presentation.
充分準備是成功的報告的最重要因素。

1. First steps 前幾步

- Check the **time** allowed for your talk and any **guidelines** you have been given. 核實規定的演講時間和要遵守的規則。
- Think about the **purpose** of your talk: is it to inform, to entertain or to persuade your audience? 考慮演講的目的：是向聽眾提供信息、是娛樂他們，還是說服他們？
- Think about the **audience**. Who are they? How much do they already know? How much do you need to tell them? What will interest them? 考慮聽眾。他們是誰？他們對話題瞭解多少？你需要告訴他們多少？什麼會引起他們的興趣？
- Decide on the **topic** if you do not know this already. If you do, decide on the specific area that you will present. Be realistic about how much you can cover in the time allowed. 如果還不知道主題，就選定主題。如果知道的話，就選定你想談的具體方面。實事求是地估計在規定的時間內能說多少內容。
- **Collect** your ideas and gather more information if you need to. 彙集自己的想法，如有必要可再收集資料。

2. Writing your talk 寫講稿

- Make notes on what you want to include. Think about what you *must* tell the audience, what you *should* tell them and what you *would like* to tell them if you have time. 將想說的東西記下來。考慮一下有什麼必須告訴聽眾，有什麼應該告訴他們，如果有時間還有什麼想告訴他們。
- Produce an outline or a plan of your talk. 寫出演講提綱。

Tips 提示

- **Structure** your talk as you would an essay: have an introduction, a middle and a conclusion. 像寫文章一樣組織演講：有引言、中間部份和總結。
- Use **headings** to show the different sections of your talk. 用標題標示出演講的各個部份。

- Some people prefer to write out the whole talk like an essay. If you do this, it is better not to read this when you give your talk, but make notes as below and talk from those. 有些人喜歡像寫文章一樣寫出整個演講內容。如果這麼做，那麼演講時最好不要讀稿子，而是按以下方式寫出綱要並照着演講。

3. Producing notes 寫綱要

- Make notes in English on cards that you can refer to while you are speaking. 在卡片上用英語寫出綱要供演講時參考。

- **Open** with an introduction to the title and an overview of what you want to say.
  開宗明義，介紹題目並概述內容：

The benefits of learning a foreign language 1	The benefits of learning a foreign language 2
Show OHT/Slide 1 Intro: **Good morning. My talk today examines** the benefits of learning a foreign language. Overview: **I intend to outline** 3 imp. benefits of learning another lang.	**Show OHT/Slide 2** **The first benefit I shall describe is** practical – communicate with other nationalities **A further benefit is** increased cultural understanding – breaks down barriers / bridges gap between cultures. **The final benefit that I shall describe is** improved cognitive skills – research shows → brain power

Number note card.
為綱要卡片編號。

Note the **number** of the visual you will show. 寫出視覺資料編號。

Write out and **highlight** key words and phrases to **guide** your audience through your talk. 寫出並突出顯示演講中引導聽眾的關鍵詞和短語。

- Try to get the attention of your audience at the beginning with e.g. a story, joke or surprising fact. 開頭講個故事、笑話或奇聞異事等，以設法抓住聽眾的注意力。
- **Close** with a summary and an invitation for people to ask questions.
  收尾時作總結並邀請大家提問。
- Some people find it helpful to write out the whole introduction and conclusion.
  有些人覺得完整地寫出引言和結論很有幫助。

4. Preparing visual aids 準備視覺資料

Visual aids help you to communicate your talk to the audience, if they are prepared carefully and used well. 準備充分並且使用得當的視覺資料有助於傳達演講內容。

Tips 提示

- If you use PowerPoint™ or OHTs (overhead transparencies), writing and diagrams must be large and clear. 如果使用幻燈片演示軟件或投影膠片，其中的文字和圖表一定要大而且清晰。
- Do not put too much information on each slide. 每張幻燈片或膠片上不要放太多內容。
- If you use posters or pictures, check that the people at the back of the room will be able to see/read them. 如果使用海報或圖片，要確保房間後排的人能看到/讀到。
- Avoid writing/drawing things on a whiteboard during your talk. 演講期間要避免在白板上寫字/畫圖。

Examples of OHTs 投影膠片示例

The benefits of learning a foreign language 2	The benefits of learning a foreign language 3
Three main benefits: • Practical uses • Increased cultural understanding • Improved cognitive skills	**1. Practical uses for:** • Travel • Work • Study

Leave lots of white space.
多留些空白。

Use headings and bullets to show the relationship between ideas. 用標題和項目符號顯示要點之間的關係。

Use notes, not sentences.
用短語，不用句子。

5. Practising your talk 練習演講

The more you practise, the more confident you will feel and the better your talk will be.
練習越多就越有自信，演講就越好。

- First, practise your talk alone several times until you can speak fluently and confidently from your notes and keep to the time allowed. 首先，獨自演練幾次，直到能在規定的時間內用講稿綱要流利而自信地演講。
- Then practise with one or more friends listening. Is the talk clear? Is your voice loud and clear? Are you looking at the audience? 然後找一兩個朋友做聽眾進行演練。演講清楚嗎？聲音響亮清晰嗎？目光注視聽眾了嗎？
- If you can, practise at least once with the equipment you will use. 如果可以的話，用所要使用的設備演練至少一次。
- Use your dictionary or dictionary DVD-ROM to check pronunciation, vocabulary and grammar. 用詞典或詞典光盤檢查讀音、詞彙和語法。

6. Preparing for questions 準備回答問題

- Try to predict some of the questions your audience may ask you and practise your answers. 嘗試估計一些聽眾可能提出的問題並練習回答。

Language bank 用語庫

Introduction 引言	**Changing the subject** 轉換話題
Good morning. My talk today examines … *The subject/title of my talk/paper is …* *Hello. Today I'm going to talk about/discuss …*	*So, I have discussed …* *Now I'd like to turn to …* *Moving on to the next/second/last benefit …*
Explaining structure 解釋結構	**Concluding** 總結
In this talk I intend to outline … *In my talk I will discuss the main features of …* *I am going to examine three benefits/advantages of …*	*So, I have talked about …* *To sum up/summarize: in my talk I have …* *In conclusion, I believe it is clear that …* *To conclude: the benefits I have described in my talk are important and therefore I consider that …*
Introducing each point 介紹各要點	**Answering difficult questions** 回答難題
The first/second/next/last point/area … I would like to discuss is … *I want to begin by looking at …* *I'd now like to look at another/the second benefit of …*	*"I'm sorry, I don't quite understand your question. Could you repeat it?"* *"Well, I'm not sure about that, but I think …"*
Clarifying 闡釋	
In other words, … *That is to say …*	

Writing a summary 撰寫摘要

A summary is a shortened version of a text containing only the key information. The aim is to present readers with a short, clear account of the ideas in the text. Summary writing is an important skill in both academic and business contexts. Follow the steps in order to write a successful summary. 摘要是僅包含文本主要信息的簡本，其目的是提供有關文章大意的簡短而清晰的報告。摘要寫作在學術和商業領域中均是一項重要技能。按以下步驟寫一份好的摘要。

Preparing to write 準備寫作

Select the key information 選擇主要信息：

- Read the text carefully, looking up words you don't know. It is important to understand the whole sequence of the argument. Ask yourself what the text is about. Think about the purpose of your summary and what your readers need to know. 仔細閱讀文章，查出不懂的生詞的含義。重要的是要理解論述的整體思路。想想文章寫的是什麼。考慮一下寫摘要的目的和讀者需要瞭解什麼。
- Highlight the **key information** (the main ideas). Omit details such as examples, quotations, information in brackets, repetitions, figures of speech and most figures and statistics. 用彩筆標示主要信息（主題思想）。略去細節，如例子、引語、括號內的信息、重複的內容、修辭以及大多數數字和統計數據。
- Underline any information which you are not sure about. Only include it in your summary if you have space. 用下畫線標示任何不確定的信息。只有當篇幅允許時才把這些信息寫到摘要裏。
- Make notes on the key information in your own words. 用自己的語言就主要信息寫筆記。

Are we living in a surveillance society?

The number of CCTV (or closed-circuit television) cameras in Britain has grown enormously in recent years. There are now more than 4 million, which makes an astonishing one camera for every 14 people.

CCTV has been used for many years for the surveillance of public areas associated with an obvious security risk, such as military installations, airports, casinos and banks. However, since the 1990s, there has been a huge increase in the surveillance of everyday locations such as city and town centres, car parks, shops and traffic. Added to this, more and more individuals are buying their own consumer CCTV systems for personal or commercial use. The most common function of these systems is to survey the area in front of a house or business and record any antisocial or criminal behaviour. People who buy these systems range from wealthy individuals who are afraid of being targeted by burglars, to people who are not wealthy at all but who live in high-crime areas, such as inner cities, and are trying to protect themselves.

For some people, the huge increase in public surveillance is a threat to the individual's civil liberties and is a sign that society is becoming increasingly authoritarian. They argue that the individual's right to privacy and right to live anonymously is an important aspect of being British. They also fear that present or future governments might abuse the information gathered by surveillance in order to manipulate, control or persecute the population, as happens in George Orwell's novel *1984*.

Individuals and groups in favour of CCTV, including the police, believe that it is a valuable weapon against crime. In fact, there is no strong evidence that CCTV reduces crime overall. It may act as a deterrent in certain locations, but the crime is displaced to another location. It is not even always a good deterrent. Many criminals aren't afraid of CCTV because they know that the cameras may not be running, or that no one is likely to be watching the screens. Few crimes are solved through CCTV. Sometimes CCTV footage is analysed retrospectively to identify criminals after a crime has taken place, but even this process is enormously time-consuming and expensive. One promising new development is the computer monitoring of CCTV, where computers are programmed to notice unusual movements, such as those of a car thief in a supermarket car park, and sound an alarm. Meanwhile we can expect the argument about the rights and wrongs of CCTV to continue.

Writing the summary 撰寫摘要

Write a first draft of your summary using the information you have selected.
用選取的信息寫摘要初稿。

- **Organize** the ideas in your notes into a logical order. This need not be the same order as in the original text, but must show the same argument. 有條理地組織摘錄的要點。不必按原文順序排列，但必須體現原文論點。
- **Condense** the information where possible. 盡可能地壓縮信息。
- **Express the ideas in your own words.** This will usually be shorter than the original. Rewrite phrases in the text, but keep any **key terms** from the subject area. 用自己的話表述要點，通常要比原文簡短。重寫原文，但要保留論題領域的關鍵術語。
- Do not give your own opinion on the topic. 不要加進自己對論題的看法。

Your own words: try using synonyms or rephrasing words and expressions such as adjective + noun phrases. Use the dictionary to help you. 自己的話：盡量用同義詞，或重寫詞語和形容詞 + 名詞短語之類的表達方式。可借助詞典。

- *everyday* → ***ordinary***
- *their own consumer CCTV systems for personal … use* → ***private systems***
- *no strong evidence* → ***no clear proof***
- *promising* → ***that may be effective***

Introduce **new terms** and concepts to condense and clarify the argument. For example, **opponents** and **supporters** can be used to refer to those against, and those in favour of, CCTV. 引入新的術語和概念以壓縮和澄清論述。例如，可以用 opponents 和 supporters 指稱反對和支持使用閉路電視的人。

Britain has a very high number of CCTV cameras. **Originally** used for locations with an obvious security risk, CCTV surveillance has **now** spread to ordinary public areas, **while** individuals are **also** buying private systems to protect themselves from crime.

Opponents of the growth in CCTV surveillance base their arguments on the threat to civil liberties and the danger of government misuse of the data acquired by surveillance.

Supporters of CCTV argue that it reduces crime, although there is no clear proof of this. If it acts as a deterrent, crime probably moves to another area. Often it is not a deterrent and it does not solve many crimes. However, the technology is developing in ways that may be effective.

Combine sentences in new ways to condense the argument, e.g. by linking the key ideas with different conjunctions and adverbs from those in the original text. 重新組合句子以壓縮論述，如使用有別於原文的連詞和副詞連接主要觀點。

Rephrase information to shorten it: try changing the verb form or the part of speech. Examples and word families in the dictionary can help. 改變措辭以簡化內容：嘗試變換動詞形式或詞類。本詞典中的示例和詞族會有助這方面的改寫。

e.g. **passive** → **active verb** 如被動式 → 主動式動詞：*Few crimes **are solved** through CCTV* → ***it does not solve many crimes***

noun → **verb** 名詞 → 動詞：*One promising new **development** is …* → ***the technology is developing***

Working on the draft 修改初稿

Ask yourself these questions 問自己以下問題：

- **Is it the right length?** 長度合適嗎？
  If there is a word limit, try to stay as close to it as possible. If your summary is too long, you can usually reduce it further by 如有字數限制，則盡可能接近這一字數。如果摘要過長，通常可以這樣縮短：
  – cutting adjectives 刪除形容詞，e.g. *locations with an obvious security risk* → *locations with a security risk; no clear proof* → *no proof*
  – replacing phrases with shorter versions 用更簡短的表達方式替換短語，e.g. *a lot of/not a lot of* → *many/few*
  If it is still too long, go back and reduce your key information.
  如果仍然過長，就從頭開始縮減主要內容。
- **Does it contain all the important points from the text?** 摘要已包括原文的所有要點嗎？
- **Does it read well?** 讀上去通順嗎？
- **Are the grammar and spelling correct?** 語法和拼寫正確嗎？

Reporting on data 報告數據

The most common types of graphs and charts are **line graphs** (showing developments over a period of time), **bar charts** (comparing the proportions or amounts of different things) and **pie charts** (comparing percentages of parts of a whole piece of data). 圖和圖表中最常見的類型是線形圖（line graph，顯示一段時間內的發展情況）、柱形圖（bar chart，比較不同事物所佔比例或量）和餅分圖（pie chart，比較完整的一批數據中各部份所佔的百分比）。

Preparing to write 準備寫作

Interpreting a line graph 解釋線形圖

It is essential that you understand the information presented in the diagram before you begin writing. 動筆之前先弄懂圖表中顯示的信息，這一點十分重要。

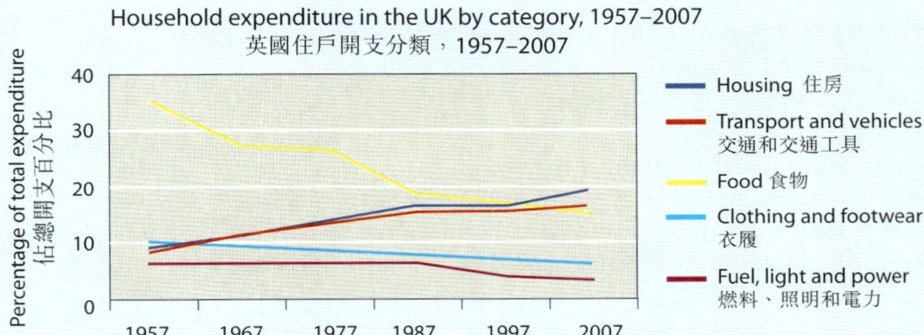

(Statistics from Office for National Statistics 統計資料來自國家統計處)

You should ask yourself these questions 應該問自己以下問題：

What is the information about? 這些信息是關於什麼的？	*the proportion of their money that UK households spent on certain things, on average, over a period of 50 years*
What do the numbers on each axis represent? 各軸上的數字代表什麼？	*horizontal axis: years; vertical axis: percentages*
What changes do the lines show? 這些線顯示出什麼變化？	*Two show an increase and three show a decrease.*
How do the lines stand in relation to each other? 這些線相互間的關係是什麼？	*Two almost always remain below the rest; expenditure is always lower.*
Which feature of the lines stands out most? 這些線最明顯的特徵是什麼？	*Expenditure on food shows a huge decrease.*
What conclusions can be drawn from the graph? 從圖表中可以得出什麼結論？	*Patterns of household expenditure have changed over 50 years; expenditure on food has changed the most.*

Writing the report 撰寫報告

- **Language: accuracy** and **clarity** are the essential features of a good report. The language you use should be plain and simple, but academic in style. 語言：好的報告最重要的特點是準確和清晰。所使用的語言應該清楚簡單，但要有學術風格。
- **Vocabulary:** the range of language you need for describing data is small. (*See the Language Bank*) 詞彙：描述數據的語言很有限。(見用語庫)
- **Organization:** organize the information so that you highlight the **main trends** or features. There is usually more than one suitable way of doing this. For example, for the graph above, you could focus on the relationship between the various spending categories, **or** you could focus on the different directions each has taken over 50 years. (*Look at the structure of the report below*) 組織：組織內容時要突出主要趨勢或特徵；這通常有不止一種適用的方法。例如，關於上頁的圖表，可集中討論各類開支之間的關係，或集中討論 50 年間各類開支所呈現的不同趨勢。(見下面的報告結構)

Summarize the information in the graph by selecting and reporting the main features and make comparisons where relevant.
通過選取和報告主要特徵來概括圖表信息並進行相關比較。

The graph shows what proportion of their total expenditure households in the UK spent, over a fifty year period, in five different categories: housing; transport and vehicles; food; clothing and footwear; and fuel, light and power.

Between 1957 and 2007 expenditure in all five categories changed to some extent, but the most marked change was in the food category.[1] At the beginning of the period the proportion of expenditure on food was more than three times as high as that in all the other categories, representing more than thirty per cent of total household expenditure.[2] However, by 2007 this figure had more than halved to around fifteen per cent, and was slightly less than expenditure on both housing and transport.[3]

The two other areas where proportions of expenditure fell over the period are clothing and footwear, and fuel, light and power.[1] However, the changes here were much less dramatic.[2] Expenditure on the former dropped steadily from ten per cent to five per cent, and on the latter from six per cent to three per cent.[3] For most of the fifty-year period, these categories used up a significantly smaller proportion of the household budget than the others.[4]

In two categories, housing and transport, the proportions of expenditure almost doubled, rising from nine and eight per cent to nineteen and sixteen per cent respectively.[1] Thus, by the end of the period, the highest proportion of household expenditure went on housing, and the lowest on fuel, light and power.[2]

In conclusion, the graph shows that the patterns of spending in UK households changed to some extent over the period 1957 to 2007, the part of the budget spent on food showing the most marked change.

Paragraph 1—Introduction
第 1 段——引言
Describes the subject of the data. 描述數據的主題。

Paragraph 2—Trends
第 2 段——趨勢
[1] a general comment on the trends shown in the graph + main trend. 概要評論圖表顯示的各種趨勢 + 主要趨勢。
[2–3] provide supporting detail on the main trend. 提供支持主要趨勢的細節。

Paragraph 3—Trends
第 3 段——趨勢
More detail on other trends where expenditure has fallen. 有關其他開支下降趨勢的更多細節。
[1, 2] a general comment, explained in detail in [3]. 概要評論，在 [3] 中詳細說明。
[4] compares these trends with other expenditure. 將這些趨勢與其他開支進行比較。

Paragraph 4—Trends
第 4 段——趨勢
[1] more detail on trends where spending rose. 關於開支上升趨勢的更多細節。
[2] summarizes the main contrast in the trends. 總結各種趨勢的主要對比。

Paragraph 5—Conclusion
第 5 段——總結
This summarizes the report with a general conclusion. 概括總結報告。

Core language for describing graphs 描述圖表的核心用語

Language bank 用語庫

General 概述 *The graph/chart shows/represents/indicates …* *The figures show/indicate (that) …* draw conclusions from e.g. 從…中得出結論，如：*The following conclusions can be drawn from the data.*	**Pie charts: describing proportions of a whole** 餅分圖：描述整體中的比例 *More/Less than* half *of the total …* *Only* a third/a quarter… *Just/Well under/over* 50% … *The biggest/smallest proportion/sector …* *The vast majority of …* *As many (people were learning French) as (Spanish).*
Bar charts: describing differences between amounts 柱形圖：描述數量之間的差別 *There were* almost *twice/three times/half as many … as* Far/Slightly/20% *fewer X … than Y …* Many/Far/A few/20% *more X … than Y …* *A greater proportion of … than of…* *20% of women …, while only 10% of men …* *80% of (adults send emails), compared to 34% (who prefer texts).*	**Graphs: describing developments over time** 線形圖：描述一段時間內的發展情況 *a* small/slight/gradual *increase/decrease* *a* significant/marked/dramatic *increase/decrease* *a* small/slight *rise/fall/dip* *steady growth* *to rise/increase/fall/decrease/decline/drop* *to rise/fall* steadily/dramatically/sharply/rapidly *Customer numbers have fluctuated. (Online sales) reached an all-time high/low.* *The graph shows a marked change in …*

Writing a report 撰寫報告

A report describes a study, an investigation, or a project. Its purpose is to provide recommendations or updates, and sometimes to persuade the readers to accept an idea. It is written by a single person or a group who has investigated the issue. It is read by people who require the information. 報告是對研究、調查或項目的描述，其目的是提供建議或報告最新情況，有時是說服讀者接受某觀點。它是由對課題進行過研究的個人或小組撰寫的，其讀者是需要瞭解有關信息的人。

Tip 提示

- Reports can vary in length but a good rule to remember is that they should be as long as necessary and as short as possible. 報告的長度不盡相同，不過要記住一條有用的原則：有必要則長，有可能則短。

Think about the reader 考慮讀者

You need to make the objective of the report clear so that the people who are reading the report know why they are reading. Thinking about the readers and what they need to know will help improve your report. 要清楚說明報告的目的，以便讀者明白他們為什麼讀。考慮讀者和他們需要知道什麼會有助於改進報告。

- Is the purpose of the report clear throughout? 報告通篇都目的明確嗎？
- Can the readers find the information they need? 讀者能找到他們想瞭解的信息嗎？
- Will diagrams or tables make the information clearer? 圖表或表格可以更清楚說明信息嗎？
- Should I just present the facts or include recommendations as well? 我應該只報告事實還是也提出建議？

Organizing your report 組織報告

A typical report should follow the structure outlined below. Shorter reports might not need all the sections but they should at least include the highlighted sections. 一篇典型的報告應該遵從下面的結構。短篇報告可能不需要包括所有部份，但至少應包括以藍色突出顯示的部份。

1 Title 標題

Your title should tell the reader exactly what the report is about. 標題應該準確說明報告主題。

2 Contents List 目錄

If your report has a number of sections it is important to include a table of contents so that the readers can find the information they want. A good way to structure a report is to use numbered headings 如果報告包括許多部份，那麼列出目錄以方便讀者查找信息，這一點很重要。好的編排方式是使用帶編號的標題：

2.0 Research
2.1 Focus groups
2.2 Technology for accessing the Internet

3 Summary 摘要

This section is often called an **Executive Summary**. It tells the reader what the objectives of the report are as well as the main findings, conclusions and any recommendations. 這部份通常稱作行政摘要（Executive Summary），其中說明報告的目的和主要發現、結論及建議。

4 Introduction 引言

This should give the reader the background to the report: why you are writing it. You should also include what the report will cover (and what it won't) and how you got the information you have based the report on. 這部份應該說明報告背景：為什麼寫報告。也應說明報告所涉及（和不涉及）的內容以及報告所根據的信息是如何收集的。

5 Body of the report 報告主體

The main body of the report will follow the structure in the Contents List. It will give precise information about the research you have carried out and what you have discovered from it. The information here should be mainly factual and not based on opinion. Tables, charts and bulleted lists can make the information clearer. Some of the more detailed information can go into Appendices and the Bibliography. 報告主體部份將依照目錄所列的結構編排。這部份給出研究的確切信息和發現；這些信息應主要基於事實而非主觀看法。表格、圖表和項目符號列表可使內容更清楚。有些較詳細的信息可放在附錄和參考書目中。

6 Conclusions 結論

This is where you give your opinions on the facts that you have discovered. 此處發表對所發現的事實的看法。

7 Recommendations 建議

If you have been asked to give recommendations, they should be based on your conclusions. You should also let the reader know what you predict will happen if your recommendations are followed. 如要求提出建議，所提建議應以自己的結論為基礎。亦應說明，如果建議被採納，你預計會出現什麼情況。

8 Appendices 附錄

In a long report, you should put very detailed information in the Appendices with cross-references to them in the body of the report. 長篇報告中應把十分詳細的信息放在附錄中，並在報告主體部份設參見項。

9 Bibliography 參考書目

If your report refers to a number of other publications, you should list these in a Bibliography. 如果報告提及一些其他出版物，就應該列入參考書目。

Executive summary 行政摘要

The summary below gives some useful language in context. In the Language bank are some other phrases that you can use in reports. Notice that the language used should be **clear**, **accurate** and **formal**. *We* and *I* are often used in internal reports, for example for describing research. 以下摘要給出了相關背景下一些有用的說法；用語庫中是其他一些可用於報告的短語。注意所使用的語言應清晰、準確和正式。We 和 I 常用於內部報告，例如，用來描述研究。

Web Page Design

The purpose of this report is to compare two different web designs. The reason for this is to decide what kind of web page is most likely to attract new customers and to encourage existing customers to buy more products from us.

We asked two developers to produce alternative web pages for our company. We asked Developer A to produce a simple, easy-to-use design and we asked Developer B to produce a more sophisticated design with lots of eye-catching graphics. We conducted our research by asking a group of twenty existing customers and twenty non-customers to use the web page over a month. The group was made up of people with a range of ages, professions, incomes, and computer expertise. We divided the group in two and asked one sub-group to use Design A and the other to use Design B. We asked each sub-group to log on once a day and to use the web page to perform certain tasks, including: buying products, getting information, returning damaged products, and tracking deliveries. We also asked the sub-groups to assess how attractive they found their designs and whether they would be encouraged to return to the web page.

In addition, we researched the technology that people had available for accessing the Internet, including the devices people used and the connection speeds available.

We found that, on the whole, people preferred to be able to purchase products quickly and easily. In conclusion, users do not visit a site such as ours for entertainment. While they initially enjoyed some of the aspects of Design B these could take a long time to load and users eventually became bored.

We recommend that we adopt Design A with two or three of the more practical features from Design B.

Language bank 用語庫

Stating objectives 説明目的

The purpose/aim/objective of this report is to …

This report aims to …

This reports presents/gives information on …

Outlining research 概述研究

We asked (*two developers*) *to …*

We conducted our research by …
(e.g. *asking a group of …*)

We examined/looked at/researched …
(e.g. *the problem/the cost/several companies*)

We surveyed … (e.g. *a total of 250 employees*)

We compared A and B.

The group was made up of …

Presenting findings 描述發現

We found that, on the whole, …

According to the majority of respondents …

Overall people preferred …

50% of those surveyed said (*that*) *…*

Giving Conclusions 作總結

In conclusion …

The research shows/demonstrates (*that*) *…*

The research shows/demonstrates + noun 名詞
(e.g. *the effect of …*)

From the research/the evidence we conclude that …

Giving recommendations 提建議

We recommend that …

It is recommended that …

The best solution is/would be to …
(e.g. *to adopt design A*)

The best solution is/would be + noun 名詞
(e.g. *a reduction in office hours*)

If we do A, we will see B.

This will have an impact on + noun 名詞
(e.g. *costs/productivity/the business*)

Writing a review of a book or film/movie 撰寫書評或影評

The main purpose of a book review is to give information to a potential reader so that they can decide whether or not they want to read the book. A review of a film/movie has the same purpose. You can approach it in the same way as a book review. 書評的主要目的是向潛在讀者提供信息，以便他們決定是否想讀這本書。影評有同樣的目的，可按書評的模式寫影評。

***Wuthering Heights* by Emily Brontë**

Is it a darkly passionate tale of love? Or should we call it a highly original gothic story? The classic novel *Wuthering* Heights by Emily Brontë is, in my opinion, a unique and gripping blend of these genres. Written in 1847, it is an epic family saga full of desire, hate, revenge and regret, focusing on the main characters of Heathcliff and Catherine. The atmospheric setting of the wild Yorkshire moors cleverly mirrors these violent emotions.

When Catherine's father adopts the starving orphan boy Heathcliff, Catherine's brother Hindley feels deeply hurt and resentful. She, on the other hand, develops an immensely strong bond with Heathcliff, which becomes an all-consuming love. Upon her father's death, Hindley becomes the head of the family and forces Heathcliff to assume the position of a servant. Despite loving Heathcliff, Catherine chooses to marry Edgar Linton, who is closer to her class and position in society. It is this decision which leads to heartbreak and tragedy, not only for them but for many others.

Heathcliff could be described as an anti-hero with his rough manners and lack of control. Likewise, Catherine displays many flaws, but the reader can still empathize with these characters. In fact, this is the main reason why I believe this novel is so brilliant. It rings with truth. The reader may be horrified at the way that Heathcliff and Catherine behave, and yet, at the same time, the writer ensures that we never hate them because the reasons for their actions are crystal clear.

The main part of the book relies on a narrator, Ellen Dean, who is a servant at Wuthering Heights and I think that this is a useful device which holds the complex plot together. However, *Wuthering Heights* is not what I would call an 'easy read'. There is dense description and some of the dialogue is written in dialect, which can be difficult to follow.

Nevertheless, I persevered and, all in all, I can highly recommend *Wuthering Heights*. I challenge you to remain unmoved after reading this exceptional book.

Asking a question is one way to engage the reader. Or you could start with a personal opinion. 提問題是吸引讀者的一種方式，亦可先提出自己的看法。

Information about the **setting** and **era** can be useful. 背景和時代信息有時很有用。

It is usual to use the present tense to describe the story. 用現在時講述故事很常見。

Most **nouns** can be enhanced with an **adjective** – but make sure it is a natural collocation. 大多數名詞可用形容詞修飾——但要確保搭配是自然的。

Linking words aid organization and can also give your opinion. 銜接詞有助於篇章組織連貫，也可以用來提出看法。

Conclusion. Restate your opinion of the book as a recommendation to read it or not to read it. 總結。重申自己的看法，說明是否推薦閱讀這本書。

The **title** and **author's name** should appear in the introductory paragraph. 標題和作者姓名應出現在引言段。

This is one of many **synonyms** of 'interesting'. Look at the note at the dictionary entry 'interesting'. 這是 interesting 的多個同義詞之一。查閱本詞典 interesting 條的用法說明。

Collocations of adverb + adjective show your vocabulary knowledge. Look up **hurt** adjective. 使用副詞 + 形容詞的搭配顯示出自己的詞彙知識。查閱形容詞 hurt。

Including information on the **style of writing** can be helpful. 加入寫作風格方面的信息會有幫助。

Writing your review 撰寫書評

1. Read or re-read the book and make notes 閱讀或重讀這本書並做筆記

Your notes should try to answer the questions a reader might have
所做筆記應盡量回答讀者可能問的問題：

- What kind of book is it? 這是一本什麼樣的書？
- What happens in the story? 故事情節是什麼？
- Who are the main characters? 主要人物是哪些？
- What is the main theme of the book? 書的主題是什麼？
- Is it well written? 這本書寫得好嗎？
- Would you recommend this book? 你會推薦閱讀這本書嗎？

2. Organize your notes 組織筆記

You can use the same plan as the model review (see below). A successful review will contain these elements, but the order can be changed. 可採用下列書評範文的提綱。成功的書評會包括這些要素，但次序可以改變。

Paragraph 1—Introduction 第 1 段——引言 General comments about the book. 對這本書的概要評論。
Paragraph 2—Plot 第 2 段——情節 A brief summary of what happens. 簡要說明故事梗概。
Paragraph 3—Characters 第 3 段——人物 Briefly describe and comment on the main characters. 簡要描述和評論主要人物。
Paragraph 4—Other information 第 4 段——其他信息 Anything else important that you want to say about the book. 你想說的關於這本書的任何其他要點。
Paragraph 5—Conclusion 第 5 段——總結 Include your personal recommendation here. 本段寫你個人的建議。

3. Write your review 撰寫書評

Remember not to include too many details and don't give away the ending of the book. The reviewer recommends this book but the review also contains some criticisms. It is a good idea to try to write about both positive and negative aspects of the book.
記住不要過於糾纏細節，也不要透露書的結局。書評作者推薦閱讀這本書，但書評中也要有所批評。最好對書的正反兩方面均加以評論。

Tips 提示

- Remember at all times that the person who reads your review has NOT read the book!
  始終記着書評讀者沒有讀過這本書！
- Use your dictionary to help you find synonyms of words such as **book** or **story**.
  在詞典中查找 book 或 story 之類單詞的同義詞。
- Find a range of adjectives to use to describe the book, plot and characters.
  找出一系列用於介紹書、情節和人物的形容詞。

Reviews of non-fiction books 非小説類圖書書評

The purpose of a non-fiction book review is basically the same as fiction but the potential reader will have different questions 非小説類圖書書評的目的與小説書評基本相同，但其潛在讀者會問不同的問題：

- What is the author's reason for writing the book? 作者寫這本書的原因是什麼？
- Is it well organized? Can you follow the argument easily and find the important information? 篇章組織得好嗎？你能輕鬆地讀懂作者的論述並找到重要信息嗎？
- Does the author support his/her findings well? 作者很好地證明了自己的研究結果嗎？
- How does it compare to other books on the same subject? 這本書與其他同一題材的書相比如何？

Language bank 用語庫

Beginnings 開頭 *It is a fascinating tale of …* (e.g. *rural life*) *This moving account of …* (e.g. *a young man's experiences*) *I found this story far-fetched and unconvincing.*	**Giving your opinion 發表看法** *The writer excels at …* (e.g. *describing …*) *I was impressed by …* *One aspect I found a little disappointing was …* *One possible flaw is that …*
Details/plot 細節／情節 *Written in …, the story begins with …* *The events unfold in …* *The tale is set in …* **Characters 人物** *The writer introduces us to …* *The principal characters are …* *My favourite character is undoubtedly …* *The story focuses on …* *We experience all this through the eyes of …*	**Conclusions 總結** *I would highly recommend this rewarding book.* *I thoroughly enjoyed this book. In fact I couldn't put it down!* *By the end of this book, you feel …* *I was left unmoved by this story.* *I would strongly advise against reading this book.*

Discussing pictures and cartoons
論述圖片和漫畫

This task may occur in written or spoken examinations. Describing photographs or pictures can be similar to interpreting cartoons. There may not be a caption or any speech, but the photo can still have a message. You can also discuss the effect it has on you. 此任務可能出現在筆試或口試中。描述照片或圖片與解釋漫畫相似。圖片中可能沒有說明文字或顯示任何人說的話，但仍然會有想要表達的信息。亦可談論它對自己的影響。

Look at the cartoon and the interpretation below. 看看下面的漫畫和說明文字。

"It is good to see people doing their bit for the environment!"

The cartoon shows a bird's-eye view of part of a European city or town. There is a large factory, several rows of houses, two vehicles and some people.[1] In the foreground, there is a rubbish collection truck, with two men collecting household waste for recycling. On the left of the cartoon, a man is putting a bottle in a street recycling bin. Watching him are two other men who are obviously managers in the local factory.[2] The caption reads "It is so good to see people doing their bit for the environment!"[3]

The caption is clearly the words that one of the factory managers is saying to his colleague, because the focus of attention is on them and also on the man with the bottle: all three of them are drawn in detail[1] and they also stand out because of the black clothing they are wearing.[2]

Another important element in the cartoon is the factory and the pollution from its chimneys. The cartoonist has exaggerated the size of the factory in relation to the surrounding houses and has also exaggerated the pollution by blackening a wide expanse of sky.[3] These aspects of the picture show the way that the pollution from the factory dominates the town and causes a serious environmental impact.

The factory itself is a symbol representing industry in general.[4] It seems that the man who is dropping off his one empty bottle in the recycling bin has driven there in his car, so he has probably damaged the environment more than if he had just thrown the bottle away. He represents ordinary people.[4]

The cartoon is about our attitude to the environment. It is clear that the cartoonist is suggesting that while people focus on small-scale activities, such as recycling household waste, they are ignoring much more serious environmental problems such as the pollution from industries and from cars.[1] He/she uses irony to show that we are becoming complacent about saving the environment. This is done by contrasting what the factory managers are saying with what is really happening all around them: serious pollution that they themselves are responsible for.

Personally, I believe that the cartoonist is right. Many people are now very good about recycling their household waste. But, because we do this, we have become complacent about pollution and feel we are doing enough to protect the environment. We need also to address other more important sources of environmental damage.

Paragraph 1—Description
第 1 段——描述
[1] General description 概要描述
[2] Detailed description 詳細描述
[3] Caption or speech bubble 說明文字或說話框

Paragraphs 2–4—Artistic techniques
第 2-4 段——藝術技巧
[1] Technique 1–detail 技巧 1—細部
[2] Technique 2–emphasis 技巧 2—突出
[3] Technique 3–exaggeration 技巧 3—誇張
[4] Technique 4–symbolism 技巧 4—象徵

Paragraph 5—Message
第 5 段——信息
[1] Use of irony 反諷手法的使用

Paragraph 6—Personal reaction 第 6 段——個人的反應

Key 標示顏色說明

(yellow) shows the key language in each section. 標示各部份的關鍵用語

(green) focuses on prepositions and phrasal verbs. 提醒注意介詞和短語動詞

Writing a description and interpretation
撰寫描述和說明

Follow these steps when you prepare for this task. Think about the questions and make notes; then, when you write, use some of the phrases in the Language banks and take note of the tips. 按照以下步驟準備這項任務。考慮這些問題並做筆記；然後，在寫作過程中，使用用語庫中的一些短語並留意提示中的建議。

Stage 1—Description
第 1 步——描述

The scene 情景：

- What is the scene in the cartoon/picture? 漫畫／圖片中的情景是什麼？
- Where is it? 在哪裏？
- What are the major features? 主要特點是什麼？

Details 細部：

- Who/What is in the picture? 畫面中有誰／什麼？
- What are they doing? 他們在做什麼？
- What is happening? 發生了什麼事？

Language bank 用語庫

The scene is of … (e.g. *a café in which two people* …)
The cartoon shows/depicts …
There is/are … (e.g. *two people who look angry.*)
In the centre of the cartoon is/are … , (*who/which* …)
At the top/bottom of the cartoon is/are …
On the left/right …
In the foreground/background …
The central feature of the cartoon is …
You can use prepositions 可使用介詞，e.g. 例如 ***behind*** *the houses*
Avoid using 避免使用：~~*I/You can see* …; *In the picture*~~ …

Tips 提示

- Only describe the details that are important for the message. 只描述對於表達有關信息很重要的細部。
- Try to avoid using short simple sentences such as: ~~*In the centre is a man. He is shouting.*~~ **Relative sentences** are particularly useful: *In the centre is a man who is shouting.* 盡量避免使用短小的簡單句，如：~~*In the centre is a man. He is shouting*~~。關係從句（relative sentence）特別有用，如：*In the centre is a man who is shouting*。

The caption or speech bubble
說明文字或說話框：

- What is written in the caption or in any speech bubbles? 說明文字或說話框中寫的是什麼？
- Who is talking and to whom? 誰在說話，對誰說？

Language bank 用語庫

The caption reads "…"
One man is saying to the other "…"
The woman is asking whether …
He/She is commenting that …
He/She is wondering whether … (*to go/he/she should go* …)

Stage 2—Interpretation
第 2 步——說明

Tip 提示

- Start a new paragraph for this section. Give evidence and reasons for your interpretation. 這部份另開新段。為自己的說明提供依據或理由。

Artistic techniques 藝術技巧：
How does the artist draw attention to important parts of the cartoon/picture? Does he/she use 畫家如何使讀者注意到漫畫／圖片中的重點部份？他／她是否使用：

- detail? Where? 細部？在哪裏？
- emphasis? What is emphasized? How? 突出？突出的是什麼？如何突出的？
- exaggeration? What is exaggerated? 誇張？誇張的是什麼？
- symbolism? Which objects or people are symbols? What do they mean? 象徵？哪些物體或人是象徵？有何含義？

Language bank 用語庫

The focus of attention is on …

X is/are drawn in detail, (which shows/to show …)

X stand(s) out because of the …

The most important element in the cartoon is …

This aspect of the cartoon indicates …

The X symbolize(s)/represent(s) …

The cartoonist has exaggerated X (in order to …/ because …)

The reason for this is that …

Use your dictionary to find synonyms so that you use a wide range of vocabulary. 在詞典中查找同義詞以豐富寫作的詞彙，e.g. 例如 *clearly/obviously; indicate/show*

Message 信息：

- What is the cartoon/picture really about? 漫畫/圖畫實際上是關於什麼的？
- What is the artist trying to say? 畫家試圖說明什麼？
- How does he/she try to persuade you? Does he/she use **irony** (contrasting the way the cartoon shows things with the way they really are) or **analogy** (using a simple situation to make a more complex situation clear)? 他/她試圖如何說服你？他/她有否使用反諷（irony，即將漫畫中的情形與真實情況相對比）或類比（analogy，即用簡單的情況解釋較複雜的情況）？

Language bank 用語庫

The cartoon is about/refers to/deals with …

The cartoon has to do with …

The cartoonist is obviously trying to show …

What the cartoon is saying is that …

I take/understand the cartoon to mean that …

Stage 3—Personal reaction
第 3 步——個人的反應

- Do you agree or disagree with the message? 你是否同意這一信息？
- Why? 為什麼？

Tip 提示

- Start a new paragraph for this section. 這部份另開新段。

Language bank 用語庫

Personally, I believe that the cartoonist is right.

I only partly/partially agree with the artist's message because …

In my opinion/view, the artist is wrong, because …

Use phrases such as 使用此類短語，例如 *I think …; In my opinion …;* or 或 *It seems to me that …*

Do not use 不要用 ~~*According to me/my opinion …*~~

Writing a formal letter 撰寫正式信函

Writing a letter of complaint 撰寫投訴信

The important things to remember about writing formal letters are the layout, which follows particular conventions, and the language, which must be formal or semi-formal and polite, even when you are complaining. 撰寫正式信函時需要記住的重點之一是格式，它有其慣用的格式，二是語言，用語必須是正式或半正式的，而且是有禮貌的，即便是表達不滿的時候亦然。

6 Fore Street
Kensington
London W8 9NW

Customer Services Manager
FlyHigh Airways
PO Box 589
London W3 5NJ

1 August 2009

Dear Sir/Madam

Booking reference: Porter POR 1359AZ

My wife and I and our two children, aged 2 and 4, were passengers on flight LZ238 from London to Orlando, USA on July 23rd 2009. I am writing to complain about a number of aspects of the service we received.

Paragraph 1 第 1 段
Explain clearly why you are writing. 清楚地說明寫信的原因。

Firstly, when the flight was delayed, the staff at the airline's information desk were very unhelpful. We were not even given a voucher for a drink or meal, when it was clear the delay would be at least seven hours. This meant that we had to spend a considerable amount of money in the restaurant.

Paragraph 2 第 2 段
Explain the problem and how you were affected. 說明問題和自己所受的影響。

Then, when we were finally able to board, families were not allowed to board first, although we had paid for this. As a result we were not able to sit together, making our children, already very tired, extremely distressed.

Paragraph 3 第 3 段
Explain any further problem and the consequences. 說明任何其他問題和後果。

It is a legal requirement for airline operators to provide suitable refreshments in the event of a long delay. I would therefore expect some compensation for your failure both to comply with this regulation and to provide us with the priority boarding for which we had paid.

Paragraph 4 第 4 段
State clearly what action you wish the company to take. 清楚提出自己希望公司採取的行動。

I enclose our boarding passes and look forward to hearing from you shortly.

Yours faithfully

S R Porter (Dr)

Ending 結束語
General comment. Say you would like a quick reply. 概要評論。說明你希望儘快得到答覆。

Key 標示顏色說明

Yellow = key language
黃色 = 關鍵用語

Writing the letter 寫信

Layout 格式

Look carefully at the layout of the model letter and note. 仔細看範文信件的格式並注意：

- Your address, but not your name, goes at the top on the right. 右上角寫上寫信人的地址，而不是姓名。
- The name and address of the person you are writing to goes on the left. 左邊寫收信人姓名和地址。
- If you do not know a name, use a position e.g. 'Customer Services Manager'. 如果不知道姓名，就使用職位，如"客戶服務部經理"。
- The date goes under either address. 日期放在左邊或右邊地址的下方均可。
- Give some kind of reference or use a heading (e.g. **Poor service levels**). 寫出所涉及的事件或使用標題（如"服務質量差"）。

Tips 提示

- **Tone:** be polite and formal, but keep your language simple and clear. 語氣：有禮貌而且正式，但語言要簡單明瞭。
- Use short sentences rather than long ones. 用短句，不用長句。
- Try not to be emotional; avoid *you/you didn't* if possible. 設法不要感情用事；如果可能，避免使用 you/you didn't。

If you are writing in **American English**, remember 如果用美式英語寫信，記住：

- Use American spelling and punctuation e.g. Mrs., Dr., etc. 用美式拼寫和標點符號，如 Mrs.、Dr. 等。
- End your letter **Sincerely**, **Sincerely yours**, or **Yours truly**,. 結尾使用 Sincerely、Sincerely yours 或 Yours truly。

Language bank 用語庫

Openings and closings 開頭和結尾套語

Dear Sir/Madam .... Yours faithfully

Dear Ms Walker .... Yours sincerely

Introducing the topic 引入話題

I am writing to complain about/to express my dissatisfaction with ...

The purpose of this letter is to express my disappointment with ...

Describing the problem 描述問題

Strong adjectives 語氣強的形容詞：*appalled, distressed, disgusted, shocked*

Less strong 較溫和的形容詞：*disappointed, dismayed, dissatisfied.*

What do you want? 你的訴求是什麼？

Definite 明確的：*a full/partial refund, a replacement, an apology*

More flexible 有商討餘地的：*compensation, reimbursement, recompense*

Endings 結束語

I look forward to your swift reply.

I look forward to hearing from you at your earliest convenience.

I look forward to hearing from you without delay.

I very much hope to hear from you shortly.

I await your prompt reply.

Writing a letter to a newspaper 給報紙寫信

This should still be a formal letter, but because it is for the public, it should show your opinion clearly or tell people something interesting or new. It can be direct and feel quite personal – you can use *I*, *we* and *you*. 這依然應為正式信件，但對象是公眾，所以應該清楚表明自己的觀點，或向人介紹有趣或新鮮的事物。可以直截了當，帶有個人色彩——可以使用 I、we 和 you。

A title attracts the readers' attention. 標題吸引讀者的注意力。

Give information about you if relevant. 如適用的話，寫出關於自己的相關信息。

Use strong adjectives. 使用語氣強的形容詞。

Exclamation marks are acceptable to show how you feel. 感歎號可用來表達感受。

A challenge to readers can be effective. 向讀者發出倡議會是有效的做法。

Ending: No finishing phrase is needed. 結尾：不需要結尾套語。

Sir

The craze for reality TV

As a student in my early twenties I am part of a key audience for TV channels. Why then, do I find so little to interest or entertain me? One trend I find particularly appalling is the increase in 'reality' TV programmes such as Survivor, Big Brother and Fear Factor, to name but a few.

'Reality' TV shows involve 'real' people performing ridiculous and often dangerous acts and generally behaving horribly towards each other. These shows appeal to that part of us which takes pleasure in watching the humiliation of others and I believe that programme-makers are being irresponsible by promoting this. It is demeaning to both the participants and the viewers.

Even worse, these programmes are having a negative effect on society, particularly on young people, who no longer feel any shame at watching or taking part in this kind of disgraceful behaviour. A national survey recently stated that one in seven British teenagers hopes to become famous by going on a show like this! The average British adult watches 26 hours of television per week. Reality TV is not only a waste of time, but it is dangerous. I believe it can and will affect our society, dragging it down into the gutter.

It is time we made a stand against reality TV, in favour of quality TV. How can we do it? Start by changing the channel.

Maria Fedora
Madrid

Paragraph 1 第 1 段
Clear introduction of the topic and the writer's opinion.
清楚地介紹主題和作者的看法。

Paragraph 2 第 2 段
Main point, with reasons. 主要觀點，並提出理由。

Paragraph 3 第 3 段
Further point to support main one, with reasons and/or examples.
支持主要觀點的進一步的觀點，附帶理由和/或例證。

Paragraph 4 第 4 段
Repeats the writer's opinion and offers a challenge.
重申作者的看法並發出倡議。

Writing emails (business and academic)
撰寫電子郵件（商務與學術類）

- Emails **vary in formality** depending on how well you know the reader and what your status is in relation to them. 根據寫信人對讀者的熟悉程度和相對於他們的地位，電子郵件的正式程度亦不盡相同。
- All emails should be polite, but they **vary in level of politeness** depending on who you are writing to and what you are asking them. 所有電子郵件都應該有禮貌，但根據收信人的身分和寫信人對他們所提的要求，其禮貌程度不盡相同。
- Writers use level of formality and politeness to achieve an appropriate **tone**. 作者以一定的正式程度和禮貌程度以達到適當的語氣。
- Emails between colleagues of a similar status can be informal and personal, but should still be polite and friendly. 地位相近的同事之間的電郵可以是非正式的並帶有個人色彩，但依然應禮貌友好。

Email etiquette 電子郵件禮節

- Always use a short, informative **subject line**, not single general words e.g. *Urgent* or *Enquiry*. 應使用簡短扼要的主題欄（subject line），不要用籠統的詞語，如 Urgent 或 Enquiry。
- Mention **attachments** and say what they contain. Don't leave the body of the email empty. 提及附件（attachment）並說明其內容。電子郵件的正文部份要有內容。
- **Acknowledge** email attachments you receive. *Thanks* + your name is often enough. 覆函告知收悉電郵附件。一般用 Thanks + 自己的名字就行了。
- **Re-read** your email before you send it to make sure it is understandable and not offensive. 電郵發出之前再讀一遍，確保行文易懂且沒有冒犯性。

Writing business emails 撰寫商務電子郵件

Formal – An enquiry to a company – *formal, polite*
正式——向一家公司的查詢——正式，有禮貌

Tips 提示

Formal business emails are shorter and less formal than letters. 正式商務電郵比信函短而且正式程度較低。

- You should **not** use very informal language, incomplete sentences, exclamation marks or emoticons. 不應使用很不正式的語言、不完整的句子、感歎號或表情符。
- You **can** use contracted verb forms, except where first impressions are important. 可以使用動詞的縮略形式，第一印象很重要的情況除外。
- You can become **less formal** as you establish a working relationship with somebody. 與某人已建立工作關係時，語氣可以變得不太正式。

Greeting: full name as this is the first contact with this company. 稱呼：完整姓氏，因為是與該公司的首次聯繫。

To: office@trainersrus.com
Cc: Andrea.penn@fgt.com
Subject: Query about training DVDs

Clear **subject line** 清楚的主題欄

Dear Mr Baxter

I am the HR assistant at FeelGood Training plc. I am contacting you to say that we have received the promo material about your sales training DVDs and are interested in purchasing some.

Opening: introduce yourself (use your position, not your name) and explain why you are writing. 開頭：作自我介紹（用職位，不用姓名）並説明寫郵件的原因。

Abbreviations: ***promo*** is acceptable in formal emails, as are ***asap*** (*as soon as possible*), ***ad*** (*advertisement*), ***re***: (*regarding*). 縮寫：在正式電郵中可使用縮寫，如 promo（promotion，促銷）。其他常見縮寫還有 asap（as soon as possible，儘快）、ad（advertisement，廣告）和 re:（regarding，關於）。

Could you please send us some more information regarding their content as we are not sure which would be the most useful for our staff.

We would also require a price list and payment terms.

We rather than *I* makes the message less personal and more formal. 用 we 而不用 I 使內容更加客觀正式。

Looking forward to your reply

Regards
Renata Klein

Ending: formal and friendly 結束語：正式而友好

Renata Klein, HR assistant
FeelGood Training plc 484 London Road,Uxbridge,UX3 6HO

www.fgt.com

Signature: give your position and contact details. 署名：寫出職位和詳細聯繫方式。

Language: formal vocabulary: ***purchase*** = *buy*, ***require*** = *need*. 語言：正式詞彙：purchase = buy（購買）、require = need（需要；要求）。

Modal verbs (***could***, ***would***) make the request more formal and polite. 情態動詞（could、would）使所提的要求更加正式和有禮貌。

Close: Most writers use one before their name. Give your full name in the first email. The reader can use *Renata* or *Ms Klein* in a reply. 結尾：大多數寫電郵的人在自己的名字前寫結尾套語。在第一封電郵中寫出完整姓名，讀者回覆可使用名（Renata）或稱謂 + 姓（Ms Klein）。

A reply – *Less formal (semi-formal), polite*
回覆——不太正式（半正式），有禮貌

Greeting and close: Jim chooses to use first names – correspondence will now tend to be less formal. 開頭稱呼和結尾：Jim 選擇稱呼對方的名字——通信將會不太正式。

Say what's in the **attachment**. 說出附件中有什麼。

Contracted forms can be used as the language is less formal now. 可使用縮略形式，因為此處的語言不太正式。

```
To: Renata.klein@fgt.com
Subject: Re: Query about training DVDs

Dear Renata

Thank you for your interest in
our training material. We're happy
to provide you with more detailed
information regarding the contents of
the DVDs. Attached you'll find a PDF
containing a brochure plus purchasing
agreement where you'll find terms and
conditions are clearly explained.

Should you need help choosing a product
to suit your company's needs, please
feel free to contact us again. Either
email me or alternatively you can speak
to one of our customer service team by
calling 05 471 375 31.

Best regards

Jim

Jim Baxter, Marketing Manager
Trainers-R-Us
j.baxter@trainersrus.com
```

Opening: a formal, polite opening sentence is appropriate for the first reply. 開頭：正式、有禮貌的起始句適合第一次回覆。

Language sets a polite, semi-formal, friendly tone. 以下用語使語氣有禮貌、半正式、友好：

- ***We're happy to*** ... OR 或 ***We're pleased to*** ...

  NOT 不可說：~~*We're delighted to*~~ ... – too formal for emails ——對於電郵而言太正式

- ***Please feel free to*** ...

  NOT 不可說：~~*Please don't hesitate to*~~ ... – too formal ——太正式

- ***Should you need help***: more formal than '***If you*** ...' 比 If you ... 的說法更正式

Language bank 用語庫

Greetings 稱呼 **Formal** 正式	**Semi-formal** 半正式	**Informal** 非正式
Dear Ms Klein/Dear Professor Smith/Dear Chris White (if you don't know the gender 假如不清楚對方性別). Do **not** use title and first name. 不要用稱謂 + 名字：~~*Dear Ms Mary.*~~	*Dear Renata*	*Hi/Hi Renata/Hello/ Hello Renata*
Dear All (to a group)	*Dear All*	*Hi everyone/Hello all*
FAO/For the attention of the Sales Manager	—	—
Closes 結尾		
Best wishes/Best regards/Regards + your full name 全名. Add position and contact details. 附上職位和詳細聯繫方式。	*All the best/Best/Yours/ Many thanks* + your first name or your full name 名字或全名. (or formal closes 或正式結尾)	*Thanks/Cheers/Speak to you soon* + your first name 名字.
Requesting action 請求 **Very polite** 很有禮貌	**Polite** 有禮貌	**Informal request** 非正式請求
Would it be possible (for you) to send me ...?/ I would be grateful if you could send me ...	*Could you (please) send me ...?*	*Can you send me ...?/ Pls can you let me have ...?*
I was wondering if you have had a chance to do it yet?	*Have you had a chance to [do it yet?] ...?*	*Have you [done it yet]?*
Would it be possible for me to come ...?	*Could I come ...?*	*Can I come ...?*
I would really appreciate your help./ I would be very grateful (indeed) for your help.	*Thank you./Many thanks*	*Thanks*

Writing academic emails 撰寫學術性電子郵件

- Academic emails are usually **personal**, not official. You are writing to a specific, named individual, not to somebody in their official role. 學術性電子郵件通常為私人而非官方通信。收信人是特定的、有名有姓的個人，而不是處在某職位的人。
- The level of **politeness** you need will vary. If you are asking a favour of an academic outside your university, you need to express a higher level of politeness than if you are asking your own teacher for a meeting. Emails between colleagues can be very **informal**. 所需要的禮貌程度亦不盡相同。請其他學校的老師幫忙要比請自己的老師與自己會面表現得更加禮貌。同事之間的電郵可以很不正式。
- Remember to use a level of formality and politeness to achieve an appropriate **tone**. 緊記採用恰當的正式程度和禮貌程度，使語氣得體。

Formal – A request from a student to an academic from a different department 正式——學生向其他學系的老師提出的請求

Low status writer to high status reader whom he does not know.
地位低的人寫信給地位高的陌生讀者。

Tone: *Personal, very formal, very polite*
語氣：私人色彩、很正式、很有禮貌

Subject: Request for statistical help

Dear Dr Barr

I am a first year PhD student in the department of linguistics and my research topic is a quantitative study of verb forms in academic writing. As I need to use advanced statistical tools for processing the data, my supervisor, Dr John Pugh, suggested I contact you to ask for advice. Would it be possible for me to come and see you to discuss what I need? I attach a copy of my draft research proposal to give you an idea of the scope of my study.

I would be very grateful indeed for your help.

Best wishes

David Samuels

Greeting: use ***Dear*** + academic title and family name, or Mr, Ms, etc. and family name 稱呼：使用 Dear + 學術頭銜和姓氏，或 Mr、Ms 等和姓氏

Introduce yourself by giving your position in the university. 通過說明自己在大學中的身分作自我介紹。

Would it be possible … Very polite. 很禮貌 **OR** 或 *Could I possibly* … (**NOT** 不可說 ~~*I kindly request*~~ – too official 公務語氣太重)

Close 結尾：**OR** 或 *Best regards, Regards.* Give your full name. Add position and contact details if necessary. 寫出全名。如果有必要應寫上職位和詳細聯繫方式。

Clear **subject** line 清楚的主題欄

Say **why you are writing**. Mention any academic contact. 說明為什麼寫信。提一下學術圈的熟人。

Be specific about what you want the reader to do. 具體說明想要讀者做什麼。

Give **supporting details**. 提供細節予以證明。

Ending: very polite 結束語：非常有禮貌 **OR** 或：*I would really appreciate your help.* (**NOT** 不可說：~~*Thank you for your time*~~ – official. 公務語氣 **NOT** 不可說：~~*Thank you for your attention*~~ – very formal spoken 很正式的口語)

Less formal – request from a student to their own supervisor
不太正式——學生向自己的導師提出的請求

Lower status writer to higher status reader whom she knows very well.
地位較低的人寫信給地位較高的熟悉的讀者。

Tone: *Personal, polite, less formal*
語氣：私人色彩、有禮貌、不太正式

Subject: use ? to show a request 主題欄：用 ? 表示請求

A polite indirect question. Use it to remind somebody of higher status about something. 有禮貌的間接問句。用於向地位較高的人提醒某事。

Close: informal – Nicole has the right to ask for a meeting 結尾：非正式—— Nicole 有權要求會面

```
Subject: Meeting this week?

Dear Ruth

I was wondering if you've had a chance
to look at my paper yet. If so, could
we have a meeting some time this week?
The best day for me would be Tues.
I start my fieldwork at the end of
the week and it would be very useful
to have some feedback before then.

Many thanks

Nicole
```

Greeting: first names can be used as they know each other well. 稱呼：可用名字，因雙方很熟悉。

Abbreviations can be used as style is less formal. 可用縮寫，因為文體風格不太正式。

***Could, would*:** Less abrupt/direct forms. Use them to make a suggestion/request to somebody of higher status. * could、would：不太唐突/直率的形式。用於向地位較高的人提出建議/請求。

Using American style in emails
美式風格的電子郵件

- If you are writing emails in an American English environment, the points about formality, politeness and tone on pages WT40–42 still apply. The language you use will be very similar. However, there are one or two things that you should be aware of, as shown below. 如果在美式英語環境中寫電子郵件，WT40–42 頁上有關正式程度、禮貌和語氣的要點仍然適用，所使用的語言會非常相似。不過，還應留意以下所列各項。

Formality 正式程度

The main difference between American and British style in emails is that US emails do not use the very formal language that British emails often do and can be more direct. 美式和英式電郵風格的主要區別在於，美式電郵不使用英式電郵通常使用的很正式的語言，而會更直率。
Look at these examples 參看以下示例：

British (formal) 英式風格（正式）	**American** 美式風格
I would be grateful if you could send your payment to …	*Please send your payment to …*
A list of fees can be found on our website.	*You can find a list of fees on our website.*
Please don't hesitate to contact me …	*Please feel free to contact me.*

Business emails 商務電子郵件

```
     To: kmiller@charitytrainers.org
   From: risai@newgreenspaces.jp
   Date: 08/19/2009
Subject: Request for customized training

Dear Ms. Miller,

I am writing to ask about the possibility
of organizing a customized training program
for a group of five of our mid-level
managers. We would be interested in having
them learn more about staff recruitment,
project management, and fundraising practices
in the American charity and nonprofit
sector. Could you please let me know
what scheduling and pricing options are
available for a week-long course fulfilling
these requirements?

Sincerely yours,
Risa Inyaka
New Green Spaces, Japan
```

Notice how the date is written. 注意日期的寫法。(BrE 英式英語寫法為：19/8/2009)

Notice the use of full stops and commas in these emails. Use full stops after abbreviations. 注意這些電郵中句號和逗號的用法。縮寫的後面用句號。

Close: *Sincerely yours*, or *Sincerely*, are good ways to close a business email. 結尾：Sincerely yours 或 Sincerely 是商務電郵結尾的不錯方式。

Use US spellings (e.g. customize, flavor, center, etc.) consistently. 使用美式拼寫（如 customize、flavor、center 等）要前後一致。

Direct but polite questions using "you" are fine when writing to Americans. 給美國人寫電郵時，可用 you 直率但有禮貌地提出請求。

Academic emails 學術性電子郵件

```
        To: jacobi@bussch.clemson.edu
      From: rwagner@stud.clemson.edu
      Date: 8/23/2009
   Subject: Proposed meeting this week
Attachments: mif.doc

Dear Dr. Jacobi,

I'm planning to submit the attached paper
to 'Markets in Focus' next week. I wonder
if it might be possible for us to meet
to discuss it before I send it off?
I'd be very grateful for your comments
and advice. I'm available every day after
3p.m., or in the mornings on either
Tuesday or Thursday.

Many thanks,

Ross Wagner
```

Short, clear subject line 簡短明確的主題欄

Attachments should be no larger than 2MB, if possible. 如果可能的話，附件大小不應超過 2MB。

Close: courteous and fairly formal 結尾：有禮貌且相當正式

Use full stops after short titles. 縮寫的頭銜之後用句點。

Writing a CV/résumé and covering letter
撰寫簡歷和附信

A well-written, well-produced, appropriate CV (*British English*) or résumé (*American English*) is vital for getting you to the interview stage for a job. Use the examples and advice here to help you. On page WT49 you will find an example of a good covering (cover) letter. 一份寫得好、製作得體、恰如其分的簡歷（英式英語稱 CV，美式英語稱 résumé）是求職者通向面試階段至關重要的一環。以下示例和建議可以有助你完成這一目的。WT49 頁上有一份很好的附信範文。

Tips 提示

- Adapt your CV/résumé so that it is appropriate for the job you are applying for.
  修改簡歷，使之適合所申請的工作。
- Keep your CV short - no more than 2 pages if possible. 簡歷要簡短——可能的話不要超過 2 頁。
- Present yourself positively and accurately. 介紹自己的優點，用詞準確。
- Make your CV attractive and easy to read: use capitals, bold type, spacing and underlining.
  將簡歷製作得有吸引力並一目瞭然：適當使用大寫字母、粗體、間距和下畫線。
- Choose a typeface such as Times New Roman, Arial or Verdana. Use at least 10 pt.
  選擇字體，如 Times New Roman、Arial 或 Verdana。至少使用 10 號字。

British style CV (curriculum vitae) – *new graduate*
英式簡歷（CV，即 curriculum vitae）——剛畢業大學生

Name Pamela Janet Mason
Address 29 Greenlands Avenue, London, SW3 6RF
Telephone 01924 786512 **Mobile** 0779 9238182
e-mail pam_mason@scapenet.com

Objective To find a role in a film or TV production company that will enable me to acquire and develop the skills required for a career in film or television.

Profile An outgoing and articulate graduate with work experience in both television and teaching

Education and qualifications

2009 - MA in Media Studies. Bristol University. Expected 2010
2005–2009 BA in Media Studies with French (2:1) Bristol University
1997–2004 Beacon School, London
3 A levels: Drama (A); French (A); German (B)
5 AS levels 9 GCSEs

Personal information. 個人信息 You can omit the labels. There is no need to mention your age, gender, nationality, race, religion or marital status. Don't send a photo unless you are asked to. 這些標籤可省略。不必提及自己的年齡、性別、國籍、種族、宗教或婚姻狀況。除非對方要求，否則不要寄照片。

Profile and objective. 簡介和目標 Some people do not include these, but they do give an employer an idea of who you are. 有些人不寫這些部份，但這些部份一定會讓雇主對自己有所瞭解。

Education. 學歷 Put the most recent first. Add prizes and awards. Omit primary school. Try to give British equivalents of your qualifications. 先列出最近的學歷，附帶列出獲獎情況。不要列出小學。盡量提供與英國相應的學歷。

Work experience

October 2007–June 2008: Language assistant in secondary school in France. Taught English to large classes and small groups. Ran a film club and a holiday dance and drama club. Assisted with school drama productions.

September 2004– August 2005: Production assistant at Oordman and Associates Filmmakers, London N16. Performed office and on-set duties.

June–September 2004: Tutor for Jacaranda Drama Workshops. Led groups of teenagers of different backgrounds in dance and drama activities.

July–August 2003: Host at Adventure Camping holiday campsite in France. Led the children's club for 4–10 year olds and performed various practical duties on the campsite.

Skills

Languages: French–near native-speaker fluency (CEF C1); German (B2).

Good keyboard skills. Familiarity with Word, Excel and film editing packages.

Clean driving licence.

Interests

Drama, both acting and directing; singing (was member of university choral society). Regular volunteer at a local centre for the homeless.

References – attached

Work experience. 工作經歷 Put this in reverse order. Experienced candidates: put this before Education and write more about your most recent post. 按倒序排列。有工作經歷的求職申請人將這部份放在學歷之前，着重寫一下最近的工作。

Skills. 技能 Your practical abilities. Include exams passed. Write more here if you are experienced. 個人的實踐能力。列出所通過的考試。如果有實踐經驗，此部份着力寫一下。

Interests. 興趣 Keep this short. Include a sport, a creative and a community activity, if you can. Avoid vague subjects such as *reading* or *travel*. 這部份要簡短。可能的話，列出一項體育運動、一項有創意的活動和一項社區活動。避免不夠具體的主題，如閱讀或旅行。

References. 推薦人 Give the names, titles, and addresses when you send your CV, either here or on a separate page. 寄簡歷時要提供他們的姓名、頭銜和地址，列在此處或放在單獨一頁上均可。

American style résumé – *new graduate*
美式簡歷（résumé）——剛畢業大學生

These are similar to British style CVs. But notice 這些項目與英式簡歷相似。不過要注意：

- For new graduates your résumé should be only one page. 剛畢業大學生的簡歷應只有一頁。
- Describe your work experience in terms of self-motivation, teamwork, organization, problem-solving, and enthusiasm. 從主動性、團隊合作、組織、解決問題和工作熱情幾方面描述工作經歷。

Tip 提示

- The standard US paper size is not A4 (210 x 297 mm) but 216 x 279 mm.
  標準美國紙張的大小不是 A4（210 x 297 mm），而是 216 x 279 mm。

Provide your college or temporary **address** if you have one. 提供大學住址或當前臨時住址(如有)。

Objective. To summarize your goals and customize your résumé for specific positions. State a realistic short-term goal and/or a job for which you are currently qualified. **目標**。概述自己的目標並按特定職位編寫簡歷。說出一個現實的短期目標和/或目前能夠勝任的工作。

Use **bold** to highlight key information. 用**粗體**字強調關鍵信息。

Use US **spelling** and **punctuation**. 用美式拼寫和標點符號。

Jane Q. Student
jqstudent@mba.nau.edu

Present Address:	Permanent Address:
508 Blackbird's Roost	50, rue de Vaugirard
Flagstaff, AZ, USA 86011	Saint-Sulpice, France 75006
Tel +1 929 555 1212	Tel +33 1234 567 890

OBJECTIVE To obtain an entry-level management position within an international hospitality organization.

EDUCATION **Masters in Business Administration (M.B.A.)**, 2006–2008
Northern Arizona University, Flagstaff, Arizona, USA
B.A. in International Hospitality, 2002–2006 Université de Savoie, Chambéry, France

EXPERIENCE **Travel Agent**, Sep. 2006-Present
Kokopelli Extreme Tours, Sedona, Arizona, USA
Organized adventure package tours for large student groups, trained and supervized new staff members, and maintained partner relationships.
Camp Counselor, Jun 2002-Aug 2006
Voyageurs Summer Camp, Voglans, France Group leader for children aged 10–15. Developed curriculum for campers and led overnight hiking trips.

HONORS Agent of the Month, Kokopelli Extreme Tours, March 2008
Voted 'Most Popular Counselor,' Voyageurs, 2005 & 2006

SKILLS & INTERESTS Fluent in French and English; conversational Spanish
Enjoy web design in HTML and Flash

Language bank 用語庫

Action verbs 動作動詞

Use action verbs to describe your achievements and make them look more dynamic. 用動作動詞描述所取得的成績從而看上去更有活力。

Examples 例子： *achieved, administered, analyzed, advised, arranged, compiled, conducted, coordinated, created, designed, developed, devised, distributed, evaluated, examined, executed, implemented, increased, introduced, instructed, liaised, managed, mentored, monitored, negotiated, organized, oversaw, prepared, recommended, reduced, researched, represented, solved, supervised, trained.*

Positive adjectives 褒義形容詞

Use positive adjectives to describe yourself. 用褒義形容詞描寫自己。

Examples 例子： *active, adaptable, committed, competent, dynamic, effective, efficient, enthusiastic, experienced, flexible, (highly) motivated, organized, professional, proficient, qualified, successful.*

Other useful phrases 其他有用的短語

Skills 技能

Native French speaker

Near-native command of English

Good spoken and written German

Computer literate *Familiar with HTML*

Experienced trainer and facilitator

Education and experience 學歷和經歷

Baccalauréat, série C (equivalent of A levels in Maths and Physics)

The qualifications described below do not have exact equivalents in the British/American system.

Four weeks' work experience at ...

Summer internship at a marketing firm.

Personal qualities 個人素質

Work well as part of a team

Work well under pressure

Able to meet deadlines

Welcome new challenges *Can-do attitude*

Writing a covering letter 撰寫附信

A covering letter (*NAmE* cover letter) accompanies a CV/résumé or an application form. In Britain and North America they are usually typed on a single page. A good letter uses formal language and presents some key arguments for why your application should be taken seriously. 簡歷或申請表須附上附信。在英國和北美，附信通常是一頁長。好的附信使用正式語言，並提出一些主要理由說明為什麼自己的申請應受到重視。

Flat 3
19 Strangelands Road
London
NE23 6ZB
Tel: 0207 337 34589
20 January 2010

Mrs F Hunter
Human Resources Manager
Timson Office Supplies
Unit 5 Males Industrial Estate
Cambridge CB7 9HD

Dear Mrs Hunter

Senior Accounts Clerk

I am writing to apply for the post of senior accounts clerk advertised in the Cambridge Evening News of 17 January.

As you will see from my enclosed CV I am currently an accounts clerk in a medium-sized printing firm. In addition to my normal bookkeeping duties, I am responsible for invoicing and chasing up late payments. I also deal with credit checks on potential customers.

I am committed to pursuing a career in management accounting and am currently studying for further professional qualifications by distance learning. I am particularly interested in your post as it would enable me to gain experience of working in a larger company with the opportunities for professional training and development that this brings. In addition to my skills and experience as an accounts clerk, I would bring to the post a proven ability to deal successfully and tactfully with customers and clients.

I am available for interview for the next three weeks.

I look forward to hearing from you.

Yours sincerely

Dilip Patel
Dilip Patel
Enc. CV

For advice on layout see Formal letters pages 有關格式方面的建議，參見"正式信函"頁。

The date could also be January 20, 2010, 20/1/10 (*BrE*), or (*NAmE*) 1/20/10. 日期亦可寫成 January 20, 2010、20/1/10（英式英語），或 1/20/10（美式英語）。

In a cover letter use the words **post**, **position** or **vacancy**, not *job*. 在附信中使用 post、position 或 vacancy，不用 job。

Avoid contracted forms such as *I'm*. 避免縮略形式，如 I'm。

Use **Yours faithfully** here if you have begun Dear Sir or Madam. 如果開頭是 Dear Sir or Madam，此處用 Yours faithfully。

Sign your name and print it in full underneath. 簽名並在下方打印全名。

Enc. or **encl.** shows you have enclosed something. * enc. 或 encl. 表示有附件。

Key phrases 關鍵短語

Paragraph 1 states your purpose for writing. Say which job you are applying for and how/where you heard about it. 第 1 段說明寫信目的。說明要申請哪份工作以及如何/從何處知悉。

Paragraph 2 outlines your current job and responsibilities. Make it relevant to the post you are applying for. 第 2 段略述目前的工作和職責。將它與所申請的工作聯繫起來。

Paragraph 3 says why you want the job and what you can bring to the company. It is very important to say what *you* can do for *them*. 第 3 段說明自己為什麼需要這份工作以及能對公司帶來什麼貢獻。說明自己能為他們做什麼，這很重要。

Paragraph 4 gives other relevant information and when you are available for interview. 第 4 段給出其他相關信息和可以參加面試的時間。

Language bank 用語庫

Since graduating from ..., I have ...
I have considerable/extensive experience in (the field of ...)
I consider/feel that my qualifications and work experience could/might be of interest to the company.
If called for (an) interview, I would be available at any time convenient for you.
Please find attached a copy of my curriculum vitae/résumé for your consideration.
I look forward to hearing from you in due course.

Visual Vocabulary Builder Contents
圖解詞彙擴充目錄

City and countryside 城市和鄉村

City 城市

1 skyscraper 摩天大樓
2 crane 起重機
3 office block (*BrE*) / office building (*NAmE*) 辦公大樓
4 dome 穹頂
5 museum 博物館
6 clock tower 鐘樓
7 hoarding (*BrE*) (*also* billboard *especially NAmE*) 大幅廣告牌
8 cinema (*BrE*) / movie theater (*NAmE*) 電影院
9 banner 旗幡
10 flag 旗
11 flagpole (*also* flagstaff) 旗杆
12 alley (*also* alleyway) 小巷
13 awning 遮陽篷；雨篷
14 fountain 噴泉
15 statue 塑像
16 shopping centre (*BrE*) shopping center (*NAmE*) 購物中心
17 arcade 拱廊
18 street light (*BrE also* street lamp) 路燈
19 lamp post (*especially BrE*) 燈柱
20 market 集市
21 market stall 集市攤位
22 road sign 路標
23 theatre (*BrE*) / theater (*especially US*) 劇院
24 shop (*BrE*) store (*NAmE*) 商店
25 cafe (*also* café) 咖啡館
26 postbox / letter box (*both BrE*) mailbox (*NAmE*) 郵筒
27 busker 街頭藝人
28 traffic lights (*NAmE also* stoplights) 交通信號燈
29 bollard 護柱
30 litter bin (*BrE*) trash can (*NAmE*) 垃圾箱
31 pedestrian precinct (*BrE*) / pedestrian mall (*NAmE*) 步行區
32 taxi rank (*BrE*) (*also* taxi stand *especially NAmE*) 出租汽車站
33 railings 護欄
34 pavement (*BrE*) sidewalk (*NAmE*) 人行道
35 kerb (*BrE*) curb (*NAmE*) 路緣
36 parking meter (*also* meter) 停車收費器
37 pedestrian crossing (*BrE*) crosswalk (*NAmE*) 人行橫道
38 cycle lane (*BrE*) bicycle lane (*NAmE*) 自行車道
39 bus stop 公交車站
40 high street (*BrE*) main street (*NAmE*) 大街

Countryside 鄉村

1 windmill 風車
2 hill 山丘
3 hay 乾草
4 haystack 乾草堆
5 vineyard 葡萄園
6 copse (*also* coppice) 矮林
7 stream 溪流
8 wood (*also* woods) 樹林
9 furrow 犁溝
10 polytunnel 塑料大棚
11 pasture 牧場
12 crops 作物
13 tractor 拖拉機
14 field 農田
15 farmyard 農家庭院
16 orchard 果園
17 footpath 人行小道
18 footbridge 人行橋
19 stile 梯磴
20 silo 筒倉
21 farmhouse 農舍
22 stable 馬廄
23 hedge 樹籬
24 signpost 路標
25 village green (*BrE*) 村鎮公共綠地
26 village 村莊
27 duck pond 養鴨池
28 farm 農場
29 meadow 草地
30 marsh 沼澤
31 reeds 蘆葦
32 fence 籬笆
33 barn 穀倉
34 hedgerow 樹籬
35 ditch 溝渠
36 livestock 家畜
37 lane 小路
38 bridge 橋
39 river 河
40 riverbank 河岸

Mountains and coast 山和海濱

Mountains 山

1 summit 山頂
2 ridge 山脊
3 glacier 冰川
4 snow 雪
5 mountain range 山脈
6 plateau 高原
7 peak 山峰
8 mountain 山
9 precipice 峭壁
10 foothills 山麓小丘
11 snowline 雪線
12 ice 冰
13 source 源頭
14 waterfall 瀑布
15 forest 森林
16 lake 湖泊
17 conifers 針葉林
18 glade (*also* clearing) 林中空地
19 tributary 支流
20 river 河
21 meander 河曲
22 pass 山口
23 slope 斜坡
24 scree 碎石坡
25 track 小路
26 boulder 巨石
27 valley 山谷
28 gorge (*also* canyon) 峽谷

Coast 海濱

1 coastal path 海濱小道
2 cave 洞穴
3 headland (*also* promontory) 岬角
4 horizon 地平線
5 sea (*BrE*) ocean (*NAmE*) 海
6 lighthouse 燈塔
7 island 島
8 cove 小海灣
9 clifftop 懸崖頂
10 dune (*also* sand dune) 沙丘
11 estuary （江河入海的）河口
12 wave 海浪
13 spit 沙嘴
14 crest 波峰
15 foam 泡沫
16 reef 礁
17 cliff 懸崖
18 sandbank 沙洲
19 wake 尾流
20 rock 岩石
21 rock pool (*BrE*) tide pool (*NAmE*) 岩石區潮水潭
22 quay 碼頭
23 beach 海灘
24 bay 海灣
25 shingle 卵石灘
26 harbour (*BrE*) harbor (*NAmE*) 港灣
27 jetty (*NAmE also* dock) 棧橋
28 sand 沙灘
29 seashore 海岸

The environment 環境

Causes of the greenhouse effect 温室效應的原因

- **Carbon dioxide** is produced by **vehicle exhaust fumes** (1) and by **burning fossil fuels** (2) from power plants (*BrE also* power stations), factories and homes. This causes temperatures to rise. Trees, which absorb carbon dioxide, are felled by logging, causing **deforestation** (3). 二氧化碳（carbon dioxide）是由車輛排放的廢氣（vehicle exhaust fumes）（圖示 1）和發電廠、工廠、住宅燃燒的化石燃料（burning fossil fuels）（圖示 2）產生的。這導致氣溫上升。吸收二氧化碳的樹木遭到砍伐，森林被毀壞（deforestation）（圖示 3）。
- **Nitrogen oxide** comes from vehicles and power plants, and from agricultural fertilizers and pesticides used in **intensive farming** (4). 氧化氮（nitrogen oxide）來自車輛和發電廠，還來自用於集約耕作（intensive farming）（圖示 4）的農業化肥和殺蟲劑。
- Many **household products**, such as **refrigerators** and **aerosols**, emit **CFCs (chlorofluorocarbons)** which damage the ozone layer. 許多家用產品（household product），如冰箱（refrigerator）和氣霧劑（aerosol），會排放破壞臭氧層的氯氟烴（CFC，或 chlorofluorocarbon）。

- **Methane gas** is released from household and industrial waste in **landfill sites** (5), and also from **cattle** (6). 處理住宅垃圾和工業廢物的填埋場（landfill site）（圖示 5），還有牛（cattle）（圖示 6），都會排出沼氣（methane gas）。
- Sunlight causes these **greenhouse gases** to undergo **chemical change** and react with **water vapour** (*BrE*) (*NAmE* **vapor**), creating **acid rain**. 這些溫室氣體（greenhouse gas）經陽光照射發生化學變化（chemical change）並與水蒸氣（water vapour，vapor）發生反應，產生了酸雨（acid rain）。

Acid rain 酸雨

- **Acid rain** (7) falls on leaves and bark, damaging trees and plants in **forests**. **Nutrients** are **leached out** of the soil, and plants die. 酸雨（acid rain）（圖示 7）落到葉子和樹皮上，毀壞森林（forest）裏的樹木和植物。土壤中的養分（nutrient）被濾掉（leached out），造成植物死亡。
- **Acid levels** build up in **lakes** and **rivers** (8), poisoning and killing fish. 湖泊（lake）和河流（river）（圖示 8）中的含酸量（acid level）上升，使魚中毒和死亡。
- **Acid corrosion** attacks buildings, eating away at metal, stone and wood. 酸腐蝕（acid corrosion）損壞建築物，腐蝕金屬、石料和木料。
- **Pollution** from **smog** (9) causes **respiratory diseases** such as **asthma** and **bronchitis**. 煙霧（smog）（圖示 9）污染（pollution）引發呼吸道疾病（respiratory disease），如哮喘（asthma）和支氣管炎（bronchitis）。

Global warming 全球氣溫變暖

- **Global warming** can cause **climate change** and **environmental disaster**. Long-term changes in **temperature**, **wind**, **pressure**, **precipitation** (rain and snow) and **humidity** present challenges to our survival. 全球氣溫變暖（global warming）可導致氣候變化（climate change）和環境災難（environmental disaster）。氣溫（temperature）、風（wind）、氣壓（pressure）、降水（precipitation，即雨和雪）以及濕度（humidity）的長期變化對我們的生存構成挑戰。
- **Environmental degradation**, such as **desertification** and **desiccation**, creates problems in many parts of the world. 沙漠化（desertification）和乾燥（desiccation）等環境惡化（environmental degradation）給世界上許多地區帶來了問題。
- **Rising temperatures** cause **ice caps** to **melt**. **Rising sea levels** lead to coastal and river **flooding** and **erosion**. 日益上升的氣溫（rising temperature）造成冰蓋（ice cap）融化（melt），逐漸上升的海平面（rising sea level）導致海濱和河流洪災（flooding）與侵蝕（erosion）。
- **Extreme events** occur, such as **storms**, **drought**, **forest fires**, **soil erosion**, **landslides**, **avalanches**, **tsunamis** and the sudden appearance of **pests** and **diseases**. 極端惡劣的情況（extreme event）發生，例如風暴（storm）、乾旱（drought）、森林大火（forest fire）、土壤侵蝕（soil erosion）、滑坡（landslide）、雪崩（avalanche）、海嘯（tsunami）以及突然出現害蟲（pest）和疾病（disease）。

1
2
3
4
5
6
7
8
9
10
11

Solutions and sustainability
解決辦法和可持續性

- **Wind turbines** (1), **solar power** and **hydroelectric power** (2) provide **alternative sources of energy** that are **renewable** and do not pollute the air. 風力發電機（wind turbine）（圖示 1）、太陽能（solar power）和水力發電（hydroelectric power）（圖示 2）提供可再生（renewable）且不污染空氣的替代能源（alternative source of energy）。
- In the home, **solar panels** (3), **insulation**, **energy-efficient light bulbs** and **biodegradable products** are **environmentally friendly**. Rubbish can be sorted for **recycling** in **bins** (4) and **bottle banks** (5), and **biodegradable waste** becomes **compost** (6). 在家中，太陽能電池板（solar panel）（圖示 3）、隔熱材料（insulation）、節能燈（energy-efficient light bulb）和可生物降解的產品（biodegradable product）均對環境無害（environmentally friendly）。垃圾可分類放進垃圾箱（bin）（圖示 4）和舊瓶回收箱（bottle bank）（圖示 5）供回收（recycle），可生物降解的廢品（biodegradable waste）可變成堆肥（compost）（圖示 6）。
- Using a **bicycle** (7), an **electric car** (8) or **public transport** (9) helps to **reduce carbon emissions**. Avoiding long-distance travel and buying local, seasonal food with **low food miles** reduces your **carbon footprint**. 騎自行車（bicycle）（圖示 7）、開電動轎車（electric car）（圖示 8）或利用公共交通（public transport）（圖示 9）有助於減少碳排放（reduce carbon emission）。避免長距離旅行和購買食物里程短（low food mile）的本地時令食物可減少碳足跡（carbon footprint）。
- **Reforestation** (10) and **organic farming** (11) help to restore the earth's balance. Trees give off **oxygen**, absorb **carbon dioxide** and provide **habitats for wildlife. Organic farming** is **chemical-free**. 重新造林（reforestation）（圖示 10）和有機耕作（organic farming）（圖示 11）有助於恢復地球的平衡。樹木釋放氧氣（oxygen），吸收二氧化碳（carbon dioxide）並為野生動植物提供棲息地（habitat for wildlife）。有機耕作不使用化學製品（chemical-free）。

SOME RECYCLABLE MATERIALS 一些可回收材料

- batteries 電池
- cans 金屬罐
- cardboard 硬紙板
- engine oil 發動機油
- fluorescent tubes 熒光燈管
- glass 玻璃
- organic garden waste 有機菜園廢料
- paper 紙
- plastic bottles 塑料瓶
- scrap metal 廢金屬
- textiles 紡織品
- timber 木材

Trees, plants and flowers 樹、植物和花

Trees 樹

foliage 枝葉
twig 細枝
branch 樹枝
limb 大枝
trunk 樹幹
roots 根
tree 樹
blossom 花朵
bud 花蕾
leaf 葉
twig 細枝
rings 年輪
wood 木
bark 樹皮
log 原木

Evergreen trees 常青樹

berry 漿果
palm 棕櫚樹
yew 紫杉
needles 針葉
cone (BrE also fir cone) 球果
fir 冷杉

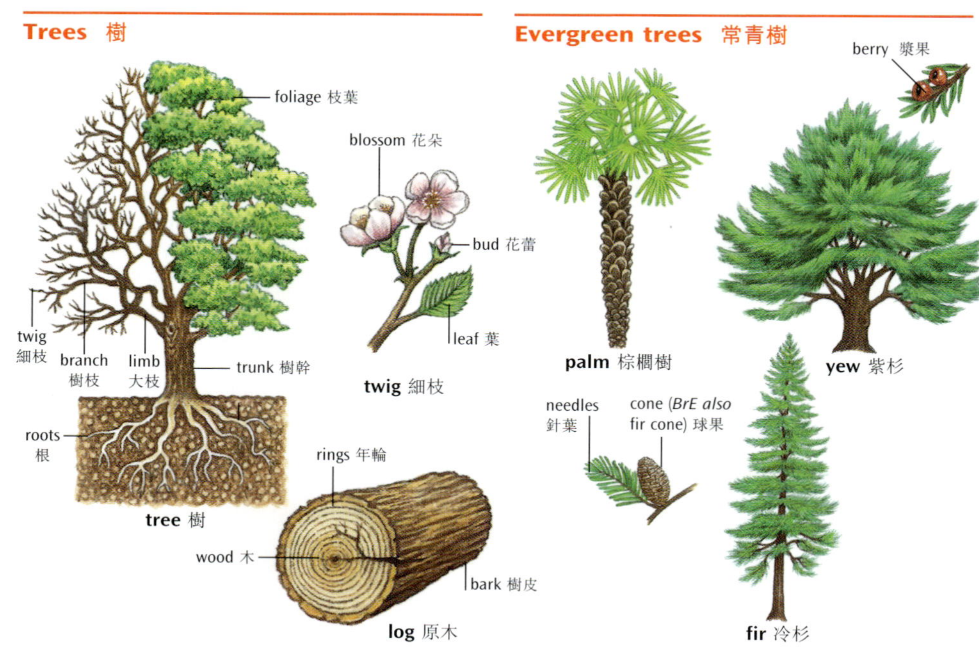

Deciduous trees 落葉樹

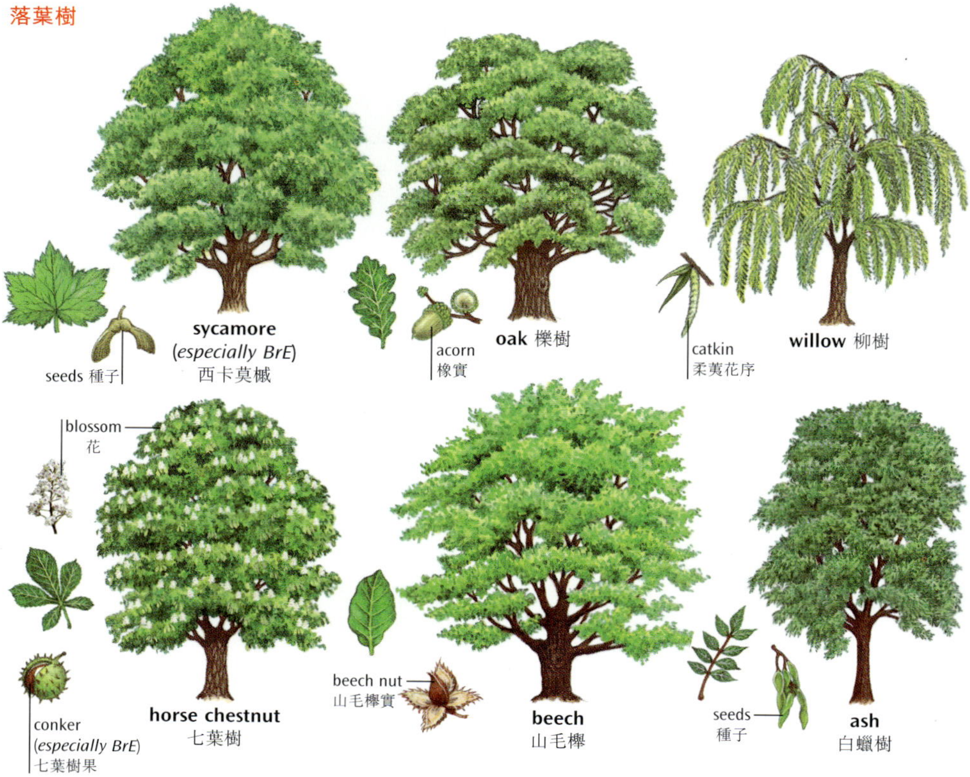

seeds 種子
sycamore (especially BrE) 西卡莫槭
acorn 橡實
oak 櫟樹
catkin 柔荑花序
willow 柳樹
blossom 花
conker (especially BrE) 七葉樹果
horse chestnut 七葉樹
beech nut 山毛櫸實
beech 山毛櫸
seeds 種子
ash 白蠟樹

flower 花朵
bud 花蕾
stalk 柄
thorn 棘刺
stem 莖
shoot 嫩芽
bulb 鱗莖
roots 根
roots
根
plant 植物
anther 花藥
stigma 柱頭
style
花柱
carpel
心皮
stamen 雄蕊
petal
花瓣
ovule
胚珠
ovary
子房
sepal 萼片
flower 花
bamboo
竹子
bulrush
燈芯草
reed
蘆葦
fern
蕨
variegated
leaves
斑葉
ivy
常春籐
dandelion clock
蒲公英絨球
moss 苔蘚
lichen 地衣
cactus 仙人掌
nettle 蕁麻
thistle 薊
dandelion 蒲公英
seed head
種球
bluebell 風鈴草
daisy 雛菊
buttercup 毛茛
primrose 報春花
poppy 罌粟
carnation
康乃馨
chrysanthemum 菊花
tendril
捲鬚
sweet pea
香豌豆
sunflower
向日葵
thorn
棘刺
rose
玫瑰
trumpet 喇叭狀花
daffodil 黃水仙
tulip 鬱金香
iris 鳶尾屬植物
lily 百合花
orchid 蘭花
lotus 蓮花

The animal kingdom 動物界

Birds 鳥類
webbed foot 蹼足
talons（猛禽的）爪
beak / bill 喙
wing 翅膀
tail 尾巴
toe 腳趾
claw 爪
finch 雀
crest 羽冠
feather 羽毛
nest 鳥巢
egg 鳥蛋
poultry and game 家禽和野禽
pheasant 野雞
duck 鴨
turkey 火雞
chicken 雞
birds of prey 猛禽
golden eagle 金雕
carrion 腐肉
vulture 禿鷲
barn owl 倉鴞
seabirds 海鳥
gull 海鷗
albatross 信天翁
puffin 海鸚
Mammals 哺乳類
coat 皮毛
mane 鬣毛
muzzle（狗馬等）口鼻部
tail 尾
lion 獅子
snout（豬等）口鼻部
paw 腳掌
claw 腳爪
whisker 鬚
antlers 鹿角
horn 角
hooves 蹄
primates 靈長類
chimpanzee (also informal chimp) 黑猩猩
prehensile tail 長捲尾
spider monkey 蜘蛛猴
rodents 齧齒類
red squirrel 紅松鼠
beaver 河狸
cetacean 鯨類
blowhole 呼吸孔
sperm whale 抹香鯨
tusk 長牙
trunk 象鼻
bat 蝙蝠
Fish 魚類
dorsal fin 背鰭
tail 尾
scales 鱗
fin 鰭
gill 鰓
ventral fin 腹鰭
trout 鱒魚
marsupials 有袋類
eucalyptus tree 桉樹
joey 幼袋鼠
pouch 育兒袋
koala (also koala bear) 樹袋熊
kangaroo (also informal roo) 袋鼠

Taxonomy 分類學

Living things are grouped on the basis of their similarities and differences into smaller and smaller groups. This scientific process of classification is called **taxonomy**. The main groups, from the largest to the smallest, are
生物根據其異同逐級分類，這種科學的分類方法叫做分類學（taxonomy）。生物從大到小的主要類別有：

- **kingdom** (animal or plant) 界（動物或植物）
- **phylum** (*plural* **phyla**) (e.g. mollusc, arthropod) 門（例如：軟體動物、節肢動物）
- **class** (e.g. mammal, gastropod, insect) 綱（例如：哺乳動物、腹足動物、昆蟲）
- **order** (e.g. primate, marsupial) 目（例如：靈長目動物、有袋目動物）
- **family** 科
- **genus** (*plural* **genera**) 屬
- **species** 種

Architecture 建築設計

geodesic dome 網格球形穹頂

gargoyle 滴水獸

obelisk 方尖碑

dome 穹頂

rotunda 圓形建築

arch 拱

vaulted ceiling 拱形天花

colonnade 柱廊

cloister 迴廊 plinth 柱基 column 柱

portico 門廊

Bridges 橋

humpback bridge (*BrE*) 拱橋

suspension bridge 懸索橋

cantilever bridge 懸臂橋

viaduct 高架橋

aqueduct 渡槽

Buildings
建築物

amphitheatre 圓形露天劇場

fort 堡壘

palace 宮殿

castle 城堡

stately home 豪華大宅

glasshouse 温室

pyramid（古埃及）金字塔

log cabin 原木小屋

pub (*BrE*) 酒吧

warehouse 倉庫

lighthouse 燈塔

oil rig
oil platform
鑽油平台

hut 棚屋

barn 穀倉

pagoda 佛塔

skyscraper
摩天大樓

Work connected with building
與建築有關的工作

	person 人員	**work** – all [U] 工作（均為不可數名詞）
building houses and other buildings 建房屋：	**builder** 建築工人	**building** 建築
designing buildings 設計房屋：	**architect** 建築師	**architecture** 建築設計
designing roads and bridges, etc. 設計公路、橋梁等：	**civil engineer** 土木工程師	**civil engineering** 土木工程
building walls, etc. with bricks 用磚砌牆等：	**bricklayer** 砌磚工	**bricklaying** 砌磚
repairing or building roofs 修或蓋屋頂：	**roofer** 蓋屋頂工人	**roofing** 蓋屋頂
making doors and window frames from wood 用木材做門窗：	**joiner** 細木工人	**joinery** 細木工作
making and repairing wooden objects and structures 製作或修理木製品和木結構：	**carpenter** 木匠	**carpentry** 木工製作
fitting glass into the frames of windows, etc. 給窗戶等安裝玻璃：	**glazier** 鑲玻璃工人	**glazing** 玻璃裝配
putting plaster on walls 用灰泥抹牆：	**plasterer** 抹灰工人	**plastering** 抹灰泥
fitting and repairing water pipes, toilets, etc. 安裝和修理水管、抽水馬桶等：	**plumber** 管子工	**plumbing** 管道工程
connecting, repairing, etc. electrical equipment 接通、修理電器設備：	**electrician** 電工	**wiring** 修理及佈線工作

Homes 住宅

semi-detached house (*BrE*)
半獨立式住宅

duplex (*especially NAmE*)
二聯式住宅

town house (*BrE*) 排房

row house (*NAmE*) 排房

terraced house (*BrE*) 排房

block of flats (*BrE*) 公寓大樓

apartment building (*NAmE*)
公寓大樓

bungalow (*BrE*) 平房

thatched cottage 茅屋

Other types of home 其他類型的住宅

- **Duplex** (*especially NAmE*) has two meanings: it is a building divided into two separate homes, each with its own entrance, or it is a flat/apartment with rooms on two floors, with a shared entrance from the street. * duplex（二聯式住宅）有兩種含義：一是指分隔為兩個獨立住宅的一棟房子，它們有各自的大門；二是指跨兩層的單元房，它們共用一個臨街入口。

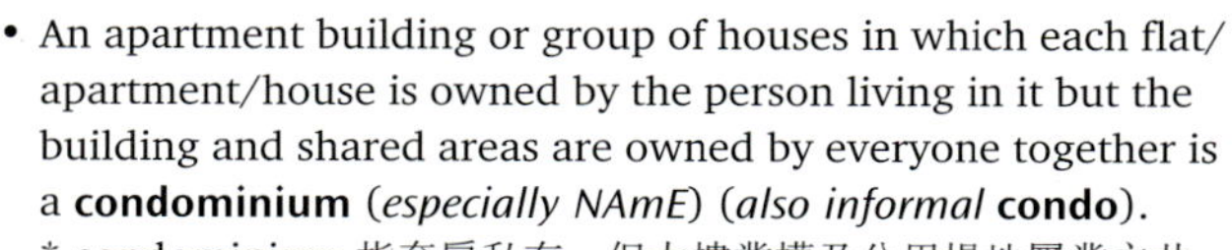

- An apartment building or group of houses in which each flat/apartment/house is owned by the person living in it but the building and shared areas are owned by everyone together is a **condominium** (*especially NAmE*) (*also informal* **condo**). * condominium 指套房私有，但大樓業權及公用場地屬業主共有的公寓（非正式亦作 condo）。
- A flat/apartment with rooms on two floors, and usually its own entrance from the street, is a **maisonette** (*BrE*). * maisonette 指複式住宅。

mobile home (*especially NAmE*)
活動住房

houseboat 水上住宅

- A house built on one level, that is very wide but not very deep from front to back, and has a roof that is not very steep, is a **ranch house** (*NAmE*) – compare **bungalow**. * ranch house 指平房住宅（與 bungalow 比較）。
- A very large house is a **mansion**. * mansion 指公館、宅第。
- An expensive and comfortable flat/apartment at the top of a tall building is a **penthouse**. * penthouse 指頂層豪華公寓。
- A set of rooms for an old person, especially in a relative's house, is called a **granny flat** (*BrE*)/ **in-law apartment/mother-in-law apartment** (*both NAmE*). * granny flat/in-law apartment/mother-in-law apartment 尤指親戚家中留出的老人套間。

House 房屋

1 chimney pot 煙囪管帽
2 chimney 煙囪
3 aerial (*BrE*) antenna (*NAmE, BrE*) 天線
4 ridge 屋脊
5 gable 山牆
6 roof 屋頂
7 skylight 天窗
8 dormer window 屋頂窗
9 eaves 屋簷
10 burglar alarm 防盜鈴
11 gutter 簷溝
12 drainpipe (*NAmE also* downspout) 雨水管
13 shutter 活動護窗
14 windowpane 窗玻璃
15 sash window 垂直推拉窗
16 casement window 平開窗
17 balcony 陽台
18 window box 窗口花壇
19 windowsill 窗台
20 porch 門廊
21 tile 瓦
22 hanging basket 吊花籃
23 door knocker 門環
24 French window (*BrE*) French door (*NAmE*) 落地窗
25 bay window 凸窗
26 letter box (*BrE*) mail slot (*NAmE*) 信箱
27 front door 正門
28 wall 牆
29 garage 車庫
30 brick 磚
31 doorstep 門階
32 basement 地下室
33 step 台階
34 drive (*also* driveway) 車道

Where you live 住處

- The area surrounding a house is the **neighbourhood** (*BrE*) / **neighborhood** (*NAmE*). * neighbourhood / neighborhood 指鄰里。
- A person who lives next or near to you is your **neighbour** (*BrE*) / **neighbor** (*NAmE*). * neighbour / neighbor 指鄰居。

  The next house, room or building is **next door**. * next door 指隔壁：
  ▸ *our next-door neighbours* 我們隔壁的鄰居
- An area where people live that is outside the main part of a city or town is called a **suburb**, or **the suburbs**. The adjective is **suburban**. * suburb 或 the suburbs 指郊區、城外，形容詞為 suburban：
  ▸ *suburban houses/streets* 郊區住宅/街道
- An area where a large number of houses are planned and built as a group is called an **estate** or a **development**. * estate 或 development 指住宅區、開發區：
  ▸ *a new housing estate/development* 新建住宅區
- If you go and live in another house, you **move**, or **move house**. You **move in/move into** a new house, then **move out/move out of** it when you stop living there. * move 或 move house 指搬家、搬遷；move in / move into 指搬入（新居）；move out / move out of 指搬出、遷出。

Buying or renting a house 買房或租房

- A house that is available to buy is **for sale** or **on the market**. * for sale 或 on the market 指待售、供出售：
  ▸ *This property has been on the market for about six weeks.* 這房產已在市場上放售約六週了。
- A person whose job is to buy and sell houses and land for other people is an **estate agent** (*BrE*) / **real estate agent** (*NAmE*). * estate agent / real estate agent 指房地產經紀人。
- When you borrow money from a bank or building society in order to buy a house, you **take out a mortgage**. * take out a mortgage 指取得按揭貸款。
- If you pay money for the use of a room, house, etc., you **rent** it (**from** sb). The money that you pay, probably each month, is **rent**. The person who rents a room, house, etc. is a **tenant** and the person who owns the property is a **landlord** (or **landlady** if it is a woman). * rent (from sb) 指（向某人）租用（房間、房屋等），房屋租金叫 rent，租用房屋等的房客或租戶叫 tenant，擁有房地產的房東或地主叫 landlord 或 landlady（女）：
  ▸ *The landlord has put the rent up again.* 房東又把租金提高了。

Garden (*BrE*) / Yard (*NAmE*) 庭園

1 greenhouse 温室
2 shed 棚屋
3 hedge 樹籬
4 bird table (*BrE*) bird feeder (*NAmE*) 鳥食平台
5 parasol / sunshade 大遮陽傘
6 conservatory (*BrE*) 暖房
7 pergola 蔓籐架
8 climber 攀緣植物
9 gate 門
10 fence 籬笆
11 sunlounger (*BrE*) (*also* lounger, *BrE, NAmE*) 日光浴椅
12 deckchair 帆布摺疊椅
13 barbecue (*also* BBQ) (戶外燒烤) 烤架
14 water butt (*BrE*) rain barrel (*NAmE*) 雨水桶
15 bench 長椅
16 trellis 攀緣架
17 stake 籬笆樁
18 deck 木製平台
19 flowerpot 花盆
20 patio 露台
21 planter 花盆
22 flower bed 花壇
23 compost bin 堆肥箱
24 border 狹長花壇
25 lawn 草坪
26 cane 莖
27 water feature 人工水景
28 pond 水池
29 cold frame (*also* frame) 冷床
30 seedling 幼苗
31 cloche 玻璃罩
32 vegetable patch / vegetable plot 小塊菜地

rakes 耙子

fork 叉

hoe 鋤頭

spade 鍬

shovel 鏟

trowel 小鏟子

hand fork 小叉子

lawnmower (*also* **mower**) 割草機

wheelbarrow (*also* **barrow**) 獨輪手推車

hose (*also* **hosepipe**) 橡皮管

watering can 灑水壺

Strimmer™ (*BrE*) 草坪修剪器

sprinkler 噴灑器

DIY, cleaning and decorating
自己動手、清潔用具和粉刷用具

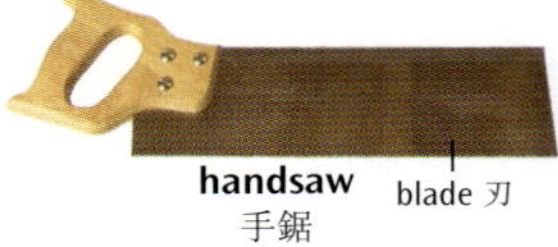

Tools 工具

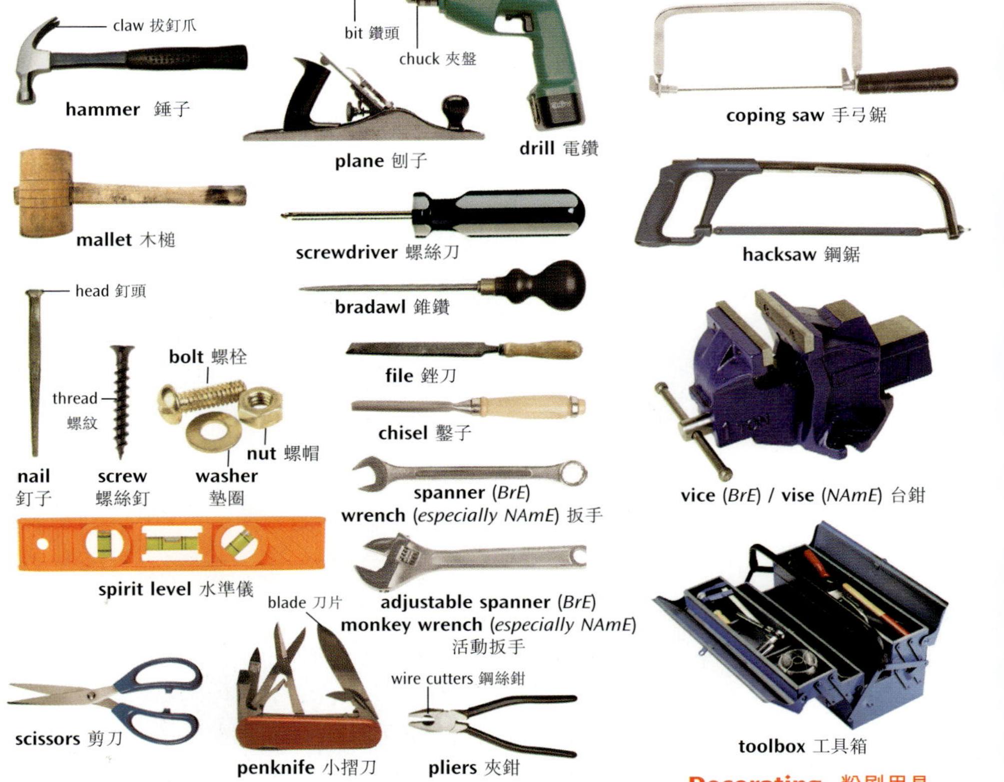

claw 拔釘爪
hammer 錘子

bit 鑽頭
chuck 夾盤
drill 電鑽

plane 刨子

coping saw 手弓鋸

mallet 木槌

screwdriver 螺絲刀

hacksaw 鋼鋸

head 釘頭
thread 螺紋
nail 釘子
screw 螺絲釘
bolt 螺栓
nut 螺帽
washer 墊圈

bradawl 錐鑽

file 銼刀

chisel 鑿子

spanner (*BrE*)
wrench (*especially NAmE*) 扳手

vice (*BrE*) / **vise** (*NAmE*) 台鉗

spirit level 水準儀

adjustable spanner (*BrE*)
monkey wrench (*especially NAmE*)
活動扳手

toolbox 工具箱

scissors 剪刀

blade 刀片
penknife 小摺刀

wire cutters 鋼絲鉗
pliers 夾鉗

Cleaning 清潔用具

bucket
(*NAmE also* **pail**) 水桶

feather duster
羽毛撣子

dustpan and brush
畚箕和刷子

duster
抹布

broom
掃把

mop
拖把

squeegee mop
膠棉拖把

iron
熨斗

squeegee
橡皮刮水刷

ironing board
燙衣板

rubber gloves
橡膠手套

vacuum cleaner
(*BrE also* **Hoover™**) 真空吸塵器

Decorating 粉刷用具

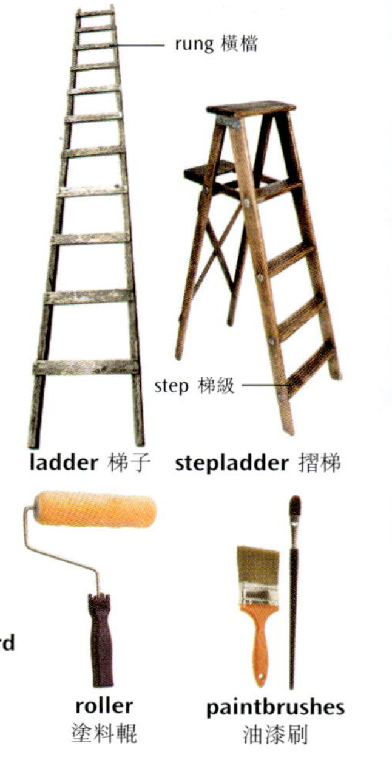

rung 橫檔

step 梯級

ladder 梯子

stepladder 摺梯

roller
塗料輥

paintbrushes
油漆刷

Living room 客廳

1 hi-fi system 高保真音響設備
2 speakers 喇叭
3 waste-paper basket (*BrE*) / wastebasket (*NAmE*) 廢紙簍
4 mantelpiece (*also* mantel *especially NAmE*) 壁爐台
5 coal scuttle 煤桶
6 fire surround 壁爐框
7 fireplace 壁爐
8 grate 爐箅
9 hearth 爐前地面
10 poker 撥火棍
11 house plant (*BrE also* pot plant) 室內盆栽植物
12 plant pot 花盆
13 armchair 扶手椅
14 rug 地毯
15 bookcase 書櫃
16 ornament (*especially BrE*) 裝飾品
17 bookend 書擋
18 flat-screen TV 平面電視
19 vase 花瓶
20 coaster 玻璃杯墊
21 footstool 腳凳
22 coffee table 茶几
23 remote control 遙控器
24 radiator 暖氣片
25 magazine rack 報刊架
26 recliner 躺椅
27 scatter cushion (*BrE*) throw pillow (*NAmE*) 小裝飾墊
28 throw 沙發罩
29 sofa / couch 長沙發
30 occasional table 臨時茶几
31 floorboards 木地板

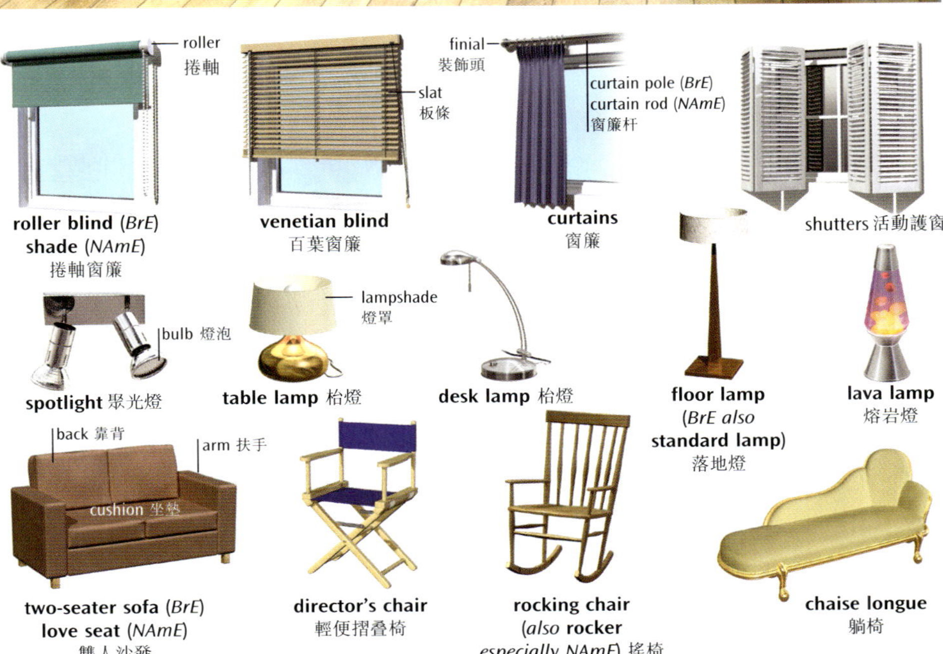

roller blind (*BrE*) **shade** (*NAmE*) 捲軸窗簾

venetian blind 百葉窗簾

curtains 窗簾

shutters 活動護窗

spotlight 聚光燈

table lamp 枱燈

desk lamp 枱燈

floor lamp (*BrE also* **standard lamp**) 落地燈

lava lamp 熔岩燈

two-seater sofa (*BrE*) **love seat** (*NAmE*) 雙人沙發

director's chair 輕便摺疊椅

rocking chair (*also* **rocker** *especially NAmE*) 搖椅

chaise longue 躺椅

Dining room 飯廳

1 fruit bowl 水果盆
2 cheeseboard 乾酪切板
3 cheese knife 乾酪刀
4 sideboard 餐具櫃
5 drawer 抽屜
6 cutlery (*especially BrE*) flatware (*NAmE*) 餐具（刀、叉和匙）
7 napkin 餐巾
8 bowl 碗
9 plate 盤子
10 place mat (*BrE also* table mat) 餐具墊
11 side plate 麵包盤
12 glass 玻璃杯
13 pepper pot (*especially BrE*) / pepper shaker (*NAmE*) 胡椒瓶
14 salt cellar (*BrE*) salt shaker (*NAmE*) 小鹽瓶
15 butter knife 黃油刀
16 butter dish 黃油碟
17 serving dish 餐盤
18 lid 蓋子
19 gravy boat 船型肉汁盤
20 candlestick 蠟燭台
21 candle 蠟燭
22 wick 燭芯
23 carafe （喇叭口）飲料瓶
24 dining chair 餐椅
25 high chair 高腳椅
26 dining table 餐桌
27 tablecloth 枱布

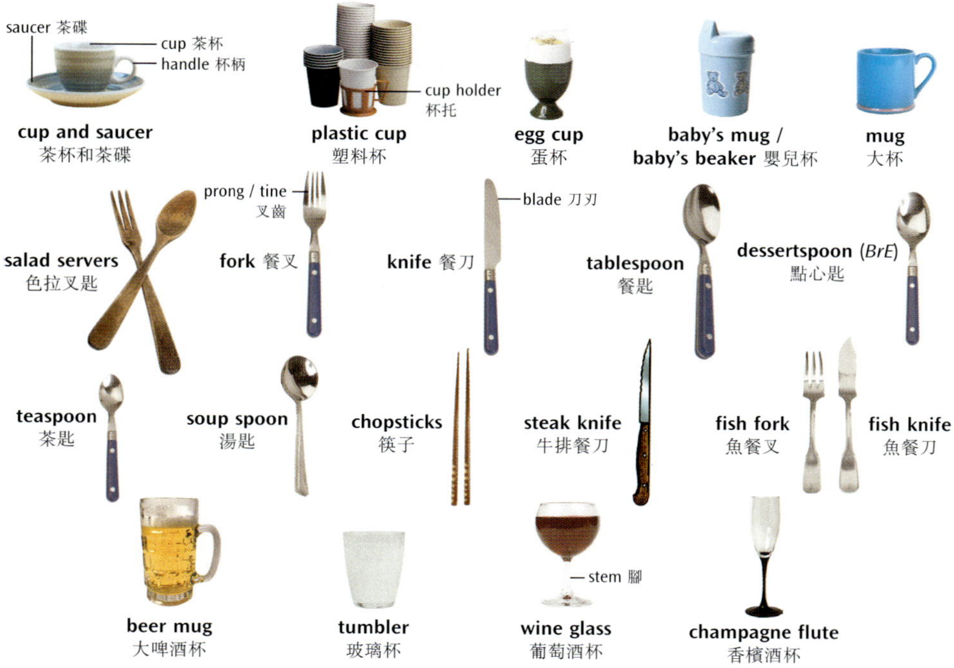

saucer 茶碟
cup 茶杯
handle 杯柄

cup and saucer
茶杯和茶碟

cup holder
杯托

plastic cup
塑料杯

egg cup
蛋杯

baby's mug / baby's beaker 嬰兒杯

mug
大杯

salad servers
色拉叉匙

prong / tine
叉齒

fork 餐叉

blade 刀刃

knife 餐刀

tablespoon
餐匙

dessertspoon (*BrE*)
點心匙

teaspoon
茶匙

soup spoon
湯匙

chopsticks
筷子

steak knife
牛排餐刀

fish fork
魚餐叉

fish knife
魚餐刀

beer mug
大啤酒杯

tumbler
玻璃杯

stem 腳

wine glass
葡萄酒杯

champagne flute
香檳酒杯

Bedroom 卧室

1 bedside table (*especially BrE*) (*NAmE usually* nightstand, night table) 牀頭櫃
2 clock radio 收音機鬧鐘
3 headboard 牀頭板
4 pillow 枕頭
5 pillowcase 枕頭套
6 bottom sheet 牀單
7 double bed 雙人牀
8 duvet 羽絨被
9 en suite (*BrE, from French*) （卧室）帶浴室的
10 built-in/fitted wardrobe (*BrE*) / closet (*especially NAmE*) 壁櫥
11 rail 橫杆
12 hanger 衣架
13 chest of drawers (*NAmE also* bureau, dresser) 五斗櫥
14 drawer 抽屜
15 full-length mirror 全身鏡
16 mirror 鏡子
17 dressing table (*NAmE also* vanity, vanity table) 梳妝枱
18 stool 凳子
19 fitted carpet (*BrE*) / wall-to-wall carpet (*NAmE*) 全室地毯
20 rug 小地毯

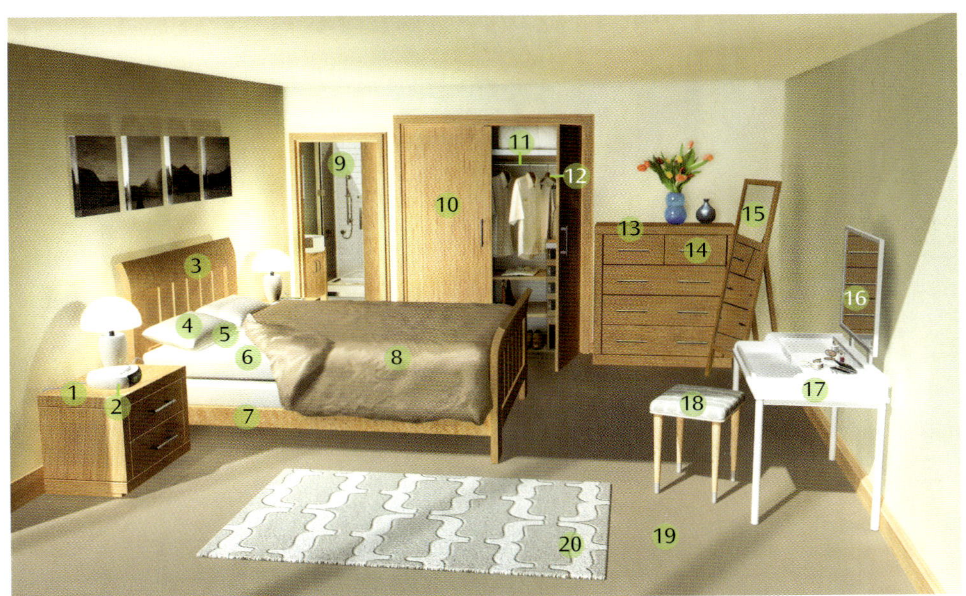

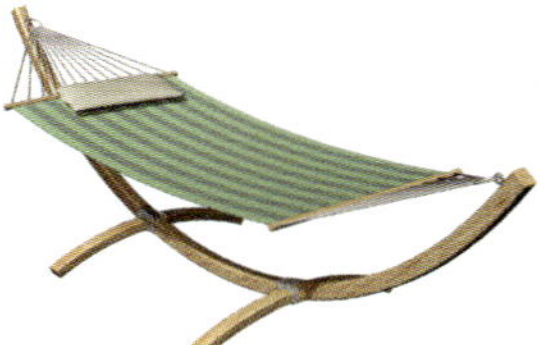

hammock 吊牀

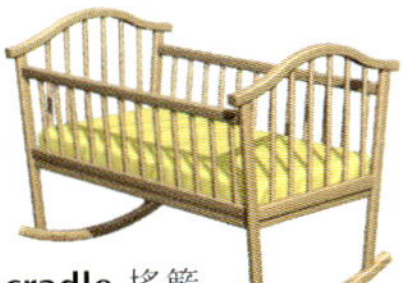

cradle 搖籃

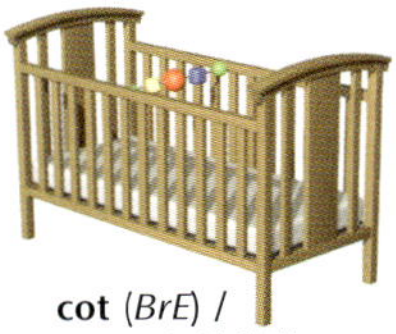

cot (*BrE*) / **crib** (*NAmE*) 幼兒牀

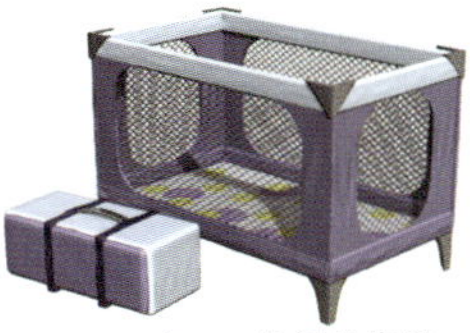

travel cot 旅行幼兒牀

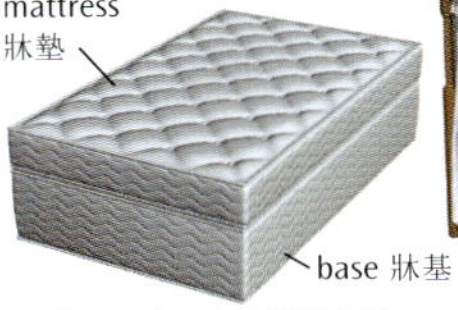

mattress 牀墊
base 牀基
divan (*BrE*) 厚墊睡榻

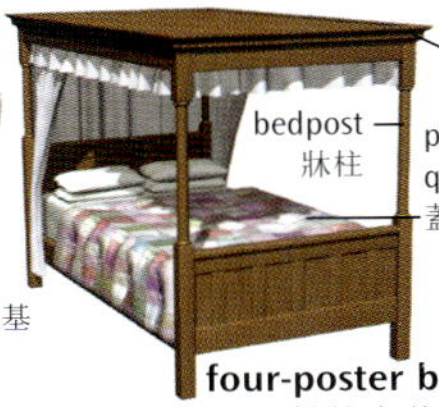

canopy 罩篷
bedpost 牀柱
patchwork quilt 拼布絎縫蓋被
four-poster bed 四帷柱大牀

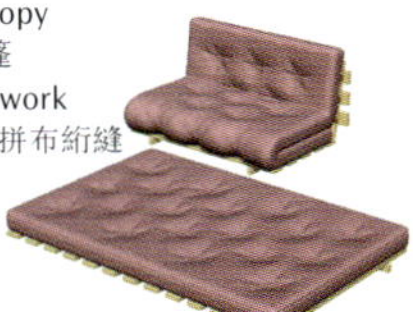

futon 日式牀墊

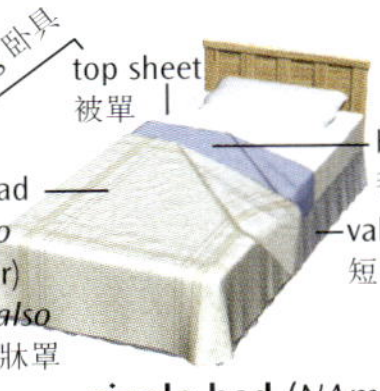

bedding 卧具
top sheet 被單
blanket 毯子
valance 短帷幔
bedspread (*BrE also* bedcover) (*NAmE also* spread) 牀罩
single bed (*NAmE also* **twin bed**) 單人牀

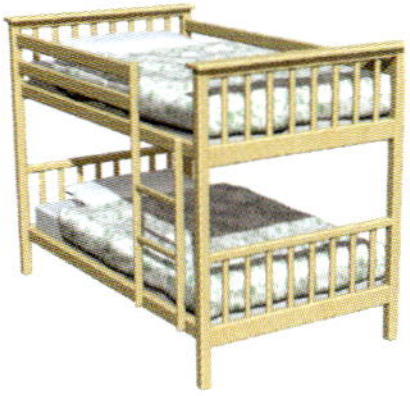

bunk beds 雙層牀

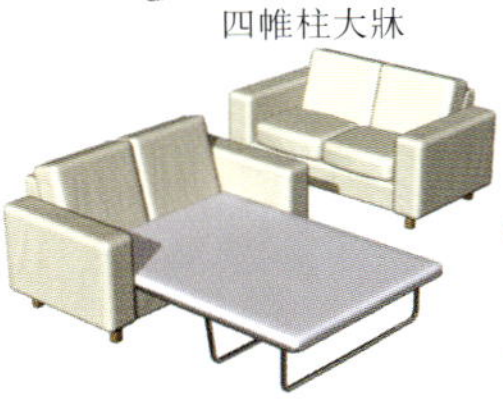

sofa bed 沙發牀

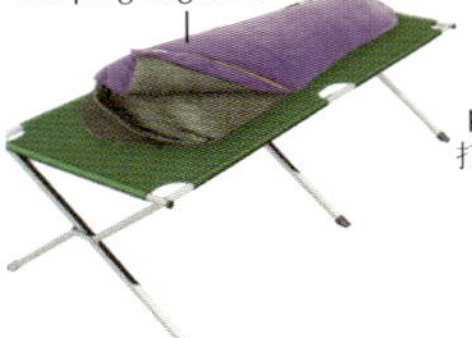

sleeping bag 睡袋
camp bed (*BrE*) **cot** (*NAmE*) 行軍牀

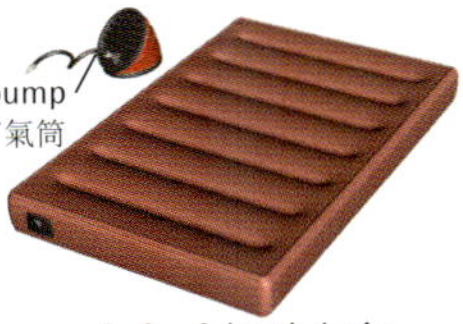

pump 打氣筒
air bed (*BrE*) / **air mattress** (*especially NAmE*) 充氣牀墊

Bathroom 浴室

1 bathroom cabinet 浴室櫃
2 toothbrush holder 牙刷架
3 beaker 塑料杯
4 mixer tap 冷熱水混合龍頭
5 washbasin 洗臉盆
6 soap dispenser 皂液瓶
7 flannel (*BrE*) / washcloth (*NAmE*) 毛巾
8 vanity unit (*BrE*) 組合式盥洗盆
9 shower cubicle 淋浴間
10 shower head 淋浴噴頭
11 soap dish 肥皂盤
12 shower tray 淋浴間底盆
13 plughole (*BrE*) drain (*US*) 排水孔
14 towel rail (*BrE*) / towel rack (*NAmE*) 毛巾架
15 hand towel 擦手巾
16 bath towel 浴巾
17 bathroom scales 浴室秤
18 bath (*BrE*) / bathtub (*especially NAmE*) 浴缸
19 bath mat 浴室腳墊
20 tiling 瓷磚面
21 bath panel 浴缸裙板
22 tap (*especially BrE*) faucet (*NAmE*) 水龍頭
23 bathrobe (*also* robe) 浴衣
24 bidet 坐浴盆
25 toilet 坐便器
26 cistern (*BrE*) 水箱
27 toilet paper 衛生紙
28 toilet brush 馬桶刷

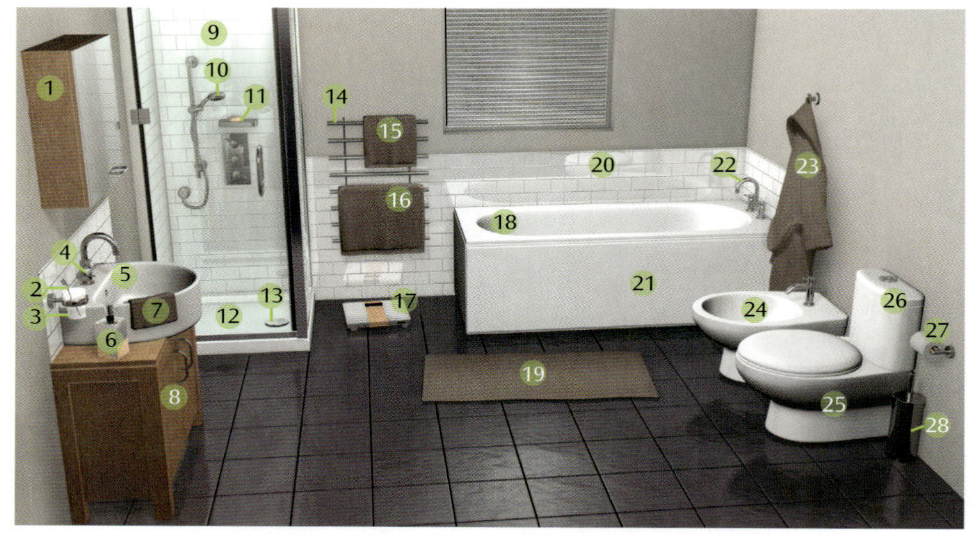

Kitchen 廚房

1 microwave 微波爐
2 worktop (*BrE*) / counter (*NAmE*) 操作枱
3 knife block 刀架
4 kitchen units 廚房組合櫃
5 cooker hood 吸油煙機
6 splashback 防濺擋板
7 gas ring (*especially BrE*) / burner (*NAmE*) 煤氣灶火圈
8 hob (*BrE*) / stovetop (*NAmE*) 爐盤
9 drawer 抽屜
10 oven glove (*also* oven mitt) 烤箱手套
11 grill (*BrE*) 烤架
12 oven 烤箱
13 fridge (*BrE*) / refrigerator (*NAmE*) 冰箱
14 breakfast bar 早餐枱
15 stool 高凳
16 toaster 烤麵包片器
17 door 門
18 shelf 擱板
19 kitchen roll holder 廚房捲紙架
20 kitchen paper (*BrE*) paper towel (*NAmE*) 廚房捲紙
21 draining board (*BrE*) drainboard (*NAmE*) 滴水板
22 dishcloth (*NAmE usually* dishrag) 洗碗布
23 sink 洗碗槽
24 tap (*especially BrE*) faucet (*NAmE*) 水龍頭
25 dishwasher 洗碗碟機
26 tea towel (*BrE*) dishtowel (*NAmE*) 茶巾

Appliances （家用）器具

blender (*BrE also* **liquidizer**) 食物攪拌器

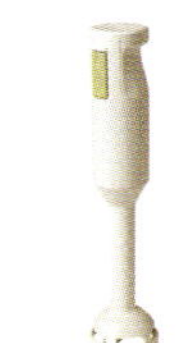
hand-held blender 手持攪拌器

food processor 食物加工器

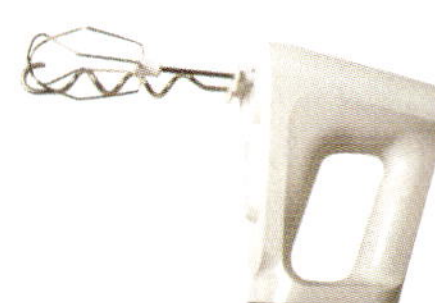
electric whisk 電動攪拌器

Coffee and tea 咖啡和茶

electric kettle 電水壺

espresso maker 蒸餾咖啡機

cafetière (*BrE*) **French press** (*NAmE*) 法式咖啡壺

coffee maker (*also* **coffee machine**) 煮咖啡機

teapot 茶壺

Kitchen utensils 廚房用具

Cutting 切削
bread knife 麪包刀
serrated blade 鋸齒刀刃
handle 柄
carving knife 切肉刀
edge 刀鋒
point 刀尖
steel 磨刀棒
cleaver 剁肉刀
peeler 削皮器
palette knife 鏟刀
chopping board (BrE) cutting board (NAmE) 砧板
paring knife 削皮刀
kitchen scissors 廚房用剪刀
Measuring 計量
measuring spoons 量匙
measuring cups 量杯
measuring jug （有刻度的）量杯
timer 計時器
Opening 開啟
corkscrew 瓶塞鑽
bottle opener 開瓶器
tin opener (BrE) can opener (NAmE) 開罐器
Crushing, grating, squeezing 搗碎，擦碎，壓榨
potato masher 土豆搗爛器
grater 磨碎器
zester 果皮刨
lemon-squeezer (BrE) juicer (NAmE) 榨汁器
garlic press (also garlic crusher) 壓蒜器
nutcracker 堅果鉗
pestle 杵
mortar 臼
pestle and mortar 杵和臼
pepper mill 胡椒研磨器
Other utensils 其他用具
colander 濾鍋
sieve (BrE) sifter (NAmE) 篩子
ladle 長柄勺
wooden spoon 木匙
whisk 打蛋器
basting brush 塗油刷
spatula 刮鏟
fish slice (BrE) spatula (NAmE) 煎魚鍋鏟
ramekin 小盤子
tongs 夾鉗
ice-cream scoop 冰淇淋勺
cake slice 蛋糕鏟
rolling pin 擀麪杖

Cooking 烹飪

flambé 法式火燒

stir-fry 炒

fry 煎

barbecue 燒烤

boil 煮

steam 蒸

bake 烤

casserole 燉

Cook 烹煮食物

- When talking generally about preparing meals, use the verb **to cook**. 泛指烹調食物用動詞 cook：
  - ▸ *When you're cooking for your family, make an extra serving.* 你給家人做飯時，多做一份。

You can **cook** food or a meal, 烹製食物或做飯均可用 cook：

- ▸ *Lucas is cooking dinner.* 盧卡斯在做飯。
- ▸ *Cook the onion gently until soft.* 用文火把洋葱煮軟。

… or the food or the meal can **cook**. 飯菜在燒煮中亦可用 cook：

- ▸ *Add the meat and let it cook for ten minutes.* 加上肉煮十分鐘。

There are different verbs for particular ways of cooking: with water or oil, or in dry heat. 有各種不同的動詞表示特定的烹飪方法，如水煮、油炸或乾烘。

Fry 煎，炸，炒

- You can **fry** meat, fish, eggs, etc. in a shallow pan of hot oil, or the meat, fish, eggs, etc. can **fry**. 在平底鍋上用油煎或炒肉、魚、蛋等用 fry。肉、魚、蛋等後亦可直接用 fry 表示煎炒的意思：
  - ▸ *Fry the onion and garlic for five minutes.* 將洋葱和大蒜炒五分鐘。
  - ▸ *The smell of frying bacon made her mouth water.* 炒燻肉的香味饞得她流口水。
- Chips (*BrE*) / French fries (*NAmE*), etc. can be completely covered in very hot oil and **deep-fried**. 油炸土豆條等可用 deep-fry。
- You can **sauté** food by frying it quickly in a little hot fat. 表示用少量油快速地嫩煎可用 sauté：
  - ▸ *new potatoes sautéed in butter and thyme* 用黃油和百里香嫩煎的早土豆

Boil 煮

- You can **boil** vegetables, eggs, rice, etc. by covering them with water and heating to **boiling point** (=100°C). 可以用水煮 (boil) 菜、蛋、米飯等，加熱至沸點 (boiling point)：
  - ▸ *Boil the potatoes until tender, then drain.* 將土豆煮軟，然後瀝掉水。

Preparation 準備

chop 切碎

dice 切成丁

slice 切成片

knead 揉麪

roll out 擀麪

mash 搗碎

grate 擦成細絲

whip 攪打

- You can also just **boil** the water, 燒開水用 boil :
  ▸ *I'm boiling the water for the pasta now.* 我在燒水準備煮意大利麪。

  ... or the container the water is in. 燒裝了水的容器亦用 boil :
  ▸ *Boil a large pan of salted water.* 燒一大鍋加了鹽的水。
- The vegetables, the water, or (in British English) the container, can **boil**. 菜、水或（在英式英語中）容器均可後接 boil 表示燒煮 :
  ▸ *The potatoes were boiling away merrily.* 土豆在咕嘟咕嘟地煮着。
  ▸ *The kettle's boiled! Do you want some tea?* (*BrE*) 壺裏的水燒開了！你想喝點茶嗎？
- If you **bring something to the boil** (*BrE*) / **a boil** (*NAmE*) you heat it until it boils; you can then **simmer** it or let it **simmer** by letting it boil gently for a period of time. 把東西加熱至沸點説 bring something to the boil / a boil，再用文火煨或燉就用 simmer :
  ▸ *Simmer the carrots in a large pan of water.* 用一大鍋水文火燉胡蘿蔔。
  ▸ *Bring to the boil and let it simmer for five minutes.* 燒開後用文火煨五分鐘。
- You can **poach** food by cooking it gently in a small amount of liquid. 在少量水中煨用 poach:
  ▸ *Gently poach the salmon fillets for eight minutes.* 將鮭魚片慢煨八分鐘。

Steam 蒸

- You can **steam** fish, vegetables, etc. by placing the food above boiling water in a covered container with holes in the bottom so the steam reaches it. 蒸魚、菜等用 steam :
  ▸ *Chinese rice is always white and usually prepared by steaming.* 中國米飯一向是白的，通常是蒸熟的。

Roast 烘，烤，焙

- You can **roast** large pieces of meat, potatoes, etc. by covering the surface of the food with oil in the heat of an oven. 將大塊肉、土豆等食物的表面抹上油在烤爐裏燒烤用 roast。

Grill 炙烤

- You can **grill** (*BrE*) / **broil** (*NAmE*) food under direct heat on a **grill pan** (*BrE*) / **broiler pan** (*NAmE*). 在烤盤（英式英語用 grill pan，美式英語用 broiler pan）上烤製食物用 grill 或 broil。

Bake 烘烤

- You can **bake** bread, cakes, potatoes, etc. in the dry heat of an oven or a fire, 在烤箱或火爐內烤麵包、蛋糕、土豆等用 bake：
  - ▶ *He baked a cake for her birthday.* 他為她的生日烤了一個蛋糕。

  … or the bread, cakes, etc. can **bake**. 麵包、蛋糕等詞後可直接用 bake：
  - ▶ *While the cake is baking, avoid opening the oven door.* 蛋糕在烘烤時不要打開烤箱門。
- **Baking** can be used for things that are baked, or for the activity of baking them. * baking 可指烘烤的食物或烘烤這活動：
  - ▶ *A nice smell of baking came from the kitchen.* 廚房裏飄來烘烤食物的香味。
  - ▶ *My grandmother always used to bake/do the baking on Saturdays.* 以前我的祖母總是在星期六烤製食物。

GRAMMAR POINT 語法説明

- The past participle (**-ed** form) of most cooking verbs can be used as an adjective before an item of food, meaning 'that has been cooked in this way'. 多數表示烹調的動詞的過去分詞（-ed 形式）可用作形容詞，置於食物名稱前，表示是用這種方法烹調的：
  - ▶ *a cooked breakfast* (*BrE*) *a warm breakfast* (*NAmE*) 煮熟的早餐
  - ▶ *a boiled egg* 煮（熟的）蛋
  - ▶ *sautéed potatoes* (*also sauté potatoes*) 嫩煎土豆
  - ▶ *BUT* 但 *roast chicken* 烤雞
- The gerund (**-ing** form) of some cooking verbs can be used as an adjective before an item of food, meaning 'suitable to be cooked in this way', 有些表示烹調的動名詞（-ing 形式）可用作形容詞，置於食物名稱前，表示宜用這種方法烹製：
  - ▶ *cooking apples* (= that must be cooked before they are eaten) 烹調用蘋果
  - ▶ *stewing steak* 宜燉煮的牛排

  … or before a piece of equipment, meaning 'suitable to be used when cooking in this way'. 或置於炊具名稱前，表示適用於這種烹調方法：
  - ▶ *a frying pan* 煎鍋
  - ▶ *a baking tray* (*BrE*) / *baking sheet* (*NAmE*) 烘烤盤

Fruit and vegetables 水果和蔬菜

- Some fruit and vegetables are always countable. 有些水果和蔬菜總是可數名詞：
  ▶ *Do you like bananas?* 你喜歡香蕉嗎？
  Some are always uncountable. 而有些總是不可數名詞：
  ▶ *Celery is usually eaten raw.* 芹菜通常生吃。
- Some may be countable or uncountable, depending on whether you are thinking of them as plants or as food and on how they are prepared as food. If you are thinking of a fruit or vegetable as a plant you are usually talking about the whole fruit or vegetable, so it will be countable. 還有些既可以是可數名詞，也可以是不可數名詞，取決於你把它視為植物還是食物，以及作為食物時如何烹製。如果把某種水果或蔬菜視為植物，通常指整個水果或整棵蔬菜，所以是可數名詞：
  ▶ *Plant the cabbages in rows.* 把捲心菜種在一行一行的地裏。
- Larger fruit or vegetables, that you do not eat whole, are uncountable as food. 較大的不能整個吃的水果或整棵吃的蔬菜作為食物時為不可數名詞：
  ▶ *duck with spring cabbage* 春甘藍煮鴨
  Others may be eaten whole (countable) … 其他可以整個吃的水果或整棵吃的蔬菜為可數名詞：
  ▶ *baked apples* 烤蘋果
  ▶ *baby carrots* 小胡蘿蔔
  … or prepared in such a way that they are not eaten whole (uncountable in British English but still countable in American English). 或以某種方式烹調而不能整個吃，在英式英語中為不可數名詞，但在美式英語中仍為可數名詞：
  ▶ *stewed apple* (*BrE*) / *stewed apples* (*NAmE*) 燉蘋果
  ▶ *grated raw carrot* (*BrE*) / *grated raw carrots* (*NAmE*) 生胡蘿蔔細絲

clove 蒜瓣
garlic
大蒜
onion
洋葱
shallots
青葱
fennel 茴香
cabbage
捲心菜
floret (BrE)
花部
cauliflower
花椰菜
leek 韭葱
Brussels sprouts
湯菜
spring onions (BrE)
green onions (NAmE)
大葱
okra 秋葵
mushrooms 蘑菇
broccoli
西蘭花
artichoke
(also globe artichoke)
洋蓟
spear 幼芽
celery 芹菜
chilli 辣椒
asparagus
蘆筍
sweet potato
甘薯
potato
馬鈴薯
corn on the cob
玉米棒子
sweetcorn (BrE)
corn (NAmE)
（甜）玉米粒
aubergine (BrE)
eggplant (NAmE)
茄子
yam 山藥
Squash 南瓜類
marrow (BrE) 西葫蘆
pumpkin 南瓜
courgette (BrE)
zucchini (NAmE)
小胡瓜
Peas and beans 豆類
pod 豆莢
green beans 四季豆
peas 豌豆
kidney beans
紅腰豆
chickpeas
(especially BrE)
garbanzos (NAmE)
鷹嘴豆
bean sprouts 豆芽
Root vegetables 根莖類蔬菜
carrot 胡蘿蔔
parsnip 歐洲防風
moolis / daikons 白蘿蔔
beetroot (BrE)
beet (NAmE)
甜菜根
swede (BrE)
rutabaga (NAmE)
蕪菁甘藍
turnip
蕪菁
Salad vegetables （生吃的）色拉蔬菜
radishes 櫻桃蘿蔔
tomato 番茄
lettuce 生菜
peppers (BrE)
bell peppers (NAmE)
燈籠椒
cucumber 黃瓜

Herbs, spices, nuts and cereals
香草、香料、堅果和穀物

Herbs 香草

bay 月桂

sage 鼠尾草

basil 羅勒

oregano 牛至

mint 薄荷

parsley 歐芹

thyme
百里香

rosemary
迷迭香

dill
蒔蘿

tarragon
龍蒿

chives
細香蔥

coriander
(*NAmE also* **cilantro**)
芫荽

Spices 香料

cloves
丁香

black peppercorns
黑胡椒粒

star anise
八角茴香

cinnamon
桂皮

cardamom
豆蔻乾籽

nutmeg
肉豆蔻

ginger
薑

saffron
番紅花

turmeric
薑黃根粉

paprika
紅辣椒粉

cumin seeds
蒔蘿籽

coriander seeds
芫荽籽

Nuts 堅果

cashew
腰果

peanut
花生

macadamia
澳洲堅果

hazelnut
(*also* **filbert** *especially NAmE*)
榛子

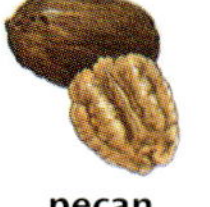
pecan
美洲山核桃

almond
杏仁

pistachio
開心果

brazil 巴西堅果

walnut 核桃

chestnut 栗子

Cereals 穀物

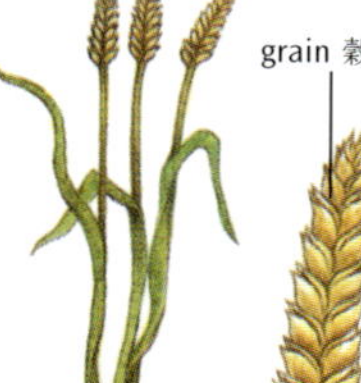
wheat
小麥

ear of wheat
麥穗

barley
大麥

maize (*BrE*)
corn (*NAmE*)
玉米

rye
黑麥

rice
稻米

oats
燕麥

millet
穀子

Packaging 包裝

multipack 合裝包

blister pack 吸塑包裝

box 盒

box (*BrE also* **packet**) 盒

matchbox 火柴盒

packet (*BrE*) **stick** (*NAmE*) 條

stick 條

packet (*BrE*) **pack** (*NAmE*) 紙包

packet (*BrE*) **package** (*NAmE*) 包

packet (*BrE*) **roll** (*NAmE*) 包；管

cap / top 蓋子

top 蓋子

tube 軟管；管

sachet (*BrE*) **packet** (*NAmE*) 小袋

roll 捲

straw 吸管

carton (*BrE*) **juice box** (*NAmE*) 果汁紙盒

carton 硬紙盒

carton (*BrE also* **pot**) 紙盒；塑料盒

tub 飯盒；食物盒

nozzle 噴嘴

top 蓋子

aerosol can 噴霧罐

can 罐

cork 軟木塞

screw-top 螺旋蓋

bottle 瓶子

lid 蓋子

tin 金屬食物盒

ring pull (*BrE*) pull tab (*NAmE*) 拉環

lid 蓋子

tin / can (*both BrE*) **/ can** (*NAmE*) 罐頭

punnet (*BrE*) 小果盒

tray 托盤

label 標籤

jar 廣口瓶

bag (*BrE also* **packet**) 袋

bag 袋

shopping bag 購物袋

carrier bag (*BrE*) 購物袋

shopping basket 購物籃

shopping trolley (*BrE*) **shopping cart** (*NAmE*) 購物手推車

Musical instruments 樂器

Playing an instrument 演奏樂器

- When talking generally about playing musical instruments, **the** is usually used before the name of the instrument. 泛指演奏樂器時通常在樂器名稱前加定冠詞 the :
  - ▸ *He played **the** trumpet in a jazz band.* 他在爵士樂隊吹小號。
  - ▸ *She decided to take up* (= start learning to play) ***the** flute.* 她決定學習吹奏長笛。
- **The** is not usually used when two or more instruments are mentioned. 涉及兩種或以上樂器時一般不用定冠詞 the :
  - ▸ *She teaches violin, cello and piano.* 她教小提琴、大提琴和鋼琴。
- The preposition **on** is used to say who is playing which instrument. 指某人演奏某種樂器用介詞 on :
  - ▸ *The CD features James Galway **on** the flute.* 這張 CD 唱片主推詹姆斯 • 高爾韋的長笛演奏。
  - ▸ *She sang and he accompanied her **on** the piano.* 她演唱，他用鋼琴伴奏。
- **The** is not usually used when you are talking about pop or jazz musicians. 指流行音樂家或爵士音樂家的演奏通常不用定冠詞 the :
  - ▸ *John Squire on guitar* 約翰 • 斯夸爾的吉他演奏
  - ▸ *Miles Davis played trumpet.* 邁爾斯 • 戴維斯吹小號。

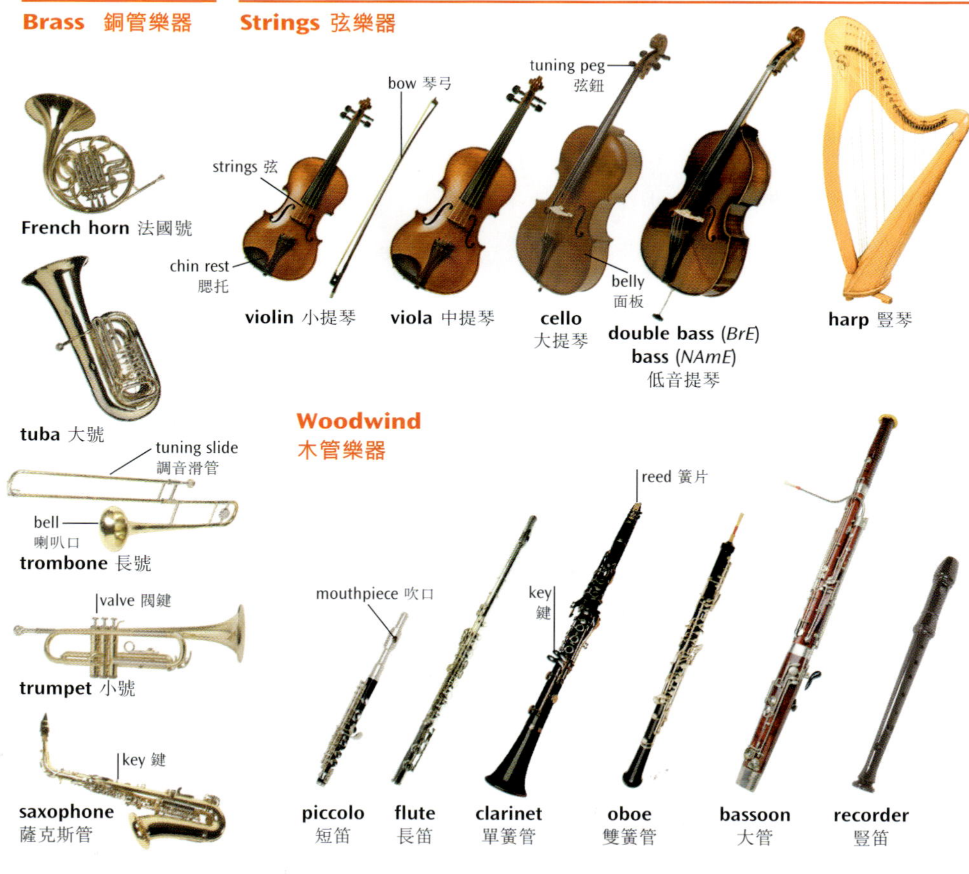

Percussion 打擊樂器

Describing instruments 描述樂器

- There are four **sections** of instruments in an **orchestra**: **strings**, **woodwind**, **brass** and **percussion**. 一個管弦樂隊（orchestra）包括四組（section）樂器：弦樂組（strings）、木管樂組（woodwind）、銅管樂組（brass）和打擊樂組（percussion）。
- Different bands or **ensembles** can be formed when instruments from the different sections play separately. 不同樂器組分別演奏時可組成不同的樂隊或合奏組（ensemble）：
  - ▸ *a brass band* 銅管樂隊
  - ▸ *a wind band* 管樂隊
  - ▸ *a string quartet* 弦樂四重奏小組
  - ▸ *a jazz trio* 爵士樂三重奏小組
- Particular adjectives are used before the names of musical instruments to describe the type of instrument it is. 在樂器名稱前用特定的形容詞表示樂器類型：
  - ▸ *a tenor saxophone* 次中音薩克斯管
  - ▸ *a classical guitar* 古典吉他
  - ▸ *a bass drum* 大鼓

GRAMMAR POINT 語法説明

- The names of instruments can be used like adjectives before other nouns. 樂器名稱可用作形容詞置於其他名詞前：
  - ▸ *a clarinet lesson* 單簧管課
  - ▸ *Chopin's Piano Concerto No. 1* 肖邦的第一鋼琴協奏曲
  - ▸ *She's going to do her cello practice.* 她要練習大提琴。

People who play instruments 樂器演奏者

- Some musical instruments have a special name, ending in **–ist** or **–er** for the people who play them. 有些樂器有特定的名稱，其後接 -ist 或 -er 時，表示演奏的人：
  - ▸ *The violinist lifted his bow.* 小提琴演奏者拿起琴弓。
  - ▸ *The South African drummer, Louis Moholo* 南非鼓手路易斯•莫霍洛
- Check near the entry for each instrument to find the correct word. If there is no special word, you use **player** after the name of the instrument. 表示某種樂器的演奏者的詞可在相關的樂器詞條附近查找，如果沒有特定名稱就在樂器名稱後加 player：
  - ▸ *the quartet's viola player* 四重奏的中提琴演奏者
- When talking about pop or jazz, people often use **player** even when there is a word for the person like **saxophonist** or **bassist**. 談及流行音樂或爵士樂時，雖然有薩克斯管吹奏者（saxophonist）或低音吉他手（bassist）等特定名稱，人們仍常用 player：
  - ▸ *A brilliant young sax player* 才華橫溢的青年薩克斯管吹奏者
  - ▸ *We're looking for a new bass player.* 我們在物色新的低音吉他手。

- In an orchestra playing classical music, **principal**, **deputy principal** (*BrE*), **associate principal** (*NAmE*) and **assistant principal** (*NAmE*) are used with the names of instruments to describe a player's position or importance. 在演奏古典音樂的管弦弦樂隊中，首席演奏者（principal）、副首席演奏者（deputy principal 或 associate principal）和助理首席演奏者（assistant principal）與樂器名稱連用表示演奏者的地位和重要性：
  - ▸ *He became principal cellist within a few years.* 他幾年內就成為首席大提琴手。
- A person who directs (or **conducts**) an orchestra is a **conductor**. The principal violinist (who **leads** the orchestra) is the **leader** (*BrE*) or the **concertmaster** (*NAmE*). 指揮（conduct）管弦樂隊的人稱作 conductor。首席小提琴手（管弦樂隊首席）稱作 leader 或 concertmaster。

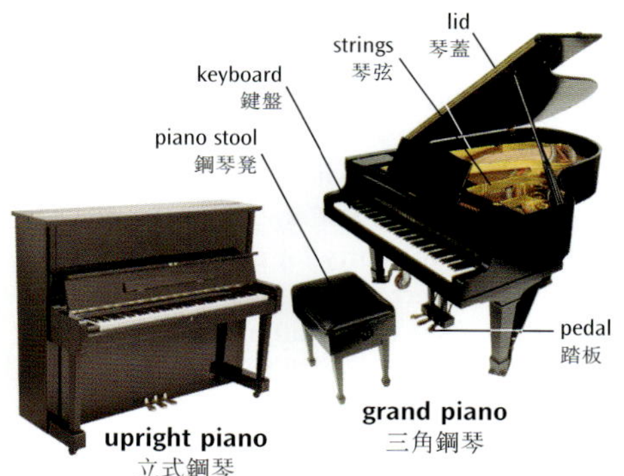

upright piano
立式鋼琴

grand piano
三角鋼琴

Music for instruments 器樂

- Music is **composed** or **written** for an instrument. In a piece of music written for a group of instruments, each has a different **part** to play. 樂曲是為某種樂器譜寫（compose 或 write）而成。合奏樂中的聲部或分譜稱為 part：
  - ▸ *There are parts for oboe and bassoon.* 有雙簧管和大管聲部。
- If there is more than one part for the same type of instrument, the terms **first** and **second**, and sometimes **third** and **fourth**, are used. 如果同種樂器有兩個或以上聲部就用第一、第二，有時用第三或第四聲部表示：
  - ▸ *She's a second violin* (= plays the second violin part). 她是第二聲部小提琴手。
  - ▸ *the deep low notes of the third horn* 法國號第三聲部的低音
- A **solo** is a part for one instrument playing alone. A **soloist** plays it. * solo 指獨奏，soloist 指獨奏者：
  - ▸ *She performs regularly as a soloist and in chamber music.* 她定期獨奏表演並參與室內樂演奏。
  - ▸ *I love the saxophone solo in this song.* 我喜歡這首歌曲中的薩克斯管獨奏。

More illustrations at ACCORDION and MUSIC.
其他插圖見 accordion 和 music 詞條。

electric guitar 電吉他 · **acoustic guitar** 原聲吉他 · **banjo** 班卓琴 · **mandolin** 曼陀林 · **balalaika** 巴拉萊卡琴 · **sitar** 西塔爾

Toys and games 玩具和遊戲

Frisbee™ 弗里斯比飛盤

kite 風箏

skipping rope (*BrE*) / **jump rope** (*NAmE*) 跳繩

sandpit (*BrE*) **sandbox** (*NAmE*) 沙坑

swing 鞦韆

slide 滑梯

trampoline 蹦床

climbing frame (*BrE*) **jungle gym** (*NAmE*) 攀爬架

teddy bear (*BrE also* **teddy**) 泰迪熊

soft toy (*BrE*) / **stuffed animal** (*especially NAmE*) 布絨玩具

rag doll 布娃娃

glove puppet (*BrE*) **hand puppet** (*NAmE*) 手偶

rocking horse 木馬

building blocks 積木

doll's house (*BrE*) / **dollhouse** (*NAmE*) 玩具小屋

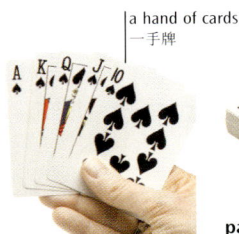

playing cards / cards 紙牌

pack of cards (*BrE*) **deck of cards** (*especially NAmE*) 一副紙牌

suits 花色

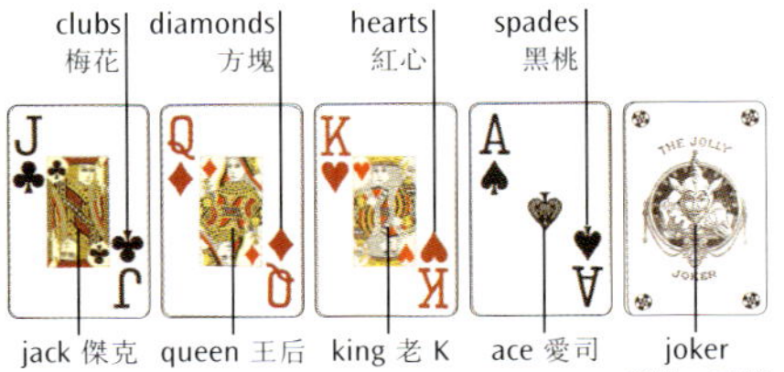

court cards (*BrE*) **face cards** (*especially NAmE*) 花牌

Cards 紙牌

- To mix the playing cards is to **shuffle** them. 洗牌叫 shuffle：
  - ▸ *Shuffle the cards well.* 好好洗牌。
  - ▸ *Shall I shuffle?* 我來洗牌好嗎？
- To give cards to each individual person who is playing the game is to **deal** them (**out**). The person who does this is called the **dealer**. 給大家發牌用 deal ... (out)。發牌人稱作 dealer：
  - ▸ *Whose turn is it to deal?* 輪到誰發牌了？
  - ▸ *Deal the cards.* 發牌。
- To divide the pack of cards into two or three parts is to **cut** them. 切牌用 cut：
  - ▸ *Cut the cards to see who starts.* 切牌看看從誰開始。
- A card which is on the table showing the picture side is **face up**. A card which is on the table so that you cannot see the picture side is **face down**. 紙牌正面朝上放為 face up，正面朝下放為 face down。
- The cards that you have in your hand when you play cards is a **hand**. 一手牌為 a hand。
  - ▸ *I knew I'd win – I had a really good hand* (=I had good cards). 我就知道我會贏的——我抓了一手特好的牌。

dominoes 多米諾骨牌

noughts and crosses (*BrE*) / tic-tac-toe (*NAmE*)
圈叉遊戲

Chinese chequers (*BrE*) / Chinese checkers (*NAmE*)
（彈子）跳棋

snakes and ladders (*BrE*) 蛇梯棋

chess 國際象棋

backgammon 十五子棋

Playing games 玩遊戲

- The official statements that tell you what you can or cannot do in a game are the **rules**; something which is not allowed in a game is **against the rules**. 遊戲規則稱作 rules，違反規則稱作 against the rules。
- To play a game in a dishonest or unfair way: **cheat**; *noun* [U]: **cheating**; a person who cheats is **a cheat**. 玩遊戲時作弊稱作 cheat，名詞形式為 cheating（不可數）；作弊者稱作 cheat：
  - ▶ *You can't do that, it's cheating.* 你不能那麼做，那是作弊。
  - ▶ *He's such a cheat.* 他真能耍賴。

Board games 棋類遊戲

- A game played on a flat hard piece of wood or cardboard is a **board game**. 棋類遊戲稱為 board game。
- A small cube with a different number of spots on each side, used in certain games, is called a **dice** (*also* **die** *especially NAmE*) (*plural* **dice**). 某些遊戲中使用的骰子稱作 dice。
- A small round flat object that is used in some games to show where a player is on the board is a **counter**. 某些遊戲中使用的棋子稱作 counter。
- To take a piece or a counter and move it to another place on the board: **move** (something). 走棋叫作 move：
  - ▶ *You can only move your counter one square in any direction.* 棋子在任何方向只能走一格。
- The time in a game when one person must do something (for example move a piece) is called a **move**, **turn**, **go** (*plural* **goes**). 下棋時輪到的走棋機會稱作 move、turn 或 go：
  - ▶ *It's your move/turn/go.* 該你走了。
  - ▶ *You've just had two goes.* 你剛才走了兩步。

Chess 國際象棋

- A stage in the game of chess when a player's king could be taken by the other person is called **check** *noun* [U]. When you are in this position, you are **in check**. 將軍的局面稱作 check（不可數名詞），被將軍為 in check。
- When one player cannot move his king out of check and the game ends is called **checkmate** *noun* [U]. 被將死或輸棋稱作 checkmate（不可數名詞）。
- The end of a game of chess when neither player can win is **stalemate** *noun* [U]. 和棋或僵局為 stalemate（不可數名詞）。

Puzzles 智力遊戲

- A game that tests your knowledge or intelligence is a **puzzle**. * puzzle 指測試知識或智力的遊戲：
  - ▶ *to do a puzzle* 做智力遊戲
  - ▶ *a mathematical puzzle* 數學智力遊戲
- A picture on cardboard or wood that is cut into small pieces which you have to join together is a **jigsaw** (**puzzle**). * jigsaw (puzzle) 指拼圖。
- A word game with black and white squares where you write the word in the white squares is a **crossword** (**puzzle**). To find the right word, you have to **solve a clue**. * crossword (puzzle) 指縱橫字謎。按提示語填出一個詞叫作 solve a clue：
  - ▶ *I can't do this crossword, the clues are too difficult.* 這個填字遊戲我做不出來，給的提示太難了。
  - ▶ *to solve a crossword puzzle* 解答縱橫字謎

sudoku 數獨

AKEHJOMNBALNIMZ
ALSKDJFHQPWOMNB
HGEFIGJLEPQMWZB
PEAPQRGLIKWZBTR
ITRBINWQMRINWJE
AKCHJOMNBALNIMZ
ALHKDJFHQPWOMNB
HGJFIGJLEPQMWZB
PEVPORGLIKWZBTR

wordsearch 文字搜索遊戲

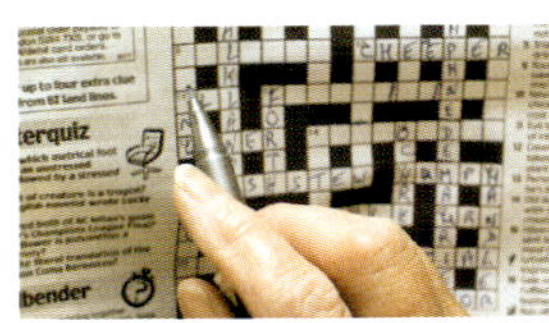

crossword (*also* **crossword puzzle**) 縱橫字謎

jigsaw (**puzzle**) (*BrE*) (*also* **puzzle** *especially NAmE*) 拼圖

Hobbies 業餘愛好

orienteering
定向運動

caving (*BrE*) / **spelunking** (*NAmE*)
洞穴探察

archery 射箭運動

ice skating 滑冰

scuba-diving
戴水肺潛水

snorkelling (*also* **snorkeling** *especially US*) 浮潛

in-line skating
直排滾軸溜冰

skateboarding 滑板運動

bowls 草地滾球遊戲

tenpin bowling 十柱保齡球

darts 擲鏢遊戲

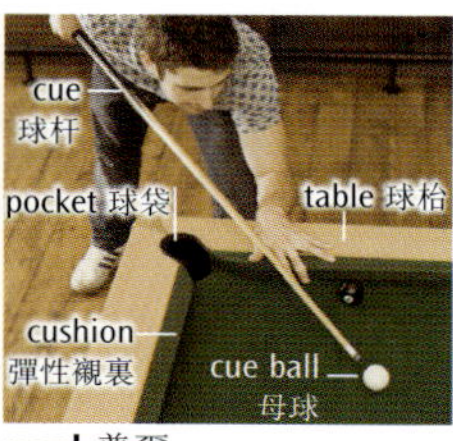

pool 普爾

golf 高爾夫球運動

Golf 高爾夫球運動

- A game of golf is called a **round of golf** (nine or eighteen **holes**). 一輪高爾夫球稱作 round of golf，打九洞或十八洞（holes）。
- At the start of each hole a player **tees off** by hitting the ball from the **tee** (= an area of flat ground). 球員從發球區（tee）開球（tee off）。
- The act of hitting the ball is called a **shot**. The swinging movement players make with their arms and body when they hit the ball is called their **swing**. 擊球的動作稱作 shot。扭動身體揮杆擊球稱作 swing：
  ▸ *My golf swing is in need of improvement.*
  我需要提高我的高爾夫球揮杆技巧。
- Players attempt to hit their ball down the **fairway** (= a long strip of short grass), avoiding the **bunker** (*NAmE also* **sand trap**, **trap**) and **the rough** (= the part of the golf course with long grass making it difficult to hit the ball), to the **green**. 球員盡力避開沙坑（bunker、sand trap、trap）和長草區（rough），將球沿球道（fairway）擊到果嶺（green）上。
- The **green** is an area of short grass on which you **putt** your ball (= hit the ball gently so that it rolls across the ground a short distance into or towards the **hole**). 在果嶺（green）推（putt）球入洞（hole）。

Snooker, pool and billiards 斯諾克、普爾和枱球

- **Snooker** is a game for two people, played on a long table covered with green cloth (**baize**). Players use **cues** to hit the **cue ball** (white) against the other balls (fifteen red, and six of other colours) in order to **pot** the coloured balls (= hit them into **pockets** at the edge of the table), in a particular order. 斯諾克（snooker）是兩人遊戲，在鋪有枱面呢（baize）的長桌上進行。玩遊戲者用球杆（cue）將白色母球（cue ball）擊向其他球（十五個紅球和六個其他顏色的球），按一定順序將不同顏色的球擊進（pot）球袋（pocket）。

- **Snooker** also refers to a position in the game of snooker in which one player has made it very difficult for the opponent to play a shot within the rules. * snooker 也指在斯諾克比賽中設障礙球。
- A game of snooker is called a **frame**. 一局斯諾克比賽稱作 frame：
  ▸ *He won the frame easily.*
  他輕鬆贏得了這局斯諾克比賽。
- **Pool** is similar to snooker, but is played with a cue ball (white), a black ball, and two sets of coloured balls (seven solid colours and seven striped balls). 普爾（pool）與斯諾克相似，但使用一個母球（白色）、一個黑球和兩組彩球（七個單色球和七個花球）。
- **Billiards** is played with three balls (one white, one white with a spot, and one red). Each player uses one of the white balls as the cue ball. Points are scored by pocketing a ball after contact with another ball, or by striking your cue ball against the other two balls. 枱球（billiards）使用三個球（一個白球、一個帶斑點的白球和一個紅球）。球手使用兩個白球之一作為母球，擊球落袋或用母球撞擊其他兩個球即得分。

photography 攝影

painting 繪畫

pottery 製陶

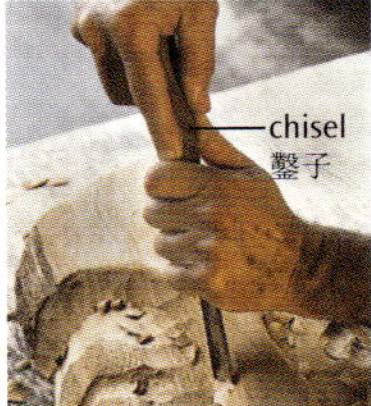

woodcarving 木雕

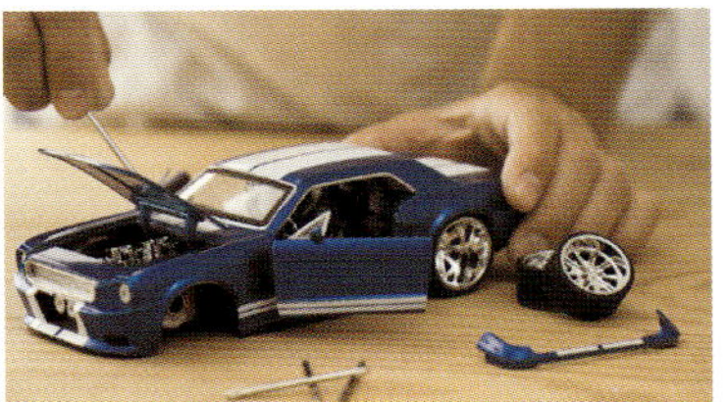
model making 製作模型

stamp collecting 集郵

gardening 園藝

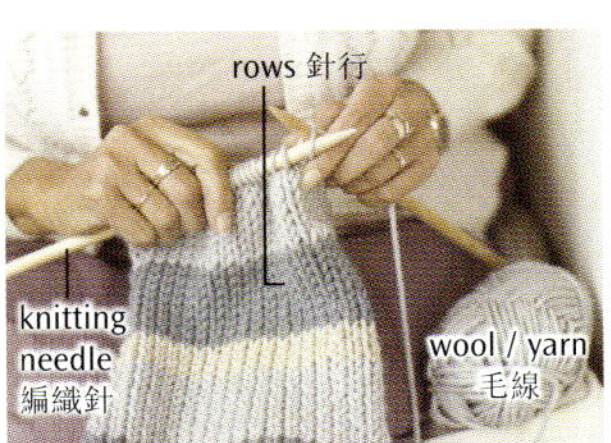

knitting 編織

crochet 鈎針編織

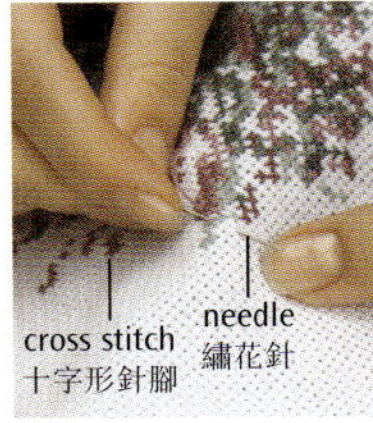

embroidery 繡花

sewing 縫紉

reel of cotton (*especially BrE*)
spool of thread (*especially NAmE*)
線軸

Keeping fit 健身

press-up (*BrE*)
push-up (*especially NAmE*)
俯卧撐

sit-up 仰卧起坐

jogging
慢跑鍛煉

yoga 瑜伽

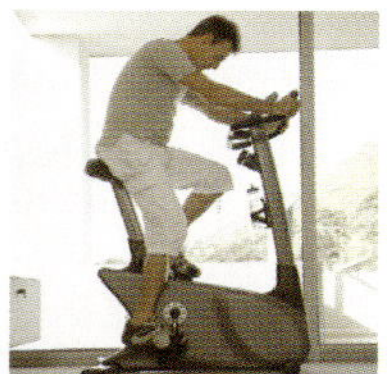

exercise bike
健身腳踏車

barbell 槓鈴

dumb-bell 啞鈴

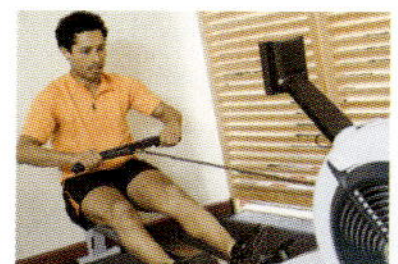

rowing machine
划船練習架

treadmill
跑步機

Staying healthy 保持健康

- If you are **fit** (*BrE*), **physically fit**, or **in shape** (*especially NAmE*), you are healthy and strong, especially as a result of diet and exercise. * fit、physically fit 或 in shape 指體格健壯，尤指通過均衡飲食和鍛煉來達到：
  - ▶ *Top athletes have to be very fit.* (*BrE*) 頂級運動員體格必須十分健壯。
  - ▶ *The doctor said I should* ***get*** *more* ***exercise*** (*BrE also ...****take*** *more* ***exercise***). 醫生說我應該加強鍛煉。
  - ▶ *No cream for me – I'm* ***on a diet.*** 我不要奶油，我在節食。
  - ▶ *She cycles up to 90 miles a day to* ***keep fit.*** (*BrE*) 她每天騎自行車 90 英里以保持健康。
  - ▶ *I still run every day to* ***stay in shape.*** (*especially NAmE*) 我仍然堅持每天跑步以保持健康。

Aerobics, step, and circuit training 有氧運動、踏板操和循環訓練

- **Aerobics** involves physical exercises to make the heart and lungs stronger, often done in classes and to music. 有氧運動（aerobics）是能增強心肺功能的體育鍛煉，常常分班組伴隨音樂進行：
  - ▶ *do an aerobics class* 上有氧運動課
- **Step** is a type of aerobics that you do by stepping on and off a raised piece of equipment called a **step**. 踏板操（step）是在踏板（step）上踏上踏下的健身操。
- **Circuit training** is a type of training in which different exercises are each done for a short time. 循環訓練（circuit training）指輪番做不同的體育運動，每種只做很短的時間。

Sports 體育運動

Talking about a particular sport 談論某項體育運動

- You can **play** a specific sport. 參加特定的體育運動可用 play：
  - ▸ *Do you play tennis?* 你打網球嗎？
- This is used particularly for competitive sports in which one team or person **plays** or **plays against** another. 這詞尤用於隊與隊或個人之間競技性的體育運動（用 play 或 play against）：
  - ▸ *We played them in last year's final.* 在去年的決賽中我們與他們對壘。
  - ▸ *Who are you playing against this afternoon?* 你今天下午同誰比賽？
- Members of a sports team **play for** their team. 為某隊效力用 play for：
  - ▸ *He used to play for the Dallas Cowboys.* 他以前效力於達拉斯牛仔隊。
- If the name of a sport or an activity ends in **–ing** we often use it with the verb **to go**. 某項體育運動或活動的名稱以 -ing 結尾時常與動詞 to go 連用：
  - ▸ *I go swimming twice a week.* 我一週游泳兩次。
  - ▸ *Have you ever been rock climbing?* 你攀過岩嗎？
- Typical sports and activities with this pattern include: **go skiing**; **go sailing**; **go riding** (*BrE*) or **go horseback riding** (*NAmE*); and **go dancing**. Check at the entry for each sport to see if it can be used in this way. 常用該句型的體育項目和活動有 go skiing（滑雪）、go sailing（乘帆船航行）、go riding 或 go horseback riding（騎馬）以及 go dancing（跳舞）。可查閱各項體育運動的詞條看是否有這一用法。

Other sports and activities can take the verbs **to do** or **to go to**. 其他一些體育項目和活動可用動詞 to do 或 to go to：

- *I do aerobics once or twice a week.* 我每週做一兩次有氧運動。
- *I go to judo* (= to my judo class) *on Mondays.* 我每星期一去練習柔道。

Where sports are played 體育運動場地

- The area that is specially marked for playing a sports game is often called a **pitch** (*BrE*), **field** or **court**, depending on the sport being played. 體育運動場地常用 pitch、field 或 court 表示，依所進行的運動類型而定：
  - ▸ *a cricket/football/rugby/hockey pitch* (*BrE*) 板球／足球／橄欖球／曲棍球場
  - ▸ *a soccer/baseball field* (*especially NAmE*) 足球／棒球場
  - ▸ *a tennis/badminton/squash/basketball court* 網球／羽毛球／壁球／籃球場
- A large sports ground surrounded by rows of seats for **spectators** is called a **stadium** (*plural* **stadiums** or **stadia**). 備有座位供觀眾觀賞比賽的大型體育場稱作 stadium，場內觀眾稱作 spectator：
  - ▸ *an all-seater stadium* 全坐席體育場

GRAMMAR POINT 語法說明

- Names of American sports teams always start with 'the'; names of British sports teams almost never do. Names of sports teams may look either singular or plural but always take a plural verb. 美國體育運動隊的名稱總是以 the 開頭，而英國的運動隊名稱幾乎從不用 the。體育運動隊的名稱看上去可能是單數，也可能是複數，但總是用複數動詞：
  - ▸ *The Jazz are playing the Chicago Bulls.* 爵士隊在與芝加哥公牛隊比賽。
  - ▸ *Aston Villa have started the season well.* 阿斯頓維拉隊在本賽季旗開得勝。
- Teams are often referred to just by the name of the place they come from. In American English this means a singular verb is used, but in British English the verb is still plural. 運動隊常常以該隊來自的地方的名稱指代。在美式英語中這就意味着要用單數動詞，但在英式英語中謂語動詞仍然用複數：
  - ▸ *Cincinnati is having a great season.* 辛辛那提隊這一賽季成績輝煌。
  - ▸ *Norwich were disappointed with the score.* 諾里奇隊對比分感到失望。

Team Sports 團隊體育運動

cricket 板球

basketball 籃球

baseball 棒球

rugby 橄欖球

soccer (*BrE also* **football**) 足球

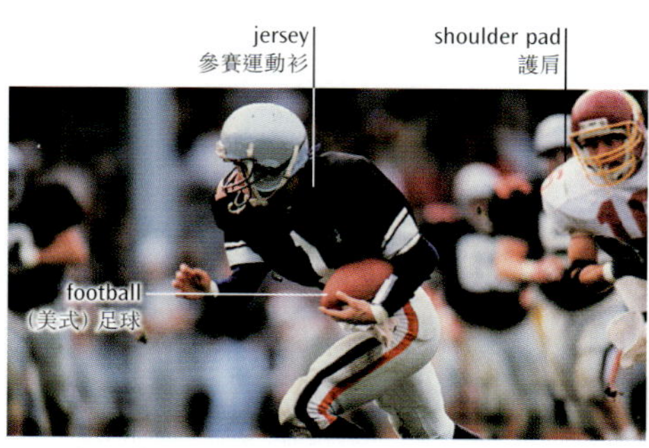

American football (*BrE*) / **football** (*NAmE*) 美式足球

hockey (*BrE*) / **field hockey** (*NAmE*) 曲棍球

ice hockey (*BrE*) / **hockey** (*NAmE*) 冰球

Swimming 游泳

crawl 自由泳

butterfly 蝶泳

backstroke 仰泳

breaststroke 蛙泳

Racket sports 球拍運動

tennis 網球

badminton 羽毛球

squash 壁球

table tennis (*BrE*) / **Ping-Pong™** (*NAmE*) 乒乓球

People who take part in sports 參加體育運動的人

- A person who **plays** a particular sport is usually called a football/tennis/basketball **player**. 參加（play）某項體育運動例如足球／網球／籃球的人通常稱作 player：
  - ▸ *Welsh rugby players could get £2000 each from a new sponsorship deal.* 威爾士橄欖球運動員可從一項新的贊助中得到 £2000 英鎊。
- Some sports have a special name for the players or people who do them. Some of these names end in **-er** but others do not follow a particular pattern. Check near the entry for each sport to find the correct word. 某些體育運動的運動員或參加這些運動的人有專門的名稱，有的以 -er 結尾，而有的則沒有特定的模式。要知道正確的詞，請在各體育運動條目查找：
  - ▸ *talented young footballers* (*BrE only*) 有才華的年輕足球運動員
  - ▸ *an Olympic boxer* 奧運拳擊手
  - ▸ *top athletes from around the world* 來自全世界的頂尖田徑運動員
  - ▸ *cyclists competing in the Tour de France* 參加環法自行車賽的車手

Field events 田賽項目

the high jump 跳高

the discus 擲鐵餅

the pole vault 撐杆跳高

the hammer 擲鏈球

the javelin 擲標槍

Field events 田賽項目

- *do the long jump* 跳遠
- *do the high jump* 跳高
- *do the pole vault* 撐杆跳高
- *do the triple jump* 三級跳遠
- *throw the javelin* 擲標槍
- *throw the discus* 擲鐵餅
- *throw the hammer* 擲鏈球
- *put the shot* 推鉛球

Equestrian sports 馬術運動

horse racing 賽馬運動

showjumping 超越障礙比賽

polo 馬球

Track events 徑賽項目

hurdling 跨欄賽跑

sprinting 短跑

starting blocks 起跑器

Track events 徑賽項目

- *run the 100 metres* 跑 100 米
- *run the relay* 跑接力賽

Talking about sports in general 一般地談論體育運動

- You can **do sport** (*BrE*), 進行體育運動可用 do sport：
  - ▶ *Do you do a lot of sport?* 你常進行體育活動嗎？

  ... or you can **play sports** (*especially NAmE*), 亦可用 play sports：
  - ▶ *We played sports together when we were kids.* 孩提時，我們曾一起進行體育活動。

  ... but these verbs are not used very often. 不過上述動詞並不很常用。It is more usual to talk about liking sport/sports or **being good at** sport/sports. 較常用的有 like sport / sports（喜歡運動）或 be good at sport / sports（擅長運動）：
  - ▶ *Are you good at sport?* (*BrE*) 你擅長體育運動嗎？
  - ▶ *Are you good at sports?* (*NAmE*) 你擅長體育運動嗎？
  - ▶ *What sports do you like best?* 你最喜歡什麼運動？
- Do **not** say that you 'practise' sport or a sport if you just mean that you do or play it. 如果只是進行體育運動不要用 practise sport 或 a sport。Say 可說：
  - ▶ *I love sport.* (*BrE*) 我喜愛體育運動。
  - ▶ *I love sports.* (*NAmE*) 我喜愛體育運動。
  (No other verb is necessary. 不用加其他動詞。)
  NOT 不可說 ~~*I love practising sport.*~~
- Say which sports you play. 談及某種體育運動項目：
  - ▶ *Every Sunday I play volleyball or badminton with my friends.* 我每個星期日都與朋友一起打排球或羽毛球。
  NOT 不可說 ~~*Every Sunday I practise sport with my friends.*~~
- However, you can use the verb 'practise', especially in American English (where it is spelt 'practice'), if it means 'to train'. 但表示練習時，可用動詞 practise，尤其在美式英語中，不過美式英語的拼法為 practice：
  - ▶ *The team is practicing for its big game.* (*NAmE*) 這個隊正在進行大賽前的訓練。
  - ▶ *The team are in training for their big match.* (*BrE*) 這個隊正在進行大賽前的訓練。

GRAMMAR POINT 語法説明

- The names of sports can be used like adjectives before other nouns. 運動項目名稱可用作形容詞，置於其他名詞前：
  - ▶ *a tennis match* 網球比賽
  - ▶ *cycling shorts* 自行車運動短褲
  - ▶ *a football team* 足球隊
- The words sports and sporting (but not 'sport') can be used in the same way. * sports 和 sporting 兩詞亦可有上述用法（但 sport 不能）：
  - ▶ *a sports club* 體育俱樂部
  - ▶ *sports shoes* 運動鞋
  - ▶ *a sporting event* 體育比賽項目
  - ▶ *sporting goods* 體育用品

cycling 自行車運動

gymnastics 體操

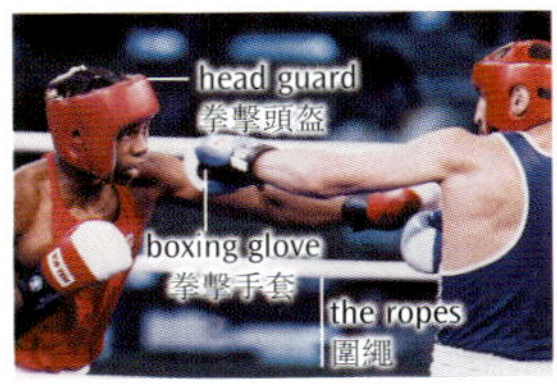

boxing 拳擊運動

fencing 擊劍運動

Winter sports 冬季運動

bobsleigh (*BrE*) / **bobsled** (*NAmE*)
大雪橇

the luge 短雪橇運動

downhill skiing 速降滑雪

cross-country skiing 越野滑雪運動

Extreme sports 極限運動

paragliding
滑翔傘運動

hang-gliding
懸掛式滑翔運動

snowboarding
單板滑雪運動

abseiling (*BrE*)
rappelling (*NAmE*)
繞繩下降運動

- Activities that involve danger or speed or both are often called **extreme sports**. Many extreme sports are done on or in water. 極限運動稱作 extreme sports，許多極限運動是在水上或水下進行。
- **Surfing** and **bodyboarding** are similar, but a surfer stands on a surfboard to ride on the waves while a bodyboarder lies on their stomach on a bodyboard. **Kitesurfing** involves riding on a type of surfboard and being pulled along by a kite. 衝浪運動（surfing）和俯伏衝浪板運動（bodysurfing）相似，但衝浪運動員是站在衝浪板上踏浪而行，俯伏衝浪板運動員則是俯卧在腹板上。風箏衝浪運動（kite surfing）是站在衝浪板上由風箏牽引行進。
- **Waterskiing** and **wakeboarding** both involve being pulled through the water by a fast boat: a waterskier wears one or two waterskis, while a wakeboarder stands sideways on a wakeboard. 水橇滑水運動（waterskiing）和尾浪滑水運動（wakeboarding）均由快艇牽引；水橇滑水運動員穿着一隻或兩隻滑水橇，尾浪滑水運動員則是側站在尾波板上滑行。
- Other extreme sports involve jumping from great heights. **Skydivers** jump from a plane and fall for as long as they safely can before opening their **parachutes**. You can jump from the side of a mountain, wearing a kind of parachute in **paragliding**, or a frame like a very large kite in **hang-gliding**. **Parasailing** and **base jumping** are both also done wearing parachutes. In parasailing you are pulled behind a fast boat and rise into the air. A base jumper jumps from the top of a tall building or bridge (BASE stands for building, antenna, span, earth). 其他一些極限運動是從高處往下跳。特技跳傘運動員（skydiver）是從飛機上往下跳，在安全的前提下盡可能延緩張傘（parachute）；做滑翔傘運動（paragliding）是繫着降落傘從山崖上往下跳；做懸掛式滑翔運動（hang-gliding）則繫着像風箏一樣的支架往下跳。帆傘運動（parasailing）和高處跳傘運動（base jumping）亦是繫着降落傘進行的。做帆傘運動由快艇牽引在空中滑翔；高處跳傘運動員則從高樓頂或橋上往下跳（BASE 由 building、antenna、span 和 earth 的首字母組成）。
- In **rock climbing**, a rope is attached to the climber and the rock for safety – this is called **belaying**. The climber wears a **harness** to which the rope is attached with a metal ring called a **karabiner**. 在攀岩運動（rock climbing）中，攀岩者用繩索牽在岩石上以保安全——這叫作 belaying。攀岩者身繫保護帶（harness），用穿索鐵鎖（karabiner）將繩索扣在保護帶上。
- **Skateboarders** and **snowboarders** may ride on a **half-pipe**: a U-shaped structure or a U-shaped channel cut into the snow. They do jumps and tricks, for example a **fakie**, an **ollie**, or a **kick-turn**. 滑板運動員（skateboarder）和滑雪板運動員（snowboarder）可在 U 形滑道（half-pipe）上做各種飛躍和技巧動作，如倒溜（fakie）、豚跳（ollie）或倒板調頭（kick-turn）。

skydiving 特技跳傘運動

bungee jumping
蹦極跳

waterskiing
水橇滑水運動

wakeboarding
尾浪滑水運動

windsurfing 帆板運動

surfing 衝浪運動

jet-skiing
噴氣式划艇運動

bodyboarding
俯伏衝浪板運動

white-water rafting
激流皮划艇運動

kitesurfing / kiteboarding
風箏衝浪運動

parkour 跑酷

Cycles 自行車；摩托車

Other types of bicycle and motorcycle 其他類型的自行車和摩托車

- An early type of bicycle with a very large front wheel and a very small back wheel is a **penny-farthing**. 早期自行車（penny-farthing）前輪很大，後輪很小。
- A stationary bicycle that is used indoors to exercise is an **exercise bike**. 健身腳踏車（exercise bike）置於室內，供人進行鍛煉。
- A motorcycle with a small engine and pedals is a **moped**. 機器腳踏車（moped）是使用小型發動機和腳踏板的摩托車。

Cars 汽車

1 rear-view mirror 後視鏡
2 visor 遮陽板
3 windscreen (*BrE*) windshield (*NAmE*) 擋風玻璃
4 windscreen wiper (*BrE*) windshield wiper (*NAmE*) 雨刮器
5 wing mirror (*BrE*) side-view mirror (*NAmE*) 側翼後視鏡
6 door handle 門把手
7 air vent 通氣孔
8 glove compartment glove box 雜物箱
9 satnav (*also* sat nav) 衛星導航儀
10 dashboard 儀表板
11 milometer (*BrE*) odometer (*NAmE*) 里程表
12 speedometer 車速計
13 rev counter 轉速計
14 fuel gauge 燃料表
15 steering wheel 方向盤
16 ignition 點火裝置
17 horn 喇叭
18 gear lever (*BrE*) gear shift (*NAmE*) 變速桿
19 clutch 離合器踏板
20 brake 刹車
21 accelerator (*BrE*) / gas pedal (*especially NAmE*) 油門
22 handbrake (*especially BrE*) / emergency brake (*NAmE*) 手閘
23 headrest 頭枕
24 passenger seat 乘客座位
25 driver's seat 駕駛座
26 seat belt 安全帶

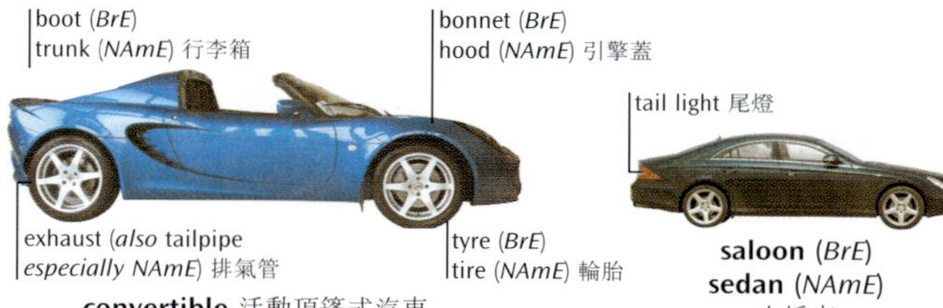

convertible 活動頂篷式汽車

saloon (*BrE*)
sedan (*NAmE*)
小轎車

hatchback 掀背式汽車

people carrier (*BrE*)
minivan (*especially NAmE*) 小型麵包車

estate car (*BrE*)
station wagon (*NAmE*)
旅行轎車

four-wheel drive
四輪驅動轎車

sports car
(*US also* **sport car**) 跑車

Verbs to talk about driving 有關駕駛的動詞

- to control the direction in which the car is going: **steer** 掌方向盤
- to change direction suddenly: **swerve** 突然轉向；急轉彎
- to signal that your car is going to turn: **indicate** 打行車轉向信號
- to make a car go faster: **speed up**, **accelerate**, **put your foot down** 加速行駛；踩油門
- to make a car go more slowly: **slow down**, **brake**, **put the brake on** 減緩車速；踩刹車
- to put the engine into a higher/lower gear as you get faster/slower: **change up/down** 換高／低擋；加／減速
- to allow another vehicle to go before you: **give way** (*BrE*) / **yield** (*NAmE*) 讓路
- to pass another vehicle because you are moving faster: **overtake** 超車
- to turn round and go back along the same road: **do/make a U-turn** * U 形轉彎；180 度轉彎
- to stop and leave the car: **park** 停車

Aircraft 航空器

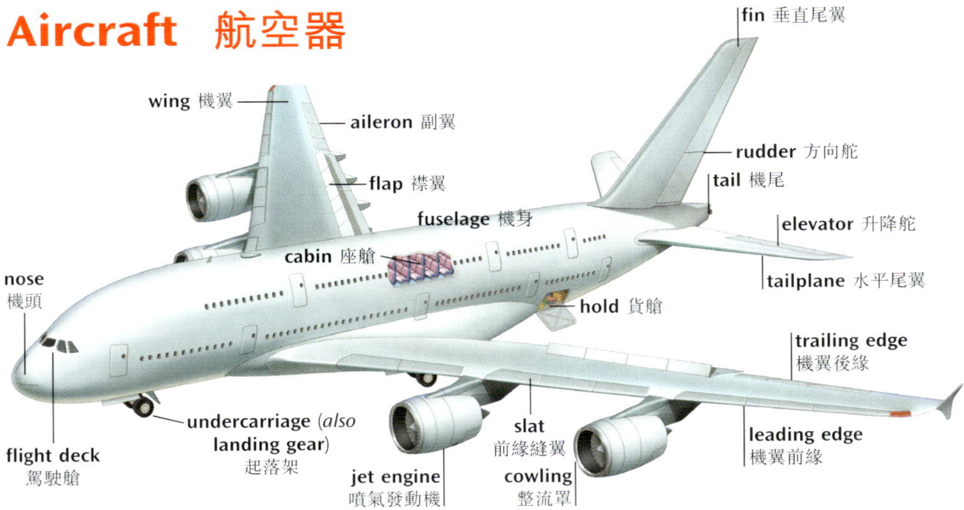

aerobatic display 特技飛行表演

light aircraft 輕型飛機

helicopter 直升機

ski-plane 滑橇起落架飛機

glider 滑翔機

microlight (*BrE*) 微型飛機

seaplane 水上飛機

fighter 戰鬥機

biplane 雙翼飛機

At the airport 在機場

- An airport building where journeys begin and end is a **terminal**. You go to the **check-in desk** and say you have arrived (**check in**). * terminal 指航空站，在登機手續辦理處（check-in desk）辦理登記手續用 check in。
- You check in the **baggage** (*especially NAmE*) that will go into the **hold** (= the part of the plane where goods are stored) but you carry your **hand luggage** (especially *BrE*) / **carry-on baggage** (*especially NAmE*) with you onto the plane. If your bags are heavier than the weight limit you have to **pay excess baggage**. * check in baggage 指託運行李，託運的行李放入貨艙（hold），但手提行李（hand luggage / carry-on baggage）隨身帶上飛機。如果行李超重需付超重行李費（pay excess baggage）。
- You wait in the **departure lounge** and when your flight **is boarding** (= is ready for passengers to get on) you leave the terminal from a **gate**. * departure lounge 指候機室，登機（board）時從登機口（gate）離開航空站。
- When you arrive at your destination in a different country you **disembark** and go through **immigration**. Collect your **luggage** (*especially BrE*) from **baggage reclaim** (*BrE*) / **baggage claim** (*NAmE*) and exit through **customs**. 到達另一國家目的地下機（disembark）後要通過移民局檢查站（immigration）。在行李提取處（baggage reclaim / baggage claim）領取行李，然後通過海關（customs）離開。

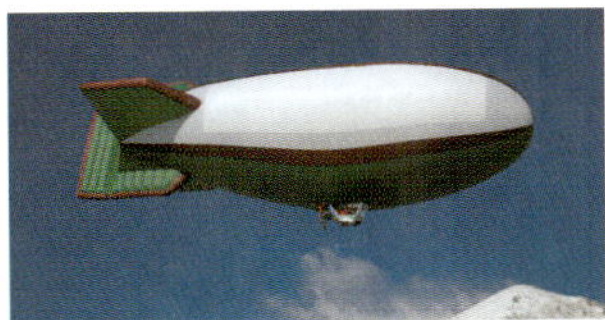
airship 飛艇

hot-air balloon 熱氣球

Boats and ships 船

container ship 集裝箱船

lifeboat 救生船

ferry 渡船

hovercraft 氣墊船

hydrofoil 水翼船

catamaran 雙體船

liner 郵輪

canal boat / narrowboat 運河船

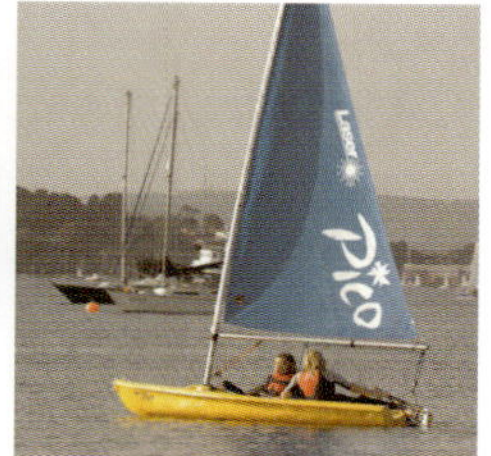
sailing dinghy (*NAmE also* **sailboat**) 小帆船

More kinds of boat 其他種類的船

- Any large boat that is used for carrying passengers or goods by sea is a **ship**, or (*formal*) a **vessel**. * ship 或（正式用語）vessel 指輪船：
  ▸ *In which country was this vessel registered?* 這艘船是在哪個國家註冊的？

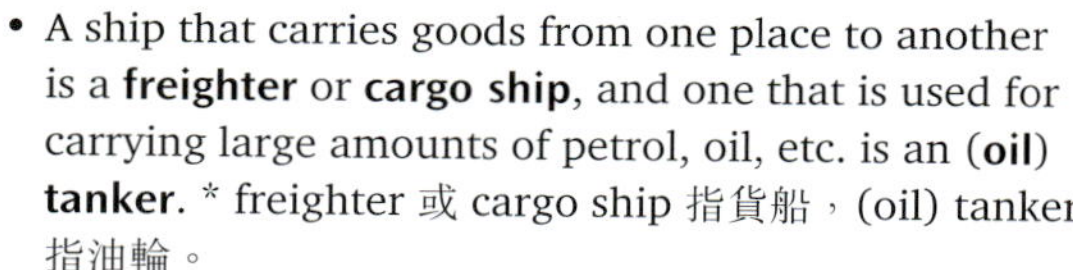

- A ship that carries goods from one place to another is a **freighter** or **cargo ship**, and one that is used for carrying large amounts of petrol, oil, etc. is an (**oil**) **tanker**. * freighter 或 cargo ship 指貨船，(oil) tanker 指油輪。

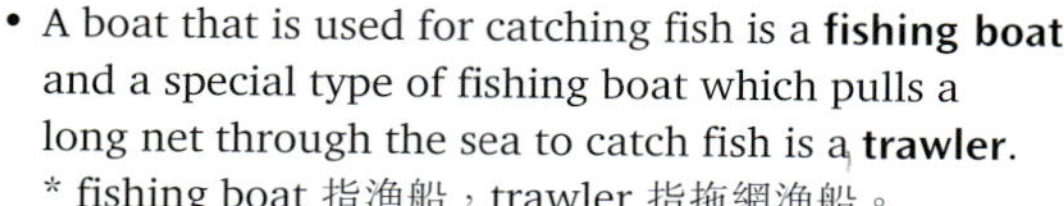

- A boat that is used for catching fish is a **fishing boat**, and a special type of fishing boat which pulls a long net through the sea to catch fish is a **trawler**. * fishing boat 指漁船，trawler 指拖網漁船。

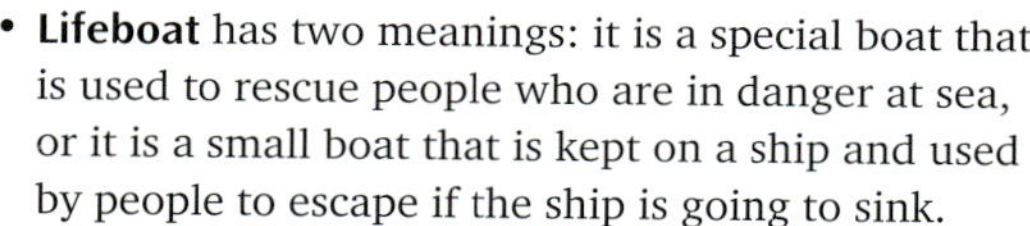

- **Lifeboat** has two meanings: it is a special boat that is used to rescue people who are in danger at sea, or it is a small boat that is kept on a ship and used by people to escape if the ship is going to sink. * lifeboat 有兩個含義：一是指派往海上救援的救生船，二是指船上備用的救生艇。
- **Raft** also has two meanings: it is a small boat made of rubber or plastic that is filled with air, or it is a flat structure made of pieces of wood tied together and used as a boat. * raft 亦有兩個含義：一是指橡皮艇、充氣船，二是指木排、筏。

paddle steamer (*BrE*) / **paddleboat** (*NAmE*) 槳輪蒸汽船

cruiser / cabin cruiser（可住宿的）艙式遊艇

speedboat 快艇

rowing boat (*BrE*) / **rowboat** (*NAmE*) 划艇

kayak (*BrE also* **canoe**)
獨木舟；單人划子

canoe 皮划艇

punt 方頭平底船

gondola 威尼斯小划船

Groups of boats 船隊

- A group of boats that sail and work together is a **fleet**. * fleet 指一起航行和作業的船隊：
  - ▶ *a fishing fleet* 捕魚船隊
- A group of boats travelling together is a **flotilla** or a **convoy**. * flotilla 或 convoy 指同行的船隊：
  - ▶ *The boats travelled* ***in convoy***. 這些船隻結隊航行。
  - ▶ *We were travelling in a flotilla of boats.* 我們隨船隊航行。

Travelling by boat 駕船／乘船旅行

- You **sail** a sailing boat or yacht, **row** a rowing boat, and **paddle** a canoe or kayak. * sail 指駕駛或乘坐（帆船或遊船）；row 指划（划艇）；paddle 指用槳划（獨木舟或單人划子）：
  - ▶ *My brother's planning to sail (his yacht) to Bermuda.* 我哥哥計劃駕（帆）船去百慕大島。
  - ▶ *They rowed (the boat) back to shore.* 他們划船回到了岸上。
- You **go sailing**, **go yachting**, **go rowing** and **go canoeing**. * go sailing 指駕船運動；go yachting 指駕快艇或帆船運動；go rowing 指划船；go canoeing 指划／乘獨木舟。
- When you get on a ship you **board** (it), or (*formal*) **embark**. * board 或（正式用語）embark 指上船：
  - ▶ *We boarded the ship at midday.* 我們正午上了船。
  - ▶ *One passenger had embarked at Alexandria.* 一名乘客在亞歷山德里亞登船了。
- When you get off a ship you **go ashore**, or (*formal*) **disembark**. * go ashore 或（正式用語）disembark 指下船（離船上岸）。
- To begin a journey by sea is to **set sail** (**from**/**to**/**for** a place). * set sail 指（從某地）起航（前往某地）：
  - ▶ *Twenty competitors set sail from Rio on the round-the-world race.* 二十名參賽者從里約熱內盧起航進行環球航行比賽。
- When you are on a ship you are **on board** or **aboard**. * on board 或 aboard 指在船上：
  - ▶ *There were a thousand passengers on board.* 船上有一千名乘客。
  - ▶ *All aboard please!* 請大家上船！
- When you are sailing on the sea in a ship, you are **at sea**. * at sea 指在海上航行。
- A holiday where you travel by boat and visit a number of places is a **cruise**. * cruise 指乘船遊覽：
  - ▶ *They're going on a cruise.* 他們正在乘船遊覽。
- A long journey by sea is a **voyage**. * voyage 指航海：
  - ▶ *Captain Cook made his first voyage to the South Pacific in 1768.* 庫克船長於 1768 年第一次航行去南太平洋。
- If a boat moves backwards and forwards it **pitches**; if it moves from side to side it **rolls**. * pitch 指船顛簸、前後搖盪；roll 指船搖擺、左右搖晃：
  - ▶ *The trawler was pitching and rolling violently in the storm.* 拖網漁船在暴風雨中劇烈地顛簸搖晃。
- To be carried along by wind or water in no particular direction is to **drift**. * drift 指隨風或隨水漂流（或漂浮）：
  - ▶ *The boat drifted out to sea.* 船向海上漂去。

Parts of boats 船的各個部位

- The side of a boat that is on the left when you are facing the front: **port** * port 指船的左舷
- The side of a boat that is on the right when you are facing the front: **starboard** * starboard 指船的右舷
- The top outside floor of a boat is called the **deck**. * deck 是甲板、艙面：
  ▸ *Let's go and sit **on deck**.* 我們去甲板上坐吧。
- The other floors are also called **decks**. * deck 亦指船的一層、（某一）層：
  ▸ *the lower deck of a ship* 船的下層
- A small room in a boat where you can sleep is a **cabin**, and a kind of bed in a cabin is a **bunk** or a **berth**. * cabin 指輪船上供休息睡覺的艙室；bunk 或 berth 指船上隔間裏的卧鋪／鋪位：
  ▸ *a cabin with four berths* 有四個鋪位的船艙
- The kitchen on a boat is the **galley** and a round window is called a **porthole**. * galley 指船上的廚房；porthole 指圓形的舷窗。

yacht (*NAmE also* **sailboat**) 帆船

Steering a boat 駕駛船隻

- A piece of wood or metal in the water at the back of a boat that is used for controlling its direction is a **rudder**. * rudder 指船尾控制方向的木製或金屬舵。
- A bar that is used to turn the rudder of a small boat in order to steer it is a **tiller**. * tiller 指小船的舵柄。
- A handle or wheel used for steering a larger boat or ship is called the **helm**. * helm 指大船的舵柄或舵輪。
- The part of a ship where the captain and other officers stand when they are controlling the ship is **the bridge**. * bridge 指船的駕駛台、船橋。

Vehicles 車輛

Buses 公交車

double-decker 雙層公交車

single-decker 單層公交車

minibus 小型公交車

school bus 校車

bus (*BrE also* **coach**)（長途）客車

Trucks, etc. 卡車等

articulated lorry (*BrE*) / **tractor-trailer** (*NAmE*)
鉸接式卡車

lorry (*BrE*) / **truck** (*especially NAmE*)
卡車

transporter
大型載重運輸車

tanker 罐車

van 厢式客貨車

forklift truck 叉車

breakdown truck (*BrE*)
tow truck (*especially NAmE*) 救險車

pickup (*also* **pickup truck**)
輕型貨車

Jeep™ 吉普車

Transporting goods 運輸貨物

- Items that are carried by lorries, trains, aeroplanes and ships are called **freight** [U]. * freight 指陸運、空運或海運的貨物：
  - ▸ *a freight train* 貨運列車
- Items that are carried by road or rail are also called **goods** (*BrE*)(*pl.*). 陸運的貨物又稱 goods：
  - ▸ *a goods vehicle* 運貨車
- Items that are carried by air and sea are also called **cargo** [C, U]. 空運或海運的貨物又稱 cargo：
  - ▸ *a cargo plane* 貨機
- Something that is being carried, usually in large amounts, is a **load**. * load 指（通常大量的）負載：
  - ▸ *A lorry shed its load* (= accidentally dropped its load) *on the motorway.* 一輛卡車在高速公路上掉下了貨物。
- A load of goods that is sent from one place to another is a **shipment**. * shipment 指運輸的大量貨物。
- A large metal box in which goods are transported by sea, rail or road is a **container**. * container 指海運或陸運集裝箱。

caravan (*BrE*) / camper (*NAmE*) 旅行拖車

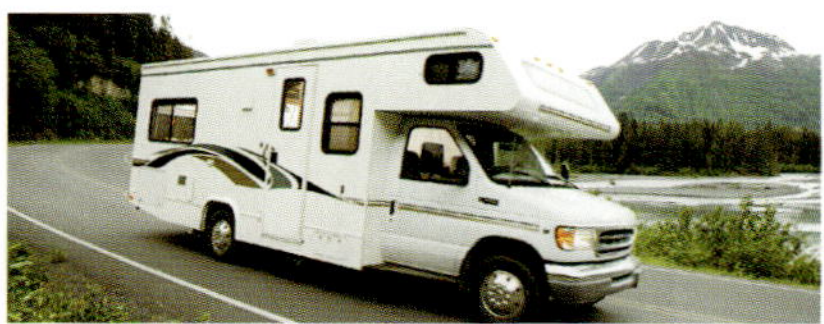

camper (*BrE*) / recreational vehicle (RV) (*NAmE*) 野營車

tractor 拖拉機

taxi (*also* cab, taxicab) 出租車

Trains, etc. 火車等

high-speed train 高速列車

freight train (*BrE also* goods train) 貨運列車

passenger train 客運列車

underground (*BrE*) / subway (*NAmE*) 地鐵

steam train 蒸汽火車

funicular 纜索鐵道

cable car（懸空的）纜車

tram (*BrE*) / streetcar (*US*) 有軌電車

Construction vehicles 建築施工車輛

excavator 挖掘機

bulldozer 推土機

cement mixer 混凝土攪拌機

dumper truck (*NAmE also* dump truck) 翻斗車

The body 身體

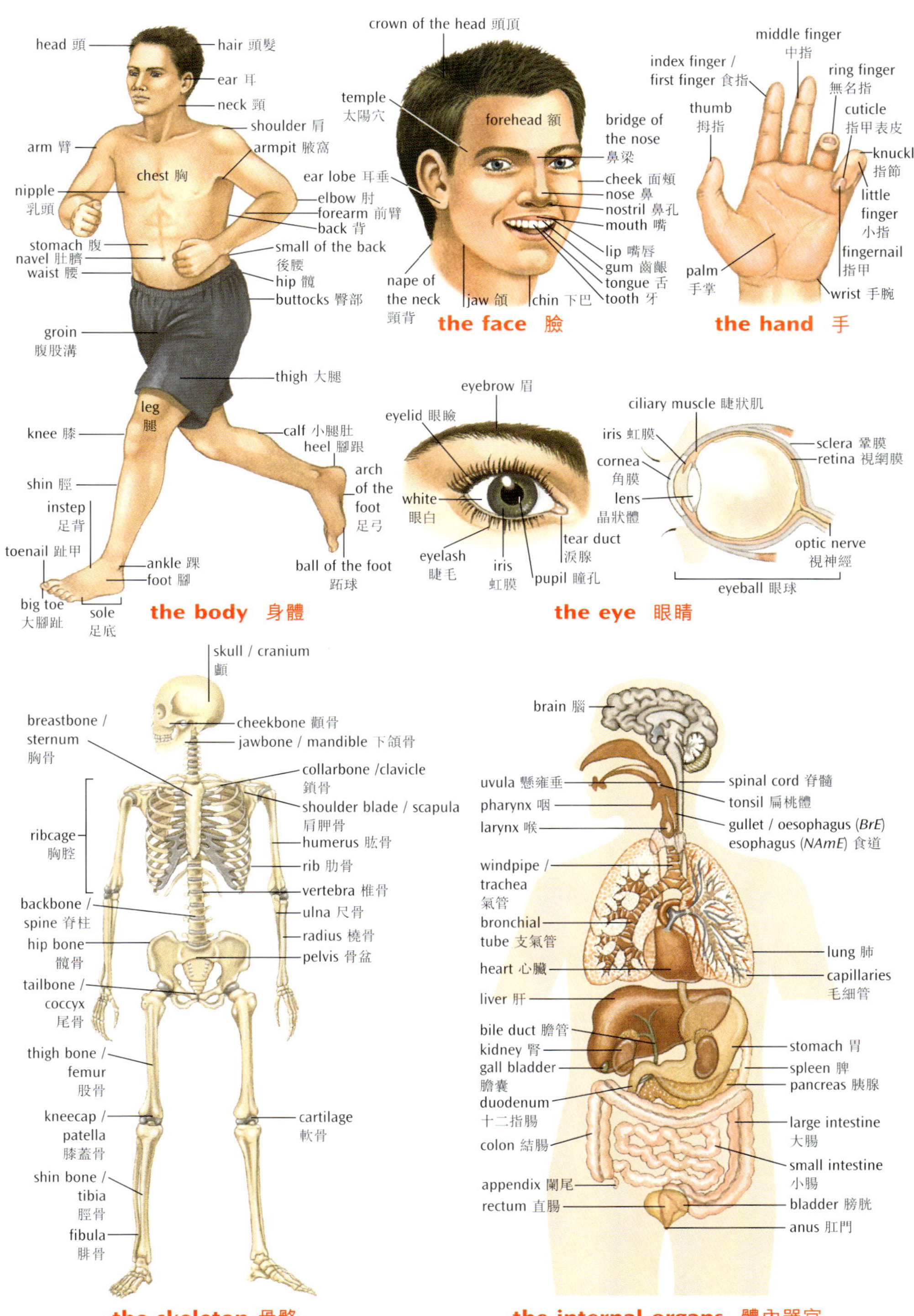

head 頭
hair 頭髮
ear 耳
neck 頸
shoulder 肩
arm 臂
armpit 腋窩
chest 胸
nipple 乳頭
elbow 肘
forearm 前臂
back 背
stomach 腹
navel 肚臍
waist 腰
small of the back 後腰
hip 髖
buttocks 臀部
groin 腹股溝
thigh 大腿
leg 腿
knee 膝
calf 小腿肚
heel 腳跟
shin 脛
instep 足背
arch of the foot 足弓
toenail 趾甲
ankle 踝
foot 腳
ball of the foot 跖球
big toe 大腳趾
sole 足底
the body 身體
crown of the head 頭頂
temple 太陽穴
forehead 額
bridge of the nose 鼻梁
ear lobe 耳垂
cheek 面頰
nose 鼻
nostril 鼻孔
mouth 嘴
lip 嘴唇
gum 齒齦
tongue 舌
tooth 牙
nape of the neck 頸背
jaw 頜
chin 下巴
the face 臉
middle finger 中指
index finger / first finger 食指
ring finger 無名指
thumb 拇指
cuticle 指甲表皮
knuckle 指節
little finger 小指
fingernail 指甲
palm 手掌
wrist 手腕
the hand 手
eyebrow 眉
eyelid 眼瞼
white 眼白
eyelash 睫毛
iris 虹膜
pupil 瞳孔
tear duct 淚腺
ciliary muscle 睫狀肌
iris 虹膜
cornea 角膜
lens 晶狀體
sclera 鞏膜
retina 視網膜
optic nerve 視神經
eyeball 眼球
the eye 眼睛
skull / cranium 顱
cheekbone 顴骨
jawbone / mandible 下頜骨
breastbone / sternum 胸骨
collarbone /clavicle 鎖骨
shoulder blade / scapula 肩胛骨
ribcage 胸腔
humerus 肱骨
rib 肋骨
vertebra 椎骨
backbone / spine 脊柱
ulna 尺骨
radius 橈骨
hip bone 髖骨
pelvis 骨盆
tailbone / coccyx 尾骨
thigh bone / femur 股骨
kneecap / patella 膝蓋骨
cartilage 軟骨
shin bone / tibia 脛骨
fibula 腓骨
the skeleton 骨骼
brain 腦
uvula 懸雍垂
spinal cord 脊髓
tonsil 扁桃體
pharynx 咽
larynx 喉
gullet / oesophagus (BrE) esophagus (NAmE) 食道
windpipe / trachea 氣管
bronchial tube 支氣管
lung 肺
heart 心臟
capillaries 毛細管
liver 肝
bile duct 膽管
kidney 腎
stomach 胃
gall bladder 膽囊
spleen 脾
pancreas 胰腺
duodenum 十二指腸
large intestine 大腸
colon 結腸
small intestine 小腸
appendix 闌尾
rectum 直腸
bladder 膀胱
anus 肛門
the internal organs 體內器官

Hair 髮型

crew cut 平頭

shaved head 剃光的頭

bald head 禿頭

receding hairline 漸禿的頭

long hair 長髮

flat-top 平頂頭

spiky 刺猬頭

dreadlocks 長髮綹

cornrows 玉米壟

bob 女式齊短髮

shoulder-length 齊肩髮

chignon 髮髻

bun 圓髮髻

French pleat (*BrE*) **French twist** (*NAmE*) 法式盤髮

long, wavy 長波浪髮

curly 鬈髮

perm 燙髮

plait (*BrE*) **braid** (*NAmE*) （一根）髮辮

French plait (*BrE*) **French braid** (*NAmE*) 法式辮子

pigtails (*BrE*) **braids** (*NAmE*) （兩根）辮子

bunches (*BrE*) **pigtails** (*NAmE*) 束髮

ponytail 馬尾辮

Make-up 化妝品

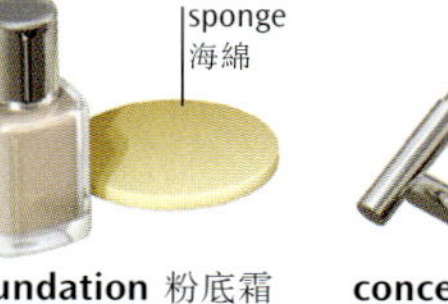

foundation 粉底霜

concealer 遮瑕膏

blusher (*NAmE also* **blush**) 胭脂

powder 撲面粉

eyeliner (*also* **liner**) 眼線筆

eyeshadow 眼影

applicator 眼影刷

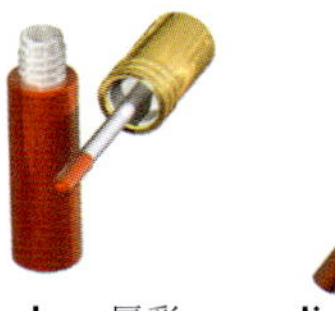

lip gloss 唇彩

lip liner 唇線筆

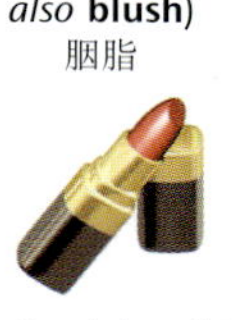

lipstick 口紅

mascara 睫毛膏

nail polish (*BrE also* **nail varnish**) 指甲油

Clothes 服裝

patterned waistcoat (*BrE*) / **vest** (*NAmE*) 印花西服背心

striped 條紋

polka dots 圓點（花樣）

tartan / plaid 花格圖案

bow ties 蝶形領結

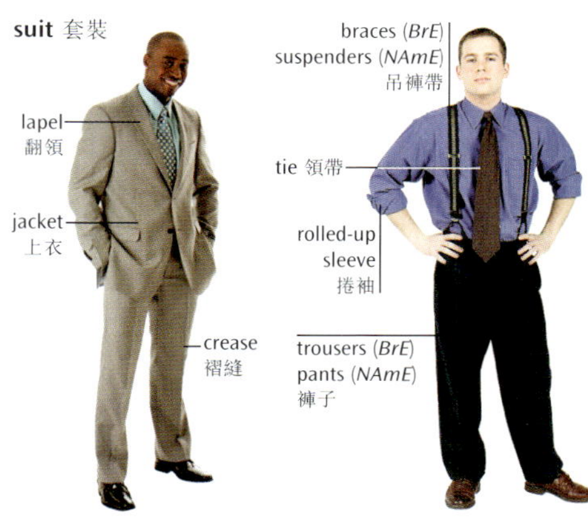

- The general word for what you wear is **clothes** (*plural*) or **clothing** [U] (*formal*). 泛指衣服用 clothes 或 clothing：
  - ▸ *She always wears such lovely clothes.* 她總是穿着這麼漂亮的衣服。
  - ▸ *a piece of clothing* 一件衣服
- A set of clothes that you wear together, especially for a particular occasion or purpose, is an **outfit**. 全套服裝（尤指為特定場合或目的而穿）用 outfit。
- Any piece of clothing worn on the top part of the body, especially by women, can be called a **top**. 上衣（尤指女人穿的）可叫做 top。
- The clothes which some children wear at school, or which some people wear at work, are called a **uniform** [C, U]. 校服或制服叫做 uniform。
- When police officers wear ordinary clothes instead of uniforms, they are in **plain clothes**. 警察穿的便衣是 plain clothes：
  - ▸ *a plain clothes police sergeant* 一名便衣警長

coats and jackets 外套和上衣

overcoat 長大衣

raincoat 雨衣

body warmer 無袖厚夾克

denim jacket 牛仔布夾克

leather jacket 皮夾克

anorak 帶帽防寒短上衣

sleeveless dress 無袖連衣裙

skirt 女裙

Describing clothes and the way people look 描述衣服和衣着

Clothes can be 形容衣服可用：

- attractive and designed well: **elegant** 漂亮雅致：elegant
- untidy and dirty: **scruffy** 不整潔、邋遢：scruffy
- clean, tidy and rather formal: **smart** (*especially BrE*) 光鮮、講究、正式：smart（尤用於英式英語）
- not formal: **casual** 隨便：casual
- fashionable and attractive: **stylish** 時髦、高雅：stylish
- very fashionable: **trendy** (*informal*) 很時髦：trendy（非正式）
- fitting closely to your body: **tight, close-fitting, skintight** 緊身：tight，close-fitting，skintight
- not fitting closely: **loose, baggy** 寬鬆：loose，baggy
- If a piece of clothing is not too big and not too small, it **fits** you. 衣服合身用 fit：
  - ▸ *These jeans don't fit me any more.* 我這條牛仔褲不合身了。
- If a piece of clothing looks good on you, it **suits** you. 衣服與人相配用 suit：
  - ▸ *It's a nice coat, but it doesn't really suit you.* 這大衣很好，但不大適合你穿。

Fastening clothes 扣／繫衣服

- To talk about fastening a piece of clothing in general, use **do** sth **up**, **fasten** sth; *opposite*: **undo** sth. 扣好或繫好用 do up、fasten，解開用 undo：
  - ▸ *Do your coat up.* 把你的外套扣上。
  - ▸ *Your shirt is undone.* 你的襯衫沒扣好。
- There are some special verbs for particular types of fastener. 有一些動詞適用於特定扣件：
  - ▸ buttons: **button** sth (**up**); *opposite:* **unbutton** sth 鈕扣：button (up)（扣上…的鈕扣），反義為 unbutton（解開…的鈕扣）
  - ▸ a zip: **zip** sth **up**; *opposite:* **unzip** sth 拉鏈：zip up（拉上…的拉鏈），反義為 unzip（拉開…的拉鏈）

British and American differences 英美服裝用語的區別

- a short piece of clothing with buttons down the front but no sleeves, usually worn over a shirt and under a jacket 西服背心：英式英語是 waistcoat，美式英語是 vest：
  British English **waistcoat**
  American English **vest**
- a piece of underwear worn under a shirt, etc. next to the skin 貼身穿的背心或汗衫：英式英語是 vest，美式英語是 undershirt：
  British English **vest**
  American English **undershirt**
- a piece of clothing that covers the body from the waist down, and is divided into two parts to cover each leg separately 褲子：英式英語是 trousers，美式英語是 pants：
  British English **trousers**
  American English **pants**
- a piece of men's underwear worn under their trousers/pants 男襯褲：英式英語是 pants（或 underpants），美式英語是 underpants：
  British English **pants** (*or* **underpants**)
  American English **underpants**
- a loose dress with no sleeves, usually worn over a shirt or blouse 通常套在襯衫外面的無袖女裝：英式英語是 pinafore，美式英語是 jumper：
  British English **pinafore**
  American English **jumper**
- a knitted woollen or cotton piece of clothing for the upper part of the body with long sleeves and no buttons 針織套衫：英式英語是 jumper，美式英語是 sweater：
  British English **jumper**
  American English **sweater**
- straps for holding trousers/pants up 吊褲帶：英式英語是 braces，美式英語是 suspenders：
  British English **braces**
  American English **suspenders**
- short elastic fastenings for holding up socks or stockings 吊襪帶：英式英語是 suspenders，美式英語是 garters：
  British English **suspenders**
  American English **garters**

cardigan 開襟毛衣

polo shirt 馬球衫

T-shirt T 恤衫

shorts 短褲

sweaters (*BrE also* jumpers) 針織套衫

polo neck (*BrE*) turtleneck sweater (*NAmE*) 高圓翻領毛衣

crew neck sweater 圓領套頭毛衣

nightdress (*BrE*) nightgown (*NAmE*) 女式睡袍

pyjamas pajamas (*especially US*) (一套) 睡衣褲

dressing gown (*BrE*) / bathrobe (*NAmE*) 晨衣

fasteners 扣件

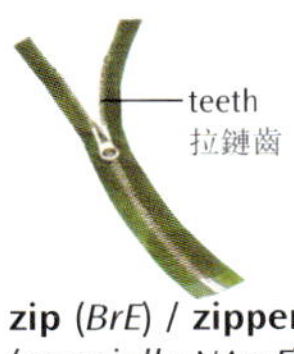

zip (*BrE*) / zipper (*especially NAmE*) 拉鏈

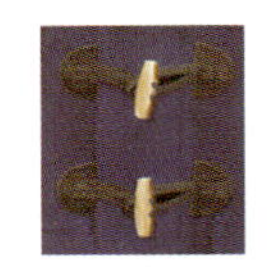

toggle 棒形鈕扣

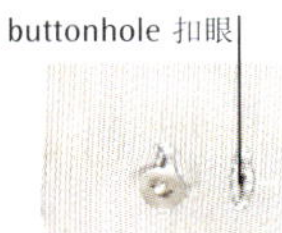

button 鈕扣

Velcro™ 維可牢搭扣

buckle 搭扣

hook and eye 鈎眼扣

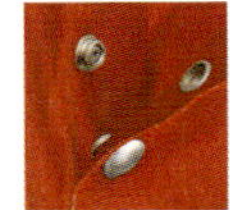

press stud / popper (*both BrE*) snap (*NAmE*) 摁扣

drawstring 拉繩

safety pin 安全別針

lace 繫帶

Accessories（服裝）配飾

Shoes 鞋

slingback
露跟女鞋

mule
女式拖鞋

court shoes (*BrE*)
pumps (*NAmE*)
半高跟女鞋

flats
(*BrE also* **pumps**)
平跟鞋

clogs
木屐

stiletto
細高跟女鞋

wedge
坡跟鞋

platform
厚底鞋

kitten heels
弧狀細矮跟鞋

slippers
便鞋

sandal
涼鞋

jelly shoe
輕便塑料鞋

flip-flops
(*NAmE also* **thongs**)
人字拖鞋

moccasins
莫卡辛軟皮鞋

lace-ups (*especially BrE*) / **oxfords** (*especially NAmE*)
繫帶鞋

brogues
（粗革）拷花皮鞋

loafer
平底便鞋

trainers (*BrE*)
sneakers (*NAmE*)
運動鞋

baseball boots
棒球鞋

boot
靴子

cowboy boot
牛仔靴

hiking boots
(*also* **walking boots**)
遠足旅行靴

wellingtons (*BrE*)
rubber boots (*NAmE*)
高筒膠靴

Bags 包

handbag (*NAmE also* **purse**)
手提包

shoulder bag
（小）挎包

clutch bag 女式小手提包

bumbag (*BrE*)
fanny pack (*NAmE*) 腰包

backpack (*BrE also* **rucksack**)
背包

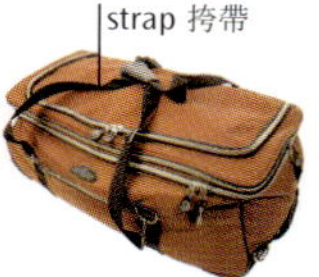

holdall (*BrE*)
duffel bag (*NAmE*)
旅行袋

purse (*especially BrE*) / **change purse** (*NAmE*)
（尤指女用）錢包

wallet (*NAmE also* **billfold**)
皮夾子

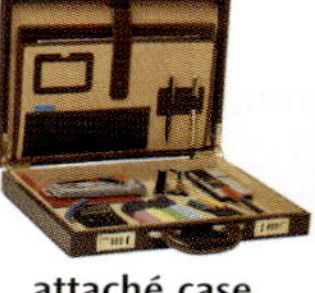

attaché case
(*also* **briefcase**)
公文包

briefcase
公文包

suitcase
手提箱

trunk 箱子

Hats 帽子

panama
巴拿馬草帽

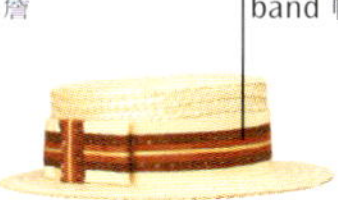

boater
平頂硬草帽

trilby
軟氈帽

cowboy hat
牛仔帽

bowler (*BrE*)
derby (*NAmE*)
常禮帽

top hat
高頂禮帽

mortar board
學位帽

cap
制服帽

cloth cap / flat cap
(*both BrE*) 布帽

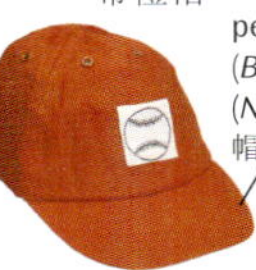

baseball cap
棒球帽

beret
貝雷帽

hard hat
安全帽

crash helmet
防護頭盔

beanie
無簷小便帽

bobble hat
絨球帽

sou'wester
防雨帽

hood
風帽

sun hats
闊邊遮陽帽

sombrero
墨西哥闊邊帽

Gloves 手套

fingerless gloves
無指手套

mitten
連指手套

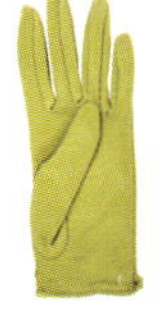
glove
（分指）手套

Scarves 圍巾

scarf
圍巾

chiffon scarf
雪紡綢圍巾

Jewellery 首飾

stud
耳飾

clip-on earring
夾式耳環

pendant
項鏈垂飾

medallion
紀念章式項鏈墜

locket
盒式項鏈墜

chain
項鏈

hoop earring
圈狀耳環

dangly earrings
垂吊式耳環

signet ring
圖章戒指

wedding ring
wedding band
結婚戒指

cufflinks
袖扣

string of beads
一串珠子

bangle
手鐲

charm bracelet
吊飾手鐲

brooch (*BrE*)
pin (*NAmE*)
飾針

badge (*also* **button** *especially NAmE*)
徽章

pearl necklace
珍珠項鏈

Computing
計算機信息處理技術

Equipment 設備

- This computer has a **processor speed** of 3 GHz (= gigahertz), 2 Gb (= gigabytes) of **RAM** (=**random access memory**) and a **hard disk capacity** of 500 Gb. 本計算機的處理器速度（processor speed）為 3 千兆赫，內存（RAM，即 random-access memory）為 2 千兆字節，硬盤容量（hard disk capacity）為 500 千兆字節。
- It comes with a 56K **modem** and a **speech recognition** system. 另配一個 56K 的調製解調器（modem）和一個語音識別（speech recognition）系統。
- The **multimedia** system includes a **sound card** with 4D stereo sound and a **graphics card** with 128 Mb of **video RAM** for a **high resolution** colour **display**. 多媒體（multimedia）系統包括 4D 音效立體聲聲卡（sound card）和帶有 128 兆字節視頻隨機存貯器（video RAM），用於高分辨率（high resolution）彩色顯示（display）的圖像顯示卡（graphics card）。
- With **DVD** (= **digital versatile disc** or **digital videodisc**) you can watch films/movies. 用 DVD（即數字多功能光盤 digital versatile disc 或數字視頻光盤 digital videodisc）可看電影。
- You pay extra for the **laser printer**, **scanner** and other **peripherals**. 激光打印機（laser printer）、掃描儀（scanner）以及其他外圍設備（peripheral）則需另外購買。
- The new **operating system** should be compatible with existing **hardware**. 新操作系統（operating system）應與現有的硬件（hardware）兼容。
- You can **download** the pictures from your **digital camera** and **burn** them to a **CD**. 可從數碼照相機（digital camera）下載（download）照片，並將它們刻錄（burn）在光盤（CD）上。
- **Wi-fi™** (= **wireless fidelity**) broadband connections are not only in computer stores but in coffee shops, public libraries and bookstores – you can log into the Internet without physically plugging into anything. 無線保真（Wi-fi™，即 wireless fidelity）寬帶連接不但電腦商店中有，咖啡店、公共圖書館和書店也有，在這些地方無需插線便可上網。

Getting started 啟動

- **PC users** should **log on** to the **network** by **entering** their **username** and **password**. 個人計算機用戶（PC user）應輸入（enter）用戶名（username）和密碼（password）登入（log on）計算機網絡（network）。
- **Load** the **program** into the computer. 將程序（program）載入（load）計算機。
- **Save** your **files** onto your **hard disk** and **back** them **up** onto **CDs** or **DVDs**. 將文件（file）存入（save）硬盤（hard disk），然後備份（back up）到光盤（CD）或數字光盤（DVD）。
- Important **data** is **archived** on the central **file server**. 重要數據（data）在中央文件服務器（file server）存檔（archive）。

When things go wrong 計算機出毛病

- I can't **log in** – the **server** is **down**. 我無法登入（log in）系統，服務器（server）停機了（down）。
- The **system** keeps **crashing** – I've lost all my files. 系統（system）不斷出故障（crash），我所有的文件都丟失了。
- You'll have to switch off and **reboot**. 必須關機，重新啟動。
- **Error**. Username contains **invalid characters**. 錯誤（error）。用戶名含無效字符（invalid character）。
- My computer can't **read** this disk. 我的計算機讀（read）不出這張磁盤。
- The **virus** in the **software** was **programmed** to **corrupt** the hard disk. 軟件（software）中的病毒（virus）編有（program）破壞（corrupt）硬盤的程序。
- A **firewall** provides essential security for your computer network. 防火牆（firewall）對計算機網絡提供基本的安全保護。
- Download and install this **patch** to fix the fault. 下載並安裝這個補丁程序（patch）修正錯誤。

Window 窗口

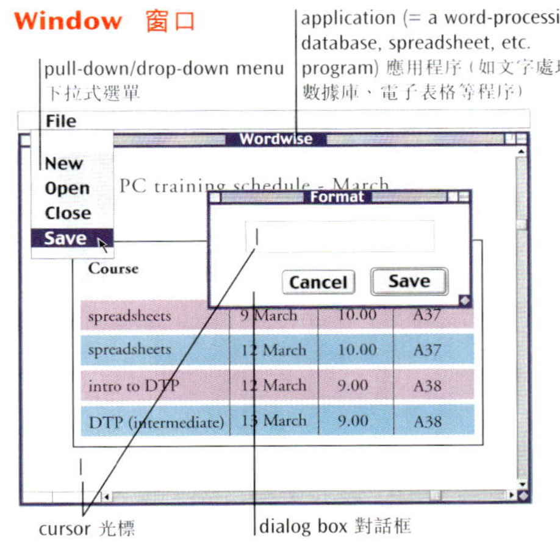

User interface 用戶界面

- **Click on** the **window** to make it **active**. 單擊（click on）窗口（window）將其激活（active）。
- You can **run** several **applications** at the same time. 可同時運行（run）幾個應用程序。
- To **create** a new **document**, **select** New from the File **menu**. 建立（create）新文檔（document），選擇（select）文件選單（menu）中的新建項。
- **Insert** the **cursor** at the beginning of the line. 在行首插入（insert）光標（cursor）。
- Use the **mouse** to **drag** the **icon** to the **desktop**. 用鼠標（mouse）拖動（drag）圖標（icon）至桌面（desktop）。
- **Scroll up** or **down** the text by clicking on the **scroll bar**. 單擊滾動條（scroll bar）使文本上下滾動（scroll up / down）。
- Search and replace **options** are **activated** from the command **prompt**. 查找和替換選項（option）從命令提示符（prompt）激活（activate）。
- **Interactive** computer **terminals** allow visitors to take an 'electronic walk' through a **virtual** Pompeii. 交互式（interactive）計算機終端（terminal）可讓訪問者"電子漫步"於虛擬（virtual）龐貝城中。

Screen 屏幕

desktop 桌面 document 文檔 scroll bar 滾動條

Wordwise

PC training schedule - March

Course	Date	Time	Room
spreadsheets	9 March	10.00	A37
spreadsheets	12 March	10.00	A37
intro to DTP	12 March	9.00	A38
DTP (intermediate)	13 March	9.00	A38

icons 圖標 windows 窗口

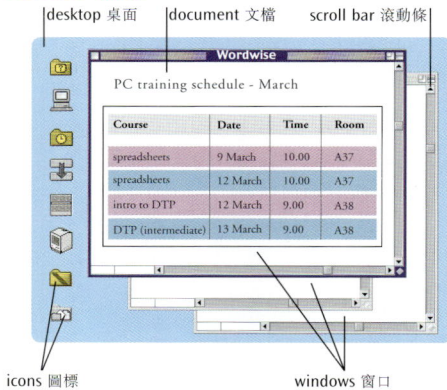

The Internet 互聯網

- There is a wide range range of **ISPs** (= **Internet Service Providers**). 有各種各樣的互聯網服務供應商（ISP，即 Internet Service Provider）。
- My free time is spent **surfing** the **net** in **Internet cafes**. 空餘時間我都在網吧（Internet cafe）上網（surf the net）。
- It's a **software package** that helps you **browse the Web**. 這是一個幫你進入互聯網瀏覽（browse the Web）的軟件包（software package）。
- This **search engine** indexes over a million **websites**. 此搜索引擎（search engine）可檢索一百多萬個網站（website）。
- **Do a search on** language schools in the UK. 查找（do a search on）英國的語言學校。
- Brief summaries are **hyperlinked** to the complete texts. 簡短摘要超鏈接到（hyperlink to）全文。
- The site's **webmaster** says it has over 100,000 **hits** a day. 這家網站的管理員（webmaster）說它每天的點擊量（hit）超過 10 萬次。
- This **chat room** is a forum for debating civil liberties issues **online**. 此聊天室（chat room）是討論公民自由的在線（online）論壇。
- My **email address** is 'joanna_smith@oup.com' (said 'joanna underscore smith at o-u-p dot com). 我的電郵地址（email address）是 joanna_smith@oup.com（讀作 joanna underscore smith at o-u-p dot com）。
- The **web address / URL** (= **uniform/ universal resource locator**) is 'www.oup.com/elt' (said 'double-U, double-U, double-U dot o-u-p dot com slash e-l-t). 本互聯網網頁地址/統一資源定位地址（web address / URL，後者即 uniform / universal resource locator）是 www.oup.com/elt（讀作 double-U, double-U, double-U dot o-u-p dot com slash e-l-t）。
- The website lets you **upload** photos, then edit and share them. 本網站可上傳（upload）照片，並進行編輯和共享。
- You can **download** images to your PC much more quickly with **broadband** than with a **dial-up** connection. 用寬帶（broadband）下載（download）圖像到個人計算機比用撥號（dial-up）連接快得多。
- **Bookmarking** a page stores the information which enables you to revisit a favourite website instantly. 為網頁做電子書籤（bookmark）可存貯信息，以便快捷訪問最喜愛的網站。
- **Cookies** are files used by some websites to gain information about their visitors, or to simplify the login process by saving usernames and passwords. 網絡餅乾（cookie）是一些網站用於獲得來訪者信息，或通過貯存用戶名和密碼以簡化登錄程序的文件。
- He maintains a personal **weblog** in which he writes (= **blogs**) extensively about film and his own film-making. 他開設了私人博客（weblog），發表網誌（blog），縱論電影和自己的電影製作。
- Most **spam** mails disguise the sender's identity. 多數垃圾電郵（spam）偽裝了發郵件者的身分。
- **VoIP** allows you to use your computer as a telephone, or use the Internet to transmit your call over ordinary phone lines. 互聯網語音協議（VoIP）使用戶可以用計算機打電話，或利用互聯網傳送從普通電話線打出的電話。

Home page 主頁

Office 辦公室

1 wall planner 壁掛式規劃表
2 noticeboard (*BrE*) bulletin board (*NAmE*) 佈告板
3 flip chart 活動掛圖
4 data projector 數據投影儀
5 laptop 膝上型電腦
6 meeting/conference room 會議室
7 water cooler 飲水冷卻機
8 desk lamp 枱燈
9 workstation / PC 工作站/個人計算機
10 partition 隔板
11 in tray (*NAmE also* in box) 收件盤
12 out tray (*BrE*) out box (*US*) 待發信件盤
13 calendar 日曆
14 pen holder 筆筒
15 mouse mat (*BrE*) mouse pad (*especially NAmE*) 鼠標墊
16 flatbed scanner 平板掃描儀
17 calculator 計算器
18 desk diary (*BrE*) datebook (*NAmE*) 枱式記事簿
19 desk 辦公桌
20 stationery tray 文具盤
21 waste-paper basket (*BrE*) / wastebasket (*NAmE*) 廢紙簍
22 swivel chair 轉椅
23 arm 扶手
24 printer 打印機
25 hard copy / printout 打印件
26 castor (*BrE*) caster (*NAmE*) 小腳輪
27 filing cabinet (*BrE*) file cabinet (*NAmE*) 文件櫃
28 suspension file 懸掛式文件夾
29 photocopier 複印機

Stationery and office supplies 文具和辦公用品

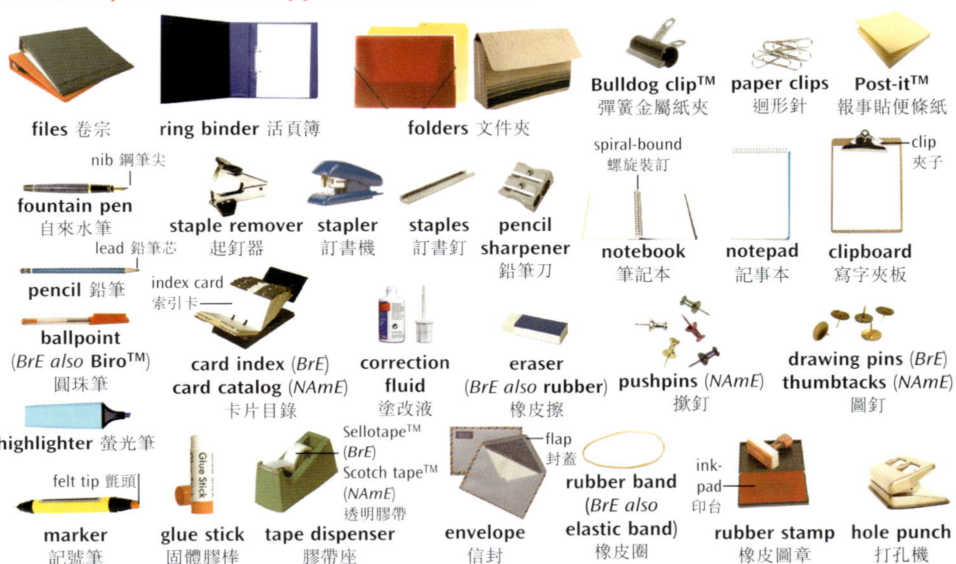

Classroom 教室

1 projector 投影儀
2 corridor (*NAmE also* hallway) 走廊
3 poster 佈告牌
4 locker 寄存櫃
5 interactive whiteboard 互動式電子白板
6 whiteboard 白板
7 board pen 白板筆
8 sports field 運動場
9 desk 書桌
10 school bag 書包
11 backpack (*BrE also* rucksack) 背包
12 textbook (*NAmE also* text) 課本
13 workbook (*BrE*) exercise book (*NAmE*) 練習冊
14 exercise book (*BrE*) notebook (*NAmE*) 練習本
15 pencil case 鉛筆盒
16 satchel 皮書包
17 protractor 量角器
18 ruler 直尺
19 set square (*BrE*) triangle (*NAmE*) 三角板

1
2
3
4
5
6
7
8
9
10
11
12
13
14
15
16
17
18
19

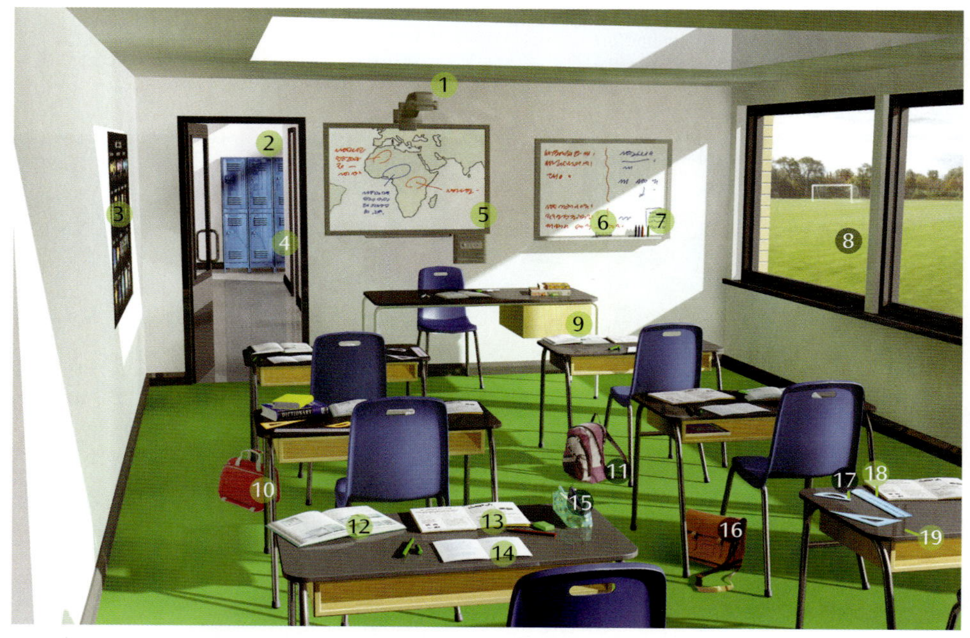

Laboratory equipment 實驗室設備

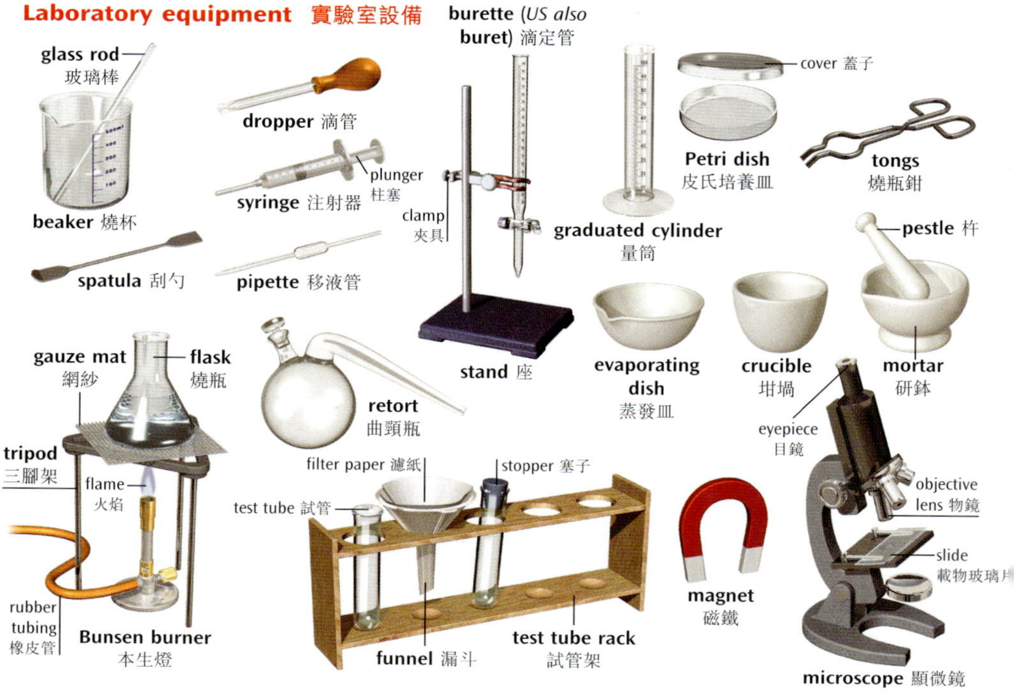

burette (*US also* buret) 滴定管
glass rod 玻璃棒
beaker 燒杯
dropper 滴管
syringe 注射器
plunger 柱塞
spatula 刮勺
pipette 移液管
clamp 夾具
stand 座
graduated cylinder 量筒
cover 蓋子
Petri dish 皮氏培養皿
tongs 燒瓶鉗
pestle 杵
mortar 研缽
evaporating dish 蒸發皿
crucible 坩堝
gauze mat 網紗
flask 燒瓶
retort 曲頸瓶
tripod 三腳架
flame 火焰
rubber tubing 橡皮管
Bunsen burner 本生燈
filter paper 濾紙
stopper 塞子
test tube 試管
funnel 漏斗
test tube rack 試管架
magnet 磁鐵
eyepiece 目鏡
objective lens 物鏡
slide 載物玻璃片
microscope 顯微鏡

Shapes, solids and angles 形狀、立體和角

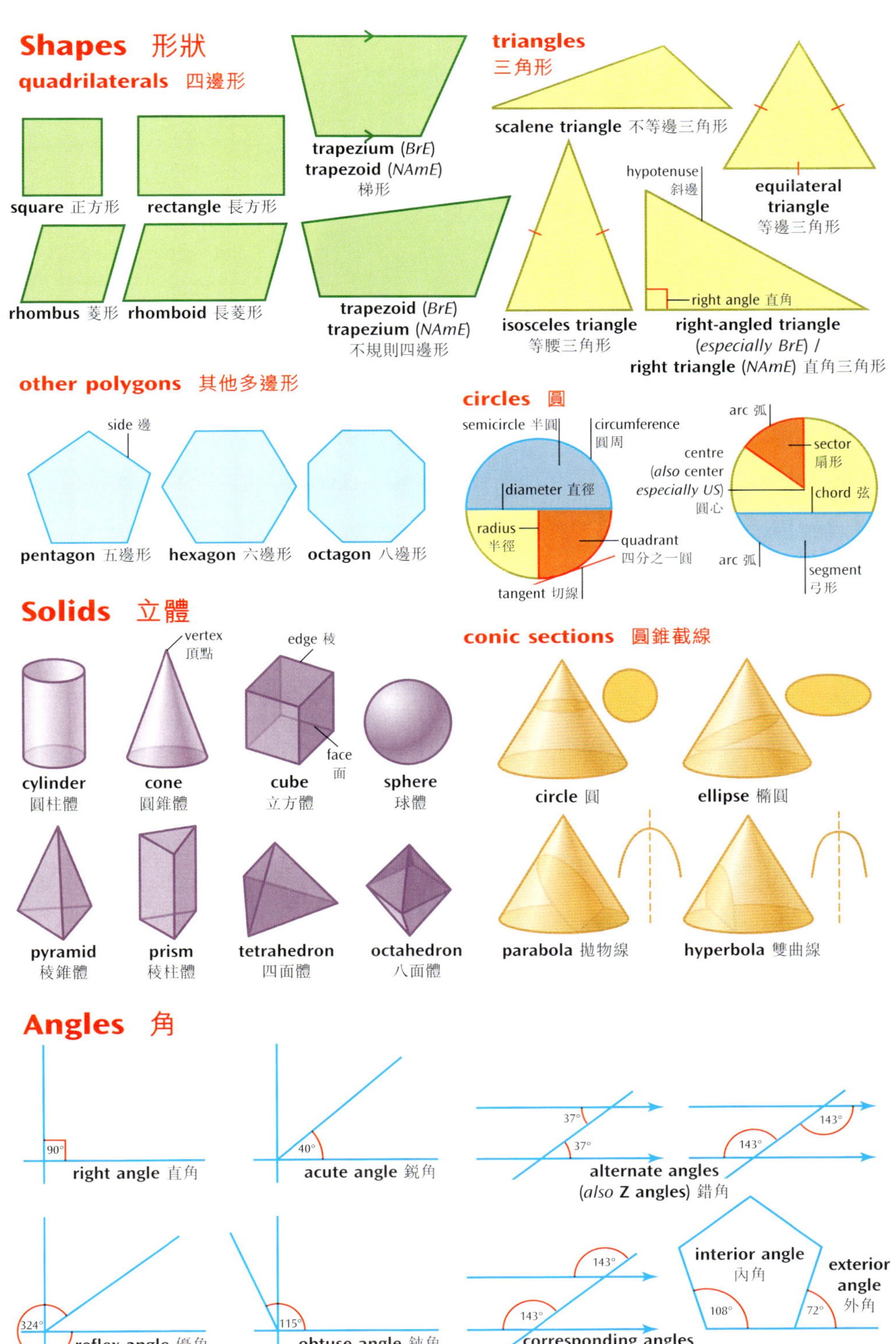

The earth and the solar system
地球和太陽系

The earth 地球

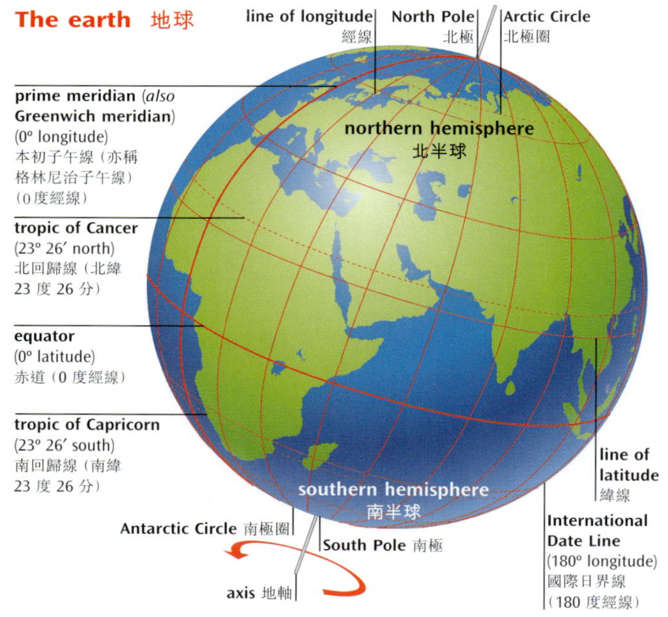

The seasons 四季

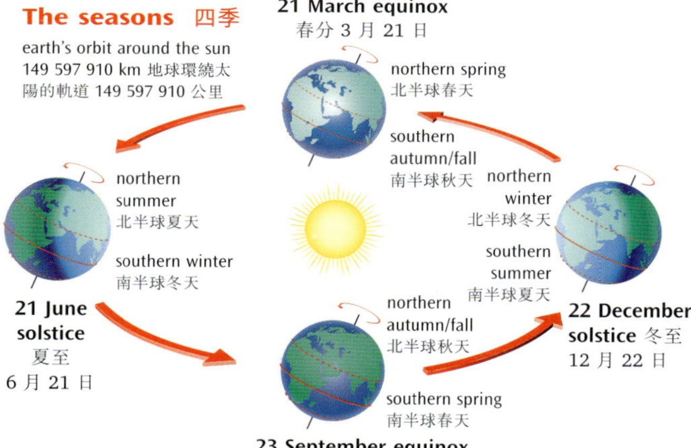

Seasons 季節

- When talking about the seasons we normally do not use **the**, but we may do if we want to talk about a particular winter, summer, etc. 指季節通常不用定冠詞 the，但指某個冬天、夏天等時要用定冠詞 the：
  - ▶ *I love spring – it's my favourite season.*
    我愛春天，這是我最喜歡的季節。
  - ▶ *That was the summer we went to Australia.*
    我們是在那個夏天去澳大利亞的。

The world 世界

- A **map** is a drawing or plan of the world or a part of the world. * map 指地圖。
- An **atlas** is a book of maps and a **globe** is a model of the earth in the shape of a ball. * atlas 指地圖冊，地圖集；globe 指地球儀。
- The planet where we live, and its surface: **earth**, **the earth** (*also* **the Earth**). * earth、the earth（亦作 the Earth）指地球，陸地。
- The earth, including all the countries, people, etc.: **world** (*often* **the world**). * world（常作 the world）指世界。
- The study of the world, including its natural and man-made features (seas, mountains, countries, cities, etc.), is **geography** [U]; *adjective*: **geographical**; *person*: **geographer**. * geography 指地理學，形容詞為 geographical，地理學家為 geographer。
- The study of the rocks, etc. which form the surface of the earth is **geology** [U]; *adjective*: **geological**; *person*: **geologist**. * geology 指地質學，形容詞為 geological，地質學家為 geologist。

The stars and planets 恒星和行星

- The planets in the solar system **orbit** (= go round) the sun. 太陽系的行星圍繞（orbit）太陽運行。
- Everything that exists, including the earth, the planets, the stars, etc. is called **the universe**. * the universe 指宇宙，天地萬物。
- A group of stars with a name is a **constellation** and a very large group of stars is a **galaxy**. * constellation 指星座；galaxy 指星系。
- A piece of rock moving through space is a **meteor** and a meteor that has landed on earth is a **meteorite**. * meteor 指流星；meteorite 指隕石。
- The scientific study of the stars, planets, etc. is **astronomy** [U]; *adjective*: **astronomical**; *person*: **astronomer**. * astronomy 指天文學，形容詞為 astronomical，天文學家為 astronomer。
- The belief that the positions and movements of the stars and planets influence what people do and what happens to them is **astrology** [U]; *adjective*: **astrological**; *person*: **astrologer**. * astrology 指占星術，形容詞為 astrological，占星家為 astrologer。

See also GEOGRAPHICAL NAMES 參看地名表

The solar system 太陽系

The British Isles 不列顛群島

Britain or **Great Britain (GB)** is a geographical area consisting of **England**, **Scotland** and **Wales** (but not **Ireland**). 不列顛（Britain）或大不列顛（Great Britain）（簡稱 GB）由英格蘭（England）、蘇格蘭（Scotland）和威爾士（Wales）組成，但不包括愛爾蘭（Ireland）。

The name **Britain** is also incorrectly used to refer to the political state, officially called the **United Kingdom of Great Britain and Northern Ireland**. This is abbreviated to the **United Kingdom** or the **UK**. 不列顛（Britain）這一名稱亦常常錯誤地用以指行政上的國家，正式名稱是大不列顛及北愛爾蘭聯合王國（United Kingdom of Great Britain and Northern Ireland），簡稱聯合王國或英國（United Kingdom 或 UK）。

The British Isles is a group of islands that includes Britain and Ireland, and a number of smaller islands. **Ireland** (formerly **Eire**) is an independent state occupying the southern part of the island of Ireland. 不列顛群島指包括不列顛、愛爾蘭以及一系列小島在內的一群島嶼。愛爾蘭（舊稱 Eire）為一獨立國家，位於愛爾蘭島的南部。

To refer to the nationality of the people of Britain or the United Kingdom, you use the adjective **British**. **English** describes people from England, and should not be used to describe people from **Ireland**, **Scotland** or **Wales**, who are **Irish**, **Scottish** and **Welsh**. There is further information in the notes at the entries for **British** and **Scottish**. 英國人的國籍用形容詞 British 表示。English 指英格蘭人，不應用以表示愛爾蘭（Ireland）、蘇格蘭（Scotland）或威爾士（Wales）的人，這些地區的人分別用 Irish、Scottish 和 Welsh 表示。本詞典在 British 和 Scottish 詞條的用法說明中有詳細說明。

There are special adjectives and nouns to describe people from some cities, for example a person from London is a **Londoner**, from Dublin a **Dubliner**, from Glasgow a **Glaswegian**, from Aberdeen an **Aberdonian**, from Manchester a **Mancunian** and from Liverpool a **Liverpudlian**. A Londoner who speaks with the local accent is also called a **Cockney**. There are also informal names for people from some cities: **Brummie** (from Birmingham); **Scouse** or **Scouser** (from Liverpool); and **Geordie** (from Tyneside, which stretches from Newcastle to the coast). 有些城市的人有專用的形容詞和名詞表示，如倫敦人叫 Londoner，都柏林人叫 Dubliner，格拉斯哥人叫 Glaswegian，阿伯丁人叫 Aberdonian，曼徹斯特人叫 Mancunian，利物浦人叫 Liverpudlian。有倫敦地方口音的倫敦人亦稱 Cockney。某些城市的人還有一些非正式的名稱，如 Brummie（伯明翰人）、Scouse 或 Scouser（利物浦人），Geordie（泰恩賽德人，指沿泰恩河從紐卡斯爾至海岸這一帶的人）。

Atlantic Ocean
大西洋
Donegal Bay 多尼戈爾灣
Mountains
多尼戈爾山
Londonderry
倫敦德里
Lough Neagh
內伊湖
Erne 厄恩河
Belfast
貝爾法斯特
Lisburn
利斯本
Mourne
Mountains
莫恩山
Newry 紐里
852m
Slieve Donard
多納德山
Lough Conn
科恩湖
Lough Mask
馬斯克湖
Lough Ree
里湖
Lough Corrib
科里布湖
Boyne 博因河
Liffey 利菲河
Dublin
都柏林
Galway 戈爾韋
Galway Bay 戈爾韋灣
Shannon
Lough Derg
德格湖
Barrow 巴羅河
Wicklow
Mountains
威克洛山
Limerick
利默里克
Suir 舒爾河
Waterford
沃特福德
Blackwater 布萊克沃特河
Dingle Bay 丁格爾灣
1041m
Carrauntoohill
卡朗圖厄爾山
Cork
科克
St. George's Channel
聖喬治海峽
IRELAND
愛爾蘭
ISLE OF
MAN
馬恩島
Douglas
道格拉斯
Irish Sea
愛爾蘭海
Anglesey
安格爾西島
Holyhead
霍利黑德
Caernarfon 卡那封
1085m
Snowdon
斯諾登山
Snowdonia
WALES
威爾士
Cardigan Bay 卡迪根灣
Aberystwyth
阿伯里斯特威斯
Cambrian Mountains
Milford Haven
米爾福德港
Swansea 斯旺西
Brecon Beacons
布雷肯山
Usk
Cardiff
加的夫
Newport
紐波特
Bristol Channel 布里斯托爾海峽
Solway Firth
Lake
District
湖區
978m
Scafell Pike
斯科費爾峰
Eden
Pennines
Tees
Swale
The
North-West
西北地區
Blackpool
布萊克浦
Preston 普雷斯頓
Bolton 博爾頓
Liverpool
利物浦
Mersey
Colwyn Bay
科爾溫灣
Chester
切斯特
Dee 迪河
Shrewsbury
什魯斯伯里
Wolverhampton
伍爾弗漢普頓
Wye
Worcester 伍斯特
Hereford 赫里福德
Gloucester
格洛斯特
Cotswold Hills
Bristol
布里斯托爾
Bath
巴斯
Avon
Exmoor
埃克斯穆爾高地
Taunton
湯頓
The
West Country
西部地區
Exe
Exeter
埃克塞特
Dartmoor
達特穆爾高地
Plymouth 普利茅斯
Truro 特魯羅
Isles of Scilly
錫利群島
Land's End
蘭茲角
Sunderland 森德蘭
Durham 達勒姆
Hartlepool 哈特爾浦
Middlesbrough 米德爾斯伯勒
North York Moors
北約克高沼
The
North-East
東北地區
York 約克
Ouse
Bradford
布拉德福德
Leeds
利茲
Blackburn
布萊克本
Aire
Huddersfield 哈德斯菲爾德
Manchester 曼徹斯特
Peak
District
皮克區
Sheffield
設菲爾德
Stoke-on-Trent
特倫特河畔斯托克
Kingston upon Hull
赫爾河畔金斯頓
Humber 亨伯河
UNITED KINGDOM
聯合王國；英國
ENGLAND
英格蘭
Lincoln 林肯
Trent
The Wash
Derby 德比
Nottingham 諾丁漢
East Midlands
The
Midlands
中部地區
Leicester
萊斯特
The Fens
芬斯（地區）
Wensum
Norwich 諾里奇
Great Yarmouth
大雅茅斯
East Anglia 東英吉利亞
Peterborough 彼得伯勒
Birmingham 伯明翰
Coventry 考文垂
Severn
Great Ouse 大烏斯河
Warwick
沃里克
Northampton
北安普敦
Cambridge 劍橋
Stratford-upon-Avon
埃文河畔斯特拉特福
Milton Keynes
米爾頓凱恩斯
Ipswich 伊普斯威奇
Stour
Stansted 斯坦斯特德
Colchester 科爾切斯特
Oxford
牛津
Luton 盧頓
Chiltern Hills
Thames
Swindon
斯溫登
Salisbury
Plain
索爾茲伯里平原
The Home Counties 倫敦周圍各郡
Thames Estuary 泰晤士河河口
Watford 沃特福德
London
倫敦
Southend-on-Sea 濱海紹森德
Margate 馬蓋特
Heathrow
Reading
雷丁
Slough
斯勞
North Downs
北部丘陵
Canterbury
坎特伯雷
Dover
多佛爾
Gatwick 蓋特威克
Salisbury
索爾茲伯里
Southampton
南安普敦
South Downs
南部丘陵
Brighton
布賴頓
Hastings
黑斯廷斯
Strait of Dover
Bournemouth
伯恩茅斯
Poole
普爾
Portsmouth
樸次茅斯
Eastbourne
伊斯特本
Isle of Wight
懷特島
English Channel 英吉利海峽
St. Peter Port
聖彼得港
Guernsey 根西島
Jersey
澤西島
Channel Islands 海峽群島
St. Helier 聖赫利爾

Canada and the United States of America
加拿大和美國
Arctic Ocean
北冰洋
USA 美國
ALASKA
阿拉斯加州
Brooks Range
布魯克斯嶺
Yukon 育空河
Mt. Mckinley
麥金利山
6194m
Alaska Range 阿拉斯加山脈
Anchorage
安克雷奇
Mt. Logan
洛根山
5951m
5489
Mt. Saint Elias
聖伊萊亞斯山
Gulf of Alaska
阿拉斯加灣
Whitehorse
懷特霍斯
Juneau
朱諾
Klondike 克朗代克河
YUKON
育空
Mackenzie Mts. 馬更些山脈
Mackenzie 馬更些河
Liard 利亞德河
BRITISH COLUMBIA
不列顛哥倫比亞省
Western Cordillera
西科迪勒拉山脈
Coast Mountains
海岸山脈
ROCK
Peace 皮斯河
ALBERTA 艾伯塔省
SASKATCHEWAN
薩斯喀徹溫省
MANITOBA
馬尼托巴省
Lake Athabasca
阿薩巴斯卡湖
Great Slave Lake
大奴湖
Yellowknife 耶洛奈夫
NORTHWEST TERRITORIES
西北地區
Great Bear Lake
大熊湖
NUNAVUT
努納武特地區
Beaufort Sea
波弗特海
Banks Island
班克斯島
Victoria Island
維多利亞島
Melville Island
梅爾維爾島
Parry Islands 帕里群島
Queen Elizabeth Island
伊麗莎白女王群島
Ellesmere Island
埃爾斯米爾島
Devon Island
德文島
Somerset Island
薩默塞特島
Prince of Wales Island
威爾士王子島
Bylot Island 拜洛特島
Baffin Island
巴芬島
Iqaluit
伊卡盧伊特
Southampton Island
南安普敦島
Hudson Bay
哈得孫灣
Belcher Islands
貝爾徹群島
CANADA 加拿大
Labrador Sea 拉布拉多海
NEWFOUNDLAND AND LABRADOR
紐芬蘭和拉布拉多省
Smallwood Reservoir
斯莫爾伍德水庫
La Grande Rivière
St. John's
聖約翰斯
Lake Superior
蘇必利爾湖
Sault Sainte Marie
蘇聖瑪麗
Greater Sudbury
大薩德伯里
Gatineau
加蒂諾
Montreal
蒙特利爾
Ottawa
渥太華
Sherbrooke
ONTARIO 安大略省
Lake Huron
休倫湖
Lake Ontario
安大略湖
Burlington
伯靈頓
Syracuse
錫拉丘茲
Toronto
多倫多
Niagara Falls
Hamilton
哈密爾頓
Rochester
羅切斯特
Albany
奧爾巴尼
NEW YORK
MICHIGAN
Green Bay
格林貝
Lake Michigan
Grand Rapids
大急流城
Detroit
底特律
London
Buffalo
布法羅
Windsor
Milwaukee
密爾沃基
Chicago
芝加哥
Toledo
Lake Erie
伊利湖
Cleveland
克利夫蘭
INDIANA
印第安納州
OHIO 俄亥俄州
Columbus 哥倫布
Indianapolis
印第安納波利斯
Dayton
代頓
Ohio
Cincinnati
辛辛那提
Charleston
WEST VIRGINIA
Allegheny Mountains
Pittsburg 匹茲堡
Baltimore
PENNSYLVANIA
賓夕法尼亞州
Philadelphia
費城
Washington D.C. 華盛頓
VIRGINIA
弗吉尼亞州
Chesapeake Bay
MARYLAND 馬里蘭州
DELAWARE 特拉華州
Wilmington
威爾明頓
NEW JERSEY
新澤西州
Princeton 普林斯頓
Newark
New York 紐約
Delaware
Hudson
Bridgeport
Hartford
哈特福德
Long Island 長島
CONNECTICUT
RHODE ISLAND
Providence
普羅維登斯
Cambridge
MASSACHUSETTS
Boston
波士頓
Cape Cod
科德角
Manchester
曼徹斯特
Portland
波特蘭
MAINE
緬因州
NEW HAMPSHIRE
VERMONT
Atlantic Ocean
大西洋
0 100 200 km
公里

UNITED STATES OF AMERICA 美國
Pacific Ocean 太平洋
Atlantic Ocean 大西洋
Gulf of Mexico 墨西哥灣
Great Lakes 五大湖
Great Plains 大平原
落基山脈
ONTARIO 安大略省
WASHINGTON 華盛頓州
OREGON 俄勒岡州
CALIFORNIA 加利福尼亞州
NEVADA 內華達州
IDAHO 愛達荷州
MONTANA 蒙大拿州
WYOMING 懷俄明州
UTAH 猶他州
ARIZONA 亞利桑那州
COLORADO 科羅拉多州
NEW MEXICO 新墨西哥州
NORTH DAKOTA 北達科他州
SOUTH DAKOTA 南達科他州
NEBRASKA 內布拉斯加州
KANSAS 堪薩斯州
OKLAHOMA 俄克拉何馬州
TEXAS 得克薩斯州
MINNESOTA 明尼蘇達州
IOWA 艾奧瓦州
MISSOURI 密蘇里州
ARKANSAS 阿肯色州
LOUISIANA 路易斯安那州
WISCONSIN 威斯康星州
ILLINOIS 伊利諾伊州
MICHIGAN 密歇根州
INDIANA 印第安納州
OHIO 俄亥俄州
KENTUCKY 肯塔基州
TENNESSEE 田納西州
MISSISSIPPI 密西西比州
ALABAMA 亞拉巴馬州
GEORGIA 佐治亞州
FLORIDA 佛羅里達州
SOUTH CAROLINA 南卡羅來納州
NORTH CAROLINA 北卡羅來納州
VIRGINIA 弗吉尼亞州
WEST VIRGINIA
PENNSYLVANIA 賓夕法尼亞州
NEW YORK 紐約州
VERMONT 佛蒙特州
NEW HAMPSHIRE 新罕布什爾州
MASSACHUSETTS 馬薩諸塞州
RHODE ISLAND 羅得島州
CONNECTICUT 康涅狄格州
NEW JERSEY 新澤西州
MARYLAND 馬里蘭州
DELAWARE 特拉華州
MAINE 緬因州
NEW BRUNSWICK
NOVA SCOTIA 新斯科舍省
PRINCE EDWARD ISLAND
HAWAII 夏威夷州
Kauai 考愛島
Oahu 瓦胡島
Honolulu 火奴魯魯（檀香山）
Maui 毛伊島
Hawaii 夏威夷島
Vancouver Island 溫哥華島
Vancouver 溫哥華
Victoria 維多利亞
Kelowna 基洛納
Calgary 卡爾加里
Saskatoon 薩斯卡通
Regina 里賈納
Winnipeg 溫尼伯
Thunder Bay 桑德貝
Seattle 西雅圖
Spokane 斯波坎
Portland 波特蘭
Salem 塞勒姆
Eugene 尤金
Columbia 哥倫比亞河
Boise 博伊西
Idaho Falls 愛達荷福爾斯
Snake 斯內克河
Great Falls 大瀑布城
Billings 畢靈斯
Missouri 密蘇里河
Bismarck 俾斯麥
Fargo 法戈
Rapid City 拉皮德城
Sioux Falls 蘇福爾斯
Sacramento 薩克拉門托
San Francisco 聖弗朗西斯科（舊金山）
Berkeley 伯克利
San José 聖何塞
Fresno 弗雷斯諾
Mt. Whitney 惠特尼山
4418m
Sierra Nevada 內華達山脈
Reno 里諾
Death Valley 死谷
Las Vegas 拉斯韋加斯
Bakersfield 貝克斯菲爾德
Los Angeles 洛杉磯
Hollywood 好萊塢
San Diego 聖迭戈
Great Salt Lake 大鹽湖
Salt Lake City 鹽湖城
Provo 普羅沃
Grand Canyon 大峽谷
Colorado 科羅拉多河
Phoenix 菲尼克斯
Mesa 梅薩
Tucson 圖森
Cheyenne 夏延
Fort Collins 柯林斯堡
Mt. Elbert 埃爾伯特山
4399m
Denver 丹佛
Colorado Springs 科羅拉多斯普林斯
Santa Fe 聖菲
Albuquerque 阿爾伯克基
El Paso 埃爾帕索
Amarillo 阿馬里洛
Lubbock 拉伯克
Fort Worth 沃思堡
Dallas 達拉斯
Austin 奧斯汀
San Antonio 聖安東尼奧
Houston 休斯頓
Corpus Christi 科珀斯克里斯蒂
Rio Grande 格蘭德河
Oklahoma City 俄克拉何馬城
Tulsa 塔爾薩
Arkansas 阿肯色河
Wichita 威奇托
Topeka 托皮卡
Kansas City 堪薩斯城
Omaha 奧馬哈
Lincoln 林肯
Des Moines 得梅因
Cedar Rapids 錫達拉皮茲
Minneapolis 明尼阿波利斯
St. Paul 聖保羅
Duluth 德盧斯
Mississippi 密西西比河
Madison
Milwaukee 密爾沃基
Chicago 芝加哥
Springfield 斯普林菲爾德
St. Louis 聖路易斯
Indianapolis 印第安納波利斯
Lake Superior 蘇必利爾湖
Lake Michigan 密歇根湖
Lake Huron 休倫湖
Lake Erie 伊利湖
Lake Ontario 安大略湖
Detroit 底特律
Toronto 多倫多
Ottawa 渥太華
Montreal 蒙特利爾
Quebec City 魁北克
Saguenay 薩格奈
St. Lawrence 聖勞倫斯河
Moncton 蒙克頓
Fredericton 弗雷德里克頓
Saint John 聖約翰
Halifax 哈利法克斯
Buffalo 布法羅
Cleveland 克利夫蘭
Pittsburgh 匹茲堡
Ohio 俄亥俄河
Hudson 哈得孫河
Delaware 特拉華河
New York 紐約
Philadelphia 費城
Washington D.C. 華盛頓
Richmond 里士滿
Chesapeake Bay 切薩皮克灣
Virginia Beach 弗吉尼亞比奇
Norfolk 諾福克
Raleigh 羅利
Charlotte 夏洛特
Columbia 哥倫比亞
Charleston 查爾斯頓
Savannah 薩凡納
Appalachian Mountains 阿巴拉契亞山脈
Louisville 路易斯維爾
Lexington 列克星頓
Knoxville 諾克斯維爾
Nashville 納什維爾
Memphis 孟菲斯
Tennessee 田納西河
Little Rock 小石城
Jackson 傑克遜
Birmingham 伯明翰
Atlanta 亞特蘭大
Augusta 奧古斯塔
Montgomery 蒙哥馬利
Mobile 莫比爾
Baton Rouge 巴吞魯日
New Orleans 新奧爾良
Tallahassee 塔拉哈西
Jacksonville 傑克遜維爾
Orlando 奧蘭多
Tampa 坦帕
The Everglades 佛羅里達大沼澤地
Fort Lauderdale 勞德代爾堡
Miami 邁阿密
Key West 基韋斯特
Florida Keys 佛羅里達群島
international boundary 國際分界線
internal boundary 國內地區分界線
capital city 首都
over 1 million inhabitants 居民超過一百萬
town or city 城鎮或城市
major airport 主要機場
river 河流
lake 湖泊
peak or highest point 山峰或標高
metres 米
5000
3000
2000
1000
500
300
200
100
sea level 海平面
0
0 250 500 km 公里

Australia and New Zealand
澳大利亞和新西蘭

international boundary 國際分界線
internal boundary 國內地區分界線
capital city 首都
over 1 million inhabitants 居民超過一百萬
town or city 城鎮或城市
major airport 主要機場
river 河流
seasonal river 季節河
lake 湖泊
seasonal lake 季節湖
metres 米
5000
3000
2000
1000
500
300
200
100
0
sea level 海平面
peak or highest point 山峰或標高
0 500 1000 km 公里
Torres Strait 托雷斯海峽
Gulf of Carpentaria 卡奔塔利亞灣
Darwin 達爾文
Arnhem Land 阿納姆地
Timor Sea 帝汶海
Kimberley Plateau 金伯利高原
Fitzroy 菲茨羅伊河
NORTHERN TERRITORY 北部地區
Barkly Tableland 巴克利台地
Tanami Desert 塔納米沙漠
AUSTRALIA 澳大利亞
Great Sandy Desert 大沙沙漠
Alice Springs 艾麗斯斯普林斯
Macdonnell Ranges 麥克唐奈山脈
Lake Mackay (salt) 麥凱湖（鹹水湖）
Hamersley Range 哈默斯利嶺
1251m
Mt. Meharry 梅哈里山
Gibson Desert 吉布森沙漠
867m
Uluru (Ayers Rock) 烏盧魯岩（艾爾斯岩）
Simpson Desert 辛普森沙漠
Musgrave Ranges 馬斯格雷夫嶺
WESTERN AUSTRALIA 西澳大利亞州
SOUTH AUSTRALIA 南澳大利亞州
Lake Eyre (salt) 艾爾湖（鹹水湖）
Great Victoria Desert 維多利亞大沙漠
Lake Torrens (salt) 托倫斯湖（鹹水湖）
Nullarbor Plain 納拉伯平原
Flinders Range
Great Australian Bight 大澳大利亞灣
Spencer Gulf
Perth 珀斯
Indian Ocean 印度洋
Adelaide 阿德萊德
Coral Sea 珊瑚海
Great Barrier Reef 大堡礁
Cairns 凱恩斯
Townsville 湯斯維爾
Great Dividing Range 大分水嶺
QUEENSLAND 昆士蘭州
Grey Range
Sunshine Coast 陽光海岸
Brisbane 布里斯班
Gold Coast 戈爾德科斯特
Darling 達令河
NEW SOUTH WALES 新南威爾士州
Newcastle 紐卡斯爾
Sydney 悉尼
Lachlan 拉克倫河
Murrumbidgee
Wollongong 伍倫貢
Canberra 堪培拉
AUSTRALIAN CAPITAL TERRITORY (ACT) 澳大利亞首都直轄區
Murray 墨累河
2230m
Mt. Kosciusko 科西阿斯科山
Snowy Mts.
Gippsland
VICTORIA 維多利亞州
Geelong 吉朗
Melbourne 墨爾本
Bass Strait 巴斯海峽
Launceston
1617m
Mt. Ossa 奧薩山
Hobart 霍巴特
TASMANIA 塔斯馬尼亞州
Tasman Sea 塔斯曼海
Lord Howe Island (Australia) 豪勳爵島（澳大利亞）
Norfolk Island (Australia) 諾福克島（澳大利亞）
Pacific Ocean 太平洋
Kermadec Islands (New Zealand) 克馬德克群島（新西蘭）
North Cape 北角
North Island 北島
Auckland 奧克蘭
Hamilton 哈密爾頓
Bay of Plenty 普倫蒂灣
Tauranga 陶朗阿
Lake Taupo 陶波湖
2797m
Mt. Ruapehu 魯阿佩胡火山
NEW ZEALAND 新西蘭
Wellington 惠靈頓
Cook Strait
Mt. Cook 庫克峰
3764m
Southern Alps
Christchurch 克賴斯特徹奇
South Island 南島
Chatham Islands (New Zealand)

Reference Section Contents
參考信息目錄

Irregular verbs 不規則動詞

This appendix lists all the verbs with irregular forms that are included in the dictionary, except for those formed with a hyphenated prefix and the modal verbs (e.g. can, must). Irregular forms that are only used in certain senses are marked with an asterisk (e.g. *abode). Full information on usage, pronunciation, etc. is given at the entry. 本附錄列出詞典中收錄的全部不規則動詞，但由前綴帶連字符構成的動詞和情態動詞（如 can、must）除外。只用於某些義項的不規則形式以星號標示（如 *abode）。有關用法、讀音等細節在各詞條內予以説明。

Infinitive 不定式	Past tense 過去式	Past participle 過去分詞
abide	abided, *abode	abided, *abode
arise	arose	arisen
awake	awoke	awoken
babysit	babysat	babysat
bear	bore	borne
beat	beat	beaten
become	became	become
befall	befell	befallen
beget	begot, *begat	begot, *begotten
begin	began	begun
behold	beheld	beheld
bend	bent	bent
beseech	beseeched, besought	beseeched, besought
beset	beset	beset
bespeak	bespoke	bespoken
bet	bet	bet
betake	betook	betaken
bid[1]	bid	bid
bid[2]	bade, bid	bidden, bid
bind	bound	bound
bite	bit	bitten
bleed	bled	bled
blow	blew	blown, *blowed
break	broke	broken
breastfeed	breastfed	breastfed
breed	bred	bred
bring	brought	brought
broadcast	broadcast	broadcast
browbeat	browbeat	browbeaten
build	built	built
burn	burnt, burned	burnt, burned
burst	burst	burst
bust	bust, busted	bust, busted
buy	bought	bought
cast	cast	cast
catch	caught	caught
choose	chose	chosen
cleave	cleaved, *cleft, *clove	cleaved, *cleft, *cloven
cling	clung	clung
come	came	come
cost	cost, *costed	cost, *costed
creep	crept	crept
cut	cut	cut
deal	dealt	dealt
dig	dug	dug
dive	dived (*NAmE also* dove)	dived
draw	drew	drawn
dream	dreamt, dreamed	dreamt, dreamed
drink	drank	drunk
drip-feed	drip-fed	drip-fed
drive	drove	driven
dwell	dwelt, dwelled	dwelt, dwelled
eat	ate	eaten
fall	fell	fallen
feed	fed	fed
feel	felt	felt
fight	fought	fought
find	found	found
fit	fitted (*NAmE usually* fit)	fitted (*NAmE usually* fit)
flee	fled	fled
fling	flung	flung
floodlight	floodlit	floodlit
fly	flew, *flied	flown, *flied
forbear	forbore	forborne
forbid	forbade	forbidden
forecast	forecast, forecasted	forecast, forecasted
foresee	foresaw	foreseen
foretell	foretold	foretold
forget	forgot	forgotten
forgive	forgave	forgiven
forgo	forwent	forgone
forsake	forsook	forsaken
forswear	forswore	forsworn
freeze	froze	frozen
gainsay	gainsaid	gainsaid
get	got	got (*NAmE, spoken* gotten)
give	gave	given
go	went	gone, *been
grind	ground	ground
grow	grew	grown
hamstring	hamstrung	hamstrung
hang	hung, *hanged	hung, *hanged
hear	heard	heard
heave	heaved, *hove	heaved, *hove
hew	hewed	hewed, hewn
hide	hid	hidden
hit	hit	hit
hold	held	held
hurt	hurt	hurt
inlay	inlaid	inlaid
input	input, inputted	input, inputted
inset	inset	inset
intercut	intercut	intercut
interweave	interwove	interwoven
keep	kept	kept

Infinitive 不定式	Past tense 過去式	Past participle 過去分詞
kneel	knelt (*NAmE also* kneeled)	knelt (*NAmE also* kneeled)
knit	knitted, *knit	knitted, *knit
know	knew	known
lay	laid	laid
lead	led	led
lean	leaned (*BrE also* leant)	leaned (*BrE also* leant)
leap	leapt, leaped	leapt, leaped
learn	learnt, learned	learnt, learned
leave	left	left
lend	lent	lent
let	let	let
lie[1]	lay	lain
light	lit, *lighted	lit, *lighted
lose	lost	lost
make	made	made
mean	meant	meant
meet	met	met
miscast	miscast	miscast
mishear	misheard	misheard
mishit	mishit	mishit
mislay	mislaid	mislaid
mislead /ˌmɪsˈli:d/	misled /ˌmɪsˈled/	misled /ˌmɪsˈled/
misread /ˌmɪsˈri:d/	misread /ˌmɪsˈred/	misread /ˌmɪsˈred/
misspell	misspelled, misspelt	misspelled, misspelt
misspend	misspent	misspent
mistake	mistook	mistaken
misunderstand	misunderstood	misunderstood
mow	mowed	mown, mowed
offset	offset	offset
outbid	outbid	outbid
outdo	outdid	outdone
outgrow	outgrew	outgrown
output	output	output
outrun	outran	outrun
outsell	outsold	outsold
outshine	outshone	outshone
overcome	overcame	overcome
overdo	overdid	overdone
overdraw	overdrew	overdrawn
overeat	overate	overeaten
overfeed	overfed	overfed
overfly	overflew	overflown
overhang	overhung	overhung
overhear	overheard	overheard
overlay	overlaid	overlaid
overlie	overlay	overlain
overpay	overpaid	overpaid
override	overrode	overridden
overrun	overran	overrun
oversee	oversaw	overseen
oversell	oversold	oversold
overshoot	overshot	overshot
oversleep	overslept	overslept
overspend	overspent	overspent
overtake	overtook	overtaken
overthrow	overthrew	overthrown
overwrite	overwrote	overwritten

Infinitive 不定式	Past tense 過去式	Past participle 過去分詞
partake	partook	partaken
pay	paid	paid
plead	pleaded (*NAmE also* pled)	pleaded (*NAmE also* pled)
preset	preset	preset
proofread /ˈpru:fri:d/	proofread /ˈpru:fred/	proofread /ˈpru:fred/
prove	proved	proved (*also* proven *especially in NAmE*)
put	put	put
quit	quit (*BrE also* quitted)	quit (*BrE also* quitted)
read /ri:d/	read /red/	read /red/
rebuild	rebuilt	rebuilt
recast	recast	recast
redo	redid	redone
redraw	redrew	redrawn
rehear	reheard	reheard
remake	remade	remade
rend	rent	rent
rerun	reran	rerun
resell	resold	resold
reset	reset	reset
resit	resat	resat
restring	restrung	restrung
retake	retook	retaken
retell	retold	retold
rethink	rethought	rethought
rewind	rewound	rewound
rewrite	rewrote	rewritten
rid	rid	rid
ride	rode	ridden
ring[2]	rang	rung
rise	rose	risen
run	ran	run
saw	sawed	sawn (*NAmE also* sawed)
say	said	said
see	saw	seen
seek	sought	sought
sell	sold	sold
send	sent	sent
set	set	set
sew	sewed	sewn, sewed
shake	shook	shaken
shear	sheared	shorn, sheared
shed	shed	shed
shine	shone, *shined	shone, *shined
shit	shit, shat (*BrE also* shitted)	shit, shat (*BrE also* shitted)
shoe	shod	shod
shoot	shot	shot
show	showed	shown, *showed
shrink	shrank, shrunk	shrunk
shut	shut	shut
simulcast	simulcast	simulcast
sing	sang	sung
sink	sank, *sunk	sunk
sit	sat	sat
slay	slew	slain
sleep	slept	slept
slide	slid	slid
sling	slung	slung

Infinitive 不定式	Past tense 過去式	Past participle 過去分詞
slink	slunk	slunk
slit	slit	slit
smell	smelled (*BrE also* smelt)	smelled (*BrE also* smelt)
smite	smote	smitten
sow	sowed	sown, sowed
speak	spoke	spoken
speed	speeded, *sped	speeded, *sped
spell	spelt, spelled	spelt, spelled
spend	spent	spent
spill	spilled (*BrE also* spilt)	spilled (*BrE also* spilt)
spin	spun	spun
spit	spat (*also* spit *especially in NAmE*)	spat (*also* spit *especially in NAmE*)
split	split	split
spoil	spoiled (*BrE also* spoilt)	spoiled (*BrE also* spoilt)
spotlight	spotlit, *spotlighted	spotlit, *spotlighted
spread	spread	spread
spring	sprang (*NAmE also* sprung)	sprung
stand	stood	stood
stave	staved, *stove	staved, *stove
steal	stole	stolen
stick	stuck	stuck
sting	stung	stung
stink	stank, stunk	stunk
strew	strewed	strewed, strewn
stride	strode	—
strike	struck	struck (*NAmE also* stricken)
string	strung	strung
strive	strove, *strived	striven, *strived
sublet	sublet	sublet
swear	swore	sworn
sweep	swept	swept
swell	swelled	swollen, swelled
swim	swam	swum

Infinitive 不定式	Past tense 過去式	Past participle 過去分詞
swing	swung	swung
take	took	taken
teach	taught	taught
tear	tore	torn
telecast	telecast	telecast
tell	told	told
think	thought	thought
throw	threw	thrown
thrust	thrust	thrust
tread	trod	trodden, trod
typecast	typecast	typecast
typeset	typeset	typeset
unbend	unbent	unbent
underbid	underbid	underbid
undercut	undercut	undercut
undergo	underwent	undergone
underlie	underlay	underlain
underpay	underpaid	underpaid
undersell	undersold	undersold
understand	understood	understood
undertake	undertook	undertaken
underwrite	underwrote	underwritten
undo	undid	undone
unfreeze	unfroze	unfrozen
unwind	unwound	unwound
uphold	upheld	upheld
upset	upset	upset
wake	woke	woken
waylay	waylaid	waylaid
wear	wore	worn
weave	wove, *weaved	woven, *weaved
wed	wedded, wed	wedded, wed
weep	wept	wept
wet	wet, wetted	wet, wetted
win	won	won
wind[2] /waɪnd/	wound /waʊnd/	wound /waʊnd/
withdraw	withdrew	withdrawn
withhold	withheld	withheld
withstand	withstood	withstood
wring	wrung	wrung
write	wrote	written

Full forms 全寫	Short forms 縮寫	Negative short forms 縮寫否定式
***be* present tense 現在式**		
I am	I'm	I'm not
you are	you're	you aren't / you're not
he is	he's	he isn't / he's not
she is	she's	she isn't / she's not
it is	it's	it isn't / it's not
we are	we're	we aren't / we're not
you are	you're	you aren't / you're not
they are	they're	they aren't / they're not
***be* past tense 過去式**		
I was	—	I wasn't
you were	—	you weren't
he was	—	he wasn't
she was	—	she wasn't
it was	—	it wasn't
we were	—	we weren't
you were	—	you weren't
they were	—	they weren't
***have* present tense 現在式**		
I have	I've	I haven't / I've not
you have	you've	you haven't / you've not
he has	he's	he hasn't / he's not
she has	she's	she hasn't / she's not
it has	it's	it hasn't / it's not
we have	we've	we haven't / we've not
you have	you've	you haven't / you've not
they have	they've	they haven't / they've not
***have* past tense (all persons) 過去式（所有人稱）**		
had	I'd you'd etc.	hadn't
***do* present tense 現在式**		
I do	—	I don't
you do	—	you don't
he does	—	he doesn't
she does	—	she doesn't
it does	—	it doesn't
we do	—	we don't
you do	—	you don't
they do	—	they don't
***do* past tense (all persons) 過去式（所有人稱）**		
did	—	didn't

	be	***do***	***have***
present participle 現在分詞	being	doing	having
past participle 過去分詞	been	done	had

be, do, have

- The negative full forms are formed by adding **not**. 全寫否定式在上述動詞後加 not 構成。

- Questions in the present and past are formed by placing the verb before the subject. 把動詞置於主語前構成現在時和過去時的疑問式：
  - ▸ *am I?* *isn't he?* *was I?* *weren't we?*
    do I? *don't you?* *did I?* *didn't I?*
    have I? *hadn't they?* etc.

- Questions using the negative full form are more formal. 疑問句用全寫否定式較為正式：
  - ▸ *has he not?* *do you not?* etc.

- The short negative question form for **I am** is **aren't**. * I am 的否定疑問式的縮寫為 aren't:
  - ▸ *aren't I?*

- When **do** or **have** is used as a main verb, questions and negative statements can be formed with **do/does/doesn't** and **did/didn't**. * do 或 have 用作主要動詞時，疑問式和否定式可由 do/does/doesn't 和 did/didn't 構成：
  - ▸ *How did you do it?*
  - ▸ *I don't do any teaching now.*
  - ▸ *Do you have any money on you?*
  - ▸ *We didn't have much time.*

- The short forms *'ve*, *'s* and *'d* are not usually used when **have** is a main verb. 當 have 為主要動詞時，通常不用縮寫 've、's 和 'd:
  - ▸ *I have a shower every morning.*
  - ▸ NOT 不可說 ~~*I've a shower every morning.*~~

- The short form *'s* can be added to other subjects. 縮寫 's 可加在主語後：
  - ▸ *Sally's ill.* *The car's been damaged.*

- The **other tenses** of **be**, **do** and **have** are formed in the same way as those of other verbs. * be、do 和 have 的其他時態與其他動詞的時態構成相同：
  - ▸ *will be* *would be* *has been*
    will do *would do* *has done*
    will have *would have* *have had;* etc.

- The **pronunciation** of each form of **be**, **do** and **have** is given at its entry in the dictionary. 關於 be、do 和 have 各種形式的讀音，參見本詞典中相關詞條。

Verbs 動詞

Transitive and intransitive 及物動詞和不及物動詞

- ▸ *He sighed.* 他歎了口氣。
  ▸ *She cut her hand.* 她割傷了手。
  ▸ *The soup tastes salty.* 這湯鹹鹹的。

Each of these sentences has a subject (**he**, **she**, **the soup**) and a verb (**sigh**, **cut**, **taste**). 以上各句均有主語（he、she、the soup）和動詞（sigh、cut、taste）。

In the first sentence, **sigh** stands alone. Verbs like this are called INTRANSITIVE. 在第一句，sigh 單獨作謂語，這類動詞稱為不及物（intransitive）動詞。

In the second sentence, **cut** is TRANSITIVE because it is used with an object (**her hand**). 在第二句，cut 為及物（transitive）動詞，其後接賓語（her hand）。

In the third sentence, **taste** has no object but it cannot be used alone without an adjective. An adjective like **salty** that gives more information about the subject of a verb is called a COMPLEMENT. Verbs that take complements are called LINKING VERBS. 在第三句，taste 後無賓語，但不能無形容詞而單獨作謂語。像 salty 這類對動詞的主語加以說明的形容詞稱為補語（complement），後接補語的動詞稱為連繫動詞（linking verb）。

Verb codes 動詞代碼

- In the dictionary, grammatical codes at the start of each meaning show you whether a verb is always transitive or always intransitive, or whether it can be sometimes transitive and sometimes intransitive. 在本詞典中，義項開頭的語法代碼表明動詞是否總是及物或不及物，或有時及物、有時不及物。

The code [I] shows you that in this meaning **change** is always intransitive. 代碼 [I] 表示，在本義項中，change 總是不及物。

change 0━ /tʃeɪndʒ/ *verb, noun*
■ *verb*
▸ **BECOME/MAKE DIFFERENT**（使）變化 **1** 0━ [I] to become different 改變；變化：*Rick hasn't changed. He looks exactly the same as he did at school.* 里克一點兒沒變，他和上學時一模一樣。◇ *changing attitudes towards education* 不斷變化的對教育的看法 ◇ *Her life changed completely when she won the lottery.* 買彩票中獎後她的生活完全變了。 **2** 0━ [T] **~ sb/sth** to make sb/sth different 使不同：*Fame hasn't really changed him.* 名聲並沒有使他有絲毫改變。◇ *Computers have changed the way people work.* 計算機已改變了人的工作方式。**3** 0━ [I, T] to pass or make sb/sth pass from one state or form into another （使）變換，改換，變成：*Wait for the traffic lights to change.* 等待交通燈變換顏色。◇ **~ (from A) to/into B** *The lights changed from red to green.* 交通燈已由紅變綠。◇ *Caterpillars change into butterflies.* 毛蟲變成蝴蝶。◇ **~ sb/sth (from A) to/into B** *With a wave of her magic wand, she changed the frog into a handsome prince.* 她魔杖一揮，把青蛙變成了英俊的王子。

The code [T] shows you that in this meaning **change** is always transitive. 代碼 [T] 表示，在本義項中，change 總是及物。

The code [I, T] shows you that in this meaning **change** is sometimes intransitive and sometimes transitive. 代碼 [I, T] 表示，在本義項中，change 有時不及物、有時及物。

Transitive verbs are the most common type of verb. A verb that is always transitive in all its meanings is just marked *verb*, and no other verb code is given. 及物動詞是最常見的動詞類型。所有義項均為及物用法的動詞只標註 verb，不再標上其他代碼。

Verb frames 動詞框架

- Transitive verbs can take different types of object – a noun, phrase or clause. Both transitive and intransitive verbs can combine with different prepositions or adverbs. Different linking verbs can take either adjectives or nouns as complements. 及物動詞可後接不同類型的賓語——名詞、短語或從句。及物動詞和不及物動詞均可與不同的介詞或副詞組合。不同的連繫動詞可後接形容詞或名詞作補語。

In the dictionary, the different patterns (or 'verb frames') in which a verb can be used are shown in **bold type**, usually just before an example showing that pattern in context. 在本詞典中，動詞的各種用法模式（或"動詞框架"）以**粗體**字表示，通常置於顯示該模式的示例前。

pro·vide /prəˈvaɪd/ *verb*
1 to give sth to sb or make it available for them to use 提供；供應；給予 SYN **supply**：**~ sth** *The hospital has a commitment to provide the best possible medical care.* 這家醫院承諾要提供最好的醫療服務。◇ *The report was not expected to provide any answers.* 不要指望這個報告能提供什麼答案。◇ *Please answer questions in the space provided.* 請在留出的空白處答題。◇ **~ sth for sb** *We are here to provide a service for the public.* 我們來這裏是為公眾服務。◇ **~ sb with sth** *We are here to provide the public with a service.* 我們來這裏是為公眾服務。◇ **~ sth to sb** *The charity aims to provide assistance to people in need.* 這家慈善機構的宗旨是向貧困者提供幫助。
2 ~ that … (*formal*) (of a law or rule 法律或規則) to state that sth will or must happen 規定 SYN **stipulate**：*The final section provides that any work produced for the company is thereafter owned by the company.* 最後一節規定，此後為公司創作的一切作品均為本公司所有。➲ see also PROVISION

If a particular verb, or one particular meaning of a verb, is always used in the same pattern, this pattern is shown in **bold type** before the definition. 如果某特定動詞或動詞的某特定義項總是使用同一模式，則將該模式以**粗體**字標示於釋義前。

Intransitive verbs [I] 不及物動詞

- Intransitive verbs do not take an object. When they are used alone after a subject, there is no verb frame. 不及物動詞後無賓語。當它們單獨用於主語後時，沒有動詞框架。

The example showing this use will usually appear first, before any other patterns and examples. 顯示這一用法的示例通常出現於其他模式和示例之前。

shiver /ˈʃɪvə(r)/ *verb, noun*
■ ***verb*** [I] (of a person 人) to shake slightly because you are cold, frightened, excited, etc. 顫抖，哆嗦（因寒冷、恐懼、激動等）：*Don't stand outside shivering—come inside and get warm!* 別站在外面凍得打哆嗦了，進來暖暖身子吧！◇ *He shivered at the thought of the cold, dark sea.* 那寒冷黑暗的大海，他想想都嚇得發抖。◇ **~ with sth** *to shiver with cold/excitement/pleasure, etc.* 冷得發抖、激動得發抖、高興得發抖等

Some intransitive verbs are often used with a particular preposition or adverb. This pattern will be shown in **bold type**, usually before an example. 有些不及物動詞常與特定介詞或副詞連用。這種模式以**粗體**字表示，通常置於示例前。

- Some intransitive verbs are always or usually used with a preposition or adverb, but not always the same one. These are often verbs showing movement in a particular direction. 有些不及物動詞總是或通常與介詞或副詞連用，但不總是用同一介詞或副詞。這類動詞常表示向特定方向運動。

▶ *A runaway car came **hurtling towards** us.*
一輛失控的汽車朝我們飛馳而來。

▶ *A group of swans **floated by**.*
一群天鵝緩緩游過。

In the dictionary this use will be shown by the frame + **adv./prep.** If a preposition or adverb is often used, but not always, there will be brackets round the frame: (+ **adv./prep.**) 在本詞典中，這一用法以框架 + adv./prep. 表示。如果常常但不總是使用介詞或副詞，該框架將置於括號內：(+ adv./prep.)

hur·tle /ˈhɜːtl; *NAmE* ˈhɜːrtl/ *verb* [I] **+ adv./prep.** to move very fast in a particular direction（向某個方向）飛馳，猛衝：*A runaway car **came hurtling** towards us.* 一輛失控的汽車朝我們飛馳而來。

Transitive verbs [T] 及物動詞

- Transitive verbs must have an object. The object can be a noun or a pronoun, a noun phrase or a clause. 及物動詞後一定接賓語，這個賓語可以是名詞、代詞、名詞短語或從句。

For information on verbs that take a clause as the object, see page R9. 有關以從句作賓語的動詞信息，另見 R9 頁。

The frames used to show a transitive verb with a noun, pronoun or noun phrase as object are **~ sb**, **~ sth** and **~ sb/sth**. 以名詞、代詞或名詞短語作賓語的及物動詞用框架 ~ sb、~ sth 和 ~ sb/sth 表示。

~ sb is used when the object is a person. 當賓語為人時，用框架 ~ sb。

ac·com·mo·date AW /əˈkɒmədeɪt; *NAmE* əˈkɑːm-/ *verb*
1 [T] **~ sb** to provide sb with a room or place to sleep, live or sit 提供住宿（或膳宿、座位等）：*The hotel can accommodate up to 500 guests.* 這家旅館可供 500 位旅客住宿。**2** [T] **~ sb/sth** to provide enough space for sb/sth 容納；提供空間：*Over 70 minutes of music can be accommodated on one CD.* 一張激光唱片可以容納 70 多分鐘的音樂。**3** [T] **~ sth** (*formal*) to consider sth, such as sb's opinion or a fact, and be influenced by it when you are deciding what to do or explaining sth 考慮到；顧及：*Our proposal tries to accommodate the special needs of minority groups.* 我們的提案盡量照顧到少數群體的特殊需要。

~ sb/sth is used when the object can be a person or a thing. 當賓語可以是人也可以是事物時，用框架 ~ sb/sth。

~ sth is used when the object is a thing. 當賓語為事物時，用框架 ~ sth。

As with intransitive verbs, some transitive verbs are often used with a preposition or an adverb. 與不及物動詞一樣，某些及物動詞常與介詞或副詞連用。

If there is a wide range of possible prepositions or adverbs a frame such as **sb/sth + adv./prep.** is used. 如果可以連用的介詞或副詞有很多，則使用 sb/sth + adv./prep. 之類的框架。

hack /hæk/ *verb, noun*
■ *verb* **1** [T, I] to cut sb/sth with rough, heavy blows 砍；劈： **~ sb/sth + adv./prep.** *I hacked the dead branches off.* 我把枯樹枝砍掉了。◇ *They were hacked to death as they tried to escape.* 他們企圖逃走時被砍死了。◇ *We had to* ***hack our way*** *through the jungle.* 我們不得不在叢林中闢路穿行。◇ **+ adv./prep.** *We hacked away at the bushes.* 我們劈開灌木叢。 **2** [T] **~ sb/sth + adv./prep.** to kick sth roughly or without control 猛踢： *He hacked the ball away.* 他把球一腳踢開。 **3** *(computing* 計) [I, T] to secretly find a way of looking at and/or changing information on sb else's computer system without permission 非法侵入（他人的計算機系統）： **~ into sth** *He hacked into the bank's computer.* 他侵入了這家銀行的計算機。◇ **~ sth** *They had hacked secret data.* 他們竊取了保密數據。

If a particular preposition or adverb is used, then it is given in the frame. 如果使用特定的介詞或副詞，框架內會標明該介詞或副詞。

Transitive verbs with two objects 後接雙賓語的動詞

■ Some verbs, like **sell** and **buy**, can be used with two objects. This is shown by the frame **~ sb sth**. 有些動詞，如 sell 和 buy，可接兩個賓語。這種情況以框架 ~ sb sth 表示：

▸ *I sold Jim a car.* 我賣給吉姆一輛車。

▸ *I bought Mary a book.* 我買給瑪麗一本書。

You can often express the same idea by using the verb as an ordinary transitive verb and adding a prepositional phrase starting with **to** or **for**. 要表達相同的意思，常常可將該動詞作一般及物動詞，後加一個以 to 或 for 開頭的介詞短語：

▸ *I* ***sold*** *a car* ***to*** *Jim.*
我賣了一輛車給吉姆。

▸ *I* ***bought*** *a book* ***for*** *Mary.*
我買了一本書給瑪麗。

These will be shown by the frames **~ to sb** and **~ for sb**. 這些情況將以框架 ~ to sb 和 ~ for sb 表示。

bake 0→ /beɪk/ *verb*
1 0→ [T, I] to cook food in an oven without extra fat or liquid; to be cooked in this way（在烤爐裏）烘烤；焙： **~ (sth)** *baked apples* 烤蘋果 ◇ *the delicious smell of baking bread* 烤製麪包的香味 ◇ **~ sth for sb** *I'm baking a birthday cake for Alex.* 我在給亞歷克斯烤生日蛋糕。◇ **~ sb sth** *I'm baking Alex a cake.* 我在給亞歷克斯烤蛋糕。 ➲ COLLOCATIONS at COOKING ➲ VISUAL VOCAB page V27

A pair of examples, with different frames, shows the same idea expressed in two different ways. 兩個一組的示例使用不同的框架，顯示兩種不同方法表達相同的意思。

Linking verbs 連繫動詞

■ ▸ *His voice sounds hoarse.*
他的聲音聽起來沙啞。

▸ *Elena became a doctor.*
埃琳娜成了醫生。

In these sentences the linking verb (**sound**, **become**) is followed by a complement, an adjective (**hoarse**) or a noun phrase (**a doctor**) that tells you more about the subject. 在上述例句中，連繫動詞（sound、become）後跟補語，即對主語作補充説明的形容詞（hoarse）或名詞短語（a doctor）。

Verbs that have an adjective as the complement have the frame **+ adj.**, and verbs with a noun phrase as the complement have the frame **+ noun**. Verbs that can take either an adjective or a noun phrase as the complement may have the frame **+ adj./noun**, or the two frames may be shown separately with an example for each. 以形容詞為補語的動詞用框架 + adj. 標示，以名詞短語為補語的動詞用框架 + noun 標示。以形容詞或名詞短語為補語的動詞用框架 + adj./noun 標示，或將這兩個框架置於各自的示例前分別標示。

be·come 0→ /bɪˈkʌm/ *verb* (**be·came** /bɪˈkeɪm/, **be·come**)
1 0→ *linking verb* to start to be sth 開始變得；變成；成為： **+ adj.** *It was becoming more and more difficult to live on his salary.* 他越來越難以靠他的工資維持生計了。◇ *It soon became apparent that no one was going to come.* 很快就很清楚，沒人會來。◇ *She was becoming confused.* 她開始糊塗了。◇ **+ noun** *She became queen in 1952.* 她於 1952 年成為女王。◇ *The bill will become law next year.* 該議案將於明年成為法律。

The linking verb **become** can be used with either an adjective or a noun phrase. 連繫動詞 become 既可與形容詞連用，也可與名詞短語連用。

There are also verbs that take both an object and a complement. 也有一些動詞既接賓語，也接補語：

▶ *She considered herself lucky.* 她覺得自己幸運。

▶ *They elected him president.* 他們選了他當主席。

The complement (**lucky**, **president**) tells you more about the object (**herself**, **him**) of the verb. The frames for these verbs are **~ sb/sth + adj.**, **sb/sth + noun** or **sb/sth + adj./noun**. 補語（lucky、president）是對動詞賓語（herself、him）的補充説明。這些動詞的框架為 ~ sb/sth + adj.、sb/sth + noun 或 sb/sth + adj./noun。

Verbs used with 'that clauses' 後接 that 從句的動詞

■ The frame **~ that ...** shows that a verb is followed by a clause beginning with **that**. 框架 ~ that ... 表示動詞後接以 that 開頭的從句：

▶ *She **replied that** she would prefer to walk.* 她回答説她寧願走路。

However, it is not always necessary to use the word **that** itself. 不過，有時 that 可以省略：

▶ *I **said that** he would come.* 我説他會來。

▶ *I **said** he would come.* 我説他會來。

These two sentences mean the same. In the dictionary they are shown by the frame **~ (that) ...** and a single example is given, using brackets. 上面兩個句子意思相同。在本詞典中，用框架 ~ (that) ... 標示，並給出一個帶括號的示例：

▶ ***I said (that)** he would come.* 我説他會來。

Some verbs can be used with both a noun phrase and a 'that clause'. The frame for verbs used like this is **~ sb that ...** or **~ sb (that) ...**. 有些動詞可同時與名詞短語和 that 從句連用，此類動詞用框架 ~ sb that ... 或 ~ sb (that) ... 標示：

▶ *Can you **remind me that** I need to buy some milk?* 你提醒我買牛奶好嗎？

▶ *I **told her (that)** I would be late.* 我告訴她我會遲到。

Verbs used with 'wh- clauses' 後接 wh- 從句的動詞

■ A 'wh-clause' (or phrase) is a clause or phrase beginning with one of the following words: **wh**ich, **wh**at, **wh**ose, **wh**y, **wh**ere, **wh**en, **wh**o, **wh**om, how, if, **wh**ether. * wh- 從句（或短語）指以下列詞開頭的從句或短語：which、what、whose、why、where、when、who、whom、how、if、whether:

▶ *I **wonder what** the new job will be like.* 我想知道那份新工作會是什麼樣。

▶ *He doesn't **care how** he looks.* 他不介意自己的外表。

▶ *Did you **see which** way they went?* 你看到他們往哪邊走了嗎？

In the dictionary, verbs used like this have a frame such as **~ how**, **what**, **etc. ...** or **~ why**, **where**, **etc. ...**. 在本詞典中，此類動詞用框架 ~ how, what, etc. ... 或 ~ why, where, etc. ... 標示。

The particular 'wh-words' given in each frame will be words that are typical for that verb, but the 'etc.' shows that other 'wh- clauses' are possible. 每個框架中特別給出的 wh- 詞為該動詞通常後接的詞，而 etc. 表示也可以後接其他 wh- 從句。

won·der /ˈwʌndə(r)/ *verb, noun*
■ ***verb*** **1** [T, I] to think about sth and try to decide what is true, what will happen, what you should do, etc. 想知道；想弄明白；琢磨： **~ who, where, etc. ...** *I wonder who she is.* 我在想她到底是誰。◇ *I was just beginning to wonder where you were.* 我剛才正琢磨你上哪兒了呢。◇ **~ (about sth)** *'Why do you want to know?' 'No particular reason. I was just wondering.'* "你為什麼想要知道？" "沒有特殊原因。我就是想搞清楚。" ◇ *We were wondering about next April for the wedding.* 我們尋思着下個四月舉行婚禮可好。◇ **+ speech** *'What should I do now?' she wondered.* "我現在該怎麼辦呢？" 她自忖道。
2 [T] **~ if, whether ...** used as a polite way of asking a question or asking sb to do sth（禮貌地提問或請人做事時説）：*I wonder if you can help me.* 不知您是否能幫我的忙？◇ *I was wondering whether you'd like to come to a party.* 不知您能否來參加聚會。

If there is no 'etc.' in the frame, then this verb or meaning can only take the particular 'wh-words' that are listed. 如果框架中沒有 etc.，那麼該動詞或義項只能使用所列出的 wh- 詞。

Some verbs can be used with both a noun phrase and a 'wh-clause'. Verbs used like this have a frame such as **~ sb where**, **when**, **etc. ...**. 有些動詞可同時與名詞短語和 wh- 從句連用，此類動詞用框架 ~ sb where, when, etc. ... 標示：

▶ *I **asked him where** the library was.* 我問他圖書館在哪兒。

▶ *I **told her when** the baby was due.* 我告訴她寶寶預計什麼時候出生。

▶ *He **teaches his students how** to research a subject thoroughly.* 他教學生如何透徹地研究一個課題。

Verbs with infinitive phrases
後接不定式短語的動詞

- **Eat** and **to eat** are both the infinitive form of the verb. **Eat** is called a BARE INFINITIVE and **to eat** is called a TO-INFINITIVE. Most verbs that take an infinitive are used with the to-infinitive. The frame for these verbs is **~ to do sth**. * eat 和 to eat 均為動詞不定式，eat 稱作原形不定式（bare infinitive），to eat 稱作帶 to 不定式（to-infinitive）。大多數後接不定式的動詞後都用帶 to 不定式。此類動詞用框架 ~ to do sth 標示：
  - ▸ *The goldfish* ***need to be fed.*** 金魚需要餵飼。
  - ▸ *She never* ***learned to read.*** 她從未學會閱讀。

Some verbs can be used with both a noun phrase and a to-infinitive. The frame for these is **~ sb to do sth**, **~ sth to do sth** or **~ sb/sth to do sth**. The noun phrase can be the object of the main verb, 有些動詞可同時與名詞短語和帶 to 不定式連用。此類動詞用框架 ~ sb to do sth、~ sth to do sth 或 ~ sb/sth to do sth 標示。名詞短語可作主要動詞的賓語：

- ▸ *Can you persuade* ***Sheila*** *to chair the meeting?* 你可以説服希拉來主持這次會議嗎？

or the noun phrase and the infinitive phrase together can be the object. 或名詞短語加動詞不定式短語作賓語：

- ▸ *I expected* ***her to pass*** *her driving test first time.* 我預計她第一次就能通過駕照考試。
- ▸ *We'd love* ***you to come*** *and visit us.* 非常歡迎你來探訪我們。

Only two groups of verbs are used with a bare infinitive (without **to**). One is the group of MODAL VERBS (or MODAL AUXILIARIES). These are the special verbs like **can**, **must** and **will** that go before a main verb and show that an action is possible, necessary, etc. These verbs have special treatment in the dictionary and are labelled *modal verb*. 只有兩類動詞與原形不定式（不帶 to）連用。一類為情態動詞（modal verb）或情態助動詞（modal auxiliary）。這類動詞（如 can、must 和 will）置於主要動詞前，表示動作的可能、必要等。本詞典將這類動詞特別處理，並標示為 modal verb。

A small group of ordinary verbs, for example **see** and **hear**, can be used with a noun phrase and a bare infinitive. The frame for these is **~ sb do sth**, **~ sth do sth** or **~ sb/sth do sth**. 一小類普通動詞（如 see 和 hear）可同時與名詞短語和原形不定式連用，此類動詞用框架 ~ sb do sth、~ sth do sth 或 ~ sb/sth do sth 標示：

- ▸ *She* ***watched him eat*** *his lunch.* 她看着他吃午餐。
- ▸ *Did you* ***hear the phone ring*** *just then?* 那時你聽到電話鈴響了嗎？

Verbs with '–*ing* phrases'
後接 –ing 短語的動詞

- An '-ing phrase' is a phrase containing a PRESENT PARTICIPLE (or GERUND). The present participle is the form of the verb that ends in *–ing*, for example **doing**, **eating** or **catching**. Sometimes the '*-ing* phrase' consists of a present participle on its own. The frame for a verb that takes an '*-ing* phrase' is **~ doing sth**. * -ing 短語指含有現在分詞（present participle）或動名詞（gerund）的短語。現在分詞是以 -ing 結尾的動詞形式，如 doing、eating 或 catching。有時 -ing 短語只含一個現在分詞。後接 -ing 短語的動詞用框架 ~ doing sth 標示：
  - ▸ *She never stops talking!* 她總是喋喋不休！
  - ▸ *I started looking for a job two years ago.* 我兩年前開始找工作。

Some verbs can be used with both a noun phrase and an '-ing phrase'. The frame for this is **~ sb doing sth**, **~ sth doing sth** or **~ sb/sth doing sth**. The noun phrase can be the object of the main verb, 有些動詞可同時與名詞短語和 -ing 短語連用。此類動詞用框架 ~ sb doing sth、~ sth doing sth 或 ~ sb/sth doing sth 標示。名詞短語可作主要動詞的賓語：

- ▸ *His comments set* ***me*** *thinking.* 他的話讓我開始思考。
- ▸ *I can smell* ***something*** *nice cooking.* 我聞到燒菜的香味。

or the noun phrase and the '*-ing* phrase' together can be the object. 或名詞短語加 -ing 短語作賓語：

- ▸ *I hate* ***him joking*** (= the fact that he jokes) *about serious things.* 我討厭他拿正經事開玩笑。

In this pattern, you can replace **him** with the possessive pronoun **his**. 在此句型中可用物主代詞 his 取代 him:

▸ *I hate **his joking** about serious things.*
我討厭他拿正經事開玩笑。

However, sentences with a possessive pronoun sound very formal and the object pronoun is more common, especially in American English. In cases where the verb itself is formal and the possessive pronoun may well be used, this is shown in the dictionary entry. 不過，用物主代詞的句子聽起來非常正式，用賓格代詞更常見，尤其在美式英語中。在動詞本身是正式用語的情況下，完全可以用物主代詞，此用法見於本詞典的詞條中。

Verbs with direct speech 與直接引語連用的動詞

- Verbs like **say**, **answer** and **demand** can be used either to report what somebody has said using a 'that clause' or to give their exact words in DIRECT SPEECH, using quotation marks (' '). Verbs that can be used with direct speech have the frame + **speech**. Compare these two sentences. * say、answer 和 demand 之類的動詞既可用 that 從句轉述某人的話，也可用直接引語（direct speech）加引號引用原話。可與直接引語連用的動詞用框架 + speech 標示。比較下列句子：

  ▸ **+ speech** *'It's snowing,' she said.*
  "下雪了。" 她說。

  ▸ **~ (that) …** *She said (that) it was snowing.*
  她說下雪了。

  Some verbs can be used with both direct speech and a noun phrase, to show who is being spoken to. The frame for this is ~ **sb** + **speech**. 有些動詞可同時與直接引語和名詞短語連用，引出說話的對象。此類動詞用框架 ~ sb + speech 標示：

  ▸ *'Tom's coming to lunch,' she **told him**.*
  她對他說："湯姆要來吃午飯。"

Verbs in the passive 用於被動語態的動詞

- Most transitive verbs can be used in the passive. 大多數及物動詞可用於被動語態：

  ▸ *Jill's behaviour **annoyed me**.*
  吉爾的行為令我惱火。

  ▸ ***I was annoyed by** Jill's behaviour.*
  我被吉爾的行為惹惱了。

If a verb can be active or passive, the same verb frame is used. If the verb is often passive, there will be an example in the passive. 如果動詞可用於主動語態或被動語態，則用同一框架標示。如果動詞常用於被動語態，則給出被動語態的示例。

con·firm AW /kən'fɜːm; *NAmE* -'fɜːrm/ *verb* **1** to state or show that sth is definitely true or correct, especially by providing evidence （尤指提供證據來）證實，證明，確認： **~ sth** *Rumours of job losses were later confirmed.* 裁員的傳言後來得到了證實。◇ *His guilty expression confirmed my suspicions.* 他內疚的表情證實了我的猜疑。◇ *Please write to confirm your reservation* (= say that it is definite). 預訂後請來函確認。◇ **~ (that)** … *Has everyone confirmed (that) they're coming?* 他們是不是每個人都確定了一定會來？◇ **~ what/when, etc.** … *Can you confirm what happened?* 你能證實一下發生了什麼事嗎？◇ **it is confirmed that** … *It has been confirmed that the meeting will take place next week.* 已經確定會議將於下個星期舉行。 **2** **~ sth | ~ sb (in sth)** to make sb feel or believe sth even more strongly 使感覺更強烈；使確信： *The walk in the mountains confirmed his fear of heights.* 在山裏步行使他更加確信自己有恐高症。 **3** to make a position, an agreement, etc. more definite or official; to establish sb/sth firmly 批准（職位、協議等）；確認；認可： **~ sth** *After a six-month*

If a pattern is *only* used in the passive, then the frame is put in the passive. This happens especially with verbs that take 'it' and a 'that clause'. 如果一個句型只能用於被動語態，那麼該框架採用被動語態的形式。這種情況尤見於同 it 和 that 從句連用的動詞。

If a transitive verb cannot be used in the passive, the label [no passive] appears before the definition. 如果及物動詞不能用於被動語態，則在釋義前標示 [no passive]。

Verbs in different patterns 不同句型的動詞

- Many verbs, for example **watch**, can be used in a number of different ways. 許多動詞如 watch 可有不同的用法：

  ▸ **~ sb/sth do sth** *I watched him eat.*
  我看着他吃了東西。

  ▸ **~ sb/sth doing sth** *I watched him eating.*
  我看着他吃東西。

  ▸ **~ sb/sth** *I watched the pianist's left hand.*
  我觀察鋼琴師的左手。

  ▸ **~ what, how, etc. …** *I watched how the pianist used her left hand.*
  我觀察鋼琴師如何用她的左手。

  The dictionary entry for each verb shows the different ways in which it can be used by giving a range of example sentences. The frame before each example shows what type of grammatical pattern is being used. When an example follows another one illustrating the same pattern, the frame is not repeated. 本詞典中每個動詞詞條均有一系列示例表明不同用法，每個示例前的框架表明語法模式。用法相同的示例框架不重複。

Sometimes patterns can combine with each other to form a longer pattern. This happens especially with patterns involving particular prepositions or adverbs; and sometimes there is a choice of two or three different prepositions or adverbs. 有時幾個句型可相互結合形成較長的模式，這尤見於涉及特定的介詞或副詞的模式；有時有兩三個不同的介詞或副詞供選用：

- **~ sth** *We shared the pizza.*
  我們把那份比薩餅分着吃了。
- **~ sth out** *We shared out the pizza.*
  我們把那份比薩餅分着吃了。
- **~ sth among sb** *We shared the pizza among the four of us.*
  我們四個人把那份比薩餅分着吃了。
- **~ sth between sb** *We shared the pizza between the four of us.*
  我們四個人把那份比薩餅分着吃了。
- **~ sth out among sb** *We shared the pizza out among the four of us.*
  我們四個人把那份比薩餅分着吃了。
- **~ sth out between sb** *We shared the pizza out between the four of us.*
  我們四個人把那份比薩餅分着吃了。

In cases like this the dictionary does not always give a separate frame and example for each different combination. It may use brackets to show where part of a long frame can be left out, and slashes to show where there is a choice between two or three different words in the frame. 此類情況下，本詞典不總是為每個不同的組合單獨給出框架和示例，而可能用括號標示長框架中可省略的部份，用斜線號標示框架中有兩三個單詞供選擇：

▸ DIVIDE BETWEEN PEOPLE 分給若干人 **2** ⊶ [T] **~ sth (out) (among/between sb)** to divide sth between two or more people 分配；分攤：*We shared the pizza between the four of us.* 我們四個人把那份比薩餅分着吃了。➲ see also JOB-SHARING, POWER-SHARING

The frame **~ (sb)**, **~ (sth)** or **~ (sb/sth)** may also be used, where a verb can be used without an object (that is, it can be intransitive), but is more commonly used with a noun phrase as object. In these cases the more common, transitive, use, is given in the first example(s), and any intransitive examples are placed after that. 也使用框架 ~ (sb)、~ (sth) 或 ~ (sb/sth)，其中的動詞後可不接賓語（即可以是不及物動詞），但更常用名詞短語作賓語。此類情況下，首先給出更常見的及物用法示例，不及物用法示例列在其後：

broad·cast ⊶ /ˈbrɔːdkɑːst; *NAmE* -kæst/ *verb, noun*
■ *verb* (**broad·cast**, **broad·cast** or **broad·cast**, **broad·casted**)
1 ⊶ [T, I] **~ (sth)** to send out programmes on television or radio 播送（電視或無線電節目）；廣播：*The concert will be **broadcast live** (= at the same time as it takes place) tomorrow evening.* 明晚的音樂會將現場直播。◇ *They began broadcasting in 1922.* 他們於 1922 年開播。
➲ COLLOCATIONS at TELEVISION

Sb and **sth** may also appear within brackets within longer frames, for example to show a verb that can take a preposition, adverb or 'that clause' either with or without a noun phrase as another object. * sb 和 sth 也可能出現於較長框架的括號中，如表示某個動詞可與介詞、副詞或 that 從句連用，這動詞後既可以接名詞短語作另一個賓語，也可以不接：

warn ⊶ /wɔːn; *NAmE* wɔːrn/ *verb*
1 ⊶ [T, I] to tell sb about sth, especially sth dangerous or unpleasant that is likely to happen, so that they can avoid it 提醒注意（可能發生的事）；使警惕：**~ sb** *I tried to warn him, but he wouldn't listen.* 我設法提醒過他，可他就是不聽。◇ *If you're thinking of getting a dog, **be warned**—they take a lot of time and money.* 如果你想養條狗，有話說在前頭，那可既費時間又費錢。◇ **~ (sb) about/against sb/sth** *He warned us against pickpockets.* 他提醒我們要提防小偷。◇ **~ (sb) of sth** *Police have warned of possible delays.* 警方已經通知交通可能受阻。◇ **~ (sb) that ...** *She was warned that if she did it again she would lose her job.* 她被警告說如果她再這樣做就會丟掉工作。◇ **~ sb what, how, etc. ...** *I had been warned what to expect.* 有人事先告訴過我要出什麼事。◇ **~ (sb) + speech** *'Beware of pickpockets,' she warned (him).* "當心扒手。" 她提醒（他）道。

Phrasal verbs 短語動詞

What are phrasal verbs? 什麼是短語動詞？

- ▸ *Jan **turned down** the chance to work abroad.* 簡回絕了到國外工作的機會。
  ▸ *Buying that new car has really **eaten into** my savings.* 買那輛新車的確耗掉我部份存款。
  ▸ *I don't think I can **put up with** his behaviour much longer.* 我想我再也不能容忍他的行為了。

PHRASAL VERBS (sometimes called MULTI-WORD VERBS) are verbs that consist of two, or sometimes three, words. The first word is a verb and it is followed by an adverb (turn **down**) or a preposition (eat **into**) or both (put **up with**). These adverbs or prepositions are sometimes called PARTICLES. 短語動詞（有時也叫多詞動詞 multi-word verb）指由兩個、有時是三個詞組成的動詞。第一個詞為動詞，其後接副詞（如 turn down）或介詞（如 eat into）或副詞加介詞（如 put up with）。此類副詞或介詞有時稱作小品詞（particle）。

- In this dictionary, phrasal verbs are listed at the end of the entry for the main verb in a section marked **PHR V**. They are listed in alphabetical order of the particles following them. 在本詞典中，短語動詞列在主要動詞詞條後段標有 **PHR V** 的地方，按後接小品詞的字母順序排列：

> **PHR V** **ˌfight ˈback (against sb/sth)** to resist strongly or attack sb who has attacked you 奮力抵抗；還擊：*Don't let them bully you. Fight back!* 別讓他們欺侮你。要還擊！◇ *It is time to fight back against street crime.* 現在是打擊街頭犯罪行為的時候了。 **ˌfight sth↔ˈback/ˈdown** to try hard not to do or show sth, especially not to show your feelings 忍住，抑制住（尤指情感）：*I was fighting back the tears.* 我強忍住眼淚。◇ *He fought down his disgust.* 他強忍住心裏的厭惡。 **ˌfight sb/sth↔ˈoff** to resist sb/sth by fighting against them/it 抵抗；擊退：*The jeweller was stabbed as he tried to fight the robbers off.* 珠寶商在試圖抵抗強盜時被刺傷了。 **ˌfight ˈout sth | ˌfight it ˈout** to fight or argue until an argument has been settled 以鬥爭方式解決；辯論出結果：*The conflict is still being fought out.* 仍在通過戰鬥解決這次衝突。◇ *They hadn't reached any agreement so we left them to fight it out.* 他們未有達成協議，所以我們讓他們爭出個結果。

Meaning of phrasal verbs 短語動詞的含義

- ▸ *He **sat down** on the bed.* 他坐到牀上。

The meaning of some phrasal verbs, such as **sit down**, is easy to guess because the verb and the particle keep their usual meaning. However, many phrasal verbs have idiomatic meanings that you need to learn. The separate meanings of **put**, **up** and **with**, for example, do not add up to the meaning of **put up with** (= tolerate). 有些短語動詞的含義很容易推斷，如 sit down，因為動詞和小品詞都保持通常的意思。但許多短語動詞卻具有習語的意思，須通過學習才知道，如 put、up 和 with 各自的意思加起來並非 put up with（容忍；忍受）的意思。

- Some particles have particular meanings that are the same when they are used with a number of different verbs. 有些小品詞具有特定的含義，與不同的動詞連用時本身意思不變：
  ▸ *I didn't see the point of **hanging around** waiting for him, so I went home.* 我覺得沒必要閒蕩着等他，就回家去了。
  ▸ *I wish you wouldn't leave all those books **lying around**.* 我希望你不要再把那些書到處亂放。

Around adds the meaning of 'with no particular purpose or aim' and is also used in a similar way with many other verbs, such as **play**, **sit** and **wait**. * around 增加了"無一定目的或目標"的含義，亦可以同樣的方式與其他許多動詞如 play、sit、wait 連用。

- The meaning of a phrasal verb can sometimes be explained with a one-word verb. However, phrasal verbs are frequently used in spoken English and, if there is a one-word equivalent, it is usually more formal in style. 短語動詞的含義有時可用另一單個動詞表達。不過，短語動詞常用於口語中，而含義相同的單個動詞通常較正式：
  ▸ *I wish my ears didn't **stick out** so much.* 真希望我的耳朵沒那麼招風。
  ▸ *The garage **projects** five metres beyond the front of the house.* 車庫在房子的正面延伸出五米。

Both **stick out** and **project** have the same meaning – 'to extend beyond a surface' – but they are very different in style. **Stick out** is used in informal contexts, and **project** in formal or technical contexts. * stick out 和 project 含義相同，均有突出、伸出之意，但語體大不相同。stick out 用於非正式語境，project 則作正式用語或術語。

Grammar of phrasal verbs
短語動詞的語法

■ Phrasal verbs can be TRANSITIVE (they take an object) or INTRANSITIVE (they have no object). Some phrasal verbs can be used in both ways. 短語動詞可以是及物（transitive），帶有賓語，也可以是不及物（intransitive），不帶賓語。有些短語動詞用於及物或不及物均可：

▶ *For heaven's sake **shut** her **up**. (transitive)*
行行好，讓她住口吧。（及物）

▶ *He told me to **shut up**. (intransitive)*
他叫我閉嘴。（不及物）

■ INTRANSITIVE phrasal verbs are written in the dictionary without **sb** (somebody) or **sth** (something) after them. This shows that they do not have an object. 在本詞典中，不及物短語動詞後沒有 sb（某人）或 sth（某物），表明其後不接賓語：

> **ˌeat ˈout** 🔑 to have a meal in a restaurant, etc. rather than at home 上館子吃飯；在外用餐：*Do you feel like eating out tonight?* 你今晚想下館子嗎？

Eat out is intransitive, and the two parts of the verb cannot be separated by any other word. * eat out 為不及物短語動詞，動詞和小品詞之間不能插進任何單詞。You can say 可說：

▶ *Shall we eat out tonight?*
我們今晚上館子好嗎？
BUT NOT 不可說 *~~Shall we eat tonight out?~~*

■ In order to use TRANSITIVE phrasal verbs correctly, you need to know where to put the object. With some phrasal verbs (often called SEPARABLE verbs), the object can go either between the verb and the particle or after the particle. 要正確使用及物短語動詞，必須知道賓語的位置。有些短語動詞（常稱作可分動詞 separable verb）的賓語既可置於動詞與小品詞之間，也可置於小品詞之後：

▶ *She **tore** the letter **up**.* 她把信撕碎了。
▶ *She **tore up** the letter.* 她把信撕碎了。

■ When the object is a long phrase, it usually comes after the particle. 賓語為較長的短語時，通常置於小品詞之後：

▶ *She **tore up** all the letters he had sent her.*
她把他寄給她的信都撕碎了。

■ When the object is a pronoun (for example *it standing for 'the letter'*), it must always go between the verb and the particle. 賓語為代詞時（如 it 代表 the letter），必須置於動詞與小品詞之間：

▶ *She read the letter and then **tore** it **up**.*
她看過信以後就把它撕毀了。

■ In the dictionary, verbs that are separable are written like this. 在本詞典中，可分的短語動詞標示為：
tear sth ↔ up

■ The double arrow between the object and the particle shows that the object may come either before or after the particle. 賓語與小品詞之間的雙箭頭表示賓語可置於小品詞之前，也可置於小品詞之後：

> **ˌcall sth↔ˈoff** 🔑 to cancel sth; to decide that sth will not happen 取消；停止進行：*to call off a deal/trip/strike* 取消交易／旅行／罷工 ◇ *They have called off their engagement* (= decided not to get married). 他們已經解除婚約。◇ *The game was called off because of bad weather.* 比賽因天氣惡劣被取消。

You can say 可說：

▶ *They **called** the deal **off**.*
他們取消了交易。
AND 和 *They **called off** the deal.*
他們取消了交易。

■ With other phrasal verbs (sometimes called INSEPARABLE verbs), the two parts of the verb cannot be separated by an object. 其他短語動詞（有時也叫不可分動詞 inseparable verb）的賓語不能置於動詞和小品詞之間：

▶ *I didn't really **take to** her husband.*
我對她的丈夫不是很有好感。
NOT 不可說 *~~I didn't really **take** her husband **to**.~~*

▶ *I didn't really **take to** him.*
我對他不是很有好感。
NOT 不可說 *~~I didn't really **take** him **to**.~~*

In the dictionary, verbs that are inseparable are written like this. 在本詞典中，不可分的短語動詞標示為：
take to sb

When you see **sb** or **sth** after the two parts of a phrasal verb, and there is no double arrow, you know that they cannot be separated by an object. 短語動詞後有 sb 或 sth，而且無雙箭頭，說明賓語不能置於動詞和小品詞之間：

> **ˌrun ˈinto sb** (*informal*) to meet sb by chance 偶然遇見，碰到（某人）：*Guess who I ran into today!* 猜猜我今天碰見誰了！

You can say 可說：

▶ *I **ran into** Joe yesterday.* 我昨天碰見喬。
BUT NOT 不可說 *~~I ran Joe into.~~*

- There are a few phrasal verbs in which the two parts of the verb must be separated by the object. 有少數短語動詞的動詞和小品詞之間必須加入賓語。You can say 可說：
  - ▸ *They changed the plans and **messed** everyone **around**.* 他們改變了計劃，給大家添了麻煩。 BUT NOT 不可說 ~~*They changed the plans and **messed around** everyone.*~~

- In the dictionary, these verbs are written like this. 在本詞典中，這類短語動詞標示為：
  mess sb around

  When you see **sb** or **sth** between the two parts of a phrasal verb and there is no double arrow, you know that they must be separated by the object. 短語動詞的動詞和小品詞之間有 sb 或 sth，而且無雙箭頭，說明賓語必須要置於兩者之間。

- Some transitive phrasal verbs can be made passive. 有些及物短語動詞可用於被動語態：
  - ▸ *The deal **has been called off**.* 交易取消了。

  When this is common, you will find an example at the dictionary entry. 如果此用法常見，在本詞典的詞條中有示例說明。

Phrasal verbs used with phrases and clauses 與短語和從句連用的短語動詞

Like other verbs, some phrasal verbs can be used with another phrase or clause. The different types of clause and phrase are explained on pages R9–11. When a phrasal verb can be used with a particular type of clause or phrase, an example is given in the dictionary entry, labelled with a special frame. 與其他動詞一樣，有些短語動詞可與另一短語或從句連用。不同類型的從句和短語見 R9–11 頁的說明。如果短語動詞可與某種類型的從句或短語連用，本詞典相關詞條中有示例予以說明，並以特別框架標示：

~ that	*We **found out** later **that** we had been at the same school.* 後來我們才弄清楚我們是校友。
~ how, what, etc ...	*I can't **figure out how** to do this.* 我弄不懂這事怎麼做。
~ to do sth	*It didn't **occur to** her **to ask** for help.* 她沒想到請人幫忙。
~ doing sth	*I didn't **bargain on finding** Matthew there as well.* 我沒想到馬修也在那裏。
+ speech	***'Help!'** he **cried out**.* "救命！" 他喊道。

Related nouns 相關名詞

A particular phrasal verb may have a noun related to it. This noun will be mentioned at the verb entry. 短語動詞可能與某個名詞相關，該名詞將在動詞詞條內提及：

ˌbreak ˈin 🔑 to enter a building by force 強行進入；破門而入：*Burglars had broken in while we were away.* 我們不在家時，竊賊闖進屋裏了。➲ related noun BREAK-IN **ˌbreak sb/sth ˈin** **1** to train sb/sth in sth new that they must do 訓練某人／某物；培訓：*to break in new recruits* 訓練新兵 ◇ *The young horse was not yet broken in* (= trained to carry a rider). 那匹剛長成的馬還沒被馴服。 **2** to wear sth, especially new shoes, until they become comfortable 把…穿得合身，使舒適自如（尤指新鞋） **ˌbreak ˈin (on sth)** to interrupt or disturb sth 打斷；攪擾：*She longed to break in on their conversation but didn't want to appear rude.* 她很想打斷他們的談話，但又不願顯得粗魯。◇ **+ speech** *'I didn't do it!' she broke in.* "不是我幹的！" 她插嘴說。 **ˌbreak ˈinto sth** **1** 🔑 to enter a building by force; to open a car, etc. by force 強行闖入；撬開（汽車等）：*We had our car broken into last week.* 我們的車上週被撬了。➲ related noun BREAK-IN **2** to begin laughing, singing, etc. suddenly 突然開始（笑、唱等）：*As the President's car drew up, the crowd broke into loud applause.* 總統的座駕停下時，人群中爆發出熱烈的掌聲。

ˌbreak ˈout 🔑 (of war, fighting or other unpleasant events 戰爭、打鬥等不愉快事件) to start suddenly 突然開始；爆發：*They had escaped to America shortly before war broke out in 1939.* *1939 年戰爭爆發前不久他們逃到了美國。◇ *Fighting had broken out between rival groups of fans.* 雙方球迷發生了打鬥。◇ *Fire broke out during the night.* 夜間突然發生了火災。➲ related noun OUTBREAK **ˌbreak ˈout (of sth)** to escape from a place or situation 逃離（某地）；擺脫（某狀況）：*Several prisoners broke out of the jail.* 幾名囚犯越獄了。◇ *She needed to break out of her daily routine and do something exciting.* 她需要從日常事務中解脫出來，找點有意思的事做。➲ related noun BREAKOUT

A noun is often related in meaning to only one or two of the phrasal verbs using a particle. **Break-in** is related to **break in** and the first meaning of **break into sth**, but not to **break sb/sth in** or **break in (on sth)**. **Breakout** is related to **break out (of sth)**, whereas the noun **outbreak** relates to **break out**.
一個名詞在意義上通常只與一個或兩個含小品詞的短語動詞相關。break-in 與 break in 以及 break into sth 的第一義相關，但與 break sb/sth in 或 break in (on sth) 不相關。breakout 與 break out (of sth) 相關，而名詞 outbreak 與 break out 相關。

Nouns and adjectives 名詞和形容詞

Nouns 名詞

Countable and uncountable 可數名詞和不可數名詞

The two biggest groups of nouns are COUNTABLE nouns (or COUNT nouns) and UNCOUNTABLE nouns (also called UNCOUNT nouns or MASS nouns). Most countable nouns are words for separate things that can be counted, like **apples**, **books** or **teachers**. Uncountable nouns are usually words for things that are thought of as a quantity or mass, like **water** or **time**. 最大的兩類名詞是可數名詞（countable noun，或稱具數名詞 count noun）和不可數名詞（uncountable noun，也稱不具數名詞 uncount noun 或整體名詞 mass noun）。多數可數名詞為可以數算的可分事物，如 apple（蘋果）、book（書）或 teacher（教師）。不可數名詞通常指以量計算或作為整體的事物，如 water（水）或 time（時間）。

However, there are some nouns in English that you might expect to be countable but which are not. For example, **furniture**, **information** and **equipment** are all uncountable nouns in English, although they are countable in some other languages. 不過，英語中一些名詞可能會被認為是可數的，其實卻不是。如 furniture（傢具）、information（信息）和 equipment（設備）。雖然這些詞在其他一些語言裏是可數的，但是在英語中為不可數名詞。

Countable nouns [C] 可數名詞

A countable noun has a singular form and a plural form. When it is singular, it must always have a DETERMINER (a word such as **a**, **the**, **both**, **each**) in front of it. In the plural it can be used with or without a determiner. 可數名詞有單、複數兩種形式。作單數時，前面一定要有限定詞（determiner），如 a、the、both、each 等；作複數時，前面有無限定詞均可：

- *I'm having **a** driving **lesson** this afternoon.*
  我今天下午上駕駛課。
- *I've had **several lessons** already.*
  我已經上了幾課。
- ***Lessons** cost £20 an hour.*
  每小時的課需付 20 英鎊。

Countable nouns are the most common type of noun. If they have only one meaning, or if all the meanings are countable, they are just marked *noun*. For nouns that have a number of meanings, some of which are not countable, each meaning that is countable is marked [C]. 可數名詞是最常見的一類名詞。如果只有一個含義或所有含義均為可數，就只標註 noun；如果有幾個含義，有些含義為不可數，則每個可數的含義都標註 [C]。

Uncountable nouns [U] 不可數名詞

An uncountable noun has only one form, not a separate singular and plural. It can be used with or without a determiner. 不可數名詞只有一種形式，無單、複數之分，前面有或沒有限定詞均可：

- *Can we make **space** for an extra chair?*
  我們能不能騰個地方再放一把椅子？
- *There isn't **much space** in this room.*
  這房間沒有多大的空間。

If an uncountable noun is the subject of a verb, the verb is singular. 如果不可數名詞是動詞的主語，該動詞用單數：

- *Extra money **has been found** for this project.*
  已有額外的款項供這個項目之用。

With nouns such as **furniture**, **information** and **equipment**, as with many other uncountable nouns, you can talk about amounts of the thing or separate parts of the thing by using phrases like **a piece of**, **three items of**, **some bits of**. Nouns like **piece**, **item** and **bit** are called PARTITIVES when used in this way. 像 furniture、information、equipment 一類的名詞與其他許多不可數名詞一樣，可用 a piece of、three items of、some bits of 等短語來表示量或件數；piece、item 和 bit 之類的名詞作此用法時稱為量詞（partitive）：

- *I picked up **some information** that might interest you.*
  我注意到一些信息，或許你會感興趣。
- *I picked up **two pieces of information** that might interest you.*
  我注意到兩則消息，或許你會感興趣。

Plural nouns [pl.] 複數名詞

Some nouns are always plural and have no singular form. Nouns that refer to things that have two parts joined together, for example **glasses**, **jeans** and **scissors**, are often plural nouns. You can usually also talk about **a pair of jeans**, **a pair of scissors**, etc. 有些名詞總是複數，無單數形式。由兩部份組成的東西，如 glasses（眼鏡）、jeans（牛仔褲）和 scissors（剪刀）等均常為複數名詞；通常亦可用 a pair of jeans、a pair of scissors 等表示：

- *I'm going to buy **some** new **jeans**.*
  我要買新的牛仔褲。
- *I'm going to buy **a** new **pair of jeans**.*
  我要買一條新牛仔褲。

An example is given in the entry for the noun to show that it can be used in this way.
在名詞詞條中有示例表明該名詞可以這樣用。

Some plural nouns, such as **police** and **cattle**, look as if they are singular. Nouns like this usually refer to a group of people or animals of a particular type, when they are considered together as one unit. They also take a plural verb. 有些複數名詞，如 police（警方）和 cattle（牛），看上去似乎是單數。這類名詞作為一個整體看待時，通常指特定的人或動物群體，謂語動詞用複數：

- ***Police are searching** for a man who escaped from Pentonville prison today.*
  警方正在搜捕一名今天從本頓維爾監獄逃跑的犯人。
- *The **cattle are fed** on barley and grass.*
  這些牛餵大麥和草。

Singular nouns [sing.] 單數名詞

Some nouns are always singular and have no plural form. Many nouns like this can be used in only a limited number of ways. For example, some singular nouns must be or are often used with a particular determiner in front of them or with a particular preposition after them. The correct determiner or preposition is shown before the definition. In the case of **fillip** the pattern given is **a ~ (to/for sth)**. 有些名詞總是單數，無複數形式，許多這樣的名詞只有幾種有限的用法。例如，有些單數名詞必須或常常前接某個特定限定詞或後接某個特定介詞。適用的限定詞或介詞列於釋義前。如 fillip 一詞顯示的模式為 a ~ (to/for sth)：

fil·lip /ˈfɪlɪp/ *noun* [sing.] **a ~ (to/for sth)** (*formal*) a thing or person that causes sth to improve suddenly 起推動作用的人（或事物）**SYN** **boost**：*A drop in interest rates gave a welcome fillip to the housing market.* 降低利率給房屋市場帶來利好刺激。

Nouns with singular or plural verbs 與單數或複數動詞連用的名詞

[sing.+sing./pl. v.] [C+sing./pl. v.] [U+sing./pl. v.]

In British English some singular nouns (or countable nouns in their singular form) can be used with a plural verb as well as a singular one. Nouns like this usually refer to a group of people, an organization, or a place, and can be thought of either as the organization, place or group (singular) or as many individual people (plural). In the dictionary an example is usually given to show agreement with a singular and a plural verb. 在英式英語中有些單數名詞（或可數名詞的單數形式）既可與單數動詞連用，也可與複數動詞連用。這類名詞通常指人的集體、機構或地點等，既可視為一個整體（單數），也可視為許多個體（複數）。本詞典中通常給出這類名詞與單數動詞和複數動詞一致的示例：

- *The **Vatican has/have** issued a further statement this morning.*
  梵蒂岡今早發表了進一步的聲明。
- *The **committee has/have** decided to dismiss him.* 委員會已決定將他免職。

These nouns are marked [sing.+sing./pl. v.] if they are always singular in form, and [C+sing./pl. v.] if they also have a plural form. The plural form always agrees with a plural verb. 這些名詞如果總是單數形式，則標示為 [sing.+sing./pl. v.]；如果亦有複數形式，則標示為 [C+sing./pl. v.]。複數形式用複數動詞。

NOTE In American English the singular form of these nouns must take a singular verb.
在美式英語中，這些名詞的單數形式必須用單數動詞：

- *The government **says it is** committed to tax reform.* 政府承諾要進行稅制改革。

Some uncountable nouns can be used with a plural verb as well as a singular one. These include some nouns that end in **-s** and therefore look as though they are plural, 有些不可數名詞既可與單數動詞連用，也可與複數動詞連用，其中包括某些以 -s 結尾而看上去像是複數的名詞：

▶ *His **whereabouts are/is** still unknown.* 他仍然下落不明。

and some nouns that refer to a group of people or things and can be thought of either as a group (singular) or as many individual people or things (plural). 另有一些名詞，既可視為集體（單數），也可視為許多個體（複數）：

▶ ***Personnel is/are** currently reviewing pay scales.* 人事部現在正審核工資標準。

Patterns with nouns 與名詞連用的句型

- Many nouns are followed by a particular preposition, adverb or other pattern. 許多名詞後接特定介詞、副詞或其他句型：
  ▶ *My comments were taken as an allegation of negligence.* 我的評論被看成指稱有人疏忽。

The correct pattern to use is shown in **bold type**, either before the definition or before an individual example. Where any part of a pattern is optional, it is given in brackets. 正確的句型在釋義或單個示例前用**粗體**字顯示，可省略的部份放在括號內。

al·le·ga·tion /ˌæləˈɡeɪʃn/ *noun* a public statement that is made without giving proof, accusing sb of doing sth that is wrong or illegal（無證據的）說法，指控 **SYN accusation**：*to investigate/deny/withdraw an allegation* 調查／否認／撤回指控 ◇ **~ of sth** *Several newspapers made allegations of corruption in the city's police department.* 有幾家報紙聲稱該市警察部門腐敗。◇ **~ (of sth) against sb** *allegations of dishonesty against him* 關於他不誠實的多種說法 ◇ **~ about sb/sth** *The committee has made serious allegations about interference in its work.* 委員會嚴正指控其工作受到了干涉。◇ **~ that …** *an allegation that he had been dishonest* 一種關於他不誠實的說法 ➲ SYNONYMS at CLAIM

The example sentences show the patterns in use. 例句表明句型的應用。

Adjectives 形容詞

- Many adjectives can be used both before a noun, 許多形容詞既可用於名詞前：
  ▶ *a serious expression* 嚴肅的表情
  ▶ *grey hair* 灰白的頭髮

  and after a LINKING VERB. 也可用於連繫動詞後：
  ▶ *She looked serious.* 她一臉嚴肅。
  ▶ *His hair had turned grey.* 他的頭髮已變得灰白。

- However, some adjectives, or particular meanings of adjectives, are always used before a noun, and cannot be used after a linking verb. They are called ATTRIBUTIVE adjectives. 但是，有些形容詞或形容詞的某些特定含義只是用於名詞前，不能用於連繫動詞後。這類形容詞稱作定語（attributive）形容詞：
  ▶ *the chief reason* 主要原因

- Others are only used after a linking verb. They are called PREDICATIVE adjectives. 另一些形容詞只用於連繫動詞後，這類形容詞稱作表語（predicative）形容詞：
  ▶ *The baby is awake.* 嬰兒醒着。

➔ For more information about LINKING VERBS, look at pages R8–9. 關於連繫動詞的詳細説明，見 R8–9 頁。

[only before noun] [usually before noun]

Attributive adjectives are labelled [only before noun]. The label [usually before noun] is used when it is rare but possible to use the adjective after a verb. 定語形容詞標註為 [only before noun]；標註為 [usually before noun] 的形容詞可用於連繫動詞後，但罕見。

Senses **1** and **3** can only be used before a noun. 第 1 義和第 3 義只能用於名詞前。

con·tin·en·tal /ˌkɒntɪˈnentl; *NAmE* ˌkɑːn-/ *adj., noun*
■ *adj.* **1** (also **Continental**) [only before noun] (*BrE*) of or in the continent of Europe, not including Britain and Ireland 歐洲大陸的（不包括英國和愛爾蘭）：*a popular continental holiday resort* 受歡迎的歐洲大陸度假勝地 ◇ *Britain's continental neighbours* 英國的歐洲大陸鄰國 **2** (*BrE*) following the customs of countries in western and southern Europe 隨（西、南歐國家）大陸風俗的：*a continental lifestyle* 西、南歐大陸的生活方式 ◇ *The shutters and the balconies make the street look almost continental.* 活動護窗和陽台使這條街看起來頗具歐洲大陸風格。**3** [only before noun] connected with the main part of the N American continent 北美大陸的：*Prices are often higher in Hawaii than in the continental United States.* 夏威夷的物價常常比美國大陸高。

Sense **2** has no grammar label because it can be used both before a noun and after a linking verb. 第 2 義沒有語法標註，因為既可用於名詞前也可用於連繫動詞後。

[not before noun]
[not usually before noun]

Predicative adjectives, labelled [not before noun], are used only after a linking verb, never before a noun. The label [not usually before noun] is used when it is rare but possible to use the adjective before a noun. 表語形容詞標註為 [not before noun]，只能用於連繫動詞後，不能用於名詞前；標註為 [not usually before noun] 的形容詞可用於名詞前，但罕見。

The grammar label straight after the *adj.* label shows that both meanings must be used after a linking verb. 在 adj. 標記後的語法標識表示兩個義項都必須用於連繫動詞後。

rife /raɪf/ *adj.* [not before noun] **1** if sth bad or unpleasant is **rife** in a place, it is very common there （壞事）盛行，普遍 **SYN** **widespread**：*It is a country where corruption is rife.* 這是個腐敗成風的國家。◇ *Rumours are rife that he is going to resign.* 到處都在傳，說他要辭職了。 **2 ~ (with sth)** full of sth bad or unpleasant 充斥，充滿（壞事）：*Los Angeles is rife with gossip about the stars' private lives.* 洛杉磯盛傳明星私生活的流言蜚語。

[after noun]

A few adjectives always follow the noun they describe. This is shown in the dictionary by the label [after noun]. 少數形容詞總是置於所修飾的名詞之後，此用法在本詞典中用 [after noun] 標示：

gal·ore /ɡəˈlɔː(r)/ *adj.* [after noun] (*informal*) in large quantities 大量；很多：*There will be games and prizes galore.* 將有很多遊戲和獎品。

Collocation 詞語搭配

What is collocation?
什麼是詞語搭配？

COLLOCATION is the way in which particular words tend to occur or belong together.
詞語搭配指比較典型或規範的詞語組合。
For example, you can say 比如，可說：

▶ *Meals will be served outside on the terrace, **weather permitting**.*
天氣許可的話，可在餐館露天座用餐。
BUT NOT 不可說 ~~*Meals will be served outside on the terrace, weather allowing.*~~

Both these sentences seem to mean the same thing: **allow** and **permit** have very similar meanings. But in this combination only **permitting** is correct. It COLLOCATES with **weather** and **allowing** does not. 上述兩句含義似乎相同。allow 和 permit 意思非常相似，但在這一組合裏只有 permitting 才是正確的，因為它可與 weather 搭配，allowing 卻不能。

Types of collocation 詞語搭配類型

In order to write and speak natural and correct English, you need to know, for example
要說寫自然和正確的英語，需要知道：

- which adjectives are used with a particular noun 哪些形容詞可與某個名詞搭配
- which nouns a particular adjective is used with 某個形容詞可與哪些名詞搭配
- which verbs are used with a particular noun 哪些動詞可與某個名詞搭配
- which adverbs are used to intensify a particular adjective 哪些副詞可用以加強某個形容詞的詞義

Collocation in this dictionary
本詞典的詞語搭配

To find out which adjectives to use with a particular noun, look at the examples at the entry for the noun. Typical adjectives used with the noun are separated by a slash (/).
查找哪些形容詞可與某個名詞搭配，見該名詞詞條的示例。與該名詞搭配的典型形容詞用斜線號 (/) 隔開：

Can you say '**pink** wine'?
可以說 pink wine 嗎？

wine 0-π /waɪn/ *noun, verb*
■ ***noun*** **1** 0-π [U, C] an alcoholic drink made from the juice of GRAPES that has been left to FERMENT. There are many different kinds of wine. 葡萄酒： *a bottle of wine* 一瓶葡萄酒 ◇ *a glass of **dry/sweet wine*** 一杯乾 / 甜葡萄酒 ◇ ***red/rosé/white wine*** 紅 / 玫瑰紅 / 白葡萄酒 ◇ ***sparkling wine*** 汽酒 ➲ see also TABLE WINE

(No, **rosé** 不能，該說 rosé)

If you look up an adjective you will see what nouns are commonly used with it. 查看形容詞詞條便可知道通常有哪些名詞可與之搭配：

Which words can be used with the adjective **heady**?
哪些詞可與形容詞 heady 搭配？

heady /ˈhedi/ *adj.* (**head·ier**, **headi·est**) **1** [usually before noun] having a strong effect on your senses; making you feel excited and confident 強烈作用於感官的；使興奮的；使有信心的 SYN **intoxicating** ： *the heady days of youth* 令人陶醉的年輕時代 ◇ *the heady scent of hot spices* 辣味香料的刺鼻氣味 ◇ *a heady mixture of desire and fear* 既期待又害怕的複雜心情 ➲ SYNONYMS at EXCITING

(**days**, **scent**, **mixture**)

Look at the examples in a noun entry to find out what verbs can be used with it. 查看名詞詞條中的示例便可得知哪些動詞可與之搭配：

Which verbs are used with **mortgage**?
哪些動詞可與 mortgage 搭配？

mort·gage /ˈmɔːɡɪdʒ; *NAmE* ˈmɔːrɡ-/ *noun, verb*
■ ***noun*** (also *informal* **ˌhome ˈloan**) a legal agreement by which a bank or similar organization lends you money to buy a house, etc., and you pay the money back over a particular number of years; the sum of money that you borrow 按揭（由銀行等提供房產抵押借款）；按揭貸款： *to **apply for/take out/pay off a mortgage*** 申請 / 取得 / 還清抵押貸款 ◇ *mortgage rates* (= of interest) 按揭貸款利率 ◇ *a mortgage on the house* 一項房產按揭 ◇ *a mortgage of £60 000* * 6 萬英鎊的按揭貸款 ◇ *monthly mortgage payments* 房貸月供 ➲ COLLOCATIONS at HOUSE

(**apply for**, **take out**, **pay off**)

If you look up an adjective, you will see which adverbs you can use to intensify it. 查看形容詞詞條便可知道哪些副詞可用以加強其詞義：

Strongly or bitterly disappointed?
用 strongly 還是 bitterly 修飾 disappointed？

dis·ap·point·ed /ˌdɪsəˈpɔɪntɪd/ *adj.* upset because sth you hoped for has not happened or been as good, successful, etc. as you expected 失望的；沮喪的；失意的：**~ (at/by sth)** *They were **bitterly disappointed** at the result of the game.* 他們對比賽結果極為失望。◇ *I was disappointed by the quality of the wine.* 這酒的質量令我失望。◇ **~ (in/with sb/sth)** *I'm disappointed in you—I really thought I could trust you!* 你真讓我失望，我原以為可以相信你的！◇ *I was very disappointed with myself.* 我對自己感到非常失望。◇ **~ (to see, hear, etc.)** *He was disappointed to see she wasn't at the party.* 看到她沒來參加晚會，他感到很失望。◇ **~ (that …)** *I'm disappointed (that) it was sold out.* 全都賣完了，我感到很失望。◇ **~ (not) to be …** *She was disappointed not to be chosen.* 她沒有被選中感到很沮喪。

(**bitterly**)

Important collocations are printed in bold type within the examples. If the meaning of the collocation is not obvious there is a short explanation after it in brackets. 重要的詞語搭配在示例中用**粗體**字顯示；如果搭配的含義並非一目瞭然，其後的括號內有簡短註釋。

hoping you will be lucky
希望自己運氣好

having unexpected luck
非常幸運，喜出望外

luck /lʌk/ *noun, verb*
■ ***noun*** [U] **1** good things that happen to you by chance, not because of your own efforts or abilities 好運；幸運；僥幸：***With (any) luck,*** *we'll be home before dark.* 如果一切順利的話，我們可在天黑前回到家。◇ (*BrE*) ***With a bit of luck,*** *we'll finish on time.* 但願我們運氣好，能夠準時完成。◇ *So far I have had no luck with finding a job.* 我找工作一直不走運。◇ ***I could hardly believe my luck*** *when he said yes.* 聽他說行，我幾乎不敢相信自己會這麼走運。◇ *It was **a stroke of luck** that we found you.* 真巧我們找到了你。◇ ***By sheer luck*** *nobody was hurt in the explosion.* 萬幸的是，沒有人在爆炸中受傷。◇ *We **wish her luck** in her new career.* 我們祝願她在新的事業中一帆風順。◇ *You're **in luck*** (= lucky)—*there's one ticket left.* 你運氣不錯，還剩一張票。◇ *You're **out of luck**. She's not here.* 真不巧，她不在。◇ *What a piece of luck!* 運氣真好！➲ see also BEGINNER'S LUCK **2** chance; the force that causes good or bad things to

not being lucky
運氣不好

being lucky
運氣好

hoping someone else will be lucky 希望別人運氣好

Idioms 習語

What are idioms? 什麼是習語？

An idiom is a phrase whose meaning is difficult or sometimes impossible to guess by looking at the meanings of the individual words it contains. For example, the phrase **be in the same boat** has a literal meaning that is easy to understand, but it also has a common idiomatic meaning. 習語是一種短語，僅憑其中各個詞的意思很難、有時甚至不可能推斷出其含義。如短語 be in the same boat 既有一個容易理解的字面含義，也有一個常見的習語含義：

▸ *I found the job difficult at first. But we were all in the same boat; we were all learning.* 開始的時候我覺得這工作挺難的，但我們處境相同，大家都在學習。

Here, **be in the same boat** means 'to be in the same difficult or unfortunate situation'. 這裏的 be in the same boat 意為處於同樣困境、境遇相同。

Some idioms are imaginative expressions such as proverbs and sayings. 有些習語是富有想像力的表達方式，如諺語和格言：

▸ *Too many cooks spoil the broth.* (= If too many people are involved in something, it will not be well done.) 廚師多了燒壞湯。(人多手雜反壞事；人多添亂)

If the expression is well known, part of it may be left out. 如果表達方式為人所熟悉，其中一部份便可以省略：

▸ *Well, I knew everything would go wrong – it's the usual story of too many cooks!* 唉，我就知道事情會搞砸，常言道，人多手雜！

Other idioms are short expressions that are used for a particular purpose. 另外一些習語比較短，用以表達特定的意思：

▸ *Hang in there!* 堅持下去！(used to encourage somebody in a difficult situation 用以鼓勵身陷困境的人)

▸ *Get lost!* 滾開！(a rude way of saying 'go away' 粗魯地叫人離開)

Many idioms, however, are not vivid in this way. They are considered as idioms because their form is fixed. 但也有許多習語並非如此生動，它們被視為習語是因為形式固定：

▸ *for certain* 肯定地

▸ *in any case* 不管怎樣

Idioms in the dictionary 本詞典中的習語

Idioms are defined at the entry for the first 'full' word (a noun, a verb, an adjective or an adverb) that they contain. This means ignoring any grammatical words such as articles and prepositions. Idioms follow the main senses of a word, in a section marked **IDM▸**. 習語的釋義在第一個實詞（名詞、動詞、形容詞或副詞）所在的詞條中，不考慮冠詞和介詞等語法詞。習語在單詞的主要義項之後標有 **IDM▸** 的地方：

> **IDM▸ in the blink of an 'eye** very quickly; in a short time 眨眼的工夫；很快 **on the 'blink** (*informal*) (of a machine 機器) no longer working correctly 失靈；出毛病

The words **in**, **the** and **on** in these idioms do not count as 'full' words, and so the idioms are not listed at the entries for these words. 兩個習語中的 in、the 和 on 不算實詞，故習語不列入這幾個單詞的詞條中。

Deciding where idioms start and stop is not always easy. 確定習語從何處開始到何處結束並不總是那麼容易。If you hear the expression 如果你聽到這樣的表達：

▸ *They decided to bury the hatchet and try to be friends again.* 他們決定捐棄前嫌，重歸於好。

you might think that **hatchet** is the only word you do not know and look that up. In fact, **bury the hatchet** is an idiomatic expression and it is defined at **bury**. At **hatchet** you will find a cross-reference directing you to **bury**. 你可能會認為你不認識的唯一單詞是 hatchet，並會去查找這個詞。事實上，bury the hatchet 為習語表達式，其釋義在 bury 詞條。在 hatchet 詞條裏可看到一個參見項指向 bury 詞條：

> **hatchet** /ˈhætʃɪt/ *noun* a small AXE (= a tool with a heavy blade for chopping things) with a short handle 短柄小斧 ➲ picture at AXE **IDM▸** see BURY

Sometimes one 'full' word of an idiom can be replaced by another. For example, in the idiom **be a bag of nerves**, **bag** can be replaced by **bundle**. This is shown as **be a bag / bundle of nerves** and the idiom is defined at the first full fixed word, **nerve**. If you try to look the phrase up at either **bag** or **bundle** you will find a cross-reference to **nerve** at the end of the idioms section. 有時習語的某個實詞可用另一實詞替換。如習語 be a bag of nerves 中的

bag 可用 bundle 替換。這種情況便用 be a bag/bundle of nerves 表示，其釋義在第一個固定不變的實詞 nerve 詞條內。如果在 bag 或 bundle 詞條中查找此短語，會在習語部份末看到參見項，指向 nerve 詞條。

IDM **not go a bundle on sb/sth** (*BrE*, *informal*) to not like sb/sth very much 不十分喜歡某人 / 某事物 ➲ more at DROP *v.*, NERVE *n.*

A few very common verbs and the adjectives **bad** and **good** have so many idioms that they cannot all be listed in the entry. Instead, there is a note telling you to look at the entry for the next noun, verb, adjective, etc. in the idiom. 一些很常見的動詞以及形容詞 bad 和 good 的習語非常多，不可能全部列入該詞條，所以有一提示引導你去查閱習語中的下一個名詞、動詞、形容詞等詞條：

IDM Most idioms containing **go** are at the entries for the nouns and adjectives in the idioms, for example **go it alone** is at **alone**. 大多數含 go 的習語，都可在該等習語中的名詞及形容詞相關詞條找到，如 go it alone 在詞條 alone 下。

In some idioms, many alternatives are possible. In the expression **disappear into thin air**, you could replace **disappear** with **vanish**, **melt** or **evaporate**. In the dictionary this is shown as **disappear, vanish, etc. into thin air**, showing that you can use other words with a similar meaning to disappear in the idiom. Since the first 'full' word of the idiom is not fixed, the expression is defined at **thin** with a cross-reference only at **air**. 有的習語可能有許多不同的替換詞，比如 disappear into thin air 中的 disappear 可用 vanish、melt 或 evaporate 替換。在本詞典中用 disappear, vanish, etc. into thin air 表示，表明在此習語中可用與 disappear 意思相似的其他詞。由於此習語中的第一個實詞並非固定不變，釋義放在 thin 詞條，只在 air 詞條中提供一個參見項。

If you cannot find an idiom in the dictionary, look it up at the entry for one of the other main words in the expression. 查不到某個習語時，可在其包含的其他主要詞的詞條中查找。

Some idioms only contain grammatical words such as **one**, **it**, or **in**. These idioms are defined at the first word that appears in them. For example, the idiom **one up on sb** is defined at the entry for **one**. 有些習語只包含 one、it 或 in 等語法詞，這類習語的釋義放在第一個詞的詞條中。如習語 one up on sb 的釋義放在 one 詞條。

Idioms are given in alphabetical order within the idioms sections. Grammatical words such as **a/an** or **the**, **sb/sth** and the possessive forms **your**, **sb's**, **his**, **her**, etc., as well as words in brackets ( ) or after a slash (/), are ignored. 習語在各詞條的習語部份按字母順序排列，語法詞（如 a/an、the 或 sb/sth）、所有格形式（如 your、sb's、his、her 等）以及括號內或斜線號後的詞不計。

Notes on usage 用法說明一覽

In the dictionary you will find many notes on various aspects of usage in English. These notes are listed below according to the type of note. 在本詞典中有許多有關英語各種用法的說明框，以下是這些說明框的分類列表。

Which Word? 詞語辨析

These notes show the differences between words that are often confused. The word in **bold** shows you the entry where you can find the note. 下列說明框為易混淆詞的辨析，**粗體**字表示所在詞條。

above / over
actual / current / present
affect / effect
agenda / diary / schedule / timetable
alone / lonely / lone
also / as well / too
although / even though / though
altogether / all together
answer / reply
around / round / about
as / like
ashamed / embarrassed
awake / awaken / wake up / waken
back – at the back / at the rear / behind
baggage / luggage
bath / bathe / swim / sunbathe
begin / start
beside / besides
besides / apart from / except
blind / blindly
borrow / lend
calm / calmness
can / may
care – take care of / look after / care for
cautious / careful
close / shut
compliment / complement
country / state
court / law court / court of law
deep / deeply
disabled / handicapped
distrust / mistrust
economic / economical
especially / specially
farther / further / farthest / furthest
firstly / first of all / at first
front – in front of / in the front of
good / goodness
hard / hardly
hate / hatred
high / tall
historic / historical
infer / imply
interested / interesting / uninterested / disinterested / uninteresting
last / take
lastly / at last
light / lighting
long – (for) long / (for) a long time
loud / loudly / aloud
near / close
next / nearest
noise / sound
old – older / elder
partly / partially
peace / peacefulness
persuade / convince
quick / quickly / fast
quite / fairly / rather / pretty
regretfully / regrettably
right / rightly
rise / raise
say / tell
sensible / sensitive
shade / shadow
slow / slowly
storey / floor
surely / certainly
tight / tightly
used to / be used to
wrong / wrongly / wrongfully

Vocabulary Building 詞彙擴充

These notes help you to choose more interesting and varied words to use and so increase your vocabulary. The word in **bold** gives you the general area of meaning of the note and shows you where to find it. 下列說明框為讀者提供更有意思、更豐富的詞彙以擴大詞彙量。**粗體**字表明該用法說明的大致內容和所在詞條。

approximately – ways of saying approximately
bad and very bad
a **bar** of chocolate
body – actions expressing emotions
break – verbs that mean 'break'
cry – verbs for ways of crying
do – household jobs: do or make?
face – expressions on your face
fat – saying that somebody is fat
good and very good
hand – verbs for ways of using your hands
laugh – verbs for different ways of laughing
learn – verbs for learning
nice and very nice
object – nouns for objects you can use
piece – words for pieces of things
rain and storms
smell – adjectives and nouns
teach and teachers – verbs and nouns

thin – saying that somebody is thin
thing – other words for thing
walk – verbs for ways of walking

Grammar Point 語法說明

These notes help make clear points of grammar that often cause problems. The word in **bold** shows you the entry where you can find the note. 下列說明框解說常見的語法疑難問題，**粗體**字表示所在詞條。

avenge / revenge
can / could / be able to / manage
dare
depend on
each / every
enjoy
half / whole / quarter
hardly / scarcely / barely / no sooner
if / whether
kind / sort
late / lately
likely
many / a lot of / lots of
modal verbs
much / a lot of / lots of
must / have (got) to / must not / don't have to
need
neither / either
none of
one / ones
per cent – expressing percentages
proportion
school
shall / will
should / ought / had better
should / would
sit
staff
used to
very / very much
well
whom
wish

British/American 英式/美式英語

These notes explain differences between British and American usage. The word in **bold** shows you the entry where you can find the note. 下列說明框闡述英式英語和美式英語的不同用法，**粗體**字表示所在詞條。

already / just / yet
bit – a bit / a little
college / university
course / program
different from / to / than
floor
have – have you got? / do you have?
holiday / vacation
hospital
inclusive / through
phone / call / ring
platform / track
post / mail
presently
rent / hire / let
rubbish / garbage / trash / refuse
school – at/in school
sea / ocean
toilet / bathroom
underground / subway / metro / tube

More About 補充說明

These notes give you more information about an aspect of life or language in Britain and America and show you the correct words to use. The word in **bold** shows you the topic of the note and the entry where you can find it. 下列說明框為英美生活或語言方面的補充說明，並提供恰當的用詞，**粗體**字表示說明框的主題和所在詞條。

American
British – describing people from Britain
course – ways of saying 'of course'
exam – words for exams and tests
gender – ways of talking about men and women
hello – greetings
lawyer – words for different kinds of lawyer
meal
name – names and titles
road
Scottish – describing things from Scotland
student – words for students at different levels
want – offers and invitations

Synonyms 同義詞辨析

These notes show the differences between groups of words with similar meanings. The words in each group are given order of frequency – from the most common to the least common. The word in **bold** shows you the entry where you can find the note. 下列說明框為近義詞辨析，每組詞按使用頻率從最常用到最不常用的順序排列，**粗體**字表示所在詞條。

action / measure / step / act / move
admit / acknowledge / recognize / concede / confess
advertisement / publicity / ad / commercial / promotion / trailer
afraid / frightened / scared / terrified / alarmed / paranoid
agree / accept / approve / go along with sb/sth / consent
almost / nearly / practically
angry / mad / indignant / cross / irate
artificial / synthetic / false / man-made / fake / imitation
ask / enquire / demand
basis / foundation / base
beat / batter / pound / lash / hammer

beautiful / pretty / handsome / attractive / lovely / good-looking / gorgeous
become / get / go / turn
big / large / great
bill / account / invoice / check
bitter / pungent / sour / acrid / sharp / acid
border / boundary / frontier
boring / dull / tedious
bottom / base / foundation / foot
bright / brilliant / vivid / vibrant
build / construct / assemble / erect / put sth up
building / property / premises / complex / structure / block
burn / char / scald / scorch / singe
call / cry out / exclaim / blurt / burst out
campaign / battle / struggle / drive / war / fight
care / caution / prudence
certain / bound / sure / definite / guaranteed
cheap / competitive / budget / affordable / reasonable / inexpensive
cheat / fool / deceive / betray / take in / trick / con
check / examine / inspect / go over sth
choice / favourite / preference / selection / pick
choose / select / pick / decide / opt / go for
claim / allegation / assertion
classic / classical
clean / wash / rinse / cleanse / dry-clean
clear / obvious / apparent / evident / plain
clothes / clothing / garment / dress / wear / gear
coast / beach / seaside / coastline / sand / seashore
cold / cool / freezing / chilly / lukewarm / tepid
collect / gather / accumulate / amass
colour / shade / hue / tint / tinge
comment / note / remark / observe
complain / protest / object / grumble / moan / whine
condition / state
consist of sb/sth / comprise / make up sth / constitute / be composed of sb/sth
continuous / continual
costs / spending / expenditure / expenses / overheads / outlay
country / landscape / countryside / terrain / land / scenery
crash / slam / collide / smash / wreck
cut / slash / cut sth back / scale sth back / rationalize / downsize
damage / hurt / harm / impair
declare / state / indicate / announce
demand / require / expect / insist / ask
difficult / hard / challenging / demanding / taxing
dirty / dusty / filthy / muddy / soiled / grubby / stained
discussion / conversation / dialogue / talk / debate / consultation / chat / gossip
disease / illness / disorder / infection / condition / ailment / bug
disgusting / foul / revolting / repulsive / offensive / gross
double / dual
economic / financial / commercial / monetary / budgetary
election / vote / poll / referendum / ballot
electric / electrical
entertainment / fun / recreation / relaxation / play / pleasure / amusement
environment / setting / surroundings / background
equipment / material / gear / kit / apparatus
essential / vital / crucial / critical / decisive / indispensable
examine / analyse / review / study / discuss
example / case / instance / specimen / illustration
excellent / outstanding / perfect / superb
excited / ecstatic / elated / euphoric / rapturous / exhilarated
exciting / dramatic / heady / thrilling / exhilarating
expensive / costly / overpriced / pricey
explode / blow up / go off / burst / erupt / detonate
fabric / cloth / material / textile
factory / plant / mill / works / yard / workshop / foundry
fast / quick / rapid
fear / terror / panic / alarm / fright
fight / clash / brawl / struggle / scuffle
floor / ground / land / earth
frighten / scare / alarm / terrify
fun / pleasure / (a) good time / enjoyment / (a) great time
funny / amusing / entertaining / witty / humorous / comic / hilarious
glad / happy / pleased / delighted / proud / relieved / thrilled
great / cool / fantastic / fabulous / terrific / brilliant / awesome
happy / satisfied / content / contented / joyful / blissful
hate / dislike / can't stand / despise / can't bear / loathe / detest
hide / conceal / cover / disguise / mask / camouflage
hit / knock / bang / strike / bump / bash
hold / hold on / cling / clutch / grip / grasp / clasp / hang on
honest / frank / direct / open / outspoken / straight / blunt
hurt / ache / burn / sting / tingle / itch / throb
identify / know / recognize / name / make sb/sth out
illness / sickness / ill health / trouble
imagine / think / see / envisage / envision
income / wage / wages / pay / salary / earnings
injure / wound / hurt / bruise / sprain / pull / strain
intelligent / smart / clever / brilliant / bright
interest / hobby / game / pastime
interesting / fascinating / compelling / stimulating / gripping / absorbing
interview / interrogation / audience / consultation
job / position / post / vacancy / appointment
label / tag / sticker
land / lot / ground / space / plot
language / vocabulary / terms / wording / terminology

lid / top / cork / cap / plug
like / love / be fond of / be keen on sth / adore
limit / restriction / control / constraint / restraint / limitation
look / watch / see / view / observe
look / glance / gaze / stare / glimpse / glare
love / like / be fond of sb / adore / be devoted to sb / care for sb / dote on sb
luck / chance / coincidence / accident / fate / destiny
mad / crazy / nuts / batty / out of your mind / (not) in your right mind
main / major / key / central / principal / chief / prime
make / do / create / develop / produce / generate / form
mark / stain / fingerprint / streak / speck / blot / smear / spot
mentally ill / insane / neurotic / psychotic / disturbed / unstable
mention / refer to sb/sth / speak / cite / quote
mistake / error / inaccuracy / slip / howler / misprint
mix / stir / mingle / blend
money / cash / change
naked / bare
narrow / thin
nervous / neurotic / on edge / jittery
notice / note / detect / observe / witness
old / elderly / aged / long-lived / mature
option / choice / alternative / possibility
order / tell / instruct / direct / command
painful / sore / raw / inflamed / excruciating / burning / itchy
patch / dot / mark / spot
payment / premium / contribution / subscription / repayment / deposit / instalment
photograph / picture / photo / shot / snapshot / snap / print
picture / painting / drawing / portrait / print / sketch
place / site / area / position / point / location / scene / spot / venue
plain / simple / stark / bare / unequivocal
pleasure / delight / joy / privilege / treat / honour
poor / disadvantaged / needy / impoverished / deprived / penniless / hard up
pressure / stress / tension / strain
price / cost / value / expense / worth
product / goods / commodity / merchandise / produce
pull / drag / draw / haul / tow / tug
purpose / aim / intention / plan / point / idea
rate / charge / fee / rent / fine / fare / toll / rental
reason / explanation / grounds / basis / excuse / motive / justification / pretext
recommend / advise / advocate / urge
regard / call / find / consider / see / view
report / story / account / version
rest / break / respite / time out / breathing space
result / consequence / outcome / repercussion
return / come back / go back / get back / turn back
rich / wealthy / prosperous / affluent / well off / comfortable
right / correct
rude / cheeky / insolent / disrespectful / impolite / impertinent / discourteous
satisfaction / happiness / pride / contentment / fulfilment
satisfying / rewarding / pleasing / gratifying / fulfilling
save / budget / economize / tighten your belt
save / rescue / bail out / redeem
see / spot / catch / glimpse
serious / grave / earnest / solemn
shine / gleam / glow / sparkle / glisten / shimmer / glitter / twinkle / glint
shock / appal / horrify / disgust / sicken / repel
shout / yell / cry / scream / cheer / bellow / raise your voice
sight / view / vision
sign / indication / symptom / symbol / indicator / signal
sit / sit down / be seated / take a seat / perch
situation / circumstances / position / conditions / things / the case / state of affairs
sleep / doze / nap / snooze
soil / mud / dust / clay / land / earth / dirt / ground
speaker / communicator / gossip / talker
speech / lecture / address / talk / sermon
spoken / oral / vocal
stand / get up / stand up / rise / get to your feet / be on your feet
stare / gaze / peer / glare
start / begin / start off / kick off / commence / open
statement / comment / announcement / remark / declaration / observation
stress / emphasize
structure / framework / form / composition / construction / fabric
student / pupil / schoolboy /schoolchild /schoolgirl
successful / profitable / commercial / lucrative / economic
sure / confident / convinced / certain / positive / clear
surprise / startle / amaze / stun / astonish / take sb aback / astound
take / lead / escort / drive / show / walk / guide / usher / direct
talk / discuss / speak / communicate / debate / consult
target / objective / goal / object / end
task / duties / mission / job / chore
tax / duty / customs / tariff / rates
terrible / awful / horrible / dreadful / vile / horrendous
thing / stuff / property / possessions / junk / belongings / goods / valuables
think / believe / feel / reckon / be under the impression
throw / toss / hurl / fling / chuck / lob / bowl / pitch

trip / journey / tour / expedition / excursion / outing / day out
true / right / correct
trust / depend on sb/sth / rely on sb/sth / count on sb/sth / believe in sb
understand / see / get / follow / grasp / comprehend
valuable / precious / priceless / irreplaceable
view / sight / scene / panorama
well / all right / OK / fine / healthy / strong / fit
wet / moist / damp / soaked / drenched / saturated
wide / broad
witness / observer / onlooker / passer-by / bystander / eyewitness
wonderful / lovely / delightful
word / term / phrase / expression / idiom
work / employment / career / profession / occupation / trade
worried / concerned / nervous / anxious / uneasy
wrong / false / mistaken / incorrect / inaccurate / misguided / untrue

Collocations 詞語搭配

These notes show useful words and phrases connected with particular topics, and a selection of verbs to use with those words and phrases. The word in **bold** shows you the entry where you can find the note. 下列說明框介紹與某特定主題相關的有用的單詞和短語以及一系列與之搭配的動詞，**粗體**字表示所在詞條。

age – The ages of life
art – Fine arts
biotechnology – Biotechnology
business – Business
child – Children
cinema – Cinema/the movies
cooking – Cooking
crime – Crime
decorate – Decorating and home improvement
diet – Diet and exercise
driving – Driving
economy – The economy
education – Education
email – Email and the Internet
environment – The environment
farming – Farming
fashion – Clothes and fashion
finance – Finance
house – Moving house
ill – Illnesses
injury – Injuries
international – International relations
job – Jobs
justice – Criminal justice
life – The living world
literature – Literature
marriage – Marriage and divorce
music – Music
phone – Phones
physical – Physical appearance
politics – Politics
race – Race and immigration
religion – Religion
restaurant – Restaurants
scientific – Scientific research
shopping – Shopping
television – Television
town – Town and country
travel – Travel and tourism
unemployment – Unemployment
vote – Voting in elections
war – War and peace
weather – The weather

Language Bank 用語庫

These notes show you how to express similar ideas in a variety of ways, particularly in writing. The word in **bold** shows you the entry where you can find the note. 下列說明框提供表達某個意思的各種不同方式，尤其是書面表達方式，**粗體**字表示所在詞條。

about – Saying what a text is about
according to – Reporting someone's opinion
addition – Adding another item
argue – Verbs for reporting an opinion
because – Explaining reasons
cause – X causes Y
conclusion – Summing up an argument
consequently – Describing the effect of something
contrast – Highlighting differences
define – Defining terms
e.g. – Giving examples
emphasis – Highlighting an important point
evidence – Giving proof
except – Making an exception
expect – Discussing predictions
fall – Describing a decrease
first – Ordering your points
generally – Ways of saying 'in general'
however – Ways of saying 'but'
i.e. – Explaining what you mean
illustrate – Referring to a chart, graph or table
impersonal – Giving opinions using impersonal language
increase – Describing an increase
nevertheless – Conceding a point and making a counter-argument
opinion – Giving your personal opinion
perhaps – Making an opinion sound less definite
process – Describing a process
proportion – Describing fractions and proportions
similarly – Making comparisons
surprising – Highlighting interesting data
therefore – Ways of saying 'For this reason ...'
vital – Saying that something is necessary

The language of literary criticism
文學批評用語

Figurative language 形象語言

Imagery is language that produces pictures in the mind. The term can be used to discuss the various stylistic devices listed below, especially **figures of speech** (= ways of using language to convey or suggest a meaning beyond the literal meaning of the words). 意象（imagery）是在心中產生形象的語言。此術語可用以討論下列各種文體手段，尤其是修辭手法（figure of speech），即用語言傳達或間接地表示字面意義所不及的含義。

Metaphor is the imaginative use of a word or phrase to describe something else, to show that the two have the same qualities. 隱喻（metaphor）是通過富於想像力的詞或短語描述另一事物來表現兩者之間具有的相同特質：

▸ *All the world's a stage*
And all the men and women merely players.
世界就是一個舞台，所有的人只是舞台上的演員。
— William Shakespeare, *As You Like It*
威廉・莎士比亞《皆大歡喜》

In **simile** the comparison between the two things is made explicit by the use of the words 'as' or 'like'. 明喻（simile）用 as 或 like 直接將兩者作比較：

▸ *I wandered lonely* ***as*** *a cloud*
我像一片雲孤獨地飄遊。
— William Wordsworth, *Daffodils*
威廉・華茲華斯《黃水仙》

▸ ***Like as*** *the waves make towards the pebbled shore,*
So *do our minutes hasten to their end.*
如同波浪向佈滿卵石的岸邊撞擊一樣，我們的歲月也匆匆流逝。
— Shakespeare, Sonnet 60
莎士比亞十四行詩第 60 首

Metonymy is the fact of referring to something by the name of something else closely connected with it, used especially as a form of shorthand for something familiar or obvious, as in 'I've been reading Shakespeare' instead of 'I've been reading the plays of Shakespeare'. 借代（metonymy）指用另一緊密相關的事物的名稱來指代某物，尤以簡略的表達方式代替人們所熟悉或不言自明的事物。如用 I've been reading Shakespeare 指代 I've been reading the plays of Shakespeare（我一直在讀莎士比亞的劇本）。

Allegory is a style of writing in which each character or event is a symbol representing a particular quality. In John Bunyan's *Pilgrim's Progress* Christian escapes from the City of Destruction, travels through the Slough of Despond, visits Vanity Fair and finally arrives at the Celestial City. He meets characters such as the Giant Despair and Mr Worldly Wiseman and is accompanied by Faithful and Hopeful. 諷喻（allegory）為一種修辭寫作，諷喻中的每個人物或事件都是一個象徵，代表特定的品質，如在約翰・班揚的《天路歷程》中，基督徒從"毀滅城"逃出，穿越"絕望的深淵"，拜訪了"名利場"，最後到達"天國"。在"忠誠卿"和"希望卿"的陪同下，他見到了"巨人絕望"和"世俗哲人先生"等人物。

Personification is the act of representing objects or qualities as human beings. 擬人（personification）是將無生命之物或特質人格化：

▸ *Love bade me welcome: yet my soul drew back,*
Guilty of dust and sin.
愛向我招手，我的靈魂卻因為骯髒和罪惡而退縮。
— George Herbert, *Love* 喬治・赫伯特《愛》

Pathetic fallacy is the effect produced when animals and things are shown as having human feelings. For example, in John Milton's poem, *Lycidas*, the flowers are shown as weeping for the dead shepherd, Lycidas. 擬人謬化（pathetic fallacy）指賦予動物或事物以人的感情時產生的效果。如在約翰・彌爾頓的詩《利西達斯》中，鮮花為死去的牧羊人——利西達斯哀悼。

Patterns of sound 音韻

Alliteration is the use of the same letter or sound at the beginning of words that are close together. It was used systematically in Old English poetry but in modern English poetry is generally only used for a particular effect. 頭韻（alliteration）指把若干相同字母或讀音開頭的詞放在一起。頭韻在古英語詩歌中經常使用，但在現代英語詩歌中一般只是為了達到特定的效果才使用：

▶ *On the **b**ald street **b**reaks the **b**lank day.*
在單調乏味的街上無聊沉悶的一天開始了。
— Alfred, Lord Tennyson, *In Memoriam*
埃爾弗雷德・丁尼生勳爵《悼念》

Assonance is the effect created when two syllables in words that are close together have the same vowel sound but different consonants, or the same consonants but different vowels. 半諧音（assonance）指若干相鄰的詞中的兩個音節元音相同，但輔音不同，或輔音相同，但元音不同而產生的效果：

▶ *It seemed that out of battle I e**scaped***
Down some profound dull tunnel long since
***scooped** …*
似乎我逃離了戰場卻又深陷於早已挖好的昏暗地道…
— Wilfred Owen, *Strange Meeting*
威爾弗雷德・歐文《奇遇》

Onomatopoeia is the effect produced when the words used contain similar sounds to the noises they describe. 擬聲（onomatopoeia）指所使用的詞語模擬所描述事物的聲音而產生的效果：

▶ *murmuring of innumerable bees*
無數蜜蜂的嗡嗡叫聲
— Tennyson, *The Princess* 丁尼生《公主》

Other stylistic effects 其他修辭效果

Irony is the use of words that say the opposite of what you really mean, often in order to make a critical comment. 反語（irony）指說與自己真實意思相反的話，通常用以達到批評的目的。

Hyperbole is the use of exaggeration. 誇張（hyperbole）指使用誇大的詞句：

▶ *An hundred years should go to praise*
Thine eyes and on thy forehead gaze
一百年的讚美應給予
您的眼睛和您深邃的凝視
— Andrew Marvell, *To His Coy Mistress*
安德魯・馬韋爾《致羞澀的情人》

An **oxymoron** is a phrase that combines two words that seem to be the opposite of each other. 逆喻（oxymoron）指將兩個看似意義相反的詞組合成短語：

▶ *Parting is such **sweet sorrow***
分離是如此甜蜜的痛苦
— Shakespeare, *Romeo and Juliet*
莎士比亞《羅密歐與朱麗葉》

A **paradox** is a statement that contains two opposite ideas or seems to be impossible. 悖論（paradox）指含兩個相互矛盾的說法或看似荒謬的說法：

▶ *The Child is father of the Man.*
兒童是成人之父。
— Wordsworth, 'My heart leaps up …'
華茲華斯"我的心激動起來…"

Poetry 詩歌

Lyric poetry is usually fairly short and expresses thoughts and feelings. Examples are Wordsworth's *Daffodils* and Dylan Thomas's *Fern Hill*. 抒情詩（lyric poetry）一般指表達思想感情的短詩。如華茲華斯的《黃水仙》和迪倫・托馬斯的《蕨山》。

Epic poetry can be much longer and deals with the actions of great men and women or the history of nations. Examples are Homer's *Iliad* and Virgil's *Aeneid*. 史詩（epic poetry）指敘述英雄事跡或民族歷史的長詩。如荷馬的《伊利亞特》和維吉爾的《埃涅阿斯記》。

Narrative poetry tells a story, like Chaucer's *Canterbury Tales*, or Coleridge's *Rime of the Ancient Mariner*. 敘事詩（narrative poetry）指敘述故事的詩篇。如喬叟的《坎特伯雷故事集》或柯爾律治的《古舟子詠》。

Dramatic poetry takes the form of a play, and includes the plays of Shakespeare (which also contain scenes in **prose**). 戲劇詩（dramatic poetry）指以劇本形式寫的詩篇，包括莎士比亞的劇本（其中某些部份以散文體（prose）寫成）。

A **ballad** is a traditional type of narrative poem with short **verses** or **stanzas** and a simple **rhyme scheme** (= pattern of rhymes). 敘事歌謠（ballad）是一種傳統的敘事詩，詩節（verse 或 stanza）短小，韻律（rhyme scheme）簡單。

An **elegy** is a type of lyric poem that expresses sadness for someone who has died. Thomas Gray's *Elegy Written in a Country Churchyard* mourns all who lived and died quietly and never had the chance to be great. 輓歌（elegy）是一種抒情詩，表達對死者的哀悼。托馬斯・格雷的《墓園輓歌》對曾經默默活在世上然後默默死去，從未有機會成為偉人的人表示哀悼。

An **ode** is a lyric poem that addresses a person or thing or celebrates an event. John Keats wrote five great odes, including *Ode to* *a Nightingale, Ode on a Grecian Urn and To Autumn*. 頌歌（ode）是一種抒情詩，對人、物或事件抒發感情。約翰·濟慈寫過五首偉大的頌歌，其中包括《夜鶯頌》、《希臘古甕頌》和《秋頌》。

Metre is the rhythm of poetry determined by the arrangement of stressed and unstressed, or long and short, syllables in each line of the poem. 格律或韻律（metre）指詩歌的輕重抑揚、長短、每行的音節等的規律。

Prosody is the theory and study of metre. 韻律學（prosody）指詩律理論和研究。

Iambic pentameter is the most common metre in English poetry. Each line consists of five **feet** (pentameter), each containing an unstressed syllable followed by a stressed syllable (iambic). 抑揚格五音步（iambic pentameter）是英詩中最常見的格律，每行為五音步（foot），每音步有一輕一重兩個音節：

▸ *The curfew tolls the knell of parting day*
— Gray's *Elegy* 格雷《輓歌》

Most lines of iambic pentameter, however, are not absolutely regular in their pattern of stresses. 不過多數抑揚格五音步詩行的重音並非絕對規則：

▸ *Shall I compare thee to a summer's day?*
— Shakespeare, Sonnet 18
莎士比亞十四行詩第 18 首

A **couplet** is a pair of lines of poetry with the same metre, especially ones that rhyme. 對句（couplet）指兩行格律相同的詩句，尤指兩行押韻的詩句：

▸ *For never was a story of more woe*
Than this of Juliet and her Romeo.
— Shakespeare, *Romeo and Juliet*
莎士比亞《羅密歐與朱麗葉》

A **sonnet** is a poem of 14 lines, in English written in iambic pentameter, and with a fixed pattern of rhyme, often ending with a rhyming couplet. 英語的十四行詩（sonnet）用抑揚格五音步寫成，韻律規範，常以押韻的對句結尾。

Blank verse is poetry written in iambic pentameters that do not rhyme. A lot of Shakespeare's dramatic verse is in blank verse, as is Milton's epic *Paradise Lost*. 無韻詩（blank verse）指以抑揚格五音步寫成的不押韻詩。與彌爾頓的史詩《失樂園》一樣，莎士比亞的許多戲劇詩都是無韻詩。

Free verse is poetry without a regular metre or rhyme scheme. Much twentieth century poetry is written in free verse, for example T. S. Eliot's *The Waste Land*. 自由詩（free verse）指無固定格律或韻律的詩歌。許多 20 世紀的詩歌都是以自由詩形式寫成，如 T. S. 艾略特的《荒原》。

Drama 戲劇

The different **genres** of drama include **comedy**, **tragedy** and **farce**. 戲劇體裁（genre）包括喜劇（comedy）、悲劇（tragedy）和鬧劇（farce）。

Catharsis is the process of releasing and providing relief from strong emotions such as pity and fear by watching the same emotions being played out on stage. 淨化（catharsis）指將強烈的情感（如憐憫和害怕）通過觀看具有相同情感的舞台演出發洩出來。

A **deus ex machina** is an unexpected power or event that suddenly appears to resolve a situation that seems hopeless. It is often used to talk about a character in a play or story who only appears at the end. 機械降神（deus ex machina）指意外介入扭轉乾坤的力量或事件。常指在劇本或故事結尾時才出現的人物或事情。

Dramatic irony is when a character's words carry an extra meaning, especially because of what is going to happen that the character does not know about. For example, King Duncan in Shakespeare's *Macbeth* is pleased to accept Macbeth's hospitality, not knowing that Macbeth is going to murder him that night. 戲劇性諷示（dramatic irony）指劇中人當時未察覺，其台詞卻帶給觀眾言外之意，尤指預示將會發生的事。如莎士比亞的《麥克佩斯》中的鄧肯王非常高興地接受了麥克佩斯的殷勤款待，卻不知道麥克佩斯那天晚上要殺害他。

Hubris is too much pride or self-confidence, especially when shown by a tragic hero or heroine who tries to defy the gods or fate. 傲慢自恃（hubris）尤表現悲劇主角傲睨神明或命運的狂妄自大。

Nemesis is what happens when the hero or heroine's past mistakes or sins finally cause his or her downfall and death. 報應（nemesis）指主角的過錯或罪孽最終招致自己的敗落和毀滅。

A **soliloquy** is a speech in a play for one character who is alone on the stage and speaks his or her thoughts aloud. The most famous soliloquy in English drama is Hamlet's beginning 'To be or not to be ...'. 獨白（soliloquy）指劇中人獨自在台上自言自語表達自己的思想感情。英語戲劇中最著名的獨白是哈姆雷特的開場白 "To be or not to be ..."。

Narrative 敘事體

A **novel** is a **narrative** (= a story) long enough to fill a complete book. The story may be told by a **first-person narrator**, who is a character in the story and relates what happens to himself or herself, or there may be an **omniscient narrator** who relates what happens to all the characters in the third person. 長篇小說（novel）指長達一本書的敘事文（narrative）或故事。敘事角度可以是第一人稱敘事者（first-person narrator）講敘，即故事的主人公敘述自己的經歷；也可以是第三人稱敘述，即由一個全知的敘述者（omniscient narrator）敘述故事中各人物的經歷。

A **short story** is a story that is short enough to be read from beginning to end without stopping. 短篇小說（short story）指可一口氣從頭讀到尾的短篇故事。

The **denouement** is the end of a book or play in which everything is explained or settled. It is often used to talk about mystery or detective stories. 結局（denouement）指書或戲劇中一切事情都得到解釋或得以解決的結尾，常用以指神秘事件或偵探故事的結局。

Stream of consciousness is a style of writing used in novels that shows the continuous flow of a character's thoughts and feelings without using the usual methods of description or conversation. It was used particularly in the twentieth century by writers such as James Joyce and Virginia Woolf. 意識流（stream of consciousness）為長篇小說的一種寫作技巧，用以表現小說中人物的思潮、感情的起伏，卻不用慣常的描寫或對話手法，20 世紀的作家如詹姆斯・喬伊斯和弗吉尼亞・吳爾夫多採用這一手法寫作。

Punctuation 標點符號用法

. full stop (*BrE*) period (*NAmE*) 句號

- at the end of a sentence that is not a question or an exclamation 用於除疑問句或感歎句以外的句子末尾：
  - ▸ *I knocked at the door. There was no reply.*
  - ▸ *I knocked again.*
- sometimes in abbreviations 有時用於縮寫後：
  - ▸ *Jan. e.g. a.m. etc.*
- in internet and email addresses (said 'dot') 用於互聯網和電子郵件地址中（讀作 dot）
  - ▸ *http://www.oup.com*

, comma 逗號

- to separate words in a list, though they are often omitted before and 用以分隔所列詞語，不過在 and 之前常常省略：
  - ▸ *a bouquet of red, pink and white roses*
  - ▸ *tea, coffee, milk or hot chocolate*
- to separate phrases or clauses 用以分隔短語或從句：
  - ▸ *If you keep calm, take your time, concentrate and think ahead, then you're likely to pass your test.*
  - ▸ *Worn out after all the excitement of the party, the children soon fell asleep.*
- before and after a clause or phrase that gives additional, but not essential, information about the noun it follows 用於給前面的名詞作非必要補充的從句或短語前後：
  - ▸ *The Pennine Hills, which are very popular with walkers, are situated between Lancashire and Yorkshire.*

  (do not use commas before and after a clause that **defines** the noun it follows 在限定性名詞從句前後不用逗號)
  - ▸ *The hills that separate Lancashire from Yorkshire are called the Pennines.*
- to separate main clauses, especially long ones, linked by a conjunction such as *and*, *as*, *but*, *for*, *or* 用以分隔由連詞 and、as、but、for、or 等連接的主句，尤其是較長的主句：
  - ▸ *We had been looking forward to our holiday all year, but unfortunately it rained every day.*
- to separate an introductory word or phrase, or an adverb or adverbial phrase that applies to the whole sentence, from the rest of the sentence 用以將引導詞或短語、修飾整個句子的副詞或副詞短語與句子的其餘部份隔開：
  - ▸ *Oh, so that's where it was.*
  - ▸ *As it happens, however, I never saw her again.*
  - ▸ *By the way, did you hear about Sue's car?*
- to separate a tag question from the rest of the sentence 用以將附加疑問句與句子的其餘部份隔開：
  - ▸ *It's quite expensive, isn't it?*
  - ▸ *You live in Bristol, right?*
- before or after 'he said', etc. when writing down conversation 書寫對話時用於 he said 等詞語前後：
  - ▸ *'Come back soon,' she said.*
- before a short quotation 用於短小的引語前：
  - ▸ *Disraeli said, 'Little things affect little minds'.*

: colon 冒號

- to introduce a list of items 用於引出下文各項：
  - ▸ *These are our options: we go by train and leave before the end of the show; or we take the car and see it all.*
- in formal writing, before a clause or phrase that gives more information about the main clause. (You can use a semicolon or a full stop, but not a comma, instead of a colon here.) 在正式書面語中，用於補充說明主句的從句或短語之前。（此處可用分號或句號代替冒號，但不可以用逗號。）
  - ▸ *The garden had been neglected for a long time: it was overgrown and full of weeds.*
- to introduce a quotation, which may be indented 用於引出引語，引語可能縮格：
  - ▸ *As Kenneth Morgan writes:*

    The truth was, perhaps, that Britain in the years from 1914 to 1983 had not changed all that fundamentally.

    Others, however, have challenged this view …

; semicolon 分號

- instead of a comma to separate parts of a sentence that already contain commas 用以代替逗號，分隔句中已含逗號的部份：
  - ▸ *She was determined to succeed whatever the cost; she would achieve her aim, whoever might suffer on the way.*
- in formal writing, to separate two main clauses, especially those not joined by a conjunction 在正式書面語中，用以分隔兩個主句，尤其是無連詞連接的兩個主句：
  - ▸ *The sun was already low in the sky; it would soon be dark.*

? question mark 問號

- at the end of a direct question 用於直接問句末尾：
  - ▸ *Where's the car?*
  - ▸ *You're leaving already?*

Do not use a question mark at the end of an indirect question. 轉述問句末尾不用問號：

  - ▸ *He asked if I was leaving.*
- especially with a date, to express doubt 尤與日期連用，表示存疑：
  - ▸ *John Marston (?1575–1634)*

! exclamation mark (*BrE*) exclamation point (*NAmE*) 感歎號

- at the end of a sentence expressing surprise, joy, anger, shock or another strong emotion 用於表示驚訝、欣喜、憤怒、震驚或其他強烈感情的句子末尾：
  - ▸ *That's marvellous!*
  - ▸ *'Never!' she cried.*
- in informal written English, you can use more than one exclamation mark, or an exclamation mark and a question mark 在非正式書面語中，可以用一個以上的感歎號或一個感歎號加一個問號：
  - ▸ *'Your wife's just given birth to triplets.' 'Triplets!?'*

' apostrophe 撇號

- with *s* to indicate that a thing or person belongs to somebody 與 s 連用表示所有格：
  - ▸ *my friend's brother*
  - ▸ *the waitress's apron*
  - ▸ *King James's crown / King James' crown*
  - ▸ *the students' books*
  - ▸ *the women's coats*
- in short forms, to indicate that letters or figures have been omitted 在縮寫中表示字母或數字的省略：
  - ▸ *I'm (I am)*
  - ▸ *they'd (they had/they would)*
  - ▸ *the summer of '89 (1989)*
- sometimes, with *s* to form the plural of a letter, a figure or an abbreviation 有時與 s 連用構成字母、數字或縮寫的複數形式：
  - ▸ *roll your r's*
  - ▸ *during the 1990's*

- hyphen 連字符；連（字）號

- to form a compound from two or more other words 將兩個或更多的詞組成複合詞：
  - ▸ *hard-hearted*
  - ▸ *fork-lift truck*
  - ▸ *mother-to-be*
- to form a compound from a prefix and a proper name 將前綴和專有名詞組成複合詞：
  - ▸ *pre-Raphaelite*
  - ▸ *pro-European*
- when writing compound numbers between 21 and 99 in words 書寫 21–99 之間的複合數字時用：
  - ▸ *seventy-three*
  - ▸ *thirty-one*
- sometimes, in British English, to separate a prefix ending in a vowel from a word beginning with the same vowel 有時在英式英語中用以將以元音結尾的前綴與以相同元音開始的詞隔開：
  - ▸ *co-operate*
  - ▸ *pre-eminent*
- after the first section of a word that is divided between one line and the next 轉行時用於單詞的前半部之後：
  - ▸ *decide what to do in order to avoid mis-takes of this kind in the future*

– dash 破折號

- in informal English, instead of a colon or semicolon, to indicate that what follows is a summary or conclusion of what has gone before 在非正式英語中，用以代替冒號或分號，表示後面所説是對前面的總結或結論：
  - ▸ *Men were shouting, women were screaming, children were crying — it was chaos.*
  - ▸ *You've admitted that you lied to me — how can I trust you again?*
- singly or in pairs to separate a comment or an afterthought from the rest of the sentence 單個或成對使用，用以將句中的評語或事後想到的補充説明與句子的其餘部份隔開：
  - ▸ *He knew nothing at all about it — or so he said.*

... dots / ellipsis 省略號

- to indicate that words have been omitted, especially from a quotation or at the end of a conversation 表示詞的省略，尤用於引語或對話末尾的省略：
  - ▸ *... challenging the view that Britain ... had not changed all that fundamentally.*

/ slash / oblique 斜線號

- to separate alternative words or phrases 用以分隔可供選擇的詞或短語：
  - ▸ *have a pudding and/or cheese*
  - ▸ *single/married/widowed/divorced*
- in internet and email addresses to separate the different elements (often said 'forward slash') 在互聯網和電子郵件地址中用以分隔各個不同的成分（通常叫做"正斜槓"）
  - ▸ *http: //www.oup.com/elt/*

' " quotation marks 引號

- to enclose words and punctuation in direct speech 用以標明引號內的詞句和標點符號為直接引語：
  - ▸ *'Why on earth did you do that?' he asked.*
  - ▸ *'I'll fetch it,' she replied.*
- to draw attention to a word that is unusual for the context, for example a slang expression, or to a word that is being used for special effect, such as irony 用以提醒注意文中的特殊詞（如俚語）或為特殊效果而使用的詞（如反語）：
  - ▸ *He told me in no uncertain terms to 'get lost'.*
  - ▸ *Thousands were imprisoned in the name of 'national security'.*
- around the titles of articles, books, poems, plays, etc. 用以標明文章、書、詩歌、劇本等的名稱：
  - ▸ *Keats's 'Ode to Autumn'*
  - ▸ *I was watching 'Match of the Day'.*
- around short quotations or sayings 用以標明短小的引語或諺語：
  - ▸ *Do you know the origin of the saying: 'A little learning is a dangerous thing'?*
- in American English, double quotation marks are used. 美式英語用雙引號：
  - ▸ *"Help! I'm drowning!"*

( ) brackets (*BrE*) parentheses (*NAmE or formal*) (圓) 括號

- to separate extra information or a comment from the rest of a sentence 用以將句中的附加信息或評語與句子的其餘部份隔開：
  - ▸ *Mount Robson (12972 feet) is the highest mountain in the Canadian Rockies.*
  - ▸ *He thinks that modern music (i.e. anything written after 1900) is rubbish.*
- to enclose cross-references 用以標明參見項：
  - ▸ *This moral ambiguity is a feature of Shakespeare's later works (see Chapter Eight).*
- around numbers or letters in text 用以標明文中號碼或字母編號：
  - ▸ *Our objectives are (1) to increase output, (2) to improve quality and (3) to maximize profits.*

[ ] square brackets (*BrE*) brackets (*NAmE*) 方括號

- around words inserted to make a quotation grammatically correct 用以標明使引語合乎語法的插入詞語：
  - ▶ *Britain in [these] years was without …*

italics 斜體字

- to show emphasis 表示強調：
  - ▶ I'm not going to do it – *you* are.
  - ▶ … proposals which we cannot accept *under any circumstances*
- to indicate the titles of books, plays, etc. 表示書、劇本等的名稱：
  - ▶ Joyce's *Ulysses*
  - ▶ the title role in Puccini's *Tosca*
  - ▶ a letter in *The Times*
- for foreign words or phrases 表示外來詞語或短語：
  - ▶ the English oak (*Quercus robur*)
  - ▶ I had to renew my *permesso di soggiorno* (residence permit).

Quoting conversation 引述對話

When you write down a conversation, you normally begin a new paragraph for each new speaker. 書寫對話時不同人說的話一般各自成段。

Quotation marks enclose the words spoken. 引號標明說話內容：

▶ *'You're sure of this?' I asked.*
He nodded grimly.
'I'm certain.'

Verbs used to indicate direct speech, for example *he said, she complained*, are separated by commas from the words spoken, unless a question mark or an exclamation mark is used. 用逗號將表示直接引語的動詞（如 he said、she complained）與說話內容隔開，除非直接引語後為問號或感歎號：

- ▶ *'That's all I know,' said Nick.*
- ▶ *Nick said, 'That's all I know.'*
- ▶ *'Why?' asked Nick.*

When *he said* or *said Nick* follows the words spoken, the comma is placed inside the quotation marks, as in the first example above. If, however, the writer puts the words *said Nick* within the actual words Nick speaks, the comma is outside the quotation marks. * he said 或 said Nick 在直接引語之後，逗號置於引號裏面，如上述第 1 例所示。若 said Nick 置於 Nick 所說內容的中間，則逗號置於引號外面：

▶ *'That', said Nick, 'is all I know.'*

Double quotation marks are used to indicate direct speech being quoted by somebody else within direct speech. 雙引號用以表示直接引語被另一人引用於直接引語中：

▶ *'But you said you loved me! "I'll never leave you, Sue, as long as I live." That's what you said, isn't it?'*

Numbers 數字用法

Writing and saying numbers 數字的讀和寫

Numbers over 20 20 以上的數字

- are written with a hyphen 書寫時用連字符：
  35 *thirty-five*
  67 *sixty-seven*

- When writing a cheque we often use words for the pounds or dollars and figures for the pence or cents. 填寫支票時常用英語詞表示英鎊或元，用阿拉伯數字表示便士或分：
  £22.45 *twenty-two pounds (and) 45 pence*
  $79.30 *seventy-nine dollars (and)* $^{30}/_{100}$

Numbers over 100 100 以上的數字

329 *three hundred and twenty nine*

- The **and** is pronounced /n/ and the stress is on the final number. * and 的發音為 /n/，重音在最後一個數字。

- In American English the **and** is sometimes left out. 美式英語有時省略 and。

Numbers over 1000 1 000 以上的數字

1100 *one thousand one hundred*
(*also informal* 非正式亦作) *eleven hundred*

2500 *two thousand five hundred*
(*also informal, especially in NAmE* 非正式，美式英語尤作)
twenty-five hundred

- These informal forms are most common for whole hundreds between 1100 and 1900. 上述非正式形式最常用於 1 100 到 1 900 之間的整百數字。

- A comma or (in *BrE*) a space is often used to divide large numbers into groups of 3 figures. 常常用逗號或英式英語用空格將數額大的數字分成 3 個數字一組：
  - ▸ *33,423* or *33 423* (*thirty three thousand four hundred and twenty three*)
  - ▸ *2,768,941* or *2 768 941* (*two million seven hundred and sixty-eight thousand nine hundred and forty-one*)

A or one? 用 a 還是用 one？

130 *a/one hundred and thirty*
1000000 *a/one million*

- **one** is more formal and more precise and can be used for emphasis * one 更正式、更準確，可表示強調：
  - ▸ *The total cost was one hundred and sixty three pounds exactly.*
  - ▸ *It cost about a hundred and fifty quid.*

- **a** can only be used at the beginning of a number * a 只能用於數字的開頭：
  1000 *a/one thousand*
  2100 *two thousand one hundred*
  ~~*two thousand a hundred*~~

- **a** is not usually used between 1100 and 1999 * 1 100 到 1 999 之間的數字一般不用 a：
  1099 *a/one thousand and ninety-nine*
  1100 *one thousand one hundred*
  1340 *one thousand three hundred and forty*
  ~~*a thousand three hundred and forty*~~

Ordinal numbers 序數詞

1st	*first*	5th	*fifth*
2nd	*second*	9th	*ninth*
3rd	*third*	12th	*twelfth*
4th	*fourth*	21st	*twenty-first*
			etc.

Fractions 分數

$^{1}/_{2}$ *a/one half*
$^{1}/_{3}$ *a/one third*
$^{1}/_{4}$ *a/one quarter* (*NAmE also* 美式英語亦作 *a/one fourth*)

(for emphasis use **one** instead of **a** 表示強調用 one 不用 a)
$^{1}/_{12}$ *one twelfth*
$^{1}/_{16}$ *one sixteenth*

$^{2}/_{3}$ *two thirds*
$^{3}/_{4}$ *three quarters* (*NAmE also* 美式英語亦作 *three fourths*)
$^{9}/_{10}$ *nine tenths*

More complex fractions 較複雜的分數

- use **over** 用 over：
  $^{19}/_{56}$ *nineteen **over** fifty-six*
  $^{31}/_{144}$ *thirty-one **over** one four four*

Whole numbers and fractions
整數和分數

- link with **and** 用 and 連接：
  2½ *two **and** a half*
  5⅔ *five **and** two thirds*
- **one** plus a fraction is followed by a plural noun * one 加分數後用複數名詞：
  1½ pts *one and a half **pints***

Fractions/percentages and noun phrases
分數／百分數和名詞短語

- use **of** 用 of 連接：
  - ▸ ***a** fifth **of** the women questioned*
  - ▸ *three quarters **of** the population*
  - ▸ *75% **of** the population*
- with **half** do not use **a**, and **of** can sometimes be omitted 表示一半（half）時不用冠詞 a，有時可省略 of：
  - ▸ *Half (of) the work is already finished.*
- do not use **of** in expressions of measurement or quantity 在表示量度或數量的短語中不用 of：
  - ▸ *How much is half a pint of milk?*
  - ▸ *It takes me half an hour by bus.*
- use **of** before pronouns 在代詞前用 of：
  - ▸ *We can't start – only half **of** us are here.*

Fractions/percentages and verbs
分數／百分數和動詞

- If a fraction/percentage is used with an uncountable or a singular noun the verb is generally singular. 分數／百分數與不可數名詞或單數名詞連用時，動詞一般為單數：
  - ▸ *Fifty per cent of the land is cultivated.*
  - ▸ *Half (of) the land is cultivated.*
- If the noun is singular but represents a group of people, the verb is singular in American English but in British English it may be singular or plural. 單數集合名詞的謂語動詞在美式英語中用單數，但在英式英語中用單、複數均可：
  - ▸ *Three quarters/75% of the workforce is/are against the strike.*
- If the noun is plural, the verb is plural. 名詞為複數，謂語動詞亦為複數：
  - ▸ *Two thirds/65% of children play computer games.*

Decimals 小數

- write and say with a point (.) (not a comma) 讀和寫均用小數點 (.)（不用逗號）表示
- say each figure after the point separately 小數點後的數字逐個讀出：
  79.3 *seventy-nine point three*
  3.142 *three point one four two*
  0.67 *(zero) point six seven*
  (BrE also 英式英語亦讀作）
  nought point six seven

Mathematical expressions
數學表達式

+	plus
−	minus
×	times/multiplied by
÷	divided by
=	equals/is
%	per cent (*NAmE* usually percent)
3^2	three squared
5^3	five cubed
6^{10}	six to the power of ten
√	square root of

The figure '0' 數字 0

The figure 0 has several different names in English, although in American English zero is commonly used in all cases. 數字 0 在英式英語中有幾個不同的名稱，而在美式英語中通常用 zero 表示：

Zero

- used in precise scientific, medical and economic contexts and to talk about temperature 用於精確的科學、醫學和經濟語境，亦用以表示溫度：
  - ▸ *It was ten degrees below zero last night.*
  - ▸ *zero inflation/growth/profit*

Nought

- used in British English to talk about a number, age, etc. 在英式英語中用以表示數字、年齡等：
  - ▸ *A million is written with six noughts.*
  - ▸ *The car goes from nought to sixty in ten seconds.*
  - ▸ *clothes for children aged nought to six*

'o' /əʊ/ *NAmE* /oʊ/

- used when saying a bank account number, telephone number, etc. 用以讀出銀行賬號、電話號碼等

Nil

- used to talk about the score in a team game, for example in football 用以表示團隊比賽（如足球賽）的比分：
  - ▸ *The final score was one nil. (1–0)*
- used to mean 'nothing at all' 用以表示完全沒有：
  - ▸ *The doctors rated her chances as nil.*

Telephone numbers 電話號碼

- All numbers are said separately. 0 is pronounced /əʊ/ (*BrE*) or /oʊ/ (*NAmE*). 每個號碼分別讀出，0 讀作 /əʊ/（英式英語）或 /oʊ/（美式英語）：
  - ▸ (01865) 556767
    o one eight six five, five five six seven six seven (or 或 *double five six seven six seven*)

Temperature 溫度

- The Celsius or Centigrade (°C) scale is officially used in Britain and for scientific purposes in the US. 攝氏溫標（°C）在英國為官方用法，在美國用於科技語境：
  - ▸ *a high of thirty-five degrees Celsius*
  - ▸ *The normal temperature of the human body is 37°C.*
- The Fahrenheit (°F) scale is used in all other contexts in the US and is also still commonly used in Britain. The words 'degrees Fahrenheit/Centigrade/Celsius' are often omitted. 華氏溫標（°F）在美國用於科技以外的其他各個方面，在英國仍普遍使用。degrees Fahrenheit/Centigrade/Celsius（華氏度／攝氏度）這些詞常常省略：
  - ▸ *Temperatures soared to over a hundred. (100°F)*
  - ▸ *She's ill in bed with a temperature of a hundred and two. (102°F)*

Money 貨幣

In Britain 在英國

- ▸ *100 pence/p = 1 British pound (£1)*
- ▸ *It costs 90p/90 pence return on the bus.*

- when talking about an individual coin 表示單枚硬幣：
  a twenty pence piece/a twenty p piece
- when talking about pounds and pence people often only say the numbers 表示英鎊和便士通常只說數字：
  It only cost five ninety nine. (£5.99)
- in informal British English 非正式英式英語：

£1	*a quid*
£5	*five quid* or 或 *a fiver*
£10	*ten quid* or 或 *a tenner*

In the US 在美國

1c	one cent	a penny 一分硬幣
5c	five cents	a nickel 五分硬幣
10c	ten cents	a dime 一角硬幣
25c	twenty-five cents	a quarter 二角五分硬幣
$1.00	one dollar	a dollar bill 一元紙幣

- in informal American English dollars are called **bucks** 在非正式美式英語中美元叫 buck：
  - ▸ *This shirt cost fifty bucks.*

Writing and saying dates 日期的讀和寫

British English 英式英語

- ▸ *14 October 1998* or 或 *14th October 1998 (14/10/98)*
- ▸ *Her birthday is on* ***the*** *ninth* ***of*** *December.*
- ▸ *Her birthday is on December* ***the*** *ninth.*

American English 美式英語

- ▸ *October 14, 1998 (10/14/98)*
- ▸ *Her birthday is December 9th.*

Years 年份

1999	*nineteen ninety-nine*
1608	*sixteen o eight* (or, less commonly 或不那麼普遍地讀作 *nineteen <u>hundred</u> and ninety-nine* and 和 *sixteen <u>hundred</u> and eight*)
1700	*seventeen hundred*
2000	*(the year) two thousand*
2002	*two thousand and two*
2015	*twenty fifteen*

AD 76 / A.D. 76 *AD seventy-six*
76 CE / 76 C.E. *seventy-six CE*

(Both these expressions mean '76 years after the beginning of the Christian calendar'. 上述兩種表示法均指公元 76 年。)

1000 BC / 1000 B.C. *one thousand BC*
1000 BCE / 1000 B.C.E *one thousand BCE*

(Both these expressions mean '1000 years before the beginning of the Christian calendar'. 上述兩種表示法均指公元前 1000 年。)

Age 年齡

- when saying a person's age use only numbers 表示一個人的年齡只用數字：
  - ▸ *Sue is ten and Tom is six.*
  - ▸ *She left home at sixteen.*
- a man/woman/boy/girl, etc. of ... * … 歲的男子／女子／男孩／女孩等：
  - ▸ *They've got a girl of three and a boy of five.*
  - ▸ *a young woman of nineteen*
- in writing, in descriptions or to emphasize sb's age use ... **years old** 書寫、描述或強調某人的年齡用 … years old：
  - ▸ *She was thirty-one years old and a barrister by profession.*
  - ▸ *He is described as white, 5ft 10 ins tall and about 50 years old.*
  - ▸ *You're forty years old — stop behaving like a teenager!*
- ... **years old** is also used for things. * ... years old 亦用以表示事物存在的時間：
  - ▸ *The monument is 120 years old.*
- You can also say **a ... year-old/month-old/week-old**, etc. * 亦可用 a ... year-old/month-old/week-old 等表示：
  - ▸ *Youth training is available to all sixteen-year-olds.*
  - ▸ *a ten week-old baby*
  - ▸ *a remarkable 1000 year-old tomb*
- Use ... **years of age** in formal or written contexts. 正式用語或書面語用 ... years of age：
  - ▸ *Not applicable to persons under eighteen years of age.*
- Use **the ... age group** to talk about people between certain ages. 表示某一年齡段的人用 the ... age group：
  - ▸ *He took first prize in the 10–16 age group.*
- To give the approximate age of a person. 表示一個人的大致年齡：

13–19	*in his/her teens*
21–29	*in his/her twenties*
31–33	*in his/her early thirties*
34–36	*in his/her mid thirties*
37–39	*in his/her late thirties*

- To refer to a particular event you can use **at/by/before, etc. the age of ...** . 特指某事情與某年齡有關可用 at/by/before etc. the age of ... ：
  - ▸ *Most smokers start smoking cigarettes before the age of sixteen.*

Numbers in time 用於時間的數字

There is often more than one way of telling the time. 表示時間的方法通常不止一種：

Half hours 半小時

6:30 *six thirty*
half past six (*BrE*)
half six (*BrE informal*)

Other times 其他時刻

5:45	*five forty-five*	*(a) quarter to six (BrE)* *(a) quarter to/of six (NAmE)*
2:15	*two fifteen*	*(a) quarter past two (BrE)* *(a) quarter after two (NAmE)*
1:10	*one ten*	*ten past one (BrE)* *ten after one (NAmE)*
3:05	*three o five*	*five past three (BrE)* *five after three (NAmE)*
1:55	*one fifty-five*	*five to two (BrE)* *five to/of two (NAmE)*

- with 5, 10, 20 and 25 the word **minutes** is not necessary, but it is used with other numbers 表示 5、10、20 和 25 分鐘不必用 minute，但表示其他分鐘要用 minute：
  10.25 *twenty-five past/after ten*
  10.17 *seventeen* ***minutes*** *past/after ten*
- use **o'clock** only for whole hours 只有表示整點才用 o'clock：
  - ▸ *It's three o'clock.*
- If it is necessary to specify the time of day use **in the morning, in the afternoon, in the evening** or **at night**. 有必要說明是上午、下午、傍晚或晚上就用 in the morning、in the afternoon、in the evening 或 at night。

- in more formal contexts use 在較正式的語境中用：
  a.m. = in the morning or after midnight 早上或午夜以後
  p.m. = in the afternoon, in the evening or before midnight 下午、晚上或午夜以前
  ▸ *He gets up at 4 a.m. to deliver the mail.*

  Do not use **o'clock** with **a.m.** or **p.m.**
  * o'clock 不與 a.m. 或 p.m. 同時用：
  ▸ ~~*He gets up at 4 o'clock a.m.*~~
  ▸ *He gets up at 4 o'clock in the morning.*
  ▸ ~~*I'll see you at 6 o'clock p.m.*~~
  ▸ *I'll see you at 6 o'clock this evening.*

Twenty-four hour clock 二十四小時制

- used for military purposes and in some other particular contexts, for example on train timetables in Britain 用於軍事和其他特定場合，如英國的火車時刻表：
  13:52 *thirteen fifty-two* (1:52 p.m.)
  22:30 *twenty-two thirty* (10:30 p.m.)
- for military purposes whole hours are said as **hundred hours** 在軍事上，整點讀作 hundred hours：
  0400 *(o) four hundred hours* (4 a.m.)
  2400 *twenty four hundred hours* (midnight)

Expressing time 表示時間

When referring to days, weeks, etc. in the past, present and future the following expressions are used, speaking from a point of view in the present. 以現在為基點說過去、現在和將來的日期、星期等，用下列詞語表示：

	past 過去	**present 現在**	**future 將來**
morning	yesterday morning	this morning	tomorrow morning
afternoon	yesterday afternoon	this afternoon	tomorrow afternoon
evening	yesterday evening	this evening	tomorrow evening
night	last night	tonight	tomorrow night
day	yesterday	today	tomorrow
week	last week	this week	next week
month	last month	this month	next month
year	last year	this year	next year

To talk about a time further back in the past or further forward in the future use
表示更遠的過去或將來的時間用：

past 過去	**future 將來**
the day before yesterday	the day after tomorrow
the week/month/year before last	the week/month/year after next
two days/weeks, etc. ago	in two days/weeks, etc. time

To talk about sth that happens regularly use expressions with '**every**'. 定期發生的事用 every 表示：

▸ *He has to work **every third** weekend.*
▸ *I wash my hair **every other** day* (= every second day).

In British English a period of two weeks is a **fortnight**. 在英式英語中，fortnight 表示兩週。

▸ *I've got a **fortnight's** holiday in Spain.*

Prepositions of time 表示時間的介詞

in (the)

parts of the day (not night) 一天中（不包括夜間）的時段	*in the morning(s), in the evening(s), etc.*
months 月份	*in February*
seasons 季節	*in (the) summer*
years 年份	*in 1995*
decades 十年	*in the 1920s*
centuries 世紀	*in the 20th century*

at (the)

clock time 鐘點	*at 5 o'clock* *at 7.45 p.m.*
night 夜晚	*at night*
holiday periods 假期	*at Christmas* *at the weekend (BrE)*

on (the)

day of the week 星期…	*on Saturdays*
dates 日期	*on (the) 20th (of) May (NAmE also* 美式英語亦作 *on May 20th)*
particular days 特定的日期	*on Good Friday* *on New Year's Day* *on my birthday* *on the following day*

Numbers in measurement in Britain and America 英美計量表示法

item being measured 計量項目	unit of measurement 計量單位	examples 示例
length of time 時間	hours (hrs) 小時 minutes (mins) 分 seconds (secs) 秒	*Cover the pan and simmer gently for one hour.* *He took just two minutes to knock out his opponent.* *The fastest time was 12 mins 26 secs.*
person's height 人的身高	feet and inches 英尺和英寸 metres and centimetres (UK) 米和厘米	*She's 1.63 metres tall.* *He's only five feet four (inches).* *He's only five foot four.*
distance by road 路程	miles 英里	*It is 42 miles to Liverpool.* *The signpost said: 'Liverpool 42'.*
speed 速度	miles per hour (mph) 每小時英里數 kilometres per hour (kph) 每小時公里數 kilometres per second, etc. 每秒（等）公里數 miles an hour *(informal)* 每小時英里數	*She was driving at 75 miles per hour.* *a speed limit of 50kph* *Light travels at 299 792 kilometres per second.* *a hundred-mile-an-hour police chase*
distance in sport 體育運動中的距離	metres 米 yards / miles (US) 碼；英里	*the women's 800 metres freestyle* *a six-mile run*
area of land (for example farmland) 土地面積（如農田）	acres / hectares 英畝；公頃	*a house with 10 acres of grounds* *a 2 000-hectare farm*
regions or areas of a country 國家的地區或區域	square miles 平方英里 square kilometres (UK) 平方公里	*Dartmoor covers an area of more than 350 square miles.* *Population density is only 24 people per square kilometre.*
area of a room/ garden, etc. 房間、庭園等的面積	square yards / feet 平方碼；平方英尺 square metres (UK) 平方米 … by … (… × …)	*5 000 square feet of office space* *15 square metres of carpet (5m × 3m)* *a carpet fifteen metres square (15m × 15m)* *a room sixteen feet by twelve (16ft × 12ft)*

item being measured 計量項目	unit of measurement 計量單位	examples 示例
weight of food **食物重量**	pounds and ounces 磅和盎司 kilograms and grams (UK) 千克和克 cups (US, in cooking) 杯（用於烹飪）	*Fold in 6 ounces of flour.* *250 grams of Brie please* *Add half a cup of sugar.*
weight of a person **人的體重**	stones and pounds (UK) 英石和磅 pounds only (US) 磅	*She weighs 8st 10lb.* *My brother weighs 183 pounds.*
weight of a baby **嬰兒的體重**	pounds and ounces 磅和盎司 kilograms (UK) 千克；公斤	*The baby weighed 6lb 4oz at birth.*
heavy items/ large amounts **重型物體；大數量**	tons / tonnes 噸；公噸 pounds 磅 kilograms (UK) 千克；公斤	*The price of copper fell by £11 a tonne* *a car packed with 140 pounds of explosive* *a 40kg sack of gravel* *Our baggage allowance is only 20 kilos.*
milk 牛奶	pints / half pints (UK) 品脫；半品脫 pints / quarts / gallons (US) 品脫；夸脫；加侖	*a one-pint carton of mil* *a quart of milk*
beer 啤酒	pints / half pints (UK) 品脫；半品脫	*a half of lager please* (= half a pint) *(informal)*
wine, bottled drinks **葡萄酒；瓶裝飲料**	litres / centilitres 升；厘升	*a litre of juice*
other liquids **其他液體**	litres (UK) 升 fluid ounces / gallons (US) 液盎司；加侖 millilitres (scientific context) 毫升（科技語境）	*half a litre of cooking oil* *5 litres of paint; 2 gallons of paint* *100 ml sulphuric acid*
liquid in cooking **用於烹飪的液體**	fluid ounces 液盎司 millilitres (UK) 毫升	*Add 8 fl oz milk and beat thoroughly.*
petrol (*BrE*) (*NAmE* **gasoline**)/ **diesel 汽油；柴油**	gallons (US) 加侖 litres (UK) 升	*My new car does over 50 miles to the gallon.*

As the table shows, both metric and non-metric systems of measurement can be used in many cases, especially in the UK. Often the choice depends on the speaker or the situation. In the UK the metric system must now be used on packaging and for displaying prices by weight or measurement in shops. The metric system is always used in a scientific context. In the US the metric system is much less widely used. 如上表所示，在許多情況下公制度量衡和非公制度量衡均可使用，尤其在英國。選擇公制度量衡還是非公制度量衡通常取決於說話者或場合。在英國，包裝上、商店裏以重量或計量標價現在必須用公制，在科技語境則總是用公制。在美國，公制的使用遠沒有這麼廣泛。

Metric measures 公制計量單位

(with approximate non-metric equivalents 附大約相當於非公制的量)

	Metric 公制		Non-metric 非公制
Length 長度	10 millimetres (mm) 毫米	= 1 centimetre (cm) 厘米	= 0.394 inch 英寸
	100 centimetres 厘米	= 1 metre (m) 米	= 39.4 inches 英寸/ 1.094 yards 碼
	1000 metres 米	= 1 kilometre (km) 千米；公里	= 0.6214 mile 英里
Area 面積	100 square metres (m^2) 平方米	= 1 are (a) 公畝	= 0.025 acre 英畝
	100 ares 公畝	= 1 hectare (ha) 公頃	= 2.471 acres 英畝
	100 hectares 公頃	= 1 square kilometre (km^2) 平方千米；平方公里	= 0.386 square mile 平方英里
Weight 重量	1000 milligrams (mg) 毫克	= 1 gram (g) 克	= 15.43 grains 格令
	1000 grams 克	= 1 kilogram (kg) 千克；公斤	= 2.205 pounds 磅
	1000 kilograms 千克；公斤	= 1 tonne 公噸	= 19.688 hundredweight 英擔
Capacity 容量	10 millilitres (ml) 毫升	= 1 centilitre 厘升	= 0.018 pint 品脫 (0.021 US pint 美制品脫)
	100 centilitres (cl) 厘升	= 1 litre (l) 升	= 1.76 pints 品脫 (2.1 US pints 美制品脫)
	10 litres 升	= 1 decalitre (dal) 十升	= 2.2 gallons 加侖 (2.63 US gallons 美制加侖)

Non-metric measures 非公制計量單位

(with approximate metric equivalents 附大約相當於公制的量)

	Non-metric 非公制		Metric 公制
Length 長度	1 inch (in) 英寸	—	= 25.4 millimetres 毫米
	12 inches 英寸	= 1 foot (ft) 英尺	= 30.48 centimetres 厘米
	3 feet 英尺	= 1 yard (yd) 碼	= 0.914 metre 米
	220 yards 碼	= 1 furlong 浪	= 201.17 metres 米
	8 furlongs 浪	= 1 mile 英里	= 1.609 kilometres 千米；公里
	1760 yards 碼	= 1 mile 英里	= 1.609 kilometres 千米；公里
Area 面積	1 square (sq) inch 平方英寸	—	= 6.452 sq centimetres (cm^2) 平方厘米
	144 sq inches 平方英寸	= 1 sq foot 平方英尺	= 929.03 sq centimetres 平方厘米
	9 sq feet 平方英尺	= 1 sq yard 平方碼	= 0.836 sq metre 平方米
	4840 sq yards 平方碼	= 1 acre 英畝	= 0.405 hectare 公頃
	640 acres 英畝	= 1 sq mile 平方英里	= 259 hectares 公頃/ 2.59 sq kilometres 平方公里
Weight 重量	437 grains 格令	= 1 ounce (oz) 盎司	= 28.35 grams 克
	16 ounces 盎司	= 1 pound (lb) 磅	= 0.454 kilogram 千克
	14 pounds 磅	= 1 stone (st) 英石	= 6.356 kilograms 千克
	8 stone 英石	= 1 hundredweight (cwt) 英擔	= 50.8 kilograms 千克
	20 hundredweight 英擔	= 1 ton 噸	= 1016.04 kilograms 千克
British capacity 英國容量單位	20 fluid ounces (fl oz) 液盎司	= 1 pint (pt) 品脫	= 0.568 litre 升
	2 pints 品脫	= 1 quart (qt) 夸脫	= 1.136 litres 升
	8 pints 品脫	= 1 gallon (gal.) 加侖	= 4.546 litres 升
American capacity 美國容量單位	16 US fluid ounces 美制液盎司	= 1 US pint 美制品脫	= 0.473 litre 升
	2 US pints 美制品脫	= 1 US quart 美制夸脫	= 0.946 litre 升
	4 US quarts 美制夸脫	= 1 US gallon 美制加侖	= 3.785 litres 升

Common first names 常見人名

Variant spellings and forms are given.
Short forms and pet names follow the name from which they are formed.
表中列出不同的拼寫形式，簡稱和昵稱列於其正式名字之後。

Female names 女子名

Abigail /'æbɪgeɪl/ 阿比蓋爾 **Abbie** /'æbi/ 阿比
Aimee /'eɪmi/ 艾梅
Aisling /'æʃlɪŋ/ *(IrishE)* 艾斯林
Alexandra /ˌælɪg'zɑːndrə; *NAmE* -'zændrə/ 亞歷山德拉 **Alex** /'ælɪks/ 亞歷克斯 **Sandy** /'sændi/ 桑迪
Alexis /æ'leksɪs/ *(NAmE)* 亞歷克西斯
Alice /'ælɪs/ 艾麗斯
Alison, *(NAmE)* **Allison** /'ælɪsn/ 艾莉森
Alyssa /æ'lɪsə/ *(NAmE)* 阿莉莎
Amanda /ə'mændə/ 阿曼達 **Mandy** /'mændi/ 曼迪
Amber /'æmbə(r)/ 安伯
Amelia /ə'miːliə/ 阿梅莉亞
Amy /'eɪmi/ 埃米
Angela /'ændʒələ/ 安傑拉
Anita /ə'niːtə/ 安妮塔
Ann, Anne /æn/ 安（妮）**Anna** /'ænə/ 安娜
Annabel, Annabelle /'ænəbel/ 安娜貝爾，安娜貝勒
Annette /æ'net/ 安妮特
Antonia /æn'təʊniə; *NAmE* -'toʊ-/ 安東尼婭
Aoife /'iːfə/ *(IrishE)* 伊弗
Ashley /'æʃli/ 阿什莉
Audrey /'ɔːdri/ 奧德麗
Ava /'eɪvə/ 阿娃
Barbara, Barbra /'bɑːbrə; *NAmE* 'bɑːrbrə/ 巴巴拉
Beatrice /'bɪətrɪs; *NAmE* 'bɪr-/ 比阿特麗斯
Becky see REBECCA
Belinda /bə'lɪndə/ 貝琳達
Bernadette /ˌbɜːnə'det; *NAmE* ˌbɜːrn-/ 貝爾納黛特
Beryl /'berəl/ 貝麗爾
Beth, Betsy, Betty see ELIZABETH
Bethany /'beθəni/ 貝薩妮
Brenda /'brendə/ 布倫達
Brianna /ˌbraɪ'ænə; ˌbrɪ'ænə/ *(NAmE)* 布里安娜
Bridget, Bridgit, Brigid /'brɪdʒɪt/ 布麗奇特
Brooke /brʊk/ 布魯克
Caitlin, Kaitlin, Kaitlyn /'keɪtlɪn/ 凱特琳
Carol, Carole /'kærəl/ 卡蘿爾
Caroline /'kærəlaɪn/ 卡羅琳 **Carolyn** /'kærəlɪn/ 卡羅琳 **Carrie** /'kæri/ 卡麗
Catherine, Katherine, Katharine, Kathryn /'kæθrɪn/ 凱瑟琳 **Cathy, Kathy** /'kæθi/ 凱西 **Kate** /keɪt/ 凱特 **Katie, Katy** /'keɪti/ 凱蒂
Cecily /'sesɪli/ 塞西莉
Charlotte /'ʃɑːlət; *NAmE* 'ʃɑːrlət/ 夏洛特
Cheryl /'ʃerəl; 'tʃe-/ 謝里爾
Chloe /'kləʊi; *NAmE* 'kloʊi/ 克洛艾
Christina /krɪ'stiːnə/ 克里斯蒂娜 **Chrissie** /'krɪsi/ 克麗茜 **Tina** /'tiːnə/ 蒂娜
Christine /'krɪstiːn/ 克里斯蒂娜 **Chris** /krɪs/ 克麗絲
Ciara /'kɪərə; *NAmE* 'kɪrə/ *(IrishE)* 西婭拉
Cindy /'sɪndi/ 辛迪
Clare, Claire /kleə(r); *NAmE* kler/ 克萊爾
Claudia /'klɔːdiə; 'klaʊdiə/ 克勞迪婭
Cleo, Clio /'kliːəʊ; *NAmE* 'kliːoʊ/ 克利奧
Constance /'kɒnstəns; *NAmE* 'kɑːn-/ 康斯坦絲 **Connie** /'kɒni; *NAmE* 'kɑːni/ 康妮
Cynthia /'sɪnθiə/ 辛西婭
Daisy /'deɪzi/ 戴西
Daphne /'dæfni/ 達夫妮
Dawn /dɔːn/ 唐
Deborah /'debrə/ 德博拉 **Debbie** /'debi/ 黛比 **Deb** /deb/ 德布
Delia /'diːliə/ 迪莉婭
Denise /də'niːz; -niːs/ 丹尼絲
Diana /daɪ'ænə/ 黛安娜 **Diane** /daɪ'æn/ 黛安 **Di** /daɪ/ 黛
Doris /'dɒrɪs; *NAmE* 'dɔːr-/ 多麗絲
Dorothy /'dɒrəθi; *NAmE* 'dɔːr-/ 多蘿西
Edith /'iːdɪθ/ 伊迪絲
Edna /'ednə/ 埃德娜
Eileen /'aɪliːn/ 艾琳
Elaine /ɪ'leɪn/ 伊萊恩
Eleanor /'elənə(r)/ 埃莉諾 **Ellie** /'eli/ 埃莉
Eliza /ɪ'laɪzə/ 伊麗莎 **Liza** /'laɪzə; 'liːzə/ 莉莎
Elizabeth, Elisabeth /ɪ'lɪzəbəθ/ 伊麗莎白 **Beth** /beθ/ 貝絲 **Betsy** /'betsi/ 貝齊 **Betty** /'beti/ 貝蒂 **Liz** /lɪz/ 莉茲 **Lizzie** /'lɪzi/ 莉齊
Ella /'elə/ 埃拉
Ellen /'elən/ 埃倫
Ellie see ELEANOR
Elspeth /'elspəθ/ 伊麗莎白
Emily /'eməli/ 埃米莉
Emma /'emə/ 埃瑪
Erin /'erɪn/ 埃琳
Ethel /'eθəl/ 埃塞爾
Eunice /'juːnɪs/ 尤妮斯
Eve /iːv/ 伊芙
Evelyn /'iːvlɪn/ 伊夫琳
Fay /feɪ/ 費伊
Felicity /fə'lɪsəti/ 費莉西蒂
Fiona /fi'əʊnə; *NAmE* -'oʊ-/ 菲奧娜
Florence /'flɒrəns; *NAmE* 'flɔːr-/ 弗洛倫絲
Frances /'frɑːnsɪs; -sɪz; *NAmE* 'fræn-/ 弗朗西絲 **Fran** /fræn/ 弗蘭
Freda /'friːdə/ 弗蕾達
Freya /'freɪə/ 弗雷亞
Georgia /'dʒɔːdʒə; *NAmE* 'dʒɔːrdʒə/ 喬治婭
Georgina /ˌdʒɔː'dʒiːnə; *NAmE* ˌdʒɔːr'dʒ-/ 喬治娜 **Georgie** /'dʒɔːdʒi; *NAmE* 'dʒɔːrdʒi/ 喬姬
Geraldine /'dʒerəldiːn/ 傑拉爾丁
Germaine /ˌdʒɜː'meɪn; *NAmE* ˌdʒɜːr'm-/ 傑曼
Gertrude /'gɜːtruːd; *NAmE* 'gɜːrt-/ 格特魯德

Gillian /ˈdʒɪliən/ 吉莉恩 **Jill, Gill** /dʒɪl/ 吉爾 **Jilly** /ˈdʒɪli/ 吉莉
Gladys /ˈglædɪs/ 格拉迪絲
Glenda /ˈglendə/ 格倫達
Grace /greɪs/ 格雷斯
Gwendoline /ˈgwendəlɪn/ 格溫德琳 **Gwen** /gwen/ 格溫
Hailey /ˈheɪli/ 黑莉
Hannah /ˈhænə/ 漢納
Harriet /ˈhæriət/ 哈麗雅特
Hazel /ˈheɪzl/ 黑茲爾
Heather /ˈheðə(r)/ 希瑟
Helen /ˈhelən/ 海倫
Hilary /ˈhɪləri/ 希拉麗
Hilda /ˈhɪldə/ 希爾達
Holly /ˈhɒli; *NAmE* ˈhɑːli/ 霍莉
Imogen /ˈɪmədʒən/ 伊莫金
Ingrid /ˈɪŋgrɪd/ 英格麗德
Irene /aɪˈriːni; ˈaɪriːn; aɪˈriːn/ 艾琳
Iris /ˈaɪrɪs/ 艾麗斯
Isabel, Isabelle, (*especially ScotE*) **Isobel** /ˈɪzəbel/ 伊莎貝爾 **Isabella** /ˌɪzəˈbelə/ 伊莎貝拉
Jacqueline /ˈdʒækəlɪn/ 傑奎琳 **Jackie** /ˈdʒæki/ 傑姬
Jade /dʒeɪd/ 傑德
Jane /dʒeɪn/ 簡
Janet /ˈdʒænɪt/ 珍妮特 **Jan** /dʒæn/ 簡
Janice, Janis /ˈdʒænɪs/ 賈尼絲 **Jan** /dʒæn/ 簡
Jasmine /ˈdʒæzmɪn/ 賈絲明
Jean /dʒiːn/ 瓊
Jeanette /dʒəˈnet/ 珍妮特
Jennifer /ˈdʒenɪfə(r)/ 珍妮弗 **Jenny** /ˈdʒeni/ 珍妮 **Jen** /dʒen/ 珍
Jessica /ˈdʒesɪkə/ 傑茜卡 **Jess** /dʒes/ 傑絲
Jill, Jilly see GILLIAN
Jo see JOANNA, JOSEPHINE
Joanna /dʒəʊˈænə; *NAmE* dʒoʊ-/ 喬安娜 **Joanne** /dʒəʊˈæn; *NAmE* dʒoʊ-/ 喬安妮 **Jo** /dʒəʊ; *NAmE* dʒoʊ/ 喬
Jocelyn /ˈdʒɒsəlɪn; *NAmE* ˈdʒɑːs-/ 喬斯琳
Jodie /ˈdʒəʊdi; *NAmE* ˈdʒoʊ-/ 喬迪
Josephine /ˈdʒəʊzəfiːn; *NAmE* ˈdʒoʊ-/ 約瑟芬 **Jo** /dʒəʊ; *NAmE* dʒoʊ/ 喬 **Josie** /ˈdʒəʊzi; *NAmE* ˈdʒoʊ-/ 喬茜
Joyce /dʒɔɪs/ 喬伊絲
Judith /ˈdʒuːdɪθ/ 朱迪絲 **Judy** /ˈdʒuːdi/ 朱迪
Julia /ˈdʒuːliə/ 朱莉婭 **Julie** /ˈdʒuːli/ 朱莉
June /dʒuːn/ 瓊
Kaitlin, Kaitlyn (*NAmE*) see CAITLIN
Karen, Karin /ˈkærən; ˈkɑːrən/ 卡倫
Katherine, Katharine, Kathryn, Kathy, Kate, Katie, Katy see CATHERINE
Kay /keɪ/ 凱
Kayla /ˈkeɪlə/ 凱拉
Kaylee /ˈkeɪli/ (*NAmE*) 凱莉
Kim /kɪm/ 金
Kirsten /ˈkɜːstən; *NAmE* ˈkɜːrs-/ 柯爾絲滕 **Kirsty** /ˈkɜːsti; *NAmE* ˈkɜːrs-/ 柯絲蒂
Laura /ˈlɔːrə/ 勞拉
Lauren /ˈlɒrən; *NAmE* ˈlɔːr-/ 勞倫
Leah /ˈliːə/ 利婭
Lesley /ˈlezli/ 萊斯莉
Lily /ˈlɪli/ 莉莉
Linda /ˈlɪndə/ 琳達
Lisa /ˈliːzə; -sə/ 莉薩
Liza see ELIZA
Liz, Lizzie see ELIZABETH
Lois /ˈləʊɪs; *NAmE* ˈloʊ-/ 洛伊絲
Lorna /ˈlɔːnə; *NAmE* ˈlɔːrnə/ 洛娜
Louise /luˈiːz/ 路易絲
Lucinda /luːˈsɪndə/ 露辛達
Lucy /ˈluːsi/ 露西
Lydia /ˈlɪdiə/ 莉迪婭
Lyn /lɪn/ 琳恩
Madeleine, (*NAmE*) **Madeline** /ˈmædlɪn/ 馬德琳
Madison /ˈmædɪsn/ (*NAmE*) 麥迪遜
Maeve /meɪv/ (*IrishE*) 梅芙
Maggie see MARGARET
Maisie /ˈmeɪzi/ 梅茜
Mandy see AMANDA
Margaret /ˈmɑːgrət; *NAmE* ˈmɑːrg-/ 瑪格麗特 **Maggie** /ˈmægi/ 瑪吉
Margery, Marjorie /ˈmɑːdʒəri; *NAmE* ˈmɑːrdʒ-/ 瑪格麗；瑪喬麗
Maria /məˈriːə/ 瑪麗亞
Marian, Marion /ˈmæriən/ 瑪麗安
Marie /məˈriː/ 瑪麗
Marilyn /ˈmærəlɪn/ 瑪麗蓮
Marion see MARIAN
Martha /ˈmɑːθə; *NAmE* ˈmɑːrθə/ 瑪莎
Martina /mɑːˈtiːnə; *NAmE* mɑːrˈt-/ 馬丁娜
Mary /ˈmeəri; *NAmE* ˈmeri/ 瑪麗
Maud /mɔːd/ 莫德
Mavis /ˈmeɪvɪs/ 梅維絲
Megan /ˈmegən/ 梅甘
Melanie /ˈmeləni/ 梅拉妮
Melinda /məˈlɪndə/ 梅琳達
Melissa /məˈlɪsə/ 梅利莎
Meryl /ˈmerəl/ 梅里爾
Mia /ˈmiːə/ 米婭
Michelle /mɪˈʃel/ 米歇爾
Millie /ˈmɪli/ 米莉
Miranda /mɪˈrændə/ 米蘭達
Miriam /ˈmɪriəm/ 米麗婭姆
Moira /ˈmɔɪrə/ 莫伊拉
Molly /ˈmɒli; *NAmE* ˈmɑːli/ 莫莉
Monica /ˈmɒnɪkə; *NAmE* ˈmɑːn-/ 莫妮卡
Morgan /ˈmɔːgən; *NAmE* ˈmɔːrg-/ 摩根
Muriel /ˈmjʊəriəl; *NAmE* ˈmjʊr-/ 繆麗爾
Nadia /ˈnædiə; ˈnɑːdiə/ 納迪婭
Nancy /ˈnænsi/ 南希
Naomi /ˈneɪəmi; neɪˈəʊmi; *NAmE* -ˈoʊ-/ 娜奧米
Natalie /ˈnætəli/ 納塔莉
Natasha /nəˈtæʃə/ 娜塔莎
Niamh /niːv/ (*IrishE*) 尼芙
Nicola /ˈnɪkələ/ 妮古拉 **Nicky** /ˈnɪki/ 尼基
Nicole /nɪˈkəʊl; -ˈkɒl; *NAmE* nɪˈkoʊl/ 妮科爾
Nora /ˈnɔːrə/ 諾拉
Norma /ˈnɔːmə; *NAmE* ˈnɔːrmə/ 諾爾瑪
Olive /ˈɒlɪv; *NAmE* ˈɑːlɪv/ 奧利芙
Olivia /əˈlɪviə/ 奧利維婭
Paige /peɪdʒ/ 佩奇

Pamela /ˈpæmələ/ 帕梅拉 **Pam** /pæm/ 帕姆

Patricia /pəˈtrɪʃə/ 帕特里夏 **Pat** /pæt/ 帕特 **Patty** /ˈpæti/ 帕蒂

Paula /ˈpɔːlə/ 葆拉

Pauline /ˈpɔːliːn/ 保利娜

Penelope /pəˈneləpi/ 佩內洛普 **Penny** /ˈpeni/ 彭妮

Philippa /ˈfɪlɪpə/ 菲莉帕 **Pippa** /ˈpɪpə/ 皮帕

Phoebe /ˈfiːbi/ 菲比

Phyllis /ˈfɪlɪs/ 菲莉絲

Polly /ˈpɒli; *NAmE* ˈpɑːli/ 波莉

Poppy /ˈpɒpi; *NAmE* ˈpɑːpi/ 波皮

Priscilla /prɪˈsɪlə/ 普麗西拉

Prudence /ˈpruːdəns/ 普魯登絲

Rachel /ˈreɪtʃəl/ 雷切爾

Rebecca /rɪˈbekə/ 麗貝卡 **Becky** /ˈbeki/ 貝姬

Robin /ˈrɒbɪn; *NAmE* ˈrɑːbɪn/ 羅賓

Roisin /rəʊˈʃiːn; *NAmE* roʊ-/ *(IrishE)* 魯瓦辛

Rosalind /ˈrɒzəlɪnd; *NAmE* ˈrɑːz-/ 羅莎琳德 **Rosalyn** /ˈrɒzəlɪn; *NAmE* ˈrɑːz-/ 羅莎琳 **Ros** /rɒz; *NAmE* rɑːz/ 羅斯

Rose /rəʊz; *NAmE* roʊz/ 羅絲 **Rosie** /ˈrəʊzi; *NAmE* ˈroʊzi/ 羅茜

Rosemary /ˈrəʊzməri; *NAmE* ˈroʊzmeri/ 羅斯瑪麗 **Rosie** /ˈrəʊzi; *NAmE* ˈroʊzi/ 羅茜

Ruby /ˈruːbi/ 魯比

Ruth /ruːθ/ 露絲

Sally /ˈsæli/ 薩莉

Samantha /səˈmænθə/ 薩曼莎 **Sam** /sæm/ 薩姆

Sandra /ˈsɑːndrə; *NAmE* ˈsæn-/ 桑德拉 **Sandy** /ˈsændi/ 桑迪

Sandy see ALEXANDRA, SANDRA

Sarah /ˈseərə; *NAmE* ˈserə/ 薩拉 **Sara** /ˈseərə; ˈsɑːrə; *NAmE also* ˈserə/ 薩拉

Shannon /ˈʃænən/ 香農

Sharon /ˈʃærən/ 莎倫

Sheila, Shelagh /ˈʃiːlə/ 希拉

Shirley /ˈʃɜːli; *NAmE* ˈʃɜːrli/ 雪莉

Sian /ʃɑːn/ *(WelshE)* 沙恩

Sibyl see SYBIL

Silvia, Sylvia /ˈsɪlviə/ 西爾維婭

Sinead /ʃɪˈneɪd/ *(IrishE)* 西內德

Siobhan /ʃɪˈvɔːn/ *(IrishE)* 西沃恩

Sophia /səˈfiːə; -ˈfaɪə/ 索菲婭 **Sophie, Sophy** /ˈsəʊfi; *NAmE* ˈsoʊfi/ 索菲

Stella /ˈstelə/ 斯特拉

Stephanie /ˈstefəni/ 斯蒂芬妮

Susan /ˈsuːzən/ 蘇珊 **Sue** /suː/ 休 **Susie, Suzy** /ˈsuːzi/ 蘇茜

Susanna(h) /suːˈzænə/ 蘇珊娜 **Suzanne** /suːˈzæn/ 蘇珊 **Susie, Suzy** /ˈsuːzi/ 蘇茜

Sybil, Sibyl /ˈsɪbl/ 西比爾

Sylvia, Silvia /ˈsɪlviə/ 西爾維婭

Taylor /ˈteɪlə(r)/ 泰勒

Teresa, Theresa /təˈriːzə; -ˈreɪzə/ 特蕾莎 **Tessa** /ˈtesə/ 特莎 **Tess** /tes/ 特絲

Thelma /ˈθelmə/ 特爾瑪

Tina see CHRISTINA

Toni /ˈtəʊni; *NAmE* ˈtoʊni/ *(NAmE)* 托妮

Tracy, Tracey /ˈtreɪsi/ 特蕾西

Ursula /ˈɜːsjələ; *NAmE* ˈɜːrs-/ 厄休拉

Valerie /ˈvæləri/ 瓦萊麗 **Val** /væl/ 瓦爾

Vanessa /vəˈnesə/ 瓦妮莎

Vera /ˈvɪərə; *NAmE* ˈvɪrə/ 薇拉

Veronica /vəˈrɒnɪkə; *NAmE* -ˈrɑːn-/ 韋羅妮卡

Victoria /vɪkˈtɔːriə/ 維多利亞 **Vicki, Vickie, Vicky, Vikki** /ˈvɪki/ 薇娅

Violet /ˈvaɪələt/ 維奧莉特

Virginia /vəˈdʒɪniə; *NAmE* vərˈdʒɪnjə/ 弗吉尼婭

Vivien, Vivienne /ˈvɪviən/ 維維恩

Wendy /ˈwendi/ 溫迪

Winifred /ˈwɪnɪfrɪd/ 威妮弗雷德 **Winnie** /ˈwɪni/ 溫妮

Yvonne /ɪˈvɒn; iːˈvɒn; *NAmE* -ˈvɑːn/ 伊馮娜

Zoe /ˈzəʊi; *NAmE* ˈzoʊi/ 佐伊

Male names 男子名

Aaron /ˈeərən; *NAmE* ˈerən/ 阿倫

Abraham /ˈeɪbrəhæm/ 亞伯拉罕

Adam /ˈædəm/ 亞當

Adrian /ˈeɪdriən/ 阿德里安

Aidan /ˈeɪdn/ 艾丹

Alan, Allan, Allen /ælən/ 艾倫

Albert /ˈælbət; *NAmE* -bərt/ 艾伯特 **Al** /æl/ 阿爾 **Bert** /bɜːt; *NAmE* bɜːrt/ 伯特

Alexander /ˌælɪɡˈzɑːndə(r); *NAmE* -ˈzæn-/ 亞歷山大 **Alex** /ˈælɪks/ 亞歷克斯 **Sandy** /ˈsændi/ 桑迪

Alfred /ˈælfrɪd/ 艾爾弗雷德 **Alfie** /ˈælfi/ 阿爾菲

Alistair, Alisdair, Alasdair /ˈælɪsteə(r); *NAmE* -ter/ 阿利斯泰爾

Allan, Allen see ALAN

Andrew /ˈændruː/ 安德魯 **Andy** /ˈændi/ 安迪

Angus /ˈæŋɡəs/ *(ScotE)* 安格斯

Anthony, Antony /ˈæntəni/ 安東尼 **Tony** /ˈtəʊni; *NAmE* ˈtoʊni/ 托尼

Archibald /ˈɑːtʃɪbɔːld; *NAmE* ˈɑːrtʃ-/ 阿奇博爾德 **Archie** /ˈɑːtʃi; *NAmE* ˈɑːrtʃi/ 阿奇

Arnold /ˈɑːnəld; *NAmE* ˈɑːrn-/ 阿諾德

Arthur /ˈɑːθə(r); *NAmE* ˈɑːrθ-/ 阿瑟

Austin /ˈɒstɪn; *NAmE* ˈɑːs-/ 奧斯汀

Barry /ˈbæri/ 巴里

Basil /ˈbæzl/ 巴茲爾

Benjamin /ˈbendʒəmɪn/ 本傑明 **Ben** /ben/ 本

Bernard /ˈbɜːnəd; *NAmE* ˈbɜːrnərd/ 伯納德 **Bernie** /ˈbɜːni; *NAmE* ˈbɜːrni/ 伯尼

Bert see ALBERT, HERBERT

Bill, Billy see WILLIAM

Bob, Bobby see ROBERT

Bradford /ˈbrædfəd; *NAmE* -fərd/ 布拉德福德 **Brad** /bræd/ *(especially NAmE)* 布拉德

Bradley /ˈbrædli/ 布拉德利

Brandon /ˈbrændən/ 布蘭登

Brendan /ˈbrendən/ *(IrishE)* 布倫丹

Brian, Bryan /ˈbraɪən/ 布賴恩

Bruce /bruːs/ 布魯斯

Bud /bʌd/ *(NAmE)* 巴德

Caleb /ˈkeɪləb/ 凱萊布

Callum /ˈkæləm/ 卡勒姆

Cameron /ˈkæmərən/ 卡梅倫
Carl /kɑːl; *NAmE* kɑːrl/ 卡爾
Cecil /ˈsesl/ 塞西爾
Charles /tʃɑːlz; *NAmE* tʃɑːrlz/ 查爾斯
 Charlie /ˈtʃɑːli; *NAmE* ˈtʃɑːrli/ 查利 **Chuck** /tʃʌk/ 查克
Christopher /ˈkrɪstəfə(r)/ 克里斯托弗
 Chris /krɪs/ 克里斯
Chuck see CHARLES
Cian /ʃɑːn/ *(IrishE)* 奇安
Ciaran /ˈkɪərən; *NAmE* ˈkɪr-/ *(IrishE)* 夏蘭
Clark /klɑːk; *NAmE* klɑːrk/ 克拉克
Clifford /ˈklɪfəd; *NAmE* -fərd/ 克利福德 **Cliff** 克利夫
Clint /klɪnt/ 克林特
Clive /klaɪv/ 克萊夫
Colin /ˈkɒlɪn; *NAmE* ˈkɑːl-; ˈkoʊl-/ 科林
Conor, *(NAmE)* **Connor** /ˈkɒnə(r); *NAmE* ˈkɑːn-/ 康納
Craig /kreɪɡ/ 克雷格
Cyril /ˈsɪrɪl/ 西里爾
Dale /deɪl/ 戴爾
Daniel /ˈdænjəl/ 丹尼爾 **Dan** /dæn/ 丹
 Danny /ˈdæni/ 丹尼
Darrell /ˈdærəl/ 達雷爾
Darren /ˈdærən/ 達倫
David /ˈdeɪvɪd/ 戴維 **Dave** /deɪv/ 戴夫
Dean /diːn/ 迪安
Dennis, **Denis** /ˈdenɪs/ 丹尼斯
Derek /ˈderɪk/ 德里克
Dermot /ˈdɜːmət; *NAmE* ˈdɜːrm-/ *(IrishE)* 德莫特
Desmond /ˈdezmənd/ 德斯蒙德
Dick see RICHARD
Dirk /dɜːk; *NAmE* dɜːrk/ 德克
Dominic /ˈdɒmɪnɪk; *NAmE* ˈdɑːm-/ 多米尼克
Donald /ˈdɒnəld; *NAmE* ˈdɑːn-/ 唐納德
Douglas /ˈdʌɡləs 道格拉斯 / **Doug** /dʌɡ/ 道格
Duane, **Dwane** /dweɪn/ *(especially NAmE)* 杜安
Duncan /ˈdʌŋkən/ 鄧肯
Dwight /dwaɪt/ *(especially NAmE)* 德懷特
Dylan /ˈdɪlən/ 迪倫
Eamonn, **Eamon** /ˈeɪmən/ *(IrishE)* 埃蒙
Ed, **Eddie**, **Eddy** see EDWARD
Edmond, **Edmund** /ˈedmənd/ 埃德蒙
Edward /ˈedwəd; *NAmE* -wərd/ 愛德華
 Ed /ed/ 埃德 **Eddie, Eddy** /ˈedi/ 埃迪 **Ted** /ted/ 特德
Edwin /ˈedwɪn/ 埃德溫
Elijah /ɪˈlaɪdʒə/ 伊萊賈
Elmer /ˈelmə(r)/ *(NAmE)* 埃爾默
Elroy /ˈelrɔɪ/ *(NAmE)* 埃爾羅伊
Emlyn /ˈemlɪn/ *(WelshE)* 埃姆林
Eric /ˈerɪk/ 埃里克
Ernest /ˈɜːnɪst; *NAmE* ˈɜːrn-/ 歐內斯特
Ethan /ˈiːθən/ 伊桑
Eugene /juːˈdʒiːn; ˈjuː-/ 尤金 **Gene** /dʒiːn/ *(NAmE)* 吉恩
Evan /ˈevən/ 埃文
Fergus /ˈfɜːɡəs; *NAmE* ˈfɜːrɡ-/ *(IrishE, ScotE)* 弗格斯
Francis /ˈfrɑːnsɪs; -sɪz; *NAmE* ˈfræn-/ 弗朗西斯
 Frank /fræŋk/ 弗蘭克
Frederick /ˈfredərɪk/ 弗雷德里克
 Fred /fred/ 弗雷德 **Freddie, Freddy** /ˈfredi/ 弗雷迪
Gabriel /ˈɡeɪbrɪəl/ 加布里埃爾
Gareth /ˈɡærəθ/ 加雷思
Gary /ˈɡæri/ 加里
Gavin /ˈɡævɪn/ 加文
Gene see EUGENE
Geoffrey, **Jeffrey** /ˈdʒefri/ 傑弗里
 Geoff, Jeff /dʒef/ 傑夫
George /dʒɔːdʒ; *NAmE* dʒɔːrdʒ/ 喬治
Geraint /ˈɡeraɪnt/ *(WelshE)* 傑蘭特
Gerald /ˈdʒerəld/ 傑拉爾德 **Gerry, Jerry** /ˈdʒeri/ 格里
Gerard /ˈdʒerɑːd; -rəd; *NAmE* ˈdʒerɑːrd/ 傑勒德
Gilbert /ˈɡɪlbət; *NAmE* -bərt/ 吉爾伯特
Glen /ɡlen/ 格倫
Godfrey /ˈɡɒdfri; *NAmE* ˈɡɑːd-/ 戈弗雷
Gordon /ˈɡɔːdn; *NAmE* ˈɡɔːrdn/ 戈登
Graham, **Grahame**, **Graeme** /ˈɡreɪəm/ 格雷厄姆
Gregory /ˈɡreɡəri/ 格雷戈里 **Greg** /ɡreɡ/ 格雷格
Guy /ɡaɪ/ 蓋伊
Harold /ˈhærəld/ 哈羅德
Harrison /ˈhærɪsən/ 哈里森
Harvey /ˈhɑːvi; *NAmE* ˈhɑːrvi/ 哈維
Henry /ˈhenri/ 亨利 **Hank** /hæŋk/ 漢克
 Harry /ˈhæri/ 哈里
Herbert /ˈhɜːbət; *NAmE* ˈhɜːrbərt/ 赫伯特
 Bert /bɜːt; *NAmE* bɜːrt/ 伯特
 Herb /hɜːb; *NAmE* hɜːrb/ 赫布
Horace /ˈhɒrɪs; *NAmE* ˈhɑːr-/ 霍勒斯
Howard /ˈhaʊəd; *NAmE* -ərd/ 霍華德
Hubert /ˈhjuːbət; *NAmE* -bərt/ 休伯特
Hugh /hjuː/ 休
Hugo /ˈhjuːɡəʊ; *NAmE* -ɡoʊ/ 雨果
Ian /ˈiːən/ 伊恩
Isaac /ˈaɪzək/ 艾薩克
Isaiah /aɪˈzaɪə; *NAmE* aɪˈzeɪə/ 以賽亞
Ivan /ˈaɪvn/ 伊萬
Ivor /ˈaɪvə(r)/ 艾弗
Jack /dʒæk/ 傑克
Jacob /ˈdʒeɪkəb/ 雅各布 **Jake** /dʒeɪk/ 傑克
James /dʒeɪmz/ 詹姆斯
 Jim /dʒɪm/ 吉姆 **Jimmy** /ˈdʒɪmi/ 吉米
 Jamie /ˈdʒeɪmi/ 傑米
Jason /ˈdʒeɪsn/ 賈森
Jasper /ˈdʒæspə(r)/ 賈思珀
Jayden /ˈdʒeɪdn/ *(NAmE)* 傑登
Jed /dʒed/ 傑德
Jeff, **Jeffrey** see GEOFFREY
Jeremy /ˈdʒerəmi/ 傑里米 **Jerry** /ˈdʒeri/ 傑里
Jerome /dʒəˈrəʊm; *NAmE* -ˈroʊm/ 傑羅姆
Jerry see GERALD, JEREMY
Jesse /ˈdʒesi/ *(especially NAmE)* 傑西
Jim, **Jimmy** see JAMES
Joe see JOSEPH
John /dʒɒn; *NAmE* dʒɑːn/ 約翰
 Johnny /ˈdʒɒni; *NAmE* ˈdʒɑːni/ 約翰尼
Jonathan /ˈdʒɒnəθən; *NAmE* ˈdʒɑːn-/ 喬納森
 Jon /dʒɒn; *NAmE* dʒɑːn/ 喬恩
Jordan /ˈdʒɔːdn; *NAmE* ˈdʒɔːrdn/ 喬丹
Joseph /ˈdʒəʊzɪf; -sɪf/ 約瑟夫 **Joe** /dʒəʊ; *NAmE* dʒoʊ/ 喬
Joshua /ˈdʒɒʃuə; *NAmE* ˈdʒɑːʃ-/ 喬舒亞
Julian /ˈdʒuːliən/ 朱利安
Justin /ˈdʒʌstɪn/ 賈斯廷
Keith /kiːθ/ 基思

Kenneth /ˈkenɪθ/ 肯尼思 **Ken** /ken/ 肯
Kenny /ˈkeni/ 肯尼

Kevin /ˈkevɪn/ 凱文

Kieran /ˈkɪərən; *NAmE* ˈkɪr-/ 基蘭

Kirk /kɜːk; *NAmE* kɜːrk/ 柯克

Kit see CHRISTOPHER

Kyle /kaɪl/ 凱爾

Lance /lɑːns; *NAmE* læns/ 蘭斯

Laurence, Lawrence /ˈlɒrəns; *NAmE* ˈlɔːr-/ 勞倫斯
Larry /ˈlæri/ 拉里 **Laurie** /ˈlɒri; *NAmE* ˈlɔːri/ 勞里

Len, Lenny see LEONARD

Leo /ˈliːəʊ; *NAmE* -oʊ/ 利奧

Leonard /ˈlenəd; *NAmE* -ərd/ 倫納德
Len /len/ 萊恩 **Lenny** /ˈleni/ 倫尼

Leslie /ˈlezli/ 萊斯利 **Les** /lez/ 萊斯

Lester /ˈlestə(r)/ 萊斯特

Lewis /ˈluːɪs/ 劉易斯 **Lew** /luː/ 盧

Liam /ˈliːəm/ 利亞姆

Logan /ˈləʊgən; *NAmE* ˈloʊ-/ *(NAmE)* 洛根
Louis /ˈluːi; ˈluːɪs/ 路易；路易斯
Lou /luː/ *(especially NAmE)* 盧

Luke /luːk/ 盧克

Malcolm /ˈmælkəm/ 馬爾科姆

Mark /mɑːk; *NAmE* mɑːrk/ 馬克

Martin /ˈmɑːtin; *NAmE* ˈmɑːrt-/ 馬丁

Matthew /ˈmæθjuː/ 馬修 **Matt** /mæt/ 馬特

Maurice, Morris /ˈmɒrɪs; *NAmE* ˈmɔːr-/ 莫里斯

Max /mæks/ 馬克斯

Michael /ˈmaɪkəl/ 邁克爾 **Mike** /maɪk/ 邁克
Mick /mɪk/ 米克 **Micky, Mickey** /ˈmɪki/ 米基

Miles, Myles /maɪlz/ 邁爾斯

Morris see MAURICE

Mort /mɔːt; *NAmE* mɔːrt/ *(NAmE)* 莫特

Murray /ˈmʌri/ *(ScotE)* 默里

Myles see MILES

Nathan /ˈneɪθən/ 內森 **Nat** /næt/ 納特

Nathaniel /nəˈθænjəl/ 納撒尼爾 **Nat** /næt/ 納特

Neil, Neal /niəl/ 尼爾

Nicholas /ˈnɪkələs/ 尼古拉斯 **Nick** /nɪk/ 尼克
Nicky /nɪki/ 尼基

Nigel /ˈnaɪdʒəl/ 奈傑爾

Noah /ˈnəʊə; *NAmE* ˈnoʊə/ 諾厄

Noel /ˈnəʊəl; *NAmE* ˈnoʊ-/ 諾埃爾

Norman /ˈnɔːmən; *NAmE* ˈnɔːrm-/ 諾曼

Oliver /ˈɒlɪvə(r); *NAmE* ˈɑːl-/ 奧利弗
Ollie /ˈɒli; *NAmE* ˈɑːli/ 奧利

Oscar /ˈɒskə(r); *NAmE* ˈɑːs-/ 奧斯卡

Owen /ˈəʊɪn; *NAmE* ˈoʊɪn/ *(WelshE)* 歐文

Patrick /ˈpætrɪk/ 帕特里克 **Pat** /pæt/ 帕特
Paddy /ˈpædi/ 帕迪

Paul /pɔːl/ 保羅

Peter /ˈpiːtə(r)/ 彼得 **Pete** /piːt/ 皮特

Philip /ˈfɪlɪp/ 菲利普 **Phil** /fɪl/ 菲爾

Ralph /rælf; reɪf/ 拉爾夫

Randolph, Randolf /ˈrændɒlf; *NAmE* -dɑːlf/ 倫道夫
Randy /ˈrændi/ *(especially NAmE)* 蘭迪

Raymond /ˈreɪmənd/ 雷蒙德 **Ray** /reɪ/ 雷

Reece /riːs/ 里斯

Rex /reks/ 雷克斯

Richard /ˈrɪtʃəd; *NAmE* -ərd/ 理查德
Rick /rɪk/ 里克 **Ricky** /ˈrɪki/ 里基 **Ritchie** /ˈrɪtʃi/ 里奇
Dick /dɪk/ 迪克

Robert /ˈrɒbət; *NAmE* ˈrɑːbərt/ 羅伯特
Rob /rɒb; *NAmE* rɑːb/ 羅布
Robbie /ˈrɒbi; *NAmE* ˈrɑːbi/ 羅比
Bob /bɒb; *NAmE* bɑːb/ 鮑勃
Bobby /ˈbɒbi; *NAmE* ˈbɑːbi/ 博比

Robin /ˈrɒbɪn; *NAmE* ˈrɑːb-/ 羅賓

Roderick /ˈrɒdərɪk; *NAmE* ˈrɑːd-/ 羅德里克

Rodney /ˈrɒdni; *NAmE* ˈrɑːd-/ 羅德尼
Rod /rɒd; *NAmE* rɑːd/ 羅德

Roger /ˈrɒdʒə(r); *NAmE* ˈrɑːdʒ-/ 羅傑

Ronald /ˈrɒnəld; *NAmE* ˈrɑːn-/ 羅納德
Ron /rɒn; *NAmE* rɑːn/ 羅恩
Ronnie /ˈrɒni; *NAmE* ˈrɑːni/ 龍尼

Rory /ˈrɔːri/ 羅里

Ross /rɒs; *NAmE* rɑːs/ 羅斯

Roy /rɔɪ/ 羅伊

Russell /ˈrʌsl/ 拉塞爾

Ryan /ˈraɪən/ 瑞安

Samuel /ˈsæmjuəl; *NAmE* -jəl/ 塞繆爾
Sam /sæm/ 薩姆 **Sammy** /ˈsæmi/ 薩米

Sandy see ALEXANDER

Scott /skɒt; *NAmE* skɑːt/ 斯科特

Seamas, Seamus /ˈʃeɪməs/ *(IrishE)* 謝默斯

Sean /ʃɔːn/ 肖恩

Sebastian /səˈbæstiən; *NAmE* -tjən/ 塞巴斯蒂安
Seb /seb/ 塞布

Sidney, Sydney /ˈsɪdni/ 悉尼 **Sid** /sɪd/ 錫德

Simon /ˈsaɪmən/ 西蒙

Stanley /ˈstænli/ 斯坦利 **Stan** /stæn/ 斯坦

Stephen, Steven /ˈstiːvən/ 斯蒂芬 **Steve** /stiːv/ 史蒂夫

Stewart, Stuart /ˈstjuːət; *NAmE* ˈstuːərt/ 斯圖爾特

Ted see EDWARD

Terence /ˈterəns/ 特倫斯 **Terry** /ˈteri/ 特里

Theodore /ˈθiːədɔː(r)/ 西奧多
Theo /ˈθiːəʊ; *NAmE* -oʊ/ 西奧

Thomas /ˈtɒməs; *NAmE* ˈtɑːm-/ 托馬斯
Tom /tɒm; *NAmE* tɑːm/ 湯姆
Tommy /ˈtɒmi; *NAmE* ˈtɑːmi/ 湯米

Timothy /ˈtɪməθi/ 蒂莫西 **Tim** /tɪm/ 蒂姆

Toby /ˈtəʊbi; *NAmE* ˈtoʊ-/ 托比

Tom, Tommy see THOMAS

Tony see ANTHONY

Trevor /ˈtrevə(r)/ 特雷弗

Tyler /ˈtaɪlə(r)/ 泰勒

Victor /ˈvɪktə(r)/ 維克托 **Vic** /vɪk/ 維克

Vincent /ˈvɪnsnt/ 文森特 **Vince** /vɪns/ 文斯

Walter /ˈwɔːltə(r)/ 沃爾特

Warren /ˈwɒrən; *NAmE* ˈwɔːr-/ 沃倫

Wayne /weɪn/ *(NAmE)* 韋恩

Wilbur /ˈwɪlbə(r)/ 威爾伯

William /ˈwɪljəm/ 威廉 **Bill** /bɪl/ 比爾 **Billy** /ˈbɪli/ 比利
Will /wɪl/ 威爾 **Willy** /ˈwɪli/ 威利

Zachary /ˈzækəri/ 扎卡里

Geographical names 地名

These lists show the spelling and pronunciation of geographical names.
下表列出各地名的拼寫和讀音。

If a country has different words for the country, adjective and person, all are given, (eg **Denmark**; **Danish**, **a Dane**). To make the plural of a word for a person from a particular country, add **–s**, except for **Swiss** and for words ending in **-ese** (eg **Japanese**), which stay the same, and for words that end in **-man** or **-woman**, which change to **-men** or **-women**. 若某國的名稱、形容詞和該國的人用不同的詞表示，此處均一併列出，如 Denmark（丹麥），Danish（丹麥的），Dane（丹麥人）。表示某國人的複數，在該詞末尾加 s 構成，但 Swiss（瑞士人）和以 -ese 結尾的詞（如 Japanese 日本人）複數同單數拼法一樣；以 -man 或 -woman 結尾的詞，複數作 -men 或 -women。

(Inclusion in this list does not imply status as a sovereign state. 本表所收錄的不一定為主權國。)

Afghanistan /æfˈgænɪstæn; -stɑːn/ 阿富汗 **Afghan** /ˈæfgæn/

Africa /ˈæfrɪkə/ 非洲 **African** /ˈæfrɪkən/

Albania /ælˈbeɪniə/ 阿爾巴尼亞 **Albanian** /ælˈbeɪniən/

Algeria /ælˈdʒɪəriə; *NAmE* -ˈdʒɪr-/ 阿爾及利亞
Algerian /ælˈdʒɪəriən; *NAmE* -ˈdʒɪr-/

America /əˈmerɪkə/ 美洲；美國 **American** /əˈmerɪkən/

Andorra /ænˈdɔːrə/ 安道爾 **Andorran** /ænˈdɔːrən/

Angola /æŋˈgəʊlə; *NAmE* -ˈgoʊ-/ 安哥拉
Angolan /æŋˈgəʊlən; *NAmE* -ˈgoʊ-/

Antarctica /ænˈtɑːktɪkə; *NAmE* -ˈtɑːrk-/ 南極洲
Antarctic /ænˈtɑːktɪk; *NAmE* -ˈtɑːrk-/

Antigua and Barbuda /æn͵tiːgə ən bɑːˈbjuːdə; *NAmE* bɑːrˈb-/ 安提瓜和巴布達 **Antiguan** /ænˈtiːgən/
Barbudan /bɑːˈbjuːdən; *NAmE* bɑːrˈb-/

(the) Arctic Ocean /͵ɑːktɪk ˈəʊʃn; *NAmE* ͵ɑːrktɪk ˈoʊʃn/ 北冰洋 **Arctic** /ˈɑːktɪk; *NAmE* ˈɑːrk-/

Argentina /͵ɑːdʒənˈtiːnə; *NAmE* ͵ɑːrdʒ-/ 阿根廷
Argentinian /͵ɑːdʒənˈtɪniən; *NAmE* ͵ɑːrdʒ-/
Argentine /ˈɑːdʒəntaɪn; *NAmE* ˈɑːrdʒ-/

Armenia /ɑːˈmiːniə; *NAmE* ɑːrˈm-/ 亞美尼亞
Armenian /ɑːˈmiːniən; *NAmE* ɑːrˈm-/

Asia /ˈeɪʒə; ˈeɪʃə/ 亞洲 **Asian** /ˈeɪʒn; ˈeɪʃn/

(the) Atlantic Ocean /ət͵læntɪk ˈəʊʃn; *NAmE* ˈoʊʃn/ 大西洋

Australasia /͵ɒstrəˈleɪʒə; -ˈleɪʃə; *NAmE* ͵ɔːstrə-/ 澳大拉西亞 **Australasian** /͵ɒstrəˈleɪʒn; -ˈleɪʃn; *NAmE* ͵ɔːstrə-/

Australia /ɒˈstreɪliə; *NAmE* ɔːˈs-/ 澳大利亞
Australian /ɒˈstreɪliən; *NAmE* ɔːˈs-/

Austria /ˈɒstriə; *NAmE* ˈɔːs-/ 奧地利 **Austrian** /ˈɒstriən; *NAmE* ˈɔːs-/

Azerbaijan /͵æzəbaɪˈdʒɑːn; *NAmE* -zərb-/ 阿塞拜疆
Azerbaijani /͵æzəbaɪˈdʒɑːni; *NAmE* -zərb-/
Azeri /əˈzeəri; *NAmE* əˈzeri/

(the) Bahamas /bəˈhɑːməz/ 巴哈馬 **Bahamian** /bəˈheɪmiən/

Bahrain /bɑːˈreɪn/ 巴林 **Bahraini** /bɑːˈreɪni/

Bangladesh /͵bæŋgləˈdeʃ/ 孟加拉國
Bangladeshi /͵bæŋgləˈdeʃi/

Barbados /bɑːˈbeɪdɒs; *NAmE* bɑːrˈbeɪdoʊs/ 巴巴多斯
Barbadian /bɑːˈbeɪdiən; *NAmE* bɑːrˈb-/

Belarus /͵beləˈruːs/ 白俄羅斯 **Belarusian** /͵beləˈruːsiən/
Belorussian /͵beləˈrʌʃn/

Belgium /ˈbeldʒəm/ 比利時 **Belgian** /ˈbeldʒən/

Belize /bəˈliːz; beˈl-/ 伯利茲 **Belizean** /bəˈliːziən; beˈl-/

Benin /beˈniːn/ 貝寧 **Beninese** /͵benɪˈniːz/

Bhutan /buːˈtɑːn/ 不丹 **Bhutanese** /͵buːtəˈniːz/

Bolivia /bəˈlɪviə/ 玻利維亞 **Bolivian** /bəˈlɪviən/

Bosnia and Herzegovina /͵bɒzniə ən ͵hɜːtsəgəˈviːnə; *NAmE* ͵bɑːzniə ən ͵hɜːrts-; ͵bɔːz-/ 波斯尼亞及黑塞哥維那
Bosnian /ˈbɒzniən; *NAmE* ˈbɑːz-; ˈbɔːz-/
Herzegovinian /͵hɜːtsəgəˈvɪniən; *NAmE* ͵hɜːrts-/

Botswana /bɒtˈswɑːnə; *NAmE* bɑːt-/ 博茨瓦納
Botswanan /bɒtˈswɑːnən; *NAmE* bɑːt-/
person **a Motswana** /mɒtˈswɑːnə; *NAmE* mɑːt-/
people **Batswana** /bætˈswɑːnə/

Brazil /brəˈzɪl/ 巴西 **Brazilian** /brəˈzɪliən/

Brunei /bruːˈnaɪ/ 文萊 **Bruneian** /bruːˈnaɪən/

Bulgaria /bʌlˈgeəriə; *NAmE* -ˈger-/ 保加利亞
Bulgarian /bʌlˈgeəriən; *NAmE* -ˈger-/

Burkina /bɜːˈkiːnə; *NAmE* bɜːrˈk-/ 布基納法索
Burkinan /͵bɜːˈkiːnən; *NAmE* ͵bɜːrˈk-/
Burkinabe /bɜː͵kiːnəˈbeɪ; *NAmE* bɜːr͵k-/

Burma /ˈbɜːmə; *NAmE* ˈbɜːrmə/ 緬甸 **Burmese** /bɜːˈmiːz; *NAmE* bɜːrˈm-/ ➲ see also **Myanmar**

Burundi /bʊˈrʊndi/ 布隆迪 **Burundian** /bʊˈrʊndiən/

Cambodia /kæmˈbəʊdiə; *NAmE* -ˈboʊ-/ 柬埔寨
Cambodian /kæmˈbəʊdiən; *NAmE* -ˈboʊ-/

Cameroon /͵kæməˈruːn/ 喀麥隆
Cameroonian /͵kæməˈruːniən/

Canada /ˈkænədə/ 加拿大 **Canadian** /kəˈneɪdiən/

Cape Verde /͵keɪp ˈvɜːd; *NAmE* ˈvɜːrd/ 佛得角
Cape Verdean /͵keɪp ˈvɜːdiən; *NAmE* ˈvɜːrd-/

(the) Caribbean Sea /͵kærəbiːən ˈsiː; kə͵rɪbiən/ 加勒比海 **Caribbean** /͵kærəˈbiːən; kə͵rɪbiən/

Central African Republic /͵sentrəl ͵æfrɪkən rɪˈpʌblɪk/ 中非共和國 **Central African** /͵sentrəl ˈæfrɪkən/

Chad /tʃæd/ 乍得 **Chadian** /ˈtʃædiən/

Chile /ˈtʃɪli/ 智利 **Chilean** /ˈtʃɪliən/

China /ˈtʃaɪnə/ 中國 **Chinese** /tʃaɪˈniːz/

Colombia /kəˈlɒmbiə; -ˈlʌm-; *NAmE* -ˈlʌm-/ 哥倫比亞
Colombian /kəˈlɒmbiən; -ˈlʌm-; *NAmE* -ˈlʌm-/

Comoros /ˈkɒmərəʊz; *NAmE* ˈkɑːməroʊz/ 科摩羅
Comoran /kəˈmɔːrən/

Congo /ˈkɒŋɡəʊ/ *NAmE* ˈkɑːŋɡoʊ/ 剛果 **Congolese** /ˌkɒŋɡəˈliːz; *NAmE* ˌkɑːŋ-/

(the) Democratic Republic of the Congo (DR Congo) /ˌdeməˌkrætɪk rɪˌpʌblɪk əv ðə ˈkɒŋɡəʊ; *NAmE* ˈkɑːŋɡoʊ/ 剛果民主共和國 **Congolese** /ˌkɒŋɡəˈliːz; *NAmE* ˌkɑːŋ-/

Costa Rica /ˌkɒstə ˈriːkə; *NAmE* ˌkɑːstə; ˌkoʊstə/ 哥斯達黎加 **Costa Rican** /ˌkɒstə ˈriːkən; *NAmE* ˌkɑːstə; ˌkoʊstə/

Côte d'Ivoire /ˌkəʊt diːˈvwɑː; *NAmE* ˌkoʊt diːˈvwɑːr/ 科特迪瓦 **Ivorian** /aɪˈvɔːriən/ ➲ see also **Ivory Coast**

Croatia /krəʊˈeɪʃə; *NAmE* kroʊ-/ 克羅地亞 **Croatian** /krəʊˈeɪʃn; *NAmE* kroʊ-/

Cuba /ˈkjuːbə/ 古巴 **Cuban** /ˈkjuːbən/

Cyprus /ˈsaɪprəs/ 塞浦路斯 **Cypriot** /ˈsɪpriət/

(the) Czech Republic /ˌtʃek rɪˈpʌblɪk/ 捷克共和國 **Czech** /tʃek/

Denmark /ˈdenmɑːk; *NAmE* -mɑːrk/ 丹麥 **Danish** /ˈdeɪnɪʃ/ **a Dane** /deɪn/

Djibouti /dʒɪˈbuːti/ 吉布提 **Djiboutian** /dʒɪˈbuːtiən/

Dominica /ˌdɒmɪˈniːkə; *NAmE* ˌdɑːməˈn-/ 多米尼加 **Dominican** /ˌdɒmɪˈniːkən; *NAmE* ˌdɑːməˈn-/

(the) Dominican Republic /dəˌmɪnɪkən rɪˈpʌblɪk/ 多米尼加共和國 **Dominican** /dəˈmɪnɪkən/

East Timor /ˌiːst ˈtiːmɔː(r)/ 東帝汶 **East Timorese** /ˌiːst tɪməˈriːz/

Ecuador /ˈekwədɔː(r)/ 厄瓜多爾 **Ecuadorian, Ecuadorean** /ˌekwəˈdɔːriən/

Egypt /ˈiːdʒɪpt/ 埃及 **Egyptian** /iˈdʒɪpʃn/

El Salvador /ˌel ˈsælvədɔː(r)/ 薩爾瓦多 **Salvadorean** /ˌsælvəˈdɔːriən/

Equatorial Guinea /ˌekwətɔːriəl ˈɡɪni/ 赤道幾內亞 **Equatorial Guinean** /ˌekwətɔːriəl ˈɡɪniən/

Eritrea /ˌerɪˈtreɪə; *NAmE* -ˈtriːə/ 厄立特里亞 **Eritrean** /ˌerɪˈtreɪən; *NAmE* -ˈtriːən/

Estonia /eˈstəʊniə; *NAmE* eˈstoʊ-/ 愛沙尼亞 **Estonian** /eˈstəʊniən; *NAmE* eˈstoʊ-/

Ethiopia /ˌiːθiˈəʊpiə; *NAmE* -ˈoʊ-/ 埃塞俄比亞 **Ethiopian** /ˌiːθiˈəʊpiən; *NAmE* -ˈoʊ-/

Europe /ˈjʊərəp; *NAmE* ˈjʊrəp/ 歐洲 **European** /ˌjʊərəˈpiːən; *NAmE* jʊrə-/

Fiji /ˈfiːdʒiː/ 斐濟 **Fijian** /fiːˈdʒiːən; *NAmE also* ˈfiːdʒiːən/

Finland /ˈfɪnlənd/ 芬蘭 **Finnish** /ˈfɪnɪʃ/ **a Finn** /fɪn/

France /frɑːns; *NAmE* fræns/ 法國 **French** /frentʃ/ **a Frenchman** /ˈfrentʃmən/ **a Frenchwoman** /ˈfrentʃwʊmən/

FYROM /ˈfaɪrɒm; *NAmE* -rɑːm/ ➲ see also **Former Yugoslav Republic of Macedonia**

Gabon /ɡæˈbɒn; *NAmE* ɡæˈboʊn/ 加蓬 **Gabonese** /ˌɡæbəˈniːz/

(the) Gambia /ˈɡæmbiə/ 岡比亞 **Gambian** /ˈɡæmbiən/

Georgia /ˈdʒɔːdʒə; *NAmE* ˈdʒɔːrdʒə/ 格魯吉亞 **Georgian** /ˈdʒɔːdʒən; *NAmE* ˈdʒɔːrdʒən/

Germany /ˈdʒɜːməni; *NAmE* ˈdʒɜːrm-/ 德國 **German** /ˈdʒɜːmən; *NAmE* ˈdʒɜːrm-/

Ghana /ˈɡɑːnə/ 加納 **Ghanaian** /ɡɑːˈneɪən/

Greece /ɡriːs/ 希臘 **Greek** /ɡriːk/

Grenada /ɡrəˈneɪdə/ 格林納達 **Grenadian** /ɡrəˈneɪdiən/

Guatemala /ˌɡwɑːtəˈmɑːlə; *BrE also* ˌɡwæt-/ 危地馬拉 **Guatemalan** /ˌɡwɑːtəˈmɑːlən; *BrE also* ˌɡwæt-/

Guinea /ˈɡɪni/ 幾內亞 **Guinean** /ˈɡɪniən/

Guinea-Bissau /ˌɡɪni bɪˈsaʊ/ 幾內亞比紹 **Guinean** /ˈɡɪniən/

Guyana /ɡaɪˈænə/ 圭亞那 **Guyanese** /ˌɡaɪəˈniːz/

Haiti /ˈheɪti/ 海地 **Haitian** /ˈheɪʃn/

Honduras /hɒnˈdjʊərəs; *NAmE* hɑːnˈdʊrəs/ 洪都拉斯 **Honduran** /hɒnˈdjʊərən; *NAmE* hɑːnˈdʊrən/

Hungary /ˈhʌŋɡəri/ 匈牙利 **Hungarian** /hʌŋˈɡeəriən; *NAmE* -ˈɡer-/

Iceland /ˈaɪslənd/ 冰島 **Icelandic** /aɪsˈlændɪk/ **an Icelander** /ˈaɪsləndə(r)/

India /ˈɪndiə/ 印度 **Indian** /ˈɪndiən/

(the) Indian Ocean /ˌɪndiən ˈəʊʃn; *NAmE* ˈoʊʃn/ 印度洋

Indonesia /ˌɪndəˈniːʒə; *BrE also* -ˈniːziə/ 印度尼西亞 **Indonesian** /ˌɪndəˈniːʒn; *BrE also* -ˈniːziən/

Iran /ɪˈrɑːn; ɪˈræn/ 伊朗 **Iranian** /ɪˈreɪniən/

Iraq /ɪˈrɑːk; ɪˈræk/ 伊拉克 **Iraqi** /ɪˈrɑːki; ɪˈræki/

Israel /ˈɪzreɪl/ 以色列 **Israeli** /ɪzˈreɪli/

Italy /ˈɪtəli/ 意大利 **Italian** /ɪˈtæliən/

(the) Ivory Coast /ˌaɪvəri ˈkəʊst; *NAmE* ˈkoʊst/ 象牙海岸 **Ivorian** /aɪˈvɔːriən/ ➲ see also **Côte d'Ivoire**

Jamaica /dʒəˈmeɪkə/ 牙買加 **Jamaican** /dʒəˈmeɪkən/

Japan /dʒəˈpæn/ 日本 **Japanese** /ˌdʒæpəˈniːz/

Jordan /ˈdʒɔːdn; *NAmE* ˈdʒɔːrdn/ 約旦 **Jordanian** /dʒɔːˈdeɪniən; *NAmE* dʒɔːrˈd-/

Kazakhstan /ˌkæzækˈstæn; -ˈstɑːn/ 哈薩克斯坦 **Kazakh** /kəˈzæk; ˈkæzæk/

Kenya /ˈkenjə; *NAmE also* ˈkiːnjə/ 肯尼亞 **Kenyan** /ˈkenjən; *NAmE also* ˈkiːnjən/

Kiribati /ˌkɪrɪˈbɑːti; -ˈbæs; *NAmE* ˈkɪrəbæs/ 基里巴斯 **Kiribati**

Korea /kəˈriə/ 朝鮮；韓國 **Korean** /kəˈriən/ ➲ see also **North Korea, South Korea**

Kuwait /kʊˈweɪt/ 科威特 **Kuwaiti** /kʊˈweɪti/

Kyrgyzstan /ˌkɜːɡɪˈstæn; ˌkɪəɡ-; -ˈstɑːn; *NAmE* ˌkɪrɡ-/ 吉爾吉斯坦 **Kyrgyz** /ˈkɜːɡɪz; ˈkɪəɡɪz; *NAmE* ˈkɪrɡɪz/

Laos /laʊs/ 老撾 **Laotian** /ˈlaʊʃn; *NAmE also* leɪˈoʊʃn/ **Lao** /laʊ/

Latvia /ˈlætviə/ 拉脫維亞 **Latvian** /ˈlætviən/

Lebanon /ˈlebənən; *NAmE also* -nɑːn/ 黎巴嫩 **Lebanese** /ˌlebəˈniːz/

Lesotho /ləˈsuːtuː/ 萊索托 person **a Mosotho** /məˈsuːtuː/ people **Basotho** /bəˈsuːtuː/

Liberia /laɪˈbɪəriə; *NAmE* -ˈbɪr-/ 利比里亞 **Liberian** /laɪˈbɪəriən; *NAmE* -ˈbɪr-/

Libya /ˈlɪbiə/ 利比亞 **Libyan** /ˈlɪbiən/

Liechtenstein /ˈlɪktənstaɪn; ˈlɪxt-/ 列支敦士登 **Liechtenstein** /ˈlɪktənstaɪn; ˈlɪxt-/ **a Liechtensteiner** /ˈlɪktenstaɪnə(r); ˈlɪxt-/

Lithuania /ˌlɪθjuˈeɪniə; *NAmE* ˌlɪθu-/ 立陶宛 **Lithuanian** /ˌlɪθjuˈeɪniən; *NAmE* ˌlɪθu-/

Luxembourg /ˈlʌksəmbɜːɡ; *NAmE* -bɜːrɡ/ 盧森堡 **Luxembourg** /ˈlʌksəmbɜːɡ; *NAmE* -bɜːrɡ/ **a Luxembourger** /ˈlʌksəmbɜːɡə(r); *NAmE* -bɜːrɡər/

(the) Former Yugoslav Republic of Macedonia /ˌfɔːmə ˌjuːɡəslɑːv rɪˌpʌblɪk əv ˌmæsəˈdəʊniə; *NAmE* ˌfɔːrmər ˌjuːɡəslɑːv rɪˌpʌblɪk əv ˌmæsəˈdoʊniə; *NAmE also* -ɡoʊ-/ 前南斯拉夫馬其頓共和國
Macedonian /ˌmæsəˈdəʊniən; *NAmE* -ˈdoʊ-/

Madagascar /ˌmædəˈɡæskə(r)/ 馬達加斯加
Madagascan /ˌmædəˈɡæskən/ **Malagasy** /ˌmæləˈɡæsi/

Malawi /məˈlɑːwi/ 馬拉維 **Malawian** /məˈlɑːwiən/

Malaysia /məˈleɪʒə; *BrE also* -ˈleɪziə/ 馬來西亞
Malaysian /məˈleɪʒn; *BrE also* -ˈleɪziən/

(the) Maldives /ˈmɔːldiːvz/ 馬爾代夫
Maldivian /mɔːlˈdɪviən/

Mali /ˈmɑːli/ 馬里 **Malian** /ˈmɑːliən/

Malta /ˈmɔːltə/ 馬耳他 **Maltese** /mɔːlˈtiːz/

(the) Marshall Islands /ˈmɑːʃl aɪləndz; *NAmE* ˈmɑːrʃl/ 馬紹爾群島 **Marshallese** /ˌmɑːʃəˈliːz; *NAmE* ˌmɑːrʃ-/

Mauritania /ˌmɒrɪˈteɪniə; *NAmE* ˌmɔːr-/ 毛里塔尼亞
Mauritanian /ˌmɒrɪˈteɪniən; *NAmE* ˌmɔːr-/

Mauritius /məˈrɪʃəs; *NAmE* mɔːˈr-/ 毛里求斯
Mauritian /məˈrɪʃn; *NAmE* mɔːˈr-/

Mexico /ˈmeksɪkəʊ; *NAmE* -koʊ/ 墨西哥
Mexican /ˈmeksɪkən/

Micronesia /ˌmaɪkrəˈniːziə; *NAmE* -ˈniːʒə/ 密克羅尼西亞
Micronesian /ˌmaɪkrəˈniːziən; *NAmE* -ˈniːʒn/

Moldova /mɒlˈdəʊvə; *NAmE* mɑːlˈdoʊvə; mɔːl-/ 摩爾多瓦
Moldovan /mɒlˈdəʊvn; *NAmE* mɑːlˈdoʊvn; mɔːl-/

Monaco /ˈmɒnəkəʊ; *NAmE* ˈmɑːnəkoʊ/ 摩納哥
Monégasque /ˌmɒnɪˈɡæsk; ˌmɒneɪˈɡ-; *NAmE* ˌmɑːn-/

Mongolia /mɒŋˈɡəʊliə; *NAmE* mɑːŋˈɡoʊ-/ 蒙古
Mongolian /mɒŋˈɡəʊliən; *NAmE* mɑːŋˈɡoʊ-/
Mongol /ˈmɒŋɡl; *NAmE* ˈmɑːŋɡl/

Montenegro /ˌmɒntɪˈniːɡrəʊ; *NAmE* ˌmɑːntəˈneɪɡroʊ; -ˈneɡ-/ 黑山
Montenegrin /ˌmɒntɪˈniːɡrɪn; *NAmE* ˌmɑːntəˈneɪɡrɪn; -ˈneɡ-/

Morocco /məˈrɒkəʊ; *NAmE* məˈrɑːkoʊ/ 摩洛哥
Moroccan /məˈrɒkən; *NAmE* -ˈrɑːk-/

Mozambique /ˌməʊzæmˈbiːk; *NAmE* ˌmoʊ-/ 莫桑比克
Mozambican /ˌməʊzæmˈbiːkən; *NAmE* ˌmoʊ-/

Myanmar /miˌænˈmɑː(r)/ 緬甸 ➲ see also **Burma**

Namibia /nəˈmɪbiə/ 納米比亞 **Namibian** /nəˈmɪbiən/

Nauru /ˈnaʊruː/ 瑙魯 **Nauruan** /naʊˈruːən/

Nepal /nəˈpɔːl/ 尼泊爾 **Nepalese** /ˌnepəˈliːz/

(the) Netherlands /ˈneðələndz; *NAmE* -ðərl-/ 荷蘭
Dutch /dʌtʃ/ **a Dutchman** /ˈdʌtʃmən/
a Dutchwoman /ˈdʌtʃwʊmən/

New Zealand (NZ) /ˌnjuː ˈziːlənd; *NAmE* ˌnuː/ 新西蘭
New Zealand, a New Zealander /ˌnjuː ˈziːləndə(r); *NAmE* ˌnuː/

Nicaragua /ˌnɪkəˈræɡjuə; *NAmE* -ɡwə/ 尼加拉瓜
Nicaraguan /ˌnɪkəˈræɡjuən; *NAmE* -ɡwən/

Niger /niːˈʒeə(r); *NAmE* -ˈʒer/ 尼日爾
Nigerien /niːˈʒeəriən; *NAmE* -ˈʒeriən/

Nigeria /naɪˈdʒɪəriə; *NAmE* -ˈdʒɪr-/ 尼日利亞
Nigerian /naɪˈdʒɪəriən; *NAmE* -ˈdʒɪr-/

North Korea /ˌnɔːθ kəˈriə; *NAmE* ˌnɔːrθ/ 朝鮮
North Korean /ˌnɔːθ kəˈriən; *NAmE* ˌnɔːrθ/

Norway /ˈnɔːweɪ; *NAmE* ˈnɔːrweɪ/ 挪威
Norwegian /nɔːˈwiːdʒən; *NAmE* nɔːrˈw-/

Oman /əʊˈmɑːn; *BrE also* -ˈmæn; *NAmE* oʊˈmɑːn/ 阿曼
Omani /əʊˈmɑːni; *BrE also* -ˈmæni; *NAmE* oʊˈmɑːni/

(the) Pacific Ocean /pəˌsɪfɪk ˈəʊʃn; *NAmE* ˈoʊʃn/ 太平洋

Pakistan /ˌpækɪˈstæn; ˌpɑːkɪ-; -ˈstɑːn/ 巴基斯坦
Pakistani /ˌpækɪˈstæni; ˌpɑːkɪ-; -ˈstɑːni/

Palau /pəˈlaʊ/ 帕勞 **Palauan** /pəˈlaʊən/

Panama /ˈpænəmɑː/ 巴拿馬 **Panamanian** /ˌpænəˈmeɪniən/

Papua New Guinea (PNG) /ˌpæpjuə ˌnjuː ˈɡɪni; *BrE also* ˌpæpuə; *NAmE* ˌpæpuə ˌnuː ˈɡɪni/ 巴布亞新幾內亞 **Papua New Guinean** /ˌpæpjuə ˌnjuː ˈɡɪniən; *BrE also* ˌpæpuə; *NAmE* ˌpæpuə ˌnuː ˈɡɪniən/

Paraguay /ˈpærəɡwaɪ/ 巴拉圭 **Paraguayan** /ˌpærəˈɡwaɪən/

Peru /pəˈruː/ 秘魯 **Peruvian** /pəˈruːviən/

(the) Philippines /ˈfɪlɪpiːnz/ 菲律賓 **Philippine** /ˈfɪlɪpiːn/
a Filipino /ˌfɪlɪˈpiːnəʊ; *NAmE* -noʊ/ **a Filipina** /ˌfɪlɪˈpiːnə/

Poland /ˈpəʊlənd; *NAmE* ˈpoʊ-/ 波蘭
Polish /ˈpəʊlɪʃ; *NAmE* ˈpoʊ-/ **a Pole** /pəʊl; *NAmE* poʊl/

Portugal /ˈpɔːtʃʊɡl; *NAmE* ˈpɔːrtʃ-/ 葡萄牙
Portuguese /ˌpɔːtʃʊˈɡiːz; *NAmE* ˌpɔːrtʃ-/

Qatar /ˈkʌtɑː(r); ˈkæt-; *NAmE* ˈkɑːtɑːr; kəˈtɑːr/ 卡塔爾
Qatari /kʌˈtɑːri; kæˈt-; *NAmE* ˈkɑːtɑːri; kəˈtɑːri/

Romania /ruˈmeɪniə/ 羅馬尼亞 **Romanian** /ruˈmeɪniən/

Russia /ˈrʌʃə/ 俄羅斯 **Russian** /ˈrʌʃn/

Rwanda /ruˈændə/ 盧旺達 **Rwandan** /ruˈændən/

Samoa /səˈməʊə; *NAmE* səˈmoʊə/ 薩摩亞
Samoan /səˈməʊən; *NAmE* səˈmoʊən/

San Marino /ˌsæn məˈriːnəʊ; *NAmE* -noʊ/ 聖馬力諾

São Tomé and Príncipe /ˌsaʊ təˌmeɪ ən ˈprɪnsɪpeɪ/ 聖多美和普林西比

Saudi Arabia /ˌsaʊdi əˈreɪbiə/ 沙特阿拉伯
Saudi /ˈsaʊdi/ **Saudi Arabian** /ˌsaʊdi əˈreɪbiən/

Senegal /ˌsenɪˈɡɔːl/ 塞內加爾 **Senegalese** /ˌsenɪɡəˈliːz/

Serbia /ˈsɜːbiə; *NAmE* ˈsɜːrb-/
Serbian /ˈsɜːbiən; *NAmE* ˈsɜːrb-/ 塞爾維亞
Serb /sɜːb; *NAmE* sɜːrb/

(the) Seychelles /seɪˈʃelz/ 塞舌爾 **Seychellois** /ˌseɪʃelˈwɑː/

Sierra Leone /siˌerə liˈəʊn; *NAmE* liˈoʊn/ 塞拉利昂
Sierra Leonean / siˌerə liˈəʊniən; *NAmE* liˈoʊniən/

Singapore /ˌsɪŋəˈpɔː(r)/ 新加坡 **Singaporean** /ˌsɪŋəˈpɔːriən/

Slovakia /sləˈvækiə; *NAmE* sloʊˈv-/ 斯洛伐克
Slovak /ˈsləʊvæk; *NAmE* ˈsloʊ-/
Slovakian /sləˈvækiən; *NAmE* sloʊˈv-/

Slovenia /sləˈviːniə; *NAmE* sloʊˈv-/ 斯洛文尼亞
Slovene /ˈsləʊviːn; *NAmE* ˈsloʊ-/
Slovenian /sləˈviːniən; *NAmE* sloʊˈv-/

(the) Solomon Islands /ˈsɒləmən aɪləndz; *NAmE* ˈsɑːl-/ 所羅門群島 **a Solomon Islander** /ˈsɒləmən aɪləndə(r); *NAmE* ˈsɑːl-/

Somalia /səˈmɑːliə/ 索馬里 **Somali** /səˈmɑːli/

South Africa /ˌsaʊθ ˈæfrɪkə/ 南非
South African /ˌsaʊθ ˈæfrɪkən/

South Korea /ˌsaʊθ kəˈriə/ 韓國
South Korean /ˌsaʊθ kəˈriən/

South Sudan /ˌsaʊθ suˈdɑːn; -ˈdæn/ 南蘇丹
South Sudanese /ˌsaʊθ suːdəˈniːz/

Spain /speɪn/ 西班牙 **Spanish** /ˈspænɪʃ/ **a Spaniard** /ˈspænjəd; *NAmE* -njərd/

Sri Lanka /ˌsri ˈlæŋkə; *NAmE also* ˈlɑːŋkə/ 斯里蘭卡 **Sri Lankan** /ˌsri ˈlæŋkən; *NAmE also* ˈlɑːŋ-/

St Kitts and Nevis /snt ˌkɪts ən ˈniːvɪs; *NAmE also* seɪnt/ 聖基茨和尼維斯 **Kittitian** /kɪˈtɪʃn/ **Nevisian** /niːˈvɪsiən; *NAmE* nəˈvɪʒn/

St Lucia /ˌsnt ˈluːʃə; *NAmE also* ˌseɪnt/ 聖盧西亞 **St Lucian** /ˌsnt ˈluːʃən; *NAmE also* ˌseɪnt/

St Vincent and the Grenadines /snt ˌvɪnsnt ən ðə ˈɡrenədiːnz; *NAmE also* seɪnt/ 聖文森特和格林納丁斯 **Vincentian** /vɪnˈsenʃn/

Sudan /suˈdɑːn; -ˈdæn/ 蘇丹 **Sudanese** /ˌsuːdəˈniːz/

Suriname /ˌsʊərɪˈnɑːm; -ˈnæm; *NAmE* ˌsʊr-/ 蘇里南 **Surinamese** /ˌsʊərɪnəˈmiːz; *NAmE* ˌsʊr-/

Swaziland /ˈswɑːzilænd/ 斯威士蘭 **Swazi** /ˈswɑːzi/

Sweden /ˈswiːdn/ 瑞典 **Swedish** /ˈswiːdɪʃ/ **a Swede** /swiːd/

Switzerland /ˈswɪtsələnd; *NAmE* -ərl-/ 瑞士 **Swiss** /swɪs/

Syria /ˈsɪriə/ 敘利亞 **Syrian** /ˈsɪriən/

Tajikistan /tæˌdʒiːkɪˈstæn; -ˈstɑːn/ 塔吉克斯坦 **Tajik** /tæˈdʒiːk/

Tanzania /ˌtænzəˈniːə/ 坦桑尼亞 **Tanzanian** /ˌtænzəˈniːən/

Thailand /ˈtaɪlænd/ 泰國 **Thai** /taɪ/

Togo /ˈtəʊɡəʊ; *NAmE* ˈtoʊɡoʊ/ 多哥 **Togolese** /ˌtəʊɡəˈliːz; *NAmE* ˌtoʊ-/

Tonga /ˈtɒŋə; ˈtɒŋɡə; *NAmE* ˈtɑːŋɡə/ 湯加 **Tongan** /ˈtɒŋən; ˈtɒŋɡən; *NAmE* ˈtɑːŋɡən/

Trinidad and Tobago /ˌtrɪnɪdæd ən təˈbeɪɡəʊ; *NAmE* -ɡoʊ/ 特立尼達和多巴哥 **Trinidadian** /ˌtrɪnɪˈdædiən/ **Tobagan** /təˈbeɪɡən/ **Tobagonian** /ˌtəʊbəˈɡəʊniən; *NAmE* ˌtoʊbəˈɡoʊ-/

Tunisia /tjuˈnɪziə; *NAmE usually* tuˈniːʒə/ 突尼斯 **Tunisian** /tjuˈnɪziən; *NAmE usually* tuˈniːʒən/

Turkey /ˈtɜːki; *NAmE* ˈtɜːrki/ 土耳其 **Turkish** /ˈtɜːkɪʃ; *NAmE* ˈtɜːrkɪʃ/ **a Turk** /tɜːk; *NAmE* tɜːrk/

Turkmenistan /tɜːkˌmenɪˈstæn; -ˈstɑːn; *NAmE* tɜːrk-/ 土庫曼斯坦 **Turkmen** /ˈtɜːkmen; *NAmE* ˈtɜːrk-/

Tuvalu /tuːˈvɑːluː/ 圖瓦盧 **Tuvaluan** /ˌtuːvɑːˈluːən/

Uganda /juːˈɡændə/ 烏干達 **Ugandan** /juːˈɡændən/

Ukraine /juːˈkreɪn/ 烏克蘭 **Ukrainian** /juːˈkreɪniən/

(the) United Arab Emirates (UAE) /juˌnaɪtɪd ˌærəb ˈemɪrəts/ 阿拉伯聯合酋長國 **Emirati** /emɪˈrɑːti/

(the) United States of America (USA) /juˌnaɪtɪd ˌsteɪts əv əˈmerɪkə/ 美利堅合眾國；美國 **American** /əˈmerɪkən/

Uruguay /ˈjʊərəɡwaɪ; *NAmE* ˈjʊr-/ 烏拉圭 **Uruguayan** /ˌjʊərəˈɡwaɪən; *NAmE* jʊr-/

Uzbekistan /ʊzˌbekɪˈstæn; -ˈstɑːn/ 烏茲別克斯坦 **Uzbek** /ˈʊzbek/

Vanuatu /ˌvænuːˈɑːtuː; ˌvænwɑːˈtuː/ 瓦努阿圖 **Vanuatuan** /ˌvænwɑːˈtuːən/

(the) Vatican City /ˌvætɪkən ˈsɪti/ 梵蒂岡城

Venezuela /ˌvenəˈzweɪlə/ 委內瑞拉 **Venezuelan** /ˌvenəˈzweɪlən/

Vietnam /ˌvjetˈnæm; ˌviːet-; -ˈnɑːm/ 越南 **Vietnamese** /ˌvjetnəˈmiːz; viːˌetnə-/

Yemen /ˈjemən/ 也門 **Yemeni** /ˈjeməni/

Zambia /ˈzæmbiə/ 贊比亞 **Zambian** /ˈzæmbiən/

Zimbabwe /zɪmˈbɑːbwi; -ˈbɑːbweɪ/ 津巴布韋 **Zimbabwean** /zɪmˈbɑːbwiən/

The British Isles /ðə ˌbrɪtɪʃ ˈaɪlz/ 不列顛群島

(the) United Kingdom (UK) /juˌnaɪtɪd ˈkɪŋdəm/ 聯合王國

Great Britain /ˌɡreɪt ˈbrɪtn/ 大不列顛

England /ˈɪŋɡlənd/ 英格蘭

Scotland /ˈskɒtlənd; *NAmE* ˈskɑːt-/ 蘇格蘭

Wales /weɪlz/ 威爾士

Northern Ireland /ˌnɔːðən ˈaɪələnd; *NAmE* ˌnɔːrðərn ˈaɪərlənd/ 北愛爾蘭

Ireland /ˈaɪələnd; *NAmE* ˈaɪərlənd/ 愛爾蘭

Towns and cities in the British Isles 不列顛群島的城鎮

Aberdeen /ˌæbəˈdiːn; *NAmE* ˌæbərˈdiːn/ 阿伯丁

Aberystwyth /ˌæbəˈrɪstwɪθ/ 阿伯里斯特威斯

Ayr /eə(r); *NAmE* er/ 艾爾

Bath /bɑːθ; *NAmE* bæθ/ 巴斯

Belfast /ˈbelfɑːst; ˌbelˈfɑːst; *NAmE* ˈbelfæst/ 貝爾法斯特

Berwick-upon-Tweed /ˌberɪk əpɒn ˈtwiːd; *NAmE* əpɑːn/ 特威德河畔貝里克

Birmingham /ˈbɜːmɪŋəm; *NAmE* ˈbɜːrmɪŋhæm/ 伯明翰

Blackburn /ˈblækbɜːn; *NAmE* ˈblækbɜːrn/ 布萊克本

Blackpool /ˈblækpuːl/ 布萊克浦

Bolton /ˈbəʊltən; *NAmE* ˈboʊ-/ 博爾頓

Bournemouth /ˈbɔːnməθ; *NAmE* ˈbɔːrn-/ 伯恩茅斯

Bradford /ˈbrædfəd; *NAmE* -fərd/ 布拉德福德

Brighton /ˈbraɪtn/ 布賴頓

Bristol /ˈbrɪstl/ 布里斯托爾

Caernarfon /kəˈnɑːvn; *NAmE* kɑːrˈnɑːrvn; kə(r)-/ 卡那封

Cambridge /ˈkeɪmbrɪdʒ/ 劍橋

Canterbury /ˈkæntəbəri; *NAmE also* -tərberi/ 坎特伯雷

Cardiff /ˈkɑːdɪf; *NAmE* ˈkɑːrdɪf/ 加的夫

Carlisle /kɑːˈlaɪl; *NAmE* ˈkɑːrlaɪl/ 卡萊爾

Chester /ˈtʃestə(r)/ 切斯特

Colchester /ˈkəʊltʃɪstə(r); *NAmE* ˈkoʊltʃestər/ 科爾切斯特

Colwyn Bay /ˌkɒlwɪn ˈbeɪ; *NAmE* ˌkɑːl-; ˌkoʊl-/ 科爾溫貝

Cork /kɔːk; *NAmE* kɔːrk/ 科克

Coventry /ˈkɒvəntri; *NAmE* ˈkɑːv-/ 考文垂

Derby /ˈdɑːbi; *NAmE* ˈdɑːrbi/ 德比

Douglas /ˈdʌɡləs/ 道格拉斯

Dover /ˈdəʊvə(r); *NAmE* ˈdoʊ-/ 多佛爾

Dublin /ˈdʌblɪn/ 都柏林

Dumfries /dʌmˈfriːs/ 鄧弗里斯

Dundee /dʌnˈdiː/ 鄧迪

Durham /ˈdʌrəm; *NAmE also* ˈdɜːr-/ 達勒姆

Eastbourne /ˈiːstbɔːn; *NAmE* -bɔːrn/ 伊斯特本

East Kilbride /ˌɪst kɪlˈbraɪd/ 東基爾布賴德

Edinburgh /ˈedɪnbrə; -bərə/ 愛丁堡

Exeter /ˈeksɪtə(r)/ 埃克塞特

Fort William /ˌfɔːt ˈwɪljəm; *NAmE* ˌfɔːrt/ 威廉堡

Galway /ˈɡɔːlweɪ/ 戈爾韋

Glasgow /ˈɡlɑːzɡəʊ; *NAmE* ˈɡlæzɡoʊ/ 格拉斯哥

Gloucester /ˈɡlɒstə(r); *NAmE* ˈɡlɑːs-; ˈɡlɔːs-/ 格洛斯特

Great Yarmouth /ˌɡreɪt ˈjɑːməθ; *NAmE* ˈjɑːrm-/ 大雅茅斯

Hartlepool /ˈhɑːtlipuːl; *NAmE* ˈhɑːrt-/ 哈特爾浦

Hastings /ˈheɪstɪŋz/ 黑斯廷斯

Hereford /ˈherɪfəd; *NAmE* -fərd/ 赫里福德

Holyhead /ˈhɒlihed; *NAmE* ˈhɑːl-/ 霍利黑德

Huddersfield /ˈhʌdəzfiːld; *NAmE* -dərz-/ 哈德斯菲爾德

Inverness /ˌɪnvəˈnes; *NAmE* -vərˈn-/ 因弗內斯

Ipswich /ˈɪpswɪtʃ/ 伊普斯威奇

John o'Groats /ˌdʒɒn ə ˈɡrəʊts; *NAmE* ˌdʒɑːn ə ˈɡroʊts/ 約翰奧格羅茨

Kilmarnock /kɪlˈmɑːnək; *NAmE* -ˈmɑːrn-/ 基爾馬諾克

Kingston upon Hull /ˌkɪŋstən əpɒn ˈhʌl; *NAmE* əpɑːn/ 赫爾河畔金斯頓

Leeds /liːdz/ 利茲

Leicester /ˈlestə(r)/ 萊斯特

Limerick /ˈlɪmərɪk/ 利默里克

Lincoln /ˈlɪŋkən/ 林肯

Lisburn /ˈlɪzbɜːn; *NAmE* -bɜːrn/ 利斯本

Liverpool /ˈlɪvəpuːl; *NAmE* -vərp-/ 利物浦

London /ˈlʌndən/ 倫敦

Londonderry /ˈlʌndənderi/ 倫敦德里

Luton /ˈluːtn/ 盧頓

Manchester /ˈmæntʃɪstə(r)/ 曼徹斯特

Margate /ˈmɑːɡeɪt; *NAmE* ˈmɑːrɡ-/ 馬蓋特

Middlesbrough /ˈmɪdlzbrə/ 米德爾斯伯勒

Milford Haven /ˌmɪlfəd ˈheɪvn; *NAmE* -fərd/ 米爾福德港

Milton Keynes /ˌmɪltn ˈkiːnz; ˌmɪltən/ 米爾頓凱恩斯

Newcastle upon Tyne /ˌnjuːkɑːsl əpɒn ˈtaɪn; *NAmE* ˌnuːkæsl əpɑːn/ 泰恩河畔紐卡斯爾

Newport /ˈnjuːpɔːt; *NAmE* ˈnuːpɔːrt/ 紐波特

Newry /ˈnjuːri; *NAmE* ˈnuː-/ 紐里

Northampton /nɔːˈθæmptən; *NAmE* nɔːrθ-/ 北安普頓

Norwich /ˈnɒrɪdʒ; *NAmE* ˈnɑːr-/ 諾里奇

Nottingham /ˈnɒtɪŋəm; *NAmE* ˈnɑːtɪŋhæm; -tɪŋəm/ 諾丁漢

Oxford /ˈɒksfəd; *NAmE* ˈɑːksfərd/ 牛津

Perth /pɜːθ; *NAmE* pɜːrθ/ 珀斯

Peterborough /ˈpiːtəbʌrə; *NAmE* ˈpiːtərbəroʊ/ 彼得伯勒

Plymouth /ˈplɪməθ/ 普利茅斯

Poole /puːl/ 普爾

Portsmouth /ˈpɔːtsməθ; *NAmE* ˈpɔːrts-/ 樸次茅斯

Preston /ˈprestən/ 普雷斯頓

Reading /ˈredɪŋ/ 雷丁

Salisbury /ˈsɔːlzbəri; *NAmE also* -beri/ 索爾茲伯里

Sheffield /ˈʃefiːld/ 設菲爾德

Shrewsbury /ˈʃrəʊzbəri; *NAmE* ˈʃroʊz-; *NAmE also* -beri/ 什魯斯伯里

Slough /slaʊ/ 斯勞

Southampton /saʊˈθæmptən/ 南安普頓

Southend-on-Sea /ˌsaʊθend ɒn ˈsiː; *NAmE* ɑːn/ 濱海紹森德

St Andrews /ˌsnt ˈændruːz; *NAmE also* ˌseɪnt/ 聖安德魯斯

St Helier /ˌsnt ˈheliə(r); *NAmE also* ˌseɪnt/ 聖赫利爾

Stirling /ˈstɜːlɪŋ; *NAmE* ˈstɜːrlɪŋ/ 斯特靈

Stoke-on-Trent /ˌstəʊk ɒn ˈtrent; *NAmE* ˌstoʊk ɑːn/ 特倫特河畔斯托克

Stornoway /ˈstɔːnəweɪ; *NAmE* ˈstɔːrn-/ 斯托諾韋

St Peter Port /snt ˈpiːtə pɔːt; *NAmE* snt ˈpiːtər pɔːrt; *NAmE also* seɪnt/ 聖彼得港

Stratford-upon-Avon /ˌstrætfəd əpɒn ˈeɪvn; *NAmE* -fərd əpɑːn/ 埃文河畔斯特拉特福

Sunderland /ˈsʌndələnd; *NAmE* -dərl-/ 森德蘭

Swansea /ˈswɒnzi; *NAmE* ˈswɑːnzi/ 斯旺西

Swindon /ˈswɪndən/ 斯溫登

Taunton /ˈtɔːntən/ 湯頓

Truro /ˈtrʊərəʊ; *NAmE* ˈtrʊroʊ/ 特魯羅

Warwick /ˈwɒrɪk; *NAmE* ˈwɑːrɪk; ˈwɔːrɪk/ 沃里克

Waterford /ˈwɔːtəfəd; *NAmE* ˈwɔːtərfərd; ˈwɑːt-/ 沃特福德

Watford /ˈwɒtfəd; *NAmE* ˈwɑːtfərd/ 沃特福德

Wolverhampton /ˌwʊlvəˈhæmptən; *NAmE* -vərˈh-/ 伍爾弗漢普頓

Worcester /ˈwʊstə(r)/ 伍斯特

York /jɔːk; *NAmE* jɔːrk/ 約克

The United States of America and Canada 美利堅合眾國和加拿大

The states of the United States of America 美利堅合眾國各州

Alabama /ˌæləˈbæmə/ 亞拉巴馬州
Alaska /əˈlæskə/ 阿拉斯加州
Arizona /ˌærɪˈzəʊnə; *NAmE* -ˈzoʊ-/ 亞利桑那州
Arkansas /ˈɑːkənsɔː; *NAmE* ˈɑːrk-/ 阿肯色州
California /ˌkæləˈfɔːniə; *NAmE* -ˈfɔːrn-/ 加利福尼亞州
Colorado /ˌkɒləˈrɑːdəʊ; *NAmE* ˌkɑːləˈrædoʊ/ 科羅拉多州
Connecticut /kəˈnetɪkət/ 康涅狄格州
Delaware /ˈdeləweə(r); *NAmE* -wer/ 特拉華州
Florida /ˈflɒrɪdə; *NAmE* ˈflɔːr-/ 佛羅里達州
Georgia /ˈdʒɔːdʒə; *NAmE* ˈdʒɔːrdʒə/ 佐治亞州
Hawaii /həˈwaɪi/ 夏威夷州
Idaho /ˈaɪdəhəʊ; *NAmE* -hoʊ/ 愛達荷州
Illinois /ˌɪləˈnɔɪ/ 伊利諾伊州
Indiana /ˌɪndiˈænə/ 印第安納州
Iowa /ˈaɪəwə/ 艾奧瓦州（衣阿華州）
Kansas /ˈkænzəs/ 堪薩斯州
Kentucky /kenˈtʌki/ 肯塔基州
Louisiana /luˌiːziˈænə/ 路易斯安那州
Maine /meɪn/ 緬因州
Maryland /ˈmeərilənd; *NAmE* ˈmerəl-/ 馬里蘭州
Massachusetts /ˌmæsəˈtʃuːsɪts/ 馬薩諸塞州
Michigan /ˈmɪʃɪgən/ 密歇根州（密執安州）
Minnesota /ˌmɪnɪˈsəʊtə; *NAmE* -ˈsoʊtə/ 明尼蘇達州
Mississippi /ˌmɪsɪˈsɪpi/ 密西西比州
Missouri /mɪˈzʊəri; *NAmE* məˈzʊri/ 密蘇里州
Montana /mɒnˈtænə; *NAmE* mɑːn-/ 蒙大拿州
Nebraska /nəˈbræskə/ 內布拉斯加州
Nevada /nəˈvɑːdə; *NAmE* nəˈvædə/ 內華達州
New Hampshire /ˌnjuː ˈhæmpʃə(r); *NAmE* ˌnuː/ 新罕布什爾州
New Jersey /ˌnjuː ˈdʒɜːzi; *NAmE* ˌnuː ˈdʒɜːrzi/ 新澤西州
New Mexico /ˌnjuː ˈmeksɪkəʊ; *NAmE* ˌnuː ˈmeksɪkoʊ/ 新墨西哥州
New York /ˌnjuː ˈjɔːk; *NAmE* ˌnuː ˈjɔːrk/ 紐約州
North Carolina /ˌnɔːθ kærəˈlaɪnə; *NAmE* ˌnɔːrθ/ 北卡羅來納州
North Dakota /ˌnɔːθ dəˈkəʊtə; *NAmE* ˌnɔːrθ dəˈkoʊtə/ 北達科他州
Ohio /əʊˈhaɪəʊ; *NAmE* oʊˈhaɪoʊ/ 俄亥俄州
Oklahoma /ˌəʊkləˈhəʊmə; *NAmE* ˌoʊkləˈhoʊmə/ 俄克拉何馬州
Oregon /ˈɒrɪgən; *NAmE* ˈɔːrəgən; ˈɑːr-/ 俄勒岡州
Pennsylvania /ˌpenslˈveɪniə/ 賓夕法尼亞州
Rhode Island /ˌrəʊd ˈaɪlənd; *NAmE* ˌroʊd/ 羅得島州
South Carolina /ˌsaʊθ kærəˈlaɪnə/ 南卡羅來納州
South Dakota /ˌsaʊθ dəˈkəʊtə; *NAmE* dəˈkoʊtə/ 南達科他州
Tennessee /ˌtenəˈsiː/ 田納西州
Texas /ˈteksəs/ 得克薩斯州
Utah /ˈjuːtɑː/ 猶他州
Vermont /vəˈmɒnt; *NAmE* vərˈmɑːnt/ 佛蒙特州
Virginia /vəˈdʒɪniə; *NAmE* vərˈdʒ-/ 弗吉尼亞州
Washington /ˈwɒʃɪŋtən; *NAmE* ˈwɑːʃ-; ˈwɔːʃ-/ 華盛頓州
West Virginia /ˌwest vəˈdʒɪniə; *NAmE* vərˈdʒ-/ 西弗吉尼亞州
Wisconsin /wɪsˈkɒnsɪn; *NAmE* -ˈkɑːn-/ 威斯康星州
Wyoming /waɪˈəʊmɪŋ; *NAmE* -ˈoʊmɪŋ/ 懷俄明州

Towns and cities in the United States 美利堅合眾國的城鎮

Albany /ˈɔːlbəni/ 奧爾巴尼
Albuquerque /ˈælbəkɜːki; *NAmE* -kɜːrki/ 阿爾伯克基
Amarillo /ˌæməˈrɪləʊ; *NAmE* -loʊ/ 阿馬里洛
Anchorage /ˈæŋkərɪdʒ/ 安克雷奇
Atlanta /ətˈlæntə; *NAmE* æt-/ 亞特蘭大
Augusta /ɔːˈgʌstə/ 奧古斯塔
Austin /ˈɒstɪn; *NAmE* ˈɔːstɪn/ 奧斯汀
Bakersfield /ˈbeɪkəzfiːld; *NAmE* -ərz-/ 貝克斯菲爾德
Baltimore /ˈbɔːltɪmɔː(r)/ 巴爾的摩
Baton Rouge /ˌbætn ˈruːʒ/ 巴吞魯日
Berkeley /ˈbɜːkli; *NAmE* ˈbɜːrkli/ 伯克利
Billings /ˈbɪlɪŋz/ 比靈斯
Birmingham /ˈbɜːmɪŋəm; *NAmE* ˈbɜːrmɪŋhæm/ 伯明翰
Bismarck /ˈbɪzmɑːk; *NAmE* -mɑːrk/ 俾斯麥
Boise /ˈbɔɪsi/ 博伊西
Boston /ˈbɒstən; *NAmE* ˈbɔːs-/ 波士頓
Bridgeport /ˈbrɪdʒpɔːt; *NAmE* -pɔːrt/ 布里奇波特
Buffalo /ˈbʌfələʊ; *NAmE* -loʊ/ 布法羅
Burlington /ˈbɜːlɪŋtən; *NAmE* ˈbɜːrl-/ 伯靈頓
Cambridge /ˈkeɪmbrɪdʒ/ 坎布里奇
Cedar Rapids /ˌsiːdə ˈræpɪdz; *NAmE* ˌsiːdər/ 錫達拉皮茲
Charleston /ˈtʃɑːlstən; *NAmE* ˈtʃɑːrl-/ 查爾斯頓
Charlotte /ˈʃɑːlət; *NAmE* ˈʃɑːrlət/ 夏洛特
Cheyenne /ʃaɪˈæn/ 夏延
Chicago /ʃɪˈkɑːgəʊ; *NAmE* -goʊ/ 芝加哥
Cincinnati /ˌsɪnsɪˈnæti/ 辛辛那提
Cleveland /ˈkliːvlənd/ 克利夫蘭
Colorado Springs /ˌkɒlərɑːdəʊ ˈsprɪŋz; *NAmE* ˌkɑːlərædoʊ/ 科羅拉多斯普林斯
Columbus /kəˈlʌmbəs/ 哥倫比亞
Corpus Christi /ˌkɔːpəs ˈkrɪsti; *NAmE* ˌkɔːrpəs/ 科珀斯克里斯蒂
Dallas /ˈdæləs/ 達拉斯
Dayton /ˈdeɪtn/ 代頓
Denver /ˈdenvə(r)/ 丹佛
Des Moines /dɪ ˈmɔɪn/ 得梅因

Detroit /dɪ'trɔɪt/ 底特律

Duluth /də'lu:θ/ 德盧斯

El Paso /el 'pæsəʊ; *NAmE* -soʊ/ 埃爾帕索

Eugene /ju:'dʒi:n/ 尤金

Fargo /'fɑ:gəʊ; *NAmE* 'fɑ:rgoʊ/ 法戈

Fort Collins /ˌfɔ:t 'kɒlɪnz; *NAmE* ˌfɔ:rt 'kɑ:lɪnz/ 柯林斯堡

Fort Lauderdale /ˌfɔ:t 'lɔ:dədeɪl; *NAmE* ˌfɔ:rt 'lɔ:dərdeɪl/ 勞德代爾堡

Fort Worth /ˌfɔ:t 'wɜ:θ; *NAmE* ˌfɔ:rt 'wɜ:rθ/ 沃思堡

Fresno /'freznəʊ; *NAmE* 'freznoʊ/ 弗雷斯諾

Grand Rapids /ˌgrænd 'ræpɪdz/ 大急流城

Great Falls /ˌgreɪt 'fɔ:lz/ 大瀑布城

Green Bay /ˌgri:n 'beɪ/ 格林貝

Hartford /'hɑ:tfəd; *NAmE* 'hɑ:rtfərd/ 哈特福德

Honolulu /ˌhɒnə'lu:lu:; *NAmE* ˌhɑ:nə-/ 火奴魯魯（檀香山）

Houston /'hju:stən/ 休斯敦

Idaho Falls /ˌaɪdəhəʊ 'fɔ:lz; *NAmE* -hoʊ/ 愛達荷福爾斯

Indianapolis /ˌɪndiə'næpəlɪs/ 印第安納波利斯

Jackson /'dʒæksən/ 傑克遜

Jacksonville /'dʒæksənvɪl/ 傑克遜維爾

Juneau /'dʒu:nəʊ; *NAmE* -noʊ/ 朱諾

Kansas City /ˌkænzəs 'sɪti/ 堪薩斯城

Key West /ˌki: 'west/ 基韋斯特

Knoxville /'nɒksvɪl; *NAmE* 'nɑ:ks-/ 諾克斯維爾

Las Vegas /ˌlæs 'veɪgəs/ 拉斯韋加斯

Lexington /'leksɪŋtən/ 列克星敦

Lincoln /'lɪŋkən/ 林肯

Little Rock /'lɪtl rɒk; *NAmE* rɑ:k/ 小石城

Los Angeles /ˌlɒs 'ændʒəli:z; *NAmE* ˌlɔ:s 'ændʒələs/ 洛杉磯

Louisville /'lu:ivɪl/ 路易斯維爾

Lubbock /'lʌbək/ 拉伯克

Madison /'mædɪsən/ 麥迪遜

Manchester /'mæntʃestə(r)/ 曼徹斯特

Memphis /'memfɪs/ 孟菲斯

Mesa /'meɪsə/ 梅薩

Miami /maɪ'æmi/ 邁阿密

Milwaukee /mɪl'wɔ:ki/ 密爾沃基

Minneapolis /ˌmɪni'æpəlɪs/ 明尼阿波利斯

Mobile /məʊ'bi:l; *NAmE* moʊ-/ 莫比爾

Montgomery /mɒnt'gɒməri; *NAmE* mənt'gɑ:m-/ 蒙哥馬利

Nashville /'næʃvɪl/ 納什維爾

New Orleans /ˌnju: ɔ:'li:ənz; *NAmE* ˌnu: 'ɔ:rlənz/ 新奧爾良

New York /ˌnju: 'jɔ:k; *NAmE* ˌnu: 'jɔ:rk/ 紐約

Newark /'nju:ək; *NAmE* 'nu:ərk/ 紐瓦克

Norfolk /'nɔ:fək; *NAmE* 'nɔ:rfək/ 諾福克

Oklahoma City /ˌəʊklə'həʊmə 'sɪti; *NAmE* ˌoʊklə'hoʊmə/ 俄克拉何馬城

Omaha /'əʊməhɑ:; *NAmE* 'oʊ-/ 奧馬哈

Orlando /ɔ:'lændəʊ; *NAmE* ɔ:r'lændoʊ/ 奧蘭多

Philadelphia /ˌfɪlə'delfiə/ 費拉德爾菲亞（費城）

Phoenix /'fi:nɪks/ 菲尼克斯

Pittsburgh /'pɪtsbɜ:g; *NAmE* -bɜ:rg/ 匹茲堡

Portland /'pɔ:tlənd; *NAmE* 'pɔ:rt-/ 波特蘭

Princeton /'prɪnstən/ 普林斯頓

Providence /'prɒvɪdəns; *NAmE* 'prɑ:v-/ 普羅維登斯

Provo /'prəʊvəʊ; *NAmE* 'proʊvoʊ/ 普羅沃

Raleigh /'rɑ:li; *NAmE* 'rɔ:li/ 羅利

Rapid City /ˌræpɪd 'sɪti/ 拉皮德城

Reno /'ri:nəʊ; *NAmE* 'ri:noʊ/ 里諾

Richmond /'rɪtʃmənd/ 里士滿

Rochester /'rɒtʃɪstə(r); *NAmE* 'rɑ:tʃəs-/ 羅切斯特

Sacramento /ˌsækrə'mentəʊ; *NAmE* -toʊ/ 薩克拉門托

Salem /'seɪləm/ 塞勒姆

Salt Lake City /ˌsɔ:lt leɪk 'sɪti/ 鹽湖城

San Antonio /ˌsæn æn'təʊniəʊ; *NAmE* æn'toʊnioʊ/ 聖安東尼奧

San Diego /ˌsæn di'eɪgəʊ; *NAmE* -goʊ/ 聖迭戈

San Francisco /ˌsæn frən'sɪskəʊ; *NAmE* -koʊ/ 聖弗朗西斯科（舊金山）

San Jose /ˌsæn həʊ'zeɪ; *NAmE* hoʊ-/ 聖何塞

Santa Fe /ˌsæntə 'feɪ/ 聖菲

Savannah /sə'vænə/ 薩凡納

Seattle /si'ætl/ 西雅圖

Sioux Falls /ˌsu: 'fɔ:lz/ 蘇福爾斯

Spokane /spəʊ'kæn; *NAmE* spoʊ-/ 斯波坎

Springfield /'sprɪŋfi:ld/ 斯普林菲爾德

St Paul /ˌsnt 'pɔ:l; *NAmE also* ˌseɪnt/ 聖保羅

St Louis /ˌsnt 'lu:ɪs; *NAmE also* ˌseɪnt/ 聖路易斯

Syracuse /'sɪrəkju:s/ 錫拉丘茲

Tallahassee /ˌtælə'hæsi/ 塔拉哈西

Tampa /'tæmpə/ 坦帕

Toledo /tə'li:dəʊ; *NAmE* -doʊ/ 托萊多

Topeka /tə'pi:kə/ 托皮卡

Tucson /'tu:sɒn; *NAmE* -sɑ:n/ 圖森

Tulsa /'tʌlsə/ 塔爾薩

Virginia Beach /vəˌdʒɪniə 'bi:tʃ; *NAmE* vərˌdʒ-/ 弗吉尼亞比奇

Washington D.C. /ˌwɒʃɪŋtən di: 'si:; *NAmE* ˌwɑ:ʃ-; ˌwɔ:ʃ-/ 華盛頓

Wichita /'wɪtʃɪtɔ:/ 威奇托

Wilmington /'wɪlmɪŋtən/ 威爾明頓

The provinces and territories of Canada 加拿大各省和地區

Alberta /æl'bɜ:tə; *NAmE* æl'bɜ:rtə/ 艾伯塔省

British Columbia /ˌbrɪtɪʃ kə'lʌmbiə/ 不列顛哥倫比亞省

Manitoba /ˌmænɪ'təʊbə; *NAmE* -'toʊ-/ 馬尼托巴省

New Brunswick /ˌnju: 'brʌnzwɪk; *NAmE* ˌnu:/ 新不倫瑞克省

Newfoundland and Labrador 紐芬蘭省 /ˌnju:fəndlənd ən 'læbrədɔ:(r); *NAmE* ˌnu:-/

Northwest Territories /ˌnɔːθwest ˈterətriz; *NAmE* ˌnɔːrθwest ˈterətɔːriz/ 西北地區

Nova Scotia /ˌnəʊvə ˈskəʊʃə; *NAmE* ˌnoʊvə ˈskoʊʃə/ 新斯科舍省

Nunavut /ˈnʊnəvʊt/ 努納武特地區

Ontario /ɒnˈteəriəʊ; *NAmE* ɑːnˈterioʊ/ 安大略省

Prince Edward Island /ˌprɪns ˈedwəd aɪlənd; *NAmE* ˈedwərd/ 愛德華王子島省

Quebec /kwɪˈbek/ 魁北克省

Saskatchewan /səˈskætʃəwən/ 薩斯喀徹溫省

(the) Yukon /ˈjuːkɒn; *NAmE* ˈjuːkɑːn/ 育空

Towns and cities in Canada 加拿大的城鎮

Calgary /ˈkælɡəri/ 卡爾加里

Edmonton /ˈedməntən/ 埃德蒙頓

Fredericton /ˈfredrɪktən/ 弗雷德里克頓

Gatineau /ˌɡætɪˈnəʊ; *NAmE* ˌɡætəˈnoʊ/ 加蒂諾

Greater Sudbury /ˌɡreɪtə ˈsʌdbəri; *NAmE* ˌɡreɪtər ˈsʌdberi/ 大薩德伯里

Halifax /ˈhælɪfæks/ 哈利法克斯

Hamilton /ˈhæmɪltən/ 哈密爾頓

Iqaluit /ɪˈkæluːɪt/ 伊卡盧伊特

Kelowna /keˈləʊnə; *NAmE* -ˈloʊ-/ 基洛納

London /ˈlʌndən/ 倫敦

Moncton /ˈmʌŋktən/ 蒙克頓

Montreal /ˌmɒntriˈɔːl; *NAmE* ˌmɑːn-/ 蒙特利爾

Niagara Falls /naɪˌæɡrə ˈfɔːlz/ 尼亞加拉瀑布城

Ottawa /ˈɒtəwə; *NAmE* ˈɑːt-/ 渥太華

Quebec City /kwɪˌbek ˈsɪti/ 魁北克

Regina /rɪˈdʒaɪnə/ 里賈納

Saguenay /ˈsæɡɪneɪ/ 薩格奈

Saint John /ˌseɪnt ˈdʒɒn; *NAmE* ˈdʒɑːn/ 聖約翰

Saskatoon /ˌsæskəˈtuːn/ 薩斯卡通

Sault Sainte Marie /ˌsuː seɪnt məˈriː/ 蘇聖瑪麗

Sherbrooke /ˈʃɜːbrʊk; *NAmE* ˈʃɜːrb-/ 舍布魯克

St John's /ˌsnt ˈdʒɒnz; *NAmE* ˌsnt ˈdʒɑːnz; *NAmE also* ˌseɪnt/ 聖約翰斯

Sydney /ˈsɪdni/ 悉尼

Thunder Bay /ˌθʌndə ˈbeɪ; *NAmE* -dər/ 桑德貝

Toronto /təˈrɒntəʊ; *NAmE* təˈrɑːntoʊ/ 多倫多

Vancouver /vænˈkuːvə(r)/ 温哥華

Victoria /vɪkˈtɔːriə/ 維多利亞

Whitehorse /ˈwaɪthɔːs; *NAmE* -hɔːrs/ 懷特霍斯

Windsor /ˈwɪnzə(r)/ 温莎

Winnipeg /ˈwɪnɪpeɡ/ 温尼伯

Yellowknife /ˈjeləʊnaɪf; *NAmE* -loʊ-/ 耶洛奈夫

Australia and New Zealand 澳大利亞和新西蘭

The states of Australia 澳大利亞各州

Australian Capital Territory (ACT) /ɒˌstreɪliən kæpɪtl ˈterətri; *NAmE* ɔːˌstreɪliən; ˈterətɔːri/ 澳大利亞首都直轄區

New South Wales /ˌnjuː saʊθ ˈweɪlz; *NAmE* ˌnuː/ 新南威爾士州

Northern Territory /ˌnɔːðən ˈterətri; *NAmE* ˌnɔːrðərn ˈterətɔːri/ 北部地區

Queensland /ˈkwiːnzlənd/ 昆士蘭州

South Australia /ˌsaʊθ ɒˈstreɪliə; *NAmE* ɔːˈstreɪliə/ 南澳大利亞州

Tasmania /tæzˈmeɪniə/ 塔斯馬尼亞州

Victoria /vɪkˈtɔːriə/ 維多利亞州

Western Australia /ˌwestən ɒˈstreɪliə; *NAmE* ˌwestərn ɔːˈstreɪliə/ 西澳大利亞州

Towns and cities in Australia and New Zealand 澳大利亞和新西蘭的城鎮

Adelaide /ˈædəleɪd/ 阿德萊德

Alice Springs /ˌælɪs ˈsprɪŋz/ 艾麗斯斯普林斯

Auckland /ˈɔːklənd/ 奥克蘭

Brisbane /ˈbrɪzbən/ 布里斯班

Cairns /keənz; *NAmE* kernz/ 凱恩斯

Canberra /ˈkænbərə; *NAmE also* -berə/ 堪培拉

Christchurch /ˈkraɪstʃɜːtʃ; *NAmE* -tʃɜːrtʃ/ 克賴斯特徹奇

Darwin /ˈdɑːwɪn; *NAmE* ˈdɑːrwɪn/ 達爾文

Dunedin /dʌˈniːdɪn/ 達尼丁

Geelong /dʒɪˈlɒŋ; *NAmE* dʒəˈlɔːŋ/ 吉朗

Gold Coast /ˈɡəʊld kəʊst; *NAmE* ˈɡoʊld koʊst/ 戈爾德科斯特

Hamilton /ˈhæmɪltən/ 哈密爾頓

Hobart /ˈhəʊbɑːt; *NAmE* ˈhoʊbɑːrt/ 霍巴特

Launceston /ˈlɒnsəstən; *NAmE* ˈlɑːn-/ 朗塞斯頓

Melbourne /ˈmelbən; *NAmE* -bərn/ 墨爾本

Newcastle /ˈnjuːkɑːsl; *NAmE* ˈnuːkæsl/ 紐卡斯爾

Perth /pɜːθ; *NAmE* pɜːrθ/ 珀斯

Sunshine Coast /ˈsʌnʃaɪn kəʊst; *NAmE* koʊst/ 陽光海岸

Sydney /ˈsɪdni/ 悉尼

Tauranga /taʊˈræŋə; təʊˈrɒŋə; *NAmE* taʊˈrɑːŋə; toʊ-/ 陶朗阿

Townsville /ˈtaʊnsvɪl/ 湯斯威爾

Wellington /ˈwelɪŋtən/ 惠靈頓

Wollongong /ˈwʊləŋɡɒŋ; *NAmE* ˈwʊləŋɡɔːŋ; -ɡɑːŋ/ 伍倫貢

British and American English
英式英語和美式英語

American English differs from British English not only in pronunciation but also in vocabulary, spelling and grammar. 美式英語與英式英語不僅在讀音上有區別，在用詞、拼寫和語法上也有所不同。

Pronunciation 讀音

- When the American pronunciation is different from the British pronunciation it is given after the British pronunciation in the dictionary. 如果美式讀音與英式讀音有差異，本詞典先給出英式讀音，然後給出美式讀音：**tomato**: /təˈmɑːtəʊ; *NAmE* təˈmeɪtoʊ/.
- Some important differences: Stressed vowels are usually longer in American English. In **packet**, for example, the /æ/ is longer. 在讀音上的一些重要差異：在美式英語中重讀元音通常發音較長，如 packet 中的 /æ/。
- In British English the consonant /r/ is pronounced only before a vowel (for example in **red** and **bedroom**). In all other cases the /r/ is silent (for example in **car**, **learn**, **over**). In American English the /r/ is always pronounced. 在英式英語中，輔音 /r/ 只是在元音之前才發音（如 red 和 bedroom），其他情況下均不發音（如 car、learn、over）。在美式英語中，/r/ 在任何位置都發音。
- In American English the t between vowels is pronounced as a soft d /d/, so that **writer** and **rider** sound similar. British English speakers usually pronounce the t as /t/. 在美式英語中，元音之間的 t 讀成弱化的 /d/，因此 writer 和 rider 聽起來相似，而說英式英語者通常將 t 讀成 /t/。

Vocabulary 詞彙

The dictionary tells you which words are used only in American English or have different meanings in British and American English, for example **cookie**, **elevator**, **trunk**. 本詞典對只用於美式英語或在英式英語和美式英語中含義不同的單詞均予以註明，如 cookie、elevator、trunk。

Spelling 拼寫

- The dictionary shows different spellings in British and American English. The following differences are particularly common. 本詞典標有英式英語和美式英語的不同拼法，常見區別如下：
- In verbs which end in *l* and are not stressed on the final syllable, the *l* is not doubled in the *-ing* form and the past participle: **cancelling**; (*NAmE*) **canceling**. 在美式英語中，以 l 結尾的動詞，如果最後一個音節為非重讀音節，該動詞的 -ing 形式和過去分詞均不雙寫 l，如 cancelling（英式拼法）；canceling（美式拼法）。
- Words which end in *-tre* are spelt *-ter* in American English: **centre**; (*NAmE*) **center**. 以 -tre 結尾的詞，美式英語拼作 -ter，如 centre（英式拼法）；center（美式拼法）。
- Words which end in *-our* are usually spelt *-or* in American English: **colour**; (*NAmE*) **color**. 以 -our 結尾的詞，美式英語通常拼作 -or，如 colour（英式拼法）；color（美式拼法）。
- Words which end in *-ogue* are usually spelt *-og* in American English: **dialogue**; (*NAmE*) **dialog**. 以 -ogue 結尾的詞，美式英語中通常拼作 -og，如 dialogue（英式拼法）；dialog（美式拼法）。
- In British English many verbs can be spelt with either *-ize* or *-ise*. In American English only the spelling with *-ize* is possible: **realize, -ise**; (*NAmE*) **realize**. 在英式英語中，許多動詞的結尾拼作 -ize 或 -ise 均可，但在美式英語中只能拼作 -ize，如 realize/realise（英式拼法）；realize（美式拼法）。

Grammar 語法

Present perfect/Simple past 現在完成時；一般過去時

In American English the simple past can be used with **already**, **just** and **yet**. In British English the present perfect is used. 在美式英語中，already、just 和 yet 可用於一般過去時；在英式英語中，這些詞只能用於現在完成時：

▸ *I have already given her the present.* (*BrE*)
我已把禮物送給她了。

- *I already gave her the present.* (*NAmE*)
  我已把禮物送給她了。
- *I've just seen her.* (*BrE*) 我剛見過她。
- *I just saw her.* (*NAmE*) 我剛見過她。
- *Have you heard the news yet?* (*BrE*)
  你聽説這消息了嗎？
- *Did you hear the news yet?* (*NAmE*)
  你聽説這消息了嗎？

Have/have got

In British English it is possible to use **have got** or **have** to express the idea of possession. In American English only **have** can be used in questions and negative sentences. 在英式英語中，表示擁有用 have got 或 have 均可；而在美式英語的疑問句和否定句中，表達此義只能用 have：

- *They have/have got two computers.* (*BrE* and *NAmE*) 他們有兩台計算機。
- *Have you got a computer? Yes, I have.* (*BrE*)
  你有計算機嗎？我有。
- *Do you have a computer? Yes, I do.* (*BrE* and *NAmE*) 你有計算機嗎？我有。

Get/gotten

In American English the past participle of **get** is **gotten**. 在美式英語中，get 的過去分詞為 gotten：

- *Your English has got better.* (*BrE*)
  你的英語進步了。
- *Your English has gotten better.* (*NAmE*)
  你的英語進步了。

Prepositions and adverbs 介詞和副詞

Some prepositions and adverbs are used differently in British and American English, for example **stay at home** (*BrE*); **stay home** (*NAmE*). 有些介詞和副詞在英式英語和美式英語中用法不同，如 stay at home（英式英語）；stay home（美式英語）。

Form of the adverb 副詞的形式

In informal American English the adverb form ending in *-ly* is often not used. 在非正式的美式英語中，副詞經常用不以 -ly 結尾的形式：

- *He looked at me really strangely.* (*BrE*)
  他用十分異樣的目光看我。
- *He looked at me really strange.* (*NAmE*)
  他用十分異樣的目光看我。

Shall

Shall is not used instead of **will** in American English for the first person singular of the future. 在美式英語中，將來時的第一人稱單數不用 shall，只用 will：

- *I shall/will be here tomorrow.* (*BrE*)
  我明天在這裏。
- *I will be here tomorrow.* (*NAmE*)
  我明天在這裏。

Nor is it used in polite offers. 表示禮貌的提議也不用 shall：

- *Shall I open the window?* (*BrE*)
  我把窗戶打開好嗎？
- *Should I open the window?* (*NAmE*)
  我把窗戶打開好嗎？

Irregular verbs 不規則動詞

In British English the past simple and past participle of many verbs can be formed with *-ed* or *-t*, for example **burned/burnt**. In American English only the forms ending in *-ed* are used. 在英式英語中，許多動詞的一般過去式和過去分詞可以由 -ed 或 -t 構成，如 burned/burnt，美式英語只用 -ed 結尾的形式：

- *They burned/burnt the documents.* (*BrE*)
  他們把文件燒了。
- *They burned the documents.* (*NAmE*)
  他們把文件燒了。

When the past participle is used as an adjective, British English prefers the *-t* form, whereas in American English the *-ed* form is preferred, with the exception of **burnt**. 在英式英語中，過去分詞用作形容詞時常用 -t 形式，在美式英語中則更常用 -ed 形式，但 burnt 除外：

- *a spoilt child* (*BrE*) 嬌慣壞了的孩子
- *a spoiled child* (*NAmE*) 嬌慣壞了的孩子
- *burnt toast* (*BrE* and *NAmE*) 烤焦了的麵包片

Go/Come and ...

In these expressions **and** is often omitted. 在下列表達方式中 and 通常省略不用：

- *Go and take a look outside.* (*BrE*)
  到外面去看看吧。
- *Go take a look outside.* (*NAmE*)
  到外面去看看吧。

On the telephone 打電話

- *Hello, is that David?* (*BrE*)
  喂，是戴維嗎？
- *Hello, is this David?* (*NAmE*)
  喂，是戴維嗎？

The Oxford 3000™

The keywords of the **Oxford 3000** have been carefully selected by a group of language experts and experienced teachers as the words which should receive priority in vocabulary study because of their importance and usefulness. The selection is based on three criteria.

The words which occur most **frequently** in English are included, based on the information in the British National Corpus and the Oxford Corpus Collection. (A corpus is an electronically held collection of written or spoken texts, often consisting of hundreds of millions of words – for more information, visit the OALD website.) However, being frequent in the corpus alone is not enough for a word to qualify as a keyword: it may be that the word is used very frequently, but only in a narrowly defined area, such as newspapers or scientific articles. In order to avoid including these restricted words, we include as keywords only those words which are frequent across a **range** of different types of text. In other words, keywords are both frequent and used in a variety of contexts. In addition, the list includes some very important words which happen not to be used frequently, even though they are very **familiar** to most users of English. These include, for example, words for parts of the body, words used in travel, and words which are useful for explaining what you mean when you do not know the exact word for something. These words were identified by consulting a panel of over seventy experts in the fields of teaching and language study.

The words of the **Oxford 3000** are shown in the main section of the dictionary in larger print, and with a key symbol 🔑 immediately following. The most useful parts of the entries (particular parts of speech, meanings, phrasal verbs and idioms) are marked with a small key symbol. The entries for keywords often have extra information in the form of more examples of use, special notes explaining synonyms or related words, or helpful illustrations. This means that the keywords make an excellent starting point for expanding your vocabulary. With most keywords, there is far more to learn about them than the first meaning in the entry: often these words have many meanings, have a large family of words derived from them, or are used in a variety of patterns.

The list covers British and American English. Some basic phrases are also included. Proper names (names of people, places, etc. beginning with a capital letter) are not included in the list.

In order to make the definitions in this dictionary easy to understand, we have written them using the keywords of the **Oxford 3000**. All words used in normal definition text are keywords, or are on the list of language study terms, shown below. Numbers and proper names are also used in definitions. When it has been necessary to use a specialist term which is not in the **Oxford 3000**, the word is shown in small capitals. If you do not know the meaning of this word, look it up in the dictionary: it will help you to understand the definition that you are interested in, and will probably be a useful word to learn because it will be related to the original word you looked up.

For more information on the **Oxford 3000**, and to download a copy of the list, visit the OALD website at **http://www.oup.com/elt/oald**.

牛津 3000 詞彙表

牛津 3000 核心詞是由一批語言專家和有經驗的教師精心挑選而成，按重要性和實用性而選為詞彙學習的重點，選詞標準有三個。

第一是根據英國國家語料庫和牛津語料庫提供的資料，收錄英語中最常用的詞彙。（語料庫指用電子方法彙集和保存的書面或口語文獻，通常由數以億萬的詞彙構成。有關語料庫的詳細信息，請訪問《牛津高階英語詞典》(OALD) 網站。）不過，在語料庫中出現頻率高還不足以選進牛津 3000 詞彙表中。有些詞或許使用頻率非常高，但只是在嚴格限定的範圍內，如報章或科技文章中。為了避免收錄這類受限詞彙，本表只包括使用頻率高且廣泛用於各種不同文體的核心詞。因此，核心詞收錄的第二個標準是既要使用頻率高，又要能用於各種不同的語境。第三，詞表中還包括一些對大多數英語使用者來說非常熟悉、但碰巧不太常用的重要詞彙，如表示身體部位的詞彙、旅行詞彙和對釋義非常有用的詞彙。這些詞彙均由教學和語言學習領域裏 70 多位專家組成的專家咨詢組確認。

牛津 3000 詞彙表的詞彙在本詞典的主體部份用較大的字體顯示，其後緊跟鑰匙符 O╖。詞條中最有用的部份（特定詞類、詞義、短語動詞和習語）以小鑰匙符標示。核心詞詞條通常有一些附加信息，如較多的用法實例、同義詞和相關詞特別註釋或一些有用的插圖，作為擴充詞彙的基礎。就多數核心詞來說，要瞭解的遠不止詞條中的第一個含義。這些詞常常具有多重含義，衍生出豐富的同族詞，或用於各種句型中。

詞彙表涵蓋英式英語和美式英語，還包括一些基本短語。專有名詞（以大寫字母開頭的人名、地名等）不包含在詞彙表內。

為使本詞典的釋義易於理解，我們用牛津 3000 核心詞來撰寫釋義，一般釋義中使用的詞彙均為牛津 3000 核心詞或下頁所列的語言學習術語詞彙表中的詞。數字和專有名詞也用於釋義中。必須使用牛津 3000 詞彙表中未收錄的專業術語時，術語會用小號的大寫字母顯示。要瞭解這些詞的含義，可在本詞典中查找，瞭解詞義之餘，因為與之前查找的詞有關聯，該詞也很值得學習。

關於牛津 3000 詞彙表的詳細信息，以及下載該詞彙表，請訪問《牛津高階英語詞典》(OALD) 網站 http://www.oup.com/elt/oald。

Language study terms
語言學習術語

Knowing these words will be useful in your study of English and will also help you to use the **Oxford Advanced Learner's Dictionary** more effectively. It includes words to do with grammar, pronunciation and punctuation. 瞭解下列詞彙有助於學習英語，並且更有效地使用《牛津高階英語詞典》(OALD)。這其中包括有關語法、讀音和標點符號的詞。

abbreviation *n.*
active *adj.*, *n.*
adjective *n.*
adverb *n.*
apostrophe *n.*
article *n.*
auxiliary (*also* auxiliary verb) *n.*
bracket *n.*
clause *n.*
colon *n.*
comma *n.*
comparative *adj.*, *n.*
compound *n.*, *adj.*
conditional *adj.*, *n.*
conjunction *n.*
consonant *n.*
contraction *n.*
countable *adj.*
continuous
➲progressive
derivative *n.*
determiner *n.*
dialect *n.*
entry *n.*
exclamation *n.*
exclamation mark (*especially BrE*) (*NAmE usually* exclamation point) *n.*
figurative *adj.*
full stop *n.* (*BrE*)
gerund *n.*
hyphen *n.*
idiom *n.*
imperative *adj.*, *n.*
indirect speech
➲reported speech
infinitive *n.*
inverted commas
➲quotation marks
ironic *adj.*
irregular *adj.*
literal *adj.*
literary *adj.*
modal *n.*
noun *n.*
object *n.*
ordinal *n.*
paragraph *n.*
parenthesis *n.*
part of speech (*also* word class) *n.*
participle *n.*
particle *n.*
passive *adj.*, *n.*
perfect *adj.*
period *n.* (*NAmE*)
phrasal verb *n.*
plural *n.*, *adj.*
possessive *adj.*, *n.*
prefix *n.*
preposition *n.*
progressive (*also* continuous) *adj.*
pronoun *n.*
punctuation *n.*
question mark *n.*
question tag (*also* tag question) *n.*
quotation marks (*BrE also* inverted commas) *n.*
reflexive *adj.*
register *n.*
regular *adj.*
relative *adj.*
reported speech (*also* indirect speech) *n.*
saying *n.*
semicolon *n.*
simple *adj.*
singular *n.*, *adj.*
slang *n.*
slash *n.*
subject *n.*
suffix *n.*
superlative *adj.*, *n.*
syllable *n.*
taboo *adj.*
tag question
➲question tag
tense *n.*
uncountable *adj.*
verb *n.*
vowel *n.*
word class
➲part of speech

The Academic Word List:

A tool for vocabulary learning

Averil Coxhead
Victoria University of Wellington New Zealand

You are holding a dictionary which contains many thousands of words. As a learner of English as a second or even third language, how can you decide which words you need to spend your valuable time on? One way you can do this is by looking at the frequency of words. That is, how often these words occur in your reading and listening material in English. What you read and listen to might depend on your purposes for learning English. If, for example, you want to study in an English-medium university, it will be important to focus on words that you will meet often at university.

How can this dictionary help you decide which words to learn for your studies? This dictionary includes words from the Academic Word List (AWL). The list was developed by analysing a corpus or body of academic written texts to find out which words occurred across a range of 28 subject areas (such as Biology, History, Marketing, and International Law) in four academic disciplines (Arts, Commerce, Law, and Science). These words were selected because of their range and frequency of occurrence. They are outside the first 2000 words of English. The AWL contains 570 word families and covers roughly 10% of a written academic text, which means that ten words in every 100 can be found in the list.

In this dictionary, you will find that words from the AWL are labelled **AW**. Words in the Oxford 3000 word list of general English are also highlighted. The AWL and the Oxford 3000 lists have some words in common because the AWL excludes the first 2000 words while the Oxford 3000 includes the first 2000 words and 1000 words more. Examples of some words that are shared include *abandon* and *academic*.

What are some other challenges for learners when it comes to academic vocabulary? First and foremost, it is important to know the meaning of a word and to recognise its meaning when the word is presented in context. Some words, such as 'require', carry roughly the same meaning in most contexts. Other words have developed very specific meanings depending on an area of study. An example is the word 'significant' which carries a particular meaning in statistical studies. You can use this dictionary to help you find out more about the meanings of words in context.

Another challenge is using tools such as this dictionary to enhance your understanding. The dictionary includes words that commonly occur with a target word, its pronunciation, and examples or sentences with the target word in it. All of this information can help you develop a fuller understanding of a word.

There is a saying which goes, 'If you don't use it, you'll lose it'. Make sure you try to use words, from the AWL for example, in your writing and speaking. That way you can get feedback and further develop your knowledge of these words. You also need useful strategies to cement your learning. If you find yourself looking up the same word more than once or you find specialised words for your studies, you may need to develop word cards or design a vocabulary notebook to help you learn.

If we think of language as a toolbox for life, this dictionary contains many useful tools for your learning. The AWL is a vocabulary tool that might help you prepare for your future studies.

You can find out more about the AWL on this website: **http://www.victoria.ac.nz/lals/staff/averil-coxhead.aspx.**

學術詞彙表

詞彙學習的工具

埃夫里爾·考克斯黑德
新西蘭惠靈頓維多利亞大學

你手頭的詞典包含成千上萬條詞彙。作為以英語為第二甚至第三語言的學習者，你如何確定哪些詞需要花費寶貴的時間來學習？方法之一是看詞的頻率，即這些詞在你的英語閱讀和聽力材料中出現的頻次。你所閱讀和聽的東西可能取決於你學習英語的目的。例如，如果想去用英語授課的大學學習，那麼要緊的是重點學習在大學中將經常遇到的詞彙。

如何借助本詞典確定學習所需要的詞彙？本詞典收錄學術詞彙表（AWL）中的詞彙。這個詞表是通過分析語料庫和大量學術文本、找出 4 個學術範疇（文學藝術、商業、法律和科學）中多達 28 個專業（如生物、歷史、營銷和國際法）中所出現的詞彙。選取這些詞彙是由於它們出現的廣泛程度和頻率。它們在最基本的 2000 個英語詞彙以外。AWL 包含 570 個詞族，覆蓋了學術文本約 10% 的內容，也就是說，每 100 個詞中就有 10 個出現在本詞彙表中。

在本詞典中，AWL 詞彙以 **AW** 標示，牛津 3000 詞彙表的常用英語詞彙也特別標示出來。AWL 和牛津 3000 詞彙表中有些詞相同，因為 AWL 不包括最基本的 2000 個英語詞彙，而牛津 3000 詞彙表除了最基本的 2000 個詞外另行收錄了 1000 個英語詞彙。如 abandon 和 academic 在這兩個詞彙表中均可找到。

學習者在學術詞彙方面還會遇到一些什麼挑戰呢？首先，重要的是要知道詞的意思並識別它在上下文中的含義。有些詞在大多數語境中的意思基本相同，如 require。另外一些詞在某一學科領域中有十分特定的含義，例如，significant 在統計學中有其特定含義。本詞典有助於進一步瞭解詞彙在上下文中的意思。

另一挑戰是利用本詞典這一類的工具書加深理解。本詞典列出與目標詞經常連用的詞語、目標詞讀音以及包含目標詞的示例或例句。這些信息均有助於更充分地理解詞語。

常言道，“不用則廢”。在寫作和口頭表達中一定要盡可能地使用詞彙，如 AWL 中的詞彙，如此便可以獲得反饋信息並進一步豐富詞彙知識。還得有行之有效的策略以鞏固所學知識。如果查閱同一個詞超過一次或遇到學習中所需要的專門用語，也許就得製作單詞卡片或設計生詞本來幫助學習。

如果我們把語言看作生活的工具箱，那麼本詞典包含了許多有用的學習工具。AWL 便是一種詞彙工具，可幫助你為未來的學習做好準備。

要瞭解 AWL 的詳細信息可登錄以下網站：http://www.victoria.ac.nz/lals/staff/averil-coxhead.aspx。

Pronunciation and phonetic symbols
讀音和音標

The British pronunciations given are those of younger speakers of General British. This includes RP (Received Pronunciation) and a range of similar accents which are not strongly regional. The American pronunciations chosen are also as far as possible the most general (not associated with any particular region). If there is a difference between British and American pronunciations of a word, the British one is given first, with *NAmE* before the American pronunciation. 本詞典標出的英式讀音為較年輕的人使用的通用英語讀音，其中包括標準讀音和一系列地方音不太重的類似口音。所選的美式讀音也是盡可能通用的（不與任何特定地區的讀音相聯繫）。如果某個詞的英式讀音和美式讀音有差異，則先給出英式讀音，再給出美式讀音，美式讀音前用 *NAmE* 標示。

Consonants 輔音

p	pen	/pen/	s	see	/siː/
b	bad	/bæd/	z	zoo	/zuː/
t	tea	/tiː/	ʃ	shoe	/ʃuː/
d	did	/dɪd/	ʒ	vision	/ˈvɪʒn/
k	cat	/kæt/	h	hat	/hæt/
g	get	/get/	m	man	/mæn/
tʃ	chain	/tʃeɪn/	n	now	/naʊ/
dʒ	jam	/dʒæm/	ŋ	sing	/sɪŋ/
f	fall	/fɔːl/	l	leg	/leg/
v	van	/væn/	r	red	/red/
θ	thin	/θɪn/	j	yes	/jes/
ð	this	/θɪs/	w	wet	/wet/

The symbol (r) indicates that British pronunciation will have /r/ only if a vowel sound follows directly at the beginning of the next word, as in **far away**; otherwise the /r/ is omitted. For American English, all the /r/ sounds should be pronounced. 符號 (r) 表示只有當後面緊跟一個以元音開頭的詞時，英式讀音的 /r/ 才發音，如 far away，否則這個 /r/ 就省略不讀。在美式英語中，所有的 /r/ 音都應讀出。

/x/ represents a fricative sound as in /lɒx/ for Scottish **loch**, Irish **lough**. * /x/ 表示摩擦音，如 /lɒx/ 讀音代表蘇格蘭英語的 loch、愛爾蘭英語的 lough。

Vowels and diphthongs
元音和雙元音

iː	see	/siː/	
i	happy	/ˈhæpi/	
ɪ	sit	/sɪt/	
e	ten	/ten/	
æ	cat	/kæt/	
ɑː	father	/ˈfɑːðə(r)/	
ɒ	got	/gɒt/	(*British English*)
ɔː	saw	/sɔː/	
ʊ	put	/pʊt/	
u	actual	/ˈæktʃuəl/	
uː	too	/tuː/	
ʌ	cup	/kʌp/	
ɜː	fur	/fɜː(r)/	
ə	about	/əˈbaʊt/	
eɪ	say	/seɪ/	
əʊ	go	/gəʊ/	(*British English*)
oʊ	go	/goʊ/	(*American English*)
aɪ	my	/maɪ/	
ɔɪ	boy	/bɔɪ/	
aʊ	now	/naʊ/	
ɪə	near	/nɪə(r)/	(*British English*)
eə	hair	/heə(r)/	(*British English*)
ʊə	pure	/pjʊə(r)/	(*British English*)

Many British speakers use /ɔː/ instead of the diphthong /ʊə/, especially in common words, so that **sure** becomes /ʃɔː(r)/, etc. 英式發音常用 /ɔː/ 代替雙元音 /ʊə/，尤其在一些常見詞彙中，如 sure 的發音就成了 /ʃɔː(r)/。

The sound /ɒ/ does not occur in American English, and words which have this vowel in British pronunciation will instead have /ɑː/ or /ɔː/ in American English. For instance, **got** is /gɒt/ in British English, but /gɑːt/ in American English, while **dog** is British /dɒg/, American /dɔːg/. 在美式英語中沒有 /ɒ/ 音，在英式讀音中有這個元音的詞彙在美式英語中以 /ɑː/ 或 /ɔː/ 取代，如 got 在英式英語中為 /gɒt/，在美式英語中則為 /gɑːt/；而 dog 在英式英語中為 /dɒg/，在美式英語中則為 /dɔːg/。

The three diphthongs /ɪə eə ʊə/ are found only in British English. In corresponding places, American English has a simple vowel followed by /r/, so **near** is /nɪr/, **hair** is /her/, and **pure** is /pjʊr/. 只有在英式英語中才有 /ɪə eə ʊə/ 這三個雙元音，美式英語則對應為一個單元音後跟一個 /r/，故 near 讀作 /nɪr/，hair 讀作 /her/，pure 讀作 /pjʊr/。

Nasalized vowels, marked with /˜/, may be retained in certain words taken from French, as in **penchant** /ˈpɒ̃ʃɒ̃/, **coq au vin** /ˌkɒk əʊ ˈvæ̃/. 標有 /˜/ 的鼻元音在某些來自法語的詞中可能保留下來，如 penchant /ˈpɒ̃ʃɒ̃/，coq au vin /ˌkɒk əʊ ˈvæ̃/。

Syllabic consonants 音節輔音

The sounds /l/ and /n/ can often be 'syllabic' – that is, they can form a syllable by themselves without a vowel. There is a syllabic /l/ in the usual pronunciation of **middle** /ˈmɪdl/, and a syllabic /n/ in **sudden** /ˈsʌdn/. */l/ 和 /n/ 音常可成音節，即沒有元音它們本身也可構成一個音節。在 middle /ˈmɪdl/ 的通常讀音中有一個成音節 /l/，sudden /ˈsʌdn/ 的通常讀音中也有一個成音節 /n/。

Weak vowels /i/ and /u/
弱元音 /i/ 和 /u/

The sounds represented by /iː/ and /ɪ/ must always be made different, as in **heat** /hiːt/ compared with **hit** /hɪt/. The symbol /i/ represents a vowel that can be sounded as either /iː/ or /ɪ/, or as a sound which is a compromise between them. In a word such as **happy** /ˈhæpi/, younger speakers use a quality more like /iː/, but short in duration. When /i/ *is followed by* /ə/ *the sequence can also be* pronounced /jə/. So the word **dubious** can be /ˈdjuːbiəs/ or /ˈdjuːdjəs/. 由 /iː/ 和 /ɪ/ 表示的音一定要區分清楚，如 heat /hiːt/ 與 hit /hɪt/。音標 /i/ 是一個元音，它聽起來像 /iː/ 或 /ɪ/，或像兩者之間的音，如在 happy /ˈhæpi/ 一詞中，年輕人的讀音更像 /iː/ 音，只是發得較短。/i/ 後接 /ə/ 時亦可讀作 /jə/，因此 dubious 一詞可讀作 /ˈdjuːbiəs/ 或 /ˈdjuːdjəs/。

In the same way, the two vowels represented /uː/ and /ʊ/ must be kept distinct but /u/ represents a weak vowel that varies between them. If /u/ is followed directly by a consonant sound, it can also be pronounced as /ə/. So **stimulate** can be /ˈstɪmjuleɪt/ or /ˈstɪmjəleɪt/. 同樣，由 /uː/ 和 /ʊ/ 表示的兩個元音必須區分清楚，但是 /u/ 是一個弱元音，介於 /uː/ 和 /ʊ/ 之間。如果 /u/ 後緊跟一個輔音，亦可讀作 /ə/，因此，stimulate 可讀作 /ˈstɪmjuleɪt/ 或 /ˈstɪmjəleɪt/。

Weak forms and strong forms
弱讀式與強讀式

Certain very common words, for example **at**, **and**, **for**, **can**, have two pronunciations. We give the usual (weak) pronunciation first. The second pronunciation (strong) must be used if the word is stressed, and also generally when the word is at the end of a sentence. 某些常用詞（如 at、and、for、can）有兩種讀音，本詞典先給出常用的弱讀式，如果強調此詞就必須用第二種讀音，即強讀；如果此詞位於句末，一般也用強讀。For example 如：

- *Can* /kən/ *you help?*
- *I'll help if I can* /kæn/.

Stress 重音

The mark /ˈ/ shows the main stress in a word. Compare **able** /ˈeɪbl/, stressed on the first syllable, with **ability** /əˈbɪləti/, stressed on the second. A stressed syllable is relatively loud, long in duration, said clearly and distinctly, and made noticeable by the pitch of the voice. 符號 /ˈ/ 表示一個詞的主重音。比較 able /ˈeɪbl/（重音在第一音節）和 ability /əˈbɪləti/（重音在第二音節）。重讀音節相對而言聲音較響，發音較長，讀得清晰，音調較高，使音節明顯。

Longer words may have one or more secondary stresses coming before the main stress. These are marked with /ˌ/ as in **abbreviation** /əˌbriːviˈeɪʃn/, **agricultural** /ˌægrɪˈkʌltʃərəl/. They feel like beats in a rhythm leading up to the main stress. 較長的詞在主重音之前可能有一個或多個次重音，以 /ˌ/ 標示，如 abbreviation /əˌbriːviˈeɪʃn/，agricultural /ˌægrɪˈkʌltʃərəl/。它們就像節奏中的拍子一樣帶出主重音。

Weak stresses coming after the main stress in a word can sometimes be heard, but they are not marked in this dictionary. 有時在單詞中的主重音後可聽到一個弱重音，不過本詞典未標出弱重音。

When two words are put together in a phrase, the main stress in the first word may shift to the place of the secondary stress to avoid a clash between two stressed syllables next to each other. For instance, **ˌafterˈnoon** has the main stress on **noon**, but in the phrase **ˌafternoon ˈtea** the stress on **noon** is missing. **ˌWell ˈknown** has the main stress on **known**, but in the phrase **ˌwell-known ˈactor** the stress on **known** is missing. 兩個單詞同在一個短語中時，第一個單詞的主重音可能轉化為次重音，以避免兩個相鄰的重音音節相衝突。如 ˌafterˈnoon 的主重音在 noon，但在短語 ˌafternoon ˈtea 中，noon 的重音就消失了。ˌwell ˈknown 的主重音在 known，但在短語 ˌwell-known ˈactor 中，known 的重音消失了。

Stress in phrasal verbs 短語動詞的重音

One type of phrasal verb has a single strong stress on the first word. Examples are **ˈcome to sth**, **ˈgo for sb**, **ˈlook at sth**. This stress pattern is kept in all situations, and the second word is never stressed. If the second word is one which normally appears in a weak form, remember that the strong form must be used at the end of a phrase. 有一種短語動詞只在第一個單詞上有一個強讀重音，如 ˈcome to sth、ˈgo for sb、ˈlook at sth。這種重音模式適用於此類短語動詞的所有情況，第二個單詞永遠不重讀。如果第二個單詞通常為弱讀式，那麼切記在短語的末尾必須強讀。

Another type of phrasal verb is shown with two stresses. The pattern shown in the dictionary, with the main stress on the second word, is the one which is used when the verb is said on its own, or when the verb as a whole is the last important word in a phrase. 另一種短語動詞標有兩個重音。本詞典中，如果短語動詞的主重音在第二個單詞上，則它只適用於兩種情況，即該短語動詞獨立出現，或其作為一個整體是某個短語中最不重要的詞：

- *What time are you ˌcoming ˈback?*
- *He ˌmade it ˈup.*
- *ˌFill them ˈin.*

But the speaker will put a strong stress on any other important word if it comes later than the verb. The stress on the second word of the verb is then weakened or lost, especially if it would otherwise be next to the other strong stress. This happens whether the important word which receives the strong stress is between the two parts of the phrasal verb, or after both of them. 但說話人可能把強讀重音放在動詞後任何一個重要單詞上。在這種情況下，短語動詞的第二個單詞的重音便弱化或消失，尤其當這個重音又靠近另一個強讀重音時。無論具有強讀重音的重要單詞是在該短語動詞的兩部份之間還是之後，都可能發生這種情況。

- *We ˌcame back ˈearly.*
- *I ˌfilled in a ˈform.*
- *ˌFill this ˈform in.*

If more than one stress pattern is possible, or the stress depends on the context, no stress is shown. 如果有可能出現兩種以上的重音模式，或重音要依據上下文來確定，本詞典就不標出重音。

Stress in idioms 習語的重音

Idioms are shown in the dictionary with at least one main stress unless more than one stress pattern is possible or the stress depends on the context. The learner should not change the position of this stress when speaking or the special meaning of the idiom may be lost. 本詞典中的習語至少標有一個主重音，除非有可能出現兩種或以上的重音模式或重音要依據上下文來確定。學習者在說話時不應改變此重音的位置，否則該習語就可能失去既定的含義。

Tapping of /t/ 輕觸音 /t/

In American English, if a /t/ sound is between two vowels, and the second vowel is not stressed, the /t/ can be pronounced very quickly, and made voiced so that it is like a brief /d/ or the r-sound of certain languages. Technically, the sound is a 'tap', and can be symbolised by /t̬/. So Americans can pronounce **potato** as /pəˈteɪt̬oʊ/, tapping the second /t/ in the word (but not the first, because of the stress). British speakers don't generally do this. 在美式英語中，如果 /t/ 音在兩個元音之間，而且第二個元音不重讀，則 /t/ 可能讀得很快，而且濁化，聽起來就像一個短 /d/ 音或某些語言中的 r 音。術語稱作輕觸音 (tap)，可用 /t̬/ 表示。因此美國人可能將 potato 讀作 /pəˈteɪt̬oʊ/，第二個 /t/ 輕輕一觸（由於重音的原因第一個 t 不讀輕觸音）。說英式英語的人一般不這樣讀。

The conditions for tapping also arise very frequently when words are put together, as in **not only**, **what I**, etc. In this case it doesn't matter whether the following vowel is stressed or not, and even British speakers can use taps in this situation, though they sound rather casual. 幾個單詞連在一起時常常出現輕觸音現象，如在 not only、what I 等中。這時，後面的元音是否重讀無關緊要，在這種情況下，甚至説英式英語的人也可能使用輕觸音，但聽起來很不正式。

The glottal stop 聲門閉塞音

In both British and American varieties of English, a /t/ which comes at the end of a word or syllable can often be pronounced as a glottal stop /ʔ/ (a silent gap produced by holding one's breath briefly) instead of a /t/. For this to happen, the next sound must not be a vowel or a syllabic /l/. So **football** can be /ˈfʊʔbɔːl/ instead of /ˈfʊtbɔːl/, and **button** can be /ˈbʌʔn/ instead of /ˈbʌtn/. But a glottal stop would not be used for the /t/ sounds in **bottle** or **better** because of the sounds which come afterwards. 在英式英語和美式英語中，單詞或音節末的 /t/ 音常用聲門閉塞音 /ʔ/（短暫的屏息產生的停頓）代替。但只有當下一個音不是元音或成音節 /l/ 時，才可能出現上述情況。因此，football 可能讀作 /ˈfʊʔbɔːl/ 而不讀 /ˈfʊtbɔːl/，button 可能讀作 /ˈbʌʔn/ 而不讀 /ˈbʌtn/。但 bottle 和 better 因為後接的音不符合這種條件，故不能用聲門閉塞音代替 /t/ 音。

ACKNOWLEDGEMENTS

Illustrations by: Julian Baker & Janet Baker (JB Illustrations) basket, dreamcatcher, gazebo, oxbow, stile, pp V2–8, V17–19, V52–53, V59, V67–68, V72 (earth, seasons); M Dunn chart; Hardlines optical illusion; K Hiscock pp V10–13, V30–32; M Jones matchstick figure; KJA-artists.com ball-and-socket joint, ball bearing, barbed wire, bevelled, blade, block and tackle, bolt, chip, cogwheel, cord, dovetail joint, elk, knot, label, money, piston, plug, rabbit, ratchet, sprocket wheel, staircase, pp V33, V63; Oxford University Press concentric, convex, ideogram, musical notation, rebus, Venn diagram, wavelength; P Schramm/ Meiklejohn Illustration bar, bow 1, bow 2, bridge, catapult, cat's cradle, curved, froth, hook, neck, ring, shade, spring, squeeze, pp V21–25, V60, V69–70; Q2AMedia ankh, broken, corrugated, edge, filter, frame, handle, hieroglyphics, key, möbius strip, peg, pipe, pushchair, rack, roundabout, scale, pp V71, V73 (solar system); G White helix

The Publishers would like to thank the following for their kind permission to reproduce photographs and other copyright material: Alamy Ltd. pp V14 (V Abbey/gargoyle, B Boston/aqueduct, curved-light/viaduct, David R Frazier Photolibrary, Inc./humpback bridge, graficart.net/portico, J Kase/cantilever bridge, H Sadura/geodesic dome), V16 (P Evans/thatched cottage, Eye Candy Images 4/houseboat, M Frost/Adams Picture Library/block of flats, KAKIMAGE/apartment building, J Kase/terraced house, philipus/duplex, M Richardson/bungalow, mobile home), V20 (D Hurst/ironing board, Image Farm Inc./bradawl), V24 (D Hurst/electric toothbrush, stockpix/nail scissors), V25 (ilian studio/electric kettle), V26 (D Amado/paring knife, D Hurst/measuring cups, J F T L IMAGES/kitchen scissors, Stockbyte/Getty Images, Inc./cake slice), V27 (discpicture/steam, A Shalamov/stir-fry, Studio EYE/ Photo Agency EYE/casserole, E Westmacott/boil), V37 (J Helgason/teddy bear, InspireStock Inc./Frisbee™, Stockbyte/Getty Images, Inc./rocking horse, THINGX/slide), V38–39 (W Heidasch/dominoes, Ilanphoto/PhotoStock-Israel/Chinese chequers, G Kollidas/backgammon, S May/sudoku, reppans/crossword, L Ryder/snakes and ladders), V40 (C Hochachka/Design Pics Inc./caving, T Kraus/tenpin bowling, TongRo Image Stock/archery, J Warrington/scuba-diving), V41 (Images-USA/photography, VStock/Tetra Images LLC/model making, I Zhorov/embroidery), V44 (A Muttitt/hockey), V49 (M-E Keith/hang-gliding, PHOVOIR/FCM Graphic/paragliding), V51 (S Sloan/scooter), V52 (Best View Stock/four-wheel drive, ilian car/convertible, sportscar, Luminis/estate car, hatchback, people carrier, I Montero/saloon), V53 (P Brogden/light aircraft, E Clendennen/aerobatic display, Thierry GRUN-Aero/biplane, A Scott/airship), V54 (Dacorum Gold/container ship, David R. Frazier Photolibrary, Inc./liner, C George/canal boat, Greece/hydrofoil, Images-USA/speedboat, J Kase/catamaran, I MacDonald/paddle steamer, R Naude/hovercraft, D Newham/ferry, I Patrick/lifeboat, A Stiop/cruiser, J Sullivan/sailing dinghy), V57 (M Dalton/single-decker bus, J Kase/articulated lorry, lorry, minibus, tanker, transporter, van, E Nguyen/US school bus, philipus/pickup, Pixoi Ltd./double-decker bus, A Schein/bus, A Stone/Jeep™), V58 (M Anderson/high-speed train, L Ashley/cab, A Bell/freight train, passenger train, I Blair/funicular, H Ibrahim/Photov.com/underground, J Kase/caravan, I MacDonald/bulldozer, Photolink Ltd./cable car, R Rayworth/steam train, M Richardson/tractor, RMT/cement mixer, Steppenwolf/tram, C Young/dumper truck), V61 (P Hakimata/suit, S Lihodeev/dress), V64 (T Large/baseball boots, T Payne/jelly shoe, P Springett/platform, SugarStock Ltd./clutch bag, H Threlfall/wedge, E Westmacott/flats), V65 (D Templeton/sou'wester), V66 (A Buckin/flash drive, CreativeAct-Technology series/digital camera, MP3 player, O Leedham/scanner, D Tolokonov/PDA), V69 (I Genkin/notepad, something else/glue stick); Corbis Corporation pp V39 (BLOOMimage/jigsaw), V45 (Floresco Productions/table tennis, Moodboard/Mike Watson Images Limited/breaststroke, tennis), V46 (Moodboard/Mike Watson Images Limited/polo), V50 (Moodboard/Mike Watson Images Limited/wakeboarding), V53 (Ben Blankenburg/glider), V58 (A Levenson/excavator, Moodboard/Mike Watson Images Limited/camper); Corel pp V14 (cloister), V15 (amphitheatre, castle, glasshouse, hut, lighthouse, log cabin, oil rig, pub, pyramid, skyscraper, stately home, warehouse), V47 (boxing), V55 (punt); Hemera Technologies Inc. all A–Z photographs, pp V15 (barn),

V19 (all except sprinkler, strimmer), V20 (all except bradawl, ironing board, mop, squeegee mop, toolbox), V22 (all except cake slice, fish knife and fork), V24 (comb, emery board, hairbrush, nail brush, nail clippers, shaver, sponge bag, toothbrush, tweezers), V25 (all except electric kettle, espresso maker), V26 (all except cake slice, fish slice, garlic press, measuring cups, measuring jug, measuring spoons, paring knife, potato masher, ramekin), V34–35 (castanets, cello, clarinet, congas, drum kit, French horn, flute, glockenspiel, harmonica, harp, maracas, recorder, saxophone, steel drum, tambourine, triangle, trombone, viola, violin), V36 (all except sitar, upright piano), V37 (glove puppet, pack of cards, suits), V38 (chess), V51 (D-lock, helmet, light, motorcycle pump), V61 (all except dress, suit), V63 (all except crew neck, nightwear, polo neck), V64 (all except baseball boots, clutch bag, flats, handbag, jelly shoe, platform, shoulder bag, wedge) V65 (all except charm bracelet, locket, sombrero, sou'wester), V69 (all except correction fluid, envelopes, glue stick, highlighter, notepad, Post-it™); Oxford University Press pp V16 (semi-detached house, PictureNet/Corbis Corporation/row house), V26 (fish slice, garlic press, potato masher), V37 (M Mason/rag doll), V40 (J Kase/Alamy Ltd./ice skating), V44 (M Karrass/Corbis Corporation/basketball), V63 (polo neck), V65 (charm bracelet, locket), V69 (correction fluid, drawing pins, highlighter), V74–75, V76–77, V78; Photolibrary Group Ltd. pp cover (R Chapple Stock/Photolibrary RF/dictionary, J Cundy/Image Source Ltd./Oxford, H Huber/Westend61 GmbH/fern, Glow Images RF/Glowimages Inc./book, Ingram Publishing Limited/steps, Y Kushima/Amana Images Inc./parasol, M Roessler/Corbis/sky, J Woodhouse/Radius Images/Masterfile Corporation/bicycle), V14 (Alanie/Life File/PhotoDisc/Getty Images, Inc./rotunda, R Chapple Stock/Photolibrary RF/vaulted ceiling, FOTOG/Tetra Images LLC/suspension bridge, D Fox/Purestock/Superstock, Inc./colonnade, Ingram Publishing RF/Ingram Publishing Limited/arch, M Milbradt/Brand X Pictures/Jupiterimages (UK) Ltd./obelisk, S Nicolas/ICONOTEC/dome), V15 (M Fife/PhotoDisc/Getty Images, Inc./fort, *hinkstock Images*/Jupiterimages (UK) Ltd./pagoda, R Kaestner/Corbis Corporation/palace), V16 (A Jones/Image Source Ltd./town house), V19 (Comstock Images/Jupiterimages (UK) Ltd./strimmer, Tetra Images LLC/sprinkler), V20 (Lynx/ICONOTEC/toolbox, Photolibrary RF/squeegee mop, Stockdisc/Stockbyte/Getty Images, Inc./mop), V22 (R McVay/PhotoDisc/Getty Images, Inc./fish knife and fork), V24 (J Atlas/Brand X Pictures/Jupiterimages (UK) Ltd./loofah, image100/Corbis Corporation/nail file, L Manning/Corbis Corporation/toothpaste, Stockbyte/Getty Images, Inc./sponge), V25 (Lynx/ICONOTEC/espresso maker), V26 (L Manning/Corbis Corporation/measuring spoons, T Northcut/PhotoDisc/Getty Images, Inc./measuring jug, Photolibrary RF/ramekin), V27 (Glow Images RF/Glow Images Inc./fry, Image Source Ltd./bake, barbecue, Jetta Productions/Dana Neely/Tetra Images LLC/flambé), V28 (J Baigrie/Digital Vision/Getty Images, Inc./grate, Ben Fink Photo Inc./Brand X Pictures/Jupiterimages (UK) Ltd./roll out, Creativ Studio Heinemann/Westend61 GmbH/mash, Fancy/Veer Incorporated/whip, image100/Corbis Corporation/dice, Image Source Ltd./chop, Jetta Productions/Dana Neely/Tetra Images LLC/knead, J Silva/Digital Vision/Getty Images, Inc./slice), V34–35 (C Squared Studios/PhotoDisc Getty Images, Inc./bassoon, double bass, kettledrum, oboe, piccolo, trumpet, xylophone, Stockbyte/Getty Images, Inc./tuba), V36 (C Squared Studios/PhotoDisc/Getty Images, Inc./sitar, Stockbyte/Getty Images, Inc./upright piano), V37 (Buccina Studios/PhotoDisc/Getty Images, Inc./doll's house, Comstock Images/Jupiterimages (UK) Ltd./building blocks, Dex Image/sandpit, G Doyle/Stockbyte/Getty Images, Inc./kite, O Drew/National Geographic/climbing frame, Dynamic Graphics/Creatas Images/Jupiterimages (UK) Ltd./playing cards, D Laurens/PhotoAlto/swing, L Manning/Corbis Corporation/soft toy, PhotoDisc/Getty Images, Inc./trampoline, RubberBall Productions/skipping rope), V38–39 (Image Source Ltd./wordsearch, Medioimages/Getty Images, Inc./noughts and crosses), V40 (Digital Vision/Getty Images, Inc./bowls, Duomo TIPS RF/ Tips Italia RF/skateboarding, Image Source Ltd./in-line skating, snorkelling, P Lee Harvey/Cultura Limited/orienteering, PhotoLink/PhotoDisc/Getty Images, Inc./darts, PNC/ Brand X Pictures/Jupiterimages (UK) Ltd./golf, Polka Dot Images/Jupiterimages (UK) Ltd./pool), V41–42 (Henry Arden/Image Source Ltd./press-up, S Baccon/

Digital Vision/ Getty Images, Inc./sewing, BananaStock/Jupiterimages (UK) Ltd./ gardening, T Grill/ Corbis Corporation/ painting, Richard Gross/Corbis Corporation/ pottery, woodcarving, J Henley/Blend Images, LLC/stamp collecting, Image Source Ltd./rowing machine, JGI/Blend Images, LLC/treadmill, R Lewine/Image Source Ltd./barbell, dumb-bell, yoga, D Madison/Digital Vision/Getty Images, Inc./jogging, S Mason/PhotoDisc/Getty Images, Inc./crochet, Moodboard/Mike Watson Images Limited/exercise bike, Photolibrary RF/sit-up, Polka Dot Images/Jupiterimages (UK) Ltd./ knitting), V44 (Duomo TIPS RF/Tips Italia RF/ice hockey, D Hammond/Design Pics Inc./baseball, rugby, Moodboard/Mike Watson Images Limited/soccer, PhotoLink/PhotoDisc/Getty Images, Inc./American football, A Somvanshi/ India Picture RF/cricket), V45 (Glow Images RF/ Glowimages Inc./backstroke, Goodshoot/ Jupiterimages (UK) Ltd./badminton, image100/ Corbis Corporation/butterfly, Image Source Ltd./squash, R Michael/Corbis Corporation/ crawl), V46–47 (B Blankenburg/Corbis Corporation/showjumping, E Calderoni/Score Royalty Free Images/Aflo Foto Agency Inc./ hammer, M Colomb/Digital Vision/Getty Images, Inc./horse racing, CS Productions/ Brand X Pictures/Jupiterimages (UK) Ltd./ javelin, pole vault, T Levine/zefa/Corbis Corporation/discus, D Madison/Photographer's Choice/Getty Images, Inc./high jump, J Oliver/ Digital Vision/Getty Images, Inc./sprinting, PhotoLink/PhotoDisc/Getty Images, Inc./ hurdling), V47–48 (K Aoki/Score Royalty Free Images/Aflo Foto Agency Inc./downhill skiing, Digital Vision/Getty Images, Inc./luge, Image Source Ltd./fencing, D Madison/Digital Vision/ Getty Images, Inc./bobsleigh, cross-country skiing, R McVay/Digital Vision/Getty Images, Inc./cycling, R Michael/Corbis Corporation/ gymnastics), V49–50 (B Blankenburg/Corbis Corporation/jet-skiing, windsurfing, Brand X Pictures/Jupiterimages (UK) Ltd./bodyboarding, Buzz Pictures/Purestock/Superstock, Inc./ surfing, Digital Vision/Getty Images, Inc./ skydiving, DLILLC/Corbis Corporation/bungee jumping, Image Source Ltd./abseiling, parkour, D Leniuk/Radius Images/Masterfile Corporation/kitesurfing, D Madison/Corbis Corporation/white-water rafting, Thinkstock Images/Jupiterimages (UK) Ltd./snowboarding, K Weatherly/PhotoDisc/Getty Images, Inc./ waterskiing), V51 (C Squared Studios/ PhotoDisc/Getty Images, Inc./bicycle, child's bicycle, tandem, tricycle, Glow Images RF/ Glowimages Inc./dirt bike, Moodboard/Mike Watson Images Limited/quad bike, J Nazz/ Corbis Corporation/racing bike, unicycle, K Weatherly/PhotoDisc/Getty Images, Inc./ mountain bike), V53 (Creatas Images/ Jupiterimages (UK) Ltd./seaplane, P Mastrovito/ Image Source Ltd./hot-air balloon, L Mayer/ Creatas Images/Jupiterimages (UK) Ltd./ ski-plane, Photolibrary RF/helicopter, StockTrek/Purestock/Superstock, Inc./fighter, P Tom/ICONOTEC/microlight), V54 (CAMP/ RelaXimages/rowing boat), V55–56 (Creatas Images/Jupiterimages (UK) Ltd./canoe, Medioimages/PhotoDisc/Getty Images, Inc./ yacht, L Riß/Westend61 GmbH/gondola, K Weatherly/PhotoDisc/Getty Images, Inc./ kayak), V57 (A Berg/Digital Vision/Getty Images, Inc./forklift truck, Thinkstock Images/ Jupiterimages (UK) Ltd./breakdown truck), V58 (Thinkstock Images/Jupiterimages (UK) Ltd./black cab), V63 (M Andersen/RubberBall Productions/nightwear, T Northcut/PhotoDisc/ Getty Images, Inc./crew-neck sweater), V64 (Stockbyte/Getty Images, Inc./handbag, shoulder bag), V65 (S Cole/ PhotoDisc Getty Images, Inc./sombrero), V66 (Y Arcurs/Tetra Images LLC/laptop, Brand X Pictures/ Jupiterimages (UK) Ltd./headset, G Doyle & C Griffin/Stockbyte/ Getty Images, Inc./router, webcam, Tetra Images LLC/PC), V69 (C Squared Studios/PhotoDisc/Getty Images, Inc./ envelopes, Stockbyte/Getty Images, Inc./ Post-it™)

V20, V27–28, V37–40, V52–57, V61–63 text adapted from Oxford Learner's Wordfinder Dictionary © Oxford University Press 1997

Maps © Oxford University Press

Design by Peter Burgess

Text capture, processing and typesetting by Oxford University Press